THE OHIO CRIMINAL LAW HANDBOOK

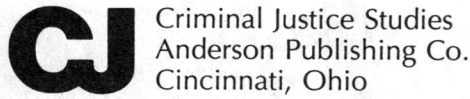

Criminal Justice Studies
Anderson Publishing Co.
Cincinnati, Ohio

© 1997 Anderson Publishing Co.
2035 Reading Road
Cincinnati, Ohio 45202
800 582-7295
FAX: 513 562-8110
E-mail: andpubmail@aol.com
World Wide Web: http://www.legalpubs.com

All rights reserved

Publisher's Staff Editor
Amy B. Brann, J.D.

ISBN: 0-87084-717-1

TABLE OF CONTENTS

PREFACE iv
TABLE OF PENALTIES A-1
DAYS OF CREDIT A-5
BAD TIME A-5
INDEX OF OFFENSES A-7
ELEMENTS OF OFFENSES A-27
Title XXIX (29)—CRIMINAL CODE 1
MISCELLANEOUS STATUTORY PROVISIONS 503
CONSTITUTION OF THE UNITED STATES 1325
CONSTITUTION OF THE STATE OF OHIO (Selected Provisions) 1337
TIME TABLE IN CRIMINAL CASES 1343
RULES OF PROCEDURE
    Ohio Rules of Criminal Procedure 1351
        Forms 1382
    Ohio Rules of Evidence 1413
    Ohio Rules of Juvenile Procedure 1429
    Ohio Traffic Rules 1453
        Forms 1463
    RULES OF COURT OF CLAIMS
        Forms 1469
GENERAL INDEX 1489

ABBREVIATIONS

Anderson Fam. L. — Anderson's Ohio Family Law
App. R. — Ohio Rules of Appellate Procedure
Civ. R. — Ohio Rules of Civil Procedure
Crim. R. — Ohio Rules of Criminal Procedure
Evid. R. — Ohio Rules of Evidence
Juv. R. — Ohio Rules of Juvenile Procedure
M.C.Sup.R. — Rules of Superintendence for Municipal Courts and County Courts
OCP&P — Anderson's Ohio Criminal Practice & Procedure
Sup. R. — Rules of Superintendence of the Supreme Court of Ohio
Traf. R. — Ohio Traffic Rules

PREFACE

This book collects in a compact format statutes, rules, and special features for the use of judges, attorneys, law enforcement officers, students, and others involved in the Ohio criminal justice process. It is designed to be a basic guide to Ohio criminal law. More detailed treatment of criminal law issues can be found in Anderson's Ohio Criminal Practice and Procedure, Third Edition.

The comments and suggestions of users have contributed immeasurably to the quality and usefulness of this handbook. There is no substitute for the experience of those who use this book, whether they use it in the courtroom, the office, the station house, or the classroom. We hope that you will continue to give us the benefit of your experience in using this book and our other publications. Please send your comments to: Amy B. Brann, Esq., Editor, Ohio Criminal Law Handbook, Anderson Publishing Company, P.O. Box 1576, Cincinnati, Ohio 45201–1576.

TABLE OF PENALTIES

(Including legislation passed through August 11, 1997)

SPECIAL FELONIES (SpecF)
(2929.02–2929.04)

Classification	Confinement	Maximum Fine	Organizational Fine (2929.31)
AGGRAVATED MURDER (2903.01)			
—death specifications	Death, life imprisonment without parole, life with parole after 20 years, life with parole after 25 years, or life with parole after 30 years	$25,000	$100,000
—no death specification	Life with parole after 20 years		
MURDER (2903.02)	15 years to life, except that, if the offender also is convicted of or pleads guilty to a sexual motivation specification and a sexually violent predator specification, life without parole	$15,000	$ 50,000

FELONIES (F)
(2929.14)

Classification	Confinement[1]	Maximum Fine	Organizational Fine (2929.31)
FELONY 1 (F1)	3, 4, 5, 6, 7, 8, 9, or 10 years (Additional 1 to 10 years for certain offenses)[2]	$20,000	$25,000
FELONY 2 (F2)	2, 3, 4, 5, 6, 7, or 8 years (Additional 1 to 10 years for certain offenses)[2]	$15,000	$20,000
FELONY 3 (F3)	1, 2, 3, 4, or 5 years	$10,000	$15,000
FELONY 4 (F4)	6, 7, 8, 9, 10, 11, 12, 13, 14, 15, 16, 17, or 18 months	$ 5,000	$10,000
FELONY 5 (F5)	6, 7, 8, 9, 10, 11, or 12 months	$ 2,500	$ 7,500

ENHANCEMENTS

A. Additional penalties for use or possession of a firearm (2929.14(D)(1)).
   1. Possession of an automatic or muffled firearm—6 additional years.
   2. Displaying, brandishing, or using firearm—3 additional years.
   3. Firearm not factor in committing the crime—1 additional year.
   4. Drive-by shooting—5 additional years plus penalty for use or possession of gun as above plus penalty for the underlying offense.
   5. The additional prison terms imposed under this section may not be reduced by §§ 2929.20, 2967.19.3, or any other provision of Chapters 2967. or 5120.
B. Additional penalties for repeat violent offenders (2929.14(D)(2)).
   - Where there is no physical harm or disfigurement, the offender shall be sentenced to any prison term specified in the range of prison terms for the specific offense.
   - Where there is physical harm with a substantial risk of death or permanent disfigurement, the offender shall be sentenced to the longest prison term specified in the range of prison terms for the specific offense.
   - If the prison terms specified for the specific offense are inadequate to punish the offender and protect the public from future crime because the offender is likely to commit future crimes and the terms are demeaning to the seriousness of the offense because the offender's conduct is more serious than normal (2929.12), the offender shall be sentenced to an additional term of 1 to 10 years.

The additional prison term imposed under this section may not be reduced by §§ 2929.20, 2967.19.3, or any other provision of Chapters 2967. or 5120.

C. Additional penalties for major drug offenders, corrupt activity, attempted forcible rape and attempted felonious sexual penetration when victim is under 13 years of age (2929.13(F), 2929.14(D)(3)).
   - Where a mandatory 10 year sentence is required and a finding is made that the term is inadequate to

---

[1] The overriding purposes of felony sentencing are (1) to protect the public from future crime by the offender and others, and (2) to punish the offender. To achieve these purposes the court is required to consider the need for incapacitating the offender, deterring the offender and others from future crime, rehabilitating the offender, and making restitution to the victim of the offense, the public, or both. A sentence imposed for a felony must be reasonably calculated to achieve the above-stated purposes, commensurate with and not demeaning to the seriousness of the offender's conduct and its impact upon the victim, and consistent with sentences imposed for similar crimes committed by other offenders with similar characteristics (2929.11). If the offender is eligible to be sentenced to community control sanctions, the court shall consider the appropriateness of imposing a financial sanction pursuant to § 2929.18 or a sanction of community service pursuant to § 2929.17 as the sole sanction for the offense. If the court is required to impose a mandatory prison term for the offense for which sentence is being imposed, the court may also impose a financial sanction pursuant to § 2929.19 but may not impose any additional sanction or combination of sanctions under §§ 2929.16 or 2929.17 (2929.13).

[2] Repeat violent offenders (2929.14(D)(2)), and Major drug offenders (2929.14(D)(3)).

punish the offender and protect the public from future crimes because the offender is likely to commit future crimes and the term is demeaning to the seriousness of the offense because the offender's conduct is more serious than normal (2929.12), the offender shall be sentenced to an additional term of 1 to 10 years.

The additional prison term imposed under this section may not be reduced by §§ 2929.20, 2967.19.3, or any other provision of Chapters 2967. or 5120.

MISDEMEANORS (M)
(2929.21) [3]

Classification	Confinement [4]	Maximum Fine [5]	Organizational Fine (2929.31)
MISDEMEANOR 1 (M1)	Maximum sentence of 6 months	$ 1,000	$ 5,000
MISDEMEANOR 2 (M2)	Maximum sentence of 90 days	$ 750	$ 4,000
MISDEMEANOR 3 (M3)	Maximum sentence of 60 days	$ 500	$ 3,000
MISDEMEANOR 4 (M4)	Maximum sentence of 30 days	$ 250	$ 2,000
MINOR MISDEMEANOR (MM)	None	$ 100	$ 1,000

[3] Committed on or after 8/30/78, restitution may also be required, R.C. § 2929.21(E) (137 v S 119). *See also* R.C. §§ 2929.22 (criteria for determining imprisonment and/or fines) and 2929.23 (electronically monitored house arrest or detention).

[4] *See also* R.C. § 2967.19.3 regarding days of credit.
Maximum reductions are set forth following this Table of Penalties.

[5] Offender required to pay towing and storage fees if convicted of theft offense involving motor vehicle or major part thereof. *See* R.C. § 2913.82.

DAYS OF CREDIT

Revised Code § 2967.19.3 allows persons confined to state correctional institutions to earn one day of credit as a deduction from the person's stated prison term for each full month during which the person productively participates in an education program, vocational training, employment in prison industries, treatment for substance abuse, treatment as a sex offender, or any other constructive program developed by the Department with specific standards for performance by prisoners. At the end of each calendar month in which a prisoner productively participates in such a program or activity, the Department of Rehabilitation and Correction shall deduct one day from the date on which the prisoner's stated prison term will expire. If the prisoner violates prison rules, the Department may deny the prisoner a credit that otherwise would have been awarded or may withdraw one or more credits previously earned by the prisoner. If a prisoner is released early by reason of credit under Revised Code § 2967.19.3, the Department shall retain control of the prisoner by means of an appropriate post-release control sanction imposed by the parole board until the end of the prisoner's stated term if the parole board imposes a post-release control sanction pursuant to section 2967.28 of the Revised Code. If the parole board is not required to impose a post-release control sanction under section 2967.28 of the Revised Code, the parole board may elect not to impose a post-release control sanction on the prisoner. No person who is serving a sentence of life imprisonment without parole imposed under Revised Code § 2929.03 or 2929.06 or who is serving a prison term or a term of life imprisonment without parole imposed pursuant to Revised Code § 2971.03 shall be awarded any days of credit.

BAD TIME

Revised Code § 2967.11 authorizes the Parole Board to punish a violation committed by the prisoner by extending the prisoner's stated prison term for a period of 15, 30, 60, or 90 days, but no stated prison term could be extended for a period longer than one-half of the stated prison term's duration for all violations occurring during the course of the prisoner's stated prison term, including violations occurring while the offender is serving extended time under this section or serving a prison term imposed for a failure to meet the conditions of a post-release control sanction imposed under section 2967.28 of the Revised Code. The extension period is referred to as "bad time."

INDEX OF OFFENSES

References are to the Revised Code and to penalty classifications abbreviated as follows:
F—Felony; M—Misdemeanor; MM—Minor Misdemeanor; SpecF—Special Felony; 1, 2, 3, 4, 5—First, Second, Third, Fourth, or Fifth Degree.

For the specific penalty of a given offense, consult the Table of Penalties, page A-1, preceding this Index.
The General Index is located at the end of this book.

ABDUCTION (2905.02), F3—*see also* KIDNAPPING

ABORTION MANSLAUGHTER (2919.13), F1—*see also* MURDER

ABORTION, PERFORMING AN UNLAWFUL PROCEDURE (2919.15), F4

ABORTION TRAFFICKING (2919.14), M1

ABORTION, UNLAWFUL (2919.12), M1
prior conviction, F4, F5

ABUSE OF CORPSE—*see* CORPSE, ABUSE OF

ACCIDENT, LEAVING SCENE OF—*see* MOTOR VEHICLES/TRAFFIC LAWS *at* accident, failure to stop after

ADULT CABARETS, OFFENSES CONCERNING (503.53, 503.59), M1, M3, F4

ADVERTISING DRUG PARAPHERNALIA (2925.14), M2

ADVERTISING VIA FACSIMILE DEVICE (4931.55), MM
prior conviction (4931.55), M1

AGGRAVATED OFFENSES—*see* specific offense

AIDING AND ABETTING—*see* COMPLICITY

AIDS
blood, contaminated, selling or donating (2927.13), F3

AIRCRAFT, AIRPORTS—*see also* CRIMINAL DAMAGING OR ENDANGERING
endangering aircraft (2909.08), M1, F5, F4
endangering airport operations (2909.08), M2, F5, F4
firearms on—*see* CARRYING CONCEALED WEAPONS

ALCOHOL—*see* INTOXICATING LIQUOR

AMPHETAMINES—*see* DRUG ABUSE

ANIMAL, DUTY TO REPORT ESCAPE OF (2927.21), M1

ARREST, RESISTING—*see* RESISTING ARREST

ARSON
defraud, to (2909.03), F4
hire, for (2909.03), F3
public buildings (2909.03), F4
public parks (2909.03), F4
without owner's consent (2903.03)
   harm or property under $500 (2909.03), M1
   harm or property more than $500 (2909.03), F4

ARSON, AGGRAVATED (2909.02), F2, F1

ASSAULT (2903.13), M1, F5, F4, F3

ASSAULT, AGGRAVATED (2903.12), F4
victim is peace officer (2903.12), F3

ASSAULT, FELONIOUS (2903.11), F2
victim is peace officer (2903.11), F1

ASSAULTING POLICE DOG OR HORSE OR HANDICAPPED ASSISTANCE DOG (2921.32.1), M2, M1, F5, F4

ASSAULT, NEGLIGENT (2903.14), M3

ATTEMPT (2923.02), 1 degree less than substantive crime[1] murder, to commit (2923.02), F1, F2, F3, F4, F5, M1, M4

BAD CHECKS, PASSING—*see* CHECKS

BARBITURATES—*see* DRUG ABUSE

BEER—*see also* INTOXICATING LIQUOR
keeping place where sold or furnished illegally (4399.09), $100-500 fine

BIGAMY (2919.01), M1

BINGO
failure to maintain records (2915.10), M1
illegally conducting (2915.09), F4, M1, MM
inspection of, interfering with (2915.10), M1
operator under 18 (2915.11), M3
operator with prior offense (2915.11), M1
without license (2915.07), F4

BLACKMAIL—*see* COERCION; EXTORTION

BLOCK PARENT SYMBOL, UNAUTHORIZED USE OF (2917.46), MM

BLOOD, CONTAMINATED, SELLING OR DONATING (2927.13), F4

BREAKING AND ENTERING (2911.13), F5

BRIBERY (2921.02), F3[2]

BURGLAR TOOLS, POSSESSION OF—*see* CRIMINAL TOOLS, POSSESSING

BURGLARY (2911.12), F2, F3, F4

BURGLARY, AGGRAVATED (2911.11), F1

BURN INJURY, FAILURE TO REPORT (2921.22), MM, M2

CABLE TELEVISION, POSSESSION OR SALE OF UNAUTHORIZED DEVICES (2913.04.1), F5, F4

CANNABIS—*see* DRUG ABUSE

CARRYING CONCEALED WEAPONS (2923.12), M1—*see also* WEAPONS OFFENSES
aboard aircraft (2923.12), F3
loaded or dangerous ordnance (2923.12), F4
prior conviction (2923.12), F4

---

[1] Attempt to commit a first, second, third, or fourth degree felony is F of the next lesser degree. Attempt to commit a fifth degree felony is M1.
[2] Upon conviction, public servant or party official is forever disqualified from holding public office, employment, or position of trust.

CARRYING CONCEALED WEAPONS—*Continued*
violation committed at a D permit premises, F3

CHEATING (2915.05), M1
value of $300 or more, or prior theft or gambling offense (2915.05), F5

CHECKS—*see also* FORGERY
passing bad—
    value under $500 (2913.11), M1
    value of $500 but under $5,000 (2913.11), F5
    value of $5,000 but under $100,000 (2913.11), F4
    value of $100,000 or more, F3
recording credit card, telephone, or social security number when presented (1349.17, 1349.99), MM

CHILD ABUSE OR NEGLECT, FALSE REPORT OF (2921.14), M1

CHILD, CONTRIBUTING TO UNRULINESS/DELINQUENCY OF (2919.24), M1

CHILD, CRIMINAL ENTICEMENT (2905.05), M1
prior conviction, F5

CHILD ENDANGERING (2919.22)[3]
abuse or neglect, M1
    prior conviction, F4
    resulting in serious physical harm, F3
administering extreme and cruel abuse or discipline, F3
    prior conviction or resulting in serious physical harm, F2
permitting/encouraging child to act/participate in pornography (2919.22), M1

CHILDREN, IMPROPER SOLICITATION OF CONTRIBUTIONS FOR MISSING (2901.32), M3

CIGARETTES, TOBACCO PRODUCTS
sale or distribution to minors prohibited (2927.02), M4
    prior conviction, M3

CIVIL RIGHTS, INTERFERING WITH (2921.45), M1

COCAINE—*see* DRUG ABUSE

COERCION (2905.12), M2

COIN MACHINES, TAMPERING WITH—*see* TAMPERING WITH COIN MACHINES

COMPELLING PROSTITUTION—*see* PROSTITUTION

COMPLICITY (2923.03), same as substantive offense

COMPOUNDING CRIME—*see* CRIME, COMPOUNDING

COMPUTER PROPERTY, UNAUTHORIZED USE OF (2913.04), F5

CONSENT AGREEMENT, VIOLATING (2919.27), M4
one prior conviction, M1
two or more prior convictions, F4

CONSPIRACY (2923.01), 1 degree less than substantive offense[4]
aggravated murder or murder, to commit (2923.01), F1

---

[3] Probation may be granted under certain conditions, R.C. § 2933.16.
[4] Conspiracy to commit a first, second, third, or fourth degree felony is F of the next lesser degree. Conspiracy to commit a fifth degree felony is M1.

CONTAMINATING SUBSTANCE FOR HUMAN CONSUMPTION OR USE (2927.24), F1
amount sufficient to cause death, F1
resulting in serious physical harm, F1

CONTRABAND
possession, concealment, transportation, receipt, purchase, sale, lease, rent, transfer (2933.42)

CONTRIBUTING TO UNRULINESS/DELINQUENCY OF A CHILD—see CHILD, CONTRIBUTING TO UNRULINESS/DELINQUENCY OF

CONTROLLED SUBSTANCES—see DRUG ABUSE; see Publisher's Note preceding R.C. § 3719.41 in Miscellaneous Statutory Provisions

CORPSE, ABUSE OF (2927.01), M2
gross abuse (2927.01), F5

CORRUPT ACTIVITY, PATTERN OF (2923.32), F1, F2
civil proceedings against violators (2923.34)
conspiracy (2923.01, 2923.32)
definitions (2923.31)
disposition of fines, civil penalties, property forfeited (2923.35)
forfeiture of property (2923.32)
lien, corrupt activity (2923.36)
penalties, additional (2923.32)
preserving reachability of property (2923.33)
proceeds, receipt and use of (2923.32)
securities, purchase on open market (2923.32)

CORRUPTING SPORTS (2915.05), F5
prior conviction (2915.05), F4

CORRUPTION OF A MINOR—see MINORS

COUNTERFEIT DRUGS—see DRUG ABUSE

COUNTERFEITING—see CRIMINAL SIMULATION; SLUGS, MAKING OR USING

COUPONS, ILLEGAL USE OF (2913.46)
value under $500, M1
value of $500 but less than $5,000, F5
value of $5,000 but less than $100,000, F4
value of $100,000 or more, F3

CREDIT CARD, MISUSE OF (2913.21), M1, F5, F4, F3
using or accepting invalid card or misrepresenting transaction to card issuer (2913.21)
    value under $500 within 90 days (2913.21), M1
    value of $500 but under $5,000 within 90 days (2913.21), F5
    value of $5,000 but under $100,000 within 90 days (2913.21), F4
    value of $100,000 or more within 90 days (2913.21), F3

CREDIT CARD NUMBER
recording when check presented (1349.17, 1349.99), MM

CREDIT CARD, THEFT OF—see THEFT

CREDIT PRACTICES, UNLAWFUL
extortionate credit extension, criminal usury (2905.22), F4
possession of record of usurious transactions (2905.22), M1

CRIME, COMPOUNDING (2921.21), M1

CRIME, FAILURE TO REPORT (2921.22), M4
doctors, by (2921.22), M2

CRIMINAL CHILD ENTICEMENT (2905.05), M1—*see also* MINORS
prior conviction, F4

CRIMINAL DAMAGING OR ENDANGERING (2909.06), M2
aircraft, involving, F5
physical harm to any person (2909.06), M1
occupied aircraft, involving, F4

CRIMINAL MISCHIEF (2909.07), M3
aircraft, involving, F5
physical harm to any person (2909.07), M1
occupied aircraft, involving, F4

CRIMINAL SIMULATION (2913.32), M1
value between $500 and $5,000, F5
value between $5,000 and $100,000, F4
value more than $100,000, F3

CRIMINAL TOOLS, POSSESSING (2923.24), M1, F5

CRIMINAL TRESPASS (2911.21), M4

CROPS, DAMAGING (901.51), MM

CROWD SAFETY, ENDANGERING (2917.40), M1[5]

CUSTODY, INTERFERENCE WITH (2919.23), M3, M1, F5, F4

DANGEROUS ORDNANCE—see WEAPONS OFFENSES

DEATH, FAILURE TO REPORT (2921.22), M4

DECEPTION TO SECURE WRITINGS
value under $500 (2913.43), M1
value of $500 but under $5,000 (2913.43), F5
value of $5,000 but under $100,000 (2913.43), F4
value of $100,000 or more (2913.43), F3

DEFRAUDING CREDITORS (2913.45), M1
value of $500 but under $5,000, F5
value of $5,000 but under $100,000, F4
value of $100,000 or more, F3

DERELICTION OF DUTY (2921.44), M2

DESECRATION (2927.11), M2 or M1

DISCLOSURE OF CONFIDENTIAL INFORMATION (2921.24), M4

DISORDERLY CONDUCT (2917.11), MM[6]—*see also* RIOT
persist after request to desist (2917.11), M4
school, near (2917.11), M4

DISRUPTING PUBLIC SERVICES (2909.04), F4

DISTURBING LAWFUL MEETING (2917.12), M4

DIVULGING CONFIDENTIAL INFORMATION
sealed record of conviction (2953.35), M4

---

[5] If physical harm to person, court must consider imprisonment, R.C. § 2917.40.
[6] Commitment of alcoholics and intoxicated persons for inpatient care, R.C. § 2935.33.

DOMESTIC VIOLENCE (2919.25), M1,[7] M4
prior conviction (2919.25), M3 or F5
violating protection order or consent agreement (2919.27), M1 or F4

DRIVER'S LICENSE—*see* MOTOR VEHICLES/TRAFFIC LAWS

DRIVING UNDER THE INFLUENCE—*see* MOTOR VEHICLES/TRAFFIC LAWS *at* D.U.I.

DRUG ABUSE—*see also* Publisher's Note preceding R.C. § 3719.41 in Miscellaneous Statutory Provisions
anabolic steroids, illegal administration or distribution of (2925.06), F4
conveyance of drug of abuse onto the grounds of detention, etc., facility (2921.36), M2
corrupting another with drugs[8]—
    marihuana (2925.02), F4
        near school premises (2925.02), F3
    schedule I or II substance (except marihuana) (2925.02), F2
        near school premises (2925.02), F1
    schedule III, IV, or V (2925.02), F2
        near school premises (2925.02), F2
counterfeit controlled substances—
    aggravated trafficking (2925.37), F4
    fraudulent advertising (2925.37), F5
        offense committed in the vicinity of school or juvenile (2925.37), F4
    possession (2925.37), M1
    promoting drug abuse (2925.37), F5
        offense committed in the vicinity of school or juvenile, F4
    trafficking (2925.37), F5
        offense committed in the vicinity of school or juvenile (2925.37), F4
cultivation of marihuana, illegal (2925.04), MM, M4, F5, F3, F2
deception to obtain dangerous drugs (2925.22)
        schedule I or II substance (except marihuana) (2925.22), F4
        schedule III, IV or V substance or marihuana (2925.22), F5
driving under the influence—*see* MOTOR VEHICLES/TRAFFIC LAWS *at* D.U.I.
drug documents, illegal processing of (2925.23)
    dangerous drug, schedule III, IV, or V substance, or marihuana (2925.23), F5
    schedule I or II substance (except marihuana) (2925.23), F4
drug samples, illegal dispensing of (2925.36)
    dangerous drug, schedule III, IV, or V substance, or marihuana (2925.36), M2
        offense committed in the vicinity of school or juvenile, M1
    schedule I or II substance (except marihuana) (2925.23), F5
        offense committed in the vicinity of school or juvenile, F4
harmful intoxicants, abusing (2925.31), M1
    prior conviction (2925.31), F5
knowingly obtain, possess, or use a controlled substance[9]—
    cocaine (2925.11), F5, F4, F3, F2, F1
    hashish (2925.11), MM, M4, F5, F3, F2
    heroin (2925.11), F5, F4, F3, F2, F1
    LSD (2925.11), F5, F4, F3, F2, F1
    marihuana (2925.11), MM, M4, F5, F3, F2
    schedule I or II substance (except marihuana, cocaine, LSD, heroin, and hashish) (2925.11), F5, F3, F2, F1
    schedule III, IV or V substance (2925.11), M3, M2, F4, F3, F2
livestock, offenses involving (2925.09), F5, F4
manufacture of drugs, illegal[10] (2925.04), F3, F2
marihuana trafficking, finding of (2925.05), F3
nitrous oxide—
    improperly dispensing or distributing (2925.32), M4, F5, F4
    possessing in motor vehicle (2925.33), M4

---

[7] *Supra* n.3. Commitment of alcoholics and intoxicated persons for inpatient care, R.C. § 2935.33.
[8] Not eligible for treatment in lieu of conviction, R.C. § 2951.04.1.
[9] *Supra* n.8.
[10] *Supra* n.8.

DRUG ABUSE—*Continued*
paraphernalia, (2925.14), M4, M2, M1
permitting vehicle or property to be used for commission of felony drug abuse offense (2925.13), M1
    offense committed in the vicinity of school or juvenile, F5
possessing drug abuse instruments (2925.12), M2
    prior conviction (2925.12), M1
trafficking, aggravated (schedule I or II substance, except marihuana, cocaine, LSD, heroin, and hashish)[11]
    (2925.03), F4, F3, F2, F1
trafficking, aggravated funding of (2925.05), F1
    possession, aggravated (schedule I or II substance, except marihuana, cocaine, LSD, heroin, and hashish)
        (2925.11), F5, F3, F2, F1
    possession of cocaine (2925.11), F5, F4, F3, F2, F1
    possession of drugs (schedule III, IV, or V substance) (2925.11), M3, M2, F4, F3, F2
    possession of hashish (2925.11), MM, M4, F5, F3, F2
    possession of heroin (2925.11), F5, F4, F3, F2, F1
    possession of LSD (2925.11), F5, F4, F3, F2, F1
    possession of marihuana (2925.11), MM, M4, F5, F3, F2
trafficking, funding of (2925.05), F2
trafficking in cocaine[12] (2925.03), F5, F4, F3, F2, F1
trafficking in drugs (schedule III, IV or V substance)[13] (2925.03), F5, F4, F3, F2, F1
trafficking in harmful intoxicants (2925.32), M4, F5, F4
trafficking in hashish[14] (2925.03), F5, F4, F3, F2, F1
trafficking in heroin[15] (2925.03), F5, F4, F3, F2, F1
trafficking in LSD[16] (2925.03), F5, F4, F3, F2, F1
trafficking in marihuana[17] (2925.03), MM, M3, F5, F4, F3, F2, F1

EAVESDROPPING—*see* INTERCEPTION OF WIRE OR ORAL COMMUNICATION; LISTENING DEVICE, UNLAWFUL

EMBEZZLEMENT—*see* THEFT

EMERGENCY, MISCONDUCT AT—*see* MISCONDUCT AT EMERGENCY

ESCAPE (2921.34), M1, F5, F3, F2
aiding (2921.35), F4

ETHNIC INTIMIDATION (2927.12)

EVIDENCE, TAMPERING WITH—*see* TAMPERING WITH EVIDENCE

EXPLOSIVES, ILLEGALLY MANUFACTURING OR PROCESSING (2923.17), F2

EXTORTION (2905.11), F3

FACSIMILE DEVICE, TRANSMITTING ADVERTISING TO (4931.55), MM
prior conviction (4931.55), M1

FAILURE TO AID LAW ENFORCEMENT OFFICER (2921.23), MM

FAILURE TO COMPLY WITH ORDER OR SIGNAL OF POLICE OFFICER (2921.33.1), M1, F4

FAILURE TO DISPERSE—*see* RIOT

FAILURE TO PERFORM VIABILITY TESTING (2919.18), M4

---

[11] *Supra* n.8.
[12] *Supra* n.8.
[13] *Supra* n.8.
[14] *Supra* n.8.
[15] *Supra* n.8.
[16] *Supra* n.8.
[17] *Supra* n.8. However, if offense involves a gift of 20 grams or less, trafficking in marihuana is a minor misdemeanor for the first offense and a misdemeanor of the third degree for any subsequent offense.

FAIR HOUSING RIGHTS, INTERFERENCE WITH (2927.03), M1

FALSE ALARMS (2917.32), M1

FALSIFICATION; IN THEFT OFFENSE; TO PURCHASE FIREARM (2921.13), M1, F5, F4, F3

FAX MACHINE—*see* FACSIMILE DEVICE

FELONIOUS ASSAULT—*see* ASSAULT, FELONIOUS

FELONIOUS SEXUAL PENETRATION
administering drug or intoxicant to prevent resistance, by (2907.12), F1
force or threat, by (2907.12), F1
victim under 13 (2907.12), F1
    by force or threat (2907.12), F1 with life imprisonment
victim's ability to resist or consent is substantially impaired by mental or physical condition or advanced age and the offender knows or has reasonable cause to believe the victim's ability to resist or consent is substantially impaired by such condition or advanced age (2907.12), F1

FIREARMS, DANGEROUS ORDNANCE—*see* WEAPONS OFFENSES

FLEEING OR ELUDING OFFICER (2921.33.1), M1, F4

FOOD ADULTERATED (3716.11), M1

FOOD STAMPS OR COUPONS
illegal use—
    value under $500, F5
    value of $500 but less than $5,000, F4
    value $5,000 but less than $100,000, F3
    value $100,000 or more, F2

FORGERY (2913.31[A]), F5—*see also* CHECKS
identification cards, offenses involving (2913.31[B]), M1
    value between $5,000 and $100,000, F4
    value over $100,000, F3

FRAUDS—*see* specific topics

FUNCTIONALLY IMPAIRED PERSON, FAILING TO PROVIDE FOR (2903.16), M1, M2, F4

GAMBLING (2915.02), M1—*see also* BINGO; CHEATING; CORRUPTING SPORTS
prior conviction (2915.02), F5

GAMBLING HOUSE, OPERATING (2915.03), M1
prior conviction (2915.03), F5

GAMING, PUBLIC (2915.04), MM
prior conviction (2915.04), M4

GARBAGE, OFFENSES INVOLVING (3767.32, 3767.99), M3

GRAND THEFT—*see* THEFT

GROSS SEXUAL IMPOSITION—*see* SEXUAL IMPOSITION, GROSS

GUNSHOT WOUND, STAB WOUND, BURN VIOLENTLY INFLICTED, FAILURE TO REPORT (2921.22), M2

HALLUCINOGENS—*see* DRUG ABUSE

HANDICAPPED PERSON—*see* FUNCTIONALLY IMPAIRED PERSON, FAILING TO PROVIDE FOR

HARASSMENT BY INMATE (2921.38), F5, F3

HARASSMENT, TELEPHONE—see TELEPHONE HARASSMENT

HARBORING CRIMINAL—see OBSTRUCTING JUSTICE

HAZING (2903.31), M4

HEROIN—see DRUG ABUSE

HIT & RUN—see MOTOR VEHICLES/TRAFFIC LAWS *at* accident, failure to stop after

HOMICIDE—see ABORTION MANSLAUGHTER; MANSLAUGHTER, INVOLUNTARY; MANSLAUGHTER, VOLUNTARY; MURDER; NEGLIGENT HOMICIDE; VEHICULAR HOMICIDE

HOUSING RIGHTS, INTERFERENCE WITH (2927.03), M1

IDENTIFICATION CARDS, FORGED (2913.31), M1

ILLEGAL CONVEYANCE OF DEADLY WEAPON OR DANGEROUS ORDNANCE INTO COURTHOUSE; ILLEGAL POSSESSION OR CONTROL IN COURTHOUSE (2923.12.3), F5, F4

ILLEGAL CONVEYANCE OF WEAPONS OR PROHIBITED ITEMS ONTO DETENTION FACILITY OR INSTITUTION (2921.36), F4, F5, M1, M2—see also WEAPONS OFFENSES

ILLEGAL CONVEYANCE OR POSSESSION OF A DEADLY WEAPON OR DANGEROUS ORDNANCE OR ILLEGAL POSSESSION OF AN OBJECT INDISTINGUISHABLE FROM A FIREARM ON SCHOOL PREMISES (2923.12.2), M1, F5, F4

IMPERSONATING PEACE OFFICER (2921.51), M4—*see also* PERSONATING AN OFFICER
arrest/detain/search (2921.51), M1
commit felony while impersonating (2921.51), F3
purpose to commit offense (2921.51), M1
to commit felony (2921.51), F4

IMPORTUNING (2907.07), M4
under age 13 or homosexual solicitation (2907.07), M1

IMPROPER SOLICITATION OF CONTRIBUTIONS FOR MISSING CHILDREN (2901.32), M3

INCITING TO VIOLENCE—see RIOT

INDECENCY—see PUBLIC INDECENCY

INMATE, HARASSMENT BY—see HARASSMENT BY INMATE

INSURANCE FRAUD (2913.47), M1, F5, F4, F3

INTERCEPTION OF WIRE OR ORAL COMMUNICATION (2933.52), F4

INTERFERENCE WITH FAIR HOUSING RIGHTS (2927.03), M1

INTERFERING WITH ACTION TO ISSUE OR MODIFY SUPPORT ORDER (2919.23.1), M1, F5

INTIMIDATION (2921.03), F3
attorney, victim or witness in a criminal case (2921.04), M1
   force or threat of harm, F3
ethnic (2927.12)

INTOXICANTS, HARMFUL—see DRUG ABUSE

INTOXICATING LIQUOR
diluted/refilled containers (4301.68, 4301.99), M1
disorderly conduct while intoxicated (2917.11), MM
   refusal to desist (2917.11), M4
driving while intoxicated—see MOTOR VEHICLES/TRAFFIC LAWS *at* D.U.I.
injunction violation (4301.74, 4301.99), M1

INTOXICATING LIQUOR—*Continued*
inspection, interference with (4301.49, 4301.99), MM
invoice, false entry (4301.48, 4301.99), MM
keeping place where sold illegally (4399.09), $100-500 fine
    subsequent offense (4399.09, 4399.99), $200-500 fine
label, forging or counterfeiting (4301.61, 4301.99), F3
manufacture, sale without permit (4301.58, 4301.99), M1
minor—
    false I.D., etc., for purchase (4301.63.5, 4301.99), M1
        furnishing (4301.63.3, 4301.99), M1
    order, etc., when under 21 (4301.63.2, 4301.99), M1
    purchase by (4301.63, 4301.99), $25-100 fine
    sold to (4301.69, 4301.99), M1
miscellaneous unspecified offenses (4301.70, 4301.99), MM
misrepresentation of quality (4301.59, 4301.99), M1
motor vehicle, consumption in (4301.64, 4301.99), M4
obstructing search (4301.66, 4301.99), M1
open container prohibited (4301.62, 4301.99), MM
possession, illegal (4301.67, 4301.99), M4
possession/sale of illegally obtained beer (4301.58, 4301.99), M1
rationing violation (4301.15, 4301.99), M4
record keeping violation (4301.47, 4301.99), MM
resale, purchase for, possession (4301.14, 4301.99), M3
sale of—
    emergency suspension (4301.25.1, 4301.99), M1
    restrictions (4301.22, 4301.99), M3
    Sunday, after-hours (4301.22, 4301.99), M4
tavern keeper permitting drunkenness (4399.16, 4399.99), $5-100 fine
transportation, illegal (4301.60, 4301.99), M1
weapons, use of—*see* WEAPONS OFFENSES

INVOLUNTARY MANSLAUGHTER—*see* MANSLAUGHTER, INVOLUNTARY

JUVENILES—*see* MINORS

KIDNAPPING (2905.01), F1—*see also* ABDUCTION; UNLAWFUL RESTRAINT
safe release (2905.01), F2

LAW ENFORCEMENT EMBLEM, UNLAWFUL DISPLAY (2913.44.1), MM

LICENSE PLATES—*see* MOTOR VEHICLES/TRAFFIC LAWS

LISTENING DEVICE, UNLAWFUL (2933.58), 1 to 3 years, and/or $1,000

LITTER, OFFENSES INVOLVING (3767.32, 3767.99), M3

MACHINE GUN, ILLEGAL POSSESSION—*see* WEAPONS OFFENSES

MANSLAUGHTER, ABORTION—*see* ABORTION MANSLAUGHTER

MANSLAUGHTER, INVOLUNTARY
in felony commission/attempt (2903.04), F1
in misdemeanor commission/attempt (2903.04), F3

MANSLAUGHTER, VOLUNTARY (2903.03), F1

MARIHUANA—*see* DRUG ABUSE

MASSAGE ESTABLISHMENTS, OFFENSES CONCERNING (503.42, 503.99), M1, M3, F4

MEDICAID FRAUD (2913.40), M1[18]

---

[18] For provisions regarding forfeiture of property, *see* R.C. §§ 2933.71-2933.75.

value of between $500 and $5,000, F5
value of between $5,000 and $100,000, F4
value of $100,000 or more, F3

MENACING (2903.22), M4
aggravated (2903.21), M1
stalking, by, (2903.21.1), M1, F5

MINORS—*see also* CHILD, CONTRIBUTING TO UNRULINESS/DELINQUENCY OF; CHILD ENDANGERING; CRIMINAL CHILD ENTICEMENT; CUSTODY, INTERFERENCE WITH
cigarettes or other tobacco products, sale or distribution to (2927.02), M4
    prior conviction, M3
corruption of (2907.04), F4
    less than 4 years difference (2907.04), M1
deception to obtain material harmful to (2907.33), M2
displaying matter harmful to juveniles (2907.31.1), M1
disseminating matter harmful to juveniles (2907.31), M1
    obscene (2907.31), F5
    obscene and juvenile under 13 (2907.31), F4
drug paraphernalia (2925.14), M1
firearms, improperly furnishing to (2923.21), F5
illegal use of in nudity-oriented material or performance (2907.32.3), F5 or F2
    prior conviction, F4
pandering obscenity involving (2907.32.1), F4, F3, F2
pandering sexually oriented matter involving (2907.32.2), F5, F4, F2

MISCONDUCT AT EMERGENCY (2917.13), MM
physical harm to person or property (2917.13), M4

MISCONDUCT INVOLVING PUBLIC TRANSPORTATION SYSTEM (2917.41), M4 or M3

MISUSE OF CREDIT CARD—*see* CREDIT CARD, MISUSE OF

MORPHINE—*see* DRUG ABUSE

MOTOR VEHICLES/TRAFFIC LAWS[19]—*see also* GENERAL INDEX
accident, failure to stop after (4549.02, 4549.99), M1[20]
    injury to person or property, when (4549.02.1, 4549.99), M1
    injury to real property, when (4549.03, 4549.99), M1
assured clear distance, (4511.21)
bumpers (4513.02.1, 4513.99), MM
    subsequent offense (4513.02.1, 4513.99), M3
certificate of registration, failure to display on commercial car (4549.18, 4549.99), MM
child restraint device required (4511.81, 4511.99), MM, M4
commercial vehicle—
    driving with impaired alertness (4511.79, 4511.99), MM
        subseqent offense (4511.99), M4
directional signals required (4513.26.1, 4513.99), MM
drag racing (4511.25.1, 4511.99), M1[21]
driver's (operator's) license—
    driving under suspension (4507.02, 4507.99), M1 with maximum 1 year suspension
    perjury or false affidavit re (4507.16, 4507.99)[22]

---

[19] Violation of R.C. §§ 4511.01-4511.76, 4511.84, 4513.03-4513.262, 4513.27-4513.37 for which no other penalty is provided is MM for a first offense, second offense within 1 year is M4, each subsequent offense within 1 year of the first offense is M3, R.C. §§ 4511.99, 4513.99.

Violation of R.C. §§ 4507.01-4507.081 or 4507.10 to 4507.37 for which no other penalty is provided is M1, R.C. § 4507.99.

[20] Court of record to suspend for not less than 30 days nor more than 3 years or revoke license, R.C. § 4507.16.
[21] *Supra* n.19.
[22] *Supra* n.19.

Motor Ohio Criminal Law Handbook A-18

MOTOR VEHICLES/TRAFFIC LAWS—*Continued*
driver's (operator's) license—*Continued*
    violation where penalty not otherwise specified (4507.99), M1
D.U.I. (driving under the influence of alcohol or drug of abuse or both) (4511.19), M1[23]
    implied consent to tests—
        chemical test shows positive results (4511.19.1)[24]
            prior D.U.I.; driving under suspension; serious physical harm to another; failure to appear; threat to public safety (4511.19.1)[25]
        informed refusal to submit to testing (4511.19.1)[26]
        no prior D.U.I. nor vehicular homicide involving D.U.I. within 6 years (4511.99)[27]
        one prior D.U.I. or vehicular homicide with D.U.I. within 6 years (4511.99)[28]
        two prior D.U.I.'s or vehicular homicide with D.U.I. within 6 years (4511.99)[29]
        three or more prior D.U.I.'s or vehicular homicide with D.U.I. within 5 years (4511.99)[30]
    vehicular homicide while—*see* VEHICULAR HOMICIDE
earphones, wearing (4511.84), MM, M4, M3
falsification of insurance claim (2921.13), M1 to F3
falsification of report of theft of (2921.13), F3

---

[23] *See* commitment of alcoholics and intoxicated persons, R.C. § 2935.33; drivers' intervention program, R.C. § 3793.10; treatment in lieu of conviction, R.C. § 2951.04.1; ignition interlock device as condition of probation, R.C. §§ 2951.02, 4511.83.

[24] Immediate seizure and 90 day suspension of license by arresting officer.

[25] Officer takes the offender's license and the suspension begins immediately.
Second offense in six-year period results in 1 year suspension.
Third offense in six-year period results in 2 years' suspension.
Fourth or more offense in six-year period results in 3 years' suspension.

[26] Officer takes the offender's license and the suspension begins immediately.
First refusal in five-year period results in 1 year suspension.
Second refusal in five-year period results in 2 years' suspension.
Third refusal in five-year period results in 3 years' suspension.
Fourth or more refusal in five-year period results in 5 years' suspension.

[27] Mandatory minimum 3 consecutive days' actual incarceration or 3-day intervention program and mandatory minimum fine of $200 to $1,000.
Mandatory minimum 6 months to 3 years' license suspension, R.C. § 4507.16; occupational driving privilege after 15 days' suspension, R.C. § 4507.16.
Work release available after mandatory minimum time served, R.C. § 4511.99.

[28] Mandatory minimum 10 consecutive days' actual incarceration or 5 days actual incarceration and a period of electronically monitored house arrest of at least 18 days and mandatory minimum fine of $300 to $1,500.
Discretionary driver's intervention program.
Immobilization and impoundment of vehicle for 90 days.
Mandatory minimum 1 to 5 years' license suspension, R.C. § 4507.16; occupational driving privilege after 30 days' suspension, R.C. § 4507.16.
Work release available after mandatory minimum time served, R.C. § 4511.99.

[29] Mandatory minimum 30 days to 1 year actual incarceration or 15 days actual incarceration and a period of electronically monitored house arrest of at least 55 days and mandatory minimum fine of $500 to $2,500.
Mandatory alcohol and drug addiction program paid by offender.
Immobilization and impoundment of vehicle for 180 days.
Mandatory minimum 1 to 10 years' license suspension, R.C. § 4507.16; occupational driving privilege after 180 days' suspension, R.C. § 4507.16.
Work release available after mandatory minimum time served, R.C. § 4511.99.

[30] Mandatory minimum 60 days to 1 year actual incarceration and mandatory minimum fine of $750 to $10,000.
Mandatory drug-and-alcohol-treatment program paid by offender.
Forfeiture of vehicle offender was driving.
Mandatory minimum 3 year to permanent license suspension, R.C. § 4507.16; occupational driving privilege after 3 years' suspension.
Work release available after mandatory minimum time served, R.C. § 4511.99.

MOTOR VEHICLES/TRAFFIC LAWS—*Continued*
  financial responsibility act, failure to comply with (4509.10.1, 4509.78, 4509.99)
  firearms re—*see* WEAPONS OFFENSES
  grand theft—*see* THEFT
  hit & run—*see* accident, failing to stop after, this entry
  junk vehicle—
    abandoning (4513.64, 4513.99), MM[31]
    noncompliance with order to remove (4513.65, 4513.99), MM
      second offense (4513.99), M4
      subsequent offenses (4513.99), M3
  license plates—
    foreign, when resident of this state (4549.12, 4549.99), MM
      subsequent offense (4549.99), M4
    operation without (4549.10, 4549.99), MM
      subsequent offense (4549.99), M4
    previous registration, driving with (4549.11), MM
      subsequent offense (4549.99), M4
    unauthorized use (4549.08, 4549.99), M4
      subsequent offense (4549.99), M3
  motorized bicycle without license or safety equipment (4511.52.1, 4511.99), MM
  odometer tampering (4549.42, 4549.99), F4
    subsequent offense (4549.99), F3
  operating a motor vehicle after under-age alcohol consumption (4511.19), M4, M3
  order, failure to comply with (2921.33.1), M1, F4
  parking on posted private property (4511.68.1, 4511.99), MM
    use of unlicensed tow truck by property owner (4513.60, 4513.99), MM
  points (4507.02, 4507.02.1), M1 with impounding of title and plates; possible 1 year additional
  resisting traffic officer (2921.33.1, 4513.36, 4513.99)
    fleeing after signal to stop (2921.33.1), M1, F4[32]
  safety belts (4513.26.2, 4513.99), MM
    second offense, M4
    subsequent offense, M3
  school buses—
    bus driver to report traffic violation conviction or license suspension or revocation (3327.10), MM
    failure to mark (4511.77, 4511.99), MM[33]
      subsequent offense (4511.99), M4
    inspection decal display (4511.76.1, 4511.99), MM[34]
      subsequent offense (4511.99), M4
    passing stopped bus (4511.75, 4511.99), $500 maximum fine[35]
    registration and identification (4511.76.4, 4511.99), MM
      subsequent offense (4511.99), M4
    use for other than school purposes (4511.76.2, 4511.99), MM[36]
      subsequent offense (4511.99), M4
    violation of regulations (4511.76.1, 4511.99), MM[37]
      subsequent offense (4511.99), M4
  speeding (4511.21, 4511.99), MM
    second offense within 1 year (4511.99), M4
      subsequent offenses within one year (4511.99), M3
    faster than 35 m.p.h. in business district (4511.99), M4
    faster than 50 m.p.h. in other than business district or municipal corporation (4511.99), M4
    faster than 35 m.p.h. in school zone during restricted hours (4511.99), M4
  stop at grade crossing (4511.63, 4511.99), MM

---

[31] Assessment of costs incurred in disposal.
[32] Court of record to suspend for not less than 30 days nor more than 3 years or revoke license, R.C. § 4507.16.
[33] Suspension for up to 3 years or revocation of license upon finding of guilty, R.C. § 4511.99.
[34] *Supra* n.33.
[35] License suspension for not more than 1 year, R.C. § 4507.16.5.
[36] *Supra* n.33.
[37] *Supra* n.33.

MOTOR VEHICLES/TRAFFIC LAWS—*Continued*
   subsequent offense (4511.99), M4
stopping when signalled (4549.01, 4549.99), MM
   subsequent offense (4549.99), M4
temporary license or windshield sticker, failure to display (4503.21, 4503.99), MM
theft—*see* THEFT
title, altering, etc., fraudulent use (4505.19, 4505.99), 6 months to 5 years and/or $5,000 maximum fine
unauthorized use of vehicle (2913.03), M1
   removal from state or for 48 hours or longer (2913.03), F5
unsafe vehicle, operation of (4513.02, 4513.99), MM
   subsequent offense (4513.99), M3
vehicle identification number or derivative, offenses re (4549.62, 4549.99), M1 to F3
vehicular homicide—*see* VEHICULAR HOMICIDE

MURDER (2903.02), SpecF[38]

MURDER, AGGRAVATED (2903.01), SpecF[39]

NARCOTICS—*see* CONTROLLED SUBSTANCES; DRUG ABUSE

NEGLIGENT ASSAULT—*see* ASSAULT, NEGLIGENT

NEGLIGENT HOMICIDE (2903.05), M1

NONSUPPORT OR CONTRIBUTING TO NONSUPPORT OF DEPENDENTS (2919.21), M1, F5, F4

NUISANCES (Ch. 3767)—*see* General Index

OBSCENITY—
deception to obtain, for minors (2907.33), M2
displaying matter harmful to juveniles (2907.31.1), M1
disseminating, harmful to minors (2907.31), M1
   illegal use of minor in nudity-oriented material or performance (2907.32.3), M1 or F2
      prior conviction, F4
   objectionable matter, compelling acceptance of (2907.34), F5
   obscene (2907.31), F5
   obscene and juvenile under 13 (2907.31), F4
   pandering (2907.32), F5, F4
      prior conviction (2907.32), F4
   pandering sexually oriented matter involving minor (2907.32.2), M1 or F2
      prior conviction, F4

OBSTRUCTING JUSTICE (2921.32), MM, M4, M3, M2, M1
aid in commission of aggravated murder, murder, or a felony of the 1st or 2nd degree, F3
aid to felon (2921.32), F5

OBSTRUCTING OFFICIAL BUSINESS (2921.31), M2

OPERATING A GAMBLING HOUSE—*see* GAMBLING HOUSE, OPERATING

OPIUM—*see* DRUG ABUSE

ORGANIZED CRIME—*see* CORRUPT ACTIVITY, PATTERN OF

PANIC, INDUCING (2917.31), M1
physical harm to any person (2917.31), F4

PARENTAL EDUCATION NEGLECT (2919.22.1), M4

PASSING BAD CHECKS—*see* CHECKS

---

[38] Not eligible for probation.
[39] *Supra* n.38.

PATIENTS
abuse of (2903.34), F4 or F3
false complaint of abuse or neglect, filing (2903.35), M1
gross neglect of (2903.34), M1 or F5
neglect of (2903.34), M2 or F5

PERJURY (2921.11), F3

PERSONATING AN OFFICER (2913.44), M1—*see also* IMPERSONATING PEACE OFFICER

PETTY THEFT—*see* THEFT

PLANTS, DAMAGING (901.51), MM

POISONS, OFFENSES INVOLVING (3719.32), MM

POSSESSING CRIMINAL TOOLS—*see* CRIMINAL TOOLS, POSSESSING

PROPERTY OFFENSES—*see* specific offense

PROSTITUTION (2907.25), M3
after positive HIV test (2907.25), F3
compelling (2907.21), F3, F2
loitering to engage in solicitation (2907.24.1), M3
   after positive HIV test (2907.24.1), F5
procuring (2907.23), M1
promoting (2907.22), F4
   minor (2907.22), F3
soliciting (2907.24), M3
   after positive HIV test (2907.24), F3

PROTECTION ORDER, VIOLATING (2919.27), M1[40]
anti-stalking (2903.27), M1
   two or more prior convictions, same subject, F5
one prior conviction, F5
two or more prior convictions, F5

PUBLIC CONTRACT, UNLAWFUL INTEREST IN (2921.42), M1
authorize/influence public contract for investment for own interest (2921.42), F4

PUBLIC GAMING—*see* GAMING, PUBLIC

PUBLIC INDECENCY (2907.09), M4, M3, M2, M1

PUBLIC SERVICES, DISRUPTING—*see* DISRUPTING PUBLIC SERVICES

PUBLIC TRANSPORTATION SYSTEM, MISCONDUCT INVOLVING—*see* MISCONDUCT INVOLVING PUBLIC TRANSPORTATION SYSTEM

RAILROADS
abandonment of track, failure to remove rails (4955.20.1, 4955.99), M1
animals, allowing into enclosures of (4999.03), 10-30 days imprisonment, $10 fine
bridges over, constructing (4999.10), $100-$1000 fine
driving on (4999.01), $5-$25 fine
freight, diverting (4999.19), 30 days imprisonment, $100 fine
out of service tracks, operation of train on (4955.37, 4955.99), M1

RAPE[41]
administering drug or intoxicant to prevent resistance, by (2907.02), F1
   force or threat, by (2907.02), F1

---

[40] *Supra* n.7.
[41] *Supra* n.38.

RAPE—*Continued*
victim's ability to resist or consent is substantially impaired because of mental or physical condition or advanced age and offender knows, or has reasonable cause to believe the victim's ability to resist or consent is substantially impaired by such condition or advanced age (2907.02), F1
    force or threat, by (2907.02), F1
victim under 13 years of age (2907.02), F1
    force or threat, by (2907.02), F1 with life imprisonment

RECEIVING STOLEN PROPERTY
value less than $300 (2913.51), M1
value of $300 but less than $5,000; or special property of R.C. § 2913.71 (2913.51), F5
value of $5,000 but less than $100,000; or motor vehicle; or dangerous drug (2913.51), F4
value of $100,000 or more, F3

RECOGNIZANCE, FAILURE TO APPEAR
original charge, felony (2937.29, 2937.99), 1 to 5 years, $5,000 fine or both
original charge, misdemeanor (2937.29, 2937.99), 1 year maximum, $1,000 or both

RECORDS, TAMPERING WITH—*see* TAMPERING WITH RECORDS

RESIDENTS OF CARE FACILITIES—*see* PATIENTS

RESISTANCE TO LAWFUL AUTHORITY—*see* ESCAPE

RESISTING ARREST (2921.33), M2, M1, F4

RESTRAINT, UNLAWFUL—*see* UNLAWFUL RESTRAINT

RETALIATION (2921.05), F3

RICO—*see* CORRUPT ACTIVITY, PATTERN OF

RIOT (2917.03), M1—*see also* DISORDERLY CONDUCT
failure to disperse (2917.04), MM
inciting to violence (2917.01), M1, F3
inmate, by (2917.02), F4, F3

RIOT, AGGRAVATED (2917.02), F5, F4, F3

ROBBERY (2911.02), F3, F2

ROBBERY, AGGRAVATED (2911.01), F1

SAFECRACKING (2911.31), F4

SCHOOL BUSES—*see* MOTOR VEHICLES/TRAFFIC LAWS

SEARCH
conducting unauthorized (2933.32), M1
    failure to prepare proper report, M4

SECURING WRITING BY DECEPTION—*see* DECEPTION TO SECURE WRITINGS

SEX OFFENDERS, HABITUAL
registration offenses (2950.99), M1
    prior conviction (2950.99), F4

SEX OFFENSES—*see* specific offense

SEXUAL BATTERY (2907.03), F4, F3

SEXUAL IMPOSITION (2907.06), M3, M1

SEXUAL IMPOSITION, GROSS (2907.05), F4
victim under 13 years of age (2907.05), F3

SEXUAL PENETRATION, FELONIOUS—see FELONIOUS SEXUAL PENETRATION

SHAM LEGAL PROCESS, USING (2921.52), M4, M1, F4, F3

SLUGS, MAKING OR USING (2913.33), M2

SOCIAL SECURITY NUMBER
recording when check presented (1349.17, 1349.99), MM

SOLICITING IMPROPER COMPENSATION (2921.43), M1 and 7 year bar from office

SOLICITING PROSTITUTION—see PROSTITUTION

SPEEDING—see MOTOR VEHICLES/TRAFFIC LAWS

SPORTS, CORRUPTING—see CORRUPTING SPORTS

SPREADING A FALSE REPORT OF CONTAMINATION (2927.24), F4

STALKING, MENACING BY (2903.21.1), M1, F5

STOLEN PROPERTY, RECEIVING—see RECEIVING STOLEN PROPERTY

TAMPERING WITH COIN MACHINES (2911.32), M1
prior conviction (2911.32), F4

TAMPERING WITH EVIDENCE (2921.12), F3

TAMPERING WITH RECORDS (2913.42), M1, F5, F4, F3

TELEPHONE HARASSMENT (2917.21), M1
facsimile device, transmitting advertising to (4931.55), MM
    prior conviction (4931.55), M1
prior conviction involving the same person recipient, or premises (2917.21), F5

TELEPHONE NUMBER
recording when check presented (1349.17, 1349.99)

TERMINATING OR ATTEMPTING TO TERMINATE HUMAN PREGNANCY AFTER VIABILITY
    (2919.17), F4

THEFT
check, (2913.02), F4
credit card (2913.02), F4
drugs, dangerous—
    no prior felony drug abuse conviction (2913.02), F4
    prior felony drug abuse conviction (2913.02), F3
firearm (2913.02), F5
motor vehicle, documents relating thereto (2913.02), F5
negotiable instruments (2913.02), F5
ordnance, dangerous (2913.02), F5
value—
    less than $500 (2913.02), M1
    $500 or more, less than $5,000 (2913.02), F5
    $5,000 or more, less than $100,000 (2913.02), F4
    $100,000 or more (2913.02), F3

THEFT IN OFFICE (2921.41), F5, F4, F3[42]

THREATS—see COERCION; EXTORTION

---

[42] Upon conviction a public servant or party official is forever disqualified from holding public office, employment, or position of trust.

TOBACCO PRODUCTS, ILLEGAL DISTRIBUTION OF (2927.02), M4
prior conviction (2927.02), M3

TRADEMARK COUNTERFEITING (2913.34), M1, F5, F4, F3

TRAFFIC CONTROL DEVICES, OFFENSES INVOLVING (4511.18)

TRAFFIC OFFENSES—*see* MOTOR VEHICLES/TRAFFIC LAWS

TRASH, OFFENSES INVOLVING (3767.32, 3767.99), M3

TREES, DAMAGING (901.51), MM

TRESPASS—*see* CRIMINAL TRESPASS

UNAUTHORIZED USE OF BLOCK PARENT SYMBOL—*see* BLOCK PARENT SYMBOL, UNAUTHORIZED USE OF

UNAUTHORIZED USE OF PROPERTY (2913.04), M4, M1, F5, F4, F3

UNAUTHORIZED USE OF VEHICLE—*see* MOTOR VEHICLES/TRAFFIC LAWS

UNLAWFUL ABORTION—*see* ABORTION, UNLAWFUL

UNLAWFUL RESTRAINT (2905.03), M3

USURY—*see* CREDIT PRACTICES, UNLAWFUL

VANDALISM
value $5,000 but less than $100,000 (2909.05), F4
value less than $5,000 (2909.05), F5 plus $2,500 fine
value $100,000 or more, F3

VEHICULAR ASSAULT, AGGRAVATED (2903.08), F4
prior conviction under 2903.06, 2903.07, 2903.08, F3
under the influence (2903.08), F4 or F3 with permanent license revocation

VEHICULAR HOMICIDE (2903.07, 4507.16), M1 with 30 days to 3 years' license suspension
prior conviction under 2903.06, 2903.07, 2903.08, F4
under the influence (2903.07), M1 with permanent license revocation

VEHICULAR HOMICIDE, AGGRAVATED (2903.06, 4507.16), F3 with 30 days to 3 years' license suspension
prior conviction under 2903.06, 2903.07, 2903.08, F2
under the influence (2903.06), F3 or F2 with permanent license revocation

VIABILITY TESTING, FAILURE TO PERFORM (2919.18), M4

VIOLENCE, INCITING TO—*see* RIOT

VOLUNTARY MANSLAUGHTER—*see* MANSLAUGHTER, VOLUNTARY

VOYEURISM (2907.08), M3

WEAPONS OFFENSES—*see also* CARRYING CONCEALED WEAPONS
conveyance into detention facility or institution (2921.36), F3
dangerous ordnance, failure to secure (2923.19), M2
dangerous ordnance, unlawful possession (2923.17), F5
drug dependent person/chronic alcoholic, use of weapon by (2923.13), F5
drug of abuse, using weapon while under influence of (2923.15), M1
firearms, improper handling in motor vehicle (2923.16), M1
    unloaded (2923.16), M4
firearms, improperly discharging at or into habitation or school, (2923.16.1), F3, F2
firearms, improperly furnishing to minor (2923.21), F5
having while under disability (2923.13), F5
if convicted of felony of the first or second degree in the previous five years, F3

WEAPONS OFFENSES—*Continued*
intoxicated, using while (2923.15), M1
liquor permit premises, possession of firearm in (2923.12.1), F5
possessing criminal tools (2923.24), M1, F5
possession of a deadly weapon while under detention (2923.13.1), M1, F5, F4, F3, F2, F1
possession of an object indistinguishable from a firearm on school premises (2923.12.2), M1
school premises or activities (2923.12.2), F5, F4
underage purchase of firearm or handgun (2913.21.1), M2
unlawful transaction in (2923.20), F3
    failure to report loss (2923.20), M4
    manufacturing, transfer (2923.20), M2

WIRETAPPING—*see* INTERCEPTION OF WIRE OR ORAL COMMUNICATION; LISTENING DEVICE, UNLAWFUL

WITNESS, BRIBING—*see* BRIBERY

WORKERS' COMPENSATION FRAUD (2913.48), M1, F5, F4, F3

ELEMENTS OF OFFENSES

	Page
Missing Children	A-28
Homicides and Assaults	A-28
Kidnapping and Extortion	A-39
Sex Offenses	A-42
Arson and Related Offenses	A-55
Robbery, Burglary, Trespass	A-61
Thefts and Frauds	A-65
Gambling	A-78
Offenses Against the Public Peace	A-85
Offenses Against the Family	A-93
Offenses Against Justice and Public Administration	A-104
Weapons/Ordnance/Conspiracy/Attempt	A-123
Drug Abuse Offenses	A-136
Miscellaneous Offenses	A-167

Explanatory Note

In this division of the Handbook, the elements of each offense in Title 29 of the Ohio Revised Code, plus other selected offenses, are set forth. Venue is included under each offense. Venue must be proved in every case, although technically it is not an element. *State v. Draggo,* 65 Ohio St. 2d 88, 19 Ohio Op. 3d 294, 418 N.E. 2d 1343 (1981). For a complete discussion, *see* Chapter 15, Anderson's Ohio Criminal Practice and Procedure, Third Edition.

The headings consist of the name of the offense, the statute in which it is defined, and the classification and degree of the offense. Felony is abbreviated **F,** misdemeanor is **M,** and minor misdemeanor is **MM.** Numbers following the abbreviations indicate the degree of the offense. Thus, **F3** denotes a felony of the third degree. Multiple classifications indicate that the offense may fall under more than one classification, depending on the circumstances of the offense or on the offender's past record. This is explained in the Penalty section under each offense.

The date on which an offense was committed may affect the prosecution of the offense. See R.C. § 2929.61.

MISSING CHILDREN

***IMPROPER SOLICITATION OF CONTRIBUTIONS FOR MISSING CHILDREN*, R.C. § 2901.32 [M3]**

Division (A):
(1) Being an organization
(2) Solicit contributions
(3) For purpose of distributing materials containing information relating to missing children
(4) Unless
    (a) For period of two years prior to time of such solicitation
        (i) Incorporated under R.C. Chapter 1702. or nonprofit corporation law of another state
        (*and*)
        (ii) Exempt from federal income taxation under I.R.C. § 501(a) and described in I.R.C. § 501(c)(3), 501(c)(4), 501(c)(8), 501(c)(10) or 501(c)(19)
        (*and*)
    (b) Does not use fund-raising counsel, professional solicitors, commercial co-venturers, or other charitable organizations as defined in R.C. § 1716.01 to solicit such contributions
(5) Venue

Division (B):
(1) Being an organization
(2) Solicit contributions for purpose of distributing materials containing information relating to missing children
(3) Expressly stating or implying in any way that it is affiliated with or soliciting contributions on behalf of an organization established to assist in the location of missing children
(4) Without the express written consent of that organization
(5) Venue

Penalty: A misdemeanor of the third degree (2929.21, 2929.31)

HOMICIDES AND ASSAULTS

***AGGRAVATED MURDER*, R.C. § 2903.01 [F]**

Division (A):
(1) Purposely
(2) With prior calculation and design
(3) (a) Cause another's death
       (*or*)
    (b) The unlawful termination of another's pregnancy
(4) Venue

Division (B):
(1) Purposely
(2) (a) Cause another's death
       (*or*)

(b) The unlawful termination of another's pregnancy
(3) While committing, attempting to commit, fleeing immediately after committing or attempting to commit
(4) Kidnapping, rape, aggravated arson, arson, aggravated robbery, robbery, aggravated burglary, burglary, or escape
(5) Venue

Division (C):
(1) Purposely
(2) Cause the death
(3) Of another who is under 13 at the time of the commission of the offense
(4) Venue

Notes: No person shall be convicted of aggravated murder unless the person is specifically found to have intended to cause the death of another or, if the case involves an alleged violation of division (A) or (B) of this section, the unlawful termination of another's pregnancy. In no case shall a jury in an aggravated murder case be instructed in such a manner that it may believe that a person who commits or attempts to commit any offense listed in division (B) of this section is to be conclusively inferred, because the person engaged in a common design with others to commit the offense by force and violence or because the offense and the manner of its commission would be likely to produce death or the unlawful termination of another's pregnancy, to have intended to cause the death of any person who is killed or the unlawful termination of another's pregnancy during the commission of, attempt to commit, or flight from the commission of or attempt to commit, the offense. If a jury in an aggravated murder case is instructed that a person who commits or attempts to commit any offense listed in division (B) of this section may be inferred, because the offender engaged in a common design with others to commit the offense by force or violence or because the offense and the manner of its commission would be likely to produce death or the unlawful termination of another's pregnancy, to have intended to cause the death of any person who is killed or the unlawful termination of another's pregnancy during the commission of, attempt to commit, or flight from the commission of or attempt to commit the offense, the jury also shall be instructed that the inference is nonconclusive, that the inference may be considered in determining intent, that it is to consider all evidence introduced by the prosecution to indicate the person's intent and by the person to indicate the person's lack of intent in determining whether the person specifically intended to cause the death of the person killed or the unlawful termination of another's pregnancy, and that the prosecution must prove the specific intent of the person to have caused the death or the unlawful termination of another's pregnancy by proof beyond a reasonable doubt.

Penalty: Death, life imprisonment without parole, life with parole after 20 years, life with parole after 25 years, or life with parole after 30 years according to R.C. §§ 2929.02, 2929.02.2, 2929.03 and 2929.04 and up to $25,000, except that persons who were not 18 years of age or older at the time of commission of the offense shall not suffer death. Indictment or count in indictment must contain one or more specifications of aggravating circumstances listed in R.C. § 2929.04(A) for capital offense, R.C. § 2901.02(B).

Organization: Up to $100,000

MURDER, R.C. § 2903.02 [F]

(1) Purposely
(2) (a) Cause another's death

§ 2903.03

  (*or*)
 (b) The unlawful termination of another's pregnancy
(3) Venue

Penalty: Indefinite term of 15 years to life except that, if the offender also is convicted of or pleads guilty to a sexual motivation specification and a sexually violent predator specification that were included in the indictment, count in the indictment, or information that charged the murder, the court shall impose upon the offender a term of life imprisonment without parole that shall be served pursuant to section 2971.03 of the Revised Code. In addition, the offender may be fined an amount fixed by the court, but not more than $15,000

 Organization: Up to $50,000

VOLUNTARY MANSLAUGHTER, R.C. § 2903.03 [F1]

(1) Knowingly
(2) (a) Cause another's death
  (*or*)
 (b) The unlawful termination of another's pregnancy
(3) While under the influence of sudden passion or in a sudden fit of rage
(4) Brought on by serious provocation occasioned by the victim
(5) Reasonably sufficient to incite the offender
(6) To use deadly force
(7) Venue

Penalty: A felony of the first degree (2929.11-2929.18, 2929.31)

INVOLUNTARY MANSLAUGHTER, R.C. § 2903.04 [F1, F3]

Division (A): [F1]
(1) (a) Cause another's death
  (*or*)
 (b) The unlawful termination of another's pregnancy
(2) As proximate result of committing or attempting to commit a felony
(3) Venue

Penalty: A felony of the first degree (2929.11-2929.18, 2929.31)

Division (B): [F3]
(1) (a) Cause another's death
  (*or*)
 (b) The unlawful termination of another's pregnancy
(2) As proximate result of committing or attempting to commit a misdemeanor of the first, second, third, or fourth degree or a minor misdemeanor
(3) Venue

Penalty: A felony of the third degree (2929.11-2929.18, 2929.31)

Notes: If offense that proximately resulted in death of victim or the unlawful termination of another's pregnancy and that is basis of violation included as an element the offender's operation or participation in the operation of a motor vehicle, motorcycle, snowmobile, locomotive, watercraft, or aircraft while under the influence of alcohol, drug of abuse, or both, driver's license shall be permanently revoked.

If conditions of preceding paragraph apply, and offender (1) has prior conviction under this statute (or substantially similar municipal ordinance) involving similar conditions, or (2) has prior conviction under R.C. §§ 1547.11, 2903.06, 2903.07, 2903.08, 4511.19, 4511.19.2, prior 4507.38 or 4507.39, or municipal ordinance substantially similar to these statutes, or (3) has accumulated 12 points under R.C. § 4507.02.1 within 1 year preceding the offense, or (4) was driving under suspension at the time of the offense, — no eligibility for a sentence to a community control sanction, for judicial release pursuant to RC § 2929.20.

See statute for provision addressing use of alcohol tests in prosecutions under this statute.

NEGLIGENT HOMICIDE, R.C. § 2903.05 [M1]

(1) Negligently
(2) (a) Cause another's death
    (or)
    (b) The unlawful termination of another's pregnancy
(3) By means of a deadly weapon or dangerous ordnance
(4) Venue

Penalty: A misdemeanor of the first degree (2929.21, 2929.31)

Definitions: "Deadly weapon," "dangerous ordnance," R.C. § 2923.11.

AGGRAVATED VEHICULAR HOMICIDE, R.C. § 2903.06 [F3, F2]

(1) Recklessly
(2) (a) Cause another's death
    (or)
    (b) The unlawful termination of another's pregnancy
(3) While operating or participating in operation of
(4) Motor vehicle, motorcycle, snowmobile, locomotive, watercraft, or aircraft
(5) Venue

Penalty: A felony of the third degree (2929.11-2929.18, 2929.31)

If previous conviction hereunder or under R.C. § 2903.04 (involving certain conditions) or 2903.07

Penalty: A felony of the second degree (2929.11-2929.18, 2929.31)

Notes: If previous conviction hereunder or under R.C. §§ 1547.11, 2903.04 (involving certain conditions), 2903.07, 2903.08, 4511.19, or 4511.19.2, 4507.02(B) or (D), 4507.38, or 4507.39 as they existed prior to Sept. 24, 1986, or municipal ordinance substantially similar to §§ 2903.04 (involving certain conditions), 2903.07, 2903.08, 4511.19, or 4511.19.2, or municipal ordinance substantially similar to 4507.38 or 4507.39 as they existed prior to Sept. 24, 1986, or accumulation of 12 points within one year of the offense or if finding that offender was driving under suspension or operating under the influence of alcohol or drug of abuse or combination thereof — the offender shall be sentenced to a mandatory prison term and have no eligibility for a sentence to a community control sanction pursuant to RC § 2923.13, judicial release pursuant to RC § 2929.20, or for a reduction of a stated prison term or a release pursuant to RC § 2967.19.3.

If finding that offender was under the influence of alcohol or drug of abuse or combination thereof—permanent revocation of license

VEHICULAR HOMICIDE, R.C. § 2903.07 [M1, F4]

(1) Negligently
(2) (a) Cause the death of another
    (or)
    (b) The unlawful termination of another's pregnancy
(3) By operating or participating in operation of
(4) Motor vehicle, motorcycle, snowmobile, locomotive, watercraft, or aircraft
(5) Venue

Penalty: A misdemeanor of the first degree (2929.21, 2929.31)

If previous conviction under this section, R.C. § 2903.04 (involving certain conditions), or 2903.06

Penalty: A felony of the fourth degree (2929.11-2929.18, 2929.31)

Notes: If previous conviction hereunder or under R.C. §§ 1547.11, 2903.04 (involving certain conditions), 2903.06, 2903.08, 4511.19, or 4511.19.2, 4507.02(B) or (D), or under 4507.38, or 4507.39, or municipal ordinance substantially similar to §§ 2903.04 (involving certain conditions), 2903.08, 4511.19, or 4511.19.2, or municipal ordinance substantially similar to 4507.38 or 4507.39 as they existed prior to Sept. 24, 1986, or accumulation of 12 points within one year of the offense or if finding that offender was driving under suspension or operating under the influence of alcohol or drug of abuse or combination thereof — the offender shall be sentenced to a mandatory prison term and have no eligibility for a sentence to a community control sanction pursuant to RC § 2923.13, judicial release pursuant to RC § 2929.20, or for a reduction of a stated prison term or a release pursuant to RC § 2967.19.3.

If finding that offender was under the influence of alcohol or drug of abuse or combination thereof—permanent revocation of license

AGGRAVATED VEHICULAR ASSAULT, R.C. § 2903.08 [F4, F3]

(1) (a) While operating
    (or)
    (b) While participating in the operation of
(2) A motor vehicle, motorcycle, snowmobile, locomotive, watercraft, or aircraft
(3) Recklessly cause
(4) Serious physical harm
(5) (a) To another person
    (or)
    (b) Another's unborn
(6) Venue

Penalty: A felony of the fourth degree (2929.11-2929.18, 2929.31)

If previous conviction under R.C. §§ 2903.04 (involving certain conditions), 2903.06, 2903.07, or 2903.08

Penalty: A felony of the third degree (2929.11-2929.18, 2929.31)

Notes: If trier of fact finds offender was under influence of alcohol, drug of abuse, or both, at time of offense — permanent revocation of license.

If offender (1) has prior conviction under this statute (or substantially similar municipal ordinance) involving similar conditions, or (2) has prior conviction under R.C. §§ 1547.11, 2903.04 (under certain conditions), 2903.06, 2903.07, 2903.08, 4511.19, 4511.19.2, prior

4507.38 or 4507.39, or municipal ordinance substantially similar to these statutes, or (3) has accumulated 12 points under R.C. § 4507.02.1 within 1 year preceding the offense, or (4) was driving under suspension at the time of the offense, — the offender shall be sentenced to a mandatory prison term and have no eligibility for a sentence to a community control sanction pursuant to RC § 2923.13, judicial release pursuant to RC § 2929.20, or for a reduction of a stated prison term or a release pursuant to RC § 2967.19.3.

See statute for provision addressing use of alcohol tests in prosecutions under this statute.

FELONIOUS ASSAULT, R.C. § 2903.11 [F2, F1]

(1) Knowingly
(2) (a) Cause serious physical harm to another or to another's unborn
    (or)
    (b) Cause or attempt to cause physical harm to another or to another's unborn by use of deadly weapon/dangerous ordnance
(3) Venue

Penalty: A felony of the second degree (2929.11-2929.18, 2929.31)

If victim is a peace officer

Penalty: A felony of the first degree (2929.11-2929.18, 2929.31)

Definitions: "Deadly weapon," "dangerous ordnance," R.C. § 2923.11.
   "Physical harm to persons," R.C. § 2901.01(C).
   "Serious physical harm to persons," R.C. § 2901.01(E).
   "Firearm," R.C. § 2923.11(B).
   "Peace officer," R.C. § 2935.01(B).

AGGRAVATED ASSAULT, R.C. § 2903.12 [F4, F3]

(1) While under
    (a) the influence of sudden passion or in a sudden fit of rage
    (or)
    (b) extreme emotional stress
(2) Brought on by serious provocation occasioned by the victim reasonably sufficient to incite him to use deadly force
(3) Knowingly
    (a) Cause serious physical harm to another or to another's unborn
    (or)
    (b) Cause or attempt to cause physical harm to another or to another's unborn by means of deadly weapon or dangerous ordnance
(4) Venue

Penalty: A felony of the fourth degree (2929.11-2929.18, 2929.31)

If the victim is a peace officer

Penalty: A felony of the third degree (2929.11-2929.18, 2929.31)

Definitions: "Deadly weapon," "dangerous ordnance," "firearm," R.C. § 2923.11.
   "Peace officer," R.C. § 2935.01(B).

ASSAULT, R.C. § 2903.13 [M1, F5, F4, F3]

Division (A):
(1) Knowingly
(2) Cause or attempt to cause
(3) Physical harm to another or to another's unborn
(4) Venue

Division (B):
(1) Recklessly
(2) Cause serious physical harm to another or to another's unborn
(3) Venue

Penalty: A misdemeanor of the first degree (2929.21, 2929.31)

If committed by a caretaker against a functionally impaired person under the caretaker's care

Penalty: A felony of the fourth degree (2929.11-2929.18, 2929.31)

If committed by a caretaker against a functionally impaired person under the caretaker's care, and if the offender has been previously convicted under R.C. § 2903.11, 2903.13, or 2903.16, and if the previous offense was against a functionally impaired person under the care of the offender, who was acting as a caretaker

Penalty: A felony of the third degree (2929.11-2929.18, 2929.31)

If committed (a) in or on the grounds of a state correctional institution or an institution of the Department of Youth Services, the victim is an employee of the Department of Rehabilitation and Correction, the Department of Youth Services, or a probation department or is on the premises of the particular institution for business purposes or as a visitor, and the offense is committed by a person incarcerated in the state correctional institution, a person institutionalized in the Department of Youth Services institution pursuant to a commitment to the Department of Youth Services, or a probationer, furloughee, or parolee; or (b) in or on the grounds of a local correctional facility, the victim is an employee of the local correctional facility or a probation department or is on the premises of the facility for business purposes or as a visitor, and the offense is committed by a person who is under custody in the facility subsequent to the person's arrest for any crime or delinquent act, subsequent to the person being charged with or convicted of any crime, or subsequent to the person being alleged to be or adjudicated a delinquent child; or (c) off the grounds of a state correctional institution and off the grounds of an institution of the Department of Youth Services, the victim is an employee of the Department of Rehabilitation and Correction, the Department of Youth Services, or a probation department, the offense occurs during the employee's official work hours and while the employee is engaged in official work responsibilities, and the offense is committed by a person incarcerated in a state correctional institution or institutionalized in the Department of Youth Services who temporarily is outside of the institution for any purpose or by a probationer, parolee, or furloughee; or (d) off the grounds of a local correctional facility, the victim is an employee of the local correctional facility or probation department, the offense occurs during the employee's official work hours and while the employee is engaged in official work responsibilities, and the offense is committed by a person who is under custody in the facility subsequent to the person's arrest for any crime or delinquent act, subsequent to the person being charged with or convicted of any crime, or subsequent to the person being alleged to be or adjudicated a deliquent child and who temporarily is outside of the facility for any purpose or by a probationer, parolee, or furloughee; or (e) on school premises, in a school building, on a school bus, or while the victim is outside of school premises or a school bus and is engaged in duties or official responsibilities associated with victim's employment as a school teacher or administrator or a school bus operator, including, but not limited to, driving, accompanying, or chaperoning students at or on class or field trips, athletic events or other school extracurricular activities or functions outside school premises

Penalty: A felony of the fifth degree (2929.11-2929.18, 2929.31)

If the victim of the offense is a peace officer, a fire fighter, or person performing emergency medical service, while in the performance of their official duties

Penalty: A felony of the fourth degree (2929.11-2929.18, 2929.31)

Definitions: "Caretaker," "functionally impaired person," R.C. § 2903.10.
   "Peace officer," R.C. § 2935.01(B).
   "School," "school building," "school premises," R.C. § 2925.01
   "School bus," R.C. § 4511.01

NEGLIGENT ASSAULT, R.C. § 2903.14 [M3]

(1) Negligently
(2) By means of a deadly weapon or dangerous ordnance
(3) Cause physical harm to another or to another's unborn
(4) Venue

Penalty: A misdemeanor of the third degree (2929.21, 2929.31)

Definitions: "Deadly weapon," "dangerous ordnance," R.C. § 2923.11.

FAILING TO PROVIDE FOR A FUNCTIONALLY IMPAIRED PERSON, R.C. § 2903.16 [M1, M2, F4]

Division (A): Knowingly Failing to Provide for a Functionally Impaired Person
(1) Being a caretaker
(2) Knowingly
(3) Fail to provide
(4) To a functionally impaired person under the caretaker's care
(5) Any treatment, care, goods, or service
(6) Necessary to maintain the health or safety of the functionally impaired person
(7) When the failure results in physical harm or serious physical harm to the functionally impaired person
(8) Venue

Penalty: A misdemeanor of the first degree (2929.21, 2929.31)

If the functionally impaired person under the offender's care suffers serious physical harm as a result of the violation

Penalty: A felony of the fourth degree (2929.11-2929.18, 2929.31)

Division (B): Recklessly Failing to Provide for a Functionally Impaired Person
(1) Being a caretaker
(2) Recklessly
(3) Fail to provide
(4) To a functionally impaired person under the caretaker's care

§ 2903.21   Ohio Criminal Law Handbook   A-36

(5) Any treatment, care, goods, or service
(6) Necessary to maintain the health or safety of the functionally impaired person
(7) When the failure results in serious physical harm to the functionally impaired person
(8) Venue

Penalty: A misdemeanor of the second degree (2929.21, 2929.31)

If the functionally impaired person under the offender's care suffers serious physical harm as a result of the violation

Penalty: A felony of the fourth degree (2929.11-2929.18, 2929.31)

Note: See R.C. § 2903.34 for similar offenses involving residents or patients of care facilities

Definitions: "Caretaker," "Functionally impaired person," R.C. § 2903.10

AGGRAVATED MENACING, R.C. § 2903.21 [M1]

(1) Knowingly
(2) Cause another to believe
(3) That the offender will cause serious physical harm to the person or property of such other person, such other person's unborn, or member of the other person's immediate family
(4) Venue

Penalty: A misdemeanor of the first degree (2929.21, 2929.31)

MENACING BY STALKING, R.C. § 2903.21.1 [M1, F5]

(1) By engaging in a pattern of conduct
(2) Knowingly
(3) (a) Cause another to believe that the offender will cause physical harm to the other person
      (or)
   (b) Cause mental distress to the other person
(4) Venue

Penalty: A misdemeanor of the first degree (2929.21, 2929.31)

If prior conviction under this statute involving same victim

Penalty: A felony of the fifth degree (2929.11-2929.18, 2929.31)

Notes: See R.C. § 2903.21.2 for special provisions concerning repeat offenders and offenders violating prior anti-stalking orders.
See R.C. § 2903.21.2 for special provisions concerning bail.
See R.C. § 2903.21.3 for special provisions concerning anti-stalking protection orders.
See R.C. § 2919.26 for special provisions concerning protection orders.
See R.C. § 2925.03 for special provisions concerning arrest and detention.

Definitions: "Pattern of conduct" means two or more actions or incidents closely related in time, regardless of whether there has been a prior conviction based on any of those actions or incidents, R.C. § 2903.21.1.

"Mental distress" means any mental illness or condition that involves some temporary substantial incapacity or mental illness or condition that would normally require psychiatric treatment, R.C. § 2903.21.1.

MENACING, R.C. § 2903.22 [M4]

(1) Knowingly
(2) Cause another to believe

(3) That the offender will cause physical harm to the person or property of such other person, such other person's unborn, or member of the other person's immediate family
(4) Venue

Penalty: A misdemeanor of the fourth degree (2929.21, 2929.31)

HAZING, R.C. § 2903.31 [M4]

Division (B)(1):
(1) Recklessly
(2) Participate in hazing
(3) Another
(4) Venue

Division (B)(2):
(1) Being an administrator, employee, or faculty member
(2) Of a public or private primary, secondary, post-secondary school, or other educational institution
(3) Recklessly
(4) Permit hazing
(5) Any person
(6) Venue

Penalty: A misdemeanor of the fourth degree (2929.21, 2929.31)

Notes: Hazing is defined as doing any act or coercing another, including the victim, to do any act of initiation into any student or other organization that causes or creates a substantial risk of causing mental or physical harm to any person. R.C. § 2903.31(A).

See R.C. § 2307.44 for provisions regarding civil liability.

PATIENT ABUSE; NEGLECT, R.C. § 2903.34 [M1, M2, F3, F4, F5]

A. PATIENT ABUSE [F4, F3]

(1) While owning, operating, administering, or an agent or employee of a care facility
(2) (a) Knowingly cause physical harm
    (or)
    (b) Recklessly cause serious physical harm
(3) To a resident or patient of the facility
(4) (a) By physical contact with the person
    (or)
    (b) By the inappropriate use of physical or chemical restraint, medication, or isolation on the person (i.e., use as punishment, for staff convenience, excessively, as substitute for treatment, or in quantities which preclude habilitation or treatment)
(5) Venue

If no prior offense under this section

Penalty: A felony of the fourth degree (2929.11-2929.18, 2929.31)

If prior offense under this section

Penalty: A felony of the third degree (2929.11-2929.18, 2929.31)

B. GROSS PATIENT NEGLECT [M1, F5]

(1) While owning, operating, administering, or an agent or employee of a care facility

(2) Knowingly
(3) Fail to provide
(4) To a resident or patient of the facility
(5) Any treatment, care, goods, or service
(6) Necessary to maintain the health or safety of the person
(7) When the failure results in physical harm or serious physical harm to the person
(8) Venue

If no prior offense under this section

Penalty: A misdemeanor of the first degree (2929.21, 2929.31)

If prior offense under this section

Penalty: A felony of the fifth degree (2929.11-2929.18, 2929.31)

C. PATIENT NEGLECT [M2, F5]

(1) While owning, operating, administering, or an agent or employee of a care facility
(2) Recklessly
(3) Fail to provide
(4) To a resident or patient of the facility
(5) Any treatment, care, goods, or service
(6) Necessary to maintain the health or safety of the person
(7) When the failure results in serious physical harm to the person
(8) Venue

If no prior offense under this section

Penalty: A misdemeanor of the second degree (2929.21, 2929.31)

If prior offense under this section

Penalty: A felony of the fifth degree (2929.11-2929.18, 2929.31)

Notes: Any individual convicted of felony violation of this statute who is required to be licensed under Ohio law shall have license revoked. R.C. § 2903.37.

Affirmative defense to charge of neglect or gross neglect that conduct in good faith solely because ordered by person with supervisory authority. *See* R.C. § 2903.34(B)(2).

Person who relies on treatment by spiritual means through prayer alone under tenets of recognized denomination not to be considered neglected under (C) above for that reason alone. *See* R.C. § 2903.34(B)(1).

Discharge, discrimination, and retaliation for filing complaint, etc. prohibited, *see* R.C. § 2903.36.

Filing false complaint, *see* R.C. § 2903.35.

Attorney General to investigate, refer, and (when appropriate) prosecute violations, *see* R.C. § 109.86.

Local officials — proceedings hereunder, *see* R.C. § 109.86.

See also R.C. §§ 2903.11, 2903.13, 2903.16 for similar offenses involving functionally impaired persons.

Definitions: "Care facility," "abuse," "gross neglect," "neglect," "inappropriate use of a physical or chemical restraint, medication, or isolation," RC § 2903.33.

FILING A FALSE PATIENT ABUSE OR NEGLECT COMPLAINT, R.C. § 2903.35 [M1]

(1) Knowingly
(2) (a) Make a false statement
    (or)
    (b) Swear or affirm the truth of a false statement previously made
(3) Alleging a violation of R.C. § 2903.34
(4) When statement made with purpose to incriminate another
(5) Venue

Penalty: A misdemeanor of the first degree (2929.21, 2929.31)

KIDNAPPING AND EXTORTION

KIDNAPPING, R.C. § 2905.01 [F1, F2]

Division (A):
(1) (a) By force, threat, or deception
    (or)
    (b) By any means where victim is under 13 or mentally incompetent
(2) (a) Remove person from the place the other person is found
    (or)
    (b) Restrain another person of the other person's liberty
(3) With a purpose to:
    (a) Hold for ransom, or as a shield or hostage
    (b) Facilitate commission of any felony or flight thereafter
    (c) Terrorize or inflict serious physical harm on the victim or another
    (d) Engage in sexual activity (R.C. § 2907.01) with the victim against the victim's will
    (e) Hinder, impede, or obstruct a function of government, or to force any action or concession on the part of governmental authority
(4) Venue

Division (B):
(1) (a) By force, threat, or deception
    (or)
    (b) By any means where victim is under 13 or mentally incompetent
(2) Knowingly
(3) Under circumstances creating a substantial risk of serious physical harm to the victim or, in the case of a minor victim, under circumstances that either create a substantial risk of serious physical harm to the victim or cause physical harm to the victim
(4) (a) Remove another from the place the other person is found
    (or)
    (b) Restrain another of the other person's liberty
    (or)
    (c) Hold another in a condition of involuntary servitude
(5) Venue

Penalty: A felony of the first degree (2929.11-2929.18, 2929.31)
If victim released in a safe place unharmed

Penalty: A felony of the second degree (2929.11-2929.18, 2929.31)

ABDUCTION, R.C. § 2905.02 [F3]

(1) Knowingly
(2) (a) Remove another by force or threat from the place where the other person is found
(*or*)
  (b) Restrain the liberty of another person by force or threat under circumstances creating a risk of physical harm to the victim or by placing the other person in fear
(*or*)
  (c) Hold another in a condition of involuntary servitude
(3) Without privilege to do so
(4) Venue

Penalty: A felony of the third degree (2929.11-2929.18, 2929.31)

UNLAWFUL RESTRAINT, R.C. § 2905.03 [M3]

(1) Knowingly
(2) Restrain another of his liberty
(3) Without privilege to do so
(4) Venue

Penalty: A misdemeanor of the third degree (2929.21, 2929.31)

CRIMINAL CHILD ENTICEMENT, R.C. § 2905.05 [M1, F5]

(1) Knowingly
(2) By any means
(3) Without privilege to do so
(4) Solicit, coax, entice, or lure
(5) Any child under 14 years of age (regardless of actor's ignorance of child's age)
(6) To enter into any vehicle as defined in R.C. § 4501.01
(7) If actor does not have express or implied consent of child's parent, guardian, or other legal custodian
(8) (a) Where actor is not either of the following
   (i) A law enforcement officer, medic, firefighter, or other person regularly providing emergency services
(*or*)
   (ii) An employee or agent of, or volunteer acting under the direction of, any board of education
(*or*)
  (b) Where actor is a person described in (a)(i) or (ii) who at the time is not acting within the scope of the actor's lawful duties in that capacity
(9) Venue

Penalty: A misdemeanor of the first degree (2929.21, 2929.31)

If prior conviction under this section 2907.02, 2907.03 or 2907.12, or 2905.01 or 2907.05 when the victim was under 17

Penalty: A felony of the fifth degree (2929.11-2929.18, 2929.31)

Note: It is an affirmative defense that the actor undertook the activity in response to a bona fide emergency situation, or in a reasonable belief that it was necessary to preserve the health, safety, or welfare of the child.

EXTORTION, R.C. § 2905.11 [F3]
(1) With a purpose to:
    (a) Obtain anything of value or valuable benefit
        (or)
    (b) To induce another to do any unlawful act
(2) (a) Threaten to commit a felony
        (or)
    (b) Threaten to commit an offense of violence
        (or)
    (c) Violate R.C. §§ 2903.21 or 2903.22
        (or)
    (d) Utter or threaten any calumny against any person
        (or)
    (e) Expose or threaten to expose any matter that tends to:
       (i) Subject any person to hatred, contempt, or ridicule
          (or)
       (ii) Damage any person's personal or business reputation
          (or)
       (iii) Impair any person's credit
(3) Venue

Penalty: A felony of the third degree (2929.11-2929.18, 2929.31)
Note: Threat includes direct threat and threat by innuendo.

COERCION, R.C. § 2905.12 [M2]
(1) With purpose to coerce another into taking or refraining from action concerning which he has a legal freedom of choice
(2) (a) Threaten to commit any offense
        (or)
    (b) Utter or threaten any calumny against any person
        (or)
    (c) Expose or threaten to expose any matter tending to:
       (i) Subject any person to hatred, contempt, or ridicule
          (or)
       (ii) Damage his personal or business repute
          (or)
       (iii) Impair his credit
          (or)
    (d) Institute or threaten criminal proceedings against any person
        (or)
    (e) Take or withhold, or threaten to take or to withhold official action, or cause or threaten to cause official action to be taken or withheld
(3) Venue

Penalty: A misdemeanor of the second degree (2929.21, 2929.31)
Notes: Threat includes direct threat and threat by innuendo.
    Affirmative defenses are set forth in the statute.

EXTORTIONATE EXTENSION OF CREDIT; CRIMINAL USURY, R.C. § 2905.22 [F4, M1]
Division (A)(1) or (2): **[F4]**
(1) Knowingly

(2) Make or participate in an extortionate extension of credit
   (*or*)
(3) Engage in criminal usury
(4) Venue

Penalty: A felony of the fourth degree (2929.11-2929.18, 2929.31)

Division (A)(3): **[M1]**
(1) Possess
(2) Any writing, paper, instrument or article used to record criminally usurious transactions
(3) Knowing that the contents record a criminally usurious transaction
(4) Venue

Penalty: A misdemeanor of the first degree (2929.21, 2929.31)

Notes: See R.C. § 2905.23 for standard of proof that an extension of credit is extortionate.

See R.C. § 2905.24 for evidence admissible to prove an implicit threat as means of collection.

Definitions: "To extend credit," "collect an extension of credit," "extortionate extension of credit," "extortionate means," "criminal usury," R.C. § 2905.21.

SEX OFFENSES

RAPE, R.C. § 2907.02 [F1]

(1) Engage in sexual conduct
(2) (a) With another by purposely compelling submission by force or threat of force
       (*or*)
    (b) With another not offender's spouse or with offender's spouse if living separate and apart, if:
       (i) For purpose of preventing resistance, offender substantially impairs victim's judgment or control by administering any drug/intoxicant surreptitiously or by force, threat of force, or deception
          (*or*)
       (ii) Victim under 13, regardless of offender's knowledge of age
          (*or*)
       (iii) Victim's ability to resist or consent is substantially impaired because of a mental or physical condition or because of advanced age and the offender knows or has reasonable cause to believe that the victim's ability to resist or consent is substantially impaired by such condition or advanced age
(3) Venue

Penalty: A felony of the first degree (2929.11-2929.18, 2929.31)

If both elements 2(a) and 2(b)(ii) apply

Penalty: Life imprisonment

Notes: Victim need not prove physical resistance.

See R.C. § 2907.02(D)-(F) for provisions re evidence of prior sexual activity of victim/offender, admissibility of evidence, and victim's right to counsel in proceeding to determine admissibility.

See R.C. § 2907.27 for provisions regarding mandatory medical tests for persons charged under this statute.

The provisions of § 7 of SB 199 (139 v —, eff 1-5-83) read as follows:

SECTION 7. Any person who commits a violation of section 2907.02 or 2907.12 of the Revised Code before July 1, 1983, and after August 27, 1975, who has previously been convicted of a violation of either section, and who is not subject to imprisonment for life under either section shall be sentenced pursuant to section 2929.11 of the Revised Code and pursuant to the version of section 2907.10 of the Revised Code as it existed immediately preceding July 1, 1983, notwithstanding the fact that section 2907.10 of the Revised Code is repealed by this act.

SEXUAL BATTERY, R.C. § 2907.03 [F3, F4]

(1) Engage in sexual conduct
(2) With a person not the spouse of the offender when the offender:
   (a) Knowingly coerced the other person to submit by any means that would prevent resistance by a person of ordinary resolution
     (or)
   (b) Knows that the other's ability to appraise the nature of or control the other person's own conduct is substantially impaired
     (or)
   (c) Knows the other person submits because the other person is unaware that the act is being committed
     (or)
   (d) Knows the other person submits because the other person mistakenly identifies the offender as the other person's spouse
     (or)
   (e) Is the other person's natural/adoptive parent, stepparent, guardian, custodian, or person in loco parentis
     (or)
   (f) Has supervisory or disciplinary authority over the other person and such person is in legal custody or a patient in a hospital or other institution
     (or)
   (g) Is a teacher, administrator, coach, or other person in authority in a school for which the state board of education prescribes minimum standards in which the other person is enrolled or attends that school and the offender is not enrolled and does not attend that school
     (or)
   (h) The other person is a minor, the offender is a teacher, administrator, coach, or other person in authority employed by or serving in an institution of higher education and the other person is enrolled in that institution
     (or)
   (i) The other person is a minor, and the offender is the other person's athletic or other type of coach, is the other person's instructor, is the leader of a scouting troop of which the other person is a member, or is a person with temporary or occasional disciplinary control over the other person
(3) Venue

§ 2907.04

Violation of divisions (a), (e), (f), (g), (h), (i)

Penalty: A felony of the third degree (2929.11-2929.18, 2929.31)

Violation of divisions (b), (c), (d) **[F4]**

Penalty: A felony of the fourth degree (2929.11-2929.18, 2929.31)

Note: See R.C. § 2907.27 for provisions regarding mandatory medical tests for persons charged under this statute.

CORRUPTION OF A MINOR, R.C. § 2907.04 [F4, M1]

(1) Being 18 or older
(2) Engage in sexual conduct
(3) With another who is not the offender's spouse when:
    (a) Offender knows the other person is 13 years of age or older, but less than 16 years of age
    (or)
    (b) Offender is reckless in this regard
(4) Venue

Penalty: A felony of the fourth degree (2929.11-2929.18, 2929.31)

If offender is less than 4 years older than the victim

Penalty: A misdemeanor of the first degree (2929.21, 2929.31)

Note: See R.C. § 2907.27 for provisions regarding mandatory medical tests for persons charged under this statute.

GROSS SEXUAL IMPOSITION, R.C. § 2907.05 [F4, F3]

(1) (a) Have sexual contact with another, not the spouse of the offender
    (or)
    (b) Cause another, not the spouse of the offender, to have sexual contact with the offender
    (or)
    (c) Cause two or more other persons to have sexual contact
(2) (a) By purposely compelling the other, or one of the others, to submit by force or threat of force
    (or)
    (b) For the purpose of preventing resistance, the offender substantially impairs the judgment or control of the other person or of one of the other persons by administering any drug or intoxicant to the other person, surreptitiously or by force, threat of force, or deception
    (or)
    (c) The offender knows that the judgment or control of the other person, or of one of the other persons is substantially impaired as a result of the influence of any drug or intoxicant administered to the other person with his consent for the purpose of any kind of medical or dental examination, treatment, or surgery
    (or)
    (d) The other person, or one of the other persons, is less than thirteen years of age whether or not the offender knows the age of that person
    (or)

(e) The ability of the other person to resist or consent or the ability of one of the other persons to resist or consent is substantially impaired because of a mental or physical condition or because of advanced age, and the offender knows or has reasonable cause to believe that the ability to resist or consent of the other person or one of the other persons is substantially impaired because of a mental or physical condition or because of advanced age

(3) Venue

Penalty: A felony of the fourth degree (2929.11-2929.18, 2929.31)

Where other person is less than 13, regardless of whether offender knows the age

Penalty: A felony of the third degree (2929.11-2929.18, 2929.31)

Notes: Victim need not prove physical resistance.

See R.C. § 2907.05(D)-(F) for provisions re evidence of prior sexual activity of victim/offender, admissibility of evidence, and victim's right to counsel in proceeding to determine admissibility.

SEXUAL IMPOSITION, R.C. § 2907.06 [M3, M1]

(1) (a) Have sexual contact with another, not the spouse of the offender
    (*or*)
  (b) Cause another, not the spouse of the offender, to have sexual contact with the offender
    (*or*)
  (c) Cause two or more other persons to have sexual contact
(2) (a) The offender knows that the sexual contact is offensive to the other person, or one of the other persons, or is reckless in that regard
    (*or*)
  (b) The offender knows that the other person's, or one of the other persons', ability to appraise the nature of or control the offender's or the touching person's conduct is substantially impaired
    (*or*)
  (c) The offender knows that the other person, or one of the other persons, submits because of being unaware of the sexual contact
    (*or*)
  (d) The other person, or one of the other persons, is 13 years of age or older, but less than 16 years of age, regardless of the offender's knowledge of this, and the offender is at least 18 and 4 or more years older than such other person.
(3) Venue

Penalty: A misdemeanor of the third degree (2929.21, 2929.31)

If prior conviction under this section or RC §§ 2907.02, 2907.03, 2907.04, 2907.05, or 2907.12

Penalty: A misdemeanor of the first degree (2929.21, 2929.31)

Note: A person may not be convicted of sexual imposition without evidence corroborating victim's testimony.

IMPORTUNING, R.C. § 2907.07 [M1, M4]

Division (A): [**M1**]
(1) Solicit a person under 13
(2) To engage in sexual activity with the offender

§ 2907.08

(3) Whether or not offender knows age of such person
(4) Venue

Division (B): [M1]
(1) Solicit person of same sex
(2) To engage in sexual activity
(3) Knowing such solicitation is offensive to the other person, or being reckless in this regard
(4) Venue
Penalty: A misdemeanor of the first degree (2929.21, 2929.31)

Division (C): [M4]
(1) Solicit another person, not the spouse of offender
(2) To engage in sexual conduct with the offender
(3) When offender is 18 or older and 4 or more years older than other person, and other person is over 12 years but not over 15 years
(4) Whether or not offender knows age of such person
(5) Venue
Penalty: A misdemeanor of the fourth degree (2929.21, 2929.31)

VOYEURISM, R.C. § 2907.08 [M3]

(1) Trespass or otherwise surreptitiously invade privacy of another
(2) To spy or eavesdrop upon another
(3) With purpose of sexually arousing or gratifying self
(4) Venue
Penalty: A misdemeanor of the third degree (2929.21, 2929.31)

PUBLIC INDECENCY, R.C. § 2907.09 [M4, M3, M2, M1]

(1) Recklessly
(2) Under circumstances likely to be viewed by and affront others not members of his or her household
(3) (a) Expose his or her private parts, or masturbate
    (*or*)
    (b) Engage in sexual conduct
    (*or*)
    (c) Engage in conduct appearing to ordinary observer to be sexual conduct or masturbation
(4) Venue
Penalty: A misdemeanor of the fourth degree (2929.21, 2929.31)
One prior conviction under this section
Penalty: A misdemeanor of the third degree (2929.21, 2929.31)
Two prior convictions under this section
Penalty: A misdemeanor of the second degree (2929.21, 2929.31)
Three or more prior convictions under this section
Penalty: A misdemeanor of the first degree (2929.21, 2929.31)

COMPELLING PROSTITUTION, R.C. § 2907.21 [F3, F2]

(1) Knowingly
(2) (a) Compel another to engage in sexual activity for hire

(or)
- (b) Induce, procure, encourage, solicit, request, or otherwise facilitate a minor to engage in sexual activity for hire, whether or not there is actual knowledge as to minor's age
(or)
- (c) Pay or agree to pay a minor, directly or through the minor's agent, so that the minor will engage in sexual activity, whether or not there is actual knowledge of the minor's age
(or)
- (d) Pay a minor, directly or through the minor's agent, for the minor having engaged in sexual activity pursuant to a prior agreement, whether or not there is actual knowledge of the minor's age
- (e) Allow a minor to engage in sexual activity for hire if the person allowing the child to engage in sexual activity for hire is the parent, guardian, custodian, person having custody or control, or person in loco parentis of the minor

(3) Venue

Penalty: A felony of the third degree (2929.11-2929.18, 2929.31)

If offender commits a violation of Division (2)(a) and the person compelled to engage in sexual activity for hire is less than 16

Penalty: A felony of the second degree (2929.11-2929.18, 2929.31)

Notes: See R.C. § 2907.26 for rules of evidence in prostitution cases.

Sentences of imprisonment for violations under 2(b), (c), and (d) above are to be served consecutively to any other sentence of imprisonment, R.C. § 2929.41.

Definitions: "Minor" means a person under the age of eighteen, R.C. § 2907.01

"Sexual activity," R.C. § 2907.01

PROMOTING PROSTITUTION, R.C. § 2907.22 [F4, F3]

(1) Knowingly
(2) (a) Establish, maintain, operate, manage, supervise, control, or have an interest in a brothel
(or)
- (b) Supervise, manage or control activities of a prostitute in engaging in sexual activity for hire
(or)
- (c) (i) Transport, or cause another to be transported
  (ii) Across the boundary of Ohio or any county in Ohio
  (iii) To facilitate the other person's engaging in sexual activity for hire
(or)
- (d) (i) Induce or procure another to engage in sexual activity for hire
  (ii) For the purpose of violating or facilitating a violation of this section

(3) Venue

Penalty: A felony of the fourth degree (2929.11-2929.18, 2929.31)

If the prostitute or the person transported, induced, or procured to engage in sexual activity for hire is a minor, regardless of whether the offender knows the age

Penalty: A felony of the third degree (2929.11-2929.18, 2929.31)

Notes: See R.C. § 2907.26 for rules of evidence in prostitution cases.

Any sentence of imprisonment imposed for an F3 conviction is to be served consecutively to any other term of imprisonment.

Definitions: "Minor" means a person under the age of eighteen, R.C. § 2907.01
"Sexual activity," R.C. § 2907.01

PROCURING, R.C. § 2907.23 [M1]

Division (A):
(1) Knowingly
(2) For gain
(3) (a) Entice or solicit another to patronize a prostitute or brothel
(or)
(b) Procure a prostitute for another to patronize
(or)
(c) Take or direct another person to place for the purpose of patronizing a prostitute as requested by such other person
(4) Venue

Division (B):
(1) While having authority/responsibility over premises
(2) Knowingly
(3) Permit the premises to be used
(4) For the purpose of engaging in sexual activity for hire
(5) Venue

Penalty: A misdemeanor of the first degree (2929.21, 2929.31)

Note: See R.C. § 2907.26 for rules of evidence in prostitution cases.

SOLICITING; AFTER POSITIVE HIV TEST, R.C. § 2907.24 [M3, F3]

Division (A): [M3]
(1) Solicit another
(2) To engage in sexual activity for hire
(3) Venue

Penalty: A misdemeanor of the third degree (2929.21, 2929.31)

Division (B): [F3]
(1) Engage in conduct in violation of Division A
(2) With knowledge that he or she has tested positive as a carrier of a virus that causes AIDS
(3) Venue

Penalty: A felony of the third degree (2929.11-2929.18, 2929.31)

Notes: See R.C. § 2907.26 for rules of evidence in prostitution cases.
See R.C. § 2907.27 for provisions regarding mandatory medical tests for persons charged under this statute.

LOITERING TO ENGAGE IN SOLICITATION; SOLICITATION AFTER A POSITIVE HIV TEST, R.C. § 2907.24.1 [M3, F5]

Division (A): [M3]
(1) (a) Beckon to, stop, or attempt to stop another
(or)
(b) Engage, or attempt to engage another in conversation

(or)
- (c) Stop or attempt to stop the operator of a vehicle or approach a stationary vehicle
  (or)
- (d) If the offender is the operator of or a passenger in a vehicle, stop, attempt to stop, beckon to, attempt to beckon to, or entice another to approach or enter the vehicle of which the offender is the operator or passenger
  (or)
- (e) Interfere with the passage of another
(2) While in or near a public place
(3) With purpose to solicit another to engage in sexual activity for hire
(4) Venue

Penalty: A misdemeanor of the third degree (2929.21, 2929.31)

Division (B): **[F5]**
(1) Engage in conduct in violation of Division (A)
(2) With knowledge that he or she has tested positive as a carrier of a virus that causes AIDS
(3) Venue

Penalty: A felony of the fifth degree (2929.11-2929.18, 2929.31)

PROSTITUTION; AFTER POSITIVE HIV TEST, R.C. § 2907.25 [M3, F3]

Division (A): **[M3]**
(1) Engage in sexual activity
(2) For hire
(3) Venue

Penalty: A misdemeanor of the third degree (2929.21, 2929.31)

Division (B): **[F3]**
(1) Engage in sexual activity
(2) For hire
(3) With knowledge that he or she has tested positive as a carrier of a virus that causes AIDS
(4) Venue

Penalty: A felony of the third degree (2929.11-2929.18, 2929.31)

Notes: See R.C. § 2907.26 for rules of evidence in prostitution cases.

See R.C. § 2907.27 for provisions regarding mandatory medical tests for persons charged under this statute.

DISSEMINATING MATTER HARMFUL TO JUVENILES, R.C. § 2907.31 [M1, F5, F4]

(1) Recklessly
(2) With knowledge of its character or content
(3) (a) Sell, deliver, furnish, disseminate, provide, exhibit, rent, or present to a juvenile any material or performance that is obscene or harmful to juveniles
   (or)
   (b) Offer or agree to sell, deliver, furnish, disseminate, provide, exhibit, rent, or present to a juvenile any material or performance that is obscene or harmful to juveniles
   (or)

§ 2907.31.1

(c) Allow any juvenile to review or peruse any material or view any live performance that is harmful to juveniles

(4) Venue

If the material or performance is harmful to juveniles but not obscene

Penalty: A misdemeanor of the first degree (2929.21, 2929.31)

If the material or performance is obscene and the juvenile is thirteen years of age or older

Penalty: A felony of the fifth degree (2929.11-2929.18, 2929.31)

If the material or performance is obscene and the juvenile is under thirteen years of age

Penalty: A felony of the fourth degree (2929.11-2929.18, 2929.31)

Note: See R.C. § 2907.31 for affirmative defenses.

Definitions: "Juvenile" means an unmarried person under the age of eighteen, R.C. § 2907.01
"Harmful to juveniles," "material," "obscene," "performance," R.C. § 2907.01

DISPLAYING MATTER HARMFUL TO JUVENILES, R.C. § 2907.31.1 [M1]

(1) Having custody, control, or supervision of a commercial establishment
(2) With knowledge of the character or content of the material involved
(3) Display at the establishment
(4) Any material that is
    (a) Harmful to juveniles
        (and)
    (b) Open to view by juveniles as part of the invited general public
(5) Venue

Penalty: A misdemeanor of the first degree (2929.21, 2929.31)

Notes: Each day of violation is a separate offense.
See R.C. § 2907.31.1 for provisions regarding "blinder racks," placing material behind counter, etc.

Definitions: "Juvenile" means an unmarried person under the age of eighteen, R.C. § 2907.01
"Harmful to juveniles," "material," "obscene," R.C. § 2907.01

PANDERING OBSCENITY, R.C. § 2907.32 [F5, F4]

(1) Knowing the character of the material or performance involved
(2) (a) (i) Create, reproduce or publish obscene material
       (ii) Knowing that the material is to be used for commercial exploitation or will be publicly disseminated or displayed, or is reckless in that regard
       (or)
   (b) (i) Promote or advertise for sale, delivery, or dissemination, or sell, deliver, or publicly disseminate, display, exhibit, present, rent, provide, or offer to do any of the foregoing
       (ii) Obscene material
       (or)
   (c) (i) Create, direct or produce
       (ii) An obscene performance
       (iii) Knowing it is to be commercially exploited or publicly presented, or being reckless in that regard

(or)
- (d) (i) Advertise or promote an obscene performance for presentation
  - (ii) Present or participate in an obscene performance
  - (iii) Which is presented publicly, or when admission is charged
  (or)
- (e) (i) Buy, procure, possess or control obscene material
  - (ii) With purpose to violate (2) (b) or (2) (d) above

(3) Venue

Penalty: A felony of the fifth degree (2929.11-2929.18, 2929.31)

Where there is a prior conviction under this section or R.C. § 2907.31

Penalty: A felony of the fourth degree (2929.11-2929.18, 2929.31)

Note: See R.C. § 2907.32 for affirmative defenses.

Definitions: "Harmful to juveniles," "material," "obscene," "performance," R.C. § 2907.01

PANDERING OBSCENITY INVOLVING A MINOR, R.C. § 2907.32.1 [F2, F3, F4]

(1) With knowledge of the character of the material or performance

(2) (a) Create, reproduce, or publish
  - (i) Any obscene material
  - (ii) That has a minor as one of its participants or portrayed observers
  - (iii) When the offender knows that it will be used for commercial exploitation or will be publicly disseminated or displayed, or is reckless in that regard
  (or)
- (b) Promote or advertise for sale or dissemination, sell, deliver, or disseminate, display, exhibit, present, rent, or provide, or offer to do any of the foregoing
  - (i) Any obscene material
  - (ii) That has a minor as one of its participants or portrayed observers
  (or)
- (c) Create, direct, or produce
  - (i) An obscene performance
  - (ii) That has a minor as one of its participants
  - (iii) When the offender knows that it will be used for commercial exploitation or will be publicly presented, or is reckless in that regard
  (or)
- (d) Advertise or promote for presentation, present, or participate in presenting
  - (i) An obscene performance
  - (ii) That has a minor as one of its participants
  - (iii) When the performance is presented publicly or admission is charged
  (or)
- (e) Buy, procure, possess, or control
  - (i) Any obscene material
  - (ii) That has a minor as one of its participants
  (or)
- (f) Bring or cause to be brought into this state
  - (i) Any obscene material
  - (ii) That has a minor as one of its participants or portrayed observers

§ 2907.32.2

(3) Venue

Violation of any provision but (e)

Penalty: A felony of the second degree (2929.11-2929.18, 2929.31)

Violation of (e)

Penalty: A felony of the fourth degree (2929.11-2929.18, 2929.31)

If prior conviction under R.C. §§ 2907.32.1—2907.32.3

Penalty: A felony of the third degree (2929.11-2929.18, 2929.31)

Notes: This section does not apply to any material or performance that is sold, disseminated, displayed, possessed, controlled, brought or caused to be brought into this state, or presented for a bona fide medical, scientific, educational, religious, governmental, judicial, or other proper purpose, by or to a physician, psychologist, sociologist, scientist, teacher, person pursuing bona fide studies or research, librarian, clergyman, prosecutor, judge, or other person having a proper interest in the material or performance.

Mistake of age is not a defense.

See R.C. § 2907.32.1 for provisions regarding permissible inferences of age by the trier of fact. A sentence of imprisonment is to be served consecutively to any other sentence of imprisonment, R.C. § 2929.41.

Definitions: "Minor" means a person under the age of eighteen, R.C. § 2907.01

"Material," "obscene," "performance," R.C. § 2907.01

PANDERING SEXUALLY ORIENTED MATTER INVOLVING A MINOR, R.C. § 2907.32.2 [F5, F4, F2]

(1) With knowledge of the character of the material or performance involved

(2) (a) Create, record, photograph, film, develop, reproduce, or publish any material
   (*or*)
   (b) Advertise for sale or dissemination, sell, distribute, transport, disseminate, exhibit, or display any material that shows
   (*or*)
   (c) Create, direct, or produce a performance that shows
   (*or*)
   (d) Advertise for presentation, present, or participate in presenting a performance that shows
   (*or*)
   (e) Solicit, receive, purchase, exchange, possess or control any material that shows
   (*or*)
   (f) Bring or cause to be brought into this state any material that shows
   (*or*)
   (g) Bring, cause to be brought, or finance the bringing of a minor into or across this state, with the intent that
   (*or*)
   (h) Bring, cause to be brought, or finance the bringing of a minor into or across this state, for the purpose of producing material containing a visual representation depicting

(3) A minor

(4) Participating or engaging in sexual activity, masturbation, or bestiality

(5) Venue

Penalty: A felony of the second degree (2929.11-2929.18, 2929.31)

Offense under 2(e), above

Penalty: A felony of the fifth degree (2929.11-2929.18, 2929.31)

Offense under 2(e) above, and prior conviction under R.C. §§ 2907.32.1—2907.32.3

Penalty: A felony of the fourth degree (2929.11-2929.18, 2929.31)

Notes: This section does not apply to materials or performances used for a proper purpose by persons having a proper interest therein. Proper purposes include bona fide medical, scientific, educational, religious, governmental, judicial, and other proper purposes; persons having a proper interest include physicians, psychologists, sociologists, scientists, teachers, persons pursuing bona fide studies or research, librarians, clergymen, prosecutors, judges, or other persons having a proper interest in the material or performance.

Mistake of age is not a defense.

See R.C. § 2907.32.2 for provisions regarding permissible inferences of age by the trier of fact.

A sentence of imprisonment is to be served consecutively to any other sentence of imprisonment.

Definitions: "Minor" means a person under the age of eighteen, R.C. § 2907.01

"Material," "performance," "sexual activity," R.C. § 2907.01

ILLEGAL USE OF MINOR IN NUDITY-ORIENTED MATERIAL OR PERFORMANCE, R.C. § 2907.32.3 [F5, F4, F2]

[A](1) (a) Photograph
  (*or*)
  (b) Create, direct, produce, or transfer any material or performance showing
(2) A minor who is not the actor's child or ward
(3) In a state of nudity
(4) Unless
  (a) The material or performance is or is to be sold, disseminated, displayed, possessed, controlled, brought or caused to be brought into this state
    (i) For a proper purpose
    (ii) By or to a person having a proper interest
    (*and*)
  (b) The minor's parents, guardian, or custodian consents in writing to the photographing of the minor, to the use of the minor in the material or performance, or to the transfer of the material and to the specific manner in which the material or performance is to be used
(5) Venue

[B](1) (a) Photograph
  (*or*)
  (b) Consent to
    (i) Photographing of
      (*or*)
    (ii) Use in any material or performance of
      (*or*)

§ 2907.33 Ohio Criminal Law Handbook A-54

  (c) Use or transfer of any material or performance using
(2) The actor's minor child or ward
(3) In a state of nudity
(4) Unless the material or performance is sold, disseminated, displayed, possessed, controlled, brought or caused to be brought into this state
  (i) For a proper purpose
  (ii) By or to a person having a proper interest
(5) Venue
[C](1) (a) Possess
  (or)
  (b) View
(2) Any material or performance showing
(3) A minor who is not the actor's child or ward
(4) In a state of nudity
(5) Unless
  (a) The material or performance is sold, disseminated, displayed, possessed, controlled, brought or caused to be brought into this state
    (i) For a proper purpose
    (ii) By or to a person having a proper interest
      (or)
  (b) The actor knows that the child's parents, guardian, or custodian has consented in writing to the photographing or use of the minor in a state of nudity, and to the manner in which the material or performance is used or transferred
(6) Venue

Penalty: A felony of the second degree (2929.11-2929.18, 2929.31)

Offense under [C], above

Penalty: A felony of the fifth degree (2929.11-2929.18, 2929.31)

Offense under [C], above, plus prior conviction under R.C. §§ 2907.32.1—2907.32.3

Penalty: A felony of the fourth degree (2929.11-2929.18, 2929.31)

Note: Under this section, a proper purpose is a bona fide artistic, medical, scientific, educational, religious, governmental, judicial, or other proper purpose; a person having a proper interest includes a physician, psychologist, sociologist, scientist, teacher, persons pursuing bona fide studies or research, librarian, clergymen, prosecutor, judge, or other person having a proper interest in the material or performance.

Definitions: "Minor" means a person under the age of eighteen, R.C. § 2907.01
  "Material," "nudity," "performance," R.C. § 2907.01

DECEPTION TO OBTAIN MATTER HARMFUL TO JUVENILES, R.C. § 2907.33 [M2]

Division (A):
(1) With purpose to enable a juvenile to obtain material, or gain admission to a performance, harmful to juveniles
(2) (a) Falsely represent that he is the juvenile's parent, guardian, or spouse
    (or)
  (b) Furnish the juvenile with identification or documents purporting to show the juvenile is 18 or over, or married

(3) Venue

Division (B):
(1) Being a juvenile
(2) For purpose of obtaining material, or gaining admission to a performance, harmful to juveniles
(3) (a) Falsely represent the juvenile is 18 or over or married
(or)
(b) Exhibit identification or documents purporting to show the juvenile is 18 or over or married
(4) Venue

Penalty: A misdemeanor of the second degree (2929.21, 2929.31)

Note: *See* "unruly child," R.C. § 2151.02.2.

Definitions: "Juvenile" means an unmarried person under the age of eighteen, R.C. § 2907.01
"Harmful to juveniles," "material," "performance," R.C. § 2907.01

COMPELLING ACCEPTANCE OF OBJECTIONABLE MATERIALS, R.C. § 2907.34 [F5]

Division (A):
(1) As a precondition to the sale, allocation, consignment, or delivery of any material or goods
(2) Over objections of the purchaser/consignee
(3) Require such purchaser/consignee
(4) To accept other material reasonably believed to be obscene, or which, if furnished/presented to a juvenile, would violate R.C. § 2907.31
(5) Venue

Division (B):
(1) (a) Deny or threaten to deny any franchise to
(or)
(b) Impose or threaten to impose any financial penalty upon
(2) Any purchaser or consignee
(3) (a) Because the purchaser or consignee failed or refused to accept any material reasonably believed to be obscene as a condition to the sale, allocation, consignment, or delivery of any other material or goods
(or)
(b) Because purchaser or consignee returned any material believed to be obscene which the purchaser or consignee initially accepted
(4) Venue

Penalty: A felony of the fifth degree (2929.11-2929.18, 2929.31)

Definitions: "Material," "obscene," R.C. § 2907.01

ARSON AND RELATED OFFENSES

AGGRAVATED ARSON, R.C. § 2909.02 [F2, F1]

(1) Knowingly
(2) (a) Create substantial risk of serious physical harm to any person other than the offender

(or)
    (b) Cause physical harm to an occupied structure
    (or)
    (c) Create, through the offer or acceptance of an agreement for hire or other consideration, a substantial risk of physical harm to any occupied structure
(3) By means of fire or explosion
(4) Venue

Violation of Division (2)(a) or (c)
Penalty: A felony of the first degree (2929.11-2929.18, 2929.31)
Violation of Division (2)(b)
Penalty: A felony of the second degree (2929.11-2929.18, 2929.31)
Notes: R.C. § 2929.28 sets forth requirements for hearings on reimbursement to agencies.
Definitions: "Create a substantial risk of serious physical harm to any person" includes the creation of a substantial risk of serious physical harm to any emergency personnel, R.C. § 2909.01.
    "Emergency personnel," R.C. § 2909.01.
    "Occupied structure," R.C. § 2909.01.
    "Political subdivision," R.C. § 2909.01.
    "State," R.C. § 2909.01.

ARSON, R.C. § 2909.03 [F4, F3, M1]

(1) Knowingly
(2) (a) Cause or create substantial risk of physical harm to any property of another without the other person's consent
    (or)
    (b) Cause or create substantial risk of physical harm to any property of the offender or another, with purpose to defraud
    (or)
    (c) Cause or create substantial risk of physical harm to statehouse, courthouse, school building, or other building or structure owned or controlled by state or any political subdivision, or any department, agency, instrumentality of either the state or a political subdivision, and used for public purpose
    (or)
    (d) Cause, or create a substantial risk of, physical harm, through the offer or the acceptance of an agreement for hire or other consideration, to any property of another without the other person's consent or to any property of the offender or another with purpose to defraud
    (e) Cause, or create a substantial risk of, physical harm to any park, preserve, wildlands, brush-covered land, cut-over land, forest, timberland, greenlands, woods, or similar real property that is owned or controlled by another person, the state, or a political subdivision without the consent of the other person, the state, or the political subdivision;
    (or)
    (f) With purpose to defraud, cause, or create a substantial risk of, physical harm to any park, preserve, wildlands, brush-covered land, cut-over land, forest, timberland, greenlands, woods, or similar real property that is owned or controlled by the offender, another person, the state, or a political subdivision
(3) By means of fire or explosion
(4) Venue

Violation of (2)(a) above, value of property or amount of physical harm less than $500
Penalty: A misdemeanor of the first degree (2929.21, 2929.31)
Violation of (2)(a) above, value of property or amount of physical harm $500 or more
Penalty: A felony of the fourth degree (2929.11-2929.18, 2929.31)
Violation of (2)(b), (c), (e), or (f)
Penalty: A felony of the fourth degree (2929.11-2929.18, 2929.31)
Violation of (2)(d)
Penalty: A felony of the third degree (2929.11-2929.18, 2929.31)
Notes: R.C. § 2929.21(A) requires restitution to governmental authorities.
  R.C. § 2909.11 sets forth requirements for findings concerning property value damage and amount of physical harm.
  R.C. § 2929.28 sets forth requirements for hearings on reimbursement to agencies.
Definitions: "Political subdivision," R.C. § 2909.01.
  "State," R.C. § 2909.01.

DISRUPTING PUBLIC SERVICES, R.C. § 2909.04 [F4]

(1) (a) Purposely by any means
    (or)
  (b) Knowingly, by damaging or tampering with property
(2) Interrupt or impair
  (a) TV, radio, telephone, telegraph, or other mass communications service
    (or)
  (b) Police, fire, other public service communications
    (or)
  (c) Radar, loran, radio, other electronic aids to air or marine navigation or communications
    (or)
  (d) Amateur or citizens band radio communications being used for public service or emergency communications
    (or)
  (e) Public transportation, including school bus transportation, water supply, gas, power, other utility service to public
    (or)
(3) Substantially impair
  (a) Ability of law enforcement officers, firemen, rescue personnel to respond to emergency or to protect and preserve any person or property from serious physical harm
(4) Venue

Penalty: A felony of the fourth degree (2929.11-2929.18, 2929.31)

VANDALISM, R.C. § 2909.05 [F5, F4, F3]

Division (A):
(1) Knowingly cause serious physical harm to
(2) Occupied structure or any of its contents
(3) Venue

Division (B)(1):
(1) Knowingly cause serious physical harm to
(2) Property owned or possessed by another and which is

§ 2909.06   Ohio Criminal Law Handbook   A-58

   (a) Used by its owner or possessor in the owner or possessor's profession, business, trade, occupation, and value of property or physical harm is $500 or more
       (or)
   (b) Such property or equivalent necessary for its owner or possessor to engage in profession, business, trade, occupation
(3) Venue

Division (B)(2):
(1) Knowingly cause serious physical harm to
(2) Property owned, leased, or controlled by a government entity
(3) Venue

Division (C):
(1) Knowingly, and without privilege to do so, cause serious physical harm to
(2) (a) Any tomb, monument, gravestone, or other similar structure used as a memorial for the dead
       (or)
    (b) Any fence, railing, curb, or other property used to protect, enclose, or ornament any place of burial
       (or)
    (c) A place of burial
(3) Venue

Division (D):
(1) Knowingly, and without privilege to do so, cause physical harm to
(2) A place of burial
(3) By breaking and entering into a tomb, crypt, casket, or other structure that is used as a memorial for the dead or as an enclosure for the dead
(4) Venue

Value of property or amount of physical harm less than $5,000
Penalty: A felony of the fifth degree (2929.11-2929.18, 2929.31) with possible additional fine of up to $2,500
Value of property or amount of physical harm more than $5,000 but less than $100,000
Penalty: A felony of the fourth degree (2929.11-2929.18, 2929.31)
Value of property or amount of physical harm more than $100,000
Penalty: A felony of the third degree (2929.11-2929.18, 2929.31)
Notes: See R.C. § 2307.70 regarding civil actions.
       See R.C. § 2909.05 for examples of "government entities."
       R.C. § 2909.11 sets forth requirements for findings concerning property value damage and amount of physical harm.
Definitions: "Occupied structure," R.C. § 2909.01.

CRIMINAL DAMAGING OR ENDANGERING, R.C. § 2909.06 [M2, M1, F5, F4]

(1) Cause or create substantial risk of physical harm to property of another without consent
(2) (a) Knowingly, by any means
       (or)
    (b) Recklessly, by fire, explosion, flood, poison gas, poison, radioactive material, caustic or corrosive material, other inherently dangerous agency or substance
(3) Venue

Penalty: A misdemeanor of the second degree (2929.21, 2929.31)

If violation creates risk of physical harm to a person

Penalty: A misdemeanor of the first degree (2929.21, 2929.31)

If the property involved in a violation of this section is an aircraft, an aircraft engine, propeller, appliance, spare part, or any other equipment or implement used or intended to be used in the operation of an aircraft and if the violation creates a risk of physical harm to any person

Penalty: A felony of the fifth degree (2929.11-2929.18, 2929.31)

If the property involved in a violation is an aircraft, an aircraft engine, propeller, appliance, spare part, or any other equipment or implement used or intended to be used in the operation of the aircraft and if the violation creates a substantial risk of physical harm to any person or if the property involved is an occupied aircraft

Penalty: A felony of the fourth degree (2929.11-2929.18, 2929.31)

Notes: R.C. § 2929.21 requires reimbursement of agencies when offense committed recklessly by fire or explosion.

R.C. § 2929.28 sets forth requirements for hearings on reimbursement to agencies.

CRIMINAL MISCHIEF, R.C. § 2909.07 [M3, M1, F5, F4]

(1) Without privilege knowingly move, deface, damage, destroy, or otherwise improperly tamper with property of another
   (or)
(2) With purpose to interfere with use or enjoyment of property of another, employ tear gas device, stink bomb, smoke generator, or other device, releasing a substance harmful or offensive to persons exposed, or that tends to cause public alarm
   (or)
(3) Without privilege to do so, knowingly move, deface, damage, destroy, or otherwise improperly tamper with bench mark, triangulation station, boundary marker, other survey station, monument, or marker
   (or)
(4) Without privilege to do so, knowingly move, deface, damage, destroy, or otherwise improperly tamper with any safety device, property of another or the offender, when required or placed for safety of others, so as to destroy or diminish its effectiveness or availability for intended purpose
(5) With purpose to interfere with the use or enjoyment of the property of another, set a fire on the land of another or place personal property that has been set on fire on the land of another, which fire or personal property is outside and apart from any building, other structure, or personal property that is on that land
(6) Venue

Penalty: A misdemeanor of the third degree (2929.21, 2929.31)

If violation creates risk of physical harm to any person

Penalty: A misdemeanor of the first degree (2929.21, 2929.31)

If the property involved in violation of this section is an aircraft, an aircraft engine, propeller, appliance, spare part, fuel, lubricant, hydraulic fluid, any other equipment, implement, or material used or intended to be used in the operation of an aircraft, or any cargo carried or intended to be carried in an aircraft and if the violation creates a risk of physical harm to any person

Penalty: A felony of the fifth degree (2929.11-2929.18, 2929.31)

If the property involved in violation of this section is an aircraft, an aircraft engine, propeller, appliance, spare part, fuel, lubricant, hydraulic fluid, any other equipment, implement, or material used or intended to be used in the operation of an aircraft, or any cargo carried or intended to be carried in an aircraft and if the violation creates a substantial risk of physical harm to any person or if property involved is an occupied aircraft

Penalty: A felony of the fourth degree (2929.11-2929.18, 2929.31)

Note: As used in this section, "safety device" means any fire extinguisher, fire hose, or fire axe, or any fire escape, emergency exit, or emergency escape equipment, or any life line, life-saving ring, life preserver, or life boat or raft, or any alarm, light, flare, signal, sign, or notice intended to warn of danger or emergency, or intended for other safety purposes, or any guard railing or safety barricade, or any traffic sign or signal, or any railroad grade crossing sign, signal, or gate, or any first aid or survival equipment, or any other device, apparatus, or equipment intended for protecting or preserving the safety of persons or property.

ENDANGERING AIRCRAFT OR AIRPORT OPERATIONS, R.C. § 2909.08 [M2, M1, F5, F4]

[A](1) Knowingly
  (2) (a) (i) Throw an object at or drop an object upon
       (ii) Any moving aircraft
     (*or*)
    (b) (i) Shoot with a bow and arrow or discharge a firearm, air gun, or spring-operated gun
       (ii) At or toward any aircraft
  (3) Venue
[B](1) Knowingly or recklessly
  (2) Shoot with a bow and arrow or discharge a firearm, air gun, or spring-operated gun
  (3) Upon or over any airport operational surface
  (4) Venue

Offense under Division [A] above [endangering aircraft]

Penalty: A misdemeanor of the first degree (2929.21, 2929.31)

If violation creates risk of physical harm

Penalty: A felony of the fifth degree (2929.11-2929.18, 2929.31)

If violation creates a substantial risk of physical harm to any person or if the aircraft is occupied

Penalty: A felony of the fourth degree (2929.11-2929.18, 2929.31)

Offense under Division [B] above [endangering airport operations]

Penalty: A misdemeanor of the second degree (2929.21, 2929.31)

If violation creates risk of physical harm

Penalty: A felony of the fifth degree (2929.11-2929.18, 2929.31)

If the violation creates a substantial risk of physical harm to any person

Penalty: A felony of the fourth degree (2929.11-2929.18, 2929.31)

Notes: Division [B] above does not apply to any federal or Ohio or other state officer, agent, or employee, or any law enforcement officer, who is authorized to discharge firearms and is acting within the scope of the officer's, agent's, or employee's duties; or to any person who, with the consent of the owner or operator of the airport operational surface or the authorized agent of either, is lawfully engaging in any hunting or sporting activity or is otherwise lawfully discharging a firearm. *See* R.C. § 2909.08(C).

R.C. § 2909.08(F) provides that any bow and arrow, air gun, spring-operated gun, or firearm used in a felony violation of this section shall be seized and forfeited, and disposed of pursuant to R.C. § 2933.41.

In addition to any other penalty or section imposed for a violation of Division [B], the hunting license or permit of the offender shall be suspended or revoked

Definitions: "Air gun," "firearm," "spring-operated gun," and "airport operational surface, (R.C. § 2909.08.")

ROBBERY, BURGLARY, TRESPASS

AGGRAVATED ROBBERY, R.C. § 2911.01 [F1]

Division (A):

(1) (a) Attempt or commit theft offense
   (*or*)
   (b) Flee immediately after the theft or attempt
(2) While
   (a) Having a deadly weapon on or about the offender's person or under the offender's control and either display the weapon, brandish it, indicate that the offender possesses it, or use it
   (*or*)
   (b) Having a dangerous ordnance on or about the offender's person or under the offender's control
   (*or*)
   (c) Inflicting or attempting to inflict serious physical harm on another
(3) Venue

Division (B):

(1) (a) Knowingly remove or attempt to remove
   (*or*)
   (b) Knowingly deprive or attempt to deprive
(2) From the person of a law enforcement officer
(3) A deadly weapon
(4) When
   (a) The law enforcement officer, at the time of the removal, attempted removal, deprivation, or attempted deprivation is acting within the course and scope of the officer's duties
   (*or*)
   (b) The offender knows or has reason to know that the law enforcement officer is a law enforcement officer
(5) Venue

Penalty: A felony of the first degree (2929.11-2929.18, 2929.31)

ROBBERY, R.C. § 2911.02 [F3, F2]

(1) (a) Attempt or commit theft offense
   (*or*)
   (b) Flee immediately after the attempt or offense
(2) While
   (a) Having a deadly weapon on or about the offender's person or under the offender's control
   (*or*)

(b) Inflicting, or attempting to inflict, or threatening to inflict physical harm on another
   (or)
(c) Use or threaten the immediate use of force against another

Violation of division (2)(a) or (b)
Penalty: A felony of the second degree (2929.11-2929.18, 2929.31)

Violation of division (2)(c)
Penalty: A felony of the third degree (2929.11-2929.18, 2929.31)

AGGRAVATED BURGLARY, R.C. § 2911.11 [F1]

(1) Trespass in
   (a) Occupied structure
      (or)
   (b) A separately secured or separately occupied portion of an occupied structure
(2) By force, stealth, or deception
(3) When another person other than an accomplice of the offender is present
(4) With purpose to commit in the structure or in the separately secured or separately occupied portion of the structure any criminal offense
(5) If any of the following apply:
   (a) The offender inflicts, attempts or threatens to inflict physical harm on another
      (or)
   (b) The offender has a deadly weapon or dangerous ordnance on or about the offender's person or under the offender's control
(6) Venue

Penalty: A felony of the first degree (2929.11-2929.18, 2929.31)
Definitions: "Occupied structure," R.C. § 2909.11
   "Weapons/ordnance," R.C. § 2923.11

BURGLARY, R.C. § 2911.12 [F2, F3, F4]

(1) By means of force, stealth, or deception
(2) Trespass
(3) (a) In an occupied structure or in a separately secured or separately occupied portion of an occupied structure, when another person other than an accomplice of the offender is present, with purpose to commit in the structure or in the separately secured or separately occupied portion of the structure any criminal offense
      (or)
   (b) In an occupied structure or in a separately secured or separately occupied portion of an occupied structure that is a permanent or temporary habitation of any person when any person other than an accomplice of the offender is present or likely to be present, with purpose to commit in the habitation any criminal offense
      (or)
   (c) In an occupied structure or in a separately secured or separately occupied portion of an occupied structure, with purpose to commit in the structure or separately secured or separately occupied portion of the structure any criminal offense
      (or)

(d) In a permanent or temporary habitation of any person when any person other than an accomplice of the offender is present or likely to be present

(4) Venue

Offense under (3)(a) or (3)(b)

Penalty: A felony of the second degree (2929.11-2929.18, 2929.31)

Offense under (3)(c)

Penalty: A felony of the third degree (2929.11-2929.18, 2929.31)

Offense under (3)(d)

Penalty: A felony of the fourth degree (2929.11-2929.18, 2929.31)

Definitions: "Occupied structure," R.C. § 2909.01

BREAKING AND ENTERING, R.C. § 2911.13 [F5]

Division (A):
(1) With purpose to commit a theft offense or any felony therein
(2) Trespass in unoccupied structure
(3) By force, stealth, or deception
(4) Venue

Division (B):
(1) With purpose to commit a felony
(2) Trespass on land or premises of another
(3) Venue

Penalty: A felony of the fifth degree (2929.11-2929.18, 2929.31)

CRIMINAL TRESPASS, R.C. § 2911.21 [M4]

(1) Without privilege to do so
(2) (a) Knowingly enter or remain on land or premises of another
(*or*)
  (b) (i) Knowingly enter or remain on land or premises of another, use of which is lawfully restricted to certain persons, purposes, modes, or hours
    (ii) When the offender knows he is violating such restrictions or is reckless in that regard
(*or*)
  (c) Recklessly enter or remain on the land or premises of another, as to which notice against unauthorized access or presence is given
    (i) By actual communication to the offender
    (*or*)
    (ii) In a manner prescribed by law
    (*or*)
    (iii) By posting in a manner reasonably calculated to come to the attention of potential intruders
    (*or*)
    (iv) By fencing or other enclosure manifestly designed to restrict access
    (*or*)
  (d) (i) Being on the land or premises of another
    (ii) Negligently failing or refusing to leave

§ 2911.21.1   Ohio Criminal Law Handbook   A-64

(iii) Upon being notified to do so by the owner or occupant, or the agent or servant of either
(3) Venue

Penalty: A misdemeanor of the fourth degree (2929.21, 2929.31)

Note: It is no defense to this charge that the premises were owned or controlled by a public agency, or that there was authority to enter when such authorization was obtained by deception.

Definitions: "Land or premises," as used in this section, includes any land, building structure, or place belonging to, controlled by, or in custody of another, and any separate enclosure or room, or portion thereof, R.C. § 2911.21.

AGGRAVATED TRESPASS, R.C. § 2911.21.1 [M1]

(1) (a) Enter
    (*or*)
    (b) Remain
(2) On the land or premises of another
(3) With purpose to commit
(4) On that land or those premises
(5) A misdemeanor the elements of which involve
(6) (a) Causing physical harm to another person
    (*or*)
    (b) Causing another person to believe that the offender will cause physical harm to him
(7) Venue

Penalty: A misdemeanor of the first degree (2929.21, 2929.31)

Notes: See R.C. § 2919.25.1 for special provisions concerning repeat offenders and offenders violating prior protection orders or consent orders.

See R.C. § 2919.25.1 for special provisions concerning bail.

See R.C. § 2919.26 for special provisions concerning protection orders.

See R.C. § 2925.03 for special provisions concerning arrest and detention.

SAFECRACKING, R.C. § 2911.31 [F4]

(1) With purpose to commit an offense
(2) Knowingly enter, force entry into or tamper with a vault, safe or strongbox
(3) Venue

Penalty: A felony of the fourth degree (2929.11-2929.18, 2929.31)

TAMPERING WITH COIN MACHINES, R.C. § 2911.32 [M1, F5]

(1) With purpose to commit a theft or to defraud
(2) Knowingly
(3) Enter, force entrance into, tamper with or insert any part of an instrument into
(4) A coin machine
(5) Venue

Penalty: A misdemeanor of the first degree (2929.21, 2929.31)

If a prior conviction under this section or of a theft offense
Penalty: A felony of the fifth degree (2929.11-2929.18, 2929.31)

THEFTS AND FRAUDS

THEFT, R.C. § 2913.02 [M1, F5, F4, F3]

(1) Knowingly
(2) Obtain or exert control over property or services
(3) With purpose to deprive the owner thereof
(4) (a) Without consent of owner or person authorized to consent
(*or*)
    (b) Beyond the scope of the express or implied consent of owner or person authorized to consent
(*or*)
    (c) By deception
(*or*)
    (d) By threat
(5) Venue

THEFT:

Penalty: A misdemeanor of the first degree (2929.21, 2929.31)

If value is $500 or more and is less than $5,000 *or* if object is one of the following listed in R.C. § 2913.71: credit card/printed form for check or other negotiable instrument which identifies the drawer, maker, or account, etc./motor vehicle license plate/temporary license placard or sticker/blank certificate of title, or manufacturer's or importer's certificate to a motor vehicle/blank form for any license listed in R.C. § 4507.01

Penalty: A felony of the fifth degree (2929.11-2929.18, 2929.31)

If value is $5,000 or more and less than $100,000 (*or*) if property is a firearm or dangerous ordnance (*or*) if property is a motor vehicle as defined in R.C. § 4501.01

Penalty: A felony of the fourth degree (2929.11-2929.18, 2929.31)

If value is $100,000 or more

Penalty: A felony of the third degree (2929.11-2929.18, 2929.31)

THEFT OF DRUGS:

If property stolen is any dangerous drug, as defined in R.C. § 4729.02, and no prior felony drug abuse conviction, as defined in R.C. § 2925.01

Penalty: A felony of the fourth degree (2929.11-2929.18, 2929.31)

If property stolen is any dangerous drug, as defined in R.C. § 4729.02, and prior felony drug abuse conviction, as defined in R.C. § 2925.01

Penalty: A felony of the third degree (2929.11-2929.18, 2929.31)

UNAUTHORIZED USE OF VEHICLE, R.C. § 2913.03 [M1, F5]

Division (A): [**M1**]
(1) Knowingly
(2) Use or operate
(3) Aircraft, motor vehicle, motorboat, other motor propelled vehicle
(4) Without consent of owner or person authorized to give consent
(5) Venue

Penalty: A misdemeanor of the first degree (2929.21, 2929.31)

Division (B): [**F5**]
(1) Knowingly
(2) Use or operate
(3) Aircraft, motor vehicle, motorcycle, motorboat, other motor propelled vehicle
(4) Without consent of owner or person authorized to give consent
(5) Remove from Ohio, or keep possession more than 48 hours
(6) Venue

Penalty: A felony of the fifth degree (2929.11-2929.18, 2929.31)

UNAUTHORIZED USE OF PROPERTY; COMPUTER PROPERTY, R.C. § 2913.04 [M4, M1, F5, F4, F3]

Division (A): [**M4, M1, F5, F4, F3**]
(1) Knowingly
(2) Use or operate
(3) Property of another
(4) Without owner's consent or consent of authorized person
(5) Venue

Penalty: A misdemeanor of the fourth degree (2929.21, 2929.31)

If committed for the purpose of devising or executing a scheme to defraud or to obtain property or services and the value of the property or services or the loss to the victim is less than $500

Penalty: A misdemeanor of the first degree (2929.21, 2929.31)

If the value of the property or services or the loss to the victim is $500 or more and is less than $5,000

Penalty: A felony of the fifth degree (2929.11-2929.18, 2929.31)

If the value of the property or services or the loss to the victim is $5,000 or more and less than $100,000

Penalty: A felony of the fourth degree (2929.11-2929.18, 2929.31)

If the value of the property or services or the loss to the victim is $100,000 or more

Penalty: A felony of the third degree (2929.11-2929.18, 2929.31)

Division (B): [**F5**]
(1) Knowingly
(2) Gain access to or cause access to be gained to
(3) Any computer, computer system, or computer network
(4) Without the consent of, or beyond the scope of the express or implied consent of,

(5) The owner of the computer, computer system, or computer network or other person authorized to give consent by the owner

Penalty: A felony of the fifth degree (2929.11-2929.18, 2929.31)

POSSESSION OR SALE OF UNAUTHORIZED CABLE TELEVISION DEVICE, R.C. § 2913.04.1 [F5, F4]

Division (A): **[F5]**
(1) Knowingly
(2) Possess any device, including any instrument, apparatus, computer chip, equipment, decoder, descrambler, converter, software, or other device specially adapted, modified, or remanufactured for gaining access to cable television service
(3) Without securing authorization from or paying the required compensation to the owner or operator of the system that provides the cable television service
(4) Venue

Penalty: A felony of the fifth degree (2929.11-2929.18, 2929.31)

Division (B): **[F4]**
(1) Knowingly
(2) Sell, distribute or manufacture any device, including any instrument, apparatus, computer chip, equipment, decoder, descrambler, converter, software, or other device specially adapted, modified, or remanufactured for gaining access to cable television service
(3) Without securing authorization from or paying the required compensation to the owner or operator of the system that provides the cable television service
(4) Venue

Penalty: A felony of the fourth degree (2929.11-2929.18, 2929.31)

PASSING BAD CHECKS, R.C. § 2913.11 [M1, F5, F4, F3]

(1) Issue, transfer or cause to be issued or transferred
(2) Check or other negotiable instrument
(3) Knowing it will be dishonored
(4) With purpose to defraud
(5) Venue

If value is $500 or less

Penalty: A misdemeanor of the first degree (2929.21, 2929.31)

If value is $500 or more, and less than $5,000

Penalty: A felony of the fifth degree (2929.11-2929.18, 2929.31)

If value is $5,000 or more and less than $100,000

Penalty: A felony of the fourth degree (2929.11-2929.18, 2929.31)

If value is $100,000 or more

Penalty: A felony of the third degree (2929.11-2929.18, 2929.31)

Note: See statute for circumstance giving rise to presumption of purpose to defraud.

MISUSE OF CREDIT CARDS, R.C. § 2913.21 [M1, F5, F4, F3]

Division (A):
(1) Procure the issuance of a credit card by deception which is relied upon

§ 2913.31(A)   Ohio Criminal Law Handbook   A-68

    (or)
- (2) Knowingly buy or sell a credit card from or to a person other than the issuer
- (3) Venue

Division (B): With a purpose to defraud
- (1) Obtain control of a credit card to secure a debt
  (or)
- (2) Obtain property or services by use of a credit card, in one or more transactions, knowing or having reasonable cause to believe the card was expired, revoked, or was obtained, retained, or being used illegally
  (or)
- (3) Furnish property or services on the presentation of a credit card, knowing the card is being used illegally
  (or)
- (4) Representing or causing it to be represented to the issuer of a credit card that property/services were furnished, knowing the representation to be false
- (5) Venue

Division (C):
- (1) With a purpose to violate this section
- (2) Receive, possess, control or dispose of a credit card
- (3) Venue

If violation of (A), (B)(1) or (C) **[M1]**

If violation of (B)(2), (3), or (4) and cumulative retail value of property and services involved in one or more violations is $500 or less and the violations involve one or more credit card accounts and occur within a period of 90 consecutive days commencing on the date of the first violation **[M1]**

Penalty: A misdemeanor of the first degree (2929.21, 2929.31)

If violation of (B)(2), (3), or (4) and cumulative retail value of property and services involved in one or more violations is $500 or more and less than $5,000 and the violations involve one or more credit card accounts and occur within a period of 90 consecutive days commencing on the date of the first violation or if offender has previous conviction of a theft offense

Penalty: A felony of the fifth degree (2929.11-2929.18, 2929.31)

If violation of (B)(2), (3), or (4) and cumulative retail value of property and services involved in one or more violations is $5,000 or more and less than $100,000 and the violations involve one or more credit card accounts and occur within a period of 90 consecutive days commencing on the date of the first violation or if offender has previous conviction of two or more theft offenses

Penalty: A felony of the fourth degree (2929.11-2929.18, 2929.31)

If violation of (B)(2), (3), or (4) and cumulative retail value of property and services in one or more violations is $100,000 or more and violations involve one or more accounts and occur within period of 90 consecutive days commencing on date of first violation

Penalty: A felony of the third degree (2929.11-2929.18, 2929.31)

FORGERY, R.C. § 2913.31(A) [F5, F4, F3]

- (1) With a purpose to defraud or knowing the person is facilitating a fraud
  - (a) Forge another's writing without the other person's authority

        (or)
    (b) Forge a writing so that it
        (i) Appears to be genuine when it actually is spurious
           (or)
        (ii) Purports to be the act of another though actually unauthorized
           (or)
        (iii) Purports to have been executed at a time or place or with different terms from what in fact was the case
           (or)
        (iv) Purports to be a copy of an original when no such original existed
           (or)
    (c) Utter, or possess with purpose to utter, any writing known to have been forged
(2) Venue

Penalty: A felony of the fifth degree (2929.11-2929.18, 2929.31)

If property or services are involved or the victim suffers a loss and if the value of the property or services or the loss to the victim is $5,000 or more and less than $100,000

Penalty: A felony of the fourth degree (2929.11-2929.18, 2929.31)

If property or services are involved or the victim suffers a loss and if the value of the property or services or the loss to the victim is $100,000 or more

Penalty: A felony of the third degree (2929.11-2929.18, 2929.31)

FORGING IDENTIFICATION CARDS
SELLING FORGED IDENTIFICATION CARDS
DISTRIBUTING FORGED IDENTIFICATION CARDS, R.C. § 2913.31(B) [M1]

    (1) Knowingly
    (2) (a) Forge an identification card
        (or)
      (b) Sell or otherwise distribute a card that purports to be an identification card, knowing it to have been forged.
    (3) Venue

Penalty: A misdemeanor of the first degree (2929.21, 2929.31)

If prior conviction under this subsection

Penalty: A misdemeanor of the first degree (2929.21, 2929.31)

Mandatory Minimum Fine: $250

Definitions: "Identification card," R.C. § 2913.31(B).

Note: See also R.C. § 4301.63.6 for offenses involving false official identification cards.

CRIMINAL SIMULATION, R.C. § 2913.32 [M1, F5, F4, F3]

    (1) With a purpose to defraud or knowing the person is facilitating a fraud
    (2) (a) Make or alter any object so that it appears to have value due to antiquity, rarity, curiosity, source, authorship but which it does not in fact possess
        (or)
      (b) Practice deception in making, retouching, editing or reproducing a photograph, movie film, video tape, phonograph record, recording tape

§ 2913.33

(or)

(c) Falsely or fraudulently make, simulate, forge, alter, or counterfeit any wrapper, label, stamp, cork, or cap prescribed by the Liquor Control Commission under Chapters 4301. and 4303., falsely or fraudulently cause to be made, simulated, forged, altered, or counterfeited any wrapper, label, stamp, cork, or cap prescribed by the Liquor Control Commission under Chapters 4301. and 4303., or use more than once any wrapper, label, stamp, cork, or cap prescribed by the Liquor Control Commission under Chapters 4301. and 4303.
(or)

(d) Utter, or possess with a purpose to utter, any object known to have been simulated as above

(3) Venue

Penalty: A misdemeanor of the first degree (2929.21, 2929.31)

If the loss to the victim is $500 or more and less than $5,000

Penalty: A felony of the fifth degree (2929.11-2929.18, 2929.31)

If the loss to the victim is $5,000 or more and less than $100,000

Penalty: A felony of the fourth degree (2929.11-2929.18, 2929.31)

If the loss to the victim is more than $100,000

Penalty: A felony of the third degree (2929.11-2929.18, 2929.31)

MAKING OR USING SLUGS, R.C. § 2913.33 [M2]

(1) (a) With purpose to defraud, insert or deposit a slug in a coin machine
(or)
(b) With purpose of enabling another to defraud by inserting or depositing in coin machine, make, possess or dispose of a slug

(2) Venue

Penalty: A misdemeanor of the second degree (2929.21, 2929.31)

TRADEMARK COUNTERFEITING, R.C. § 2913.34 [M1, F5, F4, F3]

Division (A)(1): **[F5, F4, F3]**
(1) Knowingly
(2) Attach, affix, or otherwise use
(3) A counterfeit mark
(4) In connection with the manufacture of goods or services
(5) Whether or not the goods or services are intended for sale or resale

Penalty: A felony of the fifth degree (2929.11-2929.18, 2929.31)

If the cumulative sales price of the goods or services to which or in connection with which the counterfeit mark is attached, affixed, or otherwise used in the offense is $5,000 or more but less than $100,000 or if the number of units of goods to which or in connection with which the counterfeit mark is attached, affixed, or otherwise used in the offense is more than 100 units but less than 1,000 units

Penalty: A felony of the fourt degree (2929.11-2929.18, 2929.31)

If the cumulative sales price of the goods or services to which or in connection with which the counterfeit mark is attached, affixed, or otherwise used in the offense is $100,000 or more or if the number of units of goods to which or in connection with which the counterfeit mark is attached, affixed, or otherwise used in the offense is 1,000 units or more

Penalty: A felony of the third degree (2929.11-2929.18, 2929.31)

Division (A)(2): **[M1, F5]**
(1) Knowingly
(2) Possess, sell, or offer for sale
(3) Tools, machines, instruments, materials, articles, or other items of personal property
(4) Knowing that they are designed for the production or reproduction of counterfeit marks

Penalty: A misdemeanor of the first degree (2929.21, 2929.31)

If the circumstances of the violation indicate that the tools, machines, instruments, materials, articles, or other items of personal property involved were intended for use in the commission of a felony

Penalty: A felony of the fifth degree (2929.11-2929.18, 2929.31)

Division (A)(3): **[M1, F5, F4, F3]**
(1) Knowingly
(2) Purchase or otherwise acquire goods
(3) Keep or otherwise have the goods in the person's possession
(4) Knowing that a counterfeit mark is attached to, affixed to, or otherwise used in connection with the goods
(5) With the intent to sell or otherwise dispose of the goods

Penalty: A misdemeanor of the first degree (2929.21, 2929.31)

If the cumulative sales price of the goods or services to which or in connection with which the counterfeit mark is attached, affixed, or otherwise used is $500 or more but less than $5,000

Penalty: A felony of the fifth degree (2929.11-2929.18, 2929.31)

If the cumulative sales price of the goods or services to which or in connection with which the counterfeit mark is attached, affixed, or otherwise used is $5000 or more but less than $100,000 or if the number of units of goods to which the counterfeit mark is attached, affixed, or otherwise used is more than 100 units but less than 1,000 units

Penalty: A felony of the fourth degree (2929.11-2929.18, 2929.31)

If the cumulative sales price of the goods or services to which or in connection with which the counterfeit mark is attached, affixed, or otherwise used is $100,000 or more or if the number of units of goods to which or in connection with which the counterfeit mark is attached, affixed, or otherwise used is 1,000 units or more

Penalty: A felony of the third degree (2929.11-2929.18, 2929.31)

Division (A)(4): **[M1, F5, F4, F3]**
(1) Knowingly
(2) Sell, offer for sale, or otherwise dispose of goods in the person's possession
(3) Knowing that a counterfeit mark is attached to, affixed to, or otherwise used in connection with the goods

Penalty: A misdemeanor of the first degree (2929.21, 2929.31)

If the cumulative sales price of the goods or services to which or in connection with which the counterfeit mark is attached, affixed, or otherwise used is $500 or more but less than $5,000

Penalty: A felony of the fifth degree (2929.11-2929.18, 2929.31)

If the cumulative sales price of the goods or services to which or in connection with which the counterfeit mark is attached, affixed, or otherwise used is $5000 or more but less than $100,000 or if the number of units of goods to which the counterfeit mark is attached, affixed, or otherwise used is more than 100 units but less than 1,000 units

Penalty: A felony of the fourth degree (2929.11-2929.18, 2929.31)

If the cumulative sales price of the goods or services to which or in connection with which the counterfeit mark is attached, affixed, or otherwise used is $100,000 or more or if the number of units of goods to which or in connection with which the counterfeit mark is attached, affixed, or otherwise used is 1,000 units or more

Penalty: A felony of the third degree (2929.11-2929.18, 2929.31)

Division (A)(5): **[M1, F5, F4, F3]**
(1) Knowingly
(2) Sell, offer for sale, or otherwise provide services
(3) Knowing that a counterfeit mark is used in connection with that sale, offer for sale, or other provision of services

Penalty: A misdemeanor of the first degree (2929.21, 2929.31)

If the cumulative sales price of the goods or services to which or in connection with which the counterfeit mark is attached, affixed, or otherwise used is $500 or more but less than $5,000

Penalty: A felony of the fifth degree (2929.11-2929.18, 2929.31)

If the cumulative sales price of the goods or services to which or in connection with which the counterfeit mark is attached, affixed, or otherwise used is $5000 or more but less than $100,000 or if the number of units of goods to which the counterfeit mark is attached, affixed, or otherwise used is more than 100 units but less than 1,000 units

Penalty: A felony of the fourth degree (2929.11-2929.18, 2929.31)

If the cumulative sales price of the goods or services to which or in connection with which the counterfeit mark is attached, affixed, or otherwise used is $100,000 or more or if the number of units of goods to which or in connection with which the counterfeit mark is attached, affixed, or otherwise used is 1,000 units or more

Penalty: A felony of the third degree (2929.11-2929.18, 2929.31)

MEDICAID FRAUD, R.C. § 2913.40 [M1, F5, F4, F3]

Division (B):
(1) Knowingly
(2) Make or cause to be made
(3) False or misleading statement or representation
(4) For use in obtaining reimbursement from the Medical Assistance Program
(5) Venue

Division (C)(1):
(1) (a) With purpose to commit fraud
    (*or*)
    (b) Knowing the person is facilitating a fraud
(2) Contrary to terms of provider agreement

(3) Charge, solicit, accept, or receive
(4) For goods or services the person provides under the Medical Assistance Program
(5) Any property, money or other consideration in addition to amount under Medical Assistance Program and provider agreement and authorized deductibles and co-payments
(6) Venue

Division (C)(2):
(1) (a) With purpose to commit fraud
    (or)
    (b) Knowing the person is facilitating a fraud
(2) Solicit, offer, or receive
(3) Any remuneration other than authorized deductibles or co-payments, in cash or in kind, including but not limited to kickback or rebate
(4) In connection with furnishing goods and services for which whole or partial reimbursement is or may be made under the Medical Assistance Program
(5) Venue

Division (D):
(1) Having submitted a claim for or provided goods or services under the Medical Assistance Program
(2) Knowingly
(3) Alter, falsify, destroy, conceal, or remove
(4) Any records that are necessary to fully disclose
(5) (a) Nature of all goods or services for which the claim was submitted, or for which reimbursement was received, by the person
    (or)
    (b) All income and expenditures upon which rates of reimbursements were based for the person
(6) For a period of six years after a reimbursement pursuant to that claim or a reimbursement for those goods or services is received under the Medical Assistance Program
(7) Venue

Penalty: A misdemeanor of the first degree (2929.21, 2929.31)

If value of property, services, or funds is more than $500 and less than $5,000

Penalty: A felony of the fifth degree (2929.11-2929.18, 2929.31)

If value of property, services or funds is more than $5,000 and less than $100,000

Penalty: A felony of the fourth degree (2929.11-2929.18, 2929.31)

If the value of the property, services or funds is $100,000 or more

Penalty: A felony of the third degree (2929.11-2929.18, 2929.31)

Note: Provisions of this section not intended to be exclusive remedies.

TAMPERING WITH RECORDS, R.C. § 2913.42 [M1, F5, F4, F3]

(1) (a) Falsify, destroy, remove, conceal, alter, deface, or mutilate any writing, computer software, data, computer data, or record
    (or)
    (b) Utter any writing or record knowing it has been tampered with as above

(2) Knowing the person has no privilege to do so and with a purpose to defraud or knowingly to facilitate a fraud
(3) Venue

Offense not involving data, and writing or record is not unrevoked will or record kept by or belonging to governmental agency
Penalty: A misdemeanor of the first degree (2929.21, 2929.31)

Offense not involving data, and writing or record is unrevoked will or record kept by or belonging to governmental agency
Penalty: A felony of the fifth degree (2929.11-2929.18, 2929.31)

Offense involving data and the value of the data involved or the loss to the victim is less than $500
Penalty: A misdemeanor of the first degree (2929.21, 2929.31)

Offense involving data and the value of the data involved or the loss to the victim is $500 or more and is less than $5,000
Penalty: A felony of the fifth degree (2929.11-2929.18, 2929.31)

Offense involving data and the value of the data involved or the loss to the victim is $5,000 or more and is less than $100,000
Penalty: A felony of the fourth degree (2929.11-2929.18, 2929.31)

Offense involving data and the value of the data involved or the loss to the victim is $100,000 or more or if the offense is committed for the purpose of devising or executing a scheme to defraud or to obtain property or services and the value of the property or services or the loss to the victim is $5,000 or more
Penalty: A felony of the third degree (2929.11-2929.18, 2929.31)

SECURING WRITINGS BY DECEPTION, R.C. § 2913.43 [M1, F5, F4, F3]

(1) By deception
(2) Cause another to execute a writing disposing of or encumbering property or creating pecuniary obligation
(3) Venue

Penalty: A misdemeanor of the first degree (2929.21, 2929.31)

If property or obligation value $500 or more and less than $5,000
Penalty: A felony of the fifth degree (2929.11-2929.18, 2929.31)

If property or obligation value $5,000 or more but less than $100,000
Penalty: A felony of the fourth degree (2929.11-2929.18, 2929.31)

If property or obligation value $100,000 or more
Penalty: A felony of the third degree (2929.11-2929.18, 2929.31)

PERSONATING AN OFFICER, R.C. § 2913.44 [M1]

(1) (a) With purpose to defraud or knowingly to facilitate a fraud
    (*or*)
    (b) With purpose to induce another to buy property or services
(2) Personate a law enforcement officer, inspector, investigator or agent of any governmental agency

(3) Venue

Penalty: A misdemeanor of the first degree (2929.21, 2929.31)

ILLEGAL DISPLAY OF LAW ENFORCEMENT EMBLEM, R.C. § 2913.44.1 [MM]
(1) Knowingly display on a motor vehicle
(2) Emblem of a law enforcement agency or an organization of law enforcement officers
(3) By a person who is not entitled to do so
(4) Venue

Penalty: A minor misdemeanor (2929.21, 2929.31)

DEFRAUDING CREDITORS, R.C. § 2913.45 [M1, F5, F4, F3]
(1) (a) Remove, conceal, destroy, encumber, convey, or otherwise deal with any of the person's property
    (or)
  (b) Misrepresent or refuse to disclose to fiduciary appointed to administer or manage the person's affairs or estate, the existence, amount, location of any of the person's property, or any other information regarding such property which the person is legally required to furnish fiduciary
(2) With purpose to defraud a creditor
(3) Venue

Penalty: A misdemeanor of the first degree (2929.21, 2929.31)

If the value of the property involved is $500 or more and less than $5,000

Penalty: A felony of the fifth degree (2929.11-2929.18, 2929.31)

If the value of the property involved is $5,000 or more and less than $100,000

Penalty: A felony of the fourth degree (2929.11-2929.18, 2929.31)

If the value of the property involved is $100,000 or more

Penalty: A felony of the third degree (2929.11-2929.18, 2929.31)

ILLEGAL USE OF FOOD STAMPS OR WIC PROGRAM BENEFITS, R.C. § 2913.46 [F5, F4, F3, F2]

Division (B):
(1) Individual
(2) Knowingly
(3) Possess, buy, sell, use, alter, accept, or transfer
(4) Food stamp coupons, WIC program benefits or any electronically transferred benefits
(5) In manner not authorized by Food Stamp Act of 1977 or the Child Nutrition Act of 1966
(6) Venue

Division (C)(1):
(1) Organization
(2) Knowingly
(3) Allow an employee
(4) To sell, transfer, or trade items or services the purchase of which is prohibited by the Food Stamp Act of 1977 or the Child Nutrition Act of 1966

§ 2913.47

(5) In exchange for food stamp coupons, WIC program benefits or any electronically transferred benefits
(6) Venue

Division (C)(2):
(1) Organization
(2) Negligently
(3) Allow an employee
(4) To sell, transfer, or exchange food stamp coupons, WIC program benefits or any electronically transferred benefits
(5) For anything of value
(6) Venue

If value is less than $500

Penalty: A felony of the fifth degree (2929.11-2929.18, 2929.31)

If value is $500 and less than $5,000

Penalty: A felony of the fourth degree (2929.11-2929.18, 2929.31)

If the value is $5,000 or more and is less than $100,000

Penalty: A felony of the third degree (2929.11-2929.18, 2929.31)

If the value is $100,000 or more

Penalty: A felony of the second degree (2929.11-2929.18, 2929.31)

INSURANCE FRAUD, R.C. § 2913.47 [M1, F5, F4, F3]

(1) (a) With purpose to defraud
    (*or*)
    (b) Knowing that the person is facilitating a fraud
(2) (a) Present to or cause to be presented to an insurer any written or oral statement
    (*or*)
    (b) Assist, aid, abet, solicit, procure, or conspire with another to prepare or make any written or oral statement that is intended to be presented to an insurer
(3) If the statement is part of, or in support of
(4) (a) An application for insurance
    (*or*)
    (b) A claim for payment pursuant to a policy
    (*or*)
    (c) A claim for any other benefit pursuant to a policy
(5) Knowing that the statement or any part of the statement is false or deceptive
(6) Venue

Penalty: A misdemeanor of the first degree (2929.21, 2929.31)

If the amount of the application or claim is five hundred dollars or more, but less than five thousand dollars

Penalty: A felony of the fifth degree (2929.11-2929.18, 2929.31)

If the amount of the application or claim is five thousand dollars or more, but less than one hundred thousand dollars

Penalty: A felony of the fourth degree (2929.11-2929.18, 2929.31)

If the amount of the application or claim is one hundred thousand dollars or more

Penalty: A felony of the third degree (2929.11-2929.18, 2929.31)

Note: This statute does not abrogate, waive, or modify, R.C. § 2317.02(A), concerning the attorney-client privilege.

Definitions: "Data," "deceptive," "insurer," "policy," "statement," R.C. § 2913.47

WORKERS' COMPENSATION FRAUD, R.C. § 2913.48 [M1, F5, F4, F3]

(1) (a) With purpose to defraud
     (*or*)
  (b) Knowing that the person is facilitating a fraud
(2) (a) Receive workers' compensation benefits to which the person is not entitled
     (*or*)
  (b) Make or present or cause to be made or presented a false or misleading statement with the purpose to secure payment for goods or services rendered under R.C. Ch. 4121., 4123., 4127., or 4131. or to secure workers' compensation benefits
     (*or*)
  (c) Alter, falsify, destroy, conceal, or remove any record or document that
    (i) is necessary to fully establish the validity of any claim filed with the bureau of workers' compensation or a self-insuring employer
      (*or*)
    (ii) is necessary to establish the nature of goods and services for which reimbursement or payment was received or is requested from, the bureau of workers' compensation or a self-insuring employer
     (*or*)
  (d) Enter into an agreement or conspiracy to defraud the bureau or a self-insuring employer by making or presenting or causing to be made or presented a false claim for workers' compensation benefits
     (*or*)
  (e) make or present or cause to made or presented a false or misleading statement or other misrepresentation concerning manual codes, classification of employees, payroll, or number of personnel when information of that nature is necessary to determine the actual workers' compensation premium or assessment owed to the bureau by an employer
     (*or*)
  (f) solicit, offer, or receive any remuneration in cash or in kind, including, but not limited to, a kickback or rebate, in connection with a referral for the furnishing of goods or services for which reimbursement may be made pursuant to Chapters 4121., 4123., 4127., or 4131.
     (*or*)
  (g) alter, forge, or create a workers' compensation certificate to falsely show current or correct workers' compensattion coverage
     (*or*)
  (h) fail to secure or maintain workers' compensation coverage as required by Chapter 4123.
(3) Venue

If the value of premiums and assessments unpaid pursuant to actions described in (2)(e), (g) or (h) or of goods, services, property, or money stolen is less than five hundred dollars

Penalty: A misdemeanor of the first degree (2929.21, 2929.31)

§ 2913.51

If the value of premiums and assessments unpaid pursuant to actions described in (2)(e), (g) or (h) or of goods, services, property, or money stolen is five hundred dollars or more, but less than five thousand dollars

Penalty: A felony of the fifth degree (2929.11-2929.18, 2929.31)

If the value of premiums and assessments unpaid pursuant to actions described in (2)(e), (g) or (h) or of goods, services, property, or money stolen is five thousand dollars or more, but less than one hundred thousand dollars

Penalty: A felony of the fourth degree (2929.11-2929.18, 2929.31)

If the value of premiums and assessments unpaid pursuant to actions described in (2)(e), (g) or (h) or of goods, services, property, or money stolen is one hundred thousand dollars or more

Penalty: A felony of the third degree (2929.11-2929.18, 2929.31)

Note: Division (2)(f) of this section does not apply to any contract to provide services under the bureau's health care partnership program or a qualified health plan entered into between a managed care organization and an organization formed pursuant to 4123.29(A)(4).

RECEIVING STOLEN PROPERTY, R.C. § 2913.51 [M1, F5, F4, F3]

(1) Receive, retain or dispose of property of another
(2) (a) Knowing
        (*or*)
    (b) Having reasonable cause to believe
(3) Such property has been obtained through commission of theft offense
(4) Venue

Penalty: A misdemeanor of the first degree (2929.21, 2929.31)

If value of the property involved is more than $500 but less than $5,000, *or* if object is one of the following listed in R.C. § 2913.71: credit card/printed form for check or other negotiable instrument which identifies the drawer, maker, or account, etc./firearm or dangerous ordnance/motor vehicle license plate/blank certificate of title, or manufacturer's or importer's certificate to a motor vehicle/ blank form for any license listed in R.C. § 4507.01

Penalty: A felony of the fifth degree (2929.11-2929.18, 2929.31)

If property is a motor vehicle as defined in R.C. § 4501.01, if the property involved is a dangerous drug as defined in R.C. § 4729.02, or if the value of the property is $5,000 or more and less than $100,000

Penalty: A felony of the fourth degree (2929.11-2929.18, 2929.31)

If value is $100,000 or more

Penalty: A felony of the third degree (2929.11-2929.18, 2929.31)

GAMBLING

GAMBLING, R.C. § 2915.02 [M1, F5]

(1) (a) Engage in bookmaking
        (*or*)

- (b) (i) Knowingly
  - (ii) Engage in conduct that facilitates bookmaking (i.e. aid an illegal bookmaking operation, including without limitation placing a bet with a person engaged in or facilitating illegal bookmaking)

  (or)
- (c) (i) Establish, promote, or operate
  - (ii) Any scheme or game of chance conducted for profit

  (or)
- (d) (i) Knowingly
  - (ii) Engage in conduct that facilitates any scheme or game of chance conducted for profit (i.e., in any way knowingly and in the conduct or operation of any such scheme or game, including without limitation playing the scheme or game)

  (or)
- (e) (i) Knowingly
  - (ii) Procure, transmit, exchange or engage in conduct that facilitates the procurement, transmission, or exchange of
  - (iii) Information for use in establishing odds or determining winners in connection with
  - (iv) Bookmaking or any scheme or game of chance conducted for profit

  (or)
- (f) (i) Engage in betting or in playing any scheme or game of chance, except a charitable bingo game
  - (ii) As a substantial source of income or livelihood

  (or)
- (g) (i) With purpose to violate this section as set forth above
  - (ii) Acquire, possess, control, or operate
  - (iii) Any gambling device

  (or)
- (h) (i) Receive
  - (ii) Any commission, wage, salary, tip, reward, donation, gratuity, or other form of compensation
  - (iii) Directly or indirectly
  - (iv) For operating or assisting in the operation of
  - (v) Any scheme or game of chance

(2) Venue

Penalty: A misdemeanor of the first degree (2929.21, 2929.31)

If prior gambling conviction

Penalty: A felony of the fifth degree (2929.11-2929.18, 2929.31)

Note: This section does not prohibit conduct in connection with gambling expressly permitted by law. R.C. § 2915.02(C), (D).

OPERATING GAMBLING HOUSE, R.C. § 2915.03 [M1, F5]

(1) Being an owner, lessee, or person having control/supervision of premises
(2) (a) Use or occupy premises for gambling in violation of R.C. § 2915.02

   (or)

   (b) Recklessly permit premises to be used or occupied for gambling as above

§ 2915.04

(3) Venue

Penalty: A misdemeanor of the first degree (2929.21, 2929.31)

If prior gambling conviction

Penalty: A felony of the fifth degree (2929.11-2929.18, 2929.31)

PUBLIC GAMING, R.C. § 2915.04 [MM, M4]

Division (A):
(1) While at a hotel, restaurant, tavern, store, arena, hall, or other place of public accommodation, business, amusement or resort
(2) Make a bet or play a game of chance
(3) Venue

Division (B):
(1) Being an owner, lessee, or person having control/supervision of:
   (a) Premises as listed in Division (A)(1)(a) above
(2) Recklessly permit such premises to be used or occupied for purpose of making a bet or playing a game of chance
(3) Venue

Penalty: A minor misdemeanor (2929.21, 2929.31)

If prior conviction of gambling offense

Penalty: A misdemeanor of the fourth degree (2929.21, 2929.31)

CHEATING; CORRUPTING SPORTS, R.C. § 2915.05 [M1, F5, F4]

Division (A): [M1, F5]
(1) With purpose to defraud or to facilitate a fraud
(2) Engage in conduct designed to corrupt the outcome of
(3) (a) A bet
      (or)
    (b) A contest of knowledge, skill, or endurance that is not an athletic or sporting event
      (or)
    (c) A scheme or game of chance
(4) Venue

Penalty: A misdemeanor of the first degree (2929.21, 2929.31)

If prior theft offense or gambling conviction, or the potential gain is $500 or more

Penalty: A felony of the fifth degree (2929.11-2929.18, 2929.31)

Division (B): [F5, F4]
(1) Knowingly
(2) (a) Offer, give, solicit, or accept anything of value to corrupt the outcome of an athletic or sporting event
      (or)
    (b) Engage in conduct designed to corrupt the outcome of an athletic or sporting event
(3) Venue

Penalty: A felony of the fifth degree (2929.11-2929.18, 2929.31)

If prior conviction of a gambling or theft offense

Penalty: A felony of the fourth degree (2929.11-2929.18, 2929.31)

CONDUCTING BINGO GAME, R.C. § 2915.07 [F4]

(1) Conduct or advertise
(2) Bingo game
(3) Without having obtained a bingo license pursuant to R.C. § 2915.08
(4) Venue

Penalty: A felony of the fourth degree (2929.11-2929.18, 2929.31)

Notes: This section does not apply to bingo games conducted for amusement only. R.C. § 2915.12.
See R.C. § 173.12.1 for special provisions concerning bingo games involving only persons sixty or older and conducted at certain senior centers.

ILLEGALLY CONDUCTING A BINGO GAME, R.C. § 2915.09 [F4, M1, MM]

Division (A)(2): [F4]
(1) Being a charitable organization
(2) Conduct bingo game
(3) (a) Without using all gross receipts for paying prizes or the purposes listed in its license application
   (or)
   (b) Using an amount of the receipts above the amount reasonably and customarily spent for similar purchases, leases, hiring or advertising for
   (i) purchasing, or leasing bingo cards and other equipment used in conducting the bingo game
   (or)
   (ii) hiring security personnel for the bingo game
   (or)
   (iii) advertising the bingo game
   (or)
   (iv) renting premises in which to conduct the bingo game
   (or)
   (c) For each bingo session, deducting from the gross receipts a sum in excess of the lesser of $600 or 45% of the gross receipts as consideration for the use of the premises owned by the charitable organization conducting the game
(4) Venue

Penalty: A felony of the fourth degree (2929.11-2929.18, 2929.31)

Division (A)(1): [MM]
(1) Being a charitable organization
(2) Conduct bingo game without
   (a) Owning all equipment used to conduct the bingo game
   (or)
   (b) Leasing such equipment from a licensed charitable organization at a customary and reasonable rental rate
(3) Venue

Divisions (A)(3), (4), (5): [MM]

(1) Being a charitable organization
(2) Conduct bingo game
(3) On premises not
    (a) Owned by charitable organization
    (or)
    (b) Leased from another charitable organization at a rate not exceeding $450 per session (*Note:* A charitable organization shall not lease premises that it owns to more than one other charitable organization per calendar week for the purpose of conducting bingo on the premises.)
    (or)
    (c) Leased from a person other than a charitable organization at a rental rate that is more than is customary and reasonable for premises similar in location, size, and quality, but not exceeding $450 per session. (*Note:* Lessor other than charitable organization shall lease premises only and shall not provide special personnel, services or equipment.)
    (or)
    (d) Subleased from another charitable organization that leases from a person other than a charitable organization at a rate not exceeding $450 per session
    (or)
(4) Conduct more than two bingo sessions on any premises in any calendar week except that a volunteer firefighter's organization or a volunteer rescue service organization that conducts not more than five bingo sessions in a calendar year may conduct more than two bingo sessions in a seven-day period after notifying the attorney general when it will conduct the sessions
(or)
(5) Fail to display its bingo license conspicuously at the location where the bingo game is conducted
(or)
(6) Fail to conduct the bingo in accordance with definition in R.C. § 2915.01(S)(1)
(7) Venue

Note: See R.C. § 2915.09(D) for exceptions to R.C. § 2915.09(A)(3)

Division (B): **[MM]**
(1) Being a charitable organization
(2) Conduct a bingo game and
(3) (a) (i) Pay compensation to a bingo game operator for operating a bingo game or for preparing, selling or serving food or beverages at the site of the bingo game
        (or)
    (ii) Permit any auxiliary unit or society of the charitable organization to pay compensation to any bingo game operator who prepares, sells or serves food or beverages at a bingo session
        (or)
    (iii) Permit any auxiliary unit or society of the charitable organization to prepare, sell or serve beverages at a bingo session if the auxiliary unit or society pays compensation to the bingo game operators who prepare, sell or serve the food or beverages
        (or)
    (b) Pay consulting fees to any person for any services performed in relation to the bingo game
    (or)
    (c) Pay concession fees to any person who provides refreshments to participants in the bingo game

(or)
- (d) Conduct more than two bingo sessions in any seven-day period
  (or)
- (e) Pay out more than $3,500 in prizes during any bingo session
  (or)
- (f) (i) Do so at any time during the 10 hour period between midnight and 10 a.m.
  (or)
  (ii) Do so at any time during, or within 10 hours of, a bingo game conducted for amusement only pursuant to R.C. § 2915.12
  (or)
  (iii) Do so at any location, on any day of the week, or during any time period not specified on its bingo license
  (or)
- (g) Permit any person whom the charitable organization knows, or should have known, is under the age of 18 to work as a bingo game operator
- (h) Permit any person whom the charitable organization knows, or should have known, has been convicted of a felony or gambling offense to be a bingo game operator
- (i) Permit the lessor of the premises on which bingo is conducted, if the lessor is not a charitable organization, to provide the charitable organization with bingo game operators, security personnel, concessions, bingo equipment, or any other type of service or equipment

(4) Venue

Division (C): [MM]
(1) Being a bingo game operation
(2) Receive or accept
(3) Directly or indirectly, regardless of the source
(4) Any commission, wage, salary, reward, tip, donation, gratuity or other form of compensation
(5) (a) For operating a bingo game
    (or)
    (b) For providing other work or labor at the site of the bingo game
(6) Venue

Penalty: A minor misdemeanor (2929.21, 2929.31)
If prior conviction of Division (A)(1), (3), (4) or (5) or (B), or (C)
Penalty: A misdemeanor of the first degree (2929.21, 2929.31)
Notes: This section does not apply to bingo games conducted for amusement only. R.C. § 2915.12.
See R.C. § 173.12.1 for special provisions concerning bingo games involving only persons sixty or older and conducted at certain senior centers.

FAILURE TO MAINTAIN RECORDS OF BINGO SESSION OR SCHEME OR GAME OF CHANCE FOR THREE YEARS, R.C. § 2915.10(A) [M1]

(1) Being a charitable organization
(2) Conduct bingo session or scheme or game of chance
(3) Fail to maintain the following records for at least three years from the date on which the bingo session or scheme or game of chance is conducted
   (a) An itemized list of the gross receipts of each session or scheme or game of chance
   (b) An itemized list of all expenses other than prizes that are incurred in conducting the bingo

session, the name of each person to whom the expenses are paid, and a receipt for all of the expenses

(c) A list of all prizes awarded during the bingo session or scheme or game of chance conducted by said organization and the name and address of all persons who are winners of prizes of $100 or more in value

(d) An itemized list of the charitable recipients of the proceeds of the bingo session or scheme or game of chance, including the name and address of each recipient to whom the money is distributed, and if the organization uses the proceeds of a bingo session or the money or assets received from a scheme or game of chance for any purpose set forth in R.C. § 2915.01(Z) or R.C. § 2915.02(D), a list of each purpose and an itemized list of each expenditure for each purpose

(e) The number of persons who participate in any bingo session or scheme or game of chance that is conducted by the charitable organization

(f) A list of receipts from the sale of food and beverages by the charitable organization or one of its auxiliary units or societies, if the receipts are excluded from the definition of "gross receipts" under R.C. § 2915.01(X)

(g) An itemized list of all expenses incurred at each bingo session conducted by the charitable organization in the sale of food or beverages by the charitable organization or by an auxiliary unit or society of the charitable organization, the name of each person to whom the expenses are paid, and a receipt for all of the expenses

(4) Venue

Penalty: A misdemeanor of the first degree (2929.21, 2929.31)

Notes: R.C. § 2915.10(B) provides attorney general or local law enforcement may inspect and investigate charitable organization, its officers and accounts, games in session and premises where held.

This section does not apply to bingo games conducted for amusement only. R.C. § 2915.12.

See R.C. § 173.12.1 for special provisions concerning bingo games involving only persons sixty or older and conducted at certain senior centers.

ILLEGAL ACTS RE INSPECTION OF BINGO GAME OR SCHEME OR GAME OF CHANCE, R.C. § 2915.10(C) [M1]

(1) (a) Destroy, alter, conceal, withhold, or deny access to any accounts or records of a charitable organization that have been requested for examination
    (or)
  (b) Obstruct, impede, or interfere with any inspection, audit, or observation of
    (i) a bingo game or scheme or game of chance
      (or)
    (ii) premises where a bingo game or scheme or game of chance is operated
      (or)
  (c) Refuse to comply with any reasonable request of, or obstruct, impede, or interfere with any other reasonable action undertaken by the attorney general or a local law enforcement agency pursuant to R.C. § 2915.10(B)

(2) Venue

Penalty: A misdemeanor of the first degree (2929.21, 2929.31)

Notes: This section does not apply to bingo games conducted for amusement only.

See R.C. § 173.12.1 for special provisions concerning bingo games involving only persons sixty or older and conducted at certain senior centers.

OPERATION OF BINGO GAME BY MINOR, R.C. § 2915.11(A) [M3]

(1) Being under the age of 18
(2) Operate a bingo game
(3) Venue

Penalty: A misdemeanor of the third degree (2929.21, 2929.31)

Notes: This section does not apply to bingo games conducted for amusement only.

See R.C. § 173.12.1 for special provisions concerning bingo games involving only persons sixty or older and conducted at certain senior centers.

OPERATION OF BINGO GAME BY FORMER OFFENDER, R.C. § 2915.11(B) [M1]

(1) Being a person who has been convicted in any jurisdiction of
   (a) felony
      (or)
   (b) gambling offense
(2) Operate a bingo game
(3) Venue

Penalty: A misdemeanor of the first degree (2929.21, 2929.31)

Notes: This section does not apply to bingo games conducted for amusement only.

See R.C. § 173.12.1 for special provisions concerning bingo games involving only persons sixty or older and conducted at certain senior centers.

OFFENSES AGAINST THE PUBLIC PEACE

INCITING TO VIOLENCE, R.C. § 2917.01 [M1, F3]

(1) Knowingly
(2) Engage in conduct designed to urge or incite another to commit an offense of violence
(3) Under circumstances where
   (a) The conduct creates clear and present danger that an offense of violence will result
      (or)
   (b) The conduct proximately results in an offense of violence
(4) Venue

If the offense of violence that the other person is being urged or incited to commit is a misdemeanor
Penalty: A misdemeanor of the first degree (2929.21, 2929.31)

If the offense of violence that the other person is being urged or incited to commit is a felony
Penalty: A felony of the third degree (2929.11-2929.18, 2929.31)

AGGRAVATED RIOT, R.C. § 2917.02 [F5, F4, F3]

Division (A):
(1) Participate with 4 or more others
(2) In a course of disorderly conduct contrary to R.C. § 2917.11
(3) (a) With a purpose to commit or facilitate a felony
    (or)
    (b) With purpose to commit or facilitate an offense of violence
    (or)
    (c) While the offender, or any participant to the knowledge of the offender, has a deadly weapon or dangerous ordnance on or about the offender's or participant's person or under his control, uses, or intends to use same
(4) Venue

Division (B):
(1) Being an inmate of a detention facility
(2) Violate division (A)(3)(a) or (c)
    (or)
(3) Violate division (A)(3)(b) or RC. § 2917.03
(4) Venue

A violation of division (A)(3)(a) or (c)
Penalty: A felony of the fifth degree (2929.11-2929.18, 2929.31)
A violation of division (A)(3)(b) or (B)(2)
Penalty: A felony of the fourth degree (2929.11-2929.18, 2929.31)
A violation of division (B)(3)
Penalty: A felony of the third degree (2929.11-2929.18, 2929.31)
Definitions: "Deadly weapon," "dangerous ordnance," R.C. § 2923.11.

RIOT, R.C. § 2917.03 [M1]

Division (A):
(1) Participate with 4 or more others
(2) In a course of disorderly conduct contrary to R.C. § 2917.11
(3) (a) With purpose to commit or facilitate a misdemeanor other than disorderly conduct
    (or)
    (b) With purpose to intimidate a public official or employee into taking or refraining from taking official action
    (or)
    (c) With a purpose to hinder, impede, obstruct function of government
    (or)
    (d) With a purpose to hinder, impede or obstruct the orderly administration of or instruction at an educational institution, or interfere with or disrupt its activities
(4) Venue

Division (B):
(1) Participate with 4 or more others
(2) With purpose to do an act with unlawful force or violence
(3) Although such act would otherwise be lawful

(4) Venue

Penalty: A misdemeanor of the first degree (2929.21, 2929.31)

FAILURE TO DISPERSE, R.C. § 2917.04 [MM]
(1) When five or more persons are participating in disorderly conduct in violation of R.C. § 2917.11
(2) With other persons in vicinity and whose presence creates:
    (a) A likelihood of physical harm to persons/property
        (or)
    (b) Serious public inconvenience, annoyance, or alarm
(3) And a law enforcement officer or other public official orders all of above to disperse
(4) Knowingly fail to obey such order
(5) Venue

Penalty: A minor misdemeanor (2929.21, 2929.31)

DISORDERLY CONDUCT, R.C. § 2917.11 [MM, M4]
Division (A):
(1) Recklessly
(2) Cause inconvenience, annoyance or alarm to another by means of
    (a) Fighting/threatening harm to persons or property/violent or turbulent behavior
        (or)
    (b) Making unreasonable noise/offensively coarse utterances/gestures, displays, or communicating unwarranted and grossly abusive language to others
        (or)
    (c) Insulting/taunting/challenging another under circumstances in which such conduct is likely to provoke a violent response
        (or)
    (d) Hindering or preventing movement of persons upon a public street/road/highway/right-of-way, or to or from public/private property, so as to interfere with rights of others by acts that serve no lawful/reasonable purpose
        (or)
    (e) Creating a physically offensive condition or one that presents a risk of physical harm to persons/property by acts serving no lawful reasonable purpose
(3) Venue

Division (B):
(1) While voluntarily intoxicated
(2) (a) In a public place or in the presence of 2 or more persons
        (i) Engage in conduct likely to be offensive
            (or)
        (ii) Cause inconvenience, annoyance, or alarm to persons of ordinary sensibilities, which conduct the offender, if the offender were not intoxicated, should know is likely to have that effect on others
            (or)
    (b) Engage in conduct or create a condition that presents a risk of physical harm to the offender or another, or the property of another
(3) Venue

§ 2917.12

Penalty: A minor misdemeanor (2929.21, 2929.31)

If the offender persists after a reasonable warning or request to desist, or if the offense is committed in the vicinity of a school

Penalty: A misdemeanor of the fourth degree (2929.21, 2929.31)

Note: The violation of a statute or ordinance in which an element is operating motor vehicle, locomotive, watercraft, aircraft, or other vehicle under the influence of alcohol or drugs of abuse, is not a violation of Division (B).

Definitions: "School," "school premises," "school building," R.C. §§ 2917.11, 2925.01.

DISTURBING A LAWFUL MEETING, R.C. § 2917.12 [M4]

(1) With a purpose to prevent or disrupt
(2) (a) Do anything which obstructs or interferes with the conduct of a meeting, procession, or gathering
    (or)
    (b) Make utterances, gestures, or displays which outrage the sensibilities of group
(3) Venue

Penalty: A misdemeanor of the fourth degree (2929.21, 2929.31)

MISCONDUCT AT AN EMERGENCY, R.C. § 2917.13 [MM, M4]

(1) Knowingly
    (a) Hamper lawful operations of any law enforcement officer, fireman, rescuer, medical or other authorized person, engaged in duties at a fire, accident, disaster, riot, or emergency
    (or)
    (b) Fail to obey a lawful order of any law enforcement officer engaged in duties at the scene or in connection with a fire, accident, disaster, riot, or emergency
(2) Venue

Penalty: A minor misdemeanor (2929.21, 2929.31)

Where the violation creates a risk of physical harm to persons/property

Penalty: A misdemeanor of the fourth degree (2929.21, 2929.31)

Note: Nothing in this section shall be construed to limit access or deny information to any news media representative in the lawful exercise of his duties.

TELEPHONE HARASSMENT, R.C. § 2917.21 [M1, F5]

Division (A):
(1) Knowingly
(2) (a) Make a telephone call
    (or)
    (b) Cause a telephone call to be made
    (or)
    (c) Permit a telephone call to be made from a telephone under the offender's control
(3) To another
(4) If the caller does any of the following:
    (a) Fails to identify the caller to the recipient of the telephone call and makes the telephone

call with purpose to harass, abuse, or annoy any person at the premises to which the telephone call is made, whether or not conversation takes place during the telephone call
(or)
- (b) Describes, suggests, requests, or proposes that the caller, recipient of the telephone call, or any other person engage in, any sexual activity as defined in division (C) of section 2907.01 of the Revised Code, and the recipient of the telephone call, or another person at the premises to which the telephone call is made, has requested, in a previous telephone call or in the immediate telephone call, the caller not to make a telephone call to the recipient of the telephone call or to the premises to which the telephone call is made
(or)
- (c) During the telephone call, violates section 2903.21 of the Revised Code
(or)
- (d) Knowingly states to the recipient of the telephone call that the caller intends to cause damage to or destroy public or private property, and the recipient of the telephone call, any member of the family of the recipient of the telephone call, or any other person who resides at the premises to which the telephone call is made owns, leases, resides, or works in, will at the time of the destruction or damaging be near or in, has the responsibility of protecting, or insures the property that will be destroyed or damaged
(or)
- (e) Knowingly makes the telephone call to the recipient of the telephone call, to another person at the premises to which the telephone call is made, or to the premises to which the telephone call is made, and the recipient of the telephone call, or another person at the premises to which the telephone call is made, previously has told the caller not to call the premises to which the telephone call is made or not to call any persons at the premises to which the telephone call is made

(5) Venue

Division (B):
(1) (a) Make a telephone call
   (or)
   (b) Cause a telephone call to be made
   (or)
   (c) Permit a telephone call to be made from a telephone under the offender's control
(2) With purpose to
   (a) Abuse
   (or)
   (b) Threaten
   (or)
   (c) Annoy
   (or)
   (d) Harass
(3) Another person
(4) Venue

Penalty: A misdemeanor of the first degree (2929.21, 2929.31)

If prior conviction under this section involving the same person, recipient, or premises

Penalty: A felony of the fifth degree (2929.11-2929.18, 2929.31)

INDUCING PANIC, R.C. § 2917.31 [M1, F4]

(1) Cause
(2) The evacuation of a public place or serious public inconvenience or alarm
(3) By means of
    (a) Initiating or circulating a report or warning of alleged or impending fire, explosion, crime or other catastrophe, knowing such to be false
        (or)
    (b) Threatening to commit any offense of violence
        (or)
    (c) Committing any offense with reckless disregard of the likelihood that it will cause serious public inconvenience or alarm
(4) Venue

Penalty: A misdemeanor of the first degree (2929.21, 2929.31)

Where a violation results in physical harm to another

Penalty: A felony of the fourth degree (2929.11-2929.18, 2929.31)

MAKING FALSE ALARMS, R.C. § 2917.32 [M1]

(1) (a) Initiate or circulate a report/warning of alleged or impending fire, explosion, crime, or other catastrophe
    (b) Knowing it to be both false and likely to cause public inconvenience/alarm
        (or)
(2) (a) Knowingly cause
    (b) A false alarm of fire or other emergency
    (c) To be transmitted to or within
    (d) A public or private organization dealing with emergencies which involve a risk of physical harm to persons/property
        (or)
(3) (a) Report to any law enforcement agency
    (b) Alleged offense or other incident
    (c) Knowing such did not occur
(4) Venue

Penalty: A misdemeanor of the first degree (2929.21, 2929.31)

Note: This section does not apply to any person conducting an authorized fire emergency drill.

CROWD SAFETY, R.C. § 2917.40 [M1]

Division (B)(1):
(1) (a) Sell
        (or)
    (b) Offer to sell
        (or)
    (c) Offer in return for a donation
(2) Ticket that is not numbered and that does not correspond to a specific seat for admission to
(3) (a) A live entertainment performance that is not exempted under R.C. § 2917.40(D), that is held in a restricted entertainment area, and for which more than eight thousand tickets

are offered to the public
(or)
 (b) A concert that is not exempted under R.C. § 2917.40(D) and for which more than three thousand tickets are offered to the public
(4) Venue

Division (B)(2):
(1) Advertise
(2) A live entertainment performance that is not exempted under R.C. § 2917.40(D) that is held in a restricted entertainment area, and for which more than eight thousand tickets are offered to the public
(3) Without including the words "reserved seats only"
(4) Venue

Division (C):
(1) (a) Being the owner of a restricted entertainment area
  (or)
 (b) Being the operator of a restricted entertainment area
(2) Fail to open, maintain and properly staff
(3) Number of entrances designated by R.C. § 2917.40(E)
(4) For a minimum of 90 minutes prior to the start of a live entertainment performance
(5) Held in a restricted entertainment area
(6) For which more than 3,000 tickets are
 (a) Sold
  (or)
 (b) Offered for sale
  (or)
 (c) Offered in return for a donation
(7) Venue

Division (F):
(1) Enter into contract
(2) For a live entertainment performance
(3) That does not
 (a) Require
  (or)
 (b) Permit
(4) Compliance with R.C. § 2917.40

Penalty: A misdemeanor of the first degree (2929.21, 2929.31)

Notes: If any individual suffers physical harm to his person as a result of a violation of this section, the sentencing court shall consider this factor in favor of imposing a term of imprisonment upon the offender.

 Exempted performances, see R.C. § 2917.40(D).

 Responsibility for designating number of open, staffed entrances, see R.C. § 2917.40(E).

 Performances outside the scope of R.C. § 2917.40, see R.C. § 2917.40(G).

 Municipalities may impose additional requirements, see R.C. § 2917.40(H).

MISCONDUCT INVOLVING A PUBLIC TRANSPORTATION SYSTEM, R.C. § 2917.41 [M4, M3]

Division (A): **[M4]**
(1) Evade payment
(2) Of known fares
(3) Of a public transportation system
(4) Venue

Division (B): **[M4]**
(1) Alter any transfer, pass, ticket, or token
(2) Of a public transportation system
(3) With purpose of evading the payment of fares or of defrauding the system
(4) Venue

Division (C): **[M4]**
(1) (a) Play sound equipment without proper use of a private earphone
     (or)
    (b) (i) Smoke, eat, or drink
        (ii) In any area where such activity is clearly marked as being prohibited
     (or)
    (c) Expectorate upon a facility or vehicle
(2) While in any facility or vehicle
(3) Of a public transportation system
(4) Venue

Division (D): **[M3]**
(1) Write, deface, draw, or otherwise mark
(2) On any facility or vehicle
(3) Of a public transportation system
(4) Venue

Division (E): **[M4]**
(1) Fail to comply with a lawful order
    (and)
(2) Resist, obstruct, or abuse
(3) A public transportation system police officer in the performance of the officer's duties
(4) Venue

    Offense under Division (A), (B), (C), or (E)
Penalty: A misdemeanor of the fourth degree (2929.21, 2929.31)
    Offense under Division (D)
Penalty: A misdemeanor of the third degree (2929.21, 2929.31)
Definition: "Public transportation system," R.C. § 2917.41(G).

UNAUTHORIZED USE OF BLOCK PARENT SYMBOL, R.C. § 2917.46 [MM]

(1) With intent to identify a building as a block parent home or building
(2) (a) Display the block parent symbol, unless authorized
     (or)

(b) Display a symbol that falsely gives the appearance of being the block parent symbol
(3) Venue

Penalty: A minor misdemeanor (2929.21, 2929.31)

Note: See R.C. §§ 3301.07.6, 3313.20.6 regarding adoption and use of block parent symbols.

IMPROPERLY HANDLING INFECTIOUS AGENTS, R.C. § 2917.47 [F2]

(1) Knowingly
(2) Possess, send, receive, or cause to be sent or received
(3) An isolate or derivative of an isolate of an infectious agent

Penalty: A felony of the second degree (2929.11-2929.18, 2929.31).

Note: A person may possess, send, receive, or cause to be sent or received an isolate or derivative of an isolate of an infectious agent as permitted by state or federal law, including for purposes of biomedical or biotechnical research or production, provision of health care services, or investigation of disease by public health agencies.

OFFENSES AGAINST THE FAMILY

BIGAMY, R.C. § 2919.01 [M1]

(1) Being married
(2) (a) Marry another
      (*or*)
    (b) Continue to cohabit with another in this state
(3) Venue

Penalty: A misdemeanor of the first degree (2929.21, 2929.31)

Note: It is an affirmative defense that the spouse was continuously absent for five years and was not known by the actor to be alive, R.C. § 2919.01(B)

UNLAWFUL ABORTION, R.C. § 2919.12 [M1, F4, F5]

(1) Perform or induce abortion without informed consent of pregnant woman
    (*or*)
(2) Knowingly perform or induce abortion upon woman who is pregnant, unmarried, under eighteen, and unemancipated unless:
    (a) Person performing has given 24 hours actual notice to one parent, guardian, or custodian
        (*or*)
    (b) Woman has requested to notify one of certain specified relatives in lieu of parents, guardian, or custodian, affidavits containing specified information have been filed in juvenile court, the court has notified the person performing of the filing of the affidavits, the juvenile court has been given name and address of person performing, and the person performing has given 24 hours actual notice to the specified relative
        (*or*)
    (c) One parent, guardian, or custodian has given written consent

§ 2919.13

(or)
(d) Juvenile court has authorized woman to consent without notification pursuant to R.C. § 2151.85
(or)
(e) Juvenile court or court of appeals by inaction has constructively authorized woman to consent without notification pursuant to R.C. § 2151.85 or § 2505.07.3
(or)
(f) Parent, guardian, custodian, or specified relative notified in accordance with statute clearly and unequivocably expresses he or she does not wish to consult with the woman
(or)
(g) Reasonable efforts to give actual notice to appropriate person have failed, and 48 hours constructive notice has been given in manner specified in statute

(3) Venue

Penalty: A misdemeanor of the first degree (2929.21, 2929.31)

Subsequent offenses under division (1)

Penalty: A felony of the fourth degree (2929.11-2929.18, 2929.31)

Subsequent offenses under division (2)

Penalty: A felony of the fifth degree (2929.11-2929.18, 2929.31)

Notes: Affirmative defense that woman provided false, misleading, or incorrect information on specified matters and person had no reasonable cause to disbelieve such information.

Affirmative defense that compliance not possible because immediate threat of serious risk to life or health of woman created emergency necessitating immediate performance or inducement of abortion.

Offender also liable for civil compensatory and exemplary damages.

Definitions: "Unemancipated," R.C. § 2919.12(F)

ABORTION MANSLAUGHTER, R.C. § 2919.13 [F1]

Division (A):
(1) Purposely
(2) Take the life of a child
   (a) Born by attempted abortion
   (b) Alive when removed from the uterus of the pregnant woman
(3) Venue

Division (B):
(1) Being a person performing an abortion
(2) Fail to take measures required by the exercise of medical judgment in light of the attending circumstances to preserve the life of a child who is alive when removed from the uterus of a pregnant woman
(3) Venue

Penalty: A felony of the first degree (2929.11-2929.18, 2929.31)

ABORTION TRAFFICKING, R.C. § 2919.14 [M1]

(1) (a) Experiment upon
    (or)

(b) Sell
(2) The aborted product of human conception
(3) Venue

Penalty: A misdemeanor of the first degree (2929.21, 2929.31)

Note: "Experiment" does not include autopsies pursuant to R.C. §§ 313.13, 2108.50.

PERFORMING UNLAWFUL ABORTION PROCEDURE, R.C. § 2919.15 [F4]

(1) Knowingly
(2) Perform or attempt to perform
(3) A dilation and extraction procedure
(4) On a pregnant woman
(5) Venue

Penalty: A felony of the fourth degree (2929.11-2929.18, 2929.31)

Notes: Affirmative defense that all other available abortion procedures would pose a greater risk to the health of a pregnant woman than the risk posed by the dilation and extraction procedure.

TERMINATING OR ATTEMPTING TO TERMINATE HUMAN PREGNANCY AFTER VIABILITY, R.C. § 2919.17 [F4]

Division (A):
(1) Purposely
(2) (a) Perform or induce
    (or)
    (b) Attempt to perform or induce
(3) An abortion
(4) Upon a pregnant woman
(5) If the unborn human is viable unless the abortion is performed or induced or attempted to be performed or induced by a physician and that physician determines, in good faith and in the exercise of reasonable medical judgment,
    (a) that the abortion is necessary to prevent the death of the pregnant woman or a serious risk of the substantial and irreversible impairment of a major bodily function of the pregnant woman
    (or)
    (b) after making a determination relative of the viability of the unborn human in conformity with Division (A) of R.C. § 2919.18 that the unborn human is not viable
(6) Venue

Division (B):
(1) Physician
(2) Purposely
(3) (a) Perform or induce
    (or)
    (b) Attempt to perform or induce
(4) An abortion
(5) Upon a pregnant woman when the unborn human is viable and when the physician has

determined, in good faith and reasonable medical judgment, that the abortion is necessary to prevent the death of the pregnant woman or a serious risk of the substantial and irreversible impairment of a major bodily function of the pregnant woman, unless each of the following is satisfied:
- (a) the physician certifies in writing that he has determined, in good faith and the exercise of reasonable medical judgment, that the abortion is necessary to prevent the death of the pregnant woman or a serious risk of the substantial and irreversible impairment of a major bodily function of the pregnant woman
(*and*)
- (b) the determination referred to in (5)(a) is concurred in by at least one other physician who certifies in writing that the concurring physician has determined, in good faith and the exercise of reasonable medical judgment, and following a review of the available medical records of and any available test results pertaining to the pregnant woman, that the abortion is necessary to prevent the death of the pregnant woman or a serious risk of the substantial and irreversible impairment of a major bodily function of the pregnant woman
(*and*)
- (c) the abortion is performed or induced or attempted to be performed or induced in a health care facility that has or has access to appropriate neonatal services for premature infants
(*and*)
- (d) the physician who performs or induces or attempts to perform or induce the abortion terminates or attempts to terminate the pregnancy in the manner that provides the best opportunity for the unborn human to survive, unless that physician determines, in good faith and in the exercise of reasonable medical judgment, that the termination of the pregnancy in that manner poses a significantly greater risk of the death of the pregnant woman or a serious risk of the substantial and irreversible impairment of a major bodily function of the pregnant woman than would other available methods of abortion
(*and*)
- (e) the physician who performs or induces or attempts to perform or induce the abortion has arranged for the attendance in the same room in which the abortion is to be performed or induced or attempted to be performed or induced of at least one other physician who is to take control of, provide immediate medical care for, and take all reasonable steps necessary to preserve the life and health of the unborn human immediately upon the unborn human's complete expulsion or extraction from the pregnant woman

(6) Venue

Penalty: A felony of the fourth degree (2929.11-2929.18, 2929.31)

Notes: Division (B) does not prohibit the performance or inducement or attempted performance or inducement of an abortion without prior satisfaction of each of the conditions described in Division (B)(5)(a)-(e) if the physician in good faith and reasonable medical judgment believes that a medical emergency exists that prevents compliance with one or more of those conditions.

FAILURE TO PERFORM VIABILITY TESTING, R.C. § 2919.18 [M4]

Division (A)(1):
(1) Physician
(2) (a) Perform or induce

(or)
    (b) Attempt to perform or induce
(3) An abortion
(4) Upon a pregnant woman after the beginning of her twenty-second week of pregnancy unless the physician determines in good faith and in the exercise of reasonable medical judgment, that the unborn human is not viable, and the physician makes that determination after performing a medical examination and after performing or causing the performance of gestational age, weight, lung maturity, or other tests of the unborn human that a reasonable physician making a determination as to whether an unborn human is or is not viable would perform or cause to be performed
(5) Venue

Division (A)(2):
(1) Physician
(2) (a) Perform or induce
    (or)
    (b) Attempt to perform or induce
(3) An abortion
(4) Upon a pregnant woman after the beginning of her twenty-second week of pregnancy without first entering the determination described in Division (A)(1) and the associated findings of the medical examination and tests in the medical record of the woman
(5) Venue

Penalty: A misdemeanor of the fourth degree (2929.21, 2929.31)

Notes: Divisions (A)(1) and (2) do not prohibit a physician from performing or inducing or attempting to perform or induce an abortion on a pregnant woman after the beginning of her twenty-second week of pregnancy if a medical emergency exists.

NONSUPPORT OR CONTRIBUTING TO NONSUPPORT OF DEPENDENTS, R.C. § 2919.21 [M1, F5, F4]

Division (A): **[M1, F5, F4]**
(1) Abandon or fail to support adequately according to law
(2) (a) A spouse
    (or)
    (b) A child under 18, or a mentally or physically handicapped child under 21
    (or)
    (c) An aged/infirm parent or adoptive parent who is unable to provide adequately the parent's own support
(3) Venue

Division (B): **[M1, F5, F4]**
(1) Abandon or fail to provide support as established by a court order to
(2) Another person
(3) Whom by court order or decree,
(4) The person is legally obligated to support
(5) Venue

Penalty: A misdemeanor of the first degree (2929.21, 2929.31)

If previously convicted under (A)(2)(b) or (B), above, or if the offender has failed to provide support under (A)(2)(b) or (B), above for 26 of 104 weeks

Penalty: A felony of the fifth degree (2929.11-2929.18, 2929.31)

If previously convicted of a felony violation of (A)(2)(b) or (B) of this section

Penalty: A felony of the fourth degree (2929.11-2929.18, 2929.31)

Division (C): **[M1]**
(1) Aid, abet, induce, cause, encourage, or contribute to
(2) (a) Child
    (*or*)
  (b) Ward of juvenile court
(3) (a) Becoming a dependent child as defined in R.C. § 2151.04
    (*or*)
  (b) Becoming a neglected child as defined in R.C. § 2151.03
(4) Venue

Penalty: A misdemeanor of the first degree (2929.21, 2929.31)

Notes: It is an affirmative defense to a charge under this section that the accused was unable to provide adequate support or the established support, and provided such support as was within his ability and means. In addition, it is an affirmative defense to a charge under (A)(2)(c) above, that the parent abandoned, or failed to support the accused as required by law, while the accused was under age 18, or was mentally or physically handicapped and under age 21.

It is not a defense to a charge under division (B) that the person whom a court has ordered the accused to support is being adequately supported by someone other than the accused.

Court costs and the attorney fees of adverse parties are to be assessed for a violation of a support order issued on or after 4-15-85.

Each day of violation of Division (C) is a separate offense.

ENDANGERING CHILDREN, R.C. § 2919.22 [M1, F5, F4, F3, F2]

Division (A):
(1) Being a parent, guardian, custodian, person with custody or control, or a person in loco parentis
(2) Create a substantial risk to the health or safety of
(3) A child under 18 or a mentally or physically handicapped person under 21
(4) By violating a duty of care, protection, or support
(5) Venue

Division (B):
(1) (a) Abuse a child
    (*or*)
  (b) Torture/cruelly abuse a child
    (*or*)
  (c) Administer corporal punishment or use other physical disciplinary measures, or physically restrain a child in a cruel manner or for prolonged periods in a manner excessive under the circumstances and which creates substantial risk of serious physical harm
    (*or*)
  (d) Repeatedly administer unwarranted disciplinary measures to a child involving substantial

risk that such conduct, if continued, will seriously impair or retard mental health/development if continued
   (or)
(e) Entice, coerce, permit, encourage, compel, employ, hire, use, or allow the child to act, model, or in any other way participate in, or be photographed for, the production, presentation, dissemination, or advertisement of any material or performance that he knows or reasonably should know is obscene, as defined in R.C. § 2907.01, or any material or performance that is a sexually- or nudity-oriented matter
   (or)
(2) When such child is under 18 or is a mentally or physically handicapped child under 21
(3) Venue

Division (C):
(1) Operate a vehicle, streetcar, or trackless trolley
(2) Within this state
(3) In violation of Division (A) of R.C. § 4511.19
(4) When one or more children under 18 are in the vehicle, streetcar, or trackless trolley
(5) Venue

Violation of (A) or (B)(1)
Penalty: A misdemeanor of the first degree (2929.21, 2929.31)
Where offender has previously been convicted under this section or of any offense involving neglect, abandonment, contributing to the delinquency of, or physical abuse of a child
Penalty: A felony of the fourth degree (2929.11-2929.18, 2929.31)
Where serious physical harm results to child
Penalty: A felony of the third degree (2929.11-2929.18, 2929.31)
Violation of (B)(1)(b), (c) or (d)
Penalty: A felony of the third degree (2929.11-2929.18, 2929.31)
Violation of (B)(1)(b), (c), or (d), plus serious physical harm to the child or prior conviction under this section or any offense involving neglect, abandonment, contributing to the delinquency of or physical abuse of a child
Violation of (B)(1)(e) or (f)
Penalty: A felony of the second degree (2929.11-2929.18, 2929.31)
Violation of (C) with no violation of (B)(5)(b) or (c)
Penalty: A misdemeanor of the first degree (2929.21, 2929.31)
> Up to 200 hours of supervised community service may be required
>
> Driver's or commercial driver's permit or nonresident operating privilege may be suspended for up to 90 days
>
>> Violation of (C) with no violation of (B)(5)(c) and serious physical harm results to the child or the offender has previously been convicted of an offense under this section or any offense involving neglect, abandonment, contributing to the delinquency of, or physical abuse of a child

Penalty: A felony of the fifth degree (2929.11-2929.18, 2929.31)
> Up to 200 hours of supervised community service may be required

Driver's or commercial driver's permit or nonresident operating privilege may be suspended for up to 90 days

    Violation of (C) resulting in serious physical harm to the child involved and the offender previously has been convicted of a violation of Division (C) of this section, R.C. §§ 2903.06, 2903.07, or 2903.08, or R.C. § 2903.04 in a case in which the offender was subject to the sanctions described in Division (D) of that section

Penalty: A felony of the fourth degree (2929.11-2929.18, 2929.31)

Notes: It is not a violation of a duty of care, protection or support under Division (A) where the parent, guardian, custodian, or person having custody or control of a child treats the physical or mental illness or defect of such child by spiritual means—through prayer alone, in accordance with the tenets of a recognized religious body.

    Division (B) of this section does not apply to any material or performance that is produced, presented, or disseminated for a bona fide medical, scientific, educational, religious, governmental, judicial, or other proper purpose, by or to a physician, psychologist, sociologist, scientist, teacher, person pursuing bona fide studies or research, librarian, clergyman, prosecutor, judge, or other person having a proper interest in the material or performance.

    Mistake of age is not a defense under (B)(1)(e) above.

    See R.C. § 2919.22 for provisions regarding the inference of age by the trier of fact.

    R.C. § 2933.16 provides that if an offender is convicted of or pleads guilty to a violation of R.C. § 2919.22(B), the court may suspend execution of sentence and place the offender on probation conditioned upon the participation of the offender, to the satisfaction of the court, in a program of clinically appropriate psychiatric or psychological treatment.

    Any sentence of imprisonment imposed under (B)(1)(e) above is to be served consecutively to any other sentence of imprisonment.

Definitions: "Material," "performance," and "sexual activity" have the same meanings as in section 2907.01 of the Revised Code.

    "Nudity-oriented matter" means any material or performance that shows a minor in a state of nudity and that, taken as a whole by the average person applying contemporary community standards, appeals to prurient interest. R.C. § 2919.22.

    "Sexually oriented matter" means any material or performance that shows a minor participating or engaging in sexual activity, masturbation, or bestiality. R.C. § 2919.22.

    "Prostitute" has the meaning given in R.C. § 2907.01

PARENTAL EDUCATION NEGLECT, R.C. § 2919.22.2 [M4]

(1) Fail to attend a parental education or training program
(2) The person is required to attend pursuant to a policy adopted under § 3313.66.3
(3) Venue

Penalty: A misdemeanor of the fourth degree (2929.21, 2929.31)

INTERFERENCE WITH CUSTODY, R.C. § 2919.23 [M3, M1, F5, F4]

Division (A):
(1) (a) Knowing the person is without privilege to do so
    (or)
   (b) Being reckless in that regard

(2) Entice, take, keep or harbor from parent, guardian or custodian
(3) (a) A child under 18 or mentally/physically handicapped child under 21
    (or)
    (b) A person committed by laws to an institution for delinquent, unruly, neglected, abused, or dependent children
    (or)
    (c) A person committed by laws to an institution for the mentally ill/mentally retarded
(4) Venue

Division (B):
(1) Aid, abet, induce, cause, or encourage
(2) (a) Child
    (or)
    (b) Ward of the juvenile court
(3) Who has been committed to the custody of any person, department, or public or private institution
(4) To leave the custody of that person, department, or institution
(5) Without legal consent
(6) Venue

Division (A)(3)(a)
Penalty: A misdemeanor of the first degree (2929.21, 2929.31)
If the child is removed from the state or if the offender previously has been convicted of an offense under this section
Penalty: A felony of the fifth degree (2929.11-2929.18, 2929.31)
If the child suffers physical harm as a result of the violation
Penalty: A felony of the fourth degree (2929.11-2929.18, 2929.31)

Division (A)(3)(b) or (c)
Penalty: A misdemeanor of the third degree (2929.21, 2929.31)

Division (B)
Penalty: A misdemeanor of the first degree (2929.21, 2929.31)

Notes: It is an affirmative defense to a charge of enticing or taking, under Division (A)(3)(a), above, that the actor reasonably believed that his conduct was necessary to preserve the child's health or safety. It is an affirmative defense to a charge of keeping or harboring under this section, that the actor in good faith gave notice to law enforcement or judicial authorities within a reasonable time after the child or committed person came under his shelter, protection or influence.

Each day of violation of Division (B) is a separate offense.

INTERFERING WITH ACTION TO ISSUE OR MODIFY SUPPORT ORDER, R.C. § 2919.23.1 [M1, F5]

(1) By using physical harassment or threats of violence against another person
(2) (a) Interfere with the other person's initiation or continuance of
    (or)
    (b) Attempt to prevent the other person from initiating or continuing an action to issue or modify

§ 2919.24

(3) A support order under Chapter 3115, or under R.C. § 2151.23, 2151.23.1, 2151.23.2, 2151.33, 2151.36, 2151.49, 3105.18, 3105.21, 3109.05, 3109.19, 3111.13, 3113.04, 3113.07, or 3113.31
(4) Venue

Penalty: A misdemeanor of the first degree (2929.21, 2929.31)

If prior conviction under this section or R.C. § 3111.29

Penalty: A felony of the fifth degree (2929.11-2929.18, 2929.31)

CONTRIBUTING TO THE UNRULINESS OR DELINQUENCY OF A CHILD, R.C. § 2919.24 [M1]

(1) (a) Aid, abet, induce, cause, encourage, or contribute to
    (*or*)
    (b) Act in a way tending to cause
(2) (a) Child
    (*or*)
    (b) Ward of the juvenile court
(3) (a) Becoming (to become) an unruly child, as defined in R.C. § 2151.022
    (*or*)
    (b) Becoming (to become) a delinquent child, as defined in R.C. § 2151.02
(4) Venue

Penalty: A misdemeanor of the first degree (2929.21, 2929.31)

Note: Each day of violation is a separate offense.

DOMESTIC VIOLENCE, R.C. § 2919.25 [M4, M3, M1, F5]

Division (A):
(1) Knowingly
(2) Cause or attempt to cause
(3) Physical harm
(4) To a family or household member
(5) Venue

Division (B):
(1) Recklessly
(2) Cause
(3) Serious physical harm
(4) To a family or household member
(5) Venue

Division (C):
(1) Knowingly
(2) By force or threat of force
(3) Cause
(4) A family or household member to believe
(5) The offender will cause imminent physical harm
(6) To the family or household member
(7) Venue

Division (A) or (B), no previous conviction under this section or conviction under R.C. §§ 2903.11, 2903.12, 2903.13, 2903.14, 2903.21, 2903.211, 2903.22, 2911.211, or 2919.22 involving person who was family or household member at time of violation or a violation of a municipal ordinance that is substantially similar to one of those sections involving person who was family or household member at time of violation

Penalty: A misdemeanor of the first degree (2929.21, 2929.31)

Division (A) or (B), previous conviction under this section of a violation of municipal ordinance that is substantially similar to domestic violence, or conviction under R.C. §§ 2903.11, 2903.12, 2903.13, 2903.14, 2903.21, 2903.211, 2903.22, 2911.211, or 2919.22 involving person who was family or household member at time of violation

Penalty: A felony of the fifth degree (2929.11-2929.18, 2929.31)

Division (C), no previous conviction under this section or conviction under R.C. §§ 2903.11, 2903.12, 2903.13, 2903.14, 2903.21, 2903.211, 2903.22, 2911.211, or 2919.22 involving person who was family or household member at time of violation

Penalty: A misdemeanor of the fourth degree (2929.21, 2929.31)

Division (C), no previous conviction under this section of a violation of municipal ordinance that is substantially similar to domestic violence, or conviction under R.C. §§ 2903.11, 2903.12, 2903.13, 2903.14, 2903.21, 2903.211, 2903.22, 2911.211, or 2919.22 involving person who was family or household member at time of violation or a violation of a municipal ordinance that is substantially similar to one of those sections involving person who was family or household member at time of violation

Penalty: A misdemeanor of the third degree (2929.21, 2929.31)

Notes: R.C. § 2933.16 provides that if an offender is convicted of or pleads guilty to a violation of R.C. § 2919.25, the court may suspend execution of sentence and place the offender on probation conditioned upon the participation of the offender, to the satisfaction of the court, in a program of clinically appropriate psychiatric or psychological treatment.

For bail considerations for prior offenders or persons subject to protection order or consent agreement, R.C. § 2919.25.1.

Definitions: "Family or household member," "person living as a spouse," R.C. § 2919.25(E)

"Motion for temporary protection order," R.C. § 2919.26

VIOLATING PROTECTION ORDER, CONSENT AGREEMENT OR ANTI-STALKING PROTECTION ORDER, R.C. § 2919.27 [M1, F5]

(1) Recklessly
(2) Violate any terms
(3) Of protection order issued or consent agreement approved pursuant to R.C. § 2919.26 or § 3113.31
   (*or*)
(4) Of an anti-stalking protection order issued pursuant to R.C. § 2903.21.3
(5) Of protection order issued by a court of another state
(6) Venue

Penalty: A misdemeanor of the first degree (2929.21, 2929.31)

Violation of (3)

Penalty: A misdemeanor of the first degree (2929.21, 2929.31)

If one or more prior convictions/guilty pleas under this section or two or more violations of R.C. § 2903.21.1 or 2911.21.1, involving same person who is subject of protection order or consent agreement or anti-stalking protection order

Penalty: A felony of the fifth degree (2929.11-2929.18, 2929.31)

Violation of (4)

Penalty: A misdemeanor of the first degree (2929.21, 2929.31)

If previous conviction or guilty plea to two or more violations of this section or of former R.C. § 2919.27 involving an anti-stalking protection order, two or more violations of R.C. §§ 2903.21, 2903.211, 2903.22, or 2911.211 that involve the same person who is the subject of the anti-stalking protection order, or two or more violations of R.C. § 2903.214 as it existed prior to July 1, 1996

Penalty: A felony of the fifth degree (2929.11-2929.18, 2929.31)

Note: See R.C. §§ 2919.27.1, 2937.23, concerning mental examination of defendants.

OFFENSES AGAINST JUSTICE AND PUBLIC ADMINISTRATION

BRIBERY, R.C. § 2921.02 [F3]

Division (A):
(1) With purpose to corrupt or improperly influence
(2) A public servant or party official whether before or after attaining office
(3) With respect to the discharge of his duty
(4) Promise, offer or give any valuable thing or benefit
(5) Venue

Division (B):
(1) Knowingly solicit/accept any valuable thing or benefit for himself or another person
(2) As a public servant/party official
(3) To corrupt or improperly influence him or another public servant or party official
(4) With respect to the discharge of his or the other servant's or official's duty
(5) Before or after attaining office
(6) Venue

Division (C):
(1) With purpose to corrupt a witness or improperly influence his testimony in an official proceeding
(2) Promise, offer or give any valuable thing or benefit to said witness or another person
(3) Either before or after he is subpoenaed or sworn
(4) Venue

Division (D):
(1) Knowingly solicit or accept a valuable thing or benefit for himself or another person
(2) To corrupt or improperly influence acceptor's testimony in an official proceeding
(3) Venue

Penalty: A felony of the third degree (2929.11-2929.18, 2929.31)

Note: If public servant or party official is convicted, he is forever disqualified from holding public office, employment, or position of trust in state.

INTIMIDATION, R.C. § 2921.03 [F3]

(1) Knowingly
(2) By force, unlawful threat of harm, or by filing, recording, or otherwise using a materially false or fraudulent writing with malicious purpose, in bad faith, or in a wanton and reckless manner
(3) Attempt to influence, intimidate or hinder a public servant, party official, an attorney, or witness involved in a civil action or proceeding
(4) In the discharge of the duties of the public servant, party official, attorney, or witness
(5) Venue

Penalty: A felony of the third degree (2929.11-2929.18, 2929.31)

INTIMIDATION OF ATTORNEY, VICTIM OR WITNESS IN CRIMINAL CASE, R.C. § 2921.04 [M1, F3]

Division (A): [M1]
(1) Knowingly
(2) Attempt to
(3) (a) Intimidate
    (*or*)
  (b) Hinder
(4) (a) A victim of crime
    (i) In filing of criminal charges
      (*or*)
    (ii) In prosecution of criminal charges
      (*or*)
  (b) A witness involved in a criminal action or proceeding in the discharge of the duties of the witness
(5) Venue

Division (B): [F3]
(1) Knowingly
(2) (a) By force
    (*or*)
  (b) By unlawful threat of harm to any person or property
(3) Attempt to
(4) (a) Influence
    (*or*)
  (b) Intimidate
    (*or*)
  (c) Hinder
(5) (a) A victim of crime
    (i) In filing of criminal charges
      (*or*)
    (ii) In prosecution of criminal charges
      (*or*)

§ 2921.05

(b) An attorney or witness involved in a criminal action or proceeding in the discharge of the duties of the attorney or witness

(6) Venue

Division (A):

Penalty: A misdemeanor of the first degree (2929.21, 2929.31)

Division (B):

Penalty: A felony of the third degree (2929.11-2929.18, 2929.31)

Note: Division (A) above does not apply to any person who, either prior or subsequent to the filing of the complaint, indictment, information, is either attempting to resolve a dispute pertaining to the alleged commission of a criminal offense, or is attempting to arbitrate, mediate, compromise, settle, or assist in the conciliation of that dispute pursuant to an authorization for arbitration, mediation, compromise, settlement, or conciliation of a dispute of that nature. See R.C. § 2921.04(C).

RETALIATION, R.C. § 2921.05 [F3]

Division (A):
(1) Purposely
(2) (a) By force
    (or)
    (b) By unlawful threat of harm to any person or property
(3) Retaliate against a public servant, a party official, or an attorney or witness who was involved in a civil or criminal action or proceeding
(4) Because the public servant, party official, or attorney or witness discharged the duties of the public servant, party official, attorney, or witness
(5) Venue

Division (B):
(1) Purposely
(2) (a) By force
    (or)
    (b) By unlawful threat of harm to any person or property
(3) Retaliate against the victim of a crime
(4) Because the victim filed or prosecuted criminal charges
(5) Venue

Penalty: A felony of the third degree (2929.11-2929.18, 2929.31)

PERJURY, R.C. § 2921.11 [F3]

(1) Knowingly
(2) (a) Make a false statement under oath or affirmation
    (or)
    (b) Swear or affirm the truth of a false statement previously made
(3) In an official proceeding
(4) When either statement is material to such proceeding
(5) Venue

Penalty: A felony of the third degree (2929.11-2929.18, 2929.31)

Notes: No conviction may be had under this section where proof of falsity rests solely upon contradictory testimony of one person, other than defendant. However, where contradictory statements relating to the same material fact are made by the offender under oath or affirmation and within the period of the statute of limitations for perjury, it is not necessary for the prosecution to prove which statement was false, but only that one or the other was false.

A falsification is material, regardless of its admissibility in evidence, if it can affect the course or outcome of the proceeding. It is no defense to a charge under this section that the offender mistakenly believed a falsification to be immaterial.

TAMPERING WITH EVIDENCE, R.C. § 2921.12 [F3]

(1) Knowing an official proceeding or investigation is in progress, or is about to be or is likely to be instituted
(2) (a) (i) Alter, destroy, conceal, or remove any record, document, or thing
      (ii) With purpose to impair its value or availability as evidence in such proceeding or investigation
      (*or*)
  (b) (i) Make, present, or use any record, document or thing
      (ii) Knowing it to be false
      (iii) With purpose to mislead a public official who is or may be engaged in a proceeding or investigation or with a purpose to corrupt the outcome of any proceeding or investigation
(3) Venue

Penalty: A felony of the third degree (2929.11-2929.18, 2929.31)

FALSIFICATION; IN THEFT OFFENSE; TO PURCHASE FIREARM, R.C. § 2921.13 [M1, F5, F4, F3]

Division (A):
(1) Knowingly
  (a) Make a false statement
    (*or*)
  (b) Swear or affirm the truth of a previous false statement
(2) When such is:
  (a) Made in official proceeding
    (*or*)
  (b) Made with purpose to incriminate another
    (*or*)
  (c) Made with purpose to mislead public official in performing his official function
    (*or*)
  (d) Made with a purpose to secure payment of unemployment compensation; Ohio Works First; prevention, retention, and contingency assistance; disability assistance; retirement benefits; economic development assistance as defined in § 9.66 of the Revised Code; or other benefits administered by governmental agency or paid out of public treasury
    (*or*)

- (e) Made with a purpose to secure issuance by governmental agency of license, permit, authorization, certificate, registration, release, or provider agreement
  (or)
- (f) Sworn or affirmed before notary public or other person empowered to administer oath
  (or)
- (g) In writing on or in connection with a report or return that is required or authorized by law
  (or)
- (h) In writing, and made with purpose to induce another to extend credit, employ offender; confer any degree, diploma, certificate of attainment, award of excellence, honor on offender; extend or bestow on offender any other valuable benefit or distinction when person to whom statement directed relies upon it to that person's detriment
  (or)
- (i) Made with purpose to commit or facilitate commission of theft offense
  (or)
- (j) Made to a probate court in connection with any action, proceeding, or other matter within its jurisdiction, either orally or in a written document, including but not limited to, an application, petition, complaint, or other pleading, or an inventory, account, or report
  (or)
- (k) Made on an account, record, stamp, or other writing that is required by law.
  (or)
- (l) Made in connection with the purchase of a firearm, as defined in RC § 2923.11, and in conjunction with the furnishing to the seller of the firearm of a fictitious or altered driver's or commercial driver's license or permit, a fictitious or altered identification card, or any other document that contains false information about the purchaser's identity
  (or)
- (m) Made in a document or instrument of writing that purports to be a judgment, lien, or claim of indebtedness and is filed or recorded with the secretary of state, a county recorder, or the clerk of a court of record

(3) Venue

Division (B):
(1) In connection with the purchase of a firearm
(2) Knowingly furnish to the seller of the firearm a fictitious or altered driver's or commercial driver's license or permit, a fictitious or altered identification card, or any other document that contains false information about the purchaser's identity
(3) Venue

Violation of (A)(2)(a)(b)(c)(d)(e)(f)(g)(h)(j)(k)(m)

Penalty: A misdemeanor of the first degree (2929.21, 2929.31)

Violation of (A)(2)(i) (falsification in a theft offense)

Penalty: A misdemeanor of the first degree (2929.21, 2929.31)

If the value of the property or services stolen is $500 or more and is less than $5,000

Penalty: A felony of the fifth degree (2929.11-2929.18, 2929.31)

If the value of the property or services stolen is $5,000 or more and less than $100,000

Penalty: A felony of the fourth degree (2929.11-2929.18, 2929.31)

If the value of the property or services stolen is $100,000 or more
Penalty: A felony of the third degree (2929.11-2929.18, 2929.31)
Violation of (A)(2)(l) or (B)
Penalty: A felony of the fifth degree (2929.11-2929.18, 2929.31)

FALSE REPORT OF CHILD ABUSE OR NEGLECT, R.C. § 2921.14 [M1]

(1) Knowingly
(2) (a) Make
    (*or*)
  (b) Cause another person to make
(3) A false report under R.C. § 2151.42.1(B) that any person has committed an act or omission that resulted in a child being
  (a) An abused child as defined in R.C. § 2151.03.1
    (*or*)
  (b) A neglected child as defined in R.C. § 2151.03
(4) Venue

Penalty: A misdemeanor of the first degree (2929.21, 2929.31)

COMPOUNDING A CRIME, R.C. § 2921.21 [M1]

(1) Knowingly
(2) Demand, accept, or agree to accept
(3) Anything of value
(4) In consideration for abandoning or agreeing to abandon a pending prosecution
(5) Venue

Penalty: A misdemeanor of the first degree (2929.21, 2929.31)

Note: There is no violation if pending prosecution is for a violation of R.C. § 2913.02 (theft), 2913.11 (bad checks), 2913.21(B)(2) (credit cards), or 2913.47 (insurance fraud), the actor under this section is the victim, and the thing of value received did not exceed amount which actor reasonably believed due him as restitution for loss caused by offense.

FAILURE TO REPORT A CRIME OR KNOWLEDGE OF A DEATH, OR BURN INJURY, R.C. § 2921.22 [M4, M2, MM]

Division (A): [M4] Failure to report a crime (Felony)
(1) While having knowledge that a felony has been or is being committed
(2) Knowingly
(3) Fail to report
(4) To law enforcement authorities
(5) That a felony has been or is being committed

Penalty: A misdemeanor of the fourth degree (2929.21, 2929.31)

Division (B): [M2] Failure to report a crime (Injury from offense of violence)
(1) While a physician, limited practitioner, nurse, or other person giving aid to a sick or injured person
(2) Negligently

(3) Fail to report
(4) To law enforcement authorities
(5) (a) Any gunshot wound treated or observed by the physician, limited practictioner, nurse, or person
    (or)
    (b) Any stab wound treated or observed by the physician, limited practictioner, nurse, or person
    (or)
    (c) Any serious physical harm to persons that the physician, limited practictioner, nurse, or person knows or has reasonable cause to believe resulted from an offense of violence

Penalty: A misdemeanor of the second degree (2929.21, 2929.31)

Division (C): **[M4]** Failure to report knowledge of a death
(1) (a) Having discovered the body of a person
    (or)
    (b) Having acquired the first knowledge of the death of a person
(2) Fail to report the death immediately to
(3) (a) Any physician known to be treating the deceased for a condition from which death at such time would not be unexpected
    (or)
    (b) A law enforcement officer
    (or)
    (c) An ambulance service
    (or)
    (d) An emergency squad
    (or)
    (e) The coroner in a political subdivision in which the body is discovered, the death is believed to have occurred, or knowledge concerning the death is obtained

Penalty: A misdemeanor of the fourth degree (2929.21, 2929.31)

Division (D): **[M4]** Failure to report knowledge of a death (Facts bearing on investigation of death)
(1) Fail to provide
(2) (a) Upon request of the person to whom a report under (C) above was made
    (or)
    (b) To any law enforcement officer who has reasonable cause to assert the authority to investigate the circumstances surrounding the death
(3) Any facts within the person's knowledge that may have a bearing on the facts of the death

Penalty: A misdemeanor of the fourth degree (2929.21, 2929.31)

Division (E): **[M2, MM]** Failure to report a burn injury
(1) (a) While a physician, nurse, or limited practitioner outside a hospital, sanitarium, or other medical facility who attends or treats a person who has sustained a
    (or)
    (b) While a manager, superintendent, or other person in charge of a hospital, sanitarium, or other medical facility in which a person is attended or treated for any
(2) Burn injury
(3) (a) Inflicted by an explosion or other incendiary device

  (or)
  (b) That shows evidence of having been inflicted in a violent, malicious, or criminal manner
(4) (a) Fail to report the burn injury immediately to the local arson bureau if there is one in the jurisdiction in which the person is attended or treated or otherwise to local law enforcement authorities
  (or)
  (b) Fail to file within three working days after attending or treating the victim, a written report, on a form to be provided by the state fire marshal, with the state fire marshal

Negligent violation of (E)

Penalty: A minor misdemeanor (2929.21, 2929.31)

Knowing violation of (E)

Penalty: A misdemeanor of the second degree (2929.21, 2929.31)

Note: Division (A) or (D) does not apply in privileged relationships listed in R.C. § 2921.22(F); R.C. § 2921.22(G) disallows liability for breach of privilege in disclosures under R.C. § 2921.22.

Definition: "Burn injury" means any second or third degree burns, burns to the upper respiratory tract or laryngeal edema due to the inhalation of superheated air, or any burn injury or wound that may result in death. R.C. § 2921.22(E)

FAILURE TO AID LAW ENFORCEMENT OFFICER, R.C. § 2921.23 [MM]

(1) When called upon to assist law enforcement officer in preventing/halting commission of offense, or in apprehension or detention of an offender
(2) Negligently fail or refuse to render aid
(3) When such aid can be given without substantial risk of physical harm to person called upon
(4) Venue

Penalty: A minor misdemeanor (2929.21, 2929.31)

DISCLOSURE OF CONFIDENTIAL INFORMATION, R.C. § 2921.24 [M4]

(1) Being an officer or employee
(2) (a) Of a law enforcement agency or court
  (or)
  (b) Of the office of the clerk of any court
(3) Disclose
(4) During the pendency of any criminal case
(5) The home address of any peace officer as defined in R.C. § 2935.01
(6) Who is a witness or arresting officer in the case
(7) Venue

Penalty: A misdemeanor of the fourth degree (2929.21, 2929.31)

Notes: The court in which any criminal case is pending may order the disclosure of the home address of any peace officer in the case pursuant to a written request and for good cause shown. *See* R.C. § 2921.24(C).

This section does not prohibit a peace officer from disclosing his own address, and does not apply to any person who discloses such address pursuant to a court order. *See* R.C. § 2921.24(B).

OBSTRUCTING OFFICIAL BUSINESS, R.C. § 2921.31 [M2]

(1) Perform any act which hampers/impedes a public official in the performance of his lawful duties
(2) With a purpose to prevent, obstruct, or delay performance by a public official of his authorized acts
(3) Without having a privilege to do so
(4) Venue

Penalty: A misdemeanor of the second degree (2929.21, 2929.31)

OBSTRUCTING JUSTICE, R.C. § 2921.32 [MM, M4, M3, M2, M1, F5, F3]

(1) With a purpose
    (a) To hinder the discovery, apprehension, prosecution, conviction, or punishment of another for crime
    (or)
    (b) To assist another to benefit from the commission of a crime
(2) (a) Harbor or conceal another
    (or)
    (b) Provide another with money, transportation, a weapon, disguise or other means of avoiding discovery or apprehension
    (or)
    (c) Warn another of impending discovery or apprehension
    (or)
    (d) Destroy or conceal physical evidence of a crime
    (or)
    (e) Induce anyone to withhold testimony or information, or elude legal process summoning the other person to testify or supply evidence
    (or)
    (f) Communicate false information to anyone
(3) Venue

If the person aided committed a misdemeanor, a misdemeanor of the same degree and the crime committed **[MM, M4, M3, M2, M1]**

If the person aided committed a felony:

Penalty: A felony of the fifth degree (2929.11-2929.18, 2929.31)

If the person aided committed aggravated murder, murder, or a felony of the first or second degree and if the offender knows or has reason to believe that the crime committed by the person aided is one of those offenses

Penalty: A felony of the third degree (2929.11-2929.18, 2929.31)

ASSAULTING POLICE DOG OR HORSE OR HANDICAPPED ASSISTANCE DOG, R.C. § 2921.32.1 [M2, M1, F5, F4]

Division (A):
(1) Knowingly
(2) Cause or attempt to cause
(3) Physical harm

(4) To a police dog or horse
(5) In either of the following circumstances:
   (i) the police dog or horse is assisting a law enforcement officer in the performance of the officer's official duties at the time the physical harm is caused or attempted (*or*)
   (ii) the police dog or horse is not assisting a law enforcement officer in the performance of the officer's official duties at the time the physical harm is caused or attempted, but the offender has actual knowledge that the dog or horse is a police dog or horse
(6) Venue

Division (B):
(1) Knowingly
(2) Cause or attempt to cause
(3) Physical harm
(4) To a handicapped assistance dog
(5) In either of the following circumstances:
   (i) the handicapped assistance dog is assisting a blind, deaf, or mobility impaired person at the time the physical harm is caused or attempted (*or*)
   (ii) the handicapped assistance dog is not assisting a blind, deaf, or mobility impaired person at the time the physical harm is caused or attempted, but the offender has actual knowledge that the dog is a handicapped assistance dog
(6) Venue

Where violation results in the death of the police dog or horse or handicapped assistance dog

Penalty: A felony of the fourth degree (2929.11-2929.18, 2929.31)

Where violation results in serious physical harm to the police dog or horse or handicapped assistance dog other than its death

Penalty: A felony of the fifth degree (2929.11-2929.18, 2929.31)

Where violation results in physical harm to the police dog or horse or handicapped assistance dog other than death or serious physical harm

Penalty: A misdemeanor of the first degree (2929.21, 2929.31)

Where violation does not result in death, serious harm, or physical harm to the police dog or horse or handicapped assistance dog

Penalty: A misdemeanor of the second degree (2929.21, 2929.31)

RESISTING ARREST, R.C. § 2921.33 [M2, M1, F4]

Division (A):
(1) Recklessly or by means of force
(2) Resist/interfere with lawful arrest
(3) Of the person or another
(4) Venue

Penalty: A misdemeanor of the second degree (2929.21, 2929.31)

Division (B):
(1) Recklessly or by means of force

§ 2921.33.1   Ohio Criminal Law Handbook   A-114

(2) Resist/interfere with a lawful arrest
(3) During the course of or as a result of the resistance or interference, cause physical harm to a law enforcement officer
(4) Venue

Penalty: A misdemeanor of the first degree (2929.21, 2929.31)

Division (C):
(1) Recklessly or by means of force
(2) Resist/interfere with a lawful arrest if
   (a) the offender, during the course of or as a result of the resistance or interference, recklessly causes physical harm to a law enforcement officer by means of a deadly weapon
      (*or*)
   (b) the offender, during the course of the resistance or interference, brandishes a deadly weapon
(3) Venue

Penalty: A felony of the fourth degree (2929.11-2929.18, 2929.31)

FAILURE TO COMPLY WITH ORDER OR SIGNAL OF POLICE OFFICER, R.C. § 2921.33.1 [M1, F4]

Division (A): [**M1**]
(1) Fail to comply
(2) With any lawful order or direction
(3) Of any police officer invested with authority to direct, control, or regulate traffic
(4) Venue

Penalty: A misdemeanor of the first degree (2929.21, 2929.31)

Division (B): [**M1, F4**]
(1) Operate a motor vehicle
(2) So as willfully to elude or flee
(3) A police officer
(4) After receiving a visible or audible signal
(5) From a police officer
(6) To bring his motor vehicle to a stop
(7) Venue

Penalty: A misdemeanor of the first degree (2929.21, 2929.31)

If the trier of fact finds beyond a reasonable doubt that: (1) the offense was committed while the offender was fleeing immediately after committing a felony, (2) the operation of the motor vehicle was a proximate cause of serious physical harm to persons or property, or (3) the operation of the motor vehicle caused a substantial risk of serious physical harm to persons or property

Penalty: A felony of the fourth degree (2929.11-2929.18, 2929.31)

Definitions: "Police officer," R.C. § 2921.33.1(D), 4511.01.

ESCAPE, R.C. § 2921.34 [M1, F5, F3, F2]

Division (A)(1):
(1) Knowing oneself to be under detention or being reckless in that regard

(2) (a) Purposely break or attempt to break that detention
   (or)
   (b) Purposely fail to return to detention, either following a temporary leave granted for a specific purpose or limited period, or at the time required when serving a sentence in intermittent confinement
(3) Venue

Division (A)(2):
(1) No person who is sentenced as a sexually violent predator whose sentence has been modified and is restricted to a geographic area
(2) Knowing that the person is under a geographic restriction or being reckless in that regard
(3) (a) Purposely leave the geographic area to which the restriction applies
   (or)
   (b) Purposely fail to return to that geographic area following a temporary leave granted for a specific purpose or for a specific period of time

If the offender, at the time of the commission of the offense, was under detention as an alleged or adjudicated delinquent or unruly child, if the act for which the offender was under detention would not be a felony if committed by an adult

Penalty: A misdemeanor of the first degree (2929.21, 2929.31)

If the offender, at the time of the commission of the offense, was under detention in any other manner or was a sexually violent predator for whom the requirement that the entire prison term imposed pursuant to R.C. § 2971.03(A)(3) be served in a state correctional institution has been modified pursuant to R.C. § 2971.05, when the most serious offense for which the offender was under detention or adjudicated a sexually violent predator is aggravated murder, murder, or a felony of the first or second degree or, if the person was under detention as an alleged or adjudicated delinquent child, when the most serious act for which the person was under detention would be aggravated murder, murder, or a felony of the first or second degree if committed by an adult

Penalty: A felony of the second degree (2929.11-2929.18, 2929.31)

If the offender, at the time of the commission of the offense, was under detention in any other manner or was a sexually violent predator for whom the requirement that the entire prison term imposed pursuant to R.C. § 2971.03(A)(3) be served in a state correctional institution has been modified pursuant to R.C. § 2971.05, when the most serious offense for which the offender was under detention or adjudicated a sexually violent predator is a felony of the third, fourth, or fifth degree or an unclassified felony or, if the person was under detention as an alleged or adjudicated delinquent child, when the most serious act for which the person was under detention would be a third, fourth, or fifth degree or an unclassified felony if committed by an adult

Penalty: A felony of the third degree (2929.11-2929.18, 2929.31)

If the offender at the time of the commission of the offense, was under detention in any other manner, when the most serious offense for which the offender was under detention is a misdemeanor

Penalty: A felony of the fifth degree (2929.11-2929.18, 2929.31)

If the offender at the time of the commission of the offense, was under detention in any other manner, when the person was found not guilty by reason of insanity and the person's detention consisted of hospitalization, institutionalization, or confinement in a facility under an order made pursuant to R.C. § 2945.40, 2945.401, or 2945.402

Penalty: A felony of the fifth degree (2929.11-2929.18, 2929.31)

If the offender at the time of the commission of the offense, was under detention in any other manner, when the most serious offense for which the offender was under detention is a misdemeanor and when the person fails to return to the detention at a specified time following temporary leave granted for a specific purpose or limited period or at the time required when serving a sentence in intermittent confinement

Penalty: A misdemeanor of the first degree (2929.21, 2929.31)

Definitions: "Detention," "detention facility," R.C. § 2921.01.

AIDING ESCAPE OR RESISTANCE TO AUTHORITY, R.C. § 2921.35 [F4]

Division (A):
(1) With a purpose to promote or facilitate an escape or resistance to lawful authority
(2) (a) Convey into a detention facility
      (*or*)
    (b) Provide to anyone confined therein instruments or things which may be used to escape or resist authority
(3) Venue

Division (B):
(1) Being confined in a detention facility
(2) Make, procure, conceal, unlawfully possess or give to another inmate
(3) Any instrument or thing which may be used for such purposes
(4) With a purpose to promote or facilitate escape or resistance to lawful authority
(5) Venue

Penalty: A felony of the fourth degree (2929.11-2929.18, 2929.31)

ILLEGAL CONVEYANCE OF WEAPONS OR PROHIBITED ITEMS ONTO DETENTION FACILITY OR INSTITUTION, R.C. § 2921.36 [F4, F5, M1, M2]

(1) Knowingly
    (a) Convey or attempt to convey onto the grounds of
        (*or*)
    (b) Deliver or attempt to deliver to any person who is confined in
(2) (a) A detention facility
        (*or*)
    (b) An institution under the control of the department of mental health or the department of mental retardation and developmental disabilities
(3) (a) Any deadly weapon or dangerous ordnance as defined in R.C. § 2923.11
        (*or*)
    (b) Any part of or ammunition for use in such deadly weapon or dangerous ordnance
        (*or*)
(4) Any drug of abuse as defined in R.C. § 3719.01.1
    (*or*)
(5) Any intoxicating liquor as defined in R.C. § 4301.01
    (*or*)
(6) Cash
(7) Venue

CASH [F5, M1]

If offender has not been previously convicted under division (D) of this section

Penalty: A misdemeanor of the first degree (2929.21, 2929.31)

If offender has previously been convicted under division (D) of this section

Penalty: A felony of the fifth degree (2929.11-2929.18, 2929.31)

DEADLY WEAPON/DANGEROUS ORDNANCE [F4]

Penalty: A felony of the fourth degree (2929.11-2929.18, 2929.31)

DRUG OF ABUSE [F5, F4]

If offender is not an officer or employee of the facility or institution

Penalty: A felony of the fifth degree (2929.11-2929.18, 2929.31)

If offender is an officer or employee of the facility or institution

Penalty: A felony of the fourth degree (2929.11-2929.18, 2929.31)

INTOXICATING LIQUOR [M2]

Penalty: A misdemeanor of the second degree (2929.21, 2929.31)

Notes: For exceptions to (1)(a), above, when person has written authorization, *see* R.C. § 2921.36(B). For affirmative defenses to charge involving (1)(b), above, *see* R.C. § 2921.36(D). See also R.C. § 2921.37, for arrest powers of person in charge of detention facility re violation of R.C. § 2921.36.

Definitions: "Deadly weapon," "dangerous ordnance," R.C. § 2923.11

"Drug abuse," R.C. § 3719.01.1

"Intoxicating liquor," R.C. § 4301.01

"Institution under the control of the department of mental health and mental retardation," R.C. § 5123.11.

HARASSMENT BY INMATE, R.C. § 2921.38 [F5, F3]

Division (A):
(1) Being a person confined in a detention facility
(2) Cause or attempt to cause another person to come into contact with blood, semen, urine, feces, or another bodily substance
   (a) by throwing the bodily substance at the other person
      (*or*)
   (b) by expelling the bodily substance upon the other person
      (*or*)
   (c) in any other manner
(3) With intent to harass, annoy, threaten, or alarm the other person
(4) Venue

Penalty: A felony of the fifth degree (2929.11-2929.18, 2929.31)

Division (B):

§ 2921.41   Ohio Criminal Law Handbook   A-118

(1) Being a person confined in a detention facility with knowledge that the person is
    (a) a carrier of the virus that causes AIDS
        (or)
    (b) a carrier of a hepatitis virus
        (or)
    (c) infected with tuberculosis
(2) Cause or attempt to cause another person to come into contact with blood, semen, urine, feces, or another bodily substance
    (a) by throwing the bodily substance at the other person
        (or)
    (b) by expelling the bodily substance upon the other person
        (or)
    (c) in any other manner
(3) With intent to harass, annoy, threaten, or alarm the other person
(4) Venue

Penalty: A felony of the third degree (2929.11-2929.18, 2929.31)

Notes: This section does not apply to a person who is hospitalized, institutionalized, or confined in a facility operated by the Department of Mental Health or the Department of Mental Retardation and Developmental Disabilities.

THEFT IN OFFICE, R.C. § 2921.41 [F5, F4, F3]

(1) Being a public official/party official
(2) Commit a theft offense:
    (a) Using the offender's office or permitting its use or assenting to its use in aid of such offense
        (or)
    (b) Involving property or service owned by this or any state, the United States, a county, municipal corporation, or township, or any political subdivision, department, or agency thereof, or by a political party, or which is part of a political campaign fund
(3) Venue

Penalty: A felony of the fifth degree (2929.11-2929.18, 2929.31)

If the value of the property or services stolen is $500 or more and is less than $5,000

Penalty: A felony of the fourth degree (2929.11-2929.18, 2929.31)

If the value of the property or services stolen is $5,000 or more

Penalty: A felony of the third degree (2929.11-2929.18, 2929.31)

Note: A person convicted or pleading guilty hereunder is forever barred from office of public trust. In addition to any imprisonment or fine, the court shall require restitution [R.C. § 2921.41(C)(2)]. State retirement and deferred compensation benefits may be withheld to effect restitution, and the prosecutor must notify the retirement and deferred compensation systems of the filing of charges.

HAVING UNLAWFUL INTEREST IN A PUBLIC CONTRACT, R.C. § 2921.42 [F4, M1]

Division (A): **[F4]**
(1) Being a public official

(2) Knowingly authorize or employ the authority or influence of his office
    (a) To secure authorization of a public contract in which he, his family, or business associate has an interest
    (or)
    (b) To secure the investment of public funds in any share, bond, mortgage or other security which such public official, his family member or business associate has an interest, or is an underwriter, or receives any brokerage, origination or servicing fees
(3) Venue

Penalty: A felony of the fourth degree (2929.11-2929.18, 2929.31)

Division (B):
(1) (a) Being or having been a public official, during his term or within one year thereafter occupy a position of profit in the prosecution of a public contract authorized by him or by a legislative body, commission or board of which he was a member at the time of authorization, and which was not let by competitive bidding, or if let by competitive bidding, in which his is not the lowest and best bid
    (or)
    (b) Have an interest in profits or benefits of a public contract:
        (i) Entered into by, or for the use of a political subdivision/governmental agency/instrumentality with which he is connected
        (or)
        (ii) Involving more than $150, not let by competitive bidding when so required by law
(2) Venue

Penalty: A misdemeanor of the first degree (2929.21, 2929.31)

Notes: Defenses to this violation are set forth in R.C. § 2921.42(B) and (C).

It is not a violation of this section for a prosecuting attorney to appoint assistants and employees in accordance with R.C. § 309.06 or for a chief legal officer of a municipal corporation or an official designated as prosecutor in a municipal corporation to appoint assistants and employees in accordance with R.C. § 733.62.1.

Definitions: "Public contract," "chief legal officer," R.C. § 2921.42.

SOLICITING IMPROPER COMPENSATION, R.C. § 2921.43 [M1]

Division (A):
(1) (a) Knowingly promise or give to a public servant
    (or)
    (b) Being a public servant, knowingly solicit or accept
(2) (a) Any compensation other than as allowed by law
        (i) To perform his official duties
        (or)
        (ii) To perform any other act in his public capacity
        (or)
        (iii) For the general performance of the duties of his public office or public employment
        (or)
        (iv) As a supplement to his public compensation
        (or)

(b) Additional or greater fees or costs than allowed by law to perform his official duties
(3) Venue

Division (B):
(1) (a) For one's own personal or business use (whether a public servant or not)
    (or)
    (b) For the personal or business use of a public servant or party official
(2) Solicit or accept anything of value in consideration of:
    (a) Appointing/securing/maintaining/renewing the appointment of anyone to public office, employment or agency
    (or)
    (b) Preferring/maintaining the status of any public employee with respect to his compensation, duties, placement, location, promotion or other material aspects of his employment
(3) Venue

Division (C):
(1) Coerce a contribution
(2) For the benefit of a political party, campaign committee, legislative campaign fund, or political action committee
(3) In consideration of:
    (a) Appointing/securing/maintaining/renewing the appointment of anyone to public office, employment, or agency
    (b) Preferring/maintaining the status of any public employee with respect to his compensation, duties, placement, location, promotion or other material aspects of his employment
(4) Venue

Penalty: A misdemeanor of the first degree (2929.21, 2929.31)

Note: A public servant convicted hereunder is barred from public office, employment, or position of trust for 7 years.

Definitions: R.C. § 2921.01.

DERELICTION OF DUTY, R.C. § 2921.44 [M2]

Division (A):
(1) Being a law enforcement officer
(2) Negligently fail
(3) (a) To serve a warrant without delay
    (or)
    (b) To prevent/halt the commission of an offense, or to apprehend an offender, when it is in his power to do so alone or with available assistance
(4) Venue

Division (B):
(1) Being a law enforcement, ministerial or judicial officer
(2) Negligently fail
(3) To perform one's duty in a criminal proceeding
(4) Venue

Division (C):
(1) Being an officer in charge of a detention facility

(2) Negligently
(3) (a) Allow the facility to become littered or unsanitary
    (or)
    (b) Fail to provide prisoners with adequate food, clothing, bedding, shelter or medical attention
    (or)
    (c) Fail to control an unruly prisoner or prevent intimidation of or physical harm to a prisoner
    (or)
    (d) Allow a prisoner to escape
    (or)
    (e) Fail to observe all lawful and reasonable regulations for the management of the facility
(4) Venue

Division (D):
(1) Being a public official of the state
(2) Recklessly
(3) (a) Create a deficiency
    (or)
    (b) Incur a liability
    (or)
    (c) Expend a greater sum than appropriated by general assembly for one year's use by the department, agency or institution with which the public official is connected
(4) Venue

Division (E):
(1) Being a public servant
(2) Recklessly
(3) (a) Fail to perform a duty imposed by law
    (or)
    (b) Do any act forbidden by law with respect to one's office
(4) Venue

Penalty: A misdemeanor of the second degree (2929.21, 2929.31)

INTERFERING WITH CIVIL RIGHTS, R.C. § 2921.45 [M1]

(1) Being a public servant
(2) Under color of one's office, employment or authority
(3) Knowingly
(4) Deprive, or conspire or attempt to deprive another
(5) Of a constitutional or statutory right
(6) Venue

Penalty: A misdemeanor of the first degree (2929.21, 2929.31)

IMPERSONATING PEACE OFFICER OR PRIVATE POLICEMAN, R.C. § 2921.51 [M4, M1, F4, F3]

Division (B): **[M4]**
(1) Impersonate
(2) (a) Peace officer

        (or)
    (b) Private policeman
(3) Venue

Penalty: A misdemeanor of the fourth degree (2929.21, 2929.31)

Division (C): [**M1**]
(1) By impersonation of
(2) (a) Peace officer
        (or)
    (b) Private policeman
(3) (a) Arrest or detain any person
        (or)
    (b) Search any person
        (or)
    (c) Search the property of any person
(4) Venue

Penalty: A misdemeanor of the first degree (2929.21, 2929.31)

Division (D): [**M1, F4**]
(1) Impersonate
(2) (a) Peace officer
        (or)
    (b) Private policeman
        (or)
    (c) An officer, agent or employee of the state
(3) With purpose to facilitate the commission of an offense
(4) Venue

Penalty: A misdemeanor of the first degree (2929.21, 2929.31)

If the purpose of violation of Division (D) is to commit or facilitate the commission of a felony

Penalty: A felony of the fourth degree (2929.11-2929.18, 2929.31)

Division (E):
(1) While impersonating
(2) (a) Peace officer
        (or)
    (b) Private policeman
        (or)
    (c) An officer, agent or employee of the state
(3) Commit a felony
(4) Venue

Penalty: A felony of the third degree (2929.11-2929.18, 2929.31)

Note: It is an affirmative defense to a charge under Division (B) that the impersonation of the peace officer was for a lawful purpose.

Definitions: "Peace officer," "private policeman," "impersonate," R.C. § 2921.51(A).

USING SHAM LEGAL PROCESS, R.C. § 2921.52 [M4, M1, F4, F3]
(1) Knowingly
(2) (a) Issue, display, deliver, distribute, or otherwise use sham legal process
(or)
(b) Use sham legal process to arrest, detain, search, or seize any person or the property of another
(or)
(c) Commit or facilitate the commission of an offense, using sham legal process
(or)
(d) Commit a felony by using sham legal process
(3) Venue

Division (2)(a) [**M4**]

Penalty: A misdemeanor of the fourth degree (2929.21, 2929.31)

Division (2)(b) or (c) [**M1, F4**]

Penalty: A misdemeanor of the first degree (2929.21, 2929.31)

If the purpose of the violation of Division (2)(c) is to commit or facilitate the commission of a felony

Penalty: A felony of the fourth degree (2929.11-2929.18, 2929.31)

Division (2)(d) [**F3**]

Penalty: A felony of the third degree (2929.11-2929.18, 2929.31)

WEAPONS/ORDNANCE/CONSPIRACY/ATTEMPT

CONSPIRACY, R.C. § 2923.01 [F1, M1]
(1) With purpose
(2) To commit, promote or facilitate the commission of (a) aggravated murder or murder, (b) kidnapping, (c) compelling or promoting prostitution, (d) aggravated arson, or arson, (e) aggravated robbery, or robbery, (f) aggravated burglary, or burglary, or (g) engaging in a pattern of corrupt activity, or (h) corrupting another with drugs, a felony drug trafficking, manufacturing, processing, or possession offense, theft of drugs, or illegal processing of drug documents, or (i) felony offense of unauthorized use of vehicle, or (j) violation of R.C. Chapter 3734. relating to hazardous wastes, other than R.C. § 3734.18
(3) (a) Plan or aid in planning with another person or persons the commission of any of the specified offenses
(or)
(b) Agree with another person or persons that one or more will engage in conduct which facilitates commission of any of the specified offenses
(4) The offender, or one of his co-conspirators
(a) Subsequent to the offender's entrance into the conspiracy
(b) Does an overt act

  (c) Which is in furtherance of the conspiracy, and is of a character that manifests a purpose on the part of the actor that the object of the conspiracy be completed

(5) Venue

If principal offense is aggravated murder, murder, or an offense for which the maximum penalty is imprisonment for life

Penalty: A felony of the first degree (2929.11-2929.18, 2929.31)

If element 2(g) applies

Penalty: Above, plus fine of 3 times gross value gained/loss caused, court costs, costs of investigation/prosecution, criminal forfeiture of real and personal property. *See* R.C. § 2923.32

  A conspiracy to commit a first, second, third, or fourth degree felony is a felony of the next lesser degree.

  A conspiracy relating to hazardous waste provisions is a felony punishable by a fine of not more than $25,000 or imprisonment for not more than 18 months, or both.

  A conspiracy to commit a fifth degree felony

Penalty: A misdemeanor of the first degree (2929.21, 2929.31)

Notes: When the offender knows or has reasonable cause to believe that a person with whom he conspires has also conspired or is conspiring with another to commit the same offense, then the offender is guilty of conspiracy with such other person, even though his identity may be unknown to the offender.

  It is no defense to a charge of conspiracy that, in retrospect, commission of the offense which was the object of the conspiracy was impossible under the circumstances.

  A conspiracy terminates when the offense or offenses which are its objects are committed, or when it is abandoned by all conspirators. In the absence of abandonment, it is no defense to a charge of conspiracy that no offense which was the object of the conspiracy was committed.

  A person who conspires to commit more than one offense is guilty of only one conspiracy, when such offenses are the object of the same agreement or continuous conspiratorial relationship.

  When a person is convicted of committing or attempting to commit a specific offense or a complicity in the commission of or attempt to commit such offense, he shall not be convicted of conspiracy involving the same offense.

  The testimony of a co-conspirator alone is not enough to convict of conspiracy, unless the conspiracy results in an attempt to commit an offense or in the commission of an offense.

  Affirmative defenses, *see* R.C. § 2923.01(I).

ATTEMPT, R.C. § 2923.02 [F1, F2, F3, F4, F5, M1, M4]

 (1) Purposely or knowingly (when purpose or knowledge is sufficient culpability)
 (2) Engage in conduct that, if successful, would result in an offense
 (3) Venue

Where offense attempted is aggravated murder, murder, or an offense for which the maximum penalty is imprisonment for life

Penalty: A felony of the first degree (2929.11-2929.18, 2929.31)

  An attempt to violate hazardous waste provisions, R.C. Chapter 3734, other than R.C. § 3734.18, is a felony punishable by a fine up to $25,000 or imprisonment up to 18 months, or both.

Other attempts are offenses of the next lesser degree than the offenses attempted.
An attempt to commit a felony offense not specifically classified

Penalty: A misdemeanor of the first degree (2929.21, 2929.31)

An attempt to commit a misdemeanor offense not specifically classified

Penalty: A misdemeanor of the fourth degree (2929.21, 2929.31)

Attempt to commit minor misdemeanor, or to engage in conspiracy, is no offense.

Notes: A person may not be convicted of attempt if he is convicted of committing the attempted offense, of complicity in the commission of an offense, or of conspiracy to commit an offense.

It is no defense to a charge of attempt that, in retrospect, commission of the offense which was the object of the attempt was either factually or legally impossible under the attendant circumstances, if that offense could have been committed had the attendant circumstances been as the actor believed them to be.

It is an affirmative defense that the actor abandoned his effort to commit the offense or otherwise prevented its commission, under circumstances manifesting a complete and voluntary renunciation of his criminal purpose.

COMPLICITY, R.C. § 2923.03 [Same as principal offense]

(1) Acting with the culpability required in the principal offense
(2) (a) Solicit or procure another to commit the offense
     (*or*)
    (b) Aid or abet another to commit the offense
     (*or*)
    (c) Conspire with another to commit the offense in violation of R.C. § 2923.01
     (*or*)
    (d) Cause an innocent or irresponsible person to commit the offense
(3) Venue

Penalty: Same as that for principal offense

Notes: Complicity may be charged in terms of this section or terms of the principal offense.

No person shall be convicted of complicity under this section unless an offense is actually committed, but a person may be convicted of complicity in an attempt to commit an offense in violation of R.C. § 2923.02. It is an affirmative defense to a charge of complicity that, prior to the commission of or attempt to commit the offense, the actor terminated his complicity, under circumstances manifesting a complete and voluntary renunciation of his criminal purpose. It is no defense, however, to a charge of complicity that no person with whom the accused was in complicity has been convicted as a principal offender.

CARRYING CONCEALED WEAPON, R.C. § 2923.12 [M1, F4, F3]

(1) Knowingly
(2) Carry or have concealed
(3) On the person ready at hand
(4) A deadly weapon or dangerous ordnance
(5) Venue

Penalty: A misdemeanor of the first degree (2929.21, 2929.31)

Where previous conviction under this section or offense of violence, or weapon is loaded firearm, or ammunition is ready at hand or weapon is dangerous ordnance

Penalty: A felony of the fourth degree (2929.11-2929.18, 2929.31)

If weapon is a firearm and the violation is committed at a premises for which a D permit has been issued, or if offense committed aboard aircraft or with purpose to carry concealed weapon aboard

Penalty: A felony of the third degree (2929.11-2929.18, 2929.31)

Defenses: *See* R.C. § 2923.12.

Definitions: "Dangerous ordnance," "deadly weapon," R.C. § 2923.11.

ILLEGAL POSSESSION OF FIREARM IN LIQUOR PERMIT PREMISES, R.C. § 2923.12.1 [F5]

(1) Possess
(2) Firearm
(3) In any room in which liquor is being dispensed
(4) In premises for which a D permit issued under R.C. Chapter 4303.
(5) Venue

Penalty: A felony of the fifth degree (2929.11-2929.18, 2929.31)

Defenses: *See* R.C. § 2923.12.1.

ILLEGAL CONVEYANCE OR POSSESSION OF A DEADLY WEAPON OR DANGEROUS ORDNANCE OR ILLEGAL POSSESSION OF AN OBJECT INDISTINGUISHABLE FROM A FIREARM ON SCHOOL PREMISES, R.C. § 2923.12.2 [M1, F5, F4]

Division (A) — Conveyance:

(1) Knowingly
(2) (a) Convey
    (*or*)
  (b) Attempt to convey
(3) (a) Deadly weapon
    (*or*)
  (b) Dangerous ordnance
(4) Onto school premises, into a school or school building, to a school activity, or onto a school bus
(5) Venue

Division (B) — Possession:

(1) Knowingly
(2) Possess
(3) (a) Deadly weapon
    (*or*)
  (b) Dangerous ordnance
(4) On school premises, in a school or school building, at a school activity, or on a school bus
(5) Venue

No previous conviction under this section

Penalty: A felony of the fifth degree (2929.11-2929.18, 2929.31)

Previous conviction under this section

Penalty: A felony of the fourth degree (2929.11-2929.18, 2929.31)

Division (C):
(1) Knowingly
(2) Possess
(3) An object
  (a) that is indistinguishable from a firearm, whether or not capable of being fired
      (*and*)
  (b) the person indicates that the person possesses the object and that it is a firearm, or the person knowingly displays or brandishes the object and indicates that it is a firearm
(4) In a school or school building, at a school activity, or on a school bus
(5) Venue

Penalty: A misdemeanor of the first degree (2929.21, 2929.31)

Notes: This section does not apply to officers, agents, or employees of Ohio or any other state or the United States or to law enforcement officers authorized to carry deadly weapons or dangerous ordnance and acting within the scope of their duties, to any on-duty security officer employed by the board or governing authorization to convey or possess deadly weapons or dangerous ordnance. R.C. § 2923.12.2.

In addition to the penalties listed, the driver's license, permit or nonresident operating privilege of any person who is under 19 shall be suspended for a period of 12 to 36 months.

Definitions: "Deadly weapon," "dangerous ordnance," R.C. § 2923.11.

ILLEGAL CONVEYANCE OF DEADLY WEAPON OR DANGEROUS ORDNANCE INTO COURTHOUSE; ILLEGAL POSSESSION OR CONTROL IN COURTHOUSE, R.C. § 2923.12.3 [F5, F4]

Division (A):
(1) Knowingly
(2) Convey or attempt to convey
(3) Deadly weapon or dangerous ordnance
(4) Into a
  (a) Courthouse
      (*or*)
  (b) Other building or structure in which a courtroom is located
(5) Venue

Penalty: A felony of the fifth degree (2929.11-2929.18, 2929.31)

If the offender previously has been convicted of a violation of Division (A) or (B) of this section

Penalty: A felony of the fourth degree (2929.11-2929.18, 2929.31)

Division (B):
(1) Knowingly
(2) (a) Possess
      (*or*)
    (b) Have under the person's control
(3) Deadly weapon or dangerous ordnance

(4) In a
   (a) Courthouse
       (or)
   (b) Other building or structure in which a courtroom is located
(5) Venue

Penalty: A felony of the fifth degree (2929.11-2929.18, 2929.31)

If the offender previously has been convicted of a violation of Division (A) or (B) of this section

Penalty: A felony of the fourth degree (2929.11-2929.18, 2929.31)

HAVING WEAPONS WHILE UNDER DISABILITY, R.C. § 2923.13 [F5, F3]

Division (A): **[F5]**

(1) Knowingly
(2) Acquire, have, carry, or use
(3) Firearm/dangerous ordnance
(4) While
   (a) A fugitive from justice
       (or)
   (b) Under indictment, or convicted of any felony offense of violence, or adjudicated a delinquent child for the commission of an offense that, if committed by an adult, would have been an offense of violence
       (or)
   (c) Under indictment, or previously convicted of offenses involving illegal possession, use, sale, administration, distribution, trafficking in drugs of abuse, or adjudicated a delinquent child for commission of such offense
       (or)
   (d) Drug dependent person/in danger of becoming drug dependent or a chronic alcoholic
       (or)
   (e) Adjudicated mentally incompetent
(5) Unless relieved of above disabilites under R.C. § 2923.14
(6) Venue

Penalty: A felony of the fifth degree (2929.11-2929.18, 2929.31)

Division (B):
(1) Person convicted of a first or second degree felony
(2) Knowingly
(3) Violate Division (A)
(4) Within 5 years of the date of the person's release
   (a) from imprisonment
       (or)
   (b) from post-release control that is imposed for the commission of a first or second degree felony
(5) Venue

Penalty: A felony of the third degree (2929.11-2929.18, 2929.31)

Definitions: "Dangerous ordnance," "deadly weapon," R.C. § 2923.11.
"Drug dependent/in danger of becoming drug dependent," R.C. § 3719.50.

POSSESSION OF DEADLY WEAPON WHILE UNDER DETENTION, R.C. § 2923.13.1 [M1, F5, F4, F3, F2, F1]

(1) Possess
(2) Deadly weapon
(3) While under detention at a detention facility
(4) Venue

If the offender, at the time of the commission of the offense, was under detention as an alleged or adjudicated delinquent child or unruly child and if at the time the offender commits the act for which the offender was under detention it would not be a felony if committed by an adult **[M1]**

Penalty: A misdemeanor of the first degree (2929.21, 2929.31)

If the offender, at the time of the commission of the offense, was under detention in any other manner:

When the most serious offense for which the person was under detention is aggravated murder or murder and regardless of when the aggravated murder or murder occurred, or if the person was under detention as an alleged or adjudicated delinquent child, when the most serious act for which the person was under detention would be aggravated murder or murder if committed by an adult and regardless of when that occurred **[F1]**

Penalty: A felony of the first degree (2929.11-2929.18, 2929.31)

When the most serious offense for which the person was under detention is a felony of the first degree committed on or after July 1, 1996, or an aggravated felony of the first degree committed prior to July 1, 1996 **[F2]**

Penalty: A felony of the second degree (2929.11-2929.18, 2929.31)

If the person was under detention as an alleged or adjudicated delinquent child, the most serious act for which the person was under detention was committed on or after July 1, 1996, and would be a felony of the first degree if committed by an adult, or was committed prior to July 1, 1996, and would have been an aggravated felony of the first degree if committed by an adult **[F2]**

Penalty: A felony of the second degree (2929.11-2929.18, 2929.31)

When the most serious offense for which the person was under detention is a felony of the second degree committed on or after July 1, 1996, or an aggravated felony of the second degree or a felony of the first degree committed prior to July 1, 1996 **[F3]**

Penalty: A felony of the third degree (2929.11-2929.18, 2929.31)

If the person was under detention as an alleged or adjudicated delinquent child, the most serious act for which the person was under detention was committed on or after July 1, 1996, and would be a felony of the second degree if committed by an adult, or was committed prior to July 1, 1996, and would have been an aggravated felony of the second degree or a felony of the first degree if committed by an adult **[F3]**

Penalty: A felony of the third degree (2929.11-2929.18, 2929.31)

When the most serious offense for which the person was under detention is a felony of the third degree committed on or after July 1, 1996, or an aggravated felony of the third degree or a felony of the second degree committed prior to July 1, 1996, or is a felony of the third degree committed prior to July 1, 1996, that, if it had been committed on or after July 1, 1996, also would be a felony of the third degree **[F4]**

Penalty: A felony of the fourth degree (2929.11-2929.18, 2929.31)

If the person was under detention as an alleged or adjudicated delinquent child, the most serious act for which the person was under detention was committed on or after July 1, 1996, and would be a felony of the third degree if committed by an adult, or was committed prior to July 1, 1996, and would have been an aggravated felony of the third degree or a felony of the second degree if committed by an adult, or was committed prior to July 1, 1996, would have been a felony of the third degree if committed by an adult, and, if it had been committed on or after July 1, 1996 also would be a felony of the third degree if committed by an adult **[F4]**

Penalty: A felony of the fourth degree (2929.11-2929.18, 2929.31)

When the most serious offense for which the person was under detention is a felony of the fourth or fifth degree committed on or after July 1, 1996, is a felony of the third degree committed prior to July 1, 1996, that, if committed on or after July 1, 1996, would be a felony of the fourth degree, is a felony of the fourth degree committed prior to July 1, 1996, or is an unclassified felony or misdemeanor regardless of when the unclassified felony or misdemeanor is committed **[F5]**

Penalty: A felony of the fifth degree (2929.11-2929.18, 2929.31)

If the person was under detention as an alleged or adjudicated delinquent child, the most serious act for which the person was under detention was committed on or after July 1, 1996, and would be a felony of the fourth or fifth degree if committed by an adult, was committed prior to July 1, 1996, and would have been a felony of the third degree if committed by an adult, and, if it had been committed on or after July 1, 1996, would be a felony of the fourth degree if committed by an adult, was committed prior to July 1, 1996, and would have been a felony of the fourth degree if committed by an adult, and, or would be an unclassified felony if committed by an adult regardless of when the act is committed **[F5]**

Penalty: A felony of the fifth degree (2929.11-2929.18, 2929.31)

USING WEAPONS WHILE INTOXICATED, R.C. § 2923.15 [M1]

(1) Use or carry
(2) Any firearm/dangerous ordnance
(3) While under influence of alcohol or drug of abuse
(4) Venue

Penalty: A misdemeanor of the first degree (2929.21, 2929.31)

Definitions: "Deadly weapon," "dangerous ordnance," R.C. § 2923.11.

IMPROPERLY HANDLING FIREARMS IN A MOTOR VEHICLE, R.C. § 2923.16 [M1, M4]

Division (A): **[M1]**
(1) While in or on a motor vehicle
(2) Knowingly discharge a firearm
(3) Venue

Division (B): **[M1]**
(1) Knowingly
(2) Transport or have a loaded firearm
(3) In a motor vehicle
(4) So that firearm is accessible to operator or passenger without leaving the vehicle
(5) Venue

Penalty: A misdemeanor of the first degree (2929.21, 2929.31)

Division (C): **[M4]**
(1) Knowingly
(2) Transport or have firearm
(3) In motor vehicle
(4) Unless unloaded and carried:
   (a) In closed package, box, or case
       (*or*)
   (b) In compartment accessible only by leaving vehicle
       (*or*)
   (c) In plain sight and secured in rack or holder made for that purpose
       (*or*)
   (d) In plain sight with action open or weapon stripped (if firearm will not permit this, in plain sight)
(5) Venue

Penalty: A misdemeanor of the fourth degree (2929.21, 2929.31)

Note: As used here, "unloaded" means, with respect to a firearm employing a percussion cap, flintlock, or other obsolete ignition system, when the weapon is uncapped, or when the priming charge is removed from the pan. R.C. § 2923.16(G).

IMPROPERLY DISCHARGING A FIREARM AT OR INTO A HABITATION OR SCHOOL, R.C. § 2923.16.1 [F2, F3]

(1) Without privilege to do so
(2) Knowingly
(3) Discharge a firearm
(4) At or into
   (a) Occupied structure that is a permanent or temporary habitation of any individual
       (*or*)
   (b) School (See Note below.)
(5) Venue

Penalty: A felony of the third degree (2929.11-2929.18, 2929.31)

If previous conviction under this section **[F2]**

Penalty: A felony of the second degree (2929.11-2929.18, 2929.31)

Notes: This section does not apply to any officer, agent, or employee of Ohio, any other state, or the United States, or to any law enforcement officer who discharges the firearm while acting within the scope of the officer's, agent's, or employee's duties.

As enacted, the statute refers to "an occupied structure that is a permanent or temporary habitation of any individual or a school;" it is unclear whether the "occupied structure" limitation applies to schools.

Definition: "Occupied structure," R.C. § 2901.01.

UNLAWFUL POSSESSION OF DANGEROUS ORDNANCE; ILLEGALLY MANUFACTURING OR PROCESSING EXPLOSIVES, R.C. § 2923.17 [F5, F2]

Division (A): **[F5]**
(1) Knowingly

(2) Acquire, have, carry or use
(3) Dangerous ordnance
(4) Venue

Penalty: A felony of the fifth degree (2929.11-2929.18, 2929.31)

Division (B): **[F2]**
(1) Manufacture or process an explosive
(2) At any location in this state
(3) Unless the person first has been issued a license, certificate of registration, or permit to do so from a fire official of a political subdivision of the state or from the fire marshal
(4) Venue

Penalty: A felony of the second degree (2929.11-2929.18, 2929.31)

Note: Division (A) does not apply to, among others listed in R.C. § 2923.17, the holders of a license or temporary permit issued and in effect pursuant to R.C. § 2923.18, with respect to dangerous ordnance lawfully acquired, possessed, carried, or used for the purposes and in the manner specified in such license or permit.

Definitions: "Dangerous ordnance," R.C. § 2923.11.

FAILURE TO SECURE DANGEROUS ORDNANCE, R.C. § 2923.19 [M2]

(1) Negligently
(2) Fail to take proper precautions to
(3) (a) Secure against theft, acquisition or use by unauthorized or incompetent person
    (*or*)
    (b) Insure safety of persons and property
(4) In acquiring, possessing, carrying or using
(5) Dangerous ordnance
(6) Venue

Penalty: A misdemeanor of the second degree (2929.21, 2929.31)

Definitions:"Dangerous ordnance," R.C. § 2923.11.

UNLAWFUL TRANSACTIONS IN WEAPONS, R.C. § 2923.20 [F4, M2, M4]

A. (1) Recklessly
   (2) Sell, lend, give or furnish
   (3) Firearm
   (4) To any person prohibited under R.C. §§ 2923.13 (Having weapons while under disability), 2923.15 (Using weapons while intoxicated)
   (5) Venue **[F4]**
   (*or*)
B. (1) Recklessly
   (2) Sell, lend, give or furnish
   (3) Dangerous ordnance
   (4) To any person prohibited under R.C. §§ 2923.13 (Having weapons while under disability), 2923.15 (Using weapons while intoxicated), 2923.17 (Unlawful possession of dangerous ordnance)
   (5) Venue **[F4]**

(or)
C. (1) Possess
   (2) Firearm/dangerous ordnance
   (3) With purpose to dispose of it in violation of A or B above
   (4) Venue [F4]
   (or)
D. (1) Manufacture, possess for sale, sell or furnish
   (2) To any person (other than law enforcement agency for use in police work)
   (3) Brass knuckles, cestus, billy, blackjack, sandbag, switch-blade knife, springblade knife, gravity knife or similar weapon
   (4) Venue [M2]
   (or)
E. (1) When transferring dangerous ordnance to another
   (2) Negligently
   (3) Fail to require transferee to exhibit identification, license, permit, showing him authorized to acquire dangerous ordnance under R.C. § 2923.17 (unlawful possession of dangerous ordnance)
   (4) Venue [M2]
   (or)
F. (1) When transferring dangerous ordnance to another
   (2) Negligently
   (3) Fail to take a complete record of the transaction and forthwith forward the record of the transaction to the sheriff of the county or the safety director or police chief of the municipality where the transaction takes place
   (4) Venue [M2]
   (or)
G. (1) Knowingly
   (2) Fail to report to law enforcement authority
   (3) Forthwith
   (4) Loss or theft
   (5) Firearm or dangerous ordnance under person's control
   (6) Venue [M4]

Penalty: A felony of the fourth degree (2929.11-2929.18, 2929.31)

   D, E, and F: A misdemeanor of the second degree (2929.21, 2929.31)

   G: A misdemeanor of the fourth degree (2929.21, 2929.31)

Definitions: "Firearm," "dangerous ordnance," R.C. § 2923.11.

IMPROPERLY FURNISHING FIREARMS TO MINOR, R.C. § 2923.21 [F5]

(1) Sell a firearm to person under 18
(or)
(2) Subject to Division (B) of this section, sell a handgun to person under 21
(or)
(3) Furnish firearm to a person under 18 or subject to Division (B) of the section, any handgun to a person under 21, except for purpose of lawful hunting/instruction in firearms safety, care, handling or marksmanship under direct supervision or control of responsible adult
(or)

§ 2923.21.1   Ohio Criminal Law Handbook   A-134

(4) Sell or furnish a firearm to a person 18 or older if the seller or furnisher knows, or has reason to know, that the person is purchasing or receiving the firearm for the purpose of selling or furnishing the firearm to a person under 18
   (or)
(5) Sell or furnish a handgun to a person 21 or older if the seller or furnisher knows, or has reason to know, that the person is purchasing or receiving the handgun for the purpose of selling or furnishing the handgun to a person under 21
   (or)
(6) Purchase or attempt to purchase any firearm with the intent to sell or furnish the handgun to a person under 18
   (or)
(7) Purchase or attempt to purchase any handgun with the intent to sell or furnish the handgun to a person under 21
(8) Venue

Penalty: A felony of the fifth degree (2929.11-2929.18, 2929.31)

Definitions: "Handgun," "firearm," "deadly weapon," R.C. § 2923.11.

Note: Divisions (A)(1) and (2) of this section do not apply to the sale or furnishing of a handgun to a person 18 or older and under 21 if the person is a law enforcement officer who is properly appointed or employed as a law enforcement officer and has received firearms training approved by the Ohio Peace Officer Training Council or equivalent firearms training.

UNDERAGE PURCHASE OF FIREARM OR HANDGUN, R.C. § 2923.21.1 [M2]

(A)(1) No person under 18
   (2) Shall purchase or attempt to purchase
   (3) A firearm

Penalty: If found guilty the minor is considered a delinquent child and is subject to an order of disposition as provided in R.C. § 2151.355.

(B)(1) No person under 21
   (2) Shall purchase or attempt to purchase
   (3) A handgun

Penalty: A misdemeanor of the second degree (2929.21, 2929.31)

Note: Division (B) of this section does not apply to the purchase or attempted purchase of a handgun by a person 18 or older and under 21 if the person is a law enforcement officer who is properly appointed or employed as a law enforcement officer and has received firearms training approved by the Ohio Peace Officer Training Council or equivalent firearms training.

POSSESSING CRIMINAL TOOLS, R.C. § 2923.24 [F5, M1]

(1) Have possession or control of
(2) Any substance, device, instrument, or article
(3) With purpose to use it criminally
(4) Venue

Penalty: A misdemeanor of the first degree (2929.21, 2929.31)

If the circumstances indicate that the substance, device, instrument, or article involved in the offense was intended for use in the commission of a felony

Penalty: A felony of the fifth degree (2929.11-2929.18, 2929.31)

ENGAGING IN PATTERN OF CORRUPT ACTIVITY, R.C. § 2923.32 [F1, F2]

[A](1) Being employed by or associated with any enterprise
    (2) Conduct or participate in affairs of enterprise
    (3) Directly or indirectly
    (4) (a) Through pattern of corrupt activity
          (or)
       (b) Through collection of unlawful debt
    (5) Venue
       (or)
[B](1) (a) Through pattern of corrupt activity
          (or)
       (b) Through collection of unlawful debt
    (2) Acquire or maintain
    (3) Directly or indirectly
    (4) Interest in or control of
    (5) Any enterprise or real property
    (6) Venue
       (or)
[C](1) Knowingly having received
    (2) Any proceeds
    (3) Derived
    (4) Directly or indirectly
    (5) (a) From pattern of corrupt activity
          (or)
       (b) From collection of any unlawful debt
    (6) Use or invest
    (7) Directly or indirectly
    (8) (a) Any part of those proceeds
          (or)
       (b) Any proceeds derived from use/investment of those proceeds
    (9) (a) In acquisition of any title to, right, interest, or equity in real property
          (or)
       (b) In establishment or operation of any enterprise
   (10) Venue

Penalty: A felony of the second degree (2929.11-2929.18, 2929.31)

Also, fine of 3 times gross value gained/loss caused, court costs, costs of investigation/prosecution, criminal forfeiture of real and personal property

If at least one of the incidents of corrupt activity is a felony of the first, second, or third degree, aggravated murder, or murder, if at least one of the incidents of corrupt activity was a felony under the laws of this state that was committed prior to the effective date of this amendment and that would constitute a felony of the first, second, or third degree, aggravated murder, or murder, if committed on or after the effective date of this amendment, or if at least one of the incidents of corrupt activity is a felony under the laws of the United States or of another state that, if committed in this state on or after the effective date of this amendment, would constitute a felony of the first, second, or third degree, aggravated murder, or murder under the laws of this state

Penalty: A felony of the first degree (2929.11-2929.18, 2929.31)

Also, fine of 3 times gross value gained/loss caused, court costs, costs of investigation/prosecution, criminal forfeiture of real and personal property

Definitions: Generally, R.C. § 2923.31

Notes: For preserving reachability of property, R.C. § 2923.33.

    For provisions regarding civil proceedings, R.C. § 2923.34.

    For provisions regarding corrupt activity liens, R.C. § 2923.36.

    For provisions regarding disposition of property forfeited, fines, and civil penalties, R.C. § 2923.35.

    Regarding purchase of securities on open market without intent to control issuer, R.C. § 2923.32(A)(3).

DRUG ABUSE OFFENSES

CORRUPTING ANOTHER WITH DRUGS, R.C. § 2925.02 [F1, F2, F3, F4]

Division (A)(1):
(1) Knowingly
(2) By force, threat, or deception
(3) Administer to another or induce or cause another to use
(4) A controlled substance
(5) Venue

Division (A)(2):
(1) Knowingly
(2) By any means
(3) Administer or furnish to another or induce or cause another to use
(4) A controlled substance
(5) With purpose to cause serious physical harm to the other person, or with purpose to cause the other person to become drug dependent
(6) Venue

Division (A)(3):
(1) Knowingly
(2) By any means
(3) Administer or furnish to another or induce or cause another to use
(4) A controlled substance
(5) And thereby cause serious physical harm to the other person, or cause the other person to become drug dependent
(6) Venue

Division (A)(4)(a-c):
(1) Knowingly
(2) By any means

(3) (a) Administer or furnish a controlled substance to a juvenile who is at least two years the offender's junior
   (*or*)
   (b) Induce or cause a juvenile who is at least two years the offender's junior to use a controlled substance
   (*or*)
   (c) Induce or cause a juvenile who is at least two years the offender's junior to commit a felony drug abuse offense
(4) When the offender knows the age of the juvenile or is reckless in that regard
(5) Venue

Division (A)(4)(d):
(1) Use a juvenile
(2) To perform any surveillance activity that is intended to prevent
(3) (a) The detection of the offender or any other person in the commission of
   (*or*)
   (b) The arrest of the offender or any other person for the commission of
(4) A felony drug abuse offense
(5) Whether or not the offender knows the age of the juvenile
(6) Venue

Where drug involved is schedule I or II substance (except marihuana) **[F2]**

Penalty: Mandatory prison term of 2, 3, 4, 5, 6, 7, or 8 years and up to $15,000

> Mandatory minimum fine: $7,500
>
> Organization: Up to $20,000

Where drug involved is a schedule I or II substance (except marihuana) and the offense was committed in the vicinity of a school **[F1]**

Penalty: Mandatory prison term of 3, 4, 5, 6, 7, 8, 9, or 10 years and up to $20,000

> Mandatory minimum fine: $10,000
>
> Organization: Up to $25,000

If the violation involves the sale, offer to sell, or possession of a schedule I or II controlled substance (except marihuana), and the offender, as a result of the violation, is a major drug offender, the court, in lieu of the prison term that is authorized or required, shall impose upon the offender the mandatory ten-year prison term under R.C. § 2929.14(D)(3)(a) and may impose an additional prison term under R.C. § 2929.14(D)(3)(b) of 1, 2, 3, 4, 5, 6, 7, 8, 9, or 10 years.

Where drug involved is schedule III, IV, or V substance **[F2]**

Penalty: Presumption of a prison term of 2, 3, 4, 5, 6, 7, or 8 years and up to $15,000

> Mandatory minimum fine: $7,500
>
> Organization: Up to $20,000

Where drug involved is a schedule III, IV, or V substance and the offense was committed in the vicinity of a school **[F2]**

Penalty: Mandatory prison term of 2, 3, 4, 5, 6, 7, or 8 years and up to $15,000

> Mandatory minimum fine: $7,500
>
> Organization: Up to $20,000

Where drug involved is marihuana [F4]

Penalty: R.C. § 2929.13(C) applies in determining whether to impose a prison term of 6, 7, 8, 9, 10, 11, 12, 13, 14, 15, 16, 17, or 18 months on the offender and up to $5,000

Organization: Up to $10,000

Where drug involved is marihuana and the offense was committed in the vicinity of a school [F3]

Penalty: R.C. § 2929.13(C) applies in determining whether to impose a prison term of 1, 2, 3, 4, or 5 years and up to $10,000

Mandatory minimum fine: $5,000

Organization: Up to $15,000

Notes: Laboratory report as prima-facie evidence in drug abuse cases; rights of accused in re, R.C. § 2925.51.

Manufacturers, wholesalers, practitioners, pharmacists, others are excepted from A., C., and D. under R.C. § 2925.02(B).

See statute for special provisions concerning attorneys and professionally licensed persons convicted under this statute.

See statute for provisions exempting indigents from mandatory fines.

See statute for provisions allowing revocation or suspension of driver's and commercial driver's licenses.

Note: See Publisher's Note preceding R.C. § 3719.41 in Miscellaneous Statutory Provisions.

Definitions: "Drug dependent person," R.C. § 3719.01.1

"Felony drug abuse offense," R.C. § 2925.01

"Juvenile," R.C. § 2925.01

"Professionally licensed person," R.C. § 2925.01

"School," "school building," "school premises," R.C. § 2925.01

TRAFFICKING IN DRUGS, R.C. § 2925.03 [MM, M3, F5, F4, F3, F2, F1]

(1) Knowingly
(2) Sell or offer to sell
(3) A controlled substance
(4) Venue

AGGRAVATED TRAFFICKING IN DRUGS

If the drug involved in the violation is any compound, mixture, preparation or substance included in schedule I or II (except marijuana, cocaine, LSD, heroin, and hashish) [F4]

Penalty: R.C. § 2929.13(C) applies in determining whether to impose a prison term of 6, 7, 8, 9, 10, 11, 12, 13, 14, 15, 16, 17, or 18 months and up to $5,000

Organization: Up to $10,000

If the offense was committed in the vicinity of a school, or in the vicinity of a juvenile [F3]

Penalty: R.C. § 2929.13(C) applies in determining whether to impose a prison term of 1, 2, 3, 4, or 5 years and up to $10,000

Mandatory minimum fine: $5,000

Organization: Up to $15,000

If the amount of the drug involved exceeds the bulk amount but does not exceed five times the bulk amount [F3]

Penalty: Mandatory prison term of 1, 2, 3, 4, or 5 years and up to $10,000

    Mandatory minimum fine: $5,000

    Organization: Up to $15,000

If the amount of the drug involved exceeds the bulk amount but does not exceed five times the bulk amount and the offense was committed in the vicinity of a school, or in the vicinity of a juvenile [F2]

Penalty: Mandatory prison term of 2, 3, 4, 5, 6, 7, or 8 years and up to $15,000

    Mandatory minimum fine: $7,500

    Organization: Up to $20,000

If the amount of the drug involved exceeds five times the bulk amount but does not exceed fifty times the bulk amount [F2]

Penalty: Mandatory prison term of 2, 3, 4, 5, 6, 7, or 8 years and up to $15,000

    Mandatory minimum fine: $7,500

    Organization: Up to $20,000

If the amount of the drug involved exceeds five times the bulk amount but does not exceed fifty times the bulk amount and the offense was committed in the vicinity of a school, or in the vicinity of a juvenile [F1]

Penalty: Mandatory prison term of 3, 4, 5, 6, 7, 8, 9, or 10 years and up to $20,000

    Mandatory minimum fine: $10,000

    Organization: Up to $25,000

If the amount of the drug involved exceeds fifty times the bulk amount but does not exceed one hundred times the bulk amount and regardless of whether the offense was committed in the vicinity of a school or in the vicinity of a juvenile [F1]

Penalty: Mandatory prison term of 3, 4, 5, 6, 7, 8, 9, or 10 years and up to $20,000

    Mandatory minimum fine: $10,000

    Organization: Up to $25,000

If the amount of the drug involved exceeds one hundred times the bulk amount and regardless of whether the offense was commited in the vicinity of a school or in the vicinity of a juvenile [F1]

Penalty: Mandatory prison term of 10 years and up to $20,000 and may impose an additional prison term under R.C. § 2929.14(D)(3)(b) of 1, 2, 3, 4, 5, 6, 7, 8, 9, or 10 years

    Mandatory minimum fine: $10,000

    Organization: Up to $25,000

TRAFFICKING IN DRUGS

If the drug involved in the violation is any compound, mixture, preparation or substance included in schedule III, IV, or V [F5]

Penalty: R.C. § 2929.13(C) applies in determining whether to impose a prison term of 6, 7, 8, 9, 10, 11, or 12 months and up to $2,500

    Organization: Up to $7,500

If the offense was committed in the vicinity of a school, or in the vicinity of a juvenile [F4]

§ 2925.03

Penalty: R.C. § 2929.13(C) applies in determining whether to impose a prison term of 6, 7, 8, 9, 10, 11, 12, 13, 14, 15, 16, 17, or 18 months and up to $5,000

    Organization: Up to $10,000

If the amount of the drug involved exceeds the bulk amount but does not exceed five times the bulk amount **[F4]**

Penalty: Presumption of prison term of 6, 7, 8, 9, 10, 11, 12, 13, 14, 15, 16, 17, or 18 months and up to $5,000

    Organization: Up to $10,000

If the amount of the drug involved exceeds the bulk amount but does not exceed five times the bulk amount and the offense was committed in the vicinity of a school, or in the vicinity of a juvenile **[F3]**

Penalty: Presumption of prison term of 1, 2, 3, 4, or 5 years and up to $10,000

    Mandatory minimum fine: $5,000

    Organization: Up to $15,000

If the amount of the drug involved exceeds five times the bulk amount but does not exceed fifty times the bulk amount **[F3]**

Penalty: Presumption of prison term of 1, 2, 3, 4, or 5 years and up to $10,000

    Mandatory minimum fine: $5,000

    Organization: Up to $15,000

If the amount of the drug involved exceeds five times the bulk amount but does not exceed fifty times the bulk amount and the offense was committed in the vicinity of a juvenile **[F2]**

Penalty: Presumption of prison term of 2, 3, 4, 5, 6, 7, or 8 years and up to $15,000

    Mandatory minimum fine: $7,500

    Organization: Up to $25,000

If the amount of the drug involved exceeds fifty times the bulk amount **[F2]**

Penalty: Mandatory prison term of 2, 3, 4, 5, 6, 7, or 8 years and up to $15,000

    Mandatory minimum fine: $7,500

    Organization: Up to $20,000

If the amount of the drug involved exceeds fifty times the bulk amount and the offense was committed in the vicinity of a school, or in the vicinity of a juvenile **[F1]**

Penalty: Mandatory prison term of 3, 4, 5, 6, 7, 8, 9, or 10 years and up to $20,000

    Mandatory minimum fine: $10,000

Organization: Up to $25,000

TRAFFICKING IN MARIHUANA

If the drug involved in the violation is marihuana or a compound, mixture, preparation, or substance containing marihuana other than hashish **[F5]**

Penalty: R.C. § 2929.13(C) applies in determining whether to impose a prison term of 6, 7, 8, 9, 10, 11, or 12 months and up to $2,500

    Organization: Up to $7,500

If the offense was committed in the vicinity of a school, or in the vicinity of a juvenile **[F4]**

Penalty: R.C. § 2929.13(C) applies in determining whether to impose a prison term of 6, 7, 8, 9, 10, 11, 12, 13, 14, 15, 16, 17, or 18 months and up to $5,000
    Organization: Up to $10,000

If the amount of the drug involved exceeds 200 grams but does not exceed 1,000 grams **[F4]**

Penalty: R.C. § 2929.13(C) applies in determining whether to impose a prison term of 6, 7, 8, 9, 10, 11, 12, 13, 14, 15, 16, 17, or 18 months and up to $5,000
    Organization: Up to $10,000

If the amount of the drug involved exceeds 200 grams but does not exceed 1,000 grams and the offense was committed in the vicinity of a school, or in the vicinity of a juvenile **[F3]**

Penalty: R.C. § 2929.13(C) applies in determining whether to impose a prison term of 1, 2, 3, 4, or 5 years and up to $10,000
    Mandatory minimum fine: $5,000
    Organization: Up to $15,000

If the amount of the drug involved exceeds 1,000 grams but does not exceed 5,000 grams **[F3]**

Penalty: R.C. § 2929.13(C) applies in determining whether to impose a prison term of 1, 2, 3, 4, or 5 years and up to $10,000
    Mandatory minimum fine: $5,000
    Organization: Up to $15,000

If the amount of the drug involved exceeds 1,000 grams but does not exceed 5,000 grams and the offense was committed in the vicinity of a school, or in the vicinity of a juvenile **[F2]**

Penalty: Presumption of prison term of 2, 3, 4, 5, 6, 7, or 8 years and up to $15,000
    Mandatory minimum fine: $7,500
    Organization: Up to $25,000

If the amount of the drug involved exceeds 5,000 grams but does not exceed 20,000 grams **[F3]**

Penalty: Presumption of prison term of 1, 2, 3, 4, or 5 years and up to $10,000
    Mandatory minimum fine: $5,000
    Organization: Up to $15,000

If the amount of the drug involved exceeds 5,000 grams but does not exceed 20,000 grams and the offense was committed in the vicinity of a school, or in the vicinity of a juvenile **[F2]**

Penalty: Presumption of prison term of 2, 3, 4, 5, 6, 7, or 8 years and up to $15,000
    Mandatory minimum fine: $7,500
    Organization: Up to $25,000

If the amount of the drug involved exceeds 20,000 grams **[F2]**

Penalty: Mandatory prison term of 8 years and up to $15,000
    Mandatory minimum fine: $7,500
    Organization: Up to $20,000

If the amount of the drug involved exceeds 20,000 grams and the offense was committed in the vicinity of a school, or in the vicinity of a juvenile **[F1]**

Penalty: Mandatory prison term of 10 years and up to $20,000
    Mandatory minimum fine: $10,000
    Organization: Up to $25,000

§ 2925.03   OHIO CRIMINAL LAW HANDBOOK   A-142

If the offense involves a gift of 20 grams or less and is a first offense **[MM]**
Penalty: No prison term and up to $100
    Organization: Up to $1,000

If the offense involves a gift of 20 grams or less and there is a prior offense **[M3]**
Penalty: Up to 60 days or up to $500 or both
    Organization: Up to $3,000

If the offense involves a gift of 20 grams or less and the offense was commited in the vicinity of a school, or in the vicinity of a juvenile **[M3]**
Penalty: Up to 60 days or up to $500 or both
    Organization: Up to $3,000

TRAFFICKING IN COCAINE [F5]

If the drug involved in the violation is cocaine or a compound, mixture, preparation, or substance containing cocaine
Penalty: R.C. § 2929.13(C) applies in determining whether to impose a prison term of 6, 7, 8, 9, 10, 11, or 12 months and up to $2,500
    Organization: Up to $7,500

If the offense was committed in the vicinity of a school, or in the vicinity of a juvenile **[F4]**
Penalty: R.C. § 2929.13(C) applies in determining whether to impose a prison term of 6, 7, 8, 9, 10, 11, 12, 13, 14, 15, 16, 17, or 18 months and up to $5,000
    Organization: Up to $10,000

If the amount of the drug involved exceeds five grams but does not exceed ten grams that is not crack cocaine or exceeds one gram but does not exceed five grams of crack cocaine **[F4]**
Penalty: Presumption of prison term of 6, 7, 8, 9, 10, 11, 12, 13, 14, 15, 16, 17, or 18 months and up to $5,000
    Organization: Up to $10,000

If the amount of the drug involved exceeds five grams but does not exceed ten grams that is not crack cocaine or exceeds one gram but does not exceed five grams of crack cocaine and the offense was committed in the vicinity of a school, or in the vicinity of a juvenile **[F3]**
Penalty: Presumption of prison term of 1, 2, 3, 4, or 5 years and up to $10,000
    Mandatory minimum fine: $5,000
    Organization: Up to $15,000

If the amount of the drug involved exceeds ten grams but does not exceed one hundred grams that is not crack cocaine or exceeds five grams but does not exceed ten grams of crack cocaine **[F3]**
Penalty: Mandatory prison term of 1, 2, 3, 4, or 5 years and up to $10,000
    Mandatory minimum fine: $5,000
    Organization: Up to $15,000

If the amount of the drug involved exceeds ten grams but does not exceed one hundred grams that is not crack cocaine or exceeds five grams but does not exceed ten grams of crack cocaine and the offense was committed in the vicinity of a school, or in the vicinity of a juvenile **[F2]**

Penalty: Mandatory prison term of 2, 3, 4, 5, 6, 7, or 8 years and up to $15,000
    Mandatory minimum fine: $7,500
    Organization: Up to $20,000

If the amount of the drug involved exceeds one hundred grams but does not exceed five hundred grams that is not crack cocaine or exceeds ten grams but does not exceed twenty-five grams of crack cocaine [F2]

Penalty: Mandatory prison term of 2, 3, 4, 5, 6, 7, or 8 years and up to $15,000
    Mandatory minimum fine: $7,500
    Organization: Up to $20,000

If the amount of the drug involved exceeds one hundred grams but does not exceed five hundred grams that is not crack cocaine or exceeds ten grams but does not exceed twenty-five grams of crack cocaine and the offense was committed in the vicinity of a school, or in the vicinity of a juvenile [F1]

Penalty: Mandatory prison term of 3, 4, 5, 6, 7, 8, 9, or 10 years and up to $20,000
    Mandatory minimum fine: $10,000
    Organization: Up to $25,000

If the amount of the drug involved exceeds five hundred grams but does not exceed one thousand grams that is not crack cocaine or exceeds twenty-five grams but does not exceed one hundred grams of crack cocaine [F1]

Penalty: Mandatory prison term of 3, 4, 5, 6, 7, 8, 9, or 10 years and up to $20,000
    Mandatory minimum fine: $10,000
    Organization: Up to $25,000

If the amount of the drug involved exceeds one thousand grams that is not crack cocaine or exceeds one hundred grams of crack cocaine [F1]

Penalty: Mandatory prison term of 10 years and up to $20,000 and may impose an additional prison term under R.C. § 2929.14(D)(3)(b) of 1, 2, 3, 4, 5, 6, 7, 8, 9, or 10 years
    Mandatory minimum fine: $10,000
    Organization: Up to $25,000

TRAFFICKING IN L.S.D. [F5]

If the drug involved in the violation is L.S.D. or a compound, mixture, preparation, or substance containing L.S.D.

Penalty: R.C. § 2929.13(C) applies in determining whether to impose a prison term of 6, 7, 8, 9, 10, 11, or 12 months and up to $2,500
    Organization: Up to $7,500

If the offense was committed in the vicinity of a school, or in the vicinity of a juvenile [F4]

Penalty: R.C. § 2929.13(C) applies in determining whether to impose a prison term of 6, 7, 8, 9, 10, 11, 12, 13, 14, 15, 16, 17, or 18 months and up to $5,000
    Organization: Up to $10,000

If the amount of the drug involved exceeds ten unit doses but does not exceed fifty unit doses of L.S.D. in a solid form or exceeds one gram but does not exceed five grams of L.S.D. in a liquid concentrate, liquid extract, or liquid distillate form [F4]

Penalty: Presumption of prison term of 6, 7, 8, 9, 10, 11, 12, 13, 14, 15, 16, 17, or 18 months and up to $5,000

    Organization: Up to $10,000

If the amount of the drug involved exceeds ten unit doses but does not exceed fifty unit doses of L.S.D. in a solid form or exceeds one gram but does not exceed five grams of L.S.D. in a liquid concentrate, liquid extract, or liquid distillate form, and the offense was committed in the vicinity of a school, or in the vicinity of a juvenile **[F3]**

Penalty: Presumption of prison term of 1, 2, 3, 4, or 5 years and up to $10,000

    Mandatory minimum fine: $5,000

    Organization: Up to $15,000

If the amount of the drug involved exceeds fifty unit doses but does not exceed two hundred fifty unit doses of L.S.D. in a solid form or exceeds five grams but does not exceed twenty-five grams of L.S.D. in a liquid concentrate, liquid extract, or liquid distillate form **[F3]**

Penalty: Mandatory prison term of 1, 2, 3, 4, or 5 years and up to $10,000

    Mandatory minimum fine: $5,000

    Organization: Up to $15,000

If the amount of the drug involved exceeds fifty unit doses but does not exceed two hundred fifty unit doses of L.S.D. in a solid form or exceeds five grams but does not exceed twenty-five grams of L.S.D. in a liquid concentrate, liquid extract, or liquid distillate form, and the offense was committed in the vicinity of a school, or in the vicinity of a juvenile **[F2]**

Penalty: Mandatory prison term of 2, 3, 4, 5, 6, 7, or 8 years and up to $15,000

    Mandatory minimum fine: $7,500

    Organization: Up to $20,000

If the amount of the drug involved exceeds two hundred fifty unit doses but does not exceed one thousand unit doses of L.S.D. in a solid form or exceeds twenty-five grams but does not exceed one hundred grams of L.S.D. in a liquid concentrate, liquid extract, or liquid distillate form **[F2]**

Penalty: Mandatory prison term of 2, 3, 4, 5, 6, 7, or 8 years and up to $15,000

    Mandatory minimum fine: $7,500

    Organization: Up to $20,000

If the amount of the drug involved exceeds two hundred fifty unit doses but does not exceed one thousand unit doses of L.S.D. in a solid form or exceeds twenty-five grams but does not exceed one hundred grams of L.S.D. in a liquid concentrate, liquid extract, or liquid distillate form, and the offense was committed in the vicinity of a school, or in the vicinity of a juvenile **[F1]**

Penalty: Mandatory prison term of 3, 4, 5, 6, 7, 8, 9, or 10 years and up to $20,000

    Mandatory minimum fine: $10,000

    Organization: Up to $25,000

If the amount of the drug involved exceeds one thousand unit doses but does not exceed five thousand unit doses of L.S.D. in a solid form or exceeds one hundred grams but does not exceed five hundred grams of L.S.D. in a liquid concentrate, liquid extract, or liquid distillate form, and regardless of whether the offense was committed in the vicinity of a school, or in the vicinity of a juvenile **[F1]**

Penalty: Mandatory prison term of 3, 4, 5, 6, 7, 8, 9, or 10 years and up to $20,000

    Mandatory minimum fine: $10,000

    Organization: Up to $25,000

If the amount of the drug involved exceeds five thousand unit doses of L.S.D. in a solid form or exceeds five hundred grams of L.S.D. in a liquid concentrate, liquid extract, or liquid distillate form, and regardless of whether the offense was committed in the vicinity of a school, or in the vicinity of a juvenile [F1]

Penalty: Mandatory prison term of 10 years and up to $20,000 and may impose an additional prison term under R.C. § 2929.14(D)(3)(b) of 1, 2, 3, 4, 5, 6, 7, 8, 9, or 10 years

    Mandatory minimum fine: $10,000

    Organization: Up to $25,000

TRAFFICKING IN HEROIN [F5]

If the drug involved in the violation is heroin or a compound, mixture, preparation, or substance containing heroin

Penalty: R.C. § 2929.13(C) applies in determining whether to impose a prison term of 6, 7, 8, 9, 10, 11, or 12 months and up to $2,500

    Organization: Up to $7,500

If the offense was committed in the vicinity of a school, or in the vicinity of a juvenile [F4]

Penalty: R.C. § 2929.13(C) applies in determining whether to impose a prison term of 6, 7, 8, 9, 10, 11, 12, 13, 14, 15, 16, 17, or 18 months and up to $5,000

    Organization: Up to $10,000

If the amount of the drug involved exceeds one gram but does not exceed five grams [F4]

Penalty: Presumption of prison term of 6, 7, 8, 9, 10, 11, 12, 13, 14, 15, 16, 17, or 18 months and up to $5,000

    Organization: Up to $10,000

If the amount of the drug involved exceeds one gram but does not exceed five grams and the offense was committed in the vicinity of a school, or in the vicinity of a juvenile [F3]

Penalty: Presumption of prison term of 1, 2, 3, 4, or 5 years and up to $10,000

    Mandatory minimum fine: $5,000

    Organization: Up to $15,000

If the amount of the drug involved exceeds five grams but does not exceed ten grams [F3]

Penalty: Presumption of prison term of 1, 2, 3, 4, or 5 years and up to $10,000

    Mandatory minimum fine: $5,000

    Organization: Up to $15,000

If the amount of the drug involved exceeds five grams but does not exceed ten grams and the offense was committed in the vicinity of a school, or in the vicinity of a juvenile [F2]

Penalty: Presumption of prison term of 2, 3, 4, 5, 6, 7, or 8 years and up to $15,000

    Mandatory minimum fine: $7,500

    Organization: Up to $20,000

If the amount of the drug involved exceeds ten grams but does not exceed fifty grams [F2]

Penalty: Mandatory prison term of 2, 3, 4, 5, 6, 7, or 8 years and up to $15,000

    Mandatory minimum fine: $7,500

    Organization: Up to $20,000

If the amount of the drug involved exceeds ten grams but does not exceed fifty grams and the offense was committed in the vicinity of a school, or in the vicinity of a juvenile [F1]

Penalty: Mandatory prison term of 3, 4, 5, 6, 7, 8, 9, or 10 years and up to $20,000

Mandatory minimum fine: $10,000

Organization: Up to $25,000

If the amount of the drug involved exceeds fifty grams but does not exceed two hundred fifty grams and regardless of whether the offense was committed in the vicinity of a school, or in the vicinity of a juvenile [F1]

Penalty: Mandatory prison term of 3, 4, 5, 6, 7, 8, 9, or 10 years and up to $20,000

Mandatory minimum fine: $10,000

Organization: Up to $25,000

If the amount of the drug involved exceeds two hundred fifty grams and regardless of whether the offense was committed in the vicinity of a school, or in the vicinity of a juvenile [F1]

Penalty: Mandatory prison term of 10 years and up to $20,000 and may impose an additional prison term under R.C. § 2929.14(D)(3)(b) of 1, 2, 3, 4, 5, 6, 7, 8, 9, or 10 years

Mandatory minimum fine: $10,000

Organization: Up to $25,000

TRAFFICKING IN HASHISH [F5]

If the drug involved in the violation is hashish or a compound, mixture, preparation or substance containing hashish

Penalty: R.C. § 2929.13(C) applies in determining whether to impose a prison term of 6, 7, 8, 9, 10, 11, or 12 months and up to $2,500

Organization: Up to $7,500

If the offense was committed in the vicinity of a school, or in the vicinity of a juvenile [F4]

Penalty: R.C. § 2929.13(C) applies in determining whether to impose a prison term of 6, 7, 8, 9, 10, 11, 12, 13, 14, 15, 16, 17, or 18 months and up to $5,000

Organization: Up to $10,000

If the amount of the drug involved exceeds ten grams but does not exceed fifty grams of hashish in a solid form or exceeds two grams but does not exceed ten grams of hashish in a liquid concentrate, liquid extract, or liquid distillate form [F4]

Penalty: R.C. § 2929.13(C) applies in determining whether to impose a prison term of 6, 7, 8, 9, 10, 11, 12, 13, 14, 15, 16, 17, or 18 months and up to $5,000

Organization: Up to $10,000

If the amount of the drug involved exceeds ten grams but does not exceed fifty grams of hashish in a solid form or exceeds two grams but does not exceed ten grams of hashish in a liquid concentrate, liquid extract, or liquid distillate form and the offense was committed in the vicinity of a school, or in the vicinity of a juvenile [F3]

Penalty: R.C. § 2929.13(C) applies in determining whether to impose a prison term of 1, 2, 3, 4, or 5 years and up to $10,000

Mandatory minimum fine: $5,000

Organization: Up to $15,000

If the amount of the drug involved exceeds fifty grams but does not exceed two hundred fifty grams of hashish in a solid form or exceeds ten grams but does not exceed fifty grams of hashish in a liquid concentrate, liquid extract, or liquid distillate form **[F3]**

Penalty: R.C. § 2929.13(C) applies in determining whether to impose a prison term of 1, 2, 3, 4, or 5 years and up to $10,000

    Mandatory minimum fine: $5,000

    Organization: Up to $15,000

If the amount of the drug involved exceeds fifty grams but does not exceed two hundred fifty grams of hashish in a solid form or exceeds ten grams but does not exceed fifty grams of hashish in a liquid concentrate, liquid extract, or liquid distillate form and the offense was committed in the vicinity of a school, or in the vicinity of a juvenile **[F2]**

Penalty: Presumption of prison term of 2, 3, 4, 5, 6, 7, or 8 years and up to $15,000

    Mandatory minimum fine: $7,500

    Organization: Up to $20,000

If the amount of the drug involved exceeds two hundred fifty grams but does not exceed one thousand grams of hashish in a solid form or exceeds fifty grams but does not exceed two hundred grams of hashish in a liquid concentrate, liquid extract, or liquid distillate form **[F3]**

Penalty: Presumption of prison term of 1, 2, 3, 4, or 5 years and up to $10,000

    Mandatory minimum fine: $5,000

    Organization: Up to $15,000

If the amount of the drug involved exceeds two hundred fifty grams but does not exceed one thousand grams of hashish in a solid form or exceeds fifty grams but does not exceed two hundred fifty grams of hashish in a liquid concentrate, liquid extract, or liquid distillate form and the offense was committed in the vicinity of a school, or in the vicinity of a juvenile **[F2]**

Penalty: Presumption of prison term of 2, 3, 4, 5, 6, 7, or 8 years and up to $15,000

    Mandatory minimum fine: $7,500

    Organization: Up to $20,000

If the amount of the drug involved exceeds one thousand grams of hashish in a solid form or exceeds two hundred grams of hashish in a liquid concentrate, liquid extract, or liquid distillate form **[F2]**

Penalty: Mandatory prison term of 8 years and up to $15,000

    Mandatory minimum fine: $7,500

    Organization: Up to $20,000

If the amount of the drug involved exceeds one thousand grams of hashish in a solid form or exceeds two hundred grams of hashish in a liquid concentrate, liquid extract, or liquid distillate form and the offense was committed in the vicinity of a school, or the vicinity of a juvenile **[F1]**

Penalty: Mandatory prison term of 10 years and up to $20,000

    Mandatory minimum fine: $10,000

    Organization: Up to $25,000

Notes: See statute for provisions exempting indigents from mandatory fines.

    See statute for provisions allowing revocation or suspension of driver's and commercial driver's licenses.

§ 2925.04   Ohio Criminal Law Handbook   A-148

    Laboratory report as prima-facie evidence in drug abuse cases; rights of accused in re, R.C. § 2925.51.

    Manufacturers, practitioners, pharmacists, others excepted under R.C. § 2925.03(B).

Definitions: "Controlled substance," R.C. § 3719.01(D)
              "Marihuana," R.C. § 3719.01(Q)

ILLEGAL MANUFACTURE OF DRUGS OR CULTIVATION OF MARIHUANA, R.C. § 2925.04 [MM, M4, F5, F3, F2]

(1) Knowingly
(2) Cultivate
(3) Marihuana
(4) Venue
    (*or*)
(1) Knowingly
(2) Manufacture or otherwise engage in
(3) Any part of the production of a controlled substance
(4) Venue

If the drug involved is any compound, mixture, preparation or substance included in schedule I or II (except marihuana) **[F2]**

Penalty: Mandatory prison term of 2, 3, 4, 5, 6, 7, or 8 years and up to $15,000

    Mandatory minimum fine: $7,500

    Organization: Up to $20,000

If the above violation involves the sale, offer to sell or possession of a schedule I or II controlled substance (except marijuana) and if the offender, as a result of the violation, is a major drug offender

Penalty: Mandatory prison term of 10 years, up to $15,000 and may impose under R.C. § 2929.14(D)(3)(b) an additional 1 to 10 years

    Mandatory minimum fine: $7,500

    Organization: Up to $20,000

If the drug involved is any compound, mixture, preparation or substance included in schedule III, IV, or V **[F3]**

Penalty: Presumption of prison term of 1, 2, 3, 4, or 5 years and up to $10,000

    Mandatory minimum fine: $5,000

    Organization: Up to $15,000

If the drug involved is marihuana: **[MM]**

Penalty: No prison term and up to $100

    Organization: Up to $1,000

If the amount of marihuana involved equals or exceeds one hundred grams but does not exceed two hundred grams **[M4]**

Penalty: Up to 30 days or up to $250 or both

    Organization: Up to $2,000

If the amount of marihuana involved exceeds two hundred grams but does not exceed one thousand grams **[F5]**

Penalty: R.C. § 2929.13(B) applies in determining whether to impose a prison term of 6, 7, 8, 9, 10, 11, or 12 months and up to $2,500

    Organization: Up to $7,500

If the amount of marihuana involved exceeds one thousand grams but does not exceed five thousand grams **[F3]**

Penalty: R.C. § 2929.13(C) applies in determining whether to impose a prison term of 1, 2, 3, 4, or 5 years and up to $10,000

    Mandatory minimum fine: $5,000

    Organization: Up to $15,000

If the amount of marihuana involved exceeds five thousand grams but does not exceed twenty thousand grams **[F3]**

Penalty: Presumption of prison term of 1, 2, 3, 4, or 5 years and up to $10,000

    Mandatory minimum fine: $5,000

    Organization: Up to $15,000

If the amount of marihuana involved exceeds twenty thousand grams **[F2]**

Penalty: Mandatory prison term of 8 years and up to $15,000

    Mandatory minimum fine: $7,500

    Organization: Up to $20,000

FUNDING OF DRUG OR MARIHUANA TRAFFICKING, R.C. § 2925.05 [F3, F2, F1]

(1) Knowingly
(2) Provide
(3) Money
    (*or*)
    Other items of value
(4) To another person
(5) With the purpose that the recipient of the money or items of value use them to obtain any controlled substance
(6) For the purpose of selling or offering to sell the controlled substance
    (*or*)
    For the purpose of violating R.C. § 2925.04
(7) Venue

AGGRAVATED FUNDING OF DRUG TRAFFICKING

If the drug involved is any compound, mixture, preparation, or substance included in schedule I or II (except marihuana) **[F1]**

Penalty: Mandatory prison term of 3, 4, 5, 6, 7, 8, 9, or 10 years and up to $20,000

    Mandatory minimum fine: $10,000

    Organization: Up to $25,000

If the above violation involves the sale, offer to sell or possession of a schedule I or II controlled substance (except marijuana) and if the offender, as a result of the violation, is a major drug offender

Penalty: Mandatory prison term of 10 years, up to $20,000 and may impose under R.C. § 2929.14(D)(3)(b) an additional 1 to 10 years
   Mandatory minimum fine: $10,000
   Organization: Up to $25,000

FUNDING OF DRUG TRAFFICKING

If the drug involved is any compound, mixture, preparation, or substance included in schedule III, IV, or V [F2]

Penalty: Mandatory prison term of 2, 3, 4, 5, 6, 7, or 8 years and up to $15,000
   Mandatory minimum fine: $7,500
   Organization: Up to $20,000

FUNDING OF MARIHUANA TRAFFICKING

If the drug involved is marihuana [F3]

Penalty: Mandatory prison term of 1, 2, 3, 4, or 5 years and up to $10,000
   Mandatory minimum fine: $5,000
   Organization: Up to $15,000

ILLEGAL ADMINISTRATION OR DISTRIBUTION OF ANABOLIC STEROIDS, R.C. § 2925.06 [F4]

(1) Knowingly
(2) Administer to
    (or)
    Prescribe to
    (or)
    Dispense for administration to
(3) A human being
(4) Any anabolic steroid not approved by the FDA for administration to human beings
(5) Venue

Penalty: R.C. § 2929.13(C) applies in determining whether to impose a prison term of 6, 7, 8, 9, 10, 11, 12, 13, 14, 15, 16, 17, or 18 months and up to $5,000
   Organization: Up to $10,000

OFFENSES INVOLVING UNAPPROVED DRUGS; DANGEROUS DRUG OFFENSES INVOLVING LIVESTOCK, R.C. § 2925.09 [F5, F4]

Division (A):
(1) Administer, dispense, distribute, manufacture, possess, sell, or use
(2) Any drug, other than a controlled substance, that is not approved by the United States Food and Drug Administration, or the United States Department of Agriculture, unless one of the following applies
    (a) The United States Food and Drug Administration has approved an application for investigational use in accordance with the "Federal Food, Drug, and Cosmetic Act," 52 Stat. 1040 (1938), 21 U.S.C.A. 301, as amended, and the drug is used only for the approved investigational use

(or)
- (b) The United States Department of Agriculture has approved an application for investigational use in accordance with the federal "Virus Serum-Toxin Act," 37 Stat. 832 (1913), 21 U.S.C.A. 151, as amended, and the drug is used only for the approved investigational use

(or)
- (c) A practitioner, other than a veterinarian, prescribes or combines two or more drugs as a single product for medical purposes

(or)
- (d) A pharmacist, pursuant to a prescription, compounds and dispenses two or more drugs as a single product for medical purposes

(3) Venue

Division (B)(2):
(1) Administer, dispense, distribute, manufacture, possess, sell, or use
(2) Any dangerous drug to or for livestock or any animal that is generally used for food or in the production of food, unless the drug is prescribed by a licensed veterinarian by prescription or other written order and the drug is used in accordance with the veterinarian's order or direction
(3) Venue

Penalty: A felony of the fifth degree (2929.11-2929.18, 2929.31)

Subsequent offenses [F4]

Penalty: A felony of the fourth degree (2929.11-2929.18, 2929.31)

Notes: Division (B)(2) of this section does not apply to a registered wholesale distributor of dangerous drugs, a licensed terminal distributor of dangerous drugs, or a person who possesses, possesses for sale, or sells, at retail, a drug in accordance with Chapters 3719., 4729., or 4741. of the Revised Code.

POSSESSION OF DRUGS, R.C. § 2925.11 [MM, M4, M3, F5, F4, F3, F2, F1]

(1) Knowingly
(2) Obtain, possess or use
(3) Controlled substance
(4) Venue

AGGRAVATED POSSESSION OF DRUGS

If the drug involved is a compound, mixture, preparation, or substance included in schedule I or II (except marihuana, cocaine, LSD, heroin, and hashish) [F5]

Penalty: R.C. § 2929.13(B) applies in determining whether to impose a prison term of 6, 7, 8, 9, 10, 11, or 12 months and up to $2,500

    Organization: Up to $7,500

If the amount of the drug involved exceeds the bulk amount but does not exceed five times the bulk amount [F3]

Penalty: Presumption of a prison term of 1, 2, 3, 4, or 5 years and up to $10,000

    Mandatory minimum fine: $5,000

    Organization: Up to $15,000

If the amount of the drug involved exceeds five times the bulk amount but does not exceed fifty times the bulk amount [**F2**]

Penalty: Mandatory prison term of 2, 3, 4, 5, 6, 7, or 8 years and up to $15,000

    Mandatory minimum fine: $7,500

    Organization: Up to $20,000

If the amount of the drug involved exceeds fifty times the bulk amount but does not exceed one hundred times the bulk amount [**F1**]

Penalty: Mandatory prison term of 3, 4, 5, 6, 7, 8, 9, or 10 years and up to $20,000

    Mandatory minimum fine: $10,000

    Organization: Up to $25,000

If the amount of the drug involved exceeds one hundred times the bulk amount [**F1**]

Penalty: Mandatory prison term of 10 years and up to $20,000 and may impose an additional prison term under R.C. § 2929.14(D)(3)(b) of 1, 2, 3, 4, 5, 6, 7, 8, 9, or 10 years

    Mandatory minimum fine: $10,000

    Organization: Up to $25,000

POSSESSION OF DRUGS

If the drug involved is a compound, mixture, preparation, or substance included in schedule III, IV, or V [**M3**]

Penalty: A misdemeanor of the third degree (2929.21, 2929.31)

If the offender above has previously been convicted of a drug abuse offense [**M2**]

Penalty: A misdemeanor of the second degree (2929.21, 2929.31)

If the drug involved is an anabolic steroid included in schedule III and the offense is a M3, the court may sentence the offender to conditional probation instead of imprisonment in a detention facility.

If the amount of the drug involved exceeds the bulk amount but does not exceed five times the bulk amount [**F4**]

Penalty: R.C. § 2929.13(C) applies in determining whether to impose a prison term of 6, 7, 8, 9, 10, 11, 12, 13, 14, 15, 16, 17, or 18 months and up to $5,000

    Organization: Up to $10,000

If the amount of the drug involved exceeds five times the bulk amount but does not exceed fifty times the bulk amount [**F3**]

Penalty: Presumption of a prison term of 1, 2, 3, 4, or 5 years and up to $10,000

    Mandatory minimum fine: $5,000

    Organization: Up to $15,000

If the amount of the drug involved exceeds fifty times the bulk amount [**F2**]

Penalty: Mandatory prison term of 2, 3, 4, 5, 6, 7, or 8 years and up to $15,000

    Mandatory minimum fine: $7,500

    Organization: Up to $20,000

POSSESSION OF MARIHUANA [**MM**]

If the drug involved in the violation is marihuana or a compound, mixture, preparation, or substance containing marihuana other than hashish

Penalty: A minor misdemeanor (2929.21, 2929.31)

If the amount of the drug involved equals or exceeds one hundred grams but does not exceed two hundred grams **[M4]**

Penalty: A misdemeanor of the fourth degree (2929.21, 2929.31)

If the amount of the drug involved equals or exceeds two hundred grams but does not exceed one thousand grams **[F5]**

Penalty: R.C. § 2929.13(B) applies in determining whether to impose a prison term of 6, 7, 8, 9, 10, 11, or 12 months and up to $2,500
    Organization: Up to $7,500

If the amount of the drug involved equals or exceeds one thousand grams but does not exceed five thousand grams **[F3]**

Penalty: R.C. § 2929.13(C) applies in determining whether to impose a prison term of 1, 2, 3, 4, or 5 years and up to $10,000
    Mandatory minimum fine: $5,000
    Organization: Up to $15,000

If the amount of the drug involved equals or exceeds five thousand grams but does not exceed twenty thousand grams **[F3]**

Penalty: Presumption of a prison term of 1, 2, 3, 4, or 5 years and up to $10,000
    Mandatory minimum fine: $5,000
    Organization: Up to $15,000

If the amount of the drug involved equals or exceeds twenty thousand grams **[F2]**

Penalty: Mandatory prison term of 8 years and up to $15,000
    Mandatory minimum fine: $7,500
    Organization: Up to $20,000

POSSESSION OF COCAINE [F5]

If the drug involved in the violation is cocaine or a compound, mixture, preparation, or substance containing concaine

Penalty: R.C. § 2929.13(B) applies in determining whether to impose a prison term of 6, 7, 8, 9, 10, 11, or 12 months and up to $2,500
    Organization: Up to $7,500

If the amount of the drug involved exceeds five grams but does not exceed twenty-five grams of cocaine that is not crack cocaine or exceeds one gram but does not exceed five grams of crack cocaine **[F4]**

Penalty: Presumption of a prison term of 6, 7, 8, 9, 10, 11, 12, 13, 14, 15, 16, 17, or 18 months and up to $5,000
    Organization: Up to $10,000

If the amount of the drug involved exceeds twenty-five grams but does not exceed one hundred grams of cocaine that is not crack cocaine or exceeds five grams but does not exceed ten grams of crack cocaine **[F3]**

Penalty: Mandatory prison term of 1, 2, 3, 4, or 5 years and up to $10,000
    Mandatory minimum fine: $5,000
    Organization: Up to $15,000

If the amount of the drug involved exceeds one hundred grams but does not exceed five hundred grams of cocaine that is not crack cocaine or exceeds ten grams but does not exceed twenty-five grams of crack cocaine [F2]

Penalty: Mandatory prison term of 2, 3, 4, 5, 6, 7, or 8 years and up to $15,000

    Mandatory minimum fine: $7,500

    Organization: Up to $20,000

If the amount of the drug involved exceeds five hundred grams but does not exceed one thousand grams of cocaine that is not crack cocaine or exceeds twenty-five grams but does not exceed one hundred grams of crack cocaine [F1]

Penalty: Mandatory prison term of 3, 4, 5, 6, 7, 8, 9, or 10 years and up to $20,000

    Mandatory minimum fine: $10,000

    Organization: Up to $25,000

If the amount of the drug involved exceeds one thousand grams that is not crack cocaine or exceeds one hundred grams of crack cocaine [F1]

Penalty: Mandatory prison term of 10 years and up to $20,000 and may impose an additional prison term under R.C. § 2929.14(D)(3)(b) of 1, 2, 3, 4, 5, 6, 7, 8, 9, or 10 years

    Mandatory minimum fine: $10,000

    Organization: Up to $25,000

POSSESSION OF L.S.D. [F5]

Penalty: R.C. § 2929.13(B) applies in determining whether to impose a prison term of 6, 7, 8, 9, 10, 11, or 12 months and up to $2,500

    Organization: Up to $7,500

If the amount of L.S.D. involved exceeds ten unit doses but does not exceed fifty unit doses of L.S.D. in a solid form or exceeds one gram but does not exceed five grams of L.S.D. in a liquid concentrate, liquid extract, or liquid distillate form [F4]

Penalty: R.C. § 2929.13(C) applies in determining whether to impose a prison term of 6, 7, 8, 9, 10, 11, 12, 13, 14, 15, 16, 17, or 18 months and up to $5,000

    Organization: Up to $10,000

If the amount of L.S.D. involved exceeds fifty unit doses but does not exceed two hundred fifty unit doses of L.S.D. in a solid form or exceeds five grams but does not exceed twenty-five grams of L.S.D. in a liquid concentrate, liquid extract, or liquid distillate form [F3]

Penalty: Presumption of a prison term of 1, 2, 3, 4, or 5 years and up to $10,000

    Mandatory minimum fine: $5,000

    Organization: Up to $15,000

If the amount of L.S.D. involved exceeds two hundred fifty unit doses but does not exceed one thousand unit doses of L.S.D. in a solid form or exceeds twenty-five grams but does not exceed one hundred grams of L.S.D. in a liquid concentrate, liquid extract, or liquid distillate form [F2]

Penalty: Mandatory prison term of 2, 3, 4, 5, 6, 7, or 8 years and up to $15,000

    Mandatory minimum fine: $7,500

    Organization: Up to $20,000

If the amount of L.S.D. involved exceeds one thousand unit doses but does not exceed five thousand unit doses of L.S.D. in a solid form or exceeds one hundred grams but does not exceed five hundred grams of L.S.D. in a liquid concentrate, liquid extract, or liquid distillate form [F1]
Penalty: Mandatory prison term of 3, 4, 5, 6, 7, 8, 9, or 10 years and up to $20,000
    Mandatory minimum fine: $10,000
    Organization: Up to $25,000

If the amount of L.S.D. involved exceeds five thousand unit doses of L.S.D. in a solid form or exceeds five hundred grams of L.S.D. in a liquid concentrate, liquid extract, or liquid distillate form [F1]
Penalty: Mandatory prison term of 10 years and up to $20,000 and may impose an additional prison term under R.C. § 2929.14(D)(3)(b) of 1, 2, 3, 4, 5, 6, 7, 8, 9, or 10 years
    Mandatory minimum fine: $10,000
    Organization: Up to $25,000

POSSESSION OF HEROIN [F5]

If the drug involved in the violation is heroin or a compound, mixture, preparation, or substance containing heroin
Penalty: R.C. § 2929.13(B) applies in determining whether to impose a prison term of 6, 7, 8, 9, 10, 11, or 12 months and up to $2,500
    Organization: Up to $7,500

If the amount of the drug involved exceeds one gram but does not exceed five grams [F4]
Penalty: R.C. § 2929.13(C) applies in determining whether to impose a prison term of 6, 7, 8, 9, 10, 11, 12, 13, 14, 15, 16, 17, or 18 months and up to $5,000
    Organization: Up to $10,000

If the amount of the drug involved exceeds five grams but does not exceed ten grams [F3]
Penalty: Presumption of a prison term of 1, 2, 3, 4, or 5 years and up to $10,000
    Mandatory minimum fine: $5,000
    Organization: Up to $15,000

If the amount of the drug involved exceeds ten grams but does not exceed fifty grams [F2]
Penalty: Mandatory prison term of 2, 3, 4, 5, 6, 7, or 8 years and up to $15,000
    Mandatory minimum fine: $7,500
    Organization: Up to $20,000

If the amount of the drug involved exceeds fifty grams but does not exceed two hundred fifty grams [F1]
Penalty: Mandatory prison term of 3, 4, 5, 6, 7, 8, 9, or 10 years and up to $20,000
    Mandatory minimum fine: $10,000
    Organization: Up to $25,000

If the amount of the drug involved exceeds two hundred fifty grams [F1]
Penalty: Mandatory prison term of 10 years and up to $20,000 and may impose an additional prison term under R.C. § 2929.14(D)(3)(b) of 1, 2, 3, 4, 5, 6, 7, 8, 9, or 10 years
    Mandatory minimum fine: $10,000
    Organization: Up to $25,000

POSSESSION OF HASHISH [MM]

If the drug involved in the violation is hashish or a compound, mixture, preparation, or substance containing hashish

Penalty: A minor misdemeanor (2929.21, 2929.31)

If the amount of the drug involved equals or exceeds five grams but does not exceed ten grams of hashish in a solid form or equals or exceeds one gram but does not exceed two grams of hashish in a liquid concentrate, liquid extract, or liquid distillate form [M4]

Penalty: A misdemeanor of the fourth degree (2929.21, 2929.31)

If the amount of the drug involved equals or exceeds ten grams but does not exceed fifty grams of hashish in a solid form or exceeds two grams but does not exceed ten grams of hashish in a liquid concentrate, liquid extract, or liquid distillate form [F5]

Penalty: R.C. § 2929.13(B) applies in determining whether to impose a prison term of 6, 7, 8, 9, 10, 11, or 12 months and up to $2,500

Organization: Up to $7,500

If the amount of the drug involved equals or exceeds fifty grams but does not exceed two hundred fifty grams of hashish in a solid form or equals or exceeds ten grams but does not exceed fifty grams of hashish in a liquid concentrate, liquid extract, or liquid distillate form [F3]

Penalty: R.C. § 2929.13(B) applies in determining whether to impose a prison term of 1, 2, 3, 4, or 5 years and up to $10,000

Mandatory minimum fine: $5,000

Organization: Up to $15,000

If the amount of the drug involved equals or exceeds two hundred fifty grams but does not exceed one thousand grams of hashish in a solid form or equals or exceeds fifty grams but does not exceed two hundred grams of hashish in a liquid concentrate, liquid extract, or liquid distillate form [F3]

Penalty: Presumption of a prison term of 2, 3, 4, 5, 6, 7, or 8 years and up to $15,000

Mandatory minimum fine: $5,000

Organization: Up to $15,000

If the amount of the drug involved exceeds one thousand grams of hashish in a solid form or equals or exceeds two hundred grams of hashish in a liquid concentrate, liquid extract, or liquid distillate form [F2]

Penalty: Mandatory prison term of 2, 3, 4, 5, 6, 7, or 8 years and up to $15,000

Mandatory minimum fine: $7,500

Organization: Up to $20,000

Notes: See Publisher's Note preceding R.C. § 3719.41 in Miscellaneous Statutory Provisions.

See statute for provisions exempting some parties from provisions concerning anabolic steroids.

See statute for special provisions concerning attorneys and professionally licensed persons convicted under this statute.

See statute for provisions exempting indigents from mandatory fines.

See statute for provisions allowing revocation or suspension of driver's and commercial driver's licenses.

See statute for special provisions concerning probation, treatment, and counseling.

See statute for special provisions concerning pregnant offenders.

Arrest or conviction for a minor misdemeanor violation of this section does not constitute a criminal record. R.C. § 2925.11(D).

Laboratory report as prima-facie evidence in drug abuse cases; rights of accused in re, R.C. § 2925.51.

Definitions: "Controlled substance," R.C. § 3719.01(D)
"Marihuana," R.C. § 3719.01(Q)
"Possess," R.C. § 2925.01(K)
"Professionally licensed person," R.C. § 2925.01

POSSESSING DRUG ABUSE INSTRUMENTS, R.C. § 2925.12 [M2, M1]

(1) Knowingly
(2) Make, obtain, possess, or use
(3) Any instrument, article, or thing the customary and primary purpose of which is for the administration or use of a dangerous drug, other than marihuana
(4) When the instrument involved is a hypodermic or syringe, whether or not of crude or extemporized manufacture or assembly
(*and*)
(5) The instrument, article or thing involved has been used by the offender
   (a) To unlawfully administer or use a dangerous drug, other than marihuana,
     (*or*)
   (b) To prepare a dangerous drug, other than marihuana, for unlawful administration or use
(6) Venue

Penalty: A misdemeanor of the second degree (2929.21, 2929.31)

Where previously convicted of drug abuse offense **[M1]**

Penalty: A misdemeanor of the first degree (2929.21, 2929.31)

Notes: This section does not apply to manufacturers, practitioners, pharmacists, owners of pharmacies, and other persons whose conduct was in accordance with Chapters 3719., 4715., 4729., 4731., and 4741. or section 4723.56 of the Revised Code. R.C. § 2925.12(B).

See Publisher's Note preceding R.C. § 3719.41 in Miscellaneous Statutory Provisions.

See statute for special provisions concerning attorneys and professionally licensed persons convicted under this statute.

See statute for provisions allowing revocation or suspension of driver's and commercial driver's licenses.

Definitions: "Dangerous drugs," R.C. § 4729.02(D)
"Hypodermic," R.C. § 3719.01(M)
"Professionally licensed person," R.C. § 2925.01

POSSESSION, SALE, AND DISPOSAL OF HYPODERMICS, R.C. § 3719.17.2 [F4, F3, M3, M1]

Division (B): **[M3]**
(1) (a) Being a manufacturer, distributor, dealer, owner of pharmacy, or pharmacist
    (b) Display any hypodermic for sale

(or)
(2) (a) Being authorized to possess a hypodermic under division (A)
  (i) Negligently fail to take reasonable precautions to prevent any hypodermic in his possession from theft or acquisition by any unauthorized person
(3) Venue

Penalty: Division (B): A misdemeanor of the third degree (2929.21, 2929.31)
Where previously convicted [M1]
Penalty: A misdemeanor of the first degree (2929.21, 2929.31)

Division (C): [F4]
(1) Not being a manufacturer, distributor, dealer, hospital, pharmacist, or practitioner
(2) Sell or furnish a hypodermic to another
(3) Venue

Penalty: Division (C): A felony of the fourth degree (2929.11-2929.18, 2929.31)
Where previously convicted [F3]
Penalty: A felony of the third degree (2929.11-2929.18, 2929.31)

Division (D): [F4]
(1) Sell or furnish a hypodermic
(2) To another whom he knows or has reasonable cause to believe
(3) Is not authorized by division (A) to possess a hypodermic
(4) Venue

Penalty: Division (D): A felony of the fourth degree (2929.11-2929.18, 2929.31)

Division (E): [M3]
(1) Being a pharmacist or person under the supervision of a pharmacist
(2) Furnish a hypodermic
(3) To another without a prescription without
(4) (a) Positive identification of each person to whom furnished
  (b) Written record including date, quantity and type of articles
  (c) Name, address and signature of person to whom furnished
(5) Venue

Penalty: Division (E): A misdemeanor of the third degree (2929.21, 2929.31)

PERMITTING DRUG ABUSE, R.C. § 2925.13 [M1, F5]

Division (A):
(1) Being the owner, operator, or person in charge of a locomotive, watercraft, aircraft, or other vehicle as defined in R.C. § 4501.01(A)
(2) Knowingly
(3) Permit such vehicle to be used for commission of felony drug abuse offense
(4) Venue

Division (B):
(1) Being the owner, lessee, or occupant, or having custody, control, or supervision of premises, or real estate, including vacant land
(2) Knowingly

(3) Permit premises, or real estate, including vacant land, to be used for commission of a felony drug abuse offense
(4) By another person
(5) Venue

Penalty: A misdemeanor of the first degree (2929.21, 2929.31)

If the felony drug offense in question involves corrupting another with drugs (R.C. § 2925.02), or the sale of a controlled substance [violation of R.C. § 2925.03], and was committed in the vicinity of a school or in the vicinity of a juvenile **[F5]**

Penalty: A felony of the fifth degree (2929.11-2929.18, 2929.31)

If the violation of Division (A) involves the sale, offer to sell, or possession of schedule I or II controlled substance (except marihuana) and if the offender as a result of the violation is a major drug offender, the court in lieu of the prison term otherwise authorized or required, shall impose upon the offender a mandatory 10 year prison term and may impose an additional prison term of 1 to 10 years pursuant to R.C. § 2929.14(D)(3).

Notes: See statute for special provisions concerning attorneys and professionally licensed persons convicted under this statute.

See Publisher's Note preceding R.C. § 3719.41 in Miscellaneous Statutory Provisions.

See statute for provisions allowing revocation or suspension of driver's and commercial driver's licenses.

Laboratory report as prima-facie evidence in drug abuse cases; rights of accused in re, R.C. § 2925.51.

Definitions: "Felony drug abuse offense," R.C. § 2925.01

DRUG PARAPHERNALIA, R.C. § 2925.14 [M4, M2, M1]

Illegal Use or Possession of Drug Paraphernalia [Division (C)(1)] **[M4]**
(1) Knowingly
(2) (a) Use
    (or)
    (b) Possess with purpose to use
(3) Drug paraphernalia
(4) Venue

Penalty: A misdemeanor of the fourth degree (2929.21, 2929.31)

Dealing in Drug Paraphernalia [Division (C)(2)] **[M2]**
(1) Knowingly
(2) (a) Sell
    (or)
    (b) Possess with purpose to sell
    (or)
    (c) Manufacture with purpose to sell
(3) Drug paraphernalia
(4) If the person knows or reasonably should know the equipment, product, or material will be used as drug paraphernalia
(5) Venue

§ 2925.22

Penalty: A misdemeanor of the second degree (2929.21, 2929.31)

Selling Drug Paraphernalia to Juveniles [Divisions (C)(2), (F)(3)] **[M1]**

(1) Knowingly
(2) (a) Sell
    (*or*)
    (b) Possess with purpose to sell
    (*or*)
    (c) Manufacture with purpose to sell
(3) Drug paraphernalia
(4) To a juvenile
(5) Venue

Penalty: A misdemeanor of the first degree (2929.21, 2929.31)

Illegal Advertising of Drug Paraphernalia [Division (C)(3)] **[M2]**

(1) Place an advertisement
(2) In any newspaper, magazine, handbill, or other publication that is published and printed, circulates primarily within this state
(3) Knowing that the purpose of the advertisement is to promote the illegal sale in this state of the equipment, product, or material that the offender intended or designed for use as drug paraphernalia
(4) Venue

Penalty: A misdemeanor of the second degree (2929.21, 2929.31)

Notes: See R.C. § 2925.14 for special provisions regarding seizure and disposal.

See Publisher's Note preceding R.C. § 3719.41 in Miscellaneous Statutory Provisions.

See statute for special provisions concerning attorneys and professionally licensed persons convicted under this statute.

See statute for provisions allowing revocation or suspension of driver's and commercial driver's licenses.

This statute does not apply to manufacturers, practitioners, pharmacists, owners of pharmacies, and other persons whose conduct is in accordance with Chapter 3719., 4715., 4729., 4731., or 4741. or section 4723.56 of the Revised Code.

This statute is not to be construed to prohibit the possession or use of a hypodermic as authorized by Section 3719.17.2 of the Revised Code.

Definitions: "Drug paraphernalia," R.C. § 2925.14

DECEPTION TO OBTAIN DANGEROUS DRUG, R.C. § 2925.22 [F5, F4]

(1) By deception as defined in R.C. § 2913.01
(2) (a) Procure the administration of, a prescription for, or the dispensing of, a dangerous drug
    (*or*)
    (b) Possess an uncompleted preprinted prescription blank used for writing a prescription for a dangerous drug
(3) Venue

If the drug involved is a compound, mixture, preparation, or substance included in schedule I or II (except marihuana) **[F4]**

Penalty: R.C. § 2929.13(C) applies in determining whether to impose a prison term of 6, 7, 8, 9, 10, 11, 12, 13, 14, 15, 16, 17, or 18 months and up to $5,000

Organization: Up to $10,000

If the drug involved is a compound, mixture, preparation, or substance included in schedule III, IV, or V or is marihuana [F5]

Penalty: R.C. § 2929.13(C) applies in determining whether to impose a prison term of 6, 7, 8, 9, 10, 11, or 12 months and up to $2,500

Organization: Up to $7,500

Notes: Laboratory report as prima-facie evidence in drug abuse cases; rights of accused in re, R.C. § 2925.51.

See Publisher's Note preceding R.C. § 3719.41 in Miscellaneous Statutory Provisions.

See statute for special provisions concerning attorneys and professionally licensed persons convicted under this statute.

See statute for provisions allowing revocation or suspension of driver's and commercial driver's licenses.

Definitions: "Prescription," R.C. § 3719.01(CC)

ILLEGAL PROCESSING OF DRUG DOCUMENTS, R.C. § 2925.23 [F5, F4]

Division (A):
(1) Knowingly
(2) Make a false statement in any prescription, order, report, or record required by R.C. Chapter 3719. or 4729.
(3) Venue

Division (B):
(1) (a) Intentionally make, utter, or sell
    (*or*)
    (b) Knowingly possess
(2) A false or forged
    (a) Prescription
        (*or*)
    (b) Uncompleted preprinted prescription blank used for writing a prescription
        (*or*)
    (c) Official written order
        (*or*)
    (d) License for a terminal distributor of dangerous drugs as required in R.C. § 4729.60
        (*or*)
    (e) Registration certificate for a wholesale distributor of dangerous drugs as required in R.C. § 4729.60
(3) Venue

Division (C):
(1) By theft, as defined in R.C. § 2913.02
(2) Acquire
(3) (a) A prescription
        (*or*)

§ 2925.31   Ohio Criminal Law Handbook   A-162

    (b) An uncompleted preprinted prescription blank used for writing a prescription
        (or)
    (c) An official written order
        (or)
    (d) A blank official written order
        (or)
    (e) A license or blank license for a terminal distributor of dangerous drugs as required in R.C. § 4729.60
        (or)
    (f) A registration certificate or blank registration certificate for a wholesale distributor of dangerous drugs as required in R.C. § 4729.60
(4) Venue

Division (D):
(1) Knowingly
(2) Make or affix
(3) Any false or forged label
(4) To a package or receptacle containing any dangerous drug
(5) Venue

If the drug involved is a compound, mixture, preparation, or substance included in schedule I or II (except marihuana) **[F4]**

Penalty: R.C. § 2929.13(C) applies in determining whether to impose a prison term of 6, 7, 8, 9, 10, 11, 12, 13, 14, 15, 16, 17, or 18 months and up to $5,000

    Organization: Up to $10,000

If the drug involved is a dangerous drug or a compound, mixture, preparation, or substance included in schedule III, IV, or V or is marihuana **[F5]**

Penalty: R.C. § 2929.13(C) applies in determining whether to impose a prison term of 6, 7, 8, 9, 10, 11, or 12 months and up to $2,500

    Organization: Up to $7,500

Notes: Divisions (A) and (D) do not apply to practitioners, pharmacists, owners of pharmacies, and other persons whose conduct is in accordance with R.C. Chapters 3719., 4715., 4725., 4729., 4731., and 4741.

    See Publisher's Note preceding R.C. § 3719.41 in Miscellaneous Statutory Provisions.

    See statute for special provisions concerning attorneys and professionally licensed persons convicted under this statute.

    See statute for provisions allowing revocation or suspension of driver's and commercial driver's licenses.

Definitions: "Felony drug abuse offense," R.C. § 2925.01(H)
        "Official written order," R.C. § 3719.01(U)
        "Prescription," R.C. § 3719.01(CC)

ABUSING HARMFUL INTOXICANTS, R.C. § 2925.31 [M1, F5]

(1) Except for lawful research, clinical, medical, dental, or veterinary purposes
(2) Obtain, possess, or use

(3) A harmful intoxicant
(4) With purpose to induce intoxication or similar physiological effects
(5) Venue

Penalty: A misdemeanor of the first degree (2929.21, 2929.31)

Where previously convicted of drug abuse offense [**F5**]

Penalty: A felony of the fifth degree (2929.11-2929.18, 2929.31)

Notes: Laboratory report as prima-facie evidence in drug abuse cases; rights of accused in re, R.C. § 2925.51.

See statute for special provisions concerning attorneys and professionally licensed persons convicted under this statute.

See statute for provisions allowing revocation or suspension of driver's and commercial driver's licenses.

Definitions: "Drug abuse offense," R.C. § 2925.01(G)
"Harmful intoxicant," R.C. § 2925.01(I)

TRAFFICKING IN HARMFUL INTOXICANTS; IMPROPERLY DISPENSING OR DISTRIBUTING NITROUS OXIDE, R.C. § 2925.32 [M4, F5, F4]

Division (A)(1): [**F5, F4**]
(1) Knowingly
(2) Dispense or distribute
(3) A harmful intoxicant (excluding nitrous oxide)
(4) To a person age 18 or older
(5) Believing or having reason to believe that the harmful intoxicant will be used in violation of R.C. § 2925.31
(6) Venue

Division (A)(2): [**F5, F4**]
(1) Knowingly
(2) Dispense or distribute
(3) A harmful intoxicant (excluding nitrous oxide)
(4) To a person under age 18
(5) Believing or having reason to believe that the harmful intoxicant will be used in violation of R.C. § 2925.31
(6) Venue

Division (B)(1): [**F5, F4**]
(1) Knowingly
(2) Dispense or distribute
(3) Nitrous oxide
(4) To a person age 21 or older
(5) Knowing or having reason to believe that the nitrous oxide will be used in violation of R.C. § 2925.31
(6) Venue

Division (B)(2): [**F5, F4**]
(1) Knowingly

§ 2925.33   Ohio Criminal Law Handbook   A-164

(2) Dispense or distribute
(3) Nitrous oxide
(4) To a person under 21
(5) Except for lawful medical, dental or clinical purposes
(6) Venue

Division (B)(3): [F5, F4]
(1) Sell
(2) Device that allows the purchaser to inhale nitrous oxide from cartridges or to hold nitrous oxide released from cartridges for purposes of inhalation
(3) At the time a cartridge of nitrous oxide is sold to another person
(4) Venue

Penalty: A felony of the fifth degree (2929.11-2929.18, 2929.31)

If the offender previously has been convicted of a drug abuse offense [F4]

Penalty: A felony of the fourth degree (2929.11-2929.18, 2929.31)

Division (B)(4): [M4]
(1) Being a person who dispenses or distributes nitrous oxide in cartridges
(2) Fail to comply with
(3) (a) The record-keeping requirements established under Division (F) of this section
  (or)
  (b) The labeling and transaction identification requirements established under Division (F) of this section
(4) Venue

Penalty: A misdemeanor of the fourth degree (2929.21, 2929.31)

Notes: Division (A)(2) of this section does not prohibit dispensing or distributing a harmful intoxicant to a person under 18 if a written order from the juvenile's parent or guardian is provided to the dispenser or distributor or dispensing or distributing gasoline or diesel fuel to a person under 18 if the dispenser or distributor does not know or have reason to believe the product will be used in violation of R.C. § 2925.31. A person is not required to obtain a written order from the parent or guardian of a person under age 18 in order to distribute or dispense gasoline or diesel fuel to the person.

The sale of such a device as described in Division (B)(3) constitutes a rebuttable presumption that the person knew or had reason to believe that the purchaser intended to abuse the nitrous oxide.

This section does not apply to products used in making, fabricating, assembling, transporting, or constructing a product or structure by manual labor or machinery for sale or lease to another person, or to the mining, refining, or processing of natural deposits.

In addition to any other sanction imposed for trafficking in harmful intoxicants, the court shall suspend for not less than six months or more than five years the driver's or commercial driver's license or permit of any person who is convicted of or has pleaded guilty to trafficking in harmful intoxicants. If the offender is a professionally licensed person or a person who has been admitted to the bar by order of the supreme court, in addition to any other sanction imposed, the court forthwith shall comply with R.C. § 2925.38.

POSSESSING NITROUS OXIDE IN MOTOR VEHICLE, R.C. § 2925.33 [M4]

(1) Possess
(2) An open cartridge of nitrous oxide

(3) (a) While operating or being a passenger in or on a motor vehicle on a street, highway, or other public or private property open to the public for purposes of vehicular traffic or parking
(or)
(b) While being in or on a stationary motor vehicle on a street, highway, or other public or private property open to the public for purposes of vehicular traffic or parking
(4) Unless authorized under Chapter 3719, 4715, 4729, 4731, 4741, or 4765
(5) Venue

Penalty: A misdemeanor of the fourth degree (2929.21, 2929.31)

ILLEGAL DISPENSING OF DRUG SAMPLES, R.C. § 2925.36 [M2, M1, F5, F4]

(1) Knowingly
(2) Furnish
(3) Another
(4) A sample drug
(5) Venue

If the drug involved is a compound, mixture, preparation, or substance included in schedule I or II (except marihuana) **[F5]**

Penalty: R.C. § 2929.13(C) applies in determining whether to impose a prison term of 6, 7, 8, 9, 10, 11, or 12 months and up to $2,500
    Organization: Up to $7,500

If the offense was committed in the vicinity of a school or in the vicinity of a juvenile **[F4]**

Penalty: R.C. § 2929.13(C) applies in determining whether to impose a prison term of 6, 7, 8, 9, 10, 11, 12, 13, 14, 15, 16, 17, or 18 months and up to $5,000
    Organization: Up to $10,000

If the drug involved is a dangerous drug or a compound, mixture, preparation, or substance included in schedule III, IV, or V or is marihuana **[M2]**

Penalty: A misdemeanor of the second degree (2929.21, 2929.31)

If the offense was committed in the vicinity of a school or in the vicinity of a juvenile **[M1]**

Penalty: A misdemeanor of the first degree (2929.21, 2929.31)

Notes: See statute for special provisions concerning attorneys and professionally licensed persons convicted under this statute.

See statute for provisions allowing revocation or suspension of driver's and commercial driver's licenses.

Laboratory report as prima-facie evidence in drug abuse cases; rights of accused in re, R.C. § 2925.51.

Definitions: "Dispense," R.C. § 3719.01(F)
    "Drug abuse offense," R.C. § 2925.01(G)
    "Sample drug," R.C. § 2925.01(L)

OFFENSES INVOLVING COUNTERFEIT CONTROLLED SUBSTANCES, R.C. § 2925.37 [M1, F5, F4]

Division (A):
(1) Knowingly

(2) Possess
(3) Any counterfeit controlled substance
(4) Venue

Division (B):
(1) Knowingly
(2) Make, sell, offer to sell, or deliver
(3) Any substance
(4) Knowing it is a counterfeit controlled substance
(5) Venue

Division (C):
(1) Make, possess, sell, offer to sell, or deliver
(2) Any punch, die, plate, stone, or other device
(3) Knowing or having a reason to know
(4) That it will be used to print or reproduce a trademark, trade name or other identifying mark
(5) Upon a counterfeit controlled substance
(6) Venue

Division (D):
(1) Sell, offer to sell, give, or deliver
(2) Any counterfeit controlled substance
(3) To a juvenile
(4) Venue

Division (E):
(1) Directly or indirectly represent
(2) A counterfeit controlled substance
(3) As a controlled substance
(4) By describing its effects
(5) As the physical or psychological effects associated with the use of controlled substances
(6) Venue

Division (F):
(1) Directly or indirectly falsely represent or advertise
(2) A counterfeit controlled substance
(3) As a controlled substance
(4) Venue

Division (A) Possession of counterfeit controlled substances [M1]

Penalty: A misdemeanor of the first degree (2929.21, 2929.31)

Divisions (B) or (C) Trafficking in counterfeit controlled substances [F5]

Penalty: R.C. § 2929.13(C) applies in determining whether to impose a prison term of 6, 7, 8, 9, 10, 11, or 12 months and up to $2,500

   Organization: Up to $7,500

If the offense was committed in the vicinity of a school or in the vicinity of a juvenile [F4]

Penalty: R.C. § 2929.13(C) applies in determining whether to impose a prison term of 6, 7, 8, 9, 10, 11, 12, 13, 14, 15, 16, 17, or 18 months and up to $5,000

   Organization: Up to $10,000

Division (D) Aggravated trafficking in counterfeit controlled substances [F4]
Penalty: R.C. § 2929.13(C) applies in determining whether to impose a prison term of 6, 7, 8, 9, 10, 11, 12, 13, 14, 15, 16, 17, or 18 months and up to $5,000
    Organization: Up to $10,000

Division (E) Promoting and encouraging drug abuse [F5]
Penalty: R.C. § 2929.13(C) applies in determining whether to impose a prison term of 6, 7, 8, 9, 10, 11, or 12 months and up to $2,500
    Organization: Up to $7,500

If the offense was committed in the vicinity of a school or in the vicinity of a juvenile [F4]
Penalty: R.C. § 2929.13(C) applies in determining whether to impose a prison term of 6, 7, 8, 9, 10, 11, 12, 13, 14, 15, 16, 17, or 18 months and up to $5,000
    Organization: Up to $10,000

Division (F) Fraudulent drug advertising [F5]
Penalty: R.C. § 2929.13(C) applies in determining whether to impose a prison term of 6, 7, 8, 9, 10, 11, or 12 months and up to $2,500
    Organization: Up to $7,500

If the offense was committed in the vicinity of a school or in the vicinity of a juvenile [F4]
Penalty: R.C. § 2929.13(C) applies in determining whether to impose a prison term of 6, 7, 8, 9, 10, 11, 12, 13, 14, 15, 16, 17, or 18 months and up to $5,000
    Organization: Up to $10,000

Notes: See statute for special provisions concerning attorneys and professionally licensed persons convicted under this statute.

See Publisher's Note preceding R.C. § 3719.41 in Miscellaneous Statutory Provisions.

See statute for provisions allowing revocation or suspension of driver's and commercial driver's licenses.

Definitions: "Advertise," R.C. § 2925.37.
    "Advertisement," R.C. § 3715.01.

MISCELLANEOUS OFFENSES

ABUSE OF CORPSE, R.C. § 2927.01(A) [M2]

(1) Without authority of law
(2) Treat a human corpse
(3) In a manner which the offender knows would outrage reasonable family sensibilities
(4) Venue

Penalty: A misdemeanor of the second degree (2929.21, 2929.31)

GROSS ABUSE OF A CORPSE, R.C. § 2927.01(B) [F5]

(1) Without authority of law
(2) Treat a human corpse

(3) In a manner that would outrage reasonable community sensibilities
(4) Venue

Penalty: A felony of the fifth degree (2929.11-2929.18, 2929.31)

ILLEGAL DISTRIBUTION OF CIGARETTES OR OTHER TOBACCO PRODUCTS, R.C. § 2927.02 [M4, M3]

Division (A):
(1) (a) Being a manufacturer, producer, distributor, wholesaler, or retailer of cigarettes or other tobacco products
   (or)
   (b) Being an agent, employee, or representative of any of the above
(2) (a) (i) Give, sell, or otherwise distribute
      (ii) Cigarettes or other tobacco products
      (iii) To any person under 18 years of age
      (or)
   (b) (i) Give away, sell, or distribute
      (ii) Cigarettes or other tobacco products
      (iii) In any place that does not have posted in a conspicuous place
      (iv) A sign stating that giving, selling, or otherwise distributing cigarettes or other tobacco products to a person under 18 years of age is against the law
(3) Venue

Division (B):
(1) (a) Sell
   (or)
   (b) Offer to sell
(2) Cigarettes or other tobacco products
(3) From a vending machine which is *not*
   (a) In an area within a factory, business, office, or other place not open to the general public
   (or)
   (b) In an area to which persons under the age of eighteen years are not generally permitted access
   (or)
   (c) In a place not identified in (3)(a) or (b) above, where the vending machine is
      (i) Located within the immediate vicinity, plain view, and control of the person who owns or operates the place, or an employee of such person, so that all cigarettes and other tobacco product purchases from the vending machine will be readily observed by the person who owns or operates the place or an employee of such person
      (and)
      (ii) Inaccessible to the public when the place is closed
(4) Venue

Penalty: A misdemeanor of the fourth degree (2929.21, 2929.31)

If prior conviction under this section [M3]

Penalty: A misdemeanor of the third degree (2929.21, 2929.31)

Note: For purposes of this section, a vending machine located in any unmonitored area, including an unmonitored coatroom, restroom, hallway, or outer waiting area, shall not be considered located within the immediate vicinity, plain view, and control of the person who owns or operates the place, or an employee of such person.

Definition: "Vending machine" has the same definition as "coin machine" as defined in R.C. § 2913.01.

INTERFERENCE WITH FAIR HOUSING RIGHTS, R.C. § 2927.03 [M1]

(1) Whether or not acting under color of law
(2) (a) By force
    (*or*)
    (b) By threat of force
(3) Willfully
(4) (a) Injure, intimidate, or interfere with
    (*or*)
    (b) Attempt to injure, intimidate or interfere with
(5) Any person
(6) (a) (i) Because of race, color, religion, sex, familial status, national origin, handicap, or ancestry
        (*and*)
    (ii) Because that person is or has been
        (A) Selling, purchasing, renting, financing, occupying, or contracting for any housing accommodations
            (*or*)
        (B) Negotiating for the sale, purchase, rental, financing, or occupation of any housing accommodations
            (*or*)
        (C) Applying for or participating in any service, organization, or facility relating to the business of selling or renting housing accommodations
            (*or*)
    (b) (i) (A) Because that person is or has been
            (*or*)
        (B) In order to intimidate that person or any other person or class of persons from
        (ii) (A) Participating, without discrimination on account of race, color, religion, sex, familial status, national origin, handicap, or ancestry, in any of the activities, services, organizations, or facilities described in 6(a)(ii), above
            (*or*)
        (B) Affording another person or class of persons opportunity to participate, without discrimination on account of race, color, religion, sex, familial status, national origin, handicap, or ancestry, in any of the activities, services, organizations, or facilities described in 6(a)(ii), above
            (*or*)
    (c) (i) (A) Because that person is or has been
            (*or*)
        (B) In order to discourage that person or any other person from
        (ii) (A) Lawfully aiding or encouraging other persons to participate, without discrimination on account of race, color, religion, sex, familial status, national origin, handicap,

　　　　　　or ancestry, in any of the activities, services, organizations, or facilities described in 6(a)(ii) above
　　　　　　(or)
　　　(B) Participating lawfully in speech or peaceful assembly opposing any denial of the opportunity to participate, without discrimination on account of race, color, religion, sex, familial status, national origin, handicap, or ancestry, in any of the activities, services, organizations, or facilities described in 6(a)(ii), above
(7) Venue

Penalty: A misdemeanor of the first degree (2929.21, 2929.31)

Definitions: "Familial status," "handicap," R.C. § 4112.01.

DESECRATION, R.C. § 2927.11 [M2, M1]

(1) Purposely
(2) Deface, damage, pollute or physically mistreat
(3) (a) The United States flag or the flag of Ohio
　　　(or)
　　(b) A public monument
　　　(or)
　　(c) A historical or commemorative marker, or any structure, Indian mound or earthwork, thing or site of great historical or archaeological interest
　　　(or)
　　(d) A place of worship or its furnishings, or religious artifacts or sacred texts within the place of worship
　　　(or)
　　(e) A work of art or museum piece
　　(f) Any object of reverence or devotion
(4) Without privilege to do so
(5) Venue

Penalty: A misdemeanor of the second degree (2929.21, 2929.31)

If violation of 3(d), above **[M1]**

Penalty: A misdemeanor of the first degree (2929.21, 2929.31)

Note: See R.C. § 2307.70 regarding civil damages.

ETHNIC INTIMIDATION, R.C. § 2927.12

(1) Violate R.C. § 2903.21, 2903.22, 2909.06, 2909.07, or 2917.21(A)(3), (4), or (5)
(2) By reason of the race, color, religion, or national origin
(3) Of another person or group of persons
(4) Venue

Penalty: Next higher degree than offense which is a necessary element

Note: See R.C. § 2307.70 regarding civil damages.

SELLING OR DONATING CONTAMINATED BLOOD, R.C. § 2927.13 [F4]

(1) With knowledge that the person is a carrier of a virus that causes Acquired Immune Deficiency Syndrome

(2) (a) Sell
   (or)
   (b) Donate
(3) (a) The person's blood
   (or)
   (b) The person's plasma
   (or)
   (c) A product of the person's blood
(4) If the person knows or should know that it is being accepted for the purpose of transfusion to another individual
(5) Venue

Penalty: A felony of the fourth degree (2929.11-2929.18, 2929.31)

DUTY TO REPORT ESCAPE OF ANIMAL, R.C. § 2927.21 [M1]

(1) Being the owner or keeper of animal
   (a) not indigenous to Ohio
   (or)
   (b) presenting risk of serious physical harm to persons or property
(2) Fail to report the animal's escape to appropriate law enforcement officer and to clerk of council or township clerk within one hour after one discovers the escape or reasonably should have discovered it
(3) Venue

Penalty: A misdemeanor of the first degree (2929.21, 2929.31)

Note: If the office of the clerk of a legislative authority or township clerk is closed to the public at the time a report is required by this section, then it is sufficient compliance with this section if the owner or keeper makes the report within one hour after the office is next open to the public.

CONTAMINATING SUBSTANCE FOR HUMAN CONSUMPTION OR USE; SPREADING FALSE REPORT, R.C. § 2927.24 [F1, F1, F4]

[B] (Contaminating a substance for human consumption or use) **[F1, F1]**
(1) (a) Knowingly
   (b) Mingle a poison or other harmful substance with
   (c) (i) food
      (or)
      (ii) drink
      (or)
      (iii) nonprescription drug
      (or)
      (iv) prescription drug
      (or)
      (v) pharmaceutical product
      (or)
(2) (a) Knowingly
   (b) Place a poison or other harmful substance in a

§ 2927.24   Ohio Criminal Law Handbook   A-172

    (c) (i) spring
          (or)
      (ii) well
          (or)
      (iii) reservoir
          (or)
      (iv) public water supply
(3) If the person knows or has reason to know that
(4) (a) The food
      (or)
    (b) drink
      (or)
    (c) nonprescription drug
      (or)
    (d) prescription drug
      (or)
    (e) pharmaceutical product
      (or)
    (f) water
(5) May be ingested or used by another person
(6) Venue

Penalty: A felony of the first degree (2929.11-2929.18, 2929.31)
If the offense involved an amount of poison or other harmful substance sufficient to cause death if ingested or used by a person or if the offense resulted in serious physical harm to another person, imprisonment for life and a fine not to exceed $10,000

[C] (Spreading a false report of contamination) **[F4]**
(1) Inform another person
(2) That a poison or other harmful substance
(3) Will be placed in
(4) (a) A food
      (or)
    (b) Drink
      (or)
    (c) Nonprescription drug
      (or)
    (d) Prescription drug
      (or)
    (e) Other pharmaceutical product
      (or)
    (f) Spring
      (or)
    (g) Well
      (or)
    (h) Reservoir
      (or)
    (i) Public water supply

(5) If the placement of the poison or other harmful substance would be a violation of division (B) of this section
(6) The person knows that the information is
  (a) False
      (and)
  (b) Will likely be disseminated to the public
(7) Venue

Penalty: A felony of the fourth degree (2929.11-2929.18, 2929.31)

CONDUCTING UNAUTHORIZED BODY CAVITY OR STRIP SEARCH; FAILURE TO PREPARE PROPER REPORT, R.C. § 2933.32 [M4, M1]

[A] (Conducting unauthorized body cavity or strip search) **[M1]**
(1) Being a law enforcement officer, other employee of a law enforcement agency, physician, registered nurse, or licensed practical nurse
(2) Conduct or cause to be conducted
(3) (a) A body cavity search
        (or)
    (b) A strip search
(4) Where any of the following requirements is not met
    (a) (i) (A) A law enforcement officer or employee of a law enforcement agency
            (B) Has probable cause to believe, based upon the nature of the offense with which the person is charged, the circumstances of his arrest, and his prior conviction record (if known)
            (C) That the person is concealing evidence of the commission of a criminal offense, including fruits or tools of a crime, contraband, or a deadly weapon as defined in R.C. § 2923.11
            (D) That could not otherwise be discovered
                (or)
        (ii) The search is conducted for a legitimate medical or hygienic reason
            (and)
    (b) The search is conducted
        (i) Following issuance of a search warrant authorizing the search (unless there is a legitimate medical reason or medical emergency justifying the warrantless search)
            (and)
        (ii) Under sanitary conditions
            (and)
        (iii) By a physician or registered nurse or licensed practical nurse registered or licensed to practice in this state
            (and)
        (iv) After a law enforcement officer or employee of a law enforcement agency obtains written authorization therefor from the person in command of the agency or from his specific designee (unless there is a legitimate medical reason or medical emergency making obtaining such authorization impractable)
            (and)
        (v) By a person or persons of the same sex as the person being searched
            (and)

(vi) In a manner and in a location that permits only the person(s) conducting the search and the person being searched to observe it.
(5) Venue

[B] (Failure to prepare proper report) **[M4]**
(1) Following completion of a body cavity search or strip search
(2) Being the person(s) conducting the search
(3) Fail to prepare a written report containing all of the following
   (a) The written authorization for the search by the person in command of the law enforcement agency (if required)
   (and)
   (b) The name of the person searched
   (and)
   (c) The name of the person(s) conducting the search, and the time and date of and place at which the search was conducted
   (and)
   (d) A list of items recovered during the search (if any)
   (and)
   (e) The facts upon which the law enforcement agency officer or employee based his probable cause for the search, including his review of the nature of the offense with which the person is charged, the circumstances of his arrest, and his prior conviction record (if known)
   (and)
   (f) If the search was conducted without issuance of a search warrant or without the granting of a written authorization, the legitimate medical reason or emergency that justified the warrantless search or made obtaining written authorization impracticable
(4) Venue

Division [A] [Unauthorized body cavity or strip search] **[M1]**
Penalty: A misdemeanor of the first degree (2929.21, 2929.31)

Division [B] [Failure to prepare proper search report] **[M4]**
Penalty: A misdemeanor of the fourth degree (2929.21, 2929.31)

Note: R.C. § 2933.32(C)(2) provides that a copy of the required body cavity or strip search report is to be kept on file in the law enforcement agency, and that another copy is to be given to the person searched. This section does not apply to searches of persons sentenced to and serving a term in a detention facility, as defined in R.C. § 2921.01, R.C. § 2933.32(D).

Definitions: "Body cavity search" and "strip search," R.C. § 2933.32(A)

CONTRABAND, R.C. § 2933.42

(1) (a) Possess
       (or)
   (b) Conceal
       (or)
   (c) Transport
       (or)
   (d) Receive

　　　　　　(or)
　　(e) Purchase
　　　　　　(or)
　　(f) Sell
　　　　　　(or)
　　(g) Lease
　　　　　　(or)
　　(h) Rent
　　　　　　(or)
　　(i) Otherwise transfer
(2) Any contraband
(3) Venue

Penalty: Seizure and forfeiture under certain conditions—*see* R.C. §§ 2933.42 and 2933.43.

Notes: R.C. § 2933.43 contains procedural requirements regarding seizure, custody, and disposition of contraband.

　　See statute for provisions concerning forfeiture of contraband possessed or owned by persons under eighteen.

Definition: "Contraband," R.C. §§ 2901.01, 2933.42.

INTERCEPTION OF WIRE, ORAL OR ELECTRONIC COMMUNICATION, R.C. § 2933.52 [F4]

(1) (a) Purposely
　　(b) (i) Intercept
　　　　　　(or)
　　　　(ii) Attempt to intercept
　　　　　　(or)
　　　　(iii) Procure any other person to intercept or attempt to intercept
　　(c) (i) Any wire communication
　　　　　　(or)
　　　　(ii) Any oral communication
　　　　　　(or)
　　　　(iii) any electronic communication
　　(d) Venue
　　　　　　(or)
(2) (a) Purposely
　　(b) (i) Use
　　　　　　(or)
　　　　(ii) Attempt to use
　　　　　　(or)
　　　　(iii) Procure any other person to use or attempt to use
　　(c) Any interception device which
　　　　(i) Is affixed to, or otherwise transmits a signal through a wire, cable, satellite, microwave or other similar method of connection used in wire communications
　　　　　　(or)
　　　　(ii) Transmits communications by radio, or interferes with the transmission of communication by radio

§ 2933.59(C)

    (d) To intercept any wire, oral, or electronic communication
    (e) Venue
        (or)
(3) (a) Purposely
    (b) (i) Use
           (or)
        (ii) Attempt to use
    (c) The contents of
    (d) Any wire, oral or electronic communication
    (e) Knowing or having reason to know
    (f) That the contents were obtained
    (g) Through the interception of wire, oral, or electronic communication in violation of R.C. §§ 2933.51 to 2933.66
    (h) Venue

Penalty: A felony of the fourth degree (2929.11-2929.18, 2929.31)

Notes: For exclusions, see R.C. § 2933.52.

    For provisions concerning interception warrants, see R.C. §§ 2933.53—2933.61, 2933.66.

    For provisions regarding evidentiary issues, see R.C. §§ 2933.59, 2933.62, 2933.63.

    For provisions concerning civil cause of action, see R.C. § 2933.65.

    For other provisions regarding telephone offenses, see Chapter 4931, Miscellaneous Statutory Provisions.

Definitions: Generally, R.C. § 2933.51.

PRESENTING ALTERED RECORD OF INTERCEPTED COMMUNICATION, R.C. § 2933.59(C) [F3]

(1) With intent to present the altered recording or resume
(2) (a) In any judicial proceeding
        (or)
    (b) In any proceeding under oath or affirmation
(3) Purposefully
    (a) Edit
        (or)
    (b) Alter
        (or)
    (c) Tamper with
        (or)
    (d) Attempt to alter, edit, or tamper with
(4) Any recording or resume of any intercepted wire or oral communication
(5) Present or permit presentation of any altered recording or resume
(6) (a) In any judicial proceeding
        (or)
    (b) In any proceeding under oath or affirmation
(7) Without fully indicating the nature of the changes made
(8) Venue

Penalty: A felony of the third degree (2929.11-2929.18, 2929.31)

ADULTERATED FOOD, R.C. § 3716.11 [M1]

(1) With knowledge, or having reasonable cause to believe, another may suffer physical harm or be seriously inconvenienced or annoyed:
   (a) Place a pin, needle, razor blade, glass, laxative, drug of abuse, or other harmful/hazardous object/substance in food or confections
   (*or*)
   (b) Furnish to another food or confections adulterated in violation of (a) above
(2) Venue

Penalty: A misdemeanor of the first degree (2929.21, 2929.31)

REGULATING THE SALE OF POISONS, R.C. § 3719.32 [MM]

(1) Knowingly
(2) Sell or deliver
(3) (a) To any person other than in the manner prescribed by law
   (*or*)
   (b) To a minor under 16 in the manner prescribed by law but without written order of an adult
(4) (a) Any of the substances listed in this section [includes many scheduled drugs]
   (*or*)
   (b) Any poisonous compounds, combinations, or preparations thereof
(5) Venue

Penalty: A minor misdemeanor (2929.21, 2929.31)

FIREARMS, DISCHARGING, R.C. § 3773.21 [M4]

(1) Not being the owner of the enclosure involved
(2) Discharge a firearm
(3) On a lawn, park, pleasure ground, orchard, or grounds appurtenant to a schoolhouse, church or inhabited dwelling, such being the property of another or of a charitable institution
(4) Venue

Penalty: A misdemeanor of the fourth degree (2929.21, 2929.31)

FIREARMS, DISCHARGING OVER HIGHWAY, R.C. § 3773.21.1 [M4]

(1) Discharge a firearm
(2) Upon or over a public road or highway
(3) Venue

Penalty: A misdemeanor of the fourth degree (2929.21, 2929.31)

OPENED CONTAINER, R.C. § 4301.62 [MM]

(1) Have in one's possession
(2) An opened container of beer or intoxicating liquor
(3) (a) In a state liquor store

(or)
(b) On the premises of the holder of any permit issued by the department of liquor control
(or)
(c) In any other public place
(or)
(d) While operating or being a passenger in or on a motor vehicle on any street, highway, or other public or private property open to the public for purposes of vehicular travel or parking
(or)
(e) While being in or on a stationary motor vehicle on any street, highway, or other public or private property open to the public for purposes of vehicular travel or parking
(4) Venue

Penalty: A minor misdemeanor (2929.21, 2929.31)

Note: The statute specifies exceptions for beer or intoxicating liquor which has been lawfully bought for consumption on certain permit premises or convention premises.

MOTOR VEHICLES, OPERATING WHILE UNDER THE INFLUENCE, R.C. § 4511.19 [M1]

Division (A)(1)
(1) Operate any vehicle, streetcar, or trackless trolley
(2) Within this state
(3) While under the influence of
(4) Alcohol or drug of abuse or combination thereof
(5) Venue

Division (A)(2), (3), (4)
(1) Operate any vehicle, streetcar, or trackless trolley
(2) Within this state
(3) While having a concentration of
   (a) .10 of 1% or more by weight of alcohol in the blood
   (or)
   (b) .10 of 1 gram or more by weight of alcohol per 210 liters of breath
   (or)
   (c) .14 of 1 gram or more by weight of alcohol per 100 milliliters of urine
(4) Venue

If no conviction, within six years of the offense, under this section or similar municipal ordinance, or under R.C. § 2903.04 (involuntary manslaughter) in a case in which the offender was subject to the sanctions described in division (D), R.C. § 2903.06 (aggravated vehicular homicide), R.C. § 2903.07 (vehicular homicide), R.C. § 2903.08 (aggravated vehicular assault), or municipal ordinance similar to R.C. § 2903.07, in a case in which the jury or judge found that the offender was under the influence [M1]

Penalty: Mandatory minimum imprisonment: three consecutive days (or a three day intervention program)

Mandatory fine: $200 to $1,000

If the offender has been convicted, within six years of the offense, of one offense under this section or similar municipal ordinance, or under R.C. § 2903.04 (involuntary manslaughter) in a case in which the offender was subject to the sanctions described in division (D), R.C. § 2903.06 (aggravated vehicular homicide), R.C. § 2903.07 (vehicular homicide), R.C. § 2903.08 (aggravated vehicular assault), or municipal ordinance similar to R.C. § 2903.07, in a case in which the jury or judge found that the offender was under the influence [M1]

Penalty: Mandatory minimum imprisonment: ten consecutive days (or mandatory minimum imprisonment of five consecutive days followed immediately by electronically monitored house arrest of at least 18 days)

Mandatory fine: $300 to $1,500

If the offender has been convicted, within six years of the offense, of two offenses under this section or similar municipal ordinance, or under R.C. § 2903.04 (involuntary manslaughter) in a case in which the offender was subject to the sanctions described in division (D), R.C. § 2903.06 (aggravated vehicular homicide), R.C. § 2903.07 (vehicular homicide), R.C. § 2903.08 (aggravated vehicular assault), or municipal ordinance similar to R.C. § 2903.07, in a case in which the jury or judge found that the offender was under the influence

Penalty: Mandatory minimum imprisonment: thirty consecutive days, or longer definite term of not more than one year (or mandatory minimum imprisonment of fifteen consecutive days followed immediately by electronically monitored house arrest of at least 55 days)

Mandatory fine: $500 to $2,500

Also: mandatory attendance at treatment program

If the offender has been convicted, within six years of the offense, of three or more offenses under this section or similar municipal ordinance, or under R.C. § 2903.04 (involuntary manslaughter) in a case in which the offender was subject to the sanctions described in division (D), R.C. § 2903.06 (aggravated vehicular homicide), R.C. § 2903.07 (vehicular homicide), R.C. § 2903.08 (aggravated vehicular assault), or similar municipal ordinance, in a case in which the jury or judge found that the offender was under the influence

Penalty: Mandatory minimum imprisonment: sixty consecutive days, or longer definite term of not more than one year

Mandatory fine: $750 to $10,000

Also: mandatory attendance at treatment program and criminal forfeiture of the vehicle the offender was driving

Notes: Immobilization and impoundment is provided for in R.C. § 4503.23.4.

Immediate seizure and suspension of license for refusal to submit to test or failure of test is provided for in R.C. § 4511.19.1.

License suspension, revocation, and disqualification are provided for in R.C. §§ 4507.16, 4511.19.6.

Definitions: "Three consecutive days" is defined as 72 consecutive hours, R.C. § 4511.99.1

Division (B)(1), (2), or (3)
(1) Being under 21 years of age
(2) Operate any vehicle, streetcar, or trackless trolley
(3) Within this state
(4) While having a concentration of at least
   (a) .02 of 1% but less than .10 of 1% by weight of alcohol in his blood
   (b) .02 of 1 gram but less than .10 of 1 gram by weight of alcohol per 210 liters of his breath

§ 4511.19.1

(c) .028 of 1 gram but less than .14 of 1 gram by weight of alcohol per 100 milliliters of his urine

(5) Venue

If no conviction, within one year of the offense, under this section or similar municipal ordinance, or under R.C. § 2903.04 (involuntary manslaughter) in a case in which the offender was subject to the sanctions described in division (D), R.C. § 2903.06 (aggravated vehicular homicide), R.C. § 2903.07 (vehicular homicide), R.C. § 2903.08 (aggravated vehicular assault), or municipal ordinance similar to R.C. § 2903.07, in a case in which the jury or judge found that the offender was under the influence [M4]

Penalty: Mandatory suspension of the offender's driver's or commercial driver's license or permit or nonresident operating privilege for no less than 60 days and no more than two years

If the offender has been convicted or plead guilty to, within one year of the offense, of one offense under this section or similar municipal ordinance, or under R.C. § 2903.04 (involuntary manslaughter) in a case in which the offender was subject to the sanctions described in division (D), R.C. § 2903.06 (aggravated vehicular homicide), R.C. § 2903.07 (vehicular homicide), R.C. § 2903.08 (aggravated vehicular assault), or municipal ordinance similar to R.C. § 2903.07, in a case in which the jury or judge found that the offender was under the influence [M3]

Penalty: Mandatory suspension of the offender's driver's or commercial driver's license or permit or nonresident operating privilege for no less than 60 days and no more than two years

MOTOR VEHICLE, OPERATING WHILE LICENSE SUSPENDED UNDER R.C. §§ 4511.19.1, 4511.19.2 [M1]

(1) Operate a vehicle
(2) Upon the highways or streets within this state
(3) When one's license or permit to drive has been suspended under R.C. § 4511.19.1
(4) Venue

Penalty: A misdemeanor of the first degree (2929.21, 2929.31)

Note: See R.C. § 4511.19.1 for provisions relative to suspension of the driver's license of a person under arrest for driving while under the influence of alcohol who refuses to submit to chemical tests.
See also R.C. § 4511.99.

MOTOR VEHICLES, RECKLESS DRIVING, R.C. §§ 4511.20, 4511.20.1 [MM, M4, M3]

(a) Operate a motor vehicle, trackless trolley, or streetcar
(b) On any street or highway
(c) In willful or wanton disregard of the safety of persons or property
(d) Venue
  (or)
(a) Operate a motor vehicle, trackless trolley, or streetcar
(b) On public or private property other than streets or highways
(c) In willful or wanton disregard of the safety of persons or property
(d) Venue

Penalty: [First offense]: A minor misdemeanor (2929.21, 2929.31)

Penalty: [Second offense within 1 year of first]: A misdemeanor of the fourth degree (2929.21, 2929.31)

Penalty: [Third and further offenses within 1 year of first]: A misdemeanor of the third degree (2929.21, 2929.31)

Note: Competition among vehicles with consent of property owner is excepted under R.C. § 4511.20.1.

MOTOR VEHICLES, OPERATING WITHOUT REASONABLE CONTROL, R.C. § 4511.20.2 [MM]

(1) Operate a motor vehicle, trackless trolley, or streetcar
(2) On any street, highway, or property open to the public for vehicular traffic
(3) Without being in reasonable control
(4) Of the vehicle, trackless trolley, or streetcar
(5) Venue

Penalty: A minor misdemeanor (2929.21, 2929.31)

MOTOR VEHICLES, SPEED LIMITS/ASSURED CLEAR DISTANCE, R.C. § 4511.21 [MM, M4, M3]

Speed Limits:

(1) Operate a motor vehicle, trackless trolley, or streetcar
(2) At a speed greater or less than is reasonable or proper, having due regard to the traffic, surface, and width of the street or highway and any other conditions

(*or*)

(1) Operate a motor vehicle, trackless trolley, or streetcar upon a street or highway
(2) (a) At a speed exceeding 55 miles per hour, except upon a freeway as provided in R.C. § 4511.21(B)(10)

(b) At a speed exceeding 65 miles per hour, except upon a freeway as provided in R.C. § 4511.21(B)(10) motor vehicles weighing in excess of 8,000 pounds empty or noncommercial buses are excepted from this provision and are governed by the following provision (2)(C)

(*or*)

(c) At a speed exceeding 55 miles per hour upon a freeway if the motor vehicle weighs in excess of 8,000 pounds empty or is a noncommercial bus

Assured Clear Distance

(1) Drive any motor vehicle, trackless trolley, or streetcar
(2) In and upon any street or highway
(3) At a greater speed than will permit him to bring it to a stop within the assured clear distance ahead

First offense [MM]

Penalty: A minor misdemeanor (2929.21, 2929.31)

Second offense within one year of the first [M4]

Penalty: A misdemeanor of the fourth degree (2929.21, 2929.31)

Subsequent offenses within one year of the first [M3]

Penalty: A misdemeanor of the third degree (2929.21, 2929.31)

Note: See statute for speeds considered prima-facie lawful in absence of lower limits declared by director of transportation or local authorities.

MOTOR VEHICLES, MASTER CAR KEYS, R.C. § 4549.04.2 [M1, F4]
  (1) Sell or dispose of
  (2) Master key for more than one motor vehicle
  (3) Knowing or having reasonable cause to believe key will be used to commit offense
  (4) Venue
  　　(*or*)
  (1) Buy, receive or possess
  (2) Master key for more than one motor vehicle
  (3) With purpose to use it to commit a crime
  (4) Venue

Penalty: [First offense]: A misdemeanor of the first degree (2929.21, 2929.31)

Penalty: [Subsequent offenses]: A felony of the fourth degree (2929.11-2929.18, 2929.31)

TITLE XXIX [29]
CRIMES—PROCEDURE

Chapter
2901 General Provisions
2903 Homicide and Assault
2905 Kidnapping and Extortion
2907 Sex Offenses
2909 Arson and Related Offenses
2911 Robbery, Burglary, Trespass and Safecracking
2913 Theft and Fraud
2915 Gambling
2917 Offenses Against the Public Peace
2919 Offenses Against the Family
2921 Offenses Against Justice and Public Administration
2923 Conspiracy, Attempt, and Complicity; Weapons Control; Corrupt Activity
2925 Drug Offenses
2927 Miscellaneous Offenses
2929 Penalties and Sentencing
2930 Victims' Rights
2931 Jurisdiction; Venue
2933 Peace Warrants; Search Warrants
2935 Arrest, Citation, and Disposition Alternatives
2937 Preliminary Examination; Bail
2938 Trial—Magistrate Courts
2939 Grand Juries
2941 Indictment
2943 Arraignment; Pleas
2945 Trial
2947 Judgment; Sentence
2949 Execution of Sentence
2950 Sexual Predators, Habitual Sex Offenders, Sexually Oriented Offenders
2951 Probation
2953 Appeals; Other Post-Conviction Remedies
2961 Disfranchised Convicts; Habitual Criminals
2963 Extradition
2965 Pardon; Parole [Repealed]
2967 Pardon; Parole; Probation
2969 Recovery of Offender's Profits Fund; Crime Victims Recovery Fund
2971 Sentencing of Sexually Violent Predators

Ohio Rules of Criminal Procedure

CHAPTER 2901: GENERAL PROVISIONS

Section

[IN GENERAL]

2901.01 Definitions.
2901.02 Classification of offenses.
2901.03 Common law offenses abrogated.
2901.04 Rules of construction.
2901.05 Burden and degree of proof.
2901.06 Battered woman syndrome testimony as evidence relevant to claim of self-defense.
2901.07 DNA testing of offenders sentenced to incarceration.
2901.08 Status of juvenile adjudication as prior conviction.
2901.09, 2901.10 Repealed.

[JURISDICTION, VENUE, AND LIMITATION OF PROSECUTIONS]

2901.11 Criminal law jurisdiction.
2901.12 Venue.
2901.13 Limitation of criminal prosecutions.
2901.14-2901.20 Repealed.

[CRIMINAL LIABILITY]

2901.21 Requirements for criminal liability.
2901.22 Culpable mental states.
2901.23 Organizational criminal liability.
2901.24 Personal accountability for organizational conduct.
[2901.24.1] 2901.241 Repealed.
2901.25 Repealed.
[2901.25.1, 2901.25.2] 2901.251, 2901.252 Repealed.
2901.26-2901.29 Repealed.

[MISSING CHILDREN]

2901.30 Missing child report; notice of return.
2901.31 Cooperation in locating missing children.
2901.32 Improper solicitation of contributions for missing children.
2901.33-2901.45 Repealed.

[IN GENERAL]

§ 2901.01 Definitions.

(A) As used in the Revised Code:

(1) "Force" means any violence, compulsion, or constraint physically exerted by any means upon or against a person or thing.

(2) "Deadly force" means any force that carries a substantial risk that it will proximately result in the death of any person.

(3) "Physical harm to persons" means any injury, illness, or other physiological impairment, regardless of its gravity or duration.

(4) "Physical harm to property" means any tangible or intangible damage to property that, in any degree, results in loss to its value or interferes with its use or enjoyment. "Physical harm to property" does not include wear and tear occasioned by normal use.

(5) "Serious physical harm to persons" means any of the following:

(a) Any mental illness or condition of such gravity as would normally require hospitalization or prolonged psychiatric treatment;

(b) Any physical harm that carries a substantial risk of death;

(c) Any physical harm that involves some permanent incapacity, whether partial or total, or that involves some temporary, substantial incapacity;

(d) Any physical harm that involves some permanent disfigurement, or that involves some temporary, serious disfigurement;

(e) Any physical harm that involves acute pain of such duration as to result in substantial suffering, or that involves any degree of prolonged or intractable pain.

(6) "Serious physical harm to property" means any physical harm to property that does either of the following:

(a) Results in substantial loss to the value of the property, or requires a substantial amount of time, effort, or money to repair or replace;

(b) Temporarily prevents the use or enjoyment of the property, or substantially interferes with its use or enjoyment for an extended period of time.

(7) "Risk" means a significant possibility, as contrasted with a remote possibility, that a certain result may occur or that certain circumstances may exist.

(8) "Substantial risk" means a strong possibility, as contrasted with a remote or significant possibility, that a certain result may occur or that certain circumstances may exist.

(9) "Offense of violence" means any of the following:

(a) A violation of section 2903.01, 2903.02, 2903.03, 2903.04, 2903.11, 2903.12, 2903.13, 2903.21, 2903.211 [2903.21.1], 2903.22, 2905.01, 2905.02, 2905.11, 2907.02, 2907.03, 2907.05, 2909.02, 2909.03, 2911.01, 2911.02, 2911.11, 2917.01, 2917.02, 2917.03, 2917.31, 2919.25, 2921.03, 2921.04, 2921.34, or 2923.161 [2923.16.1] or of division (A)(1), (2), or (3) of section 2911.12 of the Revised Code or felonious sexual penetration in violation of former section 2907.12 of the Revised Code;

(b) A violation of an existing or former municipal ordinance or law of this or any other state or the United States, substantially equivalent to any section or division or offense listed in division (A)(9)(a) of this section;

(c) An offense, other than a traffic offense, under an existing or former municipal ordinance or law of this or any other state or the United States, committed purposely or knowingly, and involving physical harm to persons or a risk of serious physical harm to persons;

(d) A conspiracy or attempt to commit, or complicity in committing, any offense under division (A)(9)(a), (b), or (c) of this section.

(10)(a) "Property" means any property, real or personal, tangible or intangible, and any interest or license in that property. "Property" includes, but is not limited to, cable television service, computer data, computer software, financial instruments associated with computers, and other documents associated with computers, or copies of the documents, whether in machine or human readable form. "Financial instruments associated with computers" include, but are not limited to, checks, drafts, warrants, money orders, notes of indebtedness, certificates of deposit, letters of credit, bills of credit or debit cards, financial transaction authorization mechanisms, marketable securities, or any computer system representations of any of them.

(b) As used in this division and division (A)(13) of this section, "cable television service," "computer," "computer software," "computer system," "computer network," and "data" have the same meaning as in section 2913.01 of the Revised Code.

(11) "Law enforcement officer" means any of the following:

(a) A sheriff, deputy sheriff, constable, police officer of a township or joint township police district, marshal, deputy marshal, municipal police officer, member of a police force employed by a metropolitan housing authority under division (D) of section 3735.31 of the Revised Code, or state highway patrol trooper;

(b) An officer, agent, or employee of the state or any of its agencies, instrumentalities, or political subdivisions, upon whom, by statute, a duty to conserve the peace or to enforce all or certain laws is imposed and the authority to arrest violators is conferred, within the limits of that statutory duty and authority;

(c) A mayor, in the mayor's capacity as chief conservator of the peace within the mayor's municipal corporation;

(d) A member of an auxiliary police force organized by county, township, or municipal law enforcement authorities, within the scope of the member's appointment or commission;

(e) A person lawfully called pursuant to section 311.07 of the Revised Code to aid a sheriff in keeping the peace, for the purposes and during the time when the person is called;

(f) A person appointed by a mayor pursuant to section 737.01 of the Revised Code as a special patrolling officer during riot or emergency, for the purposes and during the time when the person is appointed;

(g) A member of the organized militia of this state or the armed forces of the United States, lawfully called to duty to aid civil authorities in keeping the peace or protect against domestic violence;

(h) A prosecuting attorney, assistant prosecuting attorney, secret service officer, or municipal prosecutor;

(i) An Ohio veterans' home police officer appointed under section 5907.02 of the Revised Code;

(j) A member of a police force employed by a regional transit authority under division (Y) of section 306.35 of the Revised Code.

(12) "Privilege" means an immunity, license, or right conferred by law, bestowed by express or implied grant, arising out of status, position, office, or relationship, or growing out of necessity.

(13) "Contraband" means any property described in the following categories:

(a) Property that in and of itself is unlawful for a person to acquire or possess;

(b) Property that is not in and of itself unlawful for a person to acquire or possess, but that has been determined by a court of this state, in accordance with law, to be contraband because of its use in an unlawful activity or manner, of its nature, or of the circumstances of the person who acquires or possesses it, including, but not limited to, goods and personal property described in division (D) of section 2913.34 of the Revised Code;

(c) Property that is specifically stated to be contraband by a section of the Revised Code or by an ordinance, regulation, or resolution;

(d) Property that is forfeitable pursuant to a section of the Revised Code, or an ordinance, regulation, or resolution, including, but not limited to, forfeitable firearms, dangerous ordnance, obscene materials, and goods and personal property described in division (D) of section 2913.34 of the Revised Code;

(e) Any controlled substance, as defined in section 3719.01 of the Revised Code, or any device, paraphernalia, money as defined in section 1301.01 of the Revised Code, or other means of exchange that has been, is being, or is intended to be used in an attempt or conspiracy to violate, or in a violation of, Chapter 2925. or 3719. of the Revised Code;

(f) Any gambling device, paraphernalia, money as defined in section 1301.01 of the Revised Code, or other means of exchange that has been, is being, or is intended to be used in an attempt or conspiracy to violate, or in the violation of, Chapter 2915. of the Revised Code;

(g) Any equipment, machine, device, apparatus, vehicle, vessel, container, liquid, or substance that has been, is being, or is intended to be used in an attempt or conspiracy to violate, or in the violation of, any law of this state relating to alcohol or tobacco;

(h) Any personal property that has been, is being, or is intended to be used in an attempt or conspiracy to commit, or in the commission of, any offense or in the transportation of the fruits of any offense;

(i) Any property that is acquired through the sale or other transfer of contraband or through the proceeds of contraband, other than by a court or a law enforcement agency acting within the scope of its duties;

(j) Any computer, computer system, computer network, or computer software that is used in a conspiracy to commit, an attempt to commit, or in the commission of any offense, if the owner of the computer, computer system, computer network, or computer software is convicted of or pleads guilty to the offense in which it is used.

(14) A person is "not guilty by reason of insanity" relative to a charge of an offense only if the person proves, in the manner specified in section 2901.05 of the Revised Code, that at the time of the commission of the offense, the person did not know, as a result of a severe mental disease or defect, the wrongfulness of the person's acts.

(B)(1)(a) Subject to division (B)(2) of this section, as used in any section contained in Title XXIX [29] of the Revised Code that sets forth a criminal offense, "person" includes all of the following:

(i) An individual, corporation, business trust, estate, trust, partnership, and association;

(ii) An unborn human who is viable.

(b) As used in any section contained in Title XXIX [29] of the Revised Code that does not set forth a criminal offense, "person" includes an individual, corporation, business trust, estate, trust, partnership, and association.

(c) As used in division (B)(1)(a) of this section:

(i) "Unborn human" means an individual organism of the species homo sapiens from fertilization until live birth.

(ii) "Viable" means the stage of development of a human fetus at which there is a realistic possibility of maintaining and nourishing of a life outside the womb with or without temporary artificial life-sustaining support.

(2) Notwithstanding division (B)(1)(a) of this section, in no case shall the portion of the definition of the term "person" that is set forth in division (B)(1)(a)(ii) of this section be applied or construed in any section contained in Title XXIX [29] of the Revised Code that sets forth a criminal offense in any of the following manners:

(a) Except as otherwise provided in division (B)(2)(a) of this section, in a manner so that the offense prohibits or is construed as prohibiting any pregnant woman or her physician from performing an abortion with the consent of the pregnant woman, with the consent of the pregnant woman implied by law in a medical emergency, or with the approval of one otherwise authorized by law to consent to medical treatment on behalf of the pregnant woman. An abortion that violates the conditions described in the immediately preceding sentence may be punished as a violation of section 2903.01, 2903.02, 2903.03, 2903.04, 2903.05, 2903.06, 2903.07, 2903.08, 2903.11, 2903.12, 2903.13, 2903.14, 2903.21, or 2903.22 of the Revised Code, as applicable. An abortion that does not violate the conditions described in the second immediately preceding sentence, but that does violate section 2919.12, division (B) of section 2919.13, section 2919.15, 2919.17, or 2919.18 of the Revised Code, may be punished as a violation of section 2919.12, division (B) of section 2919.13, section 2919.15, 2919.17, or 2919.18 of the Revised Code, as applicable. Consent is sufficient under this division if it is of the type otherwise adequate to permit medical treatment to the pregnant woman, even if it does not comply with section 2919.12 of the Revised Code.

(b) In a manner so that the offense is applied or is construed as applying to a woman based on an act or omission of the woman that occurs while she is or was pregnant and that results in any of the following:

(i) Her delivery of a stillborn baby;

(ii) Her causing, in any other manner, the death in utero of a viable, unborn human that she is carrying;

(iii) Her causing the death of her child who is born alive but who dies from one or more injuries that are sustained while the child is a viable, unborn human;

(iv) Her causing her child who is born alive to sustain one or more injuries while the child is a viable, unborn human;

(v) Her causing, threatening to cause, or attempting to cause, in any other manner, an injury, illness, or other physiological impairment, regardless of its duration or gravity, or a mental illness or condition, regardless of its duration or gravity, to a viable, unborn human that she is carrying.

HISTORY: 142 v H 708 (Eff 4-19-88); 143 v S 24 (Eff 7-24-90); 144 v H 77 (Eff 9-17-91); 144 v S 144 (Eff 8-8-91); 146 v S 2 (Eff 7-1-96); 146 v S 269 (Eff 7-1-96); 146 v H 445 (Eff 9-3-96); 146 v S 239 (Eff 9-6-96); 146 v S 277. Eff 3-31-97.

Analogous to former RC § 2901.01 (134 v H 511; 139 v H 437; 139 v S 199; 140 v S 183; 140 v H 632; 140 v H 129, §§ 1, 3; 141 v H 49, §§ 1, 3; 141 v S 69, §§ 1, 3; 141 v H 428; 142 v H 231; 142 v H 261), repealed 142 v H 708, § 2, eff 12-31-87.

Not analogous to former RC § 2901.01 (RS § 6808; S&C 401; 33 v 33; 93 v 223; GC §§ 12399, 12400; 118 v 288; 120 v 413; Bureau of Code Revision, 10-1-53), repealed 134 v H 511, § 2, eff 1-1-74.

The provisions of § 9 of SB 277 (146 v —) read as follows:

SECTION 9. ° ° ° Section 2901.01 of the Revised Code is presented in this act [Sub. S.B. No. 277] as a composite of the section as amended by Am. Sub. S.B. 269, Am. Sub. H.B. 445, and Am. Sub. S.B. 239 of the 121st General Assembly, with the new language of none of those acts shown in capital letters.

° ° °

This is in recognition of the principle stated in division (B) of section 1.52 of the Revised Code that such amendments are to be harmonized where not substantively irreconcilable and constitutes a legislative finding that such is the resulting version in effect prior to the effective date of this act.

§ 2901.02 Classification of offenses.

As used in the Revised Code:

(A) Offenses include aggravated murder, murder, felonies of the first, second, third, fourth, and fifth degree, misdemeanors of the first, second, third, and fourth degree, minor misdemeanors, and offenses not specifically classified.

(B) Aggravated murder when the indictment or the count in the indictment charging aggravated murder contains one or more specifications of aggravating circumstances listed in division (A) of section 2929.04 of

[the] Revised Code, and any other offense for which death may be imposed as a penalty, is a capital offense.

(C) Aggravated murder and murder are felonies.

(D) Regardless of the penalty that may be imposed, any offense specifically classified as a felony is a felony, and any offense specifically classified as a misdemeanor is a misdemeanor.

(E) Any offense not specifically classified is a felony if imprisonment for more than one year may be imposed as a penalty.

(F) Any offense not specifically classified is a misdemeanor if imprisonment for not more than one year may be imposed as a penalty.

(G) Any offense not specifically classified is a minor misdemeanor if the only penalty that may be imposed is a fine not exceeding one hundred dollars.

HISTORY: 134 v H 511 (Eff 1-1-74); 139 v S 199 (Eff 7-1-83); 140 v H 380 (Eff 4-3-84); 146 v S 2. Eff 7-1-96.

Not analogous to former RC § 2901.02 (RS §§ 6808, 6809; S&S 268; S&C 401; 33 v 33; 60 v 17; 93 v 223; GC § 12401; Bureau of Code Revision, 10-1-53), repealed 134 v H 511, § 2, eff 1-1-74.

The effective date is set by section 6 of SB 2.

§ 2901.03 Common law offenses abrogated.

(A) No conduct constitutes a criminal offense against the state unless it is defined as an offense in the Revised Code.

(B) An offense is defined when one or more sections of the Revised Code state a positive prohibition or enjoin a specific duty, and provide a penalty for violation of such prohibition or failure to meet such duty.

(C) This section does not affect any power of the general assembly under section 8 of Article II, Ohio Constitution, nor does it affect the power of a court to punish for contempt or to employ any sanction authorized by law to enforce an order, civil judgment, or decree.

HISTORY: 134 v H 511. Eff 1-1-74.

Not analogous to former RC § 2901.03 (RS § 7388-52; 98 v 180; GC § 12402; Bureau of Code Revision, 10-1-53; 126 v 575), repealed 134 v H 511, § 2, eff 1-1-74.

The effective date is set by section 4 of HB 511.

§ 2901.04 Rules of construction.

(A) Sections of the Revised Code defining offenses or penalties shall be strictly construed against the state, and liberally construed in favor of the accused.

(B) Rules of criminal procedure and sections of the Revised Code providing for criminal procedure shall be construed so as to effect the fair, impartial, speedy, and sure administration of justice.

HISTORY: 134 v H 511. Eff 1-1-74.

Not analogous to former RC § 2901.04 (GC § 12402-1; 109 v 545; 111 v 77; Bureau of Code Revision, 10-1-53), repealed 134 v H 511, § 2, eff 1-1-74.

The effective date is set by section 4 of HB 511.

§ 2901.05 Burden and degree of proof.

(A) Every person accused of an offense is presumed innocent until proven guilty beyond a reasonable doubt, and the burden of proof for all elements of the offense is upon the prosecution. The burden of going forward with the evidence of an affirmative defense, and the burden of proof, by a preponderance of the evidence, for an affirmative defense, is upon the accused.

(B) As part of its charge to the jury in a criminal case, the court shall read the definitions of "reasonable doubt" and "proof beyond a reasonable doubt," contained in division (D) of this section.

(C) As used in this section, an "affirmative defense" is either of the following:

(1) A defense expressly designated as affirmative;

(2) A defense involving an excuse or justification peculiarly within the knowledge of the accused, on which he can fairly be required to adduce supporting evidence.

(D) "Reasonable doubt" is present when the jurors, after they have carefully considered and compared all the evidence, cannot say they are firmly convinced of the truth of the charge. It is a doubt based on reason and common sense. Reasonable doubt is not mere possible doubt, because everything relating to human affairs or depending on moral evidence is open to some possible or imaginary doubt. "Proof beyond a reasonable doubt" is proof of such character that an ordinary person would be willing to rely and act upon it in the most important of his own affairs.

HISTORY: 134 v H 511 (Eff 1-1-74); 137 v H 1168. Eff 11-1-78.

Not analogous to former RC § 2901.05 (RS § 6810; S&C 402; 33 v 33; GC § 12403; 124 v 14; Bureau of Code Revision, eff 10-1-53), repealed 134 v H 511, § 2, eff 1-1-74.

§ 2901.06 Battered woman syndrome testimony as evidence relevant to claim of self-defense.

(A) The general assembly hereby declares that it recognizes both of the following, in relation to the "battered woman syndrome:"

(1) That the syndrome currently is a matter of commonly accepted scientific knowledge;

(2) That the subject matter and details of the syndrome are not within the general understanding or experience of a person who is a member of the general populace and are not within the field of common knowledge.

(B) If a person is charged with an offense involving the use of force against another and the person, as a defense to the offense charged, raises the affirmative defense of self-defense, the person may introduce expert testimony of the "battered woman syndrome" and expert testimony that the person suffered from that syndrome as evidence to establish the requisite belief of an imminent danger of death or great bodily harm that is necessary, as an element of the affirmative defense, to justify the person's use of the force in question. The introduction of any expert testimony under this division shall be in accordance with the Ohio Rules of Evidence.

HISTORY: 143 v H 484. Eff 11-5-90.

Not analogous to former RC § 2901.06 (RS § 6811; S&C 403; 33 v 33; GC § 12404; 116 v 205; Bureau of Code Revision, 10-1-53), repealed, 134 v H 511, § 2, eff 1-1-74.

§ 2901.07 DNA testing of offenders sentenced to incarceration.

(A) As used in this section:

(1) "DNA analysis" and "DNA specimen" have the same meanings as in section 109.573 [109.57.3] of the Revised Code.

(2) "Jail" and "community-based correctional facility" have the same meanings as in section 2929.01 of the Revised Code.

(3) "Post-release control" has the same meaning as in section 2967.28 of the Revised Code.

(B)(1) A person who is convicted of or pleads guilty to a felony offense listed in division (D) of this section and who is sentenced to a prison term or to a community residential sanction in a jail or community-based correctional facility pursuant to section 2929.16 of the Revised Code, and a person who is convicted of or pleads guilty to a misdemeanor offense listed in division (D) of this section and who is sentenced to a term of imprisonment shall submit to a DNA specimen collection procedure administered by the director of rehabilitation and correction or the chief administrative officer of the jail or other detention facility in which the person is serving the term of imprisonment. If the person serves the prison term in a state correctional institution, the director of rehabilitation and correction shall cause the DNA specimen to be collected from the person during the intake process at the reception facility designated by the director. If the person serves the community residential sanction or term of imprisonment in a jail, a community-based correctional facility, or another county, multi-county, municipal, municipal-county, or multicounty-municipal detention facility, the chief administrative officer of the jail, community-based correctional facility, or detention facility shall cause the DNA specimen to be collected from the person during the intake process at the jail, community-based correctional facility, or detention facility. In accordance with division (C) of this section, the director or the chief administrative officer shall cause the DNA specimen to be forwarded to the bureau of criminal identification and investigation no later than fifteen days after the date of the collection of the DNA specimen. The DNA specimen shall be collected in accordance with division (C) of this section.

(2) If a person is convicted of or pleads guilty to an offense listed in division (D) of this section, is serving a prison term, community residential sanction, or term of imprisonment for that offense, and does not provide a DNA specimen pursuant to division (B)(1) of this section, prior to the person's release from the prison term, community residential sanction, or imprisonment, the person shall submit to, and director of rehabilitation and correction or the chief administrative officer of the jail, community-based correctional facility, or detention facility in which the person is serving the prison term, community residential sanction, or term of imprisonment shall administer, a DNA specimen collection procedure at the state correctional institution, jail, community-based correctional facility, or detention facility in which the person is serving the prison term, community residential sanction, or term of imprisonment. In accordance with division (C) of this section, the director or the chief administrative officer shall cause the DNA specimen to be forwarded to the bureau of criminal identification and investigation no later than fifteen days after the date of the collection of the DNA specimen. The DNA specimen shall be collected in accordance with division (C) of this section.

(3) If a person serving a prison term or community residential sanction for a felony is released on parole, furlough, or other release or is on post-release control, if the person is under the supervision of the adult parole authority, if the person is returned to a jail, community-based correctional facility, or state correctional institution for a violation of a condition of the parole, furlough, other release, or post-release control, if the person was or will be serving a prison term or community residential sanction for committing an offense listed in division (D) of this section, and if the person did not provide a DNA specimen pursuant to division (B)(1) or (2) of this section, the person shall submit to, and the director of rehabilitation and correction or the chief administrative officer of the jail or community-based correctional facility shall administer, a DNA specimen collection procedure at the jail, community-based correctional facility, or state correctional institution in which the person is serving the prison term or community residential sanction. In accordance with division (C) of this section, the director or the chief administrative officer shall cause the DNA specimen to be forwarded to the bureau of criminal identification and investigation no later than fifteen days after the date of the collection of the DNA specimen. The DNA specimen shall be collected from the person in accordance with division (C) of this section.

(C) A physician, registered nurse, licensed practical nurse, duly licensed clinical laboratory technician, or other qualified medical practitioner shall collect in a medically approved manner the DNA specimen required to be collected pursuant to division (B) of this section. No later than fifteen days after the date of the collection of the DNA specimen, the director of rehabilitation and correction or the chief administrative officer of the jail, community-based correctional facility, or other county, multicounty, municipal, municipal-county, or multicounty-municipal detention facility, in which the person is serving the prison term, community residential sanction, or term of imprisonment shall cause the DNA specimen to be forwarded to the bureau of criminal identification and investigation in accordance with procedures established by the superintendent of the bureau under division (H) of section 109.573 [109.57.3] of the Revised Code. The bureau shall provide the specimen vials, mailing tubes, labels, postage, and instructions needed for the collection and forwarding of the DNA specimen to the bureau.

(D) The director of rehabilitation and correction and the chief administrative officer of the jail, community-based correctional facility, or other county, multicounty, municipal, municipal-county, or multicounty-municipal detention facility shall cause a DNA specimen to be collected in accordance with divisions (B) and (C) of this section from a person in its custody who is convicted of or pleads guilty to any of the following offenses:

(1) A violation of section 2903.01, 2903.02, 2905.01, 2907.02, 2907.03, 2907.04, 2907.05, or 2911.11 of the Revised Code;

(2) A violation of section 2907.12 of the Revised Code as it existed prior to September 3, 1996;

(3) An attempt to commit a violation of section 2907.02, 2907.03, 2907.04, or 2907.05 of the Revised Code or to commit a violation of section 2907.12 of the Revised Code as it existed prior to September 3, 1996;

(4) A violation of any law that arose out of the same facts and circumstances and same act as did a charge against the person of a violation of section 2907.02, 2907.03, 2907.04, or 2907.05 of the Revised Code that previously was dismissed or as did a charge against the person of a violation of section 2907.12 of the Revised Code as it existed prior to September 3, 1996, that previously was dismissed;

(5) A violation of section 2905.02 or 2919.23 of the Revised Code that would have been a violation of section 2905.04 of the Revised Code as it existed prior to July 1, 1996, had it been committed prior to that date;

(6) A sexually oriented offense, as defined in section 2950.01 of the Revised Code, if, in relation to that offense, the offender has been adjudicated as being a sexual predator, as defined in section 2950.01 of the Revised Code.

(E) The director of rehabilitation and correction or a chief administrative officer of a jail, community-based correctional facility, or other detention facility described in division (B) of this section is not required to comply with this section until the superintendent of the bureau of criminal identification and investigation gives agencies in the criminal justice system, as defined in section 181.51 of the Revised Code, in the state official notification that the state DNA laboratory is prepared to accept DNA specimens.

HISTORY: 146 v H 5 (Eff 8-30-95); 146 v S 269 (Eff 7-1-96); 146 v H 180 (Eff 1-1-97); 146 v H 124. Eff 3-31-97.

Not analogous to former RC § 2901.07 (GC § 12401-1; 124 v 177; Bureau of Code Revision, 10-1-53), repealed 134 v H 511, § 2, eff 1-1-74.

The provisions of § 7 of HB 124 (146 v —) read in part as follows:

SECTION 7. ° ° ° Section 2901.07 of the Revised Code is presented in Section 1 of this act as a composite of the section as amended by both Am. Sub. S.B. 269 and Am. Sub. H.B. 180 of the 121st General Assembly, with the new language of neither of the acts appearing in capital letters. This is in recognition of the principle stated in division (B) of section 1.52 of the Revised Code that such amendments are to be harmonized where not substantively irreconcilable and constitutes a legislative finding that such is the resulting version in effect prior to the effective date of this act.

§ 2901.08 Status of juvenile adjudication as prior conviction.

If a person is alleged to have committed an offense and if the person previously has been adjudicated a delinquent child or juvenile traffic offender for a violation of a law or ordinance, the adjudication as a delinquent child or as a juvenile traffic offender is a conviction for a violation of the law or ordinance for purposes of determining the offense with which the person should be charged and, if the person is convicted of or pleads guilty to an offense, the sentence to be imposed upon the person relative to the conviction or guilty plea.

HISTORY: 146 v H 1. Eff 1-1-96.

Not analogous to former RC § 2901.08 (GC § 12405; RS § 6812; S&S 266; S&C 415; 58 v 65, § 34; Bureau of Code Revision, 10-1-53), repealed 134 v H 511, § 2, eff 1-1-74.

The effective date is set by section 6 of HB 1.

§§ 2901.09, 2901.10 Repealed, 134 v H 511, § 2 [RS § 6812-1, 6812-2; GC §§ 12406, 12407; Bureau of Code Revision, 10-1-53]. Eff 1-1-74.

These sections concerned taking the life of president or governor.

[JURISDICTION, VENUE, AND LIMITATION OF PROSECUTIONS]

§ 2901.11 Criminal law jurisdiction.

(A) A person is subject to criminal prosecution and punishment in this state if any of the following occur:

(1) He commits an offense under the laws of this state, any element of which takes place in this state;

(2) While in this state, he conspires or attempts to commit, or is guilty of complicity in the commission of an offense in another jurisdiction, which offense is an offense under both the laws of this state and such other jurisdiction;

(3) While out of this state, he conspires or attempts to commit, or is guilty of complicity in the commission of an offense in this state;

(4) While out of this state, he omits to perform a legal duty imposed by the laws of this state, which omission affects a legitimate interest of the state in protecting, governing, or regulating any person, property, thing, transaction, or activity in this state;

(5) While out of this state, he unlawfully takes or retains property and subsequently brings any of such property into this state;

(6) While out of this state, he unlawfully takes or entices another and subsequently brings such other person into this state.

(B) In homicide, the element referred to in division (A)(1) of this section is either the act which causes death, or the physical contact which causes death, or the death itself. If any part of the body of a homicide victim is found in this state, the death is presumed to have occurred within this state.

(C)(1) This state includes the land and water within its boundaries and the air space above that land and water, with respect to which this state has either exclusive or concurrent legislative jurisdiction. Where the boundary between this state and another state or foreign country is disputed, the disputed territory is conclusively presumed to be within this state for purposes of this section.

(2) The courts of common pleas of Adams, Athens, Belmont, Brown, Clermont, Columbiana, Gallia, Hamilton, Jefferson, Lawrence, Meigs, Monroe, Scioto, and Washington counties have jurisdiction beyond the north or northwest shore of the Ohio river extending to the opposite shore line, between the extended boundary lines of any adjacent counties or adjacent state. Each of those courts of common pleas has concurrent jurisdiction on the Ohio river with any adjacent court of common pleas that borders on that river and with any court of Kentucky or of West Virginia that borders on the Ohio river and that has jurisdiction on the Ohio river under the law of Kentucky or the law of West Virginia, whichever is applicable, or under federal law.

(D) When an offense is committed under the laws of this state, and it appears beyond a reasonable doubt that the offense or any element thereof took place either in Ohio or in another jurisdiction or jurisdictions, but it cannot reasonably be determined in which it took place, such offense or element is conclusively presumed to have taken place in this state for purposes of this section.

HISTORY: 134 v H 511 (Eff 1-1-74); 144 v S 371. Eff 1-17-93.

Not analogous to former RC § 2901.11 (RS § 7388-52; 98 v 180; GC § 12408; Bureau of Code Revision, 10-1-53; 125 v H 88; 132 v H 65; 133 v H 1), repealed 134 v H 511, § 2, eff 1-1-74.

§ 2901.12 Venue.

(A) The trial of a criminal case in this state shall be held in a court having jurisdiction of the subject matter, and in the territory of which the offense or any element of the offense was committed.

(B) When the offense or any element of the offense was committed in an aircraft, motor vehicle, train, watercraft, or other vehicle, in transit, and it cannot reasonably be determined in which jurisdiction the offense was committed, the offender may be tried in any jurisdiction through which the aircraft, motor vehicle, train, watercraft, or other vehicle passed.

(C) When the offense involved the unlawful taking or receiving of property or the unlawful taking or enticing of another, the offender may be tried in any jurisdiction from which or into which the property or victim was taken, received, or enticed.

(D) When the offense is conspiracy, attempt, or complicity cognizable under division (A)(2) of section 2901.11 of the Revised Code, the offender may be tried in any jurisdiction in which the conspiracy, attempt, complicity, or any of its elements occurred.

(E) When the offense is conspiracy or attempt cognizable under division (A)(3) of section 2901.11 of the Revised Code, the offender may be tried in any jurisdiction in which the offense that was the object of the conspiracy or attempt, or any element thereof, was intended to or could have taken place. When the offense is complicity cognizable under division (A)(3) of section 2901.11 of the Revised Code, the offender may be tried in any jurisdiction in which the principal offender may be tried.

(F) When an offense is considered to have been committed in this state while the offender was out of this state, and the jurisdiction in this state in which the offense or any material element of the offense was committed is not reasonably ascertainable, the offender may be tried in any jurisdiction in which the offense or element reasonably could have been committed.

(G) When it appears beyond a reasonable doubt that an offense or any element of an offense was committed in any of two or more jurisdictions, but it cannot reasonably be determined in which jurisdiction the offense or element was committed, the offender may be tried in any such jurisdiction.

(H) When an offender, as part of a course of criminal conduct, commits offenses in different jurisdictions, he may be tried for all of those offenses in any jurisdiction in which one of those offenses or any element of one of those offenses occurred. Without limitation on the evidence that may be used to establish such course of criminal conduct, any of the following is prima-facie evidence of a course of criminal conduct:

(1) The offenses involved the same victim, or victims of the same type or from the same group.

(2) The offenses were committed by the offender in his same employment, or capacity, or relationship to another.

(3) The offenses were committed as part of the same transaction or chain of events, or in furtherance of the same purpose or objective.

(4) The offenses were committed in furtherance of the same conspiracy.

(5) The offenses involved the same or a similar modus operandi.

(6) The offenses were committed along the offender's line of travel in this state, regardless of his point of origin or destination.

(I)(1) When the offense involves a computer, computer system, or computer network, the offender may be tried in any jurisdiction containing any location of the computer, computer system, or computer network of the victim of the offense or any jurisdiction in which the alleged offender commits any activity that is an essential part of the offense.

(2) As used in this section, "computer," "computer system," and "computer network" have the same meaning as in section 2913.01 of the Revised Code.

(J) When the offense involves the death of a person, and it cannot reasonably be determined in which jurisdiction the offense was committed, the offender may be tried in the jurisdiction in which the dead person's body or any part of the dead person's body was found.

(K) Notwithstanding any other requirement for the place of trial, venue may be changed upon motion of the prosecution, the defense, or the court, to any court having jurisdiction of the subject matter outside the county in which trial otherwise would be held, when it appears that a fair and impartial trial cannot be held in the jurisdiction in which trial otherwise would be held, or when it appears that trial should be held in another jurisdiction for the convenience of the parties and in the interests of justice.

HISTORY: 134 v H 511 (Eff 1-1-74); 141 v H 49 (Eff 6-26-86); 143 v S 64. Eff 10-26-89.

Not analogous to former RC § 2901.12 (RS § 6818; S&C 406; 33 v 33; 80 v 38; GC § 12432; 109 v 612; 118 v 611; Bureau of Code Revision, 10-1-53; 129 v 1704), repealed 134 v H 511, § 2, eff 1-1-74.

§ 2901.13 Limitation of criminal prosecutions.

(A) Except as otherwise provided in this section, a prosecution shall be barred unless it is commenced within the following periods after an offense is committed:

(1) For a felony other than aggravated murder or murder, six years;

(2) For a misdemeanor other than a minor misdemeanor, two years;

(3) For a minor misdemeanor, six months.

(B) If the period of limitation provided in division (A) of this section has expired, prosecution shall be commenced for an offense of which an element is fraud or breach of a fiduciary duty, within one year after discovery of the offense either by an aggrieved person, or by his legal representative who is not himself a party to the offense.

(C) If the period of limitation provided in division (A) of this section has expired, prosecution shall be commenced for an offense involving misconduct in office by a public servant as defined in section 2921.01 of the Revised Code, at any time while the accused remains a public servant, or within two years thereafter.

(D) An offense is committed when every element of the offense occurs. In the case of an offense of which an element is a continuing course of conduct, the period of limitation does not begin to run until such course of conduct or the accused's accountability for it terminates, whichever occurs first.

(E) A prosecution is commenced on the date an indictment is returned or an information filed, or on the date a lawful arrest without a warrant is made, or on the date a warrant, summons, citation, or other process is issued, whichever occurs first. A prosecution is not commenced by the return of an indictment or the filing of an information unless reasonable diligence is exercised to issue and execute process on the same. A prosecution is not commenced upon issuance of a warrant, summons, citation, or other process, unless reasonable diligence is exercised to execute the same.

(F) The period of limitation shall not run during any time when the corpus delicti remains undiscovered.

(G) The period of limitation shall not run during any time when the accused purposely avoids prosecution. Proof that the accused absented himself from this state or concealed his identity or whereabouts is prima-facie evidence of his purpose to avoid prosecution.

(H) The period of limitation shall not run during any time a prosecution against the accused based on the same conduct is pending in this state, even though the indictment, information, or process which commenced the prosecution is quashed or the proceedings thereon are set aside or reversed on appeal.

HISTORY: 134 v H 511. Eff 1-1-74.

Not analogous to former RC § 2901.13 (GC § 12432-1; 118 v 611; Bureau of Code Revision, 10-1-53; 134 v H 143), repealed 134 v H 511, § 2, eff 1-1-74.

The effective date is set by section 4 of HB 511.

§§ 2901.14, 2901.15, 2901.16

Repealed, 134 v H 511, § 2 [RS §§ 6813—6815; S&C 440; S&S 272; 32 v 20, §§ 1, 3, 4; 64 v 135, § 2; GC §§ 12410—12412; Bureau of Code Revision, 10-1-53]. Eff 1-1-74.

These sections concerned administering medicine while intoxicated, prescribing secret medicine, and abortion.

§§ 2901.17, 2901.18, 2901.19

Repealed, 134 v H 511, § 2 [RS §§ 6819, 6984a; S&C 411; 33 v 33, § 23; 78 v 43; 81 v 184; 83 v 27; 95 v 273 (646); GC §§ 12412-1, 12416, 12428; 101 v 210; Bureau of Code Revision, 10-1-53; 131 v 670]. Eff 1-1-74.

These sections concerned abortion, torture, and maiming.

§ 2901.20

Repealed, 134 v H 511, § 2 [RS § 6819-1; 90 v 353; 98 v 124; GC § 12417; Bureau of Code Revision, 10-1-53]. Eff 1-1-74.

This section concerned hazing.

[CRIMINAL LIABILITY]

§ 2901.21 Requirements for criminal liability.

(A) Except as provided in division (B) of this section, a person is not guilty of an offense unless both of the following apply:

(1) His liability is based on conduct which includes either a voluntary act, or an omission to perform an act or duty which he is capable of performing;

(2) He has the requisite degree of culpability for each element as to which a culpable mental state is specified by the section defining the offense.

(B) When the section defining an offense does not specify any degree of culpability, and plainly indicates a purpose to impose strict criminal liability for the conduct described in such section, then culpability is not required for a person to be guilty of the offense. When the section neither specifies culpability nor plainly indicates a purpose to impose strict liability, recklessness is sufficient culpability to commit the offense.

(C) As used in this section:

(1) Possession is a voluntary act if the possessor knowingly procured or received the thing possessed, or was aware of his control thereof for a sufficient time to have ended his possession.

(2) Reflexes, convulsions, body movements during unconsciousness or sleep, and body movements that are not otherwise a product of the actor's volition, are involuntary acts.

(3) "Culpability" means purpose, knowledge, recklessness, or negligence, as defined in section 2901.22 of the Revised Code.

HISTORY: 134 v H 511. Eff 1-1-74.

Not analogous to former RC § 2901.21 (RS § 6819-1a; 98 v 124; GC § 12418; Bureau of Code Revision, 10-1-53), repealed 134 v H 511, § 2, eff 1-1-74.

The effective date is set by section 4 of HB 511.

§ 2901.22 Culpable mental states.

(A) A person acts purposely when it is his specific intention to cause a certain result, or, when the gist of the offense is a prohibition against conduct of a certain nature, regardless of what the offender intends to accomplish thereby, it is his specific intention to engage in conduct of that nature.

(B) A person acts knowingly, regardless of his purpose, when he is aware that his conduct will probably cause a certain result or will probably be of a certain nature. A person has knowledge of circumstances when he is aware that such circumstances probably exist.

(C) A person acts recklessly when, with heedless indifference to the consequences, he perversely disregards a known risk that his conduct is likely to cause a certain result or is likely to be of a certain nature. A person is reckless with respect to circumstances when, with heedless indifference to the consequences, he perversely disregards a known risk that such circumstances are likely to exist.

(D) A person acts negligently when, because of a substantial lapse from due care, he fails to perceive or avoid a risk that his conduct may cause a certain result or may be of a certain nature. A person is negligent with respect to circumstances when, because of a substantial lapse from due care, he fails to perceive or avoid a risk that such circumstances may exist.

(E) When the section defining an offense provides that negligence suffices to establish an element thereof, then recklessness, knowledge, or purpose is also sufficient culpability for such element. When recklessness suffices to establish an element of an offense, then knowledge or purpose is also sufficient culpability for such element. When knowledge suffices to establish an element of an offense, then purpose is also sufficient culpability for such element.

HISTORY: 134 v H 511. Eff 1-1-74.

Not analogous to former RC § 2901.22 (RS § 6819-2; 90 v 353; GC § 12419; Bureau of Code Revision, 10-1-53), repealed 134 v H 511, § 2, eff 1-1-74.

The effective date is set by section 4 of HB 511.

§ 2901.23 Organizational criminal liability.

(A) An organization may be convicted of an offense under any of the following circumstances:

(1) The offense is a minor misdemeanor committed by an officer, agent, or employee of the organization acting in its behalf and within the scope of his office or employment, except that if the section defining the offense designates the officers, agents, or employees for whose conduct the organization is accountable or the circumstances under which it is accountable, such provisions shall apply.

(2) A purpose to impose organizational liability plainly appears in the section defining the offense, and the offense is committed by an officer, agent, or employee of the organization acting in its behalf and within the scope of his office or employment, except that if the section defining the offense designates the officers,

agents, or employees for whose conduct the organization is accountable or the circumstances under which it is accountable, such provisions shall apply.

(3) The offense consists of an omission to discharge a specific duty imposed by law on the organization.

(4) If, acting with the kind of culpability otherwise required for the commission of the offense, its commission was authorized, requested, commanded, tolerated, or performed by the board of directors, trustees, partners, or by a high managerial officer, agent, or employee acting in behalf of the organization and within the scope of his office or employment.

(B) When strict liability is imposed for the commission of an offense, a purpose to impose organizational liability shall be presumed, unless the contrary plainly appears.

(C) In a prosecution of an organization for an offense other than one for which strict liability is imposed, it is a defense that the high managerial officer, agent, or employee having supervisory responsibility over the subject matter of the offense exercised due diligence to prevent its commission. This defense is not available if it plainly appears inconsistent with the purpose of the section defining the offense.

(D) As used in this section, "organization" means a corporation for profit or not for profit, partnership, limited partnership, joint venture, unincorporated association, estate, trust, or other commercial or legal entity. "Organization" does not include an entity organized as or by a governmental agency for the execution of a governmental program.

HISTORY: 134 v H 511. Eff 1-1-74.

Not analogous to former RC § 2901.23 (RS § 6820; S&S 265; S&C 411; 64 v 43; GC § 12420; Bureau of Code Revision, 10-1-53), repealed 134 v H 511, § 2, eff 1-1-74.

The effective date is set by section 4 of HB 511.

§ 2901.24 Personal accountability for organizational conduct.

(A) An officer, agent, or employee of an organization as defined in section 2901.23 of the Revised Code may be prosecuted for an offense committed by such organization, if he acts with the kind of culpability required for the commission of the offense, and any of the following apply:

(1) In the name of the organization or in its behalf, he engages in conduct constituting the offense, or causes another to engage in such conduct, or tolerates such conduct when it is of a type for which he has direct responsibility;

(2) He has primary responsibility to discharge a duty imposed on the organization by law, and such duty is not discharged.

(B) When a person is convicted of an offense by reason of this section, he is subject to the same penalty as if he had acted in his own behalf.

HISTORY: 134 v H 511. Eff 1-1-74.

Not analogous to former RC § 2901.24 (RS § 6821; S&S 262; S&C 407; 62 v 77; 95 v 344; GC § 12421; Bureau of Code Revision, 10-1-53; 129 v 1704), repealed 134 v H 511, § 2, eff 1-1-74.

The effective date is set by section 4 of HB 511.

[§ 2901.24.1] § 2901.241 Repealed, 134 v H 511, § 2 [128 v 560]. Eff 1-1-74.

This section concerned assault with a dangerous or deadly weapon.

§ 2901.25 Repealed, 134 v H 511, § 2 [RS § 6823; S&S 276; 64 v 21; GC § 12423; Bureau of Code Revision, 10-1-53]. Eff 1-1-74.

This section concerned assault and battery, and menacing threats.

[§§ 2901.25.1, 2901.25.2] §§ 2901.251, 2901.252 Repealed, 134 v H 511, § 2 [131 v 670; 132 v H 996]. Eff 1-1-74.

These sections concerned throwing at or towards a person; assault and battery upon law enforcement officers and firemen.

§§ 2901.26, 2901.27, 2901.28
Repealed, 134 v H 511, § 2 [RS §§ 6824, 6830-1, 6830-2; S&S 275; 65 v 87; 79 v 132; 95 v 100; 95 v 648, § 2; GC §§ 12424, 12427, 13386; 101 v 263; 115 v PtII, 73, 90; 117 v 485; Bureau of Code Revision, 10-1-53]. Eff 1-1-74.

These sections concerned kidnapping.

§ 2901.29 Repealed, 134 v H 511, § 2 [GC § 13386-1; 115 v PtII, 90; Bureau of Code Revision, 10-1-53]. Eff 1-1-74.

This section concerned kidnapping.

[MISSING CHILDREN]

§ 2901.30 Missing child report; notice of return.

(A) As used in sections 2901.30 to 2901.32 of the Revised Code:

(1) "Information" means information that can be integrated into the computer system and that relates to the physical or mental description of a minor including, but not limited to, height, weight, color of hair and eyes, use of eyeglasses or contact lenses, skin coloring, physical or mental handicaps, special medical conditions or needs, abnormalities, problems, scars and marks, and distinguishing characteristics, and other information that could assist in identifying a minor including, but not limited to, full name and nickname, date and place of

birth, age, names and addresses of parents and other relatives, fingerprints, dental records, photographs, social security number, driver's license number, credit card numbers, bank account numbers, and clothing.

(2) "Minor" means a person under eighteen years of age.

(3) "Missing children" or "missing child" means either of the following:

(a) A minor who has run away from or who otherwise is missing from the home of, or the care, custody, and control of, the minor's parents, parent who is the residential parent and legal custodian, guardian, legal custodian, or other person having responsibility for the care of the minor;

(b) A minor who is missing and about whom there is reason to believe the minor could be the victim of a violation of section 2905.01, 2905.02, 2905.03, or 2919.23 of the Revised Code or of a violation of section 2905.04 of the Revised Code as it existed prior to the effective date of this amendment.

(B) When a law enforcement agency in this state that has jurisdiction in the matter is informed that a minor is or may be a missing child and that the person providing the information wishes to file a missing child report, the law enforcement agency shall take that report. Upon taking the report, the law enforcement agency shall take prompt action upon it, including, but not limited to, concerted efforts to locate the missing child. No law enforcement agency in this state shall have a rule or policy that prohibits or discourages the filing of or the taking of action upon a missing child report, within a specified period following the discovery or formulation of a belief that a minor is or could be a missing child.

(C) If a missing child report is made to a law enforcement agency in this state that has jurisdiction in the matter, the law enforcement agency shall gather readily available information about the missing child and integrate it into the national crime information center computer within twelve hours following the making of the report. The law enforcement agency shall make reasonable efforts to acquire additional information about the missing child following the transmittal of the initially available information, and promptly integrate any additional information acquired into such computer systems.

Whenever a law enforcement agency integrates information about a missing child into the national crime information center computer, the law enforcement agency promptly shall notify the missing child's parents, parent who is the residential parent and legal custodian, guardian, or legal custodian, or any other person responsible for the care of the missing child, that it has so integrated the information.

The parents, parent who is the residential parent and legal custodian, guardian, legal custodian, or other person responsible for the care of the missing child shall provide available information upon request, and may provide information voluntarily, to the law enforcement agency during the information gathering process. The law enforcement agency also may obtain available information about the missing child from other persons, subject to constitutional and statutory limitations.

(D) Upon the filing of a missing child report, the law enforcement agency involved promptly shall make a reasonable attempt to notify other law enforcement agencies within its county and, if the agency has jurisdiction in a municipal corporation or township that borders another county, to notify the law enforcement agency for the municipal corporation or township in the other county with which it shares the border, that it has taken a missing child report and may be requesting assistance or cooperation in the case, and provide relevant information to the other law enforcement agencies. The agency may notify additional law enforcement agencies, appropriate public children services agencies, about the case, request their assistance or cooperation in the case, and provide them with relevant information.

Upon request from a law enforcement agency, a public children services agency shall grant the law enforcement agency access to all information concerning a missing child that the agency possesses that may be relevant to the law enforcement agency in investigating a missing child report concerning that child. The information obtained by the law enforcement agency shall be used only to further the investigation to locate the missing child.

(E) Upon request, law enforcement agencies in this state shall provide assistance to, and cooperate with, other law enforcement agencies in their investigation of missing child cases.

The information in any missing child report made to a law enforcement agency shall be made available, upon request, to law enforcement personnel of this state, other states, and the federal government when the law enforcement personnel indicate that the request is to aid in identifying or locating a missing child or the possible identification of a deceased minor who, upon discovery, cannot be identified.

(F) When a missing child has not been located within thirty days after the date on which the missing child report pertaining to the child was filed with a law enforcement agency, that law enforcement agency shall request the missing child's parents, parent who is the residential parent and legal custodian, guardian, or legal custodian, or any other person responsible for the care of the missing child, to provide written consent for the law enforcement agency to contact the missing child's dentist and request the missing child's dental records. Upon receipt of such written consent, the dentist shall release a copy of the missing child's dental records to the law enforcement agency and shall provide and encode the records in such form as requested by the law enforcement agency. The law enforcement agency then shall integrate information in the records into the national crime information center computer in order to compare the records to those of unidentified deceased persons. This division does not prevent a law enforcement agency from seeking consent to obtain copies of a missing child's dental records, or prevent a missing child's parents, parent who is the residential parent and legal custodian, guardian, or legal custodian, or any other person responsible for the care of the missing child, from granting consent for the release of copies of the missing child's dental records to a law enforcement agency, at any time.

(G) A missing child's parents, parent who is the residential parent and legal custodian, guardian, or legal custodian, or any other persons responsible for the care of a missing child, immediately shall notify the law enforcement agency with which they filed the missing child report whenever the child has returned to their home or to their care, custody, and control, has been released if the missing child was the victim of an offense listed in division (A)(3)(b) of this section, or otherwise has been located. Upon such notification or upon otherwise learning that a missing child has returned to the home of, or to the care, custody, and control of the missing child's parents, parent who is the residential parent and legal custodian, guardian, legal custodian, or other person responsible for the missing child's care, has been released if the missing child was the victim of an offense listed in division (A)(3)(b) of this section, or otherwise has been located, the law enforcement agency involved promptly shall integrate the fact that the minor no longer is a missing child into the national crime information center computer.

(H) Nothing contained in this section shall be construed to impair the confidentiality of services provided to runaway minors by shelters for runaway minors pursuant to sections 5119.64 to 5119.68 of the Revised Code.

HISTORY: 140 v S 321 (Eff 4-9-85); 143 v S 3 (Eff 4-11-91); 146 v S 2 (Eff 7-1-96); 147 v H 408. Eff 10-1-97.

Not analogous to former RC § 2901.30 (GC § 13386-2; 115 v PtII, 90, § 3; Bureau of Code Revision, 10-1-53), repealed 134 v H 511, § 2, eff 1-1-74.

§ 2901.31 Cooperation in locating missing children.

Law enforcement agencies in this state shall cooperate fully with the United States attorney general in the collection of information that would assist in the identification of unidentified deceased persons and information that would assist in the location of missing persons under the "Federal Missing Children Act of 1982," 96 Stat. 1259, 28 U.S.C. 534, as amended.

Law enforcement agencies in this state that are investigating missing children cases shall utilize the records and information compiled by the United States attorney general pursuant to that act when the circumstances of an investigation indicate that the records and information may be of assistance and when the act authorizes it.

HISTORY: 140 v S 321. Eff 4-9-85.

Not analogous to former RC § 2901.31 (GC § 13386-3; 115 v PtII, 90, § 4; Bureau of Code Revision, 10-1-53), repealed 134 v H 511, § 2, eff 1-1-74.

§ 2901.32 Improper solicitation of contributions for missing children.

(A) No organization shall solicit contributions for the purpose of distributing materials containing information relating to missing children unless it complies with all of the following requirements:

(1) It has been incorporated under Chapter 1702. of the Revised Code or the nonprofit corporation law of another state for a period of two years prior to the time of the solicitation of contributions.

(2) It has been exempt from federal income taxation under subsection 501(a) and described in subsection 501(c)(3), 501(c)(4), 501(c)(8), 501(c)(10), or 501(c)(19) of the Internal Revenue Code of 1954, 68A Stat. 3, 26 U.S.C. 1, as now or hereafter amended, for a period of two years prior to the time of the solicitation of contributions.

(3) It does not use fund-raising counsel, professional solicitors, commercial co-venturers, or other charitable organizations, as these terms are defined in section 1716.01 of the Revised Code, to solicit such contributions.

(B) No organization that solicits contributions for the purpose of distributing materials containing information relating to missing children shall expressly state or imply in any way that it is affiliated with, or is soliciting contributions on behalf of, an organization established to assist in the location of missing children without the express written consent of that organization.

(C) Whoever violates division (A) or (B) of this section is guilty of improper solicitation of contributions for missing children, a misdemeanor of the third degree.

HISTORY: 140 v S 321 (Eff 4-9-85); 143 v H 486. Eff 11-7-90.

Not analogous to former RC § 2901.32 (GC § 13386-4; 115 v PtII, 90, § 5; Bureau of Code Revision, 10-1-53), repealed 134 v H 511, § 2, eff 1-1-74.

§§ 2901.33, 2901.34, 2901.35

Repealed, 134 v H 511, § 2 [RS §§ 4426-1, 4426-2, 6825; S&C 457; 73 v 207; 81 v 15, 90; 91 v 17; GC §§ 12425, 12940, 12941, 13386-5; 115 v PtII, 90; 117 v 274; Bureau of Code Revision, 10-1-53]. Eff 1-1-74.

These sections concerned kidnapping and discrimination.

§§ 2901.36, 2901.37, 2901.38

Repealed, 134 v H 511, § 2 [RS §§ 4426-2, 6828, 6830; S&S 279; S&C 431; 64 v 69; 76 v 167; 79 v 84; 81 v 15, 90; 91 v 17; GC §§ 12942, 13383, 13384; 116 v 373; Bureau of Code Revision, 10-1-53; 126 v 575]. Eff 1-1-74.

These sections referred to prosecution, libel and blackmail.

§§ 2901.39, 2901.40, 2901.41

Repealed, 134 v H 511, § 2 [RS §§ 6829, 7017-3; S&C 430; 29 v 144; 93 v 114; 98 v 98; GC §§ 12429, 12430, 13385; 111 v 85; 115 v 144; Bureau of Code Revision, 10-1-53; 126 v 429]. Eff 1-1-74.

These sections prohibited threatening letters and provided for destitute, infirm, or aged parents.

§§ 2901.42, 2901.43, 2901.44

Repealed, 134 v H 511, § 2 [RS § 7017-3; 93 v 114; 98 v 98; GC § 12431; Bureau of Code Revision, 10-1-53; 131 v 670, 671]. Eff 1-1-74.

These sections concerned duty to support destitute parent, deprivation of equal protection of law, and threats to destroy buildings or property.

§ 2901.45

Repealed, 135 v H 716, § 2 [134 v S 538]. Eff 1-1-74.

This section concerned adulterating candy or food.

CHAPTER 2903: HOMICIDE AND ASSAULT

Section

[HOMICIDE]

2903.01	Aggravated murder.
2903.02	Murder.
2903.03	Voluntary manslaughter.
2903.04	Involuntary manslaughter.
2903.05	Negligent homicide.
2903.06	Aggravated vehicular homicide.
2903.07	Vehicular homicide.
2903.08	Aggravated vehicular assault.
2903.09	Legal abortions and acts or omissions of pregnant woman excepted from liability.
2903.10	Definitions: functionally impaired person; caretaker.

[ASSAULT]

2903.11	Felonious assault.
2903.12	Aggravated assault.
2903.13	Assault.
2903.14	Negligent assault.
2903.15	Repealed.
2903.16	Failing to provide for a functionally impaired person.

[MENACING]

2903.21	Aggravated menacing.

[STALKING]

[2903.21.1] 2903.211	Menacing by stalking.
[2903.21.2] 2903.212	Consideration in setting amount and conditions of bail for violations of certain protection orders.
[2903.21.3] 2903.213	Motion for issuance of anti-stalking protection order.
[2903.21.4, 2903.21.5] 2903.214, 2903.215	Repealed.
2903.22	Menacing.
2903.31	Hazing.

[PATIENT ABUSE AND NEGLECT IN CARE FACILITIES]

2903.33	Definitions.
2903.34	Patient abuse; neglect.
2903.35	Filing false patient abuse or neglect complaints.
2903.36	Discrimination, retaliation prohibited.
2903.37	License revocation.

[HOMICIDE]

§ 2903.01 Aggravated murder.

(A) No person shall purposely, and with prior calculation and design, cause the death of another or the unlawful termination of another's pregnancy.

(B) No person shall purposely cause the death of another or the unlawful termination of another's pregnancy while committing or attempting to commit, or while fleeing immediately after committing or attempting to commit kidnapping, rape, aggravated arson or arson, aggravated robbery or robbery, aggravated burglary or burglary, or escape.

(C) No person shall purposely cause the death of another who is under thirteen years of age at the time of the commission of the offense.

(D) Whoever violates this section is guilty of aggravated murder, and shall be punished as provided in section 2929.02 of the Revised Code.

(E) No person shall be convicted of aggravated murder unless the person is specifically found to have intended to cause the death of another or, if the case involves an alleged violation of division (A) or (B) of this section, the unlawful termination of another's pregnancy. In no case shall a jury in an aggravated murder case be instructed in such a manner that it may believe that a person who commits or attempts to commit any offense listed in division (B) of this section is to be conclusively inferred, because the person engaged in a common design with others to commit the offense by force and violence or because the offense and the manner of its commission would be likely to produce death or the unlawful termination of another's pregnancy, to have intended to cause the death of any person who is killed or the unlawful termination of another's pregnancy during the commission of, attempt to commit, or flight from the commission of or attempt to commit, the offense. If a jury in an aggravated murder case is instructed that a person who commits or attempts to commit any offense listed in division (B) of this section may be inferred, because the offender engaged in a common design with others to commit the offense by force or violence or because the offense and the manner of its commission would be likely to produce death or the unlawful termination of another's pregnancy, to have intended to cause the death of any person who is killed or the unlawful termination of another's pregnancy during the commission of, attempt to commit, or flight from the commission of or attempt to commit the offense, the jury also shall be instructed that the inference is nonconclusive, that the inference may be considered in determining intent, that it is to consider all evidence introduced by the prosecution to indicate the person's intent and by the person to indicate the person's lack of intent in determining whether the person specifically intended to cause the death of the person killed or the unlawful termination of another's pregnancy, and that the prosecution must prove the specific intent of the person to have caused the death or the unlawful termination of another's pregnancy by proof beyond a reasonable doubt.

HISTORY: 134 v H 511 (Eff 1-1-74); 139 v S 1 (Eff 10-19-81); 146 v S 239 (Eff 9-6-96); 147 v S 32. Eff 8-6-97.

Not analogous to former RC § 2903.01 (GC § 12423-1; 109 v 45; 121 v 557 (572); Bureau of Code Revision, 10-1-53; 126 v 114), repealed 134 v H 511, § 2, eff 1-1-74.

§ 2903.02 Murder.

(A) No person shall purposely cause the death of

another or the unlawful termination of another's pregnancy.

(B) Whoever violates this section is guilty of murder, and shall be punished as provided in section 2929.02 of the Revised Code.

HISTORY: 134 v H 511 (Eff 1-1-74); 146 v S 239. Eff 9-6-96.

Not analogous to former RC § 2903.02 (RS § 6998; S&S 377; 59 v 65; 83 v 202; GC §§ 12962, 12963; Bureau of Code Revision, 10-1-53; 131 v 671), repealed 134 v H 511, § 2, eff 1-1-74.

The effective date is set by section 4 of HB 511.

§ 2903.03 Voluntary manslaughter.

(A) No person, while under the influence of sudden passion or in a sudden fit of rage, either of which is brought on by serious provocation occasioned by the victim that is reasonably sufficient to incite the person into using deadly force, shall knowingly cause the death of another or the unlawful termination of another's pregnancy.

(B) Whoever violates this section is guilty of voluntary manslaughter, a felony of the first degree.

HISTORY: 134 v H 511 (Eff 1-1-74); 139 v H 103 (Eff 5-19-82); 139 v S 199 (Eff 1-5-83); 146 v S 2 (Eff 7-1-96); 146 v S 239. Eff 9-6-96.

Not analogous to former RC § 2903.03 (RS § 6937; S&C 667; 54 v 196; GC § 12964; 103 v 864; Bureau of Code Revision, 10-1-53), repealed 134 v H 511, § 2, eff 1-1-74.

§ 2903.04 Involuntary manslaughter.

(A) No person shall cause the death of another or the unlawful termination of another's pregnancy as a proximate result of the offender's committing or attempting to commit a felony.

(B) No person shall cause the death of another or the unlawful termination of another's pregnancy as a proximate result of the offender's committing or attempting to commit a misdemeanor of the first, second, third, or fourth degree or a minor misdemeanor.

(C) Whoever violates this section is guilty of involuntary manslaughter. Violation of division (A) of this section is a felony of the first degree. Violation of division (B) of this section is a felony of the third degree.

(D)(1) In addition to any penalty imposed upon the offender under division (C) of this section and sections 2929.11 to 2929.18 of the Revised Code, if an offender is convicted of or pleads guilty to a violation of division (A) or (B) of this section and if the felony or misdemeanor that the offender committed or attempted to commit, that proximately resulted in the death of the other person or the unlawful termination of another's pregnancy, and that is the basis of the offender's violation of division (A) or (B) of this section included, as an element of that felony or misdemeanor offense, the offender's operation or participation in the operation of a motor vehicle, motorcycle, snowmobile, locomotive, watercraft, or aircraft while the offender was under the influence of alcohol, a drug of abuse, or alcohol and a drug of abuse, both of the following apply:

(a) The offender's driver's or commercial driver's license or permit or nonresident operating privilege shall be permanently revoked pursuant to section 4507.16 of the Revised Code;

(b) The offender is not eligible for a sentence to a community control sanction, as defined in section 2929.01 of the Revised Code, pursuant to section 2929.13, for judicial release pursuant to section 2929.20 of the Revised Code if any of the following apply relative to the offender:

(i) The offender previously has been convicted of or pleaded guilty to a violation of division (A) or (B) of this section in which the felony or misdemeanor that the offender committed or attempted to commit, that proximately resulted in the death of the other person or the unlawful termination of another's pregnancy, and that is the basis of the offender's violation of division (A) or (B) of this section included, as an element of that felony or misdemeanor offense, the offender's operation or participation in the operation of a motor vehicle, motorcycle, snowmobile, locomotive, watercraft, or aircraft while the offender was under the influence of alcohol, a drug of abuse, or alcohol and a drug of abuse;

(ii) The offender previously has been convicted of or pleaded guilty to a violation of a municipal ordinance that is substantially similar to division (A) or (B) of this section and the felony or misdemeanor that the offender committed or attempted to commit, that proximately resulted in the death of the other person or the unlawful termination of another's pregnancy, and that is the basis of the offender's violation of the municipal ordinance that is substantially similar to division (A) or (B) of this section included, as an element of that felony or misdemeanor offense, the offender's operation or participation in the operation of a motor vehicle, motorcycle, snowmobile, locomotive, watercraft, or aircraft while the offender was under the influence of alcohol, a drug of abuse, or alcohol and a drug of abuse;

(iii) The offender previously has been convicted of or pleaded guilty to a violation of section 1547.11, 2903.06, 2903.07, 2903.08, 4511.19, or 4511.192 [4511.19.2] of the Revised Code, division (B) or (D) of section 4507.02 of the Revised Code, section 4507.38 or 4507.39 of the Revised Code as those sections existed prior to September 24, 1986, a municipal ordinance that is substantially similar to section 2903.06, 2903.07, 2903.08, 4511.19, or 4511.192 [4511.19.2] of the Revised Code, or a municipal ordinance that is substantially similar to section 4507.38 or 4507.39 of the Revised Code as those sections existed prior to September 24, 1986;

(iv) The offender has accumulated twelve points pursuant to section 4507.021 [4507.02.1] of the Revised Code within one year of the offense;

(v) The offender was driving under suspension at the time he committed the offense.

(2) In determining, for purposes of division (D)(1) of this section, whether an offender was under the influence of alcohol, a drug of abuse, or alcohol and a drug of abuse at the time of the commission of the offender's violation of division (A) or (B) of this section, the trier of fact may consider as competent evidence the concentration of alcohol in the offender's blood, breath, or urine as shown by a chemical test taken pursuant to section 1547.111 [1547.11.1] or 4511.191 [4511.19.1] of the Revised Code. The offender shall be presumed to have been under the influence of alcohol if there was, at the time the bodily substance was withdrawn for the chemical test, a concentration of ten-hundredths of one per cent or more by weight of alcohol in the offender's blood, ten-hundredths of one gram or more by weight of alcohol per two hundred ten liters of the offender's breath, or fourteen-hundredths of one gram or more by weight of alcohol per one hundred milliliters of the offender's urine.

HISTORY: 134 v H 511 (Eff 1-1-74); 139 v S 199 (Eff 7-1-83); 144 v S 275 (Eff 7-1-93)†; 145 v H 236 (Eff 9-29-94); 146 v S 2 (Eff 7-1-96); 146 v S 269 (Eff 7-1-96); 146 v S 239. Eff 9-6-96.

Not analogous to former RC § 2903.04 (RS §§ 4364-38, 4364-39; 90 v 235; 91 v 311; 92 v 71; GC § 12965; 101 v 133; Bureau of Code Revision, 10-1-53), repealed 134 v H 511, § 2, eff 1-1-74.

† The provisions of §§ 4, 5 of SB 62 (145 v —) read as follows:

SECTION 4. That Section 3 of Sub. S.B. 275 of the 119th General Assembly be amended to read as follows:

"Sec. 3. Sections 1 and 2 of this act shall take effect September 1, 1993."

SECTION 5. That existing Section 3 of Sub. S.B. 275 of the 119th General Assembly is hereby repealed.

Comment, Legislative Service Commission

Sections 2903.04, 2903.06, 2903.07, and 2903.08 of the Revised Code are amended by this act [Am. Sub. S.B. 269] and Am. Sub. S.B. 239 of the 121st General Assembly. Comparison of these amendments in pursuance of section 1.52 of the Revised Code discloses that they are not irreconcilable so that they are required by that section to be harmonized to give effect to each amendment.

§ 2903.05 Negligent homicide.

(A) No person shall negligently cause the death of another or the unlawful termination of another's pregnancy by means of a deadly weapon or dangerous ordnance as defined in section 2923.11 of the Revised Code.

(B) Whoever violates this section is guilty of negligent homicide, a misdemeanor of the first degree.

HISTORY: 134 v H 511 (Eff 1-1-74); 146 v S 239. Eff 9-6-96.

Not analogous to former RC § 2903.05 (RS § 6986b; 80 v 222; GC § 12966; 103 v 864; Bureau of Code Revision, 10-1-53), repealed 134 v H 511, § 2, eff 1-1-74.

§ 2903.06 Aggravated vehicular homicide.

(A) No person, while operating or participating in the operation of a motor vehicle, motorcycle, snowmobile, locomotive, watercraft, or aircraft, shall recklessly cause the death of another or the unlawful termination of another's pregnancy.

(B) Whoever violates this section is guilty of aggravated vehicular homicide, a felony of the third degree. If the offender previously has been convicted of or pleaded guilty to an offense under this section, section 2903.07 or 2903.08 of the Revised Code, or section 2903.04 of the Revised Code in a case in which the offender was subject to the sanctions described in division (D) of that section, aggravated vehicular homicide is a felony of the second degree.

If the jury or judge as trier of fact finds that the offender was under the influence of alcohol, a drug of abuse, or alcohol and a drug of abuse, at the time of the commission of the offense, then the offender's driver's or commercial driver's license or permit or nonresident operating privilege shall be permanently revoked pursuant to section 4507.16 of the Revised Code.

When the trier of fact determines whether the offender was under the influence of alcohol, a drug of abuse, or alcohol and a drug of abuse, the concentration of alcohol in the offender's blood, breath, or urine as shown by a chemical test taken pursuant to section 1547.111 [1547.11.1] or 4511.191 [4511.19.1] of the Revised Code may be considered as competent evidence, and the offender shall be presumed to have been under the influence of alcohol if there was at the time the bodily substance was withdrawn for the chemical test a concentration of ten-hundredths of one per cent or more by weight of alcohol in the offender's blood, ten-hundredths of one gram or more by weight of alcohol per two hundred ten liters of the offender's breath, or fourteen-hundredths of one gram or more by weight of alcohol per one hundred milliliters of the offender's urine.

(C) If the offender previously has been convicted of or pleaded guilty to a violation of this section, section 2903.04 of the Revised Code in a case in which the offender was subject to the sanctions described in division (D) of that section, section 1547.11, 2903.07, 2903.08, 4511.19, or 4511.192 [4511.19.2] of the Revised Code, division (B) or (D) of section 4507.02 of the Revised Code, section 4507.38 or 4507.39 of the Revised Code as those sections existed prior to September 24, 1986, a municipal ordinance that is substantially similar to section 2903.07, 2903.08, 4511.19, or 4511.192 [4511.19.2] of the Revised Code, a municipal ordinance that is substantially similar to section 4507.38 or 4507.39 of the Revised Code as those sections existed prior to September 24, 1986, or a municipal ordinance that is substantially similar to section 2903.04 of the Revised Code in a case in which the offender would have been subject to the sanctions described in division

(D) of that section had the offender been convicted of a violation of that section, if the offender has accumulated twelve points pursuant to section 4507.021 [4507.02.1] of the Revised Code within one year of the offense, or if in the commission of the offense the offender was driving under suspension or operating a motor vehicle while under the influence of alcohol, a drug of abuse, or alcohol and a drug of abuse, the offender shall be sentenced to a mandatory prison term and shall not be eligible for a sentence to a community control sanction pursuant to section 2929.13 of the Revised Code, for judicial release pursuant to section 2929.20 of the Revised Code, or for a reduction of a stated prison term or a release pursuant to section 2967.193 [2967.19.3] of the Revised Code or any other provisions of Chapter 2967. or Chapter 5120. of the Revised Code.

(D) As used in this section, "mandatory prison term" and "community control sanction" have the same meanings as in section 2929.01 of the Revised Code.

HISTORY: 134 v H 511 (Eff 1-1-74); 135 v H 716 (Eff 1-1-74); 139 v S 432 (Eff 3-16-83); 141 v H 265 (Eff 7-24-86); 141 v S 356 (Eff 9-24-86); 141 v S 262 (Eff 3-20-87); 141 v H 428 (Eff 12-23-86); 143 v H 381 (Eff 7-1-89); 143 v S 49 (Eff 11-3-89); 143 v S 131 (Eff 7-25-90); 144 v S 275 (Eff 7-1-93)†; 146 v S 2 (Eff 7-1-96); 146 v S 269 (Eff 7-1-96); 146 v S 239. Eff 9-6-96.

Not analogous to former RC § 2903.06 (RS § 6986a; 77 v 79; GC § 12967; 103 v 864; Bureau of Code Revision, 10-1-53), repealed 134 v H 511, § 2, eff 1-1-74.

For current analogous provision to former RC § 2903.06 see RC § 2923.21.

† See provisions, §§ 4, 5 of SB 62 (145 v —) following RC § 2903.04.

See Comment, Legislative Service Commission following RC § 2903.04.

§ 2903.07 Vehicular homicide.

(A) No person, while operating or participating in the operation of a motor vehicle, motorcycle, snowmobile, locomotive, watercraft, or aircraft, shall negligently cause the death of another or the unlawful termination of another's pregnancy.

(B) Whoever violates this section is guilty of vehicular homicide, a misdemeanor of the first degree. If the offender previously has been convicted of an offense under this section, section 2903.06 or 2903.08 of the Revised Code, or section 2903.04 of the Revised Code in a case in which the offender was subject to the sanctions described in division (D) of that section, vehicular homicide is a felony of the fourth degree.

If the jury or judge as trier of fact finds that the offender was under the influence of alcohol, a drug of abuse, or alcohol and a drug of abuse, at the time of the commission of the offense, then the offender's driver's or commercial driver's license or permit or nonresident operating privileges shall be permanently revoked pursuant to section 4507.16 of the Revised Code.

When the trier of fact determines whether the offender was under the influence of alcohol, a drug of abuse, or alcohol and a drug of abuse, the concentration of alcohol in the offender's blood, breath, or urine as shown by a chemical test taken pursuant to section 1547.111 [1547.11.1] or 4511.191 [4511.19.1] of the Revised Code may be considered as competent evidence and the offender shall be presumed to have been under the influence of alcohol if there was at the time the bodily substance was withdrawn for the chemical test a concentration of ten-hundredths of one per cent or more by weight of alcohol in the offender's blood, ten-hundredths of one gram or more by weight of alcohol per two hundred ten liters of the offender's breath, or fourteen-hundredths of one gram or more by weight of alcohol per one hundred milliliters of the offender's urine.

(C) If the offender previously has been convicted of or pleaded guilty to a violation of this section, section 2903.04 of the Revised Code in a case in which the offender was subject to the sanctions described in division (D) of that section, section 1547.11, 2903.06, 2903.08, 4511.19, or 4511.192 [4511.19.2] of the Revised Code, division (B) or (D) of section 4507.02 of the Revised Code, section 4507.38 or 4507.39 of the Revised Code as those sections existed prior to September 24, 1986, a municipal ordinance that is substantially similar to this section, section 2903.08, 4511.19, or 4511.192 [4511.19.2] of the Revised Code, a municipal ordinance that is substantially similar to section 4507.38 or 4507.39 of the Revised Code as those sections existed prior to September 24, 1986, or a municipal ordinance that is substantially similar to section 2903.04 of the Revised Code in a case in which the offender would have been subject to the sanctions described in division (D) of that section had the offender been convicted of a violation of that section, if the offender has accumulated twelve points pursuant to section 4507.021 [4507.02.1] of the Revised Code within one year of the offense, or if in the commission of the offense the offender was driving under suspension or operating a motor vehicle while under the influence of alcohol, a drug of abuse, or alcohol and a drug of abuse, the offender shall be sentenced to a mandatory prison term and shall not be eligible for a sentence to a community control sanction, pursuant to section 2929.13 of the Revised Code, for judicial release pursuant to section 2929.20 of the Revised Code, or for a reduction of a stated prison term or a release pursuant to section 2967.193 [2967.19.3] of the Revised Code or any other provision of Chapter 2967. or Chapter 5120. of the Revised Code.

(D) As used in this section, "mandatory prison term" and "community control sanction" have the same meanings as in section 2929.01 of the Revised Code.

HISTORY: 134 v H 511 (Eff 1-1-74); 135 v H 716 (Eff 1-1-74); 139 v S 432 (Eff 3-16-83); 141 v H 265 (Eff 7-24-86); 141 v S 356 (Eff 9-24-86); 141 v S 262 (Eff 3-20-87); 141 v H 428 (Eff 12-23-86); 143 v H 381 (Eff 7-1-89); 143 v S 131 (Eff 7-25-90); 144 v S 275 (Eff 7-1-93)†; 146 v S 2 (Eff 7-1-96); 146 v S 269 (Eff 7-1-96); 146 v S 239. Eff 9-6-96.

Not analogous to former RC § 2903.07 (GC § 12967-1; 120 v 143; Bureau of Code Revision, 10-1-53), repealed 134 v H 511, § 2, eff 1-1-74.

For current analogous provision to former RC § 2903.07 see RC § 2923.21

† See provisions, §§ 4, 5 of SB 62 (145 v —) following RC § 2903.04.

See Comment, Legislative Service Commission following RC § 2903.04.

§ 2903.08 Aggravated vehicular assault.

(A) No person, while operating or participating in the operation of a motor vehicle, motorcycle, snowmobile, locomotive, watercraft, or aircraft, shall recklessly cause serious physical harm to another person or another's unborn.

(B) Whoever violates this section is guilty of aggravated vehicular assault, a felony of the fourth degree. If the offender previously has been convicted of an offense under this section, section 2903.06 or 2903.07 of the Revised Code, or section 2903.04 of the Revised Code in a case in which the offender was subject to the sanctions described in division (D) of that section, aggravated vehicular assault is a felony of the third degree.

If the jury or judge as trier of fact finds that the offender was under the influence of alcohol, a drug of abuse, or alcohol and a drug of abuse, at the time of the commission of the offense, then the offender's driver's or commercial driver's license or permit or non-resident operating privileges shall be permanently revoked pursuant to section 4507.16 of the Revised Code.

When the trier of fact determines whether the offender was under the influence of alcohol, a drug of abuse, or alcohol and a drug of abuse, the concentration of alcohol in the offender's blood, breath, or urine as shown by a chemical test taken pursuant to section 1547.111 [1547.11.1] or 4511.191 [4511.19.1] of the Revised Code may be considered as competent evidence and the offender shall be presumed to have been under the influence of alcohol if there was at the time the bodily substance was withdrawn for the chemical test a concentration of ten-hundredths of one per cent or more by weight of alcohol in the offender's blood, ten-hundredths of one gram or more by weight of alcohol per two hundred ten liters of the offender's breath, or fourteen-hundredths of one gram or more by weight of alcohol per one hundred milliliters of the offender's urine.

(C) If the offender previously has been convicted of or pleaded guilty to a violation of this section, section 2903.04 of the Revised Code in a case in which the offender was subject to the sanctions described in division (D) of that section, section 1547.11, 2903.06, 2903.07, 4511.19, or 4511.192 [4511.19.2] of the Revised Code, division (B) or (D) of section 4507.02 of the Revised Code, section 4507.38 or 4507.39 of the Revised Code as those sections existed prior to September 24, 1986, a municipal ordinance that is substantially similar to this section, section 2903.07, 4511.19, or 4511.192 [4511.19.2] of the Revised Code, a municipal ordinance that is substantially similar to section 4507.38 or 4507.39 of the Revised Code as those sections existed prior to September 24, 1986, or a municipal ordinance that is substantially similar to section 2903.04 of the Revised Code in a case in which the offender would have been subject to the sanctions described in division (D) of that section had the offender been convicted of a violation of that section, if the offender has accumulated twelve points pursuant to section 4507.021 [4507.02.1] of the Revised Code within one year of the offense, or if in the commission of the offense the offender was driving under suspension or operating a motor vehicle while under the influence of alcohol, a drug of abuse, or alcohol and a drug of abuse, the offender shall be sentenced to a mandatory prison term and is not eligible for a sentence to a community control sanction pursuant to section 2929.13 of the Revised Code, for judicial release pursuant to section 2929.20 of the Revised Code, or for a reduction of a stated prison term or a release pursuant to section 2967.193 [2967.19.3] of the Revised Code or any other provision of Chapter 2967. or Chapter 5120. of the Revised Code.

(D) As used in this section, "mandatory prison term" and "community control sanction" have the same meanings as in section 2929.01 of the Revised Code.

HISTORY: 143 v S 131 (Eff 7-25-90); 144 v S 275 (Eff 7-1-93)†; 145 v H 236 (Eff 9-29-94); 146 v S 2 (Eff 7-1-96); 146 v S 269 (Eff 7-1-96); 146 v S 239. Eff 9-6-96.

Not analogous to former RC § 2903.08 (RS §§ 6984a, 6985; 73 v 219, §§ 1-6; 81 v 181, 184; 83 v 27; 95 v 273; GC §§ 12970, 12971; Bureau of Code Revision, 10-1-53; 132 v S 65), repealed 134 v H 511, § 2, eff 1-1-74.

† See provisions, §§ 4, 5 of SB 62 (145 v —) following RC § 2903.04.

See Comment, Legislative Service Commission following RC § 2903.04.

§ 2903.09 Legal abortions and acts or omissions of pregnant woman excepted from liability.

As used in sections 2903.01 to 2903.08, 2903.11 to 2903.14, 2903.21, and 2903.22 of the Revised Code:

(A) "Unlawful termination of another's pregnancy" means causing the death of an unborn member of the species homo sapiens, who is or was carried in the womb of another, as a result of injuries inflicted during the period that begins with fertilization and that continues unless and until live birth occurs.

(B) "Another's unborn" or "such other person's unborn" means a member of the species homo sapiens, who is or was carried in the womb of another, during a period that begins with fertilization and that continues unless and until live birth occurs.

(C) Notwithstanding divisions (A) and (B) of this section, in no case shall the definitions of the terms "unlawful termination of another's pregnancy," "another's unborn," and "such other person's unborn" that are set forth in division (A) of this section be applied or construed in any of the following manners:

(1) Except as otherwise provided in division (C)(1) of this section, in a manner so that the offense prohibits or is construed as prohibiting any pregnant woman or her physician from performing an abortion with the actual consent of the pregnant woman, with the consent of the pregnant woman implied by law in a medical emergency, or with the approval of one otherwise authorized by law to consent to medical treatment on behalf of the pregnant woman. An abortion that violates the conditions described in the immediately preceding sentence may be punished as a violation of section 2903.01, 2903.02, 2903.03, 2903.04, 2903.05, 2903.06, 2903.07, 2903.08, 2903.11, 2903.12, 2903.13, 2903.14, 2903.21, or 2903.22 of the Revised Code, as applicable. An abortion that does not violate the conditions described in the second immediately preceding sentence, but that does violate section 2919.12, division (B) of section 2919.13, section 2919.15, 2919.17, or 2919.18 of the Revised Code, may be punished as a violation of section 2919.12, division (B) of section 2919.13, section 2919.15, 2919.17, or 2919.18 of the Revised Code, as applicable.

(2) In a manner so that the offense is applied or is construed as applying to a woman based on an act or omission of the woman that occurs while she is or was pregnant and that results in any of the following:

(a) Her delivery of a stillborn baby;

(b) Her causing, in any other manner, the death in utero of an unborn that she is carrying;

(c) Her causing the death of her child who is born alive but who dies from one or more injuries that are sustained while the child is an unborn;

(d) Her causing her child who is born alive to sustain one or more injuries while the child is an unborn;

(e) Her causing, threatening to cause, or attempting to cause, in any other manner, an injury, illness, or other physiological impairment, regardless of its duration or gravity, or a mental illness or condition, regardless of its duration or gravity, to an unborn that she is carrying.

HISTORY: 146 v S 239. Eff 9-6-96.

Not analogous to former RC § 2903.09 (GC §§ 12970-1, 12970-2; 101 v 233; 103 v 864 (907); 113 v 281; Bureau of Code Revision; 10-1-53; 132 v S 65; 133 v H 1), repealed 134 v H 511, § 2, eff 1-1-74.

§ 2903.10 Definitions: functionally impaired person; caretaker.

As used in sections 2903.13 and 2903.16 of the Revised Code:

(A) "Functionally impaired person" means any person who has a physical or mental impairment that prevents him from providing for his own care or protection or whose infirmities caused by aging prevent him from providing for his own care or protection.

(B) "Caretaker" means a person who assumes the duty to provide for the care and protection of a functionally impaired person on a voluntary basis, by contract, through receipt of payment for care and protection, as a result of a family relationship, or by order of a court of competent jurisdiction. "Caretaker" does not include a person who owns, operates, or administers, or who is an agent or employee of, a care facility, as defined in section 2903.33 of the Revised Code.

HISTORY: 142 v H 642. Eff 3-17-89.

Not analogous to former RC § 2903.10 (126 v 1039; 130 v 658; 130 v PtII, 143), repealed 134 v H 511, § 2, eff 1-1-74.

[ASSAULT]

§ 2903.11 Felonious assault.

(A) No person shall knowingly:

(1) Cause serious physical harm to another or to another's unborn;

(2) Cause or attempt to cause physical harm to another or to another's unborn by means of a deadly weapon or dangerous ordnance, as defined in section 2923.11 of the Revised Code.

(B) Whoever violates this section is guilty of felonious assault, a felony of the second degree. If the victim of the offense is a peace officer, as defined in section 2935.01 of the Revised Code, felonious assault is a felony of the first degree.

HISTORY: 134 v H 511 (Eff 1-1-74); 139 v S 199 (Eff 7-1-83); 139 v H 269 (Eff 7-1-83); 140 v S 210 (Eff 7-1-83); 146 v S 2 (Eff 7-1-96); 146 v S 239. Eff 9-6-96.

Not analogous to former RC § 2903.11 (126 v 1039; 130 v 658), repealed 133 v H 84, § 2, eff 9-15-70.

§ 2903.12 Aggravated assault.†

(A) No person, while under the influence of sudden passion or in a sudden fit of rage, either of which is brought on by serious provocation occasioned by the victim that is reasonably sufficient to incite the person into using deadly force, shall knowingly:

(1) Cause serious physical harm to another or to another's unborn;

(2) Cause or attempt to cause physical harm to another or to another's unborn by means of a deadly weapon or dangerous ordnance, as defined in section 2923.11 of the Revised Code.

(B) Whoever violates this section is guilty of aggravated assault, a felony of the fourth degree. If the victim of the offense is a peace officer, as defined in section 2935.01 of the Revised Code, aggravated assault is a felony of the third degree.

HISTORY: 134 v H 511 (Eff 1-1-74); 139 v H 103 (Eff 5-19-

82); 139 v S 199 (Eff 7-1-83); 139 v H 269 (Eff 7-1-83); 140 v S 210 (Eff 7-1-83); 140 v H 37 (Eff 6-22-84); 146 v S 239. Eff 9-6-96.

Not analogous to former RC § 2903.12 (130 v 659), repealed 134 v H 511, § 2, eff 1-1-74.

Analogous to former RC § 2901.18 (RS § 6984a; 81 v 184; 83 v 27; 95 v 273; GC § 12428; Bureau of Code Revision, 10-1-53; 131 v 670), repealed 134 v H 511, § 2, eff 1-1-74.

† In 139 v H 103 effective 5/19/82, RC § 2903.12(A) was amended as follows:

Sec. 2903.12. (A) No person, while under THE INFLUENCE OF SUDDEN PASSION OR IN A SUDDEN FIT OF RAGE, EITHER OF WHICH IS brought on by serious provocation OCCASIONED BY THE VICTIM THAT IS reasonably sufficient to incite THE PERSON into using deadly force, shall knowingly:

(1) Cause serious physical harm to another;
(2) Cause or attempt to cause physical harm to another by means of a deadly weapon or dangerous ordnance, as defined in section 2923.11 of the Revised Code.
(B) Whoever violates this section is guilty of aggravated assault, a felony of the fourth degree.

Comment

Three subsequent amendments to the section in 1983, S 199, H 269, S 210 picked up the original "extreme emotional stress" wording of division (A). The Legislative Service Commission advises that comparison of H 103 with S 199, H 269, and S 210 pursuant to section 1.52 of the Revised Code discloses that they are not irreconcilable, so that they are required by that section to be harmonized to give effect to each amendment.

The most recent amendment to subdivision (A) is H 37, an act which harmonizes "multiple prior amendments" and corrects "nonsubstantive errors." This amendment uses the "sudden passion" language.

§ 2903.13 Assault.

(A) No person shall knowingly cause or attempt to cause physical harm to another or to another's unborn.

(B) No person shall recklessly cause serious physical harm to another or to another's unborn.

(C) Whoever violates this section is guilty of assault. Except as otherwise provided in division (C)(1), (2), or (3) of this section, assault is a misdemeanor of the first degree.

(1) If the offense is committed by a caretaker against a functionally impaired person under the caretaker's care, assault is a felony of the fourth degree. If the offense is committed by a caretaker against a functionally impaired person under the caretaker's care, if the offender previously has been convicted of or pleaded guilty to a violation of this section or section 2903.11 or 2903.16 of the Revised Code, and if in relation to the previous conviction the offender was a caretaker and the victim was a functionally impaired person under the offender's care, assault is a felony of the third degree.

(2) If the offense is committed in any of the following circumstances, assault is a felony of the fifth degree:

(a) The offense occurs in or on the grounds of a state correctional institution or an institution of the department of youth services, the victim of the offense is an employee of the department of rehabilitation and correction, the department of youth services, or a probation department or is on the premises of the particular institution for business purposes or as a visitor, and the offense is committed by a person incarcerated in the state correctional institution, a person institutionalized in the department of youth services institution pursuant to a commitment to the department of youth services, or a probationer, furloughee, or parolee;

(b) The offense occurs in or on the grounds of a local correctional facility, the victim of the offense is an employee of the local correctional facility or a probation department or is on the premises of the facility for business purposes or as a visitor, and the offense is committed by a person who is under custody in the facility subsequent to the person's arrest for any crime or delinquent act, subsequent to the person's being charged with or convicted of any crime, or subsequent to the person's being alleged to be or adjudicated a delinquent child.

(c) The offense occurs off the grounds of a state correctional institution and off the grounds of an institution of the department of youth services, the victim of the offense is an employee of the department of rehabilitation and correction, the department of youth services, or a probation department, the offense occurs during the employee's official work hours and while the employee is engaged in official work responsibilities, and the offense is committed by a person incarcerated in a state correctional institution or institutionalized in the department of youth services who temporarily is outside of the institution for any purpose or by a probationer, parolee, or furloughee.

(d) The offense occurs off the grounds of a local correctional facility, the victim of the offense is an employee of the local correctional facility or a probation department, the offense occurs during the employee's official work hours and while the employee is engaged in official work responsibilities, and the offense is committed by a person who is under custody in the facility subsequent to the person's arrest for any crime or delinquent act, subsequent to the person being charged with or convicted of any crime, or subsequent to the person being alleged to be or adjudicated a delinquent child and who temporarily is outside of the facility for any purpose or by a probationer, parolee, or furloughee.

(e) The victim of the offense is a school teacher or administrator or a school bus operator, and the offense occurs on school premises, in a school building, on a school bus, or while the victim is outside of school premises or a school bus and is engaged in duties or official responsibilities associated with the victim's employment or position as a school teacher or administrator or a school bus operator, including, but not limited to, driving, accompanying, or chaperoning students at or on class or field trips, athletic events, or other school extracurricular activities or functions outside of school premises.

(3) If the victim of the offense is a peace officer, a fire fighter, or a person performing emergency medical service, while in the performance of their official duties, assault is a felony of the fourth degree.

(4) As used in this section:

(a) "Peace officer" has the same meaning as in section 2935.01 of the Revised Code.

(b) "Fire fighter" has the same meaning as in section 3937.41 of the Revised Code.

(c) "Emergency medical service" has the same meaning as in section 4765.01 of the Revised Code.

(d) "Local correctional facility" means a county, multicounty, municipal, municipal-county, or multicounty-municipal jail or workhouse, a minimum security jail established under section 341.23 or 753.21 of the Revised Code, or another county, multicounty, municipal, municipal-county, or multicounty-municipal facility used for the custody of persons arrested for any crime or delinquent act, persons charged with or convicted of any crime, or persons alleged to be or adjudicated a delinquent child.

(e) "Employee of a local correctional facility" means a person who is an employee of the political subdivision or of one or more of the affiliated political subdivisions that operates the local correctional facility and who operates or assists in the operation of the facility.

(f) "School," "school building," and "school premises" have the same meanings as in section 2925.01 of the Revised Code.

(g) "School teacher or administrator" means either of the following:

(i) A person who is employed in the public schools of the state under a contract described in section 3319.08 of the Revised Code in a position in which the person is required to have a certificate issued pursuant to sections 3319.22 to 3319.311 [3319.31.1] of the Revised Code.

(ii) A person who is employed by a nonpublic school for which the state board of education prescribes minimum standards under section 3301.07 of the Revised Code and who is certificated in accordance with section 3301.071 [3301.07.1] of the Revised Code.

(h) "School bus" has the same meaning as in section 4511.01 of the Revised Code.

HISTORY: 134 v H 511 (Eff 1-1-74); 142 v H 642 (Eff 3-17-89); 144 v H 561 (Eff 4-9-93); 145 v S 116 (Eff 9-29-94); 145 v H 571 (Eff 10-6-94); 146 v H 614 (Eff 6-16-96)†; 146 v S 2 (Eff 7-1-96); 146 v S 239 (Eff 9-6-96); 146 v H 480 (Eff 10-16-96); 147 v H 106. Eff 11-21-97.

Not analogous to former RC § 2903.13 (133 v H 84), repealed 134 v H 511, § 2, eff 1-1-74.

† The provisions of §§ 4, 5 of HB 614 (146 v —) read as follows:

SECTION 4. The text of RC 2903.13, as amended in Am. Sub. S.B. 116 and Am. Sub. H.B. 571 of the 120th General Assembly and harmonized pursuant to RC 1.52, as it should have been judicially noticed by the First District Court of Appeals of Ohio, Hamilton County, in *State v. Wilson*, No. C-950038 (November 8, 1995), reads as follows:

"Sec. 2903.13. (A) No person shall knowingly cause or attempt to cause physical harm to another.

(B) No person shall recklessly cause serious physical harm to another.

(C) Whoever violates this section is guilty of assault, a misdemeanor of the first degree.

(1) If the offense is committed by a caretaker against a functionally impaired person under his care, assault is a felony of the fourth degree. If the offense is committed by a caretaker against a functionally impaired person under his care, if the offender previously has been convicted of or pleaded guilty to a violation of this section or section 2903.11 or 2903.16 of the Revised Code, and if in relation to the previous conviction the offender was a caretaker and the victim was a functionally impaired person under the offender's care, assault is a felony of the third degree.

(2) If the offense is committed in any of the following circumstances, assault is a felony of the fourth degree, and the sentence of imprisonment imposed upon the offender shall be served consecutively to any other sentence of imprisonment imposed upon the offender:

(a) The offense occurs in or on the grounds of a state correctional institution or an institution of the department of youth services, the victim of the offense is an employee of the department of rehabilitation and correction, the department of youth services, or a probation department or is on the premises of the particular institution for business purposes or as a visitor, and the offense is committed by a person incarcerated in the state correctional institution, a person institutionalized in the department of youth services institution pursuant to a commitment to the department of youth services, or a probationer, furloughee, or parolee;

(b) The offense occurs in or on the grounds of a local correctional facility, the victim of the offense is an employee of the local correctional facility or a probation department or is on the premises of the facility for business purposes or as a visitor, and the offense is committed by a person who is under custody in the facility subsequent to his arrest for any crime or delinquent act, subsequent to his being charged with or convicted of any crime, or subsequent to his being alleged to be or adjudicated a delinquent child.

(c) The offense occurs off the grounds of a state correctional institution and off the grounds of an institution of the department of youth services, the victim of the offense is an employee of the department of rehabilitation and correction, the department of youth services, or a probation department, the offense occurs during the employee's official work hours and while he is engaged in official work responsibilities, and the offense is committed by a person incarcerated in a state correctional institution or institutionalized in the department of youth services who temporarily is outside of the institution for any purpose or by a probationer, parolee, or furloughee.

(d) The offense occurs off the grounds of a local correctional facility, the victim of the offense is an employee of the local correctional facility or a probation department, the offense occurs during the employee's official work hours and while he is engaged in official work responsibilities, and the offense is committed by a person who is under custody in the facility subsequent to his arrest for any crime or delinquent act, subsequent to his being charged with or convicted of any crime, or subsequent to his being alleged to be or adjudicated a delinquent child and who temporarily is outside of the facility for any purpose or by a probationer, parolee, or furloughee.

(3) If the victim of the offense is a peace officer, a fire fighter, or a person performing emergency medical service, while in the performance of their official duties, assault is a felony of the fourth degree.

(4) As used in this section:

(a) "Peace officer" has the same meaning as in section 2935.01 of the Revised Code.

(b) "Fire fighter" has the same meaning as in section 3937.41 of the Revised Code.

(c) "Emergency medical service" has the same meaning as in section 4765.01 of the Revised Code.

(d) "Local correctional facility" means any county, multicounty, municipal, municipal-county, or multicounty-municipal jail or workhouse, any minimum security misdemeanant jail established under section 341.23 or 753.21 of the Revised Code, or any other county, multicounty, municipal, municipal-county, or multicounty-municipal facility used for the custody of persons arrested for any crime or delinquent act, persons charged with or convicted of any crime, or persons alleged to be or adjudicated a delinquent child.

(e) "Employee of a local correctional facility" means any person who is an employee of the political subdivision or of one or more of the affiliated political subdivisions that operates the local correctional facility and who operates or assists in the operation of the facility."

SECTION 5. The presentation, in Section 4 of this act, of the harmonized text of RC 2903.13 is nonsubstantive and merely spells out the text of the section in effect at the time of the *Wilson* case as a result of the self-executing operation of RC 1.52 as applied to Am. Sub. S.B. 116 and Am. Sub. H.B. 571 of the 120th General Assembly.

The provisions of § 7 of SB 2 (146 v —) read as follows:

SECTION 7. ° ° ° Section 2903.13 of the Revised Code is presented in this act as a composite of the section as amended by both Am. Sub. H.B. 571 and Am. Sub. S.B. 116 of the 120th General Assembly, with the new language of neither of the acts shown in capital letters. ° ° ° This is in recognition of the principle stated in division (B) of section 1.52 of the Revised Code that such amendments are to be harmonized where not substantively irreconcilable and constitutes a legislative finding that such is the resulting version in effect prior to the effective date of this act.

Comment, Legislative Service Commission

° ° ° Section 2903.13 of the Revised Code is amended by this act [Am. Sub. S.B. 239] and also by Sub. H.B. 480 of the 121st General Assembly. ° ° ° Comparison of these amendments in pursuance of section 1.52 of the Revised Code discloses that they are not irreconcilable so that they are required by that section to be harmonized to give effect to each amendment.

§ 2903.14 Negligent assault.

(A) No person shall negligently, by means of a deadly weapon or dangerous ordnance as defined in section 2923.11 of the Revised Code, cause physical harm to another or to another's unborn.

(B) Whoever violates this section is guilty of negligent assault, a misdemeanor of the third degree.

HISTORY: 134 v H 511 (Eff 1-1-74); 146 v S 239. Eff 9-6-96.

Not analogous to former RC § 2903.14 (133 v H 84), repealed 134 v H 511, § 2, eff 1-1-74.

§ 2903.15 Repealed, 134 v H 511, § 2 [133 v H 84; 135 v S 62]. Eff 1-1-74.

This section concerned material and performances obscene or harmful to minors.

§ 2903.16 Failing to provide for a functionally impaired person.

(A) No caretaker shall knowingly fail to provide a functionally impaired person under the caretaker's care with any treatment, care, goods, or service that is necessary to maintain the health or safety of the functionally impaired person when this failure results in physical harm or serious physical harm to the functionally impaired person.

(B) No caretaker shall recklessly fail to provide a functionally impaired person under the caretaker's care with any treatment, care, goods, or service that is necessary to maintain the health or safety of the functionally impaired person when this failure results in serious physical harm to the functionally impaired person.

(C)(1) Whoever violates division (A) of this section is guilty of knowingly failing to provide for a functionally impaired person, a misdemeanor of the first degree. If the functionally impaired person under the offender's care suffers serious physical harm as a result of the violation of this section, a violation of division (A) of this section is a felony of the fourth degree.

(2) Whoever violates division (B) of this section is guilty of recklessly failing to provide for a functionally impaired person, a misdemeanor of the second degree. If the functionally impaired person under the offender's care suffers serious physical harm as a result of the violation of this section, a violation of division (B) of this section is a felony of the fourth degree.

HISTORY: 142 v H 642 (Eff 3-17-89); 146 v S 2. Eff 7-1-96.

Not analogous to former RC § 2903.16 (133 v H 84), repealed 134 v H 511, § 2, eff 1-1-74.

The effective date is set by section 6 of SB 2.

[MENACING]

§ 2903.21 Aggravated menacing.

(A) No person shall knowingly cause another to believe that the offender will cause serious physical harm to the person or property of such other person, such other person's unborn, or a member of the other person's immediate family.

(B) Whoever violates this section is guilty of aggra-

vated menacing, a misdemeanor of the first degree.
HISTORY: 134 v H 511 (Eff 1-1-74); 146 v S 239. Eff 9-6-96.

[STALKING]

[§ 2903.21.1] § 2903.211 Menacing by stalking.

(A) No person by engaging in a pattern of conduct shall knowingly cause another to believe that the offender will cause physical harm to the other person or cause mental distress to the other person.

(B) Whoever violates this section is guilty of menacing by stalking, a misdemeanor of the first degree. If the offender previously has been convicted of or pleaded guilty to a violation of this section involving the same person who is the victim of the current offense, menacing by stalking is a felony of the fifth degree.

(C) As used in this section:
(1) "Pattern of conduct" means two or more actions or incidents closely related in time, whether or not there has been a prior conviction based on any of those actions or incidents.
(2) "Mental distress" means any mental illness or condition that involves some temporary substantial incapacity or mental illness or condition that would normally require psychiatric treatment.

HISTORY: 144 v H 536 (Eff 11-5-92); 146 v S 2. Eff 7-1-96.

The effective date is set by section 6 of SB 2.

[§ 2903.21.2] § 2903.212 Consideration in setting amount and conditions of bail for violations of certain protection orders.

(A) Except when the complaint involves a person who is a family or household member as defined in section 2919.25 of the Revised Code, if a person is charged with a violation of section 2903.21, 2903.211 [2903.21.1], 2903.22, or 2911.211 [2911.21.1] of the Revised Code or a violation of a municipal ordinance that is substantially similar to one of those sections and if the person, at the time of the alleged violation, was subject to the terms of any order issued pursuant to section 2903.213 [2903.21.3], 2933.08, or 2945.04 of the Revised Code or previously had been convicted of or pleaded guilty to a violation of section 2903.21, 2903.211 [2903.21.1], 2903.22, or 2911.211 [2911.21.1] of the Revised Code that involves the same complainant or a violation of a municipal ordinance that is substantially similar to one of those sections and that involves the same complainant, the court shall consider all of the following, in addition to any other circumstances considered by the court and notwithstanding any provisions to the contrary contained in Criminal Rule 46, before setting the amount and conditions of the bail for the person:
(1) Whether the person has a history of violence toward the complainant or a history of other violent acts;
(2) The mental health of the person;
(3) Whether the person has a history of violating the orders of any court or governmental entity;
(4) Whether the person is potentially a threat to any other person;
(5) Whether setting bail at a high level will interfere with any treatment or counseling that the person is undergoing.

(B) Any court that has jurisdiction over violations of section 2903.21, 2903.211 [2903.21.1], 2903.22, or 2911.211 [2911.21.1] of the Revised Code or violations of a municipal ordinance that is substantially similar to one of those sections may set a schedule for bail to be used in cases involving those violations. The schedule shall require that a judge consider all of the factors listed in division (A) of this section and may require judges to set bail at a certain level or impose other reasonable conditions related to a release on bail or on recognizance if the history of the alleged offender or the circumstances of the alleged offense meet certain criteria in the schedule.

HISTORY: 144 v H 536. Eff 11-5-92.

[§ 2903.21.3] § 2903.213 Motion for issuance of anti-stalking protection order.

(A) Except when the complaint involves a person who is a family or household member as defined in section 2919.25 of the Revised Code, upon the filing of a complaint that alleges a violation of section 2903.21, 2903.211 [2903.21.1], 2903.22, or 2911.211 [2911.21.1] of the Revised Code, the complainant may file a motion that requests the issuance of an anti-stalking protection order as a pretrial condition of release of the alleged offender, in addition to any bail set under Criminal Rule 46. The motion shall be filed with the clerk of the court that has jurisdiction of the case at any time after the filing of the complaint. If the complaint involves a person who is a family or household member, the complainant may file a motion for a temporary protection order pursuant to section 2919.26 of the Revised Code.

(B) A motion for an anti-stalking protection order shall be prepared on a form that is provided by the clerk of the court, which form shall be substantially as follows:

"Motion for Anti-stalking Protection Order
.... Court
Name and address of court
State of Ohio
v.   No. ....
....
Name of Defendant

(Name of person), the complainant in the above-captioned case, moves the court to issue an anti-stalking protection order containing terms designed to ensure the safety and protection of the complainant in relation to the named defendant, pursuant to its authority to issue such an order under section 2903.213 [2903.21.3] of the Revised Code.

A complaint, a copy of which has been attached to this motion, has been filed in this court charging the named defendant with a violation of section 2903.21, 2903.211 [2903.21.1], 2903.22, or 2911.211 [2911.21.1] of the Revised Code.

I understand that I must appear before the court, at a time set by the court not later than the next day that the court is in session after the filing of this motion, for a hearing on the motion, and that any anti-stalking protection order granted pursuant to this motion is a pretrial condition of release and is effective only until the disposition of the criminal proceeding arising out of the attached complaint.

....
Signature of complainant
....
Address of complainant"

(C) As soon as possible after the filing of a motion that requests the issuance of an anti-stalking protection order, but not later than the next day that the court is in session after the filing of the motion, the court shall conduct a hearing to determine whether to issue the order. The complainant shall appear before the court and provide the court with the information that it requests concerning the basis of the motion. If the court finds that the safety and protection of the complainant may be impaired by the continued presence of the alleged offender, the court may issue an anti-stalking protection order, as a pretrial condition of release, that contains terms designed to ensure the safety and protection of the complainant, including a requirement that the alleged offender refrain from entering the residence, school, business, or place of employment of the complainant.

(D)(1) Except when the complaint involves a person who is a family or household member as defined in section 2919.25 of the Revised Code, upon the filing of a complaint that alleges a violation of section 2903.21, 2903.211 [2903.21.1], 2903.22, or 2911.211 [2911.21.1] of the Revised Code, the court, upon its own motion, may issue an anti-stalking protection order as a pretrial condition of release of the alleged offender if it finds that the safety and protection of the complainant may be impaired by the continued presence of the alleged offender.

(2) If the court issues an anti-stalking protection order under this section as an ex parte order, it shall conduct, as soon as possible after the issuance of the order but not later than the next day the court is in session after its issuance, a hearing to determine whether the order should remain in effect, be modified, or be revoked. The hearing shall be conducted under the standards set forth in division (C) of this section.

(E) An anti-stalking protection order that is issued as a pretrial condition of release under this section:

(1) Is in addition to, but shall not be construed as a part of, any bail set under Criminal Rule 46;

(2) Is effective only until the disposition of the criminal proceeding arising out of the complaint upon which it is based;

(3) Shall not be construed as a finding that the alleged offender committed the alleged offense, and shall not be introduced as evidence of the commission of the offense at the trial of the alleged offender on the complaint upon which the order is based.

(F) A person who meets the criteria for bail under Criminal Rule 46 and who, if required to do so pursuant to that rule, executes or posts bond or deposits cash or securities as bail, shall not be held in custody pending a hearing before the court on a motion requesting an anti-stalking protection order.

(G)(1) A copy of any anti-stalking protection order that is issued under this section shall be issued by the court to the complainant, to the defendant, and to all law enforcement agencies that have jurisdiction to enforce the order. The court shall direct that a copy of the order be delivered to the defendant on the same day that the order is entered.

(2) All law enforcement agencies shall establish and maintain an index for the anti-stalking protection orders delivered to the agencies pursuant to division (G)(1) of this section. With respect to each order delivered, each agency shall note on the index, the date and time of the receipt of the order by the agency.

(3) Any officer of a law enforcement agency shall enforce an anti-stalking protection order in accordance with the provisions of the order.

(H) Upon a violation of an anti-stalking protection order, the court may issue another anti-stalking protection order, as a pretrial condition of release, that modifies the terms of the order that was violated.

(I) Notwithstanding any provision of law to the contrary, no court shall charge a fee for the filing of a motion pursuant to this section.

HISTORY: 144 v H 536 (Eff 11-5-92); 145 v S 31. Eff 9-27-93.

[§§ 2903.21.4, 2903.21.5]
§§ 2903.214, 2903.215 Repealed, 146 v S 2, § 6 [144 v H 536]. Eff 7-1-96.

These sections concerned violation of anti-stalking protection order and evaluation of mental condition of defendant charged with such a violation.

§ 2903.22 Menacing.

(A) No person shall knowingly cause another to believe that the offender will cause physical harm to the person or property of such other person, such other person's unborn, or a member of the other person's immediate family.

(B) Whoever violates this section is guilty of menacing, a misdemeanor of the fourth degree.

HISTORY: 134 v H 511 (Eff 1-1-74); 146 v S 239. Eff 9-6-96.

§ 2903.31 Hazing.

(A) As used in this section, "hazing" means doing any act or coercing another, including the victim, to do any act of initiation into any student or other organization that causes or creates a substantial risk of causing mental or physical harm to any person.

(B)(1) No person shall recklessly participate in the hazing of another.

(2) No administrator, employee, or faculty member of any primary, secondary, or post-secondary school or of any other educational institution, public or private, shall recklessly permit the hazing of any person.

(C) Whoever violates this section is guilty of hazing, a misdemeanor of the fourth degree.

HISTORY: 139 v H 444. Eff 3-3-83.

[PATIENT ABUSE AND NEGLECT IN CARE FACILITIES]

§ 2903.33 Definitions.

As used in sections 2903.33 to 2903.36 of the Revised Code:

(A) "Care facility" means any of the following:

(1) Any "home" as defined in section 3721.10 or 5111.20 of the Revised Code;

(2) Any "residential facility" as defined in section 5123.19 of the Revised Code;

(3) Any institution or facility operated or provided by the department of mental health or by the department of mental retardation and developmental disabilities pursuant to sections 5119.02 and 5123.03 of the Revised Code;

(4) Any "residential facility" as defined in section 5119.22 of the Revised Code;

(5) Any unit of any hospital, as defined in section 3701.01 of the Revised Code, that provides the same services as a nursing home, as defined in section 3721.01 of the Revised Code;

(6) Any institution, residence, or facility that provides, for a period of more than twenty-four hours, whether for a consideration or not, accommodations to one individual or two unrelated individuals who are dependent upon the services of others;

(7) Any "adult care facility" as defined in section 3722.01 of the Revised Code;

(8) Any adult foster home certified by the department of aging or its designee under section 173.36 of the Revised Code;

(9) Any "community alternative home" as defined in section 3724.01 of the Revised Code.

(B) "Abuse" means knowingly causing physical harm or recklessly causing serious physical harm to a person by physical contact with the person or by the inappropriate use of a physical or chemical restraint, medication, or isolation on the person.

(C)(1) "Gross neglect" means knowingly failing to provide a person with any treatment, care, goods, or service that is necessary to maintain the health or safety of the person when the failure results in physical harm or serious physical harm to the person.

(2) "Neglect" means recklessly failing to provide a person with any treatment, care, goods, or service that is necessary to maintain the health or safety of the person when the failure results in serious physical harm to the person.

(D) "Inappropriate use of a physical or chemical restraint, medication, or isolation" means the use of physical or chemical restraint, medication, or isolation as punishment, for staff convenience, excessively, as a substitute for treatment, or in quantities that preclude habilitation and treatment.

HISTORY: 141 v H 566 (Eff 9-17-86); 142 v S 156 (Eff 7-1-88); 143 v S 2 (Eff 11-1-89); 143 v H 253 (Eff 11-15-90); 145 v H 152 (Eff 7-1-93); 145 v S 21 (Eff 10-29-93); 146 v S 2. Eff 7-1-96.

The effective date is set by section 6 of SB 2.

The provisions of § 7 of SB 2 (146 v —) read as follows:

SECTION 7. ° ° ° Section 2903.33 of the Revised Code is presented in this act as a composite of the section as amended by both Am. Sub. H.B. 152 and Am. Sub. S.B. 21 of the 120th General Assembly, with the new language of neither of the acts shown in capital letters. ° ° ° This is in recognition of the principle stated in division (B) of section 1.52 of the Revised Code that such amendments are to be harmonized where not substantively irreconcilable and constitutes a legislative finding that such is the resulting version in effect prior to the effective date of this act.

§ 2903.34 Patient abuse; neglect.

(A) No person who owns, operates, or administers, or who is an agent or employee of, a care facility shall do any of the following:

(1) Commit abuse against a resident or patient of the facility;

(2) Commit gross neglect against a resident or patient of the facility;

(3) Commit neglect against a resident or patient of the facility.

(B)(1) A person who relies upon treatment by spiritual means through prayer alone, in accordance with the tenets of a recognized religious denomination, shall not be considered neglected under division (A)(3) of this section for that reason alone.

(2) It is an affirmative defense to a charge of gross neglect or neglect under this section that the actor's conduct was committed in good faith solely because

the actor was ordered to commit the conduct by a person with supervisory authority over the actor.

(C) Whoever violates division (A)(1) of this section is guilty of patient abuse, a felony of the fourth degree. If the offender previously has been convicted of, or pleaded guilty to, any violation of this section, patient abuse is a felony of the third degree.

(D) Whoever violates division (A)(2) of this section is guilty of gross patient neglect, a misdemeanor of the first degree. If the offender previously has been convicted of, or pleaded guilty to, any violation of this section, gross patient neglect is a felony of the fifth degree.

(E) Whoever violates division (A)(3) of this section is guilty of patient neglect, a misdemeanor of the second degree. If the offender previously has been convicted of or pleaded guilty to any violation of this section, patient neglect is a felony of the fifth degree.

HISTORY: 141 v H 566 (Eff 9-17-86); 146 v S 2. Eff 7-1-96.

The effective date is set by section 6 of SB 2.

§ 2903.35 Filing false patient abuse or neglect complaints.

(A) No person shall knowingly make a false statement, or knowingly swear or affirm the truth of a false statement previously made, alleging a violation of section 2903.34 of the Revised Code, when the statement is made with purpose to incriminate another.

(B) Whoever violates this section is guilty of filing a false patient abuse or neglect complaint, a misdemeanor of the first degree.

HISTORY: 141 v H 566. Eff 9-17-86.

§ 2903.36 Discrimination, retaliation prohibited.

No care facility shall discharge or in any manner discriminate or retaliate against any person solely because such person, in good faith, filed a complaint, affidavit, or other document alleging a violation of section 2903.34 of the Revised Code.

HISTORY: 141 v H 566. Eff 9-17-86.

§ 2903.37 License revocation.

Any individual, who owns, operates, or administers, or who is an agent or employee of, a care facility, who is convicted of a felony violation of section 2903.34 of the Revised Code, and who is required to be licensed under any law of this state, shall have his license revoked in accordance with Chapter 119. of the Revised Code.

HISTORY: 141 v H 566. Eff 9-17-86.

CHAPTER 2905: KIDNAPPING AND EXTORTION

Section

[KIDNAPPING AND RELATED OFFENSES]

2905.01 Kidnapping.
2905.02 Abduction.
2905.03 Unlawful restraint.
[2905.03.1] 2905.031 Repealed.
2905.04 Repealed.
[2905.04.1] 2905.041 Repealed.
2905.05 Criminal child enticement.
2905.06-2905.10 Repealed.

[EXTORTION]

2905.11 Extortion.
2905.12 Coercion.
2905.13-2905.20 Repealed.

[EXTORTIONATE EXTENSION OF CREDIT; CRIMINAL USURY]

2905.21 Definitions.
2905.22 Extortionate extension of credit; criminal usury.
2905.23 Probable cause to believe that extension of credit was extortionate.
2905.24 Evidence of implicit threat as means of collection.
2905.25-2905.30 Repealed.
[2905.30.1] 2905.301 Repealed.
2905.31-2905.34 Repealed.
[2905.34.1-2905.34.3] 2905.341-2905.343 Repealed.
2905.35-2905.37 Repealed.
[2905.37.1] 2905.371 Repealed.
2905.38-2905.44 Repealed.

[KIDNAPPING AND RELATED OFFENSES]

§ 2905.01 Kidnapping.

(A) No person, by force, threat, or deception, or, in the case of a victim under the age of thirteen or mentally incompetent, by any means, shall remove another from the place where the other person is found or restrain the liberty of the other person, for any of the following purposes:

(1) To hold for ransom, or as a shield or hostage;

(2) To facilitate the commission of any felony or flight thereafter;

(3) To terrorize, or to inflict serious physical harm on the victim or another;

(4) To engage in sexual activity, as defined in section 2907.01 of the Revised Code, with the victim against the victim's will;

(5) To hinder, impede, or obstruct a function of government, or to force any action or concession on the part of governmental authority.

(B) No person, by force, threat, or deception, or, in the case of a victim under the age of thirteen or mentally incompetent, by any means, shall knowingly do any of the following, under circumstances that create a substantial risk of serious physical harm to the victim or, in the case of a minor victim, under circumstances that either create a substantial risk of serious physical harm to the victim or cause physical harm to the victim:

(1) Remove another from the place where the other person is found;

(2) Restrain another of his liberty;

(3) Hold another in a condition of involuntary servitude.

(C) Whoever violates this section is guilty of kidnapping, a felony of the first degree. If the offender releases the victim in a safe place unharmed, kidnapping is a felony of the second degree.

HISTORY: 134 v H 511 (Eff 1-1-74); 139 v S 199 (Eff 1-5-83); 146 v S 2. Eff 7-1-96.

Not analogous to former RC § 2905.01 (Bureau of Code Revision, 10-1-53), repealed 134 v H 511, § 2, eff 1-1-74.

The effective date is set by section 6 of SB 2.

§ 2905.02 Abduction.

(A) No person, without privilege to do so, shall knowingly do any of the following:

(1) By force or threat, remove another from the place where the other person is found;

(2) By force or threat, restrain the liberty of another person, under circumstances which create a risk of physical harm to the victim, or place the other person in fear;

(3) Hold another in a condition of involuntary servitude.

(B) Whoever violates this section is guilty of abduction, a felony of the third degree.

HISTORY: 134 v H 511 (Eff 1-1-74); 139 v S 199 (Eff 7-1-83); 146 v S 2. Eff 7-1-96.

Not analogous to former RC § 2905.02 (RS §§ 6816, 6817; S& C 404; 72 v 93; 84 v 65; 91 v 61; 92 v 54; 95 v 344; GC § 12413; Bureau of Code Revision, 10-1-53), repealed 134 v H 511, § 2, eff 1-1-74.

The effective date is set by section 6 of SB 2.

§ 2905.03 Unlawful restraint.

(A) No person, without privilege to do so, shall knowingly restrain another of his liberty.

(B) Whoever violates this section is guilty of unlawful restraint, a misdemeanor of the third degree.

HISTORY: 134 v H 511. Eff 1-1-74.

Not analogous to former RC § 2905.03 (RS §§ 6816, 6817; S& C 404; 72 v 93; 84 v 65; 91 v 61; 92 v 54; 95 v 344; GC § 12414; Bureau of Code Revision, 10-1-53), repealed 134 v H 511, § 2, eff 1-1-74.

Analogous to former RC § 2921.08 (RS § 6826; 69 v 189; 73 v 249; 95 v 69; 97 v 306; GC § 12426; Bureau of Code Revision, 10-1-53), repealed 134 v H 511, § 2, eff 1-1-74.

The effective date is set by section 4 of HB 511.

[§ 2905.03.1] § 2905.031 Repealed, 134 v H 511, § 2 [129 v 998]. Eff 1-1-74.

This section concerned rape of person under fourteen.

§ 2905.04 Repealed, 146 v S 2, §§ 2, 6 [134 v H 511; 140 v S 321]. Eff 7-1-96.

This section defined child stealing. See provisions of RC § 2905.01.

[§ 2905.04.1] § 2905.041 Repealed, 134 v H 511, § 2 [129 v 998]. Eff 1-1-74.

This section concerned attempted rape of person under fourteen.

§ 2905.05 Criminal child enticement.

(A) No person, by any means and without privilege to do so, shall knowingly solicit, coax, entice, or lure any child under fourteen years of age to enter into any vehicle, as defined in section 4501.01 of the Revised Code, whether or not the offender knows the age of the child, if both of the following apply:

(1) The actor does not have the express or implied permission of the parent, guardian, or other legal custodian of the child in undertaking the activity;

(2) The actor is not a law enforcement officer, medic, firefighter, or other person who regularly provides emergency services, and is not an employee or agent of, or a volunteer acting under the direction of, any board of education, or the actor is any of such persons, but, at the time the actor undertakes the activity, the actor is not acting within the scope of the actor's lawful duties in that capacity.

(B) It is an affirmative defense to a charge under division (A) of this section that the actor undertook the activity in response to a bona fide emergency situation or that the actor undertook the activity in a reasonable belief that it was necessary to preserve the health, safety, or welfare of the child.

(C) Whoever violates this section is guilty of criminal child enticement, a misdemeanor of the first degree. If the offender previously has been convicted of a violation of this section, section 2907.02, 2907.03, or 2907.12 of the Revised Code, or section 2905.01 or 2907.05 of the Revised Code when the victim of that prior offense was under seventeen years of age at the time of the offense, criminal child enticement is a felony of the fifth degree.

HISTORY: 140 v S 321 (Eff 4-9-85); 146 v S 2. Eff 7-1-96.

Not analogous to former RC § 2905.05 (GC § 13444-24; 113 v 123(191), ch 23, § 24; Bureau of Code Revision, 10-1-53), repealed 134 v H 511, § 2, eff 1-1-74.

The effective date is set by section 6 of SB 2.

§§ 2905.06, 2905.07, 2905.08 Repealed, 134 v H 511, § 2 [RS §§ 7019—7021; S&C 404, 405, 430, 431; 29 v 144; 33 v 33; GC §§ 13023—13025; Bureau of Code Revision, 10-1-53]. Eff 1-1-74.

These sections concerned carnal knowledge, incest, and adultery.

§§ 2905.09, 2905.10 Repealed, 134 v H 511, § 2 [RS §§ 7022, 7023; S&S 273; S&C 452; 56 v 158; 65 v 204; 82 v 209; 84 v 43; 92 v 207; GC §§ 13026, 13027; Bureau of Code Revision, 10-1-53; 126 v 575]. Eff 1-1-74.

These sections dealt with seduction under promise to marry and inducing or permitting illicit intercourse.

[EXTORTION]

§ 2905.11 Extortion.

(A) No person, with purpose to obtain any valuable thing or valuable benefit or to induce another to do an unlawful act, shall do any of the following:

(1) Threaten to commit any felony;

(2) Threaten to commit any offense of violence;

(3) Violate section 2903.21 or 2903.22 of the Revised Code;

(4) Utter or threaten any calumny against any person;

(5) Expose or threaten to expose any matter tending to subject any person to hatred, contempt, or ridicule, or to damage any person's personal or business repute, or to impair any person's credit.

(B) Whoever violates this section is guilty of extortion, a felony of the third degree.

(C) As used in this section, "threat" includes a direct threat and a threat by innuendo.

HISTORY: 134 v H 511 (Eff 1-1-74); 139 v S 199 (Eff 7-1-83); 146 v S 2. Eff 7-1-96.

Not analogous to former RC § 2905.11 (RS § 7023a; 82 v 209; GC § 13028; Bureau of Code Revision, 10-1-53), repealed 134 v H 511, § 2, eff 1-1-74.

The effective date is set by section 6 of SB 2.

§ 2905.12 Coercion.

(A) No person, with purpose to coerce another into taking or refraining from action concerning which he has a legal freedom of choice, shall do any of the following:

(1) Threaten to commit any offense;

(2) Utter or threaten any calumny against any person;

(3) Expose or threaten to expose any matter tending to subject any person to hatred, contempt, or ridicule, or to damage his personal or business repute, or to impair his credit;

(4) Institute or threaten criminal proceedings against any person;

(5) Take or withhold, or threaten to take or withhold official action, or cause or threaten to cause official action to be taken or withheld.

(B) Divisions (A)(4) and (5) of this section shall not be construed to prohibit a prosecutor or court from doing any of the following in good faith and in the interests of justice:

(1) Offering or agreeing to grant, or granting immunity from prosecution pursuant to section 2945.44 of the Revised Code;

(2) In return for a plea of guilty to one or more offenses charged or to one or more other or lesser offenses, or in return for the testimony of the accused in a case to which he is not a party, offering or agreeing to dismiss, or dismissing one or more charges pending against an accused, or offering or agreeing to impose, or imposing a certain sentence or modification of sentence;

(3) Imposing probation on certain conditions, including without limitation requiring the offender to make restitution or redress to the victim of his offense.

(C) It is an affirmative defense to a charge under division (A)(3), (4), or (5) of this section that the actor's conduct was a reasonable response to the circumstances which occasioned it, and that his purpose was limited to:

(1) Compelling another to refrain from misconduct or to desist from further misconduct;

(2) Preventing or redressing a wrong or injustice;

(3) Preventing another from taking action for which the actor reasonably believed such other person to be disqualified;

(4) Compelling another to take action which the actor reasonably believed such other person to be under a duty to take.

(D) Whoever violates this section is guilty of coercion, a misdemeanor of the second degree.

(E) As used in this section, "threat" includes a direct threat and a threat by innuendo.

HISTORY: 134 v H 511. Eff 1-1-74.

Not analogous to former RC § 2905.12 (RS § 6824; S&S 275; 65 v 87; 79 v 132; 95 v 100; GC § 13029; Bureau of Code Revision, 10-1-53), repealed 134 v H 511, § 2, eff 1-1-74.

The effective date is set by section 4 of HB 511.

§§ 2905.13, 2905.14, 2905.15

Repealed, 134 v H 511, § 2 [RS §§ 7024, 7025; S&C 879; 53 v 140; 75 v 142; 83 v 92; 85 v 137; 92 v 398; GC §§ 13030—13031-1; 101 v 50; 103 v 188; Bureau of Code Revision, 10-1-53]. Eff 1-1-74.

These sections concerned intercourse with female pupil and prostitution.

§§ 2905.16, 2905.17, 2905.18

Repealed, 134 v H 511, § 2 [GC §§ 13031-2, 13031-3, 13031-9; 101 v 50; 103 v 188; Bureau of Code Revision, 10-1-53]. Eff 1-1-74.

These sections concerned prostitution.

§§ 2905.19, 2905.20

Repealed, 134 v H 511, § 2 [GC §§ 13031-4, 13031-5; 101 v 50; 103 v 188; Bureau of Code Revision, 10-1-53]. Eff 1-1-74.

These sections concerned prostitution.

[EXTORTIONATE EXTENSION OF CREDIT; CRIMINAL USURY]

§ 2905.21 Definitions.

As used in sections 2905.21 to 2905.24 of the Revised Code:

(A) "To extend credit" means to make or renew any loan, or to enter into any agreement, express or implied, for the repayment or satisfaction of any debt or claim, regardless of whether the extension of credit is acknowledged or disputed, valid or invalid, and however arising.

(B) "Creditor" means any person who extends credit, or any person claiming by, under, or through such a person.

(C) "Debtor" means any person who receives an extension of credit, any person who guarantees the repayment of an extension of credit, or any person who in any manner undertakes to indemnify the creditor against loss resulting from the failure of any recipient to repay an extension of credit.

(D) "Repayment" of an extension of credit means the repayment, satisfaction, or discharge in whole or in part of any debt or claim, acknowledged or disputed, valid or invalid, resulting from or in connection with that extension of credit.

(E) "Collect an extension of credit" means an attempt to collect from a debtor all or part of an amount due from the extension of credit.

(F) "Extortionate extension of credit" means any extension of credit with respect to which it is the understanding of the creditor and the debtor at the time it is made that delay in making repayment or failure to make repayment will result in the use of an extortionate means or if the debtor at a later time learns that failure to make repayment will result in the use of extortionate means.

(G) "Extortionate means" is any means that involves the use, or an express or implicit threat of use, of violence or other criminal means to cause harm to the person or property of the debtor or any member of his family.

(H) "Criminal usury" means illegally charging, taking, or receiving any money or other property as interest on an extension of credit at a rate exceeding twenty-five per cent per annum or the equivalent rate for a longer or shorter period, unless either:

(1) The rate of interest is otherwise authorized by law;

(2) The creditor and the debtor, or all the creditors and all the debtors are members of the same immediate family.

(I) "Immediate family" means a person's spouse residing in the person's household, brothers and sisters of the whole or of the half blood, and children, including adopted children.

HISTORY: 137 v H 88. Eff 10-9-78.

Not analogous to former RC § 2905.21 (GC § 13031-6; 101 v 50, § 6; 103 v 188; Bureau of Code Revision, 10-1-53), repealed 134 v H 511, § 2, eff 1-1-74.

§ 2905.22 Extortionate extension of credit; criminal usury.

(A) No person shall:
(1) Knowingly make or participate in an extortionate extension of credit;
(2) Knowingly engage in criminal usury;
(3) Possess any writing, paper, instrument, or article used to record criminally usurious transactions, knowing that the contents record a criminally usurious transaction.
(B) Whoever violates division (A)(1) or (2) of this section is guilty of a felony of the fourth degree. Whoever violates division (A)(3) of this section is guilty of a misdemeanor of the first degree.

HISTORY: 137 v H 88 (Eff 10-9-78); 146 v S 2. Eff 7-1-96.

Not analogous to former RC § 2905.22 (GC § 13031-7; 101 v 50; Bureau of Code Revision, 10-1-53), repealed 134 v H 511, § 2, eff 1-1-74.

The effective date is set by section 6 of SB 2.

§ 2905.23 Probable cause to believe that extension of credit was extortionate.

In any prosecution under sections 2905.21 to 2905.24 of the Revised Code, if it is shown that any of the following factors were present in connection with the extension of credit, there is probable cause to believe that the extension of credit was extortionate:
(A) The extension of credit was made at a rate of interest in excess of that established for criminal usury;
(B) At the time credit was extended, the debtor reasonably believed that:
(1) One or more extensions of credit by the creditor were collected or attempted to be collected by extortionate means, or the nonrepayment thereof was punished by extortionate means;
(2) The creditor had a reputation for the use of extortionate means to collect extensions of credit or punish the nonrepayment thereof.

HISTORY: 137 v H 88. Eff 10-9-78.

Not analogous to former RC § 2905.23 (GC § 13031-10; 103 v 188; Bureau of Code Revision, 10-1-53), repealed 134 v H 511, § 2, eff 1-1-74.

§ 2905.24 Evidence of implicit threat as means of collection.

In any prosecution under sections 2905.21 to 2905.24 of the Revised Code, for the purpose of showing an implicit threat as a means of collection, evidence may be introduced tending to show that one or more extensions of credit by the creditor were, to the knowledge of the person against whom the implicit threat is alleged to have been made, collected, or attempted to be collected by extortionate means or that the nonrepayment thereof was punished by extortionate means.

HISTORY: 137 v H 88. Eff 10-9-78.

Not analogous to former RC § 2905.24 (GC § 13031-8; 101 v 50; Bureau of Code Revision, 10-1-53), repealed 134 v H 511, § 2, eff 1-1-74.

§§ 2905.25, 2905.26, 2905.27

Repealed, 134 v H 511, § 2 [GC §§ 13031-11, 13031-13, 13031-14; 103 v 188; 108 v PtI, 730; Bureau of Code Revision, 10-1-53; 130 v PtII, 143, 144]. Eff 1-1-74.

These sections concerned prostitution.

§§ 2905.28, 2905.29, 2905.30

Repealed, 134 v H 511, § 2 [RS § 7026; S&S 289; 59 v 32; 89 v 127; GC §§ 13031-15, 13031-17, 13032; 108 v PtI, 730; 118 v 301, 121 v 557; Bureau of Code Revision, 10-1-53; 129 v 1670; 130 v PtII, 143, 144, 659; 131 v 672]. Eff 1-1-74.

These sections concerned prostitution, indecent exposure, and obscene language.

[§ 2905.30.1] § 2905.301 Repealed,

134 v H 511, § 2 [130 v 659]. Eff 1-1-74.

This section concerned obscene language.

§§ 2905.31, 2905.32, 2905.33

Repealed, 134 v H 511, § 2 [RS §§ 7029, 7030; S&S 272; 64 v 202; GC §§ 13032-1, 13033, 13034; 118 v 428; 121 v 557(573); Bureau of Code Revision, 10-1-53]. Eff 1-1-74.

These sections concerned nudism, abortion and miscarriage.

§ 2905.34 Repealed, 134 v H 511, § 2 [RS § 7027; 73 v 158; 82 v 184; 91 v 330; GC § 13035; 118 v 420; 120 v 230; Bureau of Code Revision, 10-1-53; 131 v 672; 133 v H 84]. Eff 1-1-74.

This section prohibited the selling, exhibiting, and possessing of obscene literature or drugs for criminal purposes.

[§§ 2905.34.1, 2905.34.2, 2905.-34.3]
§§ 2905.341, 2905.342, 2905.343

Repealed, 133 v H 84, § 2 [126 v 1039]. Eff 9-15-70.

These sections prohibited conditional sales of obscene magazines, exhibition of films, and depicting public disorder.

§§ 2905.35, 2905.36, 2905.37

Repealed, 134 v H 511, § 2 [133 v H 84]. Eff 1-1-74.

These sections concerned obscene material.

[§ 2905.37.1] § 2905.371 Repealed, 133 v H 84, § 2 [129 v 1400]. Eff 9-15-70.

This section provided immunity from the provisions of former RC §§ 2905.34 to 2905.37 and RC § 2933.21.

§ 2905.38 Repealed, 134 v H 511, § 2 [133 v H 84; 135 v S 62, eff 10-31-73]. Eff 1-1-74.

This section concerned obscene matter.

§§ 2905.39, 2905.40, 2905.41

Repealed, 133 v H 84, § 2 [RS §§ 7027-1—7027-3; 86 v 320; 98 v 303; GC §§ 13039—13041; 100 v 91; Bureau of Code Revision, 10-1-53]. Eff 9-15-70.

These sections concerned lewd pictures and exhibitions.

§§ 2905.42, 2905.43, 2905.44

Repealed, 134 v H 511, § 2 [RS §§ 6989, 7018, 7021-1; S&C 404, 1396; 9 v 115; 33 v 33; 82 v 241; 86 v 251; GC §§ 13022, 13042, 13043; 121 v 417; Bureau of Code Revision, 10-1-53; 129 v 252]. Eff 1-1-74.

These sections concerned enticing to abandon marriage, bigamy, and sodomy.

CHAPTER 2907: SEX OFFENSES

Section

[IN GENERAL]

2907.01　Definitions.

[SEXUAL ASSAULTS]

2907.02　Rape.
[2907.02.1] 2907.021　Repealed.
2907.03　Sexual battery.
2907.04　Corruption of a minor.
2907.05　Gross sexual imposition.
2907.06　Sexual imposition.
2907.07　Importuning.
2907.08　Voyeurism.
[2907.08.1, 2907.08.2] 2907.081, 2907.082　Repealed.
2907.09　Public indecency.
2907.10　Repealed.
2907.11　Victim or offender may request temporary suppression of information.
2907.12　Repealed.
[2907.12.1] 2907.121　Repealed.
2907.13, 2907.14　Repealed.
[2907.14.1-2907.14.5] 2907.141-2907.145　Repealed.
2907.15　Motion for withholding of restitution needed from government deferred compensation or public retirement system payment.
2907.16-2907.20　Repealed.
[2907.20.1] 2907.201　Repealed.

[PROSTITUTION]

2907.21　Compelling prostitution.
2907.22　Promoting prostitution.
2907.23　Procuring.
2907.24　Soliciting; after positive HIV test.
[2907.24.1] 2907.241　Loitering to engage in solicitation; solicitation after positive HIV test.
2907.25　Prostitution; after positive HIV test.
2907.26　Rules of evidence in prostitution cases.
2907.27　Testing of accused for venereal diseases and HIV.

[MEDICAL ASSISTANCE FOR VICTIMS]

2907.28　Payment of cost of medical examination and test of victim or accused.
2907.29　Hospital emergency services for victims.
2907.30　Victim to be interviewed by crisis intervention trained officer.

[OBSCENITY]

2907.31　Disseminating matter harmful to juveniles.
[2907.31.1] 2907.311　Displaying matter harmful to juveniles.
2907.32　Pandering obscenity.
[2907.32.1] 2907.321　Pandering obscenity involving a minor.
[2907.32.2] 2907.322　Pandering sexually oriented matter involving a minor.
[2907.32.3] 2907.323　Illegal use of minor in nudity-oriented material or performance.
2907.33　Deception to obtain matter harmful to juveniles.
2907.34　Compelling acceptance of objectionable materials.
2907.35　Presumptions; notice.
2907.36　Declaratory judgment.
2907.37　Injunction.
2907.38-2907.40　Repealed.
2907.41　Renumbered.

Section

2907.42-2907.48　Repealed.

[IN GENERAL]

§ 2907.01　Definitions.

As used in sections 2907.01 to 2907.37 of the Revised Code:

(A) "Sexual conduct" means vaginal intercourse between a male and female; anal intercourse, fellatio, and cunnilingus between persons regardless of sex; and the insertion, however slight, of any part of the body or any instrument, apparatus, or other object into the vaginal or anal cavity of another. Penetration, however slight, is sufficient to complete vaginal or anal intercourse.

(B) "Sexual contact" means any touching of an erogenous zone of another, including without limitation the thigh, genitals, buttock, pubic region, or, if the person is a female, a breast, for the purpose of sexually arousing or gratifying either person.

(C) "Sexual activity" means sexual conduct or sexual contact, or both.

(D) "Prostitute" means a male or female who promiscuously engages in sexual activity for hire, regardless of whether the hire is paid to the prostitute or to another.

(E) Any material or performance is "harmful to juveniles," if it is offensive to prevailing standards in the adult community with respect to what is suitable for juveniles, and if any of the following apply:

(1) It tends to appeal to the prurient interest of juveniles;

(2) It contains a display, description, or representation of sexual activity, masturbation, sexual excitement, or nudity;

(3) It contains a display, description, or representation of bestiality or extreme or bizarre violence, cruelty, or brutality;

(4) It contains a display, description, or representation of human bodily functions of elimination;

(5) It makes repeated use of foul language;

(6) It contains a display, description, or representation in lurid detail of the violent physical torture, dismemberment, destruction, or death of a human being;

(7) It contains a display, description, or representation of criminal activity that tends to glorify or glamorize the activity, and that, with respect to juveniles, has a dominant tendency to corrupt.

(F) When considered as a whole, and judged with reference to ordinary adults or, if it is designed for sexual deviates or other specially susceptible group, judged with reference to that group, any material or performance is "obscene" if any of the following apply:

(1) Its dominant appeal is to prurient interest;

(2) Its dominant tendency is to arouse lust by dis-

playing or depicting sexual activity, masturbation, sexual excitement, or nudity in a way that tends to represent human beings as mere objects of sexual appetite;

(3) Its dominant tendency is to arouse lust by displaying or depicting bestiality or extreme or bizarre violence, cruelty, or brutality;

(4) Its dominant tendency is to appeal to scatological interest by displaying or depicting human bodily functions of elimination in a way that inspires disgust or revulsion in persons with ordinary sensibilities, without serving any genuine scientific, educational, sociological, moral, or artistic purpose;

(5) It contains a series of displays or descriptions of sexual activity, masturbation, sexual excitement, nudity, bestiality, extreme or bizarre violence, cruelty, or brutality, or human bodily functions of elimination, the cumulative effect of which is a dominant tendency to appeal to prurient or scatological interest, when the appeal to such an interest is primarily for its own sake or for commercial exploitation, rather than primarily for a genuine scientific, educational, sociological, moral, or artistic purpose.

(G) "Sexual excitement" means the condition of human male or female genitals when in a state of sexual stimulation or arousal.

(H) "Nudity" means the showing, representation, or depiction of human male or female genitals, pubic area, or buttocks with less than a full, opaque covering, or of a female breast with less than a full, opaque covering of any portion thereof below the top of the nipple, or of covered male genitals in a discernibly turgid state.

(I) "Juvenile" means an unmarried person under the age of eighteen.

(J) "Material" means any book, magazine, newspaper, pamphlet, poster, print, picture, figure, image, description, motion picture film, phonographic record, or tape, or other tangible thing capable of arousing interest through sight, sound, or touch.

(K) "Performance" means any motion picture, preview, trailer, play, show, skit, dance, or other exhibition performed before an audience.

(L) "Spouse" means a person married to an offender at the time of an alleged offense, except that such person shall not be considered the spouse when any of the following apply:

(1) When the parties have entered into a written separation agreement authorized by section 3103.06 of the Revised Code;

(2) During the pendency of an action between the parties for annulment, divorce, dissolution of marriage, or legal separation;

(3) In the case of an action for legal separation, after the effective date of the judgment for legal separation.

(M) "Minor" means a person under the age of eighteen.

HISTORY: 134 v H 511 (Eff 1-1-74); 136 v S 144 (Eff 8-27-75); 142 v H 51 (Eff 3-17-89); 143 v H 514 (Eff 1-1-91); 146 v H 445. Eff 9-3-96.

Not analogous to former RC § 2907.01 (RS § 6830-3; 95 v 649; GC § 13387; Bureau of Code Revision, 10-1-53), repealed 134 v H 511, § 2, eff 1-1-74.

[SEXUAL ASSAULTS]

§ 2907.02 Rape.

(A)(1) No person shall engage in sexual conduct with another who is not the spouse of the offender or who is the spouse of the offender but is living separate and apart from the offender, when any of the following applies:

(a) For the purpose of preventing resistance, the offender substantially impairs the other person's judgment or control by administering any drug or intoxicant to the other person, surreptitiously or by force, threat of force, or deception.

(b) The other person is less than thirteen years of age, whether or not the offender knows the age of the other person.

(c) The other person's ability to resist or consent is substantially impaired because of a mental or physical condition or because of advanced age, and the offender knows or has reasonable cause to believe that the other person's ability to resist or consent is substantially impaired because of a mental or physical condition or because of advanced age.

(2) No person shall engage in sexual conduct with another when the offender purposely compels the other person to submit by force or threat of force.

(B) Whoever violates this section is guilty of rape, a felony of the first degree. If the offender under division (A)(1)(b) of this section purposely compels the victim to submit by force or threat of force, whoever violates division (A)(1)(b) of this section shall be imprisoned for life.

(C) A victim need not prove physical resistance to the offender in prosecutions under this section.

(D) Evidence of specific instances of the victim's sexual activity, opinion evidence of the victim's sexual activity, and reputation evidence of the victim's sexual activity shall not be admitted under this section unless it involves evidence of the origin of semen, pregnancy, or disease, or the victim's past sexual activity with the offender, and only to the extent that the court finds that the evidence is material to a fact at issue in the case and that its inflammatory or prejudicial nature does not outweigh its probative value.

Evidence of specific instances of the defendant's sexual activity, opinion evidence of the defendant's sexual activity, and reputation evidence of the defendant's sexual activity shall not be admitted under this section unless it involves evidence of the origin of semen, pregnancy, or disease, the defendant's past sexual activity with the victim, or is admissible against the defendant under section 2945.59 of the Revised Code, and only to the extent that the court finds that the evidence is material to a fact at issue in the case and that its inflammatory or prejudicial nature does not outweigh its probative value.

(E) Prior to taking testimony or receiving evidence of any sexual activity of the victim or the defendant in a proceeding under this section, the court shall resolve the admissibility of the proposed evidence in a hearing in chambers, which shall be held at or before preliminary hearing and not less than three days before trial, or for good cause shown during the trial.

(F) Upon approval by the court, the victim may be represented by counsel in any hearing in chambers or other proceeding to resolve the admissibility of evidence. If the victim is indigent or otherwise is unable to obtain the services of counsel, the court, upon request, may appoint counsel to represent the victim without cost to the victim.

(G) It is not a defense to a charge under division (A)(2) of this section that the offender and the victim were married or were cohabiting at the time of the commission of the offense.

HISTORY: 134 v H 511 (Eff 1-1-74); 136 v S 144 (Eff 8-27-75); 139 v S 199 (Eff 7-1-83); 141 v H 475 (Eff 3-7-86); 145 v S 31 (Eff 9-27-93); 146 v S 2. Eff 7-1-96.

Not analogous to former RC § 2907.02 (RS § 6831; S&C 406; S&S 267, 268; 33 v 33; 60 v 85; 66 v 122; 83 v 81; 86 v 3; GC § 12433; 113 v 541; Bureau of Code Revision, 10-1-53; 131 v 673), repealed 134 v H 511, § 2, eff 1-1-74.

The effective date is set by section 6 of SB 2.

[§ 2907.02.1] § 2907.021 Repealed,
134 v H 511, § 2 [132 v H 179; 133 v H 1]. Eff 1-1-74.

This section concerned prohibition of manufacture, distribution or possession of fire bombs.

§ 2907.03 Sexual battery.

(A) No person shall engage in sexual conduct with another, not the spouse of the offender, when any of the following apply:

(1) The offender knowingly coerces the other person to submit by any means that would prevent resistance by a person of ordinary resolution.

(2) The offender knows that the other person's ability to appraise the nature of or control the other person's own conduct is substantially impaired.

(3) The offender knows that the other person submits because the other person is unaware that the act is being committed.

(4) The offender knows that the other person submits because the other person mistakenly identifies the offender as the other person's spouse.

(5) The offender is the other person's natural or adoptive parent, or a stepparent, or guardian, custodian, or person in loco parentis of the other person.

(6) The other person is in custody of law or a patient in a hospital or other institution, and the offender has supervisory or disciplinary authority over the other person.

(7) The offender is a teacher, administrator, coach, or other person in authority employed by or serving in a school for which the state board of education prescribes minimum standards pursuant to division (D) of section 3301.07 of the Revised Code, the other person is enrolled in or attends that school, and the offender is not enrolled in and does not attend that school.

(8) The other person is a minor, the offender is a teacher, administrator, coach, or other person in authority employed by or serving in an institution of higher education, and the other person is enrolled in or attends that institution.

(9) The other person is a minor, and the offender is the other person's athletic or other type of coach, is the other person's instructor, is the leader of a scouting troop of which the other person is a member, or is a person with temporary or occasional disciplinary control over the other person.

(B) Whoever violates this section is guilty of sexual battery. A violation of division (A)(1), (5), (6), (7), (8), or (9) of this section is a felony of the third degree. A violation of division (A)(2), (3), or (4) of this section is a felony of the fourth degree.

(C) As used in this section, "institution of higher education" means a state institution of higher education defined in section 3345.011 [3345.01.1] of the Revised Code, a private nonprofit college or university located in this state that possesses a certificate of authorization issued by the Ohio board of regents pursuant to Chapter 1713. of the Revised Code, or a school certified under Chapter 3332. of the Revised Code.

HISTORY: 134 v H 511 (Eff 1-1-74); 145 v H 454 (Eff 7-19-94); 146 v S 2 (Eff 7-1-96); 147 v S 6. Eff 6-20-97.

Not analogous to former RC § 2907.03 (GC § 12433-1; 113 v 541; Bureau of Code Revision, 10-1-53), repealed 134 v H 511, § 2, eff 1-1-74.

The effective date is set by section 6 of SB 6.

The provisions of § 6 of SB 6 (147 v —) read as follows:

SECTION 6. Except for this section and Section 4 of this act, which appropriate or relate to the appropriation of money, the codified and uncodified sections of law contained in this act are subject to the referendum. Therefore, under Ohio Constitution, Article II, Section 1c and section 1.471 of the Revised Code, the codified and uncodified sections of law contained in this act, except this section and Section 4 of this act, take effect on the ninety-first day after this act is filed with the Secretary of State. If, however, a referendum petition is filed against a section, the section, unless rejected at the referendum, takes effect at the earliest time permitted by law.

This section and Section 4 of this act, which appropriate or relate to the appropriation of money, are not subject to the referendum. Therefore, under Ohio Constitution, Article II, Section 1d and section 1.471 of the Revised Code, this section and Section 4 of this act go into immediate effect when this act becomes law.

§ 2907.04 Corruption of a minor.

(A) No person who is eighteen years of age or older

shall engage in sexual conduct with another, who is not the spouse of the offender, when the offender knows the other person is thirteen years of age or older but less than sixteen years of age, or the offender is reckless in that regard.

(B) Whoever violates this section is guilty of corruption of a minor, a felony of the fourth degree. If the offender is less than four years older than the other person, corruption of a minor is a misdemeanor of the first degree.

HISTORY: 134 v H 511 (Eff 1-1-74); 143 v H 44 (Eff 7-24-90); 146 v S 2. Eff 7-1-96.

Not analogous to former RC § 2907.04 (RS § 6832; S&C 457a, 457b; 57 v 49; GC § 12434; 113 v 541; Bureau of Code Revision, 10-1-53), repealed 134 v H 511, § 2, eff 1-1-74.

The effective date is set by section 6 of SB 2.

§ 2907.05 Gross sexual imposition.

(A) No person shall have sexual contact with another, not the spouse of the offender; cause another, not the spouse of the offender, to have sexual contact with the offender; or cause two or more other persons to have sexual contact when any of the following applies:

(1) The offender purposely compels the other person, or one of the other persons, to submit by force or threat of force.

(2) For the purpose of preventing resistance, the offender substantially impairs the judgment or control of the other person or of one of the other persons by administering any drug or intoxicant to the other person, surreptitiously or by force, threat of force, or deception.

(3) The offender knows that the judgment or control of the other person or of one of the other persons is substantially impaired as a result of the influence of any drug or intoxicant administered to the other person with his consent for the purpose of any kind of medical or dental examination, treatment, or surgery.

(4) The other person, or one of the other persons, is less than thirteen years of age, whether or not the offender knows the age of that person.

(5) The ability of the other person to resist or consent or the ability of one of the other persons to resist or consent is substantially impaired because of a mental or physical condition or because of advanced age, and the offender knows or has reasonable cause to believe that the ability to resist or consent of the other person or of one of the other persons is substantially impaired because of a mental or physical condition or because of advanced age.

(B) Whoever violates this section is guilty of gross sexual imposition. Violation of division (A)(1), (2), (3), or (5) of this section is a felony of the fourth degree. Violation of division (A)(4) of this section is a felony of the third degree.

(C) A victim need not prove physical resistance to the offender in prosecutions under this section.

(D) Evidence of specific instances of the victim's sexual activity, opinion evidence of the victim's sexual activity, and reputation evidence of the victim's sexual activity shall not be admitted under this section unless it involves evidence of the origin of semen, pregnancy, or disease, or the victim's past sexual activity with the offender, and only to the extent that the court finds that the evidence is material to a fact at issue in the case and that its inflammatory or prejudicial nature does not outweigh its probative value.

Evidence of specific instances of the defendant's sexual activity, opinion evidence of the defendant's sexual activity, and reputation evidence of the defendant's sexual activity shall not be admitted under this section unless it involves evidence of the origin of semen, pregnancy, or disease, the defendant's past sexual activity with the victim, or is admissible against the defendant under section 2945.59 of the Revised Code, and only to the extent that the court finds that the evidence is material to a fact at issue in the case and that its inflammatory or prejudicial nature does not outweigh its probative value.

(E) Prior to taking testimony or receiving evidence of any sexual activity of the victim or the defendant in a proceeding under this section, the court shall resolve the admissibility of the proposed evidence in a hearing in chambers, which shall be held at or before preliminary hearing and not less than three days before trial, or for good cause shown during the trial.

(F) Upon approval by the court, the victim may be represented by counsel in any hearing in chambers or other proceeding to resolve the admissibility of evidence. If the victim is indigent or otherwise is unable to obtain the services of counsel, the court, upon request, may appoint counsel to represent the victim without cost to the victim.

HISTORY: 134 v H 511 (Eff 1-1-74); 136 v S 144 (Eff 8-27-75); 137 v H 134 (Eff 8-8-77); 143 v H 208 (Eff 4-11-90); 145 v S 31. Eff 9-27-93.

Not analogous to former RC § 2907.05 (RS § 6833; S&C 425; 54 v 162; GC § 12435; 113 v 541; Bureau of Code Revision, 10-1-53), repealed 134 v H 511, § 2, eff 1-1-74.

§ 2907.06 Sexual imposition.

(A) No person shall have sexual contact with another, not the spouse of the offender; cause another, not the spouse of the offender, to have sexual contact with the offender; or cause two or more other persons to have sexual contact when any of the following applies:

(1) The offender knows that the sexual contact is offensive to the other person, or one of the other persons, or is reckless in that regard.

(2) The offender knows that the other person's, or one of the other person's, ability to appraise the nature of or control the offender's or touching person's conduct is substantially impaired.

(3) The offender knows that the other person, or one of the other persons, submits because of being unaware of the sexual contact.

(4) The other person, or one of the other persons, is thirteen years of age or older but less than sixteen years of age, whether or not the offender knows the age of such person, and the offender is at least eighteen years of age and four or more years older than such other person.

(B) No person shall be convicted of a violation of this section solely upon the victim's testimony unsupported by other evidence.

(C) Whoever violates this section is guilty of sexual imposition, a misdemeanor of the third degree. If the offender previously has been convicted of a violation of this section or of section 2907.02, 2907.03, 2907.04, 2907.05, or 2907.12 of the Revised Code, a violation of this section is a misdemeanor of the first degree.

HISTORY: 134 v H 511 (Eff 1-1-74); 137 v H 134 (Eff 8-8-77); 143 v H 44 (Eff 7-24-90); 146 v S 2. Eff 7-1-96.

Not analogous to former RC § 2907.06 (GC § 12435-1; 113 v 541; Bureau of Code Revision, 10-1-53), repealed 134 v H 511, § 2, eff 1-1-74.

The effective date is set by section 6 of SB 2.

§ 2907.07 Importuning.

(A) No person shall solicit a person under thirteen years of age to engage in sexual activity with the offender, whether or not the offender knows the age of such person.

(B) No person shall solicit a person of the same sex to engage in sexual activity with the offender, when the offender knows such solicitation is offensive to the other person, or is reckless in that regard.

(C) No person shall solicit another, not the spouse of the offender, to engage in sexual conduct with the offender, when the offender is eighteen years of age or older and four or more years older than the other person, and the other person is over twelve but not over fifteen years of age, whether or not the offender knows the age of the other person.

(D) Whoever violates this section is guilty of importuning. Violation of division (A) or (B) of this section is a misdemeanor of the first degree. Violation of division (C) of this section is a misdemeanor of the fourth degree.

HISTORY: 134 v H 511. Eff 1-1-74.

Not analogous to former RC § 2907.07 (RS § 6834; S&C 432; 72 v 149; GC § 12436; Bureau of Code Revision, 10-1-53), repealed 134 v H 511, § 2, eff 1-1-74.

Analogous to former RC § 2905.30 (RS § 7026; S&S 289; 59 v 32; 89 v 127; GC § 13032; 121 v 557(573); Bureau of Code Revision, 10-1-53; 129 v 1670; 130 v 659; 131 v 672), repealed 134 v H 511, § 2, eff 1-1-74.

The effective date is set by section 4 of HB 511.

§ 2907.08 Voyeurism.

(A) No person, for the purpose of sexually arousing or gratifying himself or herself, shall commit trespass or otherwise surreptitiously invade the privacy of another, to spy or eavesdrop upon another.

(B) Whoever violates this section is guilty of voyeurism, a misdemeanor of the third degree.

HISTORY: 134 v H 511. Eff 1-1-74.

Not analogous to former RC § 2907.08 (Bureau of Code Revision, 10-1-53; 132 v H 996), repealed 134 v H 511, § 2, eff 1-1-74.

The effective date is set by section 4 of HB 511.

[§§ 2907.08.1, 2907.08.2] §§ 2907.081, 2907.082 Repealed, 134 v H 511, § 2 [129 v 562; 131 v 674]. Eff 1-1-74.

These sections concerned penalty and intentional injury or damage to public or private property.

§ 2907.09 Public indecency.

(A) No person shall recklessly do any of the following, under circumstances in which his or her conduct is likely to be viewed by and affront others, not members of his or her household:

(1) Expose his or her private parts, or engage in masturbation;

(2) Engage in sexual conduct;

(3) Engage in conduct that to an ordinary observer would appear to be sexual conduct or masturbation.

(B) Whoever violates this section is guilty of public indecency. Except as otherwise provided in this division, public indecency is a misdemeanor of the fourth degree. If the offender previously has been convicted of or pleaded guilty to one violation of this section, public indecency is a misdemeanor of the third degree. If the offender previously has been convicted of or pleaded guilty to two violations of this section, public indecency is a misdemeanor of the second degree. If the offender previously has been convicted of or pleaded guilty to three or more violations of this section, public indecency is a misdemeanor of the first degree.

HISTORY: 134 v H 511 (Eff 1-1-74); 143 v H 214 (Eff 4-13-90); 146 v S 2. Eff 7-1-96.

Not analogous to former RC § 2907.09 (RS § 6835; 69 v 10; 82 v 161; 95 v 561; 96 v 14; 98 v 3; GC § 12437; 100 v 5; 101 v 128; Bureau of Code Revision, 10-1-53; 129 v 1426), repealed 134 v H 511, § 2, eff 1-1-74.

The effective date is set by section 6 of SB 2.

§ 2907.10 Repealed, 139 v S 199, § 2 [136 v S 144; 137 v H 565; 138 v H 900]. Eff 7-1-83.

This section concerned actual incarceration.

§ 2907.11 Victim or offender may request temporary suppression of information.

Upon the request of the victim or offender in a prosecution under any provision of sections 2907.02 to

2907.07 of the Revised Code, the judge before whom any person is brought on a charge of having committed an offense under a provision of one of those sections shall order that the names of the victim and offender and the details of the alleged offense as obtained by any law enforcement officer be suppressed until the preliminary hearing, the accused is arraigned in the court of common pleas, the charge is dismissed, or the case is otherwise concluded, whichever occurs first. Nothing in this section shall be construed to deny to either party in the case the name and address of the other party or the details of the alleged offense.

HISTORY: 136 v S 144 (Eff 8-27-75); 146 v H 445. Eff 9-3-96.

Not analogous to former RC § 2907.11 (RS § 6835; 69 v 10; 82 v 161; 95 v 561; 96 v 14; 98 v 3; GC § 12439; 100 v 5; Bureau of Code Revision, 10-1-53), repealed 134 v H 511, § 2, eff 1-1-74.

The provisions of § 3(E) of HB 445 (146 v —) read as follows:

(E) Section 2907.11 of the Revised Code, as amended by this act, applies to a prosecution for felonious sexual penetration committed in violation of former section 2907.12 of the Revised Code.

§ 2907.12 Repealed, 146 v H 445, § 2 [136 v S 144; 139 v S 199; 141 v H 475; 143 v S 94; 145 v S 31; 146 v S 2]. Eff 9-3-96.

This section defined felonious sexual penetration. See now section 2907.01(A).

The provisions of § 3(A)-(J) of HB 445 (146 v —) read as follows:

SECTION 3. (A) When a complaint is filed alleging that a child is a delinquent child for committing felonious sexual penetration in violation of former section 2907.12 of the Revised Code and the arresting authority, a court, or a probation officer discovers that the child or a person whom the child caused to engage in sexual activity has a communicable disease, the arresting authority, court, or probation officer shall notify the victim of the delinquent act of the nature of the disease in accordance with division (C) of section 2151.14 of the Revised Code.

As used in division (A) of Section 3 of this act:

(1) "Child" has the same meaning as in section 2151.011 of the Revised Code.

(2) "Delinquent child" has the same meaning as in section 2151.02 of the Revised Code.

(3) "Sexual activity" has the same meaning as in section 2907.01 of the Revised Code.

(B) If a child is adjudicated a delinquent child for violating any provision of former section 2907.12 of the Revised Code other than division (A)(1)(b) of that section when the insertion involved was consensual and when the victim of the violation of division (A)(1)(b) of that section was older than the delinquent child, was the same age as the delinquent child, or was less that three years younger than the delinquent child, the juvenile court with jurisdiction over the child may commit the child to the legal custody of the department of youth services pursuant to division (A)(5)(a) of section 2151.355 of the Revised Code, as amended by this act, and all provisions of the Revised Code that apply to a disposition otherwise imposed pursuant to division (A)(5)(a) of section 2151.355 of the Revised Code, as amended by this act, apply to a disposition imposed in accordance with division (B) of Section 3 of this act.

As used in division (B) of Section 3 of this act:

(1) "Child" and "legal custody" have the same meanings as in section 2151.011 of the Revised Code.

(2) "Delinquent child" has the same meaning as in section 2151.02 of the Revised Code.

(C) Section 2151.3511 of the Revised Code, as amended by this act, applies to a proceeding in juvenile court involving a complaint in which a child is charged with committing an act that if committed by an adult would be felonious sexual penetration in violation of former section 2907.12 of the Revised Code and in which an alleged victim of the act was a child who was under eleven years of age when the complaint was filed.

As used in division (C) of Section 3 of this act, "child" has the same meaning as in section 2151.011 of the Revised Code.

(D) Division (E) of section 2743.62 of the Revised Code applies to a claim for an award of reparations arising out of the commission of felonious sexual penetration in violation of former section 2907.12 of the Revised Code.

(E) Section 2907.11 of the Revised Code, as amended by this act, applies to a prosecution for felonious sexual penetration committed in violation of former section 2907.12 of the Revised Code.

(F) Division (A) of section 2907.28 and sections 2907.29 and 2907.30 of the Revised Code, as amended by this act, apply to a victim of felonious sexual penetration committed in violation of former section 2907.12 of the Revised Code.

(G) Sections 2907.41 and 2945.49 of the Revised Code, as amended by this act, apply to a trial or other proceeding involving a charge of felonious sexual penetration in violation of former section 2907.12 of the Revised Code in which an alleged victim of the offense was a child who was under eleven years of age when the complaint, indictment, or information was filed relative to the trial or other proceeding.

(H) Divisions (B) and (C) of section 2937.11 of the Revised Code, as amended by this act, apply to a case involving an alleged commission of the offense of felonious sexual penetration in violation of former section 2907.12 of the Revised Code.

(I) Notwithstanding section 2967.13 of the Revised Code, as amended by this act, a prisoner serving a term of imprisonment for life for committing the offense of felonious sexual penetration in violation of former section 2907.12 of the Revised Code becomes eligible for parole after serving a term of ten full years' imprisonment.

(J) Notwithstanding section 2967.18 of the Revised Code, as amended by this act, no reduction of sentence pursuant to division (B)(1) of section 2967.18 of the Revised Code shall be given to a person who is serving a term of imprisonment for the commission of felonious sexual penetration in violation of former section 2907.12 of the Revised Code.

[§ 2907.12.1] § 2907.121 Repealed, 134 v H 511, § 2 [132 v H 656]. Eff 1-1-74.

This section concerned forcing entry into coin-receiving device.

§§ 2907.13, 2907.14 Repealed, 134 v H 511, § 2 [RS § 6836; S&C 407, 426; 33 v 33; 78 v 28; GC § 12441; 113 v 502; Bureau of Code Revision, 10-1-53; 129 v 1812; 129 v 1426; 130 v 660]. Eff 1-1-74.

These sections concerned malicious entry and definition of financial institution.

[§§ 2907.14.1, 2907.14.2, 2907.-14.3]
§§ 2907.141, 2907.142, 2907.143 Repealed, 134 v H 511, § 2 [129 v 1812]. Eff 1-1-74.

These sections concerned unlawful entry of financial institution.

[§§ 2907.14.4, 2907.14.5]
§§ 2907.144, 2907.145 Repealed, 134 v H 511, § 2 [129 v 1812]. Eff 1-1-74.

These sections concerned unlawful entry of financial institution.

§ 2907.15 Motion for withholding of restitution needed from government deferred compensation or public retirement system payment.

(A) As used in this section:

(1) "Public retirement system" means the public employees retirement system, state teachers retirement system, school employees retirement system, police and firemen's disability and pension fund, state highway patrol retirement system, or a municipal retirement system of a municipal corporation of this state.

(2) "Government deferred compensation program" means such a program offered by the Ohio public employees deferred compensation board; a municipal corporation; or governmental unit, as defined in section 145.74 of the Revised Code.

(3) "Deferred compensation program participant" means a "participating employee" or "continuing member," as defined in section 145.71 of the Revised Code, or any other public employee who has funds in a government deferred compensation program.

(4) "Prosecutor" has the same meaning as in section 2935.01 of the Revised Code.

In any case in which a sentencing court orders restitution to the victim under section 2929.18 of the Revised Code for a violation of section 2907.02, 2907.03, 2907.04, or 2907.05 of the Revised Code and in which the offender is a government deferred compensation program participant or is a member of, or receiving a pension, benefit, or allowance, other than a survivorship benefit, from, a public retirement system and committed the offense against a child, student, patient, or other person with whom the offender had contact in the context of the offender's public employment, at the request of the victim the prosecutor shall file a motion with the sentencing court specifying the government deferred compensation program or public retirement system and requesting that the court issue an order requiring the government deferred compensation program or public retirement system to withhold the amount required as restitution from one or more of the following: any payment to be made from a government deferred compensation program or under a pension, annuity, allowance, or any other benefit, other than a survivorship benefit, that has been or is in the future granted to the offender; from any payment of accumulated employee contributions standing to the offender's credit with the government deferred compensation program or public retirement system; or from any payment of any other amounts to be paid to the offender pursuant to Chapter 145., 742., 3307., 3309., or 5505. of the Revised Code on withdrawal of contributions. The motion may be filed at any time subsequent to the conviction of the offender or entry of a guilty plea. On the filing of the motion, the clerk of the court in which the motion is filed shall notify the offender and the government deferred compensation program or public retirement system, in writing, of all of the following: that the motion was filed; that the offender will be granted a hearing on the issuance of the requested order if the offender files a written request for a hearing with the clerk prior to the expiration of thirty days after the offender receives the notice; that, if a hearing is requested, the court will schedule a hearing as soon as possible and notify the offender and the government deferred compensation program or public retirement system of the date, time, and place of the hearing; that, if a hearing is conducted, it will be limited to a consideration of whether the offender can show good cause why the order should not be issued; that, if a hearing is conducted, the court will not issue the order if the court determines, based on evidence presented at the hearing by the offender, that there is good cause for the order not to be issued; that the court will issue the order if a hearing is not requested or if a hearing is conducted but the court does not determine, based on evidence presented at the hearing by the offender, that there is good cause for the order not to be issued; and that, if the order is issued, the government deferred compensation program or public retirement system specified in the motion will be required to withhold the amount required as restitution from payments to the offender.

(B) In any case in which a motion requesting the issuance of a withholding order as described in division (A) of this section is filed, the offender may receive a hearing on the motion by delivering a written request for a hearing to the court prior to the expiration of thirty days after the offender's receipt of the notice provided pursuant to division (A) of this section. If the offender requests a hearing within the prescribed time, the court shall schedule a hearing as soon as possible after the request is made and notify the offender and the government deferred compensation program or public retirement system of the date, time, and place of the hearing. A hearing scheduled under this division shall be limited to a consideration of whether there is good cause, based on evidence presented by the offender, for the requested order not to be issued. If the court determines, based on evidence presented by the offender, that there is good cause for the order not to be issued, the court shall deny the motion and shall not issue the order. Good cause for not issuing the order includes a determination by the court that the order would severely impact the offender's ability to support the offender's dependents.

If the offender does not request a hearing within the prescribed time or the court conducts a hearing but does not determine, based on evidence presented by the offender, that there is good cause for the order not to be issued, the court shall order the government deferred compensation program or public retirement system, to withhold the amount required as restitution from one or more of the following: any payments to be made from a government deferred compensation program or under a pension, annuity, allowance, or under any other benefit, other than a survivorship benefit, that has been or is in the future granted to the offender; from any payment of accumulated employee contributions standing to the offender's credit with the government deferred compensation program or public retirement system; or from any payment of any other amounts to be paid to the offender upon withdrawal of contributions pursuant to Chapter 145., 742., 3307., 3309., or 5505. of the Revised Code and to continue the withholding for that purpose, in accordance with the order, out of each payment to be made on or after the date of issuance of the order, until further order of the court. On receipt of an order issued under this division, the government deferred compensation program or public retirement system shall withhold the amount required as restitution, in accordance with the order, from any such payments and immediately forward the amount withheld to the clerk of the court in which the order was issued for payment to the person to whom restitution is to be made. The order shall not apply to any portion of payments made from a government deferred compensation program or public retirement system to a person other than the offender pursuant to a previously issued domestic court order.

(C) Service of a notice required by division (A) or (B) of this section shall be effected in the same manner as provided in the Rules of Civil Procedure for the service of process.

(D) Upon the filing of charges under section 2907.02, 2907.03, 2907.04, or 2907.05 of the Revised Code against a person who is a deferred compensation program participant or a member of, or receiving a pension benefit, or allowance, other than a survivorship benefit, from a public retirement system for an offense against a child, student, patient, or other person with whom the offender had contact in the context of the offender's public employment, the prosecutor shall send written notice that charges have been filed against that person to the appropriate government deferred compensation program or public retirement system. The notice shall specifically identify the person charged.

HISTORY: 146 v H 668. Eff 12-6-96.

Not analogous to former RC § 2907.15 (RS § 6837; S & C 435; 52 v 28; 88 v 432; GC § 12442; 109 v 53; Bureau of Code Revision, 10-1-53; 129 v 1426), repealed 134 v H 511, § 2, eff 1-1-74.

§§ 2907.16, 2907.17 Repealed, 134 v H 511, § 2 [RS § 6839; S&C 426, 427; 29 v 144; GC §§ 12443—12444; Bureau of Code Revision, 10-1-53; 129 v 1426; 130 v 660]. Eff 1-1-74.

These sections prohibited breaking and entering.

§§ 2907.18, 2907.19, 2907.20
Repealed, 134 v H 511, § 2 [RS §§ 3107, 6840, 6856; S&C 408, 439, 1632; S&S 263, 279, 457; 47 v 21; 60 v 5, 20; 63 v 70; 66 v 341; 68 v 87; 69 v 67; GC §§ 12445—12447; 124 v 466; Bureau of Code Revision, 10-1-53; 132 v H 996; 133 v H 49]. Eff 1-1-74.

These sections prohibited breaking and entering and theft.

[§ 2907.20.1] § 2907.201 Repealed, 134 v H 511, § 2 [133 v S 346; 134 v S 302]. Eff 1-1-74.

This section concerned credit card theft and fraud.

[PROSTITUTION]

§ 2907.21 Compelling prostitution.

(A) No person shall knowingly do any of the following:

(1) Compel another to engage in sexual activity for hire;

(2) Induce, procure, encourage, solicit, request, or otherwise facilitate a minor to engage in sexual activity for hire, whether or not the offender knows the age of the minor;

(3) Pay or agree to pay a minor, either directly or through the minor's agent, so that the minor will engage in sexual activity, whether or not the offender knows the age of the minor;

(4) Pay a minor, either directly or through the minor's agent, for the minor having engaged in sexual activity, pursuant to a prior agreement, whether or not the offender knows the age of the minor;

(5) Allow a minor to engage in sexual activity for hire if the person allowing the child to engage in sexual activity for hire is the parent, guardian, custodian, person having custody or control, or person in loco parentis of the minor.

(B) Whoever violates this section is guilty of compelling prostitution. Except as otherwise provided in this division, compelling prostitution is a felony of the third degree. If the offender commits a violation of division (A)(1) of this section and the person compelled to engage in sexual activity for hire in violation of that division is less than sixteen years of age, compelling prostitution is a felony of the second degree.

HISTORY: 134 v H 511 (Eff 1-1-74); 142 v H 51 (Eff 3-17-89); 146 v S 2. Eff 7-1-96.

Not analogous to former RC § 2907.21 (GC § 12447-1; 120 v 444; 124 v 466; Bureau of Code Revision, 10-1-53; 129 v 340; 130 v 660; 133 v S 346), repealed 134 v H 511, § 2, eff 1-1-74.

The effective date is set by section 6 of SB 2.

§ 2907.22 Promoting prostitution.

(A) No person shall knowingly:
(1) Establish, maintain, operate, manage, supervise, control, or have an interest in a brothel;
(2) Supervise, manage, or control the activities of a prostitute in engaging in sexual activity for hire;
(3) Transport another, or cause another to be transported across the boundary of this state or of any county in this state, in order to facilitate the other person's engaging in sexual activity for hire;
(4) For the purpose of violating or facilitating a violation of this section, induce or procure another to engage in sexual activity for hire.
(B) Whoever violates this section is guilty of promoting prostitution, a felony of the fourth degree. If any prostitute in the brothel involved in the offense, or the prostitute whose activities are supervised, managed, or controlled by the offender, or the person transported, induced, or procured by the offender to engage in sexual activity for hire, is a minor, whether or not the offender knows the age of the minor, then promoting prostitution is a felony of the third degree.

HISTORY: 134 v H 511 (Eff 1-1-74); 142 v H 51 (Eff 3-17-89); 146 v S 2. Eff 7-1-96.

Not analogous to former RC § 2907.22 (RS § 6857; S&C 412; 33 v 33; GC § 12448; 107 v 558; 110 v 58; Bureau of Code Revision, 10-1-53), repealed 134 v H 511, § 2, eff 1-1-74.

The effective date is set by section 6 of SB 2.

§ 2907.23 Procuring.

(A) No person, knowingly and for gain, shall do either of the following:
(1) Entice or solicit another to patronize a prostitute or brothel;
(2) Procure a prostitute for another to patronize, or take or direct another at his or her request to any place for the purpose of patronizing a prostitute.
(B) No person, having authority or responsibility over the use of premises, shall knowingly permit such premises to be used for the purpose of engaging in sexual activity for hire.

(C) Whoever violates this section is guilty of procuring, a misdemeanor of the first degree.

HISTORY: 134 v H 511. Eff 1-1-74.

Not analogous to former RC § 2907.23 (GC § 12448-1; 117 v 821; Bureau of Code Revision, 10-1-53), repealed 134 v H 511, § 2, eff 1-1-74.

The effective date is set by section 4 of HB 511.

§ 2907.24 Soliciting; after positive HIV test.

(A) No person shall solicit another to engage with such other person in sexual activity for hire.
(B) No person, with knowledge that the person has tested positive as a carrier of a virus that causes acquired immunodeficiency syndrome, shall engage in conduct in violation of division (A) of this section.
(C)(1) Whoever violates division (A) of this section is guilty of soliciting, a misdemeanor of the third degree.
(2) Whoever violates division (B) of this section is guilty of engaging in solicitation after a positive HIV test. If the offender commits the violation prior to July 1, 1996, engaging in solicitation after a positive HIV test is a felony of the second degree. If the offender commits the violation on or after July 1, 1996, engaging in solicitation after a positive HIV test is a felony of the third degree.

HISTORY: 134 v H 511 (Eff 1-1-74); 146 v H 40. Eff 5-30-96.

Not analogous to former RC § 2907.24 (GC § 12448-2; 117 v 821; Bureau of Code Revision, 10-1-53), repealed 134 v H 511, § 2, eff 1-1-74.

Analogous to former RC § 2905.27 (GC § 13031-13; 108 v PtI, 730; Bureau of Code Revision, 10-1-53; 130 v PtII, 143), repealed 134 v H 511, § 2, eff 1-1-74.

[§ 2907.24.1] § 2907.241 Loitering to engage in solicitation; solicitation after positive HIV test.

(A) No person, with purpose to solicit another to engage in sexual activity for hire and while in or near a public place, shall do any of the following:
(1) Beckon to, stop, or attempt to stop another;
(2) Engage or attempt to engage another in conversation;
(3) Stop or attempt to stop the operator of a vehicle or approach a stationary vehicle;
(4) If the offender is the operator of or a passenger in a vehicle, stop, attempt to stop, beckon to, attempt to beckon to, or entice another to approach or enter the vehicle of which the offender is the operator or in which the offender is the passenger;
(5) Interfere with the free passage of another.
(B) No person, with knowledge that the person has tested positive as a carrier of a virus that causes acquired immunodeficiency syndrome, shall engage in conduct in violation of division (A) of this section.
(C) as used in this section:

(1) "Vehicle" has the same meaning as in section 4501.01 of the revised code.
(2) "Public place" means any of the following:
(a) A street, road, highway, thoroughfare, bikeway, walkway, sidewalk, bridge, alley, alleyway, plaza, park, driveway, parking lot, or transportation facility;
(b) A doorway or entrance way to a building that fronts on a place described in division (C)(2)(a) of this section;
(c) A place not described in division (C)(2)(a) or (b) of this section that is open to the public.
(D)(1) Whoever violates division (A) of this section is guilty of loitering to engage in solicitation, a misdemeanor of the third degree.
(2) Whoever violates division (B) of this section is guilty of loitering to engage in solicitation after a positive HIV test. If the offender commits the violation prior to July 1, 1996, loitering to engage in solicitation after a positive HIV test is a felony of the fourth degree. If the offender commits the violation on or after July 1, 1996, loitering to engage in solicitation after a positive HIV test is a felony of the fifth degree.

HISTORY: 146 v H 40. Eff 5-30-96.

§ 2907.25 Prostitution; after positive HIV test.

(A) No person shall engage in sexual activity for hire.
(B) No person, with knowledge that the person has tested positive as a carrier of a virus that causes acquired immunodeficiency syndrome, shall engage in sexual activity for hire.
(C)(1) Whoever violates division (A) of this section is guilty of prostitution, a misdemeanor of the third degree.
(2) Whoever violates division (B) of this section is guilty of engaging in prostitution after a positive HIV test. If the offender commits the violation prior to July 1, 1996, engaging in prostitution after a positive HIV test is a felony of the second degree. If the offender commits the violation on or after July 1, 1996, engaging in prostitution after a positive HIV test is a felony of the third degree.

HISTORY: 134 v H 511 (Eff 1-1-74); 146 v H 40. Eff 5-30-96.

Not analogous to former RC § 2907.25 (GC § 12448-3; 117 v 821; Bureau of Code Revision, 10-1-53), repealed 134 v H 511, § 2, eff 1-1-74.

Analogous to former RC § 2905.27 (GC § 13031-13; 108 v PtI, 730; Bureau of Code Revision, 10-1-53; 130 v PtII, 143), repealed 134 v H 511, § 2, eff 1-1-74.

§ 2907.26 Rules of evidence in prostitution cases.

(A) In any case in which it is necessary to prove that a place is a brothel, evidence as to the reputation of such place and as to the reputation of the persons who inhabit or frequent it, is admissible on the question of whether such place is or is not a brothel.
(B) In any case in which it is necessary to prove that a person is a prostitute, evidence as to the reputation of such person is admissible on the question of whether such person is or is not a prostitute.
(C) In any prosecution for a violation of sections 2907.21 to 2907.25 of the Revised Code, proof of a prior conviction of the accused of any such offense or substantially equivalent offense is admissible in support of the charge.
(D) The prohibition contained in division (D) of section 2317.02 of the Revised Code against testimony by a husband or wife concerning communications between them does not apply, and the accused's spouse may testify concerning any such communication, in any of the following cases:
(1) When the husband or wife is charged with a violation of section 2907.21 of the Revised Code, and the spouse testifying was the victim of the offense;
(2) When the husband or wife is charged with a violation of section 2907.22 of the Revised Code, and the spouse testifying was the prostitute involved in the offense, or the person transported, induced, or procured by the offender to engage in sexual activity for hire;
(3) When the husband or wife is charged with a violation of section 2907.23 of the Revised Code, and the spouse testifying was the prostitute involved in the offense or the person who used the offender's premises to engage in sexual activity for hire;
(4) When the husband or wife is charged with a violation of section 2907.24 or 2907.25 of the Revised Code.

HISTORY: 134 v H 511 (Eff 1-1-74); 137 v H 1. Eff 8-26-77.

Not analogous to former RC § 2907.26 (GC § 12448-4; 117 v 821; 119 v 554; Bureau of Code Revision, 10-1-53), repealed 134 v H 511, § 2, eff 1-1-74.

§ 2907.27 Testing of accused for venereal diseases and HIV.

(A)(1) If a person is charged with a violation of section 2907.02, 2907.03, 2907.04, 2907.24, 2907.241 [2907.24.1], or 2907.25 of the Revised Code or with a violation of a municipal ordinance that is substantially equivalent to any of those sections, the arresting authorities or a court, upon the request of the prosecutor in the case or upon the request of the victim, shall cause the accused to submit to one or more appropriate tests to determine if the accused is suffering from a venereal disease.
(2) If the accused is found to be suffering from a venereal disease in an infectious stage, the accused shall be required to submit to medical treatment for that disease. The cost of the medical treatment shall be charged to and paid by the accused who undergoes the treatment. If the accused is indigent, the court shall order the accused to report to a facility operated by a city health district or a general health district for treatment. If the accused is convicted of or pleads guilty

to the offense with which the accused is charged and is placed on probation, a condition of probation shall be that the offender submit to and faithfully follow a course of medical treatment for the venereal disease. If the offender does not seek the required medical treatment, the court may revoke the offender's probation and order the offender to undergo medical treatment during the period of the offender's incarceration and to pay the cost of that treatment.

(B)(1)(a) Notwithstanding the requirements for informed consent in section 3701.242 [3701.24.2] of the Revised Code, if a person is charged with a violation of section 2907.02, 2907.03, 2907.04, 2907.05, 2907.12, 2907.24, 2907.241 [2907.24.1], or 2907.25 of the Revised Code or with a violation of a municipal ordinance that is substantially equivalent to any of those sections, the court, upon the request of the prosecutor in the case, upon the request of the victim, or upon the request of any other person whom the court reasonably believes had contact with the accused in circumstances related to the violation that could have resulted in the transmission to that person of a virus that causes acquired immunodeficiency syndrome, shall cause the accused to submit to one or more tests designated by the director of health under section 3701.241 [3701.24.1] of the Revised Code to determine if the accused is a carrier of a virus that causes acquired immunodeficiency syndrome. The court, upon the request of the prosecutor in the case, upon the request of the victim with the agreement of the prosecutor, or upon the request of any other person with the agreement of the prosecutor, may cause an accused who is charged with a violation of any other section of the Revised Code or with a violation of any other municipal ordinance to submit to one or more tests so designated by the director of health if the circumstances of the violation indicate probable cause to believe that the accused, if the accused is infected with the virus that causes acquired immunodeficiency syndrome, might have transmitted the virus to any of the following persons in committing the violation:

(i) In relation to a request made by the prosecuting attorney, to the victim or to any other person;

(ii) In relation to a request made by the victim, to the victim making the request;

(iii) In relation to a request made by any other person, to the person making the request.

(b) The results of a test performed under division (B)(1)(a) of this section shall be communicated in confidence to the court, and the court shall inform the accused of the result. The court shall inform the victim that the test was performed and that the victim has a right to receive the results on request. If the test was performed upon the request of a person other than the prosecutor in the case and other than the victim, the court shall inform the person who made the request that the test was performed and that the person has a right to receive the results upon request. Additionally, regardless of who made the request that was the basis of the test being performed, if the court reasonably believes that, in circumstances related to the violation, a person other than the victim had contact with the accused that could have resulted in the transmission of the virus to that person, the court may inform that person that the test was performed and that the person has a right to receive the results of the test on request. If the accused tests positive for a virus that causes acquired immunodeficiency syndrome, the test results shall be reported to the department of health in accordance with section 3701.24 of the Revised Code and to the sheriff, head of the state correctional institution, or other person in charge of any jail or prison in which the accused is incarcerated. If the accused tests positive for a virus that causes acquired immunodeficiency syndrome and the accused was charged with, and was convicted of or pleaded guilty to, a violation of section 2907.24, 2907.241 [2907.24.1], or 2907.25 of the Revised Code or a violation of a municipal ordinance that is substantially equivalent to any of those sections, the test results also shall be reported to the law enforcement agency that arrested the accused, and the law enforcement agency may use the test results as the basis for any future charge of a violation of division (B) of any of those sections or a violation of a municipal ordinance that is substantially equivalent to division (B) of any of those sections. No other disclosure of the test results or the fact that a test was performed shall be made, other than as evidence in a grand jury proceeding or as evidence in a judicial proceeding in accordance with the Rules of Evidence. If the test result is negative, and the charge has not been dismissed or if the accused has been convicted of the charge or a different offense arising out of the same circumstances as the offense charged, the court shall order that the test be repeated not earlier than three months nor later than six months after the original test.

(2) If an accused who is free on bond refuses to submit to a test ordered by the court pursuant to division (B)(1) of this section, the court may order that the accused's bond be revoked and that the accused be incarcerated until the test is performed. If an accused who is incarcerated refuses to submit to a test ordered by the court pursuant to division (B)(1) of this section, the court shall order the person in charge of the jail or prison in which the accused is incarcerated to take any action necessary to facilitate the performance of the test, including the forcible restraint of the accused for the purpose of drawing blood to be used in the test.

(3) A state agency, a political subdivision of the state, or an employee of a state agency or of a political subdivision of the state is immune from liability in a civil action to recover damages for injury, death, or loss to person or property allegedly caused by any act or omission in connection with the performance of the duties required under division (B)(2) of this section unless the acts or omissions are with malicious purpose, in bad faith, or in a wanton or reckless manner.

HISTORY: 134 v H 511 (Eff 1-1-74); 143 v S 94 (Eff 9-27-89);

143 v S 2 (Eff 11-1-89); 145 v H 571 (Eff 10-6-94); 146 v H 40. Eff 5-30-96.

Not analogous to former RC § 2907.27 (GC § 12448-5; 117 v 821; Bureau of Code Revision, 10-1-53), repealed 134 v H 511, § 2, eff 1-1-74.

Analogous to former RC § 2905.28 (GC § 13031-17; 108 v PtI, 730; 118 v 301; Bureau of Code Revision, 10-1-53; 130 v PtII, 144), repealed 134 v H 511, § 2, eff 1-1-74.

[MEDICAL ASSISTANCE FOR VICTIMS]

§ 2907.28 Payment of cost of medical examination and test of victim or accused.

(A) Any cost incurred by a hospital or other emergency medical facility in conducting a medical examination of a victim of an offense under any provision of sections 2907.02 to 2907.06 of the Revised Code for the purpose of gathering physical evidence for a possible prosecution shall be charged to and paid by the appropriate local government as follows:

(1) Cost incurred by a county facility shall be charged to and paid by the county;

(2) Cost incurred by a municipal facility shall be charged to and paid by the municipal corporation;

(3) Cost incurred by a private facility shall be charged to and paid by the municipal corporation in which the alleged offense was committed, or charged to and paid by the county, if committed within an unincorporated area. If separate counts of an offense or separate offenses under any provisions of sections 2907.02 to 2907.06 of the Revised Code took place in more than one municipal corporation or more than one unincorporated area, or both, the local governments shall share the cost of the examination.

(B) Any cost incurred by a hospital or other emergency medical facility in conducting a medical examination and test of any person who is charged with a violation of section 2907.02, 2907.03, 2907.04, 2907.05, 2907.12,† 2907.24, 2907.241 [2907.24.1], or 2907.25 of the Revised Code or with a violation of a municipal ordinance that is substantially equivalent to any of those sections, pursuant to division (B) of section 2907.27 of the Revised Code, shall be charged to and paid by the accused who undergoes the examination and test, unless the court determines that the accused is unable to pay, in which case the cost shall be charged to and paid by the municipal corporation in which the offense allegedly was committed, or charged to and paid by the county if the offense allegedly was committed within an unincorporated area. If separate counts of an alleged offense or alleged separate offenses under section 2907.02, 2907.03, 2907.04, 2907.05, 2907.12,† 2907.24, 2907.241 [2907.24.1], or 2907.25 of the Revised Code or under a municipal ordinance that is substantially equivalent to any of those sections took place in more than one municipal corporation or more than one unincorporated area, or both, the local governments shall share the cost of the examination and test. If a hospital or other emergency medical facility has submitted charges for the cost of a medical examination and test to an accused and has been unable to collect payment for the charges after making good faith attempts to collect for a period of six months or more, the cost shall be charged to and paid by the appropriate municipal corporation or county as specified in division (B) of this section.

HISTORY: 136 v S 144 (Eff 8-27-75); 143 v S 2 (Eff 11-1-89); 146 v H 40 (Eff 5-30-96); 146 v H 445. Eff 9-3-96.

Not analogous to former RC § 2907.28 (GC § 12448-6; 117 v 821; Bureau of Code Revision, 10-1-53), repealed 134 v H 511, § 2, eff 1-1-74.

The provisions of § 3(F) of HB 445 (146 v —) read as follows:

(F) Division (A) of section 2907.28 and sections 2907.29 and 2907.30 of the Revised Code, as amended by this act, apply to a victim of felonious sexual penetration committed in violation of former section 2907.12 of the Revised Code.

† RC § 2907.12 is repealed by § 2 of HB 445 (146 v —), eff 9-3-96.

Comment, Legislative Service Commission

° ° ° Section 2907.28 of the Revised Code is amended by this act [Am. Sub. H.B. 445] and also by Sub. H.B. 40 of the 121st General Assembly. ° ° ° Comparison of these amendments in pursuance of section 1.52 of the Revised Code discloses that they are not irreconcilable so that they are required by that section to be harmonized to give effect to each amendment.

§ 2907.29 Hospital emergency services for victims.

Every hospital of this state that offers organized emergency services shall provide that a physician is available on call twenty-four hours each day for the examination of persons reported to any law enforcement agency to be victims of sexual offenses cognizable as violations of any provision of sections 2907.02 to 2907.06 of the Revised Code. The physician, upon the request of any peace officer or prosecuting attorney and with the consent of the reported victim or upon the request of the reported victim, shall examine the person for the purposes of gathering physical evidence. The public health council shall establish procedures for gathering evidence under this section.

Each reported victim shall be informed of available venereal disease, pregnancy, medical, and psychiatric services.

Notwithstanding any other provision of law, a minor may consent to examination under this section. The consent is not subject to disaffirmance because of minority, and consent of the parent, parents, or guardian of the minor is not required for an examination under this section. However, the hospital shall give written notice to the parent, parents, or guardian of a minor that an examination under this section has taken place. The parent, parents, or guardian of a minor giving consent under this section are not liable for payment for any services provided under this section without their consent.

HISTORY: 136 v S 144 (Eff 8-27-75); 146 v H 445. Eff 9-3-96.

Not analogous to former RC § 2907.29 (RS § 6818; S&C 406; 33 v 33; 80 v 38; GC § 12449; Bureau of Code Revision, 10-1-53), repealed 134 v H 511, § 2, eff 1-1-74.

See provisions, § 3(F) of HB 445 (146 v —) following RC § 2907.28.

§ 2907.30 Victim to be interviewed by crisis intervention trained officer.

(A) A victim of a sexual offense cognizable as a violation of section 2907.02 of the Revised Code who is interviewed by a law enforcement agency shall be interviewed by a peace officer employed by the agency who has had crisis intervention training, if any of the peace officers employed by the agency who have had crisis intervention training is reasonably available.

(B) When a person is charged with a violation of section 2907.02, 2907.03, 2907.04, 2907.05, or 2907.06 of the Revised Code and the law enforcement agency that arrested the person or a court discovers that the person arrested or a person whom the person arrested caused to engage in sexual activity has a communicable disease, the law enforcement agency that arrested the person or the court immediately shall notify the victim of the nature of the disease.

(C) As used in this section, "crisis intervention training" has the same meaning as in section 109.71 of the Revised Code.

HISTORY: 140 v H 435 (Eff 4-4-85); 141 v H 468 (Eff 9-17-86); 146 v H 445. Eff 9-3-96.

Not analogous to former RC § 2907.30 (RS § 6858; S&C 408, 412, 426, 439, 451; GC § 12450; 33 v 33, §§ 20, 26; 34 v 10; 37 v 74; 56 v 26; 69 v 68; 124 v 466; Bureau of Code Revision, 10-1-53), repealed 134 v H 511, § 2, eff 1-1-74.

See provisions, § 3(F) of HB 445 (146 v —) following RC § 2907.28.

[OBSCENITY]

§ 2907.31 Disseminating matter harmful to juveniles.

(A) No person, with knowledge of its character or content, shall recklessly do any of the following:

(1) Sell, deliver, furnish, disseminate, provide, exhibit, rent, or present to a juvenile any material or performance that is obscene or harmful to juveniles;

(2) Offer or agree to sell, deliver, furnish, disseminate, provide, exhibit, rent, or present to a juvenile any material or performance that is obscene or harmful to juveniles;

(3) Allow any juvenile to review or peruse any material or view any live performance that is harmful to juveniles.

(B) The following are affirmative defenses to a charge under this section that involves material or a performance that is harmful to juveniles but not obscene:

(1) The defendant is the parent, guardian, or spouse of the juvenile involved.

(2) The juvenile involved, at the time of the conduct in question, was accompanied by the juvenile's parent or guardian who, with knowledge of its character, consented to the material or performance being furnished or presented to the juvenile.

(3) The juvenile exhibited to the defendant or to the defendant's agent or employee a draft card, driver's license, birth record, marriage license, or other official or apparently official document purporting to show that the juvenile was eighteen years of age or over or married, and the person to whom that document was exhibited did not otherwise have reasonable cause to believe that the juvenile was under the age of eighteen and unmarried.

(C)(1) It is an affirmative defense to a charge under this section, involving material or a performance that is obscene or harmful to juveniles, that the material or performance was furnished or presented for a bona fide medical, scientific, educational, governmental, judicial, or other proper purpose, by a physician, psychologist, sociologist, scientist, teacher, librarian, clergyman, prosecutor, judge, or other proper person.

(2) Except as provided in division (B)(3) of this section, mistake of age is not a defense to a charge under this section.

(D) Whoever violates this section is guilty of disseminating matter harmful to juveniles. If the material or performance involved is harmful to juveniles, except as otherwise provided in this division, a violation of this section is a misdemeanor of the first degree. If the material or performance involved is obscene, except as otherwise provided in this division, a violation of this section is a felony of the fifth degree. If the material or performance involved is obscene and the juvenile to whom it is sold, delivered, furnished, disseminated, provided, exhibited, rented, or presented, the juvenile to whom the offer is made or who is the subject of the agreement, or the juvenile who is allowed to review, peruse, or view it is under thirteen years of age, violation of this section is a felony of the fourth degree.

HISTORY: 134 v H 511 (Eff 1-1-74); 142 v H 51 (Eff 3-17-89); 142 v H 790 (Eff 3-16-89); 146 v S 2. Eff 7-1-96.

Not analogous to former RC § 2907.31 (RS § 6859; S&C 1632; 47 v 21; GC § 12451; Bureau of Code Revision, 10-1-53), repealed 134 v H 511, § 2, eff 1-1-74.

The effective date is set by section 6 of SB 2.

The provisions of § 7 of SB 2 (146 v —) read as follows:

SECTION 7. ° ° ° Section 2907.31 of the Revised Code is presented in this act as a composite of the section as amended by both Sub. H.B. 51 and Am. Sub. H.B. 790 of the 117th General Assembly, with the new language of neither of the acts shown in capital letters. ° ° ° This is in recognition of the principle stated in division (B) of section 1.52 of the Revised Code that such amendments are to be harmonized where not substantively irreconcilable and constitutes a legislative finding that such is the resulting version in effect prior to the effective date of this act.

[§ 2907.31.1] § 2907.311 Displaying matter harmful to juveniles.

(A) No person who has custody, control, or supervision of a commercial establishment, with knowledge of the character or content of the material involved, shall display at the establishment any material that is harmful to juveniles and that is open to view by juveniles as part of the invited general public.

(B) It is not a violation of division (A) of this section if the material in question is displayed by placing it behind "blinder racks" or similar devices that cover at least the lower two-thirds of the material, if the material in question is wrapped or placed behind the counter, or if the material in question otherwise is covered or located so that the portion that is harmful to juveniles is not open to the view of juveniles.

(C) Whoever violates this section is guilty of displaying matter harmful to juveniles, a misdemeanor of the first degree. Each day during which the offender is in violation of this section constitutes a separate offense.

HISTORY: 142 v H 51. Eff 3-17-89.

§ 2907.32 Pandering obscenity.

(A) No person, with knowledge of the character of the material or performance involved, shall do any of the following:

(1) Create, reproduce, or publish any obscene material, when the offender knows that the material is to be used for commercial exploitation or will be publicly disseminated or displayed, or when the offender is reckless in that regard;

(2) Promote or advertise for sale, delivery, or dissemination; sell, deliver, publicly disseminate, publicly display, exhibit, present, rent, or provide; or offer or agree to sell, deliver, publicly disseminate, publicly display, exhibit, present, rent, or provide, any obscene material;

(3) Create, direct, or produce an obscene performance, when the offender knows that it is to be used for commercial exploitation or will be publicly presented, or when the offender is reckless in that regard;

(4) Advertise or promote an obscene performance for presentation, or present or participate in presenting an obscene performance, when the performance is presented publicly, or when admission is charged;

(5) Buy, procure, possess, or control any obscene material with purpose to violate division (A)(2) or (4) of this section.

(B) It is an affirmative defense to a charge under this section, that the material or performance involved was disseminated or presented for a bona fide medical, scientific, educational, religious, governmental, judicial, or other proper purpose, by or to a physician, psychologist, sociologist, scientist, teacher, person pursuing bona fide studies or research, librarian, clergyman, prosecutor, judge, or other person having a proper interest in the material or performance.

(C) Whoever violates this section is guilty of pandering obscenity, a felony of the fifth degree. If the offender previously has been convicted of a violation of this section or of section 2907.31 of the Revised Code, then pandering obscenity is a felony of the fourth degree.

HISTORY: 134 v H 511 (Eff 1-1-74); 142 v H 51 (Eff 3-17-89); 146 v S 2. Eff 7-1-96.

Not analogous to former RC § 2907.32 (RS § 6860; S&C 351; 56 v 79; 90 v 232; GC § 12452; Bureau of Code Revision, 10-1-53), repealed 134 v H 511, § 2, eff 1-1-74.

Analogous to former RC § 2905.35 (133 v H 84), repealed 134 v H 511, § 2, eff 1-1-74.

The effective date is set by section 6 of SB 2.

[§ 2907.32.1] § 2907.321 Pandering obscenity involving a minor.

(A) No person, with knowledge of the character of the material or performance involved, shall do any of the following:

(1) Create, reproduce, or publish any obscene material that has a minor as one of its participants or portrayed observers;

(2) Promote or advertise for sale or dissemination; sell, deliver, disseminate, display, exhibit, present, rent, or provide; or offer or agree to sell, deliver, disseminate, display, exhibit, present, rent, or provide, any obscene material that has a minor as one of its participants or portrayed observers;

(3) Create, direct, or produce an obscene performance that has a minor as one of its participants;

(4) Advertise or promote for presentation, present, or participate in presenting an obscene performance that has a minor as one of its participants;

(5) Buy, procure, possess, or control any obscene material, that has a minor as one of its participants;

(6) Bring or cause to be brought into this state any obscene material that has a minor as one of its participants or portrayed observers.

(B)(1) This section does not apply to any material or performance that is sold, disseminated, displayed, possessed, controlled, brought or caused to be brought into this state, or presented for a bona fide medical, scientific, educational, religious, governmental, judicial, or other proper purpose, by or to a physician, psychologist, sociologist, scientist, teacher, person pursuing bona fide studies or research, librarian, clergyman, prosecutor, judge, or other person having a proper interest in the material or performance.

(2) Mistake of age is not a defense to a charge under this section.

(3) In a prosecution under this section, the trier of

fact may infer that a person in the material or performance involved is a minor if the material or performance, through its title, text, visual representation, or otherwise, represents or depicts the person as a minor.

(C) Whoever violates this section is guilty of pandering obscenity involving a minor. Violation of division (A)(1), (2), (3), (4), or (6) of this section is a felony of the second degree. Violation of division (A)(5) of this section is a felony of the fourth degree. If the offender previously has been convicted of or pleaded guilty to a violation of this section or section 2907.322 [2907.32.2] or 2907.323 [2907.32.3] of the Revised Code, pandering obscenity involving a minor in violation of division (A)(5) of this section is a felony of the third degree.

HISTORY: 137 v S 243 (Eff 11-17-77); 140 v H 44 (Eff 9-27-84); 142 v H 51. Eff 3-17-89.

[§ 2907.32.2] § 2907.322 Pandering sexually oriented matter involving a minor.

(A) No person, with knowledge of the character of the material or performance involved, shall do any of the following:

(1) Create, record, photograph, film, develop, reproduce, or publish any material that shows a minor participating or engaging in sexual activity, masturbation, or bestiality;

(2) Advertise for sale or dissemination, sell, distribute, transport, disseminate, exhibit, or display any material that shows a minor participating or engaging in sexual activity, masturbation, or bestiality;

(3) Create, direct, or produce a performance that shows a minor participating or engaging in sexual activity, masturbation, or bestiality;

(4) Advertise for presentation, present, or participate in presenting a performance that shows a minor participating or engaging in sexual activity, masturbation, or bestiality;

(5) Solicit, receive, purchase, exchange, possess or control any material that shows a minor participating or engaging in sexual activity, masturbation, or bestiality;

(6) Bring or cause to be brought into this state any material that shows a minor participating or engaging in sexual activity, masturbation, or bestiality, or bring, cause to be brought, or finance the bringing of any minor into or across this state with the intent that the minor engage in sexual activity, masturbation, or bestiality in a performance or for the purpose of producing material containing a visual representation depicting the minor engaged in sexual activity, masturbation, or bestiality.

(B)(1) This section does not apply to any material or performance that is sold, disseminated, displayed, possessed, controlled, brought or caused to be brought into this state, or presented for a bona fide medical, scientific, educational, religious, governmental, judicial, or other proper purpose, by or to a physician, psychologist, sociologist, scientist, teacher, person pursuing bona fide studies or research, librarian, clergyman, prosecutor, judge, or other person having a proper interest in the material or performance.

(2) Mistake of age is not a defense to a charge under this section.

(3) In a prosecution under this section, the trier of fact may infer that a person in the material or performance involved is a minor if the material or performance, through its title, text, visual representation, or otherwise, represents or depicts the person as a minor.

(C) Whoever violates this section is guilty of pandering sexually oriented matter involving a minor. Violation of division (A)(1), (2), (3), (4), or (6) of this section is a felony of the second degree. Violation of division (A)(5) of this section is a felony of the fifth degree. If the offender previously has been convicted of or pleaded guilty to a violation of this section or section 2907.321 [2907.32.1] or 2907.323 [2907.32.3] of the Revised Code, pandering sexually oriented matter involving a minor in violation of division (A)(5) of this section is a felony of the fourth degree.

HISTORY: 140 v H 44 (Eff 9-27-84); 142 v H 51 (Eff 3-17-89); 146 v S 2. Eff 7-1-96.

The effective date is set by section 6 of SB 2.

[§ 2907.32.3] § 2907.323 Illegal use of minor in nudity-oriented material or performance.

(A) No person shall do any of the following:

(1) Photograph any minor who is not the person's child or ward in a state of nudity, or create, direct, produce, or transfer any material or performance that shows the minor in a state of nudity, unless both of the following apply:

(a) The material or performance is, or is to be, sold, disseminated, displayed, possessed, controlled, brought or caused to be brought into this state, or presented for a bona fide artistic, medical, scientific, educational, religious, governmental, judicial, or other proper purpose, by or to a physician, psychologist, sociologist, scientist, teacher, person pursuing bona fide studies or research, librarian, clergyman, prosecutor, judge, or other person having a proper interest in the material or performance;

(b) The minor's parents, guardian, or custodian consents in writing to the photographing of the minor, to the use of the minor in the material or performance, or to the transfer of the material and to the specific manner in which the material or performance is to be used.

(2) Consent to the photographing of the person's minor child or ward, or photograph the person's minor child or ward, in a state of nudity or consent to the use of the person's minor child or ward in a state of nudity in any material or performance, or use or transfer a material or performance of that nature, unless the material or performance is sold, disseminated, displayed,

possessed, controlled, brought or caused to be brought into this state, or presented for a bona fide artistic, medical, scientific, educational, religious, governmental, judicial, or other proper purpose, by or to a physician, psychologist, sociologist, scientist, teacher, person pursuing bona fide studies or research, librarian, clergyman, prosecutor, judge, or other person having a proper interest in the material or performance;

(3) Possess or view any material or performance that shows a minor who is not the person's child or ward in a state of nudity, unless one of the following applies:

(a) The material or performance is sold, disseminated, displayed, possessed, controlled, brought or caused to be brought into this state, or presented for a bona fide artistic, medical, scientific, educational, religious, governmental, judicial, or other proper purpose, by or to a physician, psychologist, sociologist, scientist, teacher, person pursuing bona fide studies or research, librarian, clergyman, prosecutor, judge, or other person having a proper interest in the material or performance.

(b) The person knows that the parents, guardian, or custodian has consented in writing to the photographing or use of the minor in a state of nudity and to the manner in which the material or performance is used or transferred.

(B) Whoever violates this section is guilty of illegal use of a minor in a nudity-oriented material or performance. Whoever violates division (A)(1) or (2) of this section is guilty of a felony of the second degree. Whoever violates division (A)(3) of this section is guilty of a felony of the fifth degree. If the offender previously has been convicted of or pleaded guilty to a violation of this section or section 2907.321 [2907.32.1] or 2907.322 [2907.32.2.] of the Revised Code, illegal use of a minor in a nudity-oriented material or performance in violation of division (A)(3) of this section is a felony of the fourth degree.

HISTORY: 140 v H 44 (Eff 9-27-84); 140 v S 321 (Eff 4-9-85); 142 v H 51 (Eff 3-17-89); 146 v S 2. Eff 7-1-96.

The effective date is set by section 6 of SB 2.

§ 2907.33 Deception to obtain matter harmful to juveniles.

(A) No person, for the purpose of enabling a juvenile to obtain any material or gain admission to any performance which is harmful to juveniles, shall do either of the following:

(1) Falsely represent that he is the parent, guardian, or spouse of such juvenile;

(2) Furnish such juvenile with any identification or document purporting to show that such juvenile is eighteen years of age or over or married.

(B) No juvenile, for the purpose of obtaining any material or gaining admission to any performance which is harmful to juveniles, shall do either of the following:

(1) Falsely represent that he is eighteen years of age or over or married;

(2) Exhibit any identification or document purporting to show that he is eighteen years of age or over or married.

(C) Whoever violates this section is guilty of deception to obtain matter harmful to juveniles, a misdemeanor of the second degree. A juvenile who violates division (B) of this section shall be adjudged an unruly child, with such disposition of the case as may be appropriate under Chapter 2151. of the Revised Code.

HISTORY: 134 v H 511. Eff 1-1-74.

Not analogous to former RC § 2907.33 (RS § 7071; S&C 351; 56 v 79; GC § 13127; Bureau of Code Revision, 10-1-53), repealed 134 v H 511, § 2, eff 1-1-74.

Analogous to former RC § 2903.16 (133 v H 84; 135 v S 62), repealed 134 v H 511, § 2, eff 1-1-74.

The effective date is set by section 4 of HB 511.

§ 2907.34 Compelling acceptance of objectionable materials.

(A) No person, as a condition to the sale, allocation, consignment, or delivery of any material or goods of any kind, shall require the purchaser or consignee to accept any other material reasonably believed to be obscene, or which if furnished or presented to a juvenile would be in violation of section 2907.31 of the Revised Code.

(B) No person shall deny or threaten to deny any franchise or impose or threaten to impose any financial or other penalty upon any purchaser or consignee because the purchaser or consignee failed or refused to accept any material reasonably believed to be obscene as a condition to the sale, allocation, consignment, or delivery of any other material or goods or because the purchaser or consignee returned any material believed to be obscene that the purchaser or consignee initially accepted.

(C) Whoever violates this section is guilty of compelling acceptance of objectionable materials, a felony of the fifth degree.

HISTORY: 134 v H 511 (Eff 1-1-74); 142 v H 51 (Eff 3-17-89); 146 v S 2. Eff 7-1-96.

Not analogous to former RC § 2907.34 (RS § 6842; S&C 240, 426; 55 v 84; 66 v 29; 73 v 31; 73 v 86; 78 v 186; 82 v 140; 83 v 23; 95 v 303; 97 v 67; GC § 12467; 111 v 101; 124 v 466; Bureau of Code Revision, 10-1-53), repealed 134 v H 511, § 2, eff 1-1-74.

Analogous to former RC § 2905.36 (133 v H 84), repealed 134 v H 511, § 2, eff 1-1-74.

The effective date is set by section 6 of SB 2.

§ 2907.35 Presumptions; notice.

(A) An owner or manager, or his agent or employee, of a bookstore, newsstand, theater, or other commercial establishment engaged in selling materials or exhibiting performances, who, in the course of business:

(1) Possesses five or more identical or substantially

similar obscene articles, having knowledge of their character, is presumed to possess them in violation of division (A)(5) of section 2907.32 of the Revised Code;

(2) Does any of the acts prohibited by section 2907.31 or 2907.32 of the Revised Code, is presumed to have knowledge of the character of the material or performance involved, if he has actual notice of the nature of such material or performance, whether or not he has precise knowledge of its contents.

(B) Without limitation on the manner in which such notice may be given, actual notice of the character of material or a performance may be given in writing by the chief legal officer of the jurisdiction in which the person to whom the notice is directed does business. Such notice, regardless of the manner in which it is given, shall identify the sender, identify the material or performance involved, state whether it is obscene or harmful to juveniles, and bear the date of such notice.

(C) Sections 2907.31 and 2907.32 of the Revised Code do not apply to a motion picture operator or projectionist acting within the scope of his employment as an employee of the owner or manager of a theater or other place for the showing of motion pictures to the general public, and having no managerial responsibility or financial interest in his place of employment, other than wages.

HISTORY: 134 v H 511 (Eff 1-1-74); 135 v S 62. Eff 1-1-74.

Not analogous to former RC § 2907.35 (RS § 6843; S&C 426; 37 v 74; GC § 12468; Bureau of Code Revision, 10-1-53), repealed 134 v H 511, § 2, eff 1-1-74.

§ 2907.36 Declaratory judgment.

(A) Without limitation on the persons otherwise entitled to bring an action for a declaratory judgment pursuant to sections 2721.01 to 2721.15 of the Revised Code, involving the same issue, the following persons have standing to bring such an action to determine whether particular materials or performances are obscene or harmful to juveniles:

(1) The chief legal officer of the jurisdiction in which there is reasonable cause to believe that section 2907.31 or 2907.32 of the Revised Code is being or is about to be violated;

(2) Any person who, pursuant to division (B) of section 2907.35 of the Revised Code, has received notice in writing from a chief legal officer stating that particular materials or performances are obscene or harmful to juveniles.

(B) Any party to an action for a declaratory judgment pursuant to division (A) of this section is entitled, upon his request, to trial on the merits within five days after joinder of the issues, and the court shall render judgment within five days after trial is concluded.

(C) An action for a declaratory judgment pursuant to division (A) of this section shall not be brought during the pendency of any civil action or criminal prosecution, when the character of the particular materials or performances involved is at issue in the pending case, and either of the following apply:

(1) Either of the parties to the action for a declaratory judgment is a party to the pending case;

(2) A judgment in the pending case will necessarily constitute res judicata as to the character of the materials or performances involved.

(D) A civil action or criminal prosecution in which the character of particular materials or performances is at issue, brought during the pendency of an action for a declaratory judgment involving the same issue, shall be stayed during the pendency of the action for a declaratory judgment.

(E) The fact that a violation of section 2907.31 or 2907.32 of the Revised Code occurs prior to a judicial determination of the character of the material or performance involved in the violation, does not relieve the offender of criminal liability for the violation, even though prosecution may be stayed pending the judicial determination.

HISTORY: 134 v H 511. Eff 1-1-74.

Not analogous to former RC § 2907.36 (RS § 6844; S&C 426, 1425; 37 v 74; 57 v 15; 72 v 20; GC § 12469; 124 v 466; Bureau of Code Revision, 10-1-53), repealed 134 v H 511, § 2, eff 1-1-74.

Analogous to former RC § 2905.38 (133 v H 84), repealed 134 v H 511, § 2, eff 1-1-74.

The effective date is set by section 4 of HB 511.

§ 2907.37 Injunction.

(A) Where it appears that section 2907.31 or 2907.32 of the Revised Code is being or is about to be violated, the chief legal officer of the jurisdiction in which the violation is taking place or is about to take place may bring an action to enjoin the violation. The defendant, upon his request, is entitled to trial on the merits within five days after joinder of the issues, and the court shall render judgment within five days after trial is concluded.

(B) Premises used or occupied for repeated violations of section 2907.31 or 2907.32 of the Revised Code constitute a nuisance subject to abatement pursuant to sections 3767.01 to 3767.99 of the Revised Code.

HISTORY: 134 v H 511. Eff 1-1-74.

Not analogous to former RC § 2907.37 (RS § 6845; S&C 421, 423; 42 v 49; 50 v 132; 71 v 66; 78 v 15; GC § 12470; Bureau of Code Revision, 10-1-53), repealed 134 v H 511, § 2, eff 1-1-74.

Analogous to former RC § 2905.37 (133 v H 84), repealed 134 v H 511, § 2, eff 1-1-74.

The effective date is set by section 4 of HB 511.

§§ 2907.38, 2907.39, 2907.40

Repealed, 134 v H 511, § 2 [RS § 6849a; 82 v 247; 99 v 460; GC §§ 12471, 12475, 12475-1; 124 v 360; 124 v 466; Bureau of Code Revision, 10-1-53]. Eff 1-1-74.

These sections concerned embezzlement; conversion of personal property.

§ **2907.41** Amended and renumbered RC § 2945.481 in 147 v S 53, eff 10-14-97.

§§ **2907.42, 2907.43, 2907.44**
Repealed, 134 v H 511, § 2 [RS §§ 1280, 1281, 6880; S&C 432, 1612; S&S 284; 29 v 144, 470; 56 v 72; 62 v 139; 66 v 287; 69 v 67; GC §§ 12465, 12466, 12476-2, 12490; 112 v 420; 117 v 430; Bureau of Code Revision, 10-1-53]. Eff 1-1-74.

These sections concerned conversion of personal property and destroying trees.

§§ **2907.45, 2907.46, 2907.47**
Repealed, 134 v H 511, § 2 [125 v H 457, 131 v 674]. Eff 1-1-74.

These sections concerned conversion of personal property and removal of name or serial number.

§ **2907.48** Repealed, 134 v H 511, § 2 [133 v H 49]. Eff 1-1-74.

This section prohibited shoplifting.

CHAPTER 2909: ARSON AND RELATED OFFENSES

Section
2909.01 Definitions.
2909.02 Aggravated arson.
2909.03 Arson.
2909.04 Disrupting public services.
2909.05 Vandalism.
2909.06 Criminal damaging or endangering.
2909.07 Criminal mischief.
2909.08 Endangering aircraft or airport operations.
2909.09, 2909.10 Repealed.
2909.11 Determining property value or amount of physical harm.
2909.12-2909.26 Repealed.

§ 2909.01 Definitions.

As used in sections 2909.01 to 2909.07 of the Revised Code:

(A) To "create a substantial risk of serious physical harm to any person" includes the creation of a substantial risk of serious physical harm to any emergency personnel.

(B) "Emergency personnel" means any of the following persons:

(1) A peace officer, as defined in section 2935.01 of the Revised Code;

(2) A member of a fire department or other firefighting agency of a municipal corporation, township, township fire district, joint fire district, other political subdivision, or combination of political subdivisions;

(3) A member of a private fire company, as defined in section 9.60 of the Revised Code, or a volunteer firefighter;

(4) A member of a joint ambulance district;

(5) An emergency medical technician-basic, emergency medical technician-intermediate, emergency medical technician-paramedic, ambulance operator, or other member of an emergency medical service that is owned or operated by a political subdivision or a private entity;

(6) The state fire marshal, an assistant state marshal, or an arson investigator of the office of the state fire marshal;

(7) A fire prevention officer of a political subdivision or an arson investigator or similar inspector of a political subdivision.

(C) "Occupied structure" means any house, building, outbuilding, watercraft, aircraft, railroad car, truck, trailer, tent, or other structure, vehicle, or shelter, or any portion thereof, to which any of the following applies:

(1) It is maintained as a permanent or temporary dwelling, even though it is temporarily unoccupied and whether or not any person is actually present.

(2) At the time, it is occupied as the permanent or temporary habitation of any person, whether or not any person is actually present.

(3) At the time, it is specially adapted for the overnight accommodation of any person, whether or not any person is actually present.

(4) At the time, any person is present or likely to be present in it.

(D) "Political subdivision" and "state" have the same meanings as in section 2744.01 of the Revised Code.

HISTORY: 134 v H 511 (Eff 1-1-74); 144 v H 675 (Eff 3-19-93); 146 v S 150. Eff 11-24-95.

Not analogous to former RC § 2909.01 (RS § 6863; S&S 56, 155, 162, 263, 284, 736; S&C 419, 420, 429, 430, 445, 446; 29 v 144; 43 v 92; 54 v 36; 54 v 99; 59 v 57; 60 v 20; 62 v 8; 62 v 72; 64 v 74; 64 v 128; 66 v 122; 66 v 341; 68 v 42; 68 v 87; 69 v 82; 70 v 215; 73 v 64; 73 v 94; 73 v 180; GC § 12477; Bureau of Code Revision, 10-1-53), repealed 134 v H 511, § 2, eff 1-1-74.

§ 2909.02 Aggravated arson.

(A) No person, by means of fire or explosion, shall knowingly do any of the following:

(1) Create a substantial risk of serious physical harm to any person other than the offender;

(2) Cause physical harm to any occupied structure;

(3) Create, through the offer or acceptance of an agreement for hire or other consideration, a substantial risk of physical harm to any occupied structure.

(B)(1) Whoever violates this section is guilty of aggravated arson.

(2) A violation of division (A)(1) or (3) of this section is a felony of the first degree.

(3) A violation of division (A)(2) of this section is a felony of the second degree.

HISTORY: 134 v H 511 (Eff 1-1-74); 136 v S 282 (Eff 5-21-76); 139 v S 199 (Eff 1-5-83); 146 v S 2 (Eff 7-1-96); 146 v S 269. Eff 7-1-96.

Not analogous to former RC § 2909.02 (RS § 6864; S&C 433, 437, 438, 1612; S&S 282—284; 29 v 470; 29 v 144; 59 v 27; 59 v 79; 62 v 139; 69 v 67; GC § 12478; 124 v 466; Bureau of Code Revision, 10-1-53), repealed 134 v H 511, § 2, eff 1-1-74.

The effective date is set by section 5 of SB 269.

§ 2909.03 Arson.

(A) No person, by means of fire or explosion, shall knowingly do any of the following:

(1) Cause, or create a substantial risk of, physical harm to any property of another without the other person's consent;

(2) Cause, or create a substantial risk of, physical harm to any property of the offender or another, with purpose to defraud;

(3) Cause, or create a substantial risk of, physical harm to the statehouse or a courthouse, school building, or other building or structure that is owned or controlled by the state, any political subdivision, or any department, agency, or instrumentality of the state or a political subdivision, and that is used for public purposes;

(4) Cause, or create a substantial risk of, physical harm, through the offer or the acceptance of an agreement for hire or other consideration, to any property of another without the other person's consent or to any property of the offender or another with purpose to defraud;

(5) Cause, or create a substantial risk of, physical harm to any park, preserve, wildlands, brush-covered land, cut-over land, forest, timberland, greenlands, woods, or similar real property that is owned or controlled by another person, the state, or a political subdivision without the consent of the other person, the state, or the political subdivision;

(6) With purpose to defraud, cause, or create a substantial risk of, physical harm to any park, preserve, wildlands, brush-covered land, cut-over land, forest, timberland, greenlands, woods, or similar real property that is owned or controlled by the offender, another person, the state, or a political subdivision.

(B)(1) Whoever violates this section is guilty of arson.

(2) A violation of division (A)(1) of this section is one of the following:

(a) Except as otherwise provided in division (B)(2)(b) of this section, a misdemeanor of the first degree;

(b) If the value of the property or the amount of the physical harm involved is five hundred dollars or more, a felony of the fourth degree.

(3) A violation of division (A)(2), (3), (5), or (6) of this section is a felony of the fourth degree.

(4) A violation of division (A)(4) of this section is a felony of the third degree.

HISTORY: 134 v H 511 (Eff 1-1-74); 136 v S 282 (Eff 5-21-76); 139 v S 199 (Eff 1-1-83); 144 v H 675 (Eff 3-19-93); 146 v S 2. Eff 7-1-96.

Not analogous to former RC § 2909.03 (GC § 12478-1; 106 v 104; Bureau of Code Revision, 10-1-53), repealed 134 v H 511, § 2, eff 1-1-74.

The effective date is set by section 6 of SB 2.

§ 2909.04 Disrupting public services.

(A) No person, purposely by any means, or knowingly by damaging or tampering with any property, shall do any of the following:

(1) Interrupt or impair television, radio, telephone, telegraph, or other mass communications service, or police, fire, or other public service communications, or radar, loran, radio, or other electronic aids to air or marine navigation or communications, or amateur or citizens band radio communications being used for public service or emergency communications;

(2) Interrupt or impair public transportation, including without limitation school bus transportation, or water supply, gas, power, or other utility service to the public;

(3) Substantially impair the ability of law enforcement officers, firemen, or rescue personnel to respond to an emergency, or to protect and preserve any person or property from serious physical harm.

(B) Whoever violates this section is guilty of disrupting public services, a felony of the fourth degree.

HISTORY: 134 v H 511 (Eff 1-1-74); 146 v S 2. Eff 7-1-96.

Not analogous to former RC § 2909.04 (GC § 12479; 99 v 526; Bureau of Code Revision, 10-1-53), repealed 134 v H 511, § 2, eff 1-1-74.

The effective date is set by section 6 of SB 2.

§ 2909.05 Vandalism.

(A) No person shall knowingly cause serious physical harm to an occupied structure or any of its contents.

(B)(1) No person shall knowingly cause serious physical harm to property that is owned or possessed by another, when either of the following applies:

(a) The property is used by its owner or possessor in the owner's or possessor's profession, business, trade, or occupation, and the value of the property or the amount of physical harm involved is five hundred dollars or more;

(b) Regardless of the value of the property or the amount of damage done, the property or its equivalent is necessary in order for its owner or possessor to engage in the owner's or possessor's profession, business, trade, or occupation.

(2) No person shall knowingly cause serious physical harm to property that is owned, leased, or controlled by a governmental entity. A governmental entity includes, but is not limited to, the state or a political subdivision of the state, a school district, the board of trustees of a public library or public university, or any other body corporate and politic responsible for governmental activities only in geographical areas smaller than that of the state.

(C) No person, without privilege to do so, shall knowingly cause serious physical harm to any tomb, monument, gravestone, or other similar structure that is used as a memorial for the dead; to any fence, railing, curb, or other property that is used to protect, enclose, or ornament any place of burial; or to a place of burial.

(D) No person, without privilege to do so, shall knowingly cause physical harm to a place of burial by breaking and entering into a tomb, crypt, casket, or other structure that is used as a memorial for the dead or as an enclosure for the dead.

(E) Whoever violates this section is guilty of vandalism. Except as otherwise provided in this division, vandalism is a felony of the fifth degree that is punishable by a fine of up to two thousand five hundred dollars in addition to the penalties specified for a felony of the fifth degree in sections 2929.11 to 2929.18 of the Revised Code. If the value of the property or the amount of physical harm involved is five thousand dollars or more but less than one hundred thousand dollars, vandalism is a felony of the fourth degree. If the value of the property or the amount of physical harm involved is one hundred thousand dollars or more, vandalism is a felony of the third degree.

(F) For purposes of this section, "serious physical harm" means physical harm to property that results in loss to the value of the property of five hundred dollars or more.

HISTORY: 134 v H 511 (Eff 1-1-74); 137 v H 741 (Eff 10-9-78); 138 v H 618 (Eff 7-31-80); 139 v S 199 (Eff 1-5-83); 139 v H 269 (Eff 1-5-83); 141 v S 316 (Eff 3-19-87); 144 v H 675 (Eff 3-19-93); 146 v S 2. Eff 7-1-96.

Not analogous to former RC § 2909.05 (RS § 6865; S&C 429; 29 v 144; 75 v 130; GC § 12480; Bureau of Code Revision, 10-1-53), repealed 134 v H 511, § 2, eff 1-1-74.

The effective date is set by section 6 of SB 2.

§ 2909.06 Criminal damaging or endangering.

(A) No person shall cause, or create a substantial risk of physical harm to any property of another without the other person's consent:

(1) Knowingly, by any means;

(2) Recklessly, by means of fire, explosion, flood, poison gas, poison, radioactive material, caustic or corrosive material, or other inherently dangerous agency or substance.

(B) Whoever violates this section is guilty of criminal damaging or endangering, a misdemeanor of the second degree. If a violation of this section creates a risk of physical harm to any person, criminal damaging or endangering is a misdemeanor of the first degree. If the property involved in a violation of this section is an aircraft, an aircraft engine, propeller, appliance, spare part, or any other equipment or implement used or intended to be used in the operation of an aircraft and if the violation creates a risk of physical harm to any person, criminal damaging or endangering is a felony of the fifth degree. If the property involved in a violation of this section is an aircraft, an aircraft engine, propeller, appliance, spare part, or any other equipment or implement used or intended to be used in the operation of an aircraft and if the violation creates a substantial risk of physical harm to any person or if the property involved in a violation of this section is an occupied aircraft, criminal damaging or endangering is a felony of the fourth degree.

HISTORY: 134 v H 511 (Eff 1-1-74); 140 v H 570 (Eff 3-28-85); 146 v S 2. Eff 7-1-96.

Not analogous to former RC § 2909.06 (GC § 12480-1; 102 v 297; Bureau of Code Revision, 10-1-53), repealed 134 v H 511, § 2, eff 1-1-74.

The effective date is set by section 6 of SB 2.

§ 2909.07 Criminal mischief.

(A) No person shall:

(1) Without privilege to do so, knowingly move, deface, damage, destroy, or otherwise improperly tamper with the property of another;

(2) With purpose to interfere with the use or enjoyment of property of another, employ a tear gas device, stink bomb, smoke generator, or other device releasing a substance that is harmful or offensive to persons exposed or that tends to cause public alarm;

(3) Without privilege to do so, knowingly move, deface, damage, destroy, or otherwise improperly tamper with a bench mark, triangulation station, boundary marker, or other survey station, monument, or marker;

(4) Without privilege to do so, knowingly move, deface, damage, destroy, or otherwise improperly tamper with any safety device, the property of another, or the property of the offender when required or placed for the safety of others, so as to destroy or diminish its effectiveness or availability for its intended purpose;

(5) With purpose to interfere with the use or enjoyment of the property of another, set a fire on the land of another or place personal property that has been set on fire on the land of another, which fire or personal property is outside and apart from any building, other structure, or personal property that is on that land.

(B) As used in this section, "safety device" means any fire extinguisher, fire hose, or fire axe, or any fire escape, emergency exit, or emergency escape equipment, or any life line, life-saving ring, life preserver, or life boat or raft, or any alarm, light, flare, signal, sign, or notice intended to warn of danger or emergency, or intended for other safety purposes, or any guard railing or safety barricade, or any traffic sign or signal, or any railroad grade crossing sign, signal, or gate, or any first aid or survival equipment, or any other device, apparatus, or equipment intended for protecting or preserving the safety of persons or property.

(C) Whoever violates this section is guilty of criminal mischief, a misdemeanor of the third degree. If violation of this section creates a risk of physical harm to any person, criminal mischief is a misdemeanor of the first degree. If the property involved in violation of this section is an aircraft, an aircraft engine, propeller, appliance, spare part, fuel, lubricant, hydraulic fluid, any other equipment, implement, or material used or intended to be used in the operation of an aircraft, or any cargo carried or intended to be carried in an aircraft and if the violation creates a risk of physical harm to any person, criminal mischief is a felony of the fifth degree. If the property involved in violation of this section is an aircraft, an aircraft engine, propeller, appliance, spare part, fuel, lubricant, hydraulic fluid, any other equipment, implement, or material used or intended to be used in the operation of an aircraft, or any cargo carried or intended to be carried in an aircraft and if the violation creates a substantial risk of physical harm to any person or if the property involved in a violation of this section is an occupied aircraft, criminal mischief is a felony of the fourth degree.

HISTORY: 134 v H 511 (Eff 1-1-74); 135 v H 89 (Eff 1-1-74); 140 v H 570 (Eff 3-28-85); 141 v S 316 (Eff 3-19-87); 146 v S 2. Eff 7-1-96.

Analogous to former RC § 2909.07 (RS § 6866; 69 v 81; GC

§ 12481; Bureau of Code Revision, 10-1-53), repealed 134 v H 511, § 2, eff 1-1-74.

The effective date is set by section 6 of SB 2.

§ 2909.08 Endangering aircraft or airport operations.

(A) As used in this section:

(1) "Air gun" means a hand pistol or rifle that propels its projectile by means of releasing compressed air, carbon dioxide, or other gas.

(2) "Firearm" has the same meaning as in section 2923.11 of the Revised Code.

(3) "Spring-operated gun" means a hand pistol or rifle that propels a projectile not less than four or more than five millimeters in diameter by means of a spring.

(4) "Airport operational surface" means any surface of land or water that is developed, posted, or marked so as to give an observer reasonable notice that the surface is designed and developed for the purpose of storing, parking, taxiing, or operating aircraft, or any surface of land or water that is actually being used for any of those purposes.

(B) No person shall do either of the following:

(1) Knowingly throw an object at, or drop an object upon, any moving aircraft;

(2) Knowingly shoot with a bow and arrow, or knowingly discharge a firearm, air gun, or spring-operated gun, at or toward any aircraft.

(C) No person shall knowingly or recklessly shoot with a bow and arrow, or shall knowingly or recklessly discharge a firearm, air gun, or spring-operated gun, upon or over any airport operational surface. This division does not apply to the following:

(1) An officer, agent, or employee of this or any other state or the United States, or a law enforcement officer, authorized to discharge firearms and acting within the scope of his duties;

(2) A person who, with the consent of the owner or operator of the airport operational surface or the authorized agent of either, is lawfully engaged in any hunting or sporting activity or is otherwise lawfully discharging a firearm.

(D) Whoever violates division (B) of this section is guilty of endangering aircraft, a misdemeanor of the first degree. If the violation creates a risk of physical harm to any person or if the aircraft that is the subject of the violation is occupied, endangering aircraft is a felony of the fourth degree.

(E) Whoever violates division (C) of this section is guilty of endangering airport operations, a misdemeanor of the second degree. If the violation creates a risk of physical harm to any person, endangering airport operations is a felony of the fourth degree. Whoever violates division (C) of this section while hunting shall additionally have his hunting license or permit suspended or revoked pursuant to section 1533.68 of the Revised Code.

(F) Any bow and arrow, air gun, spring-operated gun, or firearm that has been used in a felony violation of this section, shall be seized or forfeited, and shall be disposed of pursuant to section 2933.41 of the Revised Code.

HISTORY: 140 v H 570. Eff 3-28-85.

Not analogous to former RC § 2909.08 (RS § 6868; S&S 285; S&C 436; 60 v 85; GC § 12483; Bureau of Code Revision, 10-1-53; 131 v 674), repealed 134 v H 511, § 2, eff 1-1-74.

§§ 2909.09, 2909.10 Repealed, 134 v H 511, § 2 [RS §§ 6877, 6878; S&C 457b; S&S 280, 285; 63 v 8; 63 v 175; 70 v 216; GC §§ 12487, 12488; 123 v 468; Bureau of Code Revision, 10-1-53; 131 v 674]. Eff 1-1-74.

These sections concerned malicious destruction of property.

§ 2909.11 Determining property value or amount of physical harm.

(A) When a person is charged with a violation of division (A)(1) of section 2909.03 of the Revised Code involving property value or an amount of physical harm of five hundred dollars or more or with a violation of section 2909.05 of the Revised Code involving property value or an amount of physical harm of five hundred dollars or more, the jury or court trying the accused shall determine the value of the property or amount of physical harm and, if a guilty verdict is returned, shall return the finding as part of the verdict. In any such case, it is unnecessary to find or return the exact value or amount of physical harm, section 2945.75 of the Revised Code applies, and it is sufficient if either of the following applies, as appropriate, relative to the finding and return of the value or amount of physical harm:

(1) If the finding and return relate to a violation of division (A)(1) of section 2909.03 of the Revised Code† and are that the value or amount of the physical harm was five hundred dollars or more, the finding and return shall include a statement that the value or amount was five hundred dollars or more.

(2) If the finding and return relate to a violation of division section 2909.05 of the Revised Code and are that the value or amount of the physical harm was in any of the following categories, the finding and return shall include one of the following statements, as appropriate:

(a) If the finding and return are that the value or amount was one hundred thousand dollars or more, a statement that the value or amount was one hundred thousand dollars or more;

(b) If the finding and return are that the value or amount was five thousand dollars or more but less than one hundred thousand dollars a statement that the value or amount was five thousand dollars or more but less than one hundred thousand dollars;

(c) If the finding and return are that the value or amount was five hundred dollars or more but less than five thousand dollars, a statement that the value or amount was five hundred dollars or more but less than five thousand dollars.

(B) The following criteria shall be used in determining the value of property or amount of physical harm involved in a violation of division (A)(1) of section 2909.03 or section 2909.05 of the Revised Code:

(1) If the property is an heirloom, memento, collector's item, antique, museum piece, manuscript, document, record, or other thing that is either irreplaceable or is replaceable only on the expenditure of substantial time, effort, or money, the value of the property or the amount of physical harm involved is the amount that would compensate the owner for its loss.

(2) If the property is not covered under division (B)(1) of this section and the physical harm is such that the property can be restored substantially to its former condition, the amount of physical harm involved is the reasonable cost of restoring the property.

(3) If the property is not covered under division (B)(1) of this section and the physical harm is such that the property cannot be restored substantially to its former condition, the value of the property, in the case of personal property, is the cost of replacing the property with new property of like kind and quality, and, in the case of real property or real property fixtures, is the difference in the fair market value of the property immediately before and immediately after the offense.

(C) As used in this section, "fair market value" has the same meaning as in section 2913.61 of the Revised Code.

(D) Prima-facie evidence of the value of property, as provided in division (E) of section 2913.61 of the Revised Code, may be used to establish the value of property pursuant to this section.

HISTORY: 134 v H 511 (Eff 1-1-74); 137 v H 741 (Eff 10-9-78); 138 v H 618 (Eff 7-31-80); 139 v S 199 (Eff 1-5-83); 139 v H 269 (Eff 1-5-83); 144 v H 675 (Eff 3-19-93); 146 v S 2. Eff 7-1-96.

Not analogous to former RC § 2909.11 (RS § 6879; S&C 336, 433, 1313; S&S 665; 29 v 144; 36 v 104; 65 v 14; GC § 12489; **Bureau of Code Revision, 10-1-53), repealed 134 v H 511, § 2, eff 1-1-74.**

The effective date is set by section 6 of SB 2.

† So in enrolled bill.

§§ 2909.12, 2909.13, 2909.14

Repealed, 134 v H 511, § 2 [RS §§ 6862, 6883, 6885; S&S 9, 281; 64 v 127, 254; 76 v 11; 81 v 125; 84 v 81; Bureau of Code Revision, 10-1-53; 126 v 575; 131 v 675]. Eff 1-1-74.

These sections concerned offenses against property.

§§ 2909.15, 2909.16, 2909.17

Repealed, 134 v H 511, § 2 [RS §§ 6854a—6854c; 90 v 329; GC §§ 12514—12516; Bureau of Code Revision, 10-1-53]. Eff 1-1-74.

These sections concerned offenses against property.

§§ 2909.18, 2909.19, 2909.20

Repealed, 134 v H 511, § 2 [RS §§ 3713-7—3713-9; 82 v 208; 86 v 302; 92 v 157; 95 v 241; GC §§ 12518—12520; Bureau of Code Revision, 10-1-53; 129 v 582(746)]. Eff 1-1-74.

These sections concerned offenses against property.

§§ 2909.21, 2909.22, 2909.23

Repealed, 134 v H 511, § 2 [RS §§ 4905, 6880e, 6881-1; 73 v 117; 82 v 166; 91 v 224; GC §§ 12522, 12530, 12532; 102 v 88; 119 v 114; Bureau of Code Revision, 10-1-53]. Eff 1-1-74.

These sections concerned trespassing.

§§ 2909.24, 2909.25, 2909.26

Repealed, 134 v H 511, § 2 [127 v 810; 128 v 467; 132 v H 996]. Eff 1-1-74.

These sections concerned destruction of public utilities facilities, dumping of garbage, and trespassing.

CHAPTER 2911: ROBBERY, BURGLARY, TRESPASS AND SAFECRACKING

Section

[ROBBERY]
2911.01　Aggravated robbery.
2911.02　Robbery.
2911.03-2911.10　Repealed.

[BURGLARY]
2911.11　Aggravated burglary.
[2911.11.1] 2911.111　Repealed.
2911.12　Burglary.
2911.13　Breaking and entering.
[2911.13.1] 2911.131　Repealed.
2911.14, 2911.15, 2911.16　Repealed.
2911.17-2911.20　Repealed.

[TRESPASS]
2911.21　Criminal trespass.
[2911.21.1] 2911.211　Aggravated trespass.
2911.22-2911.30　Repealed.

[SAFECRACKING]
2911.31　Safecracking.
2911.32　Tampering with coin machines.
2911.33-2911.49　Repealed.
2911.71-2911.73　Repealed.

[ROBBERY]

§ 2911.01　Aggravated robbery.

(A) No person, in attempting or committing a theft offense, as defined in section 2913.01 of the Revised Code, or in fleeing immediately after the attempt or offense, shall do any of the following:

(1) Have a deadly weapon on or about the offender's person or under the offender's control and either display the weapon, brandish it, indicate that the offender possesses it, or use it;

(2) Have a dangerous ordnance on or about the offender's person or under the offender's control;

(3) Inflict, or attempt to inflict, serious physical harm on another.

(B) No person, without privilege to do so, shall knowingly remove or attempt to remove a deadly weapon from the person of a law enforcement officer, or shall knowingly deprive or attempt to deprive a law enforcement officer of a deadly weapon, when both of the following apply:

(1) The law enforcement officer, at the time of the removal, attempted removal, deprivation, or attempted deprivation, is acting within the course and scope of the officer's duties;

(2) The offender knows or has reasonable cause to know that the law enforcement officer is a law enforcement officer.

(C) Whoever violates this section is guilty of aggravated robbery, a felony of the first degree.

(D) As used in this section:

(1) "Deadly weapon" and "dangerous ordnance" have the same meanings as in section 2923.11 of the Revised Code.

(2) "Law enforcement officer" has the same meaning as in section 2901.01 of the Revised Code and also includes employees of the department of rehabilitation and correction who are authorized to carry weapons within the course and scope of their duties.

HISTORY: 134 v H 511 (Eff 1-1-74); 139 v S 199 (Eff 1-5-83); 140 v S 210 (Eff 7-1-83); 146 v S 2 (Eff 7-1-96); 147 v H 151. Eff 9-16-97.

Not analogous to former RC § 2911.01 (RS § 7076; 70 v 39; 73 v 20; 74 v 41; GC § 13104; 124 v 466; Bureau of Code Revision, 10-1-53; 129 v 344), repealed 134 v H 511, § 2, eff 1-1-74.

§ 2911.02　Robbery.

(A) No person, in attempting or committing a theft offense or in fleeing immediately after the attempt or offense, shall do any of the following:

(1) Have a deadly weapon on or about the offender's person or under the offender's control;

(2) Inflict, attempt to inflict, or threaten to inflict physical harm on another;

(3) Use or threaten the immediate use of force against another.

(B) Whoever violates this section is guilty of robbery. A violation of division (A)(1) or (2) of this section is a felony of the second degree. A violation of division (A)(3) of this section is a felony of the third degree.

(C) As used in this section:

(1) "Deadly weapon" has the same meaning as in section 2923.11 of the Revised Code.

(2) "Theft offense" has the same meaning as in section 2913.01 of the Revised Code.

HISTORY: 134 v H 511 (Eff 1-1-74); 139 v S 199 (Eff 7-1-83); 146 v S 2 (Eff 7-1-96); 146 v S 269. Eff 7-1-96.

Not analogous to former RC § 2911.02 (RS § 7075; 59 v 193; 102 v 114; GC § 13105; 124 v 466; Bureau of Code Revision, 10-1-53), repealed 134 v H 511, § 2, eff 1-1-74.

The effective date is set by section 6 of SB 2.

§§ 2911.03, 2911.04, 2911.05

Repealed, 134 v H 511, § 2 [GC §§ 13105-1, 13108, 13108-1; 111 v 257, 258; 124 v 466; Bureau of Code Revision, 10-1-53; 126 v 575]. Eff 1-1-74.

These sections concerned false statements and stock brokers.

§§ 2911.06, 2911.07, 2911.08

Repealed, 134 v H 511, § 2 [GC §§ 13108-2—13108-4; 111 v 258; Bureau of Code Revision, 10-1-53; 126 v 575]. Eff 1-1-74.

These sections concerned false statements and stock brokers.

§§ 2911.09, 2911.10 Repealed, 134 v H 511, § 2 [GC §§ 13108-5, 13108-6; 111 v 258, 259; Bureau of Code Revision, 10-1-53]. Eff 1-1-74.

These sections concerned false statements and stock brokers.

[BURGLARY]

§ 2911.11 Aggravated burglary.

(A) No person, by force, stealth, or deception, shall trespass in an occupied structure or in a separately secured or separately occupied portion of an occupied structure, when another person other than an accomplice of the offender is present, with purpose to commit in the structure or in the separately secured or separately occupied portion of the structure any criminal offense, if any of the following apply:

(1) The offender inflicts, or attempts or threatens to inflict physical harm on another;

(2) The offender has a deadly weapon or dangerous ordnance on or about the offender's person or under the offender's control.

(B) Whoever violates this section is guilty of aggravated burglary, a felony of the first degree.

(C) As used in this section:

(1) "Occupied structure" has the same meaning as in section 2909.01 of the Revised Code.

(2) "Deadly weapon" and "dangerous ordnance" have the same meanings as in section 2923.11 of the Revised Code.

HISTORY: 134 v H 511 (Eff 1-1-74); 139 v S 199 (Eff 1-5-83); 140 v S 210 (Eff 7-1-83); 146 v S 2 (Eff 7-1-96); 146 v S 269. Eff 7-1-96.

Not analogous to former RC § 2911.11 (RS § 7085; S&C 422; 50 v 132; 57 v 56; GC § 13115; Bureau of Code Revision, 10-1-53), repealed 134 v H 511, § 2, eff 1-1-74.

The effective date is set by section 6 of SB 2.

[§ 2911.11.1] § 2911.111 Repealed, 134 v H 511, § 2 [132 v S 97]. Eff 1-1-74.

This section concerned checks drawn on insufficient funds.

§ 2911.12 Burglary.

(A) No person, by force, stealth, or deception, shall do any of the following:

(1) Trespass in an occupied structure or in a separately secured or separately occupied portion of an occupied structure, when another person other than an accomplice of the offender is present, with purpose to commit in the structure or in the separately secured or separately occupied portion of the structure any criminal offense;

(2) Trespass in an occupied structure or in a separately secured or separately occupied portion of an occupied structure that is a permanent or temporary habitation of any person when any person other than an accomplice of the offender is present or likely to be present, with purpose to commit in the habitation any criminal offense;

(3) Trespass in an occupied structure or in a separately secured or separately occupied portion of an occupied structure, with purpose to commit in the structure or separately secured or separately occupied portion of the structure any criminal offense;

(4) Trespass in a permanent or temporary habitation of any person when any person other than an accomplice of the offender is present or likely to be present.

(B) As used in this section, "occupied structure" has the same meaning as in section 2909.01 of the Revised Code.

(C) Whoever violates this section is guilty of burglary. A violation of division (A)(1) or (2) of this section is a felony of the second degree. A violation of division (A)(3) of this section is a felony of the third degree. A violation of division (A)(4) of this section is a felony of the fourth degree.

HISTORY: 134 v H 511 (Eff 1-1-74); 139 v S 199 (Eff 7-1-83); 143 v H 837 (Eff 7-3-90); 146 v S 2 (Eff 7-1-96); 146 v S 269. Eff 7-1-96.

Not analogous to former RC § 2911.12 (RS § 7080; S&C 703; 70 v 40; GC § 13126; Bureau of Code Revision, 10-1-53), repealed 134 v H 511, § 2, eff 1-1-74.

The effective date is set by section 6 of SB 2.

§ 2911.13 Breaking and entering.

(A) No person[,] by force, stealth, or deception, shall trespass in an unoccupied structure, with purpose to commit therein any theft offense, as defined in section 2913.01 of the Revised Code, or any felony.

(B) No person shall trespass on the land or premises of another, with purpose to commit a felony.

(C) Whoever violates this section is guilty of breaking and entering, a felony of the fifth degree.

HISTORY: 134 v H 511 (Eff 1-1-74); 146 v S 2. Eff 7-1-96.

Not analogous to former RC § 2911.13 (RS §§ 7076-4—7076-6; 95 v 306; GC § 13130; 123 v 700; Bureau of Code Revision, 10-1-53), repealed 134 v H 511, § 2, eff 1-1-74.

The effective date is set by section 6 of SB 2.

[§ 2911.13.1] § 2911.131 Repealed, 134 v H 511, § 2 [133 v H 192]. Eff 1-1-74.

This section concerned false motor vehicle repair estimates and fraudulent charges.

§§ 2911.14, 2911.15, 2911.16

Repealed, 134 v H 511, § 2 [RS §§ 7017-4, 7017-5, 7076a—7076c, 7087; S&C 422; 44 v 34; 83 v 138; 94 v 20, 363; 99 v 115, 116; GC §§ 13131, 13143, 13145; 110 v 29; Bureau of Code Revision, 10-1-53]. Eff 1-1-74.

These sections concerned miscellaneous frauds.

§ 2911.17 Repealed, 134 v H 511, § 2 [RS § 7017-6; 95 v 68; GC § 13148; Bureau of Code Revision, 10-1-53]. Eff 1-1-74.

This section prohibited the performance of dramatic compositions without consent of owner.

§ 2911.18 Repealed, 129 v 13 (182), § 2 [RS § 6993; 66 v 93; GC § 13149; Bureau of Code Revision, 10-1-53]. Eff 7-1-62.

This section concerned taking or selling note for patent right.

§§ 2911.19, 2911.20 Repealed, 134 v H 511, § 2 [RS §§ 7076-3, 7105-1; 88 v 64; 90 v 131; GC §§ 13146, 13158; Bureau of Code Revision, 10-1-53]. Eff 1-1-74.

These sections concerned misrepresentation by married man, and furnishing false pedigree.

[TRESPASS]

§ 2911.21 Criminal trespass.

(A) No person, without privilege to do so, shall do any of the following:

(1) Knowingly enter or remain on the land or premises of another;

(2) Knowingly enter or remain on the land or premises of another, the use of which is lawfully restricted to certain persons, purposes, modes, or hours, when the offender knows he is in violation of any such restriction or is reckless in that regard;

(3) Recklessly enter or remain on the land or premises of another, as to which notice against unauthorized access or presence is given by actual communication to the offender, or in a manner prescribed by law, or by posting in a manner reasonably calculated to come to the attention of potential intruders, or by fencing or other enclosure manifestly designed to restrict access;

(4) Being on the land or premises of another, negligently fail or refuse to leave upon being notified to do so by the owner or occupant, or the agent or servant of either.

(B) It is no defense to a charge under this section that the land or premises involved was owned, controlled, or in custody of a public agency.

(C) It is no defense to a charge under this section that the offender was authorized to enter or remain on the land or premises involved, when such authorization was secured by deception.

(D) Whoever violates this section is guilty of criminal trespass, a misdemeanor of the fourth degree.

(E) As used in this section, "land or premises" includes any land, building, structure, or place belonging to, controlled by, or in custody of another, and any separate enclosure or room, or portion thereof.

HISTORY: 134 v H 511. Eff 1-1-74.

Not analogous to former RC § 2911.21 (RS §§ 7076-1, 7076-2; 84 v 213; GC § 13162; 109 v 406; Bureau of Code Revision, 10-1-53; 126 v 575), repealed 134 v H 511, § 2, eff 1-1-74.

[§ 2911.21.1] § 2911.211 Aggravated trespass.

(A) No person shall enter or remain on the land or premises of another with purpose to commit on that land or those premises a misdemeanor, the elements of which involve causing physical harm to another person or causing another person to believe that the offender will cause physical harm to him.

(B) Whoever violates this section is guilty of aggravated trespass, a misdemeanor of the first degree.

HISTORY: 144 v H 536. Eff 11-5-92.

§§ 2911.22, 2911.23, 2911.24 Repealed, 134 v H 511, § 2 [RS §§ 4355a, 7069-5; 78 v 242; 83 v 162; GC §§ 13129, 13147, 13162-1; 109 v 406; Bureau of Code Revision, 10-1-53]. Eff 1-1-74.

These sections concerned unlawful entries; sales of seed, tobacco, and wool.

§§ 2911.25, 2911.26, 2911.27 Repealed, 134 v H 511, § 2 [RS §§ 7069-3, 7069-4, 7088-2; 85 v 285; 86 v 5; 99 v 114; GC §§ 13114, 13163, 13164; 109 v 228; Bureau of Code Revision, 10-1-53; 131 v 675]. Eff 1-1-74.

These sections concerned unlawful sales of wool; insignia or badge.

§§ 2911.28, 2911.29, 2911.30 Repealed, 134 v H 511, § 2 [99 v 336; GC §§ 13163-1, 13175, 14867-21, 14867-22; 108 v PtI, 64; 109 v 312; Bureau of Code Revision, 10-1-53; 129 v 582(746)]. Eff 1-1-74.

These sections concerned unlawful wearing of insignia or badge; prospectus.

[SAFECRACKING]

§ 2911.31 Safecracking.

(A) No person, with purpose to commit an offense, shall knowingly enter, force an entrance into, or tamper with any vault, safe, or strongbox.

(B) Whoever violates this section is guilty of safecracking, a felony of the fourth degree.

HISTORY: 134 v H 511 (Eff 1-1-74); 146 v S 2. Eff 7-1-96.

Not analogous to former RC § 2911.31 (RS § 3184c; 86 v 374; 95 v 210; 97 v 499; GC § 13180; Bureau of Code Revision, 10-1-53), repealed 134 v H 511, § 2, eff 1-1-74.

Analogous to former RC § 2907.12 (RS § 6835-1; 95 v 122; GC § 12440; Bureau of Code Revision, 10-1-53), repealed 134 v H 511, § 2, eff 1-1-74.

The effective date is set by section 6 of SB 2.

§ 2911.32 Tampering with coin machines.

(A) No person, with purpose to commit theft or to defraud, shall knowingly enter, force an entrance into, tamper with, or insert any part of an instrument into any coin machine.

(B) Whoever violates this section is guilty of tampering with coin machines, a misdemeanor of the first degree. If the offender previously has been convicted of a violation of this section or of any theft offense as defined in section 2913.01 of the Revised Code, tampering with coin machines is a felony of the fifth degree.

HISTORY: 134 v H 511 (Eff 1-1-74); 146 v S 2. Eff 7-1-96.

Not analogous to former RC § 2911.32 (RS § 3231-5; 86 v 121; GC § 13181; 107 v 181; Bureau of Code Revision, 10-1-53), repealed 134 v H 511, § 2, eff 1-1-74.

Analogous to former RC § 2907.12.1 (132 v H 656), repealed 134 v H 511, § 2, eff 1-1-74.

The effective date is set by section 6 of SB 2.

§§ 2911.33, 2911.34, 2911.35

Repealed, 134 v H 511, § 2 [RS §§ 7088, 7090-1; 73 v 19; 93 v 168, 313; GC §§ 13144, 13152, 13183; 114 v 118; Bureau of Code Revision, 10-1-53]. Eff 1-1-74.

These sections concerned crockery; mails; coins; slugs.

§§ 2911.36, 2911.37, 2911.38

Repealed, 134 v H 511, § 2 [GC §§ 13184, 13184-1, 13187; 114 v 118; 115 v 247; 119 v 312; Bureau of Code Revision, 10-1-53]. Eff 1-1-74.

These sections concerned coins; slugs; batteries.

§§ 2911.39, 2911.40, 2911.41

Repealed, 134 v H 511, § 2 [GC §§ 13187-1, 13193-2, 13194-1; 103 v 43; 115 v 248; 121 v 72, 590; Bureau of Code Revision, 10-1-53; 127 v 461; 129 v 1305]. Eff 1-1-74.

These sections concerned batteries; advertising.

§§ 2911.42, 2911.43, 2911.44

Repealed, 134 v H 511, § 2 [GC § 13193-3; 121 v 590; Bureau of Code Revision, 10-1-53; 129 v 13 (179)]. Eff 1-1-74.

These sections concerned fraudulent advertising; bills of lading.

§§ 2911.45, 2911.46, 2911.47

Repealed, 134 v H 511, § 2 [129 v 13 (179)]. Eff 1-1-74.

These sections concerned bills of lading.

§§ 2911.48, 2911.49

Repealed, 134 v H 511, § 2 [129 v 13 (179)]. Eff 1-1-74.

These sections concerned bills of lading.

§§ 2911.71, 2911.72, 2911.73

Repealed, 134 v H 511, § 2 [129 v 1023; 133 v S 6]. Eff 1-1-74.

These sections concerned frauds involving electronic picture tubes, and medical fraud and misrepresentations.

CHAPTER 2913: THEFT AND FRAUD

Section

[IN GENERAL]
2913.01 Definitions.

[THEFT]
2913.02 Theft.
2913.03 Unauthorized use of a vehicle.
2913.04 Unauthorized use of property; computer property.
[2913.04.1] 2913.041 Possession or sale of unauthorized cable television device.
2913.05, 2913.06, 2913.07 Repealed.
2913.08, 2913.09, 2913.10 Repealed.

[PASSING BAD CHECKS]
2913.11 Passing bad checks.
2913.12, 2913.13, 2913.14 Repealed.
2913.15, 2913.16, 2913.17 Repealed.

[MISUSE OF CREDIT CARDS]
2913.21 Misuse of credit cards.

[FORGERY]
2913.31 Forgery.
2913.32 Criminal simulation.
2913.33 Making or using slugs.
2913.34 Trademark counterfeiting.

[FRAUDS]
2913.40 Medicaid fraud.
2913.41 Defrauding a livery or hostelry.
2913.42 Tampering with records.
2913.43 Securing writings by deception.
2913.44 Personating an officer.
[2913.44.1] 2913.441 Law enforcement emblem display.
2913.45 Defrauding creditors.
2913.46 Illegal use of food stamps or WIC program benefits.
2913.47 Insurance fraud.
2913.48 Workers' compensation fraud.

[RECEIVING]
2913.51 Receiving stolen property.

[VALUE]
2913.61 Value of stolen property.

[AGGRAVATING CIRCUMSTANCES]
2913.71 Degree of offense when certain property involved.
2913.72 Evidence of intent to commit theft of rental property.

[MISCELLANEOUS OFFENSES]
2913.81 Repealed.
2913.82 Motor vehicle theft offender to pay towing or storage costs.

[IN GENERAL]

§ 2913.01 Definitions.

As used in this chapter:

(A) "Deception" means knowingly deceiving another or causing another to be deceived by any false or misleading representation, by withholding information, by preventing another from acquiring information, or by any other conduct, act, or omission that creates, confirms, or perpetuates a false impression in another, including a false impression as to law, value, state of mind, or other objective or subjective fact.

(B) "Defraud" means to knowingly obtain, by deception, some benefit for oneself or another, or to knowingly cause, by deception, some detriment to another.

(C) "Deprive" means to do any of the following:

(1) Withhold property of another permanently, or for a period that appropriates a substantial portion of its value or use, or with purpose to restore it only upon payment of a reward or other consideration;

(2) Dispose of property so as to make it unlikely that the owner will recover it;

(3) Accept, use, or appropriate money, property, or services, with purpose not to give proper consideration in return for the money, property, or services, and without reasonable justification or excuse for not giving proper consideration.

(D) "Owner" means, unless the context requires a different meaning, any person, other than the actor, who is the owner of, who has possession or control of, or who has any license or interest in property or services, even though the ownership, possession, control, license, or interest is unlawful.

(E) "Services" include labor, personal services, professional services, public utility services, common carrier services, and food, drink, transportation, entertainment, and cable television services.

(F) "Writing" means any computer software, document, letter, memorandum, note, paper, plate, data, film, or other thing having in or upon it any written, typewritten, or printed matter, and any token, stamp, seal, credit card, badge, trademark, label, or other symbol of value, right, privilege, license, or identification.

(G) "Forge" means to fabricate or create, in whole or in part and by any means, any spurious writing, or to make, execute, alter, complete, reproduce, or otherwise purport to authenticate any writing, when the writing in fact is not authenticated by that conduct.

(H) "Utter" means to issue, publish, transfer, use, put or send into circulation, deliver, or display.

(I) "Coin machine" means any mechanical or electronic device designed to do both of the following:

(1) Receive a coin, bill, or token made for that purpose;

(2) In return for the insertion or deposit of a coin, bill, or token, automatically dispense property, provide a service, or grant a license.

(J) "Slug" means an object that, by virtue of its size, shape, composition, or other quality, is capable of being inserted or deposited in a coin machine as an improper substitute for a genuine coin, bill, or token made for that purpose.

(K) "Theft offense" means any of the following:

(1) A violation of section 2911.01, 2911.02, 2911.11, 2911.12, 2911.13, 2911.31, 2911.32, 2913.02, 2913.03, 2913.04, 2913.041 [2913.04.1], 2913.11, 2913.21, 2913.31, 2913.32, 2913.33, 2913.34, 2913.40, 2913.42, 2913.43, 2913.44, 2913.45, 2913.47, former section 2913.47 or 2913.48, or section 2913.51, 2915.05, or 2921.41 of the Revised Code;

(2) A violation of an existing or former municipal ordinance or law of this or any other state, or of the United States, substantially equivalent to any section listed in division (K)(1) of this section or a violation of section 2913.41, 2913.81, or 2915.06 of the Revised Code as it existed prior to July 1, 1996;

(3) An offense under an existing or former municipal ordinance or law of this or any other state, or of the United States, involving robbery, burglary, breaking and entering, theft, embezzlement, wrongful conversion, forgery, counterfeiting, deceit, or fraud;

(4) A conspiracy or attempt to commit, or complicity in committing any offense under division (K)(1), (2), or (3) of this section.

(L) "Computer services" includes, but is not limited to, the use of a computer system, computer network, computer program, data that is prepared for computer use, or data that is contained within a computer system or computer network.

(M) "Computer" means an electronic device that performs logical, arithmetic, and memory functions by the manipulation of electronic or magnetic impulses. "Computer" includes, but is not limited to, all input, output, processing, storage, computer program, or communication facilities that are connected, or related, in a computer system or network to an electronic device of that nature.

(N) "Computer system" means a computer and related devices, whether connected or unconnected, including, but not limited to, data input, output, and storage devices, data communications links, and computer programs and data that make the system capable of performing specified special purpose data processing tasks.

(O) "Computer network" means a set of related and remotely connected computers and communication facilities that includes more than one computer system that has the capability to transmit among the connected computers and communication facilities through the use of computer facilities.

(P) "Computer program" means an ordered set of data representing coded instructions or statements that, when executed by a computer, cause the computer to process data.

(Q) "Computer software" means computer programs, procedures, and other documentation associated with the operation of a computer system.

(R) "Data" means a representation of information, knowledge, facts, concepts, or instructions that are being or have been prepared in a formalized manner and that are intended for use in a computer system or computer network. For purposes of section 2913.47 of the Revised Code, "data" has the additional meaning set forth in division (A) of that section.

(S) "Cable television service" means any services provided by or through the facilities of any cable television system or other similar closed circuit coaxial cable communications system, or any microwave or similar transmission service used in connection with any cable television system or other similar closed circuit coaxial cable communications system.

(T) "Gain access" means to approach, instruct, communicate with, store data in, retrieve data from, or otherwise make use of any resources of a computer, computer system, or computer network.

(U) "Credit card" includes, but is not limited to, a card, code, device, or other means of access to a customer's account for the purpose of obtaining money, property, labor, or services on credit, or for initiating an electronic fund transfer at a point-of-sale terminal, an automated teller machine, or a cash dispensing machine.

(V) "Electronic fund transfer" has the same meaning as in 92 Stat. 3728, 15 U.S.C.A. 1693a, as amended.

(W) "Rented property" means personal property in which the right of possession and use of the property is for a short and possibly indeterminate term in return for consideration; the rentee generally controls the duration of possession of the property, within any applicable minimum or maximum term; and the amount of consideration generally is determined by the duration of possession of the property.

HISTORY: 134 v H 511 (Eff 1-1-74); 139 v H 437 (Eff 7-21-82); 140 v H 97 (Eff 3-20-84); 140 v S 183 (Eff 9-26-84); 141 v H 340 (Eff 5-20-86); 141 v H 49 (Eff 6-26-86); 142 v H 182 (Eff 7-7-87); 143 v H 347 (Eff 7-18-90); 146 v S 2 (Eff 7-1-96); 146 v S 277. Eff 3-31-97.

Not analogous to former RC § 2913.01 (RS § 7091; S&S 264; S&C 409; 73 v 59; GC § 13083; 101 v 206; Bureau of Code Revision, 10-1-53), repealed 134 v H 511, § 2, eff 1-1-74.

[THEFT]

§ 2913.02 Theft.

(A) No person, with purpose to deprive the owner of property or services, shall knowingly obtain or exert control over either the property or services in any of the following ways:

(1) Without the consent of the owner or person authorized to give consent;

(2) Beyond the scope of the express or implied consent of the owner or person authorized to give consent;

(3) By deception;

(4) By threat.

(B) Whoever violates this section is guilty of theft. Except as otherwise provided in this division, a violation of this section is petty theft, a misdemeanor of the first degree. If the value of the property or services stolen is five hundred dollars or more and is less than five thousand dollars if† the property stolen is any of the property listed in section 2913.71 of the Revised Code, a violation of this section is theft, a felony of the fifth degree. If the value of the property or services stolen is five thousand dollars or more and is less than one hundred thousand dollars, if the property stolen is a firearm or dangerous ordnance, as defined in section 2923.11 of the Revised Code, a violation of this section is grand theft, a felony of the fourth degree. If the property stolen is a motor vehicle, as defined in section 4501.01 of the Revised Code, a violation of this section is grand theft of a motor vehicle, a felony of the fourth degree. If the value of the property or services stolen is one hundred thousand dollars or more, a violation of this section is aggravated theft, a felony of the third degree. If the property stolen is any dangerous drug, as defined in section 4729.02 of the Revised Code, a violation of this section is theft of drugs, a felony of the fourth degree, or, if the offender previously has been convicted of a felony drug abuse offense, as defined in section 2925.01 of the Revised Code, a felony of the third degree.

HISTORY: 134 v H 511 (Eff 1-1-74); 138 v S 191 (Eff 6-20-80); 139 v S 199 (Eff 1-1-83); 140 v H 632 (Eff 3-28-85); 141 v H 49 (Eff 6-26-86); 143 v H 347 (Eff 7-18-90); 143 v S 258 (Eff 11-20-90); 146 v H 4 (Eff 11-9-95); 146 v S 2. Eff 7-1-96.

Not analogous to former RC § 2913.02 (RS § 7092; 71 v 3; GC § 13084; Bureau of Code Revision, 10-1-53), repealed 134 v H 511, § 2, eff 1-1-74.

Publisher's Note

The amendments made by HB 4 (146 v —) and SB 2 (146 v —) have been combined. Please see provisions of RC § 1.52.

The effective date is set by section 6 of SB 2.

† The wording appears as a result of combining HB 4 and SB 2.

The provisions of § 3 of HB 4 (146 v —) read as follows:

SECTION 3. Sections 2151.02, 2151.022, 2151.355, 2151.411, 2913.02, 2913.51, 2913.71, 2921.13, 2923.21, 2947.061, 2951.02, 2967.01, and 2967.15 of the Revised Code, as amended by this act, and sections 2923.211 and 2967.131 of the Revised Code, as enacted by this act, apply to any offense, delinquent act, or unruly act committed on or after the effective date of this act. Sections 2151.02, 2151.022, 2151.355, 2151.411, 2913.02, 2913.51, 2913.71, 2921.13, 2923.21, 2947.061, 2951.02, 2967.01, and 2967.15 of the Revised Code, as they existed immediately prior to the effective date of this act, apply to any offense, delinquent act, or unruly act committed before the effective date of this act.

§ 2913.03 Unauthorized use of a vehicle.

(A) No person shall knowingly use or operate an aircraft, motor vehicle, motorcycle, motorboat, or other motor-propelled vehicle without the consent of the owner or person authorized to give consent.

(B) No person shall knowingly use or operate an aircraft, motor vehicle, motorboat, or other motor-propelled vehicle without the consent of the owner or person authorized to give consent, and either remove it from this state or keep possession of it for more than forty-eight hours.

(C) The following are affirmative defenses to a charge under this section:

(1) At the time of the alleged offense, the actor, though mistaken, reasonably believed that the actor was authorized to use or operate the property.

(2) At the time of the alleged offense, the actor reasonably believed that the owner or person empowered to give consent would authorize the actor to use or operate the property.

(D) Whoever violates this section is guilty of unauthorized use of a vehicle. A violation of division (A) of this section is a misdemeanor of the first degree. A violation of division (B) of this section is a felony of the fifth degree.

HISTORY: 134 v H 511 (Eff 1-1-74); 146 v S 2. Eff 7-1-96.

Not analogous to former RC § 2913.03 (RS § 7092a; 81 v 165; GC § 13085; Bureau of Code Revision, 10-1-53), repealed 134 v H 511, § 2, eff 1-1-74.

The effective date is set by section 6 of SB 2.

§ 2913.04 Unauthorized use of property; computer property.

(A) No person shall knowingly use or operate the property of another without the consent of the owner or person authorized to give consent.

(B) No person shall knowingly gain access to, attempt to gain access to, or cause access to be gained to any computer, computer system, or computer network without the consent of, or beyond the scope of the express or implied consent of, the owner of the computer, computer system, or computer network or other person authorized to give consent by the owner.

(C) The affirmative defenses contained in division (C) of section 2913.03 of the Revised Code are affirmative defenses to a charge under this section.

(D) Whoever violates division (A) of this section is guilty of unauthorized use of property. Except as otherwise provided in this division, unauthorized use of property is a misdemeanor of the fourth degree.

If unauthorized use of property is committed for the purpose of devising or executing a scheme to defraud or to obtain property or services, unauthorized use of property is whichever of the following is applicable:

(1) Except as otherwise provided in division (D)(2), (3), or (4) of this section, a misdemeanor of the first degree.

(2) If the value of the property or services or the loss to the victim is five hundred dollars or more and is less than five thousand dollars, a felony of the fifth degree.

(3) If the value of the property or services or the loss to the victim is five thousand dollars or more and is less than one hundred thousand dollars, a felony of the fourth degree.

(4) If the value of the property or services or the loss to the victim is one hundred thousand dollars or more, a felony of the third degree.

(E) Whoever violates division (B) of this section is guilty of unauthorized use of computer property, a felony of the fifth degree.

HISTORY: 134 v H 511 (Eff 1-1-74); 141 v H 49 (Eff 6-26-86); 146 v S 2 (Eff 7-1-96); 146 v S 269. Eff 7-1-96.

Not analogous to former RC § 2913.04 (RS § 7093; S&S 57; 64 v 128; 66 v 99; 70 v 156; GC § 13086; Bureau of Code Revision, 10-1-53; 129 v 1594), repealed 134 v H 511, § 2, eff 1-1-74.

The effective date is set by section 5 of SB 269.

[§ 2913.04.1] § 2913.041 Possession or sale of unauthorized cable television device.

(A) No person shall knowingly possess any device, including any instrument, apparatus, computer chip, equipment, decoder, descrambler, converter, software, or other device specially adapted, modified, or remanufactured for gaining access to cable television service, without securing authorization from or paying the required compensation to the owner or operator of the system that provides the cable television service.

(B) No person shall knowingly sell, distribute, or manufacture any device, including any instrument, apparatus, computer chip, equipment, decoder, descrambler, converter, software, or other device specially adapted, modified, or remanufactured for gaining access to cable television service, without securing authorization from or paying the required compensation to the owner or operator of the system that provides the cable television service.

(C) Whoever violates division (A) of this section is guilty of possession of an unauthorized device, a felony of the fifth degree. Whoever violates division (B) of this section is guilty of sale of an unauthorized device, a felony of the fourth degree.

(D) A person commits a separate violation of this section with regard to each device that is sold, distributed, manufactured, or possessed in violation of division (A) or (B) of this section.

HISTORY: 146 v S 2. Eff 7-1-96.

The effective date is set by section 6 of SB 2.

§§ 2913.05, 2913.06, 2913.07

Repealed, 134 v H 511, § 2 [RS §§ 7094—7096; S&C 454; S&S 57, 286; 56 v 86; 62 v 179; 64 v 128; 66 v 99; 67 v 17; 70 v 156; GC §§ 13087—13089; 114 v 119; Bureau of Code Revision, 10-1-53; 127 v 1039(1095); 129 v 1594]. Eff 1-1-74.

These sections concerned forgery and counterfeiting.

§§ 2913.08, 2913.09, 2913.10

Repealed, 134 v H 511, § 2 [RS §§ 7098—7101; S&C 413, 455; S&S 269; 33 v 33; 56 v 86; 61 v 79; GC §§ 13091, 13094, 13096; Bureau of Code Revision, 10-1-53; 126 v 575]. Eff 1-1-74.

These sections concerned forgery and counterfeiting.

[PASSING BAD CHECKS]

§ 2913.11 Passing bad checks.

(A) No person, with purpose to defraud, shall issue or transfer or cause to be issued or transferred a check or other negotiable instrument, knowing that it will be dishonored.

(B) For purposes of this section, a person who issues or transfers a check or other negotiable instrument is presumed to know that it will be dishonored if either of the following occurs:

(1) The drawer had no account with the drawee at the time of issue or the stated date, whichever is later;

(2) The check or other negotiable instrument was properly refused payment for insufficient funds upon presentment within thirty days after issue or the stated date, whichever is later, and the liability of the drawer, indorser, or any party who may be liable thereon is not discharged by payment or satisfaction within ten days after receiving notice of dishonor.

(C) For purposes of this section, a person who issues or transfers a check, bill of exchange, or other draft is presumed to have the purpose to defraud if the drawer fails to comply with section 1349.16 of the Revised Code by doing any of the following when opening a checking account intended for personal, family, or household purposes at a financial institution:

(1) Falsely stating that the drawer has not been issued a valid driver's or commercial driver's license or identification card issued under section 4507.50 of the Revised Code;

(2) Furnishing such license or card, or another identification document that contains false information;

(3) Making a false statement with respect to the drawer's current address or any additional relevant information reasonably required by the financial institution.

(D) Whoever violates this section is guilty of passing bad checks. Except as otherwise provided in this division, passing bad checks is a misdemeanor of the first degree. If the check or other negotiable instrument is for payment of five hundred dollars or more and is for the payment of less than five thousand dollars, passing bad checks is a felony of the fifth degree. If the check or other negotiable instrument is for the payment of five thousand dollars or more and is for the payment of less than one hundred thousand dollars, passing bad checks is a felony of the fourth degree. If the check or other negotiable instrument is for the payment of one hundred thousand dollars or more, passing bad checks is a felony of the third degree.

HISTORY: 134 v H 511 (Eff 1-1-74); 139 v S 199 (Eff 1-5-83); 139 v H 269 (Eff 1-5-83); 141 v H 49 (Eff 6-26-86); 143 v H 711 (Eff 10-16-90); 146 v S 2. Eff 7-1-96.

Not analogous to former RC § 2913.11 (GC § 13097-1; 115 v 46; Bureau of Code Revision, 10-1-53), repealed 134 v H 511, § 2, eff 1-1-74.

Analogous to former RC § 2911.11.1 (132 v S 97), repealed 134 v H 511, § 2, eff 1-1-74.

The effective date is set by section 6 of SB 2.

§§ 2913.12, 2913.13, 2913.14

Repealed, 134 v H 511, § 2 [RS §§ 7102, 7103; S&C 415; S&S 270; 33 v 33; 61 v 79; GC §§ 13097-2, 13098, 13099; 115 v 226; Bureau of Code Revision, 10-1-53; 126 v 575]. Eff 1-1-74.

These sections concerned counterfeiting.

§§ 2913.15, 2913.16, 2913.17

Repealed, 134 v H 511, § 2 [RS §§ 3031, 7104, 7105; S&C 413, 415, 425; S&S 267, 450; 33 v 33; 55 v 149; 58 v 5; 63 v 70; GC §§ 13093, 13100, 13101; Bureau of Code Revision, 10-1-53]. Eff 1-1-74.

These sections concerned counterfeiting.

[MISUSE OF CREDIT CARDS]

§ 2913.21 Misuse of credit cards.

(A) No person shall do any of the following:

(1) Practice deception for the purpose of procuring the issuance of a credit card, when a credit card is issued in actual reliance thereon;

(2) Knowingly buy or sell a credit card from or to a person other than the issuer.

(B) No person, with purpose to defraud, shall do any of the following:

(1) Obtain control over a credit card as security for a debt;

(2) Obtain property or services by the use of a credit card, in one or more transactions, knowing or having reasonable cause to believe that the card has expired or been revoked, or was obtained, is retained, or is being used in violation of law;

(3) Furnish property or services upon presentation of a credit card, knowing that the card is being used in violation of law;

(4) Represent or cause to be represented to the issuer of a credit card that property or services have been furnished, knowing that the representation is false.

(C) No person, with purpose to violate this section, shall receive, possess, control, or dispose of a credit card.

(D)(1) Whoever violates this section is guilty of misuse of credit cards.

(2) A violation of division (A), (B)(1), or (C) of this section is a misdemeanor of the first degree.

(3) Except as otherwise provided in this division, a violation of division (B)(2), (3), or (4) of this section is a misdemeanor of the first degree. If the cumulative retail value of the property and services involved in one or more violations of division (B)(2), (3), or (4) of this section, which violations involve one or more credit card accounts and occur within a period of ninety consecutive days commencing on the date of the first violation, is five hundred dollars or more and is less than five thousand dollars, misuse of credit cards in violation of any of those divisions is a felony of the fifth degree. If the cumulative retail value of the property and services involved in one or more violations of division (B)(2), (3), or (4) of this section, which violations involve one or more credit card accounts and occur within a period of ninety consecutive days commencing on the date of the first violation, is five thousand dollars or more and is less than one hundred thousand dollars, misuse of credit cards in violation of any of those divisions is a felony of the fourth degree. If the cumulative retail value of the property and services involved in one or more violations of division (B)(2), (3), or (4) of this section, which violations involve one or more credit card accounts and occur within a period of ninety consecutive days commencing on the date of the first violation, is one hundred thousand dollars or more, misuse of credit cards in violation of any of those divisions is a felony of the third degree.

HISTORY: 134 v H 511 (Eff 1-1-74); 137 v S 289 (Eff 5-23-78); 139 v S 199 (Eff 1-5-83); 139 v H 269 (Eff 1-5-83); 140 v S 210 (Eff 7-1-83); 141 v H 49 (Eff 6-26-86); 146 v S 2. Eff 7-1-96.

Analogous to former RC § 2907.20.1 (133 v S 346; 134 v S 302), repealed 134 v H 511, § 2, eff 1-1-74.

The effective date is set by section 6 of SB 2.

[FORGERY]

§ 2913.31 Forgery.

(A) No person, with purpose to defraud, or knowing that the person is facilitating a fraud, shall do any of the following:

(1) Forge any writing of another without the other person's authority;

(2) Forge any writing so that it purports to be genuine when it actually is spurious, or to be the act of another who did not authorize that act, or to have been executed at a time or place or with terms different from what in fact was the case, or to be a copy of an original when no such original existed;

(3) Utter, or possess with purpose to utter, any writing that the person knows to have been forged.

(B) No person shall knowingly do either of the following:
(1) Forge an identification card;
(2) Sell or otherwise distribute a card that purports to be an identification card, knowing it to have been forged.

As used in this division, "identification card" means a card that includes personal information or characteristics of an individual, a purpose of which is to establish the identity of the bearer described on the card, whether the words "identity," "identification," "identification card," or other similar words appear on the card.

(C)(1) Whoever violates division (A) of this section is guilty of forgery. Except as otherwise provided in this division, forgery is a felony of the fifth degree. If property or services are involved in the offense or the victim suffers a loss and if the value of the property or services or the loss to the victim is five thousand dollars or more and is less than one hundred thousand dollars, forgery is a felony of the fourth degree. If property or services are involved in the offense or the victim suffers a loss and if the value of the property or services or the loss to the victim is one hundred thousand dollars or more, forgery is a felony of the third degree.

(2) Whoever violates division (B) of this section is guilty of forging identification cards or selling or distributing forged identification cards. Except as otherwise provided in this division, forging identification cards or selling or distributing forged identification cards is a misdemeanor of the first degree. If the offender previously has been convicted of a violation of division (B) of this section, forging identification cards or selling or distributing forged identification cards is a misdemeanor of the first degree and, in addition, the court shall impose upon the offender a fine of not less than two hundred fifty dollars.

HISTORY: 134 v H 511 (Eff 1-1-74); 144 v H 162 (Eff 11-11-91); 146 v S 2. Eff 7-1-96.

The effective date is set by section 6 of SB 2.

§ 2913.32 Criminal simulation.

(A) No person, with purpose to defraud, or knowing that the person is facilitating a fraud, shall do any of the following:
(1) Make or alter any object so that it appears to have value because of antiquity, rarity, curiosity, source, or authorship, which it does not in fact possess;
(2) Practice deception in making, retouching, editing, or reproducing any photograph, movie film, video tape, phonograph record, or recording tape;
(3) Falsely or fraudulently make, simulate, forge, alter, or counterfeit any wrapper, label, stamp, cork, or cap prescribed by the liquor control commission under Chapters 4301. and 4303. of the Revised Code, falsely or fraudulently cause to be made, simulated, forged, altered, or counterfeited any wrapper, label, stamp, cork, or cap prescribed by the liquor control commission under Chapters 4301. and 4303. of the Revised Code, or use more than once any wrapper, label, stamp, cork, or cap prescribed by the liquor control commission under Chapters 4301. and 4303. of the Revised Code.

(4) Utter, or possess with purpose to utter, any object that the person knows to have been simulated as provided in division (A)(1), (2), or (3) of this section.

(B) Whoever violates this section is guilty of criminal simulation. Except as otherwise provided in this division, criminal simulation is a misdemeanor of the first degree. If the loss to the victim is five hundred dollars or more and is less than five thousand dollars, criminal simulation is a felony of the fifth degree. If the loss to the victim is five thousand dollars or more and is less than one hundred thousand dollars, criminal simulation is a felony of the fourth degree. If the loss to the victim is one hundred thousand dollars or more, criminal simulation is a felony of the third degree.

HISTORY: 134 v H 511 (Eff 1-1-74); 146 v S 2. Eff 7-1-96.

The effective date is set by section 6 of SB 2.

§ 2913.33 Making or using slugs.

(A) No person shall do any of the following:
(1) Insert or deposit a slug in a coin machine, with purpose to defraud;
(2) Make, possess, or dispose of a slug, with purpose of enabling another to defraud by inserting or depositing it in a coin machine.

(B) Whoever violates this section is guilty of making or using slugs, a misdemeanor of the second degree.

HISTORY: 134 v H 511. Eff 1-1-74.

§ 2913.34 Trademark counterfeiting.

(A) No person shall knowingly do any of the following:
(1) Attach, affix, or otherwise use a counterfeit mark in connection with the manufacture of goods or services, whether or not the goods or services are intended for sale or resale;
(2) Possess, sell, or offer for sale tools, machines, instruments, materials, articles, or other items of personal property with the knowledge that they are designed for the production or reproduction of counterfeit marks;
(3) Purchase or otherwise acquire goods, and keep or otherwise have the goods in the person's possession, with the knowledge that a counterfeit mark is attached to, affixed to, or otherwise used in connection with the goods and with the intent to sell or otherwise dispose of the goods;
(4) Sell, offer for sale, or otherwise dispose of goods with the knowledge that a counterfeit mark is attached to, affixed to, or otherwise used in connection with the goods;
(5) Sell, offer for sale, or otherwise provide services with the knowledge that a counterfeit mark is used in

connection with that sale, offer for sale, or other provision of the services.

(B)(1) Whoever violates this section is guilty of trademark counterfeiting.

(2) Except as otherwise provided in this division, a violation of division (A)(1) of this section is a felony of the fifth degree. Except as otherwise provided in this division, if the cumulative sales price of the goods or services to which or in connection with which the counterfeit mark is attached, affixed, or otherwise used in the offense is five thousand dollars or more but less than one hundred thousand dollars or if the number of units of goods to which or in connection with which the counterfeit mark is attached, affixed, or otherwise used in the offense is more than one hundred units but less than one thousand units, a violation of division (A)(1) of this section is a felony of the fourth degree. If the cumulative sales price of the goods or services to which or in connection with which the counterfeit mark is attached, affixed, or otherwise used in the offense is one hundred thousand dollars or more or if the number of units of goods to which or in connection with which the counterfeit mark is attached, affixed, or otherwise used in the offense is one thousand units or more, a violation of division (A)(1) of this section is a felony of the third degree.

(3) Except as otherwise provided in this division, a violation of division (A)(2) of this section is a misdemeanor of the first degree. If the circumstances of the violation indicate that the tools, machines, instruments, materials, articles, or other items of personal property involved in the violation were intended for use in the commission of a felony, a violation of division (A)(2) of this section is a felony of the fifth degree.

(4) Except as otherwise provided in this division, a violation of division (A)(3), (4), or (5) of this section is a misdemeanor of the first degree. Except as otherwise provided in this division, if the cumulative sales price of the goods or services to which or in connection with which the counterfeit mark is attached, affixed, or otherwise used in the offense is five hundred dollars or more but less than five thousand dollars, a violation of division (A)(3), (4), or (5) of this section is a felony of the fifth degree. Except as otherwise provided in this division, if the cumulative sales price of the goods or services to which or in connection with which the counterfeit mark is attached, affixed, or otherwise used in the offense is five thousand dollars or more but less than one hundred thousand dollars or if the number of units of goods to which or in connection with which the counterfeit mark is attached, affixed, or otherwise used in the offense is more than one hundred units but less than one thousand units, a violation of division (A)(3), (4), or (5) of this section is a felony of the fourth degree. If the cumulative sales price of the goods or services to which or in connection with which the counterfeit mark is attached, affixed, or otherwise used in the offense is one hundred thousand dollars or more or if the number of units of goods to which or in connection with which the counterfeit mark is attached, affixed, or otherwise used in the offense is one thousand units or more, a violation of division (A)(3), (4), or (5) of this section is a felony of the third degree.

(C) A defendant may assert as an affirmative defense to a charge of a violation of this section defenses, affirmative defenses, and limitations on remedies that would be available in a civil, criminal, or administrative action or proceeding under the "Lanham Act," 60 Stat. 427-443 (1946), 15 U.S.C. 1051-1127, as amended, "The Trademark Counterfeiting Act of 1984," 98 Stat. 2178, 18 U.S.C. 2320, as amended, Chapter 1329. or another section of the Revised Code, or common law.

(D)(1) Law enforcement officers may seize pursuant to Criminal Rule 41 or Chapter 2933. of the Revised Code either of the following:

(a) Goods to which or in connection with which a person attached, affixed, otherwise used, or intended to attach, affix, or otherwise use a counterfeit mark in violation of this section;

(b) Tools, machines, instruments, materials, articles, vehicles, or other items of personal property that are possessed, sold, offered for sale, or used in a violation of this section or in an attempt to commit or complicity in the commission of a violation of this section.

(2) Notwithstanding any contrary provision of sections 2923.31 to 2923.35 or 2933.41 to 2933.43 of the Revised Code, if a person is convicted of or pleads guilty to a violation of this section, an attempt to violate this section, or complicity in a violation of this section, the court involved shall declare that the goods described in division (D)(1)(a) of this section and the personal property described in division (D)(1)(b) of this section are contraband and are forfeited. Prior to the court's entry of judgment under Criminal Rule 32, the owner of a registered trademark or service mark that is the subject of the counterfeit mark may recommend a manner in which the forfeited goods and forfeited personal property should be disposed of. If that owner makes a timely recommendation of a manner of disposition, the court is not bound by the recommendation. If that owner makes a timely recommendation of a manner of disposition, the court may include in its entry of judgment an order that requires appropriate persons to dispose of the forfeited goods and forfeited personal property in the recommended manner. If that owner fails to make a timely recommendation of a manner of disposition or if that owner makes a timely recommendation of the manner of disposition but the court determines to not follow the recommendation, the court shall include in its entry of judgment an order that requires the law enforcement agency that employs the law enforcement officer who seized the forfeited goods or the forfeited personal property to destroy them or cause their destruction.

(E) This section does not affect the rights of an owner of a trademark or a service mark, or the enforcement in a civil action or in administrative proceedings of the rights of an owner of a trademark or a service mark, under the "Lanham Act," 60 Stat. 427-443 (1946), 15 U.S.C. 1051-1127, as amended, "The Trademark Counterfeiting Act of 1984," 92 Stat. 2178, 18 U.S.C. 2320, as amended, Chapter 1329. or another section of the Revised Code, or common law.

(F) As used in this section:

(1)(a) Except as provided in division (F)(1)(b) of this section, "counterfeit mark" means a spurious trademark or a spurious service mark that satisfies both of the following:

(i) It is identical with or substantially indistinguishable from a mark that is registered on the principal register in the United States patent and trademark office for the same goods or services as the goods or services to which or in connection with which the spurious trademark or spurious service mark is attached, affixed, or otherwise used or from a mark that is registered with the secretary of state pursuant to sections 1329.54 to 1329.67 of the Revised Code for the same goods or services as the goods or services to which or in connection with which the spurious trademark or spurious service mark is attached, affixed, or otherwise used, and the owner of the registration uses the registered mark, whether or not the offender knows that the mark is registered in a manner described in division (F)(1)(a)(i) of this section.

(ii) Its use is likely to cause confusion or mistake or to deceive other persons.

(b) "Counterfeit mark" does not include a mark or other designation that is attached to, affixed to, or otherwise used in connection with goods or services if the holder of the right to use the mark or other designation authorizes the manufacturer, producer, or vendor of those goods or services to attach, affix, or otherwise use the mark or other designation in connection with those goods or services at the time of their manufacture, production, or sale.

(2) "Cumulative sales price" means the product of the lowest single unit sales price charged or sought to be charged by an offender for goods to which or in connection with which a counterfeit mark is attached, affixed, or otherwise used or of the lowest single service transaction price charged or sought to be charged by an offender for services in connection with which a counterfeit mark is used, multiplied by the total number of those goods or services, whether or not units of goods are sold or are in an offender's possession, custody, or control.

(3) "Registered trademark or service mark" means a trademark or service mark that is registered in a manner described in division (F)(1) of this section.

(4) "Trademark" and "service mark" have the same meanings as in section 1329.54 of the Revised Code.

HISTORY: 146 v S 277. Eff 3-31-97.

[FRAUDS]

§ 2913.40 Medicaid fraud.

(A) As used in this section:

(1) "Statement or representation" means any oral, written, electronic, electronic impulse, or magnetic communication that is used to identify an item of goods or a service for which reimbursement may be made under the medical assistance program or that states income and expense and is or may be used to determine a rate of reimbursement under the medical assistance program.

(2) "Medical assistance program" means the program established by the department of human services to provide medical assistance under section 5111.01 of the Revised Code and the medicaid program of Title XIX of the "Social Security Act," 49 Stat. 620 (1935), 42 U.S.C. 301, as amended.

(3) "Provider" means any person who has signed a provider agreement with the department of human services to provide goods or services pursuant to the medical assistance program or any person who has signed an agreement with a party to such a provider agreement under which the person agrees to provide goods or services that are reimbursable under the medical assistance program.

(4) "Provider agreement" means an oral or written agreement between the department of human services and a person in which the person agrees to provide goods or services under the medical assistance program.

(5) "Recipient" means any individual who receives goods or services from a provider under the medical assistance program.

(6) "Records" means any medical, professional, financial, or business records relating to the treatment or care of any recipient, to goods or services provided to any recipient, or to rates paid for goods or services provided to any recipient and any records that are required by the rules of the department of human services to be kept for the medical assistance program.

(B) No person shall knowingly make or cause to be made a false or misleading statement or representation for use in obtaining reimbursement from the medical assistance program.

(C) No person, with purpose to commit fraud or knowing that the person is facilitating a fraud, shall do either of the following:

(1) Contrary to the terms of the person's provider agreement, charge, solicit, accept, or receive for goods or services that the person provides under the medical assistance program any property, money, or other consideration in addition to the amount of reimbursement under the medical assistance program and the person's provider agreement for the goods or services and any deductibles or co-payments authorized by section 5111.02 of the Revised Code or by any rules adopted pursuant to that section.

(2) Solicit, offer, or receive any remuneration, other than any deductibles or co-payments authorized by section 5111.02 of the Revised Code or by any rules adopted pursuant to that section, in cash or in kind, including, but not limited to, a kickback or rebate, in

connection with the furnishing of goods or services for which whole or partial reimbursement is or may be made under the medical assistance program.

(D) No person, having submitted a claim for or provided goods or services under the medical assistance program, shall do either of the following for a period of at least six years after a reimbursement pursuant to that claim, or a reimbursement for those goods or services, is received under the medical assistance program:

(1) Knowingly alter, falsify, destroy, conceal, or remove any records that are necessary to fully disclose the nature of all goods or services for which the claim was submitted, or for which reimbursement was received, by the person;

(2) Knowingly alter, falsify, destroy, conceal, or remove any records that are necessary to disclose fully all income and expenditures upon which rates of reimbursements were based for the person.

(E) Whoever violates this section is guilty of medicaid fraud. Except as otherwise provided in this division, medicaid fraud is a misdemeanor of the first degree. If the value of property, services, or funds obtained in violation of this section is five hundred dollars or more and is less than five thousand dollars, medicaid fraud is a felony of the fifth degree. If the value of property, services, or funds obtained in violation of this section is five thousand dollars or more and is less than one hundred thousand dollars, medicaid fraud is a felony of the fourth degree. If the value of the property, services, or funds obtained in violation of this section is one hundred thousand dollars or more, medicaid fraud is a felony of the third degree.

(F) Upon application of the governmental agency, office, or other entity that conducted the investigation and prosecution in a case under this section, the court shall order any person who is convicted of a violation of this section for receiving any reimbursement for furnishing goods or services under the medical assistance program to which the person is not entitled to pay to the applicant its cost of investigating and prosecuting the case. The costs of investigation and prosecution that a defendant is ordered to pay pursuant to this division shall be in addition to any other penalties for the receipt of that reimbursement that are provided in this section, section 5111.03 of the Revised Code, or any other provision of law.

(G) The provisions of this section are not intended to be exclusive remedies and do not preclude the use of any other criminal or civil remedy for any act that is in violation of this section.

HISTORY: 141 v H 340 (Eff 5-20-86); 143 v H 672 (Eff 11-14-89); 146 v S 2. Eff 7-1-96.

The effective date is set by section 6 of SB 2.

§ 2913.41 Defrauding a livery or hostelry.

In a prosecution of a person for a theft offense that alleges that the person, with purpose to defraud or knowing that the person was facilitating a fraud, hired an aircraft, motor vehicle, motorcycle, motorboat, sailboat, camper, trailer, horse, or buggy, or kept or operated any of the same that has been hired, or engaged accommodations at a hotel, motel, inn, campground, or other hostelry, it is prima-facie evidence of purpose to defraud if the person did any of the following:

(A) Used deception to induce the rental agency to furnish the person with the aircraft, motor vehicle, motorcycle, motorboat, sailboat, camper, trailer, horse, or buggy, or used deception to induce the hostelry to furnish the person with accommodations;

(B) Hired any aircraft, motor vehicle, motorcycle, motorboat, sailboat, camper, trailer, horse, or buggy, or engaged accommodations, knowing the person was without sufficient means to pay the hire or rental;

(C) Absconded without paying the hire or rental;

(D) Knowingly failed to pay the hire or rental as required by the contract of hire or rental, without reasonable excuse for such failure;

(E) Knowingly failed to return hired property as required by the contract of hire, without reasonable excuse for the failure.

HISTORY: 134 v H 511 (Eff 1-1-74); 146 v S 2. Eff 7-1-96.

The effective date is set by section 6 of SB 2.

§ 2913.42 Tampering with records.

(A) No person, knowing the person has no privilege to do so, and with purpose to defraud or knowing that the person is facilitating a fraud, shall do any of the following:

(1) Falsify, destroy, remove, conceal, alter, deface, or mutilate any writing, computer software, data, computer data, or record;

(2) Utter any writing or record, knowing it to have been tampered with as provided in division (A)(1) of this section.

(B)(1) Whoever violates this section is guilty of tampering with records.

(2) If the offense does not involve data, tampering with records is whichever of the following is applicable:

(a) If division (B)(2)(b) of this section does not apply, a misdemeanor of the first degree;

(b) If the writing or record is a will unrevoked at the time of the offense or a record kept by or belonging to a governmental agency, a felony of the fifth degree.

(3) If the offense involves a violation of division (A) of this section involving data, tampering with records is whichever of the following is applicable:

(a) Except as otherwise provided in division (B)(3)(b), (c), or (d) of this section, a misdemeanor of the first degree;

(b) If the value of the data involved in the offense or the loss to the victim is five hundred dollars or more and is less than five thousand dollars, a felony of the fifth degree;

(c) If the value of the data involved in the offense or the loss to the victim is five thousand dollars or more and is less than one hundred thousand dollars, a felony of the fourth degree;

(d) If the value of the data involved in the offense or the loss to the victim is one hundred thousand dollars or more or if the offense is committed for the purpose of devising or executing a scheme to defraud or to obtain property or services and the value of the property or services or the loss to the victim is five thousand dollars or more, a felony of the third degree.

HISTORY: 134 v H 511 (Eff 1-1-74); 141 v H 49 (Eff 6-26-86); 141 v H 428 (Eff 12-23-86); 146 v S 2. Eff 7-1-96.

The effective date is set by section 6 of SB 2.

§ 2913.43 Securing writings by deception.

(A) No person, by deception, shall cause another to execute any writing that disposes of or encumbers property, or by which a pecuniary obligation is incurred.

(B) Whoever violates this section is guilty of securing writings by deception. Except as otherwise provided in this division, securing writings by deception is a misdemeanor of the first degree. If the value of the property or the obligation involved is five hundred dollars or more and less than five thousand dollars, securing writings by deception is a felony of the fifth degree. If the value of the property or the obligation involved is five thousand dollars or more and is less than one hundred thousand dollars, securing writings by deception is a felony of the fourth degree. If the value of the property or the obligation involved is one hundred thousand dollars or more, securing writings by deception is a felony of the third degree.

HISTORY: 134 v H 511 (Eff 1-1-74); 139 v S 199 (Eff 1-5-83); 139 v H 269 (Eff 1-5-83); 141 v H 49 (Eff 6-26-86); 146 v S 2. Eff 7-1-96.

Analogous to former RC § 2911.01 (RS § 7076; 70 v 39; 73 v 20; 74 v 41; GC § 13104; 124 v 466; Bureau of Code Revision, 10-1-53; 129 v 344), repealed 134 v H 511, § 2, eff 1-1-74.

The effective date is set by section 6 of SB 2.

§ 2913.44 Personating an officer.

(A) No person, with purpose to defraud or knowing that he is facilitating a fraud, or with purpose to induce another to purchase property or services, shall personate a law enforcement officer, or an inspector, investigator, or agent of any governmental agency.

(B) Whoever violates this section is guilty of personating an officer, a misdemeanor of the first degree.

HISTORY: 134 v H 511. Eff 1-1-74.

[§ 2913.44.1] § 2913.441 Law enforcement emblem display.

(A) No person who is not entitled to do so shall knowingly display on a motor vehicle the emblem of a law enforcement agency or an organization of law enforcement officers.

(B) Whoever violates this section is guilty of the unlawful display of the emblem of a law enforcement agency or an organization of law enforcement officers, a minor misdemeanor.

HISTORY: 136 v H 1363. Eff 1-11-77.

§ 2913.45 Defrauding creditors.

(A) No person, with purpose to defraud one or more of the person's creditors, shall do any of the following:

(1) Remove, conceal, destroy, encumber, convey, or otherwise deal with any of the person's property;

(2) Misrepresent or refuse to disclose to a fiduciary appointed to administer or manage the person's affairs or estate, the existence, amount, or location of any of the person's property, or any other information regarding such property that the person is legally required to furnish to the fiduciary.

(B) Whoever violates this section is guilty of defrauding creditors. Except as otherwise provided in this division, defrauding creditors is a misdemeanor of the first degree. If the value of the property involved is five hundred dollars or more and is less than five thousand dollars, defrauding creditors is a felony of the fifth degree. If the value of the property involved is five thousand dollars or more and is less than one hundred thousand dollars, defrauding creditors is a felony of the fourth degree. If the value of the property involved is one hundred thousand dollars or more, defrauding creditors is a felony of the third degree.

HISTORY: 134 v H 511 (Eff 1-1-74); 146 v S 2. Eff 7-1-96.

The effective date is set by section 6 of SB 2.

§ 2913.46 Illegal use of food stamps or WIC program benefits.

(A)(1) As used in this section:

(a) "Electronically transferred benefit" means the transfer of food stamp program benefits or WIC program benefits through the use of an access device.

(b) "WIC program benefits" includes money, coupons, delivery verification receipts, other documents, food, or other property received directly or indirectly pursuant to section 17 [of] the "Child Nutrition Act of 1966," 80 Stat. 885, 42 U.S.C.A. 1786, as amended.

(c) "Access device" means any card, plate, code, account number, or other means of access that can be used, alone or in conjunction with another access device, to obtain payments, allotments, benefits, money, goods, or other things of value or that can be used to initiate a transfer of funds pursuant to section 5101.33 of the Revised Code and the "Food Stamp Act of 1977," 91 Stat. 958, 7 U.S.C.A. 2011 et seq., or any supplemental food program administered by any department of this state or any county or local agency pursuant to section 17 of the "Child Nutrition Act of 1966," 80 Stat.

885, 42 U.S.C.A. 1786, as amended. An "access device" may include an electronic debit card or other means authorized by section 5101.33 of the Revised Code.

(d) "Aggregate value of the food stamp coupons, WIC program benefits, and electronically transferred benefits involved in the violation" means the total face value of any food stamps, plus the total face value of WIC program coupons or delivery verification receipts, plus the total value of other WIC program benefits, plus the total value of any electronically transferred benefit or other access device, involved in the violation.

(e) "Total value of any electronically transferred benefit or other access device" means the total value of the payments, allotments, benefits, money, goods, or other things of value that may be obtained, or the total value of funds that may be transferred, by use of any electronically transferred benefit or other access device at the time of violation.

(2) If food stamp coupons, WIC program benefits, or electronically transferred benefits or other access devices of various values are used, transferred, bought, acquired, altered, purchased, possessed, presented for redemption, or transported in violation of this section over a period of twelve months, the course of conduct may be charged as one offense and the values of food stamp coupons, WIC program benefits, or any electronically transferred benefits or other access devices may be aggregated in determining the degree of the offense.

(B) No individual shall knowingly possess, buy, sell, use, alter, accept, or transfer food stamp coupons, WIC program benefits, or any electronically transferred benefit in any manner not authorized by the "Food Stamp Act of 1977," 91 Stat. 958, 7 U.S.C.A. 2011, as amended, or section 17 of the "Child Nutrition Act of 1966," 80 Stat. 885, 42 U.S.C.A. 1786, as amended.

(C) No organization, as defined in division (D) of section 2901.23 of the Revised Code, shall do either of the following:

(1) Knowingly allow an employee or agent to sell, transfer, or trade items or services, the purchase of which is prohibited by the "Food Stamp Act of 1977," 91 Stat. 958, 7 U.S.C.A. 2011, as amended, or section 17 of the "Child Nutrition Act of 1966," 80 Stat. 885, 42 U.S.C.A. 1786, as amended, in exchange for food stamp coupons, WIC program benefits, or any electronically transferred benefit;

(2) Negligently allow an employee or agent to sell, transfer, or exchange food stamp coupons, WIC program benefits, or any electronically transferred benefit for anything of value.

(D) Whoever violates this section is guilty of illegal use of food stamps or WIC program benefits. Except as otherwise provided in this division, illegal use of food stamps or WIC program benefits is a felony of the fifth degree. If the aggregate value of the food stamp coupons, WIC program benefits, and electronically transferred benefits involved in the violation is five hundred dollars or more and is less than five thousand dollars, illegal use of food stamps or WIC program benefits is a felony of the fourth degree. If the aggregate value of the food stamp coupons, WIC program benefits, and electronically transferred benefits involved in the violation is five thousand dollars or more and is less than one hundred thousand dollars, illegal use of food stamps or WIC program benefits is a felony of the third degree. If the aggregate value of the food stamp coupons, WIC program benefits, and electronically transferred benefits involved in the violation is one hundred thousand dollars or more, illegal use of food stamps or WIC program benefits is a felony of the second degree.

HISTORY: 140 v H 291 (Eff 7-1-83); 146 v S 162 (Eff 10-29-95); 146 v H 239 (Eff 11-24-95); 146 v S 107 (Eff 5-8-96); 146 v S 2 (Eff 7-1-96); 146 v S 269 (Eff 7-1-96); 146 v S 293. Eff 9-26-96.

The provisions of § 3 of SB 107 (146 v —) read as follows:

SECTION 3. Section 2913.46 of the Revised Code is presented in this act [Am. Sub. S.B. 107] as a composite of the section as amended by both Sub. H.B. 239 and Am. Sub. S.B. 162 of the 121st General Assembly, with the new language of neither of the acts shown in capital letters. This is in recognition of the principle stated in division (B) of section 1.52 of the Revised Code that such amendments are to be harmonized where not substantively irreconcilable and constitutes a legislative finding that such is the resulting version in effect prior to the effective date of this act.

§ 2913.47 Insurance fraud.

(A) As used in this section:

(1) "Data" has the same meaning as in section 2913.01 of the Revised Code and additionally includes any other representation of information, knowledge, facts, concepts, or instructions that are being or have been prepared in a formalized manner.

(2) "Deceptive" means that a statement, in whole or in part, would cause another to be deceived because it contains a misleading representation, withholds information, prevents the acquisition of information, or by any other conduct, act, or omission creates, confirms, or perpetuates a false impression, including, but not limited to, a false impression as to law, value, state of mind, or other objective or subjective fact.

(3) "Insurer" means any person that is authorized to engage in the business of insurance in this state under Title XXXIX [39] of the Revised Code, the Ohio fair plan underwriting association created under section 3929.43 of the Revised Code, any health insuring corporation, and any legal entity that is self-insured and provides benefits to its employees or members.

(4) "Policy" means a policy, certificate, contract, or plan that is issued by an insurer.

(5) "Statement" includes, but is not limited to, any notice, letter, or memorandum; proof of loss; bill of lading; receipt for payment; invoice, account, or other financial statement; estimate of property damage; bill for services; diagnosis or prognosis; prescription; hospi-

tal, medical, or dental chart or other record; x-ray, photograph, videotape, or movie film; test result; other evidence of loss, injury, or expense; computer-generated document; and data in any form.

(B) No person, with purpose to defraud or knowing that the person is facilitating a fraud, shall do either of the following:

(1) Present to, or cause to be presented to, an insurer any written or oral statement that is part of, or in support of, an application for insurance, a claim for payment pursuant to a policy, or a claim for any other benefit pursuant to a policy, knowing that the statement, or any part of the statement, is false or deceptive;

(2) Assist, aid, abet, solicit, procure, or conspire with another to prepare or make any written or oral statement that is intended to be presented to an insurer as part of, or in support of, an application for insurance, a claim for payment pursuant to a policy, or a claim for any other benefit pursuant to a policy, knowing that the statement, or any part of the statement, is false or deceptive.

(C) Whoever violates this section is guilty of insurance fraud. Except as otherwise provided in this division, insurance fraud is a misdemeanor of the first degree. If the amount of the claim that is false or deceptive is five hundred dollars or more and is less than five thousand dollars, insurance fraud is a felony of the fifth degree. If the amount of the claim that is false or deceptive is five thousand dollars or more and is less than one hundred thousand dollars, insurance fraud is a felony of the fourth degree. If the amount of the claim that is false or deceptive is one hundred thousand dollars or more, insurance fraud is a felony of the third degree.

(D) This section shall not be construed to abrogate, waive, or modify division (A) of section 2317.02 of the Revised Code.

HISTORY: 143 v H 347 (Eff 7-18-90); 146 v S 2 (Eff 7-1-96); 146 v S 269 (Eff 7-1-96); 147 v S 67. Eff 6-4-97.

Not analogous to former RC § 2913.47 (140 v H 97), repealed 140 v H 632, § 2, eff 3-28-85.

§ 2913.48 Workers' compensation fraud.

Note: Two versions of RC § 2913.48 are presented because the status of SB 45 (147 v —) is in question until the referendum vote in November, 1997.

(A) No person, with purpose to defraud or knowing that the person is facilitating a fraud shall do any of the following:

(1) Receive workers' compensation benefits to which the person is not entitled;

(2) Make or present or cause to be made or presented a false or misleading statement with the purpose to secure payment for goods or services rendered under Chapter 4121., 4123., 4127., or 4131. of the Revised Code or to secure workers' compensation benefits;

(3) Alter, falsify, destroy, conceal, or remove any record or document that is necessary to fully establish the validity of any claim filed with, or necessary to establish the nature and validity of all goods and services for which reimbursement or payment was received or is requested from, the bureau of workers' compensation, or a self-insuring employer under Chapter 4121., 4123., 4127., or 4131. of the Revised Code;

(4) Enter into an agreement or conspiracy to defraud the bureau or a self-insuring employer by making or presenting or causing to be made or presented a false claim for workers' compensation benefits.

(B) Whoever violates this section is guilty of workers' compensation fraud. Except as otherwise provided in this division, a violation of this section is a misdemeanor of the first degree. If the value of the goods, services, property, or money stolen is five hundred dollars or more and is less than five thousand dollars, a violation of this section is a felony of the fifth degree. If the value of the goods, services, property, or money stolen is five thousand dollars or more and is less than one hundred thousand dollars, a violation of this section is a felony of the fourth degree. If the value of the goods, services, property, or money stolen is one hundred thousand dollars or more, a violation of this section is a felony of the third degree.

(C) Upon application of the governmental body that conducted the investigation and prosecution of a violation of this section, the court shall order the person who is convicted of the violation to pay the governmental body its costs of investigating and prosecuting the case. These costs are in addition to any other costs or penalty provided in the Revised Code or any other section of law.

(D) The remedies and penalties provided in this section are not exclusive remedies and penalties and do not preclude the use of any other criminal or civil remedy or penalty for any act that is in violation of this section.

(E) As used in this section:

(1) "False" means wholly or partially untrue or deceptive.

(2) "Goods" includes, but is not limited to, medical supplies, appliances, rehabilitative equipment, and any other apparatus or furnishing provided or used in the care, treatment, or rehabilitation of a claimant for workers' compensation benefits.

(3) "Services" includes, but is not limited to, any service provided by any health care provider to a claimant for workers' compensation benefits.

(4) "Claim" means any attempt to cause the bureau, an independent third party with whom the administrator or an employer contracts under section 4121.44 of the Revised Code, or a self-insuring employer to make payment or reimbursement for workers' compensation benefits.

(5) "Employment" means participating in any trade, occupation, business, service, or profession for substantial gainful remuneration.

(6) "Employer," "employee," and "self-insuring em-

ployer" have the same meanings as in section 4123.01 of the Revised Code.

(7) "Remuneration" includes, but is not limited to, wages, commissions, rebates, and any other reward or consideration.

(8) "Statement" includes, but is not limited to, any oral, written, electronic, electronic impulse, or magnetic communication notice, letter, memorandum, receipt for payment, invoice, account, financial statement, bill for services; a diagnosis, prognosis, prescription, hospital, medical, or dental chart or other record; and a computer generated document.

(9) "Records" means any medical, professional, financial, or business record relating to the treatment or care of any person, to goods or services provided to any person, or to rates paid for goods or services provided to any person, or any record that the administrator of workers' compensation requires pursuant to rule.

(10) "Workers' compensation benefits" means any compensation or benefits payable under Chapter 4121., 4123., 4127., or 4131. of the Revised Code.

HISTORY: 145 v H 107 (Eff 10-20-93); 146 v S 2. Eff 7-1-96.

Not analogous to former RC § 2913.48 (140 v H 97), repealed 140 v H 632, § 2, eff 3-28-85.

The effective date is set by section 6 of SB 2.

§ 2913.48 Workers' compensation fraud.

(A) No person, with purpose to defraud or knowing that the person is facilitating a fraud, shall do any of the following:

(1) Receive workers' compensation benefits to which the person is not entitled;

(2) Make or present or cause to be made or presented a false or misleading statement with the purpose to secure payment for goods or services rendered under Chapter 4121., 4123., 4127., or 4131. of the Revised Code or to secure workers' compensation benefits;

(3) Alter, falsify, destroy, conceal, or remove any record or document that is necessary to fully establish the validity of any claim filed with, or necessary to establish the nature and validity of all goods and services for which reimbursement or payment was received or is requested from, the bureau of workers' compensation, or a self-insuring employer under Chapter 4121., 4123., 4127., or 4131. of the Revised Code;

(4) Enter into an agreement or conspiracy to defraud the bureau or a self-insuring employer by making or presenting or causing to be made or presented a false claim for workers' compensation benefits;

(5) Make or present or cause to be made or presented a false or misleading statement or other misrepresentation concerning manual codes, classification of employees, payroll, or number of personnel, when information of that nature is necessary to determine the actual workers' compensation premium or assessment owed to the bureau by an employer;

(6) Solicit, offer, or receive any remuneration in cash or in kind, including, but not limited to, a kickback or rebate, in connection with a referral for the furnishing of goods or services for which reimbursement may be made pursuant to Chapter 4121., 4123., 4127., or 4131. of the Revised Code. Division (A)(6) of this section does not apply to any contract to provide services under the bureau's health care partnership program or a qualified health plan entered into between a managed care organization and an organization formed pursuant to division (A)(4) of section 4123.29 of the Revised Code.

(7) Alter, forge, or create a workers' compensation certificate to falsely show current or correct workers' compensation coverage;

(8) Fail to secure or maintain workers' compensation coverage as required by Chapter 4123. of the Revised Code.

(B) Whoever violates this section is guilty of workers' compensation fraud. Except as otherwise provided in this division, a violation of this section is a misdemeanor of the first degree. If the value of premiums and assessments unpaid pursuant to actions described in division (A)(5), (7) or (8) of this section, or of goods, services, property, or money stolen is five hundred dollars or more and is less than five thousand dollars, a violation of this section is a felony of the fifth degree. If the value of premiums and assessments unpaid pursuant to actions described in division (A)(5), (7), or (8) of this section, or of goods, services, property, or money stolen is five thousand dollars or more and is less than one hundred thousand dollars, a violation of this section is a felony of the fourth degree. If the value of premiums and assessments unpaid pursuant to actions described in division (A)(5), (7) or (8) of this section, or of goods, services, property, or money stolen is one hundred thousand dollars or more, a violation of this section is a felony of the third degree.

(C) Upon application of the governmental body that conducted the investigation and prosecution of a violation of this section, the court shall order the person who is convicted of the violation to pay the governmental body its costs of investigating and prosecuting the case. These costs are in addition to any other costs or penalty provided in the Revised Code or any other section of law.

(D) The remedies and penalties provided in this section are not exclusive remedies and penalties and do not preclude the use of any other criminal or civil remedy or penalty for any act that is in violation of this section.

(E) As used in this section:

(1) "False" means wholly or partially untrue or deceptive.

(2) "Goods" includes, but is not limited to, medical supplies, appliances, rehabilitative equipment, and any other apparatus or furnishing provided or used in the care, treatment, or rehabilitation of a claimant for workers' compensation benefits.

(3) "Services" includes, but is not limited to, any service provided by any health care provider to a claimant

for workers' compensation benefits and any and all services provided by the bureau as part of workers' compensation insurance coverage.

(4) "Claim" means any attempt to cause the bureau, an independent third party with whom the administrator or an employer contracts under section 4121.44 of the Revised Code, or a self-insuring employer to make payment or reimbursement for workers' compensation benefits.

(5) "Employment" means participating in any trade, occupation, business, service, or profession for substantial gainful remuneration.

(6) "Employer," "employee," and "self-insuring employer" have the same meanings as in section 4123.01 of the Revised Code.

(7) "Remuneration" includes, but is not limited to, wages, commissions, rebates, and any other reward or consideration.

(8) "Statement" includes, but is not limited to, any oral, written, electronic, electronic impulse, or magnetic communication notice, letter, memorandum, receipt for payment, invoice, account, financial statement, bill for services; a diagnosis, prognosis, prescription, hospital, medical, or dental chart or other record; and a computer generated document.

(9) "Records" means any medical, professional, financial, or business record relating to the treatment or care of any person, to goods or services provided to any person, or to rates paid for goods or services provided to any person, or any record that the administrator of workers' compensation requires pursuant to rule.

(10) "Workers' compensation benefits" means any compensation or benefits payable under Chapter 4121., 4123., 4127., or 4131. of the Revised Code.

HISTORY: 145 v H 107 (Eff 10-20-93); 146 v S 2 (Eff 7-1-96); 147 v S 45. Eff 7-22-97.

Not analogous to former RC § 2913.48 (140 v H 97), repealed 140 v H 632, § 2, eff 3-28-85.

[RECEIVING]

§ 2913.51 Receiving stolen property.

(A) No person shall receive, retain, or dispose of property of another knowing or having reasonable cause to believe that the property has been obtained through commission of a theft offense.

(B) Whoever violates this section is guilty of receiving stolen property. Except as otherwise provided in this division, receiving stolen property is a misdemeanor of the first degree. If the value of the property involved is five hundred dollars or more and is less than five thousand dollars, if the property involved is any of the property listed in section 2913.71 of the Revised Code, receiving stolen property is a felony of the fifth degree. If the property involved is a motor vehicle, as defined in section 4501.01 of the Revised Code, if the property involved is a dangerous drug, as defined in section 4729.02 of the Revised Code, or if the value of the property involved is five thousand dollars or more and is less than one hundred thousand dollars if the property involved is a firearm or dangerous ordnance, as defined in section 2923.11 of the Revised Code, stolen property is a felony of the fourth degree. If the value of the property involved is one hundred thousand dollars or more, receiving stolen property is a felony of the third degree.

HISTORY: 134 v H 511 (Eff 1-1-74); 138 v S 191 (Eff 6-20-80); 139 v S 199 (Eff 1-5-83); 139 v H 269 (Eff 1-5-83); 140 v S 210 (Eff 7-1-83); 141 v H 49 (Eff 6-26-86); 146 v H 4 (Eff 11-9-95); 146 v S 2. Eff 7-1-96.

Publisher's Note

The amendments made by HB 4 (146 v —) and SB 2 (146 v —) have been combined. Please see provisions of RC § 1.52.

The effective date is set by section 6 of SB 2.

See provisions, § 3 of HB 4 (146 v —) following RC § 2913.02.

[VALUE]

§ 2913.61 Value of stolen property.

(A) When a person is charged with a theft offense involving property or services valued at five hundred dollars or more, a theft offense involving property or services valued at five hundred dollars or more and less than five thousand dollars, a theft offense involving property or services valued at five thousand dollars or more and less than one hundred thousand dollars, or a theft offense involving property or services valued at one hundred thousand dollars or more, the jury or court trying the accused shall determine the value of the property or services as of the time of the offense and, if a guilty verdict is returned, shall return the finding of value as part of the verdict. In any case in which the jury or court determines that the value of the property or services at the time of the offense was five hundred dollars or more, it is unnecessary to find and return the exact value, and it is sufficient if the finding and return is to the effect that the value of the property or services involved was, five hundred dollars or more and less than five thousand dollars, was five thousand dollars or more and less than one hundred thousand dollars, or was one hundred thousand dollars or more.

(B) Where more than one item of property or services is involved in a theft offense, the value of the property or services involved for the purpose of determining the value as required by division (A) of this section, is the aggregate value of all property or services involved in the offense.

(C) When a series of offenses under section 2913.02 of the Revised Code is committed by the offender in the offender's same employment, capacity, or relationship to another, all such offenses shall be tried as a single offense, and the value of the property or services involved for the purpose of determining the value as required by division (A) of this section, is the aggregate value of all property and services involved in all offenses in the series. In prosecuting a single offense under this division, it is not necessary to separately allege and prove each offense in the series. It is sufficient to allege and prove that the offender, within a given span of time, committed one or more theft offenses in the offender's same employment, capacity, or relationship to another.

(D) The following criteria shall be used in determining the value of property or services involved in a theft offense:

(1) The value of an heirloom, memento, collector's item, antique, museum piece, manuscript, document, record, or other thing that has intrinsic worth to its owner and that either is irreplaceable or is replaceable only on the expenditure of substantial time, effort, or money, is the amount that would compensate the owner for its loss.

(2) The value of personal effects and household goods, and of materials, supplies, equipment, and fixtures used in the profession, business, trade, occupation, or avocation of its owner, which property is not covered under division (D)(1) of this section and which retains substantial utility for its purpose regardless of its age or condition, is the cost of replacing the property with new property of like kind and quality.

(3) The value of any property, real or personal, not covered under division (D)(1) or (2) of this section, and the value of services, is the fair market value of the property or services. As used in this section, "fair market value" is the money consideration that a buyer would give and a seller would accept for property or services, assuming that the buyer is willing to buy and the seller is willing to sell, that both are fully informed as to all facts material to the transaction, and that neither is under any compulsion to act.

(E) Without limitation on the evidence that may be used to establish the value of property or services involved in a theft offense:

(1) When the property involved is personal property held for sale at wholesale or retail, the price at which the property was held for sale is prima-facie evidence of its value.

(2) When the property involved is a security or commodity traded on an exchange, the closing price or, if there is no closing price, the asked price, given in the latest market quotation prior to the offense, is prima-facie evidence of the value of the security or commodity.

(3) When the property involved is livestock, poultry, or raw agricultural products for which a local market price is available, the latest local market price prior to the offense is prima-facie evidence of the value of the livestock, poultry, or products.

(4) When the property involved is a negotiable instrument, the face value is prima-facie evidence of the value of the instrument.

(5) When the property involved is a warehouse receipt, bill of lading, pawn ticket, claim check, or other instrument entitling the holder or bearer to receive property, the face value or, if there is no face value, the value of the property covered by the instrument less any payment necessary to receive the property, is prima-facie evidence of the value of the instrument.

(6) When the property involved is a ticket of admission, ticket for transportation, coupon, token, or other instrument entitling the holder or bearer to receive property or services, the face value or, if there is no face value, the value of the property or services that may be received thereby, is prima-facie evidence of the value of the instrument.

(7) When the services involved are gas, electricity, water, telephone, transportation, shipping, or other services for which the rate is established by law, the duly established rate is prima-facie evidence of the value of the services.

(8) When the services involved are services for which the rate is not established by law, and the offender has been notified prior to the offense of the rate for the services, either in writing, or orally, or by posting in a manner reasonably calculated to come to the attention of potential offenders, the rate contained in the notice is prima-facie evidence of the value of the services.

HISTORY: 134 v H 511 (Eff 1-1-74); 139 v S 199 (Eff 1-5-83); 139 v H 269 (Eff 1-5-83); 146 v S 2. Eff 7-1-96.

The effective date is set by section 6 of SB 2.

[AGGRAVATING CIRCUMSTANCES]

§ 2913.71 Degree of offense when certain property involved.

Regardless of the value of the property involved and regardless of whether the offender previously has been convicted of a theft offense, a violation of section 2913.02 or 2913.51 of the Revised Code is a felony of the fifth degree if the property involved is any of the following:

(A) A credit card;

(B) A printed form for a check or other negotiable instrument, that on its face identifies the drawer or maker for whose use it is designed or identifies the account on which it is to be drawn, and that has not been executed by the drawer or maker or on which the amount is blank;

(C) A motor vehicle identification license plate as prescribed by section 4503.22 of the Revised Code, a temporary license placard or windshield sticker as prescribed by section 4503.182 [4503.18.2] of the Revised Code, or any comparable license plate, placard, or sticker as prescribed by the applicable law of another state or the United States;†

(D) A blank form for a certificate of title or a manufacturer's or importer's certificate to a motor vehicle, as prescribed by section 4505.07 of the Revised Code;

(E) A blank form for any license listed in section 4507.01 of the Revised Code.

HISTORY: 134 v H 511 (Eff 1-1-74); 137 v H 1 (Eff 8-26-77); 138 v S 191 (Eff 6-20-80); 140 v H 632 (Eff 3-28-85); 146 v H 4 (Eff 11-9-95); 146 v S 2. Eff 7-1-96.

The effective date is set by section 6 of SB 2.

† The provision in former section 2913.71(C) concerning a firearm or dangerous ordnance was moved to section 2913.02(B) in HB 4 (146 v —).

Comment, Legislative Service Commission

Section 2913.71 of the Revised Code is amended by this act [Sub. H.B. 4] and also by Am. Sub. S.B. 2 of the 121st General Assembly (effective July 1, 1996). Comparison of these amendments in pursuance of section 1.52 of the Revised Code discloses that they are not irreconcilable so that they are required by that section to be harmonized to give effect to each amendment.

§ 2913.72 Evidence of intent to commit theft of rental property.

(A) Each of the following shall be considered evidence of an intent to commit theft of rented property:

(1) At the time of entering into the rental contract, the rentee presented the renter with identification that was materially false, fictitious, or not current with respect to name, address, place of employment, or other relevant information.

(2) After receiving a notice demanding the return of rented property as provided in division (B) of this section, the rentee neither returned the rented property nor made arrangements acceptable with the renter to return the rented property.

(B) To establish that a rentee has an intent to commit theft of rented property under division (A)(2) of this section, a renter may issue a notice to a rentee demanding the return of rented property. The renter shall mail the notice by certified mail, return receipt requested, to the rentee at the address the rentee gave when the rental contract was executed, or to the rentee at the last address the rentee or the rentee's agent furnished in writing to the renter.

(C) A demand for the return of rented property is not a prerequisite for the prosecution of a rentee for theft of rented property. The evidence specified in division (A) of this section does not constitute the only evidence that may be considered as evidence of intent to commit theft of rented property.

(D) As used in this section:

(1) "Renter" means a person who owns rented property.

(2) "Rentee" means a person who pays consideration to a renter for the use of rented property.

HISTORY: 146 v S 2. Eff 7-1-96.

The effective date is set by section 6 of SB 2.

[MISCELLANEOUS OFFENSES]

§ 2913.81 Repealed, 146 v S 2, § 6 [141 v H 49]. Eff 7-1-96.

This section concerned denying access to a computer system or services.

§ 2913.82 Motor vehicle theft offender to pay towing or storage costs.

If a person is convicted of a theft offense that involves a motor vehicle, as defined in section 4501.01 of the Revised Code, or any major part of a motor vehicle, and if a local authority, as defined in section 4511.01 of the Revised Code, the owner of the vehicle or major part, or a person, acting on behalf of the owner, was required to pay any towing or storage fees prior to recovering possession of the motor vehicle or major part, the court that sentences the offender, as a part of its sentence, shall require the offender to repay the fees to the local authority, the owner, or the person who paid the fees on behalf of the owner.

As used in this section, "major part" has the same meaning as in the "Motor Vehicle Theft Law Enforcement Act of 1984," 98 Stat. 2754, 15 U.S.C. 2021(7), as amended.

HISTORY: 141 v H 546. Eff 3-25-87.

CHAPTER 2915: GAMBLING

Section
2915.01 Definitions.
2915.02 Gambling.
2915.03 Operating a gambling house.
2915.04 Public gaming.
2915.05 Cheating.
2915.06 Repealed.

[BINGO]

2915.07 Conducting illegal bingo game.
2915.08 Application for license.
2915.09 Rules for conducting bingo.
2915.10 Records to be kept for three years.
2915.11 Persons prohibited from being bingo game operators.
[2915.11.1] 2915.111 Repealed.
2915.12 Bingo for amusement only.
[2915.12.1, 2915.12.2] 2915.121, 2915.122 Repealed.
2915.13-2915.21 Repealed.
2915.31-2915.37 Repealed.
2915.40 Repealed.

§ 2915.01 Definitions.

As used in this chapter:

(A) "Bookmaking" means the business of receiving or paying off bets.

(B) "Bet" means the hazarding of anything of value upon the result of an event, undertaking, or contingency, but does not include a bona fide business risk.

(C) "Scheme of chance" means a lottery, numbers game, pool, or other scheme in which a participant gives a valuable consideration for a chance to win a prize.

(D) "Game of chance" means poker, craps, roulette, a slot machine, a punch board, or other game in which a player gives anything of value in the hope of gain, the outcome of which is determined largely or wholly by chance.

(E) "Scheme or game of chance conducted for profit" means any scheme or game of chance designed to produce income for the person who conducts or operates the scheme or game of chance, but does not include a charitable bingo game.

(F) "Gambling device" means:

(1) A book, totalizer, or other equipment for recording bets;

(2) A ticket, token, or other device representing a chance, share, or interest in a scheme of chance, except a charitable bingo game, or evidencing a bet;

(3) A deck of cards, dice, gaming table, roulette wheel, slot machine, punch board, or other apparatus designed for use in connection with a game of chance;

(4) Any equipment, device, apparatus, or paraphernalia specially designed for gambling purposes.

(G) "Gambling offense" means any of the following:

(1) A violation of section 2915.02, 2915.03, 2915.04, 2915.05, 2915.07, 2915.08, 2915.09, 2915.10, or 2915.11 of the Revised Code;

(2) A violation of an existing or former municipal ordinance or law of this or any other state or the United States substantially equivalent to any section listed in division (G)(1) of this section or a violation of section 2915.06 of the Revised Code as it existed prior to the effective date of this amendment;

(3) An offense under an existing or former municipal ordinance or law of this or any other state or the United States, of which gambling is an element;

(4) A conspiracy or attempt to commit, or complicity in committing any offense under division (G)(1), (2), or (3) of this section.

(H) "Charitable organization" means any tax exempt religious, educational, veteran's, fraternal, service, nonprofit medical, volunteer rescue service, volunteer fire fighter's, senior citizen's, youth athletic, amateur athletic, or youth athletic park organization. An organization is tax exempt if the organization is, and has received from the internal revenue service a determination letter that currently is in effect stating that the organization is, exempt from federal income taxation under subsection 501(a) and described in subsection 501(c)(3), 501(c)(4), 501(c)(8), 501(c)(10), or 501(c)(19) of the Internal Revenue Code. To qualify as a charitable organization, an organization, except a volunteer rescue service or volunteer fire fighter's organization, shall have been in continuous existence as such in this state for a period of two years immediately preceding either the making of an application for a bingo license under section 2915.08 of the Revised Code or the conducting of any scheme of chance or game of chance as provided in division (C) of section 2915.02 of the Revised Code.

(I) "Religious organization" means any church, body of communicants, or group that is not organized or operated for profit and that gathers in common membership for regular worship and religious observances.

(J) "Educational organization" means any organization within this state that is not organized for profit, the primary purpose of which is to educate and develop the capabilities of individuals through instruction, and that operates or contributes to the support of a school, academy, college, or university.

(K) "Veteran's organization" means any individual post of a national veteran's association or an auxiliary unit of any individual post of a national veteran's association, which post or auxiliary unit has been incorporated as a nonprofit corporation for at least two years and has received a letter from the state headquarters of the national veteran's association indicating that the individual post or auxiliary unit is in good standing with the national veteran's association. As used in this division, "national veteran's association" means any veteran's association that has been in continuous existence as such for a period of at least ten years and either is incorporated by an act of the United States congress or has a national dues-paying membership of at least five thousand persons.

(L) "Volunteer fire fighter's organization" means any organization of volunteer fire fighters, as defined in section 146.01 of the Revised Code, that is organized and operated exclusively to provide financial support for a volunteer fire department or a volunteer fire company.

(M) "Fraternal organization" means any society, order, or association within this state, except a college or high school fraternity, that is not organized for profit, that is a branch, lodge, or chapter of a national or state organization, that exists exclusively for the common business or sodality of its members, and that has been in continuous existence in this state for a period of five years.

(N) "Volunteer rescue service organization" means any organization of volunteers organized to function as an emergency medical service organization as defined in section 4765.01 of the Revised Code.

(O) "Service organization" means any organization, not organized for profit, that is organized and operated exclusively to provide, or to contribute to the support of organizations or institutions organized and operated exclusively to provide, medical and therapeutic services for persons who are crippled, born with birth defects, or have any other mental or physical defect or those organized and operated exclusively to protect, or to contribute to the support of organizations or institutions organized and operated exclusively to protect, animals from inhumane treatment.

(P) "Nonprofit medical organization" means any organization that has been incorporated as a nonprofit corporation for at least five years and that has continuously operated and will be operated exclusively to provide, or to contribute to the support of organizations or institutions organized and operated exclusively to provide, hospital, medical, research, or therapeutic services for the public.

(Q) "Senior citizen's organization" means any private organization, not organized for profit, that is organized and operated exclusively to provide recreational or social services for persons who are fifty-five years of age or older and that is described and qualified under subsection 501(c)(3) of the Internal Revenue Code.

(R) "Charitable bingo game" means any bingo game that is conducted by a charitable organization that has obtained a bingo license pursuant to section 2915.08 of the Revised Code and the proceeds of which are used for a charitable purpose.

(S) "Bingo" means:
(1) A game with all of the following characteristics:
(a) The participants use bingo cards that are divided into twenty-five spaces arranged in five horizontal and five vertical rows of spaces, with each space, except the central space, being designated by a combination of a letter and a number and with the central space being designated as a free space.
(b) The participants cover the spaces on the bingo cards that correspond to combinations of letters and numbers that are announced by a bingo game operator.

(c) A bingo game operator announces combinations of letters and numbers that appear on objects that a bingo game operator selects by chance, either manually or mechanically, from a receptacle that contains seventy-five objects at the beginning of each game, each object marked by a different combination of a letter and a number that corresponds to one of the seventy-five possible combinations of a letter and a number that can appear on the bingo cards.
(d) The winner of the bingo game includes any participant who properly announces during the interval between the announcements of letters and numbers as described in division (S)(1)(c) of this section, that a predetermined and preannounced pattern of spaces has been covered on a bingo card being used by the participant.

(2) Any scheme or game other than a game as defined in division (S)(1) of this section with the following characteristics:
(a) The participants use cards, sheets, or other devices that are divided into spaces arranged in horizontal, vertical, or diagonal rows of spaces, with each space, except free spaces, being designated by a single letter, number, or symbol; by a combination of letters, numbers, or symbols; by a combination of a letter and a number, a letter and a symbol, or a number and a symbol; or by any combination of letters, numbers, and symbols, with some or none of the spaces being designated as a free, complimentary, or similar space.
(b) The participants cover the spaces on the cards, sheets, or devices that correspond to letters, numbers, symbols, or combinations of such that are announced by a bingo game operator or otherwise transmitted to the participants.
(c) A bingo game operator announces, or otherwise transmits to the participants, letters, numbers, symbols, or any combination of such as set forth in division (S)(2)(a) of this section that appear on objects that a bingo game operator selects by chance that correspond to one of the possible letters, numbers, symbols, or combinations of such that can appear on the bingo cards, sheets, or devices.
(d) The winner of the bingo game is any participant who properly announces that a predetermined and preannounced pattern of spaces has been covered on a card, sheet, or device being used by the participant.

(T) "Conduct" means to back, promote, organize, manage, carry on, or prepare for the operation of a scheme or game of chance but does not include any act performed by a bingo game operator.

(U) "Bingo game operator" means any person, except security personnel, who performs work or labor at the site of a bingo game including, but not limited to, collecting money from participants, handing out bingo cards or objects to cover spaces on the bingo cards, selecting from a receptacle the objects that contain the combination of letters and numbers that appear on the bingo cards, calling out the combinations of letters and numbers, distributing prizes to the winner of the bingo game, and preparing, selling, and serving food or beverages.

(V) "Participant" means any person who plays bingo by covering the spaces on a bingo card that correspond to combinations of letters and numbers that are announced by a bingo game operator.

(W) "Bingo session" means a period, not to exceed five continuous hours, during which a person conducts one or more bingo games.

(X) "Gross receipts" means all money or assets, including admission fees, that a person receives from a bingo session that the person conducts without the deduction of any amounts for prizes paid out during the session or for the expenses of conducting the bingo session. "Gross receipts" does not include any money directly taken in from the sale of food or beverages by a charitable organization conducting a bingo session, or by a bona fide auxiliary unit or society of a charitable organization, at a bingo session conducted by the charitable organization, provided all of the following apply:

(1) The auxiliary unit or society has been in existence as a bona fide auxiliary unit or society of the charitable organization for at least two years prior to the bingo session.

(2) The person who purchases the food or beverage receives nothing of value except the food or beverage and items customarily received with the purchase of that food or beverage.

(3) The food and beverages are sold at customary and reasonable prices.

(4) No person preparing, selling, or serving the food or beverages at the site of the bingo game receives directly or indirectly any form of compensation for the preparation, sale, or service of the food or beverages.

(Y) "Security personnel" includes any person who either is a sheriff, deputy sheriff, marshal, deputy marshal, township constable, or member of an organized police department of a municipal corporation or has successfully completed a peace officer's training course pursuant to sections 109.71 to 109.79 of the Revised Code and who is hired to provide security for the premises on which a bingo game is conducted.

(Z) "To use gross receipts for a charitable purpose" means that the proceeds of the bingo game are used by, or given, donated, or otherwise transferred to, any organization that is described in subsection 509(a)(1), 509(a)(2), or 509(a)(3) of the Internal Revenue Code and is either a governmental unit or an organization that is tax exempt under subsection 501(a) and described in subsection 501(c)(3) of the Internal Revenue Code; that the proceeds of the bingo game are used by, or given, donated, or otherwise transferred to a veteran's organization, as defined in division (K) of this section, that is a post, chapter, or organization of war veterans, or an auxiliary unit or society of, or a trust or foundation for, any such post, chapter, or organization organized in the United States or any of its possessions, at least seventy-five per cent of the members of which are war veterans and substantially all of the other members of which are individuals who are veterans (but not war veterans) or are cadets, or are spouses, widows or widowers of war veterans, or such individuals, provided that no part of the net earnings of such post or organization inures to the benefit of any private shareholder or individual, and further provided that the bingo game proceeds are used by the post or organization for the charitable purposes set forth in division (B)(12) of section 5739.02 of the Revised Code, are used for awarding scholarships to or for attendance at an institution mentioned in division (B)(12) of section 5739.02 of the Revised Code, are donated to a governmental agency, or are used for nonprofit youth activities, the purchase of United States or Ohio flags that are donated to schools, youth groups, or other bona fide nonprofit organizations, promotion of patriotism, or disaster relief; that the proceeds of the bingo game are used by, or given, donated, or otherwise transferred to a fraternal organization that has been in continuous existence in this state for fifteen years for use exclusively for religious, charitable, scientific, literary, or educational purposes, or for the prevention of cruelty to children or animals and contributions for such use would qualify as a deductible charitable contribution under subsection 170 of the Internal Revenue Code; or that the proceeds of the bingo game are used by a volunteer fire fighter's organization and are used by the organization for the purposes set forth in division (L) of this section.

(AA) "Internal Revenue Code" means the "Internal Revenue Code of 1986," 100 Stat. 2085, 26 U.S.C. 1, as now or hereafter amended.

(BB) "Youth athletic organization" means any organization, not organized for profit, that is organized and operated exclusively to provide financial support to, or to operate, athletic activities for persons who are twenty-one years of age or younger by means of sponsoring, organizing, operating, or contributing to the support of an athletic team, club, league, or association.

(CC) "Youth athletic park organization" means any organization, not organized for profit, that satisfies both of the following:

(1) It owns, operates, and maintains playing fields that satisfy both of the following:

(a) The playing fields are used at least one hundred days per year for athletic activities by one or more organizations, not organized for profit, each of which is organized and operated exclusively to provide financial support to, or to operate, athletic activities for persons who are eighteen years of age or younger by means of sponsoring, organizing, operating, or contributing to the support of an athletic team, club, league, or association.

(b) The playing fields are not used for any profit-making activity at any time during the year.

(2) It uses the proceeds of the bingo games it conducts exclusively for the operation, maintenance, and improvement of its playing fields of the type described in division (CC)(1) of this section.

(DD) "Amateur athletic organization" means any organization, not organized for profit, that is organized and operated exclusively to provide financial support to, or to operate, athletic activities for persons who are training for amateur athletic competition that is sanctioned by a national governing body as defined in the "Amateur Sports Act of 1978," 90 Stat. 3045, 36 U.S.C.A. 373.

HISTORY: 134 v H 511 (Eff 1-1-74); 136 v H 1 (Eff 6-13-75); 136 v S 398 (Eff 5-26-76); 136 v H 1547 (Eff 12-6-76); 137 v H 72 (Eff 12-15-77); 139 v S 91 (Eff 10-20-81); 143 v H 573 (Eff 4-10-91); 144 v S 98 (Eff 11-12-92); 146 v S 2, § 1 (Eff 7-1-96); 146 v H 143, § 1 (Eff 5-15-96); 146 v H 143, § 3. Eff 7-1-96.

Not analogous to former RC § 2915.01 (RS § 6932; S&C 662; 54 v 196; GC § 13054; Bureau of Code Revision, 10-1-53), repealed 134 v H 511, § 2, eff 1-1-74.

Analogous to former RC § 2915.16 (GC § 13066-1; 124 v 838; Bureau of Code Revision, 10-1-53), repealed 134 v H 511, § 2, eff 1-1-74.

The effective date is set by Section 5 of HB 143.

§ 2915.02 Gambling.

(A) No person shall do any of the following:

(1) Engage in bookmaking, or knowingly engage in conduct that facilitates bookmaking;

(2) Establish, promote, or operate or knowingly engage in conduct that facilitates any scheme or game of chance conducted for profit;

(3) Knowingly procure, transmit, exchange, or engage in conduct that facilitates the procurement, transmission, or exchange of information for use in establishing odds or determining winners in connection with bookmaking or with any scheme or game of chance conducted for profit;

(4) Engage in betting or in playing any scheme or game of chance, except a charitable bingo game, as a substantial source of income or livelihood;

(5) With purpose to violate division (A)(1), (2), (3), or (4) of this section, acquire, possess, control, or operate any gambling device.

(B) For purposes of division (A)(1) of this section, a person facilitates bookmaking if the person in any way knowingly aids an illegal bookmaking operation, including, without limitation, placing a bet with a person engaged in or facilitating illegal bookmaking. For purposes of division (A)(2) of this section, a person facilitates a scheme or game of chance conducted for profit if the person in any way knowingly aids in the conduct or operation of any such scheme or game, including, without limitation, playing any such scheme or game.

(C) This section does not prohibit conduct in connection with gambling expressly permitted by law.

(D) This section does not apply to any of the following:

(1) Schemes of chance conducted by a charitable organization that is, and has received from the internal revenue service a determination letter that is currently in effect stating that the organization is, exempt from federal income taxation under subsection 501(a) and described in subsection 501(c)(3) of the Internal Revenue Code, provided that all of the money or assets received from the scheme of chance after deduction only of prizes paid out during the conduct of the scheme of chance are used by, or given, donated, or otherwise transferred to, any organization that is described in subsection 509(a)(1), 509(a)(2), or 509(a)(3) of the Internal Revenue Code and is either a governmental unit or an organization that is tax exempt under subsection 501(a) and described in subsection 501(c)(3) of the Internal Revenue Code, and provided that the scheme of chance is not conducted during, or within ten hours of, a bingo game conducted for amusement purposes only pursuant to section 2915.12 of the Revised Code;

(2) Games of chance, if all of the following apply:

(a) The games of chance are not craps for money, roulette for money, or slot machines;

(b) The games of chance are conducted by a charitable organization that is, and has received from the internal revenue service a determination letter that is currently in effect, stating that the organization is, exempt from federal income taxation under subsection 501(a) and described in subsection 501(c)(3) of the Internal Revenue Code;

(c) The games of chance are conducted at festivals of the organization that are conducted either for a period of four consecutive days or less and not more than twice a year or for a period of five consecutive days not more than once a year, and are conducted on premises owned by the charitable organization for a period of no less than one year immediately preceding the conducting of the games of chance, on premises leased from a governmental unit, or on premises that are leased from a veteran's or fraternal organization and that have been owned by the lessor veteran's or fraternal organization for a period of no less than one year immediately preceding the conducting of the games of chance.

A charitable organization shall not lease premises from a veteran's or fraternal organization to conduct a festival described in division (D)(2)(c) of this section if the veteran's or fraternal organization already has leased the premises four times during the preceding year to charitable organizations for that purpose. If a charitable organization leases premises from a veteran's or fraternal organization to conduct a festival described in division (D)(2)(c) of this section, the charitable organization shall not pay a rental rate for the premises per day of the festival that exceeds the rental rate per bingo session that a charitable organization may pay under division (A)(3) of section 2915.09 of the Revised Code when it leases premises from another charitable organization to conduct bingo games.

(d) All of the money or assets received from the games of chance after deduction only of prizes paid out during the conduct of the games of chance are used by, or given, donated, or otherwise transferred to, any organization that is described in subsection 509(a)(1), 509(a)(2), or 509(a)(3) of the Internal Revenue Code and is either a governmental unit or an organization that is tax exempt under subsection 501(a) and described in subsection 501(c)(3) of the Internal Revenue Code;

(e) The games of chance are not conducted during, or within ten hours of, a bingo game conducted for amusement purposes only pursuant to section 2915.12 of the Revised Code.

No person shall receive any commission, wage, salary, reward, tip, donation, gratuity, or other form of compensation, directly or indirectly, for operating or assisting in the operation of any scheme or game of chance.

(3) Any tag fishing tournament operated under a permit issued under section 1533.92 of the Revised Code, as "tag fishing tournament" is defined in section 1531.01 of the Revised Code.

(E) Division (D) of this section shall not be construed to authorize the sale, lease, or other temporary or permanent transfer of the right to conduct schemes of chance or games of chance, as granted by division (D) of this section, by any charitable organization that is granted that right.

(F) Whoever violates this section is guilty of gambling, a misdemeanor of the first degree. If the offender previously has been convicted of any gambling offense, gambling is a felony of the fifth degree.

HISTORY: 134 v H 511 (Eff 1-1-74); 136 v S 398 (Eff 5-26-76); 136 v H 1547 (Eff 12-6-76); 137 v H 72 (Eff 12-15-77); 142 v H 514 (Eff 2-11-88); 143 v H 550 (Eff 5-3-90); 143 v H 573 (Eff 4-10-91); 145 v H 104 (Eff 10-7-93); 145 v H 336 (Eff 10-29-93); 146 v S 2 (Eff 7-1-96); 147 v S 37. Eff 7-26-97.

Not analogous to former RC § 2915.02 (GC § 13054-1; Bureau of Code Revision, 10-1-53; 125 v 544), repealed 134 v H 511, § 2, eff 1-1-74.

§ 2915.03 Operating a gambling house.

(A) No person, being the owner or lessee, or having custody, control, or supervision of premises, shall:

(1) Use or occupy such premises for gambling in violation of section 2915.02 of the Revised Code;

(2) Recklessly permit such premises to be used or occupied for gambling in violation of section 2915.02 of the Revised Code.

(B) Whoever violates this section is guilty of operating a gambling house, a misdemeanor of the first degree. If the offender previously has been convicted of a gambling offense, operating a gambling house is a felony of the fifth degree.

(C) Premises used or occupied in violation of this section constitute a nuisance subject to abatement pursuant to sections 3767.01 to 3767.99 of the Revised Code.

HISTORY: 134 v H 511 (Eff 1-1-74); 146 v S 2. Eff 7-1-96.

Not analogous to former RC § 2915.03 (GC § 13054-2; 124 v 544; Bureau of Code Revision, 10-1-53), repealed 134 v H 511, § 2, eff 1-1-74.

The effective date is set by section 6 of SB 2.

§ 2915.04 Public gaming.

(A) No person, while at a hotel, restaurant, tavern, store, arena, hall, or other place of public accommodation, business, amusement, or resort shall make a bet or play any game of chance.

(B) No person, being the owner or lessee, or having custody, control, or supervision of a hotel, restaurant, tavern, store, arena, hall, or other place of public accommodation, business, amusement, or resort shall recklessly permit such premises to be used or occupied in violation of division (A) of this section.

(C) This section does not prohibit conduct in connection with gambling expressly permitted by law.

(D) Whoever violates this section is guilty of public gaming, a minor misdemeanor. If the offender has previously been convicted of any gambling offense, public gaming is a misdemeanor of the fourth degree.

(E) Premises used or occupied in violation of division (B) of this section constitute a nuisance subject to abatement pursuant to sections 3767.01 to 3767.99 of the Revised Code.

HISTORY: 134 v H 511. Eff 1-1-74.

Not analogous to former RC § 2915.04 (RS § 6933; S&C 666; 29 v 442; GC § 13056; Bureau of Code Revision, 10-1-53), repealed 134 v H 511, § 2, eff 1-1-74.

§ 2915.05 Cheating.

(A) No person, with purpose to defraud or knowing that the person is facilitating a fraud, shall engage in conduct designed to corrupt the outcome of any of the following:

(1) The subject of a bet;

(2) A contest of knowledge, skill, or endurance that is not an athletic or sporting event;

(3) A scheme or game of chance.

(B) No person shall knowingly do any of the following:

(1) Offer, give, solicit, or accept anything of value to corrupt the outcome of an athletic or sporting event;

(2) Engage in conduct designed to corrupt the outcome of an athletic or sporting event.

(C)(1) Whoever violates division (A) of this section is guilty of cheating, a misdemeanor of the first degree. If the potential gain from the cheating is five hundred dollars or more or if the offender previously has been convicted of any gambling offense or of any theft offense, as defined in section 2913.01 of the Revised Code, cheating is a felony of the fifth degree.

(2) Whoever violates division (B) of this section is guilty of corrupting sports. Corrupting sports is a felony of the fifth degree on a first offense and a felony of the fourth degree on each subsequent offense.

HISTORY: 134 v H 511 (Eff 1-1-74); 139 v S 199 (Eff 1-1-83); 146 v S 2. Eff 7-1-96.

Not analogous to former RC § 2915.05 (RS § 6935; S&C 666; 29 v 442; GC § 13057; Bureau of Code Revision, 10-1-53), repealed 134 v H 511, § 2, eff 1-1-74.

The effective date is set by section 6 of SB 2.

§ 2915.06 Repealed, 146 v S 2, § 6 [134 v H 511]. Eff 7-1-96.

This section concerned corrupting outcome of athletic or sporting event. See now RC § 2915.05(B).

[BINGO]

§ 2915.07 Conducting illegal bingo game.

(A) No person, except a charitable organization that has obtained a bingo license pursuant to section 2915.08 of the Revised Code, shall conduct or advertise a bingo game.

(B) Whoever violates this section is guilty of conducting an illegal bingo game, a felony of the fourth degree.

HISTORY: 136 v S 398 (Eff 5-26-76); 146 v S 2. Eff 7-1-96.

Not analogous to former RC § 2915.07 (RS § 6936; S&C 665; 29 v 442; GC § 13058; Bureau of Code Revision, 10-1-53), repealed 134 v H 511, § 2, eff 1-1-74.

The effective date is set by section 6 of SB 2.

§ 2915.08 Application for license.

(A) Annually before the first day of January a charitable organization that desires to conduct bingo games shall make out and deliver to the attorney general, upon a form to be furnished by the attorney general for that purpose, an application for a license to conduct bingo and a license fee of one hundred dollars or a reduced license fee established by the attorney general pursuant to division (G) of this section. The application shall be in the form prescribed by the attorney general and shall be signed and sworn to by the applicant.

The application shall contain the following:

(1) The name and post-office address of the applicant;

(2) A statement that the applicant is a charitable organization and that it has been in continuous existence as a charitable organization in this state for two years immediately preceding the making of the application or for five years in the case of a fraternal organization or a nonprofit medical organization;

(3) The location at which the organization will conduct the bingo game, which location shall be within the county in which the principal place of business of the applicant is located, the days of the week and the times on each of those days when a bingo session will be conducted, whether the organization owns, leases, or subleases the premises, and a copy of the rental agreement if it leases or subleases the premises;

(4) A statement of the applicant's previous history, record, and association that is sufficient to establish that the applicant is a charitable organization and a copy of a determination letter that is issued by the Internal Revenue Service and states that the organization is tax exempt under subsection 501(a) and described in subsection 501(c)(3), 501(c)(4), 501(c)(8), 501(c)(10), or 501(c)(19) of the Internal Revenue Code;

(5) A statement as to whether the applicant has ever had any previous application refused, whether it previously has had a license revoked or suspended, and the reason stated by the attorney general for the refusal, revocation, or suspension;

(6) A statement of the charitable purpose for which the bingo proceeds will be used;

(7) Other necessary and reasonable information that the attorney general may require by rule adopted pursuant to section 111.15 of the Revised Code;

(8) In the case of an applicant seeking to qualify as a youth athletic park organization under division (CC) of section 2915.01 of the Revised Code, a statement issued by a board or body vested with authority under Chapter 755. of the Revised Code for the supervision and maintenance of recreation facilities in the territory in which the organization is located, certifying that the playing fields owned by the organization were used for at least one hundred days during the year in which the statement is issued, and were open for use to all residents of that territory, regardless of race, color, creed, religion, sex, or national origin, for athletic activities by youth athletic organizations, as defined in division (BB) of section 2915.01 of the Revised Code, that do not discriminate on the basis of race, color, creed, religion, sex, or national origin, and that the fields were not used for any profit-making activity at any time during the year. That type of board or body is authorized to issue the statement upon request and shall issue the statement if it finds that the applicant's playing fields were so used.

The attorney general, within thirty days after receiving a timely filed application from a charitable organization that has been issued a bingo license that has not expired and has not been revoked or suspended, shall send a temporary permit to the applicant specifying the date on which the application was filed with the attorney general and stating that, pursuant to section 119.06 of the Revised Code, the applicant may continue to conduct bingo games until a new license is granted or, if the application is rejected, until fifteen days after notice of the rejection is mailed to the applicant. The temporary permit does not affect the validity of the applicant's application and does not grant any rights to the applicant except those rights specifically granted in section 119.06 of the Revised Code. The issuance of a temporary permit by the attorney general pursuant to this paragraph does not prohibit the attorney general from rejecting the applicant's application because of acts that the applicant committed, or actions that he failed to take, before or after the issuance of the temporary permit.

(B)(1) The attorney general shall adopt rules to enforce sections 2915.01, 2915.02, and 2915.07 to 2915.12 of the Revised Code, to ensure that bingo games are conducted in accordance with those sections, and to maintain proper control over the conduct of bingo games. The rules, except rules adopted pursuant to division (A)(7) of this section, shall be adopted pursuant to Chapter 119. of the Revised Code. The attorney general shall license charitable organizations to conduct bingo games in conformance with this chapter and with the licensing provisions of Chapter 119. of the Revised Code.

(2) The attorney general may refuse to grant a bingo license to any organization, or revoke or suspend the license of any organization, that does any of the following or to which any of the following applies:

(a) Fails or has failed at any time to meet any requirement of sections 2915.07 to 2915.11 of the Revised Code, or violates or has violated any provision of sections 2915.02 or 2915.07 to 2915.12 of the Revised Code or any rule adopted by the attorney general pursuant to this section;

(b) Makes or has made an incorrect or false statement that is material to the granting of the license in an application filed pursuant to division (A) of this section;

(c) Submits or has submitted any incorrect or false information relating to an application if the information is material to the granting of the license;

(d) Maintains or has maintained any incorrect or false information that is material to the granting of the license in the records required to be kept pursuant to division (A) of section 2915.10 of the Revised Code, if applicable;

(e) The attorney general has good cause to believe will not conduct its bingo games in accordance with sections 2915.02 and 2915.07 to 2915.12 of the Revised Code or with any rule adopted by the attorney general pursuant to this section.

(3) For the purposes of this division, any action of an officer, trustee, agent, representative, or bingo game operator of an organization is an action of the organization.

(C) The attorney general may grant bingo licenses to charitable organizations that are branches, lodges, or chapters of national charitable organizations.

(D) The attorney general shall send notice in writing to the prosecuting attorney and sheriff of the county in which the organization will conduct the bingo game, as stated in its application for a license or amended license, and to any other law enforcement agency in that county that so requests, of all of the following:

(1) The issuance of the license;

(2) The issuance of the amended license;

(3) The rejection of an application for and refusal to grant a license;

(4) The revocation of any license previously issued;

(5) The suspension of any license previously issued.

(E) A bingo license issued by the attorney general shall set forth the information contained on the application of the charitable organization that the attorney general determines is relevant, including, but not limited to, the location at which the organization will conduct the bingo game and the days of the week and the times on each of those days when a bingo session will be conducted. If the attorney general refuses to grant or revokes or suspends a bingo license, he shall notify the applicant in writing and specifically identify the reason for the refusal, revocation, or suspension in narrative form and, if applicable, by identifying the section of the Revised Code violated. The failure of the attorney general to give the written notice of the reasons for the refusal, revocation, or suspension or a mistake in the written notice does not affect the validity of the attorney general's refusal to grant, or the revocation or suspension of, a bingo license. If the attorney general fails to give the written notice or if there is a mistake in the written notice, the applicant may bring an action to compel the attorney general to comply with this division or to correct the mistake, but the attorney general's order refusing to grant, or revoking or suspending, a bingo license shall not be enjoined during the pendency of the action.

(F) A charitable organization that has been issued a bingo license pursuant to division (B) of this section but that cannot conduct bingo sessions at the location, or on the day of the week or the time, specified on the license due to circumstances beyond its control may apply, without charge, in writing to the attorney general for an amended bingo license. The application shall describe in detail the causes making it impossible for the organization to conduct its bingo sessions in conformity with its license and shall indicate the location, days of the week, and times on each of those days when it desires to conduct a bingo session. If the attorney general approves the application for the amended license, he shall issue the amended license in accordance with division (E) of this section, and the organization shall surrender its original license to the attorney general. The attorney general shall refuse to grant an application for an amended bingo license according to the terms of division (B) of this section.

(G) The attorney general, by rule adopted pursuant to section 111.15 of the Revised Code, shall establish a schedule of reduced license fees for charitable organizations that desire to conduct bingo games during fewer than twenty-six weeks in any calendar year.

HISTORY: 136 v S 398 (Eff 5-26-76); 136 v H 1547 (Eff 12-6-76); 137 v H 72 (Eff 12-15-77); 139 v S 91 (Eff 10-20-81); 139 v S 550 (Eff 11-26-82); 140 v H 291 (Eff 7-1-83); 145 v H 104. Eff 10-7-93.

Not analogous to former RC § 2915.08 (RS § 6939; S&C 446; 75 v 57; GC §§ 13060, 13061; Bureau of Code Revision, 10-1-53), repealed 134 v H 511, § 2, eff 1-1-74.

The provisions of § 3 of HB 104 (145 v —) read as follows:

SECTION 3. In amending division (A)(3) of section 2915.08 and division (A)(3) of section 2915.09 of the Revised Code, the General Assembly hereby declares its intent to supersede the effect of the holding of the Court of Appeals for Montgomery County in the January 23, 1981, decision of *Shomrei Emunah Congregation v. Brown* (Case No. CA 6913) insofar as that decision relates to subleases of premises on which bingo games may be conducted by charitable organizations.

§ 2915.09 Rules for conducting bingo.

(A) A charitable organization that conducts a bingo game shall do all of the following:

(1) Own all of the equipment used to conduct the bingo game or lease that equipment from a charitable organization that is licensed to conduct a bingo game for a rental rate that is not more than is customary and reasonable for that equipment;

(2) Use all of the gross receipts from the bingo game for paying prizes, for the charitable purposes listed in its bingo license application, for purchasing or leasing bingo cards and other equipment used in conducting the bingo game, hiring security personnel for the bingo game, or advertising the bingo game, provided that the amount of the receipts so spent is not more than is customary and reasonable for a similar purchase, lease, hiring, or advertising, and for renting premises in which to conduct the bingo game, except that if the building in which the game is conducted is owned by the charitable organization conducting the game, the charitable organization may deduct from the total amount of the gross receipts from each session a sum equal to the lesser of six hundred dollars or forty-five per cent of the gross receipts from the session as consideration for the use of the premises;

(3) Conduct the bingo game on premises that are owned by the charitable organization, on premises that are owned by another charitable organization and leased from that charitable organization for a rental rate not in excess of four hundred fifty dollars per bingo session, on premises that are leased from a person other than a charitable organization for a rental rate that is not more than is customary and reasonable for premises that are similar in location, size, and quality but not in excess of four hundred fifty dollars per bingo session, or on premises that are owned by a person other than a charitable organization, that are leased from that person by another charitable organization, and that are subleased from that other charitable organization by the charitable organization for a rental rate not in excess of four hundred fifty dollars per bingo session. If the charitable organization leases from a person other than a charitable organization the premises on which it conducts bingo games, the lessor of the premises shall provide only the premises to the organization and shall not provide the organization with bingo game operators, security personnel, concessions or concession operators, bingo equipment, or any other type of service or equipment. A charitable organization shall not lease or sublease premises that it owns or leases to more than one other charitable organization per calendar week for the purpose of conducting bingo games on the premises. A person that is not a charitable organization shall not lease premises that it owns, leases, or otherwise is empowered to lease to more than one charitable organization per calendar week for conducting bingo games on the premises. In no case shall more than two bingo sessions be conducted on any premises in any calendar week.

(4) Display its bingo license conspicuously at the location where the bingo game is conducted;

(5) Conduct the bingo game in accordance with the definition of bingo set forth in division (S)(1) of section 2915.01 of the Revised Code.

(B) A charitable organization that conducts a bingo game shall not do any of the following:

(1) Pay any compensation to a bingo game operator for operating a bingo game that is conducted by the charitable organization or for preparing, selling, or serving food or beverages at the site of the bingo game, permit any auxiliary unit or society of the charitable organization to pay compensation to any bingo game operator who prepares, sells, or serves food or beverages at a bingo session conducted by the charitable organization, or permit any auxiliary unit or society of the charitable organization to prepare, sell, or serve food or beverages at a bingo session conducted by the charitable organization, if the auxiliary unit or society pays any compensation to the bingo game operators who prepare, sell, or serve the food or beverages;

(2) Pay consulting fees to any person for any services performed in relation to the bingo game;

(3) Pay concession fees to any person who provides refreshments to the participants in the bingo game;

(4) Conduct more than two bingo sessions in any seven-day period. Except that a volunteer fire fighter's organization or a volunteer rescue service organization that conducts not more than five bingo sessions in a calendar year may conduct more than two bingo sessions in a seven-day period after notifying the attorney general when it will conduct the sessions;

(5) Pay out more than three thousand five hundred dollars in prizes during any bingo session that is conducted by the charitable organization;

(6) Conduct a bingo session at any time during the ten-hour period between midnight and ten a.m., at any time during, or within ten hours of, a bingo game conducted for amusement only pursuant to section 2915.12 of the Revised Code, at any location not specified on its bingo license, or on any day of the week or during any time period not specified on its bingo license. If circumstances beyond its control make it impossible for the charitable organization to conduct a bingo session at the location specified on its bingo license or if a charitable organization wants to conduct bingo sessions on a day of the week or at a time other than the day or time specified on its bingo license, the charitable organization may apply in writing to the attorney general for an amended bingo license, pursuant to division (F) of section 2915.08 of the Revised Code. A charitable organization may apply only once in each calendar year for an amended license to conduct bingo sessions on a day of the week or at a time other than the day or time specified on its bingo license. If the amended license is granted, the organization may conduct bingo sessions at the location, on the day of the week, and at the time specified on its amended license.

(7) Permit any person whom the charitable organiza-

tion knows, or should have known, is under the age of eighteen to work as a bingo game operator;

(8) Permit any person whom the charitable organization knows, or should have known, has been convicted of a felony or gambling offense in any jurisdiction to be a bingo game operator;

(9) Permit the lessor of the premises on which bingo is conducted, if the lessor is not a charitable organization, to provide the charitable organization with bingo game operators, security personnel, concessions, bingo equipment, or any other type of service or equipment.

(C) A bingo game operator shall not receive or accept any commission, wage, salary, reward, tip, donation, gratuity, or other form of compensation, directly or indirectly, regardless of the source, for operating a bingo game or providing other work or labor at the site of the bingo game.

(D) Notwithstanding division (A)(3) of this section, a charitable organization that, prior to December 6, 1977, has entered into written agreements for the lease of premises it owns to another charitable organization or other charitable organizations for the conducting of bingo sessions so that more than two bingo sessions are conducted per calendar week on the premises, and a person that is not a charitable organization and that, prior to December 6, 1977, has entered into written agreements for the lease of premises it owns to charitable organizations for the conducting of more than two bingo sessions per calendar week on the premises, may continue to lease the premises to those charitable organizations, provided that no more than four sessions are conducted per calendar week, that the lessor organization or person has notified the attorney general in writing of the organizations that will conduct the sessions and the days of the week and the times of the day on which the sessions will be conducted, that the initial lease entered into with each organization that will conduct the sessions was filed with the attorney general prior to December 6, 1977, and that each organization that will conduct the sessions was issued a license to conduct bingo games by the attorney general prior to December 6, 1977.

(E) Whoever violates division (A)(2) of this section is guilty of illegally conducting a bingo game, a felony of the fourth degree. Whoever violates division (A)(1), (3), (4), or (5), (B), or (C) of this section is guilty of a minor misdemeanor. If the offender previously has been convicted of a violation of division (A)(1), (3), (4), or (5), (B), or (C) of this section, a violation of division (A)(1), (3), (4), or (5), (B), or (C) of this section is a misdemeanor of the first degree.

HISTORY: 136 v S 398 (Eff 5-26-76); 136 v H 1547 (Eff 12-6-76); 137 v H 72 (Eff 12-15-77); 139 v S 91 (Eff 10-20-81); 143 v H 573 (Eff 4-10-91); 145 v H 104 (Eff 10-7-93); 146 v S 70 (Eff 3-5-96); 146 v S 2. Eff 7-1-96.

Not analogous to former RC § 2915.09 (RS § 6939a; 78 v 11; GC § 13062; Bureau of Code Revision, 10-1-53; 129 v 1513), repealed 134 v H 511, § 2, eff 1-1-74.

See provisions, § 3 of HB 104 (145 v —) following RC § 2915.08.

The effective date is set by section 6 of SB 2.

Comment, Legislative Service Commission

Section 2915.09 of the Revised Code is amended by this act [Am. Sub. S.B. 70] and also by Am. Sub. S.B. 2 of the 121st General Assembly (effective July 1, 1996). Comparison of these amendments in pursuance of section 1.52 of the Revised Code discloses that they are not irreconcilable so that they are required by that section to be harmonized to give effect to each amendment.

§ 2915.10 Records to be kept for three years.

(A) A charitable organization that conducts a bingo session or scheme or game of chance pursuant to division (D) of section 2915.02 of the Revised Code, shall maintain the following records for at least three years from the date on which the bingo session or scheme or game of chance is conducted:

(1) An itemized list of the gross receipts of each session or scheme or game of chance;

(2) An itemized list of all expenses other than prizes that are incurred in conducting the bingo session, the name of each person to whom the expenses are paid, and a receipt for all of the expenses;

(3) A list of all prizes awarded during the bingo session or scheme or game of chance conducted by the charitable organization and the name and address of all persons who are winners of prizes of one hundred dollars or more in value;

(4) An itemized list of the charitable recipients of the proceeds of the bingo session or scheme or game of chance, including the name and address of each recipient to whom the money is distributed, and if the organization uses the proceeds of a bingo session, or the money or assets received from a scheme or game of chance for any purpose set forth in division (Z) of section 2915.01 or division (D) of section 2915.02 of the Revised Code, a list of each purpose and an itemized list of each expenditure for each purpose;

(5) The number of persons who participate in any bingo session or scheme or game of chance that is conducted by the charitable organization;

(6) A list of receipts from the sale of food and beverages by the charitable organization or one of its auxiliary units or societies, if the receipts were excluded from the definition of "gross receipts" under division (X) of section 2915.01 of the Revised Code;

(7) An itemized list of all expenses incurred at each bingo session conducted by the charitable organization in the sale of food and beverages by the charitable organization or by an auxiliary unit or society of the charitable organization, the name of each person to whom the expenses are paid, and a receipt for all of the expenses.

(B) The attorney general, or any local law enforcement agency, may:

(1) Investigate any charitable organization or any officer, agent, trustee, member, or employee of the organization;

(2) Examine the accounts and records of the organization;

(3) Conduct inspections, audits, and observations of bingo games or schemes or games of chance while they are in session;

(4) Conduct inspections of the premises where bingo games or schemes or games of chance are operated;

(5) Take any other necessary and reasonable action to determine if a violation of any provision of sections 2915.01, 2915.02, and 2915.07 to 2915.12 of the Revised Code has occurred and to determine whether section 2915.11 of the Revised Code has been complied with.

If any local law enforcement agency has reasonable grounds to believe that a charitable organization or an officer, agent, trustee, member, or employee of the organization has violated any provision of this chapter, the local law enforcement agency may proceed by action in the proper court to enforce this chapter, provided that the local law enforcement agency shall give written notice to the attorney general when commencing an action as described in this division.

(C) No person shall destroy, alter, conceal, withhold, or deny access to any accounts or records of a charitable organization that have been requested for examination, or obstruct, impede, or interfere with any inspection, audit, or observation of a bingo game or scheme or game of chance or premises where a bingo game or scheme or game of chance is operated, or refuse to comply with any reasonable request of, or obstruct, impede, or interfere with any other reasonable action undertaken by, the attorney general or a local law enforcement agency pursuant to division (B) of this section.

(D) Whoever violates division (A) or (C) of this section is guilty of a misdemeanor of the first degree.

HISTORY: 136 v S 398 (Eff 5-26-76); 136 v H 1547 (Eff 12-6-76); 137 v H 72 (Eff 12-15-77); 139 v S 91 (Eff 10-20-81); 146 v S 2. Eff 7-1-96.

Not analogous to former RC § 2915.10 (RS § 6930; S&S 287; 59 v 10; GC § 13063; 120 v 663; Bureau of Code Revision, 10-1-53; 129 v 1513), repealed 134 v H 511, § 2, eff 1-1-74.

The effective date is set by section 6 of SB 2.

§ 2915.11 Persons prohibited from being bingo game operators.

(A) No person shall be a bingo game operator unless he is eighteen years of age or older.

(B) No person who has been convicted of a felony or a gambling offense in any jurisdiction shall be a bingo game operator.

(C) Whoever violates division (A) of this section is guilty of a misdemeanor of the third degree.

(D) Whoever violates division (B) of this section is guilty of a misdemeanor of the first degree.

HISTORY: 136 v S 398 (Eff 5-26-76); 137 v H 72. Eff 12-15-77.

Not analogous to former RC § 2915.11 (GC § 13063-1; 120 v 663; Bureau of Code Revision, 10-1-53; 129 v 1409), repealed 134 v H 511, § 2, eff 1-1-74.

[§ 2915.11.1] § 2915.111 Repealed, 134 v H 511, § 2 [129 v 1409]. Eff 1-1-74.

This section concerned possession of "numbers game" ticket.

§ 2915.12 Bingo for amusement only.

Sections 2915.07 to 2915.11 of the Revised Code do not apply to bingo games that are conducted for the purpose of amusement only. A bingo game is conducted for the purpose of amusement only if it complies with all of the requirements specified in either division (A) or (B) of this section:

(A)(1) The participants do not pay any money or any other thing of value including an admission fee, or any fee for bingo cards, sheets, objects to cover the spaces, or other devices used in playing bingo, for the privilege of participating in the bingo game, or to defray any costs of the game, or pay tips or make donations during or immediately before or after the bingo game;

(2) All prizes awarded during the course of the game are nonmonetary, and in the form of merchandise, goods, or entitlements to goods or services only, and the total value of all prizes awarded during the game is less than one hundred dollars;

(3) No commission, wages, salary, reward, tip, donation, gratuity, or other form of compensation, either directly or indirectly, and regardless of the source, is paid to any bingo game operator for work or labor performed at the site of the bingo game;

(4) The bingo game is not conducted either during or within ten hours of:

(a) A bingo session during which a charitable bingo game is conducted pursuant to sections 2915.07 to 2915.11 of the Revised Code;

(b) A scheme or game of chance other than a bingo game conducted pursuant to this section.

(5) The number of players participating in the bingo game does not exceed fifty.

(B)(1) The participants do not pay money or any other thing of value as an admission fee, and no participant is charged more than twenty-five cents to purchase a bingo card, sheet, objects to cover the spaces, or other devices used in playing bingo;

(2) The total amount of money paid by all of the participants for bingo cards, sheets, objects to cover the spaces, or other devices used in playing bingo does not exceed one hundred dollars;

(3) All of the money paid for bingo cards, sheets, objects to cover spaces, or other devices used in playing

bingo are used only to pay winners monetary and nonmonetary prizes and to provide refreshments;

(4) The total value of all prizes awarded during the game does not exceed one hundred dollars;

(5) No commission, wages, salary, reward, tip, donation, gratuity, or other form of compensation, either directly or indirectly, and regardless of the source, is paid to any bingo game operator for work or labor performed at the site of the bingo game;

(6) The bingo game is not conducted during or within ten hours of either of the following:

(a) A bingo session during which a charitable bingo game is conducted pursuant to sections 2915.07 to 2915.11 of the Revised Code;

(b) A scheme of chance or game of chance other than a bingo game conducted pursuant to this section.

(7) All of the participants reside at the premises where the bingo game is conducted;

(8) The bingo games are conducted on different days of the week and not more than twice in a calendar week.

(C) The attorney general, or any local law enforcement agency, may investigate the conduct of a bingo game that purportedly is conducted for purposes of amusement only if there is reason to believe that the purported amusement bingo game does not comply with the requirements of either division (A) or (B) of this section. A local law enforcement agency may proceed by action in the proper court to enforce this section if the local law enforcement agency gives written notice to the attorney general when commencing the action.

HISTORY: 136 v S 398 (Eff 5-26-76); 137 v H 72 (Eff 12-15-77); 143 v H 573 (Eff 4-10-91); 146 v S 2. Eff 7-1-96.

Not analogous to former RC § 2915.12 (RS § 6931; S&S 287; 59 v 10; 70 v 123; GC § 13064; 120 v 663; Bureau of Code Revision, 10-1-53; 129 v 1409), repealed 134 v H 511, § 2, eff 1-1-74.

The effective date is set by section 6 of SB 2.

[§§ 2915.12.1, 2915.12.2]
§§ 2915.121, 2915.122
Repealed, 134 v H 511, § 2 [129 v 1408]. Eff 1-1-74.

These sections concerned schemes of chance and possessing odds ticket on athletic events.

§§ 2915.13, 2915.14, 2915.15
Repealed, 134 v H 511, § 2 [RS § 6934; S&C 662, 665; S&S 377; 54 v 196; 73 v 249; GC §§ 13064-1, 13065, 13066; 120 v 663; 124 v 838; Bureau of Code Revision, 10-1-53; 129 v 1409]. Eff 1-1-74.

These sections concerned promoting "numbers games," gambling as a profession, and gambling devices.

§§ 2915.16, 2915.17, 2915.18
Repealed, 134 v H 511, § 2 [GC §§ 13066-1—13066-3; 124 v 838; Bureau of Code Revision, 10-1-53]. Eff 1-1-74.

These sections concerned gambling devices.

§§ 2915.19, 2915.20, 2915.21
Repealed, 134 v H 511, § 2 [RS §§ 6929, 6934a; S&C 435; 49 v 105; 79 v 118; 83 v 195; GC §§ 13067—13070]. Eff 1-1-74.

These sections concerned advertising lotteries and contracts for options on commodities.

§§ 2915.31, 2915.32, 2915.33
Repealed, 134 v H 511, § 2 [RS §§ 6934a-1, 6934a-4; 86 v 12; GC §§ 13071—13074, 13079, 13080; 102 v 317; Bureau of Code Revision, 10-1-53]. Eff 1-1-74.

These sections concerned bucket shops.

§§ 2915.34, 2915.35, 2915.36
Repealed, 134 v H 511, § 2 [RS §§ 6934a-2, 6934a-3; 86 v 13, 14; GC §§ 13075—13077; 102 v 317; Bureau of Code Revision, 10-1-53]. Eff 1-1-74.

These sections concerned bucket shops.

§ 2915.37
Repealed, 134 v H 511, § 2 [RS § 6934a-5; 86 v 14; GC § 13081; Bureau of Code Revision, 10-1-53]. Eff 1-1-74.

This section concerned bucket shops.

§ 2915.40
Repealed, 134 v H 511, § 2 [133 v S 284]. Eff 1-1-74.

This section concerned coerced establishment of give-away games and penalty.

CHAPTER 2917: OFFENSES AGAINST THE PUBLIC PEACE

Section

[INCITING, RIOT, AND RELATED OFFENSES]

2917.01 Inciting to violence.
2917.02 Aggravated riot.
2917.03 Riot.
2917.04 Failure to disperse.
2917.05 Justifiable use of force to suppress riot.
2917.06-2917.10 Repealed.

[DISORDERLY CONDUCT]

2917.11 Disorderly conduct.
2917.12 Disturbing a lawful meeting.
2917.13 Misconduct at an emergency.
2917.14, 2917.15, 2917.16 Repealed.
2917.17, 2917.18, 2917.19 Repealed.
[2917.19.1] 2917.191 Repealed.
2917.20 Repealed.

[HARASSMENT]

2917.21 Telephone harassment.
[2917.21.1] 2917.211 Repealed.
2917.22-2917.30 Repealed.

[FALSE ALARMS]

2917.31 Inducing panic.
2917.32 Making false alarms.
2917.33-2917.39 Repealed.

[CROWD SAFETY]

2917.40 Required crowd safety measures at live entertainment performances.
2917.41 Misconduct involving public transportation system.
2917.42-2917.44 Repealed.
2917.45 Repealed.
2917.46 Unauthorized use of a block parent symbol.
2917.47 Improperly handling infectious agents.

[INCITING, RIOT, AND RELATED OFFENSES]

§ 2917.01 Inciting to violence.

(A) No person shall knowingly engage in conduct designed to urge or incite another to commit any offense of violence, when either of the following apply:

(1) The conduct takes place under circumstances that create a clear and present danger that any offense of violence will be committed;

(2) The conduct proximately results in the commission of any offense of violence.

(B) Whoever violates this section is guilty of inciting to violence. If the offense of violence that the other person is being urged or incited to commit is a misdemeanor, inciting to violence is a misdemeanor of the first degree. If the offense of violence that the other person is being urged or incited to commit is a felony, inciting to violence is a felony of the third degree.

HISTORY: 134 v H 511 (Eff 1-1-74); 146 v S 2. Eff 7-1-96.

Not analogous to former RC § 2917.01 (RS § 6900; S&C 432, 457, 457a; 29 v 144; 57 v 47; 70 v 155; GC §§ 12823, 12824; 102 v 129; Bureau of Code Revision, 10-1-53), repealed 134 v H 511, § 2, eff 1-1-74.

The effective date is set by section 6 of SB 2.

§ 2917.02 Aggravated riot.

(A) No person shall participate with four or more others in a course of disorderly conduct in violation of section 2917.11 of the Revised Code:

(1) With purpose to commit or facilitate the commission of a felony;

(2) With purpose to commit or facilitate the commission of any offense of violence;

(3) When the offender or any participant to the knowledge of the offender has on or about the offender's or participant's person or under the offender's or participant's control, uses, or intends to use a deadly weapon or dangerous ordnance, as defined in section 2923.11 of the Revised Code.

(B)(1) No person, being an inmate in a detention facility, shall violate division (A)(1) or (3) of this section.

(2) No person, being an inmate in a detention facility, shall violate division (A)(2) of this section or section 2917.03 of the Revised Code.

(C) Whoever violates this section is guilty of aggravated riot. A violation of division (A)(1) or (3) of this section is a felony of the fifth degree. A violation of division (A)(2) or (B)(1) of this section is a felony of the fourth degree. A violation of division (B)(2) of this section is a felony of the third degree.

(D) As used in this section, "detention facility" has the same meaning as in section 2921.01 of the Revised Code.

HISTORY: 134 v H 511 (Eff 1-1-74); 139 v S 199 (Eff 1-5-83); 140 v S 210 (Eff 7-1-83); 146 v S 2. Eff 7-1-96.

Not analogous to former RC § 2917.02 (GC § 12823-1; 122 v 130; Bureau of Code Revision, 10-1-53), repealed 134 v H 511, § 2, eff 1-1-74.

The effective date is set by section 6 of SB 2.

§ 2917.03 Riot.

(A) No person shall participate with four or more others in a course of disorderly conduct in violation of section 2917.11 of the Revised Code:

(1) With purpose to commit or facilitate the commission of a misdemeanor, other than disorderly conduct;

(2) With purpose to intimidate a public official or employee into taking or refraining from official action, or with purpose to hinder, impede, or obstruct a function of government;

(3) With purpose to hinder, impede, or obstruct the orderly process of administration or instruction at an educational institution, or to interfere with or disrupt lawful activities carried on at such institution.

(B) No person shall participate with four or more

others with purpose to do an act with unlawful force or violence, even though such act might otherwise be lawful.

(C) Whoever violates this section is guilty of riot, a misdemeanor of the first degree.

HISTORY: 134 v H 511. Eff 1-1-74.

Not analogous to former RC § 2917.03 (RS § 6899; S&C 431, 432; 29 v 144; 95 v 300; GC § 12825; Bureau of Code Revision, 10-1-53), repealed 134 v H 511, § 2, eff 1-1-74.

§ 2917.04 Failure to disperse.

(A) Where five or more persons are participating in a course of disorderly conduct in violation of section 2917.11 of the Revised Code, and there are other persons in the vicinity whose presence creates the likelihood of physical harm to persons or property or of serious public inconvenience, annoyance, or alarm, a law enforcement officer or other public official may order the participants and such other persons to disperse. No person shall knowingly fail to obey such order.

(B) Nothing in this section requires persons to disperse who are peaceably assembled for a lawful purpose.

(C) Whoever violates this section is guilty of failure to disperse, a minor misdemeanor.

HISTORY: 134 v H 511. Eff 1-1-74.

Not analogous to former RC § 2917.04 (GC § 12824-1; 101 v 100; Bureau of Code Revision, 10-1-53), repealed 134 v H 511, § 2, eff 1-1-74.

Analogous to former RC § 2923.51 (132 v H 996), repealed 134 v H 511, § 2, eff 1-1-74.

§ 2917.05 Justifiable use of force to suppress riot.

A law enforcement officer or fireman, engaged in suppressing riot or in protecting persons or property during riot:

(A) Is justified in using force, other than deadly force, when and to the extent he has probable cause to believe such force is necessary to disperse or apprehend rioters;

(B) Is justified in using force, including deadly force, when and to the extent he has probable cause to believe such force is necessary to disperse or apprehend rioters whose conduct is creating a substantial risk of serious physical harm to persons.

HISTORY: 134 v H 511. Eff 1-1-74.

Not analogous to former RC § 2917.05 (RS § 6899a; 95 v 300; GC § 12826; Bureau of Code Revision, 10-1-53), repealed 134 v H 511, § 2, eff 1-1-74.

Analogous to former RC § 2923.55 (132 v H 996), repealed 134 v H 511, § 2, eff 1-1-74.

§§ 2917.06, 2917.07, 2917.08

Repealed, 134 v H 511, § 2 [RS §§ 6899b, 6907, 6918a; S&C 258; 32 v 17; 86 v 127; 97 v 281; GC §§ 12827, 12828, 12866; 124 v 62; Bureau of Code Revision, 10-1-53; 129 v 582(746)]. Eff 1-1-74.

These sections concerned bribery.

§§ 2917.09, 2917.10 Repealed, 134 v H 511, § 2 [RS §§ 6903, 6908-1; S&C 431; 29 v 144; 93 v 411; GC §§ 12831, 12832; Bureau of Code Revision, 10-1-53]. Eff 1-1-74.

These sections concerned lynching and escape of prisoner.

[DISORDERLY CONDUCT]

§ 2917.11 Disorderly conduct.

(A) No person shall recklessly cause inconvenience, annoyance, or alarm to another, by doing any of the following:

(1) Engaging in fighting, in threatening harm to persons or property, or in violent or turbulent behavior;

(2) Making unreasonable noise or an offensively coarse utterance, gesture, or display, or communicating unwarranted and grossly abusive language to any person;

(3) Insulting, taunting, or challenging another, under circumstances in which such conduct is likely to provoke a violent response;

(4) Hindering or preventing the movement of persons on a public street, road, highway, or right-of-way, or to, from, within, or upon public or private property, so as to interfere with the rights of others, and by any act that serves no lawful and reasonable purpose of the offender;

(5) Creating a condition that is physically offensive to persons or that presents a risk of physical harm to persons or property, by any act that serves no lawful and reasonable purpose of the offender.

(B) No person, while voluntarily intoxicated, shall do either of the following:

(1) In a public place or in the presence of two or more persons, engage in conduct likely to be offensive or to cause inconvenience, annoyance, or alarm to persons of ordinary sensibilities, which conduct the offender, if the offender were not intoxicated, should know is likely to have that effect on others;

(2) Engage in conduct or create a condition that presents a risk of physical harm to the offender or another, or to the property of another.

(C) Violation of any statute or ordinance of which an element is operating a motor vehicle, locomotive, watercraft, aircraft, or other vehicle while under the influence of alcohol or any drug of abuse, is not a violation of division (B) of this section.

(D) When to an ordinary observer a person appears to be intoxicated, it is probable cause to believe that person is voluntarily intoxicated for purposes of division (B) of this section.

(E) Whoever violates this section is guilty of disorderly conduct. Except as otherwise provided in this division, disorderly conduct is a minor misdemeanor. If the offender persists in disorderly conduct after reasonable warning or request to desist or if the offense is committed in the vicinity of a school, disorderly conduct is a misdemeanor of the fourth degree.

(F) As used in this section, "committed in the vicinity of a school" has the same meaning as in section 2925.01 of the Revised Code.

HISTORY: 134 v H 511 (Eff 1-1-74); 143 v H 51 (Eff 11-8-90); 146 v S 2. Eff 7-1-96.

Not analogous to former RC § 2917.11 (RS § 6904; S&C 415, 431, 911; 29 v 144; 68 v 9; GC § 12833, Bureau of Code Revision, 10-1-53), repealed 134 v H 511, § 2, eff 1-1-74.

The effective date is set by section 6 of SB 2.

§ 2917.12 Disturbing a lawful meeting.

(A) No person, with purpose to prevent or disrupt a lawful meeting, procession, or gathering, shall do either of the following:

(1) Do any act which obstructs or interferes with the due conduct of such meeting, procession, or gathering;

(2) Make any utterance, gesture, or display which outrages the sensibilities of the group.

(B) Whoever violates this section is guilty of disturbing a lawful meeting, a misdemeanor of the fourth degree.

HISTORY: 134 v H 511. Eff 1-1-74.

Not analogous to former RC § 2917.12 (RS § 6904; S&C 415, 431, 911; 29 v 144; 68 v 9; GC § 12833; Bureau of Code Revision, 10-1-53), repealed 134 v H 511, § 2, eff 1-1-74.

§ 2917.13 Misconduct at an emergency.

(A) No person shall knowingly:

(1) Hamper the lawful operations of any law enforcement officer, fireman, rescuer, medical person, or other authorized person, engaged in his duties at the scene of a fire, accident, disaster, riot, or emergency of any kind;

(2) Fail to obey the lawful order of any law enforcement officer engaged in his duties at the scene of or in connection with a fire, accident, disaster, riot, or emergency of any kind.

(B) Nothing in this section shall be construed to limit access or deny information to any news media representative in the lawful exercise of his duties.

(C) Whoever violates this section is guilty of misconduct at an emergency, a minor misdemeanor. If violation of this section creates a risk of physical harm to persons or property, misconduct at an emergency is a misdemeanor of the fourth degree.

HISTORY: 134 v H 511 (Eff 1-1-74); 135 v H 716. Eff 1-1-74.

Not analogous to former RC § 2917.13 (RS § 6905; S&C 432; 29 v 144; GC § 12834; Bureau of Code Revision, 10-1-53), repealed 134 v H 511, § 2, eff 1-1-74.

Analogous to former RC § 2923.43 (132 v H 332), repealed 134 v H 511, § 2, eff 1-1-74.

§§ 2917.14, 2917.15, 2917.16

Repealed, 134 v H 511, § 2 [RS § 6902; S&S 287; 62 v 109; 68 v 9; 84 v 91; 97 v 120; GC §§ 12835, 12837; 123 v 223; Bureau of Code Revision, 10-1-53; 125 v H 88]. Eff 1-1-74.

These sections concerned conveying articles to prisoners.

§§ 2917.17, 2917.18, 2917.19

Repealed, 134 v H 511, § 2 [RS §§ 6827, 6902, 6947; S&C 750; S&S 287; 54 v 127; 62 v 109; 68 v 9; 73 v 249; 84 v 91; 95 v 69; 97 v 120, 307; GC §§ 12836, 12838, 12846; Bureau of Code Revision, 10-1-53; 128 v 1040; 130 v 662; 130 v PtII, 145; 134 v H 494]. Eff 1-1-74.

These sections concerned conveying articles to prisoners; escapes.

[§ 2917.19.1] § 2917.191 Repealed,

134 v H 511, § 2 [130 v 662]. Eff 1-1-74.

This section concerned attempting to persuade inmates to escape.

§ 2917.20 Repealed, 134 v H 511, § 2 [GC § 12838-1; 103 v 93; Bureau of Code Revision, 10-1-53]. Eff 1-1-74.

This section concerned soliciting money from persons confined.

[HARASSMENT]

§ 2917.21 Telephone harassment.

(A) No person shall knowingly make or cause to be made a telephone call, or knowingly permit a telephone call to be made from a telephone under the person's control, to another, if the caller does any of the following:

(1) Fails to identify the caller to the recipient of the telephone call and makes the telephone call with purpose to harass, abuse, or annoy any person at the premises to which the telephone call is made, whether or not conversation takes place during the telephone call;

(2) Describes, suggests, requests, or proposes that the caller, recipient of the telephone call, or any other person engage in, any sexual activity as defined in division (C) of section 2907.01 of the Revised Code, and the recipient of the telephone call, or another person at the premises to which the telephone call is made, has requested, in a previous telephone call or in the immediate telephone call, the caller not to make a telephone call to the recipient of the telephone call or to the premises to which the telephone call is made;

(3) During the telephone call, violates section 2903.21 of the Revised Code;

(4) Knowingly states to the recipient of the telephone call that the caller intends to cause damage to or destroy public or private property, and the recipient of the telephone call, any member of the family of the recipient of the telephone call, or any other person who resides at the premises to which the telephone call is made owns, leases, resides, or works in, will at the time of the destruction or damaging be near or in, has the

responsibility of protecting, or insures the property that will be destroyed or damaged;

(5) Knowingly makes the telephone call to the recipient of the telephone call, to another person at the premises to which the telephone call is made, or to the premises to which the telephone call is made, and the recipient of the telephone call, or another person at the premises to which the telephone call is made, previously has told the caller not to call the premises to which the telephone call is made or not to call any persons at the premises to which the telephone call is made.

(B) No person shall make or cause to be made a telephone call, or permit a telephone call to be made from a telephone under the person's control, with purpose to abuse, threaten, annoy, or harass another person.

(C) Whoever violates this section is guilty of telephone harassment, a misdemeanor of the first degree on a first offense and a felony of the fifth degree on each subsequent offense involving the same person, recipient, or premises.

HISTORY: 134 v H 511 (Eff 1-1-74); 138 v H 164 (Eff 4-9-81); 146 v S 2. Eff 7-1-96.

Not analogous to former RC § 2917.21 (RS § 6827a; 90 v 33; 95 v 69; 97 v 307; GC § 12839; Bureau of Code Revision, 10-1-53), repealed 134 v H 511, § 2, eff 1-1-74.

The effective date is set by section 6 of SB 2.

[§ 2917.21.1] § 2917.211 Repealed,
134 v H 511, § 2 [131 v 675]. Eff 1-1-74.

This section concerned prohibition against trespassing on school grounds and penalty.

§§ 2917.22, 2917.23, 2917.24
Repealed, 134 v H 511, § 2 [RS §§ 2103, 6979; S&C 412; Bates, § 1536-374; 33 v 33; 66 v 196; GC §§ 12840, 12840-1, 12841; 110 v 261; 113 v 476; Bureau of Code Revision, 10-1-53; 133 v S 460]. Eff 1-1-74.

These sections concerned harboring felons and escape from a workhouse.

§§ 2917.25, 2917.26, 2917.27
Repealed, 134 v H 511, § 2 [RS §§ 6897, 6906; S&C 405, 432, 546, 547, 607, 1171; 29 v 144; 33 v 33; 38 v 146; 39 v 13; 52 v 27; 54 v 83; 59 v 91; 68 v 27; 69 v 62; 73 v 58; GC §§ 12842—12844; 104 v 7; 112 v 177; Bureau of Code Revision, 10-1-53]. Eff 1-1-74.

These sections concerned misconduct of witnesses.

§§ 2917.28, 2917.29, 2917.30
Repealed, 134 v H 511, § 2 [RS §§ 6916, 6917; S&C 433, 434, 1398, 1401; 20 v 144; 29 v 112, 144; GC §§ 12849, 12850]. Eff 1-1-74.

These sections concerned misconduct of officers.

[FALSE ALARMS]

§ 2917.31 Inducing panic.
(A) No person shall cause the evacuation of any public place, or otherwise cause serious public inconvenience or alarm, by doing any of the following:

(1) Initiating or circulating a report or warning of an alleged or impending fire, explosion, crime, or other catastrophe, knowing that such report or warning is false;

(2) Threatening to commit any offense of violence;

(3) Committing any offense, with reckless disregard of the likelihood that its commission will cause serious public inconvenience or alarm.

(B) Division (A)(1) of this section does not apply to any person conducting an authorized fire or emergency drill.

(C) Whoever violates this section is guilty of inducing panic, a misdemeanor of the first degree. If violation of this section results in physical harm to any person, inducing panic is a felony of the fourth degree.

HISTORY: 134 v H 511. Eff 1-1-74.

Not analogous to former RC § 2917.31 (RS § 6917; S&C 434, 1398, 1401; 29 v 144; 29 v 112; GC § 12851; Bureau of Code Revision, 10-1-53), repealed 134 v H 511, § 2, eff 1-1-74.

§ 2917.32 Making false alarms.
(A) No person shall do either of the following:

(1) Initiate or circulate a report or warning of an alleged or impending fire, explosion, crime, or other catastrophe, knowing that the report or warning is false and likely to cause public inconvenience or alarm;

(2) Knowingly cause a false alarm of fire or other emergency to be transmitted to or within any organization, public or private, for dealing with emergencies involving a risk of physical harm to persons or property;

(3) Report to any law enforcement agency an alleged offense or other incident within its concern, knowing that such offense did not occur.

(B) This section does not apply to any person conducting an authorized fire or emergency drill.

(C) Whoever violates this section is guilty of making false alarms, a misdemeanor of the first degree.

HISTORY: 134 v H 511. Eff 1-1-74.

Not analogous to former RC § 2917.32 (RS § 6918; S&C 430; 29 v 144; GC § 12857; Bureau of Code Revision, 10-1-53), repealed 134 v H 511, § 2, eff 1-1-74.

§§ 2917.33, 2917.34, 2917.35
Repealed, 134 v H 511, § 2 [RS §§ 6898, 6908, 6913a; S&C 409, 427, 428; 29 v 144; 33 v 33; 97 v 319; GC §§ 12858—12860; Bureau of Code Revision, 10-1-53; 127 v 1039; 129 v 582(746)]. Eff 1-1-74.

These sections concerned resisting or impersonating an officer.

§§ 2917.36, 2917.37, 2917.38
Repealed, 134 v H 511, § 2 [RS §§ 6901, 7014; 75 v 517; 76 v 23; 79 v 30; 81 v 101; 91 v 361; GC §§ 12861—12863; 102 v 114; Bureau of Code Revision, 10-1-53]. Eff 1-1-74.

These sections concerned compounding felonies and assignment of debt for collection outside state.

§ 2917.39 Repealed, 134 v H 511, § 2 [RS § 7014; 75 v 517; 79 v 30; 91 v 361; GC § 12864; Bureau of Code Revision, 10-1-53]. Eff 1-1-74.

This section concerned assignment of debt for collection outside state.

[CROWD SAFETY]

§ 2917.40 Required crowd safety measures at live entertainment performances.

(A) As used in this section:

(1) "Live entertainment performance" means any live speech; any live musical performance, including a concert; any live dramatic performance; any live variety show; and any other live performance with respect to which the primary intent of the audience can be construed to be viewing the performers. A "live entertainment performance" does not include any form of entertainment with respect to which the person purchasing a ticket routinely participates in amusements as well as views performers.

(2) "Restricted entertainment area" means any wholly or partially enclosed area, whether indoors or outdoors, that has limited access through established entrances, or established turnstyles† or similar devices.

(3) "Concert" means a musical performance of which the primary component is a presentation by persons singing or playing musical instruments, that is intended by its sponsors mainly, but not necessarily exclusively, for the listening enjoyment of the audience, and that is held in a facility. A "concert" does not include any performance in which music is a part of the presentation and the primary component of which is acting, dancing, a motion picture, a demonstration of skills or talent other than singing or playing an instrument, an athletic event, an exhibition, or a speech.

(4) "Facility" means any structure that has a roof or partial roof and that has walls that wholly surround the area on all sides, including, but not limited to, a stadium, hall, arena, armory, auditorium, ballroom, exhibition hall, convention center, or music hall.

(5) "Person" includes, in addition to an individual or entity specified in division (C) of section 1.59 of the Revised Code, any governmental entity.

(B)(1) No person shall sell, offer to sell, or offer in return for a donation any ticket that is not numbered and that does not correspond to a specific seat for admission to either of the following:

(a) A live entertainment performance that is not exempted under division (D) of this section, that is held in a restricted entertainment area, and for which more than eight thousand tickets are offered to the public;

(b) A concert that is not exempted under division (D) of this section and for which more than three thousand tickets are offered to the public.

(2) No person shall advertise any live entertainment performance as described in division (B)(1)(a) of this section or any concert as described in division (B)(1)(b) of this section, unless the advertisement contains the words "Reserved Seats Only."

(C) Unless exempted by division (D)(1) of this section, no person who owns or operates any restricted entertainment area shall fail to open, maintain, and properly staff at least the number of entrances designated under division (E) of this section for a minimum of ninety minutes prior to the scheduled start of any live entertainment performance that is held in the restricted entertainment area and for which more than three thousand tickets are sold, offered for sale, or offered in return for a donation.

(D)(1) A live entertainment performance, other than a concert, is exempted from the provisions of divisions (B) and (C) of this section if both of the following apply:

(a) The restricted entertainment area in which the performance is held has at least eight entrances or, if both entrances and separate admission turnstyles† or similar devices are used, has at least eight turnstyles† or similar devices;

(b) The eight entrances or, if applicable, the eight turnstyles† or similar devices are opened, maintained, and properly staffed at least one hour prior to the scheduled start of the performance.

(2)(a) The chief of the police department of a township police district in the case of a facility located within the district, the officer responsible for public safety within a municipal corporation in the case of a facility located within the municipal corporation, or the county sheriff in the case of a facility located outside the boundaries of a township police district or municipal corporation may, upon application of the sponsor of a concert covered by division (B) of this section, exempt the concert from the provisions of that division if the official finds that the health, safety, and welfare of the participants and spectators would not be substantially affected by failure to comply with the provisions of that division.

In determining whether to grant an exemption, the official shall consider the following factors:

(i) The size and design of the facility in which the concert is scheduled;

(ii) The size, age, and anticipated conduct of the crowd expected to attend the concert;

(iii) The ability of the sponsor to manage and control the expected crowd.

If the sponsor of any concert desires to obtain an exemption under this division, the sponsor shall apply to the appropriate official on a form prescribed by that official. The official shall issue an order that grants or denies the exemption within five days after receipt of the application. The sponsor may appeal any order that denies an exemption to the court of common pleas of the county in which the facility is located.

(b) If an official grants an exemption under division (D)(2)(a) of this section, the official shall designate an on-duty law enforcement officer to be present at the concert. The designated officer has authority to issue orders to all security personnel at the concert to protect the health, safety, and welfare of the participants and spectators.

(3) Notwithstanding division (D)(2) of this section, in the case of a concert held in a facility located on the campus of an educational institution covered by section 3345.04 of the Revised Code, a state university law enforcement officer appointed pursuant to sections 3345.04 and 3345.21 of the Revised Code shall do both of the following:

(a) Exercise the authority to grant exemptions provided by division (D)(2)(a) of this section in lieu of an official designated in that division;

(b) If the officer grants an exemption under division (D)(3)(a) of this section, designate an on-duty state university law enforcement officer to be present at the concert. The designated officer has authority to issue orders to all security personnel at the concert to protect the health, safety, and welfare of the participants and spectators.

(E)(1) Unless a live entertainment performance is exempted by division (D)(1) of this section, the chief of the police department of a township police district in the case of a restricted entertainment area located within the district, the officer responsible for public safety within a municipal corporation in the case of a restricted entertainment area located within the municipal corporation, or the county sheriff in the case of a restricted entertainment area located outside the boundaries of a township police district or municipal corporation shall designate, for purposes of division (C) of this section, the minimum number of entrances required to be opened, maintained, and staffed at each live entertainment performance so as to permit crowd control and reduce congestion at the entrances. The designation shall be based on such factors as the size and nature of the crowd expected to attend the live entertainment performance, the length of time prior to the live entertainment performance that crowds are expected to congregate at the entrances, and the amount of security provided at the restricted entertainment area.

(2) Notwithstanding division (E)(1) of this section, a state university law enforcement officer appointed pursuant to sections 3345.04 and 3345.21 of the Revised Code shall designate the number of entrances required to be opened, maintained, and staffed in the case of a live entertainment performance that is held at a restricted entertainment area located on the campus of an educational institution covered by section 3345.04 of the Revised Code.

(F) No person shall enter into any contract for a live entertainment performance, that does not permit or require compliance with this section.

(G)(1) This section does not apply to a live entertainment performance held in a restricted entertainment area if one admission ticket entitles the holder to view or participate in three or more different games, rides, activities, or live entertainment performances occurring simultaneously at different sites within the restricted entertainment area and if the initial admittance entrance to the restricted entertainment area, for which the ticket is required, is separate from the entrance to any specific live entertainment performance and an additional ticket is not required for admission to the particular live entertainment performance.

(2) This section does not apply to a symphony orchestra performance, a ballet performance, horse races, dances, or fairs.

(H) This section does not prohibit the legislative authority of any municipal corporation from imposing additional requirements, not in conflict with this section, for the promotion or holding of live entertainment performances.

(I) Whoever violates division (B), (C), or (F) of this section is guilty of a misdemeanor of the first degree. If any individual suffers physical harm to his person as a result of a violation of this section, the sentencing court shall consider this factor in favor of imposing a term of imprisonment upon the offender.

HISTORY: 138 v S 320. Eff 3-23-81.

Not analogous to former RC § 2917.40 (RS § 7014; 75 v 517; 79 v 30; 91 v 361; GC § 12865; Bureau of Code Revision, 10-1-53), repealed 134 v H 511, § 2, eff 1-1-74.

† So in enrolled bill. Apparently, "turnstiles" was intended.

§ 2917.41 Misconduct involving public transportation system.

(A) No person shall evade the payment of the known fares of a public transportation system.

(B) No person shall alter any transfer, pass, ticket, or token of a public transportation system with the purpose of evading the payment of fares or of defrauding the system.

(C) No person shall do any of the following while in any facility or on any vehicle of a public transportation system:

(1) Play sound equipment without the proper use of a private earphone;

(2) Smoke, eat, or drink in any area where the activity is clearly marked as being prohibited;

(3) Expectorate upon a person, facility, or vehicle.

(D) No person shall write, deface, draw, or otherwise mark on any facility or vehicle of a public transportation system.

(E) No person shall fail to comply with a lawful order of a public transportation system police officer, and no person shall resist, obstruct, or abuse a public transportation police officer in the performance of the officer's duties.

(F) Whoever violates this section is guilty of misconduct involving a public transportation system.

(1) Violation of division (A) of this section is a misdemeanor of the fourth degree.

(2) Violation of division (B) of this section is a misdemeanor of the fourth degree.

(3) Violation of division (C) or (E) of this section is a misdemeanor of the fourth degree.

(4) Violation of division (D) of this section is a misdemeanor of the third degree.

(G) Notwithstanding any other provision of law, seventy-five per cent of each fine paid to satisfy a sentence imposed for a violation of this section shall be deposited into the treasury of the county in which the violation occurred and twenty-five per cent shall be deposited with the county transit board, regional transit authority, or regional transit commission that operates the public transportation system involved in the violation, unless the board of county commissioners operates the public transportation system, in which case one hundred per cent of each fine shall be deposited into the treasury of the county.

(H) As used in this section, "public transportation system" means a county transit system operated in accordance with sections 306.01 to 306.13 of the Revised Code, a regional transit authority operated in accordance with sections 306.30 to 306.71 of the Revised Code, or a regional transit commission operated in accordance with sections 306.80 to 306.90 of the Revised Code.

HISTORY: 140 v S 86 (Eff 9-20-84); 141 v H 813 (Eff 9-17-86); 146 v H 61 (Eff 10-25-95); 146 v S 2. Eff 7-1-96.

Not analogous to former RC § 2917.41 (RS § 7034a; GC § 12869; 81 v 92; Bureau of Code Revision, 10-1-53), repealed 134 v H 511, § 2, eff 1-1-74.

The effective date is set by section 6 of SB 2.

Comment, Legislative Service Commission

° ° ° Section 2917.41 of the Revised Code is amended by this act [Am. H.B. 61] and also by Am. Sub. S.B. 2 of the 121st General Assembly (effective July 1, 1996). Comparison of these amendments in pursuance of section 1.52 of the Revised Code discloses that they are not irreconcilable so that they are required by that section to be harmonized to give effect to each amendment.

§§ 2917.42, 2917.43, 2917.44

Repealed, 134 v H 511, § 2 [RS §§ 6911, 6986-1; S&C 429; 29 v 144; 98 v 99; GC §§ 12845, 12847; Bureau of Code Revision, 10-1-53; 127 v 1039; 129 v 1034; 130 v 662]. Eff 1-1-74.

These sections concerned suppression of evidence, refusal to testify, encouraging lawsuits, and reporting gunshot wounds.

§ 2917.45

Repealed, 134 v H 511, § 2 [131 v 676]. Eff 1-1-74.

This section concerned disguise.

§ 2917.46 Unauthorized use of a block parent symbol.

(A) No person shall, with intent to identify a building as a block parent home or building, display the block parent symbol adopted by the state board of education pursuant to section 3301.076 [3301.07.6] of the Revised Code unless authorized in accordance with that section or section 3313.206 [3313.20.6] of the Revised Code.

(B) No person shall, with intent to identify a building as a block parent home or building, display a symbol that falsely gives the appearance of being the block parent symbol adopted by the board of education.

(C) Whoever violates division (A) or (B) of this section is guilty of unauthorized use of a block parent symbol, a minor misdemeanor.

HISTORY: 141 v H 112 (Eff 10-17-85); 142 v H 708. Eff 4-19-88.

§ 2917.47 Improperly handling infectious agents.

As used in this section, "infectious agent" means a microorganism such as a virus, bacterium, or similar agent that causes disease or death in human beings.

(A) No person shall knowingly possess, send, receive, or cause to be sent or received an isolate or derivative of an isolate of an infectious agent, except as permitted by division (B) of this section.

(B) A person may possess, send, receive, or cause to be sent or received an isolate or derivative of an isolate of an infectious agent as permitted by state or federal law, including for purposes of biomedical or biotechnical research or production, provision of health care services, or investigation of disease by public health agencies.

(C) Whoever violates this section is guilty of improperly handling infectious agents, a felony of the second degree.

HISTORY: 146 v H 456. Eff 9-10-96.

CHAPTER 2919: OFFENSES AGAINST THE FAMILY

Section

[BIGAMY]

2919.01 Bigamy.
2919.02-2919.10 Repealed.

[ABORTION]

2919.11 Definition of abortion.
2919.12 Unlawful abortion.
2919.13 Abortion manslaughter.
2919.14 Abortion trafficking.
2919.15 Performing unlawful abortion procedure.

[POST-VIABILITY ABORTION]

2919.16 Definitions.
2919.17 Terminating or attempting to terminate human pregnancy after viability.
2919.18 Failure to perform viability testing.
2919.19, 2919.20 Repealed.

[NONSUPPORT AND RELATED OFFENSES]

2919.21 Nonsupport or contributing to nonsupport of dependents.
2919.22 Endangering children.
[2919.22.2] 2919.222 Parental education neglect.
2919.23 Interference with custody.
[2919.23.1] 2919.231 Interfering with action to issue or modify support order.
2919.24 Contributing to unruliness or delinquency of a child.

[DOMESTIC VIOLENCE]

2919.25 Domestic violence.
[2919.25.1] 2919.251 Considerations in setting bail in certain domestic violence cases; schedule.
2919.26 Motion for temporary protection order; form.
2919.27 Violating protection order, consent agreement or anti-stalking protection order.
[2919.27.1] 2919.271 Evaluation of defendant's mental condition.
[2919.27.2] 2919.272 Registration and filing of out-of-state protection order.

[BIGAMY]

§ 2919.01 Bigamy.

(A) No married person shall marry another or continue to cohabit with such other person in this state.

(B) It is an affirmative defense to a charge under this section that the actor's spouse was continuously absent for five years immediately preceding the purported subsequent marriage, and was not known by the actor to be alive within that time.

(C) Whoever violates this section is guilty of bigamy, a misdemeanor of the first degree.

HISTORY: 134 v H 511. Eff 1-1-74.

Not analogous to former RC § 2919.01 (RS § 6841; S&C 1610; 55 v 44; 80 v 43; 91 v 338; GC §§ 12873, 12874; Bureau of Code Revision, 10-1-53; 127 v 847), repealed 134 v H 511, § 2, eff 1-1-74.

§§ 2919.02, 2919.03, 2919.04

Repealed, 134 v H 511, § 2 [RS §§ 6841—6843; S&C 240, 426; 37 v 74; 55 v 44; 66 v 29; 73 v 31, 86; 78 v 186; 80 v 43; 82 v 140; 83 v 23; 91 v 338; 95 v 303; 97 v 67; GC §§ 12875—12877; 106 v 550; 124 v 466; Bureau of Code Revision, 10-1-53]. Eff 1-1-74.

These sections concerned embezzlement.

§§ 2919.05, 2919.06, 2919.07

Repealed, 134 v H 511, § 2 [RS §§ 6846, 6847, 7373; S&C 748; 41 v 74; 66 v 263; 69 v 193; 73 v 116; GC §§ 12878—12881, 12886; Bureau of Code Revision, 10-1-53]. Eff 1-1-74.

These sections concerned embezzlement and conflict of interest by public officials.

§§ 2919.08, 2919.09, 2919.10

Repealed, 134 v H 511, § 2 [RS §§ 6969, 6976; 66 v 164; 73 v 31, 43, 86; 90 v 29; 94 v 391, 406; GC §§ 12910—12912; 101 v 145; Bureau of Code Revision, 10-1-53]. Eff 1-1-74.

These sections concerned conflict of interest by public officials.

[ABORTION]

§ 2919.11 Definition of abortion.

As used in the Revised Code, "abortion" means the purposeful termination of a human pregnancy by any person, including the pregnant woman herself, with an intention other than to produce a live birth or to remove a dead fetus or embryo. Abortion is the practice of medicine or surgery for the purposes of section 4731.41 of the Revised Code.

HISTORY: 135 v H 989. Eff 9-16-74.

Not analogous to former RC § 2919.11 (134 v H 511 entitled "Criminal abortion."), repealed by 135 v H 989; and not analogous to former RC § 2919.11 (GC § 12912-1; 118 v 677; Bureau of Code Revision, 10-1-53), repealed 134 v H 511, § 2, eff 1-1-74.

§ 2919.12 Unlawful abortion.

(A) No person shall perform or induce an abortion without the informed consent of the pregnant woman.

(B)(1)(a) No person shall knowingly perform or induce an abortion upon a woman who is pregnant, unmarried, under eighteen years of age, and unemancipated unless at least one of the following applies:

(i) Subject to division (B)(2) of this section, the person has given at least twenty-four hours actual notice, in person or by telephone, to one of the woman's parents, her guardian, or her custodian as to the intention to perform or induce the abortion, provided that if the woman has requested, in accordance with division (B)(1)(b) of this section, that notice be given to a specified brother or sister of the woman who is twenty-one years of age or older or to a specified stepparent or grandparent of the woman instead of to one of her parents, her guardian, or her custodian, and if the person is notified by a juvenile court that affidavits of the type described in that division have been filed with that court, the twenty-four hours actual notice described in this division as to the intention to perform or induce the abortion shall be given, in person or by telephone, to the specified brother, sister, stepparent, or grandparent instead of to the parent, guardian, or custodian;

(ii) One of the woman's parents, her guardian, or her custodian has consented in writing to the performance or inducement of the abortion;

(iii) A juvenile court pursuant to section 2151.85 of the Revised Code issues an order authorizing the woman to consent to the abortion without notification of one of her parents, her guardian, or her custodian;

(iv) A juvenile court or a court of appeals, by its inaction, constructively has authorized the woman to consent to the abortion without notification of one of her parents, her guardian, or her custodian under division (B)(1) of section 2151.85 or division (A) of section 2505.073 [2505.07.3] of the Revised Code.

(b) If a woman who is pregnant, unmarried, under eighteen years of age, and unemancipated desires notification as to a person's intention to perform or induce an abortion on the woman to be given to a specified brother or sister of the woman who is twenty-one years of age or older or to a specified stepparent or grandparent of the woman instead of to one of her parents, her guardian, or her custodian, the person who intends to perform or induce the abortion shall notify the specified brother, sister, stepparent, or grandparent instead of the parent, guardian, or custodian for purposes of division (B)(1)(a)(i) of this section if all of the following apply:

(i) The woman has requested the person to provide the notification to the specified brother, sister, stepparent, or grandparent, clearly has identified the specified brother, sister, stepparent, or grandparent and her relation to that person, and, if the specified relative is a brother or sister, has indicated the age of the brother or sister;

(ii) The woman has executed an affidavit stating that she is in fear of physical, sexual, or severe emotional abuse from the parent, guardian, or custodian who otherwise would be notified under division (B)(1)(a)(i) of this section, and that the fear is based on a pattern of physical, sexual, or severe emotional abuse of her exhibited by that parent, guardian, or custodian, has filed the affidavit with the juvenile court of the county in which the woman has a residence or legal settlement, the juvenile court of any county that borders to any extent the county in which she has a residence or legal settlement, or the juvenile court of the county in which the hospital, clinic, or other facility in which the abortion would be performed or induced is located, and has given the court written notice of the name and address of the person who intends to perform or induce the abortion;

(iii) The specified brother, sister, stepparent, or grandparent has executed an affidavit stating that the woman has reason to fear physical, sexual, or severe emotional abuse from the parent, guardian, or custodian who otherwise would be notified under division (B)(1)(a)(i) of this section, based on a pattern of physical, sexual, or severe emotional abuse of her by that parent, guardian, or custodian, and the woman or the specified brother, sister, stepparent, or grandparent has filed the affidavit with the juvenile court in which the affidavit described in division (B)(1)(b)(ii) of this section was filed;

(iv) The juvenile court in which the affidavits described in divisions (B)(1)(b)(ii) and (iii) of this section were filed has notified the person that both of those affidavits have been filed with the court.

(c) If an affidavit of the type described in division (B)(1)(b)(ii) of this section and an affidavit of the type described in division (B)(1)(b)(iii) of this section are filed with a juvenile court and the court has been provided with written notice of the name and address of the person who intends to perform or induce an abortion upon the woman to whom the affidavits pertain, the court promptly shall notify the person who intends to perform or induce the abortion that the affidavits have been filed. If possible, the notice to the person shall be given in person or by telephone.

(2) If division (B)(1)(a)(ii), (iii), or (iv) of this section does not apply, and if no parent, guardian, or custodian can be reached for purposes of division (B)(1)(a)(i) of this section after a reasonable effort, or if notification is to be given to a specified brother, sister, stepparent, or grandparent under that division and the specified brother, sister, stepparent, or grandparent cannot be reached for purposes of that division after a reasonable effort, no person shall perform or induce such an abortion without giving at least forty-eight hours constructive notice to one of the woman's parents, her guardian, or her custodian, by both certified and ordinary mail sent to the last known address of the parent, guardian, or custodian, or if notification for purposes of division (B)(1)(a)(i) of this section is to be given to a specified brother, sister, stepparent, or grandparent, without giving at least forty-eight hours constructive notice to that specified brother, sister, stepparent, or grandparent by both certified and ordinary mail sent to the last known address of that specified brother, sister, stepparent, or grandparent. The forty-eight-hour period under this division begins when the certified mail notice is mailed. If a parent, guardian, or custodian of the woman, or if notification under division (B)(1)(a)(i) of this section is to be given to a specified brother, sister, stepparent, or

grandparent, the specified brother, sister, stepparent, or grandparent, is not reached within the forty-eight-hour period, the abortion may proceed even if the certified mail notice is not received.

(3) If a parent, guardian, custodian, or specified brother, sister, stepparent, or grandparent who has been notified in accordance with division (B)(1) or (2) of this section clearly and unequivocally expresses that he or she does not wish to consult with a pregnant woman prior to her abortion, then the abortion may proceed without any further waiting period.

(4) For purposes of prosecutions for a violation of division (B)(1) or (2) of this section, it shall be a rebuttable presumption that a woman who is unmarried and under eighteen years of age is unemancipated.

(C)(1) It is an affirmative defense to a charge under division (B)(1) or (2) of this section that the pregnant woman provided the person who performed or induced the abortion with false, misleading, or incorrect information about her age, marital status, or emancipation, about the age of a brother or sister to whom she requested notice be given as a specified relative instead of to one of her parents, her guardian, or her custodian, or about the last known address of either of her parents, her guardian, her custodian, or a specified brother, sister, stepparent, or grandparent to whom she requested notice be given and the person who performed or induced the abortion did not otherwise have reasonable cause to believe the pregnant woman was under eighteen years of age, unmarried, or unemancipated, to believe that the age of a brother or sister to whom she requested notice be given as a specified relative instead of to one of her parents, her guardian, or her custodian was not twenty-one years of age, or to believe that the last known address of either of her parents, her guardian, her custodian, or a specified brother, sister, stepparent, or grandparent to whom she requested notice be given was incorrect.

(2) It is an affirmative defense to a charge under this section that compliance with the requirements of this section was not possible because an immediate threat of serious risk to the life or physical health of the pregnant woman from the continuation of her pregnancy created an emergency necessitating the immediate performance or inducement of an abortion.

(D) Whoever violates this section is guilty of unlawful abortion. A violation of division (A) of this section is a misdemeanor of the first degree on the first offense and a felony of the fourth degree on each subsequent offense. A violation of division (B) of this section is a misdemeanor of the first degree on a first offense and a felony of the fifth degree on each subsequent offense.

(E) Whoever violates this section is liable to the pregnant woman and her parents, guardian, or custodian for civil compensatory and exemplary damages.

(F) As used in this section "unemancipated" means that a woman who is unmarried and under eighteen years of age has not entered the armed services of the United States, has not become employed and self-subsisting, or has not otherwise become independent from the care and control of her parent, guardian, or custodian.

HISTORY: 135 v H 989 (Eff 9-16-74); 141 v H 319 (Eff 3-24-86); 146 v S 2. Eff 7-1-96.

Not analogous to former RC § 2919.12 (134 v H 511 entitled "Promoting abortion."), repealed by 135 v H 989; and not analogous to former RC § 2919.12 (RS § 6910; S&C 429; 29 v 144; GC § 12915; Bureau of Code Revision, 10-1-53), repealed 134 v H 511, § 2, eff 1-1-74.

The effective date is set by section 6 of SB 2.

§ 2919.13 Abortion manslaughter.

(A) No person shall purposely take the life of a child born by attempted abortion who is alive when removed from the uterus of the pregnant woman.

(B) No person who performs an abortion shall fail to take the measures required by the exercise of medical judgment in light of the attending circumstances to preserve the life of a child who is alive when removed from the uterus of the pregnant woman.

(C) Whoever violates this section is guilty of abortion manslaughter, a felony of the first degree.

HISTORY: 135 v H 989. Eff 9-16-74.

Not analogous to former RC § 2919.13 (RS § 6909; S&C 428; 29 v 144; 70 v 61; GC §§ 12916, 12917; Bureau of Code Revision, 10-1-53), repealed 134 v H 511, § 2, eff 1-1-74.

§ 2919.14 Abortion trafficking.

(A) No person shall experiment upon or sell the product of human conception which is aborted. Experiment does not include autopsies pursuant to sections 313.13 and 2108.50 of the Revised Code.

(B) Whoever violates this section is guilty of abortion trafficking, a misdemeanor of the first degree.

HISTORY: 135 v H 989. Eff 9-16-74.

Not analogous to former RC § 2919.14 (RS § 6970; S&S 640; 66 v 57; 70 v 105; GC § 12918; 101 v 131; Bureau of Code Revision, 10-1-53), repealed 134 v H 511, § 2, eff 1-1-74.

§ 2919.15 Performing unlawful abortion procedure.

(A) As used in this section, "dilation and extraction procedure" means the termination of a human pregnancy by purposely inserting a suction device into the skull of a fetus to remove the brain. "Dilation and extraction procedure" does not include either the suction curettage procedure of abortion or the suction aspiration procedure of abortion.

(B) No person shall knowingly perform or attempt to perform a dilation and extraction procedure upon a pregnant woman.

(C)(1) It is an affirmative defense to a charge under division (B) of this section that all other available abortion procedures would pose a greater risk to the health of the pregnant woman than the risk posed by the dilation and extraction procedure.

(2) Notwithstanding section 2901.05 of the Revised Code, if a person charged with a violation of division (B) of this section presents prima facie evidence relative to the affirmative defense set forth in division (C)(1) of this section, the prosecution, in addition to proving all elements of the violation by proof beyond a reasonable doubt, has the burden of proving by proof beyond a reasonable doubt that at least one other available abortion procedure would not pose a greater risk to the health of the pregnant woman than the risk posed by the dilation and extraction procedure performed or attempted to be performed by the person charged with the violation of division (B) of this section.

(D) Whoever violates division (B) of this section is guilty of performing an unlawful abortion procedure, a felony of the fourth degree.

(E) A pregnant woman upon whom a dilation and extraction procedure is performed or attempted to be performed in violation of division (B) of this section is not guilty of an attempt to commit, complicity in the commission of, or conspiracy in the commission of a violation of that division.

HISTORY: 146 v H 135. Eff 11-15-95.

Not analogous to former RC § 2919.15 (RS §§ 17-1, 17-2; 86 v 76, §§ 1, 2; GC § 12923; Bureau of Code Revision, 10-1-53), repealed 134 v H 511, § 2, eff 1-1-74.

The provisions of § 3 of HB 135 (146 v —) read as follows:

SECTION 3. The General Assembly declares that its intent in enacting sections 2307.51 and 2919.15 and in amending section 2305.11 of the Revised Code in this act is to prevent the unnecessary use of a specific procedure used in performing an abortion. This intent is based on a state interest in preventing unnecessary cruelty to the human fetus.

[POST-VIABILITY ABORTION]

§ 2919.16 Definitions.

As used in sections 2919.16 to 2919.18 of the Revised Code:

(A) "Fertilization" means the fusion of a human spermatozoon with a human ovum.

(B) "Gestational age" means the age of an unborn human as calculated from the first day of the last menstrual period of a pregnant woman.

(C) "Health care facility" means a hospital, clinic, ambulatory surgical treatment center, other center, medical school, office of a physician, infirmary, dispensary, medical training institution, or other institution or location in or at which medical care, treatment, or diagnosis is provided to a person.

(D) "Hospital" has the same meanings as in sections 2108.01, 3701.01, and 5122.01 of the Revised Code.

(E) "Live birth" has the same meaning as in division (A) of section 3705.01 of the Revised Code.

(F) "Medical emergency" means a condition that a pregnant woman's physician determines, in good faith and in the exercise of reasonable medical judgment, so complicates the woman's pregnancy as to necessitate the immediate performance or inducement of an abortion in order to prevent the death of the pregnant woman or to avoid a serious risk of the substantial and irreversible impairment of a major bodily function of the pregnant woman that delay in the performance or inducement of the abortion would create.

(G) "Physician" has the same meaning as in section 2305.11 of the Revised Code.

(H) "Pregnant" means the human female reproductive condition, that commences with fertilization, of having a developing fetus.

(I) "Premature infant" means a human whose live birth occurs prior to thirty-eight weeks of gestational age.

(J) "Serious risk of the substantial and irreversible impairment of a major bodily function" means any medically diagnosed condition that so complicates the pregnancy of the woman as to directly or indirectly cause the substantial and irreversible impairment of a major bodily function, including, but not limited to, the following conditions:

(1) Pre-eclampsia;
(2) Inevitable abortion;
(3) Prematurely ruptured membrane;
(4) Diabetes;
(5) Multiple sclerosis.

(K) "Unborn human" means an individual organism of the species homo sapiens from fertilization until live birth.

(L) "Viable" means the stage of development of a human fetus at which in the determination of a physician, based on the particular facts of a woman's pregnancy that are known to the physician and in light of medical technology and information reasonably available to the physician, there is a realistic possibility of the maintaining and nourishing of a life outside of the womb with or without temporary artificial life-sustaining support.

HISTORY: 146 v H 135. Eff 11-15-95.

Not analogous to former RC § 2919.16 (RS 2739a; 83 v 80; GC § 12924; Bureau of Code Revision, 10-1-53), repealed 134 v H 511, § 2, eff 1-1-74.

The provisions of § 4 of HB 135 (146 v —) read as follows:

SECTION 4. The General Assembly declares that, in using the phrase "serious risk of the substantial and irreversible impairment of a major bodily function" in sections 2919.16 and 2919.17 of the Revised Code, as enacted by this act, it is the intent of the General Assembly that the phrase be construed according to the interpretation given to that phrase in *Planned Parenthood v. Casey*, 112 S.Ct. 2791, 2822 (1992), and *Planned Parenthood v. Casey*, 947 F. 2d 682, 699-702 (3rd Cir. 1991).

§ 2919.17 Terminating or attempting to terminate human pregnancy after viability.

(A) No person shall purposely perform or induce or

attempt to perform or induce an abortion upon a pregnant woman if the unborn human is viable, unless either of the following applies:

(1) The abortion is performed or induced or attempted to be performed or induced by a physician, and that physician determines, in good faith and in the exercise of reasonable medical judgment, that the abortion is necessary to prevent the death of the pregnant woman or a serious risk of the substantial and irreversible impairment of a major bodily function of the pregnant woman.

(2) The abortion is performed or induced or attempted to be performed or induced by a physician and that physician determines, in good faith and in the exercise of reasonable medical judgment, after making a determination relative to the viability of the unborn human in conformity with division (A) of section 2919.18 of the Revised Code, that the unborn human is not viable.

(B)(1) Except as provided in division (B)(2) of this section, no physician shall purposely perform or induce or attempt to perform or induce an abortion upon a pregnant woman when the unborn human is viable and when the physician has determined, in good faith and in the exercise of reasonable medical judgment, that the abortion is necessary to prevent the death of the pregnant woman or a serious risk of the substantial and irreversible impairment of a major bodily function of the pregnant woman, unless each of the following conditions is satisfied:

(a) The physician who performs or induces or attempts to perform or induce the abortion certifies in writing that that physician has determined, in good faith and in the exercise of reasonable medical judgment, that the abortion is necessary to prevent the death of the pregnant woman or a serious risk of the substantial and irreversible impairment of a major bodily function of the pregnant woman.

(b) The determination of the physician who performs or induces or attempts to perform or induce the abortion that is described in division (B)(1)(a) of this section is concurred in by at least one other physician who certifies in writing that the concurring physician has determined, in good faith, in the exercise of reasonable medical judgment, and following a review of the available medical records of and any available tests results pertaining to the pregnant woman, that the abortion is necessary to prevent the death of the pregnant woman or a serious risk of the substantial and irreversible impairment of a major bodily function of the pregnant woman.

(c) The abortion is performed or induced or attempted to be performed or induced in a health care facility that has or has access to appropriate neonatal services for premature infants.

(d) The physician who performs or induces or attempts to perform or induce the abortion terminates or attempts to terminate the pregnancy in the manner that provides the best opportunity for the unborn human to survive, unless that physician determines, in good faith and in the exercise of reasonable medical judgment, that the termination of the pregnancy in that manner poses a significantly greater risk of the death of the pregnant woman or a serious risk of the substantial and irreversible impairment of a major bodily function of the pregnant woman than would other available methods of abortion.

(e) The physician who performs or induces or attempts to perform or induce the abortion has arranged for the attendance in the same room in which the abortion is to be performed or induced or attempted to be performed or induced of at least one other physician who is to take control of, provide immediate medical care for, and take all reasonable steps necessary to preserve the life and health of the unborn human immediately upon the unborn human's complete expulsion or extraction from the pregnant woman.

(2) Division (B)(1) of this section does not prohibit the performance or inducement or an attempted performance or inducement of an abortion without prior satisfaction of each of the conditions described in divisions (B)(1)(a) to (e) of this section if the physician who performs or induces or attempts to perform or induce the abortion determines, in good faith and in the exercise of reasonable medical judgment, that a medical emergency exists that prevents compliance with one or more of those conditions.

(C) For purposes of this section, it shall be rebuttably presumed that an unborn child of at least twenty-four weeks of gestational age is viable.

(D) Whoever violates this section is guilty of terminating or attempting to terminate a human pregnancy after viability, a felony of the fourth degree.

(E) A pregnant woman upon whom an abortion is performed or induced or attempted to be performed or induced in violation of division (A) or (B) of this section is not guilty of an attempt to commit, complicity in the commission of, or conspiracy in the commission of a violation of either of those divisions.

HISTORY: 146 v H 135. Eff 11-15-95.

Not analogous to former RC § 2919.17 (RS § 6913; S & C 429; 29 v 144, § 13; GC § 12925; Bureau of Code Revision, 10-1-53), repealed 134 v H 511, § 2, eff 1-1-74.

See provisions, § 4 of HB 135 (146 v —) following RC § 2919.16.

§ 2919.18 Failure to perform viability testing.

(A)(1) Except as provided in division (A)(3) of this section, no physician shall perform or induce or attempt to perform or induce an abortion upon a pregnant woman after the beginning of her twenty-second week of pregnancy unless, prior to the performance or inducement of the abortion or the attempt to perform or induce the abortion, the physician determines, in good faith and in the exercise of reasonable medical judgment, that the unborn human is not viable, and the physician makes that determination after performing a medical examination of the pregnant woman and after performing or causing the performing of gestational age, weight, lung maturity, or other tests of the unborn human that a reasonable physician making a determination as to whether an unborn human is or is not viable would perform or cause to be performed.

(2) Except as provided in division (A)(3) of this section, no physician shall perform or induce or attempt to perform or induce an abortion upon a pregnant woman after the beginning of her twenty-second week of pregnancy without first entering the determination described in division (A)(1) of this section and the associated findings of the medical examination and tests described in that division in the medical record of the pregnant woman.

(3) Divisions (A)(1) and (2) of this section do not prohibit a physician from performing or inducing or attempting to perform or induce an abortion upon a pregnant woman after the beginning of her twenty-second week of pregnancy without making the determination described in division (A)(1) of this section or without making the entry described in division (a)(2) of this section if a medical emergency exists.

(b) Whoever violates this section is guilty of failure to provide viability testing, a misdemeanor of the fourth degree.

HISTORY: 146 v H 135. Eff 11-15-95.

Not analogous to former RC § 2919.18 (RS § 633-14; 92 v 212, § 4; GC § 12933; Bureau of Code Revision, 10-1-53), repealed 134 v H 511, § 2, eff 1-1-74).

§§ 2919.19, 2919.20 Repealed, 134 v H 511, § 2 [RS §§ 181-6, 3107-48, 3107-49, 55 v 99; 85 v 149; 92 v 50; 94 v 157; GC §§ 12893, 12934; Bureau of Code Revision, 10-1-53]. Eff 1-1-74.

These sections concerned hindering examination of state treasury and failure to prefer soldiers for appointments.

[NONSUPPORT AND RELATED OFFENSES]

§ 2919.21 Nonsupport or contributing to nonsupport of dependents.

Note: See following version, HB 352 (147 v —), effective 1-1-98.

(A) No person shall abandon, or fail to provide adequate support to:
(1) The person's spouse, as required by law;
(2) The person's child who is under age eighteen, or mentally or physically handicapped child who is under age twenty-one;
(3) The person's aged or infirm parent or adoptive parent, who from lack of ability and means is unable to provide adequately for the parent's own support;

(B) No person shall abandon, or fail to provide support as established by a court order to, another person whom, by court order or decree, the person is legally obligated to support.

(C) No person shall aid, abet, induce, cause, encourage, or contribute to a child or a ward of the juvenile court becoming a dependent child, as defined in section 2151.04 of the Revised Code, or a neglected child, as defined in section 2151.03 of the Revised Code.

(D) It is an affirmative defense to a charge of failure to provide adequate support under division (A) of this section or a charge of failure to provide support established by a court order under division (B) of this section that the accused was unable to provide adequate support or the established support but did provide the support that was within the accused's ability and means.

(E) It is an affirmative defense to a charge under division (A)(3) of this section that the parent abandoned the accused or failed to support the accused as required by law, while the accused was under age eighteen, or was mentally or physically handicapped and under age twenty-one.

(F) It is not a defense to a charge under division (B) of this section that the person whom a court has ordered the accused to support is being adequately supported by someone other than the accused.

(G)(1) Except as otherwise provided in this division, whoever violates division (A) or (B) of this section is guilty of nonsupport of dependents, a misdemeanor of the first degree. If the offender previously has been convicted of or pleaded guilty to a violation of division (A)(2) or (B) of this section or if the offender has failed to provide support under division (A)(2) or (B) of this section for a total accumulated period of twenty-six weeks out of one hundred four consecutive weeks, whether or not the twenty-six weeks were consecutive, then a violation of division (A)(2) or (B) of this section is a felony of the fifth degree. If the offender previously has been convicted of or pleaded guilty to a felony violation of this section, a violation of division (A)(2) or (B) of this section is a felony of the fourth degree. If the offender is guilty of nonsupport of dependents by reason of failing to provide support to the offender's child as required by a child support order issued on or after April 15, 1985, pursuant to section 2151.23, 2151.33, 3105.21, 3109.05, 3111.13, 3113.04, 3113.31, or 3115.22 of the Revised Code, the court, in addition to any other sentence imposed, shall assess all court costs arising out of the charge against the person and require the person to pay any reasonable attorney's fees of any adverse party other than the state, as determined by the court, that arose in relation to the charge.

(2) Whoever violates division (C) of this section is guilty of contributing to the nonsupport of dependents, a misdemeanor of the first degree. Each day of violation of division (C) of this section is a separate offense.

HISTORY: 134 v H 511 (Eff 1-1-74); 140 v H 614 (Eff 4-10-

85); 141 v H 349 (Eff 3-6-86); 141 v S 136 (Eff 9-24-86); 146 v S 2 (Eff 7-1-96); 146 v S 269 (Eff 7-1-96); 146 v H 274, §§ 1, 4. Eff 8-8-96.

Not analogous to former RC § 2919.21 (RS § 3107-48; 85 v 149; 92 v 50; 94 v 157; GC § 12894; Bureau of Code Revision, 10-1-53), repealed 134 v H 511, § 2, eff 1-1-74.

Comment, Legislative Service Commission

° ° ° Sections 2919.21 and 2919.231 of the Revised Code are amended by this act [Am. Sub. S.B. 269] and also by Sub. H.B. 274 of the 121st General Assembly. ° ° ° Comparison of these amendments in pursuance of section 1.52 of the Revised Code discloses that they are not irreconcilable so that they are required by that section to be harmonized to give effect to each amendment.

§ 2919.21 Nonsupport or contributing to nonsupport of dependents.

Note: See preceding version, HB 274 (146 v —), in effect until 1-1-98.

(A) No person shall abandon, or fail to provide adequate support to:
(1) The person's spouse, as required by law;
(2) The person's child who is under age eighteen, or mentally or physically handicapped child who is under age twenty-one;
(3) The person's aged or infirm parent or adoptive parent, who from lack of ability and means is unable to provide adequately for the parent's own support.
(B) No person shall abandon, or fail to provide support as established by a court order to, another person whom, by court order or decree, the person is legally obligated to support.
(C) No person shall aid, abet, induce, cause, encourage, or contribute to a child or a ward of the juvenile court becoming a dependent child, as defined in section 2151.04 of the Revised Code, or a neglected child, as defined in section 2151.03 of the Revised Code.
(D) It is an affirmative defense to a charge of failure to provide adequate support under division (A) of this section or a charge of failure to provide support established by a court order under division (B) of this section that the accused was unable to provide adequate support or the established support but did provide the support that was within the accused's ability and means.
(E) It is an affirmative defense to a charge under division (A)(3) of this section that the parent abandoned the accused or failed to support the accused as required by law, while the accused was under age eighteen, or was mentally or physically handicapped and under age twenty-one.
(F) It is not a defense to a charge under division (B) of this section that the person whom a court has ordered the accused to support is being adequately supported by someone other than the accused.
(G)(1) Except as otherwise provided in this division, whoever violates division (A) or (B) of this section is guilty of nonsupport of dependents, a misdemeanor of the first degree. If the offender previously has been convicted of or pleaded guilty to a violation of division (A)(2) or (B) of this section or if the offender has failed to provide support under division (A)(2) or (B) of this section for a total accumulated period of twenty-six weeks out of one hundred four consecutive weeks, whether or not the twenty-six weeks were consecutive, then a violation of division (A)(2) or (B) of this section is a felony of the fifth degree. If the offender previously has been convicted of or pleaded guilty to a felony violation of this section, a violation of division (A)(2) or (B) of this section is a felony of the fourth degree. If the offender is guilty of nonsupport of dependents by reason of failing to provide support to the offender's child as required by a child support order issued on or after April 15, 1985, pursuant to section 2151.23, 2151.231 [2151.23.1], 2151.232 [2151.23.2], 2151.33, 3105.21, 3109.05, 3111.13, 3113.04, 3113.31, or 3115.31 of the Revised Code, the court, in addition to any other sentence imposed, shall assess all court costs arising out of the charge against the person and require the person to pay any reasonable attorney's fees of any adverse party other than the state, as determined by the court, that arose in relation to the charge.

(2) Whoever violates division (C) of this section is guilty of contributing to the nonsupport of dependents, a misdemeanor of the first degree. Each day of violation of division (C) of this section is a separate offense.

HISTORY: 134 v H 511 (Eff 1-1-74); 140 v H 614 (Eff 4-10-85); 141 v H 349 (Eff 3-6-86); 141 v S 136 (Eff 9-24-86); 146 v S 2 (Eff 7-1-96); 146 v S 269 (Eff 7-1-96); 146 v H 274, §§ 1, 4 (Eff 8-8-96); 147 v H 352. Eff 1-1-98.

The effective date is set by section 4 of HB 352.

§ 2919.22 Endangering children.

(A) No person, who is the parent, guardian, custodian, person having custody or control, or person in loco parentis of a child under eighteen years of age or a mentally or physically handicapped child under twenty-one years of age, shall create a substantial risk to the health or safety of the child, by violating a duty of care, protection, or support. It is not a violation of a duty of care, protection, or support under this division when the parent, guardian, custodian, or person having custody or control of a child treats the physical or mental illness or defect of the child by spiritual means through prayer alone, in accordance with the tenets of a recognized religious body.

(B) No person shall do any of the following to a child under eighteen years of age or a mentally or physically handicapped child under twenty-one years of age:
(1) Abuse the child;
(2) Torture or cruelly abuse the child;
(3) Administer corporal punishment or other physical disciplinary measure, or physically restrain the child in a cruel manner or for a prolonged period, which punishment, discipline, or restraint is excessive under the circumstances and creates a substantial risk of serious physical harm to the child;
(4) Repeatedly administer unwarranted disciplinary measures to the child, when there is a substantial risk that such conduct, if continued, will seriously impair or retard the child's mental health or development;
(5) Entice, coerce, permit, encourage, compel, hire, employ, use, or allow the child to act, model, or in any other way participate in, or be photographed for, the production, presentation, dissemination, or advertisement of any material or performance that the offender knows or reasonably should know is obscene, is sexually

oriented matter, or is nudity-oriented matter.

(C)(1) No person shall operate a vehicle, streetcar, or trackless trolley within this state in violation of division (A) of section 4511.19 of the Revised Code when one or more children under eighteen years of age are in the vehicle, streetcar, or trackless trolley. Notwithstanding any other provision of law, a person may be convicted at the same trial or proceeding of a violation of this division and a violation of division (A) of section 4511.19 of the Revised Code that constitutes the basis of the charge of the violation of this division. For purposes of section 4511.191 [4511.19.1] of the Revised Code and all related provisions of law, a person arrested for a violation of this division shall be considered to be under arrest for operating a vehicle while under the influence of alcohol, a drug of abuse, or alcohol and a drug of abuse or for operating a vehicle with a prohibited concentration of alcohol in the blood, breath, or urine.

(2) As used in division (C)(1) of this section, "vehicle," "streetcar," and "trackless trolley" have the same meanings as in section 4511.01 of the Revised Code.

(D)(1) Division (B)(5) of this section does not apply to any material or performance that is produced, presented, or disseminated for a bona fide medical, scientific, educational, religious, governmental, judicial, or other proper purpose, by or to a physician, psychologist, sociologist, scientist, teacher, person pursuing bona fide studies or research, librarian, clergyman, prosecutor, judge, or other person having a proper interest in the material or performance.

(2) Mistake of age is not a defense to a charge under division (B)(5) of this section.

(3) In a prosecution under division (B)(5) of this section, the trier of fact may infer that an actor, model, or participant in the material or performance involved is a juvenile if the material or performance, through its title, text, visual representation, or otherwise, represents or depicts the actor, model, or participant as a juvenile.

(4) As used in this division and division (B)(5) of this section:

(a) "Material," "performance," "obscene," and "sexual activity" have the same meanings as in section 2907.01 of the Revised Code.

(b) "Nudity-oriented matter" means any material or performance that shows a minor in a state of nudity and that, taken as a whole by the average person applying contemporary community standards, appeals to prurient interest.

(c) "Sexually oriented matter" means any material or performance that shows a minor participating or engaging in sexual activity, masturbation, or bestiality.

(E)(1) Whoever violates this section is guilty of endangering children.

(2) If the offender violates division (A) or (B)(1) of this section, endangering children is one of the following:

(a) Except as otherwise provided in division (E)(2)(b) or (c) of this section, a misdemeanor of the first degree;

(b) If the offender previously has been convicted of an offense under this section or of any offense involving neglect, abandonment, contributing to the delinquency of, or physical abuse of a child, except as otherwise provided in division (E)(2)(c) of this section, a felony of the fourth degree;

(c) If the violation results in serious physical harm to the child involved, a felony of the third degree.

(3) If the offender violates division (B)(2), (3), or (4) of this section, except as otherwise provided in this division, endangering children is a felony of the third degree. If the violation results in serious physical harm to the child involved, or if the offender previously has been convicted of an offense under this section or of any offense involving neglect, abandonment, contributing to the delinquency of, or physical abuse of a child, endangering children is a felony of the second degree.

(4) If the offender violates division (B)(5) of this section, endangering children is a felony of the second degree.

(5) If the offender violates division (C) of this section, the offender shall be punished as follows:

(a) Except as otherwise provided in division (E)(5)(b) or (c) of this section, endangering children in violation of division (C) of this section is a misdemeanor of the first degree.

(b) If the violation results in serious physical harm to the child involved or the offender previously has been convicted of an offense under this section or any offense involving neglect, abandonment, contributing to the delinquency of, or physical abuse of a child, except as otherwise provided in division (E)(5)(c) of this section, endangering children in violation of division (C) of this section is a felony of the fifth degree.

(c) If the violation results in serious physical harm to the child involved and if the offender previously has been convicted of a violation of division (C) of this section, section 2903.06, 2903.07, or 2903.08 of the Revised Code, or section 2903.04 of the Revised Code in a case in which the offender was subject to the sanctions described in division (D) of that section, endangering children in violation of division (C) of this section is a felony of the fourth degree.

(d) In addition to any term of imprisonment, fine, or other sentence, penalty, or sanction it imposes upon the offender pursuant to division (E)(5)(a), (b), or (c) of this section or pursuant to any other provision of law, the court also may impose upon the offender one or both of the following sanctions:

(i) It may require the offender, as part of the offender's sentence and in the manner described in division (F) of this section, to perform not more than two hundred hours of supervised community service work under the authority of any agency, political subdivision, or charitable organization of the type described in division (F)(1) of section 2951.02 of the Revised Code, provided that the court shall not require the offender to perform supervised community service work under this division unless the offender agrees to perform the supervised community service work.

(ii) It may suspend the driver's or commercial driver's license or permit or nonresident operating privilege of the offender for up to ninety days, in addition to any suspension or revocation of the offender's driver's or commercial driver's license or permit or nonresident operating privilege under Chapter 4506., 4507., 4509., or 4511. of the Revised Code or under any other provision of law.

(e) In addition to any term of imprisonment, fine, or other sentence, penalty, or sanction imposed upon the offender pursuant to division (E)(5)(a), (b), (c), or (d) of this section or pursuant to any other provision of law for the violation of division (C) of this section, if as part of the same trial or proceeding the offender also is convicted of or pleads guilty to a separate charge charging the violation of division (A) of section 4511.19 of the Revised Code that was the basis of the charge of the violation of division (C) of this section, the offender also shall be sentenced, in accordance with section 4511.99 of the Revised Code, for that violation of division (A) of section 4511.19 of the Revised Code and also shall be subject to all other sanctions that are required or authorized by any provision of law for that violation of division (A) of section 4511.19 of the Revised Code.

(F)(1)(a) If a court, pursuant to division (E)(5)(d)(i) of this section, requires an offender to perform supervised community service work under the authority of an agency, subdivision, or charitable organization, the requirement shall be part of the community control sanction or sentence of the offender, and the court shall impose the community service in accordance with and subject to divisions (F)(1)(a) and (b) of this section. The court may require an offender whom it requires to perform supervised community service work as part of the offender's community control sanction or sentence to pay the court a reasonable fee to cover the costs of the offender's participation in the work, including, but not limited to, the costs of procuring a policy or policies of liability insurance to cover the period during which the offender will perform the work. If the court requires the offender to perform supervised community service work as part of the offender's community control sanction or sentence, the court shall do so in accordance with the following limitations and criteria:

(i) The court shall require that the community service work be performed after completion of the term of imprisonment imposed upon the offender for the violation of division (C) of this section, if applicable.

(ii) The supervised community service work shall be subject to the limitations set forth in divisions (F)(1)(a) to (c) of section 2951.02 of the Revised Code.

(iii) The community service work shall be supervised in the manner described in division (F)(1)(d) of section 2951.02 of the Revised Code by an official or person with the qualifications described in that division. The official or person periodically shall report in writing to the court concerning the conduct of the offender in performing the work.

(iv) The court shall inform the offender in writing that if the offender does not adequately perform, as determined by the court, all of the required community service work, the court may order that the offender be committed to a jail or workhouse for a period of time that does not exceed the term of imprisonment that the court could have imposed upon the offender for the violation of division (C) of this section, reduced by the total amount of time that the offender actually was imprisoned under the sentence or term that was imposed upon the offender for that violation and by the total amount of time that the offender was confined for any reason arising out of the offense for which the offender was convicted and sentenced as described in sections 2949.08 and 2967.191 [2967.19.1] of the Revised Code, and that, if the court orders that the offender be so committed, the court is authorized, but not required, to grant the offender credit upon the period of the commitment for the community service work that the offender adequately performed.

(b) If a court, pursuant to this division and division (E)(5)(d)(i) of this section, orders an offender to perform community service work as part of the offender's community control sanction or sentence and if the offender does not adequately perform all of the required community service work, as determined by the court, the court may order that the offender be committed to a jail or workhouse for a period of time that does not exceed the term of imprisonment that the court could have imposed upon the offender for the violation of division (C) of this section, reduced by the total amount of time that the offender actually was imprisoned under the sentence or term that was imposed upon the offender for that violation and by the total amount of time that the offender was confined for any reason arising out of the offense for which the offender was convicted and sentenced as described in sections 2949.08 and 2967.191 [2967.19.1] of the Revised Code. The court may order that a person committed pursuant to this division shall receive hour-for-hour credit upon the period of the commitment for the community service work that the offender adequately performed. No commitment pursuant to this division shall exceed the period of the term of imprisonment that the sentencing court could have imposed upon the offender for the violation of division (C) of this section, reduced by the total amount of time that the offender actually was imprisoned under that sentence or term and by the total amount of time that the offender was confined for any reason arising out of the offense for which the offender was convicted and sentenced as described in sections 2949.08 and 2967.191 [2967.19.1] of the Revised Code.

(2) Divisions (E)(5)(d)(i) and (F)(1) of this section do not limit or affect the authority of the court to suspend the sentence imposed upon a misdemeanor of-

fender and place the offender on probation or otherwise suspend the sentence pursuant to sections 2929.51 and 2951.02 of the Revised Code, to require the misdemeanor offender, as a condition of the offender's probation or of otherwise suspending the offender's sentence, to perform supervised community service work in accordance with division (F) of section 2951.02 of the Revised Code, or to place a felony offender under a community control sanction.

(G) If a court suspends an offender's driver's or commercial driver's license or permit or nonresident operating privilege under division (E)(5)(d)(ii) of this section, the period of the suspension shall be consecutive to, and commence after, the period of suspension or revocation of the offender's driver's or commercial driver's license or permit or nonresident operating privilege that is imposed under Chapter 4506., 4507., 4509., or 4511. of the Revised Code or under any other provision of law in relation to the violation of division (C) of this section that is the basis of the suspension under division (E)(5)(d)(ii) of this section or in relation to the violation of division (A) of section 4511.19 of the Revised Code that is the basis for that violation of division (C) of this section.

If an offender's license, permit, or privilege has been suspended under division (E)(5)(d)(ii) of this section and the offender, within the preceding seven years, has been convicted of or pleaded guilty to three or more violations of division (C) of this section, division (A) or (B) of section 4511.19 of the Revised Code, a municipal ordinance relating to operating a vehicle while under the influence of alcohol, a drug of abuse, or alcohol and a drug of abuse, a municipal ordinance relating to operating a vehicle with a prohibited concentration of alcohol in the blood, breath, or urine, section 2903.04 of the Revised Code in a case in which the offender was subject to the sanctions described in division (D) of that section, section 2903.06, 2903.07, or 2903.08 of the Revised Code or a municipal ordinance that is substantially similar to section 2903.07 of the Revised Code in a case in which the jury or judge found that the offender was under the influence of alcohol, a drug of abuse, or alcohol and a drug of abuse, or a statute of the United States or of any other state or a municipal ordinance of a municipal corporation located in any other state that is substantially similar to division (A) or (B) of section 4511.19 of the Revised Code, the offender is not entitled to request, and the court shall not grant to the offender, occupational driving privileges under this division. Any other offender whose license, permit, or nonresident operating privilege has been suspended under division (E)(5)(d)(ii) of this section may file with the sentencing court a petition alleging that the suspension would seriously affect the offender's ability to continue employment. Upon satisfactory proof that there is reasonable cause to believe that the suspension would seriously affect the offender's ability to continue employment, the court may grant the offender occupational driving privileges during the period during which the suspension otherwise would be imposed, except that the court shall not grant occupational driving privileges for employment as a driver of commercial motor vehicles to any person who is disqualified from operating a commercial motor vehicle under section 2301.374 [2301.37.4] or 4506.16 of the Revised Code.

(H)(1) If a person violates division (C) of this section and if, at the time of the violation, there were two or more children under eighteen years of age in the motor vehicle involved in the violation, the offender may be convicted of a violation of division (C) of this section for each of the children, but the court may sentence the offender for only one of the violations.

(2)(a) If a person is convicted of or pleads guilty to a violation of division (C) of this section but the person is not also convicted of and does not also plead guilty to a separate charge charging the violation of division (A) of section 4511.19 of the Revised Code that was the basis of the charge of the violation of division (C) of this section, both of the following apply:

(i) For purposes of the provisions of section 4511.99 of the Revised Code that set forth the penalties and sanctions for a violation of division (A) of section 4511.19 of the Revised Code, the conviction of or plea of guilty to the violation of division (C) of this section shall not constitute a violation of division (A) of section 4511.19 of the Revised Code;

(ii) For purposes of any provision of law that refers to a conviction of or plea of guilty to a violation of division (A) of section 4511.19 of the Revised Code and that is not described in division (H)(2)(a)(i) of this section, the conviction of or plea of guilty to the violation of division (C) of this section shall constitute a conviction of or plea of guilty to a violation of division (A) of section 4511.19 of the Revised Code.

(b) If a person is convicted of or pleads guilty to a violation of division (C) of this section and the person also is convicted of or pleads guilty to a separate charge charging the violation of division (A) of section 4511.19 of the Revised Code that was the basis of the charge of the violation of division (C) of this section, the conviction of or plea of guilty to the violation of division (C) of this section shall not constitute, for purposes of any provision of law that refers to a conviction of or plea of guilty to a violation of division (A) of section 4511.19 of the Revised Code, a conviction of or plea of guilty to a violation of division (A) of section 4511.19 of the Revised Code.

(I) As used in this section, "community control sanction" has the same meaning as in section 2929.01 of the Revised Code.

HISTORY: 134 v H 511 (Eff 1-1-74); 137 v S 243 (Eff 11-17-77); 140 v H 44 (Eff 9-27-84); 140 v S 321 (Eff 4-9-85); 141 v H 349 (Eff 3-6-86); 142 v H 51 (Eff 3-17-89); 145 v H 236 (Eff 9-29-94); 146 v S 2 (Eff 7-1-96); 146 v S 269, § 1 (Eff 7-1-96); 146 v H 353, § 1 (Eff 9-17-96); 146 v H 167 (Eff 5-15-97); 146 v S 269, § 8 (Eff 5-15-97); 146 v H 353, § 4 (Eff 5-15-97); 147 v S 60. Eff 10-21-97.

Not analogous to former RC § 2919.22 (RS § 1296-14; 98 v 90; GC § 12935; Bureau of Code Revision, 10-1-53), repealed 134 v H 511, § 2, eff 1-1-74.

[§ 2919.22.2] § 2919.222 Parental education neglect.

No person required to attend a parental education or training program pursuant to a policy adopted under division (A) or (B) of section 3313.663 [3313.66.3] of the Revised Code shall fail to attend the program. Whoever violates this section is guilty of parental education neglect, a misdemeanor of the fourth degree.

HISTORY: 146 v H 601. Eff 10-29-96.

§ 2919.23 Interference with custody.

(A) No person, knowing the person is without privilege to do so or being reckless in that regard, shall entice, take, keep, or harbor a person identified in division (A)(1), (2), or (3) of this section from the parent, guardian, or custodian of the person identified in division (A)(1), (2), or (3) of this section:

(1) A child under the age of eighteen, or a mentally or physically handicapped child under the age of twenty-one;

(2) A person committed by law to an institution for delinquent, unruly, neglected, abused, or dependent children;

(3) A person committed by law to an institution for the mentally ill or mentally retarded.

(B) No person shall aid, abet, induce, cause, or encourage a child or a ward of the juvenile court who has been committed to the custody of any person, department, or public or private institution to leave the custody of that person, department, or institution without legal consent.

(C) It is an affirmative defense to a charge of enticing or taking under division (A)(1) of this section, that the actor reasonably believed that the actor's conduct was necessary to preserve the child's health or safety. It is an affirmative defense to a charge of keeping or harboring under division (A) of this section, that the actor in good faith gave notice to law enforcement or judicial authorities within a reasonable time after the child or committed person came under the actor's shelter, protection, or influence.

(D)(1) Whoever violates this section is guilty of interference with custody.

(2) Except as otherwise provided in this division, a violation of division (A)(1) of this section is a misdemeanor of the first degree. If the child who is the subject of a violation of division (A)(1) of this section is removed from the state or if the offender previously has been convicted of an offense under this section, a violation of division (A)(1) of this section is a felony of the fifth degree. If the child who is the subject of a violation of division (A)(1) of this section suffers physical harm as a result of the violation, a violation of division (A)(1) of this section is a felony of the fourth degree.

(3) A violation of division (A)(2) or (3) of this section is a misdemeanor of the third degree.

(4) A violation of division (B) of this section is a misdemeanor of the first degree. Each day of violation of division (B) of this section is a separate offense.

HISTORY: 134 v H 511 (Eff 1-1-74); 136 v H 85 (Eff 11-28-75); 141 v H 349 (Eff 3-6-86); 143 v S 3 (Eff 4-11-91); 146 v S 2. Eff 7-1-96.

Not analogous to former RC § 2919.23 (RS § 294; 71 v 21; 81 v 153, 156; 99 v 108; GC § 12936; Bureau of Code Revision, 10-1-53), repealed 134 v H 511, § 2, eff 1-1-74.

The effective date is set by section 6 of SB 2.

[§ 2919.23.1] § 2919.231 Interfering with action to issue or modify support order.

Note: See following version, HB 352 (147 v —), effective 1-1-98.

(A) No person, by using physical harassment or threats of violence against another person, shall interfere with the other person's initiation or continuance of, or attempt to prevent the other person from initiating or continuing, an action to issue or modify a support order under Chapter 3115. or under section 2151.23, 2151.231 [2151.23.1], 2151.33, 2151.36, 2151.49, 3105.18, 3105.21, 3109.05, 3109.19, 3111.13, 3113.04, 3113.07, or 3113.31 of the Revised Code.

(B) Whoever violates this section is guilty of interfering with an action to issue or modify a support order, a misdemeanor of the first degree. If the offender previously has been convicted of or pleaded guilty to a violation of this section or of section 3111.29 of the Revised Code, interfering with an action to issue or modify a support order is a felony of the fifth degree.

HISTORY: 144 v S 10 (Eff 7-15-92); 146 v H 167 (Eff 11-15-95); 146 v S 269 (Eff 7-1-96); 146 v H 274. Eff 8-8-96.

See Comment, Legislative Service Commission, following RC § 2919.21.

[§ 2919.23.1] § 2919.231 Interfering with action to issue or modify support order.

Note: See preceding version, HB 274 (146 v —), in effect until 1-1-98.

(A) No person, by using physical harassment or threats of violence against another person, shall interfere with the other person's initiation or continuance of, or attempt to prevent the other person from initiating or continuing, an action to issue or modify a support order under Chapter 3115. or under section 2151.23, 2151.231 [2151.23.1], 2151.232 [2151.23.2], 2151.33, 2151.36, 2151.49, 3105.18, 3105.21, 3109.05, 3109.19, 3111.13, 3113.04, 3113.07, or 3113.31 of the Revised Code.

(B) Whoever violates this section is guilty of interfering with an action to issue or modify a support order, a misdemeanor of the first degree. If the offender previously has been convicted of or pleaded guilty to a violation of this section or of section 3111.29 of the Revised Code, interfering with an action to issue or modify a support order is a felony of the fifth degree.

HISTORY: 144 v S 10 (Eff 7-15-92); 146 v H 167 (Eff 11-15-95); 146 v S 269 (Eff 7-1-96); 146 v H 274 (Eff 8-8-96); 147 v H 352. Eff 1-1-98.

The effective date is set by section 4 of HB 352.

§ 2919.24 Contributing to unruliness or delinquency of a child.

(A) No person shall do either of the following:
(1) Aid, abet, induce, cause, encourage, or contribute to a child or a ward of the juvenile court becoming an unruly child, as defined in section 2151.022 [2151.02.2] of the Revised Code, or a delinquent child, as defined in section 2151.02 of the Revised Code;
(2) Act in a way tending to cause a child or a ward of the juvenile court to become an unruly child, as defined in section 2151.022 [2151.02.2] of the Revised Code, or a delinquent child, as defined in section 2151.02 of the Revised Code.
(B) Whoever violates this section is guilty of contributing to the unruliness or delinquency of a child, a misdemeanor of the first degree. Each day of violation of this section is a separate offense.

HISTORY: 141 v H 349. Eff 3-6-86.

[DOMESTIC VIOLENCE]

§ 2919.25 Domestic violence.

(A) No person shall knowingly cause or attempt to cause physical harm to a family or household member.
(B) No person shall recklessly cause serious physical harm to a family or household member.
(C) No person, by threat of force, shall knowingly cause a family or household member to believe that the offender will cause imminent physical harm to the family or household member.
(D) Whoever violates this section is guilty of domestic violence. Except as otherwise provided in this division, a violation of division (C) of this section is a misdemeanor of the fourth degree, and a violation of division (A) or (B) of this section is a misdemeanor of the first degree. If the offender previously has been convicted of domestic violence, of a violation of a municipal ordinance that is substantially similar to domestic violence, of a violation of section 2903.11, 2903.12, 2903.13, 2903.14, 2903.21, 2903.211 [2903.21.1], 2903.22, 2911.211 [2911.21.1], or 2919.22 of the Revised Code involving a person who was a family or household member at the time of the violation, or of a municipal ordinance that is substantially similar to one of those sections involving a person who was a family or household member at the time of the violation, a violation of division (A) or (B) of this section is a felony of the fifth degree, and a violation of division (C) of this section is a misdemeanor of the third degree.

(E) As used in this section and sections 2919.251 [2919.25.1] and 2919.26 of the Revised Code:
(1) "Family or household member" means any of the following:
(a) Any of the following who is residing or has resided with the offender:
(i) A spouse, a person living as a spouse, or a former spouse of the offender;
(ii) A parent or a child of the offender, or another person related by consanguinity or affinity to the offender;
(iii) A parent or a child of a spouse, person living as a spouse, or former spouse of the offender, or another person related by consanguinity or affinity to a spouse, person living as a spouse, or former spouse of the offender.
(b) The natural parent of any child of whom the offender is the other natural parent or is the putative other natural parent.
(2) "Person living as a spouse" means a person who is living or has lived with the offender in a common law marital relationship, who otherwise is cohabiting with the offender, or who otherwise has cohabited with the offender within five years prior to the date of the alleged commission of the act in question.

HISTORY: 137 v H 835 (Eff 3-27-79); 138 v H 920 (Eff 4-9-81); 140 v H 587 (Eff 9-25-84); 142 v S 6 (Eff 6-10-87); 142 v H 172 (Eff 3-17-89); 143 v S 3 (Eff 4-11-91); 144 v H 536 (Eff 11-5-92); 145 v H 335 (Eff 12-9-94); 146 v S 2 (Eff 7-1-96); 147 v S 1 (Eff 10-21-97); 147 v H 238. Eff 11-5-97.

Publisher's Note

The amendments made by SB 1 (147 v —) and HB 238 (147 v —) have been combined. Please see provisions of RC § 1.52.

[§ 2919.25.1] § 2919.251 Considerations in setting bail in certain domestic violence cases; schedule.

(A) If a person is charged with a violation of section 2919.25 of the Revised Code, a violation of a municipal ordinance that is substantially similar to that section, a violation of section 2903.11, 2903.12, 2903.13, 2903.211 [2903.21.1], or 2911.211 [2911.21.1] of the Revised Code involving a person who was a family or household member at the time of the violation, or a violation of a municipal ordinance substantially similar to section 2903.13, 2903.211 [2903.21.1], or 2911.211 [2911.21.1] of the Revised Code that involves a person who was a family or household member at the time of the violation and if the person, at the time of the alleged violation, was subject to the terms of a protection order issued or consent agreement approved pursuant to section 2919.26 or 3113.31 of the Revised Code or previously was convicted of or pleaded guilty to a violation of section 2919.25 of the Revised Code or a violation of section 2919.27 of the Revised Code involving a protection order or consent agreement of that type, a violation of a municipal ordinance that is substantially similar to either section, a violation of section 2903.11, 2903.12, 2903.13, 2903.211 [2903.21.1], or 2911.211 [2911.21.1] of the Revised Code involving a person who was a family or household member at the time of the violation, or a violation of a municipal ordinance substantially similar to section 2903.13, 2903.211 [2903.21.1], or 2911.211 [2911.21.1] of the Revised Code that involves a person who was a family or household member at the time of the violation, the court shall consider all of the following, in addition to any other circumstances considered by the court and notwithstanding any provisions to the contrary contained in Criminal Rule 46, before setting bail for the person:

(1) Whether the person has a history of domestic violence or a history of other violent acts;

(2) The mental health of the person;

(3) Whether the person has a history of violating the orders of any court or governmental entity;

(4) Whether the person is potentially a threat to any other person;

(5) Whether setting bail at a high level will interfere with any treatment or counseling that the person or the family of the person is undergoing.

(B) Any court that has jurisdiction over violations of section 2919.25 of the Revised Code, violations of a municipal ordinance that is substantially similar to that section, violations of section 2903.13, 2903.211 [2903.21.1], or 2911.211 [2911.21.1] of the Revised Code that involve persons who are family or household members at the time of the violation, or violations of a municipal ordinance substantially similar to section 2903.13, 2903.211 [2903.21.1], or 2911.211 [2911.21.1] of the Revised Code that involve persons who are family or household members at the time of the violation, may set a schedule for bail to be used in cases involving those violations. The schedule shall require that a judge consider all of the factors listed in division (A) of this section and may require judges to set bail at a certain level if the history of the alleged offender or the circumstances of the alleged offense meet certain criteria in the schedule.

HISTORY: 141 v H 475 (Eff 3-7-86); 143 v S 3 (Eff 4-11-91); 144 v H 536 (Eff 11-5-92); 146 v S 2. Eff 7-1-96.

The effective date is set by section 6 of SB 2.

§ 2919.26 Motion for temporary protection order; form.

(A)(1) Upon the filing of a complaint that alleges a violation of section 2919.25 of the Revised Code, a violation of a municipal ordinance substantially similar to that section, a violation of section 2903.11, 2903.12, 2903.13, 2903.211 [2903.21.1], or 2911.211 [2911.21.1] of the Revised Code that involves a person who was a family or household member at the time of the violation, or a violation of a municipal ordinance that is substantially similar to section 2903.13, 2903.211 [2903.21.1], or 2911.211 [2911.21.1] of the Revised Code that involves a person who was a family or household member at the time of the violation, the complainant may file, or, if in an emergency the complainant is unable to file, a person who made an arrest for the alleged violation under section 2935.03 of the Revised Code may file on behalf of the complainant, a motion that requests the issuance of a temporary protection order as a pretrial condition of release of the alleged offender, in addition to any bail set under Criminal Rule 46. The motion shall be filed with the clerk of the court that has jurisdiction of the case at any time after the filing of the complaint.

(2) For purposes of section 2930.09 of the Revised Code, all stages of a proceeding arising out of a violation specified in division (A)(1) of this section, including all proceedings on a motion for a temporary protection order, are critical stages of the case, and a complainant may be accompanied by a victim advocate or another person to provide support to the victim as provided in that section.

(B) The motion shall be prepared on a form that is provided by the clerk of the court, which form shall be substantially as follows:

"MOTION FOR TEMPORARY
PROTECTION ORDER
.... Court
Name and address of court
State of Ohio
   v.   No. ....
....
Name of Defendant
(name of person), the complainant in the above-captioned case, moves the court to issue a temporary protection order containing terms designed to ensure the safety and protection of the complainant and other family or household members, in relation to the named defendant, pursuant to its authority to issue such an order under section 2919.26 of the Revised Code.

A complaint, a copy of which has been attached to this motion, has been filed in this court charging the named defendant with at least one of the following violations of section 2919.25 of the Revised Code that constitutes "domestic violence" or a municipal ordinance that is substantially similar to that section: knowingly causing or attempting to cause physical harm to a family or household member; recklessly causing serious physical harm to a family or household member; or, by threat of force, knowingly causing a family or household member to believe that the named defendant would cause imminent physical harm to that family or household member; charging the named defendant with felonious assault, aggravated assault, or assault that involved a family or household member in violation of section 2903.11, 2903.12, or 2903.13 of the Revised Code; charging the named defendant with menacing by stalking or aggravated trespass that involves a family or household member in violation of section 2903.211 [2903.21.1] or 2911.211 [2911.21.1] of the Revised

Code; or charging the named defendant with a violation of a municipal ordinance that is substantially similar to section 2903.13, 2903.211 [2903.21.1], or 2911.211 [2911.21.1] of the Revised Code that involves a family or household member.

I understand that I must appear before the court, at a time set by the court within twenty-four hours after the filing of this motion, for a hearing on the motion or that, if I am unable to appear because of hospitalization or a medical condition resulting from the offense alleged in the complaint, a person who can provide information about my need for a temporary protection order must appear before the court in lieu of my appearing in court. I understand that any temporary protection order granted pursuant to this motion is a pretrial condition of release and is effective only until the disposition of the criminal proceeding arising out of the attached complaint, or the issuance of a civil protection order or the approval of a consent agreement, arising out of the same activities as those that were the basis of the complaint, under section 3113.31 of the Revised Code.

....

Signature of complainant
(or signature of the arresting officer who filed the motion on behalf of the complainant)

....

Address of complainant
(or office address of the arresting officer who filed the motion on behalf of the complainant)"

(C)(1) As soon as possible after the filing of a motion that requests the issuance of a temporary protection order, but not later than twenty-four hours after the filing of the motion, the court shall conduct a hearing to determine whether to issue the order. The person who requested the order shall appear before the court and provide the court with the information that it requests concerning the basis of the motion. If the person who requested the order is unable to appear and if the court finds that the failure to appear is because of the person's hospitalization or medical condition resulting from the offense alleged in the complaint, another person who is able to provide the court with the information it requests may appear in lieu of the person who requested the order. If the court finds that the safety and protection of the complainant or any other family or household member of the alleged offender may be impaired by the continued presence of the alleged offender, the court may issue a temporary protection order, as a pretrial condition of release, that contains terms designed to ensure the safety and protection of the complainant or the family or household member, including a requirement that the alleged offender refrain from entering the residence, school, business, or place of employment of the complainant or the family or household member.

(2)(a) If the court issues a temporary protection order that includes a requirement that the alleged offender refrain from entering the residence, school, business, or place of employment of the complainant or the family or household member, the order shall state clearly that the order cannot be waived or nullified by an invitation to the alleged offender from the complainant or family or household member to enter the residence, school, business, or place of employment or by the alleged offender's entry into one of those places otherwise upon the consent of the complainant or family or household member.

(b) Division (C)(2)(a) of this section does not limit any discretion of a court to determine that an alleged offender charged with a violation of section 2919.27 of the Revised Code, with a violation of a municipal ordinance substantially equivalent to that section, or with contempt of court, which charge is based on an alleged violation of a temporary protection order issued under this section, did not commit the violation or was not in contempt of court.

(D)(1) Upon the filing of a complaint that alleges a violation of section 2919.25 of the Revised Code, a violation of a municipal ordinance that is substantially similar to that section, a violation of section 2903.11, 2903.12, 2903.13, 2903.211 [2903.21.1], or 2911.211 [2911.21.1] of the Revised Code that involves a person who was a family or household member at the time of the violation, or a violation of a municipal ordinance that is substantially similar to section 2903.13, 2903.211 [2903.21.1], or 2911.211 [2911.21.1] of the Revised Code that involves a person who was a family or household member at the time of the violation, the court, upon its own motion, may issue a temporary protection order as a pretrial condition of release if it finds that the safety and protection of the complainant or other family or household member of the alleged offender may be impaired by the continued presence of the alleged offender.

(2) If the court issues a temporary protection order under this section as an ex parte order, it shall conduct, as soon as possible after the issuance of the order, a hearing in the presence of the alleged offender not later than the next day on which the court is scheduled to conduct business after the day on which the alleged offender was arrested or at the time of the appearance of the alleged offender pursuant to summons to determine whether the order should remain in effect, be modified, or be revoked. The hearing shall be conducted under the standards set forth in division (C) of this section.

(3) An order issued under this division shall contain only those terms authorized in orders issued under division (C) of this section.

(E) A temporary protection order that is issued as a pretrial condition of release under this section:
(1) Is in addition to, but shall not be construed as a part of, any bail set under Criminal Rule 46;
(2) Is effective only until the disposition of the criminal proceeding arising out of the complaint upon which

it is based, or the issuance of a protection order or the approval of a consent agreement, arising out of the same activities as those that were the basis of the complaint, under section 3113.31 of the Revised Code;

(3) Shall not be construed as a finding that the alleged offender committed the alleged offense, and shall not be introduced as evidence of the commission of the offense at the trial of the alleged offender on the complaint upon which the order is based.

(F) A person who meets the criteria for bail under Criminal Rule 46 and who, if required to do so pursuant to that rule, executes or posts bond or deposits cash or securities as bail, shall not be held in custody pending a hearing before the court on a motion requesting a temporary protection order.

(G)(1) A copy of any temporary protection order that is issued under this section shall be issued by the court to the complainant, to the defendant, and to all law enforcement agencies that have jurisdiction to enforce the order. The court shall direct that a copy of the order be delivered to the defendant on the same day that the order is entered.

(2) All law enforcement agencies shall establish and maintain an index for the temporary protection orders delivered to the agencies pursuant to division (G)(1) of this section. With respect to each order delivered, each agency shall note on the index, the date and time of the receipt of the order by the agency.

(3) A complainant who obtains a temporary protection order under this section may provide notice of the issuance of the temporary protection order to the judicial and law enforcement officials in any county other than the county in which the order is issued by registering that order in the other county in accordance with division (N) of section 3113.31 of the Revised Code and filing a copy of the registered protection order with a law enforcement agency in the other county in accordance with that division.

(4) Any officer of a law enforcement agency shall enforce a temporary protection order issued by any court in this state in accordance with the provisions of the order, including removing the defendant from the premises, regardless of whether the order is registered in the county in which the officer's agency has jurisdiction as authorized by division (G)(3) of this section.

(H) Upon a violation of a temporary protection order, the court may issue another temporary protection order, as a pretrial condition of release, that modifies the terms of the order that was violated.

(I)(1) As used in divisions (I)(1) and (2) of this section, "defendant" means a person who is alleged in a complaint to have committed a violation of the type described in division (A) of this section.

(2) If a complaint is filed that alleges that a person committed a violation of the type described in division (A) of this section, the court may not issue a temporary protection order under this section that requires the complainant or another family or household member of the defendant to do or refrain from doing an act that the court may require the defendant to do or refrain from doing under a temporary protection order unless both of the following apply:

(a) The defendant has filed a separate complaint that alleges that the complainant or other family or household member in question who would be required under the order to do or refrain from doing the act committed a violation of the type described in division (A) of this section.

(b) The court determines that both the complainant or other family or household member in question who would be required under the order to do or refrain from doing the act and the defendant acted primarily as aggressors, that neither the complainant or other family or household member in question who would be required under the order to do or refrain from doing the act nor the defendant acted primarily in self-defense, and, in accordance with the standards and criteria of this section as applied in relation to the separate complaint filed by the defendant, that it should issue the order to require the complainant or other family or household member in question to do or refrain from doing the act.

(J) Notwithstanding any provision of law to the contrary, no court shall charge a fee for the filing of a motion pursuant to this section.

(K) As used in this section, "victim advocate" means a person who provides support and assistance for a victim of an offense during court proceedings.

HISTORY: 137 v H 835 (Eff 3-27-79); 138 v H 920 (Eff 4-9-81); 140 v H 587 (Eff 9-25-84); 143 v S 3 (Eff 4-11-91); 144 v H 536 (Eff 11-5-92); 145 v H 335 (Eff 12-9-94); 147 v S 1. Eff 10-21-97.

§ 2919.27 Violating protection order, consent agreement or anti-stalking protection order.

(A) No person shall recklessly violate the terms of any of the following:

(1) A protection order issued or consent agreement approved pursuant to section 2919.26 or 3113.31 of the Revised Code;

(2) An anti-stalking protection order issued pursuant to section 2903.213 [2903.21.3] of the Revised Code;

(3) A protection order issued by a court of another state.

(B) Whoever violates this section is guilty of violating a protection order.

(1) If the offense involves a violation of division (A)(1) or (3) of this section, one of the following applies:

(a) Except as otherwise provided in division (B)(1)(b) of this section, violating a protection order is a misdemeanor of the first degree.

(b) If the offender previously has been convicted of or pleaded guilty to two or more violations of section 2903.211 [2903.21.1] or 2911.211 [2911.21.1] of the Revised Code that involved the same person who is the subject of the protection order or consent agreement or previously has been convicted of or pleaded guilty to one or more violations of this section, violating a protection order is a felony of the fifth degree.

(2) If the offense involves a violation of division (A)(2) of this section, one of the following applies:

(a) Except as otherwise provided in division (B)(2)(b) of this section, violating a protection order is a misdemeanor of the first degree.

(b) If the offender previously has been convicted of or pleaded guilty to two or more violations of this section or of former section 2919.27 of the Revised Code involving an anti-stalking protection order, two or more violations of section 2903.21, 2903.211 [2903.21.1], 2903.22, or 2911.211 [2911.21.1] of the Revised Code that involved the same person who is the subject of the anti-stalking protection order, or two or more violations of section 2903.214 [2903.21.4] of the Revised Code as it existed prior to July 1, 1996, violating a protection order is a felony of the fifth degree.

(C) It is an affirmative defense to a charge under division (A)(3) of this section that the protection order issued by a court of another state does not comply with the requirements specified in 18 U.S.C. 2265(b) for a protection order that must be accorded full faith and credit by a court of this state or that it is not entitled to full faith and credit under 18 U.S.C. 2265(c).

(D) As used in this section, "protection order issued by a court of another state" means an injunction or another order issued by a criminal court of another state for the purpose of preventing violent or threatening acts or harassment against, contact or communication with, or physical proximity to another person, including a temporary order, and means an injunction or order of that nature issued by a civil court of another state, including a temporary order and a final order issued in an independent action or as a pendente lite order in a proceeding for other relief, if the court issued it in response to a complaint, petition, or motion filed by or on behalf of a person seeking protection. "Protection order issued by a court of another state" does not include an order for support or for custody of a child.

HISTORY: 140 v H 587 (Eff 9-25-84); 141 v H 475 (Eff 3-7-86); 144 v H 536 (Eff 11-5-92); 145 v H 335 (Eff 12-9-94); 146 v S 2 (Eff 7-1-96); 147 v S 1. Eff 10-21-97.

[§ 2919.27.1] § 2919.271 Evaluation of defendant's mental condition.

(A)(1) If a defendant is charged with a violation of section 2919.27 of the Revised Code or of a municipal ordinance that is substantially similar to that section, the court may order an evaluation of the mental condition of the defendant if the court determines that either of the following criteria apply:

(a) If the alleged violation is a violation of a protection order issued or consent agreement approved pursuant to section 2919.26 or 3113.31 of the Revised Code, that the violation allegedly involves conduct by the defendant that caused physical harm to the person or property of a family or household member covered by the order or agreement, or conduct by the defendant that caused a family or household member to believe that the defendant would cause physical harm to that member or that member's property.

(b) If the alleged violation is a violation of an anti-stalking protection order issued pursuant to section 2903.213 [2903.21.3] of the Revised Code or a protection order issued by a court of another state, that the violation allegedly involves conduct by the defendant that caused physical harm to the person or property of the person covered by the order, or conduct by the defendant that caused the person covered by the order to believe that the defendant would cause physical harm to that person or that person's property.

(2) The evaluation shall be completed no later than thirty days from the date the order is entered pursuant to division (A)(1) of this section. In that order, the court shall do either of the following:

(a) Order that the evaluation of the mental condition of the defendant be preceded by an examination conducted either by a forensic center that is designated by the department of mental health to conduct examinations and make evaluations of defendants charged with violations of section 2919.27 of the Revised Code or of substantially similar municipal ordinances in the area in which the court is located, or by any other program or facility that is designated by the department of mental health or the department of mental retardation and developmental disabilities to conduct examinations and make evaluations of defendants charged with violations of section 2919.27 of the Revised Code or of substantially similar municipal ordinances, and that is operated by either department or is certified by either department as being in compliance with the standards established under division (J) of section 5119.01 of the Revised Code or division (C) of section 5123.04 of the Revised Code.

(b) Designate a center, program, or facility other than one designated by the department of mental health or the department of mental retardation and developmental disabilities, as described in division (A)(2)(a) of this section, to conduct the evaluation and preceding examination of the mental condition of the defendant.

Whether the court acts pursuant to division (A)(2)(a) or (b) of this section, the court may designate examiners other than the personnel of the center, program, facility, or department involved to make the evaluation and preceding examination of the mental condition of the defendant.

(B) If the court considers that additional evaluations of the mental condition of a defendant are necessary following the evaluation authorized by division (A) of this section, the court may order up to two additional similar evaluations. These evaluations shall be completed no later than thirty days from the date the applicable court order is entered. If more than one evaluation of the mental condition of the defendant is ordered under this division, the prosecutor and the defendant may recommend to the court an examiner whom each prefers to perform one of the evaluations and preceding examinations.

(C)(1) The court may order a defendant who has been released on bail to submit to an examination under division (A) or (B) of this section. The examination shall be conducted either at the detention facility in which the defendant would have been confined if the defendant had not been released on bail, or, if so specified by the center, program, facility, or examiners involved, at the premises of the center, program, or facility. Additionally, the examination shall be conducted at the times established by the examiners involved. If such a defendant refuses to submit to an examination or a complete examination as required by the court or the center, program, facility, or examiners involved, the court may amend the conditions of the bail of the defendant and order the sheriff to take the defendant into custody and deliver the defendant to the detention facility in which the defendant would have been confined if the defendant had not been released on bail, or, if so specified by the center, program, facility, or examiners involved, to the premises of the center, program, or facility, for purposes of the examination.

(2) A defendant who has not been released on bail shall be examined at the detention facility in which the defendant is confined or, if so specified by the center, program, facility, or examiners involved, at the premises of the center, program, facility, or facility.

(D) The examiner of the mental condition of a defendant under division (A) or (B) of this section shall file a written report with the court within thirty days after the entry of an order for the evaluation of the mental condition of the defendant. The report shall contain the findings of the examiner; the facts in reasonable detail on which the findings are based; the opinion of the examiner as to the mental condition of the defendant; the opinion of the examiner as to whether the defendant represents a substantial risk of physical harm to other persons as manifested by evidence of recent homicidal or other violent behavior, evidence of recent threats that placed other persons in reasonable fear of violent behavior and serious physical harm, or evidence of present dangerousness; and the opinion of the examiner as to the types of treatment or counseling that the defendant needs. The court shall provide copies of the report to the prosecutor and defense counsel.

(E) The costs of any evaluation and preceding examination of a defendant that is ordered pursuant to division (A) or (B) of this section shall be taxed as court costs in the criminal case.

(F) If the examiner considers it necessary in order to make an accurate evaluation of the mental condition of a defendant, an examiner under division (A) or (B) of this section may request any family or household member of the defendant to provide the examiner with information. A family or household member may, but is not required to, provide information to the examiner upon receipt of the request.

(G) As used in this section:
(1) "Bail" includes a recognizance.
(2) "Examiner" means a psychiatrist, a licensed independent social worker who is employed by a forensic center that is certified as being in compliance with the standards established under division (J) of section 5119.01 or division (C) of section 5123.04 of the Revised Code, a licensed professional clinical counselor who is employed at a forensic center that is certified as being in compliance with such standards, or a licensed clinical psychologist, except that in order to be an examiner, a licensed clinical psychologist shall meet the criteria of division (I)(1) of section 5122.01 of the Revised Code or be employed to conduct examinations by the department of mental health or by a forensic center certified as being in compliance with the standards established under division (J) of section 5119.01 or division (C) of section 5123.04 of the Revised Code that is designated by the department of mental health.
(3) "Family or household member" has the same meaning as in section 2919.25 of the Revised Code.
(4) "Prosecutor" has the same meaning as in section 2935.01 of the Revised Code.
(5) "Psychiatrist" and "licensed clinical psychologist" have the same meanings as in section 5122.01 of the Revised Code.
(6) "Protection order issued by a court of another state" has the same meaning as in section 2919.27 of the Revised Code.

HISTORY: 141 v H 475 (Eff 3-7-86); 146 v S 2 (Eff 7-1-96); 146 v S 223 (Eff 3-18-97); 147 v S 1. Eff 10-21-97.

[§ 2919.27.2] § 2919.272 Registration and filing of out-of-state protection order.

(A) As used in this section, "protection order issued by a court of another state" has the same meaning as in section 2919.27 of the Revised Code.

(B) A person who has obtained a protection order issued by a court of another state may provide notice of the issuance of the order to judicial and law enforcement officials in any county of this state by registering the order in that county and filing a copy of the registered order with a law enforcement agency in that county. To register the order, the person shall obtain a certified copy of the order from the clerk of the court that issued the order and present that certified copy to the clerk of the court of common pleas or the clerk of a municipal court or county court in the county in which the order is to be registered. Upon accepting the certified copy of the order for registration, the clerk shall place an endorsement of registration on the order and give the person a copy of the order that bears proof of registration. The person then may file with a law enforcement agency in that county a copy of the order that bears proof of registration.

(C) The clerk of each court of common pleas and the clerk of each municipal court and county court shall maintain a registry of certified copies of protection orders issued by courts of another state that have been registered with the clerk. Each law enforcement agency shall establish and maintain a registry for protection orders delivered to the agency pursuant to this section. The agency shall note in the registry the date and time that the agency received an order.

(D) An officer of a law enforcement agency shall enforce a protection order issued by a court of another state in accordance with the provisions of the order, including removing the person allegedly violating the order from the premises, regardless of whether the order is registered as authorized by division (B) of this section in the county in which the officer's agency has jurisdiction.

HISTORY: 147 v S 1. Eff 10-21-97.

CHAPTER 2921: OFFENSES AGAINST JUSTICE AND PUBLIC ADMINISTRATION

Section

[IN GENERAL]

2921.01 Definitions.

[BRIBERY AND INTIMIDATION]

2921.02 Bribery.
2921.03 Intimidation.
2921.04 Intimidation of attorney, victim or witness in criminal case.
2921.05 Retaliation.
2921.06-2921.10 Repealed.

[PERJURY]

2921.11 Perjury.
2921.12 Tampering with evidence.
2921.13 Falsification; in theft offense; to purchase firearm.
2921.14 Making or causing false report of child abuse or neglect.
2921.15-2921.18 Repealed.

[COMPOUNDING]

2921.21 Compounding a crime.
2921.22 Failure to report a crime or knowledge of a death or burn injury.
2921.23 Failure to aid a law enforcement officer.
2921.24 Disclosure of confidential information.
2921.25 Disclosure of peace officer's home address.
2921.26, 2921.27 Repealed.

[OBSTRUCTING AND ESCAPE]

2921.31 Obstructing official business.
2921.32 Obstructing justice.
[2921.32.1] 2921.321 Assaulting police dog or horse or handicapped assistance dog.
2921.33 Resisting arrest.
[2921.33.1] 2921.331 Failure to comply with order or signal of police officer.
2921.34 Escape.
2921.35 Aiding escape or resistance to authority.
2921.36 Illegal conveyance of weapons or prohibited items onto grounds of detention facility or institution.
2921.37 Arrest powers of detention facility chief.
2921.38 Harassment by inmate.

[PECULATION AND DERELICTION]

2921.41 Theft in office; restitution; withholding of retirement benefits.
2921.42 Having an unlawful interest in a public contract.
[2921.42.1] 2921.421 Conditions for prosecuting attorney's appointment of assistants and employees who are associated in the private practice of law.
2921.43 Soliciting or receiving improper compensation.
[2921.43.1] 2921.431 Repealed.
2921.44 Dereliction of duty.
2921.45 Interfering with civil rights.

[IMPERSONATING PEACE OFFICER]

2921.51 Impersonating a peace officer or private policeman.

Section

2921.52 Using sham legal process.

[IN GENERAL]

§ 2921.01 Definitions.

As used in sections 2921.01 to 2921.45 of the Revised Code:

(A) "Public official" means any elected or appointed officer, or employee, or agent of the state or any political subdivision, whether in a temporary or permanent capacity, and includes, but is not limited to, legislators, judges, and law enforcement officers.

(B) "Public servant" means any of the following:

(1) Any public official;

(2) Any person performing ad hoc a governmental function, including, but not limited to, a juror, member of a temporary commission, master, arbitrator, advisor, or consultant;

(3) A person who is a candidate for public office, whether or not the person is elected or appointed to the office for which the person is a candidate. A person is a candidate for purposes of this division if the person has been nominated according to law for election or appointment to public office, or if the person has filed a petition or petitions as required by law to have the person's name placed on the ballot in a primary, general, or special election, or if the person campaigns as a write-in candidate in any primary, general, or special election.

(C) "Party official" means any person who holds an elective or appointive post in a political party in the United States or this state, by virtue of which the person directs, conducts, or participates in directing or conducting party affairs at any level of responsibility.

(D) "Official proceeding" means any proceeding before a legislative, judicial, administrative, or other governmental agency or official authorized to take evidence under oath, and includes any proceeding before a referee, hearing examiner, commissioner, notary, or other person taking testimony or a deposition in connection with an official proceeding.

(E) "Detention" means arrest; confinement in any vehicle subsequent to an arrest; confinement in any facility for custody of persons charged with or convicted of crime or alleged or found to be a delinquent child or unruly child; hospitalization, institutionalization, or confinement in any facility that is ordered pursuant to or under the authority of section 2945.37, 2945.371 [2945.37.1], 2945.38, 2945.39, 2945.40, 2945.401 [2945.40.1], or 2945.402 [2945.40.2] of the Revised Code; confinement in any vehicle for transportation to or from any facility of any of those natures; detention for extradition or deportation; except as provided in this division, supervision by any employee of any facility of any of those natures that is incidental to hospitalization, institutionalization, or confinement in the facility but that occurs outside the facility; or supervision by an employee of the department of rehabilitation and correction of a person on any type of release from a state correctional institution. For a person confined in a county jail who participates in a county jail industry program pursuant to section 5147.30 of the Revised Code, "detention" includes time spent at an assigned work site and going to and from the work site.

(F) "Detention facility" means any place used for the confinement of a person charged with or convicted of any crime or alleged or found to be a delinquent child or unruly child.

(G) "Valuable thing or valuable benefit" includes, but is not limited to, a contribution. This inclusion does not indicate or imply that a contribution was not included in those terms before September 17, 1986.

(H) "Campaign committee," "contribution," "political action committee," "legislative campaign fund," and "political party" have the same meanings as in section 3517.01 of the Revised Code.

(I) "Provider agreement" and "medical assistance program" have the same meanings as in section 2913.40 of the Revised Code.

HISTORY: 134 v H 511 (Eff 1-1-74); 141 v H 340 (Eff 5-20-86); 141 v H 300 (Eff 9-17-86); 141 v H 428 (Eff 12-23-86); 142 v H 708 (Eff 4-19-88); 143 v H 51 (Eff 11-8-90); 144 v S 37 (Eff 7-31-92); 145 v H 42 (Eff 2-9-94); 145 v H 571 (Eff 10-6-94); 146 v S 8 (Eff 8-23-95); 146 v S 2 (Eff 7-1-96); 146 v H 154 (Eff 10-4-96); 146 v S 285. Eff 7-1-97.

The effective date is set by section 4 of SB 285.

[BRIBERY AND INTIMIDATION]

§ 2921.02 Bribery.

(A) No person, with purpose to corrupt a public servant or party official, or improperly to influence him with respect to the discharge of his duty, whether before or after he is elected, appointed, qualified, employed, summoned, or sworn, shall promise, offer, or give any valuable thing or valuable benefit.

(B) No person, either before or after he is elected, appointed, qualified, employed, summoned, or sworn as a public servant or party official, shall knowingly solicit or accept for himself or another person any valuable thing or valuable benefit to corrupt or improperly influence him or another public servant or party official with respect to the discharge of his or the other public servant's or party official's duty.

(C) No person, with purpose to corrupt a witness or improperly to influence him with respect to his testimony in an official proceeding, either before or after he is subpoenaed or sworn, shall promise, offer, or give him or another person any valuable thing or valuable benefit.

(D) No person, either before or after he is subpoenaed or sworn as a witness, shall knowingly solicit or accept for himself or another person any valuable thing or valuable benefit to corrupt or improperly influence him with respect to his testimony in an official proceeding.

(E) Whoever violates this section is guilty of bribery, a felony of the third degree.

(F) A public servant or party official who is convicted of bribery is forever disqualified from holding any public office, employment, or position of trust in this state.

HISTORY: 134 v H 511 (Eff 1-1-74); 141 v H 300. Eff 9-17-86.

Not analogous to former RC § 2921.02 (RS § 6807; S&S 261; 58 v 110; GC § 12393; Bureau of Code Revision, 10-1-53), repealed 134 v H 511, § 2, eff 1-1-74.

§ 2921.03 Intimidation.

(A) No person, knowingly and by force, by unlawful threat of harm to any person or property, or by filing, recording, or otherwise using a materially false or fraudulent writing with malicious purpose, in bad faith, or in a wanton or reckless manner, shall attempt to influence, intimidate, or hinder a public servant, party official, or witness in the discharge of the person's duty.†

(B) Whoever violates this section is guilty of intimidation, a felony of the third degree.

(C) A person who violates this section is liable in a civil action to any person harmed by the violation for injury, death, or loss to person or property incurred as a result of the commission of the offense and for reasonable attorney's fees, court costs, and other expenses incurred as a result of prosecuting the civil action commenced under this division. A civil action under this division is not the exclusive remedy of a person who incurs injury, death, or loss to person or property as a result of a violation of this section.

HISTORY: 134 v H 511 (Eff 1-1-74); 140 v S 172 (Eff 9-26-84); 146 v H 88 (Eff 9-3-96); 146 v H 644. Eff 11-6-96.

Not analogous to former RC § 2921.03 (RS § 6886; S&S 262; 58 v 110; GC § 12394; Bureau of Code Revision, 10-1-53), repealed 134 v H 511, § 2, eff 1-1-74.

† The first paragraph as amended by HB 88 (146 v —) reads as follows:

". . . a party official, or an attorney or witness involved in a civil action or proceeding in the discharge of the duties of the public servant, party official, attorney, or witness."

Division (C) was added by HB 644 (146 v —).

§ 2921.04 Intimidation of attorney, victim or witness in criminal case.

(A) No person shall knowingly attempt to intimidate or hinder the victim of a crime in the filing or prosecution of criminal charges or a witness involved in a criminal action or proceeding in the discharge of the duties of the witness.

(B) No person, knowingly and by force or by unlawful threat of harm to any person or property, shall attempt to influence, intimidate, or hinder the victim of a crime in the filing or prosecution of criminal charges or an attorney or witness involved in a criminal action or proceeding in the discharge of the duties of the attorney or witness.

(C) Division (A) of this section does not apply to any person who is attempting to resolve a dispute pertaining to the alleged commission of a criminal offense, either prior to or subsequent to the filing of a complaint, indictment, or information, by participating in the arbitration, mediation, compromise, settlement, or conciliation of that dispute pursuant to an authorization for arbitration, mediation, compromise, settlement, or conciliation of a dispute of that nature that is conferred by any of the following:

(1) A section of the Revised Code;
(2) The Rules of Criminal Procedure, the Rules of Superintendence for Municipal Courts and County Courts, the Rules of Superintendence for Courts of Common Pleas, or another rule adopted by the supreme court in accordance with Section 5 of Article IV, Ohio Constitution;
(3) A local rule of court, including, but not limited to, a local rule of court that relates to alternative dispute resolution or other case management programs and that authorizes the referral of disputes pertaining to the alleged commission of certain types of criminal offenses to appropriate and available arbitration, mediation, compromise, settlement, or other conciliation programs;
(4) The order of a judge of a municipal court, county court, or court of common pleas.

(D) Whoever violates this section is guilty of intimidation of an attorney, victim, or witness in a criminal case. A violation of division (A) of this section is a misdemeanor of the first degree. A violation of division (B) of this section is a felony of the third degree.

HISTORY: 140 v S 172 (Eff 9-26-84); 146 v H 88. Eff 9-3-96.

Not analogous to former RC § 2921.04 (RS §§ 803-1, 803-2; GC § 12395; 92 v 89, §§ 1, 2; 106 v 341; Bureau of Code Revision, 10-1-53), repealed 134 v H 511, § 2, eff 1-1-74.

§ 2921.05 Retaliation.

(A) No person, purposely and by force or by unlawful threat of harm to any person or property, shall retaliate against a public servant, a party official, or an attorney or witness who was involved in a civil or criminal action or proceeding because the public servant, party official, attorney, or witness discharged the duties of the public servant, party official, attorney, or witness.

(B) No person, purposely and by force or by unlawful threat of harm to any person or property, shall retaliate against the victim of a crime because the victim filed or prosecuted criminal charges.

(C) Whoever violates this section is guilty of retaliation, a felony of the third degree.

HISTORY: 146 v H 88. Eff 9-3-96.

Not analogous to former RC § 2921.05 (RS §§ 7017-7, 7017-8; 95 v 305; GC §§ 12396, 12397; Bureau of Code Revision, 10-1-53; 132 v H 664), repealed 134 v H 511, § 2, eff 1-1-74.

§§ 2921.06, 2921.07 Repealed, 134 v H 511, § 2 [RS § 7017-9; 95 v 305; GC §§ 12398—12398-2; 108 v PtI, 57; Bureau of Code Revision, 10-1-53]. Eff 1-1-74.

These sections concerned offenses against the state.

§§ 2921.08, 2921.09, 2921.10 Repealed, 134 v H 511, § 2 [RS §§ 218-217, 218-218, 6826; 69 v 189; 73 v 249; 76 v 187, 188; 95 v 69; 97 v 306; GC §§ 12426, 12461, 12462; Bureau of Code Revision, 10-1-53]. Eff 1-1-74.

These sections concerned offenses against the state.

[PERJURY]

§ 2921.11 Perjury.

(A) No person, in any official proceeding, shall knowingly make a false statement under oath or affirmation, or knowingly swear or affirm the truth of a false statement previously made, when either statement is material.

(B) A falsification is material, regardless of its admissibility in evidence, if it can affect the course or outcome of the proceeding. It is no defense to a charge under this section that the offender mistakenly believed a falsification to be immaterial.

(C) It is no defense to a charge under this section that the oath or affirmation was administered or taken in an irregular manner.

(D) Where contradictory statements relating to the same material fact are made by the offender under oath or affirmation and within the period of the statute of limitations for perjury, it is not necessary for the prosecution to prove which statement was false, but only that one or the other was false.

(E) No person shall be convicted of a violation of this section where proof of falsity rests solely upon contradiction by testimony of one person other than the defendant.

(F) Whoever violates this section is guilty of perjury, a felony of the third degree.

HISTORY: 134 v H 511. Eff 1-1-74.

Not analogous to former RC § 2921.11 (RS §§ 674-13, 6827b; 89 v 40; 97 v 307; GC § 12463; Bureau of Code Revision, 10-1-53), repealed 134 v H 511, § 2, eff 1-1-74.

§ 2921.12 Tampering with evidence.

(A) No person, knowing that an official proceeding or investigation is in progress, or is about to be or likely to be instituted, shall do any of the following:

(1) Alter, destroy, conceal, or remove any record, document, or thing, with purpose to impair its value or availability as evidence in such proceeding or investigation;

(2) Make, present, or use any record, document, or thing, knowing it to be false and with purpose to mislead a public official who is or may be engaged in such proceeding or investigation, or with purpose to corrupt the outcome of any such proceeding or investigation.

(B) Whoever violates this section is guilty of tampering with evidence, a felony of the third degree.

HISTORY: 134 v H 511. Eff 1-1-74.

Not analogous to former RC § 2921.12 (RS § 6882; S&S 57; S&C 192, 449; 29 v 372; 64 v 128; GC § 12491; Bureau of Code Revision, 10-1-53), repealed 134 v H 511, § 2, eff 1-1-74.

§ 2921.13 Falsification; in theft offense; to purchase firearm.

(A) No person shall knowingly make a false statement, or knowingly swear or affirm the truth of a false statement previously made, when any of the following applies:

(1) The statement is made in any official proceeding.

(2) The statement is made with purpose to incriminate another.

(3) The statement is made with purpose to mislead a public official in performing the public official's official function.

(4) The statement is made with purpose to secure the payment of unemployment compensation; Ohio works first; prevention, retention, and contingency assistance; disability assistance; retirement benefits; economic development assistance, as defined in section 9.66 of the Revised Code; or other benefits administered by a governmental agency or paid out of a public treasury.

(5) The statement is made with purpose to secure the issuance by a governmental agency of a license, permit, authorization, certificate, registration, release, or provider agreement.

(6) The statement is sworn or affirmed before a notary public or another person empowered to administer oaths.

(7) The statement is in writing on or in connection with a report or return that is required or authorized by law.

(8) The statement is in writing and is made with purpose to induce another to extend credit to or employ the offender, to confer any degree, diploma, certificate of attainment, award of excellence, or honor on the offender, or to extend to or bestow upon the offender any other valuable benefit or distinction, when the person to whom the statement is directed relies upon it to that person's detriment.

(9) The statement is made with purpose to commit or facilitate the commission of a theft offense.

(10) The statement is knowingly made to a probate court in connection with any action, proceeding, or other matter within its jurisdiction, either orally or in a written document, including, but not limited to, an application, petition, complaint, or other pleading, or an inventory, account, or report.

(11) The statement is made on an account, form, record, stamp, label, or other writing that is required by law.

(12) The statement is made in connection with the purchase of a firearm, as defined in section 2923.11 of the Revised Code, and in conjunction with the furnishing to the seller of the firearm of a fictitious or altered driver's or commercial driver's license or permit, a fictitious or altered identification card, or any other document that contains false information about the purchaser's identity.

(13) The statement is made in a document or instrument of writing that purports to be a judgment, lien, or claim of indebtedness and is filed or recorded with the secretary of state, a county recorder, or the clerk of a court of record.

(B) No person, in connection with the purchase of a firearm, as defined in section 2923.11 of the Revised Code, shall knowingly furnish to the seller of the firearm a fictitious or altered driver's or commercial driver's license or permit, a fictitious or altered identification card, or any other document that contains false information about the purchaser's identity.

(C) It is no defense to a charge under division (A)(4) of this section that the oath or affirmation was administered or taken in an irregular manner.

(D) If contradictory statements relating to the same fact are made by the offender within the period of the statute of limitations for falsification, it is not necessary for the prosecution to prove which statement was false but only that one or the other was false.

(E)(1) Whoever violates division (A)(1), (2), (3), (4), (5), (6), (7), (8), (10), (11), or (13) of this section is guilty of falsification, a misdemeanor of the first degree.

(2) Whoever violates division (A)(9) of this section is guilty of falsification in a theft offense. Except as otherwise provided in this division, falsification in a theft offense is a misdemeanor of the first degree. If the value of the property or services stolen is five hundred dollars or more and is less than five thousand dollars, falsification in a theft offense is a felony of the fifth degree. If the value of the property or services stolen is five thousand dollars or more and is less than one hundred thousand dollars, falsification in a theft offense is a felony of the fourth degree. If the value of the property or services stolen is one hundred thousand dollars or more, falsification in a theft offense is a felony of the third degree.

(3) Whoever violates division (A)(12) or (B) of this section is guilty of falsification to purchase a firearm, a felony of the fifth degree.

(F) A person who violates this section is liable in a civil action to any person harmed by the violation for injury, death, or loss to person or property incurred as a result of the commission of the offense and for reasonable attorney's fees, court costs, and other expenses incurred as a result of prosecuting the civil action commenced under this division. A civil action under this division is not the exclusive remedy of a person who incurs injury, death, or loss to person or property as a result of a violation of this section.

HISTORY: 134 v H 511 (Eff 1-1-74); 136 v S 545 (Eff 1-17-77); 140 v H 632 (Eff 3-28-85); 141 v H 340 (Eff 5-20-86); 142 v H 708 (Eff 4-19-88); 143 v S 46 (Eff 1-1-90); 143 v H 347 (Eff 7-18-90); 143 v S 3 (Eff 4-11-91); 144 v H 298 (Eff 7-26-91); 145 v H 152 (Eff 7-1-93); 145 v H 107 (Eff 10-20-93); 146 v H 249 (Eff 7-17-95); 146 v H 4 (Eff 11-9-95); 146 v S 46 (Eff 11-15-95); 146 v S 2 (Eff 7-1-96); 146 v S 269 (Eff 7-1-96); 146 v H 644 (Eff 11-6-96); 147 v H 408. Eff 10-1-97.

The provisions of § 5 of HB 249 (146 v —) read as follows:

SECTION 5. No action that may be taken under sections 329.091, 2921.13, 5101.181, 5101.182, 5101.184, and 5747.122 of the Revised Code against a former General Assistance recipient shall be initiated later than two years after the effective date of this act.

§ 2921.14 Making or causing false report of child abuse or neglect.

(A) No person shall knowingly make or cause another person to make a false report under division (B) of section 2151.421 [2151.42.1] of the Revised Code alleging that any person has committed an act or omission that resulted in a child being an abused child as defined in section 2151.031 [2151.03.1] of the Revised Code or a neglected child as defined in section 2151.03 of the Revised Code.

(B) Whoever violates this section is guilty of making or causing a false report of child abuse or child neglect, a misdemeanor of the first degree.

HISTORY: 143 v S 3. Eff 4-11-91.

Not analogous to former RC § 2921.14 (GC § 13116-1; 118 v 501; Bureau of Code Revision, 10-1-53; 126 v 575), repealed, 134 v H 511, § 2, eff 1-1-74.

§§ 2921.15, 2921.16, 2921.17

Repealed, 134 v H 511, § 2 [82 v 221; GC §§ 12506, 13116-2, 13116-3; 118 v 501; Bureau of Code Revision, 10-1-53]. Eff 1-1-74.

These sections concerned offenses against the state and the United States; prosecution; and compensation of jurors.

§ 2921.18 Repealed, 134 v H 511, § 2 [130 v 663; 132 v H 65; 133 v H 1; 134 v H 494]. Eff 1-1-74.

This section concerned imprisonment.

[COMPOUNDING]

§ 2921.21 Compounding a crime.

(A) No person shall knowingly demand, accept, or agree to accept anything of value in consideration of abandoning or agreeing to abandon a pending criminal prosecution.

(B) It is an affirmative defense to a charge under this section when both of the following apply:

(1) The pending prosecution involved is for a violation of section 2913.02 or 2913.11, division (B)(2) of section 2913.21, or section 2913.47 of the Revised Code, of which the actor under this section was the victim.

(2) The thing of value demanded, accepted, or agreed to be accepted, in consideration of abandoning or agreeing to abandon the prosecution, did not exceed an amount that the actor reasonably believed due him as restitution for the loss caused him by the offense.

(C) When a prosecuting witness abandons or agrees to abandon a prosecution under division (B) of this section, the abandonment or agreement in no way binds the state to abandoning the prosecution.

(D) Whoever violates this section is guilty of compounding a crime, a misdemeanor of the first degree.

HISTORY: 134 v H 511 (Eff 1-1-74); 135 v H 716 (Eff 1-1-74); 143 v H 347. Eff 7-18-90.

Not analogous to former RC § 2921.21 (125 v H 308), repealed 134 v H 511, § 2, eff 1-1-74.

Analogous to former RC § 2917.36 (RS § 6901; 76 v 23; 81 v 101; GC § 12861; Bureau of Code Revision, 10-1-53), repealed 134 v H 511, § 2, eff 1-1-74.

§ 2921.22 Failure to report a crime or knowledge of a death or burn injury.

(A) No person, knowing that a felony has been or is being committed, shall knowingly fail to report such information to law enforcement authorities.

(B) Except for conditions that are within the scope of division (E) of this section, no person who is a physician, limited practitioner, nurse, or other person giving aid to a sick or injured person shall negligently fail to report to law enforcement authorities any gunshot or stab wound that the physician, limited practitioner, nurse, or person treated or observed or any serious physical harm to persons that the physician, limited practitioner, nurse, or person knows or has reasonable cause to believe resulted from an offense of violence.

(C) No person who discovers the body or acquires the first knowledge of the death of a person shall fail to report the death immediately to a physician whom the person knows to be treating the deceased for a condition from which death at such time would not be unexpected, or to a law enforcement officer, ambulance service, emergency squad, or the coroner in a political subdivision in which the body is discovered, the death is believed to have occurred, or knowledge concerning the death is obtained.

(D) No person shall fail to provide upon request of the person to whom the person† a report required by division (C) of this section was made, or to any law enforcement officer who has reasonable cause to assert the authority to investigate the circumstances surrounding the death, any facts within the person's knowledge that may have a bearing on the investigation of the death.

(E)(1) As used in this division, "burn injury" means any of the following:

(a) Second or third degree burns;

(b) Any burns to the upper respiratory tract or laryngeal edema due to the inhalation of superheated air;

(c) Any burn injury or wound that may result in death.

(2) No physician, nurse, or limited practitioner who, outside a hospital, sanitarium, or other medical facility, attends or treats a person who has sustained a burn injury inflicted by an explosion or other incendiary device, or that shows evidence of having been inflicted in a violent, malicious, or criminal manner, shall fail to report the burn injury immediately to the local arson bureau, if there is such a bureau in the jurisdiction in which the person is attended or treated, or otherwise to local law enforcement authorities.

(3) No manager, superintendent, or other person in charge of a hospital, sanitarium, or other medical facility in which a person is attended or treated for any burn injury inflicted by an explosion or other incendiary device, or that shows evidence of having been inflicted in a violent, malicious, or criminal manner, shall fail to report the burn injury immediately to the local arson bureau, if there is such a bureau in the jurisdiction in which the person is attended or treated, or otherwise to local law enforcement authorities.

(4) No person who is required to report any burn injury under division (E)(2) or (3) of this section shall fail to file, within three working days after attending or treating the victim, a written report of the burn injury with the office of the state fire marshal. The report shall be made on a form provided by the state fire marshal.

(5) Anyone participating in the making of reports under division (E) of this section or anyone participating in a judicial proceeding resulting from the reports is immune from any civil or criminal liability that otherwise might be incurred or imposed as a result of such actions. Notwithstanding section 4731.22 of the Revised Code, the physician-patient relationship is not a ground for excluding evidence regarding a person's burn injury or the cause of the burn injury in any judicial proceeding resulting from a report submitted pursuant to division (E) of this section.

(F)(1) Any doctor of medicine or osteopathic medicine, hospital intern or resident, registered or licensed practical nurse, psychologist, social worker, independent social worker, social work assistant, professional clinical counselor, or professional counselor who knows or has reasonable cause to believe that a patient or client has been the victim of domestic violence, as defined in section 3113.31 of the Revised Code, shall note that knowledge or belief and the basis for it in the patient's or client's records.

(2) Notwithstanding section 4731.22 of the Revised Code, the doctor-patient privilege shall not be a ground for excluding any information regarding the report containing the knowledge or belief noted pursuant to division (F)(1) of this section, and the information may be admitted as evidence in accordance with the Rules of Evidence.

(G) Division (A) or (D) of this section does not require disclosure of information, when any of the following applies:

(1) The information is privileged by reason of the relationship between attorney and client; doctor and patient; licensed psychologist or licensed school psychologist and client; member of the clergy, rabbi, minister, or priest and any person communicating information confidentially to the clergyman,† the member of the clergy, rabbi, minister, or priest for a religious counseling purpose of a† the professional character of the member of the clergy, rabbi, minister, or priest; husband and wife; or a communications assistant and those who are a party to a telecommunications relay service call.

(2) The information would tend to incriminate a member of the actor's immediate family.

(3) Disclosure of the information would amount to revealing a news source, privileged under section 2739.04 or 2739.12 of the Revised Code.

(4) Disclosure of the information would amount to disclosure by a member of the ordained clergy of an organized religious body of a confidential communication made to the clergyman† that member of the clergy in a† that member's capacity as a clergyman by a person seeking the aid or counsel of that member of the clergy.

(5) Disclosure would amount to revealing information acquired by the actor in the course of the actor's duties in connection with a bona fide program of treatment or services for drug dependent persons or persons in danger of drug dependence, which program is maintained or conducted by a hospital, clinic, person, agency, or organization certified pursuant to section 3793.06 of the Revised Code.

(6) Disclosure would amount to revealing information acquired by the actor in the course of the actor's duties in connection with a bona fide program for providing counseling services to victims of crimes that are violations of section 2907.02 or 2907.05 of the Revised Code or to victims of felonious sexual penetration in violation of former section 2907.12 of the Revised Code. As used in this division, "counseling services" include services provided in an informal setting by a person who, by education or experience, is competent to provide such services.

(H) No disclosure of information pursuant to this section gives rise to any liability or recrimination for a breach of privilege or confidence.

(I) Whoever violates division (A) or (B) of this section is guilty of failure to report a crime. Violation of division (A) of this section is a misdemeanor of the fourth degree.

Violation of division (B) of this section is a misdemeanor of the second degree.

(J) Whoever violates division (C) or (D) of this section is guilty of failure to report knowledge of a death, a misdemeanor of the fourth degree.

(K)(1) Whoever negligently violates division (E) of this section is guilty of a minor misdemeanor.

(2) Whoever knowingly violates division (E) of this section is guilty of a misdemeanor of the second degree.

HISTORY: 134 v H 511 (Eff 1-1-74); 136 v H 750 (Eff 8-26-75); 136 v S 283 (Eff 11-26-75); 137 v H 1 (Eff 8-26-77); 137 v S 203 (Eff 1-13-78); 138 v H 284 (Eff 10-22-80); 142 v H 273 (Eff 9-10-87); 143 v H 317 (Eff 10-10-89); 144 v S 343 (Eff 3-24-93); 145 v H 335 (Eff 12-9-94); 146 v H 445 (Eff 9-3-96); 146 v S 223. Eff 3-18-97.

Not analogous to former RC § 2921.22 (125 v H 308), repealed 134 v H 511, § 2, eff 1-1-74.

Publisher's Note

The amendments made by HB 445 (146 v —) and SB 223 (146 v —) have been combined. Please see provisions of RC § 1.52.

† The wording is the result of combining HB 445 (146 v —) and SB 223 (146 v —).

§ 2921.23 Failure to aid a law enforcement officer.

(A) No person shall negligently fail or refuse to aid a law enforcement officer, when called upon for assistance in preventing or halting the commission of an offense, or in apprehending or detaining an offender, when such aid can be given without a substantial risk of physical harm to the person giving it.

(B) Whoever violates this section is guilty of failure to aid a law enforcement officer, a minor misdemeanor.

HISTORY: 134 v H 511. Eff 1-1-74.

Not analogous to former RC § 2921.23 (125 v H 308), repealed 134 v H 511, § 2, eff 1-1-74.

Analogous to former RC § 2917.32 (RS § 6918; S&C 430; 29 v 144; GC § 12857; Bureau of Code Revision, 10-1-53), repealed 134 v H 511, § 2, eff 1-1-74.

§ 2921.24 Disclosure of confidential information.

(A) No officer or employee of a law enforcement agency or court, or of the office of the clerk of any court, shall disclose during the pendency of any criminal case the home address of any peace officer, as defined in section 2935.01 of the Revised Code, who is a witness or arresting officer in the case.

(B) Division (A) of this section does not prohibit a peace officer from disclosing his own home address, and does not apply to any person who discloses the home address of a peace officer pursuant to a court-ordered disclosure under division (C) of this section.

(C) The court in which any criminal case is pending may order the disclosure of the home address of any peace officer who is a witness or arresting officer in the case, if the court determines after a written request for the disclosure that good cause exists for disclosing the home address of the peace officer.

(D) Whoever violates division (A) of this section is guilty of disclosure of confidential information, a misdemeanor of the fourth degree.

HISTORY: 140 v H 403. Eff 9-26-84.

Not analogous to former RC § 2921.24 (125 v H 308), repealed 134 v H 511, § 2, eff 1-1-74.

§ 2921.25 Disclosure of peace officer's home address.

No judge of a court of record, or mayor presiding over a mayor's court, shall order a peace officer, as defined in section 2935.01 of the Revised Code, who is a witness in a criminal case, to disclose his home address during his examination in the case, unless the judge or mayor determines that the defendant has a right to the disclosure.

HISTORY: 140 v H 403. Eff 9-26-84.

Not analogous to former RC § 2921.25 (125 v H 308; 130 v 663), repealed 134 v H 511, § 2, eff 1-1-74.

§§ 2921.26, 2921.27 Repealed, 134 v H 511, § 2 [125 v H 308]. Eff 1-1-74.

These sections concerned charge to grand jury and records not to be public.

[OBSTRUCTING AND ESCAPE]

§ 2921.31 Obstructing official business.

(A) No person, without privilege to do so and with purpose to prevent, obstruct, or delay the performance by a public official of any authorized act within his official capacity, shall do any act which hampers or impedes a public official in the performance of his lawful duties.

(B) Whoever violates this section is guilty of obstructing official business, a misdemeanor of the second degree.

HISTORY: 134 v H 511. Eff 1-1-74.

§ 2921.32 Obstructing justice.

(A) No person, with purpose to hinder the discovery, apprehension, prosecution, conviction, or punishment of another for crime, or to assist another to benefit from the commission of a crime, shall do any of the following:

(1) Harbor or conceal the other person;

(2) Provide the other person with money, transportation, a weapon, a disguise, or other means of avoiding discovery or apprehension;

(3) Warn the other person of impending discovery or apprehension;
(4) Destroy or conceal physical evidence of the crime, or induce any person to withhold testimony or information or to elude legal process summoning the person to testify or supply evidence;
(5) Communicate false information to any person.

(B)(1) Whoever violates this section is guilty of obstructing justice.
(2) If the crime committed by the person aided is a misdemeanor, obstructing justice is a misdemeanor of the same degree as the crime committed by the person aided.
(3) Except as otherwise provided in division (B)(4) of this section, if the crime committed by the person aided is a felony, obstructing justice is a felony of the fifth degree.
(4) If the crime committed by the person aided is aggravated murder, murder, or a felony of the first or second degree and if the offender knows or has reason to believe that the crime committed by the person aided is one of those offenses, obstructing justice is a felony of the third degree.

HISTORY: 134 v H 511 (Eff 1-1-74); 146 v S 2. Eff 7-1-96.

The effective date is set by section 6 of SB 2.

[§ 2921.32.1] § 2921.321 Assaulting police dog or horse or handicapped assistance dog.

(A) No person shall knowingly cause, or attempt to cause, physical harm to a police dog or horse in either of the following circumstances:
(1) The police dog or horse is assisting a law enforcement officer in the performance of the officer's official duties at the time the physical harm is caused or attempted.
(2) The police dog or horse is not assisting a law enforcement officer in the performance of the officer's official duties at the time the physical harm is caused or attempted, but the offender has actual knowledge that the dog or horse is a police dog or horse.

(B) No person shall knowingly cause, or attempt to cause, physical harm to a handicapped assistance dog in either of the following circumstances:
(1) The handicapped assistance dog is assisting a blind, deaf, or mobility impaired person at the time the physical harm is caused or attempted.
(2) The handicapped assistance dog is not assisting a blind, deaf, or mobility impaired person at the time the physical harm is caused or attempted, but the offender has actual knowledge that the dog is a handicapped assistance dog.

(C)(1) Whoever violates division (A) of this section is guilty of assaulting a police dog or horse. Except as otherwise provided in this division, assaulting a police dog or horse is a misdemeanor of the second degree. If the violation results in the death of the dog or horse, assaulting a police dog or horse is a felony of the fourth degree. If the violation results in serious physical harm to the police dog or horse other than its death, assaulting a police dog or horse is a felony of the fifth degree. If the violation results in physical harm to the police dog or horse other than death or serious physical harm, assaulting a police dog or horse is a misdemeanor of the first degree.

(2) Whoever violates division (B) of this section is guilty of assaulting a handicapped assistance dog. Except as otherwise provided in this division, assaulting a handicapped assistance dog is a misdemeanor of the second degree. If the violation results in the death of the dog, assaulting a handicapped assistance dog is a felony of the fourth degree. If the violation results in serious physical harm to the dog other than its death, assaulting a handicapped assistance dog is a felony of the fifth degree. If the violation results in physical harm to the dog other than death or serious physical harm, assaulting a handicapped assistance dog is a misdemeanor of the first degree.

(D) This section does not apply to a licensed veterinarian whose conduct is in accordance with Chapter 4741. of the Revised Code.

(E) As used in this section:
(1) "Physical harm" means any injury, illness, or other physiological impairment, regardless of its gravity or duration.
(2) "Police dog or horse" means a dog or horse that has been trained, and may be used, to assist law enforcement officers in the performance of their official duties.
(3) "Serious physical harm" means any of the following:
(a) Any physical harm that carries a substantial risk of death;
(b) Any physical harm that causes permanent maiming or that involves some temporary, substantial maiming;
(c) Any physical harm that causes acute pain of a duration that results in substantial suffering.
(4) "Handicapped assistance dog" means a dog that serves as a guide or leader for a blind person or as a listener for a deaf person or that provides support or assistance for a mobility impaired person.
(5) "Blind" and "mobility impaired person" have the same meanings as in section 955.011 [955.01.1] of the Revised Code.

HISTORY: 145 v S 116 (Eff 9-29-94); 146 v S 2. Eff 7-1-96.

The effective date is set by section 6 of SB 2.

§ 2921.33 Resisting arrest.

(A) No person, recklessly or by force, shall resist or interfere with a lawful arrest of the person or another.
(B) No person, recklessly or by force, shall resist or interfere with a lawful arrest of the person or another person and, during the course of or as a result of the resistance or interference, cause physical harm to a law enforcement officer.

(C) No person, recklessly or by force, shall resist or interfere with a lawful arrest of the person or another person if either of the following applies:

(1) The offender, during the course of or as a result of the resistance or interference, recklessly causes physical harm to a law enforcement officer by means of a deadly weapon;

(2) The offender, during the course of the resistance or interference, brandishes a deadly weapon.

(D) Whoever violates this section is guilty of resisting arrest. A violation of division (A) of this section is a misdemeanor of the second degree. A violation of division (B) of this section is a misdemeanor of the first degree. A violation of division (C) of this section is a felony of the fourth degree.

(E) As used in this section, "deadly weapon" has the same meaning as in section 2923.11 of the Revised Code.

HISTORY: 134 v H 511 (Eff 1-1-74); 146 v S 2 (Eff 7-1-96); 147 v H 151. Eff 9-16-97.

[§ 2921.33.1] § 2921.331 Failure to comply with order or signal of police officer.

(A) No person shall fail to comply with any lawful order or direction of any police officer invested with authority to direct, control, or regulate traffic.

(B) No person shall operate a motor vehicle so as willfully to elude or flee a police officer after receiving a visible or audible signal from a police officer to bring his motor vehicle to a stop.

(C) Whoever violates this section is guilty of failure to comply with an order or signal of a police officer. A violation of division (A) of this section is a misdemeanor of the first degree. A violation of division (B) of this section is a misdemeanor of the first degree, except that a violation of division (B) of this section is a felony of the fourth degree if the jury or judge as trier of fact finds any one of the following by proof beyond a reasonable doubt:

(1) In committing the offense, the offender was fleeing immediately after the commission of a felony;

(2) The operation of the motor vehicle by the offender was a proximate cause of serious physical harm to persons or property;

(3) The operation of the motor vehicle by the offender caused a substantial risk of serious physical harm to persons or property.

(D) As used in this section, "police officer" has the same meaning as in section 4511.01 of the Revised Code.

HISTORY: GC § 6307-3; 119 v 766, § 3; Bureau of Code Revision, RC § 4511.02, 10-1-53; 132 v H 380 (Eff 1-1-68); 137 v S 381 (Eff 10-19-78); RC § 2921.33.1, 143 v S 49. Eff 11-3-89.

§ 2921.34 Escape.

(A)(1) No person, knowing the person is under detention or being reckless in that regard, shall purposely break or attempt to break the detention, or purposely fail to return to detention, either following temporary leave granted for a specific purpose or limited period, or at the time required when serving a sentence in intermittent confinement.

(2) No person who is sentenced to a prison term pursuant to division (A)(3) of section 2971.03 of the Revised Code as a sexually violent predator, for whom the requirement that the entire prison term be served in a state correctional institution has been modified pursuant to section 2971.05 of the Revised Code, and who, pursuant to that modification, is restricted to a geographic area, knowing that the person is under a geographic restriction or being reckless in that regard, shall purposely leave the geographic area to which the restriction applies or purposely fail to return to that geographic area following a temporary leave granted for a specific purpose or for a limited period of time.

(B) Irregularity in bringing about or maintaining detention, or lack of jurisdiction of the committing or detaining authority, is not a defense to a charge under this section if the detention is pursuant to judicial order or in a detention facility. In the case of any other detention, irregularity or lack of jurisdiction is an affirmative defense only if either of the following occurs:

(1) The escape involved no substantial risk of harm to the person or property of another.

(2) The detaining authority knew or should have known there was no legal basis or authority for the detention.

(C) Whoever violates this section is guilty of escape.

(1) If the offender, at the time of the commission of the offense, was under detention as an alleged or adjudicated delinquent child or unruly child and if the act for which the offender was under detention would not be a felony if committed by an adult, escape is a misdemeanor of the first degree.

(2) If the offender, at the time of the commission of the offense, was under detention in any other manner or was a sexually violent predator for whom the requirement that the entire prison term imposed pursuant to division (A)(3) of section 2971.03 of the Revised Code be served in a state correctional institution has been modified pursuant to section 2971.05 of the Revised Code, escape is one of the following:

(a) A felony of the second degree, when the most serious offense for which the person was under detention or adjudicated a sexually violent predator is aggravated murder, murder, or a felony of the first or second degree or, if the person was under detention as an alleged or adjudicated delinquent child, when the most serious act for which the person was under detention would be aggravated murder, murder, or a felony of the first or second degree if committed by an adult;

(b) A felony of the third degree, when the most serious offense for which the person was under detention or adjudicated a sexually violent predator is a felony of the third, fourth, or fifth degree or an unclassified felony or, if the person was under detention as an alleged or adjudicated delinquent child, when the most serious act for which the person was under detention would be a felony of the third, fourth, or fifth degree or an unclassified felony if committed by an adult;

(c) A felony of the fifth degree, when any of the following applies:

(i) The most serious offense for which the person was under detention is a misdemeanor.†

(ii) The person was found not guilty by reason of insanity, and the person's detention consisted of hospitalization, institutionalization, or confinement in a facility under an order made pursuant to or under authority of section 2945.40, 2945.401 [2945.40.1], or 2945.402 [2945.40.2] of the Revised Code.

(d) A misdemeanor of the first degree, when the most serious offense for which the person was under detention is a misdemeanor and when the person fails to return to detention at a specified time following temporary leave granted for a specific purpose or limited period or at the time required when serving a sentence in intermittent confinement.

HISTORY: 134 v H 511 (Eff 1-1-74); 144 v H 298 (Eff 7-26-91); 144 v S 37 (Eff 7-31-92); 144 v H 725 (Eff 4-16-93); 145 v H 42 (Eff 2-9-94); 146 v S 2 (Eff 7-1-96); 146 v H 180 (Eff 1-1-97); 146 v S 285. Eff 7-1-97.

The effective date is set by section 4 of SB 285.

† So in enrolled bill. The period was added in HB 180 (146 v —), eff 1-1-97.

Comment, Legislative Service Commission

° ° ° Section 2921.34 of the Revised Code is amended by this act [Am. Sub. S.B. 285] and also by Am. Sub. H.B. 180 of the 121st General Assembly. ° ° ° Comparison of these amendments in pursuance of section 1.52 of the Revised Code discloses that they are not irreconcilable so that they are required by that section to be harmonized to give effect to each amendment.

The provisions of § 4 of HB 180 (146 v —) read as follows:

SECTION 4. Sections 2921.34, 2929.02, 2929.03, 2929.06, 2929.13, 2929.14, 2929.19, 2929.21, 2929.41, 2930.16, 2941.147, 2941.148, 2953.08, 2967.12, 2967.121, 2967.13, 2967.18, 2967.193, 2967.26, 2967.27, 2971.01, 2971.02, 2971.03, 2971.04, 2971.05, 2971.06, 2971.07, 5120.49, 5120.61, 5149.03, and 5149.10 of the Revised Code, as amended or enacted in Sections 1 and 2 of this act, shall apply only to persons who commit an offense governed by those amended and enacted sections on or after the effective date of this act.

§ 2921.35 Aiding escape or resistance to authority.

(A) No person, with purpose to promote or facilitate an escape or resistance to lawful authority, shall convey into a detention facility, or provide anyone confined therein with any instrument or thing which may be used for such purposes.

(B) No person who is confined in a detention facility, and with purpose to promote or facilitate an escape or resistance to lawful authority, shall make, procure, conceal, unlawfully possess, or give to another inmate, any instrument or thing which may be used for such purposes.

(C) Whoever violates this section is guilty of aiding escape or resistance to lawful authority, a felony of the fourth degree.

HISTORY: 134 v H 511 (Eff 1-1-74); 146 v S 2. Eff 7-1-96.

The effective date is set by section 6 of SB 2.

§ 2921.36 Illegal conveyance of weapons or prohibited items onto grounds of detention facility or institution.

(A) No person shall knowingly convey, or attempt to convey, onto the grounds of a detention facility or of an institution that is under the control of the department of mental health or the department of mental retardation and developmental disabilities, any of the following items:

(1) Any deadly weapon or dangerous ordnance, as defined in section 2923.11 of the Revised Code, or any part of or ammunition for use in such a deadly weapon or dangerous ordnance;

(2) Any drug of abuse, as defined in section 3719.011 [3719.01.1] of the Revised Code;

(3) Any intoxicating liquor, as defined in section 4301.01 of the Revised Code.

(B) Division (A) of this section does not apply to any person who conveys or attempts to convey an item onto the grounds of a detention facility or of an institution under the control of the department of mental health or the department of mental retardation and developmental disabilities pursuant to the written authorization of the person in charge of the detention facility or the institution and in accordance with the written rules of the detention facility or the institution.

(C) No person shall knowingly deliver, or attempt to deliver, to any person who is confined in a detention facility or to any patient in an institution under the control of the department of mental health or the department of mental retardation and developmental disabilities, any item listed in division (A)(1), (2), or (3) of this section.

(D) No person shall knowingly deliver, or attempt to deliver, cash to any person who is confined in a detention facility.

(E) It is an affirmative defense to a charge under division (C) of this section that the actor was not otherwise prohibited by law from delivering the item to the confined person or the patient and that either of the following applies:

(1) The actor was permitted by the written rules of the detention facility or the institution to deliver the item to the confined person or the patient.

(2) The actor was given written authorization by the person in charge of the detention facility or the institution

to deliver the item to the confined person or the patient.

(F)(1) Whoever violates division (A)(1) of this section or commits a violation of division (C) of this section involving an item listed in division (A)(1) of this section is guilty of illegal conveyance of weapons onto the grounds of a detention facility or a mental health or mental retardation and developmental disabilities institution, a felony of the fourth degree.

(2) Whoever violates division (A)(2) of this section or commits a violation of division (C) of this section involving any drug of abuse is guilty of illegal conveyance of drugs of abuse onto the grounds of a detention facility or a mental health or mental retardation and developmental disabilities institution, a felony of the fourth degree if the offender is an officer or employee of the facility or institution or a felony of the fifth degree if the offender is not such an officer or employee.

(3) Whoever violates division (A)(3) of this section or commits a violation of division (C) of this section involving any intoxicating liquor is guilty of illegal conveyance of intoxicating liquor onto the grounds of a detention facility or a mental health or mental retardation and developmental disabilities institution, a misdemeanor of the second degree.

(4) Whoever violates division (D) of this section is guilty of illegal conveyance of cash onto the grounds of a detention facility, a misdemeanor of the first degree. If the offender previously has been convicted of or pleaded guilty to a violation of division (D) of this section, illegal conveyance of cash onto the grounds of a detention facility is a felony of the fifth degree.

HISTORY: 137 v H 630 (Eff 5-23-78); 138 v H 900 (Eff 7-1-80); 143 v S 258 (Eff 11-20-90); 145 v H 571 (Eff 10-6-94); 146 v S 2. Eff 7-1-96.

The effective date is set by section 6 of SB 2.

§ 2921.37 Arrest powers of detention facility chief.

The person in charge of a detention facility shall, on the grounds of the detention facility, have the same power as a peace officer, as defined in section 2935.01 of the Revised Code, to arrest a person who violates section 2921.36 of the Revised Code.

HISTORY: 137 v H 630. Eff 5-23-78.

§ 2921.38 Harassment by inmate.

(A) No person who is confined in a detention facility, with intent to harass, annoy, threaten, or alarm another person, shall cause or attempt to cause the other person to come into contact with blood, semen, urine, feces, or another bodily substance by throwing the bodily substance at the other person, by expelling the bodily substance upon the other person, or in any other manner.

(B) No person who is confined in a detention facility, with knowledge that the person is a carrier of the virus that causes acquired immunodeficiency syndrome, is a carrier of a hepatitis virus, or is infected with tuberculosis and with intent to harass, annoy, threaten, or alarm another person, shall cause or attempt to cause the other person to come into contact with blood, semen, urine, feces, or another bodily substance by throwing the bodily substance at the other person, by expelling the bodily substance upon the other person, or in any other manner.

(C) Whoever violates this section is guilty of harassment by an inmate. A violation of division (A) of this section is a felony of the fifth degree. A violation of division (B) of this section is a felony of the third degree.

(D)(1) The court, on request of the prosecutor, or the law enforcement authority responsible for the investigation of the violation, shall cause a person who allegedly has committed a violation of this section to submit to one or more appropriate tests to determine if the person is a carrier of the virus that causes acquired immunodeficiency syndrome, is a carrier of a hepatitis virus, or is infected with tuberculosis.

(2) The court shall charge the offender with the costs of the test or tests ordered under division (D)(1) of this section unless the court determines that the accused is unable to pay, in which case the costs shall be charged to the entity that operates the detention facility in which the alleged offense occurred.

(E) This section does not apply to a person who is hospitalized, institutionalized, or confined in a facility operated by the department of mental health or the department of mental retardation and developmental disabilities.

HISTORY: 147 v H 37. Eff 6-11-97.

[PECULATION AND DERELICTION]

§ 2921.41 Theft in office; restitution; withholding of retirement benefits.

(A) No public official or party official shall commit any theft offense, as defined in division (K) of section 2913.01 of the Revised Code, when either of the following applies:

(1) The offender uses the offender's office in aid of committing the offense or permits or assents to its use in aid of committing the offense;

(2) The property or service involved is owned by this state, any other state, the United States, a county, a municipal corporation, a township, or any political subdivision, department, or agency of any of them, is owned by a political party, or is part of a political campaign fund.

(B) Whoever violates this section is guilty of theft in office. Except as otherwise provided in this division, theft in office is a felony of the fifth degree. If the value of property or services stolen is five hundred dollars or more and is less than five thousand dollars, theft in office is a felony of the fourth degree. If the value of

§ 2921.41

property or services stolen is five thousand dollars or more theft in office is a felony of the third degree.

(C)(1) A public official or party official who is convicted of or pleads guilty to theft in office is forever disqualified from holding any public office, employment, or position of trust in this state.

(2)(a) A court that imposes sentence for a violation of this section based on conduct described in division (A)(2) of this section shall require the public official or party official who is convicted of or pleads guilty to the offense to make restitution for all of the property or the service that is the subject of the offense, in addition to the term of imprisonment and any fine imposed. A court that imposes sentence for a violation of this section based on conduct described in division (A)(1) of this section and that determines at trial that this state or a political subdivision of this state if the offender is a public official, or a political party in the United States or this state if the offender is a party official, suffered actual loss as a result of the offense shall require the offender to make restitution to the state, political subdivision, or political party for all of the actual loss experienced, in addition to the term of imprisonment and any fine imposed.

(b)(i) In any case in which a sentencing court is required to order restitution under division (C)(2)(a) of this section and in which the offender, at the time of the commission of the offense or at any other time, was a member of the public employees retirement system, the police and firemen's disability and pension fund, the state teachers retirement system, the school employees retirement system, or the state highway patrol retirement system; was an electing employee, as defined in section 3305.01 of the Revised Code, participating in an alternative retirement plan provided pursuant to Chapter 3305. of the Revised Code; was a participating employee or continuing member, as defined in section 145.71 of the Revised Code, in a deferred compensation program offered by the Ohio public employees deferred compensation board; was an officer or employee of a municipal corporation who was a participant in a deferred compensation program offered by that municipal corporation; was an officer or employee of a government unit; as defined in section 145.74 of the Revised Code, who was a participant in a deferred compensation program offered by that government unit, or was a participating employee, continuing member, or participant in any deferred compensation program described in this division and a member of a retirement system specified in this division or a retirement system of a municipal corporation, the entity to which restitution is to be made may file a motion with the sentencing court specifying any retirement system, any entity providing any benefit under an alternative retirement plan, and any deferred compensation program of which the offender was a member, electing employee, participating employee, continuing member, or participant and requesting the court to issue an order requiring the specified retirement system, the specified entity providing the benefit under the alternative retirement plan, or the specified deferred compensation program, or, if more than one is specified in the motion, the applicable combination of these, to withhold the amount required as restitution from any payment that is to be made under a pension, annuity, or allowance, under a participant account, as defined in section 145.71 of the Revised Code, or under any other type of benefit, other than a survivorship benefit, that has been or is in the future granted to the offender, from any payment of accumulated employee contributions standing to the offender's credit with that retirement system, that entity providing the payment under the alternative retirement plan, or that deferred compensation program, or, if more than one is specified in the motion, the applicable combination of these, and from any payment of any other amounts to be paid to the offender upon the offender's withdrawal of the offender's contributions pursuant to Chapter 145., 742., 3307., 3309., or 5505. of the Revised Code. A motion described in this division may be filed at any time subsequent to the conviction of the offender or entry of a guilty plea. Upon the filing of the motion, the clerk of the court in which the motion is filed shall notify the offender, the specified retirement system, the specified entity providing the benefit under the alternative retirement plan, or the specified deferred compensation program, or, if more than one is specified in the motion, the applicable combination of these, in writing, of all of the following: that the motion was filed; that the offender will be granted a hearing on the issuance of the requested order if the offender files a written request for a hearing with the clerk prior to the expiration of thirty days after the offender receives the notice; that, if a hearing is requested, the court will schedule a hearing as soon as possible and notify the offender, any specified retirement system, any specified entity providing any benefit under an alternative retirement plan, and any specified deferred compensation program of the date, time, and place of the hearing; that, if a hearing is conducted, it will be limited only to a consideration of whether the offender can show good cause why the requested order should not be issued; that, if a hearing is conducted, the court will not issue the requested order if the court determines, based on evidence presented at the hearing by the offender, that there is good cause for the requested order not to be issued; that the court will issue the requested order if a hearing is not requested or if a hearing is conducted but the court does not determine, based on evidence presented at the hearing by the offender, that there is good cause for the requested order not to be issued; and that, if the requested order is issued, any retirement system, any entity providing any benefit under an alternative retirement plan, and any deferred compensation program specified in the motion will be required to withhold the amount required as restitution from payments to the offender.

(ii) In any case in which a sentencing court is required to order restitution under division (C)(2)(a) of this section and in which a motion requesting the issuance of a withholding order as described in division (C)(2)(b)(i) of this section is filed, the offender may receive a hearing on the motion by delivering a written request for a hearing to the court prior to the expiration of thirty days after the offender's receipt of the notice provided pursuant to division (C)(2)(b)(i) of this section. If a request for a hearing is made by the offender within the prescribed time, the court shall schedule a hearing as soon as possible after the request is made and shall notify the offender, the specified retirement system, the specified entity providing the benefit under the alternative retirement plan, or the specified deferred compensation program, or, if more than one is specified in the motion, the applicable combination of these, of the date, time, and place of the hearing. A hearing scheduled under this division shall be limited to a consideration of whether there is good cause, based on evidence presented by the offender, for the requested order not to be issued. If the court determines, based on evidence presented by the offender, that there is good cause for the order not to be issued, the court shall deny the motion and shall not issue the requested order. If the offender does not request a hearing within the prescribed time or if the court conducts a hearing but does not determine, based on evidence presented by the offender, that there is good cause for the order not to be issued, the court shall order the specified retirement system, the specified entity providing the benefit under the alternative retirement plan, or the specified deferred compensation program, or, if more than one is specified in the motion, the applicable combination of these, to withhold the amount required as restitution under division (C)(2)(a) of this section from any payments to be made under a pension, annuity, or allowance, under a participant account, as defined in section 145.71 of the Revised Code, or under any other type of benefit, other than a survivorship benefit, that has been or is in the future granted to the offender, from any payment of accumulated employee contributions standing to the offender's credit with that retirement system, that entity providing the benefit under the alternative retirement plan, or that deferred compensation program, or, if more than one is specified in the motion, the applicable combination of these, and from any payment of any other amounts to be paid to the offender upon the offender's withdrawal of the offender's contributions pursuant to Chapter 145., 742., 3307., 3309., or 5505. of the Revised Code, and to continue the withholding for that purpose, in accordance with the order, out of each payment to be made on or after the date of issuance of the order, until further order of the court. Upon receipt of an order issued under this division, the public employees retirement system, the police and firemen's disability and pension fund, the state teachers retirement system, the school employees retirement system, the state highway patrol retirement system, a municipal corporation retirement system, the entity providing the benefit under the alternative retirement plan, and the deferred compensation program offered by the Ohio public employees deferred compensation board, a municipal corporation, or a government unit, as defined in section 145.74 of the Revised Code, whichever are applicable, shall withhold the amount required as restitution, in accordance with the order, from any such payments and immediately shall forward the amount withheld to the clerk of the court in which the order was issued for payment to the entity to which restitution is to be made.

(iii) Service of a notice required by division (C)(2)(b)(i) or (ii) of this section shall be effected in the same manner as provided in the Rules of Civil Procedure for the service of process.

(D) Upon the filing of charges against a person under this section, the prosecutor, as defined in section 2935.01 of the Revised Code, who is assigned the case shall send written notice that charges have been filed against that person to the public employees retirement system, the police and firemen's disability and pension fund, the state teachers retirement system, the school employees retirement system, the state highway patrol retirement system, the entity providing any benefit under an alternative retirement plan, any municipal corporation retirement system in this state, and the deferred compensation program offered by the Ohio public employees deferred compensation board, a municipal corporation, or a government unit, as defined in section 145.74 of the Revised Code. The written notice shall specifically identify the person charged.

HISTORY: 134 v H 511 (Eff 1-1-74); 140 v H 265 (Eff 9-20-84); 144 v S 300 (Eff 11-5-92); 146 v S 2 (Eff 7-1-96); 146 v H 586. Eff 3-31-97.

§ 2921.42 Having an unlawful interest in a public contract.

(A) No public official shall knowingly do any of the following:

(1) Authorize, or employ the authority or influence of his office to secure authorization of any public contract in which he, a member of his family, or any of his business associates has an interest;

(2) Authorize, or employ the authority or influence of his office to secure the investment of public funds in any share, bond, mortgage, or other security, with respect to which he, a member of his family, or any of his business associates either has an interest, is an underwriter, or receives any brokerage, origination, or servicing fees;

(3) During his term of office or within one year thereafter, occupy any position of profit in the prosecution of a public contract authorized by him or by a legislative body, commission, or board of which he was a member at the time of authorization, unless the contract was let

by competitive bidding to the lowest and best bidder;

(4) Have an interest in the profits or benefits of a public contract entered into by or for the use of the political subdivision or governmental agency or instrumentality with which he is connected;

(5) Have an interest in the profits or benefits of a public contract that is not let by competitive bidding if required by law and that involves more than one hundred fifty dollars.

(B) In the absence of bribery or a purpose to defraud, a public official, member of his family, or any of his business associates shall not be considered as having an interest in a public contract or the investment of public funds, if all of the following apply:

(1) The interest of that person is limited to owning or controlling shares of the corporation, or being a creditor of the corporation or other organization, that is the contractor on the public contract involved, or that is the issuer of the security in which public funds are invested;

(2) The shares owned or controlled by that person do not exceed five per cent of the outstanding shares of the corporation, and the amount due that person as creditor does not exceed five per cent of the total indebtedness of the corporation or other organization;

(3) That person, prior to the time the public contract is entered into, files with the political subdivision or governmental agency or instrumentality involved, an affidavit giving his exact status in connection with the corporation or other organization.

(C) This section does not apply to a public contract in which a public official, member of his family, or one of his business associates has an interest, when all of the following apply:

(1) The subject of the public contract is necessary supplies or services for the political subdivision or governmental agency or instrumentality involved;

(2) The supplies or services are unobtainable elsewhere for the same or lower cost, or are being furnished to the political subdivision or governmental agency or instrumentality as part of a continuing course of dealing established prior to the public official's becoming associated with the political subdivision or governmental agency or instrumentality involved;

(3) The treatment accorded the political subdivision or governmental agency or instrumentality is either preferential to or the same as that accorded other customers or clients in similar transactions;

(4) The entire transaction is conducted at arm's length, with full knowledge by the political subdivision or governmental agency or instrumentality involved, of the interest of the public official, member of his family, or business associate, and the public official takes no part in the deliberations or decision of the political subdivision or governmental agency or instrumentality with respect to the public contract.

(D) Division (A)(4) of this section does not prohibit participation by a public employee in any housing program funded by public moneys if the public employee otherwise qualifies for the program and does not use the authority or influence of his office or employment to secure benefits from the program and if the moneys are to be used on the primary residence of the public employee. Such participation does not constitute an unlawful interest in a public contract in violation of this section.

(E) Whoever violates this section is guilty of having an unlawful interest in a public contract. Violation of division (A)(1) or (2) of this section is a felony of the fourth degree. Violation of division (A)(3), (4), or (5) of this section is a misdemeanor of the first degree.

(F) It is not a violation of this section for a prosecuting attorney to appoint assistants and employees in accordance with sections 309.06 and 2921.421 [2921.42.1] of the Revised Code, for a chief legal officer of a municipal corporation or an official designated as prosecutor in a municipal corporation to appoint assistants and employees in accordance with sections 733.621 [733.62.1] and 2921.421 [2921.42.1] of the Revised Code, or for a township law director appointed under section 504.15 of the Revised Code to appoint assistants and employees in accordance with sections 504.151 [504.15.1] and 2921.421 [2921.42.1] of the Revised Code.†

(F) This section does not apply to a public contract in which a township trustee in a township with a population of five thousand or less in its unincorporated area, a member of the township trustee's family, or one of his business associates has an interest, if all of the following apply:

(1) The subject of the public contract is necessary supplies or services for the township and the amount of the contract is less than five thousand dollars per year.

(2) The supplies or services are being furnished to the township as part of a continuing course of dealing established before the township trustee held that office with the township;

(3) The treatment accorded the township is either preferential to or the same as that accorded other customers or clients in similar transactions;

(4) The entire transaction is conducted with full knowledge by the township of the interest of the township trustee, member of his family, or his business associate.††

(G) As used in this section:

(1) "Public contract" means any of the following:

(a) The purchase or acquisition, or a contract for the purchase or acquisition, of property or services by or for the use of the state, any of its political subdivisions, or any agency or instrumentality of either, including the employment of an individual by the state, any of its political subdivisions, or any agency or instrumentality of either;

(b) A contract for the design, construction, alteration, repair, or maintenance of any public property.

(2) "Chief legal officer" has the same meaning as in section 733.621 [733.62.1] of the Revised Code.

HISTORY: 134 v H 511 (Eff 1-1-74); 144 v S 359 (Eff 12-22-

92); 145 v H 152 (Eff 7-1-93); 145 v H 285 (Eff 3-2-94); 145 v H 150. Eff 6-23-94.

† This division was changed from (E) to (F) by HB 150 (145 v —), eff 6-23-94.

†† This division (F) was added by HB 285 (145 v —), eff 3-2-94.

Comment, Legislative Service Commission

Section 2921.42 of the Revised Code is amended by this [Sub. H.B. 150] and also by Am. Sub. H.B. 285 of the 120th General Assembly. Comparison of these amendments in pursuance of section 1.52 of the Revised Code discloses that they are not irreconcilable, so that they are required by that section to be harmonized to give effect to each amendment.

[§ 2921.42.1] § 2921.421 Conditions for prosecuting attorney's appointment of assistants and employees who are associated in the private practice of law.

(A) As used in this section:

(1) "Chief legal officer" has the same meaning as in section 733.621 [733.62.1] of the Revised Code.

(2) "Political subdivision" means a county, a municipal corporation, or a township that adopts the limited self-government form of government under Chapter 504. of the Revised Code.

(B) A prosecuting attorney may appoint assistants and employees, except a member of the family of the prosecuting attorney, in accordance with division (B) of section 309.06 of the Revised Code, a chief legal officer of a municipal corporation or an official designated as prosecutor in a municipal corporation may appoint assistants and employees, except a member of the family of the chief legal officer or official designated as prosecutor, in accordance with section 733.621 [733.62.1] of the Revised Code, and a township law director appointed under section 504.15 of the Revised Code may appoint assistants and employees, except a member of the family of the township law director, in accordance with section 504.151 [504.15.1] of the Revised Code, if all of the following apply:

(1) The services to be furnished by the appointee or employee are necessary services for the political subdivision or are authorized by the legislative authority, governing board, or other contracting authority of the political subdivision.

(2) The treatment accorded the political subdivision is either preferential to or the same as that accorded other clients or customers of the appointee or employee in similar transactions, or the legislative authority, governing board, or other contracting authority of the political subdivision, in its sole discretion, determines that the compensation and other terms of appointment or employment of the appointee or employee are fair and reasonable to the political subdivision.

(3) The appointment or employment is made after prior written disclosure to the legislative authority, governing board, or other contracting authority of the political subdivision of the business relationship between the prosecuting attorney, the chief legal officer or official designated as prosecutor in a municipal corporation, or the township law director and his appointee or employee. In the case of a municipal corporation, the disclosure may be made or evidenced in an ordinance, resolution, or other document that does either or both of the following:

(a) Authorizes the furnishing of services as required under division (B)(1) of this section;

(b) Determines that the compensation and other terms of appointment or employment of the appointee or employee are fair and reasonable to the political subdivision as required under division (B)(2) of this section.

(4) The prosecuting attorney, the elected chief legal officer, or the township law director does not receive any distributive share or other portion, in whole or in part, of the earnings of his business associate, partner, or employee paid by the political subdivision to the business associate, partner, or employee for services rendered for the political subdivision.

(C) It is not a violation of this section or of section 102.03 or 2921.42 of the Revised Code for the legislative authority, the governing board, or other contracting authority of a political subdivision to engage the services of any firm that practices the profession of law upon the terms approved by the legislative authority, the governing board, or the contracting authority, or to designate any partner, officer, or employee of that firm as a nonelected public official or employee of the political subdivision, whether the public office or position of employment is created by statute, charter, ordinance, resolution, or other legislative or administrative action.

HISTORY: 145 v H 285. Eff 3-2-94.

§ 2921.43 Soliciting or receiving improper compensation.

(A) No public servant shall knowingly solicit or accept and no person shall knowingly promise or give to a public servant either of the following:

(1) Any compensation, other than as allowed by divisions (G), (H), and (I) of section 102.03 of the Revised Code or other provisions of law, to perform his official duties, to perform any other act or service in the public servant's public capacity, for the general performance of the duties of the public servant's public office or public employment, or as a supplement to the public servant's public compensation;

(2) Additional or greater fees or costs than are allowed by law to perform his official duties.

(B) No public servant for his own personal or business use and no person for his own personal or business use or for the personal or business use of a public servant or party official, shall solicit or accept anything of value in consideration of either of the following:

(1) Appointing or securing, maintaining, or renewing the appointment of any person to any public office, employment, or agency;

(2) Preferring, or maintaining the status of, any public employee with respect to his compensation, duties, placement, location, promotion, or other material aspects of his employment.

(C) No person for the benefit of a political party, campaign committee, legislative campaign fund, or political action committee shall coerce any contribution in consideration of either of the following:

(1) Appointing or securing, maintaining, or renewing the appointment of any person to any public office, employment, or agency;

(2) Preferring, or maintaining the status of, any public employee with respect to his compensation, duties, placement, location, promotion, or other material aspects of his employment.

(D) Whoever violates this section is guilty of soliciting improper compensation, a misdemeanor of the first degree.

(E) A public servant who is convicted of a violation of this section is disqualified from holding any public office, employment, or position of trust in this state for a period of seven years from the date of conviction.

(F) Divisions (A), (B), and (C) of this section do not prohibit a person from making voluntary contributions to a political party, campaign committee, legislative campaign fund, or political action committee or prohibit a political party, campaign committee, legislative campaign fund, or political action committee from accepting voluntary contributions.

HISTORY: 134 v H 511 (Eff 1-1-74); 135 v S 46 (Eff 7-23-74); 141 v H 300 (Eff 9-17-86); 146 v S 8. Eff 8-23-95.

[§ 2921.43.1] § 2921.431 Repealed, 146 v S 8, § 2 [136 v H 784]. Eff 8-23-95.

This section concerned solicitation of improper contributions by county officers. See now section 3517.09.2.

§ 2921.44 Dereliction of duty.

(A) No law enforcement officer shall negligently do any of the following:

(1) Fail to serve a lawful warrant without delay;
(2) Fail to prevent or halt the commission of an offense or to apprehend an offender, when it is in his power to do so alone or with available assistance.

(B) No law enforcement, ministerial, or judicial officer shall negligently fail to perform a lawful duty in a criminal case or proceeding.

(C) No officer, having charge of a detention facility, shall negligently do any of the following:

(1) Allow the detention facility to become littered or unsanitary;
(2) Fail to provide persons confined in the detention facility with adequate food, clothing, bedding, shelter, and medical attention;
(3) Fail to control an unruly prisoner, or to prevent intimidation of or physical harm to a prisoner by another;

(4) Allow a prisoner to escape;
(5) Fail to observe any lawful and reasonable regulation for the management of the detention facility.

(D) No public official of the state shall recklessly create a deficiency, incur a liability, or expend a greater sum than is appropriated by the general assembly for the use in any one year of the department, agency, or institution of the state with which the public official is connected.

(E) No public servant shall recklessly fail to perform a duty expressly imposed by law with respect to his office, or recklessly do any act expressly forbidden by law with respect to his office.

(F) Whoever violates this section is guilty of dereliction of duty, a misdemeanor of the second degree.

HISTORY: 134 v H 511. Eff 1-1-74.

§ 2921.45 Interfering with civil rights.

(A) No public servant, under color of his office, employment, or authority, shall knowingly deprive, or conspire or attempt to deprive any person of a constitutional or statutory right.

(B) Whoever violates this section is guilty of interfering with civil rights, a misdemeanor of the first degree.

HISTORY: 134 v H 511. Eff 1-1-74.

[IMPERSONATING PEACE OFFICER]

§ 2921.51 Impersonating a peace officer or private policeman.

(A) As used in this section:

(1) "Peace officer" means a sheriff, deputy sheriff, marshal, deputy marshal, member of the organized police department of a municipal corporation, or township constable, who is employed by a political subdivision of this state, a member of a police force employed by a metropolitan housing authority under division (D) of section 3735.31 of the Revised Code, a member of a police force employed by a regional transit authority under division (Y) of section 306.35 of the Revised Code, a state university law enforcement officer appointed under section 3345.04 of the Revised Code, an Ohio veterans' home policeman appointed under section 5907.02 of the Revised Code, or a state highway patrol trooper and whose primary duties are to preserve the peace, to protect life and property, and to enforce the laws, ordinances, or rules of the state or any of its political subdivisions.

(2) "Private policeman" means any security guard, special policeman, private detective, or other person who is privately employed in a police capacity.

(3) "Impersonate" means to act the part of, assume the identity of, wear the uniform or any part of the uniform of, or display the identification of a particular person or of a member of a class of persons with purpose

to make another person believe that the actor is that particular person or is a member of that class of persons.

(B) No person shall impersonate a peace officer or a private policeman.

(C) No person, by impersonating a peace officer or a private policeman, shall arrest or detain any person, search any person, or search the property of any person.

(D) No person, with purpose to commit or facilitate the commission of an offense, shall impersonate a peace officer, a private policeman, or an officer, agent, or employee of the state.

(E) No person shall commit a felony while impersonating a peace officer, a private policeman, or an officer, agent, or employee of the state.

(F) It is an affirmative defense to a charge under division (B) of this section that the impersonation of the peace officer was for a lawful purpose.

(G) Whoever violates division (B) of this section is guilty of a misdemeanor of the fourth degree. Whoever violates division (C) or (D) of this section is guilty of a misdemeanor of the first degree. If the purpose of a violation of division (D) of this section is to commit or facilitate the commission of a felony, a violation of division (D) is a felony of the fourth degree. Whoever violates division (E) of this section is guilty of a felony of the third degree.

HISTORY: 142 v H 708 (Eff 4-19-88); 144 v S 144 (Eff 8-8-91); 146 v S 2. Eff 7-1-96.

Analogous to former RC § 2921.51 (136 v H 1144; 137 v H 588; 140 v H 129; 142 v H 231; 142 v H 261), repealed 142 v H 708, § 2, eff 4-19-88.

The effective date is set by section 6 of SB 2.

§ 2921.52 Using sham legal process.

(A) As used in this section:

(1) "Lawfully issued" means adopted, issued, or rendered in accordance with the United States constitution, the constitution of a state, and the applicable statutes, rules, regulations, and ordinances of the United States, a state, and the political subdivisions of a state.

(2) "State" means a state of the United States, including without limitation, the state legislature, the highest court of the state that has statewide jurisdiction, the offices of all elected state officers, and all departments, boards, offices, commissions, agencies, institutions, and other instrumentalities of the state. "State" does not include the political subdivisions of the state.

(3) "Political subdivisions" means municipal corporations, townships, counties, school districts, and all other bodies corporate and politic that are organized under state law and are responsible for governmental activities only in geographical areas smaller than that of a state.

(4) "Sham legal process" means an instrument that meets all of the following conditions:

(a) It is not lawfully issued.

(b) It purports to do any of the following:

(i) To be a summons, subpoena, judgment, or order of a court, a law enforcement officer, or a legislative, executive, or administrative body.

(ii) To assert jurisdiction over or determine the legal or equitable status, rights, duties, powers, or privileges of any person or property.

(iii) To require or authorize the search, seizure, indictment, arrest, trial, or sentencing of any person or property.

(c) It is designed to make another person believe that it is lawfully issued.

(B) No person shall, knowing the sham legal process to be sham legal process, do any of the following:

(1) Knowingly issue, display, deliver, distribute, or otherwise use sham legal process;

(2) Knowingly use sham legal process to arrest, detain, search, or seize any person or the property of another person;

(3) Knowingly commit or facilitate the commission of an offense, using sham legal process;

(4) Knowingly commit a felony by using sham legal process.

(C) It is an affirmative defense to a charge under division (B)(1) or (2) of this section that the use of sham legal process was for a lawful purpose.

(D) Whoever violates this section is guilty of using sham legal process. A violation of division (B)(1) of this section is a misdemeanor of the fourth degree. A violation of division (B)(2) or (3) of this section is a misdemeanor of the first degree, except that, if the purpose of a violation of division (B)(3) of this section is to commit or facilitate the commission of a felony, a violation of division (B)(3) of this section is a felony of the fourth degree. A violation of division (B)(4) of this section is a felony of the third degree.

(E) A person who violates this section is liable in a civil action to any person harmed by the violation for injury, death, or loss to person or property incurred as a result of the commission of the offense and for reasonable attorney's fees, court costs, and other expenses incurred as a result of prosecuting the civil action commenced under this division. A civil action under this division is not the exclusive remedy of a person who incurs injury, death, or loss to person or property as a result of a violation of this section.

HISTORY: 146 v H 644. Eff 11-6-96.

CHAPTER 2923: CONSPIRACY, ATTEMPT, AND COMPLICITY; WEAPONS CONTROL; CORRUPT ACTIVITY

Section

[CONSPIRACY, ATTEMPT, AND COMPLICITY]

2923.01 Conspiracy.
[2923.01.1, 2923.01.2] 2923.011, 2923.012 Repealed.
2923.02 Attempt.
[2923.02.1] 2923.021 Repealed.
2923.03 Complicity.
2923.04 Repealed.
2923.05-2923.10 Repealed.

[WEAPONS CONTROL]

2923.11 Definitions.
2923.12 Carrying concealed weapons.
[2923.12.1] 2923.121 Illegal possession of firearm in liquor permit premises.
[2923.12.2] 2923.122 Illegal conveyance or possession of deadly weapon or dangerous ordnance or illegal possession of object indistinguishable from firearm on school premises.
[2923.12.3] 2923.123 Illegal conveyance of deadly weapon or dangerous ordnance into courthouse; illegal possession or control in courthouse.
2923.13 Having weapons while under disability.
[2923.13.1] 2923.131 Possession of deadly weapon while under detention.
2923.14 Relief from disability.
2923.15 Using weapons while intoxicated.
2923.16 Improperly handling firearms in a motor vehicle.
[2923.16.1] 2923.161 Improperly discharging a firearm at or into a habitation or school.
2923.17 Unlawful possession of dangerous ordnance.
2923.18 License or permit to possess dangerous ordnance.
2923.19 Failure to secure dangerous ordnance.
2923.20 Unlawful transaction in weapons.
2923.21 Improperly furnishing firearms to a minor.
[2923.21.1] 2923.211 Underage purchase of firearm or handgun.
2923.22 Permitted interstate transactions in firearms.
2923.23 Immunity from prosecution.
2923.24 Possessing criminal tools.
2923.25 Repealed.
[2923.25.1] 2923.251 Repealed.
2923.26-2923.30 Repealed.

[CORRUPT ACTIVITY]

2923.31 Definitions.
2923.32 Engaging in pattern of corrupt activity; forfeiture.
2923.33 Motion and order to preserve reachability of property subject to forfeit.
2923.34 Civil proceedings for relief from violation; civil penalty.
2923.35 Disposition of forfeited property, fine or civil penalty.
2923.36 Filing of corrupt activity lien notice; lis pendens.
2923.41-2923.57 Repealed.
2923.61 Repealed.
2923.99 Repealed.

[CONSPIRACY, ATTEMPT, AND COMPLICITY]

§ 2923.01 Conspiracy.

(A) No person, with purpose to commit or to promote or facilitate the commission of aggravated murder, murder, kidnapping, compelling prostitution, promoting prostitution, aggravated arson, arson, aggravated robbery, robbery, aggravated burglary, burglary, engaging in a pattern of corrupt activity, corrupting another with drugs, a felony drug trafficking, manufacturing, processing, or possession offense, theft of drugs, or illegal processing of drug documents, the commission of a felony offense of unauthorized use of a vehicle, or the commission of a violation of any provision of Chapter 3734. of the Revised Code, other than section 3734.18 of the Revised Code, that relates to hazardous wastes, shall do either of the following:

(1) With another person or persons, plan or aid in planning the commission of any of the specified offenses;

(2) Agree with another person or persons that one or more of them will engage in conduct that facilitates the commission of any of the specified offenses.

(B) No person shall be convicted of conspiracy unless a substantial overt act in furtherance of the conspiracy is alleged and proved to have been done by the accused or a person with whom the accused conspired, subsequent to the accused's entrance into the conspiracy. For purposes of this section, an overt act is substantial when it is of a character that manifests a purpose on the part of the actor that the object of the conspiracy should be completed.

(C) When the offender knows or has reasonable cause to believe that a person with whom the offender conspires also has conspired or is conspiring with another to commit the same offense, the offender is guilty of conspiring with that other person, even though the other person's identity may be unknown to the offender.

(D) It is no defense to a charge under this section that, in retrospect, commission of the offense that was the object of the conspiracy was impossible under the circumstances.

(E) A conspiracy terminates when the offense or offenses that are its objects are committed, or when it is abandoned by all conspirators. In the absence of abandonment, it is no defense to a charge under this section that no offense that was the object of the conspiracy was committed.

(F) A person who conspires to commit more than one offense is guilty of only one conspiracy, when the offenses are the object of the same agreement or continuous conspiratorial relationship.

(G) When a person is convicted of committing or attempting to commit a specific offense or of complicity in the commission of or attempt to commit the specific offense, the person shall not be convicted of conspiracy involving the same offense.

(H)(1) No person shall be convicted of conspiracy upon the testimony of a person with whom the defendant conspired, unsupported by other evidence.

(2) If a person with whom the defendant allegedly has conspired testifies against the defendant in a case in which the defendant is charged with conspiracy and if the testimony is supported by other evidence, the court, when it charges the jury, shall state substantially the following:

"The testimony of an accomplice that is supported by other evidence does not become inadmissible because of the accomplice's complicity, moral turpitude, or self-interest, but the admitted or claimed complicity of a witness may affect the witness' credibility and make the witness' testimony subject to grave suspicion, and require that it be weighed with great caution.

It is for you, as jurors, in the light of all the facts presented to you from the witness stand, to evaluate such testimony and to determine its quality and worth or its lack of quality and worth."

(3) "Conspiracy," as used in division (H)(1) of this section, does not include any conspiracy that results in an attempt to commit an offense or in the commission of an offense.

(I) The following are affirmative defenses to a charge of conspiracy:

(1) After conspiring to commit an offense, the actor thwarted the success of the conspiracy under circumstances manifesting a complete and voluntary renunciation of the actor's criminal purpose.

(2) After conspiring to commit an offense, the actor abandoned the conspiracy prior to the commission of or attempt to commit any offense that was the object of the conspiracy, either by advising all other conspirators of the actor's abandonment, or by informing any law enforcement authority of the existence of the conspiracy and of the actor's participation in the conspiracy.

(J) Whoever violates this section is guilty of conspiracy, which is one of the following:

(1) A felony of the first degree, when one of the objects of the conspiracy is aggravated murder, murder, or an offense for which the maximum penalty is imprisonment for life;

(2) A felony of the next lesser degree than the most serious offense that is the object of the conspiracy, when the most serious offense that is the object of the conspiracy is a felony of the first, second, third, or fourth degree;

(3) A felony punishable by a fine of not more than twenty-five thousand dollars or imprisonment for not more than eighteen months, or both, when the offense that is the object of the conspiracy is a violation of any provision of Chapter 3734. of the Revised Code, other than section 3734.18 of the Revised Code, that relates to hazardous wastes;

(4) A misdemeanor of the first degree, when the most serious offense that is the object of the conspiracy is a felony of the fifth degree.

(K) This section does not define a separate conspiracy offense or penalty where conspiracy is defined as an offense by one or more sections of the Revised Code, other than this section. In such a case, however:

(1) With respect to the offense specified as the object of the conspiracy in the other section or sections, division (A) of this section defines the voluntary act or acts and culpable mental state necessary to constitute the conspiracy;

(2) Divisions (B) to (I) of this section are incorporated by reference in the conspiracy offense defined by the other section or sections of the Revised Code.

(L)(1) In addition to the penalties that otherwise are imposed for conspiracy, a person who is found guilty of conspiracy to engage in a pattern of corrupt activity is subject to divisions (B)(2), (3), (4), and (5) of section 2923.32 of the Revised Code.

(2) If a person is convicted of or pleads guilty to conspiracy and if the most serious offense that is the object of the conspiracy is a felony drug trafficking, manufacturing, processing, or possession offense, in addition to the penalties or sanctions that may be imposed for the conspiracy under division (J)(2) or (4) of this section and Chapter 2929. of the Revised Code, both of the following apply:

(a) The provisions of divisions (D), (F), and (G) of section 2925.03, division (D) of section 2925.04, division (D) of section 2925.05, division (D) of section 2925.06, and division (E) of section 2925.11 of the Revised Code that pertain to mandatory and additional fines, driver's or commercial driver's license or permit revocations or suspensions, and professionally licensed persons or persons who have been admitted to the bar by order of the supreme court and that would apply under the appropriate provisions of those divisions to a person who is convicted of or pleads guilty to the felony drug trafficking, manufacturing, processing, or possession offense that is the most serious offense that is the basis of the conspiracy shall apply to the person who is convicted of or pleads guilty to the conspiracy as if the person had been convicted of or pleaded guilty to the felony drug trafficking, manufacturing, processing, or possession offense that is the most serious offense that is the basis of the conspiracy.

(b) The court that imposes sentence upon the person who is convicted of or pleads guilty to the conspiracy shall comply with the provisions identified as being applicable under division (L)(2) of this section, in addition to any other penalty or sanction that it imposes for the conspiracy under division (J)(2) or (4) of this section and Chapter 2929. of the Revised Code.

(M) As used in this section, "felony drug trafficking, manufacturing, processing, or possession offense"

means any of the following that is a felony:
 (1) A violation of section 2925.03, 2925.04, 2925.05, or 2925.06 of the Revised Code;
 (2) A violation of section 2925.11 of the Revised Code that is not a minor drug possession offense, as defined in section 2925.01 of the Revised Code.
 (M) As used in this section:
 (1) "Felony drug trafficking, manufacturing, processing, or possession offense" means any of the following that is a felony:
 (a) A violation of section 2925.03, 2925.04, 2925.05, or 2925.06 of the Revised Code;
 (b) A violation of section 2925.11 of the Revised Code that is not a minor drug possession offense.
 (2) "Minor drug possession offense" has the same meaning as in section 2925.01 of the Revised Code.†

HISTORY: 134 v H 511 (Eff 1-1-74); 136 v H 300 (Eff 7-1-76); 139 v H 108 (Eff 6-23-82); 139 v S 199 (Eff 7-1-83); 140 v S 210 (Eff 7-1-83); 140 v H 651 (Eff 10-1-84); 141 v H 5 (Eff 1-1-86); 141 v H 338 (Eff 9-17-86); 141 v H 428 (Eff 12-23-86); 146 v S 2 (Eff 7-1-96); 146 v H 125 (Eff 7-1-96); 146 v S 269. Eff 7-1-96.

Publisher's Note

The amendments made by HB 125 (146 v —) and SB 269 (146 v —) have been combined. Please see provisions of RC § 1.52.

The effective date is set by section 5 of SB 269.

† The second division (M) is the wording as enacted in SB 269 (146 v —).

[§§ 2923.01.1, 2923.01.2]
§§ 2923.011, 2923.012 Repealed, 134 v H 511, § 2 [131 v 676; 132 v H 1; 133 v H 288]. Eff 1-1-74.

These sections concerned carrying firearms, explosives and other concealed weapons.

§ 2923.02 Attempt.

(A) No person, purposely or knowingly, and when purpose or knowledge is sufficient culpability for the commission of an offense, shall engage in conduct that, if successful, would constitute or result in the offense.

(B) It is no defense to a charge under this section that, in retrospect, commission of the offense that was the object of the attempt was either factually or legally impossible under the attendant circumstances, if that offense could have been committed had the attendant circumstances been as the actor believed them to be.

(C) No person who is convicted of committing a specific offense, of complicity in the commission of an offense, or of conspiracy to commit an offense shall be convicted of an attempt to commit the same offense in violation of this section.

(D) It is an affirmative defense to a charge under this section that the actor abandoned the actor's effort to commit the offense or otherwise prevented its commission, under circumstances manifesting a complete and voluntary renunciation of the actor's criminal purpose.

(E) Whoever violates this section is guilty of an attempt to commit an offense. An attempt to commit aggravated murder, murder, or an offense for which the maximum penalty is imprisonment for life is a felony of the first degree. An attempt to commit any other offense is an offense of the next lesser degree than the offense attempted. In the case of an attempt to commit an offense other than a violation of Chapter 3734. of the Revised Code that is not specifically classified, an attempt is a misdemeanor of the first degree if the offense attempted is a felony, and a misdemeanor of the fourth degree if the offense attempted is a misdemeanor. In the case of an attempt to commit a violation of any provision of Chapter 3734. of the Revised Code, other than section 3734.18 of the Revised Code, that relates to hazardous wastes, an attempt is a felony punishable by a fine of not more than twenty-five thousand dollars or imprisonment for not more than eighteen months, or both. An attempt to commit a minor misdemeanor, or to engage in conspiracy, is not an offense under this section.

HISTORY: 134 v H 511 (Eff 1-1-74); 140 v S 210 (Eff 7-1-83); 140 v H 651 (Eff 10-1-84); 144 v H 225 (Eff 10-23-91); 146 v S 2. Eff 7-1-96.

Not analogous to former RC § 2923.02 (GC §§ 12819-1, 12819-2; 102 v 124; Bureau of Code Revision, 10-1-53), repealed 134 v H 511, § 2, eff 1-1-74.

The effective date is set by section 6 of SB 2.

[§ 2923.02.1] § 2923.021 Repealed, 134 v H 511, § 2 [125 v S 62(125)]. Eff 1-1-74.

This section concerned sale or possession of switch or spring knife.

§ 2923.03 Complicity.

(A) No person, acting with the kind of culpability required for the commission of an offense, shall do any of the following:
 (1) Solicit or procure another to commit the offense;
 (2) Aid or abet another in committing the offense;
 (3) Conspire with another to commit the offense in violation of section 2923.01 of the Revised Code;
 (4) Cause an innocent or irresponsible person to commit the offense.

(B) It is no defense to a charge under this section that no person with whom the accused was in complicity has been convicted as a principal offender.

(C) No person shall be convicted of complicity under this section unless an offense is actually committed, but a person may be convicted of complicity in an attempt to commit an offense in violation of section 2923.02 of the Revised Code.

(D) If an alleged accomplice of the defendant testifies against the defendant in a case in which the defendant is charged with complicity in the commission of or an attempt to commit an offense, an attempt to commit an offense, or an offense, the court, when it charges the jury, shall state substantially the following:

"The testimony of an accomplice does not become inadmissible because of his complicity, moral turpitude, or self-interest, but the admitted or claimed complicity of a witness may affect his credibility and make his testimony subject to grave suspicion, and require that it be weighed with great caution.

It is for you, as jurors, in the light of all the facts presented to you from the witness stand, to evaluate such testimony and to determine its quality and worth or its lack of quality and worth."

(E) It is an affirmative defense to a charge under this section that, prior to the commission of or attempt to commit the offense, the actor terminated his complicity, under circumstances manifesting a complete and voluntary renunciation of his criminal purpose.

(F) Whoever violates this section is guilty of complicity in the commission of an offense, and shall be prosecuted and punished as if he were a principal offender. A charge of complicity may be stated in terms of this section, or in terms of the principal offense.

HISTORY: 134 v H 511 (Eff 1-1-74); 141 v H 338. Eff 9-17-86.

Not analogous to former RC § 2923.03 (GC § 12819-3; 115 v 189; Bureau of Code Revision, 10-1-53; 129 v 420), repealed 134 v H 511, § 2, eff 1-1-74.

§ 2923.04
Repealed, 141 v H 5, § 2 [134 v H 511; 135 v H 716]. Eff 1-1-86.

This section concerned engaging in organized crime. See now sections 2923.31 et seq.

§§ 2923.05, 2923.06, 2923.07
Repealed, 134 v H 511, § 2 [RS § 7034; S&C 437; GC §§ 12819-6, 12819-7, 13391; 44 v 77; 67 v 25; 77 v 85; 115 v 190; Bureau of Code Revision, 10-1-53; 132 v H 45]. Eff 1-1-74.

These sections concerned offenses regarding sale of firearms, war trophies and graves robbing.

§§ 2923.08, 2923.09, 2923.10
Repealed, 134 v H 511, § 2 [RS §§ 1470, 7034; S&C 228, 437; GC §§ 12684, 13391-1, 13392; 44 v 77; 54 v 187, § 5; 67 v 25; 77 v 85; 120 v 111; Bureau of Code Revision, 10-1-53; 126 v 575; 129 v H 1]. Eff 1-1-74.

These sections concerned offenses regarding corpses.

[WEAPONS CONTROL]

§ 2923.11 Definitions.

As used in sections 2923.11 to 2923.24 of the Revised Code:

(A) "Deadly weapon" means any instrument, device, or thing capable of inflicting death, and designed or specially adapted for use as a weapon, or possessed, carried, or used as a weapon.

(B)(1) "Firearm" means any deadly weapon capable of expelling or propelling one or more projectiles by the action of an explosive or combustible propellant. "Firearm" includes an unloaded firearm, and any firearm that is inoperable but that can readily be rendered operable.

(2) When determining whether a firearm is capable of expelling or propelling one or more projectiles by the action of an explosive or combustible propellant, the trier of fact may rely upon circumstantial evidence, including, but not limited to, the representations and actions of the individual exercising control over the firearm.

(C) "Handgun" means any firearm designed to be fired while being held in one hand.

(D) "Semi-automatic firearm" means any firearm designed or specially adapted to fire a single cartridge and automatically chamber a succeeding cartridge ready to fire, with a single function of the trigger.

(E) "Automatic firearm" means any firearm designed or specially adapted to fire a succession of cartridges with a single function of the trigger. "Automatic firearm" also means any semi-automatic firearm designed or specially adapted to fire more than thirty-one cartridges without reloading, other than a firearm chambering only .22 caliber short, long, or long-rifle cartridges.

(F) "Sawed-off firearm" means a shotgun with a barrel less than eighteen inches long, or a rifle with a barrel less than sixteen inches long, or a shotgun or rifle less than twenty-six inches long overall.

(G) "Zip-gun" means any of the following:

(1) Any firearm of crude and extemporized manufacture;

(2) Any device, including without limitation a starter's pistol, that is not designed as a firearm, but that is specially adapted for use as a firearm;

(3) Any industrial tool, signalling device, or safety device, that is not designed as a firearm, but that as designed is capable of use as such, when possessed, carried, or used as a firearm.

(H) "Explosive device" means any device designed or specially adapted to cause physical harm to persons or property by means of an explosion, and consisting of an explosive substance or agency and a means to detonate it. "Explosive device" includes without limitation any bomb, any explosive demolition device, any blasting cap or detonator containing an explosive charge, and any pressure vessel that has been knowingly tampered with or arranged so as to explode.

(I) "Incendiary device" means any firebomb, and any device designed or specially adapted to cause physical harm to persons or property by means of fire, and consisting of an incendiary substance or agency and a means to ignite it.

(J) "Ballistic knife" means a knife with a detachable blade that is propelled by a spring-operated mechanism.

(K) "Dangerous ordnance" means any of the following, except as provided in division (L) of this section:

(1) Any automatic or sawed-off firearm, zip-gun, or ballistic knife;

(2) Any explosive device or incendiary device;

(3) Nitroglycerin, nitrocellulose, nitrostarch, PETN, cyclonite, TNT, picric acid, and other high explosives; amatol, tritonal, tetrytol, pentolite, pecretol, cyclotol, and other high explosive compositions; plastic explosives; dynamite, blasting gelatin, gelatin dynamite, sensitized ammonium nitrate, liquid-oxygen blasting explosives, blasting powder, and other blasting agents; and any other explosive substance having sufficient brisance or power to be particularly suitable for use as a military explosive, or for use in mining, quarrying, excavating, or demolitions;

(4) Any firearm, rocket launcher, mortar, artillery piece, grenade, mine, bomb, torpedo, or similar weapon, designed and manufactured for military purposes, and the ammunition for that weapon;

(5) Any firearm muffler or silencer;

(6) Any combination of parts that is intended by the owner for use in converting any firearm or other device into a dangerous ordnance.

(L) "Dangerous ordnance" does not include any of the following:

(1) Any firearm, including a military weapon and the ammunition for that weapon, and regardless of its actual age, that employs a percussion cap or other obsolete ignition system, or that is designed and safe for use only with black powder;

(2) Any pistol, rifle, or shotgun, designed or suitable for sporting purposes, including a military weapon as issued or as modified, and the ammunition for that weapon, unless the firearm is an automatic or sawed-off firearm;

(3) Any cannon or other artillery piece that, regardless of its actual age, is of a type in accepted use prior to 1887, has no mechanical, hydraulic, pneumatic, or other system for absorbing recoil and returning the tube into battery without displacing the carriage, and is designed and safe for use only with black powder;

(4) Black powder, priming quills, and percussion caps possessed and lawfully used to fire a cannon of a type defined in division (L)(3) of this section during displays, celebrations, organized matches or shoots, and target practice, and smokeless and black powder, primers, and percussion caps possessed and lawfully used as a propellant or ignition device in small-arms or small-arms ammunition;

(5) Dangerous ordnance that is inoperable or inert and cannot readily be rendered operable or activated, and that is kept as a trophy, souvenir, curio, or museum piece.

(6) Any device that is expressly excepted from the definition of a destructive device pursuant to the "Gun Control Act of 1968," 82 Stat. 1213, 18 U.S.C. 921(a)(4), as amended, and regulations issued under that act.

(M) "Explosive" means any chemical compound, mixture, or device, the primary or common purpose of which is to function by explosion. "Explosive" includes all materials that have been classified as class A, class B, or class C explosives by the United States department of transportation in its regulations and includes, but is not limited to, dynamite, black powder, pellet powders, initiating explosives, blasting caps, electric blasting caps, safety fuses, fuse igniters, squibs, cordeau detonant fuses, instantaneous fuses, and igniter cords and igniters. "Explosive" does not include "fireworks," as defined in section 3743.01 of the Revised Code, or any explosive that is not subject to regulation under the rules of the fire marshal adopted pursuant to section 3737.82 of the Revised Code.

HISTORY: 134 v H 511 (Eff 1-1-74); 137 v H 728 (Eff 8-22-78); 141 v H 51 (Eff 7-30-86); 142 v H 24 (Eff 7-31-87); 143 v S 96 (Eff 6-13-90); 146 v S 2. Eff 7-1-96.

Not analogous to former RC § 2923.11 (RS § 7035; 67 v 25; 78 v 131; GC § 12693; Bureau of Code Revision, 10-1-53), repealed 134 v H 511, § 2, eff 1-1-74.

The effective date is set by section 6 of SB 2.

§ 2923.12 Carrying concealed weapons.

(A) No person shall knowingly carry or have, concealed on his or her person or concealed ready at hand, any deadly weapon or dangerous ordnance.

(B) This section does not apply to officers, agents, or employees of this or any other state or the United States, or to law enforcement officers, authorized to carry concealed weapons or dangerous ordnance, and acting within the scope of their duties.

(C) It is an affirmative defense to a charge under this section of carrying or having control of a weapon other than dangerous ordnance, that the actor was not otherwise prohibited by law from having the weapon, and that any of the following apply:

(1) The weapon was carried or kept ready at hand by the actor for defensive purposes, while the actor was engaged in or was going to or from the actor's lawful business or occupation, which business or occupation was of such character or was necessarily carried on in such manner or at such a time or place as to render the actor particularly susceptible to criminal attack, such as would justify a prudent person in going armed.

(2) The weapon was carried or kept ready at hand by the actor for defensive purposes, while the actor was engaged in a lawful activity and had reasonable cause to fear a criminal attack upon the actor or a member of the actor's family, or upon the actor's home, such as would justify a prudent person in going armed.

(3) The weapon was carried or kept ready at hand by the actor for any lawful purpose and while in the actor's own home.

(4) The weapon was being transported in a motor

vehicle for any lawful purpose, and was not on the actor's person, and, if the weapon was a firearm, was carried in compliance with the applicable requirements of division (C) of section 2923.16 of the Revised Code.

(D) Whoever violates this section is guilty of carrying concealed weapons, a misdemeanor of the first degree. If the offender previously has been convicted of a violation of this section or of any offense of violence, if the weapon involved is a firearm that is either loaded or for which the offender has ammunition ready at hand, or if the weapon involved is dangerous ordnance, carrying concealed weapons is a felony of the fourth degree. If the weapon involved is a firearm and the violation of this section is committed at premises for which a D permit has been issued under Chapter 4303. of the Revised Code or if the offense is committed aboard an aircraft, or with purpose to carry a concealed weapon aboard an aircraft, regardless of the weapon involved, carrying concealed weapons is a felony of the third degree.

HISTORY: 134 v H 511 (Eff 1-1-74); 135 v H 716 (Eff 1-1-74); 141 v H 51 (Eff 7-30-86); 146 v S 2. Eff 7-1-96.

Not analogous to former RC § 2923.12 (GC § 13421-23; 108 v PtI, 189; Bureau of Code Revision, 10-1-53), repealed 134 v H 511, § 2, eff 1-1-74.

The effective date is set by section 6 of SB 2.

See provisions, § 4 of SB 210 (140 v—) following RC § 2951.02.

[§ 2923.12.1] § 2923.121 Illegal possession of firearm in liquor permit premises.

(A) No person shall possess a firearm in any room in which liquor is being dispensed in premises for which a D permit has been issued under Chapter 4303. of the Revised Code.

(B)(1) This section does not apply to officers, agents, or employees of this or any other state or the United States, or to law enforcement officers, authorized to carry firearms, and acting within the scope of their duties.

(2) This section does not apply to any room used for the accommodation of guests of a hotel, as defined in section 4301.01 of the Revised Code.

(3) This section does not prohibit any person who is a member of a veteran's organization, as defined in section 2915.01 of the Revised Code, from possessing a rifle in any room in any premises owned, leased, or otherwise under the control of the veteran's organization, if the rifle is not loaded with live ammunition and if the person otherwise is not prohibited by law from having the rifle.

(4) This section does not apply to any person possessing or displaying firearms in any room used to exhibit unloaded firearms for sale or trade in a soldiers' memorial established pursuant to Chapter 345. of the Revised Code, in a convention center, or in any other public meeting place, if the person is an exhibitor, trader, purchaser, or seller of firearms and is not otherwise prohibited by law from possessing, trading, purchasing, or selling the firearms.

(C) It is an affirmative defense to a charge under this section of illegal possession of a firearm in liquor permit premises, that the actor was not otherwise prohibited by law from having the firearm, and that any of the following apply:

(1) The firearm was carried or kept ready at hand by the actor for defensive purposes, while the actor was engaged in or was going to or from the actor's lawful business or occupation, which business or occupation was of such character or was necessarily carried on in such manner or at such a time or place as to render the actor particularly susceptible to criminal attack, such as would justify a prudent person in going armed.

(2) The firearm was carried or kept ready at hand by the actor for defensive purposes, while the actor was engaged in a lawful activity, and had reasonable cause to fear a criminal attack upon the actor or a member of the actor's family, or upon the actor's home, such as would justify a prudent person in going armed.

(D) Whoever violates this section is guilty of illegal possession of a firearm in liquor permit premises, a felony of the fifth degree.

HISTORY: 141 v H 51 (Eff 7-30-86); 141 v H 39 (Eff 2-21-87); 146 v S 2. Eff 7-1-96.

The effective date is set by section 6 of SB 2.

[§ 2923.12.2] § 2923.122 Illegal conveyance or possession of deadly weapon or dangerous ordnance or illegal possession of object indistinguishable from firearm on school premises.

(A) No person shall knowingly convey, or attempt to convey, a deadly weapon or dangerous ordnance onto school premises, into a school or school building, to a school activity, or onto a school bus.

(B) No person shall knowingly possess a deadly weapon or dangerous ordnance on school premises, in a school or school building, at a school activity, or on a school bus.

(C) No person shall knowingly possess an object on school premises, in a school or school building, at a school activity, or on a school bus if both of the following apply:

(1) The object is indistinguishable from a firearm, whether or not the object is capable of being fired.

(2) The person indicates that the person possesses the object and that it is a firearm, or the person knowingly displays or brandishes the object and indicates that it is a firearm.

(D) This section does not apply to officers, agents, or employees of this or any other state or the United States, or to law enforcement officers, authorized to carry deadly weapons or dangerous ordnance and acting within the scope of their duties, to any security officer employed by a board of education or governing body of a school during the time that the security officer is on duty pursuant to that contract of employment, or to any other person who has written authorization from the board of education or governing body of a school to convey deadly weapons or dangerous ordnance onto school premises, into a school or school building, to a school activity, or onto a school bus or to possess a deadly weapon or dangerous ordnance on school premises, in a school or school building, at a school activity, or on a school bus and who conveys or possesses the deadly weapon or dangerous ordnance in accordance with that authorization.

Division (C) of this section does not apply to premises upon which home schooling is conducted. Division (C) of this section also does not apply to a school administrator, teacher, or employee who possesses an object that is indistinguishable from a firearm for legitimate school purposes during the course of employment, a student who uses an object that is indistinguishable from a firearm under the direction of a school administrator, teacher, or employee, or any other person who with the express prior approval of a school administrator possesses an object that is indistinguishable from a firearm for a legitimate purpose, including the use of the object in a ceremonial activity, a play, reenactment, or other dramatic presentation, or a ROTC activity or another similar use of the object.

(E)(1) Whoever violates division (A) or (B) of this section is guilty of illegal conveyance or possession of a deadly weapon or dangerous ordnance on school premises. Except as otherwise provided in this division, illegal conveyance or possession of a deadly weapon or dangerous ordnance on school premises is a felony of the fifth degree. If the offender previously has been convicted of a violation of this section, illegal conveyance or possession of a deadly weapon or dangerous ordnance on school premises is a felony of the fourth degree.

(2) Whoever violates division (C) of this section is guilty of illegal possession of an object indistinguishable from a firearm on school premises. Except as otherwise provided in this division, illegal possession of an object indistinguishable from a firearm on school premises is a misdemeanor of the first degree. If the offender previously has been convicted of a violation of this section, illegal possession of an object indistinguishable from a firearm on school premises is a felony of the fifth degree.

[(E)(1) In addition to any other penalty imposed upon a person who is convicted of or pleads guilty to a violation of this section and subject to division (E)(2) of this section, if the offender has not attained nineteen years of age, regardless of whether the offender is attending or is enrolled in a school operated by a board of education or for which the state board of education prescribes minimum standards under section 3301.07 of the Revised Code, the court shall impose upon the offender whichever of the following penalties applies:

(a) If the offender has been issued a probationary driver's license, restricted license, driver's license, or probationary commercial driver's license that then is in effect, the court shall suspend for a period of not less than twelve months and not more than thirty-six months that license of the offender.

(b) If the offender has been issued a temporary instruction permit that then is in effect, the court shall revoke it and deny the offender the issuance of another temporary instruction permit, and the period of denial shall be for not less than twelve months and not more than thirty-six months.

(c) If the offender has been issued a commercial driver's license temporary instruction permit that then is in effect, the court shall suspend the offender's driver's license, revoke the commercial driver's license temporary instruction permit, and deny the offender the issuance of another commercial driver's license temporary instruction permit, and the period of suspension plus the period of denial shall total not less than twelve months and not more than thirty-six months.

(d) If, on the date the court imposes sentence upon the offender for a violation of this section, the offender has not been issued any type of license that then is in effect to operate a motor vehicle in this state or a temporary instruction permit that then is in effect, the court shall deny the offender the issuance of a temporary instruction permit for a period of not less than twelve months and not more than thirty-six months.

(e) If the offender is not a resident of this state, the court shall suspend for a period of not less than twelve months and not more than thirty-six months the nonresident operating privilege of the offender.

(2) If the offender shows good cause why the court should not suspend or revoke one of the types of licenses, permits or privileges specified in division (E)(1) of this section or deny the issuance of one of the temporary instruction permits specified in that division, the court in its discretion may choose not to impose the suspension, revocation, or denial required in that division.]†

(F) As used in this section:

(1) "School," "school building," and "school premises" have the same meanings as in section 2925.01 of the Revised Code.

(2) "School activity" means any activity held under the auspices of a board of education of a city, local, county, exempted village, joint vocational, or cooperative education school district or the governing body of a school for which the state board of education prescribes minimum standards under section 3301.07 of the Revised Code.

(3) "School bus" has the same meaning as in section 4511.01 of the Revised Code.

(4) "Object that is indistinguishable from a firearm" means an object made, constructed, or altered so that, to a reasonable person without specialized training in

firearms, the object appears to be a firearm.

HISTORY: 144 v H 154 (Eff 7-31-92); 146 v S 2 (Eff 7-1-96); 146 v H 72 (Eff 3-18-97); 146 v H 124. Eff 9-30-97.

† The second division (E) in brackets was enacted in HB 124 (146 v —).

The effective date is set by section 3 of HB 124.

[§ 2923.12.3] § 2923.123 Illegal conveyance of deadly weapon or dangerous ordnance into courthouse; illegal possession or control in courthouse.

(A) No person shall knowingly convey or attempt to convey a deadly weapon or dangerous ordnance into a courthouse or into another building or structure in which a courtroom is located.

(B) No person shall knowingly possess or have under the person's control a deadly weapon or dangerous ordnance in a courthouse or in another building or structure in which a courtroom is located.

(C) This section does not apply to any of the following:

(1) A judge of a court of record of this state or a magistrate, unless a rule of superintendence or another type of rule adopted by the supreme court pursuant to Article IV, Ohio Constitution or an applicable local rule of court prohibits all persons from conveying or attempting to convey a deadly weapon or dangerous ordnance into a courthouse or into another building or structure in which a courtroom is located or from possessing or having under one's control a deadly weapon or dangerous ordnance in a courthouse or in another building or structure in which a courtroom is located;

(2) A peace officer, or an officer of a law enforcement agency of another state, a political subdivision of another state, or the United States, who is authorized to carry a deadly weapon or dangerous ordnance, who possesses or has under that individual's control a deadly weapon or dangerous ordnance as a requirement of that individual's duties, and who is acting within the scope of that individual's duties at the time of that possession or control, unless a rule of superintendence or another type of rule adopted by the supreme court pursuant to Article IV, Ohio Constitution or an applicable local rule of court prohibits all persons from conveying or attempting to convey a deadly weapon or dangerous ordnance into a courthouse or into another building or structure in which a courtroom is located or from possessing or having under one's control a deadly weapon or dangerous ordnance in a courthouse or in another building or structure in which a courtroom is located;

(3) A person who conveys, attempts to convey, possesses, or has under the person's control a deadly weapon or dangerous ordnance that is to be used as evidence in a pending criminal or civil action or proceeding;

(4) A bailiff or deputy bailiff of a court of record of this state who is authorized to carry a firearm pursuant to section 109.77 of the Revised Code, who possesses or has under that individual's control a firearm as a requirement of that individual's duties, and who is acting within the scope of that individual's duties at the time of that possession or control, unless a rule of superintendence or another type of rule adopted by the supreme court pursuant to Article IV, Ohio Constitution, or an applicable local rule of court prohibits all persons from conveying or attempting to convey a deadly weapon or dangerous ordnance into a courthouse or into another building or structure in which a courtroom is located or from possessing or having under one's control a deadly weapon or dangerous ordnance in a courthouse or in another building or structure in which a courtroom is located;

(5) A prosecutor, or a secret service officer appointed by a county prosecuting attorney, who is authorized to carry a deadly weapon or dangerous ordnance in the performance of the individual's duties, who possesses or has under that individual's control a deadly weapon or dangerous ordnance as a requirement of that individual's duties, and who is acting within the scope of that individual's duties at the time of that possession or control, unless a rule of superintendence or another type of rule adopted by the supreme court pursuant to Article IV of the Ohio Constitution or an applicable local rule of court prohibits all persons from conveying or attempting to convey a deadly weapon or dangerous ordnance into a courthouse or into another building or structure in which a courtroom is located or from possessing or having under one's control a deadly weapon or dangerous ordnance in a courthouse or in another building or structure in which a courtroom is located.

(D)(1) Whoever violates division (A) of this section is guilty of illegal conveyance of a deadly weapon or dangerous ordnance into a courthouse. Except as otherwise provided in this division, illegal conveyance of a deadly weapon or dangerous ordnance into a courthouse is a felony of the fifth degree. If the offender previously has been convicted of a violation of division (A) or (B) of this section, illegal conveyance of a deadly weapon or dangerous ordnance into a courthouse is a felony of the fourth degree.

(2) Whoever violates division (B) of this section is guilty of illegal possession or control of a deadly weapon or dangerous ordnance in a courthouse. Except as otherwise provided in this division, illegal possession or control of a deadly weapon or dangerous ordnance in a courthouse is a felony of the fifth degree. If the offender previously has been convicted of a violation of division (A) or (B) of this section, illegal possession or control of a deadly weapon or dangerous ordnance in a courthouse is a felony of the fourth degree.

(E) As used in this section:

(1) "Magistrate" means an individual who is ap-

pointed by a court of record of this state and who has the powers and may perform the functions specified in Civil Rule 53, Criminal Rule 19, or Juvenile Rule 40.

(2) "Peace officer" and "prosecutor" have the same meanings as in section 2935.01 of the Revised Code.

HISTORY: 146 v H 88 (Eff 9-3-96); 147 v H 151. Eff 9-16-97.

§ 2923.13 Having weapons while under disability.

(A) Unless relieved from disability as provided in section 2923.14 of the Revised Code, no person shall knowingly acquire, have, carry, or use any firearm or dangerous ordnance, if any of the following apply:

(1) The person is a fugitive from justice.

(2) The person is under indictment for or has been convicted of any felony offense of violence or has been adjudicated a delinquent child for the commission of an offense that, if committed by an adult, would have been a felony offense of violence.

(3) The person is under indictment for or has been convicted of any offense involving the illegal possession, use, sale, administration, distribution, or trafficking in any drug of abuse or has been adjudicated a delinquent child for the commission of an offense that, if committed by an adult, would have been an offense involving the illegal possession, use, sale, administration, distribution, or trafficking in any drug of abuse.

(4) The person is drug dependent, in danger of drug dependence, or a chronic alcoholic.

(5) The person is under adjudication of mental incompetence.

(B) No person who has been convicted of a felony of the first or second degree shall violate division (A) of this section within five years of the date of the person's release from imprisonment or from post-release control that is imposed for the commission of a felony of the first or second degree.

(C) Whoever violates this section is guilty of having weapons while under disability. A violation of division (A) of this section is a felony of the fifth degree. A violation of division (B) of this section is a felony of the third degree.

HISTORY: 134 v H 511 (Eff 1-1-74); 146 v S 2. Eff 7-1-96.

Not analogous to former RC § 2923.13 (GC § 13421-24; 108 v PtI, 189; Bureau of Code Revision, 10-1-53; 126 v 575), repealed 134 v H 511, § 2, eff 1-1-74.

Analogous to former RC § 2923.56 (133 v H 484), repealed 134 v H 511, § 2, eff 1-1-74.

The effective date is set by section 6 of SB 2.

[§ 2923.13.1] § 2923.131 Possession of deadly weapon while under detention.

(A) "Detention" and "detention facility" have the same meanings as in section 2921.01 of the Revised Code.

(B) No person under detention at a detention facility shall possess a deadly weapon.

(C) Whoever violates this section is guilty of possession of a deadly weapon while under detention.

(1) If the offender, at the time of the commission of the offense, was under detention as an alleged or adjudicated delinquent child or unruly child and if at the time the offender commits the act for which the offender was under detention it would not be a felony if committed by an adult, possession of a deadly weapon while under detention is a misdemeanor of the first degree.

(2) If the offender, at the time of the commission of the offense, was under detention in any other manner, possession of a deadly weapon while under detention is one of the following:

(a) A felony of the first degree, when the most serious offense for which the person was under detention is aggravated murder or murder and regardless of when the aggravated murder or murder occurred or, if the person was under detention as an alleged or adjudicated delinquent child, when the most serious act for which the person was under detention would be aggravated murder or murder if committed by an adult and regardless of when that act occurred;

(b) A felony of the second degree if any of the following applies:

(i) The most serious offense for which the person was under detention is a felony of the first degree committed on or after July 1, 1996, or an aggravated felony of the first degree committed prior to July 1, 1996.

(ii) If the person was under detention as an alleged or adjudicated delinquent child, the most serious act for which the person was under detention was committed on or after July 1, 1996, and would be a felony of the first degree if committed by an adult, or was committed prior to July 1, 1996, and would have been an aggravated felony of the first degree if committed by an adult.

(c) A felony of the third degree if any of the following applies:

(i) The most serious offense for which the person was under detention is a felony of the second degree committed on or after July 1, 1996, or is an aggravated felony of the second degree or a felony of the first degree committed prior to July 1, 1996.

(ii) If the person was under detention as an alleged or adjudicated delinquent child, the most serious act for which the person was under detention was committed on or after July 1, 1996, and would be a felony of the second degree if committed by an adult, or was committed prior to July 1, 1996, and would have been an aggravated felony of the second degree or a felony of the first degree if committed by an adult.

(d) A felony of the fourth degree if any of the following applies:

(i) The most serious offense for which the person was under detention is a felony of the third degree committed on or after July 1, 1996, is an aggravated felony of the third degree or a felony of the second degree committed prior to July 1, 1996, or is a felony of the third degree committed prior to July 1, 1996, that, if it had been committed on or after July 1, 1996, also would be a felony of the third degree.

(ii) If the person was under detention as an alleged or adjudicated delinquent child, the most serious act for which the person was under detention was committed on or after July 1, 1996, and would be a felony of the third degree if committed by an adult, was committed prior to July 1, 1996, and would have been an aggravated felony of the third degree or a felony of the second degree if committed by an adult, or was committed prior to July 1, 1996, would have been a felony of the third degree if committed by an adult, and, if it had been committed on or after July 1, 1996, also would be a felony of the third degree if committed by an adult.

(e) A felony of the fifth degree if any of the following applies:

(i) The most serious offense for which the person was under detention is a felony of the fourth or fifth degree committed on or after July 1, 1996, is a felony of the third degree committed prior to July 1, 1996, that, if committed on or after July 1, 1996, would be a felony of the fourth degree, is a felony of the fourth degree committed prior to July 1, 1996, or is an unclassified felony or a misdemeanor regardless of when the unclassified felony or misdemeanor is committed.

(ii) If the person was under detention as an alleged or adjudicated delinquent child, the most serious act for which the person was under detention was committed on or after July 1, 1996, and would be a felony of the fourth or fifth degree if committed by an adult, was committed prior to July 1, 1996, would have been a felony of the third degree if committed by an adult, and, if it had been committed on or after July 1, 1996, would be a felony of the fourth degree if committed by an adult, was committed prior to July 1, 1996, and would have been a felony of the fourth degree if committed by an adult, or would be an unclassified felony if committed by an adult regardless of when the act is committed.

HISTORY: 146 v H 154. Eff 10-4-96.

§ 2923.14 Relief from disability.

(A) Any person who, solely by reason of his disability under division (A)(2) or (3) of section 2923.13 of the Revised Code, is prohibited from acquiring, having, carrying, or using firearms, may apply to the court of common pleas in the county where he resides for relief from such prohibition.

(B) The application shall recite the following:

(1) All indictments, convictions, or adjudications upon which the applicant's disability is based, the sentence imposed and served, and probation, parole, or partial or conditional pardon granted, or other disposition of each case;

(2) Facts showing the applicant to be a fit subject for relief under this section.

(C) A copy of the application shall be served on the county prosecutor, who shall cause the matter to be investigated, and shall raise before the court such objections to granting relief as the investigation reveals.

(D) Upon hearing, the court may grant the applicant relief pursuant to this section, if all of the following apply:

(1) The applicant has been fully discharged from imprisonment, probation, and parole, or, if he is under indictment, has been released on bail or recognizance;

(2) The applicant has led a law-abiding life since his discharge or release, and appears likely to continue to do so;

(3) The applicant is not otherwise prohibited by law from acquiring, having, or using firearms.

(E) Costs of the proceeding shall be charged as in other civil cases, and taxed to the applicant.

(F) Relief from disability granted pursuant to this section:

(1) Applies only with respect to indictments, convictions, or adjudications recited in the application;

(2) Applies only with respect to firearms lawfully acquired, possessed, carried, or used by the applicant;

(3) Does not apply with respect to dangerous ordnance;

(4) May be revoked by the court at any time for good cause shown and upon notice to the applicant;

(5) Is automatically void upon commission by the applicant of any offense embraced by division (A)(2) or (3) of section 2923.13 of the Revised Code, or upon the applicant's becoming one of the class of persons named in division (A)(1), (4), or (5) of such section.

HISTORY: 134 v H 511. Eff 1-1-74.

Not analogous to former RC § 2923.14 (GC § 13421-25; 108 v PtI, 189; Bureau of Code Revision, 10-1-53; 126 v 575), repealed 134 v H 511, § 2, eff 1-1-74.

Analogous to former RC § 2923.56 (133 v H 484), repealed 134 v H 511, § 2, eff 1-1-74.

§ 2923.15 Using weapons while intoxicated.

(A) No person, while under the influence of alcohol or any drug of abuse, shall carry or use any firearm or dangerous ordnance.

(B) Whoever violates this section is guilty of using weapons while intoxicated, a misdemeanor of the first degree.

HISTORY: 134 v H 511. Eff 1-1-74.

Not analogous to former RC § 2923.15 (GC § 13421-26; 108 v PtI, 189; Bureau of Code Revision, 10-1-53), repealed 134 v H 511, § 2, eff 1-1-74.

§ 2923.16 Improperly handling firearms in a motor vehicle.

(A) No person shall knowingly discharge a firearm while in or on a motor vehicle.

(B) No person shall knowingly transport or have a loaded firearm in a motor vehicle, in such manner that the firearm is accessible to the operator or any passenger without leaving the vehicle.

(C) No person shall knowingly transport or have a firearm in a motor vehicle, unless it is unloaded, and is carried in one of the following ways:

(1) In a closed package, box, or case;

(2) In a compartment which can be reached only by leaving the vehicle;

(3) In plain sight and secured in a rack or holder made for the purpose;

(4) In plain sight with the action open or the weapon stripped, or, if the firearm is of a type on which the action will not stay open or which cannot easily be stripped, in plain sight.

(D) This section does not apply to officers, agents, or employees of this or any other state or the United States, or to law enforcement officers, authorized to carry or have loaded or accessible firearms in motor vehicles, and acting within the scope of their duties.

(E) The affirmative defenses contained in division (C)(1) and (2) of section 2923.12 of the Revised Code are affirmative defenses to a charge under division (B) or (C) of this section.

(F) Whoever violates this section is guilty of improperly handling firearms in a motor vehicle. Violation of division (A) or (B) of this section is a misdemeanor of the first degree. Violation of division (C) of this section is a misdemeanor of the fourth degree.

(G) As used in this section, "unloaded" means, with respect to a firearm employing a percussion cap, flintlock, or other obsolete ignition system, when the weapon is uncapped, or when the priming charge is removed from the pan.

HISTORY: 134 v H 511 (Eff 1-1-74); 135 v H 716. Eff 1-1-74.

Not analogous to former RC § 2923.16 (RS § 7031; S&C 448, 449; 29 v 161; GC § 13390; Bureau of Code Revision, 10-1-53), repealed 134 v H 511, § 2, eff 1-1-74.

[§ 2923.16.1] § 2923.161 Improperly discharging a firearm at or into a habitation or school.

(A) No person, without privilege to do so, shall knowingly discharge a firearm at or into an occupied structure that is a permanent or temporary habitation of any individual or a school.

(B) This section does not apply to any officer, agent, or employee of this or any other state or the United States, or to any law enforcement officer, who discharges the firearm while acting within the scope of the officer's, agent's, or employee's duties.

(C) Whoever violates this section is guilty of improperly discharging a firearm at or into a habitation or school. Except as otherwise provided in this division, improperly discharging a firearm at or into a habitation or school is a felony of the third degree. If the offender previously has been convicted of or pleaded guilty to a violation of this section, improperly discharging a firearm at or into a habitation or school is a felony of the second degree.

(D) As used in this section, "occupied structure" has the same meaning as in section 2909.01 of the Revised Code.

HISTORY: 143 v S 258 (Eff 11-20-90); 146 v S 2. Eff 7-1-96.

The effective date is set by section 6 of SB 2.

§ 2923.17 Unlawful possession of dangerous ordnance.

(A) No person shall knowingly acquire, have, carry, or use any dangerous ordnance.

(B) No person shall manufacture or process an explosive at any location in this state unless the person first has been issued a license, certificate of registration, or permit to do so from a fire official of a political subdivision of this state or from the office of the fire marshal.

(C) Division (A) of this section does not apply to:

(1) Officers, agents, or employees of this or any other state or the United States, members of the armed forces of the United States or the organized militia of this or any other state, and law enforcement officers, to the extent that any such person is authorized to acquire, have, carry, or use dangerous ordnance and is acting within the scope of the person's duties;

(2) Importers, manufacturers, dealers, and users of explosives, having a license or user permit issued and in effect pursuant to the "Organized Crime Control Act of 1970," 84 Stat. 952, 18 U.S.C. 843, and any amendments or additions thereto or reenactments thereof, with respect to explosives and explosive devices lawfully acquired, possessed, carried, or used under the laws of this state and applicable federal law;

(3) Importers, manufacturers, and dealers having a license to deal in destructive devices or their ammunition, issued and in effect pursuant to the "Gun Control Act of 1968," 82 Stat. 1213, 18 U.S.C. 923, and any amendments or additions thereto or reenactments thereof, with respect to dangerous ordnance lawfully acquired, possessed, carried, or used under the laws of this state and applicable federal law;

(4) Persons to whom surplus ordnance has been sold, loaned, or given by the secretary of the army pursuant to 70A Stat. 262 and 263, 10 U.S.C. 4684, 4685, and 4686, and any amendments or additions thereto or reenactments thereof, with respect to dangerous ordnance when lawfully possessed and used for the purposes specified in such section;

(5) Owners of dangerous ordnance registered in the national firearms registration and transfer record pursuant to the act of October 22, 1968, 82 Stat. 1229, 26

U.S.C. 5841, and any amendments or additions thereto or reenactments thereof, and regulations issued thereunder.

(6) Carriers, warehousemen, and others engaged in the business of transporting or storing goods for hire, with respect to dangerous ordnance lawfully transported or stored in the usual course of their business and in compliance with the laws of this state and applicable federal law;

(7) The holders of a license or temporary permit issued and in effect pursuant to section 2923.18 of the Revised Code, with respect to dangerous ordnance lawfully acquired, possessed, carried, or used for the purposes and in the manner specified in such license or permit.

(D) Whoever violates division (A) of this section is guilty of unlawful possession of dangerous ordnance, a felony of the fifth degree.

(E) Whoever violates division (B) of this section is guilty of illegally manufacturing or processing explosives, a felony of the second degree.

HISTORY: 134 v H 511 (Eff 1-1-74); 137 v H 728 (Eff 8-22-78); 146 v S 2. Eff 7-1-96.

Not analogous to former RC § 2923.17 (RS § 6990; 73 v 154; GC § 12678; Bureau of Code Revision, 10-1-53), repealed 134 v H 511, § 2, eff 1-1-74.

Analogous to former RC § 2923.04 (GC §§ 12819-4, 12819-5; 115 v 189; Bureau of Code Revision, 10-1-53; 132 v H 43), repealed 134 v H 511, § 2, eff 1-1-74.

The effective date is set by section 6 of SB 2.

§ 2923.18 License or permit to possess dangerous ordnance.

(A) Upon application to the sheriff of the county or safety director or police chief of the municipality where the applicant resides or has his principal place of business, and upon payment of the fee specified in division (B) of this section, a license or temporary permit shall be issued to qualified applicants to acquire, possess, carry, or use dangerous ordnance, for the following purposes:

(1) Contractors, wreckers, quarrymen, mine operators, and other persons regularly employing explosives in the course of a legitimate business, with respect to explosives and explosive devices acquired, possessed, carried, or used in the course of such business;

(2) Farmers, with respect to explosives and explosive devices acquired, possessed, carried, or used for agricultural purposes on lands farmed by them;

(3) Scientists, engineers, and instructors, with respect to dangerous ordnance acquired, possessed, carried, or used in the course of bona fide research or instruction;

(4) Financial institution and armored car company guards, with respect to automatic firearms lawfully acquired, possessed, carried, or used by any such person while acting within the scope of his duties;

(5) In the discretion of the issuing authority, any responsible person, with respect to dangerous ordnance lawfully acquired, possessed, carried, or used for a legitimate research, scientific, educational, industrial, or other proper purpose.

(B) Application for a license or temporary permit under this section shall be in writing under oath to the sheriff of the county or safety director or police chief of the municipality where the applicant resides or has his principal place of business. The application shall be accompanied by an application fee of fifty dollars when the application is for a license, and an application fee of five dollars when the application is for a temporary permit. The fees shall be paid into the general revenue fund of the county or municipality. The application shall contain the following information:

(1) The name, age, address, occupation, and business address of the applicant, if he is a natural person, or the name, address, and principal place of business of the applicant, if the applicant is a corporation;

(2) A description of the dangerous ordnance for which a permit is requested;

(3) A description of the place or places where and the manner in which the dangerous ordnance is to be kept, carried, and used;

(4) A statement of the purposes for which the dangerous ordnance is to be acquired, possessed, carried, or used;

(5) Such other information as the issuing authority may require in giving effect to this section.

(C) Upon investigation, the issuing authority shall issue a license or temporary permit only if all of the following apply:

(1) The applicant is not otherwise prohibited by law from acquiring, having, carrying or using dangerous ordnance;

(2) The applicant is age twenty-one or over, if he is a natural person;

(3) It appears that the applicant has sufficient competence to safely acquire, possess, carry, or use the dangerous ordnance, and that proper precautions will be taken to protect the security of the dangerous ordnance and ensure the safety of persons and property;

(4) It appears that the dangerous ordnance will be lawfully acquired, possessed, carried, and used by the applicant for a legitimate purpose.

(D) The license or temporary permit shall identify the person to whom it is issued, identify the dangerous ordnance involved and state the purposes for which the license or temporary permit is issued, state the expiration date, if any, and list such restrictions on the acquisition, possession, carriage, or use of the dangerous ordnance as the issuing authority considers advisable to protect the security of the dangerous ordnance and ensure the safety of persons and property.

(E) A temporary permit shall be issued for the casual use of explosives and explosive devices, and other consumable dangerous ordnance, and shall expire within thirty days of its issuance. A license shall be issued for the regular use of consumable dangerous ordnance, or for any nonconsumable dangerous ordnance, which license need not specify an expiration date, but the issuing authority may specify such expiration date, not earlier than one year from the date of issuance, as it considers advisable in view of the nature of the dangerous ordnance and the purposes for which the license is issued.

(F) The dangerous ordnance specified in a license or temporary permit may be obtained by the holder anywhere in the state. The holder of a license may use such dangerous ordnance anywhere in the state. The holder of a temporary permit may use such dangerous ordnance only within the territorial jurisdiction of the issuing authority.

(G) The issuing authority shall forward to the state fire marshal a copy of each license or temporary permit issued pursuant to this section, and a copy of each record of a transaction in dangerous ordnance and of each report of lost or stolen dangerous ordnance, given to the local law enforcement authority as required by divisions (A)(4) and (5) of section 2923.20 of the Revised Code. The state fire marshal shall keep a permanent file of all licenses and temporary permits issued pursuant to this section, and of all records of transactions in, and losses or thefts of dangerous ordnance forwarded by local law enforcement authorities pursuant to this section.

HISTORY: 134 v H 511 (Eff 1-1-74); 137 v H 590. Eff 7-1-79.

Not analogous to former RC § 2923.18 (RS § 2127; Bates § 1536-740; 66 v 202; 95 v 428; GC §§ 12785, 12786; 108 v PtI, 236; Bureau of Code Revision, 10-1-53), repealed 134 v H 511, § 2, eff 1-1-74.

Analogous to former RC § 2923.04 (GC §§ 12819-4, 12819-5; 115 v 189, 190; Bureau of Code Revision, 10-1-53; 132 v H 43), repealed 134 v H 511, § 2, eff 1-1-74.

The effective date is set by section 3 of HB 590.

§ 2923.19 Failure to secure dangerous ordnance.

(A) No person, in acquiring, possessing, carrying, or using any dangerous ordnance, shall negligently fail to take proper precautions:

(1) To secure the dangerous ordnance against theft, or against its acquisition or use by any unauthorized or incompetent person;

(2) To insure the safety of persons and property.

(B) Whoever violates this section is guilty of failure to secure dangerous ordnance, a misdemeanor of the second degree.

HISTORY: 134 v H 511. Eff 1-1-74.

Not analogous to former RC § 2923.19 (RS § 6875; S&S 487; 62 v 67; 71 v 34; 73 v 63; GC § 12637; Bureau of Code Revision, 10-1-53), repealed 134 v H 511, § 2, eff 1-1-74.

§ 2923.20 Unlawful transaction in weapons.

(A) No person shall:

(1) Recklessly sell, lend, give, or furnish any firearm to any person prohibited by section 2923.13 or 2923.15 of the Revised Code from acquiring or using any firearm, or recklessly sell, lend, give, or furnish any dangerous ordnance to any person prohibited by section 2923.13, 2923.15, or 2923.17 of the Revised Code from acquiring or using any dangerous ordnance;

(2) Possess any firearm or dangerous ordnance with purpose to dispose of it in violation of division (A) of this section;

(3) Manufacture, possess for sale, sell, or furnish to any person other than a law enforcement agency for authorized use in police work, any brass knuckles, cestus, billy, blackjack, sandbag, switchblade knife, springblade knife, gravity knife, or similar weapon;

(4) When transferring any dangerous ordnance to another, negligently fail to require the transferee to exhibit such identification, license, or permit showing him to be authorized to acquire dangerous ordnance pursuant to section 2923.17 of the Revised Code, or negligently fail to take a complete record of the transaction and forthwith forward a copy of that record to the sheriff of the county or safety director or police chief of the municipality where the transaction takes place;

(5) Knowingly fail to report to law enforcement authorities forthwith the loss or theft of any firearm or dangerous ordnance in the person's possession or under the person's control.

(B) Whoever violates this section is guilty of unlawful transactions in weapons. A violation of division (A)(1) or (2) of this section is a felony of the fourth degree. A violation of division (A)(3) or (4) of this section is a misdemeanor of the second degree. A violation of division (A)(5) of this section is a misdemeanor of the fourth degree.

HISTORY: 134 v H 511 (Eff 1-1-74); 137 v H 728 (Eff 8-22-78); 146 v S 2. Eff 7-1-96.

Not analogous to former RC § 2923.20 (RS § 6875; S&S 487; 62 v 67; 71 v 34; 73 v 63; GC § 12637; Bureau of Code Revision, 10-1-53), repealed 134 v H 511, § 2, eff 1-1-74.

The effective date is set by section 6 of SB 2.

§ 2923.21 Improperly furnishing firearms to a minor.

(A) No person shall do any of the following:

(1) Sell any firearm to a person who is under eighteen years of age;

(2) Subject to division (B) of this section, sell any handgun to a person who is under twenty-one years of age;

(3) Furnish any firearm to a person who is under eighteen years of age or, subject to division (B) of this section, furnish any handgun to a person who is under twenty-one years of age, except for lawful hunting, sporting, or educational purposes, including, but not limited to, instruction in firearms or handgun safety,

care, handling, or marksmanship under the supervision or control of a responsible adult;

(4) Sell or furnish a firearm to a person who is eighteen years of age or older if the seller or furnisher knows, or has reason to know, that the person is purchasing or receiving the firearm for the purpose of selling the firearm in violation of division (A)(1) of this section to a person who is under eighteen years of age or for the purpose of furnishing the firearm in violation of division (A)(3) of this section to a person who is under eighteen years of age;

(5) Sell or furnish a handgun to a person who is twenty-one years of age or older if the seller or furnisher knows, or has reason to know, that the person is purchasing or receiving the handgun for the purpose of selling the handgun in violation of division (A)(2) of this section to a person who is under twenty-one years of age or for the purpose of furnishing the handgun in violation of division (A)(3) of this section to a person who is under twenty-one years of age;

(6) Purchase or attempt to purchase any firearm with the intent to sell the firearm in violation of division (A)(1) of this section to a person who is under eighteen years of age or with the intent to furnish the firearm in violation of division (A)(3) of this section to a person who is under eighteen years of age;

(7) Purchase or attempt to purchase any handgun with the intent to sell the handgun in violation of division (A)(2) of this section to a person who is under twenty-one years of age or with the intent to furnish the handgun in violation of division (A)(3) of this section to a person who is under twenty-one years of age.

(B) Divisions (A)(1) and (2) of this section do not apply to the sale or furnishing of a handgun to a person eighteen years of age or older and under twenty-one years of age if the person eighteen years of age or older and under twenty-one years of age is a law enforcement officer who is properly appointed or employed as a law enforcement officer and has received firearms training approved by the Ohio peace officer training council or equivalent firearms training.

(C) Whoever violates this section is guilty of improperly furnishing firearms to a minor, a felony of the fifth degree.

HISTORY: 134 v H 511 (Eff 1-1-74); 146 v H 4 (Eff 11-9-95); 146 v S 269 (Eff 7-1-96); 146 v H 124. Eff 3-31-97.

Not analogous to former RC § 2923.21 (RS § 6876; S&C 1642; 37 v 17; GC § 12638; Bureau of Code Revision, 10-1-53; 126 v 575), repealed 134 v H 511, § 2, eff 1-1-74.

See provisions, § 3 of HB 4 (146 v —) following RC § 2913.02.

[§ 2923.21.1] § 2923.211 Underage purchase of firearm or handgun.

(A) No person under eighteen years of age shall purchase or attempt to purchase a firearm.

(B) No person under twenty-one years of age shall purchase or attempt to purchase a handgun, provided that this division does not apply to the purchase or attempted purchase of a handgun by a person eighteen years of age or older and under twenty-one years of age if the person eighteen years of age or older and under twenty-one years of age is a law enforcement officer who is properly appointed or employed as a law enforcement officer and has received firearms training approved by the Ohio peace officer training council or equivalent firearms training.

(C) Whoever violates division (A) of this section is guilty of underage purchase of a firearm, is a delinquent child, and is subject to an order of disposition as provided in section 2151.355 [2151.35.5] of the Revised Code. Whoever violates division (B) of this section is guilty of underage purchase of a handgun, a misdemeanor of the second degree.

HISTORY: 146 v H 4 (Eff 11-9-95); 146 v H 124. Eff 3-31-97.

See provisions, § 3 of HB 4 (146 v —) following RC § 2913.02.

§ 2923.22 Permitted interstate transactions in firearms.

(A) Any resident of Ohio age eighteen or over, and not prohibited by section 2923.13 or 2923.15 of the Revised Code or any applicable law of another state or the United States from acquiring or using firearms, may purchase or obtain a rifle, shotgun, or ammunition therefor in Indiana, Kentucky, Michigan, Pennsylvania, or West Virginia.

(B) Any resident of Indiana, Kentucky, Michigan, Pennsylvania, or West Virginia, age eighteen or over, and not prohibited by section 2923.13 or 2923.15 of the Revised Code or the laws of his domicile or the United States from acquiring or using firearms, may purchase or obtain a rifle, shotgun, or ammunition therefor in Ohio.

(C) Any purchase and sale pursuant to this section shall be for such purposes and under such circumstances and upon such conditions as are prescribed by the "Gun Control Act of 1968," 82 Stat. 1213, 18 U.S.C. 922(b)(3), and any amendments or additions thereto or reenactments thereof.

HISTORY: 134 v H 511. Eff 1-1-74.

Not analogous to former RC § 2923.22 (RS § 6884; S&S 694; 71 v 105; 77 v 145; 79 v 131; 89 v 234; GC § 12639; Bureau of Code Revision, 10-1-53), repealed 134 v H 511, § 2, eff 1-1-74.

Analogous to former RC § 2923.57 (133 v H 484), repealed 134 v H 511, § 2, eff 1-1-74.

§ 2923.23 Immunity from prosecution.

(A) No person who acquires, possesses, or carries a firearm or dangerous ordnance in violation of section 2923.13 or 2923.17 of the Revised Code shall be prosecuted for such violation, if he reports his possession of firearms or dangerous ordnance to any law enforcement authority, describes the firearms of [or] dangerous ordnance in his possession and where they may be found, and voluntarily surrenders the firearms or dangerous ordnance to the law enforcement authority. A surrender is not voluntary if it occurs when the person is taken into custody or during a pursuit or attempt to take the person into custody under circumstances indicating that the surrender is made under threat of force.

(B) No person in violation of section 2923.13 of the Revised Code solely by reason of his being under indictment shall be prosecuted for such violation if, within ten days after service of the indictment, he voluntarily surrenders the firearms and dangerous ordnance in his possession to any law enforcement authority pursuant to division (A) of this section, for safekeeping pending disposition of the indictment or of an application for relief under section 2923.14 of the Revised Code.

(C) Evidence obtained from or by reason of an application or proceeding under section 2923.14 of the Revised Code for relief from disability, shall not be used in a prosecution of the applicant for any violation of section 2923.13 of the Revised Code.

(D) Evidence obtained from or by reason of an application under section 2923.18 of the Revised Code for a permit to possess dangerous ordnance, shall not be used in a prosecution of the applicant for any violation of section 2923.13 or 2923.17 of the Revised Code.

HISTORY: 134 v H 511. Eff 1-1-74.

Not analogous to former RC § 2923.23 (GC § 12642, repealed in 113 v 685; 115 v 70; Bureau of Code Revision, 10-1-53), repealed 134 v H 511, § 2, eff 1-1-74.

§ 2923.24 Possessing criminal tools.

(A) No person shall possess or have under the person's control any substance, device, instrument, or article, with purpose to use it criminally.

(B) Each of the following constitutes prima-facie evidence of criminal purpose:

(1) Possession or control of any dangerous ordnance, or the materials or parts for making dangerous ordnance, in the absence of circumstances indicating the dangerous ordnance, materials, or parts are intended for legitimate use;

(2) Possession or control of any substance, device, instrument, or article designed or specially adapted for criminal use;

(3) Possession or control of any substance, device, instrument, or article commonly used for criminal purposes, under circumstances indicating the item is intended for criminal use.

(C) Whoever violates this section is guilty of possessing criminal tools. Except as otherwise provided in this division, possessing criminal tools is a misdemeanor of the first degree. If the circumstances indicate that the substance, device, instrument, or article involved in the offense was intended for use in the commission of a felony, possessing criminal tools is a felony of the fifth degree.

HISTORY: 134 v H 511 (Eff 1-1-74); 146 v S 2. Eff 7-1-96.

Not analogous to former RC § 2923.24 (RS § 6928-1; 92 v 97; GC § 12779; Bureau of Code Revision, 10-1-53), repealed 134 v H 511, § 2, eff 1-1-74.

The effective date is set by section 6 of SB 2.

§ 2923.25 Repealed, 134 v H 511, § 2 [GC § 12798-6; 108 v PtI, 419; Bureau of Code Revision, 10-1-53]. Eff 1-1-74.

This section concerned obnoxious gases from burners.

[§ 2923.25.1] § 2923.251 Repealed, 134 v H 511, § 2 [127 v 459; 129 v 582]. Eff 1-1-74.

This section concerned unvented gas heaters.

§§ 2923.26, 2923.27, 2923.28

Repealed, 134 v H 511, § 2 [RS §§ 6884-2, 6995; GC §§ 13396, 13397, 13408; 76 v 191; 92 v 88; 99 v 86; 120 v 133; Bureau of Code Revision, 10-1-53; 129 v H 1]. Eff 1-1-74.

These sections concerned offenses regarding false alarms, camping on public lands and tramps.

§§ 2923.29, 2923.30 Repealed, 134 v H 511, § 2 [GC §§ 13383-1, 13410; 99 v 20; 101 v 263; 103 v 469; 115 v 334; Bureau of Code Revision, 10-1-53; 126 v 575]. Eff 1-1-74.

These sections concerned improper use of transcripts and fraud.

[CORRUPT ACTIVITY]

§ 2923.31 Definitions.

As used in sections 2923.31 to 2923.36 of the Revised Code:

(A) "Beneficial interest" means any of the following:

(1) The interest of a person as a beneficiary under a trust in which the trustee holds title to personal or real property;

(2) The interest of a person as a beneficiary under any other trust arrangement under which any other person holds title to personal or real property for the benefit of such person;

(3) The interest of a person under any other form of express fiduciary arrangement under which any other person holds title to personal or real property for the benefit of such person.

"Beneficial interest" does not include the interest of a stockholder in a corporation or the interest of a partner in either a general or limited partnership.

(B) "Costs of investigation and prosecution" and "costs of investigation and litigation" mean all of the costs incurred by the state or a county or municipal corporation under sections 2923.31 to 2923.36 of the

Revised Code in the prosecution and investigation of any criminal action or in the litigation and investigation of any civil action, and includes, but is not limited to, the costs of resources and personnel.

(C) "Enterprise" includes any individual, sole proprietorship, partnership, limited partnership, corporation, trust, union, government agency, or other legal entity, or any organization, association, or group of persons associated in fact although not a legal entity. "Enterprise" includes illicit as well as licit enterprises.

(D) "Innocent person" includes any bona fide purchaser of property that is allegedly involved in a violation of section 2923.32 of the Revised Code, including any person who establishes a valid claim to or interest in the property in accordance with division (E) of section 2923.32 of the Revised Code, and any victim of an alleged violation of that section or of any underlying offense involved in an alleged violation of that section.

(E) "Pattern of corrupt activity" means two or more incidents of corrupt activity, whether or not there has been a prior conviction, that are related to the affairs of the same enterprise, are not isolated, and are not so closely related to each other and connected in time and place that they constitute a single event.

At least one of the incidents forming the pattern shall occur on or after January 1, 1986. Unless any incident was an aggravated murder or murder, the last of the incidents forming the pattern shall occur within six years after the commission of any prior incident forming the pattern, excluding any period of imprisonment served by any person engaging in the corrupt activity.

For the purposes of the criminal penalties that may be imposed pursuant to section 2923.32 of the Revised Code, at least one of the incidents forming the pattern shall constitute a felony under the laws of this state in existence at the time it was committed or, if committed in violation of the laws of the United States or of any other state, shall constitute a felony under the law of the United States or the other state and would be a criminal offense under the law of this state if committed in this state.

(F) "Pecuniary value" means money, a negotiable instrument, a commercial interest, or anything of value, as defined in section 1.03 of the Revised Code, or any other property or service that has a value in excess of one hundred dollars.

(G) "Person" means any person, as defined in section 1.59 of the Revised Code, and any governmental officer, employee, or entity.

(H) "Personal property" means any personal property, any interest in personal property, or any right, including, but not limited to, bank accounts, debts, corporate stocks, patents, or copyrights. Personal property and any beneficial interest in personal property are deemed to be located where the trustee of the property, the personal property, or the instrument evidencing the right is located.

(I) "Corrupt activity" means engaging in, attempting to engage in, conspiring to engage in, or soliciting, coercing, or intimidating another person to engage in any of the following:

(1) Conduct defined as "racketeering activity" under the "Organized Crime Control Act of 1970," 84 Stat. 941, 18 U.S.C. 1961(1)(B), (1)(C), (1)(D), and (1)(E), as amended;

(2) Conduct constituting any of the following:

(a) A violation of section 1315.55, 1322.02, 2903.01, 2903.02, 2903.03, 2903.04, 2903.11, 2903.12, 2905.01, 2905.02, 2905.11, 2905.22, 2907.321 [2907.32.1], 2907.322 [2907.32.2], 2907.323 [2907.32.3], 2909.02, 2909.03, 2911.01, 2911.02, 2911.11, 2911.12, 2911.13, 2911.31, 2921.02, 2921.03, 2921.04, 2921.11, 2921.12, 2921.32, 2921.41, 2921.42, 2921.43, 2923.12, or 2923.17; division (F)(1)(a), (b), or (c) of section 1315.53; division (A)(1) or (2) of section 1707.042 [1707.04.2]; division (B), (C)(4), (D), (E), or (F) of section 1707.44; division (A)(1) or (2) of section 2923.20; division (J)(1) of section 4712.02; section 4719.02, 4719.05, or 4719.06; division (C), (D), or (E) of section 4719.07; section 4719.08; or division (A) of section 4719.09 of the Revised Code.

(b) Any violation of section 3769.11, 3769.15, 3769.16, or 3769.19 of the Revised Code as it existed prior to July 1, 1996, any violation of section 2915.02 of the Revised Code that occurs on or after July 1, 1996, and that, had it occurred prior to that date, would have been a violation of section 3769.11 of the Revised Code as it existed prior to that date, or any violation of section 2915.05 of the Revised Code that occurs on or after July 1, 1996, and that, had it occurred prior to that date, would have been a violation of section 3769.15, 3769.16, or 3769.19 of the Revised Code as it existed prior to that date.

(c) Any violation of section 2907.21, 2907.22, 2907.31, 2913.02, 2913.11, 2913.21, 2913.31, 2913.32, 2913.34, 2913.42, 2913.47, 2913.51, 2915.03, 2925.03, 2925.04, 2925.05, or 2925.37 of the Revised Code, any violation of section 2925.11 of the Revised Code that is a felony of the first, second, third, or fourth degree and that occurs on or after July 1, 1996, any violation of section 2915.02 of the Revised Code that occurred prior to July 1, 1996, any violation of section 2915.02 of the Revised Code that occurs on or after July 1, 1996, and that, had it occurred prior to that date, would not have been a violation of section 3769.11 of the Revised Code as it existed prior to that date, any violation of section 2915.06 of the Revised Code as it existed prior to July 1, 1996, or any violation of division (B) of section 2915.05 of the Revised Code as it exists on and after July 1, 1996, when the proceeds of the violation, the payments made in the violation, the amount of a claim for payment or for any other benefit that is false or deceptive and that is involved in the violation, or the value of the contraband or other property illegally possessed, sold, or purchased in the violation exceeds five hundred dollars, or any combination of violations described in division (I)(2)(c) of this section when the total proceeds of the combination of violations, payments made in the combination of violations, amount of the claims for payment or for other benefits that is false or deceptive and that is involved in the combination of violations, or value of the contraband or other property illegally possessed, sold, or purchased in the combination of violations exceeds five hundred dollars;

(d) Any violation of section 5743.112 [5743.11.2] of the Revised Code when the amount of unpaid tax exceeds one hundred dollars;

(e) Any violation or combination of violations of section 2907.32 of the Revised Code involving any material or performance containing a display of bestiality or of sexual conduct, as defined in section 2907.01 of the Revised Code, that is explicit and depicted with clearly visible penetration of the genitals or clearly visible penetration by the penis of any orifice when the total proceeds of the violation or combination of violations, the payments made in the violation or combination of violations, or the value of the contraband or other property illegally possessed, sold, or purchased in the violation or combination of violations exceeds five hundred dollars;

(f) Any combination of violations described in division (I)(2)(c) of this section and violations of section 2907.32 of the Revised Code involving any material or performance containing a display of bestiality or of sexual conduct, as defined in section 2907.01 of the Revised Code, that is explicit and depicted with clearly visible penetration of the genitals or clearly visible penetration by the penis of any orifice when the total proceeds of the combination of violations, payments made in the combination of violations, amount of the claims for payment or for other benefits that is false or deceptive and that is involved in the combination of violations, or value of the contraband or other property illegally possessed, sold, or purchased in the combination of violations exceeds five hundred dollars.

(3) Conduct constituting a violation of any law of any state other than this state that is substantially similar to the conduct described in division (I)(2) of this section, provided the defendant was convicted of the conduct in a criminal proceeding in the other state.

(J) "Real property" means any real property or any interest in real property, including, but not limited to, any lease of, or mortgage upon, real property. Real property and any beneficial interest in it is deemed to be located where the real property is located.

(K) "Trustee" means any of the following:

(1) Any person acting as trustee under a trust in which the trustee holds title to personal or real property;

(2) Any person who holds title to personal or real property for which any other person has a beneficial interest;

(3) Any successor trustee.

"Trustee" does not include an assignee or trustee for an insolvent debtor or an executor, administrator, administrator with the will annexed, testamentary trustee, guardian, or committee, appointed by, under the control of, or accountable to a court.

(L) "Unlawful debt" means any money or other thing of value constituting principal or interest of a debt that is legally unenforceable in this state in whole or in part because the debt was incurred or contracted in violation of any federal or state law relating to the business of gambling activity or relating to the business of lending money at an usurious rate unless the creditor proves, by a preponderance of the evidence, that the usurious rate was not intentionally set and that it resulted from a good faith error by the creditor, notwithstanding the maintenance of procedures that were adopted by the creditor to avoid an error of that nature.

HISTORY: 141 v H 5 (Eff 1-1-86); 141 v S 74 (Eff 9-3-86); 142 v H 708 (Eff 4-19-88); 142 v H 624 (Eff 3-17-89); 143 v H 347 (Eff 7-18-90); 144 v S 323 (Eff 4-16-93); 146 v S 2 (Eff 7-1-96); 146 v S 269 (Eff 7-1-96); 146 v H 333 (Eff 9-19-96); 146 v S 214, § 1 (Eff 12-5-96); 146 v S 214, § 3 (Eff 12-5-96); 146 v S 277. Eff 3-31-97.

Not analogous to former RC § 2923.31 (RS § 6983-1; 92 v 122; GC § 13411; Bureau of Code Revision, 10-1-53), repealed 134 v H 511, § 2, eff 1-1-74.

The provisions of § 9 of SB 277 (146 v —) read as follows:

SECTION 9. ° ° ° Section 2923.31 of the Revised Code is presented in this act as a composite of the section as amended by Am. Sub. H.B. 333, Am. Sub. S.B. 269, and Sub. S.B. 214 of the 121st General Assembly, with the new language of none of the acts shown in capital letters. This is in recognition of the principle stated in division (B) of section 1.52 of the Revised Code that such amendments are to be harmonized where not substantively irreconcilable and constitutes a legislative finding that such is the resulting version in effect prior to the effective date of this act.

§ 2923.32 Engaging in pattern of corrupt activity; forfeiture.

(A)(1) No person employed by, or associated with, any enterprise shall conduct or participate in, directly or indirectly, the affairs of the enterprise through a pattern of corrupt activity or the collection of an unlawful debt.

(2) No person, through a pattern of corrupt activity or the collection of an unlawful debt, shall acquire or maintain, directly or indirectly, any interest in, or control of, any enterprise or real property.

(3) No person, who knowingly has received any proceeds derived, directly or indirectly, from a pattern of corrupt activity or the collection of any unlawful debt, shall use or invest, directly or indirectly, any part of those proceeds, or any proceeds derived from the use or investment of any of those proceeds, in the acquisition of any title to, or any right, interest, or equity in, real property or in the establishment or operation of any enterprise.

A purchase of securities on the open market with intent to make an investment, without intent to control or participate in the control of the issuer, and without intent to assist another to do so is not a violation of this division, if the securities of the issuer held after the purchase by the purchaser, the members of the purchaser's immediate family, and the purchaser's or the immediate family members' accomplices in any pattern of corrupt activity or the collection of an unlawful debt do not aggregate one per cent of the outstanding securities of any one class of the issuer and do not confer, in law or in fact, the power to elect one or more directors of the issuer.

(B)(1) Whoever violates this section is guilty of engaging in a pattern of corrupt activity. Except as otherwise provided in this division, engaging in corrupt activity is a felony of the second degree. If at least one of the incidents of corrupt activity is a felony of the first, second, or third degree, aggravated murder, or murder, if at least one of the incidents was a felony under the law of this state that was committed prior to the effective date of this amendment and that would constitute a felony of the first, second, or third degree, aggravated murder, or murder if committed on or after the effective date of this amendment, or if at least one of the incidents of corrupt activity is a felony under the law of the United States or of another state that, if committed in this state on or after the effective date of this amendment, would constitute a felony of the first, second, or third degree, aggravated murder, or murder under the law of this state, engaging in a pattern of corrupt activity is a felony of the first degree. Notwithstanding any other provision of law, a person may be convicted of violating the provisions of this section as well as of a conspiracy to violate one or more of those provisions under section 2923.01 of the Revised Code.

(2) Notwithstanding the financial sanctions authorized by section 2929.18 of the Revised Code, the court may do all of the following with respect to any person who derives pecuniary value or causes property damage, personal injury other than pain and suffering, or other loss through or by the violation of this section:

(a) In lieu of the fine authorized by that section, impose a fine not exceeding the greater of three times the gross value gained or three times the gross loss caused and order the clerk of the court to pay the fine into the corrupt activity investigation and prosecution fund created in section 2923.35 of the Revised Code;

(b) In addition to the fine described in division (B)(2)(a) of this section and the financial sanctions authorized by section 2929.18 of the Revised Code, order the person to pay court costs;

(c) In addition to the fine described in division (B)(2)(a) of this section and the financial sanctions authorized by section 2929.18 of the Revised Code, order the person to pay to the state, municipal, or county law enforcement agencies that handled the investigation and prosecution the costs of investigation and prosecution that are reasonably incurred.

The court shall hold a hearing to determine the amount of fine, court costs, and other costs to be imposed under this division.

(3) In addition to any other penalty or disposition authorized or required by law, the court shall order any person who is convicted of or pleads guilty to a violation of this section or who is adjudicated delinquent by reason of a violation of this section to criminally forfeit to the state any personal or real property in which the person has an interest and that was used in the course of or intended for use in the course of a violation of this section, or that was derived from or realized through conduct in violation of this section, including any property constituting an interest in, means of control over, or influence over the enterprise involved in the violation and any property constituting proceeds derived from the violation, including all of the following:

(a) Any position, office, appointment, tenure, commission, or employment contract of any kind acquired or maintained by the person in violation of this section, through which the person, in violation of this section, conducted or participated in the conduct of an enterprise, or that afforded the person a source of influence or control over an enterprise that the person exercised in violation of this section;

(b) Any compensation, right, or benefit derived from a position, office, appointment, tenure, commission, or employment contract described in division (B)(3)(a) of this section that accrued to the person in violation of this section during the period of the pattern of corrupt activity;

(c) Any interest in, security of, claim against, or property or contractual right affording the person a source of influence or control over the affairs of an enterprise that the person exercised in violation of this section;

(d) Any amount payable or paid under any contract for goods or services that was awarded or performed in violation of this section.

(4)(a) A sentence or disposition of criminal forfeiture pursuant to division (B)(3) of this section shall not be entered unless either of the following applies:

(i) The indictment, count in the indictment, or information charging the offense, or the complaint filed in juvenile court charging the violation as a delinquent act alleges the extent of the property subject to forfeiture;

(ii) The criminal sentence or delinquency disposition requires the forfeiture of property that was not reasonably foreseen to be subject to forfeiture at the time of the indictment, count in the indictment, or information charging the offense, or the complaint filed in juvenile court charging the violation as a delinquent act, provided that the prosecuting attorney gave prompt notice to the defendant or the alleged or adjudicated delinquent child of such property not reasonably foreseen to be subject to forfeiture when it is discovered to be forfeitable.

(b) A special verdict shall be returned as to the extent of the property, if any, subject to forfeiture. When the special verdict is returned, a judgment of forfeiture shall be entered.

(5) If any property included in a special verdict of

forfeiture returned pursuant to division (B)(4) of this section cannot be located, has been sold to a bona fide purchaser for value, placed beyond the jurisdiction of the court, substantially diminished in value by the conduct of the defendant or adjudicated delinquent child, or commingled with other property that cannot be divided without difficulty or undue injury to innocent persons, or otherwise is unreachable without undue injury to innocent persons, the court shall order forfeiture of any other reachable property of the defendant or adjudicated delinquent child up to the value of the property that is unreachable.

(6) All property ordered forfeited pursuant to this section shall be held by the law enforcement agency that seized it for distribution or disposal pursuant to section 2923.35 of the Revised Code. The agency shall maintain an accurate record of each item of property so seized and held, which record shall include the date on which each item was seized, the manner and date of disposition by the agency, and if applicable, the name of the person who received the item; however, the record shall not identify or enable the identification of the individual officer who seized the property. The record is a public record open for inspection under section 149.43 of the Revised Code. Each law enforcement agency that seizes and holds in any calendar year any item of property that is ordered forfeited pursuant to this section shall prepare a report covering the calendar year that cumulates all of the information contained in all of the records kept by the agency pursuant to this division for that calendar year, and shall send the cumulative report, no later than the first day of March in the calendar year following the calendar year covered by the report, to the attorney general. Each such report so received by the attorney general is a public record open for inspection under section 149.43 of the Revised Code. The attorney general shall make copies of each such report so received, and, no later than the fifteenth day of April in the calendar year in which the reports were received, shall send a copy of each such report to the office of the president of the senate and the office of the speaker of the house of representatives.

(C) Notwithstanding the notice and procedure prescribed by division (E) of this section, an order of criminal forfeiture entered under division (B)(3) of this section shall authorize an appropriate law enforcement agency to seize the property declared forfeited under this section upon the terms and conditions, relating to the time and manner of seizure, that the court determines proper.

(D) Criminal penalties under this section are not mutually exclusive, unless otherwise provided, and do not preclude the application of any other criminal or civil remedy under this or any other section of the Revised Code. A disposition of criminal forfeiture ordered pursuant to division (B)(3) of this section in relation to a child who was adjudicated delinquent by reason of a violation of this section does not preclude the application of any other order of disposition under section 2151.355 [2151.35.5] of the Revised Code or any other civil remedy under this or any other section of the Revised Code.

(E)(1) Upon the entry of a judgment of forfeiture pursuant to division (B)(3) of this section, the court shall cause notice of the judgment to be sent by certified mail, return receipt requested, to all persons known to have, or appearing to have, an interest in the property that was acquired prior to the filing of a corrupt activity lien notice or a lis pendens as authorized by section 2923.36 of the Revised Code. If the notices cannot be given to those persons in that manner, the court shall cause publication of the notice of the judgment of forfeiture pursuant to the Rules of Civil Procedure.

(2) Within thirty days after receipt of a notice or after the date of publication of a notice under division (E)(1) of this section, any person, other than the defendant or the adjudicated delinquent child, who claims an interest in the property that is subject to forfeiture may petition the court for a hearing to determine the validity of the claim. The petition shall be signed and sworn to by the petitioner and shall set forth the nature and extent of the petitioner's interest in the property, the date and circumstances of the petitioner's acquisition of the interest, any additional allegations supporting the claim, and the relief sought. The petitioner shall furnish the prosecuting attorney with a copy of the petition.

(3) The court, to the extent practicable and consistent with the interests of justice, shall hold the hearing described under division (E)(2) of this section within thirty days from the filing of the petition. The court may consolidate the hearings on all petitions filed by third party claimants under this section. At the hearing, the petitioner may testify and present evidence on the petitioner's own behalf and cross-examine witnesses. The prosecuting attorney may present evidence and witnesses in rebuttal and in defense of the claim of the state to the property and cross-examine witnesses. The court, in making its determination, shall consider the testimony and evidence presented at the hearing and the relevant portions of the record of the criminal proceeding that resulted in the judgment of forfeiture.

(4) If at a hearing held under division (E)(3) of this section, the court, by a preponderance of the evidence, determines either that the petitioner has a legal right, title, or interest in the property that, at the time of the commission of the acts giving rise to the forfeiture of the property, was vested in the petitioner and not in the defendant or the adjudicated delinquent child or was superior to the right, title, or interest of the defendant or the adjudicated delinquent child, or that the petitioner is a bona fide purchaser for value of the right, title, or interest in the property and was at the time of the purchase reasonably without cause to believe that the property was subject to forfeiture under this section, it shall amend, in accordance with its determination, the judgment of forfeiture to protect the rights of innocent persons.

(F) Except as provided in division (E) of this section, no person claiming an interest in property that is subject to forfeiture under this section shall do either of the following:

(1) Intervene in a trial or appeal of a criminal case or a delinquency case that involves the forfeiture of the property;

(2) File an action against the state concerning the validity of his alleged interest in the property subsequent to the filing of the indictment, count in the indictment, or information, or the filing of the complaint in juvenile court, that alleges that the property is subject to forfeiture under this section.

(G) As used in this section, "law enforcement agency" includes, but is not limited to, the state board of pharmacy.

HISTORY: 141 v H 5 (Eff 1-1-86); 141 v S 74 (Eff 9-3-86); 142 v H 708 (Eff 4-19-88); 143 v H 215 (Eff 4-11-90); 143 v H 266 (Eff 9-6-90); 146 v S 2. Eff 7-1-96.

Not analogous to former RC § 2923.32 (GC § 12674; 114 v 143; Bureau of Code Revision, 10-1-53), repealed 134 v H 511, § 2, eff 1-1-74.

The effective date is set by section 6 of SB 2.

§ 2923.33 Motion and order to preserve reachability of property subject to forfeit.

(A) At any time after an indictment is filed alleging a violation of section 2923.32 of the Revised Code or a conspiracy to violate that section or after a complaint is filed in juvenile court alleging a violation of that section or a conspiracy to violate that section as a delinquent act, the prosecuting attorney may file a motion requesting the court to issue an order to preserve the reachability of any property that may be subject to forfeiture. Upon the filing of the motion, the court, after giving notice to any person who will be affected by any order issued by the court pursuant to the motion, shall hold a hearing on the motion at which all affected persons have an opportunity to be heard and, upon a showing by the prosecuting attorney by a preponderance of the evidence that the particular action is necessary to preserve the reachability of any property that may be subject to forfeiture and based upon the indictment, may enter a restraining order or injunction, require the execution of a satisfactory performance bond, or take any other necessary action, including the appointment of a receiver. The prosecuting attorney is not required to show special or irreparable injury to obtain any court action pursuant to this division. Notwithstanding the Rules of Evidence, the court's order or injunction may be based on hearsay testimony.

(B) If no indictment has been filed alleging a violation of section 2923.32 of the Revised Code or a conspiracy to violate that section and no complaint has been filed in juvenile court alleging a violation of that section or a conspiracy to violate that section as a delinquent act, the court may take any action specified in division (A) of this section if the prosecuting attorney for the county, in addition to the showing that would be required pursuant to division (A) of this section, also shows both of the following by a preponderance of the evidence:

(1) There is probable cause to believe that the property with respect to which the order is sought, in the event of a conviction or a delinquency adjudication, would be subject to criminal forfeiture under section 2923.32 of the Revised Code;

(2) The requested order would not result in irreparable harm to the party against whom the order is to be entered that outweighs the need to preserve the reachability of the property.

No order entered pursuant to this division shall be effective for more than ninety days, unless it is extended pursuant to the procedure provided in this division by the court for good cause shown or an indictment is returned alleging that the property is subject to forfeiture.

(C) Upon application by the prosecuting attorney, the court may grant a temporary restraining order to preserve the reachability of property subject to criminal forfeiture under section 2923.32 of the Revised Code without notice to any party, if all of the following occur:

(1) Either an indictment or a juvenile delinquency complaint alleging that property is subject to criminal forfeiture has been filed, or the court determines that there is probable cause to believe that property with respect to which the order is sought would be subject, in the event of a conviction or a delinquency adjudication, to criminal forfeiture;

(2) The property is in the possession or control of the party against whom the order is to be entered;

(3) The court determines that the nature of the property is such that it can be concealed, disposed of, or placed beyond the jurisdiction of the court before any party may be heard in opposition to the order.

A temporary restraining order granted without notice to any party under this division shall expire within the time, not to exceed ten days, that the court fixes, unless extended for good cause shown or unless the party against whom it is entered consents to an extension for a longer period. If a temporary restraining order is granted under this division without notice to any party, the court shall hold a hearing concerning the entry of an order under this division at the earliest practicable time prior to the expiration of the temporary order.

(D) Following sentencing and the entry of a judgment against an offender that includes a fine or an order of criminal forfeiture, or both, under section 2923.32 of the Revised Code, or following the entry of a judgment against a delinquent child that includes an order of criminal forfeiture under that section, the court may enter a restraining order or injunction, require the execution of a satisfactory performance bond, or take any other action, including the appointment of a receiver, that the court determines to be proper to protect the interests of the state or an innocent person.

HISTORY: 141 v H 5 (Eff 1-1-86); 143 v H 266. Eff 9-6-90.

Not analogous to former RC § 2923.33 (GC § 12674-1; 114 v 143, § 2; Bureau of Code Revision, 10-1-53), repealed 134 v H 511, § 2, eff 1-1-74.

§ 2923.34 Civil proceedings for relief from violation; civil penalty.

(A) The prosecuting attorney of the county in which a violation of section 2923.32 of the Revised Code, or a conspiracy to violate that section, occurs may institute a civil proceeding as authorized by this section in an appropriate court seeking relief from any person whose conduct violated section 2923.32 of the Revised Code or who conspired to violate that section.

(B) Any person who is injured or threatened with injury by a violation of section 2923.32 of the Revised Code may institute a civil proceeding in an appropriate court seeking relief from any person whose conduct violated or allegedly violated section 2923.32 of the Revised Code or who conspired or allegedly conspired to violate that section, except that the pattern of corrupt activity alleged by an injured person or person threatened with injury shall include at least one incident other than a violation of division (A)(1) or (2) of section 1707.042 [1707.04.2] or division (B), (C)(4), (D), (E), or (F) of section 1707.44 of the Revised Code, of 18 U.S.C. 1341, 18 U.S.C. 1343, 18 U.S.C. 2314, or any other offense involving fraud in the sale of securities.

(C) If the plaintiff in a civil action instituted pursuant to this section proves the violation by a preponderance of the evidence, the court, after making due provision for the rights of innocent persons, may grant relief by entering any appropriate orders to ensure that the violation will not continue or be repeated. The orders may include, but are not limited to, orders that:

(1) Require any defendant in the action to divest himself of any interest in any enterprise or in any real property;

(2) Impose reasonable restrictions upon the future activities or investments of any defendant in the action, including, but not limited to, restrictions that prohibit the defendant from engaging in the same type of endeavor as the enterprise in which he was engaged in violation of section 2923.32 of the Revised Code;

(3) Order the dissolution or reorganization of any enterprise;

(4) Order the suspension or revocation of a license, permit, or prior approval granted to any enterprise by any department or agency of the state;

(5) Order the dissolution of a corporation organized under the laws of this state, or the revocation of the authorization of a foreign corporation to conduct business within this state, upon a finding that the board of directors or an agent acting on behalf of the corporation, in conducting the affairs of the corporation, has authorized or engaged in conduct in violation of section 2923.32 of the Revised Code, and that, for the prevention of future criminal conduct, the public interest requires the corporation to be dissolved or its license revoked.

(D) Relief pursuant to division (C)(3), (4), or (5) of this section shall not be granted in any civil proceeding instituted by an injured person unless the attorney general intervenes in the civil action pursuant to this division.

Upon the filing of a civil proceeding for relief under division (C)(3), (4), or (5) of this section by an allegedly injured person other than a prosecuting attorney, the allegedly injured person immediately shall notify the attorney general of the filing. The attorney general, upon timely application, may intervene in any civil proceeding for relief under division (C)(3), (4), or (5) if the attorney general certifies that, in his opinion, the proceeding is of general public interest. In any proceeding brought by an injured person under division (C)(3), (4), or (5) of this section, the attorney general is entitled to the same relief as if the attorney general instituted the proceeding.

(E) In a civil proceeding under division (C) of this section, the court may grant injunctive relief without a showing of special or irreparable injury.

Pending final determination of a civil proceeding initiated under this section, the court may issue a temporary restraining order or a preliminary injunction upon a showing of immediate danger or significant injury to the plaintiff, including the possibility that any judgment for money damages might be difficult to execute, and, in a proceeding initiated by an aggrieved person, upon the execution of proper bond against injury for an improvidently granted injunction.

(F) In a civil proceeding under division (B) of this section, any person directly or indirectly injured by conduct in violation of section 2923.32 of the Revised Code or a conspiracy to violate that section, other than a violator of that section or a conspirator to violate that section, in addition to relief under division (C) of this section, shall have a cause of action for triple the actual damages he sustained. To recover triple damages, the plaintiff shall prove the violation or conspiracy to violate that section and actual damages by clear and convincing evidence. Damages under this division may include, but are not limited to, competitive injury and injury distinct from the injury inflicted by corrupt activity.

(G) In a civil action in which the plaintiff prevails under division (C) or (F) of this section, he shall recover reasonable attorney fees in the trial and appellate courts, and the court shall order the defendant to pay to the state, municipal, or county law enforcement agencies that handled the investigation and litigation the costs of investigation and litigation that reasonably are incurred and that are not ordered to be paid pursuant to division (B)(2) of section 2923.32 of the Revised Code or division (I) of this section.

(H) Upon application, based on the evidence presented in the case by the plaintiff, as the interests of justice may require, the trial court may grant a defendant who prevails in a civil action brought pursuant to this section all or part of his costs, including the costs of investigation and litigation reasonably incurred, and all or part of his reasonable attorney fees, unless the court finds that special circumstances, including the relative economic position of the parties, make an award unjust.

(I) If a person, other than an individual, is not convicted of a violation of section 2923.32 of the Revised Code, the prosecuting attorney may institute proceedings against the person to recover a civil penalty for conduct that the prosecuting attorney proves by clear and convincing evidence is in violation of section 2923.32 of the Revised Code. The civil penalty shall not exceed one hundred thousand dollars and shall be paid into the state treasury to the credit of the corrupt activity investigation and prosecution fund created in section 2923.35 of the Revised Code. If a civil penalty is ordered pursuant to this division, the court shall order the defendant to pay to the state, municipal, or county law enforcement agencies that handled the investigation and litigation the costs of investigation and litigation that are reasonably incurred and that are not ordered to be paid pursuant to this section.

(J) A final judgment, decree, or delinquency adjudication rendered against the defendant or the adjudicated delinquent child in a civil action under this section or in a criminal or delinquency action or proceeding for a violation of section 2923.32 of the Revised Code shall estop the defendant or the adjudicated delinquent child in any subsequent civil proceeding or action brought by any person as to all matters as to which the judgment, decree, or adjudication would be an estoppel as between the parties to the civil, criminal, or delinquency proceeding or action.

(K) Notwithstanding any other provision of law providing a shorter period of limitations, a civil proceeding or action under this section may be commenced at any time within five years after the unlawful conduct terminates or the cause of action accrues or within any longer statutory period of limitations that may be applicable. If a criminal proceeding, delinquency proceeding, civil action, or other proceeding is brought or intervened in by the state to punish, prevent, or restrain any activity that is unlawful under section 2923.32 of the Revised Code, the running of the period of limitations prescribed by this division with respect to any civil action brought under this section by a person who is injured by a violation or threatened violation of section 2923.32 of the Revised Code, based in whole or in part upon any matter complained of in the state prosecution, action, or proceeding, shall be suspended during the pendency of the state prosecution, action, or proceeding and for two years following its termination.

(L) Personal service of any process in a proceeding under this section may be made upon any person outside this state if the person was involved in any conduct constituting a violation of section 2923.32 of the Revised Code in this state. The person is deemed by his conduct in violation of section 2923.32 of the Revised Code to have submitted himself to the jurisdiction of the courts of this state for the purposes of this section.

(M) The application of any civil remedy under this section shall not preclude the application of any criminal remedy or criminal forfeiture under section 2923.32 of the Revised Code or any other provision of law, or the application of any delinquency disposition under section 2151.355 [2151.35.5] of the Revised Code or any other provision of law.

(N) As used in this section, "law enforcement agency" includes, but is not limited to, the state board of pharmacy.

HISTORY: 141 v H 5 (Eff 1-1-86); 141 v H 428 (Eff 12-23-86); 143 v H 266. Eff 9-6-90.

Not analogous to former RC § 2923.34 (GC § 12674-2; 114 v 143, § 3; Bureau of Code Revision, 10-1-53), repealed 134 v H 511, § 2, eff 1-1-74.

§ 2923.35 Disposition of forfeited property, fine or civil penalty.

(A)(1) With respect to property ordered forfeited under section 2923.32 of the Revised Code, with respect to any fine or civil penalty imposed in any criminal or civil proceeding under section 2923.32 or 2923.34 of the Revised Code, and with respect to any fine imposed for a violation of section 2923.01 of the Revised Code for conspiracy to violate section 2923.32 of the Revised Code, the court, upon petition of the prosecuting attorney, may do any of the following:

(a) Authorize the prosecuting attorney to settle claims;

(b) Award compensation to persons who provide information that results in a forfeiture, fine, or civil penalty under section 2923.32 or 2923.34 of the Revised Code;

(c) Grant petitions for mitigation or remission of forfeiture, fines, or civil penalties, or restore forfeited property, imposed fines, or imposed civil penalties to persons injured by the violation;

(d) Take any other action to protect the rights of innocent persons that is in the interest of justice and that is consistent with the purposes of sections 2923.31 to 2923.36 of the Revised Code.

(2) The court shall maintain an accurate record of the actions it takes under division (A)(1) of this section with respect to the property ordered forfeited or the fine or civil penalty. The record is a public record open for inspection under section 149.43 of the Revised Code.

(B)(1) After the application of division (A) of this section, any person who prevails in a civil action pursuant to section 2923.34 of the Revised Code has a right to any property, or the proceeds of any property, criminally forfeited to the state pursuant to section 2923.32 of the Revised Code or against which any fine under that section or civil penalty under division (I) of section 2923.34 of the Revised Code may be imposed.

The right of any person who prevails in a civil action pursuant to section 2923.34 of the Revised Code, other than a prosecuting attorney performing official duties under that section, to forfeited property, property against which fines and civil penalties may be imposed, and the proceeds of that property is superior to any right of the state, a municipal corporation, or a county to the property or the proceeds of the property, if the civil action is brought within one hundred eighty days after the entry of a sentence of forfeiture or a fine pursuant to section 2923.32 of the Revised Code or the entry of a civil penalty pursuant to division (I) of section 2923.34 of the Revised Code.

The right is limited to the total value of the treble damages, civil penalties, attorney's fees, and costs awarded to the prevailing party in an action pursuant to section 2923.34 of the Revised Code, less any restitution received by the person.

(2) If the aggregate amount of claims of persons who have prevailed in a civil action pursuant to section 2923.34 of the Revised Code against any one defendant is greater than the total value of the treble fines, civil penalties, and forfeited property paid by the person against whom the actions were brought, all of the persons who brought their actions within one hundred eighty days after the entry of a sentence or disposition of forfeiture or a fine pursuant to section 2923.32 of the Revised Code or the entry of a civil penalty pursuant to division (I) of section 2923.34 of the Revised Code, first shall receive a pro rata share of the total amount of the fines, civil penalties, and forfeited property. After the persons who brought their actions within the specified one hundred eighty-day period have satisfied their claims out of the fines, civil penalties, and forfeited property, all other persons who prevailed in civil actions pursuant to section 2923.34 of the Revised Code shall receive a pro rata share of the total amount of the fines, civil penalties, and forfeited property that remains in the custody of the law enforcement agency or in the corrupt activity investigation and prosecution fund.

(C)(1) Subject to divisions (A) and (B) of this section and notwithstanding any contrary provision of section 2933.41 of the Revised Code, the prosecuting attorney shall order the disposal of property ordered forfeited in any proceeding under sections 2923.32 and 2923.34 of the Revised Code as soon as feasible, making due provisions for the rights of innocent persons, by any of the following methods:

(a) Transfer to any person who prevails in a civil action pursuant to section 2923.34 of the Revised Code, subject to the limit set forth in division (B)(1) of this section;

(b) Public sale;

(c) Transfer to a state governmental agency for official use;

(d) Sale or transfer to an innocent person;

(e) If the property is contraband and is not needed for evidence in any pending criminal or civil proceeding, pursuant to section 2933.41 or any other applicable section of the Revised Code.

(2) Any interest in personal or real property not disposed of pursuant to this division and not exercisable by, or transferable for value to, the state shall expire and shall not revert to the person found guilty of or adjudicated a delinquent child for a violation of section 2923.32 of the Revised Code. No person found guilty of or adjudicated a delinquent child for a violation of that section and no person acting in concert with a person found guilty of or adjudicated a delinquent child for a violation of that section is eligible to purchase forfeited property from the state.

(3) Upon application of a person, other than the defendant, the adjudicated delinquent child, or a person acting in concert with or on behalf of either the defendant or the adjudicated delinquent child, the court may restrain or stay the disposal of the property pursuant to this division pending the conclusion of any appeal of the criminal case or delinquency case giving rise to the forfeiture or pending the determination of the validity of a claim to or interest in the property pursuant to division (E) of section 2923.32 of the Revised Code, if the applicant demonstrates that proceeding with the disposal of the property will result in irreparable injury, harm, or loss to the applicant.

(4) The prosecuting attorney shall maintain an accurate record of each item of property disposed of pursuant to this division, which record shall include the date on which each item came into the prosecuting attorney's custody, the manner and date of disposition, and, if applicable, the name of the person who received the item. The record shall not identify or enable the identification of the individual officer who seized the property, and the record is a public record open for inspection under section 149.43 of the Revised Code.

Each prosecuting attorney who disposes in any calendar year of any item of property pursuant to this division shall prepare a report covering the calendar year that cumulates all of the information contained in all of the records kept by the prosecuting attorney pursuant to this division for that calendar year and shall send the cumulative report, no later than the first day of March in the calendar year following the calendar year covered by the report, to the attorney general. Each report received by the attorney general is a public record open for inspection under section 149.43 of the Revised Code. The attorney general shall send a copy of the cumulative report, no later than the fifteenth day of April in the calendar year following the calendar year covered by the report, to the president of the senate and the speaker of the house of representatives.

(D)(1)(a) Ten per cent of the proceeds of all property ordered forfeited by a juvenile court pursuant to section 2923.32 of the Revised Code shall be applied to one or more alcohol and drug addiction treatment programs that are certified by the department of alcohol and drug addiction services under section 3793.06 of the Revised Code and that are specified in the order of forfeiture. A juvenile court shall not specify an alcohol or drug addiction treatment program in the order of forfeiture unless the program is a certified alcohol and drug addiction treatment program and, except as provided in division (D)(1)(a) of this section, unless the program is located in the county in which the court that orders the forfeiture is located or in a contiguous county. If no certified alcohol and drug addiction treatment program is located in any of those counties, the juvenile court may specify in the order a certified alcohol and drug addiction treatment program located anywhere within this state. The remaining ninety per cent of the proceeds shall be disposed of as provided in divisions (D)(1)(b) and (D)(2) of this section.

All of the proceeds of all property ordered forfeited by a court other than a juvenile court pursuant to section 2923.32 of the Revised Code shall be disposed of as provided in divisions (D)(1)(b) and (D)(2) of this section.

(b) The remaining proceeds of all property ordered forfeited pursuant to section 2923.32 of the Revised Code, after compliance with division (D)(1)(a) of this section when that division is applicable, and all fines and civil penalties imposed pursuant to sections 2923.32 and 2923.34 of the Revised Code shall be deposited into the state treasury and credited to the corrupt activity investigation and prosecution fund, which is hereby created.

(2) The proceeds, fines, and penalties credited to the corrupt activity investigation and prosecution fund pursuant to division (D)(1) of this section shall be disposed of in the following order:

(a) To a civil plaintiff in an action brought within the one hundred eighty-day time period specified in division (B)(1) of this section, subject to the limit set forth in that division;

(b) To the payment of the fees and costs of the forfeiture and sale, including expenses of seizure, maintenance, and custody of the property pending its disposition, advertising, and court costs;

(c) Except as otherwise provided in division (D)(2)(c) of this section, the remainder shall be paid to the law enforcement trust fund of the prosecuting attorney that is established pursuant to division (D)(1)(c) of section 2933.43 of the Revised Code and to the law enforcement trust fund of the county sheriff that is established pursuant to that division if the county sheriff substantially conducted the investigation, to the law enforcement trust fund of a municipal corporation that is established pursuant to that division if its police department substantially conducted the investigation, to the law enforcement trust fund of a township that is established pursuant to that division if the investigation was substantially conducted by a township police department, township police district police force, or office of a township constable, or to the law enforcement trust fund of a park district created pursuant to section 511.18 or 1545.01 of the Revised Code that is established pursuant to that division if the investigation was substantially conducted by its park district police force or law enforcement department. The prosecuting attorney may decline to accept any of the remaining proceeds, fines, and penalties, and, if the prosecuting attorney so declines, they shall be applied to the fund described in division (D)(2)(c) of this section that relates to the appropriate law enforcement agency that substantially conducted the investigation.

If the state highway patrol substantially conducted the investigation, the director of budget and management shall transfer the remaining proceeds, fines, and penalties to the state highway patrol for deposit into the state highway patrol contraband, forfeiture, and other fund that is created by division (D)(1)(c) of section 2933.43 of the Revised Code. If the state board of pharmacy substantially conducted the investigation, the director shall transfer the remaining proceeds, fines, and penalties to the board for deposit into the board of pharmacy drug law enforcement fund that is created by division (B)(1) of section 4729.65 of the Revised Code. If a state law enforcement agency, other than the state highway patrol or the board, substantially conducted the investigation, the director shall transfer the remaining proceeds, fines, and penalties to the treasurer of state for deposit into the peace officer training commission fund that is created by division (D)(1)(c) of section 2933.43 of the Revised Code.

The remaining proceeds, fines, and penalties that are paid to a law enforcement trust fund or that are deposited into the state highway patrol contraband, forfeiture, and other fund, the board of pharmacy drug law enforcement fund, or the peace officer training commission fund pursuant to division (D)(2)(c) of this section shall be allocated, used, and expended only in accordance with division (D)(1)(c) of section 2933.43 of the Revised Code, only in accordance with a written internal control policy adopted under division (D)(3) of that section, and, if applicable, only in accordance with division (B) of section 4729.65 of the Revised Code. The annual reports that pertain to the funds and that are required by divisions (D)(1)(c) and (3)(b) of section 2933.43 of the Revised Code also shall address the remaining proceeds, fines, and penalties that are paid or deposited into the funds pursuant to division (D)(2)(c) of this section.

(3) If more than one law enforcement agency substantially conducted the investigation, the court ordering the forfeiture shall equitably divide the remaining proceeds, fines, and penalties among the law enforcement agencies that substantially conducted the investigation, in the manner described in division (D)(2) of section 2933.43 of the Revised Code for the equitable division of contraband proceeds and forfeited moneys. The equitable shares of the proceeds, fines, and penalt-

ies so determined by the court shall be paid or deposited into the appropriate funds specified in division (D)(2)(c) of this section.

(E) As used in this section, "law enforcement agency" includes, but is not limited to, the state board of pharmacy.

HISTORY: 141 v H 5 (Eff 1-1-86); 141 v S 74 (Eff 9-3-86); 143 v H 215 (Eff 4-11-90); 143 v H 261 (Eff 7-18-90); 143 v H 266 (Eff 9-6-90); 143 v S 258 (Eff 11-20-90); 144 v S 174 (Eff 7-31-92); 145 v H 152 (Eff 7-1-93); 146 v H 1 (Eff 1-1-96); 146 v H 670. Eff 12-2-96.

Not analogous to former RC § 2923.35 (99 v 253, §§ 1, 3; GC § 12906; Bureau of Code Revision, 10-1-53), repealed 134 v H 511, § 2, eff 1-1-74.

§ 2923.36 Filing of corrupt activity lien notice; lis pendens.

(A) Upon the institution of any criminal proceeding charging a violation of section 2923.32 of the Revised Code, the filing of any complaint in juvenile court alleging a violation of that section as a delinquent act, or the institution of any civil proceeding under section 2923.32 or 2923.34 of the Revised Code, the state, at any time during the pendency of the proceeding, may file a corrupt activity lien notice with the county recorder of any county in which property subject to forfeiture may be located. No fee shall be required for filing the notice. The recorder immediately shall record the notice pursuant to section 317.08 of the Revised Code.

(B) A corrupt activity lien notice shall be signed by the prosecuting attorney who files the lien. The notice shall set forth all of the following information:

(1) The name of the person against whom the proceeding has been brought. The prosecuting attorney may specify in the notice any aliases, names, or fictitious names under which the person may be known. The prosecuting attorney also may specify any corporation, partnership, or other entity in which the person has an interest subject to forfeiture under section 2923.32 of the Revised Code and shall describe in the notice the person's interest in the corporation, partnership, or other entity.

(2) If known to the prosecuting attorney, the present residence and business addresses of the person or names set forth in the notice;

(3) A statement that a criminal or delinquency proceeding for a violation of section 2923.32 of the Revised Code or a civil proceeding under section 2923.32 or 2923.34 of the Revised Code has been brought against the person named in the notice, the name of the county in which the proceeding has been brought, and the case number of the proceeding;

(4) A statement that the notice is being filed pursuant to this section;

(5) The name and address of the prosecuting attorney filing the notice;

(6) A description of the real or personal property subject to the notice and of the interest in that property of the person named in the notice, to the extent the property and the interest of the person in it reasonably is known at the time the proceeding is instituted or at the time the notice is filed.

(C) A corrupt activity lien notice shall apply only to one person and, to the extent applicable, any aliases, fictitious names, or other names, including names of corporations, partnerships, or other entities, to the extent permitted in this section. A separate corrupt activity lien notice is required to be filed for any other person.

(D) Within seven days after the filing of each corrupt activity lien notice, the prosecuting attorney who files the notice shall furnish to the person named in the notice by certified mail, return receipt requested, to the last known business or residential address of the person, a copy of the recorded notice with a notation on it of any county in which the notice has been recorded. The failure of the prosecuting attorney to furnish a copy of the notice under this section shall not invalidate or otherwise affect the corrupt activity lien notice when the prosecuting attorney did not know and could not reasonably ascertain the address of the person entitled to notice.

After receipt of a copy of the notice under this division, the person named in the notice may petition the court to authorize the person to post a surety bond in lieu of the lien or to otherwise modify the lien as the interests of justice may require. The bond shall be in an amount equal to the value of the property reasonably known to be subject to the notice and conditioned on the payment of any judgment and costs ordered in an action pursuant to section 2923.32 or 2923.34 of the Revised Code up to the value of the bond.

(E) From the date of filing of a corrupt activity lien notice, the notice creates a lien in favor of the state on any personal or real property or any beneficial interest in the property located in the county in which the notice is filed that then or subsequently is owned by the person named in the notice or under any of the names set forth in the notice.

The lien created in favor of the state is superior and prior to the interest of any other person in the personal or real property or beneficial interest in the property, if the interest is acquired subsequent to the filing of the notice.

(F)(1) Notwithstanding any law or rule to the contrary, in conjunction with any civil proceeding brought pursuant to section 2923.34 of the Revised Code, the prosecuting attorney may file in any county, without prior court order, a lis pendens pursuant to sections 2703.26 and 2703.27 of the Revised Code. In such a case, any person acquiring an interest in the subject property or beneficial interest in the property, if the property interest is acquired subsequent to the filing of the lis pendens, shall take the property or interest subject to the civil proceeding and any subsequent judgment.

(2) If a corrupt activity lien notice has been filed, the

prosecuting attorney may name as a defendant in the lis pendens, in addition to the person named in the notice, any person acquiring an interest in the personal or real property or beneficial interest in the property subsequent to the filing of the notice. If a judgment of forfeiture is entered in the criminal or delinquency proceeding pursuant to section 2923.32 of the Revised Code in favor of the state, the interest of any person in the property that was acquired subsequent to the filing of the notice shall be subject to the notice and judgment of forfeiture.

(G) Upon a final judgment of forfeiture in favor of the state pursuant to section 2923.32 of the Revised Code, title of the state to the forfeited property shall do either of the following:

(1) In the case of real property, or a beneficial interest in it, relate back to the date of filing of the corrupt activity lien notice in the county where the property or interest is located. If no corrupt activity lien notice was filed, title of the state relates back to the date of the filing of any lis pendens under division (F) of this section in the records of the county recorder of the county in which the real property or beneficial interest is located. If no corrupt activity lien notice or lis pendens was filed, title of the state relates back to the date of the recording of the final judgment of forfeiture in the records of the county recorder of the county in which the real property or beneficial interest is located.

(2) In the case of personal property or a beneficial interest in it, relate back to the date on which the property or interest was seized by the state, or the date of filing of a corrupt activity lien notice in the county in which the property or beneficial interest is located. If the property was not seized and no corrupt activity lien notice was filed, title of the state relates back to the date of the recording of the final judgment of forfeiture in the county in which the personal property or beneficial interest is located.

(H) If personal or real property, or a beneficial interest in it, that is subject to forfeiture pursuant to section 2923.32 of the Revised Code is conveyed, alienated, disposed of, or otherwise rendered unavailable for forfeiture after the filing of either a corrupt activity lien notice, or a criminal or delinquency proceeding for a violation of section 2923.32 or a civil proceeding under section 2923.32 or 2923.34 of the Revised Code, whichever is earlier, the state may bring an action in any court of common pleas against the person named in the corrupt activity lien notice or the defendant in the criminal, delinquency, or civil proceeding to recover the value of the property or interest. The court shall enter final judgment against the person named in the notice or the defendant for an amount equal to the value of the property or interest together with investigative costs and attorney's fees incurred by the state in the action. If a civil proceeding is pending, an action pursuant to this section shall be filed in the court in which the proceeding is pending.

(I) If personal or real property, or a beneficial interest in it, that is subject to forfeiture pursuant to section 2923.32 of the Revised Code is alienated or otherwise transferred or disposed of after either the filing of a corrupt activity lien notice, or the filing of a criminal or delinquency proceeding for a violation of section 2923.32 or a civil proceeding under section 2923.32 or 2923.34 of the Revised Code, whichever is earlier, the transfer or disposal is fraudulent as to the state and the state shall have all the rights granted a creditor under Chapter 1336. of the Revised Code.

(J) No trustee, who acquires actual knowledge that a corrupt activity lien notice, a criminal or delinquency proceeding for a violation of section 2923.32 or a civil proceeding under section 2923.32 or 2923.34 of the Revised Code has been filed against any person for whom he holds legal or record title to personal or real property, shall recklessly fail to furnish promptly to the prosecuting attorney all of the following:

(1) The name and address of the person, as known to the trustee;

(2) The name and address, as known to the trustee, of all other persons for whose benefit the trustee holds title to the property;

(3) If requested by the prosecuting attorney, a copy of the trust agreement or other instrument under which the trustee holds title to the property.

Any trustee who fails to comply with this division is guilty of failure to provide corrupt activity lien information, a misdemeanor of the first degree.

(K) If a trustee transfers title to personal or real property after a corrupt activity lien notice is filed against the property, the lien is filed in the county in which the property is located, and the lien names a person who holds a beneficial interest in the property, the trustee, if he has actual notice of the notice, shall be liable to the state for the greater of the following:

(1) The proceeds received directly by the person named in the notice as a result of the transfer;

(2) The proceeds received by the trustee as a result of the transfer and distributed to the person named in the notice;

(3) The fair market value of the interest of the person named in the notice in the property transferred.

However, if the trustee transfers property for at least its fair market value and holds the proceeds that otherwise would be paid or distributed to the beneficiary, or at the direction of the beneficiary or his designee, the liability of the trustee shall not exceed the amount of the proceeds held by the trustee.

(L) The filing of a corrupt activity lien notice does not constitute a lien on the record title to personal or real property owned by the trustee, except to the extent the trustee is named in the notice.

The prosecuting attorney for the county may bring a civil action in any court of common pleas to recover from the trustee the amounts set forth in division (H) of this section. The county may recover investigative costs and attorney's fees incurred by the prosecuting attorney.

(M)(1) This section does not apply to any transfer by a trustee under a court order, unless the order is entered in an action between the trustee and the beneficiary.

(2) Unless the trustee has actual knowledge that a person owning a beneficial interest in the trust is named in a corrupt activity lien notice or otherwise is a defendant in a civil proceeding brought pursuant to section 2923.34 of the Revised Code, this section does not apply to either of the following:

(a) Any transfer by a trustee required under the terms of any trust agreement, if the agreement is a matter of public record before the filing of any corrupt activity lien notice;

(b) Any transfer by a trustee to all of the persons who own a beneficial interest in the trust.

(N) The filing of a corrupt activity lien notice does not affect the use to which personal or real property, or a beneficial interest in it, that is owned by the person named in the notice may be put or the right of the person to receive any proceeds resulting from the use and ownership, but not the sale, of the property, until a judgment of forfeiture is entered.

(O) The term of a corrupt activity lien notice is five years from the date the notice is filed, unless a renewal notice has been filed by the prosecuting attorney of the county in which the property or interest is located. The term of any renewal of a corrupt activity lien notice granted by the court is five years from the date of its filing. A corrupt activity lien notice may be renewed any number of times while a criminal or civil proceeding under section 2923.32 or 2923.34 of the Revised Code, or an appeal from either type of proceeding, is pending.

(P) The prosecuting attorney who files the corrupt activity lien notice may terminate, in whole or part, any corrupt activity lien notice or release any personal or real property or beneficial interest in the property upon any terms that he determines are appropriate. Any termination or release shall be filed by the prosecuting attorney with each county recorder with whom the notice was filed. No fee shall be imposed for the filing.

(Q)(1) If no civil proceeding has been brought by the prosecuting attorney pursuant to section 2923.34 of the Revised Code against the person named in the corrupt activity lien notice, the acquittal in a criminal or delinquency proceeding for a violation of section 2923.32 of the Revised Code of the person named in the notice or the dismissal of a criminal or delinquency proceeding for such a violation against the person named in the notice terminates the notice. In such a case, the filing of the notice has no effect.

(2) If a civil proceeding has been brought pursuant to section 2923.34 of the Revised Code with respect to any property that is the subject of a corrupt activity lien notice and if the criminal or delinquency proceeding brought against the person named in the notice for a violation of section 2923.32 of the Revised Code has been dismissed or the person named in the notice has been acquitted in the criminal or delinquency proceeding for such a violation, the notice shall continue for the duration of the civil proceeding and any appeals from the civil proceeding, except that it shall not continue any longer than the term of the notice as determined pursuant to division (O) of this section.

(3) If no civil proceeding brought pursuant to section 2923.34 of the Revised Code then is pending against the person named in a corrupt activity lien notice, any person so named may bring an action against the prosecuting attorney who filed the notice, in the county where it was filed, seeking a release of the property subject to the notice or termination of the notice. In such a case, the court of common pleas promptly shall set a date for hearing, which shall be not less than five nor more than ten days after the action is filed. The order and a copy of the complaint shall be served on the prosecuting attorney within three days after the action is filed. At the hearing, the court shall take evidence as to whether any personal or real property, or beneficial interest in it, that is owned by the person bringing the action is covered by the notice or otherwise is subject to forfeiture. If the person bringing the action shows by a preponderance of the evidence that the notice does not apply to him or that any personal or real property, or beneficial interest in it, that is owned by him is not subject to forfeiture, the court shall enter a judgment terminating the notice or releasing the personal or real property or beneficial interest from the notice.

At a hearing, the court may release from the notice any property or beneficial interest upon the posting of security, by the person against whom the notice was filed, in an amount equal to the value of the property or beneficial interest owned by the person.

(4) The court promptly shall enter an order terminating a corrupt activity lien notice or releasing any personal or real property or beneficial interest in the property, if a sale of the property or beneficial interest is pending and the filing of the notice prevents the sale. However, the proceeds of the sale shall be deposited with the clerk of the court, subject to the further order of the court.

(R) Notwithstanding any provision of this section, any person, who has perfected a security interest in personal or real property or a beneficial interest in the property for the payment of an enforceable debt or other similar obligation prior to the filing of a corrupt activity lien notice or a lis pendens in reference to the property or interest may foreclose on the property or interest as otherwise provided by law. The foreclosure, insofar as practical, shall be made so that it otherwise will not interfere with a forfeiture under section 2923.32 of the Revised Code.

HISTORY: 141 v H 5 (Eff 1-1-86); 143 v H 190 (Eff 9-25-89); 143 v H 266 (Eff 9-6-90); 143 v H 506. Eff 9-28-90.

Comment, Legislative Service Commission

Section 2923.36 of the Revised Code is amended by this

act [H.B. 506] and also by Sub. H.B. 266 of the 118th General Assembly. Comparison of these amendments in pursuance of section 1.52 of the Revised Code discloses that they are not irreconcilable, so that they are required by that section to be harmonized to give effect to each amendment.

§§ 2923.41, 2923.42, 2923.43
Repealed, 134 v H 511, § 2 [125 v S 28(211); 128 v 623; 129 v 376; 129 v 582(748); 132 v H 332; 134 v H 344]. Eff 1-1-74.

These sections concerned disturbing the peace, giving false information, and interference at emergency scenes.

§§ 2923.51, 2923.52, 2923.53
Repealed, 134 v H 511, § 2 [132 v H 996]. Eff 1-1-74.

These sections concerned riot control.

§§ 2923.54, 2923.55
Repealed, 134 v H 511, § 2 [132 v H 996]. Eff 1-1-74.

These sections concerned riot control.

§§ 2923.56, 2923.57
Repealed, 134 v H 511, § 2 [133 v H 484]. Eff 1-1-74.

These sections concerned rules and transactions regarding firearms.

§ 2923.61
Repealed, 134 v H 511, § 2 [133 v H 1219]. Eff 1-1-74.

This section concerned disrupting college activities.

§ 2923.99
Repealed, 129 v 582(990), § 2 [127 v 459]. Eff 1-10-61.

This section provided a penalty for former RC § 2923.25.1 concerning unvented gas heaters.

CHAPTER 2925: DRUG OFFENSES

Section
2925.01 Definitions.

[CORRUPTING; TRAFFICKING]
2925.02 Corrupting another with drugs.
2925.03 Trafficking in drugs.

[DRUG ABUSE]
2925.04 Illegal manufacture of drugs or cultivation of marihuana.
2925.05 Funding of drug or marihuana trafficking.
2925.06 Illegal administration or distribution of anabolic steroids.
2925.09 Offenses involving unapproved drugs; dangerous drug offenses involving livestock.
2925.11 Possession of drugs.
2925.12 Possessing drug abuse instruments.
2925.13 Permitting drug abuse.
2925.14 Drug paraphernalia offenses.

[DRUG THEFT]
2925.21 Repealed.
2925.22 Deception to obtain a dangerous drug.
2925.23 Illegal processing of drug documents.

[HARMFUL INTOXICANTS]
2925.31 Abusing harmful intoxicants.
2925.32 Trafficking in harmful intoxicants.
2925.33 Possessing nitrous oxide in motor vehicle.

[DRUG SAMPLES]
2925.36 Illegal dispensing of drug samples.
2925.37 Offenses involving counterfeit controlled substances.
2925.38 Convictions to be reported to professional licensing authorities.

[FORFEITURE OF PROPERTY RELATING TO FELONY DRUG ABUSE OFFENSE]
2925.41 Definitions.
2925.42 Forfeiture of property in connection with felony drug abuse offense or act.
2925.43 Civil forfeiture action prior to prosecution.
2925.44 Rights of law enforcement agency seizing property; disposition of forfeited property.
2925.45 Motion alleging seizure was unlawful; return of property.

[FEDERAL NARCOTIC LAWS]
2925.50 Conviction or acquittal under federal narcotic laws.

[LABORATORY EVIDENCE]
2925.51 Laboratory report as evidence; requirements; violation.

§ 2925.01 Definitions.

As used in this chapter:
(A) "Administer," "controlled substance," "dispense," "distribute," "federal drug abuse control laws," "hypodermic," "manufacturer," "official written order," "person," "pharmacist," "pharmacy," "practitioner," "prescription," "sale," "schedule I," "schedule II," "schedule III," "schedule IV," "schedule V," and "wholesaler" have the same meanings as in section 3719.01 of the Revised Code.

(B) "Drug dependent person" and "drug of abuse" have the same meanings as in section 3719.011 [3719.01.1] of the Revised Code.

(C) "Drug," "dangerous drug," and "Federal Food, Drug, and Cosmetic Act" have the same meanings as in section 4729.02 of the Revised Code.

(D) "Bulk amount" of a controlled substance means any of the following:

(1) For any compound, mixture, preparation, or substance included in schedule I, schedule II, or schedule III, with the exception of marihuana, cocaine, L.S.D., heroin, and hashish and except as provided in division (D)(2) or (5) of this section, whichever of the following is applicable:

(a) An amount equal to or exceeding ten grams or twenty-five unit doses of a compound, mixture, preparation, or substance that is or contains any amount of a schedule I opiate or opium derivative;

(b) An amount equal to or exceeding ten grams of a compound, mixture, preparation, or substance that is or contains any amount of raw or gum opium;

(c) An amount equal to or exceeding thirty grams or ten unit doses of a compound, mixture, preparation, or substance that is or contains any amount of a schedule I hallucinogen other than tetrahydrocannabinol or lysergic acid amide, or a schedule I stimulant or depressant;

(d) An amount equal to or exceeding twenty grams or five times the maximum daily dose in the usual dose range specified in a standard pharmaceutical reference manual of a compound, mixture, preparation, or substance that is or contains any amount of a schedule II opiate or opium derivative;

(e) An amount equal to or exceeding five grams or ten unit doses of a compound, mixture, preparation, or substance that is or contains any amount of phencyclidine;

(f) An amount equal to or exceeding one hundred twenty grams or thirty times the maximum daily dose in the usual dose range specified in a standard pharmaceutical reference manual of a compound, mixture, preparation, or substance that is or contains any amount of a schedule II stimulant that is in a final dosage form manufactured by a person authorized by the Federal Food, Drug, and Cosmetic Act and the federal drug abuse control laws, that is or contains any amount of a schedule II depressant substance or a schedule II hallucinogenic substance;

(g) An amount equal to or exceeding three grams of a compound, mixture, preparation, or substance that is or contains any amount of a schedule II stimulant, or any of its salts or isomers, that is not in a final dosage form manufactured by a person authorized by the Federal Food, Drug, and Cosmetic Act and the federal drug abuse control laws.

(2) An amount equal to or exceeding one hundred twenty grams or thirty times the maximum daily dose in the usual dose range specified in a standard pharmaceutical reference manual of a compound, mixture, preparation, or substance that is or contains any amount of a schedule III or IV substance other than an anabolic steroid or a schedule III opiate or opium derivative;

(3) An amount equal to or exceeding twenty grams or five times the maximum daily dose in the usual dose range specified in a standard pharmaceutical reference manual of a compound, mixture, specification, or substance that is or contains any amount of a schedule III opiate or opium derivative;

(4) An amount equal to or exceeding two hundred fifty milliliters or two hundred fifty grams of a compound, mixture, preparation, or substance that is or contains any amount of a schedule V substance;

(5) An amount equal to or exceeding two hundred solid dosage units, sixteen grams, or sixteen milliliters of a compound, mixture, preparation, or substance that is or contains any amount of a schedule III anabolic steroid.

(E) "Unit dose" means an amount or unit of a compound, mixture, or preparation containing a controlled substance that is separately identifiable and is in a form indicating† that indicates that it is the amount or unit by which the controlled substance is separately administered to or taken by an individual.

(F) "Cultivate" includes planting, watering, fertilizing, or tilling.

(G) "Drug abuse offense" means any of the following:

(1) A violation of division (A) of section 2913.02 that constitutes theft of drugs, or a violation of section 2925.02, 2925.03, 2925.04, 2925.05, 2925.06, 2925.11, 2925.12, 2925.13, 2925.22, 2925.23, 2925.31, 2925.32, 2925.36, or 2925.37 of the Revised Code;

(2) A violation of an existing or former law of this or any other state or of the United States that is substantially equivalent to any section listed in division (G)(1) of this section;

(3) An offense under an existing or former law of this or any other state, or of the United States, of which planting, cultivating, harvesting, processing, making, manufacturing, producing, shipping, transporting, delivering, acquiring, possessing, storing, distributing, dispensing, selling, inducing another to use, administering to another, using, or otherwise dealing with a controlled substance is an element;

(4) A conspiracy to commit, attempt to commit, or complicity in committing or attempting to commit, any offense under division (G)(1), (2), or (3) of this section.

(H) "Felony drug abuse offense" means any drug abuse offense that would constitute a felony under the laws of this state, any other state, or the United States.

(I) "Harmful intoxicant" does not include beer or intoxicating liquor, but means any compound, mixture, preparation, or substance the gas, fumes, or vapor of which when inhaled can induce intoxication, excitement, giddiness, irrational behavior, depression, stupefaction, paralysis, unconsciousness, asphyxiation, or other harmful physiological effects, and includes, but is not limited to, any of the following:

(1) Any volatile organic solvent, plastic cement, model cement, fingernail polish remover, lacquer thinner, cleaning fluid, gasoline, or other preparation containing a volatile organic solvent;

(2) Any aerosol propellant;

(3) Any fluorocarbon refrigerant;

(4) Any anesthetic gas.

(J) "Manufacture" means to plant, cultivate, harvest, process, make, prepare, or otherwise engage in any part of the production of a drug, by propagation, extraction, chemical synthesis, or compounding, or any combination of the same, and includes packaging, repackaging, labeling, and other activities incident to production.

(K) "Possess" or "possession" means having control over a thing or substance, but may not be inferred solely from mere access to the thing or substance through ownership or occupation of the premises upon which the thing or substance is found.

(L) "Sample drug" means a drug or pharmaceutical preparation that would be hazardous to health or safety if used without the supervision of a practitioner, or a drug of abuse, and that, at one time, had been placed in a container plainly marked as a sample by a manufacturer.

(M) "Standard pharmaceutical reference manual" means the current edition, with cumulative changes if any, of any of the following reference works:

(1) "The National Formulary";

(2) "The United States Pharmacopeia," prepared by authority of the United States Pharmacopeial Convention, Inc.;

(3) Other standard references that are approved by the state board of pharmacy.

(N) "Juvenile" means a person under eighteen years of age.

(O) "Counterfeit controlled substance" means any of the following:

(1) Any drug that bears, or whose container or label bears, a trademark, trade name, or other identifying mark used without authorization of the owner of rights to that trademark, trade name, or identifying mark;

(2) Any unmarked or unlabeled substance that is represented to be a controlled substance manufactured, processed, packed, or distributed by a person other than the person that manufactured, processed, packed, or distributed it;

(3) Any substance that is represented to be a controlled substance but is not a controlled substance or is a different controlled substance;

(4) Any substance other than a controlled substance that a reasonable person would believe to be a controlled substance because of its similarity in shape, size, and color, or its markings, labeling, packaging, distribution, or the price for which it is sold or offered for sale.

(P) An offense is "committed in the vicinity of a school" if the offender commits the offense on school premises, in a school building, or within one thousand feet of the boundaries of any school premises.

(Q) "School" means any school operated by a board of education or any school for which the state board of education prescribes minimum standards under section 3301.07 of the Revised Code, whether or not any instruction, extracurricular activities, or training provided by the school is being conducted at the time a criminal offense is committed.

(R) "School premises" means either of the following:

(1) The parcel of real property on which any school is situated, whether or not any instruction, extracurricular activities, or training provided by the school is being conducted on the premises at the time a criminal offense is committed;

(2) Any other parcel of real property that is owned or leased by a board of education of a school or the governing body of a school for which the state board of education prescribes minimum standards under section 3301.07 of the Revised Code and on which some of the instruction, extracurricular activities, or training of the school is conducted, whether or not any instruction, extracurricular activities, or training provided by the school is being conducted on the parcel of real property at the time a criminal offense is committed.

(S) "School building" means any building in which any of the instruction, extracurricular activities, or training provided by a school is conducted, whether or not any instruction, extracurricular activities, or training provided by the school is being conducted in the school building at the time a criminal offense is committed.

(T) "Disciplinary counsel" means the disciplinary counsel appointed by the board of commissioners on grievances and discipline of the supreme court under the Rules for the Government of the Bar of Ohio.

(U) "Certified grievance committee" means a duly constituted and organized committee of the Ohio state bar association or of one or more local bar associations of the state of Ohio that complies with the criteria set forth in Rule V, section 6 of the Rules for the Government of the Bar of Ohio.

(V) "Professional license" means any license, permit, certificate, registration, qualification, admission, temporary license, temporary permit, temporary certificate, or temporary registration that is described in divisions (W)(1) to (35) of this section and that qualifies a person as a professionally licensed person.

(W) "Professionally licensed person" means any of the following:

(1) A person who has obtained a license as a manufacturer of controlled substances or a wholesaler of controlled substances under Chapter 3719. of the Revised Code;

(2) A person who has received a certificate or temporary certificate as a certified public accountant or who has registered as a public accountant under Chapter 4701. of the Revised Code and who holds a live permit issued under that chapter;

(3) A person who holds a certificate of qualification to practice architecture issued or renewed and registered under Chapter 4703. of the Revised Code;

(4) A person who is registered as a landscape architect under Chapter 4703. of the Revised Code or who holds a permit as a landscape architect issued under that chapter;

(5) A person licensed as an auctioneer or apprentice auctioneer or licensed to operate an auction company under Chapter 4707. of the Revised Code;

(6) A person who has been issued a certificate of registration as a registered barber under Chapter 4709. of the Revised Code;

(7) A person licensed and regulated to engage in the business of a debt pooling company by a legislative authority, under authority of Chapter 4710. of the Revised Code;

(8) A person who has been issued a cosmetologist's license, manicurist's license, esthetician's license, managing cosmetologist's license, managing manicurist's license, managing esthetician's license, cosmetology instructor's license, manicurist instructor's license, esthetician instructor's license, or tanning facility permit under Chapter 4713. of the Revised Code;

(9) A person who has been issued a license to practice dentistry, a general anesthesia permit, a conscious intravenous sedation permit, a limited resident's license, a limited teaching license, a dental hygienist's license, or a dental hygienist's teacher's certificate under Chapter 4715. of the Revised Code;

(10) A person who has been issued an embalmer's license, a funeral director's license, or a funeral home license, or who has been registered for a funeral director's apprenticeship under Chapter 4717. of the Revised Code;

(11) A person who has been licensed as a registered nurse or practical nurse, or who has been issued a certificate for the practice of nurse-midwifery under Chapter 4723. of the Revised Code;

(12) A person who has been licensed to practice optometry or to engage in optical dispensing under Chapter 4725. of the Revised Code;

(13) A person licensed to act as a pawnbroker under Chapter 4727. of the Revised Code;

(14) A person licensed to act as a precious metals dealer under Chapter 4728. of the Revised Code;

(15) A person registered as a pharmacist, a pharmacy intern, a wholesale distributor of dangerous drugs, or a terminal distributor of dangerous drugs under Chapter 4729. of the Revised Code;

(16) A person who is authorized to practice as a physician assistant under Chapter 4730. of the Revised Code;

(17) A person who has been issued a certificate to practice medicine and surgery, osteopathic medicine and surgery, a limited branch of medicine or surgery, or podiatry under Chapter 4731. of the Revised Code;

(18) A person licensed as a psychologist or school psychologist under Chapter 4732. of the Revised Code;

(19) A person registered to practice the profession of engineering or surveying under Chapter 4733. of the Revised Code;

(20) A person who has been issued a certificate to practice chiropractic under Chapter 4734. of the Revised Code;

(21) A person licensed to act as a real estate broker, real estate salesman, limited real estate broker, or limited real estate salesman under Chapter 4735. of the Revised Code;

(22) A person registered as a registered sanitarian under Chapter 4736. of the Revised Code;

(23) A person licensed to operate or maintain a junkyard under Chapter 4737. of the Revised Code;

(24) A person who has been issued a motor vehicle salvage dealer's license under Chapter 4738. of the Revised Code;

(25) A person who has been licensed to act as a steam engineer under Chapter 4739. of the Revised Code;

(26) A person who has been issued a license or temporary permit to practice veterinary medicine or any of its branches, or who is registered as a graduate animal technician under Chapter 4741. of the Revised Code;

(27) A person who has been issued a hearing aid dealer's or fitter's license or trainee permit under Chapter 4747. of the Revised Code;

(28) A person who has been issued a class A, class B, or class C license or who has been registered as an investigator or security guard employee under Chapter 4749. of the Revised Code;

(29) A person licensed and registered to practice as a nursing home administrator under Chapter 4751. of the Revised Code;

(30) A person licensed to practice as a speech pathologist or audiologist under Chapter 4753. of the Revised Code;

(31) A person issued a license as an occupational therapist or physical therapist under Chapter 4755. of the Revised Code;

(32) A person who is licensed as a professional clinical counselor or professional counselor, licensed as a social worker or independent social worker, or registered as a social work assistant under Chapter 4757. of the Revised Code;

(33) A person issued a license to practice dietetics under Chapter 4759. of the Revised Code;

(34) A person who has been issued a license or temporary permit to practice respiratory therapy under Chapter 4761. of the Revised Code;

(35) A person who has been issued a real estate appraiser certificate under Chapter 4763. of the Revised Code.

(X) "Cocaine" means any of the following:

(1) A cocaine salt, isomer, or derivative, a salt of a cocaine isomer or derivative, or the base form of cocaine;

(2) Coca leaves or a salt, compound, derivative, or preparation of coca leaves, including ecgonine, a salt, isomer, or derivative of ecgonine, or a salt of an isomer or derivative of ecgonine;

(3) A salt, compound, derivative, or preparation of a substance identified in division (X)(1) or (2) of this section that is chemically equivalent to or identical with any of those substances, except that the substances shall not include decocainized coca leaves or extraction of coca leaves if the extractions do not contain cocaine or ecgonine.

(Y) "L.S.D." means lysergic acid diethylamide.

(Z) "Hashish" means the resin or a preparation of the resin contained in marihuana, whether in solid form or in a liquid concentrate, liquid extract, or liquid distillate form.

(AA) "Marihuana" has the same meaning as in section 3719.01 of the Revised Code, except that it does not include hashish.

(BB) An offense is "committed in the vicinity of a juvenile" if the offender commits the offense within one hundred feet of a juvenile or within the view of a juvenile, regardless of whether the offender knows the age of the juvenile, whether the offender knows the offense is being committed within one hundred feet of or within view of the juvenile, or whether the juvenile actually views the commission of the offense.

(CC) "Presumption for a prison term" or "presumption that a prison term shall be imposed" means a presumption, as described in division (D) of section 2929.13 of the Revised Code, that a prison term is a necessary sanction for a felony in order to comply with the purposes and principles of sentencing under section 2929.11 of the Revised Code.

(DD) "Major drug offender" has the same meaning as in section 2929.01 of the Revised Code.

(EE) "Minor drug possession offense" means either of the following:

(1) A violation of section 2925.11 of the Revised Code as it existed prior to July 1, 1996;

(2) A violation of section 2925.11 of the Revised Code as it exists on and after July 1, 1996 that is a misdemeanor or a felony of the fifth degree.

(FF) "Mandatory prison term" has the same meaning as in section 2929.01 of the Revised Code.

(GG) "Crack cocaine" means a compound, mixture, preparation, or substance that is or contains any amount of cocaine that is analytically identified as the base form of cocaine or that is in a form that resembles rocks or pebbles generally intended for individual use.

HISTORY: 136 v H 300 (Eff 7-1-76); 136 v S 414 (Eff 9-22-76); 137 v H 565 (Eff 11-1-78); 138 v H 900 (Eff 7-1-80); 138 v S 378 (Eff 3-23-81); 139 v H 535 (Eff 8-20-82); 139 v S 199 (Eff 7-1-83); 141 v H 281 (Eff 7-18-85); 143 v H 215 (Eff 4-11-90); 143 v S 258 (Eff 11-20-90); 144 v H 62 (Eff 5-21-91); 144 v H 322 (Eff 3-2-92); 145 v H 156 (Eff 5-19-93); 146 v S 143, § 1 (Eff 3-5-96); 146 v S 2 (Eff 7-1-96); 146 v S 143, § 5 (Eff 7-1-96); 146 v H 125 (Eff 7-1-96); 146 v S 269 (Eff 7-1-96); 146 v S 223. Eff 3-18-97.

Publisher's Note

The amendments made by HB 125 (146 v —), SB 269 (146 v —) and SB 223 (146 v —) have been combined. Please see provisions of RC § 1.52.

† The language is the result of combining HB 125 (146 v —), SB 269 (146 v —), and SB 223 (146 v —), division (E).

[CORRUPTING; TRAFFICKING]

§ 2925.02 Corrupting another with drugs.

(A) No person shall knowingly do any of the following:

(1) By force, threat, or deception, administer to another or induce or cause another to use a controlled substance;

(2) By any means, administer or furnish to another or induce or cause another to use a controlled substance with purpose to cause serious physical harm to the other person, or with purpose to cause the other person to become drug dependent;

(3) By any means, administer or furnish to another or induce or cause another to use a controlled substance, and thereby cause serious physical harm to the other person, or cause the other person to become drug dependent;

(4) By any means, do any of the following:

(a) Furnish or administer a controlled substance to a juvenile who is at least two years the offender's junior, when the offender knows the age of the juvenile or is reckless in that regard;

(b) Induce or cause a juvenile who is at least two years the offender's junior to use a controlled substance, when the offender knows the age of the juvenile or is reckless in that regard;

(c) Induce or cause a juvenile who is at least two years the offender's junior to commit a felony drug abuse offense, when the offender knows the age of the juvenile or is reckless in that regard;

(d) Use a juvenile, whether or not the offender knows the age of the juvenile, to perform any surveillance activity that is intended to prevent the detection of the offender or any other person in the commission of a felony drug abuse offense or to prevent the arrest of the offender or any other person for the commission of a felony drug abuse offense.

(B) Division (A)(1), (3), or (4) of this section does not apply to manufacturers, wholesalers, practitioners, pharmacists, owners of pharmacies, and other persons whose conduct is in accordance with Chapters 3719., 4715., 4729., 4731., and 4741. of the Revised Code or section 4723.56 of the Revised Code.

(C) Whoever violates this section is guilty of corrupting another with drugs. The penalty for the offense shall be determined as follows:

(1) Except as otherwise provided in this division, if the drug involved is any compound, mixture, preparation, or substance included in schedule I or II, with the exception of marihuana, corrupting another with drugs is a felony of the second degree, and, subject to division (E) of this section, the court shall impose as a mandatory prison term one of the prison terms prescribed for a felony of the second degree. If the drug involved is any compound, mixture, preparation, or substance included in schedule I or II, with the exception of marihuana, and if the offense was committed in the vicinity of a school, corrupting another with drugs is a felony of the first degree, and, subject to division (E) of this section, the court shall impose as a mandatory prison term one of the prison terms prescribed for a felony of the first degree.

(2) Except as otherwise provided in this division, if the drug involved is any compound, mixture, preparation, or substance included in schedule III, IV, or V, corrupting another with drugs is a felony of the second degree, and there is a presumption for a prison term for the offense. If the drug involved is any compound, mixture, preparation, or substance included in schedule III, IV, or V and if the offense was committed in the vicinity of a school, corrupting another with drugs is a felony of the second degree, and the court shall impose as a mandatory prison term one of the prison terms prescribed for a felony of the second degree.

(3) Except as otherwise provided in this division, if the drug involved is marihuana, corrupting another with drugs is a felony of the fourth degree, and division (C) of section 2929.13 of the Revised Code applies in determining whether to impose a prison term on the offender. If the drug involved in† marihuana and if the offense was committed in the vicinity of a school, corrupting another with drugs is a felony of the third degree, and division (C) of section 2929.13 of the Revised Code applies in determining whether to impose a prison term on the offender.

(D) In addition to any prison term authorized or required by division (C) or (E) of this section and sections 2929.13 and 2929.14 of the Revised Code and in addition to any other sanction imposed for the offense under this section or sections 2929.11 to 2929.18 of the Revised Code, the court that sentences an offender who is convicted of or pleads guilty to a violation of division (A) of this section or the clerk of that court shall do all of the following that are applicable regarding the offender:

(1)(a) If the violation is a felony of the first, second, or third degree, the court shall impose upon the offender the mandatory fine specified for the offense under division (B)(1) of section 2929.18 of the Revised Code unless, as specified in that division, the court determines that the offender is indigent.

(b) Notwithstanding any contrary provision of section 3719.21 of the Revised Code, any mandatory fine imposed pursuant to division (D)(1)(a) of this section and any fine imposed for a violation of this section pursuant to division (A) of section 2929.18 of the Revised Code shall be paid by the clerk of the court in accordance with and subject to the requirements of, and shall be used as specified in, division (F) of section 2925.03 of the Revised Code.

(c) If a person is charged with any violation of this section that is a felony of the first, second, or third degree, posts bail, and forfeits the bail, the forfeited bail shall be paid by the clerk of the court pursuant to division (D)(1)(b) of this section as if it were a fine imposed for a violation of this section.

(2) The court either shall revoke or, if it does not revoke, shall suspend for not less than six months or more than five years, the driver's or commercial driver's license or permit of any person who is convicted of or pleads guilty to a violation of this section that is a felony of the first degree and shall suspend for not less than six months nor more than five years the driver's or commercial driver's license or permit of any person who is convicted of or pleads guilty to any other violation of this section. If an offender's driver's or commercial driver's license or permit is revoked pursuant to this division, the offender, at any time after the expiration of two years from the day on which the offender's sentence was imposed or from the day on which the offender finally was released from a prison term under the sentence, whichever is later, may file a motion with the sentencing court requesting termination of the revocation. Upon the filing of the motion and the court's finding of good cause for the termination, the court may terminate the revocation.

(3) If the offender is a professionally licensed person or a person who has been admitted to the bar by order of the supreme court in compliance with its prescribed and published rules, in addition to any other sanction imposed for a violation of this section, the court forthwith shall comply with section 2925.38 of the Revised Code.

(E) Notwithstanding the prison term otherwise authorized or required for the offense under division (C) of this section and sections 2929.13 and 2929.14 of the Revised Code, if the violation of division (A) of this section involves the sale, offer to sell, or possession of a schedule I or II controlled substance, with the exception of marihuana, and if the offender, as a result of the violation, is a major drug offender, the court, in lieu of the prison term that otherwise is authorized or required, shall impose upon the offender the mandatory prison term specified in division (D)(3)(a) of section 2929.14 of the Revised Code and may impose an additional prison term under division (D)(3)(b) of that section.

HISTORY: 136 v H 300 (Eff 7-1-76); 143 v H 215 (Eff 4-11-90); 143 v S 258 (Eff 11-20-90); 144 v H 591 (Eff 11-2-92); 145 v H 377 (Eff 9-30-93); 145 v H 391 (Eff 7-21-94); 146 v S 2 (Eff 7-1-96); 146 v S 269. Eff 7-1-96.

The effective date is set by section 5 of SB 269.

† So in enrolled bill.

§ 2925.03 Trafficking in drugs.

(A) No person shall knowingly sell or offer to sell a controlled substance.

(B) This section does not apply to any of the following:

(1) Manufacturers, practitioners, pharmacists, owners of pharmacies, and other persons whose conduct is in accordance with Chapters 3719., 4715., 4729., 4731., and 4741. or section 4723.56 of the Revised Code;

(2) If the offense involves an anabolic steroid, any person who is conducting or participating in a research project involving the use of an anabolic steroid if the project has been approved by the United States food and drug administration;

(3) Any person who sells, offers for sale, prescribes, dispenses, or administers for livestock or other nonhuman species an anabolic steroid that is expressly intended for administration through implants to livestock or other nonhuman species and approved for that purpose under the "Federal Food, Drug, and Cosmetic Act," 52 Stat. 1040 (1938), 21 U.S.C.A. 301, as amended, and is sold, offered for sale, prescribed, dispensed, or administered for that purpose in accordance with that act.

(C) Whoever violates division (A) of this section is guilty of one of the following:

(1) If the drug involved in the violation is any compound, mixture, preparation, or substance included in schedule I or schedule II, with the exception of marihuana, cocaine, L.S.D., heroin, and hashish, whoever violates division (A) of this section is guilty of aggravated trafficking in drugs. The penalty for the offense shall be determined as follows:

(a) Except as otherwise provided in division (C)(1)(b), (c), (d), (e), or (f) of this section, aggravated trafficking in drugs is a felony of the fourth degree, and division (C) of section 2929.13 of the Revised Code applies in determining whether to impose a prison term on the offender.

(b) Except as otherwise provided in division (C)(1)(c), (d), (e), or (f) of this section, if the offense was committed in the vicinity of a school or in the vicinity of a juvenile, aggravated trafficking in drugs is a felony of the third degree, and division (C) of section 2929.13 of the Revised Code applies in determining whether to impose a prison term on the offender.

(c) Except as otherwise provided in this division, if the amount of the drug involved exceeds the bulk amount but does not exceed five times the bulk amount, aggravated trafficking in drugs is a felony of the third degree, and the court shall impose as a mandatory prison term one of the prison terms prescribed for a felony of the third degree. If the amount of the drug involved is within that range and if the offense was committed in the vicinity of a school or in the vicinity of a juvenile, aggravated trafficking in drugs is a felony of the second degree, and the court shall impose as a mandatory prison term one of the prison terms prescribed for a felony of the second degree.

(d) Except as otherwise provided in this division, if the amount of the drug involved exceeds five times the bulk amount but does not exceed fifty times the bulk amount, aggravated trafficking in drugs is a felony of the second degree, and the court shall impose as a mandatory prison term one of the prison terms prescribed for a felony of the second degree. If the amount of the drug involved is within that range and if the offense was committed in the vicinity of a school or in the vicinity of a juvenile, aggravated trafficking in drugs is a felony of the first degree, and the court shall impose as a mandatory prison term one of the prison terms prescribed for a felony of the first degree.

(e) If the amount of the drug involved exceeds fifty times the bulk amount but does not exceed one hundred times the bulk amount and regardless of whether the offense was committed in the vicinity of a school or in the vicinity of a juvenile, aggravated trafficking in drugs is a felony of the first degree, and the court shall impose as a mandatory prison term one of the prison terms prescribed for a felony of the first degree.

(f) If the amount of the drug involved exceeds one hundred times the bulk amount and regardless of whether the offense was committed in the vicinity of a school or in the vicinity of a juvenile, aggravated trafficking in drugs is a felony of the first degree, and the court shall impose as a mandatory prison term the maximum prison term prescribed for a felony of the first degree and may impose an additional prison term prescribed for a major drug offender under division (D)(3)(b) of section 2929.14 of the Revised Code.

(2) If the drug involved in the violation is any compound, mixture, preparation, or substance included in schedule III, IV, or V, whoever violates division (A) of this section is guilty of trafficking in drugs. The penalty for the offense shall be determined as follows:

(a) Except as otherwise provided in division (C)(2)(b), (c), (d), or (e) of this section, trafficking in drugs is a felony of the fifth degree, and division (C) of section 2929.13 of the Revised Code applies in determining whether to impose a prison term on the offender.

(b) Except as otherwise provided in division (C)(2)(c), (d), or (e) of this section, if the offense was committed in the vicinity of a school or in the vicinity of a juvenile, trafficking in drugs is a felony of the fourth degree, and division (C) of section 2929.13 of the Revised Code applies in determining whether to impose a prison term on the offender.

(c) Except as otherwise provided in this division, if the amount of the drug involved exceeds the bulk amount but does not exceed five times the bulk amount, trafficking in drugs is a felony of the fourth degree, and there is a presumption for a prison term for the offense. If the amount of the drug involved is within that range and if the offense was committed in the vicinity of a school or in the vicinity of a juvenile, trafficking in drugs is a felony of the third degree, and there is a presumption for a prison term for the offense.

(d) Except as otherwise provided in this division, if the amount of the drug involved exceeds five times the bulk amount but does not exceed fifty times the bulk amount, trafficking in drugs is a felony of the third degree, and there is a presumption for a prison term for the offense. If the amount of the drug involved is within that range and if the offense was committed in the vicinity of a school or in the vicinity of a juvenile, trafficking in drugs is a felony of the second degree, and there is a presumption for a prison term for the offense.

(e) Except as otherwise provided in this division, if the amount of the drug involved exceeds fifty times the bulk amount, trafficking in drugs is a felony of the second degree, and the court shall impose as a mandatory prison term one of the prison terms prescribed for a felony of the second degree. If the amount of the drug involved exceeds fifty times the bulk amount and if the offense was committed in the vicinity of a school or in the vicinity of a juvenile, trafficking in drugs is a felony of the first degree, and the court shall impose as a mandatory prison term one of the prison terms prescribed for a felony of the first degree.

(3) If the drug involved in the violation is marihuana or a compound, mixture, preparation, or substance containing marihuana other than hashish, whoever violates division (A) of this section is guilty of trafficking in marihuana. The penalty for the offense shall be determined as follows:

(a) Except as otherwise provided in division (C)(3)(b), (c), (d), (e), (f), or (g) of this section, trafficking in marihuana is a felony of the fifth degree, and division (C) of section 2929.13 of the Revised Code applies in determining whether to impose a prison term on the offender.

(b) Except as otherwise provided in division (C)(3)(c), (d), (e), (f), or (g) of this section, if the offense was committed in the vicinity of a school or in the vicinity of a juvenile, trafficking in marihuana is a felony of the fourth degree, and division (C) of section 2929.13 of the Revised Code applies in determining whether to impose a prison term on the offender.

(c) Except as otherwise provided in this division, if the amount of the drug involved exceeds two hundred grams but does not exceed one thousand grams, trafficking in marihuana is a felony of the fourth degree, and division (C) of section 2929.13 of the Revised Code applies in determining whether to impose a prison term on the offender. If the amount of the drug involved is within that range and if the offense was committed in the vicinity of a school or in the vicinity of a juvenile, trafficking in marihuana is a felony of the third degree, and division (C) of section 2929.13 of the Revised Code applies in determining whether to impose a prison term on the offender.

(d) Except as otherwise provided in this division, if the amount of the drug involved exceeds one thousand grams but does not exceed five thousand grams, trafficking in marihuana is a felony of the third degree, and division (C) of section 2929.13 of the Revised Code applies in determining whether to impose a prison term on the offender. If the amount of the drug involved is within that range and if the offense was committed in the vicinity of a school or in the vicinity of a juvenile, trafficking in marihuana is a felony of the second degree, and there is a presumption that a prison term shall be imposed for the offense.

(e) Except as otherwise provided in this division, if the amount of the drug involved exceeds five thousand grams but does not exceed twenty thousand grams, trafficking in marihuana is a felony of the third degree, and there is a presumption that a prison term shall be imposed for the offense. If the amount of the drug involved is within that range and if the offense was committed in the vicinity of a school or in the vicinity of a juvenile, trafficking in marihuana is a felony of the second degree, and there is a presumption that a prison term shall be imposed for the offense.

(f) Except as otherwise provided in this division, if the amount of the drug involved exceeds twenty thousand grams, trafficking in marihuana is a felony of the second degree, and the court shall impose as a mandatory prison term the maximum prison term prescribed for a felony of the second degree. If the amount of the drug involved exceeds twenty thousand grams and if the offense was committed in the vicinity of a school or in the vicinity of a juvenile, trafficking in marihuana is a felony of the first degree, and the court shall impose as a mandatory prison term the maximum prison term prescribed for a felony of the first degree.

(g) Except as otherwise provided in this division, if the offense involves a gift of twenty grams or less of marihuana, trafficking in marihuana is a minor misdemeanor upon a first offense and a misdemeanor of the third degree upon a subsequent offense. If the offense involves a gift of twenty grams or less of marihuana and if the offense was committed in the vicinity of a school or in the vicinity of a juvenile, trafficking in marihuana is a misdemeanor of the third degree.

(4) If the drug involved in the violation is cocaine or a compound, mixture, preparation, or substance containing cocaine, whoever violates division (A) of this section is guilty of trafficking in cocaine. The penalty for the offense shall be determined as follows:

(a) Except as otherwise provided in division (C)(4)(b), (c), (d), (e), (f), or (g) of this section, trafficking in cocaine is a felony of the fifth degree, and division (C) of section 2929.13 of the Revised Code applies in determining whether to impose a prison term on the offender.

(b) Except as otherwise provided in division (C)(4)(c), (d), (e), (f), or (g) of this section, if the offense was committed in the vicinity of a school or in the vicinity of a juvenile, trafficking in cocaine is a felony of the fourth degree, and division (C) of section 2929.13 of the Revised Code applies in determining whether to impose a prison term on the offender.

(c) Except as otherwise provided in this division, if the amount of the drug involved exceeds five grams but does not exceed ten grams of cocaine that is not crack cocaine or exceeds one gram but does not exceed five grams of crack cocaine, trafficking in cocaine is a felony of the fourth degree, and there is a presumption for a prison term for the offense. If the amount of the drug involved is within one of those ranges and if the offense was committed in the vicinity of a school or in the vicinity of a juvenile, trafficking in cocaine is a felony of the third degree, and there is a presumption for a prison term for the offense.

(d) Except as otherwise provided in this division, if the amount of the drug involved exceeds ten grams but does not exceed one hundred grams of cocaine that is not crack cocaine or exceeds five grams but does not exceed ten grams of crack cocaine, trafficking in cocaine is a felony of the third degree, and the court shall impose as a mandatory prison term one of the prison terms prescribed for a felony of the third degree. If the amount of the drug involved is within one of those ranges and if the offense was committed in the vicinity of a school or in the vicinity of a juvenile, trafficking in cocaine is a felony of the second degree, and the court shall impose as a mandatory prison term one of the prison terms prescribed for a felony of the second degree.

(e) Except as otherwise provided in this division, if the amount of the drug involved exceeds one hundred grams but does not exceed five hundred grams of cocaine that is not crack cocaine or exceeds ten grams but does not exceed twenty-five grams of crack cocaine, trafficking in cocaine is a felony of the second degree, and the court shall impose as a mandatory prison term one of the prison terms prescribed for a felony of the second degree. If the amount of the drug involved is within one of those ranges and if the offense was committed in the vicinity of a school or in the vicinity of a juvenile, trafficking in cocaine is a felony of the first degree, and the court shall impose as a mandatory prison term one of the prison terms prescribed for a felony of the first degree.

(f) If the amount of the drug involved exceeds five hundred grams but does not exceed one thousand grams of cocaine that is not crack cocaine or exceeds twenty-five grams but does not exceed one hundred grams of crack cocaine and regardless of whether the offense was committed in the vicinity of a school or in the vicinity of a juvenile, trafficking in cocaine is a felony of the first degree, and the court shall impose as a mandatory prison term one of the prison terms prescribed for a felony of the first degree.

(g) If the amount of the drug involved exceeds one thousand grams of cocaine that is not crack cocaine or exceeds one hundred grams of crack cocaine and regardless of whether the offense was committed in the vicinity of a school or in the vicinity of a juvenile, trafficking in cocaine is a felony of the first degree, and the court shall impose as a mandatory prison term the maximum prison term prescribed for a felony of the first degree and may impose an additional mandatory prison term prescribed for a major drug offender under division (D)(3)(b) of section 2929.14 of the Revised Code.

(5) If the drug involved in the violation is L.S.D. or a compound, mixture, preparation, or substance containing L.S.D., whoever violates division (A) of this section is guilty of trafficking in L.S.D. The penalty for the offense shall be determined as follows:

(a) Except as otherwise provided in division (C)(5)(b), (c), (d), (e), (f), or (g) of this section, trafficking in L.S.D. is a felony of the fifth degree, and division (C) of section 2929.13 of the Revised Code applies in determining whether to impose a prison term on the offender.

(b) Except as otherwise provided in division (C)(5)(c), (d), (e), (f), or (g) of this section, if the offense was committed in the vicinity of a school or in the vicinity of a juvenile, trafficking in L.S.D. is a felony of the fourth degree, and division (C) of section 2929.13 of the Revised Code applies in determining whether to impose a prison term on the offender.

(c) Except as otherwise provided in this division, if the amount of the drug involved exceeds ten unit doses but does not exceed fifty unit doses of L.S.D. in a solid form or exceeds one gram but does not exceed five grams of L.S.D. in a liquid concentrate, liquid extract, or liquid distillate form, trafficking in L.S.D. is a felony of the fourth degree, and there is a presumption for a prison term for the offense. If the amount of the drug involved is within that range and if the offense was committed in the vicinity of a school or in the vicinity of a juvenile, trafficking in L.S.D. is a felony of the third degree, and there is a presumption for a prison term for the offense.

(d) Except as otherwise provided in this division, if the amount of the drug involved exceeds fifty unit doses but does not exceed two hundred fifty unit doses of L.S.D. in a solid form or exceeds five grams but does not exceed twenty-five grams of L.S.D. in a liquid concentrate, liquid extract, or liquid distillate form, trafficking in L.S.D. is a felony of the third degree, and the court shall impose as a mandatory prison term one of the prison terms prescribed for a felony of the third degree. If the amount of the drug involved is within that range and if the offense was committed in the vicinity of a school or in the vicinity of a juvenile, trafficking in L.S.D. is a felony of the second degree, and the court shall impose as a mandatory prison term one of the prison terms prescribed for a felony of the second degree.

(e) Except as otherwise provided in this division, if the amount of the drug involved exceeds two hundred fifty unit doses but does not exceed one thousand unit doses of L.S.D. in a solid form or exceeds twenty-five grams but does not exceed one hundred grams of L.S.D. in a liquid concentrate, liquid extract, or liquid distillate form, trafficking in L.S.D. is a felony of the second degree, and the court shall impose as a mandatory prison term one of the prison terms prescribed for a felony of the second degree. If the amount of the drug involved is within that range and if the offense was committed in the vicinity of a school or in the vicinity of a juvenile, trafficking in L.S.D. is a felony of the first degree, and the court shall impose as a mandatory prison term one of the prison terms prescribed for a felony of the first degree.

(f) If the amount of the drug involved exceeds one thousand unit doses but does not exceed five thousand unit doses of L.S.D. in a solid form or exceeds one hundred grams but does not exceed five hundred grams of L.S.D. in a liquid concentrate, liquid extract, or liquid distillate form and regardless of whether the offense was committed in the vicinity of a school or in the vicinity of a juvenile, trafficking in L.S.D. is a felony of the first degree, and the court shall impose as a mandatory prison term one of the prison terms prescribed for a felony of the first degree.

(g) If the amount of the drug involved exceeds five thousand unit doses of L.S.D. in a solid form or exceeds five hundred grams of L.S.D. in a liquid concentrate, liquid extract, or liquid distillate form and regardless of whether the offense was committed in the vicinity of a school or in the vicinity of a juvenile, trafficking in L.S.D. is a felony of the first degree, and the court shall impose as a mandatory prison term the maximum prison term prescribed for a felony of the first degree and may impose an additional mandatory prison term prescribed for a major drug offender under division (D)(3)(b) of section 2929.14 of the Revised Code.

(6) If the drug involved in the violation is heroin or a compound, mixture, preparation, or substance containing heroin, whoever violates division (A) of this section is guilty of trafficking in heroin. The penalty for the offense shall be determined as follows:

(a) Except as otherwise provided in division (C)(6)(b), (c), (d), (e), (f), or (g) of this section, trafficking in heroin is a felony of the fifth degree, and division (C) of section 2929.13 of the Revised Code applies in determining whether to impose a prison term on the offender.

(b) Except as otherwise provided in division (C)(6)(c), (d), (e), (f), or (g) of this section, if the offense was committed in the vicinity of a school or in the vicinity of a juvenile, trafficking in heroin is a felony of the fourth degree, and division (C) of section 2929.13 of the Revised Code applies in determining whether to impose a prison term on the offender.

(c) Except as otherwise provided in this division, if the amount of the drug involved exceeds one gram but does not exceed five grams, trafficking in heroin is a felony of the fourth degree, and there is a presumption for a prison term for the offense. If the amount of the drug involved is within that range and if the offense was committed in the vicinity of a school or in the vicinity of a juvenile, trafficking in heroin is a felony of the third degree, and there is a presumption for a prison term for the offense.

(d) Except as otherwise provided in this division, if the amount of the drug involved exceeds five grams but does not exceed ten grams, trafficking in heroin is a felony of the third degree, and there is a presumption for a prison term for the offense. If the amount of the drug involved is within that range and if the offense was committed in the vicinity of a school or in the vicinity of a juvenile, trafficking in heroin is a felony of the second degree, and there is a presumption for a prison term for the offense.

(e) Except as otherwise provided in this division, if the amount of the drug involved exceeds ten grams but does not exceed fifty grams, trafficking in heroin is a felony of the second degree, and the court shall impose as a mandatory prison term one of the prison terms prescribed for a felony of the second degree. If the amount of the drug involved is within that range and if the offense was committed in the vicinity of a school or in the vicinity of a juvenile, trafficking in heroin is a felony of the first degree, and the court shall impose as a mandatory prison term one of the prison terms prescribed for a felony of the first degree.

(f) If the amount of the drug involved exceeds fifty grams but does not exceed two hundred fifty grams and regardless of whether the offense was committed in the vicinity of a school or in the vicinity of a juvenile, trafficking in heroin is a felony of the first degree, and the court shall impose as a mandatory prison term one of the prison terms prescribed for a felony of the first degree.

(g) If the amount of the drug involved exceeds two hundred fifty grams and regardless of whether the offense was committed in the vicinity of a school or in the vicinity of a juvenile, trafficking in heroin is a felony of the first degree, and the court shall impose as a mandatory prison term the maximum prison term prescribed for a felony of the first degree and may impose an additional mandatory prison term prescribed for a major drug offender under division (D)(3)(b) of section 2929.14 of the Revised Code.

(7) If the drug involved in the violation is hashish or a compound, mixture, preparation, or substance containing hashish, whoever violates division (A) of this section is guilty of trafficking in hashish. The penalty for the offense shall be determined as follows:

(a) Except as otherwise provided in division (C)(7)(b), (c), (d), (e), or (f) of this section, trafficking in hashish is a felony of the fifth degree, and division (C) of section 2929.13 of the Revised Code applies in determining whether to impose a prison term on the offender.

(b) Except as otherwise provided in division (C)(7)(c), (d), (e), or (f) of this section, if the offense was committed in the vicinity of a school or in the vicinity of a juvenile, trafficking in hashish is a felony of the fourth degree, and division (C) of section 2929.13 of the Revised Code applies in determining whether to impose a prison term on the offender.

(c) Except as otherwise provided in this division, if the amount of the drug involved exceeds ten grams but does not exceed fifty grams of hashish in a solid form or exceeds two grams but does not exceed ten grams of hashish in a liquid concentrate, liquid extract, or liquid distillate form, trafficking in hashish is a felony of the fourth degree, and division (C) of section 2929.13 of the Revised Code applies in determining whether to impose a prison term on the offender. If the amount of the drug involved is within that range and if the offense was committed in the vicinity of a school or in the vicinity of a juvenile, trafficking in hashish is a felony of the third degree, and division (C) of section 2929.13 of the Revised Code applies in determining whether to impose a prison term on the offender.

(d) Except as otherwise provided in this division, if the amount of the drug involved exceeds fifty grams but does not exceed two hundred fifty grams of hashish in a solid form or exceeds ten grams but does not exceed fifty grams of hashish in a liquid concentrate, liquid extract, or liquid distillate form, trafficking in hashish is a felony of the third degree, and division (C) of section 2929.13 of the Revised Code applies in determining whether to impose a prison term on the offender. If the amount of the drug involved is within that range and if the offense was committed in the vicinity of a school or in the vicinity of a juvenile, trafficking in hashish is a felony of the second degree, and there is a presumption that a prison term shall be imposed for the offense.

(e) Except as otherwise provided in this division, if the amount of the drug involved exceeds two hundred fifty grams but does not exceed one thousand grams of hashish in a solid form or exceeds fifty grams but does not exceed two hundred grams of hashish in a liquid concentrate, liquid extract, or liquid distillate form, trafficking in hashish is a felony of the third degree, and there is a presumption that a prison term shall be imposed for the offense. If the amount of the drug involved is within that range and if the offense was committed in the vicinity of a school or in the vicinity of a juvenile, trafficking in hashish is a felony of the second degree, and there is a presumption that a prison term shall be imposed for the offense.

(f) Except as otherwise provided in this division, if the amount of the drug involved exceeds one thousand grams of hashish in a solid form or exceeds two hundred grams of hashish in a liquid concentrate, liquid extract, or liquid distillate form, trafficking in hashish is a felony of the second degree, and the court shall impose as a mandatory prison term the maximum prison term prescribed for a felony of the second degree. If the amount of the drug involved exceeds one thousand grams of hashish in a solid form or exceeds two hundred grams of hashish in a liquid concentrate, liquid extract, or liquid distillate form and if the offense was committed in the vicinity of a school or in the vicinity of a juvenile, trafficking in hashish is a felony of the first degree, and the court shall impose as a mandatory prison term the maximum prison term prescribed for a felony of the first degree.

(D) In addition to any prison term authorized or required by division (C) of this section and sections 2929.13 and 2929.14 of the Revised Code, and in addition to any other sanction imposed for the offense under this section or sections 2929.11 to 2929.18 of the Revised Code, the court that sentences an offender who is convicted of or pleads guilty to a violation of division (A) of this section shall do all of the following that are applicable regarding the offender:

(1) If the violation of division (A) of this section is a felony of the first, second, or third degree, the court shall impose upon the offender the mandatory fine specified for the offense under division (B)(1) of section 2929.18 of the Revised Code unless, as specified in that division, the court determines that the offender is indigent. Except as otherwise provided in division (H)(1) of this section, a mandatory fine or any other fine imposed for a violation of this section is subject to division (F) of this section. If a person is charged with a violation of this section that is a felony of the first, second, or third degree, posts bail, and forfeits the bail, the clerk of the court shall pay the forfeited bail pursuant to divisions (D)(1) and (F) of this section, as if the forfeited bail was a fine imposed for a violation of this section. If any amount of the forfeited bail remains after that payment and if a fine is imposed under division (H)(1) of this section, the clerk of the court shall pay the remaining amount of the forfeited bail pursuant to divisions (H)(2) and (3) of this section, as if that remaining amount was a fine imposed under division (H)(1) of this section.

(2) The court shall revoke or suspend the driver's or commercial driver's license or permit of the offender in accordance with division (G) of this section.

(3) If the offender is a professionally licensed person or a person who has been admitted to the bar by order of the supreme court in compliance with its prescribed and published rules, the court forthwith shall comply with section 2925.38 of the Revised Code.

(E) When a person is charged with the sale of or offer to sell a bulk amount or a multiple of a bulk amount of a controlled substance, the jury, or the court trying the accused, shall determine the amount of the controlled substance involved at the time of the offense and, if a guilty verdict is returned, shall return the findings as part of the verdict. In any such case, it is unnecessary to find and return the exact amount of the controlled substance involved, and it is sufficient if the finding and return is to the effect that the amount of the controlled substance involved is the requisite amount, or that the amount of the controlled substance involved is less than the requisite amount.

(F)(1) Notwithstanding any contrary provision of section 3719.21 of the Revised Code and except as provided in division (H) of this section, the clerk of the court shall pay any mandatory fine imposed pursuant to division (D)(1) of this section and any fine other than a mandatory fine that is imposed for a violation of this section pursuant to division (A) or (B)(5) of section 2929.18 of the Revised Code to the county, township, municipal corporation, park district, as created pursuant to section 511.18 or 1545.04 of the Revised Code, or state law enforcement agencies in this state that primarily were responsible for or involved in making the arrest of, and in prosecuting, the offender. However, the clerk shall not pay a mandatory fine so imposed to a law enforcement agency unless the agency has adopted a written internal control policy under division (F)(2) of this section that addresses the use of the fine moneys that it receives. Each agency shall use the mandatory fines so paid to subsidize the agency's law enforcement efforts that pertain to drug offenses, in accordance with the written internal control policy adopted by the recipient agency under division (F)(2) of this section.

(2)(a) Prior to receiving any fine moneys under division (F)(1) of this section or division (B)(5) of section 2925.42 of the Revised Code, a law enforcement agency shall adopt a written internal control policy that addresses the agency's use and disposition of all fine moneys so received and that provides for the keeping of detailed financial records of the receipts of those fine moneys, the general types of expenditures made out of those fine moneys, and the specific amount of each general type of expenditure. The policy shall not provide for or permit the identification of any specific expenditure that is made in an ongoing investigation. All financial records of the receipts of those fine moneys, the general types of expenditures made out of those fine moneys, and the specific amount of each general type of expenditure by an agency are public records open for inspection under section 149.43 of the Revised Code. Additionally, a written internal control policy adopted under this division is such a public record, and the agency that adopted it shall comply with it.

(b) Each law enforcement agency that receives in any calendar year any fine moneys under division (F)(1) of this section or division (B)(5) of section 2925.42 of the Revised Code shall prepare a report covering the calendar year that cumulates all of the information contained in all of the public financial records kept by the agency pursuant to division (F)(2)(a) of this section for that calendar year, and shall send a copy of the cumulative report, no later than the first day of March in the calendar year following the calendar year covered by the report, to the attorney general. Each report received by the attorney general is a public record open for inspection under section 149.43 of the Revised Code. The attorney general shall make copies of each report received, and, no later than the fifteenth day of April in the calendar year in which the report is received, shall send a copy of it to the president of the senate and the speaker of the house of representatives.

(3) As used in division (F) of this section:

(a) "Law enforcement agencies" includes, but is not limited to, the state board of pharmacy and the office of a prosecutor.

(b) "Prosecutor" has the same meaning as in section 2935.01 of the Revised Code.

(G) When required under division (D)(2) of this section, the court either shall revoke or, if it does not revoke, shall suspend for not less than six months or more than five years, the driver's or commercial driver's license or permit of any person who is convicted of or pleads guilty to a violation of this section that is a felony of the first degree and shall suspend for not less than six months or more than five years the driver's or commercial driver's license or permit of any person who is convicted of or pleads guilty to any other violation of this section. If an offender's driver's or commercial driver's license or permit is revoked pursuant to this division, the offender, at any time after the expiration of two years from the day on which the offender's sentence was imposed or from the day on which the offender finally was released from a prison term under the sentence, whichever is later, may file a motion with the sentencing court requesting termination of the revocation; upon the filing of such a motion and the court's finding of good cause for the termination, the court may terminate the revocation.

(H)(1) In addition to any prison term authorized or required by division (C) of this section and sections 2929.13 and 2929.14 of the Revised Code, in addition to any other penalty or sanction imposed for the offense under this section or sections 2929.11 to 2929.181 [2929.18.1] of the Revised Code, and in addition to the forfeiture of property in connection with the offense as prescribed in sections 2925.42 to 2925.45 of the Revised Code, the court that sentences an offender who is convicted of or pleads guilty to a violation of division (A) of this section may impose upon the offender an additional fine specified for the offense in division (B)(4) of section 2929.18 of the Revised Code. A fine imposed under division (H)(1) of this section is not subject to division (F) of this section and shall be used solely for the support of one or more eligible alcohol and drug addiction programs in accordance with divisions (H)(2) and (3) of this section.

(2) The court that imposes a fine under division (H)(1) of this section shall specify in the judgment that imposes the fine one or more eligible alcohol and drug addiction programs for the support of which the fine money is to be used. No alcohol and drug addiction program shall receive or use money paid or collected in satisfaction of a fine imposed under division (H)(1) of this section unless the program is specified in the judgment that imposes the fine. No alcohol and drug addiction program shall be specified in the judgment unless the program is an eligible alcohol and drug addiction program and, except as otherwise provided in division (H)(2) of this section, unless the program is located in the county in which the court that imposes the fine is located or in a county that is immediately contiguous to the county in which that court is located. If no eligible alcohol and drug addiction program is located in any of those counties, the judgment may specify an eligible alcohol and drug addiction program that is located anywhere within this state.

(3) Notwithstanding any contrary provision of section 3719.21 of the Revised Code, the clerk of the court shall pay any fine imposed under division (H)(1) of this section to the eligible alcohol and drug addiction program specified pursuant to division (H)(2) of this section in the judgment. The eligible alcohol and drug addiction program that receives the fine moneys shall use the moneys only for the alcohol and drug addiction services identified in the application for certification under section 3793.06 of the Revised Code or in the application for a license under section 3793.11 of the Revised Code filed with the department of alcohol and drug addiction services by the alcohol and drug addiction program specified in the judgment.

(4) Each alcohol and drug addiction program that receives in a calendar year any fine moneys under division (H)(3) of this section shall file an annual report covering that calendar year with the court of common pleas and the board of county commissioners of the county in which the program is located, with the court of common pleas and the board of county commissioners of each county from which the program received the moneys if that county is different from the county in which the program is located, and with the attorney general. The alcohol and drug addiction program shall file the report no later than the first day of March in the calendar year following the calendar year in which the program received the fine moneys. The report shall include statistics on the number of persons served by the alcohol and drug addiction program, identify the types of alcohol and drug addiction services provided to those persons, and include a specific accounting of the purposes for which the fine moneys received were used. No information contained in the report shall identify, or enable a person to determine the identity of, any person served by the alcohol and drug addiction program. Each report received by a court of common pleas, a board of county commissioners, or the attorney general is a public record open for inspection under section 149.43 of the Revised Code.

(5) As used in divisions (H)(1) to (5) of this section:

(a) "Alcohol and drug addiction program" and "alcohol and drug addiction services" have the same meanings as in section 3793.01 of the Revised Code.

(b) "Eligible alcohol and drug addiction program" means an alcohol and drug addiction program that is certified under section 3793.06 of the Revised Code or licensed under section 3793.11 of the Revised Code by the department of alcohol and drug addiction services.

HISTORY: 136 v H 300 (Eff 7-1-76); 141 v S 67 (Eff 8-29-86); 143 v H 215 (Eff 4-11-90); 143 v H 261 (Eff 7-18-90); 143 v H 266 (Eff 9-6-90); 143 v S 258 (Eff 11-20-90); 144 v H 62 (Eff 5-21-91); 144 v S 174 (Eff 7-31-92); 144 v H 591 (Eff 11-2-92); 145 v H 377 (Eff 9-30-93); 145 v H 391 (Eff 7-21-94); 146 v S 2 (Eff 7-1-96); 146 v S 269 (Eff 7-1-96); 146 v S 166. Eff 10-17-96.

The provisions of § 4 of SB 166 (146 v —) read as follows:

SECTION 4. The amendments made by this act to selections 309.08, 2925.03, 2929.18, 3719.21, 3793.06, and 3793.11 of the Revised Code apply to offenses that are committed on or after the effective date of this act.

[DRUG ABUSE]

§ 2925.04 Illegal manufacture of drugs or cultivation of marihuana.

(A) No person shall knowingly cultivate marihuana or knowingly manufacture or otherwise engage in any part of the production of a controlled substance.

(B) This section does not apply to any person listed in division (B)(1), (2), or (3) of section 2925.03 of the Revised Code to the extent and under the circumstances described in those divisions.

(C)(1) Whoever commits a violation of division (A) of this section that involves any drug other than marihuana is guilty of illegal manufacture of drugs, and whoever commits a violation of division (A) of this section that involves marihuana is guilty of illegal cultivation of marihuana.

(2) If the drug involved in the violation of division (A) of this section is any compound, mixture, preparation, or substance included in schedule I or II, with the exception of marihuana, illegal manufacture of drugs is a felony of the second degree, and, subject to division (E) of this section, the court shall impose as a mandatory prison term one of the prison terms prescribed for a felony of the second degree.

(3) If the drug involved in the violation of division (A) of this section is any compound, mixture, preparation, or substance included in schedule III, IV, or V, illegal manufacture of drugs is a felony of the third degree, and there is a presumption for a prison term for the offense.

(4) If the drug involved in the violation is marihuana, the penalty for the offense shall be determined as follows:

(a) Except as otherwise provided in division (C)(4)(b), (c), (d), (e), or (f) of this section, illegal cultivation of marihuana is a minor misdemeanor.

(b) If the amount of marihuana involved equals or exceeds one hundred grams but does not exceed two hundred grams, illegal cultivation of marihuana is a misdemeanor of the fourth degree.

(c) If the amount of marihuana involved exceeds two hundred grams but does not exceed one thousand grams, illegal cultivation of marihuana is a felony of the fifth degree, and division (B) of section 2929.13 of the Revised Code applies in determining whether to impose a prison term on the offender.

(d) If the amount of marihuana involved exceeds one thousand grams but does not exceed five thousand grams, illegal cultivation of marihuana is a felony of the third degree, and division (C) of section 2929.13 of the Revised Code applies in determining whether to impose a prison term on the offender.

(e) If the amount of marihuana involved exceeds five thousand grams but does not exceed twenty thousand grams, illegal cultivation of marihuana is a felony of the third degree, and there is a presumption for a prison term for the offense.

(f) If the amount of marihuana involved exceeds twenty thousand grams, illegal cultivation of marihuana is a felony of the second degree, and the court shall impose as a mandatory prison term the maximum prison term prescribed for a felony of the second degree.

(D) In addition to any prison term authorized or required by division (C) or (E) of this section and sections 2929.13 and 2929.14 of the Revised Code and in addition to any other sanction imposed for the offense under this section or sections 2929.11 to 2929.18 of the Revised Code, the court that sentences an offender who is convicted of or pleads guilty to a violation of division (A) of this section shall do all of the following that are applicable regarding the offender:

(1) If the violation of division (A) of this section is a felony of the second or third degree, the court shall impose upon the offender the mandatory fine specified for the offense under division (B)(1) of section 2929.18 of the Revised Code unless, as specified in that division, the court determines that the offender is indigent. The clerk of the court shall pay a mandatory fine or other fine imposed for a violation of this section pursuant to division (A) of section 2929.18 of the Revised Code in accordance with and subject to the requirements of division (F) of section 2925.03 of the Revised Code. The agency that receives the fine shall use the fine as specified in division (F) of section 2925.03 of the Revised Code. If a person is charged with a violation of this section that is a felony of the second or third degree, posts bail, and forfeits the bail, the clerk shall pay the forfeited bail as if the forfeited bail were a fine imposed for a violation of this section.

(2) The court shall revoke or suspend the offender's driver's or commercial driver's license or permit in accordance with division (G) of section 2925.03 of the Revised Code. If an offender's driver's or commercial driver's license or permit is revoked in accordance with that division, the offender may request termination of, and the court may terminate, the revocation in accordance with that division.

(3) If the offender is a professionally licensed person or a person who has been admitted to the bar by order of the supreme court in compliance with its prescribed

and published rules, the court shall comply with section 2925.38 of the Revised Code.

(E) Notwithstanding the prison term otherwise authorized or required for the offense under division (C) of this section and sections 2929.13 and 2929.14 of the Revised Code, if the violation of division (A) of this section involves the sale, offer to sell, or possession of a schedule I or II controlled substance, with the exception of marihuana, and if the offender, as a result of the violation, is a major drug offender, the court, in lieu of the prison term otherwise authorized or required, shall impose upon the offender the mandatory prison term specified in division (D)(3)(a) of section 2929.14 of the Revised Code and may impose an additional prison term under division (D)(3)(b) of that section.

(F) It is an affirmative defense, as provided in section 2901.05 of the Revised Code, to a charge under this section for a fifth degree felony violation of illegal cultivation of marihuana that the marihuana that gave rise to the charge is in an amount, is in a form, is prepared, compounded, or mixed with substances that are not controlled substances in a manner, or is possessed or cultivated under any other circumstances that indicate that the marihuana was solely for personal use.

Notwithstanding any contrary provision of division (F) of this section, if, in accordance with section 2901.05 of the Revised Code, a person who is charged with a violation of illegal cultivation of marihuana that is a felony of the fifth degree sustains the burden of going forward with evidence of and establishes by a preponderance of the evidence the affirmative defense described in this division, the person may be prosecuted for and may be convicted of or plead guilty to a misdemeanor violation of illegal cultivation of marihuana.

(G) Arrest or conviction for a minor misdemeanor violation of this section does not constitute a criminal record and need not be reported by the person so arrested or convicted in response to any inquiries about the person's criminal record, including any inquiries contained in an application for employment, a license, or any other right or privilege or made in connection with the person's appearance as a witness.

HISTORY: 146 v S 2 (Eff 7-1-96); 146 v S 269. Eff 7-1-96.

The effective date is set by section 5 of SB 269.

§ 2925.05 Funding of drug or marihuana trafficking.

(A) No person shall knowingly provide money or other items of value to another person with the purpose that the recipient of the money or items of value use them to obtain any controlled substance for the purpose of selling or offering to sell the controlled substance or for the purpose of violating section 2925.04 of the Revised Code.

(B) This section does not apply to any person listed in division (B)(1), (2), or (3) of section 2925.03 of the Revised Code to the extent and under the circumstances described in those divisions.

(C)(1) If the drug involved in the violation is any compound, mixture, preparation, or substance included in schedule I or II, with the exception of marihuana, whoever violates division (A) of this section is guilty of aggravated funding of drug trafficking, a felony of the first degree, and, subject to division (E) of this section, the court shall impose as a mandatory prison term one of the prison terms prescribed for a felony of the first degree.

(2) If the drug involved in the violation is any compound, mixture, preparation, or substance included in schedule III, IV, or V, whoever violates division (A) of this section is guilty of funding of drug trafficking, a felony of the second degree, and the court shall impose as a mandatory prison term one of the prison terms prescribed for a felony of the second degree.

(3) If the drug involved in the violation is marihuana, whoever violates division (A) of this section is guilty of funding of marihuana trafficking, a felony of the third degree, and the court shall impose as a mandatory prison term one of the prison terms prescribed for a felony of the third degree.

(D) In addition to any prison term authorized or required by division (C) or (E) of this section and sections 2929.13 and 2929.14 of the Revised Code and in addition to any other sanction imposed for the offense under this section or sections 2929.11 to 2929.18 of the Revised Code, the court that sentences an offender who is convicted of or pleads guilty to a violation of division (A) of this section shall do all of the following that are applicable regarding the offender:

(1) The court shall impose the mandatory fine specified for the offense under division (B)(1) of section 2929.18 of the Revised Code unless, as specified in that division, the court determines that the offender is indigent. The clerk of the court shall pay a mandatory fine or other fine imposed for a violation of this section pursuant to division (A) of section 2929.18 of the Revised Code in accordance with and subject to the requirements of division (F) of section 2925.03 of the Revised Code. The agency that receives the fine shall use the fine in accordance with division (F) of section 2925.03 of the Revised Code. If a person is charged with a violation of this section, posts bail, and forfeits the bail, the forfeited bail shall be paid as if the forfeited bail were a fine imposed for a violation of this section.

(2) The court shall revoke or suspend the offender's driver's or commercial driver's license or permit in accordance with division (G) of section 2925.03 of the Revised Code. If an offender's driver's or commercial driver's license or permit is revoked in accordance with that division, the offender may request termination of, and the court may terminate, the revocation in accordance with that division.

(3) If the offender is a professionally licensed person or a person who has been admitted to the bar by order

of the supreme court in compliance with its prescribed and published rules, the court shall comply with section 2925.38 of the Revised Code.

(E) Notwithstanding the prison term otherwise authorized or required for the offense under division (C) of this section and sections 2929.13 and 2929.14 of the Revised Code, if the violation of division (A) of this section involves the sale, offer to sell, or possession of a schedule I or II controlled substance, with the exception of marihuana, and if the offender, as a result of the violation, is a major drug offender, the court, in lieu of the prison term otherwise authorized or required, shall impose upon the offender the mandatory prison term specified in division (D)(3)(a) of section 2929.14 of the Revised Code and may impose an additional prison term under division (D)(3)(b) of that section.

HISTORY: 146 v S 2 (Eff 7-1-96); 146 v S 269. Eff 7-1-96.

The effective date is set by section 5 of SB 269.

§ 2925.06 Illegal administration or distribution of anabolic steroids.

(A) No person shall knowingly administer to a human being, or prescribe or dispense for administration to a human being, any anabolic steroid not approved by the United States food and drug administration for administration to human beings.

(B) This section does not apply to any person listed in division (B)(1), (2), or (3) of section 2925.03 of the Revised Code to the extent and under the circumstances described in those divisions.

(C) Whoever violates division (A) of this section is guilty of illegal administration or distribution of anabolic steroids, a felony of the fourth degree, and division (C) of section 2929.13 of the Revised Code applies in determining whether to impose a prison term on the offender.

(D) In addition to any prison term authorized or required by division (C) of this section and sections 2929.13 and 2929.14 of the Revised Code and in addition to any other sanction imposed for the offense under this section or sections 2929.11 to 2929.18 of the Revised Code, the court that sentences an offender who is convicted of or pleads guilty to a violation of division (A) of this section shall do both of the following:

(1) The court shall revoke or suspend the offender's driver's or commercial driver's license or permit in accordance with division (G) of section 2925.03 of the Revised Code. If an offender's driver's or commercial driver's license or permit is revoked in accordance with that division, the offender may request termination of, and the court may terminate, the revocation in accordance with that division.

(2) If the offender is a professionally licensed person or a person who has been admitted to the bar by order of the supreme court in compliance with its prescribed and published rules, the court shall comply with section 2925.38 of the Revised Code.

(E) If a person commits any act that constitutes a violation of division (A) of this section and that also constitutes a violation of any other provision of the Revised Code, the prosecutor, as defined in section 2935.01 of the Revised Code, using customary prosecutorial discretion, may prosecute the person for a violation of the appropriate provision of the Revised Code.

HISTORY: 146 v S 2 (Eff 7-1-96); 146 v S 269. Eff 7-1-96.

The effective date is set by section 5 of SB 269.

§ 2925.09 Offenses involving unapproved drugs; dangerous drug offenses involving livestock.

(A) No person shall administer, dispense, distribute, manufacture, possess, sell, or use any drug, other than a controlled substance, that is not approved by the United States food and drug administration, or the United States department of agriculture, unless one of the following applies:

(1) The United States food and drug administration has approved an application for investigational use in accordance with the Federal Food, Drug, and Cosmetic Act,"† 52 Stat. 1040 (1938), 21 U.S.C.A. 301, as amended, and the drug is used only for the approved investigational use;

(2) The United States department of agriculture has approved an application for investigational use in accordance with the federal "Virus-Serum-Toxin Act," 37 Stat. 832 (1913), 21 U.S.C.A. as amended, 151,† as amended, and the drug is used only for the approved investigational use;

(3) A practitioner, other than a veterinarian, prescribes or combines two or more drugs as a single product for medical purposes;

(4) A pharmacist, pursuant to a prescription, compounds and dispenses two or more drugs as a single product for medical purposes.

(B)(1) As used in this division, "dangerous drug," "prescription," "sale at retail," "wholesale distributor of dangerous drugs," and "terminal distributor of dangerous drugs," have the meanings set forth in section 4729.02 of the Revised Code.

(2) Except as provided in division (B)(3) of this section, no person shall administer, dispense, distribute, manufacture, possess, sell, or use any dangerous drug to or for livestock or any animal that is generally used for food or in the production of food, unless the drug is prescribed by a licensed veterinarian by prescription or other written order and the drug is used in accordance with the veterinarian's order or direction.

(3) Division (B)(2) of this section does not apply to a registered wholesale distributor of dangerous drugs, a licensed terminal distributor of dangerous drugs, or a person who possesses, possesses for sale, or sells, at retail, a drug in accordance with Chapters 3719., 4729., or 4741. of the Revised Code.

(C) Whoever violates division (A) or (B)(2) of this

section is guilty of a felony of the fifth degree on a first offense and of a felony of the fourth degree on each subsequent offense.

HISTORY: RC § 2925.04, 146 v H 202 (Eff 6-14-95); 146 v S 269. Eff 7-1-96.

† So in enrolled bill.

§ 2925.11 Possession of drugs.

(A) No person shall knowingly obtain, possess, or use a controlled substance.

(B) This section does not apply to any of the following:

(1) Manufacturers, practitioners, pharmacists, owners of pharmacies, and other persons whose conduct was in accordance with Chapters 3719., 4715., 4729., 4731., and 4741. or section 4723.56 of the Revised Code;

(2) If the offense involves an anabolic steroid, any person who is conducting or participating in a research project involving the use of an anabolic steroid if the project has been approved by the United States food and drug administration;

(3) Any person who sells, offers for sale, prescribes, dispenses, or administers for livestock or other nonhuman species an anabolic steroid that is expressly intended for administration through implants to livestock or other nonhuman species and approved for that purpose under the "Federal Food, Drug, and Cosmetic Act," 52 Stat. 1040 (1938), 21 U.S.C.A. 301, as amended, and is sold, offered for sale, prescribed, dispensed, or administered for that purpose in accordance with that act;

(4) Any person who obtained the controlled substance pursuant to a prescription issued by a practitioner, where the drug is in the original container in which it was dispensed to such person.

(C) Whoever violates division (A) of this section is guilty of one of the following:

(1) If the drug involved in the violation is a compound, mixture, preparation, or substance included in schedule I or II, with the exception of marihuana, cocaine, L.S.D., heroin, and hashish, whoever violates division (A) of this section is guilty of aggravated possession of drugs. The penalty for the offense shall be determined as follows:

(a) Except as otherwise provided in division (C)(1)(b), (c), (d), or (e) of this section, aggravated possession of drugs is a felony of the fifth degree, and division (B) of section 2929.13 of the Revised Code applies in determining whether to impose a prison term on the offender.

(b) If the amount of the drug involved exceeds the bulk amount but does not exceed five times the bulk amount, aggravated possession of drugs is a felony of the third degree, and there is a presumption for a prison term for the offense.

(c) If the amount of the drug involved exceeds five times the bulk amount but does not exceed fifty times the bulk amount, aggravated possession of drugs is a felony of the second degree, and the court shall impose as a mandatory prison term one of the prison terms prescribed for a felony of the second degree.

(d) If the amount of the drug involved exceeds fifty times the bulk amount but does not exceed one hundred times the bulk amount, aggravated possession of drugs is a felony of the first degree, and the court shall impose as a mandatory prison term one of the prison terms prescribed for a felony of the first degree.

(e) If the amount of the drug involved exceeds one hundred times the bulk amount, aggravated possession of drugs is a felony of the first degree, and the court shall impose as a mandatory prison term the maximum prison term prescribed for a felony of the first degree and may impose an additional mandatory prison term prescribed for a major drug offender under division (D)(3)(b) of section 2929.14 of the Revised Code.

(2) If the drug involved in the violation is a compound, mixture, preparation, or substance included in schedule III, IV, or V, whoever violates division (A) of this section is guilty of possession of drugs. The penalty for the offense shall be determined as follows:

(a) Except as otherwise provided in division (C)(2)(b), (c), or (d) of this section, possession of drugs is a misdemeanor of the third degree or, if the offender previously has been convicted of a drug abuse offense, a misdemeanor of the second degree. If the drug involved in the violation is an anabolic steroid included in schedule III and if the offense is a misdemeanor of the third degree under this division, in lieu of sentencing the offender to a term of imprisonment in a detention facility, the court may place the offender on conditional probation pursuant to division (F) of section 2951.02 of the Revised Code.

(b) If the amount of the drug involved exceeds the bulk amount but does not exceed five times the bulk amount, possession of drugs is a felony of the fourth degree, and division (C) of section 2929.13 of the Revised Code applies in determining whether to impose a prison term on the offender.

(c) If the amount of the drug involved exceeds five times the bulk amount but does not exceed fifty times the bulk amount, possession of drugs is a felony of the third degree, and there is a presumption for a prison term for the offense.

(d) If the amount of the drug involved exceeds fifty times the bulk amount, possession of drugs is a felony of the second degree, and the court shall impose upon the offender as a mandatory prison term one of the prison terms prescribed for a felony of the second degree.

(3) If the drug involved in the violation is marihuana or a compound, mixture, preparation, or substance containing marihuana other than hashish, whoever violates division (A) of this section is guilty of possession of marihuana. The penalty for the offense shall be determined as follows:

(a) Except as otherwise provided in division (C)(3)(b), (c), (d), (e), or (f) of this section, possession of marihuana is a minor misdemeanor.

(b) If the amount of the drug involved equals or exceeds one hundred grams but does not exceed two hundred grams, possession of marihuana is a misdemeanor of the fourth degree.

(c) If the amount of the drug involved exceeds two hundred grams but does not exceed one thousand grams, possession of marihuana is a felony of the fifth degree, and division (B) of section 2929.13 of the Revised Code applies in determining whether to impose a prison term on the offender.

(d) If the amount of the drug involved exceeds one thousand grams but does not exceed five thousand grams, possession of marihuana is a felony of the third degree, and division (C) of section 2929.13 of the Revised Code applies in determining whether to impose a prison term on the offender.

(e) If the amount of the drug involved exceeds five thousand grams but does not exceed twenty thousand grams, possession of marihuana is a felony of the third degree, and there is a presumption that a prison term shall be imposed for the offense.

(f) If the amount of the drug involved exceeds twenty thousand grams, possession of marihuana is a felony of the second degree, and the court shall impose as a mandatory prison term the maximum prison term prescribed for a felony of the second degree.

(4) If the drug involved in the violation is cocaine or a compound, mixture, preparation, or substance containing cocaine, whoever violates division (A) of this section is guilty of possession of cocaine. The penalty for the offense shall be determined as follows:

(a) Except as otherwise provided in division (C)(4)(b), (c), (d), (e), or (f) of this section, possession of cocaine is a felony of the fifth degree, and division (B) of section 2929.13 of the Revised Code applies in determining whether to impose a prison term on the offender.

(b) If the amount of the drug involved exceeds five grams but does not exceed twenty-five grams of cocaine that is not crack cocaine or exceeds one gram but does not exceed five grams of crack cocaine, possession of cocaine is a felony of the fourth degree, and there is a presumption for a prison term for the offense.

(c) If the amount of the drug involved exceeds twenty-five grams but does not exceed one hundred grams of cocaine that is not crack cocaine or exceeds five grams but does not exceed ten grams of crack cocaine, possession of cocaine is a felony of the third degree, and the court shall impose as a mandatory prison term one of the prison terms prescribed for a felony of the third degree.

(d) If the amount of the drug involved exceeds one hundred grams but does not exceed five hundred grams of cocaine that is not crack cocaine or exceeds ten grams but does not exceed twenty-five grams of crack cocaine, possession of cocaine is a felony of the second degree, and the court shall impose as a mandatory prison term one of the prison terms prescribed for a felony of the second degree.

(e) If the amount of the drug involved exceeds five hundred grams but does not exceed one thousand grams of cocaine that is not crack cocaine or exceeds twenty-five grams but does not exceed one hundred grams of crack cocaine, possession of cocaine is a felony of the first degree, and the court shall impose as a mandatory prison term one of the prison terms prescribed for a felony of the first degree.

(f) If the amount of the drug involved exceeds one thousand grams of cocaine that is not crack cocaine or exceeds one hundred grams of crack cocaine, possession of cocaine is a felony of the first degree, and the court shall impose as a mandatory prison term the maximum prison term prescribed for a felony of the first degree and may impose an additional mandatory prison term prescribed for a major drug offender under division (D)(3)(b) of section 2929.14 of the Revised Code.

(5) If the drug involved in the violation is L.S.D., whoever violates division (A) of this section is guilty of possession of L.S.D. The penalty for the offense shall be determined as follows:

(a) Except as otherwise provided in division (C)(5)(b), (c), (d), (e), or (f) of this section, possession of L.S.D. is a felony of the fifth degree, and division (B) of section 2929.13 of the Revised Code applies in determining whether to impose a prison term on the offender.

(b) If the amount of L.S.D. involved exceeds ten unit doses but does not exceed fifty unit doses of L.S.D. in a solid form or exceeds one gram but does not exceed five grams of L.S.D. in a liquid concentrate, liquid extract, or liquid distillate form, possession of L.S.D. is a felony of the fourth degree, and division (C) of section 2929.13 of the Revised Code applies in determining whether to impose a prison term on the offender.

(c) If the amount of L.S.D. involved exceeds fifty unit doses, but does not exceed two hundred fifty unit doses of L.S.D. in a solid form or exceeds five grams but does not exceed twenty-five grams of L.S.D. in a liquid concentrate, liquid extract, or liquid distillate form, possession of L.S.D. is a felony of the third degree, and there is a presumption for a prison term for the offense.

(d) If the amount of L.S.D. involved exceeds two hundred fifty unit doses but does not exceed one thousand unit doses of L.S.D. in a solid form or exceeds twenty-five grams but does not exceed one hundred grams of L.S.D. in a liquid concentrate, liquid extract, or liquid distillate form, possession of L.S.D. is a felony of the second degree, and the court shall impose as a mandatory prison term one of the prison terms prescribed for a felony of the second degree.

(e) If the amount of L.S.D. involved exceeds one

thousand unit doses but does not exceed five thousand unit doses of L.S.D. in a solid form or exceeds one hundred grams but does not exceed five hundred grams of L.S.D. in a liquid concentrate, liquid extract, or liquid distillate form, possession of L.S.D. is a felony of the first degree, and the court shall impose as a mandatory prison term one of the prison terms prescribed for a felony of the first degree.

(f) If the amount of L.S.D. involved exceeds five thousand unit doses of L.S.D. in a solid form or exceeds five hundred grams of L.S.D. in a liquid concentrate, liquid extract, or liquid distillate form, possession of L.S.D. is a felony of the first degree, and the court shall impose as a mandatory prison term the maximum prison term prescribed for a felony of the first degree and may impose an additional mandatory prison term prescribed for a major drug offender under division (D)(3)(b) of section 2929.14 of the Revised Code.

(6) If the drug involved in the violation is heroin or a compound, mixture, preparation, or substance containing heroin, whoever violates division (A) of this section is guilty of possession of heroin. The penalty for the offense shall be determined as follows:

(a) Except as otherwise provided in division (C)(6)(b), (c), (d), (e), or (f) of this section, possession of heroin is a felony of the fifth degree, and division (B) of section 2929.13 of the Revised Code applies in determining whether to impose a prison term on the offender.

(b) If the amount of the drug involved exceeds one gram but does not exceed five grams, possession of heroin is a felony of the fourth degree, and division (C) of section 2929.13 of the Revised Code applies in determining whether to impose a prison term on the offender.

(c) If the amount of the drug involved exceeds five grams but does not exceed ten grams, possession of heroin is a felony of the third degree, and there is a presumption for a prison term for the offense.

(d) If the amount of the drug involved exceeds ten grams but does not exceed fifty grams, possession of heroin is a felony of the second degree, and the court shall impose as a mandatory prison term one of the prison terms prescribed for a felony of the second degree.

(e) If the amount of the drug involved exceeds fifty grams but does not exceed two hundred fifty grams, possession of heroin is a felony of the first degree, and the court shall impose as a mandatory prison term one of the prison terms prescribed for a felony of the first degree.

(f) If the amount of the drug involved exceeds two hundred fifty grams, possession of heroin is a felony of the first degree, and the court shall impose as a mandatory prison term the maximum prison term prescribed for a felony of the first degree and may impose an additional mandatory prison term prescribed for a major drug offender under division (D)(3)(b) of section 2929.14 of the Revised Code.

(7) If the drug involved in the violation is hashish or a compound, mixture, preparation, or substance containing hashish, whoever violates division (A) of this section is guilty of possession of hashish. The penalty for the offense shall be determined as follows:

(a) Except as otherwise provided in division (C)(7)(b), (c), (d), (e), or (f) of this section, possession of hashish is a minor misdemeanor.

(b) If the amount of the drug involved equals or exceeds five grams but does not exceed ten grams of hashish in a solid form or equals or exceeds one gram but does not exceed two grams of hashish in a liquid concentrate, liquid extract, or liquid distillate form, possession of hashish is a misdemeanor of the fourth degree.

(c) If the amount of the drug involved exceeds ten grams but does not exceed fifty grams of hashish in a solid form or exceeds two grams but does not exceed ten grams of hashish in a liquid concentrate, liquid extract, or liquid distillate form, possession of hashish is a felony of the fifth degree, and division (B) of section 2929.13 of the Revised Code applies in determining whether to impose a prison term on the offender.

(d) If the amount of the drug involved exceeds fifty grams but does not exceed two hundred fifty grams of hashish in a solid form or exceeds ten grams but does not exceed fifty grams of hashish in a liquid concentrate, liquid extract, or liquid distillate form, possession of hashish is a felony of the third degree, and division (C) of section 2929.13 of the Revised Code applies in determining whether to impose a prison term on the offender.

(e) If the amount of the drug involved exceeds two hundred fifty grams but does not exceed one thousand grams of hashish in a solid form or exceeds fifty grams but does not exceed two hundred grams of hashish in a liquid concentrate, liquid extract, or liquid distillate form, possession of hashish is a felony of the third degree, and there is a presumption that a prison term shall be imposed for the offense.

(f) If the amount of the drug involved exceeds one thousand grams of hashish in a solid form or exceeds two hundred grams of hashish in a liquid concentrate, liquid extract, or liquid distillate form, possession of hashish is a felony of the second degree, and the court shall impose as a mandatory prison term the maximum prison term prescribed for a felony of the second degree.

(D) Arrest or conviction for a minor misdemeanor violation of this section does not constitute a criminal record and need not be reported by the person so arrested or convicted in response to any inquiries about the person's criminal record, including any inquiries contained in any application for employment, license, or other right or privilege, or made in connection with the person's appearance as a witness.

(E) In addition to any prison term authorized or required by division (C) of this section and sections

2929.13 and 2929.14 of the Revised Code and in addition to any other sanction that is imposed for the offense under this section or sections 2929.11 to 2929.18 of the Revised Code, the court that sentences an offender who is convicted of or pleads guilty to a violation of division (A) of this section shall do all of the following that are applicable regarding the offender:

(1)(a) If the violation is a felony of the first, second, or third degree, the court shall impose upon the offender the mandatory fine specified for the offense under division (B)(1) of section 2929.18 of the Revised Code unless, as specified in that division, the court determines that the offender is indigent.

(b) Notwithstanding any contrary provision of section 3719.21 of the Revised Code, the clerk of the court shall pay a mandatory fine or other fine imposed for a violation of this section pursuant to division (A) of section 2929.18 of the Revised Code in accordance with and subject to the requirements of division (F) of section 2925.03 of the Revised Code. The agency that receives the fine shall use the fine as specified in division (F) of section 2925.03 of the Revised Code.

(c) If a person is charged with a violation of this section that is a felony of the first, second, or third degree, posts bail, and forfeits the bail, the clerk shall pay the forfeited bail pursuant to division (E)(1)(b) of this section as if it were a mandatory fine imposed under division (E)(1)(a) of this section.

(2) The court shall suspend for not less than six months or more than five years the driver's or commercial driver's license or permit of any person who is convicted of or has pleaded guilty to a violation of this section.

(3) If the offender is a professionally licensed person or a person who has been admitted to the bar by order of the supreme court in compliance with its prescribed and published rules, in addition to any other sanction imposed for a violation of this section, the court forthwith shall comply with section 2925.38 of the Revised Code.

(F) It is an affirmative defense, as provided in section 2901.05 of the Revised Code, to a charge of a fourth degree felony violation under this section that the controlled substance that gave rise to the charge is in an amount, is in a form, is prepared, compounded, or mixed with substances that are not controlled substances in a manner, or is possessed under any other circumstances, that indicate that the substance was possessed solely for personal use. Notwithstanding any contrary provision of this section, if, in accordance with section 2901.05 of the Revised Code, an accused who is charged with a fourth degree felony violation of division (C)(2), (4), (5), or (6) of this section sustains the burden of going forward with evidence of and establishes by a preponderance of the evidence the affirmative defense described in this division, the accused may be prosecuted for and may plead guilty to or be convicted of a misdemeanor violation of division (C)(2) of this section or a fifth degree felony violation of division (C)(4), (5), or (6) of this section respectively.

(G) When a person is charged with possessing a bulk amount or multiple of a bulk amount, division (E) of section 2925.03 of the Revised Code applies regarding the determination of the amount of the controlled substance involved at the time of the offense.

HISTORY: 138 v S 184, § 5 (Eff 6-20-84); 143 v S 258 (Eff 11-20-90); 144 v H 62 (Eff 5-21-91); 144 v H 298 (Eff 7-26-91); 145 v H 377 (Eff 9-30-93); 145 v H 391 (Eff 7-21-94); 146 v H 249 (Eff 7-17-95); 146 v S 2 (Eff 7-1-96); 146 v S 269 (Eff 7-1-96); 147 v S 2. Eff 6-20-97.

Analogous to former RC § 2925.11 (136 v H 300; 138 v S 184), repealed 138 v S 184, § 4, eff 6-20-84.

§ 2925.12 Possessing drug abuse instruments.

(A) No person shall knowingly make, obtain, possess, or use any instrument, article, or thing the customary and primary purpose of which is for the administration or use of a dangerous drug, other than marihuana, when the instrument involved is a hypodermic or syringe, whether or not of crude or extemporized manufacture or assembly, and the instrument, article, or thing involved has been used by the offender to unlawfully administer or use a dangerous drug, other than marihuana, or to prepare a dangerous drug, other than marihuana, for unlawful administration or use.

(B) This section does not apply to manufacturers, practitioners, pharmacists, owners of pharmacies, and other persons whose conduct was in accordance with Chapters 3719., 4715., 4729., 4731., and 4741. or section 4723.56 of the Revised Code.

(C) Whoever violates this section is guilty of possessing drug abuse instruments, a misdemeanor of the second degree. If the offender previously has been convicted of a drug abuse offense, a violation of this section is a misdemeanor of the first degree.

(D) In addition to any other sanction imposed for a violation of this section, the court shall suspend for not less than six months or more than five years the driver's or commercial driver's license or permit of any person who is convicted of or has pleaded guilty to a violation of this section. If the offender is a professionally licensed person or a person who has been admitted to the bar by order of the supreme court in compliance with its prescribed and published rules, in addition to any other sanction imposed for a violation of this section, the court forthwith shall comply with section 2925.38 of the Revised Code.

HISTORY: 136 v H 300 (Eff 7-1-76); 143 v S 258 (Eff 11-20-90); 145 v H 377 (Eff 9-30-93); 145 v H 391 (Eff 7-21-94); 146 v S 2 (Eff 7-1-96); 146 v S 269. Eff 7-1-96.

The effective date is set by section 5 of SB 269.

§ 2925.13 Permitting drug abuse.

(A) No person who is the owner, operator, or person

in charge of a locomotive, watercraft, aircraft, or other vehicle, as defined in division (A) of section 4501.01 of the Revised Code, shall knowingly permit the vehicle to be used for the commission of a felony drug abuse offense.

(B) No person who is the owner, lessee, or occupant, or who has custody, control, or supervision, of premises or real estate, including vacant land, shall knowingly permit the premises or real estate, including vacant land, to be used for the commission of a felony drug abuse offense by another person.

(C)(1) Whoever violates this section is guilty of permitting drug abuse.

(2) Except as provided in division (C)(3) of this section, permitting drug abuse is a misdemeanor of the first degree.

(3) Permitting drug abuse is a felony of the fifth degree, and division (C) of section 2929.13 of the Revised Code applies in determining whether to impose a prison term on the offender, if the felony drug abuse offense in question is a violation of section 2925.02 or 2925.03 of the Revised Code that was committed in the vicinity of a school or in the vicinity of a juvenile.

(D) In addition to any prison term authorized or required by division (C) of this section and sections 2929.13 and 2929.14 of the Revised Code and in addition to any other sanction imposed for the offense under this section or sections 2929.11 to 2929.18 of the Revised Code, the court that sentences a person who is convicted of or pleads guilty to a violation of division (A) of this section shall do all of the following that are applicable regarding the offender:

(1) The court shall suspend for not less than six months or more than five years the driver's or commercial driver's license or permit of the offender.

(2) If the offender is a professionally licensed person or a person who has been admitted to the bar by order of the supreme court in compliance with its prescribed and published rules, in addition to any other sanction imposed for a violation of this section, the court forthwith shall comply with section 2925.38 of the Revised Code.

(E) Notwithstanding any contrary provision of section 3719.21 of the Revised Code, the clerk of the court shall pay a fine imposed for a violation of this section pursuant to division (A) of section 2929.18 of the Revised Code in accordance with and subject to the requirements of division (F) of section 2925.03 of the Revised Code. The agency that receives the fine shall use the fine as specified in division (F) of section 2925.03 of the Revised Code.

HISTORY: 136 v H 300 (Eff 7-1-76); 143 v H 215 (Eff 4-11-90); 143 v S 258 (Eff 11-20-90); 144 v H 591 (Eff 11-2-92); 145 v H 377 (Eff 9-30-93); 146 v S 2 (Eff 7-1-96); 146 v S 269. Eff 7-1-96.

The effective date is set by section 5 of SB 269.

§ 2925.14 Drug paraphernalia offenses.

(A) As used in this section, "drug paraphernalia" means any equipment, product, or material of any kind that is used by the offender, intended by the offender for use, or designed for use, in propagating, cultivating, growing, harvesting, manufacturing, compounding, converting, producing, processing, preparing, testing, analyzing, packaging, repackaging, storing, containing, concealing, injecting, ingesting, inhaling, or otherwise introducing into the human body, a controlled substance in violation of this chapter. "Drug paraphernalia" includes, but is not limited to, any of the following equipment, products, or materials that are used by the offender, intended by the offender for use, or designed by the offender for use, in any of the following manners:

(1) A kit for propagating, cultivating, growing, or harvesting any species of a plant that is a controlled substance or from which a controlled substance can be derived;

(2) A kit for manufacturing, compounding, converting, producing, processing, or preparing a controlled substance;

(3) An isomerization device for increasing the potency of any species of a plant that is a controlled substance;

(4) Testing equipment for identifying, or analyzing the strength, effectiveness, or purity of, a controlled substance;

(5) A scale or balance for weighing or measuring a controlled substance;

(6) A diluent or adulterant, such as quinine hydrochloride, mannitol, mannite, dextrose, or lactose, for cutting a controlled substance;

(7) A separation gin or sifter for removing twigs and seeds from, or otherwise cleaning or refining, marihuana;

(8) A blender, bowl, container, spoon, or mixing device for compounding a controlled substance;

(9) A capsule, balloon, envelope, or container for packaging small quantities of a controlled substance;

(10) A container or device for storing or concealing a controlled substance;

(11) A hypodermic syringe, needle, or instrument for parenterally injecting a controlled substance into the human body;

(12) An object, instrument, or device for ingesting, inhaling, or otherwise introducing into the human body, marihuana, cocaine, hashish, or hashish oil, such as a metal, wooden, acrylic, glass, stone, plastic, or ceramic pipe, with or without a screen, permanent screen, hashish head, or punctured metal bowl; water pipe; carburetion tube or device; smoking or carburetion mask; roach clip or similar object used to hold burning material, such as a marihuana cigarette, that has become too small or too short to be held in the hand; miniature cocaine spoon, or cocaine vial; chamber pipe; carburetor pipe; electric pipe; air driver pipe; chillum; bong; or ice pipe or chiller.

(B) In determining if an object is drug paraphernalia, a court or law enforcement officer shall consider, in addition to other relevant factors, the following:

(1) Any statement by the owner, or by anyone in control, of the object, concerning its use;

(2) The proximity in time or space of the object, or of the act relating to the object, to a violation of any provision of this chapter;

(3) The proximity of the object to any controlled substance;

(4) The existence of any residue of a controlled substance on the object;

(5) Direct or circumstantial evidence of the intent of the owner, or of anyone in control, of the object, to deliver it to any person whom the owner or person in control of the object knows intends to use the object to facilitate a violation of any provision of this chapter. A finding that the owner, or anyone in control, of the object, is not guilty of a violation of any other provision of this chapter does not prevent a finding that the object was intended or designed by the offender for use as drug paraphernalia.

(6) Any oral or written instruction provided with the object concerning its use;

(7) Any descriptive material accompanying the object and explaining or depicting its use;

(8) National or local advertising concerning the use of the object;

(9) The manner and circumstances in which the object is displayed for sale;

(10) Direct or circumstantial evidence of the ratio of the sales of the object to the total sales of the business enterprise;

(11) The existence and scope of legitimate uses of the object in the community;

(12) Expert testimony concerning the use of the object.

(C)(1) No person shall knowingly use, or possess with purpose to use, drug paraphernalia.

(2) No person shall knowingly sell, or possess or manufacture with purpose to sell, drug paraphernalia, if the person knows or reasonably should know that the equipment, product, or material will be used as drug paraphernalia.

(3) No person shall place an advertisement in any newspaper, magazine, handbill, or other publication that is published and printed and circulates primarily within this state, if the person knows that the purpose of the advertisement is to promote the illegal sale in this state of the equipment, product, or material that the offender intended or designed for use as drug paraphernalia.

(D) This section does not apply to manufacturers, practitioners, pharmacists, owners of pharmacies, and other persons whose conduct is in accordance with Chapters 3719., 4715., 4729., 4731., and 4741. or section 4723.56 of the Revised Code. This section shall not be construed to prohibit the possession or use of a hypodermic as authorized by section 3719.172 [3719.17.2] of the Revised Code.

(E) Notwithstanding sections 2933.42 and 2933.43 of the Revised Code, any drug paraphernalia that was used, possessed, sold, or manufactured in a violation of this section shall be seized, after a conviction for that violation shall be forfeited, and upon forfeiture shall be disposed of pursuant to division (D)(8) of section 2933.41 of the Revised Code.

(F)(1) Whoever violates division (C)(1) of this section is guilty of illegal use or possession of drug paraphernalia, a misdemeanor of the fourth degree.

(2) Except as provided in division (F)(3) of this section, whoever violates division (C)(2) of this section is guilty of dealing in drug paraphernalia, a misdemeanor of the second degree.

(3) Whoever violates division (C)(2) of this section by selling drug paraphernalia to a juvenile is guilty of selling drug paraphernalia to juveniles, a misdemeanor of the first degree.

(4) Whoever violates division (C)(3) of this section is guilty of illegal advertising of drug paraphernalia, a misdemeanor of the second degree.

(G) In addition to any other sanction imposed for a violation of this section, the court shall suspend for not less than six months or more than five years the driver's or commercial driver's license or permit of any person who is convicted of or has pleaded guilty to a violation of this section. If the offender is a professionally licensed person or a person who has been admitted to the bar by order of the supreme court in compliance with its prescribed and published rules, in addition to any other sanction imposed for a violation of this section, the court forthwith shall comply with section 2925.38 of the Revised Code.

HISTORY: 143 v H 182 (Eff 11-2-89); 143 v S 258 (Eff 11-20-90); 145 v H 377 (Eff 9-30-93); 145 v H 391 (Eff 7-21-94); 146 v S 2 (Eff 7-1-96); 146 v S 269. Eff 7-1-96.

Analogous in part to former RC § 2925.14 (138 v S 378; 142 v H 790), repealed, 143 v H 182, § 2, eff 11-2-89.

The effective date is set by section 5 of SB 269.

[DRUG THEFT]

§ 2925.21 Repealed, 143 v S 258, § 2 [136 v H 300]. Eff 11-20-90.

This section concerned theft of drugs.

The effective date is set by section 15 of SB 258.

§ 2925.22 Deception to obtain a dangerous drug.

(A) No person, by deception, as defined in section 2913.01 of the Revised Code, shall procure the administration of, a prescription for, or the dispensing of, a dangerous drug or shall possess an uncompleted preprinted prescription blank used for writing a prescription for a dangerous drug.

(B) Whoever violates this section is guilty of deception to obtain a dangerous drug. The penalty for the offense shall be determined as follows:

(1) If the drug involved is a compound, mixture, preparation, or substance included in schedule I or II, with the exception of marihuana, deception to obtain drugs is a felony of the fourth degree, and division (C) of section 2929.13 of the Revised Code applies in determining whether to impose a prison term on the offender.

(2) If the drug involved is a dangerous drug or a compound, mixture, preparation, or substance included in schedule III, IV, or V or is marihuana, deception to obtain a dangerous drug is a felony of the fifth degree, and division (C) of section 2929.13 of the Revised Code applies in determining whether to impose a prison term on the offender.

(C) In addition to any prison term authorized or required by division (B) of this section and sections 2929.13 and 2929.14 of the Revised Code and in addition to any other sanction imposed for the offense under this section or sections 2929.11 to 2929.18 of the Revised Code, the court that sentences an offender who is convicted of or pleads guilty to a violation of division (A) of this section shall do both of the following:

(1) The court shall suspend for not less than six months or more than five years the driver's or commercial driver's license or permit of any person who is convicted of or has pleaded guilty to a violation of this section.

(2) If the offender is a professionally licensed person or a person who has been admitted to the bar by order of the supreme court in compliance with its prescribed and published rules, in addition to any other sanction imposed for a violation of this section, the court forthwith shall comply with section 2925.38 of the Revised Code.

(D) Notwithstanding any contrary provision of section 3719.21 of the Revised Code, the clerk of the court shall pay a fine imposed for a violation of this section pursuant to division (A) of section 2929.18 of the Revised Code in accordance with and subject to the requirements of division (F) of section 2925.03 of the Revised Code. The agency that receives the fine shall use the fine as specified in division (F) of section 2925.03 of the Revised Code.

HISTORY: 136 v H 300 (Eff 7-1-76); 143 v S 258 (Eff 11-20-90); 143 v H 615 (Eff 3-27-91); 145 v H 377 (Eff 9-30-93); 146 v S 2 (Eff 7-1-96); 146 v S 269. Eff 7-1-96.

The effective date is set by section 5 of SB 269.

§ 2925.23 Illegal processing of drug documents.

(A) No person shall knowingly make a false statement in any prescription, order, report, or record required by Chapter 3719. or 4729. of the Revised Code.

(B) No person shall intentionally make, utter, or sell, or knowingly possess a false or forged:

(1) Prescription;
(2) Uncompleted preprinted prescription blank used for writing a prescription;
(3) Official written order;
(4) License for a terminal distributor of dangerous drugs as required in section 4729.60 of the Revised Code;
(5) Registration certificate for a wholesale distributor of dangerous drugs as required in section 4729.60 of the Revised Code.

(C) No person, by theft as defined in section 2913.02 of the Revised Code, shall acquire any of the following:
(1) A prescription;
(2) An uncompleted preprinted prescription blank used for writing a prescription;
(3) An official written order;
(4) A blank official written order;
(5) A license or blank license for a terminal distributor of dangerous drugs as required in section 4729.60 of the Revised Code;
(6) A registration certificate or blank registration certificate for a wholesale distributor of dangerous drugs as required in section 4729.60 of the Revised Code.

(D) No person shall knowingly make or affix any false or forged label to a package or receptacle containing any dangerous drugs.

(E) Divisions (A) and (D) of this section do not apply to practitioners, pharmacists, owners of pharmacies, and other persons whose conduct is in accordance with Chapters 3719., 4715., 4725., 4729., 4731., and 4741. of the Revised Code or section 4723.56 of the Revised Code.

(F) Whoever violates this section is guilty of illegal processing of drug documents. The penalty for the offense shall be determined as follows:

(1) If the drug involved is a compound, mixture, preparation, or substance included in schedule I or II, with the exception of marihuana, illegal processing of drug documents is a felony of the fourth degree, and division (C) of section 2929.13 of the Revised Code applies in determining whether to impose a prison term on the offender.

(2) If the drug involved is a dangerous drug or a compound, mixture, preparation, or substance included in schedule III, IV, or V or is marihuana, illegal processing of drug documents is a felony of the fifth degree, and division (C) of section 2929.13 of the Revised Code applies in determining whether to impose a prison term on the offender.

(G) In addition to any prison term authorized or required by division (F) of this section and sections 2929.13 and 2929.14 of the Revised Code and in addition to any other sanction imposed for the offense under this section or sections 2929.11 to 2929.18 of the Revised Code, the court that sentences an offender who is convicted of or pleads guilty to any violation of divisions (A) to (D) of this section shall do both of the following:

(1) The court shall suspend for not less than six months or more than five years the driver's or commercial driver's license or permit of any person who is convicted of or has pleaded guilty to a violation of this section.

(2) If the offender is a professionally licensed person or a person who has been admitted to the bar by order of the supreme court in compliance with its prescribed and published rules, in addition to any other sanction imposed for a violation of this section, the court forthwith shall comply with section 2925.38 of the Revised Code.

(H) Notwithstanding any contrary provision of section 3719.21 of the Revised Code, the clerk of court shall pay a fine imposed for a violation of this section pursuant to division (A) of section 2929.18 of the Revised Code in accordance with and subject to the requirements of division (F) of section 2925.03 of the Revised Code. The agency that receives the fine shall use the fine as specified in division (F) of section 2925.03 of the Revised Code.

HISTORY: 136 v H 300 (Eff 7-1-76); 143 v S 258 (Eff 11-20-90); 144 v S 110 (Eff 5-19-92); 145 v H 377 (Eff 9-30-93); 145 v H 391 (7-21-94); 146 v S 2 (Eff 7-1-96); 146 v S 269. Eff 7-1-96.

The effective date is set by section 5 of SB 269.

[HARMFUL INTOXICANTS]

§ 2925.31 Abusing harmful intoxicants.

(A) Except for lawful research, clinical, medical, dental, or veterinary purposes, no person, with purpose to induce intoxication or similar physiological effects, shall obtain, possess, or use a harmful intoxicant.

(B) Whoever violates this section is guilty of abusing harmful intoxicants, a misdemeanor of the first degree. If the offender previously has been convicted of a drug abuse offense, abusing harmful intoxicants is a felony of the fifth degree.

(C) In addition to any other sanction imposed for a violation of this section, the court shall suspend for not less than six months or more than five years the driver's or commercial driver's license or permit of any person who is convicted of or has pleaded guilty to a violation of this section. If the offender is a professionally licensed person or a person who has been admitted to the bar by order of the supreme court in compliance with its prescribed and published rules, in addition to any other sanction imposed for a violation of this section, the court forthwith shall comply with section 2925.38 of the Revised Code.

HISTORY: 136 v H 300 (Eff 7-1-76); 143 v S 258 (Eff 11-20-90); 145 v H 377 (Eff 9-30-93); 146 v S 2 (Eff 7-1-96); 146 v H 162. Eff 1-1-97.

The effective date is set by section 3 of HB 162.

§ 2925.32 Trafficking in harmful intoxicants; improperly dispensing or distributing nitrous oxide.

(A) Divisions (A)(1) and (2) of this section do not apply to the dispensing or distributing of nitrous oxide.

(1) No person shall knowingly dispense or distribute a harmful intoxicant to a person age eighteen or older if the person who dispenses or distributes it knows or has reason to believe that the harmful intoxicant will be used in violation of section 2925.31 of the Revised Code.

(2) No person shall knowingly dispense or distribute a harmful intoxicant to a person under age eighteen if the person who dispenses or distributes it knows or has reason to believe that the harmful intoxicant will be used in violation of section 2925.31 of the Revised Code. Division (A)(2) of this section does not prohibit either of the following:

(a) Dispensing or distributing a harmful intoxicant to a person under age eighteen if a written order from the juvenile's parent or guardian is provided to the dispenser or distributor;

(b) Dispensing or distributing gasoline or diesel fuel to a person under age eighteen if the dispenser or distributor does not know or have reason to believe the product will be used in violation of section 2925.31 of the Revised Code. Division (A)(2)(a) of this section does not require a person to obtain a written order from the parent or guardian of a person under age eighteen in order to distribute or dispense gasoline or diesel fuel to the person.

(B)(1) No person shall knowingly dispense or distribute nitrous oxide to a person age twenty-one or older if the person who dispenses or distributes it knows or has reason to believe the nitrous oxide will be used in violation of section 2925.31 of the Revised Code.

(2) Except for lawful medical, dental, or clinical purposes, no person shall knowingly dispense or distribute nitrous oxide to a person under age twenty-one.

(3) No person, at the time a cartridge of nitrous oxide is sold to another person, shall sell a device that allows the purchaser to inhale nitrous oxide from cartridges or to hold nitrous oxide released from cartridges for purposes of inhalation. The sale of any such device constitutes a rebuttable presumption that the person knew or had reason to believe that the purchaser intended to abuse the nitrous oxide.

(4) No person who dispenses or distributes nitrous oxide in cartridges shall fail to comply with either of the following:

(a) The record-keeping requirements established under division (F) of this section;

(b) The labeling and transaction identification requirements established under division (G) of this section.

(C) This section does not apply to products used in making, fabricating, assembling, transporting, or constructing a product or structure by manual labor or machinery for sale or lease to another person, or to the mining, refining, or processing of natural deposits.

(D)(1) Whoever violates division (A)(1) or (2) or division (B)(1), (2), or (3) of this section is guilty of trafficking in harmful intoxicants, a felony of the fifth degree. If the offender previously has been convicted of a drug abuse offense, trafficking in harmful intoxicants is a felony of the fourth degree. In addition to any other sanction imposed for trafficking in harmful intoxicants, the court shall suspend for not less than six months or more than five years the driver's or commercial driver's license or permit of any person who is convicted of or has pleaded guilty to trafficking in harmful intoxicants. If the offender is a professionally licensed person or a person who has been admitted to the bar by order of the supreme court in compliance with its prescribed and published rules, in addition to any other sanction imposed for trafficking in harmful intoxicants, the court forthwith shall comply with section 2925.38 of the Revised Code.

(2) Whoever violates division (B)(4) (a) or (b) of this section is guilty of improperly dispensing or distributing nitrous oxide, a misdemeanor of the fourth degree.

(E) It is an affirmative defense to a charge of a violation of division (A)(2) or (B)(2) of this section that:

(1) An individual exhibited to the defendant or an officer or employee of the defendant, for purposes of establishing the individual's age, a driver's license or permit issued by this state, a commercial driver's license or permit issued by this state, an identification card issued pursuant to section 4507.50 of the Revised Code, or another document that purports to be a license, permit, or identification card described in this division;

(2) The document exhibited appeared to be a genuine, unaltered document, to pertain to the individual, and to establish the individual's age;

(3) The defendant or the officer or employee of the defendant otherwise did not have reasonable cause to believe that the individual was under the age represented.

(F) Beginning July 1, 1998, a person who dispenses or distributes nitrous oxide shall record each transaction involving the dispensing or distributing of the nitrous oxide on a separate card. The person shall require the purchaser to sign the card and provide a complete residence address. The person dispensing or distributing the nitrous oxide shall sign and date the card. The person shall retain the card recording a transaction for one year from the date of the transaction. The person shall maintain the cards at the person's business address and make them available during normal business hours for inspection and copying by officers or employees of the state board of pharmacy or of other law enforcement agencies of this state or the United States that are authorized to investigate violations of Chapter 2925., 3719., or 4729. of the Revised Code or the federal drug abuse control laws.

The cards used to record each transaction shall inform the purchaser of the following:

(1) That nitrous oxide cartridges are to be used only for purposes of preparing food;

(2) That inhalation of nitrous oxide can have dangerous health effects;

(3) That it is a violation of state law to distribute or dispense cartridges of nitrous oxide to any person under age twenty-one, punishable as a felony of the fifth degree.

(G)(1) Each cartridge of nitrous oxide dispensed or distributed in this state shall bear the following printed warning:

"Nitrous oxide cartridges are to be used only for purposes of preparing food. Nitrous oxide cartridges may not be sold to persons under age twenty-one. Do not inhale contents. Misuse can be dangerous to your health."

(2) Each time a person dispenses or distributes one or more cartridges of nitrous oxide, the person shall mark the packaging containing the cartridges with a label or other device that identifies the person who dispensed or distributed the nitrous oxide and the person's business address.

HISTORY: 136 v S 414 (Eff 9-22-76); 143 v S 258 (Eff 11-20-90); 145 v H 377 (Eff 9-30-93); 146 v S 2 (Eff 7-1-96); 146 v H 162. Eff 1-1-97.

The effective date is set by section 3 of HB 162.

The provisions of § 5 of HB 162 (146 v —) read as follows:

SECTION 5. The Department of Alcohol and Drug Addiction Services shall conduct a study of the effects of the amendments made by this act to section 2925.32 of the Revised Code with regard to the dispensing or distributing of nitrous oxide and the enactment by this act of section 2925.33 of the Revised Code prohibiting open cartridges of nitrous oxide in vehicles. The study shall include consideration of the provisions' impact on the frequency of abuse of nitrous oxide and the sale of nitrous oxide in this state. The study may include an evaluation of any other matter the Department considers relevant.

At the Department's request, the State Board of Pharmacy, the Department of Health, law enforcement agencies, prosecutors, and other state and local entities shall provide the Department with information and assistance in completing the study. All persons required to maintain records under section 2925.32 of the Revised Code shall cooperate with the Department in its conduct of the study.

The Department shall complete the study on or before April 1, 1998, and submit its findings and recommendations to the chairpersons of each of the standing committees of the Senate and House of Representatives with primary responsibility for considering legislation that pertains to health or criminal laws related to drug abuse. The Department shall make copies of the report available to the public on request.

§ 2925.33 Possessing nitrous oxide in motor vehicle.

(A) As used in this section, "motor vehicle," "street," and "highway" have the same meanings as in section 4511.01 of the Revised Code.

(B) Unless authorized under Chapter 3719., 4715., 4729., 4731., 4741., or 4765. of the Revised Code, no person shall possess an open cartridge of nitrous oxide in either of the following circumstances:

(1) While operating or being a passenger in or on a motor vehicle on a street, highway, or other public or private property open to the public for purposes of vehicular traffic or parking;

(2) While being in or on a stationary motor vehicle on a street, highway, or other public or private property open to the public for purposes of vehicular traffic or parking.

(C) Whoever violates this section is guilty of possessing nitrous oxide in a motor vehicle, a misdemeanor of the fourth degree.

HISTORY: 146 v H 162. Eff 1-1-97.

The effective date is set by section 3 of HB 162.

See provisions, § 5 of HB 162 (146 v —) following RC § 2925.32.

[DRUG SAMPLES]

§ 2925.36 Illegal dispensing of drug samples.

(A) No person shall knowingly furnish another a sample drug.

(B) Division (A) of this section does not apply to manufacturers, wholesalers, pharmacists, owners of pharmacies, dentists, doctors of medicine and surgery, doctors of osteopathic medicine and surgery, doctors of podiatry, veterinarians, and other persons whose conduct is in accordance with Chapters 3719., 4715., 4729., 4731., and 4741. of the Revised Code or to optometrists whose conduct is in accordance with a valid therapeutic pharmaceutical agents certificate issued under Chapter 4725. of the Revised Code.

(C)(1) Whoever violates this section is guilty of illegal dispensing of drug samples.

(2) If the drug involved in the offense is a compound, mixture, preparation, or substance included in schedule I or II, with the exception of marihuana, the penalty for the offense shall be determined as follows:

(a) Except as otherwise provided in division (C)(2)(b) of this section, illegal dispensing of drug samples is a felony of the fifth degree, and, subject to division (E) of this section, division (C) of section 2929.13 of the Revised Code applies in determining whether to impose a prison term on the offender.

(b) If the offense was committed in the vicinity of a school or in the vicinity of a juvenile, illegal dispensing of drug samples is a felony of the fourth degree, and, subject to division (E) of this section, division (C) of section 2929.13 of the Revised Code applies in determining whether to impose a prison term on the offender.

(3) If the drug involved in the offense is a dangerous drug or a compound, mixture, preparation, or substance included in schedule III, IV, or V, or is marihuana, the penalty for the offense shall be determined as follows:

(a) Except as otherwise provided in division (C)(3)(b) of this section, illegal dispensing of drug samples is a misdemeanor of the second degree.

(b) If the offense was committed in the vicinity of a school or in the vicinity of a juvenile, illegal dispensing of drug samples is a misdemeanor of the first degree.

(D) In addition to any prison term authorized or required by division (C) or (E) of this section and sections 2929.13 and 2929.14 of the Revised Code and in addition to any other sanction imposed for the offense under this section or sections 2929.11 to 2929.18 of the Revised Code, the court that sentences an offender who is convicted of or pleads guilty to a violation of division (A) of this section shall do both of the following:

(1) The court shall suspend for not less than six months or more than five years the driver's or commercial driver's license or permit of any person who is convicted of or has pleaded guilty to a violation of this section.

(2) If the offender is a professionally licensed person or a person who has been admitted to the bar by order of the supreme court in compliance with its prescribed and published rules, in addition to any other sanction imposed for a violation of this section, the court forthwith shall comply with section 2925.38 of the Revised Code.

(E) Notwithstanding the prison term authorized or required by division (C) of this section and sections 2929.13 and 2929.14 of the Revised Code, if the violation of division (A) of this section involves the sale, offer to sell, or possession of a schedule I or II controlled substance, with the exception of marihuana, and if the offender, as a result of the violation, is a major drug offender, the court, in lieu of the prison term otherwise authorized or required, shall impose upon the offender the mandatory prison term specified in division (D)(3)(a) of section 2929.14 of the Revised Code and may impose an additional prison term under division (D)(3)(b) of that section.

(F) Notwithstanding any contrary provision of section 3719.21 of the Revised Code, the clerk of the court shall pay a fine imposed for a violation of this section pursuant to division (A) of section 2929.18 of the Revised Code in accordance with and subject to the requirements of division (F) of section 2925.03 of the Revised Code. The agency that receives the fine shall use the fine as specified in division (F) of section 2925.03 of the Revised Code.

HISTORY: 136 v H 300 (Eff 7-1-76); 143 v H 215 (Eff 4-11-90); 143 v S 258 (Eff 11-20-90); 144 v S 110 (Eff 5-19-92); 144 v H 591 (Eff 11-2-92); 145 v H 377 (Eff 9-30-93); 145 v H 391 (Eff 7-21-94); 146 v S 2 (Eff 7-1-96); 146 v S 269. Eff 7-1-96.

The effective date is set by section 5 of SB 269.

§ 2925.37 Offenses involving counterfeit controlled substances.

(A) No person shall knowingly possess any counterfeit controlled substance.

(B) No person shall knowingly make, sell, offer to sell, or deliver any substance that the person knows is a counterfeit controlled substance.

(C) No person shall make, possess, sell, offer to sell, or deliver any punch, die, plate, stone, or other device knowing or having reason to know that it will be used to print or reproduce a trademark, trade name, or other identifying mark upon a counterfeit controlled substance.

(D) No person shall sell, offer to sell, give, or deliver any counterfeit controlled substance to a juvenile.

(E) No person shall directly or indirectly represent a counterfeit controlled substance as a controlled substance by describing its effects as the physical or psychological effects associated with use of a controlled substance.

(F) No person shall directly or indirectly falsely represent or advertise a counterfeit controlled substance as a controlled substance. As used in this division, "advertise" means engaging in "advertisement," as defined in section 3715.01 of the Revised Code.

(G) Whoever violates division (A) of this section is guilty of possession of counterfeit controlled substances, a misdemeanor of the first degree.

(H) Whoever violates division (B) or (C) of this section is guilty of trafficking in counterfeit controlled substances. Except as otherwise provided in this division, trafficking in counterfeit controlled substances is a felony of the fifth degree, and division (C) of section 2929.13 of the Revised Code applies in determining whether to impose a prison term on the offender. If the offense was committed in the vicinity of a school or in the vicinity of a juvenile, trafficking in counterfeit controlled substances is a felony of the fourth degree, and division (C) of section 2929.13 of the Revised Code applies in determining whether to impose a prison term on the offender.

(I) Whoever violates division (D) of this section is guilty of aggravated trafficking in counterfeit controlled substances. Except as otherwise provided in this division, aggravated trafficking in counterfeit controlled substances is a felony of the fourth degree, and division (C) of section 2929.13 of the Revised Code applies in determining whether to impose a prison term on the offender.

(J) Whoever violates division (E) of this section is guilty of promoting and encouraging drug abuse. Except as otherwise provided in this division, promoting and encouraging drug abuse is a felony of the fifth degree, and division (C) of section 2929.13 of the Revised Code applies in determining whether to impose a prison term on the offender. If the offense was committed in the vicinity of a school or in the vicinity of a juvenile, promoting and encouraging drug abuse is a felony of the fourth degree, and division (C) of section 2929.13 of the Revised Code applies in determining whether to impose a prison term on the offender.

(K) Whoever violates division (F) of this section is guilty of fraudulent drug advertising. Except as otherwise provided in this division, fraudulent drug advertising is a felony of the fifth degree, and division (C) of section 2929.13 of the Revised Code applies in determining whether to impose a prison term on the offender. If the offense was committed in the vicinity of a school or in the vicinity of a juvenile, fraudulent drug advertising is a felony of the fourth degree, and division (C) of section 2929.13 of the Revised Code applies in determining whether to impose a prison term on the offender.

(L) In addition to any prison term authorized or required by divisions (H) to (K) of this section and sections 2929.13 and 2929.14 of the Revised Code and in addition to any other sanction imposed for the offense under this section or sections 2929.11 to 2929.18 of the Revised Code, the court that sentences an offender who is convicted of or pleads guilty to a violation of division (B), (C), (D), (E), or (F) of this section shall do both of the following:

(1) The court shall suspend for not less than six months or more than five years the driver's or commercial driver's license or permit of any person who is convicted of or has pleaded guilty to any other violation of this section.

(2) If the offender is a professionally licensed person or a person who has been admitted to the bar by order of the supreme court in compliance with its prescribed and published rules, in addition to any other sanction imposed for a violation of this section, the court forthwith shall comply with section 2925.38 of the Revised Code.

(M) Notwithstanding any contrary provision of section 3719.21 of the Revised Code, the clerk of the court shall pay a fine imposed for a violation of this section pursuant to division (A) of section 2929.18 of the Revised Code in accordance with and subject to the requirements of division (F) of section 2925.03 of the Revised Code. The agency that receives the fine shall use the fine as specified in division (F) of section 2925.03 of the Revised Code.

HISTORY: 139 v H 535 (Eff 8-20-82); 143 v S 258 (Eff 11-20-90); 145 v H 377 (Eff 9-30-93); 146 v S 2 (Eff 7-1-96); 146 v S 269. Eff 7-1-96.

The effective date is set by section 5 of SB 269.

§ 2925.38 Convictions to be reported to professional licensing authorities.

If a person who is convicted of or pleads guilty to a violation of section 2925.02, 2925.03, 2925.04, 2925.05, 2925.06, 2925.11, 2925.12, 2925.13, 2925.14, 2925.22, 2925.23, 2925.31, 2925.32, 2925.36, or 2925.37 of the Revised Code is a professionally licensed person, in addition to any other sanctions imposed for the violation, the court forthwith shall transmit a certified copy of the judgment entry of conviction to the regulatory or licensing board or agency that has the administrative authority to suspend or revoke the offender's professional license. If a person who is convicted of or pleads guilty to a violation of any section listed in this section is a person who has been admitted to the bar by order of the supreme court in compliance with its prescribed and published rules, in addition to any other sanctions imposed for the violation, the court forthwith shall transmit a certified copy of the judgment entry of conviction to the secretary of the board of commissioners on grievances and discipline of the supreme court and to either the disciplinary counsel or the president, secretary, and chairman of each certified grievance committee.

HISTORY: 143 v S 258 (Eff 11-20-90); 146 v S 2. Eff 7-1-96.

The effective date is set by section 6 of SB 2.

[FORFEITURE OF PROPERTY RELATING TO FELONY DRUG ABUSE OFFENSE]

§ 2925.41 Definitions.

As used in sections 2925.42 to 2925.45 of the Revised Code:

(A) "Financial institution" means a bank, credit union, savings and loan association, or a licensee or registrant under Chapter 1321. of the Revised Code.

(B) "Property" includes both of the following:

(1) Real property, including, but not limited to, things growing on, affixed to, and found in the real property;

(2) Tangible and intangible personal property, including, but not limited to, rights, privileges, interests, claims, and securities.

HISTORY: 143 v S 258. Eff 11-20-90.

The effective date is set by section 15 of SB 258.

§ 2925.42 Forfeiture of property in connection with felony drug abuse offense or act.

(A)(1) In accordance with division (B) of this section, a person who is convicted of or pleads guilty to a felony drug abuse offense, and any juvenile who is found by a juvenile court to be a delinquent child for an act that, if committed by an adult, would be a felony drug abuse offense, loses any right to the possession of property and forfeits to the state any right, title, and interest the person may have in that property if either of the following applies:

(a) The property constitutes, or is derived directly or indirectly from, any proceeds that the person obtained directly or indirectly from the commission of the felony drug abuse offense or act.

(b) The property was used or intended to be used in any manner to commit, or to facilitate the commission of, the felony drug abuse offense or act.

(2) All right, title, and interest of a person in property described in division (A)(1) of this section vests in the state upon the person's commission of the felony drug abuse offense of which the person is convicted or to which the person pleads guilty and that is the basis of the forfeiture, or upon the juvenile's commission of the act that, if committed by an adult, would be a felony drug abuse offense, that is the basis of the juvenile being found to be a delinquent child, and that is the basis of the forfeiture. Subject to divisions (F)(3)(b) and (5)(b) and (G)(2) of this section, if any right, title, or interest in property is vested in this state under this division and subsequently is transferred to a person other than the offender who forfeits the right, title, or interest under division (A)(1) of this section, then, in accordance with division (B) of this section, the right, title, or interest in the property may be the subject of a special verdict of forfeiture and, after any special verdict of forfeiture, shall be ordered forfeited to this state, unless the transferee establishes in a hearing held pursuant to division (F) of this section that the transferee is a bona fide purchaser for value of the right, title, or interest in the property and that, at the time of its purchase, the transferee was reasonably without cause to believe that it was subject to forfeiture under this section.

(3) The provisions of section 2925.43 of the Revised Code that relate to the forfeiture of any right, title, or interest in property associated with a felony drug abuse offense pursuant to a civil action to obtain a civil forfeiture do not apply to the forfeiture of any right, title, or interest in property described in division (A)(1) of this section that occurs pursuant to division (B) of this section upon a person's conviction of or guilty plea to a felony drug abuse offense or upon a juvenile being found by a juvenile court to be a delinquent child for an act that, if committed by an adult, would be a felony drug abuse offense.

(4) Nothing in this section precludes a financial institution that has or purports to have a security interest in or lien on property described in division (A)(1) of this section from commencing a civil action or taking other appropriate legal action in connection with the property, prior to its disposition in accordance with section 2925.44 of the Revised Code, for the purpose of obtaining possession of the property in order to foreclose or otherwise enforce the security interest or lien. A financial institution may commence a civil action or take other appropriate legal action for that purpose prior to the disposition of the property in accordance with section 2925.44 of the Revised Code, even if a felony drug abuse offense prosecution or a delinquent child proceeding for an act that, if committed by an adult, would be a felony drug abuse offense has been or could be commenced, even if the property is or could be the subject of an order of forfeiture issued under division (B)(5) of this section, and even if the property has been seized or is subject to seizure pursuant to division (D) or (E) of this section.

If a financial institution commences a civil action or takes any other appropriate legal action as described in this division, if the financial institution subsequently causes the sale of the property prior to its seizure pursuant to division (D) or (E) of this section and its disposition pursuant to section 2925.44 of the Revised Code, and if the person responsible for the conduct of the sale has actual knowledge of the commencement of a felony drug abuse offense prosecution or of a delinquent child proceeding for an act that, if committed by an adult, would be a felony drug abuse offense, actual knowledge of a pending forfeiture proceeding under division (B) of this section, or actual knowledge of an order of forfeiture issued under division (B)(5) of this section, then the person responsible for the conduct of the sale shall dispose of the proceeds of the sale in the following order:

(a) First, to the payment of the costs of the sale and to the payment of the costs incurred by law enforcement agencies and financial institutions in connection with the seizure of, storage of, maintenance of, and provision of security for the property. As used in this division, "costs" of a financial institution do not include attorney's fees incurred by that institution in connection with the property.

(b) Second, the remaining proceeds of the sale after compliance with division (A)(4)(a) of this section, to the payment of valid security interests and liens pertaining to the property that, at the time of the vesting of the right, title, or interest of the adult or juvenile in the state under division (A)(2) of this section, are held by known secured parties and lienholders, in the order of priority of those security interests and liens;

(c) Third, the remaining proceeds of the sale after compliance with division (A)(4)(b) of this section, to the court that has or would have jurisdiction in a felony drug abuse offense prosecution or a delinquent child proceeding for an act that, if committed by an adult, would be a felony drug abuse offense, for disposition in accordance with section 2925.44 of the Revised Code.

(B)(1) A criminal forfeiture of any right, title, or interest in property described in division (A)(1) of this section is precluded unless one of the following applies:

(a) The indictment, count in the indictment, or information charging the felony drug abuse offense specifies the nature of the right, title, or interest of the alleged offender in the property described in division (A)(1) of this section that is potentially subject to forfeiture under this section, or a description of the property of the alleged offender that is potentially subject to forfeiture under this section, to the extent the right, title, or interest in the property or the property reasonably is known at the time of the filing of the indictment or information; or the complaint charging a juvenile with being a delinquent child for the commission of an act that, if committed by an adult, would be a felony drug abuse offense specifies the nature of the right, title, or interest of the juvenile in the property described in division (A)(1) of this section that is potentially subject to forfeiture under this section, or a description of the property of the juvenile that is potentially subject to forfeiture under this section, to the extent the right, title, or interest in the property or the property reasonably is known at the time of the filing of the complaint.

(b) The property in question was not reasonably foreseen to be subject to forfeiture under this section at the time of the filing of the indictment, information, or complaint, the prosecuting attorney gave prompt notice to the alleged offender or juvenile of that property when it was discovered to be subject to forfeiture under this section, and a verdict of forfeiture described in division (B)(3) of this section requires the forfeiture of that property.

(2) The specifications described in division (B)(1) of this section shall be stated at the end of the body of the indictment, count in the indictment, information, or complaint.

(3)(a) If a person is convicted of or pleads guilty to a felony drug abuse offense, or a juvenile is found to be a delinquent child for an act that, if committed by an adult, would be a felony drug abuse offense, then a special proceeding shall be conducted in accordance with this division to determine whether any property described in division (B)(1)(a) or (b) of this section will be the subject of an order of forfeiture under this section. Except as otherwise provided in division (B)(3)(b) of this section, the jury in the felony drug abuse offense criminal action or in the delinquent child action or, if that action was a nonjury action, the judge in that action shall hear and consider testimony and other evidence in the proceeding relative to whether any property described in division (B)(1)(a) or (b) of this section is subject to forfeiture under this section. If the jury or judge determines that the prosecuting attorney has established, by a preponderance of the evidence, that any property so described is subject to forfeiture under this section, the judge or juvenile judge shall render a verdict of forfeiture that specifically describes the right, title, or interest in property or the property that is subject to forfeiture under this section. The Rules of Evidence shall apply in the proceeding.

(b) If the trier of fact in a felony drug abuse offense criminal action or in a delinquent child action was a jury, then, upon the filing of a motion by the person who was convicted of or pleaded guilty to the felony drug abuse offense or upon the filing of a motion by the juvenile who was found to be a delinquent child for an act that, if committed by an adult, would be a felony drug abuse offense, the determinations in the proceeding described in this division instead shall be made by the judge in the felony drug abuse offense criminal action or the juvenile judge.

(4) In a felony drug abuse offense criminal action or in a delinquent child action, if the trier of fact is a jury, the jury shall not be informed of any specification described in division (B)(1)(a) of this section or of any property described in that division or division (B)(1)(b) of this section prior to the alleged offender being convicted of or pleading guilty to the felony drug abuse

offense or prior to the juvenile being found to be a delinquent child for the commission of an act that, if committed by an adult, would be a felony drug abuse offense.

(5)(a) If a verdict of forfeiture is entered pursuant to division (B)(3) of this section, then the court that imposes sentence upon a person who is convicted of or pleads guilty to a felony drug abuse offense, or the juvenile court that finds a juvenile to be a delinquent child for an act that, if committed by an adult, would be a felony drug abuse offense, in addition to any other sentence imposed upon the offender or order of disposition imposed upon the delinquent child, shall order that the offender or delinquent child forfeit to the state all of the offender's or delinquent child's right, title, and interest in the property described in division (A)(1) of this section. If a person is convicted of or pleads guilty to a felony drug abuse offense, or a juvenile is found by a juvenile court to be a delinquent child for an act that, if committed by an adult, would be a felony drug abuse offense, and derives profits or other proceeds from the offense or act, the court that imposes sentence or an order of disposition upon the offender or delinquent child, in lieu of any fine that the court is otherwise authorized or required to impose, may impose upon the offender or delinquent child a fine of not more than twice the gross profits or other proceeds so derived.

(b) Notwithstanding any contrary provision of section 3719.21 of the Revised Code, all fines imposed pursuant to this division shall be paid by the clerk of the court to the county, municipal corporation, township, park district, as created pursuant to section 511.18 or 1545.01 of the Revised Code, or state law enforcement agencies in this state that were primarily responsible for or involved in making the arrest of, and in prosecuting, the offender. However, no fine so imposed shall be paid to a law enforcement agency unless the agency has adopted a written internal control policy under division (F)(2) of section 2925.03 of the Revised Code that addresses the use of the fine moneys that it receives under this division and division (F)(1) of section 2925.03 of the Revised Code. The fines imposed and paid pursuant to this division shall be used by the law enforcement agencies to subsidize their efforts pertaining to drug offenses, in accordance with the written internal control policy adopted by the recipient agency under division (F)(2) of section 2925.03 of the Revised Code.

(c) As used in division (B)(5) of this section:

(i) "Law enforcement agencies" includes, but is not limited to, the state board of pharmacy and the office of a prosecutor.

(ii) "Prosecutor" has the same meaning as in section 2935.01 of the Revised Code.

(6) If any of the property that is described in division (A)(1) of this section and that is the subject of an order of forfeiture issued under division (B)(5) of this section, because of an act or omission of the person who is convicted of or pleads guilty to the felony drug abuse offense that is the basis of the order of forfeiture, or an act or omission of the juvenile found by a juvenile court to be a delinquent child for an act that, if committed by an adult, would be a felony drug abuse offense and that is the basis of the forfeiture, cannot be located upon the exercise of due diligence, has been transferred to, sold to, or deposited with a third party, has been placed beyond the jurisdiction of the court, has been substantially diminished in value, or has been commingled with other property that cannot be divided without difficulty, the court that issues the order of forfeiture shall order the forfeiture of any other property of the offender up to the value of any forfeited property described in this division.

(C) There shall be a rebuttable presumption that any right, title, or interest of a person in property described in division (A)(1) of this section is subject to forfeiture under division (B) of this section, if the state proves both of the following by a preponderance of the evidence:

(1) The right, title, or interest in the property was acquired by the offender during the period of the commission of the felony drug abuse offense or act that, if committed by an adult, would be a felony drug abuse offense, or within a reasonable time after that period.

(2) There is no likely source for the right, title, or interest in the property other than proceeds obtained from the commission of the felony drug abuse offense or act.

(D)(1) Upon the application of the prosecuting attorney who is prosecuting or has jurisdiction to prosecute the felony drug abuse offense or act, the court of common pleas or juvenile court of the county in which property subject to forfeiture under division (B) of this section is located, whichever is applicable, may issue a restraining order or injunction, an order requiring the execution of a satisfactory performance bond, or an order taking any other reasonable action necessary to preserve the availability of the property, at either of the following times:

(a) Upon the filing of an indictment, complaint, or information charging a person who has any right, title, or interest in the property with the commission of a felony drug abuse offense and alleging that the property with respect to which the order is sought will be subject to forfeiture under division (B) of this section if the person is convicted of or pleads guilty to the offense, or upon the filing of a complaint alleging that a juvenile who has any right, title, or interest in the property is a delinquent child because of the commission of an act that, if committed by an adult, would be a felony drug abuse offense and alleging that the property with respect to which the order is sought will be subject to forfeiture under division (B) of this section if the juvenile is found to be a delinquent child because of the commission of that act;

(b) Except as provided in division (D)(3) of this section, prior to the filing of an indictment, complaint, or information charging a person who has any right, title, or interest in the property with the commission of a felony drug abuse offense, or prior to the filing of a complaint alleging that a juvenile who has any right, title, or interest in the property is a delinquent child because of the commission of an act that, if committed by an adult, would be a felony drug abuse offense, if, after notice is given to all persons known to have any right, title, or interest in the property and an opportunity to have a hearing on the order is given to those persons, the court determines both of the following:

(i) There is a substantial probability that the state will prevail on the issue of forfeiture and that failure to enter the order will result in the property subject to forfeiture being destroyed, removed from the jurisdiction of the court, or otherwise being made unavailable for forfeiture.

(ii) The need to preserve the availability of the property subject to forfeiture through the entry of the requested order outweighs the hardship on any party against whom the order is to be entered.

(2) Except as provided in division (D)(3) of this section, an order issued under division (D)(1) of this section is effective for not more than ninety days, unless extended by the court for good cause shown or unless an indictment, complaint, or information charging the commission of a felony drug abuse offense or a complaint alleging that a juvenile is a delinquent child because of the commission of an act that, if committed by an adult, would be a felony drug abuse offense, is filed against any alleged adult offender or alleged delinquent child with any right, title, or interest in the property that is the subject of the order.

(3) A court may issue an order under division (D)(1)(b) of this section without giving notice or an opportunity for a hearing to persons known to have any right, title, or interest in property, if the prosecuting attorney who is prosecuting or has jurisdiction to prosecute the felony drug abuse offense or act demonstrates that there is probable cause to believe that the property will be subject to forfeiture under division (B) of this section if a person with any right, title, or interest in the property is convicted of or pleads guilty to a felony drug abuse offense or a juvenile with any right, title, or interest in the property is found by a juvenile court to be a delinquent child for an act that, if committed by an adult, would be a felony drug abuse offense, and that giving notice or an opportunity for a hearing to persons with any right, title, or interest in the property will jeopardize its availability for forfeiture. The order shall be a temporary order and expire not more than ten days after the date on which it is entered, unless it is extended for good cause shown or unless a person with any right, title, or interest in the property that is the subject of the order consents to an extension for a longer period. A hearing concerning an order issued under this division may be requested, and, if it is requested, the court shall hold the hearing at the earliest possible time prior to the expiration of the order.

(4) At any hearing held under division (D) of this section, the court may receive and consider evidence and information that is inadmissible under the Rules of Evidence. However, each hearing held under division (D) of this section shall be recorded by shorthand, by stenotype, or by any other mechanical, electronic, or video recording device. If, as a result of a hearing under division (D) of this section, property would be seized, the recording of and any transcript of the recording of that hearing shall not be a public record for purposes of section 149.43 of the Revised Code until that property has been seized pursuant to division (D) of this section. Division (D)(4) of this section shall not be construed as requiring, authorizing, or permitting, and does not require, authorize, or permit, the making available for inspection, or the copying, under section 149.43 of the Revised Code of any confidential law enforcement investigatory record or trial preparation record, as defined in that section.

(5) A prosecuting attorney or other law enforcement officer may request the court of common pleas of the county in which property subject to forfeiture under this section is located to issue a warrant authorizing the seizure of that property. The request shall be made in the same manner as provided for a search warrant. If the court determines that there is probable cause to believe that the property to be seized will be subject to forfeiture under this section when a person with any right, title, or interest in the property is convicted of or pleads guilty to a felony drug abuse offense or when a juvenile with any right, title, or interest in the property is found by a juvenile court to be a delinquent child for an act that, if committed by an adult, would be a felony drug abuse offense, and if the court determines that any order issued under division (D)(1), (2), or (3) of this section may not be sufficient to ensure the availability of the property for forfeiture, the court shall issue a warrant authorizing the seizure of the property.

(E)(1) Upon the entry of an order of forfeiture under this section, the court shall order an appropriate law enforcement officer to seize all of the forfeited property upon the terms and conditions that the court determines are proper. In addition, upon the request of the prosecuting attorney who prosecuted the felony drug abuse offense or act, the court shall enter any appropriate restraining orders or injunctions, require the execution of satisfactory performance bonds, appoint receivers, conservators, appraisers, accountants, or trustees, or take any other action to protect the interest of the state in the forfeited property. Any income accruing to or derived from property ordered forfeited under this section may be used to offset ordinary and necessary expenses related to the property that are required by law or that are necessary to protect the interest of the state or third parties.

After forfeited property is seized, the prosecuting attorney who prosecuted the felony drug abuse offense or act shall direct its disposition in accordance with section 2925.44 of the Revised Code, making due provision for the rights of any innocent persons. Any right, title, or interest in property not exercisable by, or transferable for value to, the state shall expire and shall not revert to the offender whose conviction or plea of guilty or act as a delinquent child is the basis of the order of forfeiture. Neither the adult offender or delinquent child nor any person acting in concert with or on behalf of the adult offender or delinquent child is eligible to purchase forfeited property at any sale held pursuant to section 2925.44 of the Revised Code.

Upon the application of any person other than the adult offender or delinquent child whose right, title, or interest in the property is the subject of the order of forfeiture or any person acting in concert with or on behalf of the adult offender or delinquent child, the court may restrain or stay the sale or other disposition of the property pursuant to section 2925.44 of the Revised Code pending the conclusion of any appeal of the felony drug abuse offense conviction or of the delinquent child adjudication that is the basis of the order of forfeiture, if the applicant demonstrates that proceeding with the sale or other disposition of the property will result in irreparable injury or loss to the applicant.

(2) With respect to property that is the subject of an order of forfeiture issued under this section, the court that issued the order, upon the petition of the prosecuting attorney who prosecuted the felony drug abuse offense or act, may do any of the following:

(a) Grant petitions for mitigation or remission of forfeiture, restore forfeited property to victims of a felony drug abuse offense, or take any other action to protect the rights of innocent persons that is in the interest of justice and that is not inconsistent with this section;

(b) Compromise claims that arise under this section;

(c) Award compensation to persons who provide information resulting in a forfeiture under this section;

(d) Direct the disposition by the prosecuting attorney who prosecuted the felony drug abuse offense or act, in accordance with section 2925.44 of the Revised Code, of all property ordered forfeited under this section, making due provision for the rights of innocent persons;

(e) Pending the disposition of any property that is the subject of an order of forfeiture under this section, take any appropriate measures that are necessary to safeguard and maintain the property.

(3) To facilitate the identification and location of property that is the subject of an order of forfeiture under this section and to facilitate the disposition of petitions for remission or mitigation issued under division (E)(2) of this section, after the issuance of an order of forfeiture under this section and upon application by the prosecuting attorney who prosecuted the felony drug abuse offense or act, the court may order that the testimony of any witness relating to the forfeited property be taken by deposition, and that any designated book, paper, document, record, recording, or other material that is not privileged be produced at the same time and place as the testimony, in the same manner as provided for the taking of depositions under the Rules of Civil Procedure.

(F)(1) Except as provided in divisions (F)(2) to (5) of this section, no person claiming any right, title, or interest in property subject to forfeiture under this section or section 2925.43 of the Revised Code may intervene in a criminal trial or appeal, or a delinquent child proceeding or appeal, involving the forfeiture of the property under this section or in a civil action for a civil forfeiture under section 2925.43 of the Revised Code, or may commence an action at law or equity against the state concerning the validity of the person's alleged right, title, or interest in the property subsequent to the filing of an indictment, complaint, or information alleging that the property is subject to forfeiture under this section or subsequent to the filing of a complaint alleging that a juvenile who has any right, title, or interest in the property is a delinquent child because of the commission of an act that, if committed by an adult, would be a felony drug abuse offense and alleging that the property is subject to forfeiture under this section.

(2) After the entry of an order of forfeiture under this section, the prosecuting attorney who prosecuted the felony drug abuse offense or act shall conduct or cause to be conducted a search of the appropriate public records that relate to the property, and make or cause to be made reasonably diligent inquiries, for the purpose of identifying persons who have any right, title, or interest in the property. The prosecuting attorney then shall cause a notice of the order of forfeiture, of the prosecuting attorney's intent to dispose of the property in accordance with section 2925.44 of the Revised Code, and of the manner of the proposed disposal, to be given to each person who is known, because of the conduct of the search, the making of the inquiries, or otherwise, to have any right, title, or interest in the property, by certified mail, return receipt requested, or by personal service. Additionally, the prosecuting attorney shall cause a similar notice to be published once a week for two consecutive weeks in a newspaper of general circulation in the county in which the property was seized.

(3)(a) Any person, other than the adult offender whose conviction or guilty plea or the delinquent child whose adjudication is the basis of the order of forfeiture, who asserts a legal right, title, or interest in the property that is the subject of the order may petition the court that issued the order, within thirty days after the earlier of the final publication of notice or the person's receipt of notice under division (F)(2) of this section, for a hearing to adjudicate the validity of the person's alleged right, title, or interest in the property. The petition shall be signed by the petitioner under the penalties for falsification as specified in section 2921.13 of the Revised Code and shall set forth the nature and extent of the petitioner's right, title, or interest in the property, the time and circumstances of the petitioner's acquisition of that right, title, or interest, any additional facts supporting the petitioner's claim, and the relief sought.

(b) In lieu of filing a petition as described in division (F)(3)(a) of this section, a secured party or other lienholder of record that asserts a legal right, title, or interest in the property that is the subject of the order, including, but not limited to, a mortgage, security interest, or other type of lien, may file an affidavit as described in this division to establish the validity of the alleged right, title, or interest in the property. The affidavit shall be filed within thirty days after the earlier of the final publication of notice or the receipt of notice under division (F)(2) of this section and, except as otherwise provided in this section, shall constitute prima-facie evidence of the validity of the secured party's or other lienholder's alleged right, title, or interest in the property. Unless the prosecuting attorney files a motion challenging the affidavit within ten days after its filing and unless the prosecuting attorney establishes, by a preponderance of the evidence, at a subsequent hearing before the court that issued the forfeiture order, that the secured party or other lienholder does not possess the alleged right, title, or interest in the property or that the secured party or other lienholder had actual knowledge of facts pertaining to the felony drug abuse offense or act that was the basis of the forfeiture order, the affidavit shall constitute conclusive evidence of the validity of the secured party's or other lienholder's right, title, or interest in the property and shall have the legal effect described in division (G)(2) of this section. To the extent practicable and consistent with the interests of justice, any such hearing shall be held within thirty days after the prosecuting attorney files the motion. At any such hearing, the prosecuting attorney and the secured party or other lienholder may present evidence and witnesses and cross-examine witnesses.

In order to be valid for the purposes of this division and division (G)(2) of this section, the affidavit of a secured party or other lienholder shall contain averments that the secured party or other lienholder acquired its alleged right, title, or interest in the property in the regular course of its business, for a specified valuable consideration, without actual knowledge of any facts pertaining to the felony drug abuse offense or act that was the basis of the forfeiture order, in good faith and without the intent to prevent or otherwise impede the state from seizing or obtaining a forfeiture of the property under sections 2925.41 to 2925.45 of the Revised Code, and prior to the seizure or forfeiture of the property under those sections.

(4) Upon receipt of a petition filed under division (F)(3) of this section, the court shall hold a hearing to determine the validity of the petitioner's right, title, or interest in the property that is the subject of the order of forfeiture. To the extent practicable and consistent with the interests of justice, the hearing shall be held within thirty days after the filing of the petition. The court may consolidate the hearing on the petition with a hearing on any other petition filed by a person other than the offender whose conviction or guilty plea or adjudication as a delinquent child is the basis of the order of forfeiture. At the hearing, the petitioner may testify, present evidence and witnesses on the petitioner's behalf, and cross-examine witnesses for the state. The state may present evidence and witnesses in rebuttal and in defense of its claim to the property and cross-examine witnesses for the petitioner. In addition to evidence and testimony presented at the hearing, the court shall consider the relevant portions of the record in the felony drug abuse offense or delinquent child case that resulted in the order of forfeiture.

(5)(a) The court shall amend its order of forfeiture in accordance with its determination if it determines, at the hearing, that the petitioner has established either of the following by a preponderance of the evidence:

(i) The petitioner has a legal right, title, or interest in the property that renders the order of forfeiture completely or partially invalid because it was vested in the petitioner, rather than the adult offender whose conviction or guilty plea or the delinquent child whose adjudication is the basis of the order, or was superior to any right, title, or interest of that offender, at the time of the commission of the felony drug abuse offense or act that is the basis of the order.

(ii) The petitioner is a bona fide purchaser for value of the right, title, or interest in the property and was at the time of the purchase reasonably without cause to believe that it was subject to forfeiture under this section.

(b) The court also shall amend its order of forfeiture to reflect any right, title, or interest of a secured party or other lienholder of record in the property subject to the order that was established pursuant to division (F)(3)(b) of this section by means of an affidavit, or that was established pursuant to that division by the failure of a prosecuting attorney to establish, in a hearing as described in that division, that the secured party or other lienholder did not possess the alleged right, title, or interest in the property or that the secured party or other lienholder had actual knowledge of facts pertaining to the felony drug abuse offense or act that was the basis of the order.

(G)(1) Subject to division (G)(2) of this section, if the court has disposed of all petitions filed under division (F) of this section or if no petitions are filed under that division and the time for filing petitions under that division has expired, the state shall have clear title to all property that is the subject of an order of forfeiture issued under this section and may warrant good title to any subsequent purchaser or other transferee.

(2) If an affidavit as described in division (F)(3)(b) of this section is filed in accordance with that division, if the affidavit constitutes, under the circumstances described in that division, conclusive evidence of the validity of the right, title, or interest of a secured party or

other lienholder of record in the property subject to a forfeiture order, and if any mortgage, security interest, or other type of lien possessed by the secured party or other lienholder in connection with the property is not satisfied prior to a sale or other disposition of the property pursuant to section 2925.44 of the Revised Code, then the right, title, or interest of the secured party or other lienholder in the property remains valid for purposes of sections 2925.41 to 2925.45 of the Revised Code and any subsequent purchaser or other transferee of the property pursuant to section 2925.44 of the Revised Code shall take the property subject to the continued validity of the right, title, or interest of the secured party or other lienholder in the property.

HISTORY: 143 v S 258 (Eff 11-20-90); 144 v S 174 (Eff 7-31-92); 146 v S 2. Eff 7-1-96.

The effective date is set by section 6 of SB 2.

§ 2925.43 Civil forfeiture action prior to prosecution.

(A) The following property is subject to forfeiture to the state in a civil action as described in division (E) of this section, and no person has any right, title, or interest in the following property:

(1) Any property that constitutes, or is derived directly or indirectly from, any proceeds that a person obtained directly or indirectly from the commission of an act that, upon the filing of an indictment, complaint, or information, could be prosecuted as a felony drug abuse offense or that, upon the filing of a complaint, could be the basis for finding a juvenile to be a delinquent child for committing an act that, if committed by an adult, would be a felony drug abuse offense;

(2) Any property that was used or intended to be used in any manner to commit, or to facilitate the commission of, an act that, upon the filing of an indictment, complaint, or information, could be prosecuted as a felony drug abuse offense or that, upon the filing of a complaint, could be the basis for finding a juvenile to be a delinquent child for committing an act that, if committed by an adult, would be a felony drug abuse offense.

(B)(1) All right, title, and interest in property described in division (A) of this section shall vest in the state upon the commission of the act giving rise to a civil forfeiture under this section.

(2) The provisions of section 2933.43 of the Revised Code relating to the procedures for the forfeiture of contraband do not apply to a civil action to obtain a civil forfeiture under this section.

(3) Any property taken or detained pursuant to this section is not subject to replevin and is deemed to be in the custody of the head of the law enforcement agency that seized the property.

This section does not preclude the head of a law enforcement agency that seizes property from seeking the forfeiture of that property pursuant to federal law. However, if the head of a law enforcement agency that seizes property does not seek the forfeiture of that property pursuant to federal law and if the property is subject to forfeiture under this section, the property is subject only to the orders of the court of common pleas of the county in which the property is located, and it shall be disposed of in accordance with section 2925.44 of the Revised Code.

(4) Nothing in this section precludes a financial institution that has or purports to have a security interest in or lien on property described in division (A) of this section from commencing a civil action or taking other appropriate legal action in connection with the property, prior to its disposition in accordance with section 2925.44 of the Revised Code, for the purpose of obtaining possession of the property in order to foreclose or otherwise enforce the security interest or lien. A financial institution may commence a civil action or take other appropriate legal action for that purpose prior to the disposition of the property in accordance with section 2925.44 of the Revised Code, even if a civil action to obtain a civil forfeiture has been or could be commenced under this section, even if the property is or could be the subject of an order of civil forfeiture issued under this section, and even if the property has been seized or is subject to seizure pursuant to this section.

If a financial institution commences a civil action or takes any other appropriate legal action as described in this division, if the financial institution subsequently causes the sale of the property prior to its seizure pursuant to this section and its disposition pursuant to section 2925.44 of the Revised Code, and if the person responsible for the conduct of the sale has actual knowledge of the commencement of a civil action to obtain a civil forfeiture under this section or actual knowledge of an order of civil forfeiture issued under this section, then the person responsible for the conduct of the sale shall dispose of the proceeds of the sale in the following order:

(a) First, to the payment of the costs of the sale and to the payment of the costs incurred by law enforcement agencies and financial institutions in connection with the seizure of, storage of, maintenance of, and provision of security for the property. As used in this division, "costs" of a financial institution do not include attorney's fees incurred by that institution in connection with the property;

(b) Second, the remaining proceeds of the sale after compliance with division (B)(4)(a) of this section, to the payment of valid security interests and liens pertaining to the property that, at the time of the vesting of the right, title, or interest of the adult or juvenile in the state under division (B)(1) of this section, are held by known secured parties and lienholders, in the order of priority of those security interests and liens;

(c) Third, the remaining proceeds of the sale after compliance with division (B)(4)(b) of this section, to the court that has or would have jurisdiction in a civil action to obtain a civil forfeiture under this section, for disposition in accordance with section 2925.44 of the Revised Code.

(C)(1) Any property that is subject to civil forfeiture under this section may be seized by a law enforcement officer upon process, or a warrant as described in division (C)(2) of this section, issued by a court of common pleas that has jurisdiction over the property. Additionally, a seizure of the property, without process or a warrant being so issued, may be made by a law enforcement officer when any of the following applies:

(a) The seizure is incident to an arrest, a search under a search warrant, a lawful search without a search warrant, or an inspection under an administrative inspection warrant.

(b) The property is the subject of a prior judgment in favor of the state in a restraining order, injunction, or other preservation order proceeding under section 2925.42 of the Revised Code, or is the subject of a forfeiture order issued pursuant to that section.

(c) The law enforcement officer has probable cause to believe that the property is directly or indirectly dangerous to the public health or safety.

(d) The initial intrusion by the law enforcement officer afforded him with plain view of personal property that is subject to civil forfeiture in a civil action under this section, the initial intrusion by the law enforcement officer was lawful, the discovery of the personal property by the law enforcement officer was inadvertent, and the incriminating nature of the personal property was immediately apparent to the law enforcement officer.

(2) For purposes of division (C)(1) of this section, the state may request a court of common pleas to issue a warrant that authorizes the seizure of property that is subject to civil forfeiture under this section, in the same manner as provided in Criminal Rule 41 and Chapter 2933. of the Revised Code for the issuance of a search warrant. Additionally, for purposes of division (C)(1) of this section, any proceeding before a court of common pleas that involves a request for the issuance of process, or a warrant as described in this division, authorizing the seizure of any property that is subject to civil forfeiture under this section shall be recorded by shorthand, by stenotype, or by any other mechanical, electronic, or video recording device. The recording of and any transcript of the recording of such a proceeding shall not be a public record for purposes of section 149.43 of the Revised Code until the property has been seized pursuant to the process or warrant. This division shall not be construed as requiring, authorizing, or permitting, and does not require, authorize, or permit, the making available for inspection, or the copying, under section 149.43 of the Revised Code of any confidential law enforcement investigatory record or trial preparation record, as defined in that section.

(3) If property is seized pursuant to division (C)(1) of this section and if a civil action to obtain a civil forfeiture under this section, a criminal action that could result in a criminal forfeiture under section 2925.42 of the Revised Code, or a delinquent child proceeding that could result in a criminal forfeiture under that section is not pending at the time of the seizure or previously did not occur in connection with the property, then the prosecuting attorney of the county in which the seizure occurred promptly shall commence a civil action to obtain a civil forfeiture under this section in connection with the property, unless an indictment, complaint, or information alleging the commission of a felony drug abuse offense or a complaint alleging that a juvenile is a delinquent child because of the commission of an act that, if committed by an adult, would be a felony drug abuse offense is filed prior to the commencement of the civil action. Nothing in this division precludes, or shall be construed as precluding, the filing of an indictment, complaint, or information alleging the commission of a felony drug abuse offense or the filing of a complaint alleging that a juvenile is a delinquent child because of the commission of an act that, if committed by an adult, would be a felony drug abuse offense, after the commencement of a civil action to obtain a civil forfeiture under this section.

(D)(1) The filing of an indictment, complaint, or information alleging the commission of a felony drug abuse offense that also is the basis of a civil action for a civil forfeiture under this section, or the filing of a complaint alleging that a juvenile is a delinquent child because of the commission of an act that, if committed by an adult, would be a felony drug abuse offense, and that also is the basis of a civil action for a civil forfeiture under this section, upon the motion of the prosecuting attorney of the county in which the indictment, complaint, or information or the complaint in the delinquent child proceeding is filed, shall stay the civil action.

(2) A civil action to obtain a civil forfeiture under this section may be commenced as described in division (E) of this section whether or not the adult or juvenile who committed a felony drug abuse offense or an act that, if committed by an adult, would be a felony drug abuse offense has been charged by an indictment, complaint, or information with the commission of such an offense or such an act, has pleaded guilty to or been found guilty of such an offense, has been determined to be a delinquent child for the commission of such an act, has been found not guilty of committing such an offense, or has not been determined to be a delinquent child for the alleged commission of such an act.

(E)(1) The prosecuting attorney of the county in which property described in division (A) of this section is located may commence a civil action to obtain a civil forfeiture under this section by filing, in the court of common pleas of that county, a complaint that requests the issuance of an order of civil forfeiture of the property to the state. Notices of the action shall be served and published in accordance with division (E)(2) of this section.

(2) Prior to or simultaneously with the commencement of the civil action as described in division (E)(1) of this section, the prosecuting attorney shall conduct or cause to be conducted a search of the appropriate public records that relate to the property subject to civil forfeiture, and make or cause to be made reasonably diligent inquiries, for the purpose of identifying persons who have any right, title, or interest in the property. The prosecuting attorney then shall cause a notice of the commencement of the civil action, together with a copy of the complaint filed in it, to be given to each person who is known, because of the conduct of the search, the making of the inquiries, or otherwise, to have any right, title, or interest in the property, by certified mail, return receipt requested, or by personal service. Additionally, the prosecuting attorney shall cause a similar notice to be published once a week for two consecutive weeks in a newspaper of general circulation in the county in which the property is located.

(3) The procedures specified in divisions (F)(3) to (5) of section 2925.42 of the Revised Code apply to persons claiming any right, title, or interest in property subject to civil forfeiture under this section. The references in those divisions to the adult offender whose conviction or guilty plea, or the delinquent child whose adjudication, is the basis of an order of criminal forfeiture shall be construed for purposes of this section to mean the adult or juvenile who committed the act that could be the basis of an order of civil forfeiture under this section, and the references in those divisions to an issued order of criminal forfeiture shall be inapplicable.

(4) A hearing shall be held in the civil action described in division (E)(1) of this section at least thirty days after the final publication of notice as required by division (E)(2) of this section and after the date of completion of the service of notice by personal service or certified mail, return receipt requested, as required by that division. Following the hearing, the court shall issue the requested order of civil forfeiture if the court determines that the prosecuting attorney has proven, by clear and convincing evidence, that the property in question is property as described in division (A)(1) or (2) of this section, and if the court has disposed of all petitions filed under division (E)(3) of this section or no petitions have been so filed and the time for filing them has expired. An order of civil forfeiture so issued shall state that all right, title, and interest in the property in question of the adult or juvenile who committed the act that is the basis of the order, is forfeited to the state and shall make due provision for the right, title, or interest in that property of any other person in accordance with any determinations made by the court under division (E)(3) of this section and in accordance with divisions (F)(5)(b) and (G)(2) of section 2925.42 of the Revised Code.

(5) Subject to division (G)(2) of section 2925.42 of the Revised Code, if a court of common pleas enters an order of civil forfeiture in accordance with division (E) of this section, the state shall have clear title to the property that is the subject of the order and may warrant good title to any subsequent purchaser or other transferee.

HISTORY: 143 v S 258. Eff 11-20-90.

The effective date is set by section 15 of SB 258.

§ 2925.44 Rights of law enforcement agency seizing property; disposition of forfeited property.

(A) If property is seized pursuant to section 2925.42 or 2925.43 of the Revised Code, it is deemed to be in the custody of the head of the law enforcement agency that seized it, and the head of that agency may do any of the following with respect to that property prior to its disposition in accordance with division (A)(4) or (B) of this section:

(1) Place the property under seal;

(2) Remove the property to a place that the head of that agency designates;

(3) Request the issuance of a court order that requires any other appropriate municipal corporation, county, township, park district created pursuant to section 511.18 or 1545.01 of the Revised Code, or state law enforcement officer or other officer to take custody of the property and, if practicable, remove it to an appropriate location for eventual disposition in accordance with division (B) of this section;

(4)(a) Seek forfeiture of the property pursuant to federal law. If the head of that agency seeks its forfeiture pursuant to federal law, the law enforcement agency shall deposit, use, and account for proceeds from a sale of the property upon its forfeiture, proceeds from another disposition of the property upon its forfeiture, or forfeited moneys it receives, in accordance with the applicable federal law and otherwise shall comply with that law.

(b) If the state highway patrol seized the property and if the superintendent of the state highway patrol seeks its forfeiture pursuant to federal law, the appropriate governmental officials shall deposit into the state highway patrol contraband, forfeiture, and other fund all interest or other earnings derived from the investment of the proceeds from a sale of the property upon its forfeiture, the proceeds from another disposition of the property upon its forfeiture, or the forfeited moneys. The state highway patrol shall use and account for that interest or other earnings in accordance with the applicable federal law.

(c) If the liquor enforcement unit of the department of public safety seized the property and if the director of public safety seeks its forfeiture pursuant to federal law, the appropriate governmental officials shall deposit into the liquor enforcement contraband, forfeiture, and other fund all interest or other earnings derived from the investment of the proceeds from a sale of the property upon its forfeiture, the proceeds from another disposition of the property upon its forfeiture, or the forfeited moneys. The department shall use and account for that interest or other earnings in accordance with the applicable federal law.

(d) If the food stamp fraud unit of the department of public safety seized the property and if the director of public safety seeks its forfeiture pursuant to federal law, the appropriate governmental officials shall deposit into the food stamp contraband, forfeiture, and other fund all interest or other earnings derived from the investment of the proceeds from a sale of the property upon its forfeiture, the proceeds from another disposition of the property upon its forfeiture, or the forfeited moneys. The department shall use and account for that interest or other earnings in accordance with the applicable federal law.

(e) Division (B) of this section and divisions (D)(1) to (3) of section 2933.43 of the Revised Code do not apply to proceeds or forfeited moneys received pursuant to federal law or to the interest or other earnings that are derived from the investment of proceeds or forfeited moneys received pursuant to federal law and that are described in division (A)(4)(b) of this section.

(B) In addition to complying with any requirements imposed by a court pursuant to section 2925.42 or 2925.43 of the Revised Code, and the requirements imposed by those sections, in relation to the disposition of property forfeited to the state under either of those sections, the prosecuting attorney who is responsible for its disposition shall dispose of the property as follows:

(1) Any vehicle, as defined in section 4501.01 of the Revised Code, that was used in a felony drug abuse offense or in an act that, if committed by an adult, would be a felony drug abuse offense shall be given to the law enforcement agency of the municipal corporation or county in which the offense occurred if that agency desires to have the vehicle, except that, if the offense occurred in a township or in a park district created pursuant to section 511.18 or 1545.01 of the Revised Code and a law enforcement officer employed by the township or the park district was involved in the seizure of the vehicle, the vehicle may be given to the law enforcement agency of that township or park district if that agency desires to have the vehicle, and except that, if the state highway patrol made the seizure of the vehicle, the vehicle may be given to the state highway patrol if it desires to have the vehicle.

(2) Any drug paraphernalia that was used, possessed, sold, or manufactured in a violation of section 2925.14 of the Revised Code that would be a felony drug abuse offense or in a violation of that section committed by a juvenile that, if committed by an adult, would be a felony drug abuse offense, may be given to the law enforcement agency of the municipal corporation or county in which the offense occurred if that agency desires to have and can use the drug paraphernalia, except that, if the offense occurred in a township or in a park district created pursuant to section 511.18 or 1545.01 of the Revised Code and a law enforcement officer employed by the township or the park district was involved in the seizure of the drug paraphernalia, the drug paraphernalia may be given to the law enforcement agency of that township or park district if that agency desires to have and can use the drug paraphernalia. If the drug paraphernalia is not so given, it shall be disposed of by sale pursuant to division (B)(8) of this section or disposed of in another manner that the court that issued the order of forfeiture considers proper under the circumstances.

(3) Drugs shall be disposed of pursuant to section 3719.11 of the Revised Code or placed in the custody of the secretary of the treasury of the United States for disposal or use for medical or scientific purposes under applicable federal law.

(4) Firearms and dangerous ordnance suitable for police work may be given to a law enforcement agency for that purpose. Firearms suitable for sporting use, or as museum pieces or collectors' items, may be disposed of by sale pursuant to division (B)(8) of this section. Other firearms and dangerous ordnance shall be destroyed by a law enforcement agency or shall be sent to the bureau of criminal identification and investigation for destruction by it. As used in this division, "firearms" and "dangerous ordnance" have the same meanings as in section 2923.11 of the Revised Code.

(5) Computers, computer networks, computer systems, and computer software suitable for police work may be given to a law enforcement agency for that purpose. Other computers, computer networks, computer systems, and computer software shall be disposed of by sale pursuant to division (B)(8) of this section or disposed of in another manner that the court that issued the order of forfeiture considers proper under the circumstances. As used in this division, "computers," "computer networks," "computer systems," and "computer software" have the same meanings as in section 2913.01 of the Revised Code.

(6) Obscene materials shall be destroyed.

(7) Beer, intoxicating liquor, and alcohol shall be disposed of in accordance with division (D)(4) of section 2933.41 of the Revised Code.

(8) In the case of property not described in divisions (B)(1) to (7) of this section and of property described in those divisions but not disposed of pursuant to them, the property shall be sold in accordance with division (B)(8) of this section or, in the case of forfeited moneys, disposed of in accordance with division (B)(8) of this section. If the property is to be sold, the prosecuting attorney shall cause a notice of the proposed sale of the property to be given in accordance with law, and the property shall be sold, without appraisal, at a public auction to the highest bidder for cash. The proceeds of a sale and forfeited moneys shall be applied in the following order:

(a) First, to the payment of the costs incurred in

connection with the seizure of, storage of, maintenance of, and provision of security for the property, the forfeiture proceeding or civil action, and, if any, the sale;

(b) Second, the remaining proceeds or forfeited moneys after compliance with division (B)(8)(a) of this section, to the payment of the value of any legal right, title, or interest in the property that is possessed by a person who, pursuant to division (F) of section 2925.42 of the Revised Code or division (E) of section 2925.43 of the Revised Code, established the validity of and consequently preserved that legal right, title, or interest, including, but not limited to, any mortgage, perfected or other security interest, or other lien in the property. The value of these rights, titles, or interests shall be paid according to their record or other order of priority.

(c) Third, the remaining proceeds or forfeited moneys after compliance with divisions (B)(8)(a) and (b) of this section, as follows:

(i) If the forfeiture was ordered in a juvenile court, ten per cent to one or more alcohol and drug addiction treatment programs that are certified by the department of alcohol and drug addiction services under section 3793.06 of the Revised Code and that are specified in the order of forfeiture. A juvenile court shall not specify an alcohol or drug addiction treatment program in the order of forfeiture unless the program is a certified alcohol and drug addiction treatment program and, except as provided in division (B)(8)(c)(i) of this section, unless the program is located in the county in which the court that orders the forfeiture is located or in a contiguous county. If no certified alcohol and drug addiction treatment program is located in any of those counties, the juvenile court may specify in the order a certified alcohol and drug addiction treatment program located anywhere within this state.

(ii) If the forfeiture was ordered in a juvenile court, ninety per cent, and if the forfeiture was ordered in a court other than a juvenile court, one hundred per cent to appropriate funds in accordance with divisions (D)(1)(c) and (2) of section 2933.43 of the Revised Code. The remaining proceeds or forfeited moneys so deposited shall be used only for the purposes authorized by those divisions and division (D)(3)(a)(ii) of that section.

(C)(1) Sections 2925.41 to 2925.45 of the Revised Code do not preclude a financial institution that possessed a valid mortgage, security interest, or lien that is not satisfied prior to a sale under division (B)(8) of this section or following a sale by application of division (B)(8)(b) of this section, from commencing a civil action in any appropriate court in this or another state to obtain a deficiency judgment against the debtor if the financial institution otherwise would have been entitled to do so in this or another state.

(2) Any law enforcement agency that obtains any vehicle pursuant to division (B)(1) of this section shall take the vehicle subject to the outstanding amount of any security interest or lien that attaches to the vehicle.

(3) Nothing in this section impairs a mortgage, security interest, lien, or other interest of a financial institution in property that was the subject of a forfeiture order under section 2925.42 or 2925.43 of the Revised Code and that was sold or otherwise disposed of in a manner that does not conform to the requirements of division (B) of this section, or any right of a financial institution of that nature to commence a civil action in any appropriate court in this or another state to obtain a deficiency judgment against the debtor.

(4) Following the sale under division (B)(8) of this section of any property that is required to be titled or registered under the law of this state, the prosecuting attorney responsible for the disposition of the property shall cause the state to issue an appropriate certificate of title or registration to the purchaser of the property. Additionally, if, in a disposition of property pursuant to division (B) of this section, the state or a political subdivision is given any property that is required to be titled or registered under the law of this state, the prosecuting attorney responsible for the disposition of the property shall cause the state to issue an appropriate certificate of title or registration to itself or to the political subdivision.

(D) Property that has been forfeited to the state pursuant to an order of criminal forfeiture under section 2925.42 of the Revised Code or an order of civil forfeiture under section 2925.43 of the Revised Code shall not be available for use to pay any fine imposed upon a person who is convicted of or pleads guilty to a felony drug abuse offense or upon any juvenile who is found by a juvenile court to be a delinquent child for an act that, if committed by an adult, would be a felony drug abuse offense.

(E) Sections 2925.41 to 2925.45 of the Revised Code do not prohibit a law enforcement officer from seeking the forfeiture of contraband associated with a felony drug abuse offense pursuant to section 2933.43 of the Revised Code.

HISTORY: 143 v S 258 (Eff 11-20-90); 144 v S 218 (Eff 10-11-91); 144 v S 174 (Eff 7-31-92); 146 v H 107 (Eff 6-30-95); 146 v H 1 (Eff 1-1-96); 147 v H 210. Eff 6-30-97.

The effective date is set by section 21 of HB 210.

§ 2925.45 Motion alleging seizure was unlawful; return of property.

(A) Any person who is aggrieved by an alleged unlawful seizure of property that potentially is subject to forfeiture under section 2925.42 or 2925.43 of the Revised Code may file a motion as described in division (B) of this section with whichever of the following courts is appropriate under the circumstances, within the time described in division (C) of this section:

(1) The court of common pleas in which a criminal prosecution for a felony drug abuse offense is pending;

(2) The juvenile court in which a delinquent child action for an act that, if committed by an adult, would

be a felony drug abuse offense is pending;

(3) The court of common pleas in which a civil action as described in division (E) of section 2925.43 of the Revised Code is pending;

(4) The court of common pleas of the county in which the property was seized.

(B) The motion shall specify that the seizure of specified property was unlawful, state the reasons why the movant believes the seizure was unlawful, state that the movant is lawfully entitled to possession of the seized property, and request the court of common pleas to issue an order that mandates the law enforcement agency having custody of the seized property to return it to the movant. For purposes of this division, an unlawful seizure of property includes, but is not limited to, a seizure in violation of the Fourth Amendment to the Constitution of the United States or of Section 14 of Article I, Ohio Constitution, and a seizure pursuant to sections 2925.41 to 2925.44 of the Revised Code of property other than potentially forfeitable property as described in division (A)(1) of section 2925.42 or division (A) of section 2925.43 of the Revised Code.

(C)(1) If a motion as described in division (A) of this section is filed prior to the entry of an order of forfeiture under section 2925.42 or 2925.43 of the Revised Code, the court of common pleas promptly shall schedule a hearing on the motion and cause notice of the date and time of the hearing to be given to the movant and the prosecuting attorney of the county in which the property was seized. At the hearing, the movant and the prosecuting attorney may present witnesses and evidence relative to the issues of whether the property in question was unlawfully seized and whether the movant is lawfully entitled to possession of it. If, after the hearing, the court of common pleas determines that the movant has established, by a preponderance of the evidence, that the property in question was unlawfully seized and that the movant is lawfully entitled to possession of it, the court shall issue an order that requires the law enforcement agency having custody of the seized property to return it to the movant.

(2)(a) If a motion is filed in accordance with division (C)(1) of this section and, at the time of filing or of the hearing on the motion, a criminal prosecution for a felony drug abuse offense or a delinquent child action for an act that, if committed by an adult, would be a felony drug abuse offense has been commenced by the filing of an indictment, information, or complaint, then the court of common pleas shall treat the motion as a motion to suppress evidence.

(b) If an order to return seized property is issued pursuant to division (C)(1) of this section, the returned property shall not be admissible in evidence in any pending or subsequently commenced criminal prosecution for a felony drug abuse offense if the prosecution arose or arises out of the unlawful seizure of the property, or in any pending or subsequently commenced delinquent child action for an act that, if committed by an adult, would be a felony drug abuse offense if the action arose or arises out of the unlawful seizure of the property.

HISTORY: 143 v S 258. Eff 11-20-90.

The effective date is set by section 15 of SB 258.

[FEDERAL NARCOTIC LAWS]

§ 2925.50 Conviction or acquittal under federal narcotic laws.

If a violation of this chapter is a violation of federal narcotic laws, as defined in section 3719.01 of the Revised Code, a conviction or acquittal under federal narcotic laws for the same act is a bar to prosecution in this state.

HISTORY: 136 v H 300. Eff 7-1-76.

[LABORATORY EVIDENCE]

§ 2925.51 Laboratory report as evidence; requirements; violation.

(A) In any criminal prosecution for a violation of this chapter or Chapter 3719. of the Revised Code, a laboratory report from the bureau of criminal identification and investigation, a laboratory operated by another law enforcement agency, or a laboratory established by or under the authority of an institution of higher education that has its main campus in this state and that is accredited by the association of American universities or the north central association of colleges and secondary schools, primarily for the purpose of providing scientific services to law enforcement agencies and signed by the person performing the analysis, stating that the substance which is the basis of the alleged offense has been weighed and analyzed and stating the findings as to the content, weight, and identity of the substance and that it contains any amount of a controlled substance and the number and description of unit dosages, is prima-facie evidence of the content, identity, and weight or the existence and number of unit dosages of the substance.

Attached to that report shall be a copy of a notarized statement by the signer of the report giving the name of the signer and stating that he is an employee of the laboratory issuing the report and that performing the analysis is a part of his regular duties, and giving an outline of his education, training, and experience for performing an analysis of materials included under this section. The signer shall attest that scientifically accepted tests were performed with due caution, and that the evidence was handled in accordance with established and accepted procedures while in the custody of the laboratory.

(B) The prosecuting attorney shall serve a copy of the report on the attorney of record for the accused, or on the accused if he has no attorney, prior to any proceeding in which the report is to be used against the accused other than at a preliminary hearing or grand jury proceeding where the report may be used without having been previously served upon the accused.

(C) The report shall not be prima-facie evidence of the contents, identity, and weight or the existence and number of unit dosages of the substance if the accused or his attorney demands the testimony of the person signing the report, by serving the demand upon the prosecuting attorney within seven days from the accused or his attorney's receipt of the report. The time may be extended by a trial judge in the interests of justice.

(D) Any report issued for use under this section shall contain notice of the right of the accused to demand, and the manner in which the accused shall demand, the testimony of the person signing the report.

(E) Any person who is accused of a violation of this chapter or of Chapter 3719. of the Revised Code is entitled, upon written request made to the prosecuting attorney, to have a portion of the substance that is the basis of the alleged violation preserved for the benefit of independent analysis performed by a laboratory analyst employed by the accused person, or, if he is indigent, by a qualified laboratory analyst appointed by the court. Such portion shall be a representative sample of the entire substance that is the basis of the alleged violation and shall be of sufficient size, in the opinion of the court, to permit the accused's analyst to make a thorough scientific analysis concerning the identity of the substance. The prosecuting attorney shall provide the accused's analyst with the sample portion at least fourteen days prior to trial, unless the trial is to be held in a court not of record or unless the accused person is charged with a minor misdemeanor, in which case the prosecuting attorney shall provide the accused's analyst with the sample portion at least three days prior to trial. If the prosecuting attorney determines that such a sample portion cannot be preserved and given to the accused's analyst, the prosecuting attorney shall so inform the accused person, or his attorney. In such a circumstance, the accused person is entitled, upon written request made to the prosecuting attorney, to have his privately employed or court appointed analyst present at an analysis of the substance that is the basis of the alleged violation, and, upon further written request, to receive copies of all recorded scientific data that result from the analysis and that can be used by an analyst in arriving at conclusions, findings, or opinions concerning the identity of the substance subject to the analysis.

(F) In addition to the rights provided under division (E) of this section, any person who is accused of a violation of this chapter or of Chapter 3719. of the Revised Code that involves a bulk amount of a controlled substance, or any multiple thereof, or who is accused of a violation of section 2925.11 of the Revised Code, other than a minor misdemeanor violation, that involves marihuana, is entitled, upon written request made to the prosecuting attorney, to have a laboratory analyst of his choice, or, if the accused is indigent, a qualified laboratory analyst appointed by the court, present at a measurement or weighing of the substance that is the basis of the alleged violation. Also, the accused person is entitled, upon further written request, to receive copies of all recorded scientific data that result from the measurement or weighing and that can be used by an analyst in arriving at conclusions, findings, or opinions concerning the weight, volume, or number of unit doses of the substance subject to the measurement or weighing.

HISTORY: 136 v H 300 (Eff 7-1-76); 136 v S 541 (Eff 6-28-76); 137 v S 201. Eff 11-16-77.

CHAPTER 2927: MISCELLANEOUS OFFENSES

Section
2927.01 Abuse of a corpse.
2927.02 Illegal distribution of cigarettes or other tobacco products.
2927.03 Interference with fair housing rights.
2927.11 Desecration.
2927.12 Ethnic intimidation.
2927.13 Selling or donating contaminated blood.
2927.21 Duty to report escape of certain animals.
2927.24 Contaminating substance for human consumption or use; spreading false report

§ 2927.01 Abuse of a corpse.

(A) No person, except as authorized by law, shall treat a human corpse in a way that the person knows would outrage reasonable family sensibilities.

(B) No person, except as authorized by law, shall treat a human corpse in a way that would outrage reasonable community sensibilities.

(C) Whoever violates division (A) of this section is guilty of abuse of a corpse, a misdemeanor of the second degree. Whoever violates division (B) of this section is guilty of gross abuse of a corpse, a felony of the fifth degree.

HISTORY: 134 v H 511 (Eff 1-1-74); 137 v H 741 (Eff 10-9-78); 146 v S 2. Eff 7-1-96.

The effective date is set by section 6 of SB 2.

§ 2927.02 Illegal distribution of cigarettes or other tobacco products.

(A) No manufacturer, producer, distributor, wholesaler, or retailer of cigarettes or other tobacco products, or any agent, employee, or representative of a manufacturer, producer, distributor, wholesaler, or retailer of cigarettes or other tobacco products shall do any of the following:

(1) Give, sell, or otherwise distribute cigarettes or other tobacco products to any person under eighteen years of age;

(2) Give away, sell, or distribute cigarettes or other tobacco products in any place that does not have posted in a conspicuous place a sign stating that giving, selling, or otherwise distributing cigarettes or other tobacco products to a person under eighteen years of age is prohibited by law.

(B) No person shall sell or offer to sell cigarettes or other tobacco products by or from a vending machine except in the following locations:

(1) An area either:

(a) Within a factory, business, office, or other place not open to the general public; or

(b) To which persons under the age of eighteen years are not generally permitted access;

(2) In any other place not identified in division (B)(1) of this section, upon all of the following conditions:

(a) The vending machine is located within the immediate vicinity, plain view, and control of the person who owns or operates the place, or an employee of such person, so that all cigarettes and other tobacco product purchases from the vending machine will be readily observed by the person who owns or operates the place or an employee of such person. For the purpose of this section, a vending machine located in any unmonitored area, including an unmonitored coatroom, restroom, hallway, or outer waiting area, shall not be considered located within the immediate vicinity, plain view, and control of the person who owns or operates the place, or an employee of such person.

(b) The vending machine is inaccessible to the public when the place is closed.

(C) As used in this section, "vending machine" has the same meaning as "coin machine" as defined in section 2913.01 of the Revised Code.

(D) Whoever violates this section is guilty of illegal distribution of cigarettes or other tobacco products, a misdemeanor of the fourth degree. If the offender previously has been convicted of a violation of this section, then illegal distribution of cigarettes or other tobacco products is a misdemeanor of the third degree.

HISTORY: 140 v H 152 (Eff 9-26-84); 144 v S 40. Eff 10-23-91.

§ 2927.03 Interference with fair housing rights.

(A) No person, whether or not acting under color of law, shall by force or threat of force willfully injure, intimidate, or interfere with, or attempt to injure, intimidate, or interfere with any of the following:

(1) Any person because of race, color, religion, sex, familial status, as defined in section 4112.01 of the Revised Code, national origin, handicap, as defined in that section, or ancestry and because that person is or has been selling, purchasing, renting, financing, occupying, contracting, or negotiating for the sale, purchase, rental, financing, or occupation of any housing accommodations, or applying for or participating in any service, organization, or facility relating to the business of selling or renting housing accommodations;

(2) Any person because that person is or has been, or in order to intimidate that person or any other person or any class of persons from doing either of the following:

(a) Participating, without discrimination on account of race, color, religion, sex, familial status, as defined in section 4112.01 of the Revised Code, national origin, handicap, as defined in that section, or ancestry, in any of the activities, services, organizations, or facilities described in division (A)(1) of this section;

(b) Affording another person or class of persons opportunity or protection so to participate.

(3) Any person because that person is or has been, or in order to discourage that person or any other person from, lawfully aiding or encouraging other persons to participate, without discrimination on account of race, color, religion, sex, familial status, as defined in section 4112.01 of the Revised Code, national origin, handicap, as defined in that section, or ancestry, in any of the activities, services, organizations, or facilities described in division (A)(1) of this section, or participating lawfully in speech or peaceful assembly opposing any denial of the opportunity to so participate.

(B) Whoever violates division (A) of this section is guilty of a misdemeanor of the first degree.

HISTORY: 142 v H 5 (Eff 9-28-87); 144 v H 321 (Eff 6-30-92); 146 v S 2. Eff 7-1-96.

The effective date is set by section 6 of SB 2.

§ 2927.11 Desecration.

(A) No person, without privilege to do so, shall purposely deface, damage, pollute, or otherwise physically mistreat any of the following:

(1) The flag of the United States or of this state;

(2) Any public monument;

(3) Any historical or commemorative marker, or any structure, Indian mound or earthwork, thing, or site of great historical or archaeological interest;

(4) A place of worship, its furnishings, or religious artifacts or sacred texts within the place of worship;

(5) A work of art or museum piece;

(6) Any other object of reverence or sacred devotion.

(B) Whoever violates this section is guilty of desecration. Violation of division (A)(1), (2), (3), (5), or (6) of this section is a misdemeanor of the second degree. Violation of division (A)(4) of this section is a misdemeanor of the first degree that is punishable by a fine of up to four thousand dollars in addition to the penalties specified for a misdemeanor of the first degree in section 2929.21 of the Revised Code.

HISTORY: 134 v H 511 (Eff 1-1-74); 136 v H 418 (Eff 8-24-76); 137 v H 741 (Eff 10-9-78); 141 v S 316. Eff 3-19-87.

§ 2927.12 Ethnic intimidation.

(A) No person shall violate section 2903.21, 2903.22, 2909.06, or 2909.07, or division (A)(3), (4), or (5) of section 2917.21 of the Revised Code by reason of the race, color, religion, or national origin of another person or group of persons.

(B) Whoever violates this section is guilty of ethnic intimidation. Ethnic intimidation is an offense of the next higher degree than the offense the commission of which is a necessary element of ethnic intimidation.

HISTORY: 141 v S 316. Eff 3-19-87.

§ 2927.13 Selling or donating contaminated blood.

(A) No person, with knowledge that the person is a carrier of a virus that causes acquired immune deficiency syndrome, shall sell or donate the person's blood, plasma, or a product of the person's blood, if the person knows or should know the blood, plasma, or product of the person's blood is being accepted for the purpose of transfusion to another individual.

(B) Whoever violates this section is guilty of selling or donating contaminated blood, a felony of the fourth degree.

HISTORY: 142 v H 571 (Eff 3-17-89); 146 v S 2. Eff 7-1-96.

The effective date is set by section 6 of SB 2.

§ 2927.21 Duty to report escape of certain animals.

(A) The owner or keeper of any member of a species of the animal kingdom that escapes from his custody or control and that is not indigenous to this state or presents a risk of serious physical harm to persons or property, or both, shall, within one hour after he discovers or reasonably should have discovered the escape, report it to:

(1) A law enforcement officer of the municipal corporation or township and the sheriff of the county where the escape occurred; and

(2) The clerk of the municipal legislative authority or the township clerk of the township where the escape occurred.

(B) If the office of the clerk of a legislative authority or township clerk is closed to the public at the time a report is required by division (A) of this section, then it is sufficient compliance with division (A)(2) of this section if the owner or keeper makes the report within one hour after the office is next open to the public.

(C) Whoever violates this section is guilty of a misdemeanor of the first degree.

HISTORY: 141 v H 32. Eff 9-11-85.

§ 2927.24 Contaminating substance for human consumption or use; spreading false report.

(A) As used in this section, "poison" and "drug" have the same meanings as in section 4729.02 of the Revised Code.

(B) Except as provided in division (D) of this section, no person shall knowingly mingle a poison or other harmful substance with a food, drink, nonprescription drug, prescription drug, or pharmaceutical product, or knowingly place a poison or other harmful substance in a spring, well, reservoir, or public water supply, if the person knows or has reason to know that the food, drink, nonprescription drug, prescription drug, pharmaceutical product, or water may be ingested or used by another person. For purposes of this division, a person does not know or have reason to know that water may be ingested or used by another person if it is disposed of as waste into a household drain including the drain of a toilet, sink, tub, or floor.

(C) No person shall inform another person that a poison or other harmful substance has been or will be placed in a food, drink, nonprescription drug, prescription drug, or other pharmaceutical product, spring, well, reservoir, or public water supply, if the placement of the poison or other harmful substance would be a violation of division (B) of this section, and the person knows both that the information is false and that the information likely will be disseminated to the public.

(D)(1) A person may mingle a drug with a food or drink for the purpose of causing the drug to be ingested or used in the quantity described by its labeling or prescription.

(2) A person may place a poison or other harmful substance in a spring, well, reservoir, or public water supply in such quantity as is necessary to treat the spring, well, reservoir, or water supply to make it safe for human consumption and use.

(3) The provisions of division (A) of this section shall not be applied in a manner that conflicts with any other state or federal law or rule relating to substances permitted to be applied to or present in any food, raw or processed, any milk or milk product, any meat or meat product, any type of crop, water, or alcoholic or nonalcoholic beverage.

(E)(1) Whoever violates division (B) of this section is guilty of contaminating a substance for human consumption or use, a felony of the first degree. If the offense involved an amount of poison or other harmful substance sufficient to cause death if ingested or used by a person or if the offense resulted in serious physical harm to another person, whoever violates division (B) of this section is guilty of an aggravated felony of the first degree and shall be imprisoned for life.

(2) Whoever violates division (C) of this section is guilty of spreading a false report of contamination, a felony of the fourth degree.

HISTORY: 145 v H 280 (Eff 6-29-94); 146 v S 2. Eff 7-1-96.

The effective date is set by section 6 of SB 2.

CHAPTER 2929: PENALTIES AND SENTENCING

Section

[IN GENERAL]

2929.01 Definitions.

[PENALTIES FOR MURDER]

2929.02 Penalties for murder.
[2929.02.1] 2929.021 Notice to supreme court of indictment charging aggravated murder; plea.
[2929.02.2] 2929.022 Determination of aggravating circumstances.
[2929.02.3] 2929.023 Defendant may raise matter of age.
[2929.02.4] 2929.024 Investigation services and experts for indigent.
2929.03 Imposing sentence for aggravated murder.
2929.04 Criteria for imposing death or imprisonment for a capital offense.
2929.05 Appellate review of death sentence.
2929.06 Resentencing after vacation of death sentence or life inprisonment without parole.

[PENALTIES FOR FELONY]

2929.11 Purposes of felony sentencing.
2929.12 Seriousness and recidivism factors.
2929.13 Guidance by degree of felony.
2929.14 Basic prison terms.
2929.15 Community control.
2929.16 Eligibility of felons for participation in county jail industry program.
2929.17 Nonresidential sanctions.
2929.18 Financial sanctions; restitution.
[2929.18.1] 2929.181 Repealed.
2929.19 Sentencing hearing.
2929.20 Judicial release.

[PENALTIES FOR MISDEMEANOR]

2929.21 Penalties for misdemeanor.
2929.22 Imposing sentence for misdemeanor.
[2929.22.1] 2929.221 Type of institution where term of imprisonment to be served.
[2929.22.3] 2929.223 Reimbursement for costs of confinement for an offense other than a minor misdemeanor.
2929.23 Electronically monitored house arrest; certification of devices; device fund.
2929.24 Prosecutor to notify appropriate licensing board.
2929.25 Additional fine for certain offenders; collection of fines; crime victims recovery fund.

[REIMBURSEMENT BY ARSONIST]

2929.28 Arsonist to reimburse agencies for costs of investigation and prosecution.
2929.29 Procedure for accepting peace officer's guilty plea to felony or after conviction; negotiated misdemeanor pleas.

[ORGANIZATIONAL PENALTIES]

2929.31 Organizational penalties.

[MULTIPLE SENTENCES]

2929.41 Multiple sentences.

[MODIFICATION OF SENTENCE]

2929.51 Modification of sentence.

[OFFENSES PRIOR TO JANUARY 1, 1974]

2929.61 Offense committed prior to January 1, 1974; third or fourth degree felony committed between that date and July 1, 1983.

Section

[FIREARM OFFENSES]

2929.71, 2929.72 Repealed.

[IN GENERAL]

§ 2929.01 Definitions.

As used in this chapter:

(A) "Alternative residential facility" means any facility other than an offender's home or residence in which an offender is assigned to live and that provides programs through which the offender may seek or maintain employment or may receive education, training, treatment, or habilitation. "Alternative residential facility" does not include a community-based correctional facility, jail, halfway house, or prison.

(B) "Bad time" means the time by which the parole board administratively extends an offender's stated prison term or terms pursuant to section 2967.11 of the Revised Code because the parole board finds by clear and convincing evidence that the offender, while serving the prison term or terms, committed an act that is a criminal offense under the law of this state or the United States, whether or not the offender is prosecuted for the commission of that act.

(C) "Basic supervision" means a requirement that the offender maintain contact with a person appointed to supervise the offender in accordance with sanctions imposed by the court or imposed by the parole board pursuant to section 2967.28 of the Revised Code.

(D) "Cocaine," "crack cocaine," "hashish," "L.S.D.," and "unit dose" have the same meanings as in section 2925.01 of the Revised Code.

(E) "Community-based correctional facility" means a community-based correctional facility and program or district community-based correctional facility and program developed pursuant to sections 2301.51 to 2301.56 of the Revised Code.

(F) "Community control sanction" means a sanction that is not a prison term and that is described in section 2929.15, 2929.16, 2929.17, or 2929.18 of the Revised Code.

(G) "Criminally injurious conduct" means any conduct of the type that is described in division (C)(1) or (2) of section 2743.51 of the Revised Code and that occurs on or after July 1, 1996.

(H) "Controlled substance," "marihuana," "schedule I," and "schedule II" have the same meanings as in section 3719.01 of the Revised Code.

(I) "Curfew" means a requirement that an offender during a specified period of time be at a designated place.

(J) "Day reporting" means a sanction pursuant to which an offender is required each day to report to and leave a center or other approved reporting location at specified times in order to participate in work, education or training, treatment, and other approved programs at the center or outside the center.

(K) "Deadly weapon" has the same meaning as in section 2923.11 of the Revised Code.

(L) "Drug and alcohol use monitoring" means a program under which an offender agrees to submit to random chemical analysis of the offender's blood, breath, or urine to determine whether the offender has ingested any alcohol or other drugs.

(M) "Drug treatment program" means any program under which a person undergoes assessment and treatment designed to reduce or completely eliminate the person's physical or emotional reliance upon alcohol, another drug, or alcohol and another drug and under which the person may be required to receive assessment and treatment on an outpatient basis or may be required to reside at a facility other than the person's home or residence while undergoing assessment and treatment.

(N) "Economic loss" means any economic detriment suffered by a victim as a result of criminally injurious conduct and includes any loss of income due to lost time at work because of any injury caused to the victim, and any property loss, medical cost, or funeral expense incurred as a result of the criminally injurious conduct.

(O) "Education or training" includes study at, or in conjunction with a program offered by, a university, college, or technical college or vocational study and also includes the completion of primary school, secondary school, and literacy curriculums or their equivalent.

(P) "Electronically monitored house arrest" has the same meaning as in section 2929.23 of the Revised Code.

(Q) "Eligible offender" has the same meaning as in section 2929.23 of the Revised Code except as otherwise specified in section 2929.20 of the Revised Code.

(R) "Firearm" has the same meaning as in section 2923.11 of the Revised Code.

(S) "Halfway house" means a facility licensed by the division of parole and community services of the department of rehabilitation and correction pursuant to section 2967.14 of the Revised Code as a suitable facility for the care and treatment of adult offenders.

(T) "House arrest" means a period of confinement of an eligible offender that is in the eligible offender's home or in other premises specified by the sentencing court or by the parole board pursuant to section 2967.28 of the Revised Code, that may be electronically monitored house arrest, and during which all of the following apply:

(1) The eligible offender is required to remain in the eligible offender's home or other specified premises for the specified period of confinement, except for periods of time during which the eligible offender is at the eligible offender's place of employment or at other premises as authorized by the sentencing court or by the parole board.

(2) The eligible offender is required to report periodically to a person designated by the court or parole board.

(3) The eligible offender is subject to any other restrictions and requirements that may be imposed by the sentencing court or by the parole board.

(U) "Intensive supervision" means a requirement that an offender maintain frequent contact with a person appointed by the court, or by the parole board pursuant to section 2967.28 of the Revised Code, to supervise the offender while the offender is seeking or maintaining necessary employment and participating in training, education, and treatment programs as required in the court's or parole board's order.

(V) "Jail" means a jail, workhouse, minimum security jail, or other residential facility used for the confinement of alleged or convicted offenders that is operated by a political subdivision or a combination of political subdivisions of this state.

(W) "Delinquent child" has the same meaning as in section 2151.02 of the Revised Code.

(X) "License violation report" means a report that is made by a sentencing court, or by the parole board pursuant to section 2967.28 of the Revised Code, to the regulatory or licensing board or agency that issued an offender a professional license or a license or permit to do business in this state and that specifies that the offender has been convicted of or pleaded guilty to an offense that may violate the conditions under which the offender's professional license or license or permit to do business in this state was granted or an offense for which the offender's professional license or license or permit to do business in this state may be revoked or suspended.

(Y) "Major drug offender" means an offender who is convicted of or pleads guilty to the possession of, sale of, or offer to sell any drug, compound, mixture, preparation, or substance that consists of or contains at least one thousand grams of hashish; at least one hundred grams of crack cocaine; at least one thousand grams of cocaine that is not crack cocaine; at least two hundred fifty grams of heroin; at least five thousand unit doses of L.S.D.; or at least one hundred times the amount of any other schedule I or II controlled substance other than marihuana that is necessary to commit a felony of the third degree pursuant to section 2925.03, 2925.04, 2925.05, 2925.06, or 2925.11 of the Revised Code that is based on the possession of, sale of, or offer to sell the controlled substance.

(Z) "Mandatory prison term" means either of the following:

(1) Subject to division (CC)(2)† of this section, the term in prison that must be imposed for the offenses or circumstances set forth in divisions (F)(1) to (8) of section 2929.13 and division (D) of section 2929.14 of the Revised Code. Except as provided in sections 2925.02, 2925.03, 2925.04, 2925.05, and 2925.11 of the Revised Code, unless the maximum or another specific

term is required under section 2929.14 of the Revised Code, a mandatory prison term described in this division may be any prison term authorized for the level of offense.

(2) The term of sixty days in prison that a sentencing court is required to impose for a fourth degree felony OMVI offense pursuant to division (G)(2) of section 2929.13 and division (A)(4) of section 4511.99 of the Revised Code.

(2) The term in prison imposed pursuant to section 2971.03 of the Revised Code and that term as modified or terminated pursuant to section 2971.05 of the Revised Code.††

(AA) "Monitored time" means a period of time during which an offender continues to be under the control of the sentencing court or parole board, subject to no conditions other than leading a law abiding life.

(BB) "Offender" means a person who, in this state, is convicted of or pleads guilty to a felony or a misdemeanor.

(CC) "Prison" means a residential facility used for the confinement of convicted felony offenders that is under the control of the department of rehabilitation and correction.

(DD) "Prison term" includes any of the following sanctions for an offender:

(1) A stated prison term;

(2) A term in a prison shortened by, or with the approval of, the sentencing court pursuant to section 2929.20, 2967.26, 2967.27, 5120.031 [5120.03.1], 5120.032 [5120.03.2], or 5120.073 [5120.07.3] of the Revised Code;

(3) A term in prison extended by bad time imposed pursuant to section 2967.11 of the Revised Code or imposed for a violation of post-release control pursuant to section 2967.28 of the Revised Code.

(EE) "Repeat violent offender" means a person about whom both of the following apply:

(1) The person has been convicted of or has pleaded guilty to, and is being sentenced for committing, for complicity in committing, or for an attempt to commit, aggravated murder, murder, involuntary manslaughter, a felony of the first degree other than one set forth in Chapter 2925. of the Revised Code, a felony of the first degree set forth in Chapter 2925. of the Revised Code that involved an attempt to cause serious physical harm to a person or that resulted in serious physical harm to a person, or a felony of the second degree that involved an attempt to cause serious physical harm to a person or that resulted in serious physical harm to a person.

(2) Either of the following applies:

(a) The person previously was convicted of or pleaded guilty to, and served a prison term for, any of the following:

(i) Aggravated murder, murder, involuntary manslaughter, rape, felonious sexual penetration in violation of former section 2907.12 of the Revised Code, a felony of the first or second degree that resulted in the death of a person or in physical harm to a person, or complicity in or an attempt to commit any of those offenses;

(ii) An offense under an existing or former law of this state, another state, or the United States that is or was substantially equivalent to an offense listed under division (EE)(2)(a)(i) of this section.

(b) The person previously was adjudicated a delinquent child for committing an act that if committed by an adult would have been an offense listed in division (EE)(2)(a)(i) or (ii) of this section, the person was committed to the department of youth services for that delinquent act, and the juvenile court in which the person was adjudicated a delinquent child made a specific finding that the adjudication should be considered a conviction for purposes of a determination in the future pursuant to this chapter as to whether the person is a repeat violent offender.

(FF) "Sanction" means any penalty imposed upon an offender who is convicted of or pleads guilty to an offense, as punishment for the offense. "Sanction" includes any sanction imposed pursuant to any provision of sections 2929.14 to 2929.18 of the Revised Code.

(GG) "Sentence" means the sanction or combination of sanctions imposed by the sentencing court on an offender who is convicted of or pleads guilty to a felony.

(HH) "Stated prison term" means the prison term, mandatory prison term, or combination of all prison terms and mandatory prison terms imposed by the sentencing court pursuant to section 2929.14 or 2971.03 of the Revised Code. "Stated prison term" includes any credit received by the offender for time spent in jail awaiting trial, sentencing, or transfer to prison for the offense, any time spent under house arrest or electronically monitored house arrest imposed after earning credits pursuant to section 2967.193 [2967.19.3] of the Revised Code.

(II) "Victim-offender mediation" means a reconciliation or mediation program that involves an offender and the victim of the offense committed by the offender and that includes a meeting in which the offender and the victim may discuss the offense, discuss restitution, and consider other sanctions for the offense.

†††(OO)"Fourth degree felony OMVI offense" means a violation of division (A) of section 4511.19 of the Revised Code that, under section 4511.99 of the Revised Code, is a felony of the fourth degree.

(PP) "Mandatory term of local incarceration" means the term of sixty days in a jail, a community-based correctional facility, a halfway house, or an alternative residential facility that a sentencing court is required to impose upon a person who is convicted of or pleads guilty to a fourth degree felony OMVI offense pursuant to division (G)(1) of section 2929.13 of the Revised Code and division (A)(4) of section 4511.99 of the Revised Code.

††††(OO) "Designated homicide, assault, or kidnapping offense," "sexual motivation specification," "sexually violent offense," "sexually violent predator," and

"sexually violent predator specification" have the same meanings as in section 2971.01 of the Revised Code.

(PP) "Habitual sex offender," "sexually oriented offense," and "sexual predator" have the same meanings as in section 2950.01 of the Revised Code.

HISTORY: 146 v S 2 (Eff 7-1-96); 146 v S 269 (Eff 7-1-96); 146 v H 445 (Eff 9-3-96); 146 v H 480 (Eff 10-16-96); 146 v S 166 (Eff 10-17-96); 146 v H 180. Eff 1-1-97.

Not analogous to former RC § 2929.01 (134 v H 511; 136 v H 300; 137 v H 565; 139 v S 199; 140 v S 210; 142 v H 261; 145 v H 571; 145 v S 186, repealed 146 v S 2, § 2, eff 7-1-96.

Publisher's Note

The amendments made by SB 269 (146 v —), HB 480 (146 v —), SB 166 (146 v —), HB 445 (146 v —), and HB 180 (146 v —) have been combined. Please see provisions of RC § 1.52.

The effective date is set by section 3 of HB 180.

† Division (CC) was changed to (Z) in SB 269 (146 v —).

†† The second (2) is the result of combining SB 166 (146 v —) and HB 180 (146 v —).

††† These divisions (OO) and (PP) were enacted in SB 166 (146 v —). The lettering is the result of combining SB 166 (146 v —) and SB 269 (146 v —).

†††† These divisions (OO) and (PP) were enacted in HB 180 (146 v —). The lettering is the result of combining HB 180 (146 v —) and SB 269 (146 v —).

[PENALTIES FOR MURDER]

§ 2929.02 Penalties for murder.

(A) Whoever is convicted of or pleads guilty to aggravated murder in violation of section 2903.01 of the Revised Code shall suffer death or be imprisoned for life, as determined pursuant to sections 2929.022 [2929.02.2], 2929.03, and 2929.04 of the Revised Code, except that no person who raises the matter of age pursuant to section 2929.023 [2929.02.3] or division (C) of section 2929.05 of the Revised Code and who is not found to have been eighteen years of age or older at the time of the commission of the offense shall suffer death. In addition, the offender may be fined an amount fixed by the court, but not more than twenty-five thousand dollars.

(B) Whoever is convicted of or pleads guilty to murder in violation of section 2903.02 of the Revised Code shall be imprisoned for an indefinite term of fifteen years to life, except that, if the offender also is convicted of or pleads guilty to a sexual motivation specification and a sexually violent predator specification that were included in the indictment, count in the indictment, or information that charged the murder, the court shall impose upon the offender a term of life imprisonment without parole that shall be served pursuant to section 2971.03 of the Revised Code. In addition, the offender may be fined an amount fixed by the court, but not more than fifteen thousand dollars.

(C) The court shall not impose a fine or fines for aggravated murder or murder which, in the aggregate and to the extent not suspended by the court, exceeds the amount which the offender is or will be able to pay by the method and within the time allowed without undue hardship to the offender or to the dependents of the offender, or will prevent the offender from making reparation for the victim's wrongful death.

HISTORY: 134 v H 511 (Eff 1-1-74); 139 v S 1 (Eff 10-19-81); 146 v H 180. Eff 1-1-97.

The effective date is set by section 3 of HB 180.

See provisions, § 4 of HB 180 (146 v —) following RC § 2921.34.

[§ 2929.02.1] § 2929.021 Notice to supreme court of indictment charging aggravated murder; plea.

(A) If an indictment or a count in an indictment charges the defendant with aggravated murder and contains one or more specifications of aggravating circumstances listed in division (A) of section 2929.04 of the Revised Code, the clerk of the court in which the indictment is filed, within fifteen days after the day on which it is filed, shall file a notice with the supreme court indicating that the indictment was filed. The notice shall be in the form prescribed by the clerk of the supreme court and shall contain, for each charge of aggravated murder with a specification, at least the following information pertaining to the charge:

(1) The name of the person charged in the indictment or count in the indictment with aggravated murder with a specification;

(2) The docket number or numbers of the case or cases arising out of the charge, if available;

(3) The court in which the case or cases will be heard;

(4) The date on which the indictment was filed.

(B) If the indictment or a count in an indictment charges the defendant with aggravated murder and contains one or more specifications of aggravating circumstances listed in division (A) of section 2929.04 of the Revised Code and if the defendant pleads guilty or no contest to any offense in the case or if the indictment or any count in the indictment is dismissed, the clerk of the court in which the plea is entered or the indictment or count is dismissed shall file a notice with the supreme court indicating what action was taken in the case. The notice shall be filed within fifteen days after the plea is entered or the indictment or count is dismissed, shall be in the form prescribed by the clerk of the supreme court, and shall contain at least the following information:

(1) The name of the person who entered the guilty or no contest plea or who is named in the indictment or count that is dismissed;

(2) The docket numbers of the cases in which the guilty or no contest plea is entered or in which the indictment or count is dismissed;

(3) The sentence imposed on the offender in each case.

HISTORY: 139 v S 1. Eff 10-19-81.

[§ 2929.02.2] § 2929.022 Determination of aggravating circumstances.

(A) If an indictment or count in an indictment charging a defendant with aggravated murder contains a specification of the aggravating circumstance of a prior conviction listed in division (A)(5) of section 2929.04 of the Revised Code, the defendant may elect to have the panel of three judges, if he waives trial by jury, or the trial judge, if he is tried by jury, determine the existence of that aggravating circumstance at the sentencing hearing held pursuant to divisions (C) and (D) of section 2929.03 of the Revised Code.

(1) If the defendant does not elect to have the existence of the aggravating circumstance determined at the sentencing hearing, the defendant shall be tried on the charge of aggravated murder, on the specification of the aggravating circumstance of a prior conviction listed in division (A)(5) of section 2929.04 of the Revised Code, and on any other specifications of an aggravating circumstance listed in division (A) of section 2929.04 of the Revised Code in a single trial as in any other criminal case in which a person is charged with aggravated murder and specifications.

(2) If the defendant does elect to have the existence of the aggravating circumstance of a prior conviction listed in division (A)(5) of section 2929.04 of the Revised Code determined at the sentencing hearing, then, following a verdict of guilty of the charge of aggravated murder, the panel of three judges or the trial judge shall:

(a) Hold a sentencing hearing pursuant to division (B) of this section, unless required to do otherwise under division (A)(2)(b) of this section;

(b) If the offender raises the matter of age at trial pursuant to section 2929.023 [2929.02.3] of the Revised Code and is not found at trial to have been eighteen years of age or older at the time of the commission of the offense, conduct a hearing to determine if the specification of the aggravating circumstance of a prior conviction listed in division (A)(5) of section 2929.04 of the Revised Code is proven beyond a reasonable doubt. After conducting the hearing, the panel or judge shall proceed as follows:

(i) If that aggravating circumstance is proven beyond a reasonable doubt or if the defendant at trial was convicted of any other specification of an aggravating circumstance, the panel or judge shall impose sentence according to division (E) of section 2929.03 of the Revised Code;

(ii) If that aggravating circumstance is not proven beyond a reasonable doubt and the defendant at trial was not convicted of any other specification of an aggravating circumstance, the panel or judge shall impose a sentence of life imprisonment with parole eligibility after serving twenty years of imprisonment on the offender.

(B) At the sentencing hearing, the panel of judges, if the defendant was tried by a panel of three judges, or the trial judge, if the defendant was tried by jury, shall, when required pursuant to division (A)(2) of this section, first determine if the specification of the aggravating circumstance of a prior conviction listed in division (A)(5) of section 2929.04 of the Revised Code is proven beyond a reasonable doubt. If the panel of judges or the trial judge determines that the specification of the aggravating circumstance of a prior conviction listed in division (A)(5) of section 2929.04 of the Revised Code is proven beyond a reasonable doubt or if they do not determine that the specification is proven beyond a reasonable doubt but the defendant at trial was convicted of a specification of any other aggravating circumstance listed in division (A) of section 2929.04 of the Revised Code, the panel of judges or the trial judge and trial jury shall impose sentence on the offender pursuant to division (D) of section 2929.03 and section 2929.04 of the Revised Code. If the panel of judges or the trial judge does not determine that the specification of the aggravating circumstance of a prior conviction listed in division (A)(5) of section 2929.04 of the Revised Code is proven beyond a reasonable doubt and the defendant at trial was not convicted of any other specification of an aggravating circumstance listed in division (A) of section 2929.04 of the Revised Code, the panel of judges or the trial judge shall terminate the sentencing hearing and impose a sentence of life imprisonment with parole eligibility after serving twenty years of imprisonment on the offender.

HISTORY: 139 v S 1. Eff 10-19-81.

[§ 2929.02.3] § 2929.023 Defendant may raise matter of age.

A person charged with aggravated murder and one or more specifications of an aggravating circumstance may, at trial, raise the matter of his age at the time of the alleged commission of the offense and may present evidence at trial that he was not eighteen years of age or older at the time of the alleged commission of the offense. The burdens of raising the matter of age, and of going forward with the evidence relating to the matter of age, are upon the defendant. After a defendant has raised the matter of age at trial, the prosecution shall have the burden of proving, by proof beyond a reasonable doubt, that the defendant was eighteen years of age or older at the time of the alleged commission of the offense.

HISTORY: 139 v S 1. Eff 10-19-81.

[§ 2929.02.4] § 2929.024 Investigation services and experts for indigent.

If the court determines that the defendant is indigent

and that investigation services, experts, or other services are reasonably necessary for the proper representation of a defendant charged with aggravated murder at trial or at the sentencing hearing, the court shall authorize the defendant's counsel to obtain the necessary services for the defendant, and shall order that payment of the fees and expenses for the necessary services be made in the same manner that payment for appointed counsel is made pursuant to Chapter 120. of the Revised Code. If the court determines that the necessary services had to be obtained prior to court authorization for payment of the fees and expenses for the necessary services, the court may, after the services have been obtained, authorize the defendant's counsel to obtain the necessary services and order that payment of the fees and expenses for the necessary services be made as provided in this section.

HISTORY: 139 v S 1. Eff 10-19-81.

§ 2929.03 Imposing sentence for aggravated murder.

(A) If the indictment or count in the indictment charging aggravated murder does not contain one or more specifications of aggravating circumstances listed in division (A) of section 2929.04 of the Revised Code, then, following a verdict of guilty of the charge of aggravated murder, the trial court shall impose sentence on the offender as follows:

(1) Except as provided in division (A)(2) of this section, the trial court shall impose a sentence of life imprisonment with parole eligibility after serving twenty years of imprisonment on the offender.

(2) If the offender also is convicted of or pleads guilty to a sexual motivation specification and a sexually violent predator specification that are included in the indictment, count in the indictment, or information that charged the aggravated murder, the trial court shall impose upon the offender a sentence of life imprisonment without parole that shall be served pursuant to section 2971.03 of the Revised Code.

(B) If the indictment or count in the indictment charging aggravated murder contains one or more specifications of aggravating circumstances listed in division (A) of section 2929.04 of the Revised Code, the verdict shall separately state whether the accused is found guilty or not guilty of the principal charge and, if guilty of the principal charge, whether the offender was eighteen years of age or older at the time of the commission of the offense, if the matter of age was raised by the offender pursuant to section 2929.023 [2929.02.3] of the Revised Code, and whether the offender is guilty or not guilty of each specification. The jury shall be instructed on its duties in this regard. The instruction to the jury shall include an instruction that a specification shall be proved beyond a reasonable doubt in order to support a guilty verdict on the specification, but the instruction shall not mention the penalty that may be the consequence of a guilty or not guilty verdict on any charge or specification.

(C)(1) If the indictment or count in the indictment charging aggravated murder contains one or more specifications of aggravating circumstances listed in division (A) of section 2929.04 of the Revised Code, then, following a verdict of guilty of the charge but not guilty of each of the specifications, and regardless of whether the offender raised the matter of age pursuant to section 2929.023 [2929.02.3] of the Revised Code, the trial court shall impose sentence on the offender as follows:

(a) Except as provided in division (C)(1)(b) of this section, the trial court shall impose a sentence of life imprisonment with parole eligibility after serving twenty years of imprisonment on the offender.

(b) If the offender also is convicted of or pleads guilty to a sexual motivation specification and a sexually violent predator specification that are included in the indictment, count in the indictment, or information that charged the aggravated murder, the trial court shall impose upon the offender a sentence of life imprisonment without parole that shall be served pursuant to section 2971.03 of the Revised Code.

(2)(a) If the indictment or count in the indictment contains one or more specifications of aggravating circumstances listed in division (A) of section 2929.04 of the Revised Code and if the offender is found guilty of both the charge and one or more of the specifications, the penalty to be imposed on the offender shall be one of the following:

(i) Except as provided in division (C)(2)(a)(ii) of this section, the penalty to be imposed on the offender shall be death, life imprisonment without parole, life imprisonment with parole eligibility after serving twenty-five† full years of imprisonment, or life imprisonment with parole eligibility after serving thirty full years of imprisonment.

(ii) If the offender also is convicted of or pleads guilty to a sexual motivation specification and a sexually violent predator specification that are included in the indictment, count in the indictment, or information that charged the aggravated murder, the penalty to be imposed on the offender shall be death or life imprisonment without parole that shall be served pursuant to section 2971.03 of the Revised Code.

(b) A penalty imposed pursuant to division (C)(2)(a)(i) or (ii) of this section shall be determined pursuant to divisions (D) and (E) of this section and shall be determined by one of the following:

(i) By the panel of three judges that tried the offender upon the offender's waiver of the right to trial by jury;

(ii) By the trial jury and the trial judge, if the offender was tried by jury.

(D)(1) Death may not be imposed as a penalty for aggravated murder if the offender raised the matter of age at trial pursuant to section 2929.023 [2929.02.3] of the Revised Code and was not found at trial to have been eighteen years of age or older at the time of the commission of the offense. When death may be imposed as a penalty for aggravated murder, the court shall proceed under this division. When death may be imposed as a penalty, the court, upon the request of the defendant, shall require a pre-sentence investigation to be made and, upon the request of the defendant, shall require a mental examination to be made, and shall require reports of the investigation and of any mental examination submitted to the court, pursuant to section 2947.06 of the Revised Code. No statement made or information provided by a defendant in a mental examination or proceeding conducted pursuant to this division shall be disclosed to any person, except as provided in this division, or be used in evidence against the defendant on the issue of guilt in any retrial. A pre-sentence investigation or mental examination shall not be made except upon request of the defendant. Copies of any reports prepared under this division shall be furnished to the court, to the trial jury if the offender was tried by a jury, to the prosecutor, and to the offender or the offender's counsel for use under this division. The court, and the trial jury if the offender was tried by a jury, shall consider any report prepared pursuant to this division and furnished to it and any evidence raised at trial that is relevant to the aggravating circumstances the offender was found guilty of committing or to any factors in mitigation of the imposition of the sentence of death, shall hear testimony and other evidence that is relevant to the nature and circumstances of the aggravating circumstances the offender was found guilty of committing, the mitigating factors set forth in division (B) of section 2929.04 of the Revised Code, and any other factors in mitigation of the imposition of the sentence of death, and shall hear the statement, if any, of the offender, and the arguments, if any, of counsel for the defense and prosecution, that are relevant to the penalty that should be imposed on the offender. The defendant shall be given great latitude in the presentation of evidence of the mitigating factors set forth in division (B) of section 2929.04 of the Revised Code and of any other factors in mitigation of the imposition of the sentence of death. If the offender chooses to make a statement, the offender is subject to cross-examination only if the offender consents to make the statement under oath or affirmation.

The defendant shall have the burden of going forward with the evidence of any factors in mitigation of the imposition of the sentence of death. The prosecution shall have the burden of proving, by proof beyond a reasonable doubt, that the aggravating circumstances the defendant was found guilty of committing are sufficient to outweigh the factors in mitigation of the imposition of the sentence of death.

(2) Upon consideration of the relevant evidence raised at trial, the testimony, other evidence, statement of the offender, arguments of counsel, and, if applicable, the reports submitted pursuant to division (D)(1) of this section, the trial jury, if the offender was tried by a jury, shall determine whether the aggravating circumstances the offender was found guilty of committing are sufficient to outweigh the mitigating factors present in the case. If the trial jury unanimously finds, by proof beyond a reasonable doubt, that the aggravating circumstances the offender was found guilty of committing outweigh the mitigating factors, the trial jury shall recommend to the court that the sentence of death be imposed on the offender. Absent such a finding, the jury shall recommend that the offender be sentenced to one of the following:

(a) Except as provided in division (D)(2)(b) of this section, to life imprisonment without parole, life imprisonment with parole eligibility after serving twenty-five† full years of imprisonment, or life imprisonment with parole eligibility after serving thirty full years of imprisonment;

(b) If the offender also is convicted of or pleads guilty to a sexual motivation specification and a sexually violent predator specification that are included in the indictment, count in the indictment, or information that charged the aggravated murder, to life imprisonment without parole.

If the trial jury recommends that the offender be sentenced to life imprisonment without parole, life imprisonment with parole eligibility after serving twenty-five† full years of imprisonment, or life imprisonment with parole eligibility after serving thirty full years of imprisonment, the court shall impose the sentence recommended by the jury upon the offender. If the sentence is a sentence of life imprisonment without parole imposed under division (D)(2)(b) of this section, the sentence shall be served pursuant to section 2971.03 of the Revised Code. If the trial jury recommends that the sentence of death be imposed upon the offender, the court shall proceed to impose sentence pursuant to division (D)(3) of this section.

(3) Upon consideration of the relevant evidence raised at trial, the testimony, other evidence, statement of the offender, arguments of counsel, and, if applicable, the reports submitted to the court pursuant to division (D)(1) of this section, if, after receiving pursuant to division (D)(2) of this section the trial jury's recommendation that the sentence of death be imposed, the court finds, by proof beyond a reasonable doubt, or if the panel of three judges unanimously finds, by proof beyond a reasonable doubt, that the aggravating circumstances the offender was found guilty of committing outweigh the mitigating factors, it shall impose sentence of death on the offender. Absent such a finding by the court or panel, the court or the panel shall impose one of the following sentences on the offender:

(a) Except as provided in division (D)(3)(b) of this section, one of the following:

(i) Life imprisonment without parole;

(ii) Life imprisonment with parole eligibility after serving twenty-five† full years of imprisonment;

(iii) Life imprisonment with parole eligibility after

serving thirty full years of imprisonment.

(b) If the offender also is convicted of or pleads guilty to a sexual motivation specification and a sexually violent predator specification that are included in the indictment, count in the indictment, or information that charged the aggravated murder, life imprisonment without parole that shall be served pursuant to section 2971.03 of the Revised Code.

(E) If the offender raised the matter of age at trial pursuant to section 2929.023 [2929.02.3] of the Revised Code, was convicted of aggravated murder and one or more specifications of an aggravating circumstance listed in division (A) of section 2929.04 of the Revised Code, and was not found at trial to have been eighteen years of age or older at the time of the commission of the offense, the court or the panel of three judges shall not impose a sentence of death on the offender. Instead, the court or panel shall impose one of the following sentences on the offender:

(1) Except as provided in division (E)(2) of this section, one of the following:

(a) Life imprisonment without parole;

(b) Life imprisonment with parole eligibility after serving twenty-five† full years of imprisonment;

(c) Life imprisonment with parole eligibility after serving thirty full years of imprisonment.

(2) If the offender also is convicted of or pleads guilty to a sexual motivation specification and a sexually violent predator specification that are included in the indictment, count in the indictment, or information that charged the aggravated murder, life imprisonment without parole that shall be served pursuant to section 2971.03 of the Revised Code.

(F) The court or the panel of three judges, when it imposes sentence of death, shall state in a separate opinion its specific findings as to the existence of any of the mitigating factors set forth in division (B) of section 2929.04 of the Revised Code, the existence of any other mitigating factors, the aggravating circumstances the offender was found guilty of committing, and the reasons why the aggravating circumstances the offender was found guilty of committing were sufficient to outweigh the mitigating factors. The court or panel, when it imposes life imprisonment under division (D) of this section, shall state in a separate opinion its specific findings of which of the mitigating factors set forth in division (B) of section 2929.04 of the Revised Code it found to exist, what other mitigating factors it found to exist, what aggravating circumstances the offender was found guilty of committing, and why it could not find that these aggravating circumstances were sufficient to outweigh the mitigating factors. For cases in which a sentence of death is imposed for an offense committed before January 1, 1995, the court or panel shall file the opinion required to be prepared by this division with the clerk of the appropriate court of appeals and with the clerk of the supreme court within fifteen days after the court or panel imposes sentence. For cases in which a sentence of death is imposed for an offense committed on or after January 1, 1995, the court or panel shall file the opinion required to be prepared by this division with the clerk of the supreme court within fifteen days after the court or panel imposes sentence. The judgment in a case in which a sentencing hearing is held pursuant to this section is not final until the opinion is filed.

(G)(1) Whenever the court or a panel of three judges imposes a sentence of death for an offense committed before January 1, 1995, the clerk of the court in which the judgment is rendered shall deliver the entire record in the case to the appellate court.

(2) Whenever the court or a panel of three judges imposes a sentence of death for an offense committed on or after January 1, 1995, the clerk of the court in which the judgment is rendered shall deliver the entire record in the case to the supreme court.

HISTORY: 134 v H 511 (Eff 1-1-74); 139 v S 1 (Eff 10-19-81); 146 v S 4 (Eff 9-21-95); 146 v S 2 (Eff 7-1-96); 146 v S 269 (Eff 7-1-96); 146 H 180. Eff 1-1-97.

The effective date is set by section 3 of HB 180.

See provisions, § 4 of HB 180 (146 v —) following RC § 2921.34.

The provisions of § 6 of HB 180 (146 v —) read in part as follows:

* * * Sections 2929.03 and 2929.06 of the Revised Code are presented in this act as composites of the sections as amended by both Am. Sub. S.B. 2 and Am. Sub. S.B. 4 of the 120th General Assembly, with the new language of neither of the acts shown in capital letters. This is in recognition of the principle stated in division (B) of section 1.52 of the Revised Code that such amendments are to be harmonized where not substantively irreconcilable and constitutes a legislative finding that such is the resulting version in effect prior to the effective date of this act.

The provisions of §§ 3, 4 of SB 269 read as follows:

SECTION 3. That Section 5 of Am. Sub. S.B. 2 of the 121st General Assembly be amended to read as follows:

"Sec. 5. The provisions of the Revised Code in existence prior to July 1, 1996, shall apply to a person upon whom a court imposed a term of imprisonment prior to that date and, notwithstanding division (B) of section 1.58 of the Revised Code, to a person upon whom a court, on or after that date and in accordance with the law in existence prior to that date, imposes a term of imprisonment for an offense that was committed prior to that date.

The provisions of the Revised Code in existence on and after July 1, 1996, apply to a person who commits an offense on or after that date."

SECTION 4. That existing Section 5 of Am. Sub. S.B. 2 of the 121st General Assembly is hereby repealed.

† The number was changed from twenty to twenty-five years by SB 269 (146 v —), effective 7-1-96.

Comment, Legislative Service Commission

Section 2929.03 of the Revised Code is amended by this act [Am. Sub. S.B. 269] and also by Am. Sub. H.B. 180 of the 121st General Assembly. Comparison of these amendments in pursuance of section 1.52 of the Revised Code discloses that they are not irreconcilable so that they are required by that section to be harmonized to give effect to each amendment.

§ 2929.04 Criteria for imposing death or imprisonment for a capital offense.

(A) Imposition of the death penalty for aggravated murder is precluded unless one or more of the following is specified in the indictment or count in the indictment pursuant to section 2941.14 of the Revised Code and proved beyond a reasonable doubt:

(1) The offense was the assassination of the president of the United States or a person in line of succession to the presidency, the governor or lieutenant governor of this state, the president-elect or vice president-elect of the United States, the governor-elect or lieutenant governor-elect of this state, or a candidate for any of the offices described in this division. For purposes of this division, a person is a candidate if the person has been nominated for election according to law, if the person has filed a petition or petitions according to law to have the person's name placed on the ballot in a primary or general election, or if the person campaigns as a write-in candidate in a primary or general election.

(2) The offense was committed for hire.

(3) The offense was committed for the purpose of escaping detection, apprehension, trial, or punishment for another offense committed by the offender.

(4) The offense was committed while the offender was a prisoner in a detention facility, as defined in section 2921.01 of the Revised Code.

(5) Prior to the offense at bar, the offender was convicted of an offense an essential element of which was the purposeful killing of or attempt to kill another, or the offense at bar was part of a course of conduct involving the purposeful killing of or attempt to kill two or more persons by the offender.

(6) The victim of the offense was a law enforcement officer, as defined in section 2911.01 of the Revised Code, whom the offender had reasonable cause to know or knew to be a law enforcement officer as so defined, and either the victim, at the time of the commission of the offense, was engaged in the victim's duties, or it was the offender's specific purpose to kill a law enforcement officer as so defined.

(7) The offense was committed while the offender was committing, attempting to commit, or fleeing immediately after committing or attempting to commit kidnapping, rape, aggravated arson, aggravated robbery, or aggravated burglary, and either the offender was the principal offender in the commission of the aggravated murder or, if not the principal offender, committed the aggravated murder with prior calculation and design.

(8) The victim of the aggravated murder was a witness to an offense who was purposely killed to prevent the victim's testimony in any criminal proceeding and the aggravated murder was not committed during the commission, attempted commission, or flight immediately after the commission or attempted commission of the offense to which the victim was a witness, or the victim of the aggravated murder was a witness to an offense and was purposely killed in retaliation for the victim's testimony in any criminal proceeding.

(9) The offender, in the commission of the offense, purposefully caused the death of another who was under thirteen years of age at the time of the commission of the offense, and either the offender was the principal offender in the commission of the offense or, if not the principal offender, committed the offense with prior calculation and design.

(B) If one or more of the aggravating circumstances listed in division (A) of this section is specified in the indictment or count in the indictment and proved beyond a reasonable doubt, and if the offender did not raise the matter of age pursuant to section 2929.023 [2929.02.3] of the Revised Code or if the offender, after raising the matter of age, was found at trial to have been eighteen years of age or older at the time of the commission of the offense, the court, trial jury, or panel of three judges shall consider, and weigh against the aggravating circumstances proved beyond a reasonable doubt, the nature and circumstances of the offense, the history, character, and background of the offender, and all of the following factors:

(1) Whether the victim of the offense induced or facilitated it;

(2) Whether it is unlikely that the offense would have been committed, but for the fact that the offender was under duress, coercion, or strong provocation;

(3) Whether, at the time of committing the offense, the offender, because of a mental disease or defect, lacked substantial capacity to appreciate the criminality of the offender's conduct or to conform the offender's conduct to the requirements of the law;

(4) The youth of the offender;

(5) The offender's lack of a significant history of prior criminal convictions and delinquency adjudications;

(6) If the offender was a participant in the offense but not the principal offender, the degree of the offender's participation in the offense and the degree of the offender's participation in the acts that led to the death of the victim;

(7) Any other factors that are relevant to the issue of whether the offender should be sentenced to death.

(C) The defendant shall be given great latitude in the presentation of evidence of the factors listed in division (B) of this section and of any other factors in mitigation of the imposition of the sentence of death.

The existence of any of the mitigating factors listed in division (B) of this section does not preclude the imposition of a sentence of death on the offender but shall be weighed pursuant to divisions (D)(2) and (3) of section 2929.03 of the Revised Code by the trial court, trial jury, or the panel of three judges against the aggravating circumstances the offender was found guilty of committing.

HISTORY: 134 v H 511 (Eff 1-1-74); 139 v S 1 (Eff 10-19-81); 147 v S 32 (Eff 8-6-97); 147 v H 151. Eff 9-16-97.

Publisher's Note

The amendments made by SB 32 (147 v —) and HB 151 (147 v —) have been combined. Please see provisions of RC § 1.52.

§ 2929.05 Appellate review of death sentence.

(A) Whenever sentence of death is imposed pursuant to sections 2929.03 and 2929.04 of the Revised Code, the court of appeals, in a case in which a sentence of death was imposed for an offense committed before January 1, 1995, and the supreme court shall upon appeal review the sentence of death at the same time that they review the other issues in the case. The court of appeals and the supreme court shall review the judgment in the case and the sentence of death imposed by the court or panel of three judges in the same manner that they review other criminal cases, except that they shall review and independently weigh all of the facts and other evidence disclosed in the record in the case and consider the offense and the offender to determine whether the aggravating circumstances the offender was found guilty of committing outweigh the mitigating factors in the case, and whether the sentence of death is appropriate. In determining whether the sentence of death is appropriate, the court of appeals, in a case in which a sentence of death was imposed for an offense committed before January 1, 1995, and the supreme court shall consider whether the sentence is excessive or disproportionate to the penalty imposed in similar cases. They shall also review all of the facts and other evidence to determine if the evidence supports the finding of the aggravating circumstances the trial jury or the panel of three judges found the offender guilty of committing, and shall determine whether the sentencing court properly weighed the aggravating circumstances the offender was found guilty of committing and the mitigating factors. The court of appeals, in a case in which a sentence of death was imposed for an offense committed before January 1, 1995, or the supreme court shall affirm a sentence of death only if the particular court is persuaded from the record that the aggravating circumstances the offender was found guilty of committing outweigh the mitigating factors present in the case and that the sentence of death is the appropriate sentence in the case.

A court of appeals that reviews a case in which the sentence of death is imposed for an offense committed before January 1, 1995, shall file a separate opinion as to its findings in the case with the clerk of the supreme court. The opinion shall be filed within fifteen days after the court issues its opinion and shall contain whatever information is required by the clerk of the supreme court.

(B) The court of appeals, in a case in which a sentence of death was imposed for an offense committed before January 1, 1995, and the supreme court shall give priority over all other cases to the review of judgments in which the sentence of death is imposed, and, except as otherwise provided in this section, shall conduct the review in accordance with the Appellate Rules.

(C) Whenever sentence of death is imposed pursuant to section 2929.022 [2929.02.2] or 2929.03 of the Revised Code, the court of common pleas that sentenced the offender shall, upon motion of the offender and after conducting a hearing on the motion, vacate the sentence if all of the following apply:

(1) The offender alleges in the motion and presents evidence at the hearing that the offender was not eighteen years of age or older at the time of the commission of the aggravated murder for which the offender was sentenced;

(2) The offender did not present evidence at trial pursuant to section 2929.023 [2929.02.3] of the Revised Code that the offender was not eighteen years of age or older at the time of the commission of the aggravated murder for which the offender was sentenced;

(3) The motion was filed at any time after the sentence was imposed in the case and prior to execution of the sentence;

(4) At the hearing conducted on the motion, the prosecution does not prove beyond a reasonable doubt that the offender was eighteen years of age or older at the time of the commission of the aggravated murder for which the offender was sentenced.

HISTORY: 139 v S 1 (Eff 10-19-81); 146 v S 4. Eff 9-21-95.

§ 2929.06 Resentencing after vacation of death sentence or life imprisonment without parole.

(A) If the sentence of death that is imposed upon an offender is vacated upon appeal because the court of appeals, in a case in which a sentence of death was imposed for an offense committed before January 1, 1995, or the supreme court, in cases in which the supreme court reviews the sentence upon appeal, could not affirm the sentence of death under the standards imposed by section 2929.05 of the Revised Code, is vacated upon appeal for the sole reason that the statutory procedure for imposing the sentence of death that is set forth in sections 2929.03 and 2929.04 of the Revised Code is unconstitutional, or is vacated pursuant to division (C) of section 2929.05 of the Revised Code, the trial court that sentenced the offender shall conduct a hearing to resentence the offender. At the resentencing hearing, the court shall impose one of the following sentences upon the offender:

(1) Except as provided in division (A)(2) of this section, life imprisonment without parole, life imprisonment with parole eligibility after serving twenty-five† full years of imprisonment, or life imprisonment with parole eligibility after serving thirty full years of imprisonment;

(2) If the sentence of death was imposed for an aggra-

vated murder committed on or after the effective date of this amendment and if the offender also was convicted of or pleaded guilty to a sexual motivation specification and a sexually violent predator specification that were included in the indictment, count in the indictment, or information that charged the aggravated murder, life imprisonment without parole that shall be served pursuant to section 2971.03 of the Revised Code.

(2) If the sentence of death that is imposed upon an offender is vacated upon appeal because of error that occurred in the sentencing phase of the trial and if division (A)(1) of this section does not apply, the trial court that sentenced the offender shall conduct a new hearing to resentence the offender. If the offender was tried by a jury, the trial court shall impanel a new jury for the hearing. If the offender was tried by a panel of three judges, that panel or, if necessary, a new panel of three judges, shall conduct the hearing. At the hearing, the court shall follow the procedure set forth in division (D) of section 2929.03 of the Revised Code in determining whether to impose upon the offender a sentence of death, life imprisonment without parole, life imprisonment with parole eligibility after serving twenty full years of imprisonment, or life imprisonment with parole eligibility after serving thirty full years of imprisonment.††

(B) If the sentence of life imprisonment without parole that is imposed upon an offender pursuant to section 2929.021 [2929.02.1] or 2929.03 of the Revised Code is vacated upon appeal for the sole reason that the statutory procedure for imposing the sentence of life imprisonment without parole that is set forth in sections 2929.03 and 2929.04 of the Revised Code is unconstitutional, the trial court that sentenced the offender shall conduct a hearing to resentence the offender to life imprisonment with parole eligibility after serving twenty-five† full years of imprisonment or to life imprisonment with parole eligibility after serving thirty full years of imprisonment.

HISTORY: 139 v S 1 (Eff 10-19-81); 146 v S 4 (Eff 9-21-95); 146 v S 2 (Eff 7-1-96); 146 v S 269 (Eff 7-1-96); 146 v S 258 (Eff 10-16-96); 146 v H 180. Eff 1-1-97.

Publisher's Note

The amendments made by HB 180 (146 v —), SB 258 (146 v —), and SB 269 (146 v —) have been combined. Please see provisions of RC § 1.52.

The effective date is set by section 3 of HB 180.

See provisions, § 4 of HB 180 (146 v —) following RC § 2921.34.

See provisions, § 6 of HB 180 (146 v —) following RC § 2929.03.

† The number of years was changed from twenty to twenty-five in SB 269 (146 v —), effective 7-1-96.

†† The duplication in numbering is the result of combining SB 258 (146 v —) and HB 180 (146 v —).

[PENALTIES FOR FELONY]

§ 2929.11 Purposes of felony sentencing; discrimination prohibited.

(A) A court that sentences an offender for a felony shall be guided by the overriding purposes of felony sentencing. The overriding purposes of felony sentencing are to protect the public from future crime by the offender and others and to punish the offender. To achieve those purposes, the sentencing court shall consider the need for incapacitating the offender, deterring the offender and others from future crime, rehabilitating the offender, and making restitution to the victim of the offense, the public, or both.

(B) A sentence imposed for a felony shall be reasonably calculated to achieve the two overriding purposes of felony sentencing set forth in division (A) of this section, commensurate with and not demeaning to the seriousness of the offender's conduct and its impact upon the victim, and consistent with sentences imposed for similar crimes committed by similar offenders.

(C) A court that imposes a sentence upon an offender for a felony shall not base the sentence upon the race, ethnic background, gender, or religion of the offender.

HISTORY: 146 v S 2. Eff 7-1-96.

Not analogous to former RC § 2929.11 (134 v H 511; 137 v S 119; 139 v S 199; 140 v S 210; 140 v H 265; 140 v S 4; 141 v H 284; 143 v H 51; 143 v S 258), repealed 146 v S 2, § 2, eff 7-1-96.

The effective date is set by section 6 of SB 2.

§ 2929.12 Seriousness and recidivism factors.

(A) Unless a mandatory prison term is required by division (F) of section 2929.13 or section 2929.14 of the Revised Code, a court that imposes a sentence under this chapter upon an offender for a felony has discretion to determine the most effective way to comply with the purposes and principles of sentencing set forth in section 2929.11 of the Revised Code. In exercising that discretion, the court shall consider the factors set forth in divisions (B) and (C) of this section relating to the seriousness of the conduct and the factors provided in divisions (D) and (E) of this section relating to the likelihood of the offender's recidivism and, in addition, may consider any other factors that are relevant to achieving those purposes and principles of sentencing.

(B) The sentencing court shall consider all of the following that apply regarding the offender, the offense, or the victim, and any other relevant factors, as indicating that the offender's conduct is more serious than conduct normally constituting the offense:

(1) The physical or mental injury suffered by the victim of the offense due to the conduct of the offender was exacerbated because of the physical or mental condition or age of the victim.

(2) The victim of the offense suffered serious physical, psychological, or economic harm as a result of the offense.

(3) The offender held a public office or position of

trust in the community, and the offense related to that office or position.

(4) The offender's occupation, elected office, or profession obliged the offender to prevent the offense or bring others committing it to justice.

(5) The offender's professional reputation or occupation, elected office, or profession was used to facilitate the offense or is likely to influence the future conduct of others.

(6) The offender's relationship with the victim facilitated the offense.

(7) The offender committed the offense for hire or as a part of an organized criminal activity.

(8) In committing the offense, the offender was motivated by prejudice based on race, ethnic background, gender, sexual orientation, or religion.

(C) The sentencing court shall consider all of the following that apply regarding the offender, the offense, or the victim, and any other relevant factors, as indicating that the offender's conduct is less serious than conduct normally constituting the offense:

(1) The victim induced or facilitated the offense.

(2) In committing the offense, the offender acted under strong provocation.

(3) In committing the offense, the offender did not cause or expect to cause physical harm to any person or property.

(4) There are substantial grounds to mitigate the offender's conduct, although the grounds are not enough to constitute a defense.

(D) The sentencing court shall consider all of the following that apply regarding the offender, and any other relevant factors, as factors indicating that the offender is likely to commit future crimes:

(1) At the time of committing the offense, the offender was under release from confinement before trial or sentencing, under a sanction imposed pursuant to section 2929.16, 2929.17, or 2929.18 of the Revised Code, or under post-release control pursuant to section 2967.28 or any other provision of the Revised Code for an earlier offense.

(2) The offender previously was adjudicated a delinquent child pursuant to Chapter 2151. of the Revised Code, or the offender has a history of criminal convictions.

(3) The offender has not been rehabilitated to a satisfactory degree after previously being adjudicated a delinquent child pursuant to Chapter 2151. of the Revised Code, or the offender has not responded favorably to sanctions previously imposed for criminal convictions.

(4) The offender has demonstrated a pattern of drug or alcohol abuse that is related to the offense, and the offender refuses to acknowledge that the offender has demonstrated that pattern, or the offender refuses treatment for the drug or alcohol abuse.

(5) The offender shows no genuine remorse for the offense.

(E) The sentencing court shall consider all of the following that apply regarding the offender, and any other relevant factors, as factors indicating that the offender is not likely to commit future crimes:

(1) Prior to committing the offense, the offender had not been adjudicated a delinquent child.

(2) Prior to committing the offense, the offender had not been convicted of or pleaded guilty to a criminal offense.

(3) Prior to committing the offense, the offender had led a law-abiding life for a significant number of years.

(4) The offense was committed under circumstances not likely to recur.

(5) The offender shows genuine remorse for the offense.

HISTORY: 146 v S 2 (Eff 7-1-96); 146 v S 269. Eff 7-1-96.

Analogous to former RC § 2929.12 (134 v H 511; 137 v S 119; 138 v S 384; 139 v S 199; 143 v S 258; 145 v S 186), repealed 146 v S 2, § 2, eff 7-1-96.

The effective date is set by section 5 of SB 269.

§ 2929.13 Guidance by degree of felony.

(A) Except as provided in division (E), (F), (G)† of this section and unless a specific sanction is required to be imposed or is precluded from being imposed pursuant to law, a court that imposes a sentence upon an offender for a felony may impose any sanction or combination of sanctions on the offender that are provided in sections 2929.14 to 2929.18 of the Revised Code. The sentence shall not impose an unnecessary burden on state or local government resources.

If the offender is eligible to be sentenced to community control sanctions, the court shall consider the appropriateness of imposing a financial sanction pursuant to section 2929.18 of the Revised Code or a sanction of community service pursuant to section 2929.17 of the Revised Code as the sole sanction for the offense. Except as otherwise provided in this division, if the court is required to impose a mandatory prison term for the offense for which sentence is being imposed, the court also may impose a financial sanction pursuant to section 2929.18 of the Revised Code but may not impose any additional sanction or combination of sanctions under section 2929.16 or 2929.17 of the Revised Code.

If the offender is being sentenced for a fourth degree felony OMVI offense, in addition to the mandatory term of local incarceration or the mandatory prison term required for the offense by division (G)(1) or (2)† of this section, the court shall impose upon the offender a mandatory fine in accordance with division (B)(3) of section 2929.18 of the Revised Code and may impose whichever of the following is applicable:

(1) If division (G)(1)† of this section requires that the offender be sentenced to a mandatory term of local incarceration, an additional community control sanction or combination of community control sanctions under section 2929.16 or 2929.17 of the Revised Code;

(2) If division (G)(2)† of this section requires that the offender be sentenced to a mandatory prison term, an additional prison term as described in division (D)(4) of section 2929.14 of the Revised Code.

(B)(1) Except as provided in division (B)(2), (E), (F), or (G)† of this section, in sentencing an offender for a felony of the fourth or fifth degree, the sentencing court shall determine whether any of the following apply:

(a) In committing the offense, the offender caused physical harm to a person.

(b) In committing the offense, the offender attempted to cause or made an actual threat of physical harm to a person with a deadly weapon.

(c) In committing the offense, the offender attempted to cause or made an actual threat of physical harm to a person, and the offender previously was convicted of an offense that caused physical harm to a person.

(d) The offender held a public office or position of trust and the offense related to that office or position; the offender's position obliged the offender to prevent the offense or to bring those committing it to justice; or the offender's professional reputation or position facilitated the offense or was likely to influence the future conduct of others.

(e) The offender committed the offense for hire or as part of an organized criminal activity.

(f) The offense is a sex offense that is a fourth or fifth degree felony violation of section 2907.03, 2907.04, 2907.05, 2907.22, 2907.31, 2907.321 [2907.32.1], 2907.322 [2907.32.2], 2907.323 [2907.32.3], or 2907.34 of the Revised Code.

(g) The offender previously served a prison term.

(h) The offender previously was subject to a community control sanction, and the offender committed another offense while under the sanction.

(2)(a) Except as provided in division (E), (F), or (G)† of this section, if the court makes a finding described in division (B)(1)(a), (b), (c), (d), (e), (f), (g) or, (h) of this section and if the court, after considering the factors set forth in section 2929.12 of the Revised Code, finds that a prison term is consistent with the purposes and principles of sentencing set forth in section 2929.11 of the Revised Code and finds that the offender is not amenable to an available community control sanction, the court shall impose a prison term upon the offender.

(b) If the court does not make a finding described in division (B)(1)(a), (b), (c), (d), (e), (f), (g), or (h) of this section and if the court, after considering the factors set forth in section 2929.12 of the Revised Code, finds that a community control sanction or combination of community control sanctions is consistent with the purposes and principles of sentencing set forth in section 2929.11 of the Revised Code, the court shall impose a community control sanction or combination of community control sanctions upon the offender.

(C) Except as provided in division (E) or (F) of this section, in determining whether to impose a prison term as a sanction for a felony of the third degree or a felony drug offense that is a violation of a provision of Chapter 2925. of the Revised Code and that is specified as being subject to this division for purposes of sentencing, the sentencing court shall comply with the purposes and principles of sentencing under section 2929.11 of the Revised Code and with section 2929.12 of the Revised Code.

(D) Except as provided in division (E) or (F) of this section, for a felony of the first or second degree and for a felony drug offense that is a violation of any provision of Chapter 2925., 3719., or 4729. of the Revised Code for which a presumption in favor of a prison term is specified as being applicable, it is presumed that a prison term is necessary in order to comply with the purposes and principles of sentencing under section 2929.11 of the Revised Code. Notwithstanding the presumption established under this division, the sentencing court may impose a community control sanction or a combination of community control sanctions instead of a prison term on an offender for a felony of the first or second degree or for a felony drug offense that is a violation of any provision of Chapter 2925., 3719., or 4729. of the Revised Code for which a presumption in favor of a prison term is specified as being applicable if it makes both of the following findings:

(1) A community control sanction or a combination of community control sanctions would adequately punish the offender and protect the public from future crime, because the applicable factors under section 2929.12 of the Revised Code indicating a lesser likelihood of recidivism outweigh the applicable factors under that section indicating a greater likelihood of recidivism.

(2) A community control sanction or a combination of community control sanctions would not demean the seriousness of the offense, because one or more factors under section 2929.12 of the Revised Code that indicate that the offender's conduct was less serious than conduct normally constituting the offense are applicable, and they outweigh the applicable factors under that section that indicate that the offender's conduct was more serious than conduct normally constituting the offense.

(E)(1) Except as provided in division (F) of this section, for any drug offense that is a violation of any provision of Chapter 2925. of the Revised Code and that is a felony of the third, fourth, or fifth degree, the applicability of a presumption under division (D) of this section in favor of a prison term or of division (B) or (C) of this section in determining whether to impose a prison term for the offense shall be determined as specified in section 2925.02, 2925.03, 2925.04, 2925.05, 2925.06, 2925.11, 2925.13, 2925.22, 2925.23, 2925.36, or 2925.37 of the Revised Code, whichever is applicable regarding the violation.

(2) If an offender who was convicted of or pleaded guilty to a felony drug offense in violation of a provision

of Chapter 2925., 3719., or 4729. of the Revised Code violates the conditions of a community control sanction imposed for the offense solely by possession or using a controlled substance and if the offender has not failed to meet the conditions of any drug treatment program in which the offender was ordered to participate as a sanction for the offense, the court, as punishment for the violation of the sanction, shall order that the offender participate in a drug treatment program or in alcoholics anonymous, narcotics anonymous, or a similar program if the court determines that an order of that nature is consistent with the purposes and principles of sentencing set forth in section 2929.11 of the Revised Code. If the court determines that an order of that nature would not be consistent with those purposes and principles or if the offender violated the conditions of a drug treatment program in which the offender participated as a sanction for the offense, the court may impose on the offender a sanction authorized for the violation of the sanction, including a prison term.

(F) Notwithstanding divisions (A) to (E) of this section, the court shall impose a prison term or terms under sections 2929.02 to 2929.06, section 2929.14, or section 2971.03 of the Revised Code and except as specifically provided in section 2929.20 of the Revised Code or when parole is authorized for the offense under section 2967.13 of the Revised Code, shall not reduce the terms pursuant to section 2929.20, section 2967.193 [2967.19.3], or any other provision of Chapter 2967. or Chapter 5120. of the Revised Code for any of the following offenses:

(1) Aggravated murder when death is not imposed or murder;

(2) Rape or an attempt to commit rape by force when the victim is under thirteen years of age;

(3) Gross sexual imposition or sexual battery, if the victim is under thirteen years of age, if the offender previously was convicted of or pleaded guilty to rape, felonious sexual penetration, gross sexual imposition, or sexual battery, and if the victim of the previous offense was under thirteen years of age;

(4) A felony violation of section 2903.06, 2903.07, or 2903.08 of the Revised Code if the section requires the imposition of a prison term;

(5) A first, second, or third degree felony drug offense for which section 2925.02, 2925.03, 2925.04, 2925.05, 2925.06, 2925.11, 2925.13, 2925.22, 2925.23, 2925.36, 2925.37, 3719.99, or 4729.99 of the Revised Code, whichever is applicable regarding the violation, requires the imposition of a mandatory prison term;

(6) Any offense that is a first or second degree felony and that is not set forth in division (F)(1), (2), (3), or (4) of this section, if the offender previously was convicted of or pleaded guilty to aggravated murder, murder, any first or second degree felony, or an offense under an existing or former law of this state, another state, or the United States that is or was substantially equivalent to one of those offenses;

(7) Any offense, other than a violation of section 2923.12 of the Revised Code, that is a felony, if the offender had a firearm on or about the offender's person or under the offender's control while committing the felony, with respect to a portion of the sentence imposed pursuant to division (D)(1)(a) of section 2929.14 of the Revised Code for having the firearm;

(8) Corrupt activity in violation of section 2923.32 of the Revised Code when the most serious offense in the pattern of corrupt activity that is the basis of the offense is a felony of the first degree;

(9) Any sexually violent offense for which the offender also is convicted of or pleads guilty to a sexually violent predator specification that was included in the indictment, count in the indictment, or information charging the sexually violent offense.

††(G) If an offender is being sentenced for a sexually oriented offense committed on or after the effective date of this amendment, the judge shall require the offender to submit to a DNA specimen collection procedure pursuant to section 2901.07 of the Revised Code if either of the following applies:

(1) The offense was a sexually violent offense, and the offender also was convicted of or pleaded guilty to a sexually violent predator specification that was included in the indictment, count in the indictment, or information charging the sexually violent offense.

(2) The judge imposing sentence for the sexually oriented offense determines pursuant to division (B) of section 2950.09 of the Revised Code that the offender is a sexual predator.

(H) If an offender is being sentenced for a sexually oriented offense committed on or after the effective date of this amendment, the judge shall include in the sentence a summary of the offender's duty to register pursuant to section 2950.04 of the Revised Code, the offender's duty to provide notice of a change in residence address and register the new residence address pursuant to section 2950.05 of the Revised Code, the offender's duty to periodically verify the offender's current residence address pursuant to section 2950.06 of the Revised Code, and the duration of the duties. The judge shall inform the offender, at the time of sentencing, of those duties and of their duration and, if required under division (A)(2) of section 2950.03 of the Revised Code, shall perform the duties specified in that section.

†††(G) Notwithstanding divisions (A) to (E) of this section, if an offender is being sentenced for a fourth degree felony OMVI offense, the court shall impose upon the offender a mandatory term of local incarceration or a mandatory prison term in accordance with the following:

(1) Except as provided in division (G)(2)† of this section, the court shall impose upon the offender a mandatory term of local incarceration of sixty days as specified in division (A)(4) of section 4511.99 of the Revised Code and shall not reduce the term pursuant to section 2929.20, 2967.193 [2967.19.3], or any other provision

of the Revised Code. The court that imposes a mandatory term of local incarceration under this division shall specify whether the term is to be served in a jail, a community-based correctional facility, a halfway house, or an alternative residential facility, and the offender shall serve the term in the type of facility specified by the court. The court shall not sentence the offender to a prison term and shall not specify that the offender is to serve the mandatory term of local incarceration in prison. A mandatory term of local incarceration imposed under division (G)(1)† of this section is not subject to extension under section 2967.11 of the Revised Code, to a period of post-release control under section 2967.28 of the Revised Code, or to any other Revised Code provision that pertains to a prison term.

(2) If the offender previously has been sentenced to a mandatory term of local incarceration pursuant to division (G)(1)† of this section for a fourth degree felony OMVI offense, the court shall impose upon the offender a mandatory prison term of sixty days as specified in division (A)(4) of section 4511.99 of the Revised Code and shall not reduce the term pursuant to section 2929.20, 2967.193 [2967.19.3], or any other provision of the Revised Code. In no case shall an offender who once has been sentenced to a mandatory term of local incarceration pursuant to division (G)(1)† of this section for a fourth degree felony OMVI offense be sentenced to another mandatory term of local incarceration under that division for a fourth degree felony OMVI offense. the court shall not sentence the offender to a community control sanction under section 2929.16 or 2929.17 of the Revised Code. The department of rehabilitation and correction may place an offender sentenced to a mandatory prison term under this division in an intensive program prison established pursuant to section 5120.033 [5120.03.3] of the Revised Code if the department gave the sentencing judge prior notice of its intent to place the offender in an intensive program prison established under that section and if the judge did not notify the department that the judge disapproved the placement.

HISTORY: 146 v S2 (Eff 7-1-96); 146 v S 269 (Eff 7-1-96); 146 v H 445 (Eff 9-3-96); 146 v S 166 (Eff 10-17-96); HB 180. Eff 1-1-97.

Not analogous to former RC § 2929.13 (139 v S 199), repealed 146 v S 2, § 2, eff 7-1-96.

Publisher's Note

The amendments made by SB 269 (146 v —), HB 445 (146 v —), SB 166 (146 v —) and HB 180 (146 v —) have been combined. Please see provisions of RC § 1.52.

The effective date is set by section 3 of HB 180.

† This is a reference to division (G) as enacted by SB 166 (146 v —), effective 10-16-96.

†† This division (G)(1), (2) and (H) are enacted in HB 180 (146 v —), effective 1-1-97.

††† This division (G)(1), (2) is enacted in SB 166 (146 v —), effective 10-17-96.

§ 2929.14 Basic prison terms.

(A) Except as provided in division (C), (D)(2), (D)(3) (D)(4), or (G) of this section and except in relation to an offense for which a sentence of death or life imprisonment is to be imposed, if the court imposing a sentence upon an offender for a felony elects or is required to impose a prison term on the offender pursuant to this chapter and is not prohibited by division (G)(1) of section 2929.13 of the Revised Code from imposing a prison term on the offender, the court shall impose a definite prison term that shall be one of the following:

(1) For a felony of the first degree, the prison term shall be three, four, five, six, seven, eight, nine, or ten years.

(2) For a felony of the second degree, the prison term shall be two, three, four, five, six, seven, or eight years.

(3) For a felony of the third degree, the prison term shall be one, two, three, four, or five years.

(4) For a felony of the fourth degree, the prison term shall be six, seven, eight, nine, ten, eleven, twelve, thirteen, fourteen, fifteen, sixteen, seventeen, or eighteen months.

(5) For a felony of the fifth degree, the prison term shall be six, seven, eight, nine, ten, eleven, or twelve months.

(B) Except as provided in division (C), (D)(2), (D)(3), or (G) of this section or in Chapter 2925. of the Revised Code, if the court imposing a sentence upon an offender for a felony elects or is required to impose a prison term on the offender and if the offender previously has not served a prison term, the court shall impose the shortest prison term authorized for the offense pursuant to division (A) of this section, unless the court finds on the record that the shortest prison term will demean the seriousness of the offender's conduct or will not adequately protect the public from future crime by the offender or others.

(C) Except as provided in division (G) of this section or in Chapter 2925. of the Revised Code, the court imposing a sentence upon an offender for a felony may impose the longest prison term authorized for the offense pursuant to division (A) of this section only upon offenders who committed the worst forms of the offense, upon offenders who pose the greatest likelihood of committing future crimes, upon certain major drug offenders under division (D)(3) of this section, and upon certain repeat violent offenders in accordance with division (D)(2) of this section.

(D)(1)(a)(i) Except as provided in division (D)(1)(b) of this section, if an offender who is convicted of or pleads guilty to a felony also is convicted of or pleads guilty to a specification of the type described in section 2941.144 [2941.14.4] of the Revised Code that charges the offender with having a firearm that is an automatic firearm or that was equipped with a firearm muffler or silencer on or about the offender's person or under the offender's control while committing the felony, a specification of the type described in section 2941.145 [2941.14.5] of the Revised Code that charges the offender with having a firearm on or about the offender's person or under the offender's control while committing the offense and displaying the firearm, brandishing the firearm, indicating that the offender possessed the firearm, or using it to facilitate the offense, or a specification of the type described in section 2941.141 [2941.14.1] of the Revised Code that charges the offender with having a firearm on or about the offender's person or under the offender's control while committing the felony, the court, after imposing a prison term on the offender for the felony under division (A), (D)(2), or (D)(3) of this section, shall impose an additional prison term, determined pursuant to this division, that shall not be reduced pursuant to section 2929.20, section 2967.193 [2967.19.3], or any other provision of Chapter 2967. or Chapter 5120. of the Revised Code. If the specification is of the type described in section 2941.144 [2941.14.4] of the Revised Code, the additional prison term shall be six years. If the specification is of the type described in section 2941.145 [2941.14.5] of the Revised Code, the additional prison term shall be three years. If the specification is of the type described in section 2941.141 [2941.14.1] of the Revised Code, the additional prison term shall be one year. A court shall not impose more than one additional prison term on an offender under this division for felonies committed as part of the same act or transaction. If a court imposes an additional prison term under division (D)(1)(a)(ii) of this section, the court is not precluded from imposing an additional prison term under this division.

(ii) Except as provided in division (D)(1)(b) of this section, if an offender who is convicted of or pleads guilty to a violation of section 2923.161 [2923.16.1] of the Revised Code or to a felony that includes, as an essential element, purposely or knowingly causing or attempting to cause the death of or physical harm to another, also is convicted of or pleads guilty to a specification of the type described in section 2941.146 [2941.14.6] of the Revised Code that charges the offender with committing the offense by discharging a firearm from a motor vehicle, as defined in section 4501.01 of the Revised Code, other than a manufactured home, as defined in section 4501.01 of the Revised Code, the court, after imposing a prison term on the offender for the violation of section 2923.161 [2923.16.1] of the Revised Code or for the other felony offense under division (A), (D)(2), or (D)(3) of this section, shall impose an additional prison term of five years upon the offender that shall not be reduced pursuant to section 2929.20, section 2967.193 [2967.19.3], or any other provision of Chapter 2967. or Chapter 5120. of the Revised Code. A court shall not impose more than one additional prison term on an offender under this division for felonies committed as part of the same act or transaction. If a court imposes an additional prison term on an offender under this division relative to an offense, the court also shall impose an additional prison term under division (D)(1)(a)(i) of this section relative to the same offense, provided the criteria specified in that division for imposing an additional prison term are satisfied relative to the offender and the offense.

(b) The court shall not impose any of the additional prison terms described in division (D)(1)(a) of this section upon an offender for a violation of section 2923.12 or 2923.123 [2923.12.3]† of the Revised Code. The court shall not impose any of the additional prison terms described in that division upon an offender for a violation of section 2923.13 of the Revised Code unless all of the following apply:

(i) The offender previously has been convicted of aggravated murder, murder, or any felony of the first or second degree.

(ii) Less than five years have passed since the offender was released from prison or post-release control, whichever is later, for the prior offense.

(2)(a) If an offender who is convicted of or pleads guilty to a felony also is convicted of or pleads guilty to a specification of the type described in section 2941.149 [2941.14.9] of the Revised Code that the offender is a repeat violent offender, the court shall impose a prison term from the range of terms authorized for the offense under division (A) of this section that may be the longest term in the range and that shall not be reduced pursuant to section 2929.20, section 2967.193 [2967.19.3], or any other provision of Chapter 2967. or Chapter 5120. of the Revised Code. If the court finds that the repeat violent offender, in committing the offense, caused any physical harm that carried a substantial risk of death to a person or that involved substantial permanent incapacity or substantial permanent disfigurement of a person, the court shall impose the longest prison term from the range of terms authorized for the offense under division (A) of this section.

(b) If the court imposing a prison term on a repeat violent offender imposes the longest prison term from the range of terms authorized for the offense under division (A) of this section, the court may impose on the offender an additional definite prison term of one, two, three, four, five, six, seven, eight, nine, or ten years if the court finds that both of the following apply with respect to the prison terms imposed on the offender pursuant to division (D)(2)(a) of this section and, if applicable, divisions (D)(1) and (3) of this section:

(i) The terms so imposed are inadequate to punish the offender and protect the public from future crime, because the applicable factors under section 2929.12 of the Revised Code indicating a greater likelihood of recidivism outweigh the applicable factors under that section indicating a lesser likelihood of recidivism.

(ii) The terms so imposed are demeaning to the seriousness of the offense, because one or more of the factors under section 2929.12 of the Revised Code indicating that the offender's conduct is more serious than conduct normally constituting the offense are present, and they outweigh the applicable factors under that section indicating that the offender's conduct is less serious than conduct normally constituting the offense.

(3)(a) Except when an offender commits a violation of section 2903.01 or 2907.02 of the Revised Code and the penalty imposed for the violation is life imprisonment or commits a violation of section 2903.02 of the Revised Code, if the offender commits a violation of section 2925.03, 2925.04, or 2925.11 of the Revised Code and that section requires the imposition of a ten-year prison term on the offender or if a court imposing a sentence upon an offender for a felony finds that the offender is guilty of a specification of the type described in section 2941.1410 [2941.14.10] of the Revised Code, that the offender is a major drug offender, is guilty of corrupt activity with the most serious offense in the pattern of corrupt activity being a felony of the first degree, or is guilty of an attempted forcible violation of section 2907.02 of the Revised Code with the victim being under thirteen years of age and that attempted violation is the felony for which sentence is being imposed, the court shall impose upon the offender for the felony violation a ten-year prison term that cannot be reduced pursuant to section 2929.20 or Chapter 2967. or 5120. of the Revised Code.

(b) The court imposing a prison term on an offender under division (D)(3)(a) of this section may impose an additional prison term of one, two, three, four, five, six, seven, eight, nine, or ten years, if the court, with respect to the term imposed under division (D)(3)(a) of this section and, if applicable, divisions (D)(1) and (2) of this section, makes both of the findings set forth in divisions (D)(2)(b)(i) and (ii) of this section.

(4) If the offender is being sentenced for a fourth degree felony OMVI offense and if division (G)(2) of section 2929.13 of the Revised Code requires the sentencing court to impose upon the offender a mandatory prison term, the sentencing court shall impose upon the offender a mandatory prison term in accordance with that division. In addition to the mandatory prison term, the sentencing court may sentence the offender to an additional prison term of any duration specified in division (A)(4) of this section minus the sixty days imposed upon the offender as the mandatory prison term. The total of the additional prison term imposed under division (D)(4) of this section plus the sixty days imposed as the mandatory prison term shall equal one of the authorized prison terms specified in division (A)(4) of this section. If the court imposes an additional prison term under division (D)(4) of this section, the offender shall serve the additional prison term after the offender has served the mandatory prison term required for the offense. The court shall not sentence the offender to a community control sanction under section 2929.16 or 2929.17 of the Revised Code.

(E)(1) If a mandatory prison term is imposed upon an offender pursuant to division (D)(1)(a) of this section for having a firearm on or about the offender's person or under the offender's control while committing a felony or if a mandatory prison term is imposed upon an offender pursuant to division (D)(1)(b) of this section for committing a felony specified in that division by discharging a firearm from a motor vehicle, the offender shall serve the mandatory prison term consecutively to and prior to the prison term imposed for the underlying felony pursuant to division (A), (D)(2), or (D)(3) of this section or any other section of the Revised Code and consecutively to any other prison term or mandatory prison term previously or subsequently imposed upon the offender.

(2) If an offender who is an inmate in a jail, prison, or other residential detention facility violates section 2917.02, 2917.03, 2921.34, or 2921.35 of the Revised Code, if an offender who is under detention at a detention facility commits a felony violation of section 2923.131 [2923.13.1] of the Revised Code, or if an offender who is an inmate in a jail, prison, or other residential detention facility or is under detention at a detention facility commits another felony while the offender is an escapee in violation of section 2921.34 of the Revised Code, any prison term imposed upon the offender for one of those violations shall be served by the offender consecutively to the prison term or term of imprisonment the offender was serving when the offender committed that offense and to any other prison term previously or subsequently imposed upon the offender. As used in this division, "detention" and "detention facility" have the same meanings as in section 2921.01 of the Revised Code.

(3) If a prison term is imposed for a violation of division (B) of section 2911.01 of the Revised Code, the offender shall serve that prison term consecutively to any other prison term.

(4) If multiple prison terms are imposed on an offender for convictions of multiple offenses, the court may require the offender to serve the prison terms consecutively if the court finds that the consecutive service is necessary to protect the public from future crime or to punish the offender and that consecutive sentences are not disproportionate to the seriousness of the offender's conduct and to the danger the offender poses to the public, and if the court also finds any of the following:

(a) The offender committed the multiple offenses while the offender was awaiting trial or sentencing, was under a sanction imposed pursuant to section 2929.16, 2929.17, or 2929.18 of the Revised Code, or was under post-release control for a prior offense.

(b) The harm caused by the multiple offenses was so great or unusual that no single prison term for any of the offenses committed as part of a single course of conduct adequately reflects the seriousness of the offender's conduct.

(c) The offender's history of criminal conduct demonstrates that consecutive sentences are necessary to protect the public from future crime by the offender.

(5) When consecutive prison terms are imposed pursuant to division (E)(1), (2), (3), or (4) of this section, the term to be served is the aggregate of all of the terms so imposed.

(F) If a court imposes a prison term of a type described in division (B) of section 2967.28 of the Revised Code, it shall include in the sentence a requirement that the offender be subject to a period of post-release control after the offender's release from imprisonment, in accordance with that division. If a court imposes a prison term of a type described in division (C) of that section, it shall include in the sentence a requirement that the offender be subject to a period of post-release control after the offender's release from imprisonment, in accordance with that division, if the parole board determines that a period of post-release control is necessary.

(G) If a person is convicted of or pleads guilty to a sexually violent offense and also is convicted of or pleads guilty to a sexually violent predator specification that was included in the indictment, count in the indictment, or information charging that offense, the court shall impose sentence upon the offender in accordance with section 2971.03 of the Revised Code, and Chapter 2971. of the Revised Code applies regarding the prison term or term of life imprisonment without parole imposed upon the offender and the service of that term of imprisonment.

HISTORY: 146 v S 2 (Eff 7-1-96); 146 v S 269 (Eff 7-1-96); 146 v H 88 (Eff 9-3-96); 146 v H 445 (Eff 9-3-96); 146 v H 154 (Eff 10-4-96); 146 v S 166 (Eff 10-17-96); 146 v H 180 (Eff 1-1-97); 147 v H 151. Eff 9-16-97.

Not analogous to former RC § 2929.14 (139 v S 199; 145 v S 186), repealed 146 v S 2, § 2, eff 7-1-96.

† In division (D)(1)(b), [RC § 2923.12.3] RC § 2923.123 was added by HB 88 (146 v —), but is not included in the HB 151 (147 v —) composite.

The provisions of § 3 of HB 151 (147 v —) read as follows:

SECTION 3. ° ° ° Section 2929.14 of the Revised Code is presented in this act as a composite of the section as amended by Am. Sub. H.B. 88, Am. Sub. H.B. 445, Sub. H.B. 154, Am. Sub. S.B. 166, Am. Sub. S.B. 269, and Am. Sub. H.B. 180 of the 121st General Assembly, with the new language of none of the acts shown in capital letters. Section 2953.08 of the Revised Code is presented in this act as a composite of the section as amended by both Am. Sub. S.B. 269 and Am. Sub. H.B. 180 of the 121st General Assembly, with the new language of neither of the acts shown in capital letters. This is in recognition of the principle stated in division (B) of section 1.52 of the Revised Code that such amendments are to be harmonized where not substantively irreconcilable and constitutes a legislative finding that such is the resulting version in effect prior to the effective date of this act.

See provisions, § 4 of HB 180 (146 v —) following RC § 2921.34.

§ 2929.15 Community control.

(A)(1) If in sentencing an offender for a felony the court is not required to impose a prison term, a mandatory prison term, or a term of life imprisonment upon the offender, the court may directly impose a sentence that consists of one or more community control sanctions authorized pursuant to section 2929.16, 2929.17, or 2929.18 of the Revised Code. If the court is sentencing an offender for a fourth degree felony OMVI offense and if it is required to impose on the offender a mandatory term of local incarceration pursuant to division (G)(1) of section 2929.13 of the Revised Code, in addition to the mandatory term of local incarceration and the mandatory fine required by division (B)(3) of section 2929.18 of the Revised Code, the court may impose upon the offender a community control sanction or combination of community control sanctions in accordance with sections 2929.16 and 2929.17 of the Revised Code. The duration of all community control sanctions imposed upon an offender shall not exceed five years. If the court sentences the offender to one or more nonresidential sanctions under section 2929.17 of the Revised Code, the court shall comply with division (C)(1)(b) of section 2951.02 of the Revised Code and impose the mandatory condition described in that division. The court may impose any other conditions of release under a community control sanction that the court considers appropriate. If the court is sentencing an offender for a fourth degree felony OMVI offense and if it is required to impose on the offender a mandatory prison term pursuant to division (G)(2) of section 2929.13 of the Revised Code, the court shall not impose upon the offender any community control sanction or combination of community control sanctions under section 2929.16 or 2929.17 of the Revised Code.

(2)(a) If a court sentences an offender to any community control sanction or combination of community control sanctions authorized pursuant to section 2929.16, 2929.17, or 2929.18 of the Revised Code, the court shall place the offender under the general control and supervision of a department of probation in the county that serves the court for purposes of reporting to the court a violation of any of the sanctions or the mandatory condition imposed under division (C)(1)(b) of section 2951.02 of the Revised Code. Alternatively, if the offender resides in another county and a county department of probation has been established in that county or that county is served by a multicounty probation department established under section 2301.27 of the Revised Code, the court may request the court of common pleas of that county to receive the offender into the general control and supervision of that county or multicounty department of probation for purposes of reporting to the court a violation of any of the sanctions, or the mandatory condition imposed under division (C)(1)(b) of section 2951.02 of the Revised Code subject to the jurisdiction of the trial judge over and with respect to the person of the offender, and to the rules governing that department of probation.

If there is no department of probation in the county

that serves the court, the court shall place the offender, regardless of the offender's county of residence, under the general control and supervision of the adult parole authority for purposes of reporting to the court a violation of any of the sanctions or the mandatory condition imposed under division (C)(1)(b) of section 2951.02 of the Revised Code.

(b) If the court imposing sentence upon an offender sentences the offender to any community control sanction or combination of community control sanctions authorized pursuant to section 2929.16, 2929.17, or 2929.18 of the Revised Code, and if the offender violates any of the sanctions or the mandatory condition imposed under division (C)(1)(b) of section 2951.02 of the Revised Code, the public or private person or entity that operates or administers the sanction or the program or activity that comprises the sanction shall report the violation directly to the sentencing court, or shall report the violation to the county or multicounty department of probation with general control and supervision over the offender under division (A)(2)(a) of this section or the officer of that department who supervises the offender, or, if there is no such department with general control and supervision over the offender under that division, to the adult parole authority. If the public or private person or entity that operates or administers the sanction or the program or activity that comprises the sanction reports the violation to the county or multicounty department of probation or the adult parole authority, the department's or authority's officers may treat the offender as if the offender were on probation and in violation of the probation, and shall report the violation of the sanction or the mandatory condition imposed under division (C)(1)(b) of section 2951.02 of the Revised Code to the sentencing court.

(B) If the conditions of a community control sanction or the mandatory condition imposed under division (C)(1)(b) of section 2951.02 of the Revised Code is violated, the sentencing court may impose a longer time under the same sanction if the total time under the sanctions does not exceed the five-year limit specified in division (A) of this section, may impose a more restrictive sanction under section 2929.16, 2929.17, or 2929.18 of the Revised Code, or may impose a prison term on the offender pursuant to section 2929.14 of the Revised Code. The court shall not eliminate the mandatory condition imposed under division (C)(1)(b) of section 2951.02 of the Revised Code. The prison term, if any, imposed upon a violator pursuant to this division shall be within the range of prison terms available for the offense for which the sanction that was violated was imposed and shall not exceed the prison term specified in the notice provided to the offender at the sentencing hearing pursuant to division (B)(3) of section 2929.19 of the Revised Code. The court may reduce the longer period of time that the offender is required to spend under the longer sanction, the more restrictive sanction, or a prison term imposed pursuant to this division by the time the offender successfully spent under the sanction that was initially imposed.

(C) If an offender, for a significant period of time, fulfills the conditions of a sanction imposed pursuant to section 2929.16, 2929.17, or 2929.18 of the Revised Code in an exemplary manner, the court may reduce the period of time under the sanction or impose a less restrictive sanction, but the court shall not eliminate the mandatory condition imposed under division (C)(1)(b) of section 2951.02 of the Revised Code.

HISTORY: 146 v S 2 (Eff 7-1-96); 146 v S 269 (Eff 7-1-96); 146 v S 166. Eff 10-17-96.

Not analogous to former RC § 2929.15, amended and renumbered RC § 2929.22.3 in 146 v S 2, eff 7-1-96.

Publisher's Note

The amendments made by SB 269 (146 v —) and SB 166 (146 v —) have been combined. Please see provisions of RC § 1.52.

§ 2929.16 Eligibility of felons for participation in county jail industry program.

(A) The court imposing a sentence for a felony upon an offender who is not required to serve a mandatory prison term may impose any community residential sanction or combination of community residential sanctions under this section. The court imposing a sentence for a fourth degree felony OMVI offense upon an offender who is required to serve a mandatory term of local incarceration pursuant to division (G)(1) of section 2929.13 of the Revised Code may impose upon the offender, in addition to the mandatory term of local incarceration, a community residential sanction or combination of community residential sanctions under this section, and the offender shall serve or satisfy the sanction or combination of sanctions after the offender has served the mandatory term of local incarceration required for the offense. Community residential sanctions include, but are not limited to, the following:

(1) A term of up to six months at a community-based correctional facility that serves the county;

(2) Except as otherwise provided in division (A)(3) of this section, a term of up to six months in a jail, provided that the court shall not impose a sanction under this section that consists of a term in a minimum security jail for a felony of the fourth or fifth degree that is an offense of violence;

(3) If the offender is convicted of a fourth degree felony OMVI offense and is sentenced pursuant to division (G)(1) of section 2929.13 of the Revised Code, a term of up to one year in a jail less the mandatory term of local incarceration of sixty consecutive days of imprisonment imposed pursuant to that division;

(4) A term in a halfway house;

(5) A term in an alternative residential facility.

(B) The court that assigns any offender convicted of a felony to a residential sanction under this section may authorize the offender to be released so that the offender may seek or maintain employment, receive education or training, or receive treatment. A release pursuant to this division shall be only for the duration of time that is needed to fulfill the purpose of the release and for travel that reasonably is necessary to fulfill the purposes of the release.

(C) If the court assigns an offender to a county jail that is not a minimum security misdemeanant jail in a county that has established a county jail industry program pursuant to section 5147.30 of the Revised Code, the court shall specify, as part of the sentence, whether the sheriff of that county may consider the offender for participation in the county jail industry program. During the offender's term in the county jail, the court shall retain jurisdiction to modify its specification upon a reassessment of the offender's qualifications for participation in the program.

HISTORY: 146 v S 2 (Eff 7-1-96); 146 v S 269 (Eff 7-1-96); 146 v H 480 (Eff 10-16-96); 146 v S 166 (Eff 10-17-96); 146 v H 72. Eff 3-18-97.

Analogous in part to former RC § 2929.16 (143 v H 51), repealed 146 v S 2, eff 7-1-96.

The provisions of § 5 of HB 72 (146 v —) read as follows:

SECTION 5. ° ° ° Section 2929.16 of the Revised Code is presented in this act as a composite of the section as amended by Sub. H.B. 480, Am. Sub. S.B. 166, and Am. Sub. S.B. 269 of the 121st General Assembly, with the new language of none of the acts shown in capital letters.

° ° °

This is in recognition of the principle stated in division (B) of section 1.52 of the Revised Code that such amendments are to be harmonized where not substantively irreconcilable and constitutes a legislative finding that such is the resulting version in effect prior to the effective date of this act.

§ 2929.17 Nonresidential sanctions.

The court imposing a sentence for a felony upon an offender who is not required to serve a mandatory prison term may impose any nonresidential sanction or combination of nonresidential sanctions authorized under this section. If the court imposes one or more nonresidential sanctions authorized under this section, the court shall comply with division (C)(1)(b) of section 2951.02 of the Revised Code and impose the mandatory condition described in that division. The court imposing a sentence for a fourth degree felony OMVI offense upon an offender who is required to serve a mandatory term of local incarceration under division (G)(1) of section 2929.13 of the Revised Code may impose upon the offender, in addition to the mandatory term of local incarceration, a nonresidential sanction or combination of nonresidential sanctions under this section, and the offender shall serve or satisfy the sanction or combination of sanctions after the offender has served the mandatory term of local incarceration required for the offense. Nonresidential sanctions include, but are not limited to, the following:

(A) A term of day reporting;

(B) A term of electronically monitored house arrest, a term of electronic monitoring without house arrest, or a term of house arrest without electronic monitoring;

(C) A term of community service of up to five hundred hours pursuant to division (F) of section 2951.02 of the Revised Code or, if the court determines that the offender is financially incapable of fulfilling a financial sanction described in section 2929.18 of the Revised Code, a term of community service as an alternative to a financial sanction;

(D) A term in a drug treatment program with a level of security for the offender as determined necessary by the court;

(E) A term of intensive supervision;

(F) A term of basic supervision;

(G) A term of monitored time;

(H) A term of drug and alcohol use monitoring;

(I) A curfew term;

(J) A requirement that the offender obtain employment;

(K) A requirement that the offender obtain education or training;

(L) Provided the court obtains the prior approval of the victim, a requirement that the offender participate in victim-offender mediation;

(M) A license violation report.

HISTORY: 146 v S 2 (Eff 7-1-96); 146 v S 269 (Eff 7-1-96); 146 v S 166. Eff 10-17-96.

Not analogous to former RC § 2929.17, amended and renumbered RC § 2929.24 in 146 v S 2, eff 7-1-96.

Comment, Legislative Service Commission

Section 2929.17 of the Revised Code is amended by this act [Am. Sub. S.B. 166] and also by Am. Sub. S.B. 269 of the 121st General Assembly. Comparison of these amendments in pursuance of section 1.52 of the Revised Code discloses that they are not irreconcilable so that they are required by that section to be harmonized to give effect to each amendment.

§ 2929.18 Financial sanctions; restitution.

(A) Except as otherwise provided in this division and in addition to imposing court costs pursuant to section 2947.23 of the Revised Code, the court imposing a sentence upon an offender for a felony may sentence the offender to any financial sanction or combination of financial sanctions authorized under this section or, in the circumstances specified in section 2929.25 of the Revised Code, may impose upon the offender a fine in accordance with that section. If the offender is sentenced to a sanction of confinement pursuant to section 2929.14 or 2929.16 of the Revised Code that is to be served in a facility operated by a board of county commissioners, a legislative authority of a municipal corporation, or another local governmental entity, the court imposing sentence upon an offender for a felony shall comply with division (A)(4)(b) of this section in determining whether to sentence the offender to a financial sanction described in division (A)(4)(a) of this section. Financial sanctions that may be imposed pursuant to this section include, but are not limited to, the following:

(1) Restitution by the offender to the victim of the offender's crime or any survivor of the victim, in an amount based on the victim's economic loss. The court shall order that the restitution be made to the adult probation department that serves the county on behalf of the victim, to the clerk of courts, or to another agency designated by the court, except that it may include a requirement that reimbursement be made to third parties for amounts paid to or on behalf of the victim or any survivor of the victim for economic loss resulting from the offense. If reimbursement to third parties is required, the reimbursement shall be made to any governmental agency to repay any amounts paid by the agency to or on behalf of the victim or any survivor of the victim for economic loss resulting from the offense before any reimbursement is made to any person other than a governmental agency. If no governmental agency incurred expenses for economic loss of the victim or any survivor of the victim resulting from the offense, the reimbursement shall be made to any person other than a governmental agency to repay amounts paid by that person to or on behalf of the victim or any survivor of the victim for economic loss resulting from the offense. The court shall not require an offender to repay an insurance company for any amounts the company paid on behalf of the offender pursuant to a policy of insurance. At sentencing, the court shall determine the amount of restitution to be made by the offender. All restitution payments shall be credited against any recovery of economic loss in a civil action brought by the victim or any survivor of the victim against the offender.

(2) Except as provided in division (B)(1), (3), or (4) of this section, a fine payable by the offender to the state, to a political subdivision, or as described in division (B)(2) of this section to one or more law enforcement agencies, with the amount of the fine based on a standard percentage of the offender's daily income over a period of time determined by the court and based upon the seriousness of the offense. A fine ordered under this division shall not exceed the statutory fine amount authorized for the level of the offense under division (A)(3) of this section.

(3) Except as provided in division (B)(1), (3), or (4) of this section, a fine payable by the offender to the state, to a political subdivision when appropriate for a felony, or as described in division (B)(2) of this section to one or more law enforcement agencies, in the following amount:

(a) For a felony of the first degree, not more than twenty thousand dollars;

(b) For a felony of the second degree, not more than fifteen thousand dollars;

(c) For a felony of the third degree, not more than ten thousand dollars;

(d) For a felony of the fourth degree, not more than five thousand dollars;

(e) For a felony of the fifth degree, not more than two thousand five hundred dollars.

(4)(a) Subject to division (A)(4)(b) of this section, reimbursement by the offender of any or all of the costs of sanctions incurred by the government, including the following:

(i) All or part of the costs of implementing any community control sanction;

(ii) All or part of the costs of confinement under a sanction imposed pursuant to section 2929.14 or 2929.16 of the Revised Code, provided that the amount of reimbursement ordered under this division shall not exceed ten thousand dollars or the total amount of reimbursement the offender is able to pay as determined at a hearing, whichever amount is greater;

(b) If the offender is sentenced to a sanction of confinement pursuant to section 2929.14 or 2929.16 of the Revised Code that is to be served in a facility operated by a board of county commissioners, a legislative authority of a municipal corporation, or another local governmental entity, one of the following applies:

(i) If, pursuant to section 307.93, 341.14, 341.19, 341.23, 753.02, 753.04, 753.16, 2301.56, or 2947.19 of the Revised Code, the board, legislative authority, or other local governmental entity requires prisoners convicted of an offense other than a minor misdemeanor to reimburse the county, municipal corporation, or other entity for its expenses incurred by reason of the prisoner's confinement, the court shall impose a financial sanction under division (A)(4)(a) of this section that requires the offender to reimburse the county, municipal corporation, or other local governmental entity for the cost of the confinement. In addition, the court may impose any other financial sanction under this section.

(ii) If, pursuant to any section identified in division (A)(4)(b)(i) of this section, the board, legislative authority, or other local governmental entity has adopted a resolution or ordinance specifying that prisoners convicted of felonies are not required to reimburse the county, municipal corporation, or other local governmental entity for its expenses incurred by reason of the prisoner's confinement, the court shall not impose a financial sanction under division (A)(4)(a) of this section that requires the offender to reimburse the county, municipal corporation, or other local governmental entity for the cost of the confinement, but the court may impose any other financial sanction under this section.

(iii) If neither division (A)(4)(b)(i) nor (A)(4)(b)(ii) of this section applies, the court may impose, but is not required to impose, any financial sanction under this section.

(c) Reimbursement by the offender for costs pursuant to section 2929.28 of the Revised Code.

(B)(1) For a first, second, or third degree felony violation of any provision of Chapter 2925., 3719., or 4729. of the Revised Code, the sentencing court shall impose upon the offender a mandatory fine of at least one-half of, but not more than, the maximum statutory fine amount authorized for the level of the offense pursuant to division (A)(3) of this section. If an offender alleges in an affidavit filed with the court prior to sentencing that the offender is indigent and unable to pay the mandatory fine and if the court determines the offender is an indigent person and is unable to pay the mandatory fine described in this division, the court shall not impose the mandatory fine upon the offender.

(2) Any mandatory fine imposed upon an offender under division (B)(1) of this section and any fine imposed upon an offender under division (A)(2) or (3) of this section for any fourth or fifth degree felony violation of any provision of Chapter 2925., 3719., or 4729. of the Revised Code shall be paid to law enforcement agencies pursuant to division (F) of section 2925.03 of the Revised Code.

(3) For a fourth degree felony OMVI offense, the sentencing court shall impose upon the offender a mandatory fine in the amount specified in division (A)(4) of section 4511.99 of the Revised Code. The mandatory fine so imposed shall be disbursed as provided in division (A)(4) of section 4511.99 of the Revised Code.

(4) Notwithstanding any fine otherwise authorized or required to be imposed under division (A)(2) or (3) or (B)(1) of this section or section 2929.31 of the Revised Code for a violation of section 2925.03 of the Revised Code, in addition to any penalty or sanction imposed for that offense under section 2925.03 or sections 2929.11 to 2929.18 of the Revised Code and in addition to the forfeiture of property in connection with the offense as prescribed in sections 2925.42 to 2925.45 of the Revised Code, the court that sentences an offender for a violation of section 2925.03 of the Revised Code may impose upon the offender a fine in addition to any fine imposed under division (A)(2) or (3) of this section and in addition to any mandatory fine imposed under division (B)(1) of this section. The fine imposed under division (B)(4) of this section shall be used as provided in division (H) of section 2925.03 of the Revised Code. A fine imposed under division (B)(4) of this section shall not exceed whichever of the following is applicable:

(a) The total value of any personal or real property in which the offender has an interest and that was used in the course of, intended for use in the course of, derived from, or realized through conduct in violation of section 2925.03 of the Revised Code, including any property that constitutes proceeds derived from that offense;

(b) If the offender has no interest in any property of the type described in division (B)(4)(a) of this section or if it is not possible to ascertain whether the offender has an interest in any property of that type in which the offender may have an interest, the amount of the mandatory fine for the offense imposed under division (B)(1) of this section or, if no mandatory fine is imposed under division (B)(1) of this section, the amount of the fine authorized for the level of the offense imposed under division (A)(3) of this section.

(5) Prior to imposing a fine under division (B)(4) of this section, the court shall determine whether the offender has an interest in any property of the type described in division (B)(4)(a) of this section. Except as provided in division (B)(6) or (7) of this section, a fine that is authorized and imposed under division (B)(4) of this section does not limit or affect the imposition of the penalties and sanctions for a violation of section 2925.03 prescribed under that section or sections 2929.11 to 2929.18 of the Revised Code and does not limit or affect a forfeiture of property in connection with the offense as prescribed in sections 2925.42 to 2925.45 of the Revised Code.

(6) If the sum total of a mandatory fine amount imposed for a first, second, or third degree felony violation of section 2925.03 of the Revised Code under division (B)(1) of this section plus the amount of any fine imposed under division (B)(4) of this section does not exceed the maximum statutory fine amount authorized for the level of the offense under division (A)(3) of this section or section 2929.31 of the Revised Code, the court may impose a fine for the offense in addition to the mandatory fine and the fine imposed under division (B)(4) of this section. The sum total of the amounts of the mandatory fine, the fine imposed under division (B)(4) of this section, and the additional fine imposed under division (B)(6) of this section shall not exceed the maximum statutory fine amount authorized for the level of the offense under division (A)(3) of this section or section 2929.31 of the Revised Code. The clerk of the court shall pay any fine that is imposed under division (B)(6) of this section to the county, township, municipal corporation, park district as created pursuant to section 511.18 or 1545.04 of the Revised Code, or state law enforcement agencies in this state that primarily were responsible for or involved in making the arrest of, and in prosecuting, the offender pursuant to division (F) of section 2925.03 of the Revised Code.

(7) If the sum total of the amount of a mandatory fine imposed for a first, second, or third degree felony violation of section 2925.03 of the Revised Code plus the amount of any fine imposed under division (B)(4) of this section exceeds the maximum statutory fine amount authorized for the level of the offense under division (A)(3) of this section or section 2929.31 of the Revised Code, the court shall not impose a fine under division (B)(6) of this section.

(C)(1) The offender shall pay reimbursements imposed upon the offender pursuant to division (A)(4)(a) of this section to pay the costs incurred by the department of rehabilitation and correction in operating a prison or other facility used to confine offenders pursuant to sanctions imposed under section 2929.14 or 2929.16 of the Revised Code to the treasurer of state. The treasurer of state shall deposit the reimbursements in the confinement cost reimbursement fund that is hereby created in the state treasury. The department of rehabilitation and correction shall use the amounts deposited in the fund to fund the operation of facilities used to confine offenders pursuant to sections 2929.14 and 2929.16 of the Revised Code.

(2) Except as provided in section 2951.021 [2951.02.1] of the Revised Code, the offender shall pay reimbursements imposed upon the offender pursuant to division (A)(4)(a) of this section to pay the costs incurred by a county pursuant to any sanction imposed under this section or section 2929.16 or 2929.17 of the Revised Code or in operating a facility used to confine offenders pursuant to a sanction imposed under section 2929.16 of the Revised Code to the county treasurer. The county treasurer shall deposit the reimbursements in the sanction cost reimbursement fund that each board of county commissioners shall create in its county treasury. The county shall use the amounts deposited in the fund to pay the costs incurred by the county pursuant to any sanction imposed under this section or section 2929.16 or 2929.17 of the Revised Code or in operating a facility used to confine offenders pursuant to a sanction imposed under section 2929.16 of the Revised Code.

(3) Except as provided in section 2951.021 [2951.02.1] of the Revised Code, the offender shall pay reimbursements imposed upon the offender pursuant to division (A)(4)(a) of this section to pay the costs incurred by a municipal corporation pursuant to any sanction imposed under this section or section 2929.16 or 2929.17 of the Revised Code or in operating a facility used to confine offenders pursuant to a sanction imposed under section 2929.16 of the Revised Code to the treasurer of the municipal corporation. The treasurer shall deposit the reimbursements in a special fund that shall be established in the treasury of each municipal corporation. The municipal corporation shall use the amounts deposited in the fund to pay the costs incurred by the municipal corporation pursuant to any sanction imposed under this section or section 2929.16 or 2929.17 of the Revised Code or in operating a facility used to confine offenders pursuant to a sanction imposed under section 2929.16 of the Revised Code.

(4) Except as provided in section 2951.021 [2951.02.1] of the Revised Code, the offender shall pay reimbursements imposed pursuant to division (A)(4)(a) of this section for the costs incurred by a private provider pursuant to a sanction imposed under this section or section 2929.16 or 2929.17 of the Revised Code to the provider.

(D) A financial sanction imposed pursuant to division (A) or (B) of this section is a judgment in favor of the state or a political subdivision in which the court that imposed the financial sanction is located, and the offender subject to the sanction is the judgment debtor, except that a financial sanction of reimbursement imposed pursuant to division (A)(4)(a)(ii) of this section upon an offender who is incarcerated in a state facility or a municipal jail is a judgment in favor of the state or the municipal corporation, a financial sanction of reimbursement imposed upon an offender pursuant to this section for costs incurred by a private provider of sanctions is a judgment in favor of the private provider, and a financial sanction of restitution imposed pursuant to this section is a judgment in favor of the victim of the offender's criminal act. Once the financial sanction is imposed as a judgment, the victim, private provider, state, or political subdivision may bring an action to do any of the following:

(1) Obtain execution of the judgment through any available procedure, including:

(a) An execution against the property of the judgment debtor under Chapter 2329. of the Revised Code;

(b) An execution against the person of the judgment debtor under Chapter 2331. of the Revised Code;

(c) A proceeding in aid of execution under Chapter 2333. of the Revised Code, including:

(i) A proceeding for the examination of the judgment debtor under sections 2333.09 to 2333.12 and sections 2333.15 to 2333.27 of the Revised Code;

(ii) A proceeding for attachment of the person of the judgment debtor under section 2333.28 of the Revised Code;

(iii) A creditor's suit under section 2333.01 of the Revised Code.

(d) The attachment of the property of the judgment debtor under Chapter 2715. of the Revised Code;

(e) The garnishment of the property of the judgment debtor under Chapter 2716. of the Revised Code.

(2) Obtain an order for the assignment of wages of the judgment debtor under section 1321.33 of the Revised Code.

(E) A court that imposes a financial sanction upon an offender may hold a hearing if necessary to determine whether the offender is able to pay the sanction or is likely in the future to be able to pay it.

(F) Each court imposing a financial sanction upon an offender under this section or under section 2929.25 of the Revised Code may designate a court employee to collect, or may enter into contracts with one or more public agencies or private vendors for the collection of, amounts due under the financial sanction imposed pursuant to this section or section 2929.25 of the Revised Code. Before entering into a contract for the collection of amounts due from an offender pursuant to any financial sanction imposed pursuant to this section or section 2929.25 of the Revised Code, a court shall comply with sections 307.86 to 307.92 of the Revised Code.

(G) If a court that imposes a financial sanction under division (A) or (B) of this section finds that an offender satisfactorily has completed all other sanctions imposed upon the offender and that all restitution that has been ordered has been paid as ordered, the court may suspend any financial sanctions imposed pursuant to this section or section 2929.25 of the Revised Code that have not been paid.

(H) No financial sanction imposed under this section or section 2929.25 of the Revised Code shall preclude a victim from bringing a civil action against the offender.

HISTORY: 146 v S 2 (Eff 7-1-96); 146 v S 269 (Eff 7-1-96); 146 v H 480 (Eff 10-16-96); 146 v S 166. Eff 10-17-96.

See provisions, § 4 of SB 166 (146 v —) following RC § 2925.03.

Comment, Legislative Service Commission

Section 2929.18 of the Revised Code is amended by this act [Am. Sub. S.B. 166] and also by Sub. H.B. 480 and Am. Sub. S.B. 269, both of the 121st General Assembly. Comparison of these amendments in pursuance of section 1.52 of the Revised Code discloses that they are not irreconcilable so that they are required by that section to be harmonized to give effect to each amendment.

[§ 2929.18.1] § 2929.181 Repealed, 146 v S 269, § 2 [146 v S 2]. Eff 7-1-96.

This section concerned determination of offender's ability to pay; withholding or deduction orders. See now section 2929.18(E). The repeal by SB 269 (146 v —) apparently controls over an amendment by HB 480 (146 v —), effective 10-16-96. For the text of the amendment, see Legislative Bulletin #8, page 1609.

The effective date is set by section 5 of SB 269.

§ 2929.19 Sentencing hearing.

(A)(1) The court shall hold a sentencing hearing before imposing a sentence under this chapter upon an offender who was convicted of or pleaded guilty to a felony and before resentencing an offender who was convicted of or pleaded guilty to a felony and whose case was remanded pursuant to section 2953.07 or 2953.08 of the Revised Code. At the hearing, the offender, the prosecuting attorney, the victim or the victim's representative in accordance with section 2930.14 of the Revised Code, and, with the approval of the court, any other person may present information relevant to the imposition of sentence in the case. The court shall inform the offender of the verdict of the jury or finding of the court and ask the offender whether the offender has anything to say as to why sentence should not be imposed upon the offender.

(2) Except as otherwise provided in this division, before imposing sentence on an offender who is being sentenced for a sexually oriented offense that was committed on or after the effective date of this amendment and that is not a sexually violent offense, and before imposing sentence on an offender who is being sentenced for a sexually violent offense committed on or after the effective date of this amendment and who was not charged with a sexually violent predator specification in the indictment, count in the indictment, or information charging the sexually violent offense, the court shall conduct a hearing in accordance with division (B) of section 2950.09 of the Revised Code to determine whether the offender is a sexual predator. The court shall not conduct a hearing under that division if the offender is being sentenced for a sexually violent offense and a sexually violent predator specification was included in the indictment, count in the indictment, or information charging the sexually violent offense. Before imposing sentence on an offender who is being sentenced for a sexually oriented offense, the court also shall comply with division (E) of section 2950.09 of the Revised Code.

(B)(1) At the sentencing hearing, the court, before imposing sentence, shall consider the record, any information presented at the hearing by any person pursuant to division (A) of this section, and, if one was prepared, the presentence investigation report made pursuant to section 2951.03 of the Revised Code or Criminal Rule 32.2, and any victim impact statement made pursuant to section 2947.051 [2947.05.1] of the Revised Code.

(2) The court shall impose a sentence and shall make a finding that gives its reasons for selecting the sentence imposed in any of the following circumstances:

(a) Unless the offense is a sexually violent offense for which the court is required to impose sentence pursuant to division (G) of section 2929.14 of the Revised Code, if it imposes a prison term for a felony of the fourth or fifth degree or for a felony drug offense that is a violation of a provision of Chapter 2925. of the Revised Code and that is specified as being subject to division (B) of section 2929.13 of the Revised Code for purposes of sentencing and, if the term is not a mandatory prison term imposed pursuant to division (G)(2) of section 2929.13 of the Revised Code for a felony OMVI offense, its reasons for imposing the prison term, based upon the overriding purposes and principles of felony sentencing set forth in section 2929.11 of the Revised Code, and any factors listed in divisions (B)(1)(a) to (h) of section 2929.13 of the Revised Code that it found to apply relative to the offender.

(b) If it does not impose a prison term for a felony of the first or second degree or for a felony drug offense that is a violation of a provision of Chapter 2925. of the Revised Code and for which a presumption in favor of a prison term is specified as being applicable, its reasons for not imposing the prison term and for overriding the presumption, based upon the overriding purposes and principles of felony sentencing set forth in section 2929.11 of the Revised Code, and the basis of the findings it made under divisions (D)(1) and (2) of section 2929.13 of the Revised Code.

(c) If it imposes consecutive sentences under section 2929.14 of the Revised Code, its reasons for imposing the consecutive sentences.

(d) If the sentence is for one offense and it imposes a prison term for the offense that is the maximum prison term allowed for that offense by division (A) of section 2929.14 of the Revised Code, its reasons for imposing the maximum prison term;

(e) If the sentence is for two or more offenses arising

out of a single incident and it imposes a prison term for those offenses that is the maximum prison term allowed for the offense of the highest degree by division (A) of section 2929.14 of the Revised Code, its reasons for imposing the maximum prison term.

(3) Subject to division (B)(4) of this section, if the sentencing court determines at the sentencing hearing that a prison term is necessary or required, the court shall do all of the following:

(a) Impose a stated prison term;

(b) Notify the offender that the parole board may extend the stated prison term if the offender commits any criminal offense under the laws of this state or the United States while serving the prison term, that the extension will be done administratively as part of the offender's sentence in accordance with section 2967.11 of the Revised Code and may be for thirty, sixty, or ninety days for each violation, that all extensions of any stated prison term for all violations during the course of the term may not exceed one-half of the term's duration, and that the sentence so imposed automatically includes any extension of the stated prison term by the parole board;

(c) Subject to division (B)(4) of this section, if the offender is being sentenced for a felony of the first degree, for a felony of the second degree, for a felony sex offense, as defined in section 2967.28 of the Revised Code, or for a felony of the third degree that is not a felony sex offense and in the commission of which the offender caused or threatened to cause physical harm to a person, notify the offender that a period of post-release control pursuant to section 2967.28 of the Revised Code will be imposed following the offender's release from prison;

(d) Subject to division (B)(4) of this section, if the offender is being sentenced for a felony of the third, fourth, or fifth degree that is not subject to division (B)(3)(c) of this section, notify the offender that a period of post-release control pursuant to section 2967.28 of the Revised Code may be imposed following the offender's release from prison.

(e) Notify the offender that, if a period of post-release control is imposed following the offender's release from prison, as described in division (B)(3)(c) or (d) of this section, and if the offender violates a post-release control sanction imposed as a component of the post-release control including the mandatory condition described in division (A) of section 2967.121 [2967.12.1] of the Revised Code, all of the following apply:

(i) The adult parole authority or the parole board may impose a more restrictive post-release control sanction.

(ii) The parole board may increase the duration of the post-release control subject to a specified maximum.

(iii) The more restrictive sanction that the parole board may impose may consist of a prison term, provided that the prison term cannot exceed nine months and the maximum cumulative prison term so imposed for all violations during the period of post-release control cannot exceed one-half of the stated prison term originally imposed upon the offender.

(iv) If the violation of the sanction is a felony, the offender may be prosecuted for the felony and, in addition to any sentence it imposes on the offender for the new felony, the court may impose a prison term, subject to a specified maximum, for the violation.

(4) If the offender is being sentenced for a sexually violent offense that the offender committed on or after the effective date of this amendment and the offender also is convicted of or pleads guilty to a sexually violent predator specification that was included in the indictment, count in the indictment, or information charging the sexually violent offense or if the offender is being sentenced for a sexually oriented offense that the offender committed on or after the effective date of this section and the court imposing the sentence has determined pursuant to division (B) of section 2950.09 of the Revised Code that the offender is a sexual predator, the court shall include in the offender's sentence a statement that the offender has been adjudicated as being a sexual predator and shall comply with the requirements of section 2950.03 of the Revised Code. Additionally, in the circumstances described in division (G) of section 2929.14 of the Revised Code, the court shall impose sentence on the offender as described in that division.

(5) If the sentencing court determines at the sentencing hearing that a community control sanction should be imposed and the court is not prohibited from imposing a community control sanction, the court shall impose a community control sanction. The court shall notify the offender that, if the conditions of the sanction are violated, the court may impose a longer time under the same sanction, may impose a more restrictive sanction, or may impose a prison term on the offender and shall indicate the specific prison term that may be imposed as a sanction for the violation, as selected by the court from the range of prison terms for the offense pursuant to section 2929.14 of the Revised Code.

(6) Before imposing a financial sanction under section 2929.18 of the Revised Code, the court shall consider the offender's ability to pay and other matters under section 2929.181 [2929.18.1] of the Revised Code.

(C)(1) If the offender is being sentenced for a fourth degree felony OMVI offense and if the court is required by division (G)(1) of section 2929.13 of the Revised Code to impose as a sanction a mandatory term of local incarceration, the court shall impose the mandatory term of local incarceration in accordance with that division, shall impose a mandatory fine in accordance with division (B)(3) of section 2929.18 of the Revised Code, and, in addition, may impose additional sanctions as specified in sections 2929.15, 2929.16, 2929.17, and 2929.18 of the Revised Code. The court shall not impose a prison term on the offender.

(2) If the offender is being sentenced for a fourth

degree felony OMVI offense and if the court is required by division (G)(2) of section 2929.13 of the Revised Code to impose as a sanction a mandatory prison term, the court shall impose the mandatory prison term in accordance with that division, shall impose a mandatory fine in accordance with division (B)(3) of section 2929.18 of the Revised Code, and, in addition, may impose an additional prison term as specified in section 2929.14 of the Revised Code. The court shall not impose any community control sanction on the offender.

HISTORY: 146 v S 2 (Eff 7-1-96); 146 v S 269 (Eff 7-1-96); 146 v S 166 (Eff 10-17-96); 146 v H 180. Eff 1-1-97.

The effective date is set by section 3 of HB 180.

See provisions, § 4 of HB 180 (146 v —) following RC § 2921.34.

Comment, Legislative Service Commission

Section 2929.19 of the Revised Code is amended by this act [Am. Sub. S.B. 166] and also by Am. Sub. H.B. 180 and Am. Sub. S.B. 269, both of the 121st General Assembly. Comparison of these amendments in pursuance of section 1.52 of the Revised Code discloses that they are not irreconcilable so that they are required by that section to be harmonized to give effect to each amendment.

§ 2929.20 Judicial release.

(A)(1) As used in this section, "eligible offender" means any of the following:

(a) A person who has been convicted of or pleaded guilty to a felony, who is serving a stated prison term of ten years or less, and who is not serving a mandatory prison term;

(b) A person who has been convicted of or pleaded guilty to a felony, who was sentenced to a mandatory prison term and another prison term of ten years or less, and who has served the mandatory prison term;

(c) A person who has been convicted of or pleaded guilty to a felony, who was sentenced to a mandatory prison term pursuant to division (D)(1) of section 2929.14 of the Revised Code and another prison term of ten years or less, who is required by division (E)(1) of section 2929.14 of the Revised Code to serve the mandatory prison term and the other prison term consecutively, and who has served the mandatory prison term.

(2) "Eligible offender" does not include any of the following:

(a) A person who has been convicted of or pleaded guilty to a felony, who was sentenced to a mandatory prison term pursuant to division (D)(2) or (3) of section 2929.14 of the Revised Code and another prison term of ten years or less, and who is required by division (E)(2), (3), or, (4) of section 2929.14 of the Revised Code to serve the mandatory prison term and the other prison term consecutively, whether or not the person has served the mandatory prison term.

(b) A person who has been convicted of or pleaded guilty to a felony, who was sentenced to a mandatory prison term pursuant to divisions (D)(1) and (2), or division (D)(3) of section 2929.14 of the Revised Code and another prison term of ten years or less, and who is required by division (E)(1), (2), (3), or (4) of section 2929.14 of the Revised Code to serve any of the mandatory prison terms and the other prison term consecutively, whether or not the person has served the mandatory prison terms.

(B) Upon the filing of a motion by the eligible offender or upon its own motion, a sentencing court may reduce the offender's stated prison term through a judicial release in accordance with this section. An eligible offender may file a motion for judicial release with the sentencing court within the following applicable period of time:

(1) If the stated prison term was imposed for a felony of the fourth or fifth degree, the eligible offender shall file the motion not earlier than thirty days or later than ninety days after the offender is delivered to a state correctional institution.

(2) Except as otherwise provided in division (B)(3) of this section, if the stated prison term was imposed for a felony of the first, second, or third degree, the eligible offender shall file the motion not earlier than one hundred eighty days after the offender is delivered to a state correctional institution.

(3) If the stated prison term is five years or more and less than ten years, the eligible offender shall file the motion after the eligible offender has served five years of the stated prison term.

(4) If the offender was sentenced to a mandatory prison term pursuant to division (D)(1) of section 2929.14 of the Revised Code and a consecutive prison term other than a mandatory prison term that is ten years or less, the offender shall file the motion within the time authorized under division (B)(1), (2), or (3) of this section for the felony for which the prison term other than the mandatory prison term was imposed, but the time for filing the motion does not begin to run until after the expiration of the mandatory prison term.

(C) Upon receipt of a timely motion for judicial release filed by an eligible offender under division (B) of this section or upon the sentencing court's own motion made within the appropriate time period specified in that division, the court may schedule a hearing on the motion. The court may deny the motion without a hearing but shall not grant the motion in any case without a hearing. If a court denies without a hearing a motion filed by an eligible offender or on its own motion that relates to an eligible offender, the court may consider a subsequent judicial release for that eligible offender on its own motion or a subsequent motion for judicial release filed by that eligible offender. If a court denies after a hearing a motion filed by an eligible offender or its own motion that relates to an eligible offender, the court shall not consider a subsequent motion for that eligible offender. The court shall hold only one hearing for any eligible offender.

A hearing under this section shall be conducted in

open court within sixty days after the date on which the motion is filed, provided that the court may delay the hearing for a period not to exceed one hundred eighty additional days. If the court schedules a hearing on the motion, the court shall enter a ruling on the motion within ten days after the hearing. If the court denies the motion without a hearing, the court shall enter its ruling on the motion within sixty days after the motion is filed.

(D) If a court schedules a hearing on the motion filed by an eligible offender under this section or on its own motion, the court shall notify the eligible offender of the hearing. The eligible offender promptly shall serve a copy of the notice of the hearing on the head of the state correctional institution in which the eligible offender is confined. If the court schedules a hearing for judicial release, the court promptly shall give notice of the hearing to the prosecuting attorney of the county in which the eligible offender was indicted. Upon receipt of the notice from the court, the prosecuting attorney shall notify the victim of the offense for which the stated prison term was imposed or the victim's representative, pursuant to section 2930.16 of the Revised Code, of the hearing.

(E) Prior to the date of the hearing on a motion for judicial release under this section, the head of the state correctional institution in which the eligible offender in question is confined shall send to the court a report on the eligible offender's conduct in the institution and in any institution from which the eligible offender may have been transferred. The report shall cover the eligible offender's participation in school, vocational training, work, treatment, and other rehabilitative activities and any disciplinary action taken against the eligible offender. The report shall be made part of the record of the hearing.

(F) If the court grants a hearing on a motion for judicial release under this section, the eligible offender shall attend the hearing if ordered to do so by the court. Upon receipt of a copy of the journal entry containing the order, the head of the state correctional institution in which the eligible offender is incarcerated shall deliver the eligible offender to the sheriff of the county in which the hearing is to be held. The sheriff shall convey the eligible offender to the hearing and return the offender to the institution after the hearing.

(G) At the hearing on a motion for judicial release under this section, the court shall afford the eligible offender and the eligible offender's counsel an opportunity to present written information relevant to the motion and shall afford the eligible offender, if present, and the eligible offender's attorney to present oral information relevant to the motion. The court shall afford a similar opportunity to the prosecuting attorney, the victim or the victim's representative, as defined in section 2930.01 of the Revised Code, and any other person the court determines is likely to present additional relevant information. The court shall consider any statement of a victim made pursuant to section 2930.14 or 2930.17 of the Revised Code and any victim impact statement prepared pursuant to section 2947.051 [2947.05.1] of the Revised Code. After ruling on the motion, the court shall notify the victim of the ruling in accordance with sections 2930.03 and 2930.16 of the Revised Code.

(H)(1) A court shall not grant a judicial release under this section to an eligible offender who is imprisoned for a felony of the first or second degree, or to an eligible offender who committed an offense contained in Chapter 2925. or 3719. of the Revised Code and for whom there was a presumption under section 2929.13 of the Revised Code in favor of a prison term, unless the court, with reference to factors under section 2929.12 of the Revised Code, finds both of the following:

(a) That a sanction other than a prison term would adequately punish the offender and protect the public from future criminal violations by the eligible offender because the applicable factors indicating a lesser likelihood of recidivism outweigh the applicable factors indicating a greater likelihood of recidivism;

(b) That a sanction other than a prison term would not demean the seriousness of the offense because factors indicating that the eligible offender's conduct in committing the offense was less serious than conduct normally constituting the offense outweigh factors indicating that the eligible offender's conduct was more serious than conduct normally constituting the offense.

(2) A court that grants a judicial release to an eligible offender under division (H)(1) of this section shall specify on the record both findings required in that division and also shall list all the factors described in that division that were presented at the hearing.

(I) If the court grants a motion for judicial release under this section, the court shall order the release of the eligible offender, shall place the eligible offender under an appropriate community control sanction, under a mandatory condition of the type described in division (A) of section 2967.131 [2967.13.1] of the Revised Code, and under the supervision of the department of probation serving the court, and shall reserve the right to reimpose the sentence that it reduced pursuant to the judicial release if the offender violates the sanction. If the court reimposes the reduced sentence pursuant to this reserved right, it may do so either concurrently with, or consecutive to, any new sentence imposed upon the eligible offender as a result of the violation. The period of the community control sanction shall be no longer than five years. The court, in its discretion, may reduce the period of the community control sanction by the amount of time the eligible offender spent in jail for the offense and in prison. If the court made any findings pursuant to division (H)(1) of this section, the court shall serve a copy of the findings upon counsel for the parties within fifteen days after the date on which the court grants the motion for judicial release.

Prior to being released pursuant to a judicial release

granted under this section, the eligible offender shall serve any extension of sentence that was imposed under section 2967.11 of the Revised Code.

HISTORY: 146 v S 2 (Eff 7-1-96); 146 v S 269 (Eff 7-1-96); 147 v H 151. Eff 9-16-97.

[PENALTIES FOR MISDEMEANOR]

§ 2929.21 Penalties for misdemeanor.

(A) Except as provided in division (G) of this section or in section 2929.23 of the Revised Code, whoever is convicted of or pleads guilty to a misdemeanor other than a minor misdemeanor shall be imprisoned for a definite term or fined, or both, which term of imprisonment and fine shall be fixed by the court as provided in this section.

Whoever is convicted of or pleads guilty to committing, attempting to commit, or complicity in committing a violation of section 2909.03 of the Revised Code that is a misdemeanor, or a violation of division (A)(2) of section 2909.06 of the Revised Code when the means used are fire or explosion, shall be required to reimburse agencies for their investigation or prosecution costs in accordance with section 2929.28 of the Revised Code.

(B) Except as provided in division (G) of this section, terms of imprisonment for misdemeanor shall be imposed as follows:

(1) For a misdemeanor of the first degree, not more than six months;

(2) For a misdemeanor of the second degree, not more than ninety days;

(3) For a misdemeanor of the third degree, not more than sixty days;

(4) For a misdemeanor of the fourth degree, not more than thirty days.

(C) Fines for misdemeanor shall be imposed as follows:

(1) For a misdemeanor of the first degree, not more than one thousand dollars;

(2) For a misdemeanor of the second degree, not more than seven hundred fifty dollars;

(3) For a misdemeanor of the third degree, not more than five hundred dollars;

(4) For a misdemeanor of the fourth degree, not more than two hundred fifty dollars.

(D) Whoever is convicted of or pleads guilty to a minor misdemeanor shall be fined not more than one hundred dollars.

(E) The court may require a person who is convicted of or pleads guilty to a misdemeanor to make restitution for all or part of the property damage that is caused by the offense and for all or part of the value of the property that is the subject of any theft offense, as defined in division (K) of section 2913.01 of the Revised Code, that the person committed. If the court determines that the victim of the offense was sixty-five years of age or older or permanently or totally disabled at the time of the commission of the offense, the court, regardless of whether the offender knew the age of victim, shall consider this fact in favor of imposing restitution, but this fact shall not control the decision of the court.

(F) If a person is sentenced to a term of imprisonment pursuant to this section and the term of imprisonment is to be served in a county jail in a county that has established a county jail industry program pursuant to section 5147.30 of the Revised Code, the court shall specify, as part of the sentence, whether the person may be considered by the county sheriff of that county for participation in the county jail industry program. The court shall retain jurisdiction to modify its specification made pursuant to this division during the person's term of imprisonment upon a reassessment of the person's qualifications for participation in the program.

(G) If an offender is being sentenced for a sexually oriented offense that is a misdemeanor committed on or after the effective date of this amendment and if the judge imposing sentence for the sexually oriented offense determines pursuant to division (B) of section 2950.09 of the Revised Code that the offender is a sexual predator, the judge shall include in the offender's sentence a statement that the offender has been adjudicated as being a sexual predator, shall comply with the requirements of section 2950.03 of the Revised Code, and shall require the offender to submit to a DNA specimen collection procedure pursuant to section 2901.07 of the Revised Code.

(H) Before imposing sentence on an offender who is being sentenced for a sexually oriented offense that is a misdemeanor committed on or after the effective date of this amendment, the judge shall conduct a hearing in accordance with division (B) of section 2950.09 of the Revised Code to determine whether the offender is a sexual predator. Before imposing sentence on an offender who is being sentenced for a sexually oriented offense, the court also shall comply with division (E) of section 2950.09 of the Revised Code.

(I) If an offender is being sentenced for a sexually oriented offense that is a misdemeanor committed on or after the effective date of this amendment, the judge shall include in the sentence a summary of the offender's duty to register pursuant to section 2950.04 of the Revised Code, the offender's duty to provide notice of a change in residence address and register the new residence address pursuant to section 2950.05 of the Revised Code, the offender's duty to periodically verify the offender's current residence address pursuant to section 2950.06 of the Revised Code, and the duration of the duties. The judge shall inform the offender, at the time of sentencing, of those duties and of their duration and, if required under division (A)(2) of section 2950.03 of the Revised Code, shall perform the duties specified in that section.

HISTORY: 134 v H 511 (Eff 1-1-74); 137 v S 119 (Eff 8-30-78); 141 v H 284 (Eff 3-6-86); 143 v S 131 (Eff 7-25-90); 143 v H 51 (Eff 11-8-90); 146 v H 180. Eff 1-1-97.

The effective date is set by section 3 of HB 180.

See provisions, § 4 of HB 180 (146 v —) following RC § 2921.34.

§ 2929.22 Imposing sentence for misdemeanor.

(A) In determining whether to impose imprisonment or a fine, or both, for a misdemeanor, and in determining the term of imprisonment and the amount and method of payment of a fine for a misdemeanor, the court shall consider the risk that the offender will commit another offense and the need for protecting the public from the risk; the nature and circumstances of the offense; the history, character, and condition of the offender and the offender's need for correctional or rehabilitative treatment; any statement made by the victim under sections 2930.12 to 2930.17 of the Revised Code, if the offense is a misdemeanor specified in division (A) of section 2930.01 of the Revised Code; and the ability and resources of the offender and the nature of the burden that payment of a fine will impose on the offender.

(B) The following do not control the court's discretion, but shall be considered in favor of imposing imprisonment for a misdemeanor:

(1) The offender is a repeat or dangerous offender;

(2) Regardless of whether or not the offender knew the age of the victim, the victim of the offense was sixty-five years of age or older, permanently and totally disabled, or less than eighteen years of age at the time of the commission of the offense.

(C) The criteria listed in divisions (C) and (E) of section 2929.12 of the Revised Code that mitigate the seriousness of the offense and that indicate that the offender is unlikely to commit future crimes do not control the court's discretion but shall be considered against imposing imprisonment for a misdemeanor.

(D) The criteria listed in division (B) and referred to in division (C) of this section shall not be construed to limit the matters that may be considered in determining whether to impose imprisonment for a misdemeanor.

(E) The court shall not impose a fine in addition to imprisonment for a misdemeanor unless a fine is specially adapted to deterrence of the offense or the correction of the offender, the offense has proximately resulted in physical harm to the person or property of another, or the offense was committed for hire or for purpose of gain.

(F) The court shall not impose a fine or fines that, in the aggregate and to the extent not suspended by the court, exceed the amount that the offender is or will be able to pay by the method and within the time allowed without undue hardship to the offender or the offender's dependents, or will prevent the offender from making restitution or reparation to the victim of the offender's offense.

(G) At the time of sentencing or as soon as possible after sentencing, the court shall notify the victim of the offense of the victim's right to file an application for an award of reparations pursuant to sections 2743.51 to 2743.72 of the Revised Code.

(H) As used in this section, "repeat offender" and "dangerous offender" have the same meanings as in section 2935.36 of the Revised Code.

HISTORY: 134 v H 511 (Eff 1-1-74); 137 v S 119 (Eff 8-30-78); 143 v S 258 (Eff 11-20-90); 145 v S 186 (Eff 10-12-94); 146 v S 2. Eff 7-1-96.

The effective date is set by section 6 of SB 2.

See provisions, § 5 of SB 2 (146 v —) following RC § 2929.03.

[§ 2929.22.1] § 2929.221 Type of institution where term of imprisonment to be served.

(A) A person who is convicted of or pleads guilty to aggravated murder, murder, or an offense punishable by life imprisonment and who is sentenced to a term of imprisonment pursuant to that conviction shall serve that term of imprisonment in an institution under the control of the department of rehabilitation and correction.

(B)(1) A person who is convicted of or pleads guilty to a felony other than aggravated murder, murder, or an offense punishable by life imprisonment and who is sentenced to a term of imprisonment pursuant to that conviction shall serve that term of imprisonment as follows:

(a) Subject to divisions (B)(1)(b) and (B)(2) of this section, in an institution under the control of the department of rehabilitation and correction if the term of imprisonment is a prison term or shall serve it as otherwise determined by the sentencing court pursuant to section 2929.16 of the Revised Code if the term is not a prison term;

(b) In a facility of a type described in division (G)(1) of section 2929.13 of the Revised Code, if the offender is sentenced pursuant to that division.

(2) If the term of imprisonment is a prison term, the person may be imprisoned in a jail that is not a minimum security misdemeanant jail pursuant to agreement under section 5120.161 [5120.16.1] of the Revised Code between the department of rehabilitation and correction and the local authority that operates the jail.

(C) A person who is convicted of or pleads guilty to one or more misdemeanors and who is sentenced to a term of imprisonment pursuant to the conviction or convictions shall serve that term of imprisonment in a county, multicounty, municipal, municipal-county, or multicounty-municipal jail or workhouse or, if the misdemeanor or misdemeanors are not offenses of violence, in a minimum security misdemeanant jail.

(D) Nothing in this section prohibits the commitment, referral, or sentencing of a person who is convicted of or pleads guilty to a felony to a community-based correctional facility and program or district community-based correctional facility and program in accordance with sections 2301.51 to 2301.56 of the Revised Code.

HISTORY: 139 v S 199 (Eff 7-1-83); 139 v H 269 (Eff 7-1-83); 140 v S 210 (Eff 7-1-83); 142 v H 455 (Eff 7-20-87); 143 v S 258 (Eff 11-20-90); 145 v H 571 (Eff 10-6-94); 146 v S 2 (Eff 7-1-96); 146 v S 269 (Eff 7-1-96); 146 v S 166. Eff 10-17-96.

See provisions, § 5 of SB 2 (146 v —) as amended by § 3 of SB 269 (146 v —) following RC § 2929.03.

Comment, Legislative Service Commission

Section 2929.221 of the Revised Code is amended by this act [Am. Sub. S.B. 166] and also by Am. Sub. S.B. 269 of the 121st General Assembly. Comparison of these amendments in pursuance of section 1.52 of the Revised Code discloses that they are not irreconcilable so that they are required by that section to be harmonized to give effect to each amendment.

[§ 2929.22.3] § 2929.223 Reimbursement for costs of confinement for an offense other than a minor misdemeanor.

(A) If a judge in any jurisdiction in which the appropriate authority or board requires an offender an offense other than a minor misdemeanor† to reimburse the costs of confinement pursuant to section 307.93, 341.14, 341.19, 341.23, 753.02, 753.04, 753.16, 2301.56, or 2947.19 of the Revised Code sentences an offender to a term of imprisonment in the facility that is subject to the requirement for a misdemeanor, then after that person's release from imprisonment, the judge or, if that judge no longer is sitting on that court, any judge from that court, also shall hold a hearing to determine the amount of the reimbursement and whether the offender has the ability to pay the reimbursement and the amount the person is able to pay. The offender shall have an opportunity to be heard and may be represented by counsel at the hearing, at the offender's the person's† option. A record shall be made of the hearing.

Reimbursable expenses shall include, but are not limited to, the expenses relating to the provision of food, clothing, shelter, medical care, and personal hygiene products, including, but not limited to, toothpaste, toothbrushes, and feminine hygiene items, to the offender while the offender is imprisoned and during any time that the offender is incarcerated before sentencing that is credited against the offender's term of imprisonment, and up to two hours of overtime costs the sheriff or municipal corporation incurred relating to the trial of the person.

(B) Before holding a hearing on reimbursement pursuant to division (A) of this section, the judge shall investigate or cause to be investigated the offender's ability to pay the reimbursement and possible reimbursement schedules and methods. The amount of reimbursement shall be determined at the hearing in light of the sentence of imprisonment given and according to the offender's ability to pay. However, the actual amount to be paid for reimbursable expenses other than medical expenses shall be the actual cost of the confinement or a lesser amount determined pursuant to section 307.93, 341.14, 341.19, 341.23, 753.02, 753.04, 753.16, 2301.56, or 2947.19 of the Revised Code. The actual amount to be paid for medical expenses shall not exceed forty per cent of those medical expenses. In determining the offender's ability to pay the reimbursement, all of the following shall be considered:

(1) The offender's financial resources, excluding the funds saved from wages derived from the offender's labor or employment during the period of incarceration;

(2) Any obligation to support the offender's dependents;

(3) Any obligation to make restitution to the victim of the offense of which the offender is convicted;

(4) The offender's income, assets, liabilities, ability to borrow, household expenses, and any other factor that may affect the offender's financial ability to make reimbursement.

(C) At the conclusion of the hearing held pursuant to division (A) of this section, the judge shall determine the amount of the reimbursable expenses owed by the offender who is the subject of the hearing and the amount that the offender is able to pay. If the judge determines that the offender is able to pay any of the reimbursable expenses, the judge shall issue a judgment against the offender in the amount of the reimbursable expenses that the offender is able to pay. In the judgment, the judge also shall establish a payment schedule for the reimbursement. The judgment shall state that the reimbursement shall be made to the county, municipal corporation, or township for expenses incurred by it during any time that the offender served in a local jail or workhouse. Each payment on the payment schedule shall constitute a separate judgment. The prosecuting attorney for a county, city director of law, village solicitor, or similar chief legal officer of a municipal corporation, as appropriate, may execute upon the judgment for failure to meet the payment schedule.

(D) This section does not apply to a person who is sentenced for a felony to a term of imprisonment in a facility that is subject to a requirement of the type described in division (A) of this section. Sections 2929.18 and 2929.181 [2929.18.1] of the Revised Code apply to a person who is sentenced for a felony to a term of that nature.

HISTORY: RC § 2929.15, 140 v H 363 (Eff 9-26-84); RC § 2929.22.3, 146 v S 2 (Eff 7-1-96); 146 v S 269 (Eff 7-1-96); 146 v H 480. Eff 10-16-96.

Publisher's Note

The amendments made by SB 269 (146 v —) and HB 480 (146 v —) have been combined. Please see provisions of RC § 1.52.

See provisions, § 5 of SB 2 (146 v —) as amended by § 3 of SB 269 (146 v —) following RC 2929.03.

† The wording is the result of combining SB 269 (146 v —) and HB 480 (146 v —).

§ 2929.23 **Electronically monitored house arrest; certification of devices; device fund.**

(A) As used in this section:

(1) "Electronic monitoring device" means either of the following:

(a) Any device that can be operated by electrical or battery power and that conforms with all of the following:

(i) The device has a transmitter that can be attached to a person, that will transmit a specified signal to a receiver of the type described in division (A)(1)(a)(ii) of this section if the transmitter is removed from the person, turned off, or altered in any manner without prior court approval in relation to electronically monitored house arrest or electronically monitored house detention or without prior approval of the department of rehabilitation and correction in relation to electronically monitored early release or otherwise is tampered with, that can transmit continuously and periodically a signal to that receiver when the person is within a specified distance from the receiver, and that can transmit an appropriate signal to that receiver if the person to whom it is attached travels a specified distance from that receiver.

(ii) The device has a receiver that can receive continuously the signals transmitted by a transmitter of the type described in division (A)(1)(a)(i) of this section, can transmit continuously those signals by telephone to a central monitoring computer of the type described in division (A)(1)(a)(iii) of this section, and can transmit continuously an appropriate signal to that central monitoring computer if the receiver is turned off or altered without prior court approval or otherwise tampered with.

(iii) The device has a central monitoring computer that can receive continuously the signals transmitted by telephone by a receiver of the type described in division (A)(1)(a)(ii) of this section and can monitor continuously the person to whom an electronic monitoring device of the type described in division (A)(1)(a) of this section is attached.

(b) Any device that is not a device of the type described in division (A)(1)(a) of this section and that conforms with all of the following:

(i) The device includes a transmitter and receiver that can monitor and determine the location of a subject person at any time, or at a designated point in time, through the use of a central monitoring computer or through other electronic means;

(ii) The device includes a transmitter and receiver that can determine at any time, or at a designated point in time, through the use of a central monitoring computer or other electronic means the fact that the transmitter is turned off or altered in any manner without prior approval of the court in relation to electronically monitored house arrest or electronically monitored house detention or without prior approval of the department of rehabilitation and correction in relation to electronically monitored early release or otherwise is tampered with.

(2) "Certified electronic monitoring device" means an electronic monitoring device that has been certified by the superintendent of the bureau of criminal identification and investigation pursuant to division (C)(1) of this section.

(3) "Eligible offender" means a person who has been convicted of or pleaded guilty to any offense, except that a person is not an "eligible offender" if any of the following apply in relation to the person, the offense, or the person and the offense:

(a) The person is subject to or is serving a term of life imprisonment.

(b) The person is subject to or is serving a mandatory prison term imposed under division (F) of section 2929.13, division (D) of section 2929.14, or any other section of the Revised Code, provided that, after the person has served all of the mandatory prison terms so imposed, the person may be an eligible offender unless excluded by division (A)(3)(a), (c) or (d) of this section.

(c) The offense is a violation of division (A) of section 4511.19 of the Revised Code, and the offender is sentenced for that offense pursuant to division (G)(1) of section 2929.13 of the Revised Code and is serving the mandatory term of local incarceration of sixty consecutive days of imprisonment imposed under that division, provided that, after the person has served all of the mandatory term of local incarceration so imposed, the person may be an eligible offender unless excluded by division (A)(3)(a), (b), or (d) of this section.

(d) The offense is a violation of division (A) of section 4511.19 of the Revised Code, and the person is sentenced for that offense pursuant to division (G)(2) of section 2929.13 of the Revised Code.

(4) "Electronically monitored house arrest" means a period of confinement of an eligible offender in the eligible offender's home or in other premises specified by the sentencing court, during which period of confinement all of the following apply:

(a) The eligible offender wears, otherwise has attached to the eligible offender's person, or otherwise is subject to monitoring by a certified electronic monitoring device, or the eligible offender is subject to monitoring by a certified electronic monitoring system;

(b) The eligible offender is required to remain in the eligible offender's home or other premises specified by the sentencing court for the specified period of confinement, except for periods of time during which the eligible offender is at the eligible offender's place of employment or at other premises as authorized by the sentencing court;

(c) The eligible offender is subject to monitoring by a central system that monitors the certified electronic monitoring device that is attached to the eligible offender's person or that otherwise is being used to monitor the eligible offender and that can monitor and determine the eligible offender's location at any time or at a designated point in time, or the eligible offender is required to participate in monitoring by a certified electronic monitoring system;

(d) The eligible offender is required by the sentencing court to report periodically to a person designated by the court;

(e) The eligible offender is subject to any other restrictions and requirements that may be imposed by the sentencing court.

(5) "Electronic monitoring system" means a system by which the location of an eligible offender can be verified telephonically through the use of voice-activated voice response technology that conforms with all of the following:

(a) It can be programmed to call the telephone or telephones assigned to the eligible offender who is the subject of the monitoring as often as necessary;

(b) It is equipped with a voice recognition system that can work accurately and reliably under the anticipated conditions in which it will operate;

(c) It is equipped to perform an alarm function if the eligible offender who is the subject of monitoring does not respond to system commands in the manner required.

(6) "Certified electronic monitoring system" means an electronic monitoring system that has been certified by the superintendent of the bureau of criminal identification and investigation pursuant to division (C)(1) of this section.

(7) "Electronically monitored house detention" has the same meaning as in section 2151.355 [2151.35.5] of the Revised Code.

(8) "Electronically monitored early release" has the same meaning as in section 5120.071 [5120.07.1] of the Revised Code.

(B)(1) Any court may impose as a sanction pursuant to sections 2929.15 and 2929.17 of the Revised Code a period of electronically monitored house arrest upon an eligible offender who is convicted of or pleads guilty to a felony, except that the total of any period of electronically monitored house arrest imposed upon that eligible offender plus the period of all other sanctions imposed upon the same eligible offender pursuant to sections 2929.15, 2929.16, 2929.17, and 2929.18 of the Revised Code shall not exceed five years. Any court may impose a period of electronically monitored house arrest upon an eligible offender who is convicted of or pleads guilty to a misdemeanor in addition to or in lieu of any other sentence imposed or authorized for the offense, except that the total of any period of electronically monitored house arrest imposed upon that eligible offender plus the period of any sentence of imprisonment imposed upon the same eligible offender shall not exceed the maximum term of imprisonment that could be imposed upon the eligible offender pursuant to section 2929.21 of the Revised Code and except that, if the offense for which an eligible offender is being sentenced is a violation of division (A) of section 4511.19 or of division (D)(2) of section 4507.02 of the Revised Code, the court may impose a period of electronically monitored house arrest upon the eligible offender only when authorized by and only in the circumstances described in division (A) of section 4511.99 or division (B) of section 4507.99 of the Revised Code.

If a court imposes a period of electronically monitored house arrest upon an eligible offender, it shall require the eligible offender to wear, otherwise have attached to the eligible offender's person, or otherwise be subject to monitoring by a certified electronic monitoring device or to participate in the operation of and monitoring by a certified electronic monitoring system; to remain in the eligible offender's home or other specified premises for the entire period of electronically monitored house arrest except when the court permits the eligible offender to leave those premises to go to the eligible offender's place of employment or to other specified premises; to be monitored by a central system that monitors the certified electronic monitoring device that is attached to the eligible offender's person or that otherwise is being used to monitor the eligible offender and that can monitor and determine the eligible offender's location at any time or at a designated point in time or to be monitored by the certified electronic monitoring system; to report periodically to a person designated by the court; and, in return for receiving a period of electronically monitored house arrest, to enter into a written contract with the court agreeing to comply with all restrictions and requirements imposed by the court, agreeing to pay any fee imposed by the court for the costs of the electronically monitored house arrest imposed by the court pursuant to division (E) of this section, and agreeing to waive the right to receive credit for any time served on electronically monitored house arrest toward any prison term or sentence of imprisonment imposed upon the eligible offender for the offense for which the period of electronically monitored house arrest was imposed if the eligible offender violates any of the restrictions or requirements of the period of electronically monitored house arrest, and additionally, it may impose any other reasonable restrictions and requirements upon the eligible offender.

(2) If an eligible offender violates any of the restrictions or requirements imposed upon the eligible offender as part of the eligible offender's period of electronically monitored house arrest, the eligible offender shall not receive credit for any time served on electronically monitored house arrest toward any prison term or sentence of imprisonment imposed upon the eligible offender for the offense for which the period of electronically monitored house arrest was imposed.

(C)(1) The superintendent of the bureau of criminal identification and investigation, in accordance with this section and rules adopted by the superintendent pursuant to division (C)(2) of this section, shall certify for use in cases of electronically monitored house arrest, electronically monitored house detention, and electronically monitored early release specific types and brands of electronic monitoring devices and electronic monitoring systems that comply with the requirements of this section, section 5120.073 [5120.07.3] of the Revised Code, and those rules. Any manufacturer that, pursuant to this division, seeks to obtain the certification of any type or brand of electronic monitoring device or electronic monitoring system shall submit to the superintendent an application for certification in accordance with those rules together with the application fee and costs of certification as required by those rules. The superintendent shall not certify any electronic monitoring device or electronic monitoring system pursuant to this division unless the application fee and costs have been paid to the superintendent.

(2) The superintendent, in accordance with Chapter 119. of the Revised Code, shall adopt rules for certifying specific types and brands of electronic monitoring devices and electronic monitoring systems for use in electronically monitored house arrest, electronically monitored house detention, and electronically monitored early release. The rules shall set forth the requirements for obtaining the certification, the application fee and other costs for obtaining the certification, the procedure for applying for certification, and any other requirements and procedures considered necessary by the superintendent. The rules shall require that no type or brand of electronic monitoring device or electronic monitoring system be certified unless the type or brand of device or system complies with whichever of the following is applicable, in addition to any other requirements specified by the superintendent:

(a) For electronic monitoring devices of the type described in division (A)(1)(a) of this section, the type or brand of device complies with all of the following:

(i) It has a transmitter of the type described in division (A)(1)(a)(i) of this section, a receiver of the type described in division (A)(1)(a)(ii) of this section, and a central monitoring computer of the type described in division (A)(1)(a)(iii) of this section;

(ii) Its transmitter can be worn by or attached to a person with a minimum of discomfort during normal activities, is difficult to remove, turn off, or otherwise alter without prior court approval in relation to electronically monitored house arrest or electronically monitored house detention or prior approval of the department of rehabilitation and correction in relation to electronically monitored early release, and will transmit a specified signal to the receiver if it is removed, turned off, altered, or otherwise tampered with;

(iii) Its receiver is difficult to turn off or alter and will transmit a signal to the central monitoring computer if it is turned off, altered, or otherwise tampered with;

(iv) Its central monitoring computer is difficult to circumvent;

(v) Its transmitter, receiver, and central monitoring computer work accurately and reliably under the anticipated conditions under which electronically monitored house arrest or electronically monitored house detention will be imposed by courts or under which electronically monitored early release will be used by the department of rehabilitation and correction;

(vi) It has a backup battery power supply that operates automatically when the main source of electrical or battery power for the device fails.

(b) For electronic monitoring devices of the type described in division (A)(1)(b) of this section, the type or brand of device complies with all of the following:

(i) It has a transmitter and receiver of the type described in divisions (A)(1)(b)(i) and (ii) of this section.

(ii) Its transmitter is difficult to turn off or alter without prior court approval in relation to electronically monitored house arrest or electronically monitored house detention or without prior approval of the department of rehabilitation and correction in relation to electronically monitored early release, and, if the transmitter is turned off or altered in any manner without prior approval of the court or department or otherwise is tampered with, the fact that it has been turned off, altered, or tampered with can be determined at any time, or at a designated point in time, through the use of a central monitoring computer or through other electronic means.

(iii) Its receiver is difficult to turn off or alter, and, if the receiver is turned off, altered, or otherwise tampered with, the fact that it has been turned off, altered, or tampered with can be determined at any time, or at a designated point in time, through the use of a central monitoring computer or through other electronic means.

(iv) Its central monitoring computer or other means of electronic monitoring is difficult to circumvent.

(v) Its transmitter, receiver, and central monitoring computer or other means of electronic monitoring work accurately and reliably under the anticipated conditions under which electronically monitored house arrest, electronically monitored house detention, or electronically monitored early release will be used.

(vi) If it operates on electrical or battery power, it has a backup battery power supply that operates automatically when the main source of electrical or battery power for the device fails, or, if it does not operate on electrical or battery power, it has a backup method of operation so that it will continue to operate if its main method of operation fails.

(c) For electronic monitoring systems, the type or brand of system complies with all of the following:

(i) It can be programmed to call the telephone or telephones assigned to the person who is the subject of the monitoring as often as necessary;

(ii) It is equipped with a voice recognition system that can work accurately and reliably under the anticipated conditions in which it will operate;

(iii) It is equipped to perform an alarm function if the person who is the subject of the monitoring does not respond to system commands in the manner required.

(3) The superintendent shall publish and make available to all courts and to the department of rehabilitation and correction, without charge, a list of all types and brands of electronic monitoring devices and electronic monitoring systems that have been certified by the superintendent pursuant to division (C)(1) of this section and information about the manufacturers of the certified devices and systems and places at which the devices and systems can be obtained.

(D) The superintendent of the bureau of criminal identification and investigation shall deposit all costs and fees collected pursuant to division (C) of this section into the general revenue fund.

(E)(1) Each county in which is located a court that imposes a period of electronically monitored house arrest or electronically monitored house detention as a sentencing sanction or alternative may establish in the county treasury an electronically monitored house arrest and detention fund. The clerk of each court that uses that sentencing sanction or alternative may deposit into the fund all fees collected from eligible offenders upon whom electronically monitored house arrest or detention is imposed pursuant to this section, section 2151.355 [2151.35.5], or any other section of the Revised Code that specifically authorizes the imposition of electronically monitored house arrest or detention. Each court that imposes electronically monitored house arrest or detention may adopt by local court rule a reasonable daily fee to be paid by each eligible offender upon whom a period of electronically monitored house arrest or detention is imposed as a sentencing sanction or alternative. The fee may include the actual costs of providing house arrest or detention and an additional amount necessary to enable the court to provide electronically monitored house arrest or detention to indigent eligible offenders. The fund may be used only for the payment of the costs of electronically monitored house arrest or detention, including, but not limited to, the costs of electronically monitored house arrest or detention for indigent eligible offenders.

(2) If a fee is adopted pursuant to division (E)(1) of this section, it shall be in addition to any fine specifically authorized or required by any other section of the Revised Code for an eligible offender upon whom a period of electronically monitored house arrest or detention is imposed as a sentencing sanction or alternative.

HISTORY: 143 v S 131 (Eff 7-25-90); 143 v H 51 (Eff 11-8-90); 144 v S 351 (Eff 7-1-92); 144 v H 725 (Eff 4-16-93); 144 v S 275 (Eff 7-1-93)†; 145 v S 82 (Eff 5-4-94); 146 v S 2 (Eff 7-1-96); 146 v S 269 (Eff 7-1-96); 146 v S 166 (Eff 10-17-96); 146 v H 72. Eff 3-18-97.

† See provisions, §§ 4, 5 of SB 62 (145 v —) concerning change of effective date from 7-1-93 to 9-1-93 at RC § 2903.04 in the Bound Volume.

The provisions of § 6 of HB 72 (146 v —) read as follows:

SECTION 6. Section 2929.23 of the Revised Code was amended by both Am. Sub. S.B. 269 and Am. Sub. S.B. 166 of the 121st General Assembly. Comparison of these amendments in pursuance of section 1.52 of the Revised Code discloses that while certain of the amendments of these acts are reconcilable, certain other of the amendments are substantively irreconcilable. Am. Sub. S.B. 269 and Am. Sub. S.B. 166 both were passed on May 30, 1996, Am. Sub. S.B. 166 later than Am. Sub. S.B. 269. Section 2929.23 of the Revised Code is therefore presented in this act as it results from Am. Sub. S.B. 166 and such of the amendments of Am. Sub. S.B. 269 as are not in conflict with the amendments of Am. Sub. S.B. 166. This is in recognition of the principles stated in division (B) of section 1.52 of the Revised Code that amendments are to be harmonized where not substantively irreconcilable, and that where amendments are substantively irreconcilable, the latest amendment is to prevail. This section constitutes a legislative finding that such harmonized and reconciled section was the resulting version in effect prior to the effective date of this act.

§ 2929.24 Prosecutor to notify appropriate licensing board.

(A) The prosecutor in any case against any person licensed, certified, registered, or otherwise authorized to practice under Chapter 3719., 4715., 4723., 4729., 4730., 4731., or 4741. of the Revised Code shall notify the appropriate licensing board, on forms provided by the board, of any of the following regarding the person:

(1) A plea of guilty to, or a conviction of, a felony, or a court order dismissing a felony charge on technical or procedural grounds;

(2) A plea of guilty to, or a conviction of, a misdemeanor committed in the course of practice or in the course of business, or a court order dismissing such a misdemeanor charge on technical or procedural grounds;

(3) A plea of guilty to, or a conviction of, a misdemeanor involving moral turpitude, or a court order dismissing such a charge on technical or procedural grounds.

(B) The report required by division (A) of this section shall include the name and address of the person, the nature of the offense, and certified copies of court entries in the action.

HISTORY: RC § 2929.17, 143 v H 615 (Eff 3-27-91); 146 v S143, § 1 (Eff 3-5-96); RC § 2929.24, 146 v S 2 (Eff 7-1-96); 146 v S 143, § 5. Eff 7-1-96.

The effective date is set by § 7 of SB 143.

See provisions, § 5 of SB 2 (146 v —) as amended by § 3 of SB 269 (146 v —) following RC § 2929.03.

§ 2929.25 Additional fine for certain offenders; collection of fines; crime victims recovery fund.

(A)(1) Subject to division (A)(2) of this section, notwithstanding the fines prescribed in section 2929.02 of the Revised Code for a person who is convicted of or pleads guilty to aggravated murder or murder, the fines prescribed in section 2929.18 of the Revised Code for a person who is convicted of or pleads guilty to a felony, the fines prescribed in section 2929.21 of the Revised

Code for a person who is convicted of or pleads guilty to a misdemeanor, the fines prescribed in section 2929.31 of the Revised Code for an organization that is convicted of or pleads guilty to an offense, and the fines prescribed in any other section of the Revised Code for a person who is convicted of or pleads guilty to an offense, a sentencing court may impose upon the offender a fine of not more than one million dollars if any of the following applies to the offense and the offender:

(a) There are three or more victims, as defined in section 2969.11 of the Revised Code, of the offense for which the offender is being sentenced.

(b) The offender previously has been convicted of or pleaded guilty to one or more offenses, and, for the offense for which the offender is being sentenced and all of the other offenses, there is a total of three or more victims, as defined in section 2969.11 of the Revised Code.

(c) The offense for which the offender is being sentenced is aggravated murder, murder, or a felony of the first degree that, if it had been committed prior to July 1, 1996, would have been an aggravated felony of the first degree.

(2) If the offense in question is a first, second, or third degree felony violation of any provision of Chapter 2925., 3719., or 4729. of the Revised Code, the court shall impose upon the offender the mandatory fine described in division (B) of section 2929.18 of the Revised Code, and, in addition, may impose a fine under division (A)(1) of this section, provided that the total of the mandatory fine and the fine imposed under division (A)(1) of this section shall not exceed one million dollars. the mandatory fine shall be paid as described in division (D) of section 2929.18 of the Revised Code, and the fine imposed under division (A)(1) of this section shall be deposited pursuant to division (B) of this section.

(B) If a sentencing court imposes a fine upon an offender pursuant to division (A)(1) of this section, all moneys paid in satisfaction of the fine or collected pursuant to division (C)(1) of this section in satisfaction of the fine shall be deposited into the crime victims recovery fund created by division (D) of this section and shall be distributed as described in that division.

(C)(1) Subject to division (C)(2) of this section, notwithstanding any contrary provision of any section of the Revised Code, if a sentencing court imposes a fine upon an offender pursuant to division (A)(1) of this section or pursuant to another section of the Revised Code, the fine shall be a judgment against the offender in favor of the state, and both of the following apply to that judgment:

(a) The state may collect the judgment by garnishing, attaching, or otherwise executing against any income, profits, or other real or personal property in which the offender has any right, title, or interest, including property acquired after the imposition of the fine, in the same manner as if the judgment had been rendered against the offender and in favor of the state in a civil action. If the fine is imposed pursuant to division (A)(1) of this section, the moneys collected as a result of the garnishment, attachment, or other execution shall be deposited and distributed as described in divisions (B) and (D) of this section. If the fine is not imposed pursuant to division (A)(1) of this section, the moneys collected as a result of the garnishment, attachment, or other execution shall be distributed as otherwise provided by law for the distribution of money paid in satisfaction of a fine.

(b) The provisions of Chapter 2329. of the Revised Code relative to the establishment of court judgments and decrees as liens and to the enforcement of those liens apply to the judgment.

(2) Division (C)(1) of this section does not apply to any financial sanction imposed pursuant to section 2929.18 of the Revised Code upon a person who is convicted of or pleads guilty to a felony.

(D) There is hereby created in the state treasury the crime victims recovery fund. If a sentencing court imposes a fine upon an offender pursuant to division (A)(1) of this section, all moneys paid in satisfaction of the fine and all moneys collected in satisfaction of the fine pursuant to division (C)(1) of this section shall be deposited into the fund. The fund shall be administered and the moneys in it shall be distributed in accordance with sections 2969.11 to 2969.14 of the Revised Code.

HISTORY: 146 v S 91 (Eff 11-15-95); 146 v S 269. Eff 7-1-96.

The effective date is set by section 5 of SB 269.

[REIMBURSEMENT BY ARSONIST]

§ 2929.28 Arsonist to reimburse agencies for costs of investigation and prosecution.

(A) As used in this section:

(1) "Agency" means any law enforcement agency, other public agency, or public official involved in the investigation or prosecution of the offender or in the investigation of the fire or explosion in an aggravated arson, arson, or criminal damaging or endangering case. An "agency" includes, but is not limited to, a sheriff's office, a municipal corporation, township, or township police district police department, the office of a prosecuting attorney, city director of law, village solicitor, or similar chief legal officer of a municipal corporation, the fire marshal's office, a municipal corporation, township, or township fire district fire department, the office of a fire prevention officer, and any state, county, or municipal corporation crime laboratory.

(2) "Assets" includes all forms of real or personal property.

(3) "Itemized statement" means the statement of costs described in division (B) of this section.

(4) "Offender" means the person who has been convicted of or pleaded guilty to committing, attempting

to commit, or complicity in committing a violation of section 2909.02 or 2909.03 of the Revised Code, or, when the means used are fire or explosion, division (A)(2) of section 2909.06 of the Revised Code.

(5) "Costs" means the reasonable value of the time spent by an officer or employee of an agency on the aggravated arson, arson, or criminal damaging or endangering case, any moneys spent by the agency on that case, and the reasonable fair market value of resources used or expended by the agency on that case.

(B) Prior to the sentencing of an offender, the court shall enter an order that directs agencies that wish to be reimbursed by the offender for the costs they incurred in the investigation or prosecution of the offender or in the investigation of the fire or explosion involved in the case, to file with the court within a specified time an itemized statement of those costs. The order also shall require that a copy of the itemized statement be given to the offender or his attorney within the specified time. Only itemized statements so filed and given shall be considered at the hearing described in division (C) of this section.

(C) The court shall set a date for a hearing on all the itemized statements filed with it and given to the offender or his attorney in accordance with division (B) of this section. The hearing shall be held prior to the sentencing of the offender, but may be held on the same day as his sentencing. Notice of the hearing date shall be given to the offender or his attorney and to the agencies whose itemized statements are involved. At the hearing, each agency has the burden of establishing by a preponderance of the evidence that the costs set forth in its itemized statement were incurred in the investigation or prosecution of the offender or in the investigation of the fire or explosion involved in the case, and of establishing by a preponderance of the evidence that the offender has assets available for the reimbursement of all or a portion of the costs.

The offender may cross-examine all witnesses and examine all documentation presented by the agencies at the hearing, and he may present at the hearing witnesses and documentation he has obtained without a subpoena or a subpoena duces tecum or, in the case of documentation, that belongs to him. He also may issue subpoenas and subpoenas duces tecum for, and present and examine at the hearing, witnesses and documentation, subject to the following applying to the witnesses or documentation subpoenaed:

(1) The testimony of witnesses subpoenaed or documentation subpoenaed is material to the preparation or presentation by the offender of his defense to the claims of the agencies for a reimbursement of costs;

(2) If witnesses to be subpoenaed are personnel of an agency or documentation to be subpoenaed belongs to an agency, the personnel or documentation may be subpoenaed only if the agency involved has indicated, pursuant to this division, that it intends to present the personnel as witnesses or use the documentation at the hearing. The offender shall submit, in writing, a request to an agency as described in this division to ascertain whether the agency intends to present various personnel as witnesses or to use particular documentation. The request shall indicate that the offender is considering issuing subpoenas to personnel of the agency who are specifically named or identified by title or position, or for documentation of the agency that is specifically described or generally identified, and shall request the agency to indicate, in writing, whether it intends to present such personnel as witnesses or to use such documentation at the hearing. The agency shall promptly reply to the request of the offender. An agency is prohibited from presenting personnel as witnesses or from using documentation at the hearing if it indicates to the offender it does not intend to do so in response to a request of the offender under this division, or if it fails to reply or promptly reply to such a request.

(D) Following the hearing, the court shall determine which of the agencies established by a preponderance of the evidence that costs set forth in their itemized statements were incurred as described in division (C) of this section and that the offender has assets available for reimbursement purposes. The court also shall determine whether the offender has assets available to reimburse all such agencies, in whole or in part, for their established costs, and if it determines that the assets are available, it shall order the offender, as part of his sentence, to reimburse the agencies from his assets for all or a specified portion of their established costs.

HISTORY: 141 v H 284. Eff 3-6-86.

§ 2929.29 Procedure for accepting peace officer's guilty plea to felony or after conviction; negotiated misdemeanor pleas.

(A) As used in this section:

(1) "Peace officer" has the same meaning as in section 109.71 of the Revised Code.

(2) "Felony" has the same meaning as in section 109.511 [109.51.1] of the Revised Code.

(B)(1) Prior to accepting a plea of guilty to an indictment, information, or complaint charging a felony, the court shall determine whether the defendant is a peace officer. If the court determines that the defendant is a peace officer, it shall address the defendant personally and provide the following advisement to the defendant that shall be entered in the record of the court.

"You are hereby advised that conviction of the felony offense to which you are pleading guilty will result in the termination of your employment as a peace officer and in your decertification as a peace officer pursuant to the laws of Ohio."

Upon the request of the defendant, the court shall allow the defendant additional time to consider the appropriateness of the plea of guilty in light of the advisement described in division (B)(1) of this section.

The court shall not accept a plea of guilty of a defendant who is a peace officer unless, in addition to any other procedures required under the Rules of Criminal Procedure, the court determines that the defendant voluntarily and intelligently enters that plea after being given the advisement described in division (B)(1) of this section.

(2) After accepting under division (B)(1) of this section a plea of guilty to an indictment, information, or complaint charging a felony, the court shall provide to the clerk of the court of common pleas a written notice of the plea of guilty of the defendant peace officer, the name and address of the peace officer, the law enforcement agency or other governmental entity that employs the peace officer and its address, the date of the plea, the nature of the felony offense, and certified copies of court entries in the action. Upon receiving the written notice required by division (B)(2) of this section, the clerk of the court of common pleas shall transmit to the employer of the peace officer and to the Ohio peace officer training council a report that includes the information contained in the written notice and the certified copies of the court entries in the action.

(C)(1) Upon the conviction of a defendant, after trial, of a felony, the trial judge shall determine whether the defendant is a peace officer. If the judge determines that the defendant is a peace officer or if the defendant states on the record that the defendant is a peace officer, the judge shall provide to the clerk of the court of common pleas a written notice of the conviction of the defendant peace officer, the name and address of the peace officer, the law enforcement agency or other governmental entity that employs the peace officer and its address, the date of the conviction, the nature of the felony offense, and certified copies of court entries in the action. Upon receiving the written notice required by division (C)(1) of this section, the clerk of the court of common pleas shall transmit to the employer of the peace officer and to the Ohio peace officer training council a report that includes the information contained in the written notice and the certified copies of the court entries in the action.

(2) Upon the conclusion of the final appeal of a defendant who is a peace officer and who has been convicted of a felony, upon expiration of the time period within which that peace officer may appeal the conviction if no appeal is taken, or otherwise upon the final disposition of the criminal action against that peace officer, the trial judge shall provide to the clerk of the court of common pleas a written notice of the final disposition of the action that shall include, as appropriate, notice of the final conviction of the peace officer of the felony, the acquittal of the peace officer of the felony, the conviction of the peace officer of a misdemeanor, or the dismissal of the felony charge against the peace officer. The judge also shall provide to the clerk of the court of common pleas certified copies of the court entries in the action. Upon receiving the written notice required by division (C)(2) of this section, the clerk of the court of common pleas shall transmit to the employer of the peace officer and to the Ohio peace officer training council a report that includes the information contained in the written notice and the certified copies of the court entries in the action.

(D) If pursuant to a negotiated plea agreement between a prosecuting attorney and a defendant who is a peace officer and who is charged with a felony, in which the defendant agrees to enter a plea of guilty to a misdemeanor and to surrender the certificate awarded to the defendant under section 109.77 of the Revised Code, the trial judge issues an order to the defendant to surrender that certificate, the trial judge shall provide to the clerk of the court a written notice of the order, the name and address of the peace officer, the law enforcement agency or other governmental entity that employs the peace officer and its address, the date of the plea, the nature of the misdemeanor to which the peace officer pleaded guilty, and certified copies of court entries in the action. Upon receiving the written notice required by this division, the clerk of the court shall transmit to the employer of the peace officer and to the executive director of the Ohio peace officer training council a report that includes the information contained in the written notice and the certified copies of the court entries in the action.

HISTORY: 146 v H 566. Eff 10-16-96.

[ORGANIZATIONAL PENALTIES]

§ 2929.31 Organizational penalties.

(A) Regardless of the penalties provided in sections 2929.02, 2929.14 to 2929.18, and 2929.21 of the Revised Code, an organization convicted of an offense pursuant to section 2901.23 of the Revised Code shall be fined in accordance with this section. The court shall fix the fine as follows:

(1) For aggravated murder, not more than one hundred thousand dollars;

(2) For murder, not more than fifty thousand dollars;

(3) For a felony of the first degree, not more than twenty-five thousand dollars;

(4) For a felony of the second degree, not more than twenty thousand dollars;

(5) For a felony of the third degree, not more than fifteen thousand dollars;

(6) For a felony of the fourth degree, not more than ten thousand dollars;

(7) For a felony of the fifth degree, not more than seventy-five hundred dollars;

(8) For a misdemeanor of the first degree, not more than five thousand dollars;

(9) For a misdemeanor of the second degree, not more than four thousand dollars;

(10) For a misdemeanor of the third degree, not more than three thousand dollars;

(11) For a misdemeanor of the fourth degree, not more than two thousand dollars;

(12) For a minor misdemeanor, not more than one thousand dollars;

(13) For a felony not specifically classified, not more than ten thousand dollars;

(14) For a misdemeanor not specifically classified, not more than two thousand dollars;

(15) For a minor misdemeanor not specifically classified, not more than one thousand dollars.

(B) When an organization is convicted of an offense that is not specifically classified, and the section defining the offense or penalty plainly indicates a purpose to impose the penalty provided for violation upon organizations, then the penalty so provided shall be imposed in lieu of the penalty provided in this section.

(C) When an organization is convicted of an offense that is not specifically classified, and the penalty provided includes a higher fine than the fine that is provided in this section, then the penalty imposed shall be pursuant to the penalty provided for the violation of the section defining the offense.

(D) This section does not prevent the imposition of available civil sanctions against an organization convicted of an offense pursuant to section 2901.23 of the Revised Code, either in addition to or in lieu of a fine imposed pursuant to this section.

HISTORY: 134 v H 511 (Eff 1-1-74); 139 v S 199 (Eff 7-1-83); 146 v S 2. Eff 7-1-96.

The effective date is set by section 6 of SB 2.

See provisions, § 5 of SB 2 (146 v —) following RC § 2929.03.

[MULTIPLE SENTENCES]

§ 2929.41 Multiple sentences.

(A) Except as provided in division (B) of this section, division (E) of section 2929.14, or division (D) or (E) of section 2971.03 of the Revised Code, a sentence of imprisonment shall be served concurrently with any other sentence of imprisonment imposed by a court of this state, another state, or the United States. In any case, a sentence of imprisonment for misdemeanor shall be served concurrently with a sentence of imprisonment for felony served in a state or federal correctional institution.

(B)(1) A sentence of imprisonment for a misdemeanor shall be served consecutively to any other sentence of imprisonment when the trial court specifies that it is to be served consecutively or when it is imposed for a misdemeanor violation of section 2907.322 [2907.32.2], 2921.34, or 2923.131 [2323.13.1] of the Revised Code.

(2) When consecutive sentences of imprisonment are imposed for misdemeanor, the term to be served is the aggregate of the consecutive terms imposed, except that the aggregate term to be served shall not exceed eighteen months.

HISTORY: 134 v H 511 (Eff 1-1-74); 137 v H 202 (Eff 10-9-78); 139 v S 1 (Eff 10-19-81); 139 v S 199 (Eff 1-5-83); 140 v S 210 (Eff 7-1-83); 142 v H 51 (Eff 3-17-89); 143 v S 258 (Eff 11-20-90); 144 v H 561 (Eff 4-9-93); 145 v H 571 (Eff 10-6-94); 146 v S 2 (Eff 7-1-96); 146 v H 154 (Eff 10-4-96); 146 v H 180. Eff 1-1-97.

The effective date is set by section 3 of HB 180.

See provisions, § 4 of HB 180 (146 v —) following RC § 2921.34.

Comment, Legislative Service Commission

Section 2929.41 of the Revised Code is amended by this act [Am. Sub. H.B. 180] and also by Sub. H.B. 154 of the 121st General Assembly. Comparison of these amendments in pursuance of section 1.52 of the Revised Code discloses that they are not irreconcilable so that they are required by that section to be harmonized to give effect to each amendment.

[MODIFICATION OF SENTENCE]

§ 2929.51 Modification of sentence.

(A) At the time of sentencing and after sentencing, when imprisonment is imposed for a misdemeanor, the court may do any of the following:

(1) Suspend the sentence and place the offender on probation pursuant to section 2951.02 of the Revised Code;

(2) Suspend the sentence pursuant to section 2951.02 of the Revised Code upon any terms that the court considers appropriate;

(3) Permit the offender to serve the offender's sentence in intermittent confinement, overnight, or on weekends, or both, or at any other time or times that will allow the offender to continue at the offender's occupation or care for the offender's family;

(4) Require the offender to serve a portion of the offender's sentence, which may be served in intermittent confinement, and suspend the balance of the sentence pursuant to section 2951.02 of the Revised Code upon any terms that the court considers appropriate, or suspend the balance of the sentence and place the offender on probation pursuant to that section.

(B) At the time of sentencing and after sentencing, when a term of imprisonment is imposed for a misdemeanor violation of section 2919.25 of the Revised Code, a misdemeanor violation of section 2919.27 of the Revised Code involving a protection order issued or consent agreement approved pursuant to section 2919.26 or 3113.31 of the Revised Code, or a violation of a municipal ordinance that is substantially equivalent to a misdemeanor violation of either of those sections, and when the court has reason to believe, based on an evaluation performed pursuant to section 2919.271 [2919.27.1] of the Revised Code or on the advice of a chemical dependency professional, that the offender is a drug dependent person, is in danger of becoming a drug dependent person, is an alcoholic, or is suffering from acute alcohol intoxication, as defined in section 2935.33 of the Revised Code, the court may require the offender to serve a portion of the offender's sentence and suspend the balance of the sentence and place the offender on probation pursuant to section 2951.02 of the Revised Code, with one of the conditions of probation being that the offender enter into an appropriate treatment program or facility and comply with the treatment prescribed at the program or facility. The court shall order a person to enter a particular program or facility under this division only if the court has received evidence that the program or facility has space available and that the treatment provided by the program or facility is appropriate. For purposes of this division, an appropriate treatment program or facility includes a program licensed by the director of alcohol and drug addiction services pursuant to section 3793.11 of the Revised Code, a program certified by the director of alcohol and drug addiction services pursuant to section 3793.06 of the Revised Code, a public or private hospital, the veterans administration or other agencies of the federal government, or private care or treatment rendered by a physician or a psychologist licensed in the state, a licensed independent social worker, a licensed professional clinical counselor, or a certified chemical dependency counselor. For purposes of this division, the fact that an offender is a repeat offender, as defined in section 2935.36 of the Revised Code, shall not conclusively bar the offender from conditional probation under this division if the previous offenses for which the offender was imprisoned involved misdemeanor violations of section 2919.25 of the Revised Code, misdemeanor violations of section 2919.27 of the Revised Code involving a protection order issued or consent agreement approved pursuant to section 2919.26 or 3113.31 of the Revised Code, or equivalent misdemeanor violations of substantially equivalent municipal ordinances or would have been violations of either of those sections had they been in effect at the time of the violations.

(C) At the time of sentencing and after sentencing, when a fine is imposed for a misdemeanor, the court may do either of the following:

(1) Suspend all or any portion of the fine, upon any conditions that the court imposes in the interests of justice and the correction and rehabilitation of the offender;

(2) Permit payment of all or any portion of the fine in installments, or by any other method and in any time and on any terms that the court considers just, except that the maximum time permitted for payment shall not exceed two years.

HISTORY: 134 v H 511 (Eff 1-1-74); 138 v H 1000 (Eff 4-9-81); 138 v H 682 (Eff 4-9-81); 139 v H 1 (Eff 8-5-81); 139 v S 199 (Eff 7-1-83); 141 v H 475 (Eff 3-7-86); 143 v H 317 (Eff 10-10-89); 143 v S 258 (Eff 11-20-90); 145 v H 152 (Eff 7-1-93); 146 v S 2 (Eff 7-1-96); 146 v S 269 (Eff 7-1-96); 146 v S 223. Eff 3-18-97.

See provisions, § 5 of SB 2 (146 v —) as amended by § 3 of SB 269 (146 v —) following RC § 2929.03.

Comment, Legislative Service Commission

Section 2929.51 of the Revised Code is amended by this act [Am. Sub. S.B. 223] and also by Am. Sub. S.B. 269 of the 121st General Assembly. Comparison of these amendments in pursuance of section 1.52 of the Revised Code discloses that they are not irreconcilable so that they are required by that section to be harmonized to give effect to each amendment.

[OFFENSES PRIOR TO JANUARY 1, 1974]

§ **2929.61** Offense committed prior to January 1, 1974; third or fourth degree felony committed between that date and July 1, 1983.

(A) Persons charged with a capital offense committed prior to January 1, 1974, shall be prosecuted under the law as it existed at the time the offense was committed, and, if convicted, shall be imprisoned for life, except that whenever the statute under which any such person is prosecuted provides for a lesser penalty under the circumstances of the particular case, such lesser penalty shall be imposed.

(B) Persons charged with an offense, other than a capital offense, committed prior to January 1, 1974, shall be prosecuted under the law as it existed at the time the offense was committed. Persons convicted or sentenced on or after January 1, 1974, for an offense committed prior to January 1, 1974, shall be sentenced according to the penalty for commission of the substantially equivalent offense under Amended Substitute House Bill 511 of the 109th General Assembly. If the offense for which sentence is being imposed does not have a substantial equivalent under that act, or if that act provides a more severe penalty than that originally prescribed for the offense of which the person is convicted, then sentence shall be imposed under the law as it existed prior to January 1, 1974.

(C) Persons charged with an offense that is a felony of the third or fourth degree and that was committed on or after January 1, 1974, and before July 1, 1983, shall be prosecuted under the law as it existed at the time the offense was committed. Persons convicted or sentenced on or after July 1, 1983, for an offense that is a felony of the third or fourth degree and that was committed on or after January 1, 1974, and before July 1, 1983, shall be notified by the court sufficiently in advance of sentencing that they may choose to be sentenced pursuant to either the law in effect at the time of the commission of the offense or the law in effect at the time of sentencing. This notice shall be written and shall include the differences between and possible effects of the alternative sentence forms and the effect of the person's refusal to choose. The person to be sentenced shall then inform the court in writing of his choice, and shall be sentenced accordingly. Any person choosing to be sentenced pursuant to the law in effect at the time of the commission of an offense that is a felony of the third or fourth degree shall then be eligible for parole, and this person cannot at a later date have his sentence converted to a definite sentence. If the person refuses to choose between the two possible sentences, the person shall be sentenced pursuant to the law in effect at the time of the commission of the offense.

(D) Persons charged with an offense that was a felony of the first or second degree at the time it was committed, that was committed on or after January 1, 1974, and that was committed prior to July 1, 1983, shall be prosecuted for that offense and, if convicted, shall be sentenced under the law as it existed at the time the offense was committed.

HISTORY: 134 v H 511, § 3 (Eff 1-1-74); 136 v H 1 (Eff 6-13-75); 139 v S 199 (Eff 7-1-83); 139 v H 269 (Eff 7-1-83); 140 v S 210. Eff 7-1-83.

Revised Code § 2929.61 was formerly § 3 of 134 v H 511, eff 1-1-74.

The effective date is set by section 3 of SB 210.

[FIREARM OFFENSES]

§§ 2929.71, 2929.72 Repealed, 146 v S 2, § 6 [139 v S 199; 140 v S 210; 142 v H 261; 143 v S 258; 145 v H 571]. Eff 7-1-96.

These sections concerned offenses involving firearms.

For analogous sentencing provisions, see now RC § 2929.14.

CHAPTER 2930: VICTIMS' RIGHTS

Section
2930.01 Definitions.
2930.02 Exercise of victim's rights by representative.
2930.03 Means of giving notice to victim; notice of changes.
2930.04 Information to be given to victim by investigating law enforcement agency.
2930.05 Notice of arrest of defendant; affidavit concerning violence or intimidation.
2930.06 Prosecutor to confer with victim and provide information; notice of court proceedings.
2930.07 Concealment of victim's or representative's address, telephone number and similar identifying facts.
2930.08 Notice of substantial delay in prosecution; victim's objections.
2930.09 Presence of victim at proceedings; individual providing support.
2930.10 Minimization of unwanted contact between prosecution and defense sides.
2930.11 Return or retention of victim's property.
2930.12 Notice of acquittal or conviction; inclusion of impact statement in presentence investigation report.
2930.13 Victim may make written or oral statement to person preparing impact statement.
2930.14 Victim may make statement prior to sentencing; defendant's opportunity to respond.
2930.15 Notice of filing of appeal; victim's rights after return to trial court.
2930.16 Notice of defendant's incarceration and release date; prior notice of events affecting release or of defendant's escape or death.
2930.17 Victim's statement prior to granting of judicial release.
2930.18 Prohibited actions by employer of victim.
2930.19 Prosecutor's duty to seek compliance; effect of violations; conflicting statutes; incarcerated victims.

§ 2930.01 Definitions.

As used in this chapter:

(A)(1) "Crime" means, subject to division (A)(2) of this section, any of the following:

(a) A felony;

(b) A violation of section 2903.05, 2903.07, 2903.13, 2903.21, 2903.211 [2903.21.1], 2903.22, 2907.06, 2919.25, or 2921.04 of the Revised Code or a violation of a substantially equivalent municipal ordinance.

(2) "Crime" does not mean an act for which an adjudication hearing is or may be held in a juvenile court.

(B) "Custodial agency" means the entity that has custody of a defendant who is incarcerated for a crime or who is detained after a finding of incompetence to stand trial or not guilty by reason of insanity relative to a crime, including any of the following:

(1) The department of rehabilitation and correction or the adult parole authority;

(2) A county sheriff;

(3) The entity that administers a jail, as defined in section 2929.01 of the Revised Code;

(4) The entity that administers a community-based correctional facility and program or a district community-based correctional facility and program;

(5) The department of mental health or other entity to which a defendant found incompetent to stand trial or not guilty by reason of insanity is committed.

(C) "Defendant" means a person who is alleged to be the perpetrator of a crime in a police report or in a complaint, indictment, or information that charges the commission of a crime and that provides the basis for the criminal prosecution and subsequent proceedings to which this chapter makes reference.

(D) "Member of the victim's family" means a spouse, child, stepchild, sibling, parent, stepparent, grandparent, or other relative of a victim but does not include a person who is charged with or convicted of the crime against the victim or another crime arising from the same conduct, criminal episode, or plan.

(E) "Prosecutor" has the same meaning as in section 2935.01 of the Revised Code and also includes the attorney general and, when appropriate, the employees of any person listed in section 2935.01 of the Revised Code or of the attorney general.

(F) "Public agency" means an office, agency, department, bureau, or other governmental entity of the state or of a political subdivision of the state.

(G) "Public official" has the same meaning as in section 2921.01 of the Revised Code.

(H) "Victim" means a person who is identified as the victim of a crime in a police report or in a complaint, indictment, or information that charges the commission of a crime and that provides the basis for the criminal prosecution and subsequent proceedings to which this chapter makes reference.

(I) "Victim's representative" means a member of the victim's family or another person who pursuant to the authority of section 2930.02 of the Revised Code exercises the rights of a victim under this chapter.

HISTORY: 145 v S 186 (Eff 10-12-94); 146 v S 2. Eff 7-1-96.

The effective date is set by section 6 of SB 2.

§ 2930.02 Exercise of victim's rights by representative.

(A) If a victim is a minor or is incapacitated, incompetent, or deceased, or if the victim chooses to designate another person, a member of a victim's family or another person may exercise the rights of the victim under this chapter as the victim's representative.

If more than one person seeks to act as the victim's representative for a particular victim, the court in which the crime is prosecuted shall designate one of those persons as the victim's representative. If a victim does not want to have anyone act as the victim's representative, the court shall order that only the victim may exercise the rights of a victim under this chapter.

(B) If pursuant to division (A) of this section a victim's

representative is to exercise the rights of a victim, the victim or victim's representative shall notify the prosecutor that the victim's representative is to act for the victim. When a victim or victim's representative has so notified the prosecutor, all notice under this chapter shall be sent only to the victim's representative, all rights under this chapter shall be granted only to the victim's representative, and all references in this chapter to a victim shall be interpreted as being references to the victim's representative unless the victim informs the notifying authority that the victim also wishes to receive the notices or exercise the rights. If division (B) of section 2930.03 of the Revised Code requires a victim to make a request in order to receive any notice of a type described in this division and if a victim's representative is to exercise the rights of the victim, the victim's representative shall make the request.

HISTORY: 145 v S 186 (Eff 10-12-94); 146 v S 2. Eff 7-1-96.

The effective date is set by section 6 of SB 2.

§ 2930.03 Means of giving notice to victim; notice of changes.

(A) A person or entity required or authorized under this chapter to give notice to a victim shall give the notice to the victim by any means reasonably calculated to provide prompt actual notice. Except when a provision requires that notice is to be given in a specific manner, a notice may be oral or written.

(B) Except for receipt of the initial information and notice required to be given to a victim under divisions (A) and (B) of section 2930.04, section 2930.05, and divisions (A) and (B) of section 2930.06 of the Revised Code, a victim who wishes to receive any notice authorized by this chapter shall make a request for the notice to the prosecutor or the custodial agency that is to provide the notice, as specified in this chapter. If the victim does not make a request as described in this division, the prosecutor or custodial agency is not required to provide any notice described in this chapter other than the initial information and notice required to be given to a victim under divisions (A) and (B) of section 2930.04, section 2930.05, and divisions (A) and (B) of section 2930.06 of the Revised Code.

(C) A person or agency that is required to furnish notice under this chapter shall give the notice to the victim at the address or telephone number provided to the person or agency by the victim. A victim who requests to receive notice under this chapter as described in division (B) of this section shall inform the person or agency of the name, address, or telephone number of the victim and of any change to that information.

(D) A person or agency that has furnished information to a victim in accordance with any requirement or authorization under this chapter shall notify the victim promptly of any significant changes to that information.

HISTORY: 145 v S 186 (Eff 10-12-94); 146 v S 2. Eff 7-1-96.

The effective date is set by section 6 of SB 2.

§ 2930.04 Information to be given to victim by investigating law enforcement agency.

(A) After its initial contact with a victim of a crime, the law enforcement agency responsible for investigating the crime promptly shall give to the victim, in writing, all of the following information:

(1) An explanation of the victim's rights under this chapter;

(2) Information about medical, counseling, housing, emergency, and any other services that are available to a victim;

(3) Information about compensation for victims under the reparations program in sections 2743.51 to 2743.72 of the Revised Code and the name, street address, and telephone number of the agency to contact to apply for an award of reparations under those sections;

(4) Information about protection that is available to the victim, including protective orders issued by a court.

(B) As soon as practicable after its initial contact with a victim of a crime, the law enforcement agency responsible for investigating the crime shall give to the victim all of the following information:

(1) The business telephone number of the law enforcement officer assigned to investigate the case;

(2) The office address and business telephone number of the prosecutor in the case;

(3) A statement that, if the victim is not notified of the arrest of the offender in the case within a reasonable period of time, the victim may contact the law enforcement agency to learn the status of the case.

(C) To the extent that the information required by this section is provided in the pamphlet prepared pursuant to section 109.42 of the Revised Code or in the information card or other material prepared pursuant to section 2743.71 of the Revised Code, the law enforcement agency may fulfill that portion of its obligations under this section by giving that pamphlet, information card, or other material to the victim.

HISTORY: 145 v S 186 (Eff 10-12-94); 146 v S 2. Eff 7-1-96.

The effective date is set by section 6 of SB 2.

§ 2930.05 Notice of arrest of defendant; affidavit concerning violence or intimidation.

(A) Within a reasonable period of time after the arrest of a defendant for a crime, the law enforcement agency that investigates the crime shall give the victim of the crime notice of all of the following:

(1) The arrest;

(2) The name of the defendant;

(3) Whether the defendant is eligible for pretrial release;

(4) The telephone number of the law enforcement agency;

(5) The victim's right to telephone the agency to ascertain whether the defendant has been released from custody.

(B) If a defendant has been released from custody

on a bond or personal recognizance and the prosecutor in the case has received the affidavit of a victim stating that the defendant, or someone acting at the defendant's direction, has committed or threatened to commit one or more acts of violence or intimidation against the victim, the victim's family, or the victim's representative, the prosecutor may file a motion asking the court to reconsider the conditions of the bond or personal recognizance granted to the defendant.

HISTORY: 145 v S 186 (Eff 10-12-94); 146 v S 2. Eff 7-1-96.

The effective date is set by section 6 of SB 2.

§ 2930.06 Prosecutor to confer with victim and provide information; notice of court proceedings.

(A) The prosecutor in a case, to the extent practicable, shall confer with the victim in the case before pretrial diversion is granted to the defendant in the case, before amending or dismissing an indictment, information, or complaint against that defendant, before agreeing to a negotiated plea for that defendant, or before a trial of that defendant by judge or jury. If the prosecutor fails to confer with the victim at any of those times, the court, if informed of the failure, shall note on the record the failure and the prosecutor's reasons for the failure. A prosecutor's failure to confer with a victim as required by this division does not affect the validity of an agreement between the prosecutor and the defendant in the case, a pretrial diversion of the defendant, an amendment or dismissal of an indictment, information, or complaint filed against the defendant, a plea entered by the defendant, or any other disposition in the case.

(B) After a prosecution in a case has been commenced, the prosecutor or a designee of the prosecutor other than a court or court employee, to the extent practicable, promptly shall give the victim all of the following information:

(1) The name of the offense with which the defendant in the case has been charged and the name of the defendant;

(2) The file number of the case;

(3) A brief statement regarding the procedural steps in a criminal case involving an offense similar to the offense with which the defendant has been charged and the right of the victim to be present during all proceedings held throughout the prosecution of a case;

(4) A summary of the rights of a victim under this chapter;

(5) Procedures the victim or the prosecutor may follow if the victim becomes subject to threats or intimidation by the defendant or any other person;

(6) The name and business telephone number of a person to contact for further information with respect to the case;

(7) The right of the victim to have a victim's representative exercise the victim's rights under this chapter in accordance with section 2930.02 of the Revised Code and the procedure by which a victim's representative may be designated;

(8) Notice that any notification under division (C) of this section and sections 2930.07 to 2930.19 of the Revised Code will be given to the victim only if the victim asks to receive the notification.

(C) Upon the request of the victim, the prosecutor shall give the victim notice of the date, time, and place of any scheduled court proceedings in the case and notice of any changes in those proceedings or in the schedule in the case.

(D) A victim who requests notice under division (C) of this section and who elects pursuant to division (B) of section 2930.03 of the Revised Code to receive any further notice from the prosecutor under this chapter shall keep the prosecutor informed of the victim's current address and telephone number until the case is dismissed or terminated, the defendant is acquitted or sentenced, or the appellate process is completed, whichever is the final disposition in the case.

HISTORY: 145 v S 186 (Eff 10-12-94); 146 v S 2 (Eff 7-1-96); 146 v S 269. Eff 7-1-96.

The effective date is set by section 5 of SB 269.

§ 2930.07 Concealment of victim's or representative's address, telephone number and similar identifying facts.

(A) If the prosecutor in a case determines that there are reasonable grounds for the victim in a case to be apprehensive regarding acts or threats of violence or intimidation by the defendant in the case or at the defendant's direction against the victim, the victim's family, or the victim's representative, the prosecutor may file a motion with the court requesting that the court issue an order specifying that the victim and other witnesses in the case not be compelled in any phase of the criminal proceeding to give testimony that would disclose the victim's or victim's representative's address, place of employment, or similar identifying fact without the victim's or victim's representative's consent. The court shall hold a hearing on the motion in chambers, and a court reporter shall make a record of the proceeding.

(B) If the court, pursuant to division (A) of this section, orders that the victim's or victim's representative's address, telephone number, place of employment, or other identifying fact shall be confidential, the court files or documents shall not contain that information unless it is used to identify the location of the crime. The hearing shall be recorded, and the court shall order the transcript sealed.

HISTORY: 145 v S 186 (Eff 10-12-94); 146 v S 2 (Eff 7-1-96); 146 v S 269. Eff 7-1-96.

The effective date is set by section 5 of SB 269.

§ 2930.08 Notice of substantial delay in prosecution; victim's objections.

If a motion, request, or agreement between counsel

is made in a case and the motion, request, or agreement might result in a substantial delay in the prosecution of the case, the prosecutor in the case, to the extent practicable and if the victim has requested notice pursuant to division (B) of section 2930.03 of the Revised Code, shall inform the victim that the motion, request, or agreement has been made and that it might result in a delay. If the victim objects to the delay, the prosecutor shall inform the court of the victim's objections, and the court shall consider the victim's objections in ruling on the motion, request, or agreement.

HISTORY: 145 v S 186 (Eff 10-12-94); 146 v S 2. Eff 7-1-96.

The effective date is set by section 6 of SB 2.

§ 2930.09 Presence of victim at proceedings; individual providing support.

A victim in a case may be present whenever the defendant in the case is present during any stage of the case against the defendant that is conducted on the record, other than a grand jury proceeding, unless the court determines that exclusion of the victim is necessary to protect the defendant's right to a fair trial. At any stage of the case at which the victim is present, the court, at the victim's request, shall permit the victim to be accompanied by an individual to provide support to the victim unless the court determines that exclusion of the individual is necessary to protect the defendant's right to a fair trial.

HISTORY: 145 v S 186 (Eff 10-12-94); 146 v S 2 (Eff 7-1-96); 146 v S 269. Eff 7-1-96.

The effective date is set by section 5 of SB 269.

§ 2930.10 Minimization of unwanted contact between prosecution and defense sides.

(A) The court in which a criminal case is prosecuted shall make a reasonable effort to minimize any contact between the victim in the case, members of the victim's family, the victim's representative, or witnesses for the prosecution and the defendant in the case, members of the defendant's family, or witnesses for the defense before, during, and immediately after all court proceedings.

(B) The court shall provide a waiting area for the victim, members of the victim's family, the victim's representative, or witnesses for the prosecution that is separate from the waiting area provided for the defendant, members of the defendant's family, and defense witnesses if a separate waiting area is available and the use of the area is practical.

HISTORY: 145 v S 186 (Eff 10-12-94); 146 v S 2. Eff 7-1-96.

The effective date is set by section 6 of SB 2.

§ 2930.11 Return or retention of victim's property.

(A) Except as otherwise provided in this section or in sections 2933.41 to 2933.43 of the Revised Code, the law enforcement agency responsible for investigating a crime shall promptly return to the victim of the crime any property of the victim that was taken in the course of the investigation. In accordance with Criminal Rule 26, the law enforcement agency may take photographs of the property for use as evidence. If the ownership of the property is in dispute, the agency shall not return the property until the dispute is resolved.

(B) The law enforcement agency responsible for investigating a crime shall retain any property of the victim of the crime that is needed as evidence in the case, including any weapon used in the commission of the crime, if the prosecutor certifies to the court a need to retain the property in lieu of a photograph of the property or of another evidentiary substitute for the property itself.

(C) If the defendant in a case files a motion requesting the court to order the law enforcement agency to retain property of the victim because the property is needed for the defense in the case, the agency shall retain the property until the court rules on the motion. The court, in making a determination on the motion, shall weigh the victim's need for the property against the defendant's assertion that the property has evidentiary value for the defense. The court shall rule on the motion in a timely fashion.

HISTORY: 145 v S 186 (Eff 10-12-94); 146 v S 2. Eff 7-1-96.

The effective date is set by section 6 of SB 2.

§ 2930.12 Notice of acquittal or conviction; inclusion of impact statement in presentence investigation report.

At the request of the victim in a case, the prosecutor shall give the victim notice of the defendant's acquittal or conviction. If the defendant is convicted, the notice shall include all of the following:

(A) The crimes of which the defendant was convicted;

(B) The address and telephone number of the probation office or other person, if any, that is to prepare a presentence investigation report pursuant to section 2951.03 of the Revised Code or Criminal Rule 32.2, and the address and telephone number of the person, if any, who is to prepare a victim impact statement pursuant to section 2947.051 [2947.05.1] of the Revised Code;

(C) Notice that the victim may make a statement about the impact of the offense to the probation officer or other person, if any, who prepares the presentence investigation report or to the person, if any, who prepares a victim impact statement, that a statement of the victim included in the report will be made available to the defendant unless the court exempts it from disclosure, and that the court may make the victim impact statement available to the defendant;

(D) Notice of the victim's right under section 2930.14 of the Revised Code to make a statement about the

impact of the offense before sentencing;
(E) The date, time, and place of the sentencing hearing;
(F) Any sentence imposed upon the defendant and any subsequent modification of that sentence, including modification under section 2929.20 of the Revised Code or as a result of the defendant's appeal of the sentence pursuant to section 2953.08 of the Revised Code.

HISTORY: 145 v S 186 (Eff 10-12-94); 146 v S 2. Eff 7-1-96.

The effective date is set by section 6 of SB 2.

§ 2930.13 Victim may make written or oral statement to person preparing impact statement.

(A) If the court orders the preparation of a victim impact statement pursuant to section 2947.051 [2947.05.1] of the Revised Code, the victim in the case may make a written or oral statement regarding the impact of the offense to the person whom the court orders to prepare the victim impact statement. A statement made by the victim under this section shall be included in the victim impact statement.

(B) If a probation officer or other person is preparing a presentence investigation report pursuant to section 2947.06 or 2951.03 of the Revised Code or Criminal Rule 32.2 concerning the defendant in the case, the victim may make a written or oral statement regarding the impact of the offense to the probation officer or other person. The probation officer or other person shall use the statement in preparing the presentence investigation report and, upon the victim's request, shall include a written statement submitted by the victim in the presentence investigation report.

(C) A statement made by the victim under division (A) or (B) of this section may include the following:
(1) An explanation of the nature and extent of any physical, psychological, or emotional harm suffered by the victim as a result of the crime that is the basis of the case;
(2) An explanation of the extent of any property damage or other economic loss suffered by the victim as a result of that crime;
(3) An opinion regarding the extent to which, if any, the victim needs restitution for harm caused by the defendant as a result of that crime and information about whether the victim has applied for or received any compensation for loss or damage caused by that crime;
(4) The victim's recommendation for an appropriate sanction for the defendant regarding that crime.

(D) If a statement made by a victim under division (A) of this section is included in a victim impact statement, the provision, receipt, and retention of copies of, the use of, and the confidentiality, nonpublic record character, and sealing of the victim impact statement is governed by division (C) of section 2947.051 [2947.05.1] of the Revised Code. If a statement made by a victim under division (B) of this section is included in a presentence investigation report prepared pursuant to section 2947.06 or 2951.03 of the Revised Code or Criminal Rule 32.2, the provision, receipt, and retention of copies of, the use of, and the confidentiality, nonpublic record character, and sealing of the presentence investigation report that contains the victim's statement is governed by section 2951.03 of the Revised Code.

HISTORY: 145 v S 186 (Eff 10-12-94); 146 v S 2 (Eff 7-1-96); 146 v S 269. Eff 7-1-96.

The effective date is set by section 5 of SB 269.

§ 2930.14 Victim may make statement prior to sentencing; defendant's opportunity to respond.

(A) Before imposing sentence upon a defendant for the commission of a crime, the court shall permit the victim of the crime to make a statement. The court may give copies of any written statement made by a victim to the defendant and defendant's counsel and may give any written statement made by the defendant to the victim and the prosecutor. The court may redact any information contained in a written statement that the court determines is not relevant to and will not be relied upon in the sentencing decision. The written statement of the victim or of the defendant is confidential and is not a public record as used in section 149.43 of the Revised Code. Any person to whom a copy of a written statement was released by the court shall return it to the court immediately following sentencing.

(B) The court shall consider a victim's statement made under division (A) of this section along with other factors that the court is required to consider in imposing sentence. If the statement includes new material facts, the court shall not rely on the new material facts unless it continues the sentencing proceeding or takes other appropriate action to allow the defendant an adequate opportunity to respond to the new material facts.

HISTORY: 145 v S 186 (Eff 10-12-94); 146 v S 2. Eff 7-1-96.

The effective date is set by section 6 of SB 2.

§ 2930.15 Notice of filing of appeal; victim's rights after reversal.

(A) If a defendant is convicted of committing a crime against a victim, if the victim requests notice of the filing of an appeal, and if the defendant files an appeal, the prosecutor in the case promptly shall notify the victim of the appeal. The prosecutor also shall give the victim all of the following information:
(1) A brief explanation of the appellate process, including the possible disposition of the case;
(2) Whether the defendant has been released on bail or other recognizance pending the disposition of the appeal;
(3) The time, place, and location of appellate court

proceedings and any subsequent changes in the time, place, or location of those proceedings;

(4) The result of the appeal.

(B) If the appellate court returns the defendant's case to the trial court for further proceedings, the victim may exercise all the rights that previously were available to the victim in the trial court.

HISTORY: 145 v S 186 (Eff 10-12-94); 146 v S 2. Eff 7-1-96.

The effective date is set by section 6 of SB 2.

§ 2930.16 Notice of defendant's incarceration and release date; prior notice of events affecting release or of defendant's escape or death.

(A) If a defendant is incarcerated, a victim in a case who has requested to receive notice under this section shall be given notice of the incarceration of the defendant. Promptly after sentence is imposed upon the defendant, the prosecutor in the case shall notify the victim of the date on which the defendant will be released from confinement or the prosecutor's reasonable estimate of that date. The prosecutor also shall notify the victim of the name of the custodial agency of the defendant and tell the victim how to contact that custodial agency. The victim shall keep the custodial agency informed of the victim's current address and telephone number.

(B)(1) Upon the victim's request, the prosecutor promptly shall notify the victim of any hearing for judicial release of the defendant pursuant to section 2929.20 of the Revised Code and of the victim's right to make a statement under that section. The court shall notify the victim of its ruling in each of those hearings and on each of those applications.

(2) Upon the request of a victim of a crime that is a sexually violent offense and that is committed by a sexually violent predator who is sentenced to a prison term pursuant to division (A)(3) of section 2971.03 of the Revised Code, the prosecutor promptly shall notify the victim of any hearing to be conducted pursuant to section 2971.05 of the Revised Code to determine whether to modify the requirement that the offender serve the entire prison term in a state correctional facility in accordance with division (C) of that section, whether to continue, revise, or revoke any existing modification of that requirement, or whether to terminate the prison term in accordance with division (D) of that section. The court shall notify the victim of any order issued at the conclusion of the hearing. As used in this division, "sexually violent offense" and "sexually violent predator" have the same meanings as in section 2971.01 of the Revised Code.

(C) Upon the victim's request made at any time before the particular notice would be due, the custodial agency of a defendant shall give the victim any of the following notices that is applicable:

(1) At least three weeks before the adult parole authority recommends a pardon or commutation of sentence for the defendant or at least three weeks prior to a hearing before the adult parole authority regarding a grant of parole to the defendant, notice of the victim's right to submit a statement regarding the impact of the defendant's release in accordance with section 2967.12 of the Revised Code and, if applicable, of the victim's right to appear at a full board hearing of the parole board to give testimony as authorized by section 5149.101 [5149.10.1] of the Revised Code;

(2) At least three weeks before the defendant is granted a furlough under section 2967.26 or under divisions (A)(1)(c) to (g) of section 2967.27 of the Revised Code or as soon as practicable before the defendant is granted a furlough under division (A)(1)(a) or (b) of section 2967.27 of the Revised Code, notice of the pendency of the furlough and of the victim's right under those sections to submit a statement regarding the impact of the release;

(3) At least three weeks before the defendant is permitted to serve a portion of the defendant's sentence as a period of electronically monitored early release pursuant to section 5120.073 [5120.07.3] of the Revised Code, notice of the pendency of the electronically monitored early release;

(4) Prompt notice of the defendant's escape from a facility of the custodial agency in which the defendant was incarcerated, of the defendant's absence without leave from a mental health or mental retardation and developmental disabilities facility or from other custody, and of the capture of the defendant after an escape or absence;

(5) Notice of the defendant's death while in custody;

(6) Notice of the defendant's release from confinement and the conditions of the release.

HISTORY: 145 v S 186 (Eff 10-12-94); 146 v S 2 (Eff 7-1-96); 146 v H 180. Eff 1-1-97.

The effective date is set by section 3 of HB 180.

See provisions, § 4 of HB 180 (146 v —) following RC § 2921.34.

§ 2930.17 Victim's statement prior to granting of shock probation.

(A) In determining whether to grant a judicial release to a defendant from a prison term pursuant to section 2929.20 of the Revised Code at a time before the defendant's stated prison term expires, the court shall permit a victim of a crime for which the defendant was incarcerated to make a statement, in addition to any other statement made under this chapter, concerning the effects of that crime on the victim, the circumstances surrounding the crime, the manner in which the crime was perpetrated, and the victim's opinion whether the defendant should be released. The victim may make the statement in writing or orally, at the court's discretion. The court shall give the defendant and the adult parole authority a copy of any written impact statement made by the victim under this division.

(B) In deciding whether to grant a judicial release to

the defendant, the court shall consider a statement made by the victim under division (A) of this section or section 2930.14 or 2947.051 [2947.05.1] of the Revised Code.

HISTORY: 145 v S 186 (Eff 10-12-94); 146 v S 2. Eff 7-1-96.

The effective date is set by section 6 of SB 2.

§ 2930.18 Prohibited actions by employer of victim.

No employer of a victim shall discharge, discipline, or otherwise retaliate against the victim, a member of the victim's family, or a victim's representative for participating, at the prosecutor's request, in preparation for a criminal justice proceeding or for attendance, pursuant to a subpoena, at a criminal proceeding if the attendance is reasonably necessary to protect the interests of the victim. This section generally does not require an employer to pay an employee for time lost as a result of attendance at a criminal proceeding. An employer who knowingly violates this section is in contempt of court. This section does not limit or affect the application to any person of section 2151.211 [2151.21.1], 2939.121 [2939.12.1], or 2945.451 [2945.45.1] of the Revised Code.

HISTORY: 145 v S 186 (Eff 10-12-94); 146 v S 2. Eff 7-1-96.

The effective date is set by section 6 of SB 2.

§ 2930.19 Prosecutor's duty to seek compliance; effect of violations; conflicting statutes; incarcerated victims.

(A) In a manner consistent with the duty of a prosecutor to represent the interests of the public as a whole, a prosecutor shall seek compliance with this chapter on behalf of a victim, a member of the victim's family, or the victim's representative.

(B) The failure of a public official or public agency to comply with the requirements of this chapter does not give rise to a claim for damages against that public official or public agency, except that a public agency as an employer may be held responsible for a violation of section 2930.18 of the Revised Code.

(C) The failure of any person or entity to provide a right, privilege, or notice to a victim under this chapter does not constitute grounds for declaring a mistrial or new trial, for setting aside a conviction or sentence, or for granting postconviction release to a defendant.

(D) If there is a conflict between a provision in this chapter and a specific statute governing the procedure in a case involving a capital offense, the specific statute supersedes the provision in this chapter.

(E) If the victim of a crime is incarcerated in a state or local correctional facility, the victim's rights under this chapter may be modified by court order to prevent any security risk, hardship, or undue burden upon a public official or public agency with a duty under this chapter.

HISTORY: 145 v S 186 (Eff 10-12-94); 146 v S 2. Eff 7-1-96.

The effective date is set by section 6 of SB 2.

CHAPTER 2931: JURISDICTION; VENUE

For text of the Ohio Rules of Criminal Procedure, see page 1351

Section

[JURISDICTION]

2931.01 Definition of magistrate.
2931.02 General jurisdiction.
2931.03 Jurisdiction of court of common pleas.
2931.04 Jurisdiction of municipal courts not affected.
[2931.04.1] 2931.041 Repealed.
2931.05 Repealed.
2931.06 Special constables in certain townships.
2931.07 Recognizance.
2931.08-2931.14 Repealed.
2931.15 New trial.
2931.16, 2931.17 Repealed.
2931.18 Humane society may employ attorneys.
2931.19-2931.28 Repealed.

[CHANGE OF VENUE]

2931.29 Procedure on change of venue.
2931.30 Transfer of prisoner on change of venue.
2931.31 Payment of costs and expenses on change of venue.
2931.32 Repealed.

[JURISDICTION]

§ 2931.01 Definition of magistrate.

As used in Chapters 2931. to 2953. of the Revised Code:
(A) "Magistrate" includes county court judges, police justices, mayors of municipal corporation[s], and judges of other courts inferior to the court of common pleas.
(B) "Judge" does not include the probate judge.
(C) "Court" does not include the probate court.
(D) "Clerk" does not include the clerk of the probate court.

HISTORY: GC § 13422-1; 113 v 123; 114 v 320(479); Bureau of Code Revision, 10-1-53; 127 v 1039(1096) (Eff 1-1-58); 136 v H 205. Eff 1-1-76.

The effective date is set by section 4 of HB 205.

§ 2931.02 General jurisdiction.

A judge of a county court is a conservator of the peace and has jurisdiction in criminal cases throughout his area of jurisdiction. He may hear complaints of [breach of] the peace and issue search warrants. Judges of county courts have jurisdiction on sworn complaint, to issue a warrant for the arrest of a person charged with the commission of a felony where it is made to appear that such person has fled or is outside this state and it is necessary or desirable to extradite such person. Judges of county courts have jurisdiction within their respective areas of jurisdiction in all cases of violation of any law relating to:
(A) Adulteration or deception in the sale of dairy products and other food, drink, drugs, and medicines;
(B) Prevention of cruelty to animals and children;
(C) The abandonment, nonsupport, or ill treatment of a child under eighteen years of age or a physically and mentally handicapped child under the age of eighteen years by its parents;
(D) The abandonment, or ill treatment of a child under eighteen years of age or a physically and mentally handicapped child under the age of eighteen years by its guardian;
(E) The employment of a child under fourteen years of age in public exhibitions or vocations injurious to health, life, or morals, or which will cause or permit him to suffer unnecessary physical or mental pain;
(F) The regulation, restriction, or prohibition of the employment of females and minors;
(G) The torturing, unlawfully punishing, ill treating, or depriving anyone of necessary food, clothing, or shelter;
(H) Any violation of Chapters 4301. and 4303. of the Revised Code, or keeping a place where intoxicating liquor is sold, given away, or furnished in violation of any law prohibiting such acts;
(I) The shipping, selling, using, permitting the use of, branding, or having unlawful quantities of illuminating oil for or in a mine;
(J) The sale, shipment, or adulteration of commercial feeds;
(K) The use of dust-creating machinery in workshops and factories;
(L) The conducting of a pharmacy, or retail drug or chemical store, or the dispensing or selling of drugs, chemicals, poisons, or pharmaceutical preparations therein;
(M) The failure to place and keep in a sanitary condition a bakery, confectionery, creamery, dairy barn, milk depot, laboratory, hotel, restaurant, eating house, packing house, slaughterhouse, ice cream factory, or place where a food product is manufactured, packed, stored, deposited, collected, prepared, produced, or sold for any purpose, or for the violation of any law relating to public health;
(N) Inspection of steam boilers, and of laws licensing steam engineers and boiler operators;
(O) Prevention of short weighing and measuring and all violations of the weights and measures laws;
(P) Laws relating to the practice of medicine or surgery, or any of its branches;
(Q) Laws relating to the filling or refilling of registered containers by other than the owner, or the defacing of the marks of ownership thereon;
(R) Offenses arising from or growing out of the violation of conservation laws.

HISTORY: GC § 13422-2; 113 v 123; 117 v 586; Bureau of

Code Revision, 10-1-53; 127 v 1039(1096) (Eff 1-1-58); 128 v 823(859) (Eff 11-6-59); 132 v S 65 (Eff 11-17-67); 133 v H 1 (Eff 3-18-69); 135 v S 1. Eff 1-1-74.

§ 2931.03 Jurisdiction of court of common pleas.

The court of common pleas has original jurisdiction of all crimes and offenses, except in cases of minor offenses the exclusive jurisdiction of which is vested in courts inferior to the court of common pleas.

HISTORY: GC § 13422-5; 113 v 123, § 5; Bureau of Code Revision. Eff 10-1-53.

§ 2931.04 Jurisdiction of municipal courts not affected.

Sections 2931.01 to 2931.03, inclusive, of the Revised Code, do not affect, modify, or limit the jurisdiction of municipal courts. All municipal court judges have jurisdiction within the territory for which they were elected or appointed in all cases of violation of Chapters 4301. and 4303. of the Revised Code and of prosecutions for keeping a place where intoxicating liquor is sold, given away, or furnished, in violation of any law prohibiting such acts.

HISTORY: GC § 13422-6; 113 v 123, § 6; 115 v PtII, 118(164), § 62; Bureau of Code Revision, 10-1-53; 128 v 823(861). Eff 11-6-59.

[§ 2931.04.1] § 2931.041 Repealed,
141 v H 158, § 2 [128 v 141; 129 v 582 (748)]. Eff 3-17-87.

This section concerned jurisdiction of municipal courts in criminal cases.

§ 2931.05 Repealed, 128 v 97(116), § 2 [GC § 13423-1; 113 v 123; Bureau of Code Revision, 10-1-53; 127 v 1039]. Eff 1-1-60.

This section concerned bills of exception in summary convictions.

§ 2931.06 Special constables in certain townships.

When the constables in a township situated on and consisting in whole or in part of one or more islands in a lake in this state, or in a township adjoining or abutting on lands belonging to a state or national home for disabled volunteer soldiers or a disabled volunteer soldiers' home, are insufficient to maintain the peace and enforce the laws for the preservation of order therein, a judge of the county court having jurisdiction in [such] township may appoint not more than ten special constables to be conservators of the peace within such township and with powers of constables in criminal causes. The appointing judge shall enter such appointments upon his docket and they shall continue in force for one year unless revoked by him. Such special constables shall receive like fees as are paid for similar services to regular constables.

HISTORY: GC § 13423-2; 113 v 123, ch 2, § 2; Bureau of Code Revision, 10-1-53; 127 v 1039(1097). Eff 1-1-58.

§ 2931.07 Recognizance.

Recognizances taken by a judge of a county court or other officer authorized to take them, may be returned to the court of common pleas.

Such recognizances shall be returned to such court forthwith after the commitment of the accused, or after the taking of a recognizance for his appearance before such court. The prosecuting attorney may proceed with the prosecution in such court, and the accused shall appear therein and answer to his recognizance.

HISTORY: GC §§ 13423-2a, b; 114 v 320(480), § 3; Bureau of Code Revision, 10-1-53; 127 v 1039(1098). Eff 1-1-58.

§§ 2931.08, 2931.09, 2931.10
Repealed, 141 v H 158, § 2 [GC §§ 13423-3–13423-5; 113 v 123, ch 2, §§ 3-5; Bureau of Code Revision, 10-1-53; 125 v S 361; 127 v 1039(1098); 141 v S 54]. Eff 3-17-87.

These sections concerned payment of fines to county treasury by judge of county court.

§§ 2931.11, 2931.12 Repealed, 128 v 97(116), § 2 [GC §§ 13424-1, 13424-2; 113 v 123; Bureau of Code Revision, 10-1-53]. Eff 1-1-60.

These sections provided for jury trial before a magistrate and venire of jurors in magistrate's court.

§§ 2931.13, 2931.14 Repealed, 128 v 97(116), § 2 [GC §§ 13424-3, 13424-4; 113 v 123; Bureau of Code Revision, 10-1-53]. Eff 1-1-60.

These sections concerned challenges to jurors and the need for the information or affidavit on which charge is based to indicate it is a subsequent offense.

§ 2931.15† New trial.

In prosecutions before a magistrate, a defendant who has been found guilty upon the verdict of a jury or by the decision of the magistrate without the intervention of a jury may[,] upon written application filed within three days after the verdict or decision, be granted a new trial in like manner and for like reasons as provided by sections 2945.79 to 2945.83, inclusive, of the Revised Code.

HISTORY: GC § 13424-5; 113 v 123, ch 3, § 5; Bureau of Code Revision, 10-1-53; 128 v 141. Eff 1-1-60.

† This section was repealed by the 103rd General Assembly in S 73 (128 v 97 [116]) passed July 21, 1959, filed August 7,

1959 and effective Jan. 1, 1960. However, amendment in S 133 (128 v 141) was passed July 23, 1959, filed August 12, 1959 and effective Jan. 1, 1960. Apparently, the amendment prevails.

§§ 2931.16, 2931.17 Repealed, 128 v 97 (116), § 2 [GC §§ 13424-6, 13424-7; 113 v 123; Bureau of Code Revision, 10-1-53]. Eff 1-1-60.

These sections referred to jurors' fees and security for costs of prosecution payable from county treasury.

§ 2931.18 Humane society may employ attorneys.

A humane society or its agent may employ an attorney, and may also employ one or more assistant attorneys to prosecute violations of law relating to:

(A) Prevention of cruelty to animals or children;

(B) Abandonment, nonsupport, or ill-treatment of a child by its parent;

(C) Employment of a child under fourteen years of age in public exhibitions or vocations injurious to health, life, or morals or which cause or permit such child to suffer unnecessary physical or mental pain;

(D) Neglect or refusal of an adult to support destitute parent. Such attorneys shall be paid out of the county treasury in an amount approved as just and reasonable by the board of county commissioners of that county.

HISTORY: GC § 13424-8; 113 v 123, ch 3, § 8; Bureau of Code Revision, 10-1-53; 130 v 664 (Eff 10-8-63); 142 v H 246. Eff 12-12-88.

§§ 2931.19, 2931.20, 2931.21 Repealed, 134 v H 511, § 2 [GC §§ 13426-3—13426-5; 113 v 123; Bureau of Code Revision, 10-1-53; 126 v 812]. Eff 1-1-74.

These sections concerned venue. See now RC § 2901.12 and Crim R 18.

§§ 2931.22, 2931.23, 2931.24 Repealed, 134 v H 511, § 2 [GC §§ 13426-6—13426-8; 113 v 123; Bureau of Code Revision, 10-1-53]. Eff 1-1-74.

These sections concerned venue.

§§ 2931.25, 2931.26 Repealed, 134 v H 511, § 2 [GC §§ 13426-9, 13426-10; 113 v 123; Bureau of Code Revision, 10-1-53]. Eff 1-1-74.

These sections concerned venue.

§§ 2931.27, 2931.28 Repealed, 134 v H 511, § 2 [GC §§ 13426-11, 13426-12; 113 v 123; 115 v 532; Bureau of Code Revision, 10-1-53]. Eff 1-1-74.

These sections concerned venue.

[CHANGE OF VENUE]

§ 2931.29 Procedure on change of venue.

When a change of venue is ordered pursuant to section 2901.12 of the Revised Code, the clerk of the court in which the cause is pending shall make a certified transcript of the proceedings in the case, which, with the original affidavit, complaint, indictment, or information, he shall transmit to the clerk of the court to which said case is sent for trial, and the trial shall be conducted as if the cause had originated in the jurisdiction of the latter court. The prosecuting attorney, city director of law, or other officer who would have prosecuted the case in the court in which the cause originated shall take charge of and try the cause, and the court to which the cause is sent may on application appoint one or more attorneys to assist the prosecutor in the trial, and allow the appointed attorneys reasonable compensation.

HISTORY: GC § 13427-1; 113 v 123, ch 6; Bureau of Code Revision, 10-1-53; 134 v H 511 (Eff 1-1-74); 137 v H 219. Eff 11-1-77.

§ 2931.30 Transfer of prisoner on change of venue.

When a change of venue is ordered pursuant to section 2901.12 of the Revised Code, and the accused is in jail, a warrant shall be issued by the clerk of the court in which the cause originated, directed to the proper officer, commanding him to convey the prisoner to the jail of the county or municipal corporation where the prisoner is to be tried, there to be kept until discharged. If the accused is charged with a bailable offense, and at the date of the order changing the venue is under bond for his appearance at the court from which the venue is changed, the court may fix in said order the amount of recognizance which said accused shall give for his appearance at the time the court may designate, in the court to which the venue is changed, and the clerk shall take such recognizance as in other cases, and forward the same with the record. The court shall recognize the witnesses of the prosecution to appear before the court in which the accused is to be tried.

HISTORY: GC § 13427-2; 113 v 123, ch 6, § 2; Bureau of Code Revision, 10-1-53; 134 v H 511. Eff 1-1-74.

§ 2931.31 Payment of costs and expenses on change of venue.

The reasonable expenses of the officer acting as prosecutor, incurred in consequence of a change of venue under section 2901.12 of the Revised Code, the fees of the clerk of the court to which the venue is changed, the sheriff or bailiff, and of the jury shall be allowed and paid out of the treasury of the county in which said cause originated.

HISTORY: GC § 13427-3; 113 v 123, ch 6, § 3; **Bureau of Code Revision,** 10-1-53; 134 v H 511. Eff 1-1-74.

§ 2931.32 Repealed, 134 v H 511, § 2 [GC § 13426-2; 113 v 123; Bureau of Code Revision, 10-1-53]. Eff 1-1-74.

This section concerned offenses on or near county boundaries.

CHAPTER 2933: PEACE WARRANTS; SEARCH WARRANTS

Section	
2933.01	Definition of magistrate.

[PEACE WARRANT]

Section	
2933.02	Complaint to keep the peace.
2933.03	Form of warrant to keep the peace.
2933.04	Arraignment.
2933.05	Hearing; discharge, bond, or commitment.
2933.06	Appeal; bond; transcript.
2933.07	Discharge on failure to prosecute.
2933.08	Hearing; judgment.
2933.09	Commitment to jail.
2933.10	Committing without process.

[PROBATION CONDITIONED UPON TREATMENT]

2933.16	Treatment as condition of probation after conviction of certain domestic offenses.

[SEARCH WARRANT]

2933.21	Search warrant.
2933.22	Probable cause.
2933.23	Affidavit for search warrant.
[2933.23.1] 2933.231	Request for waiver of statutory precondition for nonconsensual entry.
2933.24	Contents of search warrant; report of inspection findings.
[2933.24.1] 2933.241	Inventory of property taken.
2933.25	Form of search warrant.
2933.26	Property seized to be kept by court.
2933.27	Disposition of property before trial.
2933.28	Repealed.
2933.29	Property seized liable for fines.
2933.30	Search for dead bodies.
2933.31	Search in case of animals.
2933.32	Body cavity and strip searches; conducting unauthorized search; failure to prepare proper report.
2933.41	Disposition of property held by law enforcement agency.
2933.42	Offenses involving contraband; forfeiture of property used in committing violation.
2933.43	Procedure for seizure and forfeiture of contraband; law enforcement agency authorized to use, destroy, or sell forfeited contraband; distribution of proceeds of sale.
2933.44	Annual report by alcohol and drug treatment program receiving juvenile-related forfeiture.

[WIRETAPPING, ELECTRONIC SURVEILLANCE]

2933.51	Definitions.
2933.52	Interception of wire, oral or electronic communications.
[2933.52.1] 2933.521	Divulgence of content of communication by provider of electronic communication service.
[2933.52.2] 2933.522	Powers of common pleas court judge.
2933.53	Application for interception warrant.
2933.54	Conditions for issuance of warrant; denial; termination; finding of objective.
2933.55	Application for extension of warrant; interception concerning other than designated offenses.
2933.56	Contents of warrant; sealing of application and warrant; disclosure; retention.
2933.57	Oral order for interception without warrant.
2933.58	Instructions to investigative officers; procedure for interception; territorial validity.
[2933.58.1] 2933.581	Persons providing information, facilities or technical assistance to officer; prohibited disclosures; immunity.
2933.59	Execution of warrant or oral order; recording or resume; termination; tampering; destruction of documents; disclosure.
[2933.59.1] 2933.591	Giving warning of possible surveillance.
2933.60	Reports by judges and prosecuting attorneys.
2933.61	Service of inventory on interested persons; inspection of materials.
2933.62	Conditions for receiving results in evidence or disclosure.
2933.63	Motion to suppress evidence; appeals by state.
2933.64	Training in wiretapping and electronic surveillance.
2933.65	Civil and criminal actions for violations.
2933.66	Judge to conform proceedings to constitutions.

[MEDICAID FRAUD FORFEITURES]

2933.71	Definitions.
2933.72	Order to preserve reachability of property that may be forfeitable; temporary restraining order; post-conviction actions.
2933.73	Civil hearing; forfeiture order; petition by innocent person claiming interest in property.
2933.74	Settlement of claims; awards to informants; protection of rights of innocent persons; disposal of property; use of proceeds.
2933.75	Filing of medicaid fraud lien notice; trustees of forfeitable property.
2933.76	Authorization of pen register or trap and trace device.
2933.77	Duty to provide information, facilities or technical assistance; immunity.

§ 2933.01 Definition of magistrate.

The definition of "magistrate" set forth in section 2931.01 of the Revised Code applies to Chapter 2933. of the Revised Code.

HISTORY: Bureau of Code Revision. Eff 10-1-53.

[PEACE WARRANT]

§ 2933.02 Complaint to keep the peace.

When a complaint is made in writing and upon oath, filed with a municipal or county court or a mayor sitting as the judge of a mayor's court, and states that the complainant has just cause to fear and fears that another individual will commit an offense against the person or property of the complainant or his ward or child, a municipal or county court judge or mayor shall issue to the sheriff or to any other appropriate peace officer, as defined in section 2935.01 of the Revised Code, within the territorial jurisdiction of the court, a warrant in the name of the state that commands him forthwith to arrest and take the individual complained of before the court to answer the complaint.

HISTORY: GC § 13428-1; 113 v 123, ch 7, § 1; Bureau of Code Revision, 10-1-53; 141 v H 412. Eff 3-17-87.

§ 2933.03 Form of warrant to keep the peace.

Warrants issued under section 2933.02 of the Revised Code shall be substantially in the following form:
The state of Ohio,. . . . . . . County, ss:
To the sheriff or other appropriate peace officer, greeting:

Whereas, a complaint has been filed by one C. D., in writing and upon oath, stating that he has just cause to fear and does fear that one E. F. will (here state the threatened injury or violence according to the fact as sworn to).

These are therefore to command you to forthwith arrest E. F. and bring him before this court to show cause why he should not find surety to keep the peace and be of good behavior toward the citizens of the state generally, and C. D. especially, and for his appearance before the proper court.

Given under my hand, this . . . . . . day of . . .
    A. B., Judge,........................... County Court;
    Judge,................................Municipal Court;
    Mayor, ... Mayor's Court

HISTORY: GC § 13428-2; 113 v 123, ch 7, § 2; Bureau of Code Revision, 10-1-53; 127 v 1039(1099) (Eff 1-1-58); 141 v H 412. Eff 3-17-87.

§ 2933.04 Arraignment.

When the accused in [is] brought before the municipal, county, or mayor's court pursuant to sections 2933.02 and 2933.03 of the Revised Code, he shall be heard in his defense. If it is necessary for just cause to adjourn the hearing, the municipal or county court judge or mayor involved may order such adjournment. The judge or mayor also may direct the sheriff or other peace officer having custody of the accused to detain him in the county jail or other appropriate detention facility until the cause of delay is removed, unless a bond in a sum fixed by the judge or mayor but not to exceed five hundred dollars, with sufficient surety, is given by the accused. A delay shall not exceed two days.

HISTORY: GC § 13428-3; 113 v 123(133), ch 7, § 3; Bureau of Code Revision, 10-1-53; 141 v H 412. Eff 3-17-87.

§ 2933.05 Hearing; discharge, bond, or commitment.

The municipal or county court judge or mayor sitting as the judge of a mayor's court, upon the appearance of the parties pursuant to sections 2933.02 to 2933.04 of the Revised Code, shall hear the witnesses under oath and do one of the following:

(A) Discharge the accused, render judgment against the complainant for costs, and award execution for the costs;

(B) Order the accused to enter into a bond of not less than fifty or more than five hundred dollars, with sufficient surety, to keep the peace and be of good behavior for such time as may be just, render judgment against him for costs, and award execution for the costs.

In default of such bond, the judge or mayor shall commit the accused to the county jail or other appropriate detention facility, until such order is complied with or he is discharged.

HISTORY: RS §§ 7109, 7110; 66 v 288, §§ 3, 5; 71 v 70, § 2; GC §§ 13428-4, 13428-5; 107 v 402; 113 v 123(133), ch 7, §§ 4, 5; Bureau of Code Revision, 10-1-53; 141 v H 412. Eff 3-17-87.

§ 2933.06 Appeal; bond; transcript.

The accused under sections 2933.02 to 2933.05 of the Revised Code may appeal from the decision of a municipal or county court judge to the appropriate court of appeals or from the decision of a mayor sitting as the judge of a mayor's court to the appropriate municipal or county court. An appeal from the decision of a municipal or county court judge to the appropriate court of appeals shall be only as to questions of law and, to the extent that sections 2933.06 to 2933.09 of the Revised Code do not contain relevant provisions, shall be made and proceed in accordance with the Rules of Appellate Procedure. An appeal from the decision of a mayor sitting as the judge of a mayor's court to the appropriate municipal or county court shall be as to questions of law and fact, and shall be made and proceed in accordance with sections 2933.06 to 2933.09 of the Revised Code.

In connection with either type of appeal, the accused shall file with the clerk of the municipal, county, or mayor's court, within ten days after the decision is rendered, an appeal bond in a sum to be fixed by the judge or mayor at not less than fifty or more than five hundred dollars, with surety to be approved by the judge or mayor, conditioned that, pending the determination of the appeal, the accused will keep the peace and will be of good behavior generally and especially towards the person named in the complaint. Upon the filing of the appeal bond, the clerk of the municipal, county, or mayor's court forthwith shall make a certified transcript of the proceedings in the action, the appeal bond to be included. Upon the payment by the appellant of the fee for the transcript, the clerk immediately shall file the transcript and all the original papers in the action in the office of the clerk of the appellate court.

HISTORY: GC § 13428-6; 113 v 123(133), ch 7, § 6; Bureau of Code Revision, 10-1-53; 141 v H 412. Eff 3-17-87.

§ 2933.07 Discharge on failure to prosecute.

In the case of an appeal from the decision of a mayor

sitting as the judge of a mayor's court to the appropriate municipal or county court, no further pleadings shall be required. If the complainant fails to prosecute in such an appeal, the accused shall be discharged unless good cause to the contrary is shown, and the municipal or county court shall render judgment against the complainant for the costs of prosecution and award execution for the costs.

HISTORY: GC § 13428-7; 113 v 123(134), ch 7, § 7; Bureau of Code Revision, 10-1-53; 141 v H 412. Eff 3-17-87.

§ 2933.08 Hearing; judgment.

In the case of an appeal from the decision of a mayor sitting as the judge of a mayor's court to the appropriate municipal or county court, the municipal or county court shall set a time for the hearing of that appeal and, at that time, shall hear the witnesses under oath, and either discharge the accused, render judgment against the complainant for costs, and award execution for the costs, or order the accused to enter into a bond, for such time as may be just, to keep the peace and be of good behavior, render judgment against him for costs, and award execution for the costs.

HISTORY: GC § 13428-8; 113 v 123(134), ch 7, § 8; Bureau of Code Revision, 10-1-53; 141 v H 412. Eff 3-17-87.

§ 2933.09 Commitment to jail.

In the case of an appeal from the decision of a mayor sitting as the judge of a mayor's court to the appropriate municipal or county court, if the accused fails to enter into a bond ordered pursuant to section 2933.08 of the Revised Code, the municipal or county court shall commit the accused to jail until he enters into a bond or is discharged by law, and shall render judgment against him for costs and award execution for the costs. He shall not be imprisoned longer than one year.

After such a commitment following such an appeal, or after a commitment of not more than one year for not entering into a bond ordered pursuant to section 2933.05 of the Revised Code, if such an appeal was not taken, the court may at any time discharge the accused on his own recognizance.

HISTORY: GC § 13428-9; 113 v 123(134), ch 7, § 9; Bureau of Code Revision, 10-1-53; 141 v H 412. Eff 3-17-87.

§ 2933.10 Committing without process.

Whoever, in the presence of a municipal or county court judge, or a mayor sitting as the judge of a mayor's court, makes an affray, threatens to beat or kill another or to commit an offense against the person or property of another, or contends with angry words to the disturbance of the peace, may be ordered without process or other proof to enter into a bond under section 2933.05 of the Revised Code. In default of such a bond, the person may be committed under that section.

HISTORY: GC § 13428-10; 113 v 123(134), ch 7, § 10; Bureau of Code Revision, 10-1-53; 141 v H 412 (Eff 3-17-87); 142 v H 708. Eff 4-19-88.

[PROBATION CONDITIONED UPON TREATMENT]

§ 2933.16 Treatment as condition of probation after conviction of certain domestic offenses.

Without limiting any other power of the court to grant or revoke probation, if an offender is convicted of, or pleads guilty to, a violation of division (B) of section 2919.22, or section 2919.25 of the Revised Code, the court may suspend execution of sentence and place the offender on probation conditioned upon the participation of the offender, to the satisfaction of the court, in a program of clinically appropriate psychiatric or psychological treatment.

HISTORY: 137 v H 835. Eff 3-27-79.

[SEARCH WARRANT]

§ 2933.21 Search warrant.

A judge of a court of record may, within his jurisdiction, issue warrants to search a house or place:

(A) For property stolen, taken by robbers, embezzled, or obtained under false pretense;

(B) For weapons, implements, tools, instruments, articles or property used as a means of the commission of a crime, or when any of the objects or articles are in the possession of another person with the intent to use them as a means of committing crime;

(C) For forged or counterfeit coins, stamps, imprints, labels, trade-marks, bank bills, or other instruments of writing, and dies, plates, stamps, or brands for making them;

(D) For obscene materials and materials harmful to minors involved in a violation of section 2907.31 or 2907.32 of the Revised Code, but only so much of such materials shall be seized as are [is] necessary for evidence in a prosecution of the violation;

(E) For [any] gaming table, establishment, device, or apparatus kept or exhibited for unlawful gaming, or to win or gain money or other property, and for money or property won by unlawful gaming;

(F) For the existence of physical conditions which are or may become hazardous to the public health, safety, or welfare, when governmental inspections of property are authorized or required by law.

The enumeration of certain property and material in this section shall not affect or modify other laws for search and seizure.

HISTORY: RS § 7120; S&C 455; 56 v 86, § 4; 66 v 289, § 13;

73 v 159, § 3; GC § 13430-1; 113 v 123(136), ch 9; 120 v 230; 124 v 124; Bureau of Code Revision, 10-1-53; 133 v H 84 (Eff 9-15-70); 134 v S 397 (Eff 10-23-72); 135 v H 1 (Eff 3-22-73); 135 v H 989 (Eff 9-16-74); 136 v H 1. Eff 6-13-75.

§ 2933.22 Probable cause.

(A) A warrant of search or seizure shall issue only upon probable cause, supported by oath or affirmation particularly describing the place to be searched and the property and things to be seized.

(B) A warrant of search to conduct an inspection of property shall issue only upon probable cause to believe that conditions exist upon such property which are or may become hazardous to the public health, safety, or welfare.

HISTORY: GC § 13430-2; 113 v 123(137), ch 9, § 2; Bureau of Code Revision, 10-1-53; 134 v S 397. Eff 10-23-72.

§ 2933.23 Affidavit for search warrant.

A search warrant shall not be issued until there is filed with the judge or magistrate an affidavit that particularly describes the place to be searched, names or describes the person to be searched, and names or describes the property to be searched for and seized; that states substantially the offense in relation to the property and that the affiant believes and has good cause to believe that the property is concealed at the place or on the person; and that states the facts upon which the affiant's belief is based. The judge or magistrate may demand other and further evidence before issuing the warrant. If the judge or magistrate is satisfied that grounds for the issuance of the warrant exist or that there is probable cause to believe that they exist, he shall issue the warrant, identifying in it the property and naming or describing the person or place to be searched.

A search warrant issued pursuant to this chapter or Criminal Rule 41 also may contain a provision waiving the statutory precondition for nonconsensual entry, as described in division (C) of section 2933.231 [2933.23.1] of the Revised Code, if the requirements of that section are satisfied.

HISTORY: GC § 13430-3; 113 v 123(137), ch 9, § 3; Bureau of Code Revision, 10-1-53; 130 v 664 (Eff 10-14-63); 143 v S 258. Eff 11-20-90.

The effective date is set by section 15 of SB 258.

[§ 2933.23.1] § 2933.231 Request for waiver of statutory precondition for nonconsensual entry.

(A) As used in this section:

(1) "Law enforcement officer" has the same meaning as in section 2901.01 of the Revised Code and in Criminal Rule 2.

(2) "Prosecutor" has the same meaning as in section 2935.01 of the Revised Code, and includes any prosecuting attorney as defined in Criminal Rule 2.

(3) "Statutory precondition for nonconsensual entry" means the precondition specified in section 2935.12 of the Revised Code that requires a law enforcement officer or other authorized individual executing a search warrant to give notice of his intention to execute the warrant and then be refused admittance to a dwelling house or other building before he legally may break down a door or window to gain entry to execute the warrant.

(B) A law enforcement officer, prosecutor, or other authorized individual who files an affidavit for the issuance of a search warrant pursuant to this chapter or Criminal Rule 41 may include in the affidavit a request that the statutory precondition for nonconsensual entry be waived in relation to the search warrant. A request for that waiver shall contain all of the following:

(1) A statement that the affiant has good cause to believe that there is a risk of serious physical harm to the law enforcement officers or other authorized individuals who will execute the warrant if they are required to comply with the statutory precondition for nonconsensual entry;

(2) A statement setting forth the facts upon which the affiant's belief is based, including, but not limited to, the names of all known persons who the affiant believes pose the risk of serious physical harm to the law enforcement officers or other authorized individuals who will execute the warrant at the particular dwelling house or other building;

(3) A statement verifying the address of the dwelling house or other building proposed to be searched as the correct address in relation to the criminal offense or other violation of law underlying the request for the issuance of the search warrant;

(4) A request that, based on those facts, the judge or magistrate waive the statutory precondition for nonconsensual entry.

(C) If an affidavit for the issuance of a search warrant filed pursuant to this chapter or Criminal Rule 41 includes a request for a waiver of the statutory precondition for nonconsensual entry, if the request conforms with division (B) of this section, if division (E) of this section is satisfied, and if the judge or magistrate issues the warrant, the judge or magistrate shall include in it a provision that waives the statutory precondition for nonconsensual entry for purposes of the search and seizure authorized under the warrant only if he determines there is probable cause to believe that, if the law enforcement officers or other authorized individuals who execute the warrant are required to comply with the statutory precondition for nonconsensual entry, they will be subjected to a risk of serious physical harm and to believe that the address of the dwelling house or other building to be searched is the correct address in relation to the criminal offense or other violation of law underlying the issuance of the warrant.

(D)(1) A waiver of the statutory precondition for nonconsensual entry by a judge or magistrate pursuant to division (C) of this section does not authorize, and shall not be construed as authorizing, a law enforcement officer or other authorized individual who executes a search warrant to enter a building other than a building described in the warrant.

(2) The state or any political subdivision associated with a law enforcement officer or other authorized officer who executes a search warrant that contains a provision waiving the statutory precondition for nonconsensual entry is liable in damages in a tort action for any injury, death, or loss to person or property that is proximately caused by the officer's execution of the warrant in accordance with the waiver at an address of a dwelling house or other building that is not described in the warrant.

(E) Any proceeding before a judge or magistrate that involves a request for a waiver of the statutory precondition for nonconsensual entry shall be recorded by shorthand, by stenotype, or by any other mechanical, electronic, or video recording device. The recording of and any transcript of the recording of such a proceeding shall not be a public record for purposes of section 149.43 of the Revised Code until the search warrant is returned by the law enforcement officer or other authorized officer who executes it. This division shall not be construed as requiring, authorizing, or permitting, and does not require, authorize, or permit, the making available for inspection, or the copying, under section 149.43 of the Revised Code of any confidential law enforcement investigatory record or trial preparation record, as defined in that section.

HISTORY: 143 v S 258. Eff 11-20-90.

The effective date is set by section 15 of SB 258.

§ 2933.24 Contents of search warrant; report of inspection findings.

(A) A search warrant shall be directed to the proper law enforcement officer or other authorized individual and, by a copy of the affidavit inserted in it or annexed and referred to in it, shall show or recite all the material facts alleged in the affidavit, and particularly name or describe the property to be searched for and seized, the place to be searched, and the person to be searched. If a waiver of the statutory precondition for nonconsensual entry, as defined in division (A) of section 2933.231 [2933.23.1] of the Revised Code, has been granted pursuant to that section, the warrant also shall contain a provision as described in division (C) of that section.

The warrant shall command the officer or individual to search the place or person named or described for the property, and to bring them, together with the person, before the judge or magistrate. The command of the warrant shall be that the search be made in the daytime, unless there is urgent necessity for a search in the night, in which case a search in the night may be ordered.

The warrant shall be returned by the officer or individual holding it not later than three days after its issuance. It shall designate the judge or magistrate to whom it shall be returned, if such judge or magistrate is available.

(B) When a search warrant commands a proper law enforcement officer or other authorized individual to inspect physical conditions relating to public health, safety, or welfare, such officer or individual, upon completion of the search, shall complete a report of the conditions and file a copy of such report with his agency headquarters.

HISTORY: GC § 13430-4; 113 v 123(137), ch 9, § 4; Bureau of Code Revision, 10-1-53; 130 v 665 (Eff 10-14-63); 134 v S 397 (Eff 10-23-72); 143 v S 258. Eff 11-20-90.

The effective date is set by section 15 of SB 258.

[§ 2933.24.1] § 2933.241 Inventory of property taken.

The officer taking property under a warrant for search shall give to the person from whom or from whose premises the property was taken a copy of the warrant and a receipt for the property taken or shall leave the copy and receipt at the place from which the property was taken. The return shall be made promptly and shall be accompanied by a written inventory of any property taken. The inventory shall be made in the presence of the applicant for the warrant and the person from whose possession or premises the property was taken, if they are present, or in the presence of at least one credible person other than the applicant for the warrant or the person from whose possession or premises the property was taken and shall be verified by the officer. The judge or magistrate shall upon request deliver a copy of the inventory to the person from whom or from whose premises the property was taken and to the applicant for the warrant.

HISTORY: 130 v 665. Eff 10-14-63.

§ 2933.25 Form of search warrant.

Warrants issued under section 2933.21 of the Revised Code shall be substantially in the following form:
State of Ohio, ... County, ss:
To the sheriff (or other officer) of said County, greeting:

Whereas there has been filed with me an affidavit, of which the following is a copy (here copy the affidavit).

These are, therefore, to command you in the name of the State of Ohio, with the necessary and proper assistance, to enter, in the daytime (or in the nighttime) into (here describe the house or place as in the affidavit) of the said .... of the township of .... in the County aforesaid, and there diligently search for the said goods and chattels, or articles, to wit: (here describe the articles as in the affidavit) and that you bring the same or any part thereof, found on such search, and also the body of E. F., forthwith before me, or some other judge or magistrate of the county having cognizance thereof to be disposed of and dealt with according to law.

Given under my hand, this .... day of ....

                              A. B., Judge, County Court

HISTORY: GC § 13430-5; 113 v 123(137), ch 9, § 5; Bureau of Code Revision, 10-1-53; 127 v 1039(1099). Eff 1-1-58.

§ 2933.26 Property seized to be kept by court.

When a warrant is executed by the seizure of property or things described therein, such property or things shall be kept by the judge, clerk, or magistrate to be used as evidence.

HISTORY: GC § 13430-6; 113 v 123(138), ch 9, § 6; Bureau of Code Revision. Eff 10-1-53.

§ 2933.27 Disposition of property before trial.

If, upon examination, the judge or magistrate is satisfied that the offense charged with reference to the things seized under a search warrant has been committed, he shall keep such things or deliver them to the sheriff of the county, to be kept until the accused is tried or the claimant's right is otherwise ascertained.

HISTORY: GC § 13430-7; 113 v 123(138), ch 9, § 7; Bureau of Code Revision. Eff 10-1-53.

§ 2933.28 Repealed, 140 v H 632, § 2 [GC § 13430-8; 113 v 123(138), ch 9, § 8; Bureau of Code Revision, 10-1-53]. Eff 3-28-85.

This section concerned disposition of property after trial. See now section 2933.41.

§ 2933.29 Property seized liable for fines.

Upon conviction of a person for keeping a room or place to be used for gambling, or knowingly permitting gambling to be conducted therein, or permitting a game to be played for gain, or a gaming device for gain, money, or other property or for betting, or gambling, or permitting such device to be so used, or for being without a fixed residence and in the habit of gambling, if money or other property won in gaming is found in his possession, such money or other property is subject to seizure and payment of a judgment which may be rendered against him, growing out of such violation.

HISTORY: GC § 13430-9; 113 v 123(138), ch 9, § 9; Bureau of Code Revision. Eff 10-1-53.

§ 2933.30 Search for dead bodies.

When an affidavit is filed before a judge or magistrate, alleging that affiant has reason to believe and does believe that a dead human body, procured or obtained contrary to law, is secreted in a building or place in the county, therein particularly specified, such judge or magistrate, taking with him a judge of a county court, or if within a municipal corporation, two officers of such corporation, may enter, inspect, and search said building or place for such body. In making such search, they have the powers of officers executing warrants of search.

HISTORY: GC § 13430-10; 113 v 123(138), ch 9, § 10; Bureau of Code Revision, 10-1-53; 127 v 1039(1099). Eff 1-1-58.

§ 2933.31 Search in case of animals.

When complaint is made, on oath or affirmation to a judge or magistrate, that the complainant believes that the law relating to or affecting animals is being, or is about to be violated in a particular building or place, such judge or magistrate shall forthwith issue and deliver a warrant, directed to any sheriff, deputy sheriff, marshal, deputy marshal, watchman, police officer, or agent of a society for the prevention of cruelty to animals, authorizing him to enter and search such building or place and arrest all persons there violating, or attempting to violate, such law, and bring such persons before a judge or magistrate within the county within which such offense has been committed.

An attempt to violate such law relating to animals is a violation thereof.

HISTORY: GC § 13430-11; 113 v 123(139), ch 9, § 11; Bureau of Code Revision. Eff 10-1-53.

§ 2933.32 Body cavity and strip searches; conducting unauthorized search; failure to prepare proper report.

(A) As used in this section:

(1) "Body cavity search" means an inspection of the anal or vaginal cavity of a person that is conducted visually, manually, by means of any instrument, apparatus, or object, or in any other manner while the person is detained or arrested for the alleged commission of a misdemeanor or traffic offense.

(2) "Strip search" means an inspection of the genitalia, buttocks, breasts, or undergarments of a person that is preceded by the removal or rearrangement of some or all of the person's clothing that directly covers the person's genitalia, buttocks, breasts, or undergarments and that is conducted visually, manually, by means of any instrument, apparatus, or object, or in any other manner while the person is detained or arrested for the alleged commission of a misdemeanor or traffic offense. "Strip search" does not mean the visual observation of a person who was afforded a reasonable opportunity to secure release on bail or recognizance, who fails to secure such release, and who is to be integrated with the general population of any detention facility, while the person is changing into clothing that is required to be worn by inmates in the facility.

(B)(1) Except as authorized by this division, no law enforcement officer, other employee of a law enforcement agency, physician, or registered nurse or licensed practical nurse shall conduct or cause to be conducted a body cavity search or a strip search.

(2) A body cavity search or strip search may be conducted if a law enforcement officer or employee of a law enforcement agency has probable cause to believe that the person is concealing evidence of the commission of a criminal offense, including fruits or tools of a crime, contraband, or a deadly weapon, as defined in section 2923.11 of the Revised Code, that could not otherwise be discovered. In determining probable cause for purposes of this section, a law enforcement officer or employee of a law enforcement agency shall consider the nature of the offense with which the person to be searched is charged, the circumstances of the person's arrest, and, if known, the prior conviction record of the person.

(3) A body cavity search or strip search may be conducted for any legitimate medical or hygienic reason.

(4) Unless there is a legitimate medical reason or medical emergency justifying a warrantless search, a body cavity search shall be conducted only after a search warrant is issued that authorizes the search. In any case, a body cavity search shall be conducted under sanitary conditions and only by a physician, or a registered nurse or licensed practical nurse, who is registered or licensed to practice in this state.

(5) Unless there is a legitimate medical reason or medical emergency that makes obtaining written authorization impracticable, a body cavity search or strip search shall be conducted only after a law enforcement officer or employee of a law enforcement agency obtains a written authorization for the search from the person in command of the law enforcement agency, or from a person specifically designated by the person in command to give a written authorization for either type of search.

(6) A body cavity search or strip search shall be conducted by a person or persons who are of the same sex as the person who is being searched and the search shall be conducted in a manner and in a location that permits only the person or persons who are physically conducting the search and the person who is being searched to observe the search.

(C)(1) Upon completion of a body cavity search or strip search pursuant to this section, the person or persons who conducted the search shall prepare a written report concerning the search that shall include all of the following:

(a) The written authorization for the search obtained from the person in command of the law enforcement agency or his designee, if required by division (B)(5) of this section;

(b) The name of the person who was searched;

(c) The name of the person or persons who conducted the search, the time and date of the search, and the place at which the search was conducted;

(d) A list of the items, if any, recovered during the search;

(e) The facts upon which the law enforcement officer or employee of the law enforcement agency based his probable cause for the search, including, but not limited to, the officer or employee's review of the nature of the offense with which the searched person is charged, the circumstances of his arrest, and, if known, his prior conviction record;

(f) If the body cavity search was conducted before or without the issuance of a search warrant pursuant to division (B)(4) of this section, or if the body cavity or strip search was conducted before or without the granting of written authorization pursuant to division (B)(5) of this section, the legitimate medical reason or medical emergency that justified the warrantless search or made obtaining written authorization impracticable.

(2) A copy of the written report required by division (C)(1) of this section shall be kept on file in the law enforcement agency, and another copy of it shall be given to the person who was searched.

(D)(1) This section does not preclude the prosecution of a law enforcement officer or employee of a law enforcement agency for the violation of any other section of the Revised Code.

(2) This section does not limit, and shall not be construed to limit, any statutory or common law rights of a person to obtain injunctive relief or to recover damages in a civil action.

(3) If a person is subjected to a body cavity search or strip search in violation of this section, any person may commence a civil action to recover compensatory damages for any injury, death, or loss to person or property or any indignity arising from the violation. In the civil action, the court may award punitive damages to the plaintiffs if they prevail in the action, and it may award reasonable attorney's fees to the parties who prevail in the action.

(4) This section does not apply to body cavity searches or strip searches of persons who have been sentenced to serve a term of imprisonment and who are serving that term in a detention facility, as defined in section 2921.01 of the Revised Code.

(E)(1) Whoever violates division (B) of this section is guilty of conducting an unauthorized search, a misdemeanor of the first degree.

(2) Whoever violates division (C) of this section is guilty of failure to prepare a proper search report, a misdemeanor of the fourth degree.

HISTORY: 140 v S 268 (Eff 9-26-84); 140 v H 426. Eff 4-4-85.

§ 2933.41 Disposition of property held by law enforcement agency.

(A)(1) Any property, other than contraband that is subject to the provisions of section 2913.34 or 2933.43

of the Revised Code, other than property that is subject to section 3719.141 [3719.14.1] of the Revised Code, other than property that is forfeited under sections 2925.41 to 2925.45 of the Revised Code, other than a vehicle that is criminally forfeited under an order issued under section 4503.233 [4503.23.3] or 4503.234 [4503.23.4] of the Revised Code and that is to be disposed of under section 4503.234 [4503.23.4] of the Revised Code, other than property that has been lawfully seized under sections 2933.71 to 2933.75 of the Revised Code in relation to a medicaid fraud offense, and other than property that has been lawfully seized in relation to a violation of section 2923.32 of the Revised Code, that has been lost, abandoned, stolen, seized pursuant to a search warrant, or otherwise lawfully seized or forfeited, and that is in the custody of a law enforcement agency shall be kept safely pending the time it no longer is needed as evidence and shall be disposed of pursuant to this section. Each law enforcement agency that has custody of any property that is subject to this section shall adopt a written internal control policy that addresses the keeping of detailed records as to the amount of property taken in by the agency, that addresses the agency's disposition of the property under this section, that provides for the keeping of detailed records of the disposition of the property, and that provides for the keeping of detailed financial records of the amount and disposition of any proceeds of a sale of the property under division (D)(8) of this section and of the general types of expenditures made out of the proceeds retained by the agency and the specific amount expended on each general type of expenditure. The policy shall not provide for or permit the identification of any specific expenditure that is made in an ongoing investigation. The policy is a public record open for inspection under section 149.43 of the Revised Code.

(2)(a) Every law enforcement agency that has any lost, abandoned, stolen, seized, or forfeited property as described in division (A)(1) of this section in its custody shall comply with its written internal control policy adopted under that division relative to the property. Each agency that has any property of that nature in its custody, except for property to be disposed of under division (D)(4) of this section, shall maintain an accurate record, in accordance with its written internal control policy, of each item of the property. The record shall include the date on which each item of property came into the agency's custody, the manner in which it was disposed of, the date of its disposition, the name of the person who received the property if it was not destroyed, and all other information required by the agency's written internal control policy; however, the record shall not identify or enable the identification of the individual officer who seized any item of property. The record of any property that no longer is needed as evidence, and all financial records of the amount and disposition of any proceeds of a sale under division (D)(8) of this section and of the general types of expenditures made out of the proceeds retained by the agency and the specific amount of each general type of expenditure, shall be open to public inspection during the agency's regular business hours.

Each law enforcement agency that, during any calendar year, has any seized or forfeited property as described in division (A)(1) of this section in its custody shall prepare a report covering the calendar year that cumulates all of the information contained in all of the records kept by the agency pursuant to this division for that calendar year and shall send a copy of the cumulative report, no later than the first day of March in the calendar year following the calendar year covered by the report, to the attorney general. Each report received by the attorney general is a public record open for inspection under section 149.43 of the Revised Code. The attorney general shall make copies of each report received and, no later than the fifteenth day of April in the calendar year in which the report is received, shall send a copy of it to the president of the senate and the speaker of the house of representatives.

(b) Each law enforcement agency that receives in any calendar year any proceeds of a sale under division (D)(8) of this section shall prepare a report covering the calendar year that cumulates all of the information contained in all of the public financial records kept by the agency pursuant to division (D)(2)(a) of this section for that calendar year and shall send a copy of the cumulative report, no later than the first day of March in the calendar year following the calendar year covered by the report, to the attorney general. Each report received by the attorney general is a public record open for inspection under section 149.43 of the Revised Code. The attorney general shall make copies of each report received and, no later than the fifteenth day of April in the calendar year in which the report is received, shall send a copy of it to the president of the senate and the speaker of the house of representatives.

(B) A law enforcement agency that has property in its possession that is required to be disposed of pursuant to this section shall make a reasonable effort to locate the persons entitled to possession of the property in its custody, to notify them of when and where it may be claimed, and to return the property to them at the earliest possible time. In the absence of evidence identifying persons entitled to possession, it is sufficient notice to advertise in a newspaper of general circulation in the county, briefly describing the nature of the property in custody and inviting persons to view and establish their right to it.

(C) A person loses any right that the person may have to the possession, or the possession and ownership, of property if any of the following applies:

(1) The property was the subject, or was used in a conspiracy or attempt to commit, or in the commission, of an offense other than a traffic offense, and the person is a conspirator, accomplice, or offender with respect to the offense.

(2) A court determines that the property should be forfeited because, in light of the nature of the property or the circumstances of the person, it is unlawful for the person to acquire or possess the property.

(D) Unclaimed or forfeited property in the custody of a law enforcement agency, other than contraband that is subject to the provisions of section 2913.34 or 2933.43 of the Revised Code, other than property forfeited under sections 2925.41 to 2925.45 of the Revised Code, and other than property that has been lawfully seized in relation to a violation of section 2923.32 of the Revised Code, shall be disposed of on application to and order of any court of record that has territorial jurisdiction over the political subdivision in which the law enforcement agency has jurisdiction to engage in law enforcement activities, as follows:

(1) Drugs shall be disposed of pursuant to section 3719.11 of the Revised Code or placed in the custody of the secretary of the treasury of the United States for disposal or use for medical or scientific purposes under applicable federal law.

(2) Firearms and dangerous ordnance suitable for police work may be given to a law enforcement agency for that purpose. Firearms suitable for sporting use or as museum pieces or collectors' items may be sold at public auction pursuant to division (D)(8) of this section. Other firearms and dangerous ordnance shall be destroyed by the agency or shall be sent to the bureau of criminal identification and investigation for destruction by the bureau.

(3) Obscene materials shall be destroyed.

(4) Beer, intoxicating liquor, or alcohol seized from a person who is not the holder of a permit issued under Chapters 4301. and 4303. of the Revised Code or is an offender and forfeited to the state under section 4301.45 or 4301.53 of the Revised Code shall be sold by the division of liquor control, if the division determines that the beer, intoxicating liquor, or alcohol is fit for sale. If any tax imposed under Title XLIII [43] of the Revised Code has not been paid in relation to the beer, intoxicating liquor, or alcohol, the proceeds of the sale shall first be used to pay the tax. All other money collected under division (D)(4) of this section shall be paid into the state treasury. Any such beer, intoxicating liquor, or alcohol that the division determines to be unfit for sale shall be destroyed.

(5) Money received by an inmate of a correctional institution from an unauthorized source or in an unauthorized manner shall be returned to the sender, if known, or deposited in the inmates' industrial and entertainment fund if the sender is not known.

(6) Vehicles and vehicle parts forfeited under sections 4549.61 to 4549.63 of the Revised Code may be given to a law enforcement agency for use in the performance of its duties. Those parts may be incorporated into any other official vehicle. Parts that do not bear vehicle identification numbers or derivatives of them may be sold or disposed of as provided by rules of the director of public safety. Parts from which a vehicle identification number or derivative of it has been removed, defaced, covered, altered, or destroyed and that are not suitable for police work or incorporation into an official vehicle shall be destroyed and sold as junk or scrap.

(7)(a) Computers, computer networks, computer systems, and computer software suitable for police work may be given to a law enforcement agency for that purpose. Other computers, computer networks, computer systems, and computer software shall be disposed of pursuant to division (D)(8) of this section.

(b) As used in this section, "computers," "computer networks," "computer systems," and "computer software" have the same meanings as in section 2913.01 of the Revised Code.

(8) Other unclaimed or forfeited property, with the approval of the court, may be used by the law enforcement agency that has possession of it. If the other unclaimed or forfeited property is not used by the law enforcement agency, it may be sold, without appraisal, at a public auction to the highest bidder for cash, or, in the case of other unclaimed or forfeited moneys, disposed of in another manner that the court considers proper in the circumstances.

(E)(1)(a) If the property was in the possession of the law enforcement agency in relation to a delinquent child proceeding in a juvenile court, ten per cent of the proceeds from property disposed of pursuant to this section shall be applied to one or more alcohol and drug addiction treatment programs that are certified by the department of alcohol and drug addiction services under section 3793.06 of the Revised Code and that are specified by the court in its order issued under division (D) of this section. A juvenile court shall not specify an alcohol or drug addiction treatment program in the order unless the program is a certified alcohol and drug addiction treatment program and, except as provided in division (E)(1)(a) of this section, unless the program is located in the county in which the court that issues the orders is located or in a contiguous county. If no certified alcohol and drug addiction treatment program is located in any of those counties, the juvenile court may specify in the order a certified alcohol and drug addiction treatment program located anywhere within this state. The remaining ninety per cent of the proceeds shall be applied as provided in divisions (E)(1)(b) of this section.

If the property was in the possession of the law enforcement agency other than in relation to a delinquent child proceeding in a juvenile court, all of the proceeds from property disposed of pursuant to this section shall be applied as provided in division (E)(1)(b) of this section.

(b) Except as provided in divisions (D)(4), (5), and (E)(2) of this section and after compliance with division (E)(1)(a) of this section when that division is applicable, the proceeds from property disposed of pursuant to this section shall be placed in the general fund of the state, the county, the township, or the municipal corporation, of which the law enforcement agency involved is an agency.

(2) Each board of county commissioners that recognizes a citizens' reward program as provided in section 9.92 of the Revised Code shall notify each law enforcement agency of that county and each law enforcement agency of a township or municipal corporation wholly located in that county of the official recognition of the citizens' reward program by filing a copy of its resolution conferring that recognition with each of those law enforcement agencies. When the board of county commissioners of a county recognizes a citizens' reward program and the county includes a part, but not all, of the territory of a municipal corporation, the board shall so notify the law enforcement agency of that municipal corporation of the official recognition of the citizens' reward program only if the county contains the highest percentage of the municipal corporation's population. Upon receipt of a notice of that nature, each law enforcement agency shall pay twenty-five per cent of the proceeds from each sale of property disposed of pursuant to this section to the citizens' reward program for use exclusively for the payment of rewards. No part of those funds may be used to pay for the administrative expenses or any other expenses associated with a citizens' reward program. If a citizens' reward program that operates in more than one county or in another state or states in addition to this state receives funds pursuant to this section, the funds shall be used to pay rewards only for tips and information to law enforcement agencies concerning felonies, offenses of violence, or misdemeanors that have been committed in the county from which the funds were received.

(F) This section does not apply to the collection, storage, or disposal of abandoned junk motor vehicles. This section shall not be construed to rescind or restrict the authority of a municipal law enforcement agency to keep and dispose of lost, abandoned, stolen, seized, or forfeited property under an ordinance of the municipal corporation, provided that, when a municipal corporation that has received notice as provided in division (E)(2) of this section disposes of property under an ordinance of that nature, it shall pay twenty-five per cent of the proceeds from any sale or auction to the citizens' reward program as provided under that division.

(G) The receipt of funds by a citizens' reward program pursuant to division (E) of this section does not make it a governmental unit for purposes of section 149.43 of the Revised Code and does not subject it to the disclosure provisions of that section.

(H) For purposes of this section, "law enforcement agency" includes correctional institutions. As used in this section, "citizens' reward program" has the same meaning as in section 9.92 of the Revised Code.

HISTORY: 134 v H 511 (Eff 1-1-74); 138 v S 50 (Eff 5-29-80); 139 v H 1 (Eff 8-5-81); 140 v H 632 (Eff 3-28-85); 140 v S 65 (Eff 4-4-85); 141 v H 49 (Eff 6-26-86); 141 v S 69 (Eff 9-3-86); 141 v H 428 (Eff 12-23-86); 143 v H 215 (Eff 4-11-90); 143 v S 258 (Eff 11-20-90); 144 v S 98 (Eff 11-12-92); 144 v S 275 (Eff 7-1-93)†; 145 v H 715 (Eff 7-22-94); 146 v H 1 (Eff 1-1-96); 146 v S 277, § 1 (Eff 3-31-97); 146 v S 162 (Eff 7-1-97); 146 v S 277, § 3. Eff 7-1-97.

Analogous to former RC § 2907.43 (117 v 430; Bureau of Code Revision, 10-1-53), repealed 134 v H 511, § 2, eff 1-1-74.

† See provisions, §§ 4, 5 of SB 62 (145 v —) concerning change of effective date from 7-1-93 to 9-1-93 at RC § 2903.04 in the bound volume.

The effective date is set by section 5 of SB 277.

The provisions of § 9 of SB 277 (146 v —) read as follows:

SECTION 9. Section 2933.41 of the Revised Code is presented in Section 3 of this act [Sub. S.B. No. 277] as a composite of the section as amended by both Am. Sub. S.B. 162 and Am. Sub. H.B. 1 of the 121st General Assembly, with the new language of neither of the acts shown in capital letters.

● ● ●

This is in recognition of the principle stated in division (B) of section 1.52 of the Revised Code that such amendments are to be harmonized where not substantively irreconcilable and constitutes a legislative finding that such is the resulting version in effect prior to the effective date of this act.

§ 2933.42 Offenses involving contraband; forfeiture of property used in committing violation.

(A) No person shall possess, conceal, transport, receive, purchase, sell, lease, rent, or otherwise transfer any contraband.

(B) For purposes of section 2933.43 of the Revised Code, if a watercraft, motor vehicle, aircraft, or other personal property that is not within the scope of the definition of contraband in section 2901.01 of the Revised Code is used in a violation of division (A) of this section, the watercraft, motor vehicle, aircraft, or personal property is contraband and, if the underlying offense involved in the violation of division (A) of this section is a felony, is subject to seizure and forfeiture pursuant to section 2933.43 of the Revised Code. It is rebuttably presumed that a watercraft, motor vehicle, aircraft, or other personal property in or on which contraband is found at the time of seizure has been, is being, or is intended to be used in a violation of division (A) of this section.

(C) For purposes of sections 2901.01 and 2933.41 to 2933.43 of the Revised Code, "offense," "criminal case," "criminal violation," "criminal offense," "felony," and similar terms shall be construed to include acts committed by persons under eighteen years of age that, if committed by an adult, would be within the meaning of those terms. This division shall be liberally construed to give effect to the intent of the general assembly in enacting this division that the forfeiture and contraband provisions of sections 2901.01 and 2933.41 to 2933.43 of the Revised Code apply to property that is possessed, or possessed and owned, by persons under eighteen years of age in the same manner as those provisions apply to property that is possessed, or possessed and owned, by adults.

HISTORY: 141 v S 69 (Eff 9-3-86); 143 v S 258. Eff 8-22-90.

§ 2933.43 Procedure for seizure and forfeiture of contraband; law enforcement agency authorized to use, destroy, or sell forfeited contraband; distribution of proceeds of sale.

(A)(1) Except as provided in this division or in section 2913.34 or sections 2925.41 to 2925.45 of the Revised Code, a law enforcement officer shall seize any contraband that has been, is being, or is intended to be used in violation of division (A) of section 2933.42 of the Revised Code. A law enforcement officer shall seize contraband that is a watercraft, motor vehicle, or aircraft and that has been, is being, or is intended to be used in violation of division (A) of section 2933.42 of the Revised Code only if the watercraft, motor vehicle, or aircraft is contraband because of its relationship to an underlying criminal offense that is a felony.

Additionally, a law enforcement officer shall seize any watercraft, motor vehicle, aircraft, or other personal property that is classified as contraband under division (B) of section 2933.42 of the Revised Code if the underlying offense involved in the violation of division (A) of that section that resulted in the watercraft, motor vehicle, aircraft, or personal property being classified as contraband, is a felony.

(2) If a law enforcement officer seizes property that is titled or registered under law, including a motor vehicle, pursuant to division (A)(1) of this section, the officer or the officer's employing law enforcement agency shall notify the owner of the seizure. The notification shall be given to the owner at the owner's last known address within seventy-two hours after the seizure, and may be given orally by any means, including telephone, or by certified mail, return receipt requested.

If the officer or the officer's agency is unable to provide the notice required by this division despite reasonable, good faith efforts to do so, the exercise of the reasonable, good faith efforts constitutes fulfillment of the notice requirement imposed by this division.

(B)(1) A motor vehicle seized pursuant to division (A)(1) of this section and the contents of the vehicle may be retained for a reasonable period of time, not to exceed seventy-two hours, for the purpose of inspection, investigation, and the gathering of evidence of any offense or illegal use.

At any time prior to the expiration of the seventy-two-hour period, the law enforcement agency that seized the motor vehicle may petition the court of common pleas of the county that has jurisdiction over the underlying criminal case or administrative proceeding involved in the forfeiture for an extension of the seventy-two-hour period if the motor vehicle or its contents are needed as evidence or if additional time is needed for the inspection, investigation, or gathering of evidence. Upon the filing of such a petition, the court immediately shall schedule a hearing to be held at a time as soon as possible after the filing, but in no event at a time later than the end of the next business day subsequent to the day on which the petition was filed, and upon scheduling the hearing, immediately shall notify the owner of the vehicle, at the address at which notification of the seizure was provided under division (A) of this section, of the date, time, and place of the hearing. If the court, at the hearing, determines that the vehicle or its contents, or both, are needed as evidence or that additional time is needed for the inspection, investigation, or gathering of evidence, the court may grant the petition and issue an order authorizing the retention of the vehicle or its contents, or both, for an extended period as specified by the court in its order. An order extending a period of retention issued under this division may be renewed.

If no petition for the extension of the initial seventy-two-hour period has been filed, prior to the expiration of that period, under this division, if the vehicle was not in the custody and control of the owner at the time of its seizure, and if, at the end of that seventy-two-hour period, the owner of the vehicle has not been charged with an offense or administrative violation that includes the use of the vehicle as an element and has not been charged with any other offense or administrative violation in the actual commission of which the motor vehicle was used, the vehicle and its contents shall be released to its owner or the owner's agent, provided that the law enforcement agency that seized the vehicle may require proof of ownership of the vehicle, proof of ownership or legal possession of the contents, and an affidavit of the owner that the owner neither knew of nor expressly or impliedly consented to the use of the vehicle that resulted in its forfeiture as conditions precedent to release. If a petition for the extension of the initial seventy-two-hour period has been filed, prior to the expiration of that period, under this division but the court does not grant the petition, if the vehicle was not in the custody and control of the owner at the time of its seizure, and if, at the end of that seventy-two-hour period, the owner of the vehicle has not been charged with an offense or administrative violation that includes the use of the vehicle as an element and has not been charged with any other offense or administrative violation in the actual commission of which the motor vehicle was used, the vehicle and its contents shall be released to its owner or the owner's agent, provided that the court may require the proof and affidavit described in the preceding sentence as conditions precedent to release. If the initial seventy-two-hour period has been extended under this division, the vehicle and its contents to which the extension applies may be retained in accordance with the extension order. If, at the end of that extended period, the owner of the vehicle has not been charged with an offense or administrative violation that includes the use of the vehicle as an element and has not been charged with any other offense or administrative violation in the actual commission of which the motor vehicle was used, and if the vehicle was not in the custody and control of the owner at the time of its seizure, the vehicle and its contents shall be released to its owner or the owner's agent, provided that the court may require the proof and affidavit described in the third preceding sentence as conditions precedent to release. In cases in which the court may require proof and affidavits as conditions precedent to release, the court also may require the posting of a bond, with sufficient sureties approved by the court, in an amount equal to the value of the property to be released, as determined by the court, and conditioned upon the return of the property to the court if it is forfeited under this section, as a further condition to release. If, at the end of the initial seventy-two-hour period or at the end of any extended period granted under this section, the owner has been charged with an offense or administrative violation that includes the use of the vehicle as an element or has been charged with another offense or administrative violation in the actual commission of which the motor vehicle was used, or if the vehicle was in the custody and control of the owner at the time of its seizure, the vehicle and its contents shall be retained pending disposition of the charge, provided that upon the filing of a motion for release by the owner, if the court determines that the motor vehicle or its contents, or both, are not needed as evidence in the underlying criminal case or administrative proceeding, the court may permit the release of the property that is not needed as evidence to the owner; as a condition precedent to a release of that nature, the court may require the owner to execute a bond with the court. Any bond so required shall be in an amount equal to the value of the property to be released, as determined by the court, shall have sufficient sureties approved by the court, and shall be conditioned upon the return of the property to the court to which it is forfeited under this section.

The final disposition of a motor vehicle seized pursuant to division (A)(1) of this section shall be determined in accordance with division (C) of this section.

(2) Pending a hearing pursuant to division (C) of this section, and subject to divisions (B)(1) and (C) of this section, any property lawfully seized pursuant to division (A) of this section because it was contraband of a type described in division (A)(13)(b), (d), (e), (f), (g), (h), (i), or (j) of section 2901.01 of the Revised Code shall not be subject to replevin or other action in any court and shall not be subject to release upon request of the owner, and no judgment shall be enforced against the property. Pending the hearing, and subject to divisions (B)(1) and (C) of this section, the property shall be kept in the custody of the law enforcement agency responsible for its seizure.

Pending a hearing pursuant to division (C) of this section, and notwithstanding any provisions of division (B)(1) or (C) of this section to the contrary, any property lawfully seized pursuant to division (A) of this section because it was contraband of a type described in division (A)(13)(a) or (c) of section 2901.01 of the Revised Code shall not be subject to replevin or other action in any court and shall not be subject to release upon request of the owner, and no judgment shall be enforced against the property. Pending the hearing, and notwithstanding any provisions of division (B)(1) or (C) of this section to the contrary, the property shall be kept in the custody of the law enforcement agency responsible for its seizure.

A law enforcement agency that seizes property under division (A) of this section because it was contraband of any type described in division (A)(13) of section 2901.01 or division (B) of section 2933.42 of the Revised Code shall maintain an accurate record of each item of property so seized, which record shall include the date on which each item was seized, the manner and date of its disposition, and if applicable, the name of the person who received the item; however, the record shall not identify or enable the identification of the individual officer who seized the item. The record of property of that nature that no longer is needed as evidence shall be open to public inspection during the agency's regular business hours. Each law enforcement agency that, during any calendar year, seizes property under division (A) of this section because it was contraband shall prepare a report covering the calendar year that cumulates all of the information contained in all of the records kept by the agency pursuant to this division for that calendar year, and shall send a copy of the cumulative report, no later than the first day of March in the calendar year following the calendar year covered by the report, to the attorney general. Each report received by the attorney general is a public record open for inspection under section 149.43 of the Revised Code. The attorney general shall make copies of each report received, and, no later than the fifteenth day of April in the calendar year in which the report is received, shall send a copy of it to the president of the senate and the speaker of the house of representatives.

(C) The prosecuting attorney, village solicitor, city director of law, or similar chief legal officer who has responsibility for the prosecution of the underlying criminal case or administrative proceeding, or the attorney general if the attorney general has that responsibility, shall file a petition for the forfeiture, to the seizing law enforcement agency of the contraband seized pursuant to division (A) of this section. The petition shall be filed in the court that has jurisdiction over the underlying criminal case or administrative proceeding involved in the forfeiture. If the property was seized on the basis of both a criminal violation and an administrative regulation violation, the petition shall be filed by the officer and in the court that is appropriate in relation to the criminal case.

The petitioner shall conduct or cause to be conducted a search of the appropriate public records that relate to the seized property for the purpose of determining, and shall make or cause to be made reasonably diligent inquiries for the purpose of determining, any person having an ownership or security interest in the property. The petitioner then shall give notice of the forfeiture proceedings by personal service or by certified mail, return receipt requested, to any persons known, because of the conduct of the search, the making of the inquiries, or otherwise, to have an ownership or security interest in the property, and shall publish notice of the proceedings once each week for two consecutive weeks in a newspaper of general circulation in the county in which the seizure occurred. The notices shall be personally served, mailed, and first published at least four weeks before the hearing. They shall describe the property seized; state the date and place of seizure; name the law enforcement agency that seized the property and, if applicable, that is holding the property; list the time, date, and place of the hearing; and state that any person having an ownership or security interest in the property may contest the forfeiture.

If the property seized was determined by the seizing law enforcement officer to be contraband because of its relationship to an underlying criminal offense or administrative violation, no forfeiture hearing shall be held under this section unless the person pleads guilty to or is convicted of the commission of, or an attempt or conspiracy to commit, the offense or a different offense arising out of the same facts and circumstances or unless the person admits or is adjudicated to have committed the administrative violation or a different violation arising out of the same facts and circumstances; a forfeiture hearing shall be held in a case of that nature no later than forty-five days after the conviction or the admission or adjudication of the violation, unless the time for the hearing is extended by the court for good cause shown. The owner of any property seized because of its relationship to an underlying criminal offense or administrative violation may request the court to release the property to the owner. Upon receipt of a request of that nature, if the court determines that the property is not needed as evidence in the underlying criminal case or administrative proceeding, the court may permit the release of the property to the owner. As a condition precedent to a release of that nature, the court may require the owner to execute a bond with the court. Any bond so required shall have sufficient sureties approved by the court, shall be in a sum equal to the value of the property, as determined by the court, and shall be conditioned upon the return of the property to the court if the property is forfeited under this section. Any property seized because of its relationship to an underlying criminal offense or administrative violation shall be returned to its owner if charges are not filed in relation to that underlying offense or violation within thirty days after the seizure, if charges of that nature are filed and subsequently are dismissed, or if charges of that nature are filed and the person charged does not plead guilty to and is not convicted of the offense or does not admit and is not found to have committed the violation.

If the property seized was determined by the seizing law enforcement officer to be contraband other than because of a relationship to an underlying criminal offense or administrative violation, the forfeiture hearing under this section shall be held no later than forty-five days after the seizure, unless the time for the hearing is extended by the court for good cause shown.

Where possible, a court holding a forfeiture hearing under this section shall follow the Rules of Civil Procedure. When a hearing is conducted under this section, property shall be forfeited upon a showing, by a preponderance of the evidence, by the petitioner that the person from which the property was seized was in violation of division (A) of section 2933.42 of the Revised Code. If that showing is made, the court shall issue an order of forfeiture. If an order of forfeiture is issued in relation to contraband that was released to the owner or the owner's agent pursuant to this division or division (B)(1) of this section, the order shall require the owner to deliver the property, by a specified date, to the law enforcement agency that employed the law enforcement officer who made the seizure of the property, and the court shall deliver a copy of the order to the owner or send a copy of it by certified mail, return receipt requested, to the owner at the address to which notice of the seizure was given under division (A)(2) of this section. Except as otherwise provided in this division, all rights, interest, and title to the forfeited contraband vests in the state, effective from the date of seizure.

No property shall be forfeited pursuant to this division if the owner of the property establishes, by a preponderance of the evidence, that the owner neither knew, nor should have known after a reasonable inquiry, that the property was used, or was likely to be used, in a crime or administrative violation. No bona fide security interest shall be forfeited pursuant to this division if the holder of the interest establishes, by a preponderance of the evidence, that the holder of the interest neither knew, nor should have known after a reasonable inquiry, that the property was used, or likely to be used, in a crime or administrative violation, that the holder of the interest did not expressly or impliedly consent to the use of the property in a crime or administrative violation, and that the security interest was perfected pursuant to law prior to the seizure. If the holder of the interest satisfies the court that these requirements are met, the interest shall be preserved by the court. In a case of that nature, the court shall either order that the agency to which the property is forfeited reimburse the holder of the interest to the extent of the preserved interest or order that the holder be paid for the interest from the proceeds of any sale pursuant to division (D) of this section.

(D)(1) Contraband ordered forfeited pursuant to this section shall be disposed of pursuant to divisions (D)(1) to (7) of section 2933.41 of the Revised Code or, if the contraband is not described in those divisions, may be used, with the approval of the court, by the law enforcement agency that has custody of the contraband pursuant to division (D)(8) of that section. In the case of contraband not described in any of those divisions and of contraband not disposed of pursuant to any of those divisions, the contraband shall be sold in accordance with this division or, in the case of forfeited moneys, disposed of in accordance with this division. If the contraband is to be sold, the prosecuting attorney shall cause a notice of the proposed sale of the contraband to be given in accordance with law, and the property shall be sold, without appraisal, at a public auction to the highest bidder for cash. The proceeds of a sale and forfeited moneys shall be applied in the following order:

(a) First, to the payment of the costs incurred in connection with the seizure of, storage of, maintenance of, and provision of security for the contraband, the forfeiture proceeding, and, if any, the sale;

(b) Second, the remaining proceeds or forfeited moneys after compliance with division (D)(1)(a) of this section, to the payment of the balance due on any security interest preserved pursuant to division (C) of this section;

(c) Third, the remaining proceeds or forfeited moneys after compliance with divisions (D)(1)(a) and (b) of this section, as follows:

(i) If the forfeiture was ordered in a juvenile court, ten per cent to one or more alcohol and drug addiction treatment programs that are certified by the department of alcohol and drug addiction services under section 3793.06 of the Revised Code and that are specified in the order of forfeiture. A juvenile court shall not certify an alcohol or drug addiction treatment program in the order of forfeiture unless the program is a certified alcohol and drug addiction treatment program and, except as provided in division (D)(1)(c)(i) of this section, unless the program is located in the county in which the court that orders the forfeiture is located or in a contiguous county. If no certified alcohol and drug addiction treatment program is located in any of those counties, the juvenile court may specify in the order a certified alcohol and drug addiction treatment program located anywhere within this state.

(ii) If the forfeiture was ordered in a juvenile court, ninety per cent, and if the forfeiture was ordered in a court other than a juvenile court, one hundred per cent to the law enforcement trust fund of the prosecuting attorney and to the law enforcement trust fund of the county sheriff if the county sheriff made the seizure, to the law enforcement trust fund of a municipal corporation if its police department made the seizure, to the law enforcement trust fund of a township if the seizure was made by a township police department, township police district police force, or office of a township constable, to the law enforcement trust fund of a park district created pursuant to section 511.18 or 1545.01 of the Revised Code if the seizure was made by the park district police force or law enforcement department, to the state highway patrol contraband, forfeiture, and other fund if the state highway patrol made the seizure, to the liquor enforcement contraband, forfeiture, and other fund if the liquor enforcement unit of the department of public safety made the seizure, to the food stamp contraband, forfeiture, and other fund if the food stamp trafficking unit of the department of public safety made the seizure, to the board of pharmacy drug law enforcement fund created by division (B)(1) of section 4729.65 of the Revised Code if the board made the seizure, or to the treasurer of state for deposit into the peace officer training commission fund if a state law enforcement agency, other than the state highway patrol, the department of public safety, or the state board of pharmacy, made the seizure. The prosecuting attorney may decline to accept any of the remaining proceeds or forfeited moneys, and, if the prosecuting attorney so declines, the remaining proceeds or forfeited moneys shall be applied to the fund described in this division that relates to the law enforcement agency that made the seizure.

A law enforcement trust fund shall be established by the prosecuting attorney of each county who intends to receive any remaining proceeds or forfeited moneys pursuant to this division, by the sheriff of each county, by the legislative authority of each municipal corporation, by the board of township trustees of each township that has a township police department, township police district police force, or office of the constable, and by the board of park commissioners of each park district created pursuant to section 511.18 or 1545.01 of the Revised Code that has a park district police force or law enforcement department, for the purposes of this division. There is hereby created in the state treasury the state highway patrol contraband, forfeiture, and other fund, the liquor enforcement contraband, forfeiture, and other fund, the food stamp contraband, forfeiture, and other fund, and the peace officer training commission fund, for the purposes described in this division.

Proceeds or forfeited moneys distributed to any municipal corporation, township, or park district law enforcement trust fund shall be allocated from the fund by the legislative authority only to the police department of the municipal corporation, by the board of township trustees only to the township police department, township police district police force, or office of the constable, and by the board of park commissioners only to the park district police force or law enforcement department.

Additionally, no proceeds or forfeited moneys shall be allocated to or used by the state highway patrol, the food stamp trafficking unit or liquor enforcement unit of the department of public safety, the state board of pharmacy, or a county sheriff, prosecuting attorney, municipal corporation police department, township police department, township police district police force, office of the constable, or park district police force or law enforcement department unless the state highway patrol, department of public safety, state board of pharmacy, sheriff, prosecuting attorney, municipal corporation police department, township police department, township police district police force, office of the constable, or park district police force or law enforcement department has adopted a written internal control policy under division (D)(3) of this section that addresses the use of moneys received from the state highway patrol contraband, forfeiture, and other fund, the liquor enforcement contraband, forfeiture, and other fund, the food stamp contraband, forfeiture, and other fund, the board of pharmacy drug law enforcement fund, or the appropriate law enforcement trust fund. The state highway patrol contraband, forfeiture, and other fund, the liquor enforcement contraband, forfeiture, and other fund, the food stamp contraband, forfeiture, and other fund, and a law enforcement trust fund shall be expended only in accordance with the written internal control policy so adopted by the recipient, and, subject to the requirements specified in division (D)(3)(a)(ii) of this section, only to pay the costs of protracted or complex investigations or prosecutions, to provide reasonable technical training or expertise, to provide matching funds to obtain federal grants to aid law enforcement, in the support of DARE programs or other programs designed to educate adults or children with respect to the dangers associated with the use of drugs of abuse, or for other law enforcement purposes that the superintendent of the state highway patrol, department of public safety, prosecuting attorney, county sheriff, legislative authority, board of township trustees, or board of park commissioners determines to be appropriate. The board of pharmacy drug law enforcement fund shall be expended only in accordance with the written internal control policy so adopted by the board and only in accordance with section 4729.65 of the Revised Code. The state highway patrol contraband, forfeiture, and other fund, the liquor enforcement contraband, seizure, and other fund, the food stamp contraband, forfeiture, and other fund, the board of pharmacy drug law enforcement fund, and a law enforcement trust fund shall not be used to meet the operating costs of the state highway patrol, of the food stamp trafficking unit or liquor enforcement unit of the department of public safety, of the state board of pharmacy, of any political subdivision, or of any office of a prosecuting attorney or county sheriff that are unrelated to law enforcement.

Proceeds and forfeited moneys that are paid into the state treasury to be deposited into the peace officer training commission fund shall be used by the commission only to pay the costs of peace officer training.

Any sheriff or prosecuting attorney who receives proceeds or forfeited moneys pursuant to this division during any calendar year shall file a report with the county auditor, no later than the thirty-first day of January of the next calendar year, verifying that the proceeds and forfeited moneys were expended only for the purposes authorized by this division and division (D)(3)(a)(ii) of this section and specifying the amounts expended for each authorized purpose. Any municipal corporation police department that is allocated proceeds or forfeited moneys from a municipal corporation law enforcement trust fund pursuant to this division during any calendar year shall file a report with the legislative authority of the municipal corporation, no later than the thirty-first day of January of the next calendar year, verifying that the proceeds and forfeited moneys were expended only for the purposes authorized by this division and division (D)(3)(a)(ii) of this section and specifying the amounts expended for each authorized purpose. Any township police department, township police district police force, or office of the constable that is allocated proceeds or forfeited moneys from a township law enforcement trust fund pursuant to this division during any calendar year shall file a report with the board of township trustees of the township, no later than the thirty-first day of January of the next calendar year, verifying that the proceeds and forfeited moneys were expended only for the purposes authorized by this division and division (D)(3)(a)(ii) of this section and specifying the amounts expended for each authorized purpose. Any park district police force or law enforcement department that is allocated proceeds or forfeited moneys from a park district law enforcement trust fund pursuant to this division during any calendar year shall file a report with the board of park commissioners of the park district, no later than the thirty-first day of January of the next calendar year, verifying that the proceeds and forfeited moneys were expended only for the purposes authorized by this division and division (D)(3)(a)(ii) of this section and specifying the amounts expended for each authorized purpose. The superintendent of the state highway patrol shall file a report with the attorney general, no later than the thirty-first day of January of each calendar year, verifying that proceeds and forfeited moneys paid into the state highway patrol contraband, forfeiture, and other fund pursuant to this division during the prior calendar year were used by the state highway patrol during the prior calendar year only for the purposes authorized by this division and specifying the amounts expended for each authorized purpose. The executive director of the state board of pharmacy shall file a report with the attorney general, no later than the thirty-first day of January of each calendar year, verifying that proceeds and forfeited moneys paid into the board of pharmacy drug law enforcement fund during the prior calendar year were used only in accordance with section 4729.65 of the Revised Code and specifying the amounts expended for each authorized purpose. The peace officer training commission shall file a report with the attorney general, no later than the thirty-first day of January of each calendar year, verifying that proceeds and forfeited moneys paid into the peace officer training commission fund pursuant to this division during the prior calendar year were used by the commission during the prior calendar year only to pay the costs of peace officer training and specifying the amount used for that purpose.

(2) If more than one law enforcement agency is substantially involved in the seizure of contraband that is forfeited pursuant to this section, the court ordering the forfeiture shall equitably divide the proceeds or forfeited moneys, after calculating any distribution to the law enforcement trust fund of the prosecuting attorney pursuant to division (D)(1)(c) of this section, among any county sheriff whose office is determined by the court to be substantially involved in the seizure, any legislative authority of a municipal corporation whose police department is determined by the court to be substantially involved in the seizure, any board of township trustees whose law enforcement agency is determined by the court to be substantially involved in the seizure, any board of park commissioners of a park district whose police force or law enforcement department is determined by the court to be substantially involved in the seizure, the state board of pharmacy if it is determined by the court to be substantially involved in the seizure, the food stamp trafficking unit or liquor enforcement unit of the department of public safety if it is determined by the court to be substantially involved in the seizure, and the state highway patrol if it is determined by the court to be substantially involved in the seizure. The proceeds or forfeited moneys shall be deposited in the respective law enforcement trust funds of the county sheriff, municipal corporation, township, and park district, the board of pharmacy drug law enforcement fund, the liquor enforcement contraband, forfeiture, and other fund, the food stamp contraband, forfeiture, and other fund, or the state highway patrol contraband, forfeiture, and other fund, in accordance with division (D)(1)(c) of this section. If a state law enforcement agency, other than the state highway patrol, the food stamp trafficking unit or liquor enforcement unit of the department of public safety, or the state board of pharmacy, is determined by the court to be substantially involved in the seizure, the state agency's equitable share of the proceeds and forfeited moneys shall be paid to the treasurer of state for deposit into the peace officer training commission fund.

(3)(a)(i) Prior to being allocated or using any proceeds or forfeited moneys out of the state highway patrol contraband, forfeiture, and other fund, the liquor enforcement contraband, forfeiture, and other fund, the food stamp contraband, seizure, and other fund, the board of pharmacy drug law enforcement fund, or a law enforcement trust fund under division (D)(1)(c) of this section, the state highway patrol, the department of public safety, the state board of pharmacy, and a county sheriff, prosecuting attorney, municipal corporation police department, township police department, township police district police force, office of the constable, or park district police force or law enforcement department shall adopt a written internal control policy that addresses the state highway patrol's, department of public safety's, state board of pharmacy's, sheriff's, prosecuting attorney's, police department's, police force's, office of the constable's, or law enforcement department's use and disposition of all the proceeds and forfeited moneys received and that provides for the keeping of detailed financial records of the receipts of the proceeds and forfeited moneys, the general types of expenditures made out of the proceeds and forfeited moneys, the specific amount of each general type of expenditure, and the amounts, portions, and programs described in division (D)(3)(a)(ii) of this section. The policy shall not provide for or permit the identification of any specific expenditure that is made in an ongoing investigation.

All financial records of the receipts of the proceeds and forfeited moneys, the general types of expenditures made out of the proceeds and forfeited moneys, the specific amount of each general type of expenditure by the state highway patrol, by the department of public safety, by the state board of pharmacy, and by a sheriff, prosecuting attorney, municipal corporation police department, township police department, township police district police force, office of the constable, or park district police force or law enforcement department, and the amounts, portions, and programs described in division (D)(3)(a)(ii) of this section are public records open for inspection under section 149.43 of the Revised Code. Additionally, a written internal control policy adopted under this division is a public record of that nature, and the state highway patrol, the department of public safety, the state board of pharmacy, or the sheriff, prosecuting attorney, municipal corporation police department, township police department, township police district police force, office of the constable, or park district police force or law enforcement department that adopted it shall comply with it.

(ii) The written internal control policy of a county sheriff, prosecuting attorney, municipal corporation police department, township police department, township police district police force, office of the constable, or park district police force or law enforcement department shall provide that at least ten per cent of the first one hundred thousand dollars of proceeds and forfeited moneys deposited during each calendar year in the sheriff's, prosecuting attorney's, municipal corporation's, township's, or park district's law enforcement trust fund pursuant to division (B)(8)(c) of section 2925.44 of the Revised Code, and at least twenty per cent of the proceeds and forfeited moneys exceeding one hundred thousand dollars that are so deposited, shall be used in connection with community preventive education programs. The manner in which the described percentages are so used shall be determined by the sheriff, prosecuting attorney, department, police force, or office of the constable after the receipt and consideration of advice on appropriate community preventive education programs from the county's board of alcohol, drug addiction, and mental health services, from the county's alcohol and drug addiction services board, or through appropriate community dialogue. The financial records described in division (D)(3)(a)(i) of this section shall specify the amount of the proceeds and forfeited moneys deposited during each calendar year in the sheriff's, prosecuting attorney's, municipal corporation's, township's, or park district's law enforcement trust fund pursuant to division (B)(8)(c) of section 2925.44 of the Revised Code, the portion of that amount that was used pursuant to the requirements of this division, and the community preventive education programs in connection with which the portion of that amount was so used.

As used in this division, "community preventive education programs" includes, but is not limited to, DARE programs and other programs designed to educate adults or children with respect to the dangers associated with the use of drugs of abuse.

(b) Each sheriff, prosecuting attorney, municipal corporation police department, township police department, township police district police force, office of the constable, or park district police force or law enforcement department that receives in any calendar year any proceeds or forfeited moneys out of a law enforcement trust fund under division (D)(1)(c) of this section or uses any proceeds or forfeited moneys in its law enforcement trust fund in any calendar year shall prepare a report covering the calendar year that cumulates all of the information contained in all of the public financial records kept by the sheriff, prosecuting attorney, municipal corporation police department, township police department, township police district police force, office of the constable, or park district police force or law enforcement department pursuant to division (D)(3)(a) of this section for that calendar year, and shall send a copy of the cumulative report, no later than the first day of March in the calendar year following the calendar year covered by the report, to the attorney general.

The superintendent of the state highway patrol shall prepare a report covering each calendar year in which the state highway patrol uses any proceeds or forfeited moneys in the state highway patrol contraband, forfeiture, and other fund under division (D)(1)(c) of this section, that cumulates all of the information contained in all of the public financial records kept by the state highway patrol pursuant to division (D)(3)(a) of this section for that calendar year, and shall send a copy of the cumulative report, no later than the first day of March in the calendar year following the calendar year covered by the report, to the attorney general.

The department of public safety shall prepare a report covering each fiscal year in which the department uses any proceeds or forfeited moneys in the liquor enforcement contraband, seizure, and other fund and the food stamp contraband, forfeiture, and other fund under division (D)(1)(c) of this section that cumulates all of the information contained in all of the public financial records kept by the department pursuant to division (D)(3)(a) of this section for that fiscal year. The department shall send a copy of the cumulative report to the attorney general no later than the first day of August in the fiscal year following the fiscal year covered by the report. The director of public safety shall include in the report a verification that proceeds and forfeited moneys paid into the liquor enforcement contraband, seizure, and other fund and the food stamp contraband, forfeiture, and other fund under division (D)(1)(c) of this section during the preceding fiscal year were used by the department during that fiscal year only for the purposes authorized by that division and shall specify the amount used for each authorized purpose.

The executive director of the state board of pharmacy shall prepare a report covering each calendar year in which the board uses any proceeds or forfeited moneys in the board of pharmacy drug law enforcement fund under division (D)(1)(c) of this section, that cumulates all of the information contained in all of the public financial records kept by the board pursuant to division (D)(3)(a) of this section for that calendar year, and shall send a copy of the cumulative report, no later than the first day of March in the calendar year following the calendar year covered by the report, to the attorney general. Each report received by the attorney general is a public record open for inspection under section 149.43 of the Revised Code. The attorney general shall make copies of each report received, and, no later than the fifteenth day of April in the calendar year in which the report is received, shall send a copy of it to the president of the senate and the speaker of the house of representatives.

(4)(a) A law enforcement agency that receives pursuant to federal law proceeds from a sale of forfeited contraband, proceeds from another disposition of forfeited contraband, or forfeited contraband moneys shall deposit, use, and account for the proceeds or forfeited moneys in accordance with, and otherwise comply with, the applicable federal law.

(b) If the state highway patrol receives pursuant to federal law proceeds from a sale of forfeited contraband, proceeds from another disposition of forfeited contraband, or forfeited contraband moneys, the appropriate governmental officials shall deposit into the state highway patrol contraband, forfeiture, and other fund all interest or other earnings derived from the investment of the proceeds or forfeited moneys. The state highway patrol shall use and account for that interest or other earnings in accordance with the applicable federal law.

(c) If the liquor enforcement unit of the department of public safety receives pursuant to federal law proceeds from a sale of forfeited contraband, proceeds from another disposition of forfeited contraband, or forfeited contraband moneys, the appropriate governmental officials shall deposit into the liquor enforcement contraband, forfeiture, and other fund all interest or other earnings derived from the investment of the proceeds or forfeited moneys. The department shall use and account for that interest or other earnings in accordance with the applicable federal law.

(d) If the food stamp fraud unit of the department of public safety receives pursuant to federal law proceeds from a sale of forfeited contraband, proceeds from another disposition of forfeited contraband, or forfeited contraband moneys, the appropriate governmental officials shall deposit into the food stamp contraband, forfeiture, and other fund all interest or other earnings derived from the investment of the proceeds or forfeited moneys. The department shall use and account for that interest or other earning in accordance with the applicable federal law.

(e) Divisions (D)(1) to (3) of this section do not apply to proceeds or forfeited moneys received pursuant to federal law or to the interest or other earnings that are derived from the investment of proceeds or forfeited moneys received pursuant to federal law and that are described in division (D)(4)(b) of this section.

(E) Upon the sale pursuant to this section of any property that is required to be titled or registered under law, the state shall issue an appropriate certificate of title or registration to the purchaser. If the state is vested with title pursuant to division (C) of this section and elects to retain property that is required to be titled or registered under law, the state shall issue an appropriate certificate of title or registration.

(F) Notwithstanding any provisions of this section to the contrary, any property that is lawfully seized in relation to a violation of section 2923.32 of the Revised Code shall be subject to forfeiture and disposition in accordance with sections 2923.32 to 2923.36 of the Revised Code, and any property that is forfeited pursuant to section 2925.42 or 2925.43 of the Revised Code in relation to a felony drug abuse offense, as defined in section 2925.01 of the Revised Code, or in relation to an act that, if committed by an adult, would be a felony drug abuse offense of that nature, may be subject to forfeiture and disposition in accordance with sections 2925.41 to 2925.45 of the Revised Code or this section.

(G) Any failure of a law enforcement officer or agency, a prosecuting attorney, village solicitor, city director of law, or similar chief legal officer, a court, or the attorney general to comply with any duty imposed by this section in relation to any property seized or with any other provision of this section in relation to any property seized does not affect the validity of the seizure of the property, provided the seizure itself was made in accordance with law, and is not and shall not be considered to be the basis for the suppression of any evidence resulting from the seizure of the property, provided the seizure itself was made in accordance with law.

(H) Contraband that has been forfeited pursuant to division (C) of this section shall not be available for use to pay any fine imposed upon a person who is convicted of or pleads guilty to an underlying criminal offense or a different offense arising out of the same facts and circumstances.

HISTORY: 141 v S 69 (Eff 9-3-86); 141 v H 428 (Eff 12-23-86); 143 v H 215 (Eff 4-11-90); 143 v H 261 (Eff 7-18-90); 143 v S 258 (Eff 11-20-90); 144 v S 218 (Eff 10-11-91); 144 v S 174 (Eff 7-31-92); 144 v S 351 (Eff 7-31-92); 146 v H 107 (Eff 6-30-95); 146 v S 162 (Eff 10-29-95); 146 v H 1 (Eff 1-1-96); 146 v S 239 (Eff 9-6-96); 146 v H 670 (Eff 12-2-96); 146 v S 277 (Eff 3-31-97); 147 v H 210. Eff 6-30-97.

The effective date is set by section 21 of HB 210.

The provisions of § 27 of HB 210 (147 v —) read as follows:

SECTION 27. Section 2933.43 of the Revised Code is presented in this act as a composite of the section as amended by both Sub. H.B. 670 and Sub. S.B. 277 of the 121st General Assembly, with the new language of neither of the act shown in capital letters. ° ° ° This is in recognition of the principle stated in division (B) of section 1.52 of the Revised Code that such amendments are to be harmonized where not substantively irreconcilable and constitutes a legislative finding that such is the resulting version in effect prior to the effective date of this act.

§ 2933.44 Annual report by alcohol and drug treatment program receiving juvenile-related forfeiture.

(A) As used in this section, "juvenile-related forfeiture order" means any order of forfeiture issued by a juvenile court under section 2923.32, 2925.42, 2925.43, or 2933.43 of the Revised Code and any order of disposition of property issued by a court under section 2933.41 of the Revised Code regarding property that was in the possession of a law enforcement agency in relation to a delinquent child proceeding in a juvenile court.

(B) Each certified alcohol and drug addiction treatment program that receives in any calendar year money under division (D)(1)(a) of section 2923.35, division (B)(8)(c)(i) of section 2925.44, division (E)(1)(a) of section 2933.41, or division (D)(1)(c)(i) of section 2933.43 of the Revised Code subsequent to the issuance of any juvenile-related forfeiture order shall file an annual report for that calendar year with the attorney general and with the court of common pleas and board of county commissioners of the county in which the program is located and of any other county from which the program received money under any of those divisions subsequent to the issuance of the juvenile-related forfeiture order. The program shall file the report on or before the first day of March in the calendar year following the calendar year in which the program received the money. The report shall include statistics on the number of persons the program served, identify the types of treatment services it provided to those persons, and include a specific accounting of the purposes for which it used the money so received. No information contained in

the report shall identify, or enable a person to determine the identity of, any person served by the program.
HISTORY: 146 v H 1. Eff 1-1-96.

The effective date is set by section 6 of HB 1.

[WIRETAPPING, ELECTRONIC SURVEILLANCE]

§ 2933.51 Definitions.

As used in sections 2933.51 to 2933.66 of the Revised Code:

(A) "Wire communication" means an aural transfer that is made in whole or in part through the use of facilities for the transmission of communications by the aid of wires or similar methods of connecting the point of origin of the communication and the point of reception of the communication, including the use of a method of connecting the point of origin and the point of reception of the communication in a switching station, if the facilities are furnished or operated by a person engaged in providing or operating the facilities for the transmission of communications. "Wire communication" includes an electronic storage of a wire communication.

(B) "Oral communication" means an oral communication uttered by a person exhibiting an expectation that the communication is not subject to interception under circumstances justifying that expectation. "Oral communication" does not include an electronic communication.

(C) "Intercept" means the aural or other acquisition of the contents of any wire, oral, or electronic communication through the use of an interception device.

(D) "Interception device" means an electronic, mechanical, or other device or apparatus that can be used to intercept a wire, oral, or electronic communication. "Interception device" does not mean any of the following:

(1) A telephone or telegraph instrument, equipment, or facility, or any of its components, if the instrument, equipment, facility, or component is any of the following:

(a) Furnished to the subscriber or user by a provider of wire or electronic communication service in the ordinary course of its business and being used by the subscriber or user in the ordinary course of its business;

(b) Furnished by a subscriber or user for connection to the facilities of a provider of wire or electronic communication service and used in the ordinary course of that subscriber's or user's business;

(c) Being used by a provider of wire or electronic communication service in the ordinary course of its business or by an investigative or law enforcement officer in the ordinary course of the officer's duties that do not involve the interception of wire, oral, or electronic communications.

(2) A hearing aid or similar device being used to correct subnormal hearing to not better than normal.

(E) "Investigative officer" means any of the following:

(1) An officer of this state or a political subdivision of this state, who is empowered by law to conduct investigations or to make arrests for a designated offense;

(2) A person described in divisions (A)(11)(a) and (b) of section 2901.01 of the Revised Code;

(3) An attorney authorized by law to prosecute or participate in the prosecution of a designated offense;

(4) A secret service officer appointed pursuant to section 309.07 of the Revised Code;

(5) An officer of the United States, a state, or a political subdivision of a state who is authorized to conduct investigations pursuant to the "Electronic Communications Privacy Act of 1986," 100 Stat. 1848-1857, 18 U.S.C. 2510-2521 (1986), as amended.

(F) "Interception warrant" means a court order that authorizes the interception of wire, oral, or electronic communications and that is issued pursuant to sections 2933.53 to 2933.56 of the Revised Code.

(G) "Contents," when used with respect to a wire, oral, or electronic communication, includes any information concerning the substance, purport, or meaning of the communication.

(H) "Communications common carrier" means a person who is engaged as a common carrier for hire in intrastate, interstate, or foreign communications by wire, radio, or radio transmission of energy. "Communications common carrier" does not include, to the extent that the person is engaged in radio broadcasting, a person engaged in radio broadcasting.

(I) "Designated offense" means any of the following:

(1) A felony violation of section 1315.53, 1315.55, 2903.01, 2903.02, 2903.11, 2905.01, 2905.02, 2905.11, 2905.22, 2907.02, 2907.21, 2907.22, 2909.02, 2909.03, 2909.04, 2911.01, 2911.02, 2911.11, 2911.12, 2913.02, 2913.04, 2913.42, 2913.51, 2915.02, 2915.03, 2917.01, 2917.02, 2921.02, 2921.03, 2921.04, 2921.32, 2921.34, 2923.20, 2923.32, 2925.03, 2925.04, 2925.05, or 2925.06 or of division (B) of section 2915.05 of the Revised Code;

(2) A violation of section 2919.23 of the Revised Code that, had it occurred prior to the effective date of this amendment, would have been a violation of section 2905.04 of the Revised Code as it existed prior to that date;

(3) A felony violation of section 2925.11 of the Revised Code that is not a minor drug possession offense, as defined in section 2925.01 of the Revised Code;

(4) Complicity in the commission of a felony violation of a section listed in division (I)(1), (2), or (3) of this section;

(5) An attempt to commit, or conspiracy in the commission of, a felony violation of a section listed in division (I)(1), (2), or (3) of this section, if the attempt or conspiracy is punishable by a term of imprisonment of more than one year.

(J) "Aggrieved person" means a person who was a party to an intercepted wire, oral, or electronic communication or a person against whom the interception of the communication was directed.

(K) "Person" means a person, as defined in section 1.59 of the Revised Code, or a governmental officer, employee, or entity.

(L) "Special need" means a showing that a licensed physician, licensed practicing psychologist, attorney, practicing clergyman, journalist, or either spouse is personally engaging in continuing criminal activity, was engaged in continuing criminal activity over a period of time, or is committing, has committed, or is about to commit, a designated offense, or a showing that specified public facilities are being regularly used by someone who is personally engaging in continuing criminal activity, was engaged in continuing criminal activity over a period of time, or is committing, has committed, or is about to commit, a designated offense.

(M) "Journalist" means a person engaged in, connected with, or employed by, any news media, including a newspaper, magazine, press association, news agency, or wire service, a radio or television station, or a similar media, for the purpose of gathering, processing, transmitting, compiling, editing, or disseminating news for the general public.

(N) "Electronic communication" means a transfer of a sign, signal, writing, image, sound, datum, or intelligence of any nature that is transmitted in whole or in part by a wire, radio, electromagnetic, photoelectronic, or photo-optical system. "Electronic communication" does not mean any of the following:

(1) A wire or oral communication;

(2) A communication made through a tone-only paging device;

(3) A communication from an electronic or mechanical tracking device that permits the tracking of the movement of a person or object.

(O) "User" means a person or entity that uses an electronic communication service and is duly authorized by the provider of the service to engage in the use of the electronic communication service.

(P) "Electronic communications system" means a wire, radio, electromagnetic, photoelectronic, or photo-optical facility for the transmission of electronic communications, and a computer facility or related electronic equipment for the electronic storage of electronic communications.

(Q) "Electronic communication service" means a service that provides to users of the service the ability to send or receive wire or electronic communications.

(R) "Readily accessible to the general public" means, with respect to a radio communication, that the communication is none of the following:

(1) Scrambled or encrypted;

(2) Transmitted using a modulation technique, the essential parameters of which have been withheld from the public with the intention of preserving the privacy of the communication;

(3) Carried on a subcarrier or other signal subsidiary to a radio transmission;

(4) Transmitted over a communications system provided by a communications common carrier, unless the communication is a tone-only paging system communication;

(5) Transmitted on a frequency allocated under part 25, subpart D, E, or F of part 74, or part 94 of the Rules of the Federal Communications Commission, as those provisions existed on the effective date of this amendment, unless, in the case of a communication transmitted on a frequency allocated under part 74 that is not exclusively allocated to broadcast auxiliary services, the communication is a two-way voice communication by radio.

(S) "Electronic Storage" means a temporary, intermediate storage of a wire or electronic communication that is incidental to the electronic transmission of the communication, and a storage of a wire or electronic communication by an electronic communication service for the purpose of backup protection of the communication.

(T) "Aural transfer" means a transfer containing the human voice at a point between and including the point of origin and the point of reception.

(U) "Pen register" means a device that records or decodes electronic impulses that identify the numbers dialed, pulsed, or otherwise transmitted on telephone lines to which the device is attached.

(V) "Trap and trace device" means a device or apparatus that connects to a telephone or telegraph instrument, equipment, or facility and determines the origin of a wire communication to a telephone or telegraph instrument, equipment, or facility but does not intercept the contents of a wire communication.

(W) "Judge of a court of common pleas" means a judge of that court who is elected or appointed as a judge of general jurisdiction or as a judge who exercises both general jurisdiction and probate, domestic relations, or juvenile jurisdiction. "Judge of a court of common pleas" does not mean a judge of that court who is elected or appointed specifically as a probate, domestic relations, or juvenile judge.

HISTORY: 141 v S 222 (Eff 3-25-87); 146 v H 181, § 1 (Eff 6-13-96); 146 v S 2 (Eff 7-1-96); 146 v H 181, § 3 (Eff 7-1-96); 146 v S 269 (Eff 7-1-96); 146 v S 239 (Eff 9-6-96); 146 v H 333. Eff 9-19-96.

Comment, Legislative Service Commission

Section 2933.51 of the Revised Code is amended by this act [Am. Sub. S.B. 269] and also by Sub. H.B. 181 (effective July 1, 1996), Am. Sub. H.B. 333, and Am. Sub. S.B. 239, all of the 121st General Assembly. Comparison of these amendments in pursuance of section 1.52 of the Revised Code discloses that they are not irreconcilable so that they are required by that section to be harmonized to give effect to each amendment.

§ 2933.52 Interception of wire, oral or electronic communications.

(A) No person purposely shall do any of the following:

(1) Intercept, attempt to intercept, or procure another person to intercept or attempt to intercept a wire, oral, or electronic communication;

(2) Use, attempt to use, or procure another person to use or attempt to use an interception device to intercept a wire, oral, or electronic communication, if either of the following applies:

(a) The interception device is affixed to, or otherwise transmits a signal through, a wire, cable, satellite, microwave, or other similar method of connection used in wire communications;

(b) The interception device transmits communications by radio, or interferes with the transmission of communications by radio.

(3) Use, or attempt to use, the contents of a wire, oral, or electronic communication, knowing or having reason to know that the contents were obtained through the interception of a wire, oral, or electronic communication in violation of sections 2933.51 to 2933.66 of the Revised Code.

(B) This section does not apply to any of the following:

(1) The interception, disclosure, or use of the contents, or evidence derived from the contents, of an oral, wire, or electronic communication that is obtained through the use of an interception warrant issued pursuant to sections 2933.53 to 2933.56 of the Revised Code, that is obtained pursuant to an oral approval for an interception granted pursuant to section 2933.57 of the Revised Code, or that is obtained pursuant to an order that is issued or an interception that is made in accordance with section 802 of the "Omnibus Crime Control and Safe Streets Act of 1968," 82 Stat. 237, 254, 18 U.S.C. 2510 to 2520 (1968), as amended, the "Electronic Communications Privacy Act of 1986," 100 Stat. 1848-1857, 18 U.S.C. 2510-2521 (1986), as amended, or the "Foreign Intelligence Surveillance Act," 92 Stat. 1783, 50 U.S.C. 1801.11 (1978), as amended;

(2) An operator of a switchboard, or an officer, employee, or agent of a provider of wire or electronic communication service, whose facilities are used in the transmission of a wire or electronic communication to intercept, disclose, or use that communication in the normal course of employment while engaged in an activity that is necessary to the rendition of service or to the protection of the rights or property of the provider of that service, except that a provider of wire or electronic communication service to the public shall not utilize service observing or random monitoring except for mechanical or service quality control checks;

(3) A law enforcement officer who intercepts a wire, oral, or electronic communication, if the officer is a party to the communication or if one of the parties to the communication has given prior consent to the interception by the officer;

(4) A person who is not a law enforcement officer and who intercepts a wire, oral, or electronic communication, if the person is a party to the communication or if one of the parties to the communication has given the person prior consent to the interception, and if the communication is not intercepted for the purpose of committing a criminal offense or tortious act in violation of the laws or Constitution of the United States or this state or for the purpose of committing any other injurious act;

(5) An officer, employee, or agent of a communications common carrier providing information, facilities, or technical assistance to an investigative officer who is authorized to intercept a wire, oral, or electronic communication pursuant to sections 2933.51 to 2933.66 of the Revised Code;

(6) The use of a pen register in accordance with federal or state law;

(7) The use of a trap and trace device in accordance with federal or state law;

(8) A police, fire, or emergency communications system to intercept wire communications coming into and going out of the communications system of a police department, fire department, or emergency center, if both of the following apply:

(a) The telephone, instrument, equipment, or facility is limited to the exclusive use of the communication system for administrative purposes;

(b) At least one telephone, instrument, equipment, or facility that is not subject to interception is made available for public use at each police department, fire department, or emergency center.

(9) The interception or accessing of an electronic communication made through an electronic communication system that is configured so that the electronic communication is readily accessible to the general public.

(10) The interception of a radio communication that is transmitted by any of the following:

(a) A station for the use of the general public;

(b) Governmental, law enforcement, civil defense, private land mobile, or public safety communications system, including a police or fire system, that is readily accessible to the general public;

(c) A station operating on an authorized frequency within the bands allocated to the amateur, citizens band, or general mobile radio services;

(d) A marine or aeronautical communications system.

(11) The interception of a radio communication that relates to a ship, aircraft, vehicle, or person in distress.

(12) The interception of a wire or electronic communication the transmission of which is causing harmful interference to a lawfully operating station or consumer electronic equipment, to the extent necessary to identify the source of that interference.

(13) Other users of the same frequency to intercept a radio communication made through a system that utilizes frequencies monitored by individuals engaged in the provision or the use of that system, if the communication is not scrambled or encrypted.

(C) Whoever violates this section is guilty of interception of wire, oral, or electronic communications, a felony of the fourth degree.

HISTORY: 141 v S 222 (Eff 3-25-87); 142 v H 231 (Eff 10-5-87); 146 v H 181, § 1 (Eff 6-13-96); 146 v S 2 (Eff 7-1-96); 146 v H 181, § 3. Eff 7-1-96.

Publisher's Note

The amendments made by SB 2 (146 v —) and HB 181 (146 v —) have been combined. Please see provisions of RC § 1.52.

The effective date is set by section 5 of HB 181.

[§ 2933.52.1] § 2933.521 Divulgence of content of communication by provider of electronic communication service.

(A) Except as provided in division (B) of this section, no person or entity that provides electronic communication service to the public shall purposely divulge the content of a communication, while it is in transmission on that service, to a person or entity other than an addressee or intended recipient of the communication or an agent of an addressee or intended recipient of the communication.

(B)(1) Division (A) of this section does not apply to a communication being transmitted to the person or entity providing the electronic communication service or to an agent of that person or entity.

(2) Notwithstanding division (A) of this section, a person or entity that provides electronic communication service to the public may divulge the content of a communication that is in transmission on that service in any of the following circumstances:

(a) The divulgence is authorized by division (B)(2) of section 2933.52, by section 2933.581 [2933.58.1], by division (C) of section 2933.55, or by division (F) or (G) of section 2933.59 of the Revised Code or by a provision of the "Electronic Communications Privacy Act of 1986," 100 Stat. 1848-1857, 18 U.S.C. 2510-2521 (1986), as amended.

(b) The originator or an addressee or intended recipient of the communication has lawfully consented to the divulgence.

(c) The divulgence is made to a person who is employed or authorized, or whose facilities are used, to forward the communication to its destination.

(d) The content of the communication divulged was inadvertently obtained by the provider of the service, the content appears to pertain to the commission of a crime, and the divulgence is made to a law enforcement agency.

(C) Neither division (A) of this section nor any other provision of sections 2933.51 to 2933.66 of the Revised Code prohibits a provider of electronic communication service from recording the fact that a wire or electronic communication was initiated or completed, in order to protect the provider, another provider furnishing service toward the completion of the wire or electronic communication, or a user of the electronic communication service from fraudulent, unlawful, or abusive use of the electronic communication service.

HISTORY: 146 v H 181. Eff 6-13-96.

[§ 2933.52.2] § 2933.522 Powers of common pleas court judge.

A judge of a court of common pleas, in accordance with sections 2933.51 to 2933.66 of the Revised Code, may accept applications for interception warrants, may issue interception warrants, may accept applications for extensions of interception warrants, may order extensions of interception warrants, may accept applications for grants of oral orders for interceptions, may grant oral orders for interceptions, and may issue other orders, perform other functions, or engage in other activities authorized or required by sections 2933.51 to 2933.66 of the Revised Code.

HISTORY: 146 v H 181. Eff 6-13-96.

§ 2933.53 Application for interception warrant.

(A) The prosecuting attorney of the county in which an interception is to take place or in which an interception device is to be installed, or an assistant to the prosecuting attorney of that county who is specifically designated by the prosecuting attorney to exercise authority under this section, may authorize an application for an interception warrant to a judge of the court of common pleas of the county in which the interception is to take place or in which the interception device is to be installed. If the prosecuting attorney of a county in which an interception is to take place or in which an interception device is to be installed is the subject of an investigation, a special prosecutor appointed by a judge of the court of common pleas of the county served by the prosecuting attorney, without the knowledge of the prosecuting attorney, may apply the procedures of this section. If the subject of an investigation is employed in the office of the prosecuting attorney of the county in which an interception is to take place or in which an interception device is to be installed or the prosecuting attorney of that county believes that the subject has a conflict of interest, the approval of the prosecuting attorney shall be obtained before a special prosecutor is appointed to authorize the application for an interception warrant.

(B) Each application for an interception warrant shall be made in writing upon oath or affirmation to a judge of the court of common pleas of the county in which the interception is to take place or in which the interception device is to be installed, by a person who has received training that satisfies the minimum standards established by the attorney general and the Ohio peace officer training commission under section 2933.64 of the Revised Code. Each application shall contain all of the following:

(1) The name and office of the applicant and the name and office of the prosecuting attorney or assistant prosecuting attorney authorizing the application;

(2) The identity of the investigative officers or law enforcement agency that will intercept the wire, oral, or electronic communications;

(3) A full and complete statement of the objective in seeking the warrant, and a full and complete statement of the facts and circumstances relied on by the applicant to justify the belief that the warrant should be issued, including, but not limited to the following:

(a) The details regarding the designated offense that has been, is being, or is about to be committed;

(b) The identity of the person, if known, who has committed, is committing, or is about to commit the designated offense and whose communications are to be intercepted and the location at which the communications are sought to be intercepted;

(c) Except as provided in division (G)(1) of this section, a particular description of the nature and location of the facilities from which, or the place at which, the communication is to be intercepted;

(d) A particular description of the type of communication sought to be intercepted, and the basis for believing that evidence relating to a designated offense will be obtained through the interception.

(4) A statement as to whether the applicant, or the prosecuting attorney or assistant prosecuting attorney authorizing the application for an interception warrant, knows or has reason to know that the communications sought to be intercepted are privileged under section 2317.02 of the Revised Code, the nature of any privilege that exists, and the basis of the knowledge of the applicant or authorizing prosecuting attorney or assistant prosecuting attorney of the privileged nature of the communications;

(5) A statement of the use to which the contents of an intercepted wire, oral, or electronic communication, or the evidence derived from the communication, will be put;

(6) A statement of the period of time for which the interception is required to be maintained, and, if the nature of the investigation requires that the authorization for interception not be terminated automatically when the described type of communication first has been intercepted, a particular description of the facts establishing probable cause to believe that additional communications of the same type will occur after the first intercepted communication;

(7) A full and complete statement indicating whether other investigative procedures have been tried and have failed to produce the required evidence or indicating the reason that other investigative procedures reasonably appear to be unlikely to succeed if tried or to be too dangerous to employ in order to obtain evidence;

(8) A full and complete statement of the particular facts concerning all previous applications known to the applicant or the prosecuting attorney or assistant prosecuting attorney authorizing the application for the interception warrant, that have been made to a judge for authorization to intercept wire, oral, or electronic communications involving any of the persons, facilities, or places specified in the application, and the action of the judge with respect to each previous application;

(9) Unless the attorney general is a subject of the investigation, a written statement, signed by the attorney general or an assistant attorney general designated by the attorney general, that the attorney general or assistant attorney general has reviewed the application and either agrees or disagrees with the submission of the application to a judge of the court of common pleas of the county in which the interception is to take place or in which the interception device is to be installed. A disagreement by the attorney general or assistant attorney general does not preclude the making or consideration of an application that otherwise complies with divisions (B)(1) to (8) of this section.

(C) If an application for an interception warrant is for an extension of a warrant, the application shall include, in addition to the information and statements specified in division (B) of this section, a statement setting forth the results thus far obtained from the interceptions of wire, oral, or electronic communications, or a reasonable explanation of the failure to obtain results from the interceptions.

(D) An applicant may submit affidavits of persons other than the applicant in conjunction with the application if the affidavits support a fact or conclusion in the application. The accompanying affidavits shall be based on personal knowledge of the affiant or shall be based on information and belief and specify the source of the information and the reason for the belief. If the applicant or an affiant personally knows of the facts contained in the application or affidavit, the application or affidavit shall state the personal knowledge. If the application or affidavit states the facts based upon information and belief, the application or affidavit shall state that reliance upon information and belief and shall set forth fully the facts supporting the information and belief. If the facts contained in the application or affidavits are derived in whole or in part from the statement of a person other than the applicant or affiant, the application or affidavits shall disclose or describe the sources of the facts and shall contain facts establishing the existence and reliability of the other person or the reliability of the information supplied by the other person. The application also shall state, so far as possible, the basis of the other person's knowledge or belief. If the application or affidavit relies on hearsay to support a fact alleged on information and belief, the application or affidavit shall contain the underlying facts that establish the basis for the conclusions of the source of the hearsay and the factual basis upon which the applicant or the affiant concludes that the source of the hearsay is credible or reliable.

(E) A judge of a court of common pleas to whom an

application is made under this section may require the applicant to furnish additional sworn testimony or documentary evidence in support of the application. All sworn testimony furnished shall be recorded and transcribed and shall be made part of the application.

(F) An interception warrant is not required for any of the following:

(1) A pen register used in accordance with federal or state law;

(2) The interception of a wire, oral, or electronic communication by a law enforcement officer if the officer is a party to the communication or if one of the parties to the communication has given prior consent to the interception by the officer;

(3) The interception of a wire, oral, or electronic communication by a person who is not a law enforcement officer if the person is a party to the communication or if one of the parties to the communication has given the person prior consent to the interception, and if the communication is not intercepted for the purpose of committing a criminal offense or tortious act in violation of the laws or constitution of the United States or this state or for the purpose of committing another injurious act.

(4) A trap and trace device used in accordance with federal or state law.

(G)(1) The requirements of division (B)(3)(c) of this section and of division (A)(5) of section 2933.54 of the Revised Code that relate to the specification of facilities from which or the place at which the communication is to be intercepted do not apply if either of the following applies:

(a) In the case of an application with respect to the interception of an oral communication, the application contains a full and complete statement indicating the reason that the specification is not practical and identifies the person committing the designated offense and whose communications are to be intercepted, and the judge of a court of common pleas to whom the application is made finds that the specification is not practical.

(b) In the case of an application with respect to a wire or electronic communication, the application identifies the person believed to be committing the designated offense and whose communications are to be intercepted, the applicant makes a showing of purpose on the part of that person to thwart interception by changing facilities, and the judge of a court of common pleas to whom the application is made finds that that purpose adequately has been shown.

(2) An interception of a communication under an interception warrant with respect to which the requirements of division (B)(3)(c) of this section and division (A)(5) of section 2933.54 of the Revised Code do not apply, due to the application of division (G)(1) of this section, shall not begin until the facilities from which or the place at which the communication is to be intercepted is ascertained by the person implementing the interception warrant.

A provider of wire or electronic communication service that has received an interception warrant that does not specify the facilities from which or the place at which the communication is to be intercepted, due to the application of division (G)(1)(b) of this section, may file a motion with the court requesting the court to modify or quash the interception warrant on the ground that the provider's assistance with respect to the interception cannot be performed in a timely or reasonable manner. The court, upon notice to the applicant for the interception warrant, shall decide the motion expeditiously.

HISTORY: 141 v S 222 (Eff 3-25-87); 146 v H 181 (Eff 6-13-96); 146 v H 670. Eff 12-2-96.

§ 2933.54 Conditions for issuance of warrant; denial; termination; finding of objective.

(A) A judge of a court of common pleas to whom an application for an interception warrant is made under section 2933.53 of the Revised Code may issue an interception warrant if the judge determines, on the basis of the facts submitted by the person who made the application and all affiants, that all of the following exist:

(1) The application and affidavits comply with section 2933.53 of the Revised Code.

(2) There is probable cause to believe that a particular person is committing, has committed, or is about to commit a designated offense.

(3) There is probable cause to believe that particular communications concerning the designated offense will be obtained through the interception of wire, oral, or electronic communications.

(4) Normal investigative procedures with respect to the designated offense have been tried and have failed or normal investigative procedures with respect to the designated offense reasonably appear to be unlikely to succeed if tried or to be too dangerous to employ in order to obtain evidence.

(5) Except as provided in division (G)(1) of section 2933.53 of the Revised Code, there is probable cause to believe that the communication facilities from which the communications are to be intercepted, or the place at which oral communications are to be intercepted, are being used or are about to be used in connection with the commission of the designated offense or are leased to, listed in the name of, or commonly used by a person who is the subject of the interception warrant.

(6) The investigative officer has received training that satisfies the minimum standards established by the attorney general and the Ohio peace officer training commission under section 2933.64 of the Revised Code in order to intercept the wire, oral, or electronic communication and is able to execute the interception sought.

(B) If the communication facilities from which a wire or electronic communication is to be intercepted are public facilities, the judge of the court of common pleas to whom the application for an interception warrant is made shall not issue an interception warrant unless the judge, in addition to the findings specified in division (A) of this section, determines that there is a special need to intercept wire or electronic communications made from the facilities.

(C) If the facilities from which, or the place at which, the wire, oral, or electronic communications are to be intercepted are being used by, are about to be used by, are leased to, are listed in the name of, or are commonly used by a licensed physician, a licensed practicing psychologist, an attorney, a practicing clergyman, or a journalist or are used primarily for habitation by a husband and wife, the judge of the court of common pleas to whom the application is made shall not issue an interception warrant unless the judge, in addition to the findings specified in divisions (A) and (B) of this section, determines that there is a special need to intercept wire, oral, or electronic communications over the facilities or in those places. No otherwise privileged wire, oral, or electronic communication shall lose its privileged character because it is intercepted in accordance with or in violation of sections 2933.51 to 2933.66 of the Revised Code.

(D) If an application for an interception warrant does not comply with section 2933.53 of the Revised Code, or if the judge of a court of common pleas with whom an application is filed is not satisfied that grounds exist for issuance of an interception warrant, the judge shall deny the application.

(E) An interception warrant shall terminate when the objective of the warrant has been achieved or upon the expiration of thirty days after the date of commencement of the warrant as specified in this division, whichever occurs first, unless an extension is granted as described in this division. The date of commencement of an interception warrant is the day on which an investigative or law enforcement officer first begins to conduct an interception under the warrant, or the day that is ten days after the warrant is issued, whichever is earlier. A judge of a court of common pleas may grant extensions of a warrant pursuant to section 2933.55 of the Revised Code.

(F) If a judge of a court of common pleas issues an interception warrant, the judge shall make a finding as to the objective of the warrant.

HISTORY: 141 v S 222 (Eff 3-25-87); 142 v H 708 (Eff 4-19-88); 146 v H 181 (Eff 6-13-96); 146 v H 670. Eff 12-2-96.

§ 2933.55 Application for extension of warrant; interception concerning other than designated offenses.

(A) At any time prior to the expiration of an interception warrant, the person who made the application for the warrant may apply for an extension of the warrant. The person shall file the application for extension with a judge of the court of common pleas of the county in which the interception under the warrant was to take place. An application for extension shall comply with section 2933.53 of the Revised Code.

(B) A judge of a court of common pleas with whom an application for extension of an interception warrant is filed shall determine whether to order an extension of the interception warrant in accordance with section 2933.54 of the Revised Code and shall order an extension for a period no longer than the judge considers necessary to achieve the purposes of the extension. The extension shall terminate upon the attainment of the authorized objective or thirty days after it is granted, whichever occurs first. All provisions of sections 2933.51 to 2933.66 of the Revised Code that apply to original interception warrants apply to extensions of interception warrants.

(C)(1) When an investigative officer, while intercepting communications pursuant to an interception warrant or pursuant to an oral order for an interception granted under section 2933.57 of the Revised Code, intercepts wire, oral, or electronic communications that pertain to a criminal offense that is other than the designated offense specified in the interception warrant or oral order and that is completely unrelated to the designated offense specified in the interception warrant or oral order, the prosecuting attorney, in order to permit the disclosure or use of the contents, or evidence derived from the contents, of the intercepted communications pursuant to division (G) of section 2933.59 of the Revised Code, may file a motion with the judge who issued the warrant or granted the oral order for an order approving the interception. The judge shall enter an order approving the interception if the judge finds that the communication otherwise was intercepted in accordance with sections 2933.53 to 2933.66 of the Revised Code.

A person may disclose or use the contents, and any evidence derived from the contents, of the intercepted communications dealing with the other, unrelated offense as set forth in division (F) of section 2933.59 of the Revised Code. The person may disclose or use those contents and the evidence derived from those contents as set forth in division (G) of section 2933.59 of the Revised Code only if the issuing judge issues an order approving the interception of the communications concerning the other, unrelated offense.

(2) When an investigative officer, while intercepting communications pursuant to an interception warrant or pursuant to an oral order for an interception granted under section 2933.57 of the Revised Code, intercepts wire, oral, or electronic communications that pertain to a criminal offense that is other than the designated offense specified in the interception warrant or oral order but that is not completely unrelated to the designated offense specified in the interception warrant or oral order, the wire, oral, or electronic communications intercepted shall be treated for all purposes and without the need for further action as if the offense to which

they pertain was a designated offense specified in the interception warrant or oral order.

HISTORY: 141 v S 222 (Eff 3-25-87); 146 v H 181. Eff 6-13-96.

§ 2933.56 Contents of warrant; sealing of application and warrant; disclosure; retention.

(A) Any interception warrant or extension of an interception warrant that is issued pursuant to sections 2933.53 to 2933.55 of the Revised Code shall contain all of the following:

(1) The name and court of the judge who issued the warrant and the jurisdiction of that court;

(2) If known, the identity of each person whose communications are to be intercepted or, if the identity is unascertainable, a detailed description of each known person whose communications are to be intercepted;

(3) The nature and location of the communications facilities from which or of the place at which the authority to intercept is granted and, in the case of telephone or telegraph communications, A designation of the particular lines involved;

(4) A statement of the objective of the warrant, as found by the issuing judge, and a statement of the designated offenses for which the authority to intercept is granted;

(5) A description of the particular type of communication sought to be intercepted;

(6) The identity of the investigative officer or law enforcement agency that is authorized to intercept communications pursuant to the interception warrant and the identity of the prosecuting attorney or assistant prosecuting attorney authorizing the application for the interception warrant;

(7) The period of time during which the interception is authorized, including a statement as to whether the interception shall terminate automatically when the described communication is first intercepted;

(8) A statement that the interception warrant shall be executed as soon as practicable;

(9) A statement that the interception shall be conducted in a way that minimizes the interception of communications that are not subject to the interception warrant, provided that if the intercepted communication is in a code or a foreign language and an expert in decoding or in that foreign language is not reasonably available during the interception period, minimization may be accomplished as soon as practicable after the interception;

(10) A statement that the interception shall terminate upon attainment of the authorized objective or upon the expiration of the thirty-day period described in division (E) of section 2933.54 of the Revised Code, whichever occurs first, unless an extension of the interception warrant is granted upon application by the judge who issued the original warrant;

(11) A statement that the person who made the application for the warrant or extension and the investigative officer or law enforcement agency authorized to intercept the communications shall provide oral or written progress reports at seven-day intervals to the judge who issued the warrant showing the progress made toward achievement of the authorized objective of the warrant and the need for continued interception;

(12) An authorization to enter private premises, other than the premises of a provider of wire or electronic communication service, for the sole purposes of installing, or of removing and permanently inactivating, interception devices and, if the entry is necessary to execute the interception warrant, a requirement that the time and date of the entry and name of the individual making the entry be reported to the court;

(13) If applicable, a statement directing a provider of wire or electronic communication service, landlord, custodian, or other person forthwith to furnish the applicant all information, facilities, and technical assistance necessary to accomplish the interception unobtrusively and with a minimum of interference with the services that the provider of wire or electronic communication service, landlord, custodian, or other person is providing to the person whose communications are to be intercepted. This assistance by a provider of wire or electronic communication service shall not include assistance in supplying, installing, or removing and permanently inactivating, interception devices. Any provider of wire or electronic communication service and any landlord, custodian, or other person furnishing the facilities or technical assistance shall be compensated for them at the prevailing rates.

(B) The judge of the court of common pleas to whom the application is made or who issued the warrant shall seal all applications for interception warrants that are made and all interception warrants that are issued pursuant to sections 2933.53 to 2933.55 of the Revised Code.

The judge of a court of common pleas who received the application or issued the warrant shall specify who shall have custody of the sealed application and interception warrant. Copies of the interception warrant, together with a copy of the application, shall be delivered to and retained by the person who made the application for the warrant or extension as authority for the interception authorized by the warrant.

Except as otherwise provided in sections 2933.51 to 2933.66 of the Revised Code, the application and interception warrants shall be disclosed only upon a showing of good cause before a judge who is authorized to issue interception warrants. Upon the termination of the authorized interception, the person who made the application for the warrant or extension shall return all applications made and interception warrants issued under sections 2933.53 to 2933.55 of the Revised Code that pertain to the interception to the issuing judge, and the applications and warrants shall be sealed under the issuing judge's direction.

The applications and warrants shall be kept for at least ten years. At the expiration of the ten-year period, the issuing or denying judge may order that the applications and warrants be destroyed.

(C) A violation of division (B) of this section may be punished as contempt of court.

HISTORY: 141 v S 222 (Eff 3-25-87); 146 v H 181. Eff 6-13-96.

§ 2933.57 Oral order for interception without warrant.

(A) A judge of the court of common pleas may grant an oral order for an interception without a warrant of a wire, oral, or electronic communication. Upon receipt of an application under this division, the judge of the court of common pleas to whom the application is made may grant an oral order for an interception without a warrant, may include in the order a statement of the type described in division (A)(13) of section 2933.56 of the Revised Code, and shall condition the order upon the filing with the judge, within forty-eight hours, of an application for an interception warrant under section 2933.53 of the Revised Code and division (B) of this section, if the judge determines all of the following:

(1) There appear to be grounds upon which an interception warrant could be issued under section 2933.54 of the Revised Code.

(2) There is probable cause to believe that an emergency situation exists with respect to the investigation of a designated offense.

(3) There is probable cause to believe that the emergency situation involves an immediate danger of death or serious physical harm that justifies the authorization for immediate interception of a private wire, oral, or electronic communication before an application for an interception warrant could, with due diligence, be submitted to the judge and acted upon.

(B) No statement by the attorney general or the attorney general's designee pursuant to division (B)(9) of section 2933.53 is required prior to consideration of an application pursuant to this section.

(C) The judge of a court of common pleas to whom an application is made under division (A) of this section, the applicant, the prosecuting attorney or assistant prosecuting attorney who authorized the application, and any involved provider of wire or electronic communication service may tape record any telephone or other communications between any of them related to the application for, the approval of, and the implementation of an oral order for an interception. All of the provisions of sections 2933.51 to 2933.66 of the Revised Code concerning the sealing, distribution, use, and disclosure of an application for an interception warrant apply to any tape recording between the judge, the applicant, and the prosecuting attorney or the designated assistant concerning the application for and an oral order for an interception.

(D)(1) As soon as possible after granting an oral order for an interception without a warrant, a judge shall place upon the journal of the court an entry nunc pro tunc to record the granting of the oral order. If an interception warrant is issued pursuant to the filing of an application following the granting of an oral order for an interception under this section, the judge shall issue the warrant in accordance with section 2933.54 of the Revised Code, and the warrant shall recite the granting of the oral order and shall be retroactive to the time of the oral order.

(2) Interception pursuant to an oral order under this section shall be made in accordance with section 2933.59 of the Revised Code, except that the interception shall terminate immediately when the communication sought is obtained or when the application for a warrant is denied, whichever is earlier.

(3) If no application for a warrant is made in accordance with this section within forty-eight hours following a grant of an oral order or if an application for a warrant is made in accordance with this section following the grant of an oral order but the application is denied, the content of any private wire, oral, or electronic communication intercepted under the oral order shall be treated as having been obtained in violation of this chapter, and an inventory shall be served in accordance with section 2933.61 of the Revised Code upon the person named in the application. However, a provider of wire or electronic communication service that relies in good faith on the oral order in accordance with division (B) of section 2933.65 of the Revised Code is immune from civil or criminal liability in accordance with that section.

(4) If no application for a warrant is made within forty-eight hours following a grant of an oral order under this section or if an application for a warrant is made but is denied, the judge of a court of common pleas who granted an oral order for the interception shall prepare a journal entry reciting the grant of the oral order that includes as much of the information required to be included in an interception warrant that is practical to include. All of the provisions of sections 2933.51 to 2933.63 of the Revised Code concerning the sealing, distribution, use, and disclosure of an interception warrant apply to the journal entry required by this division. The judge who granted the oral order also shall order the person who received the oral order under this section to prepare an inventory of the recordings and resumes compiled under the oral order and shall require the tape or other recording of the intercepted communication to be delivered to, and sealed by, the judge in accordance with division (B) of section 2933.59 of the Revised Code. The court served by that judge shall retain the evidence, and no person shall use or disclose the evidence in a legal proceeding, other than a civil action brought by an aggrieved person or as otherwise authorized by the order of a judge of the court of common pleas of the county in which the interception took place. In addition to other remedies or penalties

provided by law, a failure to deliver a tape or other recording to the judge in accordance with this division shall be punishable as contempt by the judge directing the delivery.

HISTORY: 141 v S 222 (Eff 3-25-87); 146 v H 181. Eff 6-13-96.

§ 2933.58 Instructions to investigative officers; procedure for interception; territorial validity.

(A) Upon the issuance of an interception warrant pursuant to section 2933.54 of the Revised Code and prior to the execution of the warrant or upon a grant of an oral order for an interception under section 2933.57 of the Revised Code, the prosecuting attorney or assistant prosecuting attorney who authorized the application for the warrant or the oral approval shall instruct the investigative officers who are authorized to intercept the communications regarding the application and interpretation of divisions (A), (B), and (C) of section 2317.02 of the Revised Code. The prosecuting attorney or assistant prosecuting attorney who authorized the application or the oral order also shall instruct the officers to minimize the interception of communications that are not subject to the warrant or oral order and shall inform the officers of the procedures to be followed if communications concerning another offense are intercepted. If individuals operating under a contract to provide interception services as described in section 2933.59 of the Revised Code are involved in the interception, the prosecuting attorney or assistant prosecuting attorney who authorized the application for the warrant or the oral order also shall give the instructions and information under this division to those individuals.

(B) Investigative officers who are authorized to intercept communications pursuant to an interception warrant or pursuant to an oral order for an interception granted under section 2933.57 of the Revised Code and individuals who are operating under a contract to provide interception services as described in section 2933.59 of the Revised Code shall monitor the receiver of the interception device at all times during the time period for which the interception is authorized. All communications shall be intercepted only in accordance with the warrant or the oral order.

(C) An interception warrant issued pursuant to sections 2933.53 to 2933.55 of the Revised Code or an oral order for an interception granted under section 2933.57 of the Revised Code authorizes the interception of wire, oral, or electronic communications or the installation of an interception device within the jurisdiction of the court of common pleas served by the judge who issued the warrant or granted the oral order. The warrant or oral order is valid at any place if the interception device is installed within the jurisdiction of the judge who issued the warrant or granted the oral order and is then moved to another place by persons other than the investigative officers.

HISTORY: 141 v S 222 (Eff 3-25-87); 146 v H 181. Eff 6-13-96.

Not analogous to former RC § 2933.58 (133 v H 956), repealed 141 v S 222, § 2, eff 3-25-87.

[§ 2933.58.1] § 2933.581 Persons providing information, facilities or technical assistance to officer; prohibited disclosures; immunity.

(A) Notwithstanding any other provision of law, a provider of wire or electronic communication service, an officer, employee, or agent of a provider of that type, and a landlord, custodian, or other person is authorized to provide information, facilities, or technical assistance to a person who is authorized by the law of this state or the United States to intercept wire, oral, or electronic communications if both of the following apply:

(1) The provider, officer, employee, agent, landlord, custodian, or person has been provided with either of the following:

(a) An interception warrant or extension of an interception warrant that contains a statement of the type described in division (A)(13) of section 2933.56 of the Revised Code;

(b) A written representation of a judge of a court of common pleas or of a prosecuting attorney or specifically designated assistant prosecuting attorney that an oral order for an interception has been granted pursuant to section 2933.57 of the Revised Code, that no interception warrant is required by law, that all applicable statutory requirements have been satisfied, and that the oral order contains a statement of the type described in division (A)(13) of section 2933.56 of the Revised Code that directs the provision of the specified information, facilities, or technical assistance.

(2) The warrant, extension, or representation sets forth the period of time during which the provision of the information, facilities, or technical assistance is authorized and specifies the information, facilities, or technical assistance required.

(B)(1) Except as provided in division (B)(2) of this section, no provider of wire or electronic communication service, no officer, employee, or agent of a provider of that type, and no landlord, custodian, or other person who is authorized to provide information, facilities, or technical assistance under division (A) of this section shall disclose the existence of an interception or the device used to accomplish the interception with respect to which the person has been furnished an interception warrant, an extension of an interception warrant, or a written representation pursuant to that division. A person that makes a disclosure in violation of this division is liable for civil damages of the type described in section 2933.65 of the Revised Code.

(2) Division (B)(1) of this section does not prohibit the disclosure of the existence of an interception or the

disclosure of a device used to accomplish an interception when the disclosure is required by legal process, provided the person making the disclosure gives prior notification of the disclosure to the prosecuting attorney of the county in which the interception takes place or in which the interception device is installed.

(C) Except as provided in this section, a provider of wire or electronic communication service, an officer, employee, or agent of a provider of that type, and a landlord, custodian, or other specified person is immune from civil or criminal liability in any action that arises out of its providing information, facilities, or technical assistance in accordance with division (A) of this section and the terms of the interception warrant, extension of an interception warrant, or written representation provided under that division.

HISTORY: 146 v H 181. Eff 6-13-96.

§ 2933.59 Execution of warrant or oral order; recording or resume; termination; tampering; destruction of documents; disclosure.

(A) An investigative officer who is, or a member of the law enforcement agency that is, authorized by an interception warrant or a grant of an oral order for an interception pursuant to section 2933.57 of the Revised Code to intercept wire, oral, or electronic communications or an individual who is operating under a contract with that agency and is acting under the supervision of that officer or a member of that agency shall execute the interception warrant or the oral order in accordance with the terms of the warrant or oral order. The officer or member of the law enforcement agency who executes the warrant or oral order or who supervises the execution of the warrant or oral order shall have received training that satisfies the minimum standards established by the attorney general and the Ohio peace officer training commission under section 2933.64 of the Revised Code. The contents of a wire, oral, or electronic communication intercepted pursuant to an interception warrant or pursuant to a grant of an oral order for an interception, if possible, shall be recorded on tape or another similar device. If it is not possible to record the intercepted communication, a detailed resume of that communication immediately shall be reduced to writing. The recording or transcribing of the contents of any wire, oral, or electronic communication pursuant to sections 2933.51 to 2933.66 of the Revised Code shall be done in a way that will protect the recording or transcription from editing or any other alteration.

(B) Immediately upon the expiration of the period of time for which an interception warrant was authorized, or any extensions of that time period, all wire, oral, or electronic communications interceptions shall cease, and any interception device installed pursuant to the interception warrant shall be removed or permanently inactivated as soon as is reasonably practicable. Entry to remove or inactivate an interception device is authorized by the granting of an interception warrant.

Immediately upon the expiration of that period of time or the extension, the recordings or resumes of intercepted communications shall be made available to the issuing judge and shall be sealed under the judge's direction. The issuing judge shall specify who shall have custody of the sealed recordings and resumes. The recordings and resumes shall be kept for at least ten years. At the expiration of the ten-year period, the recordings and resumes may be destroyed upon the order of a judge of the court of common pleas of the county in which the interception took place. Duplicate recordings or resumes may be made for use or disclosure pursuant to divisions (F) and (G) of this section.

(C) No person, with intent to present the altered recording or resume in any judicial proceeding or proceeding under oath or affirmation, shall purposely edit, alter, or tamper with any recording or resume of any intercepted wire, oral, or electronic communications, shall attempt to edit, alter, or tamper with any recording or resume of any intercepted wire, oral, or electronic communications, or shall present or permit the presentation of any altered recording or resume in any judicial proceeding or proceeding under oath or affirmation, without fully indicating the nature of the changes made in the original state of the recording or resume.

(D)(1) Any interception warrant, the existence of lawfully installed interception devices, the application, affidavits, and return prepared in connection with the warrant, and any information concerning the application for, the granting of, or the denial of an interception warrant shall remain secret until they have been disclosed in a criminal trial or in a proceeding that is open to the public or until they have been furnished to the defendant or unless otherwise provided in sections 2933.51 to 2933.66 of the Revised Code.

(2) Any person who violates division (D)(1) of this section may be punished for contempt of court.

(E) When an order for destruction of any documents dealing with an interception warrant is issued, the person directed in the order to destroy the applications, affidavits, interception warrants, any amendments or extensions of the warrants, or recordings or resumes made pursuant to the warrants shall do so in the presence of at least one witness who is not connected with a law enforcement agency. The person who destroys the documents and each witness shall execute affidavits setting forth the facts and circumstances of the destruction. The affidavits shall be filed with and approved by the court having custody of the original materials.

(F) An investigative officer who has obtained knowledge of the contents, or of evidence derived from the contents, of a wire, oral, or electronic communication pursuant to sections 2933.51 to 2933.66 of the Revised Code may disclose the contents or evidence to another investigative officer to the extent that the disclosure is appropriate to the proper performance of the official duties of the officer making or receiving the disclosure and may use the contents or evidence to the extent appropriate to the proper performance of official duties.

(G) A person who has received, pursuant to sections 2933.51 to 2933.66 of the Revised Code, information concerning, or evidence derived from, a wire, oral, or electronic communication intercepted pursuant to an interception warrant may disclose the contents of that communication, or the evidence derived from the contents, while giving testimony under oath or affirmation in a proceeding held under the authority of the United States, this state, another state, or a political subdivision of this state or another state, except that the presence of the seal provided for in division (B) of section 2933.56 of the Revised Code and in division (B) of this section, or a satisfactory explanation of the absence of the seal, shall be a prerequisite for the use or disclosure of the contents of any wire, oral, or electronic communication or evidence derived from the contents. The contents, or evidence derived from the contents, of a wire, oral, or electronic communication intercepted pursuant to an interception warrant and in accordance with sections 2933.51 to 2933.66 of the Revised Code otherwise may be disclosed only upon a showing of good cause before a judge authorized to issue interception warrants.

(H) Whoever violates division (C) of this section is guilty of a felony of the third degree.

HISTORY: 141 v S 222 (Eff 3-25-87); 146 v H 181 (Eff 6-13-96); 146 v H 670. Eff 12-2-96.

[§ 2933.59.1] § 2933.591 Giving warning of possible surveillance.

(A) No person who knows that an application for an interception warrant has been authorized or made under section 2933.53 of the Revised Code, that an interception warrant has been issued under section 2933.54 of the Revised Code, that an application for an extension of an interception warrant has been filed under section 2933.53 of the Revised Code, that an extension of an interception warrant has been ordered under that section, that an application for a grant of an oral order for an interception has been made under section 2933.57 of the Revised Code, or that oral order for an interception has been granted under section 2933.57 of the Revised Code, with purpose to obstruct, impede, or prevent the interception in question, shall give notice or attempt to give notice of the possible interception to a person.

(B) Whoever violates division (A) of this section is guilty of giving warning of possible surveillance, a felony of the third degree.

HISTORY: 146 v H 181. Eff 6-13-96.

§ 2933.60 Reports by judges and prosecuting attorneys.

(A) Within thirty days after the expiration of an interception warrant, the expiration of an extension of an interception warrant, or the denial of an application for an interception warrant, the judge of a court of common pleas who issued the warrant or extension or denied the application shall report all of the following to the administrative office of the United States courts and to the attorney general of this state:

(1) The fact that an application was made for an interception warrant or extension of an interception warrant;

(2) The kind of interception warrant or extension for which application was made, including a statement of whether the warrant or extension was or was not one to which the requirements of division (B)(3)(c) of section 2933.53 and division (A)(5) of section 2933.54 of the Revised Code did not apply due to the application of division (G)(1) of section 2933.53 of the Revised Code;

(3) The fact that the interception warrant or extension was granted as applied for or was denied;

(4) The period of interception authorized by the interception warrant, and the number and duration of any extensions of the warrant;

(5) The designated offenses specified in the interception warrant, application, or extension;

(6) The identity of the person who made the application, any person who executed any accompanying affidavit to an application, and the prosecuting attorney or assistant prosecuting attorney who authorized the application;

(7) The nature of the facilities from which, or the place at which, communications are to be intercepted.

(B) In January of each year, the prosecuting attorney of each county shall report to the administrative office of the United States courts and to the attorney general of this state all information that is required to be reported by subsection (2) of section 2519 of the "Omnibus Crime Control and Safe Streets Act of 1968," 82 Stat. 197, 18 U.S.C. 2519 (1968), as amended.

HISTORY: 141 v S 222 (Eff 3-25-87); 146 v H 181. Eff 6-13-96.

§ 2933.61 Service of inventory on interested persons; inspection of materials.

(A) Within a reasonable time not later than ninety days after the filing of an application for an interception warrant that is denied or after the termination of the period of an interception warrant or any extensions of an interception warrant, the judge of a court of common pleas who issued the warrant or extension or denied the application shall cause to be served on the persons named in the application or the interception warrant, and on any other parties to intercepted wire, oral, or electronic communications that the judge determines in the judge's discretion should be notified in the interest of justice, an inventory that shall include notice of all of the following:

(1) The fact that an interception warrant was issued or that application for one was made;

(2) The date the interception warrant was issued and

the period of authorized, approved, or disapproved interception or the date of the denial of the application;

(3) The fact that during the stated period wire, oral, or electronic communications were or were not intercepted.

(B) A judge of the court of common pleas of the county, upon the filing of a motion for inspection, in the judge's discretion, may make available for inspection to the person filing the motion or the person's counsel any portions of intercepted wire, oral, or electronic communications, applications for interception warrants, or interception warrants that the judge determines to be in the interest of justice. Upon an ex parte showing of good cause to a judge of a court of common pleas who denied the issuance of or issued an interception warrant, the judge may postpone the serving of the inventory required by this section for a specified period of time.

HISTORY: 141 v S 222 (Eff 3-25-87); 146 v H 181. Eff 6-13-96.

§ 2933.62 Conditions for receiving results in evidence or disclosure.

(A) No part of the contents, and no evidence derived from the contents, of any intercepted wire, oral, or electronic communication shall be received in evidence in any trial, hearing, or other proceedings in or before any court, grand jury, department, officer, agency, regulatory body, legislative committee, or other authority of this state or of a political subdivision of this state, if the disclosure of that information is in violation of sections 2933.51 to 2933.66 of the Revised Code.

(B) The contents, or any evidence derived from the contents, of any wire, oral, or electronic communication intercepted pursuant to sections 2933.51 to 2933.66 of the Revised Code shall not be received in evidence or otherwise disclosed in any trial, hearing, or other proceeding held under the authority of this state, other than a proceeding or session of the grand jury, unless each party has been furnished not less than ten days before the trial, hearing, or proceeding, with a copy of the interception warrant and the related application, or a written representation of a judge of a court of common pleas or of a prosecuting attorney or specifically designated assistant prosecuting attorney that an oral order for an interception has been granted pursuant to section 2933.57 of the Revised Code, under which the interception was authorized or approved. The judge or other officer conducting the trial, hearing, or other proceeding may waive the ten-day period if the judge or officer finds that it was not possible to furnish the party with the above information at least ten days before the trial, hearing, or proceeding, and that the party will not be prejudiced by the delay in receiving the information.

HISTORY: 141 v S 222 (Eff 3-25-87); 146 v H 181. Eff 6-13-96.

§ 2933.63 Motion to suppress evidence; appeals by state.

(A) Any aggrieved person in any trial, hearing, or proceeding in or before any court, department, officer, agency, regulatory body, or other authority of this state or of a political subdivision of this state, other than a grand jury, may request the involved court, department, officer, agency, body, or authority, by motion, to suppress the contents, or evidence derived from the contents, of a wire, oral, or electronic communication intercepted pursuant to sections 2933.51 to 2933.66 of the Revised Code for any of the following reasons:

(1) The communication was unlawfully intercepted.

(2) The interception warrant under which the communication was intercepted is insufficient on its face.

(3) The interception was not made in conformity with the interception warrant or an oral order for an interception granted under section 2933.57 of the Revised Code.

(4) The communications are of a privileged character and a special need for their interception is not shown or is inadequate as shown.

(B) Any motion filed pursuant to division (A) of this section shall be made before the trial, hearing, or proceeding at which the contents, or evidence derived from the contents, is to be used, unless there was no opportunity to make the motion or the aggrieved person was not aware of the intercepted communications or the grounds of the motion. Upon the filing of the motion by the aggrieved person, the judge or other officer conducting the trial, hearing, or proceeding may make available to the aggrieved person or the person's counsel for inspection any portions of the intercepted communication or evidence derived from the intercepted communication as the judge or other officer determines to be in the interest of justice. If the judge or other officer grants the motion to suppress evidence pursuant to this section, the contents, or the evidence derived from the contents, of the intercepted wire, oral, or electronic communications shall be treated as having been obtained in violation of the law, and the contents and evidence derived from the contents shall not be received in evidence in any trial, hearing, or proceeding.

(C) In addition to any other right to appeal, the state shall have an appeal as of right from an order granting a motion to suppress the contents, or evidence derived from the contents, of a wire, oral, or electronic communication that was intercepted pursuant to an interception warrant or an oral order for an interception granted under section 2933.57 of the Revised Code, or the denial of an application for an interception warrant, if the state's representative certifies to the judge or other official who granted the motion or denied the application that the appeal is not taken for purposes of delay. Any appeal shall be taken within thirty days after the date the order was entered and shall be diligently prosecuted.

HISTORY: 141 v S 222 (Eff 3-25-87); 146 v H 181. Eff 6-13-96.

§ 2933.64 Training in wiretapping and electronic surveillance.

The attorney general and the Ohio peace officer training commission, pursuant to Chapter 109. of the Revised Code, shall establish a course of training in the legal and technical aspects of wiretapping and electronic surveillance, shall establish regulations that they find necessary and proper for the training program, and shall establish minimum standards for certification and periodic recertification for investigative officers to be eligible to conduct wiretapping or electronic surveillance under sections 2933.51 to 2933.66 of the Revised Code. The commission shall charge each investigative officer who enrolls in this training a reasonable enrollment fee to offset the cost of the training.

HISTORY: 141 v S 222 (Eff 3-25-87); 146 v H 181 (Eff 6-13-96); 146 v H 670. Eff 12-2-96.

§ 2933.65 Civil and criminal actions for violations.

(A) A person whose wire, oral, or electronic communications are intercepted, disclosed, or intentionally used in violation of sections 2933.51 to 2933.66 of the Revised Code may bring a civil action to recover from the person or entity that engaged in the violation any relief that may be appropriate and that includes, but is not limited to, the following:

(1) The preliminary and other equitable or declaratory relief that is appropriate;

(2) Whichever of the following is greater:

(a) Liquidated damages computed at a rate of two hundred dollars per day for each day of violation or liquidated damages of ten thousand dollars, whichever is greater;

(b) The sum of actual damages suffered by the plaintiff and the profits, if any, made as a result of the violation by the person or entity that engaged in the violation.

(3) Punitive damages, if appropriate;

(4) Reasonable attorney's fees and other litigation expenses that are reasonably incurred in bringing the civil action.

(B) Good faith reliance on an interception warrant, extension of an interception warrant, other court order, a grant of an oral order for an interception, a grand jury subpoena, a legislative or statutory authorization, or a good faith determination that divisions (A) and (B) of section 2933.521 of the Revised Code permitted the conduct that is the subject of a complaint is a complete defense to a civil action or criminal action that is brought under the laws of this state and that arises out of the execution of the warrant or the oral order.

(C) A claimant who brings a civil action under division (A) of this section shall commence the civil action within two years after the date on which the claimant first has a reasonable opportunity to discover the violation.

(D) The remedies and sanctions described in sections 2933.51 to 2933.66 of the Revised Code with respect to the interception of wire, oral, or electronic communications are the only judicial remedies and sanctions for violations of those sections involving those types of communications that are not violations of the constitution of the United States or of this state.

HISTORY: 141 v S 222 (Eff 3-25-87); 146 v H 181. Eff 6-13-96.

§ 2933.66 Judge to conform proceedings to constitutions.

Notwithstanding any provision of sections 2933.51 to 2933.65 of the Revised Code, a judge of a court of common pleas to whom an application for an interception warrant, an extension of an interception warrant, an oral order for an interception, or another purpose is made pursuant to sections 2933.51 to 2933.65 of the Revised Code may take evidence, make a finding, or issue an order to conform the proceedings or the issuance of an order to the constitution of the United States or of this state.

HISTORY: 141 v S 222 (Eff 3-25-87); 146 v H 181. Eff 6-13-96.

[MEDICAID FRAUD FORFEITURES]

§ 2933.71 Definitions.

As used in sections 2933.71 to 2933.75 of the Revised Code:

(A) "Medicaid fraud offense" means any of the following:

(1) Any violation of section 2913.40 of the Revised Code;

(2) Any violation of section 2921.13 of the Revised Code that involves the making of a false statement in relation to the securement of benefits or payments under the medical assistance program established under section 5111.01 of the Revised Code or the swearing or affirming of a false statement previously made in relation to the securement of any such benefits or payments;

(3) Any other criminal violation of law related to the medical assistance program established under section 5111.01 of the Revised Code;

(4) Any conspiracy to commit any violation described in division (A)(1), (2), or (3) of this section.

(B) "Forfeitable property" means any profit, money, or proceeds, and any property, real or personal, tangible, or intangible, including any interest in, security of, claim against, or property or contractual right of any kind affording a source of influence over any enterprise, that is derived from, or that is traceable to any profit, money, or proceeds obtained directly or indirectly from, any medicaid fraud offense.

(C) "Beneficial interest" means any of the following:

(1) The interest of a person as a beneficiary under a

trust in which the trustee holds title to personal or real property;

(2) The interest of a person as a beneficiary under any other trust arrangement under which any other person holds title to personal or real property for the benefit of such person;

(3) The interest of a person under any other form of express fiduciary arrangement under which any other person holds title to personal or real property for the benefit of such person.

"Beneficial interest" does not include the interest of a stockholder in a corporation or the interest of a partner in either a general or limited partnership.

(D) "Costs of investigation and prosecution" and "costs of investigation and litigation" mean all of the costs incurred by the state or a county or municipal corporation in the prosecution and investigation of the medicaid fraud offense in question, and includes, but is not limited to, the costs of resources and personnel.

(E) "Innocent person" includes any bona fide purchaser of property that allegedly is forfeitable property, including any person who establishes a valid claim to or interest in the property in accordance with division (F) of section 2933.73 of the Revised Code.

(F) "Personal property" means any personal property, any interest in personal property, or any right, including, but not limited to, bank accounts, debts, corporate stocks, patents, or copyrights. Personal property and any beneficial interest in personal property are deemed to be located where the trustee of the property, the personal property, or the instrument evidencing the right is located.

(G) "Real property" means any real property or any interest in real property, including, but not limited to, any lease of, or mortgage upon, real property. Real property and any beneficial interest in it is deemed to be located where the real property is located.

(H) "Trustee" means any of the following:

(1) Any person acting as trustee under a trust in which the trustee holds title to personal or real property;

(2) Any person who holds title to personal or real property for which any other person has a beneficial interest;

(3) Any successor trustee.

"Trustee" does not include an assignee or trustee for an insolvent debtor or an executor, administrator, administrator with the will annexed, testamentary trustee, guardian, or committee, appointed by, or under the control of, or accountable to, a court.

HISTORY: 145 v H 152. Eff 7-1-93.

§ 2933.72 Order to preserve reachability of property that may be forfeitable; temporary restraining order; post-conviction actions.

(A) At any time after an indictment is filed alleging a medicaid fraud offense, the prosecuting attorney who is prosecuting the case or the attorney general, if the attorney general is prosecuting the case, may file a motion requesting the court to issue an order to preserve the reachability of any property that may be forfeitable property. Upon the filing of the motion, the court, after giving notice to any person who will be affected by any order issued by the court pursuant to the motion, shall hold a hearing on the motion at which all affected persons have an opportunity to be heard and, upon a showing by the prosecuting attorney or attorney general by a preponderance of the evidence that the particular action is necessary to preserve the reachability of any property that may be subject to forfeiture and based upon the indictment, may enter a restraining order or injunction, require the execution of a satisfactory performance bond, or take any other necessary action, including the attachment of the property or the appointment of a receiver. The prosecuting attorney or attorney general is not required to show special or irreparable injury to obtain any court action pursuant to this division. Notwithstanding the Rules of Evidence, the court's order or injunction may be based on hearsay testimony.

(B) If no indictment has been filed alleging a medicaid fraud offense, the court may take any action specified in division (A) of this section if the prosecuting attorney for the county or the attorney general, in addition to the showing that would be required pursuant to division (A) of this section, also shows both of the following by a preponderance of the evidence:

(1) There is probable cause to believe that the property with respect to which the order is sought, in the event of a conviction, would be forfeitable property subject to forfeiture under section 2933.73 of the Revised Code;

(2) The requested order would not result in irreparable harm to the party against whom the order is to be entered that outweighs the need to preserve the reachability of the property.

No order entered pursuant to division (B) of this section shall be effective for more than ninety days, unless it is extended pursuant to the procedure provided in division (B) of this section by the court for good cause shown or an indictment is returned alleging that the property is forfeitable property subject to forfeiture.

(C) Upon application by the prosecuting attorney or attorney general, the court may grant a temporary restraining order to preserve the reachability of forfeitable property that is subject to forfeiture under section 2933.73 of the Revised Code without notice to any party, if all of the following occur:

(1) An indictment alleging that property is forfeitable property has been filed, or the court determines that there is probable cause to believe that property with respect to which the order is sought would be forfeitable property subject, in the event of a conviction, to forfeiture under section 2933.73 of the Revised Code;

(2) The property is in the possession or control of the party against whom the order is to be entered;

(3) The court determines that the nature of the property is such that it can be concealed, disposed of, or placed beyond the jurisdiction of the court before any party may be heard in opposition to the order.

A temporary restraining order granted without notice to any party under division (C) of this section shall expire within the time, not to exceed ten days, that the court fixes, unless extended for good cause shown or unless the party against whom it is entered consents to an extension for a longer period. If a temporary restraining order is granted under division (C) of this section without notice to any party, the court shall hold a hearing concerning the entry of an order under division (C) of this section at the earliest practicable time prior to the expiration of the temporary order.

(D) Following sentencing and the entry of a judgment against an offender that includes an order of forfeiture under section 2933.73 of the Revised Code, the court may enter a restraining order or injunction, require the execution of a satisfactory performance bond, or take any other action, including the appointment of a receiver, that the court determines to be proper to protect the interests of the state or an innocent person.

HISTORY: 145 v H 152 (Eff 7-1-93); 145 v H 715. Eff 7-22-94.

§ 2933.73 Civil hearing; forfeiture order; petition by innocent person claiming interest in property.

(A) In addition to any other penalty or disposition authorized or required by law, if a person is convicted of or pleads guilty to any medicaid fraud offense, the trial court shall conduct a civil forfeiture hearing to determine whether any property identified in division (B) of this section should be forfeited to the state in relation to the offense. At the hearing, the offender who was convicted of or pleaded guilty to the medicaid fraud offense has the burden of proving, by a preponderance of the evidence, that the property in question is not forfeitable property in relation to the offense. If the offender does not prove by a preponderance of the evidence that the property in question is not forfeitable property in relation to the offense, the court shall issue an order specifying that the forfeitable property is forfeited to the state. If the offender proves by a preponderance of the evidence that the property in question is not forfeitable property in relation to the offense, the court shall not issue an order specifying that the forfeitable property is forfeited to the state and, if the property has been seized, shall order that it be returned to the offender.

(B) A court shall not issue an order under division (A) of this section specifying that forfeitable property is forfeited to the state unless one of the following applies:

(1) The indictment, count in the indictment, or information charging the medicaid fraud offense specifically identified the property as forfeitable property;

(2) The property was not reasonably foreseen to be forfeitable property at the time of the indictment, count in the indictment, or information charging the offense, provided that the prosecuting attorney or attorney general who prosecuted the offense gave prompt notice to the defendant of such property not reasonably foreseen to be forfeitable property when it is discovered to be forfeitable property.

(C) If any forfeitable property included in a forfeiture order issued under division (A) of this section cannot be located, has been sold to a bona fide purchaser for value, placed beyond the jurisdiction of the court, substantially diminished in value by the conduct of the defendant, or commingled with other property that cannot be divided without difficulty or undue injury to innocent persons, or otherwise is unreachable without undue injury to innocent persons, the court shall order forfeiture of any other reachable property of the defendant up to the value of the property that is unreachable.

(D) All property ordered forfeited pursuant to this section shall be held by the law enforcement agency that seized it for distribution or disposal pursuant to section 2933.74 of the Revised Code. The agency shall maintain an accurate record of each item of property so seized and held, which record shall include the date on which each item was seized, the manner and date of disposition by the agency, and if applicable, the name of the person who received the item; however, the record shall not identify or enable the identification of the individual officer who seized the property. The record is a public record open for inspection under section 149.43 of the Revised Code. Each law enforcement agency that seizes and holds in any calendar year any item of property that is ordered forfeited pursuant to this section shall prepare a report covering the calendar year that cumulates all of the information contained in all of the records kept by the agency pursuant to this division for that calendar year, and shall send the cumulative report, no later than the first day of March in the calendar year following the calendar year covered by the report, to the attorney general. Each such report so received by the attorney general is a public record open for inspection under section 149.43 of the Revised Code. The attorney general shall make copies of each such report so received, and, no later than the fifteenth day of April in the calendar year in which the reports were received, shall send a copy of each such report to the office of the president of the senate and the office of the speaker of the house of representatives.

(E) Notwithstanding the notice and procedure prescribed by division (F) of this section, an order of forfeiture entered under division (A) of this section shall authorize an appropriate law enforcement agency to seize the forfeitable property declared forfeited under this section upon the terms and conditions, relating to the time and manner of seizure, that the court determines proper.

(F)(1) Upon the entry of a forfeiture order under division (A) of this section, the court shall cause notice of the issuance of the order to be sent by certified mail, return receipt requested, to all persons known to have, or appearing to have, an interest in the property that was acquired prior to the filing of a medicaid fraud lien notice as authorized by section 2933.75 of the Revised Code. If the notices cannot be given to those persons in that manner, the court shall cause publication of the notice of the forfeiture order pursuant to the Rules of Civil Procedure.

(2) Within thirty days after receipt of a notice or after the date of publication of a notice under division (F)(1) of this section, any person, other than the offender who was convicted of or pleaded guilty to the medicaid fraud offense, who claims an interest in the forfeitable property that is subject to forfeiture may petition the court for a hearing to determine the validity of the claim. The petition shall be signed and sworn to by the petitioner and shall set forth the nature and extent of the petitioner's interest in the property, the date and circumstances of the petitioner's acquisition of the interest, any additional allegations supporting the claim, and the relief sought. The petitioner shall furnish a copy of the petition to the prosecuting attorney or attorney general who prosecuted the offense in relation to which the forfeiture order was issued.

(3) The court, to the extent practicable and consistent with the interests of justice, shall hold the hearing described under division (F)(2) of this section within thirty days from the filing of the petition. The court may consolidate the hearings on all petitions filed by third party claimants under this section. At the hearing, the petitioner may testify and present evidence on his own behalf and cross-examine witnesses. The prosecuting attorney or attorney general who prosecuted the offense may present evidence and witnesses in rebuttal and in defense of the claim of the state to the property and cross-examine witnesses. The court, in making its determination, shall consider the testimony and evidence presented at the hearing and the relevant portions of the record of the criminal proceeding that resulted in the forfeiture order.

(4) If at a hearing held under division (F)(3) of this section, the court, by a preponderance of the evidence, determines either that the petitioner has a legal right, title, or interest in the property that, at the time of the commission of the acts giving rise to the forfeiture of the property, was vested in the petitioner and not in the offender or was superior to the right, title, or interest of the offender, or that the petitioner is a bona fide purchaser for value of the right, title, or interest in the property and was at the time of the purchase reasonably without cause to believe that the property was subject to forfeiture under this section, it shall amend, in accordance with its determination, the order of forfeiture to protect the rights of innocent persons.

(G) Except as provided in division (F) of this section, no person claiming an interest in forfeitable property that is subject to forfeiture under this section shall do either of the following:

(1) Intervene in a trial or appeal of a criminal case that involves the forfeiture of the property;

(2) File an action against the state concerning the validity of his alleged interest in the property subsequent to the filing of the indictment, count in the indictment, or information, that alleges that the property is subject to forfeiture under this section.

(H) As used in this section, "law enforcement agency" includes the state board of pharmacy.

HISTORY: 145 v H 152 (Eff 7-1-93); 145 v H 715. Eff 7-22-94.

§ 2933.74 Settlement of claims; awards to informants; protection of rights of innocent persons; disposal of property; use of proceeds.

(A)(1) With respect to forfeitable property ordered forfeited under section 2933.73 of the Revised Code, the court that issued the order, upon petition of the prosecuting attorney or attorney general who prosecuted the case, may do any of the following:

(a) Authorize the prosecuting attorney or the attorney general to settle claims;

(b) Award compensation to persons who provide information that results in a forfeiture under section 2933.73 of the Revised Code;

(c) Take any other action to protect the rights of innocent persons that is in the interest of justice and that is consistent with the purposes of sections 2933.71 to 2933.75 of the Revised Code.

(2) The court shall maintain an accurate record of the actions it takes under division (A)(1) of this section with respect to the forfeitable property ordered forfeited. The record is a public record open for inspection under section 149.43 of the Revised Code.

(B)(1) Subject to division (A) of this section and notwithstanding any contrary provision of section 2933.41 of the Revised Code, the prosecuting attorney or attorney general who prosecuted the case shall order the disposal of forfeitable property ordered forfeited in any proceeding under section 2933.73 of the Revised Code as soon as feasible, making due provisions for the rights of innocent persons, by any of the following methods:

(a) Public sale;

(b) Transfer to a state governmental agency for official use;

(c) Sale or transfer to an innocent person;

(d) If the property is contraband and is not needed for evidence in any pending criminal or civil proceeding, pursuant to section 2933.41 or any other applicable section of the Revised Code.

(2) Any interest in personal or real property not disposed of pursuant to division (B) of this section and not exercisable by, or transferable for value to, the state shall expire and shall not revert to the person who was

convicted of or pleaded guilty to the medicaid fraud offense. No person who was convicted of or pleaded guilty to the medicaid fraud offense and no person acting in concert with a person who was convicted of or pleaded guilty to the medicaid fraud offense is eligible to purchase forfeited property from the state.

(3) Upon application of a person, other than the person who was convicted of or pleaded guilty to the medicaid fraud offense or a person acting in concert with or on behalf of the person who was convicted of or pleaded guilty to the medicaid fraud offense, the court may restrain or stay the disposal of the forfeitable property pursuant to this division pending the conclusion of any appeal of the criminal case giving rise to the forfeiture or pending the determination of the validity of a claim to or interest in the property pursuant to division (F) of section 2933.73 of the Revised Code, if the applicant demonstrates that proceeding with the disposal of the property will result in irreparable injury, harm, or loss to the applicant.

(4) The prosecuting attorney or attorney general who prosecuted the case shall maintain an accurate record of each item of property disposed of pursuant to division (B) of this section, which record shall include the date on which each item came into the prosecuting attorney's or attorney general's custody, the manner and date of disposition, and, if applicable, the name of the person who received the item. The record shall not identify or enable the identification of the individual officer who seized the property, and the record is a public record open for inspection under section 149.43 of the Revised Code.

Each prosecuting attorney who disposes in any calendar year of any item of property pursuant to division (B) of this section shall prepare a report covering the calendar year that cumulates all of the information contained in all of the records the prosecuting attorney kept pursuant to this division for that calendar year and shall send the cumulative report, no later than the first day of March in the calendar year following the calendar year covered by the report, to the attorney general. No later than the first day of March in the calendar year following the calendar year covered by the report, the attorney general shall prepare a report covering the calendar year that cumulates all of the records the attorney general kept pursuant to this division for that calendar year. Each report received or prepared by the attorney general is a public record open for inspection under section 149.43 of the Revised Code. The attorney general shall send a copy of each prosecuting attorney's cumulative report and of the attorney general's own cumulative report, no later than the fifteenth day of April in the calendar year following the calendar year covered by the report, to the president of the senate and the speaker of the house of representatives.

(C)(1) The proceeds of the sale of all forfeitable property ordered forfeited pursuant to section 2933.73 of the Revised Code shall be deposited into the state treasury and credited to the medicaid fraud investigation and prosecution fund, which is hereby created.

(2) The proceeds credited to the medicaid fraud investigation and prosecution fund pursuant to division (C)(1) of this section shall be disposed of in the following order:

(a) To the payment of the fees and costs of the forfeiture and sale, including expenses of seizure, maintenance, and custody of the property pending its disposition, advertising, and court costs;

(b) Except as otherwise provided in division (C)(2)(b) of this section, the remainder shall be paid to the law enforcement trust fund of the prosecuting attorney that is established pursuant to division (D)(1)(c) of section 2933.43 of the Revised Code or to the attorney general, and to the law enforcement trust fund of the county sheriff that is established pursuant to that division if the county sheriff substantially conducted the investigation, to the law enforcement trust fund of a municipal corporation that is established pursuant to that division if its police department substantially conducted the investigation, to the law enforcement trust fund of a township that is established pursuant to that division if the investigation was substantially conducted by a township police department, township police district police force, or office of a township constable, or to the law enforcement trust fund of a park district created pursuant to section 511.18 or 1545.01 of the Revised Code that is established pursuant to that division if the investigation was substantially conducted by its park district police force or law enforcement department. The prosecuting attorney or attorney general may decline to accept any of the remaining proceeds, and, if the prosecuting attorney or attorney general so declines, they shall be applied to the fund described in division (C)(2)(b) of this section that relates to the appropriate law enforcement agency that substantially conducted the investigation.

If the state highway patrol substantially conducted the investigation, the director of budget and management shall transfer the remaining proceeds to the state highway patrol for deposit into the state highway patrol contraband, forfeiture, and other fund that is created by division (D)(1)(c) of section 2933.43 of the Revised Code. If the state board of pharmacy substantially conducted the investigation, the director shall transfer the remaining proceeds to the board for deposit into the board of pharmacy drug law enforcement fund that is created by division (B)(1) of section 4729.65 of the Revised Code. If a state law enforcement agency, other than the state highway patrol, the board, or the attorney general, substantially conducted the investigation, the director shall transfer the remaining proceeds to the treasurer of state for deposit into the peace officer training commission fund that is created by division (D)(1)(c) of section 2933.43 of the Revised Code.

The remaining proceeds that are paid to the attorney general shall be used and expended only in relation to the investigation and prosecution of medicaid fraud offenses or the activities identified in section 109.85 of the Revised Code, and those that are paid to a law enforcement trust fund or that are deposited into the state highway patrol contraband, forfeiture, and other fund, the board of pharmacy drug law enforcement fund, or the peace officer training commission fund pursuant to division (C)(2)(b) of this section shall be allocated, used, and expended only in accordance with division (D)(1)(c) of section 2933.43 of the Revised Code, only in accordance with a written internal control policy adopted under division (D)(3) of that section, and, if applicable, only in accordance with division (B)(1) of section 4729.65 of the Revised Code. The annual reports that pertain to the funds and that are required by divisions (D)(1)(c) and (3)(b) of section 2933.43 of the Revised Code also shall address the remaining proceeds that are paid or deposited into the funds pursuant to division (C)(2)(b) of this section.

(3) If more than one law enforcement agency substantially conducted the investigation, the court ordering the forfeiture shall equitably divide the remaining proceeds among the law enforcement agencies that substantially conducted the investigation, in the manner described in division (D)(2) of section 2933.43 of the Revised Code for the equitable division of contraband proceeds and forfeited moneys. The equitable shares of the proceeds so determined by the court shall be paid or deposited into the appropriate funds specified in division (C)(2)(b) of this section.

(D) As used in this section, "law enforcement agency" includes, but is not limited to, the state board of pharmacy.

HISTORY: 145 v H 152 (Eff 7-1-93); 145 v H 715 (Eff 7-22-94); 146 v H 670. Eff 12-2-96.

§ 2933.75 Filing of medicaid fraud lien notice; trustees of forfeitable property.

(A) Upon the institution of any criminal proceeding charging a medicaid fraud offense, the state, at any time during the pendency of the proceeding, may file a medicaid fraud lien notice with the county recorder of any county in which forfeitable property subject to forfeiture may be located. No fee shall be required for filing the notice. The recorder immediately shall record the notice pursuant to section 317.08 of the Revised Code.

(B) A medicaid fraud lien notice shall be signed by the prosecuting attorney or attorney general who will prosecute the case and who files the lien. The notice shall set forth all of the following information:

(1) The name of the person against whom the proceeding has been brought. The prosecuting attorney or attorney general who will prosecute the case may specify in the notice any aliases, names, or fictitious names under which the person may be known.

(2) If known to the prosecuting attorney or attorney general who will prosecute the case, the present residence and business addresses of the person or names set forth in the notice;

(3) A statement that a criminal proceeding for a medicaid fraud offense has been brought against the person named in the notice, the name of the county in which the proceeding has been brought, and the case number of the proceeding;

(4) A statement that the notice is being filed pursuant to this section;

(5) The name and address of the prosecuting attorney or attorney general filing the notice;

(6) A description of the real or personal property subject to the notice and of the interest in that property of the person named in the notice, to the extent the property and the interest of the person in it reasonably is known at the time the proceeding is instituted or at the time the notice is filed.

(C) A medicaid fraud lien notice shall apply only to one person and, to the extent applicable, any aliases, fictitious names, or other names, including names of corporations, partnerships, or other entities, to the extent permitted in this section. A separate medicaid fraud lien notice is required to be filed for any other person.

(D) Within seven days after the filing of each medicaid fraud lien notice, the prosecuting attorney or attorney general who files the notice shall furnish to the person named in the notice by certified mail, return receipt requested, to the last known business or residential address of the person, a copy of the recorded notice with a notation on it of any county in which the notice has been recorded. The failure of the prosecuting attorney or attorney general to furnish a copy of the notice under this section shall not invalidate or otherwise affect the medicaid fraud lien notice when the prosecuting attorney or attorney general did not know and could not reasonably ascertain the address of the person entitled to notice.

After receipt of a copy of the notice under this division, the person named in the notice may petition the court to authorize the person to post a surety bond in lieu of the lien or to otherwise modify the lien as the interests of justice may require. The bond shall be in an amount equal to the value of the property reasonably known to be subject to the notice and conditioned on the payment of any judgment and costs ordered in an action pursuant to section 2933.73 of the Revised Code up to the value of the bond.

(E) From the date of filing of a medicaid fraud lien notice, the notice creates a lien in favor of the state on any personal or real property or any beneficial interest in the property located in the county in which the notice is filed that then or subsequently is owned by the person named in the notice or under any of the names set forth in the notice.

The lien created in favor of the state is superior and prior to the interest of any other person in the personal or real property or beneficial interest in the property, if the interest is acquired subsequent to the filing of the notice.

(F) If a medicaid fraud lien notice has been filed, and if a forfeiture order is entered subsequent to a conviction or guilty plea in the criminal proceeding pursuant to section 2933.73 of the Revised Code in favor of the state, the interest of any person in the property that was acquired subsequent to the filing of the notice shall be subject to the notice and order of forfeiture.

(G) Upon the issuance of an order of forfeiture in favor of the state pursuant to section 2933.73 of the Revised Code, title of the state to the forfeited property shall do either of the following:

(1) In the case of real property, or a beneficial interest in it, relate back to the date of filing of the medicaid fraud lien notice in the county where the property or interest is located. If no medicaid fraud lien notice was filed, title of the state relates back to the date of the recording of the order of forfeiture in the records of the county recorder of the county in which the real property or beneficial interest is located.

(2) In the case of personal property or a beneficial interest in it, relate back to the date on which the property or interest was seized by the state, or the date of filing of a medicaid fraud lien notice in the county in which the property or beneficial interest is located. If the property was not seized and no medicaid fraud lien notice was filed, title of the state relates back to the date of the recording of the order of forfeiture in the county in which the personal property or beneficial interest is located.

(H) If personal or real property, or a beneficial interest in it, that is forfeitable property and is subject to forfeiture pursuant to section 2933.73 of the Revised Code is conveyed, alienated, disposed of, or otherwise rendered unavailable for forfeiture after the filing of either a medicaid fraud lien notice, or a criminal proceeding for a medicaid fraud offense, whichever is earlier, the state may bring an action in any court of common pleas against the person named in the medicaid fraud lien notice or the defendant in the criminal proceeding to recover the value of the property or interest. The court shall enter final judgment against the person named in the notice or the defendant for an amount equal to the value of the property or interest together with investigative costs and attorney's fees incurred by the state in the action.

(I) If personal or real property, or a beneficial interest in it, that is forfeitable property and is subject to forfeiture pursuant to section 2933.73 of the Revised Code is alienated or otherwise transferred or disposed of after either the filing of a medicaid fraud lien notice, or the filing of a criminal proceeding for a medicaid fraud offense, whichever is earlier, the transfer or disposal is fraudulent as to the state and the state shall have all the rights granted a creditor under Chapter 1336. of the Revised Code.

(J) No trustee, who acquires actual knowledge that a medicaid fraud lien notice or a criminal proceeding for a medicaid fraud offense has been filed against any person for whom he holds legal or record title to personal or real property, shall recklessly fail to furnish promptly to the prosecuting attorney or attorney general who is prosecuting the case all of the following:

(1) The name and address of the person, as known to the trustee;

(2) The name and address, as known to the trustee, of all other persons for whose benefit the trustee holds title to the property;

(3) If requested by the prosecuting attorney or attorney general who is prosecuting the case, a copy of the trust agreement or other instrument under which the trustee holds title to the property.

Any trustee who fails to comply with division (J) of this section is guilty of failure to provide medicaid fraud lien information, a misdemeanor of the first degree.

(K) If a trustee transfers title to personal or real property after a medicaid fraud lien notice is filed against the property, the lien is filed in the county in which the property is located, and the lien names a person who holds a beneficial interest in the property, the trustee, if he has actual notice of the notice, shall be liable to the state for the greater of the following:

(1) The proceeds received directly by the person named in the notice as a result of the transfer;

(2) The proceeds received by the trustee as a result of the transfer and distributed to the person named in the notice;

(3) The fair market value of the interest of the person named in the notice in the property transferred.

However, if the trustee transfers property for at least its fair market value and holds the proceeds that otherwise would be paid or distributed to the beneficiary, or at the direction of the beneficiary or his designee, the liability of the trustee shall not exceed the amount of the proceeds held by the trustee.

(L) The filing of a medicaid fraud lien notice does not constitute a lien on the record title to personal or real property owned by the trustee, except to the extent the trustee is named in the notice.

The prosecuting attorney for the county or the attorney general may bring a civil action in any court of common pleas to recover from the trustee the amounts set forth in division (H) of this section. The county or state may recover investigative costs and attorney's fees incurred by the prosecuting attorney or the attorney general.

(M)(1) This section does not apply to any transfer by a trustee under a court order, unless the order is entered in an action between the trustee and the beneficiary.

(2) Unless the trustee has actual knowledge that a person owning a beneficial interest in the trust is named in a medicaid fraud lien notice, this section does not apply to either of the following:

(a) Any transfer by a trustee required under the terms of any trust agreement, if the agreement is a matter of public record before the filing of any medicaid fraud lien notice;

(b) Any transfer by a trustee to all of the persons who own a beneficial interest in the trust.

(N) The filing of a medicaid fraud lien notice does not affect the use to which personal or real property, or a beneficial interest in it, that is owned by the person named in the notice may be put or the right of the person to receive any proceeds resulting from the use and ownership, but not the sale, of the property, until a judgment of forfeiture is entered.

(O) The term of a medicaid fraud lien notice is five years from the date the notice is filed, unless a renewal notice has been filed by the prosecuting attorney of the county in which the property or interest is located or by the attorney general. The term of any renewal of a medicaid fraud lien notice granted by the court is five years from the date of its filing. A medicaid fraud lien notice may be renewed any number of times while a criminal proceeding for a medicaid fraud offense, or an appeal from such a proceeding, is pending.

(P) The prosecuting attorney or attorney general who files the medicaid fraud lien notice may terminate, in whole or part, the notice or release any personal or real property or beneficial interest in the property upon any terms that he determines are appropriate. Any termination or release shall be filed by the prosecuting attorney or attorney general with each county recorder with whom the notice was filed. No fee shall be imposed for the filing.

(Q) The acquittal in a criminal proceeding for a medicaid fraud offense of the person named in the medicaid fraud lien notice or the dismissal of a criminal proceeding for such an offense against the person named in the notice terminates the notice. In such a case, the filing of the notice has no effect.

A person named in a medicaid fraud lien notice may bring an action against the prosecuting attorney or attorney general who filed the notice, in the county where it was filed, seeking a release of the property subject to the notice or termination of the notice. In such a case, the court of common pleas promptly shall set a date for hearing, which shall be not less than five nor more than ten days after the action is filed. The order and a copy of the complaint shall be served on the prosecuting attorney or attorney general within three days after the action is filed. At the hearing, the court shall take evidence as to whether any personal or real property, or beneficial interest in it, that is owned by the person bringing the action is covered by the notice or otherwise is subject to forfeiture. If the person bringing the action shows by a preponderance of the evidence that the notice does not apply to him or that any personal or real property, or beneficial interest in it, that is owned by him is not subject to forfeiture, the court shall enter a judgment terminating the notice or releasing the personal or real property or beneficial interest from the notice.

At a hearing, the court may release from the notice any property or beneficial interest upon the posting of security, by the person against whom the notice was filed, in an amount equal to the value of the property or beneficial interest owned by the person.

The court promptly shall enter an order terminating a medicaid fraud lien notice or releasing any personal or real property or beneficial interest in the property, if a sale of the property or beneficial interest is pending and the filing of the notice prevents the sale. However, the proceeds of the sale shall be deposited with the clerk of the court, subject to the further order of the court.

(R) Notwithstanding any provision of this section, any person who has perfected a security interest in personal or real property or a beneficial interest in the property for the payment of an enforceable debt or other similar obligation prior to the filing of a medicaid fraud lien notice in reference to the property or interest may foreclose on the property or interest as otherwise provided by law. The foreclosure, insofar as practical, shall be made so that it otherwise will not interfere with a forfeiture under section 2933.73 of the Revised Code.

HISTORY: 145 v H 152 (Eff 7-1-93); 145 v H 715. Eff 7-22-94.

§ 2933.76 Authorization of pen register of trap and trace device.

(A) As used in this section and section 2933.77 of the Revised Code, "electronic communication," "electronic communication service," "pen register," "trap and trace device," and "wire communication" have the same meanings as in section 2933.51 of the Revised Code.

(B) A judge of a court of common pleas, in accordance with this section, may issue an order authorizing or approving the installation and use, within the jurisdiction of the court, of a pen register or a trap and trace device to obtain information in connection with a criminal investigation.

(C) A law enforcement officer may make an application to a judge of a court of common pleas for an order authorizing the installation and use, within the jurisdiction of the court, of a pen register or a trap and trace device to obtain information in connection with a criminal investigation. The application shall be in writing and shall be under oath or affirmation. Each application shall contain all of the following:

(1) The name of the law enforcement officer making the application and the name of the law enforcement agency conducting the criminal investigation to which the application relates;

(2) The name, if known, of the person to whom the telephone or other line to which the pen register or trap and trace device is to be attached is leased or in whose name that telephone or other line is listed;

(3) The name, if known, of the person who is the subject of the criminal investigation to which the application relates;

(4) The number and, if known, the physical location

of the telephone or other line to which the pen register or the trap and trace device is to be attached;

(5) A statement of the offense to which the information that is likely to be obtained by the installation and use of the pen register or trap and trace device relates;

(6) A certification by the law enforcement officer making the application that the information that is likely to be obtained by the installation and use of the pen register or trap and trace device is relevant to an ongoing criminal investigation being conducted by the law enforcement agency identified under division (C)(1) of this section.

(D)(1) The judge to whom an application is made under division (C) of this section shall issue and enter an order authorizing the installation and use of a pen register or a trap and trace device if the judge finds that the information relating to an offense that is likely to be obtained by the installation and use of the pen register or trap and trace device is relevant to an ongoing criminal investigation being conducted by the law enforcement agency identified under division (C)(1) of this section. In the order, the judge shall specify a finding with respect to each of the items required by divisions (C)(1) to (6) of this section to be included in the application.

(2) If the law enforcement officer so requests, the order shall direct the appropriate provider of wire or electronic communication service, landlord, custodian, or other person to furnish the law enforcement officer with all information, facilities, and technical assistance necessary to accomplish the installation and operation of a pen register or trap and trace device unobtrusively and with a minimum of interference of service to the person with respect to whom the installation and operation are to take place. The order further shall direct the person who owns or leases the telephone or other line to which the pen register or trap and trace device is to be attached, or the provider of wire or electronic communication service, landlord, custodian, or other person who is ordered under division (D)(2) of this section to provide information, facilities, or technical assistance, not to disclose the existence of the criminal investigation or of the installation and use of the pen register or trap and trace device to the listed subscriber of the telephone or other line or to another person unless or until otherwise ordered by the court. The order shall be sealed until otherwise ordered by the court.

(E) An order issued pursuant to division (D) of this section shall authorize the installation and use of a pen register or a trap and trace device for a period not to exceed sixty days. The court may grant an extension of the sixty-day period upon application for an order in accordance with division (C) of this section and upon the judicial findings required by division (D)(1) of this section. An extension of an order issued under this division shall be in effect for a period not to exceed sixty days. The court may order further extensions of the sixty-day extended period upon compliance with this division.

(F) A good faith reliance on a court order issued under this section, a legislative authorization, or a statutory authorization is a complete defense against any claim in a civil action or any charge in a criminal action alleging a violation of the requirements of this section or section 2933.77 of the Revised Code.

HISTORY: 146 v H 181. Eff 6-13-96.

§ 2933.77 Duty to provide information, facilities or technical assistance; immunity.

(A) If an order issued under section 2933.76 of the Revised Code authorizing the installation and use of a pen register or a trap and trace device directs a provider of wire or electronic communication service, landlord, custodian, or other person to furnish information, facilities, and technical assistance to accomplish the installation and operation of the pen register or trap and trace device, that provider, landlord, custodian, or other person, in accordance with the order, shall furnish the law enforcement officer with all information, facilities, and technical assistance necessary to accomplish the installation and operation of the pen register or trap and trace device unobtrusively and with a minimum of interference with the service accorded by the provider, landlord, custodian, or other person to the person with respect to whom the installation and operation are to take place.

(B) The law enforcement agency conducting the criminal investigation to which the order issued under section 2933.76 of the Revised Code for the installation and use of a pen register or a trap and trace device relates shall provide reasonable compensation to a provider of wire or electronic communication service, landlord, custodian, or other person who furnishes facilities or technical assistance in accordance with the order for any reasonable expenses the provider, landlord, custodian, or other person incurs in furnishing the facilities or technical assistance.

(C) A provider of wire or electronic communication service, an officer, employee, or agent of that provider, or a landlord, custodian, or other specified person is immune from civil or criminal liability in any action that arises from the provision of information, facilities, or technical assistance in accordance with the terms of an order of a court issued under section 2933.76 of the Revised Code.

HISTORY: 146 v H 181. Eff 6-13-96.

CHAPTER 2935: ARREST, CITATION, AND DISPOSITION ALTERNATIVES

Section
2935.01 Definitions.
2935.02 Accused may be arrested in any county.
2935.03 Officer's authority to arrest without warrant; pursuit outside jurisdiction.
[2935.03.1] 2935.031 Policy for pursuit in motor vehicle.
[2935.03.2] 2935.032 Policies and procedures for responding to alleged domestic violence offense or violation of protection order.
2935.04 When any person may arrest.
[2935.04.1] 2935.041 Detention, arrest of shoplifters; protection of library, museum and archival institution property.
2935.05 Affidavit filed in case of arrest without warrant.
2935.06 Duty of private person making arrest.
2935.07 Person arrested without warrant shall be informed of cause of arrest.
2935.08 Issuance of warrant.
[2935.08.1] 2935.081 Administration of oaths, acknowledgment of documents by peace officer.
2935.09 Accusation by affidavit to cause arrest or prosecution.
2935.10 Procedure upon filing of affidavit or complaint.
2935.11 Failure of person summoned to appear.
2935.12 Forcible entry in making arrest or executing search warrant.
2935.13 Proceedings upon arrest.
2935.14 Rights of person arrested.
2935.15 Amount and disposition of bail.
2935.16 Prisoners held without process.
2935.17 Affidavit forms; authority of supreme court to prescribe.
2935.18 Contents of warrant, summons or notice.
2935.19 Form of affidavit.
2935.20 Right to counsel.
2935.21 Security for costs.
2935.22 Repealed.
2935.23 Felony investigation; examination of witnesses.
2935.24 Arrest by telegraph order.
2935.25 Power of arrest.
2935.26 Issuance of citation for minor misdemeanor.
2935.27 Procedure after issuance of citation; penalties for failure to appear or comply.
2935.28 Names of traffic law violators damaging real property to be provided to owner.

[UNIFORM ACT ON FRESH PURSUIT]

2935.29 Definitions of fresh pursuit and state.
2935.30 Authority of foreign police.
2935.31 Hearing before magistrate in county of arrest.
2935.32 Broadcasting information of crime.

[ALCOHOLIC TREATMENT]

2935.33 Commitment of alcoholics and intoxicated persons for inpatient care.

[PRE-TRIAL DIVERSION PROGRAM]

2935.36 Pre-trial diversion programs for certain offenders.

§ 2935.01 Definitions.

As used in this chapter:

(A) "Magistrate" has the same meaning as in section 2931.01 of the Revised Code.

(B) "Peace officer" includes, except as provided in section 2935.081 [2935.08.1] of the Revised Code, a sheriff, deputy sheriff, marshal, deputy marshal, member of the organized police department of any municipal corporation, including a member of the organized police department of a municipal corporation in an adjoining state serving in Ohio under a contract pursuant to section 737.04 of the Revised Code, member of a police force employed by a metropolitan housing authority under division (D) of section 3735.31 of the Revised Code, member of a police force employed by a regional transit authority under division (Y) of section 306.05 of the Revised Code, state university law enforcement officer appointed under section 3345.04 of the Revised Code, liquor control investigator or food stamp trafficking agent of the department of public safety, Ohio veterans' home policeman appointed under section 5907.02 of the Revised Code, police constable of any township, and police officer of a township or joint township police district, and, for the purpose of arrests within those areas, and for the purposes of Chapter 5503. of the Revised Code, and the filing of and service of process relating to those offenses witnessed or investigated by them, includes the superintendent and troopers of the state highway patrol.

(C) "Prosecutor" includes the county prosecuting attorney, any assistant prosecutor designated to assist the county prosecuting attorney, and, in the case of courts inferior to courts of common pleas, includes the village solicitor, city director of law, or similar chief legal officer of a municipal corporation, any such officer's assistants, or any attorney designated by the prosecuting attorney of the county to appear for the prosecution of a given case.

(D) "Offense," except where the context specifically indicates otherwise, includes felonies, misdemeanors, and violations of ordinances of municipal corporations and other public bodies authorized by law to adopt penal regulations.

HISTORY: 142 v H 708 (Eff 4-19-88); 144 v H 77 (Eff 9-17-91); 144 v S 144 (Eff 8-8-91); 146 v S 162 (Eff 10-29-95); 146 v S 2 (Eff 7-1-96); 146 v H 72. Eff 3-18-97.

The provisions of § 5 of HB 72 (146 v —) read as follows:

SECTION 5. Section 2935.01 of the Revised Code is presented in this act as a composite of the section as amended by both Am. Sub. S.B. 2 and Am. Sub. S.B. 162 of the 121st General Assembly, with the new language of neither of the acts shown in capital letters. ° ° ° This is in recognition of the principle stated in division (B) of section 1.52 of the Revised Code that such amendments are to be harmonized where not substantively irreconcilable and constitutes a legislative finding that such is the resulting version in effect prior to the effective date of this act.

§ 2935.02 Accused may be arrested in any county.

If an accused person flees from justice, or is not found in the county where a warrant for his arrest was issued, the officer holding the same may pursue and arrest him in any county in this state, and convey him before the magistrate or court of the county having cognizance of the case.

If such warrant directs the removal of the accused to the county in which the offense was committed, the officer holding the warrant shall deliver the accused to a court or magistrate of such county.

The necessary expense of such removal and reasonable compensation for his time and trouble, shall be paid to such officer out of the treasury of such county, upon the allowance and order of the county auditor.

HISTORY: GC § 13432-10; 113 v 123(141), ch 11, § 10; Bureau of Code Revision. Eff 10-1-53.

§ 2935.03 Officer's authority to arrest without warrant; pursuit outside jurisdiction.

(A) A sheriff, deputy sheriff, marshal, deputy marshal, municipal police officer, township constable, police officer of a township or joint township police district, member of a police force employed by a metropolitan housing authority under division (D) of section 3735.31 of the Revised Code, member of a police force employed by a regional transit authority under division (Y) of section 306.35 of the Revised Code, state university law enforcement officer appointed under section 3345.04 of the Revised Code, or Ohio veterans' home police officer appointed under section 5907.02 of the Revised Code shall arrest and detain, until a warrant can be obtained, a person found violating, within the limits of the political subdivision, metropolitan housing authority housing project, regional transit authority facilities or areas of a municipal corporation that have been agreed to by a regional transit authority and a municipal corporation located within its territorial jurisdiction, college, university, or Ohio veterans' home in which the peace officer is appointed, employed, or elected, a law of this state, an ordinance of a municipal corporation, or a resolution of a township.

(B)(1) When there is reasonable ground to believe that an offense of violence, the offense of criminal child enticement as defined in section 2905.05 of the Revised Code, the offense of public indecency as defined in section 2907.09 of the Revised Code, the offense of domestic violence as defined in section 2919.25 of the Revised Code, the offense of violating a protection order as defined in section 2919.27 of the Revised Code, the offense of menacing by stalking as defined in section 2903.211 [2903.21.1] of the Revised Code, the offense of aggravated trespass as defined in section 2911.211 [2911.21.1] of the Revised Code, a theft offense as defined in section 2913.01 of the Revised Code, or a felony drug abuse offense as defined in section 2925.01 of the Revised Code, has been committed within the limits of the political subdivision, metropolitan housing authority housing project, regional transit authority facilities or those areas of a municipal corporation that have been agreed to by a regional transit authority and a municipal corporation located within its territorial jurisdiction, college, university, or Ohio veterans' home in which the peace officer is appointed, employed, or elected, a peace officer described in division (A)(1) of this section may arrest and detain until a warrant can be obtained any person whom the peace officer has reasonable cause to believe is guilty of the violation.

(2) For purposes of division (B)(1) of this section, the execution of any of the following constitutes reasonable ground to believe that the offense alleged in the statement was committed and reasonable cause to believe that the person alleged in the statement to have committed the offense is guilty of the violation:

(a) A written statement by a person alleging that an alleged offender has committed the offense of menacing by stalking or aggravated trespass;

(b) A written statement by the administrator of the interstate compact on mental health appointed under section 5119.51 of the Revised Code alleging that a person who had been hospitalized, institutionalized, or confined in any facility under an order made pursuant to or under authority of section 2945.37, 2945.371 [2945.37.1], 2945.38, 2945.39, 2945.40, 2945.401 [2945.40.1], or 2945.402 [2945.40.2] of the Revised Code has escaped from the facility, from confinement in a vehicle for transportation to or from the facility, or from supervision by an employee of the facility that is incidental to hospitalization, institutionalization, or confinement in the facility and that occurs outside of the facility, in violation of section 2921.34 of the Revised Code;

(c) A written statement by the administrator of any facility in which a person has been hospitalized, institutionalized, or confined under an order made pursuant to or under authority of section 2945.37, 2945.371 [2945.37.1], 2945.38, 2945.39, 2945.40, 2945.401 [2945.40.1], or 2945.402 [2945.40.2] of the Revised Code alleging that the person has escaped from the facility, from confinement in a vehicle for transportation to or from the facility, or from supervision by an employee of the facility that is incidental to hospitalization, institutionalization, or confinement in the facility and that occurs outside of the facility, in violation of section 2921.34 of the Revised Code.

(3)(a) For purposes of division (B)(1) of this section, a peace officer described in that division has reasonable grounds to believe that the offense of domestic violence or the offense of violating a protection order has been committed and reasonable cause to believe that a particular person is guilty of committing the offense if any of the following occurs:

(i) A person executes a written statement alleging that the person in question has committed the offense of domestic violence or the offense of violating a protection order against the person who executes the statement or against a child of the person who executes the statement.

(ii) No written statement of the type described in division (B)(3)(a)(i) of this section is executed, but the peace officer, based upon the peace officer's own knowledge and observation of the facts and circumstances of the alleged incident of the offense of domestic violence or the alleged incident of the offense of violating a protection order or based upon any other information, including, but not limited to, any reasonably trustworthy information given to the peace officer by the alleged victim of the alleged incident of the offense or any witness of the alleged incident of the offense, concludes that there are reasonable grounds to believe that the offense of domestic violence or the offense of violating a protection order has been committed and reasonable cause to believe that the person in question is guilty of committing the offense.

(iii) No written statement of the type described in division (B)(3)(a)(i) of this section is executed, but the peace officer witnessed the person in question commit the offense of domestic violence or the offense of violating a protection order.

(b) If pursuant to division (B)(3)(a) of this section a peace officer has reasonable grounds to believe that the offense of domestic violence or the offense of violating a protection order has been committed and reasonable cause to believe that a particular person is guilty of committing the offense, it is the preferred course of action in this state that the officer arrest and detain that person pursuant to division (B)(1) of this section until a warrant can be obtained.

If pursuant to division (B)(3)(a) of this section a peace officer has reasonable grounds to believe that the offense of domestic violence or the offense of violating a protection order has been committed and reasonable cause to believe that family or household members have committed the offense against each other, it is the preferred course of action in this state that the officer, pursuant to division (B)(1) of this section, arrest and detain until a warrant can be obtained the family or household member who committed the offense and whom the officer has reasonable cause to believe is the primary physical aggressor. There is no preferred course of action in this state regarding any other family or household member who committed the offense and whom the officer does not have reasonable cause to believe is the primary physical aggressor, but, pursuant to division (B)(1) of this section, the peace officer may arrest and detain until a warrant can be obtained any other family or household member who committed the offense and whom the officer does not have reasonable cause to believe is the primary physical aggressor.

(c) If a peace officer described in division (B)(1) of this section does not arrest and detain a person whom the officer has reasonable cause to believe committed the offense of domestic violence or the offense of violating a protection order when it is the preferred course of action in this state pursuant to division (B)(3)(b) of this section that the officer arrest that person, the officer shall articulate in the written report of the incident required by section 2935.032 [2935.03.2] of the Revised Code a clear statement of the officer's reasons for not arresting and detaining that person until a warrant can be obtained.

(d) In determining for purposes of division (B)(3)(b) of this section which family or household member is the primary physical aggressor in a situation in which family or household members have committed the offense of domestic violence or the offense of violating a protection order against each other, a peace officer described in division (B)(1) of this section, in addition to any other relevant circumstances, should consider all of the following:

(i) Any history of domestic violence or of any other violent acts by either person involved in the alleged offense that the officer reasonably can ascertain;

(ii) If violence is alleged, whether the alleged violence was caused by a person acting in self-defense;

(iii) Each person's fear of physical harm, if any, resulting from the other person's threatened use of force against any person or resulting from the other person's use or history of the use of force against any person, and the reasonableness of that fear;

(iv) The comparative severity of any injuries suffered by the persons involved in the alleged offense.

(e)(i) A peace officer described in division (B)(1) of this section shall not require, as a prerequisite to arresting or charging a person who has committed the offense of domestic violence or the offense of violating a protection order, that the victim of the offense specifically consent to the filing of charges against the person who has committed the offense or sign a complaint against the person who has committed the offense.

(ii) If a person is arrested for or charged with committing the offense of domestic violence or the offense of violating a protection order and if the victim of the offense does not cooperate with the involved law enforcement or prosecuting authorities in the prosecution of the offense or, subsequent to the arrest or the filing of the charges, informs the involved law enforcement or prosecuting authorities that the victim does not wish the prosecution of the offense to continue or wishes to drop charges against the alleged offender relative to the offense, the involved prosecuting authorities, in determining whether to continue with the prosecution of the offense or whether to dismiss charges against the alleged offender relative to the offense and notwithstanding the victim's failure to cooperate or the victim's wishes, shall consider all facts and circumstances that are relevant to the offense, including, but not limited to, the statements and observations of the peace officers who responded to the incident that resulted in the arrest or filing of the charges and of all witnesses to that incident.

(f) In determining pursuant to divisions (B)(3)(a) to (g) of this section whether to arrest a person pursuant to division (B)(1) of this section, a peace officer described in division (B)(1) of this section shall not consider as a factor any possible shortage of cell space at the detention facility to which the person will be taken subsequent to the person's arrest or any possibility that the person's arrest might cause, contribute to, or exacerbate overcrowding at that detention facility or at any other detention facility.

(g) If a peace officer described in division (B)(1) of this section intends pursuant to divisions (B)(3)(a) to (g) of this section to arrest a person pursuant to division (B)(1) of this section and if the officer is unable to do so because the person is not present, the officer promptly shall seek a warrant for the arrest of the person.

(h) If a peace officer described in division (B)(1) of this section responds to a report of an alleged incident of the offense of domestic violence or an alleged incident of the offense of violating a protection order and if the circumstances of the incident involved the use or threatened use of a deadly weapon or any person involved in the incident brandished a deadly weapon during or in relation to the incident, the deadly weapon that was used, threatened to be used, or brandished constitutes contraband, and, to the extent possible, the officer shall seize the deadly weapon as contraband pursuant to section 2933.43 of the Revised Code. Upon the seizure of a deadly weapon pursuant to this division, section 2933.43 of the Revised Code shall apply regarding the treatment and disposition of the deadly weapon. For purposes of that section, the "underlying criminal offense" that was the basis of the seizure of a deadly weapon under this division and to which the deadly weapon had a relationship is any of the following that is applicable:

(i) The alleged incident of the offense of domestic violence or the alleged incident of the offense of violating a protection order to which the officer who seized the deadly weapon responded;

(ii) Any offense that arose out of the same facts and circumstances as the report of the alleged incident of the offense of domestic violence or the alleged incident of the offense of violating a protection order to which the officer who seized the deadly weapon responded.

(4) If, in the circumstances described in divisions (B)(3)(a) to (g) of this section, a peace officer described in division (B)(1) of this section arrests and detains a person pursuant to division (B)(1) of this section, or if, pursuant to division (B)(3)(h) of this section, a peace officer described in division (B)(1) of this section seizes a deadly weapon, the officer, to the extent described in and in accordance with section 9.86 or 2744.03 of the Revised Code, is immune in any civil action for damages for injury, death, or loss to person or property that arises from or is related to the arrest and detention or the seizure.

(C) When there is reasonable ground to believe that a violation of division (A), (B), or (C) of section 4506.15 or a violation of section 4511.19 of the Revised Code has been committed by a person operating a motor vehicle subject to regulation by the public utilities commission of Ohio under Title XLIX [49] of the Revised Code, a peace officer with authority to enforce that provision of law may stop or detain the person whom the officer has reasonable cause to believe was operating the motor vehicle in violation of the division or section and, after investigating the circumstances surrounding the operation of the vehicle, may arrest and detain the person.

(D) If a sheriff, deputy sheriff, marshal, deputy marshal, municipal police officer, member of a police force employed by a metropolitan housing authority under division (D) of section 3735.31 of the Revised Code, member of a police force employed by a regional transit authority under division (Y) of section 306.35 of the Revised Code, constable, police officer of a township or joint township police district, or state university law enforcement officer appointed under section 3345.04 of the Revised Code is authorized by division (A) or (B) of this section to arrest and detain, within the limits of the political subdivision, metropolitan housing authority housing project, regional transit authority facilities or those areas of a municipal corporation that have been agreed to by a regional transit authority and a municipal corporation located within its territorial jurisdiction, college, or university in which the officer is appointed, employed, or elected, a person until a warrant can be obtained, the peace officer may, outside the limits of that territory, pursue, arrest, and detain that person until a warrant can be obtained if all of the following apply:

(1) The pursuit takes place without unreasonable delay after the offense is committed.

(2) The pursuit is initiated within the limits of the political subdivision, metropolitan housing authority housing project, regional transit authority facilities or those areas of a municipal corporation that have been agreed to by a regional transit authority and a municipal corporation located within its territorial jurisdiction, college, or university in which the peace officer is appointed, employed, or elected.

(3) The offense involved is a felony, a misdemeanor of the first degree or a substantially equivalent municipal ordinance, a misdemeanor of the second degree or a substantially equivalent municipal ordinance, or any offense for which points are chargeable pursuant to division (G) of section 4507.021 [4507.02.1] of the Revised Code.

(E) In addition to the authority granted under division (A) or (B) of this section:

(1) A sheriff or deputy sheriff may arrest and detain, until a warrant can be obtained, any person found violating section 4503.11, 4503.21, or 4549.01, sections 4549.08 to 4549.12, section 4549.62, or Chapter 4511. or 4513. of the Revised Code on the portion of any street or highway that is located immediately adjacent to the boundaries of the county in which the sheriff or deputy sheriff is elected or appointed.

(2) A member of the police force of a township police

district created under section 505.48 of the Revised Code, a member of the police force of a joint township police district created under section 505.481 [505.48.1] of the Revised Code, and a township constable appointed in accordance with section 509.01 of the Revised Code, who has received a certificate from the Ohio peace officer training commission under section 109.75 of the Revised Code may arrest and detain, until a warrant can be obtained, any person found violating any section or chapter of the Revised Code listed in division (E)(1) of this section, other than sections 4513.33 and 4513.34 of the Revised Code, on the portion of any street or highway that is located immediately adjacent to the boundaries of the township police district or joint township police district, in the case of a member of a township police district or joint township police district police force, or the unincorporated territory of the township, in the case of a township constable. However, if the population of the township that created the township police district served by the member's police force, or the townships that created the joint township police district served by the member's police force, or the township that is served by the township constable, is sixty thousand or less, the member of the township police district or joint police district police force or the township constable may not make an arrest under this division on a state highway that is included as part of the interstate system.

(3) A police officer or village marshal appointed, elected, or employed by a municipal corporation may arrest and detain, until a warrant can be obtained, any person found violating any section or chapter of the Revised Code listed in division (E)(1) of this section on the portion of any street or highway that is located immediately adjacent to the boundaries of the municipal corporation in which the police officer or village marshal is appointed, elected, or employed.

(F)(1) A department of mental health special police officer or a department of mental retardation and developmental disabilities special police officer may arrest without a warrant and detain until a warrant can be obtained any person found committing on the premises of any institution under the jurisdiction of the particular department a misdemeanor under a law of the state.

A department of mental health special police officer or a department of mental retardation and developmental disabilities special police officer may arrest without a warrant and detain until a warrant can be obtained any person who has been hospitalized, institutionalized, or confined in an institution under the jurisdiction of the particular department pursuant to or under authority of section 2945.37, 2945.371 [2945.37.1], 2945.38, 2945.39, 2945.40, 2945.401 [2945.40.1], or 2945.402 [2945.40.2] of the Revised Code and who is found committing on the premises of any institution under the jurisdiction of the particular department a violation of section 2921.34 of the Revised Code that involves an escape from the premises of the institution.

(2)(a) If a department of mental health special police officer or a department of mental retardation and developmental disabilities special police officer finds any person who has been hospitalized, institutionalized, or confined in an institution under the jurisdiction of the particular department pursuant to or under authority of section 2945.37, 2945.371 [2945.37.1], 2945.38, 2945.39, 2945.40, 2945.401 [2945.40.1], or 2945.402 [2945.40.2] of the Revised Code committing a violation of section 2921.34 of the Revised Code that involves an escape from the premises of the institution, or if there is reasonable ground to believe that a violation of section 2921.34 of the Revised Code has been committed that involves an escape from the premises of an institution under the jurisdiction of the department of mental health or the department of mental retardation and developmental disabilities and if a department of mental health special police officer or a department of mental retardation and developmental disabilities special police officer has reasonable cause to believe that a particular person who has been hospitalized, institutionalized, or confined in the institution pursuant to or under authority of section 2945.37, 2945.371 [2945.37.1], 2945.38, 2945.39, 2945.40, 2945.401 [2945.40.1], or 2945.402 [2945.40.2] of the Revised Code is guilty of the violation, the special police officer, outside of the premises of the institution, may pursue, arrest, and detain that person for that violation of section 2921.34 of the Revised Code, until a warrant can be obtained, if both of the following apply:

(i) The pursuit takes place without unreasonable delay after the offense is committed.

(ii) The pursuit is initiated within the premises of the institution from which the violation of section 2921.34 of the Revised Code occurred.

(b) For purposes of division (F)(2)(a) of this section, the execution of a written statement by the administrator of the institution in which a person had been hospitalized, institutionalized, or confined pursuant to or under authority of section 2945.37, 2945.371 [2945.37.1], 2945.38, 2945.39, 2945.40, 2945.401 [2945.40.1], or 2945.402 [2945.40.2] of the Revised Code alleging that the person has escaped from the premises of the institution in violation of section 2921.34 of the Revised Code constitutes reasonable ground to believe that the violation was committed and reasonable cause to believe that the person alleged in the statement to have committed the offense is guilty of the violation.

(G) As used in this section:

(1) A "department of mental health special police officer" means a special police officer of the department of mental health designated under section 5119.14 of the Revised Code who is certified by the Ohio peace officer training commission under section 109.77 of the Revised Code as having successfully completed an approved peace officer basic training program.

(2) A "department of mental retardation and developmental disabilities special police officer" means a special police officer of the department of mental retardation and developmental disabilities designated under section

5123.13 of the Revised Code who is certified by the Ohio peace officer training council under section 109.77 of the Revised Code as having successfully completed an approved peace officer basic training program.

(3) "Deadly weapon" has the same meaning as in section 2923.11 of the Revised Code.

(4) "Family or household member" has the same meaning as in section 2919.25 of the Revised Code.

(5) "Street" or "highway" has the same meaning as in section 4511.01 of the Revised Code.

(6) "Interstate system" has the same meaning as in section 5516.01 of the Revised Code.

HISTORY: 142 v H 708 (Eff 4-19-88); 143 v H 88 (Eff 3-13-90); 143 v H 669 (Eff 1-10-91); 144 v H 77 (Eff 9-17-91); 144 v H 536 (Eff 11-5-92); 145 v H 42 (Eff 2-9-94); 145 v S 82 (Eff 5-4-94); 145 v H 335 (Eff 12-9-94); 146 v S 2 (Eff 7-1-96); 146 v S 269 (Eff 7-1-96); 146 v H 670 (Eff 12-2-96); 146 v S 285 (Eff 7-1-97); 147 v S 1. Eff 10-21-97.

Analogous to former RC § 2935.03 (GC § 13432-1; 113 v 123(140), ch 11; 115 v 530; Bureau of Code Revision, 10-1-53; 132 v S 29; 134 v H 511; 136 v H 300; 137 v H 588; 137 v H 835; 138 v S 355; 140 v S 321; 140 v H 129; 141 v S 33; 141 v H 284; 141 v S 356; 142 v H 231; 142 v H 261), repealed 142 v H 708, § 2, eff 4-19-88.

[§ 2935.03.1] § 2935.031 Policy for pursuit in motor vehicle.

Any agency, instrumentality, or political subdivision of the state that employs a sheriff, deputy sheriff, constable, marshal, deputy marshal, police officer, member of a metropolitan housing authority police force, state university law enforcement officer, or Ohio veterans' home policeman with arrest authority under section 2935.03 of the Revised Code or that employs other persons with arrest authority under the Revised Code, shall adopt a policy for the pursuit in a motor vehicle of any person who violates a law of this state or an ordinance of a municipal corporation. The chief law enforcement officer or other chief official of the agency, instrumentality, or political subdivision shall formally advise each peace officer or other person with arrest authority it employs of the pursuit policy adopted by that agency, instrumentality, or political subdivision pursuant to this section.

HISTORY: 143 v S 49. Eff 11-3-89.

[§ 2935.03.2] § 2935.032 Policies and procedures for responding to alleged domestic violence offense or violation of protection order.

(A) Not later than ninety days after the effective date of this amendment, each agency, instrumentality, or political subdivision that is served by any peace officer described in division (B)(1) of section 2935.03 of the Revised Code shall adopt, in accordance with division (E) of this section, written policies, written procedures implementing the policies, and other written procedures for the peace officers who serve it to follow in implementing division (B)(3) of section 2935.03 of the Revised Code and for their appropriate response to each report of an alleged incident of the offense of domestic violence or an alleged incident of the offense of violating a protection order. The policies and procedures shall conform to and be consistent with the provisions of divisions (B)(1) and (B)(3) of section 2935.03 of the Revised Code and divisions (B) to (D) of this section. Each policy adopted under this division shall include, but not be limited to, all of the following:

(1) Provisions specifying that, if a peace officer who serves the agency, instrumentality, or political subdivision responds to an alleged incident of the offense of domestic violence, an alleged incident of the offense of violating a protection order, or an alleged incident of any other offense, both of the following apply:

(a) If the officer determines that there are reasonable grounds to believe that a person knowingly caused serious physical harm to another or to another's unborn or knowingly caused or attempted to cause physical harm to another or to another's unborn by means of a deadly weapon or dangerous ordnance, then, regardless of whether the victim of the offense was a family or household member of the offender, the officer shall treat the incident as felonious assault, shall consider the offender to have committed and the victim to have been the victim of felonious assault, shall consider the offense that was committed to have been felonious assault in determining the manner in which the offender should be treated, and shall comply with whichever of the following is applicable:

(i) Unless the officer has reasonable cause to believe that, during the incident, the offender who committed the felonious assault and one or more other persons committed offenses against each other, the officer shall arrest the offender who committed the felonious assault pursuant to section 2935.03 of the Revised Code and shall detain that offender pursuant to that section until a warrant can be obtained, and the arrest shall be for felonious assault.

(ii) If the officer has reasonable cause to believe that, during the incident, the offender who committed the felonious assault and one or more other persons committed offenses against each other, the officer shall determine in accordance with division (B)(3)(d) of section 2935.03 of the Revised Code which of those persons is the primary physical aggressor. If the offender who committed the felonious assault is the primary physical aggressor, the officer shall arrest that offender for felonious assault pursuant to section 2935.03 of the Revised Code and shall detain that offender pursuant to that section until a warrant can be obtained, and the officer is not required to arrest but may arrest pursuant to section 2935.03 of the Revised Code any other person who committed an offense but who is not the primary physical aggressor. If the offender who committed the felonious assault is not the primary physical aggressor, the officer is not required to arrest that offender or any other person who committed an offense during the incident but may arrest any of them pursuant to section 2935.03 of the Revised Code and detain them pursuant to that section until a warrant can be obtained.

(b) If the officer determines that there are reasonable grounds to believe that a person, while under the influence of sudden passion or in a sudden fit of rage, either of which is brought on by serious provocation occasioned by the victim that is reasonably sufficient to incite the person into using deadly force, knowingly caused serious physical harm to another or to another's unborn or knowingly caused or attempted to cause physical harm to another or to another's unborn by means of a deadly weapon or dangerous ordnance, then, regardless of whether the victim of the offense was a family or household member of the offender, the officer shall treat the incident as aggravated assault, shall consider the offender to have committed and the victim to have been the victim of aggravated assault, shall consider the offense that was committed to have been aggravated assault in determining the manner in which the offender should be treated, and shall comply with whichever of the following is applicable:

(i) Unless the officer has reasonable cause to believe that, during the incident, the offender who committed the aggravated assault and one or more other persons committed offenses against each other, the officer shall arrest the offender who committed the aggravated assault pursuant to section 2935.03 of the Revised Code and shall detain that offender pursuant to that section until a warrant can be obtained, and the arrest shall be for aggravated assault.

(ii) If the officer has reasonable cause to believe that, during the incident, the offender who committed the aggravated assault and one or more other persons committed offenses against each other, the officer shall determine in accordance with division (B)(3)(d) of section 2935.03 of the Revised Code which of those persons is the primary physical aggressor. If the offender who committed the aggravated assault is the primary physical aggressor, the officer shall arrest that offender for aggravated assault pursuant to section 2935.03 of the Revised Code and shall detain that offender pursuant to that section until a warrant can be obtained, and the officer is not required to arrest but may arrest pursuant to section 2935.03 of the Revised Code any other person who committed an offense but who is not the primary physical aggressor. If the offender who committed the aggravated assault is not the primary physical aggressor, the officer is not required to arrest that offender or any other person who committed an offense during the incident but may arrest any of them pursuant to section 2935.03 of the Revised Code and detain them pursuant to that section until a warrant can be obtained.

(2) Provisions requiring the peace officers who serve the agency, instrumentality, or political subdivision to do all of the following:

(a) Respond without undue delay to a report of an alleged incident of the offense of domestic violence or the offense of violating a protection order;

(b) If the alleged offender has been granted pretrial release from custody on a prior charge of the offense of domestic violence or the offense of violating a protection order and has violated one or more conditions of that pretrial release, document the facts and circumstances of the violation in the report to the law enforcement agency that the peace officer makes pursuant to division (D) of this section;

(c) Separate the victim of the offense of domestic violence or the offense of violating a protection order and the alleged offender, conduct separate interviews with the victim and the alleged offender in separate locations, and take a written statement from the victim that indicates the frequency and severity of any prior incidents of physical abuse of the victim by the alleged offender, the number of times the victim has called peace officers for assistance, and the disposition of those calls, if known;

(d) Comply with divisions (B)(1) and (B)(3) of section 2935.03 of the Revised Code and with divisions (B), (C), and (D) of this section.

(3) Sanctions to be imposed upon a peace officer who serves the agency, instrumentality, or political subdivision and who fails to comply with any provision in the policy or with division (B)(1) or (B)(3) of section 2935.03 of the Revised Code or division (B), (C), or (D) of this section.

(4) Examples of reasons that a peace officer may consider for not arresting and detaining until a warrant can be obtained a person who allegedly committed the offense of domestic violence or the offense of violating a protection order when it is the preferred course of action in this state that the officer arrest the alleged offender, as described in division (B)(3)(b) of section 2935.03 of the Revised Code.

(B)(1) Nothing in this section or in division (B)(1) or (B)(3) of section 2935.03 of the Revised Code precludes an agency, instrumentality, or political subdivision that is served by any peace officer described in division (B)(1) of section 2935.03 of the Revised Code from including in the policy it adopts under division (A) of this section either of the following types of provisions:

(a) A provision that requires the peace officers who serve it, if they have reasonable grounds to believe that the offense of domestic violence or the offense of violating a protection order has been committed within the limits of the jurisdiction of the agency, instrumentality, or political subdivision and reasonable cause to believe that a particular person committed the offense, to arrest the alleged offender;

(b) A provision that does not require the peace officers who serve it, if they have reasonable grounds to believe that the offense of domestic violence or the offense of violating a protection order has been committed within the limits of the jurisdiction of the agency, instrumentality, or political subdivision and reasonable cause to believe that a particular person committed the offense, to arrest the alleged offender, but that grants the officers less discretion in those circumstances in deciding whether to arrest the alleged offender than peace officers are granted by divisions (B)(1) and (B)(3) of section 2935.03 of the Revised Code.

(2) If an agency, instrumentality, or political subdivision that is served by any peace officer described in division (B)(1) of section 2935.03 of the Revised Code includes in the policy it adopts under division (A) of this section a provision of the type described in division (B)(1)(a) or (b) of this section, the peace officers who serve the agency, instrumentality, or political subdivision shall comply with the provision in making arrests authorized under division (B)(1) of section 2935.03 of the Revised Code.

(C) When a peace officer described in division (B)(1) of section 2935.03 of the Revised Code investigates a report of an alleged incident of the offense of domestic violence or an alleged incident of the offense of violating a protection order, the officer shall do all of the following:

(1) Complete a domestic violence report in accordance with division (D) of this section;

(2) Advise the victim of the availability of a temporary protection order pursuant to section 2919.26 of the Revised Code or a protection order or consent agreement pursuant to section 3113.31 of the Revised Code;

(3) Give the victim the officer's name, the officer's badge number if the officer has a badge and the badge has a number, the report number for the incident if a report number is available at the time of the officer's investigation, a telephone number that the victim can call for information about the case, the telephone number of a domestic violence shelter in the area, and information on any local victim advocate program.

(D) A peace officer who investigates a report of an alleged incident of the offense of domestic violence or an alleged incident of the offense of violating a protection order shall make a written report of the incident whether or not an arrest is made. The report shall document the officer's observations of the victim and the alleged offender, any visible injuries of the victim or alleged offender, any weapons at the scene, the actions of the alleged offender, any statements made by the victim or witnesses, and any other significant facts or circumstances. If the officer does not arrest and detain until a warrant can be obtained a person who allegedly committed the offense of domestic violence or the offense of violating a protection order when it is the preferred course of action in this state pursuant to division (B)(3)(b) of section 2935.03 of the Revised Code that the alleged offender be arrested, the officer must articulate in the report a clear statement of the officer's reasons for not arresting and detaining that alleged offender until a warrant can be obtained. The officer shall submit the written report to the law enforcement agency to which the officer has been appointed, employed, or elected.

(E) Each agency, instrumentality, or political subdivision that is required to adopt policies and procedures under division (A) of this section shall adopt those policies and procedures in conjunction and consultation with shelters in the community for victims of domestic violence and private organizations, law enforcement agencies, and other public agencies in the community that have expertise in the recognition and handling of domestic violence cases.

(F) To the extent described in and in accordance with section 9.86 or 2744.03 of the Revised Code, a peace officer who arrests an offender for the offense of violating a protection order with respect to a protection order or consent agreement of this state or another state that on its face is valid is immune from liability in a civil action for damages for injury, death, or loss to person or property that allegedly was caused by or related to the arrest.

(G) Each agency, instrumentality, or political subdivision described in division (A) of this section that arrests an offender for an alleged incident of the offense of domestic violence or an alleged incident of the offense of violating a protection order shall consider referring the case to federal authorities for prosecution under 18 U.S.C. 2261 if the incident constitutes a violation of federal law.

(H) As used in this section:

(1) "Another's unborn" has the same meaning as in section 2903.09 of the Revised Code.

(2) "Dangerous ordnance" and "deadly weapon" have the same meanings as in section 2923.11 of the Revised Code.

(3) "The offense of violating a protection order" includes the former offense of violating a protection order or consent agreement or anti-stalking protection order as set forth in section 2919.27 of the Revised Code as it existed prior to the effective date of this amendment.

HISTORY: 145 v H 335 (Eff 12-9-94); 147 v S 1. Eff 10-21-97.

§ 2935.04 When any person may arrest.

When a felony has been committed, or there is reasonable ground to believe that a felony has been committed, any person without a warrant may arrest another whom he has reasonable cause to believe is guilty of the offense, and detain him until a warrant can be obtained.

HISTORY: GC § 13432-2; 113 v 123(140), ch 11, § 2; Bureau of Code Revision. Eff 10-1-53.

[§ 2935.04.1] § 2935.041 Detention, arrest of shoplifters; protection of library, museum and archival institution property.

(A) A merchant, or his employee or agent, who has probable cause to believe that items offered for sale by a mercantile establishment have been unlawfully taken by a person, may, for the purposes set forth in division (C) of this section, detain the person in a reasonable manner for a reasonable length of time within the mercantile establishment or its immediate vicinity.

(B) Any officer, employee, or agent of a library, museum, or archival institution may, for the purposes set forth in division (C) of this section or for the purpose of conducting a reasonable investigation of a belief that the person has acted in a manner described in divisions (B)(1) and (2) of this section, detain a person in a reasonable manner for a reasonable length of time within, or in the immediate vicinity of, the library, museum, or archival institution, if the officer, employee, or agent has probable cause to believe that the person has either:

(1) Without privilege to do so, knowingly moved, defaced, damaged, destroyed, or otherwise improperly tampered with property owned by or in the custody of the library, museum, or archival institution; or

(2) With purpose to deprive the library, museum, or archival institution of property owned by it or in its custody, knowingly obtained or exerted control over the property without the consent of the owner or person authorized to give consent, beyond the scope of the express or implied consent of the owner or person authorized to give consent, by deception, or by threat.

(C) An officer, agent, or employee of a library, museum, or archival institution pursuant to division (B) of this section or a merchant or his employee or agent pursuant to division (A) of this section may detain another person for any of the following purposes:

(1) To recover the property that is the subject of the unlawful taking, criminal mischief, or theft;

(2) To cause an arrest to be made by a peace officer;

(3) To obtain a warrant of arrest.

(D) The officer, agent, or employee of the library, museum, or archival institution, or the merchant or his employee or agent acting under division (A) or (B) of this section shall not search the person, search or seize any property belonging to the person detained without the person's consent, or use undue restraint upon the person detained.

(E) Any peace officer may arrest without a warrant any person that he has probable cause to believe has committed any act described in division (B)(1) or (2) of this section or that he has probable cause to believe has committed an unlawful taking in a mercantile establishment. An arrest under this division shall be made within a reasonable time after the commission of the act or unlawful taking.

(F) As used in this section:

(1) "Archival institution" means any public or private building, structure, or shelter in which are stored historical documents, devices, records, manuscripts, or items of public interest, which historical materials are stored to preserve the materials or the information in the materials, to disseminate the information contained in the materials, or to make the materials available for public inspection or for inspection by certain persons who have a particular interest in, use for, or knowledge concerning the materials.

(2) "Museum" means any public or private nonprofit institution that is permanently organized for primarily educational or aesthetic purposes, owns or borrows objects or items of public interest, and cares for and exhibits to the public the objects or items.

HISTORY: 127 v 765 (Eff 9-13-57); 131 v 676 (Eff 9-15-65); 133 v H 49 (Eff 10-30-69); 137 v H 403. Eff 7-4-78.

§ 2935.05 Affidavit filed in case of arrest without warrant.

When a person named in section 2935.03 of the Revised Code has arrested a person without a warrant, he shall, without unnecessary delay, take the person arrested before a court or magistrate having jurisdiction of the offense, and shall file or cause to be filed an affidavit describing the offense for which the person was arrested. Such affidavit shall be filed either with the court or magistrate, or with the prosecuting attorney or other attorney charged by law with prosecution of crimes before such court or magistrate and if filed with such attorney he shall forthwith file with such court or magistrate a complaint, based on such affidavit.

HISTORY: GC § 13432-3; 113 v 123(140), ch 11, § 3; Bureau of Code Revision, 10-1-53; 128 v 97. Eff 1-1-60.

§ 2935.06 Duty of private person making arrest.

A private person who has made an arrest pursuant to section 2935.04 of the Revised Code or detention pursuant to section 2935.041 [2935.04.1] of the Revised Code shall forthwith take the person arrested before the most convenient judge or clerk of a court of record or before a magistrate, or deliver such person to an officer authorized to execute criminal warrants who shall, without unnecessary delay, take such person before the court or magistrate having jurisdiction of the offense. The officer may, but if he does not, the private person shall file or cause to be filed in such court or before such magistrate an affidavit stating the offense for which the person was arrested.

HISTORY: GC § 13432-4; 113 v 123(140), ch 11, § 4; Bureau of Code Revision, 10-1-53; 128 v 97. Eff 1-1-60.

§ 2935.07 Person arrested without warrant shall be informed of cause of arrest.

When an arrest is made without a warrant by an officer, he shall inform the person arrested of such officer's authority to make the arrest and the cause of the arrest.

When an arrest is made by a private person, he shall, before making the arrest, inform the person to be arrested of the intention to arrest him and the cause of the arrest.

When a person is engaged in the commission of a

criminal offense, it is not necessary to inform him of the cause of his arrest.

HISTORY: GC § 13432-5; 113 v 123(140), ch 11, § 5; Bureau of Code Revision. Eff 10-1-53.

§ 2935.08 Issuance of warrant.

Upon the filing of an affidavit or complaint as provided in sections 2935.05 or 2935.06 of the Revised Code such judge, clerk, or magistrate shall forthwith issue a warrant to the peace officer making the arrest, or if made by a private person, to the most convenient peace officer who shall receive custody of the person arrested. All further detention and further proceedings shall be pursuant to such affidavit or complaint and warrant.

HISTORY: GC § 13432-6; 113 v 123(140), ch 11, § 6; Bureau of Code Revision, 10-1-53; 128 v 97 (Eff 1-1-60); 129 v 582(748). Eff 1-10-61.

[§ 2935.08.1] § 2935.081 Administration of oaths, acknowledgment of documents by peace officer.

(A) As used in this section, "peace officer" has the same meaning as in section 2935.01 of the Revised Code, except that "peace officer" does not include, for any purpose, the superintendent or any trooper of the state highway patrol.

(B) A peace officer who has completed a course of in-service training that includes training in the administration of oaths and the acknowledgment of documents and that is approved by the chief legal officer of the political subdivision in which the peace officer is elected or of the political subdivision or other entity in which or by which the peace officer is appointed or employed may administer oaths and acknowledge criminal and juvenile court complaints, summonses, affidavits, and returns of court orders in matters related to the peace officer's official duties.

(C) Except as authorized by division (B) of this section, no peace officer who has completed a course of in-service training of a type described in division (B) of this section shall knowingly perform any act that is specifically required of a notary public unless the peace officer has complied with Chapter 147. of the Revised Code.

HISTORY: 146 v H 72. Eff 3-18-97.

§ 2935.09 Accusation by affidavit to cause arrest or prosecution.

In all cases not provided by sections 2935.02 to 2935.08, inclusive, of the Revised Code, in order to cause the arrest or prosecution of a person charged with committing an offense in this state, a peace officer, or a private citizen having knowledge of the facts, shall file with the judge or clerk of a court of record, or with a magistrate, an affidavit charging the offense committed, or shall file such affidavit with the prosecuting attorney or attorney charged by law with the prosecution of offenses in court or before such magistrate, for the purpose of having a complaint filed by such prosecuting or other authorized attorney.

HISTORY: 128 v 97. Eff 1-1-60.

Not analogous to former RC § 2935.09 (GC § 13432-7; 113 v 123(141); Bureau of Code Revision, 10-1-53), repealed 128 v 97(116), § 2, eff 1-1-60.

The substance of former RC § 2935.09 is now found in RC § 2935.11.

§ 2935.10 Procedure upon filing of affidavit or complaint.

(A) Upon the filing of an affidavit or complaint as provided by section 2935.09 of the Revised Code, if it charges the commission of a felony, such judge, clerk, or magistrate, unless he has reason to believe that it was not filed in good faith, or the claim is not meritorious, shall forthwith issue a warrant for the arrest of the person charged in the affidavit, and directed to a peace officer; otherwise he shall forthwith refer the matter to the prosecuting attorney or other attorney charged by law with prosecution for investigation prior to the issuance of warrant.

(B) If the offense charged is a misdemeanor or violation of a municipal ordinance, such judge, clerk, or magistrate may:

(1) Issue a warrant for the arrest of such person, directed to any officer named in section 2935.03 of the Revised Code but in cases of ordinance violation only to a police officer or marshal or deputy marshal of the municipal corporation;

(2) Issue summons, to be served by a peace officer, bailiff, or court constable, commanding the person against whom the affidavit or complaint was filed to appear forthwith, or at a fixed time in the future, before such court or magistrate. Such summons shall be served in the same manner as in civil cases.

(C) If the affidavit is filed by, or the complaint is filed pursuant to an affidavit executed by, a peace officer who has, at his discretion, at the time of commission of the alleged offense, notified the person to appear before the court or magistrate at a specific time set by such officer, no process need be issued unless the defendant fails to appear at the scheduled time.

(D) Any person charged with a misdemeanor or violation of a municipal ordinance may give bail as provided in sections 2937.22 to 2937.46 of the Revised Code, for his appearance, regardless of whether a warrant, summons, or notice to appear has been issued.

(E) Any warrant, summons, or any notice issued by the peace officer shall state the substance of the charge against the person arrested or directed to appear.

(F) When the offense charged is a misdemeanor, and the warrant or summons issued pursuant to this section is not served within two years of the date of issue, a judge or magistrate may order such warrant or summons withdrawn and the case closed, when it does not appear that the ends of justice require keeping the case open.

HISTORY: 128 v 97 (Eff 1-1-60); 129 v 582(749) (Eff 1-10-61); 134 v H 511. Eff 3-23-73.

Somewhat analogous to former RC §§ 2935.10, 2935.11 (GC §§ 13432-8, 13432-9; 113 v 123(141); Bureau of Code Revision, 10-1-53; analogous to former GC §§ 13494, 13496), repealed 128 v 97(116), § 2, eff 1-1-60.

The provisions of §§ 5, 6, 7 of HB 511 (134 v —) read as follows:

SECTION 5. That existing sections 2935.10, 2935.24, 2937.18, 2945.39, 2945.70, 2947.20, and 2967.191 of the Revised Code are hereby repealed.

SECTION 6. Sections 2935.10, 2935.24, 2937.18, 2945.39, 2945.70, 2947.20, and 2967.191 of the Revised Code, as amended by this act, and section 2947.271 of the Revised Code, as enacted by this act, and Sections 4 to 7 of this act, shall become effective at the earliest time permitted by law. Persons serving a sentence of imprisonment in a penal or reformatory institution on such effective date, and persons on parole who have not obtained their final release on such effective date, shall have their minimum and maximum sentences reduced as provided in section 2967.191 of the Revised Code, as amended by this act.

SECTION 7. Sections 4 to 6 of this act constitute compliance with constitutional requirements for repeal of sections and designation of effective dates that have among their purposes the making effective at the same time as this act the amendment of sections 2935.10, 2935.24, 2937.18, 2945.39, 2945.70, 2947.20, and 2967.191, the enactment of section 2947.271, and the repeal of existing sections 2935.10, 2935.24, 2937.18, 2945.39, 2945.70, 2947.20, and 2967.191 of the Revised Code, and the making effective on January 1, 1974 the amendment, enactment, and repeal by this act of all other Revised Code sections included in this act.

§ 2935.11 Failure of person summoned to appear.

If the person summoned to appear as provided in division (B) of section 2935.10 of the Revised Code fails to appear without just cause and personal service of the summons was had upon him, he may be found guilty of contempt of court, and may be fined not to exceed twenty dollars for such contempt. Upon failure to appear the court or magistrate may forthwith issue a warrant for his arrest.

HISTORY: 128 v 97. Eff 1-1-60.

Not analogous to former RC § 2935.11 (GC § 13432-9; 113 v 123(141); Bureau of Code Revision, 10-1-53), repealed 128 v 97(116), § 2, eff 1-1-60; but see former RC § 2935.09 (GC § 13432-7; 113 v 123(141); Bureau of Code Revision, 10-1-53).

§ 2935.12 Forcible entry in making arrest or executing search warrant.

(A) When making an arrest or executing an arrest warrant or summons in lieu of an arrest warrant, or when executing a search warrant, the peace officer, law enforcement officer, or other authorized individual making the arrest or executing the warrant or summons may break down an outer or inner door or window of a dwelling house or other building, if, after notice of his intention to make the arrest or to execute the warrant or summons, he is refused admittance, but the law enforcement officer or other authorized individual executing a search warrant shall not enter a house or building not described in the warrant.

(B) The precondition for nonconsensual, forcible entry established by division (A) of this section is subject to waiver, as it applies to the execution of a search warrant, in accordance with section 2933.231 [2933.23.1] of the Revised Code.

HISTORY: 128 v 97 (Eff 1-1-60); 143 v S 258. Eff 11-20-90.

Not analogous to former RC § 2935.12 (GC § 13432-11; 113 v 123(141); Bureau of Code Revision, 10-1-53), repealed 128 v 97(116), § 2, eff 1-1-60; but see former RC § 2935.15 (GC § 13432-14; 113 v 123(142); Bureau of Code Revision, 10-1-53).

The effective date is set by section 15 of SB 258.

The substance of former RC § 2935.12 is now found in RC § 2935.13.

§ 2935.13 Proceedings upon arrest.

Upon the arrest of any person pursuant to warrant, he shall forthwith be taken before the court or magistrate issuing the same, if such court be in session or such magistrate available, and proceedings had as provided in sections 2937.01 to 2937.46, inclusive, of the Revised Code. If such court be not in session and a misdemeanor or ordinance violation is charged, he shall be taken before the clerk or deputy clerk of the court and let to bail, as provided in sections 2937.22 to 2937.46, inclusive, of the Revised Code, if the magistrate be not available, or if the defendant is arrested in a county other than that of the issuing court or magistrate he shall forthwith be taken before the most convenient magistrate, clerk, or deputy clerk of a court of record, and there let to bail for his appearance before the issuing court or magistrate within a reasonable time to be set by such clerk.

HISTORY: 128 v 97. Eff 1-1-60.

Not analogous to former RC § 2935.13 (GC § 13432-12; 113 v 123(142); Bureau of Code Revision, 10-1-53), repealed 128 v 97(116), § 2, eff 1-1-60; but see in part former RC § 2935.12 (GC § 13432-11; 113 v 123(141); Bureau of Code Revision, 10-1-53).

§ 2935.14 Rights of person arrested.

If the person arrested is unable to offer sufficient bail or, if the offense charged be a felony, he shall, prior to being confined or removed from the county of arrest, as the case may be, be speedily permitted facilities to communicate with an attorney at law of his own choice, or to communicate with at least one relative or other person for the purpose of obtaining counsel (or in cases of misdemeanors or ordinance violation for the purpose of arranging bail). He shall not thereafter be confined or removed from the county or from the situs of initial detention until such attorney has had reasonable opportunity to confer with him privately, or other person to arrange bail, under such security measures as may be necessary under the circumstances.

Whoever, being a police officer in charge of a prisoner, or the custodian of any jail or place of confinement, violates this section shall be fined not less than one hundred nor more than five hundred dollars or imprisoned not more than thirty days, or both.

HISTORY: 128 v 97. Eff 1-1-60.

Not analogous to former RC § 2935.14 (GC § 13432-13; 113 v 123(142); Bureau of Code Revision, 10-1-53), repealed 128 v 97(116), § 2, eff 1-1-60; but see in part former RC § 2935.15 (GC §§ 12856-1, 13432-15; 113 v 123(142); Bureau of Code Revision, 10-1-53) and RC § 2935.17 (GC § 13432-16; 113 v 123(143); Bureau of Code Revision, 10-1-53).

§ 2935.15 Amount and disposition of bail.

Amount of bail, and nature of security therefor in misdemeanor cases may be set by a schedule fixed by the court or magistrate, or it may be endorsed on the warrant by the magistrate or clerk of the issuing court. If the amount be not endorsed on the warrant, the schedule set by the court or magistrate before whom bail is taken shall prevail. All recognizances taken, or cash received shall be promptly transmitted to the court issuing the warrant, and further proceedings thereon shall be the same as if taken by the issuing court.

HISTORY: 128 v 97. Eff 1-1-60.

Not analogous to former RC § 2935.15 (GC § 13432-14; 113 v 123(142); Bureau of Code Revision, 10-1-53), repealed 128 v 97(116), § 2, eff 1-1-60.

The substance of former RC § 2935.15 is now found in RC § 2935.12.

§ 2935.16 Prisoners held without process.

When it comes to the attention of any judge or magistrate that a prisoner is being held in any jail or place of custody in his jurisdiction without commitment from a court or magistrate, he shall forthwith, by summary process, require the officer or person in charge of such jail or place of custody to disclose to such court or magistrate, in writing, whether or not he holds the person described or identified in the process and the court under whose process the prisoner is being held. If it appears from the disclosure that the prisoner is held solely under warrant of arrest from any court or magistrate, the judge or magistrate shall order the custodian to produce the prisoner forthwith before the court or magistrate issuing the warrant and if such be impossible for any reason, to produce him before the inquiring judge or magistrate. If it appears from the disclosure that the prisoner is held without process, such judge or magistrate shall require the custodian to produce the prisoner forthwith before him, there to be charged as provided in section 2935.06 of the Revised Code.

Whoever, being the person in temporary or permanent charge of any jail or place of confinement, violates this section shall be fined not less than one hundred nor more than five hundred dollars or imprisoned not more than ninety days, or both.

HISTORY: 128 v 97. Eff 1-1-60.

Not analogous to former RC § 2935.16 (GC § 13432-15; 113 v 123(142); Bureau of Code Revision, 10-1-53), repealed 128 v 97(116), § 2, eff 1-1-60.

The substance of former RC § 2935.16 is now found in RC § 2935.14.

§ 2935.17 Affidavit forms; authority of supreme court to prescribe.

(A) An affidavit in either of the following forms is sufficient:

(1) State of Ohio,
.... County, ss:

Before me, A.B., personally came C.D., who being duly sworn according to law deposes and says that on or about the day of ...., 19 ..., at the county of .... one E.F. (here describe the offense as nearly according to the nature thereof as the case will admit, in ordinary concise language) C.D.

Sworn to and subscribed before me this ..... day of ...., 19 ....

A.B., County Judge
   Clerk of .... Court

(2) State of Ohio,
.... County, ss:

Before me, A.B., personally came C.D., who being duly sworn according to law says that on or about the .... day of ...., 19 ..., one E.F. did: (here listing several common offenses, plainly but tersely described as: fail to stop at stop sign, pass at crest of grade, etc., with a ruled box before each, and then showing an X or distinctive mark in front of the offense claimed to be committed). C.D.

Sworn to before me and subscribed in my presence this .... day of ...., 19 ..., [.]

A.B., County Judge
   Clerk of .... Court

(B) A complaint in the following form is sufficient: State of Ohio,
.... County, ss:

The undersigned (assistant) prosecuting attorney of .... County complains that on or about the .... day of ......, 19 ..., one E.F. did (here describing the offense committed as above) based on affidavit of .... filed with me.

Prosecuting Attorney
City Director of Law

Provided, that the supreme court of Ohio, may, by rule, provide for the uniform type and language to be used in any affidavit or complaint to be filed in any court inferior to the court of common pleas for violations of the motor vehicle and traffic acts and related ordinances and in any notice to violator to appear in such courts, and may require that such forms and no other, shall be received in such courts, and issued to violators.

HISTORY: 128 v 97 (Eff 1-1-60); 137 v H 219. Eff 11-1-77.

Not analogous to former RC § 2935.17 (GC § 13432-16; 113 v 123(143); Bureau of Code Revision, 10-1-53), repealed 128 v 97(116), § 2, eff 1-1-60.

The substance of former RC § 2935.17 is now found in RC § 2935.14. See also RC § 2937.03.

§ 2935.18 Contents of warrant, summons or notice.

A warrant, summons, or notice of a peace officer shall either contain a copy of the affidavit, or recite the substance of the accusation. A warrant shall be directed to a specific officer or to a department designated by its chief, and shall command such officer or member of department to take the accused and bring him forthwith before the magistrate or court issuing such warrant, to be dealt with according to law. A summons shall be directed to the officer or department, and shall command him to notify the accused by serving a copy of such summons upon him. The following form of warrant is sufficient:

The State of Ohio,
. . . . .County, ss:
To the Sheriff (other Officer):
Greetings:

Whereas there has been filed with me an affidavit of which the following is a copy (here copy) or the substance, (here set forth the substance, omitting formal parts). These are therefore to command you to take the said E.F., if he is found in your county, or if he is not found in your county, that you pursue after him in any other county in this state and take and safely keep the said E.F. so that you have his body forthwith before me or some other magistrate of said county to answer the said complaint and be further dealt with according to law.

Given under my hand this . . . . . . day of . . . . . ., 19. . . .

A.B., Judge of. . . . . .Court
Clerk of. . . . . .Court

The following form of summons is sufficient:

The State of Ohio, ... County, ss:
To the Bailiff or . . . . Constable:

Whereas there has been filed before me an Affidavit (Complaint) of which the following is a copy (here copy) or the substance (here set forth the substance, omitting formal parts). You are commanded to summon one said E.F. to appear before me on the . . . . . . day of . . . . . ., 19. . ., at . . . . . o'clock, ... M., at . . . . . . Building, ..., Ohio, to answer to said charge.

You will make due return of this summons forthwith upon service.

A.B., Judge of . . . . . . Court
Clerk of . . . . . . Court

HISTORY: 128 v 97. Eff 1-1-60.

Not analogous to former RC § 2935.18 (GC § 13432-17; 113 v 123(143); Bureau of Code Revision, 10-1-53), repealed 128 v 97(116), § 2, eff 1-1-60; but see former RC § 2935.20 (GC § 13432-19; 113 v 123(143); Bureau of Code Revision, 10-1-53; analogous to former GC §§ 13500, 13501; RS §§ 7137, 7138; S& C 816, 1402; 35 v 87; 36 v 18; 68 v 3).

§ 2935.19 Form of affidavit.

An affidavit in the form following is sufficient:
The State of Ohio,
. . . . County, ss:

Before me, A. B., personally came C. D., who being duly sworn according to law, deposes and says that on or about the . . . . day of . . . . ., at the county of . . . . . ., one E. F. (here describe the offense committed as nearly according to the nature thereof as the case will admit, in ordinary and concise language.)

Sworn to and subscribed before me, this . . . . . day of . . . . ., 19 . . . .

A.B., Judge

HISTORY: GC § 13432-18; 113 v 123(143), ch 11, § 18; Bureau of Code Revision, 10-1-53; 127 v 1039(1100). Eff 1-1-58.

§ 2935.20 Right to counsel.

After the arrest, detention, or any other taking into custody of a person, with or without a warrant, such person shall be permitted forthwith facilities to communicate with an attorney at law of his choice who is entitled to practice in the courts of this state, or to communicate with any other person of his choice for the purpose of obtaining counsel. Such communication may be made by a reasonable number of telephone calls or in any other reasonable manner. Such person shall have a right to be visited immediately by any attorney at law so obtained who is entitled to practice in the courts of this state, and to consult with him privately. No officer or any other agent of this state shall prevent, attempt to prevent, or advise such person against the communication, visit, or consultation provided for by this section.

Whoever violates this section shall be fined not less than twenty-five nor more than one hundred dollars or imprisoned not more than thirty days, or both.

HISTORY: 131 v 677. Eff 11-1-65.

Not analogous to former RC § 2935.20 (GC § 13432-19; 113 v 123(143); Bureau of Code Revision, 10-1-53), repealed 128 v 97(116), § 2, eff 1-1-60.

§ 2935.21 Security for costs.

When the offense charged is a misdemeanor, the magistrate or court, before issuing the warrant, may require the complainant, or if the magistrate considers the complainant irresponsible, may require that said complainant procure a person to be liable for the costs if the complaint is dismissed, and the complainant or other person shall acknowledge himself so liable, and such court or magistrate shall enter such acknowledgment on his docket. Such bond shall not be required of an officer authorized to make arrests when in the discharge of his official duty, or other person or officer authorized to assist the prosecuting attorney in the prosecution of offenders.

HISTORY: GC § 13432-20; 113 v 123(144), ch 11, § 20; Bureau of Code Revision. Eff 10-1-53.

§ 2935.22 Repealed, 128 v 97(116), § 2 [GC § 13432-21; 113 v 123(144); Bureau of Code Revision, 10-1-53]. Eff 1-1-60.

This section concerned issuing subpoenas for witnesses.

§ 2935.23 Felony investigation; examination of witnesses.

After a felony has been committed, and before any arrest has been made, the prosecuting attorney of the county, or any judge or magistrate, may cause subpoenas to issue, returnable before any court or magistrate, for any person to give information concerning such felony. The subpoenas shall require the witness to appear forthwith. Before such witness is required to give any information, he must be informed of the purpose of the inquiry, and that he is required to tell the truth concerning the same. He shall then be sworn and be examined under oath by the prosecuting attorney, or the court or magistrate, subject to the constitutional rights of the witness. Such examination shall be taken in writing in any form, and shall be filed with the court or magistrate taking the testimony. Witness fees shall be paid to such persons as in other cases.

HISTORY: GC § 13432-22; 113 v 123(144), ch 11, § 22; Bureau of Code Revision, 10-1-53; 134 v H 511. Eff 1-1-74.

§ 2935.24 Arrest by telegraph order.

A judge of a court of record may, by an endorsement under his hand upon a warrant of arrest, authorize the service thereof by telegraph, teletype, wire photo, or other means whereby a written or facsimile copy may be transmitted, and thereafter a copy of such warrant may be sent by any such means to any law enforcement officer. Such copy is effectual in the hands of any law enforcement officer and he shall proceed in the same manner under it as though he held the original warrant issued by the court making the endorsement, except that a state university law enforcement officer shall not arrest for a minor misdemeanor on the basis of a written or facsimile copy of a warrant of arrest. Every officer causing copies of warrants to be sent pursuant to this section, shall certify as correct and file in the office from which such warrant was sent, a copy of such warrant and endorsement thereon, and shall return the original with a statement of his action thereunder.

HISTORY: GC § 13432-23; 113 v 123(144), ch 11, § 23; Bureau of Code Revision, 10-1-53; 134 v H 511 (Eff 3-23-73); 137 v H 588. Eff 6-19-78.

§ 2935.25 Power of arrest.

Sections 2935.02 to 2935.24, inclusive, of the Revised Code do not affect or modify the power of arrest vested by law in other persons or officers than those named in section 2935.03 of the Revised Code.

HISTORY: GC § 13432-24; 113 v 123(145), ch 11, § 24; Bureau of Code Revision. Eff 10-1-53.

§ 2935.26 Issuance of citation for minor misdemeanor.

(A) Notwithstanding any other provision of the Revised Code, when a law enforcement officer is otherwise authorized to arrest a person for the commission of a minor misdemeanor, the officer shall not arrest the person, but shall issue a citation, unless one of the following applies:

(1) The offender requires medical care or is unable to provide for his own safety.

(2) The offender cannot or will not offer satisfactory evidence of his identity.

(3) The offender refuses to sign the citation.

(4) The offender has previously been issued a citation for the commission of that misdemeanor and has failed to do one of the following:

(a) Appear at the time and place stated in the citation;
(b) Comply with division (C) of this section.

(B) The citation shall contain all of the following:

(1) The name and address of the offender;
(2) A description of the offense and the numerical designation of the applicable statute or ordinance;
(3) The name of the person issuing the citation;
(4) An order for the offender to appear at a stated time and place;
(5) A notice that the offender may comply with division (C) of this section in lieu of appearing at the stated time and place;
(6) A notice that the offender is required to do one of the following and that he may be arrested if he fails to do one of them:

(a) Appear at the time and place stated in the citation;
(b) Comply with division (C) of this section.

(C) In lieu of appearing at the time and place stated in the citation, the offender may, within seven days after the date of issuance of the citation, do either of the following:

(1) Appear in person at the office of the clerk of the court stated in the citation, sign a plea of guilty and a waiver of trial provision that is on the citation, and pay the total amount of the fine and costs;

(2) Sign the guilty plea and waiver of trial provision of

the citation, and mail the citation and a check or money order for the total amount of the fine and costs to the office of the clerk of the court stated in the citation.

Remittance by mail of the fine and costs to the office of the clerk of the court stated in the citation constitutes a guilty plea and waiver of trial whether or not the guilty plea and waiver of trial provision of the citation are signed by the defendant.

(D) A law enforcement officer who issues a citation shall complete and sign the citation form, serve a copy of the completed form upon the offender and, without unnecessary delay, file the original citation with the court having jurisdiction over the offense.

(E) Each court shall establish a fine schedule that shall list the fine for each minor misdemeanor, and state the court costs. The fine schedule shall be prominently posted in the place where minor misdemeanor fines are paid.

(F) If an offender fails to appear and does not comply with division (C) of this section, the court may issue a supplemental citation, or a summons or warrant for the arrest of the offender pursuant to the Criminal Rules. Supplemental citations shall be in the form prescribed by division (B) of this section, but shall be issued and signed by the clerk of the court at which the citation directed the offender to appear and shall be served in the same manner as a summons.

HISTORY: 137 v S 351. Eff 10-25-78.

Not analogous to former RC § 2935.26 (GC § 13434-1; 113 v 123(149); Bureau of Code Revision, 10-1-53), repealed 128 v 97, § 2, eff 1-1-60.

§ 2935.27 Procedure after issuance of citation; penalties for failure to appear or comply.

(A)(1) If a law enforcement officer issues a citation to a person pursuant to section 2935.26 of the Revised Code and if the minor misdemeanor offense for which the citation is issued is an act prohibited by Chapter 4511., 4513., or 4549. of the Revised Code or an act prohibited by any municipal ordinance that is substantially similar to any section contained in Chapter 4511., 4513., or 4549. of the Revised Code, the officer shall inform the person, if the person has a current valid Ohio driver's or commercial driver's license, of the possible consequences of the person's actions as required under division (E) of this section, and also shall inform the person that the person is required either to appear at the time and place stated in the citation or to comply with division (C) of section 2935.26 of the Revised Code.

(2) If the person is an Ohio resident who does not have a current valid Ohio driver's or commercial driver's license or if the person is a resident of a state that is not a member of the nonresident violator compact, of which this state is a member pursuant to section 4511.95 of the Revised Code, the officer shall bring the person before the court with which the citation is required to be filed for the setting of a reasonable security by the court pursuant to division (F) of this section.

(B) A person who appears before a court to have security set under division (A)(2) of this section shall be given a receipt or other evidence of the deposit of the security by the court.

(C) Upon compliance with division (C) of section 2935.26 of the Revised Code by a person who was issued a citation, the clerk of the court shall notify the court. The court shall immediately return any sum of money, license, or other security deposited in relation to the citation to the person, or to any other person who deposited the security.

(D) If a person who has a current valid Ohio driver's or commercial driver's license and who was issued a citation fails to appear at the time and place specified on the citation, fails to comply with division (C) of section 2935.26 of the Revised Code, or fails to comply with or satisfy any judgment of the court within the time allowed by the court, the court shall declare the forfeiture of the person's license. Thirty days after the declaration of forfeiture, the court shall enter information relative to the forfeiture on a form approved and furnished by the registrar of motor vehicles, and forward the form to the registrar. The registrar shall suspend the person's driver's or commercial driver's license, send written notification of the suspension to the person at the person's last known address, and order the person to surrender the person's driver's or commercial driver's license to the registrar within forty-eight hours. No valid driver's or commercial driver's license shall be granted to the person until the court having jurisdiction of the offense that led to the suspension orders that the forfeiture be terminated. The court shall so order if the person, after having failed to appear in court at the required time and place to answer the charge or after having pleaded guilty to or been found guilty of the violation and having failed within the time allowed by the court to pay the fine imposed by the court, thereafter appears to answer the charge and pays any fine imposed by the court or pays the fine originally imposed by the court. The court shall inform the registrar of the termination of the forfeiture by entering information relative to the termination on a form approved and furnished by the registrar and sending the form to the registrar. The court also shall charge and collect from the person a fifteen-dollar processing fee to cover the costs of the bureau of motor vehicles in administering this section. The clerk of the court shall transmit monthly all such processing fees to the registrar for deposit into the state bureau of motor vehicles fund created by section 4501.25 of the Revised Code.

In addition, upon receipt of the copy of the declaration of forfeiture from the court, neither the registrar nor any deputy registrar shall accept any application for the registration or transfer of registration of any motor vehicle owned or leased by the person named in the declaration of forfeiture until the court having jurisdiction of the offense that led to the forfeiture orders that the forfeiture be terminated. However, for a motor vehicle leased by a person named in a declaration of forfeiture, the registrar shall not implement the preceding sentence until the registrar adopts procedures for that implementation under section 4503.39 of the Revised Code. Upon receipt by the registrar of an order terminating the forfeiture, the registrar shall take such measures as may be necessary to permit the person to register a motor vehicle owned or leased by the person or to transfer the registration of such a motor vehicle, if the person later makes application to take such action and the person otherwise is eligible to register the motor vehicle or to transfer the registration of it.

The registrar is not required to give effect to any declaration of forfeiture or order terminating a forfeiture unless the order is transmitted to the registrar by means of an electronic transfer system.

If the person who was issued the citation fails to appear at the time and place specified on the citation and fails to comply with division (C) of section 2935.26 of the Revised Code and the person has deposited a sum of money or other security in relation to the citation under division (A)(2) of this section, the deposit immediately shall be forfeited to the court.

This section does not preclude further action as authorized by division (F) of section 2935.26 of the Revised Code.

(E) A law enforcement officer who issues a person a minor misdemeanor citation for an act prohibited by Chapter 4511., 4513., or 4549. of the Revised Code or an act prohibited by a municipal ordinance that is substantially similar to any section contained in Chapter 4511., 4513., or 4549. of the Revised Code shall inform the person that if the person does not appear at the time and place stated on the citation or does not comply with division (C) of section 2935.26 of the Revised Code, the person's driver's or commercial driver's license will be suspended, the person will not be eligible for the reissuance of the license or the issuance of a new license or the issuance of a certificate of registration for a motor vehicle owned or leased by the person, until the person appears and complies with all orders of the court. The person also is subject to any applicable criminal penalties.

(F) A court setting security under division (A)(2) of this section shall do so in conformity with sections 2937.22 and 2937.23 of the Revised Code and the Rules of Criminal Procedure.

HISTORY: 137 v S 351 (Eff 10-25-78); 141 v S 356 (Eff 9-24-86); 143 v H 381 (Eff 7-1-89); 143 v S 338 (Eff 11-28-90); 144 v S 275 (Eff 7-1-93)†; 145 v H 687 (Eff 10-12-94); 146 v H 353 (Eff 9-17-96); 146 v S 121 (Eff 11-19-96); 147 v S 85. Eff 5-15-97.

Analogous to former RC § 2935.27 (GC § 13434-2; 113 v 123(149); Bureau of Code Revision, 10-1-53), repealed 128 v 97, § 2, eff 1-1-60.

The provisions of § 5 of SB 85 (147 v —) read as follows:

SECTION 5. Sections 2935.27, 2937.221, ° ° ° of the Revised Code are presented in this act as composites of the sections as amended by both Am. Sub. H.B. 353 and Am. Sub. S.B. 121 of the 121st General Assembly, with the new language of neither of the acts shown in capital letters. This is in recognition of the principle stated in division (B) of section 1.52 of the Revised Code that such amendments are to be harmonized where not substantively irreconcilable and constitutes a legislative finding that such is the resulting version in effect prior to the effective date of this act.

† See provisions, §§ 4, 5 of SB 62 (145 v —) following RC § 2903.04.

The provisions of § 4 of SB 121 (146 v —) read as follows:

SECTION 4. The Registrar of Motor Vehicles shall not be required to give effect to the amendments contained in Section 1 of this act that prohibit the Registrar from issuing or transferring a certificate of registration for a motor vehicle when so prohibited by the amendments until six months after the effective date of this act.

§ 2935.28 Names of traffic law violators damaging real property to be provided to owner.

(A) As used in this section, "motor vehicle" has the same meaning as in section 4501.01 of the Revised Code.

(B) If damage is caused to real property by the operation of a motor vehicle in, or during the violation of any section of the Revised Code or of any municipal ordinance, the law enforcement agency that investigates the case, upon request of the real property owner, shall provide the owner with the names of the persons who are charged with the commission of the offense. If a request for the names is made, the agency shall provide the names as soon as possible after the persons are charged with the offense.

(C) The personnel of law enforcement agencies who act pursuant to division (B) of this section in good faith are not liable in damages in a civil action allegedly arising from their actions taken pursuant to that division. Political subdivisions and the state are not liable in damages in a civil action allegedly arising from the actions of personnel of their law enforcement agencies if the personnel have immunity under this division.

HISTORY: 140 v H 666. Eff 3-14-85.

Not analogous to former RC § 2935.28 (GC § 13434-3; 113 v 123(149); Bureau of Code Revision, 10-1-53), repealed 128 v 97(116), § 2, eff 1-1-60.

[UNIFORM ACT ON FRESH PURSUIT]

§ 2935.29 Definition of fresh pursuit and state.

As used in sections 2935.30 and 2935.31 of the Revised Code:

(A) "Fresh pursuit" includes fresh pursuit as defined by the common law, and also the pursuit of a person who has committed a felony or who is reasonably suspected of having committed a felony. It includes the pursuit of a person suspected of having committed a supposed felony, though no felony has actually been committed, if there is reasonable ground for believing that a felony has been committed. Fresh pursuit does not necessarily imply instant pursuit, but pursuit without unreasonable delay.

(B) "State" includes the District of Columbia.

HISTORY: GC §§ 13434-7, 13434-8; 117 v 671; Bureau of Code Revision. Eff 10-1-53.

§ 2935.30 Authority of foreign police.

Any member of an organized state, county, or municipal peace unit of another state of the United States who enters this state in fresh pursuit, and continues within this state in such fresh pursuit, of a person in order to arrest him on the ground that he is believed to have committed a felony in such other state has the same authority to arrest and hold such person in custody as has any member of any organized state, county, or municipal peace unit of this state to arrest and hold in custody a person on the ground that he is believed to have committed a felony in this state.

This section does not make unlawful any arrest in this state which would otherwise be lawful.

HISTORY: GC §§ 13434-4, 13434-6; 117 v 671; Bureau of Code Revision. Eff 10-1-53.

§ 2935.31 Hearing before magistrate in county of arrest.

If an arrest is made in this state by an officer of another state under section 2935.30 of the Revised Code, he shall without unnecessary delay take the person arrested before a magistrate of the county in which the arrest was made, who shall conduct a hearing for the purpose of determining the lawfulness of the arrest. If the magistrate determines that the arrest was lawful he shall commit the person arrested to await for a reasonable time the issuance of an extradition warrant by the governor of this state, or admit him to bail for such purposes. If the magistrate determines that the arrest was unlawful he shall discharge the person arrested.

HISTORY: GC § 13434-5; 117 v 671; Bureau of Code Revision. Eff 10-1-53.

§ 2935.32 Broadcasting information of crime.

The board of county commissioners or the prosecuting attorney of any county, with the consent of the court of common pleas, may contract with any company engaged in broadcasting by radio, for the purpose of immediate broadcasting of information concerning any violent felony, when the perpetrator thereof has escaped. The sheriff and heads of police departments, immediately upon the commission of any such felony and the escape of such perpetrator, shall furnish all information concerning said crime and the perpetrator thereof, to said company with which such contract may be made, for the purpose of broadcasting. The reasonable cost of such broadcasting shall be paid by the county, out of the county treasury, on the order of the board.

HISTORY: GC § 13431-1; 113 v 123(139), ch 10, § 1; Bureau of Code Revision. Eff 10-1-53.

[ALCOHOLIC TREATMENT]

§ 2935.33 Commitment of alcoholics and intoxicated persons for inpatient care.

(A) If a person charged with a misdemeanor is taken before a judge of a court of record and if it appears to the judge that the person is an alcoholic or is suffering from acute alcohol intoxication and that the person would benefit from services provided by an alcohol and drug addiction program certified under Chapter 3793. of the Revised Code, the judge may place the person temporarily in a program certified under that chapter in the area in which the court has jurisdiction for inpatient care and treatment for an indefinite period not exceeding five days. The commitment does not limit the right to release on bail. The judge may dismiss a charge of a violation of division (B) of section 2917.11 of the Revised Code or OF a municipal ordinance substantially equivalent to that division if the defendant complies with all the conditions of treatment ordered by the court.

The court may order that any fines or court costs collected by the court from defendants who have received inpatient care from an alcohol and drug addiction program be paid, for the benefit of the program, to the board of alcohol, drug addiction, and mental health services of the alcohol, drug addiction, and mental health service district in which the program is located or to the director of alcohol and drug addiction services.

(B) If a person is being sentenced for a violation of division (B) of section 2917.11 or section 4511.19 of the Revised Code, a misdemeanor violation of section 2919.25 of the Revised Code, a misdemeanor violation of section 2919.27 of the Revised Code involving a protection order issued or consent agreement approved pursuant to section 2919.26 or 3113.31 of the Revised Code, or a violation of a municipal ordinance substantially equivalent to that division or any of those sections and if it appears to the judge at the time of sentencing that the person is an alcoholic or is suffering from acute alcohol intoxication and that, in lieu of imprisonment, the person would benefit from services provided by an alcohol and drug addiction program certified under Chapter 3793. of the Revised Code, the court may commit the person to close supervision in any facility in the area in which the court has jurisdiction that is, or is operated by, such a program. A commitment to close supervision for a misdemeanor violation of section 2919.25 of the Revised Code, a misdemeanor violation of section 2919.27 of the Revised Code involving a protection order issued or consent agreement approved pursuant to section 2919.26 or 3113.31 of the Revised Code, or a violation of any substantially equivalent municipal ordinance shall be in accordance with division (B) of section 2929.51 of the Revised Code. Such close supervision may include outpatient services and part-time release, except that a person convicted of a violation of division (A) of section 4511.19 of the Revised Code shall be confined to the facility for at least three days and except that a person convicted of a misdemeanor violation of section 2919.25 of the Revised Code, a misdemeanor violation of section 2919.27 of the Revised Code involving a protection order issued or consent agreement approved pursuant to section 2919.26 or 3113.31 of the Revised Code, or a violation of a substantially equivalent municipal ordinance shall be confined to the facility in accordance with the order of commitment. A commitment of a person to a facility for purposes of close supervision shall not exceed the maximum term for which the person could be imprisoned.

(C) A law enforcement officer who finds a person subject to prosecution for violation of division (B) of section 2917.11 of the Revised Code or a municipal ordinance substantially equivalent to that division and who has reasonable cause to believe that the person is an alcoholic or is suffering from acute alcohol intoxication and would benefit from immediate treatment immediately may place the person in an alcohol and drug addiction program certified under Chapter 3793. of the Revised Code in the area in which the person is found, for emergency treatment, in lieu of other arrest procedures, for a maximum period of forty-eight hours. During that time, if the person desires to leave such custody, he shall be released forthwith.

(D) As used in this section:

(1) "Alcoholic" has the same meaning as in section 3793.01 of the Revised Code;

(2) "Acute alcohol intoxication" means a heavy consumption of alcohol over a relatively short period of time, resulting in dysfunction of the brain centers controlling behavior, speech, and memory and causing characteristic withdrawal symptoms.

HISTORY: 134 v H 240 (Eff 4-28-72); 136 v H 1 (Eff 6-13-75); 136 v H 907 (Eff 8-25-76); 140 v H 37 (Eff 6-22-84); 141 v H 475 (Eff 3-7-86); 143 v H 317 (Eff 10-10-89); 145 v S 82 (Eff 5-4-94); 146 v S 2. Eff 7-1-96.

The effective date is set by section 6 of SB 2.

[PRE-TRIAL DIVERSION PROGRAMS]

§ 2935.36 Pre-trial diversion programs for certain offenders.

(A) The prosecuting attorney may establish pre-trial diversion programs for adults who are accused of committing criminal offenses and whom the prosecuting attorney believes probably will not offend again. The programs shall be operated pursuant to written standards approved by journal entry by the presiding judge or, in courts with only one judge, the judge of the court of common pleas and shall not be applicable to any of the following:

(1) Repeat offenders or dangerous offenders;

(2) Persons accused of an offense of violence, of a violation of section 2903.06, 2903.07, 2907.04, 2907.05, 2907.21, 2907.22, 2907.31, 2907.32, 2907.34, 2911.31, 2919.12, 2919.13, 2919.22, 2921.02, 2921.11, 2921.12, 2921.32, or 2923.20 of the Revised Code, or of a violation of section 2905.01, 2905.02, or 2919.23 of the Revised Code that, had it occurred prior to the effective date of this amendment, would have been a violation of section 2905.04 of the Revised Code as it existed prior to that date, with the exception that the prosecuting attorney may permit persons accused of any such offense to enter a pre-trial diversion program, if the prosecuting attorney finds any of the following:

(a) The accused did not cause, threaten, or intend serious physical harm to any person;

(b) The offense was the result of circumstances not likely to recur;

(c) The accused has no history of prior delinquency or criminal activity;

(d) The accused has led a law-abiding life for a substantial time before commission of the alleged offense;

(e) Substantial grounds tending to excuse or justify the alleged offense;

(3) Persons accused of a violation of Chapter 2925. or 3719. of the Revised Code;

(4) Drug dependent persons or persons in danger of becoming drug dependent persons, as defined in section 3719.011 [3719.01.1] of the Revised Code. However, this division does not affect the eligibility of such persons for treatment in lieu of conviction pursuant to section 2951.041 [2951.04.1] of the Revised Code.

(5) Persons accused of a violation of section 4511.19 of the Revised Code or a violation of any substantially similar municipal ordinance.

(B) An accused who enters a diversion program shall do all of the following:

(1) Waive, in writing and contingent upon the accused's successful completion of the program, the accused's right to a speedy trial, the preliminary hearing, the time period within which the grand jury may consider an indictment against the accused, and arraignment, unless the hearing, indictment, or arraignment has already occurred;

(2) Agree, in writing, to the tolling while in the program of all periods of limitation established by statutes or rules of court, that are applicable to the offense with which the accused is charged and to the conditions of the diversion program established by the prosecuting attorney.

(C) The trial court, upon the application of the prosecuting attorney, shall order the release from confinement of any accused who has agreed to enter a pre-trial diversion program and shall discharge and release any existing bail and release any sureties on recognizances and shall release the accused on a recognizance bond conditioned upon the accused's compliance with the terms of the diversion program. The prosecuting attorney shall notify every victim of the crime and the arresting officers of the prosecuting attorney's intent to permit the accused to enter a pre-trial diversion program. The victim of the crime and the arresting officers shall have the opportunity to file written objections with the prosecuting attorney prior to the commencement of the pre-trial diversion program.

(D) If the accused satisfactorily completes the diversion program, the prosecuting attorney shall recommend to the trial court that the charges against the accused be dismissed, and the court, upon the recommendation of the prosecuting attorney, shall dismiss the charges. If the accused chooses not to enter the prosecuting attorney's diversion program, or if the accused violates the conditions of the agreement pursuant to which the accused has been released, the accused may be brought to trial upon the charges in the manner provided by law, and the waiver executed pursuant to division (B)(1) of this section shall be void on the date the accused is removed from the program for the violation.

(E) As used in this section:

(1) "Repeat offender" means a person who has a history of persistent criminal activity and whose character and condition reveal a substantial risk that the person will commit another offense. It is prima-facie evidence that a person is a repeat offender if any of the following applies:

(a) Having been convicted of one or more offenses of violence and having been imprisoned pursuant to sentence for any such offense, the person commits a subsequent offense of violence;

(b) Having been convicted of one or more sexually oriented offenses as defined in section 2950.01 of the Revised Code and having been imprisoned pursuant to sentence for one or more of those offenses, the person commits a subsequent sexually oriented offense;

(c) Having been convicted of one or more theft offenses as defined in section 2913.01 of the Revised Code and having been imprisoned pursuant to sentence for one or more of those theft offenses, the person commits a subsequent theft offense;

(d) Having been convicted of one or more felony drug abuse offenses as defined in section 2925.01 of the Revised Code and having been imprisoned pursuant to sentence for one or more of those felony drug abuse offenses, the person commits a subsequent felony drug abuse offense;

(e) Having been convicted of two or more felonies and having been imprisoned pursuant to sentence for one or more felonies, the person commits a subsequent offense;

(f) Having been convicted of three or more offenses of any type or degree other than traffic offenses, alcoholic intoxication offenses, or minor misdemeanors and having been imprisoned pursuant to sentence for any such offense, the person commits a subsequent offense.

(2) "Dangerous offender" means a person who has committed an offense, whose history, character, and condition reveal a substantial risk that the person will be a danger to others, and whose conduct has been characterized by a pattern of repetitive, compulsive, or aggressive behavior with heedless indifference to the consequences.

HISTORY: 137 v H 473 (Eff 6-6-78); 141 v S 262 (Eff 3-20-87); 145 v S 82 (Eff 5-4-94); 146 v S 2 (Eff 7-1-96); 146 v H 180. Eff 7-1-97.

The effective date is set by section 5 of HB 180.

The provisions of § 5 of HB 180 (146 v —) read as follows:

Section 5. Sections 109.57, 2935.36, 2950.02, 2950.04, 2950.05, 2950.06, 2950.07, 2950.08, 2950.10, 2950.11, 2950.12, 2950.13, 2950.99, 2953.35, and 2953.54 of the Revised Code, as amended or enacted in Sections 1 and 2 of this act, shall take effect on July 1, 1997. The repeal of existing sections 109.57, 2935.36, 2950.08, 2950.99, 2953.35, and 2953.54 and sections 2950.02, 2950.04, 2950.05, 2950.06, and 2950.07 of the Revised Code by Section 2 of this act shall take effect on July 1, 1997, and the provisions of those sections shall remain in effect and shall be applicable to habitual sex offenders, as defined in the version of section 2950.01 of the Revised Code that is repealed by Section 2 of this act, until that date. Notwithstanding the repeal of existing sections 2950.01 and 2950.03 of the Revised Code by Section 2 of this act, the definitions and the duty to provide notice to habitual sex offenders who are being released from correctional institutions that are contained in the versions of those sections that are so repealed shall remain applicable to habitual sex offenders, as defined in the version of section 2950.01 of the Revised Code that is so repealed, until July 1, 1997.

CHAPTER 2937: PRELIMINARY EXAMINATION; BAIL

Section
2937.01 Definitions.

[PRELIMINARY EXAMINATION]

2937.02 Announcement of charge and rights of accused by court.
2937.03 Arraignment; counsel; bail.
2937.04 Motion for dismissal.
2937.05 Discharge on motion to dismiss; amendment of complaint.
2937.06 Pleas.
2937.07 Action on pleas of "guilty" and "no contest" in misdemeanor cases.
2937.08 Action on pleas of "not guilty" or "once in jeopardy" in misdemeanor cases.
[2937.08.1] 2937.081 Repealed.
2937.09 Procedure in felony cases.
2937.10 Hearing set in felony cases.
2937.11 Presentation of state's case.
2937.12 Motion for discharge; presentation on behalf of accused; finding of court.
2937.13 Basis for finding; no appeal; further prosecution.
2937.14 Entry of reason for change in charge.
2937.15 Transcript of proceedings.
2937.16 When witnesses shall be recognized to appear.
2937.17 Recognizance for minor.
2937.18 Refusal of witness to enter into a recognizance.
2937.19 Subpoena of witnesses or documents.
2937.20 Renumbered.
2937.21 Continuance.

[BAIL AND RECOGNIZANCE]

2937.22 Forms of bail; receipt.
[2937.22.1] 2937.221 License as bond; notice of penalties.
2937.23 Amount of bail.
2937.24 Oath to surety; form of affidavit.
2937.25 Lien; form.
2937.26 Cancellation of lien; form.
2937.27 Duties of county recorder.
2937.28 Transmission of recognizance.
[2937.28.1] 2937.281 Requirements of recognizance.
2937.29 Release on own recognizance.
2937.30 Recognizance when accused discharged.
2937.31 Recognizance or deposit for appearance of accused.
2937.32 Confinement for unbailable offenses and lack of sufficient bail.
2937.33 Receipt of recognizance.
2937.34 Accused unlawfully detained; examining court to be held.
2937.35 Forfeit of bail.
2937.36 Forfeiture proceedings.
2937.37 Levy on property in judgment against surety.
2937.38 Minority no defense in forfeiture proceedings.
2937.39 Remission of penalty.
2937.40 Release of bail and sureties.
2937.41 Return of bail; notice of discharge of recognizance.
2937.42 Defect in form of recognizance.
2937.43 Failure to appear; issuance of warrant.
2937.44 Forms of recognizance.
2937.45 Forms of commitments.
2937.46 Supreme court authorized to set uniform procedures in traffic cases.
2937.99 Penalties.

§ 2937.01 Definitions.

The definition of "magistrate" set forth in section 2931.01 of the Revised Code, and the definitions of "peace officer," "prosecutor," and "offense" set forth in section 2935.01 of the Revised Code apply to Chapter 2937. of the Revised Code.

HISTORY: Bureau of Code Revision, 10-1-53; 128 v 97. Eff 1-1-60.

[PRELIMINARY EXAMINATION]

§ 2937.02 Announcement of charge and rights of accused by court.

When, after arrest, the accused is taken before a court or magistrate, or when the accused appears pursuant to terms of summons or notice, the affidavit or complaint being first filed, the court or magistrate shall, before proceeding further:

(A) Inform the accused of the nature of the charge against him and the identity of the complainant and permit the accused or his counsel to see and read the affidavit or complaint or a copy thereof;

(B) Inform the accused of his right to have counsel and the right to a continuance in the proceedings to secure counsel;

(C) Inform the accused of the effect of pleas of guilty, not guilty, and no contest, of his right to trial by jury, and the necessity of making written demand therefor;

(D) If the charge be a felony, inform the accused of the nature and extent of possible punishment on conviction and of the right to preliminary hearing. Such information may be given to each accused individually or, if at any time there exists any substantial number of defendants to be arraigned at the same session, the judge or magistrate may, by general announcement or by distribution of printed matter, advise all those accused concerning those rights general in their nature, and informing as to individual matters at arraignment.

HISTORY: 128 v 97. Eff 1-1-60.

Analogous to former RC § 2937.02 (GC § 13433-1; 113 v 123(145), ch 12; 115 v 530; Bureau of Code Revision, 10-1-53), repealed 128 v 97(116), § 2, eff 1-1-60.

§ 2937.03 Arraignment; counsel; bail.

After the announcement, as provided by section 2937.02 of the Revised Code the accused shall be arraigned by the magistrate, or clerk, or prosecutor of the court reading the affidavit or complaint, or reading its substance, omitting purely formal parts, to him unless such reading be waived. The judge or magistrate shall then inquire of the accused whether he understands the nature of the charge. If he does not indicate understanding, the magistrate shall give explanation in terms of the statute or ordinance claimed violated. If he is not represented by counsel and expresses desire to consult with an attorney at law, the judge or magistrate shall continue the case for a reasonable time to allow him to send for or consult with counsel and shall set bail for such later appearance if the offense is bailable. If the accused is not able to make bail, or the offense is not bailable, the court or magistrate shall require the officer having custody of accused forthwith to take a message to any attorney at law within the municipal corporation where accused is detained, or to make available to accused forthwith use of telephone, for calling to arrange for legal counsel or bail.

HISTORY: 128 v 97 (Eff 1-1-60); 129 v 582(749). Eff 1-10-61.

Not analogous to former RC § 2937.03 (GC § 13433-2; 113 v 123(145); Bureau of Code Revision, 10-1-53), repealed 128 v 97(116), § 2, eff 1-1-60; but see former RC § 2935.17 (GC § 13432-16; 113 v 123(143); Bureau of Code Revision, 10-1-53).

§ 2937.04 Motion for dismissal.

If accused does not desire counsel or, having engaged counsel, appears at the end of granted continuance, he may then raise, by motion to dismiss the affidavit or complaint, any exception thereto which could be asserted against an indictment or information by motion to quash, plea in abatement, or demurrer. Such motion may be made orally and ruled upon by the court or magistrate at the time of presentation, with minute of motion and ruling made in the journal (if a court of record) or on the docket (if a court not of record) or such motion may be presented in writing and set down for argument at later time. Where the motion attacks a defect in the record by facts extrinsic thereto, proof may be offered by testimony or affidavit.

HISTORY: 128 v 97. Eff 1-1-60.

Not analogous to former RC § 2937.04 (GC § 13433-3; 113 v 123(145); Bureau of Code Revision, 10-1-53), repealed 128 v 97(116), § 2, eff 1-1-60.

§ 2937.05 Discharge on motion to dismiss; amendment of complaint.

If the motion pursuant to section 2937.04 of the Revised Code be sustained, accused shall be discharged unless the court or magistrate finds that the defect can be corrected without changing the nature of the charge, in which case he may order the complaint amended or a proper affidavit filed forthwith and require the accused to plead thereto. The discharge of accused upon the sustaining of a motion to dismiss shall not be considered a bar to further prosecution either of felony or misdemeanor.

HISTORY: 128 v 97. Eff 1-1-60.

Not analogous to former RC § 2937.05 (GC § 13433-4; 113 v 123(145); Bureau of Code Revision, 10-1-53), repealed 128 v 97(116), § 2, eff 1-1-60.

§ 2937.06 Pleas.

(A) After all motions are disposed of or if no motion is presented, the court or magistrate shall require the accused to plead to the charge.

(1) In cases of felony, only a plea of not guilty or a written plea of guilty shall be received and if the defendant declines to plead, a plea of not guilty shall be entered for the defendant and further proceedings had as set forth in sections 2937.09 to 2937.12 of the Revised Code.

(2) In cases of misdemeanor, the following pleas may be received:

(a) Guilty;

(b) Not guilty;

(c) No contest;

(d) Once in jeopardy, which includes the defenses of former conviction or former acquittal.

(B) Prior to accepting a plea of guilty or a plea of no contest under division (A) of this section, the court shall comply with sections 2943.031 [2943.03.1] and 2943.032 [2943.03.2] of the Revised Code.

(C) Entry of any plea pursuant to this section shall constitute a waiver of any objection that could be taken advantage of by motion pursuant to section 2937.04 of the Revised Code.

HISTORY: 128 v 97 (Eff 1-1-60); 143 v S 95 (Eff 10-2-89); 146 v S 2. Eff 7-1-96.

The effective date is set by section 6 of SB 2.

§ 2937.07 Action on pleas of "guilty" and "no contest" in misdemeanor cases.

If the offense be a misdemeanor and the accused pleads guilty thereto, the court or magistrate shall receive and enter such plea unless he believes it made through fraud, collusion;[,] or mistake in which case he shall enter a plea of not guilty and set the matter for trial pursuant to Chapter 2938. of the Revised Code. Upon a plea of guilty being received the court or magistrate shall call for explanation of circumstances of the offense from the affiant or complainant or his representatives, and after hearing the same, together with any statement of accused, shall proceed to pronounce sentence or continue the matter for the purpose of imposing sentence or admitting the defendant to probation.

If the plea be "no contest" or words of similar import in pleading to a misdemeanor, it shall constitute a stipulation that the judge or magistrate may make finding of guilty or not guilty from the explanation of circumstances, and if guilt be found, impose or continue for sentence accordingly. Such plea shall not be construed to import an admission of any fact at issue in the criminal charge in any subsequent action or proceeding, whether civil or criminal.

HISTORY: 128 v 97. Eff 1-1-60.

Not analogous to former RC § 2937.07 (GC § 13433-6; 113 v 123(146); Bureau of Code Revision, 10-1-53), repealed 128 v 97(116), § 2, eff 1-1-60; but see former RC § 2937.10 (GC §

13433-9; 113 v 123(146); Bureau of Code Revision, 10-1-53; 127 v 1039(1100)).

§ 2937.08 Action on pleas of "not guilty" or "once in jeopardy" in misdemeanor cases.

Upon a plea of not guilty or a plea of once in jeopardy, if the charge be a misdemeanor in a court of record, the court shall proceed to set the matter for trial at a future time, pursuant to Chapter 2938. of the Revised Code, and shall let accused to bail pending such trial. Or he may, but only if both prosecutor and accused expressly consent, set the matter for trial forthwith.

Upon the entry of such pleas to a charge of misdemeanor in a court not of record, the magistrate shall forthwith set the matter for future trial or, with the consent of both state and defendant may set trial forthwith, both pursuant to Chapter 2938. of the Revised Code, provided that if the nature of the offense is such that right to jury trial exists, such matter shall not be tried before him unless the accused, by writing subscribed by him, waives a jury and consents to be tried by the magistrate.

If the defendant in such event does not waive right to jury trial, then the magistrate shall require the accused to enter into recognizance to appear before court of record in the county, set by such magistrate, and the magistrate shall thereupon certify all papers filed, together with transcript of proceedings and accrued costs to date, and such recognizance if given, to such designated court of record. Such transfer shall not require the filing of indictment or information and trial shall proceed in the transferee court pursuant to Chapter 2938. of the Revised Code.

HISTORY: 128 v 97. Eff 1-1-60.

Not analogous to former RC § 2937.08 (GC § 13433-7; 113 v 123(146); Bureau of Code Revision, 10-1-53), repealed 128 v 97(116), § 2, eff 1-1-60; but see former RC § 2937.11 (GC § 13433-10; 113 v 123(147); Bureau of Code Revision, 10-1-53; 127 v 1039(1101)).

[§ 2937.08.1] § 2937.081 Repealed, 145 v S 186, § 2 [140 v S 76]. Eff 10-12-94.

This section provided for prosecutor to notify victim or agent of date, time and place of trial or other final disposition. See now RC Chapter 2930.

§ 2937.09 Procedure in felony cases.

If the charge is a felony, the court or magistrate shall, before receiving a plea of guilty, advise the accused that such plea constitutes an admission which may be used against him at a later trial. If the defendant enters a written plea of guilty or, pleading not guilty, affirmatively waives the right to have the court or magistrate take evidence concerning the offense, the court or magistrate forthwith and without taking evidence may find that the crime has been committed and that there is probable and reasonable cause to hold the defendant for trial pursuant to indictment by the grand jury, and, if the offense is bailable, require the accused to enter into recognizance in such amount as it determines to appear before the court of common pleas pursuant to indictment, otherwise to be confined until the grand jury has considered and reported the matter.

HISTORY: 128 v 97 (Eff 1-1-60); 129 v 582(750); Eff 1-10-61.

Not analogous to former RC § 2937.09 (GC § 13433-8; 113 v 123(146); Bureau of Code Revision, 10-1-53), repealed 128 v 97(116), § 2, eff 1-1-60; but see former RC § 2937.11 (GC § 13433-10; 113 v 123(147); Bureau of Code Revision, 10-1-53; 127 v 1039(1101)).

§ 2937.10 Hearing set in felony cases.

If the charge be a felony and there be no written plea of guilty or waiver of examination, or the court or magistrate refuses to receive such waiver, the court or magistrate, with the consent of the prosecutor and the accused, may set the matter for hearing forthwith, otherwise he shall set the matter for hearing at a fixed time in the future and shall notify both prosecutor and defendant promptly of such time of hearing.

HISTORY: 128 v 97. Eff 1-1-60.

Not analogous to former RC § 2937.10 (GC § 13433-9; 113 v 123(146); Bureau of Code Revision, 10-1-53; 127 v 1039(1100)), repealed 128 v 97(116), § 2, eff 1-1-60.

§ 2937.11 Presentation of state's case.

(A)(1) As used in this section, "victim" includes any person who was a victim of a felony violation identified in division (B) of this section or a felony offense of violence or against whom was directed any conduct that constitutes, or that is an element of, a felony violation identified in division (B) of this section or a felony offense of violence.

(2) At the preliminary hearing set pursuant to section 2937.10 of the Revised Code and the Criminal Rules, the prosecutor may state, but is not required to state, orally the case for the state and shall then proceed to examine witnesses and introduce exhibits for the state. The accused and the magistrate have full right of cross examination, and the accused has the right of inspection of exhibits prior to their introduction. The hearing shall be conducted under the rules of evidence prevailing in criminal trials generally. On motion of either the state or the accused, witnesses shall be separated and not permitted in the hearing room except when called to testify.

(B) In a case involving an alleged felony violation of section 2905.05, 2907.02, 2907.03, 2907.04, 2907.05, 2907.21, 2907.24, 2907.31, 2907.32, 2907.321 [2907.32.1], 2907.322 [2907.32.2], 2907.323 [2907.32.3], or 2919.22 of the Revised Code or an alleged felony offense of violence and in which an alleged victim of the alleged violation or offense was less than thirteen years of age when the complaint or information was filed, whichever occurred earlier, upon motion of the prosecution, the testimony of the child victim at the preliminary hearing may be taken in a room other than the room in which the preliminary hearing is being conducted and be televised, by closed circuit equipment, into the room in which the preliminary hearing is being conducted, in accordance with division (C) of section 2945.481 [2945.48.1] of the Revised Code.

(C) In a case involving an alleged felony violation listed in division (B) of this section or an alleged felony offense of violence and in which an alleged victim of the alleged violation or offense was less than thirteen years of age when the complaint or information was filed, whichever occurred earlier, the court, on written motion of the prosecutor in the case filed at least three days prior to the hearing, shall order that all testimony of the child victim be recorded and preserved on videotape, in addition to being recorded for purposes of the transcript of the proceeding. If such an order is issued, it shall specifically identify the child victim concerning whose testimony it pertains, apply only during the testimony of the child victim it specifically identifies, and apply to all testimony of the child victim presented at the hearing, regardless of whether the child victim is called as a witness by the prosecution or by the defense.

HISTORY: 128 v 97 (Eff 1-1-60); 141 v H 108 (Eff 10-14-86); 146 v H 445 (Eff 9-3-96); 147 v S 53. Eff 10-14-97.

Not analogous to former RC § 2937.11 (GC § 13433-10; 113 v 123(147); Bureau of Code Revision, 10-1-53; 127 v 1039(1101)), repealed 128 v 97(116), § 2, eff 1-1-60.

The provisions of §3(H) of HB 445 (146 v —) read as follows:

SECTION 3. ° ° °

(H) Divisions (B) and (C) of section 2937.11 of the Revised Code, as amended by this act, apply to a case involving an alleged commission of the offense of felonious sexual penetration in violation of former section 2907.12 of the Revised Code.

§ 2937.12 Motion for discharge; presentation on behalf of accused; finding of court.

(A) At the conclusion of the presentation of the state's case accused may move for discharge for failure of proof or may offer evidence on his own behalf. Prior to the offering of evidence on behalf of the accused, unless accused is then represented by counsel, the court or magistrate shall advise accused:

(1) That any testimony of witnesses offered by him in the proceeding may, if unfavorable in any particular, be used against him at later trial;

(2) That accused himself may make a statement, not under oath, regarding the charge, for the purpose of explaining the facts in evidence;

(3) That he may refuse to make any statement and such refusal may not be used against him at trials [trial];

(4) That any statement he makes may be used against him at trial.

(B) Upon conclusion of all the evidence and the statement, if any, of the accused, the court or magistrate shall either:

(1) Find that the crime alleged has been committed and that there is probable and reasonable cause to hold or recognize defendant to appear before the court of common pleas of the county or any other county in which venue appears, for trial pursuant to indictment by grand jury;

(2) Find that there is probable cause to hold or recognize defendant to appear before the court of common pleas for trial pursuant to indictment or information on such other charge, felony or misdemeanor, as the evidence indicates was committed by accused;

(3) Find that a misdemeanor was committed and there is probable cause to recognize accused to appear before himself or some other court inferior to the court of common pleas for trial upon such charge;

(4) Order the accused discharged from custody.

HISTORY: 128 v 97. Eff 1-1-60.

Somewhat analogous to former RC §§ 2937.12, 2937.14 (GC §§ 13433-11, 13433-13; 113 v 123(147); Bureau of Code Revision, 10-1-53), repealed 128 v 97(116), § 2, eff 1-1-60.

§ 2937.13 Basis for finding; no appeal; further prosecution.

In entering a finding, pursuant to section 2937.12 of the Revised Code, the court, while weighing credibility of witness, shall not be required to pass on the weight of the evidence and any finding requiring accused to stand trial on any charge shall be based solely on the presence of substantial credible evidence thereof. No appeal shall lie from such decision nor shall the discharge of defendant be a bar to further prosecution by indictment or otherwise.

HISTORY: 128 v 97. Eff 1-1-60.

Not analogous to former RC § 2937.13 (GC § 13433-12; 113 v 123(147); Bureau of Code Revision, 10-1-53), repealed 128 v 97(116), § 2, eff 1-1-60.

§ 2937.14 Entry of reason for change in charge.

In any case in which accused is held or recognized to appear for trial on any charge other than the one on which he was arraigned the court or magistrate shall enter the reason for such charge on the journal of the court (if a court of record) or on the docket (if a court not of record) and shall file with the papers in the case the text of the charge found by him to be sustained by the evidence.

HISTORY: 128 v 97. Eff 1-1-60.

Not analogous to former RC § 2937.14 (GC § 13433-13; 113 v 123(147); Bureau of Code Revision, 10-1-53), repealed 128 v 97(116), § 2, eff 1-1-60.

§ 2937.15 Transcript of proceedings.

Upon the conclusion of the hearing and finding, the

magistrate, or if a court of record, the clerk of such court, shall complete all notations of appearance, motions, pleas, and findings on the criminal docket of the court, and shall transmit a transcript of the appearance docket entries, together with a copy of the original complaint and affidavits, if any, filed with the complaint, the journal or docket entry of reason for changes in the charge, if any, together with the order setting bail and the bail deposit, if any, filed, and together with the videotaped testimony, if any, prepared in accordance with division (C) of section 2937.11 of the Revised Code, to the clerk of the court in which the accused is to appear. Such transcript shall contain an itemized account of the costs accrued.

HISTORY: 128 v 97 (Eff 1-1-60); 141 v H 108. Eff 10-14-86.

Not analogous to former RC § 2937.15 (GC § 13433-14; 113 v 123(147); Bureau of Code Revision, 10-1-53), repealed 128 v 97(116), § 2, eff 1-1-60; but see former RC § 2937.19.

§ 2937.16 When witnesses shall be recognized to appear.

When an accused enters into a recognizance or is committed in default thereof, the judge or magistrate shall require such witnesses against the prisoner as he finds necessary, to enter into a recognizance to appear and testify before the proper court at a proper time, and not depart from such court without leave. If the judge or magistrate finds it necessary he may require such witnesses to give sufficient surety to appear at such court.

HISTORY: GC § 13433-15; 113 v 123(147), ch 12, § 15; Bureau of Code Revision. Eff 10-1-53.

§ 2937.17 Recognizance for minor.

A person may be liable in a recognizance for a minor to appear as a witness, or the judge or magistrate may take the minor's recognizance, in a sufficient sum, which is valid notwithstanding the disability of minority.

HISTORY: GC § 13433-16; 113 v 123(148), ch 12, § 16; Bureau of Code Revision. Eff 10-1-53.

§ 2937.18 Refusal of witness to enter into a recognizance.

If a witness ordered to give recognizance fails to comply with such order, the judge or magistrate shall commit him to such custody or open or close detention as may be appropriate under the circumstances, until he complies with the order or is discharged. Commitment of the witness may be to the custody of any suitable person or public or private agency, or to an appropriate detention facility other than a jail, or to a jail, but the witness shall not be confined in association with prisoners charged with or convicted of crime. The witness, in lieu of the fee ordinarily allowed witnesses, shall be allowed twenty-five dollars for each day of custody or detention under such order, and shall be allowed mileage as provided for other witnesses, calculated on the distance from his home to the place of giving testimony and return. All proceedings in the case or cases in which the witness is held to appear shall be given priority over other cases and had with all due speed.

HISTORY: GC § 13433-17; 113 v 123(148), ch 12, § 17; Bureau of Code Revision, 10-1-53; 134 v H 511. Eff 3-23-73.

§ 2937.19 Subpoena of witnesses or documents.

The magistrate or judge or clerk of the court in which proceedings are being had may issue subpoenas or other process to bring witnesses or documents before the magistrate or court in hearings pending before him either under Chapter 2937. or 2938. of the Revised Code.

In complaints to keep the peace a subpoena must be served within the county, or, in cases of misdemeanors and ordinance offenses, it may be served at any place in this state within one hundred miles of the place where the court or magistrate is scheduled to sit; in felony cases it may be served at any place within this state. In cases where such process is to be served outside the county, it may be issued to be served either by the bailiff or constable of the court or by a sheriff or police officer either by the county in which the court or magistrate sits or in which process is to be served.

HISTORY: 128 v 97 (Eff 1-1-60); 129 v 582(750). Eff 1-10-61.

Not analogous to former RC § 2937.19 (GC § 13433-18; 113 v 123(148); Bureau of Code Revision, 10-1-53), repealed 128 v 97(116), § 2, eff 1-1-60.

§ 2937.20 Amended and renumbered RC § 2701.03.1 in 146 v S 263. Eff 11-20-96.

§ 2937.21 Continuance.

No continuance at any stage of the proceeding, including that for determination of a motion, shall extend for more than ten days unless both the state and the accused consent thereto. Any continuance or delay in ruling contrary to the provisions of this section shall, unless procured by defendant or his counsel, be grounds for discharge of the defendant forthwith.

HISTORY: 128 v 97. Eff 1-1-60.

Not analogous to former RC § 2937.21 (GC § 13435-1; 113 v 123(149); Bureau of Code Revision, 10-1-53), repealed 128 v 97(116), § 2, eff 1-1-60.

The substance of former RC § 2937.21 is now found in RC § 2937.22.

[BAIL AND RECOGNIZANCE]

§ 2937.22 Forms of bail; receipt.

Bail is security for the appearance of an accused to

appear and answer to a specific criminal or quasi-criminal charge in any court or before any magistrate at a specific time or at any time to which a case may be continued, and not depart without leave. It may take any of the following forms:

(A) The deposit of cash by the accused or by some other person for him;

(B) The deposit by the accused or by some other person for him in form of bonds of the United States, this state, or any political subdivision thereof in a face amount equal to the sum set by the court or magistrate. In case of bonds not negotiable by delivery such bonds shall be properly endorsed for transfer.

(C) The written undertaking by one or more persons to forfeit the sum of money set by the court or magistrate, if the accused is in default for appearance, which shall be known as a recognizance.

All bail shall be received by the clerk of the court, deputy clerk of court, or by the magistrate, or by a special referee appointed by the supreme court pursuant to section 2937.46 of the Revised Code, and, except in cases of recognizances, receipt shall be given therefor by him.

HISTORY: 128 v 97. Eff 1-1-60.

Not analogous to former RC § 2937.22 (GC § 13435-2; 113 v 123(149); Bureau of Code Revision, 10-1-53), repealed 128 v 97(116), § 2, eff 1-1-60; but see former RC § 2937.21 (GC § 13435-1; 113 v 123(149); Bureau of Code Revision, 10-1-53).

The substance of former RC § 2937.22 is now found in RC § 2937.23.

[§ 2937.22.1] § 2937.221 License as bond; notice of penalties.

(A) A person arrested without warrant for any violation listed in division (B) of this section, and having a current valid Ohio driver's or commercial driver's license, if the person has been notified of the possible consequences of the person's actions as required by division (C) of this section, may post bond by depositing the license with the arresting officer if the officer and person so choose, or with the local court having jurisdiction if the court and person so choose. The license may be used as bond only during the period for which it is valid.

When an arresting officer accepts the driver's or commercial driver's license as bond, the officer shall note the date, time, and place of the court appearance on "the violator's notice to appear" and the notice shall serve as a valid Ohio driver's or commercial driver's license until the date and time appearing thereon. The arresting officer immediately shall forward the license to the appropriate court.

When a local court accepts the license as bond or continues the case to another date and time, it shall provide the person with a card in a form approved by the registrar of motor vehicles setting forth the license number, name, address, the date and time of the court appearance, and a statement that the license is being held as bond. The card shall serve as a valid license until the date and time contained in the card.

The court may accept other bond at any time and return the license to the person. The court shall return the license to the person when judgment is satisfied, including, but not limited to, compliance with any court orders, unless a suspension or revocation is part of the penalty imposed.

Neither "the violator's notice to appear" nor a court granted card shall continue driving privileges beyond the expiration date of the license.

If the person arrested fails to appear in court at the date and time set by the court or fails to satisfy the judgment of the court, including, but not limited to, compliance with all court orders within the time allowed by the court, the court may declare the forfeiture of the person's license. Thirty days after the declaration of forfeiture, the court shall forward the person's license to the registrar. The court also shall enter information relative to the forfeiture on a form approved and furnished by the registrar and send the form to the registrar who shall suspend the license and send written notification of the suspension to the person at the person's last known address. No valid driver's or commercial driver's license shall be granted to the person until the court having jurisdiction orders that the forfeiture be terminated. The court shall inform the registrar of the termination of the forfeiture by entering information relative to the termination on a form approved and furnished by the registrar and sending the form to the registrar. The court also shall charge and collect from the person a processing fee of fifteen dollars to cover the costs of the bureau of motor vehicles in administering this section. The clerk of the court shall transmit monthly all such processing fees to the registrar for deposit into the state bureau of motor vehicles fund created by section 4501.25 of the Revised Code.

In addition, upon receipt from the court of the copy of the declaration of forfeiture, neither the registrar nor any deputy registrar shall accept any application for the registration or transfer of registration of any motor vehicle owned by or leased in the name of the person named in the declaration of forfeiture until the court having jurisdiction over the offense that led to the suspension issues an order terminating the forfeiture. However, for a motor vehicle leased in the name of a person named in a declaration of forfeiture, the registrar shall not implement the preceding sentence until the registrar adopts procedures for that implementation under section 4503.39 of the Revised Code. Upon receipt by the registrar of such an order, the registrar also shall take such measures as may be necessary to permit the person to register a motor vehicle the person owns or leases or to transfer the registration of such a vehicle if the person later makes a proper application and otherwise is eligible to be issued or to transfer a motor vehicle registration.

(B) Division (A) of this section applies to persons arrested for violation of:

(1) Any of the provisions of Chapter 4511. or 4513. of the Revised Code, except sections 4511.19, 4511.20, 4511.251 [4511.25.1], and 4513.36 of the Revised Code;

(2) Any municipal ordinance substantially similar to a section included in division (B)(1) of this section;

(3) Any bylaw, rule, or regulation of the Ohio turnpike commission substantially similar to a section included in division (B)(1) of this section.

Division (A) of this section does not apply to those persons issued a citation for the commission of a minor misdemeanor under section 2935.26 of the Revised Code.

(C) No license shall be accepted as bond by an arresting officer or by a court under this section until the officer or court has notified the person that, if the person deposits the license with the officer or court and either does not appear on the date and at the time set by the officer or the court, if the court sets a time, or does not satisfy any judgment rendered, including, but not limited to, compliance with all court orders, the license will be suspended, and the person will not be eligible for reissuance of the license or issuance of a new license, or the issuance of a certificate of registration for a motor vehicle owned or leased by the person until the person appears and complies with any order issued by the court. The person also is subject to any criminal penalties that may apply to the person.

HISTORY: 135 v H 234 (Eff 9-24-73); 136 v H 1 (Eff 6-13-75); 137 v S 351 (Eff 10-25-78); 141 v S 356 (Eff 9-24-86); 143 v H 381 (Eff 7-1-89); 143 v S 49 (Eff 11-3-89); 145 v H 687 (Eff 10-12-94); 146 v H 353 (Eff 9-17-96); 146 v S 121 (Eff 11-19-96); 147 v S 85. Eff 5-15-97.

See provisions, § 5 of SB 85 (147 v —) following RC § 2935.27.

See provisions, § 4 of SB 121 (146 v —) following RC § 2935.27.

§ 2937.23 Amount of bail.

(A) In a case involving a felony, the judge or magistrate shall fix the amount of bail. In a case involving a misdemeanor or a violation of a municipal ordinance and not involving a felony, the judge, magistrate, or clerk of the court may fix the amount of bail and may do so in accordance with a schedule previously fixed by the judge or magistrate, or, in a case when the judge, magistrate, or clerk of the court is not readily available, the sheriff, deputy sheriff, marshal, deputy marshal, police officer, or jailer having custody of the person charged may fix the amount of bail in accordance with a schedule previously fixed by the judge or magistrate and shall take the bail only in the county courthouse, the municipal or township building, or the county or municipal jail. In all cases, the bail shall be fixed with consideration of the seriousness of the offense charged, the previous criminal record of the defendant, and the probability of the defendant appearing at the trial of the case.

(B) In any case involving an alleged violation of section 2919.27 of the Revised Code or of a municipal ordinance that is substantially similar to that section and in which the court finds that either of the following criteria applies, the court shall determine whether it will order an evaluation of the mental condition of the defendant pursuant to section 2919.271 [2919.27.1] of the Revised Code and, if it decides to so order, shall issue the order requiring that evaluation before it sets bail for the person charged with the violation:

(1) Regarding an alleged violation of a temporary protection order or consent agreement, that the violation allegedly involves conduct by the defendant that caused physical harm to the person or property of a family or household member covered by the order or agreement or conduct by that defendant that caused a family or household member to believe that the defendant would cause physical harm to that member or that member's property;

(2) Regarding an alleged violation of an anti-stalking protection order or a protection order issued by a court of another state, as defined in section 2919.27 of the Revised Code, that the violation allegedly involves conduct by the defendant that caused physical harm to the person or property of the person covered by the order or conduct by that defendant that caused the person covered by the order to believe that the defendant would cause physical harm to that person or that person's property.

HISTORY: 128 v 97 (Eff 1-1-60); 129 v 557 (Eff 10-18-61); 141 v H 475 (Eff 3-7-86); 144 v H 536 (Eff 11-5-92); 146 v S 2 (Eff 7-1-96); 147 v S 1. Eff 10-21-97.

Not analogous to former RC § 2937.23 (GC § 13435-3; 113 v 123(150); Bureau of Code Revision, 10-1-53), repealed 128 v 97(116), § 2, eff 1-1-60; but see former RC § 2937.22 (GC § 13435-2; 113 v 129(149); Bureau of Code Revision, 10-1-53).

The substance of former RC § 2937.23 is now found in RC § 2937.28.1.

§ 2937.24 Oath to surety; form of affidavit.

When a recognizance is offered under section 2937.22 of the Revised Code, the surety on which recognizance qualifies as a real property owner, the judge or magistrate shall require such surety to pledge to this state real property owned by the surety and located in this state. Whenever such pledge of real property has been given by any such proposed surety, he shall execute the usual form of recognizance, and in addition thereto there shall be filed his affidavit of justification of suretyship, to be attached to said recognizance as a part thereof. The surety may be required in such affidavit to depose as to whether he is, at the time of executing the same, surety upon any other recognizance and as to whether there are any unsatisfied judgments or executions against him. He may also be required to state any other fact which the court thinks relevant and material to a correct determination of the surety's sufficiency to act as bail. Such surety shall state in such affidavit where notices under section 2937.38 of the Revised Code may be served on himself, and service of notice of summons at such place is sufficient service for all purposes.

Such affidavit shall be executed by the proposed surety under an oath and may be in the following form:

"State of Ohio, County of . . . ., ss:
. . . . residing at . . . ., who offers himself as surety for . . . . being first duly sworn, says that he owns in his own legal right, real property subject to execution, located in the county of . . . ., State of Ohio, consisting of . . . . and described as follows to wit: . . . .; that the title to the same is in his own name; that the value of the same is not less than . . . . dollars, and is subject to no encumbrances whatever except . . . . . .; that he is not surety upon any unpaid or forfeited recognizance, and that he is not a party to any unsatisfied judgment upon any recognizance; that he is worth not less than . . . . dollars over and above all debts, liabilities, and lawful claims against him, and all liens, encumbrances, and lawful claims against his property."

HISTORY: GC § 13435-4; 113 v 123(150), ch 14, § 4; Bureau of Code Revision. Eff 10-1-53.

§ 2937.25 Lien; form.

Upon the execution of any recognizance in an amount in excess of two hundred dollars in the usual form, and an affidavit of justification under section 2937.24 of the Revised Code, there shall attach to the real property described in said affidavit of justification, a lien in favor of this state in the penal sum of the recognizance, which lien shall remain in full force and effect during such time as such recognizance remains effective, or until further order of the court. Upon the acceptance by the judge or magistrate of such recognizance, containing such affidavit of justification, the said recognizance shall be immediately filed with the clerk of said court, if there is a clerk, or with the magistrate. The clerk of the court or the magistrate shall forthwith, upon the filing with him of such recognizance, file with the county recorder of the county in which such real property is located, a notice or lien, in writing, in substance as follows:

"To whom it may concern:
Take notice that the hereinafter described real property, located in the county of . . . ., has been pledged for the sum of . . . . dollars, to the state of Ohio, by . . . . surety upon the recognizance of . . . . in a certain cause pending in the . . . . court of the county (or city) of . . . ., to wit: the state of Ohio, plaintiff, versus . . . . defendant, known and identified in such court as cause No. . . . .
Description of real estate: . . . . Clerk of the court for the county of . . . . or . . . . Magistrate.
Dated . . . ."

From the time of the filing and recording of such notice it is notice to everyone that the real property therein described has been pledged to this state as security for the performance of the conditions of a criminal recognizance in the penal sum set forth in said recognizance and notice. Such lien does not affect the validity of prior liens on said property.

HISTORY: GC § 13435-5; 113 v 123(151), ch 14, § 5; Bureau of Code Revision. Eff 10-1-53.

§ 2937.26 Cancellation of lien; form.

Whenever, by the order of a court, a recognizance under sections 2937.24 and 2937.25 of the Revised Code has been canceled, discharged, or set aside, or the cause in which such recognizance is taken has been dismissed or otherwise terminated the clerk of such court shall forthwith file with the county recorder of the county in which the real property is located, a notice of discharge in writing, in substance as follows:

"To whom it may concern:
Take notice that by the order of the court of . . . . (naming court) . . . . of the county (or city) of . . . ., the recognizance of . . . . as principal, and . . . . as surety, given in the cause of the State of Ohio, plaintiff, versus . . . ., defendant, known and identified as Cause No. . . . . in said court, is canceled, discharged, and set aside, and the lien of the State of Ohio on the real property therein pledged as security, is hereby waived, discharged, and set aside.
. . . . Clerk of the court.
Dated . . . ."

HISTORY: GC § 13435-6; 113 v 123(151), ch 14, § 6; Bureau of Code Revision. Eff 10-1-53.

§ 2937.27 Duties of county recorder.

The county recorder of the county in which the property of a surety on a recognizance is located, shall keep and file all notices of lien and notices of discharge which are filed with him pursuant to section 2937.26 of the Revised Code, and shall keep in addition thereto, a book or record in which he shall index notice of liens and notice of discharges, as they are filed with him. When a lien has been released or discharged for a period of one year, the county recorder may destroy all notices of such lien.

HISTORY: GC § 13435-7; 113 v 123(152), ch 14, § 7; Bureau of Code Revision, 10-1-53; 129 v 1033. Eff 10-26-61.

§ 2937.28 Transmission of recognizance.

All recognizances shall be returnable to and all deposits shall be held by or subject to the order of the court or magistrate before whom the accused is to appear initially, and upon the transfer of the case to any other court or magistrate shall be returnable to and transmitted to the transferee court or magistrate.

It is not necessary for the accused to give new recognizance for appearance in common pleas court for arraignment upon indictment or pending appeal after judgment and sentence, unless the magistrate or judge of the trial court or the court to which appeal is taken, shall, for good cause shown, increase or decrease the amount of the recognizance, but such recognizance shall continue and be in full force until trial and appeal therefrom is finally determined. When two or more charges are filed, or indictments returned, against the same person at or about the same time, the recognizance given may be made to include all offenses charged against the accused.

HISTORY: 128 v 97. Eff 1-1-60.

Not analogous to former RC § 2937.28 (GC § 13435-8; 113 v 123(150); Bureau of Code Revision, 10-1-53), repealed 128 v 97(116), § 2, eff 1-1-60.

[§ 2937.28.1] § 2937.281 Requirements of recognizance.

In cases of felony, the recognizance shall be signed by the accused and one or more adult residents of the county in which the case is pending, who shall own, in the aggregate, real property double the amount set as bail, over and above all encumbrances and liable to execution in at least that amount; or it may be signed by the accused and a surety company authorized to do business in this state.

In cases of misdemeanor, the recognizance may be signed by the accused and one or more adult residents, qualified as set forth above or as to personal property ownership, by the accused and surety company, or, if authorized by judge or magistrate, by the accused alone. In cases of misdemeanors arising under Chapters 4501., 4503., 4505., 4507., 4509., 4511., 4513., 4517., and 4549. of the Revised Code, and related ordinance offenses (except those of driving under the influence of intoxicating liquor or controlled substances and leaving the scene of an accident) the court or magistrate shall accept guaranteed arrest bond with respect to which a surety company has become surety as provided in section 3929.141 [3929.14.1] of the Revised Code in lieu of cash bail in an amount not to exceed two hundred dollars.

HISTORY: 128 v 97 (Eff 1-1-60); 129 v 1401 (Eff 9-5-61); 136 v H 300. Eff 7-1-76.

Somewhat analogous to former GC § 13524 and to RC §§ 2937.28.1 (126 v 625; 127 v 847) and 2937.23 (GC § 13435-3; 113 v 123(150); Bureau of Code Revision, 10-1-53), both repealed 128 v 97(116), § 2, eff 1-1-60. See also former RC § 4549.17.

§ 2937.29 Release on own recognizance.

When from all the circumstances the court is of the opinion that the accused will appear as required, either before or after conviction, the accused may be released on his own recognizance. A failure to appear as required by such recognizance shall constitute an offense subject to the penalty provided in section 2937.99 of the Revised Code.

HISTORY: 131 v 677. Eff 8-10-65.

Not analogous to former RC § 2937.29 (GC § 13435-9; 113 v 123(152); Bureau of Code Revision, 10-1-53), repealed 128 v 97(116), § 2, eff 1-1-60.

§ 2937.30 Recognizance when accused discharged.

When a defendant is discharged by the trial court otherwise than on a verdict or finding of acquittal, or when the appellate court reverses a conviction and orders the discharge of the defendant and the state or municipality signifies its intention to appeal therefrom, or the record is certified to the supreme court, the defendant shall not be discharged if he is in jail, nor the surety discharged or deposit released if the defendant is on bail, but the trial court, or the court to which appeal is taken may make order for his release on his own recognizance or bail, or recommit him.

HISTORY: GC § 13435-10; 113 v 123(153), ch 14, § 10; Bureau of Code Revision, 10-1-53; 128 v 97(109). Eff 1-1-60.

§ 2937.31 Recognizance or deposit for appearance of accused.

If an accused is held to answer and offers sufficient bail, a recognizance or deposit shall be taken for his appearance to answer the charge before such magistrate or before such court to which proceedings may be transferred pursuant to Chapter 2937. of the Revised Code, at a date certain, or from day to day, or in case of the common pleas court on the first day of the next term thereof, and not depart without leave.

HISTORY: GC § 13435-11; 113 v 123(153), ch 14, § 11; Bureau of Code Revision, 10-1-53; 128 v 97. Eff 1-1-60.

§ 2937.32 Confinement for unbailable offenses and lack of sufficient bail.

If an offense is not bailable or sufficient bail is not offered, the accused shall be committed to the jail of the county in which he is to be tried or, in the case of offense against a municipality, in the jail of said municipality if such there be.

HISTORY: GC § 13435-12; 113 v 123(153), ch 14, § 12; Bureau of Code Revision, 10-1-53; 128 v 97. Eff 1-1-60.

§ 2937.33 Receipt of recognizance.

When a transcript or [of] recognizance is received by the clerk of the court of common pleas, or of any court of record to which proceedings are transferred, he shall enter the same upon the appearance docket of the court, with the date of the filing of such transcript or recognizance, the date and amount of the recognizance, the names of the sureties, and the costs. Such recognizance is then of record in such court, and is proceeded on by process issuing therefrom, in a like manner as if it had been entered into before such court. When a court having recognizance of an offense takes a recognizance, it is a sufficient record thereof to enter upon the journal of such court the title of the case, the crime charged, the names of the sureties, the amount of the recognizance, and the time therein required for the appearance of the accused. In making the complete record, when required to be made, recognizances whether returned to or taken in such court shall be recorded in full, if required by the prosecutor or the accused.

HISTORY: GC § 13435-13; 113 v 123(153), ch 14, § 13; Bureau of Code Revision, 10-1-53; 128 v 97. Eff 1-1-60.

§ 2937.34 Accused unlawfully detained; examining court to be held.

When a person is committed to jail, charged with an offense for which he has not been indicted, and claims to be unlawfully detained, the sheriff on demand of the accused or his counsel shall forthwith notify the court of common pleas, and the prosecuting attorney, to attend an examining court, the time of which shall be fixed by the judge. The judge shall hear said cause or complaint, examine the witnesses, and make such order as the justice of the case requires, and for such purpose the court may admit to bail, release without bond, or recommit to jail in accordance with the commitment. In the absence of the judge of the court of common pleas, the probate judge shall hold such examining court.

HISTORY: GC § 13435-14; 113 v 123(154), ch 14, § 14; 114 v 320(479), § 2; Bureau of Code Revision. Eff 10-1-53.

§ 2937.35 Forfeit of bail.

Upon the failure of the accused or witness to appear in accordance with its terms the bail may in open court be adjudged forfeit, in whole or in part by the court or magistrate before whom he is to appear. But such court or magistrate may, in its discretion, continue the cause to a later date certain, giving notice of such date to him and the bail depositor or sureties, and adjudge the bail forfeit upon failure to appear at such later date.

HISTORY: 128 v 97. Eff 1-1-60.

Not analogous to former RC § 2937.35 (GC § 13435-15; 113 v 123(154); Bureau of Code Revision, 10-1-53), repealed 128 v 97(116), § 2, eff 1-1-60; but see former RC § 2937.38 (GC § 13435-18; 113 v 123(155); Bureau of Code Revision, 10-1-53).

§ 2937.36 Forfeiture proceedings.

Upon declaration of forfeiture, the magistrate or clerk of the court adjudging forfeiture shall proceed as follows:

(A) As to each bail, he shall proceed forthwith to deal with the sum deposited as if the same were imposed as a fine for the offense charged and distribute and account for the same accordingly provided that prior to so doing, he may satisfy accrued costs in the case out of the fund.

(B) As to any securities deposited, he shall proceed to sell the same, either at public sale advertised in the same manner as sale on chattel execution, or through any state or national bank performing such service upon the over the counter securities market and shall apply proceeds of sale, less costs or brokerage thereof as in cases of forfeited cash bail. Prior to such sale, the clerk shall give notices by ordinary mail to the depositor, at his address listed of record, if any, of his intention so to do, and such sale shall not proceed if the depositor, within ten days of mailing of such notice appears, and redeems said securities by either producing the body of the defendant in open court or posting the amount set in the recognizance in cash, to be dealt with as forfeited cash bail.

(C) As to recognizances he shall notify accused and each surety by ordinary mail at the address shown by them in their affidavits of qualification or on the record of the case, of the default of the accused and the adjudication of forfeiture and require each of them to show cause on or before a date certain to be stated in the notice, and which shall be not less than twenty nor more than thirty days from date of mailing notice, why judgment should not be entered against each of them for the penalty stated in the recognizance. If good cause by production of the body of the accused or otherwise is not shown, the court or magistrate shall thereupon enter judgment against the sureties or either of them, so notified, in such amount, not exceeding the penalty of the bond, as has been set in the adjudication of forfeiture, and shall award execution therefor as in civil cases. The proceeds of sale shall be received by the clerk or magistrate and distributed as on forfeiture of cash bail.

HISTORY: 128 v 97. Eff 1-1-60.

Not analogous to former RC § 2937.36 (GC § 13435-16; 113 v 123(154); Bureau of Code Revision, 10-1-53), repealed 128 v 97(116), § 2, eff 1-1-60; but see former RC § 2937.38 (GC § 13435-18; 113 v 123(155); Bureau of Code Revision, 10-1-53).

The substance of former RC § 2937.36 is now found in RC § 2937.40.

§ 2937.37 Levy on property in judgment against surety.

A magistrate or court of record inferior to the court of common pleas may proceed to judgment against a surety on a recognizance, and levy on his personal property, notwithstanding that the bond may exceed the monetary limitations on the jurisdiction of such court in civil cases, and jurisdiction over the person of surety shall attach from the mailing of the notice specified in section 2937.36 of the Revised Code, notwithstanding that such surety may not be within the territorial jurisdiction of the court; but levy on real property shall be made only through issuance, return, and levy made under certificate of judgment issued to the clerk of the court of common pleas pursuant to section 2329.02 of the Revised Code.

HISTORY: 128 v 97. Eff 1-1-60.

Not analogous to former RC § 2937.37 (GC § 13435-17; 113 v 123(155); Bureau of Code Revision, 10-1-53), repealed 128 v 97(116), § 2, eff 1-1-60; but see former RC § 2937.38 (GC § 13435-18; 113 v 123(155); Bureau of Code Revision, 10-1-53).

§ 2937.38 Minority no defense in forfeiture proceedings.

In any matter in which a minor is admitted to bail pursuant to Chapter 2937. of the Revised Code, the minority of the accused shall not be available as a defense to judgment against principal or surety, or against the sale of securities or transfer of cash bail, upon forfeiture.

HISTORY: 128 v 97. Eff 1-1-60.

Not analogous to former RC § 2937.38 (GC § 13435-18; 113 v 123(155); Bureau of Code Revision, 10-1-53), repealed 128 v 97(116), § 2, eff 1-1-60.

The substance of former RC § 2937.38 is now found in RC § 2937.36 (GC § 13435-16; 113 v 123(154); Bureau of Code Revision, 10-1-53) and RC § 2937.37 (GC § 13435-17; 113 v 123(155); Bureau of Code Revision, 10-1-53).

§ 2937.39 Remission of penalty.

After judgment has been rendered against surety or after securities sold or cash bail applied, the court or magistrate, on the appearance, surrender, or rearrest of the accused on the charge, may remit all or such portion of the penalty as it deems just and in the case of previous application and transfer of cash or proceeds, the magistrate or clerk may deduct an amount equal to the amount so transferred from subsequent payments to the agencies receiving such proceeds of forfeiture until the amount is recouped for the benefit of the person or persons entitled thereto under order or remission.

HISTORY: 128 v 97. Eff 1-1-60.

Not analogous to former RC § 2937.39 (GC § 13435-19; 113 v 123(155); Bureau of Code Revision, 10-1-53), repealed 128 v 97(116), § 2, eff 1-1-60; but see former RC § 2937.43 (GC § 13435-23; 113 v 123(156); Bureau of Code Revision, 10-1-53).

§ 2937.40 Release of bail and sureties.

(A) Bail of any type that is deposited under sections 2937.22 to 2937.45 of the Revised Code or Criminal Rule 46 by a person other than the accused shall be discharged and released, and sureties on recognizances shall be released, in any of the following ways:

(1) When a surety on a recognizance or the depositor of cash or securities as bail for an accused desires to surrender the accused before the appearance date, the surety is discharged from further responsibility or the deposit is redeemed in either of the following ways:

(a) By delivery of the accused into open court;

(b) When, on the written request of the surety or depositor, the clerk of the court to which recognizance is returnable or in which deposit is made issues to the sheriff a warrant for the arrest of the accused and the sheriff indicates on the return that he holds the accused in his jail.

(2) By appearance of the accused in accordance with the terms of the recognizance or deposit and the entry of judgment by the court or magistrate;

(3) By payment into court, after default, of the sum fixed in the recognizance or the sum fixed in the order of forfeiture, if it is less.

(B) When cash or securities have been deposited as bail by a person other than the accused and the bail is discharged and released pursuant to division (A) of this section, or when property has been pledged by a surety on recognizance and the surety on recognizance has been released pursuant to division (A) of this section, the court shall not deduct any amount from the cash or securities or declare forfeited and levy or execute against pledged property. The court shall not apply any of the deposited cash or securities toward, or declare forfeited and levy or execute against property pledged for a recognizance for, the satisfaction of any penalty or fine, and court costs, assessed against the accused upon his conviction or guilty plea, except upon express approval of the person who deposited the cash or securities or the surety.

(C) Bail of any type that is deposited under sections 2937.22 to 2937.45 of the Revised Code or Criminal Rule 46 by an accused shall be discharged and released to the accused, and property pledged by an accused for a recognizance shall be discharged, upon the appearance of the accused in accordance with the terms of the recognizance or deposit and the entry of judgment by the court or magistrate, except that, if the defendant is not indigent, the court may apply deposited bail toward the satisfaction of a penalty or fine, and court costs, assessed against the accused upon his conviction or guilty plea, and may declare forfeited and levy or execute against pledged property for the satisfaction of a penalty or fine, and court costs, assessed against the accused upon his conviction or guilty plea.

(D) Notwithstanding any other provision of this section, an Ohio driver's or commercial driver's license that is deposited as bond may be forfeited and otherwise handled as provided in section 2937.221 [2937.22.1] of the Revised Code.

HISTORY: 128 v 97 (Eff 1-1-60); 138 v H 402 (Eff 5-13-80); 141 v S 356 (Eff 9-24-86); 143 v H 381 (Eff 7-1-89); 143 v S 338. Eff 11-28-90.

Not analogous to former RC § 2937.40 (GC § 13435-20; 113 v 123(155); Bureau of Code Revision, 10-1-53), repealed 128 v 97(116), § 2, eff 1-1-60; but see former RC § 2937.36 (GC § 13435-16; 113 v 123(154); Bureau of Code Revision, 10-1-53).

§ 2937.41 Return of bail; notice of discharge of recognizance.

On the discharge of bail, the magistrate or clerk of the court shall return, subject to division (B) or (C) of section 2937.40 of the Revised Code, deposited cash or securities to the depositor, but the magistrate or clerk of the court may require presentation of an issued original receipt as a condition to the return. In the case of discharged recognizances, subject to division (B) or (C) of section 2937.40 of the Revised Code, the magistrate or clerk of the court shall endorse the satisfaction on the recognizance and shall forthwith transmit to the county recorder the notice of discharge provided for in section 2937.26 of the Revised Code.

HISTORY: 128 v 97 (Eff 1-1-60); 138 v H 402. Eff 5-13-80.

Not analogous to former RC § 2937.41 (GC § 13435-21; 113 v 123(155); Bureau of Code Revision, 10-1-53), repealed 128 v 97(116), § 2, eff 1-1-60.

§ 2937.42 Defect in form of recognizance.

Forfeiture of a recognizance shall not be barred or defeated or a judgment thereon reversed by the neglect or omission to note or record the default, or by a defect in the form of such recognizance, if it appears from the tenor thereof at what court the party or witness was bound to appear and that the court or officer before whom it was taken was authorized to require and take such recognizance.

HISTORY: GC § 13435-22; 113 v 123(156), ch 14, § 22; Bureau of Code Revision, 10-1-53; 128 v 97(112). Eff 1-1-60.

§ 2937.43 Failure to appear; issuance of warrant.

Should the accused fail to appear as required, after having been released pursuant to section 2937.29 of the Revised Code, the court having jurisdiction at the time of such failure may, in addition to any other action provided by law, issue a warrant for the arrest of such accused.

HISTORY: 131 v 677. Eff 8-10-65.

Not analogous to former RC § 2937.43 (GC § 13435-23; 113 v 123(156); Bureau of Code Revision, 10-1-53), repealed 128 v 97(116), § 2, eff 1-1-60.

§ 2937.44 Forms of recognizance.

Recognizances substantially in the forms following are sufficient:

RECOGNIZANCE OF THE ACCUSED
The State of Ohio, ... County, ss:

Be it remembered, that on the . . . . day of . . . . . ., in the year . . . . E. F. and G. H. personally appeared before me, and jointly and severally acknowledged themselves to owe the state of Ohio, the sum of . . . . . . dollars, to be levied on their goods, chattels, lands, and tenements, if default is made in the condition following, to wit:

The condition of this recognizance is such that if the above bound E. F. personally appears before the court of common pleas on the first day of the next term thereof, then and there to answer a charge of (here name the offense with which the accused is charged) and abide the judgment of the court and not depart without leave, then this recognizance shall be void; otherwise it shall be and remain in full force and virtue in law.

Taken and acknowledged before me, on the day and year above written.

A. B., Judge
RECOGNIZANCE OF WITNESS
The State of Ohio, ... County, ss:

Be it remembered, that on the . . . . day of . . . . . ., in the year . . . . E. F. and G. H. personally appeared before me and jointly and severally acknowledged themselves to owe the state of Ohio, the sum of . . . . . . dollars, to be levied on their goods, chattels, lands, and tenements, if default is made in the condition following, to wit:

The condition of this recognizance is such that if the above bound E. F. personally appears before the court of common pleas on the first day of the next term thereof then and there to give evidence on behalf of the state, touching such matters as shall then and there be required of him, and not depart the court without leave, then this recognizance shall be void, otherwise it shall remain in full force and virtue in law.

Taken and acknowledged before me, on the day and year above written.

A. B., Judge
TO KEEP THE PEACE
The State of Ohio, ... County, ss:

Be it remembered, that on the . . . . day of . . . . . ., in the year . . . . E. F. and G. H. personally appeared before me, and jointly and severally acknowledged themselves to owe the state of Ohio, the sum of . . . . . . dollars, to be levied on their goods, chattels, lands, and tenements, if default is made in the condition following, to wit:

The condition of this recognizance is such that if the above bound E. F. personally appears before the court of common pleas, on the first day of the next term thereof, then and there to answer unto a complaint of C. D. that he has reason to fear, and does fear, that the said E. F. will (here state the charge in the complaint), and abide the order of the court thereon, and in the meantime to keep the peace and be of good behavior toward the citizens of the state generally, and especially toward the said C. D., then this recognizance shall be void; otherwise it shall be and remain in full force and virtue in law.

Taken and acknowledged before me, on the day and year above written.

A. B., Judge

HISTORY: GC § 13435-24; 113 v 123(156), ch 14, § 24; Bureau of Code Revision, 10-1-53; 127 v 1039(1102). Eff 1-1-58.

§ 2937.45 Forms of commitments.

Commitments substantially in the forms following are sufficient:

COMMITMENT AFTER EXAMINATION
The State of Ohio, ... County, ss:
To the Keeper of the Jail of the County aforesaid, greeting:

Whereas, E. F. has been arrested, on the oath of C. D., for (here describe the offense), and has been examined by me on such charge, and required to give bail in the sum of ...... dollars for his appearance before the court of common pleas with which requisition he has failed to comply. Therefore, in the name of the state of Ohio, I command you to receive the said E. F. into your custody, in the jail of the county aforesaid, there to remain until discharged by due course of law.

Given under my hand, this .... day of ....
A. B., Judge

COMMITMENT PENDING EXAMINATION
The State of Ohio, ... County, ss:
To the Keeper of the Jail of the County aforesaid, greeting:

Whereas, E. F. has been arrested on the oath of C. D., for (here describe the offense) and has been brought before me for examination and the same has been necessarily postponed by reason of (here state the cause of delay). Therefore, I command you, in the name of the state of Ohio, to receive the said E. F. into your custody in the jail of the county aforesaid (or in such other place as the justice shall name) there to remain until discharged by due course of law.

Given under my hand, this .... day of ....
A. B., Judge

HISTORY: GC § 13435-25; 113 v 123(157), ch 14, § 25; Bureau of Code Revision, 10-1-53; 127 v 1039(1102). Eff 1-1-58.

§ 2937.46 Supreme court authorized to set uniform procedures in traffic cases.

The supreme court of Ohio may, in the interest of uniformity of procedure in the various courts, and for the purpose of promoting prompt and efficient disposition of cases arising under the traffic laws of this state and related ordinances, make uniform rules for practice and procedure in courts inferior to the court of common pleas not inconsistent with the provisions of Chapter 2937. of the Revised Code, including, but not limited to:

(A) Separation of arraignment and trial of traffic and other types of cases;

(B) Consolidation of cases for trial;

(C) Transfer of cases within the same county for the purpose of trial;

(D) Designation of special referees for hearings or for receiving pleas or bail at times when courts are not in session;

(E) Fixing of reasonable bonds, and disposition of cases in which bonds have been forfeited.

All of said rules, when promulgated by the supreme court, shall be fully binding on all courts inferior to the court of common pleas and shall effect a cancellation of any local court rules inconsistent therewith.

HISTORY: 128 v 97(112) (Eff 1-1-60); 129 v 582(750). Eff 1-10-61.

§ 2937.99 Penalties.

Whoever fails to appear as required, after having been released pursuant to section 2937.29 of the Revised Code, shall be sentenced as follows:

(A) If the release was in connection with a charge of the commission of a felony or pending appeal after conviction of a felony, he shall be fined not more than five thousand dollars or imprisoned in a state correctional institution for not less than one nor more than five years, or both.

(B) If the release was in connection with a charge of the commission of a misdemeanor or for appearance as a witness, he shall be fined not more than one thousand dollars or imprisoned not more than one year, or both.

This section does not apply to misdemeanors and related ordinance offenses arising under Chapters 4501., 4503., 4505., 4507., 4509., 4511., 4513., 4517., 4549., and 5577. of the Revised Code, except that this section does apply to violations of sections 4511.19, 4549.02, and 4549.021 [4549.02.1] of the Revised Code and ordinance offenses related to such sections.

HISTORY: 131 v 677 (Eff 8-10-65); 145 v H 571. Eff 10-6-94.

CHAPTER 2938: TRIAL—MAGISTRATE COURTS

Section
2938.01 Definitions.
2938.02 Applicability of provisions.
2938.03 Setting and continuing cases; assignment of additional judges.
2938.04 Jury trial.
2938.05 Withdrawal of claim for jury.
2938.06 Number of jurors; challenges.
2938.07 Authority of magistrate or judge.
2938.08 Presumption of innocence.
2938.09 Objection to ruling or action.
2938.10 Territorial jurisdiction.
2938.11 Order of proceedings of trial.
2938.12 When accused may be tried in his absence.
2938.13 Responsibility for prosecution.
2938.14 Venires for juries.
2938.15 Rules of evidence and procedure.

§ 2938.01 Definitions.

The definition of "magistrate" set forth in section 2931.01 of the Revised Code, and the definition of "peace officer," "prosecutor," and "offense" set forth in section 2935.01 of the Revised Code applies to Chapter 2938. of the Revised Code.

HISTORY: 128 v 97(112). Eff 1-1-60.

§ 2938.02 Applicability of provisions.

The provisions of Chapter 2938. of the Revised Code shall apply to trial on the merits of any misdemeanor, ordinance offense, prosecution for the violation of any rule or regulation of any governmental body authorized to adopt penal regulations, or to complaints to keep the peace, which may be instituted in and retained for trial on the merits in any court or before any magistrate inferior to the court of common pleas; provided that in juvenile courts, where the conduct of any person under the age of eighteen years is made the subject of inquiry and for which special provision is made by Chapter 2151. of the Revised Code, such matters shall be tried, adjudged, or disposed of pursuant to Chapter 2151. of the Revised Code.

HISTORY: 128 v 97(113). Eff 1-1-60.

§ 2938.03 Setting and continuing cases; assignment of additional judges.

The magistrate, or judge or clerk of court of record, shall set all criminal cases for a trial at a date not later than thirty days after plea is received, or in those cases in which the charge has been reduced on preliminary hearing or has been certified by another magistrate, then a date not later than thirty days from fixing of charge or receipt of transcript as the case may be. Continuances beyond such date shall be granted only upon notice to the opposing party and for good cause shown.

Criminal cases shall be given precedence over civil matters in all assignments for trial and if the volume of contested criminal matters in courts of more than one judge is such as to require it, the chief justice or presiding judge of such court shall assign additional judges from other divisions of the court to assist in the trial of such criminal matters; in the case of county courts, the presiding judge of the court of common pleas shall assign county judges from other areas of jurisdiction within the county to assist those county judges whose volume of criminal cases requires assistance.

HISTORY: 128 v 97(113). Eff 1-1-60.

§ 2938.04 Jury trial.

In courts of record right to trial by jury as defined in section 2945.17 of the Revised Code shall be claimed by making demand in writing therefor and filing the same with the clerk of the court not less than three days prior to the date set for trial or on the day following receipt of notice whichever is the later. Failure to claim jury trial as provided in this section is a complete waiver of right thereto. In courts not of record jury trial may not be had, but failure to waive jury in writing where right to jury trial may be asserted shall require the magistrate to certify such case to a court of record as provided in section 2937.08 of the Revised Code.

HISTORY: 128 v 97(113) (Eff 1-1-60); 129 v 582(751). Eff 1-10-61.

§ 2938.05 Withdrawal of claim for jury.

Claim of jury, once made, may be withdrawn by written waiver of jury but in such case the court may, if a jury has been summoned, require accused to pay all costs of mileage and fees of members of the venire for one day's service, notwithstanding the outcome of the case. No withdrawal of claim for jury shall effect any re-transfer of a case, once it has been certified to a court of record.

HISTORY: 128 v 97(113). Eff 1-1-60.

§ 2938.06 Number of jurors; challenges.

If the number of jurors to be sworn in a case is not stated in the claim, the number to be sworn shall be twelve, but the accused may stipulate for a jury of six, provided in such case the number of peremptory challenges shall be limited to two on each side.

HISTORY: 128 v 97(114). Eff 1-1-60.

§ 2938.07 Authority of magistrate or judge.

The magistrate or judge of the trial court shall control all proceedings during a criminal trial and shall limit the introduction of evidence and argument of counsel to relevant and material matters with a view to expeditious and effective ascertainment of truth regarding the matters in issue.

HISTORY: 128 v 97(114). Eff 1-1-60.

§ 2938.08 Presumption of innocence.

A defendant in a criminal action is presumed to be innocent until he is proved guilty of the offense charged, and in case of a reasonable doubt whether his guilt is satisfactorily shown, he shall be acquitted. The presumption of innocence places upon the state (or the municipality) the burden of proving him guilty beyond a reasonable doubt.

In charging a jury the trial court shall state the meaning of the presumption of innocence and of reasonable doubt in each case.

HISTORY: 128 v 97(114). Eff 1-1-60.

§ 2938.09 Objection to ruling or action.

In the trial of any criminal case, the grounds of an objection to any ruling or action of the judge or magistrate shall be stated if required by him.

HISTORY: 128 v 97(114) (Eff 1-1-60); 141 v H 412. Eff 3-17-87.

§ 2938.10 Territorial jurisdiction.

The state or municipality in all cases must prove the offense committed within the territorial jurisdiction of the court, and in ordinance cases within the municipality, except as to those offenses in which the court has county wide jurisdiction created by statute and as to those cases in which certification has been made pursuant to section 2937.08 of the Revised Code.

HISTORY: 128 v 97(114). Eff 1-1-60.

§ 2938.11 Order of proceedings of trial.

The trial of an issue shall proceed before the trial court or jury as follows:

(A) Counsel may state the case for the prosecution, including the evidence by which he expects to sustain it.

(B) Counsel for the defendant may state his defense, including the evidence which he expects to offer.

(C) The prosecution then shall produce all its evidence, and the defendant may follow with his evidence, but the court or magistrate, in the furtherance of justice and for good cause shown, may permit evidence to be offered by either side out of its order and may permit rebuttal evidence to be offered by the prosecution.

(D) When the evidence is concluded, unless the case is submitted without argument, counsel for the prosecution shall commence, defendant or his counsel follow, and counsel for the prosecution conclude his argument either to the court or jury. The judge or magistrate may impose a reasonable time limit on argument.

(E) The judge, after argument is concluded in a jury case, forthwith shall charge the jury on the law pertaining to the case and controlling their deliberations, which charge shall not be reduced to writing and taken into the jury room unless the trial judge in his discretion shall so order.

(F) Any verdict arrived at by the jury, or finding determined by the judge or magistrate in trial to the court, shall be announced and received only in open court as soon as it is determined. Any finding by the judge or magistrate shall be announced in open court not more than forty-eight hours after submission of the case to him.

HISTORY: 128 v 97(114) (Eff 1-1-60); 141 v H 412. Eff 3-17-87.

§ 2938.12 When accused may be tried in his absence.

A person being tried for a misdemeanor, either to the court, or to a jury, upon request in writing, subscribed by him, may, with the consent of the judge or magistrate, be tried in his absence, but no right shall exist in the defendant to be so tried. If after trial commences a person being tried escapes or departs without leave, the trial shall proceed and verdict or finding be received and sentence passed as if he were personally present.

HISTORY: 128 v 97(115). Eff 1-1-60.

§ 2938.13 Responsibility for prosecution.

In any case prosecuted for violation of a municipal ordinance the village solicitor or city director of law, and for a statute, he or the prosecuting attorney, shall present the case for the municipal corporation and the state respectively, but either may delegate the responsibility to some other attorney in a proper case, or, if the defendant be unrepresented by counsel may with leave of court, withdraw from the case. But the magistrate or judge shall not permit prosecution of any criminal case by private attorney employed or retained by a complaining witness.

HISTORY: 128 v 97(115) (Eff 1-1-60); 137 v H 219. Eff 11-1-77.

§ 2938.14 Venires for juries.

Venires for juries in courts of record inferior to the court of common pleas shall be drawn and summoned in the manner provided in the various acts creating such courts. But no challenge to the array shall be sustained in any case for the reason that some of the venire are not residents of the territory of the court, if it appears that the venire was regularly drawn and certified by the jury commissioners of county or municipality as the case may be.

HISTORY: 128 v 97(115) (Eff 1-1-60); 129 v 582(751). Eff 1-10-61.

§ 2938.15 Rules of evidence and procedure.

The rules of evidence and procedure, including those governing notices, proof of special matters, depositions, and joinder of defendants and offenses set forth in Chapter 2945. of the Revised Code, which are not, by their nature, inapplicable to the trial of misdemeanors, shall prevail in trials under Chapter 2938. of the Revised Code where no special provision is made in such chapter, or where no provision is made by rule of the supreme court adopted pursuant to section 2937.46 of the Revised Code.

HISTORY: 128 v 97(116) (Eff 1-1-60); 129 v 582(751). Eff 1-10-61.

CHAPTER 2939: GRAND JURIES

Section
2939.01 Definition of magistrate.
2939.02 Selection of grand jury.
2939.03 Grand jurors subject to same provisions and regulations as other jurors.
[2939.03.1] 2939.031 Selection of additional or alternate juror.
2939.04 Grand jurors; compensation.
2939.05 Repealed.
2939.06 Oath to grand jurors.
2939.07 Charge of the court.
2939.08 Duty of grand jury.
2939.09 Clerk of grand jury.
2939.10 Who shall have access to grand jury.
2939.11 Official reporters.
2939.12 Clerk to issue subpoenas for witnesses.
[2939.12.1] 2939.121 Employee may not be penalized for being subpoenaed before grand jury.
2939.13 Oath to witnesses.
2939.14 Proceedings when witness refuses to testify.
2939.15 Court may proceed against witness for contempt.
2939.16 Court may appoint grand juror in case of death.
2939.17 New grand jury may be summoned.
2939.18 Fact of indictment shall be kept secret.
2939.19 Testimony of grand jurors.
2939.20 Indictment by twelve jurors.
2939.21 A grand jury to visit the county jail.
2939.22 Proceedings when indictments are returned.
2939.23 Report to court when indictment not found.
2939.24 Disposition of person in jail and not indicted.

[ATTENDANCE OF WITNESSES FROM WITHOUT STATE]

2939.25 Definition of witness, state, and summons.
2939.26 Foreign court may compel witnesses.
2939.27 Certificate to specify time witness will be required; mileage and fees.
2939.28 Exemption from arrest.
2939.29 Construction.

§ 2939.01 Definition of magistrate.

The definition of "magistrate" set forth in section 2931.01 of the Revised Code applies to Chapter 2939. of the Revised Code.

HISTORY: Bureau of Code Revision. Eff 10-1-53.

§ 2939.02 Selection of grand jury.

Grand juries shall consist of fifteen persons who satisfy the qualifications of a juror specified in section 2313.42 of the Revised Code. Persons to serve as grand jurors in the court of common pleas of each county shall be selected from the persons whose names are contained in the annual jury list and from the ballots deposited in the jury wheel, or in the automation data processing storage drawer, or from the names contained in an automated data processing information storage device as prescribed by sections 2313.07, 2313.08, and 2313.35 of the Revised Code.

At the time of the selection of the persons who are to constitute the grand jury, the commissioners of jurors shall draw from the jury wheel, or draw by utilizing the automation data processing equipment and procedures described in section 2313.07 of the Revised Code, ballots containing the names of not less than twenty-five persons. The first fifteen persons whose names are drawn shall constitute the grand jury, if they can be located and served by the sheriff, and if they are not excused by the court or a judge of the court. If any of the first fifteen persons whose names are so drawn are not located or are unable to serve and are for that reason excused by the court or by a judge of the court, whose duty it is to supervise the impaneling of the grand jury, the judge shall then designate the person whose name next appears on the list of persons drawn, to serve in the place of the person not found or excused and shall so continue to substitute the names of the persons drawn in the order in which they were drawn, to fill all vacancies resulting from persons not being found or having been excused by the court or the judge of the court, until the necessary fifteen persons are selected to make up the grand jury. If all of the names appearing on the list of persons drawn are exhausted before the grand jury is complete, the judge shall order the commissioners of jurors to draw such additional names as the judge determines, and shall proceed to fill the vacancies from those names in the order in which they are drawn.

The judge of the court of common pleas may select any person who satisfies the qualifications of a juror and whose name is not included in the annual jury list or on a ballot deposited in the jury wheel or automation data processing storage drawer, or whose name is not contained in an automated data processing information storage device, to preside as foreman of the grand jury, in which event the grand jury shall consist of the foreman so selected and fourteen additional grand jurors selected from the jury wheel or by use of the automation data processing equipment and procedures in the manner provided in this section.

HISTORY: GC § 11419-34; 114 v 193; Bureau of Code Revision, 10-1-53; 130 v 665 (Eff 8-5-63); 131 v 678 (Eff 11-1-65); 133 v H 424 (Eff 11-25-69); 140 v H 183. Eff 10-1-84.

§ 2939.03 Grand jurors subject to same provisions and regulations as other jurors.

A grand jury is drawn and notified by the same persons, from the same jury wheel, automation data processing storage drawer, or automated data processing information storage device and in the same manner as other jurors are drawn and notified under sections 2939.02 to 2939.04, inclusive, and 2313.01 to 2313.46, inclusive, of the Revised Code. Grand jurors so drawn and notified may be excused from service for the same reasons and in the same manner as other jurors under

§ 2939.03.1

such sections, and not otherwise. They are subject to the same fines and penalties for nonattendance and otherwise as are other jurors under such sections. The duties and the powers of courts of common pleas and clerks of courts of common pleas, and of the commissioners of jurors in regard to grand jurors, in all respects are the same as in regard to other jurors.

HISTORY: GC § 11419-35; 114 v 193; Bureau of Code Revision, 10-1-53; 131 v 679 (Eff 11-1-65); 133 v H 424. Eff 11-25-69.

[§ 2939.03.1] § 2939.031 Selection of additional or alternate juror.

When it appears to the judge impaneling a grand jury that the inquiry is likely to be protracted, or upon direction of the judge, an additional or alternate juror shall be selected in the same manner as the regular jurors in the inquiry are selected. The additional or alternate juror shall be sworn and seated near the jury, with equal opportunity for seeing and hearing the proceedings, shall attend the inquiry at all times and shall obey all orders and admonitions of the court or foreman. When the jurors are ordered kept together, the alternate juror shall be kept with them. The additional or alternate juror shall be liable as a regular juror for failure to attend the inquiry or to obey any order or admonition of the court or foreman. He shall receive the same compensation as other jurors, and except as provided in this section shall be discharged upon the final submission of the bill to the foreman.

If before the final submission of the bill to the jury, a juror dies or is discharged by the judge or foreman due to incapacity, absence, or disqualification of such juror, the additional or alternate juror, upon order of the judge or foreman, shall become one of the jury and serve in all respects as though selected as an original juror during the absence or incapacity of an original juror.

HISTORY: 125 v H 112. Eff 10-14-53.

§ 2939.04 Grand jurors; compensation.

The compensation of grand jurors shall be fixed by resolution of the board of county commissioners, not to exceed ten dollars for each day's attendance, payable out of the county treasury. Except in counties of less than one hundred thousand population according to the last federal census, in which counties the judge of the court of common pleas shall make rules and regulations in his own county applicable thereto, a person who has served as a grand juror at a term of court is prohibited from serving again, either as a grand juror or petit juror, in that jury year in which the service is rendered, or in the next jury year. He is entitled to a certificate of exemption in like manner as a petit juror. The court of common pleas may order the drawing of a special jury to sit at any time public business requires it.

HISTORY: GC § 11419-36; 114 v 193(204); 116 v 371; Bureau of Code Revision, 10-1-53; 135 v S 465. Eff 3-4-75.

§ 2939.05 Repealed, 129 v 1201, § 2 [GC § 13436-1; 113 v 123(158); Bureau of Code Revision, 10-1-53]. Eff 9-11-61.

This section concerned clerk to make list of persons required to appear.

§ 2939.06 Oath to grand jurors.

When a grand jury is impaneled the court of common pleas shall appoint one of the members thereof as foreman, and shall administer, or cause to be administered, to said jurors an oath in the following words:

"You and each of you do solemnly swear that you will diligently inquire, and true presentment make of all such matters and things as shall be given you in charge or otherwise come to your knowledge, touching the present service; the counsel of the state, your own, and your fellows, you shall keep secret unless called on in a court of justice to make disclosures; and you shall present no person through malice, hatred, or ill will, nor shall you leave any person unpresented through fear, favor, or affection, or for any reward or hope thereof, but in all your presentments you shall present the truth, the whole truth, and nothing but the truth, according to the best of your skill and understanding.["]

HISTORY: GC § 13436-3; 113 v 123(158), ch 15, § 3; Bureau of Code Revision. Eff 10-1-53.

§ 2939.07 Charge of the court.

The grand jurors, after being sworn, shall be charged as to their duty by the judge of the court of common pleas, who shall call their attention particularly to the obligation of secrecy which their oaths impose, and explain to them the law applicable to such matters as may be brought before them.

HISTORY: GC § 13436-4; 113 v 123(159), ch 15, § 4; Bureau of Code Revision. Eff 10-1-53.

§ 2939.08 Duty of grand jury.

After the charge of the court of common pleas, the grand jury shall retire with the officer appointed to attend it, and proceed to inquire of and present all offenses committed within the county.

HISTORY: GC § 13436-5; 113 v 123(159), ch 15, § 8; Bureau of Code Revision. Eff 10-1-53.

§ 2939.09 Clerk of grand jury.

The grand jury may appoint one of its members to be its clerk to preserve the minutes of its proceedings and actions in all cases pending before it. Such minutes shall be delivered to the prosecuting attorney before the jury is discharged.

HISTORY: GC § 13436-6; 113 v 123(159), ch 15, § 6; Bureau of Code Revision. Eff 10-1-53.

§ 2939.10 Who shall have access to grand jury.

The prosecuting attorney or assistant prosecuting attorney may at all times appear before the grand jury to give information relative to a matter cognizable by it, or advice upon a legal matter when required. The prosecuting attorney may interrogate witnesses before the grand jury when the grand jury or the prosecuting attorney finds it necessary, but no person other than the grand jurors shall be permitted to remain in the room with the jurors while the jurors are expressing their views or giving their votes on a matter before them. In all matters or cases which the attorney general is required to investigate or prosecute by the governor or general assembly, or which a special prosecutor is required by section 177.03 of the Revised Code to investigate and prosecute, the attorney general or the special prosecutor, respectively, shall have and exercise any or all rights, privileges, and powers of prosecuting attorneys, and any assistant or special counsel designated by the attorney general or special prosecutor for that purpose, has the same authority. Proceedings in relation to such matters or cases are under the exclusive supervision and control of the attorney general or the special prosecutor.

HISTORY: GC § 13436-7; 113 v 123(159), ch 15, § 7; Bureau of Code Revision, 10-1-53; 141 v S 74. Eff 9-3-86.

§ 2939.11 Official reporters.

The official shorthand reporter of the county, or any shorthand reporter designated by the court of common pleas, at the request of the prosecuting attorney, or any such reporter designated by the attorney general in investigations conducted by him, may take shorthand notes of testimony before the grand jury, and furnish a transcript to the prosecuting attorney or the attorney general, and to no other person. The shorthand reporter shall withdraw from the jury room before the jurors begin to express their views or take their vote on the matter before them. Such reporter shall take an oath to be administered by the judge after the grand jury is sworn, imposing an obligation of secrecy to not disclose any testimony taken or heard except to the grand jury, prosecuting attorney, or attorney general, unless called upon in court to make disclosures.

HISTORY: GC § 13436-8; 113 v 123(159), ch 15, § 8; Bureau of Code Revision. Eff 10-1-53.

§ 2939.12 Clerk to issue subpoenas for witnesses.

When required by the grand jury, prosecuting attorney, or judge of the court of common pleas, the clerk of the court of common pleas shall issue subpoenas and other process to any county to bring witnesses to testify before such jury.

HISTORY: GC § 13436-9; 113 v 123(160), ch 15, § 9; Bureau of Code Revision. Eff 10-1-53.

[§ 2939.12.1] § 2939.121 Employee may not be penalized for being subpoenaed before grand jury.

No employer shall discharge or terminate from employment, threaten to discharge or terminate from employment, or otherwise punish or penalize any employee because of time lost from regular employment as a result of the employee's attendance at any proceeding before a grand jury pursuant to a subpoena. This section generally does not require and shall not be construed to require an employer to pay an employee for time lost resulting from attendance at any grand jury proceeding. However, if an employee is subpoenaed to appear at a grand jury proceeding and the proceeding pertains to an offense against the employer or an offense involving the employee during the course of his employment, the employer shall not decrease or withhold the employee's pay for any time lost as a result of compliance with the subpoena. Any employer who knowingly violates this section is in contempt of court.

HISTORY: 140 v S 172. Eff 9-26-84.

§ 2939.13 Oath to witnesses.

Before a witness is examined by the grand jury, an oath shall be administered to him by the foreman of the grand jury or by the judge of the court of common pleas or the clerk of the court of common pleas, truly to testify of such matters and things as may lawfully be inquired of before such jury. A certificate that the oath has been administered shall be indorsed on the subpoena of the witness or otherwise made by the foreman of the grand jury, judge, or clerk certifying the attendance of said witness to the clerk of the court.

HISTORY: GC § 13436-10; 113 v 123(160), ch 15, § 10; 115 v 417; Bureau of Code Revision. Eff 10-1-53.

§ 2939.14 Proceedings when witness refuses to testify.

If a witness before a grand jury refuses to answer an interrogatory, the court of common pleas shall be informed in writing, in which such interrogatory shall be stated, with the excuse for the refusal given by the witness. The court shall determine whether the witness is required to answer, and the grand jury shall be forthwith informed of such decision.

HISTORY: GC § 13436-11; 113 v 123(160), ch 15, § 11; Bureau of Code Revision. Eff 10-1-53.

§ 2939.15 Court may proceed against witness for contempt.

If the court of common pleas determines that a witness before a grand jury is required to answer an interrogatory and such witness persists in his refusal, he shall be brought before the court, which shall proceed in a like manner as if such witness had been interrogated and refused to answer in open court.

HISTORY: GC § 13436-12; 113 v 123(160), ch 15, § 12; Bureau of Code Revision. Eff 10-1-53.

§ 2939.16 Court may appoint grand juror in case of death.

In case of sickness, death, discharge, or nonattendance of a grand juror after the grand jury is sworn, the court may cause another to be sworn in his stead. The court shall charge such juror as required by section 2939.07 of the Revised Code.

HISTORY: GC § 13436-13; 113 v 123(160), ch 15, § 13; Bureau of Code Revision. Eff 10-1-53.

§ 2939.17 New grand jury may be summoned.

After the grand jury is discharged, the court of common pleas, when necessary, may order the drawing and impaneling of a new grand jury, which shall be summoned and returned as provided by section 2939.03 of the Revised Code and shall be sworn and proceed in the manner provided by sections 2939.06 to 2939.24, inclusive, of the Revised Code. Whenever the governor or general assembly directs the attorney general to conduct any investigation or prosecution, the court of common pleas or any judge thereof, on written request of the attorney general, shall order a special grand jury to be summoned, and such special grand jury may be called and discharge its duties either before, during, or after any session of the regular grand jury, and its proceedings shall be independent of the proceedings of the regular grand jury but of the same force and effect.

Whenever a witness is necessary to a full investigation by the attorney general under this section, or to secure or successfully maintain and conclude a prosecution arising out of any such investigation, the judge of the court of common pleas may grant to such witness immunity from any prosecution based on the testimony or other evidence given by the witness in the course of the investigation or prosecution other than a prosecution for perjury in giving such testimony or evidence.

HISTORY: GC § 13436-14; 113 v 123(160); Bureau of Code Revision, 10-1-53; 129 v 1201 (Eff 9-11-61); 133 v H 956. Eff 9-16-70.

§ 2939.18 Fact of indictment shall be kept secret.

No grand juror, officer of the court, or other person shall disclose that an indictment has been found against a person not in custody or under bail, before such indictment is filed and the case docketed, except by the issue of process.

HISTORY: GC § 13436-15; 113 v 123(161), ch 15, § 15; Bureau of Code Revision. Eff 10-1-53.

§ 2939.19 Testimony of grand jurors.

No grand juror may state or testify in court in what manner any member of the grand jury voted or what opinion was expressed by any juror on any question before the grand jury.

HISTORY: GC § 13436-16; 113 v 123(161), ch 15, § 16; Bureau of Code Revision. Eff 10-1-53.

§ 2939.20 Indictment by twelve jurors.

At least twelve of the grand jurors must concur in the finding of an indictment. When so found, the foreman shall indorse on such indictment the words "A true bill" and subscribe his name as foreman.

HISTORY: GC § 13436-17; 113 v 123(161), ch 15, § 17; Bureau of Code Revision. Eff 10-1-53.

§ 2939.21 A grand jury to visit the county jail.

Once every three months, the grand jurors shall visit the county jail, examine its condition, and inquire into the discipline and treatment of the prisoners, their habits, diet, and accommodations. They shall report on these matters to the court of common pleas in writing. The clerk of the court of common pleas shall forward a copy of the report to the department of rehabilitation and correction.

HISTORY: GC § 13436-20; 113 v 123(161), ch 15, § 20; Bureau of Code Revision, 10-1-53; 136 v H 390 (Eff 8-6-76); 139 v S 23. Eff 7-6-82.

§ 2939.22 Proceedings when indictments are returned.

Indictments found by a grand jury shall be presented by the foreman to the court of common pleas, and filed with the clerk of the court of common pleas, who shall indorse thereon the date of such filing and enter each case upon the appearance docket and the trial docket of the term when the persons indicted have been arrested. The court shall assign such indictments for trial under section 2945.02 of the Revised Code, and recognizances of defendants and witnesses shall be taken for their appearance in court. When a case is continued to the next term of court, such recognizance shall require the appearance of the defendants and witnesses at a time designated by the court. Secret indictments shall not be docketed by name until after the apprehension of the accused.

HISTORY: GC § 13436-21; 113 v 123(161), ch 15, § 21; Bureau of Code Revision. Eff 10-1-53.

§ 2939.23 Report to court when indictment not found.

If an indictment is not found by the grand jury, against an accused who has been held to answer, such fact shall be reported by the foreman to the court of common pleas.

HISTORY: GC § 13436-22; 113 v 123(162), ch 15, § 22; Bureau of Code Revision. Eff 10-1-53.

§ 2939.24 Disposition of person in jail and not indicted.

If a person held in jail charged with an indictable offense is not indicted at the term of court at which he is held to answer, he shall be discharged unless:

(A) He was committed on such charge after the discharge of the grand jury.
(B) The transcript has not been filed.
(C) There is not sufficient time at such term of court to investigate said cause.
(D) The grand jury, for good cause, continues the hearing of said charge until the next term of court.
(E) It appears to the court of common pleas that a witness for the state has been enticed or kept away, detained, or prevented from attending court by sickness or unavoidable accident.

HISTORY: GC § 13436-23; 113 v 123(162), ch 15, § 23; Bureau of Code Revision. Eff 10-1-53.

[ATTENDANCE OF WITNESSES FROM WITHOUT STATE]

§ 2939.25 Definition of witness, state, and summons.

As used in sections 2939.25 to 2939.29, inclusive, of the Revised Code:

(A) "Witness" includes a person whose testimony is desired in any proceeding or investigation by a grand jury or in a criminal action, prosecution, or proceeding.
(B) "State" includes any territory of the United States and District of Columbia.
(C) "Summons" includes a subpoena, order, or other notice requiring the appearance of a witness.

HISTORY: GC § 13436-24; 117 v 668; Bureau of Code Revision. Eff 10-1-53.

§ 2939.26 Foreign court may compel witnesses.

If a judge of a court of record in any state which by its laws has made provision for commanding persons within that state to attend and testify in this state, certifies under the seal of such court that there is a criminal prosecution pending in such court, or that a grand jury investigation has commenced or is about to commence, that a person being within this state is a material witness in such prosecution or grand jury investigation, and that his presence will be required for a specified number of days, upon presentation of such certificate to any judge of a court of record in the county in this state in which such person is, such judge shall fix a time and place for a hearing and shall make an order directing the witness to appear at a time and place certain for the hearing.

If at a hearing such judge determines that the witness is material and necessary, that it will not cause undue hardship to the witness to be compelled to attend and testify in the prosecution or grand jury investigation in the other state, and that the laws of the state in which the prosecution is pending, or grand jury investigation has commenced or is about to commence, and of any other state through which the witness may be required to pass by ordinary course of travel, will give to him protection from arrest and the service of civil and criminal process, he shall issue a summons, with a copy of the certificate attached, directing the witness to attend and testify in the court where the prosecution is pending, or where a grand jury investigation has commenced or is about to commence, at a time and place specified in the summons. In any such hearing the certificate is prima-facie evidence of all the facts stated therein.

If said certificate recommends that the witness be taken into immediate custody and delivered to an officer of the requesting state to assure his attendance in the requesting state, such judge may, in lieu of notification of the hearing, direct that such witness be forthwith brought before him for said hearing. If the judge at the hearing is satisfied of the desirability of such custody and delivery, for which determination the certificate is prima-facie proof of such desirability, he may, in lieu of issuing subpoena or summons, order that said witness be forthwith taken into custody and delivered to an officer of the requesting state.

If the witness, who is summoned as provided in this section, after being paid or tendered by some properly authorized person the sum of ten cents a mile for each mile by the ordinary traveled route to and from the court where the prosecution is pending and five dollars for each day, that he is required to travel and attend as a witness, fails without good cause to attend and testify as directed in the summons, he shall be punished in the manner provided for the punishment of any witness who disobeys a summons issued from a court of record in this state.

HISTORY: GC § 13436-25; 117 v 668, § 2; Bureau of Code Revision. Eff 10-1-53.

§ 2939.27 Certificate to specify time witness will be required; mileage and fees.

If a person in any state, which by its laws has made

provision for commanding persons within its borders to attend and testify in criminal prosecutions or grand jury investigations commenced or about to commence, in this state, is a material witness in a prosecution pending in a court of record in this state, or in a grand jury investigation which has commenced or is about to commence, a judge of such court may issue a certificate under the seal of the court stating these facts and specifying the number of days the witness will be required. Said certificate may include a recommendation that the witness be taken into immediate custody and delivered to an officer of this state to assure his attendance in this state. This certificate shall be presented to a judge of a court of record in the county in which the witness is found.

If the witness is summoned to attend and testify in this state he shall be tendered the sum of ten cents a mile for each mile by the ordinary traveled route to and from the court where the prosecution is pending, and five dollars for each day that he is required to travel and attend as a witness. A witness who has appeared in accordance with the summons shall not be required to remain within this state a longer period of time than the period mentioned in the certificate, unless otherwise ordered by the court. If such witness, after coming into this state, fails without good cause to attend and testify as directed in the summons, he shall be punished in the manner provided for the punishment of any witness who disobeys a summons issued from a court of record in this state.

HISTORY: GC § 13436-26; 117 v 668, § 3; Bureau of Code Revision. Eff 10-1-53.

§ 2939.28 Exemption from arrest.

If a person comes into this state in obedience to a summons directing him to attend and testify in this state, while in this state pursuant to such summons he is not subject to arrest or the service of process, civil or criminal, in connection with matters which arose before his entrance into this state under the summons.

If a person passes through this state while going to another state in obedience to a summons to attend and testify in that state or while returning therefrom, while so passing through this state he is not subject to arrest or the service of process, civil or criminal, in connection with matters which arose before his entrance into this state under the summons.

HISTORY: GC § 13436-27; 117 v 668, § 4; Bureau of Code Revision. Eff 10-1-53.

§ 2939.29 Construction.

Sections 2939.25 to 2939.28, inclusive, of the Revised Code shall be so interpreted and construed as to effectuate their general purpose, to make the law of this state uniform with the law of other states which enact similar uniform legislation.

HISTORY: GC § 13436-28; 117 v 668, § 5; Bureau of Code Revision. Eff 10-1-53.

CHAPTER 2941: INDICTMENT

Section

[FORM AND SUFFICIENCY]

2941.01 Definition of magistrate.
2941.02 Informations.
[2941.02.1] 2941.021 Prosecution by information.
2941.03 Sufficiency of indictments or informations.
2941.04 Two or more offenses in one indictment.
2941.05 Statement charging an offense.
2941.06 Form of indictment or information.
2941.07 Bill of particulars.
2941.08 Certain defects do not render indictment invalid.
2941.09 Identification of corporation.
2941.10 Indictment complete.
2941.11 Pleading prior conviction.
2941.12 Pleading a statute.
2941.13 Pleading a judgment.
2941.14 Allegations in homicide indictment.
[2941.14.1] 2941.141 Specification that offender had a firearm while committing the offense.
[2941.14.2, 2941.14.3] 2941.142, 2941.14.3 Repealed.
[2941.14.4] 2941.144 Specification that offender had an automatic firearm or a firearm equipped with a muffler or silencer.
[2941.14.5] 2941.145 Specification that offender displayed, brandished, indicated possession of or used firearm.
[2941.14.6] 2941.146 Specification that offender discharged firearm from motor vehicle.
[2941.14.7] 2941.147 Specification of sexual motivation.
[2941.14.8] 2941.148 Specification that offender is a sexually violent predator.
[2941.14.9] 2941.149 Specification that offender is repeat violent offender.
[2941.14.10] 2941.1410 Specification that offender is a major drug offender.
2941.15 Sufficiency of indictment for forgery.
2941.16 Sufficient description for forgery.
2941.17 Description by usual name or purport.
2941.18 Allegations in perjury indictment.
2941.19 Alleging intent to defraud.
2941.20 Allegations sufficient for unlawfully selling liquor.
2941.21 Averments as to joint ownership.
2941.22 Averments as to will or codicil.
2941.23 Averments as to election.
2941.24 Repealed.
2941.25 Multiple counts.
2941.26 Variance.
2941.27 Proof of dilatory plea.
2941.28 Misjoinder of parties or offenses.
2941.29 Time for objecting to defect in indictment.
2941.30 Amending an indictment.
2941.31 Record of quashed indictment.
2941.32 Proceedings when two indictments pending.
2941.33 Nolle prosequi.
2941.34 Lost or destroyed indictment.
2941.35 Prosecutions for misdemeanor.

[PROCESS ON INDICTMENTS]

2941.36 Warrant for arrest of accused.
2941.37 Warrant when accused is nonresident.
2941.38 Warrant when accused escapes.
2941.39 Indictment of convicts.

Section

2941.40 Convicts removed for sentence or trial.
[2941.40.1] 2941.401 Prisoner may request trial on pending charges.
2941.41 Warrant for removal.
2941.42 Convict to be confined.
2941.43 Disposition of prisoner following trial for another offense.
2941.44 Arrest and return of escaped convicts; expenses.
2941.45 Trial of persons serving sentence.
2941.46 Arrest of convict or prisoner violating pardon or parole.
2941.47 Summons on indictments against corporations.
2941.48 Recognizance of witnesses.

[SERVICE OF INDICTMENT AND EXCEPTIONS]

2941.49 Indictment to be served on accused.
2941.50 Repealed.
2941.51 Payment of appointed counsel.
2941.52 Repealed.
2941.53 Exceptions to an indictment.
2941.54 Motion to quash.
2941.55 Plea in abatement.
2941.56 Misnomer.
2941.57 Demurrer.
2941.58 Accused not discharged when indictment quashed.
2941.59 Waiver of defects.
2941.60 Answer to plea in abatement.
2941.61 After demurrer accused may plead.
2941.62 Hearing on motions and demurrers.
2941.63 Counsel to assist prosecutor.

[FORM AND SUFFICIENCY]

§ 2941.01 Definition of magistrate.

The definition of "magistrate" set forth in section 2931.01 of the Revised Code applies to Chapter 2941. of the Revised Code.

HISTORY: Bureau of Code Revision. Eff 10-1-53.

§ 2941.02 Informations.

All sections of the Revised Code which apply to prosecutions upon indictments, the process thereon, and the issuing and service thereof, to commitments, bails, motions, pleadings, trials, appeals, and punishments, to the execution of any sentence, and all other proceedings in cases of indictments whether in the court of original or appellate jurisdiction, apply to informations, and all prosecutions and proceedings thereon.

HISTORY: GC § 13437-1; 113 v 123(162), ch 16; Bureau of Code Revision. Eff 10-1-53.

[§ 2941.02.1] § 2941.021 Prosecution by information.

Any criminal offense which is not punishable by death

or life imprisonment may be prosecuted by information filed in the common pleas court by the prosecuting attorney if the defendant, after he has been advised by the court of the nature of the charge against him and of his rights under the constitution, is represented by counsel or has affirmatively waived counsel by waiver in writing and in open court, waives in writing and in open court prosecution by indictment.

HISTORY: 128 v 53. Eff 11-9-59.

§ 2941.03 Sufficiency of indictments or informations.

An indictment or information is sufficient if it can be understood therefrom:

(A) That it is entitled in a court having authority to receive it, though the name of the court is not stated;

(B) If it is an indictment, that it was found by a grand jury of the county in which the court was held, or if it is an information, that it was subscribed and presented to the court by the prosecuting attorney of the county in which the court was held;

(C) That the defendant is named, or, if his name cannot be discovered, that he is described by a fictitious name, with a statement that his true name is unknown to the jury or prosecuting attorney, but no name shall be stated in addition to one necessary to identify the accused;

(D) That an offense was committed at some place within the jurisdiction of the court, except where the act, though done without the local jurisdiction of the county, is triable therein;

(E) That the offense was committed at some time prior to the time of finding of the indictment or filing of the information.

HISTORY: GC § 13437-2; 113 v 123(162), ch 16, § 2; Bureau of Code Revision. Eff 10-1-53.

§ 2941.04 Two or more offenses in one indictment.

An indictment or information may charge two or more different offenses connected together in their commission, or different statements of the same offense, or two or more different offenses of the same class of crimes or offenses, under separate counts, and if two or more indictments or informations are filed in such cases the court may order them to be consolidated.

The prosecution is not required to elect between the different offenses or counts set forth in the indictment or information, but the defendant may be convicted of any number of the offenses charged, and each offense upon which the defendant is convicted must be stated in the verdict. The court in the interest of justice and for good cause shown, may order different offenses or counts set forth in the indictment or information tried separately or divided into two or more groups and each of said groups tried separately. A verdict of acquittal of one or more counts is not an acquittal of any other count.

HISTORY: GC § 13437-3; 113 v 123(162), ch 16, § 3; Bureau of Code Revision. Eff 10-1-53.

§ 2941.05 Statement charging an offense.

In an indictment or information charging an offense, each count shall contain, and is sufficient if it contains in substance, a statement that the accused has committed some public offense therein specified. Such statement may be made in ordinary and concise language without any technical averments or any allegations not essential to be proved. It may be in the words of the section of the Revised Code describing the offense or declaring the matter charged to be a public offense, or in any words sufficient to give the accused notice of the offense of which he is charged.

HISTORY: GC § 13437-4; 113 v 123(163), ch 16, § 4; Bureau of Code Revision, 10-1-53; 126 v 392. Eff 3-17-55.

§ 2941.06 Form of indictment or information.

An indictment may be substantially in the following form:

The State of Ohio,)
                 ss.
.... County)

In the Year of our Lord one thousand nine hundred and . . . . . .

The jurors of the Grand Jury of the State of Ohio, within and for the body of the County aforesaid, on their oaths, in the name and by the authority of the State of Ohio, do find and present that A.B., on the . . . . . . day of . . . . . . 19. . . at the county of . . . . . aforesaid, did . . . . (here insert the name of the offense if it has one, such as murder, arson, or the like, or if a misdemeanor having no general name, insert a brief description of it as given by law) contrary to the form of the statute in such case made and provided, and against the peace and dignity of the State of Ohio.

                .... C.D. ....
                        Prosecuting Attorney

(Indorsed) A true bill.
E.F. Foreman of the Grand Jury.

HISTORY: GC § 13437-5; 113 v 123(163), ch 16, § 5; Bureau of Code Revision, 10-1-53; 136 v H 390. Eff 8-6-76.

§ 2941.07 Bill of particulars.

Upon written request of the defendant made not later than five days prior to the date set for trial, or upon order of the court, the prosecuting attorney shall furnish a bill of particulars setting up specifically the nature of the offense charged and the conduct of the

defendant which is alleged to constitute the offense.
HISTORY: GC § 13437-6; 113 v 123(164), ch 16, § 6; Bureau of Code Revision, 10-1-53; 134 v H 511. Eff 1-1-74.

§ 2941.08 Certain defects do not render indictment invalid.

An indictment or information is not made invalid, and the trial, judgment, or other proceedings stayed, arrested, or affected:
(A) By the omission of "with force and arms," or words of similar import, or "as appears by the record";
(B) For omitting to state the time at which the offense was committed, in a case in which time is not of the essence of the offense;
(C) For stating the time imperfectly;
(D) For stating imperfectly the means by which the offense was committed except insofar as means is an element of the offense;
(E) For want of a statement of the value or price of a matter or thing, or the amount of damages or injury, where the value or price or the amount of damages or injury is not of the essence of the offense, and in such case it is sufficient to aver that the value or price of the property is less than, equals, or exceeds the certain value or price which determines the offense or grade thereof;
(F) For the want of an allegation of the time or place of a material fact when the time and place have been once stated therein;
(G) Because dates and numbers are represented by figures;
(H) For an omission to allege that the grand jurors were impaneled, sworn, or charged;
(I) For surplusage or repugnant allegations when there is sufficient matter alleged to indicate the crime and person charged;
(J) For want of averment of matter not necessary to be proved;
(K) For other defects or imperfections which do not tend to prejudice the substantial rights of the defendant upon the merits.
HISTORY: GC § 13437-7; 113 v 123(165), ch 16, § 7; Bureau of Code Revision. Eff 10-1-53.

§ 2941.09 Identification of corporation.

In any indictment or information it is sufficient for the purpose of identifying any group or association of persons, not incorporated, to state the proper name of such group or association, to state any name or designation by which the group or association has been or is known, to state the names of all persons in such group or association or of one or more of them, or to state the name of one or more persons in such group or association referring to the others as "another" or "others." It is sufficient for the purpose of identifying a corporation to state the corporate name of such corporation, or any name or designation by which such corporation has been or is known.
HISTORY: GC § 13437-8; 113 v 123(165), ch 16, § 8; Bureau of Code Revision. Eff 10-1-53.

§ 2941.10 Indictment complete.

No indictment or information for any offense created or defined by statute is objectionable for the reason that it fails to negative any exception, excuse, or proviso contained in the statute creating or defining the offense. The fact that the charge is made is an allegation that no legal excuse for the doing of the act exists in the particular case.
HISTORY: GC § 13437-9; 113 v 123(165), ch 16, § 9; Bureau of Code Revision. Eff 10-1-53.

§ 2941.11 Pleading prior conviction.

Whenever it is necessary to allege a prior conviction of the accused in an indictment or information, it is sufficient to allege that the accused was, at a certain stated time, in a certain stated court, convicted of a certain stated offense, giving the name of the offense, or stating the substantial elements thereof.
HISTORY: GC § 13437-10; 113 v 123(166), ch 16, § 10; Bureau of Code Revision. Eff 10-1-53.

§ 2941.12 Pleading a statute.

In pleading a statute or right derived therefrom it is sufficient to refer to the statute by its title, or in any other manner which identifies the statute. The court must thereupon take judicial notice of such statute.
HISTORY: GC § 13437-11; 113 v 123(166), ch 16, § 11; Bureau of Code Revision. Eff 10-1-53.

§ 2941.13 Pleading a judgment.

In pleading a judgment or other determination of, or a proceeding before, any court or officer, civil or military, it is not necessary to allege the fact conferring jurisdiction on such court or officer. It is sufficient to allege generally that such judgment or determination was given or made or such proceedings had.
HISTORY: GC § 13437-12; 113 v 123(166), ch 16, § 12; Bureau of Code Revision. Eff 10-1-53.

§ 2941.14 Allegations in homicide indictment.

(A) In an indictment for aggravated murder, murder, or voluntary or involuntary manslaughter, the manner in which, or the means by which the death was caused need not be set forth.
(B) Imposition of the death penalty for aggravated murder is precluded unless the indictment or count in the indictment charging the offense specifies one or

more of the aggravating circumstances listed in division (A) of section 2929.04 of the Revised Code. If more than one aggravating circumstance is specified to an indictment or count, each shall be in a separately numbered specification, and if an aggravating circumstance is specified to a count in an indictment containing more than one count, such specification shall be identified as to the count to which it applies.

(C) A specification to an indictment or count in an indictment charging aggravated murder shall be stated at the end of the body of the indictment or count, and may be in substantially the following form:

"SPECIFICATION (or, SPECIFICATION 1, SPECIFICATION TO THE FIRST COUNT, or SPECIFICATION 1 TO THE FIRST COUNT). The Grand Jurors further find and specify that (set forth the applicable aggravating circumstance listed in divisions (A)(1) to (9) of section 2929.04 of the Revised Code. The aggravating circumstance may be stated in the words of the subdivision in which it appears, or in words sufficient to give the accused notice of the same)."

HISTORY: GC § 13437-13; 113 v 123(166), ch 16, § 13; Bureau of Code Revision, 10-1-53; 134 v H 511 (Eff 1-1-74); 135 v H 716 (Eff 1-1-74); 139 v S 1 (Eff 10-19-81); 147 v S 32. Eff 8-6-97.

[§ 2941.14.1] § 2941.141 Specification that offender had a firearm while committing the offense.

(A) Imposition of a one-year mandatory prison term upon an offender under division (D)(1)(a)(i) of section 2929.14 of the Revised Code is precluded unless the indictment, count in the indictment, or information charging the offense specifies that the offender had a firearm on or about the offender's person or under the offender's control while committing the offense. The specification shall be stated at the end of the body of the indictment, count, or information, and shall be in substantially the following form:

"SPECIFICATION (or, SPECIFICATION TO THE FIRST COUNT).
The Grand Jurors (or insert the person's or the prosecuting attorney's name when appropriate) further find and specify that (set forth that the offender had a firearm on or about the offender's person or under the offender's control while committing the offense.)"

(B) Imposition of a one-year mandatory prison term upon an offender under division (D)(1)(a)(i) of section 2929.14 of the Revised Code is precluded if a court imposes a three-year or six-year mandatory prison term on the offender under that division relative to the same felony.

(C) As used in this section, "firearm" has the same meaning as in section 2923.11 of the Revised Code.

HISTORY: 139 v S 199 (Eff 1-5-83); 143 v S 258 (Eff 11-20-90); 143 v H 669 (Eff 1-10-91); 146 v S 2. Eff 7-1-96.

The effective date is set by section 6 of SB 2.

[§§ 2941.14.2, 2941.14.3] §§ 2941.142, 2941.143 Repealed, 146 v S 2, § 6 [140 v S 210]. Eff 7-1-96.

These sections concerned actual incarceration upon second conviction for certain felonies; specification of prior offense; and indefinite term upon second conviction where either was on offense of violence.

[§ 2941.14.4] § 2941.144 Specification that offender had an automatic firearm or a firearm equipped with a muffler or silencer.

(A) Imposition of a six-year mandatory prison term upon an offender under division (D)(1)(a)(i) of section 2929.14 of the Revised Code is precluded unless the indictment, count in the indictment, or information charging the offense specifies that the offender had a firearm that is an automatic firearm or that was equipped with a firearm muffler or silencer on or about the offender's person or under the offender's control while committing the offense. The specification shall be stated at the end of the body of the indictment, count, or information and shall be stated in substantially the following form:

"SPECIFICATION (or, SPECIFICATION TO THE FIRST COUNT). The Grand Jurors (or insert the person's or the prosecuting attorney's name when appropriate) further find and specify that (set forth that the offender had a firearm that is an automatic firearm or that was equipped with a firearm muffler or silencer on or about the offender's person or under the offender's control while committing the offense)."

(B) Imposition of a six-year mandatory prison term upon an offender under division (D)(1)(a)(i) of section 2929.14 of the Revised Code is precluded if a court imposes a three-year or one-year mandatory prison term on the offender under that division relative to the same felony.

(C) As used in this section, "firearm" and "automatic firearm" have the same meanings as in section 2923.11 of the Revised Code.

HISTORY: 143 v S 258 (Eff 11-20-90); 146 v S 2. Eff 7-1-96.

The effective date is set by section 6 of SB 2.

[§ 2941.14.5] § 2941.145 Specification that offender displayed, brandished, indicated possession of or used firearm.

(A) Imposition of a three-year mandatory prison term upon an offender under division (D)(1)(a)(i) of section 2929.14 of the Revised Code is precluded unless the indictment, count in the indictment, or information charging the offense specifies that the offender had a firearm on or about the offender's person or under the offender's control while committing the offense and displayed the firearm, brandished the firearm, indicated that the offender possessed the firearm, or used it to facilitate the offense. The specification shall be stated

at the end of the body of the indictment, county†, or information, and shall be stated in substantially the following form:
"SPECIFICATION (or, SPECIFICATION TO THE FIRST COUNT). The Grand Jurors (or insert the person's or the prosecuting attorney's name when appropriate) further find and specify that (set forth that the offender had a firearm on or about the offender's person or under the offender's control while committing the offense and displayed the firearm, brandished the firearm, indicated that the offender possessed the firearm, or used it to facilitate the offense)."

(B) Imposition of a three-year mandatory prison term upon an offender under division (D)(1)(a)(i) of section 2929.14 of the Revised Code is precluded if a court imposes a one-year or six-year mandatory prison term on the offender under that division relative to the same felony.

(C) As used in this section, "firearm" has the same meaning as in section 2923.11 of the Revised Code.

HISTORY: 146 v S 2. Eff 7-1-96.

The effective date is set by section 6 of SB 2.

† So in enrolled bill.

[§ 2941.14.6] § 2941.146 Specification that offender discharged firearm from motor vehicle.

(A) Imposition of a mandatory five-year prison term upon an offender under division (D)(1)(a)(ii) of section 2929.14 of the Revised Code for committing a violation of section 2923.161 [2923.16.1] of the Revised Code or for committing a felony that includes, as an essential element, purposely or knowingly causing or attempting to cause the death of or physical harm to another and that was committed by discharging a firearm from a motor vehicle other than a manufactured home is precluded unless the indictment, count in the indictment, or information charging the offender specifies that the offender committed the offense by discharging a firearm from a motor vehicle other than a manufactured home. The specification shall be stated at the end of the body of the indictment, count, or information, and shall be stated in substantially the following form:
"SPECIFICATION (or, SPECIFICATION TO THE FIRST COUNT). The Grand Jurors (or insert the person's or prosecuting attorney's name when appropriate) further find and specify that (set forth that the offender committed the violation of section 2923.161 [2923.16.1] of the Revised Code or the felony that includes, as an essential element, purposely or knowingly causing or attempting to cause the death of or physical harm to another and that was committed by discharging a firearm from a motor vehicle other than a manufactured home)."

(B) As used in this section:

(1) "Firearm" has the same meaning as in section 2923.11 of the Revised Code;

(2) "Motor vehicle" and "manufactured home" have the same meanings as in section 4501.01 of the Revised Code.

HISTORY: 146 v S 2. Eff 7-1-96.

The effective date is set by section 6 of SB 2.

[§ 2941.14.7] § 2941.147 Specification of sexual motivation.

(A) Whenever a person is charged with an offense that is a violation of section 2903.01, 2903.02, 2903.11, or 2905.01 of the Revised Code, a violation of division (A) of section 2903.04 of the Revised Code, an attempt to violate or complicity in violating section 2903.01, 2903.02, 2903.11, or 2905.01 of the Revised Code when the attempt or complicity is a felony, or an attempt to violate or complicity in violating division (A) of section 2903.04 of the Revised Code when the attempt or complicity is a felony, the indictment, count in the indictment, information, or complaint charging the offense may include a specification that the person committed the offense with a sexual motivation. The specification shall be stated at the end of the body of the indictment, count, information, or complaint and shall be in substantially the following form:
"SPECIFICATION (OR, SPECIFICATION TO THE FIRST COUNT). The Grand Jurors (or insert the person's or the prosecuting attorney's name when appropriate) further find and specify that the offender committed the offense with a sexual motivation."

(B) As used in this section, "sexual motivation" has the same meaning as in section 2971.01 of the Revised Code.

HISTORY: 146 v H 180. Eff 1-1-97.

The effective date is set by section 3 of HB 180.

See provisions, § 4 of HB 180 (146 v —) following RC § 2921.34.

[§ 2941.14.8] § 2941.148 Specification that offender is a sexually violent predator.

(A) The application of Chapter 2971. of the Revised Code to an offender is precluded unless the indictment, count in the indictment, or information charging the sexually violent offense or charging the designated homicide, assault, or kidnapping offense also includes a specification that the offender is a sexually violent predator. The specification shall be stated at the end of the body of the indictment, count, or information and shall be stated in substantially the following form:
"SPECIFICATION (OR, SPECIFICATION TO THE FIRST COUNT). The grand jury (or insert the person's or prosecuting attorney's name when appropriate) further find and specify that the offender is a sexually violent predator."

(B) In determining for purposes of this section whether a person is a sexually violent predator, all of the factors set forth in divisions (H)(1) to (6) of section

2971.01 of the Revised Code that apply regarding the person may be considered as evidence tending to indicate that it is likely that the person will engage in the future in one or more sexually violent offenses.

(C) As used in this section, "designated homicide, assault, or kidnapping offense," "sexually violent offense," and "sexually violent predator" have the same meanings as in section 2971.01 of the Revised Code.

HISTORY: 146 v H 180. Eff 1-1-97.

The effective date is set by section 3 of HB 180.

See provisions, § 4 of HB 180 (146 v —) following RC § 2921.34.

[§ 2941.14.9] § 2941.149 Specification that offender is repeat violent offender.

(A) The determination by a court that an offender is a repeat violent offender is precluded unless the indictment, count in the indictment, or information charging the offender specifies that the offender is a repeat violent offender. The specification shall be stated at the end of the body of the indictment, count, or information, and shall be stated in substantially the following form:

"SPECIFICATION (or, SPECIFICATION TO THE FIRST COUNT). The Grand Jurors (or insert the person's or prosecuting attorney's name when appropriate) further find and specify that (set forth that the offender is a repeat violent offender)."

(B) The court shall determine the issue of whether an offender is a repeat violent offender.

(C) As used in this section, "repeat violent offender" has the same meaning as in section 2929.01 of the Revised Code.

HISTORY: 146 v S 269. Eff 7-1-96.

The effective date is set by section 5 of SB 269.

[§ 2941.14.10] § 2941.1410 Specification that offender is a major drug offender.

(A) The determination by a court that an offender is a major drug offender is precluded unless the indictment, count in the indictment, or information charging the offender specifies that the offender is a major drug offender. The specification shall be stated at the end of the body of the indictment, count, or information, and shall be stated in substantially the following form:

"SPECIFICATION (or, SPECIFICATION TO THE FIRST COUNT). The Grand Jurors (or insert the person's or prosecuting attorney's name when appropriate) further find and specify that (set forth that the offender is a major drug offender)."

(B) The court shall determine the issue of whether an offender is a major drug offender.

(C) As used in this section, "major drug offender" has the same meaning as in section 2929.01 of the Revised Code.

HISTORY: 146 v S 269. Eff 7-1-96.

The effective date is set by section 5 of SB 269.

§ 2941.15 Sufficiency of indictment for forgery.

In an indictment or information for falsely making, altering, forging, printing, photographing, uttering, disposing of, or putting off an instrument, it is sufficient to set forth the purport and value thereof. Where the instrument is a promise to pay money conditionally, it is not necessary to allege that the condition has been performed.

HISTORY: GC § 13437-14; 113 v 123(166), ch 16, § 14; Bureau of Code Revision. Eff 10-1-53.

§ 2941.16 Sufficient description for forgery.

In an indictment or information for engraving or making the whole or part of an instrument, matter, or thing, or for using or having the unlawful custody or possession of a plate or other material upon which the whole or part of an instrument, matter, or thing was engraved or made, or for having the unlawful custody or possession of a paper upon which the whole or part of an instrument, matter, or thing was made or printed, it is sufficient to describe such instrument, matter, or thing by any name or designation by which it is usually known.

HISTORY: GC § 13437-15; 113 v 123(166), ch 16, § 15; Bureau of Code Revision. Eff 10-1-53.

§ 2941.17 Description by usual name or purport.

In all cases when it is necessary to make an averment in an indictment or information as to a writing, instrument, tool, or thing, it is sufficient to describe it by any name or designation by which it is usually known, or by the purport thereof.

HISTORY: GC § 13437-16; 113 v 123(167), ch 16, § 16; Bureau of Code Revision, 10-1-53; 134 v H 511. Eff 1-1-74.

§ 2941.18 Allegations in perjury indictment.

In an indictment or information for perjury or falsification, it is not necessary to set forth any part of a record or proceeding, or the commission or authority of the court or other authority before which perjury or falsification was committed.

HISTORY: GC § 13437-17; 113 v 123(167), ch 16, § 17; Bureau of Code Revision, 10-1-53; 134 v H 511. Eff 1-1-74.

§ 2941.19 Alleging intent to defraud.

It is sufficient in an indictment or information where it is necessary to allege an intent to defraud, to allege that the accused did the act with intent to defraud, without alleging an intent to defraud a particular person or corporation. On the trial of such an indictment or information, an intent to defraud a particular person need not be proved. It is sufficient to prove that the accused did the act charged with intent to defraud.

HISTORY: GC § 13437-18; 113 v 123(167), ch 16, § 18; Bureau of Code Revision. Eff 10-1-53.

§ 2941.20 Allegations sufficient for unlawfully selling liquor.

An indictment, information, or affidavit charging a violation of law relative to the sale, possession, transportation, buying, or giving intoxicating liquor to any person, need not allege the kind of liquor sold, nor the person by whom bought except that such charge must be sufficient to inform the accused of the particular offense with which he is charged.

HISTORY: GC § 13437-19; 113 v 123(167), ch 16, § 19; Bureau of Code Revision. Eff 10-1-53.

§ 2941.21 Averments as to joint ownership.

In an indictment or information for an offense committed upon, or in relation to, property belonging to partners or joint owners, it is sufficient to allege the ownership of such property to be in such partnership by its firm name, or in one or more of such partners or owners without naming all of them.

HISTORY: GC § 13437-20; 113 v 123(167), ch 16, § 20; Bureau of Code Revision. Eff 10-1-53.

§ 2941.22 Averments as to will or codicil.

In an indictment or information for stealing a will, codicil, or other testamentary instrument, or for forgery thereof, or, for a fraudulent purpose, keeping, destroying, or secreting it, whether in relation to real or personal property, or during the life of a testator or after his death, it is not necessary to allege the ownership or value thereof.

HISTORY: GC § 13437-21; 113 v 123(167), ch 16, § 21; Bureau of Code Revision. Eff 10-1-53.

§ 2941.23 Averments as to election.

In an indictment or information for an offense committed in relation to an election, it is sufficient to allege that such election was authorized by law, without stating the names of the officers holding it or the person voted for or the offices to be filled at the election.

HISTORY: GC § 13437-22; 113 v 123(167), ch 16, § 22; Bureau of Code Revision. Eff 10-1-53.

§ 2941.24 Repealed, 135 v H 716, § 2 [GC § 13437-23; 113 v 123(168); Bureau of Code Revision, 10-1-53]. Eff 1-1-74.

This section concerned counts for embezzlement and larceny.

§ 2941.25 Multiple counts.

(A) Where the same conduct by defendant can be construed to constitute two or more allied offenses of similar import, the indictment or information may contain counts for all such offenses, but the defendant may be convicted of only one.

(B) Where the defendant's conduct constitutes two or more offenses of dissimilar import, or where his conduct results in two or more offenses of the same or similar kind committed separately or with a separate animus as to each, the indictment or information may contain counts for all such offenses, and the defendant may be convicted of all of them.

HISTORY: 134 v H 511. Eff 1-1-74.

Not analogous to former RC § 2941.25 (GC § 13437-24; 113 v 123(168); Bureau of Code Revision, 10-1-53), repealed 134 v H 511, § 2, eff 1-1-74.

§ 2941.26 Variance.

When, on the trial of an indictment or information, there appears to be a variance between the statement in such indictment or information and the evidence offered in proof thereof, in the Christian name or surname, or other description of a person therein named or described, or in the name or description of a matter or thing therein named or described, such variance is not ground for an acquittal of the defendant unless the court before which the trial is had finds that such variance is material to the merits of the case or may be prejudicial to the defendant.

HISTORY: GC § 13437-25; 113 v 123(168), ch 16, § 25; Bureau of Code Revision. Eff 10-1-53.

§ 2941.27 Proof of dilatory plea.

No plea in abatement, or other dilatory plea to the indictment or information, shall be received by any court unless the party offering such plan proves the truth thereof by affidavit, or by some other sworn evidence.

HISTORY: GC § 13437-26; 113 v 123(168), ch 16, § 26; Bureau of Code Revision. Eff 10-1-53.

§ 2941.28 Misjoinder of parties or offenses.

No indictment or information shall be quashed, set aside, or dismissed for any of the following defects:

(A) That there is a misjoinder of the parties accused;
(B) That there is a misjoinder of the offenses charged in the indictment or information, or duplicity therein;
(C) That any uncertainty exists therein.

If the court is of the opinion that either defect referred to in division (A) or (B) of this section exists in any indictment or information, it may sever such indictment or information into separate indictments or informations or into separate counts.

If the court is of the opinion that the defect referred to in division (C) of this section exists in the indictment or information, it may order the indictment or information amended to cure such defect, provided no change is made in the name or identity of the crime charged.

HISTORY: GC § 13437-27; 113 v 123(168), ch 16, § 27; Bureau of Code Revision. Eff 10-1-53.

§ 2941.29 Time for objecting to defect in indictment.

No indictment or information shall be quashed, set aside, or dismissed, or motion to quash be sustained, or any motion for delay of sentence for the purpose of review be granted, nor shall any conviction be set aside or reversed on account of any defect in form or substance of the indictment or information, unless the objection to such indictment or information, specifically stating the defect claimed, is made prior to the commencement of the trial, or at such time thereafter as the court permits.

HISTORY: GC § 13437-28; 113 v 123(169), ch 16, § 28; Bureau of Code Revision. Eff 10-1-53.

§ 2941.30 Amending an indictment.

The court may at any time before, during, or after a trial amend the indictment, information, or bill of particulars, in respect to any defect, imperfection, or omission in form or substance, or of any variance with the evidence, provided no change is made in the name or identity of the crime charged. If any amendment is made to the substance of the indictment or information or to cure a variance between the indictment or information and the proof, the accused is entitled to a discharge of the jury on his motion, if a jury has been impaneled, and to a reasonable continuance of the cause, unless it clearly appears from the whole proceedings that he has not been misled or prejudiced by the defect or variance in respect to which the amendment is made, or that his rights will be fully protected by proceeding with the trial, or by a postponement thereof to a later day with the same or another jury. In case a jury is discharged from further consideration of a case under this section, the accused was not in jeopardy. No action of the court in refusing a continuance or postponement under this section is reviewable except after motion to and refusal by the trial court to grant a new trial therefor, and no appeal based upon such action of the court shall be sustained, nor reversal had, unless from consideration of the whole proceedings, the reviewing court finds that the accused was prejudiced in his defense or that a failure of justice resulted.

HISTORY: GC § 13437-29; 113 v 123(169), ch 16, § 29; Bureau of Code Revision. Eff 10-1-53.

§ 2941.31 Record of quashed indictment.

In criminal prosecutions, when the indictment or information has been quashed or the prosecuting attorney has entered a nolle prosequi thereon, or the cause or indictment is disposed of otherwise than upon trial, a complete record shall not be made by the clerk of the court of common pleas unless ordered to do so by the court of common pleas.

HISTORY: GC § 13437-30; 113 v 123(169), ch 16, § 30; 115 v 530; Bureau of Code Revision. Eff 10-1-53.

§ 2941.32 Proceedings when two indictments pending.

If two or more indictments or informations are pending against the same defendant for the same criminal act, the prosecuting attorney must elect upon which he will proceed, and upon trial being had upon one of them, the remaining indictments or information shall be quashed.

HISTORY: GC § 13437-31; 113 v 123(170), ch 16, § 31; Bureau of Code Revision. Eff 10-1-53.

§ 2941.33 Nolle prosequi.

The prosecuting attorney shall not enter a nolle prosequi in any cause without leave of the court, on good cause shown, in open court. A nolle prosequi entered contrary to this section is invalid.

HISTORY: GC § 13437-32; 113 v 123(170), ch 16, § 32; Bureau of Code Revision. Eff 10-1-53.

§ 2941.34 Lost or destroyed indictment.

If an indictment or information is mutilated, obliterated, lost, mislaid, destroyed, or stolen, or for any other reason cannot be produced at the arraignment or trial of the defendant, the court may substitute a copy.

HISTORY: GC § 13437-33; 113 v 123(170), ch 16, § 33; Bureau of Code Revision, 10-1-53; 127 v 847. Eff 9-16-57.

§ 2941.35 Prosecutions for misdemeanor.

Prosecutions for misdemeanors may be instituted by a prosecuting attorney by affidavit or such other method as is provided by law in such courts as have original jurisdiction in misdemeanors. Laws as to form, sufficiency, amendments, objections, and exceptions to indictments and as to the service thereof apply to such affidavits and warrants issued thereon.

HISTORY: GC § 13437-34; 113 v 123(170), ch 16, § 34; 121 v 121; Bureau of Code Revision. Eff 10-1-53.

[PROCESS ON INDICTMENTS]

§ 2941.36 Warrant for arrest of accused.

A warrant may be issued at any time by an order of a court, or on motion of a prosecuting attorney after the indictment, information, or affidavit is filed. When directed to the sheriff of the county where such indictment was found or information or affidavit filed, he may pursue and arrest the accused in any county and commit him to jail or present him in open court, if court is in session.

HISTORY: GC § 13438-1; 113 v 123(170), ch 17; Bureau of Code Revision. Eff 10-1-53.

§ 2941.37 Warrant when accused is non-resident.

When an accused resides out of the county in which the indictment was found or information filed, a warrant may issue thereon, directed to the sheriff of the county where such accused resides or is found. Such sheriff shall arrest the accused and convey him to the county from which such warrant was issued, and there commit him to jail or present him in open court, if court is in session.

HISTORY: GC § 13438-2; 113 v 123(170), ch 17, § 2; Bureau of Code Revision. Eff 10-1-53.

§ 2941.38 Warrant when accused escapes.

When an accused escapes and forfeits his recognizance after the jury is sworn, a warrant reciting the facts may issue at the request of the prosecuting attorney, to the sheriff of any county, who shall pursue, arrest, and commit the accused to the jail of the county from which such warrant issued, until he is discharged.

HISTORY: GC § 13438-3; 113 v 123(171), ch 17, § 3; Bureau of Code Revision. 10-1-53.

§ 2941.39 Indictment of convicts.

When a convict in a state correctional institution is indicted for a felony committed while confined in the correctional institution, he shall remain in the custody of the warden or superintendent of the institution subject to the order of the court of common pleas of the county in which the institution is located.

HISTORY: GC § 13438-4; 113 v 123(171), ch 17, § 4; Bureau of Code Revision, 10-1-53; 145 v H 571. Eff 10-6-94.

§ 2941.40 Convicts removed for sentence or trial.

A convict in a state correctional institution, who escaped, forfeited his recognizance before receiving sentence for a felony, or against whom an indictment or information for felony is pending, may be removed to the county in which the conviction was had or the indictment or information was pending for sentence or trial, upon the warrant of the court of common pleas of the county.

HISTORY: GC § 13438-5; 113 v 123(171), ch 17, § 5; Bureau of Code Revision, 10-1-53; 133 v H 508 (Eff 10-24-69); 145 v H 571. Eff 10-6-94.

[§ 2941.40.1] § 2941.401 Prisoner may request trial on pending charges.

When a person has entered upon a term of imprisonment in a correctional institution of this state, and when during the continuance of the term of imprisonment there is pending in this state any untried indictment, information, or complaint against the prisoner, he shall be brought to trial within one hundred eighty days after he causes to be delivered to the prosecuting attorney and the appropriate court in which the matter is pending, written notice of the place of his imprisonment and a request for a final disposition to be made of the matter, except that for good cause shown in open court, with the prisoner or his counsel present, the court may grant any necessary or reasonable continuance. The request of the prisoner shall be accompanied by a certificate of the warden or superintendent having custody of the prisoner, stating the term of commitment under which the prisoner is being held, the time served and remaining to be served on the sentence, the amount of good time earned, the time of parole eligibility of the prisoner, and any decisions of the adult parole authority relating to the prisoner.

The written notice and request for final disposition shall be given or sent by the prisoner to the warden or superintendent having custody of him, who shall promptly forward it with the certificate to the appropriate prosecuting attorney and court by registered or certified mail, return receipt requested.

The warden or superintendent having custody of the prisoner shall promptly inform him in writing of the source and contents of any untried indictment, information, or complaint against him, concerning which the warden or superintendent has knowledge, and of his right to make a request for final disposition thereof.

Escape from custody by the prisoner, subsequent to his execution of the request for final disposition, voids the request.

If the action is not brought to trial within the time provided, subject to continuance allowed pursuant to this section, no court any longer has jurisdiction thereof, the indictment, information, or complaint is void, and the court shall enter an order dismissing the action with prejudice.

This section does not apply to any person adjudged to be mentally ill or who is under sentence of life imprisonment or death, or to any prisoner under sentence of death.

HISTORY: 133 v S 355 (Eff 11-18-69); 145 v H 571. Eff 10-6-94.

§ 2941.41 Warrant for removal.

A warrant for removal specified in section 2941.40 of the Revised Code shall be in the usual form, except that it shall set forth that the accused is in a state correctional institution. The warrant shall be directed to the sheriff of the county in which the conviction was had or the indictment or information is pending. When a copy of the warrant is presented to the warden or the superintendent of a state correctional institution, he shall deliver the convict to the sheriff who shall convey him to the county and commit him to the county jail. For removing and returning the convict, the sheriff shall receive the fees allowed for conveying convicts to a state correctional institution.

HISTORY: GC § 13438-6; 113 v 123(171), ch 17, § 6; Bureau of Code Revision, 10-1-53; 139 v H 145 (Eff 5-28-81); 145 v H 571. Eff 10-6-94.

§ 2941.42 Convict to be confined.

A convict removed as provided by section 2941.41 of the Revised Code shall be kept in jail subject to be taken into court for sentence or trial. If the case is continued or the execution of the sentence is suspended, the court may order him to be returned to the state correctional institution by the sheriff, who shall deliver him, with a certified copy of the order, to the warden, who shall again deliver the convict to the sheriff upon another certified order of the court.

HISTORY: GC § 13438-7; 113 v 123(171), ch 17, § 7; Bureau of Code Revision, 10-1-53; 145 v H 571. Eff 10-6-94.

§ 2941.43 Disposition of prisoner following trial for another offense.

If the convict referred to in section 2941.40 of the Revised Code is acquitted, he shall [be]† forthwith returned by the sheriff to the state correctional institution to serve out the remainder of his sentence. If he is sentenced to imprisonment in a state correctional institution, he shall be returned to the state correctional institution by the sheriff to serve his new term. If he is sentenced to death, the death sentence shall be executed as if he were not under sentence of imprisonment in a state correctional institution.

HISTORY: GC § 13438-8; 113 v 123(172), ch 17, § 8; Bureau of Code Revision, 10-1-53; 131 v 679 (Eff 10-30-65); 134 v H 511 (Eff 1-1-74); 145 v H 571. Eff 10-6-94.

† So in enrolled bill. But see version in 134 v H 511.

§ 2941.44 Arrest and return of escaped convicts; expenses.

Sheriffs, deputy sheriffs, marshals, deputy marshals, watchmen, police officers, and coroners may arrest a convict escaping from a state correctional institution and forthwith convey him to the institution and deliver him to the warden of the institution. They shall be allowed ten cents per mile going to and returning from the institution and additional compensation that the warden finds reasonable for the necessary expense incurred.

HISTORY: GC § 13438-9; 113 v 123(172), ch 17, § 9; Bureau of Code Revision, 10-1-53; 128 v 542 (Eff 7-17-59); 145 v H 571. Eff 10-6-94.

§ 2941.45 Trial of persons serving sentence.

Any person serving a sentence in jail or the workhouse, who is indicted or informed against for another offense, may be brought before the court of common pleas upon warrant for that purpose, for arraignment and trial. Such person shall remain in the custody of the jailer or keeper of the workhouse, but may be temporarily confined in the jail, if a prisoner in the workhouse.

If such prisoner is convicted and sentenced upon trial, he shall be returned to the jail or workhouse to serve out the former sentence before the subsequent sentence is executed.

HISTORY: GC § 13438-10; 113 v 123(172), ch 17, § 10; Bureau of Code Revision. Eff 10-1-53.

§ 2941.46 Arrest of convict or prisoner violating pardon or parole.

(A) If a convict has been conditionally pardoned or a prisoner has been paroled from any state correctional institution, any peace officer may arrest the convict or prisoner without a warrant if the peace officer has reasonable ground to believe that the convict or prisoner has violated or is violating any rule governing the conduct of paroled prisoners prescribed by the adult parole authority or any of the following that is a condition of his pardon or parole:

(1) A condition that prohibits his ownership, possession, or use of a firearm, deadly weapon, ammunition, or dangerous ordnance;

(2) A condition that prohibits him from being within a specified structure or geographic area;

(3) A condition that confines him to a residence, facility, or other structure;

(4) A condition that prohibits him from contacting or communicating with any specified individual;

(5) A condition that prohibits him from associating with a specified individual.

(B) Upon making an arrest under this section, the arresting peace officer or his department or agency promptly shall notify the authority that the convict or prisoner has been arrested.

(C) Nothing in this section limits, or shall be construed to limit, the powers of arrest granted to certain law enforcement officers and citizens under sections 2935.03 and 2935.04 of the Revised Code.

(D) As used in this section:

(1) "State correctional institution," "pardon," "parole," "convict," and "prisoner" have the same meanings as in section 2967.01 of the Revised Code.

(2) "Peace officer" has the same meaning as in section 2935.01 of the Revised Code.

(3) "Firearm," "deadly weapon," and "dangerous ordnance" have the same meanings as in section 2923.11 of the Revised Code.

HISTORY: GC § 13438-11; 113 v 123(172), ch 17, § 11; 118

v 288(302), § 25; Bureau of Code Revision, 10-1-53; 130 v PtII, 146 (Eff 3-18-65); 144 v S 49 (Eff 7-21-92); 145 v H 571. Eff 10-6-94.

§ 2941.47 Summons on indictments against corporations.

When an indictment is returned or information filed against a corporation, a summons commanding the sheriff to notify the accused thereof, returnable on the seventh day after its date, shall issue on praecipe of the prosecuting attorney. Such summons with a copy of the indictment shall be served and returned in the manner provided for service of summons upon corporations in civil actions. If the service cannot be made in the county where the prosecution began, the sheriff may make service in any other county of the state, upon the president, secretary, superintendent, clerk, treasurer, cashier, managing agent, or other chief officer thereof, or by leaving a copy at a general or branch office or usual place of doing business of such corporation, with the person having charge thereof. Such corporation shall appear by one of its officers or by counsel on or before the return day of the summons served and answer to the indictment or information by motion, demurrer, or plea, and upon failure to make such appearance and answer, the clerk of the court of common pleas shall enter a plea of "not guilty." Upon such appearance being made or plea entered, the corporation is before the court until the case is finally disposed of. On said indictment or information no warrant of arrest may issue except for individuals who may be included in such indictment or information.

HISTORY: GC § 13438-12; 113 v 123(172), ch 17, § 12; Bureau of Code Revision. Eff 10-1-53.

§ 2941.48 Recognizance of witnesses.

In any case pending in the court of common pleas, the court, either before or after indictment, may require any witness designated by the prosecuting attorney to enter into a recognizance, with or without surety, in such sum as the court thinks proper for his appearance to testify in such cause. A witness failing or refusing to comply with such order shall be committed to the county jail until he gives his testimony in such case or is ordered discharged by the court. If a witness is committed to jail upon order of court for want of such recognizance, he shall be paid while so confined like fees as are allowed witnesses by section 2335.08 of the Revised Code. The trial of such case has precedence over other cases and the court shall designate any early day for such trial.

HISTORY: GC § 13438-13; 113 v 123(173), ch 17, § 13; Bureau of Code Revision. Eff 10-1-53.

[SERVICE OF INDICTMENT AND EXCEPTIONS]

§ 2941.49 Indictment to be served on accused.

Within three days after the filing of an indictment for felony and in every other case when requested, the clerk of the court of common pleas shall make and deliver to the sheriff, defendant, or the defendant's counsel, a copy of such indictment. The sheriff, on receiving such copy, shall serve it on the defendant. A defendant, without his assent, shall not be arraigned or called on to answer to an indictment until one day has elapsed after receiving or having an opportunity to receive in person or by counsel, a copy of such indictment.

HISTORY: GC § 13439-1; 113 v 123(173), ch 18; Bureau of Code Revision. Eff 10-1-53.

§ 2941.50 Repealed, 136 v H 164, § 2 [GC § 13439-2; 113 v 123(173); Bureau of Code Revision, 10-1-53; 130 v 666; 131 v 679; 132 v S 486]. Eff 1-13-76.

This section concerned assigning counsel to defend.

§ 2941.51 Payment of appointed counsel.

(A) Counsel appointed to a case or selected by an indigent person under division (E) of section 120.16 or division (E) of section 120.26 of the Revised Code, or otherwise appointed by the court, except for counsel appointed by the court to provide legal representation for a person charged with a violation of an ordinance of a municipal corporation, shall be paid for their services by the county the compensation and expenses that the trial court approves. Each request for payment shall be accompanied by an affidavit of indigency completed by the indigent person on forms prescribed by the state public defender. Compensation and expenses shall not exceed the amounts fixed by the board of county commissioners pursuant to division (B) of this section.

(B) The board of county commissioners shall establish a schedule of fees by case or on an hourly basis to be paid by the county for legal services provided by appointed counsel. Prior to establishing such schedule, the board shall request the bar association or associations of the county to submit a proposed schedule. The schedule submitted shall be subject to the review, amendment, and approval of the board of county commissioners.

(C) In a case where counsel have been appointed to conduct an appeal under Chapter 120. of the Revised Code, such compensation shall be fixed by the court of appeals or the supreme court, as provided in divisions (A) and (B) of this section.

(D) The fees and expenses approved by the court under this section shall not be taxed as part of the costs and shall be paid by the county. However, if the person represented has, or reasonably may be expected to have, the means to meet some part of the cost of the services rendered to the person, the person shall pay the county an amount that the person reasonably can be expected to pay. Pursuant to section 120.04 of the Revised Code, the county shall pay to the state public defender a percentage of the payment received from the person in an amount proportionate to the percentage of the costs of the person's case that were paid to the county by the state public defender pursuant to this section. The money paid to the state public defender shall be credited to the client payment fund created pursuant to division (B)(5) of section 120.04 of the Revised Code.

(E) The county auditor shall draw a warrant on the county treasurer for the payment of such counsel in the amount fixed by the court, plus the expenses that the court fixes and certifies to the auditor. The county auditor shall report periodically, but not less than annually, to the board and to the Ohio public defender commission the amounts paid out pursuant to the approval of the court under this section, separately stating costs and expenses that are reimbursable under section 120.35 of the Revised Code. The board, after review and approval of the auditor's report, may then certify it to the state public defender for reimbursement. The state public defender shall review the report and, in accordance with the standards, guidelines, and maximums established pursuant to divisions (B)(7) and (8) of section 120.04 of the Revised Code, pay fifty per cent of the total cost, other than costs and expenses that are reimbursable under section 120.35 of the Revised Code, if any, of paying appointed counsel in each county and pay fifty per cent of costs and expenses that are reimbursable under section 120.35 of the Revised Code, if any, to the board.

(F) If any county system for paying appointed counsel fails to maintain the standards for the conduct of the system established by the rules of the Ohio public defender commission pursuant to divisions (B) and (C) of section 120.03 of the Revised Code or the standards established by the state public defender pursuant to division (B)(7) of section 102.04 of the Revised Code, the commission shall notify the board of county commissioners of the county that the county system for paying appointed counsel has failed to comply with its rules. Unless the board corrects the conduct of its appointed counsel system to comply with the rules within ninety days after the date of the notice, the state public defender may deny all or part of the county's reimbursement from the state provided for in this section.

HISTORY: GC § 13439-3; 113 v 123(173), ch 18, § 3; 117 v 279; 122 v 301; Bureau of Code Revision, 10-1-53; 128 v 54 (Eff 11-9-59); 131 v 680 (Eff 11-11-65); 132 v H 1 (Eff 2-21-67); 136 v H 164; (Eff 1-13-76); 140 v H 291 (Eff 7-1-83); 140 v S 271 (Eff 9-26-84); 141 v H 201 (Eff 7-1-85); 146 v H 117 (Eff 6-30-95); 147 v H 215. Eff 9-29-97.

The effective date is set by section 222 of HB 215.

§ 2941.52 Repealed, 136 v H 164, § 2 [GC § 13439-4; 113 v 123(174); Bureau of Code Revision, 10-1-53]. Eff 1-13-76.

This section concerned reasonable time to except.

§ 2941.53 Exceptions to an indictment.

An accused may except to an indictment by:
(A) A motion to quash;
(B) A plea in abatement;
(C) A demurrer.

HISTORY: GC § 13439-5; 113 v 123(174), ch 18, § 5; Bureau of Code Revision. Eff 10-1-53.

§ 2941.54 Motion to quash.

A motion to quash may be made when there is a defect apparent upon the face of the record, within the meaning of sections 2941.02 to 2941.35, inclusive, of the Revised Code, including defects in the form of indictment and in the manner in which an offense is charged.

HISTORY: GC § 13439-6; 113 v 123(174), ch 18, § 6; Bureau of Code Revision. Eff 10-1-53.

§ 2941.55 Plea in abatement.

Plea in abatement may be made when there is a defect in the record shown by facts extrinsic thereto.

HISTORY: GC § 13439-7; 113 v 123(174), ch 18, § 7; Bureau of Code Revision. Eff 10-1-53.

§ 2941.56 Misnomer.

If the accused pleads in abatement that he is not indicted by his true name, he must plead his true name which shall be entered on the minutes of the court. After such entry, the trial and proceedings on the indictment shall be had against him by that name, referring also to the name by which he is indicted, as if he had been indicted by his true name.

HISTORY: GC § 13439-8; 113 v 123(174), ch 18, § 8; Bureau of Code Revision. Eff 10-1-53.

§ 2941.57 Demurrer.

The accused may demur:
(A) When the facts stated in the indictment do not constitute an offense punishable by the laws of this state;
(B) When the intent is not alleged and proof thereof is necessary to make out the offense charged;
(C) When it appears on the face of the indictment that the offense charged is not within the jurisdiction of the court.

HISTORY: GC § 13439-9; 113 v 123(174), ch 18, § 9; Bureau of Code Revision. Eff 10-1-53.

§ 2941.58 Accused not discharged when indictment quashed.

When a motion to quash or a plea in abatement is adjudged in favor of the accused, the trial court may order the case to be resubmitted to the grand jury, if then pending, or to the next succeeding grand jury. The accused then may be committed to jail or held to bail in such sum as the trial court requires for his appearance to answer at a time to be fixed by the court.

HISTORY: GC § 13439-10; 113 v 123(174), ch 18, § 10; Bureau of Code Revision. Eff 10-1-53.

§ 2941.59 Waiver of defects.

The accused waives all defects which may be excepted to by a motion to quash or a plea in abatement, by demurring to an indictment, or by pleading in bar or the general issue.

HISTORY: GC § 13439-11; 113 v 123(175), ch 18, § 11; Bureau of Code Revision. Eff 10-1-53.

§ 2941.60 Answer to plea in abatement.

The prosecuting attorney may demur to a plea in abatement if it is not sufficient in substance, or he may reply, setting forth any facts which may show there is no defect in the record as charged in the plea.

HISTORY: GC § 13439-12; 113 v 123(175), ch 18, § 12; Bureau of Code Revision. Eff 10-1-53.

§ 2941.61 After demurrer accused may plead.

After a demurrer to an indictment is overruled, the accused may plead under section 2943.03 of the Revised Code.

HISTORY: GC § 13439-13; 113 v 123(175), ch 18, § 13; Bureau of Code Revision. Eff 10-1-53.

§ 2941.62 Hearing on motions and demurrers.

Motions to quash, pleas in abatement, and demurrers shall be heard immediately upon their filing, unless the trial court, for good cause shown, sets another time for such hearing.

HISTORY: GC § 13439-14; 113 v 123(175), ch 18, § 14; Bureau of Code Revision. Eff 10-1-53.

§ 2941.63 Counsel to assist prosecutor.

The court of common pleas, or the court of appeals, whenever it is of the opinion that the public interest requires it, may appoint an attorney to assist the prosecuting attorney in the trial of a case pending in such court. The board of county commissioners shall pay said assistant to the prosecuting attorney such compensation for his services as the court approves.

HISTORY: GC § 13439-15; 113 v 123(175), ch 18, § 15; Bureau of Code Revision. Eff 10-1-53.

CHAPTER 2943: ARRAIGNMENT; PLEAS

Section
2943.01 Definition of magistrate.
2943.02 Arraignment.
2943.03 Pleas to indictment.
[2943.03.1] 2943.031 Advice as to possible deportation, exclusion or denial of naturalization upon guilty or no contest plea.
[2943.03.2] 2943.032 Advice as to possible extension of prison term.
2943.04 Form of plea.
[2943.04.1] 2943.041 Repealed.

[DOUBLE JEOPARDY]

2943.05 Form of plea of former conviction.
2943.06 Trial of issue on plea of former conviction.
2943.07 What is not former acquittal.
2943.08 What is former acquittal.
2943.09 Conviction or acquittal of a higher offense.
2943.10 Proceedings after verdict on plea in bar.

§ 2943.01 Definition of magistrate.

The definition of "magistrate" set forth in section 2931.01 of the Revised Code applies to Chapter 2943. of the Revised Code.

HISTORY: Bureau of Code Revision. Eff 10-1-53.

§ 2943.02 Arraignment.

An accused person shall be arraigned by the clerk of the court of common pleas, or his deputy, reading the indictment or information to the accused, unless the accused or his attorney waives the reading thereof. He shall then be asked to plead thereto. Arraignment shall be made immediately after the disposition of exceptions to the indictment, if any are filed, or, if no exceptions are filed, after reasonable opportunity has been given the accused to file such exceptions.

HISTORY: GC § 13440-1; 113 v 123(175), ch 19; Bureau of Code Revision. Eff 10-1-53.

§ 2943.03 Pleas to indictment.

Pleas to an indictment or information are:
(A) Guilty;
(B) Not guilty;
(C) A former judgment of conviction or acquittal of the offense;
(D) Once in jeopardy;
(E) Not guilty by reason of insanity.
A defendant who does not plead guilty may enter one or more of the other pleas. A defendant who does not plead not guilty by reason of insanity is conclusively presumed to have been sane at the time of the commission of the offense charged. The court may, for good cause shown, allow a change of plea at any time before the commencement of the trial.

HISTORY: GC § 13440-2; 113 v 123(175), ch 19, § 2; Bureau of Code Revision. Eff 10-1-53.

[§ 2943.03.1] § 2943.031 Advice as to possible deportation, exclusion or denial of naturalization upon guilty or no contest plea.

(A) Except as provided in division (B) of this section, prior to accepting a plea of guilty or a plea of no contest to an indictment, information, or complaint charging a felony or a misdemeanor other than a minor misdemeanor if the defendant previously has not been convicted of or pleaded guilty to a minor misdemeanor, the court shall address the defendant personally, provide the following advisement to the defendant that shall be entered in the record of the court, and determine that the defendant understands the advisement.

"If you are not a citizen of the United States you are hereby advised that conviction of the offense to which you are pleading guilty (or no contest, when applicable) may have the consequences of deportation, exclusion from admission to the United States, or denial of naturalization pursuant to the laws of the United States."

Upon request of the defendant, the court shall allow him additional time to consider the appropriateness of the plea in light of the advisement described in this division.

(B) The court is not required to give the advisement described in division (A) of this section if either of the following applies:

(1) The defendant enters a plea of guilty on a written form, the form includes a question asking whether the defendant is a citizen of the United States, and the defendant answers that question in the affirmative;

(2) The defendant states orally on the record that he is a citizen of the United States.

(C) Except as provided in division (B) of this section, the defendant shall not be required at the time of entering a plea to disclose to the court his legal status in the United States.

(D) Upon motion of the defendant, the court shall set aside the judgment and permit the defendant to withdraw a plea of guilty or no contest and enter a plea of not guilty by reason of insanity, if, after the effective date of this section, the court fails to provide the defendant the advisement described in division (A) of this section, the advisement is required by that division, and the defendant shows that he is not a citizen of the United States and that the conviction of the offense to which he pleaded guilty or no contest may result in his being subject to deportation, exclusion from admission to the United States, or denial of naturalization pursuant to the laws of the United States.

(E) In the absence of a record that the court provided the advisement described in division (A) of this section and if the advisement is required by that division, the defendant shall be presumed not to have received the advisement.

(F) Nothing in this section shall be construed as preventing a court, in the sound exercise of its discretion pursuant to Criminal Rule 32.1, from setting aside the judgment of conviction and permitting a defendant to withdraw his plea.

HISTORY: 143 v S 95. Eff 10-2-89.

The provisions of § 3 of S 95 (143 v —) read as follows:

SECTION 3. Section 2937.06 of the Revised Code as amended by this act and section 2943.031 of the Revised Code as enacted by this act shall apply to all felony and misdemeanor cases pending on the effective date of this act in which the court has not accepted a plea to the indictment, information, or complaint.

[§ 2943.03.2] § 2943.032 Advice as to possible extension of prison term.

Prior to accepting a guilty plea or a plea of no contest to an indictment, information, or complaint that charges a felony, the court shall inform the defendant personally that, if the defendant pleads guilty or no contest to the felony so charged or any other felony and if the court imposes a prison term upon the defendant for the felony, all of the following apply:

(A) The parole board may extend the stated prison term if the defendant commits any criminal offense under the law of this state or the United States while serving the prison term.

(B) Any such extension will be done administratively as part of the defendant's sentence in accordance with section 2967.11 of the Revised Code and may be for thirty, sixty, or ninety days for each violation.

(C) All such extensions of the stated prison term for all violations during the course of the term may not exceed one-half of the term's duration.

(D) The sentence imposed for the felony automatically includes any such extension of the stated prison term by the parole board.

(E) If the offender violates the conditions of a post-release control sanction imposed by the parole board upon the completion of the stated prison term, the parole board may impose upon the offender a residential sanction that includes a new prison term up to nine months.

HISTORY: 146 v S 2. Eff 7-1-96.

The effective date is set by section 6 of SB 2.

§ 2943.04 Form of plea.

Pleas of guilty or not guilty may be oral. Pleas in all other cases shall be in writing, subscribed by the defendant or his counsel, and shall immediately be entered upon the minutes of the court.

HISTORY: GC § 13440-3; 113 v 123(176), ch 19, § 3; Bureau of Code Revision. Eff 10-1-53.

[§ 2943.04.1] § 2943.041 Repealed, 145 v S 186, § 2 [140 v S 172; 142 v S 6; 145 v H 571]. Eff 10-12-94.

This section concerned rights of victim or representative family member present at hearing or proceeding. See now RC Chapter 2930.

[DOUBLE JEOPARDY]

§ 2943.05 Form of plea of former conviction.

If a defendant pleads that he has had former judgment of conviction or acquittal, or has been once in jeopardy, he must set forth in his plea the court, time, and place of such conviction, acquittal, or jeopardy. No claim of former judgment of conviction or acquittal, or jeopardy may be given in evidence under the plea of not guilty.

HISTORY: GC § 13440-4; 113 v 123(176), ch 19, § 4; Bureau of Code Revision. Eff 10-1-53.

§ 2943.06 Trial of issue on plea of former conviction.

If a defendant pleads a judgment of conviction, acquittal, or former jeopardy, the prosecuting attorney may reply that there is no such conviction, acquittal, or jeopardy. The issue thus made shall be tried to a jury, and on such trial the defendant must produce the record of such conviction, acquittal, or jeopardy, and prove that he is the person charged in such record, and he may also introduce other evidence to establish the identity of such offense. If the prosecuting attorney demurs to said plea and said demurrer is overruled, the prosecuting attorney may then reply to said plea.

HISTORY: GC § 13440-5; 113 v 123(176), ch 19, § 5; Bureau of Code Revision. Eff 10-1-53.

§ 2943.07 What is not former acquittal.

If a defendant was formerly acquitted on the ground of variance between the indictment or information and the proof, or if the indictment or information was dismissed, without a judgment of acquittal, upon an objection to its form or substance, or in order to hold the defendant for a higher offense, it is not an acquittal of the same offense.

HISTORY: GC § 13440-6; 113 v 123(176), ch 19, § 6; Bureau of Code Revision. Eff 10-1-53.

§ 2943.08 What is former acquittal.

Whenever a defendant is acquitted on the merits, he is acquitted of the same offense, notwithstanding any defect in form or substance in the indictment or information on which the trial was had.

HISTORY: GC § 13440-7; 113 v 123(176), ch 19, § 7; Bureau of Code Revision. Eff 10-1-53.

§ 2943.09 Conviction or acquittal of a higher offense.

When a defendant has been convicted or acquitted, or has been once in jeopardy upon an indictment or information, the conviction, acquittal, or jeopardy is a bar to another indictment or information for the offense charged in the former indictment or information, or for an attempt to commit the same offense, or for an offense necessarily included therein, of which he might have been convicted under the former indictment or information.

HISTORY: GC § 13440-8; 113 v 123(176), ch 19, § 8; Bureau of Code Revision. Eff 10-1-53.

§ 2943.10 Proceedings after verdict on plea in bar.

If the issue on the plea in bar under section 2943.06 of the Revised Code is found for the defendant he shall be discharged. If the issue is found against the defendant the case shall proceed and be disposed of upon his other pleas.

HISTORY: GC § 13440-9; 113 v 123(177), ch 19, § 9; Bureau of Code Revision. Eff 10-1-53.

CHAPTER 2945: TRIAL

Section
2945.01 Definition of magistrate.
2945.02 Setting and continuing cases.
2945.03 Control of trial.
2945.04 Orders to prevent intimidation of victim or witness; orders to prevent offenses against complainant or his ward, child or property.

[TRIAL BY COURT]
2945.05 Defendant may waive jury trial.
2945.06 Jurisdiction of judge when jury trial is waived; three-judge court.
2945.07 Repealed.

[TRIAL PROCEEDINGS]
2945.08 Prosecution in wrong county; proceeding.
2945.09 Grounds of objection to be stated.
2945.10 Order of proceedings of trial.
2945.11 Charge to the jury as to law and fact.
2945.12 When accused may be tried in his absence.
2945.13 Joint trials in felony cases.
2945.14 Mistake in charging offense.
2945.15 Discharge of defendant.
2945.16 View of the premises.

[JURY TRIAL]
2945.17 Right to trial by jury.
[2945.17.1] 2945.171 Verdict in writing.
2945.18, 2945.19 Repealed.
2945.20 Separate trial for capital offense.
2945.21 Peremptory challenges.
2945.22 Repealed.
2945.23 When peremptory challenges required.
2945.24 Juries.
2945.25 Causes of challenging of jurors.
2945.26 Challenge for cause.
2945.27 Examination of jurors by the court.
2945.28 Form of oath to jury.
2945.29 Jurors becoming unable to perform duties.
2945.30 Medical attendance of juror.
2945.31 Separation of jurors.
2945.32 Oath to officers if jury sequestered.
2945.33 Keeping and conduct of jury after case submitted.
2945.34 Admonition if jurors separate during trial.
2945.35 Papers the jury may take.
2945.36 For what cause jury may be discharged.

[COMPETENCY TO STAND TRIAL]
2945.37 Definitions; hearing on competence to stand trial.
[2945.37.1] 2945.371 Evaluations of defendant's mental condition at relevant time; separate mental retardation evaluation.
2945.38 Disposition of defendant after competency hearing; sentence reduction for confinement for evaluation.
[2945.38.1] 2945.381 Repealed.
2945.39 Proceedings after expiration of maximum time for treatment after finding of incompetency.
[2945.39.1] 2945.391 Finding of not guilty by reason of insanity.
[2945.39.2] 2945.392 Battered woman syndrome testimony.
2945.40 Procedure upon acquittal by reason of insanity.

Section
[2945.40.1] 2945.401 Continuing jurisdiction of court after incompetency finding or insanity acquittal; application of other laws; termination of commitment or change in conditions.
[2945.40.2] 2945.402 Conditional release.

[WITNESSES]
2945.41 Rules applicable in criminal cases.
2945.42 Competency of witnesses.
2945.43 Defendant may testify.
2945.44 Immunity of witnesses turning state's evidence.
2945.45 Subpoenas to issue to any county.
[2945.45.1] 2945.451 Employee may not be penalized for being subpoenaed to criminal proceeding.
2945.46 Attendance of witness enforced.
2945.47 Deposition or subpoena of prisoner.
2945.48 Witness may be placed in jail.
[2945.48.1] 2945.481 Deposition of child victim; videotaping; testimony taken outside courtroom and televised into it or replayed in courtroom.
2945.49 Testimony of deceased or absent witness; videotaped preliminary hearing testimony of child victim.
2945.50 Deposition in criminal cases.
2945.51 When defendant may be taken; expenses.
2945.52 Counsel appointed shall represent the defendant.
2945.53 Right of accused to examine witness.
2945.54 Conduct of examination.
2945.55 Testimony of previous identification.
2945.56 Rebuttal of defendant's character evidence.
2945.57 Number of witnesses to character.
2945.58 Alibi.
2945.59 Proof of defendant's motive.
2945.60-2945.63 Repealed.
2945.64 Prima-facie evidence of embezzlement.

[BILL OF EXCEPTIONS]
2945.65, 2945.66 Repealed.
2945.67 Appeal by state.
2945.68-2945.70 Repealed.

[TIME FOR TRIAL]
2945.71 Time within which hearing or trial must be held.
2945.72 Extension of time for hearing or trial.
2945.73 Discharge for delay in trial.

[VERDICT]
2945.74 Defendant may be convicted of lesser offense.
2945.75 Degree of offense; charge and verdict; prior convictions.
2945.76 Repealed.
2945.77 Polling jury.
2945.78 Recording the verdict.

[NEW TRIAL]
2945.79 Causes for new trial.
2945.80 Application for new trial.
2945.81 Causes to be sustained by affidavits.
2945.82 New trial.
2945.83 When new trial shall not be granted.
[2945.83.1] 2945.831 Motion not necessary for appellate review.
[2945.83.2] 2945.832 Repealed.

§ 2945.01 Definition of magistrate.

The definition of "magistrate" set forth in section 2931.01 of the Revised Code applies to Chapter 2945. of the Revised Code.

HISTORY: Bureau of Code Revision. Eff 10-1-53.

§ 2945.02 Setting and continuing cases.

The court of common pleas shall set all criminal cases for trial for a day not later than thirty days after the date of entry of the plea of the defendant. No continuance of the trial shall be granted except upon affirmative proof in open court, upon reasonable notice, that the ends of justice require a continuance.

No continuance shall be granted for any other time than it is affirmatively proved the ends of justice require.

Whenever any continuance is granted, the court shall enter on the journal the reason for the same.

Criminal cases shall be given precedence over civil matters and proceedings. The failure of the court to set such criminal cases for trial, as required by this section, does not operate as an acquittal, but upon notice of such failure or upon motion of the prosecuting attorney or a defendant, such case shall forthwith be set for trial within a reasonable time, not exceeding thirty days thereafter.

HISTORY: GC § 13442-1; 113 v 123(178), ch 21; Bureau of Code Revision. Eff 10-1-53.

Editor's Note

The time within which a defendant must be tried is now generally controlled by §§ 2945.71-2945.73. See also CrimR 50.

§ 2945.03 Control of trial.

The judge of the trial court shall control all proceedings during a criminal trial, and shall limit the introduction of evidence and the argument of counsel to relevant and material matters with a view to expeditious and effective ascertainment of the truth regarding the matters in issue.

HISTORY: GC § 13442-2; 113 v 123(178), ch 21, § 2; Bureau of Code Revision. Eff 10-1-53.

§ 2945.04 Orders to prevent intimidation of victim or witness; orders to prevent offenses against complainant or his ward, child or property.

(A) If a motion is filed with a court before which a criminal case is pending alleging that a person has committed or is reasonably likely to commit any act prohibited by section 2921.04 of the Revised Code in relation to the case, if the court holds a hearing on the motion, and if the court determines that the allegations made in the motion are true, the court may issue an order doing any or any combination of the following, subject to division (C) of this section:

(1) Directing the defendant in the case not to violate or to cease a violation of section 2921.04 of the Revised Code;

(2) Directing a person other than a defendant who is before the court, including, but not limited to, a subpoenaed witness or other person entering the courtroom of the court, not to violate or to cease a violation of section 2921.04 of the Revised Code;

(3) Directing the defendant or a person described in division (A)(2) of this section to maintain a prescribed geographic distance from any specified person who is before the court, including, but not limited to, the victim of the offense that is the basis of the case or a subpoenaed witness in the case;

(4) Directing the defendant or a person described in division (A)(2) of this section not to communicate with any specified person who is before the court, including, but not limited to, the victim of the offense or a subpoenaed witness in the case;

(5) Directing a specified law enforcement agency that serves a political subdivision within the territorial jurisdiction of the court to provide protection for any specified person who is before the court, including, but not limited to, the victim of the offense or a subpoenaed witness in the case;

(6) Any other reasonable order that would assist in preventing or causing the cessation of a violation of section 2921.04 of the Revised Code.

(B) If a motion is filed with a court in which a criminal complaint has been filed alleging that the offender or another person acting in concert with the offender has committed or is reasonably likely to commit any act that would constitute an offense against the person or property of the complainant, his ward, or his child, if the court holds a hearing on the motion, and if the court determines that the allegations made in the motion are true, the court may issue an order doing one or more of the following, subject to division (C) of this section:

(1) Directing the defendant in the case not to commit an act or to cease committing an act that constitutes an offense against the person or property of the complainant, his ward, or child;

(2) Directing a person other than the defendant who is before the court, including, but not limited to, a subpoenaed witness or other person entering the courtroom of the court, not to commit an act or to cease committing an act that constitutes an offense against the person or property of the complainant, his ward, or child;

(3) Directing the defendant or a person described in division (B)(2) of this section to maintain a prescribed geographic distance from any specified person who is before the court, including, but not limited to, the complainant or the victim of the offense, or a subpoenaed witness in the case;

(4) Directing the defendant or a person described in division (B)(2) of this section not to communicate with any specified person who is before the court, including, but not limited to, the complainant, the victim of the

offense, or a subpoenaed witness in the case;

(5) Directing a specified law enforcement agency that serves a political subdivision within the territorial jurisdiction of the court to provide protection for any specified person who is before the court, including, but not limited to, the complainant, the victim of the offense, or a subpoenaed witness in the case;

(6) When the complainant and the defendant cohabit with one another but the complainant is not a family or household member, as defined in section 2919.25 of the Revised Code, granting possession of the residence or household to the complainant to the exclusion of the defendant by evicting the defendant when the residence or household is owned or leased solely by the complainant or by ordering the defendant to vacate the premises when the residence or household is jointly owned or leased by the complainant and the defendant;

(7) Any other reasonable order that would assist in preventing or causing the cessation of an act that constitutes an offense against the person or property of the complainant, his ward, or child.

(C) No order issued under authority of division (A) or (B) of this section shall prohibit or be construed as prohibiting any attorney for the defendant in the case or for a person described in division (A)(2) or (B)(2) of this section from conducting any investigation of the pending criminal case, from preparing or conducting any defense of the pending criminal case, or from attempting to zealously represent his client in the pending criminal case within the bounds of the law. However, this division does not exempt any person from the prohibitions contained in section 2921.04 or any section of the Revised Code that constitutes an offense against the person or property of the complainant, his ward, or his child, or provide a defense to a charge of any violation of that section or of an offense of that nature.

(D)(1) A person who violates an order issued pursuant to division (A) of this section is subject to the following sanctions:

(a) Criminal prosecution for a violation of section 2921.04 of the Revised Code, if the violation of the court order constitutes a violation of that section;

(b) Punishment for contempt of court.

(2) A person who violates an order issued pursuant to division (B) of this section is subject to the following sanctions:

(a) Criminal prosecution for a violation of a section of the Revised Code that constitutes an offense against the person or property of the complainant, his ward, or child;

(b) Punishment for contempt of court.

(E)(1) The punishment of a person for contempt of court for violation of an order issued pursuant to division (A) of this section does not bar criminal prosecution of the person for a violation of section 2921.04 of the Revised Code.

(2) The punishment of a person for contempt of court for a violation of an order issued pursuant to division (B) of this section does not bar criminal prosecution of the person for an offense against the person or property of the complainant, his ward, or child.

(3) A person punished for contempt of court under this section is entitled to credit for the punishment imposed upon conviction of a violation of the offense arising out of the same activity, and a person convicted of such a violation shall not subsequently be punished for contempt of court arising out of the same activity.

HISTORY: 140 v S 172 (Eff 9-26-84); 145 v H 335. Eff 12-9-94.

Not analogous to former RC § 2945.04 (GC § 13442-3; 113 v 123(179); Bureau of Code Revision, 10-1-53), repealed 135 v H 716, § 2, eff 1-1-74.

[TRIAL BY COURT]

§ 2945.05 Defendant may waive jury trial.

In all criminal cases pending in courts of record in this state, the defendant may waive a trial by jury and be tried by the court without a jury. Such waiver by a defendant, shall be in writing, signed by the defendant, and filed in said cause and made a part of the record thereof. It shall be entitled in the court and cause, and in substance as follows: "I . . . ., defendant in the above cause, hereby voluntarily waive and relinquish my right to a trial by jury, and elect to be tried by a Judge of the Court in which the said cause may be pending. I fully understand that under the laws of this state, I have a constitutional right to a trial by jury."

Such waiver of trial by jury must be made in open court after the defendant has been arraigned and has had opportunity to consult with counsel. Such waiver may be withdrawn by the defendant at any time before the commencement of the trial.

HISTORY: GC § 13442-4; 113 v 123(179), ch 21, § 4; Bureau of Code Revision. Eff 10-1-53.

§ 2945.06 Jurisdiction of judge when jury trial is waived; three-judge court.

In any case in which a defendant waives his right to trial by jury and elects to be tried by the court under section 2945.05 of the Revised Code, any judge of the court in which the cause is pending shall proceed to hear, try, and determine the cause in accordance with the rules and in like manner as if the cause were being tried before a jury. If the accused is charged with an offense punishable with death, he shall be tried by a court to be composed of three judges, consisting of the judge presiding at the time in the trial of criminal cases and two other judges to be designated by the presiding judge or chief justice of that court, and in case there is neither a presiding judge nor a chief justice, by the chief justice of the supreme court. The judges or a majority of them may decide all questions of fact and law arising upon the trial; however the accused shall not be found guilty or not guilty of any offense unless the judges unanimously find the accused guilty or not guilty. If the accused pleads guilty of aggravated murder, a court composed of three judges shall examine the witnesses, determine whether the accused is guilty of aggravated murder or any other offense, and pronounce sentence accordingly. The court shall follow the procedures contained in sections 2929.03 and 2929.04 of the Revised Code in all cases in which the accused is charged with an offense punishable by death. If in the composition of the court it is necessary that a judge from another county be assigned by the chief justice, the judge from another county shall be compensated for his services as provided by section 141.07 of the Revised Code.

HISTORY: GC § 13442-5; 113 v 123(179), ch 21, § 5; 115 v 531; Bureau of Code Revision, 10-1-53; 139 v S 1. Eff 10-19-81.

§ 2945.07 Repealed, 145 v S 186, § 2 [140 v S 172; 142 v S 6; 145 v H 571]. Eff 10-12-94.

This section concerned rights of victim or representative family member present at trial. See now RC Chapter 2930.

[TRIAL PROCEEDINGS]

§ 2945.08 Prosecution in wrong county; proceeding.

If it appears, on the trial of a criminal cause, that the offense was committed within the exclusive jurisdiction of another county of this state, the court must direct the defendant to be committed to await a warrant from the proper county for his arrest, but if the offense is a bailable offense the court may admit the defendant to bail with sufficient sureties conditioned, that he will, within such time as the court appoints, render himself amenable to a warrant for his arrest from the proper county, and if not sooner arrested thereon, will appear in court at the time fixed to surrender himself upon the warrant.

The clerk of the court of common pleas shall forthwith notify the prosecuting attorney of the county in which such offense was committed, in order that proper proceedings may be had in the case. A defendant in such case shall not be committed nor held under bond for a period of more than ten days.

HISTORY: GC § 13442-6; 113 v 123(180), ch 21, § 6; Bureau of Code Revision. Eff 10-1-53.

§ 2945.09 Grounds of objection to be stated.

In the trial of any criminal case, the grounds of an objection to any ruling or action of the court shall be stated if required by the court.

HISTORY: GC § 13442-7; 113 v 123(180), ch 21, § 7; Bureau of Code Revision, Eff 10-1-53; 141 v H 412. Eff 3-17-87.

§ 2945.10 Order of proceedings of trial.

The trial of an issue upon an indictment or information shall proceed before the trial court or jury as follows:

(A) Counsel for the state must first state the case for the prosecution, and may briefly state the evidence by which he expects to sustain it.

(B) The defendant or his counsel must then state his defense, and may briefly state the evidence which he expects to offer in support of it.

(C) The state must first produce its evidence and the defendant shall then produce his evidence.

(D) The state will then be confined to rebutting evidence, but the court, for good reason, in furtherance of justice, may permit evidence to be offered by either side out of its order.

(E) When the evidence is concluded, either party may request instructions to the jury on the points of law, which instructions shall be reduced to writing if either party requests it.

(F) When the evidence is concluded, unless the case is submitted without argument, the counsel for the state shall commence, the defendant or his counsel follow, and the counsel for the state conclude the argument to the jury.

(G) The court, after the argument is concluded and before proceeding with other business, shall forthwith charge the jury. Such charge shall be reduced to writing by the court if either party requests it before the argument to the jury is commenced. Such charge, or other charge or instruction provided for in this section, when so written and given, shall not be orally qualified, modified, or explained to the jury by the court. Written charges and instructions shall be taken by the jury in their retirement and returned with their verdict into court and remain on file with the papers of the case.

The court may deviate from the order of proceedings listed in this section.

HISTORY: GC § 13442-8; 113 v 123(180), ch 21, § 8; Bureau of Code Revision. Eff 10-1-53.

§ 2945.11 Charge to the jury as to law and fact.

In charging the jury, the court must state to it all matters of law necessary for the information of the jury in giving its verdict. The court must also inform the jury that the jury is the exclusive judge of all questions of fact. The court must state to the jury that in determining the question of guilt, it must not consider the punishment but that punishment rests with the judge except in cases of murder in the first degree or burglary of an inhabited dwelling.

HISTORY: GC § 13442-9; 113 v 123(181), ch 21, § 9; Bureau of Code Revision. Eff 10-1-53.

§ 2945.12 When accused may be tried in his absence.

A person indicted for a misdemeanor, upon request in writing subscribed by him and entered in the journal, may be tried in his absence by a jury or by the court. No other person shall be tried unless personally present, but if a person indicted escapes or forfeits his recognizance after the jury is sworn, the trial shall proceed and the verdict be received and recorded. If the offense charged is a misdemeanor, judgment and sentence shall be pronounced as if he were personally present. If the offense charged is a felony, the case shall be continued until the accused appears in court, or is retaken.

HISTORY: GC § 13442-10; 113 v 123(181), ch 21, § 10; Bureau of Code Revision. Eff 10-1-53.

§ 2945.13 Joint trials in felony cases.

When two or more persons are jointly indicted for a felony, except a capital offense, they shall be tried jointly unless the court, for good cause shown on application therefor by the prosecuting attorney or one or more of said defendants, orders one or more of said defendants to be tried separately.

HISTORY: GC § 13442-11; 113 v 123(181), ch 21, § 11; Bureau of Code Revision. Eff 10-1-53.

§ 2945.14 Mistake in charging offense.

If it appears during the trial and before submission to the jury or court, that a mistake has been made in charging the proper offense in the indictment or information, the court may order a discontinuance of trial without prejudice to the prosecution. The accused, if there is good cause to detain him, may be recognized to appear at the same or next succeeding term of court, or in default thereof committed to jail. In such case the court shall recognize the witnesses for the state to appear at the same time and testify.

HISTORY: GC § 13442-12; 113 v 123(181), ch 21, § 12; Bureau of Code Revision. Eff 10-1-53.

§ 2945.15 Discharge of defendant.

When two or more are tried jointly, before any of the accused has gone into his defense the trial court may direct one or more of such accused to be discharged that he may be a witness for the state.

An accused person, when there is not sufficient evidence to put him upon his defense, may be discharged by the court, but if not so discharged, shall be entitled to the immediate verdict of the jury in his favor. Such order of discharge, in either case, is a bar to another prosecution for the same offense.

HISTORY: GC § 13442-13; 113 v 123(181), ch 21, § 13; Bureau of Code Revision. Eff 10-1-53.

§ 2945.16 View of the premises.

When it is proper for the jurors to have a view of the place at which a material fact occurred, the trial court may order them to be conducted in a body, under the charge of the sheriff or other officer, to such place, which shall be shown to them by a person designated by the court. While the jurors are absent on such view no person other than such officer and such person so appointed, shall speak to them on any subject connected with the trial. The accused has the right to attend such view by the jury, but may waive this right.

The expense of such view as approved by the court shall be taxed as other costs in the case.

HISTORY: GC § 13442-14; 113 v 123(182), ch 21, § 14; Bureau of Code Revision, 10-1-53; 129 v 1201. Eff 9-11-61.

[JURY TRIAL]

§ 2945.17 Right to trial by jury.

At any trial, in any court, for the violation of any statute of this state, or of any ordinance of any municipal corporation, except in cases in which the penalty involved does not exceed a fine of one hundred dollars, the accused has the right to be tried by a jury.

HISTORY: GC § 13443; 115 v 78; Bureau of Code Revision, 10-1-53; 134 v H 511. Eff 1-1-74.

[§ 2945.17.1] § 2945.171 Verdict in writing.

In all criminal cases the verdict of the jury shall be in writing and signed by each of the jurors concurring therein.

HISTORY: 129 v 336. Eff 9-28-61.

§ 2945.18 Repealed, 145 v H 41, § 2 [139 v S 1]. Eff 9-27-93.

This section concerned venire for jury in capital cases.

The provisions of § 3 of HB 41 (145 v —) read as follows:

SECTION 3. The provisions of this act apply to any case that is filed on or after the effective date of this act and in which the defendant is charged with the commission of a capital offense, regardless of when the alleged capital offense occurred.

§ 2945.19 Repealed, 145 v H 41, § 2 [139 v S 1]. Eff 9-27-93.

This section concerned special venire in capital cases.

§ 2945.20 Separate trial for capital offense.

When two or more persons are jointly indicted for a capital offense, each of such persons shall be tried separately. The court, for good cause shown on application therefor by the prosecuting attorney or one or more of the defendants, may order said defendants to be tried jointly.

HISTORY: GC § 13443-3; 113 v 123(183), ch 22, § 3; 116 v 301; Bureau of Code Revision. Eff 10-1-53.

§ 2945.21 Peremptory challenges.

(A)(1) In criminal cases in which there is only one defendant, each party, in addition to the challenges for cause authorized by law, may peremptorily challenge three of the jurors in misdemeanor cases and four of the jurors in felony cases other than capital cases. If there is more than one defendant, each defendant may peremptorily challenge the same number of jurors as if he were the sole defendant.

(2) Notwithstanding Criminal Rule 24, in capital cases in which there is only one defendant, each party, in addition to the challenges for cause authorized by law, may peremptorily challenge twelve of the jurors. If there is more than one defendant, each defendant may peremptorily challenge the same number of jurors as if he were the sole defendant.

(3) In any case in which there are multiple defendants, the prosecuting attorney may peremptorily challenge a number of jurors equal to the total number of peremptory challenges allowed to all of the defendants.

(B) If any indictments, informations, or complaints are consolidated for trial, the consolidated cases shall be considered, for purposes of exercising peremptory challenges, as though the defendants or offenses had been joined in the same indictment, information, or complaint.

(C) The exercise of peremptory challenges authorized by this section shall be in accordance with the procedures of Criminal Rule 24.

HISTORY: GC § 13443-4; 113 v 123(183), ch 22, § 4; 119 v 594; Bureau of Code Revision, 10-1-53; 139 v S 1. Eff 10-19-81.

§ 2945.22 Repealed, 139 v S 1, § 2 [GC § 13443-6; 113 v 123(183); Bureau of Code Revision, 10-1-53]. Eff 10-19-81.

This section concerned peremptory challenges.

§ 2945.23 When peremptory challenges required.

Except by agreement, neither the state nor the defendant shall be required to exercise any peremptory challenge until twelve jurors have been passed for cause and are in the panel.

HISTORY: GC § 13443-7; 113 v 123(183), ch 22, § 7; Bureau of Code Revision. Eff 10-1-53.

§ 2945.24 Juries.

In all criminal cases, a jury summoned and impaneled under sections 2313.01 to 2313.47 of the Revised Code shall try the accused.

HISTORY: GC § 13443-5; 113 v 123(183), ch 22, § 5; Bureau of Code Revision, 10-1-53; 136 v H 133 (Eff 6-3-76); 139 v S 1 (Eff 10-19-81); 145 v H 41. Eff 9-27-93.

See provisions, § 3 of HB 41 (145 v —) following RC § 2945.18.

§ 2945.25 Causes of challenging of jurors.

A person called as a juror in a criminal case may be challenged for the following causes:

(A) That he was a member of the grand jury that found the indictment in the case;

(B) That he is possessed of a state of mind evincing enmity or bias toward the defendant or the state; but no person summoned as a juror shall be disqualified by reason of a previously formed or expressed opinion with reference to the guilt or innocence of the accused, if the court is satisfied, from examination of the juror or from other evidence, that he will render an impartial verdict according to the law and the evidence submitted to the jury at the trial;

(C) In the trial of a capital offense, that he unequivocally states that under no circumstances will he follow the instructions of a trial judge and consider fairly the imposition of a sentence of death in a particular case. A prospective juror's conscientious or religious opposition to the death penalty in and of itself is not grounds for a challenge for cause. All parties shall be given wide latitude in voir dire questioning in this regard.

(D) That he is related by consanguinity or affinity within the fifth degree to the person alleged to be injured or attempted to be injured by the offense charged, or to the person on whose complaint the prosecution was instituted, or to the defendant;

(E) That he served on a petit jury drawn in the same cause against the same defendant, and that [petit]† jury was discharged after hearing the evidence or rendering a verdict on the evidence that was set aside;

(F) That he served as a juror in a civil case brought against the defendant for the same act;

(G) That he has been subpoenaed in good faith as a witness in the case;

(H) That he is a chronic alcoholic, or drug dependent person;

(I) That he has been convicted of a crime that by law disqualifies him from serving on a jury;

(J) That he has an action pending between him and the state or the defendant;

(K) That he or his spouse is a party to another action then pending in any court in which an attorney in the cause then on trial is an attorney, either for or against him;

(L) That he is the person alleged to be injured or attempted to be injured by the offense charged, or is the person on whose complaint the prosecution was instituted, or the defendant;

(M) That he is the employer or employee, or the spouse, parent, son, or daughter of the employer or employee, or the counselor, agent, or attorney of any person included in division (L) of this section;

(N) That English is not his native language, and his knowledge of English is insufficient to permit him to understand the facts and law in the case;

(O) That he otherwise is unsuitable for any other cause to serve as a juror.

The validity of each challenge listed in this section shall be determined by the court.

HISTORY: GC § 13443-8; 113 v 123(183), ch 22, § 8; 118 v 429; Bureau of Code Revision, 10-1-53; 138 v H 965 (Eff 4-9-81); 139 v S 1. Eff 10-19-81.

† S 1 failed to contain the word "petit" here. It was added in H 965.

§ 2945.26 Challenge for cause.

Challenges for cause shall be tried by the court on the oath of the person challenged, or other evidence, and shall be made before the jury is sworn.

HISTORY: GC § 13443-9; 113 v 123(184), ch 22, § 9; Bureau of Code Revision. Eff 10-1-53.

§ 2945.27 Examination of jurors by the court.

The judge of the trial court shall examine the prospective jurors under oath or upon affirmation as to their qualifications to serve as fair and impartial jurors, but he shall permit reasonable examination of such jurors by the prosecuting attorney and by the defendant or his counsel.

HISTORY: GC § 13443-10; 113 v 123(184), ch 22, § 10; Bureau of Code Revision, 10-1-53; 127 v 419. Eff 9-9-57.

§ 2945.28 Form of oath to jury.

In criminal cases jurors and the jury shall take the following oath to be administered by the trial court or the clerk of the court of common pleas: "You shall well and truly try, and true deliverance make between the State of Ohio and the defendant (giving his name). So help you God."

A juror shall be allowed to make affirmation and the words "this you do as you shall answer under the pains and penalties of perjury" shall be substituted for the words, "So help you God."

HISTORY: RS §§ 7281, 7282; 66 v 308, §§ 137, 138; GC §§ 13443-11, 13443-12; 113 v 123(184), ch 22, §§ 11, 12; Bureau of Code Revision. Eff 10-1-53.

§ 2945.29 Jurors becoming unable to perform duties.

If, before the conclusion of the trial, a juror becomes sick, or for other reason is unable to perform his duty, the court may order him to be discharged. In that case, if alternate jurors have been selected, one of them shall be designated to take the place of the juror so discharged. If, after all alternate jurors have been made regular jurors, a juror becomes too incapacitated to perform his duty, and has been discharged by the court, a new juror may be sworn and the trial begin anew, or the jury may be discharged and a new jury then or thereafter impaneled.

HISTORY: GC § 13443-13; 113 v 123(184), ch 22, § 13; Bureau of Code Revision. Eff 10-1-53.

§ 2945.30 Medical attendance of juror.

In case of sickness of any juror before the conclusion of the trial, the court may order that such juror receive medical attendance and shall order the payment of a reasonable charge for such medical attendance out of the judiciary fund.

HISTORY: GC § 13443-14; 113 v 123(184), ch 22, § 14; Bureau of Code Revision. Eff 10-1-53.

§ 2945.31 Separation of jurors.

After the trial has commenced, before or after the jury is sworn, the court may order the jurors to be kept in charge of proper officers, or they may be permitted to separate during the trial. If the jurors are kept in charge of officers of the court, proper arrangements shall be made for their care, maintenance, and comfort, under the orders and direction of the court. In case of necessity the court may permit temporary separation of the jurors.

HISTORY: GC § 13443-15; 113 v 123(185), ch 22, § 15; Bureau of Code Revision. Eff 10-1-53.

§ 2945.32 Oath to officers if jury sequestered.

When an order has been entered by the court of common pleas in any criminal cause, directing the jurors to be kept in charge of the officers of the court, the following oath shall be administered by the clerk of the court of common pleas to said officers: "You do solemnly swear that you will, to the best of your ability, keep the persons sworn as jurors on this trial, from separating from each other; that you will not suffer any communications to be made to them, or any of them, orally or otherwise; that you will not communicate with them, or any of them, orally or otherwise, except by the order of this court, or to ask them if they have agreed on their verdict, until they shall be discharged, and that you will not, before they render their verdict communicate to any person the state of their deliberations or the verdict they have agreed upon, so help you God." Any officer having taken such oath who willfully violates the same, or permits the same to be violated, is guilty of perjury and shall be imprisoned not less than one nor more than ten years.

HISTORY: GC § 13443-16; 113 v 123(185), ch 22, § 16; Bureau of Code Revision. Eff 10-1-53.

§ 2945.33 Keeping and conduct of jury after case submitted.

When a cause is finally submitted the jurors must be kept together in a convenient place under the charge of an officer until they agree upon a verdict, or are discharged by the court. The court, except in cases where the offense charged may be punishable by death, may permit the jurors to separate during the adjournment of court overnight, under proper cautions, or under supervision of an officer. Such officer shall not permit a communication to be made to them, nor make any himself except to ask if they have agreed upon a verdict, unless he does so by order of the court. Such officer shall not communicate to any person, before the verdict is delivered, any matter in relation to their deliberation. Upon the trial of any prosecution for misdemeanor, the court may permit the jury to separate during their deliberation, or upon adjournment of the court overnight.

In cases where the offense charged may be punished by death, after the case is finally submitted to the jury, the jurors shall be kept in charge of the proper officer and proper arrangements for their care and maintenance shall be made as under section 2945.31 of the Revised Code.

HISTORY: GC § 13448-1; 113 v 123(194), ch 27; 115 v 531; Bureau of Code Revision, 10-1-53; 131 v 681. Eff 11-9-65.

§ 2945.34 Admonition if jurors separate during trial.

If the jurors are permitted to separate during a trial, they shall be admonished by the court not to converse with, nor permit themselves to be addressed by any person, nor to listen to any conversation on the subject of the trial, nor form or express any opinion thereon, until the case is finally submitted to them.

HISTORY: GC § 13443-17; 113 v 123(185), ch 22, § 17; Bureau of Code Revision. Eff 10-1-53.

§ 2945.35 Papers the jury may take.

Upon retiring for deliberation, the jury, at the discretion of the court, may take with it all papers except depositions, and all articles, photographs, and maps which have been offered in evidence. No article or paper identified but not admitted in evidence shall be taken by the jury upon its retirement.

HISTORY: GC § 13444-26; 113 v 123(191), ch 23, § 26; Bureau of Code Revision. Eff 10-1-53.

§ 2945.36 For what cause jury may be discharged.

The trial court may discharge a jury without prejudice to the prosecution:

(A) For the sickness or corruption of a juror or other accident or calamity;

(B) Because there is no probability of such jurors agreeing;

(C) If it appears after the jury has been sworn that one of the jurors is a witness in the case;

(D) By the consent of the prosecuting attorney and the defendant.

The reason for such discharge shall be entered on the journal.

HISTORY: GC § 13443-18; 113 v 123(185), ch 22, § 18; Bureau of Code Revision. Eff 10-1-53.

[COMPETENCY TO STAND TRIAL]

§ 2945.37 Definitions; hearing on competence to stand trial.

(A) As used in sections 2945.37 to 2945.402 [2945.40.2] of the Revised Code:

(1) "Prosecutor" means a prosecuting attorney or a city director of law, village solicitor, or similar chief legal officer of a municipal corporation who has authority to prosecute a criminal case that is before the court or the criminal case in which a defendant in a criminal case has been found incompetent to stand trial or not guilty by reason of insanity.

(2) "Examiner" means either of the following:

(a) A psychiatrist or a licensed clinical psychologist who satisfies the criteria of division (I)(1) of section 5122.01 of the Revised Code or is employed by a certified forensic center designated by the department of mental health to conduct examinations or evaluations.

(b) For purposes of a separate mental retardation evaluation that is ordered by a court pursuant to division (H) of section 2945.371 [2945.37.1] of the Revised Code, a psychologist designated by the director of mental retardation and developmental disabilities pursuant to that section to conduct that separate mental retardation evaluation.

(3) "Nonsecured status" means any unsupervised, off-grounds movement or trial visit from a hospital or institution, or any conditional release, that is granted to a person who is found incompetent to stand trial and is committed pursuant to section 2945.39 of the Revised Code or to a person who is found not guilty by reason of insanity and is committed pursuant to section 2945.40 of the Revised Code.

(4) "Unsupervised, off-grounds movement" includes only off-grounds privileges that are unsupervised and that have an expectation of return to the hospital or institution on a daily basis.

(5) "Trial visit" means a patient privilege of a longer

stated duration of unsupervised community contact with an expectation of return to the hospital or institution at designated times.

(6) "Conditional release" means a commitment status under which the trial court at any time may revoke a person's conditional release and order the rehospitalization or reinstitutionalization of the person as described in division (A) of section 2945.402 [2945.40.2] of the Revised Code and pursuant to which a person who is found incompetent to stand trial or a person who is found not guilty by reason of insanity lives and receives treatment in the community for a period of time that does not exceed the maximum prison term or term of imprisonment that the person could have received for the offense in question had the person been convicted of the offense instead of being found incompetent to stand trial on the charge of the offense or being found not guilty by reason of insanity relative to the offense.

(7) "Licensed clinical psychologist," "mentally ill person subject to hospitalization by court order," and "psychiatrist" have the same meanings as in section 5122.01 of the Revised Code.

(8) "Mentally retarded person subject to institutionalization by court order" has the same meaning as in section 5123.01 of the Revised Code.

(B) In a criminal action in a court of common pleas, a county court, or a municipal court, the court, prosecutor, or defense may raise the issue of the defendant's competence to stand trial. If the issue is raised before the trial has commenced, the court shall hold a hearing on the issue as provided in this section. If the issue is raised after the trial has commenced, the court shall hold a hearing on the issue only for good cause shown or on the court's own motion.

(C) The court shall conduct the hearing required or authorized under division (B) of this section within thirty days after the issue is raised, unless the defendant has been referred for evaluation in which case the court shall conduct the hearing within ten days after the filing of the report of the evaluation or, in the case of a defendant who is ordered by the court pursuant to division (H) of section 2945.371 [2945.37.1] of the Revised Code to undergo a separate mental retardation evaluation conducted by a psychologist designated by the director of mental retardation and developmental disabilities, within ten days after the filing of the report of the separate mental retardation evaluation under that division. A hearing may be continued for good cause.

(D) The defendant shall be represented by counsel at the hearing conducted under division (C) of this section. If the defendant is unable to obtain counsel, the court shall appoint counsel under Chapter 120. of the Revised Code or under the authority recognized in division (C) of section 120.06, division (E) of section 120.16, division (E) of section 120.26, or section 2941.51 of the Revised Code before proceeding with the hearing.

(E) The prosecutor and defense counsel may submit evidence on the issue of the defendant's competence to stand trial. A written report of the evaluation of the defendant may be admitted into evidence at the hearing by stipulation, but, if either the prosecution or defense objects to its admission, the report may be admitted under sections 2317.36 to 2317.38 of the Revised Code or any other applicable statute or rule.

(F) The court shall not find a defendant incompetent to stand trial solely because the defendant is receiving or has received treatment as a voluntary or involuntary mentally ill patient under Chapter 5122. or a voluntary or involuntary mentally retarded resident under Chapter 5123. of the Revised Code or because the defendant is receiving or has received psychotropic drugs or other medication, even if the defendant might become incompetent to stand trial without the drugs or medication.

(G) A defendant is presumed to be competent to stand trial. If, after a hearing, the court finds by a preponderance of the evidence that, because of the defendant's present mental condition, the defendant is incapable of understanding the nature and objective of the proceedings against the defendant or of assisting in the defendant's defense, the court shall find the defendant incompetent to stand trial and shall enter an order authorized by section 2945.38 of the Revised Code.

(H) Municipal courts shall follow the procedures set forth in sections 2945.37 to 2945.402 [2945.40.2] of the Revised Code. Except as provided in section 2945.371 [2945.37.1] of the Revised Code, a municipal court shall not order an evaluation of the defendant's competence to stand trial or the defendant's mental condition at the time of the commission of the offense to be conducted at any hospital operated by the department of mental health. Those evaluations shall be performed through community resources including, but not limited to, certified forensic centers, court probation departments, and community mental health agencies. All expenses of the evaluations shall be borne by the legislative authority of the municipal court, as defined in section 1901.03 of the Revised Code, and shall be taxed as costs in the case. If a defendant is found incompetent to stand trial or not guilty by reason of insanity, a municipal court may commit the defendant as provided in sections 2945.38 to 2945.402 [2945.40.2] of the Revised Code.

HISTORY: 137 v H 565 (Eff 11-1-78); 138 v S 297 (Eff 4-30-80); 139 v H 694 (Eff 11-15-81); 142 v S 156 (Eff 7-1-89); 146 v S 285. Eff 7-1-97.

Analogous to former RC § 2945.37 (GC § 13441-1; 113 v 123; Bureau of Code Revision, 10-1-53; 136 v S 368), repealed 137 v H 565, § 2, eff 11-1-78.

The effective date is set by section 4 of SB 285.

[§ 2945.37.1] § 2945.371 Evaluations of defendant's mental condition at relevant time; separate mental retardation evaluation.

(A) If the issue of a defendant's competence to stand

trial is raised or if a defendant enters a plea of not guilty by reason of insanity, the court may order one or more evaluations of the defendant's present mental condition or, in the case of a plea of not guilty by reason of insanity, of the defendant's mental condition at the time of the offense charged. An examiner shall conduct the evaluation.

(B) If the court orders more than one evaluation under division (A) of this section, the prosecutor and the defendant may recommend to the court an examiner whom each prefers to perform one of the evaluations. If a defendant enters a plea of not guilty by reason of insanity and if the court does not designate an examiner recommended by the defendant, the court shall inform the defendant that the defendant may have independent expert evaluation and that, if the defendant is unable to obtain independent expert evaluation, it will be obtained for the defendant at public expense if the defendant is indigent.

(C) If the court orders an evaluation under division (A) of this section, the defendant shall be available at the times and places established by the examiners who are to conduct the evaluation. The court may order a defendant who has been released on bail or recognizance to submit to an evaluation under this section. If a defendant who has been released on bail or recognizance refuses to submit to a complete evaluation, the court may amend the conditions of bail or recognizance and order the sheriff to take the defendant into custody and deliver the defendant to a center, program, or facility operated or certified by the department of mental health or the department of mental retardation and developmental disabilities where the defendant may be held for evaluation for a reasonable period of time not to exceed twenty days.

(D) A defendant who has not been released on bail or recognizance may be evaluated at the defendant's place of detention. Upon the request of the examiner, the court may order the sheriff to transport the defendant to a program or facility operated by the department of mental health or the department of mental retardation and developmental disabilities, where the defendant may be held for evaluation for a reasonable period of time not to exceed twenty days, and to return the defendant to the place of detention after the evaluation. A municipal court may make an order under this division only upon the request of a certified forensic center examiner.

(E) If a court orders the evaluation to determine a defendant's mental condition at the time of the offense charged, the court shall inform the examiner of the offense with which the defendant is charged.

(F) In conducting an evaluation of a defendant's mental condition at the time of the offense charged, the examiner shall consider all relevant evidence. If the offense charged involves the use of force against another person, the relevant evidence to be considered includes, but is not limited to, any evidence that the defendant suffered, at the time of the commission of the offense, from the "battered woman syndrome."

(G) The examiner shall file a written report with the court within thirty days after entry of a court order for evaluation, and the court shall provide copies of the report to the prosecutor and defense counsel. The report shall include all of the following:

(1) The examiner's findings;

(2) The facts in reasonable detail on which the findings are based;

(3) If the evaluation was ordered to determine the defendant's competence to stand trial, all of the following findings or recommendations that are applicable:

(a) Whether the defendant is capable of understanding the nature and objective of the proceedings against the defendant or of assisting in the defendant's defense;

(b) If the examiner's opinion is that the defendant is incapable of understanding the nature and objective of the proceedings against the defendant or of assisting in the defendant's defense, whether the defendant presently is mentally ill or mentally retarded and, if the examiner's opinion is that the defendant presently is mentally retarded, whether the defendant appears to be a mentally retarded person subject to institutionalization by court order;

(c) If the examiner's opinion is that the defendant is incapable of understanding the nature and objective of the proceedings against the defendant or of assisting in the defendant's defense and that the defendant presently is mentally ill or mentally retarded, the examiner's recommendation as to the least restrictive treatment alternative, consistent with the defendant's treatment needs for restoration to competency and with the safety of the community;

(4) If the evaluation was ordered to determine the defendant's mental condition at the time of the offense charged, the examiner's findings as to whether the defendant, at the time of the offense charged, did not know, as a result of a severe mental disease or defect, the wrongfulness of the defendant's acts charged.

(H) If the examiner's report filed under division (G) of this section indicates that in the examiner's opinion the defendant is incapable of understanding the nature and objective of the proceedings against the defendant or of assisting in the defendant's defense and that in the examiner's opinion the defendant appears to be a mentally retarded person subject to institutionalization by court order, the court shall order the defendant to undergo a separate mental retardation evaluation conducted by a psychologist designated by the director of mental retardation and developmental disabilities. Divisions (C) to (F) of this section apply in relation to a separate mental retardation evaluation conducted under this division. The psychologist appointed under this division to conduct the separate mental retardation evaluation shall file a written report with the court within thirty days after the entry of the court order requiring the separate mental retardation evaluation, and the court shall provide copies of the report to the prosecutor and defense counsel. The report shall include all of the information described in divisions (G)(1) to (4) of this section. If the court orders a separate mental retardation evaluation of a defendant under this division, the court shall not conduct a hearing under divisions (B) to (H) of section 2945.37 of the Revised Code regarding that defendant until a report of the separate mental retardation evaluation conducted under this division has been filed. Upon the filing of that report, the court shall conduct the hearing within the period of time specified in division (C) of section 2945.37 of the Revised Code.

(I) An examiner appointed under divisions (A) and (B) of this section or under division (H) of this section to evaluate a defendant to determine the defendant's competence to stand trial also may be appointed to evaluate a defendant who has entered a plea of not guilty by reason of insanity, but an examiner of that nature shall prepare separate reports on the issue of competence to stand trial and the defense of not guilty by reason of insanity.

(J) No statement that a defendant makes in an evaluation or hearing under divisions (A) to (H) of this section relating to the defendant's competence to stand trial or to the defendant's mental condition at the time of the offense charged shall be used against the defendant on the issue of guilt in any criminal action or proceeding, but, in a criminal action or proceeding, the prosecutor or defense counsel may call as a witness any person who evaluated the defendant or prepared a report pursuant to a referral under this section. Neither the appointment nor the testimony of an examiner appointed under this section precludes the prosecutor or defense counsel from calling other witnesses or presenting other evidence on competency or insanity issues.

(K) Persons appointed as examiners under divisions (A) and (B) of this section or under division (H) of this section shall be paid a reasonable amount for their services and expenses, as certified by the court. The certified amount shall be paid by the county in the case of county courts and courts of common pleas and by the legislative authority, as defined in section 1901.03 of the Revised Code, in the case of municipal courts.

HISTORY: 137 v H 565 (Eff 11-1-78); 138 v S 297 (Eff 4-30-80); 138 v H 900 (Eff 7-1-80); 138 v H 965 (Eff 4-9-81); 146 v S 285. Eff 7-1-97.

The effective date is set by section 4 of SB 285.

§ 2945.38 Disposition of defendant after competency hearing; sentence reduction for confinement for evaluation.

(A) If the issue of a defendant's competence to stand trial is raised and if the court, upon conducting the hearing provided for in section 2945.37 of the Revised Code, finds that the defendant is competent to stand trial, the defendant shall be proceeded against as provided by law. If the court finds the defendant competent to stand trial and the defendant is receiving psychotropic drugs or other medication, the court may authorize the continued administration of the drugs or medication or other appropriate treatment in order to maintain the defendant's competence to stand trial, unless the defendant's attending physician advises the court against continuation of the drugs, other medication, or treatment.

(B) After taking into consideration all relevant reports, information, and other evidence, the court shall order a defendant who is found incompetent to stand trial to undergo treatment at a facility operated by the department of mental health or the department of mental retardation and developmental disabilities, treatment at a facility certified by either of those departments as being qualified to treat mental illness or mental retardation, treatment at a public or private community mental health or mental retardation facility, or private treatment by a psychiatrist or another mental health or mental retardation professional. The order may restrict the defendant's freedom of movement as the court considers necessary. The prosecutor in the defendant's case shall send to the chief clinical officer of the hospital or facility, the managing officer of the institution, the director of the program, or the person to which the defendant is committed copies of relevant police reports and other background information that pertains to the defendant and is available to the prosecutor unless the prosecutor determines that the release of any of the information in the police reports or any of the other background information to unauthorized persons would interfere with the effective prosecution of any person or would create a substantial risk of harm to any person.

In determining placement alternatives, the court shall consider the extent to which the person is a danger to the person and to others, the need for security, and the type of crime involved and shall order the least restrictive alternative available that is consistent with public safety and treatment goals. In weighing these factors, the court shall give preference to protecting public safety.

If the defendant is found incompetent to stand trial, if the chief clinical officer of the hospital or facility, the managing officer of the institution, the director of the program, or the person to which the defendant is committed determines that medication is necessary to restore the defendant's competency to stand trial, and if the defendant lacks the capacity to give informed consent or refuses medication, the chief clinical officer, managing officer, director, or person to which the defendant is committed may petition for, and the court may authorize, the involuntary administration of medication.

(C) No defendant shall be required to undergo treatment under this section for longer than whichever of the following periods is applicable:

(1) One year, if the most serious offense with which the defendant is charged is one of the following offenses:

(a) Aggravated murder, murder, or an offense of violence for which a sentence of death or life imprisonment may be imposed;

(b) An offense of violence that is a felony of the first or second degree;

(c) A conspiracy to commit, an attempt to commit, or complicity in the commission of an offense described in division (C)(1)(a) or (b) of this section if the conspiracy, attempt, or complicity is a felony of the first or second degree.

(2) Six months, if the most serious offense with which the defendant is charged is a felony other than a felony described in division (C)(1) of this section;

(3) Sixty days, if the most serious offense with which the defendant is charged is a misdemeanor.

(D) Any defendant who is committed pursuant to this section shall not voluntarily admit the defendant or be voluntarily admitted to a hospital or institution pursuant to section 5122.02, 5122.15, 5123.69, or 5123.76 of the Revised Code.

(E) A defendant charged with an offense and committed to a hospital or other institution by the court under this section shall not be granted unsupervised on-grounds movement, supervised off-grounds movement, or nonsecured status.

(F) The person who supervises the treatment of a defendant ordered to undergo treatment under division (B) of this section shall file a written report with the court at the following times:

(1) Whenever the person believes the defendant is capable of understanding the nature and objective of the proceedings against the defendant and of assisting in the defendant's defense;

(2) For a felony offense, fourteen days before expiration of the maximum time for treatment as specified in division (C) of this section, and, for a misdemeanor offense, ten days before the expiration of the maximum time for treatment as specified in division (C) of this section;

(3) At a minimum, after each six months of treatment.

(G) A report under division (F) of this section shall contain the examiner's findings, the facts in reasonable detail on which the findings are based, and the examiner's opinion as to the defendant's capability of understanding the nature and objective of the proceedings against the defendant and of assisting in the defendant's defense. If, in the examiner's opinion, the defendant remains incapable of understanding the nature and objective of the proceedings against the defendant or of assisting in the defendant's defense and also remains mentally ill or mentally retarded, and if the maximum time for treatment as specified in division (C) of this section has not expired, the report also shall contain the examiner's recommendation as to the least restrictive treatment alternative that is consistent with the defendant's treatment needs for restoration to competency and with the safety of the community. The court shall provide copies of the report to the prosecutor and defense counsel.

(H) Within ten days after the expiration of the maximum time for treatment as specified in division (C) of this section, within thirty days after a defendant's request for a hearing that is made after six months of treatment, or within thirty days after being advised by the treating physician that the defendant is competent to stand trial, whichever is earlier, the court shall conduct another hearing to determine if the defendant is competent to stand trial and shall do whichever of the following is applicable:

(1) If the court finds that the defendant is competent to stand trial, the defendant shall be proceeded against as provided by law.

(2) If the court finds that the defendant is incompetent to stand trial and the maximum time for treatment as specified in division (C) of this section has not expired, the court, after consideration of the examiner's recommendation, shall order that treatment be continued until the expiration of the maximum time for treatment, may change the facility or program at which the treatment is to be continued, and shall specify whether the treatment is to be continued at the same or a different facility or program.

(3) If the court finds that the defendant is incompetent to stand trial, if the defendant is charged with an offense listed in division (C)(1) of this section, and if the maximum time for treatment relative to that offense as specified in that division has expired, further proceedings shall be as provided in sections 2945.39, 2945.401 [2945.40.1], and 2945.402 [2945.40.2] of the Revised Code.

(4) If the court finds that the defendant is incompetent to stand trial, if the most serious offense with which the defendant is charged is a misdemeanor or a felony other than a felony listed in division (C)(1) of this section, and if the maximum time for treatment relative to that offense as specified in division (C) of this section has expired, the court shall dismiss the indictment, information, or complaint against the defendant. A dismissal under this division is not a bar to further prosecution based on the same conduct. The court shall discharge the defendant unless the court or prosecutor files an affidavit in probate court for civil commitment pursuant to Chapter 5122. or 5123. of the Revised Code. If an affidavit for civil commitment is filed, the court may detain the defendant for ten days pending civil commitment. All of the following provisions apply to persons charged with a misdemeanor or a felony other than a felony listed in division (C)(1) of this section who are committed by the probate court subsequent to the court's or prosecutor's filing of an affidavit for civil commitment under authority of this division:

(a) The chief clinical officer of the hospital or facility, the managing officer of the institution, the director of the program, or the person to which the defendant is committed or admitted shall do all of the following:

(i) Notify the prosecutor, in writing, of the discharge of the defendant, send the notice at least ten days prior to the discharge unless the discharge is by the probate court, and state in the notice the date on which the defendant will be discharged;

(ii) Notify the prosecutor, in writing, when the defendant is absent without leave or is granted unsupervised, off-grounds movement, and send this notice promptly after the discovery of the absence without leave or prior to the granting of the unsupervised, off-grounds movement, whichever is applicable;

(iii) Notify the prosecutor, in writing, of the change of the defendant's commitment or admission to voluntary status, send the notice promptly upon learning of the change to voluntary status, and state in the notice the date on which the defendant was committed or admitted on a voluntary status.

(b) Upon receiving notice that the defendant will be granted unsupervised, off-grounds movement, the prosecutor either shall re-indict the defendant or promptly notify the court that the prosecutor does not intend to prosecute the charges against the defendant.

(I) If a defendant is convicted of a crime and sentenced to a jail or workhouse, the defendant's sentence shall be reduced by the total number of days the defendant is confined for evaluation to determine the defendant's competence to stand trial or treatment under this section and sections 2945.37 and 2945.371 [2945.37.1] of the Revised Code or by the total number of days the defendant is confined for evaluation to determine the defendant's mental condition at the time of the offense charged.

HISTORY: GC § 13441-2; 113 v 123(177), ch 20, § 2; Bureau of Code Revision, 10-1-53; 136 v S 185 (Eff 8-29-75); 137 v H 565 (Eff 11-1-78); 138 v S 297 (Eff 4-30-80); 138 v H 900 (Eff 7-1-80); 138 v H 965 (Eff 4-9-81); 142 v S 156 (Eff 7-1-89); 146 v S 269 (Eff 7-1-96); 146 v S 285. Eff 7-1-97.

The effective date is set by section 4 of SB 285.

[§ 2945.38.1] § 2945.381 Repealed, 137 v H 565, § 2 [136 v S 185]. Eff 11-1-78.

This section concerned the disposition of a mentally ill person accused of committing a crime.

§ 2945.39 Proceedings after expiration of maximum time for treatment after finding of incompetency.

(A) If a defendant who is charged with an offense described in division (C)(1) of section 2945.38 of the Revised Code is found incompetent to stand trial, after the expiration of the maximum time for treatment as specified in division (C) of that section, one of the following applies:

(1) The court or the prosecutor may file an affidavit in probate court for civil commitment of the defendant in the manner provided in Chapter 5122. or 5123. of the Revised Code. If the court or prosecutor files an affidavit for civil commitment, the court may detain the defendant for ten days pending civil commitment. If the probate court commits the defendant subsequent to the court's or prosecutor's filing of an affidavit for civil commitment, the chief clinical officer of the hospital or facility, the managing officer of the institution, the director of the program, or the person to which the defendant is committed or admitted shall send to the prosecutor the notices described in divisions (H)(4)(a)(i) to (iii) of section 2945.38 of the Revised Code within the periods of time and under the circumstances specified in those divisions.

(2) On the motion of the prosecutor or on its own motion, the court may retain jurisdiction over the defendant if, at a hearing, the court finds both of the following by clear and convincing evidence:

(a) The defendant committed the offense with which the defendant is charged.

(b) The defendant is a mentally ill person subject to hospitalization by court order or a mentally retarded person subject to institutionalization by court order.

(B) In making its determination under division (A)(2) of this section as to whether to retain jurisdiction over the defendant, the court may consider all relevant evidence, including, but not limited to, any relevant psychiatric, psychological, or medical testimony or reports, the acts constituting the offense charged, and any history of the defendant that is relevant to the defendant's ability to conform to the law.

(C) If the court conducts a hearing as described in division (A)(2) of this section and if the court does not make both findings described in divisions (A)(2)(a) and (b) of this section by clear and convincing evidence, the court shall dismiss the indictment, information, or complaint against the defendant. Upon the dismissal, the court shall discharge the defendant unless the court or prosecutor files an affidavit in probate court for civil commitment of the defendant pursuant to Chapter 5122. or 5123. of the Revised Code. If the court or prosecutor files an affidavit for civil commitment, the court may order that the defendant be detained for up to ten days pending the civil commitment. If the probate court commits the defendant subsequent to the court's or prosecutor's filing of an affidavit for civil commitment, the chief clinical officer of the hospital or facility, the managing officer of the institution, the director of the program, or the person to which the defendant is committed or admitted shall send to the prosecutor the notices described in divisions (H)(4)(a)(i) to (iii) of section 2945.38 of the Revised Code within the periods of time and under the circumstances specified in those divisions. A dismissal of charges under this division is not a bar to further criminal proceedings based on the same conduct.

(D)(1) If the court conducts a hearing as described in division (A)(2) of this section and if the court makes the findings described in divisions (A)(2)(a) and (b) of this section by clear and convincing evidence, the court shall commit the defendant to a hospital operated by the department of mental health, a facility operated by the department of mental retardation and developmental disabilities, or another medical or psychiatric facility, as appropriate. In determining the place and nature of the commitment, the court shall order the least restrictive commitment alternative available that is consistent with public safety and the welfare of the defendant. In weighing these factors, the court shall give preference to protecting public safety.

(2) If a court makes a commitment of a defendant under division (D)(1) of this section, the prosecutor shall send to the place of commitment all reports of the defendant's current mental condition and, except as otherwise provided in this division, any other relevant information, including, but not limited to, a transcript of the hearing held pursuant to division (A)(2) of this section, copies of relevant police reports, and copies of any prior arrest and conviction records that pertain to the defendant and that the prosecutor possesses. The prosecutor shall send the reports of the defendant's current mental condition in every case of commitment, and, unless the prosecutor determines that the release of any of the other relevant information to unauthorized persons would interfere with the effective prosecution of any person or would create a substantial risk of harm to any person, the prosecutor also shall send the other relevant information. Upon admission of a defendant committed under division (D)(1) of this section, the place of commitment shall send to the board of alcohol, drug addiction, and mental health services or the community mental health board serving the county in which the charges against the defendant were filed a copy of all reports of the defendant's current mental condition and a copy of the other relevant information provided by the prosecutor under this division, including, if provided, a transcript of the hearing held pursuant to division (A)(2) of this section, the relevant police reports, and the prior arrest and conviction records that pertain to the defendant and that the prosecutor possesses.

(3) If a court makes a commitment under division (D)(1) of this section, all further proceedings shall be in accordance with sections 2945.401 [2945.40.1] and 2945.402 [2945.40.2] of the Revised Code.

HISTORY: 146 v S 285. Eff 7-1-97.

Not analogous to former RC § 2945.39 (137 v H 565; 138 v S 297; 138 v H 900; 138 v H 736; 138 v H 965; 139 v H 1; 143 v H 484), repealed 146 v S 285, § 1, eff 7-1-97.

The effective date is set by section 4 of SB 285.

[§ 2945.39.1] § 2945.391 Finding of not guilty by reason of insanity.

For purposes of sections 2945.371 [2945.37.1], 2945.40, 2945.401 [2945.40.1], and 2945.402 [2945.40.2] and Chapters 5122. and 5123. of the Revised Code, a person is "not guilty by reason of insanity" relative to a charge of an offense only as described in division (A)(14) of section 2901.01 of the Revised Code. Proof that a person's reason, at the time of the commission of an offense, was so impaired that the person did not have the ability to refrain from doing the person's act or acts, does not constitute a defense.

HISTORY: 143 v S 24 (Eff 7-24-90); 146 v S 239 (Eff 9-6-96); 146 v S 285. Eff 7-1-97.

The effective date is set by section 4 of SB 285.

[§ 2945.39.2] § 2945.392 Battered woman syndrome testimony.

(A) The declarations set forth in division (A) of section 2901.06 of the Revised Code apply in relation to this section.

(B) If a defendant is charged with an offense involving the use of force against another and the defendant enters a plea to the charge of not guilty by reason of insanity, the defendant may introduce expert testimony of the "battered woman syndrome" and expert testimony that the defendant suffered from that syndrome as evidence to establish the requisite impairment of the defendant's reason, at the time of the commission of the offense, that is necessary for a finding that the defendant is not guilty by reason of insanity. The introduction of any expert testimony under this division shall be in accordance with the Ohio Rules of Evidence.

HISTORY: 143 v H 484 (Eff 11-5-90); 146 v S 285. Eff 7-1-97.

The effective date is set by section 4 of SB 285.

§ 2945.40 Procedure upon acquittal by reason of insanity.

(A) If a person is found not guilty by reason of insanity, the verdict shall state that finding, and the trial court shall conduct a full hearing to determine whether the person is a mentally ill person subject to hospitalization by court order or a mentally retarded person subject to institutionalization by court order. Prior to the hearing, if the trial judge believes that there is probable cause that the person found not guilty by reason of insanity is a mentally ill person subject to hospitalization by court order or mentally retarded person subject to institutionalization by court order, the trial judge may issue a temporary order of detention for that person to remain in effect for ten court days or until the hearing, whichever occurs first.

Any person detained pursuant to a temporary order of detention issued under this division shall be held in a suitable facility, taking into consideration the place and type of confinement prior to and during trial.

(B) The court shall hold the hearing under division (A) of this section to determine whether the person found not guilty by reason of insanity is a mentally ill person subject to hospitalization by court order or a mentally retarded person subject to institutionalization by court order within ten court days after the finding of not guilty by reason of insanity. Failure to conduct the hearing within the ten-day period shall cause the immediate discharge of the respondent, unless the judge grants a continuance for not longer than ten court days for good cause shown or for any period of time upon motion of the respondent.

(C) If a person is found not guilty by reason of insanity, the person has the right to attend all hearings conducted pursuant to sections 2945.37 to 2945.402 [2945.40.2] of the Revised Code. At any hearing conducted pursuant to one of those sections, the court shall inform the person that the person has all of the following rights:

(1) The right to be represented by counsel and to have that counsel provided at public expense if the person is indigent, with the counsel to be appointed by the court under Chapter 120. of the Revised Code or under the authority recognized in division (C) of section 120.06, division (E) of section 120.16, division (E) of section 120.26, or section 2941.51 of the Revised Code;

(2) The right to have independent expert evaluation and to have that independent expert evaluation provided at public expense if the person is indigent;

(3) The right to subpoena witnesses and documents, to present evidence on the person's behalf, and to cross-examine witnesses against the person;

(4) The right to testify in the person's own behalf and to not be compelled to testify;

(5) The right to have copies of any relevant medical or mental health document in the custody of the state or of any place of commitment other than a document for which the court finds that the release to the person of information contained in the document would create a substantial risk of harm to any person.

(D) The hearing under division (A) of this section shall be open to the public, and the court shall conduct the hearing in accordance with the Rules of Civil Procedure. The court shall make and maintain a full transcript and record of the hearing proceedings. The court may consider all relevant evidence, including, but not limited to, any relevant psychiatric, psychological, or medical testimony or reports, the acts constituting the offense in relation to which the person was found not guilty by reason of insanity, and any history of the person that is relevant to the person's ability to conform to the law.

(E) Upon completion of the hearing under division (A) of this section, if the court finds there is not clear and convincing evidence that the person is a mentally ill person subject to hospitalization by court order or a mentally retarded person subject to institutionalization by court order, the court shall discharge the person, unless a detainer has been placed upon the person by the department of rehabilitation and correction, in which case the person shall be returned to that department.

(F) If, at the hearing under division (A) of this section, the court finds by clear and convincing evidence that the person is a mentally ill person subject to hospitalization by court order or a mentally retarded person subject to institutionalization by court order, it shall commit the person to a hospital operated by the department of mental health, a facility operated by the department of mental retardation and developmental disabilities, or another medical or psychiatric facility, as appropriate, and further proceedings shall be in accordance with sections 2945.401 [2945.40.1] and 2945.402 [2945.40.2] of the Revised Code. In determining the place and nature of the commitment, the court shall order the least restrictive commitment alternative available that is consistent with public safety and the welfare of the person. In weighing these factors, the court shall give preference to protecting public safety.

(G) If a court makes a commitment of a person under division (F) of this section, the prosecutor shall send to the place of commitment all reports of the person's current mental condition, and, except as otherwise provided in this division, any other relevant information, including, but not limited to, a transcript of the hearing held pursuant to division (A) of this section, copies of relevant police reports, and copies of any prior arrest and conviction records that pertain to the person and that the prosecutor possesses. The prosecutor shall send the reports of the person's current mental condition in every case of commitment, and, unless the prosecutor determines that the release of any of the other relevant information to unauthorized persons would interfere with the effective prosecution of any person or would create a substantial risk of harm to any person, the prosecutor also shall send the other relevant information. Upon admission of a person committed under division (F) of this section, the place of commitment shall send to the board of alcohol, drug addiction, and mental health services or the community mental health board serving the county in which the charges against the person were filed a copy of all reports of the person's current mental condition and a copy of the other relevant information provided by the prosecutor under this division, including, if provided, a transcript of the hearing held pursuant to division (A) of this section, the relevant police reports, and the prior arrest and conviction records that pertain to the person and that the prosecutor possesses.

(H) A person who is committed pursuant to this section shall not voluntarily admit the person or be voluntarily admitted to a hospital or institution pursuant to sections 5122.02, 5122.15, 5123.69, or 5123.76 of the Revised Code.

HISTORY: 137 v H 565 (Eff 11-1-78); 138 v S 297 (Eff 4-30-80); 138 v H 965 (Eff 4-9-81); 139 v H 1 (Eff 8-5-81); 142 v S 156 (Eff 7-1-89); 143 v S 24 (Eff 7-24-90); 145 v H 571 (Eff 10-6-94); 146 v H 567 (Eff 10-29-96); 146 v S 285. Eff 7-1-97.

Analogous to former RC § 2945.40 (GC § 13441-4; 113 v 123; Bureau of Code Revision, 10-1-53), repealed 137 v H 565, § 2, eff 11-1-78.

The effective date is set by section 4 of SB 285.

[§ 2945.40.1] § 2945.401 Continuing jurisdiction of court after incompetency finding or insanity acquittal; application of other laws; termination of commitment or change in conditions.

(A) A defendant found incompetent to stand trial and committed pursuant to section 2945.39 of the Revised Code or a person found not guilty by reason of insanity and committed pursuant to section 2945.40 of the Revised Code shall remain subject to the jurisdiction of the trial court pursuant to that commitment, and to the provisions of this section, until the final termination of the commitment as described in division (J)(1) of this section. If the jurisdiction is terminated under this division because of the final termination of the commitment resulting from the expiration of the maximum prison term or term of imprisonment described in division (J)(1)(b) of this section, the court or prosecutor may file an affidavit for the civil commitment of the defendant or person pursuant to Chapter 5122. or 5123. of the Revised Code.

(B) A hearing conducted under any provision of sections 2945.37 to 2945.402 [2945.40.2] of the Revised Code shall not be conducted in accordance with Chapters 5122. and 5123. of the Revised Code. Any person who is committed pursuant to section 2945.39 or 2945.40 of the Revised Code shall not voluntarily admit the person or be voluntarily admitted to a hospital or institution pursuant to section 5122.02, 5122.15, 5123.69, or 5123.76 of the Revised Code. All other provisions of Chapters 5122. and 5123. of the Revised Code regarding hospitalization or institutionalization shall apply to the extent they are not in conflict with this chapter. A commitment under section 2945.39 or 2945.40 of the Revised Code shall not be terminated and the conditions of the commitment shall not be changed except as otherwise provided in division (D)(2) of this section with respect to a mentally retarded person subject to institutionalization by court order or except by order of the trial court.

(C) The hospital, facility, or program to which a defendant or person has been committed under section 2945.39 or 2945.40 of the Revised Code shall report in writing to the trial court, at the times specified in this division, as to whether the defendant or person remains a mentally ill person subject to hospitalization by court order or a mentally retarded person subject to institutionalization by court order and, in the case of a defendant committed under section 2945.39 of the Revised Code, as to whether the defendant remains incompetent to stand trial. The hospital, facility, or program shall make the reports after the initial six months of treatment and every two years after the initial report is made. The trial court shall provide copies of the reports to the prosecutor and to the counsel for the defendant or person. Within thirty days after its receipt pursuant to this division of a report from a hospital, facility, or program, the trial court shall hold a hearing on the continued commitment of the defendant or person or on any changes in the conditions of the commitment of the defendant or person. The defendant or person may request a change in the conditions of confinement, and the trial court shall conduct a hearing on that request if six months or more have elapsed since the most recent hearing was conducted under this section.

(D)(1) Except as otherwise provided in division (D)(2) of this section, when a defendant or person has been committed under section 2945.39 or 2945.40 of the Revised Code, at any time after evaluating the risks to public safety and the welfare of the defendant or person, the chief clinical officer of the hospital, facility, or program to which the defendant or person is committed may recommend a termination of the defendant's or person's commitment or a change in the conditions of the defendant's or person's commitment.

Except as otherwise provided in division (D)(2) of this section, if the chief clinical officer recommends on-grounds unsupervised movement, off-grounds supervised movement, or nonsecured status for the defendant or person or termination of the defendant's or person's commitment, the following provisions apply:

(a) If the chief clinical officer recommends on-grounds unsupervised movement or off-grounds supervised movement, the chief clinical officer shall file with the trial court an application for approval of the movement and shall send a copy of the application to the prosecutor. Within fifteen days after receiving the application, the prosecutor may request a hearing on the application and, if a hearing is requested, shall so inform the chief clinical officer. If the prosecutor does not request a hearing within the fifteen-day period, the trial court shall approve the application by entering its order approving the requested movement or, within five days after the expiration of the fifteen-day period, shall set a date for a hearing on the application. If the prosecutor requests a hearing on the application within the fifteen-day period, the trial court shall hold a hearing on the application within thirty days after the hearing is requested. If the trial court, within five days after the expiration of the fifteen-day period, sets a date for a hearing on the application, the trial court shall hold the hearing within thirty days after setting the hearing date. At least fifteen days before any hearing is held under this division, the trial court shall give the prosecutor written notice of the date, time, and place of the hearing. At the conclusion of each hearing conducted under this division, the trial court either shall approve or disapprove the application and shall enter its order accordingly.

(b) If the chief clinical officer recommends termination of the defendant's or person's commitment at any time or if the chief clinical officer recommends the first of any nonsecured status for the defendant or person, the chief clinical officer shall send written notice of this recommendation to the trial court and to the local forensic center. The local forensic center shall evaluate the committed defendant or person and, within thirty days after its receipt of the written notice, shall submit to the trial court and the chief clinical officer a written report of the evaluation. The trial court shall provide a copy of the chief clinical officer's written notice and of the local forensic center's written report to the prosecutor and to the counsel for the defendant or person. Upon the local forensic center's submission of the report to the trial court and the chief clinical officer, all of the following apply:

(i) If the forensic center disagrees with the recommendation of the chief clinical officer, it shall inform the chief clinical officer and the trial court of its decision and the reasons for the decision. The chief clinical officer, after consideration of the forensic center's decision, shall either withdraw, proceed with, or modify and proceed with the recommendation. If the chief clinical officer proceeds with, or modifies and proceeds with, the recommendation, the chief clinical officer shall proceed in accordance with division (D)(1)(b)(iii) of this section.

(ii) If the forensic center agrees with the recommendation of the chief clinical officer, it shall inform the chief clinical officer and the trial court of its decision and the reasons for the decision, and the chief clinical officer shall proceed in accordance with division (D)(1)(b)(iii) of this section.

(iii) If the forensic center disagrees with the recommendation of the chief clinical officer and the chief clinical officer proceeds with, or modifies and proceeds with, the recommendation or if the forensic center agrees with the recommendation of the chief clinical officer, the chief clinical officer shall work with the board of alcohol, drug addiction, and mental health services or community mental health board serving the area, as appropriate, to develop a plan to implement the recommendation. If the defendant or person is on medication, the plan shall include, but shall not be limited to, a system to monitor the defendant's or person's compliance with the prescribed medication treatment plan. The system shall include a schedule that clearly states when the defendant or person shall report for a medication compliance check. The medication compliance checks shall be based upon the effective duration of the prescribed medication, taking into account the route by which it is taken, and shall be scheduled at intervals sufficiently close together to detect a potential increase in mental illness symptoms that the medication is intended to prevent.

The chief clinical officer, after consultation with the board of alcohol, drug addiction, and mental health services or the community mental health board serving the area, shall send the recommendation and plan developed under division (D)(1)(b)(iii) of this section, in writing, to the trial court, the prosecutor and the counsel for the committed defendant or person. The trial court shall conduct a hearing on the recommendation and plan developed under division (D)(1)(b)(iii) of this section. Divisions (D)(1)(c) and (d) and (E) to (J) of this section apply regarding the hearing.

(c) If the chief clinical officer's recommendation is for nonsecured status or termination of commitment, the prosecutor may obtain an independent expert evaluation of the defendant's or person's mental condition, and the trial court may continue the hearing on the recommendation for a period of not more than thirty days to permit time for the evaluation.

The prosecutor may introduce the evaluation report or present other evidence at the hearing in accordance with the Rules of Evidence.

(d) The trial court shall schedule the hearing on a chief clinical officer's recommendation for nonsecured status or termination of commitment and shall give reasonable notice to the prosecutor and the counsel for the defendant or person. Unless continued for independent evaluation at the prosecutor's request or for other good cause, the hearing shall be held within thirty days after the trial court's receipt of the recommendation and plan.

(2)(a) Division (D)(1) of this section does not apply to on-grounds unsupervised movement of a defendant or person who has been committed under section 2945.39 or 2945.40 of the Revised Code, who is a mentally retarded person subject to institutionalization by court order, and who is being provided residential habilitation, care, and treatment in a facility operated by the department of mental retardation and developmental disabilities.

(b) If, pursuant to section 2945.39 of the Revised Code, the trial court commits a defendant who is found incompetent to stand trial and who is a mentally retarded person subject to institutionalization by court order, if the defendant is being provided residential habilitation, care, and treatment in a facility operated by the department of mental retardation and developmental disabilities, if an individual who is conducting a survey for the department of health to determine the facility's compliance with the certification requirements of the medicaid program under Chapter 5111. of the Revised Code and Title XIX of the "Social Security Act," 49 Stat. 620 (1935), 42 U.S.C.A. 301, as amended, cites the defendant's receipt of the residential habilitation, care, and treatment in the facility as being inappropriate under the certification requirements, if the defendant's receipt of the residential habilitation, care, and treatment in the facility potentially jeopardizes the facility's continued receipt of federal medicaid moneys, and if as a result of the citation the chief clinical officer of the facility determines that the conditions of the defendant's commitment should be changed, the department of mental retardation and developmental disabilities may cause the defendant to be removed from the particular facility and, after evaluating the risks to public safety and the welfare of the defendant and after determining whether another type of placement is consistent with the certification requirements, may place the defendant in another facility that the department selects as an appropriate facility for the defendant's continued receipt of residential habilitation, care, and treatment and that is a no less secure setting than the facility in which the defendant had been placed at the time of the citation. Within three days after the defendant's removal and alternative placement under the circumstances described in division (D)(2)(b) of this section, the department of mental retardation and developmental disabilities shall notify the trial court and the prosecutor in writing of the removal and alternative placement.

The trial court shall set a date for a hearing on the removal and alternative placement, and the hearing shall be held within twenty-one days after the trial court's receipt of the notice from the department of mental retardation and developmental disabilities. At least ten-[sic]days before the hearing is held, the trial court shall give the prosecutor, the department of mental retardation and developmental disabilities, and the counsel for the defendant written notice of the date, time, and place of the hearing. At the hearing, the trial court shall consider the citation issued by the individual who conducted the survey for the department of health to be prima-facie evidence of the fact that the defendant's commitment to the particular facility was inappropriate under the certification requirements of the medicaid program under Chapter 5111. of the Revised Code and Title XIX of the "Social Security Act," 49 Stat. 620 (1935), 42 U.S.C.A. 301, as amended, and potentially jeopardizes the particular facility's continued receipt of federal medicaid moneys. At the conclusion of the hearing, the trial court may approve or disapprove the defendant's removal and alternative placement. If the trial court approves the defendant's removal and alternative placement, the department of mental retardation and developmental disabilities may continue the defendant's alternative placement. If the trial court disapproves the defendant's removal and alternative placement, it shall enter an order modifying the defendant's removal and alternative placement, but that order shall not require the department of mental retardation and developmental disabilities to replace the defendant for purposes of continued residential habilitation, care, and treatment in the facility associated with the citation issued by the individual who conducted the survey for the department of health.

(E) In making a determination under this section regarding nonsecured status or termination of commitment, the trial court shall consider all relevant factors, including, but not limited to, all of the following:

(1) Whether, in the trial court's view, the defendant or person currently represents a substantial risk of physical harm to the defendant or person or others;

(2) Psychiatric and medical testimony as to the current mental and physical condition of the defendant or person;

(3) Whether the defendant or person has insight into the dependant's† or person's condition so that the defendant or person will continue treatment as prescribed or seek professional assistance as needed;

(4) The grounds upon which the state relies for the proposed commitment;

(5) Any past history that is relevant to establish the defendant's or person's degree of conformity to the laws, rules, regulations, and values of society;

(6) If there is evidence that the defendant's or person's mental illness is in a state of remission, the medically suggested cause and degree of the remission and the probability that the defendant or person will continue treatment to maintain the remissive state of the defendant's or person's illness should the defendant's or person's commitment conditions be altered.

(F) At any hearing held pursuant to division (C) or (D)(1) or (2) of this section, the defendant or the person shall have all the rights of a defendant or person at a commitment hearing as described in section 2945.40 of the Revised Code.

(G) In a hearing held pursuant to division (C) or (D)(1) of this section, the prosecutor has the burden of proof as follows:

(1) For a recommendation of termination of commitment, to show by clear and convincing evidence that the defendant or person remains a mentally ill person subject to hospitalization by court order or a mentally retarded person subject to institutionalization by court order;

(2) For a recommendation for a change in the conditions of the commitment to a less restrictive status, to show by clear and convincing evidence that the proposed change represents a threat to public safety or a threat to the safety of any person.

(H) In a hearing held pursuant to division (C) or (D)(1) or (2) of this section, the prosecutor shall represent the state or the public interest.

(I) At the conclusion of a hearing conducted under division (D)(1) of this section regarding a recommendation from the chief clinical officer of a hospital, program, or facility, the trial court may approve, disapprove, or modify the recommendation and shall enter an order accordingly.

(J)(1) A defendant or person who has been committed pursuant to section 2945.39 or 2945.40 of the Revised Code continues to be under the jurisdiction of the trial court until the final termination of the commitment. For purposes of division (J) of this section, the final termination of a commitment occurs upon the earlier of one of the following:

(a) The defendant or person no longer is a mentally ill person subject to hospitalization by court order or a mentally retarded person subject to institutionalization by court order, as determined by the trial court;

(b) The expiration of the maximum prison term or term of imprisonment that the defendant or person could have received if the defendant or person had been convicted of the most serious offense with which the defendant or person is charged or in relation to which the defendant or person was found not guilty by reason of insanity;

(c) The trial court enters an order terminating the commitment under the circumstances described in division (J)(2)(a)(ii) of this section.

(2)(a) If a defendant is found incompetent to stand trial and committed pursuant to section 2945.39 of the Revised Code, if neither of the circumstances described in divisions (J)(1)(a) and (b) of this section applies to that defendant, and if a report filed with the trial court pursuant to division (C) of this section indicates that the defendant presently is competent to stand trial or if, at any other time during the period of the defendant's commitment, the prosecutor, the counsel for the defendant, or the chief clinical officer of the hospital, facility, or program to which the defendant is committed files an application with the trial court alleging that the defendant presently is competent to stand trial and requesting a hearing on the competency issue or the trial court otherwise has reasonable cause to believe that the defendant presently is competent to stand trial and determines on its own motion to hold a hearing on the competency issue, the trial court shall schedule a hearing on the competency of the defendant to stand trial, shall give the prosecutor, the counsel for the defendant, and the chief clinical officer notice of the date, time, and place of the hearing at least fifteen days before the hearing, and shall conduct the hearing within thirty days of the filing of the application or of its own motion. If, at the conclusion of the hearing, the trial court determines that the defendant presently is capable of understanding the nature and objective of the proceedings against the defendant and of assisting in the defendant's defense, the trial court shall order that the defendant is competent to stand trial and shall be proceeded against as provided by law with respect to the applicable offenses described in division (C)(1) of section 2945.38 of the Revised Code and shall enter whichever of the following additional orders is appropriate:

(i) If the trial court determines that the defendant remains a mentally ill person subject to hospitalization by court order or a mentally retarded person subject to institutionalization by court order, the trial court shall order that the defendant's commitment to the hospital, facility, or program shall be continued during the pendency of the trial on the applicable offenses described in division (C)(1) of section 2945.38 of the Revised Code.

(ii) If the trial court determines that the defendant no longer is a mentally ill person subject to hospitalization by court order or a mentally retarded person subject to institutionalization by court order, the trial court shall order that the defendant's commitment to the hospital, facility, or program shall not be continued during the pendency of the trial on the applicable offenses described in division (C)(1) of section 2945.38 of the Revised Code. This order shall be a final termination of the commitment for purposes of division (J)(1)(c) of this section.

(b) If, at the conclusion of the hearing described in division (J)(2)(a) of this section, the trial court determines that the defendant remains incapable of understanding the nature and objective of the proceedings against the defendant or of assisting in the defendant's defense, the trial court shall order that the defendant continues to be incompetent to stand trial, that the defendant's commitment to the hospital, facility, or program shall be continued, and that the defendant remains subject to the jurisdiction of the trial court pursuant to that commitment, and to the provisions of this section, until the final termination of the commitment as described in division (J)(1) of this section.

HISTORY: 146 v S 285. Eff 7-1-97.

The effective date is set by section 4 of SB 285.

† So in enrolled bill, division (E)(3). Was "defendant" intended?

[§ 2945.40.2] § 2945.402 Conditional release.

(A) In approving a conditional release, the trial court may set any conditions on the release with respect to the treatment, evaluation, counseling, or control of the defendant or person that the court considers necessary to protect the public safety and the welfare of the defendant or person. The trial court may revoke a defendant's or person's conditional release and order rehospitalization or reinstitutionalization at any time the conditions of the release have not been satisfied, provided that the revocation shall be in accordance with this section.

(B) A conditional release is a commitment. The hearings on continued commitment as described in section 2945.401 [2945.40.1] of the Revised Code apply to a defendant or person on conditional release.

(C) A person, agency, or facility that is assigned to monitor a defendant or person on conditional release immediately shall notify the trial court on learning that the defendant or person being monitored has violated the terms of the conditional release. Upon learning of any violation of the terms of the conditional release, the trial court may issue a temporary order of detention or, if necessary, an arrest warrant for the defendant or person. Within ten court days after the defendant's or person's detention or arrest, the trial court shall conduct a hearing to determine whether the conditional release should be modified or terminated. At the hearing, the defendant or person shall have the same rights as are described in division (C) of section 2945.40 of the Revised Code. The trial court may order a continuance of the ten-court-day period for no longer than ten days for good cause shown or for any period on motion of the defendant or person. If the trial court fails to conduct the hearing within the ten-court-day period and does not order a continuance in accordance with this division, the defendant or person shall be restored to the prior conditional release status.

(D) The trial court shall give all parties reasonable notice of a hearing conducted under this section. At the hearing, the prosecutor shall present the case demonstrating that the defendant or person violated the terms of the conditional release. If the court finds by a preponderance of the evidence that the defendant or person violated the terms of the conditional release, the court may continue, modify, or terminate the conditional release and shall enter its order accordingly.

HISTORY: 146 v S 285. Eff 7-1-97.

The effective date is set by section 4 of SB 285.

[WITNESSES]

§ 2945.41 Rules applicable in criminal cases.

The rules of evidence in civil causes, where applicable, govern in all criminal causes.

HISTORY: GC § 13444-1; 113 v 123(185), ch 23; Bureau of Code Revision. Eff 10-1-53.

§ 2945.42 Competency of witnesses.

No person is disqualified as a witness in a criminal prosecution by reason of the person's interest in the prosecution as a party or otherwise or by reason of the person's conviction of crime. Husband and wife are competent witnesses to testify in behalf of each other in all criminal prosecutions and to testify against each other in all actions, prosecutions, and proceedings for personal injury of either by the other, bigamy, or failure to provide for, neglect of, or cruelty to their children under eighteen years of age or their physically or mentally handicapped child under twenty-one years of age. A spouse may testify against his or her spouse in a prosecution under a provision of sections 2903.11 to 2903.13, 2919.21, 2919.22, or 2919.25 of the Revised Code for cruelty to, neglect of, or abandonment of such spouse, in a prosecution against his or her spouse under section 2903.211 [2903.21.1] or 2911.211 [2911.21.1], of the Revised Code for the commission of the offense against the spouse who is testifying, in a prosecution under section 2919.27 of the Revised Code involving a protection order issued or consent agreement approved pursuant to section 2919.26 or 3113.31 of the Revised Code for the commission of the offense against the spouse who is testifying, or in a prosecution under section 2907.02 of the Revised Code for the commission of rape or under former section 2907.12 of the Revised Code for felonious sexual penetration against such spouse in a case in which the offense can be committed against a spouse. Such interest, conviction, or relationship may be shown for the purpose of affecting the credibility of the witness. Husband or wife shall not testify concerning a communication made by one to the other, or act done by either in the presence of the other, during coverture, unless the communication was made or act done in the known presence or hearing of a third person competent to be a witness, or in case of personal injury by either the husband or wife to the other, or rape or the former offense of felonious sexual penetration in a case in which the offense can be committed against a spouse, or bigamy, or failure to provide for, or neglect or cruelty of either to their children under eighteen years of age or their physically or mentally handicapped child under twenty-one years of age, violation of a protection order or consent agreement, or neglect or abandonment of a spouse under a provision of those sections. The presence or whereabouts of the husband or wife is not an act under this section. The rule is the same if the marital relation has ceased to exist.

HISTORY: GC § 13444-2; 113 v 123(186), ch 23, § 2; Bureau of Code Revision, 10-1-53; 134 v S 312 (Eff 1-26-72); 136 v H 1 (Eff 6-13-75); 138 v H 920 (Eff 4-9-81); 141 v H 475 (Eff 3-7-86); 144 v H 536 (Eff 11-5-92); 146 v S 2 (Eff 7-1-96); 146 v H 445. Eff 9-3-96.

§ 2945.43 Defendant may testify.

On the trial of a criminal cause, a person charged with an offense may, at his own request, be a witness, but not otherwise. The failure of such person to testify may be considered by the court and jury and may be made the subject of comment by counsel.

HISTORY: GC § 13444-3; 113 v 123(186), ch 23, § 3; Bureau of Code Revision. Eff 10-1-53.

§ 2945.44 Immunity of witnesses turning state's evidence.

(A) In any criminal proceeding in this state or in any criminal or civil proceeding brought pursuant to sections 2923.31 to 2923.36 of the Revised Code, if a witness refuses to answer or produce information on the basis of his privilege against self-incrimination, the court of common pleas of the county in which the proceeding is being held, unless it finds that to do so would not further the administration of justice, shall compel the witness to answer or produce the information, if both of the following apply:

(1) The prosecuting attorney of the county in which the proceedings are being held makes a written request to the court of common pleas to order the witness to answer or produce the information, notwithstanding his claim of privilege;

(2) The court of common pleas informs the witness that by answering, or producing the information he will receive immunity under division (B) of this section.

(B) If, but for this section, the witness would have been privileged to withhold an answer or any information given in any criminal proceeding, and he complies with an order under division (A) of this section compelling him to give an answer or produce any information, he shall not be prosecuted or subjected to any criminal penalty in the courts of this state for or on account of any transaction or matter concerning which, in compliance with the order, he gave an answer or produced any information.

(C) A witness granted immunity under this section may be subjected to a criminal penalty for any violation of section 2921.11, 2921.12, or 2921.13 of the Revised Code, or for contempt committed in answering, failing to answer, or failing to produce information in compliance with the order.

HISTORY: 137 v H 491 (Eff 5-30-78); 141 v H 5. Eff 1-1-86.

Analogous to former RC § 2945.44 (134 v H 511; 136 v S 234), repealed 137 v H 491, § 2, eff 5-30-78; and RC § 2945.44 (GC § 13444-4; 113 v 123(186); Bureau of Code Revision, 10-1-53; 126 v 168), repealed 134 v H 511, § 2, eff 1-1-74.

The effective date is set by section 3 of HB 5.

§ 2945.45 Subpoenas to issue to any county.

In all criminal cases, the clerk of the court of common pleas, upon a praecipe being filed, shall issue writs of subpoena for the witnesses named therein, directed to the sheriff of such county, or the county where such witnesses reside or are found, which shall be served and returned as in other cases. Such sheriff, by writing indorsed on the writs, may depute a disinterested person to serve and return them. The person so deputed to serve such subpoenas shall make a return of the service made, and make oath thereto before a person competent to administer oaths, which shall be indorsed on the writ. The return may be forwarded through the post office, or otherwise.

HISTORY: GC § 13444-5; 113 v 123(187), ch 23, § 5; Bureau of Code Revision. Eff 10-1-53.

[§ 2945.45.1] § 2945.451 Employee may not be penalized for being subpoenaed to criminal proceeding.

No employer shall discharge or terminate from employment, threaten to discharge or terminate from employment, or otherwise punish or penalize any employee because of time lost from regular employment as a result of the employee's attendance at any proceeding in a criminal case pursuant to a subpoena. This section generally does not require and shall not be construed to require an employer to pay an employee for time lost as a result of attendance at any criminal proceeding. However, if an employee is subpoenaed to appear at a criminal proceeding and the proceeding pertains to an offense against the employer or an offense involving the employee during the course of his employment, the employer shall not decrease or withhold the employee's pay for any time lost as a result of compliance with the subpoena. Any employer who knowingly violates this section is in contempt of court.

HISTORY: 140 v S 172. Eff 9-26-84.

§ 2945.46 Attendance of witness enforced.

Civil procedure relative to compelling the attendance and testimony of witnesses, their examination, the administering of oaths and affirmations, and proceedings for contempt to enforce the remedies and protect the rights of parties, extend to criminal cases as far as applicable.

HISTORY: GC § 13444-6; 113 v 123(187), ch 23, § 6; Bureau of Code Revision. Eff 10-1-53.

§ 2945.47 Deposition or subpoena of prisoner.

(A) If it is necessary in a criminal proceeding before the court to procure the testimony of a person who is imprisoned in a workhouse, juvenile detention facility, jail, or state correctional institution within this state, or who is in the custody of the department of youth services, the court may require that the person's testimony be taken by deposition pursuant to Criminal Rule 15 at the place of the person's confinement, if the person is not a defendant in the case and if the court determines that the interests of justice do not demand that the person be brought before the court for the presentation of his testimony. All witnesses for the prosecution shall be brought before the court. The defendant may waive any right to compel the appearance of a person brought before the court pursuant to this division.

(B) If it is necessary in a criminal proceeding before the court to procure the testimony of a person who is imprisoned in a workhouse, a juvenile detention facility, or a jail within this state, the court may order a subpoena to be issued, directed to the keeper of the institution, commanding him to bring the prisoner named in the subpoena before the court.

The keeper, upon receiving the subpoena, shall take the witness before the court at the time and place named in the subpoena, and hold him until he is discharged by the court. When discharged, he shall be returned in the custody of such officer to the place of imprisonment from which he was taken, and the officer may command any assistance that he considers proper for the transportation of the witness.

(C) If it is necessary in a criminal proceeding before the court to procure the testimony of a person who is imprisoned in a state correctional institution within this state, or who is in the custody of the department of youth services, the court may order a subpoena to be issued directed to the sheriff of the county in which the indictment or grand jury proceeding is pending. When a copy of the subpoena is presented by the sheriff to the warden or superintendent of a state correctional institution, or to the person in charge of the facility in which a juvenile is confined, he shall deliver the witness at the institution or facility to the sheriff who shall take him before the court at the time and place named in the subpoena and hold him until he is discharged by the court. When discharged, he shall be returned in the custody of the sheriff to the place of imprisonment from which he was taken.

(D) The court shall, in the manner provided in Chapter 120. of the Revised Code, either assign counsel or designate a public defender to represent a juvenile subpoenaed as a witness under this section. Compensation for assigned counsel shall be made pursuant to section 2941.51 of the Revised Code.

(E) When a person's testimony is taken by deposition pursuant to division (A) of this section, the deposition shall be upon oral examination if either the prosecuting authority or the defendant who is taking the deposition requests that the deposition be upon oral examination, and may be videotaped if either the prosecuting authority or the defendant who is taking the deposition requests that it be recorded by means of videotape.

The person requesting the testimony of the person whose deposition is taken pursuant to division (A) of this section shall pay the expense of taking the deposition, except that the court may tax the expense as court costs in appropriate cases.

HISTORY: RS §§ 7290, 7291; 70 v 78; GC §§ 13444-7, 13444-8; 113 v 123(187), ch 23, §§ 7, 8; Bureau of Code Revision, 10-1-53; 129 v 322 (Eff 7-14-61); 136 v S 393 (Eff 9-27-76); 139 v H 145 (Eff 5-28-81); 139 v H 440 (Eff 11-23-81); 145 v H 571. Eff 10-6-94.

§ 2945.48 Witness may be placed in jail.

When a witness mentioned in section 2945.47 of the Revised Code is in attendance upon a court he may be placed in the jail of the county. The expenses of the officer in transporting him to and from such court, including compensation for the guard or attendant of such prisoner not exceeding the per diem salary of such guard for the time he is away from said institution, shall be allowed by the court and taxed and paid as other costs against the state.

HISTORY: GC § 13444-9; 113 v 123(188), ch 23, § 9; Bureau of Code Revision. Eff 10-1-53.

[§ 2945.48.1] § 2945.481 Deposition of child victim; videotaping; testimony taken outside courtroom and televised into it or replayed in courtroom.

(A)(1) As used in this section, "victim" includes any person who was a victim of a violation identified in division (A)(2) of this section or an offense of violence or against whom was directed any conduct that constitutes, or that is an element of, a violation identified in division (A)(2) of this section or an offense of violence.

(2) In any proceeding in the prosecution of a charge of a violation of section 2905.03, 2905.05, 2907.02, 2907.03, 2907.04, 2907.05, 2907.06, 2907.07, 2907.09, 2907.21, 2907.23, 2907.24, 2907.31, 2907.32, 2907.321 [2907.32.1], 2907.322 [2907.32.2], 2907.323 [2907.32.-3], or 2919.22 of the Revised Code or an offense of violence and in which an alleged victim of the violation or offense was a child who was less than thirteen years of age when the complaint, indictment, or information was filed, whichever occurred earlier, the judge of the court in which the prosecution is being conducted, upon motion of an attorney for the prosecution, shall order that the testimony of the child victim be taken by deposition. The prosecution also may request that the deposition be videotaped in accordance with division (A)(3) of this section. The judge shall notify the child victim whose deposition is to be taken, the prosecution, and the defense of the date, time, and place for taking the deposition. The notice shall identify the child victim who is to be examined and shall indicate whether a request that the deposition be videotaped has been made. The defendant shall have the right to attend the deposition and the right to be represented by counsel. Depositions shall be taken in the manner provided in civil cases, except that the judge shall preside at the taking of the deposition and shall rule at that time on any objections of the prosecution or the attorney for the defense. The prosecution and the attorney for the defense shall have the right, as at trial, to full examination and cross-examination of the child victim whose deposition is to be taken. If a deposition taken under this division is intended to be offered as evidence in the proceeding, it shall be filed in the court in which the action is pending and is admissible in the manner described in division (B) of this section. If a deposition of a child victim taken under this division is admitted as evidence at the proceeding under division (B) of this section, the child victim shall not be required to testify in person at the proceeding. However, at any time before the conclusion of the proceeding, the attorney for the defense may file a motion with the judge requesting that another deposition of the child victim be taken because new evidence material to the defense has been discovered that the attorney for the defense could not with reasonable diligence have discovered prior to the taking of the admitted deposition. A motion for another deposition shall be accompanied by supporting affidavits. Upon the filing of a motion for another deposition and affidavits, the court may order that additional testimony of the child victim relative to the new evidence be taken by another deposition. If the court orders the taking of another deposition under this provision, the deposition shall be taken in accordance with this division; if the admitted deposition was a videotaped deposition taken in accordance with division (A)(3) of this section, the new deposition also shall be videotaped in accordance with that division and in other cases, the new deposition may be videotaped in accordance with that division.

(3) If the prosecution requests that a deposition to be taken under division (A)(2) of this section be videotaped, the judge shall order that the deposition be videotaped in accordance with this division. If a judge issues an order that the deposition be videotaped, the judge

shall exclude from the room in which the deposition is to be taken every person except the child victim giving the testimony, the judge, one or more interpreters if needed, the attorneys for the prosecution and the defense, any person needed to operate the equipment to be used, one person chosen by the child victim giving the deposition, and any person whose presence the judge determines would contribute to the welfare and well-being of the child victim giving the deposition. The person chosen by the child victim shall not be a witness in the proceeding and, both before and during the deposition, shall not discuss the testimony of the child victim with any other witness in the proceeding. To the extent feasible, any person operating the recording equipment shall be restricted to a room adjacent to the room in which the deposition is being taken, or to a location in the room in which the deposition is being taken that is behind a screen or mirror, so that the person operating the recording equipment can see and hear, but cannot be seen or heard by, the child victim giving the deposition during the deposition. The defendant shall be permitted to observe and hear the testimony of the child victim giving the deposition on a monitor, shall be provided with an electronic means of immediate communication with the defendant's attorney during the testimony, and shall be restricted to a location from which the defendant cannot be seen or heard by the child victim giving the deposition, except on a monitor provided for that purpose. The child victim giving the deposition shall be provided with a monitor on which the child victim can observe, during the testimony, the defendant. The judge, at the judge's discretion, may preside at the deposition by electronic means from outside the room in which the deposition is to be taken; if the judge presides by electronic means, the judge shall be provided with monitors on which the judge can see each person in the room in which the deposition is to be taken and with an electronic means of communication with each person, and each person in the room shall be provided with a monitor on which that person can see the judge and with an electronic means of communication with the judge. A deposition that is videotaped under this division shall be taken and filed in the manner described in division (A)(2) of this section and is admissible in the manner described in this division and division (B) of this section, and, if a deposition that is videotaped under this division is admitted as evidence at the proceeding, the child victim shall not be required to testify in person at the proceeding. No deposition videotaped under this division shall be admitted as evidence at any proceeding unless division (B) of this section is satisfied relative to the deposition and all of the following apply relative to the recording:

(a) The recording is both aural and visual and is recorded on film or videotape, or by other electronic means.

(b) The recording is authenticated under the Rules of Evidence and the Rules of Criminal Procedure as a fair and accurate representation of what occurred, and the recording is not altered other than at the direction and under the supervision of the judge in the proceeding.

(c) Each voice on the recording that is material to the testimony on the recording or the making of the recording, as determined by the judge, is identified.

(d) Both the prosecution and the defendant are afforded an opportunity to view the recording before it is shown in the proceeding.

(B)(1) At any proceeding in a prosecution in relation to which a deposition was taken under division (A) of this section, the deposition or a part of it is admissible in evidence upon motion of the prosecution if the testimony in the deposition or the part to be admitted is not excluded by the hearsay rule and if the deposition or the part to be admitted otherwise is admissible under the Rules of Evidence. For purposes of this division, testimony is not excluded by the hearsay rule if the testimony is not hearsay under Evidence Rule 801; if the testimony is within an exception to the hearsay rule set forth in Evidence Rule 803; if the child victim who gave the testimony is unavailable as a witness, as defined in Evidence Rule 804, and the testimony is admissible under that rule; or if both of the following apply:

(a) The defendant had an opportunity and similar motive at the time of the taking of the deposition to develop the testimony by direct, cross, or redirect examination.

(b) The judge determines that there is reasonable cause to believe that, if the child victim who gave the testimony in the deposition were to testify in person at the proceeding, the child victim would experience serious emotional trauma as a result of the child victim's participation at the proceeding.

(2) Objections to receiving in evidence a deposition or a part of it under division (B) of this section shall be made as provided in civil actions.

(3) The provisions of divisions (A) and (B) of this section are in addition to any other provisions of the Revised Code, the Rules of Criminal Procedure, or the Rules of Evidence that pertain to the taking or admission of depositions in a criminal proceeding and do not limit the admissibility under any of those other provisions of any deposition taken under division (A) of this section or otherwise taken.

(C) In any proceeding in the prosecution of any charge of a violation listed in division (A)(2) of this section or an offense of violence and in which an alleged victim of the violation or offense was a child who was less than thirteen years of age when the complaint, indictment, or information was filed, whichever occurred earlier, the prosecution may file a motion with the judge requesting the judge to order the testimony of the child victim to be taken in a room other than the room in which the proceeding is being conducted and be televised, by closed circuit equipment, into the room in which the proceeding is being conducted to be viewed by the jury, if applicable, the defendant, and any other persons who are not permitted in the room in which the testimony is to be taken but who would have been present during the testimony of the child victim had it been given in the room in which the proceeding is being conducted. Except for good cause shown, the prosecution shall file a motion under this division at least seven days before the date of the proceeding. The judge may issue the order upon the motion of the prosecution filed under this section, if the judge determines that the child victim is unavailable to testify in the room in which the proceeding is being conducted in the physical presence of the defendant, for one or more of the reasons set forth in division (E) of this section. If a judge issues an order of that nature, the judge shall exclude from the room in which the testimony is to be taken every person except a person described in division (A)(3) of this section. The judge, at the judge's discretion, may preside during the giving of the testimony by electronic means from outside the room in which it is being given, subject to the limitations set forth in division (A)(3) of this section. To the extent feasible, any person operating the televising equipment shall be hidden from the sight and hearing of the child victim giving the testimony, in a manner similar to that described in division (A)(3) of this section. The defendant shall be permitted to observe and hear the testimony of the child victim giving the testimony on a monitor, shall be provided with an electronic means of immediate communication with the defendant's attorney during the testimony, and shall be restricted to a location from which the defendant cannot be seen or heard by the child victim giving the testimony, except on a monitor provided for that purpose. The child victim giving the testimony shall be provided with a monitor on which the child victim can observe, during the testimony, the defendant.

(D) In any proceeding in the prosecution of any charge of a violation listed in division (A)(2) of this section or an offense of violence and in which an alleged victim of the violation or offense was a child who was less than thirteen years of age when the complaint, indictment, or information was filed, whichever occurred earlier, the prosecution may file a motion with the judge requesting the judge to order the testimony of the child victim to be taken outside of the room in which the proceeding is being conducted and be recorded for showing in the room in which the proceeding is being conducted before the judge, the jury, if applicable, the defendant, and any other persons who would have been present during the testimony of the child victim had it been given in the room in which the proceeding is being conducted. Except for good cause shown, the prosecution shall file a motion under this division at least seven days before the date of the proceeding. The judge may issue the order upon the motion of the prosecution filed under this division, if the judge determines that the child victim is unavailable to testify in the room in which the proceeding is being conducted in the physical presence of the defendant, for one or more of the reasons set forth in division (E) of this section. If a judge issues an order of that nature, the judge shall exclude from the room in which the testimony is to be taken every person except a person described in division (A)(3) of this section. To the extent feasible, any person operating the recording equipment shall be hidden from the sight and hearing of the child victim giving the testimony, in a manner similar to that described in division (A)(3) of this section. The defendant shall be permitted to observe and hear the testimony of the child victim who is giving the testimony on a monitor, shall be provided with an electronic means of immediate communication with the defendant's attorney during the testimony, and shall be restricted to a location from which the defendant cannot be seen or heard by the child victim giving the testimony, except on a monitor provided for that purpose. The child victim giving the testimony shall be provided with a monitor on which the child victim can observe, during the testimony, the defendant. No order for the taking of testimony by recording shall be issued under this division unless the provisions set forth in divisions (A)(3)(a), (b), (c), and (d) of this section apply to the recording of the testimony.

(E) For purposes of divisions (C) and (D) of this section, a judge may order the testimony of a child victim to be taken outside the room in which the proceeding is being conducted if the judge determines that the child victim is unavailable to testify in the room in the physical presence of the defendant due to one or more of the following:

(1) The persistent refusal of the child victim to testify despite judicial requests to do so;

(2) The inability of the child victim to communicate about the alleged violation or offense because of extreme fear, failure of memory, or another similar reason;

(3) The substantial likelihood that the child victim will suffer serious emotional trauma from so testifying.

(F)(1) If a judge issues an order pursuant to division (C) or (D) of this section that requires the testimony of a child victim in a criminal proceeding to be taken outside of the room in which the proceeding is being conducted, the order shall specifically identify the child victim to whose testimony it applies, the order applies only during the testimony of the specified child victim, and the child victim giving the testimony shall not be required to testify at the proceeding other than in accordance with the order.

(2) A judge who makes any determination regarding the admissibility of a deposition under divisions (A) and (B) of this section, the videotaping of a deposition under division (A)(3) of this section, or the taking of testimony outside of the room in which a proceeding is being conducted under division (C) or (D) of this section,

shall enter the determination and findings on the record in the proceeding.

HISTORY: RC § 2907.41, 141 v H 108 (Eff 10-14-86); 146 v H 445 (Eff 9-3-96); RC § 2945.48.1, 147 v S 53. Eff 10-14-97.

§ 2945.49 Testimony of deceased or absent witness; videotaped preliminary hearing testimony of child victim.

(A)(1) As used in this section, "victim" includes any person who was a victim of a felony violation identified in division (B)(1) of this section or a felony offense of violence or against whom was directed any conduct that constitutes, or that is an element of, a felony violation identified in division (B)(1) of this section or a felony offense of violence.

(2) Testimony taken at an examination or a preliminary hearing at which the defendant is present, or at a former trial of the cause, or taken by deposition at the instance of the defendant or the state, may be used whenever the witness giving the testimony dies or cannot for any reason be produced at the trial or whenever the witness has, since giving that testimony, become incapacitated to testify. If the former testimony is contained within an authenticated transcript of the testimony, it shall be proven by the transcript, otherwise by other testimony.

(B)(1) At a trial on a charge of a felony violation of section 2905.05, 2907.02, 2907.03, 2907.04, 2907.05, 2907.21, 2907.24, 2907.31, 2907.32, 2907.321 [2907.-32.1], 2907.322 [2907.32.2], 2907.323 [2907.32.3], or 2919.22 of the Revised Code or a felony offense of violence and in which an alleged victim of the alleged violation or offense was less than thirteen years of age when the complaint or information was filed, whichever occurred earlier, the court, upon motion of the prosecutor in the case, may admit videotaped preliminary hearing testimony of the child victim as evidence at the trial, in lieu of the child victim appearing as a witness and testifying at the trial, if all of the following apply:

(a) The videotape of the testimony was made at the preliminary hearing at which probable cause of the violation charged was found;

(b) The videotape of the testimony was made in accordance with division (C) of section 2937.11 of the Revised Code;

(c) The testimony in the videotape is not excluded by the hearsay rule and otherwise is admissible under the Rules of Evidence. For purposes of this division, testimony is not excluded by the hearsay rule if the testimony is not hearsay under Evidence Rule 801, if the testimony is within an exception to the hearsay rule set forth in Evidence Rule 803, if the child victim who gave the testimony is unavailable as a witness, as defined in Evidence Rule 804, and the testimony is admissible under that rule, or if both of the following apply:

(i) The accused had an opportunity and similar motive at the preliminary hearing to develop the testimony of the child victim by direct, cross, or redirect examination;

(ii) The court determines that there is reasonable cause to believe that if the child victim who gave the testimony at the preliminary hearing were to testify in person at the trial, the child victim would experience serious emotional trauma as a result of the child victim's participation at the trial.

(2) If a child victim of an alleged felony violation of section 2905.05, 2907.02, 2907.03, 2907.04, 2907.05, 2907.21, 2907.24, 2907.31, 2907.32, 2907.321 [2907.-32.1], 2907.322 [2907.32.2], 2907.323 [2907.32.3], or 2919.22 of the Revised Code or an alleged felony offense of violence testifies at the preliminary hearing in the case, if the testimony of the child victim at the preliminary hearing was videotaped pursuant to division (C) of section 2937.11 of the Revised Code, and if the defendant in the case files a written objection to the use, pursuant to division (B)(1) of this section, of the videotaped testimony at the trial, the court, immediately after the filing of the objection, shall hold a hearing to determine whether the videotaped testimony of the child victim should be admissible at trial under division (B)(1) of this section and, if it is admissible, whether the child victim should be required to provide limited additional testimony of the type described in this division. At the hearing held pursuant to this division, the defendant and the prosecutor in the case may present any evidence that is relevant to the issues to be determined at the hearing, but the child victim shall not be required to testify at the hearing.

After the hearing, the court shall not require the child victim to testify at the trial, unless it determines that both of the following apply:

(a) That the testimony of the child victim at trial is necessary for one or more of the following reasons:

(i) Evidence that was not available at the time of the testimony of the child victim at the preliminary hearing has been discovered;

(ii) The circumstances surrounding the case have changed sufficiently to necessitate that the child victim testify at the trial.

(b) That the testimony of the child victim at the trial is necessary to protect the right of the defendant to a fair trial.

The court shall enter its finding and the reasons for it in the journal. If the court requires the child victim to testify at the trial, the testimony of the victim shall be limited to the new evidence and changed circumstances, and the child victim shall not otherwise be required to testify at the trial. The required testimony of the child victim may be given in person or, upon motion of the prosecution, may be taken by deposition in accordance with division (A) of section 2945.481 [2945.48.1] of the Revised Code provided the deposition is admitted as evidence under division (B) of that section, may be taken outside of the courtroom and televised into the courtroom in accordance with division

(C) of that section, or may be taken outside of the courtroom and recorded for showing in the courtroom in accordance with division (D) of that section.

(3) If videotaped testimony of a child victim is admitted at trial in accordance with division (B)(1) of this section, the child victim shall not be compelled in any way to appear as a witness at the trial, except as provided in division (B)(2) of this section.

(C) An order issued pursuant to division (B) of this section shall specifically identify the child victim concerning whose testimony it pertains. The order shall apply only during the testimony of the child victim it specifically identifies.

(D) As used in this section, "prosecutor" has the same meaning as in section 2935.01 of the Revised Code.

HISTORY: GC § 13444-10; 113 v 123(188), ch 23, § 10; Bureau of Code Revision, 10-1-53; 141 v H 108 (Eff 10-14-86); 146 v H 445 (Eff 9-3-96); 147 v S 53. Eff 10-14-97.

§ 2945.50 Deposition in criminal cases.

At any time after an issue of fact is joined upon an indictment, information, or an affidavit, the prosecution or the defendant may apply in writing to the court in which such indictment, information, or affidavit is pending for a commission to take the depositions of any witness. The court or a judge thereof may grant such commission and make an order stating in what manner and for what length of time notice shall be given to the prosecution or to the defendant, before such witness shall be examined.

HISTORY: RS § 7293; 70 v 145, § 144; GC § 13444-11; 103 v 443; 113 v 123(188), ch 23, § 11; Bureau of Code Revision, 10-1-53; 131 v 681. Eff 10-13-65.

§ 2945.51 When defendant may be taken; expenses.

When a deposition is to be taken in this state, and a commission is granted under section 2945.50 of the Revised Code while the defendant is confined in jail, the sheriff or deputy or other person having custody of the defendant shall be ordered by the court to take the defendant to the place of the taking of the deposition, and have him before the officer at the time of taking such deposition. Such sheriff or deputy or other person having custody of the defendant shall be reimbursed for actual reasonable traveling expenses for himself and the defendant, the bills for the same, upon the approval of the board of county commissioners, to be paid from the county treasury on the warrant of the county auditor. Such sheriff shall receive as fees therefor, one dollar for each day in attendance thereat. Such fees and traveling expenses shall be taxed and collected as other fees and costs in the case.

HISTORY: GC § 13444-12; 103 v 443; 107 v 451; 113 v 123(188), ch 23, § 12; Bureau of Code Revision, 10-1-53; 131 v 681. Eff 10-13-65.

§ 2945.52 Counsel appointed shall represent the defendant.

Counsel assigned by the court to represent the defendant may attend upon and represent the defendant at the taking of a deposition under section 2945.50 of the Revised Code, and said counsel shall be paid a reasonable fee for his services in taking such deposition, in addition to the compensation allowed for defending such defendant, to be fixed by the court. He shall also be allowed his actual expenses incurred in going to and from the place of taking the deposition.

HISTORY: GC § 13444-13; 113 v 123(189), ch 23, § 13; Bureau of Code Revision. Eff 10-1-53.

§ 2945.53 Right of accused to examine witness.

In all cases in which depositions are taken by the state or the accused, to be used by or against the accused, as provided in sections 2945.50 to 2945.52, inclusive, of the Revised Code, the court shall by proper order provide and secure to the accused the means and opportunity to be present in person and with counsel at the taking of such deposition, and to examine the witness face to face, as fully and in the same manner as if in court. All expenses necessarily incurred in the securing of such means and opportunity, and the expenses of the prosecuting attorney in attending the taking of such deposition, shall be paid out of the county treasury upon the certificate of the court making such order.

HISTORY: GC § 13444-14; 113 v 123(189), ch 23, § 14; Bureau of Code Revision. Eff 10-1-53.

§ 2945.54 Conduct of examination.

The examination of witnesses by deposition in criminal cases shall be taken and certified, and the return thereof to the court made as for taking depositions under sections 2319.05 to 2319.31, inclusive, of the Revised Code. The commissioners appointed under section 2945.50 of the Revised Code to take depositions shall receive such compensation as the court directs, to be paid out of the county treasury and taxed as part of the costs in the case.

HISTORY: GC § 13444-15; 113 v 123(189), ch 23, § 15; Bureau of Code Revision. Eff 10-1-53.

This section is referred to in section 3 of HB No. 1201, effective July 1, 1970, although it was not repealed by section 1 of such act. Section 3 reads as follows:

"That the taking effect of the Rules of Civil Procedure on July 1, 1970, is prima-facie evidence that the sections of the Revised Code to be repealed by Section 1 are in conflict with such rules and shall have no further force or effect except that for the purposes of depositions in criminal cases under section 2945.54 of the Revised Code, procedures adopted by reference to sections 2319.05 to 2319.31, inclusive, of the Revised Code, and, for the purposes of an offer to confess judgment in an appropriation case under section 163.16 of the Revised Code, procedures adopted by reference to sections 2311.14 to

2311.20, inclusive, of the Revised Code, shall continue effective without change, unless a court shall determine that one of such sections, or some part thereof, has clearly not been superseded by such rules and that in the absence of such section or part thereof being effective, there would be no applicable standard of procedure prescribed by either statutory law or rule of court. The failure to repeal or amend any other section establishes no evidence concerning its conflict with such rules."

§ 2945.55 Testimony of previous identification.

When identification of the defendant is an issue, a witness who has on previous occasion identified such person may testify to such previous identification. Such identification may be proved by other witnesses.

HISTORY: GC § 13444-16; 113 v 123(189), ch 23, § 16; Bureau of Code Revision. Eff 10-1-53.

§ 2945.56 Rebuttal of defendant's character evidence.

When the defendant offers evidence of his character or reputation, the prosecution may offer, in rebuttal thereof, proof of his previous conviction of a crime involving moral turpitude, in addition to other competent evidence.

HISTORY: GC § 13444-17; 113 v 123(189), ch 23, § 17; Bureau of Code Revision. Eff 10-1-53.

§ 2945.57 Number of witnesses to character.

The number of witnesses who are expected to testify upon the subject of character or reputation, for whom subpoenas are issued, shall be designated upon the praecipe and, except in cases of murder in the first and second degree, manslaughter, rape, assault with intent to commit rape, or selling intoxicating liquor to a person in the habit of becoming intoxicated, shall not exceed ten upon each side, unless a deposit of at least one per diem and mileage fee for each of such additional witnesses is first made with the clerk of the court of common pleas. Not more than ten witnesses upon each side shall be permitted to testify upon the question of character or reputation in a criminal cause unless their full per diem and mileage fees have been deposited or paid by the party in whose behalf they are sworn, and the clerk shall not issue a certificate for compensation to be paid out of the county treasury to a witness who has testified upon the subject of character or reputation, except as provided in this section.

HISTORY: GC § 13444-18; 113 v 123(189), ch 23, § 18; Bureau of Code Revision. Eff 10-1-53.

§ 2945.58 Alibi.

Whenever a defendant in a criminal cause proposes to offer in his defense, testimony to establish an alibi on his behalf, such defendant shall, not less than three days before the trial of such cause, file and serve upon the prosecuting attorney a notice in writing of his intention to claim such alibi. Notice shall include specific information as to the place at which the defendant claims to have been at the time of the alleged offense. If the defendant fails to file such written notice, the court may exclude evidence offered by the defendant for the purpose of proving such alibi.

HISTORY: GC § 13444-20; 113 v 123(190), ch 23, § 20; Bureau of Code Revision. Eff 10-1-53.

§ 2945.59 Proof of defendant's motive.

In any criminal case in which the defendant's motive or intent, the absence of mistake or accident on his part, or the defendant's scheme, plan, or system in doing an act is material, any acts of the defendant which tend to show his motive or intent, the absence of mistake or accident on his part, or the defendant's scheme, plan, or system in doing the act in question may be proved, whether they are contemporaneous with or prior or subsequent thereto, notwithstanding that such proof may show or tend to show the commission of another crime by the defendant.

HISTORY: GC § 13444-19; 113 v 123(190), ch 23, § 19; Bureau of Code Revision. Eff 10-1-53.

§§ 2945.60, 2945.61 Repealed, 134 v H 511, § 2 [RS § 7298; S&S 262; 58 v 110; 66 v 309; GC § 13444-21; 113 v 123; Bureau of Code Revision, 10-1-53]. Eff 1-1-74.

These sections established procedure for proof of treason and proof in case of setting on foot or providing means for an unauthorized military expedition.

§§ 2945.62, 2945.63 Repealed, 134 v H 511, § 2 [GC §§ 13444-22, 13444-23; 113 v 123; Bureau of Code Revision, 10-1-53]. Eff 1-1-74.

These sections established procedure for proof in case of perjury and proof in a trial for seduction of a female.

§ 2945.64 Prima-facie evidence of embezzlement.

Failure or refusal to pay over or produce public money by a person charged with the collection, receipt, transfer, disbursement, or safekeeping of such money, whether belonging to this state, a county, township, municipal corporation, or board of education, or other public money, or to account to or make settlement with a legal authority of the official accounts of such person, is prima-facie evidence of the embezzlement thereof. Upon the trial of such person for the embezzlement of public money, it is sufficient evidence for the purpose of showing a balance against him, to produce a transcript from the records of the auditor of state, director of budget and management, county auditor, or board of county commissioners. The refusal of such person, whether in or out of office, to pay a draft, order, or warrant drawn upon him by an authorized officer, for public money in his hands, or a refusal by a person promptly to pay over to his successor public money or securities on the legal requirement of an authorized officer of the state or county, on the trial of an indictment against him for embezzlement, is prima-facie evidence thereof.

HISTORY: GC § 13444-25; 113 v 123(191), ch 23, § 25; Bureau of Code Revision, 10-1-53; 141 v H 201. Eff 7-1-85.

[BILL OF EXCEPTIONS]

§§ 2945.65, 2945.66 Repealed, 141 v H 412, § 2 [GC §§ 13445-1-13445-2; 113 v 123(191), ch. 24; Bureau of Code Revision, 10-1-53; 125 v S 112; 128 v 141; 129 v 1398; 131 v 682; 137 v H 219]. Eff 3-17-87.

These sections described a bill of exceptions and outlined procedures for filing such bill.

§ 2945.67 Appeal by state.

(A) A prosecuting attorney, village solicitor, city director of law, or the attorney general may appeal as a matter of right any decision of a trial court in a criminal case, or any decision of a juvenile court in a delinquency case, which decision grants a motion to dismiss all or any part of an indictment, complaint, or information, a motion to suppress evidence, or a motion for the return of seized property or grants post conviction relief pursuant to sections 2953.21 to 2953.24 of the Revised Code, and may appeal by leave of the court to which the appeal is taken any other decision, except the final verdict, of the trial court in a criminal case or of the juvenile court in a delinquency case. In addition to any other right to appeal under this section or any other provision of law, a prosecuting attorney, city director of law, village solicitor, or similar chief legal officer of a municipal corporation, or the attorney general may appeal, in accordance with section 2953.08 of the Revised Code, a sentence imposed upon a person who is convicted of or pleads guilty to a felony.

(B) In any proceeding brought pursuant to division (A) of this section, the court, in accordance with Chapter 120. of the Revised Code, shall appoint the county public defender, joint county public defender, or other counsel to represent any person who is indigent, is not represented by counsel, and does not waive the person's right to counsel.

HISTORY: 137 v H 1168 (Eff 11-1-78); 146 v S 2. Eff 7-1-96.

Analogous to former RC § 2945.67 (GC § 13446-1; 113 v 123; Bureau of Code Revision, 10-1-53; 131 v 682; 137 v H 219), repealed 137 v H 1168, § 2, eff 11-1-78.

The effective date is set by section 6 of SB 2.

§§ 2945.68, 2945.69, 2945.70

Repealed, 137 v H 1168, § 2 [GC §§ 13446-2—13446-4; 113 v 123; Bureau of Code Revision, 10-1-53; 131 v 682; 134 v H 511; 137 v H 219]. Eff 11-1-78.

These sections concerned application to file bill of exceptions; appointment of attorney; decision of the court.

Note: RC § 2945.68 is also repealed by 146 v S 2, § 2. Eff 7-1-96.

[TIME FOR TRIAL]

§ 2945.71 Time within which hearing or trial must be held.

(A) A person against whom a charge is pending in a court not of record, or against whom a charge of minor misdemeanor is pending in a court of record, shall be brought to trial within thirty days after his arrest or the service of summons.

(B) A person against whom a charge of misdemeanor, other than a minor misdemeanor, is pending in a court of record, shall be brought to trial:

(1) Within forty-five days after his arrest or the service of summons, if the offense charged is a misdemeanor of the third or fourth degree, or other misdemeanor for which the maximum penalty is imprisonment for not more than sixty days;

(2) Within ninety days after his arrest or the service of summons, if the offense charged is a misdemeanor of the first or second degree, or other misdemeanor for which the maximum penalty is imprisonment for more than sixty days.

(C) A person against whom a charge of felony is pending:

(1) Notwithstanding any provisions to the contrary in Criminal Rule 5(B), shall be accorded a preliminary hearing within fifteen consecutive days after his arrest if the accused is not held in jail in lieu of bail on the pending charge or within ten consecutive days after his arrest if the accused is held in jail in lieu of bail on the pending charge;

(2) Shall be brought to trial within two hundred seventy days after his arrest.

(D) A person against whom one or more charges of minor misdemeanor and one or more charges of misdemeanor other than minor misdemeanor, all of which arose out of the same act or transaction, are pending, or against whom charges of misdemeanors of different degrees, other than minor misdemeanors, all of which arose out of the same act or transaction, are pending shall be brought to trial within the time period required for the highest degree of misdemeanor charged, as determined under division (B) of this section.

(E) For purposes of computing time under divisions (A), (B), (C)(2), and (D) of this section, each day during which the accused is held in jail in lieu of bail on the pending charge shall be counted as three days. This division does not apply for purposes of computing time under division (C)(1) of this section.

(F) This section shall not be construed to modify in any way section 2941.401 [2941.40.1], or sections 2963.30 to 2963.35 of the Revised Code.

HISTORY: 134 v H 511 (Eff 1-1-74); 135 v H 716 (Eff 1-1-74); 136 v S 83 (Eff 10-17-75); 138 v S 288 (Eff 10-22-80); 139 v S 119. Eff 3-17-82.

Analogous to RC § 2945.71 (GC § 13447-1; 113 v 123(193); Bureau of Code Revision, 10-1-53), repealed 134 v H 511, § 2, eff 1-1-74.

The provisions of section 3 of SB 119 (139 v—) read as follows:

SECTION 3. The provisions of Sections 1 and 2 of this act apply in relation to all persons who commit any felony offense on or after the effective date of this act and to all persons who commit any felony offense prior to the effective date of this act who are not arrested in relation to the offense until a time on or after the effective date of this act.

§ 2945.72 Extension of time for hearing or trial.

The time within which an accused must be brought to trial, or, in the case of felony, to preliminary hearing and trial, may be extended only by the following:

(A) Any period during which the accused is unavailable for hearing or trial, by reason of other criminal proceedings against him, within or outside the state, by reason of his confinement in another state, or by reason of the pendency of extradition proceedings, provided that the prosecution exercises reasonable diligence to secure his availability;

(B) Any period during which the accused is mentally incompetent to stand trial or during which his mental competence to stand trial is being determined, or any period during which the accused is physically incapable of standing trial;

(C) Any period of delay necessitated by the accused's lack of counsel, provided that such delay is not occasioned by any lack of diligence in providing counsel to an indigent accused upon his request as required by law;

(D) Any period of delay occasioned by the neglect or improper act of the accused;

(E) Any period of delay necessitated by reason of a plea in bar or abatement, motion, proceeding, or action made or instituted by the accused;

(F) Any period of delay necessitated by a removal or change of venue pursuant to law;

(G) Any period during which trial is stayed pursuant to an express statutory requirement, or pursuant to an order of another court competent to issue such order;

(H) The period of any continuance granted on the accused's own motion, and the period of any reasonable continuance granted other than upon the accused's own motion;

(I) Any period during which an appeal filed pursuant to section 2945.67 of the Revised Code is pending.

HISTORY: 134 v H 511 (Eff 1-1-74); 136 v H 164 (Eff 1-13-76); 136 v S 368 (Eff 9-27-76); 137 v H 1168. Eff 11-1-78.

Analogous to former RC § 2945.72 (GC § 13447-2; 113 v 123(193); Bureau of Code Revision, 10-1-53), repealed 134 v H 511, § 2, eff 1-1-74.

§ 2945.73 Discharge for delay in trial.

(A) A charge of felony shall be dismissed if the accused is not accorded a preliminary hearing within the time required by sections 2945.71 and 2945.72 of the Revised Code.

(B) Upon motion made at or prior to the commencement of trial, a person charged with an offense shall be discharged if he is not brought to trial within the time required by sections 2945.71 and 2945.72 of the Revised Code.

(C) Regardless of whether a longer time limit may be provided by sections 2945.71 and 2945.72 of the Revised Code, a person charged with misdemeanor shall be discharged if he is held in jail in lieu of bond awaiting trial on the pending charge:

(1) For a total period equal to the maximum term of imprisonment which may be imposed for the most serious misdemeanor charged;

(2) For a total period equal to the term of imprisonment allowed in lieu of payment of the maximum fine which may be imposed for the most serious misdemeanor charged, when the offense or offenses charged constitute minor misdemeanors.

(D) When a charge of felony is dismissed pursuant to division (A) of this section, such dismissal has the same effect as a nolle prosequi. When an accused is discharged pursuant to division (B) or (C) of this section, such discharge is a bar to any further criminal proceedings against him based on the same conduct.

HISTORY: 134 v H 511. Eff 1-1-74.

Analogous to former RC § 2945.73 (GC § 13447-3; 113 v 123(193); Bureau of Code Revision, 10-1-53), repealed 134 v H 511, § 2, eff 1-1-74.

[VERDICT]

§ 2945.74 Defendant may be convicted of lesser offense.

The jury may find the defendant not guilty of the offense charged, but guilty of an attempt to commit it if such attempt is an offense at law. When the indictment or information charges an offense, including different degrees, or if other offenses are included within the offense charged, the jury may find the defendant not guilty of the degree charged but guilty of an inferior degree thereof or lesser included offense.

If the offense charged is murder and the accused is convicted by confession in open court, the court shall examine the witnesses, determine the degree of the crime, and pronounce sentence accordingly.

HISTORY: GC § 13448-2; 113 v 123(194), ch 27, § 2; Bureau of Code Revision. Eff 10-1-53.

§ 2945.75 Degree of offense; charge and verdict; prior convictions.

(A) When the presence of one or more additional elements makes an offense one of more serious degree:

(1) The affidavit, complaint, indictment, or information either shall state the degree of the offense which the accused is alleged to have committed, or shall allege such additional element or elements. Otherwise such affidavit, complaint, indictment, or information is effective to charge only the least degree of the offense.

(2) A guilty verdict shall state either the degree of the offense of which the offender is found guilty, or that such additional element or elements are present. Otherwise, a guilty verdict constitutes a finding of guilty of the least degree of the offense charged.

(B) Whenever in any case it is necessary to prove a prior conviction, a certified copy of the entry of judgment in such prior conviction together with evidence sufficient to identify the defendant named in the entry as the offender in the case at bar, is sufficient to prove such prior conviction.

HISTORY: 134 v H 511. Eff 1-1-74.

Analogous to former RC § 2945.75 (GC § 13448-3; 113 v 123(194), ch 27, § 3; Bureau of Code Revision, 10-1-53), repealed 134 v H 511, § 2, eff 1-1-74.

§ 2945.76 Repealed, 134 v H 511, § 2 [GC § 13448-4; 113 v 123(194); Bureau of Code Revision, 10-1-53; 133 v H 288]. Eff 1-1-74.

This section concerned circumstances for acquittal for carrying concealed weapon.

§ 2945.77 Polling jury.

When the jurors agree upon their verdict, they must be conducted into court by the officer having them in charge.

Before the verdict is accepted, the jury may be polled at the request of either the prosecuting attorney or the defendant. If one of the jurors upon being polled declare that said verdict is not his verdict, the jury must further deliberate upon the case.

HISTORY: GC § 13448-5; 113 v 123(195), ch 27, § 5; Bureau of Code Revision. Eff 10-1-53.

§ 2945.78 Recording the verdict.

When the verdict given is such as the court may receive, it must be immediately entered in full upon the minutes.

HISTORY: GC § 13448-6; 113 v 123(195), ch 27, § 6; Bureau of Code Revision. Eff 10-1-53.

[NEW TRIAL]

§ 2945.79 Causes for new trial.

A new trial, after a verdict of conviction, may be granted on the application of the defendant for any of the following causes affecting materially his substantial rights:

(A) Irregularity in the proceedings of the court, jury, prosecuting attorney, or the witnesses for the state, or for any order of the court, or abuse of discretion by which the defendant was prevented from having a fair trial;

(B) Misconduct of the jury, prosecuting attorney, or the witnesses for the state;

(C) Accident or surprise which ordinary prudence could not have guarded against;

(D) That the verdict is not sustained by sufficient evidence or is contrary to law; but if the evidence shows the defendant is not guilty of the degree of crime for which he was convicted, but guilty of a lesser degree thereof, or of a lesser crime included therein, the court may modify the verdict or finding accordingly, without granting or ordering a new trial, and pass sentence on such verdict or finding as modified, provided that this power extends to any court to which the cause may be taken on appeal;

(E) Error of law occurring at the trial;

(F) When new evidence is discovered material to the defendant, which he could not with reasonable diligence have discovered and produced at the trial. When a motion for a new trial is made upon the ground of newly discovered evidence, the defendant must produce at the hearing of said motion, in support thereof, the affidavits of the witnesses by whom such evidence is expected to be given, and if time is required by the defendant to procure such affidavits, the court may postpone the hearing of the motion for such length of time as under all the circumstances of the case is reasonable. The prosecuting attorney may produce affidavits or other evidence to impeach the affidavits of such witnesses.

HISTORY: GC § 13449-1; 113 v 123(195), ch 28; Bureau of Code Revision. Eff 10-1-53.

§ 2945.80 Application for new trial.

Application for a new trial shall be made by motion upon written grounds, and except for the cause of newly discovered evidence material for the person applying, which he could not with reasonable diligence have discovered and produced at the trial, shall be filed within three days after the verdict was rendered, or the decision of the court where a trial by jury has been waived, unless it is made to appear by clear and convincing proof that the defendant was unavoidably prevented from filing his motion for a new trial in which case it shall be filed within three days from the order of the court finding that he was unavoidably prevented from filing such motion within the time provided herein.

Motions for new trial on account of newly discovered evidence shall be filed within one hundred twenty days following the day upon which the verdict was rendered, or the decision of the court where trial by jury has been waived. If it is made to appear by clear and convincing proof that the defendant was unavoidably prevented from the discovery of the evidence upon which he must rely, such motion shall be filed within three days from an order of the court finding that he was unavoidably prevented from discovering the evidence within the one hundred twenty day period.

HISTORY: GC § 13449-2; 113 v 123(196), ch 28, § 2; Bureau of Code Revision, 10-1-53; 128 v 141 (Eff 1-1-60); 131 v 683. Eff 11-1-65.

§ 2945.81 Causes to be sustained by affidavits.

The causes enumerated in divisions (B) and (C) of section 2945.79 of the Revised Code must be sustained by affidavit showing their truth, and may be controverted by affidavits.

HISTORY: GC § 13449-3; 113 v 123(196), ch 28, § 3; Bureau of Code Revision. Eff 10-1-53.

§ 2945.82 New trial.

When a new trial is granted by the trial court, or when a new trial is awarded on appeal, the accused shall stand for trial upon the indictment or information as though there had been no previous trial thereof.

HISTORY: GC § 13449-4; 113 v 123(196), ch 28, § 4; Bureau of Code Revision. Eff 10-1-53.

§ 2945.83 When new trial shall not be granted.

No motion for a new trial shall be granted or verdict set aside, nor shall any judgment of conviction be reversed in any court because of:

(A) An inaccuracy or imperfection in the indictment, information, or warrant, provided that the charge is sufficient to fairly and reasonably inform the accused of the nature and cause of the accusation against him;

(B) A variance between the allegations and the proof thereof unless the accused is misled or prejudiced thereby;

(C) The admission or rejection of any evidence offered against or for the accused unless it affirmatively appears on the record that the accused was or may have been prejudiced thereby;

(D) A misdirection of the jury unless the accused was or may have been prejudiced thereby;

(E) Any other cause unless it appears affirmatively from the record that the accused was prejudiced thereby or was prevented from having a fair trial.

HISTORY: GC § 13449-5; 113 v 123(196), ch 28, § 5; Bureau of Code Revision. Eff 10-1-53.

[§ 2945.83.1] § 2945.831 Motion not necessary for appellate review.

A motion for a new trial is not a necessary prerequisite to obtain appellate review of the sufficiency or weight of the evidence in the trial of a criminal case.

HISTORY: 128 v 141. Eff 1-1-60.

[§ 2945.83.2] § 2945.832 Repealed, 141 v H 412, § 2 [128 v 141]. Eff 3-17-87.

This section dealt with other sections governing exceptions.

CHAPTER 2947: JUDGMENT; SENTENCE

Section
2947.01 Definition of magistrate.

[ARREST OF JUDGMENT]

2947.02 Motion in arrest.
2947.03 When judgment not arrested.
2947.04 Effect of arrest of judgment.

[SENTENCE AND PROCEEDINGS]

2947.05 Repealed.
[2947.05.1] 2947.051 Victim impact statement to be considered in imposing sentence.
[2947.05.2] 2947.052 Repealed.
2947.06 Testimony in mitigation of sentence; presentence investigation report; psychological reports.
[2947.06.1, 2947.06.2] 2947.061, 2947.062 Repealed.
2947.07 When court to pronounce judgment.
2947.08 Time of execution in capital cases.
2947.09-2947.13 Repealed.
2947.14 Satisfaction of fine.
2947.15 Labor by jail inmates; vocational training, rehabilitation.
[2947.15.1] 2947.151 Reduction of jail sentence.
2947.16 Recognizance.
2947.17 Breach of condition of a recognizance.
2947.18 Sentence to workhouse for jail offense.
2947.19 Confinement of county prisoners in city workhouse; reimbursement by prisoner for costs of confinement.
2947.20 Submission of health insurance claims of inmates.
2947.21 Officer's warrant for detention in workhouse or jail.
2947.22 Person may be confined in jail temporarily.
2947.23 Judgment for costs and jury fees.
2947.24-2947.27 Repealed.
[2947.27.1] 2947.271 Repealed.
2947.28-2947.31 Repealed.

§ 2947.01 Definition of magistrate.

The definition of "magistrate" set forth in section 2931.01 of the Revised Code applies to Chapter 2947. of the Revised Code.

HISTORY: Bureau of Code Revision. Eff 10-1-53.

[ARREST OF JUDGMENT]

§ 2947.02 Motion in arrest.

A judgment may be arrested by the court upon motion of the defendant, or upon the court's own motion, for either of the following causes:
(A) The offense charged is not within the jurisdiction of the court;
(B) The facts stated in the indictment or information do not constitute an offense.

HISTORY: GC § 13450-1; 113 v 123(196), ch 29; Bureau of Code Revision. Eff 10-1-53.

§ 2947.03 When judgment not arrested.

A judgment shall not be arrested for a defect in form. Motions in arrest of judgment shall be made within three days after the verdict is rendered.

HISTORY: GC § 13450-2; 113 v 123(197), ch 29, § 2; Bureau of Code Revision. Eff 10-1-53.

§ 2947.04 Effect of arrest of judgment.

When a judgment is arrested, it places the defendant in a like position with respect to the prosecution as before the indictment or information was found. If, from the evidence at the trial, there is reason to believe that the defendant is guilty of an offense, the trial court shall order him to enter into a recognizance with sufficient surety for his appearance at the first day of the next term of such court, or the court having jurisdiction of the offense if within this state, otherwise the defendant shall be discharged.

HISTORY: GC § 13450-3; 113 v 123(197), ch 29, § 3; Bureau of Code Revision. Eff 10-1-53.

[SENTENCE AND PROCEEDINGS]

§ 2947.05 Repealed, 146 v S 2, § 6 [GC § 13451-1; 113 v 123 (197), ch. 30; Bureau of Code Revision, 10-1-53; 145 v S 186]. Eff 7-1-96

This section gave defendant, prosecutor and victim right to make statement prior to sentencing.

[§ 2947.05.1] § 2947.051 Victim impact statement to be considered in imposing sentence.

(A) In all criminal cases in which a person is convicted of or pleads guilty to a felony, if the offender, in committing the offense, caused, attempted to cause, threatened to cause, or created a risk of physical harm to the victim of the offense, the court, prior to sentencing the offender, shall order the preparation of a victim impact statement by the department of probation of the county in which the victim of the offense resides, by the court's own regular probation officer, or by a victim assistance program that is operated by the state, any county or municipal corporation, or any other governmental entity. The court, in accordance with sections 2929.13 and 2929.19 of the Revised Code, shall consider the victim impact statement in determining the sentence to be imposed upon the offender.
(B) Each victim impact statement prepared under this section shall identify the victim of the offense, itemize any economic loss suffered by the victim as a result of the offense, identify any physical injury suffered by the victim as a result of the offense and the

seriousness and permanence of the injury, identify any change in the victim's personal welfare or familial relationships as a result of the offense and any psychological impact experienced by the victim or the victim's family as a result of the offense, and contain any other information related to the impact of the offense upon the victim that the court requires. Each victim impact statement prepared under this section shall include any statement made by the victim pursuant to section 2930.13 of the Revised Code.

(C) A victim impact statement prepared under this section shall be kept confidential and is not a public record as defined in section 149.43 of the Revised Code. However, the court may furnish copies of the statement to both the defendant or the defendant's counsel and the prosecuting attorney. Immediately following the imposition of sentence upon the defendant, the defendant, the defendant's counsel, and the prosecuting attorney shall return to the court the copies of the victim impact statement that were made available to the defendant, the counsel, or the prosecuting attorney.

HISTORY: 138 v S 384 (Eff 10-22-80); 139 v S 199 (Eff 1-5-83); 145 v S 186 (Eff 10-12-94); 146 v S 2. Eff 7-1-96.

The effective date is set by section 6 of SB 2.

[§ 2947.05.2] § 2947.052 Repealed, 145 v S 186, § 2 [144 v H 725]. Eff 10-12-94.

This section provided that victim or representative present at sentencing may request notice of intended electronically monitored early release. See now section 2930.16.

§ 2947.06 Testimony in mitigation of sentence; presentence investigation report; psychological reports.

(A)(1) The trial court may hear testimony in mitigation of a sentence at the term of conviction or plea or at the next term. The prosecuting attorney may offer testimony on behalf of the state to give the court a true understanding of the case. The court shall determine whether sentence ought immediately to be imposed or whether, if the offense is a misdemeanor, to place the defendant on probation. The court on its own motion may direct the department of probation of the county in which the defendant resides, or its own regular probation officer, to make any inquiries and presentence investigation reports that the court requires concerning the defendant.

(2) The provisions of section 2951.03 of the Revised Code shall govern the preparation of, the provision, receipt, and retention of copies of, the use of, and the confidentiality, nonpublic record character, and sealing of a presentence investigation report prepared pursuant to division (A)(1) of this section.

(B) The court may appoint not more than two psychologists or psychiatrists to make any reports concerning the defendant that the court requires for the purpose of determining the disposition of the case. Each psychologist or psychiatrist shall receive a fee to be fixed by the court and taxed in the costs of the case. The psychologist's or psychiatrist's reports shall be made in writing, in open court, and in the presence of the defendant, except in misdemeanor cases in which sentence may be pronounced in the absence of the defendant. A copy of each report of a psychologist or psychiatrist may be furnished to the defendant, if present, who may examine the persons making the report, under oath, as to any matter or thing contained in the report.

HISTORY: GC § 13451-2; 113 v 123(197), ch 30, § 2; Bureau of Code Revision, 10-1-53; 130 v 667 (Eff 9-24-63); 142 v H 73, § 1 (Eff 10-1-87); 142 v H 73, § 5 (Eff 10-1-89); 146 v S 2 (Eff 7-1-96); 146 v S 269. Eff 7-1-96.

RC § 2947.06 was repealed in 139 v S 199, § 2, file 256, eff 1-1-83. Repeal rescinded in 1982 by 139 v H 269, § 4.

The effective date is set by section 5 of SB 269.

[§§ 2947.06.1, 2947.06.2] §§ 2947.061, 2947.062 Repealed, 146 v S 2, § 6 [131 v 684; 133 v H 686; 133 v H 1136; 136 v H 837; 139 v s 199; 139 v H 269; 140 v H 291; 145 v H 571; 145 v S 186; 146 v H 4]. Eff 7-1-96.

The repeal of RC § 2947.06.1 by SB 2 (146 v —) is confirmed in § 2 of SB 269 (146 v —), effective 7-1-96. The provisions of § 12 of SB 269 (146 v —) read as follows:

SECTION 12. The repeal by this act of section 2947.061 of the Revised Code is intended to confirm the result intended by the General Assembly in enacting Am. Sub. S.B. 2 and Sub. H.B. 4 of the 121st General Assembly. Both acts passed on June 29, 1995. Am. Sub. S.B. 2 repealed the section while Sub. H.B. 4 amended it. The existence of the section is therefore uncertain. The intention of the General Assembly was for the section to be neither continued nor revived as the result of its amendment by Sub. H.B. 4, but rather for the section to be repealed as provided in Am. Sub. S.B. 2.

These sections set regulations for probation after serving thirty days or six months of sentence—shock probation—and attendance at hearing for probation and transportation of prisoner.

§ 2947.07 When court to pronounce judgment.

If a convicted defendant does not show sufficient cause as to why judgment should not be pronounced, the court shall pronounce the judgment.

HISTORY: GC § 13451-4; 113 v 123(198), ch 30, § 4; Bureau of Code Revision. Eff 10-1-53.

§ 2947.08 Time of execution in capital cases.

In cases where the death sentence is imposed, at least one hundred twenty days shall intervene between the day of sentence and the day appointed for the execution thereof.

HISTORY: GC § 13451-5; 113 v 123(198), ch 30, § 5; Bureau of Code Revision, 10-1-53; 131 v 684. Eff 8-10-65.

§§ 2947.09, 2947.10, 2947.11

Repealed, 134 v H 511, § 2 [GC §§ 13451-6—13451-8; 113 v 123; 115 v 542; Bureau of Code Revision, 10-1-53; 133 v S 460]. Eff 1-1-74.

These sections concerned sentence to hard labor, punishment by fine and imprisonment, and conditional sentence for a misdemeanor.

§§ 2947.12, 2947.13

Repealed, 134 v H 511, § 2 [GC §§ 13451-8a—13451-8b; 113 v 123; 115 v 543; Bureau of Code Revision, 10-1-53; 134 v H 139]. Eff 1-1-74.

These sections established time and manner of payment of fine and procedure for remission or suspension of sentence.

§ 2947.14 Satisfaction of fine.

(A) If a fine is imposed as a sentence or a part of a sentence, the court or magistrate that imposed the fine may order that the offender be committed to the jail or workhouse until the fine is paid or secured to be paid, or he is otherwise legally discharged, if the court or magistrate determines at a hearing that the offender is able, at that time, to pay the fine but refuses to do so. The hearing required by this section shall be conducted at the time of sentencing.

(B) At the hearing, the offender has the right to be represented by counsel and to testify and present evidence as to his ability to pay the fine. If a court or magistrate determines after considering the evidence presented by an offender, that the offender is able to pay a fine, the determination shall be supported by findings of fact set forth in a judgment entry that indicate the offender's income, assets, and debts, as presented by the offender, and his ability to pay.

(C) If the court or magistrate has found the offender able to pay a fine at a hearing conducted in compliance with divisions (A) and (B) of this section, and the offender fails to pay the fine, a warrant may be issued for the arrest of the offender. Any offender held in custody pursuant to such an arrest shall be entitled to a hearing on the first regularly scheduled court day following the date of arrest in order to inform the court or magistrate of any change of circumstances that has occurred since the time of sentencing and that affects his ability to pay the fine. The right to the hearing on any change of circumstances may be waived by the offender.

At the hearing to determine any change of circumstances, the offender has the right to testify and present evidence as to any portion of his income, assets, or debts that has changed in such a manner as to affect his ability to pay the fine. If a court or magistrate determines, after considering any evidence presented by the offender, that the offender remains able to pay the fine, that determination shall be supported by a judgment entry that includes findings of fact upon which such a determination is based.

(D) No person shall be ordered to be committed to a jail or workhouse or otherwise be held in custody in satisfaction of a fine imposed as the whole or a part of a sentence except as provided in this section. Any person imprisoned pursuant to this section shall receive credit upon the fine at the rate of thirty dollars per day or fraction of a day. If the unpaid fine is less than thirty dollars, the person shall be imprisoned one day.

(E) No commitment pursuant to this section shall exceed six months.

HISTORY: GC § 13451-9; 113 v 123(199), ch 30, § 9; 120 v 320; Bureau of Code Revision, 10-1-53; 133 v S 460 (Eff 9-3-70); 140 v H 277 (Eff 9-20-84); 140 v H 113. Eff 1-8-85.

§ 2947.15 Labor by jail inmates; vocational training, rehabilitation.

Persons committed to jail by a judge or magistrate for nonpayment of fine, or convicts sentenced to hard labor in the county jail, shall perform labor under the direction of the board of county commissioners within or outside the jail, within the county, and the board shall adopt orders and rules in relation to the performance of labor and the sheriff or other officer having the custody of the persons or convicts shall be governed by the orders and rules. The sheriff of the county shall collect the proceeds of the labor of the persons or convicts, pay it into the county treasury, take the county treasurer's duplicate receipts for the amount paid, and forthwith deposit one of them with the county auditor. The sheriff, with the approval of the board, may provide for the vocational training and rehabilitation of prisoners confined in the county jail.

This section does not apply to prisoners participating in a county jail industry program established under section 5147.30 of the Revised Code.

HISTORY: GC § 13451-10; 113 v 123(199), ch 30, § 10; Bureau of Code Revision, 10-1-53; 125 v S 275 (Eff 10-15-53); 133 v S 460 (Eff 9-3-70); 143 v H 588 (Eff 10-31-90); 143 v H 51. Eff 11-8-90.

[§ 2947.15.1] § 2947.151 Reduction of jail sentence.

The sheriff in charge of a county jail may, upon a consideration of the quality and amount of work done in the kitchen, in the jail offices, on the jail premises, or elsewhere, allow reductions of inmates' sentences as follows:

(A) On sentences of ninety days or less, up to three days for each thirty days of sentence;

(B) On sentences longer than ninety days but not longer than six months, up to four days for each thirty days of sentence;

(C) On sentences longer than six months, up to five days for each thirty days of sentence.

The reduction of the inmate's sentence shall become effective only upon the written concurrence of the presiding or sentencing judge or magistrate of the court where the sentence was imposed.

This section shall in no way restrict any other powers vested in the presiding or sentencing judge or magistrate of the court where the sentence was imposed.

HISTORY: 128 v 595. Eff 10-1-59.

§ 2947.16 Recognizance.

A person convicted of a misdemeanor may be required by the judge or magistrate to enter into a recognizance, with sufficient surety, in such sum as the judge or magistrate finds proper, to keep the peace and be of good behavior for such time, not exceeding two years, as the court directs. The court may order such person to stand committed until such order is complied with or he is discharged by law, but the court may discharge such person at any time on his own recognizance, or cancel such recognizance.

HISTORY: GC § 13451-11; 113 v 123(199), ch 30, § 11; Bureau of Code Revision. Eff 10-1-53.

§ 2947.17 Breach of condition of a recognizance.

In case of a breach of the condition of any recognizance given under section 2947.16 of the Revised Code, the same proceedings shall be had as are prescribed in relation to forfeiture of other recognizances.

HISTORY: GC § 13451-12; 113 v 123(199), ch 30, § 12; Bureau of Code Revision, 10-1-53; 133 v H 228 (Eff 1-1-70); 138 v H 736. Eff 10-16-80.

§ 2947.18 Sentence to workhouse for jail offense.

Where the board of county commissioners of a county, or legislative authority of a municipal corporation having no workhouse, has made provisions for receiving prisoners into the workhouse of a city in any other county or district in the state, a court or magistrate, where imprisonment in jail may lawfully be imposed in such case, may sentence persons convicted of a misdemeanor, including a violation of a municipal ordinance, to such workhouse.

HISTORY: GC § 13451-13; 113 v 123(199), ch 30, § 13; Bureau of Code Revision, 10-1-53; 133 v S 460. Eff 9-3-70.

§ 2947.19 Confinement of county prisoners in city workhouse; reimbursement by prisoner for costs of confinement.

(A) In a county that has no workhouse but in which is located a city that has a workhouse maintained by the city, the board of county commissioners may agree with the proper authorities of that city upon terms under which persons convicted of misdemeanors shall be maintained in the city workhouse at the expense of the county. In the case of persons committed to the city workhouse for the violation of a law of this state, whether the commitment is from the court of common pleas, magistrate's court, or other court, the cost of maintaining those persons committed shall be paid out of the general fund of the county, on the allowance of the board of county commissioners, provided that all persons committed to the city workhouse for the violation of ordinances of the city shall be maintained in that workhouse at the sole cost of the city.

(B)(1) The board of county commissioners or the legislative authority of the city may require a person who was convicted of an offense and who is confined in the city workhouse as provided in division (A) of this section to reimburse the county or the city, as the case may be, for its expenses incurred by reason of the person's confinement, including, but not limited to, the expenses relating to the provision of food, clothing, shelter, medical care, personal hygiene products, including, but not limited to, toothpaste, toothbrushes, and feminine hygiene items, and up to two hours of overtime costs of the sheriff or municipal corporation incurred relating to the trial of the person. The amount of reimbursement may be the actual cost of the prisoner's confinement plus the authorized trial overtime costs or a lesser amount determined by the board of county commissioners for the county or the legislative authority of the city, provided that the lesser amount shall be determined by a formula that is uniformly applied to persons incarcerated in the workhouse. The court shall determine the amount of reimbursement for the person convicted of the misdemeanor at a hearing held pursuant to section 2929.18 of the Revised Code if the person is confined for a felony or section 2929.223 [2929.22.3] of the Revised Code if the person is confined for a misdemeanor. The amount or amounts paid in reimbursement by a prisoner confined for a misdemeanor or the amount recovered from a prisoner confined for a misdemeanor by executing upon the judgment obtained pursuant to section 2929.223 [2929.22.3] of the Revised Code shall be paid into the treasury of the county or city that incurred the expenses. If a person is convicted of or pleads guilty to a felony and the court imposes a sanction that requires the offender to serve a term in a city workhouse, sections 341.23, 753.02, 753.04, and 753.16 of the Revised Code govern the determination of whether the court may impose a sanction under section 2929.18 of the Revised Code that requires the offender to reimburse the expenses of confinement. If a person is confined for a felony and the court imposes a sanction under section 2929.18 of the Revised Code that requires the offender to reimburse the costs of confinement, the prosecuting attorney of the county or city director of law shall bring an action to recover the expenses of confinement in accordance with section 2929.18 of the Revised Code.

(2) The board of county commissioners or the legislative authority of the city may adopt a resolution or

ordinance specifying that a person who is convicted of a felony and who is confined in the city workhouse as provided in division (A) of this section is not required to reimburse the county or city, as the case may be, for its expenses incurred by reason of the person's confinement, including the expenses listed in division (B)(1) of this section. If the board or legislative authority adopts a resolution or ordinance of that nature, the court that sentences a person convicted of a felony shall not impose a sanction under section 2929.18 of the Revised Code that requires the person to reimburse the costs of the confinement.

(C) In lieu of requiring offenders to reimburse the county or the city for expenses incurred by reason of the person's confinement under division (A) of this section, the board of county commissioners or the legislative authority of the city may adopt a prisoner reimbursement policy for the city workhouse under this division. The workhouse administrator may appoint a reimbursement coordinator to administer the prisoner reimbursement policy. A prisoner reimbursement policy adopted under this division is a policy that requires a person confined to the workhouse to reimburse the county or city for any expenses it incurs by reason of the person's confinement in the workhouse, which expenses may include, but are not limited to, the following:

(1) A per diem fee for room and board of not more than sixty dollars per day or the actual per diem cost, whichever is less for the entire period of time the person is confined to the workhouse;

(2) Actual charges for medical and dental treatment;

(3) Reimbursement for government property damaged by the person while confined to the workhouse.

Rates charged shall be on a sliding scale determined by the board of county commissioners or the legislative authority of the city, based on the ability of the person confined in the workhouse to pay and on consideration of any legal obligation of the person to support a spouse, minor children, or other dependents and any moral obligation to support dependents to whom the person is providing or has in fact provided support.

The reimbursement coordinator or another person designated by the workhouse administrator may investigate the financial status of the confined person and obtain information necessary to investigate that status, by means that may include contacting employers and reviewing income tax records. The coordinator may work with the confined person to create a repayment plan to be implemented upon the person's release. At the end of the person's incarceration, the person shall be presented with a billing statement.

The reimbursement coordinator or another person designated by the workhouse administrator may collect, or the board of county commissioners or the legislative authority of the city may enter into a contract with one or more public agencies or private vendors to collect, any amounts remaining unpaid. Within twelve months after the date of the confined person's release, the prosecuting attorney or city director of law may file a civil action to seek reimbursement from that person for any billing amount that remains unpaid. The county or city shall not enforce any judgment obtained under this section by means of execution against the person's homestead. For purposes of this section, "homestead" has the same meaning as in division (A) of section 323.151 [323.15.1] of the Revised Code. Any reimbursement received under this section shall be credited to the general fund of the county or city that bore the expense, to be used for general fund purposes.

(D)(1) Notwithstanding any contrary provision in this section or section 2929.18 or 2929.223 [2929.22.3] of the Revised Code, the board of county commissioners or the legislative authority of the city may establish a policy that requires any person who is not indigent and who is confined in the city workhouse to pay a reasonable fee for any medical treatment or service requested by and provided to that person. This fee shall not exceed the actual cost of the treatment or service provided. No person confined to a city workhouse who is indigent shall be required to pay those fees, and no person confined to a city workhouse shall be denied any necessary medical care because of inability to pay those fees.

Upon provision of the requested medical treatment or service, payment of the required fee may be automatically deducted from a person's account record in the workhouse's business office. If the person has no funds in the person's account, a deduction may be made at a later date during the person's confinement in the workhouse if funds later become available in the person's account. If the person is released from the workhouse and has an unpaid balance of these fees, the board of county commissioners or the legislative authority may bill the person for payment of the remaining unpaid fees. Fees received for medical treatment or services shall be paid into the commissary fund, if one has been created for the workhouse, or if no commissary fund exists, into the county or city treasury.

(2) If a person confined to a city workhouse is required under division (B) of this section or section 2929.18 or 2929.223 [2929.22.3] of the Revised Code to reimburse the county or city for expenses incurred by reason of the person's confinement to the workhouse, any fees paid by the person under division (D)(1) of this section shall be deducted from the expenses required to be reimbursed under division (B) of this section or section 2929.18 or 2929.223 [2929.22.3] of the Revised Code.

HISTORY: GC § 13451-14; 113 v 123(200), ch 30, § 14; Bureau of Code Revision, 10-1-53; 136 v H 205 (Eff 1-1-76); 140 v H 363 (Eff 9-26-84); 146 v S 2 (Eff 7-1-96); 146 v S 269 (Eff 7-1-96); 146 v H 480. Eff 10-16-96.

§ 2947.20 Submission of health insurance claims of inmates.

(A) For each person who is confined in a city workhouse as provided in section 2947.19 of the Revised

Code, the county or the city, as the case may be, may make a determination as to whether the person is covered under a health insurance or health care policy, contract, or plan and, if the person has such coverage, what terms and conditions are imposed by it for the filing and payment of claims.

(B) If, pursuant to division (A) of this section, it is determined that the person is covered under a policy, contract, or plan and, while that coverage is in force, the workhouse renders or arranges for the rendering of health care services to the person in accordance with the terms and conditions of the policy, contract, or plan, then the person, county, city, or provider of the health care services, as appropriate under the terms and conditions of the policy, contract, or plan, shall promptly submit a claim for payment for the health care services to the appropriate third-party payer and shall designate, or make any other arrangement necessary to ensure, that payment of any amount due on the claim be made to the county, city, or provider, as the case may be.

(C) Any payment made to the county or the city pursuant to division (B) of this section shall be paid into the treasury of the governmental entity that incurred the expenses.

(D) This section also applies to any person who is under the custody of a law enforcement officer, as defined in section 2901.01 of the Revised Code, prior to the person's confinement in the workhouse.

HISTORY: 146 v S 163. Eff 10-16-96.

Not analogous to former RC § 2947.20 (GC § 13451-15; 113 v 123(200), ch 30, § 15; 120 v 320; Bureau of Code Revision, 10-1-53; 133 v S 460; 134 v H 511; 140 v H 277), repealed 140 v H 113, § 2, eff 1-8-85.

§ 2947.21 Officer's warrant for detention in workhouse or jail.

When a person is sentenced to a workhouse by the court of common pleas, the clerk of the court of common pleas shall make and deliver to the sheriff a certified copy of the judgment. The copy shall describe the crime charged and the sentence of the court. The sheriff shall deliver the copy to the officer in charge of the workhouse, and the copy shall be that officer's warrant for detaining the person in custody. In case of such a conviction by any other court or magistrate, the court or magistrate shall make a certified transcript of the docket in the case, which, in like manner, shall be delivered to the marshal, constable, or sheriff to be delivered by the marshal, constable, or sheriff to the proper officer in charge of the workhouse and be that officer's warrant for detaining the person in custody.

When a person is sentenced to a jail or workhouse under division (A)(3) of section 2929.51 of the Revised Code, the court shall certify a transcript of the docket in the case, and the court shall deliver the certified transcript to the proper officer in charge of the workhouse or jail, and the certified transcript is the officer's warrant for detaining the person in custody during the prescribed period or periods.

HISTORY: GC § 13451-16; 113 v 123(200), ch 30, § 16; Bureau of Code Revision, 10-1-53; 133 v H 228 (Eff 1-1-70); 138 v H 736 (Eff 10-16-80); 146 v S 2. Eff 7-1-96.

The effective date is set by section 6 of SB 2.

§ 2947.22 Person may be confined in jail temporarily.

A person sentenced to a workhouse may be confined in the jail of the county in which he was convicted, for such period as is necessary to procure the papers and make arrangements to transport him to the workhouse.

HISTORY: GC § 13451-17; 113 v 123(200), ch 30, § 17; Bureau of Code Revision. Eff 10-1-53.

§ 2947.23 Judgment for costs and jury fees.

In all criminal cases, including violations of ordinances, the judge or magistrate shall include in the sentence the costs of prosecution and render a judgment against the defendant for such costs. If a jury has been sworn at the trial of a case, the fees of the jurors shall be included in the costs, which shall be paid to the public treasury from which the jurors were paid.

HISTORY: GC § 13451-18; 113 v 123(201), ch 30, § 18; 120 v 320; Bureau of Code Revision. Eff 10-1-53.

§§ 2947.24, 2947.25 Repealed, 137 v H 565, § 2 [GC §§ 13451-19, 13451-20; 118 v 686; 121 v 443; 124 v 382; Bureau of Code Revision, 10-1-53; 125 v S 155; 126 v 392; 129 v 1448; 130 v 667; 133 v H 688; 134 v H 494; 134 v H 511; 136 v H 244; 137 v H 1]. Eff 11-1-78.

These sections defined mentally deficient offenders and required psychiatric examination before sentence. See related provisions in Revised Code Chapters 5120., 5122., and 5123.

§§ 2947.26, 2947.27 Repealed, 137 v H 565, § 2 [GC §§ 13451-21, 13451-22; 118 v 686; 121 v 443; 124 v 382; Bureau of Code Revision, 10-1-53; 125 v S 155; 132 v H 1; 132 v S 316; 133 v H 688; 133 v S 272; 134 v H 494; 136 v H 1; 137 v H 1]. Eff 11-1-78.

These sections provided for postponement of commitment, conditions for release, and procedures upon recovery or improvement of inmate. See related provisions in Revised Code Chapters 5120., 5122., and 5123.

[§ 2947.27.1] § 2947.271 Repealed, 137 v H 565, § 2 [134 v H 511; 136 v H 1]. Eff 11-1-78.

This section concerned annual case review of mentally deficient offender.

§§ 2947.28, 2947.29 Repealed, 137 v H 565, § 2 [GC §§ 13451-22a, 13451-23; 118 v 686; 121 v 443; Bureau of Code Revision, 10-1-53; 125 v S 155; 133 v H 688; 134 v H 494]. Eff 11-1-78.

These sections concerned application for release.

§§ 2947.30, 2947.31 Repealed, 134 v H 511, § 2 [132 v H 996; 133 v H 228; 134 v H 143]. Eff 1-1-74.

These sections concerned additional penalty for possessing firearms while rioting and periodic sentences.

CHAPTER 2949: EXECUTION OF SENTENCE

Section
2949.01 Definition of magistrate.

[SUSPENSION OF SENTENCE]

2949.02 Execution suspended; recognizance.
2949.03 Further suspending execution.
2949.04 Increase or decrease in bail.
2949.05 Execution of sentence.
2949.06 Escape after sentencing; resentencing.
2949.07 No credit for time absent.
2949.08 Confinement upon conviction; reduction of sentence for prior confinement.

[FINES AND COSTS]

2949.09 Execution for fine and costs.
[2949.09.1] 2949.091 Additional court costs or bail.
[2949.09.2] 2949.092 Condition for waiver of specified additional court costs.
2949.10 Execution for fine to issue to other county.
2949.11 Fines paid into county treasury.
[2949.11.1] 2949.111 Assignment of offender's payment toward satisfaction of costs, restitution, fine or supervision fees.

[TRANSPORTATION OF FELONS; COSTS]

2949.12 Delivery of convict to reception facility; assignment to institution, jail or workhouse.
2949.13 Sheriff may require assistance.
2949.14 Cost bill in case of felony.
2949.15 Writs of execution to issue.
2949.16 Repealed.
2949.17 Transportation of prisoners; expenses.
2949.18 Repealed.
2949.19 State payment of criminal costs.
2949.20 Costs in case of reversal.
[2949.20.1] 2949.201 Estimate of money needed for next biennium.

[DEATH SENTENCE]

2949.21 Conveyance to reception facility; assignment to institution.
2949.22 Execution of death sentence.
2949.23 Repealed.
2949.24 Execution and return of warrant.
2949.25 Attendance at execution.
2949.26 Disposition of body of executed convict.
2949.27 Escape, rearrest, and execution.
2949.28 Convict insane.
2949.29 Proceedings on the insanity inquiry.
2949.30 When convict restored, governor to order execution.
2949.31 Pregnant prisoners.
2949.32 When execution to be ordered.
2949.33-2949.36 Repealed.

§ 2949.01 Definition of magistrate.

The definition of "magistrate" set forth in section 2931.01 of the Revised Code applies to Chapter 2949. of the Revised Code.

HISTORY: Bureau of Code Revision. Eff 10-1-53.

[SUSPENSION OF SENTENCE]

§ 2949.02 Execution suspended; recognizance.

(A) If a person is convicted of any bailable offense, including, but not limited to, a violation of an ordinance of a municipal corporation, in a municipal or county court or in a court of common pleas and if the person gives to the trial judge or magistrate a written notice of the person's intention to file or apply for leave to file an appeal to the court of appeals, the trial judge or magistrate may suspend, subject to division (A)(2)(b) of section 2953.09 of the Revised Code, execution of the sentence or judgment imposed for any fixed time that will give the person time either to prepare and file, or to apply for leave to file, the appeal. In all bailable cases, except as provided in division (B) of this section, the trial judge or magistrate may release the person on bail in accordance with Criminal Rule 46, and the bail shall at least be conditioned that the person will appeal without delay and abide by the judgment and sentence of the court.

(B) Notwithstanding any provision of Criminal Rule 46 to the contrary, a trial judge of a court of common pleas shall not release on bail pursuant to division (A) of this section a person who is convicted of a bailable offense if the person is sentenced to imprisonment for life or if that offense is a violation of section 2903.01, 2903.02, 2903.03, 2903.04, 2903.11, 2905.01, 2905.02, 2905.11, 2907.02, 2909.02, 2911.01, 2911.02, or 2911.11 of the Revised Code or is felonious sexual penetration in violation of former section 2907.12 of the Revised Code.

(C) If a trial judge of a court of common pleas is prohibited by division (B) of this section from releasing on bail pursuant to division (A) of this section a person who is convicted of a bailable offense and not sentenced to imprisonment for life, the appropriate court of appeals or two judges of it, upon motion of such a person and for good cause shown, may release the person on bail in accordance with Appellate Rule 8 and Criminal Rule 46, and the bail shall at least be conditioned as described in division (A) of this section.

HISTORY: GC § 13453-1; 113 v 123(203), ch 32; Bureau of Code Revision, 10-1-53; 139 v S 199 (Eff 7-1-83); 141 v H 412 (Eff 3-17-87); 146 v H 445. Eff 9-3-96.

§ 2949.03 Further suspending execution.

If a judgment of conviction by a court of common pleas, municipal court, or county court is affirmed by a court of appeals and remanded to the trial court for execution of the sentence or judgment imposed, and the person so convicted gives notice of his intention to file a notice of appeal to the supreme court, the trial court, on the filing of a motion by such person within three days after the rendition by the court of appeals of the judgment of affirmation, may further suspend, subject to division (A)(2)(b) of section 2953.09 of the Revised Code, the execution of the sentence or judgment imposed for a time sufficient to give such person an opportunity to file a notice of appeal to the supreme court, but the sentence or judgment imposed shall not be suspended more than thirty days for that purpose.

HISTORY: GC § 13453-2; 113 v 123(204), ch 32, § 2; Bureau of Code Revision, 10-1-53; 141 v H 412. Eff 3-17-87.

§ 2949.04 Increase or decrease in bail.

When bail is fixed pursuant to division (B) of section 2953.03 or section 2949.02 or 2953.09 of the Revised Code in connection with an appeal, a reduction or increase in the amount of that bail or other change in that bail shall not be required of the accused during the pendency of the appeal unless the trial judge or magistrate, or the court in which the appeal is being prosecuted, finds that there is good cause to reduce or increase the amount of that bail or good cause for any other change in that bail. If the court in which the appeal is being prosecuted finds there is good cause to reduce or increase the amount of that bail or good cause for any other change in that bail, it shall order the reduction, increase, or other change in accordance with Criminal Rule 46, and the new bail shall be in the amount and form so ordered and otherwise be to the approval of and filed with the clerk of the court in which the appeal is being prosecuted.

HISTORY: GC § 13453-3; 113 v 123(204), ch 32, § 3; Bureau of Code Revision, 10-1-53; 129 v 423 (Eff 10-19-61); 141 v H 412. Eff 3-17-87.

§ 2949.05 Execution of sentence.

If no appeal is filed, if leave to file an appeal or certification of a case is denied, if the judgment of the trial court is affirmed on appeal, or if post-conviction relief under section 2953.21 of the Revised Code is denied, the trial court or magistrate shall carry into execution the sentence or judgment which had been pronounced against the defendant.

HISTORY: GC § 13453-4; 113 v 123(204), ch 32, § 4; Bureau of Code Revision, 10-1-53; 129 v 423 (Eff 10-19-61); 133 v S 354 (Eff 11-18-69); 141 v H 412. Eff 3-17-87.

§ 2949.06 Escape after sentencing; resentencing.

If a person escapes after sentence and before confinement in a state correctional institution or jail, the clerk of the trial court, upon application of the prosecuting attorney or by order of the court, shall issue a warrant stating the conviction and sentence and commanding the sheriff to pursue the person into any county of this state. The sheriff shall take into custody the person so escaping and shall make return of the warrant to the court if it is in session, and if it is not in session he shall commit the accused to the jail of the county and bring him before the court at the next session of the court.

The court shall set aside the former sentence and again pronounce judgment upon the verdict.

HISTORY: GC § 13453-5; 113 v 123(204), ch 32, § 5; Bureau of Code Revision, 10-1-53; 145 v H 571. Eff 10-6-94.

§ 2949.07 No credit for time absent.

If a convict escapes from a state correctional institution, the time the convict is absent from the institution because of his escape shall not be credited as a part of the time for which he was sentenced.

HISTORY: GC § 13453-6; 113 v 123(204), ch 32, § 6; Bureau of Code Revision, 10-1-53; 145 v H 571. Eff 10-6-94.

§ 2949.08 Confinement upon conviction; reduction of sentence for prior confinement.

(A) When a person convicted of a misdemeanor is sentenced to imprisonment in jail or the workhouse, the judge or magistrate shall order him into the custody of the sheriff or constable, who shall deliver him with the record of his conviction, to the jailer or keeper, in whose custody he shall remain until the term of his imprisonment expires or he is otherwise legally discharged.

(B) The record of the person's conviction shall specify the total number of days, if any, that the person was confined for any reason arising out of the offense for which he was convicted and sentenced prior to delivery to the jailer or keeper under this section. The record shall be used to determine any reduction of sentence under division (C) of this section.

(C) The jailer, administrator, or keeper in charge of a jail or workhouse shall reduce the sentence of a person delivered into his custody pursuant to division (A) of this section by the total number of days the prisoner was confined for any reason arising out of the offense for which the prisoner was convicted and sentenced, including confinement in lieu of bail while awaiting trial, confinement for examination to determine his competence to stand trial or to determine sanity, and confinement while awaiting transportation to the place where he is to serve his sentence.

(D) For purposes of divisions (B) and (C) of this section, a person shall be considered to have been confined for a day if the person was confined for any period or periods of time totaling more than eight hours during that day.

HISTORY: GC § 13454-1; 113 v 123(205), ch 33; Bureau of Code Revision, 10-1-53; 138 v S 23. Eff 3-27-80.

[FINES AND COSTS]

§ 2949.09 Execution for fine and costs.

When a judge or magistrate renders judgment for a fine, an execution may issue for such judgment and costs of prosecution, to be levied on the property, or in default thereof, upon the body of the defendant for nonpayment of the fine. The officer holding such writ may arrest such defendant in any county and commit him to the jail of the county in which such writ issued, until such time fine is paid or secured to be paid or he is otherwise legally discharged.

HISTORY: GC § 13454-2; 113 v 123(205), ch 33, § 2; Bureau of Code Revision, 10-1-53; 133 v S 460. Eff 9-3-70.

[§ 2949.09.1] § 2949.091 Additional court costs or bail.

(A)(1) The court, in which any person is convicted of or pleads guilty to any offense other than a traffic offense that is not a moving violation, shall impose the sum of eleven dollars as costs in the case in addition to any other court costs that the court is required by law to impose upon the offender. All such moneys shall be transmitted on the first business day of each month by the clerk of the court to the treasurer of state and deposited by the treasurer of state into the general revenue fund. The court shall not waive the payment of the additional eleven dollars court costs, unless the court determines that the offender is indigent and waives the payment of all court costs imposed upon the indigent offender.

(2) The juvenile court, in which a child is found to be a delinquent child or a juvenile traffic offender for an act which, if committed by an adult, would be an offense other than a traffic offense that is not a moving violation, shall impose the sum of eleven dollars as costs in the case in addition to any other court costs that the court is required or permitted by law to impose upon the delinquent child or juvenile traffic offender. All such moneys shall be transmitted on the first business day of each month by the clerk of the court to the treasurer of state and deposited by the treasurer of state into the general revenue fund. The eleven dollars court costs shall be collected in all cases unless the court determines the juvenile is indigent and waives the payment of all court costs, or enters an order on its journal stating that it has determined that the juvenile is indigent, that no other court costs are to be taxed in the case, and that the payment of the eleven dollars court costs is waived.

(B) Whenever a person is charged with any offense other than a traffic offense that is not a moving violation and posts bail, the court shall add to the amount of the bail the eleven dollars required to be paid by division (A)(1) of this section. The eleven dollars shall be retained by the clerk of the court until the person is convicted, pleads guilty, forfeits bail, is found not guilty, or has the charges against him dismissed. If the person is convicted, pleads guilty, or forfeits bail, the clerk shall transmit the eleven dollars to the treasurer of state, who shall deposit it into the general revenue fund. If the person is found not guilty or the charges against him are dismissed, the clerk shall return the eleven dollars to the person.

(C) No person shall be placed or held in a detention facility for failing to pay the additional eleven dollars court costs or bail that are required to be paid by this section.

(D) As used in this section:

(1) "Moving violation" and "bail" have the same meanings as in section 2743.70 of the Revised Code.

(2) "Detention facility" has the same meaning as in section 2921.01 of the Revised Code.

HISTORY: 140 v H 291 (Eff 7-1-83); 142 v H 171 (Eff 7-1-87); 143 v H 111 (Eff 7-1-89); 143 v S 131 (Eff 7-25-90); 144 v H 298. Eff 7-26-91.

[§ 2949.09.2] § 2949.092 Condition for waiver of specified additional court costs.

If a person is convicted of or pleads guilty to an offense and the court specifically is required, pursuant to section 2743.70 or 2949.091 [2949.09.1] of the Revised Code or pursuant to any other section of the Revised Code, to impose a specified sum of money as costs in the case in addition to any other costs that the court is required or permitted by law to impose in the case, the court shall not waive the payment of the specified additional court costs that the section of the Revised Code specifically requires the court to impose unless the court determines that the offender is indigent and the court waives the payment of all court costs imposed upon the offender.

HISTORY: 143 v S 131. Eff 7-25-90.

§ 2949.10 Execution for fine to issue to other county.

An execution under section 2949.09 of the Revised Code may issue to the sheriff of any county in which the defendant resides, is found, or has property, and the sheriff shall execute the writ. If the defendant is taken, the sheriff shall commit him to the jail of the county in which the writ issued and deliver a certified copy of the writ to the sheriff of such county, who shall detain the offender until he is discharged as provided in such section.

HISTORY: GC § 13454-3; 113 v 123(205), ch 33, § 3; Bureau of Code Revision. Eff 10-1-53.

§ 2949.11 Fines paid into county treasury.

Unless otherwise required in the Revised Code, an officer who collects a fine shall pay it into the treasury of the county in which such fine was assessed, within twenty days after the receipt of the fine, to the credit of the county general fund. The county treasurer shall issue duplicate receipts for the fine, and the officer making the collection shall deposit one of these receipts with the county auditor.

HISTORY: GC § 13454-4; 113 v 123(205), ch 33, § 4; Bureau of Code Revision, 10-1-53; 125 v S 361 (Eff 10-1-53); 141 v S 54. Eff 5-6-86.

[§ 2949.11.1] § 2949.111 Assignment of offender's payments toward satisfaction of costs, restitution, fine or supervision fees.

(A) As used in this section:

(1) "Costs" means any court costs that the court requires an offender to pay, any reimbursement for the costs of confinement that the court orders an offender to pay pursuant to section 2929.223 [2929.22.3] of the Revised Code, any fee for the costs of electronically monitored house arrest that an offender agrees to pay pursuant to section 2929.23 of the Revised Code, any reimbursement for the costs of an investigation or prosecution that the court orders an offender to pay pursuant to section 2929.28 of the Revised Code, or any other costs that the court orders an offender to pay.

(2) "Supervision fees" means any fees that a court, pursuant to section 2951.021 [2951.02.1] of the Revised Code and as a condition of probation, requires an offender who is placed on probation to pay for probation services or that a court, pursuant to section 2929.18 of the Revised Code, requires an offender who is under a community control sanction to pay for supervision services.

(3) "Community control sanction" has the same meaning as in section 2929.01 of the Revised Code.

(B) Unless the court, in accordance with division (C) of this section, enters in the record of the case a different method of assigning a payment toward the satisfaction of costs, restitution, a fine, or supervision fees, if a person who is charged with a misdemeanor is convicted of or pleads guilty to the offense, if the court orders the offender to pay any combination of costs, restitution, a fine, or supervision fees, and if the offender makes any payment to a clerk of court toward the satisfaction of the costs, restitution, fine, or supervision fees, the clerk of the court shall assign the offender's payment so made toward the satisfaction of the costs, restitution, fine, or supervision fees in the following manner:

(1) If the court ordered the offender to pay any costs, the offender's payment shall be assigned toward the satisfaction of the costs until the court costs have been entirely paid.

(2) If the court ordered the offender to pay any restitution and if all of the costs that the court ordered the offender to pay, if any, have been paid, the remainder of the offender's payment after any assignment required under division (B)(1) of this section shall be assigned toward the satisfaction of the restitution until the restitution has been entirely paid.

(3) If the court ordered the offender to pay any fine and if all of the costs and restitution that the court ordered the offender to pay, if any, have been paid, the remainder of the offender's payment after any assignments required under divisions (B)(1) and (2) of this section shall be assigned toward the satisfaction of the fine until the fine has been entirely paid.

(4) If the court ordered the offender to pay any supervision fees and if all of the costs, restitution, and fine that the court ordered the offender to pay, if any, have been paid, the remainder of the offender's payment after any assignments required under divisions (B)(1), (2), and (3) of this section shall be assigned toward the satisfaction of the supervision fees until the supervision fees have been entirely paid.

(C) If a person who is charged with a misdemeanor is convicted of or pleads guilty to the offense and if the court orders the offender to pay any combination of costs, restitution, a fine, or supervision fees, the court, at the time it orders the offender to pay the combination of costs, restitution, a fine, or supervision fees, may prescribe a method of assigning payments that the person makes toward the satisfaction of the costs, restitution, fine, or supervision fees that differs from the method set forth in division (B) of this section. If the court prescribes a method of assigning payments under this division, the court shall enter in the record of the case the method so prescribed. Upon the entry in the record of the case of the method of assigning payments prescribed pursuant to this division, if the offender makes any payment to a clerk of court for the costs, restitution, fine, or supervision fees, the clerk of the court shall assign the payment so made toward the satisfaction of the costs, restitution, fine, or supervision fees in the manner prescribed by the court and entered in the record of the case instead of in the manner set forth in division (B) of this section.

HISTORY: 145 v H 406 (Eff 11-11-94); 146 v S 2. Eff 7-1-96.

The effective date is set by section 6 of SB 2.

[TRANSPORTATION OF FELONS; COSTS]

§ 2949.12 Delivery of convict to reception facility; assignment to institution, jail or workhouse.

Unless the execution of sentence is suspended, a convicted felon who is sentenced to serve a term of imprisonment in a state correctional institution shall be conveyed, within five days after sentencing, excluding Saturdays, Sundays, and legal holidays, by the sheriff of the county in which the conviction was had to the facility that is designated by the department of rehabilitation and correction for the reception of convicted felons. The sheriff shall deliver the convicted felon into the custody of the managing officer of the reception facility and, at that time, shall present the managing officer with a copy of the convicted felon's sentence that clearly describes each offense for which the felon was sentenced to a correctional institution, designates each section of the Revised Code that the felon violated and that resulted in the felon's conviction and sentence to a correctional institution, designates the sentence imposed for each offense for which the felon was sentenced to a correctional institution, and, pursuant to section 2967.191 [2967.19.1] of the Revised Code, specifies the total number of days, if any, that the felon was confined for any reason prior to conviction and sentence. The sheriff, at that time, also shall present the managing officer with a copy of the indictment. The clerk of the court of common pleas shall furnish the copies of the sentence and indictment. In the case of a person under the age of eighteen years who is certified to the court of common pleas by the juvenile court, the clerk of the court of common pleas also shall attach a copy of the certification to the copy of the indictment.

The convicted felon shall be assigned to an institution or designated to be housed in a county, multicounty, municipal, municipal-county, or multicounty-municipal jail or workhouse, if authorized pursuant to section 5120.161 [5120.16.1] of the Revised Code, shall be conveyed to the institution, jail, or workhouse, and shall be kept within the institution, jail, or workhouse until the term of the felon's imprisonment expires, the felon is pardoned, paroled, or placed under a post-release control sanction, or the felon is transferred under laws permitting the transfer of prisoners. If the execution of the felon's sentence is suspended, and the judgment thereafter affirmed, the felon shall be conveyed, in the same manner as if the execution of the felon's sentence had not been suspended, to the reception facility as soon as practicable after the judge directs the execution of sentence. The trial judge or other judge of the court, in the judge's discretion and for good cause shown, may extend the time of the conveyance.

HISTORY: GC § 13455-1; 113 v 123(205), ch 34; 120 v 628; Bureau of Code Revision, 10-1-53; 135 v S 254 (Eff 8-21-73); 136 v H 685 (Eff 5-21-76); 139 v S 199 (Eff 7-1-83); 140 v S 210 (Eff 7-1-83); 140 v S 172 (Eff 9-26-84); 142 v H 455 (Eff 7-20-87); 142 v H 261 (Eff 11-1-87); 142 v H 708 (Eff 4-19-88); 145 v H 571 (Eff 10-6-94); 146 v S 2. Eff 7-1-96.

The effective date is set by section 6 of SB 2.

§ 2949.13 Sheriff may require assistance.

During the time the sheriff is conveying a convicted felon to an institution for imprisonment therein, he may secure him in a jail and demand the assistance of a sheriff, jailer, or other person in keeping such prisoner, as if he were in his own county. Such sheriff, jailer, or other person is liable, on refusal, to like penalties as if the sheriff making the demand were in his own county.

HISTORY: GC § 13455-2; 113 v 123(206), ch 34, § 2; Bureau of Code Revision. Eff 10-1-53.

§ 2949.14 Cost bill in case of felony.

Upon conviction of a nonindigent person for a felony, the clerk of the court of common pleas shall make and certify under his hand and seal of the court, a complete itemized bill of the costs made in such prosecution, including the sum paid by the board of county commissioners, certified by the county auditor, for the arrest and return of the person on the requisition of the governor, or on the request of the governor to the president of the United States, or on the return of the fugitive by a designated agent pursuant to a waiver of extradition except in cases of parole violation. Such bill of costs shall be presented by such clerk to the prosecuting attorney, who shall examine each item therein charged and certify to it if correct and legal. Upon certification by the prosecuting attorney, the clerk shall attempt to collect the costs from the person convicted.

HISTORY: GC § 13455-3; 113 v 123(206), ch 34, § 3; Bureau of Code Revision, 10-1-53; 132 v S 447 (Eff 2-5-68); 140 v H 291. Eff 7-1-83.

§ 2949.15 Writs of execution to issue.

If a nonindigent person convicted of a felony fails to pay the costs of prosecution pursuant to section 2949.14 of the Revised Code, the clerk of the court of common pleas shall forthwith issue to the sheriff of the county in which the indictment was found, and to the sheriff of any other county in which the person has property, executions against his property for fines and the costs of prosecution, which shall be served and returned within ten days, with the proceedings of such sheriff or the certification that there is no property upon which to levy, indorsed thereon.

When a levy is made upon property under such execution, a writ shall forthwith be issued by the clerk for the sale thereof, and such sheriff shall sell the property and make return thereof, and after paying the costs of conviction, execution, and sale, pay the balance to the person authorized to receive it.

HISTORY: GC § 13455-4; 113 v 123(206), ch 34, § 4; Bureau of Code Revision, 10-1-53; 140 v H 291. Eff 7-1-83.

§ 2949.16 Repealed, 140 v H 291, § 2 [GC § 13455-5; 113 v 123 (206), ch 34, § 5; Bureau of Code Revision, 10-1-53]. Eff 7-1-83.

This section concerned costs on execution for felony.

§ 2949.17 Transportation of prisoners; expenses.

The sheriff may take one guard for every two convicted felons to be transported to a correctional institution. The trial judge may authorize a larger number of guards upon written application of the sheriff, in which case a transcript of the order of the judge shall be certified by the clerk of the court of common pleas under the seal of the court, and the sheriff shall deliver the order with the convict to the person in charge of the correctional institution. In order to obtain reimbursement for the county for the expenses of transportation for indigent convicted felons, the clerk of the court of common pleas shall prepare a transportation cost bill for each indigent convicted felon transported pursuant to this section for an amount equal to ten cents a mile from the county seat to the state correctional institution and return for the sheriff and each of the guards and five cents a mile from the county seat to the state correctional institution for each prisoner. The number of miles shall be computed by the usual route of travel.

HISTORY: GC § 13455-6; 113 v 123(207), ch 34, § 6; Bureau of Code Revision, 10-1-53; 128 v 542 (Eff 7-17-59); 138 v H 204 (Eff 7-30-79); 139 v H 694 (Eff 11-15-81); 140 v H 291 (Eff 7-1-83); 145 v H 571. Eff 10-6-94.

§ 2949.18 Repealed, 140 v H 291, § 2 [GC § 13455-7; 113 v 123 (207), ch 34, § 7; Bureau of Code Revision, 10-1-53; 138 v H 204; 139 v H 694]. Eff 7-1-83.

This section concerned certification and payment of cost bill.

§ 2949.19 State payment of criminal costs.

The clerk of the court of common pleas shall report to the state public defender all cases in which an indigent person was convicted of a felony, all cases in which reimbursement is required by section 2949.20 of the Revised Code, and all cost bills for transportation that are prepared pursuant to section 2949.17 of the Revised Code. The reports shall be filed for each fiscal quarter within thirty days after the end of the quarter on a form prescribed by the state public defender and shall be accompanied by a certification of a judge of the court that in all cases listed in the report the defendant was determined to be indigent and convicted of a felony or that the case is reported pursuant to section 2949.20 of the Revised Code and that for each transportation cost bill submitted pursuant to section 2949.17 of the Revised Code that the convicted felon was determined to be indigent. The state public defender shall review the reports and prepare a transportation cost voucher and a quarterly subsidy voucher for each county for the amounts he finds to be correct. To compute the quarterly subsidy, the state public defender first shall subtract the total of all transportation cost vouchers that he approves for payment for the quarter from one-fourth of his total appropriation for criminal costs subsidy for the fiscal year of which the quarter is part. He then shall compute a base subsidy amount per case by dividing the remainder by the total number of cases from all counties he approves for subsidy for the quarter. The quarterly subsidy voucher for each county shall then be the product of the base subsidy amount times the number of cases submitted by the county and approved for subsidy for the quarter. Payment shall be made to the clerk.

The clerk shall keep a record of all cases submitted for the subsidy in which the defendant was bound over to the court of common pleas from the municipal court. Upon receipt of the quarterly subsidy, the clerk shall pay to the clerk of the municipal court, for municipal court costs in such cases, an amount that does not exceed fifteen dollars per case, shall pay foreign sheriffs for their services, and shall deposit the remainder of the subsidy to the credit of the general fund of the county. The clerk of the court of common pleas then shall stamp his records "subsidy costs satisfied."

HISTORY: GC § 13455-8; 113 v 123(207), ch 34, § 8; Bureau of Code Revision, 10-1-53; 130 v 668 (Eff 10-14-63); 138 v H 204 (Eff 7-30-79); 139 v H 694 (Eff 11-15-81); 140 v H 291 (Eff 7-1-83); 140 v H 462 (Eff 3-28-85); 141 v H 201 (Eff 7-1-85); 142 v H 171. Eff 7-1-87.

§ 2949.20 Costs in case of reversal.

In any case of final judgment of reversal as provided in section 2953.07 of the Revised Code, whenever the state of Ohio is the appellee, the clerk of the court of common pleas of the county in which sentence was imposed shall certify the case to the state public defender for reimbursement in the report required by section 2949.19 of the Revised Code.

HISTORY: GC § 13455-9; 115 v 532, § 2; Bureau of Code Revision, 10-1-53; 138 v H 204 (Eff 7-30-79); 139 v H 694 (Eff 11-15-81); 140 v H 291. Eff 7-1-83.

[§ 2949.20.1] § 2949.201 Estimate of money needed for next biennium.

On or before the first day of February of even-numbered years, the state public defender shall report to the speaker and minority leader of the house of representatives, the president and minority leader of the senate, the office of budget and management, and the legislative budget office of the legislative service commission an estimate of the amount of money that will be required for the next fiscal biennium to make the payments required by section 2949.19 of the Revised Code.

HISTORY: 139 v H 694 (Eff 11-15-81); 140 v H 291. Eff 7-1-83.

[DEATH SENTENCE]

§ 2949.21 Conveyance to reception facility; assignment to institution.

A writ for the execution of the death penalty shall be directed to the sheriff by the court issuing it, and the sheriff, within thirty days and in a private manner, shall convey the prisoner to the facility designated by the director of rehabilitation and correction for the reception of the prisoner. For conducting the prisoner to the facility, the sheriff shall receive like fees and mileage as in other cases, when approved by the warden of the facility. After the procedures performed at the reception facility are completed, the prisoner shall be assigned to an appropriate correctional institution, conveyed to the institution, and kept within the institution until the execution of his sentence.

HISTORY: GC § 13456-1; 113 v 123(207), ch 35; Bureau of Code Revision, 10-1-53; 144 v S 359 (Eff 12-22-92); 145 v H 571. Eff 10-6-94.

§ 2949.22 Execution of death sentence.

(A) Except as provided in division (B)(1) of this section, a death sentence shall be executed by causing a current of electricity, of sufficient intensity to cause death, to pass through the body of the person upon whom the sentence was imposed. The application of the current shall be continued until the person upon whom the sentence was imposed is dead. The warden of the correctional institution in which the sentence is to be executed or another person selected by the director of rehabilitation and correction shall ensure that the death sentence is executed.

(B)(1) Any person sentenced to death may elect to be executed by lethal injection instead of by electrocution as described in division (A) of this section. The election shall be made no later than one week prior to the scheduled date of execution of the person by filing a written notice of the election with the department of rehabilitation and correction. If a person sentenced to death timely files with the department a written notice of an election to be executed by lethal injection, the person's death sentence shall be executed by causing the application to the person of a lethal injection of a drug or combination of drugs of sufficient dosage to quickly and painlessly cause death instead of by electrocution as described in division (A) of this section. The application of the drug or combination of drugs shall be continued until the person is dead. The warden of the correctional institution in which the sentence is to be executed or another person selected by the director of rehabilitation and correction shall ensure that the death sentence is executed.

If a person sentenced to death does not timely file with the department a written notice of election to be executed by lethal injection, his death sentence shall be executed by electrocution in accordance with division (A) of this section.

(2) Neither a person's timely filing of a written notice of election under division (B)(1) of this section nor a person's failure to file or timely file a written notice of election under that division shall affect or waive any right of appeal or postconviction relief that may be available under the laws of this state or the United States relative to the conviction for which the sentence of death was imposed upon the person or relative to the imposition or execution of that sentence of death.

(C) A death sentence shall be executed within the walls of the state correctional institution designated by the director of rehabilitation and correction as the location for executions, within an enclosure to be prepared for that purpose, under the direction of the warden of the institution or, in his absence, a deputy warden, and on the day designated by the judge passing sentence or otherwise designated by a court in the course of any appellate or postconviction proceedings. The enclosure shall exclude public view.

(D) If a death sentence is required to be executed by lethal injection because the person sentenced to death elected to be executed by lethal injection pursuant to division (B)(1) of this section and if the execution of a death sentence by lethal injection is determined to be unconstitutional, the death sentence shall be executed by causing a current of electricity, of sufficient intensity to cause death, to pass through the body of the person upon whom the sentence was imposed. The application of the current shall be continued until the person is dead. The warden of the state correctional institution in which the sentence is to be executed or another person selected by the director of rehabilitation and correction shall ensure that the death sentence is executed.

(E) No change in the law made by this amendment constitutes a declaration by or belief of the general assembly that execution of a death sentence by electrocution is a cruel and unusual punishment proscribed by the Ohio Constitution or the United States Constitution.

HISTORY: GC § 13456-2; 113 v 123(208), ch 35, § 2; Bureau of Code Revision, 10-1-53; 144 v S 359 (Eff 12-22-92); 145 v H 11 (Eff 10-1-93); 145 v H 571. Eff 10-6-94.

§ 2949.23 Repealed, 144 v S 359, § 2 [GC § 13456-3; 113 v 123(208), ch 35, § 3; Bureau of Code Revision, 10-1-53]. Eff 12-22-92.

This section concerned time of execution. See now section 2949.22.

§ 2949.24 Execution and return of warrant.

Unless a suspension of execution is ordered by the court of appeals in which the cause is pending on appeal or the supreme court for a case in which a sentence of death is imposed for an offense committed before January 1, 1995, or by the supreme court for a case in which a sentence of death is imposed for an offense committed on or after January 1, 1995, or is ordered by two judges or four justices of that court, the warden or another person selected by the director of rehabilitation and correction shall proceed at the time and place named in the warrant to ensure that the death sentence of the prisoner under death sentence is executed in accordance with section 2949.22 of the Revised Code. The warden shall make the return to the clerk of the court of common pleas of the county immediately from which the prisoner was sentenced of the manner of the execution of the warrant. The clerk shall record the warrant and the return in the records of the case.

HISTORY: GC § 13456-4; 113 v 123(208), ch 35, § 4; Bureau of Code Revision, 10-1-53; 144 v S 359 (Eff 12-22-92); 146 v S 4. Eff 9-21-95.

§ 2949.25 Attendance at execution.

(A) At the execution of a death sentence, only the following persons may be present:
(1) The warden of the state correctional institution in which the sentence is executed or a deputy warden, any other person selected by the director of rehabilitation and correction to ensure that the death sentence is executed, any persons necessary to execute the death sentence by electrocution or lethal injection, and the number of correction officers that the warden thinks necessary;
(2) The sheriff of the county in which the prisoner was tried and convicted;
(3) The director of rehabilitation and correction, or his agent;
(4) Physicians of the state correctional institution in which the sentence is executed;
(5) The clergyman in attendance upon the prisoner, and not more than three other persons, to be designated by the prisoner, who are not confined in any state institution;
(6) Not more than three persons to be designated by the immediate family of the victim;
(7) Representatives of the news media as authorized by the director of rehabilitation and correction.

(B) The director shall authorize at least one representative of a newspaper, at least one representative of a television station, and at least one representative of a radio station to be present at the execution of the sentence under division (A)(7) of this section.

HISTORY: GC § 13456-5; 113 v 123(208), ch 35, § 5; Bureau of Code Revision, 10-1-53; 125 v S 155 (Eff 7-1-54); 134 v H 494 (Eff 7-12-72); 144 v S 359 (Eff 12-22-92); 145 v H 11 (Eff 10-1-93); 145 v H 571. Eff 10-6-94.

§ 2949.26 Disposition of body of executed convict.

The body of an executed convict shall be returned for burial in any county of the state, to friends who made written request therefor, if made to the warden the day before or on the morning of the execution. The warden may pay the transportation and other funeral expenses, not to exceed fifty dollars.

If no request is made by such friends therefor, such body shall be disposed of as provided by section 1713.34 of the Revised Code and the rules of the department of human services.

HISTORY: GC § 13456-6; 113 v 123(208), ch 35, § 6; Bureau of Code Revision, 10-1-53; 141 v H 201. Eff 7-1-85.

§ 2949.27 Escape, rearrest, and execution.

If a convicted felon escapes after sentence of death, and is not retaken before the time fixed for his execution, any sheriff may rearrest and commit him to the county jail, and make return thereof to the court in which the sentence was passed. Such court shall again fix the time for execution, which shall be carried into effect as provided in sections 2949.21 to 2949.26, inclusive, of the Revised Code.

HISTORY: GC § 13456-7; 113 v 123(209), ch 35, § 7; Bureau of Code Revision. Eff 10-1-53.

§ 2949.28 Convict insane.

If a convict sentenced to death appears to be insane, the warden or the sheriff having custody of such convict shall give notice thereof to a judge of the court of common pleas of the county in which the prisoner is confined. Said judge shall inquire into such insanity at a time and place to be fixed by said judge, or impanel a jury for that purpose and shall give immediate notice thereof to the prosecuting attorney of the county in which the prisoner was convicted. Execution of the sentence shall be suspended pending completion of the inquiry.

HISTORY: GC § 13456-8; 113 v 123(209), ch 35, § 8; Bureau of Code Revision, 10-1-53; 133 v S 354. Eff 11-18-69.

§ 2949.29 Proceedings on the insanity inquiry.

In addition to the warden or sheriff, the judge of the court of common pleas, clerk of the court of common pleas, and prosecuting attorney shall attend the inquiry commenced as provided in section 2949.28 of the Revised Code. Witnesses may be produced and examined before the judge or jury, and all findings shall be in writing signed by the judge or jury. If it is found that the convict is not insane, the sentence shall be executed at the time previously appointed, unless such time has passed pending completion of the inquiry, in which case the judge conducting the inquiry shall appoint a time for execution. If it is found that the convict is insane, the judge shall suspend the execution until the warden or sheriff receives a warrant from the governor directing such execution as provided in section 2949.30 of the Revised Code. The finding, and the order of such judge, certified by him, shall be entered on the journal of the court by the clerk.

HISTORY: GC § 13456-9; 113 v 123(209), ch 35, § 9; Bureau of Code Revision, 10-1-53; 133 v S 354. Eff 11-18-69.

§ 2949.30 When convict restored, governor to order execution.

If a convict under sentence of death is found insane under section 2949.29 of the Revised Code, and if he is subsequently restored, the warden or sheriff having custody of such convict shall forthwith transmit a copy of the finding of restoration to the governor, who, when convinced that the convict is of sound mind, shall issue a warrant appointing a time for his execution.

HISTORY: GC § 13456-10; 113 v 123(209), ch 35, § 10; Bureau of Code Revision, 10-1-53; 130 v 669. Eff 9-27-63.

§ 2949.31 Pregnant prisoners.

If a female convict sentenced to death appears to be pregnant, the warden or sheriff having custody of such convict shall give notice thereof to a judge of the court of common pleas of the county in which the prisoner is confined, and like proceedings shall be had as are provided under sections 2949.28 and 2949.29 of the Revised Code in case of an insane convict sentenced to death.

HISTORY: GC § 13456-11; 113 v 123(209), ch 35, § 11; Bureau of Code Revision. Eff 10-1-53.

§ 2949.32 When execution to be ordered.

If a jury, impaneled as provided in section 2949.28 of the Revised Code in the case of a convict who appears to be insane, finds that a female convict under sentence of death is not with child, the sentence shall be executed at the time previously appointed, unless such time has passed pending completion of the inquiry, in which case the judge conducting the inquiry shall appoint a time for execution. If the jury finds that such female convict is with child, the judge conducting the inquiry shall suspend the execution of her sentence and transmit such finding to the governor, who, when satisfied that such convict is no longer pregnant, shall issue a warrant appointing a time for her execution.

HISTORY: GC § 13456-12; 113 v 123(209), ch 35, § 12; Bureau of Code Revision, 10-1-53; 133 v S 354. Eff 11-18-69.

§§ 2949.33, 2949.34 Repealed, 135 v H 716, § 2 [GC §§ 13457-1, 13457-2; 113 v 123; Bureau of Code Revision, 10-1-53; 133 v S 460]. Eff 1-1-74.

These sections determined when cumulative sentence may be imposed and established sentencing of habitual offenders.

§§ 2949.35, 2949.36 Repealed, 135 v H 716, § 2 [GC §§ 13457-3, 13457-4; 113 v 123; Bureau of Code Revision, 10-1-53]. Eff 1-1-74.

These sections outlined exemptions for convictions under RC §§ 2949.33 and 2949.34, and provided for parole from workhouse.

CHAPTER 2950: SEXUAL PREDATORS, HABITUAL SEX OFFENDERS, SEXUALLY ORIENTED OFFENDERS

Section
2950.01 Definitions.
2950.02 Legislative determinations and intent to provide information to protect public safety.
2950.03 Notice to offender of duty to register and update address.
2950.04 Duty to register.
2950.05 Notice of change of address; registration of new address.
2950.06 Periodic verification of current address.
2950.07 Commencement of duty to register; duration.
2950.08 Persons authorized to inspect information and records.
2950.09 Classification as sexual predator; determination hearing; petition for removal from classification.
2950.10 Notice to victim of offender's registration or change of information.
2950.11 Persons to be notified within geographical area.
2950.12 Immunity.
2950.13 Duties of attorney general.
2950.14 Information to be provided to Bureau of Criminal Identification and Investigation prior to release.
2950.99 Penalty.

§ 2950.01 Definitions.

As used in this chapter, unless the context clearly requires otherwise:

(A) "Confinement" includes, but is not limited to, a community residential sanction imposed pursuant to section 2929.16 of the Revised Code.

(B) "Habitual sex offender" means a person who is convicted of or pleads guilty to a sexually oriented offense and who previously has been convicted of or pleaded guilty to one or more sexually oriented offenses.

(C) "Prosecutor" has the same meaning as in section 2935.01 of the Revised Code.

(D) "Sexually oriented offense" means any of the following offenses:

(1) Regardless of the age of the victim of the offense, a violation of section 2907.02, 2907.03, 2907.05, or 2907.12 of the Revised Code;

(2) Any of the following offenses involving a minor, in the circumstances specified:

(a) A violation of section 2905.01, 2905.02, 2905.03, 2905.04, 2905.05, or 2907.04 of the Revised Code when the victim of the offense is under eighteen years of age;

(b) A violation of section 2907.21 of the Revised Code when the person who is compelled, induced, procured, encouraged, solicited, requested, or facilitated to engage in, paid or agreed to be paid for, or allowed to engage in the sexual activity in question is under eighteen years of age;

(c) A violation of division (A)(1) or (3) of section 2907.321 [2907.32.1] or 2907.322 [2907.32.2] of the Revised Code;

(d) A violation of division (A)(1) or (2) of section 2907.323 [2907.32.3] of the Revised Code;

(e) A violation of division (B)(5) of section 2919.22 of the Revised Code when the child who is involved in the offense is under eighteen years of age.

(3) Regardless of the age of the victim of the offense, a violation of section 2903.01, 2903.02, 2903.11, or 2905.01 of the Revised Code, or of division (A) of section 2903.04 of the Revised Code, that is committed with a purpose to gratify the sexual needs or desires of the offender;

(4) A sexually violent offense;

(5) A violation of any former law of this state that was substantially equivalent to any offense listed in division (D)(1), (2), (3), or (4) of this section;

(6) A violation of an existing or former municipal ordinance or law of another state or the United States, or a violation under the law applicable in a military court, that is or was substantially equivalent to any offense listed in division (D)(1), (2), (3), or (4) of this section;

(7) An attempt to commit, conspiracy to commit, or complicity in committing any offense listed in division (D)(1), (2), (3), (4), (5), or (6) of this section.

(E) "Sexual predator" means a person who has been convicted of or pleaded guilty to committing a sexually oriented offense and is likely to engage in the future in one or more sexually oriented offenses.

(F) "Supervised release" means a release from a prison term, a term of imprisonment, or another type of confinement that satisfies either of the following conditions:

(1) The release is on parole, a conditional pardon, or probation, under a furlough, or under a post-release control sanction, and it requires the person to report to or be supervised by a parole officer, probation officer, field officer, or another type of supervising officer.

(2) The release is any type of release that is not described in division (F)(1) of this section and that requires the person to report to or be supervised by a probation officer, a parole officer, a field officer, or another type of supervising officer.

(G) An offender is "adjudicated as being a sexual predator" if any of the following applies:

(1) The offender is convicted of or pleads guilty to committing, on or after the effective date of this section, a sexually oriented offense that is a sexually violent offense and also is convicted of or pleads guilty to a sexually violent predator specification that was included in the indictment, count in the indictment, or information that charged the sexually violent offense.

(2) Regardless of when the sexually oriented offense was committed, on or after the effective date of this section, the offender is sentenced for a sexually oriented offense, and the sentencing judge determines pursuant to division (B) of section 2950.09 of the Revised Code that the offender is a sexual predator.

(3) Prior to the effective date of this section, the offender was convicted of or pleaded guilty to, and was sentenced for, a sexually oriented offense, the offender is imprisoned in a state correctional institution on or after the effective date of this section, and, prior to the offender's release from imprisonment, the court determines pursuant to division (C) of section 2950.09 of the Revised Code that the offender is a sexual predator.

(H) "Sexually violent predator specification" and "sexually violent offense" have the same meanings as in section 2971.01 of the Revised Code.

HISTORY: 146 v H 180. Eff 1-1-97.

Analogous to former RC § 2950.01 (130 v 669; 134 v H 511), repealed 146 v H 180, § 2, eff 1-1-97.

The effective date is set by § 3 of HB 180.

See provisions, § 5 of HB 180 (146 v —) following RC § 2935.36.

§ 2950.02 Legislative determinations and intent to provide information to protect public safety.

(A) The general assembly hereby determines and declares that it recognizes and finds all of the following:

(1) If the public is provided adequate notice and information about sexual predators, habitual sex offenders, and certain other offenders who commit sexually oriented offenses, members of the public and communities can develop constructive plans to prepare themselves and their children for the sexual predator's, habitual sex offender's, or other offender's release from imprisonment, a prison term, or other confinement. This allows members of the public and communities to meet with members of law enforcement agencies to prepare and obtain information about the rights and responsibilities of the public and the communities and to provide education and counseling to their children.

(2) Sexual predators and habitual sex offenders pose a high risk of engaging in further offenses even after being released from imprisonment, a prison term, or other confinement and that protection of members of the public from sexual predators and habitual sex offenders is a paramount governmental interest.

(3) The penal and mental health components of the justice system of this state are largely hidden from public view, and a lack of information from either component may result in the failure of both systems to satisfy this paramount governmental interest of public safety described in division (A)(2) of this section.

(4) Overly restrictive confidentiality and liability laws governing the release of information about sexual predators and habitual sex offenders have reduced the willingness to release information that could be appropriately released under the public disclosure laws and have increased risks of public safety.

(5) A person who is found to be a sexual predator or a habitual sex offender has a reduced expectation of privacy because of the public's interest in public safety and in the effective operation of government.

(6) The release of information about sexual predators and habitual sex offenders to public agencies and the general public will further the governmental interests of public safety and public scrutiny of the criminal and mental health systems as long as the information released is rationally related to the furtherance of those goals.

(B) The general assembly hereby declares that, in providing in this chapter for registration regarding sexual predators, habitual sex offenders, and offenders who have committed sexually oriented offenses and for community notification regarding sexual predators and habitual sex offenders who are about to be or have been released from imprisonment, a prison term, or other confinement and who will live in or near a particular neighborhood or who otherwise will live in or near a particular neighborhood, it is the general assembly's intent to protect the safety and general welfare of the people of this state. The general assembly further declares that it is the policy of this state to require the exchange in accordance with this chapter of relevant information about sexual predators and habitual sex offenders among public agencies and officials and to authorize the release in accordance with this chapter of necessary and relevant information about sexual predators and habitual sex offenders to members of the general public as a means of assuring public protection and that the exchange or release of that information is not punitive.

HISTORY: 146 v H 180. Eff 7-1-97.

Analogous to former RC § 2950.02 (130 v 669), repealed 146 v H 180, § 2, eff 7-1-97.

The effective date is set by § 5 of HB 180.

See provisions, § 5 of HB 180 (146 v —) following RC § 2935.36.

§ 2950.03 Notice to offender of duty to register and update address.

(A) Each person who has been convicted of, is convicted of, has pleaded guilty to, or pleads guilty to a sexually oriented offense and who has a duty to register pursuant to section 2950.04 of the Revised Code shall be provided notice in accordance with this section of the offender's duty to register under that section, the offender's duty to provide notice of any change in the offender's residence address and to register the new residence address pursuant to section 2950.05 of the Revised Code, and the offender's duty to periodically verify the offender's residence address pursuant to section 2950.06 of the Revised Code. The following official shall provide the notice to the offender at the following time:

(1) Regardless of when the offender committed the sexually oriented offense, if the offender is sentenced for the sexually oriented offense to a prison term, a term

of imprisonment, or any other type of confinement, and if, on or after the effective date of this section, the offender is serving that term or is under that confinement, the official in charge of the jail, workhouse, state correctional institution, or other institution in which the offender serves the prison term, term of imprisonment, or confinement, or a designee of that official, shall provide the notice to the offender at least ten days before the offender is released pursuant to any type of supervised release or at least ten days before the offender otherwise is released from the prison term, term of imprisonment, or confinement.

(2) Regardless of when the offender committed the sexually oriented offense, if the offender is sentenced for that offense on or after the effective date of this section and if division (A)(1) of this section does not apply, the judge shall provide the notice to the offender at the time of sentencing.

(3) If the offender committed the sexually oriented offense prior to the effective date of this section, if neither division (A)(1) nor division (A)(2) of this section applies, and if, immediately prior to the effective date of this section, the offender was a habitual sex offender who was required to register under Chapter 2950. of the Revised Code, the chief of police or sheriff with whom the offender most recently registered under that chapter, in the circumstances described in this division, shall provide the notice to the offender. If the offender has registered with a chief of police or sheriff under Chapter 2950. of the Revised Code as it existed prior to the effective date of this section, the chief of police or sheriff with whom the offender most recently registered shall provide the notice to the offender as soon as possible after the effective date of this section, as described in division (B)(1) of this section. If the offender has not registered with a chief of police or sheriff under that chapter, the failure to register shall constitute a waiver by the offender of any right to notice under this section. If an offender described in this division does not receive notice under this section, the offender is not relieved of the duty to register, the duty to provide notice of any change in residence address and to register the new residence address, and the duty to periodically verify the residence address, as described in division (A) of this section.

(B)(1) The notice provided under division (A) of this section shall inform the offender of the offender's duty to register under section 2950.04 of the Revised Code, to notify the appropriate officials of a change in the offender's residence address and to register the new residence address in accordance with section 2950.05 of the Revised Code, and to periodically verify a residence address under section 2950.06 of the Revised Code. The notice shall comport with the following:

(a) If the notice is provided under division (A)(3) of this section, the notice shall be on a form that is prescribed by the bureau of criminal identification and investigation and that states the offender's duties to register, to register a new residence address, and to periodically verify a residence address and that, if the offender has any questions concerning these duties, the offender may contact the chief of police or sheriff who sent the form for an explanation of the duties. If the offender appears in person before the chief of police or sheriff, the chief or sheriff shall provide the notice as described in division (B)(1)(a) of this section, and all provisions of this section that apply regarding a notice provided by an official, official's designee, or judge in that manner shall be applicable.

(b) If the notice is provided under division (A)(1) or (2) of this section, the official, official's designee, or judge shall require the offender to read and sign a form prescribed by the bureau of criminal identification and investigation, stating that the offender's duties to register, to register a new residence address, and to periodically verify a residence address have been explained to the offender. If the offender is unable to read, the official, official's designee, or judge shall certify on the form that the official, designee, or judge specifically informed the offender of those duties and that the offender indicated an understanding of those duties.

(c) For a notice provided under division (A)(1), (2), or (3) of this section, the form used shall contain all of the information required by the bureau of criminal identification and investigation, including, but not limited to, a statement as to whether the offender has been adjudicated as being a sexual predator relative to the sexually oriented offense in question, a statement as to whether the offender has been determined to be a habitual sex offender, an explanation of the periodic residence address verification process and of the frequency with which the offender will be required to verify the residence address under that process, and a statement that the offender must verify the residence address at the times specified under that process or face criminal prosecution.

(2) After an offender described in division (A)(1) or (2) of this section has signed the form described in division (B)(1) of this section or the official, official's designee, or judge has certified on it that it has been explained to the offender and that the offender indicated an understanding of the duties indicated on it, the official, official's designee, or judge shall give one copy of the form to the offender, within three days shall send one copy of the form to the bureau of criminal identification and investigation in accordance with the procedures adopted pursuant to section 2950.13 of the Revised Code, and shall send one copy of the form to the sheriff of the county in which the offender expects to reside. After a chief of police or sheriff has sent a form to an offender under division (A)(3) of this section, the chief or sheriff shall send a copy of the form to the bureau of criminal identification and investigation in accordance with the procedures adopted pursuant to section 2950.13 of the Revised Code.

(C) The official, official's designee, judge, chief of

police, or sheriff who is required to provide notice to an offender under division (A) of this section shall do all of the following:

(1) If the notice is provided under division (A)(1) or (2) of this section, the official, designee, or judge shall determine the offender's name, identifying factors, and expected future residence address, shall obtain the offender's criminal history from the bureau of criminal identification and investigation, and shall obtain a photograph and the fingerprints of the offender. The official, official's designee, or judge shall obtain this information and these items prior to giving the notice, except that a judge may give the notice prior to obtaining the offender's criminal history from the bureau. Within three days after receiving this information and these items, the official, official's designee, or judge shall forward the information and items to the bureau of criminal identification in accordance with the forwarding procedures adopted pursuant to section 2950.13 of the Revised Code and to the sheriff of the county in which the offender expects to reside. If it has not already done so, the bureau of criminal identification and investigation shall forward a copy of the fingerprints and conviction data received under this division to the federal bureau of investigation.

(2) If the notice is provided under division (A)(3) of this section, the chief of police or sheriff shall determine the offender's name, identifying factors, and residence address, shall obtain the offender's criminal history from the bureau of criminal identification and investigation, and, to the extent possible, shall obtain a photograph and the fingerprints of the offender. Within three days after receiving this information and these items, the chief or sheriff shall forward the information and items to the bureau of criminal identification and investigation in accordance with the forwarding procedures adopted pursuant to section 2950.13 of the Revised Code and, in relation to a chief of police, to the sheriff of the county in which the offender resides. If it has not already done so, the bureau of criminal identification and investigation shall forward a copy of the fingerprints and conviction data so received to the federal bureau of investigation.

HISTORY: 146 v H 180. Eff 1-1-97.

Not analogous to former RC § 2950.03 (130 v 670; 145 v H 571), repealed 146 v H 180, § 2, eff 1-1-97.

The effective date is set by section 3 of HB 180.

See provisions, § 5 of HB 180 (146 v —) following RC § 2935.36.

§ 2950.04 Duty to register.

(A) Each offender who is convicted of or pleads guilty to, or has been convicted of or pleaded guilty to, a sexually oriented offense and who is described in division (A)(1), (2), or (3) of this section shall register at the following time and with the following official:

(1) Regardless of when the sexually oriented offense was committed, if the offender is sentenced for the sexually oriented offense to a prison term, a term of imprisonment, or any other type of confinement and if, on or after the effective date of this section, the offender is released in any manner from the prison term, term of imprisonment, or confinement, within seven days of the offender's coming into any county in which the offender resides or temporarily is domiciled for more than seven days, the offender shall register with the sheriff of that county.

(2) Regardless of when the sexually oriented offense was committed, if the offender is sentenced for a sexually oriented offense on or after the effective date of this section and if division (A)(1) of this section does not apply, within seven days of the offender's coming into any county in which the offender resides or temporarily is domiciled for more than seven days, the offender shall register with the sheriff of that county.

(3) If the sexually oriented offense was committed prior to the effective date of this section, if neither division (A)(1) nor division (A)(2) of this section applies, and if, immediately prior to the effective date of this section, the offender was a habitual sex offender who was required to register under Chapter 2950. of the Revised Code, within seven days of the offender's coming into any county in which the offender resides or temporarily is domiciled for more than seven days, the offender shall register with the sheriff of that county.

(B) An offender who is required by division (A) of this section to register personally shall obtain from the sheriff or from a designee of the sheriff a registration form that conforms to division (C) of this section, shall complete and sign the form, and shall return the completed form together with the offender's photograph to the sheriff or the designee. The sheriff or designee shall sign the form and indicate on the form the date on which it is so returned. The registration required under this division is complete when the offender returns the form, containing the requisite information, photograph, signatures, and date, to the sheriff or designee.

(C) The registration form to be used under divisions (A) and (B) of this section shall contain the current residence address of the offender who is registering, the name and address of the offender's employer, if the offender is employed at the time of registration or if the offender knows at the time of registration that the offender will be commencing employment with that employer subsequent to registration, and any other information required by the bureau of criminal identification and investigation and shall include the offender's photograph. Additionally, if the offender has been adjudicated as being a sexual predator relative to the sexually oriented offense in question and the court has not subsequently determined pursuant to division (D) of section 2950.09 of the Revised Code that the offender no longer is a sexual predator or if the sentencing judge determined pursuant to division (C) of section 2950.09 of the Revised Code that the offender is a habitual sex offender, the offender shall include on the signed, written registration form all of the following information:

(1) A specific declaration that the person has been adjudicated as being a sexual predator or has been determined to be a habitual sex offender, whichever is applicable;

(2) If the offender has been adjudicated as being a sexual predator, the identification license plate number of each motor vehicle the offender owns and of each motor vehicle registered in the offender's name.

(D) After an offender registers with a sheriff pursuant to this section, the sheriff shall forward the signed, written registration form and photograph to the bureau of criminal identification and investigation in accordance with the forwarding procedures adopted pursuant to section 2950.13 of the Revised Code. The bureau shall include the information and materials forwarded to it under this division in the state registry of sex offenders established and maintained under section 2950.13 of the Revised Code.

(E) No person who is required to register pursuant to divisions (A) and (B) of this section shall fail to register as required in accordance with those divisions or that division.

(F) An offender who is required to register pursuant to divisions (A) and (B) of this section shall register pursuant to this section for the period of time specified in section 2950.07 of the Revised Code.

HISTORY: 146 v H 180. Eff 7-1-97.

Not analogous to former RC § 2950.04 (130 v 670), repealed 146 v H 180, § 2, eff 7-1-97.

The effective date is set by section 5 of HB 180.

See provisions, § 5 of HB 180 (146 v —) following RC § 2935.36.

§ 2950.05 Notice of change of address; registration of new address.

(A) If an offender is required to register pursuant to section 2950.04 of the Revised Code, the offender, at least seven days prior to changing the offender's residence address during the period during which the offender is required to register, shall provide written notice of the residence address change to the sheriff with whom the offender most recently registered under section 2950.04 of the Revised Code or under division (B) of this section.

(B) If an offender is required to provide notice of a residence address change under division (A) of this section, the offender, at least seven days prior to changing the residence address, also shall register the new residence address in the manner described in divisions (B) and (C) of section 2950.04 of the Revised Code with the sheriff of the county in which the offender's new residence address is located, subject to division (C) of this section.

(C) Divisions (A) and (B) of this section apply to a person who is required to register pursuant to section 2950.04 of the Revised Code regardless of whether the new residence address is in this state or in another state. If the new residence address is in another state, the person shall register with the appropriate law enforcement officials in that state in the manner required under the law of that state and within the earlier of the period of time required under the law of that state or at least seven days prior to changing the residence address.

(D)(1) Upon receiving from an offender pursuant to division (A) of this section notice of a change of the offender's residence address, a sheriff promptly shall forward the new residence address to the bureau of criminal identification and investigation in accordance with the forwarding procedures adopted pursuant to section 2950.13 of the Revised Code if the new residence address is in another state or, if the offender's new residence address is located in another county in this state, to the sheriff of that county. The bureau shall include all information forwarded to it under this division in the state registry of sex offenders established and maintained under section 2950.13 of the Revised Code and shall forward notice of the offender's new residence address to the appropriate officials in the other state.

(2) When an offender registers a new residence address pursuant to division (B) of this section, the sheriff with whom the offender registers and the bureau of criminal identification and investigation shall comply with division (D) of section 2950.04 of the Revised Code.

(E)(1) No person who is required to notify a sheriff of a change of address pursuant to division (A) of this section shall fail to notify the appropriate sheriff in accordance with that division.

(2) No person who is required to register a new residence address with a sheriff or with an official of another state pursuant to divisions (B) and (C) of this section shall fail to register with the appropriate sheriff or official of the other state in accordance with those divisions.

(F) An offender who is required to comply with divisions (A), (B), and (C) of this section shall do so for the period of time specified in section 2950.07 of the Revised Code.

HISTORY: 146 v H 180. Eff 7-1-97.

Analogous to former RC § 2950.05 (130 v 671), repealed 146 v H 180, § 2, eff 7-1-97.

The effective date is set by section 5 of HB 180.

See provisions, § 5 of HB 180 (146 v —) following RC § 2935.36.

§ 2950.06 Periodic verification of current address.

(A) An offender who is required to register pursuant to section 2950.04 of the Revised Code shall periodically verify the offender's current residence address in accordance with this section. The frequency of verification shall be determined in accordance with division (B) of this section, and the manner of verification shall be determined in accordance with division (C) of this section.

(B) The frequency with which an offender must verify the offender's current residence address pursuant to division (A) of this section shall be determined as follows:

(1) Regardless of when the sexually oriented offense for which the offender is required to register was committed, if the offender has been adjudicated as being a sexual predator relative to the sexually oriented offense and if the court has not subsequently entered a determination pursuant to division (D) of section 2950.09 of the Revised Code that the offender no longer is a sexual predator, the offender shall verify the offender's current residence address in accordance with division (C) of this section every ninety days after the offender's initial registration date during the period the offender is required to register.

(2) In all circumstances not described in division (B)(1) of this section, the offender shall verify the offender's current residence address in accordance with division (C) of this section on each anniversary of the offender's initial registration date during the period the offender is required to register.

(C)(1) An offender who is required to verify the offender's current residence address pursuant to division (A) of this section shall verify the address with the sheriff with whom the offender most recently registered by personally appearing before the sheriff or a designee of the sheriff, no earlier than ten days before the date on which the verification is required pursuant to division (B) of this section and no later than the date so required for verification, and completing and signing a copy of the verification form prescribed by the bureau of criminal identification and investigation. The sheriff or designee shall sign the completed form and indicate on the form the date on which it is so completed. The verification required under this division is complete when the offender personally appears before the sheriff or designee and completes and signs the form as described in this division.

(2) To facilitate the verification of an offender's current residence address under division (C)(1) of this section, the sheriff with whom the offender most recently registered may mail a nonforwardable verification form prescribed by the bureau of criminal identification and investigation to the offender's last reported address, with a notice that consciously states that the offender must personally appear before the sheriff or a designee of the sheriff to complete the form and the date by which the form must be so completed. Regardless of whether a sheriff mails a form to an offender, each offender who is required to verify the offender's current residence address pursuant to division (A) of this section shall personally appear before the sheriff or a designee of the sheriff to verify the address in accordance with division (D)(1)† of this section.

(D) The verification form to be used under division (C) of this section shall contain the current residence address of the offender, the name and address of the offender's employer if the offender is employed at the time of verification or if the offender knows at the time of verification that the offender will be commencing employment with that employer subsequent to verification, and any other information required by the bureau of criminal identification and investigation.

(E) Upon an offender's personal appearance and completion of a verification form under division (C) of this section, a sheriff promptly shall forward a copy of the verification form to the bureau of criminal identification and investigation in accordance with the forwarding procedures adopted by the attorney general pursuant to section 2950.13 of the Revised Code. The bureau shall include all information forwarded to it under this division in the state registry of sex offenders established and maintained under section 2950.13 of the Revised Code.

(F) No person who is required to verify a current residence address pursuant to divisions (A) to (C) of this section shall fail to verify a current residence address in accordance with those divisions by the date required for the verification as set forth in division (B) of this section, provided that no person shall be prosecuted for a violation of this division prior to the expiration of the period of time specified in division (G) of this section.

(G)(1) If an offender fails to verify a current residence address as required by divisions (A) to (C) of this section by the date required for the verification as set forth in division (B) of this section, the sheriff with whom the offender is required to verify the current residence address, on the day following that date required for the verification, shall send a written warning to the offender, at the offender's last known residence address, regarding the offender's duty to verify the offender's current residence address. The written warning shall identify the sheriff who sends it and the date on which it is sent and shall state conspicuously that the offender has failed to verify the offender's current residence address by the date required for the verification, that the offender has seven days from the date on which the warning is sent to verify the current residence address with the sheriff who sent the warning, that a failure to timely verify the current residence address is a felony offense, that, if the offender verifies the current residence address with that sheriff within that seven-day-period, the offender will not be prosecuted for a failure to timely verify a current residence address, and that, if the offender does not verify the current residence address with that sheriff within that seven-day-period, the offender will be arrested and prosecuted for a failure to timely verify a current residence address.

(2) If an offender fails to verify a current residence address as required by divisions (A) to (C) of this section by the date required for the verification as set forth in

division (B) of this section, the offender shall not be prosecuted for a violation of division (F) of this section unless the seven-day-period subsequent to that date that the offender is provided under division (G)(1) of this section to verify the current residence address has expired and the offender, prior to the expiration of that seven-day-period, has not verified the current residence address. Upon the expiration of the seven-day-period that the offender is provided under division (G)(1) of this section to verify the current residence address has expired, if the offender has not verified the current residence, all of the following apply:

(a) The sheriff with whom the offender is required to verify the current residence address promptly shall notify the bureau of criminal identification and investigation of the failure.

(b) The sheriff with whom the offender is required to verify the current residence address, the sheriff of the county in which the offender resides, or a deputy of the appropriate sheriff, shall locate the offender, promptly shall seek a warrant for the arrest of the offender for the violation of division (F) of this section and shall arrest the offender.

(c) The offender is subject to prosecution for the violation of division (F) of this section.

(H) A person who is required to verify the person's current residence address pursuant to divisions (A) to (C) of this section shall do so for the period of time specified in section 2950.07 of the Revised Code.

HISTORY: 146 v H 180. Eff 7-1-97.

Not analogous to former RC § 2950.06 (130 v 671), repealed 146 v H 180, § 2, eff 7-1-97.

The effective date is set by section 5 of HB 180.

See provisions, § 5 of HB 180 (146 v —) following RC § 2935.36.

† So in enrolled bill. Was (C) intended?

§ 2950.07 Commencement of duty to register; duration.

(A) The duty of an offender who is convicted of or pleads guilty to, or has been convicted of or pleaded guilty to, a sexually oriented offense to comply with sections 2950.04, 2950.05, and 2950.06 of the Revised Code commences on whichever of the following dates is applicable:

(1) If the offender's duty to register is imposed pursuant to division (A)(1) of section 2950.04 of the Revised Code, the offender's duty to comply with those sections commences on the date of the offender's release from a prison term, a term of imprisonment, or any other type of confinement or on the effective date of this section, whichever is later.

(2) If the offender's duty to register is imposed pursuant to division (A)(2) of section 2950.04 of the Revised Code, the offender's duty to comply with those sections commences on the date of entry of the judgment of conviction of the sexually oriented offense or on the effective date of this section, whichever is later.

(3) If the offender's duty to register is imposed pursuant to division (A)(3) of section 2950.04 of the Revised Code, the offender's duty to comply with those sections commences fourteen days after the effective date of this section.

(B) The duty of an offender who is convicted of or pleads guilty to, or has been convicted of or pleads guilty to, a sexually oriented offense to comply with sections 2950.04, 2950.05, and 2950.06 of the Revised Code continues, after the date of commencement, for whichever of the following periods is applicable:

(1) Except as otherwise provided in this division, if the offender has been adjudicated as being a sexual predator relative to the sexually oriented offense, the offender's duty to comply with those sections continues until the offender's death. If the judge who sentenced the offender or that judge's successor in office subsequently enters a determination pursuant to division (D) of section 2950.09 of the Revised Code that the offender no longer is a sexual predator, the offender's duty to comply with those sections continues for the period of time that otherwise would have been applicable to the offender under division (B)(2) or (3) of this section.

(2) If the judge who sentenced the offender for the sexually oriented offense determined pursuant to division (E) of section 2950.09 of the Revised Code that the offender is a habitual sex offender, the offender's duty to comply with those sections continues for twenty years.

(3) If neither division (B)(1) nor (B)(2) of this section applies, the offender's duty to comply with those sections continues for ten years.

(C) If an offender has been convicted of or pleaded guilty to a sexually oriented offense and if the offender subsequently is convicted of or pleads guilty to another sexually oriented offense, the period of time for which the offender must comply with the sections specified in division (A) of this section shall be separately calculated pursuant to divisions (A)(1), (2), and (3) of this section for each of the sexually oriented offenses, and the separately calculated periods of time shall be complied with independently.

HISTORY: 146 v H 180. Eff 7-1-97.

Not analogous to former RC § 2950.07 (130 v 671), repealed 146 v H 180, § 2, eff 7-1-97.

The effective date is set by section 5 of HB 180.

See provisions, § 5 of HB 180 (146 v —) following RC § 2935.36.

§ 2950.08 Persons authorized to inspect information and records.

The statements, information, photographs, and fingerprints required by sections 2950.04, 2950.05, and 2950.06 of the Revised Code and provided by a person who registers, who provides notice of a change of residence address and registers the new residence address, or who provides verification of a current residence address pursuant to those sections and that are in the possession of the bureau of criminal identification and investigation and the information in the possession of the bureau that was received by the bureau pursuant to section 2950.14 of the Revised Code shall not be open to inspection by the public or by any person other than the following persons:

(A) A regularly employed peace officer or other law enforcement officer;

(B) An authorized employee of the bureau of criminal identification and investigation for the purpose of providing information to a board, administrator, or person pursuant to division (F) or (G) of section 109.57 of the Revised Code.

HISTORY: 130 v 671 (Eff 10-4-63); 143 v S 140 (Eff 10-2-89); 146 v S 160 (Eff 1-27-97); 146 v H 180. Eff 7-1-97.

The effective date is set by section 5 of HB 180.

Comment, Legislative Service Commission

° ° ° Section 2950.08 of the Revised Code is amended by this act [Am. Sub. S.B. 160] and also by Am. Sub. H.B. 180 of the 121st General Assembly. Comparison of these amendments in pursuance of section 1.52 of the Revised Code descloses that they are not irreconcilable so that they are required by that section to be harmonized to give effect to each amendment.

See provisions, § 5 of HB 180 (146 v —) following RC § 2935.36.

§ 2950.09 Classification as sexual predator; determination hearing; petition for removal from classification.

(A) If a person is convicted of or pleads guilty to committing, on or after the effective date of this section, a sexually oriented offense that is a sexually violent offense and also is convicted of or pleads guilty to a sexually violent predator specification that was included in the indictment, count in the indictment, or information charging the sexually violent offense, the conviction of or plea of guilty to the specification automatically classifies the offender as a sexual predator for purposes of this chapter. In all other cases, a person who is convicted of or pleads guilty to, or has been convicted of or pleaded guilty to, a sexually oriented offense may be classified as a sexual predator for purposes of this chapter only in accordance with division (B) or (C) of this section.

(B)(1) Regardless of when the sexually oriented offense was committed, if a person is to be sentenced on or after the effective date of this section for a sexually oriented offense that is not a sexually violent offense, or if a person is to be sentenced on or after the effective date of this section for a sexually oriented offense that is a sexually violent offense and a sexually violent predator specification was not included in the indictment, count in the indictment, or information charging the sexually violent offense, the judge who is to impose sentence upon the offender shall conduct a hearing to determine whether the offender is a sexual predator. The judge shall conduct the hearing prior to sentencing and, if the sexually oriented offense is a felony, may conduct it as part of the sentencing hearing required by section 2929.19 of the Revised Code. The court shall give the offender and the prosecutor who prosecuted the offender for the sexually oriented offense notice of the date, time, and location of the hearing. At the hearing, the offender and the prosecutor shall have an opportunity to testify, present evidence, call and examine witnesses and expert witnesses, and cross-examine witnesses and expert witnesses regarding the determination as to whether the offender is a sexual predator. The offender shall have the right to be represented by counsel and, if indigent, the right to have counsel appointed to represent the offender.

(2) In making a determination under divisions (B)(1) and (3) of this section as to whether an offender is a sexual predator, the judge shall consider all relevant factors, including, but not limited to, all of the following:

(a) The offender's age;

(b) The offender's prior criminal record regarding all offenses, including, but not limited to, all sexual offenses;

(c) The age of the victim of the sexually oriented offense for which sentence is to be imposed;

(d) Whether the sexually oriented offense for which sentence is to be imposed involved multiple victims;

(e) Whether the offender used drugs or alcohol to impair the victim of the sexually oriented offense or to prevent the victim from resisting;

(f) If the offender previously has been convicted of or pleaded guilty to any criminal offense, whether the offender completed any sentence imposed for the prior offense and, if the prior offense was a sex offense or a sexually oriented offense, whether the offender participated in available programs for sexual offenders;

(g) Any mental illness or mental disability of the offender;

(h) The nature of the offender's sexual conduct, sexual contact, or interaction in a sexual context with the victim of the sexually oriented offense and whether the sexual conduct, sexual contact, or interaction in a sexual context was part of a demonstrated pattern of abuse;

(i) Whether the offender, during the commission of the sexually oriented offense for which sentence is to be imposed, displayed cruelty or made one or more threats of cruelty;

(j) Any additional behavioral characteristics that contribute to the offender's conduct.

(3) After reviewing all testimony and evidence presented at the hearing conducted under division (B)(1) of this section and the factors specified in division (B)(2) of this section, the judge shall determine by clear and convincing evidence whether the offender is a sexual predator. If the judge determines that the offender is not a sexual predator, the judge shall specify in the

offender's sentence and the judgment of conviction that contains the sentence that the judge has determined that the offender is not a sexual predator. If the judge determines by clear and convincing evidence that the offender is a sexual predator, the judge shall specify in the offender's sentence and the judgment of conviction that contains the sentence that the judge has determined that the offender is a sexual predator and shall specify that the determination was pursuant to division (B) of this section. The offender and the prosecutor who prosecuted the offender for the sexually oriented offense in question may appeal as a matter of right the judge's determination under this division as to whether the offender is, or is not, a sexual predator.

(4) A hearing shall not be conducted under division (B) of this section regarding an offender if the sexually oriented offense in question is a sexually violent offense and the indictment, count in the indictment, or information charging the offense also included a sexually violent predator specification.

(C)(1) If a person was convicted of or pleaded guilty to a sexually oriented offense prior to the effective date of this section, if the person was not sentenced for the offense on or after the effective date of this section, and if, on or after the effective date of this section, the offender is serving a term of imprisonment in a state correctional institution, prior to the offender's release from the term of imprisonment, the department of rehabilitation and correction shall determine whether to recommend that the offender be adjudicated as being a sexual predator. In making a determination under this division as to whether to recommend that the offender be adjudicated as being a sexual predator, the department shall consider all relevant factors, including, but not limited to, all of the factors specified in division (B)(2) of this section. If the department determines that it will recommend that the offender be adjudicated as being a sexual predator, it immediately shall send the recommendation to the court that sentenced the offender and shall enter its determination and recommendation in the offender's institutional record, and the court shall proceed in accordance with division (C)(2) of this section.

(2) If, pursuant to division (C)(1) of this section, the department of rehabilitation and correction sends to a court a recommendation that an offender who has been convicted of or pleaded guilty to a sexually oriented offense be adjudicated as being a sexual predator, the court is not bound by the department's recommendation and the court may conduct a hearing to determine whether the offender is a sexual predator. The court may deny the recommendation and determine that the offender is not a sexual predator without a hearing but shall not make a determination that the offender is a sexual predator in any case without a hearing. If the court determines without a hearing that the offender is not a sexual predator, it shall include its determination in the offender's institutional record.

If the court schedules a hearing under this division, the court shall give the offender and the prosecutor who prosecuted the offender for the sexually oriented offense, or that prosecutor's successor in office, notice of the date, time, and place of the hearing. The hearing shall be conducted in the manner described in division (B)(1) of this section regarding hearings conducted under that division and, in making a determination under this division as to whether the offender is a sexual predator, the court shall consider all relevant factors, including, but not limited to, all of the factors specified in division (B)(2) of this section. after reviewing all testimony and evidence presented at the hearing and the factors specified in division (B)(2) of this section, the court shall determine by clear and convincing evidence whether the offender is a sexual predator. If the court determines that the offender is not a sexual predator, it shall include its determination in the offender's institutional record. If the court determines by clear and convincing evidence that the offender is a sexual predator, it shall enter its determination in the offender's institutional record, shall attach the determination to the offender's sentence, shall specify that the determination was pursuant to division (C) of this section, and shall provide a copy of the determination to the offender, to the prosecuting attorney, and to the department of rehabilitation and correction. The offender and the prosecutor may appeal as a matter of right the judge's determination under this division as to whether the offender is, or is not, a sexual predator.

(D)(1) Upon the expiration of the applicable period of time specified in division (D)(1)(a) or (b) of this section, an offender who has been convicted of or pleaded guilty to a sexually oriented offense and who has been adjudicated as being a sexual predator relative to the sexually oriented offense in the manner described in division (B) or (C) of this section may petition the judge who made the determination that the offender was a sexual predator, or that judge's successor in office, to enter a determination that the offender no longer is a sexual predator. Upon the filing of the petition, the judge may review the prior sexual predator or determination† that comprises the sexual violent predator adjudication, and, upon consideration of all relevant evidence and information, including, but not limited to, the factors set forth in division (B)(2) of this section, either shall enter a determination that the offender no longer is a sexual predator or shall enter an order denying the petition. The court shall not enter a determination under this division that the offender no longer is a sexual predator unless the court determines by clear and convincing evidence that the offender is unlikely to commit a sexually oriented offense in the future. If the judge enters a determination under this division that the offender no longer is a sexual predator, the judge shall notify the bureau of criminal identification and investigation and the parole board of the determination. Upon receipt of the notification, the bureau promptly shall notify the sheriff with whom the offender most recently registered under section 2950.04 or 2950.05 of the Revised Code of the determination that the offender no longer is a sexual predator. If the judge enters an order denying the petition, the prior adjudication of the offender as a sexual predator shall remain in effect. An offender determined to be a sexual predator in the manner described in division (B) or (C) of this section may file a petition under this division after the expiration of the following periods of time:

(a) Regardless of when the sexually oriented offense was committed, if, on or after the effective date of this section, the offender is imprisoned or sentenced to a prison term or other confinement for the sexually oriented offense in relation to which the determination was made, the offender initially may file the petition not earlier than one year prior to the offender's release from the imprisonment, prison term, or other confinement by discharge, parole, judicial release, or any other final release. If the offender is sentenced on or after the effective date of this section for the sexually oriented offense in relation to which the determination is made and is not imprisoned or sentenced to a prison term or other confinement for the sexually oriented offense, the offender initially may file the petition upon the expiration of one year after the entry of the offender's judgment of conviction.

(b) After the offender's initial filing of a petition under division (D)(1)(a) of this section, thereafter, an offender may file a petition under this division upon the expiration of five years after the court has entered an order denying the most recent petition the offender has filed under this division.

(2) Except as otherwise provided in this division, division (D)(1) of this section does not apply to a person who is classified as a sexual predator pursuant to division (A) of this section. If a person who is so classified was sentenced to a prison term pursuant to division (A)(3) of section 2971.03 of the Revised Code and if the sentencing court terminates the offender's prison term as provided in division (D) of section 2971.05 of the Revised Code, the court's termination of the prison term automatically shall constitute a determination by the court that the offender no longer is a sexual predator. If the court so terminates the offender's prison term, the court shall notify the bureau of criminal identification and investigation and the parole board of the determination that the offender no longer is a sexual predator. Upon receipt of the notification, the bureau promptly shall notify the sheriff with whom the offender most recently registered under section 2950.04 or 2950.05 of the Revised Code that the offender no longer is a sexual predator. If an offender who is classified as a sexual predator pursuant to division (A) of this section is released from prison pursuant to a pardon or commutation, the classification of the offender as a sexual predator shall remain in effect after the offender's release, and the offender may file one or more petitions in accordance with the procedures and time limitations contained in division (D)(1) of this section for a determination that the offender no longer is a sexual predator.

(E) If a person is convicted of or pleads guilty to committing, on or after the effective date of this section, a sexually oriented offense, the judge who is to impose sentence on the offender shall determine, prior to sentencing, whether the offender previously has been convicted of or pleaded guilty to a sexually oriented offense. If the judge determines that the offender previously has not been convicted of or pleaded guilty to a sexually oriented offense, the judge shall specify in the offender's sentence that the judge has determined that the offender is not a habitual sex offender. If the judge determines that the offender previously has been convicted of or pleaded guilty to a sexually oriented offense, the judge shall specify in the offender's sentence and the judgment of conviction that contains the sentence that the judge has determined that the offender is a habitual sex offender and may impose a requirement in that sentence and judgment of conviction that the offender be subject to the community notification provisions regarding the offender's place of residence that are contained in sections 2950.10 and 2950.11 of the Revised Code. Unless the habitual sex offender also has been adjudicated as being a sexual predator relative to the sexually oriented offense in question, the offender shall not be subject to those community notification provisions if the court does not impose the requirement described in this division in the offender's sentence and the judgment of conviction.

HISTORY: 146 v H 180. Eff 1-1-97.

The effective date is set by section 3 of HB 180.

† So in enrolled bill.

§ 2950.10 Notice to victim of offender's registration or change of information.

(A)(1) If a person is convicted of or pleads guilty to, or has been convicted of or pleaded guilty to, a sexually oriented offense, if the offender has been adjudicated as being a sexual predator relative to the sexually oriented offense, and the court has not subsequently determined pursuant to division (D) of section 2950.09 of the Revised Code that the offender no longer is a sexual predator or the offender has been determined pursuant to division (E) of section 2950.09 of the Revised Code to be a habitual sex offender and the court has imposed a requirement under that division subjecting the habitual sex offender to this section, if the offender registers with a sheriff pursuant to section 2950.04 or 2950.05 of the Revised Code, and if the victim of the sexually oriented offense has made a request in accordance with rules adopted by the attorney general that specifies that the victim would like to be provided the notices described in this section, the sheriff shall notify the victim of the sexually oriented offense, in writing, that the offender has registered and shall include in the notice the offender's name and residence address or addresses. The sheriff shall provide the notice required by this division to the victim at the most recent residence address available for that victim, not later than seventy-two hours after the offender registers with the sheriff.

(2) If a person is convicted of or pleads guilty to or has been convicted of or pleaded guilty to, a sexually oriented offense, if the offender has been adjudicated as being a sexual predator relative to the sexually oriented offense or sexually violent offense and the court has not subsequently determined pursuant to division (D) of section 2950.09 of the Revised Code that the offender no longer is a sexual predator or the offender has been determined pursuant to division (E) of section 2950.09 of the Revised Code to be a habitual sex offender and the court has imposed a requirement under that division subjecting the habitual sex offender to this section, if the offender registers with a sheriff pursuant to section 2950.04 or 2950.05 of the Revised Code, if the victim of the sexually oriented offense has made a request in accordance with rules adopted by the attorney general that specifies that the victim would like to be provided the notices described in this section, and if the offender notifies the sheriff of a change of residence address pursuant to section 2950.05 of the Revised Code, the sheriff shall notify the victim of the sexually oriented offense, in writing, that the offender's residence address has changed and shall include in the notice the offender's name and new residence address or addresses. The sheriff shall provide the notice required by this division to the victim at the most recent residence address available for that victim, no later than seventy-two hours after the offender notifies the sheriff of the change in the offender's residence address.

(3) If an offender is convicted of or pleads guilty to, or has been convicted of or pleaded guilty to, a sexually oriented offense and if the offender is adjudicated as being a sexual predator relative to the sexually oriented offense or the offender is determined pursuant to division (E) of section 2950.09 of the Revised Code to be a habitual sex offender and is made subject to this section, the victim of the offense may make a request in accordance with rules adopted by the attorney general pursuant to section 2950.13 of the Revised Code that specifies that the victim would like to be provided the notices described in divisions (A)(1) and (2) of this section. If the victim makes a request in accordance with those rules, the sheriff described in divisions (A)(1) and (2) of this section shall provide the victim with the notices described in those divisions.

(4) If a victim makes a request as described in division (A)(3) of this section that specifies that the victim would like to be provided the notices described in divisions (A)(1) and (2) of this section, all information a sheriff obtains regarding the victim from or as a result of the request is confidential, and the information is not a public record open for inspection under section 149.43 of the Revised Code.

(5) The notices described in divisions (A)(1) and (2) of this section are in addition to any notices regarding the offender that the victim is entitled to receive under Chapter 2930. of the Revised Code.

(B) A victim of a sexually oriented offense is not entitled to be provided any notice described in division (A)(1) or (2) of this section unless the offender is adjudicated as being a sexual predator relative to the sexually oriented offense and the court has not subsequently determined pursuant to division (E) of section 2950.09 of the Revised Code that the offender no longer is a sexual predator or the offender has been determined pursuant to division (E) of section 2950.09 of the Revised Code to be a habitual sex offender and the court has imposed a requirement under that division subjecting the habitual sex offender to this section. A victim of a sexually oriented offense is not entitled to any notice described in division (A)(1) or (2) of this section unless the victim makes a request in accordance with rules adopted by the attorney general pursuant to section 2950.13 of the Revised Code that specifies that the victim would like to be provided the notices described in divisions (A)(1) and (2) of this section. This division does not affect any rights of a victim of a sexually oriented offense to be provided notice regarding an offender that are described in Chapter 2950. of the Revised Code.

HISTORY: 146 v H 180. Eff 7-1-97.

The effective date is set by section 5 of HB 180.

See provisions, § 5 of HB 180 (146 v —) following RC § 2935.36.

§ 2950.11 Persons to be notified within geographical area.

(A) As used in this section, "specified geographical notification area" means the geographic area or areas within which the attorney general, by rule adopted under section 2950.13 of the Revised Code, requires the notice described in division (B) of this section to be given to the persons identified in divisions (A)(2) to (8) of this section. If a person is convicted of or pleads guilty to or has been convicted of or pleaded guilty to, a sexually oriented offense, and if the offender has been adjudicated as being a sexual predator relative to the sexually oriented offense and the court has not subsequently determined pursuant to division (D) of section 2950.09 of the Revised Code that the offender no longer is a sexual predator or the offender has been determined pursuant to division (C) of section 2950.09 of the Revised Code to be a habitual sex offender and the court has imposed a requirement under that division subjecting the habitual sex offender to this section, the sheriff with whom the offender has most recently registered under section 2950.04 or 2950.05 of the Revised Code, within the period of time specified in division (C) of this section, shall provide a written notice containing the information set forth in division (B) of this section to all of the following persons:

(1) All occupants of residences adjacent to the offender's place of residence that are located within the county served by the sheriff and all additional neighbors of the offender who are within any category that the attorney general by rule adopted under section 2950.13 of the Revised Code requires to be provided the notice and who reside within the county served by the sheriff;

(2) The executive director of the public children services agency, as defined in section 2151.011 [2151.01.1] of the Revised Code, that has jurisdiction within the specified geographical notification area and that is located within the county served by the sheriff;

(3) The superintendent of each board of education of a school district that has schools within the specified geographical notification area and that is located within the county served by the sheriff;

(4) The appointing or hiring officer of each chartered nonpublic school located within the specified geographical notification area and within the county served by the sheriff or of each other school located within the specified geographical notification area and within the county served by the sheriff and that is not operated by a board of education described in division (A)(3) of this section;

(5) The director, head teacher, or elementary principal of each preschool program governed by Chapter 3301. of the Revised Code that is located within the specified geographical notification area and within the county served by the sheriff;

(6) The administrator of each child day-care center or type A family day-care home that is located within the specified geographical notification area and within the county served by the sheriff, and the provider of each certified type B family day-care home that is located within the specified geographical notification area and within the county served by the sheriff. As used in this division, "child day-care center," "type A family day-care home," and "certified type B family day-care home" have the same meanings as in section 5104.01 of the Revised Code.

(7) The president or other chief administrative officer of each institution of higher education, as defined in section 2907.03 of the Revised Code, that is located within the specified geographical notification area and within the county served by the sheriff, and the chief law enforcement officer of the state university law enforcement agency or campus police department established under section 3345.04 or 1713.50 of the Revised Code, if any, that serves that institution.

(8) The sheriff of each county that includes any portion of the specified geographical notification area.

(9) If the offender resides within the county served by the sheriff, the chief of police, marshal, or other chief law enforcement officer of the municipal corporation in which the offender resides or, if the offender resides in an unincorporated area, the constable or chief of the police department or police district police force of the township in which the offender resides.

(B) The notice required under division (A) of this section shall include all of the following information regarding the subject offender:

(1) The offender's name;

(2) The address or addresses at which the offender resides;

(3) The sexually oriented offense of which the offender was convicted or to which the offender pleaded guilty;

(4) A statement that the offender has been adjudicated as being a sexual predator and that, as of the date of the notice, the court has not entered a determination that the offender no longer is a sexual predator, or a statement that the sentencing judge has determined that the offender is a habitual sex offender.

(C) If a sheriff with whom an offender registers under section 2950.04 or 2950.05 of the Revised Code is required by division (A) of this section to provide notices regarding an offender and if, pursuant to that requirement, the sheriff provides a notice to a sheriff of one or more other counties in accordance with division (A)(8) of this section, the sheriff of each of the other counties who is provided notice under division (A)(8) of this section shall provide the notices described in divisions (A)(1) to (7) and (A)(9) of this section to each person or entity identified within those divisions that is located within the geographical notification area and within the county served by the sheriff in question.

(D)(1) A sheriff required by division (A) or (C) of this section to provide notices regarding an offender shall provide the notice to the neighbors that is described in division (A)(1) of this section and the notices to law enforcement personnel that are described in divisions (A)(8) and (9) of this section no later than seventy-two hours after the offender registers with the sheriff or, if the sheriff is required by division (C) to provide the notices, no later than seventy-two hours after the sheriff is provided the notice described in division (A)(8) of this section.

(2) A sheriff required by division (A) or (C) of this section to provide notices regarding an offender shall provide the notices to all other specified persons that are described in divisions (A)(2) to (7) of this section not later than seven days after the offender registers with the sheriff or, if the sheriff is required by division (C) to provide the notices, no later than seventy-two hours after the sheriff is provided the notice described in division (A)(8) of this section.

(E) All information that a sheriff possesses regarding a sexual predator or a habitual sex offender that is described in division (B) of this section and that must be provided in a notice required under division (A) or (C) of this section is a public record that is open to inspection under section 149.43 of the Revised Code.

(F) The notification provisions of this section do not apply regarding a person who is convicted of or pleads guilty to, or has been convicted of or pleaded guilty to, a sexually oriented offense, who has not been adjudicated as being a sexual predator relative to that sexually oriented offense, and who is determined pursuant to division (F) of section 2950.09 of the Revised Code to be a habitual sex offender unless the sentencing court imposes a requirement in the offender's sentence and in the judgment of conviction that contains the sentence that subjects the offender to the provisions of this section.

(G) The department of human services shall compile, maintain, and update in January and July of each year, a list of all agencies, centers, or homes of a type described in division (A)(2) or (6) of this section that contains the name of each agency, center, or home of that type, the county in which it is located, its address and telephone number, and the name of an administrative officer or employee of the agency, center, or home. The department of education shall compile, maintain, and update in January and July of each year, a list of all boards of education, schools, or programs of a type described in division (A)(3), (4), or (5) of this section that contains the name of each board of education, school, or program of that type, the county in which it is located, its address and telephone number, the name of the superintendent of the board or of an administrative officer or employee of the school or program, and, in relation to a board of education, the county or counties in which each of its schools is located and the address of each such school. The Ohio board of regents shall compile, maintain, and update in January and July of each year, a list of all institutions of a type described in division (A)(7) of this section that contains the name of each such institution, the county in which it is located, its address and telephone number, and the name of its president or other chief administrative officer. A sheriff required by division (A) or (C) of this section to provide notices regarding an offender, or a designee of a sheriff of that type, may request the department of human services, department of education, or Ohio board of regents, by telephone, in person, or by mail, to provide the sheriff or designee with the names, addresses, and telephone numbers of the appropriate persons and entities to whom the notices described in divisions (A)(2) to (7) of this section are to be provided. Upon receipt of a request, the department or board shall provide the requesting sheriff or designee with the names, addresses, and telephone numbers of the appropriate persons and entities to whom those notices are to be provided.

HISTORY: 146 v H 180. Eff 7-1-97.

The effective date is set by section 5 of HB 180.

See provisions, § 5 of HB 180 (146 v —) following RC § 2935.36.

§ 2950.12 Immunity.

(A) Except as provided in division (B) of this section, any of the following persons shall be immune from liability in a civil action to recover damages for injury, death, or loss to person or property allegedly caused by an act or omission in connection with a power, duty, responsibility, or authorization under this chapter or under rules adopted under authority of this chapter:

(1) An officer or employee of the bureau of criminal identification and investigation;

(2) The attorney general, a chief of police, marshal, or other chief law enforcement officer of a municipal corporation, a sheriff, a constable or chief of police of a township police department or police district police force, and a deputy, officer, or employee of the office of the attorney general, the law enforcement agency served by the marshal or the municipal or township chief, the office of the sheriff, or the constable;

(3) A prosecutor and an officer or employee of the office of a prosecutor;

(4) A supervising officer and an officer or employee of the adult parole authority of the department of rehabilitation and correction;

(5) A person identified in division (A)(2), (3), (4), (5), (6), or (7) of section 2950.11 of the Revised Code or the agent of that person.

(B) The immunity described in division (A) of this section does not apply to a person described in divisions (A)(1) to (5) of this section if, in relation to the act or omission in question, any of the following applies:

(1) The act or omission was manifestly outside the scope of the person's employment or official responsibilities.

(2) The act or omission was with malicious purpose, in bad faith, or in a wanton or reckless manner.

(3) Liability for the act or omission is expressly imposed by a section of the Revised Code.

HISTORY: 146 v H 180. Eff 7-1-97.

The effective date is set by section 5 of HB 180.

See provisions, § 5 of HB 180 (146 v —) following RC § 2935.36.

§ 2950.13 Duties of attorney general.

(A) The attorney general shall do all of the following:

(1) No later than July 1, 1997, establish and maintain a state registry of sex offenders that is housed at the bureau of criminal identification and investigation and that contains all of the registration, change of residence address, and verification information the bureau receives pursuant to sections 2950.04, 2950.05, and 2950.06 of the Revised Code regarding a person who is convicted of or pleads guilty to, or has been convicted of or pleaded guilty to, a sexually oriented offense and all of the information the bureau receives pursuant to section 2950.14 of the Revised Code;

(2) In consultation with local law enforcement representatives and no later than July 1, 1997, adopt rules that contain guidelines necessary for the implementation of this chapter;

(3) In consultation with local law enforcement representatives and no later than July 1, 1997, adopt rules for the implementation and administration of the provisions contained in section 2950.11 of the Revised Code that pertain to the notification of neighbors of a person who has committed a sexually oriented offense and has been adjudicated as being a sexually violent predator or determined to be a habitual sex offender, and rules that prescribe a manner in which victims of a sexually oriented offense committed by a person who has been adjudicated as being a sexual predator or determined to be a habitual sex offender may make a request that specifies that the victim would like to be provided the notices described in divisions (A)(1) and (2) of section 2950.10 of the Revised Code.

(4) In consultation with local law enforcement representatives and through the bureau of criminal identification and investigation, prescribe the forms to be used by judges and officials pursuant to section 2950.03 of the Revised Code to advise offenders of their duties of registration, notification of a change of residence address and registration of the new residence address, and residence address verification under sections 2950.04, 2950.05, and 2950.06 of the Revised Code, and prescribe the forms to be used by sheriffs relative to those duties of registration, change of residence address notification, and residence address verification;

(5) Make copies of the forms prescribed under division (D) of this section available to judges, officials, and sheriffs;

(6) Through the bureau of criminal identification and investigation, provide the notifications, the information, and the documents that the bureau is required to provide to appropriate law enforcement officials and to the federal bureau of investigation pursuant to sections 2950.04, 2950.05, and 2950.06 of the Revised Code;

(7) Through the bureau of criminal identification and investigation, maintain the verification forms returned under the residence address verification mechanism set forth in section 2950.06 of the Revised Code;

(8) In consultation with representatives of the officials, judges, and sheriffs, adopt procedures for officials, judges, and sheriffs to use to forward information, photographs, and fingerprints to the bureau of identification and investigation pursuant to the requirements of sections 2950.03, 2950.04, 2950.05, and 2950.06 of the Revised Code;

(9) In consultation with the director of education, the director of human services, and the director of rehabilitation and correction and no later than July 1, 1997, adopt rules that contain guidelines to be followed by boards of education of a school district, chartered nonpublic schools or other schools not operated by a board of education, preschool programs, child day-care centers, type A family day-care homes, certified type B family day-care homes, and institutions of higher education regarding the proper use and administration of information received pursuant to section 2950.11 of the Revised Code relative to a person who has been adjudicated as being a sexual predator or determined to be a habitual sex offender;

(10) In consultation with local law enforcement representatives and no later than July 1, 1997, adopt rules that designate a geographic area or areas within which the notice described in division (B) of section 2950.11 of the Revised Code must be given to the persons identified in divisions (A)(2) to (8) of that section.

(B) The attorney general, in consultation with local law enforcement representatives, may adopt rules that establish one or more categories of neighbors of an offender who, in addition to the occupants of residences adjacent to an offender's place of residence, must be given the notice described in division (B) of section 2950.11 of the Revised Code.

(C) As used in this section, "local law enforcement representatives" means representatives of the sheriffs of this state, representatives of the municipal chiefs of police and marshals of this state, and representatives of the township constables and chiefs of police of the township police departments or police district police forces of this state.

HISTORY: 146 v H 180 (Eff 7-1-97); 146 v H 72. Eff 7-1-97.

The effective date is set by section 3 of HB 72.

See provisions, § 5 of HB 180 (146 v —) following RC § 2935.36.

§ 2950.14 Information to be provided to Bureau of Criminal Identification and Investigation prior to release.

(A) Prior to releasing an offender who is under the custody and control of the department of rehabilitation and correction and who has been convicted of or pleaded guilty to committing, either prior to, on, or after the effective date of this section, any sexually oriented offense, the department shall provide all of the following information to the bureau of criminal identification and investigation regarding the offender:

(1) The offender's name and any aliases used by the offender;

(2) All identifying factors concerning the offender;

(3) The offender's anticipated future residence;

(4) The offense history of the offender;

(5) Any other information that the bureau indicates is relevant and that the department possesses.

(B) Upon receipt of the information described in division (A) of this section regarding an offender, the bureau immediately shall enter the information into the state registry of sexual offenders that the bureau maintains pursuant to section 2950.13 of the Revised Code and into the records that the bureau maintains pursuant to division (A) of section 109.57 of the Revised Code.

HISTORY: 146 v H 180. Eff 1-1-97.

The effective date is set by section 3 of HB 180.

§ 2950.99 Penalties.

Whoever violates a prohibition in section 2950.04, 2950.05, or 2950.06 of the Revised Code is guilty of a felony of the fifth degree if the most serious sexually oriented offense that was the basis of the registration, change of address notification, or address verification requirement that was violated under the prohibition is a felony, and a misdemeanor of the first degree if the most serious sexually oriented offense that was the basis of the registration, change of address notification, or address verification requirement that was violated under the prohibition is a misdemeanor. In addition to any penalty or sanction imposed for the violation, if the offender is on probation or parole, is subject to one or more post-release control sanctions, or is subject to any other type of supervised release at the time of the violation, the violation shall constitute a violation of the terms and conditions of the probation, parole, post-release control sanction, or other type of supervised release.

HISTORY: 130 v 671 (Eff 10-4-63); 134 v H 511 (Eff 1-1-74); 146 v S 2 (Eff 7-1-96); 146 v H 180. Eff 7-1-97.

The effective date is set by section 5 of HB 180.

See provisions, § 5 of HB 180 (146 v —) following RC § 2935.36.

CHAPTER 2951: PROBATION

Section
2951.01   Definition of magistrate.
[2951.01.1] 2951.011   Application of 7-1-96 amendments.
2951.02   Criteria for and against probation or suspension of sentence; conditions.
[2951.02.1] 2951.021   Offender may be required to pay monthly supervision fee.
2951.03   Presentence investigation report in felony case.
2951.04   Repealed.
[2951.04.1] 2951.041   Treatment in lieu of conviction.
2951.05   Control and supervision of offender on probation.
2951.06   Release from custody.
2951.07   Probation period.
2951.08   Arrest of person on probation or under community control sanction.
2951.09   Proceedings after arrest of probationer.
2951.10   Final order.
2951.11, 2951.12   Repealed.
2951.13   Attendance at revocation hearing.

§ 2951.01 Definition of magistrate.

The definition of "magistrate" set forth in section 2931.01 of the Revised Code applies to Chapter 2951. of the Revised Code.

HISTORY: Bureau of Code Revision. Eff 10-1-53.

[§ 2951.01.1] § 2951.011 Application of 7-1-96 amendments.

(A) Chapter 2951. of the Revised Code, as it existed prior to July 1, 1996, applies to a person upon whom a court imposed a term of imprisonment prior to July 1, 1996, and a person upon whom a court, on or after July 1, 1996, and in accordance with law existing prior to July 1, 1996, imposed a term of imprisonment for an offense that was committed prior to July 1, 1996.

(B) Chapter 2951. of the Revised Code as it exists on and after July 1, 1996, applies to a person upon whom a court imposed a stated prison term for an offense committed on or after July 1, 1996.

HISTORY: 146 v S 2. Eff 7-1-96.

The effective date is set by section 6 of SB 2.

See provisions, § 5 of SB 2 (146 v —), as amended by § 3 of SB 269 (146 v —), following RC § 2929.03.

§ 2951.02 Criteria for and against probation or suspension of sentence; conditions.

(A)(1) In determining whether to suspend a sentence of imprisonment imposed upon an offender for a misdemeanor and place the offender on probation or whether to otherwise suspend a sentence of imprisonment imposed upon an offender for a misdemeanor pursuant to division (A) of section 2929.51 of the Revised Code, the court shall consider the risk that the offender will commit another offense and the need for protecting the public from the risk, the nature and circumstances of the offense, and the history, character, and condition of the offender.

(2) An offender who has been convicted of or pleaded guilty to a misdemeanor shall not be placed on probation and shall not otherwise have the sentence of imprisonment imposed upon the offender suspended pursuant to division (A) of section 2929.51 of the Revised Code if any of the following applies:

(a) The offender is a repeat or dangerous offender, as defined in section 2935.36 of the Revised Code.

(b) The misdemeanor offense involved was not a violation of section 2923.12 of the Revised Code and was committed while the offender was armed with a firearm or dangerous ordnance, as defined in section 2923.11 of the Revised Code.

(c) Under division (C) of section 2903.07 of the Revised Code, the offender is not eligible for probation.

(B) The following do not control the court's discretion but the court shall consider them in favor of placing an offender who has been convicted of or pleaded guilty to a misdemeanor on probation or in favor of otherwise suspending the offender's sentence of imprisonment pursuant to division (A) of section 2929.51 of the Revised Code:

(1) The offense neither caused nor threatened serious harm to persons or property, or the offender did not contemplate that it would do so.

(2) The offense was the result of circumstances unlikely to recur.

(3) The victim of the offense induced or facilitated it.

(4) There are substantial grounds tending to excuse or justify the offense, though failing to establish a defense.

(5) The offender acted under strong provocation.

(6) The offender has no history of prior delinquency or criminal activity, or has led a law-abiding life for a substantial period before commission of the present offense.

(7) The offender is likely to respond affirmatively to probationary or other court-imposed treatment.

(8) The character and attitudes of the offender indicate that the offender is unlikely to commit another offense.

(9) The offender has made or will make restitution or reparation to the victim of the offender's offense for the injury, damage, or loss sustained.

(10) Imprisonment of the offender will entail undue hardship to the offender or the offender's dependents.

(C)(1)(a) When an offender who has been convicted of or pleaded guilty to a misdemeanor is placed on probation or the sentence of that type of offender otherwise is suspended pursuant to division (A) of section 2929.51 of the Revised Code, the probation or other suspension shall be at least on condition that, during the period of probation or other suspension, the offender shall abide by the law, including, but not limited to, complying with the provisions of Chapter 2923. of the Revised Code relating to the possession, sale, furnishing, transfer, disposition, purchase, acquisition, carrying, conveying, or use of, or other conduct involving, a firearm or dangerous ordnance, as defined in section 2923.11 of the Revised Code, and shall not leave the state without the permission of the court or the offender's probation officer. In the interests of doing justice, rehabilitating the offender, and ensuring the offender's good behavior, the court may impose additional requirements on the offender, including, but not limited to, requiring the offender to make restitution pursuant to section 2929.21 of the Revised Code for all or part of the property damage that is caused by the offender's offense and for all or part of the value of the property that is the subject of any theft offense, as defined in division (K) of section 2913.01 of the Revised Code, that the offender committed. Compliance with the additional requirements also shall be a condition of the offender's probation or other suspension.

(b) When an offender who has been convicted of or pleaded guilty to a felony is sentenced to a nonresidential sanction pursuant to section 2929.17 of the Revised Code, the court shall impose as a condition of the sanction that, during the period of the nonresidential sanction, the offender shall abide by the law, including, but not limited to, complying with the provisions of Chapter 2923. of the Revised Code identified in division (C)(1)(a) of this section.

(2) During the period of a misdemeanor offender's probation or other suspension or during the period of a felon's nonresidential sanction, authorized probation officers who are engaged within the scope of their supervisory duties or responsibilities may search, with or without a warrant, the person of the offender, the place of residence of the offender, and a motor vehicle, another item of tangible or intangible personal property, or other real property in which the offender has a right, title, or interest or for which the offender has the express or implied permission of a person with a right, title, or interest to use, occupy, or possess if the probation officers have reasonable grounds to believe that the offender is not abiding by the law or otherwise is not complying with the conditions of the offender's probation or other suspension or the conditions of the offender's nonresidential sanction. If a felon who is sentenced to a nonresidential sanction is under the general control and supervision of the adult parole authority, as described in division (A)(2)(a) of section 2929.15 of the Revised Code, adult parole authority field officers with supervisory responsibilities over the felon shall have the same search authority relative to the felon during the period of the sanction as is described under this division for probation officers. The court that places the offender on probation or suspends the misdemeanor offender's sentence of imprisonment pursuant to division (D)(2) or (4) of section 2929.51 of the Revised Code or that sentences the felon to a nonresidential sanction pursuant to section 2929.17 of the Revised Code shall provide the offender with a written notice that informs the offender that authorized probation officers or adult parole authority field officers with supervisory responsibilities over the offender who are engaged within the scope of their supervisory duties or responsibilities may conduct those types of searches during the period of probation or other suspension or during the period of the nonresidential sanction if they have reasonable grounds to believe that the offender is not abiding by the law or otherwise is not complying with the conditions of the offender's probation or other suspension or the conditions of the offender's nonresidential sanction.

(D) The following do not control the court's discretion but the court shall consider them against placing an offender who has been convicted of or pleaded guilty to a misdemeanor on probation and against otherwise suspending the offender's sentence of imprisonment pursuant to division (A) of section 2929.51 of the Revised Code:

(1) The offender recently violated the conditions of pardon, post-release control pursuant to section 2967.28 of the Revised Code, or a probation or suspension pursuant to division (A) of section 2929.51 of the Revised Code, previously granted the offender.

(2) There is a substantial risk that, while at liberty during the period of probation or other suspension, the offender will commit another offense.

(3) The offender is in need of correctional or rehabilitative treatment that can be provided best by the offender's commitment to a locally governed and operated residential facility.

(4) Regardless of whether the offender knew the age of the victim, the victim of the offense was sixty-five years of age or older or permanently and totally disabled at the time of the commission of the offense.

(E) The criteria listed in divisions (B) and (D) of this section shall not be construed to limit the matters that may be considered in determining whether to suspend sentence of imprisonment and place an offender who has been convicted of or pleaded guilty to a misdemeanor on probation or whether to otherwise suspend the offender's sentence of imprisonment pursuant to division (A) of section 2929.51 of the Revised Code.

(F)(1) When an offender is convicted of or pleads guilty to a misdemeanor, the court may require the offender, as a condition of probation or as a condition of otherwise suspending the offender's sentence pursuant to division (A) of section 2929.51 of the Revised Code, in addition to the conditions of probation or other suspension imposed pursuant to division (C) of this section, to perform supervised community service work under the authority of health districts, park districts, counties, municipal corporations, townships, other political subdivisions of the state, or agencies of the state or any of its political subdivisions, or under the authority of charitable organizations that render services to the community or its citizens, in accordance with this division. Supervised community service work shall not be required as a condition of probation or other suspension under this division unless the offender agrees to perform the work offered as a condition of probation or other suspension by the court. The court may require an offender who agrees to perform the work to pay to it a reasonable fee to cover the costs of the offender's participation in the work, including, but not limited to, the costs of procuring a policy or policies of liability insurance to cover the period during which the offender will perform the work.

A court may permit any offender convicted of a misdemeanor to satisfy the payment of a fine imposed for the offense by performing supervised community service work as described in this division if the offender requests an opportunity to satisfy the payment by this means and if the court determines the offender is financially unable to pay the fine.

The supervised community service work that may be imposed under this division shall be subject to the following limitations:

(a) The court shall fix the period of the work and, if necessary, shall distribute it over weekends or over other appropriate times that will allow the offender to continue at the offender's occupation or to care for the offender's family. The period of the work as fixed by the court shall not exceed an aggregate of two hundred hours.

(b) An agency, political subdivision, or charitable organization must agree to accept the offender for the work before the court requires the offender to perform the work for the entity. A court shall not require an offender to perform supervised community service work for an agency, political subdivision, or charitable organization at a location that is an unreasonable distance from the offender's residence or domicile, unless the offender is provided with transportation to the location where the work is to be performed.

(c) A court may enter into an agreement with a county department of human services for the management, placement, and supervision of offenders eligible for community service work in work activities, developmental activities, and alternative work activities under sections 5107.40 to 5107.69 of the Revised Code. If a court and a county department of human services have entered into an agreement of that nature, the clerk of that court is authorized to pay directly to the department of human services all or a portion of the fees collected by the court pursuant to this division in accordance with the terms of its agreement.

(d) Community service work that a court requires under this division shall be supervised by an official of the agency, political subdivision, or charitable organization for which the work is performed or by a person designated by the agency, political subdivision, or charitable organization. The official or designated person shall be qualified for the supervision by education, training, or experience, and periodically shall report, in writing, to the court and to the offender's probation officer concerning the conduct of the offender in performing the work.

(2) When an offender is convicted of a felony, the court may impose pursuant to sections 2929.15 and 2929.17 of the Revised Code a sanction that requires the offender to perform supervised community service work in accordance with this division and under the authority of any agency, political subdivision, or charitable organization as described in division (F)(1) of this section. The court may require an offender who is ordered to perform the work to pay to it a reasonable fee to cover the costs of the offender's participation in the work, including, but not limited to, the costs of procuring a policy or policies of liability insurance to cover the period during which the offender will perform the work.

A court may permit an offender convicted of a felony to satisfy the payment of a fine imposed for the offense pursuant to section 2929.18 of the Revised Code by performing supervised community service work as described in this division if the court determines that the offender is financially unable to pay the fine.

The supervised community service work that may be imposed under this division shall be subject to the limitations specified in divisions (F)(1)(a) to (d) of this section, except that the court is not required to obtain the agreement of the offender to impose supervised community work as a sanction. Additionally, the total of any period of supervised community service work imposed on an offender under this division plus the period of all other sanctions imposed pursuant to sections 2929.15, 2929.16, 2929.17, and 2929.18 of the Revised Code shall not exceed five years.

(G)(1) When an offender is convicted of a violation of section 4511.19 of the Revised Code, a municipal ordinance relating to operating a vehicle while under the influence of alcohol, a drug of abuse, or alcohol and a drug of abuse, or a municipal ordinance relating to operating a vehicle with a prohibited concentration of alcohol in the blood, breath, or urine or of a misdemeanor violation of section 2903.07 of the Revised Code or an equivalent violation of a municipal ordinance that is substantially similar to section 2903.07 of the Revised Code and that provides for that type of finding by a jury or judge in a case in which the jury or judge found that the offender was under the influence of alcohol at the time of the commission of the offense, the court may require, as a condition of probation in addition to the required conditions of probation and the discretionary conditions of probation that may be imposed pursuant to division (C) of this section, any suspension or revocation of a driver's or commercial driver's license or permit or nonresident operating privilege, and all other penalties provided by law or by ordinance, that the offender operate only a motor vehicle equipped with an ignition interlock device that is certified pursuant to section 4511.83 of the Revised Code.

(2) When a court requires an offender, as a condition of probation pursuant to division (G)(1) of this section, to operate only a motor vehicle equipped with an ignition interlock device that is certified pursuant to section

4511.83 of the Revised Code, the offender immediately shall surrender the offender's driver's or commercial driver's license or permit to the court. Upon the receipt of the offender's license or permit, the court shall issue an order authorizing the offender to operate a motor vehicle equipped with a certified ignition interlock device, deliver the offender's license or permit to the bureau of motor vehicles, and include in the abstract of the case forwarded to the bureau pursuant to section 4507.021 [4507.02.1] of the Revised Code the conditions of probation imposed pursuant to division (G)(1) of this section. The court shall give the offender a copy of its order, and that copy shall be used by the offender in lieu of a driver's or commercial driver's license or permit until the bureau issues a restricted license to the offender.

(3) Upon receipt of an offender's driver's or commercial driver's license or permit pursuant to division (G)(2) of this section, the bureau of motor vehicles shall issue a restricted license to the offender. The restricted license shall be identical to the surrendered license, except that it shall have printed on its face a statement that the offender is prohibited from operating a motor vehicle that is not equipped with an ignition interlock device that is certified pursuant to section 4511.83 of the Revised Code. The bureau shall deliver the offender's surrendered license or permit to the court upon receipt of a court order requiring it to do so, or reissue the offender's license or permit under section 4507.54 of the Revised Code if the registrar destroyed the offender's license or permit under that section. The offender shall surrender the restricted license to the court upon receipt of the offender's surrendered license or permit.

(4) If an offender violates a requirement of the court imposed under division (G)(1) of this section, the offender's driver's or commercial driver's license or permit or nonresident operating privilege may be suspended as provided in section 4507.16 of the Revised Code.

(5) As used in this division, "ignition interlock device" has the same meaning as in section 4511.83 of the Revised Code.

HISTORY: 134 v H 511 (Eff 1-1-74); 136 v S 144 (Eff 8-27-75); 137 v S 119 (Eff 8-30-78); 138 v H 892 (Eff 10-10-80); 138 v H 682 (Eff 4-9-81); 139 v H 1 (Eff 8-5-81); 139 v S 432 (Eff 3-16-83); 140 v S 210 (Eff 7-1-83); 142 v H 429 (Eff 6-20-88); 142 v H 322 (Eff 9-9-88); 143 v H 381 (Eff 7-1-89); 143 v S 258 (Eff 11-20-90); 145 v H 152 (Eff 7-1-93); 145 v H 571 (Eff 10-6-94); 145 v H 687 (Eff 10-12-94); 145 v H 687 (Eff 10-17-94); 146 v H 4 (Eff 11-9-95); 146 v H 167 (Eff 11-15-95); 146 v S 2 (Eff 7-1-96); 146 v S 269 (Eff 7-1-96); 147 v H 408. Eff 10-1-97.

[§ 2951.02.1] § 2951.021 Offender may be required to pay monthly supervision fee.

(A) As used in this section:

(1) "Multicounty department of probation" means a probation department established under section 2301.27 of the Revised Code to serve more than one county.

(2) "Probation agency" means a county department of probation, a multicounty department of probation, a municipal court department of probation established under section 1901.33 of the Revised Code, or the adult parole authority.

(3) "County-operated municipal court" and "legislative authority" have the same meanings as in section 1901.03 of the Revised Code.

(4) "Detention facility" has the same meaning as in section 2921.01 of the Revised Code.

(B)(1) If a court places a misdemeanor offender on probation or places a felony offender under a community control sanction under section 2929.16, 2929.17, or 2929.18 of the Revised Code and if the court places the offender under the control and supervision of a probation agency, the court may require the offender, as a condition of probation or of community control, to pay a monthly supervision fee of not more than fifty dollars for supervision services. If the court requires an offender to pay a monthly supervision fee and the offender will be under the control of a county department of probation, a multicounty department of probation, or a municipal court department of probation established under section 1901.33 of the Revised Code, the court shall specify whether the offender is to pay the fee to the probation agency that will have control over the offender or to the clerk of the court for which the supervision agency is established. If the court requires an offender to pay a monthly probation fee and the offender will be under the control of the adult parole authority, the court shall specify that the offender is to pay the fee to the clerk of the court of common pleas.

(2) No person shall be assessed, in any month, more than fifty dollars in supervision fees.

(3) The prosecuting attorney of the county or the chief legal officer of a municipal corporation in which is located the court that imposed sentence upon an offender may bring a civil action to recover unpaid monthly supervision fees that the offender was required to pay. Any amount recovered in the civil action shall be paid into the appropriate county or municipal probation services fund in accordance with division (C) of this section.

(4) The failure of an offender to comply with a condition of probation or of community control that requires the offender to pay a monthly supervision fee and that is imposed under division (B)(1) of this section shall not constitute the basis for a revocation of the offender's probation and the imposition of the offender's sentence under section 2951.09 of the Revised Code or the modification of the offender's community control sanctions pursuant to section 2929.15 of the Revised Code but may be considered with any other factors that form the basis of a revocation of probation or modification of a sanction for violating a community control sanction under those sections. If the court determines at a hearing held pursuant to section 2951.09 of the Revised Code that a misdemeanor offender on probation failed to pay

a monthly supervision fee imposed under division (B)(1) of this section and that no other factors warranting revocation of probation are present, the court shall not revoke the offender's probation, shall remand the offender to the custody of the probation agency, and may impose any additional conditions of probation upon the offender, including a requirement that the offender perform community service, as the ends of justice require. Any requirement imposed pursuant to division (B)(4) of this section that the offender perform community service shall be in addition to and shall not limit or otherwise affect any order that the offender perform community service pursuant to division (F)(1)(a) of section 2951.02 of the Revised Code.

(C) Prior to the last day of the month in each month during the period of probation or of community control, an offender who is ordered to pay a monthly supervision fee under this section shall pay the fee to the probation agency that has control and supervision over the offender or to the clerk of the court for which the probation agency is established, as specified by the court, except that, if the probation agency is the adult parole authority, the offender shall pay the fee to the clerk of the court of common pleas. Each probation agency or clerk of a court that receives any monthly supervision fees shall keep a record of the monthly supervision fees that are paid to the agency or the clerk and shall give a written receipt to each person who pays a supervision fee to the agency or clerk.

(D) Subject to division (F) of this section, all monthly supervision fees collected under this section by a probation agency or the clerk of a court shall be disposed of in the following manner:

(1) For offenders who are under the control and supervision of a county department of probation or a municipal court department of probation in a county-operated municipal court, on or before the fifth business day of each month, the chief probation officer, the chief probation officer's designee, or the clerk of the court shall pay all monthly supervision fees collected in the previous month to the county treasurer of the county in which the county department of probation or municipal court department of probation is established for deposit into the county probation services fund established in the county treasury of that county pursuant to division (A)(1)† section 321.44 of the Revised Code.

(2) For offenders who are under the control and supervision of a multicounty department of probation, on or before the fifth business day of each month, the chief probation officer, the chief probation officer's designee, or the clerk of the court shall pay all monthly supervision fees collected in the previous month to the county treasurer of the county in which is located the court of common pleas that placed the offender on probation or under a community control sanction under the control of the department for deposit into the county probation services fund established in the county treasury of that county pursuant to division (A)(1) of section 321.44 of the Revised Code and for subsequent appropriation and transfer in accordance with division (A)(2) of that section to the appropriate multicounty probation services fund established pursuant to division (B) of that section.

(3) For offenders who are under the control and supervision of a municipal court department of probation in a municipal court that is not a county-operated municipal court, on or before the fifth business day of each month, the chief probation officer, the chief probation officer's designee, or the clerk of the court shall pay all monthly supervision fees collected in the previous month to the treasurer of the municipal corporation for deposit into the municipal probation services fund established pursuant to section 737.41 of the Revised Code.

(4) For offenders who are under the control and supervision of the adult parole authority, the clerk of the court of common pleas, on or before the fifth business day of January, April, July, and October, shall pay all monthly supervision fees collected by the clerk in the previous three months to the treasurer of the county in which is located the court of common pleas that placed the offender on probation or under a community control sanction under the control of the authority for deposit into the county probation services fund established in the county treasury of that county pursuant to division (A)(1) of section 321.44 of the Revised Code and for subsequent appropriation and transfer in accordance with division (A)(2) of that section to the adult parole authority probation services fund established pursuant to section 5149.06 of the Revised Code.

(E) Not later than the first day of December of each year, each probation agency shall prepare a report regarding its use of money from a county probation services fund, a multicounty probation services fund, a municipal probation services fund, or the adult parole authority probation services fund, whichever is applicable. The report shall specify the amount appropriated from the fund to the probation agency during the current calendar year, an estimate of the amount that the probation agency will expend by the end of the year, a summary of how the amount appropriated has been expended for probation services, and an estimate of the amount of supervision fees that the probation agency will collect and pay to the appropriate treasurer for deposit in the appropriate fund in the next calendar year. The report shall be filed with one of the following:

(1) If the probation agency is a county department of probation or a municipal court department of probation in a county-operated municipal court, with the board of county commissioners of that county;

(2) If the probation agency is a multicounty department of probation, with the board of county commissioners of the county whose treasurer, in accordance with section 2301.27 of the Revised Code, is designated as the treasurer to whom supervision fees collected under this section are to be appropriated and transferred under division (A)(2) of section 321.44 of the Revised Code;

(3) If the probation agency is a department of probation of a municipal court that is not a county-operated municipal court, with the legislative authority of the municipal corporation that operates the court;

(4) If the probation agency is the adult parole authority, with the chairmen of the finance committees of the senate and the house of representatives, the directors of the office of budget and management and the legislative budget office, and the board of county commissioners in each county for which the adult parole authority provides probation services.

(F) If the clerk of a court of common pleas or the clerk of a municipal court collects any monthly supervision fees under this section, the clerk may retain up to two per cent of the fees so collected to cover any administrative costs experienced in complying with the clerk's duties under this section.

HISTORY: 145 v H 406 (Eff 11-11-94); 146 v S 2 (Eff 7-1-96); 146 v S 269. Eff 7-1-96.

The effective date is set by section 5 of SB 269.

† So in enrolled bill.

§ 2951.03 Presentence investigation report in felony case.

(A)(1) No person who has been convicted of or pleaded guilty to a felony shall be placed under a community control sanction until a written presentence investigation report has been considered by the court. If a court orders the preparation of a presentence investigation report pursuant to this section, section 2947.06 of the Revised Code, or Criminal Rule 32.2, the officer making the report shall inquire into the circumstances of the offense and the criminal record, social history, and present condition of the defendant and any other matters specified in Criminal Rule 32.2. Whenever the officer considers it advisable, the officer's investigation may include a physical and mental examination of the defendant. If, pursuant to section 2930.13 of the Revised Code, the victim of the offense of which the defendant has been convicted wishes to make a statement regarding the impact of the offense for the officer's use in preparing the presentence investigation report, the officer shall comply within the requirements of that section.

(2) If a defendant is committed to any institution, the presentence investigation report shall be sent to the institution with the entry of commitment. If a defendant is committed to any institution and a presentence investigation report is not prepared regarding that defendant pursuant to this section, section 2947.06 of the Revised Code, or Criminal Rule 32.2, the director of the department of rehabilitation and correction or the director's designee may order that an offender background investigation and report be conducted and prepared regarding the defendant pursuant to section 5120.16 of the Revised Code.

(B)(1) If a presentence investigation report is prepared pursuant to this section, section 2947.06 of the Revised Code, or Criminal Rule 32.2, the court, at a reasonable time before imposing sentence, shall permit the defendant or the defendant's counsel to read the report, except that the court shall not permit the defendant or the defendant's counsel to read any of the following:

(a) Any recommendation as to sentence;

(b) Any diagnostic opinions that, if disclosed, the court believes might seriously disrupt a program of rehabilitation for the defendant;

(c) Any sources of information obtained upon a promise of confidentiality;

(d) Any other information that, if disclosed, the court believes might result in physical harm or some other type of harm to the defendant or to any other person.

(2) Prior to sentencing, the court shall permit the defendant and the defendant's counsel to comment on the presentence investigation report and, in its discretion, may permit the defendant and the defendant's counsel to introduce testimony or other information that relates to any alleged factual inaccuracy contained in the report.

(3) If the court believes that any information in the presentence investigation report should not be disclosed pursuant to division (B)(1) of this section, the court, in lieu of making the report or any part of the report available, shall state orally or in writing a summary of the factual information contained in the report that will be relied upon in determining the defendant's sentence. The court shall permit the defendant and the defendant's counsel to comment upon the oral or written summary of the report.

(4) Any material that is disclosed to the defendant or the defendant's counsel pursuant to this section shall be disclosed to the prosecutor who is handling the prosecution of the case against the defendant.

(5) If the comments of the defendant or the defendant's counsel, the testimony they introduce, or any of the other information they introduce alleges any factual inaccuracy in the presentence investigation report or the summary of the report, the court shall do either of the following with respect to each alleged factual inaccuracy:

(a) Make a finding as to the allegation;

(b) Make a determination that no finding is necessary with respect to the allegation, because the factual matter will not be taken into account in the sentencing of the defendant.

(C) A court's decision as to the content of a summary under division (B)(3) of this section or as to the withholding of information under division (B)(1)(a), (b), (c), or (d) of this section shall be considered to be within the discretion of the court. No appeal can be taken from either of those decisions, and neither of those decisions shall be the basis for a reversal of the sentence imposed.

(D)(1) The contents of a presentence investigation

report prepared pursuant to this section, section 2947.06 of the Revised Code, or Criminal Rule 32.2 and the contents of any written or oral summary of a presentence investigation report or of a part of a presentence investigation report described in division (B)(3) of this section are confidential information and are not a public record. The court, an appellate court, authorized probation officers, investigators, and court personnel, the defendant, the defendant's counsel, the prosecutor who is handling the prosecution of the case against the defendant, and authorized personnel of an institution to which the defendant is committed may inspect, receive copies of, retain copies of, and use a presentence investigation report or a written or oral summary of a presentence investigation only for the purposes of or only as authorized by Criminal Rule 32.2 or this section, division (F)(1) of section 2953.08, section 2947.06, or another section of the Revised Code.

(2) Immediately following the imposition of sentence upon the defendant, the defendant or the defendant's counsel and the prosecutor shall return to the court all copies of a presentence investigation report and of any written summary of a presentence investigation report or part of a presentence investigation report that the court made available to the defendant or the defendant's counsel and to the prosecutor pursuant to this section. The defendant or the defendant's counsel and the prosecutor shall not make any copies of the presentence investigation report or of any written summary of a presentence investigation report or part of a presentence investigation report that the court made available to them pursuant to this section.

(3) Except when a presentence investigation report or a written or oral summary of a presentence investigation report is being used for the purposes of or as authorized by Criminal Rule 32.2 or this section, division (F)(1) of section 2953.08, section 2947.06, or another section of the Revised Code, the court or other authorized holder of the report or summary shall retain the report or summary under seal.

(E) As used in this section:

(1) "Prosecutor" has the same meaning as in section 2935.01 of the Revised Code.

(2) "Community control sanction" has the same meaning as in section 2929.01 of the Revised Code.

(3) "Public record" has the same meaning as in section 149.43 of the Revised Code.

HISTORY: GC § 13452-1a; 121 v 381; Bureau of Code Revision, 10-1-53; 130 v 672 (Eff 9-24-63); 142 v H 73, § 1 (Eff 10-1-87); 142 v H 73, § 3 (Eff 10-1-89); 143 v S 258 (Eff 11-20-90); 145 v H 571 (Eff 10-6-94); 145 v S 186 (Eff 10-12-94); 146 v S 2 (Eff 7-1-96); 146 v S 269. Eff 7-1-96.

The effective date is set by section 5 of SB 269.

§ 2951.04 Repealed, 146 v S 269, § 2 [136 v H 300; 138 v H 900; 141 v H 475; 143 v H 317; 143 v S 258; 145 v H 385; 146 v S 2]. Eff 7-1-96.

This section regulated conditional probation for treatment and rehabilitation of drug dependent persons.

The effective date is set by section 5 of SB 269.

[§ 2951.04.1] § 2951.041 Treatment in lieu of conviction.

(A) If the court has reason to believe that an offender charged with a felony or misdemeanor is a drug dependent person or is in danger of becoming a drug dependent person, the court shall accept, prior to the entry of a plea, that offender's request for treatment in lieu of conviction. If the offender requests treatment in lieu of conviction, the court shall stay all criminal proceedings pending the outcome of the hearing to determine whether the offender is a person eligible for treatment in lieu of conviction. At the conclusion of the hearing, the court shall enter its findings and accept the offender's plea.

(B) An offender who requests treatment in lieu of conviction under division (A) of this section is eligible for that treatment if the court finds that:

(1) The offender's drug dependence or danger of drug dependence was a factor leading to the criminal activity with which the offender is charged, and rehabilitation through treatment would substantially reduce the likelihood of additional criminal activity.

(2) The offender has been accepted into a program licensed by the department of alcohol and drug addiction services pursuant to section 3793.11 of the Revised Code, a program certified by the department pursuant to section 3793.06 of the Revised Code, a public or private hospital, the veterans administration or other agency of the federal government, private care or treatment rendered by a physician or a psychologist licensed in the state, or other appropriate drug treatment facility or program.

(3) If the offender is convicted of a misdemeanor, the offender would be eligible for probation under section 2951.02 of the Revised Code, except that a finding of any of the criteria listed in division (D) of that section shall cause the offender to be conclusively ineligible for treatment in lieu of conviction. If the offender is convicted of a felony, the offender would be eligible for a community control sanction.

(4) The offender is not a repeat offender or dangerous offender, as defined in section 2935.36 of the Revised Code;

(5) The offender is not charged with a violation of section 2925.02, 2925.03, 2925.04, or 2925.11 of the Revised Code that is not a minor drug possession offense, as defined in section 2925.01 of the Revised Code.

Upon a finding of that nature and if the offender enters a plea of guilty or no contest, the court may stay all criminal proceedings and order the offender to a period of rehabilitation. If a plea of not guilty is entered, a trial shall precede further consideration of the offender's request for treatment in lieu of conviction.

(C) The offender and the prosecuting attorney shall be afforded the opportunity to present evidence to establish eligibility or ineligibility for treatment in lieu of conviction, and the prosecuting attorney may make a recommendation to the court concerning whether the offender should receive treatment in lieu of conviction. Upon the request of the offender and to aid the offender in establishing the offender's eligibility for treatment in lieu of conviction, the court may refer the offender for medical and psychiatric examination to the department of mental health, to a state facility designated by the department, to a psychiatric clinic approved by the department, or to a facility or program described in division (B)(2) of this section. However, the psychiatric portion of an examination pursuant to a referral under this division shall be performed only by a court-appointed individual who has not previously treated the offender or a member of the offender's immediate family.

(D) An offender found to be eligible for treatment in lieu of conviction and ordered to a period of rehabilitation shall be placed under the control and supervision of the county probation department or the adult parole authority as provided in this chapter as if the offender were on probation or as if the offender were under a community control sanction. The court shall order a period of rehabilitation to continue for any period that the judge or magistrate determines. The period of rehabilitation may be extended, but the total period shall not exceed three years. The period of rehabilitation shall be conditioned upon the offender's voluntary entrance into an appropriate drug treatment facility or program, faithful submission to prescribed treatment, and any other conditions that the court orders.

(E) Treatment of a person ordered to a period of rehabilitation under this section may include hospitalization under close supervision or otherwise, release on an outpatient status under supervision, and other treatment or after-care that the appropriate drug treatment facility or program considers necessary or desirable to rehabilitate that person. Persons released from hospitalization or treatment but still subject to the ordered period of rehabilitation may be rehospitalized or returned to treatment at any time it becomes necessary for their treatment and rehabilitation.

(F) If the appropriate drug treatment facility or program reports to the probation officer that the offender has successfully completed treatment and is rehabilitated, the court may dismiss the charges pending against the offender. If the facility or program reports to the probation officer that the offender has successfully completed treatment and is rehabilitated or has obtained maximum benefits from treatment and that the offender has completed the period of rehabilitation and other conditions ordered by the court, the court shall dismiss the charges pending against the offender. If the facility or program reports to the probation officer that the offender has failed treatment, has failed to submit to or follow the prescribed treatment, or has become a discipline problem, if the offender does not satisfactorily complete the period of rehabilitation or the other conditions ordered by the court, or if the offender violates the conditions of the period of rehabilitation, the offender shall be arrested as provided in section 2951.08 of the Revised Code and removed from the facility or program, and the court immediately shall hold a hearing to determine if the offender failed treatment, failed to submit to or follow the prescribed treatment, did not satisfactorily complete the period of rehabilitation or any other condition ordered by the court, or violated any condition of the period of rehabilitation. If the court so determines, it immediately shall enter an adjudication of guilt and shall impose upon the offender a term of imprisonment.

At any time and for any appropriate reason, the offender, the offender's probation officer, the authority or department that has the duty to control and supervise the offender as provided for in section 2951.05 of the Revised Code, or the facility or program may petition the court to reconsider, suspend, or modify its order for treatment concerning that offender.

(G) The appropriate drug treatment facility or program shall report to the authority or department that has the duty to control and supervise the offender as provided for in section 2951.05 of the Revised Code at any periodic reporting period the court requires and whenever the offender is changed from an inpatient to an outpatient, is transferred to another treatment facility or program, fails treatment, fails to submit to or follow the prescribed treatment, becomes a discipline problem, does not satisfactorily complete the period of rehabilitation or other conditions ordered by the court, has violated the conditions of the period of rehabilitation, is rehabilitated, or obtains the maximum benefit of treatment.

(H) If, on the motion of an offender ordered to a period of rehabilitation under this section, the court finds that the offender has successfully completed the period of rehabilitation ordered by the court, is rehabilitated, is no longer drug dependent or in danger of becoming drug dependent, and has completed all other conditions, the court shall dismiss the proceeding against the offender. Successful completion of a period of rehabilitation under this section shall be without adjudication of guilt and is not a criminal conviction for purposes of disqualifications or disabilities imposed by law and upon conviction of a crime, and the court may order the sealing of records in the manner provided in sections 2953.31 to 2953.36 of the Revised Code.

(I) Any person ordered to treatment by the terms of this section shall be liable for expenses incurred during the course of treatment, and, if the offender is treated in a benevolent institution under the jurisdiction of the department of mental health, the offender is subject to Chapter 5121. of the Revised Code.

(J) An offender who is charged with a drug abuse

offense, other than a minor misdemeanor offense involving marihuana, and who otherwise is eligible for treatment in lieu of conviction may request and may be ordered to a period of rehabilitation even though the findings required by divisions (B)(1) and (2) of this section are not made. An order to rehabilitation under this division shall be subject to the conditions that the court requires but shall not be conditioned upon entry into an appropriate drug treatment facility or program.

(K) As used in this section, "community control sanction" has the same meaning as in section 2929.01 of the Revised Code.

HISTORY: 136 v H 300 (Eff 7-1-76); 138 v H 900 (Eff 7-1-80); 143 v H 317 (Eff 10-10-89); 143 v S 258 (Eff 11-20-90); 145 v H 385 (Eff 7-19-94); 146 v S 2 (Eff 7-1-96); 146 v S 269. Eff 7-1-96.

The effective date is set by section 5 of SB 269.

§ 2951.05 Control and supervision of offender on probation.

If an offender mentioned in section 2951.02 of the Revised Code resides in the county in which the trial was conducted, the court that issues an order of probation shall place the offender under the control and supervision of a department of probation in the county that serves the court. If there is no department of probation in the county that serves the court, the probation order, under section 2301.32 of the Revised Code, may place the offender on probation in charge of the adult parole authority created by section 5149.02 of the Revised Code that then shall have the powers and duties of a county department of probation. If the offender resides in a county other than the county in which the court granting probation is located and a county department of probation has been established in the county of residence or the county of residence is served by a multicounty probation department, the order of probation may request the court of common pleas of the county in which the offender resides to receive him into the control and supervision of that county or multicounty department of probation, subject to the jurisdiction of the trial judge over and with respect to the person of the offender, and to the rules governing that department of probation. If the offender's county of residence has no county or multicounty department of probation, the judge may place him on probation in charge of the adult parole authority created by section 5149.02 of the Revised Code.

As used in this section, "multicounty department of probation" means a probation department established under section 2301.27 of the Revised Code to serve more than one county.

HISTORY: GC § 13452-3; 113 v 123(201), ch 31, § 3; 121 v 381; Bureau of Code Revision, 10-1-53; 125 v S 155 (Eff 7-1-54); 128 v 959 (Eff 10-1-59); 129 v 481 (Eff 10-18-61); 130 v PtII, 146 (Eff 3-18-65); 145 v H 406. Eff 11-11-94.

§ 2951.06 Release from custody.

Upon entry in the records of the judge or magistrate, of the order for probation provided for in section 2951.02 of the Revised Code, the defendant shall be released from custody as soon as the requirements and conditions required by the judge supervising the probation, have been met. The defendant shall continue under the control and supervision of the adult parole authority created by section 5149.02 of the Revised Code, or the county department of probation, to the extent required by law, the conditions of the order of probation, and the rules and regulations governing said agency of probation.

HISTORY: GC § 13452-4; 113 v 123(202), ch 31, § 4; 121 v 381; Bureau of Code Revision, 10-1-53; 125 v S 155 (Eff 7-1-54); 129 v 481 (Eff 10-18-61); 130 v PtII, 147. Eff 3-18-65.

§ 2951.07 Probation period.

Probation under section 2951.02 of the Revised Code continues for the period that the judge or magistrate determines and, subject to division (F)(1)(a) of that section, may be extended. Except as provided in division (F)(1)(a) of that section, the total period of an offender's probation shall not exceed five years. If the probationer absconds or otherwise absents himself or herself from the jurisdiction of the court without permission from the county department of probation or the court to do so, or if the probationer is confined in any institution for the commission of any offense whatever, the probation period ceases to run until such time as the probationer is brought before the court for its further action.

HISTORY: GC § 13452-5; 113 v 123(202), ch 31, § 5; 115 v 531; Bureau of Code Revision, 10-1-53; 143 v S 258 (Eff 11-20-90); 146 v S 2 (Eff 7-1-96); 146 v S 269. Eff 7-1-96.

The effective date is set by section 5 of SB 269.

§ 2951.08 Arrest of person on probation or under community control sanction.

(A) During a period of probation or community control, any field officer or probation officer may arrest the person on probation or under a community control sanction without a warrant and bring the person before the judge or magistrate before whom the cause was pending. During a period of probation or community control, any peace officer may arrest the person on probation or under a community control sanction without a warrant upon the written order of the chief county probation officer if the person on probation or under a community control sanction is under the supervision of that county department of probation or on the order of an officer of the adult parole authority created pursuant to section 5149.02 of the Revised Code if the person on probation or under a community control sanction is under the supervision of the authority. During a period of probation or community control, any peace officer may arrest the person on probation or under a community control sanction on the warrant of the judge or magistrate before whom the cause was pending.

During a period of probation or community control, any peace officer may arrest the person on probation or under a community control sanction without a warrant if the peace officer has reasonable ground to believe the person has violated or is violating any of the following that is a condition of the person's probation or of the person's community control sanction:

(1) A condition that prohibits ownership, possession, or use of a firearm, deadly weapon, ammunition, or dangerous ordnance;

(2) A condition that prohibits the person from being within a specified structure or geographic area;

(3) A condition that confines the person to a residence, facility, or other structure;

(4) A condition that prohibits the person from contacting or communicating with any specified individual;

(5) A condition that prohibits the person from associating with a specified individual.

(B) Upon making an arrest under this section, the arresting field officer, probation officer, or peace officer or the department or agency of the arresting officer promptly shall notify the chief probation officer or the chief probation officer's designee that the person has been arrested. Upon being notified that a peace officer has made an arrest under this section, the chief probation officer or designee, or another probation officer designated by the chief probation officer, promptly shall bring the person who was arrested before the judge or magistrate before whom the cause was pending.

(C) Nothing in this section limits the powers of arrest granted to certain law enforcement officers and citizens under sections 2935.03 and 2935.04 of the Revised Code.

(D) As used in this section:

(1) "Peace officer" has the same meaning as in section 2935.01 of the Revised Code.

(2) "Firearm," "deadly weapon," and "dangerous ordnance" have the same meanings as in section 2923.11 of the Revised Code.

(3) "Community control sanction" has the same meaning as in section 2929.01 of the Revised Code.

HISTORY: GC § 13452-6; 113 v 123(202), ch 31, § 6; 121 v 381; Bureau of Code Revision, 10-1-53; 125 v S 155 (Eff 7-1-54); 129 v 481 (Eff 10-18-61); 130 v PtII, 147 (Eff 3-18-65); 144 v S 49 (Eff 7-21-92); 145 v H 406 (Eff 11-11-94); 146 v S 269. Eff 7-1-96.

The effective date is set by section 5 of SB 269.

§ 2951.09 Proceedings after arrest of probationer.

When a defendant on probation is brought before the judge or magistrate under section 2951.08 of the Revised Code, the judge or magistrate immediately shall inquire into the conduct of the defendant, and may terminate the probation and impose any sentence that originally could have been imposed or continue the probation and remand the defendant to the custody of the probation authority, at any time during the probationary period. When the ends of justice will be served and the good conduct of the defendant so held warrants it, the judge or magistrate may terminate the period of probation. At the end or termination of the period of probation, the jurisdiction of the judge or magistrate to impose sentence ceases and the defendant shall be discharged.

A probation officer shall receive necessary expenses in the performance of the officer's duties.

HISTORY: GC § 13452-7; 113 v 123(202), ch 31, § 7; 115 v 532; Bureau of Code Revision, 10-1-53; 143 v S 258 (Eff 11-20-90); 146 v S 2. Eff 7-1-96.

The effective date is set by section 6 of SB 2.

§ 2951.10 Final order.

An order suspending the imposition of sentence and placing the defendant on probation is a final order from which appeal may be prosecuted.

HISTORY: GC § 13452-9; 113 v 123(202), ch 31, § 9; Bureau of Code Revision. Eff 10-1-53.

§ 2951.11 Repealed, 134 v H 511, § 2 [GC § 13452-10; 113 v 123(203); Bureau of Code Revision, 10-1-53; 133 v S 460]. Eff 1-1-74.

This section concerned parole by board of county commissioners.

§ 2951.12 Repealed, 136 v H 1, § 2 [GC § 13452-11; 113 v 123(203); Bureau of Code Revision, 10-1-53; 133 v S 460]. Eff 6-13-75.

This section concerned recommitment for failure to comply with conditions of parole.

§ 2951.13 Attendance at revocation hearing.

A convict confined in a state correctional institution for a felony committed while the convict was under a community control sanction imposed for a former conviction may be removed from the institution for the purpose of attending a hearing on revocation of the community control sanction. When a copy of the journal entry ordering the revocation hearing is presented to the warden or superintendent of the institution where the convict is confined, the warden or superintendent shall deliver the convict to the sheriff of the county where the hearing is to be held, and the sheriff shall convey the convict to and from the hearing. The approval of the governor on the journal entry is not required.

HISTORY: 133 v H 1136 (Eff 5-26-70); 140 v H 291 (Eff 7-1-83); 145 v H 571 (Eff 10-6-94); 146 v S 2. Eff 7-1-96.

The effective date is set by section 6 of SB 2.

CHAPTER 2953: APPEALS; OTHER POSTCONVICTION REMEDIES

Section
2953.01　Definition of magistrate.
2953.02　Review of judgments.
2953.03　Motion for new trial or filing of appeal if defendant on bail.
2953.04, 2953.05　Repealed.
[2953.05.1] 2953.051　Repealed.
2953.06　Repealed.
2953.07　Disposition of appeal; setting of execution date.
2953.08　Grounds for appeal by defendant or prosecutor of sentence for felony; appeal cost oversight committee.
2953.09　Suspension of sentence in criminal cases; bail.
2953.10　Power to suspend sentence.
2953.11　Custody of defendant under suspended sentence.
2953.12　Repealed.
2953.13　Procedure when conviction is reversed.
2953.14　State may seek review.

[POSTCONVICTION REMEDIES]
2953.21　Petition for postconviction relief.
2953.22　Hearing.
2953.23　Time for filing petition; appeals.
2953.24　Repealed.

[SEALING OF RECORD OF CONVICTION]
2953.31　Definitions.
2953.32　Sealing of record of conviction or bail forfeiture.
[2953.32.1] 2953.321　Disposition and use of investigatory work product.
2953.33　Rights and privileges restored; answering questions.
2953.34　First offender may still take appeal or seek relief.
2953.35　Divulging confidential information.
2953.36　Application of preceding sections.
2953.41-2953.43　Repealed.

[SEALING OF RECORDS AFTER NOT GUILTY OR DISMISSAL]
2953.51　Definitions.
2953.52　Sealing of official records after not guilty finding, dismissal of proceedings or no bill.
2953.53　Order to seal records; index of sealed records.
2953.54　Disposition and use of specific investigatory work product; divulging confidential information.
2953.55　Inquiry as to sealed records prohibited; divulging confidential information.
2953.61　Sealing of records in cases of multiple charges.

§ 2953.01 Definition of magistrate.

The definition of "magistrate" set forth in section 2931.01 of the Revised Code applies to Chapter 2953. of the Revised Code.

HISTORY: Bureau of Code Revision. Eff 10-1-53.

§ 2953.02 Review of judgments.

In a capital case in which a sentence of death is imposed for an offense committed before January 1, 1995, and in any other criminal case, including a conviction for the violation of an ordinance of a municipal corporation, the judgment or final order of a court of record inferior to the court of appeals may be reviewed in the court of appeals. A final order of an administrative officer or agency may be reviewed in the court of common pleas. A judgment or final order of the court of appeals involving a question arising under the Constitution of the United States or of this state may be appealed to the supreme court as a matter of right. This right of appeal from judgments and final orders of the court of appeals shall extend to cases in which a sentence of death is imposed for an offense committed before January 1, 1995, and in which the death penalty has been affirmed, felony cases in which the supreme court has directed the court of appeals to certify its record, and in all other criminal cases of public or general interest wherein the supreme court has granted a motion to certify the record of the court of appeals. In a capital case in which a sentence of death is imposed for an offense committed on or after January 1, 1995, the judgment or final order may be appealed from the trial court directly to the supreme court as a matter of right. The supreme court in criminal cases shall not be required to determine as to the weight of the evidence, except that, in cases in which a sentence of death is imposed for an offense committed on or after January 1, 1995, and in which the question of the weight of the evidence to support the judgment has been raised on appeal, the supreme court shall determine as to the weight of the evidence to support the judgment and shall determine as to the weight of the evidence to support the sentence of death as provided in section 2929.05 of the Revised Code.

HISTORY: GC § 13459-1; 113 v 123(211), ch 38; Bureau of Code Revision, 10-1-53; 128 v 141 (Eff 1-1-60); 133 v S 530 (Eff 6-12-70); 139 v S 1 (Eff 10-19-81); 146 v S 4. Eff 9-21-95.

§ 2953.03 Motion for new trial or filing of appeal if defendant on bail.

(A) If a motion for a new trial is filed pursuant to Criminal Rule 33 by a defendant who is convicted of a misdemeanor under the Revised Code or an ordinance of a municipal corporation, and if that defendant was on bail at the time of the conviction of that offense, the trial judge or magistrate shall suspend execution of the sentence or judgment imposed pending the determination on the motion for a new trial and shall determine the amount and nature of any bail that is required of the defendant in accordance with Criminal Rule 46.

(B) If a notice of appeal is filed pursuant to the Rules of Appellate Procedure or Chapter 1905. of the Revised Code by a defendant who is convicted in a municipal, county, or mayor's court or a court of common pleas of a misdemeanor under the Revised Code or an ordinance of a municipal corporation, if that defendant was on bail at the time of the conviction of that offense, and if execution of the sentence or judgment imposed is suspended, the trial court or magistrate or the court in which the appeal is being prosecuted shall determine the amount and nature of any bail that is required of the defendant as follows:

(1) In the case of an appeal to a court of appeals by a defendant who is convicted in a municipal or county court or a court of common pleas, in accordance with Appellate Rule 8 and Criminal Rule 46;

(2) In the case of an appeal to a municipal or county court by a defendant who is convicted in a mayor's court, in accordance with Criminal Rule 46.

HISTORY: 141 v H 412. Eff 3-17-87.

Not analogous to former RC § 2953.03 (GC § 13459-2; 113 v 123(212), ch 38, § 2; Bureau of Code Revision, 10-1-53; 128 v 144; 129 v 305; 130 v 672; 136 v H 164), repealed 141 v H 412, § 2, eff 3-17-87.

§§ 2953.04, 2953.05 Repealed, 141 v H 412, § 2 [GC §§ 13459-3, 13459-4; 113 v 123(212), ch 38, §§ 3, 4; 116 v 104 (116, 117), § 2; Bureau of Code Revision, 10-1-53; 128 v 141]. Eff 3-17-87.

These sections concerned proceedings to review and appeal.

[§ 2953.05.1] § 2953.051 Repealed, 141 v H 412, § 2 [128 v 141]. Eff 3-17-87.

This section concerned suspension of sentence and continuance of bail.

§ 2953.06 Repealed, 141 v H 412, § 2 [GC § 13459-5; 113 v 123(212), ch 38, § 5; 116 v 104(117), § 2; Bureau of Code Revision, 10-1-53]. Eff 3-17-87.

This section concerned notice of appeal served upon prosecuting attorney.

§ 2953.07 Disposition of appeal; setting of execution date.

Upon the hearing of an appeal other than an appeal from a mayor's court, the appellate court may affirm the judgment or reverse it, in whole or in part, or modify it, and order the accused to be discharged or grant a new trial. The appellate court may remand the accused for the sole purpose of correcting a sentence imposed contrary to law, provided that, on an appeal of a sentence imposed upon a person who is convicted of or pleads guilty to a felony that is brought under section 2953.08 of the Revised Code, division (G) of that section applies to the court. If the judgment is reversed, the appellant shall recover from the appellee all court costs incurred to secure the reversal, including the cost of transcripts. In capital cases, when the judgment is affirmed and the day fixed for the execution is passed, the appellate court shall appoint a day for it, and the clerk of the appellate court shall issue a warrant under the seal of the appellate court, to the sheriff of the proper county, or the warden of the appropriate state correctional institution, commanding the sheriff or warden to carry the sentence into execution on the day so appointed. The sheriff or warden shall execute and return the warrant as in other cases, and the clerk shall record the warrant and return.

(B) As used in this section, "appellate court" means, for a case in which a sentence of death is imposed for an offense committed before January 1, 1995, both the court of appeals and the supreme court, and for a case in which a sentence of death is imposed for an offense committed on or after January 1, 1995, the supreme court.

HISTORY: GC § 13459-6; 113 v 123(213), ch 38, § 6; 116 v 104(117), § 2; Bureau of Code Revision, 10-1-53; 141 v H 412 (Eff 3-17-87); 145 v H 571 (Eff 10-6-94); 146 v S 4 (Eff 9-21-95); 146 v S 2. Eff 7-1-96.

The effective date is set by section 6 of SB 2.

See provisions, § 5 of SB 2 (146 v —) as amended by § 3 of SB 269 (146 v —), following RC § 2929.03.

See Comment, Legislative Service Commission following RC § 2929.03.

§ 2953.08 Grounds for appeal by defendant or prosecutor of sentence for felony; appeal cost oversight committee.

(A) In addition to any other right to appeal and except as provided in division (D) of this section, a defendant who is convicted of or pleads guilty to a felony may appeal as a matter of right the sentence imposed upon the defendant on one of the following grounds:

(1) The sentence consisted of or included the maximum prison term allowed for the offense by division (A) of section 2929.14 of the Revised Code and was not imposed pursuant to division (D)(3)(b) of section 2929.14 of the Revised Code, and the court imposed it under one of the following circumstances:

(a) The sentence was imposed for only one offense.

(b) The sentence was imposed for two or more offenses arising out of a single incident, and the court imposed the maximum prison term for the offense of the highest degree.

(2) The sentence consisted of or included a prison term, the offense for which it was imposed is a felony of the fourth or fifth degree or is a felony drug offense that is a violation of a provision of Chapter 2925. of the Revised Code and that is specified as being subject to division (B) of section 2929.13 of the Revised Code for purposes of sentencing, and the court did not specify at sentencing that it found one or more factors specified in divisions (B)(1)(a) to (h) of section 2929.13 of the Revised Code to apply relative to the defendant. If the court specifies that it found one or more of those factors to apply relative to the defendant, the defendant is not entitled under this division to appeal as a matter of right the sentence imposed upon the offender.

(3) The person was convicted of or pleaded guilty to

a sexually violent offense, was adjudicated as being a sexually violent predator, and was sentenced pursuant to division (A)(3) of section 2971.03 of the Revised Code, if the minimum term of the indefinite term imposed pursuant to division (A)(3) of section 2971.03 of the Revised Code is the longest term available for the offense from among the range of terms listed in section 2929.14 of the Revised Code. As used in this division, "sexually violent offense" and "sexually violent predator" have the same meanings as in section 2971.01 of the Revised Code.

(4) The sentence is contrary to law.

(5) The sentence consisted of an additional prison term of ten years imposed pursuant to division (D)(3)(b) of section 2929.14 of the Revised Code.

(B) In addition to any other right to appeal and except as provided in division (D) of this section, a prosecuting attorney, a city director of law, village solicitor, or similar chief legal officer of a municipal corporation, or the attorney general, if one of those persons prosecuted the case, may appeal as a matter of right a sentence imposed upon a defendant who is convicted of or pleads guilty to a felony or, in the circumstances described in division (B)(3) of this section the modification of a sentence imposed upon such a defendant, on any of the following grounds:

(1) The sentence did not include a prison term despite a presumption favoring a prison term for the offense for which it was imposed, as set forth in section 2929.13 or Chapter 2925. of the Revised Code.

(2) The sentence is contrary to law.

(3) The sentence is a modification under section 2929.20 of the Revised Code of a sentence that was imposed for a felony of the first or second degree.

(C) In addition to the right to appeal a sentence granted under division (A) or (B) of this section, a defendant who is convicted of or pleads guilty to a felony may seek leave to appeal a sentence imposed upon the defendant on the basis that the sentencing judge has imposed consecutive sentences under division (E)(3) or (4) of section 2929.14 of the Revised Code and that the consecutive sentences exceed the maximum prison term allowed by division (A) of that section for the most serious offense of which the defendant was convicted. Upon the filing of a motion under this division, the court of appeals may grant leave to appeal the sentence if the court determines that the allegation included as the basis of the motion is true.

(D) A sentence imposed upon a defendant is not subject to review under this section if the sentence is authorized by law, has been recommended jointly by the defendant and the prosecution in the case, and is imposed by a sentencing judge. A sentence imposed for aggravated murder or murder pursuant to sections 2929.02 to 2929.06 of the Revised Code is not subject to review under this section.

(E) A defendant, prosecuting attorney, city director of law, village solicitor, or chief municipal legal officer shall file an appeal of a sentence under this section to a court of appeals within the time limits specified in Rule 4(B) of the Rules of Appellate Procedure, provided that if the appeal is pursuant to division (B)(3) of this section, the time limits specified in that rule shall not commence running until the court grants the motion that makes the sentence modification in question. A sentence appeal under this section shall be consolidated with any other appeal in the case. If no other appeal is filed, the court of appeals may review only the portions of the trial record that pertain to sentencing.

(F) On the appeal of a sentence under this section, the record to be reviewed shall include all of the following, as applicable:

(1) Any presentence, psychiatric, or other investigative report that was submitted to the court in writing before the sentence was imposed. An appellate court that reviews a presentence investigation report prepared pursuant to section 2947.06 or 2951.03 of the Revised Code or Criminal Rule 32.2 in connection with the appeal of a sentence under this section shall comply with division (D)(3) of section 2951.03 of the Revised Code when the appellate court is not using the presentence investigation report, and the appellate court's use of a presentence investigation report of that nature in connection with the appeal of a sentence under this section does not affect the otherwise confidential character of the contents of that report as described in division (D)(1) of section 2951.03 of the Revised Code and does not cause that report to become a public record, as defined in section 149.43 of the Revised Code, following the appellate court's use of the report.

(2) The trial record in the case in which the sentence was imposed;

(3) Any oral or written statements made to or by the court at the sentencing hearing at which the sentence was imposed;

(4) Any written findings that the court was required to make in connection with the modification of the sentence pursuant to a judicial release under division (H) of section 2929.20 of the Revised Code.

(G)(1) The court hearing an appeal of a sentence under division (A) or (B)(1) or (2) of this section may increase, reduce, or otherwise modify a sentence that is appealed under this section or may vacate the sentence and remand the matter to the trial court for resentencing if the court clearly and convincingly finds any of the following:

(a) That the record does not support the sentence;

(b) That the sentence included a prison term, that the offense for which it was imposed is a felony of the fourth or fifth degree or is a felony drug offense that is a violation of a provision of Chapter 2925. of the Revised Code and that is specified as being subject to division (B) of section 2929.13 of the Revised Code for purposes of sentencing, that the court did not specify in the finding it makes at sentencing that it found one or more of the factors specified in divisions (B)(1)(a) to (h) of section 2929.13 of the Revised Code to apply relative to the defendant who brought the appeal, and either that the procedures set forth in division (B) of section 2929.13 of the Revised Code for determining whether to impose a prison term for such an offense were not followed or that those procedures were followed but there is an insufficient basis for imposing a prison term for the offense;

(c) That the sentence did not include a prison term, that the offense for which it was imposed is a felony of the first or second degree or is a felony drug offense that is a violation of a provision of Chapter 2925. of the Revised Code for which a presumption in favor of a prison term is specified as being applicable, and either that the procedures set forth in division (D) of section 2929.13 of the Revised Code that set forth the only circumstances in which the presumption may be overridden and a sanction other than a prison term may be imposed in lieu of a prison term were not followed or that those procedures were followed but there is an insufficient basis for overriding the presumption and imposing a sanction other than a prison term for the offense;

(d) That the sentence is otherwise contrary to law.

(2) The court hearing an appeal under division (B)(3) of this section of a trial court's modification pursuant to section 2929.20 of the Revised Code of a sentence that was imposed upon a defendant for a felony of a first or second degree may overturn the modification and reinstate the original sentence, or may vacate the modification of the sentence and remand the matter to the trial court for reconsideration, only if the court clearly and convincingly finds any of the following:

(a) That the record does not support the modification based on the criteria for modification set forth in division (H) of section 2929.20 of the Revised Code;

(b) That the modification was not made in accordance with the procedures set forth in section 2929.20 of the Revised Code, that the defendant was not eligible for the modification under that section, or that the modification otherwise was contrary to law.

(H) A judgment or final order of a court of appeals under this section may be appealed, by leave of court, to the supreme court.

(I)(1) There is hereby established the felony sentence appeal cost oversight committee, consisting of eight members. One member shall be the chief justice of the supreme court or a representative of the court designated by the chief justice, one member shall be a member of the senate appointed by the president of the senate, one member shall be a member of the house of representatives appointed by the speaker of the house of representatives, one member shall be the director of budget and management or a representative of the office of budget and management designated by the director, one member shall be a judge of a court of appeals, court of common pleas, municipal court, or county court appointed by the chief justice of the supreme court, one member shall be the state public defender or a representative of the office of the state public defender designated by the state public defender, one member shall be a prosecuting attorney appointed by the Ohio prosecuting attorneys association, and one member shall be a county commissioner appointed by the county commissioners association of Ohio. No more than three of the appointed members of the committee may be members of the same political party.

The president of the senate, the speaker of the house of representatives, the chief justice of the supreme court, the Ohio prosecuting attorneys association, and the county commissioners association of Ohio shall make the initial appointments to the committee of the appointed members no later than ninety days after July 1, 1996. Of those initial appointments to the committee, the members appointed by the speaker of the house of representatives and the Ohio prosecuting attorneys association shall serve a term ending two years after July 1, 1996, the member appointed by the chief justice of the supreme court shall serve a term ending three years after July 1, 1996, and the members appointed by the president of the senate and the county commissioners association of Ohio shall serve terms ending four years after July 1, 1996. Thereafter, terms of office of the appointed members shall be for four years, with each term ending on the same day of the same month as did the term that it succeeds. Members may be reappointed. Vacancies shall be filled in the same manner provided for original appointments. A member appointed to fill a vacancy occurring prior to the expiration of the term for which that member's predecessor was appointed shall hold office as a member for the remainder of the predecessor's term. An appointed member shall continue in office subsequent to the expiration date of that member's term until that member's successor takes office or until a period of sixty days has elapsed, whichever occurs first.

If the chief justice of the supreme court, the director of the office of budget and management, or the state public defender serves as a member of the committee, that person's term of office as a member shall continue for as long as that person holds office as chief justice, director of the office of budget and management, or state public defender. If the chief justice of the supreme court designates a representative of the court to serve as a member, the director of budget and management designates a representative of the office of budget and management to serve as a member, or the state public defender designates a representative of the office of the state public defender to serve as a member, the person so designated shall serve as a member of the commission for as long as the official who made the designation holds office as chief justice, director of the office of budget and management, or state public defender or until that official revokes the designation.

The chief justice of the supreme court or the representative of the supreme court appointed by the chief justice shall serve as chairperson of the committee. The committee shall meet within two weeks after all appointed members have been appointed and shall organize as necessary. Thereafter, the committee shall meet at least once every six months or more often upon the call of the chairperson or the written request of three or more members, provided that the committee shall not meet unless moneys have been appropriated to the judiciary budget administered by the supreme court specifically for the purpose of providing financial assistance to counties under division (I)(2) of this section and the moneys so appropriated then are available for that purpose.

The members of the committee shall serve without compensation, but, if moneys have been appropriated to the judiciary budget administered by the supreme court specifically for the purpose of providing financial assistance to counties under division (I)(2) of this section, each member shall be reimbursed out of the moneys so appropriated that then are available for actual and necessary expenses incurred in the performance of official duties as a committee member.

(2) The state criminal sentencing commission periodically shall provide to the felony sentence appeal cost oversight committee all data the commission collects pursuant to division (A)(5) of section 181.25 of the Revised Code. Upon receipt of the data from the state criminal sentencing commission, the felony sentence appeal cost oversight committee periodically shall review the data; determine whether any money has been appropriated to the judiciary budget administered by the supreme court specifically for the purpose of providing state financial assistance to counties in accordance with this division for the increase in expenses the counties experience as a result of the felony sentence appeal provisions set forth in this section or as a result of a postconviction relief proceeding brought under division (A)(2) of section 2953.21 of the Revised Code or an appeal of a judgment in that proceeding; if it determines that any money has been so appropriated, determine the total amount of moneys that have been so appropriated specifically for that purpose and that then are available for that purpose; and develop a recommended method of distributing those moneys to the counties. The committee shall send a copy of its recommendation to the supreme court. Upon receipt of the committee's recommendation, the supreme court shall distribute to the counties, based upon that recommendation, the moneys that have been so appropriated specifically for the purpose of providing state financial assistance to counties under this division and that then are available for that purpose.

HISTORY: 146 v S 2 (Eff 7-1-96); 146 v S 269 (Eff 7-1-96); 146 v H 180 (Eff 1-1-97); 147 v H 151. Eff 9-16-97.

See provisions, § 3 of HB 151 (147 v —) following RC § 2929.14.

The provisions of § 4 of SB 2 (146 v —) read as follows:

SECTION 4. The General Assembly hereby requests the Supreme Court to adopt rules to specify procedures for and to expedite the appeals of sentences authorized under section 2953.08 of the Revised Code, including a rule that permits a court of appeals to rule on an appeal of sentence without a hearing, without addressing issues raised by the appellant that do not have merit, and without a written opinion.

The General Assembly hereby requests the Supreme Court to adopt a rule that requires a court of common pleas to maintain, in a court file that is accessible to the public, the following information in regard to each case in which an offender is convicted of or pleads guilty to a felony: the case number, the name of the judge, and the race, ethnic background, gender, and religion of the defendant.

§ 2953.09 Suspension of sentence in criminal cases; bail.

(A)(1) Upon filing an appeal in the supreme court, the execution of the sentence or judgment imposed in cases of felony is suspended.

(2)(a) If a notice of appeal is filed pursuant to the Rules of Appellate Procedure by a defendant who is convicted in a municipal or county court or a court of common pleas of a felony or misdemeanor under the Revised Code or an ordinance of a municipal corporation, the filing of the notice of appeal does not suspend execution of the sentence or judgment imposed. However, consistent with divisions (A)(2)(b), (B), and (C) of this section, Appellate Rule 8, and Criminal Rule 46, the municipal or county court, court of common pleas, or court of appeals may suspend execution of the sentence or judgment imposed during the pendency of the appeal and shall determine whether that defendant is entitled to bail and the amount and nature of any bail that is required. The bail shall at least be conditioned that the defendant will prosecute the appeal without delay and abide by the judgment and sentence of the court.

(b)(i) A court of common pleas or court of appeals may suspend the execution of a sentence of death imposed for an offense committed before January 1, 1995, only if no date for execution has been set by the supreme court, good cause is shown for the suspension, the defendant files a motion requesting the suspension, and notice has been given to the prosecuting attorney of the appropriate county.

(ii) A court of common pleas may suspend the execution of a sentence of death imposed for an offense committed on or after January 1, 1995, only if no date for execution has been set by the supreme court, good cause is shown, the defendant files a motion requesting the suspension, and notice has been given to the prosecuting attorney of the appropriate county.

(iii) A court of common pleas or court of appeals may suspend the execution of the sentence or judgment imposed for a felony in a capital case in which a sentence of death is not imposed only if no date for execution of the sentence has been set by the supreme court, good cause is shown for the suspension, the defendant files a motion requesting the suspension, and only after notice has been given to the prosecuting attorney of the appropriate county.

(B) Notwithstanding any provision of Criminal Rule 46 to the contrary, a trial judge of a court of common pleas shall not release on bail pursuant to division (A)(2)(a) of this section a defendant who is convicted of a bailable offense if the defendant is sentenced to imprisonment for life or if that offense is a violation of section 2903.01, 2903.02, 2903.03, 2903.04, 2903.11, 2905.01, 2905.02, 2905.11, 2907.02, 2909.02, 2911.01, 2911.02, or 2911.11 of the Revised Code or is felonious sexual penetration in violation of former section 2907.12 of the Revised Code.

(C) If a trial judge of a court of common pleas is prohibited by division (B) of this section from releasing on bail pursuant to division (A)(2)(a) of this section a defendant who is convicted of a bailable offense and not sentenced to imprisonment for life, the appropriate court of appeals or two judges of it, upon motion of the defendant and for good cause shown, may release the defendant on bail in accordance with division (A)(2) of this section.

HISTORY: GC § 13459-8; 113 v 123(213), ch 38, § 8; 116 v 104(118), § 2; Bureau of Code Revision, 10-1-53; 129 v 423 (Eff 10-19-61); 139 v S 199 (Eff 7-1-83); 141 v H 412 (Eff 3-17-87); 146 v S 4 (Eff 9-21-95) 146 v H 445. Eff 9-3-96.

§ 2953.10 Power to suspend sentence.

When an appeal is taken from a court of appeals to the supreme court, the supreme court has the same power and authority to suspend the execution of sentence during the pendency of the appeal and admit the defendant to bail as does the court of appeals unless another section of the Revised Code or the Rules of Practice of the Supreme Court specify a distinct bail or suspension of sentence authority.

When an appeal in a case in which a sentence of death is imposed for an offense committed on or after January 1, 1995, is taken directly from the trial court to the supreme court, the supreme court has the same power and authority to suspend the execution of the sentence during the pendency of the appeal and admit the defendant to bail as does the court of appeals for cases in which a sentence of death is imposed for an offense committed before January 1, 1995, unless another section of the Revised Code or the Rules of Practice of the Supreme Court specify a distinct bail or suspension of sentence authority.

HISTORY: GC § 13459-8a; 123 v 748; Bureau of Code Revision, 10-1-53; 141 v H 412 (Eff 3-17-87); 146 v S 4. Eff 9-21-95.

§ 2953.11 Custody of defendant under suspended sentence.

In cases of conviction of felony, except for aggravated murder or murder, if the defendant has been committed to a state correctional institution and sentence is suspended, the clerk of the court in which the entry is made suspending the sentence under the seal of the court shall forthwith certify the suspension to the warden of the state correctional institution, who shall deliver the defendant to the sheriff of the county in which the defendant was convicted. The sheriff thereupon shall convey the defendant to the jail of the county in which the defendant was convicted and keep the defendant in custody unless admitted to bail pending the decision on the appeal or the termination of the suspension of sentence. If the judgment is affirmed or if the suspension of sentence is terminated, the sheriff shall convey the defendant to the state correctional institution to serve the balance of the defendant's term of sentence. The supreme court in the order allowing the filing of an appeal may provide that the defendant shall remain in the custody of the warden of the state correctional institution pending the decision of the court in such case.

HISTORY: GC § 13459-9; 113 v 123(213), ch 38, § 9; 116 v 104(118), § 2; Bureau of Code Revision, 10-1-53; 129 v 322 (Eff 7-14-61); 145 v H 571 (Eff 10-6-94); 146 v S 2. Eff 7-1-96.

The effective date is set by section 6 of SB 2.

See provisions, § 5 of SB 2 (146 v —), as amended by § 3 of SB 269 (146 v —), effective 7-1-96, following RC § 2929.03.

§ 2953.12 Repealed, 141 v H 412, § 2 [GC § 13459-10; 113 v 123(214), ch 38, § 10; 116 v 104(118), § 2; Bureau of Code Revision, 10-1-53]. Eff 3-17-87.

This section ruled suspending execution of sentence in misdemeanor cases did not take effect until recognizance given.

§ 2953.13 Procedure when conviction is reversed.

When a defendant has been committed to a state correctional institution and the judgment, by virtue of which the commitment was made, is reversed on appeal, and the defendant is entitled to his discharge or a new trial, the clerk of the court reversing the judgment, under the seal thereof, shall forthwith certify said reversal to the warden of the state correctional institution.

The warden, on receipt of the certificate, if a discharge of the defendant is ordered, shall forthwith discharge him from the state correctional institution.

If a new trial is ordered, the warden shall forthwith cause the defendant to be conveyed to the jail of the county in which he was convicted, and committed to the custody of the sheriff thereof.

HISTORY: GC §§ 13459-11—13459-13; 113 v 123(214), ch 38, §§ 11-13; 116 v 104(118), § 2; Bureau of Code Revision, 10-1-53; 145 v H 571. Eff 10-6-94.

§ 2953.14 State may seek review.

Whenever a court superior to the trial court renders judgment adverse to the state in a criminal action or proceeding, the state, through either the prosecuting attorney or the attorney general, may institute an appeal to reverse such judgment in the next higher court. If the conviction was for a violation of a municipal ordinance, such appeal may be brought by the village solicitor, city director of law, or other chief legal officer of the municipal corporation. Like proceedings shall be had in the higher court at the hearing of the appeal as in the review of other criminal actions or proceedings. The clerk of the court rendering the judgment sought to be reversed, on application of the prosecuting attorney, attorney general, solicitor, director of law, or other chief legal officer shall make a transcript of the docket and journal entries in the action or proceeding, and transmit it with all papers and files in the action or proceeding to the higher court.

HISTORY: GC § 13459-14; 113 v 123(214), ch 38, § 14; 116 v 104(119), § 2; Bureau of Code Revision, 10-1-53; 137 v H 219 (Eff 11-1-77); 141 v H 412. Eff 3-17-87.

[POSTCONVICTION REMEDIES]

§ 2953.21 Petition for postconviction relief.

(A)(1) Any person who has been convicted of a criminal offense or adjudicated a delinquent child and who claims that there was such a denial or infringement of the person's rights as to render the judgment void or voidable under the Ohio Constitution or the Constitution of the United States may file a petition in the court that imposed sentence, stating the grounds for relief relied upon, and asking the court to vacate or set aside the judgment or sentence or to grant other appropriate relief. The petitioner may file a supporting affidavit and other documentary evidence in support of the claim for relief.

(2) A petition under division (A)(1) of this section shall be filed no later than one hundred eighty days after the date on which the trial transcript is filed in the court of appeals in the direct appeal of the judgment of conviction or adjudication or, if the direct appeal involves a sentence of death, the date on which the trial transcript is filed in the supreme court. If no appeal is taken, the petition shall be filed no later than one hundred eighty days after the expiration of the time for filing the appeal.

(3) In a petition filed under division (A) of this section, a person upon whom a sentence of death has been imposed may ask the court to render void or voidable the judgment with respect to the conviction of aggravated murder or the specification of an aggravating circumstance.

(4) A petitioner shall state in the original or amended petition filed under division (A) of this section all grounds for relief claimed by the petitioner. Except as provided in section 2953.23 of the Revised Code, any ground for relief that is not so stated in the petition is waived.

(5) If the petitioner in a petition filed under division (A) of this section was convicted of or pleaded guilty to a felony, the petition may include a claim that the petitioner was denied the equal protection of the laws in violation of the Ohio Constitution or the United States Constitution because the sentence imposed upon the petitioner for the felony was part of a consistent pattern of disparity in sentencing by the judge who imposed the sentence, with regard to the petitioner's race, gender, ethnic background, or religion. If the supreme court adopts a rule requiring a court of common pleas to maintain information with regard to an offender's race, gender, ethnic background, or religion, the supporting evidence for the petition shall include, but shall not be limited to, a copy of that type of information relative to the petitioner's sentence and copies of that type of information relative to sentences that the same judge imposed upon other persons.

(B) The clerk of the court in which the petition is filed shall docket the petition and bring it promptly to the attention of the court. The petitioner need not serve a copy of the petition on the prosecuting attorney. The clerk of the court in which the petition is filed immediately shall forward a copy of the petition to the prosecuting attorney of that county.

(C) The court shall consider a petition that is timely filed under division (A)(2) of this section even if a direct appeal of the judgment is pending. Before granting a hearing on a petition filed under division (A) of this section, the court shall determine whether there are substantive grounds for relief. In making such a determination, the court shall consider, in addition to the petition, the supporting affidavits, and the documentary evidence, all the files and records pertaining to the proceedings against the petitioner, including, but not limited to, the indictment, the court's journal entries, the journalized records of the clerk of the court, and the court reporter's transcript. The court reporter's transcript, if ordered and certified by the court, shall be taxed as court costs. If the court dismisses the petition, it shall make and file findings of fact and conclusions of law with respect to such dismissal.

(D) Within ten days after the docketing of the petition, or within any further time that the court may fix for good cause shown, the prosecuting attorney shall respond by answer or motion. Within twenty days from the date the issues are made up, either party may move for summary judgment. The right to summary judgment shall appear on the face of the record.

(E) Unless the petition and the files and records of the case show the petitioner is not entitled to relief, the court shall proceed to a prompt hearing on the issues even if a direct appeal of the case is pending. If the court notifies the parties that it has found grounds for granting relief, either party may request an appellate court in which a direct appeal of the judgment is pending to remand the pending case to the court.

(F) At any time before the answer or motion is filed, the petitioner may amend the petition with or without leave or prejudice to the proceedings. The petitioner may amend the petition with leave of court at any time thereafter.

(G) If the court does not find grounds for granting relief, it shall make and file findings of fact and conclusions of law and shall enter judgment denying relief on the petition. If no direct appeal of the case is pending and the court finds grounds for relief or if a pending direct appeal of the case has been remanded to the court pursuant to a request made pursuant to division (E) of this section and the court finds grounds for granting relief, it shall make and file findings of fact and conclusions of law and shall enter a judgment that vacates and sets aside the judgment in question, and, in the case of a petitioner who is a prisoner in custody, shall discharge or resentence the petitioner or grant a new trial as the court determines appropriate. The court also may make supplementary orders to the relief granted, concerning such matters as rearraignment, retrial, custody, and bail. If the trial court's order granting the petition is reversed on appeal and if the direct appeal of the case has been remanded from an appellate court pursuant to a request under division (E) of this section, the appellate court reversing the order granting the petition shall notify the appellate court in which the direct appeal of the case was pending at the time of the remand of the reversal and remand of the trial court's order. Upon the reversal and remand of the trial court's order granting the petition, regardless of whether notice is sent or received, the direct appeal of the case that was remanded is reinstated.

(H) Upon the filing of a petition pursuant to division (A) of this section by a prisoner in a state correctional institution who has received the death penalty, the court may stay execution of the judgment challenged by the petition.

(I)(1) If a person who has received the death penalty intends to file a petition under this section, the court shall appoint counsel to represent the person upon a finding that the person is indigent and that the person either accepts the appointment of counsel or is unable to make a competent decision whether to accept or reject the appointment of counsel. The court may decline to appoint counsel for the person only upon a finding, after a hearing if necessary, that the person rejects the appointment of counsel and understands the legal consequences of that decision or upon a finding that the person is not indigent.

(2) The court shall not appoint as counsel under division (I)(1) of this section an attorney who represented the petitioner at trial in the case to which the petition relates unless the person and the attorney expressly request the appointment. The court shall appoint as counsel under division (I)(1) of this section only an attorney who is certified under Rule 65 of the Rules of Superintendence for Courts of Common Pleas to represent indigent defendants charged with or convicted of an offense for which the death penalty can be or has been imposed. The ineffectiveness or incompetence of counsel during proceedings under this section does not constitute grounds for relief in a proceeding under this section, in an appeal of any action under this section, or in an application to reopen a direct appeal.

(3) Division (I) of this section does not preclude attorneys who represent the state of Ohio from invoking the provisions of 28 U.S.C. 154 with respect to capital cases that were pending in federal habeas corpus proceedings prior to the effective date of this amendment insofar as the petitioners in those cases were represented in proceedings under this section by one or more counsel appointed by the court under this section or section 120.06, 120.16, 120.26, or 120.33 of the Revised Code and those appointed counsel meet the requirements of division (I)(2) of this section.

(J) Subject to the appeal of a sentence for a felony that is authorized by section 2953.08 of the Revised Code, the remedy set forth in this section is the exclusive remedy by which a person may bring a collateral challenge to the validity of a conviction or sentence in a criminal case or the validity of an adjudication of a child as a delinquent child for the commission of an act that would be a criminal offense if committed by an adult or the validity of a related order of disposition.

HISTORY: 131 v 684 (Eff 7-21-65); 132 v H 742 (Eff 12-9-67); 141 v H 412 (Eff 3-17-87); 145 v H 571 (Eff 10-6-94); 146 v S 4 (Eff 9-21-95); 146 v S 2 (Eff 7-1-96); 146 v S 269 (Eff 7-1-96); 146 v S 258. Eff 10-16-96.

Comment, Legislative Service Commission

Section 2953.21 of the Revised Code is amended by this act [Am. Sub. S.B. 269] and also by Sub. S.B. 258 of the 121st General Assembly. Comparison of these amendments in pursuance of section 1.52 of the Revised Code discloses that they are not irreconcilable so that they are required by that section to be harmonized to give effect to each amendment.

§ 2953.22 Hearing.

If a hearing is granted pursuant to section 2953.21 of the Revised Code, the petitioner shall be permitted to attend the hearing. Testimony of the prisoner or other witnesses may be offered by deposition.

If the petitioner is in a state correctional institution, he may be returned for the hearing upon the warrant of the court of common pleas of the county where the hearing is to be held. The approval of the governor on the warrant shall not be required. The warrant shall be directed to the sheriff of the county in which the hearing is to be held. When a copy of the warrant is presented to the warden or other head of a state correctional institution, he shall deliver the convict to the sheriff, who shall convey him to the county. For removing and returning the convict, the sheriff shall receive the fees allowed for conveying convicts to the correctional institution.

HISTORY: 132 v H 742 (Eff 12-9-67); 145 v H 571. Eff 10-6-94.

Analogous to former RC § 2953.22 (131 v 685), repealed 132 v H 742, § 2, eff 12-9-67.

§ 2953.23 Time for filing petition; appeals.

(A) Whether a hearing is or is not held on a petition filed pursuant to section 2953.21 of the Revised Code, a court may not entertain a petition filed after the expiration of the period prescribed in division (A) of that section or a second petition or successive petitions for similar relief on behalf of a petitioner unless both of the following apply:

(1) Either of the following applies:

(a) The petitioner shows that the petitioner was unavoidably prevented from discovery of the facts upon which the petitioner must rely to present the claim for relief.

(b) Subsequent to the period prescribed in division (A)(2) of section 2953.21 of the Revised Code or to the filing of an earlier petition, the United States Supreme Court recognized a new federal or state right that applies retroactively to persons in the petitioner's situation, and the petition asserts a claim based on that right.

(2) The petitioner shows by clear and convincing evidence that, but for constitutional error at trial, no reasonable factfinder would have found the petitioner guilty of the offense of which the petitioner was convicted or, if the claim challenges a sentence of death that, but for constitutional error at the sentencing hearing, no reasonable factfinder would have found the petitioner eligible for the death sentence.

(B) An order awarding or denying relief sought in a petition filed pursuant to section 2953.21 of the Revised Code is a final judgment and may be appealed pursuant to Chapter 2953. of the Revised Code.

HISTORY: 132 v H 742 (Eff 12-9-67); 146 v S 4. Eff 9-21-95.

Analogous to former RC § 2953.23 (131 v 685), repealed 132 v H 742, § 2, eff 12-9-67.

§ 2953.24 Repealed, 136 v H 164, § 2 [132 v H 742]. Eff 1-13-76.

This section concerned compensation of counsel.

[SEALING OF RECORD OF CONVICTION]

§ 2953.31 Definitions.

As used in sections 2953.31 to 2953.36 of the Revised Code:

(A) "First offender" means anyone who has been convicted of an offense in this state or any other jurisdiction, and who previously or subsequently has not been convicted of the same or a different offense in this state or any other jurisdiction. When two or more convictions result from or are connected with the same act, or result from offenses committed at the same time, they shall be counted as one conviction.

For purposes of, and except as otherwise provided in, this division, a conviction for a minor misdemeanor, a conviction for a violation of any section in Chapter 4511., 4513., or 4549. of the Revised Code, or a conviction for a violation of a municipal ordinance that is substantially similar to any section in those chapters, is not a previous or subsequent conviction. A conviction for a violation of section 4511.19, 4511.192 [4511.19.2], 4511.251 [4511.25.1], 4549.02, 4549.021 [4549.02.1], 4549.03, 4549.042 [4549.04.2], or 4549.07, or sections 4549.41 to 4549.46 of the Revised Code, or a conviction for a violation of a municipal ordinance that is substantially similar to any of those sections, shall be considered a previous or subsequent conviction.

(B) "Prosecutor" means the county prosecuting attorney, city director of law, village solicitor, or similar chief legal officer, who has the authority to prosecute a criminal case in the court in which the case is filed.

(C) "Bail forfeiture" means the forfeiture of bail by a defendant who is arrested for the commission of a misdemeanor, other than a defendant in a traffic case as defined in Traffic Rule 2, if the forfeiture is pursuant to an agreement with the court and prosecutor in the case.

(D) "Official records" has the same meaning as in division (D) of section 2953.51 of the Revised Code.

HISTORY: 135 v S 5 (Eff 1-1-74); 140 v H 227 (Eff 9-26-84); 142 v H 175 (Eff 6-29-88); 143 v S 49 (Eff 11-3-89); 143 v S 382 (Eff 12-31-90); 146 v H 274. Eff 8-8-96.

§ 2953.32 Sealing of record of conviction or bail forfeiture.

(A)(1) Except as provided in section 2953.61 of the Revised Code, a first offender may apply to the sentencing court if convicted in this state, or to a court of common pleas if convicted in another state or in a federal court, for the sealing of the conviction record of that offender's.† Application may be made at the expiration of three years after the offender's final discharge if convicted of a felony, or at the expiration of one year after the offender's final discharge if convicted of a misdemeanor.

(2) Any person who has been arrested for any misdemeanor offense and who has effected a bail forfeiture may apply to the court in which the misdemeanor criminal case was pending when bail was forfeited for the sealing of the† that person's record of the case. Except as provided in section 2953.61 of the Revised Code, the application may be filed at any time after the expiration of one year from the date on which the bail forfei-

ture was entered upon the minutes of the court or the journal, whichever entry occurs first.

(B) Upon the filing of an application under this section, the court shall set a date for a hearing and shall notify the prosecutor for the case of the hearing on the application. The prosecutor may object to the granting of the application by filing an objection with the court prior to the date set for the hearing. The prosecutor shall specify in the objection the reasons the prosecutor for believing a denial of the application is justified.† The court shall direct its regular probation officer, a state probation officer, or the department of probation of the county in which the applicant resides to make inquiries and written reports as the court requires concerning the applicant.

(C)(1) The court shall do each of the following:

(a) Determine whether the applicant is a first offender or whether the forfeiture of bail was agreed to by the applicant and the prosecutor in the case;

(b) Determine whether criminal proceedings are pending against the applicant;

(c) If the applicant is a first offender who applies pursuant to division (A)(1) of this section, determine whether the applicant has been rehabilitated to the satisfaction of the court;

(d) If the prosecutor has filed an objection in accordance with division (B) of this section, consider the reasons against granting the application specified by the prosecutor in the objection;

(e) Weigh the interests of the applicant in having the records pertaining to the applicant's conviction sealed against the legitimate needs, if any, of the government to maintain those records.

(2) If the court determines, after complying with division (C)(1) of this section, that the applicant is a first offender or the subject of a bail forfeiture, that no criminal proceeding is pending against the applicant, and that the interests of the applicant in having the records pertaining to the applicant's conviction or bail forfeiture sealed are not outweighed by any legitimate governmental needs to maintain those records, and that the rehabilitation of an applicant who is a first offender applying pursuant to division (A)(1) of this section has been attained to the satisfaction of the court, the court, except as provided in division (G) of this section, shall order all official records pertaining to the case sealed and, except as provided in division (F) of this section, all index references to the case deleted and, in the case of bail forfeitures, shall dismiss the charges in the case. The proceedings in the case shall be considered not to have occurred and the conviction or bail forfeiture of the person who is the subject of the proceedings shall be sealed, except that upon conviction of a subsequent offense, the sealed record of prior conviction or bail forfeiture may be considered by the court in determining the sentence or other appropriate disposition, including the relief provided for in sections 2953.31 to 2953.33 of the Revised Code.

(3) Upon the filing of an application under this section, the applicant, unless the applicant† indigent, shall pay a fee of fifty dollars. The court shall pay thirty dollars of the fee into the state treasury. It shall pay twenty dollars of the fee into the county general revenue fund if the sealed conviction or bail forfeiture was pursuant to a state statute, or into the general revenue fund of the municipal corporation involved if the sealed conviction or bail forfeiture was pursuant to a municipal ordinance.

(D) Inspection of the sealed records included in the order may be made only by the following persons or for the following purposes:

(1) By a law enforcement officer or prosecutor, or the assistants of either the law enforcement officer or prosecutor, to determine whether the nature and character of the offense with which a person is to be charged would be affected by virtue of the person's previously having been convicted of a crime;

(2) By the parole or probation officer of the person who is the subject of the records, for the exclusive use of the officer in supervising the person while the person† on parole or probation and in making inquiries and written reports as requested by the court or adult parole authority;

(3) Upon application by the person who is the subject of the records, by the persons named in the† that person's application;

(4) By a law enforcement officer who was involved in the case, for use in the officer's defense of a civil action arising out of the officer's involvement in that case;

(5) By a prosecuting attorney or the prosecuting attorney's† assistants of the prosecuting attorney to determine a defendant's eligibility to enter a pre-trial diversion program established pursuant to section 2935.36 of the Revised Code;

(6) By any law enforcement agency or any authorized employee of a law enforcement agency or by the department of rehabilitation and correction as part of a background investigation of a person who applies for employment with the agency as a law enforcement officer or with the department as a corrections officer;

(7) By any law enforcement agency or any authorized employee of a law enforcement agency, for the purposes set forth in, and in the manner provided in, section 2953.321 [2953.32.1] of the Revised Code;

(8) By the bureau of criminal identification and investigation or any authorized employee of the bureau for the purpose of providing information to a board or person pursuant to division (F) or (G) of section 109.57 of the Revised Code;

(9) By the bureau of criminal identification and investigation or any authorized employee of the bureau for the purpose of performing a criminal history records check on a person to whom a certificate as prescribed in section 109.77 of the Revised Code is to be awarded.

When the nature and character of the offense with

which a person is to be charged would be affected by the information, it may be used for the purpose of charging the person with an offense.

(E) In any criminal proceeding, proof of any otherwise admissible prior conviction may be introduced and proved, notwithstanding the fact that for any such prior conviction an order of sealing previously was issued pursuant to sections 2953.31 to 2953.36 of the Revised Code.

(F) The person or governmental agency, office, or department that maintains sealed records pertaining to convictions or bail forfeitures that have been sealed pursuant to this section may maintain a manual or computerized index to the sealed records. The index shall contain only the name of, and alphanumeric identifiers that relate to, the persons who are the subject of the sealed records, the word "sealed," and the name of the person, agency, office, or department that has custody of the sealed records, and shall not contain the name of the crime committed. The index shall be made available by the person who has custody of the sealed records only for the purposes set forth in divisions (C), (D), and (E) of this section.

(G) Notwithstanding any provision of this section or section 2953.33 of the Revised Code that requires otherwise, a board of education of a city, local, exempted village, or joint vocational school district that maintains records of an individual who has been permanently excluded under sections 3301.121 [3301.12.1] and 3313.662 [3313.66.2] of the Revised Code is permitted to maintain records regarding a conviction that was used as the basis for the individual's permanent exclusion, regardless of a court order to seal the record. An order issued under this section to seal the record of a conviction does not revoke the adjudication order of the superintendent of public instruction to permanently exclude the individual who is the subject of the sealing order. An order issued under this section to seal the record of a conviction of an individual may be presented to a district superintendent as evidence to support the contention that the superintendent should recommend that the permanent exclusion of the individual who is the subject of the sealing order be revoked. Except as otherwise authorized by this division and sections 3301.121 [3301.12.1] and 3313.662 [3313.66.2] of the Revised Code, any school employee in possession of or having access to the sealed conviction records of an individual that were the basis of a permanent exclusion of the individual is subject to section 2953.35 of the Revised Code.

HISTORY: 135 v S 5 (Eff 1-1-74); 137 v H 219 (Eff 11-1-77); 138 v H 105 (Eff 10-25-79); 140 v H 227 (Eff 9-26-84); 142 v H 8 (Eff 7-31-87); 142 v H 175 (Eff 6-29-88); 143 v S 140 (Eff 10-2-89); 144 v H 154 (Eff 7-31-92); 145 v H 571 (Eff 10-6-94); 146 v H 566 (Eff 10-16-96); 146 v S 160. Eff 1-27-97.

Publisher's Note

The amendments made by HB 566 (146 v —) and SB 160 (146 v —) have been combined. Please see provisions of RC § 1.52.

† The language is the result of combining HB 566 and SB 160, division (D)(2).

See provisions, § 3 of SB 160 (146 v —) following RC § 2950.08.

[§ 2953.32.1] § 2953.321 Disposition and use of investigatory work product.

(A) As used in this section, "investigatory work product" means any records or reports of a law enforcement officer or agency that are excepted from the definition of "official records" contained in section 2953.51 of the Revised Code and that pertain to a case the records of which have been ordered sealed pursuant to division (C)(2) of section 2953.32 of the Revised Code.

(B) Upon the issuance of an order by a court pursuant to division (C)(2) of section 2953.32 of the Revised Code directing that all official records pertaining to a case be sealed:

(1) Every law enforcement officer who possesses investigatory work product immediately shall deliver that work product to his employing law enforcement agency.

(2) Except as provided in division (B)(3) of this section, every law enforcement agency that possesses investigatory work product shall close that work product to all persons who are not directly employed by the law enforcement agency and shall treat that work product, in relation to all persons other than those who are directly employed by the law enforcement agency, as if it did not exist and never had existed.

(3) A law enforcement agency that possesses investigatory work product may permit another law enforcement agency to use that work product in the investigation of another offense if the facts incident to the offense being investigated by the other law enforcement agency and the facts incident to an offense that is the subject of the case are reasonably similar. The agency that permits the use of investigatory work product may provide the other agency with the name of the person who is the subject of the case if it believes that the name of the person is necessary to the conduct of the investigation by the other agency.

(C)(1) Except as provided in division (B)(3) of this section, no law enforcement officer or other person employed by a law enforcement agency shall knowingly release, disseminate, or otherwise make the investigatory work product or any information contained in that work product available to, or discuss any information contained in it with, any person not employed by the employing law enforcement agency.

(2) No law enforcement agency, or person employed by a law enforcement agency, that receives investigatory work product pursuant to division (B)(3) of this section shall use that work product for any purpose other than the investigation of the offense for which it was obtained from the other law enforcement agency, or disclose the

name of the person who is the subject of the work product except when necessary for the conduct of the investigation of the offense, or the prosecution of the person for committing the offense, for which it was obtained from the other law enforcement agency.

(D) Whoever violates division (C)(1) or (2) of this section is guilty of divulging confidential investigatory work product, a misdemeanor of the fourth degree.

HISTORY: 142 v H 175. Eff 6-29-88.

§ 2953.33 Rights and privileges restored; answering questions.

(A) Except as provided in division (G) of section 2953.32 of the Revised Code, an order to seal the record of a person's conviction restores the person who is the subject of the order to all rights and privileges not otherwise restored by termination of sentence or probation or by final release on parole.

(B) In any application for employment, license, or other right or privilege, any appearance as a witness, or any other inquiry, except as provided in division (E) of section 2953.32 of the Revised Code, a person may be questioned only with respect to convictions not sealed, bail forfeitures not expunged under section 2953.42 of the Revised Code as it existed prior to June 29, 1988, and bail forfeitures not sealed, unless the question bears a direct and substantial relationship to the position for which the person is being considered.

HISTORY: 135 v S 5 (Eff 1-1-74); 138 v H 105 (Eff 10-25-79); 142 v H 175 (Eff 6-29-88); 144 v H 154. Eff 7-31-92.

§ 2953.34 First offender may still take appeal or seek relief.

Nothing in sections 2953.31 to 2953.33 of the Revised Code precludes a first offender from taking an appeal or seeking any relief from his conviction or from relying on it in lieu of any subsequent prosecution for the same offense.

HISTORY: 135 v S 5, § 2. Eff 1-1-74.

§ 2953.35 Divulging confidential information.

(A) Except as authorized by divisions (D), (E), and (F) of section 2953.32 of the Revised Code or by Chapter 2950. of the Revised Code, any officer or employee of the state, or a political subdivision of the state, who releases or otherwise disseminates or makes available for any purpose involving employment, bonding, or licensing in connection with any business, trade, or profession to any person, or to any department, agency, or other instrumentality of the state, or any political subdivision of the state, any information or other data concerning any arrest, complaint, indictment, trial, hearing, adjudication, conviction, or correctional supervision the records with respect to which the officer or employee had knowledge of were sealed by an existing order issued pursuant to sections 2953.31 to 2953.36 of the Revised Code, or were expunged by an order issued pursuant to section 2953.42 of the Revised Code as it existed prior to the effective date of this amendment, is guilty of divulging confidential information, a misdemeanor of the fourth degree.

(B) Any person who, in violation of section 2953.32 of the Revised Code, uses, disseminates, or otherwise makes available any index prepared pursuant to division (F) of section 2953.32 of the Revised Code is guilty of a misdemeanor of the fourth degree.

HISTORY: 135 v S 5 (Eff 1-1-74); 136 v H 1 (Eff 6-13-75); 138 v H 105 (Eff 10-25-79); 142 v H 175 (Eff 6-29-88); 146 v H 180. Eff 7-1-97.

The effective date is set by section 5 of HB 180.

See provisions, § 5 of HB 180 (146 v —) following RC § 2935.36.

§ 2953.36 Application of preceding sections.

Sections 2953.31 to 2953.35 of the Revised Code do not apply to convictions when the offender is subject to a mandatory prison term, convictions under section 2907.02, 2907.03, 2907.04, 2907.05, 2907.06, 2907.321 [2907.32.1], 2907.322 [2907.32.2], or 2907.323 [2907.32.3], former section 2907.12, or Chapter 4507., 4511., or 4549. of the Revised Code, or a conviction for a violation of a municipal ordinance that is substantially similar to any section contained in any of those chapters, or bail forfeitures in a traffic case as defined in Traffic Rule 2.

HISTORY: 135 v S 5 (Eff 1-1-74); 142 v H 175 (Eff 6-29-88); 145 v H 335 (Eff 12-9-94); 146 v S 269 (Eff 7-1-96); 146 v H 445 (Eff 9-3-96); 146 v H 353. Eff 9-17-96.

Comment, Legislative Service Commission

Section 2953.36 of the Revised Code is amended by this act [Am. Sub. S.B. 269] and also by Am. Sub. H.B. 353 and Am. Sub. H.B. 445, both of the 121st General Assembly. Comparison of these amendments in pursuance of section 1.52 of the Revised Code discloses that they are not irreconcilable so that they are required by that section to be harmonized to give effect to each amendment.

§§ 2953.41, 2953.42, 2953.43

Repealed, 142 v H 175, § 2 [137 v S 192]. Eff 6-29-88.

These sections concerned expungement after agreed bail forfeiture. See now sections 2953.31 et seq.

[SEALING OF RECORDS AFTER NOT GUILTY OR DISMISSAL]

§ 2953.51 Definitions.

As used in sections 2953.51 to 2953.55 of the Revised Code:

(A) "No bill" means a report by the foreman or deputy foreman of a grand jury that an indictment is not found by the grand jury against a person who has been held to answer before the grand jury for the commission of an offense.

(B) "Prosecutor" has the same meaning as in section 2953.31 of the Revised Code.

(C) "Court" means the court in which a case is pending at the time a finding of not guilty in the case or a dismissal of the complaint, indictment, or information in the case is entered on the minutes or journal of the court, or the court to which the foreman or deputy foreman of a grand jury reports, pursuant to section 2939.23 of the Revised Code, that the grand jury has returned a no bill.

(D) "Official records" means all records that are possessed by any public office or agency that relate to a criminal case, including, but not limited to: the notation to the case in the criminal docket; all subpoenas issued in the case; all papers and documents filed by the defendant or the prosecutor in the case; all records of all testimony and evidence presented in all proceedings in the case; all court files, papers, documents, folders, entries, affidavits, or writs that pertain to the case; all computer, microfilm, microfiche, or microdot records, indices, or references to the case; all index references to the case; all fingerprints and photographs; all records and investigative reports pertaining to the case that are possessed by any law enforcement officer or agency, except that any records or reports that are the specific investigatory work product of a law enforcement officer or agency are not and shall not be considered to be official records when they are in the possession of that officer or agency; and all investigative records and reports other than those possessed by a law enforcement officer or agency pertaining to the case. "Official records" does not include records or reports maintained pursuant to section 2151.421 [2151.42.1] of the Revised Code by a public children services agency or the department of human services.

HISTORY: 140 v H 227 (Eff 9-26-84); 146 v H 274. Eff 8-8-96.

§ 2953.52 Sealing of official records after not guilty finding, dismissal of proceedings or no bill.

(A)(1) Any person, who is found not guilty of an offense by a jury or a court or who is the defendant named in a dismissed complaint, indictment, or information, may apply to the court for an order to seal his official records in the case. Except as provided in section 2953.61 of the Revised Code, the application may be filed at any time after the finding of not guilty or the dismissal of the complaint, indictment, or information is entered upon the minutes of the court or the journal, whichever entry occurs first.

(2) Any person, against whom a no bill is entered by a grand jury, may apply to the court for an order to seal his official records in the case. Except as provided in section 2953.61 of the Revised Code, the application may be filed at any time after the expiration of two years after the date on which the foreman or deputy foreman of the grand jury reports to the court that the grand jury has reported a no bill.

(B)(1) Upon the filing of an application pursuant to division (A) of this section, the court shall set a date for a hearing and shall notify the prosecutor in the case of the hearing on the application. The prosecutor may object to the granting of the application by filing an objection with the court prior to the date set for the hearing. The prosecutor shall specify in the objection the reasons he believes justify a denial of the application.

(2) The court shall do each of the following:

(a) Determine whether the person was found not guilty in the case, or the complaint, indictment, or information in the case was dismissed, or a no bill was returned in the case and a period of two years or a longer period as required by section 2953.61 of the Revised Code has expired from the date of the report to the court of that no bill by the foreman or deputy foreman of the grand jury;

(b) Determine whether criminal proceedings are pending against the person;

(c) If the prosecutor has filed an objection in accordance with division (B)(1) of this section, consider the reasons against granting the application specified by the prosecutor in the objection;

(d) Weigh the interests of the person in having the official records pertaining to the case sealed against the legitimate needs, if any, of the government to maintain those records.

(3) If the court determines, after complying with division (B)(2) of this section, that the person was found not guilty in the case, that the complaint, indictment, or information in the case was dismissed, or that a no bill was returned in the case and that the appropriate period of time has expired from the date of the report to the court of the no bill by the foreman or deputy foreman of the grand jury; that no criminal proceedings are pending against the person; and the interests of the person in having the records pertaining to the case sealed are not outweighed by any legitimate governmental needs to maintain such records, the court shall issue an order directing that all official records pertaining to the case be sealed and that, except as provided in section 2953.53 of the Revised Code, the proceedings in the case be deemed not to have occurred.

HISTORY: 140 v H 227 (Eff 9-26-84); 142 v H 175. Eff 6-29-88.

§ 2953.53 Order to seal records; index of sealed records.

(A) The court shall send notice of any order to seal official records issued pursuant to section 2953.52 of the Revised Code to any public office or agency that the court knows or has reason to believe may have any record of the case, whether or not it is an official record, that is the subject of the order. The notice shall be sent by certified mail, return receipt requested.

(B) A person whose official records have been sealed pursuant to an order issued pursuant to section 2953.52 of the Revised Code may present a copy of that order and a written request to comply with it, to a public office or agency that has a record of the case that is the subject of the order.

(C) An order to seal official records issued pursuant to section 2953.52 of the Revised Code applies to every public office or agency that has a record of the case that is the subject of the order, regardless of whether it receives notice of the hearing on the application for the order to seal the official records or receives a copy of the order to seal the official records pursuant to division (A) or (B) of this section.

(D) Upon receiving a copy of an order to seal official records pursuant to division (A) or (B) of this section or upon otherwise becoming aware of an applicable order to seal official records issued pursuant to section 2953.52 of the Revised Code, a public office or agency shall comply with the order and, if applicable, with the provisions of section 2953.54 of the Revised Code, except that it may maintain a record of the case that is the subject of the order if the record is maintained for the purpose of compiling statistical data only and does not contain any reference to the person who is the subject of the case and the order.

A public office or agency also may maintain an index of sealed official records, in a form similar to that for sealed records of conviction as set forth in division (F) of section 2953.32 of the Revised Code, access to which may not be afforded to any person other than the person who has custody of the sealed official records. The sealed official records to which such an index pertains shall not be available to any person, except that the official records of a case that have been sealed may be made available to the following persons for the following purposes:

(1) To the person who is the subject of the records upon written application, and to any other person named in the application, for any purpose;

(2) To a law enforcement officer who was involved in the case, for use in the officer's defense of a civil action arising out of the officer's involvement in that case;

(3) To a prosecuting attorney or his assistants to determine a defendant's eligibility to enter a pre-trial diversion program established pursuant to section 2935.36 of the Revised Code.

HISTORY: 140 v H 227 (Eff 9-26-84); 142 v H 8 (Eff 7-31-87); 142 v H 175. Eff 6-29-88.

§ 2953.54 Disposition and use of specific investigatory work product; divulging confidential information.

(A) Except as otherwise provided in Chapter 2950. of the Revised Code, upon the issuance of an order by a court under division (B) of section 2953.52 of the Revised Code directing that all official records pertaining to a case be sealed and that the proceedings in the case be deemed not to have occurred:

(1) Every law enforcement officer possessing records or reports pertaining to the case that are the officer's specific investigatory work product and that are excepted from the definition of "official records" contained in section 2953.51 of the Revised Code shall immediately deliver the records and reports to his employing law enforcement agency. Except as provided in division (A)(3) of this section, no such officer shall knowingly release, disseminate, or otherwise make the records and reports or any information contained in them available to, or discuss any information contained in them with, any person not employed by the officer's employing law enforcement agency.

(2) Every law enforcement agency that possesses records or reports pertaining to the case that are its specific investigatory work product and that are excepted from the definition of "official records" contained in section 2953.51 of the Revised Code, or that are the specific investigatory work product of a law enforcement officer it employs and that were delivered to it under division (A)(1) of this section shall, except as provided in division (A)(3) of this section, close the records and reports to all persons who are not directly employed by the law enforcement agency and shall, except as provided in division (A)(3) of this section, treat the records and reports, in relation to all persons other than those who are directly employed by the law enforcement agency, as if they did not exist and had never existed. Except as provided in division (A)(3) of this section, no person who is employed by the law enforcement agency shall knowingly release, disseminate, or otherwise make the records and reports in the possession of the employing law enforcement agency or any information contained in them available to, or discuss any information contained in them with, any person not employed by the employing law enforcement agency.

(3) A law enforcement agency that possesses records or reports pertaining to the case that are its specific investigatory work product and that are excepted from the definition of "official records" contained in division (D) of section 2953.51 of the Revised Code, or that are the specific investigatory work product of a law enforcement officer it employs and that were delivered to it under division (A)(1) of this section may permit another law enforcement agency to use the records or reports in the investigation of another offense, if the facts incident to the offense being investigated by the other law enforcement agency and the facts incident to an offense that is the subject of the case are reasonably similar. The agency that provides the records and reports may provide the other agency with the name of the person who is the subject of the case, if it believes

that the name of the person is necessary to the conduct of the investigation by the other agency.

No law enforcement agency, or person employed by a law enforcement agency, that receives from another law enforcement agency records or reports pertaining to a case the records of which have been ordered sealed pursuant to division (B) of section 2953.52 of the Revised Code shall use the records and reports for any purpose other than the investigation of the offense for which they were obtained from the other law enforcement agency, or disclose the name of the person who is the subject of the records or reports except when necessary for the conduct of the investigation of the offense, or the prosecution of the person for committing the offense, for which they were obtained from the other law enforcement agency.

(B) Whoever violates division (A)(1), (2), or (3) of this section is guilty of divulging confidential information, a misdemeanor of the fourth degree.

HISTORY: 140 v H 227 (Eff 9-26-84); 146 v H 180. Eff 7-1-97.

The effective date is set by section 5 of HB 180.

See provisions, § 5 of HB 180 (146 v —) following RC § 2935.36.

§ 2953.55 Inquiry as to sealed records prohibited; divulging confidential information.

(A) In any application for employment, license, or any other right or privilege, any appearance as a witness, or any other inquiry, a person may not be questioned with respect to any record that has been sealed pursuant to section 2953.52 of the Revised Code. If an inquiry is made in violation of this section, the person whose official record was sealed may respond as if the arrest underlying the case to which the sealed official records pertain and all other proceedings in that case did not occur, and the person whose official record was sealed shall not be subject to any adverse action because of the arrest, the proceedings, or his response.

(B) An officer or employee of the state or any of its political subdivisions who knowingly releases, disseminates, or makes available for any purpose involving employment, bonding, licensing, or education to any person or to any department, agency, or other instrumentality of the state, or of any of its political subdivisions, any information or other data concerning any arrest, complaint, indictment, information, trial, adjudication, or correctional supervision, the records of which have been sealed pursuant to section 2953.52 of the Revised Code, is guilty of divulging confidential information, a misdemeanor of the fourth degree.

HISTORY: 140 v H 227. Eff 9-26-84.

§ 2953.61 Sealing of records in cases of multiple charges.

When a person is charged with two or more offenses as a result of or in connection with the same act and at least one of the charges has a final disposition that is different than the final disposition of the other charges, the person may not apply to the court for the sealing of his record in any of the cases until such time as he would be able to apply to the court and have all of the records in all of the cases pertaining to those charges sealed pursuant to divisions (A)(1) and (2) of section 2953.32 and divisions (A)(1) and (2) of section 2953.52 of the Revised Code.

HISTORY: 142 v H 175. Eff 6-29-88.

CHAPTER 2961: DISFRANCHISED CONVICTS; HABITUAL CRIMINALS

Section
2961.01 Civil rights of convicted felons.
2961.02 Repealed.
2961.03 Revocation of license in certain cases.
2961.11-2961.13 Repealed.

§ 2961.01 Civil rights of convicted felons.

A person convicted of a felony under the laws of this or any other state or the United States, unless his conviction is reversed or annulled, is incompetent to be an elector or juror, or to hold an office of honor, trust, or profit. When any such person is granted probation, parole, or a conditional pardon, he is competent to be an elector during the period of probation or parole or until the conditions of his pardon have been performed or have transpired, and thereafter following his final discharge. The full pardon of a convict restores the rights and privileges so forfeited under this section, but a pardon shall not release a convict from the costs of his conviction in this state, unless so specified.

HISTORY: GC § 13458-1; 113 v 123(211), ch 37; Bureau of Code Revision, 10-1-53; 134 v H 511. Eff 1-1-74.

§ 2961.02 Repealed, 134 v H 511, § 2 [GC § 13458-2; 113 v 123(211); Bureau of Code Revision, 10-1-53]. Eff 1-1-74.

This section concerned convict of another state.

§ 2961.03 Revocation of license in certain cases.

Whenever a person engaged in business as a secondhand dealer, junk dealer, transient dealer, peddler, itinerant vendor, or pawnbroker, under a license issued under any law of this state or under any ordinance of a municipal corporation, is convicted and sentenced for knowingly and fraudulently buying, receiving, or concealing goods or property which has been stolen, taken by robbers, embezzled, or obtained by false pretenses, such judgment of conviction, in addition to the other penalties provided by law for such offense, acts as a cancellation and revocation of such license to conduct such business, and the court in which such conviction was had shall forthwith certify to the authority which issued such license, the fact of such conviction. A person who has been so convicted and whose license has been canceled or revoked, shall not again be licensed to engage in such business, or any of the businesses enumerated in this section, unless such person is pardoned by the governor.

HISTORY: GC § 13458-3; 113 v 123(211), ch 37, § 3; Bureau of Code Revision. Eff 10-1-53.

§§ 2961.11, 2961.12, 2961.13

Repealed, 134 v H 511, § 2 [GC §§ 13744-1—13744-3; 113 v 40; Bureau of Code Revision, 10-1-53; 132 v S 36]. Eff 1-1-74.

These sections concerned habitual criminals, see RC § 2929.11 et seq for similar provisions.

CHAPTER 2963: EXTRADITION

Section
2963.01 Definitions.

[FUGITIVE FROM ANOTHER STATE]

2963.02 Governor to deliver fugitives from justice.
2963.03 Demand for extradition.
2963.04 Demand investigated by order of governor.
2963.05 Extradition upon agreement to return prisoner.
2963.06 Governor may surrender anyone charged with crime against another state.
2963.07 Warrant for arrest.
2963.08 Authority to arrest accused.
2963.09 Mandatory hearing.
2963.10 Prisoner may be confined while enroute.
2963.11 Fugitive from justice.
2963.12 Arrest without warrant.
2963.13 Fugitive to be confined pending requisition.
2963.14 Bail.
2963.15 Release of accused.
2963.16 Forfeited recognizance.
2963.17 Governor may hold fugitive indicted in this state or surrender him.
2963.18 Guilt not to be inquired into by governor or in extradition proceedings.
2963.19 Governor may recall warrant for arrest.

[FUGITIVE FROM THIS STATE]

2963.20 Governor to demand fugitive from this state.
2963.21 Application for requisition for return of fugitive.
2963.22 Reimbursement of fees.
2963.23 Accused immune from civil suits until conviction or return home.
2963.24 Extradition hearing waived.
2963.25 Right to punish or regain custody by this state not waived.
2963.26 Extradited fugitive may be tried for other crimes committed in this state.
2963.27 Uniform interpretation.
2963.28 Request by governor for extradition of criminal.
2963.29 Governor must be satisfied by evidence of good faith.

[INTERSTATE AGREEMENT ON DETAINERS]

2963.30 Interstate agreement on detainers.
2963.31 Definitions.
2963.32 Duty to effectuate agreement.
2963.33 Repealed.
2963.34 Escape and aiding escape.
2963.35 Duty of warden.

§ 2963.01 Definitions.

As used in sections 2963.01 to 2963.27, inclusive, of the Revised Code:

(A) "Governor" includes any person performing the functions of governor by authority of the law of this state.

(B) "Executive authority" includes the governor, and any person performing the functions of governor in a state other than this state.

(C) "State," referring to a state other than this state, includes any state or territory, organized or unorganized, of the United States.

HISTORY: GC § 109-1; 117 v 588; Bureau of Code Revision. Eff 10-1-53.

[FUGITIVE FROM ANOTHER STATE]

§ 2963.02 Governor to deliver fugitives from justice.

Subject to sections 2963.01 to 2963.27, inclusive, of the Revised Code, the constitution of the United States and all acts of congress enacted in pursuance thereof, the governor shall have arrested and delivered to the executive authority of any other state of the United States, any person charged in that state with treason, felony, or other crime, who has fled from justice and is found in this state.

HISTORY: GC § 109-2; 117 v 108, § 2; Bureau of Code Revision. Eff 10-1-53.

§ 2963.03 Demand for extradition.

No demand for the extradition of a person charged with crime in another state shall be recognized by the governor unless the demand is in writing alleging, except in cases arising under section 2963.06 of the Revised Code, that the accused was present in the demanding state at the time of the commission of the alleged crime, and that thereafter he fled from the state, and unless the demand is accompanied by:

(A) A copy of an indictment found or by information supported by affidavit in the state having jurisdiction of the crime, or by a copy of an affidavit made before a magistrate there, together with a copy of any warrant which was issued thereupon;

(B) A copy of a judgment of conviction or of a sentence imposed in execution thereof, together with a statement by the executive authority of the demanding state that the person claimed has escaped from confinement or has broken the terms of his bail, probation, or parole. The indictment, information, or affidavit made before the magistrate must substantially charge the person demanded with having committed a crime under the law of that state. The copy of indictment, information, affidavit, judgment of conviction, or sentence must be authenticated by the executive authority making the demand.

HISTORY: GC § 109-3; 117 v 588, § 3; Bureau of Code Revision. Eff 10-1-53.

§ 2963.04 Demand investigated by order of governor.

When a demand is made upon the governor of this

state by the executive authority of another state for the surrender of a person charged with crime, the governor may call upon the attorney general or any prosecuting officer in this state to investigate or assist in investigating the demand, and to report to him the situation and circumstances of the person so demanded, and whether such person ought to be surrendered.

HISTORY: GC § 109-4; 117 v 588, § 4; Bureau of Code Revision. Eff 10-1-53.

§ 2963.05 Extradition upon agreement to return prisoner.

When it is desired to have returned to this state a person charged in this state with a crime, and such person is imprisoned or is held under criminal proceedings then pending against him in another state, the governor may agree with the executive authority of such other state for the extradition of such person before the conclusion of such proceedings or his term of sentence in such other state, upon condition that such person be returned to such other state at the expense of this state as soon as the prosecution in this state is terminated.

The governor may also surrender, on demand of the executive authority of any other state, any person in this state who is charged under section 2963.21 of the Revised Code with having violated the laws of the state whose executive authority is making the demand, even though such person left the demanding state involuntarily. This section shall be carried out by conforming to the procedure outlined in sections 2963.01 to 2963.27, inclusive, of the Revised Code.

HISTORY: GC § 109-5; 117 v 588, § 5; Bureau of Code Revision. Eff 10-1-53.

§ 2963.06 Governor may surrender anyone charged with crime against another state.

The governor may surrender, on demand of the executive authority of any other state, any person in this state charged in such other state in the manner provided in section 2963.03 of the Revised Code with committing an act in this state, or in a third state, intentionally resulting in a crime in the state whose executive authority is making the demand, and sections 2963.01 to 2963.27, inclusive, of the Revised Code, apply to such cases, even though the accused was not in that state at the time of the commission of the crime, and has not fled therefrom.

HISTORY: GC § 109-6; 117 v 588, § 6; Bureau of Code Revision. Eff 10-1-53.

§ 2963.07 Warrant for arrest.

If the governor decides that a demand for extradition should be complied with, he shall sign a warrant of arrest, which shall be sealed with the state seal and be directed to any peace officer or other person whom the governor finds fit to entrust with the execution thereof. The warrant must substantially recite the facts necessary to the validity of its issuance.

Such warrant shall authorize the peace officer or other person to whom directed to arrest the accused at any time and any place where he may be found within the state and to command the aid of all peace officers or other persons in the execution of the warrant, and to deliver the accused, subject to sections 2963.01 to 2963.27, inclusive, of the Revised Code, to the authorized agent of the demanding state.

HISTORY: GC §§ 109-7, 109-8; 117 v 588, §§ 7, 8; Bureau of Code Revision. Eff 10-1-53.

§ 2963.08 Authority to arrest accused.

Every peace officer or other person empowered to make an arrest under section 2963.07 of the Revised Code has the same authority, in arresting the accused, to command assistance therein as peace officers have in the execution of any criminal process directed to them, with like penalties against those who refuse their assistance.

HISTORY: GC § 109-9; 117 v 588, § 9; Bureau of Code Revision. Eff 10-1-53.

§ 2963.09 Mandatory hearing.

No person arrested upon a warrant under section 2963.07 of the Revised Code shall be delivered to the agent whom the executive authority demanding him appointed to receive him unless such person is first taken forthwith before a judge of a court of record in this state, who shall inform him of the demand made for his surrender and of the crime with which he is charged, and that he has the right to demand and procure legal counsel. If the prisoner or his counsel desires to test the legality of his arrest, the judge shall fix a reasonable time to be allowed him within which to apply for a writ of habeas corpus. When such writ is applied for, notice thereof and of the time and place of hearing thereon, shall be given to the prosecuting officer of the county in which the arrest is made and in which the accused is in custody, and to the said agent of the demanding state.

Whoever violates this section by willfully delivering a person arrested upon the governor's warrant to an agent for extradition of the demanding state before a hearing, shall be fined not more than one thousand dollars or imprisoned not more than six months, or both.

HISTORY: GC § 109-10; 117 v 588, § 10; Bureau of Code Revision. Eff 10-1-53.

§ 2963.10 Prisoner may be confined while enroute.

A peace officer or other person executing a warrant

of arrest issued by the governor, or an agent of the demanding state to whom the prisoner has been delivered, may, when necessary, confine the prisoner in the jail of any county or city through which he may pass.

The officer or agent of a demanding state to whom a prisoner has been delivered following extradition proceedings in another state, or to whom a prisoner has been delivered after waiving extradition in such other state, and who is passing through this state with such a prisoner for the purpose of immediately returning such prisoner to the demanding state may, when necessary, confine the prisoner in the jail of any county or city through which he may pass. Such officer or agent shall produce and show to the keeper of such jail his warrant and other written evidence of the fact that he is actually transporting such prisoner to the demanding state after a requisition by the executive authority of such demanding state. Such prisoner may not demand a new requisition while in this state.

The keeper of such jail must receive and safely keep a prisoner delivered to him under this section, until the officer or agent having charge of him is ready to proceed on his route. Such officer or agent is chargeable with the expense of such keeping.

HISTORY: GC § 109-12; 117 v 588, § 12; Bureau of Code Revision. Eff 10-1-53.

§ 2963.11 Fugitive from justice.

When, on the oath of a credible person before any judge or magistrate of this state, any person within this state is charged with the commission of any crime in any other state and with having fled from justice, or with having been convicted of a crime in that state and having escaped from confinement, or having broken the terms of the person's bail, probation, or parole or violated the conditions of a community control sanction imposed under section 2929.16, 2929.17, or 2929.18 of the Revised Code or of post-release control under section 2967.28 of the Revised Code, or whenever complaint has been made before any judge or magistrate in this state setting forth on the affidavit of any credible person in another state that a crime has been committed in the other state and that the accused has been charged in that state with the commission of the crime, and, has fled from justice, or with having been convicted of a crime in that state and having escaped from confinement, or having broken the terms of bail, probation, or parole, and is believed to be in this state, the judge or magistrate shall issue a warrant directed to any peace officer, commanding the peace officer to apprehend the person named in the warrant, wherever the person may be found in this state, and to bring the person before the same or any other judge, magistrate, or court which may be available in or convenient of access to the place where the arrest may be made, to answer the charge or complaint and affidavit, and a certified copy of the sworn charge or complaint and upon which the warrant is issued shall be attached to the warrant.

This section does not apply to cases arising under section 2963.06 of the Revised Code.

HISTORY: GC § 109-13; 117 v 588, § 13; Bureau of Code Revision, Eff 10-1-53; 146 v S 2. Eff 7-1-96.

The effective date is set by section 6 of SB 2.

§ 2963.12 Arrest without warrant.

An arrest may be made by any peace officer or a private person without a warrant upon reasonable information that the accused stands charged in the courts of any state with a crime punishable by death or imprisonment for a term exceeding one year. When so arrested the accused must be taken before a judge or magistrate with all practicable speed and complaint must be made against him under oath setting forth the ground for the arrest, as provided in section 2963.11 of the Revised Code. Thereafter his answer shall be heard as if he had been arrested on a warrant.

HISTORY: GC § 109-14; 117 v 588, § 14; Bureau of Code Revision. Eff 10-1-53.

§ 2963.13 Fugitive to be confined pending requisition.

If from the examination before the judge or magistrate it appears that the person held under section 2963.11 or 2963.12 of the Revised Code is the person charged with having committed the crime alleged and that he has fled from justice, the judge or magistrate must, by a warrant reciting the accusation, commit him to the county jail for such a time, not to exceed thirty days and specified in the warrant, as will enable the arrest of the accused to be made under a warrant of the governor on a requisition of the executive authority of the state having jurisdiction of the offense, unless the accused furnishes bail or until he is legally discharged.

HISTORY: GC § 109-15; 117 v 588, § 15; Bureau of Code Revision. Eff 10-1-53.

§ 2963.14 Bail.

Unless the offense with which the prisoner is charged under sections 2963.11 and 2963.12 of the Revised Code is shown to be an offense punishable by death or life imprisonment under the laws of the state in which it was committed, a judge or magistrate in this state may admit the person arrested to bail by bond, with sufficient sureties and in such sum as he deems proper, conditioned for his appearance before said judge or magistrate at a time specified in such bond, and for his surrender, to be arrested upon the warrant of the governor of this state.

HISTORY: GC § 109-16; 117 v 588, § 16; Bureau of Code Revision. Eff 10-1-53.

§ 2963.15 Release of accused.

If the accused mentioned in section 2963.14 of the

Revised Code is not arrested under warrant of the governor by the expiration of the time specified in the warrant or bond, a judge or magistrate may discharge him or may recommit him for a further period not to exceed sixty days, or a judge or magistrate may again take bail for his appearance and surrender, under said section, but within a period not to exceed sixty days after the date of such new bond.

HISTORY: GC § 109-17; 117 v 588, § 17; Bureau of Code Revision. Eff 10-1-53.

§ 2963.16 Forfeited recognizance.

If a prisoner admitted to bail under section 2963.14 of the Revised Code fails to appear and surrender himself according to the conditions of his bond, the judge or magistrate, by proper order, shall declare the bond forfeited and order his immediate arrest without warrant if he is within this state. Recovery may be had on such bond in the name of the state as in the case of other bonds given by the accused in criminal proceedings.

HISTORY: GC § 109-18; 117 v 588, § 18; Bureau of Code Revision. Eff 10-1-53.

§ 2963.17 Governor may hold fugitive indicted in this state or surrender him.

If a criminal prosecution has been instituted under the laws of this state against a person sought by another state under sections 2963.01 to 2963.27, inclusive, of the Revised Code, and is still pending, the governor may surrender him on demand of the executive authority of another state or hold him until he has been tried and discharged or convicted and punished in this state.

HISTORY: GC § 109-19; 117 v 588, § 19; Bureau of Code Revision. Eff 10-1-53.

§ 2963.18 Guilt not to be inquired into by governor or in extradition proceedings.

The guilt or innocence of an accused as to the crime of which he is charged may not be inquired into by the governor or in any proceeding after a demand for extradition accompanied by a charge of crime under section 2963.03 of the Revised Code has been presented to the governor, except as it may be involved in identifying the person held as the person charged with the crime.

HISTORY: GC § 109-20; 117 v 588, § 20; Bureau of Code Revision. Eff 10-1-53.

§ 2963.19 Governor may recall warrant for arrest.

The governor may recall his warrant of arrest issued under section 2963.07 of the Revised Code or may issue another warrant whenever he thinks is proper.

HISTORY: GC § 109-21; 117 v 588, § 21; Bureau of Code Revision. Eff 10-1-53.

[FUGITIVE FROM THIS STATE]

§ 2963.20 Governor to demand fugitive from this state.

Whenever the governor demands a person charged with crime, or with escaping from confinement, or breaking the terms of his bail, probation, or parole in this state, from the executive authority of any other state, or from the chief justice or an associate justice of the supreme court of the District of Columbia authorized to receive such demand under the laws of the United States, he shall issue a warrant under the seal of this state, to some agent, commanding him to receive the person so charged and convey such person to the proper officer of the county in which the offense was committed.

HISTORY: GC § 109-22; 117 v 588, § 22; Bureau of Code Revision. Eff 10-1-53.

§ 2963.21 Application for requisition for return of fugitive.

When the return to this state of a person charged with crime in this state is required, the prosecuting attorney shall present to the governor a written application for a requisition for the return of the person charged. The application shall state the name of the person charged, the crime charged against the person, the approximate time, place, and circumstances of its commission, the state in which the person charged is believed to be located, and the location of the person in that state at the time the application is made. The prosecuting attorney shall certify that in the prosecuting attorney's opinion the ends of justice require the arrest and return of the person charged to this state for trial and that the proceeding is not instituted to enforce a private claim.

When the return to this state is required of a person who has been convicted of a crime in this state and has escaped from confinement or broken the terms of the person's bail, probation, parole, community control sanction, or post-release control sanction, the prosecuting attorney of the county in which the offense was committed, the adult parole authority, or the warden of the institution or sheriff of the county from which escape was made shall present to the governor a written application for a requisition for the return of the person. The application shall state the person's name, the crime of which the person was convicted, the circumstances of the person's escape from confinement or of the breach of the terms of the person's bail, probation, parole, community control sanction, or post-release control sanction, the state in which the person is believed to be located, and the location of the person in that state at the time the application is made.

An application presented under this section shall be verified by affidavit, executed in duplicate, and accompanied by two certified copies of the indictment returned, of the information and affidavit filed, of the complaint made to the judge or magistrate, stating the offense with which the accused is charged, of the judgment of conviction, or of the sentence. The prosecuting attorney, adult parole authority, warden, or sheriff also may attach any other affidavits or documents in duplicate that the prosecuting attorney, adult parole authority, warden, or sheriff finds proper to be submitted with the application. One copy of the application, with the action of the governor indicated by indorsement on the application, and one of the certified copies of the indictment, complaint, information, and affidavits, of the judgment of conviction, or of the sentence shall be filed in the office of the secretary of state to remain of record in that office. The other copies of all papers shall be forwarded with the governor's requisition.

HISTORY: GC § 109-23; 117 v 588, § 23; Bureau of Code Revision, 10-1-53; 146 v S 269. Eff 7-1-96.

The effective date is set by section 5 of SB 269.

§ 2963.22 Reimbursement of fees.

The director of budget and management shall provide for reimbursement of the fees to the officers of the state on whose governor the requisition is made under section 2963.21 of the Revised Code, and all necessary travel in returning the prisoner at the rates governing travel that have been adopted pursuant to section 126.31 of the Revised Code, on the certificate of the governor of such state.

HISTORY: GC § 109-24; 117 v 588, § 24; Bureau of Code Revision, 10-1-53; 141 v H 201 (Eff 7-1-85); 143 v S 336. Eff 4-10-90.

§ 2963.23 Accused immune from civil suits until conviction or return home.

A person brought into this state by, or after waiver of, extradition based on a criminal charge is not subject to service of personal process in any civil action in this state until he has been convicted in the criminal proceeding, or, if acquitted, until he has had reasonable opportunity to return to the state from which he was extradited.

HISTORY: GC § 109-25; 117 v 588, § 25; Bureau of Code Revision. Eff 10-1-53.

§ 2963.24 Extradition hearing waived.

Any person arrested in this state charged with having committed any crime in another state or alleged to have escaped from confinement, or broken the terms of his bail, probation, or parole may waive the issuance and service of the warrant provided for in section 2963.07 of the Revised Code and all other procedure incidental to extradition proceedings, by executing or subscribing in the presence of a judge of any court of record within this state, a writing which states that he consents to return to the demanding state. Before such waiver is executed or subscribed by such person the judge in open court shall inform such person of his rights to the issuance and service of a warrant of extradition and to obtain a writ of habeas corpus as provided for in section 2963.09 of the Revised Code.

When such consent has been executed it shall forthwith be forwarded to the office of the governor and filed therein. The judge shall direct the officer having such person in custody to deliver forthwith such person to the accredited agent of the demanding state, and shall deliver to such agent a copy of such consent. This section does not limit the rights of the accused person to return voluntarily and without formality to the demanding state before any such demand has been made, nor is this waiver procedure an exclusive procedure or a limitation on the powers, rights, or duties of the officers of the demanding state or of this state.

HISTORY: GC § 109-26; 117 v 588, § 26; Bureau of Code Revision. Eff 10-1-53.

§ 2963.25 Right to punish or regain custody by this state not waived.

Sections 2963.01 to 2963.27, inclusive, of the Revised Code do not constitute a waiver by this state of its right, power, or privilege to try such demanded person for crime committed within this state, or of its right, power, or privilege to regain custody of such person by extradition proceedings or otherwise for the purpose of trial, sentence, or punishment for any crime committed within this state, nor are any proceedings had under such sections, which result in, or fail to result in, extradition, a waiver by this state of any of its rights, privileges, or jurisdiction.

HISTORY: GC § 109-27; 117 v 588, § 27; Bureau of Code Revision. Eff 10-1-53.

§ 2963.26 Extradited fugitive may be tried for other crimes committed in this state.

A person returned to this state by, or after waiver of, extradition proceedings, may be tried in this state for other crimes which he may be charged with having committed here, as well as that specified in the requisition for his extradition.

HISTORY: GC § 109-28; 117 v 588, § 28; Bureau of Code Revision. Eff 10-1-53.

§ 2963.27 Uniform interpretation.

Sections 2963.01 to 2963.26, inclusive, of the Revised Code shall be so interpreted and construed as to make

§ 2963.28 Request by governor for extradition of criminal.

If it appears to the governor by sworn evidence in writing that a person has committed a crime within this state for which such person may be delivered to the United States or its authorities by a foreign government or its authorities, because of laws of the United States, or of a treaty between the United States and a foreign government, and that such person is a fugitive from justice of this state, and may be found within the territory of such foreign government, the governor, under the great seal of Ohio, shall request the president of the United States, or the secretary of state of the United States, to take any steps necessary for the extradition of such person and his delivery to any agent of this state appointed by the governor, or to the proper officer of the county within which he is charged with the commission of such crime.

HISTORY: RS § 97-1; 81 v 208; GC § 116; Bureau of Code Revision. Eff 10-1-53.

§ 2963.29 Governor must be satisfied by evidence of good faith.

The governor shall not request the extradition of a person under section 2963.28 of the Revised Code unless he is satisfied by sworn evidence that extradition is sought in good faith for the punishment of the crime named and not for the purpose of collecting a debt or pecuniary mulct or of bringing the alleged fugitive within this state to serve him with civil process, or with criminal process other than for the crime for which his extradition is sought.

HISTORY: RS § 97-1; 81 v 208; GC § 117; Bureau of Code Revision. Eff 10-1-53.

[INTERSTATE AGREEMENT ON DETAINERS]

§ 2963.30 Interstate agreement on detainers.

The Interstate Agreement on Detainers is hereby enacted into law and entered into by this state with all other jurisdictions legally joining therein, in the form substantially as follows:

THE INTERSTATE AGREEMENT ON DETAINERS

The contracting states solemnly agree that:

Article I

The party states find that charges outstanding against a prisoner, detainers based on untried indictments, informations or complaints, and difficulties in securing speedy trials of persons already incarcerated in other jurisdictions, produce uncertainties which obstruct programs of prisoner treatment and rehabilitation. Accordingly, it is the policy of the party states and the purpose of this agreement to encourage the expeditious and orderly disposition of such charges and determination of the proper status of any and all detainers based on untried indictments, informations or complaints. The party states also find that proceedings with reference to such charges and detainers, when emanating from another jurisdiction, cannot properly be had in the absence of cooperative procedures. It is the further purpose of this agreement to provide such cooperative procedures.

Article II

As used in this agreement:

(a) "State" shall mean a state of the United States:[;] the United States of America:[;] a territory or possession of the United States:[;] the District of Columbia:[;] the Commonwealth of Puerto Rico.

(b) "Sending state" shall mean a state in which a prisoner is incarcerated at the time that he initiates a request for final disposition pursuant to Article III hereof or at the time that a request for custody or availability is initiated pursuant to Article IV hereof.

(c) "Receiving state" shall mean the state in which trial is to be had on an indictment, information or complaint pursuant to Article III or Article IV hereof.

Article III

(a) Whenever a person has entered upon a term of imprisonment in a penal or correctional institution of a party state, and whenever during the continuance of the term of imprisonment there is pending in any other party state any untried indictment, information or complaint on the basis of which a detainer has been lodged against the prisoner, he shall be brought to trial within one hundred eighty days after he shall have caused to be delivered to the prosecuting officer and the appropriate court of the prosecuting officer's jurisdiction written notice of the place of his imprisonment and his request for a final disposition to be made of the indictment, information or complaint: provided that for good cause shown in open court, the prisoner or his counsel being present, the court having jurisdiction of the matter may grant any necessary or reasonable continuance. The request of the prisoner shall be accompanied by a certificate of the appropriate official having custody of the prisoner, stating the term of commitment under which the prisoner is being held, the time already served, the time remaining to be served on the sentence, the amount of good time earned, the time of parole eligibility of the prisoner, and any decisions of the state parole agency relating to the prisoner.

(b) The written notice and request for final disposition referred to in paragraph (a) hereof shall be given or sent by the prisoner to the warden, commissioner of corrections or other official having custody of him, who shall promptly forward it together with the certificate to the appropriate prosecuting official and court by registered or certified mail, return receipt requested.

(c) The warden, commissioner of corrections or other official having custody of the prisoner shall promptly inform him of the source and contents of any detainer lodged against him and shall also inform him of his rights to make a request for final disposition of the indictment, information or complaint on which the detainer is based.

(d) Any request or [for] final disposition made by a prisoner pursuant to paragraph (a) hereof shall operate as a request for final disposition of all untried indictments, informations or complaints on the basis of which detainers have been lodged against the prisoner from the state to whose prosecuting official the request for final disposition is specifically directed. The warden, commissioner of corrections or other officials having custody of the prisoner shall forthwith notify all appropriate prosecuting officers and courts in the several jurisdictions within the state to which the prisoner's request for final disposition is being sent of the proceeding being initiated by the prisoner. Any notification sent pursuant to this paragraph shall be accompanied by copies of the prisoner's written notice, request, and the certificate. If trial is not had on any indictment, information or complaint contemplated hereby prior to the return of the prisoner to the original place of imprisonment, such indictment, information or complaint shall not be of any further force or effect, and the court shall enter an order dismissing the same with prejudice.

(e) Any request for final disposition made by a prisoner pursuant to paragraph (a) hereof shall also be deemed to be a waiver of extradition with respect to any charge or proceeding contemplated thereby or included therein by reason of paragraph (d) hereof, and a waiver of extradition to the receiving state to serve any sentence there imposed upon him, after completion of his term of imprisonment in the sending state. The request for final disposition shall also constitute a consent by the prisoner to the production of his body in any court where his presence may be required in order to effectuate the purposes of this agreement and a further consent voluntarily to be returned to the original place of imprisonment in accordance with the provisions of this agreement. Nothing in this paragraph shall prevent the imposition of a concurrent sentence if otherwise permitted by law.

(f) Escape from custody by the prisoner subsequent to his execution of the request for final disposition referred to in paragraph (a) hereof shall void the request.

Article IV

(a) The appropriate officer of the jurisdiction in which an untried indictment, information or complaint is pending shall be entitled to have a prisoner against whom he has lodged a detainer and who is serving a term of imprisonment in any party state made available in accordance with Article V (a) hereof upon presentation of a written request for temporary custody or availability to the appropriate authorities of the state in which the prisoner is incarcerated:[,] provided that the court having jurisdiction of such indictment, information or complaint shall have duly approved, recorded and transmitted the request:[,] and provided further that there shall be a period of thirty days after receipt by the appropriate authorites before the request be honored, within which period the governor of the sending state may disapprove the request for temporary custody or availability, either upon his own motion or upon motion of the prisoner.

(b) Upon receipt of the officer's written request as provided in paragraph (a) hereof, the appropriate authorities having the prisoner in custody shall furnish the officer with a certificate stating the term of commitment under which the prisoner is being held, the time already served, the time remaining to be served on the sentence, the amount of good time earned, the time of parole eligibility of the prisoner, and any decisions of the state parole agency relating to the prisoner. Said authorities simultaneously shall furnish all other officers and appropriate courts in the receiving state who have lodged detainers against the prisoner with similar certificates and with notices informing them of the request for custody or availability and of the reasons therefor.

(c) In respect of any proceeding made possible by this Article, trial shall be commenced within one hundred twenty days of the arrival of the prisoner in the receiving state, but for good cause shown in open court, the prisoner or his counsel being present, the court having jurisdiction of the matter may grant any necessary or reasonable continuance.

(d) Nothing contained in this Article shall be construed to deprive any prisoner of any right which he may have to contest the legality of his delivery as provided in paragraph (a) hereof, but such delivery may not be opposed or denied on the ground that the executive authority of the sending state has not affirmatively consented to or ordered such delivery.

(e) If trial is not had on any indictment, information or complaint contemplated hereby prior to the prisoner's being returned to the original place of imprisonment pursuant to Article V (e) hereof, such indictment, information or complaint shall not be of any further force or effect, and the court shall enter an order dismissing the same with prejudice.

Article V

(a) In response to a request made under Article III or Article IV hereof, the appropriate authority in a sending state shall offer to deliver temporary custody of such prisoner to the appropriate authority in the state where such indictment, information or complaint is pending against such person in order that speedy and efficient prosecution may be had. If the request for final disposition is made by the prisoner, the offer of temporary custody shall accompany the written notice provided for in Article III of this agreement. In the case of a federal prisoner, the appropriate authority in the receiving state shall be entitled to temporary custody as provided by this agreement or to the prisoner's presence in federal custody at the place of trial, whichever custodian arrangement may be approved by the custodian.

(b) The officer or other representative of a state accepting an offer of temporary custody shall present the following upon demand:

(1) Proper identification and evidence of his authority to act for the state into whose temporary custody the prisoner is to be given.

(2) A duly certified copy of the indictment, information or complaint on the basis of which the detainer has been lodged and on the basis of which the request for temporary custody of the prisoner has been made.

(c) If the appropriate authority shall refuse or fail to accept temporary custody of said person, or in the event that an action on the indictment, information or complaint on the basis of which the detainer has been lodged is not brought to trial within the period provided in Article III or Article IV hereof, the appropriate court of the jurisdiction where the indictment, information or complaint has been pending shall enter an order dismissing the same with prejudice, and any detainer based thereon shall cease to be of any force or effect.

(d) The temporary custody referred to in this agreement shall be only for the purpose of permitting prosecution on the charge or charges contained in one or more untried indictments, informations or complaints which form the basis of the detainer or detainers or for prosecution on any other charge or charges arising out of the same transaction,[;] except for his attendance at court and while being transported to or from any place at which his presence may be required, the prisoner shall be held in a suitable jail or other facility regularly used for persons awaiting prosecution.

(e) At the earliest practicable time consonant with the purposes of this agreement, the prisoner shall be returned to the sending state.

(f) During the continuance of temporary custody or while the prisoner is otherwise being made available for trial as required by this agreement, time being served on the sentence shall continue to run but good time shall be earned by the prisoner only if, and to the extent that, the law and practice of the jurisdiction which imposed the sentence may allow.

(g) For all purposes other than that for which temporary custody as provided in this agreement is exercised, the prisoner shall be deemed to remain in the custody of and subject to the jurisdiction of the sending state and any escape from temporary custody may be dealt with in the same manner as an escape from the original place of imprisonment or in any other manner permitted by law.

(h) From the time that a party state receives custody of a prisoner pursuant to this agreement until such prisoner is returned to the territory and custody of the sending state, the state in which the one or more untried indictments, informations or complaints are pending or in which trial is being had shall be responsible for the prisoner and shall also pay all costs of transporting, caring for, keeping and returning the prisoner,[;] the provisions of this paragraph shall govern unless the states concerned shall have entered into a supplementary agreement providing for a different allocation of costs and responsibilities as between or among themselves. Nothing herein contained shall be construed to alter or affect any internal relationship among the departments, agencies and officers of and in the government of a party state, or between a party state and its subdivisions, as to the payment of costs, or responsibilities therefor.

Article VI

(a) In determining the duration and expiration dates of the time periods provided in Articles III and IV of this agreement, the running of said time periods shall be tolled whenever and for as long as the prisoner is unable to stand trial, as determined by the court having jurisdiction of the matter.

(b) No provision of this agreement, and no remedy made available by this agreement, shall apply to any person who is adjudged to be mentally ill, or who is under sentence of death.

Article VII

Each state party to this agreement shall designate an officer who, acting jointly with like officers of other party states, shall promulgate rules and regulations to carry out more effectively the terms and provisions of this agreement, and who shall provide, within and without the state, information necessary to the effective operation of this agreement.

Article VIII

This agreement shall enter into full force and effect as to a party state when such state has enacted the same into law. A state party to this agreement may withdraw herefrom by enacting a statute repealing the same. However, the withdrawal of any state shall not affect the status of any proceedings already initiated by inmates or by state officers at the time such withdrawal takes effect, nor shall it affect their rights in respect thereof.

Article IX

This agreement shall be liberally construed so as to effectuate its purposes. The provisions of this agreement shall be severable and if any phrase, clause, sentence or provision of this agreement is declared to be contrary to the constitution of any party state or of the United States or the applicability thereof to any government, agency, person or circumstance is held invalid, the validity of the remainder of this agreement and the applicability thereof to any agreement, agency, person or circumstance shall not be affected thereby. If this agreement shall be held contrary to the constitution of any state party hereto, the agreement shall remain in full force and effect as to the remaining states and in full force and effect as to the state affected as to all severable matters.

HISTORY: 133 v S 356. Eff 11-18-69.

§ 2963.31 Definitions.

As used in section 2963.30 of the Revised Code, with reference to the courts of this state, "appropriate court" means the court of record having jurisdiction of the indictment, information, or complaint.

HISTORY: 133 v S 356. Eff 11-18-69.

§ 2963.32 Duty to effectuate agreement.

The courts, departments, agencies, and officers of this state and its political subdivisions shall do all things that are necessary to effectuate the agreement adopted pursuant to section 2963.30 of the Revised Code and that are appropriate within their respective jurisdictions and consistent with their duties and authority. The warden or other official in charge of a correctional institution in this state shall give over the person of any inmate of the institution when so required by the operation of the agreement.

HISTORY: 133 v S 356 (Eff 11-18-69); 145 v H 571. Eff 10-6-94.

§ 2963.33 Repealed, 134 v H 511, § 2 [133 v S 356]. Eff 1-1-74.

This section concerned habitual offenders.

§ 2963.34 Escape and aiding escape.

A person, while in another state pursuant to the agreement, adopted pursuant to section 2963.30 of the Revised Code, is subject to the prohibitions and penalties provided by sections 2921.34 and 2921.35 of the Revised Code.

HISTORY: 133 v S 356 (Eff 11-18-69); 134 v H 511. Eff 1-1-74.

§ 2963.35 Duty of warden.

The chief of the adult parole authority is designated as the administrator as required by Article VII of the agreement adopted pursuant to section 2963.30 of the Revised Code. The administrator, acting jointly with like officers of other party states, shall, in accordance with Chapter 119. of the Revised Code, promulgate rules and regulations to carry out the terms of the agreement. The administrator is authorized and empowered to cooperate with all departments, agencies, and officers of this state and its political subdivisions, in facilitating the proper administration of the agreement or of any supplementary agreement or agreements entered into by this state thereunder.

HISTORY: 133 v S 356. Eff 11-18-69.

CHAPTER 2965: PARDON; PAROLE [REPEALED]

§§ 2965.01, 2965.02, 2965.03 Repealed, 130 v PtII, 147, § 2 [GC §§ 2209, 2209-1, 2209-2; 118 v 288; Bureau of Code Revision, 10-1-53; 126 v 307; 128 v 960; 129 v 1667]. Eff 3-18-65.

§§ 2965.04, 2965.05, 2965.06 Repealed, 130 v PtII, 147, § 2 [GC §§ 2209-3, 2209-4, 2209-5; 118 v 288; Bureau of Code Revision, 10-1-53; 128 v 960; 129 v 1668]. Eff 3-18-65.

§§ 2965.07, 2965.08, 2965.09 Repealed, 130 v PtII, 147, § 2 [GC §§ 2209-6, 2209-7, 2209-8; 118 v 288; 123 v 862; 124 v 825; Bureau of Code Revision, 10-1-53; 125 v 289, 823; 126 v 640; 127 v 8, 383; 128 v 960; 129 v 484]. Eff 3-18-65.

§§ 2965.10, 2965.11, 2965.12 Repealed, 130 v PtII, 147, § 2 [GC §§ 2209-9, 2209-10, 2209-11; 118 v 288; Bureau of Code Revision, 10-1-53]. Eff 3-18-65.

§§ 2965.13, 2965.14, 2965.15 Repealed, 130 v PtII, 147, § 2 [GC §§ 2209-12, 2209-13, 2209-14; 118 v 288; Bureau of Code Revision, 10-1-53]. Eff 3-18-65.

§§ 2965.16, 2965.17, 2965.18 Repealed, 130 v PtII, 147, § 2 [GC §§ 2209-15, 2209-16, 2209-17; 118 v 288; Bureau of Code Revision, 10-1-53; 128 v 960]. Eff 3-18-65.

§§ 2965.19, 2965.20 Repealed, 130 v PtII, 147, § 2 [GC §§ 2209-18, 2209-19; 118 v 288; Bureau of Code Revision, 10-1-53; 127 v 118; 128 v 960; 129 v 484; 130 v 673]. Eff 3-18-65.

[§ 2965.20.1] § 2965.201 Repealed, 130 v PtII, 147, § 2 [129 v S 468]. Eff 3-18-65.

§ 2965.21 Repealed, 130 v PtII, 147, § 2 [GC § 2209-20; 118 v 288, § 21; Bureau of Code Revision, 10-1-53; 128 v 960]. Eff 3-18-65.

[§ 2965.21.1] § 2965.211 Repealed, 130 v PtII, 147, § 2 [129 v H 1093]. Eff 3-18-65.

§§ 2965.22, 2965.23 Repealed, 130 v PtII, 147, § 2 [GC §§ 2209-21, 2210-1; 114 v 530, § 2; 118 v 288 (297, 300), §§ 22, 25; 121 v 402; Bureau of Code Revision, 10-1-53]. Eff 3-18-65.

§§ 2965.31, 2965.32 Repealed, 130 v PtII, 147, § 2 [GC §§ 2210, 2210-2; 114 v 530; Bureau of Code Revision, 10-1-53; 125 v 836]. Eff 3-18-65.

§§ 2965.33, 2965.34 Repealed, 130 v PtII, 147, § 2 [GC §§ 2210-3, 108-1; 114 v 530; 117 v 596; Bureau of Code Revision, 10-1-53; 127 v 115]. Eff 3-18-65.

[§ 2965.34.1] § 2965.341 Repealed, 130 v PtII, 147, § 2 [127 v S 165]. Eff 3-18-65.

§§ 2965.35, 2965.36, 2965.37 Repealed, 130 v PtII, 147, § 2 [127 v 213; 129 v 1669; 130 v H 1 (673, 674)]. Eff 3-18-65.

See RC ch 2967: PARDON; PAROLE; PROBATION.

CHAPTER 2967: PARDON; PAROLE; PROBATION

Section
2967.01 Definitions.
2967.02 Administration of provisions; pardons.
[2967.02.1] 2967.021 Application of provisions effective 7-1-96.
2967.03 Pardon, commutation, or reprieve.
2967.04 Pardons and commutations; conditions; effect.
2967.05 Parole of dying prisoner.
2967.06 Warrants of pardon and commutation.
2967.07 Applications for executive pardon, commutation, or reprieve.
2967.08 Reprieve to a person under sentence of death.
2967.09 Warrant of reprieve.
2967.10 Confinement of prisoner during reprieve.
2967.11 Bad time added to prison term for violation; rules infraction board at each institution.
2967.12 Notice of pendency of pardon, commutation, or parole.
[2967.12.1] 2967.121 Notice of early release of certain felons.
2967.13 Parole eligibility.
[2967.13.1] 2967.131 Additional conditions of release; searches.
2967.14 Time to be served at halfway house or community residential center; licensing and reimbursement of facilities.
2967.15 Arrest and proceedings against parolee, furloughee or releasee for violation.
2967.16 Final release; restoration of rights and privileges.
2967.17 Parole authority may grant administrative release.
2967.18 Sentence reduction or early release due to overcrowding emergency.
2967.19 Repealed.
[2967.19.1] 2967.191 Reduction of prison term for prior confinement.
[2967.19.2] 2967.192 Repealed.
[2967.19.3] 2967.193 Days of credit may be earned.
2967.20 Repealed.
2967.21 Term of sentence unaffected by transfer.
2967.22 Mentally ill or retarded parolee, furloughee or probationer.
2967.23 Release of prisoner to halfway house or community-based correctional facility.
2967.25 Repealed.
2967.26 Furloughs for employment, education or other programs.
2967.27 Furloughs for trustworthy prisoners.
2967.28 Period of post-release control for certain offenders; sanctions; proceedings upon violation.
2967.31 Repealed.

§ 2967.01 Definitions.

As used in this chapter:

(A) "State correctional institution" includes any institution or facility that is operated by the department of rehabilitation and correction and that is used for the custody, care, or treatment of criminal, delinquent, or psychologically or psychiatrically disturbed offenders.

(B) "Pardon" means the remission of penalty by the governor in accordance with the power vested in the governor by the constitution.

(C) "Commutation" or "commutation of sentence" means the substitution by the governor of a lesser for a greater punishment. A stated prison term may be commuted without the consent of the convict, except when granted upon the acceptance and performance by the convict of conditions precedent. After commutation, the commuted prison term shall be the only one in existence. The commutation may be stated in terms of commuting from a named offense to a lesser included offense with a shorter prison term, in terms of commuting from a stated prison term in months and years to a shorter prison term in months and years, or in terms of commuting from any other stated prison term to a shorter prison term.

(D) "Reprieve" means the temporary suspension by the governor of the execution of a sentence or prison term. The governor may grant a reprieve without the consent of and against the will of the convict.

(E) "Parole" means, regarding a prisoner who is serving a prison term for aggravated murder or murder, who is serving a prison term of life imprisonment for rape or felonious sexual penetration, or who was sentenced prior to the effective date of this amendment, a release of the prisoner from confinement in any state correctional institution by the adult parole authority that is subject to the eligibility criteria specified in this chapter and that is under the terms and conditions, and for the period of time, prescribed by the authority in its published rules and official minutes or required by division (A) of section 2967.131 [2967.13.1] of the Revised Code or another provision of this chapter.

(F) "Head of a state correctional institution" or "head of the institution" means the resident head of the institution and the person immediately in charge of the institution, whether designated warden, superintendent, or any other name by which the head is known.

(G) "Convict" means a person who has been convicted of a felony under the laws of this state, whether or not actually confined in a state correctional institution, unless the person has been pardoned or has served the person's sentence or prison term.

(H) "Prisoner" means a person who is in actual confinement in a state correctional institution.

(I) "Parolee" means any inmate who has been released from confinement on parole by order of the adult parole authority or conditionally pardoned, who is under supervision of the adult parole authority and has not been granted a final release, and who has not been declared in violation of the inmate's parole by the authority or is performing the prescribed conditions of a conditional pardon.

(J) "Releasee" means an inmate who has been released from confinement pursuant to section 2967.28 of the Revised Code under a period of post-release control that includes one or more post-release control sanctions.

(K) "Final release" means a remission by the adult parole authority of the balance of the sentence or prison term of a parolee or prisoner or the termination by the authority of a term of post-release control of a releasee.

(L) "Parole violator" or "release violator" means any parolee or releasee who has been declared to be in violation of the condition of parole or post-release control specified in division (A) of section 2967.131 [2967.13.1] of the Revised Code or in violation of any other term, condition, or rule of the parolee's or releasee's parole or of the parolee's or releasee's post-release control sanctions, the determination of which has been made by the adult parole authority and recorded in its official minutes.

(M) "Administrative release" means a termination of jurisdiction over a particular sentence or prison term by the adult parole authority for administrative convenience.

(N) "Furloughee" means a prisoner who has been released to conditional confinement by the adult parole authority pursuant to section 2967.26 of the Revised Code or who has been released by the department of rehabilitation and correction pursuant to section 2967.27 of the Revised Code.

(O) "Post release control" and "post-release control sanction" have the same meanings as in section 2967.28 of the Revised Code.

(P) "Prison term" and "stated prison term" have the same meanings as in section 2929.01 of the Revised Code.

HISTORY: 130 v PtII, 149 (Eff 3-18-65); 131 v 685 (Eff 10-20-65); 134 v H 494 (Eff 7-12-72); 138 v S 52 (Eff 1-9-81); 139 v S 199 (Eff 7-1-83); 145 v H 571 (Eff 10-6-94); 146 v H 4 (Eff 11-9-95); 146 v S 2 (Eff 7-1-96); 146 v S 269. Eff 7-1-96.

The effective date is set by section 5 of SB 269.

The provisions of § 7(B) of SB 269 (146 v—) read as follows:

(B) Section 2967.01 of the Revised Code was amended by both Sub. H.B. 4 and Am. Sub. S.B. 2 of the 121st General Assembly. Comparison of these amendments in pursuance of section 1.52 of the Revised Code discloses that while certain of the amendments of these acts are reconcilable, certain other of the amendments are substantively irreconcilable. Sub. H.B. 4 and Am. Sub. S.B. 2 both were passed on June 29, 1995. Section 2967.01 of the Revised Code is presented in this act as it results from Sub. H.B. 4 and such of the amendments of Am. Sub. S.B. 2 as are not in conflict with the amendments of Sub. H.B. 4. This is in recognition of the principles stated in division (B) of section 1.52 of the Revised Code that amendments are to be harmonized where not substantively irreconcilable, and that where amendments are substantively irreconcilable, the latest amendment is to prevail. This division constitutes a legislative finding that such harmonized and reconciled section was the resulting version in effect prior to the effective date of this act.

See provisions, § 5 of SB 2 (146 v —), as amended by § 3 of SB 269 (146 v —), following RC § 2929.03.

See provisions, § 3 of HB 4 (146 v —) following RC § 2913.02.

§ 2967.02 Administration of provisions; pardons.

(A) Sections 2967.01 to 2967.28 of the Revised Code, and other sections of the Revised Code governing pardon, probation, post-release control, and parole, shall be administered by the adult parole authority created by section 5149.02 of the Revised Code.

(B) The governor may grant a pardon after conviction, may grant an absolute and entire pardon or a partial pardon, and may grant a pardon upon conditions precedent or subsequent.

(C) The adult parole authority shall supervise all parolees. The department of rehabilitation and correction has legal custody of a parolee until the authority grants the parolee a final release pursuant to section 2967.16 of the Revised Code.

(D) The department of rehabilitation and correction has legal custody of a releasee until the adult parole authority grants the releasee a final release pursuant to section 2967.16 of the Revised Code.

HISTORY: 130 v PtII, 150 (Eff 3-18-65); 146 v S 2. Eff 7-1-96.

The effective date is set by section 6 of SB 2.

See provisions, § 5 of SB 2 (146 v —), as amended by § 3 of SB 269 (146 v —), following RC § 2929.03.

[§ 2967.02.1] § 2967.021 Application of provisions effective 7-1-96.

(A) Chapter 2967. of the Revised Code, as it existed prior to July 1, 1996, applies to a person upon whom a court imposed a term of imprisonment prior to July 1, 1996, and a person upon whom a court, on or after July 1, 1996, and in accordance with law existing prior to July 1, 1996, imposed a term of imprisonment for an offense that was committed prior to July 1, 1996.

(B) Chapter 2967. of the Revised Code, as it exists on and after July 1, 1996, applies to a person upon whom a court imposed a stated prison term for an offense committed on or after July 1, 1996.

HISTORY: 146 v S 2. Eff 7-1-96.

The effective date is set by section 6 of SB 2.

§ 2967.03 Pardon, commutation, or reprieve.

The adult parole authority may exercise its functions and duties in relation to the pardon, commutation of sentence, or reprieve of a convict upon direction of the governor or upon its own initiative. It may exercise its functions and duties in relation to the parole of a prisoner who is eligible for parole upon the initiative of the head of the institution in which the prisoner is confined or upon its own initiative. When a prisoner becomes eligible for parole, the head of the institution in which the prisoner is confined shall notify the authority in the manner prescribed by the authority. The authority may investigate and examine, or cause the investigation and examination of, prisoners confined in state correctional institutions concerning their conduct in the institutions, their mental and moral qualities and characteristics, their knowledge of a trade or profession, their former means of livelihood, their family relationships, and any other matters affecting their fitness to be at liberty without being a threat to society.

The authority may recommend to the governor the pardon, commutation of sentence, or reprieve of any convict or prisoner or grant a parole to any prisoner for whom parole is authorized, if in its judgment there is reasonable ground to believe that granting a pardon, commutation, or reprieve to the convict or paroling the prisoner would further the interests of justice and be consistent with the welfare and security of society. However, the authority shall not recommend a pardon or commutation of sentence of, or grant a parole to, any convict or prisoner until the authority has complied with the applicable notice requirements of sections 2930.16 and 2967.12 of the Revised Code and until it has considered any statement made by a victim or a victim's representative that is relevant to the convict's or prisoner's case and that was sent to the authority pursuant to section 2930.17 of the Revised Code and any other statement made by a victim or a victim's representative that is relevant to the convict's or prisoner's case and that was received by the authority after it provided notice of the pendency of the action under sections 2930.16 and 2967.12 of the Revised Code. If a victim or victim's representative appears at a full board hearing of the parole board and gives testimony as authorized by section 5149.101 [5149.10.1] of the Revised Code, the authority shall consider the testimony in determining whether to grant a parole. The trial judge and prosecuting attorney of the trial court in which a person was convicted shall furnish to the authority, at the request of the authority, a summarized statement of the facts proved at the trial and of all other facts having reference to the propriety of recommending a pardon or commutation, or granting a parole, together with a recommendation for or against a pardon, commutation, or parole, and the reasons for the recommendation. The trial judge of the court, and the prosecuting attorney in the trial, in which a prisoner was convicted may appear at a full board hearing of the parole board and give testimony in regard to the grant of a parole to the prisoner as authorized by section 5149.101 [5149.10.1] of the Revised Code. All state and local officials shall furnish information to the authority, when so requested by it in the performance of its duties.

The adult parole authority shall exercise its functions and duties in relation to the release of prisoners who are serving a stated prison term in accordance with section 2967.28 of the Revised Code.

HISTORY: 130 v PtII, 151 (Eff 3-18-65); 140 v S 172 (Eff 9-26-84); 142 v S 6 (Eff 6-10-87); 145 v H 571 (Eff 10-6-94); 145 v S 186 (Eff 10-12-94); 146 v S 2. Eff 7-1-96.

The effective date is set by section 6 of SB 2.

The provisions of § 7 of SB 2 (146 v —) read as follows:

SECTION 7. ° ° ° Section 2967.03 of the Revised Code is presented in this act as a composite of the section as amended by both Am. Sub. H.B. 571 and Am. Sub. S.B. 186 of the 120th General Assembly, with the new language of neither of the acts shown in capital letters. ° ° ° This is in recognition of the principle stated in division (B) of section 1.52 of the Revised Code that such amendments are to be harmonized where not substantively irreconcilable and constitutes a legislative finding that such is the resulting version in effect prior to the effective date of this act.

See provisions, § 5 of SB 2 (146 v —), as amended by § 3 of SB 269 (146 v —), following RC § 2929.03.

§ 2967.04 Pardons and commutations; conditions; effect.

(A) A pardon or commutation may be granted upon such conditions precedent or subsequent as the governor may impose, which conditions shall be stated in the warrant. Such pardon or commutation shall not take effect until the conditions so imposed are accepted by the convict or prisoner so pardoned or having his sentence commuted, and his acceptance is indorsed upon the warrant, signed by him, and attested by one witness. Such witness shall go before the clerk of the court of common pleas in whose office the sentence is recorded and prove the signature of the convict. The clerk shall thereupon record the warrant, indorsement, and proof in the journal of the court, which record, or a duly certified transcript thereof, shall be evidence of such pardon or commutation, the conditions thereof, and the acceptance of the conditions.

(B) An unconditional pardon relieves the person to whom it is granted of all disabilities arising out of the conviction or convictions from which it is granted. For purposes of this section, "unconditional pardon" includes a conditional pardon with respect to which all conditions have been performed or have transpired.

HISTORY: 130 v PtII, 151 (Eff 3-18-65); 134 v H 511. Eff 1-1-74.

§ 2967.05 Parole of dying prisoner.

Upon recommendation of the director of rehabilitation and correction, accompanied by a certificate of the attending physician that a prisoner or convict is in imminent danger of death, the governor may order his release as if on parole, reserving the right to return him to the institution pursuant to this section. If, subsequent to his release, his health improves so that he is no longer in imminent danger of death, he shall be returned, by order of the governor, to the institution from which he was released. If he violates any rules or conditions applicable to him, he may be returned to an institution under the control of the department of rehabilitation and correction.

HISTORY: 132 v S 395 (Eff 12-13-67); 139 v S 199 (Eff 7-1-83); 145 v H 571. Eff 10-6-94.

Analogous to former RC § 2967.05 (130 v PtII, 152), repealed 132 v S 395, § 2, eff 12-13-67.

§ 2967.06 Warrants of pardon and commutation.

Warrants of pardon and commutation shall be issued in triplicate, one to be given to the convict, one to be filed with the clerk of the court of common pleas in whose office the sentence is recorded, and one to be filed with the head of the institution in which the convict was confined, in case he was confined.

All warrants of pardon, whether conditional or otherwise, shall be recorded by said clerk and the officer of the institution with whom such warrants and copies are filed, in a book provided for that purpose, which record shall include the indorsements on such warrants. A copy of such a warrant with all indorsements, certified by said clerk under seal, shall be received in evidence as proof of the facts set forth in such copy with indorsements.

HISTORY: 130 v PtII, 152. Eff 3-18-65.

§ 2967.07 Applications for executive pardon, commutation, or reprieve.

All applications for pardon, commutation of sentence, or reprieve shall be made in writing to the adult parole authority. Upon the filing of such application, or when directed by the governor in any case, a thorough investigation into the propriety of granting a pardon, commutation, or reprieve shall be made by the authority, which shall report in writing to the governor a brief statement of the facts in the case, together with the recommendation of the authority for or against the granting of a pardon, commutation, or reprieve, the grounds therefor and the records or minutes relating to the case.

HISTORY: 130 v PtII, 152. Eff 3-18-65.

§ 2967.08 Reprieve to a person under sentence of death.

The governor may grant a reprieve for a definite time to a person under sentence of death, with or without notices or application.

HISTORY: 130 v PtII, 153. Eff 3-18-65.

§ 2967.09 Warrant of reprieve.

On receiving a warrant of reprieve, the head of the institution, sheriff, or other officer having custody of the person reprieved, shall file it forthwith with the clerk of the court of common pleas in which the sentence is recorded, who shall thereupon record the warrant in the journal of the court.

HISTORY: 130 v PtII, 153. Eff 3-18-65.

§ 2967.10 Confinement of prisoner during reprieve.

When the governor directs in a warrant of reprieve that the prisoner be confined in a state correctional institution for the time of the reprieve or any part thereof, the sheriff or other officer having the prisoner in custody shall convey him to the state correctional institution in the manner provided for the conveyance of convicts, and the warden shall receive the prisoner and warrant and proceed as the warrant directs. At the expiration of the time specified in the warrant for the confinement of the prisoner in the state correctional institution, the warden shall deal with him according to the sentence as originally imposed, or as modified by executive clemency as shown by a new warrant of pardon, commutation, or reprieve executed by the governor.

HISTORY: 130 v PtII, 153 (Eff 3-18-65); 145 v H 571. Eff 10-6-94.

§ 2967.11 Bad time added to prison term for violation; rules infraction board at each institution.

(A) As used in this section, "violation" means an act that is a criminal offense under the law of this state or the United States, whether or not a person is prosecuted for the commission of the offense.

(B) As part of a prisoner's sentence, the parole board may punish a violation committed by the prisoner by extending the prisoner's stated prison term for a period of fifteen, thirty, sixty, or ninety days in accordance with this section. The parole board may not extend a prisoner's stated prison term for a period longer than one-half of the stated prison term's duration for all violations occurring during the course of the prisoner's stated prison term, including violations occurring while the offender is serving extended time under this section or serving a prison term imposed for a failure to meet the conditions of a post-release control sanction imposed under section 2967.28 of the Revised Code. If a prisoner's stated prison term is extended under this section, the time by which it is so extended shall be referred to as "bad time."

(C) The department of rehabilitation and correction shall establish a rules infraction board in each state correctional institution. When a prisoner in an institution is alleged by any person to have committed a violation, the institutional investigator or other appropriate official promptly shall investigate the alleged violation and promptly shall report the investigator's or other appropriate official's findings to the rules infraction board in that institution. The rules infraction board in that institution shall hold a hearing on the allegation to determine, for purposes of the parole board's possible extension of the prisoner's stated prison term under this section, whether there is evidence of a violation. At the hearing, the accused prisoner shall have the right to testify and be assisted by a member of the staff of the institution who is designated pursuant to rules adopted by the department to assist the prisoner in presenting a defense before the board in the hearing. The rules infraction board shall make an audio tape of the hearing. The board shall report its finding to the head of the institution within ten days after the date of the hearing. If the board finds any evidence of a violation, it also shall include with its finding a recommendation regarding a period of time, as specified in division (B) of this section, by which the prisoner's stated prison term should be extended as a result of the violation. If the board does not so find, the board shall terminate the matter.

(D) Within ten days after receiving from the rules infraction board a finding and a recommendation that the prisoner's stated prison term be extended, the head of the institution shall review the finding and determine whether the prisoner committed a violation. If the head of the institution determines by clear and convincing evidence that the prisoner committed a violation and concludes that the prisoner's stated prison term should be extended as a result of the violation, the head of the institution shall report the determination in a finding to the parole board within ten days after making the determination and shall include with the finding a recommendation regarding the length of the extension of the stated prison term. If the head of the institution does not determine by clear and convincing evidence that the prisoner committed the violation or does not conclude that the prisoner's stated prison term should be extended, the head of the institution shall terminate the matter.

(E) Within thirty days after receiving a report from the head of an institution pursuant to division (D) of this section containing a finding and recommendation, the parole board shall review the findings of the rules infraction board and the head of the institution to determine whether there is clear and convincing evidence that the prisoner committed the violation and, if so, to determine whether the stated prison term should be extended and the length of time by which to extend it. If the parole board determines that there is clear and convincing evidence that the prisoner committed the violation and that the prisoner's stated prison term should be extended, the board shall consider the nature of the violation, other conduct of the prisoner while in prison, and any other evidence relevant to maintaining order in the institution. After considering these factors, the board shall extend the stated prison term by either fifteen, thirty, sixty, or ninety days for the violation, subject to the maximum extension authorized by division (B) of this section. The board shall act to extend a stated prison term no later than sixty days from the date of the finding by the rules infraction board pursuant to division (C) of this section.

(F) If an accusation of a violation is made within sixty days before the end of a prisoner's stated prison term, the rules infraction board, head of the institution, and parole board shall attempt to complete the procedures required by divisions (C) to (E) of this section before the prisoner's stated prison term ends. If necessary, the accused prisoner may be held in the institution for not more than ten days after the end of the prisoner's stated prison term pending review of the violation and a determination regarding an extension of the stated prison term.

(G) This section does not preclude the department of rehabilitation and correction from referring a criminal offense allegedly committed by a prisoner to the appropriate prosecuting authority or from disciplining a prisoner through the use of disciplinary processes other than the extension of the prisoner's stated prison term.

(H) Pursuant to section 111.15 of the Revised Code, the department of rehabilitation and correction shall adopt rules establishing standards and procedures for implementing the requirements of this section and for designating state correctional institution staff members to assist prisoners in hearings conducted under division (C) of this section.

HISTORY: 146 v S 2 (Eff 7-1-96); 146 v S 269. Eff 7-1-96.

The effective date is set by section 5 of SB 269.

The provisions of § 3 of SB 2 (146 v —) read as follows:

SECTION 3. The Department of Rehabilitation and Correction shall adopt the rules required by sections 2967.11, 2967.193, and 2967.28 of the Revised Code, as amended or enacted by this act, within ninety days of the effective date of this act.

§ 2967.12 Notice of pendency of pardon, commutation, or parole.

(A) Except as provided in division (G) of this section, at least three weeks before the adult parole authority recommends any pardon or commutation of sentence, or grants any parole, the authority shall send a notice of the pendency of the pardon, commutation, or parole, setting forth the name of the person on whose behalf it is made, the offense of which the person was convicted, the time of conviction, and the term of the person's sentence, to the prosecuting attorney and the judge of the court of common pleas of the county in which the indictment against the person was found. If there is more than one judge of that court of common pleas, the authority shall send the notice to the presiding judge.

(B) If a request for notification has been made pursuant to section 2930.16 of the Revised Code, the adult parole authority also shall give notice to the victim or the victim's representative prior to recommending any pardon or commutation of sentence for, or granting any parole to, the person. The authority shall provide the notice at the same time as the notice required by division (A) of this section and shall include in the notice the information required to be set forth in that notice. The notice also shall inform the victim or the victim's

§ 2967.12.1

representative that the victim or representative may send a written statement relative to the victimization and the pending action to the adult parole authority and that, if the authority receives any written statement prior to recommending a pardon or commutation or granting a parole for a person, the authority will consider the statement before it recommends a pardon or commutation or grants a parole. If the person is being considered for parole, the notice shall inform the victim or the victim's representative that a full board hearing of the parole board may be held and that the victim or victim's representative may contact the office of victims' services for further information.

(C) When notice of the pendency of any pardon, commutation of sentence, or parole has been given as provided in division (A) of this section and a hearing on the pardon, commutation, or parole is continued to a date certain, the authority shall give notice by mail of the further consideration of the pardon, commutation, or parole to the proper judge and prosecuting attorney at least ten days before the further consideration. When notice of the pendency of any pardon, commutation, or parole has been given as provided in division (B) of this section and the hearing on it is continued to a date certain, the authority shall give notice of the further consideration to the victim or the victim's representative in accordance with section 2930.03 of the Revised Code.

(D) In case of an application for the pardon or commutation of sentence of a person sentenced to capital punishment, the governor may modify the requirements of notification and publication if there is not sufficient time for compliance with the requirements before the date fixed for the execution of sentence.

(E) If an offender is serving a prison term imposed under division (A)(3) of section 2971.03 of the Revised Code and if the parole board terminates its control over the offender's service of that term pursuant to section 2971.04 of the Revised Code, the parole board immediately shall provide written notice of its termination of control or the transfer of control to the entities and persons specified in section 2971.04 of the Revised Code.

(F) The failure of the adult parole authority to comply with the notice provisions of division (A), (B), or (C) of this section or the failure of the parole board to comply with the notice provisions of division (E) of this section do not give any rights or any grounds for appeal or post-conviction relief to the person serving the sentence.

(G) Divisions (A), (B), and (C) of this section do not apply to any release of a person that is of the type described in division (B)(2)(b) of section 5120.031 [5120.03.1] of the Revised Code.

HISTORY: 130 v PtII, 153 (Eff 3-18-65); 140 v S 172 (Eff 9-26-84); 143 v S 258 (Eff 11-20-90); 145 v S 186 (Eff 10-12-94); 146 v S 2 (Eff 7-1-96); 146 v H 180. Eff 1-1-97.

The effective date is set by section 3 of HB 180.

See provisions, § 4 of HB 180 (146 v —) following RC § 2921.34.

See provisions, § 5 of SB 2 (146 v —), as amended by § 3 of SB 269 (146 v —), following RC § 2929.03.

[§ 2967.12.1] § 2967.121 Notice of early release of certain felons.

(A) Subject to division (C) of this section, at least two weeks before any convict who is serving a sentence for committing a felony of the first, second, or third degree is released from confinement in any state correctional institution pursuant to a pardon, commutation of sentence, parole, release in accordance with section 2929.20 of the Revised Code, or completed prison term, the adult parole authority shall send notice of the release to the prosecuting attorney of the county in which the indictment of the convict was found.

(B) The notice required by division (A) of this section may be contained in a weekly list of all felons of the first, second, or third degree who are scheduled for release. The notice shall contain all of the following:

(1) The name of the convict being released;
(2) The date of the convict's release;
(3) The offense for the violation of which the convict was convicted and incarcerated;
(4) The date of the convict's conviction pursuant to which the convict was incarcerated;
(5) The sentence imposed for that conviction;
(6) The length of any supervision that the convict will be under;
(7) The name, business address, and business phone number of the convict's supervising officer;
(8) The address at which the convict will reside.

(C) Divisions (A) and (B) of this section do not apply to the release from confinement of an offender if the offender is serving a prison term imposed under division (A)(3) of section 2971.03 of the Revised Code, if the court pursuant to section 2971.05 of the Revised Code modifies the requirement that the offender serve that entire term in a state correctional institution, and if the release from confinement is pursuant to that modification. In a case of that type, the court that modifies the requirement promptly shall provide written notice of the modification and the order that modifies the requirement or revises the modification to the offender, the department of rehabilitation and correction, the prosecuting attorney, and any state agency or political subdivision that is affected by the order.

HISTORY: 140 v H 399 (Eff 9-26-84); 145 v H 571 (Eff 10-6-94); 146 v S 2 (Eff 7-1-96); 146 H 180. Eff 1-1-97.

The effective date is set by section 3 of HB 180.

See provisions, § 4 of HB 180 (146 v —) following RC § 2921.34.

See provisions, § 5 of SB 2 (146 v —), as amended by § 3 of SB 269 (146 v —), following RC § 2929.03.

§ 2967.13 Parole eligibility.

(A) Except as provided in division (M) of this section,

a prisoner serving a sentence of imprisonment for life for an offense committed on or after July 1, 1996, is not entitled to any earned credit under section 2967.193 [2967.19.3] of the Revised Code and becomes eligible for parole as follows:

(1) If a sentence of imprisonment for life was imposed for the offense of murder, at the expiration of the prisoner's minimum term;

(2) If a sentence of imprisonment for life with parole eligibility after serving twenty years of imprisonment was imposed pursuant to section 2929.022 [2929.02.2] or 2929.03 of the Revised Code, after serving a term of twenty years;

(3) If a sentence of imprisonment for life with parole eligibility after serving twenty-five full years of imprisonment was imposed pursuant to section 2929.022 [2929.02.2] or 2929.03 of the Revised Code, after serving a term of twenty-five full years;

(4) If a sentence of imprisonment for life with parole eligibility after serving thirty full years of imprisonment was imposed pursuant to section 2929.022 [2929.02.2] or 2929.03 of the Revised Code, after serving a term of thirty full years;

(5) If a sentence of imprisonment for life was imposed for rape, after serving a term of ten full years' imprisonment.

(B) Except as provided in division (M) of this section, a prisoner serving a sentence of imprisonment for life with parole eligibility after serving twenty years of imprisonment or a sentence of imprisonment for life with parole eligibility after serving twenty-five full years or thirty full years of imprisonment imposed pursuant to section 2929.022 [2929.02.2] or 2929.03 of the Revised Code for an offense committed on or after July 1, 1996, consecutively to any other term of imprisonment, becomes eligible for parole after serving twenty years, twenty† full years, or thirty full years, as applicable, as to each such sentence of life imprisonment, which shall not be reduced for earned credits under section 2967.193 [2967.19.3] of the Revised Code, plus the term or terms of the other sentences consecutively imposed or, if one of the other sentences is another type of life sentence with parole eligibility, the number of years before parole eligibility for that sentence.

(C) Except as provided in division (M) of this section, a prisoner serving consecutively two or more sentences in which an indefinite term of imprisonment is imposed becomes eligible for parole upon the expiration of the aggregate of the minimum terms of the sentences.

(D) Except as provided in division (M) of this section, a prisoner serving a term of imprisonment who is described in division (A) of section 2967.021 [2967.02.1] of the Revised Code becomes eligible for parole as described in that division or, if the prisoner is serving a definite term of imprisonment, shall be released as described in that division.

(E) A prisoner serving a sentence of life imprisonment without parole imposed pursuant to section 2929.03 or 2929.06 of the Revised Code is not eligible for parole and shall be imprisoned until death.

(F) A prisoner serving a stated prison term shall be released in accordance with section 2967.28 of the Revised Code.

(M) A prisoner serving a prison term or term of life imprisonment without parole imposed pursuant to section 2971.03 of the Revised Code never becomes eligible for parole during that term of imprisonment.††

HISTORY: 134 v H 511 (Eff 1-1-74); 139 v S 1 (Eff 10-19-81); 139 v S 199 (Eff 7-1-83); 139 v H 269 (Eff 7-1-83); 140 v S 210 (Eff 7-1-83); 142 v H 5 (Eff 9-28-87); 142 v H 261 (Eff 11-1-87); 142 v H 708 (Eff 4-19-88); 144 v S 331 (Eff 11-13-92); 145 v H 571 (Eff 10-6-94); 146 v S 2 (Eff 7-1-96); 146 v S 269 (Eff 7-1-96); 146 v H 445 (Eff 9-3-96); 146 v H 180. Eff 1-1-97.

Publisher's Note

The amendments made by SB 269 (146 v —), HB 445 (146 v —) and HB 180 (146 v —) have been combined. Please see provisions of RC § 1.52.

The effective date is set by section 3 of HB 180.

See provisions, § 4 of HB 180 (146 v —) following RC § 2921.34.

See provisions, § 5 of SB 2 (146 v —), as amended by § 3 of SB 269 (146 v —), following RC § 2929.03.

† So in enrolled bill.

†† The lettering is the result of combining SB 269 (146 v —) and HB 180 (146 v —).

[§ 2967.13.1] § 2967.131 Additional conditions of release; searches.

(A) In addition to any other terms and conditions of a conditional pardon, parole, furlough, or other form of authorized release from confinement in a state correctional institution that is granted to an individual and that involves the placement of the individual under the supervision of the adult parole authority, and in addition to any other sanctions of post-release control of a felon imposed under section 2967.28 of the Revised Code, the authority or, in the case of a conditional pardon, the governor shall include in the terms and conditions of the conditional pardon, parole, furlough, or other form of authorized release or shall include as a condition of the post-release control the condition that the parolee, furloughee, or releasee abide by the law, including, but not limited to, complying with the provisions of Chapter 2923. of the Revised Code relating to the possession, sale, furnishing, transfer, disposition, purchase, acquisition, carrying, conveying, or use of, or other conduct involving, a firearm or dangerous ordnance, as defined in section 2923.11 of the Revised Code, during the period of the parolee's, furloughee's, or releasee's conditional pardon, parole, furlough, other form of authorized release, or post-release control.

(B) During the period of a conditional pardon, parole, furlough, or other form of authorized release from confinement in a state correctional institution that is granted to an individual and that involves the placement of the individual under the supervision of the adult parole authority, and during a period of post-release control of a felon imposed under section 2967.28 of the Revised Code, authorized field officers of the authority who are engaged within the scope of their supervisory duties or responsibilities may search, with or without a warrant, the person of the parolee, furloughee, or releasee, the place of residence of the parolee, furloughee, or releasee, and a motor vehicle, another item of tangible or intangible personal property, or other real property in which the parolee, furloughee, or releasee has a right, title, or interest or for which the parolee, furloughee, or releasee has the express or implied permission of a person with a right, title, or interest to use, occupy, or possess, if the field officers have reasonable grounds to believe that the parolee, furloughee, or releasee is not abiding by the law or otherwise is not complying with the terms and conditions of the parolee's, furloughee's, or releasee's conditional pardon, parole, furlough, other form of authorized release, or post-release control. The authority shall provide each parolee, furloughee, or releasee with a written notice that informs the parolee, furloughee, or releasee that authorized field officers of the authority who are engaged within the scope of their supervisory duties or responsibilities may conduct those types of searches during the period of the conditional pardon, parole, furlough, other form of authorized release, or post-release control if they have reasonable grounds to believe that the parolee, furloughee, or releasee is not abiding by the law or otherwise is not complying with the terms and conditions of the parolee's, furloughee's, or releasee's conditional pardon, parole, furlough, other form of authorized release, or post-release control.

HISTORY: 146 v H 4 (Eff 11-9-95); 146 v S 269. Eff 7-1-96.

The effective date is set by section 5 of SB 269.

See provisions, § 3 of HB 4 (146 v —) following RC § 2913.02.

§ 2967.14 Time to be served at halfway house or community residential center; licensing and reimbursement of facilities.

(A) The adult parole authority may require a parolee or releasee to reside in a halfway house or other suitable community residential center that has been licensed by the division of parole and community services pursuant to division (C) of this section during a part or for the entire period of the parolee's conditional release or of the releasee's term of post-release control. The court of common pleas that placed an offender under a sanction consisting of a term in a halfway house or in an alternative residential sanction may require the offender to reside in a halfway house or other suitable community residential center that is designated by the court and that has been licensed by the division pursuant to division (C) of this section during a part or for the entire period of the offender's residential sanction.

(B) The division of parole and community services may enter into agreements with any public or private agency or a department or political subdivision of the state that operates a halfway house or community residential center that has been licensed by the division pursuant to division (C) of this section. An agreement under this division shall provide for housing, supervision, and other services that are required for parolees, releasees, and persons placed under a residential sanction who have been assigned to a halfway house or community residential center. An agreement under this division shall provide for per diem payments to the agency, department, or political subdivision on behalf of each parolee and releasee assigned to and each person placed under a residential sanction in a halfway house or community residential center that is operated by the agency, department, or political subdivision and that has been licensed by the division. The per diem payments shall be equal to the halfway house's or community residential center's average daily per capita costs with its facility at full occupancy. The per diem payments shall not exceed the total operating costs of the halfway house or community residential center during the term of an agreement. The director of rehabilitation and correction shall adopt rules in accordance with Chapter 119. of the Revised Code for determining includable and excludable costs and income to be used in computing the agency's average daily per capita costs with its facility at full occupancy.

The department of rehabilitation and correction may use a portion of the amount appropriated to the department each fiscal year for the halfway house and community residential center program to pay for contracts for nonresidential services for offenders under the supervision of the adult parole authority. The nonresidential services may include, but are not limited to, treatment for substance abuse, mental health counseling, and counseling for sex offenders.

(C) The division of parole and community services may license a halfway house or community residential center as a suitable facility for the care and treatment of adult offenders only if the halfway house or community residential center complies with the standards that the division adopts in accordance with Chapter 119. of the Revised Code for the licensure of halfway houses and community residential centers. The division shall annually inspect each licensed halfway house and licensed community residential center to determine if it is in compliance with the licensure standards.

HISTORY: 136 v H 637 (Eff 8-27-76); 139 v H 694 (Eff 11-15-81); 144 v S 331 (Eff 11-13-92); 145 v H 571 (Eff 10-6-94); 146 v S 2. Eff 7-1-96.

The effective date is set by section 6 of SB 2.

See provisions, § 5 of SB 2 (146 v —), as amended by § 3 of SB 269 (146 v —), following RC § 2929.03.

§ 2967.15 Arrest and proceedings against parolee, furloughee or releasee for violation.

(A) If an adult parole authority field officer has reasonable cause to believe that a person who is a parolee, furloughee, or other releasee under the supervision of the adult parole authority has violated or is violating the condition of a conditional pardon, parole, furlough, other form of authorized release, or post-release control specified in division (A) of section 2967.131 [2967.13.1] of the Revised Code or any other term or condition of the person's conditional pardon, parole, furlough, other form of authorized release, or post-release control, the field officer may arrest the person without a warrant or order a peace officer to arrest the person without a warrant. A person so arrested shall be confined in the jail of the county in which the person is arrested or in another facility designated by the chief of the adult parole authority until a determination is made regarding the person's release status. Upon making an arrest under this section, the arresting or supervising adult parole authority field officer promptly shall notify the superintendent of parole supervision or the superintendent's designee, in writing, that the person has been arrested and is in custody and submit in detail an appropriate report of the reason for the arrest.

(B) Except as otherwise provided in this division, prior to the revocation by the adult parole authority of a person's pardon, parole, furlough, or other release and prior to the imposition by the parole board or adult parole authority of a new prison term as a post-release control sanction for a person, the adult parole authority shall grant the person a hearing in accordance with rules adopted by the department of rehabilitation and correction under Chapter 119. of the Revised Code. The adult parole authority is not required to grant the person a hearing if the person is convicted of or pleads guilty to an offense that the person committed while released on a pardon, on parole, furlough, or other release, or on post-release control and upon which the revocation of the person's pardon, parole, furlough, other release, or post-release control is based.

If a person who has been pardoned is found to be a violator of the conditions of the parolee's conditional pardon or commutation of sentence, the authority forthwith shall transmit to the governor its recommendation concerning that violation, and the violator shall be retained in custody until the governor issues an order concerning that violation.

If the authority fails to make a determination of the case of a parolee or releasee alleged to be a violator of the terms and conditions of the parolee's or releasee's conditional pardon, parole, other release, or post-release control sanctions within a reasonable time, the parolee or releasee shall be released from custody under the same terms and conditions of the parolee's or releasee's original conditional pardon, parole, other release, or post-release control sanctions.

(C)(1) If a person who is a parolee, furloughee, or other releasee absconds from supervision, the superintendent shall report that fact to the authority, in writing, and the authority shall enter an order upon its official minutes declaring that person to be a violator at large. The superintendent, upon being advised of the apprehension and availability for return of a violator at large, shall recommend to the authority that the violator at large be returned to the institution or restored to parole, furlough, other form of authorized release, or post-release control. If the violator is not restored to parole, furlough, other form of authorized release, or post-release control, the violator shall be returned to a state correctional institution.

The time between the date on which a person who is a parolee, furloughee, or other releasee is declared to be a violator or violator at large and the date on which that person is returned to custody in this state under the immediate control of the adult parole authority shall not be counted as time served under the sentence imposed on that person or as a part of the term of post-release control.

(2) A furloughee or a releasee other than a person who is released on parole, conditional pardon, or post-release control is considered to be in custody while on furlough or other release, and, if the furloughee or releasee absconds from supervision, the furloughee or releasee may be prosecuted for the offense of escape.

(D) A person who is a parolee, furloughee, or other releasee and who has violated a term or condition of the person's conditional pardon, parole, furlough, other form of authorized release, or post-release control shall be declared to be a violator if the person is committed to a correctional institution outside the state to serve a sentence imposed upon the person by a federal court or a court of another state or if the person otherwise leaves the state.

(E) As used in this section, "peace officer" has the same meaning as in section 2935.01 of the Revised Code.

HISTORY: 130 v PtII, 154 (Eff 3-18-65); 144 v S 49 (Eff 7-21-92); 145 v H 571 (Eff 10-6-94); 146 v H 117 (Eff 6-30-95); 146 v H 4 (Eff 11-9-95); 146 v S 2 (Eff 7-1-96); 146 v S 269. Eff 7-1-96.

The effective date is set by section 5 of SB 269.

The provisions of § 7(C) of SB 269 (146 v —) read as follows:

(C) Section 2967.15 of the Revised Code was amended by Am. Sub. H.B. 117, Sub. H.B. 4, and Am. Sub. S.B. 2 of the 121st General Assembly. Comparison of these amendments in pursuance of section 1.52 of the Revised Code discloses that while certain of the amendments of these acts are reconcilable, certain other of the amendments are substantively irreconcilable. Am. Sub. H.B. 117 was passed on June 28, 1995; Sub. H.B. 4 and Am. Sub. S.B. 2 both were passed on June 29, 1995. Section 2967.15 of the Revised Code is presented in this act as it results from Sub. H.B. 4 and such of the amendments of Am. Sub. H.B. 117 and Am. Sub. S.B. 2 as are not in conflict with the amendments of Sub. H.B. 4. This is in recognition of the principles stated in division (B) of section 1.52 of the

Revised Code that amendments are to be harmonized where not substantively irreconcilable, and that where amendments are substantively irreconcilable, the latest amendment is to prevail. This division constitutes a legislative finding that such harmonized and reconciled section was the resulting version in effect prior to the effective date of this act.

§ 2967.16 Final release; restoration of rights and privileges.

(A) Except as provided in division (D) of this section, when a paroled prisoner has faithfully performed the conditions and obligations of the paroled prisoner's parole and has obeyed the rules and regulations adopted by the adult parole authority that apply to the paroled prisoner, the authority upon the recommendation of the superintendent of parole supervision may enter upon its minutes a final release and thereupon shall issue to the paroled prisoner a certificate of final release, but the authority shall not grant a final release earlier than one year after the paroled prisoner is released from the institution on parole, and, in the case of a paroled prisoner whose minimum sentence is life imprisonment, the authority shall not grant a final release earlier than five years after the paroled prisoner is released from the institution on parole.

(B) When a prisoner who has been released under a period of post-release control pursuant to section 2967.28 of the Revised Code has faithfully performed the conditions and obligations of the released prisoner's post-release control sanctions and has obeyed the rules and regulations adopted by the adult parole authority that apply to the released prisoner, the authority, upon the recommendation of the superintendent of parole supervision, may enter upon its minutes a final release and, upon the entry of the final release, shall issue to the released prisoner a certificate of final release. The authority shall not grant a final release earlier than one year after the released prisoner is released from the institution under a period of post-release control, and, in the case of a released prisoner whose sentence is life imprisonment, the authority shall not grant a final release earlier than five years after the released prisoner is released from the institution under a period of post-release control.

(C) The following prisoners or person shall be restored to the rights and privileges forfeited by a conviction:

(1) A prisoner who has served the entire prison term that comprises or is part of the prisoner's sentence and has not been placed under any post-release control sanctions;

(2) A prisoner who has been granted a final release by the adult parole authority pursuant to division (A) or (B) of this section;

(3) A person who has completed the period of a community control sanction or combination of community control sanctions, as defined in section 2929.01 of the Revised Code, that was imposed by the sentencing court.

(D) Division (A) of this section does not apply to a prisoner in the shock incarceration program established pursuant to section 5120.031 [5120.03.1] of the Revised Code.

(E) The adult parole authority shall record the final release of a parolee or prisoner in the official minutes of the authority.

HISTORY: 130 v PtII, 156 (Eff 3-18-65); 131 v 687 (Eff 11-1-65); 145 v H 314 (Eff 9-29-94); 146 v S 2 (Eff 7-1-96); 146 v S 269. Eff 7-1-96.

The effective date is set by section 5 of SB 269.

See provisions, § 5 of SB 2 (146 v —), as amended by section 3 of SB 269 (146 v —), following RC § 2929.03.

§ 2967.17 Parole authority may grant administrative release.

(A) The adult parole authority, in its discretion, may grant an administrative release to any of the following:

(1) A parole violator or release violator serving another felony sentence in a correctional institution within or without this state for the purpose of consolidation of the records or if justice would best be served;

(2) A parole violator at large or release violator at large whose case has been inactive for at least ten years following the date of declaration of the parole violation or the violation of a post-release control sanction;

(3) A parolee taken into custody by the immigration and naturalization service of the United States department of justice and deported from the United States.

(B) The adult parole authority shall not grant an administrative release except upon the concurrence of a majority of the parole board and approval of the chief of the adult parole authority. An administrative release does not restore for the person to whom it is granted the rights and privileges forfeited by conviction as provided in section 2961.01 of the Revised Code. Any person granted an administrative release under this section may subsequently apply for a commutation of sentence for the purpose of regaining the rights and privileges forfeited by conviction.

HISTORY: 131 v 687 (Eff 10-20-65); 145 v H 571 (Eff 10-6-94); 145 v S 242 (Eff 10-6-94); 146 v S 2. Eff 7-1-96.

The effective date is set by section 6 of SB 2.

The provisions of § 7 of SB 2 (146 v —) read as follows:

SECTION 7. ° ° ° Section 2967.17 of the Revised Code is presented in this act as a composite of the section as amended by both Am. Sub. H.B. 571 and Sub. S.B. 242 of the 120th General Assembly, with the new language of neither of the acts shown in capital letters. ° ° ° This is in recognition of the principle stated in division (B) of section 1.52 of the Revised Code that such amendments are to be harmonized where not substantively irreconcilable and constitutes a legislative finding that such is the resulting version in effect prior to the effective date of this act.

See provisions, § 5 of SB 2 (146 v —), as amended by § 3 of SB 269 (146 v —), following RC § 2929.03.

§ 2967.18 Sentence reduction or early release due to overcrowding emergency.

(A) Whenever the director of rehabilitation and correction determines that the total population of the state correctional institutions for males and females, the total population of the state correctional institutions for males, or the total population of the state correctional institutions for females exceeds the capacity of those institutions and that an overcrowding emergency exists, the director shall notify the correctional institution inspection committee of the emergency and provide the committee with information in support of the director's determination. The director shall not notify the committee that an overcrowding emergency exists unless the director determines that no other reasonable method is available to resolve the overcrowding emergency.

(B) On receipt of the notice given pursuant to division (A) of this section, the correctional institution inspection committee promptly shall review the determination of the director of rehabilitation and correction. Notwithstanding any other provision of the Revised Code or the Administrative Code that governs the lengths of criminal sentences, sets forth the time within which a prisoner is eligible for parole or within which a prisoner may apply for release, or regulates the procedure for granting parole or release to prisoners confined in state correctional institutions, the committee may recommend to the governor that the prison terms of eligible male, female, or all prisoners, as determined under division (E) of this section, be reduced by thirty, sixty, or ninety days, in the manner prescribed in that division.

(C) If the correctional institution inspection committee disagrees with the determination of the director of rehabilitation and correction that an overcrowding emergency exists, if the committee finds that an overcrowding emergency exists but does not make a recommendation pursuant to division (B) of this section, or if the committee does not make a finding or a recommendation pursuant to that division within thirty days of receipt of the notice given pursuant to division (A) of this section, the director may recommend to the governor that the action set forth in division (B) of this section be taken.

(D) Upon receipt of a recommendation from the correctional institution inspection committee or the director of rehabilitation and correction made pursuant to this section, the governor may declare in writing that an overcrowding emergency exists in all of the institutions within the control of the department in which men are confined, in which women are confined, or both. The declaration shall state that the adult parole authority shall take the action set forth in division (B) of this section. After the governor makes the declaration, the director shall file a copy of it with the secretary of state, and the copy is a public record.

The department may begin to implement the declaration of the governor made pursuant to this section on the date that it is filed with the secretary of state. The department shall begin to implement the declaration within thirty days after the date of filing. The declaration shall be implemented in accordance with division (E) of this section.

(E)(1) No reduction of sentence pursuant to division (B) of this section shall be granted to any of the following:

(a) A person who is serving a term of imprisonment for aggravated murder, murder, voluntary manslaughter, involuntary manslaughter, felonious assault, kidnapping, rape, aggravated arson, aggravated robbery, or any other offense punishable by life imprisonment or by an indefinite term of a specified number of years to life, or for conspiracy in, complicity in, or attempt to commit any of those offenses;

(b) A person who is serving a term of imprisonment for any felony other than carrying a concealed weapon that was committed while the person had a firearm, as defined in section 2923.11 of the Revised Code, on or about the offender's person or under the offender's control;

(c) A person who is serving a term of imprisonment for a violation of section 2925.03 of the Revised Code;

(d) A person who is serving a term of imprisonment for engaging in a pattern of corrupt activity;

(e) A person who is serving a prison term or term of life imprisonment without parole imposed pursuant to section 2971.03 of the Revised Code;

(f) A person who was denied parole or release pursuant to section 2929.20 of the Revised Code during the term of imprisonment the person currently is serving.

(2) A declaration of the governor that requires the adult parole authority to take the action set forth in division (B) of this section shall be implemented only by reducing the prison terms of prisoners who are not in any of the categories set forth in division (E)(1) of this section, and only by granting reductions of prison terms in the following order:

(a) Under any such declaration, prison terms initially shall be reduced only for persons who are not in any of the categories set forth in division (E)(1) of this section and who are not serving a term of imprisonment for any of the following offenses:

(i) An offense of violence that is a felony of the first, second, or third degree or that, under the law in existence prior to the effective date of this amendment, was an aggravated felony of the first, second, or third degree or a felony of the first or second degree;

(ii) An offense set forth in Chapter 2925. of the Revised Code that is a felony of the first or second degree.

(b) If every person serving a term of imprisonment at the time of the implementation of any such declaration who is in the class of persons eligible for the initial reduction of prison terms, as described in division (E)(2)(a) of this section, has received a total of ninety days of term reduction for each three years of imprisonment actually served, then prison terms may be reduced for all other persons serving a term of imprisonment at that time who are not in any of the categories set forth in division (E)(1) of this section.

(F) An offender who is released from a state correctional institution pursuant to this section is subject to post-release control sanctions imposed by the adult parole authority as if the offender was a prisoner described in division (B) of section 2967.28 of the Revised Code who was being released from imprisonment.

(G) If more than one overcrowding emergency is declared while a prisoner is serving a prison term, the total term reduction for that prisoner as the result of multiple declarations shall not exceed ninety days for each three years of imprisonment actually served.

HISTORY: 139 v S 199 (Eff 1-5-83); 139 v H 269 (Eff 3-1-83); 142 v H 262 (Eff 10-20-87); 144 v H 298 (Eff 7-26-91); 145 v H 152 (Eff 7-1-93); 145 v H 571 (Eff 10-6-94); 146 v S 2 (Eff 7-1-96); 146 v H 445 (Eff 9-3-96); 146 v H 180. Eff 1-1-97.

The effective date is set by section 3 of HB 180.

See provisions, § 4 of HB 180 (146 v —) following RC § 2921.34.

See provisions, § 5 of SB 2 (146 v —), as amended by § 3 of SB 269 (146 v —), following RC § 2929.03.

Comment, Legislative Service Commission

Section 2967.18 of the Revised Code is amended by this act [Am. Sub. H.B. 180] and also by Am. Sub. H.B. 445 of the 121st General Assembly. Comparison of these amendments in pursuance of section 1.52 of the Revised Code discloses that they are not irreconcilable so that they are required by that section to be harmonized to give effect to each amendment.

§ 2967.19 Repealed, 146 v S 2, § 6 [130 v PtII, 156; 134 v H 511; 139 v S 1; 139 v S 199; 140 v S 210; 142 v H 261; 143 v S 258; 144 v H 725; 145 v H 571]. Eff 7-1-96.

This section established procedure for calculating time off for good behavior.

[§ 2967.19.1] § 2967.191 Reduction of prison term for prior confinement.

The adult parole authority shall reduce the stated prison term of a prisoner by the total number of days that the prisoner was confined for any reason arising out of the offense for which the prisoner was convicted and sentenced, including confinement in lieu of bail while awaiting trial, confinement for examination to determine the prisoner's competence to stand trial or sanity, and confinement while awaiting transportation to the place where the prisoner is to serve the prisoner's prison term.

HISTORY: 131 v 688 (Eff 10-20-65); 134 v H 511 (Eff 3-23-73); 137 v H 565 (Eff 11-1-78); 138 v H 1000 (Eff 4-9-81); 139 v S 199 (Eff 7-1-83); 146 v S 2 (Eff 7-1-96); 146 v S 269. Eff 7-1-96.

The effective date is set by section 5 of SB 269.

See provisions, § 5 of SB 2 (146 v —), as amended by § 3 of SB 269 (146 v —), following RC § 2929.03.

[§ 2967.19.2] § 2967.192 Repealed, 146 v S 2, § 6 [139 v S 199; 139 v H 269, § 4; 142 v H 261; 145 v H 571]. Eff 7-1-96.

This section described the effect of time of offense on calculation of credit for good behavior.

[§ 2967.19.3] § 2967.193 Days of credit may be earned.

(A) Except as provided in division (C) of this section or in section 2929.13, 2929.14, or 2967.13 of the Revised Code, a person confined in a state correctional institution may earn one day of credit as a deduction from the person's stated prison term for each full month during which the person productively participates in an education program, vocational training, employment in prison industries, treatment for substance abuse, treatment as a sex offender, or any other constructive program developed by the department with specific standards for performance by prisoners. At the end of each calendar month in which a prisoner productively participates in a program or activity listed in this division, the department of rehabilitation and correction shall deduct one day from the date on which the prisoner's stated prison term will expire. If the prisoner violates prison rules, the department may deny the prisoner a credit that otherwise could have been awarded to the prisoner or may withdraw one or more credits previously earned by the prisoner.

If a prisoner is released before the expiration of the prisoner's stated prison term by reason of credit earned under this section, the department shall retain control of the prisoner by means of an appropriate post-release control sanction imposed by the parole board until the end of the stated prison term if the parole board imposes a post-release control sanction pursuant to section 2967.28 of the Revised Code. If the parole board is not required to impose a post-release control sanction under section 2967.28 of the Revised Code, the parole board may elect not to impose a post-release control sanction on the prisoner.

(B) The department of rehabilitation and correction shall adopt rules that specify the programs or activities for which credit may be earned under this section, the criteria for determining productive participation in the programs or activities and for awarding credit, and the criteria for denying or withdrawing previously earned credit as a result of a violation of prison rules.

(C) No person who is serving a sentence of life imprisonment without parole imposed pursuant to section 2929.03 or 2929.06 of the Revised Code or who is serving a prison term or a term of life imprisonment without parole imposed pursuant to section 2971.03 of the Revised Code shall be awarded any days of credit under division (A) of this section.

HISTORY: 142 v H 261 (Eff 11-1-87); 143 v S 258 (Eff 11-20-90); 144 v H 725 (Eff 4-16-93); 145 v H 571 (Eff 10-6-94); 146 v S 2 (Eff 7-1-96); 146 v S 269 (Eff 7-1-96); 146 v H 180. Eff 1-1-97.

The effective date is set by section 3 of HB 180.

See provisions, § 4 of HB 180 (146 v —) following RC § 2921.34.

See provisions, § 3 of SB 2 (146 v —) following RC § 2967.11.

See provisions, § 5 of SB 2 (146 v —), as amended by § 3 of SB 269 (146 v —), following RC § 2929.03.

Comment, Legislative Service Commission

Section 2967.193 of the Revised Code is amended by this act [Am. Sub. S.B. 269] and also by Am. Sub. H.B. 180 of the 121st General Assembly. Comparison of these amendments in pursuance of section 1.52 of the Revised Code discloses that they are not irreconcilable so that they are required by that section to be harmonized to give effect to each amendment.

§ 2967.20 Repealed, 145 v H 571, § 2 [130 v PtII, 157; 134 v H 494]. Eff 10-6-94.

This section concerned transfer of prisoners.

§ 2967.21 Term of sentence unaffected by transfer.

Any prisoner sentenced or committed to a state correctional institution may be transferred from that institution to another state correctional institution, but the prisoner shall continue to be subject to the same conditions as to the stated prison term, parole, and release as if the prisoner were confined in the institution to which the prisoner originally was sentenced or committed.

HISTORY: 130 v PtII, 157 (Eff 3-18-65); 145 v H 571 (Eff 10-6-94); 146 v S 2. Eff 7-1-96.

The effective date is set by section 6 of SB 2.

See provisions, § 5 of SB 2 (146 v —), as amended by § 3 of SB 269 (146 v —), following RC § 2929.03.

§ 2967.22 Mentally ill or retarded parolee, furloughee or probationer.

Whenever it is brought to the attention of the adult parole authority or a county department of probation that a parolee, furloughee, probationer, or releasee appears to be a mentally ill person subject to hospitalization by court order, as defined in section 5122.01 of the Revised Code, or a mentally retarded person subject to institutionalization by court order, as defined in section 5123.01 of the Revised Code, the parole or probation officer, subject to the approval of the chief of the adult parole authority, the designee of the chief of the adult parole authority, or the chief probation officer, may file an affidavit under section 5122.11 or 5123.71 of the Revised Code. A parolee, probationer, or releasee who is involuntarily detained under Chapter 5122. or 5123. of the Revised Code shall receive credit against the period of parole or probation or the term of post-release control for the period of involuntary detention.

If a parolee, probationer, furloughee, or releasee escapes from an institution or facility within the department of mental health or the department of mental retardation and developmental disabilities, the superintendent of the institution immediately shall notify the chief of the adult parole authority or the chief probation officer. Notwithstanding the provisions of section 5122.26 of the Revised Code, the procedure for the apprehension, detention, and return of the parolee, probationer, furloughee, or releasee is the same as that provided for the apprehension, detention, and return of persons who escape from institutions operated by the department of rehabilitation and correction. If the escaped parolee, furloughee, or releasee is not apprehended and returned to the custody of the department of mental health or the department of mental retardation and developmental disabilities within ninety days after the escape, the parolee, furloughee, or releasee shall be discharged from the custody of the department of mental health or the department of mental retardation and developmental disabilities and returned to the custody of the department of rehabilitation and correction. If the escaped probationer is not apprehended and returned to the custody of the department of mental health or the department of mental retardation and developmental disabilities within ninety days after the escape, the probationer shall be discharged from the custody of the department of mental health or the department of mental retardation and developmental disabilities and returned to the custody of the court that sentenced the probationer.

HISTORY: 130 v PtII, 157 (Eff 3-18-65); 134 v H 494 (Eff 7-12-72); 137 v H 565 (Eff 11-1-78); 138 v S 52 (Eff 1-9-81); 138 v H 965 (Eff 4-9-81); 143 v H 569 (Eff 7-1-91); 146 v S 2. Eff 7-1-96.

The effective date is set by section 6 of SB 2.

See provisions, § 5 of SB 2 (146 v —), as amended by § 3 of SB 269 (146 v —), following RC § 2929.03.

§ 2967.23 Release of prisoner to halfway house or community-based correctional facility.

(A) Subject to disapproval by the sentencing judge, the department of rehabilitation and correction may release a prisoner to a halfway house licensed pursuant to section 2967.14 of the Revised Code or, with the further approval of the judicial corrections board of the facility, to a community-based correctional facility and program or district community-based correctional facility and program as provided in section 2929.221 [2929.22.1] of the Revised Code for the last one hundred twenty days of the prisoner's stated prison term.

(B) At least three weeks prior to releasing a prisoner to a halfway house or a community-based correctional facility and program or district community-based correctional facility and program under this section, the department shall give notice of the pendency of the release to the court of common pleas of the county in which the indictment against the prisoner was found and of the fact that the court may disapprove the pending release. If the court disapproves of the release, the court shall notify the department of the disapproval within ten days after receipt of the notice. If the court timely disapproves the pending release, the department shall not proceed with the release. If the court does not timely disapprove the pending release, the department may proceed with plans for the release.

(C) The department of rehabilitation and correction shall adopt rules for granting releases under this section, supervising prisoners on release under this section, and administering the program of releases under this section. No prisoner shall be released under this section if the prisoner ever has been convicted of an offense of violence. A prisoner who is released under this section and who violates any rule established by the department under this section may be returned to the state correctional institution from which the prisoner was released.

HISTORY: 144 v S 331 (Eff 11-13-92); 145 v H 571 (Eff 10-6-94); 146 v S 2 (Eff 7-1-96); 146 v S 269. Eff 7-1-96.

The effective date is set by section 5 of SB 269.

See provisions, § 5 of SB 2 (146 v —), as amended by § 3 of SB 269 (146 v —), following RC § 2929.03.

§ **2967.25** Repealed, 146 v S 2, § 6 [130 v PtII, 158; 132 v H 65; 133 v H 1; 134 v H 511]. Eff 7-1-96.

This section determined parole eligibility when serving consecutive sentences.

§ 2967.26 Furloughs for employment, education or other programs.

(A)(1) Subject to disapproval by the sentencing judge, the adult parole authority may grant furloughs to trustworthy prisoners, other than those serving a prison term or term of life imprisonment without parole imposed pursuant to section 2971.03 of the Revised Code or a sentence of imprisonment for life imposed for an offense committed on or after October 19, 1981, who are confined in any state correctional institution for the purpose of employment, vocational training, educational programs, or other programs designated by the director of rehabilitation and correction within this state. The adult parole authority shall not grant a furlough under this section to a prisoner who is serving a prison term or term of life imprisonment without parole imposed pursuant to section 2971.03 of the Revised Code or a sentence of imprisonment for life imposed for an offense committed on or after October 19, 1981. Additionally, the adult parole authority shall not grant a prisoner a furlough under this section if the prisoner has more than six months of imprisonment to serve until the prisoner's parole eligibility, as determined under section 2967.13 of the Revised Code, or until the expiration of the prisoner's stated prison term.

(2) At least three weeks prior to granting a furlough to a prisoner under this section, the adult parole authority shall give notice of the pendency of the furlough to the court of common pleas of the county in which the indictment against the prisoner was found and of the fact that the court may disapprove the grant of the pending furlough. If the court disapproves of the grant of the pending furlough, the court shall notify the authority of the disapproval within ten days after receipt of the notice. If the court timely disapproves the grant of the pending furlough, the authority shall not proceed with the furlough. If the court does not timely disapprove the grant of the pending furlough, the authority may proceed with plans for the furlough.

(3) If the victim of an offense for which a prisoner was sentenced to a term of imprisonment has requested notification under section 2930.16 of the Revised Code and has provided the department of rehabilitation and correction with the victim's name and address, the adult parole authority, at least three weeks prior to granting a furlough to the prisoner pursuant to this section, shall notify the victim of the pendency of the furlough and of the victim's right to submit a statement to the authority regarding the impact of the release of the prisoner on furlough. If the victim subsequently submits a statement of that nature to the authority, the authority shall consider the statement in deciding whether to grant the furlough.

(B) The department of rehabilitation and correction shall place conditions on the release of any prisoner who is granted a furlough pursuant to this section. Each furloughed prisoner shall be confined during any period of time that the furloughed prisoner is not actually working at the furloughed prisoner's approved employment, engaged in a vocational training or other educational program, engaged in another program designated by the director pursuant to division (A) of this section, or engaged in other activities approved by the department. The confinement of the furloughed prisoner shall be in a suitable facility that has been licensed by the division of parole and community services pursuant to division (C) of section 2967.14 of the Revised Code.

The division of parole and community services may enter into agreements with any agency, public or private, or a department or political subdivision of the state, that operates a facility that has been licensed by the division pursuant to division (C) of section 2967.14 of the Revised Code. An agreement shall provide for housing, supervision, and other services that are required for furloughed prisoners who are assigned to the facility. An agreement shall provide for per diem payments to the agency, department, or political subdivision on behalf of each furloughed prisoner who is assigned to a facility that is operated by the agency, department, or political subdivision and that has been licensed by the division. The per diem payments shall be equal to the facility's average daily per capita costs with its facility at full occupancy. The per diem payments shall not exceed the total operating costs of the facility during the term of an agreement. The director of rehabilitation and correction shall adopt rules in accordance with Chapter 119. of the Revised Code for determining includable and excludable costs and income to be used in computing the agency's average daily per capita costs with its facility at full occupancy.

(C) The adult parole authority, subject to approval by the director of rehabilitation and correction, shall adopt rules for granting furloughs, supervising and confining prisoners on furlough, and administering the furlough program in accordance with this section.

(D) The adult parole authority may require the prisoner on furlough to pay to the division of parole and community services the reasonable expenses incurred by the division in supervising or confining the prisoner on furlough. Inability to pay those reasonable expenses shall not be grounds for refusing to grant a furlough to an otherwise eligible prisoner. Amounts received by the division of parole and community services under this division shall be deposited into the furlough services fund that is hereby created in the state treasury. The fund shall be used solely to pay costs related to the operation of the furlough education and work release program. The director of rehabilitation and correction shall adopt rules in accordance with section 111.15 of the Revised Code for the use of the fund.

(E) A prisoner who violates any rule established by the adult parole authority under division (C) of this section may be returned to the state correctional institution in which the prisoner had been confined prior to furlough, but the prisoner shall receive credit towards completing the prisoner's sentence for the time spent on furlough.

HISTORY: 134 v H 567 (Eff 3-7-72); 136 v H 637 (Eff 8-27-76); 139 v S 1 (Eff 10-19-81); 139 v H 694 (Eff 11-15-81); 139 v S 199 (Eff 7-1-83); 140 v S 210 (Eff 7-1-83); 142 v S 94 (Eff 7-20-88); 145 v H 152 (Eff 7-1-93); 145 v H 571 (Eff 10-6-94); 145 v S 186 (Eff 10-12-94); 146 v S 2 (Eff 7-1-96); 146 v H 180. Eff 1-1-97.

The effective date is set by section 3 of HB 180.

See provisions, § 4 of HB 180 (146 v —) following RC § 2921.34.

See provisions, § 5 of SB 2 (146 v —), as amended by § 3 of SB 269 (146 v —), following RC § 2929.03.

§ 2967.27 Furloughs for trustworthy prisoners.

(A)(1) Subject to disapproval by the sentencing judge for a furlough granted under divisions (A)(1)(c) to (g) of this section, the department of rehabilitation and correction may grant furloughs to trustworthy prisoners confined in any state correctional facility for the custody and rehabilitation of persons convicted of crime, except that the department shall not grant a furlough for any purpose other than the purposes described in division (A)(1)(a) or (b) of this section to a prisoner serving a sentence of life imprisonment that was imposed for an offense committed on or after October 19, 1981, or to a prisoner serving a prison term or term of life imprisonment without parole imposed pursuant to section 2971.03 of the Revised Code. The department may authorize furloughs under this section for the purpose of:

(a) Visiting a dying relative;

(b) Attending the funeral of a relative;

(c) Arranging for a suitable parole plan, or an educational or vocational furlough plan;

(d) Arranging for employment;

(e) Arranging for suitable residence;

(f) Visiting with family;

(g) Otherwise aiding in the rehabilitation of the inmate.

(2) At least three weeks prior to granting a furlough under divisions (A)(1)(c) to (g) of this section, the department shall give notice of the pendency of the furlough to the court of common pleas of the county in which the indictment against the prisoner was found and of the fact that the court may disapprove the grant of the pending furlough. If the court disapproves of the grant, the court shall notify the department of the disapproval within ten days after receipt of the notice. If the court timely disapproves the grant of the pending furlough, the department shall not proceed with the furlough. If the court does not timely disapprove the grant of the pending furlough, the department may proceed with plans for the furlough.

(3) If the victim of an offense for which a prisoner was sentenced to a term of imprisonment has requested notification under section 2930.16 of the Revised Code and has provided the department of rehabilitation and correction with the victim's name and address, the department, at least three weeks prior to granting a furlough to the prisoner pursuant to divisions (A)(1)(c) to (g) of this section and as soon as practicable prior to granting a furlough to the prisoner pursuant to division (A)(1)(a) or (b) of this section, shall notify the victim of the pendency of the furlough and of the victim's right to submit a statement regarding the impact of the release of the prisoner on furlough. If the victim subsequently submits a statement of that nature to the department, the department shall consider the statement in deciding whether to grant the furlough.

(B) The department of rehabilitation and correction shall adopt rules for granting furloughs under this section, supervising prisoners on furlough, and administering the furlough program. The rules shall contain the following prohibitions:

(1) No prisoner who is serving a sentence of life imprisonment that was imposed for an offense committed on or after October 19, 1981, or a prison term or term of life imprisonment without parole imposed pursuant to section 2971.03 of the Revised Code shall be eligible for a furlough for any purpose described in division (A)(1)(a) or (b) of this section unless a corrections officer

or another corrections staff person accompanies the prisoner at all times while on furlough;

(2) No prisoner shall be eligible for furlough under this section who has served less than six months in a state correctional institution, except in the situation of attending the funeral of a member of the prisoner's immediate family, or attending a bedside visit with a member of the prisoner's immediate family who is ill and bedridden.

(C) No prisoner shall be granted a furlough under this section if the prisoner is likely to pose a threat to the public safety or has a record of more than two felony commitments (including the present charge), not more than one of which may be for a crime of an assaultive nature.

(D) Furloughs may be granted under this section only upon the written approval of the director of the department of rehabilitation and correction or if the director deems it appropriate, by the assistant director of the department, or the wardens within the department.

(E) Furloughs granted under this section shall be for a period no longer than is reasonably necessary to accomplish the purposes of this section, but in no event shall a furlough extend beyond seven days, nor shall the total furlough time granted to a prisoner within any calendar year exceed fourteen days except furloughs granted under divisions (A)(1)(c) and (d) of this section.

(F) A prisoner who violates any rule established by the department of rehabilitation and correction under this section may be returned to the state correctional institution from which the prisoner was furloughed, but such a violation does not constitute cause for denial of credit toward completion of the prisoner's sentence of the time the prisoner was on furlough.

HISTORY: 135 v H 217 (Eff 9-26-74); 139 v S 1 (Eff 10-19-81); 145 v H 571 (Eff 10-6-94); 145 v S 186 (Eff 10-12-94); 146 v S 2 (Eff 7-1-96); 146 v S 269 (Eff 7-1-96); 146 v H 180. Eff 1-1-97.

The effective date is set by section 3 of HB 180.

See provisions, § 4 of HB 180 (146 v —) following RC § 2921.34.

See provisions, § 5 of SB 2 (146 v —), as amended by § 3 of SB 269 (146 v —), following RC § 2929.03.

Comment, Legislative Service Commission

Section 2967.27 of the Revised Code is amended by this act [Am. Sub. H.B. 180] and also by Am. Sub. S.B. 269 of the 121st General Assembly. Comparison of these amendments in pursuance of section 1.52 of the Revised Code discloses that they are not irreconcilable so that they are required by that section to be harmonized to give effect to each amendment.

§ 2967.28 Period of post-release control for certain offenders; sanctions; proceedings upon violation.

(A) As used in this section:

(1) "Post-release control" means a period of supervision by the adult parole authority after release from imprisonment that includes one or more post-release control sanctions imposed under this section.

(2) "Post-release control sanction" means a sanction that is authorized under sections 2929.16 to 2929.18 of the Revised Code and that is imposed upon a prisoner upon the prisoner's release from a prison term.

(3) "Monitored time" means the monitored time sanction specified in section 2929.17 of the Revised Code.

(4) "Deadly weapon" and "dangerous ordnance" have the same meanings as in section 2923.11 of the Revised Code.

(5) "Felony sex offense" means a violation of a section contained in Chapter 2907. of the Revised Code that is a felony.

(B) Each sentence to a prison term for a felony of the first degree, for a felony of the second degree, for a felony sex offense, or for a felony of the third degree that is not a felony sex offense and in the commission of which the offender caused or threatened to cause physical harm to a person shall include a requirement that the offender be subject to a period of post-release control imposed by the parole board after the offender's release from imprisonment. Unless reduced by the parole board pursuant to division (D) of this section when authorized under that division, a period of post-release control required by this division for an offender shall be of one of the following periods:

(1) For a felony of the first degree or for a felony sex offense, five years;

(2) For a felony of the second degree that is not a felony sex offense, three years;

(3) For a felony of the third degree that is not a felony sex offense and in the commission of which the offender caused or threatened physical harm to a person, three years.

(C) Any sentence to a prison term for a felony of the third, fourth, or fifth degree that is not subject to division (B)(1) or (3) of this section shall include a requirement that the offender be subject to a period of post-release control of up to three years after the offender's release from imprisonment, if the parole board, in accordance with division (D) of this section, determines that a period of post-release control is necessary for that offender.

(D)(1) Before the prisoner is released from imprisonment, the parole board shall impose upon a prisoner described in division (B) of this section, may impose upon a prisoner described in division (C) of this section, and shall impose upon a prisoner described in division (B)(2)(b) of section 5120.031 [5120.03.1] or in division (B)(1) of section 5120.032 [5120.03.2] of the Revised Code, one or more post-release control sanctions to apply during the prisoner's period of post-release control. Whenever the board imposes one or more post-release control sanctions upon a prisoner, the board, in addition to imposing the sanctions, also shall include as a condition of the post-release control the mandatory condition described in division (A) of section 2967.131 [2967.13.1] of the Revised Code. The board may impose any other conditions of release under a post-release control sanction that the board considers appropriate. Prior to the release of a prisoner for whom it will impose one or more post-release control sanctions under this division, the parole board shall review the prisoner's criminal history, all juvenile court adjudications finding the prisoner, while a juvenile, to be a delinquent child, and the record of the prisoner's conduct while imprisoned. The parole board shall consider any recommendation regarding post-release control sanctions for the prisoner made by the office of victims' services. After considering those materials, the board shall determine, for a prisoner described in division (B) of this section, division (B)(2)(b) of section 5120.031 [5120.03.1], or division (B)(1) of section 5120.032 [5120.03.2] of the Revised Code, which post-release control sanction or combination of post-release control sanctions is reasonable under the circumstances or, for a prisoner described in division (C) of this section, whether a post-release control sanction is necessary and, if so, which post-release control sanction or combination of post-release control sanctions is reasonable under the circumstances. In the case of a prisoner convicted of a felony of the fourth or fifth degree other than a felony sex offense, the board shall presume that monitored time is the appropriate post-release control sanction unless the board determines that a more restrictive sanction is warranted. A post-release control sanction imposed under this division takes effect upon the prisoner's release from imprisonment.

(2) At any time after a prisoner is released from imprisonment and during the period of post-release control applicable to the releasee, the adult parole authority may review the releasee's behavior under the post-release control sanctions imposed upon the releasee under this section. The authority may determine, based upon the review and in accordance with the standards established under division (E) of this section, that a more restrictive or a less restrictive sanction is appropriate and may impose a different sanction. Unless the period of post-release control was imposed for an offense described in division (B)(1) of this section, the authority also may recommend that the parole board reduce the duration of the period of post-release control imposed by the court. If the authority recommends that the board reduce the duration of control for an offense described in division (B)(2), (B)(3), or (C) of this section, the board shall review the releasee's behavior and may reduce the duration of the period of control imposed by the court. In no case shall the board reduce the duration of the period of control imposed by the court for an offense described in division (B)(1) of this section, and in no case shall the board eliminate the mandatory condition described in division (A) of section 2967.131 [2967.13.1] of the Revised Code.

(E) The department of rehabilitation and correction, in accordance with Chapter 119. of the Revised Code, shall adopt rules that do all of the following:

(1) Establish standards for the imposition by the parole board of post-release control sanctions under this section that are consistent with the overriding purposes and sentencing principles set forth in section 2929.11 of the Revised Code and that are appropriate to the needs of releasees;

(2) Establish standards by which the parole board can determine which prisoners described in division (C) of this section should be placed under a period of post-release control;

(3) Establish standards to be used by the parole board in reducing the duration of the period of post-release control imposed by the court when authorized under division (D) of this section, in imposing a more restrictive post-release control sanction than monitored time upon a prisoner convicted of a felony of the fourth or fifth degree other than a felony sex offense, or in imposing a less restrictive control sanction upon a releasee based on the releasee's activities including, but not limited to, remaining free from criminal activity and from the abuse of alcohol or other drugs, successfully participating in approved rehabilitation programs, maintaining employment, and paying restitution to the victim or meeting the terms of other financial sanctions;

(4) Establish standards to be used by the adult parole authority in modifying a releasee's post-release control sanctions pursuant to division (D)(2) of this section;

(5) Establish standards to be used by the adult parole authority or parole board in imposing further sanctions under division (F) of this section on releasees who violate post-release control sanctions, including standards that do the following:

(a) Classify violations according to the degree of seriousness;

(b) Define the circumstances under which formal action by the parole board is warranted;

(c) Govern the use of evidence at violation hearings;

(d) Ensure procedural due process to an alleged violator;

(e) Prescribe nonresidential community control sanctions for most misdemeanor and technical violations;

(f) Provide procedures for the return of a releasee to imprisonment for violations of post-release control.

(F)(1) If a post-release control sanction is imposed upon an offender under this section, the offender upon release from imprisonment shall be under the general jurisdiction of the adult parole authority and generally shall be supervised by the parole supervision section through its staff of parole and field officers as described in section 5149.04 of the Revised Code, as if the offender had been placed on parole. If the offender upon release from imprisonment violates the post-release control sanction or the mandatory condition described in division (A) of section 2967.131 [2967.13.1] of the Revised Code, the public or private person or entity that operates or administers the sanction or the program or activity that comprises the sanction shall report the violation directly to the adult parole authority or to the officer of the authority who supervises the offender. The authority's officers may treat the offender as if the offender were on parole and in violation of the parole, and otherwise shall comply with this section.

(2) If the adult parole authority determines that a releasee has violated a post-release control sanction or the mandatory condition described in division (A) of section 2967.131 [2967.13.1] of the Revised Code imposed upon the releasee and that a more restrictive sanction is appropriate, the authority may impose a more restrictive sanction upon the releasee, in accordance with the standards established under division (E) of this section, or may report the violation to the parole board for a hearing pursuant to division (F)(3) of this section. The authority may not, pursuant to this division, increase the duration of the releasee's post-release control, impose as a post-release control sanction a residential sanction that includes a prison term or eliminate the mandatory condition described in division (A) of section 2967.131 [2967.13.1] of the Revised Code.

(3) The parole board may hold a hearing on any alleged violation by a releasee of a post-release control sanction or the mandatory condition described in division (A) of section 2967.131 [2967.13.1] of the Revised Code imposed upon the releasee. If after the hearing the board finds that the releasee violated the sanction or mandatory condition, the board may increase the duration of the releasee's post-release control up to the maximum duration authorized by division (B) or (C) of this section or impose a more restrictive post-release control sanction, but in no case shall the board eliminate the mandatory condition described in division (A) of section 2967.131 [2967.13.1] of the Revised Code. When appropriate, the board may impose as a post-release control sanction a residential sanction that includes a prison term. The board shall consider a prison term as a post-release control sanction imposed for a violation of post-release control when the violation involves a deadly weapon or dangerous ordnance, physical harm or attempted serious physical harm to a person, or sexual misconduct, or when the releasee committed repeated violations of post-release control sanctions. The period of a prison term that is imposed as a post-release control sanction under this division shall not exceed nine months, and the maximum cumulative prison term for all violations under this section shall not exceed one-half of the stated prison term originally imposed upon the offender as part of this sentence. The period of a prison term that is imposed as a post-release control sanction under this division shall not count as, or be credited toward, the remaining period of post-release control.

(4) A releasee who has violated any post-release control sanction or the mandatory condition described in division (A) of section 2967.131 [2967.13.1] of the Revised Code imposed upon the releasee by committing a felony may be prosecuted for the new felony, and, upon conviction, the court shall impose sentence for the new felony. In addition to the sentence imposed for the new felony, the court may impose a prison term for the violation, and the term imposed for the violation shall be reduced by the prison term that is administratively imposed by the parole board or adult parole authority as a post-release control sanction. The maximum prison term for the violation shall be either the maximum period of post-release control for the earlier felony under division (B) or (C) of this section minus any time the releasee has spent under post-release control for the earlier felony or twelve months, whichever is greater. A prison term imposed for the violation shall be served consecutively to any prison term imposed for the new felony. A prison term imposed for the violation, and a prison term imposed for the new felony, shall not count as, or be credited toward, the remaining period of post-release control imposed for the earlier felony.

(5) Any period of post-release control shall commence upon an offender's actual release from prison. If an offender is serving an indefinite prison term or a life sentence in addition to a stated prison term, the offender shall serve the period of post-release control in the following manner:

(a) If a period of post-release control is imposed upon the offender and if the offender also is subject to a period of parole under a life sentence or an indefinite sentence, and if the period of post-release control ends prior to the period of parole, the offender shall be supervised on parole. The offender shall receive credit for post-release control supervision during the period of parole. The offender is not eligible for final release under section 2967.16 of the Revised Code until the post-release control period otherwise would have ended.

(b) If a period of post-release control is imposed upon the offender and if the offender also is subject to a period of parole under an indefinite sentence, and if the period of parole ends prior to the period of post-release control, the offender shall be supervised on post-release control. The requirements of parole supervision shall be satisfied during the post-release control period.

(c) If an offender is subject to more than one period of post-release control, the period of post-release control for all of the sentences shall be the period of post-release control that expires last, as determined by the parole board. Periods of post-release control shall be served concurrently and shall not be imposed consecutively to each other.

(d) The period of post-release control for a releasee who commits a felony while under post-release control for an earlier felony shall be the longer of the period of post-release control specified for the new felony under division (B) or (C) of this section or the time remaining under the period of post-release control imposed for the earlier felony as determined by the parole board.

HISTORY: 146 v S 2 (Eff 7-1-96); 146 v S 269. Eff 7-1-96.

The effective date is set by section 5 of SB 269.

See provisions, § 3 of SB 2 (146 v —) following RC § 2967.11.

§ 2967.31 Repealed, 146 v S 2, § 6 [134 v H 511; 136 v H 1; 139 v S 199; 139 v 432; 145 v H 571]. Eff 7-1-96.

This section set guidelines for shock parole.

CHAPTER 2969: RECOVERY OF OFFENDER'S PROFITS FUND; CRIME VICTIMS RECOVERY FUND

Section
2969.01 Definitions.
2969.02 Payment of proceeds of contract with offender or allied person into recovery of offender's profits fund.
2969.03 Declaratory judgment to determine application.
2969.04 Administration and distribution of funds; action by victim.
2969.05 Payment from separate account to person from whom obtained.
2969.06 Recovery of offender's profits fund.

[CRIME VICTIMS RECOVERY FUND]

2969.11 Definitions.
2969.12 Administration and distribution of crime victims recovery fund.
2969.13 Crediting of moneys collected and interest to fund.
2969.14 Payment of cost of confinement from unexpended funds; disposition of residue.

[CIVIL ACTIONS BY INMATE AGAINST GOVERNMENTAL ENTITY OR EMPLOYEE]

2969.21 Definitions.
2969.22 Deductions from inmate account and procedure when inmate sues governmental entity or employee.
2969.23 Clerk to collect fees and expenses from inmate.
2969.24 Grounds for dismissal of inmate's action or appeal; hearing.
2969.25 Inmate's affidavit as to prior actions; review of multiple actions; waiver of prepayment.
2969.26 Claims subject to grievance system.
2969.27 Deductions from judgment awarded to inmate.

§ 2969.01 Definitions.

As used in sections 2969.01 to 2969.06 of the Revised Code:

(A) "Offender" means a person who pleads guilty to, is convicted of, or is found not guilty by reason of insanity of an offense in this state or a person against whom a complaint or information has been filed or an indictment has been returned in this state.

(B) "Victim" means a person who suffers personal injury, death, or property loss as a result of any of the following, or the beneficiaries of an action for the wrongful death of any person killed as a result of any of the following:

(1) An offense;
(2) The good faith effort of a person to prevent an offense;
(3) The good faith effort of any person to apprehend a person suspected of engaging in an offense.

(C) "Member of the family of an offender" means an individual who is related by consanguinity or affinity to an offender.

HISTORY: 140 v S 172 (Eff 9-26-84); 146 v S 91. Eff 11-15-95.

§ 2969.02 Payment of proceeds of contract with offender or allied person into recovery of offender's profits fund.

(A) Except as provided in section 2969.05 of the Revised Code, a person that enters into a contract with an offender, an agent, assignee, conspirator, or accomplice of an offender, a member of the family of an offender, or an agent or assignee of a member of the family of an offender shall pay the money, and the monetary value of the property other than money, due under the contract to the clerk of the court of claims for deposit in the recovery of offender's profits fund, if the terms of the contract provide for any of the following:

(1) The reenactment or description by the offender or by a member of the family of the offender in any of the following of an offense that the offender committed:

(a) A movie, book, magazine, newspaper, article, or other form of literary expression;

(b) A program on television, radio, or another broadcasting medium;

(c) A play, speech, or another form of live entertainment, instruction, or presentation.

(2) The expression or description of the thoughts, feelings, opinions, or emotions of the offender or of a member of the family of the offender regarding or experienced during the offense in a material, performance, or program described in division (A)(1)(a), (b), or (c) of this section;

(3) The life story or a part of the life story of the offender or of a member of the family of the offender or an interview or a part of an interview with the offender, an agent, assignee, conspirator, or accomplice of the offender, a member of the family of the offender, or an agent or assignee of a member of the family of an offender that is to be used in a material, performance, or program described in division (A)(1)(a), (b), or (c) of this section, if the publication value of the story or interview results in part from the notoriety brought by the commission of an offense.

(B) An offender, an agent, assignee, conspirator, or accomplice of an offender, a member of the family of an offender, or an agent or assignee of a member of the family of an offender who enters into a contract described in division (A) of this section or a person who receives money or property other than money pursuant to a contract of that nature shall pay the money or the monetary value of the property received pursuant to the contract to the clerk of the court of claims for deposit in the recovery of offender's profits fund. If a person receives money or property pursuant to a contract described in division (A) of this section and fails to pay it or its monetary value to the clerk of the court of claims for deposit in the fund as required by this division, the state has a lien upon the money or property and upon property that is purchased or otherwise obtained with the money or property. The attorney general shall enforce the lien in the same manner as a judgment lien may be enforced by a private individual.

(C)(1) A person who fails to pay money or the monetary value of property other than money to the clerk of the court of claims for deposit as required by this section is liable to the state for the money or the monetary value of the property.

(2) If a person who is required by this section to pay money or the monetary value of property other than money to the clerk of the court of claims for deposit in the recovery of offender's profits fund fails to do so, the attorney general shall bring an action to recover the money or the monetary value of the property against the person who has possession, custody, or control of the money or property or against the person who failed to pay the money or the monetary value of the property to the clerk for deposit in the fund as required by this section. The action shall be brought in the appropriate court. If the court determines in an action brought pursuant to this division that money or the monetary value of property is to be paid to the clerk for deposit in the fund, it shall order that the money be paid to the clerk for deposit in the fund and that the property be sold and the money received from the sale be paid to the clerk for deposit in the fund.

HISTORY: 140 v S 172 (Eff 9-26-84); 141 v H 201 (Eff 7-1-85); 146 v S 91. Eff 11-15-95.

§ 2969.03 Declaratory judgment to determine application.

Any person may bring an action for a declaratory judgment to determine if section 2969.02 of the Revised Code applies to a particular contract. The action for a declaratory judgment shall be brought in the Franklin county court of common pleas.

HISTORY: 140 v S 172. Eff 9-26-84.

§ 2969.04 Administration and distribution of funds; action by victim.

(A) The clerk of the court of claims shall administer the recovery of offender's profits fund created by section 2969.06 of the Revised Code and shall maintain in the fund in the name of each offender a separate account for money received, or money received from the sale or other disposition of property, pursuant to section 2969.02 or 2969.03 of the Revised Code. The clerk shall distribute the money in each account in accordance with division (C) of this section.

If money is deposited in the fund and maintained in a separate account in the name of an offender and if the offender is found not guilty of all of the charges against the offender in this state, all of the charges against the offender in this state are dismissed, or the offender is found not guilty of some of the charges against the offender in this state and the remaining charges against the offender in this state are dismissed, the clerk shall return all of the money in the separate account plus the interest earned on the money to the persons from whom it was obtained.

(B) Notwithstanding a contrary provision of any section of the Revised Code that deals with the limitation of actions, a victim of an offense committed by an offender in whose name a separate account is maintained in the recovery of offender's profits fund may bring a civil action against the offender or the representatives of the offender, and, if money in the separate account was obtained from a member of the family of the offender or an agent or assignee of a member of the family of the offender, against the family member, agent, or assignee at any time within three years after the establishment of the separate account.

In order to recover from a separate account maintained in the fund in the name of an offender, a victim of that offender shall do all of the following:

(1) Within the three-year period or, if the action was initiated before the separate account was established, within ninety days after the separate account is established, notify the clerk of the court of claims that a civil action has been brought against the offender or the representatives of the offender and, if money in the separate account was obtained from a member of the family of the offender or an agent or assignee of a member of the family of the offender, against the family member, agent, or assignee;

(2) Notify the clerk of the court of claims of the entry of any judgment in the civil action;

(3) Within ninety days after the judgment in the civil action is final or, if the judgment was obtained before the separate account was established, within ninety days after the separate account is established, request the clerk of the court of claims to pay from the separate account the judgment that the victim is awarded in the civil action.

If a civil action is brought against an offender or the representatives of the offender and, if money in the separate account was obtained from a member of the family of the offender or an agent or assignee of a member of the family of the offender, against the family member, agent, or assignee and if the civil action is brought after the expiration of the statute of limitations that would apply to the civil action but for this division, the court shall state in a judgment in favor of the victim that the judgment may be enforced only against the separate account maintained in the name of that offender in the recovery of offender's profits fund.

(C)(1) The clerk of the court of claims shall not make a payment from the separate account maintained in the name of an offender in the recovery of offender's profits fund to a victim of the offender until the expiration of the later of the following periods:

(a) The expiration of three years after the establishment of the separate account, provided that no action of which the clerk was notified under division (B)(1) of this section is pending;

(b) If three years has elapsed since the establishment of the separate account and if one or more actions of which the clerk was notified under division (B)(1) of this section is pending at the expiration of that three-year period, the date of the final disposition of the last of those pending actions.

(2) Upon the expiration of the applicable period of time set forth in division (C)(1) of this section, the clerk of the court of claims shall make payments from the separate account maintained in the name of an offender in the recovery of offender's profits fund to any victim of the offender who has obtained a judgment against the offender or the representatives of the offender and, if money in the separate account was obtained from a member of the family of the offender or an agent or assignee of a member of the family of the offender, against the family member, agent, or assignee for damages resulting from an offense committed by the offender. The payments shall be made as provided in this division.

After an offender in whose name a separate account is maintained in the recovery of offender's profits fund is convicted of or found not guilty by reason of insanity of any offense in this state, the clerk of the court of claims shall determine on the second day of January and the first day of April, July, and October of each year the amount of money in that separate account. After the expiration of the applicable period of time set forth in division (C)(1) of this section, the clerk shall pay from that separate account any judgment for which a victim of that offender has requested payment pursuant to division (B)(3) of this section and has requested payment prior to the date of the most recent quarterly determination described in this division. If, at a time that payments would be made from that separate account, there are insufficient funds in that separate account to pay all of the applicable judgments against the offender or the representatives of the offender and, if money in the separate account was obtained from a member of the family of the offender or an agent or asignee of a member of the family of the offender, against the family member, agent, or assignee, the clerk of the court of claims shall pay the judgments on a pro rata basis.

HISTORY: 140 v S 172 (Eff 9-26-84); 141 v H 201 (Eff 7-1-85); 146 v S 91. Eff 11-15-95.

§ 2969.05 Payment from separate account to person from whom obtained.

If a separate account has been maintained in the recovery of offender's profits fund and if there is no further requirement to pay money or the monetary value of property into the fund pursuant to section 2969.02 of the Revised Code, unless otherwise ordered by a court of record in which a judgment has been rendered against the offender or the representatives of the offender and, if money in the separate account was obtained from a member of the family of the offender or an agent or assignee of a member of the family of the offender, against the family member, agent, or assignee, the clerk of the court of claims shall pay the money remaining in the separate account to the persons from whom the money was obtained, if all of the following apply:

(A) The applicable period of time that governs the making of payments from the separate account, as set forth in division (C)(1) of section 2969.04 of the Revised Code, has elapsed.

(B) None of the civil actions against the offender or the representatives of the offender and, if money in the separate account was obtained from a member of the family of the offender or an agent or assignee of a member of the family of the offender, against the family member, agent, or assignee of which the clerk of the court of claims has been notified pursuant to division (B)(1) of section 2969.04 of the Revised Code is pending.

(C) All judgments for which payment was requested pursuant to division (B)(3) of section 2969.04 of the Revised Code have been paid.

HISTORY: 140 v S 172 (Eff 9-26-84); 141 v H 201 (Eff 7-1-85); 146 v S 91. Eff 11-15-95.

§ 2969.06 Recovery of offender's profits fund.

All moneys collected pursuant to sections 2969.02 and 2969.03 of the Revised Code shall be credited by the treasurer of state to the recovery of offender's profits fund, which is hereby created in the state treasury. Except as provided in division (A) of section 2969.04 of the Revised Code, any interest earned on the money in the fund shall be credited to the fund.

HISTORY: 140 v S 172 (Eff 9-26-84); 141 v H 201. Eff 7-1-85.

[CRIME VICTIMS RECOVERY FUND]

§ 2969.11 Definitions.

As used in sections 2969.11 to 2969.14 of the Revised Code:

(A) "Crime victims recovery fund" means the fund created by division (D) of section 2929.25 of the Revised Code.

(B) "Victim" means a person who suffers personal injury, death, or property loss as a result of any of the following, or the beneficiaries of an action for the wrongful death of any person killed as a result of any of the following:

(1) An offense committed by an offender in whose name a separate account is maintained in the crime

victims recovery fund pursuant to section 2969.12 of the Revised Code;

(2) The good faith effort of a person to prevent an offense committed by an offender in whose name a separate account is maintained in the crime victims recovery fund pursuant to section 2969.12 of the Revised Code;

(3) The good faith effort of a person to apprehend a person suspected of engaging in an offense committed by an offender in whose name a separate account is maintained in the crime victims recovery fund pursuant to section 2969.12 of the Revised Code.

HISTORY: 146 v S 91. Eff 11-15-95.

§ 2969.12 Administration and distribution of crime victims recovery fund.

(A) The clerk of the court of claims shall administer the crime victims recovery fund and shall maintain in the fund in the name of each offender a separate account for money received, or money received from the sale or other disposition of property, pursuant to section 2929.25 of the Revised Code in connection with that offender. The clerk shall distribute the money in that separate account in accordance with division (C) of this section.

(B) Notwithstanding a contrary provision of any section of the Revised Code that deals with the limitation of actions, a victim of an offense committed by an offender in whose name a separate account is maintained in the crime victims recovery fund may bring a civil action against the offender or the representatives of the offender at any time within three years after the establishment of the separate account.

In order to recover from a separate account maintained in the fund in the name of an offender, a victim of that offender shall do all of the following:

(1) Within the three-year period or, if the action was initiated before the separate account was established, within ninety days after the separate account is established, notify the clerk of the court of claims that a civil action has been brought against the offender or the representatives of the offender;

(2) Notify the clerk of the court of claims of the entry of any judgment in the civil action;

(3) Within ninety days after the judgment in the civil action is final or, if the judgment was obtained before the separate account was established, within ninety days after the separate account is established, request the clerk of the court of claims to pay from the separate account the judgment that the victim is awarded in the civil action.

If a civil action is brought against an offender or the representatives of the offender after the expiration of the statute of limitations that would apply to the civil action but for this division, the court shall state in a judgment in favor of the victim that the judgment may be enforced only against the separate account maintained in the name of that offender in the crime victims recovery fund.

(C)(1) The clerk of the court of claims shall not make a payment from the separate account maintained in the name of an offender in the crime victims recovery fund to a victim of the offender until the expiration of the later of the following periods:

(a) The expiration of three years after the establishment of the separate account, provided that no action of which the clerk was notified under division (B)(1) of this section is pending;

(b) If three years has elapsed since the establishment of the separate account and if one or more actions of which the clerk was notified under division (B)(1) of this section is pending at the expiration of that three-year period, the date of the final disposition of the last of those pending actions.

(2) Upon the expiration of the applicable period of time set forth in division (C)(1) of this section, the clerk of the court of claims shall make payments from the separate account maintained in the name of the offender in the crime victims recovery fund to the victims of the offender who obtained a judgment against the offender or the representatives of the offender for damages resulting from the offense committed by the offender. The payments shall be made as provided in this division.

When a separate account is maintained in the name of an offender in the crime victims recovery fund, the clerk of the court of claims shall determine on the second day of January and the first day of April, July, and October of each year the amount of money in that separate account. After the expiration of the applicable period of time set forth in division (C)(1) of this section, the clerk shall pay from that separate account any judgment for which a victim of that offender has requested payment pursuant to division (B)(3) of this section and has requested payment prior to the date of the most recent quarterly determination described in this division. If at a time that payments would be made from that separate account there are insufficient funds in that separate account to pay all of the applicable judgments against the offender or the representatives of the offender, the clerk of the court of claims shall pay the judgments on a pro rata basis.

HISTORY: 146 v S 91. Eff 11-15-95.

§ 2969.13 Crediting of moneys collected and interest to fund.

All moneys that are collected pursuant to section 2929.25 of the Revised Code and required to be deposited in the crime victims recovery fund shall be credited by the treasurer of state to the fund. Any interest earned on the money in the fund shall be credited to the fund.

HISTORY: 146 v S 91. Eff 11-15-95.

§ 2969.14 Payment of cost of confinement from unexpended funds; disposition of residue.

(A) If a separate account has been maintained in the

name of an offender in the crime victims recovery fund and if there is no further requirement to pay into the fund money, or the monetary value of property, pursuant to section 2929.25 of the Revised Code, unless otherwise ordered by a court of record in which a judgment has been rendered against the offender or the representatives of the offender, the clerk of the court of claims shall pay the money remaining in the separate account in accordance with division (B) of this section, if all of the following apply:

(1) The applicable period of time that governs the making of payments from the separate account, as set forth in division (C)(1) of section 2969.12 of the Revised Code, has elapsed.

(2) None of the civil actions against the offender or the representatives of the offender of which the clerk of the court of claims has been notified pursuant to division (B)(1) of section 2969.12 of the Revised Code is pending.

(3) All judgments for which payment was requested pursuant to division (B)(3) of section 2969.12 of the Revised Code have been paid.

(B) If the clerk of the court of claims is required by division (A) of this section to pay the money remaining in the separate account established in the name of an offender in accordance with this division, the clerk shall pay the money as follows:

(1) If the offender was confined for a felony in a prison or other facility operated by the department of rehabilitation and correction under a sanction imposed pursuant to section 2929.14 or 2929.16 of the Revised Code, the clerk shall pay the money to the treasurer of state, in accordance with division (C)(1) of section 2929.18 of the Revised Code, to cover the costs of the confinement. If any money remains in the separate account after the payment of the costs of the confinement pursuant to this division, the clerk shall pay the remaining money in accordance with divisions (B)(2), (3), and (5) of this section.

(2) If the offender was confined for a felony in a facility operated by a county or a municipal corporation, after payment of any costs required to be paid under division (B)(1) of this section, the clerk shall pay the money to the treasurer of the county or of the municipal corporation that operated the facility, in accordance with division (C)(2) or (3) of section 2929.18 of the Revised Code, to cover the costs of the confinement. If more than one county or municipal corporation operated a facility in which the offender was confined, the clerk shall equitably apportion the money among each of those counties and municipal corporations. If any money remains in the separate account after the payment of the costs of the confinement pursuant to this division, the clerk shall pay the remaining money in accordance with divisions (B)(3) and (5) of this section.

(3) If the offender was sentenced for a felony to any community control sanction other than a sanction described in division (B)(2) of this section, after payment of any costs required to be paid under division (B)(1) or (2) of this section, the clerk shall pay the money to the treasurer of the county or of the municipal corporation that incurred costs pursuant to the sanction, in accordance with division (C)(2) or (3) of section 2929.18 of the Revised Code, to cover the costs so incurred. If more than one county or municipal corporation incurred costs pursuant to the sanction, the clerk shall equitably apportion the money among each of those counties and municipal corporations. If any money remains in the separate account after the payment of the costs of the sanction pursuant to this division, the clerk shall pay the remaining money in accordance with division (B)(5) of this section.

(4) If the offender was imprisoned or incarcerated for a misdemeanor, to the treasurer of the political subdivision that operates the facility in which the offender was imprisoned or incarcerated, to cover the costs of the imprisonment or incarceration. If more than one political subdivision operated a facility in which the offender was confined, the clerk shall equitably apportion the money among each of those political subdivisions. If any money remains in the separate account after the payment of the costs of the imprisonment or incarceration under this division, the clerk shall pay the remaining money in accordance with division (B)(5) of this section.

(5) If any money remains in the separate account after payment of any costs required to be paid under division (B)(1), (2), (3), or (4) of this section, or if no provision of division (B)(1), (2), (3), or (4) of this section applies, the clerk shall distribute the amount of the money remaining in the separate account as otherwise provided by law for the distribution of money paid in satisfaction of a fine, as if that amount was a fine paid by the offender.

HISTORY: 146 v S 91 (Eff 11-15-95); 146 v S 269. Eff 7-1-96.

The effective date is set by section 5 of SB 269.

[CIVIL ACTIONS BY INMATE AGAINST GOVERNMENTAL ENTITY OR EMPLOYEE]

§ 2969.21 Definitions.

As used in sections 2969.21 to 2969.27 of the Revised Code:

(A) "Clerk" means the elected or appointed clerk of any court in this state, except the court of claims, in which an inmate has commenced a civil action or has filed an appeal of the judgment or order in a civil action of that nature.

(B)(1) "Civil action or appeal against a government entity or employee" means any of the following:

(a) A civil action that an inmate commences against the state, a political subdivision, or an employee of the state or a political subdivision in a court of common pleas, court of appeals, county court, or municipal court or in the supreme court;

(b) An appeal of the judgment or order in a civil action of the type described in division (B)(1)(a) of this section that an inmate files in a court of appeals or in the supreme court.

(2) "Civil action or appeal against a governmental entity or employee" does not include any civil action that an inmate commences against the state, a political subdivision, or an employee of the state or a political subdivision in the court of claims or an appeal of the judgment or order entered by the court of claims in a civil action of that nature, that an inmate files in a court of appeals or the supreme court.

(C) "Employee" means an officer or employee of the state or of a political subdivision who is acting under color of state law.

(D) "Inmate" means a person who is in actual confinement in a state correctional institution or in a county, multicounty, municipal, municipal-county, or multicounty-municipal jail or workhouse.

(E) "Inmate account" means an account maintained by the department of rehabilitation and correction under rules adopted by the director of rehabilitation and correction pursuant to section 5120.01 of the Revised Code or a similar account maintained by a sheriff or any other administrator of a jail or workhouse.

(F) "Political subdivision" means a county, township, city, or village; the office of an elected officer of a county, township, city, or village; or a department, board, office, commission, agency, institution, or other instrumentality of a county, township, city, or village.

(G) "State" has the same meaning as in section 2743.01 of the Revised Code.

(H) "State correctional institution" has the same meaning as in section 2967.01 of the Revised Code.

HISTORY: 146 v H 455. Eff 10-17-96.

§ 2969.22 Deductions from inmate account and procedure when inmate sues governmental entity or employee.

(A)(1) Whenever an inmate commences a civil action or appeal against a government entity or employee on or after the effective date of this section, all of the following apply:

(a) The clerk of the court in which the civil action or appeal is filed shall notify the inmate and either the department of rehabilitation and correction or, if the inmate is confined in a jail or workhouse, the sheriff or other administrator of the jail or workhouse of the deductions and procedures required by divisions (A) to (D) of this section, and shall identify in the notice the civil action or appeal by case name, case number, name of each party, and the court in which the civil action or appeal was brought.

(b) The clerk of the court in which the civil action or appeal is filed shall charge to the inmate either the total payment of the requisite fees that are described in section 2303.20 of the Revised Code or that otherwise are applicable to actions or appeals filed in that court or, if the inmate has submitted an affidavit of indigency, all funds in the inmate account of that inmate in excess of ten dollars, and shall notify the inmate of the charge.

(c) Unless the amount charged under division (A)(1)(b) of this section constitutes the total amount of the requisite fees, all income in the inmate account of the inmate shall be forwarded to the clerk of the court during each calendar month following the month in which the inmate filed the civil action or appeal until the total payment of the requisite fees occurs. The first ten dollars in the inmate account of the inmate each month shall be excluded from that forwarding requirement. If multiple charges are assessed to an inmate account under this division, charges shall be calculated on the basis of the inmate's total income and shall be paid as described in this division until the charges exceed one hundred per cent of nonexcluded funds in the inmate account; thereafter, all unpaid fees shall be paid simultaneously from the inmate account of the inmate to the appropriate court or courts pro rata.

(d) Upon receipt of the notice of the requisite fees payable pursuant to divisions (A)(1)(a) to (c) of this section, the department, sheriff, or other administrator of the jail or workhouse shall deduct from the inmate account of the inmate and transmit to the clerk of the appropriate court the appropriate amounts of the requisite fees as described in divisions (A)(1)(b) and (c) of this section.

(2) The procedures described in this section apply notwithstanding any contrary court rule or the filing of a poverty affidavit.

(3) This section does not limit the clerk of a court of common pleas, court of appeals, county court, or municipal court or the clerk of the supreme court from considering any other inmate resources separate and apart from an inmate account of an inmate in evaluating the inmate's ability to pay court costs, fees, awards, or other amounts.

(B) An inmate who commences a civil action or appeal against a governmental entity or employee on or after the effective date of this section shall be considered to have authorized payment as the plaintiff in the civil action or the appellant in the appeal of the requisite fees that are described in section 2303.20 of the Revised Code or that otherwise are applicable to actions or appeals filed in the court in which the action or appeal is filed, using the procedures set forth in this section, until total payment of the requisite fees.

(C)(1) If an inmate files a civil action or appeal against a government entity or employee on or after the effective date of this section, upon the termination of the civil action or appeal, the clerk of the court in which the action or appeal was filed shall notify the department of rehabilitation and correction or, if the inmate is confined in a jail or workhouse, the sheriff or other administrator of the jail or workhouse of the outcome of the civil action or appeal and shall identify the civil action or appeal by case name, case number, name of each party, and the court in which the civil action or appeal was brought.

(2) The department of rehabilitation and correction or the sheriff or other administrator of a jail or workhouse shall keep in the inmate's file a record of the information supplied by the clerk of the appropriate court under division (C)(1) of this section.

(D) If an inmate is to be released from confinement prior to the total payment of the requisite fees as provided in divisions (A) and (B) of this section, the department of rehabilitation and correction or, if the confinement was in a jail or workhouse, the sheriff or other administrator of the jail or workhouse shall inform the clerk of the court of common pleas, court of appeals, county court, municipal court, or supreme court of the release. The department, sheriff, or other administrator of the jail or workhouse shall deduct from the inmate account of the inmate in the month of the inmate's release from custody an amount sufficient to pay the remainder of the requisite fees owed and transmit that amount to the clerk. If there are insufficient funds in the inmate account of the inmate to totally pay the requisite fees, the department, sheriff, or other administrator of the jail or workhouse shall deduct the balance of the account and transmit that amount to the clerk. The clerk shall inform the court of the amount of the requisite fees still owed.

HISTORY: 146 v H 455. Eff 10-17-96.

§ 2969.23 Clerk to collect fees and expenses from inmate.

If an inmate files a civil action or appeal against a government entity or employee on or after the effective date of this section and if the inmate is ordered to pay court costs, an award of reasonable attorney's fees, or any other fees or expenses the clerk of the court in which the action or appeal is filed shall collect the court costs, reasonable attorney's fees, and other fees or expenses from the inmate using the procedures set forth in section 2969.22 of the Revised Code regarding the collection of fees.

HISTORY: 146 v H 455. Eff 10-17-96.

§ 2969.24 Grounds for dismissal of inmate's action or appeal; hearing.

(A) If an inmate files a civil action or appeal against a government entity or employee, the court in which the action or appeal is filed, on its own motion or on the motion of a party, may dismiss the civil action or appeal at any stage in the proceedings if the court finds any of the following:

(1) The allegation of indigency in a poverty affidavit filed by the inmate is false.

(2) The claim that is the basis of the civil action or the issues of law that are the basis of the appeal are frivolous or malicious.

(3) The inmate filed an affidavit required by section 2969.25 or 2969.26 of the Revised Code that was materially false.

(B) For the purposes of this section, in determining whether a claim that is the basis of the civil action or the issues of law that are the basis of the appeal are frivolous or malicious, the court may consider whether any of the following applies:

(1) The claim fails to state a claim or the issues of law fail to state any issues of law.

(2) The claim has no arguable basis in law or fact or the issues of law have no arguable basis in law.

(3) It is clear that the inmate cannot prove material facts in support of the claim or in support of the issues of law.

(4) The claim that is the basis of the civil action is substantially similar to a claim in a previous civil action filed by the inmate or the issues of law that are the basis of the appeal are substantially similar to issues of law raised in a previous appeal filed by the inmate, in that the claim that is the basis of the current civil action or the issues of law that are the basis of the current appeal involve the same parties or arise from the same operative facts as the claim or issues of law in the previous civil action or appeal.

(C) If a party files a motion requesting the dismissal of a civil action or appeal under division (A) of this section, the court shall hold a hearing on the motion. If the court raises the issue of the dismissal of a civil action or appeal under division (A) of this section by its own motion, the court may hold a hearing on the motion. If practicable, the court may hold the hearing described in this division by telephone or, in the alternative, at the state correctional institution, jail, or workhouse in which the inmate is confined.

(D) On the filing of a motion for dismissal of a civil action under division (A) of this section, the court may suspend discovery relating to the civil action pending the determination of the motion.

(E) Divisions (A) to (D) of this section do not limit the authority of the court in which the civil action or appeal is filed to otherwise dismiss the civil action or appeal.

HISTORY: 146 v H 455. Eff 10-17-96.

§ 2969.25 Inmate's affidavit as to prior actions; review of multiple actions; waiver of prepayment.

(A) At the time that an inmate commences a civil action or appeal against a government entity or employee, the inmate shall file with the court an affidavit that contains a description of each civil action or appeal of a civil action that the inmate has filed in the previous five years in any state or federal court. The affidavit shall include all of the following for each of those civil actions or appeals:

(1) A brief description of the nature of the civil action or appeal;

(2) The case name, case number, and the court in which the civil action or appeal was brought;

(3) The name of each party to the civil action or appeal;

(4) The outcome of the civil action or appeal, including whether the court dismissed the civil action or appeal as frivolous or malicious under state or federal law or rule of court, whether the court made an award against the inmate or the inmate's counsel of record for frivolous conduct under section 2323.51 of the Revised Code, another statute, or a rule of court, and, if the court so dismissed the action or appeal or made an award of that nature, the date of the final order affirming the dismissal or award.

(B) If an inmate who files a civil action in a court of common pleas, court of appeals, county court, or municipal court or in the supreme court or an inmate who files an appeal from a judgment or order in a civil action in any of those courts has filed three or more civil actions or appeals of civil actions in a court of record in this state in the preceding twelve months or previously has been subject to the review procedure described in this division, the court may appoint a member of the bar to review the claim that is the basis of the civil action or the issues of law that are the basis of the appeal and to make a recommendation regarding whether the claim asserted in the action or the issues of law raised in the appeal are frivolous or malicious under section 2969.24 of the Revised Code, any other provision of law, or rule of court.

(C) If an inmate who files a civil action or appeal against a government entity or employee seeks a waiver of the prepayment of the full filing fees assessed by the court in which the action or appeal is filed, the inmate shall file with the complaint or notice of appeal an affidavit that the inmate is seeking a waiver of the prepayment of the court's full filing fees and an affidavit of indigency. The affidavit of waiver and the affidavit of indigency shall contain all of the following:

(1) A statement that sets forth the balance in the inmate account of the inmate for each of the preceding six months, as certified by the institutional cashier;

(2) A statement that sets forth all other cash and things of value owned by the inmate at that time.

HISTORY: 146 v H 455. Eff 10-17-96.

§ 2969.26 Claims subject to grievance system.

(A) If an inmate commences a civil action or appeal against a government entity or employee and if the inmate's claim in the civil action or the inmate's claim in the civil action that is being appealed is subject to the grievance system for the state correctional institution, jail, or workhouse in which the inmate is confined, the inmate shall file both of the following with the court:

(1) An affidavit stating that the grievance was filed and the date on which the inmate received the decision regarding the grievance.

(2) A copy of any written decision regarding the grievance from the grievance system.

(B) If the civil action or appeal is commenced before the grievance system process is complete, the court shall stay the civil action or appeal for a period not to exceed one hundred eighty days to permit the completion of the grievance system process.

HISTORY: 146 v H 455. Eff 10-17-96.

§ 2969.27 Deductions from judgment awarded to inmate.

If an inmate commences a civil action or appeal against a government entity or employee and is granted a judgment for damages in the civil action or appeal, the court shall order that the following be deducted and paid from the award on a pro rata basis before any payment is made to the inmate or the inmate's counsel:

(A) Any fine, court costs, or court-ordered restitution imposed upon the inmate for an offense for which the inmate is confined or for any previous offense committed by the inmate;

(B) The amount of an award of reparations made under sections 2743.51 to 2743.71 of the Revised Code to a victim of the inmate relative to the offense for which the inmate is confined or any previous offense committed by the inmate;

(C) Any other award ordered by a court against the inmate in any other criminal or civil action or proceeding in any court in this state.

HISTORY: 146 v H 455. Eff 10-17-96.

CHAPTER 2971: SENTENCING OF SEXUALLY VIOLENT PREDATORS

Section
2971.01 Definitions.
2971.02 Determination of sexually violent predator specification by court or by jury.
2971.03 Sentencing of sexually violent offender with predator specification.
2971.04 Termination of parole board's control after offender has served minimum prison term; transfer to court.
2971.05 Hearing on modification or termination of prison term after transfer of control to court; conditional release; final release.
2971.06 Detention of offender for violation of condition of modification or conditional release or upon likelihood of additional offense.
2971.07 Application of chapter; warrantless searches after modification or conditional release.

§ 2971.01 Definitions.

As used in this chapter:

(A) "Mandatory prison term" has the same meaning as in section 2929.01 of the Revised Code.

(B) "Designated homicide, assault, or kidnapping offense" means any of the following:

(1) A violation of section 2903.01, 2903.02, 2903.11, or 2905.01 of the Revised Code or a violation of division (A) of section 2903.04 of the Revised Code;

(2) An attempt to commit or complicity in committing a violation listed in division (B)(1) of this section, if the attempt or complicity is a felony.

(C) "Examiner" has the same meaning as in section 2945.371 [2945.37.1] of the Revised Code.

(D) "Peace officer" has the same meaning as in section 2935.01 of the Revised Code.

(E) "Prosecuting attorney" means the prosecuting attorney who prosecuted the case of the offender in question or the successor in office to that prosecuting attorney.

(F) "Sexually oriented offense" has the same meaning as in section 2950.01 of the Revised Code.

(G) "Sexually violent offense" means a violent sex offense, or a designated homicide, assault, or kidnapping offense for which the offender also was convicted of or pleaded guilty to a sexual motivation specification.

(H)(1) "Sexually violent predator" means a person who has been convicted of or pleaded guilty to committing, on or after the effective date of this section, a sexually violent offense and is likely to engage in the future in one or more sexually violent offenses.

(2) For purposes of division (H)(1) of this section, any of the following factors may be considered as evidence tending to indicate that there is a likelihood that the person will engage in the future in one or more sexually violent offenses:

(a) The person has been convicted two or more times, in separate criminal actions, of a sexually oriented offense. For purposes of this division, convictions that result from or are connected with the same act or result from offenses committed at the same time are one conviction, and a conviction set aside pursuant to law is not a conviction.

(b) The person has a documented history from childhood, into the juvenile developmental years, that exhibits sexually deviant behavior.

(c) Available information or evidence suggests that the person chronically commits offenses with a sexual motivation.

(d) The person has committed one or more offenses in which the person has tortured or engaged in ritualistic acts with one or more victims.

(e) The person has committed one or more offenses in which one or more victims were physically harmed to the degree that the particular victim's life was in jeopardy.

(f) Any other relevant evidence.

(I) "Sexually violent predator specification" means a specification, as described in section 2941.148 [2941.14.8] of the Revised Code, charging a person with being a sexually violent predator.

(J) "Sexual motivation" means a purpose to gratify the sexual needs or desires of the offender.

(K) "Sexual motivation specification" means a specification, as described in section 2941.147 [2941.14.7] of the Revised Code, that charges that a person charged with a designated homicide, assault, or kidnapping offense committed the offense with a sexual motivation.

(L) "Violent sex offense" means any of the following:

(1) A violation of section 2907.02, 2907.03, or 2907.12 or of division (A)(4) of section 2907.05 of the Revised Code;

(2) A felony violation of a former law of this state that is substantially equivalent to a violation listed in division (L)(1) of this section or of an existing or former law of the United States or of another state that is substantially equivalent to a violation listed in division (L)(1) of this section;

(3) An attempt to commit or complicity in committing a violation listed in division (L)(1) or (2) of this section if the attempt or complicity is a felony.

HISTORY: 146 v H 180. Eff 1-1-97.

The effective date is set by section 3 of HB 180.

See provisions, § 4 of HB 180 (146 v —) following RC § 2921.34.

§ 2971.02 Determination of sexually violent predator specification by court or by jury.

In any case in which a sexually violent predator specification is included in the indictment, count in the indictment, or information charging a sexually violent offense and in which the defendant is tried by a jury, the defendant may elect to have the court instead of the jury determine the specification. If the defendant does not elect to have the court determine the specification, the defendant shall be tried before the jury on the charge of the offense, and, following a verdict of guilty on the charge of the offense, the defendant shall be tried before the jury on the sexually violent predator specification. If the defendant elects to have the court determine the specification, the defendant shall be tried on the charge of the offense before the jury, and, following a verdict of guilty on the charge of the offense, the court shall conduct a proceeding at which it shall determine the specification.

HISTORY: 146 v H 180. Eff 1-1-97.

The effective date is set by section 3 of HB 180.

See provisions, § 4 of HB 180 (146 v —) following RC § 2921.34.

§ 2971.03 Sentencing of sexually violent offender with predator specification.

(A) Notwithstanding divisions (A), (B), (C), and (F) of section 2929.14, section 2929.02, 2929.03, 2929.06, 2929.13, or another section of the Revised Code, other than divisions (D) and (E) of section 2929.14 of the Revised Code, that authorizes or requires a specified prison term or a mandatory prison term for a person who is convicted of or pleads guilty to a felony or that specifies the manner and place of service of a prison term or term of imprisonment, the court shall impose a sentence upon a person who is convicted of or pleads guilty to a sexually violent offense and who also is convicted of or pleads guilty to a sexually violent predator specification that was included in the indictment, count in the indictment, or information charging that offense as follows:

(1) If the offense is aggravated murder and if the court does not impose upon the offender a sentence of death, it shall impose upon the offender a term of life imprisonment without parole. If the court sentences the offender to death and the sentence of death is vacated, overturned, or otherwise set aside, the court shall impose upon the offender a term of life imprisonment without parole.

(2) If the offense is murder or an offense other than aggravated murder or murder for which a term of life imprisonment may be imposed, it shall impose upon the offender a term of life imprisonment without parole.

(3) Except as otherwise provided in division (A)(4) of this section, if the offense is an offense other than aggravated murder, murder, or an offense for which a term of life imprisonment may be imposed, it shall impose an indefinite prison term consisting of a minimum term fixed by the court from among the range of terms available as a definite term for the offense, but not less than two years, and a maximum term of life imprisonment.

(4) For any offense, if the offender previously has been convicted of or pleaded guilty to a sexually violent offense and also to a sexually violent predator specification that was included in the indictment, count in the indictment, or information charging that offense, it shall impose upon the offender a term of life imprisonment without parole.

(B) If the offender is sentenced to a prison term pursuant to division (A)(3) of this section, the parole board shall have control over the offender's service of the term during the entire term unless the parole board terminates its control in accordance with section 2971.04 of the Revised Code.

(C)(1) Except as provided in division (C)(2) of this section, an offender sentenced to a prison term or term of life imprisonment without parole pursuant to division (A) of this section shall serve the entire prison term or term of life imprisonment in a state correctional institution. The offender is not eligible for judicial release under section 2929.20 of the Revised Code.

(2) For a prison term imposed pursuant to division (A)(3) of this section, the court, in accordance with section 2971.05 of the Revised Code, may terminate the prison term or modify the requirement that the offender serve the entire term in a state correctional institution if all of the following apply:

(a) The offender has served at least the minimum term imposed as part of that prison term.

(b) The parole board, pursuant to section 2971.04 of the Revised Code, has terminated its control over the offender's service of that prison term.

(c) The court has held a hearing and found, by clear and convincing evidence, one of the following:

(i) In the case of termination of the prison term, that the offender is unlikely to commit a sexually violent offense in the future;

(ii) In the case of modification of the requirement, that the offender does not represent a substantial risk of physical harm to others.

(3) An offender who has been sentenced to a term of life imprisonment without parole pursuant to division (A)(1), (2), or (4) of this section shall not be released from the term of life imprisonment or be permitted to serve a portion of it in a place other than a state correctional institution.

(D) If a court sentences an offender to a prison term or term of life imprisonment without parole pursuant to division (A) of this section and the court also imposes on the offender one or more additional prison terms pursuant to division (D) of section 2929.14 of the Revised Code, all of the additional prison terms shall be served consecutively with, and prior to, the prison term or term of life imprisonment without parole imposed upon the offender pursuant to division (A) of this section.

(E) If the offender is convicted of or pleads guilty to two or more offenses for which a prison term or term of life imprisonment without parole is required to be imposed pursuant to division (A) of this section, divisions (A) to (D) of this section shall be applied for each offense. All minimum terms imposed upon the offender pursuant to division (A)(3) of this section for those offenses shall be aggregated and served consecutively, as if they were a single minimum term imposed under that division.

(F) If an offender is convicted of or pleads guilty to a sexually violent offense and also is convicted of or pleads guilty to a sexually violent predator specification that was included in the indictment, count in the indictment, or information charging the sexually violent offense, the conviction of or plea of guilty to the specification automatically classifies the offender as a sexual predator for purposes of Chapter 2950. of the Revised Code. The classification of the offender as a sexual predator for purposes of that chapter is terminated only if the offender was sentenced to a prison term pursuant to division (A)(3) of section 2971.03 of the Revised Code and the court terminates the offender's prison term as provided in division (D) of section 2971.05 of the Revised Code, or as otherwise described in division (D)(2) of section 2950.09 of the Revised Code.

HISTORY: 146 v H 180. Eff 1-1-97.

The effective date is set by section 3 of HB 180.

See provisions, § 4 of HB 180 (146 v —) following RC § 2921.34.

§ 2971.04 Termination of parole board's control after offender has served minimum prison term; transfer to court.

(A) If an offender is serving a prison term imposed under division (A)(3) of section 2971.03 of the Revised Code, at any time after the offender has served the minimum term imposed under that sentence, the parole board may terminate its control over the offender's service of the prison term. The parole board initially shall determine whether to terminate its control over the offender's service of the prison term upon the completion of the offender's service of the minimum term under the sentence and shall make subsequent determinations at least once every two years after that first determination. The parole board shall not terminate its control over the offender's service of the prison term unless it finds at a hearing that the offender does not represent a substantial risk of physical harm to others. Prior to determining whether to terminate its control over the offender's service of the prison term, the parole board shall request the department of rehabilitation and correction to prepare pursuant to section 5120.61 of the Revised Code an update of the most recent risk assessment and report relative to the offender. The offender has the right to be present at any hearing held under this section. At the hearing, the offender and the prosecuting attorney may make a statement and present evidence as to whether the parole board should terminate its control over the offender's service of the prison term. In making its determination as to whether to terminate its control over the offender's service of the prison term, the parole board may follow the standards and guidelines adopted by the department of rehabilitation and correction under section 5120.49 of the Revised Code and shall consider the updated risk assessment and report relating to the offender prepared by the department pursuant to section 5120.61 of the Revised Code in response to the request made under division (A)(1) of this section and any statements or evidence submitted by the offender or the prosecuting attorney. If the parole board terminates its control over an offender's service of a prison term imposed under division (A)(3) of section 2971.03 of the Revised Code, it shall recommend to the court modifications to the requirement that the offender serve the entire term in a state correctional institution. The court is not bound by the recommendations submitted by the parole board.

(B) If the parole board terminates its control over an offender's service of a prison term imposed pursuant to division (A)(3) of section 2971.03 of the Revised Code, the parole board immediately shall provide written notice of its termination of control to the department of rehabilitation and correction, the court, and the prosecuting attorney, and, after the board's termination of its control, the court shall have control over the offender's service of that prison term.

After the transfer, the court shall have control over the offender's service of that prison term for the offender's entire life, subject to the court's termination of the term pursuant to section 2971.05 of the Revised Code.

(C) If control over the offender's service of the prison term is transferred to the court, all of the following apply:

(1) The offender shall not be released solely as a result of the transfer of control over the service of that prison term.

(2) The offender shall not be permitted solely as a result of the transfer to serve a portion of that term in a place other than a state correctional institution.

(3) The offender shall continue serving that term in a state correctional institution, subject to the following:

(a) A release pursuant to a pardon, commutation, or reprieve;

(b) A modification or termination of the term by the court pursuant to this chapter.

HISTORY: 146 v H 180. Eff 1-1-97.

The effective date is set by section 3 of HB 180.

See provisions, § 4 of HB 180 (146 v —) following RC § 2921.34.

§ 2971.05 Hearing on modification or termination of prison term after transfer of control to court; conditional release; final release.

(A)(1) After control over an offender's service of a prison term imposed pursuant to division (A)(3) of section 2971.03 of the Revised Code has been transferred pursuant to section 2971.04 of the Revised Code to the court, the court shall schedule, within thirty days of any of the following, a hearing on whether to modify in accordance with division (C) of this section the requirement that the offender serve the entire prison term in a state correctional institution or to terminate the prison term in accordance with division (D) of this section:

(a) Control over the offender's service of a prison term is transferred pursuant to section 2971.04 of the Revised Code to the court, and no hearing to modify the requirement has been held;

(b) Two years elapse after the most recent prior hearing held pursuant to division (A)(1) or (2) of this section;

(c) The prosecuting attorney, the department of rehabilitation and correction, or the adult parole authority requests the hearing, and recommends that the requirement be modified or that the offender's prison term be terminated.

(2) After control over the offender's service of a prison term has been transferred pursuant to section 2971.04 of the Revised Code to the court, the court, within thirty days of either of the following, shall conduct a hearing on whether to modify in accordance with division (C) of this section the requirement that the offender serve the entire prison term in a state correctional institution, whether to continue, revise, or revoke an existing modification of that requirement, or whether to terminate the term in accordance with division (D) of this section:

(a) The requirement that the offender serve the entire prison term in a state correctional institution has been modified, and the offender is taken into custody for any reason.

(b) The department of rehabilitation and correction or the prosecuting attorney notifies the court pursuant to section 2971.06 of the Revised Code regarding a known or suspected violation of a term or condition of the modification or a belief that there is a substantial likelihood that the offender has committed or is about to commit a sexually violent offense.

(3) After control over the offender's service of a prison term has been transferred pursuant to section 2971.04 of the Revised Code to the court, the court, in any of the following circumstances, may conduct a hearing within thirty days to determine whether to modify in accordance with division (C) of this section the requirement that the offender serve the entire prison term in a state correctional institution, whether to continue, revise, or revoke an existing modification of that requirement, or whether to terminate the sentence in accordance with division (D) of this section:

(a) The offender requests the hearing;

(b) Upon the court's own motion;

(c) One or more examiners who have conducted a psychological examination and assessment of the offender file a statement that states that there no longer is a likelihood that the offender will engage in the future in a sexually violent offense.

(B)(1) Before a court holds a hearing pursuant to division (A) of this section, the court shall provide notice of the date, time, place, and purpose of the hearing to the offender, the prosecuting attorney, the department of rehabilitation and correction, and the adult parole authority and shall request the department to prepare pursuant to section 5120.61 of the Revised Code an update of the most recent risk assessment and report relative to the offender. The offender has the right to be present at any hearing held under this section. At the hearing, the offender and the prosecuting attorney may make a statement and present evidence as to whether the requirement should or should not be modified, whether the existing modification of the requirement should be continued, revised, or revoked, and whether the prison term should or should not be terminated.

(2) At a hearing held pursuant to division (A) of this section, the court may and, if the hearing is held pursuant to division (A)(1)(a), (1)(b), or (3)(c) of this section, shall determine by clear and convincing evidence whether the offender is unlikely to commit a sexually violent offense in the future.

(3) At the conclusion of the hearing held pursuant to division (A) of this section, the court may order that the requirement that the offender serve the entire prison term in a state correctional institution be continued, that the requirement be modified pursuant to division (C) of this section, that an existing modification be continued, revised, or revoked pursuant to division (C) of this section, or that the prison term be terminated pursuant to division (D) of this section.

(C)(1) If, at the conclusion of a hearing held pursuant to division (A) of this section, the court determines by clear and convincing evidence that the offender will not represent a substantial risk of physical harm to others, the court may modify the requirement that the offender serve the entire prison term in a state correctional institution in a manner that the court considers appropriate.

(2) The modification of the requirement does not terminate the prison term but serves only to suspend the requirement that the offender serve the entire term in a state correctional institution. The prison term shall remain in effect for the offender's entire life unless the court terminates the prison term pursuant to division (D) of this section. The offender shall remain under the jurisdiction of the court for the offender's entire life unless the court so terminates the prison term. The modification of the requirement does not terminate the classification of the offender, as described in division (F) of section 2971.03 of the Revised Code, as a sexual predator for purposes of Chapter 2950. of the Revised Code.

(3) If the court revokes the modification under consideration, the court shall order that the offender be returned to the custody of the department of rehabilitation and correction to continue serving the prison term to which the modification applied, and section 2971.06 of the Revised Code applies regarding the offender.

(D)(1) If, at the conclusion of a hearing held pursuant to division (A) of this section, the court determines by clear and convincing evidence that the offender is unlikely to commit a sexually violent offense in the future, the court may terminate the offender's prison term imposed under division (A)(3) of section 2971.03 of the Revised Code, subject to the offender satisfactorily completing the period of conditional release required by this division. If the court terminates the prison term, the court shall place the offender on conditional release for five years, notify the adult parole authority of its determination and of the termination of the prison term, and order the adult parole authority to supervise the offender during the five-year period of conditional release. Upon receipt of a notice from a court pursuant to this division, the adult parole authority shall supervise the offender who is the subject of the notice during the five-year period of conditional release, periodically notify the court of the offender's activities during that five-year period of conditional release, and file with the court no later than thirty days prior to the expiration of the five-year period of conditional release a written recommendation as to whether the termination of the offender's prison term should be finalized, whether the period of conditional release should be extended, or whether another type of action authorized pursuant to this chapter should be taken.

Upon receipt of a recommendation of the adult parole authority filed pursuant to this division, the court shall hold a hearing to determine whether to finalize the termination of the offender's prison term, to extend the period of conditional release, or to take another type of action authorized pursuant to this chapter. The court shall hold the hearing no later than the date on which the five-year period of conditional release terminates and shall provide notice of the date, time, place, and purpose of the hearing to the offender and to the prosecuting attorney. At the hearing, the offender, the prosecuting attorney, and the adult parole authority employee who supervised the offender during the period of conditional release may make a statement and present evidence.

(2) If the court determines to extend an offender's period of conditional release, it may do so for additional periods of one year in the same manner as the original period of conditional release, and except as otherwise described in this division, all procedures and requirements that applied to the original period of conditional release apply to the additional period of extended conditional release unless the court modifies a procedure or requirement. If an offender's period of conditional release is extended as described in this division, all references to a five-year period of conditional release that are contained in division (D)(1) of this section shall be construed, in applying the provisions of that division to the extension, as being references to the one-year period of the extension of the conditional release.

If the court determines to take another type of action authorized pursuant to this chapter, it may do so in the same manner as if the action had been taken at any other stage of the proceedings under this chapter. As used in this division, "another type of action" includes the revocation of the conditional release and the return of the offender to a state correctional institution to continue to serve the prison term.

If the court determines to finalize the termination of the offender's prison term, it shall notify the department of rehabilitation and correction, the department shall enter into its records a final release and issue to the offender a certificate of final release, and the prison term thereafter shall be considered completed and terminated in every way.

The termination of the offender's prison term pursuant to division (D)(1) or (2) of this section automatically terminates the classification of the offender, as described in division (F) of section 2971.03 of the Revised Code, as a sexual predator for purposes of Chapter 2950. of the Revised Code, and the court shall comply with division (D)(2) of section 2950.09 of the Revised Code.

HISTORY: 146 v H 180. Eff 1-1-97.

The effective date is set by section 3 of HB 180.

See provisions, § 4 of HB 180 (146 v —) following RC § 2921.34.

§ 2971.06 Detention of offender for violation of condition of modification or conditional release or upon likelihood of additional offense.

If, pursuant to section 2971.05 of the Revised Code, the court modifies the requirement that the offender serve the entire prison term in a state correctional institution or places the offender on conditional release and if, at any time after the offender has been released from serving the term in an institution, the department of rehabilitation and correction or the prosecuting attorney learns or obtains information indicating that the offender has violated a term or condition of the modification or conditional release or believes there is a substantial likelihood that the offender has committed or is about to commit a sexually violent offense, all of the following apply:

(A) The department or the prosecuting attorney may contact a peace officer, parole officer, or probation officer and request the officer to take the offender into custody. If the department contacts a peace officer, parole officer, or probation officer and requests that the offender be taken into custody, the department shall notify the prosecuting attorney that it made the request and shall provide the reasons for which it made the request. Upon receipt of a request that an offender be taken into custody, a peace officer, parole officer, or probation officer shall take the offender in question into custody and promptly shall notify the department and the prosecuting attorney, in writing, that the offender was taken into custody. After the offender has been taken into custody, the department or the prosecuting attorney shall notify the court of the violation or the belief that there is a substantial likelihood that the offender has committed or is about to commit a sexually violent offense, and the prosecuting attorney may request that the court, pursuant to section 2971.05 of the Revised Code, revise the modification. An offender may be held in custody under this provision for no longer than thirty days, pending a determination pursuant to section 2971.05 of the Revised Code of whether the modification of the requirement that the offender serve the entire prison term in a state correctional institution should be revised. If the court fails to make a determination under that section regarding the prosecuting attorney's request within thirty days after the offender was taken into custody, the offender shall be released from custody and shall be subject to the same terms and conditions as existed under the then-existing modification of the requirement that the offender serve the entire prison term in a state correctional institution, provided that if the act that resulted in the offender being taken into custody under this division is a criminal offense and if the offender is arrested for that act, the offender may be retained in custody in accordance with the applicable law.

(B) If the offender is not taken into custody pursuant to division (A) of this section, the department or the prosecuting attorney shall notify the court of the known or suspected violation or of the belief that there is a substantial likelihood that the offender has committed or is about to commit a sexually violent offense. If the department provides the notification to the court, it also shall notify the prosecuting attorney that it provided the notification and shall provide the reasons for which it provided the notification. The prosecuting attorney may request that the court, pursuant to section 2971.05 of the Revised Code, revise the modification.

HISTORY: 146 v H 180. Eff 1-1-97.

The effective date is set by section 3 of HB 180.

See provisions, § 4 of HB 180 (146 v —) following RC § 2921.34.

§ 2971.07 Application of chapter; warrantless searches after modification or conditional release.

(A) This chapter does not apply to any offender unless the offender is convicted of or pleads guilty to a violent sex offense and also is convicted of or pleads guilty to a sexually violent predator specification that was included in the indictment, count in the indictment, or information charging that offense or unless the offender is convicted of or pleads guilty to a designated homicide, assault, or kidnapping offense and also is convicted of or pleads guilty to both a sexual motivation specification and a sexually violent predator specification that were included in the indictment, count in the indictment, or information charging that offense.

(B) This chapter does not limit or affect a court that sentences an offender who is convicted of or pleads guilty to a violent sex offense and also is convicted of or pleads guilty to a sexually violent predator specification or a court that sentences an offender who is convicted of or pleads guilty to a designated homicide, assault, or kidnapping offense and also is convicted of or pleads guilty to both a sexual motivation specification and a sexually violent predator specification in imposing upon the offender any financial sanction under section 2929.18 or any other section of the Revised Code, or, except as specifically provided in this chapter, any other sanction that is authorized or required for the offense by any other provision of law.

(C) If, pursuant to section 2971.05 of the Revised Code, the court modifies the requirement that the offender serve the entire prison term in a state correctional institution or places the offender on conditional release that involves the placement of the offender under the supervision of the adult parole authority, authorized field officers of the authority who are engaged within the scope of their supervisory duties or responsibilities may search, with or without a warrant, the person of the offender, the place of residence of the offender, and a motor vehicle, another item of tangible or intangible personal property, or any other real property in which the offender has the express or implied permission of a person with a right, title, or interest to use, occupy, or possess if the field officer has reasonable grounds to believe that the offender is not abiding by the law or otherwise is not complying with the terms and conditions of the offender's modification or release. The authority shall provide each offender with a written notice that informs the offender that authorized field officers of the authority who are engaged within the scope of their supervisory duties or responsibilities may conduct those types of searches during the period of the modification or release if they have reasonable grounds to believe that the offender is not abiding by the law or otherwise is not complying with the terms and conditions of the offender's modification or release.

HISTORY: 146 v H 180. Eff 1-1-97.

The effective date is set by section 3 of HB 180.

See provisions, § 4 of HB 180 (146 v —) following RC § 2921.34.

MISCELLANEOUS STATUTORY PROVISIONS

CHAPTER 1: DEFINITIONS; RULES OF CONSTRUCTION

§ 1.01 "Revised Code."

All statutes of a permanent and general nature of the state as revised and consolidated into general provisions, titles, chapters, and sections shall be known and designated as the "Revised Code," for which designation "R.C." may be substituted. Title, Chapter, and section headings and marginal General Code section numbers do not constitute any part of the law as contained in the "Revised Code."

The enactment of the Revised Code shall not be construed to affect a right or liability accrued or incurred under any section of the General Code prior to the effective date of such enactment, or an action or proceeding for the enforcement of such right or liability. Such enactment shall not be construed to relieve any person from punishment for an act committed in violation of any section of the General Code, nor to affect an indictment or prosecution therefor. For such purposes, any such section of the General Code shall continue in full force notwithstanding its repeal for the purpose of revision.

HISTORY: Bureau of Code Revision. Eff 10-1-53.

[DEFINITIONS]

§ 1.02 General definitions.

As used in the Revised Code, unless the context otherwise requires:

(A) "Whoever" includes all persons, natural and artificial; partners; principals, agents, and employees; and all officials, public or private.

(B) "Another," when used to designate the owner of property which is the subject of an offense, includes not only natural persons but also every other owner of property.

(C) "Of unsound mind" includes all forms of mental retardation or derangement.

(D) "Bond" includes an undertaking.

(E) "Undertaking" includes a bond.

(F) "And" may be read "or," and "or" may be read "and" if the sense requires it.

(G) "Registered mail" includes certified mail and "certified mail" includes registered mail.

HISTORY: Bureau of Code Revision, 10-1-53; 126 v 1164 (Eff 6-27-55); 129 v 582 (Eff 1-10-61); 133 v H 688 (Eff 11-21-69); 134 v H 607. Eff 1-3-72.

§ 1.03 Definition of "anything of value."

As used in any section of the Revised Code for the violation of which there is provided a penalty or forfeiture, unless the context otherwise requires, "anything of value" includes:

(A) Money, bank bills or notes, United States treasury notes, and other bills, bonds, or notes issued by lawful authority and intended to pass and circulate as money;

(B) Goods and chattels;

(C) Promissory notes, bills of exchange, orders, drafts, warrants, checks, or bonds given for the payment of money;

(D) Receipts given for the payment of money or other property;

(E) Rights in action;

(F) Things which savor of the realty and are, at the time they are taken, a part of the freehold, whether they are of the substance or produce thereof or affixed thereto, although there may be no interval between the severing and taking away;

(G) Any interest in realty, including fee simple and partial interests, present and future, contingent or vested interest, beneficial interests, leasehold interests, and any other interest in realty;

(H) Any promise of future employment;

(I) Every other thing of value.

HISTORY: RS § 6794; 60 v 20; 66 v 29, 341; 68 v 87; 69 v 67; GC § 12369; Bureau of Code Revision, 10-1-53; 136 v H 1040. Eff 8-27-76.

§ 1.04 Definition of standard time for Ohio.

The standard time throughout this state shall be the mean astronomical time of the seventy-fifth degree of longitude west from Greenwich. Courts, public offices, and official legal proceedings subject to the laws of this state shall be regulated thereby. Whenever the time of performance of any act, or the time of accrual or determination of any rights, is fixed or governed by the statutes of this state or by any resolutions, rules, regulations, or orders in effect under authority of such statutes, such time shall be the standard time provided in this section.

All clocks maintained in or upon public buildings, existing as such under the laws of this state, shall be set and run according to this section.

HISTORY: RS § 4446-3; 90 v 115; GC § 5979; 112 v 3; 120 v 3; Bureau of Code Revision. Eff 10-1-53.

Comment

The standard time fixed by this act shall be placed in operation at 2:00 o'clock antemeridian, by mean astronomical time of the seventy-fifth degree of longitude west from Greenwich, of the first Sunday after the enactment date of this act. (120 v 3 [4], § 2).

§ 1.05 "Imprisoned" defined.

As used in the Revised Code, unless the context otherwise requires, "imprisoned" means:

(A) Imprisoned in a county, multicounty, municipal, municipal-county, or multicounty-municipal jail or workhouse, if the offense is a misdemeanor;

(B) Imprisoned in a state correctional institution, if the offense is aggravated murder, murder, or an offense punishable by life imprisonment or if the offense is another felony for which the offender is sentenced to prison pursuant to section 2929.14 or division (G)(2) of section 2929.13 of the Revised Code;

(C) Imprisoned in a county, multicounty, municipal, municipal-county, or multicounty-municipal jail or workhouse pursuant to section 2929.16 of the Revised Code if the offense is a felony or imprisoned in a county, multicounty, municipal, municipal-county, or multicounty-municipal jail or workhouse pursuant to section 5120.161 [5120.16.1] of the Revised Code if the offense is a felony of the fourth or fifth degree and is committed by a person who previously has not been convicted of or pleaded guilty to a felony, if the offense is not an offense of violence, and if the department of rehabilitation and correction designates, pursuant to that section, that the person is to be imprisoned in the jail or workhouse;

†(D) Imprisoned in a facility of a type described in section 2929.16 or division (G)(1) of section 2929.13 of the Revised Code, if the offense is a felony and the offender is sentenced pursuant to that section or division.

(D)(1) Serving a term in a community-based correctional facility pursuant to section 2929.16 of the Revised Code and consistent with sections 2301.51 to 2301.56 of the Revised Code and the rules of the division of parole and community services, the department of rehabilitation and correction, and the facility's judicial corrections board adopted pursuant to section 2301.52 of the Revised Code;

(2) Serving a term in a halfway house or an alternative residential facility pursuant to section 2929.16 of the Revised Code and consistent with section 2967.14 of the Revised Code and the rules of the division of parole and community services and of the director of rehabilitation and correction adopted pursuant to that section.

(3) The inclusion of a community-based correctional facility, a halfway house, and an alternative residential facility in division (D) of this section does not cause the facility or house to be financially responsible for the payment of any medical or other health care expenses incurred in connection with an offender who is serving a term in the facility or house pursuant to section 2929.16 of the Revised Code. Unless another section of the Revised Code requires or authorizes a community-based correctional facility, halfway house, or alternative residential facility to pay for those types of expenses, an offender who is serving a term in the facility or house pursuant to section 2929.16 of the Revised Code shall be financially responsible for the payment of those types of expenses.

(4) As used in division (D) of this section, "community-based correctional facility," "halfway house," and "alternative residential facility" have the same meanings as in section 2929.01 of the Revised Code.

HISTORY: RS § 6794; Revised Statutes of 1880 and Codifying Commission; GC § 12370; Bureau of Code Revision, 10-1-53; 134 v H 511 (Eff 1-1-74); 139 v S 199 (Eff 1-5-83); 140 v S 210 (Eff 7-1-83); 142 v H 455 (Eff 7-20-87); 143 v S 258 (Eff 11-20-90); 145 v H 571 (Eff 10-6-94); 146 v S 2 (Eff 7-1-96); 146 v S 269 (Eff 7-1-96); 146 v S 166. Eff 10-17-96.

† This paragraph (D) is from SB 166 eff 10-17-96.

§ 1.06
Repealed, 134 v H 511, § 2 [RS § 6795; 66 v 324, § 230; GC § 12372; 121 v 125; Bureau of Code Revision, 10-1-53]. Eff 1-1-74.

This section defined felonies, misdemeanors, and minor offenses. See now RC § 2901.02.

§ 1.07 Value of written instrument or evidence of debt.

Except as provided in sections 2909.11 and 2913.61 of the Revised Code, when an evidence of debt or a written instrument is the subject of a criminal act, the amount of money due on the evidence of debt or the written instrument or secured thereby, or the amount of money or the value of property affected thereby, shall be deemed the value of the evidence of debt or the written instrument.

HISTORY: RS § 6796; 74 v 241, § 3; GC § 12373; Bureau of Code Revision, 10-1-53; 134 v H 511. Eff 1-1-74.

[CONSTRUCTION]

§ 1.10
Repealed, 134 v H 607, § 2 [Bureau of Code Revision, 10-1-53]. Eff 1-3-72.

For current analogous provisions, see RC §§ 1.42, 1.43.

§ 1.11 Liberal construction of remedial laws.

Remedial laws and all proceedings under them shall be liberally construed in order to promote their object and assist the parties in obtaining justice. The rule of the common law that statutes in derogation of the common law must be strictly construed has no application to remedial laws; but this section does not require a liberal construction of laws affecting personal liberty, relating to amercement, or of a penal nature.

HISTORY: RS § 4948; S&C 940; 51 v 57, § 2; GC 10214; Bureau of Code Revision. Eff 10-1-53.

§ 1.12 Special provision governs unless cumulative.

When a special provision is made in a remedial law

as to service, pleadings, competency of witnesses, or in any other respect inconsistent with the general provisions of sections of the Revised Code relating to procedure in the court of common pleas and procedure on appeal, the special provision shall govern, unless it appears that the provisions are cumulative.

HISTORY: RS § 4956; GC § 10222; Bureau of Code Revision. Eff 10-1-53.

§ **1.13** Repealed, 134 v H 607, § 2 [GC § 26-2; 122 v 239; Bureau of Code Revision, 10-1-53]. Eff 1-3-72.

For current analogous provisions, see RC § 1.50.

§ **1.14** **First day excluded and last day included in computing time; exceptions; legal holiday defined.**

The time within which an act is required by law to be done shall be computed by excluding the first and including the last day; except that when the last day falls on Sunday or a legal holiday, then the act may be done on the next succeeding day which is not Sunday or a legal holiday.

When a public office in which an act, required by law, is to be performed is closed to the public for the entire day which constitutes the last day for doing such act or before its usual closing time on such day, then such act may be performed on the next succeeding day which is not a Sunday or a legal holiday as defined in this section.

"Legal holiday" as used in this section means the following days:

(A) The first day of January, known as New Year's day;

(B) The third Monday in January, known as Martin Luther King day;

(C) The third Monday in February, known as Washington-Lincoln day;

(D) The day designated in the "Act of September 18, 1975," 89 Stat. 479, 5 U.S.C. 6103, as now or hereafter amended, for the commemoration of Memorial day;

(E) The fourth day of July, known as Independence day;

(F) The first Monday in September, known as Labor day;

(G) The second Monday in October, known as Columbus day;

(H) The eleventh day of November, known as Veterans' day;

(I) The fourth Thursday in November, known as Thanksgiving day;

(J) The twenty-fifth day of December, known as Christmas day;

(K) Any day appointed and recommended by the governor of this state or the president of the United States as a holiday.

If any day designated in this section as a legal holiday falls on Sunday, the next succeeding day is a legal holiday.

HISTORY: RS § 4951; S&C 1130; 51 v 57, § 597; GC § 10216; Bureau of Code Revision, 10-1-53; 129 v 1073 (Eff 10-11-61); 133 v H 5 (Eff 1-1-71); 135 v H 460 (Eff 7-1-74); 136 v S 18 (Eff 8-1-75); 138 v S 93 (Eff 4-14-81); 139 v S 68 (Eff 5-17-81); 140 v H 364. Eff 3-14-85.

The provisions of § 3 of HB 364 (140 v —) read as follows:

SECTION 3. In the case of collective bargaining agreements between private employers and bona fide labor organizations that are in effect on the effective date of sections 1.14 and 124.19 of the Revised Code as amended by this act, the day designated in the "Act of September 18, 1975," 89 Stat. 479, 5 U.S.C. 6103, as now or hereafter amended, for the commemoration of Memorial Day shall be observed as Decoration or Memorial Day unless the agreement specifically identifies another day as the one on which Decoration or Memorial Day will be observed.

§ **1.15** **Effective date; priority of legal rights.**

When an act is to take effect or become operative from and after a day named, no part of that day shall be included. If priority of legal rights depends upon the order of events on the same day, such priority shall be determined by the times in the day at which they respectively occurred.

HISTORY: Codifying Commission; GC § 10217; Bureau of Code Revision. Eff 10-1-53.

§ **1.16** Amended and renumbered § 2307.60 in 140 v H 426. Eff 4-4-85.

§§ **1.17, 1.18** Repealed, 134 v H 511, § 2 [RS §§ 6804, 6805; S&C 75, 405, 407, 412, 420-424, 434-438, 457, 457a, 544, 750; S&S 266, 269, 270-273, 281; 29 v 161; 33 v 33; 39 v 13; 42 v 49; 43 v 6; 43 v 92; 44 v 34; 44 v 77; 49 v 105; 50 v 132; 53 v 192; 54 v 127; 57 v 47; 57 v 49; 58 v 65; 60 v 85; 61 v 53; 61 v 79; 64 v 135; 64 v 150; 64 v 229; 66 v 71; 67 v 51; 68 v 9; 70 v 155; 71 v 114; 71 v 115; 72 v 15; 73 v 19; 73 v 116; 73 v 158; 73 v 207; 73 v 219; 73 v 249; GC §§ 12380, 12381; Bureau of Code Revision, 10-1-53]. Eff 1-1-74.

For current analogous provisions, see RC §§ 2923.01, 2923.03.

§§ **1.19 to 1.21** Repealed, 134 v H 607, § 2 [RS §§ 78, 79; S&C 59; S&S 1; 29 v 513; 63 v 22; GC §§ 25-26-1; 122 v 28; Bureau of Code Revision, 10-1-53]. Eff 1-3-72.

For current analogous provisions, see: RC §§ 1.57, 1.58.

§ **1.22** **Change in judicial construction does not affect prior valid obligations.**

When an officer or board of a county, township, or

municipal corporation by ordinance, resolution, order, or other proceeding, in pursuance of a statute of the state, has authorized or caused the issue and delivery of any bonds, obligations, or instruments of such county, township, or municipal corporation, or has caused any county, township, or municipal contracts, grants, franchises, rights, or privileges to be made or given, which were valid according to judicial construction and adjudication at the date of such action or proceeding, and loans or other things of value have been effected or acquired or expenditures have been made by other persons in reliance upon such construction or adjudication, such bonds, obligations, contracts, grants, franchises, rights, and privileges shall be valid and binding, notwithstanding subsequent change of such rule of judicial construction and adjudication with respect to other similar legislation.

HISTORY: RS § 22b-1; 95 v 444; GC § 22; Bureau of Code Revision. Eff 10-1-53.

§ 1.23 Construction of section references.

(A) Whereever in a penalty section reference is made to a violation of a series of sections, or of divisions or subdivisions of a section, such reference shall be construed to mean a violation of any section, division, or subdivision included in such reference.

(B) References in the Revised Code to action taken or authorized under designated sections of the Revised Code include, in every case, action taken or authorized under the applicable section of the General Code which is superseded by the Revised Code.

HISTORY: Senate Judiciary Committee; 134 v H 607 (Eff 1-3-72); 136 v H 837 (Eff 5-25-76); 137 v H 1. Eff 8-26-77.

§§ 1.24 to 1.29 Repealed, 134 v H 1, § 2
[Senate Judiciary Committee; 129 v 582; 130 v 5; 130 v Pt2, 5; 132 v H 1; 133 v H 1]. Eff 3-26-71.

For current analogous provisions, see RC § 1.30.

§ 1.30 Intent of Code revision acts is nonsubstantive.

(A) In enacting any legislation with the stated purpose of correcting nonsubstantive errors in the Revised Code, it is the intent of the general assembly not to make substantive changes in the law in effect on the date of such enactment. A section of the Revised Code affected by any such act shall be construed as a restatement and correction of, and substituted in a continuing way for, the corresponding statutory provision existing on its date of enactment.

(B) Acts of the general assembly with the purpose described in division (A) of this section include:
(1) House Bill No. 1 of the 100th general assembly;
(2) House Bill No. 1 of the 104th general assembly;
(3) House Bill No. 1 of the 105th general assembly;
(4) House Bill No. 5 of the 105th general assembly special session;
(5) House Bill No. 1 of the 107th general assembly;
(6) House Bill No. 1 of the 108th general assembly;
(7) House Bill No. 1 of the 109th general assembly;
(8) House Bill No. 1 of the 110th general assembly;
(9) House Bill No. 1 of the 111th general assembly;
(10) House Bill No. 1 of the 112th general assembly;
(11) House Bill No. 1 of the 113th general assembly;
(12) House Bill No. 1 of the 114th general assembly;
(13) House Bill No. 37 of the 115th general assembly;
(14) House Bill No. 428 of the 116th general assembly;
(15) House Bill No. 708 of the 117th general assembly.

HISTORY: 134 v H 1 (Eff 3-26-71); 135 v H 1 (Eff 3-22-73); 136 v H 1 (Eff 6-13-75); 137 v H 1 (Eff 8-26-77); 138 v H 1 (Eff 5-16-79); 139 v H 1 (Eff 8-5-81); 140 v H 37 (Eff 6-22-84); 141 v H 428 (Eff 12-23-86); 142 v H 708. Eff 4-19-88.

§ 1.41 Applicability of sections 1.41 to 1.59.

Sections 1.41 to 1.59, inclusive, of the Revised Code apply to all statutes, subject to the conditions stated in section 1.51 of the Revised Code, and to rules adopted under them.

HISTORY: 134 v H 607. Eff 1-3-72.

§ 1.42 Common and technical use.

Words and phrases shall be read in context and construed according to the rules of grammar and common usage. Words and phrases that have acquired a technical or particular meaning, whether by legislative definition or otherwise, shall be construed accordingly.

HISTORY: 134 v H 607. Eff 1-3-72.

Analogous to former RC § 1.10 (Bureau of Code Revision, 10-1-53), repealed 134 v H 607, § 2, eff 1-3-72.

§ 1.43 Singular and plural; gender; tense.

(A) The singular includes the plural, and the plural includes the singular.
(B) Words of one gender include the other genders.
(C) Words in the present tense include the future.

HISTORY: 134 v H 607. Eff 1-3-72.

Analogous to former RC § 1.10 (Bureau of Code Revision, 10-1-53), repealed 134 v H 607, § 2, eff 1-3-72.

§ 1.44 Week; year.

(A) "Week" means seven consecutive days.
(B) "Year" means twelve consecutive months.

HISTORY: 134 v H 607. Eff 1-3-72.

§ 1.45 Computation of time.

If a number of months is to be computed by counting

the months from a particular day, the period ends on the same numerical day in the concluding month as the day of the month from which the computation is begun, unless there are not that many days in the concluding month, in which case the period ends on the last day of that month.
HISTORY: 134 v H 607. Eff 1-3-72.

§ 1.46 Words govern expression of numbers.

If there is a conflict between figures and words in expressing a number, the words govern.
HISTORY: 134 v H 607. Eff 1-3-72.

§ 1.47 Intentions in the enactment of statutes.

In enacting a statute, it is presumed that:
(A) Compliance with the constitutions of the state and of the United States is intended;
(B) The entire statute is intended to be effective;
(C) A just and reasonable result is intended;
(D) A result feasible of execution is intended.
HISTORY: 134 v H 607. Eff 1-3-72.

§ 1.48 Statute presumed prospective.

A statute is presumed to be prospective in its operation unless expressly made retrospective.
HISTORY: 134 v H 607. Eff 1-3-72.

§ 1.49 Court considerations as a legislative intent.

If a statute is ambiguous, the court, in determining the intention of the legislature, may consider among other matters:
(A) The object sought to be attained;
(B) The circumstances under which the statute was enacted;
(C) The legislative history;
(D) The common law or former statutory provisions, including laws upon the same or similar subjects;
(E) The consequences of a particular construction;
(F) The administrative construction of the statute.
HISTORY: 134 v H 607. Eff 1-3-72.

§ 1.50 Severability of Code section provisions.

If any provisions of a section of the Revised Code or the application thereof to any person or circumstance is held invalid, the invalidity does not affect other provisions or applications of the section or related sections which can be given effect without the invalid provision or application, and to this end the provisions are severable.
HISTORY: 134 v H 607. Eff 1-3-72.

Analogous to former RC § 1.13 (GC § 26-2; 122 v 239; Bureau of Code Revision, 10-1-53), repealed 134 v H 607, eff 1-3-72.

§ 1.51 Special or local provision prevails over general; exception.

If a general provision conflicts with a special or local provision, they shall be construed, if possible, so that effect is given to both. If the conflict between the provisions is irreconcilable, the special or local provision prevails as an exception to the general provision, unless the general provision is the later adoption and the manifest intent is that the general provision prevail.
HISTORY: 134 v H 607. Eff 1-3-72.

§ 1.52 Irreconcilable statutes or amendments.

(A) If statutes enacted at the same or different sessions of the legislature are irreconcilable, the statute latest in date of enactment prevails.
(B) If amendments to the same statute are enacted at the same or different sessions of the legislature, one amendment without reference to another, the amendments are to be harmonized, if possible, so that effect may be given to each. If the amendments are substantively irreconcilable, the latest in date of enactment prevails. The fact that a later amendment restates language deleted by an earlier amendment, or fails to include language inserted by an earlier amendment, does not of itself make the amendments irreconcilable. Amendments are irreconcilable only when changes made by each cannot reasonably be put into simultaneous operation.
HISTORY: 134 v H 607. Eff 1-3-72.

§ 1.53 Language of enrolled act prevails in conflicts.

If the language of the enrolled act deposited with the secretary of state, including any code section number designated pursuant to section 103.131 [103.13.1] of the Revised Code, conflicts with the language of any subsequent printing or reprinting of the statute, the language and any such designated section number of the enrolled act prevails.
HISTORY: 134 v H 607. Eff 1-3-72.

§ 1.54 Continuation of prior statute.

A statute which is reenacted or amended is intended to be a continuation of the prior statute and not a new enactment, so far as it is the same as the prior statute.
HISTORY: 134 v H 607. Eff 1-3-72.

§ 1.55 Intent of reference.

A reference to any portion of a statute of this state

applies to all reenactments or amendments thereof.
HISTORY: 134 v H 607. Eff 1-3-72.

§ 1.56 Reference to series.

If a statute refers to a series of numbers or letters, the first and the last numbers or letters are included.
HISTORY: 134 v H 607. Eff 1-3-72.

§ 1.57 Repeal of repealing statute.

The repeal of a repealing statute does not revive the statute originally repealed nor impair the effect of any saving clause therein.
HISTORY: 134 v H 607. Eff 1-3-72.

Analogous to former RC § 1.19 (RS § 78; S&C 59; 29 v 513; GC § 25; Bureau of Code Revision, 10-1-53), repealed 134 v H 607, § 2, eff 1-3-72.

§ 1.58 Effect of reenactment, amendment, or repeal.

(A) The reenactment, amendment, or repeal of a statute does not, except as provided in division (B) of this section:

(1) Affect the prior operation of the statute or any prior action taken thereunder;

(2) Affect any validation, cure, right, privilege, obligation, or liability previously acquired, accrued, accorded, or incurred thereunder;

(3) Affect any violation thereof or penalty, forfeiture, or punishment incurred in respect thereto, prior to the amendment or repeal;

(4) Affect any investigation, proceeding, or remedy in respect of any such privilege, obligation, liability, penalty, forfeiture, or punishment; and the investigation, proceeding, or remedy may be instituted, continued, or enforced, and the penalty, forfeiture, or punishment imposed, as if the statute had not been repealed or amended.

(B) If the penalty, forfeiture, or punishment for any offense is reduced by a reenactment or amendment of a statute, the penalty, forfeiture, or punishment, if not already imposed, shall be imposed according to the statute as amended.
HISTORY: 134 v H 607. Eff 1-3-72.

Analogous to former RC §§ 1.20, 1.21 (RS § 79; S&S 1; 63 v 22; GC §§ 26, 26-1; 122 v 28; Bureau of Code Revision, 10-1-53), repealed 134 v H 607, § 2, eff 1-3-72.

§ 1.59 Definitions.

As used in any statute, unless another definition is provided in such statute or a related statute:

(A) "Child" includes child by adoption.

(B) "Oath" includes affirmation and "swear" includes affirm.

(C) "Person" includes an individual, corporation, business trust, estate, trust, partnership, and association.

(D) "Population" means that shown by the most recent regular federal census.

(E) "Property" means real and personal property.

(F) "Rule" includes regulation.

(G) "State," when applied to a part of the United States, includes any state, district, commonwealth, territory, insular possession thereof, and any area subject to the legislative authority of the United States of America. "This state" or "the state" means the state of Ohio.

(H) "United States" includes all the states.

(I) "Will" includes codicil.

(J) "Written" or "in writing" includes any representation of words, letters, symbols, or figures; this provision does not affect any law relating to signatures.
HISTORY: 134 v H 607. Eff 1-3-72.

§ 1.60 "State agency" defined.

As used in Title I of the Revised Code, "state agency," except as otherwise provided in the title, means every organized body, office, or agency established by the laws of the state for the exercise of any function of state government.
HISTORY: 141 v H 201. Eff 7-1-85.

CHAPTER 9: MISCELLANEOUS

§ 9.06 Contracts for private operation and management of correctional facilities.

(A) The department of rehabilitation and correction, and counties and municipal corporations to the extent authorized in sections 307.93, 341.35, 753.03, and 753.15 of the Revised Code, may contract for the private operation and management of a facility under this section. The contracts shall be for an initial term of no more than two years, with an option to renew for additional periods of two years. Any contractor who applies to operate and manage a facility shall be accredited by the American correctional association and shall, at the time of the application, operate and manage one or more facilities accredited by the American correctional association.

Before a public entity may enter into a contract under this section, the contractor shall convincingly demonstrate to the public entity that it can operate the facility with the inmate capacity required by the public entity and provide the services required in this section and realize at least a five per cent savings over the projected cost to the public entity of providing these same services to operate the facility that is the subject of the contract. No out-of-state prisoners may be housed in any facility that is the subject of a contract entered into under to† this section.

(B) Any contract entered into under this section shall include all of the following:

(1) A requirement that the contractor retain the contractor's accreditation from the American correctional association throughout the contract term;

(2) A requirement that all of the following conditions be met:

(a) The contractor begins the process of accrediting the facility with the American correctional association no later than sixty days after the facility receives its first inmate.

(b) The contractor receives accreditation of the facility within twelve months after the date the contractor applies to the American correctional association for accreditation.

(c) Once the accreditation is received, the contractor maintains it for the duration of the contract term.

(d) If the contractor does not comply with divisions (B)(2)(a) to (c) of this section, the contractor is in violation of the contract and the public entity may revoke the contract at its discretion.

(3) A requirement that the contractor comply with all rules promulgated by the department of rehabilitation and correction that apply to the operation and management of correctional facilities, including the minimum standards for jails in Ohio and policies regarding the use of force and the use of deadly force, although the public entity may require more stringent standards, and comply with any applicable laws, rules, or regulations of the federal, state, and local governments, including, but not limited to, sanitation, food service, safety, and health regulations. The contractor shall be required to send copies of reports of inspections completed by the appropriate authorities regarding compliance with rules and regulations to the director of rehabilitation and correction or the director's designee and, if contracting with a local public entity, to the governing authority of that entity.

(4) A requirement that the contractor report for investigation all crimes in connection with the facility to the public entity, to all local law enforcement agencies having jurisdiction at the facility, and, for crime committed at a state correctional institution, to the state highway patrol;

(5) A requirement that, if the facility is a state correctional institution, the contractor provide a written report within specified time limits to the director of rehabilitation and correction or the director's designee of all unusual incidents at the facility as defined in rules promulgated by the department of rehabilitation and correction or, if the facility is a local correctional institution, that the contractor provide a written report to the governing authority of the local public entity.

(6) A requirement that the contractor maintain proper control of inmates' personal funds pursuant to rules promulgated by the department of rehabilitation and correction, for state correctional institutions, or pursuant to the minimum standards for jails along with any additional standards established by the local public entity, for local correctional institutions, and that records pertaining to these funds be made available to representatives of the public entity for review or audit;

(7) A requirement that the contractor prepare and distribute to the director of rehabilitation and correction or, if contracting with a local public entity, to the governing authority of the local entity, annual budget income and expenditure statements and funding source financial reports;

(8) A requirement that the public entity appoint and supervise a full-time contract monitor, that the contractor provide suitable office space for the contract monitor at the facility, and that the contractor allow the contract monitor unrestricted access to all parts of the facility and all records of the facility except the contractor's financial records;

(9) A requirement that if the facility is a state correctional institution, designated department of rehabilitation and correction staff members be allowed access to the facility in accordance with rules promulgated by the department;

(10) A requirement that the contractor provide internal and perimeter security as agreed upon in the contract;

(11) If the facility is a state correctional institution, a requirement that the contractor impose discipline on inmates housed in a state correctional institution, only in accordance with rules promulgated by the department of rehabilitation and correction;

(12) A requirement that the facility be staffed at all times with a staffing pattern approved by the public entity and adequate both to ensure supervision of inmates and maintenance of security within the facility, and to provide for programs, transportation, security, and other operational needs. In determining security needs, the contractor shall be required to consider, among other things, the proximity of the facility to neighborhoods and schools.

(13) If the contract is with a local public entity a requirement that the contractor provide the following services and programs, consistent with the minimum standards for jails promulgated by the department of rehabilitation and correction under section 5120.10 of the Revised Code;

(14) A clear statement that no immunity from liability granted to the state, and no immunity from liability granted to political subdivisions under Chapter 2744. of the Revised Code, shall extend to the contractor or any of the contractor's employees;

(15) A statement that all documents and records relevant to the facility shall be maintained in the same manner required for, and subject to the same laws, rules, and regulations as apply to, the records of the public entity;

(16) Authorization for the public entity to impose a

fine on the contractor from a schedule of fines included in the contract for the contractor's failure to perform its contractual duties, or to cancel the contract, as the public entity considers appropriate. If a fine is imposed, the public entity may reduce the payment owed to the contractor pursuant to any invoice in the amount of the imposed fine.

(17) A statement that all services provided or goods produced at the facility shall be subject to the same regulations, and the same distribution limitations, as apply to goods and services produced at other correctional institutions;

(18) Authorization for the department to establish one or more prison industries at a facility operated and managed by a contractor for the department.

(C) No contract entered into under this section may require, authorize, or imply a delegation of the authority or responsibility of the public entity to a contractor for any of the following:

(1) Developing or implementing procedures for calculating inmate release and parole eligibility dates and recommending the granting or denying of parole, although the contractor may submit written reports that have been prepared in the ordinary course of business;

(2) Developing or implementing procedures for calculating and awarding good time, approving the type of work inmates may perform and the wage or good time, if any, that may be given to inmates engaging in such work, and granting, denying, or revoking good time;

(3) Classifying an inmate or placing an inmate in a more or a less restrictive custody than the custody ordered by the public entity;

(4) Approving inmates for work release;

(5) Contracting for local or long distance telephone services for inmates or receiving commissions from such services at a facility that is owned by or operated under a contract with the department.

(D) A contractor that has been approved to operate a facility under this section shall provide an adequate policy of insurance specifically including, but not limited to, insurance for civil rights claims as determined by a risk management or actuarial firm with demonstrated experience in public liability for state governments. The insurance policy shall provide that the state, including all state agencies, and all political subdivisions of the state with jurisdiction over the facility or in which a facility is located are named as insured, and that the state and its political subdivisions shall be sent any notice of cancellation. The contractor may not self-insure.

The contractor shall indemnify, defend, and hold harmless the state, its officers, agents, and employees, and any local government entity in the state having jurisdiction over the facility or ownership of the facility, from all of the following:

(1) Any claims or losses for services rendered by the contractor or person performing or supplying services in connection with the performance of the contract;

(2) Any failure of the contractor or its officers or employees to adhere to the laws, rules, regulations, or terms agreed to in the contract;

(3) Any constitutional, federal, state, or civil rights claim brought against the state related to the facility operated and managed by the contractor;

(4) Any claims, losses, demands, or causes of action arising out of the contractor's activities in this state;

(5) Any attorney's fees or court costs arising from any habeas corpus actions or other inmate suits that may arise from any event that occurred at the facility or was a result of such an event, or arise over the conditions, management, or operation of the facility, which fees and costs shall include, but not be limited to, attorney's fees for the state's representation and for any court-appointed representation of any inmate, and the costs of any special judge who may be appointed to hear such actions.

(E) Private correctional officers of a private contractor may carry and use firearms in the course of their employment only after being certified as satisfactorily completing an approved training program as described in division (A) of section 109.78 of the Revised Code.

(F) Upon notification by the contractor of an escape from, or of a disturbance at, the facility that is the subject of a contract entered into under this section, the department of rehabilitation and correction and state and local law enforcement agencies shall use all reasonable means to recapture escapees or quell any disturbance. Any cost incurred by the state or its political subdivisions relating to the apprehension of an escapee or the quelling of a disturbance at the facility shall be chargeable to and borne by the contractor. The contractor shall also reimburse the state or its political subdivisions for all reasonable costs incurred relating to the temporary detention of the escapee following recapture.

(G) Any offense that would be a crime if committed at a state correctional institution or jail, workhouse, prison, or other correctional facility shall be a crime if committed by or with regard to inmates at facilities operated pursuant to a contract entered into under this section.

(H) The contractor shall pay any inmate workers at the facility at the rate approved by the public entity. Inmates working at the facility shall not be considered employees of the contractor.

(I) As used in this section:

(1) "Public entity" means the department of rehabilitation and correction, or a county or municipal corporation or a combination of counties and municipal corporations, that has jurisdiction over a facility that is the subject of a contract entered into under this section.

(2) "Local public entity" means a county or municipal corporation, or a combination of counties and municipal corporations, that has jurisdiction over a jail, workhouse, or other correctional facility used only for misdemeanants that is the subject of a contract entered into under this section.

(3) "Governing authority of a local public entity" means, for a county, the board of county commissioners; for a municipal corporation, the legislative authority; for a combination of counties and municipal corporation, all the boards of county commissioners and municipal legislative authorities that joined to create the facility.

(4) "Contractor" means a person who enters into a contract under this section to operate and manage a jail, workhouse, or other correctional facility.

(5) "Facility" means the specific county, multicounty, municipal, municipal-county, or multicounty-municipal jail, workhouse, prison, or other type of correctional institution or facility used only for misdemeanants, or a state correctional institution, that is the subject of a contract entered into under this section.

HISTORY: 146 v H 117 (Eff 9-29-95); 147 v H 215. Eff 9-29-97.

The effective date is set by section 222 of HB 215.

† So in enrolled bill, division A, 2nd paragraph.

TITLE 1: STATE GOVERNMENT

CHAPTER 101: GENERAL ASSEMBLY

§ 101.44 Testimony before committee not to be used in criminal prosecution of witness; exception.

Except a person who, in writing, requests permission to appear before a committee or subcommittee of the general assembly, or of either house thereof, or who, in writing, waives the rights privileges, and immunities granted by this section, the testimony of a witness examined before a committee or subcommittee shall not be used as evidence in a criminal proceeding against such witness. This section does not exempt a witness from the penalties for perjury.

HISTORY: RS § 53; 69 v 61, § 5; 98 v 268; GC § 60; 122 v 321; Bureau of Code Revision, 10-1-53; 136 v S 545. Eff 1-17-77.

§ 101.81 Power to secure information.

(A) In order to secure information with respect to any pending or contemplated legislative action, or any alleged breach of its privileges or misconduct by its members, the general assembly may order any person in Ohio to appear and testify before it, before either of its houses, or before any of its standing or select committees, and may order such person to produce books, papers, and other tangible evidence.

(B) An order under division (A) of this section, to appear or to produce books, papers, and other tangible evidence, may be issued by the general assembly, by either of its houses, or, within the limits of its charge by the general assembly or either of its houses, by a standing or a select committee. Such order shall be in writing, and may be directed to an appropriate officer anywhere in Ohio, for service and return in the same manner as a subpoena.

(C) No person shall fail to obey an order issued under this section, or, having appeared pursuant to such order, refuse to answer a question pertinent to the matter under inquiry.

(D) Whoever violates division (C) of this section is guilty of contempt of the general assembly, a misdemeanor of the fourth degree.

HISTORY: 134 v H 511. Eff 1-1-74.

Analogous to former RC § 2917.42 (RS § 6981-1; GC § 12845; 98 v 99; Bureau of Code Revision, 10-1-53), repealed 134 v H 511, § 2, eff 1-1-74.

CHAPTER 109: ATTORNEY GENERAL

[ORGANIZATION]

§ 109.01 Election; term.

The attorney general shall be elected quadrennially, and shall hold his office for a term of four years. The term of office of the attorney general shall commence on the second Monday of January next after his election.

HISTORY: RS § 214; S&C 91; Const.Art. III, § 2; 50 v 267, § 24; GC § 331; Bureau of Code Revision, 10-1-53; 129 v 582. Eff 1-10-61.

§ 109.02 Duties as chief law officer.

The attorney general is the chief law officer for the state and all its departments and shall be provided with adequate office space in Columbus. Except as provided in division (E) of section 120.06 and in sections 3517.152 [3517.15.2] to 3517.157 [3517.15.7] of the Revised Code, no state officer or board, or head of a department or institution of the state shall employ, or be represented by, other counsel or attorneys at law. The attorney general shall appear for the state in the trial and argument of all civil and criminal causes in the supreme court in which the state is directly or indirectly interested. When required by the governor or the general assembly, the attorney general shall appear for the state in any court or tribunal in a cause in which the state is a party, or in which the state is directly interested. Upon the written request of the governor, the attorney general shall prosecute any person indicted for a crime.

HISTORY: RS § 202; S&C 88; 50 v 267, §§ 3-5; 73 v 189, 191; 93 v 127; 97 v 59; GC § 333; Bureau of Code Revision, 10-1-53; 133 v S 438 (Eff 11-17-69); 144 v H 210 (Eff 5-1-92); 146 v S 9. Eff 8-24-95.

§ 109.03 Appointment of assistant attorney general and chief counsel; duties.

The attorney general may appoint a first assistant attorney general, a chief counsel, and assistant attorneys general, each of whom shall be an attorney at law, to serve for the term for which the attorney general is elected, unless sooner discharged by him, and each shall perform such duties, not otherwise provided by law, as are assigned him by the attorney general.

HISTORY: RS § 202a; 92 v 172; 97 v 59; GC § 334; 100 v 93; 110 v 10; 114 v 53; Bureau of Code Revision. Eff 10-1-53.

§ 109.04 Powers and duties of first assistant attorney general.

During the absence or disability of the attorney general, or when so directed by the attorney general, including all the rights, privileges, and powers conferred upon the attorney general by sections 2939.10, 2939.11, and 2939.17 of the Revised Code, the first assistant attorney general shall perform the duties of the attorney general.

HISTORY: RS § 202a; 92 v 172; 97 v 59; GC § 335; 100 v 93; 101 v 97; 114 v 53; Bureau of Code Revision. Eff 10-1-53.

§ 109.05 Employees.

The attorney general may appoint such employees as are necessary.

HISTORY: RS § 202a; 92 v 172; 97 v 59; GC § 337; 100 v 93; 107 v 503; Bureau of Code Revision. Eff 10-1-53.

§ 109.06 Bond.

Before entering upon the discharge of the duties of his office, the attorney general shall give a bond to the state in the sum of five thousand dollars, with two or more sureties approved by the governor, conditioned for the faithful discharge of the duties of his office. Such bond, with the approval of the governor and the oath of office indorsed thereon, shall be deposited with the secretary of state and kept in his office.

The first assistant attorney general shall give a bond to the state in the sum of five thousand dollars, and such other employees as are designated by the attorney general shall give a bond to the state in such amounts as the attorney general determines. Such bonds shall be approved by the attorney general, conditioned for the faithful discharge of the duties of their offices, and shall be deposited with the secretary of state and kept in his office.

HISTORY: RS § 201; S&C 88; 50 v 267; GC § 332; Bureau of Code Revision. Eff 10-1-53.

§ 109.07 Special counsel.

Except under the circumstances described in division (E) of section 120.06 of the Revised Code, the attorney general may appoint special counsel to represent the state in civil actions, criminal prosecutions, or other proceedings in which the state is a party or directly interested. The special counsel shall be paid for their services from funds appropriated by the general assembly for that purpose.

HISTORY: RS § 202a; 92 v 172; 97 v 59; GC § 336; 100 v 93; Bureau of Code Revision, Eff 10-1-53; 144 v H 210. Eff 5-1-92.

§ 109.08 Special counsel to collect claims.

The attorney general may appoint special counsel to represent the state in connection with all claims of whatsoever nature which are certified to the attorney general for collection under any law or which the attorney general is authorized to collect.

Such special counsel shall be paid for their services from funds collected by them in an amount approved by the attorney general.

The attorney general shall provide to the special counsel appointed to represent the state in connection with claims arising out of Chapters 5733., 5739., 5741., and 5747. of the Revised Code the official letterhead stationery of the attorney general. The special counsel shall use the letterhead stationery, but only in connection with the collection of such claims arising out of those taxes.

HISTORY: GC § 336-1; 117 v 304; Bureau of Code Revision, 10-1-53; 143 v S 147. Eff 1-1-90.

The effective date is set by section 3 of SB 147.

[§ 109.08.1] § 109.081 Attorney general claims fund.

Nine per cent of all amounts collected by the attorney general, whether by employees or agents of the attorney general or by special counsel pursuant to section 109.08 of the Revised Code, on claims due the state shall be paid into the state treasury to the credit of the attorney general claims fund, which is hereby created. The fund shall be used for the payment of expenses incurred by the office of the attorney general.

HISTORY: 140 v H 291 (Eff 7-1-83); 141 v H 201 (Eff 7-1-85); 144 v H 298. Eff 7-26-91.

[§ 109.08.2] § 109.082 Problem resolution officers for certain taxes.

The attorney general shall appoint one or more problem resolution officers from among the employees of the office of the attorney general. These officers shall receive and review inquiries and complaints concerning collections made pursuant to Chapters 5733., 5739., 5741., and 5747. of the Revised Code regarding which the taxpayer has been unable to obtain satisfactory information after several attempts to communicate with the employee of the office assigned to the taxpayer's collection case or the employee's immediate supervisor, or the special counsel assigned to the case.

HISTORY: 143 v S 147. Eff 1-1-90.

The effective date is set by section 3 of SB 147.

§ 109.09 Action on official bonds.

When so directed, the attorney general shall bring an action on the official bond of a delinquent officer, and shall also prosecute any officer for an offense against the revenue laws of the state that come to his knowledge. Such action may be brought by him in the court of common pleas of Franklin county, or of any county in which one or more of the defendants reside, or can be summoned.

HISTORY: RS § 203; S&C 89; 50 v 267, §§ 6-8; GC § 338; Bureau of Code Revision. Eff 10-1-53.

§ 109.10 Proceedings in quo warranto.

The attorney general may prosecute a proceeding in quo warranto in the supreme court of the state, the court of appeals of Franklin county, or the court of appeals of any county wherein a defendant company has a place of business, or the officers or persons made defendants reside or may be found.

HISTORY: RS § 204; S&C 89; 50 v 267; 82 v 16, 18; GC § 339; 103 v 405; Bureau of Code Revision. Eff 10-1-53.

§ 109.11 Attorney general reimbursement fund.

There is hereby created in the state treasury the attorney general reimbursement fund that shall be used for the expenses of the office of the attorney general in providing legal services and other services on behalf of the state. All amounts received by the attorney general as reimbursement for legal services and other services that have been rendered to other state agencies shall be paid into the state treasury to the credit of the attorney general reimbursement fund. All amounts awarded by a court to the attorney general for attorney's fees, investigation costs, expert witness fees, fines, and all other costs and fees associated with representation provided by the attorney general and all amounts awarded to the attorney general by a court shall be paid into the state treasury to the credit of the attorney general reimbursement fund.

HISTORY: 144 v S 351. Eff 7-1-92.

Not analogous to former RC § 109.11 (128 v 317; 135 v S 174), repealed 143 v H 111, § 2, eff 7-1-89.

[§ 109.11.1] § 109.111 Court order fund.

There is hereby created the attorney general court order fund, which shall be in the custody of the treasurer of state but shall not be part of the state treasury. The fund shall consist of all money collected or received as a result of an order of any court to be received or secured by, or delivered to, the attorney general for transfer, distribution, disbursement, or allocation pursuant to court order. All money in the fund, including investment earnings thereon, shall be used solely to make payment as directed pursuant to court order.

HISTORY: 146 v S 310. Eff 9-19-96.

§ 109.12 Legal advice to state officers and boards.

The attorney general, when so requested, shall give legal advice to a state officer, board, commission, the warden of a state correctional institution, the superintendent, trustees, or directors of a benevolent institution of the state, and the trustees of the Ohio state university, in all matters relating to their official duties.

HISTORY: RS § 206; S&C 90; 67 v 20, § 15; 70 v 19, § 15; GC § 341; Bureau of Code Revision, 10-1-53; 145 v H 571. Eff 10-6-94.

[§ 109.12.1] § 109.121 Land title review and opinion.

Prior to the acquisition by the state of any right, title, or interest in real property, except highway rights-of-way, evidence of such right, title, or interest shall be submitted to the attorney general for his review and opinion. Such evidence shall be that customarily and generally used in the community in which the real property is situated and may consist of, but not be limited to, attorneys' opinions of title, abstracts of title, title guarantees, or title insurance.

HISTORY: 133 v S 205. Eff 11-12-69.

[§ 109.12.2] § 109.122 Expositions commission duties.

(A) The attorney general may review for form, content, and legality and provide legal advice concerning any proposed entertainment or sponsorship contracts of the Ohio expositions commission that the commission provides as required by section 991.03 of the Revised Code.

(B) The commission shall reimburse the attorney general for all legal expenses associated with reviewing proposed entertainment or sponsorship contracts under division (A) of this section.

HISTORY: 145 v H 152. Eff 7-1-93.

Not analogous to former RC § 109.122 (134 v H 1170; 135 v H 1), repealed 138 v S 76, § 2, eff 3-13-80.

§ 109.13 General assembly may require written opinions.

When so required by resolution, the attorney general shall give his written opinion on questions of law to either house of the general assembly.

HISTORY: RS § 207; S&C 90; 50 v 267, § 16; GC § 342; Bureau of Code Revision. Eff 10-1-53.

§ 109.14 Advising of prosecuting attorneys, township law directors.

When requested by them, the attorney general shall advise the prosecuting attorneys of the several counties respecting their duties in all complaints, suits, and controversies in which the state is, or may be a party, and shall advise the township law director of a township that has adopted the limited self-government form of township government under Chapter 504. of the Revised Code.

HISTORY: RS § 208; S&C 90; 50 v 267, § 17; 88 v 11; GC § 343; Bureau of Code Revision, 10-1-53; 146 v H 501. Eff 11-6-96.

§ 109.15 Forms of contracts.

The attorney general shall prepare suitable forms of contracts, obligations, and other like instruments of writing for the use of state officers, when requested by the governor, secretary of state, auditor of state, or treasurer of state.

HISTORY: RS § 209; S&C 90; 50 v 267, § 18; GC § 344; Bureau of Code Revision. Eff 10-1-53.

§ 109.16 Suits may be brought in Franklin county.

The attorney general may prosecute an action, information, or other proceeding in behalf of the state, or in which the state is interested, except prosecutions by indictment, in the proper court of Franklin county, or of any other county in which one or more of the defendants reside or may be found. No civil action, unless elsewhere specially provided, shall be commenced in Franklin county, if one or more of the defendants do not reside or cannot be found therein, unless the attorney general certifies on the writ that he believes the amount in controversy exceeds five hundred dollars.

HISTORY: RS § 210; S&C 90; 50 v 267, § 19; GC § 345; Bureau of Code Revision. Eff 10-1-53.

§ 109.17 Writs in other counties.

In all cases instituted by the attorney general under sections 109.01 to 109.22, inclusive, of the Revised Code, the writ may be sent by mail to the sheriff of any county, and returned by him in like manner. For such service, the sheriff shall be allowed the same mileage and fees as if the writ had been issued from the court of common pleas or the court of appeals of his county, and made returnable thereto.

HISTORY: RS § 211; S&C 90; 50 v 267, § 20; 82 v 16, 18; GC § 346; 103 v 405; Bureau of Code Revision. Eff 10-1-53.

§ 109.18 Service by publication.

If a writ of mesne process in proceedings in quo warranto is returned "not found" by the sheriff of the county in which the company is authorized by law to have its place of business, the clerk of the court in which the information or other proceeding is filed shall issue a notice of the filing and substance thereof, and cause it to be published once a week for six consecutive weeks in a newspaper published in and of general circulation in the county wherein such company is authorized to have its place of business. An affidavit of the publication together with a copy of the notice shall be filed in the office of the clerk. If the defendant company fails to answer or plead to such information of proceeding within thirty days from the filing of the affidavit and copy, judgment shall be given upon the default as if the writ or mesne process had been served and returned.

HISTORY: RS § 212; S&C 91; 50 v 267, § 21; GC § 347; Bureau of Code Revision, 10-1-53; 137 v H 42. Eff 10-7-77.

§ 109.19 Security for costs and verification of pleadings.

No undertaking or security is required on behalf of the state or an officer thereof, in the prosecution or defense of any action, writ, or proceeding. In an action, writ, or proceeding it is not necessary to verify the pleadings on the part of the state or any officer thereof.

HISTORY: RS § 213; S&C 91; 56 v 240, § 22; GC § 348; Bureau of Code Revision. Eff 10-1-53.

§ 109.20 Actions to be taken out of their order.

Upon motion of the attorney general, embodying a statement that the public interests require it, a civil action, brought or prosecuted by him on behalf of the state, or an officer, board, or commission thereof, or an action in which the state is a party, shall be taken out of its order upon the docket and assigned for trial at as early a day as practicable.

HISTORY: RS § 217; 75 v 125; GC § 349; Bureau of Code Revision. Eff 10-1-53.

§ 109.21 Annual report.

The attorney general shall pay all moneys collected or received by him on behalf of the state into the state treasury to the credit of the general revenue fund. Each year he shall make a report to the governor of the moneys so received and the business of his office, together with an abstract of the statistics of crime returned to him by the prosecuting attorneys of the several counties.

HISTORY: RS §§ 216, 218; S&C 91, 1233; 50 v 267, § 26; 57 v 83, § 4; GC § 350; Bureau of Code Revision. Eff 10-1-53.

§ 109.22 Registers shall be kept.

The attorney general shall keep a register of all actions, demands, complaints, writs, informations, and other proceedings, prosecuted or defended by him, noting therein the proceedings under each, and a register of all official opinions in writing given by him. He shall deliver to his successor the registers, papers, documents, books, and other property belonging to his office.

HISTORY: RS § 215; S&C 91; 50 v 267, § 25; GC § 351; Bureau of Code Revision. Eff 10-1-53.

[DUTIES CONCERNING CHARITABLE TRUSTS]

§ 109.23 Charitable trust defined.

As used in sections 109.23 to 109.33 of the Revised Code:

(A) "Charitable trust" means any fiduciary relationship with respect to property arising under the law of this state or of another jurisdiction as a result of a manifestation of intention to create it, and subjecting the person by whom the property is held to fiduciary duties to deal with the property within this state for any charitable, religious or educational purpose.

(B) "Charitable trust" includes the fiduciary relationship, the entity serving as trustee, the status as trustee, the corpus of such trust, or a combination of any or all of such meanings, regardless of the primary meaning of any use of the term, that is necessary in any circumstances to effect the purposes of such sections.

(C) An executor, administrator, guardian, or other conservator of the estate of a decedent, incompetent, or other similarly protected person is, when holding assets in which a charitable trust has a vested or contingent interest and to the extent that such sections are not clearly inapplicable, to be considered a fiduciary of a charitable trust.

(D) The fact that any person sought to be charged with fiduciary duties is a corporation, association, foundation, or any other type of organization that has, under judicial decisions or other statutes, been distinguished from a charitable trust does not provide a presumption against its being a charitable trust as defined in this section.

HISTORY: 125 v 351 (Eff 10-14-53); 136 v H 347. Eff 11-19-75.

[§ 109.23.1] § 109.231 Acts prohibited in administration.

(A) In the administration of any trust which is a "private foundation" as defined in section 509 of the internal revenue code of 1954, a trust for charitable purposes described in section 4947(a)(1) of the internal revenue code of 1954 to the extent that it is treated for federal tax purposes as such a private foundation, or a "split-interest trust" as described in section 4947(a)(2) of the internal revenue code of 1954, the following acts are prohibited:

(1) Engaging in any act of "self-dealing," as defined in section 4941(d) of the internal revenue code of 1954, which would give rise to any liability for any tax imposed by section 4941 of the internal revenue code of 1954;

(2) Retaining any "excess business holdings," as defined in section 4943(c) of the internal revenue code of 1954, which would give rise to any liability for any tax imposed by section 4943 of the internal revenue code of 1954;

(3) Making any investments which would jeopardize the carrying out of any of the exempt purposes of the trust, within the meaning of section 4944 of the internal revenue code of 1954, so as to give rise to any liability for any tax imposed by section 4944 of the internal revenue code of 1954; or

(4) Making any "taxable expenditures," as defined in section 4945(d) of the internal revenue code of 1954, which would give rise to any liability for any tax imposed by section 4945 of the internal revenue code of 1954. The prohibitions of this division do not apply to split-interest trusts, or to amounts thereof, to the extent that such prohibitions are inapplicable thereto by reason of section 4947 of the internal revenue code of 1954.

(B) In the administration of any trust which is a "private foundation" as defined in section 509 of the internal revenue code of 1954, or a trust for charitable purposes described in section 4947(a)(1) of the internal revenue code of 1954 to the extent that it is treated for federal tax purposes as such a private foundation, there shall, for the purposes specified in the governing instrument, be distributed at such time and in such manner, for each taxable year, amounts of income and principal at least sufficient to avoid liability for any tax imposed by section 4942 of the internal revenue code of 1954.

(C) Divisions (A) and (B) of this section express the continuing policy of this state with respect to charitable trust interests and are enacted to assist such trusts in maintaining various tax benefits extended to them, and apply to all trusts described therein, whether or not contrary to the provisions of the governing instrument of such a trust, provided that divisions (A) and (B) of this section do not apply to a trust in existence on the effective date of this section to the extent that the attorney general, the trustor, or any beneficiary of such trust, on or before November 30, 1971, files with the trustee of such trust a written objection to application to such trust of one or more provisions of said divisions, and if the trustee receiving such written objection commences an action on or before December 31, 1971, in the court having jurisdiction over such trust to reform, or to excuse such trust from compliance with, its governing instrument or any other instrument in order to meet the requirements of said divisions. A trustee receiving such written objection shall commence such an action, and the one or more provisions of said divisions specified in such written objection will not apply to such trust unless and until said court determines that their application to such trust is in the best interests of all parties in interest.

(D) No trustee of a trust to which division (A) or (B) of this section is applicable shall be surcharged for a violation of a prohibition or requirement of said divisions, unless he participated in such violation knowing that it was a violation, nor shall such trustee be surcharged if such violation was not willful and was due to reasonable cause, provided that this division does not exonerate a trustee from any responsibility or liability to which he is subject under any other rule of law whether or not duplicated in division (A) or (B) of this section.

(E) As used in this section, "trust" includes a trust or any other organization, other than a corporation, which is a "private foundation" as defined in section 509 of the internal revenue code of 1954, and "trustee" includes any member of the governing body of such organization.

(F) Except as provided in division (D) of this section,

nothing in this section impairs the rights and powers of the courts or the attorney general of this state with respect to any trust.

HISTORY: 134 v S 198. Eff 9-17-71.

[§ 109.23.2] § 109.232 Amendment of trust.

(A) The governing instrument of a trust described in division (A) of section 109.231 [109.23.1] of the Revised Code may be amended to permit the trust to acquire the characteristics of a trust described in section 664(D)(1) or (2) of the internal revenue code of 1954, or to conform to the requirements of, or to obtain benefits available under, section 507, 508, or 509 of the internal revenue code of 1954. Such amendment may be made by the trustee with the approval of the attorney general, of the trustor, and, if one or more beneficiaries are named in the governing instrument of such trust, of each named beneficiary. If the trustor is not then living or is not then competent to give such approval, such amendment may be made by the trustee with the approval of the attorney general and, if one or more beneficiaries are named in the governing instrument of such trust, of each named beneficiary. If one or more of said required approvals is not obtained, the trustee may apply to the court having jurisdiction over such trust for approval of such amendment. Said governing instrument may also be amended in any respect and by any method set forth therein or as otherwise provided by law.

(B) Nothing in this section impairs the rights and powers of the courts or the attorney general of this state with respect to any trust.

(C) For the purposes of sections 109.231 [109.23.1] and 109.232 [109.23.2] of the Revised Code, all references to sections of the internal revenue code of 1954 include all amendments or reenactments thereof.

HISTORY: 134 v S 198 (Eff 9-17-71); 134 v S 533. Eff 7-15-72.

§ 109.24 Administration and enforcement of charitable trusts.

The powers of the attorney general under sections 109.23 to 109.33 of the Revised Code shall be in addition to and not in limitation of his powers held at common law. The attorney general may investigate transactions and relationships of trustees of a charitable trust for the purpose of determining whether the property held for charitable, religious, or educational purposes has been and is being properly administered in accordance with fiduciary principles as established by the courts and statutes of this state. The attorney general is empowered to require the production of any books or papers which are relevant to the inquiry. Each such request shall be in writing, and shall do all of the following:

(A) Identify the person to whom the request is directed;

(B) State the specific purpose of the investigation;

(C) Describe any books and the papers to be produced with such definiteness and certainty as to permit such material to be fairly identified;

(D) Prescribe a return date which will provide at least ten days' notice within which the books or papers to be produced may be assembled;

(E) State the place where and the time within which any books or papers are to be produced, provided, however, that copies of such books and papers may be produced in lieu of the originals.

No request shall contain any requirement which would be held to be unreasonable or oppressive or which would be privileged from disclosure if contained in a subpoena duces tecum issued by a court of this state pursuant to the Rules of Civil Procedure. If the production of documents required by the request would be unduly burdensome, the person upon whom the request is served, in lieu of producing such books or papers at the place designated in the request, shall make such books or papers available for inspection, copying, or reproduction at the place where such books or papers are kept.

Whenever a request fails to meet the requirements enumerated in this section, any person upon whom the request is served may file a complaint to quash such request in the court of common pleas of the county in which the trust, institution, association, or corporation has its principal place of business in this state. The complaint shall contain a brief statement of facts entitling such person to have such requests quashed. No answer to such complaint is required. Upon the filing of the complaint, the court, on motion of the complainant, shall enter an order fixing a date for a hearing on the complaint and requiring that a copy of the complaint and a notice of the filing and of the date for hearing be given to the attorney general or his assistant in the manner in which summons is required to be served or substituted services required to be made in other cases. On the day fixed for the hearing on the complaint, the court shall determine from the complaint and from such evidence as is submitted by either party whether the person upon whom the request was served is entitled to have the request quashed. The proceeding is a special proceeding, and final orders in the proceeding may be vacated, modified, or reversed on appeal pursuant to the Rules of Appellate Procedure and, to the extent not in conflict with those rules, Chapter 2505. of the Revised Code.

The attorney general shall institute and prosecute a proper action to enforce the performance of any charitable trust, and to restrain the abuse of it whenever he considers such action advisable or if directed to do so by the governor, the supreme court, the general assembly, or either house of the general assembly. Such action may be brought in his own name, on behalf of the state, or in the name of a beneficiary of the trust, in the court of common pleas of any county in which the trust property or any part of it is situated or invested, or in which the trustee resides; provided that in the case of a charitable trust created by, arising as a result of, or funded by a will, such action may be brought in either the court of common pleas of any such county, or the probate division of it, at the election of the attorney general. No such action shall abate or discontinue by virtue of the discontinuance in office of the attorney general in whose name such actions may be brought. This section is intended to allow the attorney general full discretion concerning the manner in which the action is to be prosecuted, including the authority to settle an action when he considers that advisable.

HISTORY: 125 v 352 (Eff 10-14-53); 136 v H 347 (Eff 11-19-75); 141 v H 412. Eff 3-17-87.

§ 109.25 Necessary party to charitable trust proceedings.

The attorney general is a necessary party to and shall be served with process or with summons by registered mail in all judicial proceedings, the object of which is to:

(A) Terminate a charitable trust or distribute assets;

(B) Depart from the objects or purposes of a charitable trust as the same are set forth in the instrument creating the trust, including any proceeding for the application of the doctrine of cy pres or deviation;

(C) Construe the provisions of an instrument with respect to a charitable trust;

(D) Determine the validity of a will having provisions for a charitable trust.

A judgment rendered in such proceedings without service of process or summons upon the attorney general is void, unenforceable, and shall be set aside upon the attorney general's motion seeking such relief. The attorney general shall intervene in any judicial proceeding affecting a charitable trust when requested to do so by the court having jurisdiction of the proceeding, and may intervene in any judicial proceeding affecting a charitable trust when he determines that the public interest should be protected in such proceeding.

HISTORY: 125 v 352 (Eff 10-14-53); 129 v 582 (Eff 1-10-61); 136 v H 347. Eff 11-19-75.

§ 109.26 Register of charitable trusts.

Except as provided in this section, every charitable trust established or active in this state shall register with the attorney general. The attorney general shall prepare and maintain a register of such charitable trusts. The following are not required to register under this section:

(A) Charitable remainder trusts created after July 31, 1969, gifts to which are deductible for federal income, gift, or estate tax purposes;

(B) Charitable trusts in which all charitable interests are contingent and will vest only upon conditions which have not occurred;

(C) Decedent's estates;

(D) Such other classes of charitable trusts as the attorney general may exempt from registration by regulation pursuant to section 109.27 of the Revised Code.

County or independent agricultural societies organized under Chapter 1711. of the Revised Code are not charitable trusts.

Every charitable trust shall be registered with the attorney general in accordance with this section within six months after the effective date of this section, November 19, 1975, within six months after the creation of such trust, or within six months after occurrence of an event by reason of which such trust is required to register by this section, whichever is later, provided that all registrations of charitable trusts made prior to November 19, 1975, shall be deemed in full compliance with this section and no further registration shall be required.

No trustee of a charitable trust shall willfully fail to register such charitable trust as required by this section.

HISTORY: 125 v 353 (Eff 10-14-53); 129 v 582 (Eff 1-10-61); 136 v H 347 (Eff 11-19-75); 137 v H 1 (Eff 8-26-77); 137 v H 659. Eff 1-10-78.

§ 109.27 Rules concerning charitable trusts.

The attorney general shall make such rules subject to the provisions of sections 199.01 to 199.13 of the Revised Code, as are necessary to administer sections 109.23 to 109.33 of the Revised Code.

HISTORY: 125 v 353 (Eff 10-14-53); 136 v H 347. Eff 11-19-75.

§ 109.28 Inspection of register of charitable trusts.

The register established by section 109.26 shall be open to the inspection of any person at such reasonable times and for such legitimate purposes as the attorney general may determine; provided, however, that any investigation of a charitable trust shall not be open to public inspection.

HISTORY: 125 v 353. Eff 10-14-53.

§ 109.29 Furnish information relating to charitable trusts.

The clerk of each court of common pleas or the judge of the probate division thereof, and of each court of appeals shall furnish copies of papers and such information as to the records and files of his office relating to charitable trusts as the attorney general may require.

HISTORY: 125 v 353 (Eff 10-14-53); 136 v H 347. Eff 11-19-75.

§ 109.30 Notice to attorney general and specified persons after probate of will.

After admission to probate of a will creating or purporting to create a charitable trust that must be registered under section 109.26 of the Revised Code, or containing a gift valued in excess of one thousand dollars to any charitable trust, notice shall be given to the attorney general, as well as to the persons specified in division (A)(1) of section 2107.19 of the Revised Code, in accordance with that section. If probate of a will creating or purporting to create any charitable trust is refused by interlocutory order under section 2107.181 [2107.18.1] of the Revised Code, notice of the further hearing under that section shall be given to the attorney general as well as to the other necessary parties.

HISTORY: 136 v H 347 (Eff 11-19-75); 143 v H 346. Eff 5-31-90.

Analogous to former RC § 109.30 (125 v 353), repealed 136 v H 347, § 2, eff 11-19-75.

The provisions of § 3 of HB 346 (143 v —) read as follows:

SECTION 3. (A) Sections 1 and 2 of this act shall apply only to the estates of decedents who die on or after the effective date of this act.

(B) It is the intent of the General Assembly in the outright repeal of sections 2107.13 and 2107.14 of the Revised Code and the amendments to sections 109.30, 2107.18, 2107.19, 2107.22, 2107.27, 2107.76, 2115.16, and 2703.14 of the Revised Code by this act, to respond to the dicta of the Supreme Court in *Palazzi v. Estate of Gardner* (1987), 32 Ohio St. 3d 169 and to enact statutory provisions relating to notice of probate proceedings that are not unconstitutional as potentially violative of the due process of law rights of nonresidents of this state.

(C) Chapter 2106. of the Revised Code, as enacted by this act, shall be known as "Rights of Surviving Spouses."

§ 109.31 Trustee's report to attorney general; fees.

Except as otherwise provided by this section, the trustees of a charitable trust required to register under section 109.26 of the Revised Code shall file annual reports on forms prescribed by the attorney general, on or before the fifteenth day of the fifth month following the close of the trust's taxable year as established for federal tax purposes; or, in lieu of filing those reports, the trustees may file complete copies of all annual federal returns required to be filed by the trust with the internal revenue service for the taxable year, together with all schedules, attachments, and reports due with the return or returns. The federal returns shall be filed with the attorney general at the same time as required by the internal revenue service, taking into account any applicable extension of the federal filing date.

The annual report shall be signed by the trustee who is authorized to sign it. The annual report shall be considered certified by the trustee and his signature on the report shall have the same effect as though made under oath.

A charitable trust required to register under section 109.26 of the Revised Code is not required to file the reports required by this section if any of the following apply:

(A) It is organized and operated exclusively for religious purposes.

(B) It is an educational institution that normally maintains a regular faculty and curriculum and normally has a regularly organized body of pupils or students in attendance at the place where its educational activities are regularly carried on.

(C) For any taxable year it has gross receipts of less than five thousand dollars and at the end of which it has gross assets of less than fifteen thousand dollars.

The attorney general, by rule pursuant to section 109.27 of the Revised Code, may exempt other classes of charitable trusts from the requirements of this section.

The attorney general may institute judicial proceedings to secure compliance with this section and to secure the proper administration of any trust or other relationship to which this section applies. The willful failure of any trustee to file reports as required by this section may be grounds for judicial removal of the trustee responsible for such failure.

The attorney general shall charge the following fees for filing the annual report:

Assets	Fee
Less than $25,000	$ 0
$25,000 but less than $100,000	50
$100,000 but less than $500,000	100
$500,000 or more	200

For the purposes of this section, "assets" refers to the total fair market value of the charitable trust's assets at the end of that trust's taxable year as established for federal tax purposes.

Any charitable trust that fails to pay the fee required by this section at the time required shall pay an additional fee of two hundred dollars, except that the attorney general may waive the two-hundred dollar fee upon a showing that the trustees of the charitable trust failed to pay the fee for filing the annual report at the time required by this section for reasons that were beyond the control of the trustees of the charitable trust or of a designee of the trustees.

This section shall not be subject to section 119.12 of the Revised Code.

HISTORY: 136 v H 347 (Eff 11-19-75); 143 v H 486 (Eff 11-7-90); 145 v S 71. Eff 10-29-93.

Analogous to former RC § 109.31 (125 v 353), repealed 136 v H 347, § 2, eff 11-19-75.

§ 109.32 Moneys paid into charitable foundations fund.

All annual filing fees obtained by the attorney general pursuant to section 109.31 of the Revised Code, all receipts obtained from the sale of the charitable foundations directory, and all registration fees received by the attorney general, bond forfeitures, awards of costs and attorney's fees, and civil penalties assessed under Chapter 1716. of the Revised Code shall be paid into the state treasury to the credit of the charitable foundations fund. The charitable foundations fund shall be used insofar as its moneys are available for the expenses of the charitable foundations section of the office of the attorney general. The expenses of the charitable foundations section in excess of moneys available in the charitable foundations fund shall be paid out of regular appropriations to the office of the attorney general.

HISTORY: 136 v H 347 (Eff 11-19-75); 143 v H 486. Eff 11-7-90.

Analogous to former RC § 109.32 (125 v 354), repealed 136 v H 347, § 2, eff 11-19-75.

§ 109.33 Assistants; appointments, compensation.

The attorney general may appoint, with salaries fixed pursuant to section 124.15 or 124.152 [124.15.2] of the Revised Code, such assistants and may employ such stenographers and clerks as may be necessary to carry out sections 109.23 to 109.33 of the Revised Code. The attorney general may also employ experts for assistance in any specific matter at a reasonable rate of compensation.

HISTORY: 125 v 354 (Eff 10-14-53); 132 v H 93 (Eff 5-17-67); 137 v H 1 (Eff 8-26-77); 141 v H 831. Eff 4-9-86.

[NONPROFIT HEALTH CARE ENTITY TRANSACTIONS]

§ 109.34 Nonprofit health care entity proposing certain transactions to notify attorney general and obtain approval.

(A) As used in this section and in section 109.35 of the Revised Code:

(1) "Fair market value" means the price that the assets being transferred would bring in a competitive and open market under a fair sale with the buyer and seller acting prudently, knowledgeably, and in their own best interest and a reasonable time being allowed for exposure in the market.

(2) "Nonprofit health care entity" means any of the following that was created for any charitable or social welfare purpose related to health care:

(a) A hospital, as defined in section 3727.01 of the Revised Code, that is owned or operated by a corporation organized under Chapter 1702. of the Revised Code or the nonprofit corporation law of another state;

(b) Either of the following that is or has been exempt from taxation under section 501(a) of the Internal Revenue Code:

(i) An entity that is or has been granted a certificate of authority under Chapter 1742. of the Revised Code;

(ii) An entity that is authorized or has been authorized to transact business in this state under Title XXXIX [39] of the Revised Code, that is in the business of providing sickness and accident insurance, and that was previously a hospital service association under former Chapter 1739. of the Revised Code or Chapter 669. of the General Code, has merged or otherwise consolidated with a former hospital service association, or any of whose predecessors in interest has merged or otherwise consolidated with a former hospital service association.

(3) "Party" includes a nonprofit health care entity that is the subject of a transaction or proposed transaction, an acquiring person, and the resulting entity, if any.

(4) "Transaction" means a transfer of ownership or control of assets of a nonprofit health care entity, whether by purchase, merger, consolidation, lease, gift, joint venture, or other transfer, including any binding obligation in furtherance of the transaction, that is equal to at least twenty per cent of the assets of the entity and occurs in the twenty-four-month period prior to the date notice is submitted to the attorney general in accordance with division (B) of this section. "Transaction" also means a transfer of ownership or control of any assets of a nonprofit health care entity, whether by purchase, merger, consolidation, lease, gift, joint venture, or other transfer, including any binding obligation in furtherance of the transaction, if the entity is unable to fulfill its stated or actual purpose without the assets. "Transaction" does not include either of the following:

(a) A transfer of ownership or control of assets of a nonprofit health care entity between nonprofit health care entities and persons exempt from taxation under section 501(a) of the "Internal Revenue Code of 1986," 100 Stat. 2085, 26 U.S.C. 501,† as amended;

(b) A transfer of ownership or control of assets of a nonprofit health care entity in relation to which the nonprofit health care entity, prior to the effective date of this section, has entered into a consent decree with the attorney general that requires distribution of the charitable assets of the entity to an appropriate health-related charity. The exemption in division (A)(4)(b) of this section does not limit the authority of the attorney general to seek remedies for breaches of fiduciary duty or other violations of law.

(B) A nonprofit health care entity proposing to enter into a transaction shall provide notice of the proposed transaction to the attorney general and obtain written approval of the transaction in accordance with this section. The nonprofit health care entity shall submit the notice on forms provided by the attorney general, and the notice shall include all of the following:

(1) The names and addresses of the parties, including a list of all individuals who are or have been chosen as directors, officers, or board members of the parties;

(2) The terms of the proposed transaction, including a summary of all contracts or other agreements of the parties;

(3) The amount, source, and nature of consideration to be paid to the nonprofit health care entity, its directors, officers, board members, executives, or experts retained by the nonprofit health care entity.

(4) A statement acknowledging that the nonprofit health care entity is under a continuing duty to notify the attorney general of any changes in the information contained in the notice or other documents required by this section and that a violation of this duty may delay approval of the proposed transaction. The statement shall be signed by a representative of the nonprofit health care entity at the time the notice is submitted to the attorney general.

(C) In addition to the notice described in division (B) of this section, the nonprofit health care entity shall submit all of the following:

(1) Audited financial statements for the nonprofit health care entity for the three fiscal years prior to the date the nonprofit health care entity submitted the notice to the attorney general;

(2) A valuation statement prepared by an independent, qualified expert, including an investment banker, actuary, appraiser, certified public accountant, or other expert, that assesses the full and fair market value of the nonprofit health care entity;

(3) Copies of all contracts and other agreements between the parties or their officers, directors, board members, or other fiduciaries, including any contracts or other final agreements relating to the close of the proposed transaction;

(4) Any additional information the attorney general considers necessary to value the nonprofit health care entity's assets as required in rules adopted by the attorney general in accordance with Chapter 119. of the Revised Code.

(D) The notice and all other documents or materials submitted pursuant to this section are public records provided they meet the definition set forth in section 149.43 of the Revised Code.

(E) Not later than two business days after the discovery of any changes in information contained in the notice or other documents required by this section, the nonprofit health care entity shall provide copies to the attorney general of any documents and other material relevant to the changes. In addition to the ninety-day extension authorized by division (A) of section 109.35 of the Revised Code, the attorney general for good cause may delay approval of the proposed transaction up to thirty days following receipt of the documents and other material relevant to the changes.

(F) Not later than seven days after submitting the notice and other documents required by this section, the nonprofit health care entity shall publish notice of the proposed transaction in at least one daily newspaper of general circulation in the county where the nonprofit health care entity has its principal place of business. The notice shall state the names of the parties and a description of the proposed transaction.

(G) Notwithstanding division (A)(4)(a) of this section, as used in this division, "nonprofit combination" means a transaction between a nonprofit health care entity and another unrelated nonprofit health care entity.

Not less than sixty days before the closing of a nonprofit combination, a nonprofit health care entity that is a party to the combination and is the party to be acquired shall provide notice of the nonprofit combination to the attorney general by submitting the information described in divisions (B)(1) and (3) of this section.

Not later than seven days after the information required by this section is submitted to the attorney general, each of the nonprofit health care entities that is a party to a nonprofit combination shall publish the notice described in division (F) of this section.

HISTORY: 147 v H 242. Eff 5-7-97.

† So in enrolled bill. See RC § 109.35 where the reference is set out as 100 Stat. 2085, 26 U.S.C.A. 501.

§ 109.35 Approval or disapproval of transactions; prohibitions.

(A) Not later than sixty days after receipt of a notice and other documents required by section 109.34 of the Revised Code, the attorney general shall approve or disapprove the proposed transaction, except that the attorney general for good cause may extend this period an additional ninety days.

(B) In determining whether to approve or disapprove a proposed transaction, the attorney general shall consider:

(1) Whether the proposed transaction will result in a breach of fiduciary duty, as determined by the attorney general, including conflicts of interest related to payments or benefits to officers, directors, board members, executives, and experts employed or retained by the parties;

(2) Whether the nonprofit health care entity will receive full and fair market value for its charitable or social welfare assets;

(3) Whether the proceeds of the proposed transaction will be used consistent with the nonprofit health care entity's original charitable purpose;

(4) Any other criteria the attorney general considers necessary to determine whether the nonprofit health care entity will receive full and fair market value for its charitable or social welfare assets as required in rules adopted by the attorney general in accordance with Chapter 119. of the Revised Code.

(C) The attorney general may retain, at the nonprofit health care entity's expense, one or more independently qualified experts, including an investment banker, actuary, appraiser, certified public accountant, or other expert, as the attorney general considers reasonably necessary to provide assistance in making a decision under this section. The nonprofit health care entity shall promptly reimburse the attorney general for the cost of retaining experts. The cost of retaining an expert shall not exceed an amount that is reasonable and necessary to make a determination under this section. The contract to retain an expert is exempt from Chapter 125. of the Revised Code.

At any time while considering a proposed transaction under this section, the attorney general may request any additional information from the nonprofit health care entity that the attorney general considers appropriate to the valuation of the entity's charitable or social welfare assets. The nonprofit health care entity shall provide the information not later than ten days after the date of the request. The attorney general for good cause may delay approval of the proposed transaction up to thirty days, in addition to the ninety-day extension authorized by division (A) of this section, following receipt of documents and other material containing the information requested.

(D) The attorney general shall approve or disapprove a proposed transaction on the basis of the criteria set forth in division (B) of this section. Once a proposed transaction is approved, any substantial alteration is a new transaction subject to approval by the attorney general.

The nonprofit health care entity may resubmit a notice and other documents seeking approval of a proposed transaction disapproved by the attorney general but may not submit a notice and other documents that are identical or substantially similar to the original submission.

If the attorney general disapproves the proposed transaction, the nonprofit health care entity may appeal the disapproval pursuant to division (H) of this section.

(E) If the attorney general approves the proposed transaction, the nonprofit health care entity shall hold a public hearing to receive comment on the proposed use of the proceeds of the transaction. The hearing shall be held in the county where the nonprofit health care entity has its principal place of business not later than forty-five days after receipt of written notice of the attorney general's approval.

At least thirty days prior to the date set for the hearing, the nonprofit health care entity shall publish notice of the hearing in at least one daily newspaper of general circulation in the county where the nonprofit health care entity has its principal place of business. The notice shall include a statement that a transaction has been approved by the attorney general, the names of the parties, a description of the proposed transaction, and the date, time, and place of the hearing.

(F)(1) The proceeds of an approved transaction shall be dedicated and transferred to one or more existing or new charitable organizations exempt from taxation under section 501(a) and described in section 501(c)(3) of the "Internal Revenue Code of 1986," 100 Stat. 2085, 26 U.S.C.A. 501, as amended.

(2) The attorney general may authorize a dedication and transfer to a person exempt from taxation under section 501(a) and described in section 501(c)(4) of the "Internal Revenue Code of 1986," 100 Stat. 2085, 26 U.S.C.A. 501, as amended, if all of the following conditions are met:

(a) The attorney general determines that the dedication and transfer is necessary to ensure effective management and monetization of the equity ownership, if any, in the nonprofit health care entity;

(b) The person described in division (F)(2) of this section agrees to all of the following conditions:

(i) The person described in division (F)(2) of this section will receive from the nonprofit health care entity only the amount of proceeds of the transaction as are necessary to fund the level of activity necessary to preserve the person's tax-exempt status;

(ii) No proceeds of the transaction, or any other funds or resources controlled by the person described in division (F)(2) of this section, will be disbursed for campaign contributions, lobbying expenditures, or other political activity;

(iii) The person described in division (F)(2) of this section agrees to abide by any requirements imposed on persons exempt from taxation under section 501(a) and described in section 501(c)(3) of the "Internal Revenue Code of 1986," 100 Stat. 2085, 26 U.S.C.A. 501, as amended, that the attorney general determines appropriate.

(G)(1) No nonprofit health care entity shall enter into a transaction subject to this section without the approval of the attorney general granted in accordance with this section.

(2) No person who is an officer, director, board member, or other fiduciary of a nonprofit health care entity shall receive anything of substantial value that relates to a transaction described in this section and section 109.34 of the Revised Code and is of such a character as to manifest a substantial and improper influence on the person with respect to the person's duties.

(3) The attorney general may institute and prosecute a civil or criminal action to enforce this section and section 109.34 of the Revised Code in the court of common pleas of the county in which the nonprofit health care entity has its principal place of business or the Franklin county court of common pleas. In addition to any civil remedies that exist under common law or the Revised Code, a court may rescind the transaction, grant injunctive relief, assess a civil penalty in an amount not exceeding ten million dollars, or impose any combination of these remedies.

(H) A nonprofit health care entity that is a party to a proposed transaction that has been disapproved by the attorney general may appeal the disapproval only by following the procedure set forth in this division. The disapproval may be appealed to the court of common pleas of the county in which the nonprofit health entity has its principal place of business. The court of common pleas may reverse, vacate, or modify the attorney general's decision to disapprove a transaction if the court finds that the decision was unlawful or unreasonable. This appeal shall proceed as an appeal de novo. To bring an appeal under this division, a nonprofit health care entity shall file a notice of appeal with the court and the attorney general not later than fifteen days after the entity's receipt of notice of the attorney general's disapproval of the transaction. Not later than thirty days after receipt of the notice of appeal, the attorney general shall prepare and certify to the court of common pleas a complete record of all of the documents submitted by the nonprofit health care entity to the attorney general and any documents generated by consultants at the request of the attorney general or other materials produced by the attorney general as part of the attorney general's determination of whether to approve or disapprove the transaction.

The judgment of the court of common pleas is final unless reversed, vacated, or modified on appeal. An appeal may be taken by either the nonprofit health care entity or the attorney general, shall proceed as in the case of appeals in civil actions, and shall be pursuant to the rules of appellate procedure and, to the extent not in conflict with those rules, Chapter 2505. of the Revised Code.

(I)(1) The powers of the attorney general under this section and section 109.34 of the Revised Code are in addition to the attorney general's powers held at common law and under sections 109.23 to 109.33 of the Revised Code.

This section and section 109.34 of the Revised Code do not limit or otherwise affect any of the following:

(a) Any other civil or criminal right, claim, or defense that the attorney general or parties may assert under common law or the Revised Code;

(b) The authority of the attorney general to institute and prosecute an action to enforce sections 109.23 to 109.33 of the Revised Code;

(c) The authority of the attorney general to investigate and prosecute violations of any state or federal antitrust law.

(2) Nothing in this section shall be construed to grant to the attorney general any authority of the superintendent of insurance under Title XVII [17] or Title XXXIX [39] of the Revised Code relating to the superintendent's review of an entity described in division (A)(2)(b) of section 109.34 of the Revised Code.

(3) Nothing in this section or section 109.34 of the Revised Code shall be construed to limit the independent authority of the attorney general to protect charitable trusts and charitable assets in this state.

HISTORY: 147 v H 242. Eff 5-7-97.

[DEFENSE OF OFFICERS AND EMPLOYEES]

§ 109.36 Definitions.

As used in this section and sections 109.361 [109.36.1] to 109.366 [109.36.6] of the Revised Code:

(A)(1) "Officer or employee" means any of the following:

(a) A person who, at the time a cause of action against the person arises, is serving in an elected or appointed office or position with the state or is employed by the state.

(b) A person that, at the time a cause of action against the person, partnership, or corporation arises, is rendering medical, nursing, dental, podiatric, optometric, physical therapeutic, psychiatric, or psychological services pursuant to a personal services contract or purchased service contract with a department, agency, or institution of the state.

(c) A person that, at the time a cause of action against the person, partnership, or corporation arises, is rendering peer review, utilization review, or drug utilization review services in relation to medical, nursing, dental, podiatric, optometric, physical therapeutic, psychiatric, or psychological services pursuant to a personal services contract or purchased service contract with a department, agency, or institution of the state.

(d) A person who, at the time a cause of action against the person arises, is rendering medical services to patients in a state institution operated by the department of mental health, is a member of the institution's staff, and is performing the services pursuant to an agreement between the state institution and a board of alcohol, drug addiction, and mental health services described in section 340.021 [340.02.1] of the Revised Code.

(2) "Officer or employee" does not include any person elected, appointed, or employed by any political subdivision of the state.

(B) "State" means the state of Ohio, including but not limited to, the general assembly, the supreme court, the offices of all elected state officers, and all departments, boards, offices, commissions, agencies, institutions, and other instrumentalities of the state of Ohio. "State" does not include political subdivisions.

(C) "Political subdivisions" of the state means municipal corporations, townships, counties, school districts, and all other bodies corporate and politic responsible for governmental activities only in geographical areas smaller than that of the state.

(D) "Employer" means the general assembly, the supreme court, any office of an elected state officer, or any department, board, office, commission, agency, institution, or other instrumentality of the state of Ohio that employs or contracts with an officer or employee or to which an officer or employee is elected or appointed.

HISTORY: 138 v S 76 (Eff 3-13-80); 139 v S 204 (Eff 7-26-82); 145 v H 715 (Eff 7-22-94); 145 v H 571 (Eff 10-6-94); 146 v H 350. Eff 1-27-97.

The provisions of § 9 of HB 350 (146 v —) read as follows:

SECTION 9. Section 109.36 of the Revised Code was amended by both Sub. H.B. 715 and Am. Sub. H.B. 571 of the 120th General Assembly. Comparison of these amendments in pursuance of section 1.52 of the Revised Code discloses that while certain of the amendments of these acts are reconcilable, certain other of the amendments are substantively irreconcilable. Sub. H.B. 715 was passed on April 1, 1994; Am. Sub. H.B. 571 was passed on May 26, 1994. Section 109.36 of the Revised Code is therefore presented in this act as it results from Am. Sub. H.B. 571 and such of the amendments of Sub. H.B. 715 as are not in conflict with the amendments of Am. Sub. H.B. 571. This is in recognition of the principles stated in division (B) of section 1.52 of the Revised Code that amendments are to be harmonized where not substantively irreconcilable, and that where amendments are substantively irreconcilable, the latest amendment is to prevail. This section constitutes a legislative finding that such harmonized and reconciled section was the resulting version in effect prior to the effective date of this act.

[§ 109.36.1] § 109.361 Duty to defend state officer or employee in civil action upon request.

Upon the receipt of a written request by any officer or employee, the attorney general, except as provided in section 109.362 [109.36.2] of the Revised Code, except under the circumstances described in division (E) of section 120.06 of the Revised Code, and except for civil actions in which the state is the plaintiff, shall represent and defend the officer or employee in any civil action instituted against the officer or employee. All expenses and court costs, including the reasonable compensation of special counsel, incurred by the attorney general in the defense of an officer or employee shall be paid by the employer that employed the officer or employee at the time the alleged act or omission occurred.

The defense of the officer or employee may be rendered by the attorney general, an assistant attorney general, or any special counsel appointed by the attorney general, who, in addition to providing the defense of the officer or employee, may file counterclaims and cross-claims and engage in third-party practice on behalf of the officer or employee. If the officer or employee recovers any money pursuant to any counterclaim or cross-claim so filed, the officer or employee, to the extent of the recovery on the counterclaim or cross-claim, shall reimburse the attorney general for all expenses and court costs, including the reasonable compensation of assistant attorneys general and special counsel, incurred in bringing the counterclaim or cross-claim. The officer or employee shall cooperate fully with the attorney general's defense. Sections 109.36 to 109.366 [109.36.6] of the Revised Code do not deprive any officer or employee of the right to select counsel of his own choice or settle his case at his own expense at any time, and, except under the circumstances described in division (E) of section 120.06 of the Revised Code, do not prohibit the attorney general from entering his appearance in a case to protect the interest of the state even though no request for the appearance has been made by the officer or employee.

HISTORY: 138 v S 76 (Eff 3-13-80); 144 v H 210. Eff 5-1-92.

[§ 109.36.2] § 109.362 Investigation as to whether action was outside scope of duties or in bad faith; effect of insurance; notice of denial.

(A) Prior to undertaking any defense under section 109.361 [109.36.1] of the Revised Code, the attorney general shall conduct an investigation of the facts to determine whether the requirements of this section have been met. If the attorney general determines that any officer who holds an elective state office was acting manifestly outside the scope of his official responsibilities or that any other officer or employee was acting manifestly outside the scope of his employment or official responsibilities, with malicious purpose, in bad faith, or in a wanton or reckless manner, the attorney general shall not represent and defend the officer or employee. An initial determination to represent and defend the officer or employee does not prohibit a later determination that the requirements of this section have not been met.

(B) The attorney general shall also deny a request for representation upon a determination that the requesting officer or employee is covered by a policy of insurance purchased by the state requiring the insurer to provide counsel in the action and that the amount of the claim against the officer or employee is not in excess of the amount of coverage under the policy of insurance. If the amount of the claim against the officer or employee is in excess of the amount of coverage under the policy of insurance, the state is not the plaintiff, and the officer or employee is not otherwise prohibited by this section from being represented and defended by the attorney general, the attorney general shall represent and defend the officer or employee for the amount of the claim in excess of the amount of coverage.

(C) If the attorney general denies representation to an employee or officer who makes a request in accordance with the provisions of section 109.361 [109.36.1] of the Revised Code, the attorney general shall notify the requesting officer or employee in writing of the denial setting forth the reasons for the denial within a reasonable time after the attorney general's receipt of the written request from the officer or employee.

HISTORY: 138 v S 76. Eff 3-13-80.

[§ 109.36.3] § 109.363 Employer to provide report and information.

The employer of the defendant officer or employee shall provide the attorney general with a written report indicating the present or former position, job title, or classification of the officer or employee with the state and, citing pertinent facts, whether in its opinion the officer or employee meets the requirements of section 109.362 [109.36.2] of the Revised Code. In addition, the employer shall provide any additional information that is requested by the attorney general.

HISTORY: 138 v S 76. Eff 3-13-80.

[§ 109.36.4] § 109.364 Action to recover expenses from employer upon denial.

If the attorney general denies representation to an officer or employee who made a request for representation under section 109.361 [109.36.1] of the Revised Code, the officer or employee may, upon the termination of the action for which he requested the representation, commence an action in the court of claims against the employer pursuant to sections 2743.01 to 2743.20 of the Revised Code for the reasonable expenses incurred in providing his own defense.

An action brought pursuant to this section shall be commenced no later than two years after the cause of action arising under this section accrues. A cause of action arising under this section accrues upon the conclusion of the civil action instituted against the officer or employee for which the attorney general denied the officer's or employee's request for representation if the time for filing an appeal in the action lapses without the filing of an appeal or upon the conclusion of the final appeal in the civil action instituted against the officer or employee for which the attorney general denied the officer's or employee's request for representation if an appeal is filed in the action.

If the court of claims finds that the officer or employee was entitled to have the attorney general represent and defend him under section 109.361 [109.36.1] of the Revised Code, the court shall enter judgment against the employer in favor of the officer or employee in the amount of the reasonable expenses incurred by the officer or employee in providing his own defense and in bringing the action authorized by this section. The reasonable expenses may include, but are not limited to, payment of court costs, attorney's fees, investigative costs, and expert witness fees.

HISTORY: 138 v S 76. Eff 3-13-80.

[§ 109.36.5] § 109.365 Privileged information; no reference to decision whether to defend.

Information obtained by the attorney general pursuant to his investigation to determine whether to defend an officer or employee is privileged and is not admissible as evidence against the officer or employee in any legal action or proceeding and no reference to the information may be made in any trial or hearing. The decision of the attorney general to defend or not defend an officer or employee is not admissible as evidence in any trial or hearing. This section does not apply to any trial or hearing to determine the right of an officer or employee to reimbursement pursuant to section 109.364 [109.36.4] of the Revised Code or to any trial or hearing held as a result of an action filed pursuant to division (F) of section 9.87 of the Revised Code.

HISTORY: 138 v S 76. Eff 3-13-80.

[§ 109.36.6] § 109.366 Rules for implementation.

The attorney general may promulgate any rules that are necessary for the implementation of sections 109.36 to 109.366 [109.36.6] of the Revised Code.

HISTORY: 138 v S 76. Eff 3-13-80.

§ 109.40 Compilation and distribution of obscenity laws.

The attorney general shall compile all statutes relative to obscenity in a convenient pamphlet or paper and may distribute this compilation, without charge, to such sheriffs, police chiefs, county prosecutors, city prosecutors, mayors, constables, judges of the courts of common pleas, county court judges, municipal judges, and other interested parties, as may request such distribution, and make available a reasonable number of such compilations to fill such requests.

The attorney general shall, from time to time, supplement and keep the compilation current and he may, upon request, distribute such supplemental material in the manner provided in this section.

HISTORY: 128 v 554. Eff 11-5-59.

§ 109.41 Agent in certain escheat matters.

Whenever any state begins procedure to escheat property of any person who is an Ohio citizen, corporation, firm, or resident, or whose last known address was in Ohio, on the ground that the property has been abandoned, or on any other grounds, the attorney general may, after making diligent effort to notify the owner of the property and failing in the same, act as attorney in fact for the Ohio owner to claim the property. Upon taking custody of the property, the attorney general shall deposit same in the general fund of Ohio, or if the property be in kind, the attorney general shall cause the same to be sold pursuant to section 2113.40 of the Revised Code, and deposit the proceeds of the sale in the general fund. Claims to the property shall thereafter be made in the manner provided for in Chapter 2743. of the Revised Code.

HISTORY: 129 v 497 (Eff 10-12-61); 135 v H 800. Eff 1-1-75.

§ 109.42 Victim's bill of rights pamphlet.

(A) The attorney general shall prepare and have printed a pamphlet that contains a compilation of all statutes relative to victim's rights in which the attorney general lists and explains the statutes in the form of a victim's bill of rights. The attorney general shall distribute the pamphlet to all sheriffs, marshals, municipal corporation and township police departments, constables, and other law enforcement agencies, to all prosecuting attorneys, city directors of law, village solicitors, and other similar chief legal officers of municipal corporations, and to organizations that represent or provide services for victims of crime. The victim's bill of rights set forth in the pamphlet shall contain a description of all of the rights of victims that are provided for in Chapter 2930. or in any other section of the Revised Code and shall include, but not be limited to, all of the following:

(1) The right of a victim or a victim's representative to attend a proceeding before a grand jury, in a juvenile case, or in a criminal case pursuant to a subpoena without being discharged from the victim's or representative's employment, having the victim's or representative's employment terminated, having the victim's or representative's pay decreased or withheld, or otherwise being punished, penalized, or threatened as a result of time lost from regular employment because of the victim's or representative's attendance at the proceeding pursuant to the subpoena, as set forth in section 2151.211 [2151.21.1], 2930.18, 2939.121 [2939.12.1], or 2945.451 [2945.45.1] of the Revised Code;

(2) The potential availability pursuant to section 2151.411 [2151.41.1] of the Revised Code of a forfeited recognizance to pay damages caused by a child when the delinquency of the child or child's violation of probation is found to be proximately caused by the failure of the child's parent or guardian to subject the child to reasonable parental authority or to faithfully discharge the conditions of probation;

(3) The availability of awards of reparations pursuant to sections 2743.51 to 2743.72 of the Revised Code for injuries caused by criminal offenses;

(4) The right of the victim in certain criminal cases or a victim's representative to receive, pursuant to section 2930.06 of the Revised Code, notice of the date, time, and place of the trial in the case or, if there will not be a trial, information from the prosecutor, as defined in section 2930.01 of the Revised Code, regarding the disposition of the case;

(5) The right of the victim in certain criminal cases or a victim's representative to receive, pursuant to section 2930.04, 2930.05, or 2930.06 of the Revised Code, notice of the name of the person charged with the violation, the case or docket number assigned to the charge, and a telephone number or numbers that can be called to obtain information about the disposition of the case;

(6) The right of the victim in certain criminal cases or of the victim's representative pursuant to section 2930.13 or 2930.14 of the Revised Code, subject to any reasonable terms set by the court as authorized under section 2930.14 of the Revised Code, to make a statement about the victimization and, if applicable, a statement relative to the sentencing of the offender;

(7) The opportunity to obtain a court order, pursuant to section 2945.04 of the Revised Code, to prevent or stop the commission of the offense of intimidation of a crime victim or witness or an offense against the person or property of the complainant, or of the complainant's ward or child;

(8) The right of the victim in certain criminal cases or a victim's representative pursuant to sections 2929.20, 2930.10, 2930.16, and 2930.17 of the Revised Code to receive notice of a pending motion for judicial release of the person who committed the offense against the victim and to make an oral or written statement at the court hearing on the motion;

(9) The right of the victim in certain criminal cases or a victim's representative, pursuant to section 2930.16, 2967.12, 2967.26, or 2967.27 of the Revised Code, to receive notice of any pending commutation, pardon, parole, or furlough for the person who committed the offense against the victim or any application for release of that person and to send a written statement relative to the victimization and the pending action to the adult parole authority;

(10) The right of the victim to bring a civil action pursuant to sections 2969.01 to 2969.06 of the Revised Code to obtain money from the offender's profit fund;

(11) The right, pursuant to section 3109.09 of the Revised Code, to maintain a civil action to recover compensatory damages not exceeding ten thousand dollars and costs from the parent of a minor who willfully damages property through the commission of an act that would be a theft offense, as defined in section 2913.01 of the Revised Code, if committed by an adult;

(12) The right, pursuant to section 3109.10 of the Revised Code, to maintain a civil action to recover compensatory damages not exceeding ten thousand dollars and costs from the parent of a minor who willfully and maliciously assaults a person;

(13) The possibility of receiving restitution from an offender or a delinquent child pursuant to section 2151.355 [2151.35.5], 2929.18, or 2929.21 of the Revised Code;

(14) The right of the victim in certain criminal cases or a victim's representative, pursuant to section 2930.16 of the Revised Code, to receive notice of the escape from confinement or custody of the person who committed the offense, to receive that notice from the custodial agency of the person at the victim's last address or telephone number provided to the custodial agency, and to receive notice that, if either the victim's address or telephone number changes, it is in the victim's interest to provide the new address or telephone number to the custodial agency.

(15) The right of a victim of domestic violence to seek the issuance of a temporary protection order pursuant to section 2919.26 of the Revised Code, to seek the issuance of a civil protection order pursuant to section 3113.31 of the Revised Code, and to be accompanied by a victim advocate during court proceedings.

(16) The right of a victim of a sexually oriented offense that is committed by a person who is adjudicated as being a sexual predator or, in certain cases, by a person who is determined to be a habitual sex offender to receive, pursuant to section 2950.10 of the Revised Code, notice that the offender has registered with a sheriff under section 2950.04 or 2950.05 of the Revised

Code and notice of the offender's name and residence address or addresses, and a summary of the manner in which the victim must make a request to receive the notice. As used in this division, "sexually oriented offense," "adjudicated as being a sexual predator," and "habitual sex offender" have the same meanings as in section 2950.01 of the Revised Code.

(17) The right of a victim of certain sexually violent offenses committed by a sexually violent predator who is sentenced to a prison term pursuant to division (A)(3) of section 2971.03 of the Revised Code to receive, pursuant to section 2930.16 of the Revised Code, notice of a hearing to determine whether to modify the requirement that the offender serve the entire prison term in a state correctional facility, whether to continue, revise, or revoke any existing modification of that requirement, or whether to terminate the prison term. As used in this division, "sexually violent offense" and "sexually violent predator" have the same meanings as in section 2971.01 of the Revised Code.

(B)(1)(a) Subject to division (B)(1)(c) of this section, a prosecuting attorney, assistant prosecuting attorney, city director of law, assistant director of law, village solicitor, assistant village solicitor, or similar chief legal officer of a municipal corporation or an assistant of any such officer who prosecutes an offense committed in this state, upon first contact with the victim of the offense, the victim's family, or the victim's dependents, shall give the victim, the victim's family, or the victim's dependents a copy of the pamphlet prepared pursuant to division (A) of this section and explain, upon request, the information in the pamphlet to the victim, the victim's family, or the victim's dependents.

(b) Subject to division (B)(1)(c) of this section, a law enforcement agency that investigates an offense committed in this state shall give the victim of the offense, the victim's family, or the victim's dependents a copy of the pamphlet prepared pursuant to division (A) of this section at one of the following times:

(i) Upon first contact with the victim, the victim's family, or the victim's dependents;

(ii) If the offense is an offense of violence, if the circumstances of the offense and the condition of the victim, the victim's family or the victim's dependents indicate that the victim, the victim's family, or the victim's dependents will not be able to understand the significance of the pamphlet upon first contact with the agency, and if the agency anticipates that it will have an additional contact with the victim, the victim's family, or the victim's dependents, upon the agency's second contact with the victim, the victim's family, or the victim's dependents.

If the agency does not give the victim, the victim's family, or the victim's dependents a copy of the pamphlet upon first contact with them and does not have a second contact with the victim, the victim's family, or the victim's dependents, the agency shall mail a copy of the pamphlet to the victim, the victim's family, or the victim's dependents at their last known address.

(c) In complying on and after December 9, 1994, with the duties imposed by division (B)(1)(a) or (b) of this section, an official or a law enforcement agency shall use copies of the pamphlet that are in the official's or agency's possession on December 9, 1994, until the official or agency has distributed all of those copies. After the official or agency has distributed all of those copies, the official or agency shall use only copies of the pamphlet that contain at least the information described in division (A)(1) to (15) of this section.

(2) The failure of a law enforcement agency or of a prosecuting attorney, assistant prosecuting attorney, director of law, assistant director of law, village solicitor, assistant village solicitor, or similar chief legal officer of a municipal corporation or an assistant to any such officer to give, as required by division (B)(1) of this section, the victim of an offense, the victim's family, or the victim's dependents a copy of the pamphlet prepared pursuant to division (A) of this section does not give the victim, the victim's family, the victim's dependents, or a victim's representative any rights under section 122.95, 2743.51 to 2743.72, 2945.04, 2967.12, 2969.01 to 2969.06, 3109.09, or 3109.10 of the Revised Code or under any other provision of the Revised Code and does not affect any right under those sections.

(3) A law enforcement agency, a prosecuting attorney or assistant prosecuting attorney, or a director of law, assistant director of law, village solicitor, assistant village solicitor, or similar chief legal officer of a municipal corporation that distributes a copy of the pamphlet prepared pursuant to division (A) of this section shall not be required to distribute a copy of an information card or other printed material provided by the clerk of the court of claims pursuant to section 2743.71 of the Revised Code.

(C) The cost of printing and distributing the pamphlet prepared pursuant to division (A) of this section shall be paid out of the reparations fund, created pursuant to section 2743.191 [2743.19.1] of the Revised Code, in accordance with division (D) of that section.

(D) As used in this section:

(1) "Victim's representative" has the same meaning as in section 2930.01 of the Revised Code;

(2) "Victim advocate" has the same meaning as in section 2919.26 of the Revised Code.

HISTORY: 141 v H 657 (Eff 9-12-86); 142 v H 207 (Eff 9-24-87); 142 v H 708 (Eff 4-19-88); 143 v S 3 (Eff 4-11-91); 145 v H 152 (Eff 7-1-93); 145 v H 186 (Eff 10-12-94); 145 v H 335 (Eff 12-9-94); 146 v H 18 (Eff 11-24-95); 146 v S 2 (Eff 7-1-96); 146 v H 601 (Eff 10-29-96); 146 v H 180. Eff 1-1-97.

The effective date is set by section 3 of HB 180.

Comment, Legislative Service Commission

Section 109.42 of the Revised Code is amended by this act [Am. Sub. H.B. 180] and also by Am. Sub. H.B. 601 of the 121st General Assembly. ° ° ° Comparison of these amendments in pursuance of section 1.52 of the Revised Code discloses that they are not irreconcilable so that they are required by that section to be harmonized to give effect to each amendment.

[BUREAU OF CRIMINAL IDENTIFICATION AND INVESTIGATION]

§ 109.51 Creation of bureau of criminal identification and investigation.

There is hereby created in the office of the attorney general, a bureau of criminal identification and investigation to be located at the site of the London correctional institution. The attorney general shall appoint a superintendent of said bureau. The superintendent shall appoint, with the approval of the attorney general, such assistants as are necessary to carry out the functions and duties of the bureau as contained in sections 109.51 to 109.63, inclusive, of the Revised Code.

HISTORY: 130 v 9. Eff 9-24-63.

For provisions analogous to RC § 109.51 et seq, see former RC § 5149.01 et seq.

[§ 109.51.1] § 109.511 Felony precludes or terminates employment as investigator or special agent.

(A) As used in this section, "felony" means any of the following:

(1) An offense committed in this state that is a felony under the law of this state;

(2) An offense committed in a state other than this state, or under the law of the United States, that, if committed in this state, would be a felony under the law of this state.

(B) The superintendent of the bureau of criminal identification and investigation shall not appoint or employ any person as an investigator or a special agent on a permanent basis, on a temporary basis, for a probationary term, or on other than a permanent basis if the person previously has been convicted of or has pleaded guilty to a felony.

(C)(1) The superintendent shall terminate the employment of an investigator or a special agent who does either of the following:

(a) Pleads guilty to a felony;

(b) Pleads guilty to a misdemeanor pursuant to a negotiated plea agreement as provided in division (D) of section 2929.29 of the Revised Code in which the investigator or special agent agrees to surrender the certificate awarded to the investigator or special agent under section 109.77 of the Revised Code.

(2) The superintendent shall suspend from employment an investigator or a special agent who is convicted, after trial, of a felony. If the investigator or special agent files an appeal from that conviction and the conviction is upheld by the highest court to which the appeal is taken or if the investigator or special agent does not file a timely appeal, the superintendent shall terminate the employment of that investigator or special agent. If the investigator or special agent files an appeal that results in that investigator's or special agent's acquittal of the felony or conviction of a misdemeanor, or in the dismissal of the felony charge against the investigator or special agent, the superintendent shall reinstate that investigator or special agent. An investigator or a special agent who is reinstated under this division shall not receive any back pay unless that investigator's or special agent's conviction of the felony was reversed on appeal, or the felony charge was dismissed, because the court found insufficient evidence to convict the investigator or special agent of the felony.

(D) This section does not apply regarding an offense that was committed prior to January 1, 1997.

(E) The suspension from employment or the termination of the employment of an investigator or a special agent under division (C) of this section shall be in accordance with Chapter 119. of the Revised Code.

HISTORY: 146 v H 566. Eff 10-16-96.

§ 109.52 Operations of the bureau.

The bureau of criminal identification and investigation may operate and maintain a criminal analysis laboratory and mobile units thereof, create a staff of investigators and technicians skilled in the solution and control of crimes and criminal activity, keep statistics and other necessary data, assist in the prevention of crime, and engage in such other activities as will aid law enforcement officers in solving crimes and controlling criminal activity.

HISTORY: 130 v 9. Eff 9-24-63.

§ 109.53 Equipment and furnishings of the bureau.

The bureau of criminal identification and investigation shall be supplied with furniture, fixtures, apparatus, vehicles, and materials necessary to carry out the functions and duties of the bureau as contained in sections 109.51 to 109.63, inclusive, of the Revised Code.

HISTORY: 130 v 9. Eff 9-24-63.

§ 109.54 Intergovernmental cooperation.

(A) The bureau of criminal identification and investigation may investigate any criminal activity in this state that is of statewide or intercounty concern when requested by local authorities and may aid federal authorities, when requested, in their investigation of any criminal activity in this state. The bureau may investigate any criminal activity in this state involving drug abuse or illegal drug distribution prohibited under Chapter 3719. or 4729. of the Revised Code. The superintendent and any agent of the bureau may participate, as the director of an organized crime task force established under section 177.02 of the Revised Code or as a member of the investigatory staff of a task force established under that section, in an investigation of organized criminal activity anywhere within this state under sections 177.01 to 177.03 of the Revised Code.

(B) The bureau may provide any trained investigative personnel and specialized equipment that are requested by any sheriff or chief of police, by the authorized designee of any sheriff or chief of police, or by any other authorized law enforcement officer to aid and assist the officer in the investigation and solution of any crime or the control of any criminal activity occurring within the officer's jurisdiction. This assistance shall be furnished by the bureau without disturbing or impairing any of the existing law enforcement authority or the prerogatives of local law enforcement authorities or officers. Investigators provided pursuant to this section, or engaged in an investigation pursuant to section 109.83 of the Revised Code, may go armed in the same manner as sheriffs and regularly appointed police officers under section 2923.12 of the Revised Code.

(C)(1) The bureau shall obtain recording equipment that can be used to record depositions of the type described in division (A) of section 2151.3511 [2151.35.11] and division (A) of section 2945.481 [2945.48.1] of the Revised Code, or testimony of the type described in division (D) of section 2151.3511 [2151.35.11] and division (D) of section 2945.481 [2945.48.1] or in division (C) of section 2937.11 of the Revised Code, shall obtain closed circuit equipment that can be used to televise testimony of the type described in division (C) of section 2151.3511 [2151.35.11] and division (C) of section 2945.481 [2945.48.1] or in division (B) of section 2937.11 of the Revised Code, and shall provide the equipment, upon request, to any court for use in recording any deposition or testimony of one of those types or in televising the testimony in accordance with the applicable division.

(2) The bureau shall obtain the names, addresses, and telephone numbers of persons who are experienced in questioning children in relation to an investigation of a violation of section 2905.03, 2905.05, 2907.02, 2907.03, 2907.04, 2907.05, 2907.06, 2907.07, 2907.09, 2907.21, 2907.23, 2907.24, 2907.31, 2907.32, 2907.321 [2907.32.1], 2907.322 [2907.32.2], 2907.323 [2907.32.-3], or 2919.22 of the Revised Code or an offense of violence and shall maintain a list of those names, addresses, and telephone numbers. The list shall include a classification of the names, addresses, and telephone numbers by appellate district. Upon request, the bureau shall provide any county sheriff, chief of police, prosecuting attorney, village solicitor, city director of law, or similar chief legal officer with the name, address, and telephone number of any person contained in the list.

HISTORY: 130 v 9 (Eff 9-24-63); 141 v S 74 (Eff 9-3-86); 141 v H 108 (Eff 10-14-86); 146 v H 445 (Eff 9-3-96); 146 v H 480 (Eff 10-16-96); 147 v S 53. Eff 10-14-97.

The provisions of § 3 of SB 53 (147 v —) read as follows:

SECTION 3. Section 109.54 of the Revised Code is presented in this act as a composite of the section as amended by both Am. Sub. H.B. 445 and Sub. H.B. 480 of the 121st General Assembly, with the new language of neither of the acts shown in capital letters. This is in recognition of the principle stated in division (B) of section 1.52 of the Revised Code that such amendments are to be harmonized where not substantively irreconcilable and constitutes a legislative finding that such is the resulting version in effect prior to the effective date of this act.

[§ 109.54.1] § 109.541 Arrest authority of investigator while assisting law enforcement officer; emergency assistance.

(A) As used in this section:

(1) "Investigator" means an officer or employee of the bureau of criminal identification and investigation described in section 109.54 of the Revised Code.

(2) "Peace officer" has the same meaning as in section 2935.01 of the Revised Code.

(B) An investigator, while providing assistance to a law enforcement officer pursuant to division (B) of section 109.54 of the Revised Code, has the same arrest authority as a peace officer of the law enforcement agency served by the law enforcement officer requesting the assistance. The investigator may exercise this arrest authority only in connection with the investigation or activities for which the investigator's assistance was requested.

(C)(1) No state official shall command, order, or direct an investigator to perform any duty or service that is not authorized by law. The power and duties conferred by this section on the bureau of criminal identification and investigation are supplementary to, and in no way a limitation on, the power and duties of sheriffs or other peace officers of the state or a political subdivision of the state.

(2) An investigator, pursuant to the policy established by the superintendent of the bureau of criminal identification and investigation under division (D)(1) of this section, may render emergency assistance to any peace officer who has arrest authority under section 2935.03 of the Revised Code if both of the following apply:

(a) There is a threat of imminent physical harm to the peace officer, a threat of physical harm to another person, or any serious emergency situation.

(b) The peace officer requests emergency assistance, or it appears to the investigator that the peace officer is unable to request emergency assistance and that the circumstances reasonably indicate that emergency assistance is appropriate.

(D)(1) The superintendent of the bureau of criminal identification and investigation, not later than sixty days after the effective date of this section, shall establish a policy specifying the manner and procedures by which an investigator may render emergency assistance to a peace officer pursuant to division (C)(2) of this section.

(2) An investigator who renders assistance to a law enforcement officer pursuant to division (B) of section

109.54 of the Revised Code or renders emergency assistance to any peace officer pursuant to division (C)(2) of this section and under the policy established under division (D)(1) of this section shall be considered to be engaged in the investigator's regular employment for the purpose of compensation, retirement benefits, indemnification rights, workers' compensation, and any other rights or benefits to which the investigator may be entitled incident to the investigator's regular employment.

(3) An investigator who renders emergency assistance to a peace officer pursuant to division (C)(2) of this section and under the policy established under division (D)(1) of this section has the same authority as the peace officer to whom the assistance is rendered.

(4) An investigator who renders emergency assistance to a peace officer pursuant to division (C)(2) of this section and under the policy established under division (D)(1) of this section retains personal immunity from liability as described in sections 9.85 to 9.87 of the Revised Code, the right to defense under sections 109.36 to 109.366 [109.36.6] of the Revised Code, and the right to indemnification under section 9.87 of the Revised Code. This section does not affect the provisions of section 2743.02 of the Revised Code that pertain to the commencement of a civil action against a state officer or employee.

HISTORY: 146 v H 480. Eff 10-16-96.

§ 109.55 Coordination of law enforcement activities.

The superintendent of the bureau of criminal identification and investigation shall recommend cooperative policies for the coordination of the law enforcement work and crime prevention activities of all state and local agencies and officials having law enforcement duties to promote cooperation between such agencies and officials, to secure effective and efficient law enforcement, to eliminate duplication of work, and to promote economy of operation in such agencies.

In formulating and recommending cooperative policies, the superintendent shall emphasize the provisions of section 2901.30 of the Revised Code.

The superintendent shall develop procedures and forms to implement section 2901.30 of the Revised Code.

HISTORY: 130 v 9 (Eff 9-24-63); 140 v S 321. Eff 4-9-85.

§ 109.56 Training local law enforcement authorities.

The bureau of criminal identification and investigation shall, where practicable, assist in training local law enforcement officers in crime prevention, detection, and solution when requested by local authorities, and, where practicable, furnish instruction to sheriffs, chiefs of police, and other law officers in the establishment of efficient local bureaus of identification in their districts.

HISTORY: 130 v 9. Eff 9-24-63.

§ 109.57 Duties of superintendent of bureau.

(A)(1) As used in this section:

(a) "Designated delinquent act or juvenile offense" means any of the following:

(i) Any "category one offense" or "category two offense";

(ii) Any violation of section 2907.03, 2907.04, or 2907.05 of the Revised Code;

(iii) Any violation of section 2907.12 of the Revised Code as it existed prior to September 3, 1996;

(iv) Any attempt to commit a violation of section 2907.02, 2907.03, 2907.04, or 2907.05 of the Revised Code or to commit a violation of section 2907.12 of the Revised Code as it existed prior to September 3, 1996;

(v) A violation of any law that arose out of the same facts and circumstances as did a charge against the child of a violation of section 2907.02, 2907.03, 2907.04, or 2907.05 of the Revised Code that previously was dismissed or as did a charge against the child of a violation of section 2907.12 of the Revised Code as it existed prior to September 3, 1996, that previously was dismissed;

(iv)† Any violation of section 2905.02 or 2919.23 of the Revised Code that would have been a violation of section 2905.04 of the Revised Code as it existed prior to July 1, 1996, had the violation been committed prior to that date.

(b) "Category one offense" and "category two offense" have the same meanings as in section 2151.26 of the Revised Code.

(2) The superintendent of the bureau of criminal identification and investigation shall procure from wherever procurable and file for record photographs, pictures, descriptions, fingerprints, measurements, and other information that may be pertinent of all persons who have been convicted of committing within this state a felony or any crime constituting a misdemeanor on the first offense and a felony on subsequent offenses, of all children fourteen years of age or older and under eighteen years of age who have been adjudicated delinquent children for committing within this state a designated delinquent act or juvenile offense or who have been convicted of or pleaded guilty to committing within this state a designated delinquent act or juvenile offense, and of all well-known and habitual criminals. The person in charge of any state correctional institution and the person in charge of any state institution having custody of a person suspected of having committed a felony or any crime constituting a misdemeanor on the first offense and a felony on subsequent offenses or having custody of a child fourteen years of age or older and under eighteen years of age with respect to whom there is probable cause to believe that the child may have committed a designated delinquent act or juvenile

offense shall furnish such material to the superintendent of the bureau upon request. Fingerprints, photographs, or other descriptive information of a child who is under eighteen years of age, has not been arrested or otherwise taken into custody for committing an act that is a category one offense or a category two offense, has not been adjudicated a delinquent child for committing a designated delinquent act or juvenile offense, has not been convicted of or pleaded guilty to committing a designated delinquent act or juvenile offense, and is not a child with respect to whom there is probable cause to believe that the child may have committed a designated delinquent act or juvenile offense shall not be procured by the superintendent or furnished by any person in charge of any state correctional institution, except as authorized in section 2151.313 [2151.31.3] of the Revised Code. Every court of record in this state shall send to the superintendent of the bureau a weekly report containing a summary of each case involving a felony, involving any crime constituting a misdemeanor on the first offense and a felony on subsequent offenses, or involving an adjudication that a child under eighteen years of age is a delinquent child for committing a designated delinquent act or juvenile offense. The summary shall include the style and number of the case, the dates of arrest, commencement of trial, and conviction or adjudication of delinquency, a statement of the offense and the conduct that constituted it, and the sentence or terms of probation imposed, or other disposition of the offender or the delinquent child. If the offense involved the disarming of a law enforcement officer or an attempt to disarm a law enforcement officer, the court shall clearly state that fact in the summary, and the superintendent shall ensure that a clear statement of that fact is placed in the bureau's records.

The superintendent shall cooperate with and assist sheriffs, chiefs of police, and other law enforcement officers in the establishment of a complete system of criminal identification and in obtaining fingerprints and other means of identification of all persons arrested on a charge of a felony or any crime constituting a misdemeanor on the first offense and a felony on subsequent offenses and of all children fourteen years of age or older and under eighteen years of age arrested or otherwise taken into custody for committing a designated delinquent act or juvenile offense. The superintendent also shall file for record the fingerprint impressions of all persons confined in a workhouse, jail, or state correctional institution for the violation of state laws and of all children fourteen years of age or older and under eighteen years of age who are confined in a workhouse, jail, or state correctional institution or in any facility for delinquent children for committing a designated delinquent act or juvenile offense, and any other information that the superintendent may receive from law enforcement officials of the state and its political subdivisions.

The superintendent shall carry out Chapter 2950. of the Revised Code with respect to the registration of persons who are convicted of or plead guilty to a sexually oriented offense and with respect to all other duties imposed on the bureau under that chapter.

(B) The superintendent shall prepare and furnish to every state correctional institution and to every court of record in this state standard forms for reporting the information required under division (A)(2) of this section.

(C) The superintendent may operate a center for electronic, automated, or other data processing for the storage and retrieval of information, data, and statistics pertaining to criminals and to children under eighteen years of age who are adjudicated delinquent children for committing a designated delinquent act or juvenile offense, criminal activity, crime prevention, law enforcement, and criminal justice, and may establish and operate a statewide communications network to gather and disseminate information, data, and statistics for the use of law enforcement agencies. The superintendent may gather, store, retrieve, and disseminate information, data, and statistics that pertain to children who are under eighteen years of age and that are gathered pursuant to sections 109.57 to 109.61 of the Revised Code together with information, data, and statistics that pertain to adults and that are gathered pursuant to those sections.

(D) The information and materials furnished to the superintendent pursuant to division (A)(2) of this section and information and materials furnished to any board or person under division (F) or (G) of this section are not public records under section 149.43 of the Revised Code.

(E) The attorney general shall adopt rules, in accordance with Chapter 119. of the Revised Code, setting forth the procedure by which a person may receive or release information gathered by the superintendent pursuant to division (A)(2) of this section. A reasonable fee may be charged for this service. If a temporary employment service submits a request for a determination of whether a person the service plans to refer to an employment position has been convicted of or pleaded guilty to an offense listed in division (A)(1), (3), (4), or (5) of section 109.572 [109.57.2] of the Revised Code, the request shall be treated as a single request and only one fee shall be charged.

(F)(1) As used in division (F)(2) of this section, "head start agency" means an entity in this state that has been approved to be an agency for purposes of subchapter II of the "Community Economic Development Act," 95 Stat. 489 (1981), 42 U.S.C.A. 9831, as amended.

(2)(a) In addition to or in conjunction with any request that is required to be made under section 109.572 [109.57.2], 2151.86, 3301.32, 3301.541 [3301.54.1], 3319.39, 3701.881 [3701.88.1], 5104.012 [5104.01.2], 5104.013 [5104.01.3], 5126.28, 5126.281 [5126.28.1], or 5153.111 [5153.11.1] of the Revised Code, the board of education of any school district; any county board of mental retardation and developmental disabilities; any entity under contract with a county board of mental retardation and developmental disabilities; the chief administrator of any chartered nonpublic school; the chief administrator of any home health agency; the chief administrator of or person operating any child day-care center, type A family day-care home, or type B family day-care home licensed or certified under Chapter 5104. of the Revised Code; the administrator of any type C family day-care home certified pursuant to Section 1 of Sub. H.B. 62 of the 121st general assembly or Section 5 of Am. Sub. S.B. 160 of the 121st general assembly; the chief administrator of any head start agency; or the executive director of a public children services agency may request that the superintendent of the bureau investigate and determine, with respect to any individual who has applied for employment in any position after October 2, 1989, or any individual wishing to apply for employment with a board of education may request, with regard to the individual's own self, whether the bureau has any information gathered under division (A)(2) of this section that pertains to that individual. On receipt of the request, the superintendent shall determine whether that information exists and, upon request of the person, board, or entity requesting information, also shall request from the federal bureau of investigation any criminal records it has pertaining to that individual. Within thirty days of the date that the superintendent receives a request, the superintendent shall send to the board, entity, or person a report of any information that the superintendent determines exists, including information contained in records that have been sealed under section 2953.32 of the Revised Code, and, within thirty days of its receipt, shall send the board, entity, or person a report of any information received from the federal bureau of investigation, other than information the dissemination of which is prohibited by federal law.

(b) When a board of education is required to receive information under this section as a prerequisite to employment of an individual pursuant to section 3319.39 of the Revised Code, it may accept a certified copy of records that were issued by the bureau of criminal identification and investigation and that are presented by an individual applying for employment with the district in lieu of requesting that information itself. In such a case, the board shall accept the certified copy issued by the bureau in order to make a photocopy of it for that individual's employment application documents and shall return the certified copy to the individual. In a case of that nature, a district only shall accept a certified copy of records of that nature within one year after the date of their issuance by the bureau.

(3) The state board of education may request, with respect to any individual who has applied for employment after October 2, 1989, in any position with the state board or the department of education, any information that a school district board of education is authorized to request under division (F)(2) of this section, and the superintendent of the bureau shall proceed as if the request has been received from a school district board of education under division (F)(2) of this section.

(4) When the superintendent of the bureau receives a request for information that is authorized under section 3319.291 [3319.29.1] of the Revised Code, the superintendent shall proceed as if the request has been received from a school district board of education under division (F)(2) of this section.

(G) In addition to or in conjunction with any request that is required to be made under section 173.41, 3701.881 [3701.88.1], 3712.09, 3721.121 [3721.12.1], or 3722.151 [3722.15.1] of the Revised Code with respect to an individual who has applied for employment in a position that involves providing direct care to an older adult, the chief administrator of a PASSPORT agency that provides services through the PASSPORT program created under section 173.40 of the Revised Code, home health agency, hospice care program, home licensed under Chapter 3721. of the Revised Code, adult day-care program operated pursuant to rules adopted under section 3721.04 of the Revised Code, or adult care facility may request that the superintendent of the bureau investigate and determine, with respect to any individual who has applied after January 27, 1997, for employment in a position that does not involve providing direct care to an older adult, whether the bureau has any information gathered under division (A) of this section that pertains to that individual. On receipt of the request, the superintendent shall determine whether that information exists and, on request of the administrator requesting information, shall also request from the federal bureau of investigation any criminal records it has pertaining to that individual. Within thirty days of the date a request is received, the superintendent shall send to the administrator a report of any information determined to exist, including information contained in records that have been sealed under section 2953.32 of the Revised Code, and, within thirty days of its receipt, shall send the administrator a report of any information received from the federal bureau of investigation, other than information the dissemination of which is prohibited by federal law.

(H) Information obtained by a board, administrator, or other person under this section is confidential and shall not be released or disseminated.

(I) The superintendent may charge a reasonable fee for providing information or criminal records under division (F)(2) or (G) of this section.

HISTORY: 130 v 11 (Eff 9-24-63); 130 v 10 (Eff 10-4-63); 133 v H 956 (Eff 9-16-70); 137 v H 1 (Eff 8-26-77); 138 v H 736 (Eff 10-16-80); 140 v H 235 (Eff 6-7-84); 143 v S 140 (Eff 10-2-89); 145 v H 152 (Eff 7-1-93); 145 v H 162 (Eff 10-1-93); 145 v S 38 (Eff 10-29-93); 145 v H 571 (Eff 10-6-94); 145 v H 694 (Eff 11-11-94); 146 v H 1 (Eff 1-1-96); 146 v H 223 (Eff 11-15-95); 146 v S 160 (Eff 1-27-97); 146 v H 124, § 1 (Eff 3-31-97); 146 v H 180 (Eff 7-1-97); 146 v H 124, § 4 (Eff 7-1-97); 147 v H 151. Eff 9-16-97.

† So in enrolled bill.

The provisions of § 3 of HB 151 (147 v —) read as follows:

SECTION 3. Section 109.57 of the Revised Code is presented in this act as a composite of the section as amended by both Am. Sub. S.B. 160 and Am. Sub. H.B. 124 of the 121st General Assembly, with the new language of neither of the acts shown in capital letters. ° ° ° This is in recognition of the principle stated in division (B) of section 1.52 of the Revised Code that such amendments are to be harmonized where not substantively irreconcilable and constitutes a legislative finding that such is the resulting version in effect prior to the effective date of this act.

The provisions of § 3 of SB 160 (146 v —) read as follows:

SECTION 3. Sections 109.57, 109.572, 2950.08, 2953.32, and 3701.881 of the Revised Code, as amended by this act regarding employment of persons who provide direct care to older adults, and sections 173.41, 3712.09, 3721.121, and 3722.151 of the Revised Code, as enacted by this act, apply only to persons who apply for employment on or after the effective date of this act.

[§ 109.57.1] § 109.571 Repealed, 146 v H 670, § 2 [133 v H 956; 135 v S 174; 143 v H 552]. Eff 12-2-96.

This section created the law enforcement communications committee.

[§ 109.57.2] § 109.572 Criminal records check and fingerprinting of certain persons having contact with children, mentally retarded persons or older adults.

(A)(1) Upon receipt of a request pursuant to section 2151.86, 3301.32, 3301.541 [3301.54.1], 3319.39, 5104.012 [5104.01.2], 5104.013 [5104.01.3], or 5153.111 [5153.11.1] of the Revised Code, a completed form prescribed pursuant to division (C)(1) of this section, and a set of fingerprint impressions obtained in the manner described in division (C)(2) of this section, the superintendent of the bureau of criminal identification and investigation shall conduct a criminal records check in the manner described in division (B) of this section to determine whether any information exists that indicates that the person who is the subject of the request previously has been convicted of or pleaded guilty to any of the following:

(a) A violation of section 2903.01, 2903.02, 2903.03, 2903.04, 2903.11, 2903.12, 2903.13, 2903.16, 2903.21, 2903.34, 2905.01, 2905.02, 2905.05, 2907.02, 2907.03, 2907.04, 2907.05, 2907.06, 2907.07, 2907.08, 2907.09, 2907.21, 2907.22, 2907.23, 2907.25, 2907.31, 2907.32, 2907.321 [2907.32.1], 2907.322 [2907.32.2], 2907.323 [2907.32.3], 2911.01, 2911.02, 2911.11, 2911.12, 2919.12, 2919.22, 2919.24, 2919.25, 2923.12, 2923.13, 2923.161 [2923.16.1], 2925.02, 2925.03, 2925.04, 2925.05, 2925.06, or 3716.11 of the Revised Code, felonious sexual penetration in violation of former section 2907.12 of the Revised Code, a violation of section 2905.04 of the Revised Code as it existed prior to July 1, 1996, a violation of section 2919.23 of the Revised Code that would have been a violation of section 2905.04 of the Revised Code as it existed prior to July 1, 1996, had the violation been committed prior to that date, or a violation of section 2925.11 of the Revised Code that is not a minor drug possession offense;

(b) A violation of an existing or former law of this state, any other state, or the United States that is substantially equivalent to any of the offenses listed in division (A)(1)(a) of this section.

(2) On receipt of a request pursuant to section 5126.28 of the Revised Code with respect to an applicant for employment in any position with a county board of mental retardation and developmental disabilities or pursuant to section 5126.281 [5126.28.1] of the Revised Code with respect to an applicant for employment in a position with an entity contracting with a county board for employment in a position that involves providing service directly to individuals with mental retardation and developmental disabilities, a completed form prescribed pursuant to division (C)(1) of this section, and a set of fingerprint impressions obtained in the manner described in division (C)(2) of this section, the superintendent of the bureau of criminal identification and investigation shall conduct a criminal records check. The superintendent shall conduct the criminal records check in the manner described in division (B) of this section to determine whether any information exists that indicates that the person who is the subject of the request has been convicted of or pleaded guilty to any of the following:

(a) A violation of section 2903.01, 2903.02, 2903.03, 2903.04, 2903.11, 2903.12, 2903.13, 2903.16, 2903.21, 2903.34, 2905.01, 2905.02, 2905.04†, 2905.05, 2907.02, 2907.03, 2907.04, 2907.05, 2907.06, 2907.07, 2907.08, 2907.09, 2907.12††, 2907.21, 2907.22, 2907.23, 2907.25, 2907.31, 2907.32, 2907.321 [2907.32.1], 2907.322 [2907.32.2], 2907.323 [2907.32.3], 2911.01, 2911.02, 2911.11, 2911.12, 2919.12, 2919.22, 2919.24, 2919.25, 2923.12, 2923.13, 2923.161 [2923.16.1], 2925.02, 2925.03, or 3716.11 of the Revised Code;

(b) An existing or former law of this state, any other state, or the United States that is substantially equivalent to any of the offenses listed in division (A)(2)(a) of this section.

(3) On receipt of a request pursuant to section 173.41, 3712.09, 3721.121 [3721.12.1], or 3722.151 [3722.15.1] of the Revised Code, a completed form prescribed pursuant to division (C)(1) of this section, and a set of fingerprint impressions obtained in the manner described in division (C)(2) of this section, the superintendent of the bureau of criminal identification and investigation shall conduct a criminal records check with respect to any person who has applied for employment in a position that involves providing direct care to an older adult. The superintendent shall conduct the criminal records check in the manner described in division

(B) of this section to determine whether any information exists that indicates that the person who is the subject of the request previously has been convicted of or pleaded guilty to any of the following:

(a) A violation of section 2903.01, 2903.02, 2903.03, 2903.04, 2903.11, 2903.12, 2903.13, 2903.16, 2903.21, 2903.34, 2905.01, 2905.02, 2905.11, 2905.12, 2907.02, 2907.03, 2907.05, 2907.06, 2907.07, 2907.08, 2907.09, 2907.12††, 2907.25, 2907.31, 2907.32, 2907.321 [2907.-32.1], 2907.322 [2907.32.2], 2907.323 [2907.32.3], 2911.01, 2911.02, 2911.11, 2911.12, 2911.13, 2913.02, 2913.03, 2913.04, 2913.11, 2913.21, 2913.31, 2913.40, 2913.43, 2913.47, 2913.51, 2919.25, 2921.36, 2923.12, 2923.13, 2923.161 [2923.16.1], 2925.02, 2925.03, 2925.11, 2925.13, 2925.22, 2925.23, or 3716.11 of the Revised Code;

(b) An existing or former law of this state, any other state, or the United States that is substantially equivalent to any of the offenses listed in division (A)(3)(a) of this section.

(4) On receipt of a request pursuant to section 3701.881 [3701.88.1] of the Revised Code with respect to an applicant for employment with a home health agency as a person responsible for the care, custody, or control of a child, a completed form prescribed pursuant to division (C)(1) of this section, and a set of fingerprint impressions obtained in the manner described in division (C)(2) of this section, the superintendent of the bureau of criminal identification and investigation shall conduct a criminal records check. The superintendent shall conduct the criminal records check in the manner described in division (B) of this section to determine whether any information exists that indicates that the person who is the subject of the request previously has been convicted of or pleaded guilty to any of the following:

(a) A violation of section 2903.01, 2903.02, 2903.03, 2903.04, 2903.11, 2903.12, 2903.13, 2903.16, 2903.21, 2903.34, 2905.01, 2905.02, 2905.04†, 2905.05, 2907.02, 2907.03, 2907.04, 2907.05, 2907.06, 2907.07, 2907.08, 2907.09, 2907.12††, 2907.21, 2907.22, 2907.23, 2907.25, 2907.31, 2907.32, 2907.321 [2907.32.1], 2907.322 [2907.32.2], 2907.323 [2907.32.3], 2911.01, 2911.02, 2911.11, 2911.12, 2919.12, 2919.22, 2919.24, 2919.25, 2923.12, 2923.13, 2923.161 [2923.16.1], 2925.02, 2925.03, 2925.04, 2925.05, 2925.06, or 3716.11 of the Revised Code or a violation of section 2925.11 of the Revised Code that is not a minor drug possession offense;

(b) An existing or former law of this state, any other state, or the United States that is substantially equivalent to any of the offenses listed in division (A)(4)(a) of this section.

(5) On receipt of a request pursuant to section 3701.881 [3701.88.1] of the Revised Code with respect to an applicant for employment with a home health agency in a position that involves providing direct care to an older adult, a completed form prescribed pursuant to division (C)(1) of this section, and a set of fingerprint impressions obtained in the manner described in division (C)(2) of this section, the superintendent of the bureau of criminal identification and investigation shall conduct a criminal records check. The superintendent shall conduct the criminal records check in the manner described in division (B) of this section to determine whether any information exists that indicates that the person who is the subject of the request previously has been convicted of or pleaded guilty to any of the following:

(a) A violation of section 2903.01, 2903.02, 2903.03, 2903.04, 2903.11, 2903.12, 2903.13, 2903.16, 2903.21, 2903.34, 2905.01, 2905.02, 2905.11, 2905.12, 2907.02, 2907.03, 2907.05, 2907.06, 2907.07, 2907.08, 2907.09, 2907.12††, 2907.25, 2907.31, 2907.32, 2907.321 [2907.32.1], 2907.322 [2907.32.2], 2907.323 [2907.32.3], 2911.01, 2911.02, 2911.11, 2911.12, 2911.13, 2913.02, 2913.03, 2913.04, 2913.11, 2913.21, 2913.31, 2913.40, 2913.43, 2913.47, 2913.51, 2919.25, 2921.36, 2923.12, 2923.13, 2923.161 [2923.16.1], 2925.02, 2925.03, 2925.11, 2925.13, 2925.22, 2925.23, or 3716.11 of the Revised Code;

(b) An existing or former law of this state, any other state, or the United States that is substantially equivalent to any of the offenses listed in division (A)(5)(a) of this section.

(6) When conducting a criminal records check upon a request pursuant to section 3319.39 of the Revised Code for an applicant who is a teacher, the superintendent shall determine whether any information exists that indicates that the person who is the subject of the request previously has been convicted of or pleaded guilty to any offense specified in section 3319.31 of the Revised Code.

(7) Not later than thirty days after the date the superintendent receives the request, completed form, and fingerprint impressions, the superintendent shall send the person who made the request any information, other than information the dissemination of which is prohibited by federal law, the superintendent determines exists with respect to the person who is the subject of the request that indicates that the person previously has been convicted of or pleaded guilty to any offense listed or described in division (A)(1), (2), (3), (4), or (5) of this section. The superintendent shall send the person who made the request a copy of the list of offenses specified in division (A)(1), (2), (3), (4), or (5) of this section. If the request was made under section 3701.881 [3701.88.1] of the Revised Code with regard to an applicant who may be both responsible for the care, custody, or control of a child and involved in providing direct care to an older adult, the superintendent shall provide a list of the offenses specified in divisions (A)(4) and (5) of this section.

(B) The superintendent shall conduct any criminal records check requested under section 173.41, 2151.86, 3301.32, 3301.541 [3301.54.1], 3319.39, 3701.881

[3701.88.1], 3712.09, 3721.121 [3721.12.1], 3722.151 [3722.15.1], 5104.012 [5104.01.2], 5104.013 [5104.01.-3], 5126.28, 5126.281 [5126.28.1], or 5153.111 [5153.11.1] of the Revised Code as follows:

(1) The superintendent shall review or cause to be reviewed any relevant information gathered and compiled by the bureau under division (A) of section 109.57 of the Revised Code that relates to the person who is the subject of the request, including any relevant information contained in records that have been sealed under section 2953.32 of the Revised Code;

(2) If the request received by the superintendent asks for information from the federal bureau of investigation, the superintendent shall request from the federal bureau of investigation any information it has with respect to the person who is the subject of the request and shall review or cause to be reviewed any information the superintendent receives from that bureau.

(C)(1) The superintendent shall prescribe a form to obtain the information necessary to conduct a criminal records check from any person for whom a criminal records check is required by section 173.41, 2151.86, 3301.32, 3301.541 [3301.54.1], 3319.39, 3701.881 [3701.88.1], 3712.09, 3721.121 [3721.12.1], 3722.151 [3722.15.1], 5104.012 [5104.01.2], 5104.013 [5104.01.-3], 5126.28, 5126.281 [5126.28.1], or 5153.111 [5153.11.1] of the Revised Code.

(2) The superintendent shall prescribe standard impression sheets to obtain the fingerprint impressions of any person for whom a criminal records check is required by section 173.41, 2151.86, 3301.32, 3301.541 [3301.54.1], 3319.39, 3701.881 [3701.88.1], 3712.09, 3721.121 [3721.12.1], 3722.151 [3722.15.1], 5104.012 [5104.01.2], 5104.013 [5104.01.3], 5126.28, 5126.281 [5126.28.1], or 5153.111 [5153.11.1] of the Revised Code. Any person for whom a records check is required by any of those sections shall obtain the fingerprint impressions at a county sheriff's office, municipal police department, or any other entity with the ability to make fingerprint impressions on the standard impression sheets prescribed by the superintendent. The office, department, or entity may charge the person a reasonable fee for making the impressions.

(3) Subject to division (D) of this section, the superintendent shall prescribe and charge a reasonable fee for providing a criminal records check requested under section 173.41, 2151.86, 3301.32, 3301.541 [3301.54.1], 3319.39, 3701.881 [3701.88.1], 3712.09, 3721.121 [3721.12.1], 3722.151 [3722.15.1], 5104.012 [5104.01.-2], 5104.013 [5104.01.3], 5126.28, 5126.281 [5126.28.1], or 5153.111 [5153.11.1] of the Revised Code. The person making a criminal records request under section 173.41, 2151.86, 3301.32, 3301.541 [3301.54.1], 3319.-39, 3701.881 [3701.88.1], 3712.09, 3721.121 [3721.12.-1], 3722.151 [3722.15.1], 5104.012 [5104.01.2], 5104.-013 [5104.01.3], 5126.28, 5126.281 [5126.28.1], or 5153.111 [5153.11.1] of the Revised Code shall pay the fee prescribed pursuant to this division. A person making a request under section 3701.881 [3701.88.1] of the Revised Code for a criminal records check for an applicant who may be both responsible for the care, custody, or control of a child and involved in providing direct care to an older adult shall pay one fee for the request.

(D) A determination whether any information exists that indicates that a person previously has been convicted of or pleaded guilty to any offense listed or described in division (A)(1)(a) or (b), (A)(2)(a) or (b), (A)(3)(a) or (b), (A)(4)(a) or (b), or (A)(5)(a) or (b) of this section that is made by the superintendent with respect to information considered in a criminal records check in accordance with this section is valid for the person who is the subject of the criminal records check for a period of one year from the date upon which the superintendent makes the determination. During the period in which the determination in regard to a person is valid, if another request under this section is made for a criminal records check for that person, the superintendent shall provide the information that is the basis for the superintendent's initial determination at a lower fee than the fee prescribed for the initial criminal records check.

(E) As used in this section:

(1) "Criminal records check" means any criminal records check conducted by the superintendent of the bureau of criminal identification and investigation in accordance with division (B) of this section.

(2) "Minor drug possession offense" has the same meaning as in section 2925.01 of the Revised Code.

(3) "Older adult" means a person age sixty or older.

HISTORY: 145 v S 38 (Eff 10-29-93); 145 v H 694 (Eff 11-11-94); 146 v S 2 (Eff 7-1-96); 146 v S 269 (Eff 7-1-96); 146 v H 445 (Eff 9-3-96); 146 v S 160 (Eff 1-27-97); 147 v S 96. Eff 6-11-97.

† RC § 2905.04 repealed 7-1-96.

†† RC § 2907.12 repealed 9-3-96.

The provisions of §§ 7, 8 of SB 96 (147 v —) read as follows:

SECTION 7. Sections 109.572 ° ° ° of the Revised Code are presented in this act as composites of those sections as amended by Am. Sub. H.B. 445, Am. Sub. H.B. [S.B.] 269, and Am. Sub. S.B. 160 of the 121st General Assembly, with the new language of none of the acts shown in capital letters. This is in recognition of the principle stated in division (B) of section 1.52 of the Revised Code that such amendments are to be harmonized where not substantively irreconcilable and constitutes a legislative finding that such is the resulting version in effect prior to the effective date of this act.

SECTION 8. The amendments made by this act to sections 109.572, 173.41, 3701.881, 3712.09, 3721.121, and 3722.151 of the Revised Code do not supersede Section 3 of Am. Sub. S.B. 160 of the 121st General Assembly, which provides that those sections as amended and enacted by Am. Sub. S.B. 160 apply only to persons who apply for employment on or after January 27, 1997, the effective date of Am. Sub. S.B. 160 of the 121st General Assembly.

See provisions, § 3 of SB 160 (146 v —) following RC § 109.57.

[§ 109.57.3] § 109.573 DNA laboratory and database may be established; disclosure of information.

(A) As used in this section:

(1) "DNA" means human deoxyribonucleic acid.

(2) "DNA analysis" means a laboratory analysis of a DNA specimen to identify DNA characteristics and to create a DNA record.

(3) "DNA database" means a collection of DNA records from forensic casework or from crime scenes, specimens from anonymous and unidentified sources, and records collected pursuant to sections 2151.315 [2151.31.5] and 2901.07 of the Revised Code and a population statistics database for determining the frequency of occurrence of characteristics in DNA records.

(4) "DNA record" means the objective result of a DNA analysis of a DNA specimen, including representations of DNA fragment lengths, digital images of autoradiographs, discrete allele assignment numbers, and other DNA specimen characteristics that aid in establishing the identity of an individual.

(5) "DNA specimen" includes human blood cells or physiological tissues or body fluids.

(6) "Unidentified person database" means a collection of DNA records of unidentified human corpses, human remains, or living individuals.

(7) "Law enforcement agency" means a police department, the office of a sheriff, the state highway patrol, a county prosecuting attorney, or a federal, state, or local governmental body that enforces criminal laws and that has employees who have a statutory power of arrest.

(B)(1) The superintendent of the bureau of criminal identification and investigation may do all of the following:

(a) Establish and maintain a state DNA laboratory to perform DNA analysis of DNA specimens;

(b) Establish and maintain a DNA database;

(c) Establish and maintain an unidentified person database to aid in the establishment of the identity of unknown human corpses, human remains, or living individuals.

(2) If the bureau of criminal identification and investigation establishes and maintains a DNA laboratory and a DNA database, the bureau may use or disclose information regarding DNA records for the following purposes:

(a) The bureau may disclose information to a law enforcement agency for purposes of identification.

(b) The bureau shall disclose pursuant to a court order issued under section 3111.09 of the Revised Code any information necessary to determine the existence of a parent and child relationship in an action brought under sections 3111.01 to 3111.19 of the Revised Code.

(c) The bureau may use or disclose information from the population statistics database, for identification research and protocol development, or for quality control purposes.

(3) The bureau of criminal identification and investigation may enter into a contract with a qualified public or private laboratory to perform DNA analyses, DNA specimen maintenance, preservation, and storage, DNA record keeping, and other duties required of the bureau under this section. A public or private laboratory under contract with the bureau shall follow quality assurance and privacy requirements established by the superintendent of the bureau.

(C) The superintendent of the bureau of criminal identification and investigation shall establish procedures for entering into the DNA database the DNA records submitted pursuant to sections 2151.315 [2151.31.5] and 2901.07 of the Revised Code and for determining an order of priority for entry of the DNA records based on the types of offenses committed by the persons whose records are submitted and the available resources of the bureau.

(D) When a DNA record is derived from a DNA specimen provided pursuant to section 2151.315 [2151.31.5] or 2901.07 of the Revised Code, the bureau of criminal identification and investigation shall attach to the DNA record personal identification information that identifies the person from whom the DNA specimen was taken. The personal identification information may include the subject person's fingerprints and any other information the bureau determines necessary. The DNA record and personal identification information attached to it shall be used only for the purpose of personal identification or for a purpose specified in this section.

(E) DNA records and DNA specimens that the bureau receives pursuant to this section and sections 2151.315 [2151.31.5] and 2901.07 of the Revised Code and personal identification information attached to a DNA record are not public records under section 149.43 of the Revised Code.

(F) The bureau of criminal identification and investigation may charge a reasonable fee for providing information pursuant to this section to any law enforcement agency located in another state.

(G)(1) No person who because of the person's employment or official position has access to a DNA specimen, a DNA record, or other information contained in the DNA database that identifies an individual shall knowingly disclose that specimen, record, or information to any person or agency not entitled to receive it or otherwise shall misuse that specimen, record, or information.

(2) No person without authorization or privilege to obtain information contained in the DNA database that identifies an individual person shall purposely obtain that information.

(H) The superintendent of the bureau of criminal identification and investigation shall establish procedures for all of the following:

(1) The forwarding of DNA specimens collected pursuant to sections 2151.315 [2151.31.5] and 2901.07 of the Revised Code to the bureau;

(2) The collection, maintenance, preservation, and analysis of DNA specimens;

(3) The creation, maintenance, and operation of the DNA database;

(4) The use and dissemination of information from the DNA database;

(5) The verification of entities requesting DNA records and other DNA information from the bureau and the authority of the entity to receive the information;

(6) The operation of the bureau and responsibilities of employees of the bureau with respect to the activities described in this section.

HISTORY: 146 v H 5 (Eff 8-30-95); 146 v H 124. Eff 3-31-97.

§ 109.58 Superintendent shall prepare a standard fingerprint impression sheet.

The superintendent of the bureau of criminal identification and investigation shall prepare standard impression sheets on which fingerprints may be made in accordance with the fingerprint system of identification. The impression sheets may provide for other descriptive matter that the superintendent may prescribe. The impression sheets shall be furnished to each sheriff, chief of police, and person in charge of every workhouse or state correctional institution within the state. Upon the request of the board of education of a school district or of the principal or chief administrative officer of a nonpublic school, the superintendent shall provide standard impression sheets to the district or school for use in their fingerprinting programs under section 3313.96 of the Revised Code.

HISTORY: 130 v 11 (Eff 9-24-63); 140 v S 321 (Eff 4-9-85); 145 v H 571. Eff 10-6-94.

[§§ 109.58.1, 109.58.2]
§§ 109.581, 109.582 Repealed, 146 v H 670, § 2 [143 v H 271]. Eff 12-2-96.

These sections created the automated fingerprint identification system and advisory council.

§ 109.59 Fingerprint impression and descriptive measurement records.

The sheriff, chief of police, or other person in charge of each prison, workhouse, or state correctional institution shall send to the bureau of criminal identification and investigation, on forms furnished by the superintendent of the bureau, any fingerprint impressions and other descriptive measurements that the superintendent may require. The information shall be filed, classified, and preserved by the bureau.

HISTORY: 130 v 11 (Eff 9-24-63); 145 v H 571. Eff 10-6-94.

§ 109.60 Duty of sheriffs and police chiefs to take and forward fingerprints and descriptions.

(A) As used in this section, "designated delinquent act or juvenile offense" has the same meaning as in section 109.57 of the Revised Code.

(B) The sheriffs of the several counties and the chiefs of police of cities, immediately upon the arrest of any person for any felony, on suspicion of any felony, or for a crime constituting a misdemeanor on the first offense and a felony on subsequent offenses, and immediately upon the arrest or taking into custody of any child fourteen years of age or older and under eighteen years of age for committing a designated delinquent act or juvenile offense or upon probable cause to believe that a child of that age may have committed a designated delinquent act or juvenile offense, shall take the person's or child's fingerprints, or cause the same to be taken, according to the fingerprint system of identification on the forms furnished by the superintendent of the bureau of criminal identification and investigation, and forward them, together with any other description that may be required and with the history of the offense committed, to the bureau to be classified and filed. If an accused is found not guilty of the offense charged or a nolle prosequi is entered in any case, or if any accused child fourteen years of age or older and under eighteen years of age is found not to be a delinquent child for committing a designated delinquent act or juvenile offense or not guilty of the designated delinquent act or juvenile offense charged or a nolle prosequi is entered in that case, the fingerprints and description shall be given to the accused upon the accused's request. The superintendent shall compare the description received with those already on file in the bureau, and, if the superintendent finds that the person arrested or taken into custody has a criminal record or a record as a delinquent child for having committed an act that is a designated delinquent act or juvenile offense or is a fugitive from justice or wanted by any jurisdiction in this or another state, the United States, or a foreign country for any offense, the superintendent at once shall inform the arresting officer or the officer taking the person into custody of that fact and give appropriate notice to the proper authorities in the jurisdiction in which the person is wanted, or, if that jurisdiction is a foreign country, give appropriate notice to federal authorities for transmission to the foreign country. The names, under which each person whose identification is filed is known, shall be alphabetically indexed by the superintendent.

(C) This section does not apply to a violator of a city ordinance unless the officers have reason to believe that the violator is a past offender or the crime is one constituting a misdemeanor on the first offense and a felony on subsequent offenses, or unless it is advisable for the purpose of subsequent identification. This section does not apply to any child under eighteen years of age who was not arrested or otherwise taken into custody for committing an act that is a designated delinquent act or juvenile offense or upon probable cause to believe that a child of that age may have committed an act that is a designated delinquent act or juvenile offense, except as provided in section 2151.313 [2151.31.3] of the Revised Code.

HISTORY: 130 v 12 (Eff 9-24-63); 133 v H 956 (Eff 9-16-70); 137 v S 170 (Eff 11-16-77); 146 v H 1 (Eff 1-1-96); 146 v H 124. Eff 3-31-97.

§ 109.61 Duty of sheriffs and police chiefs to send descriptions, fingerprints, photographs and measurements to bureau.

Each sheriff or chief of police shall furnish the bureau of criminal identification and investigation with descriptions, fingerprints, photographs, and measurements of the following:

(A)(1) Persons arrested who in that sheriff's or chief of police's judgment are wanted for serious offenses, are fugitives from justice, or in whose possession at the time of arrest are found goods or property reasonably believed to have been stolen;

(2) Children arrested or otherwise taken into custody who in that sheriff's or chief of police's judgment are fourteen years of age or older and under eighteen years of age and have committed an act that is a designated delinquent act or juvenile offense, as defined in section 109.57 of the Revised Code;

(B) All persons in whose possession are found burglar outfits, burglar tools, or burglar keys, or who have in their possession high power explosives reasonably believed to be intended to be used for unlawful purposes;

(C) Persons who are in possession of infernal machines or other contrivances in whole or in part and reasonably believed by the sheriff or chief of police to be intended to be used for unlawful purposes;

(D) All persons carrying concealed firearms or other deadly weapons reasonably believed to be carried for unlawful purposes;

(E) All persons who have in their possession inks, dies, paper, or other articles necessary in the making of counterfeit bank notes or in the alteration of bank notes, or dies, molds, or other articles necessary in the making of counterfeit money and reasonably believed to be intended to be used by them for those types of unlawful purposes.

HISTORY: 130 v 12 (Eff 9-24-63); 146 v H 1 (Eff 1-1-96); 146 v H 124. Eff 3-31-97.

§ 109.62 Interstate, national, and international cooperation.

The superintendent of the bureau of criminal identification and investigation shall co-operate with bureaus in other states and with the federal bureau of investigation to develop and carry on a complete interstate, national, and international system of criminal identification and investigation.

HISTORY: 130 v 12. Eff 9-24-63.

§ 109.63 Superintendent of bureau and assistants may testify in court.

The superintendent of the bureau of criminal identification and investigation and his assistants employed in accordance with section 109.51 of the Revised Code may testify in any court in this state to the same extent as any law enforcement officer in this state.

HISTORY: 130 v 12. Eff 9-24-63.

§ 109.64 Periodic information bulletins concerning missing children.

The bureau of criminal identification and investigation shall prepare a periodic information bulletin concerning missing children whom it determines may be present in this state. The bureau shall compile the bulletin from information contained in the national crime information center computer. The bulletin shall indicate the names and addresses of these minors who are the subject of missing children cases and other information that the superintendent of the bureau considers appropriate. The bulletin shall contain a reminder to law enforcement agencies of their responsibilities under section 2901.30 of the Revised Code.

The bureau shall send a copy of each periodic information bulletin to the missing children clearinghouse established under section 109.65 of the Revised Code for use in connection with its responsibilities under division (E) of that section. Upon receipt of each periodic information bulletin from the bureau, the missing children clearinghouse shall send a copy of the bulletin to each sheriff, marshal, police department of a municipal corporation, police force of a township police district or joint township police district, and township constable in this state, to the board of education of each school district in this state, and to each nonpublic school in this state. The bureau shall provide a copy of the bulletin, upon request, to other persons or entities. The superintendent of the bureau, with the approval of the attorney general, may establish a reasonable fee for a copy of a bulletin provided to persons or entities other than law enforcement agencies in this or other states or of the federal government, the department of education, governmental entities of this state, and libraries in this state. The superintendent shall deposit all fees collected by him into the missing children fund created by section 109.65 of the Revised Code.

As used in this section, "missing children," "information," and "minor" have the same meanings as in section 2901.30 of the Revised Code.

HISTORY: 140 v S 321 (Eff 4-9-85); 145 v S 63. Eff 10-1-93.

§ 109.65 Missing children clearinghouse; educational program; fund.

(A) As used in this section, "minor," "missing child," and "missing children" have the same meanings as in section 2901.30 of the Revised Code.

(B) There is hereby created within the office of the attorney general the missing children clearinghouse. The attorney general shall administer the clearinghouse. The clearinghouse is established as a central repository of information to coordinate and improve the availability of information regarding missing children, which information shall be collected and disseminated by the clearinghouse to assist in the location of missing children. The clearinghouse shall act as an information repository separate from and in addition to law enforcement agencies within this state.

(C) The missing children clearinghouse may perform any of the following functions:

(1) The establishment of services to aid in the location of missing children that include, but are not limited to, any of the following services:

(a) Assistance in the preparation and dissemination of flyers identifying and describing missing children and their abductors;

(b) The development of informational forms for the reporting of missing children that may be used by parents, guardians, and law enforcement officials to facilitate the location of a missing child;

(c) The provision of assistance to public and private organizations, boards of education, nonpublic schools, preschools, child care facilities, and law enforcement agencies in planning and implementing voluntary programs to fingerprint children.

(2) The establishment and operation of a toll-free telephone line for supplemental reports of missing children and reports of sightings of missing children;

(3) Upon the request of any person or entity and upon payment of any applicable fee established by the attorney general under division (H) of this section, the provision to the person or entity who makes the request of a copy of any information possessed by the clearinghouse that was acquired or prepared pursuant to division (E)(3) of this section;

(4) The performance of liaison services between individuals and public and private agencies regarding procedures for handling and responding to missing children reports;

(5) The participation as a member in any networks of other missing children centers or clearinghouses;

(6) The creation and operation of an intrastate network of communication designed for the speedy collection and processing of information concerning missing children.

(D) If a board of education is notified by school personnel that a missing child is attending any school under the board's jurisdiction, or if the principal or chief administrative officer of a nonpublic school is notified by school personnel that a missing child is attending that school, the board or the principal or chief administrative officer immediately shall give notice of that fact to the missing children clearinghouse and to the law enforcement agency with jurisdiction over the area where the missing child resides.

(E)(1) The attorney general, in cooperation with the department of human services, shall establish a "missing child educational program" within the missing children clearinghouse that shall perform the functions specified in divisions (E)(1) to (3) of this section. The program shall operate under the supervision and control of the attorney general in accordance with procedures that the attorney general shall develop to implement divisions (E)(1) to (3) of this section. The attorney general shall cooperate with the department of education in developing and disseminating information acquired or prepared pursuant to division (E)(3) of this section.

(2) Upon the request of any board of education in this state or any nonpublic school in this state, the missing child educational program shall provide to the board or school a reasonable number of copies of the information acquired or prepared pursuant to division (E)(3) of this section.

Upon the request of any board of education in this state or any nonpublic school in this state that, pursuant to section 3313.96 of the Revised Code, is developing an information program concerning missing children issues and matters, the missing child educational program shall provide to the board or nonpublic school assistance in developing the information program. The assistance may include, but is not limited to, the provision of any or all of the following:

(a) If the requesting entity is a board of education of a school district, sample policies on missing and exploited children issues to assist the board in complying with section 3313.205 [3313.20.5] of the Revised Code;

(b) Suggested safety curricula regarding missing children issues, including child safety and abduction prevention issues;

(c) Assistance in developing, with local law enforcement agencies, prosecuting attorneys, boards of education, school districts, and nonpublic schools, cooperative programs for fingerprinting children;

(d) Other assistance to further the goals of the program.

(3) The missing child educational program shall acquire or prepare informational materials relating to missing children issues and matters. These issues and matters include, but are not limited to, the following:

(a) The types of missing children;

(b) The reasons why and how minors become missing children, the potential adverse consequences of a minor becoming a missing child, and, in the case of minors who are considering running away from home or from the care, custody, and control of their parents, parent who is the residential parent and legal custodian, guardian, legal custodian, or another person responsible for them, alternatives that may be available to address their concerns and problems;

(c) Offenses under federal law that could relate to missing children and other provisions of federal law that focus on missing children;

(d) Offenses under the Revised Code that could relate to missing children, including, but not limited to, kidnapping, abduction, unlawful restraint, child stealing, interference with custody, endangering children, domestic violence, abuse of a child and contributing to the dependency, neglect, unruliness, or delinquency of a child, sexual offenses, drug offenses, prostitution offenses, and obscenity offenses, and other provisions of the Revised Code that could relate to missing children;

(e) Legislation being considered by the general assembly, legislatures of other states, the congress of the United States, and political subdivisions in this or any other state to address missing children issues;

(f) Sources of information on missing children issues;

(g) State, local, federal, and private systems for locating and identifying missing children;

(h) Law enforcement agency programs, responsibilities, and investigative techniques in missing children matters;

(i) Efforts on the community level in this and other states, concerning missing children issues and matters, by governmental entities and private organizations;

(j) The identification of private organizations that, among their primary objectives, address missing children issues and matters;

(k) How to avoid becoming a missing child and what to do if one becomes a missing child;

(l) Efforts that schools, parents, and members of a community can undertake to reduce the risk that a minor will become a missing child and to quickly locate or identify a minor if he becomes a missing child, including, but not limited to, fingerprinting programs.

(F) Each year the missing children clearinghouse shall issue a report describing its performance of the functions specified in division (E) of this section and shall provide a copy of the report to the speaker of the house of representatives, the president of the senate, the governor, the superintendent of the bureau of criminal identification and investigation, and the director of human services.

(G) Any state agency or political subdivision of this state that operates a missing children program or a clearinghouse for information about missing children shall coordinate its activities with the missing children clearinghouse.

(H) The attorney general shall determine a reasonable fee to be charged for providing to any person or entity other than a state or local law enforcement agency of this or any other state, a law enforcement agency of the United States, a board of education of a school district in this state, a nonpublic school in this state, a governmental entity in this state, or a public library in this state, pursuant to division (A)(3) of this section, copies of any information acquired or prepared pursuant to division (E)(3) of this section. The attorney general shall collect the fee prior to sending or giving copies of any information to any person or entity for whom or which this division requires the fee to be charged and shall deposit the fee into the missing children fund created by division (I) of this section.

(I) There is hereby created in the state treasury the missing children fund that shall consist of all moneys awarded to the state by donation, gift, or bequest, all other moneys received for purposes of this section, and all fees collected pursuant to this section or section 109.64 of the Revised Code. The attorney general shall use the moneys in the missing children fund only for purposes of the office of the attorney general acquiring or preparing information pursuant to division (E)(3) of this section.

(J) The failure of the missing children clearinghouse to undertake any function or activity authorized in this section does not create a cause of action against the state.

HISTORY: RC § 3301.25, 140 v S 321 (Eff 4-9-85); 142 v H 231 (Eff 10-5-87); 143 v S 3 (Eff 4-11-91); RC § 109.65, 145 v S 63. Eff 10-1-93.

The provisions of § 3 of SB 63 (145 v —) read as follows:

SECTION 3. (A) There hereby is transferred to the Attorney General all books, records, documents, files, transcripts, and other materials pertaining to the Missing Child Educational Program in existence prior to the effective date of this act that are in the possession of the Department of Education, as they existed immediately prior to the effective date of this act.

(B) All moneys appropriated or reappropriated to the Department of Education or the Superintendent of Public Instruction for the performance of the duties, powers, obligations, and functions, and the exercise of the rights, that are transferred by this act to the Attorney General, or that are segregated to the Department of Education or Superintendent of Public Education pursuant to law, to the extent of the remaining unexpended or unencumbered balance of the appropriations or reappropriations, whether allocated or unallocated and whether obligated or unobligated, are hereby transferred to the Attorney General for performing the same duties, powers, obligations, and functions and exercising the rights for which the moneys originally were appropriated or reappropriated. Payments for liabilities for expenses of personal service, maintenance, and operation incurred before or after the effective date of this act shall be made on separate vouchers or certificates approved by the Attorney General.

(C) All rules, acts, determinations, approvals, and decisions of the Department of Education or the Superintendent of Public Instruction pertaining to the duties, powers, obligations, and functions that are transferred and assigned by this act to the Attorney General and that are in effect at the time of the transfer shall continue in force as rules, acts, determinations, approvals, and decisions of the Department of Education or the Superintendent of Public Instruction until they are duly modified, superseded, or repealed by the Attorney General, as appropriate.

Whenever the duties, powers, obligations, and functions of the Department of Education or the Superintendent of Public Instruction that are transferred by this act to the Attorney General are referred to or designated in any law, contract, or other document pertaining to those duties, powers, obligations, or functions, the reference or designation shall be considered, as appropriate, to be a reference or designation to the Attorney General and to the duties, powers, obligations, and functions as transferred to him.

No existing right or remedy of any character shall be lost, impaired, or affected by reason of this act, except insofar as that remedy or right shall be administered, as appropriate, by the Attorney General instead of by the Department of Education and the Superintendent of Public Instruction.

[OHIO PEACE OFFICER TRAINING COMMISSION]

§ 109.71 Creation of Ohio peace officer training commission; members; definition of peace officer.

There is hereby created in the office of the attorney general the Ohio peace officer training commission. The commission shall consist of nine members appointed by the governor with the advice and consent of the senate and selected as follows: one member representing the public; two members who are incumbent sheriffs; two members who are incumbent chiefs of police; one member from the bureau of criminal identification and investigation; one member from the state highway patrol; one member who is the special agent in charge of a field office of the federal bureau of investigation in this state; and one member from the department of education, trade and industrial education services, law enforcement training.

As used in sections 109.71 to 109.77 of the Revised Code:

(A) "Peace officer" means:

(1) A deputy sheriff, marshal, deputy marshal, member of the organized police department of a township or municipal corporation, member of a township police district or joint township police district police force, member of a police force employed by a metropolitan housing authority under division (D) of section 3735.31 of the Revised Code, or township constable, who is commissioned and employed as a peace officer by a political subdivision of this state or by a metropolitan housing authority, and whose primary duties are to preserve the peace, to protect life and property, and to enforce the laws of this state, ordinances of a municipal corporation, resolutions of a township, or regulations of a board of county commissioners or board of township trustees, or any such laws, ordinances, resolutions, or regulations;

(2) A police officer who is employed by a railroad company and appointed and commissioned by the governor pursuant to sections 4973.17 to 4973.22 of the Revised Code;

(3) Employees of the department of taxation engaged in the enforcement of Chapter 5743. of the Revised Code and designated by the tax commissioner for peace officer training for purposes of the delegation of investigation powers under section 5743.45 of the Revised Code;

(4) An undercover drug agent;

(5) Liquor control investigators of the department of public safety engaged in the enforcement of Chapters 4301. and 4303. of the Revised Code;

(6) An employee of the department of natural resources who is a park officer designated pursuant to section 1541.10, a forest officer designated pursuant to section 1503.29, a preserve officer designated pursuant to section 1517.10, a wildlife officer designated pursuant to section 1531.13, or a state watercraft officer designated pursuant to section 1547.521 [1547.52.1] of the Revised Code;

(7) An employee of a park district who is designated pursuant to section 511.232 [511.23.2] or 1545.13 of the Revised Code;

(8) An employee of a conservancy district who is designated pursuant to section 6101.75 of the Revised Code;

(9) A police officer who is employed by a hospital that employs and maintains its own proprietary police department or security department, and who is appointed and commissioned by the governor pursuant to sections 4973.17 to 4973.22 of the Revised Code;

(10) Ohio veterans' home police officers designated under section 5907.02 of the Revised Code;

(11) A police officer who is employed by a qualified nonprofit corporation police department pursuant to section 1702.80 of the Revised Code;

(12) A state university law enforcement officer appointed under section 3345.04 of the Revised Code or a person serving as a state university law enforcement officer on a permanent basis on June 19, 1978, who has been awarded a certificate by the executive director of the Ohio peace officer training council† attesting to the person's satisfactory completion of an approved state, county, municipal, or department of natural resources peace officer basic training program;

(13) A special police officer employed by the department of mental health pursuant to section 5119.14 of the Revised Code or the department of mental retardation and developmental disabilities pursuant to section 5123.13 of the Revised Code;

(14) A member of a campus police department appointed under section 1713.50 of the Revised Code;

(15) A member of a police force employed by a regional transit authority under division (Y) of section 306.35 of the Revised Code.

(16) Food stamp trafficking agents of the department of public safety designated under section 5502.14 of the Revised Code;

(17) Investigators appointed by the auditor of state pursuant to section 117.091 [117.09.1] of the Revised Code and engaged in the enforcement of Chapter 117. of the Revised Code;

(18) A special police officer designated by the superintendent of the state highway patrol pursuant to section 5503.09 of the Revised Code.

(B) "Undercover drug agent" has the same meaning as in division (B)(2) of section 109.79 of the Revised Code.

(C) "Crisis intervention training" means training in the use of interpersonal and communication skills to most effectively and sensitively interview victims of rape.

(D) "Missing children" has the same meaning as in section 2901.30 of the Revised Code.

HISTORY: 142 v H 708 (Eff 4-19-88); 143 v H 110 (Eff 5-31-90); 143 v H 271 (Eff 4-10-91); 143 v H 669 (Eff 1-10-91); 144 v H 77 (Eff 9-17-91); 144 v S 49 (Eff 7-21-92); 144 v H 758 (Eff 1-15-93); 145 v S 182 (Eff 10-20-94); 146 v S 162 (Eff 10-29-95); 146 v S 2 (Eff 7-1-96); 146 v H 445 (Eff 9-3-96); 146 v H 670 (Eff 12-2-96); 146 v H 351 (Eff 1-14-97); 146 v S 285 (Eff 3-13-97); 147 v S 60. Eff 10-21-97.

† So in enrolled bill, division (A)(12), as set out by SB 285 (146 v —). Was "commission" intended? See HB 670 (146 v —) version.

Comment, Legislative Service Commission

Section 109.71 of the Revised Code is presented in this act [SB 60] as a composite of the section as amended by Sub. H.B. 351, Sub. H.B. 670, and Am. Sub. S.B. 285 of the 121st General Assembly, with the new language of none of the acts shown in capital letters. ° ° ° This is in recognition of the principle stated in division (B) of section 1.52 of the Revised Code that such amendments are to be harmonized where not substantively irreconcilable and constitutes a legislative finding that such is the resulting version in effect prior to the effective date of this act.

§ 109.72 Terms of members; meetings.

Ohio peace officer training commission member terms shall be for three years, commencing on the twentieth day of September and ending on the nineteenth day of September. Each member shall hold office from the date of appointment until the end of the term to which the member was appointed. Any member appointed to fill a vacancy occurring prior to the expiration of the term for which the member's predecessor was appointed shall hold office for the remainder of such term. Any member shall continue in office subsequent to the expiration date of the member's term until the member's successor takes office, or until a period of sixty days has elapsed, whichever occurs first. An interim chairperson shall be appointed by the governor until such time as the commission elects a permanent chairperson.

Any member of the commission appointed pursuant to section 109.71 of the Revised Code as an incumbent sheriff, incumbent chief of police, representative of the state highway patrol, state department of education, federal bureau of investigation, and bureau of criminal identification and investigation, shall immediately, upon termination of holding such office, cease to be a member of the commission, and a successor shall be appointed.

The commission shall meet at least four times each year. Special meetings may be called by the chairperson and shall be called by the chairperson at the request of the attorney general or upon the written request of five members of the commission. The commission may establish its own requirements as to quorum and its own procedures with respect to the conduct of its meetings and other affairs; provided, that all recommendations by the commission to the attorney general pursuant to section 109.74 of the Revised Code shall require the affirmative vote of five members of the commission.

Membership on the commission does not constitute the holding of an office, and members of the commission shall not be required to take and file oaths of office before serving on the commission. The commission shall not exercise any portion of the sovereign power of the state.

The members of the commission shall receive no compensation for their services but shall be allowed their actual and necessary expenses incurred in the performance of their duties.

No member of the commission shall be disqualified from holding any public office or employment, nor shall the member forfeit any such office or employment, by reason of appointment to the commission, notwithstanding any general, special, or local law, ordinance, or city charter to the contrary.

HISTORY: 131 v 8 (Eff 9-6-65); 135 v S 131 (Eff 8-21-73); 146 v H 670. Eff 12-2-96.

§ 109.73 Commission to recommend rules; executive director; powers.

(A) The Ohio peace officer training commission shall recommend rules to the attorney general with respect to all of the following:

(1) The approval, or revocation of approval, of peace officer training schools administered by the state, counties, municipal corporations, public school districts, technical college districts, and the department of natural resources;

(2) Minimum courses of study, attendance requirements, and equipment and facilities to be required at approved state, county, municipal, and department of natural resources peace officer training schools;

(3) Minimum qualifications for instructors at approved state, county, municipal, and department of natural resources peace officer training schools;

(4) The requirements of minimum basic training that peace officers appointed to probationary terms shall complete before being eligible for permanent appointment, which requirements shall include a minimum of fifteen hours of training in the handling of the offense of domestic violence, other types of domestic violence-related offenses and incidents, and protection orders and consent agreements issued or approved under section 2919.26 or 3113.31 of the Revised Code, a minimum of six hours of crisis intervention training, and a specified amount of training in the handling of missing children and child abuse and neglect cases, and the time within which such basic training shall be completed following such appointment to a probationary term;

(5) The requirements of minimum basic training that peace officers not appointed for probationary terms but appointed on other than a permanent basis shall complete in order to be eligible for continued employ-

ment or permanent appointment, which requirements shall include a minimum of fifteen hours of training in the handling of the offense of domestic violence, other types of domestic violence-related offenses and incidents, and protection orders and consent agreements issued or approved under section 2919.26 or 3113.31 of the Revised Code, a minimum of six hours of crisis intervention training, and a specified amount of training in the handling of missing children and child abuse and neglect cases, and the time within which such basic training shall be completed following such appointment on other than a permanent basis;

(6) Categories or classifications of advanced in-service training programs for peace officers, including programs in the handling of the offense of domestic violence, other types of domestic violence-related offenses and incidents, and protection orders and consent agreements issued or approved under section 2919.26 or 3113.31 of the Revised Code, in crisis intervention, and in the handling of missing children and child abuse and neglect cases, and minimum courses of study and attendance requirements with respect to such categories or classifications;

(7) Permitting persons who are employed as members of a campus police department appointed under section 1713.50 of the Revised Code, who are employed as police officers by a qualified nonprofit corporation police department pursuant to section 1702.80 of the Revised Code, or who are appointed and commissioned as railroad police officers or hospital police officers pursuant to sections 4973.17 to 4973.22 of the Revised Code to attend approved peace officer training schools, including the Ohio peace officer training academy, and to receive certificates of satisfactory completion of basic training programs, if the private college or university that established the campus police department, qualified nonprofit corporation police department, railroad company, or hospital sponsoring the police officers pays the entire cost of the training and certification and if trainee vacancies are available;

(8) Permitting undercover drug agents to attend approved peace officer training schools, other than the Ohio peace officer training academy, and to receive certificates of satisfactory completion of basic training programs, if, for each undercover drug agent, the county, township, or municipal corporation that employs that undercover drug agent pays the entire cost of the training and certification;

(9)(a) The requirements for basic training programs for bailiffs and deputy bailiffs of courts of record of this state and for criminal investigators employed by the state public defender that those persons shall complete before they may carry a firearm while on duty;

(b) The requirements for any training received by a bailiff or deputy bailiff of a court of record of this state or by a criminal investigator employed by the state public defender prior to June 6, 1986, that is to be considered equivalent to the training described in division (A)(9)(a) of this section.

(10) Establishing minimum qualifications and requirements for certification for dogs utilized by law enforcement agencies;

(11) Establishing minimum requirements for certification of persons who are employed as correction officers in a full-service jail, five-day facility, or eight-hour holding facility or who provide correction services in such a jail or facility.

(B) The commission shall appoint an executive director, with the approval of the attorney general, who shall hold office during the pleasure of the commission. The executive director shall perform such duties as may be assigned by the commission. The executive director shall receive a salary fixed pursuant to Chapter 124. of the Revised Code and reimbursement for expenses within the amounts available by appropriation. The executive director may appoint officers, employees, agents, and consultants as the executive director considers necessary, prescribe their duties, and provide for reimbursement of their expenses within the amounts available for reimbursement by appropriation and with the approval of the commission.

(C) The commission may do all of the following:

(1) Recommend studies, surveys, and reports to be made by the executive director regarding the carrying out of the objectives and purposes of sections 109.71 to 109.77 of the Revised Code;

(2) Visit and inspect any peace officer training school that has been approved by the executive director or for which application for approval has been made;

(3) Make recommendations, from time to time, to the executive director, the attorney general, and the general assembly regarding the carrying out of the purposes of sections 109.71 to 109.77 of the Revised Code;

(4) Report to the attorney general from time to time, and to the governor and the general assembly at least annually, concerning the activities of the commission;

(5) Establish fees for the services the commission offers under sections 109.71 to 109.79 of the Revised Code, including, but not limited to, fees for training, certification, and testing.

(6) Perform such other acts as are necessary or appropriate to carry out the powers and duties of the commission as set forth in sections 109.71 to 109.77 of the Revised Code.

HISTORY: 131 v 11 (Eff 9-6-65); 132 v H 93 (Eff 5-17-67); 134 v S 396 (Eff 2-17-72); 136 v S 272 (Eff 8-19-76); 137 v H 835 (Eff 3-27-79); 139 v H 44 (Eff 5-8-81); 140 v H 759 (Eff 3-28-85); 140 v H 435 (Eff 4-4-85); 140 v S 321 (Eff 4-9-85); 141 v S 149 (Eff 6-6-86); 141 v S 364 (Eff 3-17-87); 143 v H 110 (Eff 5-31-90); 143 v S 3 (Eff 4-11-91); 143 v H 669 (Eff 1-10-91); 144 v S 359 (Eff 12-22-92); 144 v H 758 (Eff 1-15-93); 146 v H 670. Eff 12-2-96.

§ 109.74 Attorney general may adopt and promulgate rules and regulations.

The attorney general, in accordance with Chapter 119. of the Revised Code, has discretion to adopt and promulgate any or all of the rules and regulations recommended by the Ohio peace officer training commission to the attorney general pursuant to section 109.73 of the Revised Code. When the attorney general promulgates any rule or regulation recommended by the commission, the attorney general shall transmit a certified copy thereof to the secretary of state.

HISTORY: 131 v 11 (Eff 9-6-65); 146 v H 670. Eff 12-2-96.

[§ 109.74.1] § 109.741 Training in missing children, child abuse and neglect cases.

The attorney general shall adopt, in accordance with Chapter 119. or pursuant to section 109.74 of the Revised Code, rules governing the training of peace officers in the handling of missing children and child abuse and neglect cases. The rules shall specify the amount of that training necessary for the satisfactory completion of basic training programs at approved peace officer training schools, other than the Ohio peace officer training academy and the time within which a peace officer is required to receive that training, if he receives his appointment as a peace officer before receiving that training.

HISTORY: 140 v S 321 (Eff 4-9-85); 141 v S 84. Eff 4-9-85.

The effective date is set by section 3 of SB 84.

[§ 109.74.2] § 109.742 Crisis intervention training.

The attorney general shall adopt, in accordance with Chapter 119. or pursuant to section 109.74 of the Revised Code, rules governing the training of peace officers in crisis intervention. The rules shall specify six or more hours of that training for the satisfactory completion of basic training programs at approved peace officer training schools, other than the Ohio peace officer training academy.

HISTORY: 140 v H 435. Eff 4-4-85.

[§ 109.74.3] § 109.743 Rules for firearms requalification programs.

The attorney general shall adopt, in accordance with Chapter 119. of the Revised Code or pursuant to section 109.74 of the Revised Code, rules governing firearms requalification programs that are required by section 109.801 [109.80.1] of the Revised Code. At a minimum, the rules shall prohibit a firearms requalification program from being used to fulfill the requirements of section 109.801 [109.80.1] of the Revised Code until after the program is approved by the executive director of the Ohio peace officer training commission pursuant to section 109.75 of the Revised Code.

HISTORY: 143 v H 271 (Eff 4-10-91); 146 v H 670. Eff 12-2-96.

[§ 109.74.4] § 109.744 Training relating to domestic violence.

The attorney general shall adopt, in accordance with Chapter 119. of the Revised Code or pursuant to section 109.74 of the Revised Code, rules governing the training of peace officers in the handling of the offense of domestic violence, other types of domestic violence-related offenses and incidents, and protection orders and consent agreements issued or approved under section 2919.26 or 3113.31 of the Revised Code. The provisions of the rules shall include, but shall not be limited to, all of the following:

(A) A specification that fifteen or more hours of that training is required for the satisfactory completion of basic training programs at approved peace officer training schools, other than the Ohio peace officer training academy;

(B) A requirement that the training include, but not be limited to, training in all of the following:

(1) All recent amendments to domestic violence-related laws;

(2) Notifying a victim of domestic violence of his rights;

(3) Processing protection orders and consent agreements issued or approved under section 2919.26 or 3113.31 of the Revised Code.

HISTORY: 143 v S 3. Eff 4-11-91.

[§ 109.74.5] § 109.745 Repealed, 146 v H 72 [146 v S 166]. Eff 3-18-97.

This section referred to training in administering oaths and acknowledging or certifying certain documents.

See now section 2935.08.1.

The provisions of § 4 of HB 72 (146 v —) read as follows:

SECTION 4. On and after the effective date of this act, any rules adopted by the Attorney General or the Superintendent of the State Highway Patrol under authority of division (A) of section 109.745 or 5503.051 of the Revised Code, as enacted in Am. Sub. S.B. 166 of the 121st General Assembly and as repealed by this act, have no further force or effect, and the powers granted to peace officers by division (B) of section 109.745 of the Revised Code and to State Highway Patrol Troopers by division (B) of section 5503.051 of the Revised Code, as enacted in Am. Sub. S.B. 166 of the 121st General Assembly and as repealed by this act, are terminated.

§ 109.75 Powers and duties of executive director.

The executive director of the Ohio peace officer training commission, on behalf of the commission, shall have the following powers and duties, which shall be exercised with the general advice of the commission and only in accordance with section 109.751 [109.75.1] of the Revised Code and the rules adopted pursuant to that section, and with the rules adopted by the attorney general pursuant to sections 109.74, 109.741 [109.74.1],

109.742 [109.74.2], and 109.743 [109.74.3] of the Revised Code:

(A) To approve peace officer training schools and firearms requalification programs administered by the state, counties, municipal corporations, and the department of natural resources, to issue certificates of approval to approved schools, and to revoke an approval or certificate;

(B) To certify, as qualified, instructors at approved peace officer training schools, to issue appropriate certificates to these instructors, and to revoke for good cause shown certificates of these instructors;

(C) To certify, as qualified, commanders at approved peace officer training schools, to issue appropriate certificates to these commanders, and to revoke for good cause shown certificates of these commanders. As used in this division, "commander" means the director or other head of an approved peace officer training school.

(D) To certify peace officers and sheriffs who have satisfactorily completed basic training programs and to issue appropriate certificates to these peace officers and sheriffs;

(E) To cause studies and surveys to be made relating to the establishment, operation, and approval of state, county, and municipal peace officer training schools;

(F) To consult and cooperate with state, county, and municipal peace officer training schools for the development of advanced in-service training programs for peace officers;

(G) To consult and cooperate with universities, colleges, and institutes for the development of specialized courses of study in the state for peace officers in police science and police administration;

(H) To consult and cooperate with other departments and agencies of the state and federal government concerned with peace officer training;

(I) To perform any other acts that may be necessary or appropriate to carry out the executive director's powers and duties as set forth in sections 109.71 to 109.77 of the Revised Code;

(J) To report to the commission at each regular meeting of the commission and at any other times that the council† may require;

(K) To certify persons who have satisfactorily completed approved training programs for correction officers in full-service jails, five-day facilities, or eight-hour holding facilities or approved training programs for others who provide correction services in those jails or facilities and to issue appropriate certificates to those persons.

HISTORY: 131 v 11 (Eff 9-6-65); 139 v H 44 (Eff 5-8-81); 140 v H 759 (Eff 3-28-85); 140 v H 435 (Eff 4-4-85); 140 v S 321 (Eff 4-9-85); 141 v H 428 (Eff 12-23-86); 143 v H 271 (Eff 4-10-91); 143 v H 669 (Eff 1-10-91); 146 v H 566 (Eff 10-16-96); 146 v H 670. Eff 12-2-96.

† So in enrolled bill, division (J). Was "commission" intended?

Comment, Legislative Service Commission

° ° ° Sections 109.75 ° ° ° of the Revised Code are amended by this act [Sub. H.B. 670] and also by Am. Sub. H.B. 566 of the 121st General Assembly. Comparison of these amendments in pursuance of section 1.52 of the Revised Code discloses that they are not irreconcilable so that they are required by that section to be harmonized to give effect to each amendment.

[§ 109.75.1] § 109.751 Attendance of undercover drug agents, bailiffs, deputy bailiffs or public defender investigators.

(A) The executive director of the Ohio peace officer training commission shall neither approve nor issue a certificate of approval to a peace officer training school pursuant to section 109.75 of the Revised Code unless the school agrees to permit, in accordance with rules adopted by the attorney general pursuant to division (C) of this section, undercover drug agents to attend its basic training programs. The executive director shall revoke approval, and the certificate of approval of, a peace officer training school that does not permit, in accordance with rules adopted by the attorney general pursuant to division (C) of this section, undercover drug agents to attend its basic training programs.

This division does not apply to peace officer training schools for employees of conservancy districts who are designated pursuant to section 6101.75 of the Revised Code or for park officers, forest officers, preserve officers, wildlife officers, or state watercraft officers of the department of natural resources.

(B)(1) A peace officer training school is not required to permit an undercover drug agent, a bailiff or deputy bailiff of a court of record of this state, or a criminal investigator employed by the state public defender to attend its basic training programs if either of the following applies:

(a) In the case of the Ohio peace officer training academy, the employer county, township, municipal corporation, court, or state public defender or the particular undercover drug agent, bailiff, deputy bailiff, or criminal investigator has not paid the tuition costs of training in accordance with section 109.79 of the Revised Code;

(b) In the case of other peace officer training schools, the employer county, township, municipal corporation, court, or state public defender fails to pay the entire cost of the training and certification.

(2) A training school shall not permit a bailiff or deputy bailiff of a court of record of this state or a criminal investigator employed by the state public defender to attend its basic training programs unless the employing court of the bailiff or deputy bailiff or the state public defender, whichever is applicable, has authorized the bailiff, deputy bailiff, or investigator to attend the school.

(C) The attorney general shall adopt, in accordance with Chapter 119. or pursuant to section 109.74 of the Revised Code, rules governing the attendance of undercover drug agents at approved peace officer training schools, other than the Ohio peace officer training academy, and the certification of the agents upon their satisfactory completion of basic training programs.

HISTORY: 139 v H 44 (Eff 5-8-81); 140 v H 759 (Eff 3-28-85); 141 v S 149 (Eff 6-6-86); 141 v S 278 (Eff 3-6-86); 141 v H 428 (Eff 12-23-86); 145 v S 182 (Eff 10-20-94); 146 v H 670. Eff 12-2-96.

[§ 109.75.2] § 109.752 Sheriff may attend peace officer basic training programs.

Any sheriff may attend and be awarded a certificate by the executive director of the Ohio peace officer training commission attesting to the satisfactory completion of any state, county, municipal, or department of natural resources peace officer basic training program that has been approved by the executive director under section 109.75 of the Revised Code or is offered at the Ohio peace officer training academy.

HISTORY: 143 v H 271 (Eff 4-10-91); 143 v H 669 (Eff 1-10-91); 146 v H 670. Eff 12-2-96.

§ 109.76 Provisions not to exempt officers from civil service provisions.

Nothing in sections 109.71 to 109.77 of the Revised Code shall be construed to except any peace officer, or other officer or employee from the provisions of Chapter 124. of the Revised Code.

HISTORY: 131 v 12 (Eff 9-6-65); 137 v H 1. Eff 8-26-77.

§ 109.77 Certificate necessary for appointment; prohibitions.

(A) As used in this section, "felony" has the same meaning as in section 109.511 [109.51.1] of the Revised Code.

(B)(1) Notwithstanding any general, special, or local law or charter to the contrary, and except as otherwise provided in this section, no person shall receive an original appointment on a permanent basis as any of the following unless the person previously has been awarded a certificate by the executive director of the Ohio peace officer training commission attesting to the person's satisfactory completion of an approved state, county, municipal, or department of natural resources peace officer basic training program:

(a) A peace officer of any county, township, municipal corporation, regional transit authority, or metropolitan housing authority;

(b) A park officer, forest officer, preserve officer, wildlife officer, or state watercraft officer of the department of natural resources;

(c) An employee of a park district under section 511.232 [511.23.2] or 1545.13 of the Revised Code;

(d) An employee of a conservancy district who is designated pursuant to section 6101.75 of the Revised Code;

(e) A state university law enforcement officer;

(f) A special police officer employed by the department of mental health pursuant to section 5119.14 of the Revised Code or the department of mental retardation and developmental disabilities pursuant to section 5123.13 of the Revised Code;

(g) A food stamp trafficking agent of the department of public safety designated under section 5502.14 of the Revised Code.

(2) Every person who is appointed on a temporary basis or for a probationary term or on other than a permanent basis as any of the following shall forfeit the appointed position unless the person previously has satisfactorily completed or, within the time prescribed by rules adopted by the attorney general pursuant to section 109.74 of the Revised Code, satisfactorily completes a state, county, municipal, or department of natural resources peace officer basic training program for temporary or probationary officers and is awarded a certificate by the director attesting to the satisfactory completion of the program:

(a) A peace officer of any county, township, municipal corporation, regional transit authority, or metropolitan housing authority;

(b) A park officer, forest officer, preserve officer, wildlife officer, or state watercraft officer of the department of natural resources;

(c) An employee of a park district under section 511.232 [511.23.2] or 1545.13 of the Revised Code;

(d) An employee of a conservancy district who is designated pursuant to section 6101.75 of the Revised Code;

(e) A special police officer employed by the department of mental health pursuant to section 5119.14 of the Revised Code or the department of mental retardation and developmental disabilities pursuant to section 5123.13 of the Revised Code;

(f) A food stamp trafficking agent of the department of public safety designated under section 5502.14 of the Revised Code.

(3) For purposes of division (B) of this section, a state, county, municipal, or department of natural resources peace officer basic training program, regardless of whether the program is to be completed by peace officers appointed on a permanent or temporary, probationary, or other nonpermanent basis, shall include at least fifteen hours of training in the handling of the offense of domestic violence, other types of domestic violence-related offenses and incidents, and protection orders and consent agreements issued or approved under section 2919.26 or 3113.31 of the Revised Code and at least six hours of crisis intervention training. The requirement to complete fifteen hours of training in the handling of the offense of domestic violence, other types of domestic violence-related offenses and incidents, and protection orders and consent agreements issued or approved under section 2919.26 or 3113.31 of the Revised Code does not apply to any person serving as a peace officer on March 27, 1979, and the

requirement to complete six hours of training in crisis intervention does not apply to any person serving as a peace officer on April 4, 1985. Any person who is serving as a peace officer on April 4, 1985, who terminates that employment after that date, and who is subsequently hired as a peace officer by the same or another law enforcement agency shall complete the six hours of training in crisis intervention within the time prescribed by rules adopted by the attorney general pursuant to section 109.742 [109.74.2] of the Revised Code. No peace officer shall have employment as a peace officer terminated and then be reinstated with intent to circumvent this section.

(4) Division (B) of this section does not apply to any person serving on a permanent basis on March 28, 1985, as a park officer, forest officer, preserve officer, wildlife officer, or state watercraft officer of the department of natural resources or as an employee of a park district under section 511.232 [511.23.2] or 1545.13 of the Revised Code, to any person serving on a permanent basis on March 6, 1986, as an employee of a conservancy district designated pursuant to section 6101.75 of the Revised Code, to any person serving on a permanent basis on January 10, 1991, as a preserve officer of the department of natural resources, to any person employed on a permanent basis on July 2, 1992, as a special police officer by the department of mental health pursuant to section 5119.14 of the Revised Code or by the department of mental retardation and developmental disabilities pursuant to section 5123.13 of the Revised Code, or to any person serving on a permanent basis on June 19, 1978, as a state university law enforcement officer pursuant to section 3345.04 of the Revised Code and who, immediately prior to June 19, 1978, was serving as a special policeman designated under authority of that section.

(5) Division (A) of this section does not apply to any person who is appointed as a regional transit authority police officer pursuant to division (Y) of section 306.35 of the Revised Code if, on or before July 1, 1996, the person has satisfactorily completed an approved state, county, municipal, or department of natural resources peace officer basic training program and has been awarded a certificate by the executive director of the Ohio peace officer training commission attesting to the person's satisfactory completion of such an approved program and if, on July 1, 1996, the person is performing peace officer functions for a regional transit authority.

(C) No person, after September 20, 1984, shall receive an original appointment on a permanent basis as a liquor control investigator or food stamp trafficking agent of the department of public safety, engaged in the enforcement of Chapters 4301. and 4303. of the Revised Code, or as an Ohio veterans' home police officer designated under section 5907.02 of the Revised Code unless the person previously has been awarded a certificate by the executive director of the Ohio peace officer training commission attesting to the person's satisfactory completion of an approved police basic training program. Every person who is appointed on a temporary basis or for a probationary term or on other than a permanent basis as a liquor control investigator of the department of public safety, engaged in the enforcement of Chapters 4301. and 4303. of the Revised Code, or as an Ohio veterans' home police officer designated under section 5907.02 of the Revised Code shall forfeit that position unless the person previously has satisfactorily completed or, within one year from the time of appointment, satisfactorily completes an approved police basic training program.

No person shall, beginning on October 29, 1995, receive an original appointment on a permanent basis as a food stamp trafficking agent of the department of public safety authorized to enforce Chapter 5502. and sections 2913.46 and 5101.54 of the Revised Code and engaged in the enforcement of laws and rules described in section 5502.14 of the Revised Code unless the person previously has been awarded a certificate by the executive director of the Ohio peace officer training commission attesting to the person's satisfactory completion of an approved police basic training program. Every person who is appointed on a temporary or for a probationary term or on other than a permanent basis as a food stamp trafficking agent shall forfeit that position unless the person previously has satisfactorily completed, or within one year from the time of the appointment satisfactorily completes, an approved police basic training program.

(D) No bailiff or deputy bailiff of a court of record of this state and no criminal investigator who is employed by the state public defender shall carry a firearm, as defined in section 2923.11 of the Revised Code, while on duty unless the bailiff, deputy bailiff, or criminal investigator has done or received one of the following:

(1) Has been awarded a certificate by the executive director of the Ohio peace officer training commission, which certificate attests to satisfactory completion of an approved state, county, or municipal basic training program for bailiffs and deputy bailiffs of courts of record and for criminal investigators employed by the state public defender that has been recommended by the Ohio peace officer training council†;

(2) Has successfully completed a firearms training program approved by the Ohio peace officer training commission prior to employment as a bailiff, deputy bailiff, or criminal investigator;

(3) Prior to June 6, 1986, was authorized to carry a firearm by the court that employed the bailiff, deputy bailiff, or criminal investigator or by the state public defender and has received training in the use of firearms that the Ohio peace officer training commission determines is equivalent to the training that otherwise is required by this division.

(E)(1) Prior to awarding any certificate prescribed in this section, the executive director of the Ohio peace officer training commission shall request the person to whom the certificate is to be awarded to disclose, and the person shall disclose, any previous criminal conviction of or plea of guilty of that person to a felony.

(2) Prior to the award by the executive director of the commission of any certificate prescribed in this section, the prospective employer of the person to whom the certificate is to be awarded or the commander of the peace officer training school attended by that person shall request the bureau of criminal identification and investigation to conduct a criminal history records check on the person. Upon receipt of the request, the bureau promptly shall conduct a criminal history records check on the person and, upon completion of the check, promptly shall provide a copy of the criminal history records check to the prospective employer or peace officer training school commander that made the request. Upon receipt of the copy of the criminal history records check from the bureau, the prospective employer or peace officer training school commander that made the request shall submit the copy to the executive director of the Ohio peace officer training commission. The executive director shall not award any certificate prescribed in this section unless the executive director has received a copy of the criminal history records check on the person to whom the certificate is to be awarded.

(3) The executive director of the commission shall not award a certificate prescribed in this section to a person who has been convicted of or has pleaded guilty to a felony or who fails to disclose any previous criminal conviction of or plea of guilty to a felony as required under division (E)(1) of this section.

(4) The executive director of the commission shall revoke the certificate awarded to a person as prescribed in this section, and that person shall forfeit all of the benefits derived from being certified as a peace officer under this section, if the person, prior to the award of the certificate, failed to disclose any previous criminal conviction of or plea of guilty to a felony as required under division (E)(1) of this section.

(F)(1) Regardless of whether the person has been awarded the certificate or has been classified as a peace officer prior to, on, or after the effective date of this amendment, the executive director of the Ohio peace officer training commission shall revoke any certificate that has been awarded to a person as prescribed in this section if the person does either of the following:

(a) Pleads guilty to a felony committed on or after January 1, 1997.

(b) Pleads guilty to a misdemeanor committed on or after January 1, 1997, pursuant to a negotiated plea agreement as provided in division (D) of section 2929.29 of the Revised Code in which the person agrees to surrender the certificate awarded to the person under this section.

(2) The executive director of the commission shall suspend any certificate that has been awarded to a person as prescribed in this section if the person is convicted, after trial, of a felony committed on or after January 1, 1997. The executive director shall suspend the certificate pursuant to this division pending the outcome of an appeal by the person from that conviction to the highest court to which the appeal is taken or until the expiration of the period in which an appeal is required to be filed. If the person files an appeal that results in that person's acquittal of the felony or conviction of a misdemeanor, or in the dismissal of the felony charge against that person, the executive director shall reinstate the certificate awarded to the person under this section. If the person files an appeal from that person's conviction of the felony and the conviction is upheld by the highest court to which the appeal is taken or if the person does not file a timely appeal, the executive director shall revoke the certificate awarded to the person under this section.

(G)(1) If a person is awarded a certificate under this section and the certificate is revoked pursuant to division (E)(4) or (F) of this section, the person shall not be eligible to receive, at any time, a certificate attesting to the person's satisfactory completion of a peace officer basic training program.

(2) The revocation or suspension of a certificate under division (E)(4) or (F) of this section shall be in accordance with Chapter 119. of the Revised Code.

(H)(1) A person who was employed as a peace officer of a county, township, or municipal corporation of the state on January 1, 1966, and who has completed at least sixteen years of full-time active service as such a peace officer may receive an original appointment on a permanent basis and serve as a peace officer of a county, township, or municipal corporation, or as a state university law enforcement officer, without complying with the requirements of division (B) of this section.

(2) Any person who held an appointment as a state highway trooper on January 1, 1966, may receive an original appointment on a permanent basis and serve as a peace officer of a county, township, or municipal corporation, or as a state university law enforcement officer, without complying with the requirements of division (B) of this section.

(I) No person who is appointed as a peace officer of a county, township, or municipal corporation on or after April 9, 1985, shall serve as a peace officer of that county, township, or municipal corporation unless the person has received training in the handling of missing children and child abuse and neglect cases from an approved state, county, township, or municipal police basic training program or receives the training within the time prescribed by rules adopted by the attorney general pursuant to section 109.741 [109.74.1] of the Revised Code.

(J) No part of any approved state, county, or municipal basic training program for bailiffs and deputy bailiffs of courts of record and no part of any approved state, county, or municipal basic training program for criminal investigators employed by the state public defender shall be used as credit toward the completion by a peace officer of any part of the approved state, county, or municipal peace officer basic training program that the peace officer is required by this section to complete satisfactorily.

(K) This section does not apply to any member of the police department of a municipal corporation in an adjoining state serving in this state under a contract pursuant to section 737.04 of the Revised Code.

HISTORY: 142 v H 708 (Eff 4-19-88); 143 v H 271 (Eff 4-10-91); 143 v S 3 (Eff 4-11-91); 143 v H 669 (Eff 1-10-91); 144 v S 49 (Eff 7-21-92); 145 v S 182 (Eff 10-20-94); 146 v S 162 (Eff 10-29-95); 146 v S 2 (Eff 7-1-96); 146 v S 269 (Eff 7-1-96); 146 v H 566 (Eff 10-16-96); 146 v H 670 (Eff 12-2-96); 146 v S 285. Eff 3-13-97.

† So in enrolled bill, division (D)(1).

Comment, Legislative Service Commission

° ° ° Sections 109.77 ° ° ° of the Revised Code are amended by this act [Sub. H.B. 670] and also by Am. Sub. S.B. 285 of the 121st General Assembly. Comparison of these amendments in pursuance of section 1.52 of the Revised Code discloses that they are not irreconcilable so that they are required by that section to be harmonized to give effect to each amendment.

The provisions of § 3 of SB 285 (146 v —) read as follows:

SECTION 3. Section 109.77 of the Revised Code is presented in this act as a composite of the section as amended by both Am. Sub. S.B. 269 and Am. Sub. H.B. 566 of the 121st General Assembly, with the new language of neither of the acts shown in capital letters. ° ° ° This is in recognition of the principle stated in division (B) of section 1.52 of the Revised Code that such amendments are to be harmonized where not substantively irreconcilable and constitutes a legislative finding that such is the resulting version of those sections in effect prior to the effective date of this act.

§ 109.78 Certification of special policemen, security guards, private police; firearms training; private security fund.

(A) The executive director of the Ohio peace officer training commission, on behalf of the commission and in accordance with rules promulgated by the attorney general, shall certify persons who have satisfactorily completed approved training programs designed to qualify persons for positions as special police, security guards, or persons otherwise privately employed in a police capacity and issue appropriate certificates to such persons. Application for approval of a training program designed to qualify persons for such positions shall be made to the commission. An application for approval shall be submitted to the commission with a fee of one hundred twenty-five dollars, which fee shall be refunded if the application is denied. Such programs shall cover only duties and jurisdiction of such security guards and special police privately employed in a police capacity when such officers do not qualify for training under section 109.71 of the Revised Code. A person attending an approved basic training program administered by the state shall pay to the agency administering the program the cost of the person's participation in the program as determined by the agency. A person attending an approved basic training program administered by a county or municipal corporation shall pay the cost of the person's participation in the program, as determined by the administering subdivision, to the county or the municipal corporation. A person who is issued a certificate for satisfactory completion of an approved basic training program shall pay to the commission a fee of fifteen dollars. A duplicate of a lost, spoliated, or destroyed certificate may be issued upon application and payment of a fee of fifteen dollars. Such certificate or the completion of twenty years of active duty as a peace officer shall satisfy the educational requirements for appointment or commission as a special police officer or special deputy of a political subdivision of this state.

(B)(1) The executive director of the Ohio peace officer training commission, on behalf of the commission and in accordance with rules promulgated by the attorney general, shall certify basic firearms training programs, and shall issue certificates to class A, B, or C licensees or prospective class A, B, or C licensees under Chapter 4749. of the Revised Code and to registered or prospective employees of such class A, B, or C licensees who have satisfactorily completed a basic firearms training program of the type described in division (A)(1) of section 4749.10 of the Revised Code.

Application for approval of a basic firearms training program shall be made to the commission. An application shall be submitted to the commission with a fee of one hundred dollars, which fee shall be refunded if the application is denied.

A person who is issued a certificate for satisfactory completion of an approved basic firearms training program shall pay a fee of ten dollars to the commission. A duplicate of a lost, spoliated, or destroyed certificate may be issued upon application and payment of a fee of five dollars.

(2) The executive director, on behalf of the commission and in accordance with rules promulgated by the attorney general, also shall certify firearms requalification training programs and instructors for the annual requalification of class A, B, or C licensees under Chapter 4749. of the Revised Code and registered or prospective employees of such class A, B, or C licensees who are authorized to carry a firearm under section 4749.10 of the Revised Code. Application for approval of a training program or instructor for such purpose shall be made to the commission. Such an application shall be submitted to the commission with a fee of fifty dollars, which fee shall be refunded if the application is denied.

(3) The executive director, upon request, also shall review firearms training received within three years prior to November 23, 1985, by any class A, B, or C licensee or prospective class A, B, or C licensee, or by any registered of† prospective employee of any class A, B, or C licensee under Chapter 4749. of the Revised

Code to determine if the training received is equivalent to a basic firearms training program that includes twenty hours of handgun training and five hours of training in the use of other firearms, if any other firearm is to be used. If the executive director determines the training was received within the three-year period and that it is equivalent to such a program, the executive director shall issue written evidence of approval of the equivalency training to the licensee or employee.

(C) There is hereby established in the state treasury the peace officer private security fund, which shall be used by the Ohio peace officer training commission to administer the training program to qualify persons for positions as special police, security guards, or other private employment in a police capacity, as described in division (A) of this section, and the training program in basic firearms and the training program for firearms requalification, both as described in division (B) of this section. All fees paid to the commission by applicants for approval of a training program designed to qualify persons for such private police positions, basic firearms training program, or a firearms requalification training program or instructor, as required by division (A) or (B) of this section, by persons who satisfactorily complete a private police training program or a basic firearms training program, as required by division (A) or (B) of this section, or by persons who satisfactorily requalify in firearms use, as required by division (B)(2) of section 4749.10 of the Revised Code, shall be transmitted to the treasurer of state for deposit in the fund. The fund shall be used only for the purpose set forth in this division.

(D) No public or private educational institution, port authority, or superintendent of the state highway patrol shall employ a person as a special police officer, security guard, or other position in which such person goes armed while on duty, who has not received a certificate of having satisfactorily completed an approved basic peace officer training program, unless the person has completed twenty years of active duty as a peace officer.

HISTORY: 133 v H 575 (Eff 11-21-69); 134 v H 1 (Eff 3-26-71); 134 v H 633 (Eff 4-3-72); 135 v S 192 (Eff 9-23-74); 137 v S 194 (Eff 7-8-77); 141 v H 402 (Eff 11-27-85); 141 v H 428 (Eff 12-23-86); 142 v H 419 (Eff 7-1-87); 146 v S 2 (Eff 7-1-96); 146 v H 670. Eff 12-2-96.

† So in enrolled bill, division (B)(3).

§ 109.79 Training academy.

(A) The Ohio peace officer training commission shall establish and conduct a training school for law enforcement officers of any political subdivision of the state or of the state public defender's office. The school shall be known as the Ohio peace officer training academy. No bailiff or deputy bailiff of a court of record of this state and no criminal investigator employed by the state public defender shall be permitted to attend the academy for training unless the employing court of the bailiff or deputy bailiff or the state public defender, whichever is applicable, has authorized the bailiff, deputy bailiff, or investigator to attend the academy.

The Ohio peace officer training commission shall develop the training program, which shall include courses in both the civil and criminal functions of law enforcement officers, a course in crisis intervention with six or more hours of training, and training in the handling of missing children and child abuse and neglect cases, and shall establish rules governing qualifications for admission to the academy. The commission may require competitive examinations to determine fitness of prospective trainees, so long as the examinations or other criteria for admission to the academy are consistent with the provisions of Chapter 124. of the Revised Code.

The Ohio peace officer training commission shall determine tuition costs which shall be sufficient in the aggregate to pay the costs of operating the academy. The costs of acquiring and equipping the academy shall be paid from appropriations made by the general assembly to the Ohio peace officer training commission for that purpose, or from gifts or grants received for that purpose.

The law enforcement officers, during the period of their training, shall receive compensation as determined by the political subdivision that sponsors them or, if the officer is a criminal investigator employed by the state public defender, as determined by the state public defender. The political subdivision may pay the tuition costs of the law enforcement officers they sponsor and the state public defender may pay the tuition costs of criminal investigators of that office who attend the academy.

If trainee vacancies exist, the academy may train and issue certificates of satisfactory completion to peace officers who are employed by a campus police department pursuant to section 1713.50 of the Revised Code, by a qualified nonprofit corporation police department pursuant to section 1702.80 of the Revised Code, or by a railroad company or who are hospital police officers appointed and commissioned by the governor pursuant to sections 4973.17 to 4973.22 of the Revised Code, provided that no such officer shall be trained at the academy unless the officer meets the qualifications established for admission to the academy and the qualified nonprofit corporation police department, railroad company, or hospital or the private college or university that established the campus police department prepays the entire cost of the training. A qualified nonprofit corporation police department, railroad company, or hospital or a private college or university that has established a campus police department is not entitled to reimbursement from the state for any amount paid for the cost of training the railroad company's peace officers or the peace officers of the qualified nonprofit corporation police department, campus police department, or hospital.

The academy shall permit investigators employed by the state medical board to take selected courses that the board determines are consistent with its responsibilities for initial and continuing training of investigators as required under division (C) of section 4731.05 of the Revised Code. The board shall pay the entire cost of training that investigators receive at the academy.

(B) As used in this section:

(1) "Law enforcement officers" include any undercover drug agent, any bailiff or deputy bailiff of a court of record, and any criminal investigator who is employed by the state public defender.

(2) "Undercover drug agent" means any person who:

(a) Is employed by a county, township, or municipal corporation for the purposes set forth in division (B)(2)(b) of this section but who is not an employee of a county sheriff's department, of a township constable, or of the police department of a municipal corporation or township;

(b) In the course of the person's employment by a county, township, or municipal corporation, investigates and gathers information pertaining to persons who are suspected of violating Chapter 2925. or 3719. of the Revised Code, and generally does not wear a uniform in the performance of the person's duties.

(3) "Crisis intervention training" has the same meaning as in section 109.71 of the Revised Code.

(4) "Missing children" has the same meaning as in section 2901.30 of the Revised Code.

HISTORY: 133 v H 1160 (Eff 8-31-70); 136 v S 272 (Eff 8-19-76); 138 v H 83 (Eff 9-26-79); 139 v H 44 (Eff 5-8-81); 140 v H 435 (Eff 4-4-85); 140 v S 321 (Eff 4-9-85); 141 v S 149 (Eff 6-6-86); 141 v H 769 (Eff 3-17-87); 141 v S 364 (Eff 3-17-87); 142 v H 708 (Eff 4-19-88); 143 v H 110 (Eff 5-31-90); 144 v H 758 (Eff 1-15-93); 146 v H 670. Eff 12-2-96.

§ 109.80 Basic training course for sheriffs; continuing education required.

(A) The Ohio peace officer training commission shall develop and conduct a basic training course lasting at least three weeks for sheriffs appointed or elected on or after January 1, 1988 and shall establish criteria for what constitutes successful completion of the course. The basic training course shall include instruction in contemporary law enforcement, criminal investigations, the judicial process, civil rules, corrections, and other topics relevant to the duties and operations of the office of sheriff. The commission shall offer the course every four years within six months after the general election of sheriffs in each county and at other times when it is needed to permit sheriffs to attend within six months after appointment or election. The course shall be conducted by the Ohio peace officer training academy. The council shall provide that not less than two weeks of the course conducted within six months after the general election of sheriffs in each county shall be conducted prior to the first Monday in January next after that general election.

(B) The attorney general shall appoint a continuing education committee, consisting of not fewer than five nor more than seven members, including but not limited to, members of the Ohio peace officer training commission and sheriffs. The commission and the committee jointly shall determine the type of continuing education required for sheriffs to complete the requirements of division (E) of section 311.01 of the Revised Code and shall establish criteria for what constitutes successful completion of the requirement. The committee shall approve the courses that sheriffs may attend to complete the continuing education requirement and shall publish an approved list of those courses. The commission shall maintain a list of approved training schools that sheriffs may attend to complete the continuing education requirement. Upon request, the committee may approve courses other than those courses conducted as part of a certified law enforcement manager program.

(C) Upon presentation of evidence by a sheriff that because of medical disability or for other good cause that† the sheriff is unable to complete the basic or continuing education requirement, the commission may waive the requirement until the disability or cause terminates.

(D) As used in this section, "newly elected sheriff" means a person who did not hold the office of sheriff of a county on the date the person was elected sheriff of that county.

HISTORY: 141 v H 683 (Eff 3-11-87); 142 v H 708 (Eff 4-19-88); 146 v H 670 (Eff 12-2-96); 146 v H 351. Eff 1-14-97.

† The language is the result of combining HB 670 (146 v —) and HB 351 (146 v —).

Comment, Legislative Service Commission

Sections ° ° ° 109.80 of the Revised Code is amended by this act [Sub. H.B. 670] and also by Sub. H.B. 351 of the 121st General Assembly. Comparison of these amendments in pursuance of section 1.52 of the Revised Code discloses that they are not irreconcilable so that they are required by that section to be harmonized to give effect to each amendment.

[§ 109.80.1] § 109.801 Annual firearms requalification program.

(A)(1) Each year the following persons shall successfully complete a firearms requalification program approved by the executive director of the Ohio peace officer training commission in accordance with rules adopted by the attorney general pursuant to section 109.743 [109.74.3] of the Revised Code: any sheriff, deputy sheriff, marshal, deputy marshal, township constable, chief of police or member of an organized police department of a municipal corporation or township, chief of police or member of a township police district police force, superintendent of the state highway patrol, state highway patrol trooper, chief of police of a university or college police department or state university law enforcement officer appointed under section 3345.04

of the Revised Code, parole or probation officer who carries a firearm in the course of official duties, or employee of the department of natural resources who is a park officer, forest officer, preserve officer, wildlife officer, or state watercraft officer who carries a firearm in the course of official duties.

(2) No person listed in division (A)(1) of this section shall carry a firearm during the course of official duties if the person does not comply with division (A)(1) of this section.

(B) The hours that a sheriff spends attending a firearms requalification program required by division (A) of this section are in addition to the sixteen hours of continuing education that are required by division (E) of section 311.01 of the Revised Code.

(C) As used in this section, "firearm" has the same meaning as in section 2923.11 of the Revised Code.

HISTORY: 143 v H 271 (Eff 4-10-91); 145 v S 182 (Eff 10-20-94); 145 v H 406 (Eff 11-11-94); 146 v H 670. Eff 12-2-96.

[§ 109.80.2] § 109.802 Law enforcement assistance fund to pay reimbursement for law enforcement training.

(A) There is hereby created in the state treasury the law enforcement assistance fund. The fund shall be used to pay reimbursements for law enforcement training as provided in this section and section 109.803 [109.80.3] of the Revised Code, the compensation of any employees of the attorney general required to administer those sections, and any other administrative costs incurred by the attorney general to administer those sections.

(B) The attorney general shall adopt rules in accordance with Chapter 119. of the Revised Code establishing application procedures, standards, and guidelines, and prescribing an application form, for the reimbursement of sheriffs, constables, chiefs of police of organized municipal and township police departments, chiefs of police of township police district police forces, and chiefs of police of university or college police departments for the costs of peace officer basic training programs, advanced peace officer training programs, basic jailer training programs, and firearms requalification programs successfully completed by them or the peace officers under their supervision, for the reimbursement of the superintendent of the state highway patrol and the director of natural resources for the costs of peace officer basic training programs, advanced peace officer training programs, and basic jailer training programs successfully completed by them or the peace officers under their supervision, and for the reimbursement of the chief of the adult parole authority and the chief probation officer of a county probation department, multicounty probation department, and municipal court department of probation for the costs of basic firearm training programs and firearms requalification programs successfully completed by them or by parole or probation officers under their supervision. The rules shall include, but are not limited to, all of the following:

(1) A requirement that applications for reimbursement be submitted on a fiscal year basis;

(2) The documentation required to substantiate any costs for which the applicant seeks reimbursement;

(3) The procedure for prorating reimbursements if the amount of money appropriated for reimbursement for any fiscal year is not sufficient to pay all of the costs approved for reimbursement for that fiscal year;

(4) Any other requirements necessary for the proper administration of the reimbursement program.

(C) Each sheriff, constable, and chief of police of an organized municipal or township police department, township police district police force, or university or college police department may apply each fiscal year to the peace officer training commission for reimbursement for the costs of peace officer basic training programs, advanced peace officer training programs, basic jailer training programs, and firearms requalification training programs that are successfully completed by the sheriff, constable, or chief or a peace officer under the sheriff's, constable's, or chief's supervision. The superintendent of the state highway patrol and the director of natural resources may apply each fiscal year to the peace officer training commission for reimbursement for the costs of peace officer basic training programs, advanced peace officer training programs, and basic jailer training programs successfully completed by the superintendent or director or the peace officers under the superintendent's or director's supervision. The chief of the adult parole authority and each chief probation officer of a county probation department, multicounty probation department, or municipal court department of probation may apply each fiscal year to the peace officer training commission for reimbursement for the costs of basic firearm training programs and firearms requalification programs successfully completed by that sucht chief or by parole or probation officers under the chief's supervision. Each application shall be made in accordance with, on an application form prescribed in, and be supported by the documentation required by, the rules adopted by the attorney general pursuant to division (B) of this section.

(D) As used in this section and section 109.803 [109.80.3] of the Revised Code:

(1) "Peace officer" includes a sheriff, deputy sheriff, marshal, deputy marshal, chief of police and member of a municipal or township police department, chief of police or member of a township police district police force, chief of police of a university or college police department, state university law enforcement officer appointed under section 3345.04 of the Revised Code, superintendent of the state highway patrol, state highway patrol trooper, and employee of the department of natural resources who is a park officer, forest officer, preserve officer, wildlife officer, or state watercraft officer.

(2) "Chief of police of an organized municipal police

department" includes the chief of police of a village police department.

(3) "Chief of police of a village police department" means the village marshal.

(4) "Chief of police of a university or college police department" means the person who has direct supervisory authority over the state university law enforcement officers who are appointed for the university or college pursuant to section 3345.04 of the Revised Code by the board of trustees of the university or college.

HISTORY: 143 v H 271 (Eff 4-10-91); 145 v S 182 (Eff 10-20-94); 145 v H 406 (Eff 11-11-94); 146 v H 566 (Eff 10-16-96); 146 v H 670. Eff 12-2-96.

Publisher's Note

The amendments made by HB 566 (146 v —) and HB 670 (146 v —) have been combined. Please see provisions of RC § 1.52.

† The wording is the result of combining HB 566 (146 v —) and HB 670 (146 v —).

[§ 109.80.3] § 109.803 Program for reimbursing local law enforcement organizations for costs of training programs.

(A) The Ohio peace officer training commission shall administer a program for reimbursing sheriffs, constables, and chiefs of police of organized municipal and township police departments, township police district police forces, and university and college police departments for the costs of peace officer basic training programs, advanced peace officer training programs, basic jailer training programs, and firearms requalification training programs that are successfully completed by them or by peace officers under their supervision, for reimbursing the superintendent of the state highway patrol and the director of natural resources for the costs of peace officer basic training programs, advanced peace officer training programs, and basic jailer training programs that are successfully completed by them or the peace officers under their supervision, and for reimbursing the chief of the adult parole authority and the chief probation officer of a county probation department, multicounty probation department, or municipal court department of probation for the costs of basic firearm training programs and firearms requalification programs that are successfully completed by them or by parole or probation officers under their supervision. The commission shall administer the reimbursement program in accordance with rules adopted by the attorney general pursuant to division (B) of section 109.802 [109.80.2] of the Revised Code.

(B)(1) The commission, in accordance with the rules of the attorney general, shall review each application for reimbursement to determine if the applicant is entitled to reimbursement for the programs for which the applicant seeks reimbursement. It shall approve for reimbursement any program for which reimbursement is authorized in the rules of the attorney general, if the program was successfully completed by the applicant or a peace officer, parole officer, or probation officer supervised by the applicant. The actual amount of reimbursement for each authorized program shall be determined pursuant to divisions (B)(2), (3), (4), and (5) of this section.

(2) The commission shall prepare a basic peace officer training reimbursement voucher for each applicant for whom it approves reimbursement for all or some of the peace officer basic training programs, basic jailer training programs, basic firearms training programs, and firearms requalification programs for which the applicant applied for reimbursement. To compute the amount of the voucher for each applicant, the commission shall do all of the following:

(a) For each application for reimbursement for a peace officer basic training program, the commission shall approve an amount equal to seventy-five per cent of the costs, not to exceed eight hundred dollars, of each approved program successfully completed by the applicant or a peace officer under the applicant's supervision.

(b) For each application for reimbursement for a basic jailer training program, the commission shall approve an amount equal to seventy-five per cent of the costs, not to exceed four hundred dollars, for each approved program successfully completed by the applicant or a peace officer under the applicant's supervision.

(c) For each application by a sheriff, constable, or chief of police for reimbursement for a firearms requalifications program, the commission shall approve an amount equal to the full amount of the costs, not to exceed fifty dollars, for each approved program successfully completed by the applicant or a peace officer under the applicant's supervision.

(d) For each application by the chief of the adult parole authority or a chief probation officer of a county probation department, multicounty probation department, or municipal court department of probation for reimbursement for a basic firearm training program or a firearms requalification program, the commission shall approve an amount equal to the full amount of the costs, not to exceed fifty dollars, for each approved program successfully completed by the applicant or a parole or probation officer under the applicant's supervision.

(e) Add the total of all amounts approved under divisions (B)(2)(a), (b), (c), and (d) of this section for all approved programs for each applicant and, subject to division (B)(3) of this section, prepare a peace officer training reimbursement voucher for the applicant for that total amount.

(3) If the amount of money appropriated by the general assembly in any fiscal year to reimburse the costs of basic peace officer training programs, basic jailer training programs, basic firearm training programs, and firearms requalification programs is not sufficient to pay all peace officer training reimbursement vouchers

prepared pursuant to division (B)(2)(e) of this section, the commission shall reduce all of the vouchers by a pro rata amount.

(4) The commission shall prepare an advanced peace officer training reimbursement voucher for each applicant for whom it approves reimbursement for all or some of the advanced peace officer training programs for which the applicant applied for reimbursement. To compute the amount of the voucher for each applicant, the commission shall do all of the following:

(a) Determine the number of full-time peace officers, parole officers, or probation officers working for each applicant;

(b) For a twenty-six week period designated by the attorney general in the rules adopted pursuant to division (B) of section 109.802 [109.80.2] of the Revised Code, determine the total number of hours worked by peace officers, parole officers, or probation officers who are under the supervision of the applicant, are not considered full-time peace officers, parole officers, or probation officers, and are not included in division (B)(4)(a) of this section and divide that number by five hundred twenty.

(c) Determine a total number of shares for each applicant by adding the two numbers determined for the applicant in divisions (B)(4)(a) and (b) of this section.

(d) Determine the reimbursement amount to be paid per share by dividing the total amount of money appropriated in the fiscal year for the reimbursement of the costs of advanced training programs by the total number of all shares receivable by all applicants for the fiscal year.

(e) Subject to division (B)(5) of this section, determine the amount of the advanced peace officer training reimbursement voucher by multiplying the total number of shares for each applicant determined under division (B)(4)(c) of this section by the reimbursement amount per share determined under division (B)(4)(d) of this section.

(5) The advanced peace officer training reimbursement voucher for each applicant shall not exceed seventy-five per cent of the total costs expended by the applicant for all advanced peace officer training programs that were approved under division (B)(4) of this section and were successfully completed by the applicant and the peace officers under the applicant's supervision.

HISTORY: 143 v H 271 (Eff 4-10-91); 145 v H 406 (Eff 11-11-94); 146 v H 670. Eff 12-2-96.

[ANTITRUST SECTION IN OFFICE OF ATTORNEY GENERAL]

§ 109.81 Antitrust cases; special counsel.

(A) The attorney general shall act as the attorney at law in any antitrust case for the state. He may act as the attorney at law in any antitrust case for any political subdivision of the state, for the governing body of any political subdivision of the state, or, as parens patriae, for any natural person residing in the state. The attorney general shall do all things necessary under the laws of any state or the federal government to properly conduct any antitrust case in which he acts as attorney at law, including the bringing of an action for equitable relief or for the recovery of damages.

(B) The attorney general may appoint special counsel to act as attorney at law in any antitrust case described in division (A) of this section. A special counsel appointed under this section shall be paid in either or both of the following ways:

(1) At an hourly rate determined by the attorney general;

(2) At a percentage determined by the attorney general of the monetary relief or economic benefit recovered from conducting the antitrust case.

HISTORY: 132 v H 556 (Eff 12-14-67); 145 v H 152. Eff 7-1-93.

§ 109.82 Antitrust section.

There is hereby created in the office of the attorney general a section of antitrust. Ten per cent of all recoveries obtained by the attorney general pursuant to section 109.81 of the Revised Code by settlement or by judgment in any court and the full amount of all related civil penalties, attorney's fees, and reimbursements of investigative, litigation, or expert witness costs shall be paid into the state treasury to the credit of the attorney general antitrust fund, which is hereby created. The fund shall be used for expenses of the antitrust section. The expenses of the antitrust section in excess of the money available in the fund shall be paid out of the regular appropriation to the office of the attorney general.

HISTORY: 132 v H 556 (Eff 12-14-67); 137 v S 221 (Eff 11-23-77); 141 v H 201 (Eff 7-1-85); 144 v H 298 (Eff 7-26-91); 144 v S 351. Eff 7-1-92.

§ 109.83 Investigation of organized criminal activity.

(A) When directed by the governor or general assembly, the attorney general may investigate any organized criminal activity in this state.

When it appears to the attorney general, as a result of an investigation conducted pursuant to this division, that there is cause to prosecute for the commission of a crime, he shall refer the evidence to the prosecuting attorney having jurisdiction of the matter, to a regular grand jury drawn and impaneled pursuant to sections 2939.01 to 2939.24 of the Revised Code, or to a special grand jury drawn and impaneled pursuant to section 2939.17 of the Revised Code. When the crime or the elements of the crime were committed in two or more counties, the referral shall be to the prosecuting attorney, the regular grand jury, or a special grand jury of the county in which the most significant portion of the crime or the elements of the crime occurred or, if it is not possible to determine that county, the county with the largest population. When evidence is referred directly to a grand jury pursuant to this section, the attorney general and any assistant or special counsel designated by him has the exclusive right to appear at any time before such grand jury to give information relative to a legal matter cognizable by it, or to advise upon a legal matter when required, and may exercise all rights, privileges, and powers of prosecuting attorneys in such cases.

(B)(1) When information is referred to the attorney general by an organized crime task force or the organized crime investigations commission pursuant to section 177.03 of the Revised Code, the attorney general shall review the information and if he determines that there is cause to prosecute for the commission of a crime, he shall refer the information as evidence to a regular or special grand jury in the manner described in, and in the county determined in accordance with the provisions of, division (A) of this section, or shall initiate a criminal action or proceeding in a court of proper jurisdiction. If an indictment is returned by a grand jury pursuant to a referral made under this division, the attorney general has sole responsibility to prosecute the accused offender.

(2) The attorney general, and any assistant or special counsel designated by him who appears under this division in any county for the prosecution of any crime has the same powers and authority as a prosecuting attorney, including, but not limited to, powers relating to attendance before the courts and grand juries of the county, preparation and trial of indictments for crimes, and representation of the state in any criminal proceeding or in any appeal from a criminal case in any court of this state.

(C) When proceeding under the authority of this section, the attorney general may appear for the state in any court or tribunal of proper jurisdiction for the purpose of conducting investigations under division (A) of this section, or for the purpose of conducting criminal proceedings or any other proceeding that is necessary to promote and safeguard the public interests of the citizens of this state.

(D) This section shall not be construed to prevent the attorney general and prosecuting attorneys or special prosecutors from cooperating in the investigation and prosecution of offenses under this section. However, in cases in which information was referred to the attorney general by an organized crime task force because the office of a prosecuting attorney was implicated by an investigation conducted by the task force, the attorney general shall not inform the implicated prosecutor of the investigation or referral and shall not cooperate with the prosecutor on the matter.

(E) As used in this section, "organized criminal activity" has the same meaning as in section 177.01 of the Revised Code.

HISTORY: 133 v H 956 (Eff 9-16-70); 141 v S 74. Eff 9-3-86.

§ 109.84 Investigation and prosecution of violation of law.

(A) Upon the written request of the governor, the industrial commission, the administrator of workers' compensation, or upon the attorney general's becoming aware of criminal or improper activity related to Chapter 4121. or 4123. of the Revised Code, the attorney general shall investigate any criminal or civil violation of law related to Chapter 4121. or 4123. of the Revised Code.

(B) When it appears to the attorney general, as a result of an investigation under division (A) of this section, that there is cause to prosecute for the commission of a crime or to pursue a civil remedy, he may refer the evidence to the prosecuting attorney having jurisdiction of the matter, or to a regular grand jury drawn and impaneled pursuant to sections 2939.01 to 2939.24 of the Revised Code, or to a special grand jury drawn and impaneled pursuant to section 2939.17 of the Revised Code, or he may initiate and prosecute any necessary criminal or civil actions in any court or tribunal of competent jurisdiction in this state. When proceeding under this section, the attorney general has all rights, privileges, and powers of prosecuting attorneys, and any assistant or special counsel designated by him for that purpose has the same authority.

(C) The attorney general shall be reimbursed by the bureau of workers' compensation for all actual and necessary costs incurred in conducting investigations requested by the governor, the commission, or the administrator and all actual and necessary costs in conducting the prosecution arising out of such investigation.

HISTORY: 136 v S 545 (Eff 1-17-77); 143 v H 222. Eff 11-3-89.

§ 109.85 Medicaid investigations.

(A) Upon the written request of the governor, the general assembly, the auditor of state, the director of human services, the director of health, or the director of budget and management, or upon the attorney general's becoming aware of criminal or improper activity related to Chapter 3721. and the medical assistance program established under section 5111.01 of the Revised Code, the attorney general shall investigate any criminal or civil violation of law related to Chapter 3721. of the Revised Code or the medical assistance program.

(B) When it appears to the attorney general, as a result of an investigation under division (A) of this section, that there is cause to prosecute for the commission of a crime or to pursue a civil remedy, he may refer the evidence to the prosecuting attorney having jurisdiction of the matter, or to a regular grand jury drawn and impaneled pursuant to sections 2939.01 to 2939.24 of the Revised Code, or to a special grand jury drawn and impaneled pursuant to section 2939.17 of the Revised Code, or he may initiate and prosecute any necessary criminal or civil actions in any court or tribunal of competent jurisdiction in this state. When proceeding under this section, the attorney general, and any assistant or special counsel designated by him for that purpose, have all rights, privileges, and powers of prosecuting attorneys. The attorney general shall have exclusive supervision and control of all investigations and prosecutions initiated by him under this section. The forfeiture provisions of sections 2933.71 to 2933.75 of the Revised Code apply in relation to any such criminal action initiated and prosecuted by the attorney general.

(C) Nothing in this section shall prevent a county prosecuting attorney from investigating and prosecuting criminal activity related to Chapter 3721. of the Revised Code and the medical assistance program established under section 5111.01 of the Revised Code. The forfeiture provisions of sections 2933.71 to 2933.75 of the Revised Code apply in relation to any prosecution of criminal activity related to the medical assistance program undertaken by the prosecuting attorney.

HISTORY: 137 v S 159 (Eff 4-24-78); 138 v H 176 (Eff 7-1-80); 141 v H 201 (Eff 7-1-85); 143 v H 672 (Eff 11-14-89); 145 v H 152. Eff 7-1-93.

§ 109.86 Investigation of abuse or neglect of care facility patient; prosecution.

(A) The attorney general shall investigate any activity he has reasonable cause to believe is in violation of section 2903.34 of the Revised Code. Upon written request of the governor, the general assembly, the auditor of state, or the director of health, human services, aging, mental health, or mental retardation and developmental disabilities, the attorney general shall investigate any activity these persons believe is in violation of section 2903.34 of the Revised Code. If after an investigation the attorney general has probable cause to prosecute for the commission of a crime, he shall refer the evidence to the prosecuting attorney, director of law, or other similar chief legal officer having jurisdiction over the matter. If the prosecuting attorney decides to present the evidence to a grand jury, he shall notify the attorney general in writing of the decision within thirty days after referral of the matter and shall present the evidence prior to the discharge of the next regular grand jury. If the director of law or other chief legal officer decides to prosecute the case, he shall notify the attorney general in writing of the decision within thirty days and shall initiate prosecution within sixty days after the matter was referred to him.

(B) If the prosecuting attorney, director of law, or other chief legal officer fails to notify the attorney general or to present evidence or initiate prosecution in accordance with division (A) of this section, the attorney general may present the evidence to a regular grand jury drawn and impaneled pursuant to sections 2939.01 to 2939.24 of the Revised Code, or to a special grand jury drawn and impaneled pursuant to section 2939.17 of the Revised Code, or he may initiate and prosecute any action in any court or tribunal of competent jurisdiction in this state. The attorney general, and any assistant or special counsel designated by him, have all the powers of a prosecuting attorney, director of law, or other chief legal officer when proceeding under this section. Nothing in this section shall limit or prevent a prosecuting attorney, director of law, or other chief legal officer from investigating and prosecuting criminal activity committed against a resident or patient of a care facility.

HISTORY: 141 v H 566. Eff 9-17-86.

[CRIME VICTIMS ASSISTANCE]

§ 109.91 Crime victims assistance office; state victims assistance advisory committee.

(A) There is hereby established within the office of the attorney general the crime victims assistance office.

(B) There is hereby established the state victims assistance advisory committee. The committee shall consist of a chairperson, to be appointed by the attorney general, four ex officio members, and fifteen members to be appointed by the attorney general as follows: one member who represents the Ohio victim-witness association; three members who represent local victim assistance programs, including one from a municipally operated program and one from a county-operated program; one member who represents the interests of elderly victims; one member who is a board member of any statewide or local organization that exists primarily to aid victims of domestic violence, or who is an employee of, or counselor for, such an organization; one member who is an employee or officer of a county probation department or a probation department operated by the department of rehabilitation and correction; one member who is a county prosecuting attorney; one member who is a city law director; one member who is a county sheriff; one member who is a member or officer of a township or municipal police department; one member who is a court of common pleas judge; one member who is a municipal court judge or county court judge; and two members who are private citizens and are not government employees.

The committee shall include the following ex officio, nonvoting members: the chief justice of the supreme court, the attorney general, one member of the senate to be designated by the president of the senate, and one member of the house of representatives to be designated by the speaker of the house.

Members of the committee shall serve without compensation, but shall be reimbursed for travel and other necessary expenses that are incurred in the conduct of their official duties as members of the committee. The chairperson and members of the committee appointed by the attorney general shall serve at the pleasure of the attorney general. The chief justice of the supreme court and the attorney general shall serve on the committee until the end of the term of office that qualified them for membership on the committee. The member of the senate and the member of the house of representatives shall serve at the pleasure of the president of the senate and the speaker of the house of representatives, respectively.

(C) The victims assistance advisory committee shall perform both of the following duties:

(1) Advise the crime victims assistance office in determining crime and delinquency victim service needs, determining crime and delinquency victim policies for the state, and improving and exercising leadership in the quality of crime and delinquency victim programs in the state;

(2) Review and recommend to the crime victims assistance office the victim assistance programs that should be considered for the receipt of state financial assistance pursuant to section 109.92 of the Revised Code. The financial assistance allocation recommendations of the committee shall be based on the following priorities:

(a) Programs in existence on July 1, 1985, shall be given first priority;

(b) Programs offering or proposing to offer the broadest range of services and referrals to the community served, including medical, psychological, financial, educational, vocational, and legal services that were not in existence on July 1, 1985, shall be given second priority;

(c) Other qualified programs shall be given last priority.

(D) As used in this section and section 109.92 of the Revised Code, "victim assistance program" includes, but is not limited to a program that provides at least one of the following:

(1) Services to victims of any offense of violence or delinquent act that would be an offense of violence if committed by an adult;

(2) Financial assistance or property repair services to victims of crime or delinquent acts;

(3) Assistance to victims of crime or delinquent acts in judicial proceedings;

(4) Assistance to victims of crime or delinquent acts under the operation of any political subdivision of the state or a branch of the criminal justice system set forth in division (B)(1), (2), or (3) of section 181.51 of the Revised Code;

(5) Technical assistance to persons or organizations that provide services to victims of crime or delinquent acts under the operation of a branch of the criminal justice system set forth in divisions (B)(1), (2), and (3) of section 181.51 of the Revised Code.

A victim assistance program does not include the program for the reparation of crime victims established pursuant to Chapter 2743. of the Revised Code.

HISTORY: 140 v S 195 (Eff 7-1-85); 142 v H 171 (Eff 7-1-87); 142 v H 231 (Eff 10-5-87); 145 v H 152 (Eff 7-1-93); 146 v H 670. Eff 12-2-96.

§ 109.92 Financial assistance to victim assistance programs.

(A) Appropriations may be made by the general assembly to the office of the attorney general for the purpose of providing state financial assistance to victim assistance programs that operate in the state. The director of budget and management shall transfer amounts equal to such appropriations from the reparations fund established by section 2743.191 [2743.19.1] of the Revised Code to the fund or funds from which such appropriations are made. All amounts so appropriated and transferred shall be used to provide financial assistance to victim assistance programs in accordance with section 109.91 of the Revised Code and this section. The program for the provision of such financial assistance shall be administered by the crime victims assistance office established pursuant to section 109.91 of the Revised Code.

(B) A victim assistance program may apply to the crime victims assistance office for state financial assistance out of funds appropriated to the office of the attorney general for that purpose by the general assembly. Each application for such financial assistance shall include all of the following information:

(1) Evidence that the program is incorporated in this state as a nonprofit corporation or is a program established by a unit of state or local government;

(2) The proposed budget of the program for the period during which the financial assistance is sought;

(3) A summary of services offered by the program;

(4) An estimate of the number of persons served by the program.

(C) Within thirty days of receipt of an application for financial assistance from a victim assistance program in accordance with division (B) of this section, the crime victims assistance office, based in part on the recommendations of the victim assistance advisory board made pursuant to section 109.91 of the Revised Code, shall notify the program in writing whether it is eligible for financial assistance and, if eligible, estimate the amount that will be made available to the program and the time when the financial assistance will be made available.

(D) Each victim assistance program that receives any financial assistance pursuant to this section shall use the financial assistance only to provide the services identified in its application for such assistance as being services it offered and to cover a reasonable cost of administration of the program. Each victim assistance program that receives any such financial assistance shall make a good faith effort to minimize its costs of administration.

HISTORY: 140 v S 195 (Eff 7-1-85); 143 v H 111. Eff 7-1-89.

§ 109.93 Attorney general education fund.

The attorney general education fund is hereby created in the custody of the treasurer of state. The fund shall consist of gifts and grants received by the attorney general for the purposes of the fund. The fund shall be administered by the attorney general and shall be used to support various educational programs. These educational programs may include programs for consumer protection, victims of crime, environmental protection, drug abuse, child abuse, peace officer training, crime prevention, and law. The fund may also be used to pay costs associated with the solicitation of gifts and grants for the purposes of the fund, and the costs of administering the fund. The fund shall not be used to replace money spent by local programs for similar purposes.

HISTORY: 144 v S 351. Eff 7-1-92.

Not analogous to former RC § 109.93 renumbered from RC § 122.21 in 142 v H 171 and renumbered to RC § 122.21 in 142 v H 231, eff 10-5-87.

§ 109.94
Former § 122.22, amended and renumbered in 142 v H 171, eff. 7-1-87. Amended and renumbered § 122.22 in 142 v H 231. Effective 10-5-87.

[§§ 109.94.1, 109.94.2]
§§ 109.941, 109.942
Former §§ 122.23, 122.24, amended and renumbered in 142 v H 171, eff. 7-1-87. Amended and renumbered §§ 122.23, 122.24 in 142 v H 231. Effective 10-5-87.

§§ 109.95 to 109.97
Former §§ 122.25 to 122.27, amended and renumbered in 142 v H 171, eff. 7-1-87. Amended and renumbered §§ 122.25 to 122.27 in 142 v H 231. Effective 10-5-87.

§ 109.98
Repealed, 142 v H 231, § 2 [142 v H 171]. Eff 10-5-87.

This section placed the office of criminal justice services in the office of the attorney general.

§ 109.99 Penalty.

(A) Whoever violates section 109.26 of the Revised Code shall be fined not less than five hundred nor more than ten thousand dollars or be imprisoned not less than one month nor more than one year, or both.

(B) Whoever violates division (G)(1) of section 109.573 [109.57.3] of the Revised Code is guilty of unlawful disclosure of DNA database information, a misdemeanor of the first degree.

(C) Whoever violates division (G)(2) of section 109.573 [109.57.3] of the Revised Code is guilty of unlawful possession of DNA database information, a misdemeanor of the first degree.

(D)(1) Whoever violates division (G)(1) of section 109.35 of the Revised Code is guilty of entering into a transaction involving a nonprofit health care entity without the approval of the attorney general, a felony of the third degree.

(2) Whoever violates division (G)(2) of section 109.35 of the Revised Code is guilty of receiving improper compensation relating to a transaction involving a nonprofit health care entity, a felony of the third degree.

HISTORY: 125 v 354 (Eff 10-14-53); 146 v H 5 (Eff 8-30-95); 147 v H 242. Eff 5-7-97.

CHAPTER 120: PUBLIC DEFENDERS

[OHIO PUBLIC DEFENDER COMMISSION]

§ 120.01 Ohio public defender commission.

There is hereby created the Ohio public defender commission to provide, supervise, and coordinate legal representation at state expense for indigent and other persons. The commission shall consist of nine members, one of whom shall be chairman. The chairman shall be appointed by the governor with the advice and consent of the senate. Four members shall be appointed by the governor, two of whom shall be from each of the two major political parties. Four members shall be appointed by the supreme court, two of whom shall be from each of the two major political parties. The chairman, and not less than two of the members appointed by the governor, and not less than two of the members appointed by the supreme court shall be attorneys admitted to the practice of law in this state.

Within thirty days after the effective date of this section, the governor and the supreme court shall make initial appointments to the commission. Of the intial appointments made to the commission by the governor, the appointment of the chairman shall be for a term of two years. Of the other four appointments, one shall be for a term ending one year after the effective date of this section, one shall be for a term ending two years after that date, one shall be for a term ending three years after that date, and one shall be for a term ending four years after that date. Of the initial appointments made to the commission by the supreme court, one shall be for a term ending one year after the effective date of this section, one shall be for a term ending two years after that date, one shall be for a term ending three years after that date, and one shall be for a term ending four years after that date. Thereafter, terms of office shall be for four years, each term ending on the same day of the same month of the year as did the term which it succeeds. Any member appointed to fill a vacancy occurring prior to the expiration of the term for which his predecessor was appointed shall hold office for the remainder of such term. Any member shall continue in office subsequent to the expiration date of his term until his successor takes office or until a period of sixty days has elapsed, whichever occurs first.

HISTORY: 136 v H 164. Eff 1-13-76.

The provisions of § 4 of HB 164 (136 v —) read as follows:

SECTION 4. The following appropriations to the Ohio Public Defender Commission are contingent upon the availability of, and shall be made available for use from general revenue fund moneys appropriated to the Emergency Purposes Fund of the controlling board in Item 911-401 in Am. Sub. H.B. No. 155 of the 111th General Assembly, moneys available from LEAA and other federal programs, and moneys available from other sources.

OHIO PUBLIC DEFENDER COMMISSION

		1975-1976	1976-1977	Biennium
Operating Expenses Subsidy		$300,000	$ 800,000	$1,100,000
019-501	County & Joint County Public Defender Systems	$500,000	$1,200,000	$1,700,000
Total		$800,000	$2,000,000	$2,800,000

The foregoing appropriations shall be used to implement the provisions of this act in accordance with this section.

The foregoing subsidy appropriation, 'County and Joint County Public Defender Systems', shall be used to meet the initial costs of establishing and operating the offices of the county and joint county public defender commissions. The Ohio public defender commission shall secure budget requests from county and joint county public defender commissions, to be used with moneys from other sources so as to maximize the implementation of this act: The Ohio public defender commission, in consultation with the office of budget and management, shall have authority to develop forms and procedures necessary for finalizing the preceding budget recommendations, to take recommendations for reallocations of moneys, and for the biennial period beginning July 1, 1975 notwithstanding any other provisions of this act, to determine which matching requirements, if any, shall apply to the foregoing subsidy appropriation. The expenditure of the appropriation shall be subject to provisions applicable to appropriations made in section 2, Am. Sub. H.B. 155, 111th general assembly, that are not in conflict with provisions of this act.

§ 120.02 Meetings; compensation.

The members of the Ohio public defender commission shall meet at least quarterly, and shall meet at other times pursuant to the call of the chairman of the commission or at the request of the state public defender. The members of the commission shall receive an amount fixed pursuant to section 124.14 of the Revised Code per diem for every meeting of the commission that they attend, together with the actual and necessary expenses that they incur, and mileage for each mile necessarily traveled, in connection with every meeting of the commission that they attend.

HISTORY: 136 v H 164 (Eff 1-13-76); 144 v H 210. Eff 5-1-92.

§ 120.03 Powers and duties.

(A) The Ohio public defender commission shall appoint the state public defender, who shall serve at the pleasure of the commission.

(B) The Ohio public defender commission shall establish rules for the conduct of the offices of the county and joint county public defenders and for the conduct of county appointed counsel systems in the state. These rules shall include, but are not limited to, the following:

(1) Standards of indigency and minimum qualifications for legal representation by a public defender or appointed counsel. In establishing standards of indigency and determining who is eligible for legal representation by a public defender or appointed counsel, the commission shall consider an indigent person to be an individual who at the time his need is determined is unable to provide for the payment of an attorney and all other necessary expenses of representation. Release on bail shall not prevent a person from being determined to be indigent.

(2) Standards for the hiring of outside counsel;

(3) Standards for contracts by a public defender with law schools, legal aid societies, and nonprofit organizations for providing counsel;

(4) Standards for the qualifications, training, and size of the legal and supporting staff for a public defender, facilities, and other requirements needed to maintain and operate an office of a public defender;

(5) Minimum caseload standards;

(6) Procedures for the assessment and collection of the costs of legal representation that is provided by public defenders or appointed counsel;

(7) Standards and guidelines for determining whether a client is able to make an up-front contribution toward the cost of his legal representation;

(8) Procedures for the collection of up-front contributions from clients who are able to contribute toward the cost of their legal representation, as determined pursuant to the standards and guidelines developed under division (B)(7) of this section. All of such up-front contributions shall be paid into the appropriate county fund.

(9) Standards for contracts between a board of county commissioners, a county public defender commission, or a joint county public defender commission and a municipal corporation for the legal representation of indigent persons charged with violations of the ordinances of the municipal corporation.

(C) The Ohio public defender commission shall adopt rules prescribing minimum qualifications of counsel appointed pursuant to this chapter or appointed by the courts. Without limiting its general authority to prescribe different qualifications for different categories of appointed counsel, the commission shall prescribe, by rule, special qualifications for counsel and co-counsel appointed in capital cases.

(D) In administering the office of the Ohio public defender commission:

(1) The commission shall do the following:

(a) Approve an annual operating budget;

(b) Make an annual report to the governor, the general assembly, and the supreme court of Ohio on the operation of the state public defender's office, the county appointed counsel systems, and the county and joint county public defenders' offices.

(2) The commission may do the following:

(a) Accept the services of volunteer workers and consultants at no compensation other than reimbursement of actual and necessary expenses;

(b) Prepare and publish statistical and case studies and other data pertinent to the legal representation of indigent persons;

(c) Conduct programs having a general objective of training and educating attorneys and others in the legal representation of indigent persons.

(E) There is hereby established in the state treasury the public defender training fund for the deposit of fees received by the Ohio public defender commission from educational seminars, and the sale of publications, on topics concerning criminal law and procedure. Expenditures from this fund shall be made only for the operation of activities authorized by division (D)(2)(c) of this section.

(F)(1) In accordance with sections 109.02, 109.07, and 109.361 [109.36.1] to 109.366 [109.36.6] of the Revised Code, but subject to division (E) of section 120.06 of the Revised Code, the attorney general shall represent or provide for the representation of the Ohio public defender commission, the state public defender, assistant state public defenders, and other employees of the commission or the state public defender.

(2) Subject to division (E) of section 120.06 of the Revised Code, the attorney general shall represent or provide for the representation of attorneys described in division (C) of section 120.41 of the Revised Code in malpractice or other civil actions or proceedings that arise from alleged actions or omissions related to responsibilities derived pursuant to this chapter, or in civil actions that are based upon alleged violations of the constitution or statutes of the United States, including section 1983 of Title 42 of the United States Code, 93 Stat. 1284 (1979), 42 U.S.C.A. 1983, as amended, and that arise from alleged actions or omissions related to responsibilities derived pursuant to this chapter. For purposes of the representation, sections 109.361 [109.36.1] to 109.366 [109.36.6] of the Revised Code shall apply to an attorney described in division (C) of section 120.41 of the Revised Code as if he were an officer or employee, as defined in section 109.36 of the Revised Code, and the Ohio public defender commission or the state public defender, whichever contracted with the attorney, shall be considered his employer.

HISTORY: 136 v H 164 (Eff 1-13-76); 138 v H 204 (Eff 7-30-79); 139 v H 694 (Eff 11-15-81); 140 v H 291 (Eff 7-1-83); 140 v S 271 (Eff 9-26-84); 141 v H 201 (Eff 7-1-85); 144 v H 210 (Eff 5-1-92); 145 v H 152. Eff 7-1-93.

§ 120.04 State public defender; powers and duties.

(A) The state public defender shall serve at the pleasure of the Ohio public defender commission and shall be an attorney with a minimum of four years of experience in the practice of law and be admitted to the practice of law in this state at least one year prior to appointment.

(B) The state public defender shall do all of the following:

(1) Maintain a central office in Columbus. The central office shall be provided with a library of adequate size, considering the needs of the office and the accessibility of other libraries, and other necessary facilities and equipment.

(2) Appoint assistant state public defenders, all of whom shall be attorneys admitted to the practice of law in this state, and other personnel necessary for the operation of the state public defender office. Assistant state public defenders shall be appointed on a full-time basis. The state public defender, assistant state public defenders, and employees appointed by the state public defender shall not engage in the private practice of law.

(3) Supervise the compliance of county public defender offices, joint county public defender offices, and county appointed counsel systems with standards established by rules of the Ohio public defender commission pursuant to division (B) of section 120.03 of the Revised Code;

(4) Keep and maintain financial records of all cases handled and develop records for use in the calculation of direct and indirect costs, in the operation of the office, and report periodically, but not less than annually, to the commission on all relevant data on the operations of the office, costs, projected needs, and recommendations for legislation or amendments to court rules, as may be appropriate to improve the criminal justice system;

(5) Collect all moneys due the state for reimbursement for legal services under this chapter and under section 2941.51 of the Revised Code and institute any actions in court on behalf of the state for the collection of such sums that the state public defender considers advisable. Except as provided otherwise in division (D) of section 120.06 of the Revised Code, all moneys collected by the state public defender under this chapter and section 2941.51 of the Revised Code shall be deposited in the state treasury to the credit of the client payment fund, which is hereby created. All moneys credited to the fund shall be used by the state public defender to appoint assistant state public defenders and to provide other personnel, equipment, and facilities

necessary for the operation of the state public defender office, to reimburse counties for the operation of county public defender offices, joint county public defender offices, and county appointed counsel systems pursuant to sections 120.18, 120.28, and 120.33 of the Revised Code, or to provide assistance to counties in the operation of county indigent defense systems.

(6) With respect to funds appropriated to the commission to pay criminal costs, perform the duties imposed by section 2949.19 of the Revised Code;

(7) Establish standards and guidelines for the reimbursement, pursuant to sections 120.18, 120.28, 120.33, 2941.51, and 2949.19 of the Revised Code, of counties for the operation of county public defender offices, joint county public defender offices, and county appointed counsel systems and for other costs related to felony prosecutions;

(8) Establish maximum amounts that the state will reimburse the counties pursuant to sections 120.18, 120.28, 120.33, and 2941.51 of the Revised Code;

(9) Establish maximum amounts that the state will reimburse the counties pursuant to section 120.33 of the Revised Code for each specific type of legal service performed by a county appointed counsel system;

(10) Administer sections 120.18, 120.28, 120.33, 2941.51, and 2949.19 of the Revised Code and make reimbursements pursuant to those sections;

(11) Administer the program established pursuant to sections 120.51 to 120.55 of the Revised Code for the charitable public purpose of providing financial assistance to legal aid societies. Neither the state public defender nor any of the state public defender's employees who is responsible in any way for the administration of that program and who performs those administrative responsibilities in good faith is in any manner liable if a legal aid society that is provided financial assistance under the program uses the financial assistance other than in accordance with sections 120.51 to 120.55 of the Revised Code or fails to comply with the requirements of those sections.

(12) Establish an office for the handling of appeal and postconviction matters;

(13) Provide technical aid and assistance to county public defender offices, joint county public defender offices, and other local counsel providing legal representation to indigent persons, including representation and assistance on appeals.

(C) The state public defender may do any of the following:

(1) In providing legal representation, conduct investigations, obtain expert testimony, take depositions, use other discovery methods, order transcripts, and make all other preparations which are appropriate and necessary to an adequate defense or the prosecution of appeals and other legal proceedings;

(2) Seek, solicit, and apply for grants for the operation of programs for the defense of indigent persons from any public or private source, and may receive donations, grants, awards, and similar funds from any lawful source. Such funds shall be deposited in the state treasury to the credit of the public defender gifts and grants fund, which is hereby created.

(3) Make all the necessary arrangements to coordinate the services of the office with any federal, county, or private programs established to provide legal representation to indigent persons and others, and to obtain and provide all funds allowable under any such programs;

(4) Consult and cooperate with professional groups concerned with the causes of criminal conduct, the reduction of crime, the rehabilitation and correction of persons convicted of crime, the administration of criminal justice, and the administration and operation of the state public defender's office;

(5) Accept the services of volunteer workers and consultants at no compensation other than reimbursement for actual and necessary expenses;

(6) Prescribe any forms that are necessary for the uniform operation of this chapter;

(7) Contract with a county public defender commission or a joint county public defender commission to provide all or any part of the services that a county public defender or joint county public defender is required or permitted to provide by this chapter, or contract with a board of county commissioners of a county that is not served by a county public defender commission or a joint county public defender commission for the provision of services in accordance with section 120.33 of the Revised Code. All money received by the state public defender pursuant to such a contract shall be credited to the county representation fund created pursuant to division (D) of section 120.06 of the Revised Code.

(8) Authorize persons employed as criminal investigators to attend the Ohio peace officer training academy or any other peace officer training school for training;

(9) Procure a policy or policies of malpractice insurance that provide coverage for the state public defender and assistant state public defenders in connection with malpractice claims that may arise from their actions or omissions related to responsibilities derived pursuant to this chapter.

(D) No person employed by the state public defender as a criminal investigator shall attend the Ohio peace officer training academy or any other peace officer training school unless authorized to do so by the state public defender.

HISTORY: 136 v H 164 (Eff 1-13-76); 138 v H 204 (Eff 7-30-79); 139 v H 694 (Eff 11-15-81); 140 v H 291 (Eff 7-1-83); 140 v S 271 (Eff 9-26-84); 140 v S 219 (Eff 1-8-85); 141 v H 201 (Eff 7-1-85); 141 v S 149 (Eff 6-6-86); 141 v H 428 (Eff 12-23-86); 142 v H 171 (Eff 7-1-87); 144 v H 210 (Eff 5-1-92); 147 v H 215. Eff 9-29-97.

The provisions of § 191 of HB 215 (147 v —) read as follows:

SECTION 191. The client payment fund, which the public defender reimbursement fund was renamed in this act through the amendments to sections 120.04, 120.33, and 2941.51 of

§ 120.05 Determination of indigency.

(A) The determination of indigency shall be made by the state public defender, subject to review by the court. This section does not apply in relation to sections 120.51 to 120.55 of the Revised Code.

(B) The state public defender shall investigate the financial status of each person to be represented, at the earliest time the circumstances permit, and may require the person represented to disclose the records of public or private income sources and property, otherwise confidential, which may be of aid in determining indigency. The state public defender may obtain information from any public record contained in any office of the state, or any political subdivision or agency thereof, on request without payment of any fees ordinarily required by law. He shall make the results of the investigation available to the court upon request. The court, before whom a person seeking representation is taken, may determine the person's eligibility for legal representation by the state public defender.

(C) If a determination of eligibility cannot be made before the time when the first services are to be rendered by the state public defender, he shall render such services on a provisional basis. If the state public defender, or the court on review, subsequently determines that the person receiving the services is ineligible, the public defender shall notify the person of the termination of his services.

(D) Where the person represented has, or may reasonably be expected to have, the means to meet some part of the cost of the services rendered to him, he shall reimburse the state public defender in an amount which he can reasonably be expected to pay.

(E) If it is determined by the state public defender, or by the court, that the legal representation was provided to a person not entitled thereto, the person may be required to reimburse the public defender for the costs of the representation provided. Any action filed by the state public defender to collect legal fees hereunder, must be brought within two years from the last date legal representation was provided.

HISTORY: 136 v H 164 (Eff 1-13-76); 140 v S 219. Eff 1-8-85.

§ 120.06 State public defender to provide representation to indigents; defense of malpractice and similar actions.

(A)(1) The state public defender, when designated by the court or requested by a county public defender or joint county public defender, may provide legal representation in all courts throughout the state to indigent adults and juveniles who are charged with the commission of an offense or act for which the penalty or any possible adjudication includes the potential loss of liberty.

(2) The state public defender may provide legal representation to any indigent person who, while incarcerated in any state correctional institution, is charged with a felony offense, for which the penalty or any possible adjudication that may be imposed by a court upon conviction includes the potential loss of liberty.

(3) The state public defender may provide legal representation to any person incarcerated in any correctional institution of the state, in any matter in which the person asserts the person is unlawfully imprisoned or detained.

(4) The state public defender, in any case in which the state public defender has provided legal representation or is requested to do so by a county public defender or joint county public defender, may provide legal representation on appeal.

(5) The state public defender, when designated by the court or requested by a county public defender, joint county public defender, or the director of rehabilitation and correction, shall provide legal representation in parole and probation revocation matters, unless the state public defender finds that the alleged parole or probation violator has the financial capacity to retain the alleged violator's own counsel.

(6) If the state public defender contracts with a county public defender commission, a joint county public defender commission, or a board of county commissioners for the provision of services, under authority of division (C)(7) of section 120.04 of the Revised Code, the state public defender shall provide legal representation in accordance with the contract.

(B) The state public defender shall not be required to prosecute any appeal, postconviction remedy, or other proceeding pursuant to division (A)(3), (4), or (5) of this section, unless the state public defender first is satisfied that there is arguable merit to the proceeding.

(C) A court may appoint counsel or allow an indigent person to select the indigent's own personal counsel to assist the state public defender as co-counsel when the interests of justice so require. When co-counsel is appointed to assist the state public defender, the co-counsel shall receive any compensation that the court may approve, not to exceed the amounts provided for in section 2941.51 of the Revised Code.

(D) When the state public defender is designated by the court or requested by a county public defender or joint county public defender to provide legal representation for an indigent person in any case, other than pursuant to a contract entered into under authority of division (C)(7) of section 120.04 of the Revised Code, the state public defender shall send to the county in which the case is filed an itemized bill for fifty per cent of the actual cost of the representation. The county, upon receipt of an itemized bill from the state public defender pursuant to this division, shall pay fifty per cent of the actual cost of the legal representation as set forth in the itemized bill. There is hereby created in the state treasury the county representation fund for the deposit of moneys received from counties under this division. All moneys credited to the fund shall be used by the state public defender to provide legal representation for indigent persons when designated by the court or requested by a county or joint county public defender.

(E)(1) Notwithstanding any contrary provision of sections 109.02, 109.07, 109.361 [109.36.1] to 109.366 [109.36.6], and 120.03 of the Revised Code that pertains to representation by the attorney general, an assistant attorney general, or special counsel of an officer or employee, as defined in section 109.36 of the Revised Code, or of an entity of state government, the state public defender may elect to contract with, and to have the state pay pursuant to division (E)(2) of this section for the services of, private legal counsel to represent the Ohio public defender commission, the state public defender, assistant state public defenders, other employees of the commission or the state public defender, and attorneys described in division (C) of section 120.41 of the Revised Code in a malpractice or other civil action or proceeding that arises from alleged actions or omissions related to responsibilities derived pursuant to this chapter, or in a civil action that is based upon alleged violations of the constitution or statutes of the United States, including section 1983 of Title 42 of the United States Code, 93 Stat. 1284 (1979), 42 U.S.C.A. 1983, as amended, and that arises from alleged actions or omissions related to responsibilities derived pursuant to this chapter, if the state public defender determines, in good faith, that the defendant in the civil action or proceeding did not act manifestly outside the scope of the defendant's employment or official responsibilities, with malicious purpose, in bad faith, or in a wanton or reckless manner. If the state public defender elects not to contract pursuant to this division for private legal counsel in a civil action or proceeding, then, in accordance with sections 109.02, 109.07, 109.361 [109.36.1] to 109.366 [109.36.6], and 120.03 of the Revised Code, the attorney general shall represent or provide for the representation of the Ohio public defender commission, the state public defender, assistant state public defenders, other employees of the commission or the state public defender, or attorneys described in division (C) of section 120.41 of the Revised Code in the civil action or proceeding.

(2)(a) Subject to division (E)(2)(b) of this section, payment from the state treasury for the services of private legal counsel with whom the state public defender has contracted pursuant to division (E)(1) of this section shall be accomplished only through the following procedure:

(i) The private legal counsel shall file with the attorney general a copy of the contract; a request for an award of legal fees, court costs, and expenses earned or incurred in connection with the defense of the Ohio public defender commission, the state public defender, an assistant state public defender, an employee, or an attorney in a specified civil action or proceeding; a written itemization of those fees, costs, and expenses, including the signature of the state public defender and the state public defender's attestation that the fees, costs, and expenses were earned or incurred pursuant to division (E)(1) of this section to the best of the state public defender's knowledge and information; a written statement whether the fees, costs, and expenses are for all legal services to be rendered in connection with that defense, are only for legal services rendered to the date of the request and additional legal services likely will have to be provided in connection with that defense, or are for the final legal services rendered in connection with that defense; a written statement indicating whether the private legal counsel previously submitted a request for an award under division (E)(2) of this section in connection with that defense and, if so, the date and the amount of each award granted; and, if the fees, costs, and expenses are for all legal services to be rendered in connection with that defense or are for the final legal services rendered in connection with that defense, a certified copy of any judgment entry in the civil action or proceeding or a signed copy of any settlement agreement entered into between the parties to the civil action or proceeding.

(ii) Upon receipt of a request for an award of legal fees, court costs, and expenses and the requisite supportive documentation described in division (E)(2)(a)(i) of this section, the attorney general shall review the request and documentation; determine whether any of the limitations specified in division (E)(2)(b) of this section apply to the request; and, if an award of legal fees, court costs, or expenses is permissible after applying the limitations, prepare a document awarding legal fees, court costs, or expenses to the private legal counsel. The document shall name the private legal counsel as the recipient of the award; specify the total amount of the award as determined by the attorney general; itemize the portions of the award that represent legal fees, court costs, and expenses; specify any limitation applied pursuant to division (E)(2)(b) of this section to reduce the amount of the award sought by the private legal counsel; state that the award is payable from the state treasury pursuant to division (E)(2)(a)(iii) of this section; and be approved by the inclusion of the signatures of the attorney general, the state public defender, and the private legal counsel.

(iii) The attorney general shall forward a copy of the document prepared pursuant to division (E)(2)(a)(ii) of this section to the director of budget and management. The director shall make application for the payment of the award of legal fees, court costs, or expenses out of the emergency purposes account or any other appropriation for emergencies or contingencies, and payments out of that account or any other appropriation for emergencies or contingencies shall be authorized if there are sufficient moneys greater than the sum total of then pending emergency purposes account requests, or requests for releases from the other appropriation. If sufficient moneys exist in the emergency purposes account or other appropriation for emergencies or contingencies to pay the award, the director shall cause payment of the award to be made to the private legal counsel. If sufficient moneys do not exist in the emergency purposes account or other appropriation for emergencies or contingencies to pay the award, the private legal counsel shall request the general assembly to make an appropriation sufficient to pay the award, and no payment shall be made until the appropriation has been made. The private legal counsel shall make the request during the current biennium and during each succeeding biennium until a sufficient appropriation is made.

(b) An award of legal fees, court costs, and expenses pursuant to division (E) of this section is subject to the following limitations:

(i) The maximum award or maximum aggregate of a series of awards of legal fees, court costs, and expenses to the private legal counsel in connection with the defense of the Ohio public defender commission, the state public defender, an assistant state public defender, an employee, or an attorney in a specified civil action or proceeding shall not exceed fifty thousand dollars.

(ii) The private legal counsel shall not be awarded legal fees, court costs, or expenses to the extent the fees, costs, or expenses are covered by a policy of malpractice or other insurance.

(iii) The private legal counsel shall be awarded legal fees and expenses only to the extent that the fees and expenses are reasonable in light of the legal services rendered by the private legal counsel in connection with the defense of the Ohio public defender commission, the state public defender, an assistant state public defender, an employee, or an attorney in a specified civil action or proceeding.

(c) If, pursuant to division (E)(2)(a) of this section, the attorney general denies a request for an award of legal fees, court costs, or expenses to private legal counsel because of the application of a limitation specified in division (E)(2)(b) of this section, the attorney general shall notify the private legal counsel in writing of the denial and of the limitation applied.

(d) If, pursuant to division (E)(2)(c) of this section, a private legal counsel receives a denial of an award notification or if a private legal counsel refuses to approve a document under division (E)(2)(a)(ii) of this section because of the proposed application of a limitation specified in division (E)(2)(b) of this section, the private legal counsel may commence a civil action against the attorney general in the court of claims to prove the private legal counsel's entitlement to the award sought, to prove that division (E)(2)(b) of this section does not prohibit or otherwise limit the award sought, and to recover a judgment for the amount of the award sought. A civil action under division (E)(2)(d) of this section shall be commenced no later than two years after receipt of a denial of award notification or, if the private legal counsel refused to approve a document under division (E)(2)(a)(ii) of this section because of the proposed application of a limitation specified in division (E)(2)(b) of this section, no later than two years after the refusal. Any judgment of the court of claims in favor of the private legal counsel shall be paid from the state treasury in accordance with division (E)(2)(a) of this section.

(F) If a court appoints the office of the state public defender to represent a petitioner in a postconviction relief proceeding under section 2953.21 of the Revised Code, the petitioner has received a sentence of death, and the proceeding relates to that sentence, all of the attorneys who represent the petitioner in the proceeding pursuant to the appointment, whether an assistant state public defender, the state public defender, or another attorney, shall be certified under Rule 65 of the Rules of Superintendence for Common Pleas Courts to represent indigent defendants charged with or convicted of an offense for which the death penalty can be or has been imposed.

HISTORY: 136 v H 164 (Eff 1-13-76); 138 v H 204 (Eff 7-30-79); 139 v H 694 (Eff 11-15-81); 140 v H 291 (Eff 7-1-83); 140 v S 271 (Eff 9-26-84); 141 v H 201 (Eff 7-1-85); 144 v H 210 (Eff 5-1-92); 145 v H 571 (Eff 10-6-94); 146 v S 258. Eff 10-16-96.

[COUNTY PUBLIC DEFENDER COMMISSION]

§ 120.13 County public defender commission.

(A) The county commissioners in any county may establish a county public defender commission. The commission shall have five members, three of whom shall be appointed by the board of county commissioners, and two by the judge, or the presiding judge if there is one, of the court of common pleas of the county. At least one member appointed by each of these appointing bodies shall be an attorney admitted to the practice of law in this state.

(B) The board of county commissioners shall select a specific day for the county public defender commission to be established and on which all members' appointments shall take effect, and shall notify the Ohio public defender commission of the date.

(C) Of the initial appointments made to the county public defender commission, two appointments by the county commissioners and one appointment by the court shall be for a term of two years ending two years after the date the commission is established, and one appointment by each of the appointing bodies shall be for a term ending four years after the date the commission is established. Thereafter, terms of office shall be for four years, each term ending on the same day of the same month of the year as did the term which it succeeds. Each member shall hold office from the date of his appointment until the end of the term for which he was appointed. Any member appointed to fill a vacancy occurring prior to the expiration of the term for which his predecessor was appointed shall hold office for the remainder of such term. Any member shall continue in office subsequent to the expiration date of his term until his successor takes office, or until a period of sixty days has elapsed, whichever occurs first.

(D) The members of the commission shall choose as chairman one of the commission members, who shall serve as chairman for two years. Meetings shall be held at least quarterly and at such other times as called by the chairman or by request of the county public defender. Members of the commission may receive an amount fixed by the county commissioners, but not in excess of the amounts set for the members of the Ohio public defender commission pursuant to section 124.14 of the Revised Code per diem for every meeting of the board they attend, and necessary expenses including mileage for each mile necessarily traveled.

(E) The county commissioners may terminate the county public defender commission at any time if at least ninety days prior to termination, the commissioners notify the Ohio public defender commission in writing of the termination date. Upon the termination date all pending county public defender matters shall be transferred to the state public defender, a joint county public defender, or appointed counsel.

(F) Fifty per cent of the cost of representation in all matters assumed by the state public defender shall be charged to the counties in accordance with division (D) of section 120.06 of the Revised Code.

HISTORY: 136 v H 164 (Eff 1-13-76); 139 v H 694. Eff 11-15-81.

§ 120.14 Powers and duties.

(A)(1) Except as provided in division (A)(2) of this section, the county public defender commission shall appoint the county public defender and may remove him from office only for good cause.

(2) If a county public defender commission contracts with the state public defender or with one or more nonprofit organizations for the state public defender or the organizations to provide all of the services that the county public defender is required or permitted to provide by this chapter, the commission shall not appoint a county public defender.

(B) The commission shall determine the qualifications and size of the supporting staff and facilities and other requirements needed to maintain and operate the office of the county public defender.

(C) In administering the office of county public defender, the commission shall:

(1) Recommend to the county commissioners an annual operating budget which is subject to the review, amendment, and approval of the board of county commissioners;

(2)(a) Make an annual report to the county commissioners and the Ohio public defender commission on the operation of the county public defender's office, including complete and detailed information on finances and costs that separately states costs and expenses that are reimbursable under section 120.35 of the Revised Code, and any other data and information requested by the state public defender;

(b) Make monthly reports relating to reimbursement and associated case data pursuant to the rules of the Ohio public defender commission to the board of county commissioners and the Ohio public defender commission on the total costs of the public defender's office.

(3) Cooperate with the Ohio public defender commission in maintaining the standards established by rules of the Ohio public defender commission pursuant to divisions (B) and (C) of section 120.03 of the Revised Code, and cooperate with the state public defender in his programs providing technical aid and assistance to county systems.

(D) The commission may accept the services of volunteer workers and consultants at no compensation except reimbursement for actual and necessary expenses.

(E) The commission may contract with any municipal corporation, within the county served by the county public defender, for the county public defender to provide legal representation for indigent persons who are charged with a violation of the ordinances of the municipal corporation.

(F) A county public defender commission, with the approval of the board of county commissioners regarding all provisions that pertain to the financing of defense counsel for indigent persons, may contract with the state public defender or with any nonprofit organization, the primary purpose of which is to provide legal representation to indigent persons, for the state public defender or the organization to provide all or any part of the services that a county public defender is required or permitted to provide by this chapter. A contract entered into pursuant to this division may provide for payment for the services provided on a per case, hourly, or fixed contract basis. The state public defender and any nonprofit organization that contracts with a county public defender commission pursuant to this division shall do all of the following:

(1) Comply with all standards established by the rules of the Ohio public defender commission;

(2) Comply with all standards established by the state public defender;

(3) Comply with all statutory duties and other laws applicable to county public defenders.

HISTORY: 136 v H 164 (Eff 1-13-76); 140 v H 291 (Eff 7-1-83); 140 v S 271. Eff 9-26-84.

§ 120.15 County public defender; powers and duties; determination of indigency.

(A) The county public defender shall be appointed

by the county public defender commission for a term not to exceed four years. He shall be an attorney with a minimum of two years experience in the practice of law and be admitted to the practice of law in Ohio at least one year prior to his appointment.

(B) In carrying out the responsibilities and performing the duties of his office, the county public defender shall:

(1) Maintain an office, approved by the commission, provided with a library of adequate size, considering the needs of the office and the accessibility of other libraries, and other necessary facilities and equipment;

(2) Keep and maintain financial records of all cases handled and develop records for use in the calculation of direct and indirect costs in the operation of the office and report monthly pursuant to the rules of the Ohio public defender commission to the county public defender commission and to the Ohio public defender commission on all relevant data on the operations of the office, costs, projected needs, and recommendations for legislation or amendments to court rules, as may be appropriate to improve the criminal justice system;

(3) Collect all moneys due from contracts with municipal corporations or for reimbursement for legal services under this chapter and institute such actions in court for the collection of such sums as he considers advisable. All moneys collected or received by the public defender shall be paid into the county treasury to the credit of the general revenue fund.

(4) Appoint assistant county public defenders and all other personnel necessary to the functioning of the county public defender's office, subject to the authority of the county public defender commission to determine the size and qualifications of the staff pursuant to division (B) of section 120.14 of the Revised Code. All assistant county public defenders shall be admitted to the practice of law in Ohio, and may be appointed on a full or part-time basis.

(C) The county public defender may exercise the rights authorized in division (C) of section 120.04 of the Revised Code.

(D) The county public defender shall determine indigency of persons, subject to review by the court, in the same manner as provided in section 120.05 of the Revised Code. Each monthly report submitted to the board of county commissioners and the state public defender shall include a certification by the county public defender that all persons provided representation by the county public defender's office during the month covered by the report were indigent under the standards of the Ohio public defender commission.

HISTORY: 136 v H 164 (Eff 1-13-76); 140 v S 271. Eff 9-26-84.

§ 120.16 When representation to be provided; notice to accused.

(A)(1) The county public defender shall provide legal representation to indigent adults and juveniles who are charged with the commission of an offense or act that is a violation of a state statute and for which the penalty or any possible adjudication includes the potential loss of liberty and in postconviction proceedings as defined in this section.

(2) The county public defender may provide legal representation to indigent adults and juveniles charged with the violation of an ordinance of a municipal corporation for which the penalty or any possible adjudication includes the potential loss of liberty, if the county public defender commission has contracted with the municipal corporation to provide legal representation for indigent persons charged with a violation of an ordinance of the municipal corporation.

(B) The county public defender shall provide the legal representation authorized by division (A) of this section at every stage of the proceedings following arrest, detention, service of summons, or indictment.

(C) The county public defender may request the state public defender to prosecute any appeal or other remedy before or after conviction that the county public defender decides is in the interests of justice, and may provide legal representation in parole and probation revocation matters.

(D) The county public defender shall not be required to prosecute any appeal, postconviction remedy, or other proceeding, unless the county public defender is first satisfied there is arguable merit to the proceeding.

(E) Nothing in this section shall prevent a court from appointing counsel other than the county public defender or from allowing an indigent person to select the indigent person's own personal counsel to represent the indigent person. A court may also appoint counsel or allow an indigent person to select the indigent person's own personal counsel to assist the county public defender as co-counsel when the interests of justice so require.

(F) Information as to the right to legal representation by the county public defender or assigned counsel shall be afforded to an accused person immediately upon arrest, when brought before a magistrate, or when formally charged, whichever occurs first.

(G) If a court appoints the office of the county public defender to represent a petitioner in a postconviction relief proceeding under section 2953.21 of the Revised Code, the petitioner has received a sentence of death, and the proceeding relates to that sentence, all of the attorneys who represent the petitioner in the proceeding pursuant to the appointment, whether an assistant county public defender or the county public defender, shall be certified under Rule 65 of the Rules of Superintendence for Common Pleas Courts to represent indigent defendants charged with or convicted of an offense for which the death penalty can be or has been imposed.

HISTORY: 136 v H 164 (Eff 1-13-76); 138 v H 204 (Eff 7-30-79); 140 v S 271 (Eff 9-26-84); 146 v S 258. Eff 10-16-96.

§ 120.17 County public defender precludes representation by state public defender; exceptions.

In any county in which the county commissioners choose to establish a county public defender's office, the Ohio public defender shall not be required to defend indigent persons in that county, except as set forth in division (A) of section 120.06 of the Revised Code, or if the court finds that it is required in the interests of justice.

HISTORY: 136 v H 164. Eff 1-13-76.

§ 120.18 Cost of county public defender's office; reimbursement.

(A) The county public defender commission's report to the board of county commissioners shall be audited by the county auditor. The board of county commissioners, after review and approval of the audited report, may then certify it to the state public defender for reimbursement. If a request for the reimbursement of any operating expenditure incurred by a county public defender office is not received by the state public defender within sixty days after the end of the calendar month in which the expenditure is incurred, the state public defender shall not pay the requested reimbursement, unless the county has requested, and the state public defender has granted, an extension of the sixty-day time limit. Each request for reimbursement shall include a certification by the county public defender that the persons provided representation by the county public defender's office during the period covered by the report were indigent. The state public defender shall also review the report and, in accordance with the standards, guidelines, and maximums established pursuant to divisions (B)(7) and (8) of section 120.04 of the Revised Code, prepare a voucher for fifty per cent of the total cost of each county public defender's office for the period of time covered by the certified report and a voucher for fifty per cent of the costs and expenses that are reimbursable under section 120.35 of the Revised Code, if any, or, if the amount of money appropriated by the general assembly to reimburse counties for the operation of county public defender offices, joint county public defender offices, and county appointed counsel systems is not sufficient to pay fifty per cent of the total cost of all of the offices and systems, for the lesser amount required by section 120.34 of the Revised Code. For the purposes of this section, "total cost" means total expenses minus costs and expenses reimbursable under section 120.35 of the Revised Code and any funds received by the county public defender commission pursuant to a contract, except a contract entered into with a municipal corporation pursuant to division (E) of section 120.14 of the Revised Code, gift, or grant.

(B) If the county public defender fails to maintain the standards for the conduct of the office established by rules of the Ohio public defender commission pursuant to divisions (B) and (C) of section 120.03 or the standards established by the state public defender pursuant to division (B)(7) of section 120.04 of the Revised Code, the Ohio public defender commission shall notify the county public defender commission and the board of county commissioners of the county that the county public defender has failed to comply with its rules or the standards of the state public defender. Unless the county public defender commission or the county public defender corrects the conduct of his office to comply with the rules and standards within ninety days after the date of the notice, the state public defender may deny payment of all or part of the county's reimbursement from the state provided for in division (A) of this section.

HISTORY: 136 v H 164 (Eff 1-13-76); 138 v H 204 (Eff 7-30-79); 139 v H 694 (Eff 11-15-81); 140 v H 291 (Eff 7-1-83); 140 v S 271 (Eff 9-26-84); 141 v H 201 (Eff 7-1-85); 146 v H 117. Eff 6-30-95.

[JOINT COUNTY PUBLIC DEFENDER COMMISSION]

§ 120.23 Joint county public defender commission.

(A) The boards of county commissioners in two or more adjoining or neighboring counties may form themselves into a joint board and proceed to organize a district for the establishment of a joint county public defender commission. The commission shall have three members from each county, who shall be appointed by the board of county commissioners of the county.

(B) The boards shall agree on a specific date for the joint county public defender commission to be established, on which date the appointments of all members shall take effect. The joint board shall notify the Ohio public defender commission of the date.

(C) Of the initial appointments made by each county to the joint county public defender commission, one appointment shall be for a term of one year ending one year after the date the commission is established, one appointment shall be for a term of two years ending two years after the date the commission is established, and one appointment shall be for a period of three years, ending three years after the date the commission is established. Thereafter, terms of office shall be for three years, each term ending on the same day of the same month of the year as did the term which it succeeds. Each member shall hold office from the date of his appointment until the end of the term for which he was appointed. Any member appointed to fill a vacancy occurring prior to the expiration of the term for which his predecessor was appointed shall hold office for the remainder of the term. Any member shall continue in office subsequent to the expiration date of his term until his successor takes office, or until a period of sixty days has elapsed, whichever occurs first.

(D) The members of the commission shall choose as chairman one of the commission members, who shall serve as chairman for two years. Meetings shall be held at least quarterly and at such other times as called by the chairman or by request of the joint county public defender. Members of the commission may receive an amount fixed by the agreement of the boards of commissioners of the counties in the district, but not in excess of the amount set for the members of the Ohio public defender commission pursuant to section 124.14 of the Revised Code per diem for every meeting of the commission they attend, and necessary expenses including mileage for each mile necessarily traveled.

(E) The agreement of the boards of county commissioners establishing the joint county public defender commission shall provide for the allocation of the proportion of expenses to be paid by each county, which may be based upon population, number of cases, or such other factors as the commissioners determine to be appropriate. The county commissioners may amend their agreement from time to time to provide for a different allocation of the proportion of expenses to be paid by each county.

(F) The county auditor of the county, with the greatest population is herey designated as the fiscal officer of a joint county public defender district organized under this section. The county auditors of the several counties composing the joint county public defender commission district shall meet at the commission office not less than once in each six months, to adjust accounts and to transact such other duties in connection with the commission as pertain to the business of their office.

(G) Each member of the board of county commissioners who meets by appointment to consider the organization of a joint county public defender commission shall, upon presentation of properly certified accounts, be paid his necessary expenses upon a warrant drawn by the county auditor of his county.

(H) The board of county commissioners of any county within a joint county public defender commission district may withdraw from the district. Such withdrawal shall not be effective until at least ninety days after the board has notified the Ohio public defender commission, the joint county public defender commission of the district, and each board of county commissioners in the district, in writing of the termination date. The failure of a board of county commissioners to approve an annual operating budget for the office of the joint county public defender as provided in division (C)(1) of section 120.24 of the Revised Code constitutes a notice of withdrawal by the county from the district, effective on the ninetieth day after commencement of the next fiscal year. Upon the termination date, all joint county public defender matters relating to the withdrawing county shall be transferred to the state public defender, a county public defender, or appointed counsel.

(I) Fifty per cent of the cost of representation in all matters assumed by the state public defender shall be charged to the counties in accordance with division (D) of section 120.06 of the Revised Code.

Members of the joint county public defender commission who are residents of a county withdrawing from such district are deemed to have resigned their positions upon the completion of the withdrawal procedure provided by this section. Vacancies thus created shall not be filled.

If two or more counties remain within the district after the withdrawal, the boards of county commissioners of the remaining adjoining or neighboring counties may agree to continue the operation of the joint county public defender commission and to reallocate the proportionate share of expenses to be paid by each participating county.

HISTORY: 136 v H 164 (Eff 1-13-76); 139 v H 694. Eff 11-15-81.

§ 120.24 Powers and duties.

(A)(1) Except as provided in division (A)(2) of this section, the joint county public defender commission shall appoint the joint county public defender and may remove him from office only for good cause.

(2) If a joint county public defender commission contracts with the state public defender or with one or more nonprofit organizations for the state public defender or the organizations to provide all of the services that the joint county public defender is required or permitted to provide by this chapter, the commission shall not appoint a joint county public defender.

(B) The commission shall determine the qualifications and size of the supporting staff and facilities and other requirements needed to maintain and operate the office.

(C) In administering the office of joint county public defender, the commission shall:

(1) Recommend to the boards of county commissioners in the district an annual operating budget which is subject to the review, amendment, and approval of the boards of county commissioners in the district;

(2)(a) Make an annual report to the boards of county commissioners in the district and the Ohio public defender commission on the operation of the public defender's office, including complete and detailed information on finances and costs that separately states costs and expenses that are reimbursable under section 120.35 of the Revised Code, and such other data and information requested by the state public defender;

(b) Make monthly reports relating to reimbursement and associated case data pursuant to the rules of the Ohio public defender commission to the boards of county commissioners in the district and the Ohio public defender commission on the total costs of the public defender's office.

(3) Cooperate with the Ohio public defender com-

mission in maintaining the standards established by rules of the Ohio public defender commission pursuant to divisions (B) and (C) of section 120.03 of the Revised Code, and cooperate with the state public defender in his programs providing technical aid and assistance to county systems.

(D) The commission may accept the services of volunteer workers and consultants at no compensation except reimbursement for actual and necessary expenses.

(E) The commission may contract with any municipal corporation, within the counties served by the joint county public defender, for the joint county public defender to provide legal representation for indigent persons who are charged with a violation of the ordinances of the municipal corporation.

(F) A joint county public defender commission, with the approval of each participating board of county commissioners regarding all provisions that pertain to the financing of defense counsel for indigent persons, may contract with the state public defender or with any nonprofit organization, the primary purpose of which is to provide legal representation to indigent persons, for the state public defender or the organization to provide all or any part of the services that a joint county public defender is required or permitted to provide by this chapter. A contract entered into pursuant to this division may provide for payment for the services provided on a per case, hourly, or fixed contract basis. The state public defender and any nonprofit organization that contracts with a joint county public defender commission pursuant to this division shall do all of the following:

(1) Comply with all standards established by the rules of the Ohio public defender commission;

(2) Comply with all standards established by the Ohio public defender;

(3) Comply with all statutory duties and other laws applicable to joint county public defenders.

HISTORY: 136 v H 164 (Eff 1-13-76); 140 v H 291 (Eff 7-1-83); 140 v S 271. Eff 9-26-84.

§ 120.25 Joint county public defender; powers and duties; determination of indigency.

(A) The joint county public defender shall be appointed by the joint county public defender commission for a term not to exceed four years. He shall be an attorney with a minimum of two years experience in the practice of law and be admitted to the practice of law in Ohio at least one year prior to his appointment.

(B) In carrying out the responsibilities and performing the duties of his office, the joint county public defender shall:

(1) Maintain an office, approved by the commission, provided with a library of adequate size, considering the needs of the office and the accessibility of other libraries, and other necessary facilities and equipment;

(2) Keep and maintain financial records of all cases handled and develop records for use in the calculation of direct and indirect costs in the operation of the office, and report monthly pursuant to the rules of the Ohio public defender commission to the joint county defender commission and to the Ohio public defender commission on all relevant data on the operations of the office, costs, projected needs, and recommendations for legislation or amendments to court rules, as may be appropriate to improve the criminal justice system;

(3) Collect all moneys due from contracts with municipal corporations or for reimbursement for legal services under this chapter and institute such actions in court for the collection of such sums as he considers advisable. The public defender shall pay into the treasury of each county in the district, to the credit of the general revenue fund, the county's proportionate share of all moneys collected or received by him.

(4) Appoint assistant joint county public defenders and all other personnel necessary to the functioning of the joint county public defender office, subject to the authority of the joint county public defender commission to determine the size and qualifications of the staff pursuant to division (B) of section 120.24 of the Revised Code. All assistant joint county public defenders shall be admitted to the practice of law in Ohio, and may be appointed on a full or part-time basis.

(C) The joint county public defender may exercise the rights authorized in division (C) of section 120.04 of the Revised Code.

(D) The joint county public defender shall determine indigency of persons, subject to review by the court, in the same manner as provided in section 120.05 of the Revised Code. Each monthly report submitted to the board of county commissioners and the state public defender shall include a certification by the joint county public defender that all persons provided representation by the joint county public defender's office during the month covered by the report were indigent under the standards of the Ohio public defender commission.

HISTORY: 136 v H 164 (Eff 1-13-76); 140 v S 271. Eff 9-26-84.

§ 120.26 When representation to be provided; notice to accused.

(A)(1) The joint county public defender shall provide legal representation to indigent adults and juveniles who are charged with the commission of an offense or act that is a violation of a state statute and for which the penalty or any possible adjudication includes the potential loss of liberty and in postconviction proceedings as defined in this section.

(2) The joint county public defender may provide legal representation to indigent adults and juveniles charged with the violation of an ordinance of a municipal corporation for which the penalty or any possible adjudication includes the potential loss of liberty, if the joint county public defender commission has contracted

with the municipal corporation to provide legal representation for indigent persons charged with a violation of an ordinance of the municipal corporation.

(B) The joint county public defender shall provide the legal representation authorized by division (A) of this section at every stage of the proceedings following arrest, detention, service of summons, or indictment.

(C) The joint county public defender may request the Ohio public defender to prosecute any appeal or other remedy before or after conviction that the joint county public defender decides is in the interests of justice and may provide legal representation in parole and probation revocation matters.

(D) The joint county public defender shall not be required to prosecute any appeal, postconviction remedy, or other proceeding, unless the joint county public defender is first satisfied that there is arguable merit to the proceeding.

(E) Nothing in this section shall prevent a court from appointing counsel other than the joint county public defender or from allowing an indigent person to select the indigent person's own personal counsel to represent the indigent person. A court may also appoint counsel or allow an indigent person to select the indigent person's own personal counsel to assist the joint county public defender as co-counsel when the interests of justice so require.

(F) Information as to the right to legal representation by the joint county public defender or assigned counsel shall be afforded to an accused person immediately upon arrest, when brought before a magistrate, or when formally charged, whichever occurs first.

(G) If a court appoints the office of the joint county public defender to represent a petitioner in a postconviction relief proceeding under section 2953.21 of the Revised Code, the petitioner has received a sentence of death, and the proceeding relates to that sentence, all of the attorneys who represent the petitioner in the proceeding pursuant to the appointment, whether an assistant joint county defender or the joint county public defender, shall be certified under Rule 65 of the Rules of Superintendence for Common Pleas Courts to represent indigent defendants charged with or convicted of an offense for which the death penalty can be or has been imposed.

HISTORY: 136 v H 164 (Eff 1-13-76); 138 v H 204 (Eff 7-30-79); 140 v S 271 (Eff 9-26-84); 146 v S 258. Eff 10-16-96.

§ 120.27 Joint county public defender precludes representation by state public defender.

In any counties in which the boards of county commissioners choose to establish a joint county public defender's office, the Ohio public defender shall not be required to defend indigent persons in those counties, except as set forth in division (A) of section 120.06 of the Revised Code, or if the court finds that it is required in the interests of justice.

HISTORY: 136 v H 164. Eff 1-13-76.

§ 120.28 Cost of joint county public defender's office; reimbursement.

(A) The joint county public defender commission's report to the joint board of county commissioners shall be audited by the fiscal officer of the district. The joint board of county commissioners, after review and approval of the audited report, may then certify it to the state public defender for reimbursement. If a request for the reimbursement of any operating expenditure incurred by a joint county public defender office is not received by the state public defender within sixty days after the end of the calendar month in which the expenditure is incurred, the state public defender shall not pay the requested reimbursement, unless the joint board of county commissioners has requested, and the state public defender has granted, an extension of the sixty-day time limit. Each request for reimbursement shall include a certification by the joint county public defender that all persons provided representation by the joint county public defender's office during the period covered by the request were indigent. The state public defender shall also review the report and, in accordance with the standards, guidelines, and maximums established pursuant to divisions (B)(7) and (8) of section 120.04 of the Revised Code, prepare a voucher for fifty per cent of the total cost of each joint county public defender's office for the period of time covered by the certified report and a voucher for fifty per cent of the costs and expenses that are reimbursable under section 120.35 of the Revised Code, if any, or, if the amount of money appropriated by the general assembly to reimburse counties for the operation of county public defender offices, joint county public defender offices, and county appointed counsel systems is not sufficient to pay fifty per cent of the total cost of all of the offices and systems, for the lesser amount required by section 120.34 of the Revised Code. For purposes of this section, "total cost" means total expenses minus costs and expenses reimbursable under section 120.35 of the Revised Code and any funds received by the joint county public defender commission pursuant to a contract, except a contract entered into with a municipal corporation pursuant to division (E) of section 120.24 of the Revised Code, gift, or grant. Each county in the district shall be entitled to a share of such state reimbursement in proportion to the percentage of the total cost it has agreed to pay.

(B) If the joint county public defender fails to maintain the standards for the conduct of the office established by the rules of the Ohio public defender commission pursuant to divisions (B) and (C) of section 120.03 or the standards established by the state public defender pursuant to division (B)(7) of section 120.04 of the Revised Code, the Ohio public defender commission shall notify the joint county public defender commission and the board of county commissioners of each county in the district that the joint county public defender has failed to comply with its rules or the standards of the state public defender. Unless the joint public defender commission or the joint county public defender corrects the conduct of his office to comply with the rules and standards within ninety days after the date of the notice, the state public defender may deny all or part of the counties' reimbursement from the state provided for in division (A) of this section.

HISTORY: 136 v H 164 (Eff 1-13-76); 138 v H 204 (Eff 7-30-79); 139 v H 694 (Eff 11-15-81); 140 v H 291 (Eff 7-1-83); 140 v S 271 (Eff 9-26-84); 141 v H 201 (Eff 7-1-85); 146 v H 117. Eff 6-30-95.

[COUNTY APPOINTED COUNSEL SYSTEM]

§ 120.33 County appointed counsel system.

(A) In lieu of using a county public defender or joint county public defender to represent indigent persons in the proceedings set forth in division (A) of section 120.16 of the Revised Code, the board of county commissioners of any county may adopt a resolution to pay counsel who are either personally selected by the indigent person or appointed by the court. The resolution shall include those provisions the board of county commissioners considers necessary to provide effective representation of indigent persons in any proceeding for which counsel is provided under this section. The resolution shall include provisions for contracts with any municipal corporation under which the municipal corporation shall reimburse the county for counsel appointed to represent indigent persons charged with violations of the ordinances of the municipal corporation.

(1) In a county that adopts a resolution to pay counsel, an indigent person shall have the right to do either of the following:

(a) To select the person's own personal counsel to represent the person in any proceeding included within the provisions of the resolution;

(b) To request the court to appoint counsel to represent the person in such a proceeding.

(2) The court having jurisdiction over the proceeding in a county that adopts a resolution to pay counsel shall, after determining that the person is indigent and entitled to legal representation under this section, do either of the following:

(a) By signed journal entry recorded on its docket, enter the name of the lawyer selected by the indigent person as counsel of record;

(b) Appoint counsel for the indigent person if the person has requested the court to appoint counsel and, by signed journal entry recorded on its dockets, enter the name of the lawyer appointed for the indigent person as counsel of record.

(3) The board of county commissioners shall establish a schedule of fees by case or on an hourly basis to be paid to counsel for legal services provided pursuant to a resolution adopted under this section. Prior to establishing the schedule, the board of county commissioners shall request the bar association or associations of the county to submit a proposed schedule. The schedule submitted shall be subject to the review, amendment, and approval of the board of county commissioners.

(4) Counsel selected by the indigent person or appointed by the court at the request of an indigent person in a county that adopts a resolution to pay counsel, except for counsel appointed to represent a person charged with any violation of an ordinance of a municipal corporation that has not contracted with the county commissioners for the payment of appointed counsel, shall be paid by the county and shall receive the compensation and expenses the court approves. Each request for payment shall be accompanied by an affidavit of indigency completed by the indigent person on forms prescribed by the state public defender. Compensation and expenses shall not exceed the amounts fixed by the board of county commissioners in the schedule adopted pursuant to division (A)(3) of this section. No court shall approve compensation and expenses that exceed the amount fixed pursuant to division (A)(3) of this section.

The fees and expenses approved by the court shall not be taxed as part of the costs and shall be paid by the county. However, if the person represented has, or may reasonably be expected to have, the means to meet some part of the cost of the services rendered to the person, the person shall pay the county an amount that the person reasonably can be expected to pay. Pursuant to section 120.04 of the Revised Code, the county shall pay to the state public defender a percentage of the payment received from the person in an amount proportionate to the percentage of the costs of the person's case that were paid to the county by the state public defender pursuant to this section. The money paid to the state public defender shall be credited to the client payment fund created pursuant to division (B)(5) of section 120.04 of the Revised Code.

The county auditor shall draw a warrant on the county treasurer for the payment of counsel in the amount fixed by the court, plus the expenses the court fixes and certifies to the auditor. The county auditor shall report periodically, but not less than annually, to the board of county commissioners and to the Ohio public defender commission the amounts paid out pursuant to the approval of the court. The board of county commissioners, after review and approval of the auditor's report, may then certify it to the state public defender for reimbursement. If a request for reimbursement is not accompanied by an affidavit of indigency completed by the indigent person on forms prescribed by the state public defender, the state public defender shall not pay the requested reimbursement. If a request for the reimbursement of the cost of counsel in any case is not received by the state public defender within ninety days after the end of the calendar month in which the case is finally disposed of by the court, unless the county has requested and the state public defender has granted an extension of the ninety-day limit, the state public defender shall not pay the requested reimbursement. The state public defender shall also review the report and, in accordance with the standards, guidelines, and maximums established pursuant to divisions (B)(7) and (8) of section 120.04 of the Revised Code, prepare a voucher for fifty per cent of the total cost of each county appointed counsel system in the period of time covered by the certified report and a voucher for fifty per cent of the costs and expenses that are reimbursable under section 120.35 of the Revised Code, if any, or, if the amount of money appropriated by the general assembly to reimburse counties for the operation of county public defender offices, joint county public defender offices, and county appointed counsel systems is not sufficient to pay fifty per cent of the total cost of all of the offices and systems other than costs and expenses that are reimbursable under section 120.35 of the Revised Code, for the lesser amount required by section 120.34 of the Revised Code.

(5) If any county appointed counsel system fails to maintain the standards for the conduct of the system established by the rules of the Ohio public defender commission pursuant to divisions (B) and (C) of section 120.03 or the standards established by the state public defender pursuant to division (B)(7) of section 120.04 of the Revised Code, the Ohio public defender commission shall notify the board of county commissioners of the county that the county appointed counsel system has failed to comply with its rules or the standards of the state public defender. Unless the board of county commissioners corrects the conduct of its appointed counsel system to comply with the rules and standards within ninety days after the date of the notice, the state public defender may deny all or part of the county's reimbursement from the state provided for in division (A)(4) of this section.

(B) In lieu of using a county public defender or joint county public defender to represent indigent persons in the proceedings set forth in division (A) of section 120.16 of the Revised Code, and in lieu of adopting the resolution and following the procedure described in division (A) of this section, the board of county commissioners of any county may contract with the state public defender for the state public defender's legal representation of indigent persons. A contract entered into pursuant to this division may provide for payment for the services provided on a per case, hourly, or fixed contract basis.

(C) If a court appoints an attorney pursuant to this section to represent a petitioner in a postconviction relief proceeding under section 2953.21 of the Revised Code, the petitioner has received a sentence of death, and the proceeding relates to that sentence, the attorney who represents the petitioner in the proceeding pursuant to the appointment shall be certified under Rule 65 of the Rules of Superintendence for Common Pleas Courts to represent indigent defendants charged with or convicted of an offense for which the death penalty can be or has been imposed.

HISTORY: 136 v H 164 (Eff 1-13-76); 138 v H 204 (Eff 7-30-79); 139 v H 694 (Eff 11-15-81); 140 v H 291 (Eff 7-1-83); 140 v S 271 (Eff 9-26-84); 141 v H 201 (Eff 7-1-85); 146 v H 117 (Eff 6-30-95); 146 v S 258 (Eff 10-16-96); 147 v H 215. Eff 9-29-97.

The effective date is set by section 222 of HB 215.

See provisions, § 191 of HB 215 (147 v —) following RC § 120.04.

§ 120.34 Total reimbursement not to exceed appropriation; pro rata reduction when funds insufficient; annual estimate.

The total amount of money paid to all counties in any fiscal year pursuant to sections 120.18, 120.28, and 120.33 of the Revised Code for the reimbursement of a percentage of the counties' cost of operating county public defender offices, joint county public defender offices, and county appointed counsel systems shall not exceed the total amount appropriated for that fiscal year by the general assembly for the reimbursement of the counties for the operation of the offices and systems. If the amount appropriated by the general assembly in any fiscal year is insufficient to pay fifty per cent of the total cost in the fiscal year of all county public defender offices, all joint county public defender offices, and all county appointed counsel systems, the amount of money paid in that fiscal year pursuant to sections 120.18, 120.28, and 120.33 of the Revised Code to each county for the fiscal year shall be reduced proportionately so that each county is paid an equal percentage of its total cost in the fiscal year for operating its county public defender system, its joint county public defender system, and its county appointed counsel system.

The total amount of money paid to all counties in any fiscal year pursuant to section 120.35 of the Revised Code for the reimbursement of a percentage of the counties' costs and expenses of conducting the defense in capital cases shall not exceed the total amount appropriated for that fiscal year by the general assembly for the reimbursement of the counties for conducting the defense in capital cases. If the amount appropriated by the general assembly in any fiscal year is insufficient to pay fifty per cent of the counties' total costs and expenses of conducting the defense in capital cases in the fiscal year, the amount of money paid in that fiscal year pursuant to section 120.35 of the Revised Code to each county for the fiscal year shall be reduced proportionately so that each county is paid an equal percentage of its costs and expenses of conducting the defense in capital cases in the fiscal year.

If any county receives an amount of money pursuant to section 120.18, 120.28, 120.33, or 120.35 of the Revised Code that is in excess of the amount of reimbursement it is entitled to receive pursuant to this section, the state public defender shall request the board of county commissioners to return the excess payment and the board of county commissioners, upon receipt of the request, shall direct the appropriate county officer to return the excess payment to the state.

Within thirty days of the end of each fiscal quarter, the state public defender shall provide to the office of budget and management and the legislative budget office of the legislative service commission an estimate of the amount of money that will be required for the balance of the fiscal year to make the payments required by sections 120.18, 120.28, 120.33, and 120.35 of the Revised Code.

HISTORY: 138 v H 204 (Eff 7-30-79); 140 v H 291. Eff 7-1-83.

§ 120.35 Reimbursement in capital cases.

The state public defender shall, pursuant to section 120.18, 120.28, 120.33, or 2941.51 of the Revised Code, reimburse fifty per cent of all costs and expenses of conducting the defense in capital cases. If appropriations are insufficient to pay fifty per cent of such costs and expenses, the state public defender shall reimburse such costs and expenses as provided in section 120.34 of the Revised Code.

HISTORY: 140 v H 291. Eff 7-1-83.

§ 120.38 Attorney-client privilege applicable.

(A) All information obtained by a public defender when determining if a person is indigent, shall be held confidential within the ethical standards of attorney-client communications, unless previously on public record, or made available to the court as provided in section 120.05 of the Revised Code.

(B) All communications between the individual defendant and a public defender shall be fully protected by the attorney-client privilege to the same extent and degree as though counsel had been privately engaged.

HISTORY: 136 v H 164. Eff 1-13-76.

§ 120.39 Restrictions.

(A) Except as provided in division (B) of this section, counsel appointed by the court, co-counsel appointed to assist the state public defender or a county or joint county public defender, and any public defender, county public defender, or joint county defender, or member of their offices, shall not be a partner or employee of any prosecuting attorney, city director of law, village solicitor, or similar chief legal officer.

(B) A partner or employee of a village solicitor or of a law firm, legal professional association, or legal clinic with which the village solicitor is affiliated may be appointed by the court, assist a public defender, or serve as public defender in any criminal proceedings in which the village solicitor is not acting as prosecuting attorney.

(C) No prosecuting attorney, city director of law or similar officer of their assistants and employees, and no judge or court employee shall serve on the state public defender commission, or any county or joint county public defender commission.

HISTORY: 136 v H 164 (Eff 1-13-76); 137 v H 219 (Eff 11-1-77); 139 v S 38. Eff 3-15-82.

§ 120.40 Pay ranges; limitation.

The pay ranges established by the board of county commissioners for the county public defender and staff, and those established by the joint board of county commissioners for the joint county public defender and staff, shall not exceed the pay ranges assigned under section 124.14 of the Revised Code for comparable positions of the Ohio public defender and staff.

HISTORY: 136 v H 164. Eff 1-13-76.

§ 120.41 Indemnification of public defenders in malpractice action.

(A) In connection with any malpractice action filed against a state, county, or joint county public defender or assistant public defender, the state, or the county or district in which the defender office is located, when the action is brought against a county or joint county public defender or assistant public defender, shall indemnify the attorney, if he acted in good faith and in the scope of his employment, for any judgment awarded in the malpractice action or amount negotiated in settlement of the malpractice claim asserted in the action, and for any court costs or legal fees incurred in the defense of the malpractice claim asserted in the action.

(B)(1) In connection with any malpractice action filed against an attorney who was either personally selected by an indigent person or appointed by a court pursuant to section 120.33 of the Revised Code, the attorney shall be indemnified in accordance with division (B) of this section for any judgment awarded in the malpractice action or amount negotiated in settlement of the malpractice claim asserted in the action, and for any court costs or legal fees incurred in defense of the malpractice claim asserted in the action.

(2) Subject to division (B)(3) of this section, an indemnification as described in division (B)(1) of this section shall be accomplished only through the following procedure:

(a) The attorney who was either personally selected by an indigent person or appointed by a court pursuant to section 120.33 of the Revised Code, or his counsel in the malpractice action, shall file with the attorney general a request for indemnification pursuant to division (B)(1) of this section, which shall be accompanied by the following types of supportive documentation to the extent that they relate to the request for indemnification:

(i) A certified copy of the judgment entry in the malpractice action;

(ii) A signed copy of any settlement agreement entered into between the parties to the malpractice action;

(iii) A written itemization of all court costs and legal

fees incurred in the defense of the malpractice claim asserted in the action.

(b) Upon receipt of a request for indemnification and the requisite supportive documentation required by division (B)(2)(a) of this section, the attorney general shall review the request and documentation; determine whether any of the limtations specified in division (B)(3) of this section apply to the requested indemnification; and, if an indemnification in any amount is permitted under division (B)(1) of this section after applying those limitations, prepare an indemnity agreement. The indemnity agreement shall specify whether the indemnification will be for a judgment awarded in a malpractice action, an amount negotiated in settlement of the malpractice claim asserted in a malpractice action, court costs or legal fees incurred in the defense of the malpractice claim asserted in a malpractice action, or a combination of those items. The indemnity agreement additionally shall specify the total amount of permissible indemnification as determined by the attorney general; itemize the portions of the permissible indemnification that represent the judgment, settlement, court costs, or legal fees covered by the indemnity agreement; specify any limitations applied pursuant to division (B)(3) of this section to reduce the amount of indemnification sought by the attorney involved; name the persons to whom the entire permissible indemnification or portions of it will be paid; state that the permissible indemnification is payable from the state treasury pursuant to division (B)(2)(c) of this section; and be approved by the inclusion of the signatures of the attorney general and the attorney involved.

(c) The attorney general shall forward a copy of the indemnity agreement prepared pursuant to division (B)(2)(b) of this section to the director of budget and management. The director shall make application for the payment of the amount of the permissible indemnification out of the emergency purposes account or any other appropriation for emergencies or contingencies, and payment out of that account or any other appropriation for emergencies or contingencies shall be authorized if there are sufficient moneys greater than the sum total of then pending emergency purposes account requests, or requests for releases from the other appropriation. If sufficient moneys exist in the emergency purposes account or any other appropriation for emergencies or contingencies to pay the permissible indemnification, the director shall cause payment of the appropriate amounts specified in the indemnity agreement to be made to the persons named in it. If sufficient moneys do not exist in the emergency purposes account or any other appropriation for emergencies or contingencies to pay the permissible indemnification, the attorney involved or his counsel in the malpractice action shall request the general assembly to make an appropriation sufficient to pay the indemnification, and no payment shall be made until the appropriation has been made. The attorney involved or his counsel in the malpractice action shall make the request during the current biennium and during each succeeding biennium until a sufficient appropriation is made.

(3) An indemnification pursuant to divisions (B)(1) and (2) of this section is subject to the following limitations:

(a) The maximum aggregate amount of the indemnification, whether paid to or on behalf of the attorney who was either personally selected by an indigent person or appointed by a court pursuant to section 120.33 of the Revised Code, shall be one million dollars per occurrence, regardless of the number of persons who suffer injury, death, or loss to person or property as a result of the malpractice involved.

(b) The attorney described in division (B)(3)(a) of this section shall not be indemnified to the extent of any amounts covered by a policy of malpractice insurance, for any portion of a judgment that represents punitive or exemplary damages, for any portion of an amount negotiated in settlement of a malpractice claim that is unreasonable, or for any amount described in division (B)(1) of this section unless he acted in good faith and in the scope of his employment.

(c) The attorney described in division (B)(3)(a) of this section shall be indemnified only for the portion of legal fees that is reasonable.

(4) If, pursuant to division (B)(2) of this section, the attorney general denies any indemnification to an attorney who was either personally selected by an indigent person or appointed by a court pursuant to section 120.33 of the Revised Code because of the application of a limitation specified in division (B)(3) of this section, he shall notify that attorney or his counsel in the malpractice action in writing of the denial and of the limitation applied.

(5) If, pursuant to division (B)(4) of this section an attorney who was either personally selected by an indigent person or appointed by a court pursuant to section 120.33 of the Revised Code or his counsel in the malpractice action receives a denial of indemnification notification, or if that attorney refuses to approve an indemnity agreement under division (B)(2) of this section because of the proposed application of a limitation specified in division (B)(3) of this section, the attorney may commence a civil action against the attorney general in the court of claims to prove his entitlement to the indemnification sought, to prove that division (B)(3) of this section does not prohibit or otherwise limit the indemnification sought, and to recover a judgment for the amount of indemnification sought. A civil action under this division shall be commenced no later than two years after the receipt of a denial of indemnification notification or, if the attorney refused to approve an indemnity agreement under division (B)(2) of this section because of the proposed application of a limitation specified in division (B)(3) of this section, no later than two years after the refusal. Any judgment of the court of claims in favor of the attorney shall be paid from the state treasury in

accordance with division (B)(2) of this section.

(C) In connection with any malpractice action filed against an attorney who has contracted with the Ohio public defender commission or the state public defender, pursuant to authority granted by this chapter, to provide legal services to indigent or other persons, the state shall indemnify the attorney, if he acted in good faith and in the scope of his employment, for any judgment awarded in the malpractice action or amount negotiated in settlement of the malpractice claim asserted in the action, and for any court costs or legal fees incurred in the defense of the malpractice claim asserted in the action.

HISTORY: 139 v H 694 (Eff 11-15-81); 144 v H 210. Eff 5-1-92.

[LEGAL AID SOCIETY FUNDING]

§ 120.51 Definitions.

As used in sections 120.51 to 120.55 of the Revised Code:

(A) "Legal aid society" means a nonprofit corporation that satisfies all of the following:

(1) It is chartered to provide general legal services to the poor, it is incorporated and operated exclusively in this state, its primary purpose or function is to provide civil legal services, without charge, to indigents, and, in addition to providing civil legal services to indigents, it may provide legal training or legal technical assistance to other legal aid societies in this state.

(2) It has a board of trustees, a majority of its board of trustees are attorneys, and at least one-third of its board of trustees, when selected, are eligible to receive legal services from the legal aid society.

(3) It receives funding from the legal services corporation or otherwise provides civil legal services to indigents.

(B) "Indigent" means a person or persons whose income is not greater than one hundred twenty-five per cent of the current poverty threshold established by the United States office of management and budget.

(C) "Fee generating case" means any case or matter which, if undertaken on behalf of an indigent by an attorney in private practice, reasonably would be expected to result in payment of a fee for legal services from an award to a client, from public funds, or from the opposing party. A case shall not be considered a fee generating case if adequate representation is unavailable or if any of the following circumstances exist concerning the case:

(1) The legal aid society that represents the indigent in the case has determined that free referral is not possible for any of the following reasons:

(a) The case has been rejected by the local lawyer referral service, or if there is no such service, by two attorneys in private practice who have experience in the subject matter of the case.

(b) Neither the local lawyer referral service, if one exists, nor any attorney will consider the case without payment of a consultation fee.

(c) The case is of a type that attorneys in private practice in the area ordinarily do not accept, or do not accept without prepayment of a fee.

(d) Emergency circumstances compel immediate action before referral can be made, but the client is advised that, if appropriate and consistent with professional responsibility, referral will be attempted at a later time.

(2) Recovery of damages is not the principal object of the case and a request for damages is merely ancillary to an action for equitable or other nonpecuniary relief, or inclusion of a counterclaim requesting damages is necessary for effective defense or because of applicable rules governing joinder of counterclaims.

(3) A court has appointed a legal aid society or its employee to represent the indigent in the case pursuant to a statute, or a court rule or practice of equal applicability to all attorneys in the jurisdiction.

(4) The case involves the rights of a claimant under a publicly supported benefit program for which entitlement is based on need.

HISTORY: 140 v S 219 (Eff 1-8-85); 145 v H 152 (Eff 7-1-93); 146 v H 151. Eff 12-4-95.

§ 120.52 Legal aid fund.

There is hereby established in the state treasury the legal aid fund, which shall be for the charitable public purpose of providing financial assistance to legal aid societies that provide civil legal services to indigents. The fund shall contain all funds credited to it by the treasurer of state pursuant to sections 1901.26, 1907.24, 2303.201 [2303.20.1], 4705.09 and 4705.10 of the Revised Code and income from investment credited to it by the treasurer of state in accordance with this section.

The treasurer of state may invest moneys contained in the legal aid fund in any manner authorized by the Revised Code for the investment of state moneys. However, no such investment shall interfere with any apportionment, allocation, or payment of moneys in January and July of each calendar year, as required by section 120.53 of the Revised Code. All income earned as a result of any such investment shall be credited to the fund.

The state public defender, through the Ohio legal assistance foundation, shall administer the payment of moneys out of the fund. Four and one-half per cent of the moneys in the fund shall be reserved for the actual, reasonable costs of administering sections 120.51 to 120.55 and sections 4705.09 and 4705.10 of the Revised Code. Moneys that are reserved for administrative costs but that are not used for actual, reasonable administrative costs shall be set aside for use in the manner described in division (A) of section 120.521 [120.52.1] of the Revised Code. The remainder of the moneys in the fund shall be distributed in accordance with section 120.53 of the Revised Code. The Ohio legal assistance foundation shall establish rules governing the administration of the legal aid fund, including the program established under sections 4705.09 and 4705.10 of the Revised Code regarding interest on interest-bearing trust accounts of an attorney, law firm, or legal professional association.

HISTORY: 140 v S 219 (Eff 1-8-85); 141 v H 201 (Eff 7-1-85); 141 v H 201, § 12 (Eff 1-1-87); 142 v H 708 (Eff 4-19-88); 145 v H 152 (Eff 7-1-93); 146 v H 117 (Eff 6-30-95); 146 v H 151. Eff 12-4-95.

§ 120.53 Legal aid society may apply for financial assistance; allocation and distribution of funds; annual reports.

(A) A legal aid society that operates within the state may apply to the Ohio legal assistance foundation for financial assistance from the legal aid fund established by section 120.52 of the Revised Code to be used for the funding of the society during the calendar year following the calendar year in which application is made.

(B) An application for financial assistance made under division (A) of this section shall be submitted by the first day of November of the calendar year preceding the calendar year for which financial assistance is desired and shall include all of the following:

(1) Evidence that the applicant is incorporated in this state as a nonprofit corporation;

(2) A list of the trustees of the applicant;

(3) The proposed budget of the applicant for these funds for the following calendar year;

(4) A summary of the services to be offered by the applicant in the following calendar year;

(5) A specific description of the territory or constituency served by the applicant;

(6) An estimate of the number of persons to be served by the applicant during the following calendar year;

(7) A general description of the additional sources of the applicant's funding;

(8) The amount of the applicant's total budget for the calendar year in which the application is filed that it will expend in that calendar year for legal services in each of the counties it serves;

(9) A specific description of any services, programs, training, and legal technical assistance to be delivered by the applicant or by another person pursuant to a contract with the applicant, including, but not limited to, by private attorneys or through reduced fee plans, judicare panels, organized pro bono programs, and mediation programs.

(C) The Ohio legal assistance foundation shall determine whether each applicant that filed an application for financial assistance under division (A) of this section in a calendar year is eligible for financial assistance under this section. To be eligible for such financial assistance, an applicant shall satisfy the criteria for being a legal aid society and shall be in compliance with the provisions of sections 120.51 to 120.55 of the Revised Code and with the rules and requirements the foundation establishes pursuant to section 120.52 of the Revised Code. The Ohio legal assistance foundation then, on or before the fifteenth day of December of the calendar year in which the application is filed, shall notify each such applicant, in writing, whether it is eligible for financial assistance under this section, and if it is eligible, estimate the amount that will be available for that applicant for each six-month distribution period, as determined under division (D) of this section.

(D) The Ohio legal assistance foundation shall allocate moneys contained in the legal aid fund twice each year for distribution to applicants that filed their applications in the previous calendar year and were determined to be eligible applicants.

All moneys contained in the fund on the first day of January of a calendar year shall be allocated, after deduction of the costs of administering sections 120.51 to 120.55 and sections 4705.09 and 4705.10 of the Revised Code that are authorized by section 120.52 of the Revised Code, according to this section and shall be distributed accordingly on the thirty-first day of January of that calendar year, and all moneys contained in the fund on the first day of July of that calendar year shall be allocated, after deduction of the costs of administering those sections that are authorized by section 120.52 of the Revised Code, according to this section and shall be distributed accordingly on the thirty-first day of July of that calendar year. In making the allocations under this section, the moneys in the fund that were generated pursuant to sections 1901.26, 1907.24, 2303.201 [2303.20.1], 4705.09 and 4705.10 of the Revised Code and all income generated from the investment of such moneys shall be apportioned as follows:

(1) After deduction of the amount authorized and used for actual, reasonable administrative costs under section 120.52 of the Revised Code:

(a) Five per cent of the moneys remaining in the fund, plus any moneys reserved for administrative costs under that section that are not used for actual, reasonable administrative costs, shall be reserved for distribution to legal aid societies that provide assistance to special population groups of their eligible clients, engage in special projects that have a substantial impact on their local service area or on significant segments of the state's poverty population, or provide legal training or support to other legal aid societies in the state;

(b) After deduction of the amount described in division (D)(1)(a) of this section, one and three-quarters per cent of the moneys remaining in the fund shall be apportioned among entities that received financial assistance from the legal aid fund prior to the effective date of this amendment but that, on and after the effective date of this amendment, no longer qualify as a legal aid society that is eligible for financial assistance under this section.

(2) After deduction of the actual, reasonable administrative costs under section 120.52 of the Revised Code and after deduction of the amounts identified in division

(D)(1)(a) and (b) of this section, the remaining moneys shall be apportioned among the counties that are served by eligible legal aid societies that have applied for financial assistance under this section so that each such county is apportioned a portion of those moneys, based upon the ratio of the number of indigents who reside in that county to the total number of indigents who reside in all counties of this state that are served by eligible legal aid societies that have applied for financial assistance under this section. Subject to division (E) of this section, the moneys apportioned to a county under this division then shall be allocated to the eligible legal aid society that serves the county and that has applied for financial assistance under this section. For purposes of this division, the source of data identifying the number of indigent persons who reside in a county shall be the most recent decennial census figures from the United States department of commerce, division of census.

(E) If the Ohio legal assistance foundation, in attempting to make an allocation of moneys under division (D)(2) of this section, determines that a county that has been apportioned money under that division is served by more than one eligible legal aid society that has applied for financial assistance under this section, the Ohio legal assistance foundation shall allocate the moneys that have been apportioned to that county under division (D)(2) of this section among all eligible legal aid societies that serve that county and that have applied for financial assistance under this section on a pro rata basis, so that each such eligible society is allocated a portion based upon the amount of its total budget expended in the prior calendar year for legal services in that county as compared to the total amount expended in the prior calendar year for legal services in that county by all eligible legal aid societies that serve that county and that have applied for financial assistance under this section.

(F) Moneys allocated to eligible applicants under this section shall be paid twice annually, on the thirty-first day of January and on the thirty-first day of July of the calendar year following the calendar year in which the application is filed.

(G)(1) A legal aid society that receives financial assistance in any calendar year under this section shall file an annual report with the Ohio legal assistance foundation detailing the number and types of cases handled, and the amount and types of legal training, legal technical assistance, and other service provided, by means of that financial assistance. No information contained in the report shall identify or enable the identification of any person served by the legal aid society or in any way breach client confidentiality.

(2) The Ohio legal assistance foundation shall make an annual report to the governor, the general assembly, and the supreme court on the distribution and use of the legal aid fund. The foundation also shall include in the annual report an audited financial statement of all gifts, bequests, donations, contributions, and other moneys the foundation receives. No information contained in the report shall identify or enable the identification of any person served by a legal aid society, or in any way breach confidentiality.

(H) A legal aid society may enter into agreements for the provision of services, programs, training, or legal technical assistance for the legal aid society or to indigent persons.

HISTORY: 140 v S 219 (Eff 1-8-85); 141 v H 201 (Eff 7-1-85); 141 v H 201, § 17 (Eff 3-1-87); 142 v H 708 (Eff 4-19-88); 145 v H 152 (Eff 7-1-93); 146 v H 117. Eff 6-30-95.

§ 120.54 Permitted uses of financial assistance.

(A) A legal aid society that receives financial assistance from the legal aid fund under section 120.53 of the Revised Code shall use the financial assistance for only the following purposes:

(1) To defray the costs of providing legal services to indigents;

(2) To provide legal training and legal technical assistance to other eligible legal aid societies; and

(3) If the legal aid society has entered into an agreement pursuant to division (H) of section 120.53 of the Revised Code and in accordance with the description and list of conditions set forth in its application pursuant to division (B)(9) of that section, to provide funds for the services, programs, training, and legal technical assistance provided to the legal aid society under the contract.

(B) No financial assistance received by a legal aid society from the legal aid fund pursuant to section 120.53 of the Revised Code shall be used for the provision of legal services in relation to any criminal case or proceeding or in relation to the provision of legal assistance in any fee generating case.

HISTORY: 140 v S 219 (Eff 1-8-85); 145 v H 152 (Eff 7-1-93); 146 v H 117. Eff 6-30-95.

§ 120.55 Conditions to be ensured by society.

In providing legal assistance, each legal aid society that receives financial assistance from the legal aid fund under section 120.53 of the Revised Code shall ensure all of the following:

(A) The maintenance of quality service and professional standards;

(B) That no person shall interfere with any attorney funded in whole or in part by sections 120.51 to 120.55 of the Revised Code in carrying out his professional responsibility to his client as established by the rules of professional responsibility;

(C) The expenditure of the financial assistance only in accordance with sections 120.51 to 120.55 of the Revised Code;

(D) The preservation of client confidentiality.

HISTORY: 140 v S 219 (Eff 1-8-85); 146 v H 117. Eff 6-30-95.

CHAPTER 149: DOCUMENTS, REPORTS, AND RECORDS

§ 149.43 Availability of public records.

(A) As used in this section:

(1) "Public record" means any record that is kept by any public office, including, but not limited to, state, county, city, village, township, and school district units, except that "public record" does not mean any of the following:

(a) Medical records;

(b) Records pertaining to probation and parole proceedings;

(c) Records pertaining to actions under section 2151.85 of the Revised Code and to appeals of actions arising under that section;

(d) Records pertaining to adoption proceedings, including the contents of an adoption file maintained by the department of health under section 3705.12 of the Revised Code;

(e) Information in a record contained in the putative father registry established by section 3107.062 [3107.06.2] of the Revised Code, regardless of whether the information is held by the department of human services or, pursuant to section 5101.313 [5101.31.3] of the Revised Code, the division of child support in the department or a child support enforcement agency;

(f) Records listed in division (A) of section 3107.42 of the Revised Code or specified in division (A) of section 3107.52 of the Revised Code;

(g) Trial preparation records;

(h) Confidential law enforcement investigatory records;

(i) Records containing information that is confidential under section 2317.023 [2317.02.3] or 4112.05 of the Revised Code;

(j) *DNA* records stored in the *DNA* database pursuant to section 109.573 [109.57.3] of the Revised Code;

(k) Inmate records released by the department of rehabilitation and correction to the department of youth services or a court of record pursuant to division (E) of section 5120.21 of the Revised Code;

(l) Records maintained by the department of youth services pertaining to children in its custody released by the department of youth services to the department of rehabilitation and correction pursuant to section 5139.05 of the Revised Code;

(m) Intellectual property records;

(n) Donor profile records;

(o) Records the release of which is prohibited by state or federal law.

(2) "Confidential law enforcement investigatory record" means any record that pertains to a law enforcement matter of a criminal, quasi-criminal, civil, or administrative nature, but only to the extent that the release of the record would create a high probability of disclosure of any of the following:

(a) The identity of a suspect who has not been charged with the offense to which the record pertains, or of an information source or witness to whom confidentiality has been reasonably promised;

(b) Information provided by an information source or witness to whom confidentiality has been reasonably promised, which information would reasonably tend to disclose the source's or witness's identity;

(c) Specific confidential investigatory techniques or procedures or specific investigatory work product;

(d) Information that would endanger the life or physical safety of law enforcement personnel, a crime victim, a witness, or a confidential information source.

(3) "Medical record" means any document or combination of documents, except births, deaths, and the fact of admission to or discharge from a hospital, that pertains to the medical history, diagnosis, prognosis, or medical condition of a patient and that is generated and maintained in the process of medical treatment.

(4) "Trial preparation record" means any record that contains information that is specifically compiled in reasonable anticipation of, or in defense of, a civil or criminal action or proceeding, including the independent thought processes and personal trial preparation of an attorney.

(5) "Intellectual property record" means a record, other than a financial or administrative record, that is produced or collected by or for faculty or staff of a state institution of higher learning in the conduct of or as a result of study or research on an educational, commercial, scientific, artistic, technical, or scholarly issue, regardless of whether the study or research was sponsored by the institution alone or in conjunction with a governmental body or private concern, and that has not been publicly released, published, or patented.

(6) "Donor profile record" means all records about donors or potential donors to a public institution of higher education except the names and reported addresses of the actual donors and the date, amount, and conditions of the actual donation.

(B) All public records shall be promptly prepared and made available for inspection to any person at all reasonable times during regular business hours. Upon request, a person responsible for public records shall make copies available at cost, within a reasonable period of time. In order to facilitate broader access to public records, governmental units shall maintain public records in a manner that they can be made available for inspection in accordance with this division.

(C) If a person allegedly is aggrieved by the failure of a governmental unit to promptly prepare a public record and to make it available to the person for inspection in accordance with division (B) of this section, or if a person who has requested a copy of a public record allegedly is aggrieved by the failure of a person responsible for the public record to make a copy available to the person allegedly aggrieved in accordance with division (B) of this section, the person allegedly aggrieved may commence a mandamus action to obtain a judgment that orders the governmental unit or the person responsible for the public record to comply with division (B) of this section and that awards reasonable attorney's fees to the person that instituted the mandamus action. The mandamus action may be commenced in the court of common pleas of the county in which division (B) of this section allegedly was not complied with, in the supreme court pursuant to its original jurisdiction under Section 2 of Article IV, Ohio Constitution, or in the court of appeals for the appellate district in which division (B) of this section allegedly was not complied with pursuant to its original jurisdiction under Section 3 of Article IV, Ohio Constitution.

(D) Chapter 1347. of the Revised Code does not limit the provisions of this section.

(E)(1) The bureau of motor vehicles may adopt rules pursuant to Chapter 119. of the Revised Code to reasonably limit the number of bulk commercial special extraction requests made by a person for the same records or for updated records during a calendar year. The rules may include provisions for charges to be made for bulk commercial special extraction requests for the actual cost of the bureau, plus special extraction costs, plus ten per cent. The bureau may charge for expenses for redacting information, the release of which is prohibited by law.

(2) As used in division (E)(1) of this section:

(a) "Actual cost" means the cost of depleted supplies, records storage media costs, actual mailing and alternative delivery costs, or other transmitting costs, and any direct equipment operating and maintenance costs, including actual costs paid to private contractors for copying services.

(b) "Bulk commercial special extraction request" means a request for copies of a record for information in a format other than the format already available, or information that cannot be extracted without examination of all items in a records series, class of records, or data base by a person who intends to use or forward the copies for surveys, marketing, solicitation, or resale for commercial purposes. "Bulk commercial special extraction request" does not include a request by a person who gives assurance to the bureau that the person making the request does not intend to use or forward the requested copies for surveys, marketing, solicitation, or resale for commercial purposes.

(c) "Commercial" means profit-seeking production, buying, or selling of any good, service, or other product.

(d) "Special extraction costs" means the cost of the time spent by the lowest paid employee competent to perform the task, the actual amount paid to outside private contractors employed by the bureau, or the actual cost incurred to create computer programs to make the special extraction. "Special extraction costs" include any charges paid to a public agency for computer or records services.

(3) For purposes of divisions (E)(1) and (2) of this section, "commercial surveys, marketing, solicitation, or resale" shall be narrowly construed and does not include reporting or gathering news, reporting or gathering information to assist citizen oversight or understanding of the operation or activities of government, or nonprofit educational research.

HISTORY: 130 v 155 (Eff 9-27-63); 138 v S 62 (Eff 1-18-80); 140 v H 84 (Eff 3-19-85); 141 v H 238 (Eff 7-1-85); 141 v H 319 (Eff 3-24-86); 142 v S 275 (Eff 10-15-87); 145 v H 152 (Eff 7-1-93); 146 v H 5 (Eff 8-30-95); 146 v S 269 (Eff 7-1-96); 146 v H 353 (Eff 9-17-96); 146 v H 419 (Eff 9-18-96); 146 v S 277, § 1 (Eff 3-31-97); 146 v H 438, § 3 (Eff 7-1-97); 146 v S 277, § 6. Eff 7-1-97.

The effective date is set by section 8 of SB 277.

The provisions of § 9 of SB 277 (146 v —) read as follows:

SECTION 9. ° ° ° Section 149.43 of the Revised Code is presented in Section 6 of this act as a composite of the section as amended by Am. Sub. H.B. 419, Am. Sub. H.B. 353, Am. Sub. S.B. 269, and Am. Sub. H.B. 438 of the 121st General Assembly, with the new language of none of those acts shown in capital letters. ° ° ° This is in recognition of the principle stated in division (B) of section 1.52 of the Revised Code that such amendments are to be harmonized where not substantively irreconcilable and constitutes a legislative finding that such is the resulting version in effect prior to the effective date of this act.

CHAPTER 173: DEPARTMENT OF AGING

[§ 173.12.1] § 173.121 Center may conduct bingo games.

(A) As used in this section, "bingo," "bingo game operator," and "participant" have the same meanings as in section 2915.01 of the Revised Code.

(B) Notwithstanding sections 2915.07 to 2915.12 of the Revised Code, a multipurpose senior center may conduct bingo games, but only if it complies with all of the following requirements:

(1) All bingo games are conducted only on the premises of the facility;

(2) All participants are sixty years of age or older;

(3) All bingo game operators are sixty years of age or older and receive no compensation for serving as operators;

(4) No participant is charged an admission fee and no participant is charged more than twenty-five cents to purchase a bingo card or a card, sheet, or other device described in division (S)(2)(a) of section 2915.01 of the Revised Code;

(5) All proceeds from games are used only for any of the following:

(a) To pay winners monetary or nonmonetary prizes;

(b) To provide refreshments;

(c) To defray any costs directly related to conducting the games;

(d) To defray costs of services the facility provides in accordance with section 173.12 of the Revised Code.
HISTORY: 143 v H 573. Eff 4-10-91.

CHAPTER 177: INVESTIGATION AND PROSECUTION OF ORGANIZED CRIMINAL ACTIVITY

§ 177.01 Organized crime investigations commission created.

(A) The organized crime investigations commission, consisting of seven members, is hereby established in the office of the attorney general. One of the members shall be the attorney general. Of the remaining members, each of whom shall be appointed by the governor with the advice and consent of the senate, two shall be prosecuting attorneys, two shall be county sheriffs, and two shall be chief municipal law enforcement officers. No more than four members of the commission shall be members of the same political party.

Of the initial appointments to the commission, one member who is a prosecuting attorney and one who is a county sheriff each shall be appointed for terms ending September 3, 1987, one member who is a prosecuting attorney and one who is a chief municipal law enforcement officer each shall be appointed for terms ending September 3, 1988, and one member who is a county sheriff and one who is a chief municipal law enforcement officer each shall be appointed for terms ending September 3, 1989. Thereafter, terms of office of persons appointed to the commission shall be for three years, with each term ending on the same day of the same month of the year as did the term that it succeeds. Members may be reappointed. Each appointed member shall hold office from the date of the member's appointment until the end of the term for which the member was appointed, except that an appointed member who ceases to hold the office or position of prosecuting attorney, county sheriff, or chief municipal law enforcement officer prior to the expiration of the member's term of office on the commission shall cease to be a member of the commission on the date that the member ceases to hold the office or position. Vacancies shall be filled in the manner provided for original appointments. Any member appointed to fill a vacancy occurring prior to the expiration of the term for which the member's predecessor was appointed shall take office on the commission when the member is confirmed by the senate and shall hold office for the remainder of such term. Any member shall continue in office subsequent to the expiration date of the member's term until the member's successor takes office, or until a period of sixty days has elapsed, whichever occurs first.

The attorney general shall become a member of the commission on September 3, 1986. Successors in office to that attorney general shall become members of the commission on the day they assume the office of attorney general. An attorney general's term of office as a member of the commission shall continue for as long as the person in question holds the office of attorney general.

Each member of the commission may designate, in writing, another person to represent the member on the commission. If a member makes such a designation, either the member or the designee may perform the member's duties and exercise the member's authority on the commission. If a member makes such a designation, the member may revoke the designation by sending written notice of the revocation to the commission. Upon such a revocation, the member may designate a different person to represent the member on the commission by sending written notice of the designation to the commission at least two weeks prior to the date on which the new designation is to take effect.

The attorney general or a person the attorney general designates pursuant to this division to represent the attorney general on the commission shall serve as chairman of the commission. The commission shall meet within two weeks after all appointed members have been appointed, at a time and place determined by the governor. The commission shall organize by selecting a vice-chairman and other officers who are necessary and shall adopt rules to govern its procedures. Thereafter, the commission shall meet at least once every six months, or more often upon the call of the chairman or the written request of two or more members. Each member of the commission shall have one vote. Four members constitute a quorum, and four votes are required to validate an action of the commission.

The members of the commission shall serve without compensation, but each member shall be reimbursed for actual and necessary expenses incurred in the performance of official duties. In the absence of the chairman, the vice-chairman shall perform the duties of the chairman.

(B) The commission shall coordinate investigations of organized criminal activity and perform all of the functions and duties relative to the investigations that are set forth in section 177.02 of the Revised Code, and it shall cooperate with departments and officers of the government of the United States in the suppression of organized criminal activity.

(C) The commission shall appoint and fix the compensation of a director and such technical and clerical employees who are necessary to exercise the powers and carry out the duties of the commission, and may enter into contracts and purchase any equipment necessary to the performance of its duties. The director and employees of the commission shall be members of the unclassified service as defined in section 124.11 of the Revised Code. The commission shall require the director and each employee, prior to commencing employment with the commission and at least once each year thereafter for the duration of the director's or employee's employment with the commission, to undergo an investigation for the purpose of obtaining a security clearance. The investigation shall include, but is not limited to, a polygraph examination and shall be conducted by an organization designated by the commission.

(D) An appointed commission member may be removed from office as a member of the commission by the vote of four members of the commission or by the governor for any of the following reasons:

(1) Neglect of duty, misconduct, incompetence, or malfeasance in office;

(2) Conviction of or a plea of guilty to a felony or an offense of moral turpitude;

(3) Being mentally ill or mentally incompetent;

(4) Being the subject of an investigation by a task force established by the commission or another law enforcement agency, where the proof of criminal activity is evident or the presumption great;

(5) Engaging in any activity or associating with any persons or organization inappropriate to the member's position as a member of the commission.

(E) As used in sections 177.01 to 177.03 of the Revised Code:

(1) "Organized criminal activity" means any combination or conspiracy to engage in activity that constitutes "engaging in a pattern of corrupt activity;" any violation, combination of violations, or conspiracy to commit one or more violations of section 2925.03, 2925.04, 2925.05, 2925.06, or 2925.11 of the Revised Code other than a violation of section 2925.11 of the Revised Code that is a minor drug possession offense; or any criminal activity that relates to the corruption of a public official, as defined in section 2921.01 of the Revised Code, or of a public servant of the type described in division (B)(3) of that section.

(2) A person is engaging in an activity that constitutes "engaging in a pattern of corrupt activity" if any of the following apply:

(a) The person is or was employed by, or associated with, an enterprise and the person conducts or participates in, directly or indirectly, the affairs of the enterprise through a pattern of corrupt activity or the collection of an unlawful debt.

(b) The person, through a pattern of corrupt activity or the collection of an unlawful debt, acquires or maintains, directly or indirectly, an interest in, or control of, an enterprise or real property.

(c) The person knowingly has received proceeds derived, directly or indirectly, from a pattern of corrupt activity or the collection of an unlawful debt and the person uses or invests, directly or indirectly, a part of those proceeds, or proceeds derived from the use or investment of any of those proceeds, in the acquisition of title to, or a right, interest, or equity in, real property or the establishment or operation of an enterprise. A purchase of securities on the open market with intent to make an investment, without intent to control or participate in the control of the issuer, and without intent to assist another to do so is not an activity that constitutes "engaging in a pattern of corrupt activity" if the securities of the issuer held after the purchase by the purchaser, the members of the purchaser's immediate family, and the purchaser's or members' accomplices in any pattern of corrupt activity or the collection of an unlawful debt, do not aggregate one per cent of the outstanding securities of any one class of the issuer and do not confer, in law or in fact, the power to elect one or more directors of the issuer.

(3) "Pattern of corrupt activity" means two or more incidents of corrupt activity, whether or not there has been a prior conviction, that are related to the affairs of the same enterprise, are not isolated, and are not so closely related to each other and connected in time and place that they constitute a single event. At least one of the incidents forming the pattern shall occur on or after September 3, 1986. Unless any incident was an aggravated murder or murder, the most recent of the incidents forming the pattern shall occur within six years after the commission of any prior incident forming the pattern, excluding any period of imprisonment served by any person engaging in the corrupt activity.

(4) "Corrupt activity," "unlawful debt," "enterprise," "person," "real property," and "beneficial interest" have the same meanings as in section 2923.31 of the Revised Code.

(5) "Minor drug possession offense" has the same meaning as in section 2925.01 of the Revised Code.

HISTORY: 141 v S 74 (Eff 9-3-86); 142 v H 708 (Eff 4-19-88); 143 v H 215 (Eff 4-11-90); 144 v H 298 (Eff 7-26-91); 146 v S 2. Eff 7-1-96.

The effective date is set by section 6 of SB 2.

[§ 177.01.1] § 177.011 Organized crime commission fund.

There is hereby created in the state treasury the organized crime commission fund. The fund shall consist of moneys paid to the treasurer of state pursuant to the judgment of a court in a criminal case as reimbursement of expenses that the organized crime investigations commission or an organized crime task force established by the commission incurred in the investigation of the criminal activity upon which the prosecution of the criminal case was based. All investment earnings on moneys in the fund shall be credited to the fund. The organized crime investigations commission shall use the moneys in the fund to reimburse political subdivisions for the expenses the political subdivisions incur when their law enforcement officers participate in an organized crime task force.

HISTORY: 147 v H 215. Eff 6-30-97.

§ 177.02 **Complaint alleging organized criminal activity; task force established; investigatory staff; confidentiality.**

(A) Any person may file with the organized crime investigations commission a complaint that alleges that organized criminal activity has occurred in a county. A person who files a complaint under this division also may file with the commission information relative to the complaint.

(B) Upon the filing of a complaint under division (A) of this section or upon its own initiative, the commission may establish an organized crime task force to investigate organized criminal activity in a county or in two or more adjacent counties if it determines, based upon the complaint filed and the information relative to it or based upon any information that it may have received, that there is reason to believe that organized criminal activity has occurred and continues to occur in the county or in each of the adjacent counties. The commission shall not establish an organized crime task force to investigate organized criminal activity in any county unless it makes the determination required under this division relative to that county, and shall not establish an organized crime task force to investigate organized criminal activity in two or more adjacent counties unless it makes the determination required under this division relative to each of the adjacent counties. The commission, at any time, may terminate an organized crime task force it has established under this section.

(C)(1) If the commission establishes an organized crime task force to investigate organized criminal activity in a county or in two or more adjacent counties pursuant to division (B) of this section, the commission initially shall appoint a task force director to directly supervise the investigation. The task force director shall be either the sheriff or a deputy sheriff of any county in the state, the chief law enforcement officer or a member of a law enforcement agency of any municipal corporation or township in the state, or an agent of the bureau of criminal identification and investigation. No person shall be appointed as task force director without his consent, and, if applicable, the consent of his employing sheriff or law enforcement agency, or the superintendent of the bureau of criminal identification and investigation if he is an employee of the bureau. Upon appointment of a task force director, the commission shall meet with the director and establish the scope and limits of the investigation to be conducted by the task force and the size of the task force investigatory staff to be appointed by the task force director. The commission, at any time, may remove a task force director appointed under this division and may replace any director so removed according to the guidelines for the initial appointment of a director.

(2) A task force director appointed under this section shall assemble a task force investigatory staff, of a size determined by the commission and the director, to conduct the investigation. Unless it appears to the commission and the director, based upon the complaint filed and any information relative to it or based upon any information that the commission may have received, that there is reason to believe that the office of the prosecuting attorney of the county or one of the counties served by the task force is implicated in the organized criminal activity to be investigated, one member of the investigatory staff shall be the prosecuting attorney or an assistant prosecuting attorney of the county or one of the counties served by the task force. If a prosecuting attorney or assistant prosecuting attorney is not included in the task force because of such a determination, the attorney general shall provide legal assistance to the task force upon request. Each of the other members of the investigatory staff shall be either the sheriff or a deputy sheriff of any county in the state, the chief law enforcement officer or a member of a law enforcement agency of any municipal corporation or township in the state, or an agent of the bureau of criminal identification and investigation. No person shall be appointed to the investigatory staff without his consent, and, if applicable, the consent of his employing sheriff or law enforcement agency, or the superintendent of the bureau of criminal identification and investigation if he is an employee of the bureau. To the extent possible, the investigatory staff shall be composed of persons familiar with investigatory techniques that generally would be utilized in an investigation of organized criminal activity. To the extent practicable, the investigatory staff shall be assembled in such a manner that numerous law enforcement agencies within the county or the counties served by the task force are represented on the investigatory staff. The investigatory staff shall be assembled in such a manner that at least one sheriff, deputy sheriff, municipal corporation law enforcement officer, or township law enforcement officer from each of the counties served by the task force is represented on the investigatory staff. A task force director, at any time, may remove any member of the investigatory staff he has assembled under this division and may replace any member so removed according to the guidelines for the initial assembly of the investigatory staff.

(3) The commission may provide an organized crime task force established under this section with technical and clerical employees and with equipment necessary to efficiently conduct its investigation into organized criminal activity.

(4) Upon the establishment of a task force, the commission shall issue to the task force director and each member of the task force investigatory staff appropriate credentials that identify him, his position, and his authority.

(D) A task force investigatory staff, during the period of the investigation for which it is assembled, is responsible only to the task force director and shall operate under his direction and control. Any necessary and actual expenses incurred by a task force director or investigatory staff, including any such expenses incurred for food, lodging, or travel, and any other necessary and actual expenses of an investigation into organized criminal activity conducted by a task force, shall be paid by the commission. For purposes of workers' compensation and the allocation of liability for any death, injury, or damage they may cause in the performance of their duties, a task force director and investigatory staff, during the period of the investigation for which the task force is assembled, shall be considered to be employees of the commission and of the state. However, for purposes of compensation, pension or indemnity fund rights, and other rights and benefits to which they may be entitled, a task force director and investigatory staff, during the period of the performance of their duties as director and investigatory staff, shall be considered to be performing their duties in their normal capacity as prosecuting attorney, assistant prosecuting attorney, sheriff, deputy sheriff, chief law enforcement officer or member of a law enforcement agency of a municipal corporation or township, or agent of the bureau of criminal identification and investigation.

(E) Except as provided in this division, upon the establishment of a task force, the commission shall provide the prosecuting attorney of each of the counties served by the task force with written notice that the task force has been established to investigate organized criminal activity in that county. Such notice shall not be provided to a prosecuting attorney if it appears to the commission, based upon the complaint filed and any information relative to it or based upon any information that the commission may have received, that there is reason to believe that the office of that prosecuting attorney is implicated in the organized criminal activity to be investigated.

(F) The filing of a complaint alleging organized criminal activity, the establishment of an organized crime task force, the appointment of a task force director and his identity, the assembly of an investigatory staff and the identity of its members, the conduct of an investigation into organized criminal activity, and the identity of any person who is being or is expected to be investigated by the task force shall be kept confidential by the commission and its director and employees, and by the task force and its director, investigatory staff, and employees until an indictment is returned or a criminal action or proceeding is initiated in a court of proper jurisdiction.

(G) For purposes of divisions (C) and (E) of this section, the office of a prosecuting attorney shall be considered as being implicated in organized criminal activity only if the prosecuting attorney, one or more of his assistants, or one or more of his employees has committed or attempted or conspired to commit, is committing or attempting or conspiring to commit, or has engaged in or is engaging in complicity in the commission of, organized criminal activity.

HISTORY: 141 v S 74. Eff 9-3-86.

§ 177.03 Authority and powers of task force; notice to local law enforcement agency; action on results of investigation; special prosecutor.

(A) An organized crime task force established under section 177.02 of the Revised Code to investigate organized criminal activity in a county or in two or more adjacent counties shall investigate organized criminal activity within the county or counties in accordance with the scope and limits established by the organized crime investigations commission and the task force director. For purposes of the investigation, the task force director and investigatory staff shall have the powers of a peace officer throughout the county or counties in which the investigation is to be undertaken. However, the authority and powers granted to the director and investigatory staff under this section do not supplant or diminish the authority and power provided by the Revised Code to other law enforcement agencies or their officers or investigators.

An organized crime task force, in the conduct of its investigation, may issue subpoenas and subpoenas duces tecum. The task force may compel the attendance of witnesses and the production of records and papers of all kinds and description that are relevant to the investigation, including, but not limited to, any books, accounts, documents, and memoranda pertaining to the subject of the investigation. Upon the failure of any person to comply with any lawful order of the task force, the task force may apply to the court of common pleas of the proper county for a contempt order, as in the case of disobedience of the requirements of a subpoena issued from the court of common pleas, or a refusal to testify thereon.

(B) This section and section 177.02 of the Revised Code do not prevent an organized crime task force from cooperating with other law enforcement agencies of this state, a political subdivision of this state, another state, a political subdivision of another state, or the United States, or their officers or investigators in the investigation and prosecution of any offenses comprising organized criminal activity.

(C)(1) If an organized crime task force, either prior to the commencement of or during the course of its investigation of organized criminal activity in a county or in two or more adjacent counties, has reason to believe that the investigation will require it to engage in substantial investigative activities in a particular municipal corporation or township in the county or any of the adjacent counties, the task force director shall notify the commission chairman of that belief and the reasons for that belief. The chairman shall present that belief and those reasons to the commission, and if the commission determines that there is a compelling reason to notify a local law enforcement agency that has jurisdiction within that municipal corporation or township that the task force will be engaging in investigative activities in the municipal corporation or township, the commission, subject to division (C)(2) of this section, shall provide written notice of that fact as follows:

(a) If the investigative activities will be engaged in a township or in a municipal corporation that does not have a police department or similar law enforcement agency, the notice shall be provided to the sheriff of the county in which the township or municipal corporation is located;

(b) If the investigative activities will be engaged in in a municipal corporation that has a police department or similar law enforcement agency, the notice shall be provided to the chief law enforcement officer of the department or agency.

(2) The notice described in division (C)(1) of this section shall not be provided to a sheriff or chief law enforcement officer if it appears to the commission, based upon the complaint filed and any information relative to it or based upon any information that the commission may have received, that there is reason to believe that the office of that sheriff or chief law enforcement officer is implicated in the organized criminal activity being investigated.

(D)(1) If an organized crime task force determines, pursuant to its investigation of organized criminal activity in a county or in two or more adjacent counties, that there is not reasonable cause to believe that organized criminal activity has occurred or is occurring in the county or in any of the counties, it shall report its determination to the commission, terminate its task force activities, and disband.

(2)(a) If a task force determines, pursuant to its investigation of organized criminal activity in a county or in two or more adjacent counties, that there is reasonable cause to believe that organized criminal activity has occurred or is occurring in the county or in any of the counties, it shall report its determination to the commission and, except as provided in division (D)(3) of this section, shall refer a copy of all of the information gathered during the course of the investigation to the prosecuting attorney who has jurisdiction over the matter and inform the prosecuting attorney that he has thirty days to decide whether he should present the information to a grand jury and that if he intends to make such a presentation, he has to give the commission written notice of that intention. If the organized criminal activity occurred or is occurring in two or more counties, the referral of the information shall be to the prosecuting attorney of the county in which the most significant portion of the activity occurred or is occurring or, if it is not possible to determine that county, the county with the largest population.

If a prosecuting attorney who has been referred information under this division fails to notify the commission in writing, within thirty days after the referral, that he will present the information to the grand jury of his county, the task force, except as provided in division (D)(2)(b) of this section, shall refer a copy of all of the information to the attorney general, who shall proceed according to division (B) of section 109.83 of the Revised Code. If the prosecuting attorney fails to notify the commission in writing within that time that he will present the information to the grand jury, he promptly shall return all of the information that the task force referred to him under this division.

If a prosecuting attorney who has been referred information under this division notifies the commission in writing, within thirty days after the referral, of his intention to present the information referred to him to the grand jury of his county, he shall proceed promptly to present the information as evidence to the grand jury and shall notify the commission of the grand jury's final actions, findings of indictments, or reports. The prosecuting attorney may disclose to the attorney general any matters occurring before the grand jury that are disclosed to the prosecuting attorney for use in the performance of his duties. The information shall be presented as evidence to the grand jury prior to the discharge of the next regular grand jury. If the prosecuting attorney fails to present the information as evidence within that time, the commission, except as provided in division (D)(2)(b) of this section, shall notify the attorney general, the task force shall refer a copy of all of the information to the attorney general, and the attorney general may proceed as if the prosecuting attorney had declined under this division to accept the matter. If the prosecuting attorney fails to present the information as evidence within that time, he promptly shall return to the task force all of the information that the task force had referred to him under this division.

(b) If a prosecuting attorney who has been referred information under division (D)(2)(a) of this section fails to notify the commission in accordance with that division that he will present the information to the grand jury, and the task force that conducted the investigation determines, pursuant to its investigation, that the office of the attorney general is implicated in organized criminal activity, the task force shall not contact or refer any information to the attorney general, but shall report its determinations and refer all of the information to the commission. If a prosecuting attorney who has been referred information under division (D)(2)(a) of this section notifies the commission in accordance with that division that he intends to present the information to the grand jury but fails to do so prior to the discharge of the next regular grand jury, and the task force that conducted the investigation determines, pursuant to the investigation, that the office of the attorney general is implicated in organized criminal activity, neither the commission nor the task force shall contact or refer any information to the attorney general. Instead, the task force shall report its determinations and refer all of the information gathered during the course of the investigation to the commission.

In either such case, the commission shall review the information, and if a majority of the members of the commission determine that the office of the attorney general is implicated, the chairman of the commission shall appear before the presiding judge of the court of common pleas or of the court of appeals for the county in which the prosecuting attorney who was referred the information serves and request the appointment of a special prosecutor to handle the matter. If the presiding judge finds that there is reasonable cause to believe that organized criminal activity has occurred or is occurring in the county or in any of the counties served by the task force and that the office of the attorney general is implicated, the judge shall appoint a special prosecutor to perform the functions of prosecuting attorney of the county in relation to the matter. The commission shall refer a copy of all of the information gathered during the course of the investigation to the special prosecutor. The special prosecutor shall review the information and if he determines that there is cause to prosecute for the commission of a crime, he shall proceed promptly to present the information referred to him to the grand jury and shall notify the commission of the grand jury's final actions, findings of indictments, or reports. A special prosecutor appointed under this division shall not inform the attorney general of the investigation or referral of information and shall not cooperate with the attorney general on the matter.

(3) If a task force determines, pursuant to its investigation of organized criminal activity in a county or in two or more adjacent counties, that there is reasonable cause to believe that organized criminal activity has occurred or is occurring in the county or in any of the counties, and that the office of a prosecuting attorney who normally would be referred the information gathered during the course of the investigation pursuant to division (D)(2) of this section is implicated by the information in organized criminal activity, it shall not contact or refer any information to the prosecuting attorney. Instead it shall report its determinations and refer all of the information gathered during the course of the investigation to the commission. The commission shall review the information, and if a majority of the members of the commission determine that the office of the prosecuting attorney is implicated in organized criminal activity, the chairman of the commission shall appear before the presiding judge of the court of common pleas or of the court of appeals for the county in which that prosecuting attorney serves and request the appointment of a special prosecutor to handle the matter. If the presiding judge finds that there is reasonable cause to believe that organized criminal activity has occurred or is occurring in the county or in any of the counties served by the task force and that the office of the prosecuting attorney in question is implicated in organized criminal activity, the judge shall appoint a special prosecutor to perform the functions of prosecuting attorney of the county in relation to the matter, and the commission shall refer a copy of all of the information gathered during the course of the investigation to the special prosecutor. It shall inform the special prosecutor that he has thirty days to decide whether he should present the information to a grand jury and that if he intends to make such a presentation, he has to give the commission written notice of that intention. A special prosecutor appointed under this division shall not inform the implicated prosecuting attorney of the investigation or referral of information and shall not cooperate with the prosecutor on the matter.

If a special prosecutor who has been referred information under this division fails to notify the commission in writing, within thirty days after the referral, that he will present the information to the grand jury of the county, or if the presiding judge is requested pursuant to this division to appoint a special prosecutor but the judge does not do so, the commission shall refer a copy of all of the information to the attorney general, who shall proceed according to division (B) of section 109.83 of the Revised Code. Upon such a failure of a special prosecutor to notify the commission, the special prosecutor promptly shall return to the commission all of the information that the commission had referred to the special prosecutor under this division.

If a special prosecutor who has been referred information under this division notifies the commission in writing, within thirty days after the referral, of his intention to present the information referred to him to the grand jury of the county, he shall proceed promptly to present the information as evidence to the grand jury and shall notify the commission of the grand jury's final actions, findings of indictments, or reports. The special prosecutor may disclose to the attorney general any matters occurring before the grand jury that are disclosed to the special prosecutor for use in the performance of his duties. The information shall be presented as evidence to the grand jury prior to the discharge of the next regular grand jury. If the special prosecutor fails to present the information as evidence within that time, the commission shall notify the attorney general and refer a copy of all of the information to the attorney general, the attorney general may proceed as if the special prosecutor had declined under this division to accept the matter, and the special prosecutor promptly shall return to the commission all of the information that the commission had referred to the special prosecutor under this division.

(4) The referral of information by a task force to a prosecuting attorney, to the attorney general, to the commission, or to a special prosecutor under this division, the content, scope, and subject of any information so referred, and the identity of any person who was investigated by the task force shall be kept confidential by the task force and its director, investigatory staff, and employees, by the commission and its director and employees, by the prosecuting attorney and his assistants and employees, by the special prosecutor and his assistants and employees, and by the attorney general and his assistants and employees until an indictment is returned or a criminal action or proceeding is initiated in a court of proper jurisdiction.

(5) Any information gathered by a task force during the course of its investigation that is in the possession of the task force, a prosecuting attorney, the attorney general, the commission, or a special prosecutor, and any record that pertains to any such information and that is maintained by the task force, a prosecuting attorney, the attorney general, the commission, or a special prosecutor is a confidential law enforcement investigatory record for purposes of section 149.43 of the Revised Code. However, no provision contained in this division or that section affects or limits or shall be construed as affecting or limiting any right of discovery granted to any person under the Revised Code, the Rules of Criminal Procedure, or the Rules of Juvenile Procedure.

(6) In no case shall the commission, a task force, a prosecuting attorney, a special prosecutor, or the attorney general publicly issue a report or summary that identifies or enables the identification of any person who has been or is being investigated under sections 177.01 to 177.03 of the Revised Code unless an indictment is returned against the person or a criminal action or proceeding is initiated against the person in a court of proper jurisdiction.

(7) For purposes of divisions (C) and (D) of this section, the office of a prosecuting attorney, the attorney general, a sheriff, or a chief law enforcement officer shall be considered as being implicated in organized criminal activity only if the prosecuting attorney, attorney general, sheriff, or chief law enforcement officer, one or more of his assistants, deputies, or officers, or one or more of his employees has committed or attempted or conspired to commit, is committing or attempting or conspiring to commit, or has engaged in or is engaging in complicity in the commission of, organized criminal activity.

(8) For purposes of this section, notification by a prosecuting attorney or special prosecutor may be accomplished by certified mail or such other documentation as is agreed upon by the prosecuting attorney or special prosecutor and the commission or their representatives. Notice by certified mail is complete upon mailing.

(E) If an organized crime task force has probable cause to believe, pursuant to its investigation of organized criminal activity in a county or in two or more adjacent counties, that a law of another state or the United States has been or is being violated, the task force director shall notify the commission chairman of that belief and the reasons for that belief. The chairman shall present that belief and those reasons to the commission, and if the commission determines that there is probable cause to believe that such a law has been or is being violated, the commission may refer the matter to the attorney general of the other state or to the appropriate United States attorney, whichever is applicable, and provide him with a copy of relevant information.

HISTORY: 141 v S 74. Eff 9-3-86.

CHAPTER 181: STATE COORDINATING COUNCIL

§ **181.25** Duties of council if sentencing structure is enacted.

(A) If the comprehensive criminal sentencing structure that it recommends to the general assembly pursuant to section 181.24 of the Revised Code or any aspects of that sentencing structure are enacted into law, the state criminal sentencing council shall do all of the following:

(1) Assist the general assembly in the implementation of those aspects of the sentencing structure that are enacted into law;

(2) Monitor the operation of the aspects of the sentencing structure that are enacted into law and report to the general assembly no later than January 1, 1997, and biennially thereafter, on all of the following matters:

(a) The impact of the sentencing structure in effect on and after July 1, 1996, on political subdivisions and other relevant aspects of local government in this state, including all of the following information:

(i) The number and type of offenders who were being imprisoned in a state correctional institution under the law in effect prior to July 1, 1996, but who are being punished under a community control sanction, as defined in section 2929.01 of the Revised Code, under the law in effect on and after July 1, 1996;

(ii) The fiscal and other impact of the law in effect on and after July 1, 1996, on political subdivisions and other relevant aspects of local government in this state, including law enforcement agencies, the court system, prosecutors, as defined in section 2935.01 of the Revised Code, the public defender and assigned counsel system, jails and workhouses, probation departments, the drug and alcohol abuse intervention and treatment system, and the mental health intervention and treatment system;

(b) The impact of the sentencing structure in effect on and after July 1, 1996, on the population of state correctional institutions, including information regarding the number and types of offenders who are being imprisoned under the law in effect on and after July 1, 1996, and the amount of space in state correctional institutions that is necessary to house those offenders;

(c) The impact of the sentencing structure and the sentence appeal provisions in effect on and after July 1, 1996, on the appellate courts of this state, including information regarding the number of sentence-based appeals, the cost of reviewing appeals of that nature, whether a special court should be created to review sentences, and whether changes should be made to ensure that sentence-based appeals are conducted expeditiously.

(3) Review all bills that are introduced in the general

assembly that provide for new criminal offenses or that change the penalty for any criminal offense, determine if those bills are consistent with the sentencing policy adopted under division (B) of section 181.23 of the Revised Code, determine the impact of those bills upon the correctional resources of the state, and recommend to the general assembly any necessary amendments to those bills. When the council recommends any amendment for a bill before the general assembly, it shall do so in a manner that is consistent with the requirements of section 181.24 of the Revised Code.

(4) Study criminal sentencing structures in this state, other states, and the federal government, recommend necessary changes to the sentencing structure of the state, and determine the costs and effects of any proposed changes in the sentencing structure of the state;

(5) Collect and maintain data that pertains to the cost to counties of the felony sentence appeal provisions set forth in section 2953.08 of the Revised Code, of the postconviction relief proceeding provisions set forth in division (A)(2) of section 2953.21 of the Revised Code, and of appeals from judgments entered in such postconviction relief proceedings. The data so collected and maintained shall include, but shall not be limited to, the increase in expenses that counties experience as a result of those provisions and those appeals and the number of felony sentence appeals made, postconviction relief proceedings filed, and appeals of postconviction relief proceeding judgments made in each county under those provisions. The council periodically shall provide to the felony sentence appeal cost oversight committee, in accordance with division (I) of section 2953.08 of the Revised Code, all data the council collects pursuant to this division.

(B) In addition to its duties set forth in section 181.24 of the Revised Code and division (A) of this section, the state criminal sentencing council shall review all forfeiture statutes in Titles XXIX [29] and XLV [45] of the Revised Code and, not later than July 1, 2001, recommend to the general assembly any necessary changes to those statutes.

HISTORY: 143 v S 258 (Eff 8-22-90); 146 v S 2 (Eff 7-1-96); 146 v H 670. Eff 12-2-96.

§ 181.26 Additional duties of council concerning juveniles.

(A) In addition to its duties set forth in sections 181.23 to 181.25 of the Revised Code, the state criminal sentencing commission† shall do all of the following:

(1) Review all statutes governing delinquent child, unruly child, and juvenile traffic offender dispositions in this state;

(2) Review state and local resources, including facilities and programs, used for delinquent child, unruly child, and juvenile traffic offender dispositions and profile the populations of youthful offenders in the facilities and programs;

(3) Report to the general assembly no later than September 1, 1997, a comprehensive plan containing recommendations based on the reviews required under divisions (A)(1) and (2) of this section. The recommendations shall do all of the following:

(a) Assist in the managing of the number of persons in, and costs of, the facilities, the programs, and other resources used in delinquent child, unruly child, and juvenile traffic offender dispositions;

(b) Foster rehabilitation, public safety, sanctions, accountability, and other reasonable goals;

(c) Provide greater certainty, proportionality, uniformity, fairness, and simplicity in delinquent child, unruly child, and juvenile traffic offender dispositions while retaining reasonable judicial discretion;

(d) Provide for the restoration of victims of juvenile offenses.

(B) The commission† shall project the impact of the comprehensive plan recommended by the commission† under this section on state and local resources used in delinquent child, unruly child, and juvenile traffic offender dispositions. The commission† shall determine whether any additional facilities, programs, or other resources are needed to implement the comprehensive plan.

(C) If the general assembly enacts all or a substantial part of the comprehensive plan recommended by the commission† under this section, the commission† shall do all of the following:

(1) Assist in the implementation of the enacted plan;

(2) Monitor the operation of the plan, periodically report to the general assembly on the plan's operation and the plan's impact on resources used in delinquent child, unruly child, and juvenile traffic offender dispositions, and periodically recommend changes in the plan to the general assembly based on this monitoring;

(3) Review all bills that are introduced in the general assembly that relate to delinquent child, unruly child, and juvenile traffic offender dispositions and assist the general assembly in making legislation consistent with the plan.

HISTORY: 146 v H 591. Eff 3-13-97.

† The title of this organization was changed from commission to council in HB 670 (146 v —), effective 12-2-96.

[CRIMINAL JUSTICE SERVICES]

§ 181.51 Definitions.

As used in sections 181.51 to 181.56 of the Revised Code:

(A) "Federal criminal justice acts" means any federal law that authorizes financial assistance and other forms of assistance to be given by the federal government to the states to be used for the improvement of the criminal and juvenile justice systems of the states.

(B)(1) "Criminal justice system" includes all of the functions of the following:

(a) The state highway patrol, county sheriff offices, municipal and township police departments, and all other law enforcement agencies;

(b) The courts of appeals, courts of common pleas, municipal courts, county courts, and mayor's courts, when dealing with criminal cases;

(c) The prosecuting attorneys, city directors of law, village solicitors, and other prosecuting authorities when prosecuting or otherwise handling criminal cases and the county and joint county public defenders and other public defender agencies or offices;

(d) The department of rehabilitation and correction, probation departments, county and municipal jails and workhouses, and any other department, agency, or facility that is concerned with the rehabilitation or correction of criminal offenders;

(e) Any public or private agency whose purposes include the prevention of crime or the diversion, adjudication, detention, or rehabilitation of criminal offenders;

(f) Any public or private agency, the purposes of which include assistance to crime victims or witnesses.

(2) The inclusion of any public or private agency, the purposes of which include assistance to crime victims or witnesses, as part of the criminal justice system pursuant to division (B)(1) of this section does not limit, and shall not be construed as limiting, the discretion or authority of the attorney general with respect to crime victim assistance and criminal justice programs.

(C) "Juvenile justice system" includes all of the functions of the juvenile courts, the department of youth services, any public or private agency whose purposes include the prevention of delinquency or the diversion, adjudication, detention, or rehabilitation of delinquent children, and any of the functions of the criminal justice system that are applicable to children.

(D) "Comprehensive plan" means a document that coordinates, evaluates, and otherwise assists, on an annual or multi-year basis, all of the functions of the criminal and juvenile justice systems of the state or a specified area of the state, that conforms to the priorities of the state with respect to criminal and juvenile justice systems, and that conforms with the requirements of all federal criminal justice acts. These functions include, but are not limited to, all of the following:

(1) Crime and delinquency prevention;

(2) Identification, detection, apprehension, and detention of persons charged with criminal offenses or delinquent acts;

(3) Assistance to crime victims or witnesses, except that the comprehensive plan does not include the functions of the attorney general pursuant to sections 109.91 and 109.92 of the Revised Code;

(4) Adjudication or diversion of persons charged with criminal offenses or delinquent acts;

(5) Custodial treatment of criminal offenders and delinquent children;

(6) Institutional and noninstitutional rehabilitation of criminal offenders and delinquent children.

(E) "Metropolitan county criminal justice services agency" means an agency that is established pursuant to division (A) of section 181.54 of the Revised Code.

(F) "Administrative planning district" means a district that is established pursuant to division (A) of section 181.56 of the Revised Code.

(G) "Criminal justice coordinating council" means a criminal justice services agency that is established pursuant to division (B) of section 181.56 of the Revised Code.

(H) "Local elected official" means any person who is a member of a board of county commissioners or township trustees or of a city or village council, judge of the court of common pleas, a municipal court, or a county court, sheriff, county coroner, prosecuting attorney, city director of law, village solicitor, or mayor.

HISTORY: RC § 122.21, 137 v H 1277 (Eff 12-14-78); 139 v H 440 (Eff 11-23-81); RC § 109.93, 142 v H 171 (Eff 7-1-87); RC § 122.21, 142 v H 231 (Eff 10-5-87); 142 v H 708 (Eff 4-19-88); 144 v H 298 (Eff 7-26-91); RC § 181.51, 145 v H 152. Eff 7-1-93.

§ 181.52 Creation and duties of office of criminal justice services.

(A) There is hereby created an office of criminal justice services. The governor shall appoint a director of the office, and the director may appoint, within the office, any professional and technical personnel and other employees that are necessary to enable the office to comply with sections 181.51 to 181.56 of the Revised Code. The director and the assistant director of the office, and all professional and technical personnel employed within the office who are not public employees as defined in section 4117.01 of the Revised Code, shall be in the unclassified civil service, and all other persons employed within the office shall be in the classified civil service. The director may enter into any contracts, except contracts governed by Chapter 4117. of the Revised Code, that are necessary for the operation of the office.

(B) Subject to division (D) of this section and subject to divisions (D) to (F) of section 5120.09 of the Revised Code insofar as those divisions relate to federal criminal justice acts that the governor requires the department of rehabilitation and correction to administer, the office of criminal justice services shall do all of the following:

(1) Serve as the state criminal justice services agency and perform criminal and juvenile justice system planning in the state, including any planning that is required by any federal law;

(2) Collect, analyze, and correlate information and data concerning the criminal and juvenile justice systems in the state;

(3) Cooperate with and provide technical assistance to state departments, administrative planning districts, metropolitan county criminal justice services agencies,

criminal justice coordinating councils, agencies, offices, and departments of the criminal and juvenile justice systems in the state, and other appropriate organizations and persons;

(4) Encourage and assist agencies, offices, and departments of the criminal and juvenile justice systems in the state and other appropriate organizations and persons to solve problems that relate to the duties of the office;

(5) Administer within the state any federal criminal justice acts or juvenile justice acts that the governor requires it to administer;

(6) Implement the state comprehensive plans;

(7) Audit grant activities of agencies, offices, organizations, and persons that are financed in whole or in part by funds granted through the office;

(8) Monitor or evaluate the performance of criminal and juvenile justice systems projects and programs in the state that are financed in whole or in part by funds granted through the office;

(9) Apply for, allocate, disburse, and account for grants that are made available pursuant to federal criminal justice acts or juvenile justice acts, or made available from other federal, state, or private sources, to improve the criminal and juvenile justice systems in the state;

(10) Contract with federal, state, and local agencies, foundations, corporations, businesses, and persons when necessary to carry out the duties of the office;

(11) Oversee the activities of metropolitan county criminal justice services agencies, administrative planning districts, and criminal justice coordinating councils in the state;

(12) Advise the general assembly and governor on legislation and other significant matters that pertain to the improvement and reform of criminal and juvenile justice systems in the state;

(13) Prepare and recommend legislation to the general assembly and governor for the improvement of the criminal and juvenile justice systems in the state;

(14) Assist, advise, and make any reports that are requested or required by the governor, attorney general, or general assembly;

(15) Adopt rules pursuant to Chapter 119. of the Revised Code.

(C) Division (B) of this section does not limit the discretion or authority of the attorney general with respect to crime victim assistance and criminal justice programs.

(D) Nothing in this section is intended to diminish or alter the status of the office of the attorney general as a criminal justice services agency.

HISTORY: RC § 122.22, 137 v H 1277 (Eff 12-14-78); 139 v H 536 (Eff 8-12-82); RC § 109.94, 142 v H 171 (Eff 7-1-87); RC § 122.22, 142 v H 231 (Eff 10-5-87); 142 v H 708 (Eff 4-19-88); 143 v S 258 (Eff 8-22-90); 144 v H 298 (Eff 7-26-91); RC § 181.52, 145 v H 152 (Eff 7-1-93); 145 v H 715 (Eff 7-22-94); 147 v H 215. Eff 9-29-97.

The effective date is set by section 222 of HB 215.

§ 181.53 Advisory committees.

The governor may appoint any advisory committees to assist the office of criminal justice services that he considers appropriate or that are required under any state or federal law.

HISTORY: RC § 122.24, 137 v H 1277 (Eff 12-14-78); RC § 109.94.2, 142 v H 171 (Eff 7-1-87); RC § 122.24, 142 v H 231 (Eff 10-5-87); 142 v H 708 (Eff 4-19-88); 144 v H 298 (Eff 7-26-91); RC § 181.53, 145 v H 152. Eff 7-1-93.

§ 181.54 Metropolitan county criminal justice services agency; formation, powers, duties.

(A) A county may enter into an agreement with the largest city within the county to establish a metropolitan county criminal justice services agency, if the population of the county exceeds five hundred thousand or the population of the city exceeds two hundred fifty thousand.

(B) A metropolitan county criminal justice services agency shall do all of the following:

(1) Accomplish criminal and juvenile justice systems planning within its services area;

(2) Collect, analyze, and correlate information and data concerning the criminal and juvenile justice systems within its services area;

(3) Cooperate with and provide technical assistance to all criminal and juvenile justice agencies and systems and other appropriate organizations and persons within its services area;

(4) Encourage and assist agencies of the criminal and juvenile justice systems and other appropriate organizations and persons to solve problems that relate to its duties;

(5) Administer within its services area any federal criminal justice acts or juvenile justice acts that the office of criminal justice services administers within the state;

(6) Implement the comprehensive plans for its services area;

(7) Monitor or evaluate, within its services area, the performance of the criminal and juvenile justice systems projects and programs that are financed in whole or in part by funds granted through it;

(8) Apply for, allocate, and disburse grants that are made available pursuant to any federal criminal justice acts, or pursuant to any other federal, state, or private sources for the purpose of improving the criminal and juvenile justice systems;

(9) Contract with federal, state, and local agencies, foundations, corporations, and other businesses or persons to carry out the duties of the agency.

HISTORY: RC § 122.25, 137 v H 1277 (Eff 12-14-78); RC § 109.95, 142 v H 171 (Eff 7-1-87); RC § 122.25, 142 v H 231 (Eff 10-5-87); 144 v H 298 (Eff 7-26-91); RC § 181.54, 145 v H 152. Eff 7-1-93.

§ 181.55 Funding, comprehensive plan, supervisory board for metropolitan county agency.

(A) When funds are available for this purpose, the

office of criminal justice services shall provide funds to metropolitan county criminal justice services agencies for the purpose of developing, coordinating, evaluating, and implementing comprehensive plans within their respective counties. The office of criminal justice services shall provide funds to an agency only if it complies with the conditions of division (B) of this section.

(B) A metropolitan county criminal justice services agency shall do all of the following:

(1) Submit, in a form that is acceptable to the office of criminal justice services, a comprehensive plan for the county;

(2) Establish a metropolitan county criminal justice services supervisory board whose members shall include a majority of the local elected officials in the county and representatives from law enforcement agencies, courts, prosecuting authorities, public defender agencies, rehabilitation and correction agencies, community organizations, juvenile justice services agencies, professionals, and private citizens in the county, and that shall have the authority set forth in division (C) of this section;

(3) Organize in the manner provided in sections 167.01 to 167.03, 302.21 to 302.24, or 713.21 to 713.27 of the Revised Code, unless the board created pursuant to division (B)(2) of this section organizes pursuant to these sections.

(C) A metropolitan county criminal justice services supervisory board shall do all of the following:

(1) Exercise leadership in improving the quality of the criminal and juvenile justice systems in the county;

(2) Review, approve, and maintain general oversight of the comprehensive plans for the county and the implementation of the plans;

(3) Review and comment on the overall needs and accomplishments of the criminal and juvenile justice systems in the county;

(4) Establish, as required to comply with this division, task forces, ad hoc committees, and other committees, whose members shall be appointed by the chairman of the board;

(5) Establish any rules that the board considers necessary and that are consistent with the federal criminal justice acts and section 181.52 of the Revised Code.

HISTORY: RC § 122.26, 137 v H 1277 (Eff 12-14-78); 139 v H 536 (Eff 8-12-82); RC § 109.96, 142 v H 171 (Eff 7-1-87); RC § 122.26, 142 v H 231 (Eff 10-5-87); 144 v H 298 (Eff 7-26-91); RC § 181.55, 145 v H 152. Eff 7-1-93.

§ 181.56 Administrative planning districts; criminal justice coordinating councils.

(A) In counties in which a metropolitan county criminal justice services agency does not exist, the office of criminal justice services shall discharge the office's duties by establishing administrative planning districts. An administrative planning district shall contain a group of contiguous counties in which no county has a metropolitan county criminal justice services agency.

(B) Any county or any combination of contiguous counties within an administrative planning district may form a criminal justice coordinating council, if the county or the group of counties has a total population in excess of two hundred fifty thousand. The council shall comply with the conditions set forth in divisions (B) and (C) of section 181.55 of the Revised Code, and exercise within its jurisdiction the powers and duties set forth in division (B) of section 181.54 of the Revised Code.

HISTORY: RC § 122.27, 137 v H 1277 (Eff 12-14-78); RC § 109.97, 142 v H 171 (Eff 7-1-87); RC § 122.27, 142 v H 231 (Eff 10-5-87); 142 v H 708 (Eff 4-19-88); RC § 181.56, 145 v H 152. Eff 7-1-93.

TITLE 3: COUNTIES

CHAPTER 306: COUNTY TRANSIT SYSTEM; REGIONAL TRANSIT AUTHORITY; REGIONAL TRANSIT COMMISSION

§ 306.35 Powers and duties of authority.

Upon the creation of a regional transit authority as provided by section 306.32 of the Revised Code, and upon the qualifying of its board of trustees and the election of a president and a vice-president, the authority shall exercise in its own name all the rights, powers, and duties vested in and conferred upon it by sections 306.30 to 306.53 of the Revised Code. Subject to any reservations, limitations, and qualifications that are set forth in those sections, the regional transit authority:

(A) May sue or be sued in its corporate name;

(B) May make contracts in the exercise of the rights, powers, and duties conferred upon it;

(C) May adopt and at will alter a seal and use such seal by causing it to be impressed, affixed, reproduced, or otherwise used, but failure to affix the seal shall not affect the validity of any instrument;

(D) May adopt, amend, and repeal bylaws for the administration of its affairs and rules for the control of the administration and operation of transit facilities under its jurisdiction, and for the exercise of all of its rights of ownership in those transit facilities;

(E) May fix, alter, and collect fares, rates, and rentals and other charges for the use of transit facilities under its jurisdiction to be determined exclusively by it for the purpose of providing for the payment of the expenses of the regional transit authority, the acquisition, construction, improvement, extension, repair, maintenance, and operation of transit facilities under its jurisdiction, the payment of principal and interest on its obligations, and to fulfill the terms of any agreements made with purchasers or holders of any such obligations, or with any person or political subdivision;

(F) Shall have jurisdiction, control, possession, and supervision of all property, rights, easements, licenses, moneys, contracts, accounts, liens, books, records, maps, or other property rights and interests conveyed, delivered, transferred, or assigned to it;

(G) May acquire, construct, improve, extend, repair, lease, operate, maintain, or manage transit facilities within or without its territorial boundaries, considered necessary to accomplish the purposes of its organization and make charges for the use of transit facilities;

(H) May levy and collect taxes as provided in sections 306.40 and 306.49 of the Revised Code;

(I) May issue bonds secured by its general credit as provided in section 306.40 of the Revised Code;

(J) May hold, encumber, control, acquire by donation, by purchase for cash or by installment payments, by lease-purchase agreement, by lease with option to purchase, or by condemnation, and may construct, own, lease as lessee or lessor, use, and sell, real and personal property, or any interest or right in real and personal property, within or without its territorial boundaries, for the location or protection of transit facilities and improvements and access to transit facilities and improvements, the relocation of buildings, structures, and improvements situated on lands acquired by the regional transit authority, or for any other necessary purpose, or for obtaining or storing materials to be used in constructing, maintaining, and improving transit facilities under its jurisdiction;

(K) May exercise the power of eminent domain to acquire property or any interest in property, within or without its territorial boundaries, that is necessary or proper for the construction or efficient operation of any transit facility or access to any transit facility under its jurisdiction in accordance with section 306.36 of the Revised Code;

(L) May provide by agreement with any county, including the counties within its territorial boundaries, or any municipal corporation or any combination of counties or municipal corporations for the making of necessary surveys, appraisals, and examinations preliminary to the acquisition or construction of any transit facility and the amount of the expense for the surveys, appraisals, and examinations to be paid by each such county or municipal corporation;

(M) May provide by agreement with any county, including the counties within its territorial boundaries, or any municipal corporation or any combination of those counties or municipal corporations for the acquisition, construction, improvement, extension, maintenance, or operation of any transit facility owned or to be owned and operated by it or owned or to be owned and operated by any such county or municipal corporation and the terms on which it shall be acquired, leased, constructed, maintained, or operated, and the amount of the cost and expense of the acquisition, lease, construction, maintenance, or operation to be paid by each such county or municipal corporation;

(N) May issue revenue bonds for the purpose of acquiring, replacing, improving, extending, enlarging, or constructing any facility or permanent improvement that it is authorized to acquire, replace, improve, extend, enlarge, or construct, including all costs in connection with and incidental to the acquisition, replacement, improvement, extension, enlargement, or construction, and their financing, as provided by section 306.37 of the Revised Code;

(O) May enter into and supervise franchise agreements for the operation of a transit system;

(P) May accept the assignment of and supervise an

existing franchise agreement for the operation of a transit system;

(Q) May exercise a right to purchase a transit system in accordance with the acquisition terms of an existing franchise agreement; and in connection with the purchase the regional transit authority may issue revenue bonds as provided by section 306.37 of the Revised Code or issue bonds secured by its general credit as provided in section 306.40 of the Revised Code;

(R) May apply for and accept grants or loans from the United States, the state, or any other public body for the purpose of providing for the development or improvement of transit facilities, mass transportation facilities, equipment, techniques, methods, or services, and grants or loans needed to exercise a right to purchase a transit system pursuant to agreement with the owner of those transit facilities, or for providing lawful financial assistance to existing transit systems; and may provide any consideration that may be required in order to obtain those grants or loans from the United States, the state, or other public body, either of which grants or loans may be evidenced by the issuance of revenue bonds as provided by section 306.37 of the Revised Code or general obligation bonds as provided by section 306.40 of the Revised Code;

(S) May employ and fix the compensation of consulting engineers, superintendents, managers, and such other engineering, construction, accounting and financial experts, attorneys, and other employees and agents necessary for the accomplishment of its purposes;

(T) May procure insurance against loss to it by reason of damages to its properties resulting from fire, theft, accident, or other casualties or by reason of its liability for any damages to persons or property occurring in the construction or operation of transit facilities under its jurisdiction or the conduct of its activities;

(U) May maintain funds that it considers necessary for the efficient performance of its duties;

(V) May direct its agents or employees, when properly identified in writing, after at least five days' written notice, to enter upon lands within or without its territorial boundaries in order to make surveys and examinations preliminary to the location and construction of transit facilities, without liability to it or its agents or employees except for actual damage done;

(W) On its own motion, may request the appropriate zoning board, as defined in section 4563.03 of the Revised Code, to establish and enforce zoning regulations pertaining to any transit facility under its jurisdiction in the manner prescribed by sections 4563.01 to 4563.21 of the Revised Code;

(X) If it acquires any existing transit system, shall assume all the employer's obligations under any existing labor contract between the employees and management of the system. If the board acquires, constructs, controls, or operates any such facilities, it shall negotiate arrangements to protect the interests of employees affected by the acquisition, construction, control, or operation. The arrangements shall include, but are not limited to:

(1) The preservation of rights, privileges, and benefits under existing collective bargaining agreements or otherwise, the preservation of rights and benefits under any existing pension plans covering prior service, and continued participation in social security in addition to participation in the public employees retirement system as required in Chapter 145. of the Revised Code;

(2) The continuation of collective bargaining rights;

(3) The protection of individual employees against a worsening of their positions with respect to their employment;

(4) Assurances of employment to employees of those transit systems and priority reemployment of employees terminated or laid off;

(5) Paid training or retraining programs;

(6) Signed written labor agreements.

The arrangements may include provisions for the submission of labor disputes to final and binding arbitration.

(Y) May provide for and maintain security operations, including a transit police department, subject to section 306.352 [306.35.2] of the Revised Code. Regional transit authority police officers shall have the power and duty to act as peace officers within transit facilities owned, operated, or leased by the transit authority to protect the transit authority's property and the person and property of passengers, to preserve the peace, and to enforce all laws of the state and ordinances and regulations of political subdivisions in which the transit authority operates. Regional transit authority police officers also shall have the power and duty to act as peace officers when they render emergency assistance outside their jurisdiction to any other peace officer who is not a regional transit authority police officer and who has arrest authority under section 2935.03 of the Revised Code. Regional transit authority police officers may render emergency assistance if there is a threat of imminent physical danger to the peace officer, a threat of physical harm to another person, or any other serious emergency situation and if either the peace officer who is assisted requests emergency assistance or it appears that the peace officer who is assisted is unable to request emergency assistance and the circumstances observed by the regional transit authority police officer reasonably indicate that emergency assistance is appropriate.

Before exercising powers of arrest and the other powers and duties of a peace officer, each regional transit authority police officer shall take an oath and give bond to the state in a sum that the board of trustees prescribes for the proper performance of the officer's duties.

Persons employed as regional transit authority police officers shall complete training for the position to which they have been appointed as required by the Ohio peace officer training commission as authorized in section 109.77 of the Revised Code, or be otherwise qualified. The cost of the training shall be provided by the regional transit authority.

(Z) May procure a policy or policies insuring members of its board of trustees against liability on account of damages or injury to persons and property resulting from any act or omission of a member in the member's official capacity as a member of the board or resulting solely out of the member's membership on the board;

(AA) May enter into any agreement for the sale and leaseback or lease and leaseback of transit facilities, which agreement may contain all necessary covenants for the security and protection of any lessor or the regional transit authority including, but not limited to, indemnification of the lessor against the loss of anticipated tax benefits arising from acts, omissions, or misrepresentations of the regional transit authority. In connection with that transaction, the regional transit authority may contract for insurance and letters of credit and pay any premiums or other charges for the insurance and letters of credit. The fiscal officer shall not be required to furnish any certificate under section 5705.41 of the Revised Code in connection with the execution of any such agreement.

(BB) In regard to any contract entered into on or after March 19, 1993, for the rendering of services or the supplying of materials or for the construction, demolition, alteration, repair, or reconstruction of transit facilities in which a bond is required for the faithful performance of the contract, may permit the person awarded the contract to utilize a letter of credit issued by a bank or other financial institution in lieu of the bond;

(CC) May enter into agreements with municipal corporations located within the territorial jurisdiction of the regional transit authority permitting regional transit authority police officers employed under division (Y) of this section to exercise full arrest powers, as provided in section 2935.03 of the Revised Code, for the purpose of preserving the peace and enforcing all laws of the state and ordinances and regulations of the municipal corporation within the areas that may be agreed to by the regional transit authority and the municipal corporation.

HISTORY: 131 v 192 (Eff 11-1-65); 133 v S 125 (Eff 8-25-70); 136 v S 427 (Eff 8-9-76); 137 v S 194 (Eff 7-8-77); 139 v S 543 (Eff 5-24-82); 144 v S 164 (Eff 3-19-93); 146 v S 2 (Eff 7-1-96); 146 v S 269 (Eff 7-1-96); 146 v H 566 (Eff 10-16-96); 146 v H 670 (Eff 12-2-96); 147 v H 228. Eff 5-7-97.

[§ 306.35.2] § 306.352 Felony precludes or terminates employment as police officer.

(A) As used in this section, "felony" has the same meaning as in section 109.511 [109.51.1] of the Revised Code.

(B)(1) In the exercise of its authority under division (Y) of section 306.35 of the Revised Code, a regional transit authority shall not employ a person as a regional transit authority police officer on a permanent basis, on a temporary basis, for a probationary term, or on other than a permanent basis if the person previously has been convicted of or has pleaded guilty to a felony.

(2)(a) The transit authority shall terminate the employment of a person as a regional transit authority police officer if the person does either of the following:

(i) Pleads guilty to a felony;

(ii) Pleads guilty to a misdemeanor pursuant to a negotiated plea agreement as provided in division (D) of section 2929.29 of the Revised Code in which the police officer agrees to surrender the certificate awarded to that police officer under section 109.77 of the Revised Code.

(b) The transit authority shall suspend from employment a person designated as a regional transit authority police officer if that person is convicted, after trial, of a felony. If the police officer files an appeal from that conviction and the conviction is upheld by the highest court to which the appeal is taken or if the police officer does not file a timely appeal, the transit authority shall terminate the employment of that police officer. If the police officer files an appeal that results in the police officer's acquittal of the felony or conviction of a misdemeanor, or in the dismissal of the felony charge against the police officer, the transit authority shall reinstate that police officer. A police officer who is reinstated under division (B)(2)(b) of this section shall not receive any back pay unless that officer's conviction of the felony was reversed on appeal, or the felony charge was dismissed, because the court found insufficient evidence to convict the police officer of the felony.

(3) Division (B) of this section does not apply regarding an offense that was committed prior to January 1, 1997.

(4) The suspension from employment, or the termination of the employment, of a regional transit authority police officer under division (B)(2) of this section shall be in accordance with Chapter 119. of the Revised Code.

HISTORY: 146 v H 566. Eff 10-16-95.

CHAPTER 307: BOARD OF COUNTY COMMISSIONERS—POWERS

§ 307.62 Appropriations and grants for crime victim assistance programs.

(A) As used in this section:

(1) "County agency" includes any department, authority, commission, office, or board of the county.

(2) "Crisis intervention services" means short-term emotional or psychological aid provided in the form of counseling or referral for crime victims.

(3) "Emergency services" means the provision of aid including temporary shelter for victims who cannot safely remain in their current lodgings, repair of locks or boarding up of windows to prevent the immediate

reburglarization of a home or an apartment, or provision of petty cash for meeting immediate needs related to transportation, food, shelter, and other necessities.

(4) "Support services" includes follow-up counseling, guidance for resolution of problems caused by the crime, and assistance in obtaining aid and services from social service agencies, criminal justice agencies, and the police.

(5) "Court-related services" means services calculated to assist crime victims in participating in criminal justice proceedings involving crimes committed against such victims, including transportation to court, child care while in court or at a court-related proceeding, escort services, and the filing of requests for restraining orders. "Court-related services" does not include the provision of an attorney to represent the crime victim in any criminal prosecution based upon the crime committed against such victim.

(6) "Crime prevention services" means educational programs and materials to help avoid and prevent the commission of criminal acts in the future.

(7) "Victim and offender mediation services" means services designed to provide victims the opportunity for a meeting to ask questions, express feelings, or discuss restitution agreements with the convicted offenders or delinquent juveniles involved in the crimes against such victims.

(B) In addition to any money from another source appropriated for the same purpose, the board of county commissioners of any county may appropriate to a county agency, or grant to a private, nonprofit corporation or association, the money derived from a tax levied pursuant to division (II) of section 5705.19 of the Revised Code, for the public purpose of providing and maintaining in the county a crime victim assistance program offering crisis intervention services, emergency services, support services, court-related services, crime prevention services, or victim and offender mediation services. Money appropriated or granted under this section may be used to pay the salaries of employees of the county agency or of the private, nonprofit corporation or association who provide those services to clients of the agency, corporation, or association, but shall not be used to pay the fees of attorneys, doctors, mental health counselors, or other professionals who are not employees of the agency, corporation, or association.

All or some of the money may be given by the board in the form of a grant to a private, nonprofit corporation or association, if such corporation or association applies, on an application form prescribed by the board, for a grant to provide and maintain a crime victim assistance program. The board shall evaluate the application, and if such application is approved, the board shall enter into an agreement with the corporation or association granting all or some of the money. The agreement shall specify the following conditions for use of the money granted:

(1) That the recipient of the grant money shall keep current and accurate accounts of its use of the grant money;

(2) That, in accordance with rules adopted by the auditor of state pursuant to section 117.20 of the Revised Code, at least annually the recipient shall audit its crime victim assistance program. The recipient may contract with private auditors for performance of these audits. The cost of the audits shall be paid out of the grant money, except that no more than ten thousand dollars of the grant money may be expended per year on audits. A copy of the fiscal audit report shall be provided to the director of the recipient providing the crime victim assistance program, the board, the auditor of state, and the county auditor.

(3) That the recipient is liable to repay to the board any grant money that is improperly used;

(4) That the recipient shall repay to the board all grant money remaining unused at the end of the fiscal year or other accounting period for which the board granted the money. However, when the recipient is to receive grant money in the next succeeding fiscal year or other accounting period following the fiscal year or other accounting period for which the board granted the money, the recipient need not repay the grant money remaining unused.

(5) That a summary of program activities offered under the recipient crime victim assistance program annually be provided to the board.

The board shall not expend any money granted under this section until it has received a written agreement, signed by an officer or agent of the recipient authorized to legally bind the recipient, embodying all conditions stated in division (B) of this section and any other conditions specified in the agreement, regarding the use of the money granted by the board.

Upon discovering that money granted under this section is being or has been improperly used, the board, by resolution, shall demand that the recipient repay the improperly used money and shall transmit a certified copy of the resolution to the recipient. If the recipient does not repay the improperly used money within a reasonable period of time, the board shall direct the prosecuting attorney to bring a civil action to recover the improperly used money.

HISTORY: 144 v S 32. Eff 7-1-92.

Not analogous to former RC § 307.62 (RS §§ 633-12, 633-13; 92 v 212; GC §§ 2498, 2499; Bureau of Code Revision, 10-1-53), repealed 139 v S 114, § 2, eff 10-27-81.

CHAPTER 309: PROSECUTING ATTORNEY

§ 309.01 Election of prosecuting attorney.

There shall be elected quadrennially in each county, a prosecuting attorney, who shall hold his office for four years, beginning on the first Monday of January next after his election.

HISTORY: RS § 1267; S & C 1225; 50 v 215, 78 v 260; 93 v 125; 98 v 273; GC § 2909; 116 v Pt II 184; Bureau of Code Revision. Eff 10-1-53.

§ 309.02 Qualifications of candidate for prosecuting attorney.

No person shall be eligible as a candidate for the office of prosecuting attorney, or shall be elected to such office, who is not an attorney at law licensed to practice law in this state. No prosecuting attorney shall be a member of the general assembly of this state or mayor of a municipal corporation.

HISTORY: RS § 1268; S & C 1227; 77 v 42; GC § 2910; Bureau of Code Revision, Eff 10-1-53; 144 v S 243. Eff 8-19-92.

§ 309.03 Bond of prosecuting attorney; oath.

Before entering upon the discharge of his duties, the prosecuting attorney shall give a bond, signed by a bonding or surety company approved by the court of common pleas or the probate court and authorized to do business in this state, or, at his option, signed by two or more freeholders having real estate in the value of double the amount of the bond over and above all encumbrances to the state. Such bond shall be in a sum not less than one thousand dollars, to be fixed by the court of common pleas or the probate court and conditioned that such prosecuting attorney will faithfully discharge all the duties enjoined upon him by law, and pay over all moneys received by him in his official capacity. The expense or premium for such bond shall be paid by the board of county commissioners, and shall be charged to the general fund of the county. Such bond, with the approval of such court and the oath of office required by sections 3.22 and 3.23 of the Revised Code indorsed thereon, shall be deposited with the county treasurer.

HISTORY: RS § 1269; S & C 1225; 50 v 215, § 3; GC § 2911; 112 v 111; Bureau of Code Revision. Eff 10-1-53.

§ 309.05 Removal of prosecuting attorney for neglect or misconduct.

On complaint, in writing, signed by one or more taxpayers, containing distinct charges and specifications of wanton and willful neglect of duty or gross misconduct in office by the prosecuting attorney, and filed in the court of common pleas, the court shall assign the complaint for hearing and shall cause reasonable notice of such hearing to be given to the prosecuting attorney of the time fixed by the court for the hearing. At the time so fixed, or to which the court adjourns the hearing, such court shall hear the evidence adduced by the complainants and the prosecuting attorney. If it appears that the prosecuting attorney has willfully and wantonly neglected to perform his duties, or has been guilty of gross misconduct in office, the court shall remove him from office and declare such office vacant. Otherwise the complaint shall be dismissed, and the court shall render judgment against the losing party for costs.

HISTORY: RS § 1272; S & C 1227; 50 v 215, § 8; GC § 2913; Bureau of Code Revision. Eff 10-1-53.

§ 309.06 Assistant prosecuting attorneys; clerks; stenographers.

(A) On or before the first Monday in January of each year, the judge of the court of common pleas or, if there is more than one judge, the judges of the court of common pleas in joint session may fix an aggregate sum to be expended for the incoming year for the compensation of assistants, clerks, and stenographers of the prosecuting attorney's office.

The prosecuting attorney may appoint any assistants, clerks, and stenographers who are necessary for the proper performance of the duties of his office and fix their compensation, not to exceed, in the aggregate, the amount fixed by the judges of the court of common pleas. The compensation, after being so fixed, shall be paid to the assistants, clerks, and stenographers bi-weekly from the general fund of the county treasury, upon the warrant of the county auditor.

(B) Subject to section 2921.421 [2921.42.1] of the Revised Code, a prosecuting attorney may appoint, as an assistant prosecuting attorney, clerk, stenographer, or other employee, a person who is an associate or partner of, or who is employed by, the prosecuting attorney or an assistant prosecuting attorney in the private practice of law in a partnership, professional association, or other law business arrangement.

HISTORY: RS § 1271; 75 v 520; 77 v 319; 79 v 79; 86 v 4; 86 v 66; 90 v 73; 92 v 37; 94 v 30; 95 v 240; 97 v 315; GC §§ 2914, 2915; Bureau of Code Revision, 10-1-53; 139 v S 114 (Eff 10-27-81); 144 v S 359 (Eff 12-22-92); 145 v H 285. Eff 3-2-94.

§ 309.07 Appointment of secret service officer.

The prosecuting attorney may appoint secret service officers whose duty it shall be to aid him in the collection and discovery of evidence to be used in the trial of criminal cases and matters of a criminal nature. Such appointment shall be made for such term as the prosecuting attorney deems advisable, and subject to termination at any time by such prosecuting attorney. The compensation of said officers shall be fixed by the judge of the court of common pleas, or, if there is more than one judge, such compensation shall be fixed by the judges of such court in joint session, and shall not be less than one hundred twenty-five dollars per month for the time actually occupied in such service nor more than seventy-five per cent of the salary of the prosecuting attorney for a year. Such salary shall be payable monthly, out of the county fund, upon the warrant of the county auditor.

HISTORY: GC § 2915-1; 102 v 77, 78; 103 v 501; Bureau of Code Revision, 10-1-53; 133 v S 94. Eff 10-24-69.

§ 309.08 Powers and duties of prosecuting attorney; rewards for information as to drug-related offenses.

(A) The prosecuting attorney may inquire into the commission of crimes within the county. The prosecuting attorney shall prosecute, on behalf of the state, all complaints, suits, and controversies in which the state is a party, except for those required to be prosecuted by a special prosecutor pursuant to section 177.03 of the Revised Code or by the attorney general pursuant to section 109.83 of the Revised Code, and other suits, matters, and controversies that the prosecuting attorney is required to prosecute within or outside the county, in the probate court, court of common pleas, and court of appeals. In conjunction with the attorney general, the prosecuting attorney shall prosecute in the supreme court cases arising in the prosecuting attorney's county, except for those cases required to be prosecuted by a special prosecutor pursuant to section 177.03 of the Revised Code or by the attorney general pursuant to section 109.83 of the Revised Code.

In every case of conviction, the prosecuting attorney forthwith shall cause execution to be issued for the fine and costs, or costs only, as the case may be, and faithfully shall urge the collection until it is effected or found to be impracticable to collect. The prosecuting attorney forthwith shall pay to the county treasurer all moneys belonging to the state or county which come into the prosecuting attorney's possession.

The prosecuting attorney or an assistant prosecuting attorney of a county may participate, as a member of the investigatory staff of an organized crime task force established under section 177.02 of the Revised Code that has jurisdiction in that county, in an investigation of organized criminal activity under sections 177.01 to 177.03 of the Revised Code.

(B) The prosecuting attorney may pay a reward to a person who has volunteered any tip or information to a law enforcement agency in the county concerning a drug-related offense that is planned to occur, is occurring, or has occurred, in whole or in part, in the county. The prosecuting attorney may provide for the payment, out of the following sources, of rewards to a person who has volunteered tips and information to a law enforcement agency in the county concerning a drug-related offense that is planned to occur, is occurring, or has occurred, in whole or in part, in the county:

(1) The law enforcement trust fund established by the prosecuting attorney pursuant to division (D)(1)(c) of section 2933.43 of the Revised Code;

(2) The portion of any mandatory fines imposed pursuant to divisions (B)(1) and (2) of section 2929.18 or Chapter 2925. of the Revised Code that is paid to the prosecuting attorney pursuant to that division or chapter, the portion of any additional fines imposed under division (B)(5) of section 2929.18 of the Revised Code that is paid to the prosecuting attorney pursuant to that division, or the portion of any double fines imposed pursuant to division (B)(5) of section 2925.42 of the Revised Code that is paid to the prosecuting attorney pursuant to that division;

(3) The furtherance of justice fund allowed to the prosecuting attorney under section 325.12 of the Revised Code or any additional funds allowed to the prosecuting attorney under section 325.13 of the Revised Code;

(4) Any other moneys lawfully in the possession or control of the prosecuting attorney.

(C) As used in division (B) of this section, "drug-related offense" means any violation of Chapter 2925. or 3719. of the Revised Code or any violation of a municipal ordinance that is substantially equivalent to any section in either of those chapters.

HISTORY: RS § 1273; S&C 1125, 1185; 33 v 44, §§ 1, 2, 3; 50 v 215, § 2; 82 v 27; 98 v 160; GC § 2916; 102 v 77; 103 v 405(419); Bureau of Code Revision, 10-1-53; 141 v S 74 (Eff 9-3-86); 143 v S 258 (Eff 11-20-90); 145 v H 152 (Eff 7-1-93); 146 v S 2 (Eff 7-1-96); 146 v S 166. Eff 10-17-96.

This section was amended in 102 v 77. The amending statute was held to be an entire act; and, accordingly, since GC § 2915-1, which was 102 v 77 (78), was held to be unconstitutional, it was held that original GC § 2916 was still in force. See State ex rel McGannon v. Sayre, 12 NP(NS) 13, 22 OD 234.

The provisions of § 4 of SB 166 read as follows:

SECTION 4. The amendments made by this act to sections 309.08, 2925.03, 2929.18, 3719.21, 3793.06, and 3793.11 of the Revised Code apply to offenses that are committed on or after the effective date of this act.

§ 309.09 Legal adviser; additional counsel.

(A) The prosecuting attorney shall be the legal adviser of the board of county commissioners, board of elections, and all other county officers and boards, including all tax-supported public libraries, and any of them may require written opinions or instructions from the prosecuting attorney in matters connected with their official duties. The prosecuting attorney shall prosecute and defend all suits and actions which any such officer or board directs or to which it is a party, and no county officer may employ any other counsel or attorney at the expense of the county, except as provided in section 305.14 of the Revised Code.

(B) Such prosecuting attorney shall be the legal adviser for all township officers, unless the township has adopted the limited self-government form of township government pursuant to Chapter 504. of the Revised Code and has not entered into a contract to have the prosecuting attorney serve as the township law director, in which case the township law director, whether serving full-time or part-time, shall be the legal adviser for all township officers. When the board of township trustees finds it advisable or necessary to have additional legal counsel it may employ an attorney other than the township law director or the prosecuting attorney of the county, either for a particular matter or on an annual basis, to represent the township and its officers in their official capacities and to advise them on legal matters. No such counsel or attorney may be employed, except on the order of the board of township trustees, duly entered upon its journal, in which the compensation to be paid for such legal services shall be fixed. Such compensation shall be paid from the township fund.

Nothing in this division confers any of the powers or duties of a prosecuting attorney under section 309.08 of the Revised Code upon a township law director.

(C) Whenever the board of county commissioners employs an attorney other than the prosecuting attorney of the county, without the authorization of the court of common pleas as provided in section 305.14 of the Revised Code, either for a particular matter or on an annual basis, to represent the board of county commissioners in its official capacity and to advise it on legal matters, the board of county commissioners shall enter upon its journal an order of the board in which the compensation to be paid for such legal services shall be fixed. The compensation shall be paid from the county general fund. The total compensation paid, in any year, by the board of county commissioners for legal services under this division shall not exceed the total annual compensation of the prosecuting attorney for that county.

(D) The prosecuting attorney and the board of county commissioners jointly may contract with a board of park commissioners under section 1545.07 of the Revised Code for the prosecuting attorney to provide legal services to the park district the board of park commissioners operates. All moneys received pursuant to such a contract shall be deposited into the prosecuting attorney's legal services fund, which shall be established in the county treasury of each county in which such a contract exists. Moneys in that fund may be appropriated only to the prosecuting attorney for the purpose of providing legal services under a contract entered into under this division.

HISTORY: RS § 1274; 98 v 160; GC § 2917; Bureau of Code Revision, 10-1-53; 125 v H 251 (Eff 10-2-53); 128 v 597 (Eff 11-9-59); 129 v 1557 (Eff 10-27-61); 137 v H 316 (Eff 10-25-78); 141 v H 428 (Eff 12-23-86); 144 v H 77 (Eff 9-17-91); 146 v H 268 (Eff 5-8-96); 146 v H 268 (Eff 5-8-96); 146 v H 501. Eff 11-6-96.

§ 309.10 Provisions for other counsel.

Sections 309.08 and 309.09 of the Revised Code do not prevent a school board from employing counsel to represent it, but such counsel, when so employed, shall be paid by such school board from the school fund. Such sections do not prevent a county board of mental retardation and developmental disabilities from employing counsel to represent it, but such counsel, when so employed, shall be employed in accordance with division (C) of section 305.14 and paid in accordance with division (A)(7) of section 5126.05 of the Revised Code.

Sections 309.08 and 309.09 of the Revised Code do not prevent a board of county hospital trustees from employing counsel with the approval of the county commissioners to bring legal action for the collection of delinquent accounts of such hospital, but such counsel, when so employed, shall be paid from the hospital's funds. Such sections do not prevent a board of library trustees from employing counsel when the prosecuting attorney is unable to serve or is adversely interested or when legal action is between two or more boards of library trustees in the same county, but such counsel, when so employed, shall be paid from the library's funds. Such sections do not prevent the appointment and employment of assistants, clerks, and stenographers, to the prosecuting attorney as provided in sections 309.01 to 309.16 of the Revised Code, or the appointment by the court of common pleas or the court of appeals of an attorney to assist the prosecuting attorney in the trial of a criminal cause pending in such court, or the board of county commissioners from paying such services.

HISTORY: RS § 1274; 98 v 160; GC § 2918; Bureau of Code Revision, 10-1-53; 127 v 440; 128 v 597 (Eff 11-9-59); 142 v S 155 (Eff 6-24-88); 143 v H 569 (Eff 11-11-90); 145 v H 694 (Eff 11-11-94); 146 v H 629. Eff 3-13-97.

§ 309.11 Official bonds.

The prosecuting attorney shall prepare, in legal form, the official bonds for all county officers, and shall see that the acceptance of such bonds by the proper authorities, the signing thereof, and all the indorsements thereon, are in conformity to law, and that they are deposited with the proper officer. No bond shall be accepted or approved for any county officer by the person or tribunal authorized to approve it, until the prosecuting attorney has inspected it, and certified thereon that such bond is sufficient. In case of a vacancy in the office of prosecuting attorney or of the absence or disability of the prosecuting attorney, such duties shall be discharged by the probate judge.

HISTORY: RS § 1276; S & S 634; S & C 1226; 62 v 173, § 5; 81 v 198; GC § 2920; Bureau of Code Revision. Eff 10-1-53.

§ 309.12 Protection of public funds.

Upon being satisfied that funds of the county, or public moneys in the hands of the county treasurer or belonging to the county, are about to be or have been misapplied, or that any such public moneys have been illegally drawn or withheld from the county treasury, or that a contract, in contravention of law, has been executed or is about to be entered into, or that such a contract was procured by fraud or corruption, or that any property, real or personal, belonging to the county is being illegally used or occupied, or that such property is being used or occupied in violation of contract, or that the terms of a contract made by or on behalf of the county are being or have been violated, or that money is due the county, the prosecuting attorney may, by civil action in the name of the state, apply to a court of competent jurisdiction, to restrain such contemplated misapplication of funds, or the completion of such illegal contract, or to recover, for the use of the county, all public moneys so misapplied or illegally drawn or withheld from the county treasury, or to recover damages, for the benefit of the county, resulting from the execution of such illegal contract, or to recover, for the benefit of the county, such real or personal property so used or occupied, or to recover for the benefit of the county, damages resulting from the nonperformance of the terms of such contract, or to otherwise enforce it, or to recover such money as is due the county.

HISTORY: RS § 1277; 70 v 38, § 1; 93 v 408; 95 v 558; GC § 2921; Bureau of Code Revision. Eff 10-1-53.

§ 309.13 Taxpayer's suit.

If the prosecuting attorney fails, upon the written request of a taxpayer of the county, to make the application or institute the civil action contemplated in section 309.12 of the Revised Code, the taxpayer may make such application or institute such civil action in the name of the state, or, in any case wherein the prosecuting attorney is authorized to make such application, such taxpayer may bring any suit or institute any such proceedings against any county officer or person who holds or has held a county office, for misconduct in office or neglect of his duty, to recover money illegally drawn or illegally withheld from the county treasury, and to recover damages resulting from the execution of such illegal contract.

If such prosecuting attorney fails upon the written request of a taxpayer of the county, to bring such suit or institute such proceedings, or if for any reason the prosecuting attorney cannot bring such action, or if he has received and unlawfully withheld moneys belonging to the county, or has received or drawn public moneys out of the county treasury which he is not lawfully entitled to demand and receive, a taxpayer, upon securing the costs, may bring such suit or institute such proceedings, in the name of the state. Such action shall be for the benefit of the county, as if brought by the prosecuting attorney.

If the court hearing such case is satisfied that such taxpayer is entitled to the relief prayed for in his petition, and judgment is ordered in his favor, he shall be allowed his costs, including a reasonable compensation to his attorney.

HISTORY: RS §§ 1278a, 1278; 70 v 38, § 2; 92 v 337; 93 v 408; GC §§ 2922, 2923; 106 v 105; Bureau of Code Revision. Eff 10-1-53.

§ 309.14 Injuries to timber.

When trees standing or growing on any land belonging to the state, or to any school district, are, without lawful authority, cut down, or in any way injured, the prosecuting attorney shall prosecute the wrongdoer, and shall seize all timber so cut down, if it can be found, and sell it at public vendue, on five days' notice. The prosecuting attorney shall pay the proceeds of such sale into the state treasury to the credit of the general revenue fund, or into the county treasury to the credit of the school district, as the case may be.

HISTORY: RS § 1279; S&C 442, 445; 40 v 57, §§ 1, 3; GC § 2924; Bureau of Code Revision, 10-1-53; 141 v H 201. Eff 7-1-85.

§ 309.15 Annual report to attorney general.

On or before the first day of September in each year, if so required by the attorney general by a written notice given on or before the first day of August, the prosecuting attorney shall transmit to the attorney general a report of all crimes prosecuted by indictment or information in his county for the year ending the first day of July, specifying:

(A) Under the head of felonies:
(1) The number convicted;
(2) The number acquitted;
(3) The amount of costs incurred;
(4) The amount of costs collected.
(B) Under the head of misdemeanors:
(1) The number convicted;
(2) The number acquitted;
(3) The amount of fines imposed;
(4) The amount of fines collected;
(5) The amount of costs incurred;
(6) The amount of costs collected.
(C) Such other information as the attorney general requires.

The attorney general may prepare and forward to the prosecuting attorney the necessary blanks and instructions for such annual reports. Prosecuting attorneys shall furnish to the attorney general any information he requires in the execution of his office, whenever such information is requested by him.

HISTORY: RS § 1282; 90 v 225; GC § 2925; Bureau of Code Revision. Eff 10-1-53.

§ 309.16 Annual report to county commissioners; certain information to be transmitted to state fire marshal.

(A) On the first Monday of September in each year,

each prosecuting attorney shall make a certified statement to the board of county commissioners specifying:

(1) The number of criminal prosecutions pursued to final conviction and sentence under his official care, during the year next preceding the time of making such statement. In such statement the prosecuting attorney shall name the parties to each prosecution, the amount of fine assessed in each case, the number of recognizances forfeited, and the amount of money collected in each case.

(2) With respect to the offenses set forth in sections 2909.02 and 2909.03 of the Revised Code, such statement shall also include the following information:

(a) The number of fires occurring in the county for which the state fire marshal or an assistant state fire marshal has determined there was evidence sufficient to charge a person with aggravated arson or arson;

(b) The number of cases under sections 2909.02 and 2909.03 of the Revised Code presented by the prosecuting attorney to the grand jury for indictment;

(c) The number of indictments under such sections returned by the grand jury;

(d) The number of cases under such sections prosecuted either by indictment or by information by the prosecuting attorney;

(e) The number of cases under such sections resulting in final conviction and sentence and the number of cases resulting in acquittals;

(f) The number of cases under such sections dismissed or terminated without a final adjudication as to guilt or innocence.

(B) The prosecuting attorney shall also transmit to the state fire marshal on or before the first Monday of September in each year all information relative to the crimes under such sections required to be reported to the board of county commissioners pursuant to division (A)(2) of this section.

(C) For purposes of divisions (A)(2) and (B) of this section, sections 2909.02 and 2909.03 of the Revised Code include a conspiracy or attempt to commit, or complicity in the commission of, arson or aggravated arson under sections 2923.01 to 2923.03 of the Revised Code.

(D) If the prosecuting attorney fails to make reports at the time and in the manner required by this section, he shall forfeit and pay not less than one hundred nor more than five hundred dollars, to be recovered in a civil action in the name of the board.

HISTORY: RS § 881; S&S 90; S&C 248; 58 v 69; GC § 2926; Bureau of Code Revision, 10-1-53; 138 v S 198. Eff 7-31-80.

§ 309.17 Action to reclaim property.

When the prosecuting attorney of a county is informed that a person has in his possession money or other property belonging to a person found dead within such county, upon whose estate no letters of administration have been issued, the prosecuting attorney, by notice in writing, shall require the person having such money or other property to deposit it with the probate court. If within fifteen days such person does not comply with such requirement, the prosecuting attorney shall bring suit in the court of common pleas, in the name of the state, for the recovery thereof, and, when recovered, it shall be at the disposition of the probate court.

HISTORY: RS § 1229; S & C 1405; 53 v 48, § 6; GC § 2865; Bureau of Code Revision. Eff 10-1-53.

§ 309.18 Victim to be notified of escape of violent offender.

If a prosecuting attorney of a county receives notice from the department of rehabilitation and correction pursuant to section 5120.14 of the Revised Code that a person indicted in that county for an offense of violence that is a felony has escaped from a correctional institution under the control of the department or otherwise has escaped from the custody of the department, receives notice from the sheriff of the county pursuant to section 341.011 [341.01.1] of the Revised Code that a person indicted for or otherwise charged with an offense of violence that is a felony and that was committed in the county has escaped from the county jail or workhouse or otherwise has escaped from the custody of the sheriff, or receives notice from a chief of police or other chief law enforcement officer of a municipal corporation pursuant to section 753.19 of the Revised Code that a person indicted for or otherwise charged with an offense of violence that is a felony and that was committed in the county has escaped from a jail or workhouse of that municipal corporation or otherwise has escaped from the custody of that municipal corporation, the prosecuting attorney shall notify each victim of an offense of violence that is a felony committed by that person of the person's escape and, if applicable, of his subsequent apprehension. The notice of escape shall be given as soon as possible after receipt of the notice from the department, sheriff, or chief law enforcement officer of the municipal corporation and shall be given by telephone or in person, except that, if a prosecuting attorney tries and fails to give the notice of escape by telephone at the victim's last known telephone number or tries and fails to give the notice of escape in person at the victim's last known address, the notice of escape shall be given to the victim at his last known address by certified mail, return receipt requested. The notice of apprehension shall be given as soon as possible after the person is apprehended and shall be given in the same manner as is the notice of escape.

Any prosecuting attorney who fails to give any notice required by this section is immune from civil liability for any injury, death, or loss to person or property that might be incurred as a result of that failure to give notice.

HISTORY: 142 v H 207 (Eff 9-24-87); 145 v H 571. Eff 10-6-94.

CHAPTER 311: SHERIFF

§ 311.01 Qualifications for sheriff; basic training course; continuing education.

(A) A sheriff shall be elected quadrennially in each county. A sheriff shall hold office for a term of four years, beginning on the first Monday of January next after the sheriff's election.

(B) On and after January 1, 1988, except as otherwise provided in this section, no person is eligible to be a candidate for sheriff and no person shall be elected or appointed to the office of sheriff unless that person meets all of the following requirements:

(1) The person is a citizen of the United States;

(2) The person has been a resident of the county in which the person is a candidate for or is appointed to the office of sheriff for at least one year immediately prior to the qualification date;

(3) The person has the qualifications of an elector as specified in section 3503.01 of the Revised Code and has complied with all applicable election laws;

(4) The person has been awarded a high school diploma or a certificate of high school equivalence issued for achievement of specified minimum scores on the general educational development test of the American council on education;

(5) The person has not been convicted of or pleaded guilty to a felony or any offense involving moral turpitude under the laws of this or any other state or the United States, and has not been convicted of or pleaded guilty to an offense that is a misdemeanor of the first degree under the laws of this state or an offense under the laws of any other state or the United States that carries a penalty that is substantially equivalent to the penalty for a misdemeanor of the first degree under the laws of this state;

(6) The person has been fingerprinted and has been the subject of a search of local, state, and national fingerprint files to disclose any criminal record. Such fingerprints shall be taken under the direction of the administrative judge of the court of common pleas who, prior to the applicable qualification date, shall notify the board of elections, board of county commissioners, or county central committee of the proper political party, as applicable, of the judge's findings.

(7) The person has prepared a complete history of the person's places of residence for a period of six years immediately preceding the qualification date and a complete history of the person's places of employment for a period of six years immediately preceding the qualification date, indicating the name and address of each employer and the period of time employed by that employer. The residence and employment histories shall be filed with the administrative judge of the court of common pleas of the county, who shall forward them with the findings under division (B)(6) of this section to the appropriate board of elections, board of county commissioners, or county central committee of the proper political party prior to the applicable qualification date.

(8) The person meets at least one of the following conditions:

(a) Has obtained or held, within the four-year period ending immediately prior to the qualification date, a valid basic peace officer certificate of training issued by the Ohio peace officer training council or has been issued a certificate of training pursuant to section 5503.05 of the Revised Code, and, within the four-year period ending immediately prior to the qualification date, has been employed as an appointee pursuant to section 5503.01 of the Revised Code or as a full-time peace officer as defined in section 109.71 of the Revised Code performing duties related to the enforcement of statutes, ordinances, or codes;

(b) Has obtained or held, within the three-year period ending immediately prior to the qualification date, a valid basic peace officer certificate of training issued by the Ohio peace officer training council and has been employed for at least the last five years prior to the qualification date as a full-time law enforcement officer as defined in division (K) of section 2901.01 of the Revised Code performing duties related to the enforcement of statutes, ordinances, or codes.

(9) The person meets at least one of the following conditions:

(a) Has at least two years of supervisory experience as a peace officer at the rank of corporal or above, or has been appointed pursuant to section 5503.01 of the Revised Code and served at the rank of sergeant or above, in the five-year period ending immediately prior to the qualification date;

(b) Has completed satisfactorily at least two years of post-secondary education or the equivalent in semester or quarter hours in a college or university authorized to confer degrees by the Ohio board of regents or the comparable agency of another state in which the college or university is located.

(C) Persons who meet the requirements of division (B) of this section, except the requirement of division (B)(2) of this section, may take all actions otherwise necessary to comply with division (B) of this section. If, on the applicable qualification date, no person has met all the requirements of division (B) of this section, then persons who have complied with and meet the requirements of division (B) of this section, except the requirement of division (B)(2) of this section, shall be considered qualified candidates under division (B) of this section.

(D) Newly elected sheriffs shall attend a basic training course conducted by the Ohio peace officer training council pursuant to division (A) of section 109.80 of the Revised Code. A newly elected sheriff shall complete not less than two weeks of this course before the first

Monday in January next after the sheriff's election. While attending the basic training course, a newly elected sheriff may, with the approval of the board of county commissioners, receive compensation, paid for from funds established by the sheriff's county for this purpose, in the same manner and amounts as if carrying out the powers and duties of the office of sheriff.

Appointed sheriffs shall attend the first basic training course conducted by the Ohio peace officer training commission pursuant to division (A) of section 109.80 of the Revised Code within six months following the date of appointment or election to the office of sheriff. While attending the basic training course, appointed sheriffs shall receive regular compensation in the same manner and amounts as if carrying out their regular powers and duties.

Five days of instruction at the basic training course shall be considered equal to one week of work. The costs of conducting the basic training course and the costs of meals, lodging, and travel of appointed and newly elected sheriffs attending the course shall be paid from state funds appropriated to the commission for this purpose.

(E) Beginning in the second calendar year of the term of appointed and newly elected sheriffs appointed or elected on or after January 1, 1988, and beginning in calendar year 1988 for other sheriffs, and in each calendar year thereafter, each sheriff shall attend and successfully complete at least sixteen hours of continuing education approved under division (B) of section 109.80 of the Revised Code. A sheriff who receives a waiver of the continuing education requirement from the commission under division (C) of section 109.80 of the Revised Code because of medical disability or for other good cause shall complete the requirement at the earliest time after the disability or cause terminates.

(F)(1) Each person who is a candidate for election to or who is under consideration for appointment to the office of sheriff shall swear before the administrative judge of the court of common pleas as to the truth of any information the person provides to verify the person's qualifications for the office. A person who violates this requirement is guilty of falsification under section 2921.13 of the Revised Code.

(2) Each board of elections shall certify whether or not a candidate for the office of sheriff who has filed a declaration of candidacy, a statement of candidacy, or a declaration of intent to be a write-in candidate meets the qualifications specified in divisions (B) and (C) of this section.

(G) The office of a sheriff who is required to comply with division (D) or (E) of this section and who fails to successfully complete the courses pursuant to those divisions is hereby deemed to be vacant.

(H) As used in this section:

(1) "Qualification date" means the last day on which a candidate for the office of sheriff can file a declaration of candidacy, a statement of candidacy, or a declaration of intent to be a write-in candidate, as applicable, in the case of a primary election for the office of sheriff; the last day on which a person may be appointed to fill a vacancy in a party nomination for the office of sheriff under Chapter 3513. of the Revised Code, in the case of a vacancy in the office of sheriff; or a date thirty days after the day on which a vacancy in the office of sheriff occurs, in the case of an appointment to such a vacancy under section 305.02 of the Revised Code.

(2) "Newly elected sheriff" means a person who did not hold the office of sheriff of a county on the date the person was elected sheriff of that county.

HISTORY: RS § 1202; S&C 1403; 55 v 150; 93 v 351; GC § 2823; 116 v PtII, 184; Bureau of Code Revision, 10-1-53; 141 v H 683 (Eff 3-11-87); 146 v S 2 (Eff 7-1-96); 146 v H 670 (Eff 12-2-96); 146 v H 351. Eff 1-14-97.

Publisher's Note

The amendments made by HB 670 (146 v —) and HB 351 (146 v —) have been combined. Please see provisions of RC § 1.52.

§ 311.02 Bond.

The sheriff shall, within ten days after receiving his commission and before the first Monday of January next after his election, give a bond, signed by a bonding or surety company authorized to do business in this state and to be approved by the board of county commissioners, or, at the option of such sheriff, signed by two or more freeholders having real estate in the value of double the amount of the bond, over and above all encumbrances to the state, in a sum not less than five thousand nor more than fifty thousand dollars, which sum shall be fixed by the board, and such bond shall be conditioned for the faithful performance of the duties of his office. The expense or premium for such bond shall be paid by the board and charged to the general fund of the county. Such bonds, with the approval of the board and the oath of office required by sections 3.22 and 3.23 of the Revised Code, and Section 7 of Article XV, Ohio Constitution, indorsed thereon, shall be filed with the county auditor and kept in his office.

The board may require the sheriff, at any time during his term of office, to give additional sureties on his bond, or to give a new bond.

No judge or clerk of any court or attorney at law shall be received as surety on such bond.

If the sheriff fails to give a bond within the time required, or fails to give additional sureties on such bond or a new bond within ten days after he has received written notice that the board so requires, the board shall declare the office of such sheriff vacant.

HISTORY: RS §§ 1203 to 1206; S & C 190, 191, 1404; 51 v 301, §§ 1-7; 55 v 150, § 3; GC §§ 2824 to 2827; 112 v 111; Bureau of Code Revision, 10-1-53; 129 v 1365. Eff 10-12-61.

§ 311.03 Disability or absence.

When the sheriff, by reason of absence, sickness,

or other disability, is incapable of serving any process required to be served, or by reason of interest is incompetent to serve it, the court of common pleas, if in session, or, if not in session, a judge of such court may appoint a suitable person to serve such process or to perform the duties of sheriff during the continuance of such disability. Such appointee shall give such bond as the court or judge requires, conditioned for the faithful performance of his duties, and take the oath of office.

HISTORY: RS § 1208; S&C 539, 1402; 29 v 410, §§ 1, 2; 50 v 311, § 35; 84 v 208; GC § 2828; 121 v 343; Bureau of Code Revision, 10-1-53; 126 v 205 (Eff 1-1-56); 129 v 582 (625) (Eff 1-10-61); 129 v 1365. Eff 10-12-61.

§ 311.04 Deputy sheriffs.

(A) As used in this section, "felony" has the same meaning as in section 109.511 [109.51.1] of the Revised Code.

(B)(1) Subject to division (C) of this section, the sheriff may appoint, in writing, one or more deputies. At the time of the appointment, the sheriff shall file the writing upon which the appointment is made with the clerk of the court of common pleas, and the clerk of the court shall enter it upon the journal of the court. The sheriff shall pay the clerk's fees for the filing and journal entry of the writing. In cases of emergency, the sheriff may request of the sheriff of another county the aid of qualified deputies serving in those other counties of the state, and, if the consent of the sheriff of that other county is received, the deputies while so assigned shall be considered to be the deputies of the sheriff of the county requesting aid. No judge of a county court or mayor shall be appointed a deputy.

(2) Notwithstanding section 2335.33 of the Revised Code, the sheriff shall retain the fee charged pursuant to division (B) of section 311.37 of the Revised Code for the purpose of training deputies appointed pursuant to this section.

(C)(1) The sheriff shall not appoint a person as a deputy sheriff pursuant to division (B)(1) of this section on a permanent basis, on a temporary basis, for a probationary term, or on other than a permanent basis if the person previously has been convicted of or has pleaded guilty to a felony.

(2)(a) The sheriff shall terminate the employment of a deputy sheriff appointed under division (B)(1) of this section if the deputy sheriff does either of the following:

(i) Pleads guilty to a felony;

(ii) Pleads guilty to a misdemeanor pursuant to a negotiated plea agreement as provided in division (D) of section 2929.29 of the Revised Code in which the deputy sheriff agrees to surrender the certificate awarded to the deputy sheriff under section 109.77 of the Revised Code.

(b) The sheriff shall suspend from employment any deputy sheriff appointed under division (B)(1) of this section if the deputy sheriff is convicted, after trial, of a felony. If the deputy sheriff files an appeal from that conviction and the conviction is upheld by the highest court to which the appeal is taken or if the deputy sheriff does not file a timely appeal, the sheriff shall terminate the employment of that deputy sheriff. If the deputy sheriff files an appeal that results in that deputy sheriff's acquittal of the felony or conviction of a misdemeanor, or in the dismissal of the felony charge against the deputy sheriff, the sheriff shall reinstate that deputy sheriff. A deputy sheriff who is reinstated under division (C)(2)(b) of this section shall not receive any back pay unless that deputy sheriff's conviction of the felony was reversed on appeal, or the felony charge was dismissed, because the court found insufficient evidence to convict the deputy sheriff of the felony.

(3) Division (C) of this section does not apply regarding an offense that was committed prior to January 1, 1997.

(4) The suspension from employment, or the termination of the employment, of a deputy sheriff under division (C)(2) of this section shall be in accordance with Chapter 119. of the Revised Code.

HISTORY: RS § 1209; S&C 500; 29 v 410, § 4; 66 v 35, § 3; 83 v 29; GC § 2830; Bureau of Code Revision, 10-1-53; 127 v 1039 (Eff 1-1-58); 128 v 688 (Eff 10-1-59); 133 v H 1106 (Eff 9-7-70); 141 v S 247 (Eff 7-9-86); 146 v H 566. Eff 10-16-96.

§ 311.05 Conduct of deputies.

The sheriff shall only be responsible for the neglect of duty or misconduct in office of any of his deputies if he orders, has prior knowledge of, participates in, acts in reckless disregard of, or ratifies the neglect of duty or misconduct in office of the deputy.

HISTORY: RS § 1210; S&C 500; 29 v 410, §§ 4, 5; GC § 2831; Bureau of Code Revision, 10-1-53; 140 v H 273. Eff 10-5-83.

§ 311.06 Location of sheriff's office.

The sheriff's office shall be maintained at the seat of justice, in such rooms as the board of county commissioners provides for that purpose. Such office shall be furnished with all necessary furniture, blankbooks, stationery, and blanks at the expense of the county.

HISTORY: RS § 1217; 70 v 292; GC § 2832; Bureau of Code Revision. Eff 10-1-53.

§ 311.07 General powers and duties of the sheriff.

(A) Each sheriff shall preserve the public peace and cause all persons guilty of any breach of the peace, within his knowledge or view, to enter into recognizance with sureties to keep the peace and to appear at the succeeding term of the court of common pleas, and the sheriff shall commit such persons to jail in case they refuse to do so. He shall return a transcript of all his proceedings with the recognizance so taken to such court. He shall, except as provided in division (C) of this section, execute all warrants, writs, and other process directed to him by any proper and lawful authority of this state, and those issued by a proper and lawful authority of any other state. He shall attend upon the court of common pleas and the court of appeals during their sessions, and, when required, shall attend upon the probate court. In the execution of the duties required of him, the sheriff may call to his aid such persons or power of the county as is necessary. Under the direction and control of the board of county commissioners, such sheriff shall have charge of the court house. A sheriff or deputy sheriff of a county may participate, as the director of an organized crime task force established under section 177.02 of the Revised Code or as a member of the investigatory staff of such a task force, in an investigation of organized criminal activity in any county or counties in this state under sections 177.01 to 177.03 of the Revised Code.

(B) The sheriff of a county may call upon the sheriff of any adjoining county, the mayor or other chief executive of any municipal corporation within his county or in adjoining counties, and the chairman of the board of township trustees of any township within his county or in adjoining counties, to furnish such law enforcement or fire protection personnel, or both, together with appropriate equipment and apparatus, as may be necessary to preserve the public peace and protect persons and property in the requesting sheriff's county in the event of riot, insurrection, or invasion. Such aid shall be furnished to the sheriff requesting it, insofar as possible without withdrawing from the political subdivision furnishing such aid the minimum police and fire protection appearing necessary under the circumstances. In such case, law enforcement and fire protection personnel acting outside the territory of their regular employment shall be considered as performing services within the territory of their regular employment for the purposes of compensation, pension or indemnity fund rights, workers' compensation, and other rights or benefits to which they may be entitled as incidents of their regular employment. The county receiving such aid shall reimburse the political subdivision furnishing it the cost of furnishing such aid, including compensation of personnel, expenses incurred by reason of the injury or death of any such personnel while rendering such aid, expenses of furnishing equipment and apparatus, compensation for damage to or loss of equipment or apparatus while in service outside the territory of its regular use, and such other reasonable expenses as may be incurred by any such political subdivision in furnishing such aid. Nothing in this section shall be construed as superseding or modifying in any way any provision of a contract entered into pursuant to section 311.29 of the Revised Code. Law enforcement officers acting pursuant to this section outside the territory of their regular employment have the same authority to enforce the law as when acting within the territory of their regular employment.

(C) The sheriff shall not execute process that is issued in a state other than this state, unless the process contains either of the following:

(1) A certification by the judge of the court that issued the process stating that the issuing court has jurisdiction to issue the process and that the documents being forwarded conform to the laws of the state in which the court is located;

(2) If the process is an initial summons to appear and defend issued after the filing of a complaint commencing an action, a certification by the clerk of the court that issued the process stating that the process was issued in conformance with the laws of the state in which the court is located.

(D) As used in this section and section 311.08 of the Revised Code, "proper and lawful authority" means any authority authorized by law to issue any process and "process" means those documents issued in this state in accordance with section 7.01 of the Revised Code and those documents, other than executions of judgments or decrees, issued in a state other than this state that conform to the laws of the state of issuance governing the issuance of process in that state.

HISTORY: RS § 1211; S&C 1229, 1397; 29 v 112, § 2; 29 v 315, § 6; 82 v 16, 26; GC § 2833; 103 v 405(419); Bureau of Code Revision, 10-1-53; 132 v H 996 (Eff 6-13-68); 136 v S 545 (Eff 1-17-77); 138 v H 278 (Eff 6-12-80); 140 v S 23 (Eff 7-29-83); 141 v S 74. Eff 9-3-86.

§ 311.08 Execution and return of process.

(A) The sheriff shall, except as provided in division (B) of this section, execute every summons, order, or other process directed to him by a proper and lawful authority of this state or issued by a proper and lawful authority of any other state, make return thereof, and exercise the powers conferred and perform the duties enjoined upon him by statute and by the common law.

In an action in which the sheriff is a party, or is interested, process shall be directed to and executed by a person appointed by the court of common pleas or a judge of the court of common pleas.

(B) The sheriff shall not execute process that is issued in a state other than this state, unless the process contains either of the following:

(1) A certification by the judge of the court that issued the process stating that the issuing court has jurisdiction to issue the process and that the documents being forwarded conform to the laws of the state in which the court is located;

(2) If the process is an initial summons to appear and defend issued after the filing of a complaint commencing an action, a certification by the clerk of the court that issued the process stating that the process was issued in conformance with the laws of the state in which the court is located.

HISTORY: RS §§ 4967, 4970; S&C 1128, 1130; S&S 572; 51 v 57, §§ 582, 593, 594; 65 v 96, § 592; GC §§ 2834, 2835; Bureau of Code Revision, 10-1-53; 138 v H 278 (Eff 6-12-80); 139 v S 114. Eff 10-27-81.

§ 311.09 Indorsement on writs.

The sheriff shall indorse upon every writ or order the day and hour such writ or order was received by him.

HISTORY: RS § 4966; S & C 1130; 51 v 57, § 591; GC § 2836; Bureau of Code Revision. Eff 10-1-53.

§ 311.10 Foreign execution docket.

(A) There shall be kept in the office of the sheriff a foreign execution docket, furnished by the county, in which, on the receipt by the sheriff of any execution, order of sale, or other process issuing from any court of any county, other than the county in which he resides, the sheriff shall make an entry of the date of such writ, when it was received by him, from what court and county it was issued, and the date and amount of the judgment or decree. The sheriff shall copy in such book, the same as indorsed upon or contained in such writ, the full description of the property and real estate that he levies upon or offers for sale. He shall also copy into such book his return on such writ when he makes a return, and shall include the bill of costs. The sheriff shall make a direct and reverse index of each case entered in such book. The entries shall be notice to subsequent purchasers and creditors of the matters contained in them, but if the lien of any judgment is kept alive in the county of rendition beyond the period of five years, purchasers and creditors in such foreign county shall not be deemed to have notice of such lien unless written notice of it is filed by the judgment creditor with the sheriff of the foreign county, who shall certify such fact upon the foreign execution docket and index such notice at the place of the original entry.

(B) The sheriff shall also enter in the foreign execution docket the receipt of any process issued by a proper and lawful authority of a state other than this state, the date of issuance and the date of his receipt of the process, the court and state in which the process was issued, and the nature of the process. The sheriff shall also enter in the docket all action taken in relation to such process by his office.

(C) For making such entries the sheriff shall receive twenty-five cents in each case, to be taxed in the fee bill.

(D) For the use of the persons entitled to such fees, the sheriff shall retain all fees due in such cases to residents of his county, and, on demand, he shall pay them to such persons.

HISTORY: RS §§ 1212, 1213; S&C 1402; 36 v 18, § 3; 57 v 6, § 2; 84 v 208, 209; GC §§ 2837, 2838; 111 v 31; Bureau of Code Revision, 10-1-53; 128 v 542 (Eff 7-17-59); 138 v H 278. Eff 6-12-80.

§ 311.11 Cashbook.

There shall be kept in the office of the sheriff a cashbook, to be furnished by the county, in which, on receipt by him of any money in his official capacity, the sheriff shall make an entry of the date, the amount thereof, the title of the cause, and the name and number of the writ or process on which such money was received. If such money is received on the sale of real estate, in partition or otherwise, where the sale has been for part cash and other evidences of indebtedness are taken for part of the purchase money, such sheriff shall make an entry on such book of the date, number, and amount of such evidences of indebtedness.

HISTORY: RS § 1214; S & S 734; 65 v 115; 84 v 208, 209; GC § 2839; Bureau of Code Revision. Eff 10-1-53.

This section was shown as repealed in GC § 2296-23, but evidently "2739" was intended.

§ 311.12 Inspection of books; certified copies of entries.

The books required to be kept by sections 311.01 to 311.23 of the Revised Code, shall be open to the search and inspection of all persons. The sheriff shall furnish a certified copy of any entry in such books upon request and shall charge and collect a fee of twenty-five cents for each such certification or copy thereof.

HISTORY: RS § 1216; S&C 1402; 36 v 18, § 4; 84 v 208, 209; GC § 2841; Bureau of Code Revision, 10-1-53; 128 v 542 (Eff 7-17-59); 139 v S 114. Eff 10-27-81.

§ 311.13 Books to be delivered to successor.

The books required to be kept by sections 311.01 to 311.23 of the Revised Code, shall not be removed from the sheriff's office. Such books shall be delivered over, without mutilation, as public property to each succeeding sheriff. No sheriff shall willfully fail to comply with this section or section 311.11 of the Revised Code.

HISTORY: RS § 1215; S&S 734; 65 v 115, §§ 2, 4, 5; 84 v 208; 86 v 239; GC § 2840; Bureau of Code Revision, 10-1-53; 139 v S 114. Eff 10-27-81.

§ 311.14 Moneys, books, and papers to be delivered to successor.

Upon retiring from office, the sheriff shall pay over to his successor in office all moneys received by such sheriff and remaining in his hands. He shall deliver to his successor all evidences of indebtedness and all books, blanks, and stationery belonging to his office. Each sheriff shall demand and receive such books and papers from his predecessor.

HISTORY: RS § 1218; S & C 1402; 36 v 18, § 5; 69 v 168, § 5; 84 v 208, 210; GC § 2842; Bureau of Code Revision. Eff 10-1-53.

§ 311.15 Process, goods, and prisoners to be delivered to successor.

When the term of office for which a sheriff has been

elected expires, or he resigns or moves outside the county, such sheriff shall deliver all writs of execution and all other processes, of whatever description, whether executed or not, and all goods and chattels taken by him, in execution or on attachment, which remain in his hands, together with all bonds, to the person elected or appointed and qualified to discharge the duties of sheriff, and he shall make the necessary and proper return upon each such writ or other process so far as executed. Such sheriff shall also deliver to his successor all prisoners in the county jail or otherwise in his custody, with all bail bonds taken by him and remaining in his possession. The new sheriff shall receive all such prisoners, writs, or other processes, and he shall execute such writs and processes as remain unexecuted in whole or in part as if they had been directed to him originally. No process shall be directed to or executed by a sheriff whose term of office has expired.

HISTORY: RS § 1219; S & C 1390; 29 v 112, § 8; 84 v 208, 210; GC § 2843; Bureau of Code Revision. Eff 10-1-53.

§ 311.16 Annual report of sheriff.

On the first Monday in September of each year, the sheriff shall make a certified statement to the board of county commissioners of all fines and costs in criminal prosecutions collected by him, on execution or otherwise, during the year next preceding such date, and he shall also report in such statement the amount of fines and costs so collected and paid over to the clerk of the court of common pleas or to the county treasurer.

If the sheriff fails to make reports at the time and in the manner required by this section, he shall forfeit and pay not less than fifty nor more than one hundred dollars, to be recovered in a civil action in the name of the board.

HISTORY: RS § 884; S&S 91; 58 v 70, § 3; GC § 2844; Bureau of Code Revision. Eff 10-1-53.

§ 311.17 Fees.

For the services specified in this section, the sheriff shall charge the following fees, which the court or clerk thereof shall tax in the bill of costs against the judgment debtor or those legally liable therefor:

(A) For the service and return of the following writs and orders:

(1) Execution:

(a) When money is paid without levy or when no property is found, five dollars;

(b) When levy is made on real property, for the first tract, twenty dollars, and for each additional tract, five dollars;

(c) When levy is made on goods and chattels, including inventory, twenty-five dollars;

(2) Writ of attachment of property, except for purpose of garnishment, twenty dollars;

(3) Writ of attachment for the purpose of garnishment, five dollars;

(4) Writ of replevin, twenty dollars;

(5) Warrant to arrest, for each person named in the writ, five dollars;

(6) Attachment for contempt, for each person named in the writ, three dollars;

(7) Writ of possession or restitution, twenty dollars;

(8) Subpoena, for each person named in the writ, if in a civil case three dollars, if in a criminal case one dollar;

(9) Venire, for each person named in the writ, if in a civil case three dollars, if in a criminal case one dollar;

(10) Summoning each juror, other than on venire, if in a civil case three dollars, if in a criminal case one dollar;

(11) Writ of partition, fifteen dollars;

(12) Order of sale on partition, for the first tract, twenty-five dollars, and for each additional tract, five dollars;

(13) Other order of sale of real property, for the first tract, twenty dollars, and for each additional tract, five dollars;

(14) Administering oath to appraisers, one dollar and fifty cents each;

(15) Furnishing copies for advertisements, fifty cents for each hundred words;

(16) Copy of indictment, for each defendant, two dollars;

(17) All summons, writs, orders, or notices, for the first name, three dollars, and for each additional name, fifty cents.

(B) In addition to the fee for service and return, the sheriff may charge:

(1) On each summons, writ, order, or notice, a fee of fifty cents per mile for the first mile, and twenty cents per mile for each additional mile, going and returning, actual mileage to be charged on each additional name;

(2) Taking bail bond, one dollar;

(3) Jail fees, as follows:

(a) For receiving a prisoner, four dollars, and for discharging or surrendering a prisoner, four dollars;

(b) Taking a prisoner before a judge or court, per day, three dollars;

(c) Calling action, fifty cents;

(d) Calling jury, one dollar;

(e) Calling each witness, one dollar;

(f) Bringing prisoner before court on habeas corpus, four dollars;

(4) Poundage on all moneys actually made and paid to the sheriff on execution, decree, or sale of real estate, one per cent;

(5) Making and executing a deed of land sold on execution, decree, or order of the court, to be paid by the purchaser, twenty-five dollars.

When any of the foregoing services are rendered by an officer or employee, whose salary or per diem compensation is paid by the county, the legal fees provided for such service in this section shall be taxed in the costs in the case, and when such fees are collected they shall be paid into the general fund of the county.

The sheriff shall charge the same fees for the execution of process issued in any other state as he charges for the execution of process of a substantively similar nature that is issued in this state.

HISTORY: RS § 1230; S&S 364; S&C 639; 73 v 127, § 11; 76 v 117, § 20; 77 v 116; GC § 2845; 102 v 277; 108 v PtII 1203(1214); Bureau of Code Revision, 10-1-53; 128 v 542 (Eff 7-17-59); 135 v S 208 (Eff 12-17-73); 138 v H 278 (Eff 6-12-80); 140 v H 897. Eff 12-26-84.

§ 311.18 Mileage fees on foreign process.

When a sheriff returns, in any manner other than by himself or his deputy personally, any process issued from the court of common pleas or other court of a county other than that in which he resides, such sheriff shall receive only mileage on such return of process, to be computed from his office to the place of service and back to his office.

HISTORY: RS § 1232; 73 v 127, § 14; 76 v 117, § 22; GC § 2847; Bureau of Code Revision. Eff 10-1-53.

§ 311.19 Fees of appraisers.

In all cases in which an attachment is issued, the freeholders required to be called by the sheriff to appraise property shall be allowed such fees for their services as the court directs.

HISTORY: RS § 1233; S & C 634; 73 v 127, § 15; 76 v 117, § 23; GC § 2848; 102 v 277; Bureau of Code Revision. Eff 10-1-53.

§ 311.20 Allowance for prisoners.

On or before the twenty-first day of June of each year, the sheriff shall prepare and submit to the board of county commissioners a budget estimating the cost of operating the jail and feeding its inmates for the ensuing fiscal year.

On the fifth day of each month the sheriff shall render to the board an itemized and accurate account, with all bills attached, showing the actual cost of keeping and feeding prisoners and other persons placed in his charge and the number of meals served to each such prisoner or other person during the preceding month. The number of days for which allowance shall be made shall be computed on the basis of one day for each three meals actually served.

HISTORY: RS § 1235; S&S 366, 441; S&C 635; 62 v 60; 73 v 127, § 17; 76 v 117, § 25; 92 v 288; 98 v 255; GC § 2850; 112 v 62; 121 v 335; Bureau of Code Revision, 10-1-53; 125 v H 198 (Eff 10-2-53); 131 v 207 (Eff 9-6-65); 139 v S 23. Eff 7-6-82.

§ 311.21 Fees in cases relating to dower.

The sheriff shall be allowed fees as follows for service relating to dower: For summoning and swearing the board of county commissioners, traveling fees, to be computed from the place of return of his proceedings to the place where the land lies in which dower is to be assigned, at the rate of ten cents per mile.

HISTORY: RS § 1237; S & C 642; 73 v 127, § 37; 76 v 117, § 27; GC § 2852; Bureau of Code Revision. Eff 10-1-53.

§ 311.22 Service of process.

The court or judge may, for good cause, appoint a person to serve a particular process or order, and such person shall have the same power to execute such process or order which the sheriff has. Such person may be appointed on the motion of the party who obtains the process or order, and the return must be verified by affidavit. He shall be entitled to the fees allowed to the sheriff for similar services.

HISTORY: RS § 4968; S & C 1128; 51 v 57, § 583; GC § 2854; Bureau of Code Revision. Eff 10-1-53.

§ 311.23 Adjournment of court.

If the judge of the court of common pleas, or a quorum of the judges of the court of appeals, fails to attend at the time and place appointed for holding such court, or if, after the calling of the court, the judge of the court of common pleas or a quorum of the judges of the court of appeals is unable, on account of sickness or from any other cause, to attend the daily sessions of such court, the sheriff shall adjourn the court from day to day, until such judge attends or such quorum is convened.

HISTORY: RS § 4969; S & C 1130; 51 v 57, § 593; 79 v 15; 82 v 16, 31; GC § 2855; 103 v 405 (419); Bureau of Code Revision, 10-1-53; 136 v H 390. Eff 8-6-76.

§ 311.24 Repealed, 139 v S 114, § 2 [GC §§ 2855-1, 2855-2; 101 v 109; Bureau of Code Revision, 10-1-53]. Eff 10-27-81.

This section concerned lynching; removal of sheriff by governor.

[SHERIFFS' STANDARD CAR-MARKING AND UNIFORM COMMISSION]

§ 311.25 Sheriffs' standard car-marking and uniform commission.

A commission is hereby established to be known as the county sheriffs' standard car-marking and uniform commission. It shall consist of three members, not more than two of whom shall be members of the same political party. To be eligible for appointment a person shall be an elected and acting county sheriff. Each member shall be appointed by the governor, with the advice and consent of the senate, and shall serve at the pleasure of the governor.

HISTORY: 128 v 310. Eff 10-23-59.

§ 311.26 Organization.

The county sheriffs' standard car-marking and uniform commission shall elect one of its members as president, who shall preside at its meetings and who may call meetings. The commission may make its own bylaws.

HISTORY: 128 v 310 (Eff 10-23-59); 129 v 582 (626) (Eff 1-10-61); 130 v 199. Eff 9-27-63.

§ 311.27 No compensation.

The members of the county sheriffs' standard car-marking and uniform commission shall receive no compensation for their services.

HISTORY: 128 v 310 (Eff 10-23-59); 129 v 582 (626) (Eff 1-10-61); 130 v 199. Eff 9-27-63.

§ 311.28 Duties.

The county sheriffs' standard car-marking and uniform commission shall prescribe a uniform of standard design and color for the use of all county sheriffs and shall prescribe a standard color and design of car-marking for all motor vehicles used by county sheriffs.

On and after January 1, 1961, the standard uniform shall be worn by the county sheriffs and their deputies and the standard car-markings shall be used on all cars operated by the county sheriffs and their deputies while in the performance of their duties.

HISTORY: 128 v 310 (Eff 10-23-59); 129 v 582 (626). Eff 1-10-61.

[§ 311.28.1] § 311.281 Use of sheriff's uniform and vehicle markings prohibited.

(A) No person, except a county sheriff or the deputies of a county sheriff, shall wear the badge, the standard uniform, or any distinctive part of the standard uniform prescribed for county sheriffs and their deputies by the county sheriffs' standard car-marking and uniform commission.

(B) No person, except a county sheriff or the deputies of a county sheriff, shall mark a motor vehicle in a manner similar to that prescribed for county sheriffs and their deputies by the county sheriffs' standard car-marking and uniform commission.

(C) Whoever violates division (A) of this section is guilty of a violation of section 2921.51 of the Revised Code. Whoever violates division (B) of this section is guilty of a violation of section 2913.441 [2913.44.1] of the Revised Code.

HISTORY: 133 v H 625 (Eff 11-21-69); 146 v S 2. Eff 7-1-96.

The effective date is set by section 6 of SB 2.

§ 311.29 Contracts to perform police functions; payments; deputy sheriffs.

(A) As used in this section, "Chautauqua assembly" has the same meaning as in section 4511.90 of the Revised Code.

(B) The sheriff may, from time to time, enter into contracts with any municipal corporation, township, township police district, metropolitan housing authority, port authority, water or sewer district, school district, library district, health district, park district created pursuant to section 511.18 or 1545.01 of the Revised Code, soil and water conservation district, water conservancy district, or other taxing district or with the board of county commissioners of any contiguous county with the concurrence of the sheriff of the other county, and such subdivisions, authorities, and counties may enter into agreements with the sheriff pursuant to which the sheriff undertakes and is authorized by the contracting subdivision, authority, or county to perform any police function, exercise any police power, or render any police service in behalf of the contracting subdivision, authority, or county, or its legislative authority, that the subdivision, authority, or county, or its legislative authority, may perform, exercise, or render.

Upon the execution of an agreement under this division and within the limitations prescribed by it, the sheriff may exercise the same powers as the contracting subdivision, authority, or county possesses with respect to such policing that by the agreement the sheriff undertakes to perform or render, and all powers necessary or incidental thereto, as amply as such powers are possessed and exercised by the contracting subdivision, authority, or county directly.

Any agreement authorized by this section shall not suspend the possession by a contracting subdivision, authority, or county of any police power performed or exercised or police service rendered in pursuance to the agreement nor limit the authority of the sheriff.

(C) The sheriff may enter into contracts with any Chautauqua assembly that has grounds located within the county, and the Chautauqua assembly may enter into agreements with the sheriff pursuant to which the sheriff undertakes to perform any police function, exercise any police power, or render any police service upon the grounds of the Chautauqua assembly that the sheriff is authorized by law to perform, exercise, or render in any other part of the county within his territorial jurisdiction. Upon the execution of an agreement under this division, the sheriff may, within the limitations prescribed by the agreement, exercise such powers with respect to such policing upon the grounds of the Chautauqua assembly, provided that any limitation contained in the agreement shall not be construed to limit the authority of the sheriff.

(D) Contracts entered into under this section shall provide for the reimbursement of the county for the costs incurred by the sheriff for such policing including, but not limited to, the salaries of deputy sheriffs assigned to such policing, the current costs of funding retirement pensions and of providing workers' compensation, the cost of training, and the cost of equipment and supplies used in such policing, to the extent that such equipment and supplies are not directly furnished by the contracting subdivision, authority, county, or Chautauqua assembly. Each contract shall provide for the ascertainment of such costs and shall be of any duration, not in excess of four years, and may contain any other terms that may be agreed upon. All payments pursuant to any such contract in reimbursement of the costs of such policing shall be made to the treasurer of the county to be credited to a special fund to be known as the "sheriff's policing revolving fund," hereby created. Any moneys coming into the fund shall be used for the purposes provided in this section and paid out on vouchers by the county commissioners as other funds coming into their possession. Any moneys credited to the fund and not obligated at the termination of the contract shall be credited to the county general fund.

The sheriff shall assign the number of deputies as may be provided for in any contract made pursuant to this section. The number of deputies regularly assigned to such policing shall be in addition to and an enlargement of the sheriff's regular number of deputies. Nothing in this section shall preclude the sheriff from temporarily increasing or decreasing the deputies so assigned as emergencies indicate a need for shifting assignments to the extent provided by the contracts.

All such deputies shall have the same powers and duties, the same qualifications, and be appointed and paid and receive the same benefits and provisions and be governed by the same laws as all other deputy sheriffs.

Such contracts may be entered into jointly with the board of county commissioners, and sections 307.14 to 307.19 of the Revised Code apply to this section insofar as they may be applicable.

HISTORY: 129 v 1362 (Eff 8-18-61); 130 v 199 (Eff 1-23-63); 133 v H 1 (Eff 3-18-69); 136 v S 545 (Eff 1-17-77); 137 v S 221 (Eff 11-23-77); 138 v H 948 (Eff 5-22-80); 144 v S 174 (Eff 7-31-92); 145 v S 200. Eff 12-7-93.

§ 311.30 Parking enforcement unit.

(A) The board of county commissioners may establish, by resolution, a parking enforcement unit within the office of the sheriff to operate in the unincorporated areas of the county, and may provide for the regulation of parking enforcement officers. The sheriff shall be the executive head of the parking enforcement unit, shall make all appointments and removals of parking enforcement officers, subject to any general rules prescribed by the board of county commissioners by resolution, and shall prescribe rules for the organization, training, administration, control, and conduct of the parking enforcement unit. The sheriff may appoint parking enforcement officers who agree to serve for nominal compensation, and persons with physical disabilities may receive appointments as parking enforcement officers.

(B) The authority of the parking enforcement officers shall be limited to the enforcement of section 4511.69 of the Revised Code and any other parking laws specified in the resolution creating the parking enforcement unit. Parking enforcement officers shall have no other powers.

(C) The training the parking enforcement officers shall receive shall include instruction in general administrative rules and procedures governing the parking enforcement unit, the role of the judicial system as it relates to parking regulation and enforcement, proper techniques and methods relating to the enforcement of parking laws, human interaction skills, and first aid.

HISTORY: 143 v S 174. Eff 7-13-90.

Not analogous to former RC § 311.30 (131 v 208; 133 v S 218), repealed 134 v H 24, § 2, eff 10-6-71.

[§ 311.30.1] § 311.301 Repealed, 134 v H 24, § 2 [133 v S 218]. Eff 10-6-71.

This section provided procedure for disposal of junk vehicle.

§§ 311.32 to 311.34 Repealed, 134 v H 24, § 2 [131 v 208; 133 v S 218; 133 v H 920]. Eff 10-6-71.

These sections referred to sale of unclaimed vehicles.

§ 311.37 Transient vendors to file information and bond; municipal regulation.

(A) No transient vendor, as defined in section 5739.17 of the Revised Code, who obtains a transient vendor's license pursuant to section 5739.17 of the Revised Code, intending to provide goods and services of a retail value of more than five hundred dollars, shall negligently fail to file with the county sheriff all of the following before doing business as a transient vendor anywhere in that county:

(1) Proof of the transient vendor's identity and proof that a transient vendor's license has been obtained in this state;

(2) A statement describing the goods or services to be provided by the transient vendor and an estimate of the amount of the goods or services that the vendor expects to sell in that county, as documented by invoices indicating the wholesale value of goods to be sold;

(3) The transient vendor's permanent business address;

(4) The times and days during which, and the temporary places of business, as defined in section 5739.17 of the Revised Code, at which the transient vendor plans to do business in that county.

(B) The sheriff shall maintain a record of the information required under division (A) of this section for a period of two years, which shall be open to the inspection of any person. The sheriff shall be allowed a fee of up to one hundred dollars for collection of the bond required by this section. The bond shall be fifty per cent of the wholesale value of the goods and services provided, but in no case shall the bond exceed ten thousand dollars. The bond shall be in a form approved by the attorney general. The bond shall remain in effect for two years after the transient vendor last does business in that county.

(C) No transient vendor, as defined in section 5739.17 of the Revised Code, intending to provide goods and services of a retail value of more than five hundred dollars, shall negligently fail to file a bond within ten days before doing business as a transient vendor anywhere in that county.

(D) The bond filed by any transient vendor pursuant to this section shall be given to the attorney general by the county sheriff within ten working days after a transient vendor ceases to do business in that county, and shall be in favor of the state for the benefit of any person who suffers loss or damage as a result of the purchase of goods from the transient vendor or as the result of the negligent or intentionally tortious acts of the transient vendor in the conduct of business in the county. The bond may be used to compensate any state or local agency for damages caused by the transient vendor, for costs incurred by the agency for the illegal acts of the transient vendor, or for failure to pay any amount owed by the transient vendor to the state or local agency. The bond also may be used to compensate the state for any sales tax not paid by the transient vendor. Except for the amount of unpaid sales taxes to be deducted from the bond, if any, the attorney general shall pay any portion of the bond to any person or agency in accordance with the order of a court without making an independent finding as to the amount of the bond that is payable to that person or agency.

(E) This section does not apply to any of the following:

(1) A limited vendor, as defined in section 5739.17 of the Revised Code, or a transient vendor making retail sales at a temporary exhibition, show, fair, world trade center, flea market, or similar event, as permitted by section 5739.17 of the Revised Code;

(2) Any nonprofit corporation, community chest, fund, or foundation organized and operated exclusively for religious, charitable, scientific, literary, or educational purposes when no part of the entity's earnings benefit any private shareholder or individual;

(3) Any person who operates a permanent business in this state, occupies temporary premises, and prominently displays the permanent business' name and permanent address while business is conducted from the temporary premises.

(4) Any person who sells goods by sample, brochure, or catalog for future delivery or any person who makes sales as the result of the invitation of an owner or occupant of a residence to the person.

(5) Any person who sells handmade or handcrafted items, or who sells fresh farm produce.

Nothing in this section shall prohibit the legislative authority of a municipal corporation from adopting an ordinance regulating transient vendors, as defined in section 5739.17 of the Revised Code, except that a municipal corporation may not require a transient vendor who obtains a bond in compliance with this section to obtain or pay for any additional bond or require that persons exempt pursuant to division (E) of this section obtain a bond. A municipal corporation may require that a transient vendor exhibit his transient vendor's license and any proof of bond required to such officer or employee of the municipal corporation as the municipal corporation designates by ordinance.

HISTORY: 141 v S 247 (Eff 7-9-86); 142 v H 153. Eff 10-20-87.

§ 311.99 Penalties.

(A) Whoever violates section 311.13 of the Revised Code shall be fined not more than one thousand dollars and imprisoned in the county jail not less than thirty days or more than two years.

(B) Whoever violates division (A) or (C) of section 311.37 of the Revised Code is guilty of failure to file a transient vendor's information or bond, a minor misdemeanor. If the offender previously has been convicted of a violation of division (A) of section 311.37 of the Revised Code, failure to file a transient vendor's information or bond is a misdemeanor of the second degree. If the offender previously has been convicted of two or more violations of division (A) of section 311.37 of the Revised Code, failure to file a transient vendor's information or bond is a misdemeanor of the first degree. A sheriff or police officer in a municipal corporation may enforce this division. The prosecuting attorney of a county shall inform the tax commissioner of any instance when a complaint is brought against a transient or limited vendor pursuant to this division.

HISTORY: Bureau of Code Revision, 10-1-53; 133 v H 625 (Eff 11-21-69); 133 v H 926 (Eff 7-14-70); 134 v H 24 (Eff 10-6-71); 141 v S 247 (Eff 7-9-86); 141 v H 683 (Eff 3-11-87); 146 v S 2. Eff 7-1-96.

The effective date is set by section 6 of SB 2.

CHAPTER 313: CORONER

§ 313.09 Records.

The coroner shall keep a complete record of and shall fill in the cause of death on the death certificate, in all cases coming under his jurisdiction. All records shall be kept in the office of the coroner, but, if no such office is maintained, then such records shall be kept in the office of the clerk of the court of common pleas. Such records shall be properly indexed, and shall state the name, if known, of every deceased person as described in section 313.12 of the Revised Code, the place where the body was found, date of death, cause of death, and all other available information. The report of the coroner and the detailed findings of the autopsy shall be attached to the report of each case. The coroner shall promptly deliver, to the prosecuting attorney of the county in which such death occurred, copies of all necessary records relating to every death in which, in the judgment of the coroner or prosecuting attorney, further investigation is advisable. The sheriff of the county, the police of the city, the constable of the township, or marshal of the village in which the death occurred may be requested to furnish more information or make further investigation when requested by the coroner or his deputy. The prosecuting attorney may obtain copies of records and such other information as is necessary from the office of the coroner. All records of the coroner are the property of the county.

HISTORY: GC § 2855-10; 121 v 591; Bureau of Code Revision, 10-1-53; 136 v H 750. Eff 8-26-75.

§ 313.10 Records to be public; certified copies as evidence.

The records of the coroner, made by himself or by anyone acting under his direction or supervision are public records, and such records, or transcripts, or photostatic copies thereof, certified by the coroner, shall be received as evidence in any criminal or civil court in this state, as to the facts contained in such records.

All records in the coroner's office shall be open to inspection by the public, and any person may receive a copy of any such record or part thereof upon demand in writing, accompanied by payment of the transcript fee, at the rate of fifteen cents per hundred words, or a minimum fee of one dollar.

HISTORY: GC § 2855-11; 121 v 591; Bureau of Code Revision. Eff 10-1-53.

§ 313.11 Removal or disturbing of body or effects prohibited.

(A) No person, without an order from the coroner, any deputy coroner, or an investigator or other person designated by the coroner as having authority to issue an order under this section, shall purposely remove or disturb the body of any person who has died in the manner described in section 313.12 of the Revised Code, or purposely and without such an order disturb the clothing or any article upon or near such a body or any of the possessions that the coroner has a duty to store under section 313.14 of the Revised Code.

(B) It is an affirmative defense to a charge under this section that the offender attempted in good faith to rescue or administer life-preserving assistance to the deceased person, even though it is established he was dead at the time of the attempted rescue or assistance.

(C) Whoever violates this section is guilty of unlawfully disturbing a body, a misdemeanor of the fourth degree.

HISTORY: 136 v H 750 (Eff 8-26-75); 139 v H 55 (Eff 8-19-82); 143 v H 639. Eff 9-26-90.

Analogous to former RC § 313.11 (121 v 591; Bureau of Code Revision, 10-1-53), repealed 134 v H 511. Eff 1-1-74.

§ 313.12 Notice to coroner of violent, suspicious, unusual or sudden death.

When any person dies as a result of criminal or other violent means, by casualty, by suicide, or in any suspicious or unusual manner, or when any person, including a child under two years of age, dies suddenly when in apparent good health, the physician called in attendance, or any member of an ambulance service, emergency squad, or law enforcement agency who obtains knowledge thereof arising from his duties, shall immediately notify the office of the coroner of the known facts concerning the time, place, manner, and circumstances of the death, and any other information which is required pursuant to sections 313.01 to 313.22 of the Revised Code. In such cases, if a request is made for cremation, the funeral director called in attendance shall immediately notify the coroner.

HISTORY: GC § 2855-5; 121 v 591; Bureau of Code Revision, 10-1-53; 136 v H 750 (Eff 8-26-75); 144 v H 244. Eff 11-1-92.

[§ 313.12.1] § 313.121 Death of apparently healthy child under age of two to be reported; autopsy; supportive services for parents; information on sudden infant death syndrome.

(A) As used in this section, "parent" means either parent, except that if one parent has been designated the residential parent and legal custodian of the child, "parent" means the designated residential parent and legal custodian, and if a person other than a parent is the child's legal guardian, "parent" means the legal guardian.

(B) If a child under two years of age dies suddenly when in apparent good health, the death shall be reported immediately to the coroner of the county in which the death occurred, as required by section 313.12

of the Revised Code. Except as provided in division (C) of this section, the coroner or deputy coroner shall perform an autopsy on the child. The autopsy shall be performed in accordance with public health council rules adopted under section 313.122 [313.12.2] of the Revised Code. The coroner or deputy coroner may perform research procedures and tests when performing the autopsy.

(C) A coroner or deputy coroner is not required to perform an autopsy if the coroner of the county in which the death occurred or a court with jurisdiction over the deceased body determines under section 313.131 [313.13.1] of the Revised Code that an autopsy is contrary to the religious beliefs of the child. If the coroner or the court makes such a determination, the coroner shall notify the health district or department of health with jurisdiction in the area in which the child's parent resides. For purposes of this division, the religious beliefs of the parents of a child shall be considered to be the religious beliefs of the child.

(D) If the child's parent makes a written or verbal request for the preliminary results of the autopsy after the results are available, the coroner, or a person designated by him, shall give the parent an oral statement of the preliminary results.

The coroner, within a reasonable time after the final results of the autopsy are reported, shall send written notice of the results to the state department of health, the health district or department with jurisdiction in the area in which the child's parent resides, and, upon the request of a parent of the child, to the child's attending physician. Upon the written request of a parent of the child and the payment of the transcript fee required by section 313.10 of the Revised Code, the coroner shall send written notice of the final results to that parent. The notice sent to the state department of health shall include all of the information specified by rule of the public health council adopted under section 313.122 [313.12.2] of the Revised Code.

(E) On the occurrence of any of the following, the health district or department with jurisdiction in the area in which the child's parent resides shall offer the parent any counseling or other supportive services it has available:

(1) When it learns through any source that an autopsy is being performed on a child under two years of age who died suddenly when in apparent good health;

(2) When it receives notice that the final result of an autopsy performed pursuant to this section concluded that the child died of sudden infant death syndrome;

(3) When it is notified by the coroner that, pursuant to division (C) of this section, an autopsy was not performed.

(F) When a health district or department receives notice that the final result of an autopsy performed pursuant to this section concluded that the child died of sudden infant death syndrome or that, pursuant to division (C) of this section, an autopsy was not performed but sudden infant death syndrome may have been the cause of death, it shall offer the child's parent information about sudden infant death syndrome. The state department of health shall ensure that current information on sudden infant death syndrome is available for distribution by health districts and departments.

HISTORY: 144 v H 244. Eff 11-1-92.

The effective date is set by section 4 of HB 244.

[§ 313.12.2] § 313.122 Protocol for autopsies after sudden infant death.

The public health council, after reviewing and considering any recommendations made by the Ohio state coroners association, shall adopt rules in accordance with Chapter 119. of the Revised Code establishing a protocol governing the performance of autopsies under section 313.121 [313.12.1] of the Revised Code. The rules shall specify the information derived from an autopsy that a coroner is required to report to the state department of health. The public health council shall not amend the rules adopted under this section unless it notifies the Ohio state coroners association of the proposed changes and consults with the association.

HISTORY: 144 v H 244. Eff 11-1-92.

The effective date is set by section 4 of HB 244.

The provisions of § 5 of HB 244 (144 v —) read as follows:
SECTION 5. The Ohio State Coroners Association, no later than sixty days after the effective date of this act, may submit to the Public Health Council recommendations regarding the adoption of rules under section 313.122 of the Revised Code establishing a protocol governing the performance of autopsies on children who die suddenly when in apparent good health and the information derived from such autopsies that a coroner is required to report to the Department of Health.

§ 313.13 Autopsy; blood test of decedent killed in motor vehicle accident.

(A) The coroner, any deputy coroner, an investigator appointed pursuant to section 313.05 of the Revised Code, or any other person the coroner designates as having the authority to act under this section may go to the dead body and take charge of it. Whether and when an autopsy is performed shall be determined under sections 313.121 [313.12.1] and 313.131 [313.13.1] of the Revised Code. If an autopsy is performed by the coroner, deputy coroner, or pathologists, a detailed description of the observations written during the progress of such autopsy, or as soon after such autopsy as reasonably possible, and the conclusions drawn from the observations shall be filed in the office of the coroner.

If he takes charge of and decides to perform, or performs, an autopsy on a dead body under section 313.121 [313.12.1] or 313.131 [313.13.1] of the Revised Code, the coroner, or in his absence, any deputy coroner, under division (E) of section 2108.02 of the Revised

Code, may waive his paramount right to any donated part of the dead body.

(B) If the office of the coroner is notified that a person who was the operator of a motor vehicle that was involved in an accident or crash was killed in the accident or crash or died as a result of injuries suffered in it, the coroner, deputy coroner, or pathologist shall go to the dead body and take charge of it and administer a chemical test to the blood of the deceased person to determine the alcohol, drug, or alcohol and drug content of the blood. This division does not authorize the coroner, deputy coroner, or pathologist to perform an autopsy, and does not affect and shall not be construed as affecting the provisions of section 313.131 [313.13.1] of the Revised Code that govern the determination of whether and when an autopsy is to be performed.

HISTORY: GC § 2855-6; 121 v 591; Bureau of Code Revision, 10-1-53; 136 v H 1182 (Eff 5-4-76); 141 v S 283 (Eff 3-25-87); 143 v S 131 (Eff 7-25-90); 143 v H 639 (Eff 9-26-90); 144 v H 244. Eff 11-1-92.

The effective date is set by section 4 of HB 244.

The provisions of § 3 of HB 244 (144 v —) read as follows:

SECTION 3. Section 313.13 of the Revised Code is presented in this act as a composite of the section as amended by both Sub. H.B. 639 and Am. Sub. S.B. 131 of the 118th General Assembly, with the new language of neither of the acts shown in capital letters. This is in recognition of the principle stated in division (B) of section 1.52 of the Revised Code that such amendments are to be harmonized where not substantively irreconcilable and constitutes a legislative finding that such is the resulting version in effect prior to the effective date of this act.

[§ 313.13.1] § 313.131 Procedure when autopsy is contrary to decedent's religious belief.

(A) As used in this section:

(1) "Friend" means any person who maintained regular contact with the deceased person, and who was familiar with the deceased person's activities, health, and religious beliefs at the time of the deceased person's death, any person who assumes custody of the body for burial, and any person authorized by written instrument executed by the deceased person to make burial arrangements.

(2) "Relative" means any of the following persons: the deceased person's surviving spouse, children, parents, or siblings.

(B) The coroner, deputy coroner, or pathologist shall perform an autopsy if, in the opinion of the coroner, or, in his absence, in the opinion of the deputy coroner, an autopsy is necessary, except for certain circumstances provided for in this section where a relative or friend of the deceased person informs the coroner that an autopsy is contrary to the deceased person's religious beliefs, or the coroner otherwise has reason to believe that an autopsy is contrary to the deceased person's religious beliefs. The coroner has such reason to believe an autopsy is contrary to the deceased person's religious beliefs if a document signed by the deceased and stating an objection to an autopsy is found on the deceased's person or in his effects. For the purposes of this division, a person is a relative or friend of the deceased person if the person presents an affidavit stating that he is a relative or friend as defined in division (A) of this section.

(C)(1) Except as provided in division (F) of this section, if a relative or friend of the deceased person informs the coroner that an autopsy is contrary to the deceased person's religious beliefs, or the coroner otherwise has reason to believe that an autopsy is contrary to the deceased person's religious beliefs, and the coroner concludes the autopsy is a compelling public necessity, no autopsy shall be performed for forty-eight hours after the coroner takes charge of the deceased person. An autopsy is a compelling public necessity if it is necessary to the conduct of an investigation by law enforcement officials of a homicide or suspected homicide, or any other criminal investigation, or is necessary to establish the cause of the deceased person's death for the purpose of protecting against an immediate and substantial threat to the public health. During the forty-eight hour period, the objecting relative or friend may file suit to enjoin the autopsy, and shall give notice of any such filing to the coroner. The coroner may seek an order waiving the forty-eight hour waiting period. If the coroner seeks such an order, the court shall give notice of the coroner's motion, by telephone if necessary, to the objecting relative or friend, or, if none objected, to all of the deceased person's relatives whose addresses or telephone numbers can be obtained through the exercise of reasonable diligence. The court may grant the coroner's motion if the court determines that no friend or relative of the deceased person objects to the autopsy or if the court is satisfied that any objections of a friend or relative have been heard, and if it also determines that the delay may prejudice the accuracy of the autopsy, or if law enforcement officials are investigating the deceased person's death as a homicide and suspect the objecting party committed the homicide or aided or abetted in the homicide. If no friend or relative files suit within the forty-eight hour period, the coroner may proceed with the autopsy.

(2) The court shall hear a petition to enjoin an autopsy within forty-eight hours after the filing of the petition. The Rules of Civil Procedure shall govern all aspects of the proceedings, except as otherwise provided in division (C)(2) of this section. The court is not bound by the rules of evidence in the conduct of the hearing. The court shall order the autopsy if the court finds that under the circumstances the coroner has demonstrated a need for the autopsy. If the court enjoins the autopsy, the coroner shall immediately proceed under section 313.14 of the Revised Code.

(D)(1) If a relative or friend of the decedent informs the coroner that an autopsy is contrary to the deceased person's religious beliefs, or the coroner otherwise has reason to believe that an autopsy is contrary to the deceased person's religious beliefs, and the coroner concludes the autopsy is necessary, but not a compelling public necessity, the coroner may file a petition in a court of common pleas seeking a declaratory judgment authorizing the autopsy. Upon the filing of the petition, the court shall schedule a hearing on the petition, and shall issue a summons to the objecting relative or friend, or, if none objected, to all of the deceased person's relatives whose addresses can be obtained through the exercise of reasonable diligence. The court shall hold the hearing no later than forty-eight hours after the filing of the petition. The court shall conduct the hearing in the manner provided in division (C)(2) of this section.

(2) Each person claiming to be a relative or friend of the deceased person shall immediately upon receipt of the summons file an affidavit with the court stating the facts upon which the claim is based. If the court finds that any person is falsely representing himself as a relative or friend of the deceased person, the court shall dismiss the person from the action. If after dismissal no objecting party remains, and the coroner does not have reason to believe that an autopsy is contrary to the deceased person's religious beliefs, the court shall dismiss the action and the coroner may proceed with the autopsy. The court shall order the autopsy after hearing the petition if the court finds that under the circumstances the coroner has demonstrated a need for the autopsy. The court shall waive the payment of all court costs in the action. If the petition is denied, the coroner shall immediately proceed under section 313.14 of the Revised Code.

Any autopsy performed pursuant to a court order granting an autopsy shall be performed using the least intrusive procedure.

(E) For purposes of divisions (B), (C)(1), and (D)(1) of this section, any time the friends or relatives of a deceased person disagree about whether an autopsy is contrary to the deceased person's religious beliefs, the coroner shall consider only the information provided to him by the person of highest priority, as determined by which is listed first among the following:

(1) The deceased person's surviving spouse;
(2) An adult son or daughter of the deceased person;
(3) Either parent of the deceased person;
(4) An adult brother or sister of the deceased person;
(5) The guardian of the person of the deceased person at the time of death;
(6) A person other than those listed in divisions (E)(1) to (5) of this section who is a friend as defined in division (A) of this section.

If two or more persons of equal priority disagree about whether an autopsy is contrary to the deceased person's religious beliefs, and those persons are also of the highest priority among those who provide the coroner with information the coroner has reason to believe that an autopsy is contrary to the deceased person's religious beliefs.

(F)(1) Divisions (C)(1) and (2) of this section do not apply in any case involving aggravated murder, suspected aggravated murder, murder, suspected murder, manslaughter offenses, or suspected manslaughter offenses.

(2) This section does not prohibit the coroner, deputy coroner, or pathologist from administering a chemical test to the blood of a deceased person to determine the alcohol, drug, or alcohol and drug content of the blood, when required by division (B) of section 313.13 of the Revised Code, and does not limit the coroner, deputy coroner, or pathologist in the performance of his duties in administering a chemical test under that division.

HISTORY: 141 v S 283 (Eff 3-25-87); 143 v S 131. Eff 7-25-90.

§ 313.14 Notice to relatives; disposition of property.

The coroner shall notify any known relatives of a deceased person who meets death in the manner described by section 313.12 of the Revised Code by letter or otherwise. The next of kin, other relatives, or friends of the deceased person, in the order named, shall have prior right as to disposition of the body of such deceased person. If relatives of the deceased are unknown, the coroner shall make a diligent effort to ascertain the next of kin, other relatives, or friends of the deceased person. The coroner shall take charge and possession of all moneys, clothing, and other valuable personal effects of such deceased person, found in connection with or pertaining to such body, and shall store such possessions in the county coroner's office or such other suitable place as is provided for such storage by the board of county commissioners. If the coroner considers it advisable, he may[,] after taking adequate precautions for the security of such possessions, store the possessions where he finds them until other storage space becomes available. After using such of the clothing as is necessary in the burial of the body, in case the cost of the burial is paid by the county, the coroner shall sell at public auction the valuable personal effects of such deceased persons, found in connection with or pertaining to the unclaimed dead body, except firearms, which shall be disposed of as provided by section 313.141 [313.14.1] of the Revised Code, and he shall make a verified inventory of such effects. Such effects shall be sold within eighteen months after burial, or after delivery of such body in accordance with section 1713.34 of the Revised Code. All moneys derived from such sale shall be deposited in the county treasury. A notice of such sale shall be given in one newspaper of general circulation in the county, for five days in succession, and the sale shall be held immediately thereafter. The cost of such advertisement and notices shall be paid by the board upon the submission of a verified statement therefor, certified to the coroner.

This section does not invalidate section 1713.34 of the Revised Code.

HISTORY: GC § 2855-13; 121 v 591; 123 v 766; Bureau of Code Revision, 10-1-53; 136 v H 750 (Eff 8-26-75); 136 v H 1182 (Eff 8-1-76); 139 v H 55. Eff 8-19-82.

[§ 313.14.1] § 313.141 Firearms in personal effects of deceased person.

If firearms are included in the valuable personal effects of a deceased person who met death in the manner described by section 313.12 of the Revised Code, the coroner shall deliver the firearms to the chief of police of the municipal corporation within which the body is found, or to the sheriff of the county if the body is not found within a municipal corporation. The firearms shall be used for law enforcement purposes only or they shall be destroyed. Upon delivery of the firearms to the chief of police or the sheriff, the law enforcement officer to whom the delivery is made shall give the coroner a receipt for the firearms that states the date of delivery and an accurate description of the firearms.

HISTORY: 136 v H 1182. Eff 8-1-76.

§ 313.15 Determination of responsibility for death.

All dead bodies in the custody of the coroner shall be held until such time as the coroner, after consultation with the prosecuting attorney, or with the police department of a municipal corporation, if the death occurred in a municipal corporation, or with the sheriff, has decided that it is no longer necessary to hold such body to enable him to decide on a diagnosis giving a reasonable and true cause of death, or to decide that such body is no longer necessary to assist any of such officials in his duties.

HISTORY: GC § 2855-14; 121 v 591; Bureau of Code Revision. Eff 10-1-53.

§ 313.17 Subpoenas; oath and testimony of witnesses.

The coroner or deputy coroner may issue subpoenas for such witnesses as are necessary, administer to such witnesses the usual oath, and proceed to inquire how the deceased came to his death, whether by violence to self or from any other persons, by whom, whether as principals or accessories before or after the fact, and all circumstances relating thereto. The testimony of such witnesses shall be reduced to writing and subscribed to by them, and with the findings and recognizances mentioned in this section, shall be kept on file in the coroner's office, unless the county fails to provide such an office, in which event all such records, findings and recognizances shall be kept on file in the office of the clerk of the court of common pleas. The coroner may cause such witnesses to enter into recognizance, in such sum as is proper, for their appearance to give testimony concerning the matter. He may require any such witnesses to give security for their attendance, and, if any of them fails to comply with his requirements he shall commit such person to the county jail until discharged by due course of law. In case of the failure of any person to comply with such subpoena, or on the refusal of a witness to testify to any matter regarding which he may lawfully be interrogated, the probate judge, or a judge of the court of common pleas, on application of the coroner, shall compel obedience to such subpoena by attachment proceedings as for contempt. A report shall be made from the personal observation by the coroner or his deputy of the corpse, from the statements of relatives or other persons having any knowledge of the facts, and from such other sources of information as are available, or from the autopsy.

HISTORY: GC § 2855-7; 121 v 591; 123 v 769; Bureau of Code Revision, 10-1-53; 136 v H 390. Eff 8-6-76.

§ 313.18 Disinterment of body.

The prosecuting attorney or coroner may order the disinterment of any dead body, under the direction and supervision of the coroner, and may authorize the removal of such body by the coroner to the quarters established for the use of such coroner, for the purpose of examination and autopsy.

HISTORY: GC § 2855-8; 121 v 591; Bureau of Code Revision. Eff 10-1-53.

§ 313.19 Coroner's verdict the legally accepted cause of death.

The cause of death and the manner and mode in which the death occurred, as delivered by the coroner and incorporated in the coroner's verdict and in the death certificate filed with the division of vital statistics, shall be the legally accepted manner and mode in which such death occurred, and the legally accepted cause of death, unless the court of common pleas of the county in which the death occurred, after a hearing, directs the coroner to change his decision as to such cause and manner and mode of death.

HISTORY: GC § 2855-16; 121 v 591; Bureau of Code Revision. Eff 10-1-53.

§ 313.20 Coroner's writs.

The coroner may issue any writ required by sections 313.01 to 313.22, of the Revised Code, to any constable of the county in which a body is found as described in section 313.12 of the Revised Code, or if the emergency so requires, to any discreet person of the county, and such person is entitled to receive for the services rendered the same fees as elected constables. Every constable, or other person so appointed, who fails to execute any warrant directed to him, shall forfeit and pay twenty-five dollars, which amount shall be recovered upon the complaint of the coroner, before any court having jurisdiction thereof. All such forfeitures shall be for the use of the county.

HISTORY: RS § 1223; 75 v 570, § 11; GC § 2858; 106 v 448; Bureau of Code Revision, 10-1-53; 136 v H 750. Eff 8-26-75.

§ 313.21 Testing for suspected toxic substances or for law enforcement purposes; records.

(A) The coroner may use or may allow the use of the coroner's laboratory and facilities for tests in an emergency involving suspected toxic substances or for law enforcement-related testing, and may direct his assistants and other personnel to perform such testing in addition to testing performed in execution of their duties as set forth in sections 313.01 to 313.22 of the Revised Code. Nothing in this division shall permit such testing except in compliance with state and federal quality assurance requirements for medical laboratories.

(B) The coroner shall keep a complete record of all chemical tests and other tests performed each fiscal year pursuant to division (A) of this section, the public agency, hospital, or person for whom the test was performed, and the cost incurred for each test. This record shall be kept in the office of the coroner.

HISTORY: 137 v H 1118 (Eff 3-8-79); 142 v H 499, §§ 1, 3 (Eff 6-30-87); 143 v H 332 (Eff 8-5-89); 144 v S 233. Eff 11-15-91.

Somewhat analogous to former RC § 313.21 (Bureau of Code Revision, 10-1-53; 132 v H 1), repealed 134 v H 511, § 2, eff 1-1-74.

CHAPTER 341: JAILS

[DUTIES OF SHERIFFS]

§ 341.01 Sheriff to have charge of jail.

The sheriff shall have charge of the county jail and all persons confined therein. He shall keep such persons safely, attend to the jail, and govern and regulate the jail according to the minimum standards for jails in Ohio promulgated by the department of rehabilitation and correction.

The sheriff's responsibilities under this section do not extend to a jail or workhouse that is the subject of a contract entered into under section 9.06 of the Revised Code.

HISTORY: RS § 7368; S&S 746; S&C 1398; 29 v 112, § 4; 41 v 74, § 5; GC § 3157; Bureau of Code Revision, 10-1-53; 139 v S 23 (Eff 7-6-82); 146 v H 117. Eff 9-29-95.

The effective date is set by section 197 of HB 117.

[§ 341.01.1] § 341.011 Notice of escape of violent offender.

If a person who was convicted of or pleaded guilty to an offense of violence that is a felony or was indicted or otherwise charged with the commission of an offense of violence that is a felony escapes from a county jail or workhouse or otherwise escapes from the custody of the sheriff of that county, the sheriff immediately after the escape shall cause notice of the escape to be published in a newspaper of general circulation in the county. The sheriff also immediately after the escape shall give notice of the escape by telephone and in writing to the prosecuting attorney of the county. Upon the apprehension of the escaped person, the sheriff shall give notice of the apprehension of the escaped person by telephone and in writing to the prosecuting attorney.

HISTORY: 142 v H 207. Eff 9-24-87.

§ 341.02 Jail register; operational policies and procedures; prisoner rules of conduct.

The sheriff shall make the following entries in a suitable book, which shall be known as the "jail register," kept in the office of the jailer, and delivered to the successor in office of such jailer:

(A) The name of each prisoner, and the date and cause of his commitment;

(B) The date and manner of his discharge.

The sheriff or jail administrator shall prepare written operational policies and procedures and prisoner rules of conduct, and maintain the records prescribed by these policies and procedures in accordance with the minimum standards for jails in Ohio promulgated by the department of rehabilitation and correction.

The court of common pleas shall review the jail's operational policies and procedures and prisoner rules of conduct. If the court approves the policies, procedures, and rules of conduct, they shall be adopted.

HISTORY: RS § 7369; S&C 746; 41 v 74, § 6; GC § 3158; Bureau of Code Revision, 10-1-53; 131 v 229 (Eff 9-6-65); 139 v S 23. Eff 7-6-82.

§ 341.03 Repealed, 140 v H 363, § 2 [RS § 7370; S&C 747; 41 v 74, § 7; GC § 3159; Bureau of Code Revision, 10-1-53]. Eff 9-26-84.

This section concerned jail reports.

§ 341.04 Sheriff shall visit jail.

The sheriff shall visit the county jail and examine the condition of each prisoner, at least once during each month.

HISTORY: RS § 7371; S&C 748; 41 v 74, § 12; GC § 3160; Bureau of Code Revision, 10-1-53; 139 v S 114 (Eff 10-27-81); 139 v S 23. Eff 7-6-82.

§ 341.05 Assignment, compensation of staff; administrator; civilian officers; female staff.

(A) The sheriff shall assign sufficient staff to ensure the safe and secure operation of the county jail, but staff shall be assigned only to the extent such staff can be provided with funds appropriated to the sheriff at the discretion of the board of county commissioners. The staff may include any of the following:

(1) An administrator for the jail;

(2) Jail officers, including civilian jail officers who are not sheriff's deputies, to conduct security duties;

(3) Other necessary employees to assist in the operation of the county jail.

(B) The sheriff shall employ a sufficient number of female staff to be available to perform all reception and release procedures for female prisoners. These female employees shall be on duty for the duration of the confinement of the female prisoners.

(C) The jail administrator and civilian jail officers appointed by the sheriff shall have all the powers of police officers on the jail grounds as are necessary for the proper performance of the duties relating to their positions at the jail and as are consistent with their level of training.

(D) The sheriff may authorize civilian jail officers to wear a standard uniform consistent with their prescribed authority, in accordance with section 311.281 [311.28.1] of the Revised Code. Civilian jail officer uniforms shall be differentiated clearly from the uniforms worn by sheriff's deputies.

(E) The compensation of jail staff shall be payable from the general fund of the county, upon the warrant of the auditor, in accordance with standard county payroll procedures.

HISTORY: RS § 7372; S&C 748; 41 v 74, § 13; GC § 3161; Bureau of Code Revision, 10-1-53; 139 v S 23 (Eff 7-6-82); 146 v H 480. Eff 10-16-96.

[RULES AND REGULATIONS]

§ 341.06 Prisoner reimbursement policy; coordinator; medical treatment or service.

(A)(1) In lieu of requiring offenders to reimburse the county for expenses incurred by reason of the person's confinement under section 341.14 or 341.19 of the Revised Code, the board of county commissioners, in an agreement with the sheriff, may adopt a prisoner reimbursement policy for the jail pursuant to this section to be administered in the jail under the sheriff's direction. The sheriff may appoint a reimbursement coordinator to administer the jail's prisoner reimbursement policy.

(2) A prisoner reimbursement policy adopted under this section is a policy that requires a person confined to the jail to reimburse the county for any expenses it incurs by reason of the person's confinement in the jail, which expenses may include, but are not limited to, the following:

(a) A per diem fee for room and board of not more than sixty dollars per day or the actual per diem cost, whichever is less, for the entire period of time the person is confined to the jail;

(b) Actual charges for medical and dental treatment;

(c) Reimbursement for county property damaged by the person while confined to the jail.

Rates charged shall be on a sliding scale determined by the sheriff with the approval of the board of county commissioners based on the ability of the person confined to the jail to pay and on consideration of any legal obligation of the person to support a spouse, minor children, or other dependents and any moral obligation to support dependents to whom the person is providing or has in fact provided support.

The reimbursement coordinator or another person designated by the sheriff may investigate the financial status of the confined person and obtain information necessary to investigate that status, by means that may include contacting employers and reviewing income tax records. The coordinator may work with the confined person to create a repayment plan to be implemented upon the person's release. At the end of the person's incarceration, the person shall be presented with a billing statement signed by the sheriff.

(3) The reimbursement coordinator or another person designated by the sheriff may collect, or the sheriff may enter into a contract with one or more public agencies or private vendors to collect, any amounts remaining unpaid. Within twelve months after the date of the confined person's release, the prosecuting attorney may file a civil action to seek reimbursement from that person for any billing amount that remains unpaid. The county shall not enforce any judgment obtained under this section by means of execution against the person's homestead. For purposes of this section, "homestead" has the same meaning as in division (A) of section 323.151 [323.15.1] of the Revised Code.

(4) Any reimbursement received under division (A)(3) of this section shall be credited to the county's general fund to be used for general fund purposes.

(B)(1) Notwithstanding any contrary provision in this section or section 341.14, 341.19, 2929.18, or 2929.223 [2929.22.3] of the Revised Code, the board of county commissioners may establish a policy that requires any person who is not indigent and who is confined in the county's jail under section 341.14 or 341.19 of the Revised Code to pay a reasonable fee for any medical treatment or service requested by and provided to that person. This fee shall not exceed the actual cost of the treatment or service provided. No person confined to the jail under either section who is indigent shall be required to pay those fees, and no person who is confined to the jail under either section shall be denied any necessary medical care because of inability to pay those fees.

Upon provision of the requested medical treatment or service, payment of the required fee may be automatically deducted from a person's account record in the jail's business office. If the person has no funds in the person's account, a deduction may be made at a later date during the person's confinement in the jail if funds later become available in the person's account. If the person is released from the jail and has an unpaid balance of these fees, the board of county commissioners may bill the person for payment of the remaining unpaid fees. Fees received for medical treatment or services shall be paid into the commissary fund, if one has been created for the jail, or if no commissary fund exists, into the county treasury.

(2) If a person confined to the jail under section 341.14 or 341.19 of the Revised Code is required under division (A) of this section or section 341.14, 341.19, 2929.18, or 2929.223 [2929.22.3] of the Revised Code to reimburse the county for expenses incurred by reason of the person's confinement to the jail, any fees paid by the person under division (B)(1) of this section shall be deducted from the expenses required to be reimbursed under division (A) of this section or section 341.14, 341.19, 2929.18, or 2929.223 [2929.22.3] of the Revised Code.

HISTORY: 146 v H 480. Eff 10-16-96.

Not analogous to former RC § 341.06 (RS § 7374; S&C 745; 41 v 74; GC § 3162; Bureau of Code Revision, 10-1-53), repealed 140 v H 363, § 2, eff 9-26-84.

§ 341.07 Copies of minimum standards for jails; notice of prisoner rules of conduct.

The department of rehabilitation and correction shall provide a copy of the minimum standards for jails in Ohio to the board of county commissioners, the common pleas court, and the sheriff.

The sheriff shall ensure that the prisoner rules of conduct are placed in a conspicuous location within each jail confinement area or are given to each prisoner in written form.

HISTORY: RS §§ 7375, 7376; S&C 746; 41 v 74, §§ 2, 3; GC §§ 3163, 3164; Bureau of Code Revision, 10-1-53; 139 v S 23. Eff 7-6-82.

§ 341.08 Minimum standards may be revised, altered or amended.

The department of rehabilitation and correction may, by rule, revise, alter, or amend the minimum standards for jails in Ohio to reflect changes in case law or public policy. Such revised, altered, or amended standards shall be printed and distributed to the board of county commissioners, the court of common pleas, and the sheriff in the manner directed by section 341.07 of the Revised Code.

HISTORY: RS § 7377; S&C 746; 41 v 74, § 4; GC § 3165; Bureau of Code Revision, 10-1-53; 139 v S 23. Eff 7-6-82.

§ 341.09 Separation of prisoners in county jails.

When the design of a county jail will permit, the separation of prisoners shall be as required in the minimum standards for jails in Ohio.

The department of rehabilitation and correction shall, when necessary, initiate appropriate judicial proceedings for the enforcement of this section.

HISTORY: RS §§ 7377-1, 7377-2; 88 v 150, §§ 1, 2; GC §§ 3166, 3167; Bureau of Code Revision, 10-1-53; 139 v S 23. Eff 7-6-82.

§ 341.10 Separate confinement in new county jails.

County officers having charge of the construction of a new jail shall provide for the separate confinement of prisoners, as required by section 341.09 of the Revised Code.

HISTORY: RS § 7377-3; 88 v 150, § 3; GC § 3168; Bureau of Code Revision, 10-1-53.

§ 341.11 Confinement of minors.

Except as provided in division (C) of section 2151.311 [2151.31.1] of the Revised Code, no child taken into custody shall be held in a county, multicounty, or municipal jail or workhouse or other place for the confinement of adults convicted of crime, under arrest, or charged with crime.

Except as provided in division (C) of section 2151.311 [2151.31.1] of the Revised Code, a child confined pursuant to section 2151.311 [2151.31.1] of the Revised Code shall be held in a room or cell totally separate and removed by sight and sound from all adult prisoners.

HISTORY: RS § 7377-4; 80 v 102; GC § 3169; Bureau of Code Revision, 10-1-53; 139 v S 23 (Eff 7-6-82); 143 v H 166 (Eff 2-14-90); 146 v H 480. Eff 10-16-96.

[USE OF OTHER JAILS]

§ 341.12 Confinement of persons in custody in jail of another county.

In a county not having a sufficient jail or staff, the sheriff shall convey any person charged with the commission of an offense, sentenced to imprisonment in the county jail, or in custody upon civil process, to a jail in any county which the sheriff considers most convenient and secure.

The sheriff may call such aid as is necessary in guarding, transporting, or returning such person. Whoever neglects or refuses to render such aid, when so called upon, shall forfeit and pay the sum of ten dollars, to be recovered by an action in the name and for the use of the county.

Such sheriff and his assistants shall receive such compensation for their services as the county auditor of the county from which such person was removed considers reasonable. The compensation shall be paid from the county treasury on the warrant of the auditor.

HISTORY: RS § 7382; S&C 1399; 29 v 112, § 5; 93 v 131; GC § 3170; Bureau of Code Revision, 10-1-53; 139 v S 23. Eff 7-6-82.

§ 341.13 Sheriffs of adjoining counties to receive prisoners.

The sheriff of the county to which a prisoner has been removed as provided by section 341.12 of the Revised Code, shall, on being furnished a copy of the process or commitment, receive such prisoner into his custody, and shall be liable for escapes or other neglect of duty in relation to such prisoner, as in other cases. Such sheriff shall receive from the treasury of the county from which the prisoner was removed, such fees as are allowed in other cases.

HISTORY: RS § 7383; S&C 1399; 29 v 112, § 6; GC § 3171; Bureau of Code Revision, 10-1-53.

§ 341.14 Advance deposit of prisoner costs; reimbursement by prisoner.

(A) The sheriff of an adjoining county shall not receive prisoners as provided by section 341.12 of the Revised Code unless there is deposited weekly with the sheriff an amount equal to the actual cost of keeping and feeding each prisoner so committed for the use of the jail of that county, and the same amount for a period of time less than one week. If a prisoner is discharged before the expiration of the term for which the prisoner was committed, the excess of the amount advanced shall be refunded.

(B)(1) The board of county commissioners of the county that receives pursuant to section 341.12 of the Revised Code for confinement in its jail, a prisoner who was convicted of an offense, may require the prisoner to reimburse the county for its expenses incurred by reason of the prisoner's confinement, including, but not limited to, the expenses relating to the provision of food, clothing, shelter, medical care, person hygiene products, including, but not limited to, toothpaste, toothbrushes, and feminine hygiene items, and up to two hours of overtime costs the sheriff or municipal corporation incurred relating to the trial of the person. The amount of reimbursement may be the actual cost of the prisoner's confinement plus the authorized trial overtime costs or a lesser amount determined by the board of county commissioners of the county, provided that the lesser amount shall be determined by a formula that is uniformly applied to persons incarcerated in the jail. The amount of reimbursement shall be determined by a court at a hearing held pursuant to section 2929.18 of the Revised Code if the prisoner is confined for a felony or section 2929.223 [2929.22.3] of the Revised Code if the prisoner is confined for a misdemeanor. The amount or amounts paid in reimbursement by a prisoner confined for a misdemeanor or the amount recovered from a prisoner confined for a misdemeanor by executing upon the judgment obtained pursuant to section 2929.223 [2929.22.3] of the Revised Code shall be paid into the county treasury. If a prisoner is confined for a felony and the court imposes a sanction under section 2929.18 of the Revised Code that requires the prisoner to reimburse the costs of confinement, the prosecuting attorney shall bring an action to recover the expenses of confinement, 2929.18† of the Revised Code.

(2) The board of county commissioners of the county that receives, pursuant to section 341.12 of the Revised Code for confinement in its jail a prisoner who was convicted of a felony may adopt a resolution specifying that prisoners convicted of felonies are not required to reimburse the county for its expenses incurred by reason of the prisoner's confinement, including the expenses listed in division (B)(1) of this section. If the board adopts a resolution of that nature, the board shall provide a copy to the court of common pleas of the county, and the court that sentences a person convicted of a felony shall not impose a sanction under section 2929.18 of the Revised Code that requires the person to reimburse the costs of the confinement.

(C) Divisions (A) and (B) of section 341.06 of the Revised Code apply regarding a prisoner confined in a jail as described in division (B) of this section.

HISTORY: RS § 7384; S&C 748; 50 v 212; GC § 3172; Bureau of Code Revision, 10-1-53; 140 v H 363 (Eff 9-26-84); 146 v S 269 (Eff 7-1-96); 146 v H 480. Eff 10-16-96.

Publisher's Note

The amendments made by SB 269 (146 v —) and HB 480 (146 v —) have been combined. Please see provisions of RC § 1.52.

† The wording is the result of combining HB 480 (146 v —) and SB 269 (146 v —).

§ 341.15 Quarterly account of fees of sheriff.

At the end of each quarter, of each calendar year, the sheriff shall account for and pay to the county treasurer all money received by him as provided by sections 341.13 and 341.14 of the Revised Code.

HISTORY: RS § 7385; S&C 740; 50 v 212, § 2; GC § 3173; Bureau of Code Revision. Eff 10-1-53.

§ 341.16 Process for the return of prisoner.

The prosecuting attorney of the county from which a person charged with the commission of an offense has been removed for safekeeping, may file a praecipe with the clerk of the court of common pleas thereof, directing that a warrant be issued to the sheriff having the custody of such person, and commanding him to deliver the prisoner to the sheriff of the county from which the prisoner was removed, or to the sheriff of the county in which the trial is to take place upon change of venue.

HISTORY: RS § 7386; S&C 1399; 29 v 112, § 7; 93 v 132; GC § 3174; Bureau of Code Revision. Eff 10-1-53.

§ 341.17 Payment of costs of habeas corpus.

When a writ of habeas corpus is issued for a person removed and confined in a county jail as provided by section 341.12 of the Revised Code, the county from which such person was sent shall pay all the costs of such proceeding. Upon the presentation of the certificate of the clerk of the court of common pleas, showing the amount of such costs, to the county auditor of the county from which such person was sent, the auditor shall draw his order for such costs on the county treasurer in favor of such clerk, or in favor of such person as the clerk orders, and the clerk shall pay such costs to the persons entitled to them.

HISTORY: RS § 7387; S&C 749; 50 v 212, § 3; GC § 3175; Bureau of Code Revision. Eff 10-1-53.

§ 341.18 County using jail of another county liable for damages.

The county in which a prisoner was confined as provided by sections 341.12 and 341.13 of the Revised Code, shall have a right of action against the county from which such prisoner was sent, for damages done by him to the jail or other property of the county.

HISTORY: RS § 7388; S&C 749; 50 v 212, § 4; GC § 3176; Bureau of Code Revision. Eff 10-1-53.

[MISCELLANEOUS]

§ 341.19 Reimbursement of county by convict.

(A)(1) The board of county commissioners may require a person who was convicted of an offense and who is confined in the county jail to reimburse the county for its expenses incurred by reason of the person's confinement, including, but not limited to, the expenses relating to the provision of food, clothing, shelter, medical care, personal hygiene products, including, but not limited to, toothpaste, toothbrushes, and feminine hygiene items, and up to two hours of overtime costs the sheriff or municipal corporation incurred relating to the trial of the person. The amount of reimbursement may be the actual cost of the prisoner's confinement plus the authorized trial overtime costs or a lesser amount determined by the board of county commissioners of the county, provided that the lesser amount shall be determined by a formula that is uniformly applied to persons incarcerated in the jail. The amount of reimbursement shall be determined by a court at a hearing held pursuant to section 2929.18 of the Revised Code if the prisoner person† is confined for a felony or section 2929.223 [2929.22.3] of the Revised Code if the prisoner person† is confined for a misdemeanor. The amount or amounts paid in reimbursement by a prisoner confined for a misdemeanor or the amount recovered from a prisoner person†† confined for a misdemeanor by executing upon the judgment obtained pursuant to section 2929.223 [2929.22.3] of the Revised Code shall be paid into the county treasury. If a prisoner person† is confined for a felony and the court imposes a sanction under section 2929.18 of the Revised Code that requires the prisoner person† to reimburse the costs of confinement, the prosecuting attorney shall bring an action to recover the expenses of confinement 2929.18 of the Revised Code.†

(2) The board of county commissioners may adopt a resolution specifying that a person who is convicted of a felony and who is confined in the county jail is not required to reimburse the county for its expenses incurred by reason of the person's confinement, including the expenses listed in division (A)(1) of this section. If the board adopts a resolution of that nature, the board shall provide a copy to the court of common pleas of the county, and the court that sentences a person convicted of a felony shall not impose a sanction under section 2929.18 of the Revised Code that requires the person to reimburse the costs of the confinement.

(B) Divisions (A) and (B) of section 341.06 of the Revised Code apply regarding a prisoner confined in a jail as described in division (A) of this section.††

HISTORY: RS § 7378; S&C 747; 41 v 74, § 10; 87 v 186; GC § 3177; Bureau of Code Revision, 10-1-53; 131 v 230 (Eff 9-6-65); 140 v H 363 (Eff 9-26-84); 146 v S 2 (Eff 7-1-96); 146 v S 269 (Eff 7-1-96); 146 v H 480. Eff 10-16-96.

Publisher's Note

The amendments made by SB 269 (146 v —) and HB 480 (146 v —) have been combined. Please see provisions of RC § 1.52.

† The wording is the result of combining HB 480 (146 v —) and SB 269 (146 v —).

†† This division (A)(2) appears as division (B) in S 269 (146 v —).

[§ 341.19.1] § 341.191 Submission of health insurance claims for jail inmates.

(A) For each person who is confined in a county jail, the county may make a determination as to whether the person is covered under a health insurance or health care policy, contract, or plan and, if the person has such coverage, what terms and conditions are imposed by it for the filing and payment of claims.

(B) If, pursuant to division (A) of this section, it is determined that the person is covered under a policy, contract, or plan and, while that coverage is in force, the county jail renders or arranges for the rendering of health care services to the person in accordance with the terms and conditions of the policy, contract, or plan, then the person, county, or provider of the health care services, as appropriate under the terms and conditions of the policy, contract, or plan, shall promptly submit a claim for payment for the health care services to the appropriate third-party payer and shall designate, or make any other arrangement necessary to ensure, that payment of any amount due on the claim be made to the county or the provider, as the case may be.

(C) Any payment made to the county pursuant to division (B) of this section shall be paid into the county treasury.

(D) This section also applies to any person who is under the custody of a law enforcement officer, as defined in section 2901.01 of the Revised Code, prior to the person's confinement in the county jail.

HISTORY: 146 v S 163. Eff 10-16-96.

§ 341.20 Contracts for food, medical, other services; cook.

The board of county commissioners, with the consent of the sheriff, may contract with commercial providers for the provision to prisoners and other persons of food services, medical services, and other programs and services necessary for the care and welfare of prisoners and other persons placed in the sheriff's charge.

In the absence of a commercial food service contract, the sheriff shall appoint a cook who shall have charge over the preparation of food for the feeding of prisoners and other persons placed in the sheriff's charge. The cook need not, but may be, required to perform other staff duties provided for in this section. The compensation of the cook shall be payable semimonthly from the general fund of the county, upon the warrant of the county auditor.

HISTORY: RS § 7388a; 93 v 577; 95 v 467, § 7388a; 97 v 86; GC § 3178; 108 v PtII, 1125; 120 v 706; 123 v 370; Bureau of Code Revision, 10-1-53; 125 v H 273 (Eff 10-2-53); 131 v 231 (Eff 9-6-65); 132 v S 117 (Eff 10-13-67); 138 v H 965 (Eff 4-9-81); 139 v S 23 (Eff 7-6-82); 146 v H 480. Eff 10-16-96.

§ 341.21 Confinement of federal or state prisoners in jail; prisoner fee for medical treatment or service.

(A) The board of county commissioners may direct the sheriff to receive into custody prisoners charged with or convicted of crime by the United States, and to keep such prisoners until discharged.

The board of the county in which prisoners charged with or convicted of crime by the United States may be so committed may negotiate and conclude any contracts with the United States for the use of the jail as provided by this section and as the board sees fit.

A prisoner so committed shall be supported at the expense of the United States during the prisoner's confinement in the county jail. No greater compensation shall be charged by a sheriff for the subsistence of that type of prisoner than is provided by section 311.20 of the Revised Code to be charged for the subsistence of state prisoners.

A sheriff or jailer who neglects or refuses to perform the services and duties directed by the board by reason of this division, shall be liable to the same penalties, forfeitures, and actions as if the prisoner had been committed under the authority of this state.

(B) Prior to the acceptance for housing into the county jail of persons who are designated by the department of rehabilitation and correction, who plead guilty to or are convicted a felony of the fourth or fifth degree, and who satisfy the other requirements listed in section 5120.161 [5120.16.1] of the Revised Code, the board of county commissioners shall enter into an agreement with the department of rehabilitation and correction under section 5120.161 [5120.16.1] of the Revised Code for the housing in the county jail of persons designated by the department who plead guilty to or are convicted of a felony of the fourth or fifth degree and who satisfy the other requirements listed in that section in exchange for a per diem fee per person. Persons incarcerated in the county jail pursuant to an agreement entered into under this division shall be subject to supervision and control in the manner described in section 5120.161 [5120.16.1] of the Revised Code. This division does not affect the authority of a court to directly sentence a person who is convicted of or pleads guilty to a felony to the county jail in accordance with section 2929.16 of the Revised Code.

(C)(1) Notwithstanding any contrary provision in the Revised Code, the board of county commissioners may establish a policy that requires any person who is not indigent and who is confined in the jail under division (B) of this section to pay a reasonable fee for any medical treatment or service requested by and provided to that person. This fee shall not exceed the actual cost of the treatment or service provided. No person confined to the jail who is indigent shall be required to pay those fees, and no person confined to the jail shall be denied any necessary medical care because of inability to pay those fees.

Upon provision of the requested medical treatment or service, payment of the required fee may be automatically deducted from a person's account record in the jail's business office. If the person has no funds in the person's account, a deduction may be made at a later date during the person's confinement in the jail if funds later become available in the person's account. If the person is released from the jail and has an unpaid balance of these fees, the board of county commissioners may bill the person for payment of the remaining unpaid fees. Fees received for medical treatment or services shall be paid into the commissary fund, if one has been established for the jail or if no such fund exists, into the county treasury.

(2) If a person confined to the jail is required under

section 341.06, 2929.18, or 2929.223 [2929.22.3] of the Revised Code to reimburse the county for expenses incurred by reason of the person's confinement to the jail, any fees paid by the person under division (C)(1) of this section shall be deducted from the expenses required to be reimbursed under section 341.06, 2929.18, or 2929.223 [2929.22.3] of the Revised Code.

HISTORY: RS § 7381; S&C 749; 57 v 108; GC § 3179; 113 v 35; Bureau of Code Revision, 10-1-53; 139 v S 199 (Eff 1-1-83); 146 v S 2 (Eff 7-1-96); 146 v H 480. Eff 10-16-96.

§ 341.22 Religious services and welfare work in county jail.

Each administrative board or other authority in the state, having control of a county jail, shall provide for the holding of religious services and the conducting of other welfare work in such jail, by such persons or organizations, and at such times, as the probate judge directs.

HISTORY: 99 v 225, § 3; GC § 3180; 109 v 526; Bureau of Code Revision. Eff 10-1-53.

§ 341.23 Confinement of misdemeanants from county or municipal corporations having no workhouse; prisoner reimbursement policy.

(A) The board of county commissioners of any county or the legislative authority of any municipal corporation in which there is no workhouse, may agree with the legislative authority of any municipal corporation or other authority having control of the workhouse of any other city, or with the directors of any district of a joint city and county workhouse or county workhouse, upon terms on which persons convicted of a misdemeanor by any court or magistrate of a county or municipal corporation having no workhouse, may be received into such workhouse, under sentence of the court or magistrate. Such board or legislative authority may pay the expenses incurred under the agreement out of the general fund of such county or municipal corporation, upon the certificate of the proper officer of the workhouse.

(B) The sheriff or other officer transporting any person to such workhouse shall receive six cents per mile for the sheriff or officer, going and returning, five cents per mile for transporting the convict, and five cents per mile, going and coming, for the service of each deputy, to be allowed as in cases in which a person is transported to a state correctional institution. The number of miles shall be computed by the usual routes of travel and, in state cases, shall be paid out of the general fund of the county, on the allowance of the board, and for the violation of the ordinances of any municipal corporation, shall be paid by such municipal corporation on the order of its legislative authority.

(C)(1) The board of county commissioners, the directors of the district of a joint city and county workhouse or county workhouse, or the legislative authority of the municipal corporation may require a person who was convicted of an offense and who is confined in a workhouse as provided in division (A) of this section, to reimburse the county, district, or municipal corporation, as the case may be, for its expenses incurred by reason of the person's confinement, including, but not limited to, the expenses relating to the provision of food, clothing, shelter, medical care, personal hygiene products, including, but not limited to, toothpaste, toothbrushes, and feminine hygiene items, and up to two hours of overtime costs the sheriff or municipal corporation incurred relating to the trial of the person. The amount of reimbursement may be the actual cost of the prisoner's confinement plus the authorized trial overtime costs or a lesser amount determined by the board of county commissioners of the county, the directors of the district of the joint city or county workhouse, or the legislative authority of the municipal corporation, provided that the lesser amount shall be determined by a formula that is uniformly applied to persons incarcerated in the workhouse. The amount of reimbursement shall be determined by a court at a hearing held pursuant to section 2929.18 of the Revised Code if the person is confined for a felony or section 2929.223 [2929.22.3] of the Revised Code if the person is confined for a misdemeanor. The amount or amounts paid in reimbursement by a person confined for a misdemeanor or the amount recovered from a person confined for a misdemeanor by executing upon the judgment obtained pursuant to section 2929.223 [2929.22.3] of the Revised Code shall be paid into the treasury of the county, district, or municipal corporation that incurred the expenses. If a person is confined for a felony and the court imposes a sanction under section 2929.18 of the Revised Code that requires the person to reimburse the costs of confinement, the prosecuting attorney or the municipal chief legal officer shall bring an action to recover the expenses of confinement 2929.18 of the Revised Code.†

(2) The board of county commissioners, the directors of the district of a joint city and county workhouse or county workhouse, or the legislative authority of the municipal corporation may adopt a resolution or ordinance specifying that a person who is convicted of a felony and who is confined in a workhouse as provided in division (A) of this section is not required to reimburse the county, district, or municipal corporation, as the case may be, for its expenses incurred by reason of the person's confinement, including the expenses listed in division (C)(1) of this section. If the board, directors, or legislative authority adopts a resolution or ordinance of that nature, the board, directors, or legislative authority shall provide a copy to the court of common pleas of the county, and the court that sentences a person convicted of a felony shall not impose a sanction under section 2929.18 of the Revised Code that requires the person to reimburse the costs of the confinement.

(D) In lieu of requiring offenders to reimburse the

political subdivision for expenses incurred by reason of the person's confinement under division (C) of this section, the board of county commissioners, the directors of the district of joint city and county workhouse or county workhouse, or the legislative authority of the municipal corporation having control of the workhouse may adopt a prisoner reimbursement policy for the workhouse under this division. A reimbursement coordinator may be appointed to administer the prisoner reimbursement policy. A prisoner reimbursement policy adopted under this division is a policy that requires a person confined to the workhouse to reimburse the political subdivision responsible for paying prisoner expenses for any expenses it incurs by reason of the person's confinement in the workhouse, which expenses may include, but are not limited to, the following:

(1) A per diem fee for room and board of not more than sixty dollars per day or the actual per diem cost, whichever is less, for the entire period of time the person is confined to the workhouse;

(2) Actual charges for medical and dental treatment;

(3) Reimbursement for government property damaged by the person while confined to the workhouse.

Rates charged shall be on a sliding scale determined by the board of county commissioners, the directors of the district of joint city and county workhouse or county workhouse, or the legislative authority of the municipal corporation having control of the workhouse, based on the ability of the person confined to the workhouse to pay and on consideration of any legal obligation of the person to support a spouse, minor children, or other dependents and any moral obligation to support dependents to whom the person is providing or has in fact provided support.

The reimbursement coordinator or another person designated by the administrator of the workhouse may investigate the financial status of the person and obtain information necessary to investigate that status, by means that may include contacting employers and reviewing income tax records. The coordinator may work with the confined person to create a repayment plan to be implemented upon the person's release. At the end of the person's incarceration, the person shall be presented with a billing statement.

The reimbursement coordinator or another appointed person may collect, or the board of county commissioners, the directors of the district of joint city and county workhouse or county workhouse, or the legislative authority of the municipal corporation having control of the workhouse may enter into a contract with one or more public agencies or private vendors to collect, any amounts remaining unpaid. Within twelve months after the date of the confined person's release, the prosecuting attorney, city director of law, village solicitor, or attorney for the district may file a civil action to seek reimbursement from that person for any billing amount that remains unpaid. The political subdivision shall not enforce any judgment obtained under this section by means of execution against the person's homestead. For purposes of this section, "homestead" has the same meaning as in division (A) of section 323.151 [323.15.1] of the Revised Code. Any reimbursement received under this section shall be credited to the general fund of the political subdivision that bore the expense, to be used for general fund purposes.

(E)(1) Notwithstanding any contrary provision in this section or section 2929.18 or 2929.223 [2929.22.3] of the Revised Code, the appropriate board of county commissioners and legislative authorities may include in their agreement entered into under division (A) of this section a policy that requires any person who is not indigent and who is confined in the county, city, district, or joint city and county workhouse under this section to pay a reasonable fee for any medical treatment or service requested by and provided to that person. This fee shall not exceed the actual cost of the treatment or service provided. No person confined to a county, city, district, or joint city and county workhouse under this section who is indigent shall be required to pay those fees, and no person confined to any workhouse of that type shall be denied any necessary medical care because of inability to pay those fees.

Upon provision of the requested medical treatment or service, payment of the required fee may be automatically deducted from a person's account record in the workhouse's business office. If the person has no funds in the person's account, a deduction may be made at a later date during the person's confinement in the workhouse if funds later become available in the person's account. If the person is released from the workhouse and has an unpaid balance of these fees, the appropriate board of county commissioners and legislative authorities may bill the person for payment of the remaining unpaid fees in the same proportion as those expenses were borne by the political subdivision issuing the billing statement. Fees received for medical treatment or services shall be paid into the commissary fund, if one has been created for the workhouse, or if no such fund exists, into the treasuries of the political subdivisions that incurred the expenses of those treatments or services in the same proportion as those expenses were borne by these political subdivisions.

(2) If a person confined to a county, city, district, or joint city and county workhouse is required under division (C) or (D) of this section or section 2929.18 or 2929.223 [2929.22.3] of the Revised Code to reimburse a county or municipal corporation for expenses incurred by reason of the person's confinement to the workhouse, any fees paid by the person under division (E)(1) of this section shall be deducted from the expenses required to be reimbursed under division (C) or (D) of this section or section 2929.18 or 2929.223 [2929.22.3] of the Revised Code.

HISTORY: 84 v 136, 139; 91 v 180; GC § 14564; Bureau of Code Revision, 10-1-53; 140 v H 363 (Eff 9-26-84); 145 v H 571 (Eff 10-6-94); 146 v S 2 (Eff 7-1-96); 146 v S 269 (Eff 7-1-96); 146 v H 480. Eff 10-16-96.

Publisher's Note

The amendments made by SB 269 (146 v —) and HB 480 (146 v —) have been combined. Please see provisions of RC § 1.52.

† The wording is the result of combining SB 269 (146 v —) and HB 480 (146 v —).

§ 341.24 Submission of health insurance claims for workhouse inmates.

(A) For each person who is confined in a workhouse as provided in section 341.23 of the Revised Code, the county, district, or municipal corporation, as the case may be, may make a determination as to whether the person is covered under a health insurance or health care policy, contract, or plan and, if the person has such coverage, what terms and conditions are imposed by it for the filing and payment of claims.

(B) If, pursuant to division (A) of this section, it is determined that the person is covered under a policy, contract, or plan and, while that coverage is in force, the workhouse renders or arranges for the rendering of health care services to the person in accordance with the terms and conditions of the policy, contract, or plan, then the person, county, district, municipal corporation, or provider of the health care services, as appropriate under the terms and conditions of the policy, contract, or plan, shall promptly submit a claim for payment for the health care services to the appropriate third-party payer and shall designate, or make any other arrangement necessary to ensure, that payment of any amount due on the claim be made to the county, district, municipal corporation, or provider, as the case may be.

(C) Any payment made to the county, district, or municipal corporation pursuant to division (B) of this section shall be paid into the treasury of the governmental entity that incurred the expenses.

(D) This section also applies to any person who is under the custody of a law enforcement officer, as defined in section 2901.01 of the Revised Code, prior to the person's confinement in the workhouse.

HISTORY: 146 v S 163. Eff 10-16-96.

§ 341.25 Commissary; fund.

(A) The sheriff may establish a commissary for the jail. The commissary may be established either in-house or by another arrangement. If a commissary is established, all persons incarcerated in the jail shall receive commissary privileges. A person's purchases from the commissary shall be deducted from the person's account record in the jail's business office. The commissary shall provide for the distribution to indigent persons incarcerated in the jail necessary hygiene articles and writing materials.

(B) If a commissary is established, the sheriff shall establish a commissary fund for the jail. The management of funds in the commissary fund shall be strictly controlled in accordance with procedures adopted by the auditor of state. Commissary fund revenue over and above operating costs and reserve shall be considered profits. All profits from the commissary fund shall be used to purchase supplies and equipment, and to provide life skills training and education or treatment services, or both, for the benefit of persons incarcerated in the jail. The sheriff shall adopt rules for the operation of any commissary fund the sheriff establishes.

HISTORY: 146 v H 480 (Eff 10-16-96); 147 v H 215. Eff 6-30-97.

[REHABILITATION WORK CAMPS]

§ 341.31 County rehabilitation work camps.

In addition to its other powers, the board of county commissioners of any county may construct, maintain, equip, furnish, appoint the necessary personnel of, and supervise the operation of county rehabilitation work camps for the purpose of the rehabilitation of persons who have been sentenced to imprisonment for a misdemeanor.

HISTORY: 128 v 1043 (Eff 11-5-59); 143 v S 258. Eff 8-22-90.

§ 341.32 Agreement with other counties and municipal corporations.

The board of county commissioners of any county not having a county rehabilitation work camp or the legislative authority of any municipal corporation may agree upon the terms on which persons convicted of a misdemeanor by any court or magistrate of such county or municipal corporation may be received into a county rehabilitation work camp under sentence of such court or magistrate. Such board or legislative authority may pay the expenses, including the cost of transportation of prisoners, incurred under such agreement out of the general fund of such county or municipal corporation, upon the certificate of the proper officer of such county work rehabilitation camp.

HISTORY: 128 v 1043. Eff 11-5-59.

§ 341.33 Use of county rehabilitation work camps by municipal corporations.

Imprisonment under the ordinances of a municipal corporation, in addition to the manner provided for in section 1905.35 of the Revised Code, may be in a county rehabilitation work camp, provided an agreement for the use of such camp has been entered into between the board of county commissioners of the county wherein such camp is located and the legislative authority of such municipal corporation.

HISTORY: 128 v 1043. Eff 11-5-59.

§ 341.34 Minimum security jails.

(A) As used in this section, "building or structure" includes, but is not limited to, a modular unit, building, or structure and a movable unit, building, or structure.

(B)(1) The board of county commissioners of any county, by resolution, may dedicate and permit the use, as a minimum security jail, of any vacant or abandoned public building or structure owned by the county that has not been dedicated to or is not then in use for any county or other public purpose, or any building or structure rented or leased by the county. The board of county commissioners of any county, by resolution, also may dedicate and permit the use, as a minimum security jail, of any building or structure purchased by or constructed by or for the county. Subject to divisions (B)(3) and (C) of this section, upon the effective date of such a resolution, the specified building or structure shall be used, in accordance with this section, for the confinement of persons who meet one of the following conditions:

(a) The person is sentenced to a term of imprisonment for a traffic violation or a misdemeanor that is not an offense of violence and the person is under the jurisdiction of the county and for the confinement of persons convicted of a felony who are sentenced to a residential sanction in the minimum security misdemeanant†† jail pursuant to section 2929.11 to 2929.19 of the Revised Code.†, or the person is sentenced to a term in the jail for a felony of the fourth or fifth degree that is not an offense of violence;

(b) The person is an inmate transferred by order of a judge of the sentencing court upon the request of the sheriff, administrator, jailer, or other person responsible for operating the jail other than a contractor as defined in division (H) of section 9.06 of the Revised Code, who is named in the request as being suitable for confinement in a minimum security facility.

(2) The board of county commissioners of any county, by resolution, may affiliate with one or more adjacent counties, or with one or more municipal corporations located within the county or within an adjacent county, and dedicate and permit the use, as a minimum security jail, of any vacant or abandoned public building or structure owned by any of the affiliating counties or municipal corporations that has not been dedicated to or is not then in use for any public purpose, or any building or structure rented or leased by any of the affiliating counties or municipal corporations. The board of county commissioners of any county, by resolution, also may affiliate with one or more adjacent counties or with one or more municipal corporations located within the county or within an adjacent county and dedicate and permit the use, as a minimum security jail, of any building or structure purchased by or constructed by or for any of the affiliating counties or municipal corporations. Any counties and municipal corporations that affiliate for purposes of this division shall enter into an agreement that establishes the responsibilities for the operation and for the cost of operation of the minimum security jail. Subject to divisions (B)(3) and (C) of this section, upon the effective date of a resolution adopted under this division, the specified building or structure shall be used, in accordance with this section, for the confinement of persons who meet one of the following conditions:

(a) The person is sentenced to a term of imprisonment for a traffic violation, a misdemeanor that is not an offense of violence, or, if a municipal corporation is involved, an ordinance of the municipal corporation that is not an offense of violence and the person is under the jurisdiction of any of the affiliating counties or municipal corporations, and for the confinement of persons convicted of a felony who are sentenced to a residential sanction in the minimum security misdemeanant†† jail pursuant to sections 2929.11 to 2929.19 of the Revised Code†, or the person is sentenced to a term in the jail for a felony of the fourth or fifth degree that is not an offense of violence;

(b) The person is an inmate transferred by order of a judge of the sentencing court upon the request of the sheriff, administrator, jailer, or other person responsible for operating the jail other than a contractor as defined in division (H) of section 9.06 of the Revised Code, who is named in the request as being suitable for confinement in a minimum security facility.

(3) No person shall be confined in a building or structure dedicated as a minimum security jail under division (B)(1) or (2) of this section unless the judge who sentenced the person to the term of imprisonment for the traffic violation or the misdemeanor or who sentenced the person to the residential sanction for the felony specifies that the term of imprisonment or residential sanction is to be served in that jail. If a rented or leased building or structure is so dedicated, the building or structure may be used as a minimum security jail only during the period that it is rented or leased by the county or by an affiliated county or municipal corporation. If a person convicted of a misdemeanor is confined to a building or structure dedicated as a minimum security jail under division (B)(1) or (2) of this section and the sheriff, administrator, jailer, or other person responsible for operating the jail other than a contractor as defined in division (H) of section 9.06 of the Revised Code determines that it would be more appropriate for the person so confined to be confined in another jail or workhouse facility, the sheriff, administrator, jailer, or other person may transfer the person so confined to a more appropriate jail or workhouse facility.

(C) All of the following apply to a building or structure that is dedicated pursuant to division (B)(1) or (2) of this section for use as a minimum security jail:

(1) To the extent that the use of the building or structure as a minimum security jail requires a variance from any county, municipal corporation, or township zoning regulations or ordinances, the variance shall be granted.

(2) Except as provided in this section, the building or structure shall not be used to confine any person unless it is in substantial compliance with any applicable housing, fire prevention, sanitation, health, and safety codes, regulations, or standards.

(3) Unless such satisfaction or compliance is required under the standards described in division (C)(4) of this section, and notwithstanding any other provision of state or local law to the contrary, the building or structure need not satisfy or comply with any state or local building standard or code in order to be used to confine a person for the purposes specified in division (B) of this section.

(4) The building or structure shall not be used to confine any person unless it is in compliance with all minimum standards and minimum renovation, modification, and construction criteria for minimum security jails that have been proposed by the department of rehabilitation and correction, through its bureau of adult detention, under section 5120.10 of the Revised Code.

(5) The building or structure need not be renovated or modified into a secure detention facility in order to be used solely to confine a person for the purposes specified in divisions (B)(1)(a) and (B)(2)(a) of this section.

(6) The building or structure shall be used, equipped, furnished, and staffed in the manner necessary to provide adequate and suitable living, sleeping, food service or preparation, drinking, bathing and toilet, sanitation, and other necessary facilities, furnishings, and equipment.

(D) Except as provided in this section, a minimum security jail dedicated and used under this section shall be considered to be part of the jail, workhouse, or other correctional facilities of the county or the affiliated counties and municipal corporations for all purposes under the law. All persons confined in such a minimum security jail shall be and shall remain, in all respects, under the control of the county authority that has responsibility for the management and operation of the jail, workhouse, or other correctional facilities of the county or, if it is operated by any affiliation of counties or municipal corporations, under the control of the specified county or municipal corporation with that authority, provided that, if the person was convicted of a felony and is serving a residential sanction in the facility, all provisions of law that pertain to persons convicted of a felony that would not by their nature clearly be inapplicable apply regarding the person. A minimum security jail dedicated and used under this section shall be managed and maintained in accordance with policies and procedures adopted by the board of county commissioners or the affiliated counties and municipal corporations governing the safe and healthful operation of the jail, the confinement and supervision of the persons sentenced to it, and their participation in work release or similar rehabilitation programs. In addition to other rules of conduct and discipline, the rights of ingress and egress of persons confined in a minimum security jail dedicated and used under this section shall be subject to reasonable restrictions. Every person confined in a minimum security jail dedicated and used under this section shall be given verbal and written notification, at the time of the person's admission to the jail, that purposely leaving, or purposely failing to return to, the jail without proper authority or permission constitutes the felony offense of escape.

HISTORY: 143 v S 131 (Eff 7-25-90); 143 v H 837 (Eff 7-25-90); 143 v S 258 (Eff 8-22-90); 144 v S 351 (Eff 7-1-92); 146 v H 117 (Eff 9-29-95); 146 v S 269 (Eff 7-1-96); 146 v H 480. Eff 10-16-96.

Publisher's Note

The amendments made by SB 269 (146 v —) and HB 480 (146 v —) have been combined. Please see provisions of RC § 1.52.

† The wording is the result of combining HB 480 (146 v —) and SB 269 (146 v —).

†† The word "misdemeanant" was deleted throughout HB 480 (146 v —).

§ 341.35 Contract for private operation of facility.

The board of county commissioners of a county with a county jail, workhouse, minimum security misdemeanant jail, or other correctional facility may enter into a contract under section 9.06 of the Revised Code for the private operation and management of that facility, but only if the facility is used to house only misdemeanant inmates.

HISTORY: 146 v H 117. Eff 9-29-95.

The effective date is set by section 197 of HB 117.

§ 341.41 Prisoner access to exercise equipment or participation in fighting skills programs.

(A) As used in this section:

(1) "Free weight exercise equipment" means any equipment or device that is designed to increase the muscle mass and physical strength of the person using it. "Free weight exercise equipment" includes, but is not limited to, barbells, dumbbells, weight plates, and similar free weight-type equipment and other devices that the department of rehabilitation and correction, in rules adopted under section 5120.423 [5120.42.3] of the Revised Code, designates as enabling a person to increase muscle mass and physical strength.

(2) "Fixed weight exercise equipment" means any equipment, machine, or device that is not designed primarily to increase muscle mass and physical strength but rather to keep a person in relatively good physical condition. "Fixed weight exercise equipment" includes, but is not limited to, weight machines that utilize weight plates, tension bands, or similar devices that provide

weight training resistance like universal and nautilus equipment. "Fixed weight exercise equipment" includes machines that are usually assembled as a unit, are not readily dismantled, and have been specifically modified for prison use so as to make them secure and immobile.

(3) "County correctional officer" means a person who is employed by a county as an employee or officer of a county jail, county workhouse, minimum security jail, joint city and county workhouse, municipal-county correctional center, multicounty-municipal correctional center, municipal-county jail or workhouse, or multicounty-municipal jail or workhouse.

(4) "Multicounty-municipal" has the same meaning as in section 307.93 of the Revised Code.

(B) No county correctional officer shall do any of the following:

(1) Provide a prisoner access to free weight or fixed weight exercise equipment;

(2) Allow a prisoner to provide or receive instruction in boxing, wrestling, karate, judo, or another form of martial arts, or any other program that the department of rehabilitation and correction, in rules adopted under section 5120.423 [5120.42.3] of the Revised Code, designates as enabling a person to improve fighting skills.

(C) Nothing in this section prohibits a county correctional officer from allowing a prisoner to participate in jogging, basketball, stationary exercise bicycling, supervised calisthenics, or other physical activities that are not designed to increase muscle mass and physical strength or improve fighting skills.

HISTORY: 146 v H 152. Eff 10-4-96.

The provisions of § 6 of HB 152 read as follows:

SECTION 6. On and after the effective date of this act, no moneys in the treasury of the state, or moneys coming lawfully into the possession or custody of the Treasurer of State, except moneys donated by gift, devise, or bequest specifically for this purpose, shall be used to purchase any fixed weight exercise equipment authorized by the act, and no moneys in the treasury of any subdivision of the state, or moneys coming lawfully into the possession or custody of the treasurer of any subdivision, shall be used to purchase any fixed weight exercise equipment for use at any facility described in Section 5 of this act.

TITLE 5: TOWNSHIPS

CHAPTER 503: GENERAL PROVISIONS

[MASSAGE ESTABLISHMENTS]

§ 503.40 Definitions.

As used in sections 503.40 to 503.49 of the Revised Code:

(A) "Massage" means any method of exerting pressure on, stroking, kneading, rubbing, tapping, pounding, vibrating, or stimulating the external soft tissue of the body with the hands, or with the aid of any mechanical or electrical apparatus or appliance.

(B) "Massage establishment" means any fixed place of business where a person offers massages:

(1) In exchange for anything of value; or

(2) In connection with the provision of another legitimate service.

(C) "Masseur" or "masseuse" means any individual who performs massages at a massage establishment.

(D) "Sexual or genital area" includes the genitalia, pubic area, anus, perineum of any person, and the breasts of a female.

HISTORY: 144 v H 247. Eff 6-3-92.

§ 503.41 Resolution regulating massage establishments and their employees; licensed health professionals excepted.

(A) A board of township trustees, by resolution, may regulate and require the registration of massage establishments and their employees within the unincorporated territory of the township. In accordance with sections 503.40 to 503.49 of the Revised Code, for that purpose, the board, by a majority vote of all members, may adopt, amend, administer, and enforce regulations within the unincorporated territory of the township.

(B) A board may adopt regulations and amendments under this section only after public hearing at not fewer than two regular sessions of the board. The board shall cause to be published in at least one newspaper of general circulation in the township notice of the public hearings, including the time, date, and place, once a week for two weeks immediately preceding the hearings. The board shall make available proposed regulations or amendments to the public at the office of the board.

(C) Regulations or amendments adopted by the board are effective thirty days after the date of adoption unless, within thirty days after the adoption of the regulations or amendments, the township clerk receives a petition, signed by a number of qualified electors residing in the unincorporated area of the township equal to not less than ten per cent of the total vote cast for all candidates for governor in the area at the most recent general election at which a governor was elected, requesting the board to submit the regulations or amendments to the electors of the area for approval or rejection at the next primary or general election occurring at least seventy-five days after the board receives the petition.

No regulation or amendment for which the referendum vote has been requested is effective unless a majority of the vote cast on the issue is in favor of the regulation or amendment. Upon certification by the board of elections that a majority of the votes cast on the issue was in favor of the regulation or amendment, the regulation or amendment takes immediate effect.

(D) The board shall make available regulations it adopts or amends to the public at the office of the board and shall cause to be published a notice of the availability of the regulations in at least one newspaper of general circulation in the township within ten days after their adoption or amendment.

(E) Nothing in sections 503.40 to 503.49 of the Revised Code shall be construed to allow a board of township trustees to regulate the practice of any limited branch of medicine or surgery in accordance with sections 4731.15 and 4731.16 of the Revised Code or the practice of providing therapeutic massage by a licensed physician, a licensed chiropractor, a licensed podiatrist, a licensed nurse, or any other licensed health professional. As used in this division, "licensed" means licensed, certified, or registered to practice in this state.

HISTORY: 144 v H 247 (Eff 6-3-92); 146 v H 99. Eff 8-22-95.

§ 503.42 Permit to operate establishment; masseur or masseuse's license; prohibited activities.

If a board of township trustees has adopted a resolution under section 503.41 of the Revised Code:

(A) No person shall engage in, conduct or carry on, or permit to be engaged in, conducted or carried on in the unincorporated areas of the township, the operation of a massage establishment without first having obtained a permit from the board of township trustees as provided in section 503.43 of the Revised Code.

(B) No individual shall act as a masseur or masseuse for a massage establishment located in the unincorporated areas of the township without first having obtained a license from the board of township trustees as provided in section 503.45 of the Revised Code.

(C) No owner or operator of a massage establishment located in the unincorporated areas of the township shall knowingly do any of the following:

(1) Employ an unlicensed masseur or masseuse;

(2) Refuse to allow appropriate state or local authori-

ties, including police officers, access to the massage establishment for any health or safety inspection conducted pursuant to a regulation adopted by the township under section 503.41 of the Revised Code;

(3) Operate during the hours designated as prohibited hours of operation by the board of township trustees;

(4) Employ any person under the age of eighteen.

(D) No person employed in a massage establishment located in the unincorporated area of the township shall knowingly do any of the following in the performance of duties at the massage establishment:

(1) Place his or her hand upon, touch with any part of his or her body, fondle in any manner, or massage the sexual or genital area of any other person;

(2) Perform, offer, or agree to perform any act which would require the touching of the sexual or genital area of any other person;

(3) Touch, offer, or agree to touch the sexual or genital area of any other person with any mechanical or electrical apparatus or appliance;

(4) Wear unclean clothing, no clothing, transparent clothing, or clothing that otherwise reveals the sexual or genital areas of the masseur or masseuse;

(5) Uncover or allow the sexual or genital area of any other person to be uncovered while providing massages.

(E) No licensed masseur or masseuse shall accept or continue employment at a massage establishment that does not have a current, valid permit issued by the board of township trustees.

HISTORY: 144 v H 247. Eff 6-3-92.

§ 503.43 Application for permit; contents and expiration of permit.

If a board of township trustees has adopted a resolution under section 503.41 of the Revised Code, the application for a permit to operate a massage establishment shall be made to the board and shall include the following:

(A) An initial, nonrefundable filing fee of two hundred fifty dollars and an annual nonrefundable renewal fee of one hundred twenty-five dollars;

(B) A health and safety report of an inspection of the premises performed within thirty days of the application to determine compliance with applicable health and safety codes, which inspection appropriate state or local authorities acting pursuant to an agreement with the board shall perform;

(C) The full name and address of any person applying for a permit, including any partner or limited partner of a partnership applicant, any officer or director of a corporate applicant, and any stockholder holding more than two per cent of the stock of a corporate applicant, the date of birth and social security number of each individual, and the federal identification number of any partnership or corporation;

(D) Authorization for an investigation into the criminal record of any person applying for a permit;

(E) Any other information determined by the board to be necessary.

A permit issued under this section to a massage establishment shall expire one year after the date of issuance, except that no massage establishment shall be required to discontinue business because of the failure of the board to act on a renewal application filed in a timely manner and pending before the board on the expiration date of the establishment's permit. Each permit shall contain the name of the applicant, the address of the massage establishment, and the expiration date of the permit.

HISTORY: 144 v H 247. Eff 6-3-92.

§ 503.44 Reasons for denial or revocation of permit.

If a board of township trustees has adopted a resolution under section 503.41 of the Revised Code, it shall deny any application for a permit to operate a massage establishment or revoke a previously issued permit, for any of the following reasons:

(A) Falsification of any of the information required for the application or failure to fully complete the application;

(B) Failure to cooperate with any required health or safety inspection;

(C) Any one of the persons named on the application is under the age of eighteen;

(D) Any one of the persons named on the application has been convicted of or pleaded guilty to any violation of Chapter 2907. of the Revised Code, or violation of any municipal ordinance that is substantially equivalent to any offense contained in Chapter 2907. of the Revised Code, within five years preceding the application;

(E) Any masseur or masseuse employed at the licensed massage establishment has been convicted of or pleaded guilty to a violation of division (D) of section 503.42 of the Revised Code.

HISTORY: 144 v H 247. Eff 6-3-92.

§ 503.45 Application for license as masseur or masseuse; contents and expiration of license.

If a board of township trustees has adopted a resolution under section 503.41 of the Revised Code, the application for a license as a masseur or masseuse shall be made to the board and shall include the following:

(A) An initial, nonrefundable filing fee of one hundred dollars and an annual nonrefundable renewal fee of fifty dollars;

(B) The results of a physical examination performed by a licensed physician within thirty days of the application certifying that the applicant is free from communicable diseases;

(C) The full name, date of birth, address, and social security number of the applicant;

(D) The results of an investigation by appropriate police agencies into the criminal record of the applicant, including a photograph taken no later than thirty days prior to the application, fingerprints, and background investigation;

(E) Any other information determined by the board to be necessary.

A license issued under this section to a masseur or masseuse shall expire one year after the date of issuance, except that no masseur or masseuse shall be required to discontinue performing massages because of the failure of the board to act on a renewal application filed in a timely manner and pending before the board on the expiration date of the person's license. Each license shall contain the full name of the applicant, a color photograph and a brief description of the person, and the expiration date of the license.

HISTORY: 144 v H 247. Eff 6-3-92.

§ 503.46 Reasons for denial or revocation of license.

If a board of township trustees has adopted a resolution under section 503.41 of the Revised Code, it shall deny the application for a masseur or masseuse license or revoke a previously issued license for any of the following reasons:

(A) Falsification of any of the information required for the application or failure to fully complete the application;

(B) The applicant is under the age of twenty-one.

(C) The applicant has been convicted of or pleaded guilty to any violation of Chapter 2907. of the Revised Code, or violation of any municipal ordinance that is substantially equivalent to any offense contained in Chapter 2907. of the Revised Code, within five years preceding the application.

(D) The applicant has been convicted of or pleaded guilty to a violation of division (D) of section 503.42 of the Revised Code.

HISTORY: 144 v H 247. Eff 6-3-92.

§ 503.47 Requirements that may be adopted.

If a board of township trustees has adopted a resolution under section 503.41 of the Revised Code, the regulations adopted for that purpose may require any of the following:

(A) A massage establishment to display its current permit in an area open to the public;

(B) Each masseur or masseuse to display his or her license at all times in the areas where the licensee is providing massages;

(C) Massage establishments to undergo periodic health and safety inspections to determine continual compliance with applicable health and safety codes;

(D) Masseurs and masseuses to undergo periodic physical examinations performed by a licensed physician certifying that the masseur or masseuse continues to be free from communicable diseases;

(E) Any other requirement reasonably thought necessary by the board.

HISTORY: 144 v H 247. Eff 6-3-92.

§ 503.48 Hearing not required; record of proceedings; appeals.

A board of township trustees acting under sections 503.40 to 503.49 of the Revised Code need not hold any hearing in connection with an order denying or revoking a permit to operate a massage establishment or masseur or masseuse license. The board shall maintain a complete record of each proceeding and shall notify the applicant in writing of its order. Any person adversely affected by an order of the board denying or revoking a permit to operate a massage establishment or masseur or masseuse license may appeal from the order of the board to the court of common pleas of the county in which the township is located, the place of business of the permit holder is located, or the person is a resident. The appeal shall be in accordance with Chapter 2506. of the Revised Code.

HISTORY: 144 v H 247. Eff 6-3-92.

§ 503.49 Deposit and use of fees.

If a board of township trustees has adopted a resolution under section 503.41 of the Revised Code, the board shall deposit the fees collected by the township for massage establishment permits and masseur and masseuse licenses in the township general fund and first use the fees for the cost of administering and enforcing regulations adopted under section 503.41 of the Revised Code.

HISTORY: 144 v H 247. Eff 6-3-92.

§ 503.50 Penalties.

(A) Whoever violates division (A) or (B) of section 503.42 of the Revised Code is guilty of a misdemeanor of the first degree.

(B) Whoever violates division (C), (D), or (E) of section 503.42 of the Revised Code is guilty of a misdemeanor of the third degree.

HISTORY: 144 v H 247 (Eff 6-3-92); 146 v S 2. Eff 7-1-96.

The effective date is set by section 6 of SB 2.

[ADULT CABARETS]

§ 503.51 Definitions.

As used in sections 503.51 to 503.59 of the Revised Code:

(A) "Adult cabaret" means a nightclub, bar, restaurant, or similar establishment in which persons appear in a state of nudity in the performance of their duties.

(B) "Nudity" means the showing of either of the following:

(1) The human male or female genitals, pubic area, or buttocks with less than a fully opaque covering;

(2) The female breast with less than a fully opaque covering on any part of the nipple.

HISTORY: 145 v H 3. Eff 10-1-93.

§ 503.52 Resolution to regulate and require registration of adult cabarets; procedure for adopting regulations, amendments.

(A) A board of township trustees, by resolution, may regulate and require the registration of adult cabarets within the unincorporated territory of the township. In accordance with sections 503.51 to 503.59 of the Revised Code, for that purpose, the board, by a majority vote of all members, may adopt, amend, administer, and enforce regulations within the unincorporated territory of the township.

(B) A board may adopt regulations and amendments under this section only after public hearing at not fewer than two regular sessions of the board. The board shall cause to be published in at least one newspaper of general circulation in the township notice of the public hearings, including the time, date, and place, once a week for two weeks immediately preceding the hearings. The board shall make available proposed regulations or amendments to the public at the office of the board.

(C) Regulations or amendments adopted by the board are effective thirty days after the date of adoption unless, within thirty days after the adoption of the regulations or amendments, the township clerk receives a petition, signed by a number of qualified electors residing in the unincorporated area of the township equal to not less than ten per cent of the total number of votes cast in that area for all candidates for the office of governor at the most recent general election for that office, requesting the board to submit the regulations or amendments to the electors of the area for approval or rejection at the next primary or general election occurring at least seventy-five days after the board receives the petition.

No regulation or amendment for which the referendum vote has been requested is effective unless a majority of the votes cast on the issue is in favor of the regulation or amendment. Upon certification by the board of elections that a majority of the votes cast on the issue was in favor of the regulation or amendment, the regulation or amendment takes immediate effect.

(D) The board shall make available regulations it adopts or amends to the public at the office of the board and shall cause to be published a notice of the availability of the regulations in at least one newspaper of general circulation in the township within ten days after their adoption or amendment.

HISTORY: 145 v H 3. Eff 10-1-93.

§ 503.53 Duty to obtain permit; prohibitions.

If a board of township trustees has adopted a resolution under section 503.52 of the Revised Code:

(A) No person shall engage in, conduct or carry on, or permit to be engaged in, conducted or carried on in the unincorporated areas of the township, the operation of an adult cabaret without first having obtained a permit from the board of township trustees as provided in section 503.54 of the Revised Code.

(B) No owner or operator of an adult cabaret located in the unincorporated areas of the township shall knowingly do any of the following:

(1) Refuse to allow appropriate state or local authorities, including police officers, access to the adult cabaret for any health or safety inspection, or any other inspection conducted to ensure compliance with sections 503.52 to 503.59 of the Revised Code and regulations adopted by the township under sections 503.52 or 503.56 of the Revised Code;

(2) Operate during the hours designated as prohibited hours of operation by the board of township trustees;

(3) Employ any person under the age of eighteen;

(4) Establish or operate an adult cabaret within five hundred feet from the boundaries of a parcel of real estate having situated on it a school, church, library, public playground, or township park.

(C) No person employed in an adult cabaret located in the unincorporated area of the township shall knowingly do any of the following in the performance of duties at the adult cabaret:

(1) Place his or her hand upon, touch with any part of his or her body, fondle in any manner, or massage the genitals, pubic area, or buttocks of any other person or the breasts of any female or, if the employee is a female, of any other female;

(2) Perform, offer, or agree to perform any act that would require the touching of the genitals, pubic area, or buttocks of any other person or the breasts of any female or, if the employee is a female, of any other female;

(3) Uncover the genitals, pubic area, or buttocks of any other person or the breasts of any female or, if the employee is a female, of any other female.

HISTORY: 145 v H 3. Eff 10-1-93.

§ 503.54 Application for permit; expiration.

If a board of township trustees has adopted a resolution under section 503.52 of the Revised Code, the application for a permit to operate an adult cabaret shall be made to the board and shall include all of the following:

(A) An initial, nonrefundable filing fee of two hundred fifty dollars and an annual nonrefundable renewal fee of one hundred twenty-five dollars;

(B) A health and safety report of an inspection of the

premises performed within thirty days of the application to determine compliance with applicable health and safety codes. Appropriate state or local authorities acting pursuant to an agreement with the board shall perform this inspection;

(C) The full name and address of any person applying for a permit, including any partner or limited partner of a partnership applicant, any officer or director of a corporate applicant, and any stock holder holding more than two per cent of the stock of a corporate applicant, the date of birth and social security number of each individual, and the federal identification number of any partnership or corporation;

(D) Authorization for an investigation into the criminal record of any person applying for a permit;

(E) Any other information determined by the board to be necessary.

A permit issued under this section to an adult cabaret shall expire one year after the date of issuance, except that no adult cabaret shall be required to discontinue business because of the failure of the board to act on a renewal application filed in a timely manner and pending before the board on the expiration date of the establishment's permit. Each permit shall contain the name of the applicant, the address of the adult cabaret, and the expiration date of the permit.

HISTORY: 145 v H 3. Eff 10-1-93.

§ 503.55 Reasons for denial or revocation of permit.

If a board of township trustees has adopted a resolution under section 503.52 of the Revised Code, it shall deny any application for a permit to operate an adult cabaret or revoke a previously issued permit, for any of the following reasons:

(A) Any of the information required for the application has been falsified or the application has not been fully completed.

(B) There has been a failure to cooperate with any required health or safety inspection.

(C) Any one of the persons named on the application has been convicted of or pleaded guilty to any violation of Chapter 2907. of the Revised Code, or any violation of any municipal ordinance or any law of another state that is substantially equivalent to any offense contained in Chapter 2907. of the Revised Code.

(D) Any person employed at the licensed adult cabaret has been convicted of or pleaded guilty to a violation of division (C) of section 503.53 of the Revised Code.

(E) The liquor control commission has revoked, under section 4301.25 of the Revised Code, a permit held by any one of the persons named on the application.

HISTORY: 145 v H 3. Eff 10-1-93.

§ 503.56 Requirements that may be imposed on cabaret.

If a board of township trustees has adopted a resolution under section 503.52 of the Revised Code, the regulations adopted for that purpose may require an adult cabaret to do any of the following:

(A) Display its current permit in an area open to the public;

(B) Undergo periodic health and safety inspections to determine continual compliance with applicable health and safety codes;

(C) Be open for business only during specified hours;

(D) Comply with any other requirement reasonably thought necessary by the board.

HISTORY: 145 v H 3. Eff 10-1-93.

§ 503.57 Hearing on denial or revocation not required; record, notice of proceedings; appeals.

A board of township trustees acting under sections 503.51 to 503.59 of the Revised Code need not hold any hearing in connection with an order denying or revoking a permit to operate an adult cabaret. The board shall maintain a complete record of each proceeding and shall notify the applicant in writing of its order. Any person adversely affected by an order of the board denying or revoking a permit to operate an adult cabaret may appeal from the order of the board to the court of common pleas of the county in which the place of business of the applicant or permit holder is to be located or is located, as appropriate. The appeal shall be in accordance with Chapter 2506. of the Revised Code.

HISTORY: 145 v H 3. Eff 10-1-93.

§ 503.58 Deposit, use of fees.

If a board of township trustees has adopted a resolution under section 503.52 of the Revised Code, the board shall deposit the fees collected by the township for adult cabaret permits in the township general fund and first use the fees for the cost of administering and enforcing regulations adopted under sections 503.52 and 503.56 of the Revised Code.

HISTORY: 145 v H 3. Eff 10-1-93.

§ 503.59 Penalties.

(A) Whoever violates division (A) of section 503.53 of the Revised Code is guilty of a misdemeanor of the first degree for a first offense, and a felony of the fourth degree for a second offense.

(B) Whoever violates division (B) or (C) of section 503.53 of the Revised Code is guilty of a misdemeanor of the third degree.

HISTORY: 145 v H 3. Eff 10-1-93.

CHAPTER 504: OPTIONAL LIMITED SELF-GOVERNMENT

§ 504.04 Exercise of powers of self-government; limitation; officers; conflicts with municipal or county laws.

(A) A township that adopts the limited self-government form of government, by resolution, may do all of the following, provided that any such resolution, other than a resolution to supply water in accordance with sections 504.18 and 504.19 of the Revised Code, may be enforced only by the imposition of civil fines as authorized in this chapter:

(1) Exercise all powers of local self-government within the unincorporated area of the township, other than powers that are in conflict with general laws, except that the township shall comply with the requirements and prohibitions of this chapter, and shall enact no taxes other than those authorized by general law, and except that no resolution adopted pursuant to this chapter shall encroach upon the powers, duties, and privileges of elected township officers or change, alter, combine, eliminate, or otherwise modify the form or structure of the township government unless the change is required by this chapter;

(2) Adopt and enforce within the unincorporated area of the township such local police, sanitary, and other similar regulations as are not in conflict with general laws or otherwise prohibited by division (B) of this section;

(3) Supply water to users within the unincorporated area of the township in accordance with sections 504.18 and 504.19 of the Revised Code.

(B) No resolution adopted pursuant to this chapter shall:

(1) Create a criminal offense or impose criminal penalties;

(2) Impose civil fines other than as authorized by this chapter;

(3) Establish or revise subdivision regulations, road construction standards, sewer regulations, urban sediment rules, or storm water and drainage regulations;

(4) Establish or revise building standards, building codes, and other standard codes except as provided in section 504.13 of the Revised Code;

(5) Increase, decrease, or otherwise alter the powers or duties of a township under any other chapter of the Revised Code relative to agriculture or the conservation or development of natural resources;

(6) Establish regulations affecting hunting, trapping, fishing, or the possession, use, or sale of firearms;

(7) Establish or revise water regulations, except in accordance with sections 504.18 and 504.19 of the Revised Code.

Nothing in this chapter shall be construed as affecting the powers of counties with regard to the subjects listed in divisions (B)(3) to (5) of this section.

(C) Under the limited self-government form of township government all officers shall have the qualifications, and be nominated, elected, or appointed, as provided in Chapter 505. of the Revised Code, except that the board of township trustees shall appoint a full-time or part-time law director pursuant to section 504.15 of the Revised Code.

(D) In case of conflict between resolutions enacted by a board of township trustees and municipal ordinances or resolutions, the ordinance or resolution enacted by the municipal corporation prevails. In case of conflict between resolutions enacted by a board of township trustees and any county resolution, the resolution enacted by the board of township trustees prevails.

HISTORY: 144 v H 77 (Eff 9-17-91); 145 v H 579. Eff 7-13-94.

§ 504.05 Civil fine for violation.

The board of township trustees may impose a civil fine for a violation of a resolution adopted pursuant to this chapter, and may graduate the amount of the fine based on the number of previous violations of the resolution. No fine shall exceed one thousand dollars. Any resolution that imposes a fine shall clearly state the amount of the fine for the first and for subsequent violations.

HISTORY: 144 v H 77. Eff 9-17-91.

§ 504.06 Citation issued to violator.

(A) Peace officers serving the township pursuant to section 504.16 of the Revised Code may issue citations to persons who violate township resolutions adopted pursuant to this chapter. Each such citation shall contain provisions that:

(1) Advise the person upon whom it is served that the person must answer in relation to the violation charged in the citation within fourteen days after the citation is served upon him;

(2) Indicate the allowable answers that may be made and that the person will be afforded a court hearing if he denies in his answer that he committed the violation;

(3) Specify that the answer must be made in person or by mail to the township clerk;

(4) Indicate the amount of the fine that arises from the violation.

(B) A peace officer who issues a citation for a violation of a township resolution shall complete the citation by identifying the violation charged and by indicating the date, time, and place of the violation charged. The officer shall sign the citation, affirm the facts that it contains, and without unnecessary delay file the original citation with the court having jurisdiction over the violation. A copy of a citation issued pursuant to this section shall be served pursuant to the Rules of Civil Procedure upon the person who violated the resolution. No peace officer is entitled to receive witness fees in a cause prosecuted under a township resolution adopted pursuant to this chapter.

HISTORY: 144 v H 77. Eff 9-17-91.

§ 504.07 Answer; scheduling of hearing; judgment or default judgment; appeal.

(A)(1) A person who is served with a citation pursuant to division (B) of section 504.06 of the Revised Code shall answer the charge by personal appearance before, or by mail addressed to, the township clerk, who shall immediately notify the township law director. An answer shall be made within fourteen days after the citation is served upon the person and shall be in one of the following forms:

(a) An admission that the person committed the violation, by payment of any fine arising from the violation. Payment of a fine pursuant to division (A)(1)(a) of this section shall be payable to the clerk of the township and deposited by the clerk into the township general fund.

(b) A denial that the person committed the violation.

(2) Whenever a person pays a fine pursuant to division (A)(1)(a) of this section or whenever a person answers by denying the violation or does not submit payment of the fine within the time required by division (A)(1) of this section, the township clerk shall notify the court having jurisdiction over the violation.

(B) If a person answers by denying the violation or does not submit payment of the fine within the time required by division (A)(1) of this section, the court having jurisdiction over the violation shall, upon receiving the notification required by division (A)(2) of this section, schedule a hearing on the violation and send notice of the date and time of the hearing to the person charged with the violation and to the township law director. If the person charged with the violation fails to appear for the scheduled hearing, the court may hold him in contempt, or issue a summons or a warrant for his arrest pursuant to Criminal Rule 4. If the court issues a summons and the person charged with the violation fails to appear, the court may enter a default judgment against the person and require him to pay the fine arising from the violation.

(C) The court shall hold the scheduled hearing in accordance with the Rules of Civil Procedure and the rules of the court, and shall determine whether the township has established, by a preponderance of the evidence, that the person committed the violation. If the court determines that the person committed the violation, it shall enter a judgment against the person requiring him to pay the fine arising from the violation.

If the court determines that the township has not established, by a preponderance of the evidence, that the person committed the violation, the court shall enter judgment against the township whose resolution allegedly was violated, shall dismiss the charge of the violation against the person, and shall assess costs against the township.

(D) Payment of any judgment or default judgment entered against a person pursuant to this section shall be made to the clerk of the court that entered the judgment, within ten days after the date of entry. All money paid in satisfaction of a judgment or default judgment shall be disbursed by the clerk as required by law and the clerk shall enter the fact of payment of the money and its disbursement in the records of the court. If payment of a judgment or default judgment is not made within this time period, execution may be levied, and such other measures may be taken for its collection as are authorized for the collection of an unpaid money judgment in a civil action rendered in that court. The municipal or county court shall assess costs against the judgment debtor, to be paid upon satisfaction of the judgment.

(E) Any person against whom a judgment or default judgment is entered pursuant to this section and any township against which a judgment is entered pursuant to this section may appeal the judgment or default judgment to the court of appeals within whose territorial jurisdiction the resolution allegedly was violated. An appeal shall be made by filing a notice of appeal with the trial court and with the court of appeals within thirty days after the entry of judgment by the trial court and by the payment of such reasonable costs as the court requires. Upon the filing of an appeal, the court shall schedule a hearing date and notify the parties of the date, time, and place of the hearing. The hearing shall be held by the court in accordance with the rules of the court. Service of a notice of appeal under this division does not stay enforcement and collection of the judgment or default judgment from which appeal is taken by the person unless the person who files the appeal posts bond with the trial court, in the amount of the judgment, plus court costs, at or before service of the notice of appeal.

Notwithstanding any other provision of law, the judgment on appeal of the court of appeals is final.

HISTORY: 144 v H 77. Eff 9-17-91.

CHAPTER 505: TRUSTEES

§ 505.17 Regulations for engine noise and vehicle parking.

(A) Except in a township or portion thereof that is within the limits of a municipal corporation, the board of township trustees may make such regulations and orders as are necessary to control passenger car, motorcycle, and internal combustion engine noise, as permitted under section 4513.221 [4513.22.1] of the Revised Code, and all vehicle parking in the township. This authorization includes, among other powers, the power to regulate parking on established roadways proximate to buildings on private property as necessary to provide access to the property by public safety vehicles and equipment, if the property is used for commercial purposes, the public is permitted to use such parking area, and accommodation for more than ten motor vehicles is provided, and the power to authorize the issuance of orders limiting or prohibiting parking on any township street or highway during as now emergency declared pursuant to a snow-emergency authorization adopted under this division. All such regulations and orders shall be subject to the limitations, restrictions, and exceptions in sections 4511.01 to 4511.76 and 4513.02 to 4513.37 of the Revised Code.

A board of township trustees may adopt a general snow-emergency authorization, which becomes effective under division (B)(1) of this section, allowing the president of the board or some other person specified in the authorization to issue an order declaring a snow emergency and limiting or prohibiting parking on any township street or highway during the snow emergency. Any such order becomes effective under division (B)(2) of this section. Each general snow-emergency authorization adopted under this division shall specify the weather conditions under which a snow emergency may be declared in that township.

(B)(1) All regulations and orders, including any snow-emergency authorization established by the board under this section, except for an order declaring a snow emergency as provided in division (B)(2) of this section, shall be posted by the township clerk in five conspicuous public places in the township for thirty days before becoming effective, and shall be published in a newspaper of general circulation in the township for three consecutive weeks. In addition to these requirements, no general snow-emergency authorization shall become effective until permanent signs giving notice that parking is limited or prohibited during a snow emergency are properly posted, in accordance with any applicable standards adopted by the department of transportation, along streets or highways specified in the authorization.

(2) Pursuant to the adoption of a snow-emergency authorization under this section, an order declaring a snow emergency becomes effective two hours after the president of the board or the other person specified in the general snow-emergency authorization makes an announcement of a snow emergency to the local news media. The president or other specified person shall request the local news media to announce that a snow emergency has been declared, the time the declaration will go into effect, and whether the snow emergency will remain in effect for a specified period of time or indefinitely until canceled by a subsequent announcement to the local news media by the president or other specified person.

(C) Such regulations and orders may be enforced where traffic control devices conforming to section 4511.09 of the Revised Code are prominently displayed. Parking regulations authorized by this section do not apply to any state highway unless the parking regulations are approved by the director of transportation.

(D) A board of township trustees or its designated agent may order into storage any vehicle parked in violation of a township parking regulation or order, if the violation is not one that is required to be handled pursuant to Chapter 4521. of the Revised Code. The owner or any lienholder of a vehicle ordered into storage may claim the vehicle upon presentation of proof of ownership, which may be evidenced by a certificate of title to the vehicle, and payment of all expenses, charges, and fines incurred as a result of the parking violation and removal and storage of the vehicle.

(E) Whoever violates any regulation or order adopted pursuant to this section is guilty of a minor misdemeanor, unless the township has enacted a regulation pursuant to division (A) of section 4521.02 of the Revised Code, that specifies that the violation shall not be considered a criminal offense and shall be handled pursuant to Chapter 4521. of the Revised Code. Fines levied and collected under this section shall be paid into the township general revenue fund.

HISTORY: GC § 3287; 123 v 265; Bureau of Code Revision, 10-1-53; 135 v H 200 (Eff 9-23-73); 135 v H 300 (Eff 1-1-74); 138 v S 257 (Eff 6-25-80); 139 v H 707 (Eff 1-1-83); 141 v H 131 (Eff 6-26-86); 142 v H 113. Eff 6-20-88.

Not analogous to former GC § 3287 [RS § 1487], repealed in 112 v 364(385), § 21.

[§ 505.37.3] § 505.373 Adoption of standard code.

The township board of trustees may, by resolution, adopt by incorporation by reference a standard code pertaining to fire, fire hazards and fire prevention, prepared and promulgated by the state, or any department, board, or other agency thereof, or any such code prepared and promulgated by a public or private organization that publishes a model or standard code.

After the adoption of such a code by the board, a notice clearly identifying the code, stating the purpose of the code, and stating that a complete copy of the code is on file with the township clerk for inspection by the public and also on file in the law library of the county in which the township is located and that the clerk has copies available for distribution to the public at cost, shall be posted by the township clerk in five conspicuous places in the township for thirty days before becoming effective. The notice required by this section shall also be published in a newspaper of general circulation in the township for three consecutive weeks. If the adopting township amends or deletes any provision of the code, the notice shall contain a brief summary of the deletion or amendment.

If the agency that originally promulgated or published the code thereafter amends the code, any township that had adopted the code pursuant to this section may adopt the amendment or change by incorporation by reference in the same manner as provided for adoption of the original code.

HISTORY: 135 v H 739. Eff 7-26-74.

[§ 505.37.4] § 505.374 Prohibition.

No person shall violate a provision of a standard code or regulation adopted under section 505.373 [505.37.3] or division (C) of section 505.375 [505.37.5] of the Revised Code. Each day of continued violation of this section shall constitute a separate offense.

HISTORY: 135 v H 739 (Eff 7-26-74); 146 v H 192. Eff 11-21-95.

[TOWNSHIP POLICE DISTRICTS]

§ 505.48 Township police districts.

(A) The board of township trustees of any township may, by resolution adopted by two-thirds of the members of the board, create a township police district comprised of all or a portion of the unincorporated territory of the township as the resolution may specify. If the township police district does not include all of the unincorporated territory of the township, the resolution creating the township police district shall contain a complete and accurate description of the territory of the district. The territorial limits of the township police district may be altered by a resolution adopted by a two-thirds vote of the board of township trustees at any time one hundred twenty days or more after the district has been created and is operative. If the township police district imposes a tax, any territory proposed for addition to the district shall become part of the district only after all of the following have occurred:

(1) Adoption by two-thirds vote of the board of township trustees of a resolution approving the expansion of the territorial limits of the district;

(2) Adoption by a two-thirds vote of the board of township trustees of a resolution recommending the extension of the tax to the additional territory;

(3) Approval of the tax by the electors of the territory proposed for addition to the district.

Each resolution of the board adopted under division (A)(2) of this section shall state the name of the police district, a description of the territory to be added, and the rate and termination date of the tax, which shall be the rate and termination date of the tax currently in effect in the police district.

(B) The board of trustees shall certify each resolution adopted under division (A)(2) of this section to the board of elections in accordance with section 5705.19 of the Revised Code. The election required under division (A)(3) of this section shall be held, canvassed, and certified in the manner provided for the submission of tax levies under section 5705.25 of the Revised Code, except that the question appearing on the ballot shall read:

"Shall the territory within .... (description of the proposed territory to be added) be added to .... township police district, and a property tax at a rate of taxation not exceeding .... (here insert tax rate) be in effect for .... (here insert the number of years the tax is to be in effect or "a continuing period of time," as applicable)?" If the question is approved by at least a majority of the electors voting on it, the joinder shall be effective as of the first day of January of the year following approval, and on that date, the township police district tax shall be extended to the taxable property within the territory that has been added.

A township police district comprising only a part of the unincorporated territory of the township shall be given a separate and distinct name in the resolution authorizing its creation.

HISTORY: 130 v 211 (Eff 9-24-63); 141 v H 743. Eff 3-10-87.

[§ 505.48.1] § 505.481 Joint township police district board.

The boards of township trustees of any two or more contiguous townships, whether or not within the same county, may, by a two-thirds favorable vote of each such board, form themselves into a joint township police district board, and such townships shall be a part of a joint township police district.

Such joint township police district board shall organize within thirty days after the favorable vote by the last board of trustees joining itself into the joint township police district board. The president of the board of township trustees of the most populous participating township shall give notice of the time and place of organization to each member of the board of township trustees of each participating township. Such notice shall be signed by the president of the board of township trustees of the most populous participating township, and shall be sent by certified mail to each member of the board of township trustees of each participating township, at least five days prior to the organization meeting, which meeting shall be held in one of the participating townships. All members of the boards of township trustees of the participating townships constitute the joint township police district board. Two-thirds of all the township trustees of the participating townships constitutes a quorum. Such members of the boards of township trustees shall, at the organization meeting of the joint township police district board, proceed with the election of a president, a secretary, and a treasurer, and such other officers as they consider necessary and proper, and shall transact such other business as properly comes before the board.

In the formation of such a police district, such action may be taken by or on behalf of part of a township, by excluding that portion of the township lying within a municipal corporation. The joint township police district board may exercise the same powers as are granted to a board of township trustees in the operation of a township police district under sections 505.49 to 505.55 of the Revised Code, including, but not limited to, the power to employ, train, and discipline personnel, to acquire equipment and buildings, to levy a tax, to issue bonds and notes, and to dissolve the district.

HISTORY: 144 v H 77. Eff 9-17-91.

§ 505.49 Contract for police protection; status of police department members.

(A) As used in this section, "felony" has the same meaning as in section 109.511 [109.51.1] of the Revised Code.

(B)(1) The township trustees by a two-thirds vote of the board may adopt rules necessary for the operation of the township police district, including a determination of the qualifications of the chief of police, patrol officers, and others to serve as members of the district police force.

(2) Except as otherwise provided in division (E) of this section and subject to division (D) of this section, the township trustees by a two-thirds vote of the board shall appoint a chief of police for the district, determine the number of patrol officers and other personnel required by the district, and establish salary schedules and other conditions of employment for the employees of the township police district. The chief of police of the district shall serve at the pleasure of the township trustees and shall appoint patrol officers and other personnel that the district may require, subject to division (D) of this section and to the rules and limits as to qualifications, salary ranges, and numbers of personnel established by the township board of trustees. The township trustees may include in the township police district and under the direction and control of the chief of police, any constable appointed pursuant to section 509.01 of the Revised Code, or may designate the chief of police or any patrol officer appointed by the chief of police as a constable, as provided for in section 509.01 of the Revised Code, for the township police district.

(3) Except as provided in division (D) of this section, a patrol officer, other police district employee, or police constable, who has been awarded a certificate attesting to the satisfactory completion of an approved state, county, or municipal police basic training program, as required by section 109.77 of the Revised Code, may be removed or suspended only under the conditions and by the procedures in sections 505.491 [505.49.1] to 505.495 [505.49.5] of the Revised Code. Any other patrol officer, police district employee, or police constable shall serve at the pleasure of the township trustees. In case of removal or suspension of an appointee by the board of township trustees, that appointee may appeal the decision of the board to the court of common pleas of the county in which the district is situated to determine the sufficiency of the cause of removal or suspension. The appointee shall take the appeal within ten days of written notice to the appointee of the decision of the board.

(C) Division (B) of this section does not apply to a township that has a population of ten thousand or more persons residing within the township and outside of any municipal corporation, that has its own police department employing ten or more full-time paid employees, and that has a civil service commission established under division (B) of section 124.40 of the Revised Code. That type of township shall comply with the procedures for the employment, promotion, and discharge of police personnel provided by Chapter 124. of the Revised Code, except that the board of township trustees of the township may appoint the chief of police, and a person so appointed shall be in the unclassified service under section 124.11 of the Revised Code and shall serve at the pleasure of the board. A person appointed chief of police under these conditions who is removed by the board or who resigns from the position shall be entitled to return to the classified service in the township police department, in the position that person held previous to the person's appointment as chief of police. The board of township trustees shall determine the number of personnel required and establish salary schedules and conditions of employment not in conflict with Chapter 124. of the Revised Code. Persons employed as police personnel in that type of township on the date a civil service commission is appointed pursuant to division (B) of section 124.40 of the Revised Code, without being required to pass a competitive examination or a police training program, shall retain their employment and any rank previously granted them by action of the township trustees or otherwise, but those persons are eligible for promotion only by compliance with Chapter 124. of the Revised Code. This division does not apply to constables appointed pursuant to section 509.01 of the Revised Code. This division is subject to division (D) of this section.

(D)(1) The board of township trustees shall not appoint or employ a person as a chief of police, and the chief of police shall not appoint or employ a person as a patrol officer or other peace officer of a township police district or a township police department, on a permanent basis, on a temporary basis, for a probationary term, or on other than a permanent basis if the person previously has been convicted of or has pleaded guilty to a felony.

(2)(a) The board of township trustees shall terminate the appointment or employment of a chief of police, patrol officer, or other peace officer of a township police district or township police department who does either of the following:

(i) Pleads guilty to a felony;

(ii) Pleads guilty to a misdemeanor pursuant to a negotiated plea agreement as provided in division (D) of section 2929.29 of the Revised Code in which the chief of police, patrol officer, or other peace officer of a township police district or township police department agrees to surrender the certificate awarded to that chief of police, patrol officer, or other peace officer under section 109.77 of the Revised Code.

(b) The board shall suspend the appointment or employment of a chief of police, patrol officer, or other peace officer of a township police district or township police department who is convicted, after trial, of a felony. If the chief of police, patrol officer, or other peace officer of a township police district or township police department files an appeal from that conviction and the conviction is upheld by the highest court to which the appeal is taken or if no timely appeal is filed, the board shall terminate the appointment or employment of that chief of police, patrol officer, or other peace officer. If the chief of police, patrol officer, or other peace officer of a township police district or township police department files an appeal that results in that chief of police's, patrol officer's, or other peace officer's acquittal of the felony or conviction of a misdemeanor, or in the dismissal of the felony charge against the chief of police, patrol officer, or other peace officer, the board shall reinstate that chief of police, patrol officer, or other peace officer. A chief of police, patrol officer, or other peace officer of a township police district or township police department who is reinstated under division (D)(2)(b) of this section shall not receive any back pay unless the conviction of that chief of police, patrol officer, or other peace officer of the felony was reversed on appeal, or the felony charge was dismissed, because the court found insufficient evidence to convict the chief of police, patrol officer, or other peace officer of the felony.

(3) Division (D) of this section does not apply regarding an offense that was committed prior to January 1, 1997.

(4) The suspension or termination of the appointment or employment of a chief of police, patrol officer, or other peace officer under division (D)(2) of this section shall be in accordance with Chapter 119. of the Revised Code.

(E) The board of township trustees may enter into a contract under section 505.43 or 505.50 of the Revised Code to obtain all police protection for the township police district from one or more municipal corporations, county sheriffs, or other townships. If the board enters into such a contract, subject to division (D) of this section, it may, but is not required to, appoint a police chief for the district.

(F) The members of the police force of a township police district of a township that adopts the limited self-government form of township government shall serve as peace officers for the township territory included in the district.

(G) A chief of police or patrol officer of a township police district, or of a township police department, may participate, as the director of an organized crime task force established under section 177.02 of the Revised Code or as a member of the investigatory staff of that task force, in an investigation of organized criminal activity in any county or counties in this state under sections 177.01 to 177.03 of the Revised Code.

HISTORY: 130 v 211 (Eff 9-24-63); 132 v H 191 (Eff 11-24-67); 135 v H 513 (Eff 8-9-74); 137 v H 671 (Eff 1-13-78); 137 v H 1074 (Eff 4-20-78); 141 v S 74 (Eff 9-3-86); 144 v H 77 (Eff 9-17-91); 144 v S 125 (Eff 4-16-93); 146 v H 566. Eff 10-16-96.

[§ 505.49.1] § 505.491 Trustees to prefer charges against delinquent police personnel.

Except as provided in division (D) of section 505.49 or in division (C) of section 509.01 of the Revised Code, if the board of trustees of a township has reason to believe that a chief of police, patrol officer, or other township police district employee appointed under division (B) of section 505.49 of the Revised Code or a police constable appointed under division (B) of section 509.01 of the Revised Code has been guilty, in the performance of the official duty of that chief of police, patrol officer, other township police district employee, or police constable, of bribery, misfeasance, malfeasance, nonfeasance, misconduct in office, neglect of duty, gross immorality, habitual drunkenness, incompetence, or failure to obey orders given that person by the proper authority, the board immediately shall file written charges against that person, setting forth in detail a statement of the alleged guilt and, at the same time, or as soon thereafter as possible, serve a true copy of those charges upon the person against whom they are made. The service may be made on the person or by leaving a copy of the charges at the office or residence of that person. Return of the service shall be made to the board in the same manner that is provided for the return of the service of summons in a civil action.

HISTORY: 132 v H 191 (Eff 11-24-67); 133 v H 1 (Eff 3-18-69); 135 v H 513 (Eff 8-9-74); 146 v H 566. Eff 10-16-96.

[§ 505.49.2] § 505.492 Hearing of charges; action of township trustees.

Charges filed by the township trustees under section

505.491 [505.49.1] of the Revised Code shall be heard at the next regular meeting thereof, unless the board extends the time for the hearing, which shall be done only on the application of the accused. The accused may appear in person and by counsel, examine all witnesses, and answer all charges against him.

HISTORY: 132 v H 191. Eff 11-24-67.

[§ 505.49.3] § 505.493 Suspension of accused pending hearing.

Pending any proceedings under sections 505.491 [505.49.1] and 505.492 [505.49.2] of the Revised Code, an accused person may be suspended by the board of township trustees, but such suspension shall be for a period not longer than fifteen days, unless the hearing of such charges is extended upon the application of the accused, in which event the suspension shall not exceed thirty days.

HISTORY: 132 v H 191. Eff 11-24-67.

[§ 505.49.4] § 505.494 Power of township trustees as to process.

For the purpose of investigating charges filed pursuant to section 505.491 [505.49.1] of the Revised Code, the board of township trustees may issue subpoenas or compulsory process to compel the attendance of persons and the production of books and papers before it and provide by resolution for exercising and enforcing this section.

HISTORY: 132 v H 191. Eff 11-24-67.

[§ 505.49.5] § 505.495 Oaths; compulsory testimony; costs.

In all cases in which the attendance of witnesses may be compelled for an investigation, under section 505.494 [505.49.4] of the Revised Code, any member of the board of township trustees may administer the requisite oaths. The board has the same power to compel the giving of testimony by attending witnesses as is conferred upon courts. In all such cases, witnesses shall be entitled to the same privileges, immunities, and compensation as are allowed witnesses in civil cases, and the costs of all such proceedings shall be payable from the general fund of the township.

HISTORY: 132 v H 191. Eff 11-24-67.

§ 505.50 Acquisition of equipment and buildings; emergency police protection.

The township trustees may purchase or otherwise acquire any police apparatus, equipment, including a public communications system, or materials that the township police district requires and may build, purchase, or lease any building or buildings and site of the building or buildings that are necessary for the operations of the district.

The boards of trustees of any two or more contiguous townships, may, by joint agreement, unite in the joint purchase, maintenance, use, and operation of police equipment, for any other police purpose designated in sections 505.48 to 505.55 of the Revised Code, and to prorate the expense of such joint action on such terms as are mutually agreed upon by the trustees in each affected township.

The board of trustees of any township may enter into a contract with one or more townships, a municipal corporation, a park district created pursuant to section 511.18 or 1545.01 of the Revised Code, or the county sheriff upon any terms that are mutually agreed upon for the provision of police protection services or additional police protection services either on a regular basis or for additional protection in times of emergency. The contract shall be agreed to in each instance by the respective board or boards of township trustees, the county commissioners, the board of park commissioners, or the legislative authority of the municipal corporation involved. Such contract may provide for a fixed annual charge to be paid at the time agreed upon in the contract.

Chapter 2744. of the Revised Code, insofar as it is applicable to the operation of police departments, applies to the contracting political subdivisions and police department members when such members are serving outside their own subdivision pursuant to such contract. Police department members acting outside the subdivision in which they are employed may participate in any pension or indemnity fund established by their employer and are entitled to all the rights and benefits of Chapter 4123. of the Revised Code, to the same extent while performing services within the subdivision.

HISTORY: 130 v 212 (Eff 9-24-63); 141 v H 176 (Eff 11-20-85); 141 v H 743 (Eff 12-10-86); 144 v S 174. Eff 7-31-92.

§ 505.51 Police district tax levy authorized.

The board of trustees of a township police district may levy a tax upon all of the taxable property in the township police district pursuant to sections 5705.19 and 5705.25 of the Revised Code to defray all or a portion of expenses of the district in providing police protection.

HISTORY: 130 v 213. Eff 9-24-63.

[§ 505.51.1] § 505.511 Fee for false alarm due to security alarm malfunction.

(A) The board of trustees of a township police district may, after the township police, a law enforcement agency with which the township contracts for police services, and the county sheriff or his deputy have answered a combined total of three false alarms resulting from the malfunction of the same commercial or residential security alarm system within the township in the same calendar year, cause the township clerk to mail the manager of the commercial establishment or the occupant, lessee, agent, or tenant of the residence, a bill for twenty-five dollars for each subsequent false alarm from the same alarm system during that year, to defray the costs incurred. If payment of the bill is not received within thirty days, the clerk shall send a notice by certified mail to the manager and to the owner, if different, of the real estate of which the commercial establishment is a part, or to the occupant, lessee, agent, or tenant and to the owner, if different, of the real estate of which the residence is a part, indicating that failure to pay the bill within thirty days, or to show just cause why the bill should not be paid, will result in the assessment of a twenty-five dollar lien upon the real estate. If payment is not received within thirty days or if just cause is not shown, the sum of twenty-five dollars shall be entered upon the tax duplicate, shall be a lien upon the real estate from the date of the entry, and shall be collected as other taxes and returned to the township general fund. The board of trustees of a township police district shall not cause the township clerk to send a bill pursuant to this division if a bill has already been sent pursuant to division (B) of this section for the same false alarm.

(B) The county sheriff may, after he or his deputy, the township police, and a law enforcement agency with which the township contracts for police services have answered a combined total of three false alarms resulting from the malfunction of the same commercial or residential security alarm system within the unincorporated area of the county in the same calendar year, mail the manager of the commercial establishment or the occupant, lessee, agent, or tenant of the residence a bill for twenty-five dollars for each subsequent false alarm from the same alarm system during that year, to defray the costs incurred. If payment of the bill is not received within thirty days, the sheriff shall send a notice by certified mail to the manager and to the owner, if different, of the real estate of which the commercial establishment is a part, or to the occupant, lessee, agent, or tenant and to the owner, if different, of the real estate of which the residence is a part, indicating that the failure to pay the bill within thirty days, or to show just cause why the bill should not be paid, will result in the assessment of a twenty-five dollar lien upon the real estate. If payment is not received within thirty days or if just cause is not shown, the sum of twenty-five dollars shall be entered upon the tax duplicate, shall be a lien upon the real estate from the date of the entry, and shall be collected as other taxes and returned to the county treasury. The sheriff shall not send a bill pursuant to this division if a bill has already been sent pursuant to division (A) of this section for the same false alarm.

(C) As used in this section, "commercial establishment" has the same meaning as in section 505.391 [505.39.1] of the Revised Code.

HISTORY: 141 v H 150 (Eff 9-17-86); 142 v H 420. Eff 6-14-88.

§ 505.52 Bond issues by police district.

The board of trustees of a township police district may issue bonds for the purpose of buying police equipment in the manner provided for in section 133.18 and pursuant to Chapter 133. of the Revised Code. The proceeds of the bonds issued under this section, other than any premium and accrued interest which is credited to the sinking fund, shall be placed in the township treasury to the credit of a fund to be known as the "police equipment fund." Money from the police equipment fund shall be paid out only upon order of the township board of trustees of the township police district.

HISTORY: 130 v 213 (Eff 9-24-63); 143 v H 230. Eff 10-30-89.

§ 505.53 Issuance of notes by police district.

The board of trustees of a township police district may issue notes for a period not to exceed three years for the purpose of buying police equipment or a building or site to house police equipment. One-third of the purchase price of the equipment, building, or site shall be paid at the time of purchase, and the remainder of the purchase price shall be covered by notes maturing in two and three years respectively. Notes may bear interest not to exceed the rate determined as provided in section 9.95 of the Revised Code, and shall not be subject to Chapter 133. of the Revised Code. Such notes shall be offered for sale on the open market or given to a vendor if no sale is made.

HISTORY: 130 v 213 (Eff 9-24-63); 138 v H 275 (Eff 11-1-79); 139 v H 95 (Eff 5-13-81); 143 v H 230. Eff 10-30-89.

§ 505.54 Additional training for police district personnel.

The board of trustees of the township may, upon nomination by the chief of police, send one or more of the officers, patrolmen, or other employees of the township police district to a school of instruction designed to provide additional training or skills related to the employees work assignment in the district. The trustees may make advance tuition payments for any employee so nominated and may defray all or a portion of the employee's expenses while receiving this instruction.

HISTORY: 130 v 213. Eff 9-24-63.

[§ 505.54.1] § 505.541 Parking enforcement unit.

(A) The board of township trustees may establish, by

resolution, a parking enforcement unit within a township police district, and provide for the regulation of parking enforcement officers. The chief of police of the district shall be the executive head of the parking enforcement unit, shall make all appointments and removals of parking enforcement officers, subject to any general rules prescribed by the board of township trustees by resolution, and shall prescribe rules for the organization, training, administration, control, and conduct of the parking enforcement unit. The chief of police may appoint parking enforcement officers who agree to serve for nominal compensation, and persons with physical disabilities may receive appointments as parking enforcement officers.

(B) The authority of the parking enforcement officers shall be limited to the enforcement of section 4511.69 of the Revised Code and any other parking laws specified in the resolution creating the parking enforcement unit. Parking enforcement officers shall have no other powers.

(C) The training the parking enforcement officers shall receive shall include instruction in general administrative rules and procedures governing the parking enforcement unit, the role of the judicial system as it relates to parking regulation and enforcement, proper techniques and methods relating to the enforcement of parking laws, human interaction skills, and first aid.

HISTORY: 143 v S 174. Eff 7-13-90.

§ 505.55 Dissolution of police district.

In the event that need for a township police district ceases to exist, the township trustees by a two-thirds vote of the board shall adopt a resolution specifying the date that the township police district shall cease to exist and provide for the disposal of all property belonging to the district by public sale. Such sale must be by public auction and upon notice thereof being published once a week for three weeks in a newspaper published, or of general circulation in such township, the last of such publications to be at least five days before the date of the sale. Any moneys remaining after the dissolution of the district or received from the public sale of property shall be paid into the treasury of the township and may be expended for any public purpose when duly authorized by the township board of trustees.

HISTORY: 130 v 213. Eff 9-24-63.

§ 505.73 Standard code for repair and maintenance of structures and premises.

The board of township trustees may, by resolution, adopt by incorporation by reference, administer, and enforce within the unincorporated area of the township an existing structures code pertaining to the repair and continued maintenance of structures and the premises of such structures. For such purpose, the board shall adopt any model or standard code prepared and promulgated by the state, any department, board, or other agency of the state, or any public or private organization that publishes a recognized model or standard code on the subject. The board shall ensure that the code adopted is fully compatible with the local residential building code and with the rules of the board of building standards adopted pursuant to section 3781.10 of the Revised Code.

The board shall assign the duties of administering and enforcing the code to a township officer or employee who is trained and qualified for such duties and shall establish by resolution the minimum qualifications necessary for performance of such duties.

After the board adopts a code, the township clerk shall post a notice which shall clearly identify the code, state the purpose of the code, state that a complete copy of the code is on file for inspection by the public with the township clerk and in the law library of the county in which the township is located, and state that the clerk has copies available for distribution to the public at cost. The township clerk shall post the notice in five conspicuous places in the township for thirty days before the code becomes effective. The clerk shall also publish the notice in a newspaper of general circulation in the township for three consecutive weeks. If the adopting township amends or deletes any provision of the code, the notice shall contain a brief summary of the deletion or amendment.

If the agency that originally promulgated or published the code thereafter amends the code, any township that has adopted the code pursuant to this section may adopt the amendment or change by incorporation by reference in the same manner as provided for adoption of the original code.

HISTORY: 142 v H 285. Eff 10-20-87.

§ 505.74 Violations prohibited.

No person shall violate a standard existing structures code as adopted pursuant to section 505.73 of the Revised Code. Each day of continued violation of this section constitutes a separate offense.

HISTORY: 142 v H 285. Eff 10-20-87.

[TOWNSHIP BUILDING CODE]

§ 505.75 Township building code; building regulation department; inspector.

(A) A board of township trustees may, by resolution, adopt by incorporation by reference, administer, and enforce a standard code pertaining to the erection, construction, repair, alteration, and maintenance of single-family, two-family, and three-family dwellings promulgated by the state, or any department, board, or other agency thereof, or by any municipal corporation or county in this state, within the unincorporated territory of the township, or establish districts in any part of the unincorporated territory and adopt, administer, and enforce such standard code in the affected districts. When adopted, all regulations contained in such code, including those establishing service charges, shall be uniform within all districts in which building codes are established, except that more stringent regulations may be imposed in flood hazard areas in order to prevent or reduce the hazard resulting from flooding. In no case shall regulations exceed the scope of regulating the safety, health, and sanitary conditions of such buildings. Any person adversely affected by a resolution of the board adopting, amending, or rescinding a regulation may seek a declaratory judgment pursuant to Chapter 2721. of the Revised Code on the ground that the board failed to comply with the law in adopting, amending, rescinding, publishing, or distributing the regulation, or that the regulation, as adopted or amended by the board, is unreasonable or unlawful, or that the revision of the regulation was unreasonable or unlawful.

A township building code may include regulations that are necessary for participation in the national flood insurance program and are not in conflict with the Ohio building code, governing the prohibition, location, erection, construction, or floodproofing of new buildings or structures, or substantial improvements to existing buildings or structures, in unincorporated territory within flood hazard areas identified under the "Flood Disaster Protection Act of 1973," 87 Stat. 975, 42 U.S.C. 4002, as amended, including, but not limited to, residential, commercial, or industrial buildings or structures.

(B) Regulations or amendments may be adopted under this section only after public hearing at not fewer than two regular sessions of the board. The board shall cause to be published in a newspaper of general circulation in the township notice of the public hearings, including time, date, and place, once a week for two weeks immediately preceding the hearings. The proposed regulations or amendments shall be made available by the board to the public at the board office.

The township building code shall be adopted if it is approved by an affirmative vote of all members of the board of township trustees.

The building code and any amendments to the building code adopted by the board become effective thirty days after the date of adoption unless, within thirty days after the adoption of the building code or amendments, there is presented to the board a petition, signed by a number of qualified voters residing in the unincorporated area of the township equal to not less than eight per cent of the total vote cast for all candidates for governor in the area at the most recent general election at which a governor was elected, requesting the board to submit the building code or amendments to the electors of such area for approval or rejection at the next primary or general election.

No building code or amendments for which the referendum vote has been requested shall be put into effect unless a majority of the vote cast on the issue is in favor of the building code or amendments. Upon certification by the board of elections they take immediate effect.

(C) The board of township trustees may establish a building regulation department and employ personnel to enforce building regulations. Upon certification of the building department under section 3781.10 of the Revised Code, the board of trustees may direct the township building department to exercise enforcement authority and to accept and approve plans pursuant to sections 3781.03 and 3791.04 of the Revised Code for any other kind or class of building in the unincorporated territory of the township.

For the purposes of administering and enforcing the regulations, the board of township trustees may create, establish, fill, and fix the compensation of the position of township building inspector. The inspector shall be the chief administrative officer of the township building regulation department and shall administer and enforce the building regulations. In lieu of the creation of the position of township building inspector, the board may assign the duties of the inspector to an existing township officer.

(D) The board of township trustees may contract with any municipal corporation or with a board of county commissioners for the administration and enforcement of building regulations, and any municipal corporation or board of county commissioners may contract with a board of township trustees for the administration and enforcement of the building regulations of the municipal corporation or county.

HISTORY: 137 v S 155 (Eff 11-16-77); 146 v H 99. Eff 8-22-95.

§ 505.76 Availability of regulations; publication of notice.

(A) Building regulations adopted or amended by a board of township trustees under sections 505.75 to 505.77 of the Revised Code shall be made available to the public at the office of the board, and the section headings and numbers and a notice of the availability of the regulations shall be published in at least one newspaper of general townshipwide circulation within ten days after their adoption or amendment.

(B) In a county in which the board of county commissioners has adopted building regulations, no township shall adopt such regulations pursuant to sections 505.75 to 505.77 of the Revised Code.

HISTORY: 137 v S 155. Eff 11-16-77.

§ 505.77 Prohibitions.

(A) No person shall erect, construct, alter, repair, or maintain any single-family, two-family, or three-family dwellings, within the unincorporated portion of any township, if the board of township trustees has adopted a standard code under section 505.75 of the Revised

Code, without complying with the building regulations. No person shall erect, construct, alter, repair, or maintain any residential, commercial, or industrial buildings or structures within the unincorporated area of any township, if a board of township trustees has enacted building regulations under section 505.75 of the Revised Code that are necessary for participation in the national flood insurance program, without complying with such regulations. If any building is being erected, constructed, altered, repaired, or maintained in violation of the building regulations, the board or the township building inspector, or any adjacent, contiguous, or neighboring property owner who would be especially damaged by such violation, in addition to the remedies provided by law, may institute a suit for injunction, abatement, or other appropriate action to prevent the violation of the regulations relating to the erection, construction, alteration, repair, or maintenance of such building.

(B) Sections 505.75 to 505.77 of the Revised Code do not confer any power on any board with respect to the location, erection, construction, reconstruction, change, alteration, maintenance, removal, use, or enlargement of any buildings or structures of any public utility or railroad, whether publicly or privately owned, or the use of land by any public utility or railroad for the operation of its business. Regulations or amendments adopted by the board shall not affect buildings or structures which exist or on which construction has begun on or before the date on which the regulations or amendments are adopted by the board.

(C) No person shall violate any regulation of the board adopted under section 505.75 of the Revised Code. Each day during which an illegal location, erection, construction, flood-proofing, repair, alteration, or maintenance continues may be considered a separate offense.

HISTORY: 137 v S 155. Eff 11-16-77.

§ 505.99 Penalty.

Whoever violates section 505.374 [505.37.4], 505.74, 505.75, 505.76, 505.77, or 505.94 of the Revised Code is guilty of a minor misdemeanor.

HISTORY: 135 v H 739 (Eff 7-26-74); 137 v S 155 (Eff 11-16-77); 139 v S 80 (Eff 3-15-82); 141 v H 85 (Eff 3-6-86); 142 v H 285 (Eff 10-20-87); 146 v S 2. Eff 7-1-96.

The effective date is set by section 6 of SB 2.

CHAPTER 509: CONSTABLES

§ 509.01 Constables; compensation.

(A) As used in this section, "felony" has the same meaning as in section 109.511 [109.51.1] of the Revised Code.

(B) Subject to division (C) of this section, the board of township trustees may designate any qualified persons as police constables and may provide them with the automobiles, communication systems, uniforms, and police equipment that the board considers necessary. Except as provided in division (C) of this section, police constables designated under this division, who have been awarded a certificate attesting to the satisfactory completion of an approved state, county, or municipal police basic training program, as required by section 109.77 of the Revised Code, may be removed or suspended only under the conditions and by the procedures in sections 505.491 [505.49.1] to 505.495 [505.49.5] of the Revised Code. Any other police constable shall serve at the pleasure of the township trustees. In case of removal or suspension of a police constable by the board of township trustees, that police constable may appeal the decision of the board to the court of common pleas of the county to determine the sufficiency of the cause of removal or suspension. The police constable shall take the appeal within ten days of written notice to the police constable of the decision of the board. The board may pay each police constable, from the general funds of the township, the compensation that the board by resolution prescribes for the time actually spent in keeping the peace, protecting property, and performing duties as a police constable, including duties as an ex officio deputy bailiff of a municipal court pursuant to section 1901.32 of the Revised Code and duties as a ministerial officer of a county court. The police constable shall not be paid fees in addition to the compensation allowed by the board for services rendered as a police constable, including services as an ex officio deputy bailiff of a municipal court pursuant to section 1901.32 of the Revised Code and as a ministerial officer of a county court. All constable fees provided for by section 509.15 of the Revised Code, if due for services rendered while the police constable performing those services is being compensated as a police constable for that performance, shall be paid into the general fund of the township.

(C)(1) The board of township trustees shall not designate a person as a police constable pursuant to division (B) of this section on a permanent basis, on a temporary basis, for a probationary term, or on other than a permanent basis if the person previously has been convicted of or has pleaded guilty to a felony.

(2)(a) The board of township trustees shall terminate the employment of a police constable designated under division (B) of this section if the police constable does either of the following:

(i) Pleads guilty to a felony;

(ii) Pleads guilty to a misdemeanor pursuant to a negotiated plea agreement as provided in division (D) of section 2929.29 of the Revised Code in which the police constable agrees to surrender the certificate awarded to the police constable under section 109.77 of the Revised Code.

(b) The board shall suspend from employment a police constable designated under division (B) of this section if the police constable is convicted, after trial, of a felony. If the police constable files an appeal from that conviction and the conviction is upheld by the highest court to which the appeal is taken or if the police constable does not file a timely appeal, the board shall terminate the employment of that police constable. If the police constable files an appeal that results in that police constable's acquittal of the felony or conviction of a misdemeanor, or in the dismissal of the felony charge against the police constable, the board shall reinstate that police constable. A police constable who is reinstated under division (C)(2)(b) of this section shall not receive any back pay unless that police constable's conviction of the felony was reversed on appeal, or the felony charge was dismissed, because the court found insufficient evidence to convict the police constable of the felony.

(3) Division (C) of this section does not apply regarding an offense that was committed prior to January 1, 1997.

(4) The suspension from employment, or the termination of the employment, of a police constable under division (C)(2) of this section shall be in accordance with Chapter 119. of the Revised Code.

HISTORY: 128 v 823 (Eff 11-6-59); 132 v H 191 (Eff 11-24-67); 141 v H 159 (Eff 3-19-87); 146 v H 566. Eff 10-16-96.

Not analogous to former RC § 509.01 (RS §§ 1442, 1448; S&S 914; S&C 85, 802, 1566, 1567; 51 v 179, § 182; 51 v 489, §§ 5, 8; 56 v 156; 65 v 87, § 7; 83 v 28; 85 v 131; 86 v 94; 87 v 118; 89 v 65; 89 v 195; 90 v 144; 97 v 39; 97 v 62; 97 v 187; 98 v 171; 98 v 172; GC § 3327; Bureau of Code Revision, 10-1-53), repealed 128 v 823(862), § 2, eff 11-6-59.

§ 509.02 Bond.

Each constable, before entering upon the discharge of his duties, shall give bond to the state in a sum of not less than five hundred nor more than two thousand dollars, conditioned for the faithful and diligent discharge of his duties, and with sureties resident of the township. The amount of such bond and its sureties shall be approved by the board of township trustees. Such bond shall be deposited with the township clerk.

HISTORY: RS § 1516; S&C 802, 1567; 51 v 179, §§ 183 to 185; 51 v 489, § 9; GC § 3328; Bureau of Code Revision. Eff 10-1-53.

§ 509.03
Repealed, 128 v 823, § 2 [RS §§ 6683, 6684; S&C 802; 51 v 179, § 187; 56 v 19, § 186; GC §§ 3329, 3330; Bureau of Code Revision, 10-1-53]. Eff 11-6-59.

This section concerned a vacancy in the constable's office.

§ 509.04 Parking enforcement unit.

(A) The board of township trustees may establish, by resolution, a parking enforcement unit within the office of a township constable, and provide for the regulation of parking enforcement officers. The board of township trustees shall appoint a police constable as executive head of the parking enforcement unit, who shall make all appointments and removals of parking enforcement officers, subject to any general rules prescribed by the board of township trustees by resolution, and shall prescribe rules for the organization, training, administration, control, and conduct of the parking enforcement unit. The executive head of the parking enforcement unit may appoint parking enforcement officers who agree to serve for nominal compensation, and persons with physical disabilities may receive appointments as parking enforcement officers.

(B) The authority of the parking enforcement officers shall be limited to the enforcement of section 4511.69 of the Revised Code and any other parking laws specified in the resolution creating the parking enforcement unit. Parking enforcement officers shall have no other powers.

(C) The training the parking enforcement officers shall receive shall include instruction in general administrative rules and procedures governing the parking enforcement unit, the role of the judicial system as it relates to parking regulation and enforcement, proper techniques and methods relating to the enforcement of parking laws, human interaction skills, and first aid.

HISTORY: 143 v S 174. Eff 7-13-90.

Not analogous to former RC § 509.04 (RS §§ 6685-6687; S&C 803; 51 v 179, §§ 188-190; GC §§ 3331-3333; 124 v 353; Bureau of Code Revision, 10-1-53), repealed 128 v 823, § 2, eff 11-6-59.

§ 509.05 Sheriffs and constables ministerial officers of county court; powers and duties of constables.

In addition to the county sheriff, constables shall be ministerial officers of the county court in all cases in their respective townships, and in criminal cases, they shall be such officers within the county. They shall apprehend and bring to justice felons and disturbers of the peace, suppress riots, and keep and preserve the peace within the county. They may execute all writs and process, in criminal cases, throughout the county in which they reside, and in which they were elected or appointed. If a person charged with the commission of a crime or offense flees from justice, any constable of the county wherein such crime or offense was committed shall pursue and arrest such fugitive in any other county of the state and convey him before the county court of the county where such crime or offense was committed.

Such constables shall serve and execute all warrants, writs, precepts, executions, and other process directed and delivered to them, and shall do all things pertaining to the office of constable.

The authority of a constable in serving any process, either civil or criminal, and in doing his duties generally shall extend throughout the county in which he is appointed, and in executing and serving process issued by a judge of the county court, he may exercise the same authority and powers over goods and chattels, and the persons of parties, as is granted to a sheriff or coroner, under like process issued from courts of record.

A constable may participate, as the director of an organized crime task force established under section 177.02 of the Revised Code or as a member of the investigatory staff of such a task force, in an investigation of organized criminal activity in any county or counties in this state under sections 177.01 to 177.03 of the Revised Code.

HISTORY: 127 v 1039 (Eff 1-1-58); 141 v S 74. Eff 9-3-86.

Analogous to former RC § 509.05 (RS §§ 6689, 6699, 6995; S&C 803, 804, 814; 35 v 87, § 25; 51 v 179, §§ 192, 198; GC §§ 3335, 3341, 3345; Bureau of Code Revision, 10-1-53), repealed in 127 v 978, § 2, eff 1-1-58.

§ 509.06 Aid of sheriff.

Constables, marshals, chiefs of police, and other police officers, in discharging their duties, may call the sheriff or a deputy sheriff to their aid in state cases.

HISTORY: RS § 6690; S&C 803; 51 v 179, § 193; GC § 3336; 108 v Pt II 1203; Bureau of Code Revision. Eff 10-1-53.

§ 509.07 Return of process.

Each constable shall, at the proper office and on the proper return day, make due return of all process directed and delivered to him. If the judgment upon which such constable has an execution is docketed in the court of common pleas, appealed, or stayed, on notice to return the execution, he shall state such fact on the execution.

HISTORY: RS § 6691; S&C 803; 51 v 179, § 194; GC § 3337; Bureau of Code Revision. Eff 10-1-53.

§ 509.08 Time of receiving writ.

Each constable, on the receipt of any writ or other process, except subpoenas, shall note thereon the time of receiving it. He shall also state in his return on such writ or process the time and manner of executing it.

HISTORY: RS § 6692; S&C 804; 51 v 179, § 195; GC § 3338; Bureau of Code Revision. Eff 10-1-53.

§ 509.09 Return of "not found."

No constable shall make a return on any process of "not found," as to any defendant, unless he has been to the usual place of residence of the defendant at least once, if such defendant has a residence in the county.

HISTORY: RS § 6693; S&C 804; 51 v 179, § 196; GC § 3339; Bureau of Code Revision. Eff 10-1-53.

§ 509.10 Arrest on view or warrant; keep the peace.

Each constable shall apprehend, on view or warrant, and bring to justice, all felons, disturbers, and violators of the criminal laws of this state, and shall suppress all riots, affrays, and unlawful assemblies which come to his knowledge, and shall generally keep the peace in his township.

HISTORY: RS § 6694; S&C 804; 51 v 179, § 197; GC § 3340; Bureau of Code Revision, 10-1-53; 128 v 823. Eff 11-6-59.

§ 509.11 Copy of process to be left with jailer.

When it becomes the duty of the constable to take a person to the county jail, such constable shall deliver to the sheriff or jailer a certified copy of the execution, commitment, or other process, whereby he holds such person in custody, and shall return the original to the judge who issued it. Such copy is sufficient authority to the sheriff or jailer to keep the prisoner in jail until discharged.

HISTORY: RS § 6696; S&C 804; 51 v 179, § 199; GC § 3342; Bureau of Code Revision, 10-1-53; 132 v H 2. Eff 2-14-67.

§ 509.12 Payment of moneys.

A constable shall pay over to the party entitled thereto, all moneys received by such constable in his official capacity, if demand is made by such party, his agent, or attorney, at any time before the constable returns the writ upon which he has received such moneys. If the money is not paid over by that time, the constable shall pay it to the judge of the county court when he returns the writ.

HISTORY: RS § 6697; S&C 804; 51 v 179, § 200; GC § 3343; Bureau of Code Revision, 10-1-53; 128 v 823. Eff 11-6-59.

§ 509.13 Forfeiture.

Constables shall be liable to a ten per cent forfeiture upon the amount of damages for which judgment may be entered against them, for failing to make return, making a false return, or failing to pay over money collected or received by them in their official capacity. Such judgment must include, in addition to the damages and costs, the forfeiture provided by this section.

HISTORY: RS § 6698; S&C 804; 51 v 179, § 201; GC § 3344; Bureau of Code Revision. Eff 10-1-53.

§ 509.14 Repealed, 139 v S 114, § 2 [RS § 1534; 75 v 48; GC § 3346; Bureau of Code Revision, 10-1-53]. Eff 10-27-81.

This section concerned compensation for advertising elections.

§ 509.15 Fees of constables.

The following fees and expenses shall be taxed as costs, collected from the judgment debtor, and paid to the general fund of the appropriate township or district as compensation due for services rendered by township constables or members of the police force of a township police district or joint police district:

(A) Serving and making return of each of the following:

(1) Order to commit to jail, order on jailer for prisoner, or order of ejectment, including copies to complete service, one dollar for each defendant named therein;

(2) Search warrant or warrant of arrest, for each person named in the writ, five dollars;

(3) Writ of attachment of property, except for purpose of garnishment, twenty dollars;

(4) Writ of attachment for the purpose of garnishment, five dollars;

(5) Writ of possession or restitution, twenty dollars;

(6) Attachment for contempt, for each person named in the writ, three dollars;

(7) Writ of replevin, twenty dollars;

(8) Summons and writs, subpoena, venire, and notice to garnishee, including copies to complete service, three dollars for each person named therein;

(9) Execution against property or person, eighty cents, and six per cent of all money thus collected;

(10) Any other writ, order, or notice required by law, for each person named therein, including copies to complete service, three dollars for the first name and fifty cents for each additional name.

(B) Mileage for the distance actually and necessarily traveled in serving and returning any of the preceding writs, orders, and notices, fifty cents for the first mile and for each additional mile, twenty cents;

(C) For attending a criminal case during the trial or hearing and having charge of prisoners, each case, two dollars and fifty cents, but, when so acting, such constable shall not be entitled to a witness fee if called upon to testify;

(D) For attending civil court during a jury trial, each case, two dollars;

(E) For attending civil court during a trial without jury, each case, one dollar and fifty cents;

(F) The actual amount paid solely for the transportation, meals, and lodging of prisoners, and for the moving and storage of goods and the care of animals taken on any legal process, such expense shall be specifically itemized on the back of the writs and sworn to;

(G) For summoning and swearing appraisers, each case, two dollars;

(H) For advertising property for sale, by posting, taken on any legal process, one dollar;

(I) For taking and making return of any bond required by law, eighty cents.

Notwithstanding anything to the contrary in this section, if any comparable fee or expense specified under section 311.17 of the Revised Code is increased to an amount greater than that set forth in this section, the board of township trustees, board of trustees of the township police district, or joint township police district board, as appropriate, may require that the amount taxed as costs under this section equal the amount specified under section 311.17 of the Revised Code.

HISTORY: RS § 622; S&S 368; S&C 638; 62 v 89, § 2; GC § 3347; 108 v PtII, 1203; 109 v 303; Bureau of Code Revision, 10-1-53; 130 v 214 (Eff 8-19-63); 146 v H 56. Eff 8-23-95.

§ 509.16 Repealed, 128 v 823 (862), § 2 [RS § 6688a; 94 v 43; GC § 3348; 121 v 608; 122 v 685; 124 v 353; Bureau of Code Revision, 10-1-53]. Eff 11-6-59.

This section was about the designation and compensation of police constables and related fees.

TITLE 7: MUNICIPAL CORPORATIONS

CHAPTER 715: GENERAL POWERS

[PEACE AND MORALS]

§ 715.48 Regulation by license of shows and games; trafficking in tickets; exceptions.

Any municipal corporation may:
(A) Regulate, by license or otherwise, restrain, or prohibit theatrical exhibitions, public shows, and athletic games, of whatever name or nature, for which money or other reward is demanded or received;
(B) Regulate, by license or otherwise, the business of trafficking in theatrical tickets, or other tickets of licensed amusements, by parties not acting as agents of those issuing them.

Public school entertainments, lecture courses, and lectures on historic, literary, or scientific subjects do not come within this section.

HISTORY: Bates § 1536-100; 96 v 22, § 7-7; 97 v 505, § 7-7; 99 v 5, § 7g; GC § 3657; 102 v 88; Bureau of Code Revision. Eff 10-1-53.

§ 715.49 Preservation of peace and protection of property.

(A) Any municipal corporation may prevent riot, gambling, noise and disturbance, and indecent and disorderly conduct or assemblages, preserve the peace and good order, and protect the property of the municipal corporation and its inhabitants.
(B) Anytime a noise ordinance of a municipal corporation is violated, but the source of the noise is located outside the borders of that municipal corporation in an adjoining municipal corporation, the municipal corporation with the ordinance may enforce the ordinance against that source as long as there is a written agreement between the two municipal corporations permitting such enforcement.

HISTORY: Bates § 1536-100; 96 v 22, § 7-1; 97 v 504, § 7-1; 99 v 5, § 7a; GC § 3658; Bureau of Code Revision, 10-1-53; 145 v S 264. Eff 9-29-94.

§ 715.50 Police jurisdiction outside municipal corporation.

A municipal corporation owning and using lands beyond its limits for a municipal purpose may provide, by ordinance or resolution, all needful police or sanitary regulations for the protection of such property and may prosecute violations thereof in the municipal court of such municipal corporation.

HISTORY: GC § 3658-1; 120 v 150; Bureau of Code Revision, 10-1-53; 136 v H 205. Eff 1-1-76.

§ 715.51 Billiards, pool, and gambling.

Any municipal corporation may:
(A) Regulate billiard and pool tables, nine or ten pin alleys or tables, and shooting and ball alleys;
(B) Authorize the destruction of instruments or devices used for the purpose of gambling.

HISTORY: Bates § 1536-100; 96 v 22, § 7-2; 97 v 505, § 7-2; 99 v 5, § 7b; GC § 3659; Bureau of Code Revision. Eff 10-1-53.

§ 715.52 Houses of ill fame.

Any municipal corporation may:
(A) Suppress and restrain disorderly houses and houses of ill fame;
(B) Provide for the punishment of all lewd and lascivious behavior in the streets and other public places.

HISTORY: Bates § 1536-100; 96 v 22, § 7-5; 97 v 505, § 7-5; 99 v 5, § 7d; GC § 3660; Bureau of Code Revision. Eff 10-1-53.

§ 715.53 Taverns.

Any municipal corporation may regulate taverns and other houses for public entertainment.

HISTORY: Bates § 1536-100; 96 v 22, § 7-6; 97 v 505, § 7-6; 99 v 5, § 7f; GC § 3662; Bureau of Code Revision. Eff 10-1-53.

§ 715.54 Vicious literature.

Any municipal corporation may restrain and prohibit the distribution, sale, and exposure for sale of books, papers, pictures, and periodicals or advertising matters of an obscene or immoral nature.

HISTORY: Bates § 1536-100; 96 v 25, § 7-24; 97 v 509, § 7-24; 99 v 9, § 7x; GC § 3663; Bureau of Code Revision. Eff 10-1-53.

§§ 715.55 to 715.58 Repealed, 146 v S 2, § 6 [RS §§ 2108-2111; S&C 1554, 1555; Bates §§ 1536-318—1536-321; 66 v 183, §§ 200-202; 67 v 75, § 203; GC §§ 3664-3667; 103 v 168; 111 v 17; 120 v 320; Bureau of Code Revision, 10-1-53; 133 v S 460; 140 v H 277; 140 v H 113]. Eff 7-1-96.

These sections concerned punishment for disturbance of public peace, punishment of breaches of peace, imprisonment for refusal or neglect to pay fine, rate of credit upon fine, and regulation as to prison labor.

§ 715.59 Hospitals for diseased prisoners.

The legislative authority of a municipal corporation may provide suitable hospitals for the reception and care of such prisoners as are diseased or disabled, under such regulations and the charge of such persons as the legislative authority directs.

HISTORY: RS § 2112; S&C 1555; Bates § 1536-322; 66 v 183, § 204; GC § 3668; Bureau of Code Revision. Eff 10-1-53.

[LICENSES]

§ 715.60 Regulation of explosives.

Any municipal corporation may regulate the transportation, keeping, and sale of gunpowder and other explosives or dangerous combustibles and materials, and provide or license magazines therefor.

HISTORY: Bates § 1536-100; 96 v 23, § 7-11; 97 v 506, § 7-11; 99 v 6, § 7k; GC § 3669; Bureau of Code Revision. Eff 10-1-53.

§ 715.61 Regulation and licensing of certain occupations and premises.

Any municipal corporation may regulate and license manufacturers and dealers in explosives, chattel mortgage and salary loan brokers, peddlers, public ballrooms, scavengers, intelligence officers, billiard rooms, bowling alleys, livery, sale, and boarding stables, dancing or riding academies or schools, race courses, ball grounds, street musicians, secondhand dealers, junk shops, and all persons engaged in the trade, business, or profession of manicuring, massaging, or chiropody. In the granting of any license a municipal corporation may charge such fees as the legislative authority deems proper and expedient.

HISTORY: Bates § 1536-100; 97 v 509, § 7-30; 99 v 9, § 7dd; GC § 3670; 101 v 232; Bureau of Code Revision, 10-1-53; 145 v H 376. Eff 7-22-94.

§ 715.62 Evidence.

In the trial of any action brought under section 715.61 of the Revised Code, the fact that any party to such action represented himself as engaged in any business or occupation, for the transaction of which a license is required, or as the keeper, proprietor, or manager of the thing for which a license is required, or that such party exhibits a sign indicating such business or calling, or such proprietorship or management, shall be conclusive evidence of the liability of the party to pay such license fee.

HISTORY: Bates § 1536-100; 97 v 509, § 7-30; 99 v 9, § 7dd; GC § 3671; Bureau of Code Revision. Eff 10-1-53.

§ 715.63 License power; exception.

Any municipal corporation may license exhibitors of shows or performances of any kind, hawkers, peddlers, auctioneers of horses and other animals on the highways or public grounds of the municipal corporation, vendors of gunpowder and other explosives, taverns, houses of public entertainment, and hucksters in the public streets or markets. The municipal corporation may, in granting such license, charge such fee as is reasonable. No municipal corporation may require of the owner of any product of his own raising, or the manufacturer of any article manufactured by him, a license to vend or sell, by himself or his agent, any such article or product. The legislative authority of such municipal corporation may delegate to the mayor of the municipal corporation the authority to grant, issue, and revoke licenses.

HISTORY: RS § 2669; Bates § 1536-327; 66 v 223, § 447; 76 v 167, § 1; 77 v 74; 82 v 148; 86 v 164; GC § 3672; 101 v 37; Bureau of Code Revision. Eff 10-1-53.

§ 715.64 Licensing transient dealers and solicitors.

Any municipal corporation may license transient dealers, persons who temporarily open stores or places for the sale of goods, wares, or merchandise, and each person who, on the streets or traveling from place to place about such municipal corporation, sells, bargains to sell, or solicits orders for goods, wares, or merchandise by retail. Such license shall be granted as provided by section 715.63 of the Revised Code.

This section does not apply to persons selling by sample only, nor to any agricultural articles or products offered or exposed for sale by the producer.

HISTORY: RS §§ 2669b, 2670-1 (Bates' Edition, 1902); Bates §§ 1536-328, 1536-331; 86 v 244; 87 v 100, § 1; 90 v 311; GC §§ 3673, 3676; Bureau of Code Revision. Eff 10-1-53.

§ 715.65 Licensing of advertising mediums and matters.

Any municipal corporation may license bill-posters, advertising sign painters, bill distributors, card tackers, and advertising matter of any article or compound which has not been manufactured or compounded within such municipal corporation. In granting such license the legislative authority of such municipal corporation may fix such license fees as are expedient, and may delegate to the mayor thereof the authority to grant, issue, and revoke such license.

This section does not authorize such legislative authority to charge merchants doing business therein a license fee for advertising their own business.

HISTORY: RS § 2669c; Bates § 1536-329; 91 v 362; GC § 3674; Bureau of Code Revision. Eff 10-1-53.

§ 715.66 Vehicle license; money to be used for street repairs.

Any municipal corporation may license the owners of vehicles used for the transportation of persons or property, for hire, and all undertakers and owners of hearses.

The owners of such vehicles may be made liable for the breach of any ordinance regulating the conduct of the drivers thereof.

All moneys and receipts, in any municipal corporation, which are derived from the enforcement of any ordinance or law requiring the payment of a vehicle license fee, shall be credited and paid into a separate fund, which fund shall be known as "the public service street repair fund." All moneys and receipts credited to such fund shall be used for the sole purpose of repairing streets, avenues, alleys, and lanes within such municipal corporation.

HISTORY: RS § 2670; Bates § 1536-330; 66 v 224, § 448; GC § 3675; 101 v 147; Bureau of Code Revision. Eff 10-1-53.

[MISDEMEANOR]

§ 715.67 Violation of ordinances may be made a misdemeanor.

Any municipal corporation may make the violation of any of its ordinances a misdemeanor, and provide for the punishment thereof by fine or imprisonment, or both. The fine, imposed under authority of this section, shall not exceed five hundred dollars and imprisonment shall not exceed six months.

HISTORY: Bates § 1536-100; 96 v 25, 7-29; 97 v 509, § 7-29; 99 v 9, § 7cc; GC § 3628; Bureau of Code Revision. Eff 10-1-53.

CHAPTER 731: ORGANIZATION

§ 731.36 Prohibited practices relative to petitions.

No person shall, directly or indirectly:

(A) Willfully misrepresent the contents of any initiative or referendum petition;

(B) Pay or offer to pay any elector anything of value for signing an initiative or referendum petition;

(C) Promise to help another person to obtain appointment to any office provided for by the constitution or laws of this state or by the ordinances of any municipal corporation, or to any position or employment in the service of the state or any political subdivision thereof as a consideration for obtaining signatures to an initiative or referendum petition;

(D) Obtain signatures to any initiative or referendum petition as a consideration for the assistance or promise of assistance of another person in securing an appointment to any office or position provided for by the constitution or laws of this state or by the ordinance of any municipal corporation therein, or employment in the service of the state or any subdivision thereof;

(E) Alter, add to, or erase any signatures or names on the parts of a petition after such parts have been filed with the city auditor or village clerk;

(F) Fail to file the sworn itemized statement required in section 731.35 of the Revised Code.

HISTORY: GC § 4227-10; 106 v 443; 104 v 238; Bureau of Code Revision. Eff 10-1-53.

§ 731.38 Prohibition against accepting premium for signing.

No person shall accept anything of value for signing an initiative or referendum petition.

HISTORY: GC § 4227-11; 104 v 238; Bureau of Code Revision. Eff 10-1-53.

§ 731.39 Repealed, 146 v S 2, § 6 [GC § 4227-11; 104 v 238; Bureau of Code Revision, 10-1-53]. Eff 7-1-96.

This set set out prohibition against destruction of petition during circulation of initiative or referendum.

§ 731.40 Prohibition against threats in securing signatures.

No person shall, directly or indirectly, by intimidation or threats, influence or seek to influence any person to sign or abstain from signing, or to solicit signatures to or abstain from soliciting signatures to an initiative or referendum petition.

HISTORY: GC § 4227-11; 104 v 238; Bureau of Code Revision. Eff 10-1-53.

§ 731.99 Penalties.

(A) Whoever violates section 731.36 of the Revised Code shall be fined not less than one hundred nor more than five hundred dollars.

(B) Whoever violates section 731.40 of the Revised Code is guilty of a minor misdemeanor.

(C) Whoever violates section 731.38 of the Revised Code shall be fined not more than twenty-five dollars.

HISTORY: Bureau of Code Revision, 10-1-53; 126 v 575 (Eff 10-6-55); 138 v H 1062 (Eff 3-23-81); 139 v S 199 (Eff 1-1-83); 146 v S 2. Eff 7-1-96.

The effective date is set by section 6 of SB 2.

CHAPTER 733: OFFICERS

§ 733.51 Powers and duties of city director of law.

The city director of law shall prepare all contracts, bonds, and other instruments in writing in which the city is concerned, and shall serve the several directors and officers provided in Title VII [7] of the Revised Code as legal counsel and attorney.

The director of law shall be prosecuting attorney of the mayor's court. When the legislative authority of the city allows assistants to the director of law, he may designate the assistants to act as prosecuting attorneys of the mayor's court. The person designated shall be subject to the approval of the legislative authority.

HISTORY: RS Bates § 1536-663; 96 v 65, § 137; 99 v 458, § 137; GC §§ 4305, 4306; 102 v 131; Bureau of Code Revision, 10-1-53; 136 v H 205 (Eff 1-1-76); 137 v H 219. Eff 11-1-77.

§ 733.52 Prosecuting attorney of mayor's court.

The city director of law as prosecuting attorney of the mayor's court shall prosecute all cases brought before the court, and perform the same duties, as far as they are applicable thereto, as required of the prosecuting attorney of the county.

The director of law or the assistants whom he designates to act as prosecuting attorneys of the mayor's court shall receive such compensation for the service provided by this section as the legislative authority of the city prescribes, and such additional compensation as the board of county commissioners allows.

HISTORY: RS § 1813; Bates § 1536-844; S&C 1536; 66 v 179, § 191; 84 v 26, 28; 95 v 86; GC § 4307; 102 v 131; Bureau of Code Revision, 10-1-53; 136 v H 205 (Eff 1-1-76); 137 v H 219. Eff 11-1-77.

§ 733.53 Duties as to suits.

The city director of law, when required to do so by resolution of the legislative authority of the city, shall prosecute or defend on behalf of the city, all complaints, suits, and controversies in which the city is a party, and such other suits, matters, and controversies as he is, by resolution or ordinance, directed to prosecute. He shall not be required to prosecute any action before the mayor of the city for the violation of an ordinance without first advising such action.

HISTORY: RS § 1774; Bates § 1536-664; 66 v 175, § 157; 85 v 249; 90 v 132; GC § 4308; Bureau of Code Revision, 10-1-53; 137 v H 219. Eff 11-1-77.

§ 733.54 City director of law shall give opinions.

When an officer of a city entertains doubts concerning the law in any matter before him in his official capacity, and desires the opinion of the city director of law, he shall clearly state to the director of law, in writing, the question upon which the opinion is desired, and thereupon the director of law shall, within a reasonable time, reply orally or in writing to such inquiry. The right conferred upon such officers by this section extends to the legislative authority of the city, and to each board provided for in Title VII [7] of the Revised Code.

HISTORY: RS § 1775; Bates § 1536-665; 85 v 225; GC § 4309; Bureau of Code Revision, 10-1-53; 137 v H 219. Eff 11-1-77.

[MISCONDUCT IN OFFICE]

§ 733.72 Charges against municipal officers filed with probate judge; proceedings.

When a complaint under oath is filed with the probate judge of the county in which a municipal corporation or the larger part thereof is situated, by any elector of the municipal corporation, signed and approved by four other electors thereof, the judge shall forthwith issue a citation to any person charged in the complaint for his appearance before the judge within ten days from the filing thereof, and shall also furnish the accused and the village solicitor or city director of law with a copy thereof. The complaint shall charge any of the following:

(A) That a member of the legislative authority of the municipal corporation has received, directly or indirectly, compensation for his services as a member thereof, as a committeeman, or otherwise, contrary to law;

(B) That a member of the legislative authority or an officer of the municipal corporation is or has been interested, directly or indirectly, in the profits of a contract, job, work, or service, or is or has been acting as a commissioner, architect, superintendent, or engineer in work undertaken or prosecuted by the municipal corporation, contrary to law;

(C) That a member of the legislative authority or an officer of the municipal corporation has been guilty of misfeasance or malfeasance in office.

Before acting upon such complaint, the judge shall require the party complaining to furnish sufficient security for costs.

HISTORY: RS § 1732; Bates § 1536-989; 68 v 113, § 1; GC § 4670; Bureau of Code Revision, 10-1-53; 137 v H 219. Eff 11-1-77.

§ 733.73 Appearance of counsel; jury.

On the day fixed by the probate judge for the return of the citation issued pursuant to section 733.72 of the Revised Code, the village solicitor or city director of law shall appear on behalf of the complainant to conduct the prosecution, and the accused may also appear by counsel. A time shall be set for hearing the case, which shall be not more than ten days after such return. If a jury is demanded by either party, the probate judge shall direct the summoning of twelve men [jurors] in the manner provided by sections 2313.19 to 2313.26 of the Revised Code. In a municipal corporation having no village solicitor or city director of law, or in case the village solicitor or city director of law is accused of any misfeasance or malfeasance in his office, the prosecuting attorney shall appear on behalf of the complainant to conduct the prosecution.

HISTORY: RS § 1733; Bates § 1536-990; 68 v 113, § 2; GC § 4671; Bureau of Code Revision, 10-1-53; 129 v 582(641) (Eff 1-10-61); 131 v 269 (Eff 1-1-66); 137 v H 219. Eff 11-1-77.

CHAPTER 737: PUBLIC SAFETY

[DEPARTMENT OF PUBLIC SAFETY IN CITY]

§ 737.01 Director of public safety.

In each city there shall be a department of public safety, which shall be administered by a director of public safety. The director shall be appointed by the mayor and need not be a resident of the city at the time of his appointment but shall become a resident thereof within six months after his appointment unless such residence requirement is waived by ordinance.

HISTORY: RS Bates § 1536-682; 96 v 68, § 146; 99 v 564, § 146; GC § 4367; Bureau of Code Revision, 10-1-53; 133 v H 279. Eff 10-2-69.

§ 737.02 General duties; records; contracts.

Under the direction of the mayor, the director of public safety shall be the executive head of the police and fire departments and the chief administrative authority of the charity, correction, and building departments. He shall have all powers and duties connected with and incident to the appointment, regulation, and government of such departments except as otherwise provided by law. He shall keep a record of his proceedings, a copy of which, certified by him, shall be competent evidence in all courts.

Such director shall make all contracts in the name of the city with reference to the management of such departments, for the erection or repair of all buildings or improvements in connection therewith, and for the purchase of all supplies necessary for such departments.

HISTORY: RS Bates §§ 1536-683, 1536-684; 1536-686; 96 v 69, §§ 147, 148; 96 v 70, § 150; 99 v 564, § 147; GC §§ 4368, 4369; Bureau of Code Revision. Eff 10-1-53.

[§ 737.02.1] § 737.021 Division of traffic engineering and safety in department of public safety.

The legislative authority of a city may create and abolish, by ordinance, a division of traffic engineering and safety within the department of public safety. The director of public safety of such city shall be the executive head of such division. He shall have all powers and duties connected with and incident to the appointment, regulation, and government of such division, and shall make such rules and regulations as he may deem necessary for the government and operation of the division. He shall keep a record of all his proceedings in connection with the administration of such division. A copy of such proceedings, when certified by him, shall be competent evidence in all courts. Such division may be staffed by traffic and safety engineers and such other employees as determined by the legislative authority.

HISTORY: 131 v 274. Eff 11-1-65.

[§ 737.02.2] § 737.022 Authority of director to promulgate certain traffic regulations.

When authorized by ordinance of the legislative authority of a city, and in order to expedite the flow and direction of traffic, to eliminate congestion on streets, alleys, and highways, and to provide for the safety of passengers in motor vehicles and pedestrians, the director of public safety may make and issue rules and regulations concerning:

(A) The number, type, and location of traffic control devices and signs;

(B) The regulation or prohibition of parking on streets, alleys, highways, or public property;

(C) The regulation of the right-of-way at intersections of streets, alleys, and highways;

(D) The regulation or prohibition of turns at intersections;

(E) The creation, abolition, and regulation of through routes and truck routes;

(F) The creation, abolition, and regulation of pedestrian crosswalk and safety zones;

(G) The creation, abolition, and regulation of bus loading and unloading zones and business loading zones;

(H) The creation, abolition, and regulation of traffic lanes, and passing zones;

(I) The regulation of the direction of traffic on streets, alleys, and highways and the creation and abolition of one way streets;

(J) Such other subjects as may be provided by ordinance, which shall not be limited by the specific enumeration of subjects by this section.

Such rules and regulations shall be issued in the

manner and subject to the conditions and limitations as prescribed by ordinance of the legislative authority of such city. Copies of such rules and regulations, when certified by the director of public safety, shall be competent evidence in all courts. Violation of such rules and regulations shall be a misdemeanor and shall be punishable as provided by the ordinances of such city.

HISTORY: 131 v 275. Eff 11-1-65.

§ 737.03 Management of certain institutions; contracts.

The director of public safety shall manage, and make all contracts with reference to the police stations, fire houses, reform schools, infirmaries, hospitals, workhouses, farms, pesthouses, and all other charitable and reformatory institutions. In the control and supervision of such institutions, the director shall be governed by Title VII [7] of the Revised Code relating to such institutions.

Such director may make all contracts and expenditures of money for acquiring lands for the erection or repairing of station houses, police stations, fire department buildings, fire cisterns, and plugs, that are required, for the purchase of engines, apparatus, and all other supplies necessary for the police and fire departments, and for other undertakings and departments under his supervision, but no obligation involving an expenditure of more than ten thousand dollars shall be created unless first authorized and directed by ordinance. In making, altering, or modifying such contracts, the director shall be governed by sections 735.05 to 735.09 of the Revised Code, except that all bids shall be filed with and opened by such director. He shall make no sale or disposition of any property belonging to the city without first being authorized by resolution or ordinance of the city legislative authority.

HISTORY: Bates §§ 1536-683, 1536-690; 96 v 69, § 147, 96 v 71, § 154; 97 v 388, § 154; 99 v 564, §§ 147, 154; GC §§ 4370, 4371; 123 v 495; Bureau of Code Revision, 10-1-53; 132 v S 378 (Eff 4-29-68); 136 v H 8 (Eff 8-11-75); 138 v H 371 (Eff 3-14-80); 142 v H 527. Eff 3-17-89.

[CONTRACT FOR POLICE PROTECTION]

§ 737.04 Mutual aid contracts with other political subdivisions for law enforcement purposes.

The legislative authority of any municipal corporation, in order to obtain police protection or to obtain additional police protection, may enter into contracts with one or more municipal corporations, townships, township police districts, or county sheriffs in this state, with one or more park districts created pursuant to section 511.18 or 1545.01 of the Revised Code, or with a contiguous municipal corporation in an adjoining state, upon any terms that are agreed upon, for services of police departments or the use of police equipment or for the interchange of services of police departments or police equipment within the several territories of the contracting subdivisions.

Chapter 2744. of the Revised Code, insofar as it applies to the operation of police departments, shall apply to the contracting political subdivisions and to the police department members when they are rendering service outside their own subdivisions pursuant to the contracts.

Police department members acting outside the subdivision in which they are employed, pursuant to a contract entered into under this section, shall be entitled to participate in any indemnity fund established by their employer to the same extent as while acting within the employing subdivision. Those members shall be entitled to all the rights and benefits of Chapter 4123. of the Revised Code, to the same extent as while performing service within the subdivision.

The contracts may provide for:

(A) A fixed annual charge to be paid at the times agreed upon and stipulated in the contract;

(B) Compensation based upon:

(1) A stipulated price for each call or emergency;

(2) The number of members or pieces of equipment employed;

(3) The elapsed time of service required in each call or emergency.

(C) Compensation for loss or damage to equipment while engaged in rendering police services outside the limits of the subdivision owning and furnishing the equipment;

(D) Reimbursement of the subdivision in which the police department members are employed for any indemnity award or premium contribution assessed against the employing subdivision for workers' compensation benefits for injuries or death of its police department members occurring while engaged in rendering police services pursuant to the contract.

HISTORY: GC § 4371-1; 122 v 288; Bureau of Code Revision, 10-1-53; 136 v S 545 (Eff 1-17-77); 138 v H 279 (Eff 10-26-79); 139 v H 738 (Eff 6-25-82); 141 v H 201 (Eff 7-1-85); 141 v H 176 (Eff 11-20-85); 144 v S 174. Eff 7-31-92.

[§ 737.04.1] § 737.041 Resolution to provide police services without a contract.

The police department of any municipal corporation may provide police protection to any county, municipal corporation, township, or township police district of this state, to a park district created pursuant to section 511.18 or 1545.01 of the Revised Code, or to a governmental entity of an adjoining state without a contract to provide police protection, upon the approval, by resolution, of the legislative authority of the municipal corporation in which the department is located and upon authorization by an officer or employee of the police department providing the police protection who is designated by title of office or position, pursuant to the resolution of the legislative authority of the municipal corporation, to give the authorization.

Chapter 2744. of the Revised Code, insofar as it applies to the operation of police departments, shall apply to any municipal corporation and to members of its police department when the members are rendering police services pursuant to this section outside the municipal corporation by which they are employed.

Police department members acting, as provided in this section, outside the municipal corporation by which they are employed shall be entitled to participate in any pension or indemnity fund established by their employer to the same extent as while acting within the municipal corporation by which they are employed. Those members shall be entitled to all the rights and benefits of Chapter 4123. of the Revised Code to the same extent as while performing services within the municipal corporation by which they are employed.

HISTORY: 138 v S 98 (Eff 10-6-80); 139 v H 103 (Eff 5-19-82); 141 v H 176 (Eff 11-20-85); 144 v S 174. Eff 7-31-92.

[POLICE AND FIRE DEPARTMENTS IN CITY]

§ 737.05 Composition and control of police department.

The police department of each city shall be composed of a chief of police and such other officers, patrolmen, and employees as the legislative authority thereof provides by ordinance.

The director of public safety of such city shall have the exclusive management and control of all other officers, surgeons, secretaries, clerks, and employees in the police department as provided by ordinances or resolution of such legislative authority. He may commission private policemen, who may not be in the classified list of the department, under such rules and regulations as the legislative authority prescribes.

HISTORY: RS Bates § 1536-685; 96 v 70, § 149; GC §§ 4374, 4375; 118 v 319; Bureau of Code Revision. Eff 10-1-53.

[§ 737.05.1] § 737.051 City auxiliary police unit; parking enforcement unit.

(A) The legislative authority of a city may establish, by ordinance, an auxiliary police unit within the police department of the city, and provide for the regulation of auxiliary police officers. The director of public safety shall be the executive head of the auxiliary police unit, shall make all appointments and removals of auxiliary police officers, subject to any general rules prescribed by the legislative authority by ordinance, and shall prescribe rules for the organization, training, administration, control, and conduct of the auxiliary police unit. Members of the auxiliary police unit shall not be in the classified service of the city.

(B)(1) The legislative authority of a city may establish, by ordinance, a parking enforcement unit within the police department of the city, and provide for the regulation of parking enforcement officers. The director of public safety shall be the executive head of the parking enforcement unit, shall make all appointments and removals of parking enforcement officers, subject to any general rules prescribed by the legislative authority by ordinance, and shall prescribe rules for the organization, training, administration, control, and conduct of the parking enforcement unit. The director may appoint parking enforcement officers who agree to serve for nominal compensation, and persons with physical disabilities may receive appointments as parking enforcement officers.

(2) The authority of the parking enforcement officers shall be limited to the enforcement of ordinances governing parking in handicapped parking locations and fire lanes and any other parking ordinances specified in the ordinance creating the parking enforcement unit. Parking enforcement officers shall have no other powers.

(3) The training the parking enforcement officers shall receive shall include instruction in general administrative rules and procedures governing the parking enforcement unit, the role of the judicial system as it relates to parking regulation and enforcement, proper techniques and methods relating to the enforcement of parking ordinances, human interaction skills, and first aid.

HISTORY: 130 v 241 (Eff 5-6-63); 141 v H 201 (Eff 7-1-85); 143 v S 174. Eff 7-13-90.

[§ 737.05.2] § 737.052 Felony precludes or terminates employment as chief, police officer or auxiliary officer.

(A) As used in this section, "felony" has the same meaning as in section 109.511 [109.51.1] of the Revised Code.

(B)(1) The director of public safety shall not appoint a person as a chief of police, a member of the police department of the municipal corporation, or an auxiliary police officer on a permanent basis, on a temporary basis, for a probationary term, or on other than a permanent basis if the person previously has been convicted of or has pleaded guilty to a felony.

(2)(a) The director of public safety shall terminate the employment of a chief of police, member of the police department, or auxiliary police officer who does either of the following:

(i) Pleads guilty to a felony;

(ii) Pleads guilty to a misdemeanor pursuant to a negotiated plea agreement as provided in division (D) of section 2929.29 of the Revised Code in which the chief of police, member of the police department, or auxiliary police officer agrees to surrender the certificate awarded to the chief of police, member of the police department, or auxiliary police officer under section 109.77 of the Revised Code.

(b) The director shall suspend from employment a chief of police, member of the police department, or auxiliary police officer who is convicted, after trial, of a felony. If the chief of police, member of the police department, or auxiliary police officer files an appeal from that conviction and the conviction is upheld by the highest court to which the appeal is taken or if the chief of police, member of the police department, or auxiliary police officer does not file a timely appeal, the director shall terminate that person's employment. If the chief of police, member of the police department, or auxiliary police officer files an appeal that results in that person's acquittal of the felony or conviction of a misdemeanor, or in the dismissal of the felony charge against that person, the director shall reinstate that person. A chief of police, member of the police department, or auxiliary police officer who is reinstated under division (B)(2)(b) of this section shall not receive any back pay unless that person's conviction of the felony was reversed on appeal, or the felony charge was dismissed, because the court found insufficient evidence to convict that person of the felony.

(3) Division (B) of this section does not apply regarding an offense that was committed prior to January 1, 1997.

(4) The suspension from employment, or the termination of the employment, of the chief of police, member of the police department, or auxiliary police officer under division (B)(2) of this section shall be in accordance with Chapter 119. of the Revised Code.

HISTORY: 146 v H 566. Eff 10-16-96.

§ 737.06 Chief of police.

The chief of police shall have exclusive control of the stationing and transfer of all patrolmen, auxiliary police officers, and other officers and employees in the police department, and police auxiliary unit, under such general rules and regulations as the director of public safety prescribes.

HISTORY: RS Bates § 1536-684; 96 v 69, § 148; GC § 4372; Bureau of Code Revision, 10-1-53; 130 v 242. Eff 5-6-63.

§ 737.07 Hours of work for policemen in cities; leave of absence.

In each city, except in case of necessary appearances in court and emergency special duty assignments not to exceed eight hours constitute a day's work and not to exceed forty-four hours constitute a week's work for policemen. Annually, in each city, each policeman shall be given not less than two weeks' leave of absence with full pay.

HISTORY: GC § 4374-1; 119 v 132; Bureau of Code Revision, 10-1-53; 133 v S 28. Eff 11-19-69.

§ 737.08 Composition and control of city fire department.

(A) The fire department of each city shall be composed of a chief of the fire department and such other officers, firefighters, and employees as provided by ordinance.

(B) No person shall, after July 1, 1970, be appointed as a permanent full-time paid member, whose duties include firefighting, of the fire department of any city, unless either of the following applies:

(1) The person has received a certificate issued under former section 3303.07 of the Revised Code or division (C)(1) or (2) of section 4765.55 of the Revised Code evidencing satisfactory completion of a firefighter training program;

(2) The person began serving as a permanent full-time paid firefighter with the fire department of a village or other city prior to July 2, 1970, and receives a certificate issued under division (C)(3) of section 4765.55 of the Revised Code.

(C) No person who is appointed as a volunteer firefighter of a city fire department after July 1, 1979, shall remain in such a position, unless either of the following applies:

(1) Within one year of the appointment the person has received a certificate issued under former section 3303.07 of the Revised Code or division (C)(1) or (2) of section 4765.55 of the Revised Code evidencing satisfactory completion of a firefighter training program;

(2) The person began serving as a permanent full-time paid firefighter with the fire department of a village or other city prior to July 2, 1970, or as a volunteer firefighter with the fire department of a township, fire district, village, or other city prior to July 2, 1979, and receives a certificate issued under division (C)(3) of section 4765.55 of the Revised Code.

(D) The director of public safety shall have the exclusive management and control of such other surgeons, secretaries, clerks, and employees, as are provided by ordinance or resolution of the legislative authority of such city.

HISTORY: RS Bates § 1536-686; 96 v 70, § 150; GC § 4377; 118 v 320; Bureau of Code Revision, 10-1-53; 133 v S 226 (Eff 11-19-69); 137 v H 590 (Eff 7-1-79); 144 v S 98 (Eff 11-12-92); 146 v H 405. Eff 10-1-96.

§ 737.09 Chief of fire department.

The chief of the fire department shall have exclusive control of the stationing and transferring of all firemen and other officers and employees in the department, under such general rules and regulations as the director of public safety prescribes.

HISTORY: RS Bates § 1536-686; 96 v 70, § 150; GC § 4376; Bureau of Code Revision. Eff 10-1-53.

§ 737.10 Additional patrolmen and firemen in emergency situation.

In case of riot or other like emergency, the mayor may appoint additional patrolmen and officers for temporary service in the police department, or additional firemen and officers for temporary service in the fire department, who need not be in the classified list of such department. Such additional persons shall be employed only for the time during which the emergency exists.

The mayor may call upon the sheriff of the county in which all or part of the municipal corporation lies or the sheriff of any adjoining county, the mayor or other chief executive of any municipal corporation in the same or any adjoining county, and the chairman of the board of township trustees of any township in the same or any adjoining county, to furnish such law enforcement or fire protection personnel, or both, together with appropriate equipment and apparatus, as may be necessary to preserve the public peace and protect persons and property in the requesting municipal corporation in the event of riot. Such aid shall be furnished to the mayor requesting it, insofar as possible without withdrawing from the political subdivision furnishing such aid the minimum police and fire protection appearing necessary under the circumstances. In such case, law enforcement and fire protection personnel acting outside the territory of their regular employment shall be considered as performing services within the territory of their regular employment for purposes of compensation, pension or indemnity fund rights, workers' compensation, and other rights or benefits to which they may be entitled as incidents of their regular employment. The municipal corporation receiving such aid shall reimburse the political subdivision furnishing it the cost of furnishing such aid, including compensation of personnel, expenses incurred by reason of the injury or death of any such personnel while rendering such aid, expenses of furnishing equipment and apparatus, compensation for damage to or loss of equipment or apparatus while in service outside the territory of its regular use, and such other reasonable expenses as may be incurred by any such political subdivision in furnishing such aid. Nothing in this section shall be construed as superseding or modifying in any way any provision of a contract entered into pursuant to section 737.04 of the Revised Code. Law enforcement officers acting pursuant to this section outside the territory of their regular employment have the same authority to enforce the law as when acting within the territory of their regular employment.

HISTORY: RS Bates § 1536-684; 96 v 69, § 148; GC § 4373; Bureau of Code Revision, 10-1-53; 132 v H 996 (Eff 6-13-68); 136 v S 545. Eff 1-17-77.

§ 737.11 General duties of police and fire departments.

The police force of a municipal corporation shall preserve the peace, protect persons and property, and obey and enforce all ordinances of the legislative authority of the municipal corporation, all criminal laws of the state and the United States, all court orders issued and consent agreements approved pursuant to sections 2919.26 and 3113.31 of the Revised Code, all anti-stalking protection orders issued pursuant to section 2903.213 [2903.21.3] of the Revised Code, and protection orders issued by courts of another state, as defined in section 2919.27 of the Revised Code. The fire department shall protect the lives and property of the people in case of fire. Both the police and fire departments shall perform any other duties that are provided by ordinance. The police and fire departments in every city shall be maintained under the civil service system.

A chief or officer of a police force of a municipal corporation may participate, as the director of an organized crime task force established under section 177.02 of the Revised Code or as a member of the investigatory staff of such a task force, in an investigation of organized criminal activity in any county or counties in this state under sections 177.01 to 177.03 of the Revised Code.

HISTORY: RS Bates § 1536-687; 96 v 71, § 151 GC § 4378; Bureau of Code Revision, 10-1-53; 137 v H 835 (Eff 3-27-79); 141 v S 74 (Eff 9-3-86); 144 v H 536 (Eff 11-5-92); 147 v S 1. Eff 10-21-97.

[§ 737.11.1] § 737.111 Disposition of funds received by police department.

All fines imposed as discipline or punishment upon members of the police department of a municipal corporation by the authority having charge or control thereof, all rewards, fees, or proceeds of gifts and emoluments allowed by such authority paid and given for or on account of any extraordinary service of any member of the department, and moneys arising from the sale of unclaimed property or money, after deducting all expenses incident thereto, shall be credited to the general fund of the municipal corporation.

HISTORY: RS Bates § 1536-597(c); 95 v 227, § 22(c); 97 v 247, § 2(c); GC § 4623; 120 v 248; Bureau of Code Revision, RC § 741.41, 10-1-53; 131 v 285 (Eff 11-5-65); RC § 737.111, 141 v H 201. Eff 7-1-85.

[§ 737.11.2] § 737.112 Disposition of funds received by fire department.

All fines imposed as discipline or punishment upon members of the fire department of a municipal corporation by the authority having charge or control thereof, the proceeds of all suits for penalties for the violation of state statutes and municipal ordinances with the execution of which such department is charged, license fees or other fees payable thereunder, and fees received by such municipal corporation for any services performed or inspections made by the fire department, except fees charged and received by the municipal corporation from other subdivisions for fire protection or fire fighting therein shall be credited to the general fund of the municipal corporation.

HISTORY: RS Bates § 1536-596(c); 95 v 224, § 1(c); 97 v 243, § 1(c); GC § 4607; 118 v 283; Bureau of Code Revision, RC §

741.10, 10-1-53; 131 v 278 (Eff 11-5-65); RC § 737.112, 141 v H 201. Eff 7-1-85.

§ 737.12 Suspension of police and fire personnel.

Except as provided in section 737.052 [737.05.2] of the Revised Code, the chief of police and the chief of the fire department have the exclusive right to suspend any of the deputies, officers, or employees in their respective departments and under their management and control, for incompetence, gross neglect of duty, gross immorality, habitual drunkenness, failure to obey orders given them by the proper authority, or for any other reasonable and just cause.

If an employee is suspended under this section, the chief of police or the chief of the fire department, as the case may be, shall forthwith certify that fact in writing, together with the cause for the suspension, to the director of public safety, who, within five days from the receipt of that certification, shall proceed to inquire into the cause of the suspension and render judgment on it. If the charge is sustained, the judgment may be for the person's suspension, reduction in rank, or dismissal from the department. The judgment shall be final except as otherwise provided by law.

The director, in any investigation of charges against a member of the police or fire department, shall have the same powers to administer oaths and to secure the attendance of witnesses and the production of books and papers that are conferred upon the mayor.

HISTORY: RS Bates § 1536-688; 96 v 71, § 152; GC §§ 4379, 4380; 101 v 297; Bureau of Code Revision (Eff 10-1-53); 146 v H 566. Eff 10-16-96.

§ 737.13 Classification of service; rules and regulations.

The director of public safety of a city shall classify the service in the police and fire departments in conformity with the ordinance of the legislative authority thereof determining the number of persons to be employed in the departments, and shall make all rules for the regulation and discipline of such departments, except as otherwise provided by law.

HISTORY: RS Bates § 1536-689; 96 v 71, § 153; 99 v 564, § 153; GC § 4382; Bureau of Code Revision. Eff 10-1-53.

§ 737.14 Relief for members of police or fire department.

The legislative authority of a municipal corporation may provide by general ordinance for the relief, out of the police or fire funds, of members of either department temporarily or permanently disabled in the discharge of their duty. This section does not impair, restrict, or repeal any law authorizing the levy of taxes in municipal corporations to provide for firemen, police, and sanitary police pension funds, and to create and perpetuate boards of trustees for the administration of such funds.

HISTORY: RS Bates § 1536-691; 96 v 72, § 155; GC § 4383; Bureau of Code Revision. Eff 10-1-53.

[VILLAGE MARSHAL]

§ 737.15 Appointment of village marshal.

Each village shall have a marshal, designated chief of police, appointed by the mayor with the advice and consent of the legislative authority of the village, who need not be a resident of the village at the time of his appointment but shall become a resident thereof within six months after his appointment by the mayor and confirmation by the legislative authority unless such residence requirement is waived by ordinance, and who shall continue in office until removed therefrom as provided by section 737.171 [737.17.1] of the Revised Code.

No person shall receive an appointment under this section after January 1, 1970, unless, not more than sixty days prior to receiving such appointment, he has passed a physical examination, given by a licensed physician, showing that he meets the physical requirements necessary to perform the duties of village marshal as established by the legislative authority of the village. The appointing authority shall, prior to making any such appointment, file with the police and firemen's disability and pension fund a copy of the report or findings of said licensed physician. The professional fee for such physical examination shall be paid for by such legislative authority.

HISTORY; RS Bates §§ 1536-860, 1536-978; 96 v 86, § 206; 98 v 172, § 222; GC § 4384; 119 v 699; Bureau of Code Revision, 10-1-53; 130 v 242 (Eff 9-16-63); 131 v 276 (Eff 9-6-65); 133 v S 86. Eff 10-24-69.

§ 737.16 Deputy marshals and policemen.

The mayor shall, when provided for by the legislative authority of a village, and subject to its confirmation, appoint all deputy marshals, policemen, night watchmen, and special policemen. All such officers shall continue in office until removed therefrom for the cause and in the manner provided by section 737.19 of the Revised Code.

No person shall receive an appointment under this section after January 1, 1970, unless he has, not more than sixty days prior to receiving such appointment, passed a physical examination given by a licensed physician, showing that he meets the physical requirements necessary to perform the duties of the position to which he is to be appointed as established by the legislative authority of the village. The appointing authority shall, prior to making any such appointment, file with the police and firemen's disability and pension fund a copy of the report or findings of said licensed physician. The professional fee for such physical examination shall be paid for by the legislative authority.

HISTORY: GC § 4384-1; 119 v 699; Bureau of Code Revision, 10-1-53; 130 v 242 (Eff 9-6-63); 133 v S 86 (Eff 10-24-69); 137 v H 812. Eff 8-1-78.

[§ 737.16.1] § 737.161 Village auxiliary police unit; parking enforcement unit.

(A) The legislative authority of a village may establish, by ordinance, an auxiliary police unit within the police department of the village, and provide for the regulation of auxiliary police officers. The mayor shall be the executive head of the auxiliary police unit, shall make all appointments and removals of auxiliary police officers, subject to any general rules prescribed by the legislative authority by ordinance, and shall prescribe rules for the organization, training, administration, control, and conduct of the auxiliary police unit. The village marshal shall have exclusive control of the stationing and transferring of all auxiliary police officers, under such general rules as the mayor prescribes.

(B)(1) The legislative authority of a village may establish, by ordinance, a parking enforcement unit within the police department of the village, and provide for the regulation of parking enforcement officers. The mayor shall be the executive head of the parking enforcement unit, shall make all appointments and removals of parking enforcement officers, subject to any general rules prescribed by the legislative authority by ordinance, and shall prescribe rules for the organization, training, administration, control, and conduct of the parking enforcement unit. The mayor may appoint parking enforcement officers who agree to serve for nominal compensation, and persons with physical disabilities may receive appointments as parking enforcement officers.

(2) The authority of the parking enforcement officers shall be limited to the enforcement of ordinances governing parking in handicapped parking locations and fire lanes and any other parking ordinances specified in the ordinance creating the parking enforcement unit. Parking enforcement officers shall have no other powers.

(3) The training the parking enforcement officers shall receive shall include instruction in general administrative rules and procedures governing the parking enforcement unit, the role of the judicial system as it relates to parking regulation and enforcement, proper techniques and methods relating to the enforcement of parking ordinances, human interaction skills, and first aid.

HISTORY: 130 v 242 (Eff 5-6-63); 141 v H 201 (Eff 7-1-85); 143 v S 174. Eff 7-13-90.

[§ 737.16.2] § 737.162 Felony precludes or terminates employment in law enforcement capacity.

(A) As used in this section, "felony" has the same meaning as in section 109.511 [109.51.1] of the Revised Code.

(B)(1) The mayor shall not appoint a person as a marshal, a deputy marshal, a police officer, a night watchperson, a special police officer, or an auxiliary police officer on a permanent basis, on a temporary basis, for a probationary term, or on other than a permanent basis if the person previously has been convicted of or has pleaded guilty to a felony.

(2)(a) The mayor shall terminate the employment of a marshal, deputy marshal, police officer, night watchperson, special police officer, or auxiliary police officer who does either of the following:

(i) Pleads guilty to a felony;

(ii) Pleads guilty to a misdemeanor pursuant to a negotiated plea agreement as provided in division (D) of section 2929.29 of the Revised Code in which the marshal, deputy marshal, police officer, night watchperson, special police officer, or auxiliary police officer agrees to surrender the certificate awarded to that person under section 109.77 of the Revised Code.

(b) The mayor shall suspend from employment a marshal, deputy marshal, police officer, night watchperson, special police officer, or auxiliary police officer who is convicted, after trial, of a felony. If the marshal, deputy marshal, police officer, night watchperson, special police officer, or auxiliary police officer files an appeal from that conviction and the conviction is upheld by the highest court to which the appeal is taken or if that person does not file a timely appeal, the mayor shall terminate that person's employment. If the marshal, deputy marshal, police officer, night watchperson, special police officer, or auxiliary police officer files an appeal that results in that person's acquittal of the felony or conviction of a misdemeanor, or in the dismissal of the felony charge against that person, the mayor shall reinstate that person. A marshal, deputy marshal, police officer, night watchperson, special police officer, or auxiliary police officer who is reinstated under division (B)(2)(b) of this section shall not receive any back pay unless that person's conviction of the felony was reversed on appeal, or the felony charge was dismissed, because the court found insufficient evidence to convict that person of the felony.

(3) Division (B) of this section does not apply regarding an offense that was committed prior to January 1, 1997.

(4) The suspension from employment, or the termination of the employment, of a marshal, deputy marshal, police officer, night watchperson, special police officer, or auxiliary police officer under division (B)(2) of this section shall be in accordance with Chapter 119. of the Revised Code.

HISTORY: 146 v H 566. Eff 10-16-96.

§ 737.17 Probationary period; final appointment.

All appointments made under sections 737.15 and

737.16 of the Revised Code shall be for a probationary period of six months' continuous service, and none shall be finally made until the appointee has satisfactorily served his probationary period. At the end of the probationary period the mayor shall transmit to the legislative authority of the village a record of such employee's service with his recommendations thereon and he may, with the concurrence of the legislative authority, remove or finally appoint the employee.

HISTORY: GC § 4384-2; 119 v 699; Bureau of Code Revision. Eff 10-1-53.

[§ 737.17.1] § 737.171 Removal proceedings; suspension; appeals.

Except as provided in section 737.162 [737.16.2] of the Revised Code, if the mayor of a village has reason to believe that a duly appointed marshal of the village has been guilty of incompetency, inefficiency, dishonesty, drunkenness, immoral conduct, insubordination, discourteous treatment of the public, neglect of duty, or any other acts of misfeasance, malfeasance, or nonfeasance in the performance of the marshal's official duty, the mayor shall file with the legislative authority of the village written charges against that person setting forth in detail the reason for the charges, and immediately shall serve a true copy of the charges upon the person against whom they are made.

Charges filed under this section shall be heard at the next regular meeting of the legislative authority occurring not less than five days after the date those charges have been served on the person against whom they are made. The person against whom those charges are filed may appear in person and by counsel at the hearing, examine all witnesses, and answer all charges against that person.

At the conclusion of the hearing, the legislative authority may dismiss the charges, suspend the accused from office for not more than sixty days, or remove the accused from office.

Action of the legislative authority removing or suspending the accused from office requires the affirmative vote of two-thirds of all members elected to it.

In the case of removal from office, the person so removed may appeal on questions of law and fact the decision of the legislative authority to the court of common pleas of the county in which the village is situated. The person shall take the appeal within ten days from the date of the finding of the legislative authority.

HISTORY: 130 v 243 (Eff 9-16-63); 130 v Pt II, 57 (Eff 12-16-64); 137 v H 812 (Eff 8-1-78); 146 v H 566. Eff 10-16-96.

§ 737.18 General powers of village police officers.

The marshal shall be the peace officer of a village and the executive head, under the mayor, of the police force. The marshal, and the deputy marshals, policemen, or night watchmen under him shall have the powers conferred by law upon police officers in all villages of the state, and such other powers, not inconsistent with the nature of their offices, as are conferred by ordinance.

A marshal, deputy marshal, or police officer of a village may participate, as the director of an organized crime task force established under section 177.02 of the Revised Code or as a member of the investigatory staff of such a task force, in an investigation of organized criminal activity in any county or counties in this state under sections 177.01 to 177.03 of the Revised Code.

HISTORY: RS Bates § 1536-860; 96 v 86, § 206; GC § 4385; Bureau of Code Revision, 10-1-53; 141 v S 74. Eff 9-3-86.

§ 737.19 Powers and duties of marshal.

(A) The marshal of a village has exclusive authority over the stationing and transfer of all deputies, officers, and employees within the police department of the village, under the general rules that the mayor prescribes.

(B) Except as provided in section 737.162 [737.16.2] of the Revised Code, the marshal of a village has the exclusive right to suspend any of the deputies, officers, or employees in the village police department who are under the management and control of the marshal for incompetence, gross neglect of duty, gross immorality, habitual drunkenness, failure to obey orders given them by the proper authority, or for any other reasonable or just cause.

If an employee is suspended under this section, the marshal immediately shall certify this fact in writing, together with the cause for the suspension, to the mayor of the village and immediately shall serve a true copy of the charges upon the person against whom they are made. Within five days after receiving this certification, the mayor shall inquire into the cause of the suspension and shall render a judgment on it. If the mayor sustains the charges, the judgment of the mayor may be for the person's suspension, reduction in rank, or removal from the department.

Suspensions of more than three days, reduction in rank, or removal from the department under this section may be appealed to the legislative authority of the village within five days from the date of the mayor's judgment. The legislative authority shall hear the appeal at its next regularly scheduled meeting. The person against whom the judgment has been rendered may appear in person and by counsel at the hearing, examine all witnesses, and answer all charges against that person.

At the conclusion of the hearing, the legislative authority may dismiss the charges, uphold the mayor's judgment, or modify the judgment to one of suspension for not more than sixty days, reduction in rank, or removal from the department.

Action of the legislative authority removing or suspending the accused from the department requires the affirmative vote of two-thirds of all members elected to it.

In the case of removal from the department, the person so removed may appeal on questions of law and fact the decision of the legislative authority to the court of common pleas of the county in which the village is situated. The person shall take the appeal within ten days from the date of the finding of the legislative authority.

(C) The marshal of a village shall suppress all riots, disturbances, and breaches of the peace, and to that end may call upon the citizens to aid the marshal. The marshal shall arrest all disorderly persons in the village and pursue and arrest any person fleeing from justice in any part of the state. The marshal shall arrest any person in the act of committing an offense against the laws of the state or the ordinances of the village and forthwith bring that person before the mayor or other competent authority for examination or trial. The marshal shall receive and execute proper authority for the arrest and detention of criminals fleeing or escaping from other places or states.

In the discharge of the marshal's duties, the marshal shall have the powers and be subject to the responsibilities of constables, and, for services performed by the marshal or the marshal's deputies, the same fees and expenses shall be taxed as are allowed constables.

HISTORY: RS §§ 1849, 1850; Bates §§ 1536-862, 1536-863; 66 v 173, §§ 142, 143; GC §§ 4386, 4387; 108 v PtII, 1203; Bureau of Code Revision, 10-1-53; 137 v H 812 (Eff 8-1-78); 146 v H 566. Eff 10-16-96.

§ 737.20 Disposition of fines and penalties.

All fees, costs, fines, and penalties collected by the marshal shall immediately be paid to the mayor, who shall report to the legislative authority of the village monthly the amount thereof, from whom, and for what purpose collected, and when paid to the mayor.

HISTORY: RS § 1851; Bates § 1536-864; 66 v 173, § 144; GC § 4388; Bureau of Code Revision. Eff 10-1-53.

§ 737.27 Investigation of fires.

The legislative authority of a municipal corporation may invest any officer of the fire or police department with the power, and impose on him the duty, to be present at all fires, investigate the cause thereof, examine witnesses, compel the attendance of witnesses and the production of books and papers, and to do and perform all other acts necessary to the effective discharge of such duties.

Such officer may administer oaths, make arrests, and enter, for the purpose of examination, any building which, in his opinion, is in danger from fire. The officer shall report his proceedings to the legislative authority at such times as are required.

HISTORY: RS §§ 2474, 2475; Bates §§ 1536-873, 1536-874; 66 v 205, §§ 330, 331; GC §§ 4396, 4397; Bureau of Code Revision. Eff 10-1-53.

[PROPERTY RECOVERED BY POLICE; DISPOSITION]

§ 737.29 Property recovered by police.

Stolen or other property recovered by members of the police force of a municipal corporation shall be deposited and kept in a place designated by the mayor. Each such article shall be entered in a book kept for that purpose, with the name of the owner, if ascertained, the person from whom taken, the place where found with general circumstances, the date of its receipt, and the name of the officer receiving it.

An inventory of all money or other property shall be given to the party from whom taken, and in case it is not claimed by some person within thirty days after arrest and seizure it shall be delivered to the person from whom taken, and to no other person, either attorney, agent, factor, or clerk, except by special order of the mayor.

HISTORY: RS § 6858-1; 98 v 60; GC §§ 4398, 4399; Bureau of Code Revision. Eff 10-1-53.

§ 737.30 Deposit [of] stolen property; prohibition.

No officer, patrolman, or other member of the police force in a municipal corporation shall neglect or refuse to deposit property taken or found by him in possession of a person arrested. Any conviction for a violation of this section shall vacate the office of the person so convicted.

HISTORY: RS § 6858-2; 98 v 61; GC § 12937; Bureau of Code Revision. Eff 10-1-53.

§ 737.31 Disposition to claimant.

If, within thirty days, the money or property recovered under section 737.29 of the Revised Code is claimed by any other person, it shall be retained by the custodian thereof until after the discharge or conviction of the person from whom it was taken and so long as it is required as evidence in any case in court. If such claimant establishes to the satisfaction of the court that he is the rightful owner, the money or property shall be restored to him, otherwise it shall be returned to the accused person, personally, and not to any attorney, agent, factor, or clerk of such accused person, except upon special order of the mayor after all liens and claims in favor of the municipal corporation have first been discharged and satisfied.

HISTORY: RS § 6858-1; 98 v 60; GC § 4400; Bureau of Code Revision. Eff 10-1-53.

§ 737.32 Sale of unclaimed property; motor vehicles worth less than $200; disposition of proceeds.

Property, unclaimed for the period of ninety days, shall be sold by the chief of police of the municipal corporation, marshal of the village, or licensed auctioneer at public auction, after giving due notice thereof by advertisement, published once a week for three successive weeks in a newspaper of general circulation in the county. The proceeds shall be paid to the treasurer of the municipal corporation and be credited to the general fund.

HISTORY: RS § 6858-3; 98 v 61; GC § 4401; 112 v 254; Bureau of Code Revision, 10-1-53; 125 v 346 (Eff 10-1-53); 131 v 276 (Eff 9-29-69); 133 v H 13 (Eff 7-14-69); 134 v H 24. Eff 10-6-71.

§ 737.33 Expenses of storage and sale; notice.

Upon the sale of any unclaimed or impounded property as provided in section 737.32 of the Revised Code, if any such unclaimed or impounded property was ordered removed to a place of storage or stored, or both, by or under the direction of a chief of police of the municipal corporation or marshal of the village, any expenses or charges for such removal or storage, or both, and costs of sale, provided the same are approved by such chief of police or marshal, shall first be paid from the proceeds of such sale. Notice shall be given by registered mail, thirty days before the date of such sale, to the owner and mortgagee, or other lien holder, at their last known address.

HISTORY: GC § 4401-1; 124 v 377; Bureau of Code Revision. Eff 10-1-53.

[PUBLIC BUILDINGS, INSPECTION FOR FIRE SAFETY]

§§ 737.34, 737.35, 737.36
Repealed, 146 v S 293, § 2 [RS §§ 2568, 2572a, 2572b; Bates §§ 1536-308, 1536-313, 1536-314; S & S 636; 62 v 139, § 3; 74 v 61; 86 v 46, 47; 87 v 279; 88 v 85; 90 v 3, 4; 92 v 409; 93 v 35; GC §§ 4648, 4655, 4657; Burea of Code Revision, 10-1-53; 146 v S 162]. Eff 9-26-96.

These sections provided for fire safety examinations of public buildings.

§ 737.37 Power of legislative authority to regulate.

The legislative authority of a municipal corporation may make such regulations pertaining to public buildings as it considers necessary for the public safety.

HISTORY: RS Bates § 1536-317f; 97 v 266, § 6; GC § 4664; Bureau of Code Revision. Eff 10-1-53.

§ 737.41 Municipal probation services fund.

(A) The legislative authority of a municipal corporation in which is established a municipal court, other than a county-operated municipal court, that has a department of probation shall establish in the municipal treasury a municipal probation services fund. The fund shall contain all moneys paid to the treasurer of the municipal corporation under section 2951.021 [2951.02.1] of the Revised Code for deposit into the fund. The treasurer of the municipal corporation shall disburse the money contained in the fund at the request of the municipal court department of probation, for use only by that department for specialized staff, purchase of equipment, purchase of services, reconciliation programs for offenders and victims, other treatment programs, including alcohol and drug addiction programs certified under section 3793.06 of the Revised Code, determined to be appropriate by the chief probation officer, and other similar probation-related expenses.

(B) Any money in a municipal probation services fund at the end of a fiscal year shall not revert to the treasury of the municipal corporation but shall be retained in the fund.

(C) As used in this section, "county-operated municipal court" has the same meaning as in section 1901.03 of the Revised Code.

HISTORY: 145 v H 406. Eff 11-11-94.

§ 737.99 Penalty.

Whoever violates section 737.30 of the Revised Code shall be fined not less than twice the value of any property not deposited as provided by such section, but not more than three thousand dollars, or imprisoned not more than thirty days, or both.

HISTORY: Bureau of Code Revision, 10-1-53; 127 v 285, § 2 (Eff 9-7-57); 133 v H 290 (Eff 7-14-70); 134 v H 24. Eff 10-6-71.

CHAPTER 753: REFORMATORY INSTITUTIONS

[PRISONS AND STATION HOUSES]

§ 753.02 Municipal liability for sustaining inmates in prison or station house; reimbursement by inmate.

(A) The legislative authority of a municipal corporation shall provide by ordinance for sustaining all persons sentenced to or confined in a prison or station house at the expense of the municipal corporation, and in counties where prisons or station houses are in quarters leased from the board of county commissioners, may contract with the board for the care and maintenance of such persons by the sheriff or other person charged with the care and maintenance of county prisoners. On the presentation of bills for food, sustenance, and necessary supplies, to the proper officer, certified by such person as the legislative authority designates, the officer shall audit the bills under the rules prescribed by the legislative authority, and draw the officer's order on the treasurer of the municipal corporation in favor of the person presenting the bill.

(B)(1) The legislative authority of the municipal corporation may require a person who was convicted of an offense and who is confined in a prison or station house as provided in division (A) of this section, or a person who was convicted of an offense and who is confined in the county jail as provided in section 1905.35 of the Revised Code, to reimburse the municipal corporation for its expenses incurred by reason of the person's confinement, including, but not limited to, the expenses relating to the provision of food, clothing, shelter, medical care, personal hygiene products, including, but not limited to, toothpaste, toothbrushes, and feminine hygiene items, and up to two hours of overtime costs the sheriff or municipal corporation incurred relating to the trial of the person. The amount of reimbursement may be the actual cost of the prisoner's confinement plus the authorized trial overtime costs or a lesser amount determined by the legislative authority of the municipal corporation, provided that the lesser amount shall be determined by a formula that is uniformly applied to persons incarcerated in the prison, station house, or county jail. The amount of reimbursement shall be determined by a court at a hearing held pursuant to section 2929.18 of the Revised Code if the person† prisoner is confined for a felony or section 2929.223 [2929.22.3] of the Revised Code if the person† prisoner is confined for a misdemeanor. The amount or amounts paid in reimbursement by a prisoner confined for a misdemeanor or the amount recovered from a prisoner confined for a misdemeanor by executing upon the judgment obtained pursuant to section 2929.223 [2929.22.3] of the Revised Code shall be paid into the treasury of the municipal corporation. If a person† prisoner is confined for a felony and the court imposes a sanction under section 2929.18 of the Revised Code that requires the person† prisoner to reimburse the costs of confinement, the village solicitor, city director of law, or other chief legal officer shall bring an action to recover the expenses of confinement in accordance with section 2929.18 of the Revised Code.

(2) The legislative authority of the municipal corporation may adopt an ordinance specifying that a person who is convicted of a felony and who is confined in a prison or station house as provided in division (A) of this section is not required to reimburse the municipal corporation for its expenses incurred by reason of the person's confinement, including the expenses listed in division (B)(1) of this section. If the legislative authority adopts an ordinance of that nature, the legislative authority shall provide a copy to the court of common pleas of the county, and the court that sentences a person convicted of a felony shall not impose a sanction under section 2929.18 of the Revised Code that requires the person to reimburse the costs of the confinement.

(C) In lieu of requiring offenders to reimburse the municipal corporation for expenses incurred by reason of the person's confinement under division (B) of this section, the legislative authority of the municipal corporation may adopt a prisoner reimbursement policy for the prison or station house under this division. The prison or station house administrator may appoint a reimbursement coordinator to administer the prisoner reimbursement policy. A prisoner reimbursement policy adopted under this division is a policy that requires a person confined to the prison or station house to reimburse the municipal corporation for any expenses it incurs by reason of the person's confinement in the prison or station house, which expenses may include, but are not limited to, the following:

(1) A per diem fee for room and board of not more than sixty dollars per day or the actual per diem cost, whichever is less, for the entire period of time the person is confined to the prison or station house;

(2) Actual charges for medical and dental treatment;

(3) Reimbursement for municipal property damaged by the person while confined to the prison or station house.

Rates charged shall be on a sliding scale determined by the legislative authority of the municipal corporation, based on the ability of the person confined to the prison or station house to pay and on consideration of any legal obligation of the person to support a spouse, minor children, or other dependents and any moral obligation to support dependents to whom the person is providing or has in fact provided support.

The reimbursement coordinator or another appointed person may investigate the financial status of the confined person and obtain information necessary to investigate that status, by means that may include contacting employers and reviewing income tax records.

The coordinator may work with the confined person to create a repayment plan to be implemented upon the person's release. At the end of the person's incarceration, the person shall be presented with a billing statement.

The reimbursement coordinator or another appointed person may collect, or the legislative authority of the municipal corporation may enter into a contract with one or more public agencies or private vendors to collect, any amounts remaining unpaid. Within twelve months after the date of the confined person's release, the city director of law, village solicitor, or other attorney for the municipal corporation may file a civil action to seek reimbursement from that person for any billing amount that remains unpaid. The municipal corporation shall not enforce any judgment obtained under this section by means of execution against the person's homestead. For purposes of this section, "homestead" has the same meaning as in division (A) of section 323.151 [323.15.1] of the Revised Code. Any reimbursement received under this section shall be credited to the general fund of the municipal corporation that bore the expense, to be used for general fund purposes.

(D)(1) Notwithstanding any contrary provision in this section or section 2929.18 or 2929.223 [2929.22.3] of the Revised Code, the legislative authority of the municipal corporation may establish a policy that requires any person who is not indigent and who is confined in a prison or station house to pay a reasonable fee for any medical treatment or service requested by and provided to that person. This fee shall not exceed the actual cost of the treatment or service provided. No person confined to a prison or station house who is indigent shall be required to pay those fees, and no person confined to a prison or station house shall be denied any necessary medical care because of inability to pay those fees.

Upon provision of the requested medical treatment or service, payment of the required fee may be automatically deducted from a person's account record in the prison or station house's business office. If the person has no funds in the person's account, a deduction may be made at a later date during the person's confinement in the prison or station house if funds later become available in the person's account. If the person is released from the prison or station house and has an unpaid balance of these fees, the legislative authority may bill the person for payment of the remaining unpaid fees. Fees received for medical treatment or services shall be paid into the commissary fund, if one has been created for the prison or station house, or if no such fund exists, into the municipal treasury.

(2) If a person confined to a prison or station house is required under division (B) or (C) of this section or section 2929.18 or 2929.223 [2929.22.3] of the Revised Code to reimburse the municipal corporation for expenses incurred by reason of the person's confinement to the prison or station house, any fees paid by the person under division (D)(1) of this section shall be deducted from the expenses required to be reimbursed under division (B) or (C) of this section or section 2929.18 or 2929.223 [2929.22.3] of the Revised Code.

HISTORY: RS § 2093; Bates § 1536-367; 66 v 186, § 217; GC § 4126; 107 v 502; 124 v 127; Bureau of Code Revision, 10-1-53; 134 v H 172 (Eff 11-25-71); 140 v H 363 (Eff 9-26-84); 146 v S 2 (Eff 7-1-96); 146 v S 269 (Eff 7-1-96); 146 v H 480. Eff 10-16-96.

Publisher's Note

The amendments made by SB 269 (146 v —) and HB 480 (146 v —) have been combined. Please see provisions of RC § 1.52.

† Added by SB 269 (146 v —), eff 7-1-96.

[§ 753.02.1] § 753.021 Submission of health insurance claims for inmates.

(A) For each person who is confined in a prison or station house as provided in section 753.02 of the Revised Code or in a county jail as provided in section 1905.35 of the Revised Code, the municipal corporation may make a determination as to whether the person is covered under a health insurance or health care policy, contract, or plan and, if the person has such coverage, what terms and conditions are imposed by it for the filing and payment of claims.

(B) If, pursuant to division (A) of this section, it is determined that the person is covered under a policy, contract, or plan and, while that coverage is in force, the prison, station house, or county jail renders or arranges for the rendering of health care services to the person, in accordance with the terms and conditions of the policy, contract, or plan, then the person, municipal corporation, or provider of the health care services, as appropriate under the terms and conditions of the policy, contract, or plan, shall promptly submit a claim for payment for the health care services to the appropriate third-party payer and shall designate, or make any other arrangement necessary to ensure, that payment of any amount due on the claim be made to the municipal corporation or the provider, as the case may be.

(C) Any payment made to the municipal corporation pursuant to division (B) of this section shall be paid into the treasury of the municipal corporation.

(D) This section also applies to any person who is under the custody of a law enforcement officer, as defined in section 2901.01 of the Revised Code, prior to the person's confinement in the prison, station house, or county jail.

HISTORY: 146 v S 163. Eff 10-16-96.

§ 753.03 Disposition of prisoners sentenced for misdemeanors.

A municipal legislative authority may, by ordinance, provide for the keeping of persons convicted and sentenced for misdemeanors, during the term of their imprisonment, at such place as the legislative authority determines, provided that the place selected is in substantial compliance with the minimum standards for jails in Ohio promulgated by the department of rehabilitation and correction. The legislative authority may enter into a contract under section 9.06 of the Revised Code for the private operation and management of any municipal correctional facility, but only if the facility is used to house only misdemeanant inmates.

HISTORY: RS § 2094; Bates § 1536-368; 66 v 186, § 218; GC § 4127; Bureau of Code Revision, 10-1-53; 139 v S 23 (Eff 7-6-82); 146 v H 117. Eff 9-29-95.

The effective date is set by section 197 of HB 117.

[WORKHOUSES]

§ 753.04 Commitment to workhouse.

(A) When a person over sixteen years of age is convicted of an offense under the law of this state or an ordinance of a municipal corporation, and the tribunal before which the conviction is had is authorized by law to commit the offender to the county jail or municipal corporation prison, the court, mayor, or judge of the county court, as the case may be, may sentence the offender to a workhouse.

When a commitment is made from a municipal corporation or township in the county, other than in a municipal corporation having a workhouse, the legislative authority of the municipal corporation or the board of township trustees shall transmit with the mittimus a sum of money equal to not less than seventy cents per day for the time of the commitment, to be placed in the hands of the superintendent of a workhouse for the care and maintenance of the prisoner.

(B)(1) The legislative authority of the municipal corporation or the board of township trustees may require a person who is convicted of an offense and who is confined in a workhouse as provided in division (A) of this section, to reimburse the municipal corporation or the township, as the case may be, for its expenses incurred by reason of the person's confinement, including, but not limited to, the expenses relating to the provision of food, clothing, shelter, medical care, personal hygiene products, including, but not limited to, toothpaste, toothbrushes, and feminine hygiene items, and up to two hours of overtime costs the sheriff or municipal corporation incurred relating to the trial of the person. The amount of reimbursement may be the actual cost of the prisoner's confinement plus the authorized trial overtime costs or a lesser amount determined by the legislative authority of the municipal corporation or board of township trustees, provided that the lesser amount shall be determined by a formula that is uniformly applied to persons incarcerated in the workhouse. The amount of reimbursement shall be determined by a court at a hearing held pursuant to section 2929.18 of the Revised Code if the prisoner person† is confined for a felony or section 2929.223 [2929.22.3] of the Revised Code if the prisoner is confined for a misdemeanor. The amount or amounts paid in reimbursement by a prisoner confined for a misdemeanor or the amount recovered from a prisoner confined for a misdemeanor by executing upon the judgment obtained pursuant to section 2929.223 [2929.22.3] of the Revised Code shall be paid into the treasury of the municipal corporation or township that incurred the expenses. If a prisoner person† is confined for a felony and the court imposes a sanction under section 2929.18 of the Revised Code that requires the prisoner person† to reimburse the costs of confinement, the city director of law, village solicitor, or other chief legal officer shall bring an action to recover the expenses of confinement in accordance with section 2929.18 of the Revised Code.

(2) The legislative authority of a municipal corporation or the board of township trustees may adopt an ordinance or resolution specifying that a person who is convicted of a felony and who is confined in a workhouse as provided in division (A) of this section is not required to reimburse the municipal corporation or the township, as the case may be, for its expenses incurred by reason of the person's confinement, including the expenses listed in division (B)(1) of this section. If the legislative authority or board adopts a resolution of that nature, the legislative authority or board shall provide a copy to the court of common pleas of the county, and the court that sentences a person convicted of a felony shall not impose a sanction under section 2929.18 of the Revised Code that requires the person to reimburse the costs of the confinement.

(C) In lieu of requiring offenders to reimburse the political subdivision for expenses incurred by reason of the person's confinement in a municipal workhouse under division (B) of this section or under division (C) of section 753.16 of the Revised Code, the legislative authority of the municipal corporation may adopt a prisoner reimbursement policy for the workhouse under this division. A reimbursement coordinator may be appointed to administer the prisoner reimbursement policy. A prisoner reimbursement policy adopted under this division is a policy that requires a person confined to the municipal workhouse to reimburse any expenses it incurs by reason of the person's confinement in the workhouse, which expenses may include, but are not limited to, the following:

(1) A per diem fee for room and board of not more than sixty dollars per day or the actual per diem cost, whichever is less, for the entire period of time the person is confined to the workhouse;

(2) Actual charges for medical and dental treatment;

(3) Reimbursement for municipal property damaged by the person while confined to the workhouse.

Rates charged shall be on a sliding scale determined by the legislative authority of the municipal corporation based on the ability of the person confined to the workhouse to pay and on consideration of any legal obligation of the person to support a spouse, minor children, or other dependents and any moral obligation to support dependents to whom the person is providing or has in fact provided support.

The reimbursement coordinator or another workhouse employee may investigate the financial status of the confined person and obtain information necessary to investigate that status, by means that may include contacting employers and reviewing income tax records. The coordinator may work with the confined person to create a repayment plan to be implemented upon the person's release. At the end of the person's incarceration, the person shall be presented with a billing statement.

The reimbursement coordinator or another workhouse employee may collect, or the legislative authority of the municipal corporation may enter into a contract with one or more public agencies or private vendors to collect, any amounts remaining unpaid. Within twelve months after the date of the confined person's release, the city director of law, village solicitor, or other attorney for the municipal corporation may file a civil action to seek reimbursement from that person for any billing amount that remains unpaid. The municipal corporation shall not enforce any judgment obtained under this section by means of execution against the person's homestead. For purposes of this section, "homestead" has the same meaning as in division (A) of section 323.151 [323.15.1] of the Revised Code. Any reimbursement received under this section shall be credited to the general fund of the political subdivision that bore the expense, to be used for general fund purposes.

(D)(1) Notwithstanding any contrary provision in this section or section 2929.18 or 2929.223 [2929.22.3] of the Revised Code, the legislative authority of the municipal corporation or board of township trustees may establish a policy that requires any person who is not indigent and who is confined in the workhouse under division (A) of this section to pay a reasonable fee for any medical treatment or service requested by and provided to that person. This fee shall not exceed the actual cost of the treatment or service provided. No person confined to a workhouse who is indigent shall be required to pay those fees, and no person confined to a workhouse shall be denied any necessary medical care because of inability to pay those fees.

Upon provision of the requested medical treatment or service, payment of the required fee may be automatically deducted from a person's account record in the workhouse's business office. If the person has no funds in the person's account, a deduction may be made at a later date during the person's confinement in the center if funds later become available in the person's account. If the person is released from the workhouse and has an unpaid balance of these fees, the legislative authority or board of township trustees may bill the person for payment of the remaining unpaid fees. Fees received for medical treatment or services shall be paid into the commissary fund, if one has been created for the workhouse, or if no such fund exists, into the treasury of the municipal corporation or township.

(2) If a person confined to a workhouse under division (A) of this section is required under division (B) of this section or section 2929.18 or 2929.223 [2929.22.3] of the Revised Code to reimburse medical expenses incurred by reason of the person's confinement to the workhouse, any fees paid by the person under division (C)(1) of this section shall be deducted from the expenses required to be reimbursed under division (B) of this section or section 2929.18 or 2929.223 [2929.22.3] of the Revised Code.

HISTORY: RS § 2099; Bates § 1536-369; 99 v 125; 73 v 211, § 275; GC § 4128; 110 v 12; Bureau of Code Revision, 10-1-53; 126 v 320; 127 v 1039 (Eff 1-1-58); 140 v H 363 (Eff 9-26-84); 146 v S 2 (Eff 7-1-96); 146 v S 269 (Eff 7-1-96); 146 v H 480. Eff 10-16-96.

Publisher's Note

The amendments made by SB 269 (146 v —) and HB 480 (146 v —) have been combined. Please see provisions of RC § 1.52.

† Added by SB 269 (146 v —), eff 7-1-96.

[§ 753.04.1] § 753.041 Submission of health insurance claims for workhouse inmates.

(A) For each person who is confined in a workhouse as provided in section 753.04 of the Revised Code, the municipal corporation or the township, as the case may be, may make a determination as to whether the person is covered under a health insurance or health care policy, contract, or plan and, if the person has such coverage, what terms and conditions are imposed by it for the filing and payment of claims.

(B) If, pursuant to division (A) of this section, it is determined that the person is covered under a policy, contract, or plan and, while that coverage is in force, the workhouse renders or arranges for the rendering of health care services to the person in accordance with the terms and conditions of the policy, contract, or plan, then the person, municipal corporation, township, or provider of the health care services, as appropriate under the terms and conditions of the policy, contract, or plan, shall promptly submit a claim for payment for the health care services to the appropriate third-party payer and shall designate, or make any other arrangement necessary to ensure, that payment of any amount due on the claim be made to the municipal corporation, township, or provider, as the case may be.

(C) Any payment made to the municipal corporation or township pursuant to division (B) of this section shall be paid into the treasury of the governmental entity that incurred the expenses.

(D) This section also applies to any person who is under the custody of a law enforcement officer, as de-

fined in section 2901.01 of the Revised Code, prior to the person's confinement in the workhouse.
HISTORY: 146 v S 163. Eff 10-16-96.

§ 753.05 Employment of prisoners.

A person sentenced under section 753.04 of the Revised Code shall be received into the workhouse, and shall be kept and confined at labor therein, or if such labor cannot be furnished he may be employed at labor elsewhere when such employment is authorized by ordinance, and shall be subject to the rules, regulations, and discipline thereof until the expiration of his sentence, when he shall be discharged.
HISTORY; RS § 2100; Bates § 1536-370; 66 v 195, § 276; 82 v 117; GC § 4129; 110 v 12; Bureau of Code Revision. Eff 10-1-53.

§ 753.08 Prompt commitment; fees.

The officer having the execution of the final sentence of a court, magistrate, or mayor shall cause the convicted person to be conveyed to the workhouse as soon as practicable after the sentence is pronounced, and all officers shall be paid the fees therefor allowed by law for similar services in other cases. Such fees shall be paid, when the sentence is by the court, from the county treasury, and when by the magistrate, from the township treasury.
HISTORY: RS § 2101; Bates § 1536-372; 66 v 196, § 277; GC § 4132; Bureau of Code Revision. Eff 10-1-53.

§ 753.09 Discharge.

The director of public safety may discharge, for good and sufficient cause, a person committed to the workhouse. A record of all such discharges shall be kept and reported to the legislative authority of the municipal corporation in the annual report of such director, with a brief statement of the reasons therefor.
HISTORY: RS § 2102; Bates § 1536-373; 66 v 196, § 278; 97 v 488; GC § 4133; Bureau of Code Revision. Eff 10-1-53.

§ 753.10 Parole of inmates.

The director of public safety may establish rules and regulations under which, and specify the conditions on which, a prisoner may be allowed to go upon parole outside of the buildings and enclosures of the workhouse. While on parole such person shall remain in the legal custody and under the control of such director, and subject at any time to be taken back within the enclosure of the institution. Full power to enforce the rules, regulations, and conditions, and to retake and reimprison any convict so paroled, is hereby conferred upon such director, whose written order shall be sufficient warrant for all officers named therein to authorize them to return to actual custody any conditionally released or paroled prisoner. All such officers shall execute such order the same as ordinary criminal process.

No parole shall be granted by such director without previous notice thereof to the trial judge.
HISTORY: RS § 2102; Bates § 1536-373; 66 v 196, § 278; 97 v 488; GC § 4134; Bureau of Code Revision. Eff 10-1-53.

§ 753.11 Violation of parole.

The director of public safety may employ or authorize any person to see that the conditions of a parole are not violated, and in case of violation to return to the workhouse any prisoner so violating his parole. The time between the violation of the conditions of such parole, or conditional release by whatever name, as entered by order of such director on the records of the workhouse, and the reimprisonment or return of the prisoner, shall not be counted as any part or portion of time served under his sentence.
HISTORY: RS § 2102; Bates § 1536-373; 66 v 196, § 278; 97 v 488; GC § 4135; Bureau of Code Revision. Eff 10-1-53.

§ 753.13 Joint municipal and county workhouse.

The board of county commissioners may unite with any municipal corporation located in the county in the acquisition or erection, management, and maintenance of a workhouse for the joint use of such county and municipal corporation, upon such terms as they may agree, and the board may levy and collect the necessary funds therefor from the taxable property of the county.
HISTORY: RS § 2107; Bates § 1536-377; 68 v 114; 81 v 129; 97 v 448; GC § 4139; Bureau of Code Revision. Eff 10-1-53.

Analogous to RS §§ 2107a to 2107w, 2107-1 to 2107-17.

§ 753.14 Withdrawal from support and maintenance of joint workhouse.

In any county in which, prior to May 20, 1920, there has been constructed and maintained a joint municipal and county workhouse, either the municipal corporation or the county may withdraw therefrom, may decline to further participate in the expense of maintaining such institution, and may sell its interest in such institution.

In the event of a sale thereof by such municipal corporation or county, the proceeds thereof shall be used in the payment of such indebtedness as was incurred in behalf of such municipal corporation or county in the management, control, and operation of such workhouse, and any balance remaining shall be placed in the general fund of such municipal corporation or county.
HISTORY: GC § 4139-1; 108 v PtII 1232; Bureau of Code Revision. Eff 10-1-53.

§ 753.15 Workhouses; management by joint board; privatization.

(A) Except as provided in division (B) of this section,

in a city, a workhouse erected for the joint use of the city and the county in which such city is located shall be managed and controlled by a joint board composed of the board of county commissioners and the board of control of the city, and in a village by the board of county commissioners and the board of trustees of public affairs. Such joint board shall have all the powers and duties in the management, control, and maintenance of such workhouse as are conferred upon the director of public safety in cities, and in addition thereto it may construct sewers for such workhouse and pay therefor from funds raised by taxation for the maintenance of such institution.

The joint board may lease or purchase suitable property and buildings for a workhouse, or real estate for the purpose of erecting and maintaining a workhouse thereon, but it shall not expend more than ten thousand dollars for any such purpose unless such amount is approved by a majority of the voters of the county, exclusive of the municipal corporation, voting at a general election.

(B) In lieu of forming a joint board to manage and control a workhouse erected for the joint use of the city and the county in which the city is located, the board of county commissioners and the legislative authority of the city may enter into a contract for the private operation and management of the workhouse as provided in section 9.06 of the Revised Code, but only if the workhouse is used solely for misdemeanant inmates. In order to enter into a contract under section 9.06 of the Revised Code, both the board and the legislative authority shall approve and be parties to the contract.

HISTORY: RS § 2107; Bates § 1536-377; 68 v 114, § 1; 81 v 129; 97 v 448; GC § 4140; 101 v 240; Bureau of Code Revision, 10-1-53; 146 v H 117. Eff 9-29-95.

The effective date is set by section 197 of HB 117.

§ 753.16 Workhouse may receive prisoners from other counties or state prisoners.

(A) Any city or district having a workhouse may receive as inmates of the workhouse persons sentenced or committed to it from counties other than the one in which the workhouse is situated, upon such terms and during such length of time as agreed upon by the boards of county commissioners of such counties, or by the legislative authority of a municipal corporation in such counties and the legislative authority of the city, or the board of the district workhouse, or other authority having the management and control of the workhouse. Prisoners so received shall in all respects be and remain under the control of such authority, and subject to the rules and discipline of the workhouse the same as other prisoners detained there.

(B) Prior to the acceptance for housing into a jail or workhouse of persons who are designated by the department of rehabilitation and correction, who plead guilty to or are convicted of a felony of the fourth or fifth degree, and who satisfy the other requirements listed in section 5120.161 [5120.16.1] of the Revised Code, the legislative authority of a municipal corporation having a jail or workhouse, or the joint board managing and controlling a workhouse for the joint use of a municipal corporation and a county shall enter into an agreement with the department of rehabilitation and correction under section 5120.161 [5120.16.1] of the Revised Code for the housing in the jail or workhouse of persons who are designated by the department, who plead guilty to or are convicted of a felony of the fourth or fifth degree, and who satisfy the other requirements listed in that section, in exchange for a per diem fee per person. Persons incarcerated in the jail or workhouse pursuant to such an agreement shall be subject to supervision and control in the manner described in section 5120.161 [5120.16.1] of the Revised Code. This division does not affect the authority of a court to directly sentence a person who is convicted of or pleads guilty to a felony to the jail or workhouse in accordance with section 2929.16 of the Revised Code.

(C)(1) The board of county commissioners, the legislative authority of the municipal corporation, or the board or other managing authority of the district workhouse may require a person who was convicted of an offense and who is confined in the workhouse as provided in division (A) of this section, to reimburse the county, municipal corporation, or district, as the case may be, for its expenses incurred by reason of the person's confinement, including, but not limited to, the expenses relating to the provision of food, clothing, shelter, medical care, personal hygiene products, including, but not limited to, toothpaste, toothbrushes, and feminine hygiene items, and up to two hours of overtime costs the sheriff or municipal corporation incurred relating to the trial of the person. The amount of reimbursement may be the actual cost of the prisoner's confinement plus the authorized trial overtime costs or a lesser amount determined by the board of county commissioners for the county, the legislative authority of the municipal corporation, or the board or other managing authority of the district workhouse, provided that the lesser amount shall be determined by a formula that is uniformly applied to persons incarcerated in the workhouse. The amount of reimbursement shall be determined by a court at a hearing held pursuant to section 2929.18 of the Revised Code if the prisoner person† is confined for a felony or section 2929.223 [2929.22.3] of the Revised Code if the prisoner person† is confined for a misdemeanor. The amount or amounts paid in reimbursement by a prisoner confined for a misdemeanor or the amount recovered from a prisoner confined for a misdemeanor by executing upon the judgment obtained pursuant to section 2929.223 [2929.22.3] of the Revised Code shall be paid into the treasury of the county, municipal corporation, or district that incurred the expenses. If a prisoner person† is confined for a felony and the court imposes a sanction under section 2929.18 of the Revised Code that requires the prisoner person† to reimburse the costs of confinement, the prosecuting attorney or municipal chief legal officer shall bring an action to recover the expenses of confinement in accordance with section 2929.18 of the Revised Code.

(2) The board of county commissioners, the legislative authority of the municipal corporation, or the board or other managing authority of the district workhouse may adopt a resolution or ordinance specifying that a person who is convicted of a felony and who is confined in the workhouse as provided in division (A) of this section is not required to reimburse the county, municipal corporation, or district, as the case may be, for its expenses incurred by reason of the person's confinement, including the expenses listed in division (C)(1) of this section. If the board, legislative authority, or managing authority adopts a resolution of that nature, the board, legislative authority or managing authority shall provide a copy to the court of common pleas of the county, and the court that sentences a person convicted of a felony shall not impose a sanction under section 2929.18 of the Revised Code that requires the person to reimburse the costs of the confinement.

(D)(1) Notwithstanding any contrary provision in this section or section 2929.223 [2929.22.3] of the Revised Code, the board of county commissioners, the legislative authority of a municipal corporation, or the board or other managing authority of the district workhouse may establish a policy that requires any person who is not indigent and who is confined in the jail or workhouse under division (A) or (B) of this section to pay a reasonable fee for any medical treatment or service requested by and provided to that person. This fee shall not exceed the actual cost of the treatment or service provided. No person who is indigent shall be required to pay those fees, and no person shall be denied any necessary medical care because of inability to pay those fees.

Upon provision of the requested medical treatment or service, payment of the required fee may be automatically deducted from a person's account record in the jail or workhouse's business office. If the person has no funds in the person's account, a deduction may be made at a later date during the person's confinement in the jail or workhouse if funds later become available in that person's account. If the person is released from the jail or workhouse and has an unpaid balance of these fees, the board of county commissioners, the legislative authority of the municipal corporation, or the board or other managing authority of the district workhouse may bill the person for payment of the remaining unpaid fees. Fees received for medical treatment or services shall be paid into the commissary fund, if one has been created for the workhouse, or if no such fund exists, into the treasury of each applicable political subdivision.

(2) If a person confined to a jail or workhouse is required under division (C) of this section or section 2929.18 or 2929.223 [2929.22.3] of the Revised Code to reimburse medical expenses incurred by reason of the person's confinement to the jail or workhouse, any fees paid by the person under division (D)(1) of this section shall be deducted from the expenses required to be reimbursed under division (C) of this section or section 2929.18 or 2929.223 [2929.22.3] of the Revised Code.

HISTORY: RS § 2107a; Bates § 1536-378; 80 v 220; GC § 4141; 110 v 12; Bureau of Code Revision, 10-1-53; 139 v S 23 (Eff 7-6-82); 139 v S 199 (Eff 1-1-83); 140 v H 363 (Eff 9-26-84); 146 v S 2 (Eff 7-1-96); 146 v S 269 (Eff 7-1-96); 146 v H 480. Eff 10-16-96.

Publisher's Note

The amendments made by SB 269 (146 v —) and HB 480 (146 v —) have been combined. Please see provisions of RC § 1.52.

† Added by SB 269 (146 v —), eff 7-1-96.

[§ 753.16.1] § 753.161 Submission of health insurance claims of out-of-county inmates.

(A) For each person who is confined in a workhouse as provided in section 753.16 of the Revised Code, the county, municipal corporation, or district, as the case may be, may make a determination as to whether the person is covered under a health insurance or health care policy, contract, or plan and, if the person has such coverage, what terms and conditions are imposed by it for the filing and payment of claims.

(B) If, pursuant to division (A) of this section, it is determined that the person is covered under a policy, contract, or plan and, while that coverage is in force, the workhouse renders or arranges for the rendering of health care services to the person in accordance with the terms and conditions of the policy, contract, or plan, then the person, county, municipal corporation, district, or provider of the health care services, as appropriate under the terms and conditions of the policy, contract, or plan, shall promptly submit a claim for payment for the health care services to the appropriate third-party payer and shall designate, or make any other arrangement necessary to ensure, that payment of any amount due on the claim be made to the county, municipal corporation, district, or provider, as the case may be.

(C) Any payment made to the county, municipal corporation, or district pursuant to division (B) of this section shall be paid into the treasury of the governmental entity that incurred the expenses.

(D) This section also applies to any person who is under the custody of a law enforcement officer, as defined in section 2901.01 of the Revised Code, prior to the person's confinement in the workhouse.

HISTORY: 146 v S 163. Eff 10-16-96.

§ 753.17 Officers to have police powers.

The superintendent, assistant superintendent, and each guard of a workhouse shall have such powers of policemen as are necessary for the proper performance of the duties of their positions.

HISTORY: RS § 2105; Bates § 1536-375; 66 v 196, § 281; GC § 4137; Bureau of Code Revision. Eff 10-1-53.

[RELIGIOUS SERVICES]

§ 753.18 Religious services in jail or workhouse.

Each administrative board or other authority in the state having charge or control of a city jail or workhouse shall provide for holding religious services therein each week, and may employ a clergyman or religious organization to conduct such services. Any expense so incurred by such board or authority shall be paid from the general fund of the city.

HISTORY: GC § 4153; 99 v 225, § 3; Bureau of Code Revision, 10-1-53; 139 v S 23. Eff 7-6-82.

§ 753.19 Notice of escape of violent offender.

If a person who was convicted of or pleaded guilty to an offense of violence that is a felony or was indicted or otherwise charged with the commission of an offense of violence that is a felony escapes from a jail or workhouse of a municipal corporation or otherwise escapes from the custody of a municipal corporation, the chief of police or other chief law enforcement officer of that municipal corporation immediately after the escape shall cause notice of the escape to be published in a newspaper of general circulation in the municipal corporation and in a newspaper of general circulation in each county in which part of the municipal corporation is located. The chief law enforcement officer also immediately after the escape shall give notice of the escape by telephone and in writing to the prosecuting attorney of the county in which the offense was committed. Upon the apprehension of the escaped person, the chief law enforcement officer shall give notice of the apprehension of the escaped person by telephone and in writing to the prosecuting attorney.

HISTORY: 142 v H 207. Eff 9-24-87.

§ 753.21 Minimum security jails.

(A) As used in this section, "building or structure" includes, but is not limited to, a modular unit, building, or structure and a movable unit, building, or structure.

(B)(1) The legislative authority of a municipal corporation, by ordinance, may dedicate and permit the use, as a minimum security jail, of any vacant or abandoned public building or structure owned by the municipal corporation that has not been dedicated to or is not then in use for any municipal or other public purpose, or any building or structure rented or leased by the municipal corporation. The legislative authority of a municipal corporation, by ordinance, also may dedicate and permit the use, as a minimum security jail, of any building or structure purchased by or constructed by or for the municipal corporation. Subject to divisions (B)(3) and (C) of this section, upon the effective date of such an ordinance, the specified building or structure shall be used, in accordance with this section, for the confinement of persons who meet one of the following conditions:

(a) The person is sentenced to a term of imprisonment for a traffic violation, a misdemeanor that is not an offense of violence, or a violation of a municipal ordinance that is not an offense of violence and the person is under the jurisdiction of the municipal corporation, and for the confinement of persons convicted of a felony who are sentenced to a residential sanction in the minimum security misdemeanant† jail pursuant to sections 2929.11 to 2929.19 of the Revised Code.†† or the person is sentenced to a term in the jail for a felony of the fourth or fifth degree that is not an offense of violence;

(b) The person is an inmate transferred by order of a judge of the sentencing court upon the request of the sheriff, administrator, jailer, or other person responsible for operating the jail other than a contractor as defined in division (H) of section 9.06 of the Revised Code, who is named in the request as being suitable for confinement in a minimum security facility.

(2) The legislative authority of a municipal corporation, by ordinance, may affiliate with the county in which it is located, with one or more counties adjacent to the county in which it is located, or with one or more municipal corporations located within the county in which it is located or within an adjacent county, and dedicate and permit the use, as a minimum security jail, of any vacant or abandoned public building or structure owned by any of the affiliating counties or municipal corporations that has not been dedicated to or is not then in use for any public purpose, or any building or structure rented or leased by any of the affiliating counties or municipal corporations. The legislative authority of a municipal corporation, by ordinance, also may affiliate with one or more counties adjacent to the county in which it is located or with one or more municipal corporations located within the county in which it is located or within an adjacent county and dedicate and permit the use, as a minimum security jail, of any building or structure purchased by or constructed by or for any of the affiliating counties or municipal corporations. Any counties and municipal corporations that affiliate for purposes of this division shall enter into an agreement that establishes the responsibilities for the operation and for the cost of operation of the minimum security jail. Subject to divisions (B)(3) and (C) of this section, upon the effective date of an ordinance adopted under this division, the specified building or structure

shall be used, in accordance with this section, for the confinement of persons who meet one of the following conditions:

(a) The person is sentenced to a term of imprisonment for a traffic violation, a misdemeanor that is not an offense of violence, or an ordinance of a municipal corporation that is not an offense of violence and the person is under the jurisdiction of any of the affiliating counties or municipal corporations, and for the confinement of persons convicted of a felony who are sentenced to a residential sanction in the minimum security misdemeanant† jail pursuant to sections 2929.11 to 2929.19 of the Revised Code,†† or the person is sentenced to a term in the jail for a felony of the fourth or fifth degree that is not an offense of violence;

(b) The person is an inmate transferred by order of a judge of the sentencing court upon the request of the sheriff, administrator, jailer, or other person responsible for operating the jail other than a contractor as defined in division (H) of section 9.06 of the Revised Code, who is named in the request as being suitable for confinement in a minimum security facility.

(3) No person shall be confined in a building or structure dedicated as a minimum security jail under division (B)(1) or (2) of this section unless the judge who sentenced the person to the term of imprisonment for the traffic violation or the misdemeanor or who sentenced the person to the residential sanction for the felony specifies that the term of imprisonment or the residential sanction is to be served in that jail. If a rented or leased building or structure is so dedicated, the building or structure may be used as a minimum security jail only during the period that it is rented or leased by the municipal corporation or by an affiliated county or municipal corporation. If a person convicted of a misdemeanor† is confined to a building or structure dedicated as a minimum security jail under division (B)(1) or (2) of this section and the sheriff, administrator, jailer, or other person responsible for operating the jail other than a contractor as defined in division (H) of section 9.06 of the Revised Code determines that it would be more appropriate for the person so confined to be confined in another jail or workhouse facility, the sheriff, administrator, jailer, or other person may transfer the person so confined to a more appropriate jail or workhouse facility.

(C) All of the following apply in relation to a building or structure that is dedicated pursuant to division (B)(1) or (2) of this section for use as a minimum security jail:

(1) To the extent that the use of the building or structure as a minimum security jail requires a variance from any municipal corporation, county, or township zoning ordinances or regulations, the variance shall be granted.

(2) Except as provided in this section, the building or structure shall not be used to confine any person unless it is in substantial compliance with any applicable housing, fire prevention, sanitation, health, and safety codes, regulations, or standards.

(3) Unless such satisfaction or compliance is required under the standards described in division (C)(4) of this section, and notwithstanding any other provision of state or local law to the contrary, the building or structure need not satisfy or comply with any state or local building standard or code in order to be used to confine a person for the purposes specified in division (B) of this section.

(4) The building or structure shall not be used to confine any person unless it is in compliance with all minimum standards and minimum renovation, modification, and construction criteria for minimum security jails that have been proposed by the department of rehabilitation and correction, through its bureau of adult detention, under section 5120.10 of the Revised Code.

(5) The building or structure need not be renovated or modified into a secure detention facility in order to be used solely to confine a person for the purposes specified in divisions (B)(1)(a) and (B)(2)(a) of this section.

(6) The building or structure shall be used, equipped, furnished, and staffed to provide adequate and suitable living, sleeping, food service or preparation, drinking, bathing and toilet, sanitation, and other necessary facilities, furnishings, and equipment.

(D) Except as provided in this section, a minimum security jail dedicated and used under this section shall be considered to be part of the jail, workhouse, or other correctional facilities of the municipal corporation or the affiliated counties and municipal corporations for all purposes under the law. All persons confined in such a minimum security jail shall be and shall remain, in all respects, under the control of the authority of the municipal corporation that has responsibility for the management and operation of the jail, workhouse, or other correctional facilities of the municipal corporation or, if it is operated by any affiliation of counties or municipal corporations, under the control of the specified county or municipal corporation with that authority, provided that, if the person was convicted of a felony and is serving a residential sanction in the facility, all provisions of law that pertain to persons convicted of a felony that would not by their nature clearly be inapplicable apply regarding the person. A minimum security jail dedicated and used under this section shall be managed and maintained in accordance with policies and procedures adopted by the legislative authority of the municipal corporation or the affiliated counties and municipal corporations governing the safe and healthful operation of the jail, the confinement and supervision of the persons sentenced to it, and their participation in work release or similar rehabilitation programs. In addition to other rules of conduct and discipline, the rights of ingress and egress of persons confined in a minimum security jail dedicated and used under this section shall be subject to reasonable restrictions. Every person confined in a minimum security jail dedicated and used under this section shall be given verbal and written notification, at the time of the person's admission to the jail, that purposely leaving, or purposely failing to return to, the jail without proper authority or permission constitutes the felony offense of escape.

HISTORY: 143 v S 131 (Eff 7-25-90); 143 v H 837 (Eff 7-25-90); 143 v S 258 (Eff 8-22-90); 144 v S 351 (Eff 7-1-92); 146 v H 117 (Eff 9-29-95); 146 v S 269 (Eff 7-1-96); 146 v H 480. Eff 10-16-96.

Publisher's Note

The amendments made by SB 269 (146 v —) and HB 480 (146 v —) have been combined. Please see provisions of RC § 1.52.

† The word "misdemeanant" was deleted throughout HB 480 (146 v —); however, it appears as new material in SB 269 (146 v —).

†† The punctuation results from the combination of SB 269 (146 v —) and HB 480 (146 v —).

§ 753.22 Commissary; fund.

(A) The director of public safety or the joint board established pursuant to section 753.15 of the Revised Code may establish a commissary for the workhouse. The commissary may be established either in-house or by another arrangement. If a commissary is established, all persons incarcerated in the workhouse shall receive commissary privileges. A person's purchases from the commissary shall be deducted from the person's account record in the workhouse's business office. The commissary shall provide for the distribution to indigent persons incarcerated in the workhouse necessary hygiene articles and writing materials.

(B) If a commissary is established, the director of public safety or the joint board established pursuant to section 753.15 of the Revised Code shall establish a commissary fund for the workhouse. The management of funds in the commissary fund shall be strictly controlled in accordance with procedures adopted by the auditor of state. Commissary fund revenue over and above operating costs and reserve shall be considered profits. All profits from the commissary fund shall be used to purchase supplies and equipment for the benefit of persons incarcerated in the workhouse. The director of public safety or the joint board established pursuant to section 753.15 of the Revised Code shall adopt rules and regulations for the operation of any commissary fund the director or the joint board establishes.

HISTORY: 146 v H 480. Eff 10-16-96.

§ 753.31 Prisoner access to exercise equipment or participation in fighting skills programs.

(A) As used in this section:

(1) "Free weight exercise equipment" means any equipment or device that is designed to increase the muscle mass and physical strength of the person using it. "Free weight exercise equipment" includes, but is not limited to, barbells, dumbbells, weight plates, and similar free weight-type equipment and other devices that the department of rehabilitation and correction, in rules adopted under section 5120.423 [5120.42.3] of the Revised Code, designates as enabling a person to increase muscle mass and physical strength.

(2) "Fixed weight exercise equipment" means any equipment, machine, or device that is not designed primarily to increase muscle mass and physical strength but rather to keep a person in relatively good physical condition. "Fixed weight exercise equipment" includes, but is not limited to, weight machines that utilize weight plates, tension bands, or similar devices that provide weight training resistance like universal and nautilus equipment. "Fixed weight exercise equipment" includes machines that are usually assembled as a unit, are not readily dismantled, and have been specifically modified for prison use so as to make them secure and immobile.

(3) "Municipal correctional officer" means a person who is employed by a municipal corporation as an employee or officer of a municipal jail, municipal workhouse, minimum security jail, joint city and county workhouse, municipal-county correctional center, multicounty-municipal correctional center, municipal-county jail or workhouse, or multicounty-municipal jail or workhouse.

(4) "Multicounty-municipal" has the same meaning as in section 307.93 of the Revised Code.

(B) No municipal correctional officer shall do any of the following:

(1) Provide a prisoner access to free weight or fixed weight exercise equipment;

(2) Allow a prisoner to provide or receive instruction in boxing, wrestling, karate, judo, or another form of martial arts, or any other program that the department of rehabilitation and correction, in rules adopted under section 5120.423 [5120.42.3] of the Revised Code, designates as enabling a person to improve fighting skills.

(C) Nothing in this section prohibits a municipal correctional officer from allowing a prisoner to participate in jogging, basketball, stationary exercise bicycling, supervised calisthenics, or other physical activities that are not designed to increase muscle mass and physical strength or improve fighting skills.

HISTORY: 146 v H 152. Eff 10-4-96.

TITLE 9: AGRICULTURE—ANIMALS—FENCES

CHAPTER 951: ANIMALS RUNNING AT LARGE; STRAYS

[ANIMALS RUNNING AT LARGE]

§ 951.01 Prohibition against animals running at large.

No person, who is the owner or keeper of a stallion, jackass, bull, boar, ram, or buck, shall permit it to go or be at large out of its own enclosure.

HISTORY: RS § 4201; S&S 11; S&C 70; 29 v 467, §§ 1, 2, 3; 70 v 286; GC § 5808; Bureau of Code Revision, 10-1-53; 129 v 582(661) (Eff 1-10-61); 137 v H 531. Eff 11-3-78.

§ 951.02 Animals running at large on public roads; grazing on another's land.

No person, who is the owner or keeper of horses, mules, cattle, sheep, goats, swine, or geese, shall permit them to run at large in the public road, highway, street, lane, or alley, or upon unenclosed land, or cause such animals to be herded, kept, or detained for the purpose of grazing on premises other than those owned or lawfully occupied by the owner or keeper of such animals.

The running at large of any such animal in or upon any of the places mentioned in this section is prima-facie evidence that it is running at large in violation of this section.

HISTORY: RS §§ 4202, 4207; S&S 7, 8; S&C 76; 56 v 77, §§ 1, 2, 3; 62 v 185; 72 v 170; 78 v 18; 81 v 105; 93 v 129; 98 v 334; GC §§ 5809, 5818; 110 v 119; Bureau of Code Revision, 10-1-53; 137 v H 531. Eff 11-3-78.

§ 951.99 Penalty.

Whoever violates section 951.01 or 951.02 of the Revised Code is guilty of a misdemeanor of the fourth degree.

HISTORY: Bureau of Code Revision, 10-1-53; 137 v H 531. Eff 11-3-78.

Comment

This section was derived from GC § 12938. See also RC § 951.03.

CHAPTER 955: DOGS

[DOG AND KENNEL LICENSES]

§ 955.01 Registration of dogs.

(A)(1) Except as otherwise provided in this section or in sections 955.011 [955.01.1] and 955.16 of the Revised Code, every person who owns, keeps, or harbors a dog more than three months of age, shall, on or after the first day of the preceding December but before the twentieth day of January of each year, file in the office of the county auditor of the county in which the dog is kept or harbored, an application for registration for the following year, beginning the twentieth day of January of that year. The board of county commissioners may, in case of an emergency, extend the period for filing the application. The application shall state the age, sex, color, character of hair, whether short or long, breed, if known, and the name and address of the owner of the dog. A registration fee of two dollars for each dog shall accompany the application, unless a greater fee has been established under division (A)(2) of this section or under section 955.14 of the Revised Code.

(2) A board of county commissioners may establish a registration fee higher than the one provided for in division (A)(1) of this section for dogs more than nine months of age that have not been spayed or neutered, except that the higher registration fee permitted by this division shall not apply if a person registering a dog furnishes with the application either a certificate from a licensed veterinarian verifying that the dog should not be spayed or neutered because of its age or medical condition or because the dog is used or intended for use for show or breeding purposes or a certificate from the owner of the dog declaring that the owner holds a valid hunting license issued by the division of wildlife of the department of natural resources and that the dog is used or intended for use for hunting purposes. If the board establishes such a fee, the application for registration shall state whether the dog is spayed or neutered, and whether a licensed veterinarian has certified that the dog should not be spayed or neutered or the owner has stated that the dog is used or intended to be used for hunting purposes. The board may require a person who is registering a spayed or neutered dog to furnish with the application a certificate from a licensed veterinarian verifying that the dog is spayed or neutered. No person shall furnish a certificate under this division which he knows to be false.

(B) If the application for registration is not filed and the registration fee paid, on or before the twentieth day of January of each year or, in case of an emergency, the date established by the board, the auditor shall assess a penalty in an amount equal to the registration fee upon the owner, keeper, or harborer, which must be paid with the registration fee.

HISTORY: RS § 2833; 74 v 177, §§ 1, 3; 76 v 85, § 14; 87 v

160; 97 v 275; 98 v 87; 99 v 484; GC § 5652; 107 v 534; 108 v PtI 534; 112 v 347; 124 v 428; Bureau of Code Revision, 10-1-53; 127 v 444 (Eff 7-18-57); 127 v 681 (Eff 9-13-57); 130 v 275 (Eff 10-10-63); 135 v H 152 (Eff 11-21-73); 137 v H 775 (Eff 1-1-79); 141 v H 454 (Eff 11-1-85); 142 v H 246. Eff 12-12-88.

§ 955.10 Tags to be worn.

No owner of a dog, except a dog constantly confined to a registered kennel, shall fail to require the dog to wear, at all times, a valid tag issued in connection with a certificate of registration. A dog's failure at any time to wear a valid tag shall be prima-facie evidence of lack of registration and shall subject any dog found not wearing such tag to impounding, sale, or destruction.

HISTORY: GC § 5652-6; 107 v 534; Bureau of Code Revision, 10-1-53; 142 v H 246. Eff 12-12-88.

§ 955.11 Transfer of ownership or possession of dog.

(A) As used in this section:

(1)(a) "Dangerous dog" means a dog that, without provocation, and subject to division (A)(1)(b) of this section, has chased or approached in either a menacing fashion or an apparent attitude of attack, or has attempted to bite or otherwise endanger any person, while that dog is off the premises of its owner, keeper, or harborer and not under the reasonable control of its owner, keeper, harborer, or some other responsible person, or not physically restrained or confined in a locked pen which has a top, locked fenced yard, or other locked enclosure which has a top.

(b) "Dangerous dog" does not include a police dog that has chased or approached in either a menacing fashion or an apparent attitude of attack, or has attempted to bite or otherwise endanger any person while the police dog is being used to assist one or more law enforcement officers in the performance of their official duties.

(2) "Menacing fashion" means that a dog would cause any person being chased or approached to reasonably believe that the dog will cause physical injury to that person.

(3) "Police dog" means a dog that has been trained, and may be used, to assist one or more law enforcement officers in the performance of their official duties.

(4)(a) "Vicious dog" means a dog that, without provocation and subject to division (A)(4)(b) of this section, meets any of the following:

(i) Has killed or caused serious injury to any person;

(ii) Has caused injury, other than killing or serious injury, to any person, or has killed another dog.

(iii) Belongs to a breed that is commonly known as a pit bull dog. The ownership, keeping, or harboring of such a breed of dog shall be prima-facie evidence of the ownership, keeping, or harboring of a vicious dog.

(b) "Vicious dog" does not include either of the following:

(i) A police dog that has killed or caused serious injury to any person or that has caused injury, other than killing or serious injury, to any person while the police dog is being used to assist one or more law enforcement officers in the performance of their official duties;

(ii) A dog that has killed or caused serious injury to any person while a person was committing or attempting to commit a trespass or other criminal offense on the property of the owner, keeper, or harborer of the dog.

(5) "Without provocation" means that a dog was not teased, tormented, or abused by a person, or that the dog was not coming to the aid or the defense of a person who was not engaged in illegal or criminal activity and who was not using the dog as a means of carrying out such activity.

(B) Upon the transfer of ownership of any dog, the seller of the dog shall give the buyer a transfer of ownership certificate that shall be signed by the seller. The certificate shall contain the registration number of the dog, the name of the seller, and a brief description of the dog. Blank forms of the certificate may be obtained from the county auditor. A transfer of ownership shall be recorded by the auditor upon presentation of a transfer of ownership certificate that is signed by the former owner of a dog and that is accompanied by a fee of twenty-five cents.

(C) Prior to the transfer of ownership or possession of any dog, upon the buyer's or other transferee's request, the seller or other transferor of the dog shall give to the person a written notice relative to the behavior and propensities of the dog.

(D) Within ten days after the transfer of ownership or possession of any dog, if the seller or other transferor of the dog has knowledge that the dog is a dangerous or vicious dog, he shall give to the buyer or other transferee, the board of health for the district in which the buyer or other transferee resides, and the dog warden of the county in which the buyer or other transferee resides, a completed copy of a written form on which the seller shall furnish the following information:

(1) The name and address of the buyer or other transferee of the dog;

(2) The age, sex, color, breed, and current registration number of the dog.

In addition, the seller shall answer the following questions which shall be specifically stated on the form as follows:

"Has the dog ever chased or attempted to attack or bite a person? if yes, describe the incident(s) in which the behavior occurred."

"Has the dog ever bitten a person? if yes, describe the incident(s) in which the behavior occurred."

"Has the dog ever seriously injured or killed a person? if yes, describe the incident(s) in which the behavior occurred."

The dog warden of the county in which the seller

resides shall furnish the form to the seller at no cost.

(E) No seller or other transferor of a dog shall fail to comply with the applicable requirements of divisions (B) to (D) of this section.

HISTORY: GC § 5652-7c; 112 v 347; Bureau of Code Revision, 10-1-53; 135 v H 152 (Eff 11-21-73); 142 v H 352. Eff 7-10-87.

§ 955.22 Confinement or restraint of dog; liability insurance.

(A) As used in this section, "dangerous dog" and "vicious dog" have the same meanings as in section 955.11 of the Revised Code.

(B) No owner, keeper, or harborer of any female dog shall permit it to go beyond the premises of the owner, keeper, or harborer at any time the dog is in heat, unless the dog is properly in leash.

(C) No owner, keeper, or harborer of any dog shall fail at any time to keep it either physically confined or restrained upon the premises of the owner, keeper, or harborer by a leash, tether, adequate fence, supervision, or secure enclosure to prevent escape, or under reasonable control of some person, except when the dog is lawfully engaged in hunting accompanied by the owner, keeper, or harborer or a handler.

(D) No owner, keeper, or harborer of a dangerous or vicious dog shall fail to do either of the following, except when the dog is lawfully engaged in hunting or training for the purpose of hunting, accompanied by the owner, keeper, harborer, or a handler:

(1) While that dog is on the premises of the owner, keeper, or harborer, securely confine it at all times in a locked pen which has a top, locked fenced yard, or other locked enclosure which has a top, except that a dangerous dog may, in the alternative, be tied with a leash or tether so that the dog is adequately restrained;

(2) While that dog is off the premises of the owner, keeper, or harborer, keep it on a chain-link leash or tether that is not more than six feet in length and additionally do at least one of the following:

(a) Keep that dog in a locked pen which has a top, locked fenced yard, or other locked enclosure which has a top;

(b) Have the leash or tether controlled by a person who is of suitable age and discretion or securely attach, tie, or affix the leash or tether to the ground or a stationary object or fixture so that the dog is adequately restrained and station such a person in close enough proximity to that dog so as to prevent it from causing injury to any person;

(c) Muzzle that dog.

(E) No owner, keeper, or harborer of a vicious dog shall fail to obtain liability insurance with an insurer authorized to write liability insurance in this state providing coverage in each occurrence, subject to a limit, exclusive of interest and costs, of not less than fifty thousand dollars because of damage or bodily injury to or death of a person caused by the vicious dog.

HISTORY: GC § 5652-14a; 112 v 347; Bureau of Code Revision, 10-1-53; 131 v 387 (Eff 9-1-65); 142 v H 352. Eff 7-10-87.

[§ 955.22.1] § 955.221 Local ordinances or resolutions to control dogs.

(A) For the purposes of this section, ordinances or resolutions to control dogs include, but are not limited to, ordinances or resolutions concerned with the ownership, keeping, or harboring of dogs, the restraint of dogs, dogs as public nuisances, and dogs as a threat to public health, safety, and welfare, except that such ordinances or resolutions as permitted in division (B) of this section shall not prohibit the use of any dog which is lawfully engaged in hunting or training for the purpose of hunting while accompanied by a licensed hunter. However, such dogs at all other times and in all other respects shall be subject to the ordinance or resolution permitted by this section, unless actually in the field and engaged in hunting or in legitimate training for such purpose.

(B)(1) A board of county commissioners may adopt and enforce resolutions to control dogs within the unincorporated areas of the county that are not otherwise in conflict with any other provision of the Revised Code.

(2) A board of township trustees may adopt and enforce resolutions to control dogs within the township that are not otherwise in conflict with any other provision of the Revised Code, if the township is located in a county where the board of county commissioners has not adopted resolutions to control dogs within the unincorporated areas of the county under this section. In the event that the board of county commissioners adopts resolutions to control dogs in the county after a board of township trustees has adopted resolutions to control dogs within the township, the resolutions adopted by the county board of commissioners prevail over the resolutions adopted by the board of township trustees.

(3) A municipal corporation may adopt and enforce ordinances to control dogs within the municipal corporation that are not otherwise in conflict with any other provision of the Revised Code.

(C) No person shall violate any resolution or ordinance adopted under this section.

HISTORY: 142 v H 352 (Eff 7-10-87); 143 v H 291. Eff 6-21-90.

§ 955.25 Unlawful tag.

No person shall own, keep, or harbor a dog wearing a fictitious, altered, or invalid registration tag or a registration tag not issued by the county auditor in connection with the registration of such animal.

HISTORY: GC § 5652-15; 107 v 534; 108 v PtI, 534; 112 v 347; Bureau of Code Revision. Eff 10-1-53.

§ 955.26 Confinement of dogs.

Whenever, in the judgment of the director of health, any city or general health district board of health, or persons performing the duties of a board of health, rabies is prevalent, the director of health, the board, or those persons shall declare a quarantine of all dogs in the health district or in a part of it. During the quarantine, the owner, keeper, or harborer of any dog shall keep it confined on the premises of the owner, keeper, or harborer, or in a suitable pound or kennel, at the expense of the owner, keeper, or harborer, except that a dog may be permitted to leave the premises of its owner, keeper, or harborer if it is under leash or under the control of a responsible person. The quarantine order shall be considered an emergency and need not be published.

When the quarantine has been declared, the director of health, the board, or those persons may require vaccination for rabies of all dogs within the health district or part of it. Proof of rabies vaccination within a satisfactory period shall be demonstrated to the county auditor before any registration is issued under section 955.01 of the Revised Code for any dog that is required to be vaccinated.

The public health council shall determine appropriate methods of rabies vaccination and satisfactory periods for purposes of quarantines under this section.

When a quarantine of dogs has been declared in any health district or part of a health district, the county dog warden and all other persons having the authority of police officers shall assist the health authorities in enforcing the quarantine order. When rabies vaccination has been declared compulsory in any health district or part of a health district, the dog warden shall assist the health authorities in enforcing the vaccination order.

Notwithstanding the provisions of this section, a city or general health district board of health may make orders pursuant to sections 3709.20 and 3709.21 of the Revised Code requiring the vaccination of dogs.

HISTORY: GC § 5652-16; 112 v 347; 124 v 413; Bureau of Code Revision, 10-1-53; 128 v 295 (Eff 9-18-59); 129 v 582(662) (Eff 1-10-61); 129 v 1190 (Eff 9-26-61); 142 v H 352. Eff 7-10-87.

[§ 955.26.1] § 955.261 Duties after dog bites person; quarantine.

(A)(1) No person shall remove a dog that has bitten any person from the county in which the bite occurred until a quarantine period as specified in division (B) of this section has been completed. No person shall transfer a dog that has bitten any person until a quarantine period as specified in division (B) of this section has been completed, except that a person may transfer the dog to the county dog warden or to any other animal control authority.

(2)(a) Subject to division (A)(2)(b) of this section, no person shall kill a dog that has bitten any person until a quarantine period as specified in division (B) of this section has been completed.

(b) Division (A)(2)(a) of this section does not apply to the killing of a dog in order to prevent further injury or death or if the dog is diseased or seriously injured.

(3) No person who has killed a dog that has bitten any person in order to prevent further injury or death or if the dog is diseased or seriously injured shall fail to do both of the following:

(a) Immediately after the killing of the dog, notify the board of health for the district in which the bite occurred of the facts relative to the bite and the killing;

(b) Hold the body of the dog until that board of health claims it to perform tests for rabies.

(B) The quarantine period for a dog that has bitten any person shall be ten days or another period that the board of health for the district in which the bite occurred determines is necessary to observe the dog for rabies.

(C)(1) To enable persons to comply with the quarantine requirements specified in divisions (A) and (B) of this section, boards of health shall make provision for the quarantine of individual dogs under the circumstances described in those divisions.

(2) Upon the receipt of a notification pursuant to division (A)(3) of this section that a dog that has bitten any person has been killed, the board of health for the district in which the bite occurred shall claim the body of the dog from its killer and then perform tests on the body for rabies.

HISTORY: 142 v H 352. Eff 7-10-87.

§ 955.39 Prohibition against violating a rabies quarantine.

No person shall violate a rabies quarantine order issued under section 955.26 of the Revised Code.

HISTORY: Bureau of Code Revision. Eff 10-1-53.
Comment

This section was derived from GC § 5652-16. See also RC § 955.26.

§ 955.99 Penalties.

(A)(1) Whoever violates division (E) of section 955.11 of the Revised Code because of a failure to comply with division (B) of that section is guilty of a minor misdemeanor.

(2) Whoever violates division (E) of section 955.11 of the Revised Code because of a failure to comply with division (C) or (D) of that section is guilty of a minor misdemeanor on a first offense and of a misdemeanor of the fourth degree on each subsequent offense.

(B) Whoever violates section 955.10, 955.23, 955.24, or 955.25 of the Revised Code is guilty of a minor misdemeanor.

(C) Whoever violates section 955.261 [955.26.1], 955.39, or 955.50 of the Revised Code is guilty of a minor misdemeanor on a first offense and of a misdemeanor of the fourth degree on each subsequent offense.

(D) Whoever violates division (F) of section 955.16 or division (B) of section 955.43 of the Revised Code is guilty of a misdemeanor of the fourth degree.

(E)(1) Whoever violates section 955.21 or division (B) or (C) of section 955.22 of the Revised Code shall be fined not less than twenty-five dollars or more than one hundred dollars on a first offense, and on each subsequent offense shall be fined not less than seventy-five dollars or more than two hundred fifty dollars and may be imprisoned for not more than thirty days.

(2) In addition to the penalties prescribed in division (E)(1) of this section, if the offender is guilty of a violation of division (B) or (C) of section 955.22 of the Revised Code, the court may order the offender to personally supervise the dog that he owns, keeps, or harbors, to cause that dog to complete dog obedience training, or to do both.

(F) If a violation of division (D) of section 955.22 of the Revised Code involves a dangerous dog, whoever violates that division is guilty of a misdemeanor of the fourth degree on a first offense and of a misdemeanor of the third degree on each subsequent offense. Additionally, the court may order the offender to personally supervise the dangerous dog that he owns, keeps, or harbors, to cause that dog to complete dog obedience training, or to do both, and the court may order the offender to obtain liability insurance pursuant to division (E) of section 955.22 of the Revised Code. The court, in the alternative, may order the dangerous dog to be humanely destroyed by a licensed veterinarian, the county dog warden, or the county humane society.

(G) If a violation of division (D) of section 955.22 of the Revised Code involves a vicious dog, whoever violates that division is guilty of one of the following:

(1) A felony of the fourth degree on a first or subsequent offense if the dog kills or seriously injures a person. Additionally, the court shall order that the vicious dog be humanely destroyed by a licensed veterinarian, the county dog warden, or the county humane society.

(2) A misdemeanor of the first degree on a first offense and a felony of the fourth degree on each subsequent offense. Additionally, the court may order the vicious dog to be humanely destroyed by a licensed veterinarian, the county dog warden, or the county humane society.

(3) A misdemeanor of the first degree if the dog causes injury other than killing or serious injury, to any person.

(H) Whoever violates division (E) of section 955.22 of the Revised Code is guilty of a misdemeanor of the first degree.

(I) Whoever violates division (C) of section 955.221 [955.22.1] of the Revised Code is guilty of a minor misdemeanor. Each day of continued violation of division (C) of section 955.221 [955.22.1] of the Revised Code constitutes a separate offense. Fines levied and collected for violations of division (C) of section 955.221 [955.22.1] of the Revised Code shall be distributed by the mayor or clerk of the municipal or county court in accordance with section 733.40, division (F) of section 1901.31, or division (C) of section 1907.20 of the Revised Code to the treasury of the county, township, or municipal corporation whose resolution or ordinance was violated.

HISTORY: Bureau of Code Revision, 10-1-53; 133 v S 514 (Eff 7-16-70); 134 v H 511 (Eff 1-1-74); 136 v S 256 (Eff 6-4-76); 138 v H 854 (Eff 1-1-81); 141 v H 454 (Eff 11-1-85); 141 v H 428 (Eff 12-23-86); 142 v H 352 (Eff 7-10-87); 142 v H 246 (Eff 12-12-88); 143 v H 291. Eff 6-21-90.

CHAPTER 959: OFFENSES RELATING TO DOMESTIC ANIMALS

§ 959.01 Abandoning animals.

No owner or keeper of a dog, cat, or other domestic animal, shall abandon such animal.

HISTORY: GC § 13368; 124 v 428, § 2; Bureau of Code Revision. Eff 10-1-53.

§ 959.02 Injuring animals.

No person shall maliciously, or willfully, and without the consent of the owner, kill or injure a horse, mare, foal, filly, jack, mule, sheep, goat, cow, steer, bull, heifer, ass, ox, swine, dog, cat, or other domestic animal that is the property of another. This section does not apply to a licensed veterinarian acting in an official capacity.

HISTORY: RS § 6851; S&C 74, 75; 53 v 192, §§ 1, 2; 54 v 126, §§ 1, 2; GC § 13361; 124 v 428, § 1; Bureau of Code Revision. Eff 10-1-53.

§ 959.03 Poisoning animals.

No person shall maliciously, or willfully and without the consent of the owner, administer poison, except a licensed veterinarian acting in such capacity, to a horse, mare, foal, filly, jack, mule, sheep, goat, cow, steer, bull, heifer, ass, ox, swine, dog, cat, poultry, or any other domestic animal that is the property of another; and no person shall, willfully and without the consent of the owner, place any poisoned food where it may be easily found and eaten by any of such animals, either upon his own lands or the lands of another.

HISTORY: RS § 6852; S&C 75; 53 v 192, § 3; GC § 13362; 108 v PtII 1231; 124 v 428; Bureau of Code Revision. Eff 10-1-53.

§ 959.04 Trespassing animals.

Sections 959.02 and 959.03 of the Revised Code do not extend to a person killing or injuring an animal or attempting to do so while endeavoring to prevent it from trespassing upon his enclosure, or while it is so trespassing, or while driving it away from his premises; provided within fifteen days thereafter, payment is made for damages done to such animal by such killing or injuring, less the actual amount of damage done by such animal while so trespassing, or a sufficient sum of money is deposited with the nearest judge of a county court or judge of a municipal court having jurisdiction within such time to cover such damages. Such deposit shall remain in the custody of such judge until there is a determination of the damages resulting from such killing or injury and from such trespass. Such judge and his bondsmen shall be responsible for the safekeeping of such money and for the payment thereof as for money collected upon a judgment.

HISTORY: RS § 6853; S&C 74, 75; 53 v 192, § 4; 54 v 126, § 3; 90 v 140; GC § 13363; Bureau of Code Revision, 10-1-53; 129 v 582 (662). Eff 1-10-61.

§ 959.05 Drugging animal prior to competition restricted.

No person shall administer to any animal within forty-eight hours prior to the time that the animal competes at a fair or exhibition conducted by a county or independent agricultural society authorized under Chapter 1711. of the Revised Code or by the Ohio expositions commission any drug or medicament not specifically permitted under rules of the state racing commission promulgated pursuant to Chapter 3769. of the Revised Code or under rules of the society, in respect to a county or independent agricultural society, or of the Ohio expositions commission, in respect to the Ohio state fair. This section does not apply to any horse racing meeting conducted under a permit issued pursuant to Chapter 3769. of the Revised Code.

HISTORY: 136 v H 894. Eff 2-26-76.

Not analogous to former RC § 959.05 (RS § 6855; S&S 11; S&C 71; 54 v 14; 64 v 207; GC § 13364; Bureau of Code Revision, 10-1-53), repealed 132 v H 842, § 2, eff 12-14-67.

§ 959.06 Prohibited methods of destroying domestic animals.

(A) No person shall destroy any domestic animal by the use of a high altitude decompression chamber or by any method other than a method that immediately and painlessly renders the domestic animal initially unconscious and subsequently dead.

(B) This section does not apply to or prohibit the slaughtering of livestock under Chapter 945. of the Revised Code, or the taking of any wild animal, as defined in section 1531.01 of the Revised Code, when taken in accordance with Chapter 1533. of the Revised Code.

HISTORY: 138 v H 854. Eff 1-1-81.

Not analogous to former RC § 959.06 (RS § 4211-26; 85 v 336; GC § 13365; Bureau of Code Revision, 10-1-53), repealed 132 v H 842, § 2, eff 12-14-67.

The effective date is set by section 3 of HB 854.

§ 959.12 Alteration of brands.

No person shall maliciously alter or deface an artificial earmark or brand upon a horse, mare, foal, filly, jack, mule, sheep, goat, cow, steer, bull, heifer, ass, ox, swine, that is the property of another.

HISTORY: RS § 6850; S&C 430; 29 v 144, § 20; GC § 13375; Bureau of Code Revision. Eff 10-1-53.

§ 959.13 Cruelty to animals.

(A) No person shall:

(1) Torture an animal, deprive one of necessary sustenance, unnecessarily or cruelly beat, needlessly mutilate or kill, or impound or confine an animal without supplying it during such confinement with a sufficient quantity of good wholesome food and water;

(2) Impound or confine an animal without affording it, during such confinement, access to shelter from wind, rain, snow, or excessive direct sunlight if it can reasonably be expected that the animals would otherwise become sick or in some other way suffer. Division (A)(2) of this section does not apply to animals impounded or confined prior to slaughter. For the purpose of this section, shelter means a man-made enclosure, windbreak, sunshade, or natural windbreak or sunshade that is developed from the earth's contour, tree development, or vegetation.[;]

(3) Carry or convey an animal in a cruel or inhuman[e] manner;

(4) Keep animals other than cattle, poultry or fowl, swine, sheep, or goats in an enclosure without wholesome exercise and change of air, †nor or feed cows on food that produces impure or unwholesome milk;

(5) Detain livestock in railroad cars or compartments longer than twenty-eight hours after they are so placed without supplying them with necessary food, water, and attention, nor permit such stock to be so crowded as to overlie, crush, wound, or kill each other.

(B) Upon the written request of the owner or person in custody of any particular shipment of livestock, which written request shall be separate and apart from any printed bill of lading or other railroad form, the length of time in which such livestock may be detained in any cars or compartment without food, water, and attention, may be extended to thirty-six hours without penalty therefor. This section does not prevent the dehorning of cattle.

(C) All fines collected for violations of this section shall be paid to the society or association for the prevention of cruelty to animals, if there be such in the county, township, or municipal corporation where such violation occurred.

HISTORY: RS § 6951; 72 v 129, §§ 1, 2, 4, 5, 6, 8, 22; 78 v 134; 89 v 140; 93 v 15; GC § 13376; 101 v 118; 109 v 152 (Eff 10-1-53); Bureau of Code Revision, 10-1-53; 136 v H 858. Eff 1-17-77.

† So in 136 v H 858.

§ 959.14 Horse tails.

No owner or person having the custody, control, or

possession of a horse, mare, gelding, foal, or filly, nor an agent or employee of such owner or custodian, shall cut off or cause to be cut off or amputated the skin, flesh, muscles, bone, or integuments of the dock or tail thereof, in order to shorten its natural length or proportions; nor shall any such owner, person, or the agent or employee of either pull out the hairs of the foretop, mane, or withers thereof. This section does not prohibit the cutting or amputation of the dock or tail of a horse, mare, gelding, foal, or filly when necessary because of accident, malformation, or disease affecting such dock or tail.

HISTORY: RS § 6951-1; 90 v 138; GC § 13377; Bureau of Code Revision. Eff 10-1-53.

§ 959.15 Animal fights.

No person shall knowingly engage in or be employed at cockfighting, bearbaiting, or pitting an animal against another; no person shall receive money for the admission of another to a place kept for such purpose; no person shall use, train, or possess any animal for seizing, detaining, or maltreating a domestic animal. Any person who knowingly purchases a ticket of admission to such place, or is present thereat, or witnesses such spectacle, is an aider and abettor.

HISTORY: RS § 6952; S&C 449; 29 v 161, §§ 11, 12; 72 v 129, §§ 7, 10, 22; GC § 13378; Bureau of Code Revision, 10-1-53; 138 v S 233. Eff 6-10-80.

§ 959.16 Dogfighting offenses; investigations; confiscation of dogs and equipment.

(A) No person shall knowingly do any of the following:
(1) Promote, engage in, or be employed at dogfighting;
(2) Receive money for the admission of another person to a place kept for dogfighting;
(3) Sell, purchase, possess, or train a dog for dogfighting;
(4) Use, train, or possess a dog for seizing, detaining, or maltreating a domestic animal;
(5) Purchase a ticket of admission to or be present at a dogfight;
(6) Witness a dogfight if it is presented as a public spectacle.
(B) The department of agriculture may investigate complaints and follow up rumors of dogfighting activities and may report any information so gathered to an appropriate prosecutor or law enforcement agency.
(C) Any peace officer, as defined in section 2935.01 of the Revised Code, shall confiscate any dogs that have been, are, or are intended to be used in dogfighting and any equipment or devices used in training such dogs or as part of dogfights.

HISTORY: 138 v S 233. Eff 6-10-80.

Not analogous to former RC § 959.16 (RS § 6854; S&S 279; 65 v 200; GC § 13379; Bureau of Code Revision, 10-1-53), repealed 134 v H 511, § 2, eff 1-1-74.

§ 959.17 Trapshooting.

Live birds or fowl shall not be used as targets in trapshooting.

HISTORY: RS §§ 6952-1, 6952-2; 95 v 254, §§ 1, 2; GC § 13380; Bureau of Code Revision. Eff 10-1-53.

§ 959.18 Prohibition against killing a carrier pigeon.

No person who is not the owner thereof, shall shoot, kill, or maim an Antwerp or homing pigeon, commonly known as "carrier" pigeon, nor shall such person entrap, catch, or detain a carrier pigeon, provided it has the name of the owner stamped upon its wing or tail, or has a band with the owner's name, initial, or number on its leg.

HISTORY: RS § 7017-2; 93 v 218; GC § 13381; Bureau of Code Revision. Eff 10-1-53.

§ 959.19 Prohibtion against servicing mare in public street.

No owner of a stallion or jack or the agent of such owner, shall permit it to serve a mare within thirty feet of a public street or alley in a municipal corporation.

HISTORY: RS § 7038-1; 88 v 394; GC § 13414; Bureau of Code Revision. Eff 10-1-53.

§ 959.20 Use of certain devices on animals prohibited.

As used in this section:
(A) "Work animal" includes a horse, pony, mule, donkey, mare, ox, bull, gelding, or other animal used or intended to be used for a work purpose.
(B) "Work purpose" means the performance by a work animal of some work or labor, including showing, performing, or being used in any exhibition, show, circus, rodeo, or similar use.
(C) "Owner" includes any person, firm, association, or corporation owning or having a proprietary interest in or possession, custody, or charge of a work animal.

No person shall directly or indirectly or by aiding, abetting, or permitting the doing thereof put, place, fasten, use, or fix upon or to any work animal used or readied for use for a work purpose, twisted wire snaffles, unpadded bucking straps, unpadded flank straps, electric or other prods, or similar devices.

The commission or performance of any act prohibited by this section is the act of the owner of the work animal upon or to which such act was done.

HISTORY: 131 v 387 (Eff 10-8-65); 141 v H 797. Eff 7-24-86.

§ 959.99 Penalties.

(A) Whoever violates section 959.01, 959.18, or

959.19 of the Revised Code is guilty of a minor misdemeanor.

(B) Except as otherwise provided in this division, whoever violates section 959.02 of the Revised Code is guilty of a misdemeanor of the second degree. If the value of the animal killed or the injury done amounts to three hundred dollars or more, whoever violates section 959.02 of the Revised Code is guilty of a misdemeanor of the first degree.

(C) Whoever violates section 959.03, 959.06, 959.12, 959.15, or 959.17 of the Revised Code is guilty of a misdemeanor of the fourth degree.

(D) Whoever violates division (A) of section 959.13 of the Revised Code is guilty of a misdemeanor of the second degree. In addition, the court may order the offender to forfeit the animal or livestock and may provide for its disposition including, but not limited to, the sale of the animal or livestock. If an animal or livestock is forfeited and sold pursuant to this division, the proceeds from the sale first shall be applied to pay the expenses incurred with regard to the care of the animal from the time it was taken from the custody of the former owner. The balance of the proceeds from the sale, if any, shall be paid to the former owner of the animal.

(E) Whoever violates section 959.14 of the Revised Code is guilty of a misdemeanor of the second degree on a first offense and a misdemeanor of the first degree on each subsequent offense.

(F) Whoever violates section 959.05 or 959.20 of the Revised Code is guilty of a misdemeanor of the first degree.

(G) Whoever violates section 959.16 of the Revised Code is guilty of a felony of the fifth degree.

HISTORY: Bureau of Code Revision, 10-1-53; 125 v 215 (Eff 10-2-53); 131 v 387 (Eff 10-8-65); 132 v H 1 (Eff 2-21-67); 132 v H 842 (Eff 12-14-67); 134 v H 511 (Eff 1-1-74); 136 v H 894 (Eff 2-26-76); 138 v S 233 (Eff 6-10-80); 138 v H 854 (Eff 1-1-81); 139 v S 199 (Eff 7-1-83); 143 v H 12 (Eff 9-15-89); 146 v S 2. Eff 7-1-96.

The effective date is set by section 6 of SB 2.

TITLE 11: FINANCIAL INSTITUTIONS

CHAPTER 1127: BANKS—CRIMES AND PROHIBITED ACTIVITIES

§ 1127.08 Falsification, forgery or counterfeiting.

No person, for the purpose of influencing in any manner the actions or decisions of the superintendent of financial institutions in the superintendent's capacity as chief executive officer of the division of financial institutions, shall knowingly make or provide to the superintendent or any employee or agent of the division, or knowingly invite reliance by any of them upon, a statement, document, or other thing the person knows to be false, misleading, forged, or counterfeit.

HISTORY: 146 v H 538. Eff 1-1-97.

The effective date is set by section 10 of HB 538.

§ 1127.09 False communications.

No person shall knowingly make, publish, or otherwise communicate any statement, report, information, or data relating to the financial or other condition of any bank or trust company that the person knows to be false or misleading.

HISTORY: 146 v H 538. Eff 1-1-97.

The effective date is set by section 10 of HB 538.

§ 1127.11 Concealment of assets or placing beyond official's reach; impeding official.

No person shall knowingly do any of the following:

(A) Conceal or attempt to conceal an asset or property from a conservator, receiver, or liquidating agent appointed by the superintendent of financial institutions with respect to any asset acquired or liability assumed by the conservator, receiver, or liquidating agent;

(B) Impede or attempt to impede the functions of the conservator, receiver, or liquidating agent;

(C) Place or attempt to place any asset or property beyond the reach of the conservator, receiver, or liquidating agent.

HISTORY: 146 v H 538. Eff 1-1-97.

The effective date is set by section 10 of HB 538.

§ 1127.99 Penalties.

(A) Whoever violates section 1127.06, 1127.08, or 1127.11 of the Revised Code is guilty of a felony of the third degree.

(B) Whoever violates section 1127.02 or 1127.03 of the Revised Code is guilty of a felony of the fourth degree.

(C) Whoever violates section 1127.09 of the Revised Code is guilty of a felony of the fifth degree.

HISTORY: 146 v H 538. Eff 1-1-97.

The effective date is set by section 10 of HB 538.

CHAPTER 1153: SAVINGS AND LOAN ASSOCIATIONS-

MISCELLANEOUS PROVISIONS

§ 1153.01 Repealed, 146 v S 2, § 6 [99 v 536, § 46; GC § 12472; Bureau of Code Revision, 10-1-53; 134 v H 511]. Eff 7-1-96.

This section described unauthorized acts by association officer.

§ 1153.03 Declaration of excessive dividend.

No director of a building and loan association shall vote to declare, and no financial or first secretary of such an association shall declare or advise its board of directors to declare, for the purpose of deceiving the people or defrauding the members of the association, a greater dividend than has been actually earned by such association.

HISTORY: 99 v 536, § 46; GC § 13189; Bureau of Code Revision. Eff 10-1-53.

§ 1153.06 Failure to make reports; unlawful solicitation of business.

No officer of a building and loan association shall fail to make the reports required of him by the laws provided for the organization, regulation, and inspection of building and loan associations, and no person shall solicit business for such association, or aid it to do business, contrary to such laws, or without having complied therewith.

HISTORY: 99 v 536, § 46; GC § 13192; Bureau of Code Revision. 10-1-53.

§ 1153.07 Civil liabilities for violations.

Suit under section 1.16 of the Revised Code, based on a violation of sections 1153.03 and 1153.06 of the

Revised Code, may be brought against the violator and the sureties on the bond given by the violator to the savings and loan association for the faithful performance of his duty.

HISTORY: GC § 13193; 99 v 536, § 46; Bureau of Code Revision, 10-1-53; 134 v H 511 (Eff 1-1-74); 136 v H 1 (Eff 6-13-75); 146 v S 2. Eff 7-1-96.

The effective date is set by section 6 of SB 2.

§ 1153.99 Penalties.

(A) Whoever violates section 1153.03 of the Revised Code is guilty of a felony of the fifth degree.

(B) Whoever violates section 1153.06 of the Revised Code is guilty of a misdemeanor of the first degree.

HISTORY: Bureau of Code Revision, 10-1-53; 134 v H 511 (Eff 1-1-74); 136 v H 1 (Eff 6-13-75); 146 v S 2. Eff 7-1-96.

The effective date is set by section 6 of SB 2.

TITLE 13: COMMERCIAL TRANSACTIONS

CHAPTER 1315: TRANSMITTERS OF MONEY; CHECK-CASHING BUSINESSES

§ 1315.53 Duty to report transactions, keep records; money laundering prohibitions.

(A) A money transmitter that is required to file a report regarding business conducted in this state pursuant to the "Currency and Foreign Transactions Reporting Act," 84 Stat. 1118 (1970), 31 U.S.C.A. 5311 to 5326 and 31 C.F.R. part 103 or 12 C.F.R. 21.11, shall file a duplicate of that report with the attorney general.

(B) All persons engaged in a trade or business, who receive more than ten thousand dollars in money in one transaction or who receive more than ten thousand dollars in money through two or more related transactions, and who are required to file returns under 26 U.S.C.A. 6050I and 26 C.F.R. 1.6050I, shall complete and file with the attorney general the information required by 26 U.S.C.A. 6050I and C.F.R. 1.6050I.

(C) A money transmitter that is regulated under the "Currency and Foreign Transactions Reporting Act," 84 Stat. 1118 (1970), 31 U.S.C.A. 5325 and 31 C.F.R. part 103 and that is required to make available prescribed records to the secretary of the United States department of treasury upon request at any time shall follow the same prescribed procedures and create and maintain the same prescribed records relating to a transaction and shall make those records available to the attorney general on request at any time.

(D)(1) The good faith filing of a report required by this section with the appropriate federal agency shall be considered compliance with the reporting requirements of this section.

(2) This section does not preclude a money transmitter or a person engaged in a trade or business, in their discretion, from instituting contact with, and thereafter communicating with and disclosing customer financial records to, appropriate state or local law enforcement agencies if the money transmitter or person has information that may be relevant to a possible violation of a section of the Revised Code or a municipal ordinance or to the evasion or attempted evasion of a reporting requirement of this section.

(3) A money transmitter, a person engaged in a trade or business, or an officer, employee, agent, or authorized delegate of an entity or person of that nature, or a public official or governmental employee who keeps or files a record pursuant to this section or who communicates or discloses information or records under division (D)(2) of this section is not liable to its customer, a state or local agency, or a person for loss or damage caused in whole or in part by the making, filing, or governmental use of the report or of information contained in that report.

(E)(1) The attorney general may report possible violations indicated by analysis of the reports required by this section to an appropriate law enforcement agency for use in the proper discharge of its official duties. The attorney general shall provide copies of the reports required by this section to an appropriate prosecutorial or law enforcement agency upon being provided with a written request for records relating to a specific individual or entity and stating that the agency has an articulable suspicion that the specific individual or entity has committed an offense to which the reports appear to be relevant.

(2) No person shall release information received pursuant to division (E) of this section, except in the proper discharge of the person's official duties.

(F)(1) No person shall do any of the following:

(a) Purposely violate or fail to comply with this section;

(b) With the intent to conceal or disguise the fact that money or a payment instrument is the proceeds of unlawful activity, or to promote, manage, establish, carry on, or facilitate the promotion, management, establishment, or carrying on of an unlawful activity, knowingly furnish or provide to a money transmitter, a person engaged in a trade or business, an officer, employee, agent, or authorized delegate of a money transmitter or person engaged in a trade or business, or the attorney general, false, inaccurate, or incomplete information or knowingly conceal a material fact in connection with a transaction for which a report is required to be filed pursuant to this section;

(c) With the intent to conceal or disguise the fact that money or a payment instrument is the proceeds of unlawful activity, or to promote, manage, establish, carry on, or facilitate the promotion, management, establishment, or carrying on of unlawful activity, or to avoid the making or filing of a report required under this section, or to cause the making or filing of a report required under this section that contains a material omission or misstatement, conduct or structure or attempt to conduct or structure a transaction by or through one or more money transmitters or persons engaged in a trade or business.

(2) In addition to the criminal sanctions imposed under section 1315.99 of the Revised Code, the sentencing court may impose upon a person who violates division (F)(1) of this section an additional fine of three times the value of the property involved in the transaction or, if no transaction is involved, five thousand dollars. The fine shall be paid to the state treasury to the credit of the general revenue fund.

(G) Notwithstanding any other section of the Revised

Code, each transaction conducted or attempted to be conducted and each exemption from reporting claimed in violation of this section constitutes a separate, punishable offense.

(H) A report, record, information, analysis, or request obtained by the attorney general or an agency pursuant to this section is not a public record subject to section 149.43 of the Revised Code and is not subject to disclosure.

HISTORY: 146 v H 333. Eff 9-19-96.

§ 1315.54 Investigations.

(A) The attorney general may conduct investigations within or outside this state to determine if a money transmitter or person engaged in a trade or business has failed to file a report required by section 1315.53 of the Revised Code or has engaged or is engaging in an act, practice, or transaction that constitutes a violation of a provision of sections 1315.51 to 1315.55 of the Revised Code.

(B) On request of the attorney general, a money transmitter shall make the money transmitter's books and records available to the attorney general during normal business hours for inspection and examination in connection with an investigation conducted under this section. No person shall purposely fail to comply with this division.

(C) Any record or other document or information obtained by the attorney general pursuant to an investigation conducted under this section is not a public record subject to section 149.43 of the Revised Code and is not subject to disclosure.

(D) This section does not apply to any bank, bank holding company, or affiliate of a bank or bank holding company, that is subject to examination by the comptroller of the currency, the federal reserve, or the federal deposit insurance corporation, or to any savings and loan association, savings and loan holding company, or affiliate of a savings and loan association or savings and loan holding company, that is subject to examination by the office of thrift supervision.

HISTORY: 146 v H 333. Eff 9-19-96.

§ 1315.55 Additional money laundering prohibitions.

(A)(1) No person shall conduct or attempt to conduct a transaction knowing that the property involved in the transaction is the proceeds of some form of unlawful activity with the purpose of committing or furthering the commission of corrupt activity.

(2) No person shall conduct or attempt to conduct a transaction knowing that the property involved in the transaction is the proceeds of some form of unlawful activity with the intent to conceal or disguise the nature, location, source, ownership, or control of the property or the intent to avoid a transaction reporting requirement under section 1315.53 of the Revised Code or federal law.

(3) No person shall conduct or attempt to conduct a transaction with the purpose to promote, manage, establish, carry on, or facilitate the promotion, management, establishment, or carrying on of corrupt activity.

(4) No person shall conduct or structure or attempt to conduct or structure a transaction that involves the proceeds of corrupt activity that is of a value greater than ten thousand dollars if the person knows or has reasonable cause to know that the transaction involves the proceeds of corrupt activity.

(5) No person shall conduct or attempt to conduct a transaction that involves what has been represented to the person by a law enforcement officer or another person at the direction of or with the approval of a law enforcement officer to be the proceeds of corrupt activity or property used to conduct or facilitate corrupt activity with the intent to promote, manage, establish, carry on, or facilitate promotion, management, establishment, or carrying on of corrupt activity, to conceal or disguise the nature, location, source, ownership, or control of the property believed to be the proceeds of corrupt activity, or to avoid a transaction reporting requirement under section 1315.53 of the Revised Code or federal law.

(B) In addition to the criminal sanctions imposed under section 1315.99 of the Revised Code, the sentencing court may impose upon a person who violates division (A) of this section an additional fine of three times the value of the property involved in the transaction. The fine shall be paid to the state treasury to the credit of the general revenue fund.

(C) For the purposes of division (A) of this section, a person shall be considered to know or have reasonable cause to know that proceeds are from corrupt activity if either of the following apply:

(1) The person knows or has reasonable cause to know that the proceeds are from some form of activity that constitutes corrupt activity, though not necessarily which form of corrupt activity;

(2) As a part of a covert investigation, a law enforcement officer in his undercover capacity represents to the person that the proceeds are from some form of activity that constitutes corrupt activity.

HISTORY: 146 v H 333. Eff 9-19-96.

§ 1315.99 Penalties.

Whoever violates section 1315.11, section 1315.17, division (A) or (B) of section 1315.28, or section 1315.41 or division (E)(2) of section 1315.53 of the Revised Code is guilty of a misdemeanor of the first degree.

HISTORY: RC § 1310.99, 126 v 756 (Eff 10-13-55); 137 v H 1134 (Eff 7-1-79); 144 v H 332 (Eff 10-6-92); RC § 1315.99, 144 v H 693 (Eff 11-6-92); 145 v H 266 (Eff 7-30-93); 146 v H 313 (Eff 12-5-95); 146 v H 333 (Eff 9-19-96); 146 v H 538. Eff 1-1-97.

The effective date is set by section 10 of HB 538.

CHAPTER 1333: TRADE PRACTICES

[PYRAMID SALES PLAN OR PROGRAM]

§ 1333.91 Definitions.

As used in sections 1333.91 to 1333.94 of the Revised Code:

(A) "Pyramid sales plan or program" means any scheme, whether or not for the disposal or distribution of property, whereby a person pays a consideration for the chance or opportunity to receive compensation, regardless of whether he also receives other rights or property, under either of the following circumstances:

(1) For introducing one or more persons into participation in the plan or program;

(2) When another participant has introduced a person into participation in the plan or program.

(B) "Compensation" means money, financial benefit, or anything of value. Compensation does not include payment based upon sales made to persons who are not participants in a pyramid sales plan or program, and who are not purchasing in order to participate in the plan or program.

(C) "Consideration" does not include:

(1) Payment for sales demonstration equipment and materials furnished at cost, whereby no profit, commission, fee, rebate or other benefit is realized by any person in the sales plan, for use in making sales and not for resale;

(2) Payment for promotional and administrative fees not to exceed twenty-five dollars when computed on an annual basis.

(D) "Participant" means a person who purchases, proposes, plans, prepares, or offers the opportunity to take part in, or advance into, a pyramid sales plan or program.

HISTORY: 135 v H 609. Eff 9-27-74.

§ 1333.92 Prohibited.

No person shall propose, plan, prepare, or operate a pyramid sales plan or program.

HISTORY: 135 v H 609. Eff 9-27-74.

§ 1333.93 Contract void; civil action recovery.

Any contract made in violation of section 1333.92 of the Revised Code is void. Any person who has paid consideration for the chance or opportunity to participate in a pyramid sales plan or program may recover, in a civil action, the amount of the consideration paid, together with reasonable attorney fees, from any participant who has received compensation under either of the following circumstances:

(A) For introducing the person into participation in a pyramid sales plan or program;

(B) When another participant has introduced the person into participation in a pyramid sales plan or program.

HISTORY: 135 v H 609. Eff 9-27-74.

§ 1333.94 Temporary restraining order.

Whenever it appears that a person is violating or about to violate section 1333.92 of the Revised Code, the attorney general may bring an action in the court of common pleas to enjoin the violation. Upon a proper showing, a temporary restraining order, or a preliminary or permanent injunction shall be granted without bond. The court may impose a penalty of not more than five thousand dollars for each day of violation of a temporary restraining order or preliminary or permanent injunction issued under this section.

HISTORY: 135 v H 609. Eff 9-27-74.

§ 1333.95 Additional remedies.

The remedies in sections 1333.91 to 1333.95 of the Revised Code are in addition to remedies otherwise available.

HISTORY: 135 v H 609. Eff 9-27-74.

§ 1333.99 Penalties.

(A) Whoever violates sections 1333.01 to 1333.04 of the Revised Code is guilty of a minor misdemeanor.

(B) Whoever violates section 1333.12 of the Revised Code is guilty of a misdemeanor of the fourth degree.

(C) Whoever violates section 1333.36 of the Revised Code is guilty of a misdemeanor of the third degree.

(D) A prosecuting attorney may file an action to restrain any person found in violation of section 1333.36 of the Revised Code. Upon the filing of such an action, the common pleas court may receive evidence of such violation and forthwith grant a temporary restraining order as may be prayed for, pending a hearing on the merits of said cause.

(E) Whoever violates division (A)(1) of section 1333.52 or section 1333.81 of the Revised Code is guilty of a misdemeanor of the first degree.

(F) Whoever violates division (A)(2) or (B) of section 1333.52 or division (F) or (H) of section 1333.96 of the Revised Code is guilty of a misdemeanor of the second degree.

(G) Except as otherwise provided in this division, whoever violates section 1333.92 of the Revised Code is guilty of a misdemeanor of the first degree. If the value of the compensation is five hundred dollars or more and less than five thousand dollars, whoever violates section 1333.92 of the Revised Code is guilty of a felony of the fifth degree. If the value of the compensation is five thousand dollars or more and less than one hundred thousand dollars, whoever violates section 1333.92 of the Revised Code is guilty of a felony of the fourth degree. If the value of the compensation is one hundred thousand dollars or more, whoever violates section 1333.92 of the Revised Code is guilty of a felony of the third degree.

(H) Whoever violates division (B), (C), or (I) of section 1333.96 of the Revised Code is guilty of a misdemeanor of the third degree.

(I) Any person not registered as a travel agency or tour promoter as provided in divisions (B) and (C) of section 1333.96 of the Revised Code who states that the person is so registered is guilty of a misdemeanor of the first degree.

HISTORY: Bureau of Code Revision, 10-1-53; 129 v H 342 (Eff 10-24-61); 132 v H 730 (Eff 11-14-67); 134 v H 511 (Eff 1-1-74); 135 v H 609 (Eff 9-27-74); 136 v H 159 (Eff 5-10-76); 137 v H 478 (Eff 11-8-77); 137 v H 1147 (Eff 1-5-79); 139 v S 199 (Eff 7-1-83); 139 v H 269 (Eff 1-5-83); 146 v S 2. Eff 7-1-96.

The effective date is set by section 6 of SB 2.

CHAPTER 1345: CONSUMER SALES PRACTICES

§ 1345.23 Writing required; contents, warning.

(A) Every home solicitation shall be evidenced by a written agreement or offer to purchase in the same language as that principally used in the oral sales presentation and shall contain the name and address of the seller. The seller shall present the writing to the buyer and obtain the buyer's signature to it. The writing shall state the date on which the buyer actually signs. The seller shall leave with the buyer a copy of the writing which has been signed by the seller and complies with division (B) of this section.

(B) In connection with every home solicitation sale:

(1) The following statement shall appear clearly and conspicuously on the copy of the contract left with the buyer in bold-face type of the minimum size of ten points, in substantially the following form and in immediate proximity to the space reserved in the contract for the signature of the buyer: "You, the buyer, may cancel this transaction at any time prior to midnight of the third business day after the date of this transaction. See the attached notice of cancellation for an explanation of this right."

(2) A completed form, in duplicate, captioned "notice of cancellation", shall be attached to the contract signed by the buyer and be easily detachable, and shall contain in ten-point, boldface type, the following information and statements in the same language as that used in the contract:

NOTICE OF CANCELLATION

(enter date of transaction)
.... (Date)

You may cancel this transaction, without any penalty or obligation, within three business days from the above date.

If you cancel, any property traded in, any payments made by you under the contract or sale, and any negotiable instrument executed by you will be returned within ten business days following receipt by the seller of your cancellation notice, and any security interest arising out of the transaction will be cancelled. If you cancel, you must make available to the seller at your residence, in substantially as good condition as when received, any goods delivered to you under this contract or sale; or you may if you wish, comply with the instructions of the seller regarding the return shipment of the goods at the seller's expense and risk.

If you do make the goods available to the seller and the seller does not pick them up within twenty days of the date of your notice of cancellation, you may retain or dispose of the goods without any further obligation. If you fail to make the goods available to the seller, or if you agree to return the goods to the seller and fail to do so, then you remain liable for performance of all obligations under the contract.

To cancel this transaction, mail or deliver a signed and dated copy of this cancellation notice or any other written notice, or send a telegram, to (Name of seller), at (address of seller's place of business)   not later than midnight of .... (Date)

I hereby cancel this transaction.

.... (Date)

..........................(Buyer's signature)..........

(3) Before furnishing copies of the notice of cancellation to the buyer, the seller shall complete both copies by entering the name of the seller, the address of the seller's place of business, the date of the transaction which is the date the buyer signed the contract and the date, not earlier than the third business day following the date of the transaction, by which the buyer may give notice of cancellation.

(4) A home solicitation sales contract which contains the notice of buyer's right to cancel and notice of cancellation in the form and language provided in the federal trade commission's trade regulation rule providing a cooling-off period for door-to-door sales shall be deemed to comply with the requirements of divisions (B)(1), (2), and (3) of this section with respect to the form and language of such notices so long as the federal trade commission language provides at least equal information to the consumer concerning his right to cancel as is required by divisions (B) (1), (2), and (3) of this section.

(C) Until the seller has complied with divisions (A) and (B) of this section the buyer may cancel the home solicitation sale by notifying the seller by mailing, delivering, or telegraphing written notice to the seller of his intention to cancel. The three day period prescribed by section 1345.22 of the Revised Code begins to run from the time the seller complies with divisions (A) and (B) of this section.

(D) In connection with any home solicitation sale, no seller shall:

(1) Include in any home solicitation sales contract, any confession of judgment or any waiver of any rights to which the buyer is entitled under this section, including specifically his right to cancel the sale in accordance with this section.

(2) Fail to inform each buyer orally, at the time he signs the contract for the goods or services, of his right to cancel.

(3) Misrepresent in any manner the buyer's right to cancel.

(4) Fail or refuse to honor any valid notice of cancellation by a buyer and within ten business days after receipt of such notice to:

(a) Refund all payments made under the contract or sale;

(b) Return any goods or property traded in, in substantially as good condition as when received by the seller;

(c) Cancel and return any note, negotiable instrument, or other evidence of indebtedness executed by the buyer in connection with the contract or sale and take any action necessary or appropriate to reflect the termination of any security interest or lien created under the sale or offer to purchase.

(5) Negotiate, transfer, sell, or assign any note or other evidence of indebtedness to a finance company or other third party prior to midnight of the fifth business day following the day the contract for the goods or services was signed.

(6) Fail to notify the buyer, within ten business days of receipt of the buyer's notice of cancellation, whether the seller intends to repossess or abandon any shipped or delivered goods.

HISTORY: 134 v 24 (Eff 1-1-73); 135 v H 241. Eff 9-30-74.

§ 1345.24 Seller to retain notice of cancellation.

In a home solicitation sale, the seller shall retain, for the period in which an action to enforce the sale could be commenced, any notice of cancellation made pursuant to section 1345.22 of the Revised Code. The seller shall also retain the envelope in which any notice of cancellation is sent or delivered. If the date of delivery is not indicated or recorded on the notice of cancellation or on the envelope, the seller shall record the date of delivery on the notice of cancellation.

HISTORY: 134 v S 24 (Eff 1-1-73); 135 v H 241. Eff 9-30-74.

§ 1345.99 Penalty.

Whoever violates section 1345.23 or 1345.24 of the Revised Code is guilty of a minor misdemeanor.

HISTORY: 134 v S 24 (Eff 1-1-73); 135 v H 241. Eff 9-30-74.

CHAPTER 1349: CONSUMER PROTECTION

§ 1349.17 Restrictions on recording credit card, telephone or social security numbers.

(A) No person shall record or cause to be recorded either of the following:

(1) A credit card account number of the other party to a transaction, when a check, bill of exchange, or other draft is presented for payment;

(2) The telephone number or social security account number of the other party to a transaction, when payment is made by credit card charge agreement, check, bill of exchange, or other draft.

(B) Division (A) of this section does not apply to a transaction, if all of the following conditions are met:

(1) The credit card account number, social security account number, or telephone number is recorded for a legitimate business purpose, including collection purposes.

(2) The other party to the transaction consents to the recording of the credit card account number, social security account number, or telephone number.

(3) The credit card account number, social security account number, or telephone number that is recorded during the course of the transaction is not disclosed to any third party for any purposes other than collection purposes and is not used to market goods or services unrelated to the goods or services purchased in the transaction.

(C) Nothing in this section prohibits the recording of the number of a credit card account when given in lieu of a deposit to secure payment in the event of default, loss, damage, or other occurrence, or requires a person to accept a check presented for payment, if the other party to the transaction refuses to consent to the recording of the number of the party's social security account or license to operate a motor vehicle.

HISTORY: 144 v H 20 (Eff 8-20-91); 145 v H 266. Eff 7-30-93.

§ 1349.99 Penalty

Whoever violates section 1349.17 of the Revised Code is guilty of a minor misdemeanor.

HISTORY: 144 v H 20. Eff 8-20-91.

TITLE 15: CONSERVATION OF NATURAL RESOURCES

CHAPTER 1531: DIVISION OF WILDLIFE

§ 1531.02 State ownership of wild animals; prohibitions.

The ownership of and the title to all wild animals in this state, not legally confined or held by private ownership legally acquired, is in the state, which holds such title in trust for the benefit of all the people. Individual possession shall be obtained only in accordance with the Revised Code or division rules. No person at any time of the year shall take in any manner or possess any number or quantity of wild animals, except such wild animals as the Revised Code or division rules permit to be taken, hunted, killed, or had in possession, and only at such time and place, and in such manner, as the Revised Code or division rules prescribe. No person shall buy, sell, or offer any part of wild animals for sale, or transport any part of wild animals, except as permitted by the Revised Code or division rules. No person shall possess or transport a wild animal which has been taken unlawfully outside the state.

A person doing anything prohibited or neglecting to do anything required by this chapter or chapter 1533. of the Revised Code or contrary to any division rule violates this section. A person who counsels, aids, shields, or harbors an offender under such chapters or any division rule, or who knowingly shares in the proceeds of such a violation, or receives or possesses any wild animal in violation of the Revised Code or division rule, violates this section. No person shall hunt a wild bird or wild quadruped, except coyotes, fox, groundhogs, or migratory waterfowl as defined in the "Migratory Bird Hunting Stamp Act," 48 Stat. 452 (1934), 16 U.S.C.A. 718, as amended, and except as provided in sections 1533.73 and 1533.731 [1533.73.1] of the Revised Code, on Sunday or use a rifle, at any time, in taking migratory game birds.

HISTORY: GC § 1391; 108 v PtI, 577, § 2; 116 v 310; 119 v 369; 123 v 84 (129), § 2; Bureau of Code Revision, 10-1-53; 130 v H 573 (Eff 9-30-63); 130 v PtII, 102 (Eff 12-16-64); 131 v 514 (Eff 11-9-65); 132 v H 1 (Eff 2-21-67); 141 v H 848 (Eff 2-27-87); 142 v S 256 (Eff 7-20-88); 145 v S 182. Eff 10-20-94.

§ 1531.07 Jurisdiction of division.

All lakes, reservoirs, and state lands dedicated to the use of the public for park and pleasure resort purposes shall be under the supervision and control of the chief of the division of wildlife with respect to the enforcement of all laws relating to the protection of birds, fish, and game. All laws for the protection of fish in inland rivers and streams of the state, and all laws for the protection of the birds, fish, and game and fur-bearing animals, shall apply to all such state reservoirs and lakes. No person shall disturb, injure, or destroy a tree, plant, lawn, embankment, decoration, or other property or kill, injure, or disturb a waterfowl, water animal, bird, or game or fur-bearing animal, kept as a semidomestic pet upon an island or within the boundary lines of Buckeye Lake, Indian Lake, The Portage Lakes, Lake St. Marys, Guilford Lake, and Lake Loramie, or any other territory over which the state has jurisdiction or an embankment or state land adjacent thereto. No person shall take or disturb fish in any lagoon or any other portion of any of the waters over which the state has jurisdiction and which have been set aside by the chief for the propagation of fish.

HISTORY: GC § 1446; 108 v PtI, 577 (601), § 56; 113 v 551 (588); 118 v 83 (96); 123 v 84 (158), § 2; Bureau of Code Revision, 10-1-53; 130 v H 573. Eff 9-30-63.

[§ 1531.20.1] § 1531.201 Action to recover possession or value of wild animal.

The chief of the division of wildlife or his authorized representative may bring a civil action to recover possession of or the value of any wild animal held, taken, or possessed in violation of this chapter or Chapter 1533. of the Revised Code or any division rule against any person who held, took, possessed, or exercised control over the wild animal. Except as otherwise provided by division rule, the following shall be presumed to be the minimum value to the state of wild animals illegally held, taken, or possessed:

(A)	Each whitetail deer	$400.00
(B)	Each fur-bearing animal	50.00
(C)	Each game bird	50.00
(D)	Each nongame bird	25.00
(E)	Each eagle	1,000.00
(F)	Each osprey	750.00
(G)	Each hawk or owl	100.00
(H)	Each game quadruped	50.00
(I)	Each fish	10.00
(J)	Each wild turkey	300.00
(K)	Each endangered or threatened species	1,000.00
(L)	Each other wild animal	200.00

Nothing in this section affects the right of seizure under any other section of the Revised Code.

HISTORY: 141 v H 848 (Eff 2-27-87); 145 v S 182. Eff 10-20-94.

§ 1531.23 Judgment for costs and fine or forfeiture; failure to pay.

If the defendant in a prosecution or condemnation proceeding under a division rule or this chapter or Chapter 1533. of the Revised Code is convicted, judgment shall be rendered against him for costs in addition to the fine imposed or forfeiture declared. The judgment shall be the first lien upon the property of the person convicted, and no exemption shall be claimed or allowed against that lien. If he fails to pay the fine and costs imposed or if execution issued is returned unsatisfied, the person convicted shall be committed to the county jail or to a workhouse and there confined one day for the amount of the fine adjudged against him, determined as provided in section 2747.14 of the Revised Code. The person convicted shall not be discharged or paroled therefrom by any board or officer except upon payment of the fine remaining unpaid or upon written permission of the chief of the division of wildlife.

HISTORY: GC § 1453; 108 v PtI, 577 (604), § 63; 113 v 551 (590); 123 v 84 (160), § 2; Bureau of Code Revision, 10-1-53; 130 v PtII, 108 (Eff 12-16-64); 132 v H 195 (Eff 8-31-67); 133 v 460 (Eff 9-3-70); 135 v H 453 (Eff 11-20-73); 140 v H 113 (Eff 1-8-85); 145 v S 182. Eff 10-20-94.

§ 1531.25 Protection of species threatened with statewide extinction.

The chief of the division of wildlife, with the approval of the wildlife council, shall adopt and may modify and repeal rules, in accordance with Chapter 119. of the Revised Code, restricting the taking or possession of native wildlife, or any eggs or offspring thereof, that he finds to be threatened with statewide extinction. The rules shall identify the common and scientific names of each endangered species and shall be modified from time to time to include all species on the list of endangered fish and wildlife pursuant to Section 4 of the "Endangered Species Act of 1973," 87 Stat. 884, 16 U.S.C. 1531, as amended, and that are native to this state, or that migrate or are otherwise reasonably likely to occur within the state.

The rules shall provide for the taking of species threatened with statewide extinction, for zoological, educational, and scientific purposes, and for propagation in captivity to preserve the species, under written permits from the chief. The rules shall in no way restrict the taking or possession of species listed on such United States list for zoological, educational, or scientific purposes, or for propagation in captivity to preserve the species, under a permit or license from the United States or any instrumentality thereof.

No person shall violate any rule adopted pursuant to this section.

HISTORY: 135 v S 35 (Eff 1-1-74); 140 v H 5 (Eff 10-14-83); 142 v S 256. Eff 7-20-88.

Not analogous to former RC § 1531.25 (GC § 1435-2; 109 v 326; 113 v 551; 118 v 83; 123 v 84; Bureau Code Revision, 10-1-53) repealed 130 v H 573, § 2, eff 9-30-63.

§ 1531.29 Polluting state land or water.

No person shall place or dispose of in any manner, any garbage, waste, peelings of vegetables or fruits, rubbish, ashes, cans, bottles, wire, paper, cartons, boxes, parts of automobiles, wagons, furniture, glass, oil, or anything else of an unsightly or unsanitary nature on any state owned, controlled, or administered land, or in any ditch, stream, river, lake, pond, or other watercourse, except those waters which do not combine or effect a junction with natural surface or underground waters, or upon the bank thereof where the same is liable to be washed into the water either by ordinary flow or floods. This section does not apply to any substance placed under authority of a permit issued under section 6111.04 of the Revised Code or exempted by such section from its terms.

HISTORY: 133 v H 503 (Eff 10-30-69); 135 v H 453. Eff 11-20-73.

§ 1531.99 Penalties.

(A) Whoever violates section 1531.02 of the Revised Code, or any division rule, other than a rule adopted under section 1531.25 of the Revised Code, is guilty of a misdemeanor of the fourth degree.

(B) Whoever violates section 1531.02 of the Revised Code concerning the taking or possession of deer or section 1531.07 or 1531.29 of the Revised Code is guilty of a misdemeanor of the third degree on a first offense; on each subsequent offense, that person is guilty of a misdemeanor of the first degree.

(C) Whoever violates section 1531.25 of the Revised Code is guilty of a misdemeanor of the first degree.

(D) Whoever violates section 1531.02 of the Revised Code concerning the selling or offering for sale of any wild animals or parts of wild animals, the minimum value of which animals or parts, in the aggregate, is more than one thousand dollars as established under section 1531.201 [1531.20.1] of the Revised Code, is guilty of a felony of the fifth degree.

(E) A court that imposes sentence for a violation of any section of this chapter governing the holding, taking, or possession of wild animals, including, without limitation, section 1531.11 of the Revised Code, shall require the person who is convicted of or pleads guilty to the offense, in addition to any fine, term of imprisonment, seizure, and forfeiture imposed, to make restitution for the minimum value of the wild animal illegally held, taken, or possessed as established under section 1531.201 [1531.20.1] of the Revised Code. An officer who collects moneys paid as restitution under this section shall pay those moneys to the treasurer of state who shall deposit them in the state treasury to the credit of the wildlife fund established under section 1531.17 of the Revised Code.

HISTORY: Bureau of Code Revision, 10-1-53; 129 v 1310 (Eff 10-12-61); 131 v 519 (Eff 9-1-65); 131 v 520 (Eff 11-4-65); 133 v H 503 (Eff 10-30-69); 135 v S 35 (Eff 1-1-74); 135 v H 453 (Eff 1-1-74); 136 v H 1316 (Eff 8-31-76); 141 v H 848 (Eff 2-27-87); 145 v S 182 (Eff 10-20-94); 146 v S 2. Eff 7-1-96.

The effective date is set by section 6 of SB 2.

CHAPTER 1547: WATERCRAFT AND WATERWAYS

§ 1547.01 Definitions.

(A) As used in sections 1541.03, 1547.25, 1547.26, 1547.39, 1547.40, 1547.53, 1547.54, 1547.541 [1547.54.1], 1547.542 [1547.54.2], 1547.543 [1547.54.3], 1547.56, 1547.57, 1547.66, 3733.21, and 5311.01 of the Revised Code, "watercraft" means any of the following when used or capable of being used for transportation on the water:

(1) A boat operated by machinery either permanently or temporarily affixed;

(2) A sailboat other than a sailboard;

(3) An inflatable, manually propelled boat having a hull identification number meeting the requirements of the United States coast guard;

(4) A canoe or row boat.

"Watercraft" does not include ferries as referred to in Chapter 4583. of the Revised Code.

Watercraft subject to section 1547.54 of the Revised Code shall be divided into five classes as follows:

Class A: Less than sixteen feet in length;

Class 1: At least sixteen feet, but less than twenty-six feet in length;

Class 2: At least twenty-six feet, but less than forty feet in length;

Class 3: At least forty feet, but less than sixty-five feet in length;

Class 4: At least sixty-five feet in length.

(B) As used in this chapter:

(1) "Vessel" includes every description of watercraft, including nondisplacement craft and seaplanes, used or capable of being used as a means of transportation on water.

(2) "Rowboat" means any vessel designed to be rowed and that is propelled by human muscular effort by oars or paddles and upon which no mechanical propulsion device, electric motor, internal combustion engine, or sail has been affixed or is used for the operation of the vessel.

(3) "Sailboat" means any vessel, equipped with mast and sails, dependent upon the wind to propel it in the normal course of operation.

(a) Any sailboat equipped with an inboard engine is deemed a powercraft with auxiliary sail.

(b) Any sailboat equipped with detachable motor is deemed a sailboat with auxiliary power.

(c) Any sailboat being propelled by mechanical power, whether under sail or not, is deemed a powercraft and subject to all laws and rules governing powercraft operation.

(4) "Powercraft" means any vessel propelled by machinery, fuel, rockets, or similar device.

(5) "Person" includes any legal entity defined as a person in section 1.59 of the Revised Code and any body politic, except the United States and this state, and includes any agent, trustee, executor, receiver, assignee, or other representative thereof.

(6) "Owner" includes any person who claims lawful possession of a vessel by virtue of legal title or equitable interest therein that entitled the person to that possession.

(7) "Operator" includes any person who navigates or has under the person's control a vessel, or vessel and detachable motor, on the waters in this state.

(8) "Visible" means visible on a dark night with clear atmosphere.

(9) "Waters in this state" means all streams, rivers, lakes, ponds, marshes, watercourses, waterways, and other bodies of water, natural or humanmade, that are situated wholly or partially within this state or within its jurisdiction and are used for recreational boating.

(10) "Navigable waters" means waters that come under the jurisdiction of the department of the army of the United States and any waterways within or adjacent to this state, except inland lakes having neither a navigable inlet nor outlet.

(11) "In operation" in reference to a vessel means that the vessel is being navigated or otherwise used on the waters in this state.

(12) "Sewage" means human body wastes and the wastes from toilets and other receptacles intended to receive or retain body waste.

(13) "Canoe" means a narrow vessel of shallow draft, pointed at both ends and propelled by human muscular effort and includes kayaks.

(14) "Coast guard approved" means bearing an approval number assigned by the United States coast guard.

(15) "Type one personal flotation device" means a device that is designed to turn an unconscious person floating in water from a face downward position to a vertical or slightly face upward position and that has at least nine kilograms, approximately twenty pounds, of buoyancy.

(16) "Type two personal flotation device" means a device that is designed to turn an unconscious person in the water from a face downward position to a vertical or slightly face upward position and that has at least seven kilograms, approximately fifteen and four-tenths pounds, of buoyancy.

(17) "Type three personal flotation device" means a device that is designed to keep a conscious person in a vertical or slightly face upward position and that has at least seven kilograms, approximately fifteen and four-tenths pounds, of buoyancy.

(18) "Type four personal flotation device" means a device that is designed to be thrown to a person in the water and not worn and that has at least seven and five-tenths kilograms, approximately sixteen and five-tenths pounds, of buoyancy.

(19) "Type five personal flotation device" means a device that, unlike other personal flotation devices, has limitations on its approval by the United States coast guard, including, without limitation, all of the following:

(a) The approval label on the type five personal flotation device indicates that the device is approved for the activity in which the vessel is being used or as a substitute for a personal flotation device of the type required on the vessel in use;

(b) The personal flotation device is used in accordance with any requirements on the approval label;

(c) The personal flotation device is used in accordance with requirements in its owner's manual if the approval label refers to such a manual.

(20) "Inflatable watercraft" means any vessel constructed of rubber, canvas, or other material that is designed to be inflated with any gaseous substance, constructed with two or more air cells, and operated as a vessel. Inflatable watercraft propelled by a motor shall be classified as powercraft and shall be registered by length.

(21) "Idle speed" means the slowest possible speed needed to maintain steerage or maneuverability.

(22) "Diver's flag" means a red flag not less than one foot square having a diagonal white stripe extending from the masthead to the opposite lower corner that when displayed indicates that divers are in the water.

(23) "Muffler" means an acoustical suppression device or system that is designed and installed to abate the sound of exhaust gases emitted from an internal combustion engine and that prevents excessive or unusual noise.

(24) "Law enforcement vessel" means any vessel used in law enforcement and under the command of a law enforcement officer.

(25) "Personal watercraft" means a vessel, less than sixteen feet in length, that is propelled by machinery and designed to be operated by an individual sitting, standing, or kneeling on the vessel rather than by an individual sitting or standing inside the vessel.

(26) "No wake" has the same meaning as "idle speed."

(C) Unless otherwise provided, this chapter applies to all vessels operating on the waters in this state. Nothing in this chapter shall be construed in contravention of any valid federal act or rule, but is in addition to the act or rule where not inconsistent.

The state reserves to itself the exclusive right to regulate the minimum equipment requirements of watercraft and vessels operated on the waters in this state.

HISTORY: 128 v 1004 (Eff 3-5-59); 129 v 582(694) (Eff 1-10-61); 129 v 1350 (Eff 11-2-61); 133 v H 1002 (Eff 9-4-70); 136 v H 957 (Eff 9-3-76); 137 v S 387 (Eff 3-15-79); 138 v S 65 (Eff 1-1-80); 139 v H 782 (Eff 3-4-83); 140 v H 682 (Eff 3-28-85); 141 v H 400 (Eff 6-12-85); 143 v H 522 (Eff 6-13-90); 146 v H 117 (Eff 6-30-95); 146 v S 295. Eff 3-18-97.

§ 1547.06 Restrictions on child operators; duty of supervisory adult.

(A) Except as otherwise provided in this division, no person under sixteen years of age shall operate a personal watercraft on the waters in this state. A person who is not less than twelve, nor more than fifteen years of age may operate a personal watercraft if a supervising person eighteen years of age or older is aboard the personal watercraft.

(B) No person under twelve years of age shall operate any vessel that is not a personal watercraft on the waters in this state unless the person is under the direct visual and audible supervision, during the operation, of a person eighteen years of age or older. If the vessel is a powercraft powered by more than ten horsepower, the supervising person shall be aboard the powercraft.

(C) No supervising person eighteen years of age or older shall permit any person who is under the supervising person's supervision and who is operating a vessel on the waters in this state to violate any section of this chapter or a rule adopted under it.

HISTORY: 128 v 1004 (Eff 8-5-59); 136 v H 957 (Eff 9-3-76); 139 v H 782 (Eff 3-4-83); 143 v H 522 (Eff 6-13-90); 146 v S 295. Eff 3-18-97.

§ 1547.07 Reckless operation.

(A) Any person who operates any vessel or manipulates any water skis, aquaplane, or similar device on the waters in this state carelessly or heedlessly, or in disregard of the rights or safety of any person, vessel, or property, or without due caution, at a rate of speed or in a manner so as to endanger any person, vessel, or property is guilty of reckless operation of the vessel or other device.

(B) No person shall operate or permit the operation of a vessel in an unsafe manner. A vessel shall be operated in a reasonable and prudent manner at all times.

Unsafe vessel operation includes, without limitation, any of the following:

(1) A vessel becoming airborne or completely leaving the water while crossing the wake of another vessel at a distance of less than one hundred feet, or at an unsafe distance, from the vessel creating the wake;

(2) Operating at such a speed and proximity to another vessel or to a person attempting to ride on one or more water skis, surfboard, inflatable device, or similar device being towed by a vessel so as to require the operator of either vessel to swerve or turn abruptly to avoid collision;

(3) Operating less than two hundred feet directly behind a person water skiing or attempting to water ski;

(4) Weaving through congested traffic.

HISTORY: 128 v 1004 (Eff 8-5-59); 133 v H 1002 (Eff 9-4-70); 139 v H 782 (Eff 3-4-83); 143 v H 522 (Eff 6-13-90); 146 v S 295. Eff 3-18-97.

[§ 1547.07.1] § 1547.071 Authority of officer when especially hazardous condition exists.

(A) If a law enforcement officer observes a vessel being used and determines that at least one of the unsafe conditions identified in division (C) of this section is present and that an especially hazardous condition exists, the officer may direct the operator of the vessel to take whatever immediate and reasonable actions are necessary for the safety of the persons aboard the vessel, including directing the operator to return the vessel to mooring and remain there until the situation creating the hazardous condition is corrected or has ended.

For the purposes of this section, an especially hazardous condition is one in which a reasonably prudent person would believe that the continued operation of a vessel would create a special hazard to the safety of the persons aboard the vessel.

(B) The refusal by an operator of a vessel to terminate use of the vessel after being ordered to do so by a law enforcement officer under division (A) of this section is prima-facie evidence of a violation of section 1547.07 of the Revised Code.

(C) For the purposes of this section, any of the following is an unsafe condition:

(1) Insufficient personal flotation devices;

(2) Insufficient fire extinguishers;

(3) Overloaded, insufficient freeboard for the water conditions in which the vessel is operating;

(4) Improper display of navigation lights;

(5) Fuel leaks, including fuel leaking from either the engine or the fuel system;

(6) Accumulation of or an abnormal amount of fuel in the bilges;

(7) Inadequate backfire flame control;

(8) Improper ventilation.

(D) This section does not apply to any of the following:

(1) Foreign vessels temporarily using waters that are subject to the jurisdiction of the United States;

(2) Military vessels, vessels owned by the state or a political subdivision, or other public vessels, except those that are used for recreation;

(3) A ship's lifeboats, as defined in section 1548.01 of the Revised Code;

(4) Vessels that are solely commercial and that are carrying more than six passengers for hire.

HISTORY: 146 v S 295. Eff 3-18-97.

§ 1547.10 Operator to stop and furnish information upon accident or collision.

In case of accident to or collision with persons or property on the waters of this state, due to the operation of any vessel, the operator having knowledge of the accident or collision shall immediately stop the vessel at the scene of the accident or collision, to the extent that it is safe and practical, and shall remain at the scene of the accident or collision until he has given his name and address and, if he is not the owner, the name and address of the owner of the vessel, together with the registration number of the vessel, if any, to any person injured in the accident or collision or to the operator, occupant, owner, or attendant of any vessel damaged in the accident or collision, or to any law enforcement officer at the scene of the accident or collision.

If the injured person is unable to comprehend and record the information required to be given by this section, the other operator involved in the accident or collision shall forthwith notify the nearest law enforcement agency having authority concerning the location of the accident or collision, and his name, address, and the registration number, if any, of the vessel he was operating, and then remain at the scene of the accident or collision or at the nearest location from which notification is possible until a law enforcement officer arrives, unless removed from the scene by an emergency vehicle operated by the state or a political subdivision or by an ambulance.

If the accident or collision is with an unoccupied or unattended vessel, the operator so colliding with the vessel shall securely attach the information required to be given in this section, in writing, to a conspicuous place in or on the unoccupied or unattended vessel.

HISTORY: 140 v H 682 (Eff 3-28-85); 143 v H 522. Eff 6-13-90.

Not analogous to former RC § 1547.10 (128 v 1004; 133 v H 1002), repealed 136 v H 957, § 2, eff 9-3-76.

§ 1547.11 Operating under influence of alcohol, drugs prohibited; test analysis.

(A) No person shall operate or be in physical control of any vessel underway or shall manipulate any water skis, aquaplane, or similar device on the waters in this state if any of the following applies:

(1) The person is under the influence of alcohol or a drug of abuse, or the combined influence of alcohol and a drug of abuse;

(2) The person has a concentration of ten-hundredths of one per cent or more by weight of alcohol in the person's blood;

(3) The person has a concentration of fourteen-hundredths of one gram or more by weight of alcohol per one hundred milliliters of the person's urine;

(4) The person has a concentration of ten-hundredths of one gram or more by weight of alcohol per two

hundred ten liters of the person's breath.

(B) No person under twenty-one years of age shall operate or be in physical control of any vessel underway or shall manipulate any water skis, aquaplane, or similar device on the waters in this state if any of the following applies:

(1) The person has a concentration of at least two-hundredths of one per cent, but less than ten-hundredths of one per cent by weight of alcohol in the person's blood;

(2) The person has a concentration of at least twenty-eight one-thousandths of one gram, but less than fourteen-hundredths of one gram by weight of alcohol per one hundred milliliters of the person's urine;

(3) The person has a concentration of at least two-hundredths of one gram, but less than ten-hundredths of one gram by weight of alcohol per two hundred ten liters of the person's breath.

(C) In any proceeding arising out of one incident, a person may be charged with a violation of division (A)(1) and a violation of division (B)(1), (2), or (3) of this section, but the person shall not be convicted of more than one violation of those divisions.

(D) In any criminal prosecution for a violation of this section or of an ordinance of any municipal corporation relating to operating a vessel or using any water skis, aquaplane, or similar device while under the influence of alcohol or a drug of abuse, the court may admit evidence on the concentration of alcohol or a drug of abuse in the defendant's blood, urine, or breath at the time of the alleged violation as shown by chemical analysis of the defendant's blood, urine, or breath taken within two hours of the time of the alleged violation.

When a person submits to a blood test, only a physician, registered nurse, or qualified technician or chemist shall withdraw blood for the purpose of determining its alcohol or drug of abuse content. This limitation does not apply to the taking of breath or urine specimens. A physician, registered nurse, or qualified technician or chemist may refuse to withdraw blood for the purpose of determining its alcohol or drug of abuse content if in the opinion of the physician, nurse, or technician or chemist, the physical welfare of the person would be endangered by the withdrawing of blood.

The blood, urine, or breath shall be analyzed in accordance with methods approved by the director of health by an individual possessing a valid permit issued by the director pursuant to section 3701.143 [3701.14.3] of the Revised Code.

If there was at the time the blood, urine, or breath was taken a concentration of less than ten-hundredths of one per cent by weight of alcohol in the defendant's blood, less than fourteen-hundredths of one gram by weight of alcohol per one hundred milliters of the defendant's urine, or less than ten-hundredths of one gram by weight of alcohol per two hundred ten liters of the defendant's breath, that fact may be considered with other competent evidence in determining the guilt or innocence of the defendant.

Upon the request of the person who was tested, the results of the test shall be made available to the person or the person's attorney or agent immediately upon the completion of the test analysis.

The person tested may have a physician, registered nurse, or qualified technician or chemist of the person's own choosing administer a chemical test or tests in addition to any administered at the direction of a law enforcement officer, and shall be so advised. The failure or inability to obtain an additional test by a person shall not preclude the admission of evidence relating to the test or tests taken at the direction of a law enforcement officer.

A physician, registered nurse, or qualified technician or chemist who withdraws blood from a person pursuant to this section, and a hospital, first-aid station, or clinic at which blood is withdrawn from a person pursuant to this section, is immune from criminal liability, and from civil liability that is based upon a claim of assault and battery or based upon any other claim that is not in the nature of a claim of malpractice, for any act performed in withdrawing blood from the person.

(E) For the purposes of this section, "operate" means that a vessel is being used on the waters in this state when the vessel is not securely affixed to a dock or to shore or to any permanent structure to which the vessel has the right to affix or that a vessel is not anchored in a designated anchorage area or boat camping area that is established by the United States coast guard, this state, or a political subdivision and in which the vessel has the right to anchor.

HISTORY: 128 v 1004 (Eff 8-5-59); 133 v H 1002 (Eff 9-4-70); 136 v H 957 (Eff 9-3-76); 139 v H 782 (Eff 3-4-83); 141 v H 265 (Eff 7-24-86); 143 v H 522 (Eff 6-13-90); 146 v S 295. Eff 3-18-97.

[§ 1547.11.1] § 1547.111 Implied consent.

(A) Any person who operates a vessel or uses any water skis, aquaplane, or similar device upon any waters in this state shall be deemed to have given consent to a chemical test or tests of his blood, breath, or urine for the purpose of determining its alcohol or drug of abuse content if arrested for the offense of operating a vessel or using any water skis, aquaplane, or similar device in violation of section 1547.11 of the Revised Code. The test or tests shall be administered at the direction of a law enforcement officer having reasonable grounds to believe the person to have been operating a vessel or using any water skis, aquaplane, or similar device in violation of section 1547.11 of the Revised Code. The law enforcement agency by which the officer is employed shall designate which of the tests shall be administered.

(B) Any person who is dead, unconscious, or who is otherwise in a condition rendering him incapable of refusal shall be deemed not to have withdrawn consent provided by division (A) of this section and the test or tests may be administered, subject to sections 313.12 to 313.16 of the Revised Code.

(C) Any person under arrest for the offense of operating a vessel or using any water skis, aquaplane, or similar device in violation of section 1547.11 of the Revised Code shall be advised of the consequences of his refusal to submit to a chemical test designated by the law enforcement agency as provided in division (A) of this section. The advice shall be in a written form prescribed by the chief of the division of watercraft and shall be read to the person. The form shall contain a statement that the form was shown to the person under arrest and read to him in the presence of the arresting officer and either another law enforcement officer, civilian law enforcement employee, or an employee of a hospital, first-aid station, or clinic, if any, to which the person has been taken for first-aid or medical treatment. The witnesses shall certify to this fact by signing the form.

(D) If a person under arrest for the offense of operating a vessel or using any water skis, aquaplane, or similar device in violation of section 1547.11 of the Revised Code refuses upon the request of a law enforcement officer to submit to a chemical test designated by the law enforcement agency as provided in division (A) of this section, after first having been advised of the consequences of his refusal as provided in division (C) of this section, no chemical test shall be given, but the chief of the division of watercraft, upon receipt of a sworn statement of the law enforcement officer that he had reasonable grounds to believe the arrested person had been operating a vessel or using any water skis, aquaplane, or similar device while under the influence of alcohol or a drug of abuse, the combined influence of alcohol and a drug of abuse, or with a prohibited concentration of alcohol in his blood, urine, or breath, and that the person refused to submit to the chemical test upon the request of the law enforcement officer, and upon receipt of the form as provided in division (C) of this section certifying that the arrested person was advised of the consequences of his refusal, shall inform the person by written notice that he is prohibited from operating a vessel or using any water skis, aquaplane, or similar device, and is prohibited from registering any watercraft in accordance with section 1547.54 of the Revised Code, for one year following the date of the alleged violation of section 1547.11 of the Revised Code. The suspension of these operation, use, and registration privileges shall continue for the entire one-year period, subject to review as provided in this section.

If the person under arrest is the owner of the vessel involved in the alleged violation, the chief of the division of watercraft, in addition to informing him by written notice that he is prohibited from operating a vessel or using any water skis, aquaplane, or similar device, and from registering any watercraft in accordance with section 1547.54 of the Revised Code, for one year following the date of the alleged violation, shall impound the registration certificate and tags issued to the person in accordance with sections 1547.54 and 1547.57 of the Revised Code, for a period of one year following the date of the alleged violation. The registration certificate and tags may be impounded on the date of the alleged violation and such impoundment shall continue for the entire one-year period, subject to review as provided in this section.

(E) Upon suspending a person's operation, use, and registration privileges in accordance with division (D) of this section, the chief of the division of watercraft shall notify the person in writing, at his last known address, and inform him that he may petition for a hearing in accordance with division (F) of this section. If a person whose operation, use, and registration privileges have been suspended petitions for a hearing or appeals any decision that is adverse to him, the suspension of privileges shall begin at the termination of any hearing or appeal unless the hearing or appeal resulted in a decision favorable to the person.

(F) Any person who has been notified by the chief of the division of watercraft that he is prohibited from operating a vessel or using any water skis, aquaplane, or similar device, and from registering any watercraft in accordance with section 1547.54 of the Revised Code, or who has had the registration certificate and tags of his watercraft impounded pursuant to division (D) of this section, may, within twenty days of the notification or impoundment, file a petition in the municipal court or the county court, or in case the person is a minor in juvenile court, in whose jurisdiction the arrest occurred, agreeing to pay the cost of the proceedings and alleging error in the action taken by the chief of the division of watercraft under division (D) of this section or alleging one or more of the matters within the scope of the hearing as provided in this section, or both. The petitioner shall notify the chief of the division of watercraft of the filing of the petition and send him a copy of the petition.

The scope of the hearing is limited to the issues of whether the law enforcement officer had reasonable grounds to believe the petitioner was operating a vessel or using any water skis, aquaplane, or similar device while under the influence of alcohol or a drug of abuse, the combined influence of alcohol and a drug of abuse, or with a prohibited concentration of alcohol or a drug of abuse in his blood, urine, or breath, whether the petitioner was placed under arrest, whether the petitioner refused to submit to the chemical test upon request of the officer, and whether he was advised of the consequences of his refusal.

(G)(1) The chief of the division of watercraft shall furnish the court a copy of the affidavit as provided in division (C) of this section and any other relevant information requested by the court.

(2) In hearing the matter and in determining whether the person has shown error in the decision taken by the chief of the division of watercraft as provided in

division (D) of this section, the court shall decide the issue upon the relevant, competent, and material evidence submitted by the chief of the division of watercraft or the person whose operation, use, and registration privileges have been suspended.

(3) If the court finds from the evidence submitted that the person has failed to show error in the action taken by the chief of the division of watercraft under division (D) of this section or in one or more of the matters within the scope of the hearing as provided in division (F) of this section, or both, then the court shall assess the cost of the proceeding against the person and shall uphold the suspension of the operation, use, and registration privileges provided in division (D) of this section. If the court finds that the person has shown error in the action taken by the chief of the division of watercraft under division (D) of this section or in one or more of the matters within the scope of the hearing as provided in division (F) of this section, or both, the cost of the proceedings shall be paid out of the county treasury of the county in which the proceedings were held, the operation, use, and registration privileges of the person shall be reinstated without charge, and the registration certificate and tags, if impounded, shall be returned without charge.

(4) The court shall give information in writing of any action taken under this section to the chief of the division of watercraft.

(H) At the end of any period of suspension or impoundment imposed under this section, and upon request of the person whose operation, use, and registration privileges were suspended or whose registration certificate and tags were impounded, the chief of the division of watercraft shall reinstate the person's operation, use, and registration privileges by written notice and return the certificate and tags.

(I) No person who has received written notice from the chief of the division of watercraft that he is prohibited from operating a vessel or using any water skis, aquaplane, or similar device, and from registering a watercraft, or who has had the registration certificate and tags of his watercraft impounded, in accordance with division (D) of this section, shall operate a vessel or use any water skis, aquaplane, or similar device for a period of one year following the date of his alleged violation of section 1547.11 of the Revised Code.

HISTORY: 141 v H 265 (Eff 7-24-86); 143 v H 522. Eff 6-13-90.

§ 1547.12 Incapacitated operators prohibited.

No person shall operate any vessel if such person is so mentally or physically incapacitated as to be unable to operate the vessel in a safe and competent manner.

HISTORY: 128 v 1004 (Eff 8-5-59); 143 v H 522. Eff 6-13-90.

§ 1547.13 Failure to comply with law enforcement order; fleeing.

(A) No person shall fail to comply with any lawful order or direction of any law enforcement officer having authority to direct, control, or regulate the operation or use of vessels.

(B) No person shall operate any vessel so as to purposely elude or flee from a law enforcement officer after receiving a visible or audible signal from a law enforcement officer to bring the vessel to a stop.

HISTORY: 143 v H 522. Eff 6-13-90.

Not analogous to former RC § 1547.13 (128 v 1004; 129 v 582; 133 v H 1002), repealed 134 v H 511, § 2, eff 1-1-74.

[§ 1547.13.1] § 1547.131 Duty upon approach of law enforcement vessel.

Upon the approach of a law enforcement vessel with at least one blue flashing, rotating, or oscillating light, the operator of any vessel shall stop if followed or give way in any crossing, head-on, or overtaking situation, and shall remain in such position until the law enforcement vessel has passed, except when otherwise directed by a law enforcement officer. If traffic conditions warrant, a siren or other sound producing device also may be operated as an additional signaling device. This section does not relieve the operator of any law enforcement vessel from the duty to operate with due regard for the safety of all persons and property on the waters in this state.

HISTORY: 143 v H 522. Eff 6-13-90.

§ 1547.14 Water skiing confined to ski zones.

(A) Except on the waters of Lake Erie, the Ohio River, and immediately connected harbors and anchorage facilities, any person who rides or attempts to ride upon one or more water skis, surfboard, or similar device, or who engages or attempts to engage in barefoot skiing, and any person who operates a vessel towing a person riding or attempting to ride on one or more water skis, surfboard, or similar device, or engaging or attempting to engage in barefoot skiing, shall confine that activity to the water area within a designated ski zone on all bodies of water whereon a ski zone has been established.

(B) On all bodies of water designated as "open zone," that is, having a combined speed and ski zone, the activities described in division (A) of this section shall be confined to the open zone.

HISTORY: 128 v 1004 (Eff 8-5-59); 139 v H 782 (Eff 3-4-83); 140 v H 682 (Eff 3-28-85); 143 v H 522. Eff 6-13-90.

§ 1547.15 Observer required when towing skier.

Any person who operates a vessel towing any person riding or attempting to ride upon one or more water skis, surfboard, or similar device, or engaging or attempting to engage in barefoot skiing, on the waters in this state shall have present in the vessel a person or persons other than the operator, ten years of age or older, who shall at all times observe the progress of the person being towed. The operator of the towing vessel shall at all times observe the traffic pattern toward which the vessel is approaching.

HISTORY: 128 v 1004 (Eff 8-5-59); 133 v H 1002 (Eff 9-4-70); 139 v H 782 (Eff 3-4-83); 140 v H 682 (Eff 3-28-85); 143 v H 522. Eff 6-13-90.

§ 1547.16 Water skiing after dark prohibited.

No person shall ride or attempt to ride upon water skis, surfboard, or similar device, or engage or attempt to engage in barefoot skiing, or use or operate any vessel to tow any person thereon on the waters in this state during that period of the day between sunset and sunrise, except upon special permit issued by the state department, conservancy district, or political subdivision having jurisdiction and control of such water.

HISTORY: 128 v 1004 (Eff 8-5-59); 139 v H 782 (Eff 3-4-83); 140 v H 682 (Eff 3-28-85); 143 v H 522. Eff 6-13-90.

§ 1547.18 Personal flotation device required for skiers.

(A) No person shall ride or attempt to ride on one or more water skis, surfboard, inflatable device, or similar device being towed by a vessel without wearing an adequate and effective coast guard approved type one, two, or three personal flotation device or type five personal flotation device specifically designed for water skiing, in good and serviceable condition and of appropriate size, except upon special permit issued by the state department, conservancy district, or political subdivision having jurisdiction and control of the water.

(B) No person shall engage or attempt to engage in barefoot skiing without wearing an adequate and effective coast guard approved type one, two, or three personal flotation device or type five personal flotation device specifically designed for water skiing, in good and serviceable condition and of appropriate size, or a wet suit specifically designed for barefoot skiing.

(C) No operator of a vessel shall tow any person who fails to comply with division (A) or (B) of this section.

HISTORY: 128 v 1004 (Eff 8-5-59); 129 v 582(695) (Eff 1-10-61); 133 v H 1002 (Eff 9-4-70); 136 v H 957 (Eff 9-3-76); 140 v H 682 (Eff 3-28-85); 143 v H 522 (Eff 6-13-90); 146 v S 295. Eff 3-18-97.

§ 1547.24 Children under 10 must wear appropriate size personal flotation device.

No person shall operate or permit to be operated any vessel under eighteen feet in length while there is present in the vessel any person under ten years of age, not wearing a coast guard approved type one, two, or three personal flotation device in good and serviceable condition of appropriate size securely attached to the person under ten years of age.

HISTORY: 128 v 1004 (Eff 8-5-59); 136 v H 957 (Eff 9-3-76); 143 v H 522. Eff 6-13-90.

§ 1547.25 Operation without personal flotation devices prohibited.

(A) No person shall operate or permit to be operated any watercraft on the waters in this state:

(1) Sixteen feet or greater in length without carrying aboard one type one, two, or three personal flotation device for each person aboard and one type four personal flotation device;

(2) Less than sixteen feet in length, including canoes and kayaks of any length, without carrying aboard one type one, two, or three personal flotation device for each person aboard.

(B) A type five personal flotation device may be carried in lieu of a type one, two, or three personal flotation device required under division (A) of this section.

(C) Each personal flotation device carried aboard a watercraft pursuant to this section shall be coast guard approved and in good and serviceable condition, of appropriate size for the wearer, and readily accessible to each person aboard the watercraft at all times.

HISTORY: 128 v 1004 (Eff 8-5-59); 129 v 1712 (Eff 3-31-62); 133 v H 1002 (Eff 9-4-70); 136 v H 957 (Eff 9-3-76); 137 v S 173 (Eff 5-20-77); 139 v H 782 (Eff 3-4-83); 143 v H 522 (Eff 6-13-90); 146 v S 295. Eff 3-18-97.

[§ 1547.52.3] § 1547.523 Felony precludes or terminates employment as state watercraft officer.

(A) As used in this section, "felony" has the same meaning as in section 109.511 [109.51.1] of the Revised Code.

(B)(1) The chief of the division of watercraft shall not appoint a person as a state watercraft officer on a permanent basis, on a temporary basis, for a probationary term, or on other than a permanent basis if the person previously has been convicted of or has pleaded guilty to a felony.

(2)(a) The chief of the division of watercraft shall terminate the employment of a state watercraft officer who does either of the following:

(i) Pleads guilty to a felony;

(ii) Pleads guilty to a misdemeanor pursuant to a negotiated plea agreement as provided in division (D) of section 2929.29 of the Revised Code in which the state watercraft officer agrees to surrender the certificate awarded to that officer under section 109.77 of the Revised Code.

(b) The chief shall suspend from employment a state watercraft officer who is convicted, after trial, of a felony. If the state watercraft officer files an appeal from that conviction and the conviction is upheld by the highest court to which the appeal is taken or if the state watercraft officer does not file a timely appeal, the chief shall terminate the employment of that state watercraft officer. If the state watercraft officer files an appeal that results in the state watercraft officer's acquittal of the felony or conviction of a misdemeanor, or in the dismissal of the felony charge against the state watercraft officer, the chief shall reinstate that state watercraft officer. A state watercraft officer who is reinstated under division (B)(2)(b) of this section shall not receive any back pay unless that state watercraft officer's conviction of the felony was reversed on appeal, or the felony charge was dismissed, because the court found insufficient evidence to convict the state watercraft officer of the felony.

(3) Division (B) of this section does not apply regarding an offense that was committed prior to January 1, 1997.

(4) The suspension from employment, or the termination of the employment, of a state watercraft officer under division (B)(2) of this section shall be in accordance with Chapter 119. of the Revised Code.

HISTORY: 146 v H 566. Eff 10-16-96.

§ 1547.63 Enforcement.

Every sheriff, deputy sheriff, marshal, deputy marshal, member of the organized police department of any municipal corporation, police constable of any township, wildlife officer, park officer, preserve officer, conservancy district police officer, and other law enforcement officer, within the area of his authority, may enforce this chapter and rules adopted by the chief of the division of watercraft and, in the exercise thereof, may stop and board any vessel subject to this chapter and rules adopted under it.

HISTORY: 129 v 582(702) (Eff 1-10-61); 131 v 546 (Eff 11-1-65); 143 v H 522 (Eff 6-13-90); 145 v S 182. Eff 10-20-94.

§ 1547.69 Firearms offenses; signaling devices.

(A) As used in this section:

(1) "Firearm" has the same meaning as in section 2923.11 of the Revised Code.

(2) "Unloaded" has the same meaning as in section 2923.16 of the Revised Code.

(B) No person shall knowingly discharge a firearm while in or on a vessel.

(C) No person shall knowingly transport or have a loaded firearm in a vessel, in such a manner that the firearm is accessible to the operator or any passenger.

(D) No person shall knowingly transport or have a firearm in a vessel, unless it is unloaded and is carried in one of the following ways:

(1) In a closed package, box, or case;

(2) In plain sight with the action opened or the weapon stripped; or, if the firearm is of a type on which the action will not stay open or which cannot easily be stripped, in plain sight.

(E) The affirmative defense contained in divisions (C)(1) and (2) of section 2923.12 of the Revised Code are affirmative defenses to a charge under division (C) or (D) of this section.

(F) Divisions (B), (C), and (D) of this section do not apply to the possession or discharge of a United States coast guard approved signaling device required to be carried aboard a vessel under section 1547.251 [1547.25.1] of the Revised Code when the signaling device is possessed or used for the purpose of giving a visual distress signal. No person shall knowingly transport or possess any such signaling device in or on a vessel in a loaded condition at any time other than immediately prior to the discharge of the signaling device for the purpose of giving a visual distress signal.

(G) This section does not apply to officers, agents, or employees of this or any other state or of the United States or to law enforcement officers when authorized to carry or have loaded or accessible firearms in a vessel and acting within the scope of their duties, nor to persons legally engaged in hunting.

HISTORY: 143 v H 522. Eff 6-13-90.

§ 1547.91 Wrecking.

No person, with purpose to unlawfully damage, ground, or sink a vessel afloat, shall do any of the following:

(A) Employ any false signal, buoy, or other aid to navigation;

(B) Tamper with any signal, buoy, or other aid to navigation;

(C) Do any act which creates an imminent and substantial risk that any vessel afloat will be damaged, grounded, sunk, or scuttled.

HISTORY: 134 v H 511 (Eff 1-1-74); 143 v H 522. Eff 6-13-90.

§ 1547.92 Tampering with navigation aid or vessel prohibited.

No person shall knowingly:

(A) Damage, remove, or tamper with any signal, buoy, or other aid to navigation;

(B) Sever the mooring lines of, set adrift, or tamper with any vessel that is moored or tied up on the waters in this state.

HISTORY: 139 v H 782 (Eff 3-4-83); 143 v H 522. Eff 6-13-90.

Analogous to former RC § 1547.92 (134 v H 511), repealed in 136 v H 957, § 2, eff 9-3-76.

§ 1547.99 Penalties.

(A) Whoever violates section 1547.91 of the Revised Code is guilty of a felony of the fourth degree.

(B) Whoever violates section 1547.10, division (I) of section 1547.111 [1547.11.1], section 1547.13, or section 1547.66 of the Revised Code is guilty of a misdemeanor of the first degree.

(C) Whoever violates a provision of this chapter or a rule adopted thereunder, for which no penalty is otherwise provided, is guilty of a minor misdemeanor.

(D) Whoever violates section 1547.07 or 1547.12 of the Revised Code without causing injury to persons or damage to property is guilty of a misdemeanor of the fourth degree.

(E) Whoever violates section 1547.07 or 1547.12 of the Revised Code causing injury to persons or damage to property is guilty of a misdemeanor of the third degree.

(F) Whoever violates division (M) of section 1547.54, division (G) of section 1547.30, or section 1547.131 [1547.13.1], 1547.25, 1547.33, 1547.38, 1547.39, 1547.40, 1547.69, or 1547.92 of the Revised Code or a rule adopted under division (A)(2) of section 1547.52 of the Revised Code is guilty of a misdemeanor of the fourth degree.

(G) Whoever violates section 1547.11 of the Revised Code is guilty of a misdemeanor of the first degree and shall be punished as provided in division (G)(1), (2), or (3) of this section.

(1) Except as otherwise provided in division (G)(2) or (3) of this section, the court shall sentence the offender to a term of imprisonment of three consecutive days and may sentence the offender pursuant to section 2929.21 of the Revised Code to a longer term of imprisonment. In addition, the court shall impose upon the offender a fine of not less than one hundred fifty nor more than one thousand dollars.

The court may suspend the execution of the mandatory three consecutive days of imprisonment that it is required to impose by division (G)(1) of this section if the court, in lieu of the suspended term of imprisonment, places the offender on probation and requires the offender to attend, for three consecutive days, a drivers' intervention program that is certified pursuant to section 3793.10 of the Revised Code. The court also may suspend the execution of any part of the mandatory three consecutive days of imprisonment that it is required to impose by division (G)(1) of this section if the court places the offender on probation for part of the three consecutive days; requires the offender to attend, for that part of the three consecutive days, a drivers' intervention program that is certified pursuant to section 3793.10 of the Revised Code; and sentences the offender to a term of imprisonment equal to the remainder of the three consecutive days that the offender does not spend attending the drivers' intervention program. The court may require the offender, as a condition of probation, to attend and satisfactorily complete any treatment or education programs, in addition to the required attendance at a drivers' intervention program, that the operators of the drivers' intervention program determine that the offender should attend and to report periodically to the court on the offender's progress in the programs. The court also may impose any other conditions of probation on the offender that it considers necessary.

(2) If, within five years of the offense, the offender has been convicted of or pleaded guilty to one violation of section 1547.11 of the Revised Code, of a municipal ordinance relating to operating a watercraft or manipulating any water skis, aquaplane, or similar device while under the influence of alcohol, a drug of abuse, or alcohol and a drug of abuse, of a municipal ordinance relating to operating a watercraft or manipulating any water skis, aquaplane, or similar device with a prohibited concentration of alcohol in the blood, breath, or urine, or of section 2903.06 or 2903.07 of the Revised Code in a case in which the jury or judge found that the offender was under the influence of alcohol, a drug of abuse, or alcohol and a drug of abuse, the court shall sentence the offender to a term of imprisonment of ten consecutive days and may sentence the offender pursuant to section 2929.21 of the Revised Code to a longer term of imprisonment. In addition, the court shall impose upon the offender a fine of not less than one hundred fifty nor more than one thousand dollars.

In addition to any other sentence that it imposes upon the offender, the court may require the offender to attend a drivers' intervention program that is certified pursuant to section 3793.10 of the Revised Code.

(3) If, within five years of the offense, the offender has been convicted of or pleaded guilty to more than one violation of section 1547.11 of the Revised Code, of a municipal ordinance relating to operating a watercraft or manipulating any water skis, aquaplane, or similar device while under the influence of alcohol, a drug of abuse, or alcohol and a drug of abuse, of a municipal ordinance relating to operating a watercraft or manipulating any water skis, aquaplane, or similar device with a prohibited concentration of alcohol in the blood, breath, or urine, or of section 2903.06 or 2903.07 of the Revised Code in a case in which the jury or judge found that the offender was under the influence of alcohol, a drug of abuse, or alcohol and a drug of abuse, the court shall sentence the offender to a term of imprisonment of thirty consecutive days and may sentence the offender to a longer term of imprisonment of not more than one year. In addition, the court shall impose upon the offender a fine of not less than one hundred fifty nor more than one thousand dollars.

In addition to any other sentence that it imposes upon the offender, the court may require the offender to attend a drivers' intervention program that is certified pursuant to section 3793.10 of the Revised Code.

(4) Upon a showing that imprisonment would seriously affect the ability of an offender sentenced pursuant to division (G)(1), (2), or (3) of this section to continue the offender's employment, the court may authorize that the offender be granted work release from

imprisonment after the offender has served the three, ten, or thirty consecutive days of imprisonment that the court is required by division (G)(1), (2), or (3) of this section to impose. No court shall authorize work release from imprisonment during the three, ten, or thirty consecutive days of imprisonment that the court is required by division (G)(1), (2), or (3) of this section to impose. The duration of the work release shall not exceed the time necessary each day for the offender to commute to and from the place of employment and the place of imprisonment and the time actually spent under employment.

(5) Notwithstanding any section of the Revised Code that authorizes the suspension of the imposition or execution of a sentence or the placement of an offender in any treatment program in lieu of imprisonment, no court shall suspend the ten or thirty consecutive days of imprisonment required to be imposed by division (G)(2) or (3) of this section or place an offender who is sentenced pursuant to division (G)(2) or (3) of this section in any treatment program in lieu of imprisonment until after the offender has served the ten or thirty consecutive days of imprisonment required to be imposed pursuant to division (G)(2) or (3) of this section. Notwithstanding any section of the Revised Code that authorizes the suspension of the imposition or execution of a sentence or the placement of an offender in any treatment program in lieu of imprisonment, no court, except as specifically authorized by division (G)(1) of this section, shall suspend the three consecutive days of imprisonment required to be imposed by division (G)(1) of this section or place an offender who is sentenced pursuant to division (G)(1) of this section in any treatment program in lieu of imprisonment until after the offender has served the three consecutive days of imprisonment required to be imposed pursuant to division (G)(1) of this section.

(H) Whoever violates section 1547.304 [1547.30.4] of the Revised Code is guilty of a misdemeanor of the fourth degree and also shall be assessed any costs incurred by the state or a county, township, municipal corporation, or other political subdivision in disposing of an abandoned junk vessel or outboard motor, less any money accruing to the state, county, township, municipal corporation, or other political subdivision from that disposal.

(I) Whoever violates division (B) or (C) of section 1547.49 of the Revised Code is guilty of a minor misdemeanor.

(J) Whoever violates section 1547.31 of the Revised Code is guilty of a misdemeanor of the fourth degree on a first offense. On each subsequent offense, the person is guilty of a misdemeanor of the third degree.

HISTORY: 128 v 1004 (Eff 8-5-59); 129 v 582(703) (Eff 1-10-61); 129 v 1388 (Eff 1-1-62); 131 v 547 (Eff 11-1-65); 134 v S 397 (Eff 10-23-72); 134 v H 511 (Eff 1-1-74); 137 v H 1 (Eff 8-26-77); 139 v H 782 (Eff 3-4-83); 140 v H 682 (Eff 3-28-85); 141 v H 265 (Eff 7-24-86); 141 v H 428 (Eff 12-23-86); 143 v H 317 (Eff 10-10-89); 143 v H 522 (Eff 6-13-90); 146 v S 2 (Eff 7-1-96); 146 v S 295. Eff 3-18-97.

CHAPTER 1548: WATERCRAFT CERTIFICATES OF TITLE

§ 1548.01 Definition of watercraft; application of chapter; forms.

(A) As used in this chapter, "watercraft" means any of the following when used or capable of being used as a means of transportation on the water:

(1) A boat operated by machinery either permanently or temporarily affixed;

(2) A sailboat other than a sailboard;

(3) An inflatable, manually propelled boat having a hull identification number meeting the requirements of the United States coast guard. "Watercraft" does not include ferries as referred to in Chapter 4583. of the Revised Code.

(B) This chapter does not apply to any of the following:

(1) A watercraft covered by a marine document in effect that has been assigned to it by the United States government pursuant to federal law;

(2) A watercraft from a country other than the United States temporarily using the waters in this state;

(3) A watercraft whose owner is the United States, a state, or a political subdivision thereof;

(4) A ship's lifeboat. As used in division (B)(4) of this section, "lifeboat" means a watercraft that is held aboard another vessel and used exclusively for emergency purposes.

(5) A canoe, kayak, or rowboat;

(6) Watercraft less than fourteen feet in length;

(7) Outboard motors of less than ten horsepower as determined by the manufacturer's rating.

(C) The various certificates, applications, and assignments necessary to provide certificates of title for watercraft and outboard motors shall be made on appropriate forms approved by the chief of the division of watercraft.

HISTORY: 130 v H 289 (Eff 10-10-63); 131 v 548 (Eff 9-9-65); 134 v S 350 (Eff 12-21-71); 139 v H 782 (Eff 3-4-83); 143 v H 522 (Eff 6-13-90); 145 v S 182 (Eff 10-20-94); 146 v S 295. Eff 3-18-97.

§ 1548.18 Prohibitions.

No person shall:

(A) Operate in this state a watercraft for which a certificate of title is required or watercraft powered by an outboard motor for which a certificate of title is required without having such certificate, or a valid temporary permit and number, in accordance with Chapter 1548. of the Revised Code;

(B) Operate in this state a watercraft for which a

certificate of title is required or watercraft powered by an outboard motor for which a certificate of title is required upon which the certificate of title has been canceled;

(C) Fail to surrender any certificate of title upon cancellation of the same by the chief of the division of watercraft and notice thereof as prescribed in Chapter 1548. of the Revised Code;

(D) Fail to surrender the certificate of title to the clerk of the court of common pleas as provided in Chapter 1548. of the Revised Code, in case of the destruction or dismantling or change of a watercraft or outboard motor in such respect that it is not the watercraft or outboard motor described in the certificate of title;

(E) Violate sections 1548.01 to 1548.21 of the Revised Code, for which no penalty is otherwise provided, or any lawful rules or regulations promulgated pursuant to such sections.

HISTORY: 130 v H 289 (Eff 10-10-63); 131 v 556 (Eff 9-9-65); 134 v S 350 (Eff 12-21-71); 135 v S 251. Eff 1-1-74.

§ 1548.19 Dealing with stolen watercraft or motor.

No person shall:

(A) Procure or attempt to procure a certificate of title to a watercraft or outboard motor, or pass or attempt to pass a certificate of title or any assignment thereof to a watercraft or outboard motor, knowing or having reason to believe that such watercraft or outboard motor has been stolen;

(B) Sell or offer for sale in this state a watercraft or outboard motor on which the manufacturer's or assigned serial number has been destroyed, removed, covered, altered, or defaced with knowledge of such destruction, removal, covering, alteration, or defacement of such manufacturer's or assigned serial number;

(C) Sell or transfer a watercraft or outboard motor without delivering to the purchaser or transferee thereof a certificate of title, or a manufacturer's or importer's certificate thereto, assigned to such purchaser as provided for in such sections.

HISTORY: 130 v H 289 (Eff 10-10-63); 134 v H 511 (Eff 1-1-74); 135 v S 251 (Eff 1-1-74); 137 v S 387 (Eff 3-15-79); 138 v S 65. Eff 1-1-80.

§ 1548.99 Penalties.

(A) Whoever violates section 1548.18 of the Revised Code is guilty of a misdemeanor of the fourth degree.

(B) Whoever violates section 1548.19 of the Revised Code is guilty of a felony of the fifth degree.

HISTORY: 130 v H 289 (Eff 10-10-63); 143 v H 522 (Eff 6-13-90); 146 v S 2. Eff 7-1-96.

The effective date is set by section 6 of SB 2.

TITLE 19:
COURTS—MUNICIPAL—MAYOR'S—COUNTY

CHAPTER 1901: MUNICIPAL COURT

§ 1901.20 Criminal and traffic jurisdiction.

(A) The municipal court has jurisdiction of the violation of any ordinance of any municipal corporation within its territory, unless the violation is required to be handled by a parking violations bureau or joint parking violations bureau pursuant to Chapter 4521. of the Revised Code, and of the violation of any misdemeanor committed within the limits of its territory. The municipal court has jurisdiction of the violation of a vehicle parking or standing resolution or regulation if a local authority, as defined in division (D) of section 4521.01 of the Revised Code, has specified that it is not to be considered a criminal offense, if the violation is committed within the limits of the court's territory, and if the violation is not required to be handled by a parking violations bureau or joint parking violations bureau pursuant to Chapter 4521. of the Revised Code. The municipal court, if it has a housing or environmental division, has jurisdiction of any criminal action over which the housing or environmental division is given jurisdiction by section 1901.181 [1901.18.1] of the Revised Code, provided that, except as specified in division (B) of that section, no judge of the court other than the judge of the division shall hear or determine any action over which the division has jurisdiction. In all such prosecutions and cases, the court shall proceed to a final determination of the prosecution or case.

(B) The municipal court has jurisdiction to hear felony cases committed within its territory. In all felony cases, the court may conduct preliminary hearings and other necessary hearings prior to the indictment of the defendant or prior to the court's finding that there is probable and reasonable cause to hold or recognize the defendant to appear before a court of common pleas and may discharge, recognize, or commit the defendant.

(C) A municipal court has jurisdiction of an appeal from a judgment or default judgment entered pursuant to Chapter 4521. of the Revised Code, as authorized by division (D) of section 4521.08 of the Revised Code. The appeal shall be placed on the regular docket of the court and shall be determined by a judge of the court.

HISTORY: GC § 1598; 124 v 589; Bureau of Code Revision, 10-1-53; 128 v 823 (Eff 11-6-59); 139 v H 707 (Eff 1-1-83); 141 v H 159 (Eff 3-19-87); 144 v S 105 (Eff 3-24-92); 146 v H 350 (Eff 1-27-97); 146 v H 438. Eff 7-1-97.

The effective date is set by section 3 of HB 438.

§ 1901.21 Criminal and civil procedure; bond.

(A) In a criminal case or proceeding, the practice, procedure, and mode of bringing and conducting prosecutions for offenses shall be as provided in the Criminal Rules, and the power of the court in relation to the prosecution is the same as the power that is conferred upon county courts.

In any civil case or proceeding for which no special provision is made in this chapter, the practice and procedure in the case or proceeding shall be the same as in courts of common pleas. If no practice or procedure for the case or proceeding is provided for in the courts of common pleas, then the practice or procedure of county courts shall apply.

(B) In the Cleveland municipal court, all bonds for the appearance of a defendant charged with an offense, when the offense is bailable, shall be entered into before the clerk of the municipal court and approved by him; and the surety in them shall be qualified by the clerk.

One surety in every such bond shall be a resident within the jurisdiction of the court; the sureties shall own property worth double the sum to be secured and shall have real estate within Cuyahoga county liable to execution of a value equal to the sum to be secured; and when two or more sureties are offered to the same bond, they shall have in the aggregate the qualification prescribed. The bond shall require the defendant to appear before the court to answer the charge against him, or before the court of common pleas when the defendant is held to the grand jury.

The bond shall clearly disclose the full name of each surety, together with the residence address, and there shall be indorsed on it a brief, but pertinent, description of the real estate owned by each surety.

When the bond is entered into, approved, and accepted, it becomes a subsisting lien on the real estate of the surety in it, upon which he has qualified, until the bond has been exonerated or discharged.

A copy of every such bond, certified under the seal of the court by the clerk as a true copy, shall be filed by him with the county recorder of Cuyahoga county forthwith unless in the meantime the defendant has been acquitted or discharged by the court. The recorder shall provide a suitable record book, properly indexed, in which he shall record all bonds certified to him. The recorder shall be entitled to receive from the clerk, such fees and record charges as are now authorized by law for recording deeds and mortgages; and such fees and charges shall be taxed by the clerk in the costs of the respective cases, and shall be paid to the recorder by the clerk from funds in his hands upon certified vouchers or bills rendered by the recorder.

The clerk shall transmit to the recorder each day a

certified list, under the seal of the court, of all bonds which have been exonerated or discharged, and the recorder shall note on the margin of the record of each bond the discharge or satisfaction of it, and the lien on the real estate of the surety in such bond shall thereby be canceled and discharged.

The clerk shall not approve or accept as surety, on any such bond, any person who is then liable on any bond previously executed in the municipal court, unless it appears to the satisfaction of the clerk that the person offering himself as surety has sufficient equity in his real estate over and above his liability on the prior bonds, to justify the subsequent bond, or unless the prior bonds have been exonerated and discharged.

The clerk may tax in the costs of the case, such fees for making the copies and certificates required in this section as the court by rule provides.

In all misdemeanor cases, the clerk, in lieu of the sureties required by this section, may accept a deposit of money, in United States legal tender, in an amount equal to the penal sum stipulated in the bond, and in any felony case a judge of the municipal court may direct the clerk to accept such a deposit in an amount fixed by the judge, which amount shall be the sum stipulated in the bond, and such deposit shall be retained by the clerk as security on it until the bond has been exonerated and discharged. If any such bond is forfeited, the clerk shall apply the money so deposited in satisfaction of any judgment that may be rendered on the bond, and the depositor of such fund shall surrender and forfeit all right in and to the deposit to the extent of such judgment.

HISTORY: GC § 1599; 124 v 589; Bureau of Code Revision, 10-1-53; 125 v 903(952); 128 v 823 (Eff 11-6-59); 129 v 423 (Eff 10-19-61); 135 v H 1 (Eff 3-22-73); 136 v H 205 (Eff 1-1-76); 141 v H 412 (Eff 3-17-87); 141 v H 159 (Eff 3-19-87); 142 v H 708. Eff 4-19-88.

§ 1901.23 Issuance of writs and process.

Writs and process in a municipal court shall be served, returned, and publication made in the manner provided for service, return, and publication of summons, writs, and process in the court of common pleas.

In any civil action or proceeding in which the subject matter of the action or proceeding is located within the territory or a defendant resides or is served with summons within the territory, the court may issue summons, orders of interpleader, all other writs, and mesne and final process, including executions necessary or proper for the complete adjudication of the issues and determination of the action, to the bailiff for service in the county or counties in which the court is situated and to the sheriff of any other county against one or more of the remaining defendants.

All warrants, executions, subpoenas, writs, and processes in all criminal and quasi-criminal cases may be issued to the bailiff of the court, a police officer of the appropriate municipal corporation, or to the sheriff of the appropriate county.

In any civil action in which the bailiff is a party or is interested, writs and process shall be directed to the sheriff. If both of these officers are interested, the writs and process shall be directed to and executed by a person appointed by the court or a judge of the court, and that person has the same power to execute the writs and process that the bailiff has. The return of the appointee shall be verified by affidavit, and he is entitled to the fees allowed to the bailiff for similar service.

HISTORY: GC § 1603; 124 v 589; Bureau of Code Revision, 10-1-53; 128 v 823 (Eff 11-6-59); 141 v H 159. Eff 3-19-87.

§ 1901.24 Jury demand; number of jurors; verdict.

(A) A jury trial in a municipal court shall be demanded in the manner prescribed in the Rules of Civil Procedure or the Rules of Criminal Procedure. The number of persons composing a jury and the verdicts of jurors shall be governed by those rules.

(B) The right of a person to a jury trial in a municipal court is waived under the circumstances prescribed in the Rules of Civil Procedure or the Rules of Criminal Procedure.

HISTORY: 141 v H 159. Eff 3-19-87.

Analogous in part to former RC § 1901.24 (GC § 1604; 124 v 589; Bureau of Code Revision, 10-1-53; 125 v 903(954); 129 v 423; 130 v 605; 130 v PtII, 138; 140 v H 183), repealed 141 v H 159, § 2, eff 3-19-87.

§ 1901.25 Selection and impaneling of a jury.

A municipal court may provide by rule the manner in which jurors shall be chosen, and may provide that jurors to be used in the court may be chosen and summoned by the jury commissioners of the county as provided in sections 2313.01 to 2313.26 of the Revised Code. Selection shall be made from residents within the territory and those appearing to reside outside the territory shall be returned to the jury wheel, to the automation data processing storage drawer, or to any other automated data processing information storage device used pursuant to division (C) of section 2313.21 of the Revised Code. Jurors shall be impaneled in the same manner, shall have the same qualifications, shall be challenged for the same causes, and shall receive the same fees as jurors in the court of common pleas. The fees of jurors in any criminal case involving violation of state law shall be paid out of the county treasury. The fees of jurors in any criminal case involving a violation of a municipal ordinance shall be paid out of the treasury of the municipal corporation in which the violation occurred.

HISTORY: GC § 1604; 124 v 589; Bureau of Code Revision, 10-1-53; 131 v 605 (Eff 11-1-65); 133 v H 424 (Eff 11-25-69); 141 v H 159. Eff 3-19-87.

§ 1901.26 Costs.

(A) Subject to division (C)† of this section, costs in a municipal court shall be fixed and taxed as follows:

(1) The municipal court shall require an advance deposit for the filing of any new civil action or proceeding when required by division (A)(9) of this section, and in all other cases, by rule, shall establish a schedule of fees and costs to be taxed in any civil or criminal action or proceeding.

(2) The municipal court, by rule, may require an advance deposit for the filing of any civil action or proceeding and publication fees as provided in section 2701.09 of the Revised Code. The court may waive the requirement for advance deposit upon affidavit or other evidence that a party is unable to make the required deposit.

(3) When a jury trial is demanded in any civil action or proceeding, the party making the demand may be required to make an advance deposit as fixed by rule of court, unless, upon affidavit or other evidence, the court concludes that the party is unable to make the required deposit. If a jury is called, the fees of a jury shall be taxed as costs.

(4) In any civil or criminal action or proceeding, witnesses' fees shall be fixed in accordance with sections 2335.06 and 2335.08 of the Revised Code.

(5) A reasonable charge for driving, towing, carting, storing, keeping, and preserving motor vehicles and other personal property recovered or seized in any proceeding may be taxed as part of the costs in a trial of the cause, in an amount that shall be fixed by rule of court.

(6) Chattel property seized under any writ or process issued by the court shall be preserved pending final disposition for the benefit of all persons interested and may be placed in storage when necessary or proper for that preservation. The custodian of any chattel property so stored shall not be required to part with the possession of the property until a reasonable charge, to be fixed by the court, is paid.

(7) The municipal court, as it determines, may refund all deposits and advance payments of fees and costs, including those for jurors and summoning jurors, when they have been paid by the losing party.

(8) Charges for the publication of legal notices required by statute or order of court may be taxed as part of the costs, as provided by section 7.13 of the Revised Code.

(B)(1) The municipal court may determine that, for the efficient operation of the court, additional funds are necessary to acquire and pay for special projects of the court including, but not limited to, the acquisition of additional facilities or the rehabilitation of existing facilities, the acquisition of equipment, the hiring and training of staff, community service programs, mediation or dispute resolution services, the employment of magistrates, and other related services. Upon that determination, the court by rule may charge a fee, in addition to all other court costs, on the filing of each criminal cause, civil action or proceeding, or judgment by confession.

If the municipal court offers a special program or service in cases of a specific type, the municipal court by rule may assess an additional charge in a case of that type, over and above court costs, to cover the special program or service. The municipal court shall adjust the special assessment periodically, but not retroactively, so that the amount assessed in those cases does not exceed the actual cost of providing the service or program.

All moneys collected under division (B) of this section shall be paid to the county treasurer if the court is a county-operated municipal court or to the city treasurer if the court is not a county-operated municipal court for deposit into either a general special projects fund or a fund established for a specific special project. Moneys from a fund of that nature shall be disbursed upon an order of the court in an amount no greater than the actual cost to the court of a project. If a specific fund is terminated because of the discontinuance of a program or service established under division (B) of this section, the municipal court may order that moneys remaining in the fund be transferred to an account established under this division for a similar purpose.

(2) As used in division (B) of this section:

(a) "Criminal cause" means a charge alleging the violation of a statute or ordinance, or subsection of a statute or ordinance, that requires a separate finding of fact or a separate plea before disposition and of which the defendant may be found guilty, whether filed as part of a multiple charge on a single summons, citation, or complaint or as a separate charge on a single summons, citation, or complaint. "Criminal cause" does not include separate violations of the same statute or ordinance, or subsection of the same statute or ordinance, unless each charge is filed on a separate summons, citation, or complaint.

(b) "Civil action or proceeding" means any civil litigation that must be determined by judgment entry.

(C) Prior to January 1, 1993, and on and after January 1, 2003, the municipal court shall collect the sum of four dollars as additional filing fees in each new civil action or proceeding for the charitable public purpose of providing financial assistance to legal aid societies that operate within the state. From January 1, 1993, through December 31, 2002, the municipal court shall collect in all its divisions except the small claims division the sum of fifteen dollars as additional filing fees in each new civil action or proceeding for the charitable public purpose of providing financial assistance to legal aid societies that operate within the state. From January 1, 1993, through December 31, 2002, the municipal court shall collect in its small claims division the sum of seven dollars as additional filing fees in each new civil action or proceeding for the charitable public purpose of providing financial assistance to legal aid societies that operate within the state. This division does not apply to any execution on a judgment, proceeding in aid of execution, or other post-judgment proceeding arising out of a civil action. The filing fees required to be collected under this division shall be in addition to any other court costs imposed in the action or proceeding and shall be collected at the time of the filing of the action or proceeding. The court shall not waive the payment of the additional filing fees in a new civil action or proceeding unless the court waives the advanced payment of all filing fees in the action or proceeding. All such moneys shall be transmitted on the first business day of each month by the clerk of the court to the treasurer of state. The moneys then shall be deposited by the treasurer of state to the credit of the legal aid fund established under section 120.52 of the Revised Code.

The court may retain up to one per cent of the moneys it collects under this division to cover administrative costs, including the hiring of any additional personnel necessary to implement this division.

(D) In the Cleveland municipal court, reasonable charges for investigating titles of real estate to be sold or disposed of under any writ or process of the court may be taxed as part of the costs.

(C) Under the circumstances described in sections 2969.21 to 2969.27 of the Revised Code, the clerk of the municipal court shall charge the fee and perform the other duties specified in those sections.††

HISTORY: GC § 1605; 124 v 589; Bureau of Code Revision, 10-1-53; 140 v S 219 (Eff 2-22-85); 141 v H 201 (Eff 7-1-85); 141 v H 201, § 14 (Eff 1-1-87); 141 v H 159, § 3 (Eff 1-1-87); 141 v H 159 (Eff 3-19-87); 142 v H 171 (Eff 7-1-87); 143 v H 111 (Eff 7-1-89); 144 v H 298 (Eff 7-26-91); 144 v H 405 (Eff 1-1-93); 146 v H 455 (Eff 10-17-96); 146 v H 423 (Eff 10-31-96); 146 v H 438. Eff 7-1-97.

The effective date is set by section 3 of HB 438.

† This is a reference to division (C) as enacted in HB 455 (146 v —), eff 10-17-96 and which is placed following division (D), formerly division (B).

†† This is division (C) as enacted in HB 455 (146 v —), effective 10-17-96.

Comment, Legislative Service Commission

Sections 1901.26 and 1907.24 of the Revised Code are amended by this act [Sub. H.B. 455] and also by Sub. H.B. 423 of the 121st General Assembly. ° ° ° Comparison of these amendments in pursuance of section 1.52 of the Revised Code discloses that they are not irreconcilable so that they are required by that section to be harmonized to give effect to each amendment.

§ 1901.30 Appeals.

Appeals from the municipal court may be taken as follows:

(A) To the court of appeals in accordance with the Rules of Appellate Procedure and any relevant sections of the Revised Code, including, but not limited to, Chapter 2505. of the Revised Code to the extent it is not in conflict with those rules.

(B) When an appeal is taken from the municipal court, the clerk of the municipal court shall transmit, pursuant to the Rules of Appellate Procedure, the record on appeal to the clerk of the appellate court to be filed.

(C) In all appeal proceedings relating to judgments or orders of a municipal court, the reviewing courts shall take judicial notice of all rules relating to pleadings, practice, or procedure of the municipal court.

HISTORY: GC § 1609; 124 v 589; Bureau of Code Revision, 10-1-53; 128 v 823 (Eff 11-6-59); 131 v 606 (Eff 11-1-65); 133 v S 530 (Eff 6-12-70); 137 v H 1168 (Eff 11-1-78); 141 v H 412 (Eff 3-17-87); 141 v H 159 (Eff 3-19-87); 142 v H 708. Eff 4-19-88.

§ 1901.33 Court employees; department of probation.

(A) The judge or judges of a municipal court may appoint one or more interpreters, one or more mental health professionals, one or more probation officers, an assignment commissioner, deputy assignment commissioners, and other court aides on a full-time, part-time, hourly, or other basis. Each appointee shall receive the compensation out of the city treasury that the legislative authority prescribes, except that in a county-operated municipal court they shall receive the compensation out of the treasury of the county in which the court is located that the board of county commissioners prescribes. Probation officers have all the powers of regular police officers and shall perform any duties that are designated by the judge or judges of the court. Assignment commissioners shall assign cases for trial and perform any other duties that the court directs.

The judge or judges may appoint one or more typists, stenographers, statistical clerks, and official court reporters, each of whom shall be paid the compensation out of the city treasury that the legislative authority prescribes, except that in a county-operated municipal court they shall be paid the compensation out of the treasury of the county in which the court is located that the board of county commissioners prescribes.

(B) If a municipal court appoints one or more probation officers, those officers shall constitute the municipal court department of probation unless the court designates other employees as the department of probation for the court.

(C) The chief probation officer may grant permission to a probation officer to carry firearms when required in the discharge of the probation officer's official duties, provided that any probation officer who is granted permission to carry firearms in the discharge of the probation officer's official duties, within six months of receiving permission to carry a firearm, shall successfully complete a basic firearm training program that is conducted at a training school approved by the Ohio peace officer training commission and that is substantially similar to the basic firearm training program for peace officers conducted at the Ohio peace officer training academy and receive a certificate of satisfactory completion of that program from the executive director of the Ohio peace officer training commission. Any probation officer who does not successfully complete a basic firearm training program within the six-month period after receiving permission to carry a firearm shall not carry, after the expiration of that six-month period, a firearm in the discharge of the probation officer's official duties until the probation officer has successfully completed a basic firearm training program. A probation officer who has received a certificate of satisfactory completion of a basic firearm training program, to maintain the right to carry a firearm in the discharge of the probation officer's official duties, annually shall successfully complete a firearms requalification program in accordance with section 109.801 [109.80.1] of the Revised Code.

HISTORY: GC § 1612; 124 v 589; Bureau of Code Revision, 10-1-53; 125 v 903 (Eff 10-1-53); 137 v H 517 (Eff 1-16-78); 141 v H 159 (Eff 3-19-87); 145 v H 406 (Eff 11-11-94); 146 v H 670 (Eff 12-2-96); 146 v H 438. Eff 7-1-97.

The effective date is set by section 3 of HB 438.

Comment, Legislative Service Commission

° ° ° Section 1901.33 of the Revised Code is amended by this act [Sub. H.B. 670] and also by Am. Sub. H.B. 438 of the 121st General Assembly. ° ° ° Comparison of these amendments in pursuance of section 1.52 of the Revised Code discloses that they are not irreconcilable so that they are required by that section to be harmonized to give effect to each amendment.

§ 1901.34 Criminal prosecution; compensation of prosecuting officers.

(A) Except as provided in divisions (B) and (D) of this section, the village solicitor, city director of law, or similar chief legal officer for each municipal corporation within the territory of a municipal court shall prosecute all cases brought before the municipal court for criminal offenses occurring within the municipal corporation for which he is the solicitor, director of law, or similar chief legal officer. Except as provided in division (B) of this section, the village solicitor, city director of law, or similar chief legal officer of the municipal corporation in which a municipal court is located shall prosecute all criminal cases brought before the court arising in the unincorporated areas within the territory of the municipal court.

(B) The Auglaize county, Clermont county, Hocking county, Jackson county, Ottawa county, and Portage county prosecuting attorneys shall prosecute in municipal court all violations of state law arising in their respective counties. The Crawford county, Hamilton county, Madison county, and Wayne county prosecuting attorneys shall prosecute all violations of state law arising within the unincorporated areas of their respective counties.

The prosecuting attorney of any county given the duty of prosecuting in municipal court violations of state law shall receive no additional compensation for assuming these additional duties, except that the prosecuting attorney of Hamilton, Portage, and Wayne counties shall receive compensation at the rate of four thousand eight hundred dollars per year, and the prosecuting attorney of Auglaize county shall receive compensation at the rate of one thousand eight hundred dollars per year, each payable from the county treasury of the respective counties in semimonthly installments.

(C) The village solicitor, city director of law, or similar chief legal officer shall perform the same duties, insofar as they are applicable to him, as are required of the prosecuting attorney of the county. He or his assistants whom he may appoint shall receive for such services additional compensation to be paid from the treasury of the county as the board of county commissioners prescribes.

(D) The prosecuting attorney of any county, other than Auglaize, Clermont, Hocking, Jackson, Ottawa, or Portage county, may enter into an agreement with any municipal corporation in the county in which he serves pursuant to which the prosecuting attorney prosecutes all criminal cases brought before the municipal court that has territorial jurisdiction over that municipal corporation for criminal offenses occurring within the municipal corporation. The prosecuting attorney of Auglaize, Clermont, Hocking, Jackson, Ottawa, or Portage county may enter into an agreement with any municipal corporation in the county in which he serves pursuant to which the respective prosecuting attorney prosecutes all cases brought before the Auglaize, Clermont, Hocking, Jackson, Ottawa, or Portage county municipal court for violations of the ordinances of the municipal corporation or for criminal offenses other than violations of state law occurring within the municipal corporation. For prosecuting these cases, the prosecuting attorney and the municipal corporation may agree upon a fee to be paid by the municipal corporation, which fee shall be paid into the county treasury, to be used to cover expenses of the office of the prosecuting attorney.

HISTORY: GC § 1613; 124 v 589; Bureau of Code Revision, 10-1-53; 125 v 496; 132 v H 361 (Eff 7-25-67); 132 v S 493 (Eff 6-11-68); 133 v H 749 (Eff 11-19-69); 136 v H 205 (Eff 1-1-76); 136 v H 1558 (Eff 1-17-77); 137 v H 219 (Eff 11-1-77); 137 v H 312 (Eff 1-1-78); 137 v H 517 (Eff 1-16-78); 138 v H 961 (Eff 9-29-80); 138 v S 357 (Eff 1-9-81); 139 v H 1 (Eff 8-5-81); 141 v H 159 (Eff 3-19-87); 144 v H 200 (Eff 7-8-91); 145 v H 21. Eff 2-4-94.

CHAPTER 1905: MAYOR'S COURT

§ 1905.01 Jurisdiction in ordinance cases and traffic violations.

(A) In all municipal corporations not being the site of a municipal court nor a place where a judge of the Auglaize county, Crawford county, Jackson county, Miami county, Portage county, or Wayne county municipal court sits as required pursuant to section 1901.021 [1901.02.1] of the Revised Code or by designation of the judges pursuant to section 1901.021 [1901.02.1] of the Revised Code, the mayor of the municipal corporation has jurisdiction, except as provided in divisions (B), (C), and (E) of this section and subject to the limitation contained in section 1905.03 and the limitation contained in section 1905.031 [1905.03.1] of the Revised Code, to hear and determine any prosecution for the violation of an ordinance of the municipal corporation, to hear and determine any case involving a violation of a vehicle parking or standing ordinance of the municipal corporation unless the violation is required to be handled by a parking violations bureau or joint parking violations bureau pursuant to Chapter 4521. of the Revised Code, and to hear and determine all criminal causes involving any moving traffic violation occurring on a state highway located within the boundaries of the municipal corporation, subject to the limitations of sections 2937.08 and 2938.04 of the Revised Code.

(B)(1) In all municipal corporations not being the site of a municipal court nor a place where a judge of a court listed in division (A) of this section sits as required pursuant to section 1901.021 [1901.02.1] of the Revised Code or by designation of the judges pursuant to section 1901.021 [1901.02.1] of the Revised Code, the mayor of the municipal corporation has jurisdiction, subject to the limitation contained in section 1905.03 of the Revised Code, to hear and determine prosecutions involving a violation of an ordinance of the municipal corporation relating to operating a vehicle while under the influence of alcohol, a drug of abuse, or alcohol and a drug of abuse or relating to operating a vehicle with a prohibited concentration of alcohol in the blood, breath, or urine, and to hear and determine criminal causes involving a violation of section 4511.19 of the Revised Code that occur on a state highway located within the boundaries of the municipal corporation, subject to the limitations of sections 2937.08 and 2938.04 of the Revised Code, only if the person charged with the violation, within six years of the date of the violation charged, has not been convicted of or pleaded guilty to any of the following:

(a) A violation of an ordinance of any municipal corporation relating to operating a vehicle while under the influence of alcohol, a drug of abuse, or alcohol and a drug of abuse or relating to operating a vehicle with a prohibited concentration of alcohol in the blood, breath, or urine;

(b) A violation of section 4511.19 of the Revised Code;

(c) A violation of any ordinance of any municipal corporation or of any section of the Revised Code that regulates the operation of vehicles, streetcars, and trackless trolleys upon the highways or streets, in relation to which all of the following apply:

(i) The person, in the case in which the conviction was obtained or the plea of guilty was entered, had been charged with a violation of an ordinance of any municipal corporation relating to operating a vehicle while under the influence of alcohol, a drug of abuse, or alcohol and a drug of abuse or relating to operating a vehicle with a prohibited concentration of alcohol in the blood, breath, or urine, or with a violation of section 4511.19 of the Revised Code;

(ii) The charge of the violation described in division (B)(1)(c)(i) of this section was dismissed or reduced;

(iii) The violation of which the person was convicted or to which the person pleaded guilty arose out of the same facts and circumstances and the same act as did the charge that was dismissed or reduced.

(d) A violation of a statute of the United States or of any other state or a municipal ordinance of a municipal corporation located in any other state that is substantially similar to section 4511.19 of the Revised Code.

(2) The mayor of a municipal corporation does not have jurisdiction to hear and determine any prosecution or criminal cause involving a violation described in division (B)(1)(a) or (b) of this section, regardless of where the violation occurred, if the person charged with the violation, within five years of the violation charged, has been convicted of or pleaded guilty to any violation listed in division (B)(1)(a), (b), (c), or (d) of this section.

If the mayor of a municipal corporation, in hearing a prosecution involving a violation of an ordinance of the municipal corporation the mayor serves relating to operating a vehicle while under the influence of alcohol, a drug of abuse, or alcohol and a drug of abuse or relating to operating a vehicle with a prohibited concentration of alcohol in the blood, breath, or urine, or in hearing a criminal cause involving a violation of section 4511.19 of the Revised Code, determines that the person charged, within five years of the violation charged, has been convicted of or pleaded guilty to any violation listed in division (B)(1)(a), (b), (c), or (d) of this section, the mayor immediately shall transfer the case to the county court or municipal court with jurisdiction over the violation charged, in accordance with section 1905.032 [1905.03.2] of the Revised Code.

(C)(1) In all municipal corporations not being the site of a municipal court and not being a place where a judge of a court listed in division (A) of this section sits as required pursuant to section 1901.021 [1901.02.1] of the Revised Code or by designation of the judges pursuant to section 1901.021 [1901.02.1] of the Revised

Code, the mayor of the municipal corporation, subject to sections 1901.031 [1901.03.1], 2937.08, and 2938.04 of the Revised Code, has jurisdiction to hear and determine prosecutions involving a violation of a municipal ordinance that is substantially equivalent to division (B)(1) or (D)(2) of section 4507.02 of the Revised Code and to hear and determine criminal causes that involve a moving traffic violation, that involve a violation of division (B)(1) or (D)(2) of section 4507.02 of the Revised Code, and that occur on a state highway located within the boundaries of the municipal corporation only if all of the following apply regarding the violation and the person charged:

(a) Regarding a violation of division (B)(1) of section 4507.02 of the Revised Code or a violation of a municipal ordinance that is substantially equivalent to that division, the person charged with the violation, within five years of the date of the violation charged, has not been convicted of or pleaded guilty to any of the following:

(i) A violation of division (B)(1) of section 4507.02 of the Revised Code;

(ii) A violation of a municipal ordinance that is substantially equivalent to division (B)(1) of section 4507.02 of the Revised Code;

(iii) A violation of any municipal ordinance or section of the Revised Code that regulates the operation of vehicles, streetcars, and trackless trolleys upon the highways or streets, in a case in which, after a charge against the person of a violation of a type described in division (C)(1)(a)(i) or (ii) of this section was dismissed or reduced, the person is convicted of or pleads guilty to a violation that arose out of the same facts and circumstances and the same act as did the charge that was dismissed or reduced.

(b) Regarding a violation of division (D)(2) of section 4507.02 of the Revised Code or a violation of a municipal ordinance that is substantially equivalent to that division, the person charged with the violation, within five years of the date of the violation charged, has not been convicted of or pleaded guilty to any of the following:

(i) A violation of division (D)(2) of section 4507.02 of the Revised Code;

(ii) A violation of a municipal ordinance that is substantially equivalent to division (D)(2) of section 4507.02 of the Revised Code;

(iii) A violation of any municipal ordinance or section of the Revised Code that regulates the operation of vehicles, streetcars, and trackless trolleys upon the highways or streets in a case in which, after a charge against the person of a violation of a type described in division (C)(1)(b)(i) or (ii) of this section was dismissed or reduced, the person is convicted of or pleads guilty to a violation that arose out of the same facts and circumstances and the same act as did the charge that was dismissed or reduced.

(2) The mayor of a municipal corporation does not have jurisdiction to hear and determine any prosecution or criminal cause involving a violation described in division (C)(1)(a)(i) or (ii) of this section if the person charged with the violation, within five years of the violation charged, has been convicted of or pleaded guilty to any violation listed in division (C)(1)(a)(i), (ii), or (iii) of this section and does not have jurisdiction to hear and determine any prosecution or criminal cause involving a violation described in division (C)(1)(b)(i) or (ii) of this section if the person charged with the violation, within five years of the violation charged, has been convicted of or pleaded guilty to any violation listed in division (C)(1)(b)(i), (ii), or (iii) of this section.

(3) If the mayor of a municipal corporation, in hearing a prosecution involving a violation of an ordinance of the municipal corporation the mayor serves that is substantially equivalent to division (B)(1) or (D)(2) of section 4507.02 of the Revised Code or a violation of division (B)(1) or (D)(2) of section 4507.02 of the Revised Code, determines that, under division (C)(2) of this section, mayors do not have jurisdiction of the prosecution, the mayor immediately shall transfer the case to the county court or municipal court with jurisdiction over the violation in accordance with section 1905.032 [1905.03.2] of the Revised Code.

(D) If the mayor of a municipal corporation has jurisdiction pursuant to division (B)(1) of this section to hear and determine a prosecution or criminal cause involving a violation described in division (B)(1)(a) or (b) of this section, the authority of the mayor to hear or determine the prosecution or cause is subject to the limitation contained in division (C) of section 1905.03 of the Revised Code. If the mayor of a municipal corporation has jurisdiction pursuant to division (A) or (C) of this section to hear and determine a prosecution or criminal cause involving a violation other than a violation described in division (B)(1)(a) or (b) of this section, the authority of the mayor to hear or determine the prosecution or cause is subject to the limitation contained in division (C) of section 1905.031 [1905.03.1] of the Revised Code.

(E)(1) The mayor of a municipal corporation does not have jurisdiction to hear and determine any prosecution or criminal cause involving any of the following:

(a) A violation of section 2919.25 or 2919.27 of the Revised Code;

(b) A violation of section 2903.11, 2903.12, 2903.13, 2903.211 [2903.21.1], or 2911.211 [2911.21.1] of the Revised Code that involves a person who was a family or household member of the defendant at the time of the violation;

(c) A violation of a municipal ordinance that is substantially equivalent to an offense described in division (E)(1)(a) or (b) of this section and that involves a person who was a family or household member of the defendant at the time of the violation.

(2) The mayor of a municipal corporation does not have jurisdiction to hear and determine a motion filed

pursuant to section 2919.26 of the Revised Code or filed pursuant to a municipal ordinance that is substantially equivalent to that section or to issue a protection order pursuant to that section or a substantially equivalent municipal ordinance.

(3) As used in this section, "family or household member" has the same meaning as in section 2919.25 of the Revised Code.

(F) In keeping a docket and files, the mayor, and a mayor's court magistrate appointed under section 1905.05 of the Revised Code, shall be governed by the laws pertaining to county courts.

HISTORY: RS § 1816; Bates § 1536-776; 66 v 169, § 114; 69 v 192, § 117; GC § 4527; 109 v PtII, 1203; Bureau of Code Revision, 10-1-53; 128 v 823 (Eff 11-6-59); 130 v 608 (Eff 10-14-63); 132 v H 361 (Eff 7-25-67); 136 v H 205 (Eff 1-1-76); 137 v H 312 (Eff 1-1-78); 139 v H 707 (Eff 1-1-83); 143 v S 131 (Eff 7-25-90); 143 v H 837 (Eff 7-25-90); 145 v S 62 (Eff 9-1-93); 146 v H 353 (Eff 9-17-96); 146 v H 670 (Eff 12-2-96); 147 v S 1 (Eff 10-21-97); 147 v S 60. Eff 10-21-97.

Publisher's Note

The amendments made by SB 1 (147 v —) and SB 60 (147 v —) have been combined. Please see provisions of RC § 1.52.

§ 1905.02 County court provisions.

The provisions of Chapter 1907. of the Revised Code, insofar as they are relevant, apply in proceedings in a mayor's court, if the municipal corporation in which the mayor's court is located is within the jurisdiction of a county court.

HISTORY: 141 v H 158. Eff 3-17-87.

Not analogous to former RC § 1905.02 (RS § 1817; Bates § 1536-777; 66 v 169; 69 v 192; GC § 4528; 108 v PtII 1203; 109 v 173; Bureau of Code Revision, 10-1-53), repealed 128 v 823(862), § 2, eff 11-6-59.

The effective date is set by section 4 of HB 158.

§ 1905.03 Supreme Court rules prescribing educational standards for mayor wishing to exercise OMVI jurisdiction; continuing education.

(A) The supreme court may adopt rules prescribing educational standards for mayors of municipal corporations who conduct a mayor's court and who wish to exercise the jurisdiction granted by section 1905.01 of the Revised Code over a prosecution or criminal cause involving a violation of section 4511.19 of the Revised Code, a violation of any ordinance of the municipal corporation relating to operating a vehicle while under the influence of alcohol, a drug of abuse, or alcohol and a drug of abuse, or a violation of any ordinance of the municipal corporation relating to operating a vehicle with a prohibited concentration of alcohol in the blood, breath, or urine. Any educational standards prescribed by rule under authority of this division shall be for the purpose of assisting mayors of municipal corporations who conduct a mayor's court and who wish to exercise the jurisdiction granted by section 1905.01 of the Revised Code over such a prosecution or cause in the handling of such a prosecution or cause, and shall include, but shall not be limited to, all of the following:

(1) Provisions for basic training in the general principles of law that apply to the hearing and determination of such prosecutions and causes and provisions for periodic continuing education in those general principles;

(2) Provisions for basic training in the laws of this state that apply relative to persons who are convicted of or plead guilty to any such violation, particularly as those laws apply relative to a person who is convicted of or pleads guilty to any such violation in a prosecution or cause that is within the jurisdiction of a mayor's court as specified in section 1905.01 of the Revised Code, and provisions for periodic continuing education in those laws;

(3) Provisions specifying whether periodic continuing education for a mayor who conducts a mayor's court, who wishes to exercise the jurisdiction granted by section 1905.01 of the Revised Code over such a prosecution or cause, and who has received basic training in the principles and laws described in divisions (A)(1) and (2) of this section will be required on an annual or biennial basis;

(4) Provisions specifying the number of hours of basic training that a mayor who conducts a mayor's court and who wishes to exercise the jurisdiction granted by section 1905.01 of the Revised Code over such a prosecution or cause will have to obtain to comply with the educational standards and provisions specifying the number of hours of periodic continuing education that such a mayor will have to obtain within each time period specified under authority of division (A)(3) of this section to comply with the educational standards;

(5) Provisions establishing an exemption, for a reasonable period of time, from the basic training requirements for mayors who initially take office on or after July 1, 1991, and who wish to conduct a mayor's court and exercise the jurisdiction granted by section 1905.01 of the Revised Code over such a prosecution or cause.

(B) If the supreme court adopts rules under authority of division (A) of this section prescribing educational standards for mayors of municipal corporations who conduct a mayor's court and who wish to exercise the jurisdiction granted by section 1905.01 of the Revised Code over a prosecution or criminal cause involving a violation described in division (A) of this section, the court may formulate a basic training course and a periodic continuing education course that such a mayor may complete to satisfy those educational standards, and may offer or provide for the offering of the basic training course and the periodic continuing education course to mayors of municipal corporations.

If the supreme court offers or provides for the offering of a basic training course and a periodic continuing education course formulated under this division, the court may prescribe a reasonable fee to cover the cost associated with formulating, offering, and teaching the particular course, which fee would have to be paid by each mayor who attends the particular course or the municipal corporation served by the mayor.

If the supreme court offers or provides for the offering of a basic training course and a periodic continuing education course formulated under this division, the court or other entity that offers either course shall issue to each mayor who successfully completes the particular course a certificate attesting to the mayor's satisfactory completion of the particular course.

(C) Notwithstanding section 1905.01 of the Revised Code, if the supreme court adopts rules under authority of division (A) of this section, if the supreme court formulates a basic training course and a periodic continuing education course under division (B) of this section, and if the supreme court offers or provides for the offering of the basic training course and the periodic continuing education course to mayors, a mayor shall not hear or determine, on or after July 1, 1991, any prosecution or criminal cause involving a violation described in division (A) of this section unless the exemption under the provisions described in division (A)(5) of this section applies to the mayor, or unless, prior to hearing the prosecution or criminal cause, the mayor successfully has completed the basic training course offered or provided for by the supreme court and has been issued a certificate attesting to satisfactory completion of the basic training course and also successfully has completed any periodic continuing education course offered or provided for by the supreme court that is applicable to the mayor under the rules and has been issued a certificate attesting to satisfactory completion of the periodic continuing education course.

This division does not affect and shall not be construed as affecting the authority of a mayor to appoint a mayor's court magistrate under section 1905.05 of the Revised Code. If a mayor is prohibited from hearing or determining a prosecution or criminal cause involving a violation described in division (A) of this section due to the operation of this division, the prohibition against the mayor hearing or determining the prosecution or cause does not affect and shall not be construed as affecting the jurisdiction or authority of a mayor's court magistrate appointed under that section to hear and determine the prosecution or cause in accordance with that section.

HISTORY: 143 v S 131 (Eff 7-25-90); 143 v H 211 (Eff 4-11-91); 146 v H 670. Eff 12-2-96.

Not analogous to former RC § 1905.03 (RS § 1818; Bates § 1536-779; 66 v 169, § 114; 69 v 192, § 117; GC § 4530; Bureau of Code Revision, 10-1-53; 128 v 823(835)), repealed 130 v 1675, § 2, eff 10-14-63.

[§ 1905.03.1] § 1905.031 Rules providing standards for exercise of jurisdiction in prosecutions other than OMVI.

(A) The supreme court may adopt rules prescribing educational standards and procedural and operational standards for mayors of municipal corporations who conduct a mayor's court and who wish to exercise the jurisdiction granted by section 1905.01 of the Revised Code over a prosecution or criminal cause other than a prosecution or cause within the scope of the standards described in section 1905.03 of the Revised Code. Any educational standards and procedural and operational standards prescribed by rule under authority of this division shall be for the purpose of assisting mayors of municipal corporations who conduct a mayor's court, and shall include, but shall not be limited to, all of the following:

(1) Provisions for basic training in the general principles of law that apply to the hearing and determination of prosecutions and causes that are within the jurisdiction of a mayor's court as specified in section 1905.01 of the Revised Code, other than prosecutions and causes that are within the scope of the standards described in section 1905.03 of the Revised Code, provisions for basic training in the procedural and operational standards prescribed by the court under this division, and provisions for periodic continuing education in those general principles and in those procedural and operational standards;

(2) Provisions for basic training in the laws of this state that apply relative to persons who are convicted of or plead guilty to any violation of a statute or ordinance, particularly as those laws apply relative to a person who is convicted of or pleads guilty to any such violation in a prosecution or cause that is within the jurisdiction of a mayor's court as specified in section 1905.01 of the Revised Code, other than prosecutions and causes that are within the scope of the standards described in section 1905.03 of the Revised Code, and provisions for periodic continuing education in those laws;

(3) Provisions specifying whether periodic continuing education for a mayor who conducts a mayor's court, who wishes to exercise the jurisdiction granted by section 1905.01 of the Revised Code over a prosecution or cause, and who has received basic training in the principles and laws described in divisions (A)(1) and (2) of this section will be required on an annual or biennial basis;

(4) Provisions specifying the number of hours of basic training that a mayor who conducts a mayor's court and who wishes to exercise the jurisdiction granted by section 1905.01 of the Revised Code over a prosecution or cause, other than a prosecution or cause that is within the scope of the standards described in section 1905.03 of the Revised Code, will have to obtain to comply with the educational standards and provisions specifying the number of hours of periodic continuing education that such a mayor will have to obtain within each time period specified under authority of division (A)(3) of this section to comply with the educational standards;

(5) Provisions establishing an exemption, for a reasonable period of time, from the basic training require-

ments for mayors who initially take office on or after July 1, 1992, and who wish to conduct a mayor's court and exercise the jurisdiction granted by section 1905.01 of the Revised Code over a prosecution or cause other than a prosecution or cause within the scope of the standards described in section 1905.03 of the Revised Code;

(6) Provisions establishing procedural and operational standards for mayor's courts.

(B) If the supreme court adopts rules under authority of division (A) of this section prescribing educational standards and procedural and operational standards for mayors of municipal corporations who conduct a mayor's court and who wish to exercise the jurisdiction granted by section 1905.01 of the Revised Code over a prosecution or criminal cause, other than a prosecution or cause that is within the scope of the standards described in section 1905.03 of the Revised Code, the court may formulate a basic training course and a periodic continuing education course that such a mayor may complete to satisfy the basic training and periodic continuing education required relative to those standards, and may offer or provide for the offering of the basic training course and the periodic continuing education course to mayors of municipal corporations.

If the supreme court offers or provides for the offering of a basic training course and a periodic continuing education course formulated under this division, the court may prescribe a reasonable fee to cover the cost associated with formulating, offering, and teaching the particular course, which fee would have to be paid by each mayor who attends the particular course or the municipal corporation served by the mayor.

If the supreme court offers or provides for the offering of a basic training course and a periodic continuing education course formulated under this division, the court or other entity that offers either course shall issue to each mayor who successfully completes the particular course a certificate attesting to the mayor's satisfactory completion of the particular course.

(C) Notwithstanding section 1905.01 of the Revised Code, if the supreme court adopts rules under authority of division (A) of this section on or before July 1, 1991, if the supreme court formulates a basic training course and a periodic continuing education course under division (B) of this section, and if the supreme court offers or provides for the offering of the basic training course and the periodic continuing education course to mayors within a reasonable period of time after the adoption of the rules, a mayor shall not hear or determine, on or after July 1, 1992, any prosecution or criminal cause involving a violation described in division (A) of this section unless the exemption under the provisions described in division (A)(5) of this section applies to the mayor, or unless, prior to hearing the prosecution or criminal cause, the mayor has successfully completed the basic training course offered or provided for by the supreme court and has been issued a certificate attesting to satisfactory completion of the basic training course and also has successfully completed any periodic continuing education course offered or provided for by the supreme court that is applicable to the mayor under the rules and has been issued a certificate attesting to satisfactory completion of the periodic continuing education course.

This division does not affect and shall not be construed as affecting the authority of a mayor to appoint a mayor's court magistrate under section 1905.05 of the Revised Code. If a mayor is prohibited from hearing or determining a prosecution or criminal cause involving a violation described in division (A) of this section due to the operation of this division, the prohibition against the mayor hearing or determining the prosecution or cause does not affect and shall not be construed as affecting the jurisdiction or authority of a mayor's court magistrate appointed under that section to hear and determine the prosecution or cause in accordance with that section.

HISTORY: 143 v S 131 (Eff 7-25-90); 143 v H 837 (Eff 7-25-90); 143 v H 211 (Eff 4-11-91); 146 v H 670. Eff 12-2-96.

[§ 1905.03.2] § 1905.032 Transfer of prosecution to another court; recognizance.

(A) If a person who is charged with a violation of a law or an ordinance is brought before a mayor's court and the violation charged is not within the jurisdiction of the court, as set forth in section 1905.01 of the Revised Code, the mayor promptly shall transfer the case to the municipal court, county court, or court of common pleas with jurisdiction over the alleged violation and shall require the person to enter into a recognizance to appear before that court.

If a person who is charged with a violation of a law or an ordinance is brought before a mayor's court and the violation charged is within the jurisdiction of the court, as set forth in section 1905.01 of the Revised Code, the mayor, at any time prior to the final disposition of the case, may transfer it to the municipal court, county court, or court of common pleas with concurrent jurisdiction over the alleged violation. If a mayor transfers a case under this provision, the mayor shall require the person charged to enter into a recognizance to appear before the court to which the case is transferred.

(B) Upon the transfer of a case by a mayor under division (A) of this section, all of the following apply:

(1) The mayor shall certify all papers filed in the case, together with a transcript of all proceedings, accrued costs to date, and the recognizance given, to the court to which the case is transferred.

(2) All further proceedings under the charge, complaint, information, or indictment in the transferred case shall be discontinued in the mayor's court and shall be conducted in the court to which the case is transferred, in accordance with the provisions governing proceedings in that court.

(3) If the case is transferred to a municipal court that has an environmental division and the case is within the jurisdiction of the environmental division, as set forth in division (A)(1) of section 1901.181 [1901.18.1] of the Revised Code, the case thereafter shall be within the exclusive jurisdiction of the environmental division of the municipal court to which it is transferred. In all other situations, the case thereafter shall be within the exclusive jurisdiction of the court to which it is transferred.

HISTORY: 143 v S 131 (Eff 7-25-90); 144 v S 105 (Eff 3-24-92); 146 v H 438. Eff 7-1-97.

The effective date is set by section 3 of HB 438.

§ 1905.04 Clerk, deputy and magistrate of mayor's court must be disinterested.

Neither the clerk of a mayor's court, nor his deputy, nor a mayor's court magistrate, shall be concerned as counsel or agent in the prosecution or defense of any case before the mayor's court.

HISTORY: RS § 1817a; Bates § 1536-778; 78 v 50; GC § 4529; Bureau of Code Revision, 10-1-53; 143 v S 131. Eff 7-25-90.

§ 1905.05 Appointment of mayor's court magistrate.

(A) A mayor of a municipal corporation that has a mayor's court may appoint a person as mayor's court magistrate to hear and determine prosecutions and criminal causes in the mayor's court that are within the jurisdiction of the mayor's court, as set forth in section 1905.01 of the Revised Code. No person shall be appointed as a mayor's court magistrate unless the person has been admitted to the practice of law in this state and, for a total of at least three years preceding the person's appointment or the commencement of the person's service as magistrate, has been engaged in the practice of law in this state or served as a judge of a court of record in any jurisdiction in the United States, or both.

A person appointed as a mayor's court magistrate under this division is entitled to hear and determine prosecutions and criminal causes in the mayor's court that are within the jurisdiction of the mayor's court, as set forth in section 1905.01 of the Revised Code. If a mayor is prohibited from hearing or determining a prosecution or cause that charges a person with a violation of section 4511.19 of the Revised Code or with a violation of a municipal ordinance relating to operating a vehicle while under the influence of alcohol, a drug of abuse, or alcohol and a drug of abuse or relating to operating a vehicle with a prohibited concentration of alcohol in the blood, breath, or urine due to the operation of division (C) of section 1905.03 of the Revised Code, or is prohibited from hearing or determining any other prosecution or cause due to the operation of division (C) of section 1905.031 [1905.03.1] of the Revised Code, the prohibition against the mayor hearing or determining the prosecution or cause does not affect and shall not be construed as affecting the jurisdiction or authority of a person appointed as a mayor's court magistrate under this division to hear and determine the prosecution or cause in accordance with this section. In hearing and determining such prosecutions and causes, the magistrate has the same powers, duties, and authority as does a mayor who conducts a mayor's court to hear and determine prosecutions and causes in general, including, but not limited to, the power and authority to decide the prosecution or cause, enter judgment, and impose sentence; the powers, duties, and authority granted to mayors of mayor's courts by this chapter, in relation to the hearing and determination of prosecutions and causes in mayor's courts; and the powers, duties, and authority granted to mayors of mayor's courts by any other provision of the Revised Code, in relation to the hearing and determination of prosecutions and causes in mayor's courts. A judgment entered and a sentence imposed by a mayor's court magistrate do not have to be reviewed or approved by the mayor who appointed the magistrate, and have the same force and effect as if they had been entered or imposed by the mayor.

A person appointed as a mayor's court magistrate under this division is not entitled to hear or determine any prosecution or criminal cause other than prosecutions and causes that are within the jurisdiction of the mayor's court, as set forth in section 1905.01 of the Revised Code.

The compensation for the services of a mayor's court magistrate shall be a fixed annual salary set by the legislative authority of the municipal corporation that the magistrate serves and shall be paid by the municipal corporation.

(B) The appointment of a person as a mayor's court magistrate under division (A) of this section does not preclude the mayor that appointed the magistrate, subject to the limitation contained in section 1905.03 and the limitation contained in section 1905.031 [1905.03.1] of the Revised Code, from also hearing and determining prosecutions and criminal causes in the mayor's court that are within the jurisdiction of the mayor's court, as set forth in section 1905.01 of the Revised Code.

HISTORY: 143 v S 131 (Eff 7-25-90); 146 v H 670. Eff 12-2-96.

Not analogous to former RC § 1905.05 (RS § 1819; Bates § 1536-780; 66 v 169, § 114; 69 v 192, § 117; GC § 4531; Bureau of Code Revision, 10-1-53), repealed 129 v S 367, § 2, eff 10-19-61.

§§ 1905.06, 1905.07 Repealed, 128 v 823(862), § 2 [RS §§ 1820, 1821; Bates §§ 1536-781, 1536-782; 66 v 169; 69 v 192; GC §§ 4532, 4533; Bureau of Code Revision, 10-1-53]. Eff 11-6-59. Also repealed by 128 v 97(116), § 2, effective 1-1-60.

These sections provided for jury trial and recognizance in misdemeanor cases.

§ 1905.08 Duties of police chief or marshal; fees.

The chief of police of the city or village or a police officer of the city or village designated by him, or the marshal of a village shall attend the sittings of the mayor's court to execute the orders and process of the court, and to preserve order in it. The chief of police, other police officer, or marshal shall execute and return all writs and process directed to him by the mayor. The jurisdiction of the chief of police, other police officer, or marshal in the execution of such writs and process is coextensive with the county in criminal cases and in cases of violations of ordinances of the municipal corporation. In serving such writs and process and taxing costs on them, the chief of police, other police officer, or marshal shall be governed by the laws pertaining to constables. The fees of the mayor are the same as those allowed in the municipal or county court within whose jurisdiction the municipal corporation is located. There shall be allowed and taxed for services of the chief of police, other police officer, or marshal, the same fees and expense as those allowed constables.

HISTORY: RS § 1822; Bates § 1536-783; 66 v 169, § 114; 69 v 192, § 117; GC § 4534; 102 v 476; 108 v PtII 1203; Bureau of Code Revision, 10-1-53; 128 v 823 (Eff 11-6-59); 130 v 609 (Eff 10-14-63); 141 v H 158. Eff 3-1-87.

The effective date is set by section 4 of H 158.

§ 1905.09
Repealed, 130 v 1675, § 2 [RS § 1823; Bates § 1536-875; 66 v 169, § 114; 69 v 192, § 117; GC § 4535; 108 v PtII 1203; Bureau of Code Revision, 10-1-53; 128 v 823(835)]. Eff 10-14-63.

This section established jurisdiction of Village Mayors in ordinance cases.

§ 1905.10
Repealed, 128 v 823(862), § 2 [RS § 1824; Bates § 1536-876; 66 v 169; 69 v 192; GC § 4536; 108 v PtII 1203; 109 v 173; Bureau of Code Revision, 10-1-53]. Eff 11-6-59.

This section established the jurisdiction of Village Mayors in misdemeanor cases, except where accused entitled to jury trial.

§ 1905.11
Repealed, 130 v 1675, § 2 [RS § 1825; Bates § 1536-877; 66 v 169, § 114; 69 v 192, § 117; GC § 4537; Bureau of Code Revision, 10-1-53; 128 v 823(835)]. Eff 10-14-63.

This section provided for jurisdiction of Village Mayors where jury trial waived.

§§ 1905.12, 1905.13
Repealed, 128 v 97(116), § 2 [RS §§ 1826, 1827; Bates §§ 1536-878, 1536-879; 66 v 169, § 114; 69 v 192, § 117; GC §§ 4538, 4539; Bureau of Code Revision, 10-1-53]. Eff 1-1-60.

Section 1905.12 provided for jury trial in ordinance cases, while section 1905.13 provided mayor with power to refuse jury trial, discharge accused or recognize accused to the court of common pleas.

§§ 1905.14, 1905.15
Repealed, 128 v 823(862), § 2 [RS §§ 1828, 1829; Bates §§ 1536-880, 1536-881; 66 v 169; 69 v 192; 89 v 362; GC §§ 4540, 4541; Bureau of Code Revision, 10-1-53]. Eff 11-6-59. Also repealed by 128 v 97(116), § 2, effective 1-1-60.

Section 1905.14 provided for jury trial in misdemeanor cases, while section 1905.15 provided mayor with power to refuse jury trial, discharge accused or recognize accused to the court of common pleas.

§ 1905.16
Repealed, 129 v 423, § 2 [RS §§ 1830, 1848; Bates §§ 1536-882, 1536-861; 66 v 169, § 114; 69 v 192, § 117; 71 v 76, § 141; GC § 4542; 108 v PtII 1203; Bureau of Code Revision, 10-1-53; 128 v 823(835)]. Eff 10-19-61.

This section provided for jurisdiction of village mayor in felonies, duties of marshal and deputies in the execution and return of process together with jurisdiction therein, and the taxing of costs thereon.

§ 1905.17 Boundary line between villages adjoining each other.

When two villages adjoin each other on opposite sides of the line of any railroad, the boundary line between such villages, except where otherwise established by law is along the middle of the right of way of such railroad.

HISTORY: RS § 1830-1; Bates § 1536-883; GC § 4543; 78 v 93; 88 v 242; Bureau of Code Revision. Eff 10-1-53.

§§ 1905.18, 1905.19
Repealed, 130 v 1675, § 2 [RS § 1744; Bates §§ 1536-773, 1536-886, 1536-887; 66 v 169, § 114; 96 v 86, 87, § 208; GC §§ 4546-4548; Bureau of Code Revision, 10-1-53; 128 v 823(836)]. Eff 10-14-63.

Section 1905.18 provided for police courts of villages, and specified that mayor, as judge, clerk and other court employees be elected or appointed. Section 1905.19 designated mayors of municipalities as conservators of the peace, together with specification of jurisdiction.

§ 1905.20 Powers of mayors and magistrates in criminal matters.

The mayor of a municipal corporation has, within the corporate limits, all the powers conferred upon sheriffs to suppress disorder and keep the peace.

The mayor of a municipal corporation shall award and issue all writs and process that are necessary to enforce the administration of justice throughout the municipal corporation. The mayor shall subscribe his name and affix his official seal to all writs, process, transcripts, and other official papers. A mayor's court magistrate, in hearing and determining prosecutions and criminal causes that are within the scope of his authority under section 1905.05 of the Revised Code, has the same powers and duties as are granted to or imposed upon a mayor under this division.

(C) The mayor of a municipal corporation shall be disqualified in any criminal case in which he was the arresting officer, assisted in the arrest, or was present at the time of arrest, and shall not hear the case.

HISTORY: RS § 1837; Bates § 1536-773a; 66 v 169, § 118; GC § 4549; Bureau of Code Revision, 10-1-53; 125 v 297; 128 v 823(836) (Eff 11-6-59); 141 v H 158, (Eff 3-1-87); 143 v S 131. Eff 7-25-90.

[§ 1905.20.1] § 1905.201 License suspension or revocation in OMVI cases.

The mayor of a municipal corporation that has a mayor's court, and a mayor's court magistrate, are entitled to suspend or revoke, and shall suspend or revoke, in accordance with division (B) of section 4507.16 of the Revised Code, the driver's or commercial driver's license or permit or nonresident operating privilege of any person who is convicted of or pleads guilty to a violation of division (A) of section 4511.19 of the Revised Code, of a municipal ordinance relating to operating a vehicle while under the influence of alcohol, a drug of abuse, or alcohol and a drug of abuse, or of a municipal ordinance relating to operating a vehicle with a prohibited concentration of alcohol in the blood, breath, or urine that is substantially equivalent to division (A) of section 4511.19 of the Revised Code. The mayor of a municipal corporation that has a mayor's court, and a mayor's court magistrate, are entitled to suspend, and shall suspend, in accordance with division (E) of section 4507.16 of the Revised Code, the driver's, or commercial driver's license or permit or nonresident operating privilege of any person who is convicted of or pleads guilty to a violation of division (B) of section 4511.19 of the Revised Code or of a municipal ordinance relating to operating a vehicle with a prohibited concentration of alcohol in the blood, breath, or urine that is substantially equivalent to division (B) of section 4511.19 of the Revised Code.

Suspension of a commercial driver's license under this section shall be concurrent with any period of disqualification under section 2301.374 [2301.37.4] or 4506.16 of the Revised Code. No person who is disqualified for life from holding a commercial driver's license under section 4506.16 of the Revised Code shall be issued a driver's license under Chapter 4507. of the Revised Code during the period for which the commercial driver's license was suspended under this section, and no person whose commercial driver's license is suspended under this section shall be issued a driver's license under Chapter 4507. of the Revised Code during the period of the suspension.

HISTORY: 142 v H 303 (Eff 10-20-87); 143 v H 381 (Eff 7-1-89); 143 v S 131 (Eff 7-25-90); 144 v S 275 (Eff 7-1-93)†; 145 v S 82 (Eff 5-4-94); 146 v H 167. Eff 5-15-97.

The effective date is set by section 8(C) of HB 167.

† The provisions of §§ 4, 5 of SB 62 (145 v —) read as follows:

SECTION 4. That Section 3 of Sub. S.B. 275 of the 119th General Assembly be amended to read as follows:

"Sec. 3. Sections 1 and 2 of this act shall take effect September 1, 1993."

SECTION 5. That existing Section 3 of Sub. S.B. 275 of the 119th General Assembly is hereby repealed.

§ 1905.21 Docket; disposition of receipts; salary; office; seal.

The mayor of a municipal corporation and a mayor's court magistrate shall keep a docket. Neither the mayor of a municipal corporation nor a mayor's court magistrate shall retain or receive for his own use any of the fines, forfeitures, fees, or costs he collects. A mayor's court magistrate shall account for all such fines, forfeitures, fees, and costs he collects and transfer them to the mayor. The mayor shall account for and dispose of all such fines, forfeitures, fees, and costs he collects, including all such fines, forfeitures, fees, and costs that are transferred to him by a mayor's court magistrate, as provided in section 733.40 of the Revised Code.

The mayor of a municipal corporation shall be paid such fixed annual salary as the legislative authority of the municipal corporation provides under sections 731.08 and 731.13 of the Revised Code, and a mayor's court magistrate shall receive compensation as provided in section 1905.05 of the Revised Code.

The mayor of a municipal corporation shall keep an office, provided by the legislative authority of the municipal corporation, at a convenient place in the municipal corporation, and shall be furnished by the legislative authority with the corporate seal of the municipal corporation. In the center of such seal shall be the words, "Mayor of the city of . . . . . ," or "Mayor of the village of . . . ."

HISTORY: RS § 1745; Bates § 1536-774; 66 v 169, § 115; GC § 4550; Bureau of Code Revision, 10-1-53; 125 v 297 (Eff 10-13-53); 143 v S 131. Eff 7-25-90.

§ 1905.22 Appeals.

Appeals from a mayor's court may be taken to the municipal court or county court having jurisdiction within the municipal corporation.

HISTORY: 133 v S 530. Eff 6-12-70.

Analogous in part to former RC § 1905.22 (RS § 1752; Bates § 1536-775; 66 v 170, 72 v 42; GC § 4551; 116 v 122; Bureau of Code Revision, 10-1-53; 128 v 836; 129 v 425) repealed 133 v S 530, § 2, eff 6-12-70.

§ 1905.23 Notice of appeal.

Within ten days from the time a mayor renders judgment, the appellant shall file with the mayor's court a written notice of appeal designating the order or judgment appealed from and the court to which the appeal is taken.

All further proceedings in the mayor's court shall be stayed from the time of filing the notice of appeal with the mayor's court.

HISTORY: 133 v S 530. Eff 6-12-70.

Not analogous to former RC § 1905.23 (RS § 1839; Bates § 1536-786; 66 v 180; GC § 4552; Bureau of Code Revision, 10-1-53) repealed 130 v 1675, § 2, eff 10-14-63.

§ 1905.24 Transcript for appeal.

Upon filing of the notice of appeal, the clerk of the mayor's court shall make a certified transcript of the proceedings and deliver such transcript together with the original papers used on the trial, to the court to which the appeal is taken, within fifteen days from the rendition of the judgment appealed from.

Upon receipt of the transcript and the papers mentioned in this section, the clerk of the court to which the appeal is taken shall file them and docket the appeal.

HISTORY: 133 v S 530. Eff 6-12-70.

Not analogous to former RC § 1905.24 (RS § 1840; Bates § 1536-787; 66 v 180; GC § 4553; Bureau of Code Revision, 10-1-53) repealed 130 v 1675, § 2, eff 10-14-63.

§ 1905.25 Appeal; trial de novo.

An appeal from the mayor's court to the municipal court or county court shall proceed as a trial de novo.

HISTORY: 133 v S 530. Eff 6-12-70.

Not analogous to former RC § 1905.25 (RS § 1841; Bates § 1536-788; 66 v 180; GC § 4554; 108 v PtII, 1203; 109 v 174; Bureau of Code Revision, 10-1-53) repealed 130 v 1675, § 2, eff 10-14-63.

§ 1905.26 Fees of witnesses.

In cases for the violation of ordinances, the fees of witnesses shall be paid, on the certificate of the officer presiding at the trial, from the treasury of the municipal corporation.

HISTORY: RS § 1842; Bates § 1536-789; 66 v 180, § 196; GC § 4555; Bureau of Code Revision, 10-1-53; 128 v 823(837). Eff 11-6-59.

§ 1905.27 Repealed, 141 v H 158, § 2 [RS § 1843; Bates § 1536-790; 66 v 180, § 197; GC § 4556; 109 v PtII 1203; 109 v 173; Bureau of Code Revision, 10-1-53; 126 v 392; 128 v 823(837)]. Eff 3-17-87.

This section concerned fees of officers.

§ 1905.28 Contempts; rules.

The mayor or mayor's court magistrate presiding at any trial under this chapter may punish contempts, compel the attendance of jurors and witnesses, and establish rules for the examination and trial of all cases brought before him, in the same manner as judges of county courts.

HISTORY: RS § 1844; Bates § 1536-791; 66 v 180, § 198; GC § 4557; Bureau of Code Revision, 10-1-53; 128 v 823(837) (Eff 11-6-59); 143 v S 131. Eff 7-25-90.

§ 1905.29 Temporary use of municipal prison by neighboring township.

The mayor of a municipal corporation, and in his absence, the president of the legislative authority of the municipal corporation, may grant to officials of adjoining or contiguous townships the temporary use of the municipal corporation prison, station house, or watchhouse, to confine criminals, or other persons dangerous to the peace of the community, until they can be safely removed to the county jail, or other place of security.

HISTORY: RS § 1845; Bates § 1536-792; 66 v 170, § 120; GC § 4558; Bureau of Code Revision, 10-1-53; 143 v S 131. Eff 7-25-90.

§ 1905.30 Offender may be confined until fine paid.

When a fine is the whole or part of a sentence, the mayor's court may order the person sentenced to remain confined in the county jail, workhouse, or prison of the municipal corporation, until the fine is paid or secured to be paid, or the offender is legally discharged.

HISTORY: RS § 1846; Bates § 1536-793; S&S 610; 60 v 66; 66 v 314, § 180; GC § 4559; Bureau of Code Revision, 10-1-53; 133 v S 460. Eff 9-3-70.

§ 1905.31 Jurisdiction over railroad forming part of boundary line.

When the line of a railroad adjoins or forms a part of the boundary line of a municipal corporation, such municipal corporation has jurisdiction over the entire width of the right of way of the line of such railroad for the punishment of the violation of the ordinances of such municipal corporation.

HISTORY: RS § 1830-2; Bates § 1536-884; 92 v 428; GC § 4560; Bureau of Code Revision. Eff 10-1-53.

§ 1905.32 Fines and forfeitures recovered.

Fines, penalties, and forfeitures may, in all cases, and in addition to any other mode provided, be recovered by action before any judge of a county court, or other court of competent jurisdiction, in the name of the proper municipal corporation, and for its use. In any action in which a pleading is necessary, it is sufficient if the petition sets forth generally the amount claimed to be due in respect to the violation of the ordinance of the municipal corporation. Such petition shall refer to the title of such ordinance, state the date of its adoption or passage, and show, as near as is practicable, the true time of the alleged violation.

HISTORY: RS § 1864; Bates § 1536-627; 66 v 167, § 108; GC § 4561; Bureau of Code Revision, 10-1-53; 128 v 823(837). Eff 11-6-59.

§ **1905.33** Repealed, 134 v H 511, § 2 [RS § 1865; Bates § 1536-628; 66 v 167; GC § 4562; Bureau of Code Revision, 10-1-53; 133 v S 4]. Eff 1-1-74.

This section concerned that actions for recovery of fines, penalties, etc. must be commenced within one year.

§ **1905.34** Party committed in default of payment.

When a fine imposed for the violation of an ordinance of a municipal corporation is not paid, the party convicted may, by order of the mayor of the municipal corporation, or other proper authority, or on process issued for the purpose, be committed until such fine and the costs of prosecution are paid, or until the party convicted is legally discharged.

HISTORY: RS § 1866; Bates § 1536-629; 66 v 168, § 110; GC § 4563; Bureau of Code Revision, 10-1-53; 136 v H 205. Eff 8-19-75.

§ **1905.35** Imprisonment.

Imprisonment under the ordinances of a municipal corporation shall be in the workhouse or other jail of the municipal corporation. Any municipal corporation not provided with a workhouse, or other jail, may, for the purpose of imprisonment, use the county jail, at the expense of the municipal corporation, until the municipal corporation is provided with a prison, house of correction, or workhouse. Persons so imprisoned in the county jail are under the charge of the sheriff. Such sheriff shall receive and hold such persons in the manner prescribed by the ordinances of the municipal corporation, until such persons are legally discharged.

HISTORY: RS § 1867; Bates § 1536-630; 66 v 168, § 111; GC § 4564; Bureau of Code Revision. Eff 10-1-53.

§ **1905.36** Use of county jail prohibited.

The board of county commissioners, at such board's discretion, on giving ninety days' written notice to the legislative authority of any municipal corporation, may prohibit the use of the county jail for the purpose authorized in section 1905.35 of the Revised Code.

HISTORY: RS § 1868; Bates § 1536-631; 66 v 168, § 112; GC § 4565; Bureau of Code Revision. Eff 10-1-53.

§ **1905.37** Limit of prohibition.

If, within ninety days after the notice mentioned in section 1905.36 of the Revised Code is given, the legislative authority of the municipal corporation provides by ordinance and the necessary contracts for the immediate erection of a prison, workhouse, or house of correction, the municipal corporation, notwithstanding the notice and prohibition provided for in such section, shall continue to have the use of the county jail for the purpose of imprisonment, until such prison, workhouse, or house of correction is erected and ready for use.

HISTORY: RS § 1869; Bates § 1536-632; 66 v 168, § 113; GC § 4566; Bureau of Code Revision. Eff 10-1-53.

TITLE 21: COURTS—PROBATE—JUVENILE

CHAPTER 2108: HUMAN BODIES OR PARTS THEREOF

§ 2108.30 Death defined.

An individual is dead if he has sustained either irreversible cessation of circulatory and respiratory functions or irreversible cessation of all functions of the brain, including the brain stem, as determined in accordance with accepted medical standards. If the respiratory and circulatory functions of a person are being artificially sustained, under accepted medical standards a determination that death has occurred is made by a physician by observing and conducting a test to determine that the irreversible cessation of all functions of the brain has occurred.

A physician who makes a determination of death in accordance with this section and accepted medical standards is not liable for damages in any civil action or subject to prosecution in any criminal proceeding for his acts or the acts of others based on that determination.

Any person who acts in good faith in reliance on a determination of death made by a physician in accordance with this section and accepted medical standards is not liable for damages in any civil action or subject to prosecution in any criminal proceeding for his actions.

HISTORY: 139 v S 98. Eff 3-15-82.

CHAPTER 2151: JUVENILE COURT

§ 2151.01 Construction; purpose.

The sections in Chapter 2151. of the Revised Code, with the exception of those sections providing for the criminal prosecution of adults, shall be liberally interpreted and construed so as to effectuate the following purposes:

(A) To provide for the care, protection, and mental and physical development of children subject to Chapter 2151. of the Revised Code;

(B) To protect the public interest in removing the consequences of criminal behavior and the taint of criminality from children committing delinquent acts and to substitute therefor a program of supervision, care, and rehabilitation;

(C) To achieve the foregoing puroses, whenever possible, in a family environment, separating the child from its parents only when necessary for his welfare or in the interests of public safety;

(D) To provide judicial procedures through which Chapter 2151. of the Revised Code is executed and enforced, and in which the parties are assured of a fair hearing, and their constitutional and other legal rights are recognized and enforced.

HISTORY: 133 v H 320. Eff 11-19-69.

Not analogous to former RC § 2151.01 (GC § 1639-1; 117 v 520; 121 v 557; Bureau of Code Revision, 10-1-53), repealed, 133 v H 320. For an analogous provision to former RC § 2151.01, see now RC § 2151.01.1

[§ 2151.01.1] § 2151.011 Definitions.

(A) As used in the Revised Code:

(1) "Juvenile court" means the division of the court of common pleas or a juvenile court separately and independently created having jurisdiction under this chapter.

(2) "Juvenile judge" means a judge of a court having jurisdiction under this chapter.

(3) "Private child placing agency" means any association, as defined in section 5103.02 of the Revised Code, that is certified pursuant to sections 5103.03 to 5103.05 of the Revised Code to accept temporary, permanent, or legal custody of children and place the children for either foster care or adoption.

(4) "Private noncustodial agency" means any person, organization, association, or society certified by the department of human services that does not accept temporary or permanent legal custody of children, that is privately operated in this state, and that does one or more of the following:

(a) Receives and cares for children for two or more consecutive weeks;

(b) Participates in the placement of children in family foster homes;

(c) Provides adoption services in conjunction with a public children services agency or private child placing agency.

(B) As used in this chapter:

(1) "Adequate parental care" means the provision by a child's parent or parents, guardian, or custodian of adequate food, clothing, and shelter to ensure the child's health and physical safety and the provision by a child's parent or parents of specialized services warranted by the child's physical or mental needs.

(2) "Adult" means an individual who is eighteen years of age or older.

(3) "Agreement for temporary custody" means a voluntary agreement authorized by section 5103.15 of the Revised Code that transfers the temporary custody of a child to a public children services agency or a private child placing agency.

(4) "Babysitting care" means care provided for a child

while the parents, guardian, or legal custodian of the child are temporarily away.

(5) "Certified family foster home" means a family foster home operated by persons holding a certificate in force, issued under section 5103.03 of the Revised Code.

(6)(a) "Child" means a person who is under eighteen years of age, except as otherwise provided in divisions (B)(6)(b) to (f) of this section.

(b) Subject to division (B)(6)(c) of this section, any person who violates a federal or state law or municipal ordinance prior to attaining eighteen years of age shall be deemed a "child" irrespective of that person's age at the time the complaint is filed or the hearing on the complaint is held.

(c) Any person who, while under eighteen years of age, commits an act that would be a felony if committed by an adult and who is not taken into custody or apprehended for that act until after the person attains twenty-one years of age is not a child in relation to that act.

(d) Any person whose case is transferred for criminal prosecution pursuant to division (B) or (C) of section 2151.26 of the Revised Code shall after the transfer be deemed not to be a child in the transferred case.

(e) Subject to division (B)(6)(f) of this section, any person whose case is transferred for criminal prosecution pursuant to division (B) or (C) of section 2151.26 of the Revised Code and who subsequently is convicted of or pleads guilty to a felony in that case shall after the transfer be deemed not to be a child in any case in which the person is alleged to have committed prior to or subsequent to the transfer an act that would be an offense if committed by an adult. Division (B)(6)(e) of this section applies to a case regardless of whether the prior or subsequent act that is alleged in the case and that would be an offense if committed by an adult allegedly was committed in the same county in which the case was transferred or in another county and regardless of whether the complaint in the case involved was filed in the same county in which the case was transferred or in another county. Division (B)(6)(e) of this section applies to a case that involves an act committed prior to the transfer only when the prior act alleged in the case has not been disposed of by a juvenile court or trial court.

(f) Notwithstanding division (B)(6)(e) of this section, if a person's case is transferred for criminal prosecution pursuant to division (B) or (C) of section 2151.26 of the Revised Code and if the person subsequently is convicted of or pleads guilty to a felony in that case, thereafter, the person shall be considered a child solely for the following purposes in relation to any act the person subsequently commits that would be an offense if committed by an adult:

(i) For purposes of the filing of a complaint alleging that the child is a delinquent child for committing the act that would be an offense if committed by an adult;

(ii) For purposes of the juvenile court conducting a hearing under division (B) of section 2151.26 of the Revised Code relative to the complaint described in division (B)(6)(f)(i) of this section to determine whether division (B)(1) of section 2151.26 of the Revised Code applies and requires that the case be transferred for criminal prosecution to the appropriate court having jurisdiction of the offense.

(7) "Child day camp," "child day-care," "child day-care center," "part-time child day-care center," "type A family day-care home," "certified type B family day-care home," "type B home," "administrator of a child day-care center," "administrator of a type A family day-care home," "in-home aide," and "authorized provider" have the same meanings as in section 5104.01 of the Revised Code.

(8) "Child day-care provider" means an individual who is a child-care staff member or administrator of a child day-care center, a type A family day-care home, or a type B family day-care home, or an in-home aide or an individual who is licensed, is regulated, is approved, operates under the direction of, or otherwise is certified by the department of human services, department of mental retardation and developmental disabilities, or the early childhood programs of the department of education.

(9) "Commit" means to vest custody as ordered by the court.

(10) "Counseling" includes both of the following:

(a) General counseling services performed by a public children services agency or shelter for victims of domestic violence to assist a child, a child's parents, and a child's siblings in alleviating identified problems that may cause or have caused the child to be an abused, neglected, or dependent child.

(b) Psychiatric or psychological therapeutic counseling services provided to correct or alleviate any mental or emotional illness or disorder and performed by a licensed psychiatrist, licensed psychologist, or a person licensed under Chapter 4757. of the Revised Code to engage in social work or professional counseling.

(11) "Custodian" means a person who has legal custody of a child or a public children services agency or private child placing agency that has permanent, temporary, or legal custody of a child.

(12) "Detention" means the temporary care of children pending court adjudication or disposition, or execution of a court order, in a public or private facility designed to physically restrict the movement and activities of children.

(13) "Developmental disability" has the same meaning as in section 5123.01 of the Revised Code.

(14) "Family foster home" means a private residence in which children are received apart from their parents, guardian, or legal custodian by an individual for hire, gain, or reward for nonsecure care, supervision, or training twenty-four hours a day. "Family foster home" does not include babysitting care provided for a child in the home of a person other than the home of the parents,

guardian, or legal custodian of the child.

(15) "Foster home" means a family home in which any child is received apart from the child's parents for care, supervision, or training.

(16) "Guardian" means a person, association, or corporation that is granted authority by a probate court pursuant to Chapter 2111. of the Revised Code to exercise parental rights over a child to the extent provided in the court's order and subject to the residual parental rights of the child's parents.

(17) "Legal custody" means a legal status that vests in the custodian the right to have physical care and control of the child and to determine where and with whom the child shall live, and the right and duty to protect, train, and discipline the child and to provide the child with food, shelter, education, and medical care, all subject to any residual parental rights, privileges, and responsibilities. An individual granted legal custody shall exercise the rights and responsibilities personally unless otherwise authorized by any section of the Revised Code or by the court.

(18) "Long-term foster care" means an order of a juvenile court pursuant to which both of the following apply:
(a) Legal custody of a child is given to a public children services agency or a private child placing agency without the termination of parental rights.
(b) The agency is permitted to make an appropriate placement of the child and to enter into a written long-term foster care agreement with a foster care provider or with another person or agency with whom the child is placed.

(19) "Mental illness" and "mentally ill person subject to hospitalization by court order" have the same meanings as in section 5122.01 of the Revised Code.

(20) "Mental injury" means any behavioral, cognitive, emotional, or mental disorder in a child caused by an act or omission that is described in section 2919.22 of the Revised Code and is committed by the parent or other person responsible for the child's care.

(21) "Mentally retarded person" has the same meaning as in section 5123.01 of the Revised Code.

(22) "Nonsecure care, supervision, or training" means care, supervision, or training of a child in a facility that does not confine or prevent movement of the child within the facility or from the facility.

(23) "Organization" means any institution, public, semipublic, or private, and any private association, society, or agency located or operating in the state, incorporated or unincorporated, having among its functions the furnishing of protective services or care for children, or the placement of children in foster homes or elsewhere.

(24) "Out-of-home care" means detention facilities, shelter facilities, foster homes, certified foster homes, placement in a prospective adoptive home prior to the issuance of a final decree of adoption, organizations, certified organizations, child day-care centers, type A family day-care homes, child day-care provided by type B family day-care home providers and by in-home aides, group home providers, group homes, institutions, state institutions, residential facilities, residential care facilities, residential camps, day camps, hospitals, and medical clinics that are responsible for the care, physical custody, or control of children.

(25) "Out-of-home care child abuse" means any of the following when committed by a person responsible for the care of a child in out-of-home care:
(a) Engaging in sexual activity with a child in the person's care;
(b) Denial to a child, as a means of punishment, of proper or necessary subsistence, education, medical care, or other care necessary for a child's health;
(c) Use of restraint procedures on a child that cause injury or pain;
(d) Administration of prescription drugs or psychotropic medication to the child without the written approval and ongoing supervision of a licensed physician;
(e) Commission of any act, other than by accidental means, that results in any injury to or death of the child in out-of-home care or commission of any act by accidental means that results in an injury to or death of a child in out-of-home care and that is at variance with the history given of the injury or death.

(26) "Out-of-home care child neglect" means any of the following when committed by a person responsible for the care of a child in out-of-home care:
(a) Failure to provide reasonable supervision according to the standards of care appropriate to the age, mental and physical condition, or other special needs of the child;
(b) Failure to provide reasonable supervision according to the standards of care appropriate to the age, mental and physical condition, or other special needs of the child, that results in sexual or physical abuse of the child by any person;
(c) Failure to develop a process for all of the following:
(i) Administration of prescription drugs or psychotropic drugs for the child;
(ii) Assuring that the instructions of the licensed physician who prescribed a drug for the child are followed;
(iii) Reporting to the licensed physician who prescribed the drug all unfavorable or dangerous side effects from the use of the drug.
(d) Failure to provide proper or necessary subsistence, education, medical care, or other individualized care necessary for the health or well-being of the child;
(e) Confinement of the child to a locked room without monitoring by staff;
(f) Failure to provide ongoing security for all prescription and nonprescription medication;
(g) Isolation of a child for a period of time when there is substantial risk that the isolation, if continued, will impair or retard the mental health or physical well-being of the child.

(27) "Permanent custody" means a legal status that vests in a public children services agency or a private child placing agency, all parental rights, duties, and obligations, including the right to consent to adoption, and divests the natural parents or adoptive parents of all parental rights, privileges, and obligations, including all residual rights and obligations.

(28) "Permanent surrender" means the act of the parents or, if a child has only one parent, of the parent of a child, by a voluntary agreement authorized by section 5103.15 of the Revised Code, to transfer the permanent custody of the child to a public children services agency or a private child placing agency.

(29) "Person responsible for a child's care in out-of-home care" means any of the following:

(a) Any foster parent, in-home aide, or provider;

(b) Any administrator, employee, or agent of any of the following: a public or private detention facility; shelter facility; organization; certified organization; child day-care center; type A family day-care home; certified type B family day-care home; group home; institution; state institution; residential facility; residential care facility; residential camp; day camp; hospital; or medical clinic;

(c) Any other person who performs a similar function with respect to, or has a similar relationship to, children.

(30) "Physically impaired" means having one or more of the following conditions that substantially limit one or more of an individual's major life activities, including self-care, receptive and expressive language, learning, mobility, and self-direction:

(a) A substantial impairment of vision, speech, or hearing;

(b) A congenital orthopedic impairment;

(c) An orthopedic impairment caused by disease, rheumatic fever or any other similar chronic or acute health problem, or amputation or another similar cause.

(31) "Placement for adoption" means the arrangement by a public children services agency or a private child placing agency with a person for the care and adoption by that person of a child of whom the agency has permanent custody.

(32) "Placement in foster care" means the arrangement by a public children services agency or a private child placing agency for the out-of-home care of a child of whom the agency has temporary custody or permanent custody.

(33) "Practice of social work" and "practice of professional counseling" have the same meanings as in section 4757.01 of the Revised Code.

(34) "Probation" means a legal status created by court order following an adjudication that a child is a delinquent child, a juvenile traffic offender, or an unruly child, whereby the child is permitted to remain in the parent's, guardian's, or custodian's home subject to supervision, or under the supervision of any agency designated by the court and returned to the court for violation of probation at any time during the period of probation.

(35) "Protective supervision" means an order of disposition pursuant to which the court permits an abused, neglected, dependent, unruly, or delinquent child or a juvenile traffic offender to remain in the custody of the child's parents, guardian, or custodian and stay in the child's home, subject to any conditions and limitations upon the child, the child's parents, guardian, or custodian, or any other person that the court prescribes, including supervision as directed by the court for the protection of the child.

(36) "Psychiatrist" has the same meaning as in section 5122.01 of the Revised Code.

(37) "Psychologist" has the same meaning as in section 4732.01 of the Revised Code.

(38) "Residential camp" means a public or private facility that engages or accepts the care, physical custody, or control of children during summer months and that is licensed, regulated, approved, operated under the direction of, or otherwise certified by the department of health or the American camping association.

(39) "Residential care facility" means an institution, residence, or facility that is licensed by the department of mental health under section 5119.22 of the Revised Code and that provides care for a child.

(40) "Residential facility" means a home or facility that is licensed by the department of mental retardation and developmental disabilities under section 5123.19 of the Revised Code and in which a child with a developmental disability resides.

(41) "Residual parental rights, privileges, and responsibilities" means those rights, privileges, and responsibilities remaining with the natural parent after the transfer of legal custody of the child, including, but not necessarily limited to, the privilege of reasonable visitation, consent to adoption, the privilege to determine the child's religious affiliation, and the responsibility for support.

(42) "Secure correctional facility" means a facility under the direction of the department of youth services that is designed to physically restrict the movement and activities of children and used for the placement of children after adjudication and disposition.

(43) "Sexual activity" has the same meaning as in section 2907.01 of the Revised Code.

(44) "Shelter" means the temporary care of children in physically unrestricted facilities pending court adjudication or disposition.

(45) "Shelter for victims of domestic violence" has the same meaning as in section 3113.33 of the Revised Code.

(46) "Temporary custody" means legal custody of a child who is removed from the child's home, which custody may be terminated at any time at the discretion of the court or, if the legal custody is granted in an agreement for temporary custody, by the person who executed the agreement.

HISTORY: 142 v H 403 (Eff 1-1-89); 143 v H 257 (Eff 8-3-89); 143 v H 38 (Eff 7-10-90); 144 v H 155 (Eff 7-22-91); 144 v H 356 (Eff 3-15-93); 145 v H 152 (Eff 7-1-93); 145 v S 21 (Eff 10-29-

93); 145 v H 715 (Eff 7-22-94); 146 v H 1 (Eff 1-1-96); 146 v S 2 (Eff 7-1-96); 146 v H 274, §§ 1, 4 (Eff 8-8-96); 146 v H 265 (Eff 3-3-97); 146 v S 223 (Eff 3-18-97); 146 v H 124 (Eff 3-31-97); 147 v H 408. Eff 10-1-97.

Analogous to former RC § 2151.01.1 (133 v H 320; 138 v H 695; 139 v H 440; 140 v S 210; 141 v H 428; 142 v H 399; 142 v S 89), repealed, 142 v H 403, § 2, eff 1-1-89.

The effective date is set by section 26 of HB 408.

The provisions of § 25 of HB 408 (147 v —) read as follows:

SECTION 25. ° ° ° Section 2151.011 of the Revised Code is presented in this act as a composite of the section as amended by Am. Sub. H.B. 124, Sub. H.B. 265, and Sub. S.B. 223 of the 121st General Assembly, with the new language of none of the acts shown in capital letters. ° ° ° This is in recognition of the principle stated in division (B) of section 1.52 of the Revised Code that such amendments are to be harmonized where not substantively irreconcilable and constitutes a legislative finding that such is the resulting version in effect prior to the effective date of this act.

The provisions of § 3 of HB 1 (146 v —) read as follows:

SECTION 3. (A) The General Assembly hereby declares that its purpose in enacting the language of division (A)(2) of section 2151.18 and division (D)(2) of section 2151.355 of the Revised Code that exists on and after the effective date of this act is to recognize the holding of the Supreme Court in In re Russell (1984), 12 Ohio St. 3d 304.

(B) The General Assembly hereby declares that its purpose in enacting the language in division (B) of section 2151.011 and divisions (B) and (C) of section 2151.26 of the Revised Code that exists on and after the effective date of this act is to overrule the holding in State v. Adams (1982), 69 Ohio St. 2d 120, regarding the effect of binding a child over for trial as an adult.

(C) The amendments made by this act to section 2151.358 of the Revised Code apply to persons who were adjudicated juvenile traffic offenders or charged with being juvenile traffic offenders prior to the effective date of this act, regardless of their age on that date. A person who was adjudicated a juvenile traffic offender or charged with being a juvenile traffic offender prior to the effective date of this act may file an application in accordance with division (D) or (F) of section 2151.358 of the Revised Code on or after the effective date of this act for the sealing of the record of the person's adjudication as a juvenile traffic offender or the expungement of the record of the case in which the person was adjudicated not guilty of being a juvenile traffic offender or the charges of being a juvenile traffic offender were dismissed, and the juvenile court involved shall proceed with a hearing on the application in accordance with division (D) or (F) of that section. A juvenile court is not required to send the notice described in division (C)(1)(b) of section 2151.358 of the Revised Code to a person who was adjudicated a juvenile traffic offender prior to the effective date of this act if, on the effective date of this act, more than ninety days has expired after the expiration of the two-year period described in division (C)(1) of section 2151.358 of the Revised Code.

§ 2151.02 Delinquent child defined.

Note: See following version, HB 25 (147 v —), effective 1-12-98.

As used in this chapter, "delinquent child" includes any of the following:

(A) Any child who violates any law of this state or the United States, or any ordinance or regulation of a political subdivision of the state, that would be a crime if committed by an adult, except as provided in section 2151.021 [2151.02.1] of the Revised Code;

(B) Any child who violates any lawful order of the court made under this chapter;

(C) Any child who violates division (A) of section 2923.211 [2923.21.1] of the Revised Code.

HISTORY: GC § 1639-2; 117 v 520; Bureau of Code Revision, 10-1-53; 127 v 547 (Eff 9-14-57); 133 v H 320 (Eff 11-19-69); 146 v H 4. Eff 11-9-95.

The provisions of § 3 of HB 4 (146 v —) read as follows:

SECTION 3. Sections 2151.02, 2151.022, 2151.355, 2151.411, 2913.02, 2913.51, 2913.71, 2921.13, 2923.21, 2947.061, 2951.02, 2967.01, and 2967.15 of the Revised Code, as amended by this act, and sections 2923.211 and 2967.131 of the Revised Code, as enacted by this act, apply to any offense, delinquent act, or unruly act committed on or after the effective date of this act. Sections 2151.02, 2151.022, 2151.355, 2151.411, 2913.02, 2913.51, 2913.71, 2921.13, 2923.21, 2947.061, 2951.02, 2967.01, and 2967.15 of the Revised Code, as they existed immediately prior to the effective date of this act, apply to any offense, delinquent act, or unruly act committed before the effective date of this act.

Text of § 3 of HB 161 (127 v 547), eff 9-14-57.

The several sections, parts of sections, sentences, and parts of sentences of this act (amending RC §§ 2151.02, 2151.18, 2151.23, 2151.27 and 2151.35, and enacting RC § 2151.02.1) are declared to be separate and independent sections, parts of sections, sentences, and parts of sentences, and a decision holding any section, part of section, sentence, or part of sentence thereof for any reason to be unconstitutional and void shall not affect the validity of the remaining portions of the act (127 v 547 (551), § 3).

§ 2151.02 Delinquent child defined.

Note: See preceding version, HB 4 (146 v —), in effect until 1-12-98.

As used in this chapter, "delinquent child" includes any of the following:

(A) Any child who violates any law of this state or the United States, or any ordinance or regulation of a political subdivision of the state, that would be a crime if committed by an adult, except as provided in section 2151.021 [2151.02.1] of the Revised Code;

(B) Any child who violates any lawful order of the court made under this chapter;

(C) Any child who violates division (A) of section 2923.211 [2923.21.1] of the Revised Code;

(D) Any child who violates division (A)(1) or (2) of section 3730.07 of the Revised Code.

HISTORY: GC § 1639-2; 117 v 520; Bureau of Code Revision, 10-1-53; 127 v 547 (Eff 9-14-57); 133 v H 320 (Eff 11-19-69); 146 v H 4 (Eff 11-9-95); 147 v H 25. Eff 1-12-98.

The effective date is set by section 3 of HB 25.

[§ 2151.02.1] § 2151.021 Juvenile traffic offender defined.

A child who violates any traffic law, traffic ordinance, or traffic regulation of this state, the United States, or any political subdivision of this state, other than a resolution, ordinance, or regulation of a political subdivision of this state the violation of which is required to be handled by a parking violations bureau or a joint parking violations bureau pursuant to Chapter 4521. of the Revised Code, shall be designated as a "juvenile traffic offender."

HISTORY: 127 v 547 (Eff 9-14-57); 133 v H 320 (Eff 11-19-69); 139 v H 707. Eff 1-1-83.

[§ 2151.02.2] § 2151.022 Unruly child defined.

As used in this chapter, "unruly child" includes any of the following:

(A) Any child who does not subject himself or herself to the reasonable control of his or her parents, teachers, guardian, or custodian, by reason of being wayward or habitually disobedient;

(B) Any child who is an habitual truant from home or school;

(C) Any child who so deports himself or herself as to injure or endanger his or her health or morals or the health or morals of others;

(D) Any child who attempts to enter the marriage relation in any state without the consent of his or her parents, custodian, or legal guardian or other legal authority;

(E) Any child who is found in a disreputable place, visits or patronizes a place prohibited by law, or associates with vagrant, vicious, criminal, notorious, or immoral persons;

(F) Any child who engages in an occupation prohibited by law or is in a situation dangerous to life or limb or injurious to his or her health or morals or the health or morals of others;

(G) Any child who violates a law, other than division (A) of section 2923.211 [2923.21.1] of the Revised Code, that is applicable only to a child.

HISTORY: 133 v H 320 (Eff 11-19-69); 146 v H 4. Eff 11-9-95.

See provisions, § 3 of HB 4 (146 v —) following RC § 2151.02.

§ 2151.03 Neglected child defined; failure to provide medical care for religious reasons.

(A) As used in this chapter, "neglected child" includes any child:

(1) Who is abandoned by the child's parents, guardian, or custodian;

(2) Who lacks adequate parental care because of the faults or habits of the child's parents, guardian, or custodian;

(3) Whose parents, guardian, or custodian neglects the child or refuses to provide proper or necessary subsistence, education, medical or surgical care or treatment, or other care necessary for the child's health, morals, or well being;

(4) Whose parents, guardian, or custodian neglects the child or refuses to provide the special care made necessary by the child's mental condition;

(5) Whose parents, legal guardian, or custodian have placed or attempted to place the child in violation of sections 5103.16 and 5103.17 of the Revised Code;

(6) Who, because of the omission of the child's parents, guardian, or custodian, suffers physical or mental injury that harms or threatens to harm the child's health or welfare;

(7) Who is subjected to out-of-home care child neglect.

(B) Nothing in this chapter shall be construed as subjecting a parent, guardian, or custodian of a child to criminal liability when, solely in the practice of religious beliefs, the parent, guardian, or custodian fails to provide adequate medical or surgical care or treatment for the child. This division does not abrogate or limit any person's responsibility under section 2151.421 [2151.42.1] of the Revised Code to report known or suspected child abuse, known or suspected child neglect, and children who are known to face or are suspected of facing a threat of suffering abuse or neglect and does not preclude any exercise of the authority of the state, any political subdivision, or any court to ensure that medical or surgical care or treatment is provided to a child when the child's health requires the provision of medical or surgical care or treatment.

HISTORY: GC § 1639-3; 117 v 520; Bureau of Code Revision, 10-1-53; 133 v H 320 (Eff 11-19-69); 143 v H 257 (Eff 8-3-89); 146 v H 274. Eff 8-8-96.

[§ 2151.03.1] § 2151.031 Abused child defined.

As used in this chapter, an "abused child" includes any child who:

(A) Is the victim of "sexual activity" as defined under Chapter 2907. of the Revised Code, where such activity would constitute an offense under that chapter, except that the court need not find that any person has been convicted of the offense in order to find that the child is an abused child;

(B) Is endangered as defined in section 2919.22 of the Revised Code, except that the court need not find that any person has been convicted under that section in order to find that the child is an abused child;

(C) Exhibits evidence of any physical or mental injury or death, inflicted other than by accidental means, or an injury or death which is at variance with the history given of it. Except as provided in division (D) of this section, a child exhibiting evidence of corporal punishment or other physical disciplinary measure by a parent, guardian, custodian, person having custody or control, or person in loco parentis of a child is not an abused child under this division if the measure is not prohibited under section 2919.22 of the Revised Code.

(D) Because of the acts of his parents, guardian, or custodian, suffers physical or mental injury that harms or threatens to harm the child's health or welfare.

(E) Is subjected to out-of-home care child abuse.

HISTORY: 136 v H 85 (Eff 11-28-75); 142 v S 89 (Eff 1-1-89); 143 v H 257. Eff 8-3-89.

§ 2151.04 Dependent child defined.

As used in this chapter, "dependent child" means any child:

(A) Who is homeless or destitute or without adequate parental care, through no fault of the child's parents, guardian, or custodian;

(B) Who lacks adequate parental care by reason of the mental or physical condition of the child's parents, guardian, or custodian;

(C) Whose condition or environment is such as to warrant the state, in the interests of the child, in assuming the child's guardianship;

(D) To whom both of the following apply:

(1) The child is residing in a household in which a parent, guardian, custodian, or other member of the household committed an act that was the basis for an adjudication that a sibling of the child or any other child who resides in the household is an abused, neglected, or dependent child.

(2) Because of the circumstances surrounding the abuse, neglect, or dependency of the sibling or other child and the other conditions in the household of the child, the child is in danger of being abused or neglected by that parent, guardian, custodian, or member of the household.

HISTORY: GC § 1639-4; 117 v 520; Bureau of Code Revision, 10-1-53; 129 v 1778 (Eff 10-27-61); 133 v H 320 (Eff 11-19-69); 142 v S 89 (Eff 1-1-89); 146 v H 274. Eff 8-8-96.

§ 2151.05 Child without proper parental care.

Under sections 2151.01 to 2151.54 of the Revised Code, a child whose home is filthy and unsanitary; whose parents, stepparents, guardian, or custodian permit him to become dependent, neglected, abused, or delinquent; whose parents, stepparents, guardian, or custodian, when able, refuse or neglect to provide him with necessary care, support, medical attention, and educational facilities; or whose parents, stepparents, guardian, or custodian fail to subject such child to necessary discipline is without proper parental care or guardianship.

HISTORY: GC § 1639-5; 117 v 520; Bureau of Code Revision, 10-1-53; 136 v H 85. Eff 11-28-75.

§ 2151.06 Residence or legal settlement.

Under sections 2151.01 to 2151.54, inclusive, of the Revised Code, a child has the same residence or legal settlement as his parents, legal guardian of his person, or his custodian who stands in the relation of loco parentis.

HISTORY: GC § 1639-6; 117 v 520; 121 v 557; Bureau of Code Revision. Eff 10-1-53.

[ESTABLISHMENT AND JURISDICTION]

§ 2151.07 Creation and powers of juvenile court.

The juvenile court is a court of record and within the division of domestic relations or probate of the court of common pleas, except that the juvenile courts of Cuyahoga county and Hamilton county shall be separate divisions of the court of common pleas. The juvenile court has and shall exercise the powers and jurisdiction conferred in sections 2151.01 to 2151.99 of the Revised Code.

Whenever the juvenile judge of the juvenile court is absent from the county, or is unable to attend court, or the volume of cases pending in court necessitates it, upon the request of said judge, the presiding judge of the court of common pleas shall assign a judge of the court of common pleas of the county to act in his place or in conjunction with him. If no such judge is available for said purpose, the chief justice of the supreme court shall assign a judge of the court of common pleas, a juvenile judge, or a probate judge from some other county to act in the place of such judge or in conjunction with him, who shall receive such compensation and expenses for his services as is provided by law for judges assigned to hold court in courts of common pleas.

HISTORY: GC § 1639-7; 117 v 520; 122 v 390; Bureau of Code Revision, 10-1-53; 127 v 847 (Eff 9-16-57); 133 v H 320 (Eff 11-19-69); 134 v H 574. Eff 6-29-72.

§ 2151.08 Juvenile court in Hamilton county.

In Hamilton county the powers and jurisdiction of the juvenile court as conferred by Chapter 2151. of the Revised Code shall be exercised by that judge of the court of common pleas whose term begins on January 1, 1957, and his successors and that judge of the court of common pleas whose term begins on February 14, 1967, and his successors as provided by section 2301.03 of the Revised Code. This conferral of powers and jurisdiction on such judges shall be deemed a creation of a separately and independently created and established juvenile court in Hamilton county, Ohio. Such judges shall serve in each and every position where the statutes permit or require a juvenile judge to serve.

HISTORY: GC § 1639-8; 117 v 520; Bureau of Code Revision, 10-1-53; 127 v 847 (Eff 9-16-57); 131 v 631. Eff 11-16-65.

§ 2151.09 Separate building and site may be purchased or leased.

Upon the advice and recommendation of the juvenile judge, the board of county commissioners may provide by purchase, lease, or otherwise a separate building and site to be known as "the juvenile court" at a convenient location within the county which shall be appropriately constructed, arranged, furnished, and maintained for the convenient and efficient transaction of the business of the court and all parts thereof and its employees, including adequate facilities to be used as laboratories, dispensaries, or clinics for the use of scientific specialists connected with the court.

HISTORY: GC § 1639-15; 117 v 520; Bureau of Code Revision. Eff 10-1-53.

§ 2151.10 Appropriation for court expenses and care of children.

The juvenile judge shall annually submit a written request for an appropriation to the board of county commissioners that shall set forth estimated administrative expenses of the juvenile court that the judge considers reasonably necessary for the operation of the court, including reasonably necessary expenses of the judge and such officers and employees as the judge may designate in attending conferences at which juvenile or welfare problems are discussed, and such sum each year as will provide for the maintenance and operation of the detention home, the care, maintenance, education, and support of neglected, abused, dependent, and delinquent children, other than children eligible to participate in the Ohio works first program established under Chapter 5107. of the Revised Code, and for necessary orthopedic, surgical, and medical treatment, and special care as may be ordered by the court for any neglected, abused, dependent, or delinquent children. The board shall conduct a public hearing with respect to the written request submitted by the judge and shall appropriate such sum of money each year as it determines, after conducting the public hearing and considering the written request of the judge, is reasonably necessary to meet all the administrative expenses of the court. All disbursements from such appropriations shall be upon specifically itemized vouchers, certified to by the judge.

If the judge considers the appropriation made by the board pursuant to this section insufficient to meet all the administrative expenses of the court, the judge shall commence an action under Chapter 2731. of the Revised Code in the court of appeals for the judicial district for a determination of the duty of the board of county commissioners to appropriate the amount of money in dispute. The court of appeals shall give priority to the action filed by the juvenile judge over all cases pending on its docket. The burden shall be on the juvenile judge to prove that the appropriation requested is reasonably necessary to meet all administrative expenses of the court. If, prior to the filing of an action under Chapter 2731. of the Revised Code or during the pendency of the action, the judge exercises the judge's contempt power in order to obtain the sum of money in dispute, the judge shall not order the imprisonment of any member of the board of county commissioners notwithstanding sections 2705.02 to 2705.06 of the Revised Code.

HISTORY: GC § 1639-57; 117 v 520; 119 v 731; 121 v 557; Bureau of Code Revision, 10-1-53; 136 v H 85 (Eff 11-28-75); 138 v S 63 (Eff 7-26-79); 147 v H 408. Eff 10-1-97.

The effective date is set by section 26 of HB 408.

§ 2151.11 Assignment of court employees to combat juvenile delinquency.

A juvenile court may participate with other public or private agencies of the county served by the court in programs which have as their objective the prevention and control of juvenile delinquency. The juvenile judge may assign employees of the court, as part of their regular duties, to work with organizations concerned with combatting conditions known to contribute to delinquency, providing adult sponsors for children who have been found delinquent, and developing wholesome youth programs.

The juvenile judge may accept and administer on behalf of the court gifts, grants, bequests, and devises made to the court for the purpose of preventing delinquency.

HISTORY: 131 v 631. Eff 11-11-65.

Not analogous to former RC § 2151.11, (GC § 1639-7a; 122 v 390; 123 v 3; Bureau of Code Revision, 10-1-53), repealed in 129 v 1072, eff 2-8-61.

§ 2151.12 Clerk; bond; judge as clerk.

(A) Except as otherwise provided in this division, whenever a court of common pleas, division of domestic relations, exercises the powers and jurisdictions conferred in Chapter 2151. of the Revised Code, the judge or judges of that division or, if applicable, the judge of that division who specifically is designated by section 2301.03 of the Revised Code as being responsible for administering sections 2151.13, 2151.16, 2151.17, and 2151.18 of the Revised Code shall be the clerk of the court for all records filed with the court pursuant to Chapter 2151. of the Revised Code or pursuant to any other section of the Revised Code that requires documents to be filed with a juvenile judge or a juvenile court. If, in a division of domestic relations of a court of common pleas that exercises the powers and jurisdiction conferred in Chapter 2151. of the Revised Code, the judge of the division, both judges in a two-judge division, or a majority of the judges in a division with three or more judges and the clerk of the court of common pleas agree in an agreement that is signed by the agreeing judge or judges and the clerk and entered into formally in the journal of the court, the clerk of courts of common pleas shall keep the records filed with the court pursuant to Chapter 2151. of the Revised Code or pursuant to any other section of the Revised Code that requires documents to be filed with a juvenile judge or a juvenile court.

Whenever the juvenile judge, or a majority of the juvenile judges of a multi-judge juvenile division, of a court of common pleas, juvenile division, and the clerk of the court of common pleas agree in an agreement that is signed by the judge and the clerk and entered formally in the journal of the court, the clerks of courts of common pleas shall keep the records of such courts. In all other cases, the juvenile judge shall be the clerk of the judge's own court.

(B) In counties in which the juvenile judge is clerk of the judge's own court, before entering upon the duties of office as such clerk, the judge shall execute and file with the county treasurer a bond in a sum to be determined by the board of county commissioners, with sufficient surety to be approved by the board, conditioned for the faithful performance of duties as clerk. The bond shall be given for the benefit of the county, the state, or any person who may suffer loss by reason of a default in any of the conditions of the bond.

HISTORY: GC § 1639-17; 117 v 520; Bureau of Code Revision, 10-1-53; 137 v S 336 (Eff 3-3-78); 146 v H 423. Eff 10-31-96.

§ 2151.13 Employees; compensation; bond.

The juvenile judge may appoint such bailiffs, probation officers, and other employees as are necessary and may designate their titles and fix their duties, compensation, and expense allowances. The juvenile court may by entry on its journal authorize any deputy clerk to administer oaths when necessary in the discharge of his duties. Such employees shall serve during the pleasure of the judge.

The compensation and expenses of all employees and the salary and expenses of the judge shall be paid in semimonthly installments by the county treasurer from the money appropriated for the operation of the court, upon the warrant of the county auditor, certified to by the judge.

The judge may require any employee to give bond in the sum of not less than one thousand dollars, conditioned for the honest and faithful performance of his duties. The sureties on such bonds shall be approved in the manner provided by section 2151.12 of the Revised Code. The judge shall not be personally liable for the default, misfeasance, or nonfeasance of any employee from whom a bond has been required.

HISTORY: GC § 1639-18; 117 v 520; 121 v 557; Bureau of Code Revision. Eff 10-1-53.

§ 2151.14 Duties and powers of probation department; records; command assistance.

(A) The chief probation officer, under the direction of the juvenile judge, shall have charge of the work of the probation department. The department shall make any investigations that the judge directs, keep a written record of the investigations, and submit the record to the judge or deal with them as the judge directs. The department shall furnish to any person placed on probation a statement of the conditions of probation and shall instruct the person regarding them. The department shall keep informed concerning the conduct and condition of each person under its supervision and shall report on their conduct and condition to the judge as the judge directs. Each probation officer shall use all suitable methods to aid persons on probation and to bring about improvement in their conduct and condition. The department shall keep full records of its work, keep accurate and complete accounts of money collected from persons under its supervision, give receipts for the money, and make reports on the money as the judge directs.

(B) Except as provided in division (C) or (D) of this section, the reports and records of the department shall be considered confidential information and shall not be made public. A probation officer may serve the process of the court within or without the county, make arrests without warrant upon reasonable information or upon view of the violation of this chapter, detain the person arrested pending the issuance of a warrant, and perform any other duties, incident to the office, that the judge directs. All sheriffs, deputy sheriffs, constables, marshals, deputy marshals, chiefs of police, municipal corporation and township police officers, and other peace officers shall render assistance to probation officers in the performance of their duties when requested to do so by any probation officer.

(C) When a complaint has been filed alleging that a child is delinquent by reason of having committed an act that would constitute a violation of section 2907.02, 2907.03, 2907.04, 2907.05, or 2907.06 of the Revised Code if committed by an adult and the arresting authority, a court, or a probation officer discovers that the child or a person whom the child caused to engage in sexual activity, as defined in section 2907.01 of the Revised Code, has a communicable disease, the arresting authority, court, or probation officer immediately shall notify the victim of the delinquent act of the nature of the disease.

(D)(1) In accordance with division (D)(2) of this section, subject to the limitation specified in division (D)(4) of this section, and in connection with a disposition pursuant to section 2151.354 [2151.35.4] of the Revised Code when a child has been found to be an unruly child, a disposition pursuant to section 2151.355 [2151.35.5] of the Revised Code when a child has been found to be a delinquent child, or a disposition pursuant to section 2151.356 [2151.35.6] of the Revised Code when a child has been found to be a juvenile traffic offender, the court may issue an order requiring boards of education, governing bodies of chartered nonpublic schools, public children services agencies, private child placing agencies, probation departments, law enforcement agencies, and prosecuting attorneys that have records related to the child in question to provide copies of one or more specified records, or specified information in one or more specified records, that the individual or entity has with respect to the child to any of the following individuals or entities that request the records in accordance with division (D)(3)(a) of this section:

(a) The child;

(b) The attorney or guardian ad litem of the child;

(c) A parent, guardian, or custodian of the child;

(d) A prosecuting attorney;

(e) A board of education of a public school district;

(f) A probation department of a juvenile court;

(g) A public children services agency or private child placing agency that has custody of the child, is providing services to the child or the child's family, or is preparing a social history or performing any other function for the juvenile court;

(h) The department of youth services when the department has custody of the child or is performing any services for the child that are required by the juvenile court or by statute;

(i) The individual in control of a juvenile detention or rehabilitation facility to which the child has been committed;

(j) An employee of the juvenile court that found the child to be an unruly child, a delinquent child, or a juvenile traffic offender;

(k) Any other entity that has custody of the child or is providing treatment, rehabilitation, or other services for the child pursuant to a court order, statutory requirement, or other arrangement.

(2) Any individual or entity listed in divisions (D)(1)(a) to (k) of this section may file a motion with the court that requests the court to issue an order as described in division (D)(1) of this section. If such a motion is filed, the court shall conduct a hearing on it. If at the hearing the movant demonstrates a need for one or more specified records, or for information in one or more specified records, related to the child in question and additionally demonstrates the relevance of the information sought to be obtained from those records, and if the court determines that the limitation specified in division (D)(4) of this section does not preclude the provision of a specified record or specified information to the movant, then the court may issue an order to a designated individual or entity to provide the movant with copies of one or more specified records or with specified information contained in one or more specified records.

(3)(a) Any individual or entity that is authorized by an order issued pursuant to division (D)(1) of this section to obtain copies of one or more specified records, or specified information, related to a particular child may file a written request for copies of the records or for the information with any individual or entity required by the order to provide copies of the records or the information. The request shall be in writing, describe the type of records or the information requested, explain the need for the records or the information, and be accompanied by a copy of the order.

(b) If an individual or entity that is required by an order issued pursuant to division (D)(1) of this section to provide one or more specified records, or specified information, related to a child receives a written request for the records or information in accordance with division (D)(3)(a) of this section, the individual or entity immediately shall comply with the request to the extent it is able to do so, unless the individual or entity determines that it is unable to comply with the request because it is prohibited by law from doing so, or unless the requesting individual or entity does not have authority to obtain the requested records or information. If the individual or entity determines that it is unable to comply with the request, it shall file a motion with the court that issued the order requesting the court to determine the extent to which it is required to comply with the request for records or information. Upon the filing of the motion, the court immediately shall hold a hearing on the motion, determine the extent to which the movant is required to comply with the request for records or information, and issue findings of fact and conclusions of law in support of its determination. The determination of the court shall be final. If the court determines that the movant is required to comply with the request for records or information, it shall identify the specific records or information that must be supplied to the individual or entity that requested the records or information.

(c) If an individual or entity is required to provide copies of one or more specified records pursuant to division (D) of this section, the individual or entity may charge a fee for the copies that does not exceed the cost of supplying them.

(4) Division (D) of this section does not require, authorize, or permit the dissemination of any records or any information contained in any records if the dissemination of the records or information generally is prohibited by any provision of the Revised Code and a specific provision of the Revised Code does not specifically authorize or permit the dissemination of the records or information pursuant to division (D) of this section.

HISTORY: GC § 1639-19; 117 v 520; Bureau of Code Revision, 10-1-53; 141 v H 468 (Eff 9-17-86); 143 v S 258 (Eff 8-22-90); 146 v H 445. Eff 9-3-96.

The provisions of § 3(A) of HB 445 (146 v —) read as follows:

SECTION 3. (A) When a complaint is filed alleging that a child is a delinquent child for committing felonious sexual penetration in violation of former section 2907.12 of the Revised Code and the arresting authority, a court, or a probation officer discovers that the child or a person whom the child caused to engage in sexual activity has a communicable disease, the arresting authority, court, or probation officer shall notify the victim of the delinquent act of the nature of the disease in accordance with division (C) of section 2151.14 of the Revised Code.

As used in division (A) of Section 3 of this act:

(1) "Child" has the same meaning as in section 2151.011 of the Revised Code.

(2) "Delinquent child" has the same meaning as in section 2151.02 of the Revised Code.

(3) "Sexual activity" has the same meaning as in section 2907.01 of the Revised Code.

[§ 2151.14.1] § 2151.141 Request for copies of records concerning child alleged to be abused, neglected or dependent.

(A) If a complaint filed with respect to a child pursuant to section 2151.27 of the Revised Code alleges that a child is an abused, neglected, or dependent child, any individual or entity that is listed in divisions (D)(1)(a) to (k) of section 2151.14 of the Revised Code and that is investigating whether the child is an abused, neglected, or dependent child, has custody of the child, is preparing a social history for the child, or is providing any services for the child may request any board of education, governing body of a chartered nonpublic school, public children services agency, private child placing agency, probation department, law enforcement agency, or prosecuting attorney that has any records related to the child to provide the individual or entity with a copy of the records. The request shall be in writing, describe the type of records requested, explain the need for the records, be accompanied by a copy of the complaint, and describe the relationship of the requesting individual or entity to the child. The individual or entity shall provide a copy of the request to the child in question, the attorney or guardian ad litem of the child, and the parent, guardian, or custodian of the child.

(B)(1) Any board of education, governing body of a chartered nonpublic school, public children services agency, private child placing agency, probation department, law enforcement agency, or prosecuting attorney that has any records related to a child who is the subject of a complaint as described in division (A) of this section and that receives a request for a copy of the records pursuant to division (A) of this section shall comply with the request, unless the individual or entity determines that it is unable to do so because it is prohibited by law from complying with the request, the request does not comply with division (A) of this section, or a complaint as described in division (A) of this section has not been filed with respect to the child who is the subject of the requested records. If the individual or entity determines that it is unable to comply with the request, it shall file a motion with the court in which the complaint as described in division (A) of this section was filed or was alleged to have been filed requesting the court to determine the extent to which it is required to comply with the request for records. Upon the filing of the motion, the court immediately shall hold a hearing on the motion, determine the extent to which the movant is required to comply with the request for records, and issue findings of fact and conclusions of law in support of its determination. The determination of the court shall be final. If the court determines that the movant is required to comply with the request for records, it shall identify the specific records that must be supplied to the individual or entity that requested them.

(2) In addition to or in lieu of the motion described in division (B)(1) of this section, a law enforcement agency or prosecuting attorney that receives a request for a copy of records pursuant to division (A) of this section may file a motion for a protective order as described in this division with the court in which the complaint as described in division (A) of this section was filed or alleged to have been filed. Upon the filing of such a motion, the court shall conduct a hearing on the motion. If at the hearing the law enforcement agency or prosecuting attorney demonstrates that any of the following applies and if, after considering the purposes for which the records were requested pursuant to division (A) of this section, the best interest of the child, and any demonstrated need to prevent specific information in the records from being disclosed, the court determines that the issuance of a protective order is necessary, then the court shall issue a protective order that appropriately limits the disclosure of one or more specified records or specified information in one or more specified records:

(a) The records or information in the records relate to a case in which the child is alleged to be a delinquent child or a case in which a child is bound over for trial as an adult pursuant to section 2151.26 of the Revised Code and Juvenile Rule 30, and the adjudication hearing in the case, the trial in the case, or other disposition of the case has not been concluded.

(b) The records in question, or the records containing the information in question, are confidential law enforcement investigatory records, as defined in section 149.43 of the Revised Code.

(c) The records or information in the records relate to a case in which the child is or was alleged to be a delinquent child or to a case in which a child is or was bound over for trial as an adult pursuant to section 2151.26 of the Revised Code and Juvenile Rule 30; another case is pending against any child or any adult in which the child is alleged to be a delinquent child, the child is so bound over for trial as an adult, or the adult is alleged to be a criminal offender; the allegations in the case to which the records or information relate and the allegations in the other case are based on the same act or transaction, are based on two or more connected transactions or constitute parts of a common scheme or plan, or are part of a course of criminal conduct; and the adjudication hearing in, trial in, or other disposition of the other case has not been concluded.

(C) If an individual or entity is required to provide copies of records pursuant to this section, the individual or entity may charge a fee for the copies that does not exceed the cost of supplying them.

(D) This section shall not be construed to require, authorize, or permit, and does not require, authorize, or permit, the dissemination of any records or any information contained in any records if the dissemination of the records or information generally is prohibited by any provision of the Revised Code and a specific provision of the Revised Code does not specifically authorize or permit the dissemination of the records or information pursuant to this section.

HISTORY: 143 v S 258. Eff 8-22-90.

§ 2151.15 Powers and duties vested in county department of probation.

When a county department of probation has been established in the county and the juvenile judge does not establish a probation department within the juvenile court as provided in section 2151.14 of the Revised Code, all powers and duties of the probation department provided for in sections 2151.01 to 2151.54, inclusive, of the Revised Code, shall vest in and be imposed upon such county department of probation.

In counties in which a county department of probation has been or is hereafter established the judge may transfer to such department all or any part of the powers and duties of his own probation department; provided that all juvenile cases shall be handled within a county department of probation exclusively by an officer or division separate and distinct from the officers or division handling adult cases.

HISTORY: GC § 1639-20; 117 v 520; 121 v 557; Bureau of Code Revision. Eff 10-1-53.

[§ 2151.15.1] § 2151.151 Contract for services for children on probation.

(A) The juvenile judge may contract with any agency, association, or organization, which may be of a public or private, or profit or nonprofit nature, or with any individual for the provision of supervisory or other services to children placed on probation who are under the custody and supervision of the juvenile court.

(B) The juvenile judges of two or more adjoining or neighboring counties may join together for purposes of contracting with any agency, association, or organization, which may be of a public or private, or profit or nonprofit nature, or with any individual for the provision of supervisory or other services to children placed on probation who are under the custody and supervision of the juvenile court of any of the counties that joins [join] together.

HISTORY: 139 v H 440. Eff 11-23-81.

[§ 2151.15.2] § 2151.152 Reimbursement of court for costs of children in custody of court.

The juvenile judge may enter into an agreement with the department of human services pursuant to section 5101.11 of the Revised Code for the purpose of reimbursing the court for foster care maintenance costs and associated administrative and training costs incurred on behalf of a child in the temporary or permanent custody of the court and eligible for payments under Title IV-E of the "Social Security Act," 94 Stat. 501, 42 U.S.C.A. 670 (1980). The agreement shall govern the responsibilities and duties the court shall perform in providing services to the child.

HISTORY: 146 v H 274. Eff 8-8-96.

§ 2151.16 Referees; powers and duties.

The juvenile judge may appoint and fix the compensation of referees who shall have the usual power of masters in chancery cases, provided, in all such cases submitted to them by the juvenile court, they shall hear the testimony of witnesses and certify to the judge their findings upon the case submitted to them, together with their recommendation as to the judgment or order to be made in the case in question. The court, after notice to the parties in the case of the presentation of such findings and recommendation, may make the order recommended by the referee, or any other order in the judgment of the court required by the findings of the referee, or may hear additional testimony, or may set aside said findings and hear the case anew. In appointing a referee for the trial of females, a female referee shall be appointed where possible.

HISTORY: GC § 1639-21; 117 v 520; Bureau of Code Revision. Eff 10-1-53.

§ 2151.17 Rules governing practice and procedure.

Except as otherwise provided by rules promulgated by the supreme court, the juvenile court may prescribe rules regulating the docketing and hearing of causes, motions, and demurrers, and such other matters as are necessary for the orderly conduct of its business and the prevention of delay, and for the government of its officers and employees, including their conduct, duties, hours, expenses, leaves of absence, and vacations.

HISTORY: GC § 1639-11; 117 v 520; 121 v 557; Bureau of Code Revision, 10-1-53; 133 v H 320. Eff 11-19-69.

§ 2151.18 Records; weekly report of case summaries; annual summary and report.

(A)(1) The juvenile court shall maintain records of all official cases brought before it, including an appearance docket, a journal, and a cashbook. The court shall maintain a separate docket for traffic cases and shall record all traffic cases on the separate docket instead of on the general appearance docket. The parents of any child affected, if they are living, or the nearest of kin of the child, if the parents are deceased, may inspect these records, either in person or by counsel during the hours in which the court is open.

(2) The juvenile court shall send to the superintendent of the bureau of criminal identification and investigation, pursuant to section 109.57 of the Revised Code, a weekly report containing a summary of each case that has come before it and that involves an adjudication that a child is a delinquent child for committing a designated delinquent act or juvenile offense, as defined in section 109.57 of the Revised Code.

(B) The clerk of the court shall maintain a statistical record that includes all of the following:

(1) The number of complaints that are filed with the court that allege that a child is a delinquent child, in relation to which the court determines under division (D) of section 2151.27 of the Revised Code that the victim of the alleged delinquent act was sixty-five years of age or older or permanently and totally disabled at the time of the alleged commission of the act;

(2) The number of complaints described in division (B)(1) of this section that result in the child being adjudicated a delinquent child;

(3) The number of complaints described in division (B)(2) of this section in which the act upon which the delinquent child adjudication is based caused property damage or would be a theft offense, as defined in division (K) of section 2913.01 of the Revised Code, if committed by an adult;

(4) The number of complaints described in division (B)(3) of this section that result in the delinquent child being required as an order of disposition made under division (A)(8)(b) of section 2151.355 [2151.35.5] of the Revised Code to make restitution for all or part of the property damage caused by his delinquent act or for all or part of the value of the property that was the subject of the delinquent act that would be a theft offense if committed by an adult;

(5) The number of complaints described in division (B)(2) of this section in which the act upon which the delinquent child adjudication is based would have been an offense of violence if committed by an adult;

(6) The number of complaints described in division (B)(5) of this section that result in the delinquent child being committed as an order of disposition made under division (A)(3), (4), (5), (6), or (7) of section 2151.355 [2151.35.5] of the Revised Code to any facility for delinquent children operated by the county, a district, or a private agency or organization or to the department of youth services;

(7) The number of complaints described in division (B)(1) of this section that result in the case being transferred for criminal prosecution to an appropriate court having jurisdiction of the offense under section 2151.26 of the Revised Code.

(C) The clerk of the court shall compile an annual summary covering the preceding calendar year showing all of the information for that year contained in the statistical record maintained under division (B) of this section. The statistical record and the annual summary shall be public records open for inspection. Neither the statistical record nor the annual summary shall include the identity of any party to a case.

(D) Not later than June of each year, the court shall prepare an annual report covering the preceding calendar year showing the number and kinds of cases that have come before it, the disposition of the cases, and any other data pertaining to the work of the court that the juvenile judge directs. The court shall file copies of the report with the board of county commissioners. With the approval of the board, the court may print or cause to be printed copies of the report for distribution to persons and agencies interested in the court or community program for dependent, neglected, abused, or delinquent children and juvenile traffic offenders. The court shall include the number of copies ordered printed and the estimated cost of each printed copy on each copy of the report printed for distribution.

HISTORY: GC § 1639-13; 117 v 520; 121 v 557; 123 v 367; Bureau of Code Revision, 10-1-53; 127 v 547 (Eff 9-14-57); 136 v H 85 (Eff 11-28-75); 138 v H 394 (Eff 9-26-79); 139 v H 440 (Eff 11-23-81); 140 v S 5 (Eff 9-26-84); 143 v S 268 (Eff 6-28-90); 145 v H 152 (Eff 7-1-93); 146 v H 1 (Eff 1-1-96); 146 v H 124. Eff 3-31-97.

The provisions of § 3 of HB 1 (146 v —) read as follows:

SECTION 3. (A) The General Assembly hereby declares that its purpose in enacting the language of division (A)(2) of section 2151.18 and division (D)(2) of section 2151.355 of the Revised Code that exists on and after the effective date of this act is to recognize the holding of the Supreme Court in *In re Russell* (1984), 12 Ohio St. 3d 304.

(B) The General Assembly hereby declares that its purpose in enacting the language in division (B) of section 2151.011 and divisions (B) and (C) of section 2151.26 of the Revised Code that exists on and after the effective date of this act is to overrule the holding in *State v. Adams* (1982), 69 Ohio St. 2d 120, regarding the effect of binding a child over for trial as an adult.

(C) The amendments made by this act to section 2151.358 of the Revised Code apply to persons who were adjudicated juvenile traffic offenders or charged with being juvenile traffic offenders prior to the effective date of this act, regardless of their age on that date. A person who was adjudicated a juvenile traffic offender or charged with being a juvenile traffic offender prior to the effective date of this act may file an application in accordance with division (D) or (F) of section 2151.358 of the Revised Code on or after the effective date of this act for the sealing of the record of the person's adjudication as a juvenile traffic offender or the expungement of the record of the case in which the person was adjudicated not guilty of being a juvenile traffic offender or the charges of being a juvenile traffic offender were dismissed, and the juvenile court involved shall proceed with a hearing on the application in accordance with division (D) or (F) of that section. A juvenile court is not required to send the notice described in division (C)(1)(b) of section 2151.358 of the Revised Code to a person who was adjudicated a juvenile traffic offender prior to the effective date of this act if, on the effective date of this act, more than ninety days has expired after the expiration of the two-year period described in division (C)(1) of section 2151.358 of the Revised Code.

§ 2151.19 Summons; expense.

The summons, warrants, citations, subpoenas, and other writs of the juvenile court may issue to a probation officer of any such court or to the sheriff of any county or any marshal, constable, or police officer, and the provisions of law relating to the subpoenaing of witnesses in other cases shall apply in so far as they are applicable.

When a summons, warrant, citation, subpoena, or other writ is issued to any such officer, other than a probation officer, the expense in serving the same shall be paid by the county, township, or municipal corporation in the manner prescribed for the payment of sheriffs, deputies, assistants, and other employees.

HISTORY: GC §§ 1639-52, 1639-53; 117 v 520; Bureau of Code Revision. Eff 10-1-53.

§ 2151.20 Seal of court; dimensions.

Juvenile courts within the probate court shall have a seal which shall consist of the coat of arms of the state within a circle one and one-fourth inches in diameter and shall be surrounded by the words "juvenile court . . . county."

The seal of other courts exercising the powers and jurisdiction conferred in sections 2151.01 to 2151.54, inclusive, of the Revised Code, shall be attached to all writs and processes.

HISTORY: GC § 1639-9; 117 v 520; Bureau of Code Revision, 10-1-53; 132 v H 164. Eff 12-15-67.

§ 2151.21 Jurisdiction in contempt.

The juvenile court has the same jurisdiction in contempt as courts of common pleas.

HISTORY: GC § 1639-10; 117 v 520; Bureau of Code Revision. Eff 10-1-53.

[§ 2151.21.1] § 2151.211 Employee may not be penalized for being subpoenaed in delinquency case.

No employer shall discharge or terminate from employment, threaten to discharge or terminate from employment, or otherwise punish or penalize any employee because of time lost from regular employment as a result of the employee's attendance at any proceeding in a delinquency case pursuant to a subpoena. This section generally does not require and shall not be construed to require an employer to pay an employee for time lost as a result of attendance at any proceeding in a delinquency case. However, if an employee is subpoenaed to appear at a proceeding in a delinquency case and the proceeding pertains to an offense against the employer or an offense involving the employee during the course of his employment, the employer shall not decrease or withhold the employee's pay for any time lost as a result of compliance with the subpoena. Any employer who knowingly violates this section is in contempt of court.

HISTORY: 140 v S 172. Eff 9-26-84.

§ 2151.22 Terms of court; sessions.

The term of any juvenile or domestic relations court, whether a division of the court of common pleas or an independent court, is one calendar year. All actions and other business pending at the expiration of any term of court is automatically continued without further order. The judge may adjourn court or continue any case whenever, in his opinion, such continuance is warranted.

Sessions of the court may be held at such places throughout the county as the judge shall from time to time determine.

HISTORY: GC § 1639-12; 117 v 520; Bureau of Code Revision, 10-1-53; 136 v H 390. Eff 8-6-76.

§ 2151.23 Jurisdiction of juvenile court.

(A) The juvenile court has exclusive original jurisdiction under the Revised Code as follows:

(1) Concerning any child who on or about the date specified in the complaint is alleged to be a juvenile traffic offender or a delinquent, unruly, abused, neglected, or dependent child;

(2) Subject to division (V) of section 2301.03 of the Revised Code, to determine the custody of any child not a ward of another court of this state;

(3) To hear and determine any application for a writ of habeas corpus involving the custody of a child;

(4) To exercise the powers and jurisdiction given the probate division of the court of common pleas in Chapter 5122. of the Revised Code, if the court has probable cause to believe that a child otherwise within the jurisdiction of the court is a mentally ill person subject to hospitalization by court order, as defined in section 5122.01 of the Revised Code;

(5) To hear and determine all criminal cases charging adults with the violation of any section of this chapter;

(6) To hear and determine all criminal cases in which an adult is charged with a violation of division (C) of section 2919.21, division (B)(1) of section 2919.22, division (B) of section 2919.23, or section 2919.24 of the Revised Code, provided the charge is not included in an indictment that also charges the alleged adult offender with the commission of a felony arising out of the same actions that are the basis of the alleged violation of division (C) of section 2919.21, division (B)(1) of section 2919.22, division (B) of section 2919.23, or section 2919.24 of the Revised Code;

See text of § 3 of HB 161 [127 v 547] following RC § 2151.02.

(7) Under the interstate compact on juveniles in section 2151.56 of the Revised Code;

(8) Concerning any child who is to be taken into custody pursuant to section 2151.31 of the Revised Code, upon being notified of the intent to take the child into custody and the reasons for taking the child into custody;

(9) To hear and determine requests for the extension of temporary custody agreements, and requests for court approval of permanent custody agreements, that are filed pursuant to section 5103.15 of the Revised Code;

(10) To hear and determine applications for consent to marry pursuant to section 3101.04 of the Revised Code;

(11) Subject to division (V) of section 2301.03 of the Revised Code, to hear and determine a request for an order for the support of any child if the request is not ancillary to an action for divorce, dissolution of marriage, annulment, or legal separation, a criminal or civil action involving an allegation of domestic violence, or an action for support brought under Chapter 3115. of the Revised Code;

(12) Concerning an action commenced under section 121.38 of the Revised Code;

(13) Concerning an action commenced under section 2151.55 of the Revised Code.

(B) The juvenile court has original jurisdiction under the Revised Code:

(1) To hear and determine all cases of misdemeanors charging adults with any act or omission with respect to any child, which act or omission is a violation of any state law or any municipal ordinance;

(2) To determine the paternity of any child alleged to have been born out of wedlock pursuant to sections 3111.01 to 3111.19 of the Revised Code;

(3) Under the uniform reciprocal enforcement of support act in Chapter 3115. of the Revised Code;

(4) To hear and determine an application for an order for the support of any child, if the child is not a ward of another court of this state.

(C) The juvenile court, except as to juvenile courts that are a separate division of the court of common pleas or a separate and independent juvenile court, has jurisdiction to hear, determine, and make a record of any action for divorce or legal separation that involves the custody or care of children and that is filed in the court of common pleas and certified by the court of common pleas with all the papers filed in the action to the juvenile court for trial, provided that no certification of that nature shall be made to any juvenile court unless the consent of the juvenile judge first is obtained. After a certification of that nature is made and consent is obtained, the juvenile court shall proceed as if the action originally had been begun in that court, except as to awards for spousal support or support due and unpaid at the time of certification, over which the juvenile court has no jurisdiction.

(D) The juvenile court has jurisdiction to hear and determine all matters as to custody and support of children duly certified by the court of common pleas to the juvenile court after a divorce decree has been granted, including jurisdiction to modify the judgment and decree of the court of common pleas as the same relate to the custody and support of children.

(E) The juvenile court has jurisdiction to hear and determine the case of any child certified to the court by any court of competent jurisdiction if the child comes within the jurisdiction of the juvenile court as defined by this section.

(F)(1) The juvenile court shall exercise its jurisdiction in child custody matters in accordance with sections 3109.04, 3109.21 to 3109.36, and 5103.20 to 5103.28 of the Revised Code.

(2) The juvenile court shall exercise its jurisdiction in child support matters in accordance with section 3109.05 of the Revised Code.

(G)(1) Each order for child support made or modified by a juvenile court on or after December 31, 1993, shall include as part of the order a general provision, as described in division (A)(1) of section 3113.21 of the Revised Code, requiring the withholding or deduction of wages or assets of the obligor under the order as described in division (D) of section 3113.21 of the Revised Code, or another type of appropriate requirement as described in division (D)(6), (D)(7), or (H) of that section, to ensure that withholding or deduction from the wages or assets of the obligor is available from the commencement of the support order for collection of the support and of any arrearages that occur; a statement requiring all parties to the order to notify the child support enforcement agency in writing of their current mailing address, their current residence address, and any changes in either address; and a notice that the requirement to notify the child support enforcement agency of all changes in either address continues until further notice from the court. Any juvenile court that makes or modifies an order for child support on or after April 12, 1990, shall comply with sections 3113.21 to 3113.219 [3113.21.9] of the Revised Code. If any person required to pay child support under an order made by a juvenile court on or after April 15, 1985, or modified on or after December 1, 1986, is found in contempt of court for failure to make support payments under the order, the court that makes the finding, in addition to any other penalty or remedy imposed, shall assess all court costs arising out of the contempt proceeding against the person and require the person to pay any reasonable attorney's fees of any adverse party, as determined by the court, that arose in relation to the act of contempt.

(2) Notwithstanding section 3109.01 of the Revised Code, if a juvenile court issues a child support order under this chapter, the order shall remain in effect beyond the child's eighteenth birthday as long as the child continuously attends on a full-time basis any recog-

nized and accredited high school. Any parent ordered to pay support under a child support order issued under this chapter shall continue to pay support under the order, including during seasonal vacation periods, until the order terminates.

(H) If a child who is charged with an act that would be an offense if committed by an adult was fourteen years of age or older and under eighteen years of age at the time of the alleged act and if the case is transferred for criminal prosecution pursuant to section 2151.26 of the Revised Code, the juvenile court does not have jurisdiction to hear or determine the case subsequent to the transfer. The court to which the case is transferred for criminal prosecution pursuant to that section has jurisdiction subsequent to the transfer to hear and determine the case in the same manner as if the case originally had been commenced in that court, including, but not limited to, jurisdiction to accept a plea of guilty or another plea authorized by Criminal Rule 11 or another section of the Revised Code and jurisdiction to accept a verdict and to enter a judgment of conviction pursuant to the Rules of Criminal Procedure against the child for the commission of the offense that was the basis of the transfer of the case for criminal prosecution, whether the conviction is for the same degree or a lesser degree of the offense charged, for the commission of a lesser-included offense, or for the commission of another offense that is different from the offense charged.

(I) If a person under eighteen years of age allegedly commits an act that would be a felony if committed by an adult and if the person is not taken into custody or apprehended for that act until after the person attains twenty-one years of age, the juvenile court does not have jurisdiction to hear or determine any portion of the case charging the person with committing that act. In those circumstances, divisions (B) and (C) of section 2151.26 of the Revised Code do not apply regarding the act, the case charging the person with committing the act shall be a criminal prosecution commenced and heard in the appropriate court having jurisdiction of the offense as if the person had been eighteen years of age or older when the person committed the act, all proceedings pertaining to the act shall be within the jurisdiction of the court having jurisdiction of the offense, and the court having jurisdiction of the offense has all the authority and duties in the case as it has in other criminal cases commenced in that court.

HISTORY: 133 v H 320 (Eff 11-19-69); 133 v H 931 (Eff 8-27-70); 136 v H 85 (Eff 11-28-75); 136 v H 244 (Eff 8-26-76); 137 v S 135 (Eff 10-25-77); 139 v H 1 (Eff 8-5-81); 139 v H 515 (Eff 6-1-82); 140 v H 93 (Eff 3-19-84); 140 v H 614 (Eff 4-10-85); 141 v H 509 (Eff 12-1-86); 141 v H 476 (Eff 9-24-86); 141 v H 428 (Eff 12-23-86); 142 v S 89 (Eff 1-1-89); 143 v H 591 (Eff 4-12-90); 143 v H 514 (Eff 1-1-91); 143 v S 258 (Eff 8-22-90); 143 v S 3 (Eff 4-11-91); 144 v S 10 (Eff 7-15-92); 145 v S 21 (Eff 10-29-93); 145 v H 173 (Eff 12-31-93); 146 v H 1 (Eff 1-1-96); 146 v S 269 (Eff 7-1-96); 146 v H 274 (Eff 8-8-96); 146 v H 377 (Eff 10-17-96); 146 v H 124 (Eff 3-31-97); 147 v H 215. Eff 6-30-97.

Analogous in part to former RC § 2151.23 (GC § 1639-16; 117 v 520; 121 v 557; Bureau of Code Revision, 10-1-53; 127 v 547; 130 v 620), repealed, 133 v H 320, eff 11-19-69.

[§ 2151.23.1] § 2151.231 Child support order without regard to marital status of parents.

The parent, guardian, or custodian of a child, the person with whom a child resides, or the child support enforcement agency of the county in which the child, parent, guardian, or custodian of the child resides may bring an action in a juvenile court under this section requesting the court to issue an order requiring a parent of the child to pay an amount for the support of the child without regard to the marital status of the child's parents.

The parties to an action under this section may raise the issue of the existence or nonexistence of a parent-child relationship, unless a final and enforceable determination of the issue has been made with respect to the parties pursuant to Chapter 3111. of the Revised Code. If a complaint is filed under this section and an issue concerning the existence or nonexistence of a parent-child relationship is raised, the court shall treat the action as an action pursuant to sections 3111.01 to 3111.19 of the Revised Code. An order issued in an action under this section does not preclude a party to the action from bringing a subsequent action pursuant to sections 3111.01 to 3111.19 of the Revised Code if the issue concerning the existence or nonexistence of the parent-child relationship was not determined with respect to the party. An order issued pursuant to this section shall remain effective until an order is issued pursuant to sections 3111.01 to 3111.19 of the Revised Code that a parent-child relationship does not exist between the alleged father of the child and the child or until the occurrence of an event described in division (G)(4)(a) of section 3113.21 of the Revised Code that would require the order to terminate.

HISTORY: 144 v S 10 (Eff 7-15-92); 146 v H 167. Eff 6-11-96.†

† The effective date of HB 167 is changed from 11-15-96 to 6-11-96 by section 7 of HB 710 (146 v —), effective 6-11-96.

§ 2151.24 Separate room for hearings.

The board of county commissioners shall provide a special room not used for the trial of criminal or adult cases, when available, for the hearing of the cases of dependent, neglected, abused, and delinquent children.

HISTORY: GC § 1639-14; 117 v 520; Bureau of Code Revision, 10-1-53; 136 v H 85. Eff 11-28-75.

[PROCEDURE IN CHILDREN'S CASES]

§ 2151.25 Case to be initiated in or transferred to juvenile court.

When a child is arrested under any charge, complaint,

affidavit, or indictment for a felony or a misdemeanor, proceedings regarding the child initially shall be in the juvenile court in accordance with this chapter. If the child is taken before a judge of a county court, a mayor, a judge of a municipal court, or a judge of a court of common pleas other than a juvenile court, the judge of the county court, mayor, judge of the municipal court, or judge of the court of common pleas shall transfer the case to the juvenile court, and, upon the transfer, the proceedings shall be in accordance with this chapter. Upon the transfer, all further proceedings under the charge, complaint, information, or indictment shall be discontinued in the court of the judge of the county court, mayor, municipal judge, or judge of the court of common pleas other than a juvenile court subject to section 2151.26 of the Revised Code, and the case relating to the child then shall be within the exclusive jurisdiction of the juvenile court subject to section 2151.26 of the Revised Code.

HISTORY: GC § 1639-29; 117 v 520; 121 v 557; Bureau of Code Revision, 10-1-53; 129 v 582 (738) (Eff 1-10-61); 133 v H 320 (Eff 11-19-69); 136 v H 205 (Eff 1-1-76); 146 v H 1. Eff 1-1-96.

The effective date is set by section 6 of HB 1.

§ 2151.26 Transfer of case for criminal prosecution.

(A) As used in this section:
(1) "Category one offense" means any of the following:
(a) A violation of section 2903.01 or 2903.02 of the Revised Code;
(b) A violation of section 2923.02 of the Revised Code involving an attempt to commit aggravated murder or murder.
(2) "Category two offense" means any of the following:
(a) A violation of section 2903.03, 2905.01, 2907.02, 2909.02, 2911.01, or 2911.11 of the Revised Code;
(b) A violation of section 2903.04 of the Revised Code that is a felony of the first degree;
(c) A violation of section 2907.12 of the Revised Code as it existed prior to September 3, 1996.
(3) "Firearm" has the same meaning as in section 2923.11 of the Revised Code.
(4) "Act charged" means the act that a child allegedly committed and that is identified in a complaint alleging that the child is a delinquent child as the act that is the basis of the child being a delinquent child.
(B) After a complaint has been filed alleging that a child is a delinquent child for committing an act that would be an offense if committed by an adult, the court at a hearing shall transfer the case for criminal prosecution to the appropriate court having jurisdiction of the offense if the child was fourteen years of age or older at the time of the act charged, if there is probable cause to believe that the child committed the act charged, and if one or more of the following applies to the child or the act charged:
(1) A complaint previously was filed in a juvenile court alleging that the child was a delinquent child for committing an act that would be an offense if committed by an adult, the juvenile court transferred the case pursuant to division (B) or (C) of this section for criminal prosecution to the appropriate court having jurisdiction of the offense, and the child was convicted of or pleaded guilty to a felony in that case.
(2) The child is domiciled in another state, and, if the act charged had been committed in that other state, the child would be subject to criminal prosecution as an adult under the law of that other state without the need for a transfer of jurisdiction from a juvenile, family, or similar noncriminal court to a criminal court.
(3) The act charged is a category one offense, and either or both of the following apply to the child:
(a) The child was sixteen years of age or older at the time of the act charged.
(b) The child previously was adjudicated a delinquent child for committing an act that is a category one offense or a category two offense and was committed to the legal custody of the department of youth services upon the basis of that adjudication.
(4) The act charged is a category two offense, other than a violation of section 2905.01 of the Revised Code, the child was sixteen years of age or older at the time of the commission of the act charged, and either or both of the following apply to the child:
(a) The child previously was adjudicated a delinquent child for committing an act that is a category one offense or a category two offense and was committed to the legal custody of the department of youth services upon the basis of that adjudication.
(b) The child is alleged to have had a firearm on or about the child's person or under the child's control while committing the act charged and to have displayed the firearm, brandished the firearm, indicated possession of the firearm, or used the firearm to facilitate the commission of the act charged.
(C)(1) Except as provided in division (B) of this section and subject to division (C)(4) of this section, after a complaint has been filed alleging that a child is a delinquent child for committing an act that would be a felony if committed by an adult, the court at a hearing may transfer the case for criminal prosecution to the appropriate court having jurisdiction of the offense, after considering the factors specified in division (C)(2) of this section and after making all of the following determinations:
(a) The child was fourteen years of age or older at the time of the act charged.
(b) There is probable cause to believe that the child committed the act charged.
(c) After an investigation, including a mental examination of the child made by a public or private agency or a person qualified to make the examination, and after

consideration of all relevant information and factors, including any factor required to be considered under division (C)(2) of this section, that there are reasonable grounds to believe that both of the following criteria are satisfied:

(i) The child is not amenable to care or rehabilitation or further care or rehabilitation in any facility designed for the care, supervision, and rehabilitation of delinquent children.

(ii) The safety of the community may require that the child be placed under legal restraint, including, if necessary, for the period extending beyond the child's majority.

(2) Subject to division (C)(4) of this section, when determining whether to order the transfer of a case for criminal prosecution to the appropriate court having jurisdiction of the offense pursuant to division (C)(1) of this section, the court shall consider all of the following factors in favor of ordering the transfer of the case:

(a) A victim of the act charged was five years of age or younger, regardless of whether the child who is alleged to have committed that act knew the age of that victim;

(b) A victim of the act charged sustained physical harm to the victim's person during the commission of or otherwise as a result of the act charged.

(c) The act charged is not a violation of section 2923.12 of the Revised Code, and the child is alleged to have had a firearm on or about the child's person or under the child's control while committing the act charged and to have displayed the firearm, brandished the firearm, indicated possession of the firearm, or used the firearm to facilitate the commission of the act charged.

(d) The child has a history indicating a failure to be rehabilitated following one or more commitments pursuant to division (A)(3), (4), (5), (6), or (7) of section 2151.355 [2151.35.5] of the Revised Code.

(e) A victim of the act charged was sixty-five years of age or older or permanently and totally disabled at the time of the commission of the act charged, regardless of whether the child who is alleged to have committed that act knew the age of that victim.

(3) A child whose case is being considered for possible transfer for criminal prosecution to the appropriate court having jurisdiction of the offense under division (C)(1) of this section may waive the examination required by division (C)(1)(c) of this section, if the court finds the waiver is competently and intelligently made. Refusal to submit to a mental and physical examination by the child constitutes a waiver of the examination.

(4) If one or more complaints are filed alleging that a child is a delinquent child for committing two or more acts that would be offenses if committed by an adult, if a motion is filed or made alleging that division (B)(2), (3), or (4) of this section applies and requires that the case or cases involving one or more of the acts charged be transferred for criminal prosecution to the appropriate court having jurisdiction over the offense, and if a motion also is filed or made requesting that the case or cases involving one or more of the acts charged be transferred for criminal prosecution to the appropriate court having jurisdiction of the offense pursuant to division (C)(1) of this section, the court, in deciding the motions, shall proceed in the following manner:

(a) Initially, the court shall decide the motion alleging that division (B)(2), (3), or (4) of this section applies and requires that the case or cases involving one or more of the acts charged be transferred for criminal prosecution to the appropriate court having jurisdiction over the offense.

(b) If, pursuant to division (C)(4)(a) of this section, the court determines that division (B)(2), (3), or (4) of this section applies and requires that the case or cases involving one or more of the acts charged be transferred for criminal prosecution to the appropriate court having jurisdiction over the offense, the court shall transfer the case or cases in accordance with the applicable division. After the transfer pursuant to division (B)(2), (3), or (4) of this section, the court shall decide, in accordance with division (C)(4)(b) of this section, whether to grant the motion requesting that the case or cases involving one or more of the acts charged be transferred for criminal prosecution to the appropriate court having jurisdiction of the offense pursuant to division (C)(1) of this section. In making its decision regarding the motion requesting a transfer pursuant to division (C)(1) of this section, the court at a hearing may transfer the subject case to the appropriate court having jurisdiction of the offense if the act charged in the case would be a felony if committed by an adult, if the child was fourteen years of age or older at the time of the act charged, and if there is probable cause to believe that the child committed the act charged. Notwithstanding divisions (C)(1) to (3) of this section, prior to transferring a case pursuant to division (C)(4)(b) of this section, the court is not required to consider any factor specified in division (C)(2) of this section or to conduct an investigation or make a determination of the type described in division (C)(1)(c) of this section.

(c) If the court determines pursuant to division (C)(4)(a) of this section, that divisions (B)(2), (3), and (4) of this section do not apply and that none of those divisions requires that the case or cases involving one or more of the acts charged be transferred for criminal prosecution to the appropriate court having jurisdiction over the offense, the court shall decide in accordance with divisions (C)(1) to (3) of this section whether to grant the motion requesting that the case or cases involving one or more of the acts charged be transferred for criminal prosecution to the appropriate court having jurisdiction of the offense pursuant to division (C)(1) of this section.

(D) The court shall give notice in writing of the time, place, and purpose of any hearing held pursuant to division (B) or (C) of this section to the child's parents, guardian, or other custodian and to the child's counsel at least three days prior to the hearing.

(E) No person, either before or after reaching eighteen years of age, shall be prosecuted as an adult for an offense committed prior to becoming eighteen years of age, unless the person has been transferred as provided in division (B) or (C) of this section or unless division (G) of this section applies. Any prosecution that is had in a criminal court on the mistaken belief that the person who is the subject of the case was eighteen years of age or older at the time of the commission of the offense shall be deemed a nullity, and the person shall not be considered to have been in jeopardy on the offense.

(F) Upon the transfer of a case for criminal prosecution to the appropriate court having jurisdiction of the offense under division (B) or (C) of this section, the juvenile court shall state the reasons for the transfer and order the child to enter into a recognizance with good and sufficient surety for the child's appearance before the appropriate court for any disposition that the court is authorized to make for a similar act committed by an adult. The transfer abates the jurisdiction of the juvenile court with respect to the delinquent acts alleged in the complaint, and, upon the transfer, all further proceedings pertaining to the act charged shall be discontinued in the juvenile court, and the case then shall be within the jurisdiction of the court to which it is transferred as described in division (H) of section 2151.23 of the Revised Code.

(G) If a person under eighteen years of age allegedly commits an act that would be a felony if committed by an adult and if the person is not taken into custody or apprehended for that act until after the person attains twenty-one years of age, the juvenile court does not have jurisdiction to hear or determine any portion of the case charging the person with committing that act, divisions (B) and (C) of this section do not apply regarding that act, the case charging the person with committing that act shall be a criminal prosecution commenced and heard in the appropriate court having jurisdiction of the offense as if the person had been eighteen years of age or older when the person committed that act, all proceedings pertaining to that act shall be within the jurisdiction of the court having jurisdiction of the offense, and the court having jurisdiction of the offense has all the authority and duties in the case as it has in other criminal cases commenced in that court.

HISTORY: 133 v H 320 (Eff 11-19-69); 134 v S 325 (Eff 1-14-72); 137 v S 119 (Eff 8-30-78); 139 v H 440 (Eff 11-23-81); 140 v S 210 (Eff 7-1-83); 141 v H 499 (Eff 3-11-87); 144 v H 27 (Eff 10-10-91); 146 v H 1 (Eff 1-1-96); 146 v S 2 (Eff 7-1-96); 146 v S 269 (Eff 7-1-96); 146 v H 124. Eff 3-31-97.

Analogous in part to former RC § 2151.26 (GC § 1639-32; 117 v 520; Bureau of Code Revision, 10-1-53; 132 v H 343), repealed 133 v H 320, eff 11-19-69.

The provisions of § 3 of HB 1 (146 v —) read as follows:

SECTION 3. (A) The General Assembly hereby declares that its purpose in enacting the language of division (A)(2) of section 2151.18 and division (D)(2) of section 2151.355 of the Revised Code that exists on and after the effective date of this act is to recognize the holding of the Supreme Court in *In re Russell* (1984), 12 Ohio St. 3d 304.

(B) The General Assembly hereby declares that its purpose in enacting the language in division (B) of section 2151.011 and divisions (B) and (C) of section 2151.26 of the Revised Code that exists on and after the effective date of this act is to overrule the holding in *State v. Adams* (1982), 69 Ohio St. 2d 120, regarding the effect of binding a child over for trial as an adult.

(C) The amendments made by this act to section 2151.358 of the Revised Code apply to persons who were adjudicated juvenile traffic offenders or charged with being juvenile traffic offenders prior to the effective date of this act, regardless of their age on that date. A person who was adjudicated a juvenile traffic offender or charged with being a juvenile traffic offender prior to the effective date of this act may file an application in accordance with division (D) or (F) of section 2151.358 of the Revised Code on or after the effective date of this act for the sealing of the record of the person's adjudication as a juvenile traffic offender or the expungement of the record of the case in which the person was adjudicated not guilty of being a juvenile traffic offender or the charges of being a juvenile traffic offender were dismissed, and the juvenile court involved shall proceed with a hearing on the application in accordance with division (D) or (F) of that section. A juvenile court is not required to send the notice described in division (C)(1)(b) of section 2151.358 of the Revised Code to a person who was adjudicated a juvenile traffic offender prior to the effective date of this act if, on the effective date of this act, more than ninety days has expired after the expiration of the two-year period described in division (C)(1) of section 2151.358 of the Revised Code.

§ 2151.27 Complaint.

(A) Any person having knowledge of a child who appears to be a juvenile traffic offender or to be a delinquent, unruly, abused, neglected, or dependent child may file a sworn complaint with respect to that child in the juvenile court of the county in which the child has a residence or legal settlement or in which the traffic offense, delinquency, unruliness, abuse, neglect, or dependency allegedly occurred. If an alleged abused, neglected, or dependent child is taken into custody pursuant to division (D) of section 2151.31 of the Revised Code or is taken into custody pursuant to division (A) of section 2151.31 of the Revised Code without the filing of a complaint and placed into shelter care pursuant to division (C) of that section, a sworn complaint shall be filed with respect to the child before the end of the next day after the day on which the child was taken into custody. The sworn complaint may be upon information and belief, and, in addition to the allegation that the child is a delinquent, unruly, abused, neglected, or dependent child or a juvenile traffic offender, the complaint shall allege the particular facts upon which the allegation that the child is a delinquent, unruly, abused, neglected, or dependent child or a juvenile traffic offender is based.

(B) If a child, before arriving at the age of eighteen years, allegedly commits an act for which the child may be adjudicated a delinquent child, an unruly child, or a juvenile traffic offender and if the specific complaint alleging the act is not filed or a hearing on that specific complaint is not held until after the child arrives at the age of eighteen years, the court has jurisdiction to hear and dispose of the complaint as if the complaint were filed and the hearing held before the child arrived at the age of eighteen years.

(C) If the complainant in a case in which a child is alleged to be an abused, neglected, or dependent child desires permanent custody of the child or children, temporary custody of the child or children, whether as the preferred or an alternative disposition, or the placement of the child in long-term foster care, the complaint shall contain a prayer specifically requesting permanent custody, temporary custody, or the placement of the child in long-term foster care.

(D) For purposes of the record to be maintained by the clerk under division (B) of section 2151.18 of the Revised Code, when a complaint is filed that alleges that a child is a delinquent child, the court shall determine if the victim of the alleged delinquent act was sixty-five years of age or older or permanently and totally disabled at the time of the alleged commission of the act.

(E) Any person with standing under applicable law may file a complaint for the determination of any other matter over which the juvenile court is given jurisdiction by section 2151.23 of the Revised Code. The complaint shall be filed in the county in which the child who is the subject of the complaint is found or was last known to be found.

(F) Within ten days after the filing of a complaint, the court shall give written notice of the filing of the complaint and of the substance of the complaint to the superintendent of a city, local, exempted village, or joint vocational school district if the complaint alleges that a child committed an act that would be a criminal offense if committed by an adult, that the child was sixteen years of age or older at the time of the commission of the alleged act, and that the alleged act is any of the following:

(1) A violation of section 2923.122 [2923.12.2] of the Revised Code that relates to property owned or controlled by, or to an activity held under the auspices of, the board of education of that school district;

(2) A violation of section 2923.12 of the Revised Code, of a substantially similar municipal ordinance, or of section 2925.03 of the Revised Code that was committed on property owned or controlled by, or at an activity held under the auspices of, the board of education of that school district;

(3) A violation of section 2925.11 of the Revised Code that was committed on property owned or controlled by, or at an activity held under the auspices of, the board of education of that school district, other than a violation of that section that would be a minor drug possession offense, as defined in section 2925.01 of the Revised Code, if committed by an adult;

(4) A violation of section 2903.01, 2903.02, 2903.03, 2903.04, 2903.11, 2903.12, 2907.02, or 2907.05 of the Revised Code, or a violation of former section 2907.12 of the Revised Code, that was committed on property owned or controlled by, or at an activity held under the auspices of, the board of education of that school district, if the victim at the time of the commission of the alleged act was an employee of the board of education of that school district.

(5) Complicity in any violation described in division (F)(1), (2), (3), or (4) of this section that was alleged to have been committed in the manner described in division (F)(1), (2), (3), or (4) of this section, regardless of whether the act of complicity was committed on property owned or controlled by, or at an activity held under the auspices of, the board of education of that school district.

(G) A public children services agency, acting pursuant to a complaint or an action on a complaint filed under this section, is not subject to the requirements of section 3109.27 of the Revised Code.

HISTORY: 133 v H 320 (Eff 11-19-69); 136 v H 85 (Eff 11-28-75); 140 v S 5 (Eff 9-26-84); 142 v S 89 (Eff 1-1-89); 144 v H 154 (Eff 7-31-92); 146 v H 2 (Eff 7-1-96); 146 v H 274, §§ 1, 4 (Eff 8-8-96); 146 v H 445. Eff 9-3-96.

Analogous in part to former RC § 2151.27 (GC § 1639-23; 117 v 520; 121 v 557; Bureau of Code Revision, 10-1-53; 127 v 547), repealed 133 v H 320, eff 11-19-69.

Comment, Legislative Service Commission

Sections ° ° ° 2151.86, ° ° ° of the Revised Code are amended by this act [Am. Sub. H.B. 445] and also by Am. Sub. S.B. 269 of the 121st General Assembly. Section 2151.27 of the Revised Code is amended by this act [Am. Sub. H.B. 445] and also by Sub. H.B. 274 of the 121st General Assembly (effective August 8, 1996). Section 2151.355 of the Revised Code is amended by this act [Am. Sub. H.B. 445] and also by Sub. H.B. 274 (effective August 8, 1996) and Am. Sub. S.B. 269, both of the 121st General Assembly. ° ° ° Comparison of these amendments in pursuance of section 1.52 of the Revised Code discloses that they are not irreconcilable so that they are required by that section to be harmonized to give effect to each amendment.

[§ 2151.27.1] § 2151.271 Transfer to juvenile court of another county.

If the child resides in a county of the state and the proceeding is commenced in a juvenile court of another county, that court, on its own motion or a motion of a party, may transfer the proceeding to the county of the child's residence upon the filing of the complaint or after the adjudicatory, or dispositional hearing, for such further proceeding as required. The court of the child's residence shall then proceed as if the original complaint had been filed in that court. Transfer may also be made if the residence of the child changes. The proceeding shall be so transferred if other proceedings involving the child are pending in the juvenile court of the county of his residence.

Whenever a case is transferred to the county of the child's residence and it appears to the court of that county that the interests of justice and the convenience of the parties requires that the adjudicatory hearing be had in the county wherein the complaint was filed, the court may return the proceeding to the county wherein the complaint was filed for the purpose of such adjudicatory hearing. The court may thereafter proceed as to the transfer to the county of the child's legal residence as provided in this section.

Certified copies of all legal and social records pertaining to the case shall accompany the transfer.

HISTORY: 133 v H 320. Eff 11-19-69.

§ 2151.28 Adjudicatory hearing; shelter care determination; summons.

(A) No later than seventy-two hours after the complaint is filed, the court shall fix a time for an adjudicatory hearing. The court shall conduct the adjudicatory hearing within one of the following periods of time:

(1) If the complaint alleged that the child is a delinquent or unruly child or a juvenile traffic offender, the adjudicatory hearing shall be held and may be continued in accordance with the Juvenile Rules.

(2) If the complaint alleged that the child is an abused, neglected, or dependent child, the adjudicatory hearing shall be held no later than thirty days after the complaint is filed, except that, for good cause shown, the court may continue the adjudicatory hearing for either of the following periods of time:

(a) For ten days beyond the thirty-day deadline to allow any party to obtain counsel;

(b) For a reasonable period of time beyond the thirty-day deadline to obtain service on all parties or any necessary evaluation, except that the adjudicatory hearing shall not be held later than sixty days after the date on which the complaint was filed.

(B) At an adjudicatory hearing held pursuant to division (A)(2) of this section, the court, in addition to determining whether the child is an abused, neglected, or dependent child, shall determine whether the child should remain or be placed in shelter care until the dispositional hearing. When the court makes the shelter care determination, all of the following apply:

(1) The court shall determine whether there are any relatives of the child who are willing to be temporary custodians of the child. If any relative is willing to be a temporary custodian, the child otherwise would remain or be placed in shelter care, and the appointment is appropriate, the court shall appoint the relative as temporary custodian of the child, unless the court appoints another relative as custodian. If it determines that the appointment of a relative as custodian would not be appropriate, it shall issue a written opinion setting forth the reasons for its determination and give a copy of the opinion to all parties and the guardian ad litem of the child.

The court's consideration of a relative for appointment as a temporary custodian does not make that relative a party to the proceedings.

(2) The court shall make the determination and issue the written finding of facts required by section 2151.419 [2151.41.9] of the Revised Code.

(3) The court shall schedule the date for the dispositional hearing to be held pursuant to section 2151.35 of the Revised Code. The parents of the child have a right to be represented by counsel; however, in no case shall the dispositional hearing be held later than ninety days after the date on which the complaint was filed.

(C) The court shall direct the issuance of a summons directed to the child except as provided by this section, the parents, guardian, custodian, or other person with whom the child may be and any other persons that appear to the court to be proper or necessary parties to the proceedings, requiring them to appear before the court at the time fixed to answer the allegations of the complaint. The summons shall contain the name and telephone number of the court employee designated by the court pursuant to section 2151.314 [2151.31.4] of the Revised Code to arrange for the prompt appointment of counsel for indigent persons. A child alleged to be an abused, neglected, or dependent child shall not be summoned unless the court so directs. A summons issued for a child who is under fourteen years of age and who is alleged to be a delinquent child, unruly child, or a juvenile traffic offender shall be served on the parent, guardian, or custodian of the child in the child's behalf.

If the person who has physical custody of the child, or with whom the child resides, is other than the parent or guardian, then the parents and guardian also shall be summoned. A copy of the complaint shall accompany the summons.

(D) If the complaint contains a prayer for permanent custody, temporary custody, whether as the preferred or an alternative disposition, or long-term foster care in a case involving an alleged abused, neglected, or dependent child, the summons served on the parents shall contain as is appropriate an explanation that the granting of permanent custody permanently divests the parents of their parental rights and privileges, an explanation that an adjudication that the child is an abused, neglected, or dependent child may result in an order of temporary custody that will cause the removal of the child from their legal custody until the court terminates the order of temporary custody or permanently divests the parents of their parental rights, or an explanation that the issuance of an order for long-term foster care will cause the removal of the child from the legal custody of the parents if any of the conditions listed in divisions (A)(5)(a) to (c) of section 2151.353 [2151.35.3] of the Revised Code are found to exist.

(E) The court may endorse upon the summons an

order directing the parents, guardian, or other person with whom the child may be to appear personally at the hearing and directing the person having the physical custody or control of the child to bring the child to the hearing.

(F)(1) The summons shall contain a statement advising that any party is entitled to counsel in the proceedings and that the court will appoint counsel or designate a county public defender or joint county public defender to provide legal representation if the party is indigent.

(2) In cases in which the complaint alleges a child to be an abused, neglected, or dependent child and no hearing has been conducted pursuant to division (A) of section 2151.314 [2151.31.4] of the Revised Code with respect to the child or a parent, guardian, or custodian of the child does not attend the hearing, the summons also shall contain a statement advising that a case plan may be prepared for the child, the general requirements usually contained in case plans, and the possible consequences of failure to comply with a journalized case plan.

(G) If it appears from an affidavit filed or from sworn testimony before the court that the conduct, condition, or surroundings of the child are endangering the child's health or welfare or those of others, that the child may abscond or be removed from the jurisdiction of the court, or that the child will not be brought to the court, notwithstanding the service of the summons, the court may endorse upon the summons an order that a law enforcement officer serve the summons and take the child into immediate custody and bring the child forthwith to the court.

(H) A party, other than the child, may waive service of summons by written stipulation.

(I) Before any temporary commitment is made permanent, the court shall fix a time for hearing in accordance with section 2151.414 [2151.41.4] of the Revised Code and shall cause notice by summons to be served upon the parent or guardian of the child and the guardian ad litem of the child, or published, as provided in section 2151.29 of the Revised Code. The summons shall contain an explanation that the granting of permanent custody permanently divests the parents of their parental rights and privileges.

(J) Any person whose presence is considered necessary and who is not summoned may be subpoenaed to appear and testify at the hearing. Any one summoned or subpoenaed to appear who fails to do so may be punished, as in other cases in the court of common pleas, for contempt of court. Persons subpoenaed shall be paid the same witness fees as are allowed in the court of common pleas.

(K) The failure of the court to hold an adjudicatory hearing within any time period set forth in division (A)(2) of this section does not affect the ability of the court to issue any order under this chapter and does not provide any basis for attacking the jurisdiction of the court or the validity of any order of the court.

(L) If the court, at an adjudicatory hearing held pursuant to division (A) of this section upon a complaint alleging that a child is an abused, neglected, dependent, delinquent, or unruly child or a juvenile traffic offender, determines that the child is a dependent child, the court shall incorporate that determination into written findings of fact and conclusions of law and enter those findings of fact and conclusions of law in the record of the case. The court shall include in those findings of fact and conclusions of law specific findings as to the existence of any danger to the child and any underlying family problems that are the basis for the court's determination that the child is a dependent child.

HISTORY: 133 v H 320 (Eff 11-19-69); 136 v H 85 (Eff 11-28-75); 136 v H 164 (Eff 1-13-76); 142 v S 89 (Eff 1-1-89); 146 v H 274 (Eff 8-8-96); 146 v H 419. Eff 9-18-96.

Analogous in part to former RC § 2151.28 (GC § 1639-24; 117 v 520; 121 v 557; Bureau of Code Revision, 10-1-53), repealed 133 v H 320, eff 11-19-69.

[§ 2151.28.1] § 2151.281 Guardian ad litem.

(A) The court shall appoint a guardian ad litem to protect the interest of a child in any proceeding concerning an alleged or adjudicated delinquent child or unruly child when either of the following applies:

(1) The child has no parent, guardian, or legal custodian.

(2) The court finds that there is a conflict of interest between the child and the child's parent, guardian, or legal custodian.

(B)(1) The court shall appoint a guardian ad litem to protect the interest of a child in any proceeding concerning an alleged abused or neglected child and in any proceeding held pursuant to section 2151.414 [2151.41.4] of the Revised Code. The guardian ad litem so appointed shall not be the attorney responsible for presenting the evidence alleging that the child is an abused or neglected child and shall not be an employee of any party in the proceeding.

(2) The guardian ad litem appointed for an alleged or adjudicated abused or neglected child may bring a civil action against any person, who is required by division (A)(1) of section 2151.421 [2151.42.1] of the Revised Code to file a report of known or suspected child abuse or child neglect, if that person knows or suspects that the child for whom the guardian ad litem is appointed is the subject of child abuse or child neglect and does not file the required report and if the child suffers any injury or harm as a result of the known or suspected child abuse or child neglect or suffers additional injury or harm after the failure to file the report.

(C) In any proceeding concerning an alleged or adjudicated delinquent, unruly, abused, neglected, or dependent child in which the parent appears to be mentally incompetent or is under eighteen years of age, the court shall appoint a guardian ad litem to protect the interest of that parent.

(D) The court shall require the guardian ad litem to faithfully discharge the guardian ad litem's duties and, upon the guardian ad litem's failure to faithfully discharge the guardian ad litem's duties, shall discharge the guardian ad litem and appoint another guardian ad litem. The court may fix the compensation for the service of the guardian ad litem, which compensation shall be paid from the treasury of the county.

(E) A parent who is eighteen years of age or older and not mentally incompetent shall be deemed sui juris for the purpose of any proceeding relative to a child of the parent who is alleged or adjudicated to be an abused, neglected, or dependent child.

(F) In any case in which a parent of a child alleged or adjudicated to be an abused, neglected, or dependent child is under eighteen years of age, the parents of that parent shall be summoned to appear at any hearing respecting the child, who is alleged or adjudicated to be an abused, neglected, or dependent child.

(G) In any case involving an alleged or adjudicated abused or neglected child or an agreement for the voluntary surrender of temporary or permanent custody of a child that is made in accordance with section 5103.15 of the Revised Code, the court shall appoint the guardian ad litem in each case as soon as possible after the complaint is filed, the request for an extension of the temporary custody agreement is filed with the court, or the request for court approval of the permanent custody agreement is filed. In any case involving an alleged dependent child in which the parent of the child appears to be mentally incompetent or is under eighteen years of age, there is a conflict of interest between the child and the child's parents, guardian, or custodian, or the court believes that the parent of the child is not capable of representing the best interest of the child, the court shall appoint a guardian ad litem for the child. The guardian ad litem or the guardian ad litem's replacement shall continue to serve until any of the following occur:

(1) The complaint is dismissed or the request for an extension of a temporary custody agreement or for court approval of the permanent custody agreement is withdrawn or denied;

(2) All dispositional orders relative to the child have terminated;

(3) The legal custody of the child is granted to a relative of the child, or to another person;

(4) The child is placed in an adoptive home or, at the court's discretion, a final decree of adoption is issued with respect to the child;

(5) The child reaches the age of eighteen if the child is not mentally retarded, developmentally disabled, or physically impaired or the child reaches the age of twenty-one if the child is mentally retarded, developmentally disabled, or physically impaired;

(6) The guardian ad litem resigns or is removed by the court and a replacement is appointed by the court.

If a guardian ad litem ceases to serve a child pursuant to division (G)(4) of this section and the petition for adoption with respect to the child is denied or withdrawn prior to the issuance of a final decree of adoption or prior to the date an interlocutory order of adoption becomes final, the juvenile court shall reappoint a guardian ad litem for that child. The public children services agency or private child placing agency with permanent custody of the child shall notify the juvenile court if the petition for adoption is denied or withdrawn.

(H) If the guardian ad litem for an alleged or adjudicated abused, neglected, or dependent child is an attorney admitted to the practice of law in this state, the guardian ad litem also may serve as counsel to the ward. If a person is serving as guardian ad litem and counsel for a child and either that person or the court finds that a conflict may exist between the person's roles as guardian ad litem and as counsel, the court shall relieve the person of duties as guardian ad litem and appoint someone else as guardian ad litem for the child. If the court appoints a person who is not an attorney admitted to the practice of law in this state to be a guardian ad litem, the court also may appoint an attorney admitted to the practice of law in this state to serve as counsel for the guardian ad litem.

(I) The guardian ad litem for an alleged or adjudicated abused, neglected, or dependent child shall perform whatever functions are necessary to protect the best interest of the child, including, but not limited to, investigation, mediation, monitoring court proceedings, and monitoring the services provided the child by the public children services agency or private child placing agency that has temporary or permanent custody of the child, and shall file any motions and other court papers that are in the best interest of the child.

The guardian ad litem shall be given notice of all hearings, administrative reviews, and other proceedings in the same manner as notice is given to parties to the action.

(J)(1) When the court appoints a guardian ad litem pursuant to this section, it shall appoint a qualified volunteer whenever one is available and the appointment is appropriate.

(2) Upon request, the department of human services shall provide for the training of volunteer guardians ad litem.

HISTORY: 133 v H 320 (Eff 11-19-69); 136 v H 85 (Eff 11-28-75); 138 v H 695 (Eff 10-24-80); 140 v S 321 (Eff 4-9-85); 141 v H 529 (Eff 3-11-87); 142 v S 89 (Eff 1-1-89); 146 v H 274 (Eff 8-8-96); 146 v H 419. Eff 9-18-96.

The provisions of § 12 of HB 274 (146 v —) read as follows:

SECTION 12. Section 2151.281 of the Revised Code as amended by this act shall take effect the earliest time permitted by law, but division (G)(4) and the last unnumbered paragraph of division (G) of the section as amended or added by Am. Sub. H.B. 419 of the 121st General Assembly shall not be applied until the later of the earliest time permitted by law or September 18, 1996.

§ 2151.29 Service of summons.

Service of summons, notices, and subpoenas, prescribed by section 2151.28 of the Revised Code, shall be made by delivering a copy to the person summoned, notified, or subpoenaed, or by leaving a copy at his usual place of residence. If the juvenile judge is satisfied that such service is impracticable, he may order service by registered or certified mail. If the person to be served is without the state but he can be found or his address is known, or his whereabouts or address can with reasonable diligence be ascertained, service of the summons may be made by delivering a copy to him personally or mailing a copy to him by registered or certified mail.

Whenever it appears by affidavit that after reasonable effort the person to be served with summons cannot be found or his post-office address ascertained, whether he is within or without a state, the clerk shall publish such summons once in a newspaper of general circulation throughout the county. The summons shall state the substance and the time and place of the hearing, which shall be held at least one week later than the date of the publication. A copy of the summons and the complaint shall be sent by registered or certified mail to the last known address of the person summoned unless it is shown by affidavit that a reasonable effort has been made, without success, to obtain such address.

A copy of the advertisement, summons, and complaint, accompanied by the certificate of the clerk that such publication has been made and that such summons and complaint have been mailed as required by this section, is sufficient evidence of publication and mailing. When a period of one week from the time of publication has elapsed, the juvenile court shall have full jurisdiction to deal with such child as provided by sections 2151.01 to 2151.99, inclusive, of the Revised Code.

HISTORY: 133 v H 320. Eff 11-19-69.

Analogous in part to former RC § 2151.29 (GC § 1639-25; 121 v 557; Bureau of Code Revision, 10-1-53), repealed 133 v H 320, eff 11-19-69.

§ 2151.30 Issuance of warrant.

In any case when it is made to appear to the juvenile judge that the service of a citation under section 2151.29 of the Revised Code will be ineffectual or the welfare of the child requires that he be brought forthwith into the custody of the juvenile court, a warrant may be issued against the parent, custodian, or guardian, or against the child himself.

HISTORY: GC § 1639-26; 117 v 520; Bureau of Code Revision. Eff 10-1-53.

§ 2151.31 Apprehension, custody, and detention.

(A) A child may be taken into custody in any of the following ways:

(1) Pursuant to an order of the court under this chapter;

(2) Pursuant to the laws of arrest;

(3) By a law enforcement officer or duly authorized officer of the court when any of the following conditions are present:

(a) There are reasonable grounds to believe that the child is suffering from illness or injury and is not receiving proper care, as described in section 2151.03 of the Revised Code, and the child's removal is necessary to prevent immediate or threatened physical or emotional harm;

(b) There are reasonable grounds to believe that the child is in immediate danger from the child's surroundings and that the child's removal is necessary to prevent immediate or threatened physical or emotional harm;

(c) There are reasonable grounds to believe that a parent, guardian, custodian, or other household member of the child's household has abused or neglected another child in the household and to believe that the child is in danger of immediate or threatened physical or emotional harm from that person.

(4) By an enforcement official, as defined in section 4109.01 of the Revised Code, under the circumstances set forth in section 4109.08 of the Revised Code;

(5) By a law enforcement officer or duly authorized officer of the court when there are reasonable grounds to believe that the child has run away from the child's parents, guardian, or other custodian;

(6) By a law enforcement officer or duly authorized officer of the court when any of the following apply:

(a) There are reasonable grounds to believe that the conduct, conditions, or surroundings of the child are endangering the health, welfare, or safety of the child;

(b) A complaint has been filed with respect to the child under section 2151.27 of the Revised Code and there are reasonable grounds to believe that the child may abscond or be removed from the jurisdiction of the court;

(c) The child is required to appear in court and there are reasonable grounds to believe that the child will not be brought before the court when required.

(B)(1) The taking of a child into custody is not and shall not be deemed an arrest except for the purpose of determining its validity under the constitution of this state or of the United States.

(2) Except as provided in division (C) of section 2151.311 [2151.31.1] of the Revised Code, a child taken into custody shall not be held in any state correctional institution, county, multicounty, or municipal jail or workhouse, or any other place where any adult convicted of crime, under arrest, or charged with crime is held.

(C) A child taken into custody shall not be confined in a place of juvenile detention or placed in shelter care prior to the implementation of the court's final order of disposition, unless detention or shelter care is required to protect the child from immediate or threatened physical or emotional harm, because the child may abscond or be removed from the jurisdiction of the court, because the child has no parents, guardian, or custodian or other person able to provide supervision and care for the child and return the child to the court when required, or because an order for placement of the child in detention or shelter care has been made by the court pursuant to this chapter.

(D) Upon receipt of notice from a person that the person intends to take an alleged abused, neglected, or dependent child into custody pursuant to division (A)(3) of this section, a juvenile judge or a designated referee may grant by telephone an ex parte emergency order authorizing the taking of the child into custody if there is probable cause to believe that any of the conditions set forth in divisions (A)(3)(a) to (c) of this section are present. The judge or referee shall journalize any ex parte emergency order issued pursuant to this division. If an order is issued pursuant to this division and the child is taken into custody pursuant to the order, a sworn complaint shall be filed with respect to the child before the end of the next business day after the day on which the child is taken into custody and a hearing shall be held pursuant to division (E) of this section and the Juvenile Rules. A juvenile judge or referee shall not grant an emergency order by telephone pursuant to this division until after the judge or referee determines that reasonable efforts have been made to notify the parents, guardian, or custodian of the child that the child may be placed into shelter care and of the reasons for placing the child into shelter care, except that, if the requirement for notification would jeopardize the physical or emotional safety of the child or result in the child being removed from the court's jurisdiction, the judge or referee may issue the order for taking the child into custody and placing the child into shelter care prior to giving notice to the parents, guardian, or custodian of the child.

(E) If a judge or referee pursuant to division (D) of this section issues an ex parte emergency order for taking a child into custody, the court shall hold a hearing to determine whether there is probable cause for the emergency order. The hearing shall be held before the end of the next business day after the day on which the emergency order is issued, except that it shall not be held later than seventy-two hours after the emergency order is issued.

If the court determines at the hearing that there is not probable cause for the issuance of the emergency order issued pursuant to division (D) of this section, it shall order the child released to the custody of the child's parents, guardian, or custodian. If the court determines at the hearing that there is probable cause for the issuance of the emergency order issued pursuant to division (D) of this section, the court shall do all of the following:

(1) Ensure that a complaint is filed or has been filed;
(2) Hold a hearing pursuant to section 2151.314 [2151.31.4] of the Revised Code to determine if the child should remain in shelter care;

(3) At the hearing held pursuant to section 2151.314 [2151.31.4] of the Revised Code, make the determination and issue the written finding of facts required by section 2151.419 [2151.41.9] of the Revised Code.

(F) If the court determines at the hearing held pursuant to division (E) of this section that there is probable cause to believe that the child is an abused child, as defined in division (A) of section 2151.031 [2151.03.1] of the Revised Code, the court may do any of the following:

(1) Upon the motion of any party, the guardian ad litem, the prosecuting attorney, or an employee of the public children services agency, or its own motion, issue reasonable protective orders with respect to the interviewing or deposition of the child;

(2) Order that the child's testimony be videotaped for preservation of the testimony for possible use in any other proceedings in the case;

(3) Set any additional conditions with respect to the child or the case involving the child that are in the best interest of the child.

(G) This section is not intended, and shall not be construed, to prevent any person from taking a child into custody, if taking the child into custody is necessary in an emergency to prevent the physical injury, emotional harm, or neglect of the child.

HISTORY: 133 v H 320 (Eff 11-19-69); 137 v H 883 (Eff 1-12-79); 142 v S 89 (Eff 1-1-89); 143 v H 166 (Eff 2-14-90); 145 v H 571 (Eff 10-6-94); 147 v H 408. Eff 10-1-97.

Analogous in part to former RC § 2151.31 (GC § 1639-27; 117 v 520; 121 v 557; Bureau of Code Revision, 10-1-53), repealed, 133 v H 320, eff 11-19-69.

The effective date is set by section 26 of HB 408.

[§ 2151.31.1] § 2151.311 Procedure upon apprehension.

(A) A person taking a child into custody shall, with all reasonable speed and in accordance with division (C) of this section, either:

(1) Release the child to the child's parents, guardian, or other custodian, unless the child's detention or shelter care appears to be warranted or required as provided in section 2151.31 of the Revised Code;

(2) Bring the child to the court or deliver the child to a place of detention or shelter care designated by the court and promptly give notice thereof, together with a statement of the reason for taking the child into custody, to a parent, guardian, or other custodian and to the court.

(B) If a parent, guardian, or other custodian fails, when requested by the court, to bring the child before the court as provided by this section, the court may issue its warrant directing that the child be taken into custody and brought before the court.

(C)(1) Before taking any action required by division

(A) of this section, a person taking a child into custody may hold the child for processing purposes in a county, multicounty, or municipal jail or workhouse, or other place where an adult convicted of crime, under arrest, or charged with crime is held for either of the following periods of time:

(a) For a period not to exceed six hours, if all of the following apply:

(i) The child is alleged to be a delinquent child for the commission of an act that would be a felony if committed by an adult;

(ii) The child remains beyond the range of touch of all adult detainees;

(iii) The child is visually supervised by jail or workhouse personnel at all times during the detention;

(iv) The child is not handcuffed or otherwise physically secured to a stationary object during the detention.

(b) For a period not to exceed three hours, if all of the following apply:

(i) The child is alleged to be a delinquent child for the commission of an act that would be a misdemeanor if committed by an adult or is alleged to be an unruly child or a juvenile traffic offender;

(ii) The child remains beyond the range of touch of all adult detainees;

(iii) The child is visually supervised by jail or workhouse personnel at all times during the detention;

(iv) The child is not handcuffed or otherwise physically secured to a stationary object during the detention.

(2) If a child has been transferred to an adult court for prosecution for the alleged commission of a criminal offense, subsequent to the transfer, the child may be held as described in division (C) of section 2151.312 [2151.31.2] or division (B) of section 5120.16 of the Revised Code.

(D) As used in division (C)(1) of this section, "processing purposes" means all of the following:

(1) Fingerprinting, photographing, or fingerprinting and photographing the child in a secure area of the facility;

(2) Interrogating the child, contacting the child's parent or guardian, arranging for placement of the child, or arranging for transfer or transferring the child, while holding the child in a nonsecure area of the facility.

HISTORY: 133 v H 320 (Eff 11-19-69); 133 v H 931 (Eff 8-27-70); 134 v S 445 (Eff 6-29-72); 143 v H 166 (Eff 2-14-90); 145 v H 571 (Eff 10-6-94); 146 v H 480 (Eff 10-16-96); 146 v H 124. Eff 3-31-97.

[§ 2151.31.2] § 2151.312 Place of detention.

(A) Except as provided in divisions (B) and (F) of this section, a child alleged to be or adjudicated a delinquent child, an unruly child, or a juvenile traffic offender may be held only in the following places:

(1) A certified family foster home or a home approved by the court;

(2) A facility operated by a certified child welfare agency;

(3) Any other suitable place designated by the court.

(B) In addition to the places listed in division (A) of this section, a child alleged to be or adjudicated a delinquent child may be held in a detention home or center for delinquent children that is under the direction or supervision of the court or other public authority or of a private agency and approved by the court.

(C)(1) Except as provided under division (C)(1) of section 2151.311 [2151.31.1] of the Revised Code or division (A)(6) of section 2151.356 [2151.35.6] of the Revised Code, a child alleged to be or adjudicated a neglected child, an abused child, a dependent child, an unruly child, or a juvenile traffic offender may not be held in any of the following facilities:

(a) A state correctional institution, county, multicounty, or municipal jail or workhouse, or other place in which an adult convicted of crime, under arrest, or charged with a crime is held.

(b) A secure correctional facility.

(2) Except as provided under sections 2151.56 to 2151.61 and division (A)(6) of section 2151.356 [2151.35.6] of the Revised Code and division (C)(3) of this section, a child alleged to be or adjudicated an unruly child or a juvenile traffic offender may not be held for more than twenty-four hours in a detention home. A child alleged to be or adjudicated a neglected child, an abused child, or a dependent child shall not be held in a detention home.

(3) A child who is alleged to be or who is adjudicated an unruly child and who is taken into custody on a Saturday, Sunday, or legal holiday, as listed in section 1.14 of the Revised Code, may be held in a detention home until the next succeeding day that is not a Saturday, Sunday, or legal holiday.

(D) Except as provided in division (C) of this section or in division (C) of section 2151.311 [2151.31.1], in division (C)(3) of section 5139.06 and section 5120.162 [5120.16.2], or in division (B) of section 5120.16 of the Revised Code, a child who is alleged to be or is adjudicated a delinquent child may not be held in a state correctional institution, county, multicounty, or municipal jail or workhouse, or other place where an adult convicted of crime, under arrest, or charged with crime is held.

(E) Unless the detention is pursuant to division (C) of this section or division (C) of section 2151.311 [2151.31.1], division (C)(3) of section 5139.06 and section 5120.162 [5120.16.2], or division (B) of section 5120.16 of the Revised Code, the official in charge of the institution, jail, workhouse, or other facility shall inform the court immediately when a child, who is or appears to be under the age of eighteen years, is received at the facility, and shall deliver the child to the court upon request or transfer the child to a detention facility designated by the court.

(F) If a case is transferred to another court for criminal prosecution pursuant to section 2151.26 of the Revised Code, the child may be transferred for detention pending the criminal prosecution in a jail or other facility in accordance with the law governing the detention of persons charged with crime. Any child so held shall be confined in a manner that keeps the child beyond the range of touch of all adult detainees. The child shall be supervised at all times during the detention.

HISTORY: 133 v H 320 (Eff 11-19-69); 136 v H 85 (Eff 11-28-75); 139 v H 440 (Eff 11-23-81); 143 v H 166 (Eff 2-14-90); 144 v S 331 (Eff 11-13-92); 145 v H 152 (Eff 7-1-93); 145 v H 571 (Eff 10-6-94); 146 v H 265 (Eff 3-3-97); 146 v H 124. Eff 3-31-97.

Publisher's Note

The amendments made by HB 265 (146 v —) and HB 124 (146 v —) have been combined. Please see provisions of RC § 1.52.

[§ 2151.31.3] § 2151.313 Fingerprints and photographs.

(A)(1) Except as provided in division (A)(2) of this section and in sections 109.57, 109.60, and 109.61 of the Revised Code, no child shall be fingerprinted or photographed in the investigation of any violation of law without the consent of the juvenile judge.

(2) Subject to division (A)(3) of this section, a law enforcement officer may fingerprint and photograph a child without the consent of the juvenile judge when the child is arrested or otherwise taken into custody for the commission of an act that would be a felony if committed by an adult, and there is probable cause to believe that the child may have been involved in the commission of the act. A law enforcement officer who takes fingerprints or photographs of a child under division (A)(2) of this section immediately shall inform the juvenile court that the fingerprints or photographs were taken and shall provide the court with the identity of the child, the number of fingerprints and photographs taken, and the name and address of each person who has custody and control of the fingerprints or photographs or copies of the fingerprints or photographs.

(3) This section does not apply to a child who is fourteen years of age or older and under eighteen years of age and to whom either of the following applies:

(a) The child has been arrested or otherwise taken into custody for committing, has been adjudicated a delinquent child for committing, or has been convicted of or pleaded guilty to committing a designated delinquent act or juvenile offense, as defined in section 109.57 of the Revised Code.

(b) There is probable cause to believe that the child may have committed a designated delinquent act or juvenile offense, as defined in section 109.57 of the Revised Code.

(B)(1) Subject to divisions (B)(4), (5), and (6) of this section, all fingerprints and photographs of a child obtained or taken under division (A)(1) or (2) of this section, and any records of the arrest or custody of the child that was the basis for the taking of the fingerprints or photographs, initially may be retained only until the expiration of thirty days after the date taken, except that the court may limit the initial retention of fingerprints and photographs of a child obtained under division (A)(1) of this section to a shorter period of time and except that, if the child is adjudicated a delinquent child for the commission of an act described in division (B)(3) of this section or is convicted of or pleads guilty to a criminal offense for the commission of an act described in division (B)(3) of this section, the fingerprints and photographs, and the records of the arrest or custody of the child that was the basis for the taking of the fingerprints and photographs, shall be retained in accordance with division (B)(3) of this section. During the initial period of retention, the fingerprints and photographs of a child, copies of the fingerprints and photographs, and records of the arrest or custody of the child shall be used or released only in accordance with division (C) of this section. At the expiration of the initial period for which fingerprints and photographs of a child, copies of fingerprints and photographs of a child, and records of the arrest or custody of a child may be retained under this division, if no complaint is pending against the child in relation to the act for which the fingerprints and photographs originally were obtained or taken and if the child has neither been adjudicated a delinquent child for the commission of that act nor been convicted of or pleaded guilty to a criminal offense based on that act subsequent to a transfer of the child's case for criminal prosecution pursuant to section 2151.26 of the Revised Code, the fingerprints and photographs of the child, all copies of the fingerprints and photographs, and all records of the arrest or custody of the child that was the basis of the taking of the fingerprints and photographs shall be removed from the file and delivered to the juvenile court.

(2) If, at the expiration of the initial period of retention set forth in division (B)(1) of this section, a complaint is pending against the child in relation to the act for which the fingerprints and photographs originally were obtained or the child either has been adjudicated a delinquent child for the commission of an act other than an act described in division (B)(3) of this section or has been convicted of or pleaded guilty to a criminal offense for the commission of an act other than an act described in division (B)(3) of this section subsequent to transfer of the child's case, the fingerprints and photographs of the child, copies of the fingerprints and photographs, and the records of the arrest or custody of the child that was the basis of the taking of the fingerprints and photographs may further be retained, subject to division (B)(4) of this section, until the earlier of the expiration of two years after the date on which the fingerprints or photographs were taken or the child attains eighteen years of age, except that, if the child is adjudicated a delinquent child for the commission of

an act described in division (B)(3) of this section or is convicted of or pleads guilty to a criminal offense for the commission of an act described in division (B)(3) of this section, the fingerprints and photographs, and the records of the arrest or custody of the child that was the basis for the taking of the fingerprints and photographs, shall be retained in accordance with division (B)(3) of this section.

Except as otherwise provided in division (B)(3) of this section, during this additional period of retention, the fingerprints and photographs of a child, copies of the fingerprints and photographs of a child, and records of the arrest or custody of a child shall be used or released only in accordance with division (C) of this section. At the expiration of the additional period, if no complaint is pending against the child in relation to the act for which the fingerprints originally were obtained or taken or in relation to another act for which the fingerprints were used as authorized by division (C) of this section and that would be a felony if committed by an adult, the fingerprints of the child, all copies of the fingerprints, and all records of the arrest or custody of the child that was the basis of the taking of the fingerprints shall be removed from the file and delivered to the juvenile court, and, if no complaint is pending against the child concerning the act for which the photographs originally were obtained or taken or concerning an act that would be a felony if committed by an adult, the photographs and all copies of the photographs, and, if no fingerprints were taken at the time the photographs were taken, all records of the arrest or custody that was the basis of the taking of the photographs shall be removed from the file and delivered to the juvenile court. In either case, if, at the expiration of the applicable additional period, such a complaint is pending against the child, the photographs and copies of the photographs of the child, or the fingerprints and copies of the fingerprints of the child, whichever is applicable, and the records of the arrest or custody of the child may be retained, subject to division (B)(4) of this section, until final disposition of the complaint, and upon final disposition of the complaint, they shall be removed from the file and delivered to the juvenile court, except that, if the child is adjudicated a delinquent child for the commission of an act described in division (B)(3) of this section or is convicted of or pleads guilty to a criminal offense for the commission of an act described in division (B)(3) of this section, the fingerprints and photographs, and the records of the arrest or custody of the child that was the basis for the taking of the fingerprints and photographs, shall be retained in accordance with division (B)(3) of this section.

(3) If a child is adjudicated a delinquent child for the commission of an act in violation of, or is convicted of or pleads guilty to a criminal offense for the commission of an act that is a violation of, section 2903.01, 2903.02, 2903.03, 2903.04, 2903.11, 2903.12, 2903.13, 2903.21, 2903.22, 2905.01, 2905.02, 2905.11, 2907.02, 2907.03, 2907.05, 2909.02, 2909.03, 2911.01, 2911.02, 2911.11, 2911.12, 2911.13, 2921.34, or 2921.35 of the Revised Code, section 2913.02 of the Revised Code involving the theft of a motor vehicle, former section 2907.12 of the Revised Code, or an existing or former municipal ordinance or law of this state, another state, or the United States that is substantially equivalent to any of those sections, both of the following apply:

(a) Originals and copies of fingerprints and photographs of the child obtained or taken under division (A)(1) of this section, and any records of the arrest or custody that was the basis for the taking of the fingerprints or photographs, may be retained for the period of time specified by the juvenile judge in that judge's grant of consent for the taking of the fingerprints or photographs. Upon the expiration of the specified period, all originals and copies of the fingerprints, photographs, and records shall be delivered to the juvenile court or otherwise disposed of in accordance with any instructions specified by the juvenile judge in that judge's grant of consent. During the period of retention of the photographs and records, all originals and copies of them shall be retained in a file separate and apart from all photographs taken of adults. During the period of retention of the fingerprints, all originals and copies of them may be maintained in the files of fingerprints taken of adults. If the juvenile judge who grants consent for the taking of fingerprints and photographs under division (A)(1) of this section does not specify a period of retention in that judge's grant of consent, originals and copies of the fingerprints, photographs, and records may be retained in accordance with this section as if the fingerprints and photographs had been taken under division (A)(2) of this section.

(b) Originals and copies of fingerprints and photographs taken under division (A)(2) of this section, and any records of the arrest or custody that was the basis for the taking of the fingerprints or photographs, may be retained for the period of time and in the manner specified in division (B)(3)(b) of this section. Prior to the child's attainment of eighteen years of age, all originals and copies of the photographs and records shall be retained and shall be kept in a file separate and apart from all photographs taken of adults. During the period of retention of the fingerprints, all originals and copies of them may be maintained in the files of fingerprints taken of adults. Upon the child's attainment of eighteen years of age, all originals and copies of the fingerprints, photographs, and records shall be disposed of as follows:

(i) If the juvenile judge issues or previously has issued an order that specifies a manner of disposition of the originals and copies of the fingerprints, photographs, and records, they shall be delivered to the juvenile court or otherwise disposed of in accordance with the order.

(ii) If the juvenile judge does not issue and has not previously issued an order that specifies a manner of disposition of the originals and copies of the fingerprints not maintained in adult files, photographs, and records, the law enforcement agency, in its discretion, either shall remove all originals and copies of them from the file in which they had been maintained and transfer them to the files that are used for the retention of fingerprints and photographs taken of adults who are arrested for, otherwise taken into custody for, or under investigation for the commission of a criminal offense or shall remove them from the file in which they had been maintained and deliver them to the juvenile court. If the originals and copies of any fingerprints of a child who attains eighteen years of age are maintained in the files of fingerprints taken of adults or if pursuant to division (B)(3)(b)(ii) of this section the agency transfers the originals and copies of any fingerprints not maintained in adult files, photographs, or records to the files that are used for the retention of fingerprints and photographs taken of adults who are arrested for, otherwise taken into custody for, or under investigation for the commission of a criminal offense, the originals and copies of the fingerprints, photographs, and records may be maintained, used, and released after they are maintained in the adult files or after the transfer as if the fingerprints and photographs had been taken of, and as if the records pertained to, an adult who was arrested for, otherwise taken into custody for, or under investigation for the commission of a criminal offense.

(4) If a sealing or expungement order issued under section 2151.358 [2151.35.8] of the Revised Code requires the sealing or destruction of any fingerprints or photographs of a child obtained or taken under division (A)(1) or (2) of this section or of the records of an arrest or custody of a child that was the basis of the taking of the fingerprints or photographs prior to the expiration of any period for which they otherwise could be retained under division (B)(1), (2), or (3) of this section, the fingerprints, photographs, and arrest or custody records that are subject to the order and all copies of the fingerprints, photographs, and arrest or custody records shall be sealed or destroyed in accordance with the order.

(5) All fingerprints of a child, photographs of a child, records of an arrest or custody of a child, and copies delivered to a juvenile court in accordance with division (B)(1), (2), or (3) of this section shall be destroyed by the court.

(6)(a) All photographs of a child and records of an arrest or custody of a child retained pursuant to division (B) of this section and not delivered to a juvenile court shall be kept in a file separate and apart from fingerprints, photographs, and records of an arrest or custody of an adult. All fingerprints of a child retained pursuant to division (B) of this section and not delivered to a juvenile court may be maintained in the files of fingerprints taken of adults.

(b) If a child who is the subject of photographs or fingerprints is adjudicated a delinquent child for the commission of an act that would be a felony if committed by an adult or is convicted of or pleads guilty to a criminal offense that is a felony, all fingerprints not maintained in the files of fingerprints taken of adults and all photographs of the child, and all records of the arrest or custody of the child that is the basis of the taking of the fingerprints or photographs, that are retained pursuant to division (B) of this section and not delivered to a juvenile court shall be kept in a file separate and apart from fingerprints, photographs, and arrest and custody records of children who have not been adjudicated a delinquent child for the commission of an act that would be a felony if committed by an adult and have not been convicted of or pleaded guilty to a criminal offense that is a felony.

(C) Until they are delivered to the juvenile court or sealed, transferred in accordance with division (B)(3)(b) of this section, or destroyed pursuant to a sealing or expungement order, the originals and copies of fingerprints and photographs of a child that are obtained or taken pursuant to division (A)(1) or (2) of this section, and the records of the arrest or custody of the child that was the basis of the taking of the fingerprints or photographs, shall be used or released only as follows:

(1) During the initial thirty-day period of retention, originals and copies of fingerprints and photographs of a child, and records of the arrest or custody of a child, shall be used, prior to the filing of a complaint against the child in relation to the act for which the fingerprints and photographs were originally obtained or taken, only for the investigation of that act and shall be released, prior to the filing of the complaint, only to a court that would have jurisdiction of the child's case under this chapter. Subsequent to the filing of a complaint, originals and copies of fingerprints and photographs of a child, and records of the arrest or custody of a child, shall be used or released during the initial thirty-day period of retention only as provided in division (C)(2)(a), (b), or (c) of this section.

(2) Originals and copies of fingerprints and photographs of a child, and records of the arrest or custody of a child, that are retained beyond the initial thirty-day period of retention subsequent to the filing of a complaint, a delinquent child adjudication, or a conviction of or guilty plea to a criminal offense shall be used or released only as follows:

(a) Originals and copies of photographs of a child, and, if no fingerprints were taken at the time the photographs were taken, records of the arrest or custody of the child that was the basis of the taking of the photographs, may be used only as follows:

(i) They may be used for the investigation of the act for which they originally were obtained or taken; if the child who is the subject of the photographs is a suspect in the investigation, for the investigation of any act that would be an offense if committed by an adult; and for arresting or bringing the child into custody.

(ii) If the child who is the subject of the photographs is adjudicated a delinquent child for the commission of an act that would be a felony if committed by an adult or is convicted of or pleads guilty to a criminal offense that is a felony as a result of the arrest or custody that was the basis of the taking of the photographs, a law enforcement officer may use the photographs for a photo line-up conducted as part of the investigation of any act that would be a felony if committed by an adult, whether or not the child who is the subject of the photographs is a suspect in the investigation. No later than ninety days after a law enforcement officer uses the photographs in a photo line-up, the officer shall return them to the file from which the officer obtained them.

(b) Originals and copies of fingerprints of a child, and records of the arrest or custody of the child that was the basis of the taking of the fingerprints, may be used only for the investigation of the act for which they originally were obtained or taken; if a child is a suspect in the investigation, for the investigation of another act that would be an offense if committed by an adult; and for arresting or bringing the child into custody.

(c) Originals and copies of fingerprints, photographs, and records of the arrest or custody that was the basis of the taking of the fingerprints or photographs shall be released only to the following:

(i) Law enforcement officers of this state or a political subdivision of this state, upon notification to the juvenile court of the name and address of the law enforcement officer or agency to whom or to which they will be released;

(ii) A court that has jurisdiction of the child's case under Chapter 2151. of the Revised Code or subsequent to a transfer of the child's case for criminal prosecution pursuant to section 2151.26 of the Revised Code.

(D) No person shall knowingly do any of the following:

(1) Fingerprint or photograph a child in the investigation of any violation of law other than as provided in division (A)(1) or (2) of this section or in sections 109.57, 109.60, and 109.61 of the Revised Code;

(2) Retain fingerprints or photographs of a child obtained or taken under division (A)(1) or (2) of this section, copies of fingerprints or photographs of that nature, or records of the arrest or custody that was the basis of the taking of fingerprints or photographs of that nature other than in accordance with division (B) of this section;

(3) Use or release fingerprints or photographs of a child obtained or taken under division (A)(1) or (2) of this section, copies of fingerprints or photographs of that nature, or records of the arrest or custody that was the basis of the taking of fingerprints or photographs of that nature other than in accordance with division (B) or (C) of this section.

HISTORY: 133 v H 320 (Eff 11-19-69); 135 v S 1 (Eff 1-1-74); 137 v H 315 (Eff 3-15-78); 140 v H 258 (Eff 9-26-84); 144 v H 198 (Eff 10-6-92); 146 v H 1 (Eff 1-1-96); 146 v H 445 (Eff 9-3-96); 146 v H 124. Eff 3-31-97.

[§ 2151.31.4] § 2151.314 Detention hearing.

(A) When a child is brought before the court or delivered to a place of detention or shelter care designated by the court, the intake or other authorized officer of the court shall immediately make an investigation and shall release the child unless it appears that the child's detention or shelter care is warranted or required under section 2151.31 of the Revised Code.

If the child is not so released, a complaint under section 2151.27 of the Revised Code shall be filed and an informal detention or shelter care hearing held promptly, not later than seventy-two hours after the child is placed in detention or shelter care, to determine whether detention or shelter care is required. Reasonable oral or written notice of the time, place, and purpose of the detention or shelter care hearing shall be given to the child and, if they can be found, to the child's parents, guardian, or custodian. In cases in which the complaint alleges a child to be an abused, neglected, or dependent child, the notice given the parents, guardian, or custodian shall inform them that a case plan may be prepared for the child, the general requirements usually contained in case plans, and the possible consequences of the failure to comply with a journalized case plan.

Prior to the hearing, the court shall inform the parties of their right to counsel and to appointed counsel or to the services of the county public defender or joint county public defender, if they are indigent, of the child's right to remain silent with respect to any allegation of delinquency, and of the name and telephone number of a court employee who can be contacted during the normal business hours of the court to arrange for the prompt appointment of counsel for any party who is indigent. Unless it appears from the hearing that the child's detention or shelter care is required under the provisions of section 2151.31 of the Revised Code, the court shall order the child's release as provided by section 2151.311 [2151.31.1] of the Revised Code. If a parent, guardian, or custodian has not been so notified and did not appear or waive appearance at the hearing, upon the filing of an affidavit stating these facts, the court shall rehear the matter without unnecessary delay.

(B) When the court conducts a hearing pursuant to division (A) of this section, all of the following apply:

(1) The court shall determine whether an alleged abused, neglected, or dependent child should remain or be placed in shelter care;

(2) The court shall determine whether there are any relatives of the child who are willing to be temporary custodians of the child. If any relative is willing to be a temporary custodian, the child would otherwise be placed or retained in shelter care, and the appointment is appropriate, the court shall appoint the relative as temporary custodian of the child, unless the court appoints another relative as temporary custodian. If it determines that the appointment of a relative as custodian would not be appropriate, it shall issue a written opinion setting forth the reasons for its determination and give a copy of the opinion to all parties and to the guardian ad litem of the child.

The court's consideration of a relative for appointment as a temporary custodian does not make that relative a party to the proceedings.

(3) The court shall make the determination and issue the written finding of facts required by section 2151.419 [2151.41.9] of the Revised Code.

(C) If a child is in shelter care following the filing of a complaint pursuant to section 2151.27 of the Revised Code or following a hearing held pursuant to division (A) of this section, any party, including the public children services agency, and the guardian ad litem of the child may file a motion with the court requesting that the child be released from shelter care. The motion shall state the reasons why the child should be released from shelter care and, if a hearing has been held pursuant to division (A) of this section, any changes in the situation of the child or the parents, guardian, or custodian of the child that have occurred since that hearing and that justify the release of the child from shelter care. Upon the filing of the motion, the court shall hold a hearing in the same manner as under division (A) of this section.

(D) Each juvenile court shall designate one court employee to assist persons who are indigent in obtaining appointed counsel. The court shall include in each notice given pursuant to division (A) or (C) of this section and in each summons served upon a party pursuant to this chapter, the name and telephone number at which the designated employee can be contacted during the normal business hours of the court to arrange for prompt appointment of counsel for indigent persons.

HISTORY: 133 v H 320 (Eff 11-19-69); 136 v H 164 (Eff 1-13-76); 142 v S 89 (Eff 1-1-89); 146 v H 274. Eff 8-8-96.

[§ 2151.31.5] § 2151.315 DNA testing of adjudicated delinquents.

(A) As used in this section, "DNA analysis" and "DNA specimen" have the same meanings as in section 109.573 [109.57.3] of the Revised Code.

(B)(1) A child who is adjudicated a delinquent child for committing an act listed in division (D) of this section and who is committed to the custody of the department of youth services or to a school, camp, institution, or other facility for delinquent children described in division (A)(3) of section 2151.355 [2151.35.5] of the Revised Code shall submit to a DNA specimen collection procedure administered by the director of youth services if committed to the department or by the chief administrative officer of the school, camp, institution, or other facility for delinquent children to which the child was committed. If the court commits the child to the department of youth services, the director of youth services shall cause the DNA specimen to be collected from the child during the intake process at an institution operated by or under the control of the department. If the court commits the child to a school, camp, institution, or other facility for delinquent children, the chief administrative officer of the school, camp, institution, or facility to which the child is committed shall cause the DNA specimen to be collected from the child during the intake process for the school, camp, institution, or facility. In accordance with division (C) of this section, the director or the chief administrative officer shall cause the DNA specimen to be forwarded to the bureau of criminal identification and investigation no later than fifteen days after the date of the collection of the DNA specimen. The DNA specimen shall be collected from the child in accordance with division (C) of this section.

(2) If a child is adjudicated a delinquent child for committing an act listed in division (D) of this section, is committed to the department of youth services or to a school, camp, institution, or other facility for delinquent children, and does not submit to a DNA specimen collection procedure pursuant to division (B)(1) of this section, prior to the child's release from the custody of the department of youth services or from the custody of the school, camp, institution, or facility, the child shall submit to, and the director of youth services or the chief administrator† of the school, camp, institution, or facility to which the child is committed shall administer, a DNA specimen collection procedure at the institution operated by or under the control of the department of youth services or at the school, camp, institution, or facility to which the child is committed. In accordance with division (C) of this section, the director or the chief administrative officer shall cause the DNA specimen to be forwarded to the bureau of criminal identification and investigation no later than fifteen days after the date of the collection of the DNA specimen. The DNA specimen shall be collected in accordance with division (C) of this section.

(C) A physician, registered nurse, licensed practical nurse, duly licensed clinical laboratory technician, or other qualified medical practitioner shall collect in a medically approved manner the DNA specimen required to be collected pursuant to division (B) of this section. No later than fifteen days after the date of the collection of the DNA specimen, the director of youth services or the chief administrative officer of the school, camp, institution, or other facility for delinquent children to which the child is committed shall cause the DNA specimen to be forwarded to the bureau of criminal identification and investigation in accordance with procedures established by the superintendent of the bureau under division (H) of section 109.573 [109.57.3] of the Revised Code. The bureau shall provide the specimen vials, mailing tubes, labels, postage, and instruction needed for the collection and forwarding of the DNA specimen to the bureau.

(D) The director of youth services and the chief administrative officer of a school, camp, institution, or other facility for delinquent children shall cause a DNA specimen to be collected in accordance with divisions (B) and (C) of this section from each child in its custody who is adjudicated a delinquent child for committing any of the following acts:

(1) A violation of section 2903.01, 2903.02, 2905.01, 2907.02, 2907.03, 2907.04, 2907.05, or 2911.11 of the Revised Code;

(2) A violation of section 2907.12 of the Revised Code as it existed prior to September 3, 1996;

(3) An attempt to commit a violation of section 2907.02, 2907.03, 2907.04, or 2907.05 of the Revised Code or to commit a violation of section 2907.12 of the Revised Code as it existed prior to September 3, 1996;

(4) A violation of any law that arose out of the same facts and circumstances and same act as did a charge against the child of a violation of section 2907.02, 2907.03, 2907.04, or 2907.05 of the Revised Code that previously was dismissed or as did a charge against the child of a violation of section 2907.12 of the Revised Code as it existed prior to September 3, 1996, that previously was dismissed;

(5) A violation of section 2905.02 or 2919.23 of the Revised Code that would have been a violation of section 2905.04 of the Revised Code as it existed prior to July 1, 1996, had the violation been committed prior to that date.

(E) The director of youth services and the chief administrative officer of a school, camp, institution, or other facility for delinquent children is not required to comply with this section until the superintendent of the bureau of criminal identification and investigation gives agencies in the juvenile justice system, as defined in section 181.51 of the Revised Code, in the state official notification that the state DNA laboratory is prepared to accept DNA specimens.

HISTORY: 146 v H 5 (Eff 8-30-95); 146 v S 269 (Eff 7-1-96); 146 v H 124. Eff 3-31-97.

† So in enrolled bill, division (B)(2). Others changed to "chief administrative officer" herein.

§ 2151.32 Selection of custodian.

In placing a child under any guardianship or custody other than that of its parent, the juvenile court shall, when practicable, select a person or an institution or agency governed by persons of like religious faith as that of the parents of such child, or in case of a difference in the religious faith of the parents, then of the religious faith of the child, or if the religious faith of the child is not ascertained, then of either of the parents.

HISTORY: GC § 1639-33; 117 v 520(531); Bureau of Code Revision. Eff 10-1-53.

§ 2151.33 Temporary care; emergency medical treatment; reimbursement.

(A) Pending hearing of a complaint filed under section 2151.27 of the Revised Code or a motion filed or made under division (B) of this section and the service of citations, the juvenile court may make any temporary disposition of any child that it considers necessary to protect the best interest of the child and that can be made pursuant to division (B) of this section. Upon the certificate of one or more reputable practicing physicians, the court may summarily provide for emergency medical and surgical treatment that appears to be immediately necessary to preserve the health and well-being of any child concerning whom a complaint or an application for care has been filed, pending the service of a citation upon the child's parents, guardian, or custodian. The court may order the parents, guardian, or custodian, if the court finds the parents, guardian, or custodian able to do so, to reimburse the court for the expense involved in providing the emergency medical or surgical treatment. Any person who disobeys the order for reimbursement may be adjudged in contempt of court and punished accordingly.

If the emergency medical or surgical treatment is furnished to a child who is found at the hearing to be a nonresident of the county in which the court is located and if the expense of the medical or surgical treatment cannot be recovered from the parents, legal guardian, or custodian of the child, the board of county commissioners of the county in which the child has a legal settlement shall reimburse the court for the reasonable cost of the emergency medical or surgical treatment out of its general fund.

(B)(1) After a complaint, petition, writ, or other document initiating a case dealing with an alleged or adjudicated abused, neglected, or dependent child is filed and upon the filing or making of a motion pursuant to division (C) of this section, the court, prior to the final disposition of the case, may issue any of the following temporary orders to protect the best interest of the child:

(a) An order granting temporary custody of the child to a particular party;

(b) An order for the taking of the child into custody pursuant to section 2151.31 of the Revised Code pending the outcome of the adjudicatory and dispositional hearings;

(c) An order granting, limiting, or eliminating visitation rights with respect to the child;

(d) An order requiring a party to vacate a residence that will be lawfully occupied by the child;

(e) An order requiring a party to attend an appropriate counseling program that is reasonably available to that party;

(f) Any other order that restrains or otherwise controls the conduct of any party which conduct would not be in the best interest of the child.

(2) Prior to the final disposition of a case subject to division (B)(1) of this section, the court shall do both of the following:

(a) Issue an order pursuant to sections 3113.21 to 3113.219 [3113.21.9] of the Revised Code requiring the parents, guardian, or person charged with the child's support to pay support for the child.

(b) Issue an order requiring the parents, guardian, or person charged with the child's support to continue to maintain any health insurance coverage for the child that existed at the time of the filing of the complaint, petition, writ, or other document, or to obtain health insurance coverage pursuant to section 3113.217 [3113.21.7] of the Revised Code.

(C)(1) A court may issue an order pursuant to division (B) of this section upon its own motion or if a party files a written motion or makes an oral motion requesting the issuance of the order and stating the reasons for it. Any notice sent by the court as a result of a motion pursuant to this division shall contain a notice that any party to a juvenile proceeding has the right to be represented by counsel and to have appointed counsel if the person is indigent.

(2) If a child is taken into custody pursuant to section 2151.31 of the Revised Code and placed in shelter care, the public children services agency or private child placing agency with which the child is placed in shelter care shall file or make a motion as described in division (C)(1) of this section before the end of the next day immediately after the date on which the child was taken into custody and, at a minimum, shall request an order for temporary custody under division (B)(1)(a) of this section.

(3) Any court that issues an order pursuant to division (B)(1)(b) of this section shall make the determination and issue the written finding of facts required by section 2151.419 [2151.41.9] of the Revised Code.

(D) The court may grant an ex parte order upon its own motion or a motion filed or made pursuant to division (C) of this section requesting such an order if it appears to the court that the best interest and the welfare of the child require that the court issue the order immediately. The court, if acting on its own motion, or the person requesting the granting of an ex parte order, to the extent possible, shall give notice of its intent or of the request to the parents, guardian, or custodian of the child who is the subject of the request. If the court issues an ex parte order, the court shall hold a hearing to review the order within seventy-two hours after it is issued or before the end of the next day after the day on which it is issued, whichever occurs first. The court shall give written notice of the hearing to all parties to the action and shall appoint a guardian ad litem for the child prior to the hearing.

The written notice shall be given by all means that are reasonably likely to result in the party receiving actual notice and shall include all of the following:

(1) The date, time, and location of the hearing;

(2) The issues to be addressed at the hearing;

(3) A statement that every party to the hearing has a right to counsel and to court appointed counsel, if the party is indigent;

(4) The name, telephone number, and address of the person requesting the order;

(5) A copy of the order, except when it is not possible to obtain it because of the exigent circumstances in the case.

If the court does not grant an ex parte order pursuant to a motion filed or made pursuant to division (C) of this section or its own motion, the court shall hold a shelter care hearing on the motion within ten days after the motion is filed. The court shall give notice of the hearing to all affected parties in the same manner as set forth in the Juvenile Rules.

(E) The court, pending the outcome of the adjudicatory and dispositional hearings, shall not issue an order granting temporary custody of a child to a public children services agency or private child placing agency pursuant to this section, unless the court determines and specifically states in the order that the continued residence of the child in the child's current home will be contrary to the child's best interest and welfare and makes the determination and issues the written finding of facts required by section 2151.419 [2151.41.9] of the Revised Code.

(F) Each public children services agency and private child placing agency that receives temporary custody of a child pursuant to this section shall maintain in the child's case record written documentation that it has placed the child, to the extent that it is consistent with the best interest, welfare, and special needs of the child, in the most family-like setting available and in close proximity to the home of the parents, custodian, or guardian of the child.

(G) For good cause shown, any court order that is issued pursuant to this section may be reviewed by the court at any time upon motion of any party to the action or upon the motion of the court.

HISTORY: GC § 1639-28; 117 v 520; 119 v 731; 121 v 557; Bureau of Code Revision, 10-1-53; 142 v S 89 (Eff 1-1-89); 146 v H 274. Eff 8-8-96.

[§ 2151.33.1] § 2151.331 Placement options for alleged or adjudicated abused, neglected, dependent or unruly child.

A child alleged to be or adjudicated an abused, neglected, dependent, or unruly child or a juvenile traffic offender may be detained after a complaint is filed in a certified family foster home for a period not exceeding sixty days or until the final disposition of the case, whichever comes first. The court also may arrange with a public children services agency or private child placing agency to receive, or with a private noncustodial agency for temporary care of, the child within the jurisdiction of the court. A child alleged to be or adjudicated an unruly child also may be assigned to an alternative diversion program established by the court for a period not exceeding sixty days after a complaint is filed or until final disposition of the case, whichever comes first.

If the court arranges for the board of a child temporarily detained in a certified family foster home or arranges for the board of a child through a private child placing agency, the board of county commissioners shall pay a reasonable sum, which the court shall fix, for the board of the child. In order to have certified family foster homes available for service, an agreed monthly subsidy may be paid in addition to a fixed rate per day for care of a child actually residing in the certified family foster home.

HISTORY: 146 v H 265. Eff 3-3-97.

[DISTRICT DETENTION HOMES]

§ 2151.34 Confinement of alleged or adjudicated delinquent child; county or district detention home.

A child who is alleged to be or adjudicated a delinquent child may be confined in a place of juvenile detention for a period not to exceed ninety days, during which time a social history may be prepared to include court record, family history, personal history, school and attendance records, and any other pertinent studies and material that will be of assistance to the juvenile court in its disposition of the charges against that juvenile offender.

Upon the advice and recommendation of the judge, the board of county commissioners shall provide, by purchase, lease, construction, or otherwise, a place to be known as a detention home that shall be within a convenient distance of the juvenile court and shall not be used for the confinement of adults charged with criminal offenses and in which delinquent children may be detained until final disposition. Upon the joint advice and recommendation of the juvenile judges of two or more adjoining or neighboring counties, the boards of county commissioners of the counties shall form themselves into a joint board and proceed to organize a district for the establishment and support of a detention home for the use of the juvenile courts of those counties, in which delinquent children may be detained until final disposition, by using a site or buildings already established in one of the counties or by providing for the purchase of a site and the erection of the necessary buildings on the site.

A child who is adjudicated to be a juvenile traffic offender for having committed a violation of division (A) of section 4511.19 of the Revised Code or of a municipal ordinance that is substantially comparable to that division may be confined in a detention home or district detention home pursuant to division (A)(6) of section 2151.356 [2151.35.6] of the Revised Code, provided the child is kept separate and apart from alleged delinquent children.

The county or district detention home shall be maintained as provided in sections 2151.01 to 2151.54 of the Revised Code. In any county in which there is no detention home or that is not served by a district detention home, the board of county commissioners shall provide funds for the boarding of such children temporarily in private homes. Children who are alleged to be or have been adjudicated delinquent children may be detained after a complaint is filed in the detention home until final disposition of their cases or in certified family foster homes or in any other home approved by the court, if any are available, for a period not exceeding sixty days or until final disposition of their cases, whichever comes first. The court also may arrange with any public children services agency or private child placing agency to receive, or private noncustodial agency for temporary care of, the children within the jurisdiction of the court. A district detention home approved for such purpose by the department of youth services under section 5139.281 [5139.28.1] of the Revised Code may receive children committed to its temporary custody under section 2151.355 [2151.35.5] of the Revised Code and provide the care, treatment, and training required.

If a detention home is established as an agency of the court or a district detention home is established by the courts of several counties as provided in this section, it shall be furnished and carried on, as far as possible, as a family home in charge of a superintendent or matron in a nonpunitive neutral atmosphere. The judge, or the directing board of a district detention home, may appoint a superintendent, a matron, and other necessary employees for the home and fix their salaries. During the school year, when possible, a comparable educational program with competent and trained staff shall be provided for those children of school age. A sufficient number of trained recreational personnel shall be included among the staff to assure wholesome and profitable leisure-time activities. Medical and mental health services shall be made available to ensure the courts all possible treatment facilities shall be given to those children placed under their care. In the case of a county detention home, the salaries shall be paid in the same manner as is provided by section 2151.13 of the Revised Code for other employees of the court, and the necessary expenses incurred in maintaining the detention home shall be paid by the county. In the case of a district detention home, the salaries and the necessary expenses incurred in maintaining the district detention home shall be paid as provided in sections 2151.341 [2151.34.1] to 2151.3415 [2151.34.15] of the Revised Code.

If the court arranges for the board of children temporarily detained in family foster homes or arranges for the board of those children through any private child placing agency, a reasonable sum to be fixed by the court for the board of those children shall be paid by the county. In order to have family foster homes available for service, an agreed monthly subsidy may be paid and a fixed rate per day for care of children actually residing in the family foster home.

HISTORY: GC § 1639-22; 117 v 520; 121 v 557; Bureau of Code Revision, 10-1-53; 128 v 1211 (Eff 11-2-59); 133 v S 49 (Eff 8-13-69); 133 v H 320 (Eff 11-19-69); 133 v H 931 (Eff 8-27-70); 136 v H 85 (Eff 11-28-75); 136 v H 1196 (Eff 8-9-76); 139 v H 440 (Eff 11-23-81); 141 v H 428 (Eff 12-23-86); 142 v S 89 (Eff 1-1-89); 143 v H 166 (Eff 2-14-90); 143 v S 131 (Eff 7-25-90); 143

v H 837 (Eff 7-25-90); 145 v H 152 (Eff 7-1-93); 146 v H 265. Eff 3-3-97.

[§ 2151.34.1] § 2151.341 Application for financial assistance; tax assessment for operation of district detention home.

A board of county commissioners that provides a detention home and the board of trustees of a district detention home may make application to the department of youth services under section 5139.281 [5139.28.1] of the Revised Code for financial assistance in defraying the cost of operating and maintaining the home. Such application shall be made on forms prescribed and furnished by the department. The joint boards of county commissioners of district detention homes shall make annual assessments of taxes sufficient to support and defray all necessary expenses of such home not paid from funds made available under section 5139.281 [5139.28.1] of the Revised Code.

HISTORY: 128 v 1211 (Eff 11-2-59); 136 v H 1196 (Eff 8-9-76); 137 v S 221 (Eff 11-23-77); 139 v H 440. Eff 11-23-81.

[§ 2151.34.2] § 2151.342 District detention home may receive donations and bequests.

When any person donates or bequeaths his real or personal estate or any part thereof, to the use and benefit of a district detention home, the board of trustees of the home may accept and use such donation or bequest as they deem for the best interests of the institution, and consistent with the conditions of such bequest.

HISTORY: 128 v 1211. Eff 11-2-59.

[§ 2151.34.3] § 2151.343 District detention home trustees.

Immediately upon the organization of the joint board of county commissioners as provided by section 2151.34 of the Revised Code, or so soon thereafter as practicable, such joint board of county commissioners shall appoint a board of not less than five trustees, which shall hold office and perform its duties until the first annual meeting after the choice of an established site and buildings, or after the selection and purchase of a building site, at which time such joint board of county commissioners shall appoint a board of not less than five trustees, one of whom shall hold office for a term of one year, one for the term of two years, one for the term of three years, half of the remaining number for the term of four years, and the remainder for the term of five years. Annually thereafter, the joint board of county commissioners shall appoint one or more trustees, each of whom shall hold office for the term of five years, to succeed the trustee or trustees whose term of office shall expire. A trustee may be appointed to succeed himself upon such board of trustees, and all appointments to such board of trustees shall be made from persons who are recommended and approved by the juvenile court judge or judges of the county of which such person is resident. The annual meeting of the board of trustees shall be held on the first Tuesday in May each year.

HISTORY: 128 v 1211. Eff 11-2-59.

[§ 2151.34.4] § 2151.344 Meetings.

A majority of the board of trustees appointed under section 2151.343 [2151.34.3] of the Revised Code constitutes a quorum. Board meetings shall be held at least quarterly. The juvenile court judge of each of the counties of the district organized pursuant to section 2151.34 of the Revised Code shall attend such meetings, or shall designate a member of his staff to do so. The members of the board shall receive no compensation for their services, except their actual traveling expenses, which, when properly certified, shall be allowed and paid by the treasurer.

HISTORY: 128 v 1211. Eff 11-2-59.

[§ 2151.34.5] § 2151.345 Superintendent of district detention home; duties.

The board of trustees of a district detention home shall appoint the superintendent thereof. Before entering upon his duties such superintendent shall give bond to the board, in such sum as it fixes, with sufficient surety, conditioned upon the full and faithful accounting of the funds and properties coming into his hands.

The superintendent shall appoint all employees, who, except for the superintendent, shall be in the classified civil service.

The superintendent under the supervision and subject to the rules and regulations of the board, shall control, manage, operate, and have general charge of the home, and shall have the custody of its property, files, and records.

The children to be admitted for care in such home, the period during which they shall be cared for in such home, and the removal and transfer of children from such home shall be determined by the juvenile courts of the respective counties.

HISTORY: 128 v 1211. Eff 11-2-59.

[§ 2151.34.6] § 2151.346 District detention homes operated in same manner as county detention homes.

District detention homes shall be established, operated, maintained, and managed in the same manner so far as applicable as county detention homes.

HISTORY: 128 v 1211. Eff 11-2-59.

[§ 2151.34.7] § 2151.347 Selection of site.

When the board of trustees appointed under section 2151.343 [2151.34.3] of the Revised Code does not choose an established institution in one of the counties of this district, it may select a suitable site for the erection of a district detention home. Such site must be easily accessible, and when, in the judgment of the board, it is equally conducive to health, economy in purchasing or in building, and to the general interest of the home and inmates, such site shall be as near as practicable to the geographical center of the district. When only two counties form such district the site shall be as near as practicable to the dividing line between such counties.

HISTORY: 128 v 1211. Eff 11-2-59.

[§ 2151.34.8] § 2151.348 Each county shall be represented on board of trustees.

Each county in the district, organized under section 2151.34 of the Revised Code, shall be entitled to one trustee, and in districts composed of but two counties, each county shall be entitled to not less than two trustees. In districts composed of more than four counties, the number of trustees shall be sufficiently increased so that there shall always be an uneven number of trustees constituting such board. The county in which a district detention home is located shall have not less than two trustees, who, in the interim period between the regular meetings of the board of trustees, shall act as an executive committee in the discharge of all business pertaining to the home.

HISTORY: 128 v 1211. Eff 11-2-59.

[§ 2151.34.9] § 2151.349 Removal of trustees.

The joint board of county commissioners organized under section 2151.34 of the Revised Code may remove any trustee appointed under section 2151.343 [2151.34.3] of the Revised Code, but no such removal shall be made on account of the religious or political opinion of such trustee. The trustee appointed to fill any vacancy shall hold his office for the unexpired term of his predecessor.

HISTORY: 128 v 1211. Eff 11-2-59.

[§ 2151.34.10] § 2151.3410 Interim powers of board of trustees.

In the interim, between the selection and purchase of a site, and the erection and occupancy of the district detention home, the joint board of county commissioners provided by section 2151.34 of the Revised Code may delegate to the board of trustees appointed under section 2151.343 [2151.34.3] of the Revised Code, such powers and duties as, in its judgment, will be of general interest or aid to the institution. Such joint board of county commissioners may appropriate a trustees' fund, to be expended by the board of trustees in payment of such contracts, purchases, or other expenses necessary to the wants or requirements of the home, which are not otherwise provided for. The board of trustees shall make a complete settlement with the joint board of county commissioners once each six months, or quarterly if required, and shall make a full report of the condition of the home and inmates, to the board of county commissioners and to the juvenile court of each of the counties.

HISTORY: 128 v 1211 (Eff 11-2-59); 129 v 582 (738). Eff 1-10-61.

Style deviations in this section were corrected by the amendment in HB 1 (129 v 582). No change in the law was intended; see RC § 1.25.

[§ 2151.34.11] § 2151.3411 Joint board of county commissioners; powers and duties.

The choice of an established site and buildings, or the purchase of a site, stock, implements, and general farm equipment, should there be a farm, the erection of buildings, and the completion and furnishing of the district detention home for occupancy, shall be in the hands of the joint board of county commissioners organized under section 2151.34 of the Revised Code. Such joint board of county commissioners may delegate all or a portion of these duties to the board of trustees provided for under section 2151.343 [2151.34.3] of the Revised Code, under such restrictions and regulations as the joint board of county commissioners imposes.

HISTORY: 128 v 1211. Eff 11-2-59.

[§ 2151.34.12] § 2151.3412 Appraisal of district detention home's site and buildings; funding of expenses.

When an established site and buildings are used for a district detention home the joint board of county commissioners organized under section 2151.34 of the Revised Code shall cause the value of such site and buildings to be properly appraised. This appraisal value, or in case of the purchase of a site, the purchase price and the cost of all betterments and additions thereto, shall be paid by the counties comprising the district, in proportion to the taxable property of each county, as shown by its tax duplicate. The current expenses of maintaining the home not paid from funds made available under section 5139.281 [5139.28.1] of the Revised Code, and the cost of ordinary repairs thereto shall be paid by each such county in accordance with one of the following methods as approved by the joint board of county commissioners:

(A) In proportion to the number of children from

such county who are maintained in the home during the year;

(B) By a levy submitted by the joint board of county commissioners under division (A) of section 5705.19 of the Revised Code and approved by the electors of the district;

(C) In proportion to the taxable property of each county, as shown by its tax duplicate;

(D) In any combination of the methods for payment described in division (A), (B), or (C) of this section.

HISTORY: 128 v 1211 (Eff 11-2-59); 134 v H 258 (Eff 1-27-72); 136 v H 1196 (Eff 8-9-76); 142 v H 365. Eff 6-14-88.

[§ 2151.34.13] § 2151.3413 Withdrawal by county from detention home district; continuity of district tax levy.

The board of county commissioners of any county within a detention home district may, upon the recommendation of the juvenile court of such county, withdraw from such district and dispose of its interest in such home by selling or leasing its right, title, and interest in the site, buildings, furniture, and equipment to any counties in the district, at such price and upon such terms as are agreed upon among the boards of county commissioners of the counties concerned. Section 307.10 of the Revised Code does not apply to this section. The net proceeds of any such sale or lease shall be paid into the treasury of the withdrawing county.

Any county withdrawing from such district or from a combined district organized under sections 2151.34 and 2151.65 of the Revised Code shall continue to have levied against its tax duplicate any tax levied by the district during the period in which the county was a member of the district for current operating expenses, permanent improvements, or the retirement of bonded indebtedness. Such levy shall continue to be a levy against such duplicate of the county until such time that it expires or is renewed.

Members of the board of trustees of a district detention home who are residents of a county withdrawing from such district are deemed to have resigned their positions upon the completion of the withdrawal procedure provided by this section. Vacancies then created shall be filled according to sections 2151.343 [2151.34.3] and 2151.349 [2151.34.9] of the Revised Code.

HISTORY: 128 v 1211 (Eff 11-2-59); 134 v H 258. Eff 1-27-72.

[§ 2151.34.14] § 2151.3414 Designation of fiscal officer of detention home district; adjustment of accounts.

The county auditor of the county having the greatest population, or, with the unanimous concurrence of the county auditors of the counties composing a district, the auditor of the county wherein the detention home is located, shall be the fiscal officer of a detention home district or a combined district organized under sections 2151.34 and 2151.65 of the Revised Code. The county auditors of the several counties composing a detention home district shall meet at the district detention home, not less than once in six months, to review accounts and to transact such other duties in connection with the institution as pertain to the business of their office.

HISTORY: 128 v 1211 (Eff 11-2-59); 134 v H 258 (Eff 1-27-72); 135 v H 1033. Eff 10-2-74.

[§ 2151.34.15] § 2151.3415 Board of county commissioners; expenses.

Members of the board of county commissioners who meet by appointment to consider the organization of a district detention home shall, upon presentation of properly certified accounts, be paid their necessary expenses upon a warrant drawn by the county auditor of their county.

HISTORY: 128 v 1211. Eff 11-2-59.

[§ 2151.34.16] § 2151.3416 Financial assistance for home.

The board of county commissioners of each county which participates in the establishment of a district detention home may apply to the department of youth services for financial assistance to defray the county's share of the cost of acquisition or construction of such home, as provided in section 5139.271 [5139.27.1] of the Revised Code. Application shall be made in accordance with rules adopted by the department. No county shall be reimbursed for expenses incurred in the acquisition or construction of a district detention home which serves a district having a population of less than one hundred thousand.

HISTORY: 133 v H 1135 (Eff 9-16-70); 139 v H 440. Eff 11-23-81.

§ 2151.35 Hearing procedure; recording of proceedings; dispositional hearing.

(A) The juvenile court may conduct its hearings in an informal manner and may adjourn its hearings from time to time. In the hearing of any case, the general public may be excluded and only those persons admitted who have a direct interest in the case.

All cases involving children shall be heard separately and apart from the trial of cases against adults. The court may excuse the attendance of the child at the hearing in cases involving abused, neglected, or dependent children. The court shall hear and determine all cases of children without a jury.

If the court at the adjudicatory hearing finds from clear and convincing evidence that the child is an abused, neglected, or dependent child, the court shall proceed, in accordance with division (B) of this section, to hold a dispositional hearing and hear the evidence as to the proper disposition to be made under section 2151.353 [2151.35.3] of the Revised Code. If the court at the adjudicatory hearing finds beyond a reasonable doubt that the child is a delinquent or unruly child or a juvenile traffic offender, the court shall proceed immediately, or at a postponed hearing, to hear the evidence as to the proper disposition to be made under sections 2151.352 [2151.35.2] to 2151.355 [2151.35.5] of the Revised Code. If the court does not find the child to be an abused, neglected, dependent, delinquent, or unruly child or a juvenile traffic offender, it shall order that the complaint be dismissed and that the child be discharged from any detention or restriction theretofore ordered.

A record of all testimony and other oral proceedings in juvenile court shall be made in all proceedings that are held pursuant to section 2151.414 [2151.41.4] of the Revised Code or in which an order of disposition may be made pursuant to division (A)(4) of section 2151.353 [2151.35.3] of the Revised Code, and shall be made upon request in any other proceedings. The record shall be made as provided in section 2301.20 of the Revised Code.

(B)(1) If the court at an adjudicatory hearing determines that a child is an abused, neglected, or dependent child, the court shall not issue a dispositional order until after the court holds a separate dispositional hearing. The court may hold the dispositional hearing for an adjudicated abused, neglected, or dependent child immediately after the adjudicatory hearing if all parties were served prior to the adjudicatory hearing with all documents required for the dispositional hearing. The dispositional hearing may not be held more than thirty days after the adjudicatory hearing is held. The court, upon the request of any party or the guardian ad litem of the child, may continue a dispositional hearing for a reasonable time not to exceed the time limits set forth in this division to enable a party to obtain or consult counsel. The dispositional hearing shall not be held more than ninety days after the date on which the complaint in the case was filed.

If the dispositional hearing is not held within the period of time required by this division, the court, on its own motion or the motion of any party or the guardian ad litem of the child, shall dismiss the complaint without prejudice.

(2) The dispositional hearing shall be conducted in accordance with all of the following:

(a) The judge or referee who presided at the adjudicatory hearing shall preside, if possible, at the dispositional hearing;

(b) The court may admit any evidence that is material and relevant, including, but not limited to, hearsay, opinion, and documentary evidence;

(c) Medical examiners and each investigator who prepared a social history shall not be cross-examined, except upon consent of the parties, for good cause shown,

or as the court in its discretion may direct. Any party may offer evidence supplementing, explaining, or disputing any information contained in the social history or other reports that may be used by the court in determining disposition.

(3) After the conclusion of the dispositional hearing, the court shall enter an appropriate judgment within seven days and shall schedule the date for the hearing to be held pursuant to section 2151.415 [2151.41.5] of the Revised Code. The court may make any order of disposition that is set forth in section 2151.353 [2151.35.3] of the Revised Code. A copy of the judgment shall be given to each party and to the child's guardian ad litem. If the judgment is conditional, the order shall state the conditions of the judgment. If the child is not returned to the child's own home, the court shall determine which school district shall bear the cost of the child's education and shall comply with section 2151.36 of the Revised Code.

(4) As part of its dispositional order, the court may issue any order described in division (B) of section 2151.33 of the Revised Code.

(C) The court shall give all parties to the action and the child's guardian ad litem notice of the adjudicatory and dispositional hearings in accordance with the Juvenile Rules.

(D) If the court issues an order pursuant to division (A)(4) of section 2151.353 [2151.35.3] of the Revised Code committing a child to the permanent custody of a public children services agency or a private child placing agency, the parents of the child whose parental rights were terminated cease to be parties to the action upon the issuance of the order. This division is not intended to eliminate or restrict any right of the parents to appeal the permanent custody order issued pursuant to division (A)(4) of section 2151.353 [2151.35.3] of the Revised Code.

(E) Each juvenile court shall schedule its hearings in accordance with the time requirements of this chapter.

(F) In cases regarding abused, neglected, or dependent children, the court may admit any statement of a child that the court determines to be excluded by the hearsay rule if the proponent of the statement informs the adverse party of the proponent's intention to offer the statement and of the particulars of the statement, including the name of the declarant, sufficiently in advance of the hearing to provide the party with a fair opportunity to prepare to challenge, respond to, or defend against the statement, and the court determines all of the following:

(1) The statement has circumstantial guarantees of trustworthiness;

(2) The statement is offered as evidence of a material fact;

(3) The statement is more probative on the point for which it is offered than any other evidence that the proponent can procure through reasonable efforts;

(4) The general purposes of the evidence rules and

the interests of justice will best be served by the admission of the statement into evidence.

(G) If a child is alleged to be an abused child, the court may order that the testimony of the child be taken by deposition. On motion of the prosecuting attorney, guardian ad litem, or any party, or in its own discretion, the court may order that the deposition be videotaped. Any deposition taken under this division shall be taken with a judge or referee present.

If a deposition taken under this division is intended to be offered as evidence at the hearing, it shall be filed with the court. Part or all of the deposition is admissible in evidence if counsel for all parties had an opportunity and similar motive at the time of the taking of the deposition to develop the testimony by direct, cross, or redirect examination and the judge determines that there is reasonable cause to believe that if the child were to testify in person at the hearing, the child would experience emotional trauma as a result of participating at the hearing.

HISTORY: 133 v H 320 (Eff 11-19-69); 136 v H 85 (Eff 11-28-75); 138 v H 695 (Eff 10-24-80); 142 v S 89 (Eff 1-1-89); 146 v H 1 (Eff 1-1-96); 146 v H 274 (Eff 8-8-96); 146 v H 124. Eff 3-31-97.

Analogous in part to former RC § 2151.35 [GC § 1639-30; 117 v 520; 119 v 731; 121 v 557; Bureau of Code Revision, 10-1-53; 125 v 324; 127 v 547; 130 v 621; 130 v 623; 132 v S 278; 133 v S 49 (eff 8-13-69)] repealed in 133 v H 320, § 2, eff 11-19-69.

See also analogous provisions now contained in RC §§ 2151.35.2, 2151.35.3, 2151.35.5, 2151.35.6.

[§ 2151.35.1] § 2151.351 Repealed, 146 v H 265, § 2 [139 v H 440]. Eff 3-3-97.

This section concerned confinement of non-delinquent children. See now sections 2151.33.1, 2151.35.3 and 2151.35.4.

[§ 2151.35.2] § 2151.352 Right to counsel.

A child, his parents, custodian, or other person in loco parentis of such child is entitled to representation by legal counsel at all stages of the proceedings and if, as an indigent person, he is unable to employ counsel, to have counsel provided for him pursuant to Chapter 120. of the Revised Code. If a party appears without counsel, the court shall ascertain whether he knows of his right to counsel and of his right to be provided with counsel if he is an indigent person. The court may continue the case to enable a party to obtain counsel or to be represented by the county public defender or the joint county public defender and shall provide counsel upon request pursuant to Chapter 120. of the Revised Code. Counsel must be provided for a child not represented by his parent, guardian, or custodian. If the interests of two or more such parties conflict, separate counsel shall be provided for each of them.

Section 2935.14 of the Revised Code applies to any child taken into custody. The parents, custodian, or guardian of such child, and any attorney at law representing them or the child, shall be entitled to visit such child at any reasonable time, be present at any hearing involving the child, and be given reasonable notice of such hearing.

Any report or part thereof concerning such child, which is used in the hearing and is pertinent thereto, shall for good cause shown be made available to any attorney at law representing such child and to any attorney at law representing the parents, custodians, or guardian of such child, upon written request prior to any hearing involving such child.

HISTORY: 133 v H 320 (Eff 11-19-69); 136 v H 164. Eff 1-13-76.

[§ 2151.35.3] § 2151.353 Disposition of abused, neglected or dependent child.

(A) If a child is adjudicated an abused, neglected, or dependent child, the court may make any of the following orders of disposition:

(1) Place the child in protective supervision;

(2) Commit the child to the temporary custody of a public children services agency, a private child placing agency, either parent, a relative residing within or outside the state, or a probation officer for placement in a certified family foster home or in any other home approved by the court;

(3) Award legal custody of the child to either parent or to any other person who, prior to the dispositional hearing, files a motion requesting legal custody of the child;

(4) Commit the child to the permanent custody of a public children services agency or private child placing agency, if the court determines in accordance with division (E) of section 2151.414 [2151.41.4] of the Revised Code that the child cannot be placed with one of the child's parents within a reasonable time or should not be placed with either parent and determines in accordance with division (D) of section 2151.414 [2151.41.4] of the Revised Code that the permanent commitment is in the best interest of the child. If the court grants permanent custody under this division, the court, upon the request of any party, shall file a written opinion setting forth its findings of fact and conclusions of law in relation to the proceeding.

(5) Place the child in long-term family foster care with a public children services agency or private child placing agency, if a public children services agency or private child placing agency requests the court to place the child in long-term family foster care and if the court finds, by clear and convincing evidence, that long-term foster care is in the best interest of the child and that one of the following exists:

(a) The child, because of physical, mental, or psychological problems or needs, is unable to function in a family-like setting and must remain in residential or institutional care;

(b) The parents of the child have significant physical, mental, or psychological problems and are unable to care for the child because of those problems, adoption is not in the best interest of the child, as determined in accordance with division (D) of section 2151.414 [2151.41.4] of the Revised Code, and the child retains a significant and positive relationship with a parent or relative;

(c) The child is sixteen years of age or older, has been counseled on the permanent placement options available to the child, is unwilling to accept or unable to adapt to a permanent placement, and is in an agency program preparing the child for independent living.

(6) Order the removal from the child's home until further order of the court of the person who committed abuse as described in section 2151.031 [2151.03.1] of the Revised Code against the child, who caused or allowed the child to suffer neglect as described in section 2151.03 of the Revised Code, or who is the parent, guardian, or custodian of a child who is adjudicated a dependent child and order any person not to have contact with the child or the child's siblings.

(B) No order for permanent custody or temporary custody of a child or the placement of a child in long-term foster care shall be made pursuant to this section unless the complaint alleging the abuse, neglect, or dependency contains a prayer requesting permanent custody, temporary custody, or the placement of the child in long-term foster care as desired, the summons served on the parents of the child contains as is appropriate a full explanation that the granting of an order for permanent custody permanently divests them of their parental rights, a full explanation that an adjudication that the child is an abused, neglected, or dependent child may result in an order of temporary custody that will cause the removal of the child from their legal custody until the court terminates the order of temporary custody or permanently divests the parents of their parental rights, or a full explanation that the granting of an order for long-term foster care will result in the removal of the child from their legal custody if any of the conditions listed in divisions (A)(5)(a) to (c) of this section are found to exist, and the summons served on the parents contains a full explanation of their right to be represented by counsel and to have counsel appointed pursuant to Chapter 120. of the Revised Code if they are indigent.

If after making disposition as authorized by division (A)(2) of this section, a motion is filed that requests permanent custody of the child, the court may grant permanent custody of the child to the movant in accordance with section 2151.414 [2151.41.4] of the Revised Code.

(C) If the court issues an order for protective supervision pursuant to division (A)(1) of this section, the court may place any reasonable restrictions upon the child, the child's parents, guardian, or custodian, or any other person, including, but not limited to, any of the following:

(1) Order a party, within forty-eight hours after the issuance of the order, to vacate the child's home indefinitely or for a specified period of time;

(2) Order a party, a parent of the child, or a physical custodian of the child to prevent any particular person from having contact with the child;

(3) Issue an order restraining or otherwise controlling the conduct of any person which conduct would not be in the best interest of the child.

(D) As part of its dispositional order, the court shall journalize a case plan for the child. The journalized case plan shall not be changed except as provided in section 2151.412 [2151.41.2] of the Revised Code.

(E)(1) The court shall retain jurisdiction over any child for whom the court issues an order of disposition pursuant to division (A) of this section or pursuant to section 2151.414 [2151.41.4] or 2151.415 [2151.41.5] of the Revised Code until the child attains the age of eighteen if the child is not mentally retarded, developmentally disabled, or physically impaired, the child attains the age of twenty-one if the child is mentally retarded, developmentally disabled, or physically impaired, or the child is adopted and a final decree of adoption is issued, except that the court may retain jurisdiction over the child and continue any order of disposition under division (A) of this section or under section 2151.414 [2151.41.4] or 2151.415 [2151.41.5] of the Revised Code for a specified period of time to enable the child to graduate from high school or vocational school. The court shall make an entry continuing its jurisdiction under this division in the journal.

(2) Any public children services agency, any private child placing agency, the department of human services, or any party, other than any parent whose parental rights with respect to the child have been terminated pursuant to an order issued under division (A)(4) of this section, by filing a motion with the court, may at any time request the court to modify or terminate any order of disposition issued pursuant to division (A) of this section or section 2151.414 [2151.41.4] or 2151.415 [2151.41.5] of the Revised Code. The court shall hold a hearing upon the motion as if the hearing were the original dispositional hearing and shall give all parties to the action and the guardian ad litem notice of the hearing pursuant to the Juvenile Rules.

(F) Any temporary custody order issued pursuant to division (A) of this section shall terminate one year after the earlier of the date on which the complaint in the case was filed or the child was first placed into shelter care, except that, upon the filing of a motion pursuant to section 2151.415 [2151.41.5] of the Revised Code, the temporary custody order shall continue and not terminate until the court issues a dispositional order under that section.

(G)(1) No later than one year after the earlier of the date the complaint in the case was filed or the child was first placed in shelter care, a party may ask the court to extend an order for protective supervision for six months or to terminate the order. A party requesting extension or termination of the order shall file a written request for the extension or termination with the court and give notice of the proposed extension or termination in writing before the end of the day after the day of filing it to all parties and the child's guardian ad litem. If a public children services agency or private child placing agency requests termination of the order, the agency shall file a written status report setting out the facts supporting termination of the order at the time it files the request with the court. If no party requests extension or termination of the order, the court shall notify the parties that the court will extend the order for six months or terminate it and that it may do so without a hearing unless one of the parties requests a hearing. All parties and the guardian ad litem shall have seven days from the date a notice is sent pursuant to this division to object to and request a hearing on the proposed extension or termination.

(a) If it receives a timely request for a hearing, the court shall schedule a hearing to be held no later than thirty days after the request is received by the court. The court shall give notice of the date, time, and location of the hearing to all parties and the guardian ad litem. At the hearing, the court shall determine whether extension or termination of the order is in the child's best interest. If termination is in the child's best interest, the court shall terminate the order. If extension is in the child's best interest, the court shall extend the order for six months.

(b) If it does not receive a timely request for a hearing, the court may extend the order for six months or terminate it without a hearing and shall journalize the order of extension or termination not later than fourteen days after receiving the request for extension or termination or after the date the court notifies the parties that it will extend or terminate the order. If the court does not extend or terminate the order, it shall schedule a hearing to be held no later than thirty days after the expiration of the applicable fourteen-day time period and give notice of the date, time, and location of the hearing to all parties and the child's guardian ad litem. At the hearing, the court shall determine whether extension or termination of the order is in the child's best interest. If termination is in the child's best interest, the court shall terminate the order. If extension is in the child's best interest, the court shall issue an order extending the order for protective supervision six months.

(2) If the court grants an extension of the order for protective supervision pursuant to division (G)(1) of this section, a party may, prior to termination of the extension, file with the court a request for an additional extension of six months or for termination of the order. The court and the parties shall comply with division (G)(1) of this section with respect to extending or terminating the order.

(3) If a court grants an extension pursuant to division (G)(2) of this section, the court shall terminate the order for protective supervision at the end of the extension.

(H) The court shall not issue a dispositional order pursuant to division (A) of this section that removes a child from the child's home unless the court makes the determination required by section 2151.419 [2151.41.9] of the Revised Code and includes in the dispositional order the finding of facts required by that section.

(I) If a motion or application for an order described in division (A)(6) of this section is made, the court shall not issue the order unless, prior to the issuance of the order, it provides to the person all of the following:

(1) Notice and a copy of the motion or application;

(2) The grounds for the motion or application;

(3) An opportunity to present evidence and witnesses at a hearing regarding the motion or application;

(4) An opportunity to be represented by counsel at the hearing.

(J) The jurisdiction of the court shall terminate one year after the date of the award or, if the court takes any further action in the matter subsequent to the award, the date of the latest further action subsequent to the award, if the court awards legal custody of a child to either of the following:

(1) A legal custodian who, at the time of the award of legal custody, resides in a county of this state other than the county in which the court is located;

(2) A legal custodian who resides in the county in which the court is located at the time of the award of legal custody, but moves to a different county of this state prior to one year after the date of the award or, if the court takes any further action in the matter subsequent to the award, one year after the date of the latest further action subsequent to the award.

The court in the county in which the legal custodian resides then shall have jurisdiction in the matter.

HISTORY: 133 v H 320 (Eff 11-19-69); 136 v H 85 (Eff 11-28-75); 138 v H 695 (Eff 10-24-80); 139 v H 440 (Eff 11-23-81); 141 v H 428 (Eff 12-23-86); 142 v S 89 (Eff 1-1-89); 145 v H 152 (Eff 7-1-93); 146 v H 274 (Eff 8-8-96); 146 v H 419 (Eff 9-18-96); 146 v H 265. Eff 3-3-97.

[§ 2151.35.4] § 2151.354 Disposition of unruly child.

(A) If the child is adjudicated an unruly child, the court may:

(1) Make any of the dispositions authorized under section 2151.353 [2151.35.3] of the Revised Code;

(2) Place the child on probation under any conditions that the court prescribes;

(3) Suspend or revoke the driver's license issued to the child and suspend or revoke the registration of all motor vehicles registered in the name of the child;

(4) Commit the child to the temporary or permanent custody of the court;

(5) If, after making a disposition under division (A)(1), (2), or (3) of this section, the court finds upon further hearing that the child is not amenable to treat-

ment or rehabilitation under that disposition, make a disposition otherwise authorized under divisions (A)(1), (2), and (A)(7) to (11) of section 2151.355 [2151.35.5] of the Revised Code, except that the child may not be committed to or placed in a secure correctional facility, and commitment to or placement in a detention home may not exceed twenty-four hours unless authorized by division (C)(3) of section 2151.312 [2151.31.2] or sections 2151.56 to 2151.61 of the Revised Code.

(B) If a child is adjudicated an unruly child for committing any act that, if committed by an adult, would be a drug abuse offense, as defined in section 2925.01 of the Revised Code, or a violation of division (B) of section 2917.11 of the Revised Code, then, in addition to imposing, in its discretion, any other order of disposition authorized by this section, the court shall do both of the following:

(1) Require the child to participate in a drug abuse or alcohol abuse counseling program;

(2) Suspend or revoke the temporary instruction permit or probationary operator's license issued to the child until the child attains the age of eighteen years or, at the discretion of the court, attends and satisfactorily completes a drug abuse or alcohol abuse education, intervention, or treatment program specified by the court. During the time the child is attending the program, the court shall retain any temporary instruction permit or probationary license issued to the child and shall return the permit or license when the child satisfactorily completes the program.

HISTORY: 133 v H 320 (Eff 11-19-69); 142 v H 643 (Eff 3-17-89); 143 v H 330 (Eff 6-30-89); 143 v H 381 (Eff 7-1-89); 143 v S 131 (Eff 7-25-90); 143 v S 258 (Eff 8-22-90); 144 v H 154 (Eff 7-31-92); 146 v H 274 (Eff 8-8-96); 146 v H 265. Eff 3-3-97.

[§ 2151.35.5] § 2151.355 Disposition of delinquent child.

(A) If a child is adjudicated a delinquent child, the court may make any of the following orders of disposition:

(1) Any order that is authorized by section 2151.353 [2151.35.3] of the Revised Code;

(2) Place the child on probation under any conditions that the court prescribes. If the child is adjudicated a delinquent child for violating section 2909.05, 2909.06, or 2909.07 of the Revised Code and if restitution is appropriate under the circumstances of the case, the court shall require the child to make restitution for the property damage caused by the child's violation as a condition of the child's probation. If the child is adjudicated a delinquent child because the child violated any other section of the Revised Code, the court may require the child as a condition of the child's probation to make restitution for the property damage caused by the child's violation and for the value of the property that was the subject of the violation the child committed if it would be a theft offense, as defined in division (K) of section 2913.01 of the Revised Code, if committed by an adult. The restitution may be in the form of a cash reimbursement paid in a lump sum or in installments, the performance of repair work to restore any damaged property to its original condition, the performance of a reasonable amount of labor for the victim approximately equal to the value of the property damage caused by the child's violation or to the value of the property that is the subject of the violation if it would be a theft offense if committed by an adult, the performance of community service or community work, any other form of restitution devised by the court, or any combination of the previously described forms of restitution.

If the child is adjudicated a delinquent child for violating a law of this state or the United States, or an ordinance or regulation of a political subdivision of this state, that would be a crime if committed by an adult or for violating division (A) of section 2923.211 [2923.21.1] of the Revised Code, the court, in addition to all other required or permissive conditions of probation that the court imposes upon the delinquent child pursuant to division (A)(2) of this section, shall require the child as a condition of the child's probation to abide by the law during the period of probation, including, but not limited to, complying with the provisions of Chapter 2923. of the Revised Code relating to the possession, sale, furnishing, transfer, disposition, purchase, acquisition, carrying, conveying, or use of, or other conduct involving a firearm or dangerous ordnance, as defined in section 2923.11 of the Revised Code.

(3) Commit the child to the temporary custody of any school, camp, institution, or other facility operated for the care of delinquent children by the county, by a district organized under section 2151.34 or 2151.65 of the Revised Code, or by a private agency or organization, within or without the state, that is authorized and qualified to provide the care, treatment, or placement required;

(4) If the child is adjudicated a delinquent child for committing an act that would be a felony of the third, fourth, or fifth degree if committed by an adult or for violating division (A) of section 2923.211 [2923.21.1] of the Revised Code, commit the child to the legal custody of the department of youth services for institutionalization for an indefinite term consisting of a minimum period of six months and a maximum period not to exceed the child's attainment of twenty-one years of age;

(5)(a) If the child is adjudicated a delinquent child for violating section 2903.03, 2905.01, 2909.02, or 2911.01 or division (A) of section 2903.04 of the Revised Code or for violating any provision of section 2907.02 of the Revised Code other than division (A)(1)(b) of that section when the sexual conduct or insertion involved was consensual and when the victim of the violation of division (A)(1)(b) of that section was older than the delinquent child, was the same age as the delinquent child, or was less than three years younger than the delinquent child, commit the child to the legal custody of the department of youth services for institutionalization in a secure facility for an indefinite term consisting of a minimum period of one to three years, as prescribed by the court, and a maximum period not to exceed the child's attainment of twenty-one years of age;

(b) If the child is adjudicated a delinquent child for violating section 2923.02 of the Revised Code and if the violation involves an attempt to commit a violation of section 2903.01 or 2903.02 of the Revised Code, commit the child to the legal custody of the department of youth services for institutionalization in a secure facility for an indefinite term consisting of a minimum period of six to seven years, as prescribed by the court, and a maximum period not to exceed the child's attainment of twenty-one years of age;

(c) If the child is adjudicated a delinquent child for committing an act that is not described in division (A)(5)(a) or (b) of this section and that would be a felony of the first or second degree if committed by an adult, commit the child to the legal custody of the department of youth services for institutionalization in a secure facility for an indefinite term consisting of a minimum period of one year and a maximum period not to exceed the child's attainment of twenty-one years of age;

(6) If the child is adjudicated a delinquent child for committing a violation of section 2903.01 or 2903.02 of the Revised Code, commit the child to the legal custody of the department of youth services for institutionalization in a secure facility until the child's attainment of twenty-one years of age;

(7)(a) If the child is adjudicated a delinquent child for committing an act, other than a violation of section 2923.12 of the Revised Code, that would be a felony if committed by an adult and is committed to the legal custody of the department of youth services pursuant to division (A)(4), (5), or (6) of this section and if the court determines that the child, if the child was an adult, would be guilty of a specification of the type set forth in section 2941.141 [2941.14.1], 2941.144 [2941.14.4], 2941.145 [2941.14.5], or 2941.146 [2941.14.6] of the Revised Code in relation to the act for which the child was adjudicated a delinquent child, commit the child to the legal custody of the department of youth services for institutionalization in a secure facility for the following period of time, subject to division (A)(7)(b) of this section:

(i) If the child would be guilty of a specification of the type set forth in section 2941.141 [2941.14.1] of the Revised Code, a period of one year;

(ii) If the child would be guilty of a specification of the type set forth in section 2941.144 [2941.14.4], 2941.145 [2941.14.5], or 2941.146 [2941.14.6] of the Revised Code, a period of three years.

(b) The court shall not commit a child to the legal custody of the department of youth services pursuant to division (A)(7)(a) of this section for a period of time that exceeds three years. The period of commitment imposed pursuant to division (A)(7)(a) of this section shall be in addition to, and shall be served consecutively with and prior to, a period of commitment ordered pursuant to division (A)(4), (5), or (6) of this section, provided that the total of all the periods of commitment shall not exceed the child's attainment of twenty-one years of age.

(8)(a) Impose a fine and costs in accordance with the schedule set forth in section 2151.3512 [2151.35.12] of the Revised Code;

(b) Require the child to make restitution for all or part of the property damage caused by the child's delinquent act and for all or part of the value of the property that was the subject of any delinquent act the child committed that would be a theft offense, as defined in division (K) of section 2913.01 of the Revised Code, if committed by an adult. If the court determines that the victim of the child's delinquent act was sixty-five years of age or older or permanently and totally disabled at the time of the commission of the act, the court, regardless of whether or not the child knew the age of the victim, shall consider that fact in favor of imposing restitution, but that fact shall not control the decision of the court. The restitution may be in the form of a cash reimbursement paid in a lump sum or in installments, the performance of repair work to restore any damaged property to its original condition, the performance of a reasonable amount of labor for the victim, the performance of community service or community work, any other form of restitution devised by the court, or any combination of the previously described forms of restitution.

(9) Subject to division (D) of this section, suspend or revoke the driver's license or temporary instruction permit issued to the child or suspend or revoke the registration of all motor vehicles registered in the name of the child;

(10) If the child is adjudicated a delinquent child for committing an act that, if committed by an adult, would be a criminal offense that would qualify the adult as an eligible offender pursuant to division (A)(3) of section 2929.23 of the Revised Code, impose a period of electronically monitored house detention in accordance with division (I) of this section that does not exceed the maximum sentence of imprisonment that could be imposed upon an adult who commits the same act;

(11) Commit the child to the temporary or permanent custody of the court;

(12) Make any further disposition that the court finds proper, except that the child shall not be placed in any of the following:

(a) A state correctional institution, a county, multi-county, or municipal jail or workhouse, or another place in which an adult convicted of a crime, under arrest, or charged with a crime is held;

(b) A community corrections facility, if the child would be covered by the definition of public safety beds for purposes of sections 5139.41 to 5139.45 of the Revised Code if the court exercised its authority to commit the child to the legal custody of the department of youth services for institutionalization or institutionalization in a secure facility pursuant to division (A)(4), (5), or (6) of this section. As used in division (A)(12)(b) of this section, "community corrections facility" and "public safety beds" have the same meanings as in section 5139.01 of the Revised Code.

(B)(1) If a child is adjudicated a delinquent child for violating section 2923.32 of the Revised Code, the court, in addition to any order of disposition it makes for the child under division (A) of this section, shall enter an order of criminal forfeiture against the child, in accordance with divisions (B)(3), (4), (5), and (6) and (C) to (F) of section 2923.32 of the Revised Code.

(2) If a child is adjudicated a delinquent child for committing two or more acts that would be felonies if committed by an adult and if the court entering the delinquent child adjudication orders the commitment of the child, for two or more of those acts, to the legal custody of the department of youth services for institutionalization or institutionalization in a secure facility pursuant to division (A)(4), (5), or (6) of this section, the court may order that all of the periods of commitment imposed under those divisions for those acts be served consecutively in the legal custody of the department of youth services and, if applicable, be in addition to and commence immediately following the expiration of a period of commitment that the court imposes pursuant to division (A)(7) of this section. A court shall not commit a delinquent child to the legal custody of the department of youth services under division (B)(2) of this section for a period that exceeds the child's attainment of twenty-one years of age.

(C) If a child is adjudicated a delinquent child for committing an act that, if committed by an adult, would be a drug abuse offense, as defined in section 2925.01 of the Revised Code, or for violating division (B) of section 2917.11 of the Revised Code, in addition to imposing in its discretion any other order of disposition authorized by this section, the court shall do both of the following:

(1) Require the child to participate in a drug abuse or alcohol abuse counseling program;

(2) Suspend or revoke the temporary instruction permit or probationary operator's license issued to the child until the child attains eighteen years of age or attends, at the discretion of the court, and satisfactorily completes, a drug abuse or alcohol abuse education, intervention, or treatment program specified by the court. During the time the child is attending the program, the court shall retain any temporary instruction permit or probationary license issued to the child, and the court shall return the permit or license when the child satisfactorily completes the program.

(D) If a child is adjudicated a delinquent child for violating section 2923.122 [2923.12.2] of the Revised Code, the court, in addition to any order of disposition it makes for the child under division (A), (B), or (C) of this section, shall revoke the temporary instruction permit and deny the child the issuance of another temporary instruction permit in accordance with division (E)(1)(b) of section 2923.122 [2923.12.2] of the Revised Code or shall suspend the probationary driver's license, restricted license, or nonresident operating privilege of the child or deny the child the issuance of a probationary driver's license, restricted license, or temporary instruction permit in accordance with division (E)(1)(a), (c), (d), or (e) of section 2923.122 [2923.12.2] of the Revised Code.

(E)(1) At the dispositional hearing and prior to making any disposition pursuant to division (A) of this section, the court shall determine whether a victim of the delinquent act committed by the child was five years of age or younger at the time the delinquent act was committed, whether a victim of the delinquent act sustained physical harm to the victim's person during the commission of or otherwise as a result of the delinquent act, whether a victim of the delinquent act was sixty-five years of age or older or permanently and totally disabled at the time the delinquent act was committed, and whether the delinquent act would have been an offense of violence if committed by an adult. If the victim was five years of age or younger at the time the delinquent act was committed, sustained physical harm to the victim's person during the commission of or otherwise as a result of the delinquent act, or was sixty-five years of age or older or permanently and totally disabled at the time the act was committed, regardless of whether the child knew the age of the victim, and if the act would have been an offense of violence if committed by an adult, the court shall consider those facts in favor of imposing commitment under division (A)(3), (4), (5), or (6) of this section, but those facts shall not control the court's decision.

(2) At the dispositional hearing and prior to making any disposition pursuant to division (A)(4), (5), or (6) of this section, the court shall determine whether the delinquent child previously has been adjudicated a delinquent child for a violation of a law or ordinance. If the delinquent child previously has been adjudicated a delinquent child for a violation of a law or ordinance, the court, for purposes of entering an order of disposition for the delinquent child under this section, shall consider the previous delinquent child adjudication as a conviction of a violation of the law or ordinance in determining the degree of offense the current delinquent act would be had it been committed by an adult.

(F)(1) When a juvenile court commits a delinquent child to the custody of the department of youth services pursuant to this section, the court shall not designate the specific institution in which the department is to place the child but instead shall specify that the child is to be institutionalized or that the institutionalization is to be in a secure facility if that is required by division (A) of this section.

(2) When a juvenile court commits a delinquent child to the custody of the department of youth services, the court shall provide the department with the child's social history, the child's medical records, a copy of the report of any mental examination of the child ordered by the court, the section or sections of the Revised Code violated by the child and the degree of the violation, the warrant to convey the child to the department, and a copy of the court's journal entry ordering the commitment of the child to the legal custody of the department. The department may refuse to accept physical custody of a delinquent child who is committed to the legal custody of the department until the court provides to the department the documents specified in division (F)(2) of this section. No officer or employee of the department who refuses to accept physical custody of a delinquent child who is committed to the legal custody of the department shall be subject to prosecution or contempt of court for the refusal if the court fails to provide the documents specified in division (F)(2) of this section at the time the court transfers the physical custody of the child to the department.

(3) Within five working days after the juvenile court commits a delinquent child to the custody of the department of youth services, the court shall provide the department with a copy of the arrest record pertaining to the act for which the child was adjudicated a delinquent child, a copy of any victim impact statement pertaining to that act, and any other information concerning the child that the department reasonably requests. Within twenty working days after the department of youth services receives physical custody of a delinquent child from a juvenile court, the court shall provide the department with a certified copy of the child's birth certificate or the child's social security number, or, if the court made all reasonable efforts to obtain the information but was unsuccessful, the court shall provide the department with documentation of the efforts it made to obtain the information.

(4) When a juvenile court commits a delinquent child to the custody of the department of youth services, the court shall give notice to the school attended by the child of the child's commitment by sending to that school a copy of the court's journal entry ordering the commitment. As soon as possible after receipt of the notice described in this division, the school shall provide the department with the child's school transcript. However, the department shall not refuse to accept a child committed to it, and a child committed to it shall not be held in a county or district detention home, because of a school's failure to provide the school transcript that it is required to provide under division (F)(4) of this section.

(5) The department of youth services shall provide the court and the school with an updated copy of the child's school transcript and shall provide the court with a summary of the institutional record of the child when it releases the child from institutional care. The department also shall provide the court with a copy of any portion of the child's institutional record that the court specifically requests within five working days of the request.

(6) When a juvenile court commits a delinquent child to the custody of the department of youth services pursuant to division (A)(4) or (5) of this section, the court shall state in the order of commitment the total number of days that the child has been held, as of the date of the issuance of the order, in detention in connection with the delinquent child complaint upon which the order of commitment is based. The department shall reduce the minimum period of institutionalization or minimum period of institutionalization in a secure facility specified in division (A)(4) or (5) of this section by both the total number of days that the child has been so held in detention as stated by the court in the order of commitment and the total number of any additional days that the child has been held in detention subsequent to the order of commitment but prior to the transfer of physical custody of the child to the department.

(G)(1) At any hearing at which a child is adjudicated a delinquent child or as soon as possible after the hearing, the court shall notify all victims of the delinquent act, who may be entitled to a recovery under any of the following sections, of the right of the victims to recover, pursuant to section 3109.09 of the Revised Code, compensatory damages from the child's parents; of the right of the victims to recover, pursuant to section 3109.10 of the Revised Code, compensatory damages from the child's parents for willful and malicious assaults committed by the child; and of the right of the victims to recover an award of reparations pursuant to sections 2743.51 to 2743.72 of the Revised Code.

(2) If a child is adjudicated a delinquent child for committing an act that, if committed by an adult, would be aggravated murder, murder, rape, felonious sexual penetration in violation of former section 2907.12 of the Revised Code, involuntary manslaughter, a felony of the first or second degree resulting in the death of or physical harm to a person, complicity in or an attempt to commit any of those offenses, or an offense under an existing or former law of this state that is or was substantially equivalent to any of those offenses and if the court in its order of disposition for that act commits the child to the custody of the department of youth services, the court may make a specific finding that the adjudication should be considered a conviction for purposes of a determination in the future, pursuant to Chapter 2929. of the Revised Code, as to whether the child is a repeat violent offender as defined in section 2929.01 of the Revised Code. If the court makes a specific finding as described in this division, it shall include the specific finding in its order of disposition and in the record in the case.

(H)(1) If a child is adjudicated a delinquent child for committing an act that would be a felony if committed by an adult and if the child caused, attempted to cause, threatened to cause, or created the risk of physical harm to the victim of the act, the court, prior to issuing an order of disposition under this section, shall order the preparation of a victim impact statement by the probation department of the county in which the victim of the act resides, by the court's own probation department, or by a victim assistance program that is operated by the state, a county, a municipal corporation, or another governmental entity. The court shall consider the victim impact statement in determining the order of disposition to issue for the child.

(2) Each victim impact statement shall identify the victim of the act for which the child was adjudicated a delinquent child, itemize any economic loss suffered by the victim as a result of the act, identify any physical injury suffered by the victim as a result of the act and the seriousness and permanence of the injury, identify any change in the victim's personal welfare or familial relationships as a result of the act and any psychological impact experienced by the victim or the victim's family as a result of the act, and contain any other information related to the impact of the act upon the victim that the court requires.

(3) A victim impact statement shall be kept confidential and is not a public record, as defined in section 149.43 of the Revised Code. However, the court may furnish copies of the statement to the department of youth services pursuant to division (F)(3) of this section or to both the adjudicated delinquent child or the adjudicated delinquent child's counsel and the prosecuting attorney. The copy of a victim impact statement furnished by the court to the department pursuant to division (F)(3) of this section shall be kept confidential and is not a public record, as defined in section 149.43 of the Revised Code. The copies of a victim impact statement that are made available to the adjudicated delinquent child or the adjudicated delinquent child's counsel and the prosecuting attorney pursuant to division (H)(3) of this section shall be returned to the court by the person to whom they were made available immediately following the imposition of an order of disposition for the child under this section.

(I)(1) As used in this division, "felony drug abuse offense" has the same meaning as in section 2925.01 of the Revised Code.

(2) Sections 2925.41 to 2925.45 of the Revised Code apply to children who are adjudicated or could be adjudicated by a juvenile court to be delinquent children for an act that, if committed by an adult, would be a felony drug abuse offense. Subject to division (B) of section 2925.42 and division (E) of section 2925.43 of the Revised Code, a delinquent child of that nature loses any right to the possession of, and forfeits to the state any right, title, and interest that the delinquent child may have in, property as defined in section 2925.41 and further described in section 2925.42 or 2925.43 of the Revised Code.

(J)(1) As used in this section:
(a) "Electronic monitoring device," "certified electronic monitoring device," "electronic monitoring system," and "certified electronic monitoring system" have the same meanings as in section 2929.23 of the Revised Code.

(b) "Electronically monitored house detention" means a period of confinement of a child in the child's home or in other premises specified by the court, during which period of confinement all of the following apply:

(i) The child wears, otherwise has attached to the child's person, or otherwise is subject to monitoring by a certified electronic monitoring device or is subject to monitoring by a certified electronic monitoring system.

(ii) The child is required to remain in the child's home or other premises specified by the court for the specified period of confinement, except for periods of time during which the child is at school or at other premises as authorized by the court.

(iii) The child is subject to monitoring by a central system that monitors the certified electronic monitoring device that is attached to the child's person or that otherwise is being used to monitor the child and that can monitor and determine the child's location at any time or at a designated point in time, or the child is required to participate in monitoring by a certified electronic monitoring system.

(iv) The child is required by the court to report periodically to a person designated by the court.

(v) The child is subject to any other restrictions and requirements that may be imposed by the court.

(2) A juvenile court, pursuant to division (A)(10) of this section, may impose a period of electronically monitored house detention upon a child who is adjudicated a delinquent child for committing an act that, if committed by an adult, would be a criminal offense that would qualify the adult as an eligible offender pursuant to division (A)(3) of section 2929.23 of the Revised Code. The court may impose a period of electronically monitored house detention in addition to or in lieu of any other dispositional order imposed upon the child, except that any period of electronically monitored house detention shall not extend beyond the child's eighteenth birthday. If a court imposes a period of electronically monitored house detention upon a child, it shall require the child to wear, otherwise have attached to the child's person, or otherwise be subject to monitoring by a certified electronic monitoring device or to participate in the operation of and monitoring by a certified electronic monitoring system; to remain in the child's home or other specified premises for the entire period of electronically monitored house detention except when the court permits the child to leave those premises to go to school or to other specified premises; to be monitored by a central system that monitors the certified electronic monitoring device that is attached to the child's person or that otherwise is being used to monitor the child and that can monitor and determine the child's

location at any time or at a designated point in time or to be monitored by the certified electronic monitoring system; to report periodically to a person designated by the court; and, in return for receiving a dispositional order of electronically monitored house detention, to enter into a written contract with the court agreeing to comply with all restrictions and requirements imposed by the court, agreeing to pay any fee imposed by the court for the costs of the electronically monitored house detention imposed by the court pursuant to division (E) of section 2929.23 of the Revised Code, and agreeing to waive the right to receive credit for any time served on electronically monitored house detention toward the period of any other dispositional order imposed upon the child for the act for which the dispositional order of electronically monitored house detention was imposed if the child violates any of the restrictions or requirements of the dispositional order of electronically monitored house detention. The court also may impose other reasonable restrictions and requirements upon the child.

(3) If a child violates any of the restrictions or requirements imposed upon the child as part of the child's dispositional order of electronically monitored house detention, the child shall not receive credit for any time served on electronically monitored house detention toward any other dispositional order imposed upon the child for the act for which the dispositional order of electronically monitored house detention was imposed.

(K) Within ten days after completion of the adjudication, the court shall give written notice of an adjudication that a child is a delinquent child to the superintendent of a city, local, exempted village, or joint vocational school district if the basis of the adjudication was the commission of an act that would be a criminal offense if committed by an adult and that was committed by the delinquent child when the child was sixteen years of age or older and if the act is any of the following:

(1) A violation of section 2923.122 [2923.12.2] of the Revised Code that relates to property owned or controlled by, or to an activity held under the auspices of, the board of education of that school district;

(2) A violation of section 2923.12 of the Revised Code or of a substantially similar municipal ordinance that was committed on property owned or controlled by, or at an activity held under the auspices of, the board of education of that school district;

(3) A violation of division (A) of section 2925.03 or 2925.11 of the Revised Code that was committed on property owned or controlled by, or at an activity held under the auspices of, the board of education of that school district and that is not a minor drug possession offense as defined in section 2925.01 of the Revised Code;

(4) A violation of section 2903.01, 2903.02, 2903.03, 2903.04, 2903.11, 2903.12, 2907.02, or 2907.05 of the Revised Code, or a violation of former section 2907.12 of the Revised Code, that was committed on property owned or controlled by, or at an activity held under the auspices of, the board of education of that school district, if the victim at the time of the commission of the act was an employee of the board of education of that school district;

(5) Complicity in any violation described in division (K)(1), (2), (3), or (4) of this section that was alleged to have been committed in the manner described in division (K)(1), (2), (3), or (4) of this section, regardless of whether the act of complicity was committed on property owned or controlled by, or at an activity held under the auspices of, the board of education of that school district.

(L) During the period of a delinquent child's probation granted under division (A)(2) of this section, authorized probation officers who are engaged within the scope of their supervisory duties or responsibilities may search, with or without a warrant, the person of the delinquent child, the place of residence of the delinquent child, and a motor vehicle, another item of tangible or intangible personal property, or other real property in which the delinquent child has a right, title, or interest or for which the delinquent child has the express or implied permission of a person with a right, title, or interest to use, occupy, or possess if the probation officers have reasonable grounds to believe that the delinquent child is not abiding by the law or otherwise is not complying with the conditions of the delinquent child's probation. The court that places a delinquent child on probation under division (A)(2) of this section shall provide the delinquent child with a written notice that informs the delinquent child that authorized probation officers who are engaged within the scope of their supervisory duties or responsibilities may conduct those types of searches during the period of probation if they have reasonable grounds to believe that the delinquent child is not abiding by the law or otherwise is not complying with the conditions of the delinquent child's probation. The court also shall provide the written notice described in division (C)(2)(b) of section 2151.411 [2151.41.1] of the Revised Code to each parent, guardian, or custodian of the delinquent child who is described in division (C)(2)(a) of that section.

HISTORY: 133 v H 320 (Eff 11-19-69); 133 v H 931 (Eff 8-27-70); 134 v H 494 (Eff 7-12-72); 135 v S 324 (Eff 12-19-73); 135 v H 1067 (Eff 4-8-74); 136 v H 1196 (Eff 8-9-76); 137 v H 1 (Eff 8-26-77); 137 v S 119 (Eff 8-30-78); 137 v H 565 (Eff 11-1-78); 139 v H 440 (Eff 11-23-81); 139 v H 209 (Eff 7-6-82); 140 v S 210 (Eff 7-1-83); 142 v H 643 (Eff 3-17-89); 143 v H 330 (Eff 6-30-89); 143 v H 381 (Eff 7-1-89); 143 v H 166 (Eff 2-14-90); 143 v H 513 (Eff 7-18-90); 143 v S 131 (Eff 7-25-90); 143 v H 266 (Eff 9-6-90); 143 v H 51 (Eff 11-8-90); 143 v S 258 (Eff 8-22-90); 144 v H 154 (Eff 7-31-92); 144 v S 331 (Eff 11-13-92); 144 v H 725 (Eff 4-16-93); 145 v H 571 (Eff 10-6-94); 146 v H 4 (Eff 11-9-95); 146 v H 1 (Eff 1-1-96); 146 v S 2 (Eff 7-1-96); 146 v S 269 (Eff 7-1-96); 146 v H 274, §§ 1, 4 (Eff 8-8-96); 146 v H 445 (Eff 9-3-96); 146 v H 124 (Eff 9-30-97); 147 v H 215, § 1 (Eff 9-29-97); 147 v H 215, § 7. Eff 9-30-97.

The effective date is set by section 9 of HB 215.

[§ 2151.35.6] § 2151.356 Disposition of juvenile traffic offender.

(A) Unless division (C) of this section applies, if a child is adjudicated a juvenile traffic offender, the court may make any of the following orders of disposition:

(1) Impose a fine and costs in accordance with the schedule set forth in section 2151.3512 [2151.35.12] of the Revised Code;

(2) Suspend the child's probationary operator's license or the registration of all motor vehicles registered in the name of the child for the period that the court prescribes;

(3) Revoke the child's probationary driver's license or the registration of all motor vehicles registered in the name of the child;

(4) Place the child on probation;

(5) Require the child to make restitution for all damages caused by the child's traffic violation or any part of the damages;

(6) If the child is adjudicated a juvenile traffic offender for committing a violation of division (A) of section 4511.19 of the Revised Code or of a municipal ordinance that is substantially comparable to that division, commit the child, for not longer than five days, to the temporary custody of a detention home or district detention home established under section 2151.34 of the Revised Code, or to the temporary custody of any school, camp, institution, or other facility for children operated in whole or in part for the care of juvenile traffic offenders of that nature by the county, by a district organized under section 2151.34 or 2151.65 of the Revised Code, or by a private agency or organization within the state that is authorized and qualified to provide the care, treatment, or placement required. If an order of disposition committing a child to the temporary custody of a home, school, camp, institution, or other facility of that nature is made under division (A)(6) of this section, the length of the commitment shall not be reduced or diminished as a credit for any time that the child was held in a place of detention or shelter care, or otherwise was detained, prior to entry of the order of disposition.

(7) If, after making a disposition under divisions (A)(1) to (6) of this section, the court finds upon further hearing that the child has failed to comply with the orders of the court and the child's operation of a motor vehicle constitutes the child a danger to the child and to others, the court may make any disposition authorized by divisions (A)(1), (2), and (A)(7) to (11) of section 2151.355 [2151.35.5] of the Revised Code, except that the child may not be committed to or placed in a secure correctional facility unless authorized by division (A)(6) of this section, and commitment to or placement in a detention home may not exceed twenty-four hours.

(B) If a child is adjudicated a juvenile traffic offender for violating division (A) of section 4511.19 of the Revised Code, the court shall suspend or revoke the temporary instruction permit or probationary driver's license issued to the child until the child attains eighteen years of age or attends, at the discretion of the court, and satisfactorily completes a drug abuse or alcohol abuse education, intervention, or treatment program specified by the court. During the time the child is attending the program, the court shall retain any temporary instruction permit or probationary license issued to the child and shall return the permit or license when the child satisfactorily completes the program. If a child is adjudicated a juvenile traffic offender for violating division (B) of section 4511.19 of the Revised Code, the court shall suspend the temporary instruction permit or probationary driver's license issued to the child for the shorter period of sixty days or until the child attains eighteen years of age.

(C) If a child is adjudicated a juvenile traffic offender for violating division (B)(1) or (2) of section 4513.263 [4513.26.3] of the Revised Code, the court shall impose the appropriate fine set forth in section 4513.99 of the Revised Code. If a child is adjudicated a juvenile traffic offender for violating division (B)(3) of section 4513.263 [4513.26.3] of the Revised Code and if the child is sixteen years of age or older, the court shall impose the fine set forth in division (G) of section 4513.99 of the Revised Code. If a child is adjudicated a juvenile traffic offender for violating division (B)(3) of section 4513.263 [4513.26.3] of the Revised Code and if the child is under sixteen years of age, the court shall not impose a fine but may place the child on probation.

(D) A juvenile traffic offender is subject to sections 4509.01 to 4509.78 of the Revised Code.

HISTORY: 133 v H 320 (Eff 11-19-69); 133 v H 931 (Eff 8-27-70); 137 v H 1 (Eff 8-26-77); 137 v H 222 (Eff 10-4-77); 141 v S 54 (Eff 5-6-86); 141 v H 428 (Eff 12-23-86); 142 v H 643 (Eff 3-17-89); 143 v H 330 (Eff 6-30-89); 143 v H 381 (Eff 7-1-89); 143 v S 131 (Eff 7-25-90); 144 v H 118 (Eff 6-1-92); 144 v H 154 (Eff 7-31-92); 144 v S 98 (Eff 11-12-92); 146 v H 1 (Eff 1-1-96); 146 v H 265. Eff 3-3-97.

[§ 2151.35.7] § 2151.357 School district liability for cost of education; state subsidy where placement is in private facility.

In the manner prescribed by division (C)(2) of section 3313.64 of the Revised Code, the court, at the time of making any order that removes a child from the child's own home or that vests legal or permanent custody of the child in a person other than the child's parent or a government agency, shall determine the school district that is to bear the cost of educating the child. The court shall make the determination a part of the order that provides for the child's placement or commitment.

Whenever a child is placed in a detention home established under section 2151.34 of the Revised Code or a juvenile facility established under section 2151.65 of the Revised Code, the child's school district as determined by the court shall pay the cost of educating the child based on the per capita cost of the educational facility within the detention home or juvenile facility.

Whenever a child is placed by the court in a private institution, school, or residential treatment center or any other private facility, the state shall pay to the court a subsidy to help defray the expense of educating the child in an amount equal to the product of the daily per capita educational cost of the private facility, as determined pursuant to this section, and the number of days the child resides at the private facility, provided that the subsidy shall not exceed twenty-five hundred dollars per year per child. The daily per capita educational cost of a private facility shall be determined by dividing the actual program cost of the private facility or twenty-five hundred dollars, whichever is less, by three hundred sixty-five days or by three hundred sixty-six days for years that include February twenty-ninth. The state shall pay seventy-five per cent of the total subsidy for each year quarterly to the court. The state may adjust the remaining twenty-five percent of the total subsidy to be paid to the court for each year to an amount that is less than twenty-five per cent of the total subsidy for that year based upon the availability of funds appropriated to the department of education for the purpose of subsidizing courts that place a child in a private institution, school, or residential treatment center or any other private facility and shall pay that adjusted amount to the court at the end of the year.

HISTORY: 133 v H 320 (Eff 11-19-69); 133 v S 518 (Eff 7-16-70); 139 v S 140 (Eff 7-1-81); 146 v H 117. Eff 6-30-95.

[§ 2151.35.8] § 2151.358 Sealing or expungement of record; judgment does not impose civil disabilities; admission of judgment in other proceedings.

(A) As used in this section, "seal a record" means to remove a record from the main file of similar records and to secure it in a separate file that contains only sealed records and that is accessible only to the juvenile court. A record that is sealed shall be destroyed by all persons and governmental bodies except the juvenile court.

(B) The department of youth services and any other institution or facility that unconditionally discharges a person who has been adjudicated a delinquent child, an unruly child, or a juvenile traffic offender shall immediately give notice of the discharge to the court that committed the person. The court shall note the date of discharge on a separate record of discharges of those natures.

(C)(1) Two years after the termination of any order made by the court or two years after the unconditional discharge of a person from the department of youth services or another institution or facility to which the person may have been committed, the court that issued the order or committed the person shall do one of the following:

(a) If the person was adjudicated an unruly child, order the record of the person sealed;

(b) If the person was adjudicated a delinquent child or a juvenile traffic offender, either order the record of the person sealed or send the person notice of the person's right to have the† that record sealed.

(2) The court shall send the notice described in division (C)(1)(b) of this section within ninety days after the expiration of the two-year period described in division (C)(1) of this section by certified mail, return receipt requested, to the person at the person's last known address. The notice shall state that the person may apply to the court for an order to seal the person's record, explain what sealing a record means, and explain the possible consequences of not having the person's record sealed.

(D) At any time after the two-year period described in division (C)(1) of this section has elapsed, any person who has been adjudicated a delinquent child or a juvenile traffic offender may apply to the court for an order to seal the person's record. The court shall hold a hearing on each application within sixty days after the application is received. Notice of the hearing on the application shall be given to the prosecuting attorney and to any other public office or agency known to have a record of the prior adjudication. If the court finds that the rehabilitation of the person who was adjudicated a delinquent child or a juvenile traffic offender has been attained to a satisfactory degree, the court may order the record of the person sealed.

(E) If the court orders the adjudication record of a person sealed pursuant to division (C) or (D) of this section, the court shall order that the proceedings in the case in which the person was adjudicated a juvenile traffic offender, a delinquent child, or an unruly child be deemed never to have occurred. All index references to the case and the person shall be deleted, and the person and the court properly may reply that no record exists with respect to the person upon any inquiry in the matter. Inspection of records that have been ordered sealed may be permitted by the court only upon application by the person who is the subject of the sealed records and only by the persons that are named in the† that application.

(F) Any person who has been arrested and charged with being a delinquent child or a juvenile traffic offender and who is adjudicated not guilty of the charges in the case or has the charges in the case dismissed may apply to the court for an expungement of the record in the case. The application may be filed at any time after the person is adjudicated not guilty or the charges against the person are dismissed. The court shall give notice to the prosecuting attorney of any hearing on the application. The court may initiate the expungement proceedings on its own motion.

Any person who has been arrested and charged with being an and† who is adjudicated not guilty of the charges in the case or has the charges in the case dismissed may apply to the court for an expungement of the record in the case. The court shall initiate the expungement proceedings on its own motion if an application for expungement is not filed.

If the court upon receipt of an application for expungement or upon its own motion determines that the charges against any person in any case were dismissed or that any person was adjudicated not guilty in any case, the court shall order that the records of the case be expunged and that the proceedings in the case be deemed never to have occurred. If the applicant for the expungement order, with the written consent of the applicant's parents or guardian if the applicant is a minor and with the written approval of the court, waives in writing the applicant's right to bring any civil action based on the arrest for which the expungement order is applied, the court shall order the appropriate persons and governmental agencies to delete all index references to the case; destroy or delete all court records of the case; destroy all copies of any pictures and fingerprints taken of the person pursuant to the expunged arrest; and destroy, erase, or delete any reference to the arrest that is maintained by the state or any political subdivision of the state, except a record of the arrest that is maintained for compiling statistical data and that does not contain any reference to the person.

If the applicant for an expungement order does not waive in writing the right to bring any civil action based on the arrest for which the expungement order is applied, the court, in addition to ordering the deletion, destruction, or erasure of all index references and court records of the case and of all references to the arrest that are maintained by the state or any political subdivision of the state, shall order that a copy of all records of the case, except fingerprints held by the court or a law enforcement agency, be delivered to the court. The court shall seal all of the records delivered to the court in a separate file in which only sealed records are maintained. The sealed records shall be kept by the court until the statute of limitations expires for any civil action based on the arrest, any pending litigation based on the arrest is terminated, or the applicant files a written waiver of the right to bring a civil action based on the arrest. After the expiration of the statute of limitations, the termination of the pending litigation, or the filing of the waiver, the court shall destroy the sealed records.

After the expungement order has been issued, the court shall, and the person may properly, reply that no record of the case with respect to the person exists.

(G) The court shall send notice of the order to expunge or seal to any public office or agency that the court has reason to believe may have a record of the expunged or sealed record. Except as provided in division (K) of this section, an order to seal or expunge under this section applies to every public office or agency that has a record of the prior adjudication or arrest, regardless of whether it receives notice of the hearing on the expungement or sealing of the record or a copy of the order to expunge or seal the record. Except as provided in division (K) of this section, upon the written request of a person whose record has been expunged or sealed and the presentation of a copy of the order to expunge or seal, a public office or agency shall destroy its record of the prior adjudication or arrest, except a record of the adjudication or arrest that is maintained for compiling statistical data and that does not contain any reference to the person who is the subject of the order to expunge or seal.

(H) The judgment rendered by the court under this chapter shall not impose any of the civil disabilities ordinarily imposed by conviction of a crime in that the child is not a criminal by reason of the adjudication. And no† child shall be charged with or convicted of a crime in any court except as provided by this chapter. The disposition of a child under the judgment rendered or any evidence given in court shall not operate to disqualify a child in any future civil service examination, appointment, or application. Evidence of a judgment rendered and the disposition of a child under the judgment is not admissible to impeach the credibility of the child in any action or proceeding. Otherwise, the disposition of a child under the judgment rendered or any evidence given in court is admissible as evidence for or against the child in any action or proceeding in any court in accordance with the Rules of Evidence and also may be considered by any court as to the matter of sentence or to the granting of probation, and a court may consider the judgment rendered and the disposition of a child under that judgment for purposes of determining whether the child, for a future criminal conviction or guilty plea, is a repeat violent offender, as defined in section 2929.01 of the Revised Code.

(I) In any application for employment, license, or other right or privilege, any appearance as a witness, or any other inquiry, a person may not be questioned with respect to any arrest for which the records were expunged. If an inquiry is made in violation of this division, the person may respond as if the expunged arrest did not occur, and the person shall not be subject to any adverse action because of the arrest or the response.

(J) An officer or employee of the state or any of its political subdivisions who knowingly releases, disseminates, or makes available for any purpose involving employment, bonding, licensing, or education to any person or to any department, agency, or other instrumentality of the state or of any of its political subdivisions any information or other data concerning any arrest, complaint, trial, hearing, adjudication, or correctional supervision, the records of which have been expunged or sealed pursuant to this section, is guilty of divulging confidential information, a misdemeanor of the fourth degree.

(K) Notwithstanding any provision of this section that requires otherwise, a board of education of a city, local, exempted village, or joint vocational school district that maintains records of an individual who has been permanently excluded under sections 3301.121 [3301.12.1] and 3313.662 [3313.66.2] of the Revised Code is permitted to maintain records regarding an adjudication that the individual is a delinquent child that was used as the basis for the individual's permanent exclusion, regardless of a court order to seal the record. An order issued under this section to seal the record of an adjudication that an individual is a delinquent child does not revoke the adjudication order of the superintendent of public instruction to permanently exclude the individual who is the subject of the sealing order. An order issued under this section to seal the record of an adjudication that an individual is a delinquent child may be presented to a district superintendent as evidence to support the contention that the superintendent should recommend that the permanent exclusion of the individual who is the subject of the sealing order be revoked. Except as otherwise authorized by this division and sections 3301.121 [3301.12.1] and 3313.662 [3313.66.2] of the Revised Code, any school employee in possession of or having access to the sealed adjudication records of an individual that were the basis of a permanent exclusion of the individual is subject to division (J) of this section.

HISTORY: 133 v H 320 (Eff 11-19-69); 137 v H 315 (Eff 3-15-78); 139 v H 440 (Eff 11-23-81); 140 v H 37 (Eff 6-22-84); 144 v H 27 (Eff 10-10-91); 144 v H 154 (Eff 7-31-92); 146 v H 1 (Eff 1-1-96); 146 v S 2. Eff 7-1-96.

Publisher's Note

The amendments made by SB 2 (146 v —) and HB 1 (146 v —) have been combined. Please see provisions of RC § 1.52.

The effective date is set by section 6 of SB 2.

† The language is the result of combining SB 2 (146 v —) and HB 1 (146 v —).

The provisions of § 3 of HB 1 (146 v —) read as follows:

SECTION 3. (A) The General Assembly hereby declares that its purpose in enacting the language of division (A)(2) of section 2151.18 and division (D)(2) of section 2151.355 of the Revised Code that exists on and after the effective date of this act is to recognize the holding of the Supreme Court in *In re Russell* (1984), 12 Ohio St. 3d 304.

(B) The General Assembly hereby declares that its purpose in enacting the language in division (B) of section 2151.011 and divisions (B) and (C) of section 2151.26 of the Revised Code that exists on and after the effective date of this act is to overrule the holding in *State v. Adams* (1982), 69 Ohio St. 2d 120, regarding the effect of binding a child over for trial as an adult.

(C) The amendments made by this act to section 2151.358 of the Revised Code apply to persons who were adjudicated juvenile traffic offenders or charged with being juvenile traffic offenders prior to the effective date of this act, regardless of their age on that date. A person who was adjudicated a juvenile traffic offender or charged with being a juvenile traffic offender prior to the effective date of this act may file an application in accordance with division (D) or (F) of section 2151.358 of the Revised Code on or after the effective date of this act for the sealing of the record of the person's adjudication as a juvenile traffic offender or the expungement of the record of the case in which the person was adjudicated not guilty of being a juvenile traffic offender or the charges of being a juvenile traffic offender were dismissed, and the juvenile court involved shall proceed with a hearing on the application in accordance with division (D) or (F) of that section. A juvenile court is not required to send the notice described in division (C)(1)(b) of section 2151.358 of the Revised Code to a person who was adjudicated a juvenile traffic offender prior to the effective date of this act if, on the effective date of this act, more than ninety days has expired after the expiration of the two-year period described in division (C)(1) of section 2151.358 of the Revised Code.

[§ 2151.35.9] § 2151.359 Control of conduct of parent, guardian, or custodian.

In any proceeding wherein a child has been adjudged delinquent, unruly, abused, neglected, or dependent, on the application of a party, or the court's own motion, the court may make an order restraining or otherwise controlling the conduct of any parent, guardian, or other custodian in the relationship of such individual to the child if the court finds that such an order is necessary to:

(A) Control any conduct or relationship that will be detrimental or harmful to the child;

(B) Where such conduct or relationship will tend to defeat the execution of the order of disposition made or to be made.

Due notice of the application or motion and the grounds therefor, and an opportunity to be heard shall be given to the person against whom such order is directed.

HISTORY: 133 v H 320 (Eff 11-19-69); 136 v H 85. Eff 11-28-75.

[§ 2151.35.10] § 2151.3510 Notice of intended commitment order.

Before a juvenile court issues an order of disposition pursuant to division (A)(1) of section 2151.354 [2151.35.4] or 2151.355 [2151.35.5] of the Revised Code committing an unruly or delinquent child to the custody of a public children services agency, it shall give the agency notice in the manner prescribed by the Juvenile Rules of the intended dispositional order.

HISTORY: 144 v H 298 (Eff 7-26-91); 146 v H 274. Eff 8-8-96.

[§ 2151.35.11] § 2151.3511 Deposition of child victim; videotaping; testimony taken outside courtroom and televised into it or replayed in courtroom.

(A)(1) As used in this section, "victim" includes any of the following persons:

(a) A person who was a victim of a violation identified in division (A)(2) of this section or an act that would be an offense of violence if committed by an adult;

(b) A person against whom was directed any conduct that constitutes, or that is an element of, a violation identified in division (A)(2) of this section or an act that would be an offense of violence if committed by an adult.

(2) In any proceeding in juvenile court involving a complaint in which a child is charged with a violation of section 2905.03, 2905.05, 2907.02, 2907.03, 2907.04, 2907.05, 2907.06, 2907.07, 2907.09, 2907.21, 2907.23, 2907.24, 2907.31, 2907.32, 2907.321 [2907.32.1], 2907.322 [2907.32.2], 2907.323 [2907.32.3], or 2919.22 of the Revised Code or an act that would be an offense of violence if committed by an adult and in which an alleged victim of the violation or act was a child who was less than thirteen years of age when the complaint was filed, the juvenile judge, upon motion of an attorney for the prosecution, shall order that the testimony of the child victim be taken by deposition. The prosecution also may request that the deposition be videotaped in accordance with division (A)(3) of this section. The judge shall notify the child victim whose deposition is to be taken, the prosecution, and the attorney for the child who is charged with the violation or act of the date, time, and place for taking the deposition. The notice shall identify the child victim who is to be examined and shall indicate whether a request that the deposition be videotaped has been made. The child who is charged with the violation or act shall have the right to attend the deposition and the right to be represented by counsel. Depositions shall be taken in the manner provided in civil cases, except that the judge in the proceeding shall preside at the taking of the deposition and shall rule at that time on any objections of the prosecution or the attorney for the child charged with the violation or act. The prosecution and the attorney for the child charged with the violation or act shall have the right, as at an adjudication hearing, to full examination and cross-examination of the child victim whose deposition is to be taken. If a deposition taken under this division is intended to be offered as evidence in the proceeding, it shall be filed in the juvenile court in which the action is pending and is admissible in the manner described in division (B) of this section. If a deposition of a child victim taken under this division is admitted as evidence at the proceeding under division (B) of this section, the child victim shall not be required to testify in person at the proceeding. However, at any time before the conclusion of the proceeding, the attorney for the child charged with the violation or act may file a motion with the judge requesting that another deposition of the child victim be taken because new evidence material to the defense of the child charged has been discovered that the attorney for the child charged could not with reasonable diligence have discovered prior to the taking of the admitted deposition. Any motion requesting another deposition shall be accompanied by supporting affidavits. Upon the filing of the motion and affidavits, the court may order that additional testimony of the child victim relative to the new evidence be taken by another deposition. If the court orders the taking of another deposition under this provision, the deposition shall be taken in accordance with this division; if the admitted deposition was a videotaped deposition taken in accordance with division (A)(3) of this section, the new deposition also shall be videotaped in accordance with that division, and, in other cases, the new deposition may be videotaped in accordance with that division.

(3) If the prosecution requests that a deposition to be taken under division (A)(2) of this section be videotaped, the juvenile judge shall order that the deposition be videotaped in accordance with this division. If a juvenile judge issues an order to video tape† the deposition, the judge shall exclude from the room in which the deposition is to be taken every person except the child victim giving the testimony, the judge, one or more interpreters if needed, the attorneys for the prosecution and the child who is charged with the violation or act, any person needed to operate the equipment to be used, one person chosen by the child victim giving the deposition, and any person whose presence the judge determines would contribute to the welfare and well-being of the child victim giving the deposition. The person chosen by the child victim shall not be a witness in the proceeding and, both before and during the deposition, shall not discuss the testimony of the child victim with any other witness in the proceeding. To the extent feasible, any person operating the recording equipment shall be restricted to a room adjacent to the room in which the deposition is being taken, or to a location in the room in which the deposition is being taken that is behind a screen or mirror so that the person operating the recording equipment can see and hear, but cannot be seen or heard by, the child victim giving the deposition during the deposition. The child who is charged with the violation or act shall be permitted to observe and hear the testimony of the child victim giving the deposition on a monitor, shall be provided with an electronic means of immediate communication with the attorney of the child who is charged with the violation or act during the testimony, and shall be restricted to a location from which the child who is charged with the violation or act cannot be seen or heard by the child victim giving the deposition, except on a monitor provided for that purpose. The child victim giving the deposition shall be provided with a monitor on which the child victim can observe, while giving testimony, the child who is charged with the violation or act. The judge, at the judge's discretion, may preside at the deposition by electronic means from outside the room in which the deposition is to be taken; if the judge presides by electronic means, the judge shall be provided with monitors on which the judge can see each person in the room in which the deposition is to be taken and with an electronic means of communication with each person in that room, and each person in the room shall be provided with a monitor on which that person can see the judge and with an electronic means of communication with the judge. A deposition

that is videotaped under this division shall be taken and filed in the manner described in division (A)(2) of this section and is admissible in the manner described in this division and division (B) of this section, and, if a deposition that is videotaped under this division is admitted as evidence at the proceeding, the child victim shall not be required to testify in person at the proceeding. No deposition videotaped under this division shall be admitted as evidence at any proceeding unless division (B) of this section is satisfied relative to the deposition and all of the following apply relative to the recording:

(a) The recording is both aural and visual and is recorded on film or videotape, or by other electronic means.

(b) The recording is authenticated under the Rules of Evidence and the Rules of Criminal Procedure as a fair and accurate representation of what occurred, and the recording is not altered other than at the direction and under the supervision of the judge in the proceeding.

(c) Each voice on the recording that is material to the testimony on the recording or the making of the recording, as determined by the judge, is identified.

(d) Both the prosecution and the child who is charged with the violation or act are afforded an opportunity to view the recording before it is shown in the proceeding.

(B)(1) At any proceeding in relation to which a deposition was taken under division (A) of this section, the deposition or a part of it is admissible in evidence upon motion of the prosecution if the testimony in the deposition or the part to be admitted is not excluded by the hearsay rule and if the deposition or the part to be admitted otherwise is admissible under the Rules of Evidence. For purposes of this division, testimony is not excluded by the hearsay rule if the testimony is not hearsay under Evidence Rule 801; if the testimony is within an exception to the hearsay rule set forth in Evidence Rule 803; if the child victim who gave the testimony is unavailable as a witness, as defined in Evidence Rule 804, and the testimony is admissible under that rule; or if both of the following apply:

(a) The child who is charged with the violation or act had an opportunity and similar motive at the time of the taking of the deposition to develop the testimony by direct, cross, or redirect examination.

(b) The judge determines that there is reasonable cause to believe that, if the child victim who gave the testimony in the deposition were to testify in person at the proceeding, the child victim would experience serious emotional trauma as a result of the child victim's participation at the proceeding.

(2) Objections to receiving in evidence a deposition or a part of it under division (B) of this section shall be made as provided in civil actions.

(3) The provisions of divisions (A) and (B) of this section are in addition to any other provisions of the Revised Code, the Rules of Juvenile Procedure, the Rules of Criminal Procedure, or the Rules of Evidence that pertain to the taking or admission of depositions in a juvenile court proceeding and do not limit the admissibility under any of those other provisions of any deposition taken under division (A) of this section or otherwise taken.

(C) In any proceeding in juvenile court involving a complaint in which a child is charged with a violation listed in division (A)(2) of this section or an act that would be an offense of violence if committed by an adult and in which an alleged victim of the violation or offense was a child who was less than thirteen years of age when the complaint was filed, the prosecution may file a motion with the juvenile judge requesting the judge to order the testimony of the child victim to be taken in a room other than the room in which the proceeding is being conducted and be televised, by closed circuit equipment, into the room in which the proceeding is being conducted to be viewed by the child who is charged with the violation or act and any other persons who are not permitted in the room in which the testimony is to be taken but who would have been present during the testimony of the child victim had it been given in the room in which the proceeding is being conducted. Except for good cause shown, the prosecution shall file a motion under this division at least seven days before the date of the proceeding. The juvenile judge may issue the order upon the motion of the prosecution filed under this division, if the judge determines that the child victim is unavailable to testify in the room in which the proceeding is being conducted in the physical presence of the child charged with the violation or act, due to one or more of the reasons set forth in division (E) of this section. If a juvenile judge issues an order of that nature, the judge shall exclude from the room in which the testimony is to be taken every person except a person described in division (A)(3) of this section. The judge, at the judge's discretion, may preside during the giving of the testimony by electronic means from outside the room in which it is being given, subject to the limitations set forth in division (A)(3) of this section. To the extent feasible, any person operating the televising equipment shall be hidden from the sight and hearing of the child victim giving the testimony, in a manner similar to that described in division (A)(3) of this section. The child who is charged with the violation or act shall be permitted to observe and hear the testimony of the child victim giving the testimony on a monitor, shall be provided with an electronic means of immediate communication with the attorney of the child who is charged with the violation or act during the testimony, and shall be restricted to a location from which the child who is charged with the violation or act cannot be seen or heard by the child victim giving the testimony, except on a monitor provided for that purpose. The child victim giving the testimony shall be provided with a monitor on which the child victim can observe, while giving testimony, the child who is charged with the violation or act.

(D) In any proceeding in juvenile court involving a complaint in which a child is charged with a violation listed in division (A)(2) of this section or an act that would be an offense of violence if committed by an adult and in which an alleged victim of the violation or offense was a child who was less than thirteen years of age when the complaint was filed, the prosecution may file a motion with the juvenile judge requesting the judge to order the testimony of the child victim to be taken outside of the room in which the proceeding is being conducted and be recorded for showing in the room in which the proceeding is being conducted before the judge, the child who is charged with the violation or act, and any other persons who would have been present during the testimony of the child victim had it been given in the room in which the proceeding is being conducted. Except for good cause shown, the prosecution shall file a motion under this division at least seven days before the date of the proceeding. The juvenile judge may issue the order upon the motion of the prosecution filed under this division, if the judge determines that the child victim is unavailable to testify in the room in which the proceeding is being conducted in the physical presence of the child charged with the violation or act, due to one or more of the reasons set forth in division (E) of this section. If a juvenile judge issues an order of that nature, the judge shall exclude from the room in which the testimony is to be taken every person except a person described in division (A)(3) of this section. To the extent feasible, any person operating the recording equipment shall be hidden from the sight and hearing of the child victim giving the testimony, in a manner similar to that described in division (A)(3) of this section. The child who is charged with the violation or act shall be permitted to observe and hear the testimony of the child victim giving the testimony on a monitor, shall be provided with an electronic means of immediate communication with the attorney of the child who is charged with the violation or act during the testimony, and shall be restricted to a location from which the child who is charged with the violation or act cannot be seen or heard by the child victim giving the testimony, except on a monitor provided for that purpose. The child victim giving the testimony shall be provided with a monitor on which the child victim can observe, while giving testimony, the child who is charged with the violation or act. No order for the taking of testimony by recording shall be issued under this division unless the provisions set forth in divisions (A)(3)(a), (b), (c), and (d) of this section apply to the recording of the testimony.

(E) For purposes of divisions (C) and (D) of this section, a juvenile judge may order the testimony of a child victim to be taken outside of the room in which a proceeding is being conducted if the judge determines that the child victim is unavailable to testify in the room in the physical presence of the child charged with the violation or act due to one or more of the following circumstances:

(1) The persistent refusal of the child victim to testify despite judicial requests to do so;

(2) The inability of the child victim to communicate about the alleged violation or offense because of extreme fear, failure of memory, or another similar reason;

(3) The substantial likelihood that the child victim will suffer serious emotional trauma from so testifying.

(F)(1) If a juvenile judge issues an order pursuant to division (C) or (D) of this section that requires the testimony of a child victim in a juvenile court proceeding to be taken outside of the room in which the proceeding is being conducted, the order shall specifically identify the child victim to whose testimony it applies, the order applies only during the testimony of the specified child victim, and the child victim giving the testimony shall not be required to testify at the proceeding other than in accordance with the order. The authority of a judge to close the taking of a deposition under division (A)(3) of this section or a proceeding under division (C) or (D) of this section is in addition to the authority of a judge to close a hearing pursuant to section 2151.35 of the Revised Code.

(2) A juvenile judge who makes any determination regarding the admissibility of a deposition under divisions (A) and (B) of this section, the videotaping of a deposition under division (A)(3) of this section, or the taking of testimony outside of the room in which a proceeding is being conducted under division (C) or (D) of this section, shall enter the determination and findings on the record in the proceeding.

HISTORY: 141 v H 108 (Eff 10-14-86); 146 v H 445 (Eff 9-3-96); 147 v S 53. Eff 10-14-97.

† So in enrolled bill, division (A)(3).

The provisions of § 3(C) of HB 445 (146 v —) read as follows:

(C) Section 2151.3511 of the Revised Code, as amended by this act, applies to a proceeding in juvenile court involving a complaint in which a child is charged with committing an act that if committed by an adult would be felonious sexual penetration in violation of former section 2907.12 of the Revised Code and in which an alleged victim of the act was a child who was under eleven years of age when the complaint was filed.

As used in division (C) of Section 3 of this act, "child" has the same meaning as in section 2151.011 of the Revised Code.

[§ 2151.35.12] § 2151.3512 Schedule of fines and costs.

If a child is adjudicated a delinquent child or is adjudicated a juvenile traffic offender, the court may make an order of disposition of the child under division (A)(8)(a) of section 2151.355 [2151.35.5] or under division (A)(1) of section 2151.356 [2151.35.6] of the Revised Code, whichever is applicable, by imposing a fine and costs in accordance with the following schedule:

(A) If the child was adjudicated a delinquent child

or a juvenile traffic offender for committing an act that would be a minor misdemeanor or an unclassified misdemeanor if committed by an adult, a fine not to exceed fifty dollars and costs;

(B) If the child was adjudicated a delinquent child or a juvenile traffic offender for committing an act that would be a misdemeanor of the fourth degree if committed by an adult, a fine not to exceed seventy-five dollars and costs;

(C) If the child was adjudicated a delinquent child or a juvenile traffic offender for committing an act that would be a misdemeanor of the third degree if committed by an adult, a fine not to exceed one hundred twenty-five dollars and costs;

(D) If the child was adjudicated a delinquent child or a juvenile traffic offender for committing an act that would be a misdemeanor of the second degree if committed by an adult, a fine not to exceed one hundred seventy-five dollars and costs;

(E) If the child was adjudicated a delinquent child or a juvenile traffic offender for committing an act that would be a misdemeanor of the first degree if committed by an adult, a fine not to exceed two hundred twenty-five dollars and costs;

(F) If the child was adjudicated a delinquent child or a juvenile traffic offender for committing an act that would be a felony of the fifth degree or an unclassified felony if committed by an adult, a fine not to exceed three hundred dollars and costs;

(G) If the child was adjudicated a delinquent child or a juvenile traffic offender for committing an act that would be a felony of the fourth degree if committed by an adult, a fine not to exceed four hundred dollars and costs;

(H) If the child was adjudicated a delinquent child or a juvenile traffic offender for committing an act that would be a felony of the third degree if committed by an adult, a fine not to exceed seven hundred fifty dollars and costs;

(I) If the child was adjudicated a delinquent child or a juvenile traffic offender for committing an act that would be a felony of the second degree if committed by an adult, a fine not to exceed one thousand dollars and costs;

(J) If the child was adjudicated a delinquent child or a juvenile traffic offender for committing an act that would be a felony of the first degree if committed by an adult, a fine not to exceed one thousand four hundred fifty dollars and costs;

(K) If the child was adjudicated a delinquent child for committing an act that would be aggravated murder or murder if committed by an adult, a fine not to exceed one thousand eight hundred dollars and costs.

HISTORY: 146 v H 1 (Eff 1-1-96); 146 v S 269. Eff 7-1-96.

The effective date is set by section 5 of SB 269.

§ 2151.36 Support of child.

When a child has been committed as provided by this chapter, the juvenile court shall issue an order pursuant to sections 3113.21 to 3113.219 [3113.21.9] of the Revised Code requiring that the parent, guardian, or person charged with the child's support pay for the care, support, maintenance, and education of the child. The juvenile court shall order that the parents, guardian, or person pay for the expenses involved in providing orthopedic, medical, or surgical treatment for, or for special care of, the child, enter a judgment for the amount due, and enforce the judgment by execution as in the court of common pleas.

Any expenses incurred for the care, support, maintenance, education, orthopedic, medical, or surgical treatment, and special care of a child who has a legal settlement in another county shall be at the expense of the county of legal settlement if the consent of the juvenile judge of the county of legal settlement is first obtained. When the consent is obtained, the board of county commissioners of the county in which the child has a legal settlement shall reimburse the committing court for the expenses out of its general fund. If the department of human services considers it to be in the best interest of any delinquent, dependent, unruly, abused, or neglected child who has a legal settlement in a foreign state or country that the child be returned to the state or country of legal settlement, the juvenile court may commit the child to the department for the child's return to that state or country.

Any expenses ordered by the court for the care, support, maintenance, education, orthopedic, medical, or surgical treatment, or special care of a dependent, neglected, abused, unruly, or delinquent child or of a juvenile traffic offender under this chapter, except the part of the expense that may be paid by the state or federal government or paid by the parents, guardians, or person charged with the child's support pursuant to this section, shall be paid from the county treasury upon specifically itemized vouchers, certified to by the judge. The court shall not be responsible for any expenses resulting from the commitment of children to any home, public children services agency, private child placing agency, or other institution, association, or agency, unless the court authorized the expenses at the time of commitment.

HISTORY: GC § 1639-34; 117 v 520; 119 v 731; 121 v 557; Bureau of Code Revision, 10-1-53; 133 v S 49 (Eff 8-13-69); 133 v H 320 (Eff 11-19-69); 136 v H 85 (Eff 11-28-75); 141 v H 428 (Eff 12-23-86); 142 v S 89 (Eff 1-1-89); 146 v H 274. Eff 8-9-96.

§ 2151.37 Institution receiving children required to make report.

At any time the juvenile judge may require from an association receiving or desiring to receive children, such reports, information, and statements as he deems necessary. He may at any time require from an association or institution reports, information, or statements concerning any child committed to it by such judge under sections 2151.01 to 2151.54, inclusive, of the Revised Code.

HISTORY: GC § 1639-36; 117 v 520(532); Bureau of Code Revision. Eff 10-1-53.

§ 2151.38 Effect of dispositional order; early release or assignment to treatment or rehabilitation facility; proceedings prior to release.

(A) When a child is committed to the legal custody of the department of youth services, the jurisdiction of the juvenile court with respect to the child so committed shall cease and terminate at the time of commitment, except as provided in divisions (B) and (C) of this section and except that, if the department of youth services makes a motion to the court for the termination of permanent custody, the court upon the motion, after notice and hearing and for good cause shown, may terminate permanent custody at any time prior to the child's attainment of eighteen years of age. The court shall make disposition of the matter in whatever manner will serve the best interests of the child. Subject to divisions (B) and (C) of this section, sections 2151.353 [2151.35.3] and 2151.411 [2151.41.1] to 2151.421 [2151.42.1] of the Revised Code, and any other provision of law that specifies a different duration for a dispositional order, all other dispositional orders made by the court shall be temporary and shall continue for a period that is designated by the court in its order, until terminated or modified by the court or until the child attains twenty-one years of age.

(B)(1)(a) If a child is committed to the department of youth services pursuant to division (A)(4) or (5) of section 2151.355 [2151.35.5] of the Revised Code, except as provided in division (B)(1)(b) and (c) of this section and in section 5139.38 of the Revised Code, the department shall not release the child from institutional care or institutional care in a secure facility and as a result shall not discharge the child, order the child's release on parole, or assign the child to a family home, group care facility, or other place for treatment or rehabilitation, prior to the expiration of the prescribed minimum period of institutionalization or institutionalization in a secure facility, unless the department, the child, or the child's parent requests an early release from institutional care or institutional care in a secure facility from the court that committed the child and the court approves the early release in a journal entry, or unless the court on its own motion grants an early release. A request for early release by the department, the child, or the child's parent shall be made only in accordance with division (B)(2) of this section.

If a child is committed to the department of youth services pursuant to division (A)(6) of section 2151.355 [2151.35.5] of the Revised Code, except as provided in division (B)(1)(b) and (c) of this section and in section 5139.38 of the Revised Code, the department shall not release the child from institutional care in a secure facility, and as a result shall not discharge the child, order the child's release on parole, or assign the child to a family home, group care facility, or other place for treatment or rehabilitation, prior to the child's attainment of twenty-one years of age, unless the department, the child, or the child's parent requests an early release from institutional care in a secure facility from the court that committed the child and the court approves the early release in a journal entry, or unless the court on its own motion grants an early release. A request for early release by the department, the child, or the child's parent shall be made only in accordance with division (B)(2) of this section.

(b) If a child is committed to the department of youth services pursuant to division (A)(7) of section 2151.355 [2151.35.5] of the Revised Code, the department shall not release the child from institutional care in a secure facility, and as a result shall not discharge the child, order the child's release on parole, or assign the child to a family home, group care facility, or other place for treatment or rehabilitation, prior to the expiration of the period of commitment required to be imposed by that division and prior to the expiration of the prescribed minimum period of institutionalization or institutionalization in a secure facility under division (A)(4) or (5) of that section if either of those divisions applies or prior to the child's attainment of twenty-one years of age if division (A)(6) of that section applies, unless the department, the child, or the child's parent requests an early release from institutional care or institutional care in a secure facility from the court that committed the child, and the court approves the early release in a journal entry, or unless the court on its own motion grants an early release. The department, the child, or the child's parent shall make a request for early release only in accordance with division (B)(2) of this section.

(c) If a child is adjudicated a delinquent child for committing two or more acts that would be felonies if committed by an adult, if the court entering the delinquent child adjudication ordered the commitment of the child to the legal custody of the department of youth services for institutionalization or institutionalization in a secure facility pursuant to division (A)(4), (5), or (6) of section 2151.355 [2151.35.5] of the Revised Code, and if pursuant to division (B)(2) of that section the court ordered the periods of commitment imposed under division (A)(4), (5), or (6) of that section for each of those delinquent acts to be served consecutively in the legal custody of the department, the department shall not release the child from institutional care or institutional care in a secure facility, and as a result shall not discharge the child, order the child's release on parole, or assign the child to a family home, group care facility, or other place for treatment or rehabilitation, prior to the expiration of any period of commitment imposed under division (A)(7) of that section and prior to the earlier of the expiration of the prescribed minimum periods or prescribed periods of institutionalization or institutionalization in a secure facility imposed under division (A)(4), (5), or (6) of that section for each of those delinquent acts or the child's attainment of twenty-one years of age, unless the department, the child, or the child's parent requests an early release from institutional care or institutional care in a secure facility from the court that committed the child, and the court approves the early release in a journal entry, or unless the court on its own motion grants an early release. The department, the child, or the child's parent shall make a request for early release only in accordance with division (B)(2) of this section.

(2)(a) If the department of youth services desires to release a child committed to it pursuant to division (A)(4) or (5) of section 2151.355 [2151.35.5] of the Revised Code from institutional care or institutional care in a secure facility prior to the expiration of the prescribed minimum periods of institutionalization, if it desires to release a child committed to it pursuant to division (A)(6) of that section from institutional care in a secure facility prior to the child's attainment of twenty-one years of age, if it desires to release a child committed to it pursuant to division (A)(7) of that section from institutional care in a secure facility prior to the expiration of the period of commitment required to be imposed by that division and prior to the expiration of the prescribed minimum period of institutionalization or institutionalization in a secure facility under division (A)(4) or (5) of that section if either of those divisions applies or prior to the child's attainment of twenty-one years of age if division (A)(6) of that section applies, or if it desires to release a child committed to it under the circumstances described in division (B)(1)(c) of this section prior to the expiration of the prescribed minimum periods or prescribed periods of institutionalization or institutionalization in a secure facility described in that division, except as provided in section 5139.38 of the Revised Code, it shall request the court that committed the child for an early release from institutional care or institutional care in a secure facility.

Upon receipt of a request for a child's early release filed by the department under this section at any time or upon its own motion at any time, the court that committed the child to the department shall approve the early release from institutional care or institutional care in a secure facility by journal entry, shall schedule a time within thirty days for a hearing on whether the child is to be released, or shall reject the request by journal entry without conducting a hearing.

(b) If a child who has been committed to the department pursuant to division (A)(4), (5), (6), or (7) of section 2151.355 [2151.35.5] of the Revised Code or the parents of a child so committed seek the child's early release from institutional care or institutional care in a secure facility as described in division (B)(1)(a), (b), or (c) of this section, the child or the child's parent shall request the court that committed the child to grant an early release. No request of that type initially may be made prior to the expiration of thirty days from the day on which the child began institutional care or institutional care in a secure facility. Upon the filing of an initial request for early release, the court shall approve the early release by journal entry, shall schedule a time within thirty days for a hearing on whether the child is to be released, or shall reject the request by journal entry without conducting a hearing. If an initial request for early release is rejected, the child or the child's parent may make one or more subsequent requests for early release but may make no more than one request for early release during each period of ninety days that the child is institutionalized or institutionalized in a secure facility after the filing of a prior request for early release. Upon the filing of any request for early release subsequent to an initial request, the court shall either approve or disapprove the early release by journal entry or schedule a time within thirty days for a hearing on whether the child is to be released.

(c) If a court schedules a hearing to determine whether a child committed to the department should be granted an early release, either upon receipt of a request filed by the department under division (B)(2)(a) of this section or filed by the child or the child's parent in accordance with the time periods prescribed in division (B)(2)(b) of this section, or upon its own motion, it may order the department to deliver the child to the court on the date set for the hearing and shall order the department to present to the court at that time a treatment plan for the child's post-institutional care. The court may conduct the hearing without the child being present. The court shall determine at the hearing whether the child should be released from institutionalization or institutionalization in a secure facility. If the court approves the early release, the department shall prepare a written treatment and rehabilitation plan for the child pursuant to division (D) of this section that shall include the terms and conditions of the child's release. It shall send the committing court and the juvenile court of the county in which the child is placed a copy of the plan and the terms and conditions that it fixed. The court of the county in which the child is placed may adopt the terms and conditions set by the department as an order of the court and may add any additional consistent terms and conditions it considers appropriate. If a child is released under this division and the court of the county in which the child is placed has reason to believe that the child has not deported self in accordance with any post-release terms and conditions established by the court in its journal entry, the court of the county in which the child is placed shall schedule a time for a hearing on whether the child violated any of the post-release terms and conditions. If the court of the county in which the child is placed determines at the hearing that the child violated any of the post-release terms and conditions established by the court in its journal entry, the court, if it determines that the violation of the terms and conditions was a serious violation, may order the child to be returned to the department for institutionalization or institutionalization in a secure facility, consistent with the original order of commitment of the child, or in any case may make any other disposition of the child authorized by law that the court considers proper. If the court of the county in which the child is placed orders the child to be returned to a department of youth services institution, the time during which the child was institutionalized or institutionalized in a secure facility prior to the child's early release shall be considered as time served in fulfilling the prescribed minimum period or prescribed period of institutionalization or institutionalization in a secure facility that is applicable to the child under the child's original order of commitment. If the court orders the child returned to a department of youth services institution, the child shall remain in institutional care for a minimum period of three months or until the child successfully completes a specialized parole revocation program of a duration of not less than thirty days operated either by the department or by an entity with whom the department has contracted to provide a specialized parole revocation program.

(C) If a child is committed to the department of youth services pursuant to division (A)(4) or (5) of section 2151.355 [2151.35.5] of the Revised Code and the child has been institutionalized or institutionalized in a secure facility for the prescribed minimum periods of time under those divisions, the department, without approval of the court that committed the child, may release the child from institutional care or discharge the child. If the department releases the child from institutional care and then orders the child's release on parole or assigns the child to a family home, group care facility, or other place for treatment or rehabilitation, the department also shall prepare a written treatment and rehabilitation plan for the child pursuant to division (D) of this section that shall include the terms and conditions of the child's release or assignment, and shall send the committing court and the juvenile court of the county in which the child is placed a copy of the plan and the terms and conditions that it fixed. The court of the county in which the child is placed may adopt the terms and conditions as an order of the court and may add any additional consistent terms and conditions it considers appropriate. The release, discharge, release on parole, or assignment shall be in accordance with division (C) of section 5139.06 of the Revised Code. Upon notification of a pending release, discharge, release on parole, or assignment in accordance with that division, the committing court shall enter the notification in its journal. If a child is released on parole or is assigned subject to specified terms and conditions and the court of the county in which the child is placed has reason to believe that the child has not deported self in accordance with any post-release terms and conditions established by the court in its journal entry, the court of the county in which the child is placed, in its discretion, may schedule a time for a hearing on whether the child violated any of the post-release terms and conditions. If the court of the county in which the child is placed conducts a hearing and determines at the hearing that the child violated any of the post-release terms and conditions established in its journal entry, the court, if it determines that the violation of the terms and conditions was a serious violation, may order the child to be returned to the department of youth services for institutionalization, or in any case may make any other disposition of the child authorized by law that the court considers proper. If the court of the county in which the child is placed orders the child to be returned to a department of youth services institution, the child shall remain institutionalized for a minimum period of three months or until the child successfully completes a specialized parole revocation program of a duration of not less than thirty days operated either by the department or by an entity with whom the department has contracted to provide a specialized parole revocation program.

(D) The department of youth services, prior to the release of a child pursuant to division (B) or (C) of this section, shall do all of the following:

(1) After reviewing the child's rehabilitative progress history and medical and educational records, prepare a written treatment and rehabilitation plan for the child that shall include terms and conditions of the release;

(2) Completely discuss the terms and conditions of the plan prepared pursuant to division (D)(1) of this section and the possible penalties for violation of the plan with the child and the child's parents, guardian, or legal custodian;

(3) Have the plan prepared pursuant to division (D)(1) of this section signed by the child, the child's parents, legal guardian, or custodian, and any authority or person that is to supervise, control, and provide supportive assistance to the child at the time of the child's release pursuant to division (B) or (C) of this section;

(4) File a copy of the treatment plan prepared pursuant to division (D)(1) of this section, prior to the child's release, with the committing court and the juvenile court of the county in which the child is to be placed.

(E) The department of youth services shall file a written progress report with the committing court regarding each child released pursuant to division (B) or (C) of this section, at least once every thirty days unless specifically directed otherwise by the court. The report shall indicate the treatment and rehabilitative progress of the child and the child's family, if applicable, and shall include any suggestions and recommendations for alteration of the program, custody, living arrangements, or treatment. The department shall retain legal custody of a child so released until it discharges the child or until the custody is terminated as otherwise provided by law.

HISTORY: GC § 1639-35; 117 v 520; 121 v 557; Bureau of Code Revision, 10-1-53; 130 v 625 (Eff 10-7-63); 133 v S 49 (Eff 8-13-69); 133 v H 320 (Eff 11-19-69); 138 v H 695 (Eff 10-24-

80); 139 v H 1 (Eff 8-5-81); 139 v H 440 (Eff 11-23-81); 140 v H 291 (Eff 7-1-83); 141 v H 428 (Eff 12-23-86); 142 v S 89 (Eff 1-1-89); 144 v S 241 (Eff 4-9-93); 145 v H 152 (Eff 7-1-93); 145 v H 715 (Eff 7-22-94); 145 v H 314 (Eff 9-29-94); 146 v H 1 (Eff 1-1-96); 146 v H 124. Eff 3-31-97.

§ 2151.39 Placement of children from other states.

No person, association or agency, public or private, of another state, incorporated or otherwise, shall place a child in a family home or with an agency or institution within the boundaries of this state, either for temporary or permanent care or custody or for adoption, unless such person or association has furnished the department of human services with a medical and social history of the child, pertinent information about the family, agency, association, or institution in this state with whom the sending party desires to place the child, and any other information or financial guaranty required by the department to determine whether the proposed placement will meet the needs of the child. The department may require the party desiring the placement to agree to promptly receive and remove from the state a child brought into the state whose placement has not proven satisfactorily responsive to the needs of the child at any time until the child is adopted, reaches majority, becomes self-supporting or is discharged with the concurrence of the department. All placements proposed to be made in this state by a party located in a state which is a party to the interstate compact on the placement of children shall be made according to the provisions of sections 5103.20 to 5103.28 of the Revised Code.

HISTORY: GC § 1639-37; 117 v 520; Bureau of Code Revision, 10-1-53; 126 v 1165 (Eff 10-17-55); 136 v H 247 (Eff 1-1-76); 141 v H 428. Eff 12-23-86.

§ 2151.40 Cooperation with court.

Every county, township, or municipal official or department, including the prosecuting attorney, shall render all assistance and co-operation within his jurisdictional power which may further the objects of sections 2151.01 to 2151.54 of the Revised Code. All institutions or agencies to which the juvenile court sends any child shall give to the court or to any officer appointed by it such information concerning such child as said court or officer requires. The court may seek the co-operation of all societies or organizations having for their object the protection or aid of children.

On the request of the judge, when the child is represented by an attorney, or when a trial is requested the prosecuting attorney shall assist the court in presenting the evidence at any hearing or proceeding concerning an alleged or adjudicated delinquent, unruly, abused, neglected, or dependent child or juvenile traffic offender.

HISTORY: GC § 1639-55; 117 v 520; Bureau of Code Revision, 10-1-53; 133 v H 320 (Eff 11-19-69); 136 v H 85. Eff 11-28-75.

§ 2151.41 Repealed, 141 v H 349, § 2 [GC § 1639-45; 117 v 520; Bureau of Code Revision, 10-1-53; 133 v H 320]. Eff 3-6-86.

This section concerned abusing or contributing to delinquency of a child. See now RC § 2919.24.

[§ 2151.41.1] § 2151.411 Parent or custodian charged with control of child; liability and searches during probation period; order to exercise control.

(A) A parent of a child whose marriage to the other parent of the child has not been terminated by divorce, dissolution of marriage, or annulment, a parent who has parental rights and responsibilities for the care of a child and is the residential parent and legal custodian of the child, a guardian who has custody of a child, or any other custodian of a child is charged with the control of the child and shall have the power to exercise parental control and authority over the child.

(B) If a child is adjudicated a delinquent child and placed on probation, if a parent of the child whose marriage to the other parent of the child has not been terminated by divorce, dissolution of marriage, or annulment or the parent who has parental rights and responsibilities for the care of the child and is the residential parent and legal custodian of the child was notified prior to the adjudication hearing of the provisions of this division and of the possibility that the provisions may be applied to the parent, and if the court finds at the hearing that the parent has failed or neglected to subject the child to reasonable parental control and authority and that that parent's failure or neglect is the proximate cause of the act or acts of the child upon which the delinquent child adjudication is based, the court may require that parent to enter into a recognizance with sufficient surety, in an amount of not more than five hundred dollars, conditioned upon the faithful discharge of the conditions of probation of the child. If the child then commits a second act and is adjudicated a delinquent child for the commission of the second act or violates the conditions of probation and if the court finds at the hearing that the failure or neglect of a parent of the child whose marriage to the other parent of the child has not been terminated by divorce, dissolution of marriage, or annulment or the parent who has parental rights and responsibilities for the care of the child and is the residential parent and legal custodian of the child to subject the child to reasonable parental control and authority or faithfully to discharge the conditions of probation of the child on the part of that parent is the proximate cause of the act or acts of the child upon which the second delinquent child adjudication is based or upon which the child is found to have violated the conditions of the child's probation, the court may declare all or a part of the recognizance forfeited. The proceeds of the forfeited recognizance shall be used to pay any damages caused by the child, and the proceeds of the forfeited recognizance remaining after the payment of any damages shall be paid into the county treasury.

(C)(1) If a child is adjudicated a delinquent child, the court may issue an order requiring either parent or both parents of the child whose marriage to the other parent of the child has not been terminated by divorce, dissolution of marriage, or annulment, the parent who has parental rights and responsibilities for the care of the child and is the residential parent and legal custodian of the child, or the guardian or other custodian of the child to exercise appropriate and necessary control and authority over the child to ensure that the child complies with the terms and conditions of probation imposed upon the child, treatment or testing that the child is required to take part in, and the terms of any other order of disposition that the court imposed upon the child pursuant to section 2151.355 [2151.35.5] of the Revised Code. The court shall give a copy of the order to the child and to the parent, guardian, or custodian who is the subject of the order and shall notify that parent, guardian, or custodian that a willful failure to comply with the order is contempt of court. If the court determines that any parent, guardian, or custodian willfully has failed to comply with an order issued pursuant to division (C)(1) of this section, it may punish the parent, guardian, or custodian for contempt of court or take other action that it determines is necessary to ensure that the child will comply with the terms and conditions of the order of disposition made pursuant to section 2151.355 [2151.35.5] of the Revised Code.

(2)(a) If a child is adjudicated a delinquent child and is granted probation under division (A)(2) of section 2151.355 [2151.35.5] of the Revised Code, the court that places the child on probation shall provide the written notice described in division (C)(2)(b) of this section to the following individuals:

(i) To each parent of the child whose marriage to the other parent of the child has not been terminated by divorce, dissolution of marriage, or annulment;

(ii) To the parent of the child who has parental rights and responsibilities for the care of the child and who is the residential parent and legal custodian of the child and, if the court knows or is able to determine through the exercise of reasonable diligence the identity and residence address of the parent of the child who does not have parental rights and responsibilities for the care of the child and who is not the residential parent and legal custodian of the child, to that parent;

(iii) To the guardian who has custody of the child;

(iv) To the other custodian of the child.

(b) The court that places the child on probation shall provide the appropriate individuals described in division (C)(2)(a) of this section with a written notice that informs them that authorized probation officers who are engaged within the scope of their supervisory duties or responsibilities may conduct searches as described in division (L) of section 2151.355 [2151.35.5] of the Revised Code during the period of probation if they have reasonable grounds to believe that the child is not abiding by the law or otherwise is not complying with the conditions of the child's probation. The notice shall specifically state that a permissible search might extend to a motor vehicle, another item of tangible or intangible personal property, or a place of residence or other real property in which a notified parent, guardian, or custodian has a right, title, or interest and that the parent, guardian, or custodian expressly or impliedly permits the child to use, occupy, or possess.

(D) The provisions of this section dealing with the failure or neglect of parents to subject a child to reasonable parental control and authority are in addition to and not in substitution for any other provision of this chapter dealing with the failure or neglect of a person to exercise parental control or authority over a child. The provisions of division (B) of this section do not apply to foster parents.

HISTORY: 127 v 21 (Eff 9-13-57); 143 v S 258 (Eff 8-22-90); 143 v S 3 (Eff 4-11-91); 146 v H 4 (Eff 11-9-95); 146 v H 124. Eff 9-30-97.

The effective date is set by section 3 of HB 124.

See provisions, § 3 of HB 4 (146 v —) following RC § 2151.02.

[§ 2151.41.2] § 2151.412 Case plan for each child; changes; priorities.

(A) Each public children services agency and private child placing agency shall prepare and maintain a case plan for any child to whom the agency is providing services and to whom any of the following applies:

(1) The agency filed a complaint pursuant to section 2151.27 of the Revised Code alleging that the child is an abused, neglected, or dependent child;

(2) The agency has temporary or permanent custody of the child;

(3) The child is living at home subject to an order for protective supervision;

(4) The child is in long-term foster care.

Except as provided by division (A)(2) of section 5103.153 [5103.15.3] of the Revised Code, a private child placing agency providing services to a child who is the subject of a voluntary permanent custody surrender agreement entered into under division (B)(2) of section 5103.15 of the Revised Code is not required to prepare and maintain a case plan for that child.

(B)(1) The department of human services shall adopt rules pursuant to Chapter 119. of the Revised Code setting forth the content and format of case plans required by division (A) of this section and establishing procedures for developing, implementing, and changing the case plans. The rules shall at a minimum comply with the requirements of Title IV-E of the "Social Security Act," 94 Stat. 501, 42 U.S.C. 671 (1980), as amended.

(2) The department of human services shall adopt

rules pursuant to Chapter 119. of the Revised Code requiring public children services agencies and private child placing agencies to maintain case plans for children and their families who are receiving services in their homes from the agencies and for whom case plans are not required by division (A) of this section. The agencies shall maintain case plans as required by those rules; however, the case plans shall not be subject to any other provision of this section except as specifically required by the rules.

(C) Each public children services agency and private child placing agency that is required by division (A) of this section to maintain a case plan shall file the case plan with the court prior to the child's adjudicatory hearing but no later than thirty days after the earlier of the date on which the complaint in the case was filed or the child was first placed into shelter care. If the agency does not have sufficient information prior to the adjudicatory hearing to complete any part of the case plan, the agency shall specify in the case plan the additional information necessary to complete each part of the case plan and the steps that will be taken to obtain that information. All parts of the case plan shall be completed by the earlier of thirty days after the adjudicatory hearing or the date of the dispositional hearing for the child.

(D) Any agency that is required by division (A) of this section to prepare a case plan shall attempt to obtain an agreement among all parties, including, but not limited to, the parents, guardian, or custodian of the child and the guardian ad litem of the child regarding the content of the case plan. If all parties agree to the content of the case plan and the court approves it, the court shall journalize it as part of its dispositional order. If the agency cannot obtain an agreement upon the contents of the case plan or the court does not approve it, the parties shall present evidence on the contents of the case plan at the dispositional hearing. The court, based upon the evidence presented at the dispositional hearing and the best interest of the child, shall determine the contents of the case plan and journalize it as part of the dispositional order for the child.

(E)(1) All parties, including the parents, guardian, or custodian of the child, are bound by the terms of the journalized case plan. A party that fails to comply with the terms of the journalized case plan may be held in contempt of court.

(2) Any party may propose a change to a substantive part of the case plan, including, but not limited to, the child's placement and the visitation rights of any party. A party proposing a change to the case plan shall file the proposed change with the court and give notice of the proposed change in writing before the end of the day after the day of filing it to all parties and the child's guardian ad litem. All parties and the guardian ad litem shall have seven days from the date the notice is sent to object to and request a hearing on the proposed change.

(a) If it receives a timely request for a hearing, the court shall schedule a hearing pursuant to section 2151.417 [2151.41.7] of the Revised Code to be held no later than thirty days after the request is received by the court. The court shall give notice of the date, time, and location of the hearing to all parties and the guardian ad litem. The agency may implement the proposed change after the hearing, if the court approves it. The agency shall not implement the proposed change unless it is approved by the court.

(b) If it does not receive a timely request for a hearing, the court may approve the proposed change without a hearing. If the court approves the proposed change without a hearing, it shall journalize the case plan with the change not later than fourteen days after the change is filed with the court. If the court does not approve the proposed change to the case plan, it shall schedule a hearing to be held pursuant to section 2151.417 [2151.41.7] of the Revised Code no later than thirty days after the expiration of the fourteen-day time period and give notice of the date, time, and location of the hearing to all parties and the guardian ad litem of the child. If, despite the requirements of division (E)(2) of this section, the court neither approves and journalizes the proposed change nor conducts a hearing, the agency may implement the proposed change not earlier than fifteen days after it is submitted to the court.

(3) If an agency has reasonable cause to believe that a child is suffering from illness or injury and is not receiving proper care and that an appropriate change in the child's case plan is necessary to prevent immediate or threatened physical or emotional harm, to believe that a child is in immediate danger from the child's surroundings and that an immediate change in the child's case plan is necessary to prevent immediate or threatened physical or emotional harm to the child, or to believe that a parent, guardian, custodian, or other member of the child's household has abused or neglected the child and that the child is in danger of immediate or threatened physical or emotional harm from that person unless the agency makes an appropriate change in the child's case plan, it may implement the change without prior agreement or a court hearing and, before the end of the next day after the change is made, give all parties, the guardian ad litem of the child, and the court notice of the change. Before the end of the third day after implementing the change in the case plan, the agency shall file a statement of the change with the court and give notice of the filing accompanied by a copy of the statement to all parties and the guardian ad litem. All parties and the guardian ad litem shall have ten days from the date the notice is sent to object to and request a hearing on the change.

(a) If it receives a timely request for a hearing, the court shall schedule a hearing pursuant to section 2151.417 [2151.41.7] of the Revised Code to be held no later than thirty days after the request is received by the court. The court shall give notice of the date, time, and location of the hearing to all parties and the guardian ad litem. The agency shall continue to administer the case plan with the change after the hearing, if the court approves the change. If the court does not approve the change, the court shall make appropriate changes to the case plan and shall journalize the case plan.

(b) If it does not receive a timely request for a hearing, the court may approve the change without a hearing. If the court approves the change without a hearing, it shall journalize the case plan with the change within fourteen days after receipt of the change. If the court does not approve the change to the case plan, it shall schedule a hearing under section 2151.417 [2151.41.7] of the Revised Code to be held no later than thirty days after the expiration of the fourteen-day time period and give notice of the date, time, and location of the hearing to all parties and the guardian ad litem of the child.

(F)(1) All case plans for children in temporary custody shall have the following general goals:

(a) Consistent with the best interest and special needs of the child, to achieve an out-of-home placement in the least restrictive, most family-like setting available and in close proximity to the home from which the child was removed or the home in which the child will be permanently placed;

(b) To do either of the following:

(i) With all due speed eliminate the need for the out-of-home placement so that the child can return home;

(ii) If return to the child's home is not imminent and desirable, develop and implement an alternative permanent living arrangement for the child.

(2) The department of human services shall adopt rules pursuant to Chapter 119. of the Revised Code setting forth the general goals of case plans for children subject to dispositional orders for protective supervision, long-term foster care, or permanent custody.

(G) In the agency's development of a case plan and the court's review of the case plan, the agency and the court shall be guided by the following general priorities:

(1) A child who is residing with or can be placed with the child's parents within a reasonable time should remain in their legal custody even if an order of protective supervision is required for a reasonable period of time;

(2) If both parents of the child have abandoned the child, have relinquished custody of the child, have become incapable of supporting or caring for the child even with reasonable assistance, or have a detrimental effect on the health, safety, and best interest of the child, the child should be placed in the legal custody of a suitable member of the child's extended family;

(3) If a child described in division (G)(2) of this section has no suitable member of the child's extended family to accept legal custody, the child should be placed in the legal custody of a suitable nonrelative who shall be made a party to the proceedings after being given legal custody of the child;

(4) If the child has no suitable member of the child's extended family to accept legal custody of the child and no suitable nonrelative is available to accept legal custody of the child and, if the child temporarily cannot or should not be placed with the child's parents, guardian, or custodian, the child should be placed in the temporary custody of a public children services agency or a private child placing agency;

(5) If the child cannot be placed with either of the child's parents within a reasonable period of time or should not be placed with either, if no suitable member of the child's extended family or suitable nonrelative is available to accept legal custody of the child, and if the agency has a reasonable expectation of placing the child for adoption, the child should be committed to the permanent custody of the public children services agency or private child placing agency;

(6) If the child is to be placed for adoption or foster care, the placement shall not be delayed or denied solely on the basis of the child's or adoptive or foster family's race, color, or national origin.

(H) The case plan for a child in temporary custody shall include at a minimum the following requirements if the child is or has been the victim of abuse or neglect or if the child witnessed the commission in the child's household of abuse or neglect against a sibling of the child, a parent of the child, or any other person in the child's household:

(1) A requirement that the child's parents, guardian, or custodian participate in mandatory counseling;

(2) A requirement that the child's parents, guardian, or custodian participate in any supportive services that are required by or provided pursuant to the child's case plan.

HISTORY: 142 v H 403 (Eff 1-1-89); 146 v H 274 (Eff 8-8-96); 146 v H 419. Eff 9-18-96.

Analogous to former RC § 2151.41.2 (138 v H 695; 141 v H 428; 142 v H 399; 142 v S 89), repealed, 142 v H 403, § 2, eff 1-1-89.

[§ 2151.41.3] § 2151.413 Agency may file motion requesting permanent custody.

(A) A public children services agency or private child placing agency that, pursuant to an order of disposition under division (A)(2) of section 2151.353 [2151.35.3] of the Revised Code or under any version of section 2151.353 [2151.35.3] of the Revised Code that existed prior to January 1, 1989, is granted temporary custody of a child who is not abandoned or orphaned or of an abandoned child whose parents have been located may file a motion in the court that made the disposition of the child requesting permanent custody of the child.

(B) A public children services agency or private child placing agency that, pursuant to an order of disposition under division (A)(2) of section 2151.353 [2151.35.3] of the Revised Code or under any version of section 2151.353 [2151.35.3] of the Revised Code that existed prior to January 1, 1989, is granted temporary custody of a child who is abandoned or orphaned may file a motion in the court that made the disposition of the child requesting permanent custody of the child, if the child is abandoned, whenever it can show the court that the parents cannot be located and, if the child is orphaned, whenever it can show that no relative of the child is able to take legal custody of the child.

(C) A public children services agency or private child placing agency that, pursuant to an order of disposition under division (A)(5) of section 2151.353 [2151.35.3] of the Revised Code, places a child in long-term foster care may file a motion in the court that made the disposition of the child requesting permanent custody of the child.

(D) Any agency that files a motion for permanent custody under this section shall include in the case plan of the child who is the subject of the motion, a specific plan of the agency's actions to seek an adoptive family for the child and to prepare the child for adoption.

HISTORY: 138 v H 695 (Eff 10-24-80); 142 v S 89 (Eff 1-1-89); 146 v H 419. Eff 9-18-96.

The effective date is set by section 3 of HB 419.

[§ 2151.41.4] § 2151.414 Hearing on motion for permanent custody; notice; determinations necessary for granting motion.

(A)(1) Upon the filing of a motion pursuant to section 2151.413 [2151.41.3] of the Revised Code for permanent custody of a child by a public children services agency or private child placing agency that has temporary custody of the child or has placed the child in long-term foster care, the court shall schedule a hearing and give notice of the filing of the motion and of the hearing, in accordance with section 2151.29 of the Revised Code, to all parties to the action and to the child's guardian ad litem. The notice also shall contain a full explanation that the granting of permanent custody permanently divests the parents of their parental rights, a full explanation of their right to be represented by counsel and to have counsel appointed pursuant to Chapter 120. of the Revised Code if they are indigent, and the name and telephone number of the court employee designated by the court pursuant to section 2151.314 [2151.31.4] of the Revised Code to arrange for the prompt appointment of counsel for indigent persons.

The court shall conduct a hearing in accordance with section 2151.35 of the Revised Code to determine if it is in the best interest of the child to permanently terminate parental rights and grant permanent custody to the agency that filed the motion. The adjudication that the child is an abused, neglected, or dependent child and the grant of temporary custody to the agency that filed the motion or placement into long-term foster care shall not be readjudicated at the hearing and shall not be affected by a denial of the motion for permanent custody.

(2) The court shall hold the hearing scheduled pursuant to division (A)(1) of this section not later than one hundred twenty days after the agency files the motion for permanent custody, except that, for good cause shown, the court may continue the hearing for a reasonable period of time beyond the one-hundred-twenty-day deadline. The court shall issue an order that grants, denies, or otherwise disposes of the motion for permanent custody, and journalize the order, not later than two hundred days after the agency files the motion.

The failure of the court to comply with the time periods set forth in division (A)(2) of this section does not affect the authority of the court to issue any order under this chapter and does not provide any basis for attacking the jurisdiction of the court or the validity of any order of the court.

(B) The court may grant permanent custody of a child to a movant if the court determines at the hearing held pursuant to division (A) of this section, by clear and convincing evidence, that it is in the best interest of the child to grant permanent custody of the child to the agency that filed the motion for permanent custody and that any of the following apply:

(1) The child is not abandoned or orphaned and the child cannot be placed with either of the child's parents within a reasonable time or should not be placed with the child's parents;

(2) The child is abandoned and the parents cannot be located;

(3) The child is orphaned and there are no relatives of the child who are able to take permanent custody.

(C) In making the determinations required by this section or division (A)(4) of section 2151.353 [2151.35.3] of the Revised Code, a court shall not consider the effect the granting of permanent custody to the agency would have upon any parent of the child. A written report of the guardian ad litem of the child shall be submitted to the court prior to or at the time of the hearing held pursuant to division (A) of this section or section 2151.35 of the Revised Code but shall not be submitted under oath.

If the court grants permanent custody of a child to a movant under this division, the court, upon the request of any party, shall file a written opinion setting forth its findings of fact and conclusions of law in relation to the proceeding. The court shall not deny an agency's motion for permanent custody solely because the agency failed to implement any particular aspect of the child's case plan.

(D) In determining the best interest of a child at a hearing held pursuant to division (A) of this section or for the purposes of division (A)(4) or (5) of section 2151.353 [2151.35.3] or division (C) of section 2151.415 [2151.41.5] of the Revised Code, the court shall consider all relevant factors, including, but not limited to, the following:

(1) The interaction and interrelationship of the child with the child's parents, siblings, relatives, foster parents

and out-of-home providers, and any other person who may significantly affect the child;

(2) The wishes of the child, as expressed directly by the child or through the child's guardian ad litem, with due regard for the maturity of the child;

(3) The custodial history of the child;

(4) The child's need for a legally secure permanent placement and whether that type of placement can be achieved without a grant of permanent custody to the agency.

(E) In determining at a hearing held pursuant to division (A) of this section or for the purposes of division (A)(4) of section 2151.353 [2151.35.3] of the Revised Code whether a child cannot be placed with either parent within a reasonable period of time or should not be placed with the parents, the court shall consider all relevant evidence. If the court determines, by clear and convincing evidence, at a hearing held pursuant to division (A) of this section or for the purposes of division (A)(4) of section 2151.353 [2151.35.3] of the Revised Code that one or more of the following exist as to each of the child's parents, the court shall enter a finding that the child cannot be placed with either parent within a reasonable time or should not be placed with either parent:

(1) Following the placement of the child outside the child's home and notwithstanding reasonable case planning and diligent efforts by the agency to assist the parents to remedy the problems that initially caused the child to be placed outside the home, the parent has failed continuously and repeatedly to substantially remedy the conditions causing the child to be placed outside the child's home. In determining whether the parents have substantially remedied those conditions, the court shall consider parental utilization of medical, psychiatric, psychological, and other social and rehabilitative services and material resources that were made available to the parents for the purpose of changing parental conduct to allow them to resume and maintain parental duties.

(2) Chronic mental illness, chronic emotional illness, mental retardation, physical disability, or chemical dependency of the parent that is so severe that it makes the parent unable to provide an adequate permanent home for the child at the present time and, as anticipated, within one year after the court holds the hearing pursuant to division (A) of this section or for the purposes of division (A)(4) of section 2151.353 [2151.35.3] of the Revised Code;

(3) The parent committed any abuse as described in section 2151.031 [2151.03.1] of the Revised Code against the child, caused the child to suffer any neglect as described in section 2151.03 of the Revised Code, or allowed the child to suffer any neglect as described in section 2151.03 of the Revised Code between the date that the original complaint alleging abuse or neglect was filed and the date of the filing of the motion for permanent custody;

(4) The parent has demonstrated a lack of commitment toward the child by failing to regularly support, visit, or communicate with the child when able to do so, or by other actions showing an unwillingness to provide an adequate permanent home for the child;

(5) The parent is incarcerated for an offense committed against the child or a sibling of the child;

(6) The parent violated section 2903.11, 2903.12, 2903.13, 2903.16, 2903.21, 2903.34, 2905.01, 2905.02, 2905.03, 2905.04†, 2905.05, 2907.02, 2907.03, 2907.04, 2907.05, 2907.06, 2907.07, 2907.08, 2907.09, 2907.12††, 2907.21, 2907.22, 2907.23, 2907.25, 2907.31, 2907.32, 2907.321 [2907.32.1], 2907.322 [2907.32.2], 2907.323 [2907.32.3], 2911.01, 2911.02, 2911.11, 2911.12, 2919.12, 2919.22, 2919.24, 2919.25, 2923.12, 2923.13, 2923.161 [2923.16.1], 2925.02, or 3716.11 of the Revised Code and the child or a sibling of the child was a victim of the violation or the parent violated section 2903.01, 2903.02, 2903.03, or 2903.04 of the Revised Code, a sibling of the child was the victim of the violation, and the parent who committed the violation poses an ongoing danger to the child or a sibling of the child.

(7) The parent is incarcerated at the time of the filing of the motion for permanent custody or the dispositional hearing of the child and will not be available to care for the child for at least eighteen months after the filing of the motion for permanent custody or the dispositional hearing;

(8) The parent is repeatedly incarcerated and the repeated incarceration prevents the parent from providing care for the child;

(9) The parent for any reason is unwilling to provide food, clothing, shelter, and other basic necessities for the child or to prevent the child from suffering physical, emotional, or sexual abuse or physical, emotional, or mental neglect;

(10) The parent has committed abuse as described in section 2151.031 [2151.03.1] of the Revised Code against the child or caused or allowed the child to suffer neglect as described in section 2151.03 of the Revised Code and the court determines that the seriousness, nature, or likelihood of recurrence of the abuse or neglect makes the child's placement with the child's parent a threat to the child's safety;

(11) The parent committed abuse as described in section 2151.031 [2151.03.1] of the Revised Code against the child or caused or allowed the child to suffer neglect as described in section 2151.03 of the Revised Code and a sibling of the child previously has been permanently removed from the home of the child's parents because the parent abused or neglected the sibling.

(12) Any other factor the court considers relevant.

(F) The parents of a child for whom the court has issued an order granting permanent custody pursuant to this section, upon the issuance of the order, cease to be parties to the action. This division is not intended to eliminate or restrict any right of the parents to appeal the granting of permanent custody of their child to a movant pursuant to this section.

HISTORY: 138 v H 695 (Eff 10-24-80); 142 v S 89 (Eff 1-1-89); 146 v H 274 (Eff 8-8-96); 146 v H 419. Eff 9-18-96.

See provisions, § 10 of HB 274 (146 v —) following RC § 2151.28.

† Repealed 7-1-96.

†† Repealed 9-3-96.

[§ 2151.41.5] § 2151.415 Motion requesting disposition order upon expiration of temporary custody order; extension.

(A) Any public children services agency or private child placing agency that has been given temporary custody of a child pursuant to section 2151.353 [2151.35.3] of the Revised Code, not later than thirty days prior to the earlier of the date for the termination of the custody order pursuant to division (F) of section 2151.353 [2151.35.3] of the Revised Code or the date set at the dispositional hearing for the hearing to be held pursuant to this section, shall file a motion with the court that issued the order of disposition requesting that any of the following orders of disposition of the child be issued by the court:

(1) An order that the child be returned home and the custody of the child's parents, guardian, or custodian without any restrictions;

(2) An order for protective supervision;

(3) An order that the child be placed in the legal custody of a relative or other interested individual;

(4) An order permanently terminating the parental rights of the child's parents;

(5) An order that the child be placed in long-term foster care;

(6) In accordance with division (D) of this section, an order for the extension of temporary custody.

(B) Upon the filing of a motion pursuant to division (A) of this section, the court shall hold a dispositional hearing on the date set at the dispositional hearing held pursuant to section 2151.35 of the Revised Code, with notice to all parties to the action in accordance with the Juvenile Rules. After the dispositional hearing or at a date after the dispositional hearing that is not later than one year after the earlier of the date on which the complaint in the case was filed or the child was first placed into shelter care, the court, in accordance with the best interest of the child as supported by the evidence presented at the dispositional hearing, shall issue an order of disposition as set forth in division (A) of this section, except that all orders for permanent custody shall be made in accordance with sections 2151.413 [2151.41.3] and 2151.414 [2151.41.4] of the Revised Code.

(C)(1) If an agency pursuant to division (A) of this section requests the court to place a child into long-term foster care, the agency shall present evidence to indicate why long-term foster care is appropriate for the child, including, but not limited to, evidence that the agency has tried or considered all other possible dispositions for the child. A court shall not place a child in long-term foster care, unless it finds, by clear and convincing evidence, that long-term foster care is in the best interest of the child and that one of the following exists:

(a) The child, because of physical, mental, or psychological problems or needs, is unable to function in a family-like setting and must remain in residential or institutional care;

(b) The parents of the child have significant physical, mental, or psychological problems and are unable to care for the child because of those problems, adoption is not in the best interest of the child, as determined in accordance with division (D) of section 2151.414 [2151.41.4] of the Revised Code, and the child retains a significant and positive relationship with a parent or relative;

(c) The child is sixteen years of age or older, has been counseled on the permanent placement options available, is unwilling to accept or unable to adapt to a permanent placement, and is in an agency program preparing for independent living.

(2) If the court issues an order placing a child in long-term foster care, both of the following apply:

(a) The court shall issue a finding of fact setting forth the reasons for its finding;

(b) The agency may make any appropriate placement for the child and shall develop a case plan for the child that is designed to assist the child in finding a permanent home outside of the home of the parents.

(D)(1) If an agency pursuant to division (A) of this section requests the court to grant an extension of temporary custody for a period of up to six months, the agency shall include in the motion an explanation of the progress on the case plan of the child and of its expectations of reunifying the child with its family, or placing the child in a permanent placement, within the extension period. The court shall schedule a hearing on the motion, give notice of its date, time, and location to all parties and the guardian ad litem of the child, and at the hearing consider the evidence presented by the parties and the guardian ad litem. The court may extend the temporary custody order of the child for a period of up to six months, if it determines at the hearing, by clear and convincing evidence, that the extension is in the best interest of the child, there has been significant progress on the case plan of the child, and there is reasonable cause to believe that the child will be reunified with one of the parents or otherwise permanently placed within the period of extension. If the court extends the temporary custody of the child pursuant to this division, upon request it shall issue findings of fact.

(2) Prior to the end of the extension granted pursuant to division (D)(1) of this section, the agency that received the extension shall file a motion with the court

requesting the issuance of one of the orders of disposition set forth in divisions (A)(1) to (5) of this section or requesting the court to extend the temporary custody order of the child for an additional period of up to six months. If the agency requests the issuance of an order of disposition under divisions (A)(1) to (5) of this section or does not file any motion prior to the expiration of the extension period, the court shall conduct a hearing in accordance with division (B) of this section and issue an appropriate order of disposition.

If the agency requests an additional extension of up to six months of the temporary custody order of the child, the court shall schedule and conduct a hearing in the manner set forth in division (D)(1) of this section. The court may extend the temporary custody order of the child for an additional period of up to six months if it determines at the hearing, by clear and convincing evidence, that the additional extension is in the best interest of the child, there has been substantial additional progress since the original extension of temporary custody in the case plan of the child, there has been substantial additional progress since the original extension of temporary custody toward reunifying the child with one of the parents or otherwise permanently placing the child, and there is reasonable cause to believe that the child will be reunified with one of the parents or otherwise placed in a permanent setting before the expiration of the additional extension period. If the court extends the temporary custody of the child for an additional period pursuant to this division, upon request it shall issue findings of fact.

(3) Prior to the end of the extension of a temporary custody order granted pursuant to division (D)(2) of this section, the agency that received the extension shall file a motion with the court requesting the issuance of one of the orders of disposition set forth in divisions (A)(1) to (5) of this section. Upon the filing of the motion by the agency or, if the agency does not file the motion prior to the expiration of the extension period, upon its own motion, the court, prior to the expiration of the extension period, shall conduct a hearing in accordance with division (B) of this section and issue an appropriate order of disposition.

(4) No court shall grant an agency more than two extensions of temporary custody pursuant to division (D) of this section.

(E) After the issuance of an order pursuant to division (B) of this section, the court shall retain jurisdiction over the child until the child attains the age of eighteen if the child is not mentally retarded, developmentally disabled, or physically impaired, the child attains the age of twenty-one if the child is mentally retarded, developmentally disabled, or physically impaired, or the child is adopted and a final decree of adoption is issued, unless the court's jurisdiction over the child is extended pursuant to division (E) of section 2151.353 [2151.35.3] of the Revised Code.

(F) The court, on its own motion or the motion of the agency or person with legal custody of the child, the child's guardian ad litem, or any other party to the action, may conduct a hearing with notice to all parties to determine whether any order issued pursuant to this section should be modified or terminated or whether any other dispositional order set forth in divisions (A)(1) to (5) of this section should be issued. After the hearing and consideration of all the evidence presented, the court, in accordance with the best interest of the child, may modify or terminate any order issued pursuant to this section or issue any dispositional order set forth in divisions (A)(1) to (5) of this section.

(G) If the court places a child in long-term foster care with a public children services agency or a private child placing agency pursuant to this section, the agency with which the child is placed in long-term foster care shall not remove the child from the residential placement in which the child is originally placed pursuant to the case plan for the child or in which the child is placed with court approval pursuant to this division, unless the court and the guardian ad litem are given notice of the intended removal and the court issues an order approving the removal or unless the removal is necessary to protect the child from physical or emotional harm and the agency gives the court notice of the removal and of the reasons why the removal is necessary to protect the child from physical or emotional harm immediately after the removal of the child from the prior setting.

(H) If the hearing held under this section takes the place of an administrative review that otherwise would have been held under section 2151.416 [2151.41.6] of the Revised Code, the court at the hearing held under this section shall do all of the following in addition to any other requirements of this section:

(1) Determine the continued necessity for and the appropriateness of the child's placement;

(2) Determine the extent of compliance with the child's case plan;

(3) Determine the extent of progress that has been made toward alleviating or mitigating the causes necessitating the child's placement in foster care;

(4) Project a likely date by which the child may be returned to his home or placed for adoption or legal guardianship;

(5) Determine the future status of the child.

HISTORY: 142 v S 89 (Eff 1-1-89); 146 v H 274. Eff 8-8-96.

[§ 2151.41.6] § 2151.416 Administrative reviews of case plan; annual report.

(A) Each agency that is required by section 2151.412 [2151.41.2] of the Revised Code to prepare a case plan for a child shall complete a semiannual administrative review of the case plan no later than six months after the earlier of the date on which the complaint in the case was filed or the child was first placed in shelter care. After the first administrative review, the agency shall complete semiannual administrative reviews no later than every six months. If the court issues an order pursuant to section 2151.414 [2151.41.4] or 2151.415 [2151.41.5] of the Revised Code, the agency shall complete an administrative review no later than six months after the court's order and continue to complete administrative reviews no later than every six months after the first review, except that the court hearing held pursuant to section 2151.417 [2151.41.7] of the Revised Code may take the place of any administrative review that would otherwise be held at the time of the court hearing.

(B) Each administrative review required by division (A) of this section shall be conducted by a review panel of at least three persons, including, but not limited to, both of the following:

(1) A caseworker with day-to-day responsibility for, or familiarity with, the management of the child's case plan;

(2) A person who is not responsible for the management of the child's case plan or for the delivery of services to the child or the parents, guardian, or custodian of the child.

(C) Each semiannual administrative review shall include, but not be limited to, a joint meeting by the review panel with the parents, guardian, or custodian of the child, the guardian ad litem of the child, and the child's foster care provider and shall include an opportunity for those persons to submit any written materials to be included in the case record of the child. If a parent, guardian, custodian, guardian ad litem, or foster care provider of the child cannot be located after reasonable efforts to do so or declines to participate in the administrative review after being contacted, the agency does not have to include them in the joint meeting.

(D) The agency shall prepare a written summary of the semiannual administrative review that shall include, but not be limited to, all of the following:

(1) A conclusion regarding the appropriateness of the child's foster care placement;

(2) The extent of the compliance with the case plan of all parties;

(3) The extent of progress that has been made toward alleviating the circumstances that required the agency to assume temporary custody of the child;

(4) An estimated date by which the child may be returned to the child's home or placed for adoption or legal custody;

(5) An updated case plan that includes any changes that the agency is proposing in the case plan;

(6) The recommendation of the agency as to which agency or person should be given custodial rights over the child for the six-month period after the administrative review;

(7) The names of all persons who participated in the administrative review.

(E) The agency shall file the summary with the court no later than seven days after the completion of the administrative review. If the agency proposes a change to the case plan as a result of the administrative review, the agency shall file the proposed change with the court at the time it files the summary. The agency shall give notice of the summary and proposed change in writing before the end of the next day after filing them to all parties and the child's guardian ad litem. All parties and the guardian ad litem shall have seven days after the date the notice is sent to object to and request a hearing on the proposed change.

(1) If the court receives a timely request for a hearing, the court shall schedule a hearing pursuant to section 2151.417 [2151.41.7] of the Revised Code to be held not later than thirty days after the court receives the request. The court shall give notice of the date, time, and location of the hearing to all parties and the guardian ad litem. The agency may implement the proposed change after the hearing, if the court approves it. The agency shall not implement the proposed change unless it is approved by the court.

(2) If the court does not receive a timely request for a hearing, the court may approve the proposed change without a hearing. If the court approves the proposed change without a hearing, it shall journalize the case plan with the change not later than fourteen days after the change is filed with the court. If the court does not approve the proposed change to the case plan, it shall schedule a review hearing to be held pursuant to section 2151.417 [2151.41.7] of the Revised Code no later than thirty days after the expiration of the fourteen-day time period and give notice of the date, time, and location of the hearing to all parties and the guardian ad litem of the child. If, despite the requirements of this division and division (D) of section 2151.417 [2151.41.7] of the Revised Code, the court neither approves and journalizes the proposed change nor conducts a hearing, the agency may implement the proposed change not earlier than fifteen days after it is submitted to the court.

(F) The department of human services may adopt rules pursuant to Chapter 119. of the Revised Code for procedures and standard forms for conducting administrative reviews pursuant to this section.

(G) The juvenile court that receives the written summary of the administrative review, upon determining, either from the written summary, case plan, or otherwise, that the custody or care arrangement is not in the best interest of the child, may terminate the custody of an agency and place the child in the custody of another institution or association certified by the department of human services under section 5103.03 of the Revised Code.

(H) The department of human services shall report annually to the public and to the general assembly on the results of the review of case plans of each agency and on the results of the summaries submitted to the department under section 3107.10 of the Revised Code. The annual report shall include any information that is required by the department, including, but not limited to, all of the following:

(1) A statistical analysis of the administrative reviews conducted pursuant to this section and section 2151.417 [2151.41.7] of the Revised Code;

(2) The number of children in temporary or permanent custody for whom an administrative review was conducted, the number of children whose custody status changed during the period, the number of children whose residential placement changed during the period, and the number of residential placement changes for each child during the period;

(3) An analysis of the utilization of public social services by agencies and parents or guardians, and the utilization of the adoption listing service of the department pursuant to section 5103.154 [5103.15.4] of the Revised Code;

(4) A compilation and analysis of data submitted to the department under section 3107.10 of the Revised Code.

HISTORY: RC § 5103.15.1, 136 v H 156 (Eff 1-1-77); 137 v H 832 (Eff 3-13-79); 138 v H 695 (Eff 10-24-80); 141 v H 428 (Eff 12-23-86); RC § 2151.41.6, 142 v S 89 (Eff 1-1-89); 146 v H 274 (Eff 8-8-96); 146 v H 419. Eff 9-18-96.

See provisions, § 10 of HB 274 (146 v —) following RC § 2151.28.

[§ 2151.41.7] § 2151.417 Court review of child's placement or custody arrangement; continuing jurisdiction; citizen's review board.

(A) Any court that issues a dispositional order pursuant to section 2151.353 [2151.35.3], 2151.414 [2151.41.4], or 2151.415 [2151.41.5] of the Revised Code may review at any time the child's placement or custody arrangement, the case plan prepared for the child pursuant to section 2151.412 [2151.41.2] of the Revised Code, the actions of the public children services agency or private child placing agency in implementing that case plan, and any other aspects of the child's placement or custody arrangement. In conducting the review, the court shall determine the appropriateness of any agency actions, the appropriateness of continuing the child's placement or custody arrangement, and whether any changes should be made with respect to the child's placement or custody arrangement or with respect to the actions of the agency under the child's placement or custody arrangement. Based upon the evidence presented at a hearing held after notice to all parties and the guardian ad litem of the child, the court may require the agency, the parents, guardian, or custodian of the child, and the physical custodians of the child to take any reasonable action that the court determines is necessary and in the best interest of the child or to discontinue any action that it determines is not in the best interest of the child.

(B) If a court issues a dispositional order pursuant to section 2151.353 [2151.35.3], 2151.414 [2151.41.4], or 2151.415 [2151.41.5] of the Revised Code, the court has continuing jurisdiction over the child as set forth in division (E)(1) of section 2151.353 [2151.35.3] of the Revised Code. The court may amend a dispositional order in accordance with division (E)(2) of section 2151.353 [2151.35.3] of the Revised Code at any time upon its own motion or upon the motion of any interested party.

(C) Any court that issues a dispositional order pursuant to section 2151.353 [2151.35.3], 2151.414 [2151.41.4], or 2151.415 [2151.41.5] of the Revised Code shall hold a review hearing one year after the earlier of the date on which the complaint in the case was filed or the child was first placed into shelter care to review the case plan prepared pursuant to section 2151.412 [2151.41.2] of the Revised Code and to review the child's placement or custody arrangement. The court shall schedule the review hearing at the time that it holds the dispositional hearing pursuant to section 2151.35 of the Revised Code.

The court shall hold a similar review hearing no later than every twelve months after the initial review hearing until the child is adopted, returned to the parents, or the court otherwise terminates the child's placement or custody arrangement, except that the dispositional hearing held pursuant to section 2151.415 [2151.41.5] of the Revised Code shall take the place of the first review hearing to be held under this section. The court shall schedule each subsequent review hearing at the conclusion of the review hearing immediately preceding the review hearing to be scheduled.

(D) If, within fourteen days after a written summary of an administrative review is filed with the court pursuant to section 2151.416 [2151.41.6] of the Revised Code, the court does not approve the proposed change to the case plan filed pursuant to division (E) of section 2151.416 [2151.41.6] of the Revised Code or a party or the guardian ad litem requests a review hearing pursuant to division (E) of that section, the court shall hold a review hearing in the same manner that it holds review hearings pursuant to division (C) of this section, except that if a review hearing is required by this division and if a hearing is to be held pursuant to division (C) of this section or section 2151.415 [2151.41.5] of the Revised Code, the hearing held pursuant to division (C) of this section or section 2151.415 [2151.41.5] of the Revised Code shall take the place of the review hearing required by this division.

(E) The court shall give notice of the review hearings held pursuant to this section to every interested party, including, but not limited to, the appropriate agency employees who are responsible for the child's care and planning, the child's parents, any person who had guardianship or legal custody of the child prior to the custody order, the child's guardian ad litem, and the child. The court shall summon every interested party to appear at the review hearing and give them an opportunity to testify and to present other evidence with respect to the child's custody arrangement, including, but not limited to, the case plan for the child, the actions taken by the child's custodian, the need for a change in the child's custodian or caseworker, or the need for any specific action to be taken with respect to the child. The court shall require any interested party to testify or present other evidence when necessary to a proper determination of the issues presented at the review hearing.

(F) After the review hearing, the court shall take the following actions based upon the evidence presented:

(1) Determine whether the conclusions of the administrative review are supported by a preponderance of the evidence and approve or modify the case plan based upon that evidence;

(2) If the child is in temporary custody, do all of the following:

(a) Determine whether the child can and should be returned home with or without an order for protective supervision;

(b) If the child can and should be returned home with or without an order for protective supervision, terminate the order for temporary custody;

(c) If the child cannot or should not be returned home with an order for protective supervision, determine whether the agency currently with custody of the child should retain custody or whether another public children services agency, private child placing agency, or an individual should be given custody of the child.

(3) If the child is in permanent custody, determine what actions are required by the custodial agency and of any other organizations or persons in order to facilitate an adoption of the child and make any appropriate orders with respect to the custody arrangement or conditions of the child, including, but not limited to, a transfer of permanent custody to another public children services agency or private child placing agency;

(4) Journalize the terms of the updated case plan for the child.

(G) The court may appoint a referee or a citizens review board to conduct the review hearings that the court is required by this section to conduct, subject to the review and approval by the court of any determinations made by the referee or citizens review board. If the court appoints a citizens review board to conduct the review hearings, the board shall consist of one member representing the general public and four members who are trained or experienced in the care or placement of children and have training or experience in the fields of medicine, psychology, social work, education, or any related field. Of the initial appointments to the board, two shall be for a term of one year, two shall be for a term of two years, and one shall be for a term of three years, with all the terms ending one year after the date on which the appointment was made. Thereafter, all terms of the board members shall be for three years and shall end on the same day of the same month of the year as did the term that they succeed. Any member appointed to fill a vacancy occurring prior to the expiration of the term for which the member's predecessor was appointed shall hold office for the remainder of the term.

(H) A copy of the court's determination following any review hearing held pursuant to this section shall be sent to the custodial agency, the guardian ad litem of the child who is the subject of the review hearing, and, if that child is not the subject of a permanent commitment hearing, the parents of the child.

(I) If the hearing held under this section takes the place of an administrative review that otherwise would have been held under section 2151.416 [2151.41.6] of the Revised Code, the court at the hearing held under this section shall do all of the following in addition to any other requirements of this section:

(1) Determine the continued necessity for and the appropriateness of the child's placement;

(2) Determine the extent of compliance with the child's case plan;

(3) Determine the extent of progress that has been made toward alleviating or mitigating the causes necessitating the child's placement in foster care;

(4) Project a likely date by which the child may be returned home or placed for adoption or legal guardianship;

(5) Determine the future status of the child.

HISTORY: 142 v S 89 (Eff 1-1-89); 146 v H 274. Eff 8-8-96.

[§ 2151.41.8] § 2151.41.8 Application of zoning laws to foster or family foster home.

Any foster home or family foster home shall be considered to be a residential use of property for purposes of municipal, county, and township zoning and shall be a permitted use in all zoning districts in which residential uses are permitted. No municipal, county, or township zoning regulation shall require a conditional permit or any other special exception certification for any foster home or family foster home.

HISTORY: 142 v S 89 (Eff 1-1-89); 145 v H 152. Eff 7-1-93.

[§ 2151.41.9] § 2151.419 Determination as to whether agency made reasonable efforts to prevent removal or to return child to home.

(A) At any hearing held pursuant to section 2151.28, division (E) of section 2151.31, or section 2151.314 [2151.31.4], 2151.33, or 2151.353 [2151.35.3] of the Revised Code at which the court removes a child from his home or continues the removal of a child from his home, the court shall determine whether the public children services agency or private child placing agency that filed the complaint in the case, removed the child from his home, has custody of the child, or will be given custody of the child has made reasonable efforts to prevent the removal of the child from his home, to eliminate the continued removal of the child from his home, or to make it possible for the child to return home. The agency shall have the burden of proving that it has made those reasonable efforts. If the agency removed the child from his home during an emergency in which the child could not safely remain at home and the agency did not have prior contact with the child, the court is not prohibited, solely because the agency did not make the reasonable efforts during the emergency to prevent the removal of the child, from determining that the agency made those reasonable efforts.

(B) The court shall issue written finding of facts setting forth its determination under division (A) of this section. In its written finding of facts, the court shall briefly describe the relevant services provided by the agency to the family of the child and why those services did not prevent the removal of the child from his home or enable the child to return home.

HISTORY: 142 v S 89. Eff 1-1-89.

The effective date is set by section 9 of SB 89.

§ **2151.42** Repealed, 134 v H 511, § 2 [GC § 1639-46; 117 v 520; 119 v 731; 121 v 557; Bureau of Code Revision, 10-1-53; 130 v 625]. Eff 1-1-74.

This section concerned prohibition against neglecting or mistreating child.

[§ 2151.42.1] § 2151.421 Duty to report child abuse or neglect; investigation and followup procedures.

(A)(1)(a) No person described in division (A)(1)(b) of this section who is acting in an official or professional capacity and knows or suspects that a child under eighteen years of age or a mentally retarded, developmentally disabled, or physically impaired child under twenty-one years of age has suffered or faces a threat of suffering any physical or mental wound, injury, disability, or condition of a nature that reasonably indicates abuse or neglect of the child, shall fail to immediately report that knowledge or suspicion to the public children services agency or a municipal or county peace officer in the county in which the child resides or in which the abuse or neglect is occurring or has occurred.

(b) Division (A)(1)(a) of this section applies to any a†person who is an attorney; physician, including a hospital intern or resident; dentist; podiatrist; practitioner of a limited branch of medicine or surgery as defined in section 4731.15 of the Revised Code; registered nurse; licensed practical nurse; visiting nurse; other health care professional; licensed psychologist; licensed school psychologist; speech pathologist or audiologist; coroner; administrator or employee of a child day-care center; administrator or employee of a certified child care agency or other public or private children services agency; school teacher; school employee; school authority; person engaged in social work or the practice of professional counseling; or a person rendering spiritual treatment through prayer in accordance with the tenets of a well-recognized religion.

(2) An attorney or a physician is not required to make a report pursuant to division (A)(1) of this section concerning any communication the attorney or physician receives from a client or patient in an attorney-client or physician-patient relationship, if, in accordance with division (A) or (B) of section 2317.02 of the Revised Code, the attorney or physician could not testify with respect to that communication in a civil or criminal proceeding, except that the client or patient is deemed to have waived any testimonial privilege under division (A) or (B) of section 2317.02 of the Revised Code with respect to that communication and the attorney or physician shall make a report pursuant to division (A)(1) of this section with respect to that communication, if all of the following apply:

(a) The client or patient, at the time of the communication, is either a child under eighteen years of age or a mentally retarded, developmentally disabled, or physically impaired person under twenty-one years of age.

(b) The attorney of†† physician knows or suspects, as a result of the communication or any observations made during that communication, that the client or patient has suffered or faces a threat of suffering any physical or mental wound, injury, disability, or condition of a nature that reasonably indicates abuse or neglect of the client or patient.

(c) The attorney-client or physician-patient relationship does not arise out of the client's or patient's attempt to have an abortion without the notification of her parents, guardian, or custodian in accordance with section 2151.85 of the Revised Code.

(B) Anyone, who knows or suspects that a child under eighteen years of age or a mentally retarded, developmentally disabled, or physically impaired person under twenty-one years of age has suffered or faces a threat of suffering any physical or mental wound, injury, disability, or other condition of a nature that reasonably indicates abuse or neglect of the child, may report or cause reports to be made of that knowledge or suspicion to the public children services agency or to a municipal or county peace officer.

(C) Any report made pursuant to division (A) or (B) of this section shall be made forthwith either by telephone or in person and shall be followed by a written report, if requested by the receiving agency or officer. The written report shall contain:

(1) The names and addresses of the child and the child's parents or the person or persons having custody of the child, if known;

(2) The child's age and the nature and extent of the child's known or suspected injuries, abuse, or neglect or of the known or suspected threat of injury, abuse, or neglect, including any evidence of previous injuries, abuse, or neglect;

(3) Any other information that might be helpful in establishing the cause of the known or suspected injury, abuse, or neglect or of the known or suspected threat of injury, abuse, or neglect.

Any person, who is required by division (A) of this section to report known or suspected child abuse or child neglect, may take or cause to be taken color photographs of areas of trauma visible on a child and, if medically indicated, cause to be performed radiological examinations of the child.

(D)(1) Upon the receipt of a report concerning the possible abuse or neglect of a child or the possible threat of abuse or neglect of a child, the municipal or county peace officer who receives the report shall refer the report to the appropriate public children services agency.

(2) On receipt of a report pursuant to this division or division (A) or (B) of this section, the public children services agency shall comply with section 2151.422 [2151.42.2] of the Revised Code.

(E) No township, municipal, or county peace officer shall remove a child about whom a report is made pursuant to this section from the child's parents, stepparents, or guardian or any other persons having custody of the child without consultation with the public children services agency, unless, in the judgment of the officer, and, if the report was made by physician, the physician, immediate removal is considered essential to protect the child from further abuse or neglect. The agency that must be consulted shall be the agency conducting the investigation of the report as determined pursuant to section 2151.422 [2151.42.2] of the Revised Code.

(F)(1) Except as provided in section 2151.422 [2151.42.2] of the Revised Code, the public children services agency shall investigate, within twenty-four hours, each report of known or suspected child abuse or child neglect and of a known or suspected threat of child abuse or child neglect that is referred to it under this section to determine the circumstances surrounding the injuries, abuse, or neglect or the threat of injury, abuse, or neglect, the cause of the injuries, abuse, neglect, or threat, and the person or persons responsible. The investigation shall be made in cooperation with the law enforcement agency and in accordance with the memorandum of understanding prepared under division (J) of this section. A failure to make the investigation in accordance with the memorandum is not grounds for, and shall not result in, the dismissal of any charges or complaint arising from the report or the suppression of any evidence obtained as a result of the report and does not give, and shall not be construed as giving, any rights or any grounds for appeal or postconviction relief to any person. The public children services agency shall report each case to a central registry which the state department of human services shall maintain in order to determine whether prior reports have been made in other counties concerning the child

or other principals in the case. The agency shall submit a report of its investigation, in writing to the law enforcement agency.

(2) The public children services agency shall make any recommendations to the county prosecuting attorney or city director of law that it considers necessary to protect any children that are brought to its attention.

(G)(1) Except as provided in division (H)(3) of this section, anyone or any hospital, institution, school, health department, or agency participating in the making of reports under division (A) of this section, anyone or any hospital, institution, school, health department, or agency participating in good faith in the making of reports under division (B) of this section, and anyone participating in good faith in a judicial proceeding resulting from the reports, shall be immune from any civil or criminal liability for injury, death, or loss to person or property that otherwise might be incurred or imposed as a result of the making of the reports or the participation in the judicial proceeding. Notwithstanding section 4731.22 of the Revised Code, the physician-patient privilege shall not be a ground for excluding evidence regarding a child's injuries, abuse, or neglect, or the cause of the injuries, abuse, or neglect in any judicial proceeding resulting from a report submitted pursuant to this section.

(2) In any civil or criminal action or proceeding in which it is alleged and proved that participation in the making of a report under this section was not in good faith or participation in a judicial proceeding resulting from a report made under this section was not in good faith, the court shall award the prevailing party reasonable attorney's fees and costs and, if a civil action or proceeding is voluntarily dismissed, may award reasonable attorney's fees and costs to the party against whom the civil action or proceeding is brought.

(H)(1) Except as provided in divisions (H)(4), (M), and (N) of this section, a report made under this section is confidential. The information provided in a report made pursuant to this section and the name of the person who made the report shall not be released for use, and shall not be used, as evidence in any civil action or proceeding brought against the person who made the report. In a criminal proceeding, the report is admissible in evidence in accordance with the Rules of Evidence and is subject to discovery in accordance with the Rules of Criminal Procedure.

(2) No person shall permit or encourage the unauthorized dissemination of the contents of any report made under this section.

(3) A person who knowingly makes or causes another person to make a false report under division (B) of this section that alleges that any person has committed an act or omission that resulted in a child being an abused child or a neglected child is guilty of a violation of section 2921.14 of the Revised Code.

(4) A public children services agency shall advise a person alleged to have inflicted abuse or neglect on a

child who is the subject of a report made pursuant to this section of the disposition of the investigation. The agency shall not provide to the person any information that identifies the person who made the report, statements of witnesses, or police or other investigative reports.

(I) Any report that is required by this section shall result in protective services and emergency supportive services being made available by the public children services agency on behalf of the children about whom the report is made, in an effort to prevent further neglect or abuse, to enhance their welfare, and, whenever possible, to preserve the family unit intact. The agency required to provide the services shall be the agency conducting the investigation of the report pursuant to section 2151.422 [2151.42.2] of the Revised Code.

(J)(1) Each public children services agency shall prepare a memorandum of understanding that is signed by all of the following:
(a) If there is only one juvenile judge in the county, the juvenile judge of the county or the juvenile judge's representative;
(b) If there is more than one juvenile judge in the county, a juvenile judge or the juvenile judges' representative selected by the juvenile judges or, if they are unable to do so for any reason, the juvenile judge who is senior in point of service or the senior juvenile judge's representative;
(c) The county peace officer;
(d) All chief municipal peace officers within the county;
(e) Other law enforcement officers handling child abuse and neglect cases in the county;
(f) The prosecuting attorney of the county;
(g) If the public children services agency is not the county department of human services, the county department of human services.

(2) A memorandum of understanding shall set forth the normal operating procedure to be employed by all concerned officials in the execution of their respective responsibilities under this section and division (C) of section 2919.21, division (B)(1) of section 2919.22, division (B) of section 2919.23, and section 2919.24 of the Revised Code and shall have as two of its primary goals the elimination of all unnecessary interviews of children who are the subject of reports made pursuant to division (A) or (B) of this section and, when feasible, providing for only one interview of a child who is the subject of any report made pursuant to division (A) or (B) of this section. A failure to follow the procedure set forth in the memorandum by the concerned officials is not grounds for, and shall not result in, the dismissal of any charges or complaint arising from any reported case of abuse or neglect or the suppression of any evidence obtained as a result of any reported child abuse or child neglect and does not give, and shall not be construed as giving, any rights or any grounds for appeal or post-conviction relief to any person.

(3) A memorandum of understanding shall include all of the following:
(a) The roles and responsibilities for handling emergency and non-emergency cases of abuse and neglect;
(b) Standards and procedures to be used in handling and coordinating investigations of reported cases of child abuse and reported cases of child neglect, methods to be used in interviewing the child who is the subject of the report and who allegedly was abused or neglected, and standards and procedures addressing the categories of persons who may interview the child who is the subject of the report and who allegedly was abused or neglected.

(K)(1) Except as provided in division (K)(4) of this section a person who is required to make a report pursuant to division (A) of this section may make a reasonable number of requests of the public children services agency that receives or is referred the report to be provided with the following information:
(a) Whether the agency has initiated an investigation of the report;
(b) Whether the agency is continuing to investigate the report;
(c) Whether the agency is otherwise involved with the child who is the subject of the report;
(d) The general status of the health and safety of the child who is the subject of the report;
(e) Whether the report has resulted in the filing of a complaint in juvenile court or of criminal charges in another court.

(2) A person may request the information specified in division (K)(1) of this section only if, at the time the report is made, the person's name, address, and telephone number are provided to the person who receives the report.

When a municipal or county peace officer or employee of a public children services agency receives a report pursuant to division (A) or (B) of this section the recipient of the report shall inform the person of the right to request the information described in division (K)(1) of this section. The recipient of the report shall include in the initial child abuse or child neglect report that the person making the report was so informed and, if provided at the time of the making of the report, shall include the person's name, address, and telephone number in the report.

Each request is subject to verification of the identity of the person making the report. If that person's identity is verified, the agency shall provide the person with the information described in division (K)(1) of this section a reasonable number of times, except that the agency shall not disclose any confidential information regarding the child who is the subject of the report other than the information described in those divisions.

(3) A request made pursuant to division (K)(1) of this section is not a substitute for any report required to be made pursuant to division (A) of this section.

(4) If an agency other than the agency that received

or was referred the report is conducting the investigation of the report pursuant to section 2151.422 [2151.42.2] of the Revised Code, the agency conducting the investigation shall comply with the requirements of division (K).

(L) The department of human services shall adopt rules in accordance with Chapter 119. of the Revised Code to implement this section. The department may enter into a plan of cooperation with any other governmental entity to aid in ensuring that children are protected from abuse and neglect. The department shall make recommendations to the attorney general that the department determines are necessary to protect children from child abuse and child neglect.

(M) No later than the end of the day following the day on which a public children services agency receives a report of alleged child abuse or child neglect, or a report of an alleged threat of child abuse or child neglect, that allegedly occurred in or involved an out-of-home care entity, the agency shall provide written notice of the allegations contained in and the person named as the alleged perpetrator in the report to the administrator, director, or other chief administrative officer of the out-of-home care entity that is the subject of the report unless the administrator, director, or other chief administrative officer is named as an alleged perpetrator in the report. If the administrator, director, or other chief administrative officer of an out-of-home care entity is named as an alleged perpetrator in a report of alleged child abuse or child neglect, or a report of an alleged threat of child abuse or child neglect, that allegedly occurred in or involved the out-of-home care entity, the agency shall provide the written notice to the owner or governing board of the out-of-home care entity that is the subject of the report. The agency shall not provide witness statements or police or other investigative reports.

(N) No later than three days after the day on which a public children services agency that conducted the investigation as determined pursuant to section 2151.422 [2151.42.2] of the Revised Code makes a disposition of an investigation involving a report of alleged child abuse or child neglect, or a report of an alleged threat of child abuse or child neglect, that allegedly occurred in or involved an out-of-home care entity, the agency shall send written notice of the disposition of the investigation to the administrator, director, or other chief administrative officer and the owner or governing board of the out-of-home care entity. The agency shall not provide witness statements or police or other investigative reports.

HISTORY: 130 v 625 (Eff 10-10-63); 131 v 632 (Eff 11-11-65); 133 v S 49 (Eff 8-13-69); 133 v H 338 (Eff 11-25-69); 136 v H 85 (Eff 11-28-75); 137 v H 219 (Eff 11-1-77); 140 v S 321 (Eff 4-9-85); 141 v H 349 (Eff 3-6-86); 141 v H 528 (Eff 7-9-86); 141 v H 529 (Eff 3-11-87); 143 v H 257 (Eff 8-3-89); 143 v H 44 (Eff 7-24-90); 143 v S 3 (Eff 4-11-91); 144 v H 154 (Eff 7-31-92); 146 v S 269 (Eff 7-1-96); 146 v H 274 (Eff 8-8-96); 146 v S 223 (Eff 3-18-97); 147 v H 215 (6-30-97); 147 v H 408. Eff 10-1-97.

Publisher's Note

The amendments made by HB 215 (147 v —) and HB 408 (147 v —) have been combined. Please see provisions of RC § 1.52.

† Wording reflects the combining of the HB 215 (147 v —) and HB 408 (147 v —) versions of this section.

†† So in enrolled bill, division (A)(2)(b).

[§ 2151.42.2] § 2151.422 Procedure where child is living in domestic violence or homeless shelter; homeless shelter to obtain last known residence information.

(A) As used in this section, "homeless shelter" means a facility that provides accommodations to homeless individuals.

(B) On receipt of a notice pursuant to division (A), (B), or (D) of section 2151.421 [2151.42.1] of the Revised Code, the public children services agency shall determine whether the child subject to the report is living in a shelter for victims of domestic violence or a homeless shelter and whether the child was brought to that shelter pursuant to an agreement with a shelter in another county. If the child is living in a shelter and was brought there from another county, the agency shall immediately notify the public children services agency of the county from which the child was brought of the report and all the information contained in the report. On receipt of the notice pursuant to this division, the agency of the county from which the child was brought shall conduct the investigation of the report required pursuant to section 2151.421 [2151.42.1] of the Revised Code and shall perform all duties required of the agency under this chapter with respect to the child who is the subject of the report. If the child is not living in a shelter or the child was not brought to the shelter from another county, the agency that received the report pursuant to division (A), (B), or (D) of section 2151.421 [2151.42.1] of the Revised Code shall conduct the investigation required pursuant to section 2151.421 [2151.42.1] of the Revised Code and shall perform all duties required of the agency under this chapter with respect to the child who is the subject of the report. The agency of the county in which the shelter is located in which the child is living and the agency of the county from which the child was brought may ask the shelter to provide information concerning the child's residence address and county of residence to the agency.

(C) If a child is living in a shelter for victims of domestic violence or a homeless shelter and the child was brought to that shelter pursuant to an agreement with a shelter in another county, the public children services agency of the county from which the child was brought shall provide services to or take custody of the child if services or custody are needed or required under this Chapter or section 5153.16 of the Revised Code.

(D) When a homeless shelter provides accommodations to a person, the shelter, on admitting the person to the shelter, shall determine, if possible, the person's last known residential address and county of residence. The information concerning the address and county of residence is confidential and may only be released to a public children services agency pursuant to this section.

HISTORY: 147 v H 215. Eff 6-30-97

Not analogous to former RC § 2151.42.2 (132 v S 316), repealed 137 v H 565, § 2, eff 11-1-78.

[PROCEDURE IN ADULT CASES]

§ 2151.43 Charges against adults; defendant bound over to grand jury.

In cases against an adult under sections 2151.01 to 2151.54 of the Revised Code, any person may file an affidavit with the clerk of the juvenile court setting forth briefly, in plain and ordinary language, the charges against the accused who shall be tried thereon. When the child is a recipient of aid pursuant to Chapter 5107. or 5115. of the Revised Code, the county department of human services shall file charges against any person who fails to provide support to a child in violation of section 2919.21 of the Revised Code, unless the department files charges under section 3113.06 of the Revised Code, or unless charges of nonsupport are filed by a relative or guardian of the child, or unless action to enforce support is brought under Chapter 3115. of the Revised Code.

In such prosecution an indictment by the grand jury or information by the prosecuting attorney shall not be required. The clerk shall issue a warrant for the arrest of the accused, who, when arrested, shall be taken before the juvenile judge and tried according to such sections.

The affidavit may be amended at any time before or during the trial.

The judge may bind such adult over to the grand jury, where the act complained of constitutes a felony.

HISTORY: GC § 1639-39; 117 v 520(533); 119 v 731; Bureau of Code Revision, 10-1-53; 127 v 847 (Eff 9-16-57); 132 v H 390 (Eff 11-7-67); 133 v H 361 (Eff 9-23-69); 134 v H 511 (Eff 1-1-74); 141 v H 428 (Eff 12-23-86); 144 v H 298 (Eff 7-26-91); 146 v H 249. Eff 7-17-95.

§ 2151.44 Complaint after hearing.

If it appears at the hearing of a child that any person has abused or has aided, induced, caused, encouraged, or contributed to the dependency, neglect, or delinquency of a child or acted in a way tending to cause delinquency in such child, or that a person charged with the care, support, education, or maintenance of any child has failed to support or sufficiently contribute toward the support, education, and maintenance of such child, the juvenile judge may order a complaint filed against such person and proceed to hear and dispose of the case as provided in sections 2151.01 to 2151.54, inclusive, of the Revised Code.

On the request of the judge, the prosecuting attorney shall prosecute all adults charged with violating such sections.

HISTORY: GC §§ 1639-40, 1639-42; 117 v 520(533, 534); Bureau of Code Revision. Eff 10-1-53.

Comment

The prosecuting attorney may be called upon to prosecute all adults charged with violating the juvenile code. This means all persons eighteen years of age or over.

§ 2151.45 Expense of extradition.

When a person charged with the violation of sections 2151.01 to 2151.54, inclusive, of the Revised Code, has fled to another state or territory, and the governor has issued a requisition for such person, the board of county commissioners shall pay from the general expense fund of the county to the agent designated in such requisition all necessary expenses incurred in pursuing and returning such prisoner.

HISTORY: GC § 1639-41; 117 v 520(533); Bureau of Code Revision. Eff 10-1-53.

§ 2151.46 Bail.

Sections 2937.21 to 2937.45, inclusive, of the Revised Code, relating to bail in criminal cases in the court of common pleas, shall apply to adults committed or held under sections 2151.01 to 2151.54, inclusive, of the Revised Code.

HISTORY: GC § 1639-43; 117 v 520(534); Bureau of Code Revision. Eff 10-1-53.

Comment

Bail applies only to adults, that is, persons eighteen years of age or over.

§ 2151.47 Jury trial; procedure.

Any adult arrested under sections 2151.01 to 2151.54, inclusive, of the Revised Code, may demand a trial by jury, or the juvenile judge upon his own motion may call a jury. A demand for a jury trial must be made in writing in not less than three days before the date set for trial, or within three days after counsel has been retained, whichever is later. Sections 2945.17 and 2945.22 to 2945.36, inclusive, of the Revised Code, relating to the drawing and impaneling of jurors in criminal cases in the court of common pleas, other than in capital cases, shall apply to such jury trial. The compensation of jurors and costs of the clerk and sheriff shall be taxed and paid as in criminal cases in the court of common pleas.

HISTORY: GC § 1639-44; 117 v 520(534); Bureau of Code Revision, 10-1-53; 132 v S 55 (Eff 10-24-67); 133 v H 1. Eff 3-18-69.

§ 2151.48 Commitment of adult females.

When any female over the age of eighteen years is found guilty of a misdemeanor under this chapter, the juvenile judge may order the female committed to the department of rehabilitation and correction for the same term for which the female could be committed to a workhouse or jail.

HISTORY: GC § 1639-48; 117 v 520(535); Bureau of Code Revision, 10-1-53; 145 v H 571. Eff 10-6-94.

§ 2151.49 Suspension of sentence.

In every case of conviction under sections 2151.01 to 2151.54 of the Revised Code, where imprisonment is imposed as part of the punishment, the juvenile judge may suspend sentence, before or during commitment, upon such condition as he imposes. In the case of conviction for non-support of a child who is receiving aid under Chapter 5107. or 5115. of the Revised Code, if the juvenile judge suspends sentence on condition that the person make payments for support, the payment shall be made to the county department of human services rather than to the child or custodian of the child.

HISTORY: GC § 1639-49; 117 v 520(535); Bureau of Code Revision, 10-1-53; 132 v H 390 (Eff 11-7-67); 141 v H 428 (Eff 12-23-86); 144 v H 298 (Eff 7-26-91); 146 v H 249. Eff 7-17-95.

§ 2151.50 Forfeiture of bond.

When, as a condition of suspension of sentence under section 2151.49 of the Revised Code, bond is required and given, upon the failure of a person giving such bond to comply with the conditions thereof, such bond may be forfeited, the suspension terminated by the juvenile judge, the original sentence executed as though it had not been suspended, and the term of any sentence imposed in such case shall commence from the date of imprisonment of such person after such forfeiture and termination of suspension. Any part of such sentence which may have been served shall be deducted from any such period of imprisonment. When such bond is forfeited the judge may issue execution thereon without further proceedings.

HISTORY: GC § 1639-50; 117 v 520(535); Bureau of Code Revision. Eff 10-1-53.

§ 2151.51 Provision for dependent children of person sentenced to workhouse or jail.

When an adult is sentenced to imprisonment for any violation of section 2919.21 or 2919.22 of the Revised Code, the county from which such person is sentenced, on the order of the juvenile judge, shall pay from the general revenue fund fifty cents for each day such prisoner is confined to the juvenile court of such county, for the maintenance of the dependent children of such prisoner. Such expenditure shall be made under the direction of the judge, who shall designate an employee for such purpose. The board of county commissioners of such county shall make an appropriation for such cases, and allowances therefrom shall be paid from the county treasury upon the warrant of the county auditor.

HISTORY: GC § 1639-47; 117 v 520(535); Bureau of Code Revision, 10-1-53; 136 v H 1. Eff 6-13-75.

§ 2151.52 Appeals on questions of law.

The sections of the Revised Code and rules relating to appeals on questions of law from the court of common pleas shall apply to prosecutions of adults under this chapter, and from such prosecutions an appeal on a question of law may be taken to the court of appeals of the county under laws or rules governing appeals in other criminal cases to such court of appeals.

HISTORY: GC § 1639-51; 117 v 520(536); Bureau of Code Revision, 10-1-53; 129 v 290 (Eff 10-2-61); 141 v H 412. Eff 3-17-87.

[GENERAL PROVISIONS]

§ 2151.53 Physical and mental examinations; records of examination; expenses.

Any person coming within sections 2151.01 to 2151.54, inclusive, of the Revised Code, may be subjected to a physical and mental examination by competent physicians, psychologists, and psychiatrists to be appointed by the juvenile court. Whenever any child is committed to any institution by virtue of such sections, a record of such examinations shall be sent with the commitment to such institution. The compensation of such physicians, psychologists, and psychiatrists and the expenses of such examinations shall be paid by the county treasurer upon specifically itemized vouchers, certified by the juvenile judge.

HISTORY: GC § 1639-54; 117 v 520(536); Bureau of Code Revision. Eff 10-1-53.

§ 2151.54 Fees and costs.

The juvenile court shall tax and collect the same fees and costs as are allowed the clerk of the court of common pleas for similar services. No fees or costs shall be taxed in cases of delinquent, unruly, dependent, abused, or neglected children except as required by section 2743.70 or 2949.091 [2949.09.1] of the Revised Code or when specifically ordered by the court. The expense of transportation of children to places to which they have been committed, and the transportation of children to and from another state by police or other officers, acting upon order of the court, shall be paid from the county treasury upon specifically itemized vouchers certified to by the judge.

If a child is adjudicated to be a delinquent child or a juvenile traffic offender and the juvenile court specifically is required, by section 2743.70 or 2949.091

[2949.09.1] of the Revised Code or any other section of the Revised Code, to impose a specified sum of money as court costs in addition to any other court costs that the court is required or permitted by law to impose, the court shall not waive the payment of the specified additional court costs that the section of the Revised Code specifically requires the court to impose unless the court determines that the child is indigent and the court either waives the payment of all court costs or enters an order in its journal stating that no court costs are to be taxed in the case.

HISTORY: GC § 1639-56; 117 v 520(537); 119 v 731; Bureau of Code Revision, 10-1-53; 133 v H 931 (Eff 8-27-70); 136 v H 85 (Eff 11-28-75); 138 v H 238 (Eff 8-8-80); 143 v S 131. Eff 7-25-90.

[§ 2151.54.1] § 2151.541 Additional fees to pay for computerizing court or office of clerk or for computerized legal research services.

(A)(1) The juvenile judge may determine that, for the efficient operation of the juvenile court, additional funds are required to computerize the court, to make available computerized legal research services, or both. Upon making a determination that additional funds are required for either or both of those purposes, the judge shall do one of the following:

(a) If he is clerk of the court, charge one additional fee not to exceed three dollars on the filing of each cause of action or appeal under division (A), (Q), or (U) of section 2303.20 of the Revised Code;

(b) If the clerk of the court of common pleas serves as the clerk of the juvenile court pursuant to section 2151.12 of the Revised Code, authorize and direct the clerk to charge one additional fee not to exceed three dollars on the filing of each cause of action or appeal under division (A), (Q), or (U) of section 2303.20 of the Revised Code.

(2) All moneys collected under division (A)(1) of this section shall be paid to the county treasurer. The treasurer shall place the moneys from the fees in a separate fund to be disbursed, upon an order of the juvenile judge, in an amount no greater than the actual cost to the court of procuring and maintaining computerization of the court, computerized legal research services, or both.

(3) If the court determines that the funds in the fund described in division (A)(2) of this section are more than sufficient to satisfy the purpose for which the additional fee described in division (A)(1) of this section was imposed, the court may declare a surplus in the fund and expend those surplus funds for other appropriate technological expenses of the court.

(B)(1) If the juvenile judge is the clerk of the juvenile court, he may determine that, for the efficient operation of his court, additional funds are required to computerize the clerk's office and, upon that determination, may charge an additional fee, not to exceed ten dollars, on the filing of each cause of action or appeal, on the filing, docketing, and endorsing of each certificate of judgment, or on the docketing and indexing of each aid in execution or petition to vacate, revive, or modify a judgment under divisions (A), (P), (Q), (T), and (U) of section 2303.20 of the Revised Code. Subject to division (B)(2) of this section, all moneys collected under this division shall be paid to the county treasurer to be disbursed, upon an order of the juvenile judge and subject to appropriation by the board of county commissioners, in an amount no greater than the actual cost to the juvenile court of procuring and maintaining computer systems for the clerk's office.

(2) If the juvenile judge makes the determination described in division (B)(1) of this section, the board of county commissioners may issue one or more general obligation bonds for the purpose of procuring and maintaining the computer systems for the office of the clerk of the juvenile court. In addition to the purposes stated in division (B)(1) of this section for which the moneys collected under that division may be expended, the moneys additionally may be expended to pay debt charges on and financing costs related to any general obligation bonds issued pursuant to this division as they become due. General obligation bonds issued pursuant to this division are Chapter 133. securities.

HISTORY: 144 v H 405 (Eff 1-1-93); 144 v S 246. Eff 3-24-93.

§ 2151.55 Procedure for placement in foster home in another county; school superintendent may seek removal.

(A) This section shall have no effect on and after the date the Supreme Court adopts, pursuant to its authority under Section 5 of Article IV, Ohio Constitution, rules governing procedure in the juvenile courts of the state that address the placement of a child in a foster home in a county other than the county in which the child resided at the time of being removed from home.

(B) Prior to placing a child in a foster home in a county other than the county in which the child resided at the time of being removed from home, the private or government entity responsible for the placement shall communicate directly with all of the following and notify them of the intended placement: the intended foster caregiver, the juvenile court of the county in which the foster home is located, and, if the child will attend the schools of the district in which the foster home is located, the school district's board of education. The private or government entity shall provide any information it has in its possession concerning the reasons the child is being placed in the foster home if that information may be disclosed under federal and state law.

(C) If a child is placed in a foster home in a county other than the county in which the child resided at the time the child was removed from home, the superintendent of the school district in which the child resides in a foster home may file, in the juvenile court of the county in which the school district is located, a complaint requesting that the child be removed from the county because the child is causing a significant and unreasonable disruption to the educational process in the school the child is attending.

(D) The court shall hold a hearing as soon as possible, but no later than thirty days after the complaint is filed. No later than five days before the date on which the court hearing is to be held, the court shall send to the entity that placed the child in a foster home in the county and to the superintendent written notice by first class mail of the date, time, place, and purpose of the court hearing. The hearing shall be limited to determining whether the child is causing a significant and unreasonable disruption to the educational process. At the conclusion of the hearing, the court shall determine whether the child is causing such a disruption. If the court determines the child is causing such a disruption, the court shall order the entity that placed the child in a foster home in the county to remove the child from the county. If the court determines the child is not causing such a disruption, the court shall dismiss the complaint.

(E) If the court orders the removal of a child, the court shall send written notice of the removal order to the juvenile court that journalized a case plan as part of its dispositional order pursuant to section 2151.35 of the Revised Code or issued any order pursuant to Chapter 2151. of the Revised Code requiring placement of the child in a foster home in the county from which the child is ordered removed. On receipt of the removal notice, the juvenile court receiving the removal notice shall enter the notice on its journal and shall do one of the following:

(1) If a case plan was journalized as part of the dispositional order, the court shall schedule a hearing under section 2151.417 [2151.41.7] of the Revised Code to be held no later than ten days after the removal notice was received. The court shall give notice of the date, time, and location of the hearing to all parties and the guardian ad litem. At the hearing, the court shall make appropriate changes to the case plan consistent with the removal order and journalize the case plan.

(2) If no case plan was journalized as part of the dispositional order, the court shall immediately issue a new order concerning the child's placement pursuant to Chapter 2151. of the Revised Code that is consistent with the removal order.

(F) This section does not affect the jurisdiction of a court with respect to a child for which the court issued a dispositional order pursuant to Chapter 2151. of the Revised Code.

HISTORY: 147 v H 215. Eff 6-30-97.

Not analogous to former RC § 2151.55 (GC § 1639-59; 117 v 520(537); Bureau of Code Revision, 10-1-53), repealed 130 v 1682, § 2, eff 10-7-63.

[INTERSTATE COMPACT ON JUVENILES]

§ 2151.56 Interstate compact on juveniles.

The governor is hereby authorized to execute a compact on behalf of this state with any other state or states legally joining therein in the form substantially as follows:

THE INTERSTATE COMPACT ON JUVENILES

The contracting states solemnly agree:

Article I—Findings and Purposes

That juveniles who are not under proper supervision and control, or who have absconded, escaped or run away, are likely to endanger their own health, morals and welfare, and the health, morals and welfare of others. The cooperation of the states party to this compact is therefore necessary to provide for the welfare and protection of juveniles and of the public with respect to (1) cooperative supervision of delinquent juveniles on probation or parole; (2) the return, from one state to another, of delinquent juveniles who have escaped or absconded; (3) the return, from one state to another, of nondelinquent juveniles who have run away from home; and (4) additional measures for the protection of juveniles and of the public, which any two or more of the party states may find desirable to undertake cooperatively. In carrying out the provisions of this compact the party states shall be guided by the noncriminal, reformative and protective policies which guide their laws concerning delinquent, neglected or dependent juveniles generally. It shall be the policy of the states party to this compact to cooperate and observe their respective responsibilities for the prompt return and acceptance of juveniles and delinquent juveniles who become subject to the provisions of this compact. The provisions of this compact shall be reasonably and liberally construed to accomplish the foregoing purposes.

Article II—Existing Rights and Remedies

That all remedies and procedures provided by this compact shall be in addition to and not in substitution for other rights, remedies and procedures, and shall not be in derogation of parental rights and responsibilities.

Article III—Definitions

That, for the purposes of this compact, "delinquent juvenile" means any juvenile who has been adjudged delinquent and who, at the time the provisions of this compact are invoked, is still subject to the jurisdiction of the court that has made such adjudication or to the jurisdiction or supervision of an agency or institution pursuant to an order of such court; "probation or parole" means any kind of conditional release of juveniles authorized under the laws of the states party hereto; "court" means any court having jurisdiction over delinquent, neglected or dependent children; "state" means any state, territory or possessions of the United States, the District of Columbia, and the commonwealth of Puerto Rico; and "residence" or any variant thereof means a place at which a home or regular place of abode is maintained.

Article IV—Return of Runaways

(a) That the parent, guardian, person or agency entitled to legal custody of a juvenile who has not been adjudged delinquent but who has run away without the consent of such parent, guardian, person or agency may petition the appropriate court in the demanding state for the issuance of a requisition for his return. The petition shall state the name and age of the juvenile, the name of the petitioner and the basis of entitlement to the juvenile's custody, the circumstances of his running away, his location if known at the time application is made, and such other facts as may tend to show that the juvenile who has run away is endangering his own welfare or the welfare of others and is not an emancipated minor. The petition shall be verified by affidavit, shall be executed in duplicate, and shall be accompanied by two certified copies of the document or documents on which the petitioner's entitlement to the juvenile's custody is based, such as birth records, letters of guardianship, or custody decrees. Such further affidavits and other documents as may be deemed proper may be submitted with such petition. The judge of the court to which this application is made may hold a hearing thereon to determine whether for the purposes of this compact the petitioner is entitled to the legal custody of the juvenile, whether or not it appears that the juvenile has in fact run away without consent, whether or not he is an emancipated minor, and whether or not it is in the best interest of the juvenile to compel his return to the state. If the judge determines, either with or without a hearing, that the juvenile should be returned, he shall present to the appropriate court or to the executive authority of the state where the juvenile is alleged to be located a written requisition for the return of such juvenile. Such requisition shall set forth the name and age of the juvenile, the determination of the court that the juvenile has run away without the consent of a parent, guardian, person or agency entitled to his legal custody, and that it is in the best interest and for the protection of such juvenile that he be returned. In the event that a proceeding for the adjudication of the juvenile as a delinquent, neglected or dependent juvenile is pending in the court at the time when such juvenile runs away, the court may issue a requisition for the return of such juvenile upon its own motion, regardless of the consent of the parent, guardian, person or agency entitled to legal custody, reciting therein the nature and circumstances of the pending proceeding. The requisition shall in every case be executed in duplicate and shall be signed by the judge. One copy of the requisition shall be filed with the compact administrator of the demanding state, there to remain on file subject to the provisions of law governing records of such court. Upon the receipt of a requisition demanding the return of a juvenile who has run away, the court or the executive authority to whom the requisition is addressed shall issue an order to any peace officer or other appropriate person directing him to take into custody and detain such juvenile. Such detention order must substantially recite the facts necessary to the validity of its issuance hereunder. No juvenile detained upon such order shall be delivered over to the officer whom the court demanding him shall have appointed to receive him, unless he shall first be taken forthwith before a judge of a court in the state, who shall inform him of the demand made for his return, and who may appoint counsel or guardian ad litem for him. If the judge of such court shall find that the requisition is in order, he shall deliver such juvenile over to the officer whom the court demanding him shall have appointed to receive him. The judge, however, may fix a reasonable time to be allowed for the purpose of testing the legality of the proceeding.

Upon reasonable information that a person is a juvenile who has run away from another state party to this compact without the consent of a parent, guardian, person or agency entitled to his legal custody, such juvenile may be taken into custody without a requisition and brought forthwith before a judge of the appropriate court who may appoint counsel or guardian ad litem for such juvenile and who shall determine after a hearing whether sufficient cause exists to hold the person, subject to the order of the court, for his own protection and welfare, for such a time not exceeding ninety days as will enable his return to another state party to this compact pursuant to a requisition for his return from a court of that state. If, at the time when a state seeks the return of a juvenile who has run away, there is pending in the state wherein he is found any criminal charge, or any proceeding to have him adjudicated a delinquent juvenile for an act committed in such state, or if he is suspected of having committed within such state a criminal offense or an act of juvenile delinquency, he shall not be returned without the consent of such state until discharged from prosecution or other form of proceeding, imprisonment, detention or supervision for such offense or juvenile delinquency. The duly accredited officers of any state party to this compact, upon the establishment of their authority and the identity of the juvenile being returned, shall be permitted to transport such juvenile through any and all states party to this compact, without interference. Upon his return to the state from which he ran away, the juvenile shall be subject to such further proceedings as may be appropriate under the laws of that state.

(b) That the state to which a juvenile is returned under this Article shall be responsible for payment of the transportation costs of such return.

(c) That "juvenile" as used in this Article means any

person who is a minor under the law of the state of residence of the parent, guardian, person or agency entitled to the legal custody of such minor.

Article V—Return of Escapees and Absconders

(a) That the appropriate person or authority from whose probation or parole supervision a delinquent juvenile has absconded or from whose institutional custody he has escaped shall present to the appropriate court or to the executive authority of the state where the delinquent juvenile is alleged to be located a written requisition for the return of such delinquent juvenile. Such requisition shall state the name and age of the delinquent juvenile, the particulars of his adjudication as a delinquent juvenile, the circumstances of the breach of the terms of his probation or parole or of his escape from an institution or agency vested with his legal custody or supervision, and the location of such delinquent juvenile, if known, at the time the requisition is made. The requisition shall be verified by affidavit, shall be executed in duplicate, and shall be accompanied by two certified copies of the judgment, formal adjudication, or order of commitment which subjects such delinquent juvenile to probation or parole or to the legal custody of the institution or agency concerned. Such further affidavits and other documents as may be deemed proper may be submitted with such requisition. One copy of the requisition shall be filed with the compact administrator of the demanding state, there to remain on file subject to the provisions of law governing records of the appropriate court. Upon the receipt of a requisition demanding the return of a delinquent juvenile who has absconded or escaped, the court or the executive authority to whom the requisition is addressed shall issue an order to any peace officer or other appropriate person directing him to take into custody and detain such delinquent juvenile. Such detention order must substantially recite the facts necessary to the validity of its issuance hereunder. No delinquent juvenile detained upon such order shall be delivered over to the officer whom the appropriate person or authority demanding him shall have appointed to receive him, unless he shall first be taken forthwith before a judge of an appropriate court in the state, who shall inform him of the demand made for his return and who may appoint counsel or guardian ad litem for him. If the judge of such court shall find that the requisition is in order, he shall deliver such delinquent juvenile over to the officer whom the appropriate person or authority demanding him shall have appointed to receive him. The judge, however, may fix a reasonable time to be allowed for the purpose of testing the legality of the proceeding.

Upon reasonable information that a person is a delinquent juvenile who has absconded while on probation or parole, or escaped from an institution or agency vested with his legal custody or supervision in any state party to this compact, such person may be taken into custody in any other state party to this compact without a requisition. But in such event, he must be taken forthwith before a judge of the appropriate court, who may appoint counsel or guardian ad litem for such person and who shall determine, after a hearing, whether sufficient cause exists to hold the person subject to the order of the court for such a time, not exceeding ninety days, as will enable his detention under a detention order issued on a requisition pursuant to this Article. If, at the time when a state seeks the return of a delinquent juvenile who has either absconded while on probation or parole or escaped from an institution or agency vested with his legal custody or supervision, there is pending in the state wherein he is detained any criminal charge or any proceeding to have him adjudicated a delinquent juvenile for an act committed in such state, or if he is suspected of having committed within such state a criminal offense or an act of juvenile delinquency, he shall not be returned without the consent of such state until discharged from prosecution or other form of proceeding, imprisonment, detention or supervision for such offense or juvenile delinquency. The duly accredited officers of any state party to this compact, upon the establishment of their authority and the identity of the delinquent juvenile being returned, shall be permitted to transport such delinquent juvenile through any and all states party to this compact, without interference. Upon his return to the state from which he escaped or absconded, the delinquent juvenile shall be subject to such further proceedings as may be appropriate under the laws of that state.

(b) That the state to which a delinquent juvenile is returned under this Article shall be responsible for the payment of the transportation costs of such return.

Article VI—Voluntary Return Procedure

That any delinquent juvenile who has absconded while on probation or parole, or escaped from an institution or agency vested with his legal custody or supervision in any state party to this compact, and any juvenile who has run away from any state party to this compact, who is taken into custody without a requisition in another state party to this compact under the provisions of Article IV (a) or of Article V (a), may consent to his immediate return to the state from which he absconded, escaped or ran away. Such consent shall be given by the juvenile or delinquent juvenile and his counsel or guardian ad litem if any, by executing or subscribing a writing, in the presence of a judge of the appropriate court, which states that the juvenile or delinquent juvenile and his counsel or guardian ad litem, if any, consent to his return to the demanding state. Before such consent shall be executed or subscribed, however, the judge, in the presence of counsel or guardian ad litem, if any, shall inform the juvenile or delinquent juvenile of his rights under this compact. When the consent has been duly executed, it shall be forwarded to and filed with the compact administrator of the state in which the court is located and the judge shall direct the officer having the juvenile or delinquent juvenile in custody to deliver him to the duly accredited officer or officers of the state demanding his return, and shall cause to be delivered to such officer or officers a copy of the consent. The court may, however, upon the request of the state to which the juvenile or delinquent juvenile is being returned, order him to return unaccompanied to such state and shall provide him with a copy of such court order; in such event a copy of the consent shall be forwarded to the compact administrator of the state to which said juvenile or delinquent juvenile is ordered to return.

Article VII—Cooperative Supervision of Probationers and Parolees

(a) That the duly constituted judicial and administrative authorities of a state party to this compact (herein called "sending state") may permit any delinquent juvenile within such state, placed on probation or parole, to reside in any other state party to this compact (herein called "receiving state") while on probation or parole, and the receiving state shall accept such delinquent juvenile, if the parent, guardian or person entitled to the legal custody of such delinquent juvenile is residing or undertakes to reside within the receiving state. Before granting such permission, opportunity shall be given to the receiving state to make such investigations as it deems necessary. The authorities of the sending state shall send to the authorities of the receiving state copies of pertinent court orders, social case studies and all other available information which may be of value to and assist the receiving state in supervising a probationer or parolee under this compact. A receiving state, in its discretion, may agree to accept supervision of a probationer or parolee in cases where the parent, guardian or person entitled to the legal custody of the delinquent juvenile is not a resident of the receiving state, and if so accepted the sending state may transfer supervision accordingly.

(b) That each receiving state will assume the duties of visitation and of supervision over any such delinquent juvenile and in the exercise of those duties will be governed by the same standards of visitation and supervision that prevail for its own delinquent juveniles released on probation or parole.

(c) That, after consultation between the appropriate authorities of the sending state and of the receiving state as to the desirability and necessity of returning such a delinquent juvenile, the duly accredited officers of a sending state may enter a receiving state and there apprehend and retake any such delinquent juvenile on probation or parole. For that purpose, no formalities will be required, other than establishing the authority of the officer and the identity of the delinquent juvenile to be retaken and returned. The decision of the sending state to retake a delinquent juvenile on probation or parole shall be conclusive upon and not reviewable within the receiving state, but if, at the time the sending state seeks to retake a delinquent juvenile on probation or parole, there is pending against him within the receiving state any criminal charge or any proceeding to have him adjudicated a delinquent juvenile for any act committed in such state, or if he is suspected of having committed within such state a criminal offense or an act of juvenile delinquency, he shall not be returned without the consent of the receiving state until discharged from prosecution or other form of proceeding, imprisonment, detention or supervision for such offense or juvenile delinquency. The duly accredited officers of the sending state shall be permitted to transport delinquent juveniles being so returned through any and all states party to this compact, without interference.

(d) That the sending state shall be responsible under this Article for paying the costs of transporting any delinquent juvenile to the receiving state or of returning any delinquent juvenile to the sending state.

Article VIII—Responsibility for Costs

(a) That the provisions of Articles IV(b), V(b) and VII(d) of this compact shall not be construed to alter or affect any internal relationship among the departments, agencies and officers of and in the government of a party state, or between a party state and its subdivisions, as to the payment of costs, or responsibilities therefor.

(b) That nothing in this compact shall be construed to prevent any party state or subdivision thereof from asserting any right against any person, agency or other entity in regard to costs for which such party state or subdivision thereof may be responsible pursuant to Articles IV(b), V(b) or VII(d) of this compact.

Article IX—Detention Practices

That, to every extent possible, it shall be the policy of states party to this compact that no juvenile or delinquent juvenile shall be placed or detained in any prison, jail or lockup nor be detained or transported in association with criminal, vicious or dissolute persons.

Article X—Supplementary Agreements

That the duly constituted administrative authorities of a state party to this compact may enter into supplementary agreements with any other state or states party hereto for the cooperative care, treatment and rehabilitation of delinquent juveniles whenever they shall find that such agreements will improve the facilities or programs available for such care, treatment and rehabilitation. Such care, treatment and rehabilitation may be provided in an institution located within any state entering into such supplementary agreement. Such supplementary agreements shall (1) provide the rates to be paid for the care, treatment and custody of such delinquent juveniles, taking into consideration the character of facilities, services and subsistence furnished; (2) provide that the delinquent juvenile shall be given a court hearing prior to his being sent to another state for care, treatment and custody; (3) provide that the state receiving such a delinquent juvenile in one of its institutions shall act solely as agent for the state sending such delinquent juvenile; (4) provide that the sending state shall at all times retain jurisdiction over delinquent juveniles sent to an institution in another state; (5) provide for reasonable inspection of such institutions by the sending state; (6) provide that the consent of the parent, guardian, person or agency entitled to the legal custody of said delinquent juvenile shall be secured prior to his being sent to another state; and (7) make provision for such other matters and details as shall be necessary to protect the rights and equities of such delinquent juveniles and of the cooperating states.

Article XI—Acceptance of Federal and Other Aid

That any state party to this compact may accept any and all donations, gifts and grants of money, equipment and services from the federal or any local government, or any agency thereof and from any person, firm or corporation, for any of the purposes and functions of this compact, and may receive and utilize the same subject to the terms, conditions and regulations governing such donations, gifts and grants.

Article XII—Compact Administrators

That the governor of each state party to this compact shall designate an officer who, acting jointly with like officers of other party states, shall promulgate rules and regulations to carry out more effectively the terms and provisions of this compact.

Article XIII—Execution of Compact

That this compact shall become operative immediately upon its execution by any state as between it and any other state or states so executing. When executed it shall have the full force and effect of law within such state, the form of execution to be in accordance with the laws of the executing state.

Article XIV—Renunciation

That this compact shall continue in force and remain binding upon each executing state until renounced by it. Renunciation of this compact shall be by the same authority which executed it, by sending six months' notice in writing of its intention to withdraw from the compact to the other states party hereto. The duties and obligations of a renouncing state under Article VII hereof shall continue as to parolees and probationers residing therein at the time of withdrawal until retaken or finally discharged. Supplementary agreements entered into under Article X hereof shall be subject to renunciation as provided by such supplementary agreements, and shall not be subject to the six months' renunciation notice of the present Article.

Article XV—Severability

That the provisions of this compact shall be severable and if any phrase, clause, sentence or provision of this compact is declared to be contrary to the constitution of any participating state or of the United States or the applicability thereof to any government, agency, person or circumstance is held invalid, the validity of the remainder of this compact and the applicability thereof to any government, agency, person or circumstance shall not be affected thereby. If this compact shall be held contrary to the constitution of any state participating therein, the compact shall remain in full force and effect as to the remaining states and in full force and effect as to the state affected as to all severable matters.

HISTORY: 127 v 530 (Eff 9-17-57); 142 v H 790. Eff 3-16-89.

The effective date is set by section 4 of HB 790.

§ 2151.57 Compact administrator; powers and duties.

Pursuant to section 2151.56 of the Revised Code, the governor is hereby authorized and empowered, with the advice and consent of the senate, to designate an officer who shall be the compact administrator and who, acting jointly with like officers of other party states, shall promulgate rules and regulations to carry out more effectively the terms of the compact. Such compact administrator shall serve subject to the pleasure of the governor. The compact administrator is hereby authorized, empowered and directed to cooperate with all departments, agencies and officers of and in the government of this state and its subdivisions in facilitating the proper administration of the compact or of any supplementary agreement or agreements entered into by this state thereunder.

HISTORY: 127 v 530. Eff 9-17-57.

§ 2151.58 Supplementary agreements.

The compact administrator is hereby authorized and empowered to enter into supplementary agreements with appropriate officials of other states pursuant to the compact. In the event that such supplementary agreement shall require or contemplate the use of any institution or facility of this state or require or contemplate the provision of any service by this state, said supplementary agreement shall have no force or effect until approved by the head of the department or agency under whose jurisdiction the institution or facility is operated or whose department or agency will be charged with the rendering of such service.

HISTORY: 127 v 530. Eff 9-17-57.

§ 2151.59 Financial obligations.

The compact administrator, subject to the approval of the director of budget and management, may make or arrange for any payments necessary to discharge any financial obligations imposed upon this state by the compact or by any supplementary agreement entered into thereunder.

HISTORY: 127 v 530 (Eff 9-17-57); 141 v H 201. Eff 7-1-85.

§ 2151.60 Enforcement by agencies of state and subdivisions.

The courts, departments, agencies and officers of this state and its subdivisions shall enforce this compact and shall do all things appropriate to the effectuation of its purposes and intent which may be within their respective jurisdictions.

HISTORY: 127 v 530. Eff 9-17-57.

§ 2151.61 Additional article.

In addition to any procedure provided in Articles IV and VI of the compact for the return of any runaway juvenile, the particular states, the juvenile or his parents, the courts, or other legal custodian involved may agree upon and adopt any other plan or procedure legally authorized under the laws of this state and the other respective party states for the return of any such runaway juvenile.

Article XVI—Additional Article

The governor is hereby authorized and directed to execute, with any other state or states legally joining in the same, an amendment to the interstate compact on juveniles in substantially the following form:

"(a) That this Article shall provide additional remedies, and shall be binding only as among and between those party states which specifically execute the same.

(b) For the purposes of Article XVI(c), "child," as used herein, means any minor within the jurisdictional age limits of any court in the home state.

(c) When any child is brought before a court of a state of which such child is not a resident, and such state is willing to permit such child's return to the home state of such child, such home state, upon being so advised by the state in which such proceeding is pending, shall immediately institute proceedings to determine the residence and jurisdictional facts as to such child in such home state, and upon finding that such child is in fact a resident of said state and subject to the jurisdiction of the court thereof, shall within five days authorize the return of such child to the home state, and to the parent or custodial agency legally authorized to accept such custody in such home state, and at the expense of such home state, to be paid from such funds as such home state may procure, designate, or provide, prompt action being of the essence.

(d) All provisions and procedures of Articles V and VI of the interstate compact on juveniles shall be construed to apply to any juvenile charged with being a delinquent juvenile for the violation of any criminal law. Any juvenile charged with being a delinquent juvenile for violating any criminal law shall be returned to the requesting state upon a requisition to the state where the juvenile may be found. A petition in the case shall be filed in a court of competent jurisdiction in the requesting state where the violation of criminal law is alleged to have been committed. The petition may be filed regardless of whether the juvenile has left the state before or after the filing of the petition. The requisition described in Article V of the compact shall be forwarded by the judge of the county in which the petition has been filed."

HISTORY: 127 v 530 (Eff 9-17-57); 144 v H 154. Eff 7-31-92.

[TRAINING AND REHABILITATION]

§ 2151.65 Single-county and joint-county juvenile facilities.

Upon the advice and recommendation of the juvenile judge, the board of county commissioners may provide by purchase, lease, construction, or otherwise a school, forestry camp, or other facility or facilities where delinquent, as defined in section 2151.02 of the Revised Code, dependent, abused, unruly, as defined in section 2151.022 [2151.02.2] of the Revised Code, or neglected children or juvenile traffic offenders may be held for training, treatment, and rehabilitation. Upon the joint advice and recommendation of the juvenile judges of two or more adjoining or neighboring counties, the boards of county commissioners of such counties may form themselves into a joint board and proceed to organize a district for the establishment and support of a school, forestry camp, or other facility or facilities for the use of the juvenile courts of such counties, where delinquent, dependent, abused, unruly, or neglected children, or juvenile traffic offenders may be held for treatment, training, and rehabilitation, by using a site or buildings already established in one such county, or by providing for the purchase of a site and the erection of the necessary buildings thereon. Such county or district school, forestry camp, or other facility or facilities shall be maintained as provided in sections 2151.01 to 2151.80 of the Revised Code. Children who are adjudged to be delinquent, dependent, neglected, abused, unruly, or juvenile traffic offenders, may be committed to and held in any such school, forestry camp, or other facility or facilities for training, treatment, and rehabilitation.

The juvenile court shall determine:

(A) The children to be admitted to any school, forestry camp, or other facility maintained under this section;

(B) The period such children shall be trained, treated, and rehabilitated at such facility;

(C) The removal and transfer of children from such facility.

HISTORY: 130 v 626 (Eff 10-14-63); 136 v H 85 (Eff 11-28-75); 138 v S 168. Eff 10-2-80.

[§ 2151.65.1] § 2151.651 State assistance for juvenile facilities.

The board of county commissioners of a county which, either separately or as part of a district, is planning to establish a school, forestry camp, or other facility under section 2151.65 of the Revised Code, to be used exclusively for the rehabilitation of children between the ages of twelve to eighteen years, other than psychotic or mentally retarded children, who are designated delinquent, as defined in section 2151.02 of the Revised Code, or unruly, as defined in section 2151.022 [2151.02.2] of the Revised Code, by order of a juvenile court, may make application to the department of youth services, created under division (B) of section 5139.01 of the Revised Code, for financial assistance in defraying the county's share of the cost of acquisition or construction of such school, camp, or other facility, as provided in section 5139.27 of the Revised Code. Such application shall be made on forms prescribed and furnished by the department.

HISTORY: 131 v 633 (Eff 8-10-65); 138 v S 168 (Eff 10-2-80); 139 v H 440. Eff 11-23-81.

[§ 2151.65.2] § 2151.652 State assistance for operation and maintenance.

The board of county commissioners of a county or the board of trustees of a district maintaining a school, forestry camp, or other facility established under section 2151.65 of the Revised Code, used exclusively for the rehabilitation of children between the ages of twelve to eighteen years, other than psychotic or mentally retarded children, who are designated delinquent, as defined in section 2151.02 of the Revised Code, or unruly, as defined in section 2151.022 [2151.02.2] of the Revised Code, by order of a juvenile court, may make application to the department of youth services, created under division (B) of section 5139.01 of the Revised Code, for financial assistance in defraying the cost of operating and maintaining such school, forestry camp, or other facility, as provided in section 5139.28 of the Revised Code.

Such application shall be made on forms prescribed and furnished by the department.

HISTORY: 131 v 633 (Eff 8-10-65); 138 v S 168 (Eff 10-2-80); 139 v H 440. Eff 11-23-81.

[§ 2151.65.3] § 2151.653 Education of youths.

The board of county commissioners of a county or the board of trustees of a district maintaining a school, forestry camp, or other facility established under section 2151.65 of the Revised Code, shall provide a program of education for the youths admitted to such school, forestry camp, or other facility. Either of such boards and the board of education of any school district may enter into an agreement whereby such board of education provides teachers for such school, forestry camp, or other facility, or permits youths admitted to such school, forestry camp, or other facility to attend a school or schools within such school district, or both. Either of such boards may enter into an agreement with the appropriate authority of any university, college, or vocational institution to assist in providing a program of education for the youths admitted to such school, forestry camp, or other facility.

HISTORY: 131 v 634. Eff 8-10-65.

[§ 2151.65.4] § 2151.654 Nonresident admission.

The board of county commissioners of a county or the board of trustees of a district maintaining a school, forestry camp, or other facility established under section 2151.65 of the Revised Code, may enter into an agreement with the board of county commissioners of a county which does not maintain such a school, forestry camp, or other facility, to admit to such school, forestry camp, or other facility a child from the county not maintaining such a school, forestry camp, or other facility.

HISTORY: 131 v 634. Eff 8-10-65.

[§ 2151.65.5] § 2151.655 Taxing authority of county may issue general obligation securities to pay cost of acquiring or acquiring sites for schools, detention homes, forestry camps, or other facilities.

The taxing authority of a county may issue general obligation securities of the county under Chapter 133. of the Revised Code to pay such county's share, either separately or as a part of a district, of the cost of acquiring schools, detention homes, forestry camps, or other facilities, or any combination thereof, under section 2151.34 or 2151.65 of the Revised Code, or of acquiring sites for and constructing, enlarging, or otherwise improving such schools, detention homes, forestry camps, other facilities, or combinations thereof.

(B) The taxing authority of a detention home district, or a district organized under section 2151.65 of the Revised Code, or of a combined district organized under sections 2151.34 and 2151.65 of the Revised Code, may submit to the electors of the district the question of issuing general obligation bonds of the district to pay the cost of acquiring, constructing, enlarging, or otherwise improving sites, buildings, and facilities for any purposes for which the district was organized. The election on such question shall be submitted and held under section 133.18 of the Revised Code.

HISTORY: RC § 133.15.1, 131 v 74 (Eff 8-10-65); 133 v H 1135 (Eff 9-16-70); 134 v H 258 (Eff 1-27-72); RC § 2151.65.5, 143 v H 230. Eff 10-30-89.

§ 2151.66 District tax levies.

The joint boards of county commissioners of district schools, forestry camps, or other facility or facilities created under section 2151.65 of the Revised Code, shall make annual assessments of taxes sufficient to support and defray all necessary expenses of such

school, forestry camp, or other facility or facilities.
HISTORY: 130 v 627. Eff 10-14-63.

§ 2151.67 Gifts and bequests.

The board of county commissioners of a county or the board of trustees of a district maintaining a school, forestry camp, or other facility established or to be established under section 2151.65 of the Revised Code may receive gifts, grants, devises, and bequests, either absolutely or in trust, and may receive any public moneys made available to it. Each of such boards shall use such gifts, grants, devises, bequests, and public moneys in whatever manner it determines is most likely to carry out the purposes for which such school, forestry camp, or other facility was or is to be established.
HISTORY: 131 v 635 (Eff 8-10-65); 132 v H 1. Eff 2-21-67.

Analogous to former RC § 2151.67 (130 v 627), repealed in 131 v 2019, § 2, eff 8-10-65.

§ 2151.68 Appointment of district boards of trustees.

Immediately upon the organization of the joint board of county commissioners as provided by section 2151.65 of the Revised Code, or so soon thereafter as practicable, such joint board of county commissioners shall appoint a board of not less than five trustees, which shall hold office and perform its duties until the first annual meeting after the choice of an established site and buildings, or after the selection and purchase of a building site, at which time such joint board of county commissioners shall appoint a board of not less than five trustees, one of whom shall hold office for a term of one year, one for the term of two years, one for the term of three years, half of the remaining number for the term of four years, and the remainder for the term of five years. Annually thereafter, the joint board of county commissioners shall appoint one or more trustees, each of whom shall hold office for the term of five years, to succeed any trustee whose term of office expires. A trustee may be appointed to succeed himself upon such board of trustees, and all appointments to such board of trustees shall be made from persons who are recommended and approved by the juvenile court judge or judges of the county of which such person is a resident. The annual meeting of the board of trustees shall be held on the first Tuesday in May in each year.
HISTORY: 130 v 627. Eff 10-14-63.

§ 2151.69 Procedures of district boards of trustees.

A majority of the trustees appointed under section 2151.68 of the Revised Code constitutes a quorum. Board meetings shall be held at least quarterly. The presiding juvenile court judge of each of the counties of the district organized pursuant to section 2151.65 of the Revised Code shall attend such meetings, or shall designate a member of his staff to do so. The members of the board shall receive no compensation for their services, except their actual traveling expenses, which, when properly certified, shall be allowed and paid by the treasurer.
HISTORY: 130 v 628. Eff 10-14-63.

§ 2151.70 Employees of juvenile facilities.

The judge, in a county maintaining a school, forestry camp, or other facility or facilities created under section 2151.65 of the Revised Code, shall appoint the superintendent of any such facility. In the case of a district facility created under such section, the board of trustees shall appoint the superintendent. A superintendent, before entering upon his duties, shall give bond with sufficient surety to the judge or to the board, as the case may be, in such amount as may be fixed by the judge or the board, such bond being conditioned upon the full and faithful accounting of the funds and properties coming into his hands.

Compensation of the superintendent and other necessary employees of a school, forestry camp, or other facility or facilities shall be fixed by the judge in the case of a county facility, or by the board of trustees in the case of a district facility. Such compensation and other expenses of maintaining the facility shall be paid in the manner prescribed in section 2151.13 of the Revised Code in the case of a county facility, or in accordance with rules and regulations provided for in section 2151.77 of the Revised Code in the case of a district facility.

The superintendent of a facility shall appoint all employees of such facility. All such employees, except the superintendent, shall be in the classified civil service.

The superintendent of a school, forestry camp, or other facility shall have entire executive charge of such facility, under supervision of the judge, in the case of a county facility, or under supervision of the board of trustees, in the case of a district facility. The superintendent shall control, manage, and operate the facility, and shall have custody of its property, files, and records.
HISTORY: 130 v 628. Eff 10-14-63.

§ 2151.71 Manner of operating facilities.

District schools, forestry camps, or other facilities created under section 2151.65 of the Revised Code shall be established, operated, maintained, and managed in the same manner, so far as applicable, as county schools, forestry camps, or other facilities.
HISTORY: 130 v 629. Eff 10-14-63.

§ 2151.72 Selection of site for district facility.

When the board of trustees appointed under section

2151.68 of the Revised Code does not choose an established institution in one of the counties of the district, it may select a suitable site for the erection of a district school, forestry camp, or other facility or facilities created under section 2151.65 of the Revised Code.

HISTORY: 130 v 629. Eff 10-14-63.

§ 2151.73 Apportionment of board of trustees posts; executive committee.

Each county in the district, organized under section 2151.65 of the Revised Code, shall be entitled to one trustee, and in districts composed of but two counties, each county shall be entitled to not less than two trustees. In districts composed of more than four counties, the number of trustees shall be sufficiently increased so that there shall always be an uneven number of trustees constituting such board. The county in which a district school, forestry camp, or other facility created under section 2151.65 of the Revised Code is located shall have not less than two trustees, who, in the interim period between the regular meetings of the board of trustees, shall act as an executive committee in the discharge of all business pertaining to the school, forestry camp, or other facility.

HISTORY: 130 v 629. Eff 10-14-63.

§ 2151.74 Removal of trustees.

The joint board of county commissioners organized under section 2151.65 of the Revised Code may remove any trustee appointed under section 2151.68 of the Revised Code, but no such removal shall be made on account of the religious or political convictions of such trustee. The trustee appointed to fill any vacancy shall hold his office for the unexpired term of his predecessor.

HISTORY: 130 v 630. Eff 10-14-63.

§ 2151.75 Interim duties of trustees; trustees' fund; reports.

In the interim, between the selection and purchase of a site, and the erection and occupancy of a district school, forestry camp, or other facility or facilities created under section 2151.65 of the Revised Code, the joint board of county commissioners provided by section 2151.65 of the Revised Code may delegate to a board of trustees appointed under section 2151.68 of the Revised Code, such powers and duties as, in its judgment, will be of general interest or aid to the institution. Such joint board of county commissioners may appropriate a trustees' fund, to be expended by the board of trustees in payment of such contracts, purchases, or other expenses necessary to the wants or requirements of the school, forestry camp, or other facility or facilities which are not otherwise provided for. The board of trustees shall make a complete settlement with the joint board of county commissioners once each six months, or quarterly if required, and shall make a full report of the condition of the school, forestry camp, or other facility or facilities and inmates, to the board of county commissioners, and to the juvenile court of each of the counties.

HISTORY: 130 v 630. Eff 10-14-63.

§ 2151.76 Authority for choice, construction, and furnishing of district facility.

The choice of an established site and buildings, or the purchase of a site, stock, implements, and general farm equipment, should there be a farm, the erection of buildings, and the completion and furnishing of the district school, forestry camp, or other facility or facilities for occupancy, shall be in the hands of the joint board of county commissioners organized under section 2151.65 of the Revised Code. Such joint board of county commissioners may delegate all or a portion of these duties to the board of trustees provided for under section 2151.68 of the Revised Code, under such restrictions and regulations as the joint board of county commissioners imposes.

HISTORY: 130 v 630. Eff 10-14-63.

§ 2151.77 Capital and current expenses of district.

When an established site and buildings are used for a district school, forestry camp, or other facility or facilities created under section 2151.65 of the Revised Code the joint board of county commissioners organized under section 2151.65 of the Revised Code shall cause the value of such site and buildings to be properly appraised. This appraisal value, or in case of the purchase of a site, the purchase price and the cost of all betterments and additions thereto, shall be paid by the counties comprising the district, in proportion to the taxable property of each county, as shown by its tax duplicate. The current expenses of maintaining the school, forestry camp, or other facility or facilities and the cost of ordinary repairs thereto shall be paid by each such county in accordance with one of the following methods as approved by the joint board of county commissioners:

(A) In proportion to the number of children from such county who are maintained in the school, forestry camp, or other facility or facilities during the year;

(B) By a levy submitted by the joint board of county commissioners under division (A) of section 5705.19 of the Revised Code and approved by the electors of the district;

(C) In proportion to the taxable property of each county, as shown by its tax duplicate;

(D) In any combination of the methods for payment described in division (A), (B), or (C) of this section.

The board of trustees shall, with the approval of the joint board of county commissioners, adopt rules for the management of funds used for the current expenses of maintaining the school, forestry camp, or other facility or facilities.

HISTORY: 130 v 631 (Eff 10-14-63); 134 v H 258 (Eff 1-27-72); 142 v H 365. Eff 6-14-88.

§ 2151.78 Withdrawal of county from district; continuity of district tax levy.

The board of county commissioners of any county within a school, forestry camp, or other facility or facilities district may, upon the recommendation of the juvenile court of such county, withdraw from such district and dispose of its interest in such school, forestry camp, or other facility or facilities selling or leasing its right, title, and interest in the site, buildings, furniture, and equipment to any counties in the district, at such price and upon such terms as are agreed upon among the boards of county commissioners of the counties concerned. Section 307.10 of the Revised Code does not apply to this section. The net proceeds of any such sale or lease shall be paid into the treasury of the withdrawing county.

Any county withdrawing from such district or from a combined district organized under sections 2154.34 and 2151.65 of the Revised Code shall continue to have levied against its tax duplicate any tax levied by the district during the period in which the county was a member of the district for current operating expenses, permanent improvements, or the retirement of bonded indebtedness. Such levy shall continue to be a levy against such duplicate of the county until such time that it expires or is renewed.

Members of the board of trustees of a district school, forestry camp, or other facility or facilities who are residents of a county withdrawing from such district are deemed to have resigned their positions upon the completion of the withdrawal procedure provided by this section. Vacancies then created shall be filled according to sections 2151.68 and 2151.74 of the Revised Code.

HISTORY: 130 v 631 (Eff 10-14-63); 134 v H 258. Eff 1-27-72.

§ 2151.79 Designation of fiscal officer of district; duties of county auditors in district.

The county auditor of the county having the greatest population, or, with the unanimous concurrence of the county auditors of the counties composing a facilities district, the auditor of the county wherein the facility is located, shall be the fiscal officer of a district organized under section 2151.65 of the Revised Code or a combined district organized under sections 2151.34 and 2151.65 of the Revised Code. The county auditors of the several counties composing a school, forestry camp, or other facility or facilities district, shall meet at the district school, forestry camp, or other facility or facilities not less than once in each six months, to review accounts and to transact such other duties in connection with the institution as pertain to the business of their office.

HISTORY: 130 v 631 (Eff 10-14-63); 134 v H 258 (Eff 1-27-72); 135 v H 1033. Eff 10-2-74.

§ 2151.80 Expenses of members of boards of county commissioners.

Each member of the board of county commissioners who meets by appointment to consider the organization of a district school, forestry camp, or other facility or facilities shall, upon presentation of properly certified accounts, be paid his necessary expenses upon a warrant drawn by the county auditor of his county.

HISTORY: 130 v 632. Eff 10-14-63.

§ 2151.85 Unmarried minor may seek abortion without notice to parent, guardian or custodian.

(A) A woman who is pregnant, unmarried, under eighteen years of age, and unemancipated and who wishes to have an abortion without the notification of her parents, guardian, or custodian may file a complaint in the juvenile court of the county in which she has a residence or legal settlement, in the juvenile court of any county that borders to any extent the county in which she has a residence or legal settlement, or in the juvenile court of the county in which the hospital, clinic, or other facility in which the abortion would be performed or induced is located, requesting the issuance of an order authorizing her to consent to the performance or inducement of an abortion without the notification of her parents, guardian, or custodian.

The complaint shall be made under oath and shall include all of the following:

(1) A statement that the complainant is pregnant;

(2) A statement that the complainant is unmarried, under eighteen years of age, and unemancipated;

(3) A statement that the complainant wishes to have an abortion without the notification of her parents, guardian, or custodian;

(4) An allegation of either or both of the following:

(a) That the complainant is sufficiently mature and well enough informed to intelligently decide whether to have an abortion without the notification of her parents, guardian, or custodian;

(b) That one or both of her parents, her guardian, or her custodian was engaged in a pattern of physical, sexual, or emotional abuse against her, or that the notification of her parents, guardian, or custodian otherwise is not in her best interest.

(5) A statement as to whether the complainant has retained an attorney and, if she has retained an attorney, the name, address, and telephone number of her attorney.

(B)(1) The court shall fix a time for a hearing on any

complaint filed pursuant to division (A) of this section and shall keep a record of all testimony and other oral proceedings in the action. The court shall hear and determine the action and shall not refer any portion of it to a referee. The hearing shall be held at the earliest possible time, but not later than the fifth business day after the day that the complaint is filed. The court shall enter judgment on the complaint immediately after the hearing is concluded. If the hearing required by this division is not held by the fifth business day after the complaint is filed, the failure to hold the hearing shall be considered to be a constructive order of the court authorizing the complainant to consent to the performance or inducement of an abortion without the notification of her parent, guardian, or custodian, and the complainant and any other person may rely on the constructive order to the same extent as if the court actually had issued an order under this section authorizing the complainant to consent to the performance or inducement of an abortion without such notification.

(2) The court shall appoint a guardian ad litem to protect the interests of the complainant at the hearing that is held pursuant to this section. If the complainant has not retained an attorney, the court shall appoint an attorney to represent her. If the guardian ad litem is an attorney admitted to the practice of law in this state, the court also may appoint him to serve as the complainant's attorney.

(C)(1) If the complainant makes only the allegation set forth in division (A)(4)(a) of this section and if the court finds, by clear and convincing evidence, that the complainant is sufficiently mature and well enough informed to decide intelligently whether to have an abortion, the court shall issue an order authorizing the complainant to consent to the performance or inducement of an abortion without the notification of her parents, guardian, or custodian. If the court does not make the finding specified in this division, it shall dismiss the complaint.

(2) If the complainant makes only the allegation set forth in division (A)(4)(b) of this section and if the court finds, by clear and convincing evidence, that there is evidence of a pattern of physical, sexual, or emotional abuse of the complainant by one or both of her parents, her guardian, or her custodian, or that the notification of the parents, guardian, or custodian of the complainant otherwise is not in the best interest of the complainant, the court shall issue an order authorizing the complainant to consent to the performance or inducement of an abortion without the notification of her parents, guardian, or custodian. If the court does not make the finding specified in this division, it shall dismiss the complaint.

(3) If the complainant makes both of the allegations set forth in divisions (A)(4)(a) and (b) of this section, the court shall proceed as follows:

(a) The court first shall determine whether it can make the finding specified in division (C)(1) of this section and, if so, shall issue an order pursuant to that division. If the court issues such an order, it shall not proceed pursuant to division (C)(3)(b) of this section. If the court does not make the finding specified in division (C)(1) of this section, it shall proceed pursuant to division (C)(3)(b) of this section.

(b) If the court pursuant to division (C)(3)(a) of this section does not make the finding specified in division (C)(1) of this section, it shall proceed to determine whether it can make the finding specified in division (C)(2) of this section and, if so, shall issue an order pursuant to that division. If the court does not make the finding specified in division (C)(2) of this section, it shall dismiss the complaint.

(D) The court shall not notify the parents, guardian, or custodian of the complainant that she is pregnant or that she wants to have an abortion.

(E) If the court dismisses the complaint, it immediately shall notify the complainant that she has a right to appeal under section 2505.073 [2505.07.3] of the Revised Code.

(F) Each hearing under this section shall be conducted in a manner that will preserve the anonymity of the complainant. The complaint and all other papers and records that pertain to an action commenced under this section shall be kept confidential and are not public records under section 149.43 of the Revised Code.

(G) The clerk of the supreme court shall prescribe complaint and notice of appeal forms that shall be used by a complainant filing a complaint under this section and by an appellant filing an appeal under section 2505.073 [2505.07.3] of the Revised Code. The clerk of each juvenile court shall furnish blank copies of the forms, without charge, to any person who requests them.

(H) No filing fee shall be required of, and no court costs shall be assessed against, a complainant filing a complaint under this section or an appellant filing an appeal under section 2505.073 [2505.07.3] of the Revised Code.

(I) As used in this section, "unemancipated" means that a woman who is unmarried and under eighteen years of age has not entered the armed services of the United States, has not become employed and self-subsisting, or has not otherwise become independent from the care and control of her parent, guardian, or custodian.

HISTORY: 141 v H 319. Eff 3-24-86.

§ 2151.86 Criminal records check and fingerprinting of employees responsible for out-of-home child care and prospective adoptive or foster parents.

(A)(1) The appointing or hiring officer of any entity that employs any person responsible for a child's care in out-of-home care shall request the superintendent of the bureau of criminal identification and investigation to conduct a criminal records check with respect to any applicant who has applied to the entity for employment as a person responsible for a child's care in out-of-home care. The administrative director of any entity that designates a person as a prospective adoptive parent or as a prospective foster parent shall request the superintendent to conduct a criminal records check with respect to that person. If the applicant, prospective adoptive parent, or prospective foster parent does not present proof that the applicant or prospective adoptive or foster parent has been a resident of this state for the five-year period immediately prior to the date upon which the criminal records check is requested or does not provide evidence that within that five-year period the superintendent has requested information about the applicant or prospective adoptive or foster parent from the federal bureau of investigation in a criminal records check, the appointing or hiring officer or administrative director shall request that the superintendent obtain information from the federal bureau of investigation as a part of the criminal records check. If the applicant, prospective adoptive parent, or prospective foster parent presents proof that the applicant or prospective adoptive or foster parent has been a resident of this state for that five-year period, the appointing or hiring officer or administrator may request that the superintendent include information from the federal bureau of investigation in the criminal records check.

(2) Any person required by division (A)(1) of this section to request a criminal records check shall provide to each applicant, prospective adoptive parent, or prospective foster parent a copy of the form prescribed pursuant to division (C)(1) of section 109.572 [109.57.2] of the Revised Code and a standard impression sheet to obtain fingerprint impressions prescribed pursuant to division (C)(2) of section 109.572 [109.57.2] of the Revised Code, obtain the completed form and impression sheet from each applicant, prospective adoptive parent, or prospective foster parent, and forward the completed form and impression sheet to the superintendent of the bureau of criminal identification and investigation at the time the person requests a criminal records check pursuant to division (A)(1) of this section.

(3) Any applicant, prospective adoptive parent, or prospective foster parent who receives pursuant to division (A)(2) of this section a copy of the form prescribed pursuant to division (C)(1) of section 109.572 [109.57.2] of the Revised Code and a copy of an impression sheet prescribed pursuant to division (C)(2) of that section and who is requested to complete the form and provide a set of fingerprint impressions shall complete the form or provide all the information necessary to complete the form and shall provide the impression sheet with the impressions of the applicant's or prospective adoptive or foster parent's fingerprints. If an applicant, prospective adoptive parent, or prospective foster parent, upon request, fails to provide the information necessary to complete the form or fails to provide impressions of the applicant's or prospective adoptive or foster parent's fingerprints, the entity shall not employ that applicant for any position for which a criminal records check is required by division (A)(1) of this section and shall not consider the prospective adoptive parent or prospective foster parent as an adoptive parent or foster parent.

(B)(1) Except as provided in rules adopted by the department of human services in accordance with division (E) of this section, no entity shall employ a person as a person responsible for a child's care in out-of-home care or permit a person to become an adoptive parent or foster parent if the person previously has been convicted of or pleaded guilty to any of the following:

(a) A violation of section 2903.01, 2903.02, 2903.03, 2903.04, 2903.11, 2903.12, 2903.13, 2903.16, 2903.21, 2903.34, 2905.01, 2905.02, 2905.05, 2907.02, 2907.03, 2907.04, 2907.05, 2907.06, 2907.07, 2907.08, 2907.09, 2907.21, 2907.22, 2907.23, 2907.25, 2907.31, 2907.32, 2907.321 [2907.32.1], 2907.322 [2907.32.2], 2907.323 [2907.32.3], 2911.01, 2911.02, 2911.11, 2911.12, 2919.12, 2919.22, 2919.24, 2919.25, 2923.12, 2923.13, 2923.161 [2923.16.1], 2925.02, 2925.03, 2925.04, 2925.05, 2925.06, or 3716.11 of the Revised Code, a violation of section 2905.04 of the Revised Code as it existed prior to July 1, 1996, a violation of section 2919.23 of the Revised Code that would have been a violation of section 2905.04 of the Revised Code as it existed prior to July 1, 1996, had the violation been committed prior to that date, a violation of section 2925.11 of the Revised Code that is not a minor drug possession offense, or felonious sexual penetration in violation of former section 2907.12 of the Revised Code;

(b) A violation of an existing or former law of this state, any other state, or the United States that is substantially equivalent to any of the offenses described in division (B)(1)(a) of this section.

(2) An out-of-home care entity may employ an applicant conditionally until the criminal records check required by this section is completed and the entity receives the results of the criminal records check. If the results of the criminal records check indicate that, pursuant to division (B)(1) of this section, the applicant does not qualify for employment, the entity shall release the applicant from employment.

(C)(1) The out-of-home care entity shall pay to the bureau of criminal identification and investigation the fee prescribed pursuant to division (C)(3) of section 109.572 [109.57.2] of the Revised Code for each criminal records check conducted in accordance with that section upon a request pursuant to division (A)(1) of this section.

(2) An out-of-home care entity may charge an applicant, prospective adoptive parent, or prospective foster parent a fee for the costs it incurs in obtaining a criminal records check under this section. A fee charged under this division shall not exceed the amount of fees the entity pays under division (C)(1) of this section. If a fee is charged under this division, the entity shall notify the applicant, prospective adoptive parent, or prospec-

tive foster parent at the time of the person's initial application for employment or for becoming an adoptive parent or foster parent of the amount of the fee and that, unless the fee is paid, the entity will not consider the person for employment or as an adoptive parent or foster parent.

(D) The report of any criminal records check conducted by the bureau of criminal identification and investigation in accordance with section 109.572 [109.57.2] of the Revised Code and pursuant to a request made under division (A)(1) of this section is not a public record for the purposes of section 149.43 of the Revised Code and shall not be made available to any person other than the applicant, prospective adoptive parent, or prospective foster parent who is the subject of the criminal records check or the applicant's or prospective adoptive or foster parent's representative; the entity requesting the criminal records check or its representative; the state department of human services or a county department of human services; and any court, hearing officer, or other necessary individual involved in a case dealing with the denial of employment to the applicant or the denial of consideration as an adoptive parent or foster parent.

(E) The department of human services shall adopt rules pursuant to Chapter 119. of the Revised Code to implement this section, including rules specifying circumstances under which an out-of-home care entity may hire a person who has been convicted of an offense listed in division (B)(1) of this section but who meets standards in regard to rehabilitation set by the department.

(F) Any person required by division (A)(1) of this section to request a criminal records check shall inform each person, at the time of the person's initial application for employment with an entity as a person responsible for a child's care in out-of-home care or the person's initial application for becoming an adoptive parent or foster parent, that the person is required to provide a set of impressions of the person's fingerprints and that a criminal records check is required to be conducted and satisfactorily completed in accordance with section 109.572 [109.57.2] of the Revised Code if the person comes under final consideration for appointment or employment as a precondition to employment for that position or if the person is to be given final consideration as an adoptive parent or foster parent.

(G) As used in this section:
(1) "Applicant" means a person who is under final consideration for appointment or employment as a person responsible for a child's care in out-of-home care.

(2) "Person responsible for a child's care in out-of-home care" has the same meaning as in section 2151.011 [2151.01.1] of the Revised Code, except that it does not include a prospective employee of the department of youth services or a person responsible for a child's care in a hospital or medical clinic other than a children's hospital.

(3) "Children's hospital" means any of the following:
(a) A hospital registered under section 3701.07 of the Revised Code that provides general pediatric medical and surgical care, and in which at least seventy-five per cent of annual inpatient discharges for the preceding two calendar years were individuals less than eighteen years of age;

(b) A distinct portion of a hospital registered under section 3701.07 of the Revised Code that provides general pediatric medical and surgical care, has a total of at least one hundred fifty registered pediatric special care and pediatric acute care beds, and in which at least seventy-five per cent of annual inpatient discharges for the preceding two calendar years were individuals less than eighteen years of age;

(c) A distinct portion of a hospital, if the hospital is registered under section 3701.07 of the Revised Code as a children's hospital and the children's hospital meets all the requirements of division (G)(3)(a) of this section.

(4) "Criminal records check" has the same meaning as in section 109.572 [109.57.2] of the Revised Code.

(5) "Minor drug possession offense" has the same meaning as in section 2925.01 of the Revised Code.

HISTORY: 145 v S 38 (Eff 10-29-93); 146 v S 2 (Eff 7-1-96); 146 v S 269 (Eff 7-1-96); 146 v H 445. Eff 9-3-96.

See Comment, Legislative Service Commission following RC § 2151.27.

§ 2151.99 Penalties.

(A) Whoever violates division (D)(2) or (3) of section 2151.313 [2151.31.3] or division (A)(1) or (H)(2) of section 2151.421 [2151.42.1] of the Revised Code is guilty of a misdemeanor of the fourth degree.

(B) Whoever violates division (D)(1) of section 2151.313 [2151.31.3] of the Revised Code is guilty of a minor misdemeanor.

HISTORY: Bureau of Code Revision, 10-1-53; 130 v 632 (Eff 10-10-63); 133 v H 320 (Eff 11-19-69); 134 v H 511 (Eff 1-1-74); 140 v H 258 (Eff 9-26-84); 141 v H 349 (Eff 3-6-86); 141 v H 529 (Eff 3-11-87); 143 v H 257. Eff 8-3-89.

TITLE 23: COURTS—COMMON PLEAS

CHAPTER 2301: ORGANIZATION

[BAILIFF]

§ 2301.15 Duties of criminal bailiff; costs.

The criminal bailiff shall act for the sheriff in criminal cases and matters of a criminal nature in the court of common pleas and the probate court of the county. Under the direction of the sheriff, he shall be present during trials of criminal cases in those courts and during such trials perform all the duties as are performed by the sheriff. The criminal bailiff shall conduct prisoners to and from the jail of the county and for that purpose shall have access to the jail and to the courtroom, whenever ordered by such courts, and have care and charge of such prisoners when so doing. Under the direction of the sheriff, the criminal bailiff shall convey to state correctional institutions all persons sentenced thereto. He shall receive and collect from the treasurer of state all costs in such criminal cases in the same manner as the sheriff is required to do, and pay the amount so collected to the sheriff of such county.

HISTORY: RS § 474-2; 76 v 54, § 2; GC § 1543; Bureau of Code Revision, 10-1-53; 145 v H 571. Eff 10-6-94.

§ 2301.16 Bailiff shall give bond.

Before entering upon the discharge of his duties, the criminal bailiff shall give a bond to the sheriff in the sum of five thousand dollars, with good and sufficient sureties, conditioned for the faithful discharge of his duties. The judges of the court of common pleas shall fix a compensation for his services, payable monthly from the fee fund, upon the warrant of the county auditor.

HISTORY: RS § 474-4; 76 v 54; 90 v 162, § 4; GC § 1545; Bureau of Code Revision. Eff 10-1-53.

§ 2301.17 Additional temporary bailiff.

On the application of the sheriff, in a criminal case, if the court of common pleas is satisfied that the administration of justice requires an additional criminal bailiff to execute process, it may appoint such additional bailiff, whose powers and duties shall cease when such case is determined.

HISTORY: RS § 474-3; 76 v 54, § 3; GC § 1544; Bureau of Code Revision. Eff 10-1-53.

[DEPARTMENT OF PROBATION]

§ 2301.27 County or multicounty department of probation or contract for probation services.

(A)(1) The court of common pleas may establish a county department of probation. The establishment of the department shall be entered upon the journal of the court, and the clerk of the court of common pleas shall certify a copy of the journal entry establishing the department to each elective officer and board of the county. The department shall consist of a chief probation officer and the number of other probation officers and employees, clerks, and stenographers that is fixed from time to time by the court. The court shall appoint those individuals, fix their salaries, and supervise their work. The court shall not appoint as a probation officer any person who does not possess the training, experience, and other qualifications prescribed by the adult parole authority created by section 5149.02 of the Revised Code. Probation officers have all the powers of regular police officers and shall perform any duties that are designated by the judge or judges of the court. All positions within the department of probation shall be in the classified service of the civil service of the county.

(2) If two or more counties desire to jointly establish a probation department for those counties, the judges of the courts of common pleas of those counties may establish a probation department for those counties. If a probation department is established pursuant to division (A)(2) of this section to serve more than one county, the judges of the courts of common pleas that established the department shall designate the county treasurer of one of the counties served by the department as the treasurer to whom probation fees paid under section 2951.021 [2951.02.1] of the Revised Code are to be appropriated and transferred under division (A)(2) of section 321.44 of the Revised Code for deposit into the multicounty probation services fund established under division (B) of section 321.44 of the Revised Code.

The cost of the administration and operation of a probation department established for two or more counties shall be prorated to the respective counties on the basis of population.

(3) Probation officers shall receive, in addition to their respective salaries, their necessary and reasonable travel and other expenses incurred in the performance of their duties. Their salaries and expenses shall be paid monthly from the county treasury in the manner provided for the payment of the compensation of other appointees of the court.

(B)(1) In lieu of establishing a county department of probation under division (A) of this section and in lieu of entering into an agreement with the adult parole authority as described in division (B) of section 2301.32 of the Revised Code, the court of common pleas may request the board of county commissioners to contract with, and upon that request the board may contract with, any nonprofit, public or private agency, association, or organization for the provision of probation services and supervisory services for persons placed under community control sanctions. The contract shall specify that each individual providing the probation services and supervisory services shall possess the training, experience, and other qualifications prescribed by the adult parole authority. The individuals who provide the probation services and supervisory services shall not be included in the classified or unclassified civil service of the county.

(2) In lieu of establishing a county department of probation under division (A) of this section and in lieu of entering into an agreement with the adult parole authority as described in division (B) of section 2301.32 of the Revised Code, the courts of common pleas of two or more adjoining counties jointly may request the boards of county commissioners of those counties to contract with, and upon that request the boards of county commissioners of two or more adjoining counties jointly may contract with, any nonprofit, public or private agency, association, or organization for the provision of probation services and supervisory services for persons placed under community control sanctions for those counties. The contract shall specify that each individual providing the probation services and supervisory services shall possess the training, experience, and other qualifications prescribed by the adult parole authority. The individuals who provide the probation services and supervisory services shall not be included in the classified or unclassified civil service of any of those counties.

(C) The chief probation officer may grant permission to a probation officer to carry firearms when required in the discharge of official duties, provided that any probation officer who is granted permission to carry firearms in the discharge of official duties, within six months of receiving permission to carry a firearm, shall successfully complete a basic firearm training program that is conducted at a training school approved by the Ohio peace officer training commission and that is substantially similar to the basic firearm training program for peace officers conducted at the Ohio peace officer training academy and receive a certificate of satisfactory completion of that program from the executive director of the Ohio peace officer training commission. Any probation officer who does not successfully complete a basic firearm training program within the six-month period after receiving permission to carry a firearm shall not carry, after the expiration of that six-month period, a firearm in the discharge of official duties until the probation officer has successfully completed a basic firearm training program. A probation officer who has received a certificate of satisfactory completion of a basic firearm training program, to maintain the right to carry a firearm in the discharge of official duties, annually shall successfully complete a firearms requalification program in accordance with section 109.801 [109.80.1] of the Revised Code.

(D) As used in this section, "community control sanction" has the same meaning as in section 2929.01 of the Revised Code.

HISTORY: GC § 1554-1; 111 v 423; Bureau of Code Revision, 10-1-53; 125 v 327 (Eff 10-13-53); 129 v 481 (Eff 10-18-61); 130 v 647 (Eff 1-23-63); 130 v PtII, 138 (Eff 3-18-65); 145 v H 152 (Eff 7-1-93); 145 v H 406 (Eff 11-11-94); 146 v S 269 (Eff 7-1-96); 146 v H 670. Eff 12-2-96.

§ 2301.28 Supervision over persons on probation, conditionally pardoned, or paroled.

The court of common pleas of a county in which a county department of probation has been established under division (A) of section 2301.27 of the Revised Code, in addition to employing the department in investigation and in the administration of its own orders of probation, shall receive into the legal control or supervision of the department any person who is a resident of the county and who has been placed on probation by order of any other court exercising criminal jurisdiction in this state, whether within or without the county in which the department of probation is located, upon the request of the other court and subject to its continuing jurisdiction. The court of common pleas also shall receive into the legal custody or supervision of the department any person who is paroled or conditionally pardoned from a state correctional institution and who resides or remains in the county, if requested by the adult parole authority created by section 5149.02 of the Revised Code or other authority having power to parole from any institution of that nature.

HISTORY: GC § 1554-2; 111 v 424; Bureau of Code Revision, 10-1-53; 129 v 481 (Eff 10-18-61); 130 v PtII, 139 (Eff 3-18-65); 145 v H 152 (Eff 7-1-93); 145 v H 571. Eff 10-6-94.

§ 2301.29 Rules of adult parole authority to govern; local court rules.

In all cases in which the county department of probation provided for in division (A) of section 2301.27 of the Revised Code acquires legal custody of or supervision over a person who is granted a conditional pardon or a parole from a state correctional institution, the court of common pleas and the department shall be governed by the rules of the adult parole authority created by section 5149.02 of the Revised Code that are applicable to those cases and by the laws of the state applicable to those cases. In the case of other persons placed in its legal control or under its supervision, the department shall administer the orders and conditions of the authority so placing those persons. The court may exercise supervision over the department by adopting rules that are not inconsistent with law or with the rules of the adult parole authority and that shall be observed and enforced by the probation officers of the department.

As used in this section "pardon," "parole," and "state

correctional institution" have the same meanings as in section 2967.01 of the Revised Code.

HISTORY: GC § 1554-3; 111 v 424; 118 v 288(300), § 25; Bureau of Code Revision, 10-1-53; 130 v PtII, 140 (Eff 3-18-65); 145 v H 152 (Eff 7-1-93); 145 v H 571. Eff 10-6-94.

§ 2301.30 Duties of probation department.

The court of common pleas of a county in which a county department of probation is established under division (A) of section 2301.27 of the Revised Code shall require the department, in the rules through which the supervision of the department is exercised or otherwise, to do all of the following:

(A) Furnish to each person on probation or parole under its supervision or in its custody, a written statement of the conditions of probation or parole and instruct him regarding the conditions;

(B) Keep informed concerning the conduct and condition of each person in its custody or under its supervision by visiting, the requiring of reports, and otherwise;

(C) Use all suitable methods, not inconsistent with the conditions of probation or parole, to aid and encourage the persons under its supervision or in its custody and to bring about improvement in their conduct and condition;

(D) Keep detailed records of the work of the department, keep accurate and complete accounts of all moneys collected from persons under its supervision or in its custody, and keep or give receipts for those moneys;

(E) Make reports to the adult parole authority created by section 5149.02 of the Revised Code that it requires.

HISTORY: GC § 1554-5; 111 v 425; Bureau of Code Revision, 10-1-53; 130 v PtII, 140 (Eff 3-18-65); 145 v H 152. Eff 7-1-93.

§ 2301.31 Arrest of parolees.

(A) If a person on parole is in the custody of a county department of probation provided for in division (A) of section 2301.27 of the Revised Code, any probation officer of that department may arrest the person without a warrant for any violation of any condition of parole, as defined in section 2967.01 of the Revised Code, or of any rule governing persons on parole. If a person on parole is in the custody of a county department of probation provided for in division (A) of section 2301.27 of the Revised Code, any probation officer or peace officer shall arrest the person without a warrant for any violation of any condition of parole or any rule governing persons on parole upon the written order of the chief probation officer of that department. Any peace officer may arrest the person without a warrant, in accordance with section 2941.46 of the Revised Code, if the peace officer has reasonable ground to believe that the person has violated or is violating any of the following that is a condition of his parole:

(1) a condition that prohibits his ownership, possession, or use of a firearm, deadly weapon, ammunition, or dangerous ordnance;

(2) a condition that prohibits him from being within a specified structure or geographic area;

(3) a condition that confines him to a residence, facility, or other structure;

(4) a condition that prohibits him from contacting or communicating with any specified individual;

(5) a condition that prohibits him from associating with a specified individual.

(B) A person who is arrested as provided in this section may be confined in the jail or juvenile detention home, as the case may be, of the county in which he is arrested, until released or removed to the proper institution. Upon making an arrest under this section, the arresting probation officer or peace officer or his department or agency promptly shall notify the chief probation officer of the county department of probation with custody of the person or the chief probation officer's designee that the person has been arrested.

Upon the written order of the chief probation officer of the county department with custody of the person, the person may be released on parole or reimprisoned or recommitted to the proper institution. An appeal from an order of reimprisonment or recommitment may be taken to the adult parole authority created by section 5149.02 of the Revised Code, and the decision of the authority on the appeal shall be final. The manner of taking an appeal of that nature and the disposition of the appellant pending the making and determination of the appeal shall be governed by the rules and orders of the adult parole authority.

(C) Nothing in this section limits the powers of arrest granted to certain law enforcement officers and citizens under sections 2935.03 and 2935.04 of the Revised Code.

(D) As used in this section:

(1) "Peace officer" has the same meaning as in section 2935.01 of the Revised Code.

(2) "Firearm," "deadly weapon," and "dangerous ordnance" have the same meanings as in section 2923.11 of the Revised Code.

HISTORY: GC § 1554-6; 111 v 425; 118 v 288(300), § 25; Bureau of Code Revision, 10-1-53; 130 v Pt2, 141 (Eff 3-12-65); 144 v S 49 (Eff 7-21-92); 145 v H 152. Eff 7-1-93.

§ 2301.32 Agreement for supervision of persons on parole or probation.

(A) In any county in which a county department of probation has been established under division (A) of section 2301.27 of the Revised Code and complies with standards and conditions prescribed by the adult parole authority created by section 5149.02 of the Revised Code, an agreement may be entered into between the court of common pleas and the authority under which the county department of probation may receive supplemental investigation or supervisory services from the authority.

(B) In any county in which a county department of probation has not been established under division (A) of section 2301.27 of the Revised Code, an agreement may be entered into between the court of common pleas of that county and the adult parole authority under which the court of common pleas may place defendants on probation in charge of the authority, and, in consideration of those placements, the county shall pay to the state from time to time the amounts that are provided for in the agreement.

HISTORY: GC § 1554-7; 121 v 381; Bureau of Code Revision, 10-1-53; 128 v 959 (Eff 10-1-59); 129 v 481 (Eff 10-18-61); 130 v PtII, 141 (Eff 3-18-65); 145 v H 152 (Eff 7-1-93); 145 v H 571 (Eff 10-6-94); 145 v H 406. Eff 11-11-94.

Comment, Director, Legislative Service Commission

* * * Sections 2301.32, * * * of the Revised Code are [is] amended by this act [Am. Sub. H.B. 406] and also by Am. Sub. H.B. 571 of the 120th General Assembly. Comparison of these amendments in pursuance of section 1.52 of the Revised Code discloses that they are not irreconcilable, so that they are required by that section to be harmonized to give effect to each amendment.

CHAPTER 2305: JURISDICTION; LIMITATION OF ACTIONS

[UNIFORM DUTIES TO DISABLED PERSONS]

§ 2305.40 Immunity of owner, lessee or renter of real property as to self-defense or defense of others.

(A) As used in this section:

(1) "Firearm" has the same meaning as in section 2923.11 of the Revised Code.

(2) "Tort action" means a civil action for damages for injury, death, or loss to person or property other than a civil action for damages for a breach of contract or another agreement between persons.

(3) "Vehicle" has the same meaning as in section 4501.01 of the Revised Code.

(B)(1) The owner, lessee, or renter of real property or a member of the owner's, lessee's, or renter's family who resides on the property is not liable in damages to a trespasser on the property, to a member of the family of the trespasser, or to any other person in a tort action for injury, death, or loss to person or property of the trespasser that allegedly is caused by the owner, lessee, renter, or family member if, at the time the injury, death, or loss to person or property allegedly is caused, all of the following apply:

(a) The owner, lessee, renter, or family member is inside a building or other structure on the property that is maintained as a permanent or temporary dwelling;

(b) The trespasser has made, is making, or is attempting to make an unlawful entry into the building or other structure described in division (B)(1)(a) of this section;

(c) The owner, lessee, renter, or family member uses reasonably necessary force to repel the trespasser from the building or other structure described in division (B)(1)(a) of this section or to prevent the trespasser from making the unlawful entry into that building or other structure.

(2) For purposes of the immunity created by division (B)(1) of this section, reasonably necessary force to repel a trespasser from a building or other structure that is maintained as a permanent or temporary dwelling or to prevent a trespasser from making an unlawful entry into a building or other structure of that nature may include the taking of or attempting to take the trespasser's life, or causing or attempting to cause physical harm or serious physical harm to the person of the trespasser, if the owner, lessee, or renter of real property or a member of the owner's, lessee's, or renter's family who resides on the property has a reasonable good faith belief that the owner, lessee, or renter or a member of the owner's, lessee's, or renter's family is in imminent danger of death or serious physical harm to person and that the only means to escape from the imminent danger is to use deadly force or other force that likely will cause physical harm or serious physical harm to the person of the trespasser, even if the owner, lessee, renter, or family member is mistaken as to the existence or imminence of the danger of death or serious physical harm to person.

(3) In order to qualify for the immunity created by division (B)(1) of this section, an owner, lessee, or renter of real property or a member of the owner's, lessee's, or renter's family who resides on the property is not required to retreat from a building or other structure that is maintained as a permanent or temporary dwelling prior to using reasonably necessary force to repel a trespasser from the building or other structure or to prevent a trespasser from making an unlawful entry into the building or other structure.

(C) The owner, lessee, or renter of real property or a member of the owner's, lessee's, or renter's family who resides on the property is not liable in damages to a trespasser on the property, to a member of the family of the trespasser, or to any other person in a tort action for injury, death, or loss to person or property of the trespasser that allegedly is caused by the owner, lessee, renter, or family member under circumstances not covered by division (B)(1) of this section if, at the time the injury, death, or loss to person or property allegedly is caused, none of the following applies:

(1) The injury, death, or loss to person or property

is caused by a physical assault of the owner, lessee, renter, or family member upon the trespasser other than in self-defense or defense of a third person.

(2) Self-defense or defense of a third person is not involved, and the injury, death, or loss to person or property is caused by a vehicle driven or otherwise set in motion, a firearm shot, or any other item of tangible personal property held, driven, set in motion, projected, or thrown by the owner, lessee, renter, or family member with the intent to cause injury, death, or loss to person or property of the trespasser or with the intent to cause the trespasser to believe that the owner, lessee, renter, or family member would cause injury, death, or loss to person or property of the trespasser.

(3) Under circumstances not described in division (C)(1) or (2) of this section, self-defense or defense of a third person is not involved, and the owner, lessee, renter, or family member intends to create a risk of injury, death, or loss to person or property of any trespasser by direct or indirect means, including, but not limited to, the use of spring guns, traps, or other dangerous instrumentalities.

(D)(1) This section does not create a new cause of action or substantive legal right against the owner, lessee, or renter of real property or a member of the owner's, lessee's, or renter's family who resides on the property.

(2) This section does not affect any civil liability under another section of the Revised Code or the common law of this state of an owner, lessee, or renter of real property or a member of the owner's, lessee's, or renter's family who resides on the property with respect to individuals other than trespassers, including, but not limited to, civil liability to invitees or licensees.

(3) This section does not affect any immunities from or defenses to civil liability established by another section of the Revised Code or available at common law to which the owner, lessee, or renter of real property or a member of the owner's, lessee's, or renter's family who resides on the property may be entitled with respect to individuals other than trespassers, including, but not limited to, immunities from or defenses to civil liability to invitees or licensees.

(4) This section does not affect any criminal liability that the owner, lessee, or renter of real property or a member of the owner's, lessee's, or renter's family who resides on the property may have for injury, death, or loss to person or property of a trespasser, invitee, or licensee on the property.

(5) This section does not affect any immunities or defenses to civil liability established by another section of the Revised Code or available at common law to which an individual other than the owner, lessee, or renter of real property or a member of the owner's, lessee's, or renter's family who resides on the property may be entitled in connection with injury, death, or loss to person or property of a trespasser on real property owned, leased, or rented by another person, including, but not limited to, self-defense or defense of third persons.

HISTORY: 146 v H 447. Eff 3-18-97.

The provisions of § 2 of HB 447 (146 v —) read as follows:

SECTION 2. The immunities from tort liability that are contained in section 2305.40 of the Revised Code, as enacted by this act, shall apply only to causes of action for injury, death, or loss to person or property allegedly caused to a trespasser on or after the effective date of this act by the owner, lessee, or renter of real property or a member of the owner's, lessee's, or renter's family who resides on the property. With respect to causes of action for injury, death, or loss to person or property allegedly caused to a trespasser prior to the effective date of this act by the owner, lessee, or renter of real property or a member of the owner's, lessee's, or renter's family who resides on the property, the liability or immunity from liability of, and any defenses available to, the owner, lessee, renter, or family member shall be determined as if this act had not been enacted.

§ 2305.41 Definitions.

As used in sections 2305.41 to 2305.49 of the Revised Code:

(A) "Disabled condition" means the condition of being unconscious, semiconscious, incoherent, or otherwise incapacitated to communicate.

(B) "Disabled person" means a person in a disabled condition.

(C) "Emergency symbol" means the caduceus inscribed within a six-barred cross used by the American medical association to denote emergency information.

(D) "Identifying device" means an identifying bracelet, necklace, metal tag, or similar device bearing the emergency symbol and the information needed in an emergency.

(E) "Identification card" means any card containing the holder's name, type of medical condition, physician's name, and other medical information. "Identification card" does not include any license or permit issued pursuant to Chapter 4507. of the Revised Code.

(F) "Medical practitioner" means an individual who holds a current valid certificate issued under Chapter 4731. of the Revised Code authorizing the practice of medicine and surgery or osteopathic medicine and surgery.

(G) "Paramedic" has the meaning given in section 4765.01 of the Revised Code.

HISTORY: 136 v H 1217 (Eff 9-30-76); 144 v S 98. Eff 11-12-92.

§ 2305.42 Disabled person to wear identifying device.

(A) A person who suffers from epilepsy, diabetes, a cardiac condition, or any other type of illness that causes temporary blackouts, semiconscious periods, or complete unconsciousness, or who suffers from a condition requiring specific medication or medical treatment, is allergic to certain medications or items used in medical treatment, wears contact lenses, has religious objections to certain forms of medication or medical treatment, or is unable to communicate coherently or effectively in the English language, is authorized and encouraged to wear an identifying device.

(B) any person may carry an identification card.

(C) By wearing an identifying device a person gives his consent for any law enforcement officer or medical practitioner who finds him in a disabled condition to make a reasonable search of his clothing or other effects for an identification card.

HISTORY: 136 v H 1217. Eff 9-30-76.

§ 2305.43 Law enforcement officer's duties to disabled person.

(A) A law enforcement officer shall make a diligent effort to determine whether any disabled person he finds is an epileptic or a diabetic, or suffers from some other type of illness that would cause the condition. Whenever feasible, this effort shall be made before the person is charged with a crime or taken to a place of detention.

(B) In seeking to determine whether a disabled person suffers from an illness, a law enforcement officer may make a reasonable search for an identifying device and an identification card and examine them for emergency information. The law enforcement officer may not search for an identifying device or an identification card in a manner or to an extent that would appear to a reasonable person in the circumstances to cause an unreasonable risk of worsening the disabled person's condition.

(C) A law enforcement officer who finds a disabled person without an identifying device of identification card is not relieved of his duty to that person to make a diligent effort to ascertain the existence of any illness causing the disabled condition.

(D) A cause of action against a law enforcement officer does not arise from his making a reasonable search of the disabled person to locate an identifying device or identification card, even though the person is not wearing an identifying device or carrying an identification card.

(E) A law enforcement officer who determines or has reason to believe that a disabled person is suffering from an illness causing his condition shall promptly notify the person's physician, if practicable. If the officer is unable to ascertain the physician's identity or to communicate with him, the officer shall make a reasonable effort to cause the disabled person to be transported immediately to a medical practitioner or to a facility where medical treatment is available. If the officer believes it unduly dangerous to move the disabled person, he shall make a reasonable effort to obtain the assistance of a medical practitioner.

HISTORY: 136 v H 1217. Eff 9-30-76.

§ 2305.44 Medical practitioner's duty re search for device.

(A) A medical practitioner or a trained paramedic, in discharging his duty to a disabled person whom he has undertaken to examine or treat, shall make a reasonable search for an identifying device or identification card and examine them for emergency information.

(B) A cause of action against a medical practitioner or a trained paramedic does not arise from his making a reasonable search of a disabled person to locate an identifying device or identification card, even though the person is not wearing an identifying device or carrying an identification card.

HISTORY: 136 v H 1217. Eff 9-30-76.

§ 2305.45 Search by unauthorized person.

(A) A person, other than a law enforcement officer, medical practitioner, or a trained paramedic, who finds a disabled person shall make a reasonable effort to notify a law enforcement officer or medical practitioner. If a law enforcement officer or medical practitioner is not present, a person who finds a disabled person may:

(1) Make a reasonable search for an identifying device;

(2) If the identifying device is found, make a reasonable search for an identification card.

If a device or card is located, the person making the search shall attempt promptly to bring its contents to the attention of a law enforcement officer or medical practitioner.

(B) A cause of action does not arise from a reasonable search to locate an identifying device or identification card as authorized by division (A) of this section.

HISTORY: 136 v H 1217. Eff 9-30-76.

§ 2305.46 False identification prohibited.

(A) No person, with purpose to deceive, shall provide, wear, use, or possess a false identifying device or identification card.

(B) Whoever violates division (A) of this section is guilty of a misdemeanor of the third degree.

HISTORY: 136 v H 1217. Eff 9-30-76.

§ 2305.47 Duties.

The duties imposed by sections 2305.41 to 2305.49 of the Revised Code are in addition to, and not in limitation of, other duties existing under the law of this state.

HISTORY: 136 v H 1217. Eff 9-30-76.

§ 2305.48 Construction.

Sections 2305.41 to 2305.49 of the Revised Code shall be so applied and construed as to effectuate its [their] general purpose to make uniform among the

states the law with respect to duties to disabled persons.
HISTORY: 136 v H 1217. Eff 9-30-76.

§ 2305.49 Cite of uniform act.

Sections 2305.41 to 2305.49 of the Revised Code may be cited as the "uniform duties to disabled persons act."

HISTORY: 136 v H 1217. Eff 9-30-76.

CHAPTER 2307: CIVIL ACTIONS

§ 2307.51 Civil liability for performing or attempting dilation and extraction procedure.

(A) As used in this section:
(1) "Dilation and extraction procedure" has the same meaning as in section 2919.15 of the Revised Code.
(2) "Frivolous conduct" has the same meaning as in section 2323.51 of the Revised Code.
(B)(1) A woman upon whom a dilation and extraction procedure is performed in violation of division (B) of section 2919.15 of the Revised Code has and may commence a civil action for compensatory damages, punitive or exemplary damages if authorized by section 2315.21 of the Revised Code, and court costs and reasonable attorney's fees against the person who performed the dilation and extraction procedure.
(2) A woman upon whom a dilation and extraction procedure is attempted in violation of division (B) of section 2919.15 of the Revised Code has and may commence a civil action for compensatory damages, punitive or exemplary damages if authorized by section 2315.21 of the Revised Code, and court costs and reasonable attorneys† fees against the person who attempted to perform the dilation and extraction procedure.
(C) It is an affirmative defense in a civil action commenced pursuant to division (B)(1) or (2) of this section that all other available abortion procedures would pose a greater risk to the health of the woman upon whom the dilation and extraction procedure was performed or attempted to be performed than the risk posed by the dilation and extraction procedure that was performed or attempted to be performed.
(D) If a judgment is rendered in favor of the defendant in a civil action commenced pursuant to division (B)(1) or (2) of this section and the court finds, upon the filing of a motion under section 2323.51 of the Revised Code, that the commencement of the civil action constitutes frivolous conduct and that the defendant was adversely affected by the frivolous conduct, the court shall award in accordance with section 2323.51 of the Revised Code reasonable attorney's fees to the defendant.

HISTORY: 146 v H 135. Eff 11-15-95.

See provisions, § 3 of HB 135 (146 v —) following RC § 2305.11.

† So in enrolled bill.

§ 2307.52 Civil liability for terminating or attempting termination of pregnancy after viability.

(A) As used in this section:
(1) "Frivolous conduct" has the same meaning as in section 2323.51 of the Revised Code.
(2) "Viable" has the same meaning as in section 2919.16 of the Revised Code.
(B)(1) A woman upon whom an abortion is purposely performed or induced or attempted to be performed or induced in violation of division (A) of section 2919.17 of the Revised Code has and may commence a civil action for compensatory damages, punitive or exemplary damages if authorized by section 2315.21 of the Revised Code, and court costs and reasonable attorney's fees against the person who purposely performed or induced or attempted to perform or induce the abortion in violation of division (A) of section 2919.17 of the Revised Code.
(2) A woman upon whom an abortion is purposely performed or induced or attempted to be performed or induced in violation of division (B) of section 2919.17 of the Revised Code has and may commence a civil action for compensatory damages, punitive or exemplary damages if authorized by section 2315.21 of the Revised Code, and court costs and reasonable attorney's fees against the person who purposely performed or induced or attempted to perform or induce the abortion in violation of division (B) of section 2919.17 of the Revised Code.
(C) If a judgment is rendered in favor of the defendant in a civil action commenced pursuant to division (B)(1) or (2) of this section and the court finds, upon the filing of a motion under section 2323.51 of the Revised Code, that the commencement of the civil action constitutes frivolous conduct and that the defendant was adversely affected by the frivolous conduct, the court shall award in accordance with section 2323.51 of the Revised Code reasonable attorney's fees to the defendant.

HISTORY: 146 v H 135. Eff 11-15-95.

§ 2307.62 Action by cable television owner or operator to recover damages.

(A) As used in this section:
(1) "Trier of fact" means the jury or, in a nonjury trial, the court.

(2) "Profits" derived from a violation of division (A) or (B) of section 2913.041 [2913.04.1] of the Revised Code are equal to whichever of the following applies:

(a) The gross revenue derived from the violation by the persons who violated division (A) or (B) of section 2913.041 [2913.04.1] of the Revised Code, as established by a preponderance of the evidence by the owner or operator of the cable television system or other similar closed circuit coaxial cable communications system who is aggrieved by the violation;

(b) The gross revenue derived from the violation by the persons who violated division (A) or (B) of section 2913.041 [2913.04.1] of the Revised Code, as established by a preponderance of the evidence by the owner or operator of the cable television system or other similar closed circuit coaxial cable communications system who is aggrieved by the violation, minus deductible expenses and other elements of profit that are not attributable to the violation of division (A) or (B) of section 2913.041 [2913.04.1] of the Revised Code, as established by a preponderance of the evidence by the persons who violated either or both of those divisions.

(B)(1) An owner or operator of a cable television system or other similar closed circuit coaxial cable communications system who is aggrieved by conduct that is prohibited by division (A) or (B) of section 2913.041 [2913.04.1] of the Revised Code may elect to commence a civil action for damages in accordance with section 2307.60 or 2307.61 of the Revised Code or to commence a civil action under this section in the appropriate municipal court, county court, or court of common pleas to recover damages and other specified moneys described in division (B)(1)(a), (b), or (c) of this section and, if applicable, damages described in division (B)(2) of this section from the persons who violated division (A) or (B) of section 2913.041 [2913.04.1] of the Revised Code. If the owner or operator elects to commence a civil action for damages and other specified moneys under this section, the owner or operator shall specify in its complaint which of the following categories of damages and other specified moneys the owner or operator seeks to recover from the persons who violated division (A) or (B) of section 2913.041 [2913.04.1] of the Revised Code:

(a) Full compensatory damages, punitive or exemplary damages if authorized by section 2315.21 of the Revised Code, and the reasonable attorney's fees, court costs, and other reasonable expenses incurred in maintaining the civil action under this section.

(b) Damages equal to the actual loss suffered by the owner or operator as a proximate result of the conduct that violated division (A) or (B) of section 2913.041 [2913.04.1] of the Revised Code and, in addition, damages equal to the profits derived by the persons who violated either or both of those divisions as a proximate result of the prohibited conduct.

(c) Liquidated damages in an amount of not less than two hundred fifty dollars and not more than ten thousand dollars, as determined by the trier of fact, for each separate violation of division (A) or (B) of section 2913.041 [2913.04.1] of the Revised Code as described in division (D) of that section.

(2) The trier of fact shall determine the amount of any compensatory damages to be awarded pursuant to division (B)(1)(a) of this section, and the court shall determine the amount of any punitive or exemplary damages authorized by section 2315.21 of the Revised Code and the amount of reasonable attorney's fees, court costs, and other reasonable expenses to be awarded pursuant to division (B)(1)(a) of this section. The trier of fact shall determine the amount of damages to be awarded to the owner or operator under division (B)(1)(b) of this section.

(3) In a civil action under this section, if an owner or operator of a cable television system or other similar closed circuit coaxial cable communications system establishes by a preponderance of the evidence that the persons who violated division (A) or (B) of section 2913.041 [2913.04.1] of the Revised Code engaged in the prohibited conduct for the purpose of direct or indirect commercial advantage or private financial gain, the trier of fact may award to the owner or operator damages in an amount not to exceed fifty thousand dollars in addition to any amount recovered pursuant to division (B)(1)(a), (b), or (c) of this section, whichever of those divisions applies to the owner or operator.

(C) A person may join a civil action under this section with a civil action under Chapter 2737. of the Revised Code to recover any property of the owner or operator of a cable television system or other similar closed circuit coaxial cable communications system that was the subject of the violation of division (A) or (B) of section 2913.041 [2913.04.1] of the Revised Code. A person may commence a civil action under this section regardless of whether any person who allegedly violated either or both of those divisions has pleaded guilty to or has been convicted of a violation of either or both of those divisions or has been adjudicated a delinquent child for the commission of any act that constitutes a violation of either or both of those divisions.

HISTORY: 146 v S 2. Eff 7-1-96.

The effective date is set by section 6 of SB 2.

CHAPTER 2313: COMMISSIONERS OF JURORS

§ 2313.41 Array may be set aside.

A challenge to the array may be made and the whole array set aside by the court when the jury, grand or petit, was not selected, drawn, or summoned, or when the officer who executed the venire did not proceed as prescribed by law. No challenge to the array shall be made or the whole array set aside by the court, by reason of the misnomer of a juror; but on challenge, a juror may be set aside by reason of a misnomer in his name; but such challenge shall only be made before the jury is impaneled and sworn, and no indictment shall be quashed or verdict set aside for any such irregularity or misnomer if the jurors who formed the same possessed the requisite qualifications to act as jurors.

HISTORY: GC § 11419-50; 114 v 193(207); Bureau of Code Revision. Eff 10-1-53.

§ 2313.42 Causes for challenge of persons called as jurors; examination under oath.

Any person called as a juror for the trial of any cause shall be examined under oath or upon affirmation as to his qualifications. A person is qualified to serve as a juror if he is an elector of the county and has been certified by the board of elections pursuant to section 2313.06 of the Revised Code. A person also is qualified to serve as a juror if he is eighteen years of age or older, is a resident of the county, would be an elector if he were registered to vote, regardless of whether he actually is registered to vote, and has been certified by the registrar of motor vehicles pursuant to section 2313.06 of the Revised Code or otherwise as having a valid and current driver's or commercial driver's license.

The following are good causes for challenge to any person called as a juror:

(A) That he has been convicted of a crime which by law renders him disqualified to serve on a jury;

(B) That he has an interest in the cause;

(C) That he has an action pending between him and either party;

(D) That he formerly was a juror in the same cause;

(E) That he is the employer, the employee, or the spouse, parent, son, or daughter of the employer or employee, counselor, agent, steward, or attorney of either party;

(F) That he is subpoenaed in good faith as a witness in the cause;

(G) That he is akin by consanguinity or affinity within the fourth degree, to either party, or to the attorney of either party;

(H) That he or his spouse, parent, son, or daughter is a party to another action then pending in any court in which an attorney in the cause then on trial is an attorney, either for or against him;

(I) That he, not being a regular juror of the term, has already served as a talesman in the trial of any cause, in any court of record in the county within the preceding twelve months;

(J) That he discloses by his answers that he cannot be a fair and impartial juror or will not follow the law as given to him by the court.

Each challenge listed in this section shall be considered as a principal challenge, and its validity tried by the court.

HISTORY: GC § 11419-51; 114 v 193(207); 117 v 72; Bureau of Code Revision, 10-1-53; 127 v 419 (Eff 9-9-57); 133 v H 104 (Eff 9-12-69); 140 v H 183 (Eff 10-1-84); 143 v H 381. Eff 7-1-89.

§ 2313.43 Challenge of petit juror.

In addition to the causes listed under section 2313.42 of the Revised Code, any petit juror may be challenged on suspicion of prejudice against or partiality for either party, or for want of a competent knowledge of the English language, or other cause that may render him at the time an unsuitable juror. The validity of such challenge shall be determined by the court and be sustained if the court has any doubt as to the juror's being entirely unbiased.

HISTORY: GC § 11419-52; 114 v 193(208); Bureau of Code Revision. Eff 10-1-53.

CHAPTER 2317: EVIDENCE

§ 2317.01 Competent witnesses.

All persons are competent witnesses except those of unsound mind and children under ten years of age who appear incapable of receiving just impressions of the facts and transactions respecting which they are examined, or of relating them truly.

In a hearing in an abuse, neglect, or dependency case, any examination made by the court to determine whether a child is a competent witness shall be conducted by the court in an office or room other than a courtroom or hearing room, shall be conducted in the presence of only those individuals considered necessary by the court for the conduct of the examination or the well-being of the child, and shall be conducted with a court reporter present. The court may allow the prosecutor, guardian ad litem, or attorney for any party to submit questions for use by the court in determining whether the child is a competent witness.

HISTORY: RS § 5240; S&C 1035; 51 v 57, § 310; 67 v 113, § 314; GC § 11493; Bureau of Code Revision, 10-1-53; 142 v S 89. Eff 1-1-89.

§ 2317.02 Privileged communications.

The following persons shall not testify in certain respects:

(A) An attorney, concerning a communication made †the attorney by a †the attorney's client in that relation or the attorney's advice to †the a client, except that the attorney may testify by express consent of the client or, if the client is deceased, by the express consent of the surviving spouse or the executor or administrator of the estate of the deceased client and except that, if the client voluntarily testifies or is deemed by section 2151.421 [2151.42.1] of the Revised Code to have waived any testimonial privilege under this division, the attorney may be compelled to testify on the same subject;

(B)(1) A physician or a dentist concerning a communication made †the physician or dentist by a †the physician's or dentist's patient in that relation or the physician's or dentist's advice to †the a patient, except as otherwise provided in this division, division (B)(2), and division (B)(3) of this section, and except that, if the patient is deemed by section 2151.421 [2151.42.1] of the Revised Code to have waived any testimonial privilege under this division, the physician may be compelled to testify on the same subject.

The testimonial privilege under this division does not apply, and a physician or dentist may testify or may be compelled to testify in any of the following circumstances:

(a) In any civil action, in accordance with the discovery provisions of the Rules of Civil Procedure in connection with a civil action, or in connection with a claim under Chapter 4123. of the Revised Code, under any of the following circumstances:

(i) If the patient or the guardian or other legal representative of the patient gives express consent;

(ii) If the patient is deceased, the spouse of the patient or the executor or administrator of the patient's estate gives express consent;

(iii) If a medical claim, dental claim, chiropractic claim, or optometric claim, as defined in section 2305.11 of the Revised Code, an action for wrongful death, any other type of civil action, or a claim under Chapter 4123. of the Revised Code is filed by the patient, the personal representative of the estate of the patient if deceased, or the patient's guardian or other legal representative.

(b) In any criminal action concerning any test or the results of any test that determines the presence or concentration of alcohol, a drug of abuse, or alcohol and a drug of abuse in the patient's blood, breath, urine, or other bodily substance at any time relevant to the criminal offense in question.

(2)(a) If any law enforcement officer submits a written statement to a health care provider that states that an official criminal investigation has begun regarding a specified person or that a criminal action or proceeding has been commenced against a specified person, that requests the provider to supply to the officer copies of any records the provider possesses that pertain to any test or the results of any test administered to the specified person to determine the presence or concentration of alcohol, a drug of abuse, or alcohol and a drug of abuse in the person's blood, breath, or urine at any time relevant to the criminal offense in question, and that conforms to section 2317.022 [2317.02.2] of the Revised Code, the provider, except to the extent specifically prohibited by any law of this state or of the United States, shall supply to the officer a copy of any of the requested records the provider possesses. If the health care provider does not possess any of the requested records, the provider shall give the officer a written statement that indicates that the provider does not possess any of the requested records.

(b) If a health care provider possesses any records of the type described in division (B)(2)(a) of this section regarding the person in question at any time relevant to the criminal offense in question, in lieu of personally testifying as to the results of the test in question, the custodian of the records may submit a certified copy of the records, and, upon its submission, the certified copy is qualified as authentic evidence and may be admitted as evidence in accordance with the Rules of Evidence. Division (A) of section 2317.422 [2317.42.2] of the Revised Code does not apply to any certified copy of records submitted in accordance with this division. Nothing in this division shall be construed to limit the right of any party to call as a witness the person who administered the test to which the records pertain, the person under whose supervision the test was administered, the custodian of the records, the person who made the records, or the person under whose supervision the records were made.

(3)(a) If the testimonial privilege described in division (B)(1) of this section does not apply as provided in division (B)(1)(a)(iii) of this section, a physician or dentist may be compelled to testify or to submit to discovery under the Rules of Civil Procedure only as to a communication made †the physician or dentist by the patient in question in that relation, or the physician's or dentist's advice to the patient in question, that related causally or historically to physical or mental injuries that are relevant to issues in the medical claim, dental claim, chiropractic claim, or optometric claim, action for wrongful death, other civil action, or claim under Chapter 4123. of the Revised Code.

(b) If the testimonial privilege described in division (B)(1) of this section does not apply to a physician or dentist as provided in division (B)(1)(b) of this section, the physician or dentist, in lieu of personally testifying as to the results of the test in question, may submit a certified copy of those results, and, upon its submission, the certified copy is qualified as authentic evidence and may be admitted as evidence in accordance with the Rules of Evidence. Division (A) of section 2317.422 [2317.42.2] of the Revised Code does not apply to any certified copy of results submitted in accordance with this division. Nothing in this division shall be construed to limit the right of any party to call as a witness the person who administered the test in question, the person under whose supervision the test was administered, the custodian of the results of the test, the person who compiled the results, or the person under whose supervision the results were compiled.

(4)(a) As used in divisions (B)(1) to (3) of this section, "communication" means acquiring, recording, or transmitting any information, in any manner, concerning any facts, opinions, or statements necessary to enable a physician or dentist to diagnose, treat, prescribe, or act for a patient. A "communication" may include, but is not limited to, any medical or dental, office, or hospital communication such as a record, chart, letter, memorandum, laboratory test and results, x-ray, photograph, financial statement, diagnosis, or prognosis.

(b) As used in division (B)(2) of this section, "health care provider" has the same meaning as in section 3729.01 of the Revised Code.

(5) Divisions (B)(1), (2), (3), and (4) of this section apply to doctors of medicine, doctors of osteopathic medicine, doctors of podiatry, and dentists.

(6) Nothing in divisions (B)(1) to (5) of this section affects, or shall be construed as affecting, the immunity from civil liability conferred by section 2305.33 of the Revised Code upon physicians who report an employee's use of a drug of abuse, or a condition of an employee other than one involving the use of a drug of abuse, to the employer of the employee in accordance with division (B) of that section. As used in this division, "employee," "employer," and "physician" have the same meanings as in section 2305.33 of the Revised Code.

(C) A member of the clergy, rabbi, priest, or regularly ordained, accredited, or licensed minister of an established and legally cognizable church, denomination, or sect, when the cleric, rabbi, priest, or minister remains accountable to the authority of that church, denomination, or sect, concerning a confession made, or any information confidentially communicated, †the clergyman, rabbi, priest, or minister for a religious counseling purpose in †the clergyman's, rabbi's, priest's, or minister's professional character; however, the cleric, rabbi, priest, or minister may testify by express consent of the person making the communication, except when the disclosure of the information is in violation of a †the clergyman's, rabbi's, priest's, or minister's sacred trust.

(D) Husband or wife, concerning any communication made by one to the other, or an act done by either in the presence of the other, during coverture, unless the communication was made, or act done, in the known presence or hearing of a third person competent to be a witness; and such rule is the same if the marital relation has ceased to exist.

(E) A person who assigns a claim or interest, concerning any matter in respect to which the person would not, if a party, be permitted to testify;

(F) A person who, if a party, would be restricted under section 2317.03 of the Revised Code, when the property or thing is sold or transferred by an executor, administrator, guardian, trustee, heir, devisee, or legatee, shall be restricted in the same manner in any action or proceeding concerning the property or thing.

(G)(1) A school guidance counselor who holds a valid educator's license from the state board of education as provided for in section 3319.22 of the Revised Code, a person licensed under Chapter 4757. of the Revised Code as a professional clinical counselor, professional counselor, social worker, or independent social worker, or registered under Chapter 4757. of the Revised Code as a social work assistant concerning a confidential communication such person received from a †such person's client in that relation or the such† person's advice to a the† client unless any of the following applies:

(a) The communication or advice indicates clear and present danger to the client or other persons. For the purposes of this division, cases in which there are indications of present or past child abuse or neglect of the client constitute a clear and present danger.

(b) The client gives express consent to the testimony.

(c) If the client is deceased, the surviving spouse or the executor or administrator of the estate of the deceased client gives express consent.

(d) The client voluntarily testifies, in which case the school guidance counselor or person licensed or registered under Chapter 4757. of the Revised Code may be compelled to testify on the same subject.

(e) The court in camera determines that the information communicated by the client is not germane to the counselor-client or social worker-client relationship.

(f) A court, in an action brought against a school, its administration, or any of its personnel by the client, rules after an in-camera inspection that the testimony of the school guidance counselor is relevant to that action.

(2) Nothing in division (G)(1) of this section shall relieve a school guidance counselor or a person licensed or registered under Chapter 4757. of the Revised Code from the requirement to report information concerning child abuse or neglect under section 2151.421 [2151.42.1] of the Revised Code.

(H) A mediator acting under a mediation order issued under division (A) of section 3109.052 [3109.05.2] of the Revised Code or otherwise issued in any proceeding for divorce, dissolution, legal separation, annulment, or the allocation of parental rights and responsibilities for the care of children, in any action or proceeding, other than a criminal, delinquency, child abuse, child neglect, or dependent child action or proceeding, that is brought by or against either parent who takes part in mediation in accordance with the order and that pertains to the mediation process, to any information discussed or presented in the mediation process, to the allocation of parental rights and responsibilities for the care of the parents' children, or to the awarding of visitation rights in relation to their children.

(I) A communications assistant, acting within the scope of †the that assistant's authority, when providing telecommunications relay service pursuant to section 4931.35 of the Revised Code or Title II of the "Communications Act of 1934," 104 Stat. 366 (1990), 47 U.S.C. 225, concerning a communication made through a telecommunications relay service.

Nothing in this section shall limit any immunity or privilege granted under federal law or regulation. Nothing in this section shall limit the obligation of a communications assistant to divulge information or testify when mandated by federal law or regulation or pursuant to subpoena in a criminal proceeding.

HISTORY: RS § 5241; S&S 558; S&C 1038; 51 v 57, § 315; 67

v 113, § 314; GC § 11494; Bureau of Code Revision, 10-1-53; 125 v 313 (Eff 10-13-53); 136 v H 682 (Eff 7-28-75); 136 v H 1426 (Eff 7-1-76); 138 v H 284 (Eff 10-22-80); 140 v H 205 (Eff 10-10-84); 141 v H 528 (Eff 7-9-86); 141 v H 529 (Eff 3-11-87); 142 v H 1 (Eff 1-5-88); 143 v S 2 (Eff 11-1-89); 143 v H 615 (Eff 3-27-91); 143 v S 3 (Eff 4-11-91); 144 v S 343 (Eff 3-24-93); 145 v S 121 (Eff 10-29-93); 145 v H 335 (Eff 12-9-94); 146 v S 230 (Eff 10-29-96); 146 v S 223. Eff 3-18-97.

Publisher's Note

The amendments made by SB 230 (146 v —) and SB 223 (146 v —) have been combined. Please see provisions of RC § 1.52.

† The wording is the result of combining SB 230 (146 v —) and SB 223 (146 v —).

[§ 2317.02.1] § 2317.021 "Client" defined; application of attorney-client privilege to dissolved corporation or association.

As used in division (A) of section 2317.02 of the Revised Code:

"Client" means a person, firm, partnership, corporation, or other association that, directly or through any representative, consults an attorney for the purpose of retaining the attorney or securing legal service or advice from him in his professional capacity, or consults an attorney employee for legal service or advice, and who communicates, either directly or through an agent, employee, or other representative, with such attorney; and includes an incompetent whose guardian so consults the attorney in behalf of the incompetent.

Where a corporation or association is a client having the privilege and it has been dissolved, the privilege shall extend to the last board of directors, their successors or assigns, or to the trustees, their successors or assigns.

This section shall be construed as in addition to, and not in limitation of, other laws affording protection to communications under the attorney-client privilege.

HISTORY: 130 v 649. Eff 10-14-63.

[§ 2317.02.2] § 2317.022 Request to health care provider for results of alcohol or drug tests for use in criminal proceedings.

(A) As used in this section, "health care provider" has the same meaning as in section 3729.01 of the Revised Code.

(B) If an official criminal investigation has begun regarding a person or if a criminal action or proceeding is commenced against a person, any law enforcement officer who wishes to obtain from any health care provider a copy of any records the provider possesses that pertain to any test or the results of any test administered to the person to determine the presence or concentration of alcohol, a drug of abuse, or alcohol and a drug of abuse in the person's blood, breath, or urine at any time relevant to the criminal offense in question shall submit to the health care facility a written statement in the following form:

"WRITTEN STATEMENT REQUESTING THE RELEASE OF RECORDS

To: . . . . (insert the name of the health care provider in question).

I hereby state that an official criminal investigation has begun regarding, or a criminal action or proceeding has been commenced against, ... (insert the name of the person in question), and that I believe that one or more tests has been administered to him by this health care provider to determine the presence or concentration of alcohol, a drug of abuse, or alcohol and a drug of abuse in his blood, breath, or urine at a time relevant to the criminal offense in question. Therefore, I hereby request that, pursuant to division (B)(2) of section 2317.02 of the Revised Code, this health care provider supply me with copies of any records the provider possesses that pertain to any test or the results of any test administered to the person specified above to determine the presence or concentration of alcohol, a drug of abuse, or alcohol and a drug of abuse in his blood, breath, or urine at any time relevant to the criminal offense in question.

. . . .
(Name of officer)
. . . .
(Officer's title)
. . . .
(Officer's employing agency)
. . . .
(Officer's telephone number)
. . . .
. . . .
. . . .
(Agency's address)
. . . .
(Date written statement submitted)"

(C) A health care provider that receives a written statement of the type described in division (B) of this section shall comply with division (B)(2) of section 2317.02 of the Revised Code relative to the written statement.

HISTORY: 145 v H 335. Eff 12-9-94.

[§ 2317.02.3] § 2317.023 Disclosure of mediation communication.

(A) As used in this section:

(1) "Mediation" means a nonbinding process for the resolution of a dispute in which both of the following apply:

(a) A person who is not a party to the dispute serves as mediator to assist the parties to the dispute in negotiating contested issues.

(b) A court, administrative agency, not-for-profit community mediation provider, or other public body appoints the mediator or refers the dispute to the mediator, or the parties, engage the mediator.

(2) "Mediation communication" means a communication made in the course of and relating to the subject matter of a mediation.

(B) A mediation communication is confidential. Except as provided in division (C) of this section, no person shall disclose a mediation communication in a civil proceeding or in an administrative proceeding.

(C) Division (B) of this section does not apply in the following circumstances:

(1) Except as provided in division (H) of section 2317.02 and division (C) of section 3109.052 [3109.05.2] of the Revised Code, to the disclosure by any person of a mediation communication made by a mediator if all parties to the mediation and the mediator consent to the disclosure;

(2) To the disclosure by a person other than the mediator of a mediation communication made by a person other than the mediator if all parties consent to the disclosure;

(3) To the disclosure of a mediation communication if disclosure is required pursuant to section 2921.22 of the Revised Code;

(4) To the disclosure of a mediation communication if a court, after a hearing, determines that the disclosure does not circumvent Evidence Rule 408, that the disclosure is necessary in the particular case to prevent a manifest injustice, and that the necessity for disclosure is of sufficient magnitude to outweigh the importance of protecting the general requirement of confidentiality in mediation proceedings.

(D) This section does not prevent or inhibit the disclosure, discovery, or admission into evidence of a statement, document, or other matter that is a mediation communication but that, prior to its use in a mediation proceeding, was subject to discovery or admission under law or a rule of evidence or was subject to disclosure as a public record pursuant to section 149.43 of the Revised Code. This section does not affect the admissibility of a written settlement agreement signed by the parties to a mediation or the status of a written settlement agreement as a public record under section 149.43 of the Revised Code.

HISTORY: 146 v H 438 (Eff 7-1-97); 146 v H 350, § 14. Eff 1-27-97.

The provisions of § 14 of HB 350 (146 v —) read as follows:

SECTION 14. That Section 3 of Am. Sub. H.B. 438 of the 121st General Assembly be amended to read as follows:

"SECTION 3. Sections 1 and 2 of Am. Sub. H.B. 438 of the 121st General Assembly shall take effect on July 1, 1997, except that section 2317.023 of the Revised Code, as amended by Am. Sub. H.B. 438 of the 121st General Assembly, shall take effect on the effective date of Am. Sub. H.B. 350 [1-27-97] of the 121st General Assembly."

§ 2317.03 Cases in which a party shall not testify.

A party shall not testify when the adverse party is the guardian or trustee of either a deaf and dumb or an insane person or of a child of a deceased person, or is an executor or administrator, or claims or defends as heir, grantee, assignee, devisee, or legatee of a deceased person except:

(A) As to facts which occurred after the appointment of the guardian or trustee of an insane person, and, in the other cases, after the time the decedent, grantor, assignor, or testator died;

(B) When the action or proceeding relates to a contract made through an agent by a person since deceased, and the agent is competent to testify as a witness, a party may testify on the same subject;

(C) If a party, or one having a direct interest, testifies to transactions or conversations with another party, the latter may testify as to the same transactions or conversations;

(D) If a party offers evidence of conversations or admissions of the opposite party, the latter may testify concerning the same conversations or admissions; and, if evidence or declarations against interest made by an insane, incompetent, or deceased person has been admitted, then any oral or written declaration made by such insane, incompetent, or deceased person concerning the same subject to which any such admitted evidence relates, and which but for this provision would be excluded as self-serving, shall be admitted in evidence if it be proved to the satisfaction of the trial judge that the declaration was made at a time when the declarant was competent to testify, concerning a subject matter in issue, and, when no apparent motive to misrepresent appears;

(E) In an action or proceeding by or against a partner or joint contractor, the adverse party shall not testify to transactions with, or admissions by, a partner or joint contractor since deceased, unless they were made in the presence of the surviving partner or joint contractor, and this rule applies without regard to the character in which the parties sue or are sued;

(F) If the claim or defense is founded on a book account, a party may testify that the book is his account book, that it is a book of original entries, that the entries therein were made in the regular course of business by himself, a person since deceased, or a disinterested person, and the book is then competent evidence in any case, without regard to the parties, upon like proof by any competent witness;

(G) If after testifying orally, a party dies, the evidence may be proved by either party on a further trial of the case, whereupon the opposite party may testify to the same matters;

(H) If a party dies and his deposition is offered in evidence, the opposite party may testify as to all competent matters therein.

This section does not apply to actions for causing death, or actions or proceedings involving the validity of a deed, will or codicil. When a case is plainly within the reason and spirit of this section and sections 2317.01

and 2317.02 of the Revised Code, though not within the strict letter, their principles shall be applied.

HISTORY: RS § 5242; S&S 557; S&C 1037; 51 v 374; 74 v 161, § 313; 82 v 125; GC § 11495; 111 v 33; Bureau of Code Revision, 10-1-53; 126 v 39. Eff 10-4-55.

§ 2317.04 Impartial report of proceedings privileged.

The publication of a fair and impartial report of the proceedings before state or municipal legislative bodies, or before state or municipal executive bodies, boards, or officers, or the whole or a fair synopsis of any bill, ordinance, report, resolution, bulletin, notice, petition, or other document presented, filed, or issued in any proceeding before such legislative or executive body, board, or officer, shall be privileged, unless it is proved that such publication was made maliciously.

HISTORY: GC § 11343-1; 102 v 95; Bureau of Code Revision. Eff 10-1-53.

§ 2317.05 Impartial report of indictment, warrant, affidavit, or arrest privileged.

The publication of a fair and impartial report of the return of any indictment, the issuing of any warrant, the arrest of any person accused of crime, or the filing of any affidavit, pleading, or other document in any criminal or civil cause in any court of competent jurisdiction, or of a fair and impartial report of the contents thereof, is privileged, unless it is proved that the same was published maliciously, or that defendant has refused or neglected to publish in the same manner in which the publication complained of appeared, a reasonable written explanation or contradiction thereof by the plaintiff, or that the publisher has refused, upon request of the plaintiff, to publish the subsequent determination of such suit or action. This section and section 2317.04 of the Revised Code do not authorize the publication of blasphemous or indecent matter.

HISTORY: GC § 11343-2; 102 v 95; Bureau of Code Revision. Eff 10-1-53.

§ 2317.06 Proving testimony of absent witness.

(A) If a party or witness, after testifying orally, dies, is beyond the jurisdiction of the court, cannot be found after diligent search, is insane, because of any physical or mental infirmity is unable to testify, or has been summoned but appears to have been kept away by the adverse party and if the evidence of the party or witness has been taken down by an official stenographer, the evidence so taken may be read in evidence by either party on the further trial of the case and shall be prima-facie evidence of what the deceased party or witness testified to orally on the former trial. If the evidence has not been taken by an official stenographer, it may be proved by witnesses who were present at the former trial, having knowledge of the testimony. All testimony so offered shall be open to all objections that might be taken if the witness was personally present.

(B)(1) If it is necessary in a civil action before the court to procure the testimony of a person who is imprisoned in a workhouse, juvenile detention facility, jail, or state correctional institution within this state, or who is in the custody of the department of youth services, the court shall require that the person's testimony be taken by deposition pursuant to the Civil Rules at the place of the person's confinement, unless the court determines that the interests of justice demand that the person be brought before the court for the presentation of his testimony.

(2) If the court determines that the interests of justice demand that a person specified in division (B)(1) of this section be brought before the court for the presentation of his testimony, the court shall order the person to be brought before it under the procedures set forth in division (B) or (C) of section 2945.47 of the Revised Code.

(C) When a person's deposition is taken pursuant to division (B)(1) of this section, the person shall remain in the custody of the officer who is in charge of the person, and the officer shall provide reasonable facilities for the taking of the deposition.

(D) The person requesting the testimony of the person whose deposition is taken pursuant to division (B)(1) of this section shall pay the expense of taking the deposition, except that the court may tax the expense as court costs in appropriate cases.

HISTORY: RS § 5242a; 89 v 143; GC § 11496; Bureau of Code Revision, 10-1-53; 139 v H 145 (Eff 5-28-81); 139 v H 440 (Eff 11-23-81); 145 v H 571. Eff 10-6-94.

§ 2317.07 Examination of parties.

At the instance of the adverse party, a party may be examined as if under cross-examination, orally, by way of deposition, like any other witness, by way of written interrogatories filed in the action or proceeding, or by any one or more of such methods. The party calling for such examination shall not thereby be concluded but may rebut it by evidence.

HISTORY: RS § 5243; S&C 1037; 51 v 57, § 312; 91 v 86; GC § 11497; 101 v 139; Bureau of Code Revision, 10-1-53; 125 v 35 (Eff 10-2-53); 131 v 658 (Eff 9-28-65); 132 v S 25 (Eff 7-24-67); 133 v H 1 (Eff 3-18-69); 133 v H 1201 (Eff 7-1-71); 134 v H 602, §§ 1, 2. Eff 6-30-71.

§§ 2317.08 to 2317.20 Repealed, 133 v H 1201, § 1 [RS §§ 5244-5252; S&C 472, 555-557, 1038-1040, 1046; 29 v 123; 45 v 54; 48 v 35; 48 v 69; 51 v 57, §§ 316-322, 330, 362; 74 v 217, § 4; 77 v 216; 82 v 221; 88 v 42; 90 v 234; 91 v 132; GC §§ 11498-11510; Bureau of Code Revision, 10-1-53; 125 v 258]. Eff 7-1-71.

Former RC §§ 2317.08, 2317.09 concerned proving written

or common law of other states or countries, see now CivR 44.1, CrimR 27; RC § 2317.10 concerned copies of certain documents as evidence, see now CivR 44, CrimR 27, EvR 901, 902; RC §§ 2317.11-2317.20 concerned subpoenas, see now CivR 45, CrimR 17.

[MEANS OF SECURING ATTENDANCE]

§ 2317.21 Attachment of witness who disobeys subpoena.

When a witness, except a witness who has demanded and has not been paid his traveling fees and fee for one day's attendance when a subpoena is served upon him, as authorized by the provisions of section 2317.18† of the Revised Code, fails to obey a subpoena personally served, the court or officer, before whom his attendance is required, may issue to the sheriff or a constable of the county, a writ of attachment, commanding him to arrest and bring the person named in the writ before such court or officer at the time and place the writ fixes, to give his testimony and answer for the contempt. If such writ does not require the witness to be immediately brought, he may give bond for a sum fixed by the court of common pleas or the court which issued the subpoena, with surety, for his appearance, which sum shall be endorsed on the back of the writ, except that, if no sum is so endorsed, it shall be one hundred dollars. When the witness was not personally served, the court, by a rule, may order him to show cause why such writ should not issue against him.

HISTORY: RS § 5253; S&C 1039; 51 v 57, § 323; GC § 11511; Bureau of Code Revision, 10-1-53; 129 v 325 (Eff 10-2-61); 139 v S 114. Eff 10-27-81.

† Repealed, 133 v H 1201.

§ 2317.22 Punishment for contempt.

Punishment for the acts of contempt specified in section 2317.20† of the Revised Code shall be as follows: When the witness fails to attend in obedience to a subpoena, the court or officer may fine him not more than fifty dollars; in other cases, not more than fifty dollars nor less than five dollars; or the court or officer may imprison such witness in the county jail, there to remain until he submits to be sworn, testifies, or gives his deposition.

HISTORY: RS § 5254; S&C 1039; 77 v 42, 45; GC § 11512; Bureau of Code Revision. Eff 10-1-53.

† Repealed, 133 v H 1201.

§ 2317.23 Disposition of fines.

A fine imposed under section 2317.22 of the Revised Code by the court shall be paid into the county treasury; that imposed by an officer shall be for the use of the party for whom the witness was subpoenaed. The witness also shall be liable to the party injured for any damages occasioned by his failure to attend, or refusal to be sworn, to testify, or to give his deposition.

HISTORY: RS § 5254; S&C 1039; 77 v 42, 45; GC § 11513; Bureau of Code Revision. Eff 10-1-53.

§ 2317.24 Release of witness from imprisonment.

A witness imprisoned by an officer under section 2317.22 of the Revised Code may apply to a judge of the supreme court, court of appeals, court of common pleas, or probate court, who may discharge him if it appears that such imprisonment is illegal.

HISTORY: RS § 5255; S&C 1040; 51 v 57, § 325; 82 v 16, 33; GC § 11514; 103 v 405(426); Bureau of Code Revision. Eff 10-1-53.

§ 2317.25 Contents of attachment or order to commit.

Every attachment for the arrest or order to commit a witness to prison by a court or officer, pursuant to sections 2317.21 and 2317.22 of the Revised Code, must be under seal of the court or official seal of the officer, if he has one, and must particularly specify the cause of the arrest or commitment. When committed for a refusal to answer a question, the question must be stated in the order.

HISTORY: RS § 5256; S&C 1040; 51 v 57, § 326; GC § 11515; Bureau of Code Revision. Eff 10-1-53.

§ 2317.26 Order of commitment.

The order of commitment mentioned in section 2317.25 of the Revised Code may be directed to the sheriff or a constable of the county where the witness resides, or is at the time, and shall be executed by committing him to the jail of such county, and delivering a copy of it to the jailer.

HISTORY: RS § 5256; S&C 1040; 51 v 57, § 326; GC § 11516; Bureau of Code Revision, 10-1-53; 139 v S 114. Eff 10-27-81.

§§ 2317.27, 2317.28 Repealed, 133 v H 1201, § 1 [RS §§ 5257, 5258; S&C 1040; 51 v 57, §§ 327, 328; GC §§ 11517, 11518; Bureau of Code Revision, 10-1-53]. Eff 7-1-71.

These sections concerned testimony of prisoner. See now CivR 30, 45 and CrimR 15, 17.

§ 2317.29 May not sue or serve witness out of his county.

A witness shall not be liable to be sued, in a county in which he does not reside, by being served with a summons in such county while going, returning or attending in obedience to a subpoena.

HISTORY: RS § 5259; S&C 1040; 51 v 57, § 329; GC § 11519; Bureau of Code Revision. Eff 10-1-53.

§ 2317.30 Oath of witness.

Before testifying, a witness shall be sworn to testify the truth, the whole truth, and nothing but the truth.

HISTORY: RS § 5260; S&C 1040; 51 v 57, § 331; GC § 11520; Bureau of Code Revision. Eff 10-1-53.

§§ 2317.31 to 2317.35 Repealed, 133 v H 1201, § 1 [RS §§ 5288-5292; S&C 1045, 1046; 51 v 57, §§ 359-361; 54 v 23, § 360; GC §§ 11550-11554; Bureau of Code Revision, 10-1-53]. Eff 7-1-71.

Former RC § 2317.31 concerned request for admission of genuineness of document, see now CivR 36, 37; RC §§ 2317.32-2317.35 concerned production, inspection and copies of books and writings, see now CivR 34, 37.

[COMPOSITE REPORTS]

§ 2317.36 Admissible reports.

A written report or finding of facts prepared by an expert who is not a party to the cause, nor an employee of a party, except for the purpose of making such report or finding, nor financially interested in the result of the controversy, and containing the conclusions resulting wholly or partly from written information furnished by the co-operation of several persons acting for a common purpose, shall, in so far as the same is relevant, be admissible when testified to by the person, or one of the persons, making such report or finding without calling as witnesses the persons furnishing the information, and without producing the books or other writings on which the report for finding is based, if, in the opinion of the court, no substantial injustice will be done the opposite party.

HISTORY: GC § 12102-17; 118 v 663; Bureau of Code Revision. Eff 10-1-53.

§ 2317.37 Cross-examination by adverse party.

Any person who has furnished information on which a report or finding mentioned in section 2317.36 of the Revised Code is based may be cross-examined by the adverse party, but the fact that his testimony is not obtainable shall not render the report or finding inadmissible, unless the trial court finds that substantial injustice would be done to the adverse party by its admission.

HISTORY: GC § 12102-18; 118 v 663, § 2; Bureau of Code Revision. Eff 10-1-53.

§ 2317.38 Notice of intention to offer report.

The report or finding mentioned in section 2317.36 of the Revised Code is not admissible unless the party offering it has given notice to the adverse party a reasonable time before trial of his intention to offer it, together with a copy of the report or finding, or so much thereof as relates to the controversy, and has afforded him a reasonable opportunity to inspect and copy any records or other documents in the offering party's possession or control, on which the report or finding was based, and also the names of all persons furnishing facts upon which the report or finding was based.

This section and sections 2317.36 and 2317.37 of the Revised Code shall be so interpreted and construed as to effectuate their general purpose to make the law of this state uniform with those states which enact similar legislation.

HISTORY: GC §§ 12102-19, 12102-20; 118 v 663, §§ 3, 4; Bureau of Code Revision. Eff 10-1-53.

§ 2317.39 Report of investigations conducted by court made available to all parties.

Whenever an investigation into the facts of any case, civil or criminal, pending at the time of such investigation in any court, is made, conducted, or participated in, directly or indirectly, by any court or any department thereof, through public employees, paid private investigators, social workers, friends of the court, or any other persons, and a report of such investigation is prepared for submission to the court, the contents of such report shall not be considered by any judge of the court wherein such case is pending either before the trial of the case or at any stage of the proceedings prior to final disposition thereof, unless the full contents of such report have been made readily available and accessible to all parties to the case or their counsel. The parties or their counsel shall be notified in writing of the fact that an investigation has been made, that a report has been submitted, and that the contents of the report are available for examination. Such notice shall be given at least five days prior to the time the contents of any report are to be considered by any judge of the court wherein the case is pending. In the event that a report following any investigation is prepared for submission orally, such oral report shall be reduced to writing prior to the issuance of notice of the availability of such report for examination.

This section does not apply only to the utilization of the contents of such reports as testimony, but shall prevent any judge from familiarizing himself with such contents in any manner unless this section has been fully complied with.

HISTORY: GC § 11521-1; 124 v 412; Bureau of Code Revision. Eff 10-1-53.

[BUSINESS RECORDS]

§ 2317.40 Records as evidence.

As used in this section "business" includes every kind of business, profession, occupation, calling, or operation of institutions, whether carried on for profit or not.

A record of an act, condition, or event, in so far as relevant, is competent evidence if the custodian or the person who made such record or under whose supervision such record was made testifies to its identity and the mode of its preparation, and if it was made in the regular course of business, at or near the time of the act, condition, or event, and if, in the opinion of the court, the sources of information, method, and time of preparation were such as to justify its admission.

This section shall be so interpreted and construed as to effectuate its general purpose to make the law of this state uniform with those states which enact similar legislation.

HISTORY: GC §§ 12102-22-12102-24; 118 v 662, §§ 1, 2; Bureau of Code Revision, 10-1-53; 127 v 847. Eff 9-16-57.

§ 2317.41 Photographic copies of records admissible in evidence.

"Photograph" as used in this section includes but is not limited to microphotograph, a roll or strip of film, a roll or strip of microfilm, a photostatic copy, or an optically-imaged copy.

To the extent that a record would be competent evidence under section 2317.40 of the Revised Code, a photograph of such record shall be competent evidence if the custodian of the photograph or the person who made such photograph or under whose supervision such photograph was made testifies to the identity of and the mode of making such photograph, and if, in the opinion of the trial court, the record has been destroyed or otherwise disposed of in good faith in the regular course of business, and the mode of making such photograph was such as to justify its admission. If a photograph is admissible under this section, the court may admit the whole or a part thereof.

Such photograph shall be admissible only if the party offering it has delivered a copy of it, or so much thereof as relates to the controversy, to the adverse party a reasonable time before trial, unless in the opinion of the court the adverse party has not been unfairly surprised by the failure to deliver such copy. No such photograph need be submitted to the adverse party as prescribed in this section unless the original instrument would be required to be so submitted.

HISTORY: GC § 12102-23a; 122 v 290; Bureau of Code Revision, 10-1-53; 146 v H 495. Eff 10-4-96.

[OFFICIAL REPORTS]

§ 2317.42 Reports or certified copies to be admitted.

Official reports made by officers of this state, or certified copies of the same, on a matter within the scope of their duty as defined by statute, shall, in so far as relevant, be admitted as evidence of the matters stated therein.

HISTORY: GC §§ 12102-26, 12102-27; 118 v 665, §§ 1, 2; Bureau of Code Revision, 10-1-53; 133 v H 1201 (Eff 7-1-71); 134 v H 602, §§ 1, 2. Eff 6-30-71.

[MEDICAL BILLS AND RECORDS]

[§ 2317.42.1] § 2317.421 Personal injury or wrongful death action.

In an action for damages arising from personal injury or wrongful death, a written bill or statement, or any relevant portion thereof, itemized by date, type of service rendered, and charge, shall, if otherwise admissible, be prima-facie evidence of the reasonableness of any charges and fees stated therein for medication and prosthetic devices furnished, or medical, dental, hospital, and funeral services rendered by the person, firm, or corporation issuing such bill or statement, provided, that such bill or statement shall be prima-facie evidence of reasonableness only if the party offering it delivers a copy of it, or the relevant portion thereof, to the attorney of record for each adverse party not less than five days before trial.

HISTORY: 133 v S 352. Eff 6-1-70.

[§ 2317.42.2] § 2317.422 Qualification of nursing, rest, community alternative home and adult care facilities records.

(A) Notwithstanding sections 2317.40 and 2317.41 of the Revised Code but subject to division (B) of this section, the records, or copies or photographs of the records, of a hospital, homes required to be licensed pursuant to section 3721.01 and of adult care facilities required to be licensed pursuant to Chapter 3722. of the Revised Code, and community alternative homes licensed pursuant to section 3724.03 of the Revised Code, in lieu of the testimony in open court of their custodian, person who made them, or person under whose supervision they were made, may be qualified as authentic evidence if any such person endorses thereon his verified certification identifying such records, giving the mode and time of their preparation, and stating that they were prepared in the usual course of the business of the institution. Such records, copies, or photographs may not be qualified by certification as provided in this section unless the party intending to offer them delivers a copy of them, or of their relevant portions, to the attorney of record for each adverse party not less than five days before trial. Nothing in this section shall be construed to limit the right of any party to call the custodian, person who made such records, or person under whose supervision they were made, as a witness.

(B) Division (A) of this section does not apply to any certified copy of the results of any test given to determine the presence or concentration of alcohol, a drug of abuse, or alcohol and a drug of abuse in a patient's blood, breath, or urine at any time relevant to a criminal offense that is submitted in a criminal action or proceeding in accordance with division (B)(2)(b) or (B)(3)(b) of section 2317.02 of the Revised Code.

HISTORY: 135 v H 614 (Eff 9-30-74); 143 v S 2 (Eff 11-1-89); 143 v H 253 (Eff 11-15-90); 145 v H 335. Eff 12-9-94.

The provisions of § 3 of HB 335 (145 v —) read as follows:

SECTION 3. Section 2317.422 of the Revised Code is presented in this act as a composite of the section as amended by both Am. Sub. H.B. 253 and Am. Sub. S.B. 2 of the 118th General Assembly, with the new language of neither of the acts shown in capital letters.

∘ ∘ ∘

This is in recognition of the principle stated in division (B) of section 1.52 of the Revised Code that such amendments are to be harmonized where not substantively irreconcilable and constitutes a legislative finding that such is the resulting version in effect prior to the effective date of this act.

§§ 2317.43, 2317.44 Repealed, 133 v H 1201, § 1 [GC §§ 12102-28, 12102-29, 12102-31-12102-33; 118 v 665, §§ 3, 4; 118 v 678, §§ 1-3; Bureau of Code Revision, 10-1-53; 132 v S 26]. Eff 7-1-71.

Former RC § 2317.43 concerned cross-examination of person making official reports, see now CivR 44; RC § 2317.44 concerned judicial notice of foreign law, see now CivR 44.1.

[§ 2317.44.1] § 2317.441 Repealed, 133 v H 1201, § 1 [132 v H 438]. Eff 7-1-71.

This section concerned judicial notice of municipal ordinances, see now CivR 44.1.

§ 2317.45 Consideration of collateral benefits in tort actions.

(A) As used in this section:

(1) "Collateral benefits" means benefits that are paid by any source, including workers' compensation benefits, to or on behalf of the plaintiff as a result of an injury or loss to person or property, regardless of whether there is an obligation to pay back the money or other benefits, in whole or in part, upon recovery in a tort action. "Collateral benefits" does not include life insurance proceeds.

(2) "Tort action" means a civil action for damages for injury, death, or loss to person or property. "Tort action" includes a product liability claim but does not include a civil action for damages for a breach of contract or another agreement between persons.

(3) "Trier of fact" means the jury or, in a nonjury action, the court.

(B) In determining the amount of the compensatory damages that are recoverable by the plaintiff in a tort action, the trier of fact shall consider, if presented in the tort action, relevant collateral benefits that have been paid, or that the source of the benefits has acknowledged are payable, from insurance other than insurance for which the plaintiff, spouse of the plaintiff, or parent of the plaintiff if the plaintiff is a minor, has paid a premium, insurance that is subject to a right of subrogation, workers' compensation benefits that are subject to a right of subrogation, or insurance that has any other obligation of repayment, including, but not limited to, evidence of the amount of the collateral benefit and of the costs, premiums, or charges for the collateral benefits.

(C) This section does not apply as follows:

(1) In tort actions against the state in the court of claims. Division (D) of section 2743.02 or division (B)(2) of section 3345.40 of the Revised Code applies to collateral recoveries or sources of plaintiffs in those tort actions.

(2) In tort actions against political subdivisions of this state that are commenced under or are subject to Chapter 2744. of the Revised Code. Division (B) of section 2744.05 of the Revised Code applies to collateral sources of plaintiffs in those tort actions.

(D) This section shall be considered to be purely remedial in operation and shall be applied in a remedial manner in any civil action commenced on or after January 27, 1997, in which this section is relevant, regardless of when the cause of action accrued and notwithstanding any other section of the Revised Code or prior rule of law of this state, but shall not be construed to apply to any civil action pending prior to January 27, 1997.

HISTORY: 142 v H 1 (Eff 1-5-88); 146 v H 350 (Eff 1-27-97); 147 v H 363. Eff 9-29-97.

Not analogous to former RC § 2317.45 (GC § 12102-34; 118 v 678, § 4; Bureau of Code Revision, 10-1-53; 132 v S 26), repealed 133 v H 1201, § 1, eff 7-1-71.

§ 2317.46 Expert witness contingent fee agreements prohibited in tort actions; evidence of liability insurance of expert defense witness.

(A) As used in this section:

(1) "Contingent fee agreement" means an agreement for the provision of testimony or other evidence and related services by an expert witness that specifies both of the following:

(a) The payment of compensation to the expert witness for the testimony, other evidence, and services is contingent, in whole or in part, upon a judgment being rendered in favor of the plaintiff or defendant in a tort action, upon a favorable settlement being obtained by the plaintiff or defendant in a tort action, or upon the plaintiff in a tort action being awarded in a judgment or settlement damages in at least a specified amount.

(b) Upon satisfaction of the contingency described in division (A)(1)(a) of this section, the compensation to be paid to the expert witness is in a fixed amount or an amount to be determined by a specified formula, including, but not limited to, a percentage of a judgment rendered in favor of the plaintiff or a percentage of a favorable settlement obtained by the plaintiff.

(2) "Tort action" means a civil action for damages for injury, death, or loss to person or property. "Tort action" includes a product liability claim but does not include a civil action for damages for a breach of contract or another agreement between persons.

(B) A plaintiff or defendant in a tort action shall not engage an expert witness by means of a contingent fee agreement.

(C) If a defendant presents testimony or other evidence in a tort action by means of an expert witness, evidence of a common insurer of liability of the defendant and the expert witness or evidence of a potential financial impact of the action on the amount of liability insurance premiums paid by the expert witness is inadmissible to prove bias, interest, or prejudice of the expert witness unless the party offering the evidence proves that the probative value of the evidence outweighs the evidence's potential prejudicial effect.

HISTORY: 146 v H 350. Eff 1-27-97.

Not analogous to former RC § 2317.46 (GC §§ 12102-35, 12102-36; 118 v 678, §§ 5, 6; Bureau of Code Revision, 10-1-53; 132 v H 438), repealed 133 v H 1201, § 1, eff 7-1-71.

The provisions of §§ 5(N), 6(L) of HB 350 (146 v —) read as follows:

SECTION 5. ° ° °

(N) In enacting division (C) of section 2317.46 of the Revised Code in this act, the General Assembly declares that it is the public policy of the state of Ohio that evidence of a common insurer of liability of the defendant and an expert witness in an action upon a medical, dental, optometric, or chiropractic claim or evidence of a potential financial impact of the action on the amount of liability insurance premiums paid by the expert witness is not admissible to prove bias, interest, or prejudice of the expert witness unless the party offering the evidence proves that probative value of the evidence outweighs the evidence's potential prejudicial effect. ° ° °

SECTION 6. ° ° °

(L) Section 2317.46 of the Revised Code, as enacted by this act, shall apply only to tort actions, as defined in that section, that are commenced on or after the effective date of this act. ° ° °

[BLOOD TESTS]

§ 2317.47 Blood tests by court order.

Whenever it is relevant in a civil or criminal action or proceeding to determine the paternity or identity of any person, the trial court on motion shall order any party to the action and any person involved in the controversy or proceeding to submit to one or more blood-grouping tests, to be made by qualified physicians or other qualified persons not to exceed three, to be selected by the court and under such restrictions or directions as the court or judge deems proper. In cases where exclusion is established, the results of the tests together with the findings of the experts of the fact of nonpaternity are receivable in evidence. Such experts shall be subject to cross-examination by both parties after the court has caused them to disclose their findings to the court or to the court and jury. Whenever the court orders such blood-grouping tests to be taken and one of the parties refuses to submit to such test, such fact shall be disclosed upon the trial unless good cause is shown to the contrary. The court shall determine how and by whom the costs of such examination shall be paid.

HISTORY: GC § 12122-2; 118 v 570; Bureau of Code Revision. Eff 10-1-53.

[DISCOVERY]

§ 2317.48 Action for discovery.

When a person claiming to have a cause of action or a defense to an action commenced against him, without the discovery of a fact from the adverse party, is unable to file his complaint or answer, he may bring an action for discovery, setting forth in his complaint in the action for discovery the necessity and the grounds for the action, with any interrogatories relating to the subject matter of the discovery that are necessary to procure the discovery sought. Unless a motion to dismiss the action is filed under Civil Rule 12, the complaint shall be fully and directly answered under oath by the defendant. Upon the final disposition of the action, the costs of the action shall be taxed in the manner the court deems equitable.

HISTORY: RS § 5293; S&C 1151; 64 v 23, § 3; GC § 11555; Bureau of Code Revision, 10-1-53; 140 v S 47. Eff 4-4-85.

§§ 2317.49 to 2317.51 Repealed, 133 v H 1201, § 1 [RS §§ 5294-5296; S&C 987, 989; 51 v 57, §§ 131-133; GC §§ 11556-11558; Bureau of Code Revision, 10-1-53]. Eff 7-1-71.

These sections concerned variance. See now CivR 15(B).

[AGENTS]

§ 2317.52 Cross-examination of agents.

When the action or proceeding relates to a transaction or occurrence in which it has been shown or it is admitted that the adverse party acted either in whole or in part through an agent or employee, such agent or employee of the adverse party may be called as a witness and examined as if under cross-examination upon any matters at issue between the parties which are shown or admitted to have been within the scope of such agent's or employee's authority or employment.

The party calling for such examination shall not thereby be concluded but may rebut such agent's or employee's testimony by counter testimony.

The party whose agent or employee is called as a witness by the adverse party and whose agent or employee is examined as if under cross-examination shall not thereby be concluded but may rebut such agent's or employee's testimony by counter testimony.

HISTORY: 127 v 95, § 1. Eff 9-13-57.

[PATIENT'S INFORMED CONSENT]

§ 2317.54 Consent to surgical or medical procedure; requirements.

No hospital, home health agency, or provider of a hospice care program shall be held liable for a physician's failure to obtain an informed consent from his patient prior to a surgical or medical procedure or course of procedures, unless the physician is an employee of the hospital, home health agency, or provider of a hospice care program.

Written consent to a surgical or medical procedure or course of procedures shall, to the extent that it fulfills all the requirements in divisions (A), (B), and (C) of this section, be presumed to be valid and effective, in the absence of proof by a preponderance of the evidence that the person who sought such consent was not acting in good faith, or that the execution of the consent was induced by fraudulent misrepresentation of material facts, or that the person executing the consent was not able to communicate effectively in spoken and written english or any other language in which the consent is written. Except as herein provided, no evidence shall be admissible to impeach, modify, or limit the authorization for performance of the procedure or procedures set forth in such written consent.

(A) The consent sets forth in general terms the nature and purpose of the procedure or procedures, and what the procedures are expected to accomplish, together with the reasonably known risks, and, except in emergency situations, sets forth the names of the physicians who shall perform the intended surgical procedures.

(B) The person making the consent acknowledges that such disclosure of information has been made and that all questions asked about the procedure or procedures have been answered in a satisfactory manner.

(C) The consent is signed by the patient for whom the procedure is to be performed, or, if the patient for any reason including, but not limited to, competence, infancy, or the fact that, at the latest time that the consent is needed, the patient is under the influence of alcohol, hallucinogens, or drugs, lacks legal capacity to consent, by a person who has legal authority to consent on behalf of such patient in such circumstances.

Any use of a consent form that fulfills the requirements stated in divisions (A), (B), and (C) of this section has no effect on the common law rights and liabilities, including the right of a physician to obtain the oral or implied consent of a patient to a medical procedure, that may exist as between physicians and patients on July 28, 1975.

As used in this section the term "hospital" has the meaning set forth in division (D) of section 2305.11 of the Revised Code; "home health agency" has the meaning set forth in division (A) of section 3701.88 of the Revised Code; and "hospice care program" has the meaning set forth in division (A) of section 3712.01 of the Revised Code. The provisions of this division apply to hospitals, doctors of medicine, doctors of osteopathic medicine, and doctors of podiatric medicine.

HISTORY: 136 v H 682 (Eff 7-28-75); 136 v H 1426 (Eff 7-1-76); 137 v H 213 (Eff 11-24-77); 141 v S 22. Eff 3-1-87.

§ 2317.56 Information to be provided to woman prior to abortion; consent form; medical emergency or necessity; liability of noncomplying physician and employer; publication of informational materials.

(A) As used in this section:

(1) "Medical emergency" means a condition of a pregnant woman that, in the reasonable judgment of the physician who is attending the woman, creates an immediate threat of serious risk to the life or physical health of the woman from the continuation of her pregnancy necessitating the immediate performance or inducement of an abortion.

(2) "Medical necessity" means a medical condition of a pregnant woman that, in the reasonable judgment of the physician who is attending the woman, so complicates the pregnancy that it necessitates the immediate performance or inducement of an abortion.

(3) "Probable gestational age of the embryo or fetus" means the gestational age that, in the judgment of a physician, is, with reasonable probability, the gestational age of the embryo or fetus at the time that the physician informs a pregnant woman pursuant to division (B)(1)(b) of this section.

(B) Except when there is a medical emergency or medical necessity, an abortion shall be performed or induced only if all of the following conditions are satisfied:

(1) At least twenty-four hours prior to the performance or inducement of the abortion, a physician informs the pregnant woman, verbally or by other non-written means of communication, of all of the following:

(a) The nature and purpose of the particular abortion procedure to be used and the medical risks associated with that procedure;

(b) The probable gestational age of the embryo or fetus;

(c) The medical risks associated with the pregnant woman carrying her pregnancy to term.

(2) A physician provides the pregnant woman with the information described in division (B)(1) of this section in an individual, private setting and gives her an

adequate opportunity to ask questions about the abortion that will be performed or induced;

(3) At least twenty-four hours prior to the performance or inducement of the abortion, one or more physicians or one or more agents of one or more physicians do each of the following in person, by telephone, by certified mail, return receipt requested, or by regular mail evidenced by a certificate of mailing:

(a) Inform the pregnant woman of the name of the physician who is scheduled to perform or induce the abortion;

(b) Give the pregnant woman copies of the published materials described in division (C) of this section;

(c) Inform the pregnant woman that the materials given to her pursuant to division (B)(3)(b) of this section are provided by the state and that they describe the embryo or fetus and list agencies that offer alternatives to abortion. The pregnant woman may choose to examine or not to examine the materials. A physician or an agent of a physician may disassociate himself from the materials and may choose to comment or not comment on the materials.

(4) Prior to the performance or inducement of the abortion, the pregnant woman signs a form consenting to the abortion and certifies both of the following on that form:

(a) She has received the information and materials described in divisions (B)(1), (2), and (3) of this section, and her questions about the abortion that will be performed or induced have been answered in a satisfactory manner.

(b) She consents to the particular abortion voluntarily, knowingly, intelligently, and without coercion by any person, and she is not under the influence of any drug of abuse or alcohol.

(5) Prior to the performance or inducement of the abortion, the physician who is scheduled to perform or induce the abortion or his agent receives a copy of the pregnant woman's signed form on which she consents to the abortion and that includes the certification required by division (B)(4) of this section.

(C) The department of health shall cause to be published in English and in Spanish, in a typeface large enough to be clearly legible, and in an easily comprehensible format, the following materials:

(1) Materials that inform the pregnant woman about family planning information, of publicly funded agencies that are available to assist her in family planning, and of public and private agencies and services that are available to assist her through her pregnancy, upon childbirth, and while her child is dependent, including, but not limited to, adoption agencies. The materials shall be geographically indexed; include a comprehensive list of the available agencies, a description of the services offered by the agencies, and the telephone numbers and addresses of the agencies; and inform the pregnant woman about available medical assistance benefits for prenatal care, childbirth, and neonatal care and about the support obligations of the father of a child who is born alive. The department shall ensure that the materials described in division (C)(1) of this section are comprehensive and do not directly or indirectly promote, exclude, or discourage the use of any agency or service described in this division.

(2) Materials that inform the pregnant woman of the probable anatomical and physiological characteristics of the zygote, blastocyte, embryo, or fetus at two-week gestational increments for the first sixteen weeks of her pregnancy and at four-week gestational increments from the seventeenth week of her pregnancy to full term, including any relevant information regarding the time at which the fetus possibly would be viable. The department shall cause these materials to be published only after it consults with the Ohio state medical association and the Ohio section of the American college of obstetricians and gynecologists relative to the probable anatomical and physiological characteristics of a zygote, blastocyte, embryo, or fetus at the various gestational increments. The materials shall use language that is understandable by the average person who is not medically trained, shall be objective and nonjudgmental, and shall include only accurate scientific information about the zygote, blastocyte, embryo, or fetus at the various gestational increments. If the materials use a pictorial, photographic, or other depiction to provide information regarding the zygote, blastocyte, embryo, or fetus, the materials shall include, in a conspicuous manner, a scale or other explanation that is understandable by the average person and that can be used to determine the actual size of the zygote, blastocyte, embryo, or fetus at a particular gestational increment as contrasted with the depicted size of the zygote, blastocyte, embryo, or fetus at that gestational increment.

(D) Upon the submission of a request to the department of health by any person, hospital, physician, or medical facility for one or more copies of the materials published in accordance with division (C) of this section, the department shall make the requested number of copies of the materials available to the person, hospital, physician, or medical facility that requested the copies.

(E) If a medical emergency or medical necessity compels the performance or inducement of an abortion, the physician who will perform or induce the abortion, prior to its performance or inducement if possible, shall inform the pregnant woman of the medical indications supporting his judgment that an immediate abortion is necessary. Any physician who performs or induces an abortion without the prior satisfaction of the conditions specified in division (B) of this section because of a medical emergency or medical necessity shall enter the reasons for his conclusion that a medical emergency or medical necessity exists in the medical record of the pregnant woman.

(F) If the conditions specified in division (B) of this section are satisfied, consent to an abortion shall be presumed to be valid and effective.

(G) The performance or inducement of an abortion without the prior satisfaction of the conditions specified in division (B) of this section does not constitute, and shall not be construed as constituting, a violation of division (A) of section 2919.12 of the Revised Code. The failure of a physician to satisfy the conditions of division (B) of this section prior to performing or inducing an abortion upon a pregnant woman may be the basis of both of the following:

(1) A civil action for compensatory and exemplary damages as described in division (H) of this section;

(2) Disciplinary action under section 4731.22 of the Revised Code.

(H)(1) Subject to divisions (H)(2) and (3) of this section, any physician who performs or induces an abortion with actual knowledge that the conditions specified in division (B) of this section have not been satisfied or with a heedless indifference as to whether those conditions have been satisfied is liable in compensatory and exemplary damages in a civil action to any person, or the representative of the estate of any person, who sustains injury, death, or loss to person or property as a result of the failure to satisfy those conditions. In the civil action, the court additionally may enter any injunctive or other equitable relief that it considers appropriate.

(2) The following shall be affirmative defenses in a civil action authorized by division (H)(1) of this section:

(a) The physician performed or induced the abortion under the circumstances described in division (E) of this section.

(b) The physician made a good faith effort to satisfy the conditions specified in division (B) of this section.

(c) The physician or an agent of the physician requested copies of the materials published in accordance with division (C) of this section from the department of health, but the physician was not able to give a pregnant woman copies of the materials pursuant to division (B)(3) of this section and to obtain a certification as described in divisions (B)(4) and (5) of this section because the department failed to make the requested number of copies available to the physician or his agent in accordance with division (D) of this section.

(3) An employer or other principal is not liable in damages in a civil action authorized by division (H)(1) of this section on the basis of the doctrine of respondeat superior unless either of the following applies:

(a) The employer or other principal had actual knowledge or, by the exercise of reasonable diligence, should have known that his employee or agent performed or induced an abortion with actual knowledge that the conditions specified in division (B) of this section had not been satisfied or with a heedless indifference as to whether those conditions had been satisfied.

(b) The employer or other principal negligently failed to secure the compliance of his employee or agent with division (B) of this section.

(4) Notwithstanding division (E) of section 2919.12 of the Revised Code, the civil action authorized by division (H)(1) of this section shall be the exclusive civil remedy for persons, or the representatives of estates of persons, who allegedly sustain injury, death, or loss to person or property as a result of a failure to satisfy the conditions specified in division (B) of this section.

(I) The department of human services shall prepare and conduct a public information program to inform women of all available governmental programs and agencies that provide services or assistance for family planning, prenatal care, child care, or alternatives to abortion.

HISTORY: 144 v H 108 (Eff 5-28-92); 145 v H 715. Eff 7-22-94.

§ 2317.62 Evidence of cost of annuity as to future damages in tort actions.

(A) As used in this section:

(1) "Annuity" means an annuity that would be purchased from either of the following types of insurance companies:

(a) An insurance company that the A.M. Best Company, in its most recently published rating guide of life insurance companies, has rated A or better and has rated XII or higher as to financial size or strength;

(b)(i) An insurance company that the superintendent of insurance, under rules adopted pursuant to Chapter 119. of the Revised Code for purposes of implementing this division, determines is licensed to do business in this state and, considering the factors described in division (A)(1)(b)(ii) of this section, is a stable insurance company that issues annuities that are safe and desirable.

(ii) In making determinations as described in division (A)(1)(b)(i) of this section, the superintendent shall be guided by the principle that the trier of fact in a tort action should be presented only with evidence as to the cost of annuities that are safe and desirable for the plaintiffs in the action who are awarded damages. In making the determinations, the superintendent shall consider the financial condition, general standing, operating results, profitability, leverage, liquidity, amount and soundness of reinsurance, adequacy of reserves, and the management of a particular insurance company and also may consider ratings, grades, and classifications of any nationally recognized rating services of insurance companies and any other factors relevant to the making of the determinations.

(2) "Future damages" means damages that result from an injury or loss to person or property that is a subject of a tort action and that will accrue after the verdict or determination of liability by the trier of fact is rendered in that tort action.

(3) "Tort action" means a civil action for damages for injury, death, or loss to person or property. "Tort action" includes a product liability claim but does not include a civil action for damages for a breach of contract or another agreement between persons.

(4) "Trier of fact" means the jury or, in a nonjury action, the court.

(B) Subject to division (A)(3)(b)(ii) of section 2125.02 of the Revised Code and consistent with the Rules of Evidence, any party to a tort action may present evidence of the cost of an annuity in connection with any issue of recoverable future damages. If that evidence is presented, the trier of fact may consider that evidence in determining the future damages suffered by reason of an injury or loss to person or property that is a subject of the tort action. If that evidence is presented, the present value in dollars of any annuity is its cost.

HISTORY: 142 v H 1 (Eff 1-5-88); 146 v H 350. Eff 1-27-97.

CHAPTER 2335: FEES; COSTS

§ 2335.08 Witness fees in criminal cases.

Each witness attending, under recognizance or subpoena issued by order of the prosecuting attorney or defendant, before the grand jury or any court of record, in criminal causes, shall be allowed the same fees as provided by section 2335.06 of the Revised Code in civil causes, to be taxed in only one cause when such witness is attending in more causes than one on the same days, unless otherwise directed by special order of the court. When certified to the county auditor by the clerk of the court, such fees shall be paid from the county treasury, and except as to the grand jury, taxed in the bill of costs. Each witness attending before a judge of a county court, magistrate, or mayor, under subpoena in criminal cases, shall be allowed the fees provided by such section for witnesses in the court of common pleas. In state cases such fees shall be paid out of the county treasury, and in ordinance cases they shall be paid out of the treasury of the municipal corporation, upon the certificates of the judge or magistrate, and they shall be taxed in the bill of costs.

When the fees enumerated by this section have been collected from the judgment debtor, they shall be paid to the public treasury from which such fees were advanced.

HISTORY: RS § 1302; S&C 631; 73 v 95, § 2; 73 v 127, § 25; 81 v 58, 59; GC § 3014; 108 v PtII 1203; Bureau of Code Revision, 10-1-53; 127 v 1039 (Eff 1-1-58); 136 v H 205. Eff 1-1-76.

§ 2335.11 Payment of fees and costs in felonies and minor state cases.

In felony cases in which the defendant is convicted, the fees of the various magistrates and their officers, the witness fees, and interpreter's fees shall be inserted in the judgment of conviction and, when collected shall be disbursed by the clerk of the court of common pleas to the persons entitled thereto. In minor state cases, which have come to the court of common pleas through such magistrate's courts, the fees enumerated by this section shall be inserted in the judgment of conviction and, when collected shall be disbursed by the clerk to the persons entitled thereto. In both felonies and minor state cases, such clerk shall pay the witness and interpreter's fees into the county treasury, monthly.

In all cases in which recognizances are taken, forfeited, and collected, the amount recovered shall be paid into the county treasury, and if no conviction is had, such costs shall be paid by the county upon the allowance of the county auditor.

HISTORY: RS § 1306; 75 v 50; 78 v 201; 97 v 11; GC § 3016; 109 v 173; Bureau of Code Revision. Eff 10-1-53.

TITLE 27: COURTS—GENERAL PROVISIONS—SPECIAL REMEDIES

CHAPTER 2701: COURTS OF RECORD—GENERAL PROVISIONS

[§ 2701.03.1] § 2701.031 Disqualification of municipal or county court judge.

(A) If a judge of a municipal or county court allegedly is interested in a proceeding pending before the judge, allegedly is related to or has a bias or prejudice for or against a party to a proceeding pending before the judge or to a party's counsel, or allegedly otherwise is disqualified to preside in a proceeding pending before the judge, any party to the proceeding or the party's counsel may file an affidavit of disqualification with the clerk of the court in which the proceeding is pending.

(B) An affidavit of disqualification shall be filed under this section with the clerk of the court in which the proceeding is pending not less than seven calendar days before the day on which the next hearing in the proceeding is scheduled and shall include all of the following:

(1) The specific allegations on which the claim of interest, bias, prejudice, or disqualification is based and the facts to support each of those allegations;

(2) The jurat of a notary public or another person authorized to administer oaths or affirmations;

(3) A certificate indicating that a copy of the affidavit has been served on the judge of the municipal or county court against whom the affidavit is filed and on all other parties or their counsel;

(4) The date of the next scheduled hearing in the proceeding or, if there is no hearing scheduled, a statement that there is no hearing scheduled.

(C)(1) Except as provided in division (C)(2) of this section, when an affidavit of disqualification is presented to the clerk of a municipal or county court for filing under division (B) of this section, the clerk shall enter the fact of the filing on the docket in that proceeding and shall provide notice of the filing of the affidavit to one of the following:

(a) The presiding judge of the court of common pleas of the county;

(b) If there is no presiding judge of the court of common pleas of the county, a judge of the court of common pleas of the county.

(2) The clerk of the municipal or county court in which a proceeding is pending shall not accept an affidavit of disqualification presented for filing under division (B) of this section if it is not timely presented for filing or does not satisfy the requirements of divisions (B)(2), (3), and (4) of this section.

(D)(1) Except as provided in divisions (D)(2) to (4) of this section, if the clerk of the municipal or county court in which a proceeding is pending accepts an affidavit of disqualification for filing under divisions (B) and (C) of this section, the affidavit deprives the judge of a municipal or county court against whom the affidavit was filed of any authority to preside in the proceeding until the judge who was notified pursuant to division (C)(1) of this section rules on the affidavit pursuant to division (E) of this section.

(2) A judge of a municipal or county court against whom an affidavit of disqualification has been filed under divisions (B) and (C) of this section may preside in the proceeding if, based on the scheduled hearing date, the affidavit was not timely filed.

(3) A judge of a municipal or county court against whom an affidavit of disqualification has been filed under divisions (B) and (C) of this section may determine a matter that does not affect a substantive right of any of the parties.

(4) If the clerk of a municipal or county court accepts an affidavit of disqualification for filing under divisions (B) and (C) of this section, if the judge who is notified pursuant to division (C)(1) of this section of the filing of the affidavit of disqualification denies the affidavit pursuant to division (E) of this section, and if, after the denial, a second or subsequent affidavit of disqualification regarding the same judge and the same proceeding is filed by the same party who filed or on whose behalf was filed the affidavit that was denied or by counsel for the same party who filed or on whose behalf was filed the affidavit that was denied, the judge of a municipal or county court against whom the second or subsequent affidavit is filed may preside in the proceeding prior to the ruling, by the judge who is notified pursuant to division (C)(1) of this section, on the second or subsequent affidavit pursuant to division (E) of this section.

(E) If the clerk of a municipal or county court accepts an affidavit of disqualification for filing under division (B) and (C) of this section and if the judge who is notified pursuant to division (C)(1) of this section of the filing of the affidavit determines that the interest, bias, prejudice, or disqualification alleged in the affidavit does not exist, the judge who is so notified shall issue an entry denying the affidavit of disqualification. If the judge who is notified pursuant to division (C)(1) of this section of the filing of the affidavit determines that the interest, bias, prejudice, or disqualification alleged in the affidavit exists, the judge who is so notified shall issue an entry that disqualifies the judge against whom the affidavit was filed from presiding in the proceeding and designate another judge of the municipal or county court, or of the court of common pleas, to preside in the proceeding in place of the disqualified judge.

HISTORY: GC § 13433-19; 113 v 123(148), ch 12, § 9; Bureau

of Code Revision, 10-1-53; 127 v 423 (Eff 8-27-57); 146 v H 151 (Eff 12-4-95); RC § 2701.03.1, 146 v S 263. Eff 11-20-96.

See provisions, § 3 of SB 263 (146 v —) following RC § 2701.03.

CHAPTER 2705: CONTEMPT OF COURT

§ 2705.01 Summary punishment for contempt.

A court, or judge at chambers, may summarily punish a person guilty of misbehavior in the presence of or so near the court or judge as to obstruct the administration of justice.

HISTORY: RS § 5639; S&C 258; 32 v 17; GC § 12136; Bureau of Code Revision. Eff 10-1-53.

[INDIRECT]

§ 2705.02 Acts in contempt of court.

A person guilty of any of the following acts may be punished as for a contempt:

(A) Disobedience of, or resistance to, a lawful writ, process, order, rule, judgment, or command of a court or an officer;

(B) Misbehavior of an officer of the court in the performance of official duties, or in official transactions;

(C) A failure to obey a subpoena duly served, or a refusal to be sworn or to answer as a witness, when lawfully required;

(D) The rescue, or attempted rescue, of a person or of property in the custody of an officer by virtue of an order or process of court held by the officer;

(E) A failure upon the part of a person recognized to appear as a witness in a court to appear in compliance with the terms of the person's recognizance;

(F) A failure to comply with an order issued pursuant to section 3111.20, 3111.21, 3111.22, or 3111.241 [3111.24.1] of the Revised Code or a withholding or deduction notice issued under section 3111.23 of the Revised Code.

HISTORY: RS § 5640; S&S 97; S&C 258; 32 v 17; 59 v 31; GC § 12137; Bureau of Code Revision, 10-1-53; 146 v H 167. Eff 6-11-96.†

† The effective date of RC § 2705.02 has been changed from 11-15-96 to 6-11-96 by Section 7 of Sub. H.B. 710 (146 v —), effective 6-11-96.

§ 2705.03 Hearing.

In cases under section 2705.02 of the Revised Code, a charge in writing shall be filed with the clerk of the court, an entry thereof made upon the journal, and an opportunity given to the accused to be heard, by himself or counsel. This section does not prevent the court from issuing process to bring the accused into court, or from holding him in custody, pending such proceedings.

HISTORY: RS § 5641; 75 v 745, § 3; GC § 12138; Bureau of Code Revision. Eff 10-1-53.

[§ 2705.03.1] § 2705.031 Contempt action for failure to pay support or comply with visitation order.

(A) As used in this section, "Title IV-D case" has the same meaning as in section 3113.21 of the Revised Code.

(B)(1) Any party who has a legal claim to any support ordered for a child, spouse, or former spouse may initiate a contempt action for failure to pay the support. In Title IV-D cases, the contempt action for failure to pay support also may be initiated by an attorney retained by the party who has the legal claim, the prosecuting attorney, or an attorney of the department of human services or the child support enforcement agency.

(2) Any person who is granted visitation rights under a visitation order or decree issued pursuant to section 3109.051 [3109.05.1], 3109.11, or 3109.12 of the Revised Code or pursuant to any other provision of the Revised Code, or any other person who is subject to any visitation order or decree, may initiate a contempt action for a failure to comply with, or an interference with, the order or decree.

(C) In any contempt action initiated pursuant to division (B) of this section, the accused shall appear upon the summons and order to appear that is issued by the court. The summons shall include all of the following:

(1) Notice that failure to appear may result in the issuance of an order of arrest, and in cases involving alleged failure to pay support, the issuance of an order for the payment of support by withholding an amount from the personal earnings of the accused or by withholding or deducting an amount from some other asset of the accused;

(2) Notice that the accused has a right to counsel, and that if the accused believes that he is indigent, the accused must apply for a public defender or court appointed counsel within three business days after receipt of the summons;

(3) Notice that the court may refuse to grant a continuance at the time of the hearing for the purpose of the accused obtaining counsel, if the accused fails to make a good faith effort to retain counsel or to obtain a public defender;

(4) Notice of the potential penalties that could be imposed upon the accused, if the accused is found guilty of contempt for failure to pay support or for a failure to comply with, or an interference with, a visitation order or decree.

(D) If the accused is served as required by the Rules of Civil Procedure or by any special statutory proceedings that are relevant to the case, the court may order the attachment of the person of the accused upon failure to appear as ordered by the court.

(E) The imposition of any penalty for contempt under section 2705.05 of the Revised Code shall not eliminate any obligation of the accused to pay any past, present, or future support obligation or any obligation of the accused to comply with or refrain from interfering with the visitation order or decree. The court shall have jurisdiction to make a finding of contempt for the failure to pay support and to impose the penalties set forth in section 2705.05 of the Revised Code in all cases in which past due support is at issue even if the duty to pay support has terminated, and shall have jurisdiction to make a finding of contempt for a failure to comply with, or an intereference with, a visitation order or decree and to impose the penalties set forth insection 2705.05 of the Revised Code in all cases in which the failure or interference is at issue even if the visitation order or decree no longer is in effect.

HISTORY: 141 v H 509 (Eff 12-1-86); 142 v H 231 (Eff 10-5-87); 142 v H 708 (Eff 4-19-88); 143 v S 3. Eff 4-11-91.

§ 2705.04 Right of accused to bail.

In proceedings under section 2705.02 of the Revised Code, if the writ is not returnable forthwith, the court may fix the amount of a bond to be given by the accused, with surety to the satisfaction of the sheriff. Upon the return of a writ, when it is not convenient to hear the charge without delay, the court shall fix the amount of a bond to be given, with surety to the satisfaction of the clerk of the court, for the appearance of the accused to answer the charge.

On the execution of such bond, the accused shall be released from custody.

HISTORY: RS §§ 5642, 5643; 75 v 746, §§ 4, 5; GC §§ 12139, 12140; Bureau of Code Revision. Eff 10-1-53.

[TRIAL; PUNISHMENT]

§ 2705.05 Hearing; penalties; duty of garnishee under support order.

(A) In all contempt proceedings, the court shall conduct a hearing. At the hearing, the court shall investigate the charge and hear any answer or testimony that the accused makes or offers and shall determine whether the accused is guilty of the contempt charge. If the accused is found guilty, the court may impose any of the following penalties:

(1) For a first offense, a fine of not more than two hundred fifty dollars, a definite term of imprisonment of not more than thirty days in jail, or both;

(2) For a second offense, a fine of not more than five hundred dollars, a definite term of imprisonment of not more than sixty days in jail, or both;

(3) For a third or subsequent offense, a fine of not more than one thousand dollars, a definite term of imprisonment of not more than ninety days in jail, or both.

(B) In all contempt proceedings initiated pursuant to section 2705.031 [2705.03.1] of the Revised Code against an employer, the bureau of workers' compensation, an employer that is paying workers' compensation benefits, a board, board of trustees, or other governing entity of a retirement system, person paying or distributing income to an obligor under a support order, or financial institution that is ordered to withhold or deduct an amount of money from the income or other assets of a person required to pay support and that fails to withhold or deduct the amount of money as ordered by the support order, the court also may require the employer, the bureau of workers' compensation, an employer that is paying workers' compensation benefits, a board, board of trustees, or other governing entity of a retirement system, person paying or distributing income to an obligor under a support order, or financial institution to pay the accumulated support arrearages.

HISTORY: RS §§ 5644, 5645; 75 v 746, §§ 6, 7; GC §§ 12141, 12142; Bureau of Code Revision, 10-1-53; 141 v H 509. Eff 12-1-86.

The effective date of HB 509 is set by section 6 of the act.

§ 2705.06 Imprisonment until order obeyed.

When the contempt consists of the omission to do an act which the accused yet can perform, he may be imprisoned until he performs it.

HISTORY: RS § 5646; 75 v 746, § 8; GC § 12143; Bureau of Code Revision. Eff 10-1-53.

§ 2705.07 Proceedings when party released on bail fails to appear.

If the party released on bail under section 2705.04 of the Revised Code fails to appear upon the day named, the court may issue another order of arrest, or order the bond for his appearance to be prosecuted, or both. If the bond is prosecuted, the measure of damages in the action is the extent of loss or injury sustained by the aggrieved party by reason of the misconduct for which the contempt was prosecuted, and the costs of the proceeding. Such recovery is for the benefit of the party injured.

HISTORY: RS § 5647; 75 v 746, § 9; GC § 12144; Bureau of Code Revision. Eff 10-1-53.

§ 2705.08 Release of prisoner committed for contempt.

When a person is committed to jail for contempt, the court or judge who made the order may discharge him from imprisonment when it appears that the public interest will not suffer thereby.

HISTORY: RS § 5648; 75 v 746, § 10; GC § 12145; Bureau of Code Revision. Eff 10-1-53.

[APPEAL]

§ 2705.09 Judgment final.

The judgment and orders of a court or officer made

in cases of contempt may be reviewed on appeal. Appeal proceedings shall not suspend execution of the order or judgment until the person in contempt files a bond in the court rendering the judgment, or in the court or before the officer making the order, payable to the state, with sureties to the acceptance of the clerk of that court, in an amount fixed by the reviewing court, or a judge thereof, conditioned that if judgment is rendered against such person he will abide by and perform the order or judgment.

HISTORY: RS § 5649; 75 v 746, § 11; GC § 12146; Bureau of Code Revision. Eff 10-1-53.

§ 2705.10 Alternative remedy.

This chapter furnishes a remedy in cases not provided for by another section of the Revised Code.

HISTORY: RS § 5650; 75 v 746, § 12; GC § 12147; Bureau of Code Revision, 10-1-53; 141 v H 158. Eff 3-17-87.

CHAPTER 2725: HABEAS CORPUS

§ 2725.01 Persons entitled to writ of habeas corpus.

Whoever is unlawfully restrained of his liberty, or entitled to the custody of another, of which custody such person is unlawfully deprived, may prosecute a writ of habeas corpus, to inquire into the cause of such imprisonment, restraint, or deprivation.

HISTORY: RS § 5726; S&C 681; 29 v 164; GC § 12161; Bureau of Code Revision. Eff 10-1-53.

§ 2725.02 Courts authorized to grant writ.

The writ of habeas corpus may be granted by the supreme court, court of appeals, court of common pleas, probate court, or by a judge of any such court.

HISTORY: RS § 5727; S&C 681, 1213; 29 v 164; 51 v 167, § 3; 82 v 16, 36; GC § 12162; 103 v 405(429); Bureau of Code Revision. Eff 10-1-53.

§ 2725.03 Jurisdiction for production or discharge of inmate of institution.

If a person restrained of his liberty is an inmate of a state benevolent or correctional institution, the location of which is fixed by statute and at the time is in the custody of the officers of the institution, no court or judge other than the courts or judges of the county in which the institution is located has jurisdiction to issue or determine a writ of habeas corpus for his production or discharge. Any writ issued by a court or judge of another county to an officer or person in charge at the state institution to compel the production or discharge of an inmate thereof is void.

HISTORY: RS § 5727a; 97 v 318; GC § 12163; Bureau of Code Revision, 10-1-53; 145 v H 571. Eff 10-6-94.

§ 2725.04 Application for writ.

Application for the writ of habeas corpus shall be by petition, signed and verified either by the party for whose relief it is intended, or by some person for him, and shall specify:

(A) That the person in whose behalf the application is made is imprisoned, or restrained of his liberty;

(B) The officer, or name of the person by whom the prisoner is so confined or restrained; or, if both are unknown or uncertain, such officer or person may be described by an assumed appellation and the person who is served with the writ is deemed the person intended;

(C) The place where the prisoner is so imprisoned or restrained, if known;

(D) A copy of the commitment or cause of detention of such person shall be exhibited, if it can be procured without impairing the efficiency of the remedy; or, if the imprisonment or detention is without legal authority, such fact must appear.

HISTORY: RS § 5728; S&C 681, 684, 685; 29 v 164; 45 v 45, §§ 4, 5; GC § 12164; Bureau of Code Revision. Eff 10-1-53.

§ 2725.05 Writ not allowed.

If it appears that a person alleged to be restrained of his liberty is in the custody of an officer under process issued by a court or magistrate, or by virtue of the judgment or order of a court of record, and that the court or magistrate had jurisdiction to issue the process, render the judgment, or make the order, the writ of habeas corpus shall not be allowed. If the jurisdiction appears after the writ is allowed, the person shall not be discharged by reason of any informality or defect in the process, judgment, or order.

HISTORY: RS § 5729; S&C 681, 684; 29 v 164; 32 v 23; GC § 12165; Bureau of Code Revision. Eff 10-1-53.

§ 2725.06 Writ must be granted.

When a petition for a writ of habeas corpus is presented, if it appears that the writ ought to issue, a court or judge authorized to grant the writ must grant it forthwith.

HISTORY: RS § 5730; S&C 681; 29 v 164; GC § 12166; Bureau of Code Revision. Eff 10-1-53.

§ 2725.07 Clerk shall issue writ.

When a writ of habeas corpus is granted, the clerk of the court which granted the writ shall forthwith issue said writ under the seal of such court. In case of emergency, the judge who allowed the writ may issue it under his own hand, and depute any officer or other person to serve it.

HISTORY: RS § 5731; S&C 681; 29 v 164; GC § 12167; Bureau of Code Revision. Eff 10-1-53.

§ 2725.08 Designation of prisoner.

The person to be produced upon a writ of habeas corpus shall be designated by his name, if known, and if his name is not known, or is uncertain, such person may be described in any other way so as to make known who is intended.

HISTORY: RS § 5732; S&C 685; 45 v 45, § 5; GC § 12168; Bureau of Code Revision. Eff 10-1-53.

§ 2725.09 Requisites of writ.

In case of confinement, imprisonment, or detention of a person by an officer, a writ of habeas corpus shall be directed to him, and command him to have such person before the court or judge designated in the writ, at a time and place therein specified.

HISTORY: RS § 5733; S&C 684; 45 v 45; GC § 12169; Bureau of Code Revision. Eff 10-1-53.

§ 2725.10 Form of writ when prisoner not in custody of an officer.

In case of confinement, imprisonment, or detention by a person not an officer, the writ of habeas corpus shall be in the following form:

The State of Ohio, ... County, ss.:
To the sheriff of our several counties, greeting:
We command you that the body of . . . . of . . . . . . by . . . . of . . . ., imprisoned and restrained of his liberty, as it is said, you take and have before . . . ., a judge of our . . . . court, or, in case of his absence or disability, before some other judge of the same court, at . . . ., forthwith to do and receive what our said judge shall then and there consider . . . . concerning him in his behalf; and summon the said . . . . then and there to appear before our said judge, to show the cause of the taking and detention of the said . . . .
(Seal) Witness . . . ., at . . . ., this . . . . day of . . . ., in the year . . . .

HISTORY: RS § 5734; S&C 684; 45 v 45; GC § 12170; Bureau of Code Revision. Eff 10-1-53.

§ 2725.11 Service of writ.

The writ of habeas corpus may be served in any county by the sheriff of that or any other county or by a person deputed by the court or judge issuing the writ.

HISTORY: RS § 5735; S&C 684; 45 v 45, § 2; GC § 12171; Bureau of Code Revision. Eff 10-1-53.

[RETURN]

§ 2725.12 Execution and return of writ.

The officer or person to whom a writ of habeas corpus is directed shall convey the person imprisoned or detained, and named in the writ, before the judge granting the writ, or, in case of his absence or disability, before some other judge of the same court, on the day specified in the writ. Said officer or person shall make due return of the writ, together with the day and the cause of the caption and detention of such person, according to its command.

HISTORY: RS § 5736; S&C 682; 29 v 164, § 2; GC § 12172; Bureau of Code Revision. Eff 10-1-53.

§ 2725.13 Return of writ to another judge.

When a writ of habeas corpus is issued by a court in session, if the court has adjourned when the writ is returned, it shall be returned before any judge of the same court. When the writ is returned before one judge, at a time when the court is in session, he may adjourn the case into the court, there to be heard and determined.

HISTORY: RS § 5737; S&C 684; 45 v 45, § 3; GC § 12173; Bureau of Code Revision. Eff 10-1-53.

§ 2725.14 Contents of the return.

When the person to be produced under a writ of habeas corpus is imprisoned or restrained by an officer, the person who makes the return shall state therein, and in other cases the person in whose custody the prisoner is found shall state, in writing, to the court or judge before whom the writ is returnable, plainly and unequivocally:

(A) Whether or not he has the prisoner in his custody or power or under restraint.

(B) If the prisoner is in his custody or power or under restraint, he shall set forth, at large, the authority, and the true and whole cause, of such imprisonment and restraint, with a copy of the writ, warrant, or other process upon which the prisoner is detained.

(C) If such prisoner was in his custody or power or under restraint, and such custody or restraint was transferred to another, he shall state particularly to whom, at what time, for what cause, and by what authority such transfer was made.

HISTORY: RS § 5738; S&C 685; 45 v 45, § 6; GC § 12174; Bureau of Code Revision. Eff 10-1-53.

§ 2725.15 Return must be signed and sworn to.

The return or statement referred to in section 2725.14 of the Revised Code shall be signed by the person who makes it, and shall be sworn to by him, unless he is a sworn public officer and makes the return in his official capacity.

HISTORY: RS § 5739; S&C 685; 45 v 45, § 7; GC § 12175; Bureau of Code Revision. Eff 10-1-53.

§ 2725.16 Continuance of cause.

The court or judge to whom a writ of habeas corpus is returned, or the court into which it is adjourned, for good cause shown, may continue the cause, and, in that event, shall make such order for the safekeeping of the person imprisoned or detained as the nature of the case requires.

HISTORY: RS § 5740; S&C 685; 45 v 45, § 9; GC § 12176; Bureau of Code Revision. Eff 10-1-53.

§ 2725.17 Discharge of prisoner.

When the judge has examined the cause of caption and detention of a person brought before him as provided in section 2725.12 of the Revised Code, and is satisfied that such person is unlawfully imprisoned or detained, he shall forthwith discharge such person from confinement. On such examination, the judge may disregard matters of form or technicalities in any mittimus or order of commitment by a court or officer authorized by law to commit.

HISTORY: RS § 5741; S&C 682; 29 v 164, § 3; 78 v 113; GC § 12177; Bureau of Code Revision. Eff 10-1-53.

§ 2725.18 Prisoner may be committed or let to bail.

When the person brought before a judge under section 2725.12 of the Revised Code is confined or detained in a legal manner on a charge of having committed a crime or offense which is bailable, the judge may recommit him or let him to bail. If such person is let to bail, the judge shall require him to enter into a recognizance, with sufficient surety, in such sum as the judge finds reasonable, after considering the circumstances of the prisoner and the nature of the offense charged, and conditioned for his appearance at the court where the offense is properly cognizable. The judge forthwith shall certify his proceedings, together with any recognizance, to the proper court. If the person charged fails to give such recognizance, he shall be committed to prison by the judge.

HISTORY: RS § 5742; S&C 682; 29 v 164, § 3; GC § 12178; Bureau of Code Revision. Eff 10-1-53.

§ 2725.19 Mandatory commitment for capital offense.

If a prisoner brought before a judge under section 2725.12 of the Revised Code was committed by a judge, and is plainly and specifically charged in the warrant of commitment with a felony the punishment for which is capital, he shall not be removed, discharged, or let to bail.

HISTORY: RS § 5743; S&C 683; 29 v 164, § 8; GC § 12179; Bureau of Code Revision, 10-1-53; 129 v 582(745). Eff 1-10-61.

§ 2725.20 Return as evidence or plea.

If a prisoner brought before a judge under section 2725.12 of the Revised Code is in custody under a warrant or commitment in pursuance of law, the return of the writ of habeas corpus is prima-facie evidence of the cause of detention. If such prisoner is restrained of his liberty by alleged private authority, the return is only a plea of the facts therein set forth, and the party claiming the custody shall be held to make proof of such facts. Upon the final disposition of a case, the court or judge shall make such order as to costs as it requires.

HISTORY: RS § 5744; S&C 685; 45 v 45, § 8; GC § 12180; Bureau of Code Revision. Eff 10-1-53.

§ 2725.21 Forfeiture by clerk for refusal to issue writ.

A clerk of a court who refuses to issue a writ of habeas corpus, after an allowance of such writ and a demand therefor, shall forfeit to the party aggrieved the sum of five hundred dollars.

HISTORY: RS § 5745; S&C 682; 29 v 164, § 5; GC § 12181; Bureau of Code Revision. Eff 10-1-53.

§ 2725.22 Failure to obey writ.

No person to whom a writ of habeas corpus is directed shall neglect or refuse to obey or make return of it according to the command thereof, or make a false return, or upon demand made by the prisoner, or by any person on his behalf, refuse to deliver to the person demanding, within six hours after demand therefor, a true copy of the warrant of commitment and detainer of the prisoner.

Whoever violates this section shall forfeit to the party aggrieved two hundred dollars for a first offense; for a second offense such person shall forfeit four hundred dollars, and, if an officer, shall be incapable of holding his office.

HISTORY: RS § 5746; S&C 682; 29 v 164, § 4; GC § 12182; Bureau of Code Revision. Eff 10-1-53.

§ 2725.23 Persons at large upon writ not to be again imprisoned.

A person who is set at large upon a writ of habeas

corpus shall not be imprisoned again for the same offense, unless by the legal order or process of the court in which he is bound by recognizance to appear, or other court having jurisdiction of the cause or offense.

No person shall knowingly, contrary to sections 2725.01 to 2725.28, inclusive, of the Revised Code, recommit, imprison, or cause to be recommitted or imprisoned, for the same offense, or pretended offense, a person so set at large, or knowingly aid or assist therein.

Whoever violates this section shall forfeit to the party aggrieved five hundred dollars, notwithstanding any colorable pretense or variation in the warrant or commitment.

HISTORY: RS § 5747; S&C 682; 29 v 164, § 6; GC § 12183; Bureau of Code Revision. Eff 10-1-53.

§ 2725.24 Prisoner shall not be removed from custody of one officer to another.

A person committed to prison, or in the custody of an officer for a criminal matter, shall not be removed therefrom into the custody of another officer, unless by legal process, or unless the prisoner is delivered to an inferior officer to be taken to jail, or, by order of the proper court, is removed from one place to another within this state for trial, or in case of fire, infection, or other necessity.

A person who, after such commitment, makes, signs, or countersigns a warrant for such removal contrary to this section shall forfeit to the party aggrieved five hundred dollars.

HISTORY: RS § 5748; S&C 683; 29 v 164, § 7; GC § 12184; Bureau of Code Revision. Eff 10-1-53.

§ 2725.25 No prisoner to be sent out of state.

No person shall be sent as a prisoner to a place out of this state, for a crime or offense committed within it.

A person imprisoned in violation of this section may maintain an action for false imprisonment against the person by whom he was so imprisoned or transported, and against a person who contrives, writes, signs, seals, or countersigns a writing for such imprisonment or transportation, or aids or assists therein.

HISTORY: RS §§ 5749, 5750; S&S 387; S&C 683; 65 v 165, § 9; GC §§ 12185, 12186; Bureau of Code Revision. Eff 10-1-53.

§ 2725.26 Record of writs.

The proceedings upon a writ of habeas corpus must be recorded by the clerk of the court in which such proceedings were had, and may be reviewed on appeal as in other cases.

HISTORY: RS § 5751; S&C 685; 45 v 45, § 10; GC § 12187; Bureau of Code Revision. Eff 10-1-53.

§ 2725.27 Recovery of forfeitures; limitations.

The forfeitures mentioned in sections 2725.21 to 2725.24, inclusive, of the Revised Code, may be recovered by the party aggrieved or his executors or administrators against the offender or his executors or administrators by civil action in a court having cognizance thereof.

Actions for violations of sections 2725.21 to 2725.25, inclusive, of the Revised Code, shall be brought within two years after the offense is committed, except in cases of imprisonment of the party aggrieved, when action may be brought within two years after his delivery out of prison, or after his decease if he dies in prison.

HISTORY: RS § 5752; S&C 683; 29 v 164, § 10; GC § 12188; Bureau of Code Revision. Eff 10-1-53.

§ 2725.28 Fees and costs.

The fees of officers and witnesses shall be taxed by the judge, on return of the proceedings on a writ of habeas corpus, and collected as a part of the original costs in the case. When the prisoner is discharged, the costs shall be taxed to the state, and paid out of the county treasury, upon the warrant of the county auditor. No officer or person shall demand payment in advance for any fees to which he is entitled by virtue of the proceedings, when the writ is demanded or issued for the discharge from custody of a person confined under color of proceedings in a criminal case. When a person in custody by virtue or under color of proceedings in a civil case is discharged, costs shall be taxed against the party at whose instance he was so in custody. If he is remanded to custody, costs shall be taxed against him.

HISTORY: RS § 5753; S&C 685; 45 v 45, § 11; GC § 12189; Bureau of Code Revision. Eff 10-1-53.

CHAPTER 2743: COURT OF CLAIMS

[§ 2743.19.1] § 2743.191 Reparations fund.

(A) There is hereby created in the state treasury the reparations fund, which shall be used only for the payment of awards of reparations that are granted by the court of claims commissioners, the compensation of the court of claims commissioners, the compensation of judges necessary to hear and determine appeals from the commissioners, the compensation of any personnel needed by the court of claims to administer sections 2743.51 to 2743.72 of the Revised Code, the compensation of witnesses as provided in division (B) of section 2743.65 of the Revised Code, other administrative costs of hearing and determining claims for an award of reparations by the court of claims commissioners and of hearing and determining appeals from the commissioners by the court of claims, the costs of administering sections 2969.01 to 2969.06 of the Revised Code, the costs of investigation and recommendation as certified by the attorney general, the provision of state financial assistance to victim assistance programs in accordance with sections 109.91 and 109.92 of the Revised Code, the cost of printing and distributing the pamphlet prepared by the attorney general pursuant to section 109.42 of the Revised Code, and, subject to division (D) of section 2743.71 of the Revised Code, the costs associated with the printing and providing of information cards or other printed materials to law enforcement agencies and prosecuting authorities and with publicizing the availability of awards of reparations pursuant to section 2743.71 of the Revised Code. All costs paid pursuant to section 2743.70 of the Revised Code, the fifty-dollar portions of license reinstatement fees mandated by division (L)(2)(b) of section 4511.191 [4511.19.1] of the Revised Code to be credited to the fund, the portions of the proceeds of the sale of a forfeited vehicle specified in division (D)(2) of section 4503.234 [4503.23.4] of the Revised Code, payments collected by the department of rehabilitation and correction from prisoners who voluntarily participate in an approved work and training program pursuant to division (C)(8)(b)(ii) of section 5145.16 of the Revised Code, and all moneys collected by the state pursuant to its right of subrogation provided in section 2743.72 of the Revised Code shall be deposited in the fund.

(B) In making an award of reparations, a single commissioner or a panel of court of claims commissioners shall render the award against the state and the director of budget and management as its agent for payment of the award. The award shall be accomplished only through the following procedure, which may be enforced by writ of mandamus directed to the appropriate official:

(1) The clerk of the court of claims shall forward a certified copy of the order granting the award to the director for payment.

(2) Upon receipt of the certified copy of the order granting the award from the clerk of the court of claims pursuant to division (B)(1) of this section, the director shall provide for payment of the claimant, an assignee of the claimant, or the claimant and the claimant's assignee in the amount of the award set forth in the certified copy of the order.

If the award is to be paid in installments, the director shall provide for payment of the amount of the award that will fall due during the current appropriation period.

(3) The expense shall be charged against all available unencumbered moneys in the fund.

(4) If the director determines that sufficient unencumbered moneys do not exist in the fund, the director shall make application for payment of the award out of the emergency purposes account or any other appropriation for emergencies or contingencies, and payment out of this account or other appropriation shall be authorized if there are sufficient moneys greater than the sum total of then pending emergency purposes account requests or requests for releases from the other appropriations.

(5) If sufficient moneys do not exist in the account or any other appropriation for emergencies or contingencies to pay the award, the director shall request the general assembly to make an appropriation sufficient to pay the award, and no payment shall be made until the appropriation has been made. The director shall make this appropriation request during the current biennium and during each succeeding biennium until a sufficient appropriation is made. If, prior to the time that an appropriation is made by the general assembly pursuant to this division, the fund has sufficient unencumbered funds to pay the award or part of the award, the available funds shall be used to pay the award or part of the award, and the appropriation request shall be amended to request only sufficient funds to pay that part of the award that is unpaid.

(C) No order granting an award shall be forwarded by the clerk of the court of claims to the director until all appeals have been determined and all rights to appeal exhausted, except as otherwise provided in this section. If any party to a claim for an award of reparations appeals from only a portion of an award, and a remaining portion provides for the payment of money by the state, a certified copy of the order, together with a copy of the notice of appeal, shall be forwarded to the director, and that part of the award calling for the payment of money by the state and not a subject of the appeal shall be processed for payment as described in this section.

(D) The attorney general shall submit to the clerk of the court of claims itemized bills for the costs of printing and distributing the pamphlet the attorney general prepares pursuant to section 109.42 of the Revised Code. The itemized bills shall set forth the name and address of the persons owed the amounts set forth in them. Upon submission of the itemized bills, the clerk shall provide for their payment.

HISTORY: 136 v H 82 (Eff 9-29-76); 137 v S 221 (Eff 11-23-77); 138 v H 238 (Eff 8-8-80); 139 v S 30 (Eff 3-18-83); 140 v S 172 (Eff 9-26-84); 141 v H 201 (Eff 7-1-85); 141 v H 657 (Eff 9-12-86); 142 v S 308 (Eff 3-14-89); 143 v H 111 (Eff 7-1-89); 144 v S 275 (Eff 7-1-93)†; 145 v H 152 (Eff 7-1-93); 146 v H 117 (Eff 6-30-95); 146 v H 353. Eff 9-17-96.

† The provisions of §§ 4, 5 of SB 62 (145 v —) read as follows:

SECTION 4. That Section 3 of Sub. S.B. 275 of the 119th General Assembly be amended to read as follows:

"Sec. 3, Sections 1 and 2 of this act shall take effect September 1, 1993."

SECTION 5. That existing Section 3 of Sub. S.B. 275 of the 119th General Assembly is hereby repealed.

TITLE 31: DOMESTIC RELATIONS—CHILDREN

CHAPTER 3107: ADOPTION

§ 3107.17 Hearings to be closed; confidentiality of information; indexing of proceedings.

(A) All hearings held under sections 3107.01 to 3107.19 of the Revised Code shall be held in closed court without the admittance of any person other than essential officers of the court, the parties, the witnesses of the parties, counsel, persons who have not previously consented to an adoption but who are required to consent, and representatives of the agencies present to perform their official duties.

(B)(1) Except as provided in divisions (B)(2) and (D) of this section and sections 3107.39 to 3107.44 and 3107.60 to 3107.68 of the Revised Code, no person or governmental entity shall knowingly reveal any information contained in a paper, book, or record pertaining to a placement under section 5103.16 of the Revised Code or to an adoption that is part of the permanent record of a court or maintained by the department of human services, an agency, or attorney without the consent of a court.

(2) An agency or attorney may examine the agency's or attorney's own papers, books, and records pertaining to a placement or adoption without a court's consent for official administrative purposes. The department of human services may examine its own papers, books, and records pertaining to a placement or adoption, or such papers, books, and records of an agency, without a court's consent for official administrative, certification, and eligibility determination purposes.

(C) The petition, the interlocutory order, the final decree of adoption, and other adoption proceedings shall be recorded in a book kept for such purposes and shall be separately indexed. The book shall be a part of the records of the court, and all consents, affidavits, and other papers shall be properly filed.

(D) All forms that pertain to the social or medical histories of the biological parents of an adopted person and that were completed pursuant to section 3107.09 or 3107.091 [3107.09.1] of the Revised Code shall be filed only in the permanent record kept by the court. During the minority of the adopted person, only the adoptive parents of the person may inspect the forms. When an adopted person reaches majority, only the adopted person may inspect the forms. Under the circumstances described in this division, an adopted person or the adoptive parents are entitled to inspect the forms upon requesting the clerk of the court to produce them.

(E)(1) The department of human services shall prescribe a form that permits any person who is authorized by division (D) of this section to inspect forms that pertain to the social or medical histories of the biological parents and that were completed pursuant to section 3107.09 or 3107.091 [3107.09.1] of the Revised Code to request notice if any correction or expansion of either such history, made pursuant to division (D) of section 3107.09 of the Revised Code, is made a part of the permanent record kept by the court. The form shall be designed to facilitate the provision of the information and statements described in division (E)(3) of this section. The department shall provide copies of the form to each court. A court shall provide a copy of the request form to each adoptive parent when a final decree of adoption is entered and shall explain to each adoptive parent at that time that an adoptive parent who completes and files the form will be notified of any correction or expansion of either the social or medical history of the biological parents of the adopted person made during the minority of the adopted person that is made a part of the permanent record kept by the court, and that, during the adopted person's minority, the adopted person may inspect the forms that pertain to those histories. Upon request, the court also shall provide a copy of the request form to any adoptive parent during the minority of the adopted person and to an adopted person who has reached the age of majority.

(2) Any person who is authorized to inspect forms pursuant to division (D) of this section who wishes to be notified of corrections or expansions pursuant to division (D) of section 3107.09 of the Revised Code that are made a part of the permanent record kept by the court shall file with the court, on a copy of the form prescribed by the department of human services pursuant to division (E)(1) of this section, a request for such notification that contains the information and statements required by division (E)(3) of this section. A request may be filed at any time if the person who files the request is authorized at that time to inspect forms that pertain to the social or medical histories.

(3) A request for notification as described in division (E)(2) of this section shall contain all of the following information:

(a) The adopted person's name and mailing address at that time;

(b) The name of each adoptive parent, and if the adoptive person is a minor at the time of the filing of the request, the mailing address of each adoptive parent at that time;

(c) The adopted person's date of birth;

(d) The date of entry of the final decree of adoption;

(e) A statement requesting the court to notify the person who files the request, at the address provided in the request, if any correction or expansion of either the social or medical history of the biological parents is made a part of the permanent record kept by the court;

(f) A statement that the person who files the request is authorized, at the time of the filing, to inspect the forms that pertain to the social and medical histories of the biological parents;

(g) The signature of the person who files the request.

(4) Upon the filing of a request for notification in accordance with division (E)(2) of this section, the clerk of the court in which it is filed immediately shall insert the request in the permanent record of the case. A person who has filed the request and who wishes to update it with respect to a new mailing address may inform the court in writing of the new address. Upon its receipt, the court promptly shall insert the new address into the permanent record by attaching it to the request. Thereafter, any notification described in this division shall be sent to the new address.

(5) Whenever a social or medical history of a biological parent is corrected or expanded and the correction or expansion is made a part of the permanent record kept by the court, the court shall ascertain whether a request for notification has been filed in accordance with division (E)(2) of this section. If such a request has been filed, the court shall determine whether, at that time, the person who filed the request is authorized, under division (D) of this section, to inspect the forms that pertain to the social or medical history of the biological parents. If the court determines that the person who filed the request is so authorized, it immediately shall notify the person that the social or medical history has been corrected or expanded, that it has been made a part of the permanent record kept by the court, and that the forms that pertain to the records may be inspected in accordance with division (D) of this section.

HISTORY: 136 v H 156 (Eff 1-1-77); 137 v S 340 (Eff 8-29-78); 137 v H 832 (Eff 3-13-79); 140 v H 84 (Eff 3-19-85); 146 v H 419. Eff 9-18-96.

Analogous to former RC § 3107.14, repealed 136 v H 156.

The effective date is set by section 3 of HB 419.

§ 3107.99 Penalty.

Whoever violates division (B)(1) of section 3107.17 of the Revised Code is guilty of a misdemeanor of the third degree.

HISTORY: 146 v H 419. Eff 9-18-96.

The effective date is set by section 3 of HB 419.

CHAPTER 3109: CHILDREN

§ 3109.09 Liability of parents for destructive acts or theft by their children.

(A) As used in this section, "parent" means one of the following:

(1) Both parents unless division (A)(2) or (3) of this section applies;

(2) The parent designated the residential parent and legal custodian pursuant to an order issued under section 3109.04 of the Revised Code that is not a shared parenting order;

(3) The custodial parent of a child born out of wedlock with respect to whom no custody order has been issued.

(B) Any owner of property, including any board of education of a city, local, exempted village, or joint vocational school district, may maintain a civil action to recover compensatory damages not exceeding ten thousand dollars and court costs from the parent of a minor if the minor willfully damages property belonging to the owner or commits acts cognizable as a "theft offense," as defined in section 2913.01 of the Revised Code, involving the property of the owner. The action may be joined with an action under Chapter 2737. of the Revised Code against the minor, or the minor and the minor's parent, to recover the property regardless of value, but any additional damages recovered from the parent pursuant to this section shall be limited to compensatory damages not exceeding ten thousand dollars, as authorized by this section. A finding of willful destruction of property or of committing acts cognizable as a theft offense is not dependent upon a prior finding that the child is a delinquent child or upon the child's conviction of any criminal offense.

(C)(1) If a court renders a judgment in favor of a board of education of a city, local, exempted village, or joint vocational school district in an action brought pursuant to division (B) of this section, if the board of education agrees to the parent's performance of community service in lieu of full payment of the judgment, and if the parent who is responsible for the payment of the judgment agrees to voluntarily participate in the performance of community service in lieu of full payment of the judgment, the court may order the parent to perform community service in lieu of providing full payment of the judgment.

(2) If a court, pursuant to division (C)(1) of this section, orders a parent to perform community service in lieu of providing full payment of a judgment, the court shall specify in its order the amount of the judgment, if any, to be paid by the parent, the type and number of hours of community service to be performed by the parent, and any other conditions necessary to carry out the order.

(D) This section shall not apply to a parent of a minor if the minor was married at the time of the commission of the acts or violations that would otherwise give rise to a civil action commenced under this section.

(E) Any action brought pursuant to this section shall be commenced and heard as in other civil actions.

(F) The monetary limitation upon compensatory damages set forth in this section does not apply to a civil action brought pursuant to section 2307.70 of the Revised Code.

HISTORY: 131 v 689 (Eff 10-6-65); 132 v H 257 (Eff 10-24-67); 133 v S 10 (Eff 9-15-69); 137 v H 456 (Eff 5-23-78); 141 v H 158 (Eff 3-17-87); 141 v S 316 (Eff 3-19-87); 142 v H 708 (Eff 4-19-88); 143 v S 3 (Eff 4-11-91); 144 v H 154 (Eff 7-31-92); 146 v H 601. Eff 10-29-96.

§ 3109.10 Liability of parents for assaults by their children.

As used in this section, "parent" has the same meaning as in section 3109.09 of the Revised Code.

Any person is entitled to maintain an action to recover compensatory damages in a civil action, in an amount not to exceed ten thousand dollars and costs of suit in a court of competent jurisdiction, from the parent of a child under the age of eighteen if the child willfully and maliciously assaults the person by a means or force likely to produce great bodily harm. A finding of willful and malicious assault by a means or force likely to produce great bodily harm is not dependent upon a prior finding that the child is a delinquent child.

Any action brought pursuant to this section shall be commenced and heard as in other civil actions for damages.

The monetary limitation upon compensatory damages set forth in this section does not apply to a civil action brought pursuant to section 2307.70 of the Revised Code.

HISTORY: 133 v S 11 (Eff 9-15-69); 141 v S 316 (Eff 3-19-87); 143 v S 3 (Eff 4-11-91); 146 v H 18 (Eff 11-24-95); 146 v H 601. Eff 10-29-96.

CHAPTER 3111: PARENTAGE

§ 3111.29 Interference with establishment of paternity.

No person, by using physical harassment or threats of violence against another person, shall interfere with the other person in his initiation or continuance of, or attempt to prevent the other person from initiating or continuing, an action under sections 3111.01 to 3111.19 of the Revised Code.

HISTORY: 144 v S 10. Eff 7-15-92.

§ 3111.99 Penalties.

(A) For purposes of this section, "administrative support order" and "obligor" have the same meaning as in section 3111.20 of the Revised Code.

(B) Whoever violates section 3111.29 of the Revised Code is guilty of interfering with the establishment of paternity, a misdemeanor of the first degree.

(C) An obligor who violates division (B)(1)(c) of section 3111.23 of the Revised Code shall be fined not more than fifty dollars for a first offense, not more than one hundred dollars for a second offense, and not more than five hundred dollars for each subsequent offense.

(D) An obligor who violates division (E)(2) of section 3111.23 of the Revised Code shall be fined not more than fifty dollars for a first offense, not more than one hundred dollars for a second offense, and not more than five hundred dollars for each subsequent offense.

(E) A fine imposed pursuant to division (C) or (D) of this section shall be paid to the child support enforcement agency administering the obligor's child support order. The amount of the fine that does not exceed the amount of arrearage the obligor owes under the administrative support order shall be disbursed in accordance with the support order. The amount of the fine that exceeds the amount of the arrearage under the support order shall be used by the agency for the administration of its program for child support enforcement.

HISTORY: 144 v S 10 (Eff 7-15-92); 146 v S 2 (Eff 7-1-96); 146 v H 167. Eff 6-11-96.

The effective date of HB 167 (146 v —) is changed from 11-15-96 to 6-11-96 by section 7 of HB 710 (146 v —).

CHAPTER 3113: NEGLECT, ABANDONMENT, OR DOMESTIC VIOLENCE

§ 3113.04 Suspension of sentence on posting bond.

(A) Sentence may be suspended if a person, after conviction under section 2919.21 of the Revised Code and before sentence under that section, appears before the court of common pleas in which the conviction took place and enters into bond to the state in a sum fixed by the court at not less than five hundred nor more than one thousand dollars, with sureties approved by the court, conditioned that the person will furnish the child or other dependent with necessary or proper home, care, food, and clothing, or will pay promptly each week for such purpose to the child support enforcement agency, a sum to be fixed by the agency. The child support enforcement agency shall comply with sections 3113.21 to 3113.219 [3113.21.9] of the Revised Code when it fixes the sum to be paid.

(B) Each order for child support made or modified under this section on or after December 31, 1993, shall include as part of the order a general provision, as described in division (A)(1) of section 3113.21 of the Revised Code, requiring the withholding or deduction of wages or assets of the obligor under the order as described in division (D) of section 3113.21 of the Revised Code or another type of appropriate requirement as described in division (D)(6), (D)(7) or (H) of that section, to ensure that withholding or deduction from the wages or assets of the obligor is available from the commencement of the support order for collection of the support and of any arrearages that occur; a statement requiring all parties to the order to notify the child support enforcement agency in writing of their current mailing address, their current residence address, and any changes in either address, and a notice that the requirement to notify the agency of all changes in either address continues until further notice from the court. If any person required to pay child support under an order made under this section on or after April 15, 1985, or modified on or after December 1, 1986, is found in contempt of court for failure to make support payments under the order, the court that makes the finding, in addition to any other penalty or remedy imposed, shall assess all court costs arising out of the contempt proceeding against the person and require the person to pay any reasonable attorney's fees of any adverse party, as determined by the court, that arose in relation to the act of contempt.

(C) Notwithstanding section 3109.01 of the Revised Code, if a court issues a child support order under this section, the order shall remain in effect beyond the child's eighteenth birthday as long as the child continuously attends on a full-time basis any recognized and accredited high school. Any parent ordered to pay support under a child support order issued under this section shall continue to pay support under the order, including during seasonal vacation periods, until the order terminates.

HISTORY: GC § 13010; 99 v 228; Bureau of Code Revision, 10-1-53; 134 v H 511 (Eff 1-1-74); 137 v S 87 (Eff 1-1-79); 140 v H 614 (Eff 4-10-85); 141 v H 509 (Eff 12-1-86); 142 v H 231 (Eff 10-5-87); 142 v H 708 (Eff 4-19-88); 143 v H 591 (Eff 4-12-90); 144 v S 10 (Eff 7-15-92); 145 v H 173. Eff 12-31-93.

The effective date is set by section 4 of HB 173.

§ 3113.06 Failure to pay maintenance cost.

No father, or mother when she is charged with the maintenance, of a child under eighteen years of age, or a mentally or physically handicapped child under age twenty-one, who is legally a ward of a public children services agency or is the recipient of aid pursuant to Chapter 5107. or 5115. of the Revised Code, shall neglect or refuse to pay such agency the reasonable cost of maintaining such child when such father or mother is able to do so by reason of property, labor, or earnings.

An offense under this section shall be held committed in the county in which the agency is located. The agency shall file charges against any parent who violates this section, unless the agency files charges under section 2919.21 of the Revised Code, or unless charges of nonsupport are filed by a relative or guardian of the child, or unless an action to enforce support is brought under Chapter 3115. of the Revised Code.

HISTORY: GC §§ 13012, 13014; 99 v 228; 121 v 538; Bureau of Code Revision, 10-1-53; 132 v H 390 (Eff 11-7-67); 133 v S 49 (Eff 8-13-69); 133 v H 361 (Eff 9-23-69); 134 v H 511 (Eff 1-1-74); 141 v H 428 (Eff 12-23-86); 144 v H 298 (Eff 7-26-91); 146 v H 249 (Eff 7-17-95); 146 v H 274 (Eff 8-8-96); 147 v H 408. Eff 10-1-97.

The effective date is set by section 26 of HB 408.

§ 3113.07 Suspension of sentence; bond.

As used in this section, "executive director" has the same meaning as in section 5153.01 of the Revised Code.

Sentence may be suspended, if a person, after conviction under section 3113.06 of the Revised Code and before sentence thereunder, appears before the court of common pleas in which such conviction took place and enters into bond to the state in a sum fixed by the court at not less than five hundred dollars, with sureties approved by such court, conditioned that such person will pay, so long as the child remains a ward of the public children services agency or a recipient of aid pursuant to Chapter 5107. or 5115. of the Revised Code, to the executive director thereof or to a trustee to be named by the court, for the benefit of such agency or if the child is a recipient of aid pursuant to Chapter 5107. or 5115. of the Revised Code, to the county department of human services, the reasonable cost of keeping such child. The amount of such costs and the time of payment shall be fixed by the court.

HISTORY: GC § 13013; 99 v 228; 121 v 538; Bureau of Code Revision, 10-1-53; 132 v H 390 (Eff 11-7-67); 133 v S 49 (Eff 8-13-69); 141 v H 428 (Eff 12-23-86); 144 v H 82 (Eff 9-10-91); 144 v H 298 (Eff 7-26-91); 146 v H 249 (Eff 7-17-95); 147 v H 408. Eff 10-1-97.

The effective date is set by section 26 of HB 408.

§ 3113.08 Failure to give bond; arrest.

Upon failure of the father or mother of a child under eighteen years of age, or of a physically or mentally handicapped child under twenty-one years of age, or the husband of a pregnant woman to comply with any order and undertaking provided for in sections 3113.01 to 3113.14, inclusive, of the Revised Code, such person may be arrested by the sheriff or other officer, on a warrant issued on the praecipe of the prosecuting attorney, and brought before the court of common pleas for sentence. Thereupon the court may pass sentence, or for good cause shown, may modify the order as to the time and amount of payments, or take a new undertaking and further suspend sentence, whichever is for the best interests of such child or pregnant woman and of the public.

HISTORY: GC § 13015; 99 v 229, § 5; Bureau of Code Revision, Eff 10-1-53; 146 v H 274. Eff 8-8-96.

§ 3113.09 Duties of trustee.

The trustee appointed by the court of common pleas under sections 3113.04 and 3113.07 of the Revised Code, shall make quarterly reports of the receipts and expenditures of all moneys coming into his hands as provided in sections 3113.01 to 3113.14 of the Revised Code, such reports to be made to the board of county commissioners of the county from which the person described in section 3113.01 of the Revised Code was sentenced, or to the department of human services. The court may require such trustee to enter into a good and sufficient bond for the faithful performance of the duties imposed on him.

HISTORY: GC § 13016; 99 v 229, § 7; Bureau of Code Revision, 10-1-53; 141 v H 428. Eff 12-23-86.

§ 3113.10 Humane society may act as trustee.

A humane society, incorporated and existing under the laws of this state, and willing to render its services without compensation, may be appointed by the court of common pleas as trustee under sections 3113.04 and 3113.07 of the Revised Code.

HISTORY: GC § 13017; 99 v 229, § 6; Bureau of Code Revision. Eff 10-1-53.

§ 3113.11 Amount credited convict paid to trustee.

When a person is convicted, sentenced, and confined in a workhouse, under sections 3113.01 to 3113.14, inclusive, of the Revised Code, the county from which he is so convicted, sentenced, and confined upon the warrant of the county auditor of such county, and out of the general revenue fund thereof, shall pay monthly fifty cents for each day he is so confined, to the trustee appointed by the court under such sections, to be expended by such trustee for the maintenance of the child under sixteen years of age.

HISTORY: GC § 13018; 99 v 229, § 7; 103 v 864(913); Bureau of Code Revision. Eff 10-1-53.

§ 3113.13 Trustee to be named in mittimus.

When a person is imprisoned in a workhouse or state correctional institution under sections 3113.01 to 3113.14 of the Revised Code, the name and post-office address of the trustee appointed by the court of common pleas under sections 3113.04 and 3113.07 of the Revised Code shall appear in the mittimus.

HISTORY: GC § 13020; 99 v 229, § 7; Bureau of Code Revision, 10-1-53; 145 v H 571. Eff 10-6-94.

§ 3113.14 Continuance of citizenship.

Citizenship once acquired in this state by a father or mother of a child living in this state, for the purpose of sections 3113.01 to 3113.14 of the Revised Code, shall continue until the child has arrived at the age of sixteen years, provided the child continues to live in this state.

HISTORY: GC § 13021; 99 v 229, § 4; Bureau of Code Revision, 10-1-53; 146 v H 274. Eff 8-8-96.

§ 3113.16 Withholding from prisoner earnings.

(A) As used in this section:

(1) "Child support order" has the same meaning as in section 2301.373 [2301.37.3] of the Revised Code.

(2) "Default," "obligor," and "obligee" have the same meanings as in section 2301.34 of the Revised Code.

(3) "Prison," "prison term," and "jail" have the same meanings as in section 2929.01 of the Revised Code.

(B) Notwithstanding any other section of the Revised Code, including sections 5145.16 and 5147.30 of the Revised Code, twenty-five per cent of any money earned pursuant to section 5145.16 or 5147.30 of the Revised Code by a prisoner in a prison or jail who has a dependent child receiving assistance under Chapter 5107. of the Revised Code, shall be paid to the state department of human services.

(C) Notwithstanding any other section of the revised code, including sections 5145.16 and 5147.30 of the Revised Code, and except as provided in division (B) of this section, twenty-five per cent of any money earned pursuant to section 5145.16 or 5147.30 of the Revised Code by a prisoner in a prison or jail who is an obligor in default under a child support order according to the records of the child support enforcement agency administering the order, shall be paid to the agency for distribution to the obligee under the order pursuant to sections 3111.23 to 3111.28 or sections 3113.21 to 3113.219 [3113.21.9] of the Revised Code.

HISTORY: 147 v S 52. Eff 9-3-97.

[SUPPORT ORDER TO WITHHOLD EARNINGS]

§ 3113.21 Withholding or deduction requirements to enforce support order; order to obligor to give cash bond; order to seek employment.

(A)(1) In any action in which support is ordered under Chapter 3115. or under section 2151.23, 2151.33, 2151.36, 2151.49, 3105.18, 3105.21, 3109.05, 3109.19, 3111.13, 3113.04, 3113.07, 3113.216 [3113.21.6], or 3113.31 of the Revised Code, the court shall require the withholding or deduction of wages or assets of the obligor in accordance with division (D) of this section or require the issuance of another type of appropriate court order in accordance with division (D)(6) or (7) or (H) of this section to ensure that withholding or deduction from the wages or assets of the obligor is available from the commencement of the support order for the collection of the support and any arrearages that occur. The court shall determine the specific withholding or deduction requirements or other appropriate requirements applicable to the obligor under the support order in accordance with divisions (D) and (H) of this section and section 2301.371 [2301.37.1] of the Revised Code and shall include the specific requirements in the notices described in divisions (A)(2) and (D) of this section or in the court orders described in divisions (A)(2), (D)(6) or (7), and (H) of this section. Any person required to comply with any withholding or deduction requirement shall determine the manner of withholding or deducting from the specific requirement included in the notices described in those divisions without the need for any amendment to the support order, and any person required to comply with a court order described in division (D)(6), (D)(7), or (H) of this section shall comply with the court order without the need for any amendment to the support order. The court shall include in any action in which support is ordered as described in division (A)(1) of this section a general provision that states the following:

"All child support and spousal support under this order shall be withheld or deducted from the wages or assets of the obligor pursuant to a withholding or deduction notice or appropriate court order issued in accordance with section 3113.21 of the Revised Code and shall be forwarded to the obligee in accordance with sections 3113.21 to 3113.214 [3113.21.4] of the Revised Code."

(2) In any action in which support is ordered or modified as described in division (A)(1) of this section, the court shall determine in accordance with divisions (D) and (H) of this section the types of withholding or deduction requirements or other appropriate requirements that should be imposed relative to the obligor under the support order to collect the support due under the order. Within fifteen days after the obligor under the support order is located subsequent to the issuance of the support order or within fifteen days after the default under the support order, whichever is applicable, the court or the child support enforcement agency, as determined by agreement of the court and the agency, shall send a notice by regular mail to each person required to comply with a withholding or deduction requirement. The notice shall specify the withholding or deduction requirement and shall contain all of the information set forth in division (D)(1)(b), (2)(b), (3)(b), (4)(b), or (5)(b) of this section that is applicable to the requirement. If the appropriate requirement is an order of the type described in division (D)(6), (D)(7), or (H) of this section, the court shall issue and send a court order in accordance with that division. The notices and court orders, and the notices provided by the court or child support enforcement agency that require the obligor to notify the agency of any change in the obligor's employment status or of any other change in the status of the obligor's assets, are final and are enforceable by the court. When the court or agency issues a notice, it shall provide the notice to the obligor in accordance with division (D)(1)(c), (D)(2)(c), (D)(3)(c), (D)(4)(c), or (D)(5)(c) of this section, whichever is applicable, and shall include with the notice the additional notices described in the particular division that is applicable.

(3)(a) If support is ordered or modified on or after December 31, 1993, under Chapter 3115. or under section 2151.23, 2151.33, 2151.36, 2151.49, 3105.18, 3105.21, 3109.05, 3109.19, 3111.13, 3113.04, 3113.07, 3113.216 [3113.21.6], or 3113.31 of the Revised Code, if the court has determined in accordance with division (A)(2) of this section the types of withholding or deduction requirements or other appropriate requirements that should be imposed relative to the obligor under the support order to collect the support due under the order, if the court or a child support enforcement agency has mailed the appropriate notice to the person required to comply with the withholding or deduction requirements that the court has determined should be imposed or the court has issued and sent a court order described in division (D)(6), (D)(7), or (H) of this section containing the other appropriate requirements that the court determined should be imposed, and if the child support enforcement agency is notified or otherwise determines that the employment status or other circumstances of the obligor have changed and that it is more appropriate to impose another type of or an additional withholding or deduction requirement or another type of or additional court order containing another appropriate requirement, the agency immediately shall comply with section 3113.212 [3113.21.2] of the Revised Code. The notices and court orders issued under this division and section 3113.212 [3113.21.2] of the Revised Code, and the notices provided by the court or child support enforcement agency that require the obligor to notify the agency of any change in the obligor's employment status or of any other change in the status of the obligor's assets, are final and are enforceable by the court.

(b) If support has been ordered prior to December 31, 1993, under Chapter 3115. or under section 2151.23, 2151.33, 2151.36, 2151.49, 3105.18, 3105.21, 3109.05, 3109.19, 3111.13, 3113.04, 3113.07, 3113.216 [3113.21.6], or 3113.31 of the Revised Code, if the support order has not been modified on or after December 31, 1993, if division (B) of this section has not been applied on or after December 31, 1993, regarding a default under the order, if the support order includes a provision that is substantively comparable to the general provision described in division (A)(1) of this section that must be included in all support orders issued or modified on or after December 31, 1993, and if the child support enforcement agency is notified or otherwise determines that the employment status or other circumstances of the obligor under the support order have changed so that it is appropriate to impose a withholding or deduction requirement or another type of or additional appropriate requirement as described in division (D) of this section to collect the support due under the order, the agency shall comply with section 3113.212 [3113.21.2] of the Revised Code as if the support order had been issued or modified on or after December 31, 1993, and as if it included the general provision described in division (A)(1) of this section that must be included in all support orders issued or modified on or after that date. The notices and court orders issued under this provision and section 3113.212 [3113.21.2] of the Revised Code, and the notices provided by the court or child support enforcement agency that require the obligor to notify the agency of any change in the obligor's employment status or of any other change in the status of the obligor's assets, are final and are enforceable by the court.

(c) If support has been ordered prior to December 31, 1993, under Chapter 3115. or under section 2151.23, 2151.33, 2151.36, 2151.49, 3105.18, 3105.21, 3109.05, 3109.19, 3111.13, 3113.04, 3113.07, 3113.216 [3113.21.6], or 3113.31 of the Revised Code, if the support order has not been modified on or after December 31, 1993, if division (B) of this section has not been applied on or after December 31, 1993, regarding a default under the order, if the support order does not include a provision that is substantively comparable to the general provision described in division (A)(1) of this section that must be included in all support orders issued or modified on or after December 31, 1993, and if the child support enforcement agency is notified or otherwise determines that the employment status or other circumstances of the obligor under the support order have changed so that it is appropriate to impose a withholding or deduction requirement or another type of or additional appropriate requirement as described in division (D) of this section to collect the support due under the order, the agency may request the court to reissue the support order in question to be identical to the support order except for a general provision as described in division (A) of this section requiring the withholding or deduction of wages or assets of the obligor in accordance with division (D) of this section or requiring the issuance of a court order containing another type of appropriate requirement in accordance with division (D)(6), (D)(7), or (H) of this section to ensure that withholding or deduction from the wages or assets of the obligor is available for the collection of current support and any arrearages that occur. Upon the receipt of a request from an agency, the court may reissue the order in accordance with this division. If the court reissues the order, the general provision for the withholding or deduction of wages or assets to be included in the reissued support order specifically shall include the statement prescribed in division (B)(1) of this section. Except for the inclusion of the general provision, the provisions of a reissued order under this division shall be identical to the support order in question, and the court or child support enforcement agency shall issue one or more notices requiring withholding or deduction of wages or assets of the obligor in accordance with divisions (A)(2) and (D) of this section, or the court shall issue one or more court orders imposing other appropriate requirements in accordance with division (A)(2) and division (D)(6), (D)(7), or (H) of this section. The notices shall be mailed within fifteen days after the obligor under the support order is located or within fifteen days after the default under the support order, whichever is applicable. Thereafter, section 3113.212 [3113.21.2] of the Revised Code applies to the issuance of notices and court orders under those divisions with respect to that support order. The notices and court orders issued under this division and section 3113.212 [3113.21.2] of the Revised Code, and the notices provided by the court or child support enforcement agency that require the obligor to notify the agency of any change in the obligor's employment status or of any other change in the status of the obligor's assets, are final and are enforceable by the court.

(4) The department of human services shall adopt standard forms for the support withholding and deduction notices that are prescribed by divisions (A)(1) to (3) and (B) of this section. All courts and child support enforcement agencies shall use the forms in issuing withholding and deduction notices in compliance with this section.

(B)(1)(a) In any action in which support is ordered under Chapter 3115. or under section 2151.23, 2151.33, 2151.36, 2151.49, 3105.18, 3105.21, 3109.05, 3109.19, 3111.13, 3111.20, 3111.21, 3111.22, 3113.04, 3113.07, 3113.216 [3113.21.6], or 3113.31 of the Revised Code and in which there has been a default under the order, the court shall comply with divisions (B)(1) to (6) of this section.

If the support was ordered prior to December 31, 1993, or pursuant to section 3111.20, 3111.21, or 3111.22 of the Revised Code, the court shall reissue the support order under which there has been a default and shall include in the reissued order a general provision as described in this division requiring the withholding or deduction of wages or assets of the obligor in accordance with division (D) of this section or requiring the issuance of a court order containing another type of appropriate requirement in accordance with division (D)(6), (D)(7), or (H) of this section to ensure that withholding or deduction from the wages or assets is available for the collection of current support and any arrearages that occur. If the support was ordered pursuant to section 3111.20, 3111.21, or 3111.22 of the Revised Code and the support order includes a general provision similar to the one described in this division, the court shall replace the similar general provision with the general provision described in this division. Except for the inclusion or replacement of the general provision, the provisions of the reissued order required under this division shall be identical to those of the support order under which there has been a default.

Regardless of when the support was ordered, when support has been ordered under any chapter or section described in this division, the child support enforcement agency shall initiate support withholding when the order is in default. Immediately after the identification of a default under the support order, the child support enforcement agency shall conduct the investigation described in division (B)(1)(b) of this section. Additionally, within fifteen calendar days after the identification of a default under the support order, the child support enforcement agency shall investigate the default and send advance notice to the obligor. The advance notice shall include a notice describing the actions that may be taken against the obligor pursuant to sections 2301.373 [2301.37.3] and 2301.374 [2301.37.4] of the Revised Code if the court or agency makes a final and enforceable determination that the obligor is in default pursuant to this division. If the location of the obligor is unknown at the time of the identification of a default under the support order, the agency shall send the advance notice to the obligor within fifteen days after the agency locates the obligor. The general provision for the withholding or deduction of wages or assets to be included in the reissued support order specifically shall include the following statement:

"All child support and spousal support under this order shall be withheld or deducted from the wages or assets of the obligor pursuant to a withholding or deduction notice or appropriate court order issued in accordance with section 3113.21 of the Revised Code and shall be forwarded to the obligee in accordance with sections 3113.21 to 3113.214 [3113.21.4] of the Revised Code."

(b) After the identification of a default under a support order as described in division (B)(1)(a) of this section, the child support enforcement agency immediately shall conduct an investigation to determine the employment status of the obligor, the obligor's social security number, the name and business address of the obligor's employer, whether the obligor is in default under a support order, the amount of any arrearages, and any other information necessary to enable the court or agency to impose any withholding or deduction requirements and issue the related notices described in division (D) of this section or to issue any court orders described in division (D)(6) or (7) of this section. The agency also shall conduct an investigation under this division when required by division (C)(1)(a) or (b) of this section, shall complete the investigation within twenty days after the obligor or obligee files the motion with the court under division (C)(1)(a) of this section or the court orders the investigation under division (C)(1)(b) of this section, and shall conduct an investigation under this division when required by section 3113.214 [3113.21.4] of the Revised Code.

(2) An advance notice to an obligor required by division (B)(1) of this section shall contain all of the following:

(a) A statement of the date on which the advance notice is sent, the amount of arrearages owed by the obligor as determined by the court or the child support enforcement agency, the types of withholding or deduction requirements and related notices described in division (D) of this section or the types of court orders described in division (D)(6), (D)(7), or (H) of this section that will be issued to pay support and any arrearages, and the amount that will be withheld or deducted pursuant to those requirements;

(b) A statement that any notice for the withholding or deduction of an amount from personal earnings or other income or assets apply to all subsequent employers of the obligor, financial institutions in which the obligor has an account, and other persons or entities who pay or distribute income to the obligor and that any withholding or deduction requirement and related notice described in division (D) of this section or any court order described in division (D)(6), (D)(7), or (H) of this section that is issued will not be discontinued solely because the obligor pays any arrearages;

(c) An explanation of the administrative and court action that will take place if the obligor contests the inclusion of any of the provisions;

(d) A statement that the contents of the advance notice are final and are enforceable by the court unless the obligor files with the child support enforcement agency, within seven days after the date on which the advance notice is sent, a written request for an administrative hearing to determine if a mistake of fact was made in the notice.

(3) If the obligor requests a hearing regarding the advance notice in accordance with division (B)(2)(d) of this section, the child support enforcement agency shall conduct an administrative hearing no later than ten days after the date on which the obligor files the request for the hearing. No later than five days before the date on which the hearing is to be conducted, the agency shall send the obligor and the obligee written notice of the date, time, place, and purpose of the hearing. The notice to the obligor and obligee also shall indicate that the obligor may present testimony and evidence at the hearing only in regard to the issue of whether a mistake of fact was made in the advance notice.

At the hearing, the child support enforcement agency shall determine whether a mistake of fact was made in the advance notice. If it determines that a mistake of fact was made, the agency shall determine the provisions that should be changed and included in a corrected notice and shall correct the advance notice accordingly. The agency shall send its determinations to the obligor. The agency's determinations are final and are enforceable by the court unless, within seven days after the agency makes its determinations, the obligor files a written motion with the court for a court hearing to determine if a mistake of fact still exists in the advance notice or corrected advance notice.

(4) If, within seven days after the agency makes its determinations under division (B)(3) of this section, the obligor files a written motion for a court hearing to determine if a mistake of fact still exists in the advance notice or the corrected advance notice, the court shall hold a hearing on the request as soon as possible, but no later than ten days, after the request is filed. If the obligor requests a court hearing, no later than five days before the date on which the court hearing is to be held, the court shall send the obligor and the obligee written notice by ordinary mail of the date, time, place, and purpose of the court hearing. The hearing shall be limited to a determination of whether there is a mistake of fact in the advance notice or the corrected advance notice.

If, at a hearing conducted under this division, the court detects a mistake of fact in the advance notice or the corrected advance notice, it immediately shall correct the notice.

(5) Upon exhaustion of all rights of the obligor to contest the withholding or deduction on the basis of a mistake of fact and no later than the expiration of forty-five days after the issuance of the advance notice under division (B)(1) of this section, the court or child support enforcement agency shall issue one or more notices requiring withholding or deduction of wages or assets of the obligor in accordance with divisions (A)(2) and (D) of this section, or the court shall issue one or more court orders imposing other appropriate requirements in accordance with division (A)(2) and division (D)(6), (D)(7), or (H) of this section. Thereafter, section 3113.212 [3113.21.2] of the Revised Code applies in relation to the issuance of the notices and court orders. The notices and court orders issued under this division or section 3113.212 [3113.21.2] of the Revised Code are final and are enforceable by the court. The court or agency shall send to the obligor by ordinary mail a copy of the withholding or deduction notice, in accordance with division (D) of this section. The failure of the court or agency to give the notice required by this division does not affect the ability of any court to issue any notice or order under this section or any other section of the Revised Code for the payment of support, does not provide any defense to any notice or order for the payment of support that is issued under this section or any other section of the Revised Code, and does not affect any obligation to pay support.

(6) The department of human services shall adopt standard forms for the advance notice prescribed by divisions (B)(1) to (5) of this section. All courts and child support enforcement agencies shall use those forms, and the support withholding and deduction notice forms adopted under division (A)(4) of this section, in complying with this section.

(C)(1) In any action in which support is ordered under Chapter 3115. or under section 2151.23, 2151.33, 2151.36, 2151.49, 3105.18, 3105.21, 3109.05, 3109.19, 3111.13, 3113.04, 3113.07, 3113.216 [3113.21.6], or 3113.31 of the Revised Code, all of the following apply:

(a) The obligor or obligee under the order may file a motion with the court that issued the order requesting the issuance of one or more withholding or deduction notices as described in division (D) of this section to pay the support due under the order. The motion may be filed at any time after the support order is issued. Upon the filing of a motion pursuant to this division, the child support enforcement agency immediately shall conduct, and shall complete within twenty days after the motion is filed, an investigation in accordance with division (B)(1)(b) of this section. Upon the completion of the investigation and the filing of the agency's report under division (B)(1)(b) of this section, the court shall issue one or more appropriate orders described in division (D) of this section.

(b) If any proceedings involving the support order that was issued before, on, or after December 1, 1986, are commenced in the court and if the court prior to the effective date of this amendment has not issued any orders under division (D) of this section with respect to the support order, if the court determines that any orders issued prior to the effective date of this amendment under division (D) of this section no longer are appropriate, if the court on or after the effective date of this amendment has not modified or reissued the support order under division (A) or (B) of this section and issued any notices under division (D) or court orders under division (D)(6) or (7) of this section, or if the court on or after the effective date of this amendment has modified or reissued the support order under division (A) or (B) of this section and issued one or more notices under division (D) or one or more court orders under division (D)(6) or (7) of this section but determines that the notices or court orders no longer are appropriate, the court, prior to or during any hearings held with respect to the proceedings and prior to the conclusion of the proceedings, shall order the child support enforcement agency to conduct an investigation pursuant to division (B)(1)(b) of this section. Upon the filing of the findings of the agency following the investigation, the court, as necessary, shall issue one or more notices described in division (D) or one or more court orders described in division (D)(6) or (7) of this section or modify any notices previously issued under division (D) or any court orders previously issued under division (D)(6) or (7) of this section.

(c)(i) If a child support enforcement agency, in accordance with section 3113.216 [3113.21.6] of the Revised Code, requests the court to issue a revised child support order in accordance with a revised amount of child support calculated by the agency, the court shall proceed as described in this division. If neither the obligor nor the obligee requests a court hearing on the revised amount of child support, the court shall issue a revised child support order requiring the obligor to pay the revised amount of child support calculated by the agency. However, if the obligor or the obligee requests a court hearing on the revised amount of child support calculated by the agency, the court, in accordance with division (C)(1)(c)(ii) of this section, shall schedule and conduct a hearing to determine if the revised amount of child support is the appropriate amount and if the amount of child support being paid under the child support order otherwise should be revised.

(ii) If the court is required to schedule and conduct a hearing pursuant to division (C)(1)(c)(i) of this section, the court shall give the obligor, obligee, and agency at least thirty days' notice of the date, time, and location of the hearing; order the obligor to provide the court with a copy of the obligor's federal income tax return from the previous year, a copy of all pay stubs obtained by the obligor within the preceding six months, and a copy of all other records evidencing the receipt of any other salary, wages, or compensation by the obligor within the preceding six months, if the obligor failed to provide any of those documents to the agency, and order the obligee to provide the court with a copy of the obligee's federal income tax return from the previous year, a copy of all pay stubs obtained by the obligee within the preceding six months, and a copy of all other records evidencing the receipt of any other salary, wages, or compensation by the obligee within the preceding six months, if the obligee failed to provide any of those documents to the agency; give the obligor and the obligee notice that any willful failure to comply with that court order is contempt of court and, upon a finding by the court that the party is in contempt of court, the court and the agency will take any action necessary to obtain the information or make any reasonable assumptions necessary with respect to the income of the person in contempt of court to ensure a fair and equitable review of the child support order; issue a revised child support order requiring the obligor to pay the revised amount of child support calculated by the agency, if the court determines at the hearing that the revised amount of child support calculated by the agency is the appropriate amount; and determine the appropriate amount of child support and, if necessary, issue a revised child support order requiring the obligor to pay the amount of child support determined by the court, if the court determines that the revised amount of child support calculated by the agency is not the appropriate amount.

(iii) In determining, at a hearing conducted under divisions (C)(1)(c)(i) and (ii) of this section, the appropriate amount of child support to be paid by the obligor, the court shall consider, in addition to all other factors required by law to be considered, the cost of health insurance which the obligor, the obligee, or both the obligor and the obligee have been ordered to obtain for the children specified in the order.

(d) On or after July 1, 1990, the court shall issue any order required by section 3113.217 [3113.21.7] of the Revised Code.

(e)(i) On or after July 1, 1990, an obligee under a child support order may file a motion with the court that issued the order requesting the court to modify the order to require the obligor to obtain health insurance coverage for the children who are the subject of the order, and on or after July 1, 1990, an obligor under a child support order may file a motion with the court that issued the order requesting the court to modify the order to require the obligee to obtain health insurance coverage for those children. Upon the filing of such a motion, the court shall order the child support enforcement agency to conduct an investigation to determine whether the obligor or obligee has satisfactory health insurance coverage for the children. Upon completion of its investigation, the agency shall inform the court, in writing, of its determination. If the court determines that neither the obligor nor the obligee has satisfactory health insurance coverage for the children, it shall issue an order in accordance with section 3113.217 [3113.21.7] of the Revised Code.

(ii) On or after July 1, 1990, an obligor or obligee under a child support order may file a motion with the court that issued the order requesting the court to modify the amount of child support required to be paid under the order because that amount does not adequately cover the medical needs of the child. Upon the filing of such a motion, the court shall determine whether the amount of child support required to be paid under the order adequately covers the medical needs of the child and whether to modify the order, in accordance with division (B)(4) of section 3113.215 [3113.21.5] of the Revised Code.

(f) Whenever a court modifies, reviews, or otherwise reconsiders a child support order, it may reconsider which parent may claim the children who are the subject of the child support order as dependents for federal income tax purposes as set forth in section 151 of the "Internal Revenue Code of 1986," 100 Stat. 2085, 26 U.S.C. 1, as amended, and shall issue its determination on this issue as part of the child support order. The court in its order may permit the parent who is not the residential parent and legal custodian to claim the children as dependents for federal income tax purposes only if the payments for child support are current in full as ordered by the court for the year in which the children will be claimed as dependents. If the court determines that the parent who is not the residential parent and legal custodian may claim the children as dependents for federal income tax purposes, it shall order the residential parent to take whatever action is necessary pursuant to section 152 of the "Internal Revenue Code of 1986," 100 Stat. 2085, 26 U.S.C. 1, as amended, to enable the parent who is not the residential parent and legal custodian to claim the children as dependents for federal income tax purposes in accordance with the order of the court. Any willful failure of the residential parent to comply with the order of the court is contempt of court.

(g) If the order is a child support order issued on or after July 1, 1990, or if the order modifies, on or after July 1, 1990, a prior child support order, the court shall include in the order all of the requirements, specifications, and statements described in division (B) of section 3113.218 [3113.21.8] of the Revised Code.

(2) In any action in which a support order is issued, on or after December 1, 1986, under Chapter 3115. or under section 2151.23, 2151.33, 2151.36, 2151.49, 3105.18, 3105.21, 3109.05, 3109.19, 3111.13, 3113.04, 3113.07, 3113.216 [3113.21.6], or 3113.31 of the Revised Code, the court issuing the order also shall conduct a hearing, prior to or at the time of the issuance of the support order, to determine the employment status of the obligor, the obligor's social security number, the name and business address of the obligor's employer, and any other information necessary to enable the court or a child support enforcement agency to issue any withholding or deduction notice described in division (D) of this section or for the court to issue a court order described in division (D)(6) or (7) of this section. The court, prior to the hearing, shall give the obligor notice of the hearing that shall include the date on which the notice is given and notice that the obligor is subject to a requirement for the withholding of a specified amount from personal earnings if employed and to one or more other types of withholding or deduction requirements described in division (D) or one or more types of court orders described in division (D)(6) or (7) of this section and that the obligor may present evidence and testimony at the hearing to prove that any of the requirements would not be proper because of a mistake of fact.

The court or child support enforcement agency, immediately upon the court's completion of the hearing, shall issue one or more of the types of notices described in division (D) of this section imposing a withholding or deduction requirement, or the court shall issue one or more types of court orders described in division (D)(6) or (7) of this section.

(D) If a court or child support enforcement agency is required under division (A), (B), or (C) of this section or any other section of the Revised Code to issue one or more withholding or deduction notices described in this division or court orders described in division (D)(6) or (7) of this section, the court shall issue one or more of the following types of notices or court orders, or the agency shall issue one or more of the following types of notices to pay the support required under the support order in question and also, if required by any of those divisions, any other section of the Revised Code, or the court, to pay any arrearages:

(1)(a) If the court or the child support enforcement agency determines that the obligor is employed, the court or agency shall require the obligor's employer to withhold from the obligor's personal earnings a specified amount for support in satisfaction of the support order, to begin the withholding no later than the first pay period that occurs after fourteen working days following the date the notice was mailed to the employer under divisions (A)(2) or (B) and (D)(1)(b) of this section, to send the amount withheld to the child support enforcement agency for that county, to send that amount to the agency immediately but not later than ten days after the date the obligor is paid, and to continue the withholding at intervals specified in the notice until further notice from the court or agency. To the extent possible, the amount specified in the notice to be withheld shall satisfy the amount ordered for support in the support order plus any arrearages that may be owed by the obligor under any prior support order that pertained to the same child or spouse, notwithstanding the limitations of sections 2329.66, 2329.70, 2716.02, and 2716.05 of the Revised Code. However, in no case shall the sum of the amount specified in the notice to be withheld and any fee withheld by the employer as a charge for its services exceed the maximum amount permitted under section 303(b) of the "Consumer Credit Protection Act," 15 U.S.C. 1673(b).

(b) If the court or agency imposes a withholding requirement under division (D)(1)(a) of this section, it, within the applicable period of time specified in division (A), (B), or (C) of this section, shall send to the obligor's employer by regular mail a notice that contains all of the information set forth in divisions (D)(1)(b)(i) to (xi) of this section. The notice is final and is enforceable by the court. The notice shall contain all of the following:

(i) The amount to be withheld from the obligor's wages and a statement that the amount actually withheld for support and other purposes, including the fee described in division (D)(1)(b)(xi) of this section, shall not be in excess of the maximum amounts permitted under section 303(b) of the "Consumer Credit Protection Act," 15 U.S.C. 1673(b);

(ii) A statement that the employer is required to send the amount withheld to the child support enforcement agency immediately, but not later than ten working days, after the obligor is paid by the employer and is required to report to the agency the date on which the amount was withheld from the obligor's wages;

(iii) A statement that the withholding is binding upon the employer until further notice from the agency;

(iv) A statement that the employer is subject to a fine to be determined under the law of this state for discharging the obligor from employment, refusing to employ the obligor, or taking any disciplinary action against the obligor because of the withholding requirement;

(v) A statement that, if the employer fails to withhold wages in accordance with the provisions of the notice, the employer is liable for the accumulated amount the employer should have withheld from the obligor's wages;

(vi) A statement that the withholding in accordance

with the notice and under the provisions of this section has priority over any other legal process under the law of this state against the same wages;

(vii) The date on which the notice was mailed and a statement that the employer is required to implement the withholding no later than the first pay period that occurs after fourteen working days following the date the notice was mailed and is required to continue the withholding at the intervals specified in the notice;

(viii) A requirement that the employer promptly notify the child support enforcement agency, in writing, within ten working days after the date of any termination of the obligor's employment, any layoff of the obligor, any leave of absence of the obligor without pay, or any other situation in which the employer ceases to pay personal earnings in an amount sufficient to comply with the order to the obligor, provide the agency with the obligor's last known address, notify the agency of the obligor's new employer, if known, and provide the agency with the new employer's name, address, and telephone number, if known;

(ix) A requirement that the employer identify in the notification given under division (D)(1)(b)(viii) of this section any types of benefits other than personal earnings that the obligor is receiving or is eligible to receive as a benefit of employment or as a result of the obligor's termination of employment, including, but not limited to, unemployment compensation, workers' compensation benefits, severance pay, sick leave, lump-sum payments of retirement benefits or contributions, and bonuses or profit-sharing payments or distributions, and the amount of such benefits, and include in the notification the obligor's last known address and telephone number, date of birth, social security number, and court case number and, if known, the name and business address of any new employer of the obligor;

(x) A requirement that, no later than the earlier of forty-five days before the lump-sum payment is to be made or, if the obligor's right to the lump-sum payment is determined less than forty-five days before it is to be made, the date on which that determination is made, the employer notify the child support enforcement agency of any lump-sum payments of any kind of five hundred dollars or more that are to be paid to the obligor, hold the lump-sum payments of five hundred dollars or more for thirty days after the date on which the lump-sum payments otherwise would have been paid to the obligor, if the lump-sum payments are workers' compensation benefits, severance pay, sick leave, lump-sum payments of retirement benefits or contributions, annual bonuses, or profit-sharing payments or distributions, and, upon order of the court, pay any specified amount of the lump-sum payment to the child support enforcement agency;

(xi) A statement that, in addition to the amount withheld for support, the employer may withhold a fee from the obligor's earnings as a charge for its services in complying with the notice and a specification of the amount that may be withheld.

(c) The court or agency shall send the notice described in division (D)(1)(b) of this section to the obligor and shall attach to the notice an additional notice requiring the obligor immediately to notify the child support enforcement agency, in writing, of any change in employment, including self-employment, and of the availability of any other sources of income that can be the subject of any withholding or deduction requirement described in division (D) of this section. The court or agency shall serve the notices upon the obligor at the same time as service of the support order or, if the support order previously has been issued, shall send the notices to the obligor by regular mail at the last known address at the same time that it sends the notice described in division (D)(1)(b) of this section to the employer. The notification required of the obligor shall include a description of the nature of any new employment, the name and business address of any new employer, and any other information reasonably required by the court. No obligor shall fail to give the notification required by division (D)(1)(c) of this section.

(2)(a) If the court or the child support enforcement agency determines that the obligor is receiving workers' compensation payments, the court or agency may require the bureau of workers' compensation or the employer that has been granted the privilege of paying compensation directly and that is paying workers' compensation benefits to the obligor to withhold from the obligor's workers' compensation payments a specified amount for support in satisfaction of the support order, to begin the withholding no later than the date of the first payment that occurs after fourteen working days following the date the notice was mailed to the bureau or employer under divisions (A)(2) or (B) and (D)(2)(b) of this section, to send the amount withheld to the child support enforcement agency for that county, to send that amount to the agency immediately but not later than ten days after the date the payment is made to the obligor, to provide the date on which the amount was withheld, and to continue the withholding at intervals specified in the notice until further notice from the court or agency. To the extent possible, the amount specified in the notice to be withheld shall satisfy the amount ordered for support in the support order plus any arrearages that may be owed by the obligor under any prior support order that pertained to the same child or spouse, notwithstanding the limitations of section 4123.67 of the Revised Code. However, in no case shall the sum of the amount specified in the notice to be withheld and any fee withheld by an employer as a charge for its services exceed the maximum amount permitted under section 303(b) of the "Consumer Credit Protection Act," 15 U.S.C. 1673(b).

(b) If the court or agency imposes a withholding requirement under division (D)(2)(a) of this section, it, within the applicable period of time specified in division (A), (B), or (C) of this section, shall send to the bureau of workers' compensation or the employer that is paying the obligor's workers' compensation benefits by regular mail a notice that contains all of the information set forth in divisions (D)(2)(b)(i) to (x) of this section. The notice is final and is enforceable by the court. The notice shall contain all of the following:

(i) The amount to be withheld from the obligor's worker's compensation payments and a statement that the amount actually withheld for support and other purposes, including the fee described in division (D)(2)(b)(x) of this section, if applicable, shall not be in excess of the maximum amounts permitted under section 303(b) of the "Consumer Credit Protection Act," 15 U.S.C. 1673(b);

(ii) A statement that the bureau or employer is required to send the amount withheld to the child support enforcement agency immediately, but not later than ten working days, after the payment is made to the obligor and is required to report to the agency the date on which the amount was withheld from the obligor's payments;

(iii) A statement that the withholding is binding upon the bureau or employer until further notice from the court or agency;

(iv) If the notice is sent to an employer who is paying the obligor's worker's compensation benefits, a statement that, if the employer fails to withhold from the obligor's worker's compensation payments in accordance with the provisions of the notice, the employer is liable for the accumulated amount the employer should have withheld from the obligor's payments;

(v) A statement that the withholding in accordance with the notice and under the provisions of this section has priority over any other legal process under the law of this state against the same payment of benefits;

(vi) The date on which the notice was mailed and a statement that the bureau or employer is required to implement the withholding no later than the date of the first payment that occurs after fourteen working days following the date the notice was mailed and is required to continue the withholding at the intervals specified in the notice;

(vii) A requirement that the bureau or employer promptly notify the child support enforcement agency, in writing, within ten working days after the date of any termination of the obligor's workers' compensation benefits;

(viii) A requirement that the bureau or employer include in all notices the obligor's last known mailing address, last known residence address, and social security number;

(ix) A requirement that, no later than the earlier of forty-five days before the lump-sum payment is to be made or, if the obligor's right to the lump-sum payment is determined less than forty-five days before it is to be made, the date on which that determination is made, the bureau or employer notify the child support enforcement agency of any lump-sum payment of any kind of five hundred dollars or more that is to be paid to the obligor, hold the lump-sum payment for thirty days after the date on which the lump-sum payment otherwise would be paid to the obligor, and, upon order of the court, pay any specified amount of the lump-sum payment to the agency;

(x) If the notice is sent to an employer who is paying the obligor's workers' compensation benefits, a statement that, in addition to the amount withheld for support, the employer may withhold a fee from the obligor's benefits as a charge for its services in complying with the notice and a specification of the amount that may be withheld.

(c) The court or agency shall send the notice described in division (D)(2)(b) of this section to the obligor and shall attach to the notice an additional notice requiring the obligor to immediately notify the child support enforcement agency, in writing, of any change in the obligor's workers' compensation payments, of the obligor's commencement of employment, including self-employment, and of the availability of any other sources of income that can be the subject of any withholding or deduction requirement described in division (D) of this section. The court or agency shall serve the notices upon the obligor at the same time as service of the support order or, if the support order previously has been issued, shall send the notices to the obligor by regular mail at the obligor's last known address at the same time that it sends the notice described in division (D)(2)(b) of this section to the bureau or employer. The additional notice also shall notify the obligor that upon commencement of employment the obligor may request the court or the child support enforcement agency to cancel its workers' compensation payment withholding notice and instead issue a notice requiring the withholding of an amount from the obligor's personal earnings for support in accordance with division (D)(1) of this section and that upon commencement of employment the court may cancel its workers' compensation payment withholding notice and instead will issue a notice requiring the withholding of an amount from the obligor's personal earnings for support in accordance with division (D)(1) of this section. The notification required of the obligor shall include a description of the nature of any new employment, the name and business address of any new employer, and any other information reasonably required by the court.

(3)(a) If the court or child support enforcement agency determines that the obligor is receiving any pension, annuity, allowance, or other benefit or is to receive or has received a warrant refunding the individual account from the public employees retirement system, a municipal retirement system established subject to sections 145.01 to 145.58 of the Revised Code, the police and firemen's disability and pension fund, the state teachers retirement system, the school employees retirement system, or the state highway patrol retirement system, the court or agency may require the public employees retirement board, the board, board of trustees, or other governing entity of any municipal retirement system, the board of trustees of the police and firemen's disability and pension fund, the state teachers retirement board, the school employees retirement board, or the state highway patrol retirement board to withhold from the obligor's pension, annuity, allowance, other benefit, or warrant a specified amount for support in satisfaction of the support order, to begin the withholding no later than the date of the first payment that occurs after fourteen working days following the date the notice was mailed to the board, board of trustees, or other entity under divisions (A)(2) or (B) and (D)(3)(b) of this section, to send the amount withheld to the child support enforcement agency for that county, to send that amount to the agency immediately but not later than ten days after the date the payment is made to the obligor, to provide the date on which the amount was withheld, and to continue the withholding at intervals specified in the notice until further notice from the court or agency. To the extent possible, the amount specified in the notice to be withheld shall satisfy the amount ordered for support in the support order plus any arrearages that may be owed by the obligor under any prior support order that pertained to the same child or spouse, notwithstanding the limitations of sections 2329.66, 2329.70, and 2716.13 of the Revised Code. However, in no case shall the sum of the amount specified in the notice to be withheld and any fee withheld by the board, board of trustees, or other entity as a charge for its services exceed the maximum amount permitted under section 303(b) of the "Consumer Credit Protection Act," 15 U.S.C. 1673(b).

(b) If the court or agency imposes a withholding requirement under division (D)(3)(a) of this section, it, within the applicable period of time specified in division (A), (B), or (C) of this section, shall send to the board, board of trustees, or other entity by regular mail a notice that contains all of the information set forth in divisions (D)(3)(b)(i) to (ix) of this section. The notice is final and is enforceable by the court. The notice shall contain all of the following:

(i) The amount to be withheld from the obligor's pension, annuity, allowance, other benefit, or warrant and a statement that the amount actually withheld for support and other purposes, including the fee described in division (D)(3)(b)(ix) of this section, shall not be in excess of the maximum amounts permitted under section 303(b) of the "Consumer Credit Protection Act," 15 U.S.C. 1673(b);

(ii) A statement that the board, board of trustees, or other entity is required to send the amount withheld to the child support enforcement agency immediately, but not later than ten working days, after the payment is made to the obligor and is required to report to the agency the date on which the amount was withheld from the obligor's payments;

(iii) A statement that the withholding is binding upon the board, board of trustees, or other entity until further notice from the court or agency;

(iv) A statement that the withholding in accordance with the notice and under the provisions of this section has priority over any other legal process under the law of this state against the same payment of the pension, annuity, allowance, other benefit, or warrant;

(v) The date on which the notice was mailed and a statement that the board, board of trustees, or other entity is required to implement the withholding no later than the date of the first payment that occurs after fourteen working days following the date the notice was mailed and is required to continue the withholding at the intervals specified in the notice;

(vi) A requirement that the board, board of trustees, or other entity promptly notify the child support enforcement agency, in writing, within ten working days after the date of any termination of the obligor's pension, annuity, allowance, or other benefit;

(vii) A requirement that the board, board of trustees, or other entity include in all notices the obligor's last known mailing address, last known residence address, and social security number;

(viii) A requirement that, no later than the earlier of forty-five days before the lump-sum payment is to be made or, if the obligor's right to the lump-sum payment is determined less than forty-five days before it is to be made, the date on which that determination is made, the board, board of trustees, or other entity notify the child support enforcement agency of any lump-sum payment of any kind of five hundred dollars or more that is to be paid to the obligor, hold the lump-sum payment for thirty days after the date on which the lump-sum payment would otherwise be paid to the obligor, if the lump-sum payments are lump-sum payments of retirement benefits or contributions, and, upon order of the court, pay any specified amount of the lump-sum payment to the agency;

(ix) A statement that, in addition to the amount withheld for support, the board, board of trustees, or other entity may withhold a fee from the obligor's pension, annuity, allowance, other benefit, or warrant as a charge for its services in complying with the notice and a specification of the amount that may be withheld.

(c) The court or agency shall send the notice described in division (D)(3)(b) of this section to the obligor and shall attach to the notice an additional notice requiring the obligor immediately to notify the child support enforcement agency, in writing, of any change in pension, annuity, allowance, or other benefit, of the commencement of employment, including self-employment, and of the availability of any other sources of income that can be the subject of any withholding or deduction requirement described in division (D) of this section. The court or agency shall serve the notices upon the obligor at the same time as service of the support order or, if the support order previously has been issued, shall send the notices to the obligor by regular mail at the last known address at the same time that it sends the notice described in division (D)(3)(b) of this section to the board, board of trustees, or other entity. The additional notice also shall specify that upon commencement of employment the obligor may request the court or the child support enforcement agency to issue a notice requiring the withholding of an amount from personal earnings for support in accordance with division (D)(1) of this section and that upon commencement of employment the court may cancel its withholding notice under division (D)(3)(b) of this section and instead will issue a notice requiring the withholding of an amount from personal earnings for support in accordance with division (D)(1) of this section. The notification required of the obligor shall include a description of the nature of any new employment, the name and business address of any new employer, and any other information reasonably required by the court.

(4)(a) If the court or child support enforcement agency determines that the obligor is receiving any form of income, including, but not limited to, disability or sick pay, insurance proceeds, lottery prize awards, federal, state, or local government benefits to the extent that the benefits can be withheld or deducted under any law governing the benefits, any form of trust fund or endowment fund, vacation pay, commissions and draws against commissions that are paid on a regular basis, bonuses or profit-sharing payments or distributions, or any lump-sum payments, the court or agency may require the person who pays or otherwise distributes the income to the obligor to withhold from the obligor's income a specified amount for support in satisfaction of the support order, to begin the withholding no later than the date of the first payment that occurs after fourteen working days following the date the notice was mailed to the person paying or otherwise distributing the obligor's income under divisions (A)(2) or (B) and (D)(4)(b) of this section, to send the amount withheld to the child support enforcement agency for that county, to send that amount to the agency immediately but not later than ten days after the date the payment is made to the obligor, to provide the date on which the amount was withheld, and to continue the withholding at intervals specified in the notice until further notice from the court or agency. To the extent possible, the amount specified in the notice to be withheld shall satisfy the amount ordered for support in the support order plus any arrearages that may be owed by the obligor under any prior support order that pertained to the same child or spouse, notwithstanding the limitations of sections 2329.66, 2329.70, and 2716.13 of the Revised Code. However, in no case shall the sum of the amount specified in the notice to be withheld and any fee withheld by the person paying or otherwise distributing the obligor's income as a charge for its services exceed the maximum amount permitted under section 303(b) of the "Consumer Credit Protection Act," 15 U.S.C. 1673(b).

(b) If the court or agency imposes a withholding requirement under division (D)(4)(a) of this section, it, within the applicable period of time specified in division (A), (B), or (C) of this section, shall send to the person paying or otherwise distributing the obligor's income by regular mail a notice that contains all of the information set forth in divisions (D)(4)(b)(i) to (ix) of this section. The notice is final and is enforceable by the court. The notice shall contain all of the following:

(i) The amount to be withheld from the obligor's income and a statement that the amount actually withheld for support and other purposes, including the fee described in division (D)(4)(b)(ix) of this section, shall not be in excess of the maximum amounts permitted under section 303(b) of the "Consumer Credit Protection Act," 15 U.S.C. 1673(b);

(ii) A statement that the person paying or otherwise distributing the obligor's income is required to send the amount withheld to the child support enforcement agency immediately, but not later than ten working days, after the payment is made to the obligor and is required to report to the agency the date on which the amount was withheld from the obligor's payments;

(iii) A statement that the withholding is binding upon the person paying or otherwise distributing the obligor's income until further notice from the court or agency;

(iv) A statement that the withholding in accordance with the notice and under the provisions of this section has priority over any other legal process under the law of this state against the same payment of the income;

(v) A statement that the person paying or otherwise distributing the obligor's income is required to implement the withholding no later than the date of the first payment that occurs after fourteen working days following the date the notice was mailed and is required to continue the withholding at the intervals specified in the notice;

(vi) A requirement that the person paying or otherwise distributing the obligor's income promptly notify the child support enforcement agency, in writing, within ten days after the date of any termination of the obligor's income;

(vii) A requirement that the person paying or otherwise distributing the obligor's income include in all notices the obligor's last known mailing address, last known residence address, and social security number;

(viii) A requirement that, no later than the earlier of forty-five days before the lump-sum payment is to be made or, if the obligor's right to the lump-sum payment is determined less than forty-five days before it is to be made, the date on which that determination is made, the person paying or otherwise distributing the obligor's income notify the child support enforcement agency of any lump-sum payment of any kind of five hundred dollars or more that is to be paid to the obligor, hold the lump-sum payment for thirty days after the date on which the lump-sum payment would otherwise be paid to the obligor, if the lump-sum payment is sick pay, lump-sum payment of retirement benefits or contributions, or profit-sharing payments or distributions, and, upon order of the court, pay any specified amount of the lump-sum payment to the child support enforcement agency;

(ix) A statement that, in addition to the amount withheld for support, the person paying or otherwise distributing the obligor's income may withhold a fee from the obligor's income as a charge for its services in complying with the order and a specification of the amount that may be withheld.

(c) The court or agency shall send the notice described in division (D)(4)(b) of this section to the obligor and shall attach to the notice an additional notice requiring the obligor immediately to notify the child support enforcement agency, in writing, of any change in income to which the withholding notice applies, of the commencement of employment, including self-employment, and of the availability of any other sources of income that can be the subject of any withholding or deduction requirement described in division (D) of this section. The court or agency shall serve the notices upon the obligor at the same time as service of the support order or, if the support order previously has been issued, shall send the notices to the obligor by regular mail at the last known address at the same time that it sends the notice described in division (D)(4)(b) of this section to the person paying or otherwise distributing the obligor's income. The additional notice also shall specify that upon commencement of employment the obligor may request the court or child support enforcement agency to issue a notice requiring the withholding of an amount from the obligor's personal earnings for support in accordance with division (D)(1) of this section and that upon commencement of employment the court may cancel its withholding notice under division (D)(4)(b) of this section and instead will issue a notice requiring the withholding of an amount from personal earnings for support in accordance with division (D)(1) of this section. The notification required of the obligor shall include a description of the nature of any new employment, the name and business address of any new employer, and any other information reasonably required by the court.

(5)(a) If the court or child support enforcement agency determines that the obligor has funds on deposit in any account in a financial institution under the jurisdiction of the court, the court or agency may require any financial institution in which the obligor's funds are on deposit to deduct from the obligor's account a specified amount for support in satisfaction of the support order, to begin the deduction no later than fourteen working days following the date the notice was mailed to the financial institution under divisions (A)(2) or (B) and (D)(5)(b) of this section, to send the amount deducted to the child support enforcement agency for that county, to send that amount to the agency immediately but not later than ten days after the date the latest deduction was made, to provide the date on which the amount was deducted, and to continue the deduction at intervals specified in the notice until further notice from the court or agency. To the extent possible, the amount specified in the notice to be deducted shall satisfy the amount ordered for support in the support order plus any arrearages that may be owed by the obligor under any prior support order that pertained to the same child or spouse, notwithstanding the limitations of sections 2329.66, 2329.70, and 2716.13 of the Revised Code. However, in no case shall the sum of the amount specified in the notice to be deducted and the fee deducted by the financial institution as a charge for its services exceed the maximum amount permitted under section 303(b) of the "Consumer Credit Protection Act," 15 U.S.C. 1673(b).

(b) If the court or agency imposes a withholding requirement under division (D)(5)(a) of this section, it, within the applicable period of time specified in division (A), (B), or (C) of this section, shall send to the financial institution by regular mail a notice that contains all of the information set forth in divisions (D)(5)(b)(i) to (viii) of this section. The notice is final and is enforceable by the court. The notice shall contain all of the following:

(i) The amount to be deducted from the obligor's account and a statement that the amount actually deducted for support and other purposes, including the fee described in division (D)(5)(b)(viii) of this section, shall not be in excess of the maximum amounts permitted under section 303(b) of the "Consumer Credit Protection Act," 15 U.S.C. 1673(b);

(ii) A statement that the financial institution is required to send the amount deducted to the child support enforcement agency immediately, but not later than ten working days, after the date the last deduction was made and is required to report to the agency the date on which the amount was deducted from the obligor's account;

(iii) A statement that the deduction is binding upon the financial institution until further notice from the court or agency;

(iv) A statement that the withholding in accordance with the notice and under the provisions of this section has priority over any other legal process under the law of this state against the same account;

(v) The date on which the notice was mailed and a statement that the financial institution is required to implement the deduction no later than fourteen working days following the date the notice was mailed and is required to continue the deduction at the intervals specified in the notice;

(vi) A requirement that the financial institution promptly notify the child support enforcement agency, in writing, within ten days after the date of any termination of the account from which the deduction is being made and notify the agency, in writing, of the opening of a new account at that financial institution, the account number of the new account, the name of any other known financial institutions in which the obligor has any accounts, and the numbers of those accounts;

(vii) A requirement that the financial institution include in all notices the obligor's last known mailing address, last known residence address, and social security number;

(viii) A statement that, in addition to the amount deducted for support, the financial institution may deduct a fee from the obligor's account as a charge for its services in complying with the notice and a specification of the amount that may be deducted.

(c) The court or agency shall send the notice described in division (D)(5)(b) of this section to the obligor and shall attach to the notice an additional notice requiring the obligor immediately to notify the child support enforcement agency, in writing, of any change in the status of the account from which the amount of support is being deducted or the opening of a new account with any financial institution, of commencement of employment, including self-employment, or of the availability of any other sources of income that can be the subject of any withholding or deduction requirement described in division (D) of this section. The court or agency shall serve the notices upon the obligor at the same time as service of the support order or, if the support order previously has been issued, shall send the notices to the obligor by regular mail at the last known address at the same time that it sends the notice described in division (D)(5)(b) of this section to the financial institution. The additional notice also shall specify that upon commencement of employment, the obligor may request the court or child support enforcement agency to cancel its financial institution account deduction notice and instead issue a notice requiring the withholding of an amount from personal earnings for support in accordance with division (D)(1) of this section and that upon commencement of employment the court may cancel its financial institution account deduction notice under division (D)(5)(b) of this section and instead will issue a notice requiring the withholding of an amount from personal earnings for support in accordance with division (D)(1) of this section. The notification required of the obligor shall include a description of the nature of any new accounts opened at a financial institution under the jurisdiction of the court, the name and business address of that financial institution, a description of the nature of any new employment, the name and business address of any new employer, and any other information reasonably required by the court.

(6) The court may issue an order requiring the obligor to enter into a cash bond with the court. The court shall issue the order as part of the support order or, if the support order previously has been issued, as a separate order. Any cash bond so required shall be in a sum fixed by the court at not less than five hundred nor more than ten thousand dollars, conditioned that the obligor will make payment as previously ordered and will pay any arrearages under any prior support order that pertained to the same child or spouse. The order, along with an additional order requiring the obligor to immediately notify the child support enforcement agency, in writing, of commencement of employment, including self-employment, shall be attached to, and shall be served upon the obligor at the same time as service of, the support order or, if the support order previously has been issued, as soon as possible after the issuance of the order under this division. The additional order also shall specify that upon commencement of employment the obligor may request the court to cancel its bond order and instead issue a notice requiring the withholding of an amount from personal earnings for support in accordance with division (D)(1) of this section and that upon commencement of employment the court will proceed to collect on the bond, if the court determines that payments due under the support order have not been made and that the amount that has not been paid is at least equal to the support owed for one month under the support order, and will issue a notice requiring the withholding of an amount from personal earnings for support in accordance with division (D)(1) of this section. The notification required of the obligor shall include a description of the nature of any new employment, the name and business address of any new employer, and any other information reasonably required by the court.

The court shall not order an obligor to post a cash bond under this division unless the court determines that the obligor has the ability to do so. A child support enforcement agency shall not issue an order of the type described in this division. If a child support enforcement agency is required to issue a withholding or deduction notice under division (D) of this section but the agency determines that no notice of the type described in division (D)(1) to (5) of this section would be appropriate, the agency may request the court to issue a court order under this division, and, upon the request, the court may issue an order as described in this division.

(7) If the obligor is unemployed, has no income, and does not have an account at any financial institution, the court shall issue an order requiring the obligor to seek employment if the obligor is able to engage in employment and immediately to notify the child support enforcement agency upon obtaining employment, upon obtaining any income, or upon obtaining ownership of any asset with a value of five hundred dollars or more. The court shall issue the notice as part of the support order or, if the support order previously has been issued, as a separate notice. A child support enforcement agency shall not issue a notice of the type described in this division. If a child support enforcement agency is required to issue a withholding or deduction notice under division (D) of this section but the agency determines that no notice of the type described in division (D)(1) to (5) of this section would be appropriate, the agency may request the court to issue a court order under this division, and, upon the request, the court may issue an order as described in this division.

(E) If a court or child support enforcement agency is required under division (A), (B), or (C) of this section or any other section of the Revised Code to issue one or more notices or court orders described in division (D) of this section, the court or agency to the extent possible shall issue a sufficient number of notices or court orders under division (D) of this section to provide that the aggregate amount withheld or deducted under those notices or court orders satisfies the amount ordered for support in the support order plus any arrearages that may be owed by the obligor under any prior support order that pertained to the same child or spouse, notwithstanding the limitations of sections 2329.66, 2329.70, 2716.13, and 4123.67 of the Revised Code. However, in no case shall the aggregate amount withheld or deducted and any fees withheld or deducted as a charge for services exceed the maximum amount permitted under section 303(b) of the "Consumer Credit Protection Act," 15 U.S.C. 1673(b).

(F)(1) Any withholding or deduction requirement that is contained in a notice described in division (D) of this section and that is required to be issued by division (A), (B), or (C) of this section or any other section of the Revised Code has priority over any order of attachment, any order in aid of execution, and any other legal process issued under state law against the same earnings, payments, or account.

(2) When two or more withholding or deduction notices that are described in division (D) of this section and that are required to be issued by division (A), (B), or (C) of this section or any other section of the Revised Code are received by an employer, the bureau of workers' compensation, an employer that is paying more than one person's workers' compensation benefits, the public employees retirement board, the board, board of trustees, or other governing entity of any municipal retirement system, the board of trustees of the police and firemen's disability and pension fund, the state teachers retirement board, the school employees retirement board, the state highway patrol retirement board, a person paying or otherwise distributing income for more than one obligor, or a financial institution, the employer, bureau of workers' compensation, employer paying workers' compensation benefits, board, board of trustees, or other governing entity of a retirement system, person paying or distributing income to an obligor, or financial institution shall comply with all of the requirements contained in the notices to the extent that the total amount withheld from the obligor's personal earnings, payments, pensions, annuities, allowances, benefits, other sources of income, or savings does not exceed the maximum amount permitted under section 303(b) of the "Consumer Credit Protection Act," 15 U.S.C. 1673(b), withhold or deduct amounts in accordance with the allocation set forth in divisions (F)(2)(a) and (b) of this section, notify each court or child support enforcement agency that issued one of the notices of the allocation, and give priority to amounts designated in each notice as current support in the following manner:

(a) If the total of the amounts designated in the notices as current support exceeds the amount available for withholding under section 303(b) of the "Consumer Credit Protection Act," 15 U.S.C. 1673(b), the employer, bureau of workers' compensation, employer paying workers' compensation benefits, board, board of trustees, or other governing entity of a municipal retirement system, person paying or distributing income to an obligor, or financial institution shall allocate to each notice an amount for current support equal to the amount designated in that notice as current support multiplied by a fraction in which the numerator is the amount of personal earnings, payments, pensions, annuities, allowances, benefits, other sources of income, or savings available for withholding and the denominator is the total amount designated in all of the notices as current support.

(b) If the total of the amounts designated in the notices as current support does not exceed the amount available for withholding under section 303(b) of the "Consumer Credit Protection Act," 15 U.S.C. 1673(b), the persons and entities listed in division (F)(2)(a) of this section shall pay all of the amounts designated as current support in the notices and shall allocate to each notice an amount for past-due support equal to the amount designated in that notice as past-due support multiplied by a fraction in which the numerator is the amount of personal earnings, payments, pensions, annuities, allowances, benefits, other sources of income, or savings remaining available for withholding after the payment of current support and the denominator is the total amount designated in all of the notices as past-due support.

(G)(1) Except when a provision specifically authorizes or requires service other than as described in this division, service of any notice on any party, the bureau of workers' compensation, an employer that is paying a person's workers' compensation benefits, the public employees retirement board, the board, board of trustees, or other governing entity of any municipal retirement system, the board of trustees of the police and firemen's disability and pension fund, the state teachers retirement board, the school employees retirement board, the state highway patrol retirement board, a person paying or otherwise distributing an obligor's income, a financial institution, or an employer, for purposes of division (A), (B), (C), or (D) of this section, may be made by personal service or ordinary first class mail directed to the addressee at the last known address, or, in the case of a corporation, at its usual place of doing business. Any service of notice by ordinary first class mail shall be evidenced by a certificate of mailing filed with the clerk of the court.

(2) Each party to a support order shall notify the child support enforcement agency of the party's current mailing address and current residence address at the time of the issuance or modification of the order and, until further notice of the court that issues the order,

shall notify the agency of any change in either address immediately after the change occurs. Any willful failure to comply with this division is contempt of court. No person shall fail to give the notice required by division (G)(2) of this section.

(3) Each support order, or modification of a support order, that is subject to this section shall contain a statement requiring each party to the order to notify the child support enforcement agency in writing of the party's current mailing address, the party's current residence address, and of any changes in either address and a notice that the requirement to notify the agency of all changes in either address continues until further notice from the court and that a willful failure to supply a correct mailing address or residence address or to provide the agency with all changes in either address is contempt of court.

(4)(a) The parent who is the residential parent and legal custodian of a child for whom a support order is issued or the person who otherwise has custody of a child for whom a support order is issued immediately shall notify, and the obligor under a support order may notify, the child support enforcement agency of any reason for which the support order should terminate, including, but not limited to, death, marriage, emancipation, enlistment in the armed services, deportation, or change of legal or physical custody of the child. A willful failure to notify the child support enforcement agency as required by this division is contempt of court. Upon receipt of a notice pursuant to this division, the agency immediately shall conduct an investigation to determine if any reason exists for which the support order should terminate. If the agency so determines, it immediately shall notify the court that issued the support order of the reason for which the support order should terminate.

(b) Upon receipt of a notice given pursuant to division (G)(4)(a) of this section, the court shall impound any funds received for the child pursuant to the support order and set the case for a hearing for a determination of whether the support order should be terminated or modified or whether the court should take any other appropriate action.

(c) If the court terminates a support order pursuant to divisions (G)(4)(a) and (b) of this section, the termination of the support order also terminates any withholding or deduction order as described in division (D) or (H) of this section that was issued relative to the support order prior to December 31, 1993, and any withholding or deduction notice as described in division (D) or court order as described in division (D)(6), (D)(7), or (H) of this section that was issued relative to the support order on or after December 31, 1993. Upon the termination of any withholding or deduction order or any withholding or deduction notice, the court immediately shall notify the appropriate child support enforcement agency that the order or notice has been terminated, and the agency immediately shall notify each employer, financial institution, or other person or entity that was required to withhold or deduct a sum of money for the payment of support under the terminated withholding or deduction order or the terminated withholding or deduction notice that the order or notice has been terminated and that it is required to cease all withholding or deduction under the order or notice.

(d) The department of human services shall adopt rules that provide for both of the following:

(i) The return to the appropriate person of any funds that a court has impounded under division (G)(4)(b) of this section if the support order under which the funds were paid has been terminated pursuant to divisions (G)(4)(a) and (b) of this section;

(ii) The return to the appropriate person of any other payments made pursuant to a support order if the payments were made at any time after the support order under which the funds were paid has been terminated pursuant to divisions (G)(4)(a) and (b) of this section.

(5) If any party to a support order requests a modification of the order or if any obligee under a support order or any person on behalf of the obligee files any action to enforce a support order, the court shall notify the child support enforcement agency that is administering the support order or that will administer the order after the court's determination of the request or the action, of the request or the filing.

(6) When a child support enforcement agency receives any notice under division (G) of section 2151.23, section 2301.37, division (E) of section 3105.18, division (C) of section 3105.21, division (A) of section 3109.05, division (F) of section 3111.13, division (B) of section 3113.04, section 3113.21, section 3113.211 [3113.21.1], section 3113.212 [3113.21.2], division (K) of section 3113.31, or division (D) of section 3115.22 of the Revised Code, it shall issue the most appropriate notices under division (D) of this section. Additionally, it shall do all of the following:

(a) If the obligor is subject to a withholding notice issued under division (D)(1) of this section and the notice relates to the obligor's change of employment, send a withholding notice under that division to the new employer of the obligor as soon as the agency obtains knowledge of that employer;

(b) If the notification received by the agency specifies that a lump-sum payment of five hundred dollars or more is to be paid to the obligor, notify the court of the receipt of the notice and its contents;

(c) Comply with section 3113.212 [3113.21.2] of the Revised Code, as appropriate.

(H)(1)(a) For purposes of division (D)(1) of this section, when a person who fails to comply with a support order that is subject to that division derives income from self-employment or commission, is employed by an employer not subject to the jurisdiction of the court, or is in any other employment situation that makes the application of that division impracticable, the court may require the person to enter into a cash bond to the court in a sum fixed by the court at not less than five hundred nor more than ten thousand dollars, conditioned that the person will make payment as previously ordered.

(b) When a court determines at a hearing conducted under division (B) of this section, or a child support enforcement agency determines at a hearing or pursuant to an investigation conducted under division (B) of this section, that the obligor under the order in relation to which the hearing or investigation is conducted is unemployed and has no other source of income and no assets so that the application of divisions (B) and (D) of this section would be impracticable, the court shall issue an order as described in division (D)(7) of this section and shall order the obligor to notify the child support enforcement agency in writing immediately upon commencement of employment, including self-employment, of the receipt of workers' compensation payments, of the receipt of any other source of income, or of the opening of an account in a financial institution, and to include in the notification a description of the nature of the employment, the name and business address of the employer, and any other information reasonably required by the court.

(2) When a court determines, at a hearing conducted under division (C)(2) of this section, that an obligor is unemployed, is not receiving workers' compensation payments, does not have an account in a financial institution, and has no other source of income and no assets so that the application of divisions (C)(2) and (D) of this section would be impracticable, the court shall issue an order as described in division (D)(7) of this section and shall order the obligor to notify the child support enforcement agency, in writing, immediately upon commencement of employment, including self-employment, of the receipt of workers' compensation payments, of the receipt of any other source of income, or of the opening of an account in a financial institution, and to include in the notification a description of the nature of the employment, the name and business address of the employer or the name and address of the financial institution, and any other information reasonably required by the court.

(3)(a) Upon receipt of a notice from a child support enforcement agency under division (G)(6) of this section that a lump-sum payment of five hundred dollars or more is to be paid to the obligor, the court shall do either of the following:

(i) If the obligor is in default under the support order or has any unpaid arrearages under the support order, issue an order requiring the transmittal of the lump-sum payment to the child support enforcement agency.

(ii) If the obligor is not in default under the support order and does not have any unpaid arrearages under the support order, issue an order directing the person who gave the notice to the court to immediately pay the full amount of the lump-sum payment to the obligor.

(b) Upon receipt of any moneys pursuant to division (H)(3)(a) of this section, a child support enforcement agency shall pay the amount of the lump-sum payment that is necessary to discharge all of the obligor's arrearages to the obligee and, within two business days after its receipt of the money, any amount that is remaining after the payment of the arrearages to the obligor.

(c) Any court that issued an order prior to December 1, 1986, requiring an employer to withhold an amount from an obligor's personal earnings for the payment of support shall issue a supplemental order that does not change the original order or the related support order requiring the employer to do all of the following:

(i) No later than the earlier of forty-five days before a lump-sum payment is to be made or, if the obligor's right to a lump-sum payment is determined less than forty-five days before it is to be made, the date on which that determination is made, notify the child support enforcement agency of any lump-sum payment of any kind of five hundred dollars or more that is to be paid to the obligor;

(ii) Hold the lump-sum payment for thirty days after the date on which it would otherwise be paid to the obligor, if the lump-sum payment is sick pay, a lump-sum payment of retirement benefits or contributions, or profit-sharing payments or distributions;

(iii) Upon order of the court, pay any specified amount of the lump-sum payment to the child support enforcement agency.

(d) If an employer knowingly fails to notify the child support enforcement agency in accordance with division (D) of this section of any lump-sum payment to be made to an obligor, the employer is liable for any support payment not made to the obligee as a result of its knowing failure to give the notice as required by that division.

(I)(1) Any support order, or modification of a support order, that is subject to this section shall contain the date of birth and social security number of the obligor.

(2) No withholding or deduction notice described in division (D) or court order described in division (D)(6) or (7) of this section shall contain any information other than the information specifically required by division (A), (B), (C), or (D) of this section or by any other section of the Revised Code and any additional information that the issuing court determines may be necessary to comply with the notice.

(J) No withholding or deduction notice described in division (D) or court order described in division (D)(6) or (7) of this section and issued under division (A), (B), or (C) of this section or any other section of the Revised Code shall be terminated solely because the obligor pays any part or all of the arrearages under the support order.

(K)(1) Except as provided in division (K)(2) of this section and section 2301.42 of the Revised Code and the rules adopted pursuant to division (C) of that section, if child support arrearages are owed by an obligor to the obligee and to the department of human services, any payments received on the arrearages by the child support enforcement agency first shall be paid to the obligee until the arrearages owed to the obligee are paid in full.

(2) Division (K)(1) of this section does not apply to the collection of past-due child support from refunds of paid federal taxes pursuant to section 5101.32 of the Revised Code or of overdue child support from refunds of paid state income taxes pursuant to sections 5101.321 [5101.32.1] and 5747.121 [5747.12.1] of the Revised Code.

(L)(1) Each court with jurisdiction to issue support orders shall establish rules of court to ensure that the following percentage of all actions to establish a support requirement or to modify a previously issued support order be completed within the following time limits:

(a) Ninety per cent of all of the actions shall be completed within three months after they were initially filed;

(b) Ninety-eight per cent of all of the actions shall be completed within six months after they were initially filed;

(c) One hundred per cent of all of the actions shall be completed within twelve months after they were initially filed.

(2) If a case involves complex legal issues requiring full judicial review, the court shall issue a temporary support order within the time limits set forth in division (L)(1) of this section, which temporary order shall be in effect until a final support order is issued in the case. All cases in which the imposition of a notice or order under division (D) of this section is contested shall be completed within the period of time specified by law for completion of the case. The failure of a court to complete a case within the required period does not affect the ability of any court to issue any order under this section or any other section of the Revised Code for the payment of support, does not provide any defense to any order for the payment of support that is issued under this section or any other section of the Revised Code, and does not affect any obligation to pay support.

(3)(a) In any Title IV-D case, the judge, when necessary to satisfy the federal requirement of expedited process for obtaining and enforcing support orders, shall appoint referees to make findings of fact and recommendations for the judge's approval in the case. All referees appointed pursuant to this division shall be attorneys admitted to the practice of law in this state. If the court appoints a referee pursuant to this division, the court may appoint any additional administrative and support personnel for the referee.

(b) Any referee appointed pursuant to division (L)(3)(a) of this section may perform any of the following functions:

(i) The taking of testimony and keeping of a record in the case;

(ii) The evaluation of evidence and the issuance of recommendations to establish, modify, and enforce support orders;

(iii) The acceptance of voluntary acknowledgments of support liability and stipulated agreements setting the amount of support to be paid;

(iv) The entering of default orders if the obligor does not respond to notices in the case within a reasonable time after the notices are issued;

(v) Any other functions considered necessary by the court.

(4) The child support enforcement agency may conduct administrative reviews of support orders to obtain voluntary notices or court orders under division (D) of this section and to correct any errors in the amount of any arrearages owed by an obligor. The obligor and the obligee shall be notified of the time, date, and location of the administrative review at least fourteen days before it is held.

(M)(1) The termination of a support obligation or a support order does not abate the power of any court to collect overdue and unpaid support or to punish any person for a failure to comply with an order of the court or to pay any support as ordered in the terminated support order and does not abate the authority of a child support enforcement agency to issue, in accordance with this section, any notice described in division (D) of this section or of a court to issue, in accordance with this section, any court order as described in division (D)(6) or (7) of this section, to collect any support due or arrearage under the support order.

(2) Any court that has the authority to issue a support order shall have all powers necessary to enforce that support order, and all other powers, set forth in this section.

(3) Except as provided in division (M)(4) of this section, a court may not retroactively modify an obligor's duty to pay a delinquent support payment.

(4) A court with jurisdiction over a support order may modify an obligor's duty to pay a support payment that becomes due after notice of a petition to modify the support order has been given to each obligee and to the obligor before a final order concerning the petition for modification is entered.

(N) If an obligor is in default under a support order and has a claim against another person of more than one thousand dollars, the obligor shall notify the child support enforcement agency of the claim, the nature of the claim, and the name of the person against whom the claim exists. If an obligor is in default under a support order and has a claim against another person or is a party in an action for any judgment, the child support enforcement agency or the agency's attorney, on behalf of the obligor, immediately shall file with the court in which the action is pending a motion to intervene in the action or a creditor's bill. The motion to intervene shall be prepared and filed pursuant to Civil Rules 5 and 24(A) and (C).

Nothing in this division shall preclude an obligee from filing a motion to intervene in any action or a creditor's bill.

(O) If an obligor is receiving unemployment compensation benefits, an amount may be deducted from those benefits for purposes of child support, in accordance with section 2301.371 [2301.37.1] and division (D)(4) of section 4141.28 of the Revised Code. Any deduction from a source in accordance with those provisions is in addition to, and does not preclude, any withholding or deduction for purposes of support under divisions (A) to (N) of this section.

(P) As used in this section, and in sections 3113.211 [3113.21.1] to 3113.217 [3113.21.7] of the Revised Code:

(1) "Financial institution" means a bank, savings and loan association, or credit union, or a regulated investment company or mutual fund in which a person who is required to pay child support has funds on deposit that are not exempt under the law of this state or the United States from execution, attachment, or other legal process.

(2) "Title IV-D case" means any case in which the child support enforcement agency is enforcing the child support order pursuant to Title IV-D of the "Social Security Act," 88 Stat. 2351 (1975), 42 U.S.C. 651, as amended.

(3) "Obligor" means the person who is required to pay support under a support order.

(4) "Obligee" means the person who is entitled to receive the support payments under a support order.

(5) "Support order" means an order for the payment of support and, for orders issued or modified on or after December 31, 1993, includes any notices described in division (D) or (H) of this section that are issued in accordance with this section.

(6) "Support" means child support, spousal support, and support for a spouse or former spouse.

(7) "Personal earnings" means compensation paid or payable for personal services, however denominated, and includes, but is not limited to, wages, salary, commissions, bonuses, draws against commissions, profit sharing, and vacation pay.

(8) "Default" has the same meaning as in section 2301.34 of the Revised Code.

HISTORY: GC § 8007-15; 124 v 112; Bureau of Code Revision, RC § 3115.09, 10-1-53; RC § 3115.23, 132 v H 471; 133 v H 361; RC § 3113.21, 134 v H 504 (Eff 10-27-71); 138 v H 674 (Eff 9-28-79); 138 v H 736 (Eff 10-16-80); 139 v H 515 (Eff 6-1-82); 139 v H 245 (Eff 6-29-82); 139 v H 254 (Eff 8-26-82); 140 v H 614 (Eff 4-10-85); 141 v H 509 (Eff 12-1-86); 142 v H 164 (Eff 4-1-87); 142 v H 231 (Eff 10-5-87); 142 v H 708 (Eff 4-19-88); 142 v H 242 (Eff 6-24-88); 143.v H 591 (Eff 4-12-90); 143 v H 514 (Eff 1-1-91); 143 v S 3 (Eff 4-1-91); 144 v S 331 (Eff 11-13-92); 145 v H 173 (Eff 12-31-93); 146 v H 167 (Eff 6-11-96); 146 v H 274, §§ 1, 7 (Eff 8-8-96); 146 v S 292 (Eff 11-06-96); 147 v H 408. Eff 10-1-97.

The effective date is set by section 26 of HB 408.

The effective date of HB 167 (146 v —) is changed from 11-15-96 to 6-11-96 by section 7 of HB 710 (146 v —).

The effective date of HB 274, § 7 (146 v —) is changed from 11-15-96 to 8-8-96 by section 8 of HB 710 (146 v —).

The provisions of §§ 7, 8, 9, and 15(A), (B) of HB 710 (146 v —) set out below describe the changes made to accelerate effective dates.

SECTION 7. Sections 2151.231, 2301.34, 2301.35, 2301.351, 2301.358, 2705.02, 3111.20, 3111.21, 3111.22, 3111.23, 3111.241, 3111.242, 3111.27, 3111.28, 3111.99, 3113.21, 3113.214, 3113.215, 3113.99, 4723.07, and 4723.09 of the Revised Code, as amended by Sub. H. B. 167 of the 121st General Assembly, shall take effect on the effective date of this act.

SECTION 8. That Section 9 of Sub. H. B. 274 of the 121st General Assembly be amended to read as follows:

"Sec. 9. Sections 7 and 8 of Sub. H. B. 274 of the 121st General Assembly shall take effect on the later of the effective date of Sub. H.B. 274 or the effective date of Sub. H.B 710 of the 121st General Assembly."

SECTION 9. That existing Section 9 of Sub. H. B. 274 of the 121st General Assembly is hereby repealed.

◦ ◦ ◦

SECTION 15. The intent of the General Assembly in enacting Sections 5 to 14 of this act is to accelerate the effective dates of the amendments to sections 2151.231, 2301.34, 2301.35, 2301.351, 2301.358, 2705.02, 3111.20, 3111.21, 3111.22, 3111.23, 3111.241, 3111.242, 3111.27, 3111.28, 3111.99, 3113.21, 3113.214, 3113.215, 3113.99, 4723.07, and 4723.09 of the Revised Code by Sub. H.B. 167 of the 121st General Assembly. The effect of Sections 9 to 14 of this act is as follows:

(A) The amendments to sections 2151.231, 2301.34, 2301.35, 2301.351, 2301.358, 2705.02, 3111.20, 3111.21, 3111.22, 3111.23, 3111.241, 3111.242, 3111.27, 3111.28, 3111.99, 3113.21, 3113.214, 3113.215, 3113.99, 4723.07, and 4723.09 of the Revised Code by Sub. H.B. 167 of the 121st General Assembly take effect, and their existing interim versions are correspondingly repealed, on the date this act takes effect and not on November 15, 1996;

(B) The amendments to sections 2301.34, 2301.35, 2301.351, 3113.21, 3113.214, and 3113.215 of the Revised Code by Sections 7 and 8 of Sub. H.B. 274 of the 121st General Assembly take effect on the later of the effective date of Sub. H.B. 274 or the effective date of this act, and not on November 15, 1996;

◦ ◦ ◦

[§ 3113.21.1] § 3113.211 Garnishee may also deduct fee; forwarding of payment; distribution to obligee.

(A)(1) For purposes of this section, a withholding or deduction order that was issued prior to December 31, 1993, under division (D)(1), (2), (3), (4), or (5) of section 3113.21 of the Revised Code as the division existed prior to that date and that has not been terminated on or after December 31, 1993, shall be considered to be a withholding or deduction notice issued under division (D)(1), (2), (3), (4), or (5) of section 3113.21 of the Revised Code.

(2) An employer ordered to withhold a specified amount from the personal earnings of an employee under a withholding notice issued under division (A), (B), (C), or (D)(1) of section 3113.21 of the Revised Code for purposes of support also may deduct from the personal earnings of the person, in addition to the

amount withheld for purposes of support, a fee of two dollars or an amount not to exceed one per cent of the amount withheld for purposes of support, whichever is greater, as a charge for its services in complying with the withholding requirement included in the withholding notice. An employer that is paying a person's workers' compensation benefits and that is required to withhold a specified amount from a person's workers' compensation benefits under a withholding notice issued under division (D)(2) of section 3113.21 of the Revised Code for purposes of support also may deduct from the workers' compensation benefits, in addition to the amount withheld for purposes of support, a fee of two dollars or an amount not to exceed one per cent of the amount withheld for purposes of support, whichever is greater, as a charge for its services in complying with the withholding requirement included in the withholding notice. A financial institution required to deduct funds from an account under a deduction notice issued under division (D)(5) of section 3113.21 of the Revised Code for purposes of support may deduct from the account of the person, in addition to the amount deducted for purposes of support, a fee of five dollars or an amount not to exceed the lowest rate that it charges, if any, for a debit transaction in a similar account, whichever is less, as a charge for its service in complying with the deduction requirement included in the deduction notice. The public employees retirement board, the board, board of trustees, or other governing entity of any municipal retirement system, the board of trustees of the police and firemen's disability and pension fund, the state teachers retirement board, the school employees retirement board, the state highway patrol retirement board, and a person paying or otherwise distributing an obligor's income required to withhold or deduct a specified amount from an obligor's pension, annuity, allowance, other benefit, or other source of income under a withholding or deduction notice issued under division (D)(3) or (4) of section 3113.21 of the Revised Code for purposes of support also may deduct from the obligor's pension, annuity, allowance, other benefit, or other source of income, a fee of two dollars or an amount not to exceed one per cent of the amount withheld or deducted, whichever is less, as a charge for its services in complying with the withholding or deduction requirement included in the withholding or deduction notice.

The entire amount withheld or deducted pursuant to a withholding or deduction notice issued under division (D) of section 3113.21 of the Revised Code for purposes of support shall be forwarded to the child support enforcement agency of the county in which that court is located immediately, but not later than ten working days after, the withholding or deduction, as directed in the withholding or deduction notice.

(B) If an employer, a financial institution, an employer that is paying an obligor's workers' compensation benefits, the public employees retirement board, the board, board of trustees, or other governing entity of any municipal retirement system, the board of trustees of the police and firemen's disability and pension fund, the state teachers retirement board, the school employees retirement board, the state highway patrol retirement board, the person paying or otherwise distributing an obligor's income, or the bureau of workers' compensation is required to withhold or deduct a specified amount from the personal earnings, payments, pensions, annuities, allowances, benefits, other sources of income, or savings of more than one obligor under a withholding or deduction notice issued under division (D) of section 3113.21 of the Revised Code and is required to forward the amounts withheld or deducted to the same child support enforcement agency, the employer, the public employees retirement board, the board, board of trustees, or other governing entity of any municipal retirement system, the board of trustees of the police and firemen's disability and pension fund, the state teachers retirement board, the school employees retirement board, the state highway patrol retirement board, the person paying or otherwise distributing an obligor's income, the financial institution, the employer that is paying an obligor's workers' compensation benefits, or the bureau of workers' compensation may combine all of the amounts to be forwarded in one payment, provided the payment is accompanied by a list that clearly identifies each obligor who is covered by the payment and the portion of the payment that is attributable to that obligor.

(C) Upon receipt of any amount forwarded from an employer, a financial institution, an employer that is paying a person's workers' compensation benefits, the public employees retirement board, the board, board of trustees, or other governing entity of any municipal retirement system, the board of trustees of the police and firemen's disability and pension fund, the state teachers retirement board, the school employees retirement board, the state highway patrol retirement board, the person paying or otherwise distributing an obligor's income, or the bureau of workers' compensation under this section, a clerk of court or child support enforcement agency shall distribute the amount to the obligee within two business days of its receipt of the amount forwarded. The department of human services may adopt, revise, or amend rules under Chapter 119. of the Revised Code to assist the clerk of court or child support enforcement agency in the implementation of this division.

HISTORY: 141 v H 509 (Eff 12-1-86); 142 v H 708 (Eff 4-19-88); 142 v H 503 (Eff 9-9-88); 143 v S 3 (Eff 4-11-91); 145 v H 173. Eff 12-31-93.

The effective date is set by section 4 of HB 173.

[§ 3113.21.2] § 3113.212 Change in status of obligor; investigation; new order; enforcement by contempt proceedings.

(A) When a court has issued a support order, when

the court or a child support enforcement agency has issued one or more notices containing one or more of the requirements described in division (D) of section 3113.21 of the Revised Code or when a court has issued one or more court orders described in division (D)(6) or (7) of that section, and when either the child support enforcement agency receives a notification as described in division (D), (G), or (H) of section 3113.21 of the Revised Code that pertains to a change in the employment status, status of the workers' compensation payments, status of the pension, annuity, allowance, benefit, or other source of income, or status of accounts in a financial institution of the obligor or the child support enforcement agency otherwise determines that the employment status, status of the workers' compensation payments, status of the pension, annuity, allowance, benefit, or other source of income, or status of accounts in a financial institution of the obligor has changed, the child support enforcement agency immediately shall conduct an investigation to determine the obligor's present employment status, his employer's address, whether he has any other source of income or assets, and the obligor's address and social security number and shall issue one or more notices described in division (D) of section 3113.21 of the Revised Code that it determines are appropriate. If the agency determines that no notice of the type described in division (D)(1) to (5) of that section would be appropriate, the agency may request the court to issue a court order under division (D)(6) or (7) of that section, and, upon the request, the court may issue an order as described in that division. The notices and court orders are final and are enforceable by the court. The notices shall be mailed within fifteen days after the obligor under the support order is located or within fifteen days after the default under the support order, whichever is applicable.

If the court or child support enforcement agency previously has issued one or more notices containing one or more of the requirements described in division (D) of section 3113.21 of the Revised Code or the court previously has issued one or more court orders described in division (D)(6) or (7) of that section and the child support enforcement agency determines that any of the requirements or court orders no longer are appropriate due to the change, the agency immediately shall cancel any previously issued notice, and the court shall cancel any previously issued court order that no longer is appropriate, the agency shall send written notice of the cancellation by regular mail to the person who was required to comply with the withholding, deduction, or other requirement contained in the canceled notice or court order, and the agency shall issue one or more new notices containing one or more requirements described in division (D) of section 3113.21 of the Revised Code that it determines are appropriate. If the agency determines that no notice of the type described in division (D)(1) to (5) of that section would be appropriate, the agency may request the court to issue a court order under division (D)(6) or (7) of that section, and, upon the request, the court may issue an order as described in that division. The notices and court orders are final and are enforceable by the court. The notices shall be mailed within fifteen days after the obligor under the support order is located or within fifteen days after the default under the support order, whichever is applicable.

(B) When a court or child support enforcement agency has issued one or more notices containing one or more of the requirements described in division (D)(2), (3), (4), or (5) of section 3113.21 of the Revised Code or a court has issued one or more court orders described in division (D)(6) or (7) of that section and the agency is informed that the obligor has commenced employment, the agency shall issue a notice requiring the withholding of an amount from the person's personal earnings for support, in accordance with division (D)(1) of section 3113.21 of the Revised Code. The notice is final and is enforceable by the court. Additionally, if the court or agency determines that payments due under the support order have not been made and that the amount that has not been paid is at least equal to the support owed for one month under the support order, the court shall proceed to collect on any cash bond.

(C) If a child support enforcement agency sends a notice imposing a withholding or deduction requirement or a court sends a court order imposing any other appropriate requirement to a person under division (A) or (B) of this section, the notice or court order, for purposes of sections 3113.21 to 3113.219 [3113.21.9] of the Revised Code, also shall be considered to have been issued under division (D) of section 3113.21 of the Revised Code. The notice or court order is final and is enforceable by the court.

(D) If a child support enforcement agency sends a notice imposing a withholding or deduction requirement or any other appropriate requirement to a person under division (A) or (B) of this section or under section 3113.21 of the Revised Code and if the employer, the financial institution, the employer that is paying the obligor's workers' compensation benefits, the public employees retirement board, the board, board of trustees, or other governing entity of the municipal retirement system, the board of trustees of the police and firemen's disability and pension fund, the state teachers retirement board, the school employees retirement board, the state highway patrol retirement board, the person paying or otherwise distributing an obligor's income, or the bureau of workers' compensation that is sent the withholding, deduction, or other appropriate notice fails to comply with the notice, the child support enforcement agency shall request the court to issue a court order requiring the employer, the financial institution, the employer that is paying the obligor's workers' compensation benefits, the public employees retirement board, the board, board of trustees, or other governing entity of the municipal retirement system, the board of trustees of the police and firemen's disability and pension fund, the state teachers retirement board, the school employees retirement board, the state highway patrol retirement board, the person paying or otherwise distributing an obligor's income, or the bureau of workers' compensation to comply with the withholding, deduction, or other appropriate notice sent by the agency immediately or be held in contempt of court. If the court issues the requested order and if the employer, the financial institution, the employer that is paying the obligor's workers' compensation benefits, the public employees retirement board, the board, board of trustees, or other governing entity of the municipal retirement system, the board of trustees of the police and firemen's disability and pension fund, the state teachers retirement board, the school employees retirement board, the state highway patrol retirement board, the person paying or otherwise distributing an obligor's income, or the bureau of workers' compensation does not comply with the withholding, deduction, or other appropriate order of the agency that is the subject of the court order immediately, it is in contempt of court.

HISTORY: 141 v H 509 (Eff 12-1-86); 142 v H 231 (Eff 10-5-87); 142 v H 708 (Eff 4-19-88); 145 v H 173. Eff 12-31-93.

The effective date is set by section 4 of HB 173.

[§ 3113.21.3] § 3113.213 Default and liability of garnishee; fine; prohibited employment actions.

(A)(1) For purposes of this section, a withholding or deduction order that was issued prior to December 31, 1993, under division (D)(1), (2), (4), or (5) of section 3113.21 of the Revised Code as the division existed prior to that date and that has not been terminated on or after December 31, 1993, shall be considered to be a withholding or deduction notice issued under division (D)(1), (2), (4), or (5) of section 3113.21 of the Revised Code.

(2) The failure of any person to send any notification required by division (D) or (H) of section 3113.21 of the Revised Code shall be considered as contempt of court.

(B) An employer that fails to withhold an amount from an obligor's personal earnings for support in accordance with a withholding requirement included in a withholding notice issued under division (D)(1) of section 3113.21 of the Revised Code, an employer that is paying an obligor's workers' compensation benefits and that fails to withhold the obligor's workers' compensation benefits for support in accordance with a withholding requirement included in a withholding notice issued under division (D)(2) of section 3113.21 of the Revised Code, a financial institution that fails to deduct funds from an obligor's account for support in accordance with a deduction requirement included in a deduction notice issued under division (D)(5) of section 3113.21 of the Revised Code, or any other person that fails to withhold or deduct an amount from the income of an obligor in accordance with a withholding or deduction requirement included in a withholding or deduction notice issued under division (D)(4) of section 3113.21 of the Revised Code is liable for the amount that was not withheld or deducted, provided that no employer whose normal pay and disbursement cycles make it impossible to comply with a withholding requirement contained in a withholding notice issued under division (D)(1) of section 3113.21 of the Revised Code shall be liable for the amount not withheld if the employer, as soon as possible after the employer's receipt of the withholding notice, provides the court or child support enforcement agency that issued the notice with written notice of the impossibility and the reasons for the impossibility. An employer who is liable under this provision for an amount that was not withheld shall be ordered by the court to pay that amount to the clerk of the court or the child support enforcement agency, to be disbursed in accordance with the support order for the benefit of the child or spouse.

(C) The court may fine an employer not more than two hundred dollars for failure to withhold personal earnings or to notify the court or child support enforcement agency that an obligor has terminated employment, has been laid off, has taken a leave of absence without pay, has entered into another situation in which the employer has ceased to pay personal earnings in an amount sufficient to comply with the order to the obligor, or is receiving or is eligible to receive a benefit of employment other than personal earnings, as required by a withholding notice issued under division (D)(1) of section 3113.21 of the Revised Code. The court may fine an employer that is paying an obligor's workers' compensation benefits not more than two hundred dollars for failure to withhold an obligor's workers' compensation benefits or to notify the court or child support enforcement agency of any termination in the payment of the obligor's workers' compensation benefits, as required by a withholding notice issued under division (D)(2) of section 3113.21 of the Revised Code. The court may fine a person who is paying or otherwise distributing the income of an obligor not more than two hundred dollars for failure to withhold or deduct an amount from the income of the obligor or to notify the court or child support enforcement agency of the termination of that income, as required by a withholding or deduction notice issued under division (D)(4) of section 3113.21 of the Revised Code. The court may fine a financial institution not more than two hundred dollars for failure to deduct funds from an account or to notify the court or child support enforcement agency of the termination of an account from which funds are being deducted or the opening of a new account, as required by a deduction notice issued under division (D)(5) of section 3113.21 of the Revised Code.

(D) No employer may use a requirement to withhold

personal earnings contained in a withholding notice issued under division (D)(1) of section 3113.21 of the Revised Code, as a basis for a discharge of, or for any disciplinary action against, an employee, or as a basis for a refusal to employ a person. The court may fine an employer who so discharges or takes disciplinary action against an employee, or refuses to employ a person, not more than five hundred dollars.

HISTORY: 141 v H 509 (Eff 12-1-86); 142 v H 708 (Eff 4-19-88); 145 v H 173. Eff 12-31-93.

The effective date is set by section 4 of HB 173.

[§ 3113.21.4] § 3113.214 Enforcement of support order issued by another state.

(A) Every court and child support enforcement agency shall give full faith and credit to any order of a court or authorized administrative agency of another state that requires the payment of any form of support, including any order of a type that may be issued pursuant to Chapter 3115. or section 2151.23, 2151.33, 2151.36, 2151.49, 3105.18, 3105.21, 3109.05, 3109.19, 3111.13, 3111.20, 3111.21, 3111.22, 3113.04, 3113.07, 3113.21, or 3113.31 of the Revised Code or pursuant to any similar provision of law.

(B)(1) Upon receiving a request for interstate income withholding from a Title IV-D agency of another state that is based upon an order of a court or authorized administrative agency of the other state that requires the payment of any form of support and is the type of order described in division (A) of this section and upon receiving the support order and other supporting documents relative to the request, the state department of human services shall examine the order and the supporting documents in accordance with federal child support regulations. If the department determines, upon completion of the examination, that the order and documents are in compliance with those federal regulations, the department shall prepare findings to that effect and shall transmit a copy of the findings and a copy of the order and documents to the child support enforcement agency in the appropriate county, as determined in accordance with rules adopted under division (C) of this section.

A child support enforcement agency that receives a copy of the findings of the department and a copy of the related support order and supporting documents pursuant to this division shall treat the order in the same manner as it would treat any support order issued by a court of this state. The agency shall proceed in accordance with division (B)(1)(b) of section 3113.21 of the Revised Code to conduct an investigation relative to the support order issued by a court or authorized administrative agency of another state and to issue a recommendation to the appropriate court in this state, as determined in accordance with rules adopted under division (C) of this section, that the court issue a separate order containing a general requirement of the type described in division (B)(2) of this section and a recommendation of one or more types of withholding or deduction requirements described in division (D) of section 3113.21 of the Revised Code that should be imposed to provide for the payment of support by the obligor under the support order that was issued by a court or authorized administrative agency of another state.

(2) When the child support enforcement agency issues its recommendations to the court, it shall file with the court its findings and its recommendations and shall file with the court at the same time a certified copy of the support order of the court or authorized administrative agency of the other state that requires the payment of the support and an advance notice of the type described in divisions (B)(1) and (2) of section 3113.21 of the Revised Code. Upon receipt of the agencies† recommendations, the court shall issue an order, separate and apart from the support order of the court or authorized administrative agency of the other state, requiring the withholding or deduction of wages or assets of the obligor in accordance with division (D) of section 3113.21 of the Revised Code or requiring the issuance of another type of appropriate order in accordance with division (D)(6), (D)(7), or (H) of that section to ensure that withholding or deduction from the wages or assets is available from the commencement of the support order of the court or authorized administrative agency of the other state for the collection of the support and any arrearages that occur. The court or agency shall determine the specific withholding or deduction requirements or other appropriate requirements applicable to the obligor under the support order in accordance with divisions (D) and (H) of section 3113.21 of the Revised Code and section 2301.371 [2301.37.1] of the Revised Code and shall include the specific requirements in the notices described in division (A)(2) of section 3113.21 of the Revised Code or in the court orders described in divisions (A)(2), (D)(6) or (7), and (H) of that section. Any person required to comply with the withholding or deduction requirements shall determine the manner of withholding or deducting an amount of the wages or assets of the obligor in accordance with the specific requirements included in the notices described in those divisions without the need for any amendment to the support order, and any person required to comply with a court order described in division (D)(6), (D)(7), or (H) of section 3113.21 of the Revised Code shall comply with the court order without the need for any amendment to the support order. The notices issued under this division, and the notices provided by the court or child support enforcement agency that require the obligor to notify the agency of any change in the obligor's employment status or of any other change in the status of the obligor's assets, are final and are enforceable by the court. If the obligor fails to request a hearing pursuant to divisions (B)(2)(d) and (3) of section 3113.21 of the Revised Code to deter-

mine whether, because of a mistake of fact, it is not proper to include an amount to pay arrearages in the withholding or deduction notice recommended by the agency pursuant to division (B)(1) of this section, the court or the child support enforcement agency, as determined by agreement of the court and the agency, shall issue one or more notices containing one or more of the withholding or deduction requirements described in division (D) of section 3113.21 of the Revised Code or one or more court orders containing other appropriate requirements described in division (D)(6) or (7) or (H) of that section, for the payment of support and arrearages by the obligor under the support order. If the obligor fails to timely request a hearing pursuant to divisions (B)(2)(d) and (3) of section 3113.21 of the Revised Code to determine whether, because of a mistake of fact, it is not proper to include an amount to pay arrearages in the withholding or deduction notices issued under this division, the notices or court orders shall include an amount for arrearages. If the obligor timely requests a hearing pursuant to those divisions to determine whether, because of a mistake of fact, it is not proper to include an amount to pay arrearages in the withholding or deduction notices or court orders issued under this division, the court shall conduct the hearing and shall include in the notices and court orders an amount for arrearages as it determines appropriate at the hearing. The court shall issue and enforce the notices and court orders described in this division in accordance with section 3113.21 of the Revised Code as if the support order to which they pertain had been issued in this state on or after the effective date of this amendment.

(3) The order that a court is required to issue under division (B)(2) of this section, separate and apart from the support order of the court or authorized administrative agency of the other state, specifically shall include the following statement:

"All child support and spousal support that is ordered by the support order of a state other than Ohio and to which this order pertains shall be withheld or deducted from the wages or assets of the obligor pursuant to a withholding or deduction notice or appropriate court order issued in accordance with section 3113.21 of the Revised Code and shall be forwarded to the obligee in accordance with sections 3113.21 to 3113.214 [3113.21.4] of the Revised Code."

(C) The state department of human services shall adopt rules in accordance with Chapter 119. of the Revised Code to aid in the implementation of this section.

(D) As used in this section:

(1) "Authorized administrative agency of another state" means an administrative agency of the state in question that is authorized by the law of that state to issue an order requiring the payment of any form of support, including any order of a type that may be issued pursuant to Chapter 3115. or section 2151.23, 2151.33, 2151.36, 2151.49, 3105.08, 3105.21, 3109.05, 3109.19, 3111.13, 3111.20, 3111.21, 3111.22, 3113.04, 3113.07, 3113.21, 3113.216 [3113.21.6], or 3113.31 of the Revised Code or pursuant to any similar provision of law.

(2) "Title IV-D agency of another state" means the state department, agency, or other governmental entity of the state in question that administers the state's program of child support enforcement that meets the requirements of Title IV-D of the "Social Security Act," 88 Stat. 2351 (1975), 42 U.S.C. 651, as amended.

HISTORY: 144 v H 298 (Eff 7-26-91); 145 v H 173 (Eff 12-31-93); 146 v H 167 (Eff 6-11-96); 146 v H 274, §§1, 7. Eff 8-8-96.

Not analogous to former RC § 3113.21.4 (141 v H 509; 143 v S 3), repealed, 144 v H 298, § 2, eff 7-26-91.

The effective date of HB 167 (146 v —) is changed from 11-15-96 to 6-11-96 by section 7 of HB 710 (146 v —).

The effective date of HB 274, § 7 (146 v —) is changed from 11-15-96 to 8-8-96 by section 8 of HB 710 (146 v —).

See provisions, §§ 7, 8, 9 and 15(A), (B) from HB 710 (146 v —) following RC § 3113.21.

† So in enrolled bill.

[§ 3113.21.5] § 3113.215 Calculation of amount of child support obligation; deviations; requests for modification; schedule; worksheet; advisory council.

(A) As used in this section:

(1) "Income" means either of the following:

(a) For a parent who is employed to full capacity, the gross income of the parent;

(b) For a parent who is unemployed or underemployed, the sum of the gross income of the parent, and any potential income of the parent.

(2) "Gross income" means, except as excluded in this division, the total of all earned and unearned income from all sources during a calendar year, whether or not the income is taxable, and includes, but is not limited to, income from salaries, wages, overtime pay and bonuses to the extent described in division (B)(5)(d) of this section, commissions, royalties, tips, rents, dividends, severance pay, pensions, interest, trust income, annuities, social security benefits, workers' compensation benefits, unemployment insurance benefits, disability insurance benefits, benefits received by and in the possession of the veteran who is the beneficiary for any service-connected disability under a program or law administered by the United States department of veterans' affairs or veterans' administration, spousal support actually received from a person not a party to the support proceeding for which actual gross income is being determined, and all other sources of income; income of members of any branch of the United States armed services or national guard, including, but not limited to, amounts representing base pay, basic allowance for quarters, basic allowance for subsistence, supplemental subsis-

tence allowance, cost of living adjustment, specialty pay, variable housing allowance, and pay for training or other types of required drills; self-generated income; and potential cash flow from any source.

"Gross income" does not include any of the following:

(a) Benefits received from means-tested public assistance programs, including, but not limited to, Ohio works first; prevention, retention, and contingency; supplemental security income; food stamps; or disability assistance;

(b) Benefits for any service-connected disability under a program or law administered by the United States department of veterans' affairs or veterans' administration that have not been distributed to the veteran who is the beneficiary of the benefits and that are in the possession of the United States department of veterans' affairs or veterans' administration;

(c) Child support received for children who were not born or adopted during the marriage at issue;

(d) Amounts paid for mandatory deductions from wages other than taxes, social security, or retirement in lieu of social security, including, but not limited to, union dues;

(e) Nonrecurring or unsustainable income or cash flow items.

(3) "Self-generated income" means gross receipts received by a parent from self-employment, proprietorship of a business, joint ownership of a partnership or closely held corporation, and rents minus ordinary and necessary expenses incurred by the parent in generating the gross receipts. "Self-generated income" includes expense reimbursements or in-kind payments received by a parent from self-employment, the operation of a business, or rents, including, but not limited to, company cars, free housing, reimbursed meals, and other benefits, if the reimbursements are significant and reduce personal living expenses.

(4)(a) "Ordinary and necessary expenses incurred in generating gross receipts" means actual cash items expended by the parent or the parent's business and includes depreciation expenses of replacement business equipment as shown on the books of a business entity.

(b) Except as specifically included in "ordinary and necessary expenses incurred in generating gross receipts" by division (A)(4)(a) of this section, "ordinary and necessary expenses incurred in generating gross receipts" does not include depreciation expenses and other noncash items that are allowed as deductions on any federal tax return of the parent or the parent's business.

(5) "Potential income" means both of the following for a parent that the court, or a child support enforcement agency pursuant to sections 3111.20, 3111.21, and 3111.22 of the Revised Code, determines is voluntarily unemployed or voluntarily underemployed:

(a) Imputed income that the court or agency determines the parent would have earned if fully employed as determined from the parent's employment potential and probable earnings based on the parent's recent work history, the parent's occupational qualifications, and the prevailing job opportunities and salary levels in the community in which the parent resides;

(b) Imputed income from any nonincome-producing assets of a parent, as determined from the local passbook savings rate or another appropriate rate as determined by the court or agency, not to exceed the rate of interest specified in division (A) of section 1343.03 of the Revised Code, if the income is significant.

(6) "Child support order" means an order for the payment of child support.

(7) "Combined gross income" means the combined gross income of both parents.

(8) "Split parental rights and responsibilities" means a situation in which there is more than one child who is the subject of an allocation of parental rights and responsibilities and each parent is the residential parent and legal custodian of at least one of those children.

(9) "Schedule" means the basic child support schedule set forth in division (D) of this section.

(10) "Worksheet" means the applicable worksheet that is used to calculate a parent's child support obligation and that is set forth in divisions (E) and (F) of this section.

(11) "Nonrecurring or unsustainable income or cash flow item" means any income or cash flow item that the parent receives in any year or for any number of years not to exceed three years and that the parent does not expect to continue to receive on a regular basis. "Nonrecurring or unsustainable income or cash flow item" does not include a lottery prize award that is not paid in a lump sum or any other item of income or cash flow that the parent receives or expects to receive for each year for a period of more than three years or that the parent receives and invests or otherwise utilizes to produce income or cash flow for a period of more than three years.

(12) "Extraordinary medical expenses" means any uninsured medical expenses that are incurred for a child during a calendar year and that exceed one hundred dollars for that child during that calendar year.

(B)(1) In any action in which a child support order is issued or modified under Chapter 3115. or section 2151.23, 2151.33, 2151.36, 2151.49, 3105.18, 3105.21, 3109.05, 3109.19, 3111.13, 3113.04, 3113.07, 3113.216 [3113.21.6], or 3113.31 of the Revised Code, in any other proceeding in which the court determines the amount of child support that will be ordered to be paid pursuant to a child support order, or when a child support enforcement agency determines the amount of child support that will be paid pursuant to an administrative child support order issued pursuant to sections 3111.20, 3111.21, and 3111.22 of the Revised Code, the court or agency shall calculate the amount of the obligor's child support obligation in accordance with the basic child support schedule in division (D) of this section, the applicable worksheet in division (E) or (F) of this section, and the other provisions of this section, shall specify the support obligation as a monthly amount due, and shall order the support obligation to be paid in periodic increments as it determines to be in the best interest of the children. In performing its duties under this section, the court or agency is not required to accept any calculations in a worksheet prepared by any party to the action or proceeding. In any action or proceeding in which the court determines the amount of child support that will be ordered to be paid pursuant to a child support order or when a child support enforcement agency determines the amount of child support that will be paid pursuant to an administrative child support order issued pursuant to sections 3111.20, 3111.21, and 3111.22 of the Revised Code, the amount of child support that would be payable under a child support order, as calculated pursuant to the basic child support schedule in division (D) of this section and pursuant to the applicable worksheet in division (E) of this section, through line 24, or in division (F) of this section, through line 23, is rebuttably presumed to be the correct amount of child support due, and the court or agency shall order that amount to be paid as child support unless both of the following apply with respect to an order issued by a court:

(a) The court, after considering the factors and criteria set forth in division (B)(3) of this section, determines that the amount calculated pursuant to the basic child support schedule and pursuant to the applicable worksheet in division (E) of this section, through line 24, or in division (F) of this section, through line 23, would be unjust or inappropriate and would not be in the best interest of the child.

(b) The court enters in the journal the amount of child support calculated pursuant to the basic child support schedule and pursuant to the applicable worksheet in division (E) of this section, through line 24, or in division (F) of this section, through line 23, its determination that that amount would be unjust or inappropriate and would not be in the best interest of the child, and findings of fact supporting that determination.

(2) In determining the amount of child support to be paid under any child support order, the court, upon its own recommendation or upon the recommendation of the child support enforcement agency, shall or the child support enforcement agency, pursuant to sections 3111.20, 3111.21, and 3111.22 of the Revised Code, shall do all of the following:

(a) If the combined gross income of both parents is less than six thousand six hundred dollars per year, the court or agency shall determine the amount of the obligor's child support obligation on a case-by-case basis using the schedule as a guideline. The court or agency shall review the obligor's gross income and living expenses to determine the maximum amount of child support that it reasonably can order without denying the obligor the means for self-support at a minimum subsistence level and shall order a specific amount of child support, unless the obligor proves to the court or agency that the obligor is totally unable to pay child support and the court or agency determines that it would be unjust or inappropriate to order the payment of child support and enters its determination and supporting findings of fact in the journal.

(b) If the combined gross income of both parents is greater than one hundred fifty thousand dollars per year, the court or agency shall determine the amount of the obligor's child support obligation on a case-by-case basis and shall consider the needs and the standard of living of the children who are the subject of the child support order and of the parents. When the court or agency determines the amount of the obligor's child support obligation for parents with a combined gross income greater than one hundred fifty thousand dollars, the court or agency shall compute a basic combined child support obligation that is no less than the same percentage of the parents' combined annual income that would have been computed under the basic child support schedule and under the applicable worksheet in division (E) of this section, through line 24, or in division (F) of this section, through line 23, for a combined gross income of one hundred fifty thousand dollars, unless the court or agency determines that it would be unjust or inappropriate and would not be in the best interest of the child, obligor, or obligee to order that amount and enters in the journal the figure, determination, and findings.

(c) The court shall not order an amount of child support that deviates from the amount of child support that would otherwise result from the use of the basic child support schedule and the applicable worksheet in division (E) of this section, through line 24, or in division (F) of this section, through line 23, unless both of the following apply:

(i) The court, after considering the factors and criteria set forth in division (B)(3) of this section, determines that the amount calculated pursuant to the basic child support schedule and pursuant to the applicable worksheet in division (E) of this section, through line 24, or in division (F) of this section, through line 23, would be unjust or inappropriate and would not be in the best interest of the child;

(ii) The court enters in the journal the amount of child support calculated pursuant to the basic child support schedule and pursuant to the applicable worksheet in division (E) of this section, through line 24, or in division (F) of this section, through line 23, its determination that that amount would be unjust or inappropriate and would not be in the best interest of the child, and findings of fact supporting that determination.

(3) The court, in accordance with divisions (B)(1) and (2)(c) of this section, may deviate from the amount of support that otherwise would result from the use of the schedule and the applicable worksheet in division (E)

of this section, through line 24, or in division (F) of this section, through line 23, in cases in which the application of the schedule and the applicable worksheet in division (E) of this section, through line 24, or in division (F) of this section, through line 23, would be unjust or inappropriate and would not be in the best interest of the child. In determining whether that amount would be unjust or inappropriate and would not be in the best interest of the child, the court may consider any of the following factors and criteria:

(a) Special and unusual needs of the children;

(b) Extraordinary obligations for minor children or obligations for handicapped children who are not stepchildren and who are not offspring from the marriage or relationship that is the basis of the immediate child support determination;

(c) Other court-ordered payments;

(d) Extended times of visitation or extraordinary costs associated with visitation, provided that this division does not authorize and shall not be construed as authorizing any deviation from the schedule and the applicable worksheet in division (E) of this section, through line 24, or in division (F) of this section, through line 23, or any escrowing, impoundment, or withholding of child support because of a denial of or interference with a right of companionship or visitation granted by court order;

(e) The obligor obtains additional employment after a child support order is issued in order to support a second family;

(f) The financial resources and the earning ability of the child;

(g) Disparity in income between parties or households;

(h) Benefits that either parent receives from remarriage or sharing living expenses with another person;

(i) The amount of federal, state, and local taxes actually paid or estimated to be paid by a parent or both of the parents;

(j) Significant in-kind contributions from a parent, including, but not limited to, direct payment for lessons, sports equipment, schooling, or clothing;

(k) The relative financial resources, other assets and resources, and needs of each parent;

(l) The standard of living and circumstances of each parent and the standard of living the child would have enjoyed had the marriage continued or had the parents been married;

(m) The physical and emotional condition and needs of the child;

(n) The need and capacity of the child for an education and the educational opportunities that would have been available to the child had the circumstances requiring a court order for support not arisen;

(o) The responsibility of each parent for the support of others;

(p) Any other relevant factor.

The court may accept an agreement of the parents that assigns a monetary value to any of the factors and criteria listed in division (B)(3) of this section that are applicable to their situation.

(4) If an obligor or obligee under a child support order requests the court to modify the amount of support required to be paid pursuant to the child support order, the court shall recalculate the amount of support that would be required to be paid under the support order in accordance with the schedule and pursuant to the applicable worksheet in division (E) of this section, through line 24, or in division (F) of this section, through line 23, and if that amount as recalculated is more than ten per cent greater than or more than ten per cent less than the amount of child support that is required to be paid pursuant to the existing child support order, the deviation from the recalculated amount that would be required to be paid under the schedule and the applicable worksheet in division (E) of this section, through line 24, or in division (F) of this section, through line 23, shall be considered by the court as a change of circumstance that is substantial enough to require a modification of the amount of the child support order. In determining pursuant to this division the recalculated amount of support that would be required to be paid under the support order for purposes of determining whether that recalculated amount is more than ten per cent greater than or more than ten per cent less than the amount of child support that is required to be paid pursuant to the existing child support order, the court shall consider, in addition to all other factors required by law to be considered, the cost of health insurance which the obligor, the obligee, or both the obligor and the obligee have been ordered to obtain for the children specified in the order. Additionally, if an obligor or obligee under a child support order requests the court to modify the amount of support required to be paid pursuant to the child support order and if the court determines that the amount of support does not adequately meet the medical needs of the child, the inadequate coverage shall be considered by the court as a change of circumstance that is substantial enough to require a modification of the amount of the child support order. If the court determines that the amount of child support required to be paid under the child support order should be changed due to a substantial change of circumstances that was not contemplated at the time of the issuance of the original child support order or the last modification of the child support order, the court shall modify the amount of child support required to be paid under the child support order to comply with the schedule and the applicable worksheet in division (E) of this section, through line 24, or in division (F) of this section, through line 23, unless the court determines that the amount calculated pursuant to the basic child support schedule and pursuant to the applicable worksheet in division (E) of this section, through line 24, or in division (F) of this section, through line 23, would be unjust or inappropriate and would

not be in the best interest of the child and enters in the journal the figure, determination, and findings specified in division (B)(2)(c) of this section.

(5) When a court computes the amount of child support required to be paid under a child support order or a child support enforcement agency computes the amount of child support to be paid pursuant to an administrative child support order issued pursuant to section 3111.20, 3111.21, or 3111.22 of the Revised Code, all of the following apply:

(a) The parents shall verify current and past income and personal earnings with suitable documents, including, but not limited to, paystubs, employer statements, receipts and expense vouchers related to self-generated income, tax returns, and all supporting documentation and schedules for the tax returns.

(b) The amount of any pre-existing child support obligation of a parent under a child support order and the amount of any court-ordered spousal support paid to a former spouse shall be deducted from the gross income of that parent to the extent that payment under the child support order or that payment of the court-ordered spousal support is verified by supporting documentation.

(c) If other minor children who were born to the parent and a person other than the other parent who is involved in the immediate child support determination live with the parent, the court or agency shall deduct an amount from that parent's gross income that equals the number of such minor children times the federal income tax exemption for such children less child support received for them for the year, not exceeding the federal income tax exemption.

(d) When the court or agency calculates the gross income of a parent, it shall include the lesser of the following as income from overtime and bonuses:

(i) The yearly average of all overtime and bonuses received during the three years immediately prior to the time when the person's child support obligation is being computed;

(ii) The total overtime and bonuses received during the year immediately prior to the time when the person's child support obligation is being computed.

(e) When the court or agency calculates the gross income of a parent, it shall not include any income earned by the spouse of that parent.

(f) The court shall not order an amount of child support for reasonable and ordinary uninsured medical or dental expenses in addition to the amount of the child support obligation determined in accordance with the schedule. The court shall issue a separate order for extraordinary medical or dental expenses, including, but not limited to, orthodontia, psychological, appropriate private education, and other expenses, and may consider the expenses in adjusting a child support order.

(g) When a court or agency calculates the amount of child support to be paid pursuant to a child support order or an administrative child support order, if the combined gross income of both parents is an amount that is between two amounts set forth in the first column of the schedule, the court or agency may use the basic child support obligation that corresponds to the higher of the two amounts in the first column of the schedule, use the basic child support obligation that corresponds to the lower of the two amounts in the first column of the schedule, or calculate a basic child support obligation that is between those two amounts and corresponds proportionally to the parents' actual combined gross income.

(h) When the court or agency calculates gross income, the court or agency, when appropriate, may average income over a reasonable period of years.

(6)(a) If the court issues a shared parenting order in accordance with section 3109.04 of the Revised Code, the court shall order an amount of child support to be paid under the child support order that is calculated in accordance with the schedule and with the worksheet set forth in division (E) of this section, through line 24, except that, if the application of the schedule and the worksheet, through line 24, would be unjust or inappropriate to the children or either parent and would not be in the best interest of the child because of the extraordinary circumstances of the parents or because of any other factors or criteria set forth in division (B)(3) of this section, the court may deviate from the amount of child support that would be ordered in accordance with the schedule and worksheet, through line 24, shall consider those extraordinary circumstances and other factors or criteria if it deviates from that amount, and shall enter in the journal the amount of child support calculated pursuant to the basic child support schedule and pursuant to the applicable worksheet, through line 24, its determination that that amount would be unjust or inappropriate and would not be in the best interest of the child, and findings of fact supporting that determination.

(b) For the purposes of this division, "extraordinary circumstances of the parents" includes, but is not limited to, all of the following:

(i) The amount of time that the children spend with each parent;

(ii) The ability of each parent to maintain adequate housing for the children;

(iii) Each parent's expenses, including, but not limited to, child care expenses, school tuition, medical expenses, and dental expenses.

(7)(a) In any action in which a child support order is issued or modified under Chapter 3115. or section 2151.23, 2151.33, 2151.36, 2151.49, 3105.18, 3105.21, 3109.05, 3109.19, 3111.13, 3113.04, or 3113.31 of the Revised Code or in any other proceeding in which the court determines the amount of child support that will be ordered to be paid pursuant to a child support order and except as otherwise provided in this division, the court shall issue a minimum support order requiring the obligor to pay a minimum amount of fifty dollars a month for child support under the child support order. The court, in its discretion and in appropriate circumstances, may issue a minimum support order requiring the obligor to pay an amount of child support that is less than fifty dollars a month or not requiring the obligor to pay an amount for support. The appropriate circumstances for which a court may issue a minimum support order requiring an obligor to pay an amount of child support that is less than fifty dollars a month or not requiring the obligor to pay an amount for support include, but are not limited to, the nonresidential parent's medically verified or documented physical or mental disability or institutionalization in a facility for persons with a mental illness. If the court issues a minimum support order pursuant to this division and the obligor under the support order is the recipient of need-based public assistance, any unpaid amounts of support due under the support order shall accrue as arrearages from month to month, the obligor's current obligation to pay the support due under the support order is suspended during any period of time that the obligor is receiving need-based public assistance and is complying with any seek work orders issued pursuant to division (D)(7) of section 3113.21 of the Revised Code, and the court, obligee, and child support enforcement agency shall not enforce the obligation of the obligor to pay the amount of support due under the support order during any period of time that the obligor is receiving need-based public assistance and is complying with any seek work orders issued pursuant to division (D)(7) of section 3113.21 of the Revised Code.

(b) Notwithstanding division (B)(7)(a) of this section, if the amount of support payments that federal law requires or permits to be disregarded in determining eligibility for aid under Chapter 5107. of the Revised Code exceeds fifty dollars, instead of fifty dollars the amount of a minimum support order described in division (B)(7)(a) of this section shall be the amount federal law requires or permits to be disregarded.

(C) Except when the parents have split parental rights and responsibilities, a parent's child support obligation for a child for whom the parent is the residential parent and legal custodian shall be presumed to be spent on that child and shall not become part of a child support order, and a parent's child support obligation for a child for whom the parent is not the residential parent and legal custodian shall become part of a child support order. If the parents have split parental rights and responsibilities, the child support obligations of the parents shall be offset, and the court shall issue a child support order requiring the parent with the larger child support obligation to pay the net amount pursuant to the child support order. If neither parent of a child who is the subject of a child support order is the residential parent and legal custodian of the child and the child resides with a third party who is the legal custodian of the child, the court shall issue a child support order requiring each parent to pay that parent's child support obligation pursuant to the child support order.

Whenever a court issues a child support order, it shall include in the order specific provisions for regular, holiday, vacation, and special visitation in accordance with section 3109.05, 3109.11, or 3109.12 of the Revised Code or in accordance with any other applicable section of the Revised Code. The court shall not authorize or permit the escrowing, impoundment, or withholding of any child support payment because of a denial of or interference with a right of visitation included as a specific provision of the child support order or as a method of enforcing the specific provisions of the child support order dealing with visitation.

(D) The following basic child support schedule shall be used by all courts and child support enforcement agencies when calculating the amount of child support that will be paid pursuant to a child support order or an administrative child support order, unless the combined gross income of the parents is less than sixty-six hundred dollars or more than one hundred fifty thousand dollars:

Basic Child Support Schedule
Number of Children

Combined Gross Income	One	Two	Three	Four	Five	Six
6600	600	600	600	600	600	600
7200	600	600	600	600	600	600
7800	600	600	600	600	600	600
8400	600	600	600	600	600	600
9000	849	859	868	878	887	896
9600	1259	1273	1287	1301	1315	1329
10200	1669	1687	1706	1724	1743	1761
10800	2076	2099	2122	2145	2168	2192
11400	2331	2505	2533	2560	2588	2616
12000	2439	2911	2943	2975	3007	3039
12600	2546	3318	3354	3390	3427	3463
13200	2654	3724	3765	3806	3846	3887
13800	2761	4029	4175	4221	4266	4311
14400	2869	4186	4586	4636	4685	4735

Basic Child Support Schedule
Number of Children

Combined Gross Income	One	Two	Three	Four	Five	Six
15000	2976	4342	4996	5051	5105	5159
15600	3079	4491	5321	5466	5524	5583
16200	3179	4635	5490	5877	5940	6003
16800	3278	4780	5660	6254	6355	6423
17400	3378	4924	5830	6442	6771	6843
18000	3478	5069	5999	6629	7186	7262
18600	3578	5213	6169	6816	7389	7682
19200	3678	5358	6339	7004	7592	8102
19800	3778	5502	6508	7191	7796	8341
20400	3878	5647	6678	7378	7999	8558
21000	3977	5790	6847	7565	8201	8774
21600	4076	5933	7015	7750	8402	8989
22200	4176	6075	7182	7936	8602	9204
22800	4275	6216	7345	8116	8798	9413
23400	4373	6357	7509	8297	8994	9623
24000	4471	6498	7672	8478	9190	9832
24600	4570	6639	7836	8658	9386	10042
25200	4668	6780	8000	8839	9582	10251
25800	4767	6920	8163	9020	9778	10461
26400	4865	7061	8327	9200	9974	10670
27000	4963	7202	8490	9381	10170	10880
27600	5054	7332	8642	9548	10351	11074
28200	5135	7448	8776	9697	10512	11246
28800	5216	7564	8911	9845	10673	11418
29400	5297	7678	9045	9995	10833	11592
30000	5377	7792	9179	10143	10994	11764
30600	5456	7907	9313	10291	11154	11936
31200	5535	8022	9447	10439	11315	12107
31800	5615	8136	9581	10587	11476	12279
32400	5694	8251	9715	10736	11636	12451
33000	5774	8366	9849	10884	11797	12623
33600	5853	8480	9983	11032	11957	12794
34200	5933	8595	10117	11180	12118	12966
34800	6012	8709	10251	11328	12279	13138
35400	6091	8824	10385	11476	12439	13310
36000	6171	8939	10519	11624	12600	13482
36600	6250	9053	10653	11772	12761	13653
37200	6330	9168	10787	11920	12921	13825
37800	6406	9275	10913	12058	13071	13988
38400	6447	9335	10984	12137	13156	14079
39000	6489	9395	11055	12215	13242	14170
39600	6530	9455	11126	12294	13328	14261
40200	6571	9515	11197	12373	13413	14353
40800	6613	9575	11268	12451	13499	14444
41400	6653	9634	11338	12529	13583	14534
42000	6694	9693	11409	12607	13667	14624
42600	6735	9752	11479	12684	13752	14714
43200	6776	9811	11549	12762	13836	14804
43800	6817	9871	11619	12840	13921	14894
44400	6857	9930	11690	12917	14005	14985
45000	6898	9989	11760	12995	14090	15075
45600	6939	10049	11830	13073	14174	15165
46200	6978	10103	11897	13146	14251	15250
46800	7013	10150	11949	13203	14313	15316

Basic Child Support Schedule
Number of Children

Combined Gross Income	One	Two	Three	Four	Five	Six
47400	7048	10197	12000	13260	14375	15382
48000	7083	10245	12052	13317	14437	15448
48600	7117	10292	12103	13374	14498	15514
49200	7152	10339	12155	13432	14560	15580
49800	7187	10386	12206	13489	14622	15646
50400	7222	10433	12258	13546	14684	15712
51000	7257	10481	12309	13603	14745	15778
51600	7291	10528	12360	13660	14807	15844
52200	7326	10575	12412	13717	14869	15910
52800	7361	10622	12463	13774	14931	15976
53400	7396	10669	12515	13832	14992	16042
54000	7431	10717	12566	13889	15054	16108
54600	7468	10765	12622	13946	15120	16178
55200	7524	10845	12716	14050	15232	16298
55800	7582	10929	12814	14159	15350	16425
56400	7643	11016	12918	14273	15474	16558
57000	7704	11104	13021	14388	15598	16691
57600	7765	11192	13125	14502	15722	16824
58200	7825	11277	13225	14613	15842	16953
58800	7883	11361	13324	14723	15961	17079
59400	7941	11445	13423	14832	16079	17206
60000	8000	11529	13522	14941	16197	17333
60600	8058	11612	13620	15050	16315	17460
61200	8116	11696	13719	15160	16433	17587
61800	8175	11780	13818	15269	16552	17714
62400	8233	11864	13917	15378	16670	17840
63000	8288	11945	14011	15481	16783	17958
63600	8344	12024	14102	15582	16893	18075
64200	8399	12103	14194	15683	17002	18193
64800	8454	12183	14285	15784	17111	18310
65400	8510	12262	14376	15885	17220	18427
66000	8565	12341	14468	15986	17330	18544
66600	8620	12421	14559	16087	17439	18661
67200	8676	12500	14650	16188	17548	18778
67800	8731	12579	14741	16289	17657	18895
68400	8786	12659	14833	16390	17767	19012
69000	8842	12738	14924	16491	17876	19129
69600	8897	12817	15015	16592	17985	19246
70200	8953	12897	15107	16693	18094	19363
70800	9008	12974	15196	16791	18201	19476
71400	9060	13047	15281	16885	18302	19585
72000	9111	13120	15366	16979	18404	19694
72600	9163	13194	15451	17073	18506	19803
73200	9214	13267	15536	17167	18608	19912
73800	9266	13340	15621	17261	18709	20021
74400	9318	13413	15706	17355	18811	20130
75000	9369	13487	15791	17449	18913	20239
75600	9421	13560	15876	17543	19015	20347
76200	9473	13633	15961	17636	19116	20456
76800	9524	13707	16046	17730	19218	20565
77400	9576	13780	16131	17824	19320	20674
78000	9627	13853	16216	17918	19422	20783
78600	9679	13927	16300	18012	19523	20892
79200	9731	14000	16385	18106	19625	21001

Basic Child Support Schedule
Number of Children

Combined Gross Income	One	Two	Three	Four	Five	Six
79800	9782	14073	16470	18200	19727	21109
80400	9834	14147	16555	18294	19829	21218
81000	9885	14220	16640	18387	19930	21326
81600	9936	14292	16723	18480	20030	21434
82200	9987	14364	16807	18573	20131	21541
82800	10038	14439	16891	18665	20235	21651
83400	10090	14514	16979	18762	20340	21763
84000	10142	14589	17066	18859	20444	21875
84600	10194	14663	17154	18956	20549	21987
85200	10246	14738	17241	19052	20653	22099
85800	10298	14813	17329	19149	20758	22211
86400	10350	14887	17417	19246	20863	22323
87000	10403	14962	17504	19343	20967	22435
87600	10455	15037	17592	19440	21072	22547
88200	10507	15111	17679	19537	21176	22659
88800	10559	15186	17767	19633	21281	22771
89400	10611	15261	17855	19730	21386	22883
90000	10663	15335	17942	19827	21490	22995
90600	10715	15410	18030	19924	21595	23107
91200	10767	15485	18118	20021	21700	23219
91800	10819	15559	18205	20118	21804	23331
92400	10872	15634	18293	20215	21909	23443
93000	10924	15709	18380	20311	22013	23555
93600	10976	15783	18468	20408	22118	23667
94200	11028	15858	18556	20505	22223	23779
94800	11080	15933	18643	20602	22327	23891
95400	11132	16007	18731	20699	22432	24003
96000	11184	16082	18818	20796	22536	24115
96600	11236	16157	18906	20892	22641	24227
97200	11289	16231	18994	20989	22746	24339
97800	11341	16306	19081	21086	22850	24451
98400	11393	16381	19169	21183	22955	24563
99000	11446	16450	19255	21279	23062	24676
99600	11491	16516	19334	21366	23156	24777
100200	11536	16583	19413	21453	23250	24878
100800	11581	16649	19491	21539	23345	24978
101400	11625	16714	19569	21625	23437	25077
102000	11670	16779	19646	21710	23530	25177
102600	11714	16844	19724	21796	23623	25276
103200	11759	16909	19801	21881	23715	25375
103800	11803	16974	19879	21967	23808	25475
104400	11847	17039	19956	22052	23901	25574
105000	11892	17104	20034	22138	23994	25673
105600	11934	17167	20108	22220	24083	25769
106200	11979	17232	20186	22305	24176	25868
106800	12023	17297	20263	22391	24269	25968
107400	12068	17362	20341	22476	24361	26067
108000	12110	17425	20415	22559	24451	26162
108600	12155	17490	20493	22644	24543	26262
109200	12199	17555	20570	22730	24636	26361
109800	12243	17620	20648	22815	24729	26460
110400	12286	17683	20722	22897	24818	26556
111000	12331	17748	20800	22983	24911	26655
111600	12375	17813	20877	23068	25004	26755

Basic Child Support Schedule
Number of Children

Combined Gross Income	One	Two	Three	Four	Five	Six
112200	12419	17878	20955	23154	25096	26854
112800	12462	17941	21029	23236	25186	26949
113400	12506	18006	21107	23322	25278	27049
114000	12551	18071	21184	23407	25371	27148
114600	12595	18136	21262	23493	25464	27247
115200	12640	18202	21339	23578	25557	27347
115800	12682	18264	21414	23660	25646	27442
116400	12727	18329	21491	23746	25739	27542
117000	12771	18394	21569	23831	25832	27641
117600	12815	18460	21646	23917	25924	27740
118200	12858	18522	21721	23999	26013	27836
118800	12902	18587	21798	24084	26106	27935
119400	12947	18652	21876	24170	26199	28034
120000	12991	18718	21953	24256	26292	28134
120600	13034	18780	22028	24338	26381	28229
121200	13078	18845	22105	24423	26474	28329
121800	13123	18910	22183	24509	26567	28428
122400	13167	18976	22260	24594	26659	28527
123000	13210	19038	22335	24676	26749	28623
123600	13254	19103	22412	24762	26841	28722
124200	13299	19168	22490	24847	26934	28821
124800	13343	19234	22567	24933	27027	28921
125400	13386	19296	22642	25015	27116	29016
126000	13430	19361	22719	25101	27209	29115
126600	13474	19426	22797	25186	27302	29215
127200	13519	19492	22874	25272	27395	29314
127800	13561	19554	22949	25354	27484	29410
128400	13606	19619	23026	25439	27576	29509
129000	13650	19684	23104	25525	27669	29608
129600	13695	19750	23181	25610	27762	29708
130200	13739	19815	23259	25696	27855	29807
130800	13783	19879	23335	25780	27946	29905
131400	13828	19945	23414	25868	28041	30007
132000	13874	20012	23494	25955	28136	30108
132600	13919	20079	23573	26043	28231	30210
133200	13963	20143	23649	26127	28323	30308
133800	14008	20210	23729	26215	28418	30410
134400	14054	20276	23808	26302	28513	30511
135000	14099	20343	23887	26390	28608	30613
135600	14143	20407	23964	26474	28699	30711
136200	14188	20474	24043	26561	28794	30813
136800	14234	20541	24123	26649	28889	30914
137400	14279	20607	24202	26737	28984	31016
138000	14323	20671	24278	26821	29075	31114
138600	14368	20738	24358	26908	29170	31215
139200	14414	20805	24437	26996	29265	31317
139800	14459	20872	24516	27083	29361	31419
140400	14503	20936	24593	27168	29452	31517
141000	14549	21002	24672	27255	29547	31618
141600	14594	21069	24751	27343	29642	31720
142200	14639	21136	24831	27430	29737	31822
142800	14683	21200	24907	27515	29828	31920
143400	14729	21267	24986	27602	29923	32021
144000	14774	21333	25066	27690	30018	32123

Basic Child Support Schedule
Number of Children

Combined Gross Income	One	Two	Three	Four	Five	Six
144600	14820	21400	25145	27777	30113	32225
145200	14865	21467	25225	27865	30208	32327
145800	14909	21531	25301	27949	30300	32424
146400	14963	21596	25377	28041	30396	32526
147000	15006	21659	25452	28124	30486	32622
147600	15049	21722	25527	28207	30576	32718
148200	15090	21782	25599	28286	30662	32810
148800	15133	21845	25674	28369	30752	32907
149400	15176	21908	25749	28452	30842	33003
150000	15218	21971	25823	28534	30931	33099

(E) When a court or child support enforcement agency calculates the amount of child support that will be required to be paid pursuant to a child support order or an administrative child support order in a proceeding in which one parent is the residential parent and legal custodian of all of the children who are the subject of the child support order or the court issues a shared parenting order, the court or child support enforcement agency shall use a worksheet that is identical in content and form to the following worksheet:

"Worksheet

.... County Domestic Relations Court (or)
.... County Child Support Enforcement Agency
Child Support Computation
Sole Residential Parent or
Shared Parenting Order

Name of parties........................
Case No. ....

Number of minor children ...... The following parent was designated as the residential parent and legal custodian (disregard if shared parenting order):
.... mother; .... father.
Father has .... pay periods annually; mother has .... pay periods annually.

	Column I Father	Column II Mother	Column III Combined
1a. Annual gross income from employment or, when determined appropriate by the court or agency, average annual gross income from employment over a reasonable period of years (exclude overtime and bonuses)..........	$..................	$..................	
b. Amount of overtime and bonuses	Father	Mother	
Yr. 3 (Three years ago)	$..................	$..................	
Yr. 2 (Two years ago)	$..................	$..................	
Yr. 1 (Last calendar year)	$..................	$..................	
Average:	$..................	$..................	

(Include in Column I and/or Column II the average of the three years or the year 1 amount, whichever is less, if there exists a reasonable expectation that the total earnings from overtime and/or bonuses during the current calendar year will meet or exceed the amount that is the lower of the average of the three years or the year 1 amount. If, however, there exists a reasonable expectation that the total earnings from overtime/bonuses during the current calendar year will be less than the lower of the average of the three years or the year 1 amount, include only the amount reasonably expected to be earned this year.) .... $.................. $..................
2. Annual income from interest and dividends (whether or not taxable) $.................. $..................
3. Annual income from unemployment compensation .... $.................. $..................

	Column I Father	Column II Mother	Column III Combined

4. Annual income from workers' compensation or disability insurance benefits .... $............ $............
5. Other annual income (identify) .... $............ $............
6. Total annual gross income (add lines 1-5) .... $............ $............
7. Annual court-ordered support paid for other children .... $............ $............
8. Adjustment for minor children born to either parent and another parent, which children are living with this parent (number of children times federal income tax exemption less child support received for the year, not to exceed the federal tax exemption) .... $............ $............
9. Annual court-ordered spousal support paid to a former spouse .... $............ $............
10. Amount of local income taxes actually paid or estimated to be paid ...... $............ $............
11. For self-employed individuals, deduct 5.6% of adjusted gross income or the actual marginal difference between the actual rate paid by the self-employed individual and the F.I.C.A. rate .... $............ $............
12. For self-employed individuals, deduct ordinary and necessary business expenses .... $............ $............
13. Total gross income adjustments (add lines 7-12) .... $............ $............
14. Adjusted annual gross income (subtract line 13 from line 6) .... $............ $............
15. Combined annual income that is basis for child support order (add line 14, Col. I and Col. II) .... $............
16. Percentage parent's income to total income
    a. Father (divide line 14, Col. I by line 15, Col. III) .... %
    b. Mother (divide line 14, Col. II by line 15, Col. III) .... +............ % =100%
17. Basic combined child support obligation (Refer to basic child support schedule in division (D) of section 3113.215 [3113.21.5] of the Revised Code; in the first column of the schedule, locate the sum that is nearest to the combined annual income listed in line 15, Col. III of this worksheet, then refer to the column of the schedule that corresponds to the number of children in this family. If the income of the parents is more than one sum, and less than another sum, in the first column of the schedule, you may calculate the basic combined child support obligation based upon the obligation for those two sums.) .... $............
18. Annual child care expenses for the children who are the subject of this order that are work, employment training, or education related, as approved by the court or agency (deduct the tax credit from annual cost, whether or not claimed) .... $............ $............
19. Marginal, out-of-pocket costs, necessary to provide for health insurance for the children who are the subject of this order .... $............ $............
20. Total child care and medical expenses (add lines 18 and 19, Column I and Column II) .... $............ $............
21. Combined annual child support obligation for this family (add lines 17 and 20, Column I and Column II) .... $............
22. Annual support obligation/parent
    a. Father (multiply line 21, Col. III, by line 16a) .... $............
    b. Mother (multiply line 21, Col. III, by line 16b) .... $............
23. Adjustment for actual expenses paid for annual child care expenses and marginal, out-of-pocket costs, necessary to provide for health insurance (enter number from line 18 or 19 if applicable) .... $............ $............
24. Actual annual obligation (subtract line 23 from line 22a or 22b) .... $............ $............
25. Gross household income per party after exchange of child support (add lines 14 and 24 Column I or II for residential parent or, in the case of shared parenting order, the parent to whom child support will be paid; subtract line 24 Column I or II from line 14 for parent who is not the residential parent or, in the case of shared parenting order, the parent who will pay child support) .... $............ $............
26. Comments, rebuttal, or adjustments to correct figures in lines 24, Column I and 24, Column II if they would be unjust or inappropriate and would

	Column I Father	Column II Mother	Column III Combined

not be in best interest of the child or children (specific facts to support adjustments must be included).. $................ $................

....

(Addendum sheet may be attached)

27. Final figure (this amount reflects final annual child support obligation) $................ father/mother obligor
28. For decree: child support per child per week or per month (divide obligor's annual share, line 27, by 12 or 52 and by number of children)................ $................
29. For deduction order: child support per pay period (calculate support per pay period from figure on line 28) plus appropriate poundage .... $................

Calculations have been reviewed.

Signatures ....

Father
I do/do not consent.

Sworn to before me and subscribed in my presence, this ...... day of ...., 19....

....

Notary Public

....

Mother
I do/do not consent.

Sworn to before me and subscribed in my presence, this ...... day of ...., 19....

....

Notary Public

....
Attorney for father   Attorney for mother"

(F) When a court or child support enforcement agency calculates the amount of child support that will be required to be paid pursuant to a child support order in a proceeding in which both parents have split parental rights and responsibilities with respect to the children who are the subject of the child support order, the court or child support enforcement agency shall use a worksheet that is identical in content and form to the following worksheet:

"Worksheet
.... County Domestic Relations Court (or)
.... County Child Support Enforcement Agency
Child Support Computation
Split Parental Rights and Responsibilities

Name of parties ....
Case No. ....
Number of minor children ...... The following parent was designated residential parent and legal custodian:
.... mother; .... father.
Father has ...... pay periods annually; mother has ...... pay periods annually.

	Column I Father	Column II Mother	Column III Combined

1a. Annual gross income from employment or, when determined to be appropriate by the court or agency, average annual gross income from employment over a reasonable period of years (exclude overtime and bonuses) $................ $................
b. Amount of overtime and bonuses

	Father	Mother	

Yr. 3
(Three years ago) $................ $................
Yr. 2
(Two years ago) $................ $................

	Column I Father	Column II Mother	Column III Combined
Yr. 1 (Last calendar year)	$..................	$..................	
Average:	$..................	$..................	

(Include in Column I and/or Column II the average of the three years or the year 1 amount, whichever is less, if there exists a reasonable expectation that the total earnings from overtime and/or bonuses during the current calendar year will meet or exceed the amount that is the lower of the average of the three years or the year 1 amount. If, however, there exists a reasonable expectation that the total earnings from overtime/bonuses during the current calendar year will be less than the lower of the average of the three years or the year 1 amount, include only the amount reasonably expected to be earned this year.) .... $.................. $..................

2. Annual income from interest and dividends (whether or not taxable) .... $.................. $..................
3. Annual income from unemployment compensation .... $.................. $..................
4. Annual income from workers' compensation or disability insurance benefits .... $.................. $..................
5. Other annual income (identify) .... $.................. $..................
6. Total annual gross income (add lines 1-5) .... $.................. $..................
7. Annual court-ordered support paid for other children .... $.................. $..................
8. Adjustment for minor children born to either parent and another parent, which children are living with this parent (number of children times federal income tax exemption less child support received for the year, not to exceed the federal tax exemption) .... $.................. $..................
9. Annual court-ordered spousal support paid to a former spouse .... $.................. $..................
10. Amount of local income taxes actually paid or estimated to be paid ...... $.................. $..................
11. For self-employed individuals, deduct 5.6% of adjusted gross income or the actual marginal difference between the actual rate paid by the self-employed individual and the F.I.C.A. rate .... $.................. $..................
12. For self-employed individuals, deduct ordinary and necessary business expenses .... $.................. $..................
13. Total gross income adjustments (add lines 7-12) .... $.................. $..................
14. Adjusted annual gross income (subtract line 13 from line 6) .... $.................. $..................
15. Combined annual income that is basis for child support order (add line 14, Col. I and Col. II) .... $..................
16. Percentage parent's income to total income
  a. Father (divide line 14, Col. I by line 15, Col. III) .... %
  b. Mother (divide line 14, Col. II by line 15, Col. III) .... + ... % =100%
17. Basic combined child support obligation/household
  a. For children for whom the father is the residential parent and legal custodian (Refer to basic child support schedule in division (D) of section 3113.215 [3113.21.5] of the Revised Code; in the first column of the schedule, locate the sum that is nearest to the combined annual income listed in line 15, Col. III of this worksheet, then refer to the column of the schedule that corresponds to the number of children for whom the father is the residential parent and legal custodian. If the income of the parents is more than one sum, and less than another sum, in the first column of the schedule, you may calculate the basic combined child support obligation based upon the obligation for those two sums.) .... $..................
  b. For children for whom the mother is the residential parent and the legal custodian. (Refer to basic child support schedule in division (D) of section 3113.215 [3113.21.5] of the Revised Code; in the first column of the schedule, locate the sum that is nearest to the combined annual income listed in line 15, Col. III of this worksheet, then refer to the column of the schedule that corresponds to the number of children for whom the mother is the residential parent and the legal custodian. If the income of the parents is more than one sum, and less than another sum, in the first column of the schedule, you may calculate the basic combined child support obligation based upon the obligation for those two sums.) .... $..................
18. Annual child care expenses for the children who are the subject of this order that are work, employment training, or education related, as approved by the court or agency (deduct the tax credit from annual cost, whether or not claimed)
  a. Expenses paid by the father .... $..................

	Column I Father	Column II Mother	Column III Combined
b. Expenses paid by the mother...		$...................	
19. Marginal, out-of-pocket costs, necessary to provide for health insurance for the children who are the subject of this order			
a. Costs paid by the father..	$...................		
b. Costs paid by the mother...		$...................	
20. Total annual child care and medical expenses			
a. Of father (add lines 18a and 19a)...	$...................		
b. Of mother (add lines 18b and 19b)..		$...................	
21. Total annual child support obligation			
a. Of father for child(ren) for whom the mother is the residential parent and legal custodian (add lines 20a and 17b and multiply by line 16a)	$...................		
b. Of mother for child(ren) for whom the father is the residential parent and legal custodian (add lines 20b and 17a and multiply by line 16b)		$...................	
22. Adjustment for actual expenses paid for annual child care expenses, and marginal, out-of-pocket costs, necessary to provide for health insurance			
a. For father (enter number from line 20a).....................................	$...................		
b. For mother (enter number from line 20b)...................................		$...................	
23. Actual annual obligation (subtract line 22a from line 21a and insert in Column I; subtract line 22b from line 21b and insert in Column II).....	$...................	$...................	
24. Net annual support obligation (greater amount on line 23 Column I or line 23 Column II minus lesser amount on line 23 Column I or line 23 Column II)	$...................	$...................	
25. Gross household income per party after exchange of child support (add line 14 and line 24 for the parent receiving a child support payment; subtract line 24 from line 14 for the parent making a child support payment)..	$...................	$...................	
26. Comments, rebuttal, or adjustments to correct figures in lines 24, Column I and 24, Column II if they would be unjust or inappropriate and would not be in best interest of the children (specific facts to support adjustments must be included)..	$...................	$...................	

....

(Addendum sheet may be attached)

27. Final figure (this amount reflects final annual child support obligation) $................... father/mother obligor
28. For decree: child support per child per week or per month (divide obligor's annual share, line 27, by 12 or 52 and by the number of children)........ $...................
29. For deduction order: child support per day (calculate support per pay period from figure on line 28) and add appropriate poundage................. $...................

Calculations have been reviewed.

Signatures   ....

Father
I do/do not consent.

Sworn to before me and subscribed in my presence, this ...... day of ...., 19....

....
Notary Public

....
Mother
I do/do not consent.

Sworn to before me and subscribed in my presence, this ...... day of ...., 19....

....
Notary Public

....
Attorney for father   Attorney for mother"

(G) At least once every four years, the department of human services shall review the basic child support schedule set forth in division (D) of this section to determine whether support orders issued in accordance with the schedule and the applicable worksheet in division (E) of this section, through line 24, or in division (F) of this section, through line 23, adequately provide for the needs of the children who are subject to the support orders, prepare a report of its review, and submit a copy of the report to both houses of the general assembly. For each review, the department shall establish a child support guideline advisory council to assist the department in the completion of its reviews and reports. Each council shall be composed of obligors, obligees, judges of courts of common pleas who have jurisdiction over domestic relations cases, attorneys whose practice includes a significant number of domestic relations cases, representatives of child support enforcement agencies, other persons interested in the welfare of children, three members of the senate appointed by the president of the senate, no more than two of whom are members of the same party, and three members of the house of representatives appointed by the speaker of the house, no more than two of whom are members of the same party. The department shall consider input from the council prior to the completion of any report under this section. The advisory council shall cease to exist at the time that it submits its report to the general assembly. Any expenses incurred by an advisory council shall be paid by the department.

On or before March 1, 1993, the department shall submit its initial report under this division to both houses of the general assembly. On or before the first day of March of every fourth year after 1993, the department shall submit a report under this division to both houses of the general assembly.

HISTORY: 143 v H 591 (Eff 4-12-90); 143 v H 514 (Eff 1-1-91); 143 v S 3 (Eff 4-11-91); 145 v S 115 (Eff 10-12-93); 145 v H 173 (Eff 10-12-93); 145 v H 415 (Eff 11-9-94); 145 v S 355 (Eff 12-9-94); 146 v H 249 (Eff 7-17-95); 146 v H 167 (Eff 6-11-96); 146 v H 274, §§ 1, 7 (Eff 8-8-96); 146 v H 670 (Eff 12-2-96); 147 v H 408. Eff 10-1-97.

[§ 3113.21.6] § 3113.216 Rules for review of existing child support orders; hearings.

(A) As used in this section, "obligor" and "obligee" have the same meanings as in section 3113.21 of the Revised Code.

(B) No later than October 13, 1990, the department of human services shall adopt rules pursuant to Chapter 119. of the Revised Code establishing a procedure for determining when existing child support orders should be reviewed to determine whether it is necessary and in the best interest of the children who are the subject of the child support order to change the child support order. The rules shall include, but are not limited to, all of the following:

(1) Any procedures necessary to comply with section 666(a)(10) of Title 42 of the U.S. Code, "Family Support Act of 1988," 102 Stat. 2346, 42 U.S.C. 666(a)(10), as amended, and any regulations adopted pursuant to, or to enforce, that section;

(2) Procedures for determining what child support orders are to be subject to review upon the request of either the obligor or the obligee or periodically by the child support enforcement agency administering the child support order;

(3) Procedures for the child support enforcement agency to periodically review and to review, upon the request of the obligor or the obligee, any child support order that is subject to review to determine whether the amount of child support paid under the child support order should be adjusted in accordance with the basic child support schedule set forth in division (D) of section 3113.215 [3113.21.5] of the Revised Code;

(4) Procedures for giving obligors and obligees notice of their right to request a review of a child support order that is determined to be subject to review, notice of any proposed revision of the amount of child support to be paid under the child support order, notice of the procedures for requesting a hearing on any proposed revision of the amount of child support to be paid under a child support order, notice of any administrative hearing to be held on a proposed revision of the amount of child support to be paid under a child support order, at least sixty days' prior notice of any review of their child support order, and notice that a failure to comply with any request for documents or information to be used in the review of a child support order is contempt of court;

(5) Procedures for obtaining the necessary documents and information necessary to review child support orders and for holding administrative hearings on a proposed revision of the amount of child support to be paid under a child support order;

(6) Procedures for adjusting child support orders in accordance with the basic child support schedule set forth in division (D) of section 3113.215 [3113.21.5] of the Revised Code and the applicable worksheet in division (E) of that section, through line 24 or in division (F) of that section, through line 23.

(C)(1) If a child support enforcement agency, periodically or upon request of an obligor or obligee, plans to review a child support order in accordance with the rules adopted pursuant to division (B) of this section or otherwise plans to review a child support order, it shall do all of the following prior to formally beginning the review:

(a) Establish a date certain upon which the review will formally begin;

(b) At least sixty days before formally beginning the review, send the obligor and the obligee notice of the planned review and of the date when the review will formally begin;

(c) Request the obligor to provide the agency, no later than the scheduled date for formally beginning the review, with a copy of the obligor's federal income tax return from the previous year, a copy of all pay stubs obtained by the obligor within the preceding six months, a copy of all other records evidencing the receipt of any other salary, wages, or compensation by the obligor within the preceding six months, and any other information necessary to properly review the child support order, and request the obligee to provide the agency, no later than the scheduled date for formally beginning the review, with a copy of the obligee's federal income tax return from the previous year, a copy of all pay stubs obtained by the obligee within the preceding six months, a copy of all other records evidencing the receipt of any other salary, wages, or compensation by the obligee within the preceding six months, and any other information necessary to properly review the child support order;

(d) Include in the notice sent pursuant to division (C)(1)(b) of this section, a notice that a willful failure to provide the documents and other information requested pursuant to division (C)(1)(c) of this section is contempt of court.

(2) If either the obligor or the obligee fails to comply with a request for information made pursuant to division (C)(1)(c) of this section, it is contempt of court, and the agency shall notify the court of the failure to comply with the request for information. The agency may request the court to issue an order requiring the obligor or the obligee to provide the information as requested or take whatever action is necessary to obtain the information and make any reasonable assumptions necessary with respect to the income of the person in contempt of court to ensure a fair and equitable review of the child support order. If the agency decides to conduct the review based upon reasonable assumptions with respect to the income of the person in contempt of court, it shall proceed under division (C)(3) of this section in the same manner as if all requested information has been received.

(3) Upon the date established pursuant to division (C)(1)(a) of this section for formally beginning the review of a child support order, the agency shall review the child support order and shall do all of the following:

(a) Calculate a revised amount of child support to be paid under the child support order;

(b) Give the obligor and obligee notice of the revised amount of child support to be paid under the child support order, of their right to request an administrative hearing on the revised amount of child support, of the procedures and time deadlines for requesting the hearing, and that the revised amount of child support will be submitted to the court for inclusion in a revised child support order unless the obligor or obligee requests an administrative hearing on the proposed change within thirty days after receipt of the notice under this division;

(c) If neither the obligor nor the obligee timely requests an administrative hearing on the revised amount of child support to be paid under the child support order, submit the revised amount of child support to the court for inclusion in a revised child support order;

(d) If the obligor or the obligee timely requests an administrative hearing on the revised amount of child support to be paid under the child support order, the agency shall schedule a hearing on the issue, give the obligor and obligee notice of the date, time, and location of the hearing, conduct the hearing in accordance with the rules adopted under division (B) of this section, redetermine at the hearing a revised amount of child support to be paid under the child support order, and give notice of all of the following to the obligor and obligee:

(i) The revised amount of child support to be paid under the child support order;

(ii) That they may request a court hearing on the revised amount of child support;

(iii) That the agency will submit the revised amount of child support to the court for inclusion in a revised child support order, if neither the obligor nor the obligee requests a court hearing on the revised amount of child support.

(e) If neither the obligor nor the obligee requests a court hearing on the revised amount of child support to be paid under the child support order, submit the revised amount of child support to the court for inclusion in a revised child support order.

(4) In calculating a revised amount of child support to be paid under a child support order under division (C)(3)(a) of this section, and in redetermining, at an administrative hearing conducted under division (C)(3)(d) of this section, a revised amount of child support to be paid under a child support order, the child support enforcement agency shall consider, in addition to all other factors required by law to be considered, the cost of health insurance which the obligor, the obligee, or both the obligor and the obligee have been ordered to obtain for the children specified in the order.

(D) If an obligor or obligee files a request for a court hearing on a revised amount of child support to be paid under a child support order in accordance with division (C) of this section and the rules adopted under division (B) of this section, the court shall conduct a hearing in accordance with division (C)(1)(c) of section 3113.21 of the Revised Code.

(E) A child support enforcement agency is not required to review a child support order pursuant to this section if the review is not otherwise required by section 666(a)(10) of Title 42 of the U.S. Code, "Family Support Act of 1988," 102 Stat. 2346, 42 U.S.C. 666(a)(10), as amended, and any regulations adopted pursuant to, or to enforce, that section and if either of the following apply:

(1) The obligee has made an assignment under section 5107.20 of the Revised Code of the right to receive child support payments, the agency determines that the review would not be in the best interest of the children who are the subject of the child support order, and neither the obligor nor the obligee has requested that the review be conducted;

(2) The obligee has not made an assignment under section 5107.20 of the Revised Code of the right to receive child support payments, neither the obligor nor the obligee has requested that the review be conducted.

HISTORY: 143 v H 591 (Eff 4-12-90); 145 v S 115 (Eff 10-12-93); 145 v H 173 (Eff 12-31-93); 147 v H 408. Eff 10-1-97.

The effective date is set by section 26 of HB 408.

[§ 3113.21.7] § 3113.217 Order requiring obligor or obligee under support order to obtain health insurance for children; duty of employer and insurer.

(A) As used in this section:

(1) "Obligor" and "obligee" have the same meanings as in section 3113.21 of the Revised Code.

(2) "Insurer" means any person that is authorized to engage in the business of insurance in this state under Title XXXIX [39] of the Revised Code, any health insuring corporation, and any legal entity that is self-insured and provides benefits to its employees or members.

(B) In any action or proceeding in which a child support order is issued or modified on or after July 1, 1990, under Chapter 3115. or section 2151.23, 2151.231 [2151.23.1], 2151.33, 2151.36, 2151.49, 3105.18, 3105.21, 3109.05, 3109.19, 3111.13, 3113.04, 3113.07, 3113.216 [3113.21.6], or 3113.31 of the Revised Code, the child support enforcement agency shall determine whether the obligor or obligee has satisfactory health insurance coverage, other than medical assistance under Title XIX of the "Social Security Act," 49 Stat. 620 (1935), 42 U.S.C. 301, as amended, for the children who are the subject of the child support order. If the agency determines that neither the obligor nor the obligee has satisfactory health insurance coverage for the children, it shall file a motion with the court requesting the court to issue an order in accordance with divisions (C) to (K) of this section.

(C) In any action or proceeding in which a child support order is issued or modified on or after July 1, 1990, under Chapter 3115. or section 2151.23, 2151.231 [2151.23.1], 2151.33, 2151.36, 2151.49, 3105.18, 3105.21, 3109.05, 3109.19, 3111.13, 3113.04, 3113.07, 3113.216 [3113.21.6], or 3113.31 of the Revised Code, in addition to any requirements in those sections, the court also shall issue a separate order that includes all of the following:

(1) A requirement that the obligor under the child support order obtain health insurance coverage for the children who are the subject of the child support order from an insurer that provides a group health insurance or health care policy, contract, or plan that is specified in the order and a requirement that the obligor, no later than thirty days after the issuance of the order under division (C)(1) of this section, furnish written proof to the child support enforcement agency that the required health insurance coverage has been obtained, if that coverage is available at a reasonable cost through a group health insurance or health care policy, contract, or plan offered by the obligor's employer or through any other group health insurance or health care policy, contract, or plan available to the obligor and if health insurance coverage for the children is not available for a more reasonable cost through a group health insurance or health care policy, contract, or plan available to the obligee under the child support order;

(2) If the obligor is required under division (C)(1) of this section to obtain health insurance coverage for the children who are the subject of the child support order, a requirement that the obligor supply the obligee with information regarding the benefits, limitations, and exclusions of the health insurance coverage, copies of any insurance forms necessary to receive reimbursement, payment, or other benefits under the health insurance coverage, and a copy of any necessary insurance cards, a requirement that the obligor submit a copy of the court order issued pursuant to division (C) of this section to the insurer at the time that the obligor makes application to enroll the children in the health insurance or health care policy, contract, or plan, and a requirement that the obligor, no later than thirty days after the issuance of the order under division (C)(2) of this section, furnish written proof to the child support enforcement agency that division (C)(2) of this section has been complied with;

(3) A requirement that the obligee under the child support order obtain health insurance coverage for the children who are the subject of the child support order from an insurer that provides a group health insurance or health care policy, contract, or plan that is specified in the order and a requirement that the obligee, no later than thirty days after the issuance of the order under division (C)(1) of this section, furnish written proof to the child support enforcement agency that the required health insurance coverage has been obtained, if that coverage is available through a group health insurance or health care policy, contract, or plan offered by the obligee's employer or through any other group health insurance or health care policy, contract, or plan available to the obligee and if that coverage is available at a more reasonable cost than health insurance coverage for the children through a group health insurance or health care policy, contract, or plan available to the obligor;

(4) If the obligee is required under division (C)(3) of this section to obtain health insurance coverage for the children who are the subject of the child support order, a requirement that the obligee submit a copy of the court order issued pursuant to division (C) of this section to the insurer at the time that the obligee makes application to enroll the children in the health insurance or health care policy, contract, or plan;

(5) A list of the group health insurance and health care policies, contracts, and plans that the court determines are available at a reasonable cost to the obligor or to the obligee and the name of the insurer that issues each policy, contract, or plan;

(6) A statement setting forth the name, address, and telephone number of the individual who is to be reimbursed for out-of-pocket medical, optical, hospital, dental, or prescription expenses paid for each child who is the subject of the support order and a statement that the insurer that provides the health insurance coverage for the children may continue making payment for medical, optical, hospital, dental, or prescription services

directly to any health care provider in accordance with the applicable health insurance or health care policy, contract, or plan;

(7) A requirement that the obligor and the obligee designate the children who are the subject of the child support order as covered dependents under any health insurance or health care policy, contract, or plan for which they contract;

(8) A requirement that the obligor, the obligee, or both of them under a formula established by the court pay co-payment or deductible costs required under the health insurance or health care policy, contract, or plan that covers the children;

(9) If health insurance coverage for the children who are the subject of the order is not available at a reasonable cost through a group health insurance or health care policy, contract, or plan offered by the obligor's employer or through any other group health insurance or health care policy, contract, or plan available to the obligor and is not available at a reasonable cost through a group health insurance or health care policy, contract, or plan offered by the obligee's employer or through any other group health insurance or health care policy, contract, or plan available to the obligee, a requirement that the obligor and the obligee share liability for the cost of the medical and health care needs of the children who are the subject of the order, under an equitable formula established by the court, and a requirement that if, after the issuance of the order, health insurance coverage for the children who are the subject of the order becomes available at a reasonable cost through a group health insurance or health care policy, contract, or plan offered by the obligor's or obligee's employer or through any other group health insurance or health care policy, contract, or plan available to the obligor or obligee, the obligor or obligee to whom the coverage becomes available immediately inform the court of that fact;

(10) A notice that, if the obligor is required under divisions (C)(1) and (2) of this section to obtain health insurance coverage for the children who are the subject of the child support order and if the obligor fails to comply with the requirements of those divisions, the court immediately shall issue an order to the employer of the obligor, upon written notice from the child support enforcement agency, requiring the employer to take whatever action is necessary to make application to enroll the obligor in any available group health insurance or health care policy, contract, or plan with coverage for the children who are the subject of the child support order, to submit a copy of the court order issued pursuant to division (C) of this section to the insurer at the time that the employer makes application to enroll the children in the health insurance or health care policy, contract, or plan, and, if the obligor's application is accepted, to deduct any additional amount from the obligor's earnings necessary to pay any additional cost for that health insurance coverage;

(11) A notice that during the time that an order under this section is in effect, the employer of the obligor is required to release to the obligee or the child support enforcement agency upon written request any necessary information on the health insurance coverage of the obligor, including, but not limited to, the name and address of the insurer and any policy, contract, or plan number, and to otherwise comply with this section and any court order issued under this section;

(12) A statement setting forth the full name and date of birth of each child who is the subject of the child support order;

(13) A requirement that the obligor and the obligee comply with any requirement described in division (C)(1), (2), (3), (4), or (7) of this section that is contained in the order issued under this section no later than thirty days after the issuance of the order.

(D) In any action in which a child support order is issued or modified on or after July 1, 1990, under Chapter 3115. or section 2151.23, 2151.231 [2151.23.1], 2151.33, 2151.36, 2151.49, 3105.18, 3105.21, 3109.05, 3109.19, 3111.13, 3113.04, 3113.07, 3113.216 [3113.21.6], or 3113.31 of the Revised Code, the court, in addition to any requirements in those sections and in lieu of an order issued under division (C) of this section, may issue a separate order requiring both the obligor and the obligee to obtain health insurance coverage for the children who are the subject of the child support order, if health insurance coverage is available for the children and if the court determines that the coverage is available at a reasonable cost to both the obligor and the obligee and that the dual coverage by both parents would provide for coordination of medical benefits without unnecessary duplication of coverage. If the court issues an order under this division, it shall include in the order any of the requirements, notices, and information set forth in divisions (C)(1) to (13) of this section that are applicable.

(E) Any order issued under this section shall be binding upon the obligor and the obligee, their employers, and any insurer that provides health insurance coverage for either of them or their children. The court shall send a copy of any order issued under this section that contains any requirement or notice described in division (C)(1), (2), (3), (4), (7), (8), or (10) of this section by ordinary mail to the obligor, the obligee, and any employer that is subject to the order. The court shall send a copy of any order issued under this section that contains any requirement contained in division (C)(9) of this section by ordinary mail to the obligor and obligee.

(F) If an obligor does not comply with any order issued under this section that contains any requirement or notice described in division (C)(1), (2), (4), (7), (8), or (10) of this section within thirty days after the order is issued, the child support enforcement agency shall notify the court in writing of the failure of the obligor to comply with the order. Upon receipt of the notice from the agency, the court shall issue an order to the employer of the obligor requiring the employer to take whatever action is necessary to make application to enroll the obligor in any available group health insurance or health care policy, contract, or plan with coverage for the children who are the subject of the child support order, to submit a copy of the court order issued pursuant to division (C) of this section to the insurer at the time that the employer makes application to enroll the children in the health insurance or health care policy, contract, or plan, and, if the obligor's application is accepted, to deduct from the wages or other income of the obligor the cost of the coverage for the children. Upon receipt of any order under this division, the employer shall take whatever action is necessary to comply with the order.

During the time that any order issued under this section is in effect and after the employer has received a copy of the order, the employer of the obligor who is the subject of the order shall comply with the order and, upon request from the obligee or agency, shall release to the obligee and the child support enforcement agency all information about the obligor's health insurance coverage that is necessary to ensure compliance with this section or any order issued under this section, including, but not limited to, the name and address of the insurer and any policy, contract, or plan number. Any information provided by an employer pursuant to this division shall be used only for the purpose of the enforcement of an order issued under this section.

Any employer who receives a copy of an order issued under this section shall notify the child support enforcement agency of any change in or the termination of the obligor's health insurance coverage that is maintained pursuant to an order issued under this section.

(G) Any insurer that receives a copy of an order issued under this section shall comply with this section and any order issued under this section, regardless of the residence of the children. If an insurer provides health insurance coverage for the children who are the subject of a child support order in accordance with an order issued under this section, the insurer shall reimburse the parent, who is designated to receive reimbursement in the order issued under this section, for covered out-of-pocket medical, optical, hospital, dental, or prescription expenses incurred on behalf of the children subject to the order.

(H) If an obligee under a child support order is eligible for medical assistance under Chapter 5111. or 5115. of the Revised Code and the obligor has obtained health insurance coverage pursuant to an order issued under division (C) of this section, the obligee shall notify any physician, hospital, or other provider of medical services for which medical assistance is available of the name and address of the obligor's insurer and of the number of the obligor's health insurance or health care policy, contract, or plan. Any physician, hospital, or other provider of medical services for which medical assistance is available under Chapter 5111. or 5115. of the Revised Code who is notified under this division of the existence of a health insurance or health care policy, contract, or plan with coverage for children who are eligible for medical assistance first shall bill the insurer for any services provided for those children. If the insurer fails to pay all or any part of a claim filed under this division by the physician, hospital, or other medical services provider and the services for which the claim is filed are covered by Chapter 5111. or 5115. of the Revised Code, the physician, hospital, or other medical services provider shall bill the remaining unpaid costs of the services in accordance with Chapter 5111. or 5115. of the Revised Code.

(I) Any obligor who fails to comply with an order issued under this section is liable to the obligee for any medical expenses incurred as a result of the failure to comply with the order.

(J) Whoever violates an order issued under this section may be punished as for contempt under Chapter 2705. of the Revised Code. If an obligor is found in contempt under that chapter for failing to comply with an order issued under this section and if the obligor previously has been found in contempt under that chapter, the court shall consider the obligor's failure to comply with the court's order as a change in circumstances for the purpose of modification of the amount of support due under the child support order that is the basis of the order issued under this section.

(K) Nothing in this section shall be construed to require an insurer to accept for enrollment any child who does not meet the underwriting standards of the health insurance or health care policy, contract, or plan for which application is made.

(L) Notwithstanding section 3109.01 of the Revised Code, if a court issues an order under this section requiring a parent to obtain health insurance coverage for the children who are the subject of a child support order, the order shall remain in effect beyond the child's eighteenth birthday as long as the child continuously attends on a full-time basis any recognized and accredited high school. Any parent ordered to obtain health insurance coverage for the children who are the subject of a child support order shall continue to obtain the coverage for the children under the order, including during seasonal vacation periods, until the order terminates.

HISTORY: 143 v H 591 (Eff 4-12-90); 143 v H 737 (Eff 4-11-91); 143 v S 3 (Eff 4-11-91); 144 v S 10 (Eff 7-15-92); 145 v H 173 (Eff 12-31-93); 146 v H 249 (Eff 7-17-95); 146 v H 167 (Eff 11-15-95); 146 v H 274 (Eff 8-8-96); 147 v S 67 (Eff 6-4-97); 147 v H 408. Eff 10-1-97.

The effective date is set by section 26 of HB 408.

[§ 3113.21.8] § 3113.218 Administration of orders on monthly basis; exceptions.

(A) As used in this section, "child support order" has the same meaning as in section 3113.215 [3113.21.5] of the Revised Code.

(B) In any action or proceeding in which a child support order is issued or modified on or after July 1, 1990, under Chapter 3115. or section 2151.23, 2151.33, 2151.36, 2151.49, 3105.18, 3105.21, 3109.05, 3109.19, 3111.13, 3113.04, 3113.07, 3113.216 [3113.21.6], or 3113.31 of the Revised Code, the court that issues or modifies the order shall include in the order, in addition to any provision required by any of those sections or by any other section of the Revised Code, all of the following:

(1) A requirement that, regardless of the frequency or amount of child support payments to be made under the order, the child support enforcement agency that is required to administer the order shall administer it on a monthly basis, in accordance with this section;

(2) A specification of the monthly amount due under the child support order for purposes of its monthly administration, as determined under division (D) of this section;

(3) A statement that payments under the order are to be made in the manner ordered by the court, and that if the payments are to be made other than on a monthly basis, the required monthly administration by the agency does not affect the frequency or the amount of the child support payments to be made under the order.

(C) If a child support enforcement agency is required by statute or court order to administer a child support order that was issued or modified on or after July 1, 1990, the agency shall administer the order on a monthly basis, in accordance with the provisions of the order that contain the information described in division (B) of this section.

(D) If a court issues or modifies a child support order on or after July 1, 1990, and if the child support payments due under the order are to be made other than on a monthly basis, the court shall calculate a monthly amount due under the child support order, for purposes of its monthly administration, in the following manner:

(1) If the child support order is to be paid weekly, multiply the weekly amount of child support due under the order by fifty-two and divide the resulting product by twelve;

(2) If the child support order is to be paid biweekly, multiply the biweekly amount of child support due under the order by twenty-six and divide the resulting product by twelve;

(3) If the child support order is to be paid periodically but is not to be paid weekly, biweekly, or monthly, multiply the periodic amount of child support due by an appropriate number to obtain the annual amount of child support due under the order and divide the annual amount of child support due by twelve.

(E) If the payments under a child support order are to be made other than on a monthly basis, the required monthly administration of the order by a child support enforcement agency pursuant to this section shall not affect the frequency or the amount of the child support payments to be made under the order.

(F) The provisions of this section do not apply in relation to a child support order unless the order was issued or modified on or after July 1, 1990.

HISTORY: 143 v H 591 (Eff 4-12-90); 145 v H 173 (Eff 12-31-93); 146 v H 167 (Eff 11-15-95); 146 v H 274 (Eff 8-8-96); 147 v H 408. Eff 10-1-97.

The effective date is set by section 26 of HB 408.

[§ 3113.21.9] § 3113.219 Interest on unpaid support; order for payment of costs of action.

(A) On or after July 1, 1992, when a court issues or modifies a support order under Chapter 3115. or section 2151.23, 2151.231 [2151.23.1], 2151.33, 2151.36, 2151.49, 3105.18, 3105.21, 3109.05, 3109.19, 3111.13, 3113.04, 3113.07, 3113.216 [3113.21.6], or 3113.31 of the Revised Code or in any proceeding in which a court determines the amount of support to be paid pursuant to a support order, the court shall determine the date the obligor failed to pay the support required under the support order and the amount of support the obligor failed to pay. If the court determines the obligor has failed at any time to comply with a support order, the court shall issue a new order requiring the obligor to pay support. If the court determines that the failure to pay was willful, the court shall assess interest on the amount of support the obligor failed to pay from the date the court specifies as the original date the obligor failed to comply with the order requiring the payment of support to the date the court issues the new order requiring the payment of support and shall compute the interest at the rate specified in division (A) of section 1343.03 of the Revised Code. The court shall specify in the support order the amount of interest the court assessed against the obligor and incorporate the amount of interest into the new monthly payment plan.

(B) On or after July 1, 1992, when a court issues or modifies a support order under Chapter 3115. or section 2151.23, 2151.231 [2151.23.1], 2151.33, 2151.36, 2151.49, 3105.18, 3105.21, 3109.05, 3109.19, 3111.13, 3113.04, 3113.07, 3113.216 [3113.21.6], or 3113.31 of the Revised Code or in any proceeding in which a court determines the amount of support to be paid pursuant to a support order, the court may include in the support order a statement ordering either party to pay the costs of the action, including, but not limited to, attorney's fees, fees for genetic tests in contested actions under sections 3111.01 to 3111.19 of the Revised Code, and court costs.

HISTORY: 144 v S 10 (Eff 7-15-92); 145 v H 173 (Eff 12-31-93); 146 v H 167 (Eff 11-15-96); 146 v H 274 (Eff 8-8-96); 146 v H 350. Eff 1-27-97.

The provisions of § 6(A) of HB 350 (146 v —) read as follows:

SECTION 6(A) The amendments to sections ° ° ° 3313.219†, ° ° ° of the Revised Code that are made in this act and that pertain to judgment interest shall apply only to civil actions based on tortious conduct and not settled by agreement of the parties that are commenced on or after the effective date of this act. ° ° °

† Presumably, 3113.21.9 was intended.

[§ 3113.21.10] § 3113.2110 Judgment for unpaid support.

Whenever an obligor fails to make any payment required by a child support order, the obligee or a child support enforcement agency acting on behalf of the obligee may bring an action in the court of common pleas that issued the support order to obtain a judgment on the unpaid amount. Any judgment obtained under this section may be enforced in the same manner as any other judgment of a court of this state.

HISTORY: 144 v S 331. Eff 11-13-92.

[DOMESTIC VIOLENCE]

§ 3113.31 Definitions; jurisdiction; petition; hearing; protection orders, consent agreements.

(A) As used in this section:

(1) "Domestic violence" means the occurrence of one or more of the following acts against a family or household member:

(a) Attempting to cause or recklessly causing bodily injury;

(b) Placing another person by the threat of force in fear of imminent serious physical harm or committing a violation of section 2903.211 [2903.21.1] or 2911.211 [2911.21.1] of the Revised Code;

(c) Committing any act with respect to a child that would result in the child being an abused child, as defined in section 2151.031 [2151.03.1] of the Revised Code.

(2) "Court" means the domestic relations division of the court of common pleas in counties that have a domestic relations division, and the court of common pleas in counties that do not have a domestic relations division.

(3) "Family or household member" means any of the following:

(a) Any of the following who is residing with or has resided with the respondent:

(i) A spouse, a person living as a spouse, or a former spouse of the respondent;

(ii) A parent or a child of the respondent, or another person related by consanguinity or affinity to the respondent;

(iii) A parent or a child of a spouse, person living as a spouse, or former spouse of the respondent, or another person related by consanguinity or affinity to a spouse, person living as a spouse, or former spouse of the respondent.

(b) The natural parent of any child of whom the respondent is the other natural parent or is the putative other natural parent.

(4) "Person living as a spouse" means a person who is living or has lived with the respondent in a common law marital relationship, who otherwise is cohabiting with the respondent, or who otherwise has cohabited with the respondent within five years prior to the date of the alleged occurrence of the act in question.

(5) "Victim advocate" means a person who provides support and assistance for a person who files a petition under this section.

(B) The court has jurisdiction over all proceedings under this section. The petitioner's right to relief under this section is not affected by the petitioner's leaving the residence or household to avoid further domestic violence.

(C) A person may seek relief under this section on the person's own behalf, or any parent or adult household member may seek relief under this section on behalf of any other family or household member, by filing a petition with the court. The petition shall contain or state:

(1) An allegation that the respondent engaged in domestic violence against a family or household member of the respondent, including a description of the nature and extent of the domestic violence;

(2) The relationship of the respondent to the petitioner, and to the victim if other than the petitioner;

(3) A request for relief under this section.

(D)(1) If a person who files a petition pursuant to this section requests an ex parte order, the court shall hold an ex parte hearing on the same day that the petition is filed. The court, for good cause shown at the ex parte hearing, may enter any temporary orders, with or without bond, including, but not limited to, an order described in division (E)(1)(a), (b), or (c) of this section, that the court finds necessary to protect the family or household member from domestic violence. Immediate and present danger of domestic violence to the family or household member constitutes good cause for purposes of this section. Immediate and present danger includes, but is not limited to, situations in which the respondent has threatened the family or household member with bodily harm or in which the respondent previously has been convicted of or pleaded guilty to an offense that constitutes domestic violence against the family or household member.

(2)(a) If the court, after an ex parte hearing, issues an order described in division (E)(1)(b) or (c) of this section, the court shall schedule a full hearing for a date that is within seven court days after the ex parte hearing. If any other type of protection order that is authorized under division (E) of this section is issued by the court after an ex parte hearing, the court shall schedule a full hearing for a date that is within ten court days after the ex parte hearing. The court shall give the respondent notice of, and an opportunity to be heard at, the full hearing. The court shall hold the full hearing on the date scheduled under this division unless the court grants a continuance of the hearing in accordance with this division. Under any of the following circumstances or for any of the following reasons, the court may grant a continuance of the full hearing to a reasonable time determined by the court:

(i) Prior to the date scheduled for the full hearing under this division, the respondent has not been served with the petition filed pursuant to this section and notice of the full hearing.

(ii) The parties consent to the continuance.

(iii) The continuance is needed to allow a party to obtain counsel.

(iv) The continuance is needed for other good cause.

(b) An ex parte order issued under this section does not expire because of a failure to serve notice of the full hearing upon the respondent before the date set for the full hearing under division (D)(2)(a) of this section or because the court grants a continuance under that division.

(3) If a person who files a petition pursuant to this section does not request an ex parte order, or if a person requests an ex parte order but the court does not issue an ex parte order after an ex parte hearing, the court shall proceed as in a normal civil action and grant a full hearing on the matter.

(E)(1) After an ex parte or full hearing, the court may grant any protection order, with or without bond, or approve any consent agreement to bring about a cessation of domestic violence against the family or household members. The order or agreement may:

(a) Direct the respondent to refrain from abusing the family or household members;

(b) Grant possession of the residence or household to the petitioner or other family or household member, to the exclusion of the respondent, by evicting the respondent, when the residence or household is owned or leased solely by the petitioner or other family or household member, or by ordering the respondent to vacate the premises, when the residence or household is jointly owned or leased by the respondent, and the petitioner or other family or household member;

(c) When the respondent has a duty to support the petitioner or other family or household member living in the residence or household and the respondent is the sole owner or lessee of the residence or household, grant possession of the residence or household to the petitioner or other family or household member, to the exclusion of the respondent, by ordering the respondent to vacate the premises, or, in the case of a consent agreement, allow the respondent to provide suitable, alternative housing;

(d) Temporarily allocate parental rights and responsibilities for the care of, or establish temporary visitation rights with regard to, minor children, if no other court has determined, or is determining, the allocation of parental rights and responsibilities for the minor children or visitation rights;

(e) Require the respondent to maintain support, if the respondent customarily provides for or contributes to the support of the family or household member, or if the respondent has a duty to support the petitioner or family or household member;

(f) Require the respondent, petitioner, victim of domestic violence, or any combination of those persons, to seek counseling;

(g) Require the respondent to refrain from entering the residence, school, business, or place of employment of the petitioner or family or household member;

(h) Grant other relief that the court considers equitable and fair, including, but not limited to, ordering the respondent to permit the use of a motor vehicle by the petitioner or other family or household member and the apportionment of household and family personal property.

(2) If a protection order has been issued pursuant to this section in a prior action involving the respondent and the petitioner or one or more of the family or household members, the court may include in a protection order that it issues a prohibition against the respondent returning to the residence or household. If it includes a prohibition against the respondent returning to the residence or household in the order, it also shall include in the order provisions of the type described in division (E)(7) of this section. This division does not preclude the court from including in a protection order or consent agreement, in circumstances other than those described in this division, a requirement that the respondent be evicted from or vacate the residence or household or refrain from entering the residence, school, business, or place of employment of the petitioner or a family or household member, and, if the court includes any requirement of that type in an order or agreement, the court also shall include in the order provisions of the type described in division (E)(7) of this section.

(3)(a) Any protection order issued or consent agreement approved under this section shall be valid until a date certain, but not later than five years from the date of its issuance or approval.

(b) Subject to the limitation on the duration of an order or agreement set forth in division (E)(3)(a) of this section, any order under division (E)(1)(d) of this section shall terminate on the date that a court in an action for divorce, dissolution of marriage, or legal separation brought by the petitioner or respondent issues an order allocating parental rights and responsibilities for the care of children or on the date that a juvenile court in an action brought by the petitioner or respondent issues an order awarding legal custody of minor children. Subject to the limitation on the duration of an order or agreement set forth in division (E)(3)(a) of this section, any order under division (E)(1)(e) of this section shall terminate on the date that a court in an action for divorce, dissolution of marriage, or legal separation brought by the petitioner or respondent issues a support order or on the date that a juvenile court in an action brought by the petitioner or respondent issues a support order.

(c) Any protection order issued or consent agreement approved pursuant to this section may be renewed in the same manner as the original order or agreement was issued or approved.

(4) A court may not issue a protection order that requires a petitioner to do or to refrain from doing an act that the court may require a respondent to do or to refrain from doing under division (E)(1)(a), (b), (c), (d), (e), (g), or (h) of this section unless all of the following apply:

(a) The respondent files a separate petition for a protection order in accordance with this section.

(b) The petitioner is served notice of the respondent's petition at least forty-eight hours before the court holds a hearing with respect to the respondent's petition, or the petitioner waives the right to receive this notice.

(c) If the petitioner has requested an ex parte order pursuant to division (D) of this section, the court does not delay any hearing required by that division beyond the time specified in that division in order to consolidate the hearing with a hearing on the petition filed by the respondent.

(d) After a full hearing at which the respondent presents evidence in support of the request for a protection order and the petitioner is afforded an opportunity to defend against that evidence, the court determines that the petitioner has committed an act of domestic violence or has violated a temporary protection order issued pursuant to section 2919.26 of the Revised Code, that both the petitioner and the respondent acted primarily as aggressors, and that neither the petitioner nor the respondent acted primarily in self-defense.

(5) No protection order issued or consent agreement approved under this section shall in any manner affect title to any real property.

(6)(a) If a petitioner, or the child of a petitioner, who obtains a protection order or consent agreement pursuant to division (E)(1) of this section or a temporary protection order pursuant to section 2919.26 of the Revised Code and is the subject of a visitation or companionship order issued pursuant to section 3109.051 [3109.05.1], 3109.11, or 3109.12 of the Revised Code or division (E)(1)(d) of this section granting visitation or companionship rights to the respondent, the court may require the public children services agency of the county in which the court is located to provide supervision of the respondent's exercise of visitation or companionship rights with respect to the child for a period not to exceed nine months, if the court makes the following findings of fact:

(i) The child is in danger from the respondent;

(ii) No other person or agency is available to provide the supervision or other services.

(b) A court that requires an agency to provide supervision or other services pursuant to division (E)(6)(a) of this section shall order the respondent to reimburse the agency for the cost of providing the supervision or other services, if it determines that the respondent has sufficient income or resources to pay that cost.

(7)(a) If a protection order issued or consent agreement approved under this section includes a requirement that the respondent be evicted from or vacate the residence or household or refrain from entering the residence, school, business, or place of employment of the petitioner or a family or household member, the order or agreement shall state clearly that the order or agreement cannot be waived or nullified by an invitation to the respondent from the petitioner or other family or household member to enter the residence, school, business, or place of employment or by the respondent's entry into one of those places otherwise upon the consent of the petitioner or other family or household member.

(b) Division (E)(7)(a) of this section does not limit any discretion of a court to determine that a respondent charged with a violation of section 2919.27 of the Revised Code, with a violation of a municipal ordinance substantially equivalent to that section, or with contempt of court, which charge is based on an alleged violation of a protection order issued or consent agreement approved under this section, did not commit the violation or was not in contempt of court.

(F)(1) A copy of any protection order, or consent agreement, that is issued or approved under this section shall be issued by the court to the petitioner, to the respondent, and to all law enforcement agencies that have jurisdiction to enforce the order or agreement. The court shall direct that a copy of an order be delivered to the respondent on the same day that the order is entered.

(2) All law enforcement agencies shall establish and maintain an index for the protection orders and the approved consent agreements delivered to the agencies pursuant to division (F)(1) of this section. With respect to each order and consent agreement delivered, each agency shall note on the index, the date and time that it received the order or consent agreement.

(3) Regardless of whether the petitioner has registered the order or agreement in the county in which the officer's agency has jurisdiction pursuant to division (N) of this section, any officer of a law enforcement agency shall enforce a protection order issued or consent agreement approved by any court in this state in accordance with the provisions of the order or agreement, including removing the respondent from the premises, if appropriate.

(G) Any proceeding under this section shall be conducted in accordance with the Rules of Civil Procedure, except that an order under this section may be obtained with or without bond. An order issued under this section, other than an ex parte order, that grants a protection order or approves a consent agreement, or that refuses to grant a protection order or approve a consent agreement, is a final, appealable order. The remedies and procedures provided in this section are in addition to, and not in lieu of, any other available civil or criminal remedies.

(H) The filing of proceedings under this section does not excuse a person from filing any report or giving any notice required by section 2151.421 [2151.42.1] of the Revised Code or by any other law. When a petition under this section alleges domestic violence against minor children, the court shall report the fact, or cause reports to be made, to a county, township, or municipal peace officer under section 2151.421 [2151.42.1] of the Revised Code.

(I) Any law enforcement agency that investigates a domestic dispute shall provide information to the family or household members involved regarding the relief available under this section and section 2919.26 of the Revised Code.

(J) Notwithstanding any provision of law to the contrary, no court shall charge a fee for the filing of a petition pursuant to this section.

(K)(1) Each order for support made or modified under this section on or after December 31, 1993, shall include as part of the order a general provision, as described in division (A)(1) of section 3113.21 of the Revised Code, requiring the withholding or deduction of wages or assets of the obligor under the order as described in division (D) of section 3113.21 of the Revised Code or another type of appropriate requirement as described in division (D)(6), (D)(7), or (H) of that section, to ensure that withholding or deduction from the wages or assets of the obligor is available from the commencement of the support order for collection of the support and of any arrearages that occur; a statement requiring all parties to the order to notify the child support enforcement agency in writing of their current mailing address, their current residence address, and any changes in either address; and a notice that the requirement to notify the agency of all changes in either address continues until further notice from the court. The court shall comply with sections 3113.21 to 3113.219 [3113.21.9] of the Revised Code when it makes or modifies an order for child support under this section on or after April 12, 1990.

If any person required to pay child support under an order made under this section on or after April 15, 1985, or modified under this section on or after December 31, 1986, is found in contempt of court for failure to make support payments under the order, the court that makes the finding, in addition to any other penalty or remedy imposed, shall assess all court costs arising out of the contempt proceeding against the person and require the person to pay any reasonable attorney's fees of any adverse party, as determined by the court, that arose in relation to the act of contempt.

(2) Notwithstanding section 3109.01 of the Revised Code, if a court issues a child support order under this section, the order shall remain in effect beyond the child's eighteenth birthday as long as the child continuously attends on a full-time basis any recognized and accredited high school. Any parent ordered to pay support under a child support order issued under this section shall continue to pay support under the order, including during seasonal vacation periods, until the order terminates.

(L)(1) A person who violates a protection order issued or a consent agreement approved under this section is subject to the following sanctions:

(a) Criminal prosecution for a violation of section 2919.27 of the Revised Code, if the violation of the protection order or consent agreement constitutes a violation of that section;

(b) Punishment for contempt of court.

(2) The punishment of a person for contempt of court for violation of a protection order issued or a consent agreement approved under this section does not bar criminal prosecution of the person for a violation of section 2919.27 of the Revised Code. However, a person punished for contempt of court is entitled to credit for the punishment imposed upon conviction of a violation of that section, and a person convicted of a violation of that section shall not subsequently be punished for contempt of court arising out of the same activity.

(M) In all stages of a proceeding under this section, a petitioner may be accompanied by a victim advocate.

(N)(1) A petitioner who obtains a protection order or consent agreement under this section or a temporary protection order under section 2919.26 of the Revised Code may provide notice of the issuance or approval of the order or agreement to the judicial and law enforcement officials in any county other than the county in which the order is issued or the agreement is approved by registering that order or agreement in the other county pursuant to division (N)(2) of this section and filing a copy of the registered order or registered agreement with a law enforcement agency in the other county in accordance with that division. A person who obtains a protection order issued by a court of another state may provide notice of the issuance of the order to the judicial and law enforcement officials in any county of this state by registering the order in that county pursuant to section 2919.272 [2919.27.2] of the Revised Code and filing a copy of the registered order with a law enforcement agency in that county.

(2) A petitioner may register a temporary protection order, protection order, or consent agreement in a county other than the county in which the court that issued the order or approved the agreement is located in the following manner:

(a) The petitioner shall obtain a certified copy of the order or agreement from the clerk of the court that issued the order or approved the agreement and present that certified copy to the clerk of the court of common pleas or the clerk of a municipal court or county court in the county in which the order or agreement is to be registered.

(b) Upon accepting the certified copy of the order or agreement for registration, the clerk of the court of common pleas, municipal court, or county court shall place an endorsement of registration on the order or agreement and give the petitioner a copy of the order or agreement that bears that proof of registration.

(3) The clerk of each court of common pleas, the clerk of each municipal court, and the clerk of each county court shall maintain a registry of certified copies of temporary protection orders, protection orders, or consent agreements that have been issued or approved by courts in other counties and that have been registered with the clerk.

(4) If a petitioner who obtains a protection order or consent agreement under this section or a temporary protection order under section 2919.26 of the Revised Code wishes to register the order or agreement in any county other than the county in which the order was issued or the agreement was approved, pursuant to divisions (N)(1) to (3) of this section, and if the petitioner is indigent, both of the following apply:

(a) If the petitioner submits to the clerk of the court that issued the order or approved the agreement satisfactory proof that the petitioner is indigent, the clerk may waive any fee that otherwise would be required for providing the petitioner with a certified copy of the order or agreement to be used for purposes of divisions (N)(1) to (3) of this section;

(b) If the petitioner submits to the clerk of the court of common pleas or the clerk of a municipal court or county court in the county in which the order or agreement is to be registered satisfactory proof that the petitioner is indigent, the clerk may waive any fee that otherwise would be required for accepting for registration a certified copy of the order or agreement, for placing an endorsement of registration on the order or agreement, or for giving the petitioner a copy of the order or agreement that bears the proof of registration.

HISTORY: 137 v H 835 (Eff 3-27-79); 138 v H 920 (Eff 4-9-81); 140 v H 587 (Eff 9-25-84); 140 v H 614 (Eff 4-10-85); 140 v H 113 (Eff 1-8-85); 141 v H 509 (Eff 12-1-86); 141 v H 428 (Eff 12-23-86); 142 v H 231 (Eff 10-5-87); 142 v H 708 (Eff 4-19-88); 142 v H 172 (Eff 3-17-89); 143 v H 591 (Eff 4-12-90); 143 v S 3 (Eff 4-11-91); 144 v S 10 (Eff 7-15-92); 144 v H 536 (Eff 11-5-92); 145 v H 173 (Eff 12-31-93); 145 v H 335 (Eff 12-9-94); 146 v H 274 (Eff 8-8-96); 146 v H 438 (Eff 7-1-97); 147 v S 1. Eff 10-21-97.

The provisions of § 4 of HB 335 (145 v —) read as follows:

SECTION 4. The General Assembly hereby requests the Supreme Court, in consultation with the Department of Human Services, to prescribe a form that is to be filed by a petitioner seeking a civil protection order under section 3113.31 of the Revised Code and that makes reference to all the forms of relief that a court is authorized to grant under division (E) of section 3113.31 of the Revised Code, as amended by this act, contains space for the petitioner to request any of those forms of relief, and includes instructions for completing the form so that a petitioner may file the form without the assistance of an attorney.

§ 3113.32 Records of domestic dispute and violence problems; annual statistical report.

(A) The sheriff of a county, constable or chief of police of a township, and chief of police of a city or village shall keep a separate record of domestic dispute and domestic violence problems on a form prepared and distributed by the superintendent of the bureau of criminal identification and investigation. The forms shall contain spaces for the reporting of all information that the superintendent determines to be relevant to domestic dispute and domestic violence problems, including, but not limited to, the number of domestic dispute and domestic violence problems reported to the law enforcement agency for which the record is kept, the relationship of the complainant and the person allegedly the victim of the domestic violence, if different, to the alleged offender, and the relationship of all other persons involved in the domestic dispute or domestic violence problem, and the action taken by the law enforcement officers who handled the domestic dispute or domestic violence problem. A copy of the record shall be submitted to the bureau each month.

(B) The superintendent of the bureau of criminal identification and investigation shall receive copies of monthly records of domestic dispute and domestic violence problems kept by local law enforcement agencies and submitted to him under division (A) of this section. The superintendent shall compile the data and annually produce a statistical public report on the incidence of domestic disputes and violence in this state and its political subdivisions. The report shall be prepared in such a manner that there is no identifying data, including the names and addresses of the persons involved in the domestic dispute and domestic violence problems, that would enable any person to determine the identity of any of the persons involved.

(C) The attorney general shall oversee the statistical reporting required pursuant to this section to ensure that it is complete and accurate.

HISTORY: 140 v H 587. Eff 9-25-84.

Analogous to former RC § 3113.32 (137 v H 835), repealed 137 v H 835, § 3, eff 3-27-83.

[SHELTERS FOR DOMESTIC VIOLENCE VICTIMS]

§ 3113.33 Definitions.

As used in sections 3113.33 to 3113.40 of the Revised Code:

(A) "Domestic violence" means attempting to cause or causing bodily injury to a family or household member, or placing a family or household member by threat of force in fear of imminent physical harm.

(B) "Family or household member" means any of the following:

(1) Any of the following who is residing or has resided

with the person committing the domestic violence:

(a) A spouse, a person living as a spouse, or a former spouse of the person committing the domestic violence;

(b) A parent or child of the person committing the domestic violence, or another person related by consanguinity or affinity to the person committing the domestic violence;

(c) A parent or a child of a spouse, person living as a spouse, or former spouse of the person committing the domestic violence, or another person related by consanguinity or affinity to a spouse, person living as a spouse, or former spouse of the person committing the domestic violence;

(d) The dependents of any person listed in division (B)(1)(a), (b), or (c) of this section.

(2) The natural parent of any child of whom the person committing the domestic violence is the other natural parent or is the putative other natural parent.

(C) "Shelter for victims of domestic violence" or "shelter" means a facility that provides temporary residential service or facilities to family or household members who are victims of domestic violence.

(D) "Person living as a spouse" means a person who is living or has lived with the person committing the domestic violence in a common law marital relationship, who otherwise is cohabiting with the person committing the domestic violence, or who otherwise has cohabited with the person committing the domestic violence within five years prior to the date of the alleged occurrence of the act in question.

HISTORY: 138 v S 46 (Eff 1-18-80); 138 v H 920 (Eff 4-9-81); 140 v H 587 (Eff 9-25-84); 142 v H 172 (Eff 3-17-89); 145 v H 335 (Eff 12-9-94); 147 v H 215 (Eff 6-30-97); 147 v S 1. Eff 10-21-97.

Publisher's Note

The amendments made by HB 215 (147 v —) and SB 1 (147 v —) have been combined. Please see provisions of RC § 1.52.

§ 3113.34 Additional fee for marriage license; fees to assist shelters for domestic violence victims.

In addition to any fee established under section 2101.16 of the Revised Code for the issuance of a marriage license, the probate court shall collect and deposit in the county treasury a fee of seventeen dollars for each marriage license issued. This fee, plus the thirty-two-dollar fee collected under division (D) of section 2303.201 [2303.20.1] of the Revised Code as additional costs in each new action or proceeding for annulment, divorce, or dissolution of marriage, shall be retained in a special fund and shall be expended only to provide financial assistance to shelters for victims of domestic violence and only as provided in sections 3113.35 to 3113.39 of the Revised Code.

HISTORY: 138 v S 46 (Eff 1-18-80); 140 v H 319 (Eff 12-26-84); 145 v H 335. Eff 12-9-94.

§ 3113.35 Shelter may apply to county for release of fees collected for marriage licenses and as additional costs in certain actions.

(A) A shelter for victims of domestic violence may apply to the board of county commissioners of the county in which it is located or of an adjoining county, the population of which is or will be served by the shelter, for the release of funds to be collected as fees for the issuance of marriage licenses pursuant to section 3113.34 or fees as additional costs in annulment, divorce, or dissolution of marriage actions and proceedings pursuant to division (D) of section 2303.201 [2303.20.1] of the Revised Code and that are to be used for the funding of the shelter. All applications for funds shall be submitted by the first day of October of the year preceding the calendar year for which the funding is desired, and shall include all of the following:

(1) Evidence that the shelter is incorporated in this state as a nonprofit corporation;

(2) A list of the trustees of the corporation, and a list of the trustees of the shelter, if different;

(3) The proposed budget of the shelter for the following calendar year;

(4) A summary of the services proposed to be offered in the following calendar year;

(5) An estimate of the number of persons to be served during the following calendar year.

(B) Upon receipt of an application for funds from a shelter that meets the criteria set forth in section 3113.36 of the Revised Code, the board of county commissioners shall, on or before the fifteenth day of November of the year in which the application is filed, notify the shelter, in writing, whether it is eligible for funds, and if the shelter is eligible, estimate the amount available for that shelter from the fees to be collected under section 3113.34 or division (D) of section 2303.201 [2303.20.1] of the Revised Code.

(C) Funds collected as fees for the issuance of marriage licenses pursuant to section 3113.34 or fees as additional costs in annulment, divorce, or dissolution of marriage actions and proceedings pursuant to division (D) of section 2303.201 [2303.20.1] of the Revised Code that are allocated to shelters under this section shall be paid to the shelters twice annually. Funds collected from the first day of January through the thirtieth day of June of the calendar year following the year in which the application is filed shall be allocated to the shelters by the fifteenth day of July of the year following the year in which the application is filed. Funds collected from the first day of July through the thirty-first day of December of the calendar year following the year in which the application is filed shall be allocated to the shelters by the fifteenth day of January of the year following the end of the collection period.

HISTORY: 138 v S 46 (Eff 1-18-80); 138 v H 736 (Eff 10-16-80); 141 v H 569 (Eff 4-15-86); 145 v H 335. Eff 12-9-94.

§ 3113.36 Requirements for qualifying for funds; disqualification.

(A) To qualify for funds under section 3113.35 of the Revised Code, a shelter for victims of domestic violence shall meet all of the following requirements:

(1) Be incorporated in this state as a nonprofit corporation;

(2) Have trustees who represent the racial, ethnic, and socioeconomic diversity of the community to be served, including at least one person who is or has been a victim of domestic violence;

(3) Receive at least twenty-five per cent of its funds from sources other than funds distributed pursuant to section 3113.35 of the Revised Code. These other sources may be public or private, and may include funds distributed pursuant to section 3113.37 of the Revised Code, and contributions of goods or services, including materials, commodities, transportation, office space, or other types of facilities or personal services.

(4) Provide residential service or facilities for children when accompanied by a parent, guardian, or custodian who is a victim of domestic violence and who is receiving temporary residential service at the shelter;

(5) Require persons employed by or volunteering services to the shelter to maintain the confidentiality of any information that would identify individuals served by the shelter.

(B) A shelter for victims of domestic violence does not qualify for funds if it discriminates in its admissions or provision of services on the basis of race, religion, color, age, marital status, national origin, or ancestry. A shelter does not qualify for funds in the second half of any year if its application projects the provision of residential service and such service has not been provided in the first half of that year; such a shelter does not qualify for funds in the following year.

HISTORY: 138 v S 46. Eff 1-18-80.

§ 3113.37 Deposit of unallocated funds in state treasury to credit of domestic violence shelters fund.

(A) If in any calendar year a board of county commissioners does not allocate all of the funds collected that year under section 3113.34 or division (D) of section 2303.201 [2303.20.1] of the Revised Code to a shelter for victims of domestic violence that applied for them, or if a board receives no application in that year from a shelter that is qualified to receive funds as determined under section 3113.36 of the Revised Code, the funds shall be deposited, on or before the thirty-first day of December of that year, in the state treasury to the credit of the domestic violence shelters fund, which is hereby created. The fund shall be administered by the attorney general for the purpose of providing financial assistance to shelters.

(B) A shelter located in this state may apply to the attorney general for funds. All applications for funds shall be submitted by the first day of February of the year for which the funds are requested and shall contain all of the information set forth in division (A) of section 3113.35 of the Revised Code.

(C) Upon receipt of an application for funds from a shelter that meets the criteria set forth in section 3113.36 of the Revised Code, the attorney general, on or before the fifteenth day of March of the year in which the application is received, shall notify the shelter, in writing, whether it is eligible for funds and, if the shelter is eligible, specify the amount available for that shelter.

(D) Funds allocated under this section shall be paid once annually, on or before the thirtieth day of April of the year in which the application is received.

HISTORY: 138 v S 46 (Eff 1-18-80); 141 v H 201 (Eff 7-1-85); 145 v H 335. Eff 12-9-94.

§ 3113.38 Priorities for allocating funds.

If a board of county commissioners or the attorney general receives applications from more than one qualified shelter for victims of domestic violence, and the requests for funds exceed the amount of funds available, funds shall be allocated on the basis of the following priorities:

(A) To shelters in existence on the effective date of this section;

(B) The shelters offering or proposing to offer the broadest range of services and referrals to the community served, including medical, psychological, financial, educational, vocational, child care services, and legal services;

(C) To other qualified shelters.

HISTORY: 138 v S 46. Eff 1-18-80.

§ 3113.39 Annual report by shelter; attorney general to compile reports.

(A) A shelter for victims of domestic violence that receives funds pursuant to section 3113.35 or 3113.37 of the Revised Code shall file an annual report with the board of county commissioners of the county in which it is located and of the county from which it is receiving funds, if different, and with the attorney general on or before the thirty-first day of March of the year following the year in which funds were received. The annual report shall include statistics on the number of persons served by the shelter, the relationship of the victim of domestic violence to the abuser, the number of referrals made for medical, psychological, financial, educational, vocational, child care services, or legal services, and shall include a compilation report of an independent accountant. No information contained in the report shall identify any person served by the shelter, or enable any person to determine the identity of any such person.

(B) The attorney general shall compile the reports

filed pursuant to division (A) of this section annually.

HISTORY: 138 v S 46 (Eff 1-18-80); 140 v H 587. Eff 9-25-84.

§ 3113.40 Shelter to obtain last known residence information.

When a shelter for victims of domestic violence provides accommodations to a person, the shelter, on admitting the person, shall determine, if possible, the person's last known residential address and county of residence. The information concerning the address and county of residence is confidential and may be released only to a public children services agency pursuant to section 2151.422 [2151.42.2] of the Revised Code.

HISTORY: 147 v H 215. Eff 6-30-97.

§ 3113.99 Penalties.

(A) For purposes of this section:

(1) "Child support order" means an order for support issued or modified under Chapter 3115. or section 2151.23, 2151.36, 2151.49, 3105.18, 3105.21, 3109.05, 3111.13, 3113.04, 3113.07, 3113.216 [3113.21.6], or 3113.31 of the Revised Code.

(2) "Obligor" means a person who is required to pay support under a child support order.

(B) Whoever violates section 3113.06 of the Revised Code is guilty of a misdemeanor of the first degree. If the offender previously has been convicted of or pleaded guilty to a violation of section 3113.06 of the Revised Code or if the court finds that the offender has failed to pay the cost of child maintenance under section 3113.06 of the Revised Code for a total accumulated period of twenty-six weeks out of one hundred four consecutive weeks, whether or not the twenty-six weeks were consecutive, a violation of section 3113.06 of the Revised Code is a felony of the fifth degree.

(C) An obligor who violates division (D)(1)(c) of section 3113.21 of the Revised Code shall be fined not more than fifty dollars for a first offense, not more than one hundred dollars for a second offense, and not more than five hundred dollars for each subsequent offense.

(D) An obligor who violates division (G)(2) of section 3113.21 of the Revised Code shall be fined not more than fifty dollars for a first offense, not more than one hundred dollars for a second offense, and not more than five hundred dollars for each subsequent offense.

(E) A fine amount imposed pursuant to division (C) or (D) of this section shall be paid to the child support enforcement agency administering the obligor's child support order. The amount of the fine that does not exceed the amount of arrearage under the child support order shall be disbursed in accordance with the child support order. The amount of the fine that exceeds the amount of the arrearage order shall be used by the agency for the administration of its program for child support enforcement.

HISTORY: Bureau of Code Revision, 10-1-53; 134 v H 511 (Eff 1-1-74); 146 v S 2 (Eff 7-1-96); 146 v H 167. Eff 6-11-96.

The effective date of HB 167 (146 v —) was changed from 11-15-96 to 6-11-96 in section 7 of HB 710 (146 v —).

Comment, Legislative Service Commission

° ° ° Sections 3111.99, 3113.99, ° ° ° of the Revised Code are amended by this act [Am. Sub. S.B. 2] (effective July 1, 1996) and also by Sub. H.B. 167 of the 121st General Assembly (November 15, 1996). ° ° ° Comparison of these amendments in pursuance of section 1.52 of the Revised Code discloses that they are not irreconcilable so that they are required by that section to be harmonized to give effect to each amendment.

TITLE 33: EDUCATION—LIBRARIES

CHAPTER 3301: DEPARTMENT OF EDUCATION

[§ 3301.12.1] § 3301.121 Adjudication procedure to determine whether to permanently exclude pupil.

(A) In addition to the duties and responsibilities of the superintendent of public instruction set forth in section 3301.12 of the Revised Code, the superintendent, in accordance with this section and section 3313.662 [3313.66.2] of the Revised Code, shall conduct an adjudication procedure to determine whether to permanently exclude from attending any of the public schools of this state any pupil who is the subject of a resolution forwarded to the superintendent by a board of education pursuant to division (D) of section 3313.662 [3313.66.2] of the Revised Code.

(B)(1) Except as provided in division (B)(3) of this section, within fourteen days after receipt of a resolution forwarded by a board of education pursuant to division (D) of section 3313.662 [3313.66.2] of the Revised Code, the superintendent of public instruction or the superintendent's designee shall provide the pupil who is the subject of the resolution and that pupil's parent, guardian, or custodian with a notice of an opportunity for an adjudication hearing on the proposed permanent exclusion of the pupil from attending any of the public schools of this state. The notice shall include all of the following:

(a) The date, time, and place of the permanent exclusion adjudication hearing;

(b) A statement informing the pupil and the pupil's parent, guardian, or custodian that the pupil may attend the adjudication hearing at the date, time, and place set forth in the notice, that the failure of the pupil or the pupil's parent, guardian, or custodian to attend the adjudication hearing will result in a waiver of the pupil's right to present evidence, testimony, and factors in mitigation of the pupil's permanent exclusion at an adjudication hearing on the proposed permanent exclusion, and that the pupil shall be accorded all of the following rights:

(i) The right to testify, to present evidence and the testimony of witnesses, and to confront, cross-examine, and compel the attendance of witnesses;

(ii) The right to a record of the hearing;

(iii) The right to written findings.

(c) A statement informing the pupil and the pupil's parent, guardian, or custodian that the pupil has the right to be represented by counsel at the adjudication hearing.

(d) A statement informing the pupil and the pupil's parent, guardian, or custodian that, if the pupil by failing to attend the hearing waives the pupil's right to present evidence, testimony, and factors in mitigation of the pupil's permanent exclusion at an adjudication hearing on the proposed permanent exclusion, the superintendent is required to review the information relevant to the permanent exclusion that is available to the superintendent and is permitted to enter an order requiring the pupil's permanent exclusion from attending any of the public schools of this state at any time within seven days after the conclusion of the adjudication hearing.

(2) The superintendent or the superintendent's designee shall provide the notice required by division (B)(1) of this section to the pupil and to the pupil's parent, guardian, or custodian by certified mail or personal service.

(3)(a) If a pupil who is the subject of a resolution forwarded to the superintendent of public instruction by a board of education pursuant to section 3313.662 [3313.66.2] of the Revised Code is in the custody of the department of youth services pursuant to a disposition under division (A)(4), (5), or (7) of section 2151.355 [2151.35.5] of the Revised Code at the time the resolution is forwarded, the department shall notify in writing the superintendent of public instruction and the board of education that forwarded the resolution of that fact. Upon receipt of the notice, the superintendent shall delay providing the notice required by division (B)(1) of this section and the adjudication of the request for permanent exclusion until the superintendent receives further notice from the department pursuant to division (B)(3)(b) of this section.

(b) At least sixty days before a pupil described in division (B)(3)(a) of this section will be released from institutionalization or institutionalization in a secure facility by the department of youth services, the department shall notify in writing the superintendent of public instruction and the board of education that forwarded the resolution pursuant to section 3313.662 [3313.66.2] of the Revised Code of the impending release and shall provide in that notice information regarding the extent of the education the pupil received while in the custody of the department, including whether the pupil has obtained a certificate of high school equivalence.

If the pupil has not obtained a certificate of high school equivalence while in the custody of the department of youth services, the superintendent of public instruction shall provide the notice required by division (B)(1) of this section and, at least thirty days before the pupil is to be released from institutionalization or institutionalization in a secure facility, conduct an adjudication procedure to determine whether to permanently exclude the pupil from attending the public schools of this state in accordance with this section. If the pupil has obtained a certificate of high school equivalence while in the custody of the department, the superintendent, in the superintendent's discretion, may conduct the adjudication.

(C)(1) Except as provided in division (B)(3) of this section, the date of the adjudication hearing set forth in the notice required by division (B)(1) of this section shall be a date no less than fourteen days nor more than twenty-one days from the date the superintendent sends the notice by certified mail or initiates personal service of the notice.

(2) The superintendent, for good cause shown on the written request of the pupil or the pupil's parent, guardian, or custodian, or on the superintendent's own motion, may grant reasonable continuances of any adjudication hearing held under this section but shall not grant either party total continuances in excess of ten days.

(3) If a pupil or the pupil's parent, guardian, or custodian does not appear at the adjudication hearing on a proposed permanent exclusion, the superintendent or the referee appointed by the superintendent shall proceed to conduct an adjudication hearing on the proposed permanent exclusion on the date for the adjudication hearing that is set forth in the notice provided pursuant to division (B)(1) of this section or on the date to which the hearing was continued pursuant to division (C)(2) of this section.

(D)(1) The superintendent or a referee appointed by the superintendent may conduct an adjudication hearing to determine whether to permanently exclude a pupil in one of the following counties:

(a) The county in which the superintendent holds the superintendent's office;

(b) Upon the request of the pupil or the pupil's parent, guardian, custodian, or attorney, in the county in which the board of education that forwarded the resolution requesting the permanent exclusion is located if the superintendent, in the superintendent's discretion and upon consideration of evidence of hardship presented on behalf of the requesting pupil, determines that the hearing should be conducted in that county.

(2) The superintendent of public instruction or a referee appointed by the superintendent shall conduct an adjudication hearing on a proposed permanent exclusion of a pupil. The referee may be an attorney admitted to the practice of law in this state but shall not be an attorney that represents the board of education that forwarded the resolution requesting the permanent exclusion.

(3) The superintendent or referee who conducts an adjudication hearing under this section may administer oaths, issue subpoenas to compel the attendance of witnesses and evidence, and enforce the subpoenas by a contempt proceeding in the court of common pleas as provided by law. The superintendent or referee may require the separation of witnesses and may bar from the proceedings any person whose presence is not essential to the proceedings.

(4) The superintendent of public instruction shall request the department of rehabilitation and correction, the sheriff, the department of youth services, or any publicly funded out-of-home care entity that has legal custody of a pupil who is the subject of an adjudication hearing held pursuant to this section to transport the pupil to the place of the adjudication hearing at the time and date set for the hearing. The department, sheriff, or publicly funded out-of-home care entity that receives the request shall provide transportation for the pupil who is the subject of the adjudication hearing to the place of the hearing at the time and date set for the hearing. The department, sheriff, or entity shall pay the cost of transporting the pupil to and from the hearing.

(E)(1) An adjudication hearing held pursuant to this section shall be adversary in nature, shall be conducted fairly and impartially, and may be conducted without the formalities of a criminal proceeding. A pupil whose permanent exclusion is being adjudicated has the right to be represented by counsel at the adjudication hearing. If the pupil has the financial capacity to retain counsel, the superintendent or the referee is not required to provide counsel for the pupil. At the adjudication hearing, the pupil also has the right to cross-examine witnesses against the pupil, to testify, to present evidence and the testimony of witnesses on the pupil's behalf, and to raise factors in mitigation of the pupil's being permanently excluded.

(2) In an adjudication hearing held pursuant to this section and section 3313.662 [3313.66.2] of the Revised Code, a representative of the school district of the board of education that adopted and forwarded the resolution requesting the permanent exclusion of the pupil shall present the case for permanent exclusion to the superintendent or the referee. The representative of the school district may be an attorney admitted to the practice of law in this state. At the adjudication hearing, the representative of the school district shall present evidence in support of the requested permanent exclusion. The superintendent or the superintendent's designee shall consider the entire school record of the pupil who is the subject of the adjudication and shall consider any of the following information that is available:

(a) The academic record of the pupil and a record of any extracurricular activities in which the pupil previously was involved;

(b) The disciplinary record of the pupil and any available records of the pupil's prior behavioral problems other than the behavioral problems contained in the disciplinary record;

(c) The social history of the pupil;

(d) The pupil's response to the imposition of prior discipline and sanctions imposed for behavioral problems;

(e) Evidence regarding the seriousness of and any aggravating factors related to the offense that is the basis of the resolution seeking permanent exclusion;

(f) Any mitigating circumstances surrounding the offense that gave rise to the request for permanent exclusion;

(g) Evidence regarding the probable danger posed to the health and safety of other pupils or of school employees by the continued presence of the pupil in a public school setting;

(h) Evidence regarding the probable disruption of the teaching of any school district's graded course of study by the continued presence of the pupil in a public school setting;

(i) Evidence regarding the availability of alternative sanctions of a less serious nature than permanent exclusion that would enable the pupil to remain in a public school setting without posing a significant danger to the health and safety of other pupils or of school employees and without posing a threat of the disruption of the teaching of any district's graded course of study.

(3) In any adjudication hearing conducted pursuant to this section and section 3313.662 [3313.66.2] of the Revised Code, a court order that proves the adjudication or conviction that is the basis for the resolution of the board of education seeking permanent exclusion is sufficient evidence to prove that the pupil committed a violation as specified in division (F)(1) of this section.

(4) The superintendent or the referee shall make or cause to be made a record of any adjudication hearing conducted pursuant to this section.

(5) A referee who conducts an adjudication hearing pursuant to this section shall promptly report the referee's findings in writing to the superintendent at the conclusion of the adjudication hearing.

(F) If an adjudication hearing is conducted or a determination is made pursuant to this section and section 3313.662 [3313.66.2] of the Revised Code, the superintendent shall review and consider the evidence presented, the entire school record of the pupil, and any available information described in divisions (E)(2)(a) to (i) of this section and shall not enter an order of permanent exclusion unless the superintendent or the superintendent's appointed referee finds, by a preponderance of the evidence, both of the following:

(1) That the pupil was convicted of or adjudicated a delinquent child for committing a violation listed in division (A) of section 3313.662 [3313.66.2] of the Revised Code and that the violation was committed when the child was sixteen years of age or older;

(2) That the pupil's continued attendance in the public school system may endanger the health and safety of other pupils or school employees.

(G)(1) Within seven days after the conclusion of an adjudication hearing that is conducted pursuant to this section, the superintendent of public instruction shall enter an order in relation to the permanent exclusion of the pupil who is the subject of the hearing or determination.

(2) If the superintendent or a referee makes the findings described in divisions (F)(1) and (2) of this section, the superintendent shall issue a written order that permanently excludes the pupil from attending any of the public schools of this state and immediately shall send a written notice of the order to the board of education that forwarded the resolution, to the pupil who was the subject of the resolution, to that pupil's parent, guardian, or custodian, and to that pupil's attorney, that includes all of the following:

(a) A copy of the order of permanent exclusion;

(b) A statement informing the pupil and the pupil's parent, guardian, or custodian of the pupil's right to appeal the order of permanent exclusion pursuant to division (H) of this section and of the possible revocation of the permanent exclusion pursuant to division (I) of this section if a final judicial determination reverses the conviction or adjudication that was the basis for the permanent exclusion;

(c) A statement informing the pupil and the pupil's parent, guardian, or custodian of the provisions of divisions (F), (G), and (H) of section 3313.662 [3313.66.2] of the Revised Code.

(3) If the superintendent or a referee does not make the findings described in divisions (F)(1) and (2) of this section, the superintendent shall issue a written order that rejects the resolution of the board of education and immediately shall send written notice of that fact to the board of education that forwarded the resolution, to the pupil who was the subject of the proposed resolution, and to that pupil's parent, guardian, or custodian.

(H) A pupil may appeal an order of permanent exclusion made by the superintendent of public instruction pursuant to this section and section 3313.662 [3313.66.2] of the Revised Code to the court of common pleas of the county in which the board of education that forwarded the resolution requesting the permanent exclusion is located. The appeal shall be conducted in accordance with Chapter 2505. of the Revised Code.

(I) If a final judicial determination reverses the conviction or adjudication that is the basis of a permanent exclusion ordered under this section, the superintendent of public instruction, upon receipt of a certified copy of an order reflecting that final determination from the pupil or that pupil's parent, guardian, custodian, or attorney, shall revoke the order of permanent exclusion.

(J) As used in this section:

(1) "Permanently exclude" and "permanent exclusion" have the same meanings as in section 3313.662 [3313.66.2] of the Revised Code.

(2) "Out-of-home care" and "legal custody" have the same meanings as in section 2151.011 [2151.01.1] of the Revised Code.

(3) "Certificate of high school equivalence" has the same meaning as in section 4109.06 of the Revised Code.

HISTORY: 144 v H 154 (Eff 7-31-92); 146 v H 1. Eff 1-1-96.

The effective date is set by section 6 of HB 1.

§ 3301.32 Criminal records check for head start employees responsible for children; employment of certain offenders prohibited.

(A)(1) The chief administrator of any head start agency shall request the superintendent of the bureau of criminal identification and investigation to conduct a criminal records check with respect to any applicant who has applied to the head start agency for employment as a person responsible for the care, custody, or control of a child. If the applicant does not present proof that the applicant has been a resident of this state for the five-year period immediately prior to the date upon which the criminal records check is requested or does not provide evidence that within that five-year period the superintendent has requested information about the applicant from the federal bureau of investigation in a criminal records check, the chief administrator shall request that the superintendent obtain information from the federal bureau of investigation as a part of the criminal records check for the applicant. If the applicant presents proof that the applicant has been a resident of this state for that five-year period, the chief administrator may request that the superintendent include information from the federal bureau of investigation in the criminal records check.

(2) Any person required by division (A)(1) of this section to request a criminal records check shall provide to each applicant a copy of the form prescribed pursuant to division (C)(1) of section 109.572 [109.57.2] of the Revised Code, provide to each applicant a standard impression sheet to obtain fingerprint impressions prescribed pursuant to division (C)(2) of section 109.572 [109.57.2] of the Revised Code, obtain the completed form and impression sheet from each applicant, and forward the completed form and impression sheet to the superintendent of the bureau of criminal identification and investigation at the time the chief administrator requests a criminal records check pursuant to division (A)(1) of this section.

(3) Any applicant who receives pursuant to division (A)(2) of this section a copy of the form prescribed pursuant to division (C)(1) of section 109.572 [109.57.2] of the Revised Code and a copy of an impression sheet prescribed pursuant to division (C)(2) of that section and who is requested to complete the form and provide a set of fingerprint impressions shall complete the form or provide all the information necessary to complete the form and shall provide the impression sheets with the impressions of the applicant's fingerprints. If an applicant, upon request, fails to provide the information necessary to complete the form or fails to provide impressions of the applicant's fingerprints, the head start agency shall not employ that applicant for any position for which a criminal records check is required by division (A)(1) of this section.

(B)(1) Except as provided in rules adopted by the department of human services in accordance with division (E) of this section, no head start agency shall employ a person as a person responsible for the care, custody, or control of a child if the person previously has been convicted of or pleaded guilty to any of the following:

(a) A violation of section 2903.01, 2903.02, 2903.03, 2903.04, 2903.11, 2903.12, 2903.13, 2903.16, 2903.21, 2903.34, 2905.01, 2905.02, 2905.05, 2907.02, 2907.03, 2907.04, 2907.05, 2907.06, 2907.07, 2907.08, 2907.09, 2907.21, 2907.22, 2907.23, 2907.25, 2907.31, 2907.32, 2907.321 [2907.32.1], 2907.322 [2907.32.2], 2907.323 [2907.32.3], 2911.01, 2911.02, 2911.11, 2911.12, 2919.12, 2919.22, 2919.24, 2919.25, 2923.12, 2923.13, 2923.161 [2923.16.1], 2925.02, 2925.03, 2925.04, 2925.05, 2925.06, or 3716.11 of the Revised Code, a violation of section 2905.04 of the Revised Code as it existed prior to July 1, 1996, a violation of section 2919.23 of the Revised Code that would have been a violation of section 2905.04 of the Revised Code as it existed prior to July 1, 1996, had the violation occurred prior to that date, a violation of section 2925.11 of the Revised Code that is not a minor drug possession offense, or felonious sexual penetration in violation of former section 2907.12 of the Revised Code;

(b) A violation of an existing or former law of this state, any other state, or the United States that is substantially equivalent to any of the offenses or violations described in division (B)(1)(a) of this section.

(2) A head-start agency may employ an applicant conditionally until the criminal records check required by this section is completed and the agency receives the results of the criminal records check. If the results of the criminal records check indicate that, pursuant to division (B)(1) of this section, the applicant does not qualify for employment, the agency shall release the applicant from employment.

(C)(1) Each head start agency shall pay to the bureau of criminal identification and investigation the fee prescribed pursuant to division (C)(3) of section 109.572 [109.57.2] of the Revised Code for each criminal records check conducted in accordance with that section upon the request pursuant to division (A)(1) of this section of the chief administrator of the head start agency.

(2) A head start agency may charge an applicant a fee for the costs it incurs in obtaining a criminal records check under this section. A fee charged under this division shall not exceed the amount of fees the agency pays under division (C)(1) of this section. If a fee is charged under this division, the agency shall notify the applicant at the time of the applicant's initial application for employment of the amount of the fee and that, unless the fee is paid, the head start agency will not consider the applicant for employment.

(D) The report of any criminal records check conducted by the bureau of criminal identification and investigation in accordance with section 109.572 [109.57.2] of the Revised Code and pursuant to a request made under division (A)(1) of this section is not a public record for the purposes of section 149.43 of the Revised Code and shall not be made available to any person other than the applicant who is the subject of the criminal records check or the applicant's representative, the head start agency requesting the criminal records check or its representative, and any court, hearing officer, or other necessary individual involved in a case dealing with the denial of employment to the applicant.

(E) The department of human services shall adopt rules pursuant to Chapter 119. of the Revised Code to implement this section, including rules specifying circumstances under which a head start agency may hire a person who has been convicted of an offense listed in division (B)(1) of this section but who meets standards in regard to rehabilitation set by the department.

(F) Any person required by division (A)(1) of this section to request a criminal records check shall inform each person, at the time of the person's initial application for employment, that the person is required to provide a set of impressions of the person's fingerprints and that a criminal records check is required to be conducted and satisfactorily completed in accordance with section 109.572 [109.57.2] of the Revised Code if the person comes under final consideration for appointment or employment as a precondition to employment for that position.

(G) As used in this section:

(1) "Applicant" means a person who is under final consideration for appointment or employment in a position with a head start agency as a person responsible for the care, custody, or control of a child.

(2) "Head start agency" has the same meaning as in section 3301.31 of the Revised Code.

(3) "Criminal records check" has the same meaning as in section 109.572 [109.57.2] of the Revised Code.

(4) "Minor drug possession offense" has the same meaning as in section 2925.01 of the Revised Code.

HISTORY: 145 v S 38 (Eff 10-29-93); 145 v H 694 (Eff 11-11-94); 146 v S 2 (Eff 7-1-96); 146 v S 269 (Eff 7-1-96); 146 v H 445. Eff 9-3-96.

Publisher's Note

The amendments made by SB 269 (146 v —) and HB 445 (146 v —) have been combined. Please see provisions of RC § 1.52.

[§ 3301.54.1] § 3301.541 Criminal records check for preschool employees responsible for children; employment of certain offenders prohibited.

(A)(1) The director, head teacher, or elementary principal of a preschool program shall request the superintendent of the bureau of criminal identification and investigation to conduct a criminal records check with respect to any applicant who has applied to the preschool program for employment as a person responsible for the care, custody, or control of a child. If the applicant does not present proof that the applicant has been a resident of this state for the five-year period immediately prior to the date upon which the criminal records check is requested or does not provide evidence that within that five-year period the superintendent has requested information about the applicant from the federal bureau of investigation in a criminal records check, the director, head teacher, or elementary principal shall request that the superintendent obtain information from the federal bureau of investigation as a part of the criminal records check for the applicant. If the applicant presents proof that the applicant has been a resident of this state for that five-year period, the director, head teacher, or elementary principal may request that the superintendent include information from the federal bureau of investigation in the criminal records check.

(2) Any director, head teacher, or elementary principal required by division (A)(1) of this section to request a criminal records check shall provide to each applicant a copy of the form prescribed pursuant to division (C)(1) of section 109.572 [109.57.2] of the Revised Code, provide to each applicant a standard impression sheet to obtain fingerprint impressions prescribed pursuant to division (C)(2) of section 109.572 [109.57.2] of the Revised Code, obtain the completed form and impression sheet from each applicant, and forward the completed form and impression sheet to the superintendent of the bureau of criminal identification and investigation at the time the person requests a criminal records check pursuant to division (A)(1) of this section.

(3) Any applicant who receives pursuant to division (A)(2) of this section a copy of the form prescribed pursuant to division (C)(1) of section 109.572 [109.57.2] of the Revised Code and a copy of an impression sheet prescribed pursuant to division (C)(2) of that section and who is requested to complete the form and provide a set of fingerprint impressions shall complete the form or provide all the information necessary to complete the form and provide the impression sheet with the impressions of the applicant's fingerprints. If an applicant, upon request, fails to provide the information necessary to complete the form or fails to provide impressions of the applicant's fingerprints, the preschool program shall not employ that applicant for any position for which a criminal records check is required by division (A)(1) of this section.

(B)(1) Except as provided in rules adopted by the department of education in accordance with division (E) of this section, no preschool program shall employ a person as a person responsible for the care, custody, or control of a child if the person previously has been convicted of or pleaded guilty to any of the following:

(a) A violation of section 2903.01, 2903.02, 2903.03, 2903.04, 2903.11, 2903.12, 2903.13, 2903.16, 2903.21, 2903.34, 2905.01, 2905.02, 2905.05, 2907.02, 2907.03, 2907.04, 2907.05, 2907.06, 2907.07, 2907.08, 2907.09, 2907.21, 2907.22, 2907.23, 2907.25, 2907.31, 2907.32,

2907.321 [2907.32.1], 2907.322 [2907.32.2], 2907.323 [2907.32.3], 2911.01, 2911.02, 2911.11, 2911.12, 2919.12, 2919.22, 2919.24, 2919.25, 2923.12, 2923.13, 2923.161 [2823.16.1], 2925.02, 2925.03, 2925.04, 2925.05, 2925.06, or 3716.11 of the Revised Code, a violation of section 2905.04 of the Revised Code as it existed prior to July 1, 1996, a violation of section 2919.23 of the Revised Code that would have been a violation of section 2905.04 of the Revised Code as it existed prior to July 1, 1996, had the violation occurred prior to that date, a violation of section 2925.11 of the Revised Code that is not a minor drug possession offense, or felonious sexual penetration in violation of former section 2907.12 of the Revised Code;

(b) A violation of an existing or former law of this state, any other state, or the United States that is substantially equivalent to any of the offenses or violations described in division (B)(1)(a) of this section.

(2) A preschool program may employ an applicant conditionally until the criminal records check required by this section is completed and the preschool program receives the results of the criminal records check. If the results of the criminal records check indicate that, pursuant to division (B)(1) of this section, the applicant does not qualify for employment, the preschool program shall release the applicant from employment.

(C)(1) Each preschool program shall pay to the bureau of criminal identification and investigation the fee prescribed pursuant to division (C)(3) of section 109.572 [109.57.2] of the Revised Code for each criminal records check conducted in accordance with that section upon the request pursuant to division (A)(1) of this section of the director, head teacher, or elementary principal of the preschool program.

(2) A preschool program may charge an applicant a fee for the costs it incurs in obtaining a criminal records check under this section. A fee charged under this division shall not exceed the amount of fees the preschool program pays under division (C)(1) of this section. If a fee is charged under this division, the preschool program shall notify the applicant at the time of the applicant's initial application for employment of the amount of the fee and that, unless the fee is paid, the applicant will not be considered for employment.

(D) The report of any criminal records check conducted by the bureau of criminal identification and investigation in accordance with section 109.572 [109.57.2] of the Revised Code and pursuant to a request under division (A)(1) of this section is not a public record for the purposes of section 149.43 of the Revised Code and shall not be made available to any person other than the applicant who is the subject of the criminal records check or the applicant's representative, the preschool program requesting the criminal records check or its representative, and any court, hearing officer, or other necessary individual in a case dealing with the denial of employment to the applicant.

(E) The department of education shall adopt rules pursuant to Chapter 119. of the Revised Code to implement this section, including rules specifying circumstances under which a preschool program may hire a person who has been convicted of an offense listed in division (B)(1) of this section but who meets standards in regard to rehabilitation set by the department.

(F) Any person required by division (A)(1) of this section to request a criminal records check shall inform each person, at the time of the person's initial application for employment, that the person is required to provide a set of impressions of the person's fingerprints and that a criminal records check is required to be conducted and satisfactorily completed in accordance with section 109.572 [109.57.2] of the Revised Code if the person comes under final consideration for appointment or employment as a precondition to employment for that position.

(G) As used in this section:

(1) "Applicant" means a person who is under final consideration for appointment or employment in a position with a preschool program as a person responsible for the care, custody, or control of a child, except that "applicant" does not include a person already employed by a board of education or chartered nonpublic school in a position of care, custody, or control of a child who is under consideration for a different position with such board or school.

(2) "Criminal records check" has the same meaning as in section 109.572 [109.57.2] of the Revised Code.

(3) "Minor drug possession offense" has the same meaning as in section 2925.01 of the Revised Code.

(H) If the board of education of a local school district adopts a resolution requesting the assistance of the educational service center in which the local district has territory in conducting criminal records checks of substitute teachers under this section, the appointing or hiring officer of such educational service center governing board shall serve for purposes of this section as the appointing or hiring officer of the local board in the case of hiring substitute teachers for employment in the local district.

HISTORY: 145 v S 38 (Eff 10-29-93); 145 v H 694 (Eff 11-11-94); 146 v H 117 (Eff 9-29-95); 146 v S 2 (Eff 7-1-96); 146 v S 269 (Eff 7-1-96); 146 v H 445. Eff 9-3-96.

Comment, Legislative Service Commission

Sections ° ° ° 3301.541 ° ° ° of the Revised Code are amended by this act [Am. Sub. H.B. 445] and also by Am. Sub. S.B. 269 of the 121st General Assembly. ° ° ° Comparison of these amendments in pursuance of section 1.52 of the Revised Code discloses that they are not irreconcilable so that they are required by that section to be harmonized to give effect to each amendment.

CHAPTER 3313: BOARDS OF EDUCATION

§ 3313.20 **Rules; locker searches; employee attendance at professional meetings.**

(A) The board of education of a school district or the governing board of an educational service center shall make any rules that are necessary for its government and the government of its employees, pupils of its schools, and all other persons entering upon its school grounds or premises. Rules regarding entry of persons other than students, staff, and faculty upon school grounds or premises shall be posted conspicuously at or near the entrance to the school grounds or premises, or near the perimeter of the school grounds or premises, if there are no formal entrances, and at the main entrance to each school building.

(B)(1) The board of education of each city, local, exempted village, or joint vocational school district may adopt a written policy that authorizes principals of public schools within the district or their designees to do one or both of the following:

(a) Search any pupil's locker and the contents of the locker that is searched if the principal reasonably suspects that the locker or its contents contains evidence of a pupil's violation of a criminal statute or of a school rule;

(b) Search any pupil's locker and the contents of any pupil's locker at any time if the board of education posts in a conspicuous place in each school building that has lockers available for use by pupils a notice that the lockers are the property of the board of education and that the lockers and the contents of all the lockers are subject to random search at any time without regard to whether there is a reasonable suspicion that any locker or its contents contains evidence of a violation of a criminal statute or a school rule.

(2) A board of education's adoption of or failure to adopt a written policy pursuant to division (B)(1) of this section does not prevent the principal of any school from searching at any time the locker of any pupil and the contents of any locker of any pupil in the school if an emergency situation exists or appears to exist that immediately threatens the health or safety of any person, or threatens to damage or destroy any property, under the control of the board of education and if a search of lockers and the contents of the lockers is reasonably necessary to avert that threat or apparent threat.

(C) Any employee may receive compensation and expenses for days on which he is excused, in accordance with the policy statement of the board, by the superintendent of such board or by a responsible administrative official designated by the superintendent for the purpose of attending professional meetings as defined by the board policy, and the board may provide and pay the salary of a substitute for such days. The expenses thus incurred by an employee shall be paid by the board from the appropriate fund of the school district or the educational service center governing board fund provided that statements of expenses are furnished in accordance with the policy statement of the board.

(D) Each city, local, and exempted village school district shall adopt a written policy governing the attendance of employees at professional meetings.

HISTORY: GC § 4834-5; 120 v 475 (519); 123 v 659; Bureau of Code Revision, 10-1-53; 125 v 903 (989); 127 v 552 (Eff 9-16-57); 131 v S 21 (Eff 9-1-65); 135 v S 436 (Eff 9-23-74); 140 v S 385 (Eff 4-10-85); 144 v H 154 (Eff 7-31-92); 145 v S 29 (Eff 9-1-94); 146 v H 117. Eff 9-29-95.

The effective date is set by section 197 of HB 117.

§ 3313.66 **Suspension, expulsion or permanent exclusion; removal from curricular or extracurricular activities.**

(A) Except as provided under division (B)(2) of this section, the superintendent of schools of a city, exempted village, or local school district, or the principal of a public school may suspend a pupil from school for not more than ten school days. If at the time a suspension is imposed there are fewer than ten school days remaining in the school year in which the incident that gives rise to the suspension takes place, the superintendent may apply any remaining part or all of the period of the suspension to the following school year. No pupil shall be suspended unless prior to the suspension such superintendent or principal does both of the following:

(1) Gives the pupil written notice of the intention to suspend him and the reasons for the intended suspension and, if the proposed suspension is based on a violation listed in division (A) of section 3313.662 [3313.66.2] of the Revised Code and if the pupil is sixteen years of age or older, includes in the notice a statement that the superintendent may seek to permanently exclude the pupil if he is convicted of or adjudicated a delinquent child for that violation;

(2) Provides the pupil an opportunity to appear at an informal hearing before the principal, assistant principal, superintendent, or superintendent's designee and challenge the reason for the intended suspension or otherwise to explain his actions.

(B)(1) Except as provided under division (B)(2) or (3) of this section, the superintendent of schools of a city, exempted village, or local school district may expel a pupil from school for a period not to exceed the greater of eighty school days or the number of school days remaining in the semester or term in which the incident that gives rise to the expulsion takes place, unless the expulsion is extended pursuant to division (F) of this section. If at the time an expulsion is imposed there are fewer than eighty school days remaining in the school year in which the incident that gives rise to the expulsion takes place, the superintendent may apply any remaining part or all of the period of the expulsion to the following school year.

(2) Unless a pupil is permanently excluded pursuant to section 3313.662 [3313.66.2] of the Revised Code, the superintendent of schools of a city, exempted village, or local school district shall expel a pupil from school for a period of one year for bringing a firearm to a school operated by the board of education of the district or on to any other property owned or controlled by the board, except that the superintendent may reduce this requirement on a case-by-case basis in accordance with the policy adopted by the board under section 3313.661 [3313.66.1] of the Revised Code. Any such expulsion shall extend, as necessary, into the school year following the school year in which the incident that gives rise to the expulsion takes place. As used in this division, "firearm" has the same meaning as provided pursuant to the "Gun-Free Schools Act of 1994," 108 Stat. 270, 20 U.S.C. 8001(a)(2).

(3) The board of education of a city, exempted village, or local school district may adopt a resolution authorizing the superintendent of schools to expel a pupil from school for a period not to exceed one year for bringing a knife to a school operated by the board or onto any other property owned or controlled by the board or for possessing a firearm or knife at a school or on any other property owned or controlled by the board which firearm or knife was initially brought onto school board property by another person. The resolution may authorize the superintendent to extend such an expulsion, as necessary, into the school year following the school year in which the incident that gives rise to the expulsion takes place.

(4) No pupil shall be expelled under division (B)(1), (2), or (3) of this section unless, prior to his expulsion, the superintendent does both of the following:

(a) Gives the pupil and his parent, guardian, or custodian written notice of the intention to expel the pupil;

(b) Provides the pupil and his parent, guardian, custodian, or representative an opportunity to appear in person before the superintendent or his designee to challenge the reasons for the intended expulsion or otherwise to explain the pupil's actions.

The notice required in this division shall include the reasons for the intended expulsion, notification of the opportunity of the pupil and his parent, guardian, custodian, or representative to appear before the superintendent or his designee to challenge the reasons for the intended expulsion or otherwise to explain the pupil's action, and notification of the time and place to appear. The time to appear shall not be earlier than three nor later than five school days after the notice is given, unless the superintendent grants an extension of time at the request of the pupil or his parent, guardian, custodian, or representative. If an extension is granted after giving the original notice, the superintendent shall notify the pupil and his parent, guardian, custodian, or representative of the new time and place to appear. If the proposed expulsion is based on a violation listed in division (A) of section 3313.662 [3313.66.2] of the Revised Code and if the pupil is sixteen years of age or older, the notice shall include a statement that the superintendent may seek to permanently exclude the pupil if he is convicted of or adjudicated a delinquent child for that violation.

(C) If a pupil's presence poses a continuing danger to persons or property or an ongoing threat of disrupting the academic process taking place either within a classroom or elsewhere on the school premises, the superintendent or a principal or assistant principal may remove a pupil from curricular or extracurricular activities or from the school premises, and a teacher may remove a pupil from curricular or extracurricular activities under his supervision, without the notice and hearing requirements of division (A) or (B) of this section. As soon as practicable after making such a removal, the teacher shall submit in writing to the principal the reasons for such removal.

If a pupil is removed under this division from a curricular or extracurricular activity or from the school premises, written notice of the hearing and of the reason for the removal shall be given to the pupil as soon as practicable prior to the hearing, which shall be held within three school days from the time the initial removal is ordered. The hearing shall be held in accordance with division (A) of this section unless it is probable that the pupil may be subject to expulsion, in which case a hearing in accordance with division (B) of this section shall be held, except that the hearing shall be held within three school days of the initial removal. The individual who ordered, caused, or requested the removal to be made shall be present at the hearing.

If the superintendent or the principal reinstates a pupil in a curricular or extracurricular activity under the teacher's supervision prior to the hearing following a removal under this division, the teacher, upon request, shall be given in writing the reasons for such reinstatement.

(D) The superintendent or principal, within one school day after the time of a pupil's expulsion or suspension, shall notify in writing the parent, guardian, or custodian of the pupil and the treasurer of the board of education of the expulsion or suspension. The notice shall include the reasons for the expulsion or suspension, notification of the right of the pupil or his parent, guardian, or custodian to appeal the expulsion or suspension to the board of education or to its designee, to be represented in all appeal proceedings, to be granted a hearing before the board or its designee in order to be heard against the suspension or expulsion, and to request that the hearing be held in executive session, notification that the expulsion may be subject to extension pursuant to division (F) of this section if the pupil is sixteen years of age or older, and notification that the superintendent may seek the pupil's permanent exclusion if the suspension or expulsion was based on a violation listed in division (A) of section 3313.662 [3313.66.2] of the Revised Code that was committed when the child was sixteen years of age or older and if the pupil is convicted of or adjudicated a delinquent child for that violation.

Any superintendent expelling a pupil under this section for more than twenty school days or for any period of time if the expulsion will extend into the following semester or school year shall, in the notice required under this division, provide the pupil and his parent, guardian, or custodian with information about services or programs offered by public and private agencies that work toward improving those aspects of the pupil's attitudes and behavior that contributed to the incident that gave rise to the pupil's expulsion. The information shall include the names, addresses, and phone numbers of the appropriate public and private agencies.

(E) A pupil or his parent, guardian, or custodian may appeal his expulsion or suspension by a superintendent or principal to the board of education or to its designee. The pupil or his parent, guardian, or custodian may be represented in all appeal proceedings and shall be granted a hearing before the board or its designee in order to be heard against the suspension or expulsion. At the request of the pupil or of his parent, guardian, custodian, or attorney, the board or its designee may hold the hearing in executive session but shall act upon the suspension or expulsion only at a public meeting. The board, by a majority vote of its full membership or by the action of its designee, may affirm the order of suspension or expulsion, reinstate the pupil, or otherwise reverse, vacate, or modify the order of suspension or expulsion.

The board or its designee shall make a verbatim record of hearings held under this division. The decisions of the board or its designee may be appealed under Chapter 2506. of the Revised Code.

This section shall not be construed to require notice and hearing in accordance with division (A), (B), or (C) of this section in the case of normal disciplinary procedures in which a pupil is removed from a curricular or extracurricular activity for a period of less than one school day and is not subject to suspension or expulsion.

(F)(1) If a pupil is expelled pursuant to division (B) of this section for committing any violation listed in division (A) of section 3313.662 [3313.66.2] of the Revised Code and he was sixteen years of age or older at the time he committed the violation, if a complaint is filed pursuant to section 2151.27 of the Revised Code alleging that the pupil is a delinquent child based upon the commission of the violation or the pupil is prosecuted as an adult for the commission of the violation, and if the resultant juvenile court or criminal proceeding is pending at the time that the expulsion terminates, the superintendent of schools that expelled the pupil may file a motion with the court in which the proceeding is pending requesting an order extending the expulsion for the lesser of an additional eighty days or the number of school days remaining in the school year. Upon the filing of the motion, the court immediately shall schedule a hearing and give written notice of the time, date, and location of the hearing to the superintendent and to the pupil and his parent, guardian, or custodian. At the hearing, the court shall determine whether there is reasonable cause to believe that the pupil committed the alleged violation that is the basis of the expulsion and, upon determining that reasonable cause to believe he committed the violation does exist, shall grant the requested extension.

(2) If a pupil has been convicted of or adjudicated a delinquent child for a violation listed in division (A) of section 3313.662 [3313.66.2] of the Revised Code for an act that was committed when the child was sixteen years of age or older, if the pupil has been expelled pursuant to division (B) of this section for that violation, and if the board of education of the school district of the school from which he was expelled has adopted a resolution seeking his permanent exclusion, the superintendent may file a motion with the court that convicted the pupil or adjudicated the pupil a delinquent child requesting an order to extend the expulsion until an adjudication order or other determination regarding permanent exclusion is issued by the superintendent of public instruction pursuant to section 3301.121 [3301.12.1] and division (D) of section 3313.662 [3313.66.2] of the Revised Code. Upon the filing of the motion, the court immediately shall schedule a hearing and give written notice of the time, date, and location of the hearing to the superintendent of the school district, the pupil, and his parent, guardian, or custodian. At the hearing, the court shall determine whether there is reasonable cause to believe the pupil's continued attendance in the public school system may endanger the health and safety of other pupils or school employees and, upon making that determination, shall grant the requested extension.

(G) The failure of the superintendent or the board of education to provide the information regarding the possibility of permanent exclusion in the notice required by divisions (A), (B), and (D) of this section is not jurisdictional, and the failure shall not affect the validity of any suspension or expulsion procedure that is conducted in accordance with this section or the validity of a permanent exclusion procedure that is conducted in accordance with sections 3301.121 [3301.12.1] and 3313.662 [3313.66.2] of the Revised Code.

(H) With regard to suspensions and expulsions pursuant to divisions (A) and (B) of this section by the board of education of any city, exempted village, or local school district, this section shall apply to any student, whether or not the student is enrolled in the district, attending or otherwise participating in any curricular program provided in a school operated by the board or provided on any other property owned or controlled by the board.

(I) Whenever a student is expelled under this section, the expulsion shall result in removal of the student from the student's regular school setting. However, during the period of the expulsion, the board of education of the school district that expelled the student or any board of education admitting the student during that expulsion period may provide educational services to the student in an alternative setting.

(J)(1) Notwithstanding section 3313.64 or 3313.65 of the Revised Code, any school district, after offering an opportunity for a hearing, may temporarily deny admittance to any pupil if the pupil has been expelled from the schools of another district under division (B) of this section and the period of the expulsion, as established under that division or as extended under division (F) of this section, has not expired. If a pupil is temporarily denied admission under this division, the pupil shall be admitted to school in accordance with section 3313.64 or 3313.65 of the Revised Code no later than upon expiration of such expulsion period.

(2) Notwithstanding section 3313.64 or 3313.65 of the Revised Code, any school district, after offering an opportunity for a hearing, may temporarily deny admittance to any pupil if the pupil has been expelled or otherwise removed for disciplinary purposes from a public school in another state and the period of expulsion or removal has not expired. If a pupil is temporarily denied admission under this division, the pupil shall be admitted to school in accordance with section 3313.64 or 3313.65 of the Revised Code no later than the earlier of the following:

(a) Upon expiration of the expulsion or removal period imposed by the out-of-state school;

(b) Upon expiration of a period established by the district, beginning with the date of expulsion or removal from the out-of-state school, that is no greater than the period of expulsion that the pupil would have received under the policy adopted by the district under section 3313.661 [3313.66.1] of the Revised Code had the offense that gave rise to the expulsion or removal by the out-of-state school been committed while the pupil was enrolled in the district.

(K) As used in this section, "permanently exclude" and "permanent exclusion" have the same meanings as in section 3313.662 [3313.66.2] of the Revised Code.

HISTORY: GC § 4838-4; 120 v 475(530); Bureau of Code Revision, 10-1-53; 127 v 104 (Eff 9-9-57); 129 v 239 (Eff 7-28-61); 136 v H 421 (Eff 6-4-76); 138 v H 1 (Eff 5-16-79); 141 v H 666 (Eff 3-25-87); 144 v S 51 (Eff 10-29-91); 144 v H 154 (Eff 7-31-92); 145 v H 152 (Eff 7-1-93); 146 v H 64 (Eff 9-14-95); 146 v H 81. Eff 6-5-96.

[§ 3313.66.1] § 3313.661 Policy regarding suspension, expulsion, removal and permanent exclusion; community service.

(A) The board of education of each city, exempted village, and local school district shall adopt a policy regarding suspension, expulsion, removal, and permanent exclusion that specifies the types of misconduct for which a pupil may be suspended, expelled, or removed. The policy shall specify the reasons for which the superintendent of the district may reduce the expulsion requirement in division (B)(2) of section 3313.66 of the Revised Code. If a board of education adopts a resolution pursuant to division (B)(3) of section 3313.66 of the Revised Code, the policy shall define the term "knife" or "firearm," as applicable, for purposes of expulsion under that resolution and shall specify any reasons for which the superintendent of the district may reduce any required expulsion period on a case-by-case basis. The policy also shall set forth the acts listed in section 3313.662 [3313.66.2] of the Revised Code for which a pupil may be permanently excluded.

A copy of the policy shall be posted in a central location in the school and made available to pupils upon request. No pupil shall be suspended, expelled, or removed except in accordance with the policy adopted by the board of education of the school district in which the pupil attends school, and no pupil shall be permanently excluded except in accordance with sections 3301.121 [3301.12.1] and 3313.662 [3313.66.2] of the Revised Code.

(B) A board of education may establish a program and adopt guidelines under which a superintendent may require a pupil to perform community service in conjunction with a suspension or expulsion imposed under section 3313.66 of the Revised Code or in place of a suspension or expulsion imposed under section 3313.66 of the Revised Code except for an expulsion imposed pursuant to division (B)(2) of that section. If a board adopts guidelines under this division, they shall permit, except with regard to an expulsion pursuant to division (B)(2) of section 3313.66 of the Revised Code, a superintendent to impose a community service requirement beyond the end of the school year in lieu of applying the suspension or expulsion into the following school year. Any guidelines adopted shall be included in the policy adopted under this section.

(C) The written policy of each board of education that is adopted pursuant to section 3313.20 of the Revised Code shall be posted in a central location in each school that is subject to the policy and shall be made available to pupils upon request.

(D) Any policy, program, or guideline adopted by a board of education under this section with regard to suspensions or expulsions pursuant to divisions (A) or (B) of section 3313.66 of the Revised Code shall apply to any student, whether or not the student is enrolled in the district, attending or otherwise participating in any curricular program provided in a school operated by the board or provided on any other property owned or controlled by the board.

(E) As used in this section, "permanently exclude" and "permanent exclusion" have the same meanings as in section 3313.662 [3313.66.2] of the Revised Code.

HISTORY: 136 v H 421 (Eff 6-4-76); 144 v S 51 (Eff 10-29-91); 144 v H 154 (Eff 7-31-92); 145 v H 152 (Eff 7-1-93); 146 v H 64 (Eff 9-14-95); 146 v H 81. Eff 6-5-96.

[§ 3313.66.2] § 3313.662 Adjudication order permanently excluding pupil from public schools; board of education resolution requesting permanent exclusion; revocation; probationary admission.

(A) The superintendent of public instruction, pursuant to this section and the adjudication procedures of section 3301.121 [3301.12.1] of the Revised Code, may issue an adjudication order that permanently excludes a pupil from attending any of the public schools of this state if the pupil is convicted of, or adjudicated a delinquent child for, committing, when the pupil was sixteen years of age or older, an act that would be a criminal offense if committed by an adult and if the act is any of the following:

(1) A violation of section 2923.122 [2923.12.2] of the Revised Code;

(2) A violation of section 2923.12 of the Revised Code, of a substantially similar municipal ordinance, or of section 2925.03 of the Revised Code that was committed on property owned or controlled by, or at an activity held under the auspices of, a board of education of a city, local, exempted village, or joint vocational school district;

(3) A violation of section 2925.11 of the Revised Code, other than a violation of that section that would be a minor drug possession offense, that was committed on property owned or controlled by, or at an activity held under the auspices of, the board of education of a city, local, exempted village, or joint vocational school district;

(4) A violation of section 2903.01, 2903.02, 2903.03, 2903.04, 2903.11, 2903.12, 2907.02, or 2907.05 or of former section 2907.12 of the Revised Code that was committed on property owned or controlled by, or at an activity held under the auspices of, a board of education of a city, local, exempted village, or joint vocational school district, if the victim at the time of the commission of the act was an employee of that board of education.

(5) Complicity in any violation described in division (A)(1), (2), (3), or (4) of this section that was alleged to have been committed in the manner described in division (A)(1), (2), (3), or (4) of this section, regardless of whether the act of complicity was committed on property owned or controlled by, or at an activity held under the auspices of, a board of education of a city, local, exempted village, or joint vocational school district.

(B) A pupil may be suspended or expelled in accordance with section 3313.66 of the Revised Code prior to being permanently excluded from public school attendance under this section and section 3301.121 [3301.12.1] of the Revised Code.

(C)(1) If the superintendent of a city, local, exempted village, or joint vocational school district in which a pupil attends school obtains or receives proof that the pupil has been convicted of committing when the pupil was sixteen years of age or older a violation listed in division (A) of this section or adjudicated a delinquent child for the commission when the pupil was sixteen years of age or older of a violation listed in division (A) of this section, the superintendent may issue to the board of education of the school district a request that the pupil be permanently excluded from public school attendance, if both of the following apply:

(a) After obtaining or receiving proof of the conviction or adjudication, the superintendent or the superintendent's designee determines that the pupil's continued attendance in school may endanger the health and safety of other pupils or school employees and gives the pupil and the pupil's parent, guardian, or custodian written notice that the superintendent intends to recommend to the board of education that the board adopt a resolution requesting the superintendent of public instruction to permanently exclude the pupil from public school attendance.

(b) The superintendent or the superintendent's designee forwards to the board of education the superintendent's written recommendation that includes the determinations the superintendent or designee made pursuant to division (C)(1)(a) of this section and a copy of the proof the superintendent received showing that the pupil has been convicted of or adjudicated a delinquent child for a violation listed in division (A) of this section that was committed when the pupil was sixteen years of age or older.

(2) Within fourteen days after receipt of a recommendation from the superintendent pursuant to division (C)(1)(b) of this section that a pupil be permanently excluded from public school attendance, the board of education of a city, local, exempted village, or joint vocational school district, after review and consideration of all of the following available information, may adopt a resolution requesting the superintendent of public instruction to permanently exclude the pupil who is the subject of the recommendation from public school attendance:

(a) The academic record of the pupil and a record of any extracurricular activities in which the pupil previously was involved;

(b) The disciplinary record of the pupil and any available records of the pupil's prior behavioral problems other than the behavioral problems contained in the disciplinary record;

(c) The social history of the pupil;

(d) The pupil's response to the imposition of prior discipline and sanctions imposed for behavioral problems;

(e) Evidence regarding the seriousness of and any aggravating factors related to the offense that is the basis of the resolution seeking permanent exclusion;

(f) Any mitigating circumstances surrounding the offense that gave rise to the request for permanent exclusion;

(g) Evidence regarding the probable danger posed

to the health and safety of other pupils or of school employees by the continued presence of the pupil in a public school setting;

(h) Evidence regarding the probable disruption of the teaching of any school district's graded course of study by the continued presence of the pupil in a public school setting;

(i) Evidence regarding the availability of alternative sanctions of a less serious nature than permanent exclusion that would enable the pupil to remain in a public school setting without posing a significant danger to the health and safety of other pupils or of school employees and without posing a threat of the disruption of the teaching of any district's graded course of study.

(3) If the board does not adopt a resolution requesting the superintendent of public instruction to permanently exclude the pupil, it immediately shall send written notice of that fact to the superintendent who sought the resolution, to the pupil who was the subject of the proposed resolution, and to that pupil's parent, guardian, or custodian.

(D)(1) Upon adoption of a resolution under division (C) of this section, the board of education immediately shall forward to the superintendent of public instruction the written resolution, proof of the conviction or adjudication that is the basis of the resolution, a copy of the pupil's entire school record, and any other relevant information and shall forward a copy of the resolution to the pupil who is the subject of the recommendation and to that pupil's parent, guardian, or custodian.

(2) The board of education that adopted and forwarded the resolution requesting the permanent exclusion of the pupil to the superintendent of public instruction promptly shall designate a representative of the school district to present the case for permanent exclusion to the superintendent or the referee appointed by the superintendent. The representative of the school district may be an attorney admitted to the practice of law in this state. At the adjudication hearing held pursuant to section 3301.121 [3301.12.1] of the Revised Code, the representative of the school district shall present evidence in support of the requested permanent exclusion.

(3) Upon receipt of a board of education's resolution requesting the permanent exclusion of a pupil from public school attendance, the superintendent of public instruction, in accordance with the adjudication procedures of section 3301.121 [3301.12.1] of the Revised Code, promptly shall issue an adjudication order that either permanently excludes the pupil from attending any of the public schools of this state or that rejects the resolution of the board of education.

(E) Notwithstanding any provision of section 3313.64 of the Revised Code or an order of any court of this state that otherwise requires the admission of the pupil to a school, no school official in a city, local, exempted village, or joint vocational school district knowingly shall admit to any school in the school district a pupil who has been permanently excluded from public school attendance by the superintendent of public instruction.

(F)(1)(a) Upon determining that the school attendance of a pupil who has been permanently excluded from public school attendance no longer will endanger the health and safety of other students or school employees, the superintendent of any city, local, exempted village, or joint vocational school district in which the pupil desires to attend school may issue to the board of education of the school district a recommendation, including the reasons for the recommendation, that the permanent exclusion of a pupil be revoked and the pupil be allowed to return to the public schools of the state.

If any violation which in whole or in part gave rise to the permanent exclusion of any pupil involved the pupil's bringing a firearm to a school operated by the board of education of a school district or on to any other property owned or operated by such a board, no superintendent shall recommend under this division an effective date for the revocation of the pupil's permanent exclusion that is less than one year after the date on which the last such firearm incident occurred. However, on a case-by-case basis, a superintendent may recommend an earlier effective date for such a revocation for any of the reasons for which he may reduce the one-year expulsion requirement in division (B)(2) of section 3313.66 of the Revised Code.

(b) Upon receipt of the recommendation of the superintendent that a permanent exclusion of a pupil be revoked, the board of education of a city, local, exempted village, or joint vocational school district may adopt a resolution by a majority vote of its members requesting the superintendent of public instruction to revoke the permanent exclusion of the pupil. Upon adoption of the resolution, the board of education shall forward a copy of the resolution, the reasons for the resolution, and any other relevant information to the superintendent of public instruction.

(c) Upon receipt of a resolution of a board of education requesting the revocation of a permanent exclusion of a pupil, the superintendent of public instruction, in accordance with the adjudication procedures of Chapter 119. of the Revised Code, shall issue an adjudication order that revokes the permanent exclusion of the pupil from public school attendance or that rejects the resolution of the board of education.

(2)(a) A pupil who has been permanently excluded pursuant to this section and section 3301.121 [3301.12.1] of the Revised Code may request the superintendent of any city, local, exempted village, or joint vocational school district in which the pupil desires to attend school to admit the pupil on a probationary basis for a period not to exceed ninety school days. Upon receiving the request, the superintendent may enter into discussions with the pupil and with the pupil's parent, guardian, or custodian or a person designated by the pupil's parent, guardian, or custodian to develop a probationary admission plan designed to assist the pupil's probationary admission to the school. The plan may include a treatment program, a behavioral modification program, or any other program reasonably designed to meet the educational needs of the child and the disciplinary requirements of the school.

If any violation which in whole or in part gave rise to the permanent exclusion of the pupil involved the pupil's bringing a firearm to a school operated by the board of education of any school district or on to any other property owned or operated by such a board, no plan developed under this division for the pupil shall include an effective date for the probationary admission of the pupil that is less than one year after the date on which the last such firearm incident occurred except that on a case-by-case basis, a plan may include an earlier effective date for such an admission for any of the reasons for which the superintendent of the district may reduce the one-year expulsion requirement in division (B)(2) of section 3313.66 of the Revised Code.

(b) If the superintendent of a school district, a pupil, and the pupil's parent, guardian, or custodian or a person designated by the pupil's parent, guardian, or custodian agree upon a probationary admission plan prepared pursuant to division (F)(2)(a) of this section, the superintendent of the school district shall issue to the board of education of the school district a recommendation that the pupil be allowed to attend school within the school district under probationary admission, the reasons for the recommendation, and a copy of the agreed upon probationary admission plan. Within fourteen days after the board of education receives the recommendation, reasons, and plan, the board may adopt the recommendation by a majority vote of its members. If the board adopts the recommendation, the pupil may attend school under probationary admission within that school district for a period not to exceed ninety days or any additional probationary period permitted under divisions (F)(2)(d) and (e) of this section in accordance with the probationary admission plan prepared pursuant to division (F)(2)(a) of this section.

(c) If a pupil who is permitted to attend school under probationary admission pursuant to division (F)(2)(b) of this section fails to comply with the probationary admission plan prepared pursuant to division (F)(2)(a) of this section, the superintendent of the school district immediately may remove the pupil from the school and issue to the board of education of the school district a recommendation that the probationary admission be revoked. Within five days after the board of education receives the recommendation, the board may adopt the recommendation to revoke the pupil's probationary admission by a majority vote of its members. If a majority of the board does not adopt the recommendation to revoke the pupil's probationary admission, the pupil shall continue to attend school in compliance with the pupil's probationary admission plan.

(d) If a pupil who is permitted to attend school under probationary admission pursuant to division (F)(2)(b) of this section complies with the probationary admission plan prepared pursuant to division (F)(2)(a) of this section, the pupil or the pupil's parent, guardian, or custodian, at any time before the expiration of the ninety-day probationary admission period, may request the superintendent of the school district to extend the terms and period of the pupil's probationary admission for a period not to exceed ninety days or to issue a recommendation pursuant to division (F)(1) of this section that the pupil's permanent exclusion be revoked and the pupil be allowed to return to the public schools of this state.

(e) If a pupil is granted an extension of the pupil's probationary admission pursuant to division (F)(2)(d) of this section, the pupil or the pupil's parent, guardian, or custodian, in the manner described in that division, may request, and the superintendent and board, in the manner described in that division, may recommend and grant, subsequent probationary admission periods not to exceed ninety days each. If a pupil who is permitted to attend school under an extension of a probationary admission plan complies with the probationary admission plan prepared pursuant to the extension, the pupil or the pupil's parent, guardian, or custodian may request a revocation of the pupil's permanent exclusion in the manner described in division (F)(2)(d) of this section.

(f) Any extension of a probationary admission requested by a pupil or a pupil's parent, guardian, or custodian pursuant to divisions (F)(2)(d) or (e) of this section shall be subject to the adoption and approval of a probationary admission plan in the manner described in divisions (F)(2)(a) and (b) of this section and may be terminated as provided in division (F)(2)(c) of this section.

(g) If the pupil has complied with any probationary admission plan and the superintendent issues a recommendation that seeks revocation of the pupil's permanent exclusion pursuant to division (F)(1) of this section, the pupil's compliance with any probationary admission plan may be considered along with other relevant factors in any determination or adjudication conducted pursuant to division (F)(1) of this section.

(G)(1) Except as provided in division (G)(2) of this section, any information regarding the permanent exclusion of a pupil shall be included in the pupil's official records and shall be included in any records sent to any school district that requests the pupil's records.

(2) When a pupil who has been permanently excluded from public school attendance reaches the age of twenty-two or when the permanent exclusion of a pupil has been revoked, all school districts that maintain records regarding the pupil's permanent exclusion shall remove all references to the exclusion from the pupil's file and shall destroy them.

A pupil who has reached the age of twenty-two or whose permanent exclusion has been revoked may send a written notice to the superintendent of any school district maintaining records of the pupil's permanent exclusion requesting the superintendent to ensure that the records are removed from the pupil's file and destroyed. Upon receipt of the request and a determination that the pupil is twenty-two years of age or older or that the pupil's permanent exclusion has been revoked, the superintendent shall ensure that the records are removed from the pupil's file and destroyed.

(H)(1) This section does not apply to any of the following:

(a) An institution that is a residential facility, that receives and cares for children, that is maintained by the department of youth services, and that operates a school chartered by the state board of education under section 3301.16 of the Revised Code;

(b) Any on-premises school operated by an out-of-home care entity that is chartered by the state board of education under section 3301.16 of the Revised Code;

(c) Any school operated in connection with an out-of-home care entity or a nonresidential youth treatment program that enters into a contract or agreement with a school district for the provision of educational services in a setting other than a setting that is a building or structure owned or controlled by the board of education of the school district during normal school hours.

(2) This section does not prohibit any person who has been permanently excluded pursuant to this section and section 3301.121 [3301.12.1] of the Revised Code from seeking a certificate of high school equivalence. A person who has been permanently excluded may be permitted to participate in a course of study in preparation for the tests of general educational development, except that the person shall not participate during normal school hours in that course of study in any building or structure owned or controlled by the board of education of a school district.

(3) This section does not relieve any school district from any requirement under section 2151.357 [2151.35.7] or 3313.64 of the Revised Code to pay for the cost of educating any child who has been permanently excluded pursuant to this section and section 3301.121 [3301.12.1] of the Revised Code.

(I) As used in this section:

(1) "Permanently exclude" means to forever prohibit an individual from attending any public school in this state that is operated by a city, local, exempted village, or joint vocational school district.

(2) "Permanent exclusion" means the prohibition of a pupil forever from attending any public school in this state that is operated by a city, local, exempted village, or joint vocational school district.

(3) "Out-of-home care" has the same meaning as in section 2151.011 [2151.01.1] of the Revised Code.

(4) "Certificate of high school equivalence" has the same meaning as in section 4109.06 of the Revised Code.

(5) "Nonresidential youth treatment program" means a program designed to provide services to persons under the age of eighteen in a setting that does not regularly provide long-term overnight care, including settlement houses, diversion and prevention programs, run-away centers, and alternative education programs.

(6) "Firearm" has the same meaning as provided pursuant to the "Gun-Free Schools Act of 1994," 108 Stat. 270, 20 U.S.C. 8001(a)(2).

(7) "Minor drug possession offense" has the same meaning as in section 2925.01 of the Revised Code.

HISTORY: 144 v H 154 (Eff 7-31-92); 146 v H 64 (Eff 9-14-95); 146 v S 2 (Eff 7-1-96); 146 v H 445. Eff 9-3-96.

[§ 3313.75.2] § 3313.752 Posting of warning concerning anabolic steroids.

As used in this section, "anabolic steroid" has the same meaning as in section 3719.41 of the Revised Code.

The board of education of each city, local, exempted village, and joint vocational school district shall require the following warning to be conspicuously posted in the locker rooms of each of the district's school buildings that includes any grade higher than sixth grade:

"Warning: Improper use of anabolic steroids may cause serious or fatal health problems, such as heart disease, stroke, cancer, growth deformities, infertility, personality changes, severe acne, and baldness. Possession, sale, or use of anabolic steroids without a valid prescription is a crime punishable by a fine and imprisonment."

HISTORY: 144 v H 62. Eff 5-21-91.

CHAPTER 3319: SCHOOLS—SUPERINTENDENT; TEACHERS; EMPLOYEES

§ 3319.20 Prosecutor to notify board of nonlicensed employee's guilty plea or conviction of certain offenses.

Whenever an employee of a board of education, other than an employee who is a license holder to whom section 3319.52 of the Revised Code applies, is convicted of or pleads guilty to a felony, a violation of section 2907.04 or 2907.06 or of division (A) or (C) of section 2907.07 of the Revised Code, an offense of violence, theft offense, or drug abuse offense that is not a minor misdemeanor, or a violation of an ordinance of a municipal corporation that is substantively comparable to a felony or to a violation or offense of that nature, the prosecutor in the case, on forms prescribed and furnished by the state board of education, shall notify the employing board of education of the employee's name and residence address, the fact that the employee was convicted of or pleaded guilty to the specified offense, the section of the Revised Code or the municipal ordinance violated, and the sentence imposed by the court.

The prosecutor shall give the notification required by this section no earlier than the fifth day following the expiration of the period within which the employee may file a notice of appeal from the judgment of the trial court under Appellate Rule 4(B) and no later than the eighth day following the expiration of that period. The notification also shall indicate whether the employee appealed the conviction, and, if applicable, the court in which the appeal will be heard. If the employee is permitted, by leave of court pursuant to Appellate Rule 5, to appeal the judgment of the trial court subsequent to the expiration of the period for filing a notice of appeal under Appellate Rule 4(B), the prosecutor promptly shall notify the employing board of education of the appeal and the court in which the appeal will be heard.

As used in this section, "theft offense" has the same meaning as in section 2913.01 of the Revised Code, "drug abuse offense" has the same meaning as in section 2925.01 of the Revised Code, and "prosecutor" has the same meaning as in section 2935.01 of the Revised Code.

HISTORY: 140 v H 109 (Eff 9-27-83); 145 v H 152 (Eff 7-1-93); 146 v S 2 (Eff 7-1-96); 146 v S 230. Eff 10-29-96.

Not analogous to former RC § 3319.20 (GC § 4857; 120 v 475(587); Bureau of Code Revision, 10-1-53), repealed 126 v 655 (697), § 2, eff 1-3-56.

CHAPTER 3321: SCHOOL ATTENDANCE

[FAILURE TO SEND CHILD TO SCHOOL]

§ 3321.38 Failure to send child to school.

(A) No parent, guardian, or other person having care of a child of compulsory school age shall violate section 3321.01, 3321.03, 3321.04, 3321.07, or 3321.10, division (A) or (B) of section 3321.19, or section 3321.20 or 3331.14 of the Revised Code. The court may require a person convicted of violating this division to give bond in the sum of one hundred dollars with sureties to the approval of the court, conditioned that the person will cause the child under the person's charge to attend upon instruction as provided by law, and remain as a pupil in the school or class during the term prescribed by law.

(B) This section does not relieve from prosecution and conviction any parent, guardian, or other person upon further violation of such sections; nor shall forfeiture of the bond relieve such person from prosecution and conviction upon further violation of such sections.

Section 4109.13 of the Revised Code applies to this section.

HISTORY: RS §§ 4022-1, 4022-2; 86 v 333, 334; 87 v 143; 87 v 316; 89 v 389; 90 v 285; 95 v 615; 97 v 365; GC §§ 12974, 12975; Bureau of Code Revision, 10-1-53; 126 v 655(684) (Eff 1-3-56); 129 v 582(781) (Eff 1-10-61); 137 v H 883 (Eff 1-12-79); 143 v S 140 (Eff 10-2-89); 146 v S 2. Eff 7-1-96.

The effective date is set by section 6 of SB 2.

§ 3321.99 Penalty.

Whoever violates division (A) of section 3321.38 of the Revised Code shall be fined not less than five nor more than twenty dollars.

HISTORY: Bureau of Code Revision, 10-1-53; 132 v S 191 (Eff 11-14-67); 146 v S 2. Eff 7-1-96.

The effective date is set by section 6 of SB 2.

CHAPTER 3345: STATE UNIVERSITIES—GENERAL POWERS

§ 3345.41 Posting of warning concerning anabolic steroids.

(A) As used in this section:

(1) "Anabolic steroid" has the same meaning as in section 3719.41 of the Revised Code.

(2) "State university or college" has the same meaning as in section 3345.32 of the Revised Code.

(B) The board of trustees of each state university or college shall require the following warning to be conspicuously posted in locker rooms of recreational and athletic facilities operated by the state university or college for use by students:

"Warning: Improper use of anabolic steroids may cause serious or fatal health problems, such as heart disease, stroke, cancer, growth deformities, infertility, personality changes, severe acne, and baldness. Possession, sale, or use of anabolic steroids without a valid prescription is a crime punishable by a fine and imprisonment."

HISTORY: 144 v H 62. Eff 5-21-91.

TITLE 35: ELECTIONS

CHAPTER 3599: OFFENSES AND PENALTIES

§ 3599.01 Bribery.

(A) No person shall before, during, or after any primary, convention, or election:

(1) Give, lend, offer, or procure or promise to give, lend, offer, or procure any money, office, position, place or employment, influence, or any other valuable consideration to or for a delegate, elector, or other person;

(2) Attempt by intimidation, coercion, or other unlawful means to induce such delegate or elector to register or refrain from registering or to vote or refrain from voting at a primary, convention, or election for a particular person, question, or issue;

(3) Advance, pay, or cause to be paid or procure or offer to procure money or other valuable thing to or for the use of another, with the intent that it or part thereof shall be used to induce such person to vote or to refrain from voting.

(B) Whoever violates this section is guilty of bribery, a felony of the fourth degree; and if he is a candidate he shall forfeit the nomination he received, or if elected to any office he shall forfeit the office to which he was elected at the election with reference to which such offense was committed.

HISTORY: GC § 4785-190; 113 v 307(399), § 190; Bureau of Code Revision, 10-1-53; 126 v 575 (Eff 10-6-55); 139 v S 199. Eff 1-1-83.

The effective date of SB 199 is set by section 11 of the act.

§ 3599.02 Sale of vote by voter.

No person shall before, during, or after any primary, convention, or election solicit, request, demand, receive, or contract for any money, gift, loan, property, influence, position, employment, or other thing of value for himself or another:

(A) For registering or refraining from registering;

(B) For agreeing to register or to refrain from registering;

(C) For agreeing to vote or refraining from voting;

(D) For voting or refraining from voting at any primary, convention, or election for a particular person, question, or issue;

(E) For registering or voting, or refraining from registering or voting, or voting or refraining from voting for a particular person, question, or issue.

Whoever violates this section is guilty of bribery, and shall be fined not less than one hundred nor more than five hundred dollars or imprisoned not more than one year, or both, and shall be excluded from the right of suffrage and holding any public office for five years next succeeding such conviction.

HISTORY: GC § 4785-191; 113 v 307(399), § 191; Bureau of Code Revision. Eff 10-1-53.

§ 3599.03 Limitations on use of corporate or union funds or property for political purposes.

(A) Except to carry on activities specified in sections 3517.082 [3517.08.2] and 3599.031 [3599.03.1] of the Revised Code and except as provided in divisions (D), (E), and (F) of this section, no corporation, no nonprofit corporation, and no labor organization, directly or indirectly, shall pay or use, or offer, advise, consent, or agree to pay or use, the corporation's money or property, or the labor organization's money, including dues, initiation fees, or other assessments paid by members, or property, for or in aid of or opposition to a political party, a candidate for election or nomination to public office, a political action committee, a legislative campaign fund, or any organization that supports or opposes any such candidate, or for any partisan political purpose, shall violate any law requiring the filing of an affidavit or statement respecting such use of those funds, or shall pay or use the corporation's or labor organization's money for the expenses of a social fund-raising event for its political action committee if an employee's or labor organization member's right to attend such an event is predicated on the employee's or member's contribution to the corporation's or labor organization's political action committee.

Whoever violates division (A) of this section shall be fined not less than five hundred nor more than five thousand dollars.

(B) No officer, stockholder, attorney, or agent of a corporation or nonprofit corporation, no member, including an officer, attorney, or agent, of a labor organization, and no candidate, political party official, or other individual shall knowingly aid, advise, solicit, or receive money or other property in violation of division (A) of this section.

Whoever violates division (B) of this section shall be fined not more than one thousand dollars, or imprisoned not more than one year, or both.

(C) A corporation, a nonprofit corporation, or a labor organization may use its funds or property for or in aid of or opposition to a proposed or certified ballot issue. Such use of funds or property shall be reported on a form prescribed by the secretary of state. Reports of contributions in connection with statewide ballot issues shall be filed with the secretary of state. Reports of contributions in connection with local issues shall be filed with the board of elections of the most populous county of the district in which the issue is submitted or to be submitted to the electors. Reports made pursuant to this division shall be filed by the times specified in divisions (A)(1) and (2) of section 3517.10 of the Revised Code.

(D) Any gift made pursuant to section 3517.101 [3517.10.1] of the Revised Code does not constitute a violation of this section or of any other section of the Revised Code.

(E) Any compensation or fees paid by a financial institution to a state political party for services rendered pursuant to division (B) of section 3517.19 of the Revised Code do not constitute a violation of this section or of any other section of the Revised Code.

(F) The use by a nonprofit corporation of its money or property for communicating information for a purpose specified in division (A) of this section is not a violation of that division if the stockholders, members, donors, trustees, or officers of the nonprofit corporation are the predominant recipients of the communication.

(G) In addition to the laws listed in division (A) of section 4117.10 of the Revised Code that prevail over conflicting agreements between employee organizations and public employers, this section prevails over any conflicting provisions of agreements between labor organizations and public employers entered into pursuant to Chapter 4117. of the Revised Code.

(H) As used in this section, "labor organization" has the same meaning as in section 3517.01 of the Revised Code.

HISTORY: GC § 4785-192; 113 v 307(400), § 192; Bureau of Code Revision, 10-1-53; 138 v H 1062 (Eff 3-23-81); 142 v H 354 (Eff 9-22-87); 143 v S 6 (Eff 10-30-89); 146 v S 8. Eff 8-23-95.

[§ 3599.03.1] § 3599.031 Payroll deduction of political contributions.

(A) Notwithstanding any section of the Revised Code and subject to divisions (C) and (H) of this section, any employer may deduct from the wages and salaries of its employees amounts for an account described in division (C) of this section, a separate segregated fund, a political action committee of the employer, a political action committee of a labor organization of the employer's employees, a political action committee of an association of which the employer is a member, a political party, or a ballot issue that the employee by written authorization may designate and shall transmit any amounts so deducted as a separate written authorization described in division (C) of this section shall direct. Any authorization authorizing a deduction from an employee's wages or salary may be on a form that is used to apply for or authorize membership in or authorize payment of dues or fees to any organization, but the authorization for a deduction shall be stated and signed separately from the application for membership or the authorization for the payment of dues or fees. The employer either may deduct from the amount to be so transmitted a uniform amount determined by the employer to be necessary to defray the actual cost of making such deduction and transmittal, or may utilize its own funds in an amount it determines is necessary to defray the actual administrative cost, including making the deduction and transmittal.

(B) Any person who solicits an employee to authorize a deduction from his wages or salary pursuant to division (A) of this section shall inform the employee at the time of the solicitation that he may refuse to authorize a deduction, and that he may at any time revoke his authorization, without suffering any reprisal.

(C) If an employer establishes a separate account in the name of an employee for the purpose of depositing into the account amounts deducted from the wages and salary of the employee pursuant to division (A) of this section or amounts directly given by the employee to the employer for the support of a candidate, a separate segregated fund, a political action committee of the employer, a political action committee of a labor organization of the employer's employees, a political action committee of an association of which the employer is a member, a political party, a legislative campaign fund, or a ballot issue, the employee shall sign a written authorization designating the recipient of a disbursement from that account. The written authorization required under this division is separate and distinct from a written authorization required under division (A) of this section. The authorization required under this division shall clearly identify and designate the candidate, separate segregated fund, political action committee of the employer, political action committee of a labor organization of the employer's employees, political action committee of an association of which the employer is a member, political party, a legislative campaign fund, or ballot issue that is to receive any disbursement from the account established pursuant to this division. No person shall designate the recipient of a disbursement from the account except the employee from whose account the disbursement is made. No employer shall make a disbursement from the account of an employee established under this division unless the employer has received the written authorization required under this division.

(D) An employer shall furnish the recipient of any amount transmitted pursuant to this section with the employer's full name and the full name of the labor organization of which the employee whose amount is being transmitted is a member, if any. An employer shall keep and maintain the authorization forms of all its employees from whose wages and salaries any amounts were deducted pursuant to division (A) of this section and the authorizations of disbursements from accounts established under division (C) of this section for a period of at least six years after the year in which the deductions and disbursements were made.

(E) An employee who has made an authorization pursuant to division (A) or (C) of this section may revoke that authorization at any time. A revocation of the authorization does not affect any deduction already made from an employee's wages and salary or any amounts already transmitted or disbursed under this section.

(F) For purposes of this section and for the purpose of the information required to be filed under division

(B)(4)(b)(iii) of section 3517.10 of the Revised Code:

(1) If an employer is a corporation, each subsidiary of a parent corporation shall be considered an entity separate and distinct from any other subsidiary and separate and distinct from the parent corporation.

(2) Each national, regional, state, and local affiliate of a labor organization shall be considered a distinct entity.

(G) Whoever violates division (C) of this section shall be fined not less than fifty nor more than five hundred dollars for each disbursement made in violation of that division.

(H) No public employer shall deduct from the wages and salaries of its employees any amounts for the support of any candidate, separate segregated fund, political action committee, legislative campaign fund, political party, or ballot issue.

(I) In addition to the laws listed in division (A) of section 4117.10 of the Revised Code that prevail over conflicting agreements between employee organizations and public employers, this section prevails over any conflicting provisions of agreements between labor organizations and public employers entered into pursuant to Chapter 4117. of the Revised Code.

(J) As used in this section:

(1) "Labor organization" and "separate segregated fund" have the same meanings as in section 3517.01 of the Revised Code.

(2) "Public employer" means an employer that is the state or a state agency, authority, commission, or board, a political subdivision of the state, a school district or state institution of higher learning, a public or special district, or any other public employer.

(3) "Employee" includes only an employee who is a resident of or is employed in this state.

HISTORY: 135 v S 46 (Eff 7-23-74); 136 v H 1379 (Eff 6-23-76); 142 v H 354 (Eff 9-22-87); 146 v S 8. Eff 8-23-95.

§ 3599.04 Contributions for illegal purposes.

No person shall, directly or indirectly, in connection with any election, pay, lend, or contribute or offer or promise to pay, lend, or contribute any money or other valuable consideration in the election or defeat of any candidate or the adoption or defeat of any question or issue for any purposes other than those enumerated in sections 3517.08 and 3517.12 of the Revised Code.

Whoever violates this section is guilty of corrupt practices and shall be fined not less than twenty-five nor more than five hundred dollars.

HISTORY: GC § 4785-193; 133 v 307(400), § 193; Bureau of Code Revision. Eff 10-1-53.

§ 3599.05 Employer shall not influence political action of employee.

No employer or his agent or a corporation shall print or authorize to be printed upon any pay envelopes any statements intended or calculated to influence the political action of his or its employees; or post or exhibit in the establishment or anywhere in or about the establishment any posters, placards, or hand bills containing any threat, notice, or information that if any particular candidate is elected or defeated work in the establishment will cease in whole or in part, or other threats expressed or implied, intended to influence the political opinions or votes of his or its employees.

Whoever violates this section is guilty of corrupt practices, and shall be punished by a fine of not less than five hundred nor more than one thousand dollars.

HISTORY: GC § 4785-194; 113 v 307(400), § 194; Bureau of Code Revision. Eff 10-1-53.

§ 3599.06 Employer shall not interfere with employee on election day.

No employer, his officer or agent, shall discharge or threaten to discharge an elector for taking a reasonable amount of time to vote on election day; or require or order an elector to accompany him to a voting place upon such day; or refuse to permit such elector to serve as an election official on any registration or election day; or indirectly use any force or restraint or threaten to inflict any injury, harm, or loss; or in any other manner practice intimidation in order to induce or compel such person to vote or refrain from voting for or against any person or question or issue submitted to the voters.

Whoever violates this section shall be fined not less than fifty nor more than five hundred dollars.

HISTORY: GC § 4785-195; 113 v 307(400), § 195; Bureau of Code Revision. Eff 10-1-53.

§ 3599.07 Repealed, 135 v S 46, § 2 [GC § 4785-196; 113 v 307(401); Bureau of Code Revision, 10-1-53]. Eff 7-23-74.

These sections concerned excessive expenditures.

§ 3599.08 Influencing candidates and voters by publications.

No owner, editor, writer, or employee of any newspaper, magazine, or other publication of any description, whether published regularly or irregularly, shall use the columns of any such publication for the printing of any threats, direct or implied, in the columns of any such publication for the purpose of controlling or intimidating candidates for public office. Such person shall not directly or indirectly solicit, receive, or accept any payment, promise, or compensation for influencing or attempting to influence votes through any printing matter, except through matter inserted in such publication as "paid advertisement" and so designated.

Whoever violates this section is guilty of a corrupt

practice and shall be fined not less than five hundred nor more than one thousand dollars.

HISTORY: GC § 4785-197; 113 v 307(401), § 197; Bureau of Code Revision. Eff 10-1-53.

§ 3599.09 Amended and renumbered RC § 3517.20 in 146 v S 9, eff 8-24-95; in 146 v H 99, eff 8-22-95.

[§§ 3599.09.1, 3599.09.2]
§§ 3599.091, 3599.092 Amended and renumbered RC §§ 3517.21, 3517.22 in 146 v S 9. Eff 8-24-95.

§ 3599.10 Candidate for general assembly shall not be asked to pledge vote on legislation.

No person, firm, or corporation shall demand of any candidate for the general assembly any pledge concerning his vote on any legislation, question, or proposition that may come before the general assembly; provided that this shall not be understood to prohibit a reasonable inquiry as to such candidate's views on such question or legislation.

Whoever violates this section is guilty of a corrupt practice and shall be fined not less than five hundred nor more than one thousand dollars.

HISTORY: GC § 4785-200; 113 v 307(402), § 200; Bureau of Code Revision. Eff 10-1-53.

§ 3599.11 False registration; penalty.

(A) No person shall knowingly register or make application or attempt to register in a precinct in which the person is not a qualified voter; or knowingly aid or abet any person to so register; or attempt to register or knowingly induce or attempt to induce any person to so register; or fraudulently impersonate another or write or assume the name of another, real or fictitious, in registering or attempting to register; or by false statement or other unlawful means procure, aid, or attempt to procure the erasure or striking out on the register or duplicate list of the name of a qualified elector therein; or fraudulently induce or attempt to induce a registrar or other election authority to refuse registration in a precinct to an elector thereof; or willfully or corruptly swear or affirm falsely upon a lawful examination by or before any registrar or registering officer; or make, print, or issue any false or counterfeit certificate of registration or fraudulently alter any certificate of registration.

No person shall knowingly register under more than one name or knowingly induce any person to so register.

No person shall knowingly make any false statement on any form for registration or change of registration or upon any application or return envelope for an absent voter's ballot.

Whoever violates this division is guilty of a felony of the fifth degree.

(B) No person who helps another person register outside an official voter registration place shall knowingly destroy, or knowingly help another person to destroy, any completed registration form, or knowingly fail to return any registration form entrusted to that person to the board of elections on or before the thirtieth day before the election.

Whoever violates this division is guilty of a misdemeanor of the first degree.

HISTORY: GC § 4785-201; 113 v 307(402), § 201; Bureau of Code Revision, 10-1-53; 134 v S 460 (Eff 3-23-72); 137 v S 125 (Eff 5-27-77); 137 v H 1209 (Eff 11-3-78); 146 v S 2. Eff 7-1-96.

The effective date is set by section 6 of SB 2.

§ 3599.12 Illegal voting.

No person shall vote or attempt to vote in any primary, special, or general election in a precinct in which he is not a legally qualified voter; or vote or attempt to vote more than once at the same election; or impersonate or sign the name of another person, real or fictitious, living or dead, and vote or attempt to vote as such person in any such election; or vote or attempt to vote at any primary the ballot of a political party with which he has not been affiliated, as required by section 3513.19 of the Revised Code, or with which he did not vote at the last election; or cast a ballot at any such election after objection has been made and sustained to his vote; or knowingly vote or attempt to vote a ballot other than the official ballot.

Whoever violates this section is guilty of a felony of the fourth degree.

HISTORY: GC § 4785-202; 113 v 307(403), § 202; Bureau of Code Revision, 10-1-53; 139 v S 199. Eff 1-1-83.

The effective date of SB 199 is set by section 11 of the act.

§ 3599.13 Unqualified persons signing petitions.

No person shall sign an initiative, supplementary, referendum, recall, or nominating petition knowing that he is not at the time qualified to sign it; or knowingly sign such petition more than once; or sign a name other than his own; or accept anything of value for signing such petition; or seek by intimidation or threats to influence any person to sign or refrain from signing such petition, or from circulating or abstaining from circulating such petition; or sign a nominating petition for a candidate of a party with which he is not affiliated, as required by section 3513.05 of the Revised Code; or make a false affidavit or statement concerning the signatures on any such petition.

Whoever violates this section shall be fined not less than fifty nor more than five hundred dollars or imprisoned not less than three nor more than six months, or both.

HISTORY: GC § 4785-203; 113 v 307(403), § 203; Bureau of Code Revision, 10-1-53; 138 v H 1062. Eff 3-23-81.

§ 3599.14 Prohibitions relating to petitions.

(A) No person shall knowingly, directly or indirectly, do any of the following in connection with an initiative, supplementary, referendum, recall, local option, or nominating petition:

(1) Misrepresent the contents, purport, or effect of the petition for the purpose of persuading a person to sign or refrain from signing the petition;

(2) Pay or offer to pay anything of value for signing or refraining from signing the petition;

(3) Promise to assist any person to obtain appointment to an office or position as a consideration for obtaining or preventing signatures to the petition;

(4) Obtain or prevent signatures to the petition as a consideration for the assistance or promise of assistance of a person in securing appointment to an office or position;

(5) Circulate or cause to be circulated the petition knowing it to contain false, forged, or fictitious names;

(6) Add signatures or names except his or her own name on the petition;

(7) Make a false certification or statement concerning the petition;

(8) File with the election authorities the petition knowing it to contain false, forged, or fictitious names;

(9) Fail to fill out truthfully and file all itemized statements required by law in connection† the petition.

(B) As used in division (A) of this section, "referendum petition" includes a referendum petition that is described in and subject to sections 305.31 to 305.41 of the Revised Code.

(C) Whoever violates division (A) of this section shall be fined not less than one hundred nor more than five hundred dollars, imprisoned not more than six months, or both.

HISTORY: GC § 4785-204; 113 v 307(403), § 204; Bureau of Code Revision, 10-1-53; 138 v H 1062 (Eff 3-23-81); 143 v H 405 (Eff 4-11-91); 146 v S 2. Eff 7-1-96.

The effective date is set by section 6 of SB 2.

† So in enrolled bill.

§ 3599.15 Sale, theft, destruction, or mutilation of petitions.

No person shall purchase, steal, attempt to steal, sell, attempt to sell, or willfully destroy or mutilate any initiative, supplementary, referendum, recall, or nominating petition, or any part of a petition, that is being or has been lawfully circulated; provided that the words "purchase" and "sell" do not apply to persons paying or receiving pay for soliciting signatures to or circulating a petition or petition paper.

Whoever violates this section is guilty of a felony of the fifth degree.

HISTORY: GC § 4785-205; 113 v 307(404), § 205; Bureau of Code Revision, 10-1-53; 139 v S 199 (Eff 1-1-83); 146 v S 2. Eff 7-1-96.

The effective date is set by section 6 of SB 2.

§ 3599.16 Misconduct of members or employees of board of elections.

No member, director, or employee of a board of elections shall:

(A) Willfully or negligently violate or neglect to perform any duty imposed upon him by law, or willfully perform or neglect to perform it in such a way as to hinder the objects of the law, or willfully disobey any law incumbent upon him so to do;

(B) Willfully or knowingly report as genuine a false or fraudulent signature on a petition or registration form, or willfully or knowingly report as false or fraudulent any such genuine signature;

(C) Willfully add to or subtract from the votes actually cast at an election in any official returns, or add to or take away or attempt to add to or take away any ballot from those legally polled at such election;

(D) Carry away, destroy, or mutilate any registration cards or forms, pollbooks, or other records of any election;

(E) Act as an election official in any capacity in an election, except as specifically authorized in his official capacity;

(F) In any other way willfully and knowingly or unlawfully violate or seek to prevent the enforcement of any other provisions of the election laws.

Whoever violates this section shall be dismissed from his position as a member or employee of the board and is guilty of a felony of the fourth degree.

HISTORY: GC § 4785-206; 113 v 307(404), § 206; Bureau of Code Revision, 10-1-53; 138 v H 1062 (Eff 3-23-81); 139 v S 199. Eff 1-1-83.

The effective date of SB 199 is set by section 11 of the act.

[§ 3599.16.1] § 3599.161 Prohibiting inspection of election records.

(A) The director of elections, deputy director of elections, or an employee of the board of elections designated by the director or deputy director shall be available during normal office hours to provide any person with access to the public records filed in the office of the board of elections.

(B) No director of elections, deputy director of elections, or employee of the board of elections designated by the director or deputy director shall knowingly prevent or prohibit any person from inspecting, under reasonable regulations established and posted by the board of elections, the public records filed in the office of the board of elections. Records relating to the declination of a person to register to vote and to the identity of a voter registration agency through which any particular person registered to vote are not public records for purposes of this section.

(C) Whoever violates division (B) of this section is guilty of prohibiting inspection of election records, a minor misdemeanor, and shall, upon conviction, be dismissed from his position as director of elections, deputy director of elections, or employee of the board of elections.

HISTORY: 137 v H 86 (Eff 8-26-77); 145 v S 300. Eff 1-1-95.

The effective date is set by section 3 of SB 300.

§ 3599.17 Failure of registrars, judges, and clerks to perform duties.

No registrar or judge or clerk of elections shall fail to appear before the board of elections, or its representative, after notice has been served personally upon him or left at his usual place of residence, for examination as to his qualifications; or fail to appear at the polling place to which he is assigned at the hour and during the hours set for the registration or election; or fail to take the oath prescribed by section 3501.31 of the Revised Code, unless excused by such board; or refuse or sanction the refusal of another registrar or judge of elections to administer an oath required by law; or fail to send notice to the board of the appointment of a judge or clerk to fill a vacancy; or act as registrar, judge, or clerk without having been appointed and having received a certificate of appointment, except a judge or clerk appointed to fill a vacancy caused by absence or removal; or in any other way fail to perform any duty imposed by law.

Whoever violates this section shall be fined not less than twenty-five nor more than one hundred dollars or imprisoned not more than fifteen days, or both.

HISTORY: GC § 4785-207; 113 v 307(405), § 207; Bureau of Code Revision. Eff 10-1-53.

§ 3599.18 Misconduct of registrars and police officers.

No registrar of electors or police officer shall refuse, neglect, or unnecessarily delay, hinder, or prevent the registration of a qualified voter, who in a lawful manner applies for registration; or enter or consent to the entry of a fictitious name for registration; or alter the name or remove or destroy the registration card or form of any qualified voter; or willfully neglect or corruptly execute or fail to execute any duty enjoined upon him as a registrar.

Whoever violates this section shall be fined not less than one hundred nor more than five hundred dollars or imprisoned not more than one year, or both.

HISTORY: GC § 4785-208; 113 v 307(405), § 208; Bureau of Code Revision, 10-1-53; 136 v H 1. Eff 6-13-75.

§ 3599.19 Misconduct of judges and clerks of elections in polling place.

No judge or clerk of elections shall unlawfully open or permit to be opened the sealed package containing registration lists, ballots, blanks, pollbooks, and other papers and material to be used in the election; or unlawfully misplace, carry away, negligently lose or permit to be taken from him, fail to deliver, or destroy any such packages, papers, or material; or knowingly receive or sanction the reception of a ballot from a person not a qualified elector or from a person who refused to answer a question in accordance with the election law; or refuse to receive or sanction the rejection of a ballot from a person, knowing him to be a qualified elector; or knowingly permit a fraudulent ballot to be placed in the ballot box; or place or permit to be placed in any ballot box any ballot known by him to be improperly or fraudulently marked; or knowingly count or permit to be counted any illegal or fraudulent ballot; or mislead an elector who is physically unable to prepare his ballot; or mark a ballot for such elector otherwise than as directed by him; or disclose to any person, except when legally required to do so, how such elector voted; or when counting the ballots alter or mark or permit any alteration or marking on any ballot; or wrongfully count or tally or sanction the wrongful counting or tallying of votes; or after the counting of votes commences, as required by law, postpone or sanction the postponement of the counting of votes, adjourn at any time or to any place, or remove the ballot box from the place of voting, or from the custody or presence of all the judges and clerks of such elections; or permit any ballot to remain or to be in the ballot box at the opening of the polls, or to be put therein during the counting of the ballots, or to be left therein without being counted; or admit or sanction the admission to the polling room at an election during the receiving, counting, and certifying of votes of any person not qualified by law to be so admitted; or refuse to admit or sanction the refusal to admit any person, upon lawful request therefor, who is legally qualified to be present; or permit or sanction the counting of the ballots contrary to the manner prescribed by law; or willfully neglect or corruptly execute any duty enjoined upon him by law.

Whoever violates this section shall be fined not less than one hundred nor more than five hundred dollars or imprisoned not less than three nor more than six months, or both.

HISTORY: GC § 4785-209; 113 v 307(405), § 209; Bureau of Code Revision. Eff 10-1-53.

§ 3599.20 Secret ballot.

No person shall attempt to induce an elector to show how he marked his ballot at an election; or, being an elector, allow his ballot to be seen by another, except as provided by section 3505.24 of the Revised Code, with the apparent intention of letting it be known how he is about to vote; or make a false statement as to his ability to mark his ballot; or purposely mark his ballot so it may be identified after it has been cast; or attempt to interfere with an elector in the voting booth when marking his ballot; or willfully destroy or mutilate a lawful ballot; or remove from the polling place or be found in unlawful possession of a lawful ballot outside the enclosure provided for voting; or willfully hinder or delay the delivery of a lawful ballot to a person entitled to receive it; or give to an elector a ballot printed or written contrary to law; or forge or falsely make an official indorsement on a ballot.

Whoever violates this section shall be fined not less than twenty-five nor more than five hundred dollars or imprisoned not more than six months, or both.

HISTORY: GC § 4785-210; 113 v 307(406), § 210; Bureau of Code Revision. Eff 10-1-53.

§ 3599.21 Absent voter's ballot.

No person shall impersonate another, or make a false representation in order to obtain an absent voter's ballot; or knowingly connive to help a person to vote an absent voter's ballot illegally; or being an election official open, destroy, steal, mark, or mutilate any absent voter's ballot; or abet another to open, destroy, steal, mark, or mutilate any absent voter's ballot after the ballot has been voted; or delay the delivery of any such ballot with a view to preventing its arrival in time to be counted; or hinder or attempt to hinder the delivery or counting of such absent voter's ballot.

Whoever violates this section is guilty of a felony of the fourth degree.

HISTORY: GC § 4785-211; 113 v 307(406), § 211; Bureau of Code Revision, 10-1-53; 139 v S 199. Eff 1-1-83.

The effective date of SB 199 is set by section 11 of the act.

§ 3599.22 Printing of ballots.

No person employed to print or engage in printing the official ballots shall print or cause or permit to be printed an official ballot other than according to the copy furnished him by the board of elections or a false or fraudulent ballot; or print or permit to be printed more ballots than are delivered to the board; or appropriate, give, deliver, or knowingly permit to be taken away any of such ballots by a person other than the person authorized by law to do so; or print such ballots on paper other than that provided in the contract with the board; or willfully seal up or cause or permit to be sealed up in packages or deliver to the board a less number of ballots than the number indorsed thereon.

Whoever violates this section shall be fined not less than two hundred nor more than one thousand dollars or imprisoned not more than six months, or both.

HISTORY: GC § 4785-212; 113 v 307(407), § 212; Bureau of Code Revision. Eff 10-1-53.

§ 3599.23 Unlawful opening; penalty.

No printer or other person entrusted with the printing, custody, or delivery of registration cards or forms, ballots, blanks, pollbooks, cards of instruction, or other required papers shall unlawfully open or permit to be opened a sealed package containing ballots or other printed forms; or give or deliver to another not lawfully entitled thereto, or unlawfully misplace or carry away, or negligently lose or permit to be taken from him, or fail to deliver, or destroy any such forms or packages of ballots, or a ballot, pollbooks, cards of instruction, or other required papers.

No person entrusted with the preparation, custody, or delivery of marking devices shall unlawfully open or permit to be opened a sealed package containing marking devices, or give or deliver to another not lawfully entitled thereto, or unlawfully or carelessly use or negligently lose or permit to be taken from him and fail to deliver or destroy, any such marking devices.

Whoever violates this section shall be fined not less than one hundred dollars or imprisoned not more than one year, or both.

HISTORY: GC § 4785-213; 113 v 307(407), § 213; Bureau of Code Revision, 10-1-53; 129 v 1653. Eff 6-29-61.

§ 3599.24 Interference with conduct of election.

(A) No person shall do any of the following:

(1) By force, fraud, or other improper means, obtain or attempt to obtain possession of the ballots, ballot boxes, or pollbooks;

(2) Recklessly destroy any property used in the conduct of elections;

(3) Attempt to intimidate an election officer, or prevent an election official from performing the official's duties;

(4) Knowingly tear down, remove, or destroy any of the registration lists or sample ballots furnished by the board of elections at the polling place;

(5) Loiter in or about a registration or polling place during registration or the casting and counting of ballots so as to hinder, delay, or interfere with the conduct of the registration or election;

(6) Remove from the voting place the pencils, cards of instruction, supplies, or other conveniences furnished to enable the voter to mark the voter's ballot.

(B) Whoever violates division (A)(1) or (2) of this section is guilty of a felony of the fifth degree. Whoever violates division (A)(3) or (4) of this section is guilty of a misdemeanor of the first degree. Whoever violates division (A)(5) or (6) of this section is guilty of a minor misdemeanor.

HISTORY: GC § 4785-214; 113 v 307(407), § 214; Bureau of Code Revision, 10-1-53; 138 v H 1062 (Eff 3-23-81); 146 v S 2. Eff 7-1-96.

The effective date is set by section 6 of SB 2.

§ 3599.25 Inducing illegal voting.

No person shall counsel or advise another to vote at an election, knowing that he is not a qualified voter; or advise, aid, or assist another person to go or come into a precinct for the purpose of voting therein, knowing that such person is not qualified to vote therein; or counsel, advise, or attempt to induce an election officer to permit a person to vote, knowing such person is not a qualified elector.

Whoever violates this section shall be fined not less than one hundred nor more than five hundred dollars or imprisoned not less than one nor more than six months, or both.

HISTORY: GC § 4785-215; 113 v 307(408), § 215; Bureau of Code Revision. Eff 10-1-53.

§ 3599.26 Tampering with ballots.

No person shall fraudulently put a ballot or ticket into a ballot box; or knowingly and willfully vote a ballot other than an official ballot lawfully obtained by the person from the precinct election authorities; or fraudulently or deceitfully change a ballot of an elector, by which such elector is prevented from voting for such candidates or on an issue as the elector intends to do; or mark a ballot of an elector except as authorized by section 3505.24 of the Revised Code; or hand a marked ballot to an elector to vote, with intent to ascertain how the elector voted; or furnish a ballot to an elector who cannot read, knowingly informing the elector that it contains a name different from the one that is printed or written thereon, to induce the elector to vote contrary to the elector's intentions; or unduly delay or hinder an elector from applying for registration, registering, or from attempting to vote or voting; or knowingly print or distribute a ballot contrary to law.

Whoever violates this section is guilty of a felony of the fifth degree.

HISTORY: GC § 4785-216; 113 v 307(408), § 216; 124 v 478; Bureau of Code Revision, 10-1-53; 139 v S 199 (Eff 1-1-83); 146 v S 2. Eff 7-1-96.

The effective date is set by section 6 of SB 2.

§ 3599.27 Possession of voting machine, tabulating equipment, or marking device prohibited; tampering; penalty.

No unauthorized person shall have in the person's possession any voting machine that may be owned or leased by any county or any of the parts or the keys thereof. No person shall tamper or attempt to tamper with, deface, impair the use of, destroy, or otherwise injure in any manner any voting machine.

No unauthorized person shall have in the person's possession any marking device, automatic tabulating equipment, or any of the parts, appurtenances, or accessories thereof. No person shall tamper or attempt to tamper with, deface, impair the use of, destroy, or otherwise change or injure in any manner any marking device, automatic tabulating equipment, or any appurtenances or accessories thereof.

Whoever violates this section is guilty of a felony of the fifth degree.

HISTORY: GC § 4785-217; 113 v 307(408), § 217; Bureau of Code Revision, 10-1-53; 126 v 575 (Eff 10-6-55); 129 v 1653 (Eff 6-29-61); 139 v S 199 (Eff 1-1-83); 146 v S 2. Eff 7-1-96.

The effective date is set by section 6 of SB 2.

§ 3599.28 False signatures.

No person, with intent to defraud or deceive, shall write or sign the name of another person to any document, petition, registration card, or other book or record authorized or required by Title XXXV [35] of the Revised Code.

Whoever violates this section is guilty of a felony of the fifth degree.

HISTORY: GC § 4785-219; 113 v 307(409), § 219; Bureau of Code Revision, 10-1-53; 139 v S 199 (Eff 1-1-83); 146 v S 2. Eff 7-1-96.

The effective date is set by section 6 of SB 2.

§ 3599.29 Possession of false records.

No person shall have in the person's possession a falsely made, altered, forged, or counterfeited registration card, form, or list, pollbook, tally sheet, or list of election returns of an election, knowing it to be such, with intent to hinder, defeat, or prevent a fair expression of the popular will at such election.

Whoever violates this section is guilty of a felony of the fifth degree.

HISTORY: GC § 4785-220; 113 v 307(409), § 220; Bureau of Code Revision, 10-1-53; 139 v S 199 (Eff 1-1-83); 146 v S 2. Eff 7-1-96.

The effective date is set by section 6 of SB 2.

§ 3599.30 Congregating at polls.

No person, being one of two or more persons congregating in or about a voting place during the receiving of ballots, so as to hinder or delay an elector in registering or casting his ballot, having been ordered by the registrar or judge of elections to disperse shall refuse to do so.

Whoever violates this section shall be fined not less than twenty nor more than three hundred dollars or imprisoned not more than six months, or both.

HISTORY: GC § 4785-221; 113 v 307(409), § 221; Bureau of Code Revision. Eff 10-1-53.

§ 3599.31 Failure of officer of law to assist election officers.

No officer of the law shall fail to obey forthwith an order of the presiding judge and aid in enforcing a lawful order of the presiding judges at an election, against persons unlawfully congregating or loitering within one hundred feet of a polling place, hindering or delaying an elector from reaching or leaving the polling place, soliciting or attempting, within one hundred feet of the polling place, to influence an elector in casting his vote, or interfering with the registration of voters or casting and counting of the ballots.

Whoever violates this section shall be fined not less than fifty nor more than one thousand dollars or imprisoned not more than thirty days, or both.

HISTORY: GC § 4785-218; 113 v 307(408), § 218; Bureau of Code Revision. Eff 10-1-53.

§ 3599.32 Failure of election official to enforce law.

No official upon whom a duty is imposed by an election law for the violation of which no penalty is otherwise provided shall willfully disobey such election law.

Whoever violates this section shall be fined not less than fifty nor more than one thousand dollars or imprisoned not more than one year, or both.

HISTORY: GC § 4785-222; 113 v 307(410), § 222; Bureau of Code Revision. Eff 10-1-53.

§ 3599.33 Fraudulent writing on ballots or election records.

No person, from the time ballots are cast or counted until the time has expired for using them as evidence in a recount or contest of election, shall willfully and with fraudulent intent make any mark or alteration on any ballot; or inscribe, write, or cause to be inscribed or written in or upon a registration form or list, pollbook, tally sheet, or list, lawfully made or kept at an election, or in or upon a book or paper purporting to be such, or upon an election return, or upon a book or paper containing such return the name of a person not entitled to vote at such election or not voting thereat, or a fictitious name, or, within such time, wrongfully change, alter, erase, or tamper with a name, word, or figure contained in such pollbook, tally sheet, list, book, or paper; or falsify, mark, or write thereon with intent to defeat, hinder, or prevent a fair expression of the will of the people at such election.

Whoever violates this section is guilty of a felony of the fifth degree.

HISTORY: GC § 4785-223; 113 v 307(410), § 223; Bureau of Code Revision, 10-1-53; 139 v S 199 (Eff 1-1-83); 146 v S 2. Eff 7-1-96.

The effective date is set by section 6 of SB 2.

§ 3599.34 Destruction of election records before expiration of time for contest.

No person, from the time ballots are cast or voted until the time has expired for using them in a recount or as evidence in a contest of election, shall unlawfully destroy or attempt to destroy the ballots, or permit such ballots or a ballot box or pollbook used at an election to be destroyed; or destroy, falsify, mark, or write in a name on any such ballot that has been voted.

Whoever violates this section is guilty of a felony of the fifth degree.

HISTORY: GC § 4785-224; 113 v 307(410), § 224; Bureau of Code Revision, 10-1-53; 139 v S 199 (Eff 1-1-83); 146 v S 2. Eff 7-1-96.

The effective date is set by section 6 of SB 2.

§ 3599.35 Proxies shall not be given by party representatives; impersonation of representatives.

No party committeeman or party delegate or alternate chosen at an election, or a delegate or alternate appointed to a convention provided by law, shall give or issue a proxy or authority to another person to act or vote in his stead.

No person shall knowingly or fraudulently act or vote or attempt to impersonate, act, or vote in place of such committeeman or delegate.

Whoever violates this section shall be fined not less than fifty nor more than five hundred dollars or imprisoned not more than sixty days, or both.

HISTORY: GC § 4785-225; 113 v 307(410), § 225; Bureau of Code Revision. Eff 10-1-53.

§ 3599.36 Perjury in matters relating to elections.

No person, either orally or in writing, on oath lawfully administered or in a statement made under penalty of election falsification, shall purposely state a falsehood as to a material matter relating to an election in a proceeding before a court, tribunal, or officer created by law, or in a matter in relation to which an oath or statement under penalty of election falsification is authorized by law, including a statement required for verifying or filing a nominating, initiative, supplementary, referendum, or recall petition, or petition paper.

Whoever violates this section is guilty of election falsification, which is a misdemeanor of the first degree.

Every paper, card, or other document relating to any election matter which calls for a statement to be made under penalty of election falsification shall be accompanied by the following statement in bold face capital letters: "The penalty for election falsification is imprisonment for not more than six months, or a fine of not more than one thousand dollars, or both."

HISTORY: GC § 4785-226; 113 v 307(411), § 226; Bureau of Code Revision, 10-1-53; 128 v S 204 (Eff 8-28-59); 135 v S 429 (Eff 7-26-74); 135 v H 662 (Eff 9-27-74); 138 v H 1062. Eff 3-23-81.

§ 3599.37 Refusal to appear or testify concerning violation of election laws.

No person having been subpoenaed or ordered to appear before a grand jury, court, board, or officer in a proceeding or prosecution upon a complaint, information, affidavit, or indictment for an offense under an election law shall fail to appear or, having appeared, refuse to answer a question pertinent to the matter under inquiry or investigation; or refuse to produce, upon reasonable notice, any material, books, papers, documents, or records in his possession or under his control.

Whoever violates this section shall, unless he claims his constitutional rights, be fined not less than one hundred nor more than one thousand dollars or imprisoned not less than thirty days nor more than six months.

HISTORY: GC § 4785-227; 113 v 307(411), § 227; 114 v 679(713); Bureau of Code Revision. Eff 10-1-53.

§ 3599.38 Election officials shall not influence voters.

No judge, clerk, witness, deputy sheriff, special deputy sheriff, police officer, or other election officer, while performing the duties of his office, shall wear any badge, sign, or other insignia or thing indicating his preference for any candidate or for any question submitted or influence or attempt to influence any voter to cast his ballot for or against any candidate or issue submitted at such election.

Whoever violates this section shall be fined not less than fifty nor more than one hundred dollars and imprisoned not less than thirty days nor more than six months.

HISTORY: GC § 4785-228; 113 v 307(411), § 228; Bureau of Code Revision. Eff 10-1-53.

§ 3599.39 Second offense under election laws.

Any person convicted of a violation of any provisions of Title XXXV [35] of the Revised Code, who is again convicted of a violation of any such provisions, whether such conviction is for the same offense or not, shall on such second conviction be fined not less than five hundred nor more than one thousand dollars or imprisoned not less than one nor more than five years, or both, and in addition, such person shall be disfranchised.

HISTORY: GC § 4785-230; 113 v 307(412), § 230; Bureau of Code Revision, 10-1-53; 126 v 575. Eff 10-6-55.

§ 3599.40 General penalty.

Whoever violates any provision of Title XXXV [35] of the Revised Code, unless otherwise provided in such title, is guilty of a misdemeanor of the first degree.

HISTORY: GC § 4785-232; 113 v 307(412), § 232; Bureau of Code Revision, 10-1-53; 134 v H 511. Eff 1-1-74.

The effective date of H 511 is set by section 4 of the act.

§ 3599.41 Person violating election laws may testify against other violators.

A person violating any provision of Title XXXV [35] of the Revised Code is a competent witness against another person so offending, and may attend and testify at a trial, hearing, or investigation thereof.

HISTORY: GC § 4785-229; 113 v 307(411), § 229; 114 v 679(713); Bureau of Code Revision. Eff 10-1-53.

§ 3599.42 Prima-facie case of fraud.

A violation of any provision of Title XXXV [35] of the Revised Code constitutes a prima-facie case of fraud within the purview of such title.

HISTORY: GC § 4785-231; 113 v 307(412), § 231; Bureau of Code Revision. Eff 10-1-53.

§ 3599.43 Communications purporting to be from boards of elections; penalty.

No person, not authorized by a board of elections, shall send or transmit to any other person any written or oral communication which purports to be a communication from a board of elections, or which reasonably construed appears to be a communication from such a board and which was intended to be so construed.

Whoever violates this section shall be fined not less than one hundred nor more than one thousand dollars or imprisoned not more than six months or both.

HISTORY: 130 v 845. Eff 9-16-63.

§ 3599.44 Repealed, 135 v S 46, § 2 [133 v H 1040]. Eff 7-23-74.

This section concerned penalties for violations of sections in Chapter 3517.

§ 3599.45 Accepting contributions from medicaid providers prohibited.

(A) No candidate for the office of attorney general or county prosecutor or his campaign committee shall knowingly accept any contribution from a provider of services or goods under contract with the department of human services pursuant to the medicaid program of Title XIX of the "Social Security Act," 49 Stat. 620 (1935), 42 U.S.C. 301, as amended, or from any person having an ownership interest in the provider.

As used in this section "candidate," "campaign committee," and "contribution" have the same meaning as in section 3517.01 of the Revised Code.

(B) Whoever violates this section is guilty of a misdemeanor of the first degree.

HISTORY: 137 v S 159 (Eff 4-24-78); 141 v H 428. Eff 12-23-86.

TITLE 37: HEALTH—SAFETY—MORALS

CHAPTER 3707: BOARD OF HEALTH

§ 3707.50 Posting of warning concerning anabolic steriods in athletic facility locker rooms.

(A) As used in this section:

(1) "Anabolic steroid" has the same meaning as in section 3719.41 of the Revised Code.

(2) "Athletic facility" means both of the following:

(a) A privately owned athletic training, exercise, or sports facility or stadium that is open to the public;

(b) A publicly owned sports facility or stadium.

(B) The following warning shall be conspicuously posted in each locker room of every athletic facility:

"Warning: Improper use of anabolic steroids may cause serious or fatal health problems, such as heart disease, stroke, cancer, growth deformities, infertility, personality changes, severe acne, and baldness. Possession, sale, or use of anabolic steroids without a valid prescription is a crime punishable by a fine and imprisonment."

(C) No privately owned athletic facility shall fail to post the warning required by this section.

(D) Any person who violates division (C) of this section is guilty of a misdemeanor of the fourth degree.

HISTORY: 144 v H 62. Eff 5-21-91.

Not analogous to former RC § 3707.50 (Bureau of Code Revision, 10-1-53), repealed 134 v H 511, § 2, eff 1-1-74.

CHAPTER 3712: HOSPICE CARE

§ 3712.09 Criminal records check for prospective employees providing direct care to older adult.

(A) As used in this section:

(1) "Applicant" means a person who is under final consideration for employment with a hospice care program in a full-time, part-time, or temporary position that involves providing direct care to an older adult. "Applicant" does not include a person who provides direct care as a volunteer without receiving or expecting to receive any form of remuneration other than reimbursement for actual expenses.

(2) "Criminal records check" and "older adult" have the same meanings as in section 109.572 [109.57.2] of the Revised Code.

(B)(1) Except as provided in division (I) of this section, the chief administrator of a hospice care program shall request that the superintendent of the bureau of criminal identification and investigation conduct a criminal records check with respect to each applicant. If the applicant does not present proof of having been a resident of this state for the five-year period immediately prior to the date the criminal records check is requested or provide evidence that within that five-year period the superintendent has requested information about the applicant from the federal bureau of investigation in a criminal records check, the chief administrator shall request that the superintendent obtain information from the federal bureau of investigation as part of the criminal records check of the applicant. Even if the applicant presents proof of having been a resident of this state for the five-year period, the chief administrator may request that the superintendent include information from the federal bureau of investigation in the criminal records check.

(2) A person required by division (B)(1) of this section to request a criminal records check shall do both of the following:

(a) Provide to each applicant a copy of the form prescribed pursuant to division (C)(1) of section 109.572 [109.57.2] of the Revised Code and a standard fingerprint impression sheet prescribed pursuant to division (C)(2) of that section, and obtain the completed form and impression sheet from the applicant;

(b) Forward the completed form and impression sheet to the superintendent of the bureau of criminal identification and investigation.

(3) An applicant provided the form and fingerprint impression sheet under division (B)(2)(a) of this section who fails to complete the form or provide fingerprint impressions shall not be employed in any position for which a criminal records check is required by this section.

(C)(1) Except as provided in rules adopted by the public health council in accordance with division (F) of this section, no hospice care program shall employ a person in a position that involves providing direct care to an older adult if the person has been convicted of or pleaded guilty to any of the following:

(a) A violation of section 2903.01, 2903.02, 2903.03, 2903.04, 2903.11, 2903.12, 2903.13, 2903.16, 2903.21, 2903.34, 2905.01, 2905.02, 2905.11, 2905.12, 2907.02, 2907.03, 2907.05, 2907.06, 2907.07, 2907.08, 2907.09, 2907.12†, 2907.25, 2907.31, 2907.32, 2907.321 [2907.32.1], 2907.322 [2907.32.2], 2907.323 [2907.32.3], 2911.01, 2911.02, 2911.11, 2911.12, 2911.13, 2913.02, 2913.03, 2913.04, 2913.11, 2913.21, 2913.31, 2913.40, 2913.43, 2913.47, 2913.51, 2919.25, 2921.36, 2923.12, 2923.13, 2923.161 [2923.16.1], 2925.02, 2925.03, 2925.11, 2925.13, 2925.22, 2925.23, or 3716.11 of the Revised Code.

(b) An existing or former law of this state, any other

state, or the United States that is substantially equivalent to any of the offenses listed in division (C)(1)(a) of this section.

(2) A hospice care program may employ an applicant conditionally prior to obtaining the results of a criminal records check regarding the individual. The program shall request a criminal records check in accordance with division (B)(1) of this section not later than five business days after the individual begins conditional employment. The program shall terminate the individual's employment if the results of the criminal records check, other than the results of any request for information from the federal bureau of investigation, are not obtained within the period ending sixty days after the date the request is made. Regardless of when the results of the criminal records check are obtained, if the results indicate that the individual has been convicted of or pleaded guilty to any of the offenses listed or described in division (C)(1) of this section, the program shall terminate the individual's employment unless the program chooses to employ the individual pursuant to division (F) of this section. Termination of employment under this division shall be considered just cause for discharge for purposes of division (D)(2) of section 4141.29 of the Revised Code if the individual makes any attempt to deceive the program about the individual's criminal record.

(D)(1) Each hospice care program shall pay to the bureau of criminal identification and investigation the fee prescribed pursuant to division (C)(3) of section 109.572 [109.57.2] of the Revised Code for each criminal records check conducted pursuant to this section.

(2) A hospice care program may charge an applicant a fee not exceeding the amount the program pays under division (D)(1) of this section. A program may collect a fee only if both of the following apply:

(a) The program notifies the person at the time of initial application for employment of the amount of the fee and that, unless the fee is paid, the person will not be considered for employment;

(b) The medical assistance program established under Chapter 5111. of the Revised Code does not reimburse the program the fee it pays under division (D)(1) of this section.

(E) The report of a criminal records check conducted pursuant to a request made under this section is not a public record for the purposes of section 149.43 of the Revised Code and shall not be made available to any person other than the following:

(1) The individual who is the subject of the criminal records check or the individual's representative;

(2) The chief administrator of the program requesting the criminal records check or the administrator's representative;

(3) The administrator of any other facility, agency, or program that provides direct care to older adults that is owned or operated by the same entity that owns or operates the hospice care program;

(4) A court, hearing officer, or other necessary individual involved in a case dealing with a denial of employment of the applicant.

(F) The public health council shall adopt rules in accordance with Chapter 119. of the Revised Code to implement this section. The rules shall specify circumstances under which a hospice care program may employ a person who has been convicted of or pleaded guilty to an offense listed or described in division (C)(1) of this section but meets personal character standards set by the council.

(G) The chief administrator of a hospice care program shall inform each individual, at the time of initial application for a position that involves providing direct care to an older adult, that the individual is required to provide a set of fingerprint impressions and that a criminal records check is required to be conducted if the individual comes under final consideration for employment.

(H) In a tort or other civil action for damages that is brought as the result of an injury, death, or loss to person or property caused by an individual who a hospice care program employs in a position that involves providing direct care to older adults, the following shall apply:

(1) If the program employed the individual in good faith and reasonable reliance on the report of a criminal records check requested under this section, the program shall not be found negligent solely because of its reliance on the report, even if the information in the report is determined later to have been incomplete or inaccurate;

(2) If the program employed the individual in good faith on a conditional basis pursuant to division (C)(2) of this section, the program shall not be found negligent solely because it employed the individual prior to receiving the report of a criminal records check requested under this section;

(3) If the program in good faith employed the individual according to the personal character standards established in rules adopted under division (F) of this section, the program shall not be found negligent solely because the individual prior to being employed had been convicted of or pleaded guilty to an offense listed or described in division (C)(1) of this section.

(I) The chief administrator is not required to request that the superintendent of the bureau of criminal identification and investigation conduct a criminal records check of an applicant if the applicant has been referred to the hospice care program by an employment service that supplies full-time, part-time, or temporary staff for positions involving the direct care of older adults and both of the following apply:

(1) The chief administrator receives from the employment service or the applicant a report of the results of a criminal records check regarding the applicant that has been conducted by the superintendent within the one-year period immediately preceding the applicant's referral;

(2) The report of the criminal records check demonstrates that the person has not been convicted of or pleaded guilty to an offense listed or described in division (C)(1) of this section.

HISTORY: 146 v S 160 (Eff 1-27-97); 147 v S 96. Eff 6-11-97.

† RC § 2907.12 repealed 9-3-96.

CHAPTER 3716: LABELING OF HAZARDOUS SUBSTANCES

§ 3716.11 Placing harmful objects in food or confection.

No person shall do either of the following, knowing or having reasonable cause to believe that any person may suffer physical harm or be seriously inconvenienced or annoyed thereby:

(A) Place a pin, needle, razor blade, glass, laxative, drug of abuse, or other harmful or hazardous object or substance in any food or confection;

(B) Furnish to any person any food or confection which has been adulterated in violation of division (A) of this section.

HISTORY: 135 v H 716. Eff 1-1-74.

The effective date is set by section 1 of HB 716.

§ 3716.99 Penalties.

(A) Whoever violates section 3716.02 of the Revised Code is guilty of a misdemeanor of the third degree on a first offense. On each subsequent offense such person is guilty of a misdemeanor of the second degree.

(B) No person is subject to prosecution for a violation of division (A) of section 3716.02 of the Revised Code with respect to any hazardous substance shipped or delivered for shipment for export to any foreign country, in a package marked for export and branded in accordance with the specifications of the foreign purchaser and in accordance with the laws of the foreign country.

(C) Whoever violates section 3716.11 of the Revised Code is guilty of a misdemeanor of the first degree.

HISTORY: 128 v 484 (Eff 11-4-59); 129 v 582(816) (Eff 1-10-61); 135 v H 716. Eff 1-1-74.

The effective date is set by section 1 of HB 716.

CHAPTER 3719: CONTROLLED SUBSTANCES

[UNIFORM CONTROLLED SUBSTANCES ACT]

[NOTE: For *criminal drug abuse* provisions (formerly contained in RC Chapter 3719.), see RC Chapter 2925.]

§ 3719.01 Definitions.

As used in this chapter:

(A) "Administer" means the direct application of a drug, whether by injection, inhalation, ingestion, or any other means to a person or an animal.

(B) "Board" means the state board of pharmacy established by section 4729.01 of the Revised Code.

(C) "Drug enforcement administration" means the drug enforcement administration of the United States department of justice or its successor agency.

(D) "Controlled substance" means a drug, compound, mixture, preparation, or substance included in schedule I, II, III, IV, or V.

(E) "Dangerous drug" has the same meaning as in section 4729.02 of the Revised Code.

(F) "Dispense" means to sell, leave with, give away, dispose of, or deliver.

(G) "Distribute" means to deal in, ship, transport, or deliver but does not include administering or dispensing a drug.

(H) "Drug" has the same meaning as in section 4729.02 of the Revised Code.

(I) "Drug abuse offense," "felony drug abuse offense," "cocaine," and "hashish" have the same meanings as in section 2925.01 of the Revised Code.

(J) "Federal drug abuse control laws" means the "Comprehensive Drug Abuse Prevention and Control Act of 1970," 84 Stat. 1242, 21 U.S.C. 801, as amended.

(K) "Hospital" means an institution for the care and treatment of the sick and injured that is certified by the department of health and approved by the state board of pharmacy as proper to be entrusted with the custody of controlled substances and the professional use of controlled substances under the direction of a practitioner or pharmacist.

(L) "Hypodermic" means a hypodermic syringe or needle, or other instrument or device for the injection of medication.

(M) "Isomer", except as otherwise expressly stated, means the optial isomer.†

(N) "Laboratory" means a laboratory approved by the state board of pharmacy as proper to be entrusted with the custody of controlled substances and the use of controlled substances for scientific and clinical purposes and for purposes of instruction.

(O) "Manufacturer" means a person who plants, cultivates, harvests, processes, makes, prepares, or otherwise engages in any part of the production of a controlled substance by propagation, compounding, conversion, or processing, either directly or indirectly by extraction from substances of natural origin, or independently by means of chemical synthesis, or by a combination of extraction and chemical synthesis, and includes any packaging or repackaging of the substance or labeling or relabeling of its container and other activities incident to production, except that a "manufacturer" does not include a pharmacist who prepares, compounds, packages, or labels a controlled substance as an incident to dispensing a controlled substance in accordance with a prescription and in the usual course of professional practice.

(P) "Marihuana" means all parts of a plant of the genus cannabis, whether growing or not; the seeds of a plant of that type; the resin extracted from a part of a plant of that type; and every compound, manufacture, salt, derivative, mixture, or preparation of a plant of that type or of its seeds or resin. "Marihuana" does not include the mature stalks of the plant, fiber produced from the stalks, oils or cake made from the seeds of the plant, or any other compound, manufacture, salt, derivative, mixture, or preparation of the mature stalks, except the resin extracted from the mature stalks, fiber, oil or cake, or the sterilized seed of the plant that is incapable of germination.

(Q) "Narcotic drugs" means coca leaves, opium, isonipecaine, amidone, isoamidone, ketobemidone, as defined in this division, and every substance not chemically distinguished from them and every drug, other than cannabis, that may be included in the meaning of "narcotic drug" under the federal drug abuse control laws. "Coca leaves" includes cocaine and any compound, manufacture, salt, derivative, mixture, or preparation of coca leaves, except derivatives of coca leaves, that do not contain cocaine, ecgonine, or substances from which cocaine or ecgonine may be synthesized or made. "Isonipecaine" means any substance identified chemically as 1-methyl-4-phenyl-piperidine-4-carboxylic acid ethyl ester, or any salt thereof, by whatever trade name designated. "Amidone" means any substance identified chemically as 4-4-diphenyl-6-dimethylamino-heptanone-3, or any salt thereof, by whatever trade name designated. "Isoamidone" means any substance identified chemically as 4-4-diphenyl-5-methyl-6-dimethylaminohexanone-3, or any salt thereof, by whatever trade name designated. "Ketobemidone" means any substance identified chemically as 4-(3-hydroxyphenyl)-1-methyl-4-piperidyl ethyl ketone hydrochloride, or any salt thereof, by whatever trade name designated.

(R) "Nurse" means a person licensed to engage in the practice of nursing in this state.

(S) "Official written order" means an order written on a form provided for that purpose by the director of the United States drug enforcement administration, under any laws of the United States making provision for the order, if the order forms are authorized and required by federal law.

(T) "Opiate" means any substance having an addiction-forming or addiction-sustaining liability similar to morphine or being capable of conversion into a drug having addiction-forming or addiction-sustaining liability. "Opiate" does not include, unless specifically designated as controlled under section 3719.41 of the Revised Code, the dextrorotatory isomer of 3-methoxy-N-methylmorphinian and its salts (dextro-methorphan). "Opiate" does include its racemic and levoratory forms.

(U) "Opium poppy" means the plant of the species papaver somniferum L., except its seeds.

(V) "Person" means any individual, corporation, government, governmental subdivision or agency, business trust, estate, trust, partnership, association, or other legal entity.

(W) "Pharmacist" means a person registered with the board as a compounder and dispenser of drugs.

(X) "Pharmacy" means any area, room, rooms, place of business, department, or portion of any of the foregoing, where prescriptions are filled or where drugs, dangerous drugs, or poisons are compounded, sold, offered, or displayed for sale, dispensed, or distributed to the public.

(Y) "Poppy straw" means all parts, except the seeds, of the opium poppy, after mowing.

(Z) "Practitioner" means the following:
(1) A person who is licensed pursuant to Chapter 4715., 4731., or 4741. of the Revised Code and authorized by law to write prescriptions for drugs or dangerous drugs;
(2) An advanced practice nurse authorized under section 4723.56 of the Revised Code to prescribe drugs and therapeutic devices.

(AA) "Prescription" means a written or oral order for a controlled substance for the use of a particular person or a particular animal given by a practitioner in the course of professional practice and in accordance with the regulations promulgated by the director of the United States drug enforcement administration, pursuant to the federal drug abuse control laws.

(BB) "Registry number" means the number assigned to each person registered under the federal drug abuse control laws.

(CC) "Sale" includes delivery, barter, exchange, transfer, or gift, or offer thereof, and each transaction of those natures made by any person, whether as principal, proprietor, agent, servant, or employee.

(DD) "Schedule I," "schedule II," "schedule III," "schedule IV," and "schedule V" mean controlled substance schedules I, II, III, IV, and V, respectively, established pursuant to section 3719.41 of the Revised Code, as amended pursuant to section 3719.43 or 3719.44 of the Revised Code.

(EE) "Wholesaler" means a person who, on official written orders other than prescriptions, supplies controlled substances that the person has not manufactured, produced, or prepared personally and includes a "wholesale distributor of dangerous drugs" as defined in section 4729.02 of the Revised Code.

(FF) "Animal shelter" means a facility operated by a humane society or any society organized under Chapter 1717. of the Revised Code or a dog pound operated pursuant to Chapter 955. of the Revised Code.

(GG) "Terminal distributor of dangerous drugs" has the same meaning as in section 4729.02 of the Revised Code.

(HH) "Category III license" means a license issued to a terminal distributor of dangerous drugs as set forth in section 4729.54 of the Revised Code.

(JJ)†† "Prosecutor" has the same meaning as in section 2935.01 of the Revised Code.

HISTORY: 136 v H 300 (Eff 7-1-76); 136 v S 414 (Eff 9-22-76); 137 v H 1 (Eff 8-26-77); 145 v H 88 (Eff 6-29-94); 145 v H 391 (Eff 7-21-94); 146 v S 2 (Eff 7-1-96); 146 v S 269 (Eff 7-1-96); 146 v H 162. Eff 1-1-97.

Analogous to former RC § 3719.01 (123 v 266; Bureau of Code Revision, 10-1-53; 126 v 178; 133 v H 874; 134 v H 924), repealed 136 v H 300, eff 7-1-76.

The effective date is set by section 3 of HB 162.

† So in enrolled bill; optical isomer referred to in 3719.41.

†† Division lettering reflects the combination of SB 269 (146 v —) and HB 162 (146 v —).

Comment, Legislative Service Commission

Section 3719.01 of the Revised Code is amended by this act [Am. Sub. H.B. 162] and also by Am. Sub. S.B. 269 of the 121st General Assembly. Comparison of these amendments in pursuance of section 1.52 of the Revised Code discloses that they are not irreconcilable so that they are required by that section to be harmonized to give effect to each amendment.

[§ 3719.01.1] § 3719.011 Definitions.

As used in the Revised Code:

(A) "Drug of abuse" means any controlled substance as defined in section 3719.01 of the Revised Code, any harmful intoxicant as defined in section 2925.01 of the Revised Code, and any dangerous drug as defined in section 4729.02 of the Revised Code.

(B) "Drug dependent person" means any person who, by reason of the use of any drug of abuse, is physically, psychologically, or physically and psychologically dependent upon the use of such drug, to the detriment of his health or welfare.

(C) "Person in danger of becoming a drug dependent person" means any person who, by reason of his habitual or incontinent use of any drug of abuse, is in imminent danger of becoming a drug dependent person.

HISTORY: 133 v H 874 (Eff 9-16-70); 134 v S 141 (Eff 12-31-71); 136 v H 300. Eff 7-1-76.

[§ 3719.01.2] § 3719.012 Minor may give consent to treatment for condition caused by drug or alcohol abuse.

(A) Notwithstanding any other provision of law, a minor may give consent for the diagnosis or treatment by a physician licensed to practice in this state of any condition which it is reasonable to believe is caused by a drug of abuse, beer, or intoxicating liquor. Such consent shall not be subject to disaffirmance because of minority.

(B) A physician licensed to practice in this state, or any person acting at his direction, who in good faith renders medical or surgical services to a minor giving consent under division (A) of this section, shall not be subject to any civil or criminal liability for assault, battery, or assault and battery.

(C) The parent or legal guardian of a minor giving consent under division (A) of this section is not liable for the payment of any charges made for medical or surgical services rendered such minor, unless the parent or legal guardian has also given consent for the diagnosis or treatment.

HISTORY: 134 v S 406 (Eff 2-9-72); 139 v H 357. Eff 10-1-82.

§ 3719.02 Manufacturer of controlled substances; license.

A person may cultivate, grow, or by other process produce or manufacture, and a person on land owned, occupied, or controlled by such person may knowingly allow to be cultivated, grown, or produced, any controlled substance if the person first obtains a license as a manufacturer of controlled substances from the state board of pharmacy.

All licenses issued pursuant to this section shall be for a period of one year from the last day of June and may be renewed for a like period annually according to the standard renewal procedure of sections 4745.01 to 4745.03 of the Revised Code.

The annual license fee shall be thirty-seven dollars and fifty cents and shall accompany each application for a license or renewal thereof. A license that has not been renewed by the first day of August in any year may be reinstated upon payment of the renewal fee and a penalty of fifty-five dollars.

The state board of pharmacy, subject to the approval of the controlling board, may establish a fee in excess of the amount provided in this section, provided that the fee does not exceed the amount established by this section by more than fifty per cent.

HISTORY: GC § 12672-2; 116 v 491, § 2; Bureau of Code Revision, 10-1-53; 126 v 178 (Eff 9-16-55); 132 v H 911 (Eff 6-11-68); 133 v H 742 (Eff 11-21-69); 136 v H 300 (Eff 7-1-76); 143 v H 111 (Eff 7-1-89); 146 v H 117 (Eff 6-30-95); 147 v H 215. Eff 6-30-97.

[§ 3719.02.1] § 3719.021 Wholesalers of controlled substances; license.

Persons other than a licensed manufacturer, pharmacist, or owner of a pharmacy who possess for sale, sell, or dispense controlled substances at wholesale shall first obtain a license as a wholesaler of controlled substances from the state board of pharmacy.

All licenses issued pursuant to this section shall be for a period of one year from the thirtieth day of June and may be renewed for a like period annually according to the standard renewal procedure of sections 4745.01 to 4745.03 of the Revised Code.

The annual license fee shall be thirty-seven dollars and fifty cents and shall accompany each application for such license or renewal thereof. All such renewal fees shall be paid in advance by the renewal applicant to the treasurer of state, and entered by the treasurer of state on the records of the state board of pharmacy. A license that has not been renewed by the first day of August in any year may be reinstated upon payment of the renewal fee and a penalty of fifty-five dollars.

The state board of pharmacy, subject to the approval of the controlling board, may establish a fee in excess of the amount provided in this section, provided that the fee does not exceed the amount established by this section by more than fifty per cent.

HISTORY: 126 v 178 (Eff 9-16-55); 132 v H 911 (Eff 6-11-68); 133 v H 742 (Eff 11-21-69); 136 v H 300 (Eff 7-1-76); 143 v H 111 (Eff 7-1-89); 146 v H 117 (Eff 6-30-95); 147 v H 215. Eff 6-30-97.

§ 3719.03 Qualification of applicant for license; revocation.

No license shall be issued under section 3719.02 or 3719.021 [3719.02.1] of the Revised Code unless and until the applicant therefor has furnished proof satisfactory to the state board of pharmacy:

(A) That the applicant is of good moral character or, if the applicant be an association or corporation, that the managing officers are of good moral character;

(B) That the applicant is equipped as to land, buildings, and paraphernalia properly to carry on the business described in his application;

(C) That the applicant's trade connections are such that there is a reasonable probability that he will apply all controlled substances grown, cultivated, processed, produced, or possessed by him to scientific, experimental, medicinal, or instructive purposes;

(D) That the applicant is in sufficiently good financial condition to carry out his obligation;

(E) That the applicant has satisfactorily shown that the granting of such license is in the public interest.

No license shall be granted to any person who has, within five years, been convicted of a drug abuse offense as defined in section 3719.01 of the Revised Code, or to any person who is a drug dependent person.

The board may suspend or revoke, for cause, any license issued under section 3719.02 or 3719.021 [3719.02.1] of the Revised Code.

HISTORY: GC § 12672-3; 116 v 491, § 3; Bureau of Code Revision, 10-1-53; 126 v 178 (Eff 9-16-55); 136 v H 300. Eff 7-1-76.

The effective date is set by section 4 of HB 300.

§ 3719.04 Sale of schedule II substances by manufacturer or wholesaler.

(A) A licensed manufacturer or wholesaler of controlled substances may sell at wholesale controlled substances to any of the following persons and subject to the following conditions:

(1) To a licensed manufacturer or wholesaler of controlled substances, or a terminal distributor of dangerous drugs having a category III license;

(2) To a person in the employ of the United States government or of any state, territorial, district, county, municipal, or insular government, purchasing, receiving, possessing, or dispensing controlled substances by reason of his official duties;

(3) To a master of a ship or a person in charge of any aircraft upon which no physician is regularly employed, for the actual medical needs of persons on board the ship or aircraft, when not in port; provided such controlled substances shall be sold to the master of the ship or person in charge of the aircraft only in pursuance of a special official written order approved by a commissioned medical officer or acting assistant surgeon of the United States public health service;

(4) To a person in a foreign country, if the federal drug abuse control laws are complied with.

(B) An official written order for any schedule II controlled substances shall be signed in triplicate by the person giving the order or by his authorized agent. The original shall be presented to the person who sells or dispenses the schedule II controlled substances named in the order and, if that person accepts the order, each party to the transaction shall preserve his copy of the order for a period of two years in such a way as to be readily accessible for inspection by any public officer or employee engaged in the enforcement of Chapter 3719. of the Revised Code. Compliance with the federal drug abuse control laws, respecting the requirements governing the use of a special official written order constitutes compliance with this division.

HISTORY: GC § 12672-4; 116 v 491, § 4; Bureau of Code Revision, 10-1-53; 126 v 178 (Eff 9-16-55); 134 v H 924 (Eff 10-26-71); 137 v H 1 (Eff 8-26-77); 145 v H 88. Eff 6-29-94.

§ 3719.05 Dispensing by pharmacist; sale of stock.

(A) As used in this section and section 3719.06 of the Revised Code:

(1) "Dentist" means a person licensed under Chapter 4715. of the Revised Code to practice dentistry.

(2) "Physician" means a person holding a valid certificate issued under Chapter 4731. of the Revised Code authorizing him to practice medicine and surgery, osteopathic medicine and surgery, or podiatry.

(3) "Veterinarian" means a person licensed under Chapter 4741. of the Revised Code to practice veterinary medicine.

(B) A pharmacist may dispense schedule II controlled

substances to any person upon a written prescription given by a dentist, physician, or veterinarian and schedule III or IV controlled substances to any person upon a written or oral prescription given by a practitioner. Each written prescription shall be properly executed, dated, and signed by the person prescribing on the day when issued and bearing the full name and address of the patient for whom, or of the owner of the animal for which, the schedule II controlled substance is dispensed, and the full name, address, and registry number under the federal drug abuse control laws of the person prescribing. If the prescription is for an animal, it shall state the species of animal for which the drug is prescribed. The prescription shall be retained on file by the owner of the pharmacy in which it is filled for a period of two years, so as to be readily accessible for inspection by any public officer or employee engaged in the enforcement of Chapter 2925., 3719., or 4719. of the Revised Code. Each oral prescription shall be recorded by the pharmacist and such record shall show the name and address of the patient for whom, or of the owner of the animal for which the schedule III or IV controlled substance is dispensed, the full name, address, and registry number under the federal drug abuse control laws of the practitioner prescribing, the name of the schedule III or IV controlled substance dispensed, the amount dispensed, and the date when dispensed. Such record shall be retained on file by the owner of the pharmacy in which it is filled for a period of two years. No prescription for a schedule II controlled substance shall be refilled. Prescriptions for schedule III and IV controlled substances may be refilled not more than five times in a six month period from the date the prescription is given by a practitioner.

(C) The legal owner of any stock of schedule II controlled substances in a pharmacy, upon discontinuance of dealing in said drugs, may sell said stock to a manufacturer, wholesaler, or owner of a pharmacy registered under the federal drug abuse control laws pursuant to an official written order.

(D) A pharmacist may dispense, upon an official written order to a practitioner in quantities not exceeding one ounce at any one time, aqueous or oleaginous solutions of which the content of narcotic drugs does not exceed a proportion greater than twenty per cent of the complete solution, to be used for medicinal purposes.

(E) Notwithstanding division (B) of this section, schedule II controlled substances may be dispensed orally and without the written prescription of a dentist, physician, or veterinarian in emergency situations as prescribed under the federal drug abuse control laws.

HISTORY: GC § 12672-5; 116 v 491, § 5; Bureau of Code Revision, 10-1-53; 126 v 178 (Eff 9-16-55); 134 v H 924 (Eff 10-26-71); 136 v H 300 (Eff 7-1-76); 145 v H 391. Eff 7-21-94.

§ 3719.06 Prescribing, dispensing and administering by dentist, physician, veterinarian or advanced practice nurse.

(A) A dentist or physician licensed to prescribe, dispense, and administer controlled substances to a human being in the course of his professional practice may do the following:

(1) Prescribe schedule II controlled substances by a written prescription;

(2) Prescribe schedule III or IV controlled substances by a written or oral prescription;

(3) Administer or dispense schedule II, III, or IV controlled substances;

(4) Cause schedule II, III, and IV controlled substances to be administered under his direction and supervision.

No dentist or physician shall prescribe, dispense, or administer a schedule III anabolic steroid for the purpose of human muscle building or enhancing human athletic performance unless it has been approved for that purpose under the "Federal Food, Drug, and Cosmetic Act," 52 Stat. 1040 (1938), 21 U.S.C.A. 301, as amended. Each written prescription shall be dated and signed by the dentist or physician prescribing on the day when issued and shall bear the full name and address of the person for whom the controlled substance is prescribed and the full name, address, and registry number under the federal drug abuse control laws of the person prescribing.

(B) A veterinarian licensed to prescribe, dispense, and administer controlled substances to an animal in the course of his professional practice may do the following:

(1) Prescribe schedule II controlled substances by a written prescription ;

(2) Prescribe schedule III or IV controlled substances by a written or oral prescription;

(3) Administer and dispense schedule II, III, or IV controlled substances;

(4) Cause schedule II, III, and IV controlled substances to be administered by an assistant or orderly under his direction and supervision.

Each written prescription shall be dated and signed by the veterinarian prescribing on the day when issued and shall bear the full name and address of the owner of the animal, the species of the animal for which the controlled substance is prescribed, and the full name, address, and registry number under the federal drug abuse control laws of the veterinarian prescribing.

(C) An advanced practice nurse approved under section 4723.56 of the Revised Code to prescribe controlled substances may prescribe by written or oral prescription any schedule III or IV controlled substance that is recommended by the formulary committee for advanced practice nurses and included in the formulary established by rules adopted under section 4723.58 of the Revised Code. No advanced practice nurse shall prescribe a schedule III anabolic steroid for the purpose of human muscle building or enhancing human athletic performance unless it is approved for that purpose under the "Federal Food, Drug, and Cosmetic Act," 52 Stat. 1040 (1938), 21 U.S.C.A. 301, as amended. Each written prescription shall be dated and signed by the advanced practice nurse issuing the prescription on the day issued and shall bear the full name and address of the person for whom the controlled substance is prescribed and the advanced practice nurse's full name, address, and registry number under the federal drug abuse control laws.

Any person, who has obtained from a practitioner any controlled substance for administration to a human being or an animal during the absence of such practitioner, shall return to such practitioner any unused portion of such drug, when it is no longer required by such human being or animal.

HISTORY: GC § 12672-6; 116 v 491, § 6; Bureau of Code Revision, 10-1-53; 126 v 178 (Eff 9-16-55); 134 v H 924 (Eff 10-26-71); 136 v H 300 (Eff 7-1-76); 144 v H 62 (Eff 5-21-91); 145 v H 391. Eff 7-21-94.

§ 3719.07 Records of controlled substances.

(A) Every practitioner, or other person who is authorized to administer or use controlled substances, shall keep a record of all such drugs received by him, and a record of all such drugs administered, dispensed, or used by him, otherwise than by prescription in accordance with the provisions of division (E) of this section. The keeping of a record of the quantity, character, and potency of solutions or other preparations purchased or made up by a practitioner or other person using small quantities of solutions or other preparations of controlled substances for local application, and of the dates when purchased or made up, without keeping a record of the amount of such solution or other preparation applied by him to individual patients is a sufficient compliance with this division.

No record need be kept of schedule V controlled substances administered, dispensed, or used in the treatment of any one person or animal, when the amount administered, dispensed, or used for that purpose does not exceed in any forty-eight consecutive hours:

(1) One hundred twenty-five milligrams of opium;

(2) Thirty milligrams of morphine or of any of its salts;

(3) Two hundred fifty milligrams of codeine or any of its salts;

(4) One hundred twenty-five milligrams of dihydrocodeine or any of its salts;

(5) Thirty milligrams of ethylmorphine or any of its salts;

(6) A quantity of any other schedule V controlled substances or any combination of schedule V controlled substances that does not exceed in pharmacologic potency any one of the drugs named above in the quantity stated.

(B) Manufacturers and wholesalers shall keep records of all controlled substances compounded, mixed, cultivated, grown, or by any other process produced or prepared by them, and of all controlled substances received or dispensed by them, in accordance with division (F) of this section.

(C) Every category III terminal distributor of dangerous drugs shall keep records of all controlled substances received or dispensed by them, in accordance with division (G) of this section.

(D) Every person who purchases for resale, or who dispenses schedule V controlled substances exempted by section 3719.15 of the Revised Code shall keep a record showing the quantities and kinds thereof received, dispensed, or disposed of otherwise, in accordance with divisions (E), (F), and (G) of this section.

(E) Every practitioner or other person, except a pharmacist, manufacturer, or wholesaler, authorized to administer or use controlled substances shall keep a record of all controlled substances received, administered, dispensed, or used which shall contain:

(1) The description of all controlled substances received, the name and address of the person from whom received, and the date of receipt;

(2) The description of controlled substances administered, dispensed, or used, the date of administering, dispensing, or using, the name and address of the person to whom, or for whose use, or the owner and species of the animal for which the controlled substance was administered, dispensed, or used.

(F) Every manufacturer and wholesaler shall keep a record of all controlled substances compounded, mixed, cultivated, grown, or by any other process produced or prepared, received, or dispensed by him which shall contain:

(1) The description of all drugs produced or prepared, the name and address of the person from whom received, and the date of receipt;

(2) The description of controlled substances dispensed, the name and address of each person to whom a controlled substance is dispensed, the amount of the controlled substance dispensed to each person, and the date it was so dispensed.

(G) Every category III terminal distributor of dangerous drugs shall keep a record of all controlled substances received or dispensed by him which shall contain:

(1) The description of controlled substances received, the name and address of the person from whom controlled substances are received, and the date of receipt;

(2) The name and place of residence of each person to whom controlled substances including those otherwise exempted by section 3719.15 of the Revised Code are dispensed, the description of such controlled substances dispensed to each person, the date such controlled substances are dispensed to each person, and the name and address of the practitioner prescribing drugs to the person to whom they are dispensed.

Every such record shall be kept for a period of two years and the date of the transaction recorded.

The keeping of a record required by or under the federal drug abuse control laws, containing substantially the same information as specified in this section, constitutes compliance with this section.

Every person who purchases for resale or who sells controlled substance preparations exempted by section 3719.15 of the Revised Code shall keep the record required by or under the federal drug abuse control law.

As used in this section, "description" means the dosage form, strength, and quantity, and the brand name, if any, or the generic name of a drug or controlled substance.

HISTORY: GC § 12672-8; 116 v 491, § 8; Bureau of Code Revision, 10-1-53; 126 v 178; 127 v 290; 128 v 1044 (Eff 10-22-59); 129 v 1796 (Eff 10-13-61); 134 v H 924 (Eff 10-26-71); 136 v H 300 (Eff 7-1-76); 140 v H 208 (Eff 9-20-84); 145 v H 88. Eff 6-29-94.

§ 3719.08 Labeling.

(A) Whenever a manufacturer dispenses a controlled substance, and whenever a wholesaler dispenses controlled substance in a package prepared by him, he shall securely affix to each package in which such controlled substance is contained a label showing in legible English the name and address of the vendor and the quantity, kind, and form of controlled substance contained therein. No person, except a pharmacist for the purpose of filling a prescription under Chapter 3719. of the Revised Code shall alter, deface, or remove any label so affixed.

(B) Whenever a pharmacist dispenses any controlled substance on a prescription issued by a practitioner, or a practitioner dispenses any controlled substance in the course of his practice, he shall affix to the container in which such controlled substance is dispensed, a label showing:

(1) His own name and address, or the name and address of the owner of the pharmacy for whom he is acting;

(2) The name of the patient for whom the controlled substance is prescribed or, if the patient is an animal, the name of the owner and the species of the animal;

(3) The name of the practitioner by whom the prescription was written or by whom the drug was dispensed;

(4) Such directions as may be stated on the prescription or provided by the practitioner on usage of the drug;

(5) The date on which the prescription was filled or refilled, whichever date is later.

The requirements of division (B) of this section do not apply when a controlled substance is prescribed for administration to an ultimate user who is institutionalized.

(C) No person shall alter, deface, or remove any label so affixed as long as any of the original contents remain.

(D) Every label for a schedule II, III, or IV drug shall contain the following warning:

"Caution: federal law prohibits the transfer of this drug to any person other than the patient for whom it was prescribed."

HISTORY: GC § 12672-9; 116 v 491, § 9; Bureau of Code Revision, 10-1-53; 126 v 178 (Eff 9-16-55); 134 v H 924 (Eff 10-26-71); 136 v H 300. Eff 7-1-76.

The effective date is set by section 4 of HB 300.

§ 3719.09 When possession of controlled substances is authorized.

Possession or control of controlled substances is authorized in the following instances and subject to the following conditions:

(A) Possession of controlled substances in the course of business by a manufacturer, wholesaler, practitioner, pharmacist, category III terminal distributor of dangerous drugs, or other person authorized to administer, dispense, or possess controlled substances under Chapter 3719. or 4729. of the Revised Code;

(B) Possession by any person of any schedule V narcotic drug exempted under section 3719.15 of the Revised Code, where the quantity of the drug does not exceed two grains of opium, one-half grain of morphine or any of its salts, four grains of codeine or any of its salts, two grains of dihydrocodeine or any of its salts, or one-half grain of ethylmorphine or any of its salts, or, in the case of any other schedule V controlled substance or any combination of narcotic drugs, where the quantity does not exceed in pharmacologic potency any one of the drugs named above in the quantity stated;

(C) Possession by any person of any controlled substance that the person obtained pursuant to a prescription issued by a practitioner or that was obtained for the person pursuant to a prescription issued by a practitioner, when the drug is in a container regardless of whether the container is the original container in which the drug was dispensed directly or indirectly to that person;

(D) Possession in the course of business of combination drugs that contain pentobarbital and at least one noncontrolled substance active ingredient, in a manufactured dosage form, the only indication of which is for euthanizing animals, or other substance that the state veterinary medical licensing board and the state board of pharmacy both approve under division (A) of section 4729.532 [4729.53.2] of the Revised Code, by an agent or employee of an animal shelter who is authorized by the licensure of the animal shelter with the state board of pharmacy to purchase and possess the drug solely for use as specified in that section. As used in this division, "in the course of business" means possession or use at an establishment described in a license issued under section 4729.54 of the Revised Code, or outside that establishment when necessary because of a risk to the health or safety of any person, provided that the substance is in a quantity no greater than reasonably could be used to alleviate the risk, is in the original manufacturer's container, and is returned to the establishment as soon as possible after the risk has passed.

HISTORY: 138 v S 184, § 5 (Eff 6-20-84); 145 v H 88 (Eff 6-29-94); 146 v S 2. Eff 7-1-96.

Analogous to former RC § 3719.09 (GC § 12672-10, 116 v 491, § 10; Bureau of Code Revision, 10-1-53; 126 v 178; 128 v 1044; 129 v 1796; 133 v H 874; 136 v H 300; 138 v S 184), repealed 138 v S 184, § 4, eff 6-20-84.

The effective date is set by section 6 of SB 2.

§ 3719.10 Nuisance.

Premises or real estate, including vacant land, on which a felony violation of Chapter 2925. or 3719. of the Revised Code occurs constitute a nuisance subject to abatement pursuant to Chapter 3767. of the Revised Code.

HISTORY: 136 v H 300. Eff 7-1-76.

Analogous to former RC § 3719.10 (GC § 12672-12; 116 v 491; Bureau of Code Revision, 10-1-53), repealed 136 v H 300, eff 7-1-76.

The effective date is set by section 4 of HB 300.

[§ 3719.10.1] § 3719.101 Repealed, 136 v H 300, § 2 [126 v 178]. Eff 7-1-76.

This section concerned prohibited use of buildings or vehicles.

§ 3719.11 Forfeiture and disposition of controlled substances.

All controlled substances, the lawful possession of which is not established or the title to which cannot be ascertained, which have come into the custody of a peace officer, shall be forfeited pursuant to sections 2925.41 to 2925.45, 2933.41, or 2933.43 of the Revised Code, and, unless any such section provides for a different manner of disposition, shall be disposed of as follows:

(A) The court or magistrate having jurisdiction shall order the controlled substances forfeited and destroyed. The agency served by the peace officer who obtained or took custody of the controlled substances may destroy them or may send them to the bureau of criminal identification and investigation for destruction by it. A record of the place where the controlled substances were seized, of the kinds and quantities of controlled substances so destroyed, and of the time, place, and manner of destruction, shall be kept, and a return under oath, reporting the destruction, shall be made by the officer who destroys them to the court or magistrate and to the United States director, bureau of narcotics and dangerous drugs.

(B) Upon written application by the department of health, the court or magistrate that ordered the forfeiture of the controlled substances may order the delivery of any of them, except heroin and its salts and derivatives, to the department for distribution or destruction as provided in this section.

(C) Upon application by any hospital within this state that is not operated for private gain, the department of health may deliver any controlled substances that have come into its custody pursuant to this section to the applicant for medicinal use. The department may deliver excess stocks of the controlled substances to the United States director, bureau of narcotics and dangerous drugs, or may destroy the excess stocks.

(D) The department of health shall keep a complete record of all controlled substances received pursuant to this section and of all controlled substances disposed of pursuant to this section, showing all of the following:

(1) The exact kinds, quantities, and forms of the controlled substances;

(2) The persons from whom they were received and to whom they were delivered;

(3) By whose authority they were received, delivered, or destroyed;

(4) The dates of their receipt, delivery, or destruction.

(E) The record required by this section shall be open to inspection by all federal and state officers charged with the enforcement of federal and state narcotic and drug abuse control laws.

HISTORY: GC § 12672-13; 116 v 491, § 13; Bureau of Code Revision, 10-1-53; 134 v H 924 (Eff 10-26-71); 136 v H 300 (Eff 7-1-76); 141 v S 69 (Eff 9-3-86); 143 v H 215 (Eff 4-11-90); 143 v S 258. Eff 11-20-90.

[§ 3719.11.1] § 3719.111 Repealed, 136 v H 300, § 2 [126 v 178]. Eff 7-1-76.

This section concerned forfeiture of vehicles.

§ 3719.12 Report of conviction to licensing board.

Unless a report has been made pursuant to section 2929.24 of the Revised Code, on the conviction of a manufacturer, wholesaler, practitioner, pharmacist, physician assistant, or nurse of the violation of this chapter or Chapter 2925. of the Revised Code, the prosecutor in the case, on forms provided by the board, promptly shall report the conviction to the board that licensed, certified, or registered the manufacturer, wholesaler, practitioner, pharmacist, physician assistant, or nurse to practice or to carry on business. Within thirty days of the receipt of this information, the board shall initiate action in accordance with Chapter 119. of the Revised Code to determine whether to suspend or revoke the license, certificate, or registration.

HISTORY: GC § 12672-14; 116 v 491, § 14; Bureau of Code Revision, 10-1-53; 126 v 178 (Eff 9-16-55); 134 v H 924 (Eff 10-26-71); 136 v H 300 (Eff 7-1-76); 143 v H 615 (Eff 3-27-91); 146 v S 2 (Eff 7-1-96); 146 v S 143, § 1 (Eff 3-5-96); 146 v S 143, § 5. Eff 7-1-96.

The effective date is set by section 7 of SB 143.

[§ 3719.12.1] § 3719.121 Suspension of licensed or registered person addicted to or improperly distributing controlled substances.

(A) Except as otherwise provided in section 4723.28 or 4731.22 of the Revised Code, the license, certificate, or registration of any practitioner, nurse, physician assistant, pharmacist, manufacturer, or wholesaler, who is or becomes addicted to the use of controlled substances, shall be suspended by the board that authorized the person's license, certificate, or registration until the person offers satisfactory proof to the board that the person no longer is addicted to the use of controlled substances.

(B) If the board under which a person has been issued a license, certificate or evidence of registration determines that there is clear and convincing evidence that continuation of the person's professional practice or method of distributing controlled substances presents a danger of immediate and serious harm to others, the board may suspend the person's license, certificate, or registration without a hearing. Except as otherwise provided in sections 4715.30, 4723.281 [4723.28.1], 4730.25, and 4731.22 of the Revised Code, the board shall follow the procedure for suspension without a prior hearing in section 119.07 of the Revised Code. The suspension shall remain in effect, unless removed by the board, until the board's final adjudication order becomes effective, except that if the board does not issue its final adjudication order within ninety days after the hearing, the suspension shall be void on the ninety-first day after the hearing.

(C) On receiving notification pursuant to section 2929.24 or 3719.12 of the Revised Code, the board under which a person has been issued a license, certificate or evidence of registration immediately shall suspend the license, certificate, or registration of that person on a plea of guilty to, a finding by a jury or court of the person's guilt of, or conviction of a felony drug abuse offense; a finding by a court of the person's eligibility for treatment in lieu of conviction; a plea of guilty to, or a finding by a jury or court of the person's guilt of, or the person's conviction of an offense in another jurisdiction that is essentially the same as a felony drug abuse offense; or a finding by a court of the person's eligibility for treatment in lieu of conviction in another jurisdiction. The board shall notify the holder of the license, certificate, or registration of the suspension, which shall remain in effect until the board holds an adjudicatory hearing under Chapter 119. of the Revised Code.

HISTORY: 126 v 178 (Eff 9-16-55); 129 v 582(816) (Eff 1-10-61); 136 v H 300 (Eff 7-1-76); 143 v H 615 (Eff 3-27-91); 146 v S 2 (Eff 7-1-96); 146 v S 143, § 1 (Eff 3-5-96); 146 v S 143, § 5. Eff 7-1-96.

§ 3719.13 Inspection of prescriptions, orders, records, and stock.

Prescriptions, orders, and records, required by Chapter 3719. of the Revised Code, and stocks of dangerous drugs and controlled substances, shall be open for inspection only to federal, state, county, and municipal officers, and employees of the state board of pharmacy whose duty it is to enforce the laws of this state or of the United States relating to controlled substances. Such prescriptions, orders, records, and stocks shall be open for inspection by employees of the state medical board for purposes of enforcing Chapter 4731. of the Revised Code. No person having knowledge of any such prescription, order, or record shall divulge such knowledge, except in connection with a prosecution or proceeding in court or before a licensing or registration board or officer, to which prosecution or proceeding the person to whom such prescriptions, orders, or records relate is a party.

HISTORY: GC § 12672-15; 116 v 491, § 15; Bureau of Code Revision, 10-1-53; 136 v H 300 (Eff 7-1-76); 140 v H 208 (Eff 9-20-84); 141 v H 769. Eff 3-17-87.

§ 3719.14 Exemptions.

(A) A common carrier or warehouser while engaged in lawfully transporting or storing any controlled substance or an employee of a common carrier or warehouser of that nature who is acting within the scope of the employee's employment may control and possess any controlled substance.

(B) Any law enforcement official may purchase, collect, or possess any controlled substance or may offer to sell any controlled substance, or any counterfeit controlled substance as defined in section 2925.01 of the Revised Code, when the purchase, collection, possession, or offer to sell is necessary to do so in the performance of the official's official duties. This division does not permit a law enforcement official to sell any controlled substance in the performance of the official's official duties. A peace officer, as defined in section 3719.141 [3719.14.1] of the Revised Code, may sell a controlled substance in the performance of the officer's official duties only as provided in that section.

(C) Any employee or agent of a person who is entitled to possession of a controlled substance or whose possession of a controlled substance is for the purpose of aiding any law enforcement official in the official's official duties temporarily may possess any controlled substance.

HISTORY: 136 v H 300 (Eff 7-1-76); 143 v H 215 (Eff 4-11-90); 146 v H 125. Eff 7-1-96.

Analogous to former RC § 3719.14 (GC § 12672-11; 116 v 491; Bureau of Code Revision, 10-1-53), repealed 136 v H 300, eff 7-1-76.

The effective date is set by section 3 of HB 125.

[§ 3719.14.1] § 3719.141 Sales of controlled substances by peace officers.

(A) A peace officer may sell any controlled substance

in the performance of the officer's official duties only if either of the following applies:

(1) A peace officer may sell any controlled substance in the performance of the officer's official duties if all of the following apply:

(a) Prior approval for the sale has been given by the prosecuting attorney of the county in which the sale takes place, in any manner described in division (B) of this section;

(b) The peace officer who makes the sale determines that the sale is necessary in the performance of the officer's official duties;

(c) Any of the following applies:

(i) The person to whom the sale is made or any other person who is involved in the sale does not know that the officer who makes the sale is a peace officer, and the peace officer who makes the sale determines that the sale is necessary to prevent the person from determining or suspecting that the officer who makes the sale is a peace officer.

(ii) The peace officer who makes the sale determines that the sale is necessary to preserve an identity that the peace officer who makes the sale has assumed in the performance of the officer's official duties.

(iii) The sale involves a controlled substance that, during the course of another sale, was intercepted by the peace officer who makes the sale or any other peace officer who serves the same agency served by the peace officer who makes the sale; the intended recipient of the controlled substance in the other sale does not know that the controlled substance has been so intercepted; the sale in question is made to the intended recipient of the controlled substance in the other sale and is undertaken with the intent of obtaining evidence of a drug abuse offense against the intended recipient of the controlled substance; and the sale in question does not involve the transfer of any money or other thing of value to the peace officer who makes the sale or any other peace officer who serves the same agency served by the peace officer who makes the sale in exchange for the controlled substance.

(d) If the sale is made under the circumstances described in division (A)(1)(c)(i) or (ii) of this section, no person is charged with any criminal offense or any delinquent act based upon the sale unless both of the following apply:

(i) The person also is charged with a criminal offense or a delinquent act that is based upon an act or omission that is independent of the sale but that either is connected together with the sale, or constitutes a part of a common scheme or plan with the sale, or is part of a course of criminal conduct involving the sale.

(ii) The criminal offense or delinquent act based upon the sale and the other criminal offense or delinquent act are charged in the same indictment, information, or complaint.

(e) The sale is not part of a continuing course of conduct involving the sale of controlled substances by the peace officer who makes the sale.

(f) The amount of the controlled substance sold and the scope of the sale of the controlled substance is as limited as possible under the circumstances.

(g) Prior to the sale, the law enforcement agency served by the peace officer who makes the sale has adopted a written internal control policy that does all of the following:

(i) Addresses the keeping of detailed records as to the amount of money or other things of value obtained in the sale in exchange for the controlled substance;

(ii) Addresses the delivery of all moneys or things of value so obtained to the prosecuting attorney pursuant to division (D) of this section;

(iii) Addresses the agency's use and disposition of all such moneys or things of value that are deposited in the law enforcement trust fund of the sheriff, municipal corporation, or township, pursuant to division (D) of this section, and that are used by the sheriff, are allocated to the police department of the municipal corporation by its legislative authority, or are allocated by the board of township trustees to the township police department, township police district police force, or office of the constable;

(iv) Provides for the keeping of detailed financial records of the receipts of the proceeds, the general types of expenditures made out of the proceeds received, and the specific amount of each general type of expenditure. The policy shall not provide for or permit the identification of any peace officer involved in the sale, any information that is or may be needed in an ongoing investigation, or any specific expenditure that is made in an ongoing investigation.

(2) A peace officer may sell any controlled substance in the performance of the officer's official duties if all of the following apply:

(a) Prior approval for the sale has been given by the prosecuting attorney of the county in which the sale takes place, in any manner described in division (B) of this section;

(b) Prior to the sale, the law enforcement agency served by the peace officer has adopted a written internal control policy that does the things listed in divisions (A)(1)(g)(i) to (iv) of this section;

(c) The purchaser of the controlled substance acquires possession of it in the presence of the peace officer who makes the sale.

(d) Upon the consummation of the sale, either of the following occurs:

(i) The peace officer arrests the purchaser of the controlled substance, recovers it and the proceeds of the sale, and secures it and the proceeds as evidence to be used in a subsequent prosecution.

(ii) The peace officer makes a reasonable, good faith effort to arrest the purchaser of the controlled substance and to recover the controlled substance and the proceeds of the sale, but the officer is unable to make the arrest and recover all of the controlled substance and proceeds for reasons beyond the officer's control, and the peace officer secures all of the controlled substance recovered and all of the proceeds recovered as evidence to be used in a subsequent prosecution.

(B) The approval of a prosecuting attorney required by division (A)(1)(a) or (2)(a) of this section may be in either of the following forms:

(1) A general approval that is given by the prosecuting attorney to the peace officer who makes the sale or to the law enforcement agency served by that peace officer, that grants approval only to that peace officer, and that grants approval for any such sale that may be necessary, after the approval has been granted, under the standards described in division (A)(1) or (2) of this section;

(2) A specific approval that is given by the prosecuting attorney to the peace officer who makes the sale or to the law enforcement agency served by that peace officer, and that grants approval only to that peace officer and only for the particular sale in question, under the standards described in division (A)(1) or (2) of this section.

(C) If a peace officer sells a controlled substance in the performance of the officer's official duties under division (A)(1) or (2) of this section, the peace officer, within a reasonable time after the sale, shall provide the prosecuting attorney who granted approval for the sale with a written summary that identifies the amount and type of controlled substance sold, the circumstances of the sale, and the amount of any money or other thing of value obtained in the sale in exchange for the controlled substance. The summary shall not identify or enable the identification of any peace officer involved in the sale and shall not contain any information that is or may be needed in an ongoing investigation.

(D)(1) Except as provided in division (D)(2) of this section, if a peace officer sells a controlled substance in the performance of the officer's official duties under division (A)(1) or (2) of this section, the peace officer, as soon as possible after the sale, shall deliver all money or other things of value obtained in the sale in exchange for the controlled substance to the prosecuting attorney who granted approval for the sale. The prosecuting attorney shall safely keep all money and other things of value the prosecuting attorney receives under this division for use as evidence in any criminal action or delinquency proceeding based upon the sale. All money so received by a prosecuting attorney that no longer is needed as evidence in any criminal action or delinquency proceeding shall be deposited by the prosecuting attorney in the law enforcement trust fund of the sheriff if the peace officer who made the sale is the sheriff or a deputy sheriff or the law enforcement trust fund of a municipal corporation or township if it is served by the peace officer who made the sale, as established pursuant to section 2933.43 of the Revised Code, and upon deposit shall be expended only as provided in that section. All other things of value so received by a prosecuting attorney that no longer are needed as evidence in any criminal action or delinquency proceeding shall be disposed of, without appraisal, at a public auction to the highest bidder for cash; the proceeds of the sale shall be deposited by the prosecuting attorney in the law enforcement trust fund of the sheriff if the peace officer who made the sale is the sheriff or a deputy sheriff or the law enforcement trust fund of a municipal corporation or township if it is served by the peace officer who made the sale, as established pursuant to section 2933.43 of the Revised Code, and upon deposit shall be expended only as provided in that section. Each law enforcement agency that uses any money that was deposited in a law enforcement trust fund pursuant to this division shall comply with the written internal control policy adopted by the agency, as required by division (A)(1)(g) or (2)(b) of this section, in its use of the money.

(2) Division (D)(1) of this section does not apply in relation to a peace officer who sells a controlled substance in the performance of the officer's official duties under division (A)(1) of this section in any of the following circumstances:

(a) The person to whom the sale is made or any other person who is involved in the sale does not know that the officer is a peace officer, and, if the officer were to retain and deliver the money or other things of value to the prosecuting attorney, the person would determine or suspect that the officer is a peace officer.

(b) If the officer were to retain and deliver the money or other things of value to the prosecuting attorney, an identity that has been assumed in the performance of the officer's official duties would not be preserved.

(c) The sale is made under the circumstances described in division (A)(1)(c)(iii) of this section.

(3) If division (D)(1) of this section does not apply in relation to a peace officer who sells a controlled substance in the performance of the officer's official duties under division (A)(1) of this section due to the operation of division (D)(2) of this section, the peace officer, as soon as possible after the sale, shall deliver to the prosecuting attorney who granted approval for the sale a written summary that describes the circumstances of the sale and the reason for which division (D)(1) of this section does not apply. The summary shall not identify or enable the identification of any peace officer involved in the sale and shall not contain any information that is or may be needed in an ongoing investigation.

(E)(1) A written internal control policy adopted by a law enforcement agency that is served by a peace officer who sells a controlled substance under division (A)(1) or (2) of this section, as required by division (A)(1)(g) or (2)(b) of this section, is a public record open for inspection under section 149.43 of the Revised Code. Each law enforcement agency that adopts a written internal control policy of that nature shall comply with it in relation to any sale of a controlled substance under division (A)(1) or (2) of this section. All records as to the amount of money or things of value obtained in the sale of a controlled substance, in exchange for the controlled substance, and all financial records of the receipts of the proceeds, the general types of expenditures made out of the proceeds received, and the specific amounts of each general type of expenditure by a law enforcement agency in relation to any sale of a controlled substance under division (A)(1) or (2) of this section are public records open for inspection under section 149.43 of the Revised Code.

(2) A summary required by division (C) or (D)(3) of this section is a public record open for inspection under section 149.43 of the Revised Code.

(F)(1) Each prosecuting attorney who grants approval for a sale of controlled substances by a peace officer and who receives in any calendar year one or more summaries under division (C) of this section relative to the sale of a controlled substance by a peace officer shall prepare a report covering the calendar year that cumulates all of the information contained in each of the summaries so received in the calendar year and shall send the cumulative report, no later than the first day of March in the calendar year following the calendar year covered by the report, to the attorney general.

(2) Each prosecuting attorney who receives any money or any other thing of value under division (D)(1) of this section shall keep detailed financial records of the receipts and dispositions of all such moneys or things of value so received. No record of that nature shall identify, or enable the identification of, any person from whom money or another thing of value was received as a result of the sale of a controlled substance under division (A)(1) or (2) of this section or contain any information that is or may be needed in an ongoing investigation. Each record of that nature is a public record open for inspection under section 149.43 of the Revised Code and shall include, but is not limited to, all of the following information:

(a) The identity of each law enforcement agency that has so delivered any money or other thing of value to the prosecuting attorney;

(b) The total amount of money or other things of value so received from each law enforcement agency;

(c) The disposition made under this section of all money or other things of value so received.

(G) Divisions (A) to (F) of this section do not apply to any peace officer, or to any officer, agent, or employee of the United States, who is operating under the management and direction of the United States department of justice. Any peace officer, or any officer, agent, or employee of the United States, who is operating under the management and direction of the United States department of justice may sell a controlled substance in the performance of the officer's, agent's, or employee's official duties if the sale is made in accordance with federal statutes and regulations.

(H) As used in this section, "peace officer" has the same meaning as in section 2935.01 of the Revised Code and also includes a special agent of the bureau of criminal identification and investigation.

HISTORY: 143 v H 215 (Eff 4-11-90); 143 v H 588 (Eff 10-31-90); 143 v S 258 (Eff 11-20-90); 146 v S 2 (Eff 7-1-96); 146 v H 125. Eff 7-1-96.

§ 3719.15 Substances exempted.

Except as specifically provided in Chapters 2925. and 3719. of the Revised Code, such chapters shall not apply to the following cases:

(A) Where a practitioner administers or dispenses; or where a pharmacist or owner of a pharmacy sells at retail any medicinal preparation that contains in one fluid ounce, or if a solid or semisolid preparation, in one avoirdupois ounce:

(1) Not more than two grains of opium;

(2) Not more than one quarter of a grain of morphine or of any of its salts;

(3) Not more than one grain of codeine or of any of its salts;

(4) Not more than one-half grain of dihydrocodeine or any of its salts;

(5) Not more than one-quarter grain of ethylmorphine or any of its salts.

Each preparation mentioned in divisions (A)(1), (2), (3), (4), and (5) of this section shall in addition contain one or more nonnarcotic active medicinal ingredients in sufficient proportion to confer upon the preparation valuable medicinal qualities other than those possessed by the narcotic drug alone.

(6) Pharmaceutical preparations in solid form containing not more than two and five-tenths milligrams diphenoxylate and not less than twenty-five micrograms atropine sulfate per dosage unit.

(B) Where a practitioner administers or dispenses; or where a pharmacist sells at retail, liniments, ointments, and other preparations, that are susceptible of external use only and that contain narcotic drugs in such combination as prevent their being readily extracted from such liniments, ointments, or preparations, except that such sections shall apply to all liniments, ointments, and other preparations, that contain coca leaves in any quantity or combination.

The medicinal preparation, or the liniment, ointment, or other preparation susceptible of external use only, prescribed, administered, dispensed, or sold, shall contain, in addition to the narcotic drug in it, some drug or drugs conferring upon it medicinal qualities other than those possessed by the narcotic drug alone. Such preparation shall be prescribed, administered, compounded, dispensed, and sold in good faith as a medicine, and not for the purpose of evading such sections.

HISTORY: GC § 12672-7; 116 v 491, § 7; **Bureau of Code Revision,** 10-1-53; 126 v 178 (Eff 9-16-55); 129 v 1796 (Eff 10-13-61); 134 v H 924 (Eff 10-26-71); 136 v H 300. Eff 7-1-76.

The effective date is set by section 4 of of HB 300.

§ 3719.16 Dispensing of excepted substances.

No person shall dispense or sell, under the exemptions of section 3719.15 of the Revised Code to any one person, or for the use of any one person or animal, any preparation included within such section, when he knows, or can by reasonable diligence ascertain, that such dispensing or selling will provide the person to whom or for whose use, or the owner of the animal for the use of which, such preparation is dispensed or sold, within any forty-eight consecutive hours, with more than two grains of opium, or more than one-half of a grain of morphine or any of its salts, or more than four grains of codeine or any of its salts, or more than two grains of dihydrocodeine or any of its salts, or more than one-half grain of ethylmorphine or any of its salts, or will provide such person or the owner of such animal, within forty-eight consecutive hours, with more than one preparation exempted by the provisions of section 3719.15 of the Revised Code.

No person shall obtain or attempt to obtain, under the exemptions of section 3719.15e of the Revised Code, more than one preparation exempted by the provisions of that section within forty-eight consecutive hours.

HISTORY: GC § 12672-7; 116 v 491, § 7; Bureau of Code Revision, 10-1-53; 126 v 178; 127 v 290; 128 v 1044 (Eff 10-22-59); 129 v 1796 (Eff 10-13-61); 134 v H 924. Eff 10-26-71.

[§ 3719.16.1] § 3719.161 Alteration to increase concentration prohibited.

No person shall alter any controlled substance from the original compounded form by evaporation or other means to increase the concentration of narcotic drug contained therein. Altered preparations having a greater concentration of schedule V narcotic drug content than specified under provisions of section 3719.15 of the Revised Code, shall be classified as a schedule III narcotic drug.

HISTORY: 128 v 1044 (Eff 10-22-59); 134 v H 924 (Eff 10-26-71); 136 v H 300. Eff 7-1-76.

The effective date is set by section 4 of HB 300.

§ 3719.17 Repealed, 136 v H 300, § 2 [GC § 12672-16; 116 v 491; Bureau of Code Revision, 10-1-53; 126 v 178; 130 v 853]. Eff 7-1-76.

This section concerned illegal procurement of narcotic drugs.

[§ 3719.17.1] § 3719.171 Repealed, 136 v H 300, § 2 [126 v 178]. Eff 7-1-76.

This section concerned illegal prescriptions, written orders, records, labels.

[§ 3719.17.2] § 3719.172 Possession, sale, and disposal of hypodermics.

(A) Possession of a hypodermic is authorized for:

(1) Any manufacturer or distributor of, or dealer in, hypodermics or medication packaged in hypodermics, and any authorized agent or employee of such manufacturer, distributor, or dealer, in the regular course of business;

(2) A hospital, owner of a pharmacy, or pharmacist, in the regular course of business;

(3) Any practitioner, nurse, or other person authorized to administer injections, in the regular course of the person's profession or employment;

(4) Any person, when the hypodermic was lawfully obtained and is kept and used for the purpose of self-administration of insulin or other drug prescribed by a practitioner for the treatment of disease;

(5) Any person whose use of a hypodermic is for legal research, clinical, educational, or medicinal purposes;

(6) Any farmer, for the lawful administration of a drug to an animal;

(7) Any person whose use of a hypodermic is for lawful professional, mechanical, trade, or craft purpose.

(B) No manufacturer or distributor of, or dealer in, hypodermics or medication packaged in hypodermics, or their authorized agents or employees, and no owner of a pharmacy, or pharmacist, shall display any hypodermic for sale. No person authorized to possess a hypodermic pursuant to division (A) of this section shall negligently fail to take reasonable precautions to prevent any hypodermic in the person's possession from theft or acquisition by any unauthorized person.

(C) No person other than one of the following shall sell or furnish a hypodermic to another person:

(1) A manufacturer or distributor of, or dealer in, hypodermics or medication packaged in hypodermics, or their authorized agents or employees;

(2) A hospital;

(3) A pharmacist or person under the direct supervision of a pharmacist;

(4) A practitioner in the regular course of business and as permitted by law;

(5) An individual who holds a current license, certificate, or registration issued under Title 47 of the Revised Code and has been certified to conduct diabetes education by a national certifying body specified in rules adopted by the state board of pharmacy under section 4729.68 of the Revised Code, but only if diabetes education is within the individual's scope of practice under statutes and rules regulating the individual's profession.

(D) No person shall sell or furnish a hypodermic to another whom the person knows or has reasonable cause to believe is not authorized by division (A) of this section to possess a hypodermic.

(E) A pharmacist or person under the direct supervision of a pharmacist may furnish hypodermics to another without a prescription by a practitioner, but the pharmacist or person being supervised shall require positive identification of each person to whom hypodermics are furnished, and shall keep a written record of each transaction, including the date, the type and quantity of the articles furnished, and the name, address, and signature of the person to whom such articles are furnished. Such record shall be retained in the same manner as the exempt narcotics register. No pharmacist or person under a pharmacist's supervision shall fail to comply with this division in furnishing hypodermics.

HISTORY: 134 v H 521 (Eff 10-19-72); 136 v H 300 (Eff 7-1-76); 146 v S 246. Eff 11-6-96.

Not analogous to former RC § 3719.17.2 (126 v 178), repealed 134 v H 521, eff 10-19-72.

§ 3719.18 Enforcement officers; co-operation with agencies.

(A) The state board of pharmacy, its officers, agents, inspectors, and representatives, and all officers within the state, and all prosecuting attorneys, shall enforce Chapters 2925. and 3719. of the Revised Code, except those specifically delegated, and cooperate with all agencies charged with the enforcement of the laws of the United States, of this state, and of all other states, relating to controlled substances.

(B) Nothing in this chapter shall be construed to require the state board of pharmacy to enforce minor violations of Chapters 2925. and 3719. of the Revised Code if the board determines that the public interest is adequately served by a notice or warning to the alleged offender.

HISTORY: GC § 12672-18; 116 v 491, § 18; Bureau of Code Revision, 10-1-53; 136 v H 300 (Eff 7-1-76); 140 v H 208. Eff 9-20-84.

§ 3719.19 Persons not subject to prosecution.

No person shall be prosecuted for a violation of Chapter 3719. of the Revised Code, if such person has been acquitted or convicted under the federal narcotic laws of the same act or omission which, it is alleged, constitutes a violation of this chapter.

HISTORY: GC § 12672-20; 116 v 491, § 20; Bureau of Code Revision, 10-1-53; 136 v H 300. Eff 7-1-76.

The effective date is set by section 4 of HB 300.

§ 3719.20
Repealed, 136 v H 300, § 2 [GC § 12672-22; 116 v 491; Bureau of Code Revision, 10-1-53; 126 v 178; 134 v H 924.] Eff 7-1-76.

This section concerned narcotic drug prohibitions.

§ 3719.21 Disposition of fines and forfeited bail.

Except as provided in divisions (D)(1), (F), and (H) of section 2925.03, division (D)(1) of section 2925.02, 2925.04, or 2925.05, division (E)(1) of section 2925.11, division (F) of section 2925.13 or 2925.36, division (D) of section 2925.22, division (H) of section 2925.23, division (M) of section 2925.37, division (B)(5) of section 2925.42, division (B) of section 2929.18, division (D) of section 3719.99, division (B)(1) of section 4729.65, and division (E)(3) of section 4729.99 of the Revised Code, the clerk of the court shall pay all fines or forfeited bail assessed and collected under prosecutions or prosecutions commenced for violations of this chapter or Chapter 2925. of the Revised Code, within thirty days, to the executive director of the state board of pharmacy, and the executive director shall deposit the fines into the state treasury to the credit of the occupational licensing and regulatory fund.

HISTORY: GC § 12672-19; 116 v 491, § 19; Bureau of Code Revision, 10-1-53; 136 v H 300 (Eff 7-1-76); 138 v H 204 (Eff 7-30-79); 143 v H 266 (Eff 9-6-90); 143 v S 258 (Eff 11-20-90); 145 v H 715 (Eff 7-22-94); 146 v S 2 (Eff 7-1-96); 146 v S 269 (Eff 7-1-96); 146 v S 166. Eff 10-17-96.

The provisions of § 4 of SB 166 (146 v —) read as follows:

SECTION 4. The amendments made by this act to sections 309.08, 2925.03, 2929.18, 3719.21, 3793.06, and 3793.11 of the Revised Code apply to offenses that are committed on or after the effective date of this act.

Comment, Legislative Service Commission

° ° ° Sections ° ° ° 3719.21, ° ° ° of the Revised Code are amended by this act [Am. Sub. S.B. 269] and also by Am. Sub. S.B. 166 of the 121st General Assembly. ° ° ° Comparison of these amendments in pursuance of section 1.52 of the Revised Code discloses that they are not irreconcilable so that they are required by that section to be harmonized to give effect to each amendment.

§§ 3719.22, 3719.23, 3719.24

Repealed, 136 v H 300, § 2 [GC §§ 12672-17, 12673, 12673-1; 116 v 491; 123 v 174; Bureau of Code Revision, 10-1-53; 130 v 854, 855; 130 v Pt.II, 193; 133 v H 90]. Eff 7-1-76.

These sections concerned power to search for narcotics; proof and arrest; definitions; and prohibitions against delivery of barbiturates or amphetamines under certain circumstances.

§§ 3719.25, 3719.26
Repealed, 136 v H 300, § 2 [GC §§ 12673-2, 12673-3; 123 v 174; Bureau of Code Revision, 10-1-53; 130 v 856; 133 v H 90]. Eff 7-1-76.

These sections concerned exceptions to regulation of delivery of barbiturates and amphetamines; and handling of records and prescriptions.

§ 3719.27 Inspection and checking of files and records.

Persons required, by Chapter 3719. of the Revised Code, to keep files or records shall, upon the written request of an officer or employee designated by the state board of pharmacy, make such files or records available to such officer or employee, at all reasonable hours, for inspection and copying, and accord to such officer or employee full opportunity to check the correctness of such files or records, including opportunity to make inventory of all stocks of controlled substances on hand. No person shall fail to make such files or records available or to accord such opportunity to check their correctness.

HISTORY: GC § 12673-4; 123 v 174, § 5; Bureau of Code Revision, 10-1-53; 133 v H 90 (Eff 11-19-69); 136 v H 300. Eff 7-1-76.

The effective date is set by section 4 of HB 300.

§ 3719.28 Rules for administration and enforcement.

(A) The state board of pharmacy, pursuant to Chapter 119. of the Revised Code, shall adopt rules for administration and enforcement of Chapter 3719. of the Revised Code and prescribing the manner of keeping and the form and content of records to be kept by persons authorized to manufacture, distribute, dispense, conduct research in, prescribe, administer, or otherwise deal with controlled substances. Such rules shall be designed to:

(1) Facilitate surveillance of traffic in drugs, to prevent the improper acquisition or use of controlled substances or their diversion into illicit channels;

(2) Aid the state board of pharmacy and state, local, and federal law enforcement officers in enforcing the laws of this state and the federal government dealing with drug abuse and control of drug traffic.

(B) Rules adopted pursuant to this section shall not provide any less stringent requirements with respect to records than the requirements of the federal drug abuse control laws and regulations adopted thereunder. To the extent that records kept under the federal drug abuse control laws and regulations adopted thereunder fulfill requirements for similar records under rules adopted pursuant to this section, compliance with the federal law and regulations shall constitute compliance with the law and rules of this state with respect to such records.

HISTORY: 136 v H 300. Eff 7-1-76.

Analogous to former RC § 3719.28 (GC § 12673-5; 123 v 174, § 6; Bureau of Code Revision, 10-1-53; 126 v 178), repealed 136 v H 300, eff 7-1-76.

The effective date is set by section 4 of HB 300.

§ 3719.29 Repealed, 136 v H 300, § 2 [GC § 12673-6; 123 v 174; Bureau of Code Revision, 10-1-53]. Eff 7-1-76.

This section concerned disposition of fines.

[POISON]

§ 3719.30 Prohibition against depositing poison on thoroughfares.

No person shall leave or deposit poison or a substance containing poison in a common, street, alley, lane, or thoroughfare, or a yard or enclosure occupied by another.

Whoever violates this section shall be liable to the person injured for all damages sustained thereby.

HISTORY: RS § 6958; 74 v 13; GC § 12663; Bureau of Code Revision. Eff 10-1-53.

§ 3719.31 Prohibition against careless distribution of samples containing drug or poison.

No person shall leave, throw, or deposit upon the doorstep or premises owned or occupied by another, or hand, give, or deliver to any person, except in a place where it is kept for sale, a patent or proprietary medicine, preparation, pill, tablet, powder, cosmetic, disinfectant, or antiseptic, or a drug or medicine that contains poison or any ingredient that is deleterious to health, as a sample or for the purpose of advertising.

As used in this section "drug," "medicine," "patent or proprietary medicine," "pill," "tablet," "powder," "cosmetic," "disinfectant," or "antiseptic" includes all remedies for internal or external use.

HISTORY: RS §§ 4238-34, 4238-35, 4238-36; 95 v 146, §§ 1, 2, 3; GC §§ 12664, 12665; 102 v 87; Bureau of Code Revision. Eff 10-1-53.

§ 3719.32 Regulating the sale of poisons.

No person shall knowingly sell or deliver to any person otherwise than in the manner prescribed by laws, or sell or deliver to a minor under sixteen years of age in the manner prescribed by law but without the written order of an adult, any of the following substances or any poisonous compounds, combinations, or preparations thereof: the compounds and salts of antimony, arsenic, chromium, copper, lead, mercury, and zinc; the concentrated mineral acids; oxalic and hydrocyanic acids and their salts, and carbolic acid; yellow phosphorus; the essential oils of almonds, pennyroyal, tansy, and savin, croton oil, creosote, chloroform, chloral hydrate, and cantharides; aconite, belladonna, bitter almonds, colchicum, cotton root, cocculus indicus, conium, digitalis, hyoscyamus, ignatia, lobelia, nux vomica, opium, physostigma, phytolacca, strophanthus, stramonium, veratum viride, or any of the poisonous alkaloids or alkaloidal salts or other poisonous principles derived from such alkaloids, or other poisonous alkaloids or their salts; or other virulent poison.

HISTORY: RS §§ 4238-29, 4238-32; 95 v 280; 95 v 282, § 4; GC § 12666; Bureau of Code Revision, 10-1-53; 125 v 903; 130 v Pt II, 194 (Eff 12-16-64); 136 v H 300. Eff 7-1-76.

The effective date is set by section 4 of HB 300.

§ 3719.33 Labeling poisons.

No person shall sell or deliver to another a substance named in section 3719.32 of the Revised Code without having first learned by due inquiry that such person is aware of the poisonous character of such substance and that it is desired for a lawful purpose; or without plainly labeling "poison," and the names of two or more antidotes therefor, upon the box, bottle, or package containing it; or deliver such substance without recording in a book kept for the purpose, the name thereof, the quantity delivered, the purpose for which it is alleged to be used, the date of its delivery, the name and address of the purchaser, and the name of the dispenser; or fail to preserve said book for five years and submit it at all times for inspection to proper officers of the law.

HISTORY: RS §§ 4238-29, 4238-32; 95 v 280, 282, §§ 1, 4; GC § 12667; Bureau of Code Revision. Eff 10-1-53.

§ 3719.34 Poisons not labeled.

Sections 3719.32 and 3719.33 of the Revised Code do not apply to substances dispensed to or upon the order or prescription of persons believed by the dispenser to be lawfully authorized practitioners of medicine or dentistry. The record of sale and delivery mentioned in section 3719.33 of the Revised Code is not required of manufacturers and wholesalers selling any of the substances mentioned in section 3719.32 of the Revised Code at wholesale, if the box, bottle, or package containing such substance when sold at wholesale, is labeled with the name of the substance, "Poison," and the name and address of the manufacturer or wholesaler.

HISTORY: RS § 4238-30; 95 v 281, § 2; GC § 12668; Bureau of Code Revision. Eff 10-1-53.

§ 3719.35 Preparations not labeled poison.

It is not necessary to place a poison label upon, nor record the delivery of:

(A) Preparations containing substances named in section 3719.32 of the Revised Code when a single box, bottle, or other package of the bulk of one-half fluid ounce or the weight of one-half avoirdupois ounce does not contain more than an adult medicinal dose of such poisonous substance;

(B) The sulphide of antimony, the oxide or carbonate of zinc, or colors ground in oil and intended for use as paints;

(C) Calomel, paregoric, or other preparations of opium containing less than two grains of opium to the fluid ounce;

(D) Preparations recommended in good faith for diarrhea or cholera, when each bottle or package is accompanied by specific directions for use and a caution against the habitual use thereof;

(E) Liniments or ointments when plainly labeled "for external use only";

(F) Preparations put up and sold in the form of pills, tablets, or lozenges and intended for internal use, when the dose recommended does not contain more than one fourth of an adult medicinal dose of such poisonous substance.

HISTORY: RS § 4238-30; 95 v 281, § 2; GC §§ 12669, 12670, 12671; Bureau of Code Revision. Eff 10-1-53.

§ 3719.36 Board of pharmacy shall enforce laws relating to poison; fines.

The state board of pharmacy or anyone acting in its behalf shall enforce sections 3719.30 to 3719.35 of the Revised Code. If such board has information that any of such sections has been violated, it shall investigate, and upon probable cause appearing, shall file a complaint and prosecute the offender.

Fines assessed and collected under prosecutions commenced by such board shall be paid to the secretary of the state board of pharmacy, and by him paid into the state treasury to the credit of the occupational licensing and regulatory fund.

HISTORY: GC § 12671-1; 109 v 100; 122 v 70; Bureau of Code Revision, 10-1-53; 145 v H 715. Eff 7-22-94.

[REGULATIONS; NAMES]

§ 3719.40 Controlled substances included by designated name.

The controlled substances included or to be included in the schedules in section 3719.41 of the Revised Code are included by whatever official, common, usual, chemical, or trade name designated.

HISTORY: 136 v H 300. Eff 7-1-76.

Not analogous to former RC § 3719.40 (132 v S 74; 133 v H 874), repealed 136 v H 300, eff 7-1-76.

The effective date is set by section 4 of HB 300.

§ 3719.41 Schedules.

See Ohio State Board of Pharmacy Schedule of Controlled Substances beginning on page 950.

Controlled substance schedules I, II, III, IV, and V are hereby established, which schedules include the following, subject to amendment pursuant to section 3719.43 or 3719.44 of the Revised Code.

SCHEDULE I

(A) Narcotics-opiates

Any of the following opiates, including their isomers, esters, ethers, salts, and salts of isomers, esters, and ethers, unless specifically excepted under federal drug abuse control laws, whenever the existence of these isomers, esters, ethers, and salts is possible within the specific chemical designation:

(1) Acetyl-alpha-methylfentanyl (N-[1-(1-methyl-2-phenethyl)-4-piperidinyl]-N-phenylacetamide);

(2) Acetylmethadol;

(3) Allylprodine;
(4) Alphacetylmethadol (except levo-alphacetylmethadol, also known as levo-alpha-acetyl-methadol, levemethadyl acetate, or LAAM);
(5) Alphameprodine;
(6) Alphamethadol;
(7) Alpha-methylfentanyl (N-[1-(alpha-methyl-beta-phenyl)ethyl-4-piperidyl] propionanilide; 1-(1-methyl-2-phenylethyl)-4-(N-propanilido) piperidine);
(8) Alpha-methylthiofentanyl (N-[1-methyl-2- (2-thienyl) ethyl-4-piperidinyl]-N-phenylpropanamide);
(9) Benzethidine;
(10) Betacetylmethadol;
(11) Beta-hydroxyfentanyl (N-[1-(2-hydroxy-2-phenethyl-4-piperidinyl]-N-phenylpropanamide);
(12) Beta-hydroxy-3-methylfentanyl (other name: N-[1-(2-hydroxy-2-phenethyl)-3-methyl-4-piperidinyl]-N-phenylpropanamide);
(13) Betameprodine;
(14) Betamethadol;
(15) Betaprodine;
(16) Clonitazene;
(17) Dextromoramide;
(18) Diampromide;
(19) Diethylthiambutene;
(20) Difenoxin;
(21) Dimenoxadol;
(22) Dimepheptanol;
(23) Dimethylthiambutene;
(24) Dioxaphetyl butyrate;
(25) Dipipanone;
(26) Ethylmethylthiambutene;
(27) Etonitazene;
(28) Etoxeridine;
(29) Furethidine;
(30) Hydroxypethidine;
(31) Ketobemidone;
(32) Levomoramide;
(33) Levophenacylmorphan;
(34) 3-methylfentanyl (N-[3-methyl-1-(2-phenyl-ethyl)-4-piperidyl]-N-phenylpropanamide);
(35) 3-methylthiofentanyl (N-[3-methyl-1-[2- (thienyl)ethyl]-4-piperidinyl]-N-phenylpropanamide);
(36) Morpheridine;
(37) MPPP (1-methyl-4-phenyl-4-propionoxypiperidine);
(38) Noracymethadol;
(39) Norlevorphanol;
(40) Normethadone;
(41) Norpipanone;
(42) Para-fluorofentanyl (N-(4-fluorophenyl)-N-[1-(2-phenethyl)-4-piperidinyl]propanamide;
(43) PEPAP (1-(2-phenethyl)-4-phenyl-4-acetoxy-piperidine;
(44) Phenadoxone;
(45) Phenampromide;
(46) Phenomorphan;
(47) Phenoperidine;
(48) Piritramide;
(49) Proheptazine;
(50) Properidine;
(51) Propiram;
(52) Racemoramide;
(53) Thiofentanyl (N-phenyl-N-[1-(2-thienyl) ethyl-4-piperidinyl]-propanamide;
(54) Tilidine;
(55) Trimeperidine.

(B) Narcotics-opium derivatives

Any of the following opium derivatives, including their salts, isomers, and salts of isomers, unless specifically excepted under federal drug abuse control laws, whenever the existence of these salts, isomers, and salts of isomers is possible within the specific chemical designation:

(1) Acetorphine;
(2) Acetyldihydrocodeine;
(3) Benzylmorphine;
(4) Codeine methylbromide;
(5) Codeine-n-oxide;
(6) Cyprenorphine;
(7) Desomorphine;
(8) Dihydromorphine;
(9) Drotebanol;
(10) Etorphine (except hydrochloride salt);
(11) Heroin;
(12) Hydromorphinol;
(13) Methyldesorphine;
(14) Methyldihydromorphine;
(15) Morphine methylbromide;
(16) Morphine methylsulfonate;
(17) Morphine-n-oxide;
(18) Myrophine;
(19) Nicocodeine;
(20) Nicomorphine;
(21) Normorphine;
(22) Pholcodine;
(23) Thebacon.

(C) Hallucinogens

Any material, compound, mixture, or preparation that contains any quantity of the following hallucinogenic substances, including their salts, isomers, and salts of isomers, unless specifically excepted under federal drug abuse control laws, whenever the existence of these salts, isomers, and salts of isomers is possible within the specific chemical designation. For the purposes of this division only, "isomer" includes the optical isomers, position isomers, and geometric isomers.

(1) 4-bromo-2,5-dimethoxyamphetamine (some trade or other names: 4-bromo-2,5-dimethoxy-alpha-methyphenethylamine; 4-bromo-2,5-DMA);
(2) 2,5-dimethoxyamphetamine (some trade or other names: 2,5-dimethoxy-alpha-methylphenethylamine; 2,5-DMA);
(3) 2,5-dimethoxy-4-ethylamphetamine (some trade or other names: DOET);
(4) 4-methoxyamphetamine (some trade or other

names: 4-methoxy-alpha-methylphenethylamine; para-methoxyamphetamine; PMA);

(5) 5-methoxy-3,4-methylenedioxy-amphetamine;

(6) 4-methyl-2,5-dimethoxy-amphetamine (some trade or other names: 4-methyl-2,5-dimethoxy-alpha-methyl-phenethylamine; "DOM" and "STP");

(7) 3,4-methylenedioxy amphetamine;

(8) 3,4-methylenedioxymethamphetamine (MDMA);

(9) 3,4-methylenedioxy-N-ethylamphetamine (also known as N-ethyl-alpha-methyl-3,4(methylenedioxy)-phenethylamine, N-ethyl MDA, MDE, MDEA);

(10) N - hydroxy - 3, 4 - methylenedioxyamphetamine (also known as N-hydroxy-alpha-methyl-3,4(methylenedioxy) phenethylamine and N-hydroxy MDA);

(11) 3,4,5-trimethoxy amphetamine;

(12) Bufotenine (some trade or other names: 3-(beta-dimethylaminoethyl)-5-hydroxyindole; 3-(2-dimethyl-aminoethyl)-5-indolol; N, N-dimethylserotonin; 5-hy-droxy-N, N-dimethyltryptamine; mappine);

(13) Diethyltryptamine (some trade or other names: N, N-diethyltryptamine; DET);

(14) Dimethyltryptamine (some trade or other names: DMT);

(15) Ibogaine (some trade or other names: 7-ethyl-6,6beta,7,8,9,10,12,13-octahydro-2-methoxy-6,9-methano-5H-pyrido [1',2':1,2] azepino [5,4-B] indole; tabernanthe iboga);

(16) Lysergic acid diethylamide;

(17) Marihuana;

(18) Mescaline;

(19) Parahexyl (some trade or other names: 3-hexyl-1-hydroxy-7,8,9,10-tetrahydro-6,6,9-trimethyl-6H-dibenzo[b,d]pyran; synhexyl);

(20) Peyote (meaning all parts of the plant presently classified botanically as "Lophophora williamsii Lemaire," whether growing or not, the seeds of that plant, any extract from any part of that plant, and every compound, manufacture, salts, derivative, mixture, or preparation of that plant, its seeds, or its extracts);

(21) N-ethyl-3-piperidyl benzilate;

(22) N-methyl-3-piperidyl benzilate;

(23) Psilocybin;

(24) Psilocyn;

(25) Tetrahydrocannabinols (synthetic equivalents of the substances contained in the plant, or in the resinous extractives of Cannabis, sp. and/or synthetic substances, derivatives, and their isomers with similar chemical structure and pharmacological activity such as the following: delta-1-cis or trans tetrahydrocannabinol, and their optical isomers; delta-6-cis or trans tetrahydrocannabinol, and their optical isomers; delta-3,4-cis or trans tetrahydrocannabinol, and its optical isomers. (Since nomenclature of these substances is not internationally standardized, compounds of these structures, regardless of numerical designation of atomic positions, are covered.));

(26) Ethylamine analog of phencyclidine (some trade or other names: N-ethyl-1-phenylcyclohexylamine; (1-phenylcyclohexyl) ethylamine; N-(1-phenylcyclohexyl) ethylamine; cyclohexamine; PCE);

(27) Pyrrolidine analog of phencyclidine (some trade or other names: 1-(1-phenylcyclohexyl)pyrrolidine; PCPY; PHP);

(28) Thiophene analog of phencyclidine (some trade or other names: 1-[1-(2-thienyl)-cyclohexyl]-piperidine; 2-thienyl analog of phencyclidine; TPCP; TCP);

(29) 1-[1-(2-thienyl)cyclohexyl]pyrrolidine;

(30) Hashish.

(D) Depressants

Any material, compound, mixture, or preparation that contains any quantity of the following substances having a depressant effect on the central nervous system, including their salts, isomers, and salts of isomers, unless specifically excepted under federal drug abuse control laws, whenever the existence of these salts, isomers, and salts of isomers is possible within the specific chemical designation:

(1) Mecloqualone;

(2) Methaqualone.

(E) Stimulants

Unless specifically excepted or unless listed in another schedule, any material, compound, mixture, or preparation that contains any quantity of the following substances having a stimulant effect on the central nervous system, including their salts, isomers, and salts of isomers:

(1) Aminorex (some other names: aminoxaphen; 2-amino- 5-phenyl- 2-oxazoline; or 4,5-dihydro- 5-phenyl-2-oxazolamine);

(2) Cathinone;

(3) Fenethylline;

(4) Methcathinone (some other names: 2-(methylamino)-propiophenone; alpha-(methylamino) propiophenone; 2-methylamino)-1-phenylpropan-1-one; alpha-N-methylaminopropiophenone; monomethylpropion; ephedrone; N-methylcathinone; methylcathinone; AL-464; AL-422; AL-463; and UR1432), its salts, optical isomers, and salts of optical isomers;

(5) (+/−)CIS-4-methylaminorex ((+/−)CIS-4,5-dihydro-4-methyl-5-phenyl-2-oxazolamine);

(6) N-ethylamphetamine;

(7) N,N-dimethylamphetamine (also known as N,N-alpha-trimethyl-benzeneethanamine; N,N-alpha-trimethylphenethylamine).

SCHEDULE II

(A) Narcotics-opium and opium derivatives

Unless specifically excepted under federal drug abuse control laws or unless listed in another schedule, any of the following substances whether produced directly or indirectly by extraction from substances of vegetable origin, independently by means of chemical synthesis, or by a combination of extraction and chemical synthesis:

(1) Opium and opiate, and any salt, compound, derivative, or preparation of opium or opiate, excluding apo-

morphine, thebaine-derived butorphanol, dextrorphan, nalbuphine, nalmefene, naloxone, and naltrexone, and their respective salts, but including the following:
(a) Raw opium;
(b) Opium extracts;
(c) Opium fluid extracts;
(d) Powdered opium;
(e) Granulated opium;
(f) Tincture of opium;
(g) Codeine;
(h) Ethylmorphine;
(i) Etorphine hydrochloride;
(j) Hydrocodone;
(k) Hydromorphone;
(l) Metopon;
(m) Morphine;
(n) Oxycodone;
(o) Oxymorphone;
(p) Thebaine.
(2) Any salt, compound, derivative, or preparation thereof that is chemically equivalent to or identical with any of the substances referred to in division (A)(1) of this schedule, except that these substances shall not include the isoquinoline alkaloids of opium;
(3) Opium poppy and poppy straw;
(4) Coca leaves and any salt, compound, derivative, or preparation of coca leaves (including cocaine and ecgonine, their salts, isomers, and derivatives, and salts of those isomers and derivatives), and any salt, compound, derivative, or preparation thereof that is chemically equivalent to or identical with any of these substances, except that the substances shall not include decocainized coca leaves or extraction of coca leaves, which extractions do not contain cocaine or ecgonine;
(5) Concentrate of poppy straw (the crude extract of poppy straw in either liquid, solid, or powder form that contains the phenanthrene alkaloids of the opium poppy).
(B) Narcotics-opiates
Unless specifically excepted under federal drug abuse control laws or unless listed in another schedule, any of the following opiates, including their isomers, esters, ethers, salts, and salts of isomers, esters, and ethers, whenever the existence of these isomers, esters, ethers, and salts is possible within the specific chemical designation, but excluding dextrorphan and levopropoxyphene:
(1) Alfentanil;
(2) Alphaprodine;
(3) Anileridine;
(4) Bezitramide;
(5) Bulk dextropropoxyphene (non-dosage forms);
(6) Carfentanil;
(7) Dihydrocodeine;
(8) Diphenoxylate;
(9) Fentanyl;
(10) Isomethadone;
(11) Levo-alphacetylmethadol (some other names: levo-alpha-acetylmethadol, levomethadyl acetate, LAAM);
(12) Levomethorphan;
(13) Levorphanol;
(14) Metazocine;
(15) Methadone;
(16) Methadone-intermediate, 4-cyano-2-dimethyl-amino-4,4-diphenyl butane;
(17) Moramide-intermediate, 2-methyl- 3-morpholino-1, 1-diphenylpropane-carboxylic acid;
(18) Pethidine (meperidine);
(19) Pethidine-intermediate-A, 4-cyano-1-methyl-4-phenylpiperidine;
(20) Pethidine-intermediate-B, ethyl-4-phenylpiperidine-4-carboxylate;
(21) Pethidine-intermediate-C, 1-methyl-4-phenyl-piperidine-4-carboxylic acid;
(22) Phenazocine;
(23) Piminodine;
(24) Racemethorphan;
(25) Racemorphan;
(26) Sufentanil.
(C) Stimulants
Unless specifically excepted under federal drug abuse control laws or unless listed in another schedule, any material, compound, mixture, or preparation that contains any quantity of the following substances having a stimulant effect on the central nervous system:
(1) Amphetamine, its salts, its optical isomers, and salts of its optical isomers;
(2) Methamphetamine, its salts, its isomers, and salts of its isomers;
(3) Methylphenidate;
(4) Phenmetrazine and its salts.
(D) Depressants
Unless specifically excepted under federal drug abuse control laws or unless listed in another schedule, any material, compound, mixture, or preparation that contains any quantity of the following substances having a depressant effect on the central nervous system, including their salts, isomers, and salts of isomers, whenever the existence of these salts, isomers, and salts of isomers is possible within the specific chemical designation:
(1) Amobarbital;
(2) Glutethimide;
(3) Phencyclidine (some trade or other names: 1-(1-phenylcyclohexyl)piperidine; PCP);
(4) Pentobarbital;
(5) Secobarbital;
(6) 1-aminophenylcyclohexane and all N-mono-substituted and/or all N-N-disubstituted analogs, including, but not limited to, the following:
(a) 1-phenylcyclohexylamine;
(b) (1-phenylcyclohexyl) methylamine;
(c) (1-phenylcyclohexyl) dimethylamine;
(d) (1-phenylcyclohexyl) methylethylamine;
(e) (1-phenylcyclohexyl) isopropylamine;
(f) 1-(1-phenylcyclohexyl) morpholine.

(E) Hallucinogenic substances

(1) Dronabinol (synthetic) in sesame oil and encapsulated in a soft gelatin capsule in a United States food and drug administration approved drug product (some other names for dronabinol: (6aR-trans)-6a,7,8,10a-tetrahydro-6,6,9-trimethyl-3-pentyl-6H-dibenzo[b,d]pyran-1-ol, or (–)-delta-9-(trans)-tetrahydrocannabinol);

(2) Nabilone (another name for nabilone: (+)-trans-3-(1,1-dimethylheptyl)-6,6a,7,8,10,10a- hexahydro-1-hydroxy-6,6-dimethyl-9H-dibenzo[b,d]pyran-9-one).

(F) Immediate precursors

Unless specifically excepted under federal drug abuse control laws or unless listed in another schedule, any material, compound, mixture, or preparation that contains any quantity of the following substances:

(1) Immediate precursor to amphetamine and methamphetamine:

(a) Phenylacetone (some trade or other names: phenyl-2-propanone; P2P; benzyl methyl ketone; methyl benzyl ketone);

(2) Immediate precursors to phencyclidine (PCP):

(a) 1-phenylcyclohexylamine;

(b) 1-piperidinocyclohexanecarbonitrile (PCC).

SCHEDULE III

(A) Stimulants

Unless specifically excepted under federal drug abuse control laws or unless listed in another schedule, any material, compound, mixture, or preparation that contains any quantity of the following substances having a stimulant effect on the central nervous system, including their salts, their optical isomers, position isomers, or geometric isomers, and salts of these isomers, whenever the existence of these salts, isomers, and salts of isomers is possible within the specific chemical designation:

(1) All stimulant compounds, mixtures, and preparations included in schedule III pursuant to the federal drug abuse control laws and regulations adopted under those laws;

(2) Benzphetamine;

(3) Chlorphentermine;

(4) Clortermine;

(5) Phendimetrazine.

(B) Depressants

Unless specifically excepted under federal drug abuse control laws or unless listed in another schedule, any material, compound, mixture, or preparation that contains any quantity of the following substances having a depressant effect on the central nervous system:

(1) Any compound, mixture, or preparation containing amobarbital, secobarbital, pentobarbital, or any salt of any of these drugs, and one or more other active medicinal ingredients that are not listed in any schedule;

(2) Any suppository dosage form containing amobarbital, secobarbital, pentobarbital, or any salt of any of these drugs and approved by the food and drug administration for marketing only as a suppository;

(3) Any substance that contains any quantity of a derivative of barbituric acid or any salt of a derivative of barbituric acid;

(4) Chlorhexadol;

(5) Lysergic acid;

(6) Lysergic acid amide;

(7) Methyprylon;

(8) Sulfondiethylmethane;

(9) Sulfonethylmethane;

(10) Sulfonmethane;

(11) Tiletamine, zolazepam, or any salt of tiletamine or zolazepam (some trade or other names for a tiletamine-zolazepam combination product: Telazol); (some trade or other names for tiletamine: 2-(ethylamino)-2-(2-thienyl)-cyclohexanone); (some trade or other names for zolazepam: 4-(2-fluorophenyl)-6,8-dihydro-1,3,8-trimethylpyrazolo-[3,4-E][1,4]-diazepin- 7(1H)-one; flupyrazapon).

(C) Narcotic antidotes

(1) Nalorphine.

(D) Narcotics-narcotic preparations

Unless specifically excepted under federal drug abuse control laws or unless listed in another schedule, any material, compound, mixture, or preparation that contains any of the following narcotic drugs, or their salts calculated as the free anhydrous base or alkaloid, in limited quantities as set forth below:

(1) Not more than 1.8 grams of codeine per 100 milliliters or not more than 90 milligrams per dosage unit, with an equal or greater quantity of an isoquinoline alkaloid of opium;

(2) Not more than 1.8 grams of codeine per 100 milliliters or not more than 90 milligrams per dosage unit, with one or more active, nonnarcotic ingredients in recognized therapeutic amounts;

(3) Not more than 300 milligrams of dihydrocodeinone per 100 milliliters or not more than 15 milligrams per dosage unit, with a fourfold or greater quantity of an isoquinoline alkaloid of opium;

(4) Not more than 300 milligrams of dihydrocodeinone per 100 milliliters or not more than 15 milligrams per dosage unit, with one or more active, nonnarcotic ingredients in recognized therapeutic amounts;

(5) Not more than 1.8 grams of dihydrocodeine per 100 milliliters or not more than 90 milligrams per dosage unit, with one or more active, nonnarcotic ingredients in recognized therapeutic amounts;

(6) Not more than 300 milligrams of ethylmorphine per 100 milliliters or not more than 15 milligrams per dosage unit, with one or more active, nonnarcotic ingredients in recognized therapeutic amounts;

(7) Not more than 500 milligrams of opium per 100 milliliters or per 100 grams or not more than 25 milligrams per dosage unit, with one or more active, nonnarcotic ingredients in recognized therapeutic amounts;

(8) Not more than 50 milligrams of morphine per 100 milliliters or per 100 grams, with one or more active, nonnarcotic ingredients in recognized therapeutic amounts.

(E) Anabolic steroids

Unless specifically excepted under federal drug abuse control laws or unless listed in another schedule, any material, compound, mixture, or preparation that contains any quantity of the following substances, including their salts, esters, isomers, and salts of esters and isomers, whenever the existence of these salts, esters, and isomers is possible within the specific chemical designation:

(1) Anabolic steroids. Except as otherwise provided in division (E)(1) of schedule III, "anabolic steroids" means any drug or hormonal substance that is chemically and pharmacologically related to testosterone (other than estrogens, progestins, and corticosteroids) and that promotes muscle growth. "Anabolic steroids" does not include an anabolic steroid that is expressly intended for administration through implants to cattle or other nonhuman species and that has been approved by the United States secretary of health and human services for that administration, unless a person prescribes, dispenses, or distributes this type of anabolic steroid for human use. "Anabolic steroid" includes, but is not limited to, the following:

(a) Boldenone;
(b) Chlorotestosterone (4-chlortestosterone);
(c) Clostebol;
(d) Dehydrochlormethyltestosterone;
(e) Dihydrotestosterone (4-dihydrotestosterone);
(f) Drostanolone;
(g) Ethylestrenol;
(h) Fluoxymesterone;
(i) Formebulone (Formebolone);
(j) Mesterolone;
(k) Methandienone;
(l) Methandranone;
(m) Methandriol;
(n) Methandrostenolone;
(o) Methenolone;
(p) Methyltestosterone;
(q) Mibolerone;
(r) Nandrolone;
(s) Norethandrolone;
(t) Oxandrolone;
(u) Oxymesterone;
(v) Oxymetholone;
(w) Stanolone;
(x) Stanozolol;
(y) Testolactone;
(z) Testosterone;
(aa) Trenbolone;

(bb) Any salt, ester, isomer, or salt of an ester or isomer of a drug or hormonal substance described or listed in division (E)(1) of schedule III if the salt, ester, or isomer promotes muscle growth.

SCHEDULE IV

(A) Narcotic drugs

Unless specifically excepted by federal drug abuse control laws or unless listed in another schedule, any material, compound, mixture, or preparation that contains any of the following narcotic drugs, or their salts calculated as the free anhydrous base or alkaloid, in limited quantities as set forth below:

(1) Not more than one milligram of difenoxin and not less than 25 micrograms of atropine sulfate per dosage unit;

(2) Dextropropoxyphene (alpha-(+)-4-dimethylamino-1,2-diphenyl-3-methyl-2-propionoxybutane) [final dosage forms].

(B) Depressants

Unless specifically excepted under federal drug abuse control laws or unless listed in another schedule, any material, compound, mixture, or preparation that contains any quantity of the following substances, including their salts, isomers, and salts of isomers, whenever the existence of these salts, isomers, and salts of isomers is possible within the specific chemical designation:

(1) Alprazolam;
(2) Barbital;
(3) Bromazepam;
(4) Camazepam;
(5) Chloral betaine;
(6) Chloral hydrate;
(7) Chlordiazepoxide;
(8) Clobazam;
(9) Clonazepam;
(10) Clorazepate;
(11) Clotiazepam;
(12) Cloxazolam;
(13) Delorazepam;
(14) Diazepam;
(15) Estazolam;
(16) Ethchlorvynol;
(17) Ethinamate;
(18) Ethyl loflazepate;
(19) Fludiazepam;
(20) Flunitrazepam;
(21) Flurazepam;
(22) Halazepam;
(23) Haloxazolam;
(24) Ketazolam;
(25) Loprazolam;
(26) Lorazepam;
(27) Lormetazepam;
(28) Mebutamate;
(29) Medazepam;
(30) Meprobamate;
(31) Methohexital;
(32) Methylphenobarbital (mephobarbital);
(33) Midazolam;
(34) Nimetazepam;
(35) Nitrazepam;
(36) Nordiazepam;
(37) Oxazepam;
(38) Oxazolam;
(39) Paraldehyde;
(40) Petrichloral;

(41) Phenobarbital;
(42) Pinazepam;
(43) Prazepam;
(44) Quazepam;
(45) Temazepam;
(46) Tetrazepam;
(47) Triazolam;
(48) Zolpidem.

(C) Fenfluramine

Any material, compound, mixture, or preparation that contains any quantity of the following substances, including their salts, their optical isomers, position isomers, or geometric isomers, and salts of these isomers, whenever the existence of these salts, isomers, and salts of isomers is possible within the specific chemical designation:

(1) Fenfluramine.

(D) Stimulants

Unless specifically excepted under federal drug abuse control laws or unless listed in another schedule, any material, compound, mixture, or preparation that contains any quantity of the following substances having a stimulant effect on the central nervous system, including their salts, their optical isomers, position isomers, or geometric isomers, and salts of these isomers, whenever the existence of these salts, isomers, and salts of isomers is possible within the specific chemical designation:

(1) Cathine ((+)-norpseudoephedrine);
(2) Diethylpropion;
(3) Fencamfamin;
(4) Fenproporex;
(5) Mazindol;
(6) Mefenorex;
(7) Pemoline (including organometallic complexes and chelates thereof);
(8) Phentermine;
(9) Pipradrol;
(10) Spa[(−)-1-dimethylamino-1, 2-diphenylethane].

(E) Other substances

Unless specifically excepted under federal drug abuse control laws or unless listed in another schedule, any material, compound, mixture, or preparation that contains any quantity of the following substances, including their salts:

(1) Pentazocine.

SCHEDULE V

(A) Narcotic drugs

Unless specifically excepted under federal drug abuse control laws or unless listed in another schedule, any material, compound, mixture, or preparation that contains any of the following narcotic drugs, and their salts, as set forth below:

(1) Buprenorphine.

(B) Narcotics-narcotic preparations

Narcotic drugs containing non-narcotic active medicinal ingredients. Any compound, mixture, or preparation that contains any of the following narcotic drugs, or their salts calculated as the free anhydrous base or alkaloid, in limited quantities as set forth below, and that includes one or more nonnarcotic active medicinal ingredients in sufficient proportion to confer upon the compound, mixture, or preparation valuable medicinal qualities other than those possessed by narcotic drugs alone:

(1) Not more than 200 milligrams of codeine per 100 milliliters or per 100 grams;
(2) Not more than 100 milligrams of dihydrocodeine per 100 milliliters or per 100 grams;
(3) Not more than 100 milligrams of ethylmorphine per 100 milliliters or per 100 grams;
(4) Not more than 2.5 milligrams of diphenoxylate and not less than 25 micrograms of atropine sulfate per dosage unit;
(5) Not more than 100 milligrams of opium per 100 milliliters or per 100 grams;
(6) Not more than 0.5 milligram of difenoxin and not less than 25 micrograms of atropine sulfate per dosage unit.

(C) Stimulants

Unless specifically exempted or excluded under federal drug abuse control laws or unless listed in another schedule, any material, compound, mixture, or preparation that contains any quantity of the following substances having a stimulant effect on the central nervous system, including their salts, isomers, and salts of isomers:

(1) Ephedrine, except as provided in division (K) of section 3719.44 of the Revised Code;
(2) Pyrovalerone.

HISTORY: 136 v H 300 (Eff 7-1-76); 144 v H 62 (Eff 5-21-91); 145 v H 156 (Eff 5-19-93); 145 v H 391 (Eff 7-21-94); 146 v S 269. Eff 7-1-96.

Not analogous to former RC § 3719.41 (132 v S 74), repealed 136 v H 300, eff 7-1-76.

The provisions of §§ 3, 9 of HB 156 (145 v —) read as follows:

SECTION 3. (A) In amending section 3719.41 of the Revised Code in this act, it is the intent of the General Assembly to codify the following in controlled substances Schedules I to V:

(1) The automatic addition of various compounds, mixtures, preparations, or substances to those schedules pursuant to section 3719.43 of the Revised Code following action taken by the United States Attorney General on or after July 1, 1976, and the addition of various compounds, mixtures, preparations, or substances to those schedules on or after July 1, 1976, by the State Board of Pharmacy pursuant to section 3719.44 of the Revised Code;

(2) The automatic transfer of various compounds, mixtures, preparations, or substances within those schedules, and the automatic removal of various compounds, mixtures, preparations, or substances from those schedules, pursuant to section 3719.43 of the Revised Code following action taken by the United States Attorney General on or after July 1, 1976;

(3) The transfer of various compounds, mixtures, preparations, or substances within those schedules, and the removal

of various compounds, mixtures, preparations, or substances from those schedules on or after July 1, 1976, by the State Board of Pharmacy pursuant to section 3719.44 of the Revised Code.

(B) The General Assembly hereby declares that, in amending section 3719.41 of the Revised Code in Am. Sub. H.B. 62 of the 119th General Assembly, it solely intended to legislatively add anabolic steroids to controlled substances Schedule III and did not intend to affect controlled substances Schedules I to V insofar as, prior to May 21, 1991, various compounds, mixtures, preparations, or substances had been added to, transferred within, or removed from those schedules pursuant to sections 3719.43 and 3719.44 of the Revised Code.

SECTION 9. This act is hereby declared to be an emergency measure necessary for the immediate preservation of the public peace, health, and safety. The primary reason for the necessity is that the version of section 3719.41 of the Revised Code amended by Am. Sub. H.B. 62 of the 119th General Assembly and effective May 21, 1991, did not include certain compounds, mixtures, preparations, or substances that automatically had been added to controlled substances Schedules I to V pursuant to section 3719.43 of the Revised Code following action taken by the United States Attorney General on or after July 1, 1976, and did not reflect the automatic transfer of various compounds, mixtures, preparations, or substances within those schedules pursuant to section 3719.43 of the Revised Code following action taken by the United States Attorney General on or after July 1, 1976. The clarification of the status of controlled substances Schedules I to V is necessary to eliminate any uncertainty as to the nature of the controlled substances that may be the subject of offenses under Chapters 2925. and 3719. of the Revised Code. Therefore, this act shall go into immediate effect.

> Publisher's Note: See RC § 3719.41

OHIO STATE BOARD OF PHARMACY

77 S. High St., 17th Floor; Columbus, Ohio 43266-0320
Telephone: 614/466-4143   FAX: 614/752-4836
TTY/TDD Ohio Relay Service: 1-800/750-0750
-Equal Opportunity Employer and Service Provider-

SUMMARY OF CHANGES MADE IN OHIO'S SCHEDULES OF CONTROLLED SUBSTANCES

Contact Persons: Frank Wickham and Sandie Butler

EFFECTIVE 01/06/94:

Temporary* Placement of 4-bromo-2,5-dimethoxyphenethylamine Into Schedule I by the Federal Government (3719.43, O.R.C.).

EFFECTIVE 03/12/94:

Extension (6 months) of Temporary* Placement of Alpha-ethyltryptamine Into Schedule I by the Federal Government (3719.43, O.R.C.).

EFFECTIVE 03/18/94:

Placement of Aminorex Into Schedule I by the Federal Governement (3719.43, O.R.C.). Has been in Schedule I under Temporary Placement since 09/21/92.

EFFECTIVE 07/21/94:

Placement of Ephedrine Into Schedule V by the Ohio Legislature (Sub. H.B. 391).

EFFECTIVE 09/12/94:

Placement of Alpha-ethyltryptamine Into Schedule I by the Federal Government (3719.43, O.R.C.). Has been in Schedule I under Temporary Placement since 03/12/93.

EFFECTIVE 06/02/95:

Placement of 4-Bromo-2,5-dimethoxyphenethylamine Into Schedule I by the Federal Government (3719.43, O.R.C.). Has been in Schedule I under Temporary Placement since 01/06/94.

EFFECTIVE 01/10/96:

Ephedrine exceptions to Schedule V added by the Board (3719.44, O.R.C.).

❖   ❖   ❖

---

*   Placement will expire at the end of one year from the effective date; may be extended six months. Emergency scheduling is intended to apply to "designer drugs".

INTRODUCTION TO

OHIO'S SCHEDULES OF CONTROLLED SUBSTANCES

The following is a compilation of substances scheduled pursuant to Sections 3719.41 (07/01/76, 05/19/93, 07/21/94), 3719.43, and 3719.44 of the Ohio Revised Code (ORC). This compilation has been prepared by the Ohio Board of Pharmacy to assist health professionals and law enforcement officers in determining:

(1) whether or not a drug or drug product is a controlled substance;

(2) which schedule a substance has been placed in;

(3) whether or not the substance was placed in, added to, or transferred to a different schedule according to Section 3719.41, 3719.43, and/or 3719.44 of the Revised Code; and

(4) the date that each substance was added to or transferred from one schedule to another.

Following each substance, in **parenthesis or brackets**, are the **dates** that the substance was **placed** in that schedule.

The **date in parentheses ( )** indicates the date that a substance was **placed** in the schedule **by the federal government** (pursuant to Section 3719.43, ORC). **A date PRIOR to July 1, 1976**, the original enactment date of Section 3719.41, ORC, indicates the date that the substance was **controlled under federal law ONLY** (i.e.-Comprehensive Drug Abuse Prevention and Control Act of 1970; 21 U.S.C. 801-966).

The **date in brackets [ ]** indicates the date that the substance was **added** or **transferred** to the schedule **by the Board** pursuant to Section 3719.44, ORC.

Substances printed in **bolded type** were **added or transferred** to the schedule **by the federal government** (Section 3719.43, ORC) **AND/OR by the Board** (Section 3719.44, ORC) since the last amendment by the Ohio Legislature to Section 3719.41 of the Ohio Revised Code.

Footnotes are used to provide additional information.

(07/21/94)

OHIO'S SCHEDULES OF CONTROLLED SUBSTANCES   Page 1

THE FOLLOWING IS A COMPILATION OF SUBSTANCES SCHEDULED PURSUANT TO SECTIONS 3719.41, 3719.43, AND 3719.44 OF THE OHIO REVISED CODE.

SCHEDULE I

(A) Narcotics-opiates

Any of the following opiates, including their isomers, esters, ethers, salts, and salts of isomers, esters, and ethers, unless specifically excepted under federal drug abuse control laws, whenever the existence of these isomers, esters, ethers, and salts is possible within the specific chemical designation:

(1) Acetyl-alpha-methylfentanyl (N-[1-(1-methyl-2-phenethyl)-4-piperidinyl]-N-phenylacetamide); (11-29-85)
(2) Acetylmethadol; (05-01-71)
(3) Allylprodine; (05-01-71)
(4) Alphacetylmethadol (except levo-alphacetylmethadol also known as levo-alpha-acetylmethadol, levomethadyl acetate, or LAAM); (05-01-71) (08-18-93) ❶
(5) Alphameprodine; (05-01-71)
(6) Alphamethadol; (05-01-71)
(7) Alpha-methylfentanyl (N- [1-(alpha-methyl-beta-phenyl)ethyl-4-piperidyl] propionanilide; 1-(1-methyl-2-phenylethyl)-4-(N-propanilido) piperidine); (09-22-81)
(8) Alpha-methylthiofentanyl (N-[1-methyl-2-(2-thienyl)ethyl-4-piperidinyl]-N-phenylpropanamide); (11-29-85)
(9) Benzethidine; (05-01-71)
(10) Betacetylmethadol; (05-01-71)
(11) Beta-hydroxyfentanyl (N-[1-(2-hydroxy-2-phenethyl-4-piperidinyl]-N-phenylpropanamide); (11-29-85)
(12) Beta-hydroxy-3-methylfentanyl (other name: N-[1-(2-hydroxy-2-phenethyl)-3-methyl-4-piperidinyl]-N-phenylpropanamide); (01-08-88)
(13) Betameprodine; (05-01-71)
(14) Betamethadol; (05-01-71)
(15) Betaprodine; (05-01-71)
(16) Clonitazene; (05-01-71)
(17) Dextromoramide; (05-01-71)
(18) Diampromide; (05-01-71)
(19) Diethylthiambutene; (05-01-71)
(20) Difenoxin; (06-01-75) [04-01-78]

---

❶ *Levo-alphacetylmethadol was transferred to Schedule II by the Federal Government pursuant to Section 3719.43 of the Ohio Revised Code on August 18, 1993.*

PAGE LAST REVISED: 08/18/93

OHIO'S SCHEDULES OF CONTROLLED SUBSTANCES

(21) Dimenoxadol; (05-01-71)
(22) Dimepheptanol; (05-01-71)
(23) Dimethylthiambutene; (05-01-71)
(24) Dioxaphetyl butyrate; (05-01-71)
(25) Dipipanone; (05-01-71)
(26) Ethylmethylthiambutene; (05-01-71).
(27) Etonitazene; (05-01-71)
(28) Etoxeridine; (05-01-71)
(29) Furethidine; (05-01-71)
(30) Hydroxypethidine; (05-01-71)
(31) Ketobemidone; (05-01-71)
(32) Levomoramide; (05-01-71)
(33) Levophenacylmorphan; (05-01-71)
(34) 3-methylfentanyl (N-[3-methyl-1-(2-phenylethyl)-4-piperidyl]-N-phenylpropanamide); (04-25-85)
(35) 3-methylthiofentanyl (N-[3-methyl-1-[2-(thienyl)ethyl]-4-piperidinyl]-N-phenylpropanamide); (11-29-85)
(36) Morpheridine; (05-01-71)
(37) MPPP (1-methyl-4-phenyl-4-propionoxypiperidine); (08-12-85)
(38) Noracymethadol; (05-01-71)
(39) Norlevorphanol; (05-01-71)
(40) Normethadone; (05-01-71)
(41) Norpipanone; (05-01-71)
(42) Para-fluorofentanyl (N-(4-fluorophenyl)-N-[1-(2-phenethyl)-4-piperidinyl]propanamide; (03-10-86)
(43) PEPAP (1-(2-phenethyl)-4-phenyl-4-acetoxypiperidine; (08-12-85)
(44) Phenadoxone; (05-01-71)
(45) Phenampromide; (05-01-71)
(46) Phenomorphan; (05-01-71)
(47) Phenoperidine; (05-01-71)
(48) Piritramide; (05-01-71)
(49) Proheptazine; (05-01-71)
(50) Properidine; (05-01-71)
(51) Propiram; (02-28-72)
(52) Racemoramide; (05-01-71)
(53) Thiofentanyl (N-phenyl-N-[1-(2-thienyl)ethyl-4-piperidinyl]-propanamide; (11-29-85)
(54) Tilidine; (12-01-80)
(55) Trimeperidine. (05-01-71)

(B) Narcotics-opium derivatives

Any of the following opium derivatives, their salts, isomers, and salts of isomers, unless specifically excepted under federal drug abuse control laws, whenever the existence of these salts, isomers, and salts of isomers is possible within the specific chemical designation:

PAGE LAST REVISED: 03/10/86

OHIO'S SCHEDULES OF CONTROLLED SUBSTANCES

(1) Acetorphine; (05-01-71)
(2) Acetyldihydrocodeine; (05-01-71)
(3) Benzylmorphine; (05-01-71)
(4) Codeine methylbromide; (05-01-71)
(5) Codeine-n-oxide; (05-01-71)
(6) Cyprenorphine; (05-01-71)
(7) Desomorphine; (05-01-71)
(8) Dihydromorphine; (05-01-71)
(9) Drotebanol; (08-06-73)
(10) Etorphine (except hydrochloride salt); (05-01-71)
(11) Heroin; (05-01-71)
(12) Hydromorphinol; (05-01-71)
(13) Methyldesorphine; (05-01-71)
(14) Methyldihydromorphine; (05-01-71)
(15) Morphine methylbromide; (05-01-71)
(16) Morphine methylsulfonate; (05-01-71)
(17) Morphine-n-oxide; (05-01-71)
(18) Myrophine; (05-01-71)
(19) Nicocodeine; (05-01-71)
(20) Nicomorphine; (05-01-71)
(21) Normorphine; (05-01-71)
(22) Pholcodine; (05-01-71)
(23) Thebacon. (05-01-71)

(C) Hallucinogens

Any material, compound, mixture, or preparation that contains any quantity of the following hallucinogenic substances, their salts, isomers, and salts of isomers, unless specifically excepted under federal drug abuse control laws, whenever the existence of these salts, isomers, and salts of isomers is possible within the specific chemical designation. For the purposes of this division only, the term "isomer" includes the optical isomers, position isomers, and geometric isomers.

(1) Alpha-ethyltryptamine (some trade or other names: etryptamine; Monase; α-ethyl-1H-indole-3-ethanamine; 3-(2-aminobutyl) indole; α-ET; and AET); (09-12-94) ❶

(2) 4-bromo-2,5-dimethoxy-amphetamine (some trade or other names: 4-bromo-2,5-dimethoxy-alpha-methyphenethylamine; 4-bromo-2,5-DMA); (09-21-73)

---

❶ *Originally placed in Schedule I on 03/12/93 under the Temporary Scheduling provisions of the Federal Government.*

OHIO'S SCHEDULES OF CONTROLLED SUBSTANCES

(3) 4-bromo-2,5-dimethoxyphenethylamine (some trade or other names: 2-(4-bromo-2,5-dimethoxyphenyl)-1-aminoethane; alpha-desmethyl DOB; 2C-B, Nexus). (06-02-95) ❶

(4) 2,5-dimethoxyamphetamine (some trade or other names: 2,5-dimethoxy-alpha-methylphenethylamine; 2,5-DMA); (09-21-73)

(5) 2,5-dimethoxy-4-ethylamphetamine (some trade or other names: DOET); (02-16-93)

(6) 4-methoxyamphetamine (some trade or other names: 4-methoxy-alpha-methylphenethylamine; paramethoxyamphetamine; PMA); (09-21-73)

(7) 5-methoxy-3,4-methylenedioxy-amphetamine; (05-01-71)

(8) 4-methyl-2,5-dimethoxy-amphetamine (some trade or other names: 4-methyl-2,5-dimethoxy-alpha-methylphenethylamine; "DOM" and "STP"); (05-01-71)

(9) 3,4-methylenedioxy amphetamine; (05-01-71)

(10) 3,4-methylenedioxymethamphetamine (MDMA); (07-01-85)

(11) 3,4-methylenedioxy-N-ethylamphetamine (also known as N-ethyl-alpha-methyl-3,4(methylenedioxy)phenethylamine, N-ethyl MDA, MDE, MDEA); (10-15-87)

(12) N-hydroxy-3,4-methylenedioxyamphetamine (also known as N-hydroxy-alpha-methyl-3,4(methylenedioxy)phenethylamine and N-hydroxy MDA); (10-15-87)

(13) 3,4,5-trimethoxy amphetamine; (05-01-71)

(14) Bufotenine (some trade or other names: 3-(beta-dimethylaminoethyl)-5-hydroxyindole; 3-(2-dimethylaminoethyl)-5-indolol; N, N-dimethyl-serotonin; 5-hydroxy-N,N-dimethyltryptamine; mappine); (05-01-71)

(15) Diethyltryptamine (some trade or other names: N, N-diethyltryptamine; DET); (05-01-71)

(16) Dimethyltryptamine (some trade or other names: DMT); (05-01-71)

---

❶ *Originally placed in Schedule I on 01/06/94 under the Temporary Scheduling provisions of the Federal Government.*

PAGE LAST REVISED: 06/02/95

OHIO'S SCHEDULES OF CONTROLLED SUBSTANCES

(17) Ibogaine (some trade or other names: 7-ethyl-6,6beta,7,8,9,10,12,13-octahydro-2-methoxy-6,9-methano-5H-pyrido [1',2':1,2] azepino [5,4-b] indole; tabernanthe iboga); (05-01-71)

(18) Lysergic acid diethylamide; (05-01-71)

(19) Marihuana; (05-01-71)

(20) Mescaline; (05-01-71)

(21) Parahexyl (some trade or other names: 3-hexyl-1-hydroxy-7,8,9,10-tetrahydro-6,6,9-trimethyl-6H-dibenzo [b,d] pyran; synhexyl); (12-22-82)

(22) Peyote (meaning all parts of the plant presently classified botanically as "Lophophora williamsii Lemaire," whether growing or not, the seeds of that plant, any extract from any part of that plant, and every compound, manufacture, salts, derivative, mixture, or preparation of that plant, its seeds, or its extracts); (05-01-71) (01-21-76) (10-01-76)

(23) N-ethyl-3-piperidyl benzilate; (05-01-71)

(24) N-methyl-3-piperidyl benzilate; (05-01-71)

(25) Psilocybin; (05-01-71)

(26) Psilocyn; (05-01-71)

(27) Tetrahydrocannabinols (synthetic equivalents of the substances contained in the plant, or in the resinous extractives of Cannabis, sp. and/or synthetic substances, derivatives, and their isomers with similar chemical structure and pharmacological activity such as the following: delta-1-cis or trans tetrahydrocannabinol, and their optical isomers; delta-6-cis or trans tetrahydrocannabinol, and their optical isomers; delta-3,4-cis or trans tetrahydrocannabinol, and its optical isomers. (Since nomenclature of these substances is not internationally standardized, compounds of these structures, regardless of numerical designation of atomic positions, are covered.)); (05-01-71)

OHIO'S SCHEDULES OF CONTROLLED SUBSTANCES

(28) Ethylamine analog of phencyclidine (some trade or other names: N-ethyl-1-phenylcyclohexylamine; (1-phenylcyclohexyl)ethylamine; N-(1-phenylcyclohexyl)-ethylamine; cyclohexamine; PCE); (10-25-78) ❶

(29) Pyrrolidine analog of phencyclidine (some trade or other names: 1-(1-phenyl-cyclohexyl)pyrrolidine; PCPy; PHP); (10-25-78) ❶

(30) Thiophene analog of phencyclidine (some trade or other names: 1-[1-(2-thienyl)-cyclohexyl]-piperidine; 2-thienyl analog of phencyclidine; TPCP; TCP); (08-11-75) [04-01-78]

(31) 1-[1-(2-thienyl)cyclohexyl]pyrrolidine. (07-06-89)

(D) Depressants

Any material, compound, mixture, or preparation that contains any quantity of the following substances having a depressant effect on the central nervous system, including their salts, isomers, and salts of isomers, unless specifically excepted under federal drug abuse control laws, whenever the existence of these salts, isomers, and salts of isomers is possible within the specific chemical designation:

(1) Mecloqualone; (07-10-75) [04-01-78]
(2) Methaqualone. (08-27-84) ❷

---

❶ Placed in Schedule II by the Board of Pharmacy pursuant to Section 3719.44 of the Revised Code on July 1, 1978.

❷ Methaqualone was previously placed by the Federal Government into Schedule II effective 10-04-73 and was moved, pursuant to Section 3719.43 of the Ohio Revised Code, to Schedule I effective 08-27-84.

OHIO'S SCHEDULES OF CONTROLLED SUBSTANCES — Page 7

(E) Stimulants

Unless specifically excepted or unless listed in another schedule, any material, compound, mixture, or preparation that contains any quantity of the following substances having a stimulant effect on the central nervous system, including their salts, isomers, and salts of isomers:

(1) Aminorex (some other names: aminoxaphen; 2-amino-5-phenyl-2-oxazoline; or 4,5-dihydro-5-phenyl-2-oxazolamine); (03-18-94) ❶
(2) Cathinone (some trade or other names: 2-amino-1-phenyl-1-propanone, alpha-aminopropiophenone, 2-aminopropiophenone, and norephedrone); (02-16-93)
(3) Fenethylline; (08-20-81)
(4) Methcathinone (some other names: 2-(methylamino)propiophenone; alpha-(methylamino)propiophenone; 2-(methylamino)-1-phenylpropan-1-one; alpha-N-methylaminopropiophenone; monomethylpropion; ephedrone; N-methylcathinone; methylcathinone; AL-464; AL-422; AL-463 and UR1432), its salts, optical isomers, and salts of optical isomers; (10-15-93) ❷
(5) (+/-)cis-4-methylaminorex ((+/-)cis-4,5-dihydro-4-methyl-5-phenyl-2-oxazolamine); (10-15-87)
(6) N-ethylamphetamine; (01-07-82)
(7) N,N-dimethylamphetamine (also known as N,N-alpha-trimethyl-benzeneethanamine; N,N-alpha-trimethylphenethylamine). (08-03-88)

---

❶ *Originally placed in Schedule I on 09/21/92 under the Temporary Scheduling provisions of the Federal Government.*

❷ *Originally placed in Schedule I on 05/01/92 under the Temporary Scheduling provisions of the Federal Government.*

PAGE LAST REVISED: 03/18/94

OHIO'S SCHEDULES OF CONTROLLED SUBSTANCES

(F) Temporary Listing Of Substances Subject To Emergency Scheduling ❶

Any material, compound, mixture or preparation which contains any quantity of the following substances:

(1) N-[1-benzyl-4-piperidyl]-N-phenylpropanamide (benzylfentanyl), its optical isomers, salts and salts of isomers; (11-29-85)
(2) N-[1-(2-thienyl)methyl-4-piperidyl]-N-phenylpropanamide (thenylfentanyl), its optical isomers, salts and salts of isomers; (11-29-85)

---

❶ *Temporary scheduling is under federal law only. It is included here as a service and is not an actual part of Section 3719.41 of the Revised Code. All Schedule I restrictions and controls still apply to the substances listed until temporary placement expires or permanent placement occurs. Temporary placement will expire at the end of one year from the effective date but may be extended six months (noted by a second effective date). Emergency scheduling is intended to apply to "designer drugs".*

OHIO'S SCHEDULES OF CONTROLLED SUBSTANCES

SCHEDULE II

(A) Narcotics-opium and opium derivatives

Unless specifically excepted under federal drug abuse control laws or unless listed in another schedule, any of the following substances whether produced directly or indirectly by extraction from substances of vegetable origin, independently by means of chemical synthesis, or by a combination of extraction and chemical synthesis:

(1) Opium and opiate, and any salt, compound, derivative, or preparation of opium or opiate, excluding apomorphine (06-28-76) [04-01-78], thebaine-derived butorphanol (07-14-92), dextrorphan (10-01-76), nalbuphine (10-01-76) [04-01-78], nalmefene (11-04-85), naloxone, and naltrexone (03-06-75) [04-01-78], and their respective salts, but including the following:

  (a) Raw opium; (05-01-71)
  (b) Opium extracts; (05-01-71)
  (c) Opium fluid extracts; (05-01-71)
  (d) Powdered opium; (05-01-71)
  (e) Granulated opium; (05-01-71)
  (f) Tincture of opium; (05-01-71)
  (g) Codeine; (05-01-71)
  (h) Ethylmorphine; (05-01-71)
  (i) Etorphine hydrochloride; (04-18-74)
  (j) Hydrocodone; (05-01-71)
  (k) Hydromorphone; (05-01-71)
  (l) Metopon; (05-01-71)
  (m) Morphine; (05-01-71)
  (n) Oxycodone; (05-01-71)
  (o) Oxymorphone; (05-01-71)
  (p) Thebaine; (05-01-71)

(2) Any salt, compound, derivative, or preparation thereof that is chemically equivalent to or identical with any of the substances referred to in division (A)(1) of this schedule, except that these substances shall not include the isoquinoline alkaloids of opium; (05-01-71)

(3) Opium poppy and poppy straw; (05-01-71)

(4) Coca leaves and any salt, compound, derivative, or preparation of coca leaves (including cocaine and ecgonine, their salts, isomers, and derivatives, and salts of those isomers and derivatives), and any salt, compound, derivative, or preparation thereof that is chemically equivalent to or identical with any of these substances, except that the substances shall not include decocainized coca leaves or extraction of coca leaves, which extractions do not contain cocaine or ecgonine; (05-01-71) (04-23-86)

OHIO'S SCHEDULES OF CONTROLLED SUBSTANCES

    (5) Concentrate of poppy straw (the crude extract of poppy straw in either liquid, solid, or powder form that contains the phenanthrene alkaloids of the opium poppy). (02-14-75)

(B) Narcotics-opiates

Unless specifically excepted under federal drug abuse control laws or unless listed in another schedule, any of the following opiates, including their isomers, esters, ethers, salts, and salts of isomers, esters, and ethers whenever the existence of these isomers, esters, ethers, and salts is possible within the specific chemical designation, but excluding dextrorphan and levopropoxyphene: (09-22-80)

  (1) Alfentanil; (01-23-87) ❶
  (2) Alphaprodine; (05-01-71)
  (3) Anileridine; (05-01-71)
  (4) Bezitramide; (05-01-71)
  (5) Bulk dextropropoxyphene (non-dosage forms); (09-22-80) ❷
  (6) Carfentanil; (10-28-88)
  (7) Dihydrocodeine; (05-01-71)
  (8) Diphenoxylate; (05-01-71)
  (9) Fentanyl; (05-01-71)
 (10) Isomethadone; (05-01-71)
 (11) Levo-alphacetylmethadol (some other names: levo-alpha-acetylmethadol, levomethadyl acetate, LAAM); (08-18-93) ❸
 (12) Levomethorphan; (05-01-71)
 (13) Levorphanol; (05-01-71)
 (14) Metazocine; (05-01-71)
 (15) Methadone; (05-01-71)
 (16) Methadone-intermediate, 4-cyano-2-dimethylamino-4,4-diphenyl butane; (05-01-71)
 (17) Moramide-intermediate, 2-methyl-3-morpholino-1,1-diphenylpropane-carboxylic acid; (05-01-71)

---

❶ *Alfentanil was previously placed by the Federal Government, pursuant to Section 3719.43 of the Ohio Revised Code, into Schedule I effective 08-24-84, and was moved to Schedule II effective 01-23-87.*

❷ *Dextropropoxyphene (final dosage forms) was reclassified in Schedule IV as a narcotic drug under federal drug abuse control laws on July 24, 1980. Bulk dextropropoxyphene (non-dosage forms) was placed in Schedule II on the same date.*

❸ *Levo-alphacetylmethadol was previously placed by the Federal Government, pursuant to Section 3719.43 of the Ohio Revised Code, into Schedule I effective 05-01-71, and was moved to Schedule II effective 08-18-93.*

PAGE LAST REVISED: 08/18/93

OHIO'S SCHEDULES OF CONTROLLED SUBSTANCES   Page 10

(18) Pethidine (meperidine); (05-01-71)
(19) Pethidine-intermediate-A, 4-cyano-1-methyl-4-phenylpiperidine; (05-01-71)
(20) Pethidine-intermediate-B, ethyl-4-phenylpiperidine-4-carboxylate; (05-01-71)
(21) Pethidine-intermediate-C, 1-methyl-4-phenylpiperidine-4-carboxylic acid; (05-01-71)
(22) Phenazocine; (05-01-71)
(23) Piminodine; (05-01-71)
(24) Racemethorphan; (05-01-71)
(25) Racemorphan; (05-01-71)
(26) Sufentanil. (05-25-84) ❶

(C) Stimulants

Unless specifically excepted under federal drug abuse control laws or unless listed in another schedule, any material, compound, mixture, or preparation that contains any quantity of the following substances having a stimulant effect on the central nervous system: (07-07-71)

(1) Amphetamine, its salts, its optical isomers, and salts of its optical isomers; (07-07-71)
(2) Methamphetamine, its salts, its isomers, and salts of its isomers; (07-07-71)
(3) Methylphenidate; (10-28-71)
(4) Phenmetrazine and its salts. (10-28-71)

(D) Depressants

Unless specifically excepted under federal drug abuse control laws or unless listed in another schedule, any material, compound, mixture, or preparation that contains any quantity of the following substances having a depressant effect on the central nervous system, including their salts, isomers, and salts of isomers whenever the existence of these salts, isomers, and salts of isomers is possible within the specific chemical designation:

(1) Amobarbital; (12-17-73)

(2) Glutethimide; (03-21-91) ❷

---

❶ *Sufentanil was previously placed by the Federal Government, pursuant to Section 3719.43 of the Ohio Revised Code, into Schedule I effective 12-1-80, and was moved to Schedule II effective 5-25-84.*

❷ *Glutethimide was placed in Schedule III by the Federal Government on 05-01-71 and was moved to Schedule II by the Federal Government, pursuant to Section 3719.43 of the Ohio Revised Code, effective 03-21-91.*

OHIO'S SCHEDULES OF CONTROLLED SUBSTANCES

(3) Phencyclidine (some trade or other names: 1-(1-phenylcyclohexyl)piperidine; PCP); (02-24-78) [07-01-78]

(4) Pentobarbital; (12-17-73)

(5) Secobarbital; (12-17-73)

(6) 1-aminophenylcyclohexane and all N-mono-substituted and/or all N-N-disubstituted analogs, including, but not limited to, the following: ❶

    (a) 1-phenylcyclohexylamine; [07-01-78]
    (b) (1-phenylcyclohexyl) methylamine; [07-01-78]
    (c) (1-phenylcyclohexyl) dimethylamine; [07-01-78]
    (d) (1-phenylcyclohexyl) methylethylamine; [07-01-78]
    (e) (1-phenylcyclohexyl) isopropylamine; [07-01-78]
    (f) 1-(1-phenylcyclohexyl) morpholine. [07-01-78]

(E) Hallucinogenic substances

(1) Dronabinol (synthetic) in sesame oil and encapsulated in a soft gelatin capsule in a United States food and drug administration approved drug product (some other names for dronabinol: (6aR-trans)-6a,7,8,10a-tetrahydro-6,6,9-trimethyl-3-pentyl-6H-dibenzo [b,d]pyran-1-ol, or (-)-delta-9-(trans)-tetrahydrocannabinol); (05-13-86)

(2) Nabilone (another name for nabilone: (+)-trans-3-(1,1-dimethylheptyl)-6,6a,7,8,10,10a-hexahydro-1-hydroxy-6,6-dimethyl-9H-dibenzo [b,d]pyran-9-one). (04-07-87)

---

❶ *(1-phenylcyclohexyl) ethylamine and 1-(1-phenylcyclohexyl) pyrrolidine were placed in Schedule II by the Board of Pharmacy on 07-01-78 and were moved to Schedule I by the Federal Government on 10-25-78.*

PAGE LAST REVISED: 04/07/87

OHIO'S SCHEDULES OF CONTROLLED SUBSTANCES   Page 12

(F) Immediate precursors

Unless specifically excepted under federal drug abuse control laws or unless listed in another schedule, any material, compound, mixture, or preparation that contains any quantity of the following substances:

(1) Immediate precursor to amphetamine and methamphetamine:

    (a) Phenylacetone (some trade or other names: phenyl-2-propanone; P2P; benzyl methyl ketone; methyl benzyl ketone); (02-11-80)

(2) Immediate precursors to phencyclidine (PCP):

    (a) 1-phenylcyclohexylamine; (06-16-78)

    (b) 1-piperidinocyclohexanecarbonitrile (PCC). (06-16-78)

OHIO'S SCHEDULES OF CONTROLLED SUBSTANCES   Page 13

SCHEDULE III

(A) Stimulants

Unless specifically excepted under federal drug abuse control laws or unless listed in another schedule, any material, compound, mixture, or preparation that contains any quantity of the following substances having a stimulant effect on the central nervous system, including their salts, their optical isomers, position isomers, or geometric isomers, and salts of these isomers whenever the existence of these salts, isomers, and salts of isomers is possible within the specific chemical designation:

(1) All stimulant compounds, mixtures, and preparations included in schedule III pursuant to the federal drug abuse control laws and regulations adopted under those laws; (06-15-73)
(2) Benzphetamine; (06-15-73)
(3) Chlorphentermine; (06-15-73)
(4) Clortermine; (06-15-73)
(5) Phendimetrazine. (06-15-73)

(B) Depressants

Unless specifically excepted under federal drug abuse control laws or unless listed in another schedule, any material, compound, mixture, or preparation that contains any quantity of the following substances having a depressant effect on the central nervous system: (11-08-73)

(1) Any compound, mixture, or preparation containing amobarbital, secobarbital, pentobarbital, or any salt of any of these drugs, and one or more other active medicinal ingredients that are not listed in any schedule; (11-08-73)
(2) Any suppository dosage form containing amobarbital, secobarbital, pentobarbital, or any salt of any of these drugs and approved by the food and drug administration for marketing only as a suppository; (11-08-73)
(3) Any substance that contains any quantity of a derivative of barbituric acid or any salt of a derivative of barbituric acid; (05-01-71)
(4) Chlorhexadol; (05-01-71)
(5) Lysergic acid; (05-01-71)
(6) Lysergic acid amide; (05-01-71)
(7) Methyprylon; (05-01-71)
(8) Sulfondiethylmethane; (05-01-71)
(9) Sulfonethylmethane; (05-01-71)
(10) Sulfonmethane; (05-01-71)
(11) Tiletamine, zolazepam, or any salt of tiletamine or zolazepam (some trade or other names for a tiletamine-zolazepam combination product: Telazol); (some trade or other names for tiletamine: 2-(ethylamino)-2-(2-thienyl)-cyclohexanone); (some trade or other names for zolazepam: 4-(2-fluorophenyl)-6,8-dihydro-1,3,8-trimethylpyrazolo-[3,4-e] [1,4]-diazepin-7(1H)-one; flupyrazapon). (02-20-87)

PAGE LAST REVISED: 03/21/91   III-1

OHIO'S SCHEDULES OF CONTROLLED SUBSTANCES Page 14

(C) Narcotic antidotes

   (1) Nalorphine. (05-01-71)

(D) Narcotics-narcotic preparations

Unless specifically excepted under federal drug abuse control laws or unless listed in another schedule, any material, compound, mixture, or preparation that contains any of the following narcotic drugs, or their salts calculated as the free anhydrous base or alkaloid, in limited quantities as set forth below: (07-26-79)

   (1) Not more than 1.8 grams of codeine per 100 milliliters or not more than 90 milligrams per dosage unit, with an equal or greater quantity of an isoquinoline alkaloid of opium; (05-01-71)

   (2) Not more than 1.8 grams of codeine per 100 milliliters or not more than 90 milligrams per dosage unit, with one or more active, nonnarcotic ingredients in recognized therapeutic amounts; (05-01-71)

   (3) Not more than 300 milligrams of dihydrocodeinone per 100 milliliters or not more than 15 milligrams per dosage unit, with a fourfold or greater quantity of an isoquinoline alkaloid of opium; (05-01-71)

   (4) Not more than 300 milligrams of dihydrocodeinone per 100 milliliters or not more than 15 milligrams per dosage unit, with one or more active, nonnarcotic ingredients in recognized therapeutic amounts; (05-01-71)

   (5) Not more than 1.8 grams of dihydrocodeine per 100 milliliters or not more than 90 milligrams per dosage unit, with one or more active, nonnarcotic ingredients in recognized therapeutic amounts; (05-01-71)

   (6) Not more than 300 milligrams of ethylmorphine per 100 milliliters or not more than 15 milligrams per dosage unit, with one or more active, nonnarcotic ingredients in recognized therapeutic amounts; (05-01-71)

   (7) Not more than 500 milligrams of opium per 100 milliliters or per 100 grams or not more than 25 milligrams per dosage unit, with one or more active, nonnarcotic ingredients in recognized therapeutic amounts; (05-01-71)

   (8) Not more than 50 milligrams of morphine per 100 milliliters or per 100 grams, with one or more active, nonnarcotic ingredients in recognized therapeutic amounts. (05-01-71)

PAGE LAST REVISED: 07/26/79

OHIO'S SCHEDULES OF CONTROLLED SUBSTANCES   Page 15

(E) Anabolic steroids

Unless specifically excepted under federal drug abuse control laws or unless listed in another schedule, any material, compound, mixture, or preparation that contains any quantity of the following substances, including their salts, esters, isomers, and salts of esters and isomers whenever the existence of these salts, esters, and isomers is possible within the specific chemical designation:

(1) Anabolic steroids (02-27-91) ❶ Except as otherwise provided in division (E)(1) of schedule III, "anabolic steroids" means any drug or hormonal substance that is chemically and pharmacologically related to testosterone (other than estrogens, progestins, and corticosteroids) and that promotes muscle growth. "Anabolic steroids" does not include an anabolic steroid that is expressly intended for administration through implants to cattle or other nonhuman species and that has been approved by the United States secretary of health and human services for that administration, unless a person prescribes, dispenses, or distributes this type of anabolic steroid for human use. "Anabolic steroid" includes, but is not limited to, the following:

(a) Boldenone;
(b) Chlorotestosterone (4-chlortestosterone);
(c) Clostebol;
(d) Dehydrochlormethyltestosterone;
(e) Dihydrotestosterone (4-dihydrotestosterone);
(f) Drostanolone;
(g) Ethylestrenol;
(h) Fluoxymesterone;
(i) Formebulone (formebolone);
(j) Mesterolone;
(k) Methandienone;
(l) Methandranone;
(m) Methandriol;
(n) Methandrostenolone;
(o) Methenolone;
(p) Methyltestosterone;
(q) Mibolerone;
(r) Nandrolone;
(s) Norethandrolone;
(t) Oxandrolone;
(u) Oxymesterone;
(v) Oxymetholone;

---

❶ *Anabolic steroids was also added to Schedule III by the Ohio Legislature effective 05/21/91; a "cleanup" bill was passed by the Ohio Legislature on 05/19/93.*

OHIO'S SCHEDULES OF CONTROLLED SUBSTANCES

(w) Stanolone;
(x) Stanozolol;
(y) Testolactone;
(z) Testosterone;
(aa) Trenbolone;
(bb) Any salt, ester, isomer, or salt of an ester or isomer of a drug or hormonal substance described or listed in division (E)(1) of schedule III if the salt, ester, or isomer promotes muscle growth.

OHIO'S SCHEDULES OF CONTROLLED SUBSTANCES   Page 17

SCHEDULE IV

(A) Narcotic drugs

Unless specifically excepted by federal drug abuse control laws or unless listed in another schedule, any material, compound, mixture, or preparation that contains any of the following narcotic drugs, or their salts calculated as the free anhydrous base or alkaloid, in limited quantities as set forth below: (07-26-79)

(1) Not more than one milligram of difenoxin and not less than 25 micrograms of atropine sulfate per dosage unit; (09-27-78)

(2) Dextropropoxyphene (alpha-(+)-4-dimethylamino-1,2-diphenyl-3-methyl-2-propionoxybutane) [final dosage forms]. (03-14-77) (07-24-80) ❶

(B) Depressants

Unless specifically excepted under federal drug abuse control laws or unless listed in another schedule, any material, compound, mixture, or preparation that contains any quantity of the following substances, including their salts, isomers, and salts of isomers whenever the existence of these salts, isomers, and salts of isomers is possible within the specific chemical designation:

(1) Alprazolam; (11-12-81)
(2) Barbital; (05-01-71)
(3) Bromazepam; (11-05-84)
(4) Camazepam; (11-05-84)
(5) Chloral betaine; (05-01-71)
(6) Chloral hydrate; (05-01-71)
(7) Chlordiazepoxide; (07-02-75) [04-01-78]
(8) Clobazam; (11-05-84)
(9) Clonazepam; (07-02-75) [04-01-78]
(10) Clorazepate; (07-02-75) [04-01-78]
(11) Clotiazepam; (11-05-84)
(12) Cloxazolam; (11-05-84)
(13) Delorazepam; (11-05-84)
(14) Diazepam; (07-02-75) [04-01-78]
(15) Estazolam; (11-05-84)

---

❶ *Dextropropoxyphene (final dosage forms) was reclassified in Schedule IV as a narcotic drug under federal drug abuse control laws on 07-24-80. Bulk dextropropoxyphene (non-dosage forms) was placed in Schedule II on the same date.*

PAGE LAST REVISED: 11/05/84

OHIO'S SCHEDULES OF CONTROLLED SUBSTANCES   Page 18

    (16) Ethchlorvynol; (05-01-71)
    (17) Ethinamate; (05-01-71)
    (18) Ethyl loflazepate; (11-05-84)
    (19) Fludiazepam; (11-05-84)
    (20) Flunitrazepam; (11-05-84)
    (21) Flurazepam; (07-02-75) [04-01-78]
    (22) Halazepam; (10-29-81)
    (23) Haloxazolam; (11-05-84)
    (24) Ketazolam; (11-05-84)
    (25) Loprazolam; (11-05-84)
    (26) Lorazepam; (10-03-77)
    (27) Lormetazepam; (11-05-84)
    (28) Mebutamate; (01-30-75)
    (29) Medazepam; (11-05-84)
    (30) Meprobamate; (05-01-71)
    (31) Methohexital; (05-01-71)
    (32) Methylphenobarbital (mephobarbital); (05-01-71)
    (33) Midazolam; (03-25-86)
    (34) Nimetazepam; (11-05-84)
    (35) Nitrazepam; (11-05-84)
    (36) Nordiazepam; (11-05-84)
    (37) Oxazepam; (07-02-75) [04-01-78]
    (38) Oxazolam; (11-05-84)
    (39) Paraldehyde; (05-01-71)
    (40) Petrichloral; (05-01-71)
    (41) Phenobarbital; (05-01-71)
    (42) Pinazepam; (11-05-84)
    (43) Prazepam; (12-17-86)
    (44) Quazepam; (03-25-86)
    (45) Temazepam; (04-07-81)
    (46) Tetrazepam; (11-05-84)
    (47) Triazolam; (12-28-82)
    (48) Zolpidem. (02-05-93)

(C) Fenfluramine

Any material, compound, mixture, or preparation that contains any quantity of the following substances, including their salts, their optical isomers, position isomers, or geometric isomers, and salts of these isomers whenever the existence of these salts, isomers, and salts of isomers is possible within the specific chemical designation:

    (1) Fenfluramine. (06-15-73)

OHIO'S SCHEDULES OF CONTROLLED SUBSTANCES

(D) Stimulants

Unless specifically excepted under federal drug abuse control laws or unless listed in another schedule, any material, compound, mixture, or preparation that contains any quantity of the following substances having a stimulant effect on the central nervous system, including their salts, their optical isomers, position isomers, or geometric isomers, and salts of these isomers whenever the existence of these salts, isomers, and salts of isomers is possible within the specific chemical designation:

   (1)   Cathine ((+)-norpseudoephedrine); (06-16-88)
   (2)   Diethylpropion; (09-01-73)
   (3)   Fencamfamin; (06-16-88)
   (4)   Fenproporex; (06-16-88)
   (5)   Mazindol; (11-27-81) ❶
   (6)   Mefenorex; (06-16-88)
   (7)   Pemoline (including organometallic complexes and chelates thereof); (01-28-75)
   (8)   Phentermine; (09-01-73)
   (9)   Pipradrol; (12-01-80)
  (10) SPA [(-)-1-dimethylamino-1,2-diphenylethane]. (12-01-80)

(E) Other substances

Unless specifically excepted under federal drug abuse control laws or unless listed in another schedule, any material, compound, mixture or preparation that contains any quantity of the following substances, including their salts:

   (1)   Pentazocine. (02-09-79)

---

❶ *Mazindol was previously placed by the Federal Government into Schedule III effective 06-15-73 and was moved, pursuant to Section 3719.43 of the Ohio Revised Code, to Schedule IV effective 11-27-81.*

OHIO'S SCHEDULES OF CONTROLLED SUBSTANCES   Page 20

SCHEDULE V

(A) Narcotic drugs

Unless specifically excepted under federal drug abuse control laws or unless listed in another schedule, any material, compound, mixture, or preparation that contains any of the following narcotic drugs, and their salts, as set forth below:

　(1)　Buprenorphine. (04-01-85)

(B) Narcotics-narcotic preparations

Narcotic drugs containing nonnarcotic active medicinal ingredients. Any compound, mixture, or preparation that contains any of the following narcotic drugs, or their salts calculated as the free anhydrous base or alkaloid, in limited quantities as set forth below, and that includes one or more nonnarcotic active medicinal ingredients in sufficient proportion to confer upon the compound, mixture, or preparation valuable medicinal qualities other than those possessed by narcotic drugs alone: (07-26-79)

　(1)　Not more than 200 milligrams of codeine per 100 milliliters or per 100 grams; (05-01-71) (06-20-74)

　(2)　Not more than 100 milligrams of dihydrocodeine per 100 milliliters or per 100 grams; (05-01-71) (06-20-74)

　(3)　Not more than 100 milligrams of ethylmorphine per 100 milliliters or per 100 grams; (05-01-71) (06-20-74)

　(4)　Not more than 2.5 milligrams of diphenoxylate and not less than 25 micrograms of atropine sulfate per dosage unit; (05-01-71) (06-20-74)

　(5)　Not more than 100 milligrams of opium per 100 milliliters or per 100 grams; (05-01-71) (06-20-74)

　(6)　Not more than 0.5 milligram of difenoxin and not less than 25 micrograms of atropine sulfate per dosage unit. (09-27-78)

PAGE LAST REVISED: 04/01/85   V-1

OHIO'S SCHEDULES OF CONTROLLED SUBSTANCES   Page 21

(C) Stimulants

Unless specifically exempted or excluded under federal drug abuse control laws or unless listed in another schedule, any material, compound, mixture, or preparation that contains any quantity of the following substances having a stimulant effect on the central nervous system, including their salts, isomers, and salts of isomers:

(1) Ephedrine, except as provided in division (K) of section 3719.44 of the Revised Code;❶
(2) Pyrovalerone. (05-04-88)

---

❶ *Ephedrine was added by the Ohio Legislature (Sub. H.B. 391) effective 07/21/94. Division (K) of Section 3719.44 of the Revised Code states:*

A drug product containing ephedrine that is known as one of the following and is in the form specified shall not be considered a schedule V controlled substance:
(1) Amesec capsules;
(2) Bronitin tablets;
(3) Bronkotabs;
(4) Bronkolixir;
(5) Bronkaid tablets;
(6) Efedron nasal jelly;
(7) Guiaphed elixir;
(8) Haysma;
(9) Pazo hemorrhoid ointment and suppositories;
(10) Primatene "M" formula tablets;
(11) Primatene "P" formula tablets;
(12) Tedrigen tablets;
(13) Tedral tablets, suspension, and elixir;
(14) T.E.P.;
(15) Vatronol nose drops.

At the request of any person, the board may except any other drug product containing ephedrine from being included as a schedule V controlled substance if it determines that the product does not contain any other controlled substance. The board shall make the determination in accordance with this section and by rules adopted in accordance with Chapter 119. of the Revised Code.

Board exceptions pursuant to Rule 4729-12-09 of the Administrative Code:

(A) All products that contain the isomer known as pseudoephedrine or its salts, but do not also contain any of the isomer known as ephedrine or its salts. *(excepted by emergency rule of the Board effective 08/24/94, and by permanent rule of the Board effective 12/15/94)*
(B) "Breathe Easy®" herb tea. *(exception effective 01/10/96)*
(C) "Bronkaid® Dual Action" caplets. *(exception effective 01/10/96)*
(D) "Hydrosal®" hemorrhoidal ointment. *(exception effective 01/10/96)*
(E) "Primatene® Dual Action Formula" tablets. *(exception effective 01/10/96)*
(F) "Primatene®" tablets. *(exception effective 01/10/96)*

PAGE LAST REVISED: 01/10/96   V-2

§ 3719.42 Annual meeting of state pharmacy board.

The state pharmacy board shall meet in Columbus at least once each fiscal year for the purpose of carrying out its duties pursuant to Chapter 3719. of the Revised Code.

HISTORY: 136 v H 300. Eff 7-1-76.

Not analogous to former RC § 3719.42 (132 v S 74), repealed 136 v H 300, eff 7-1-76.

The effective date is set by section 4 of HB 300.

§ 3719.43 Addition, transfer, removal of substance by attorney general of United States; effect.

When pursuant to the federal drug abuse control laws the attorney general of the United States adds a compound, mixture, preparation, or substance to a schedule of the laws, transfers any of the same between one schedule of the laws to another, or removes a compound, mixture, preparation, or substance from the schedules of the laws then such addition, transfer, or removal is automatically effected in the corresponding schedule or schedules in section 3719.41 of the Revised Code, subject to amendment pursuant to section 3719.44 of the Revised Code.

HISTORY: 136 v H 300. Eff 7-1-76.

Not analogous to former RC § 3719.43 (132 v S 74), repealed 136 v H 300, eff 7-1-76.

The effective date is set by section 4 of HB 300.

§ 3719.44 Authority of board of pharmacy to change schedules.

(A) Pursuant to this section, and by rule adopted pursuant to Chapter 119. of the Revised Code, the state board of pharmacy may do any of the following with respect to schedules I, II, III, IV, and V established in section 3719.41 of the Revised Code:

(1) Add a previously unscheduled compound, mixture, preparation, or substance to any schedule;

(2) Transfer a compound, mixture, preparation, or substance from one schedule to another, provided the transfer does not have the effect under Chapter 3719. of the Revised Code of providing less stringent control of the compound, mixture, preparation, or substance than is provided under federal narcotic laws;

(3) Remove a compound, mixture, preparation, or substance from the schedules where the board had previously added the compound, mixture, preparation, or substance to the schedules, provided that the removal shall not have the effect under Chapter 3719. of the Revised Code of providing less stringent control of the compound, mixture, preparation, or substance than is provided under federal narcotic laws.

(B) In making a determination to add, remove, or transfer pursuant to division (A) of this section, the board shall consider the following:

(1) The actual or relative potential for abuse;

(2) The scientific evidence of the pharmacological effect of the substance, if known;

(3) The state of current scientific knowledge regarding the substance;

(4) The history and current pattern of abuse;

(5) The scope, duration, and significance of abuse;

(6) The risk to the public health;

(7) The potential of the substance to produce psychic or physiological dependence liability;

(8) Whether the substance is an immediate precursor.

(C) The board may add or transfer a compound, mixture, preparation, or substance to schedule I when it appears that there is a high potential for abuse, that it has no accepted medical use in treatment in this state, or lacks accepted safety for use in treatment under medical supervision.

(D) The board may add or transfer a compound, mixture, preparation, or substance to schedule II when it appears that there is a high potential for abuse, that it has a currently accepted medical use in treatment in this state, or currently accepted medical use in treatment with severe restrictions, and that its abuse may lead to severe physical or severe psychological dependence.

(E) The board may add or transfer a compound, mixture, preparation, or substance to schedule III when it appears that there is a potential for abuse less than the substances included in schedules I and II, that it has a currently accepted medical use in treatment in this state, and that its abuse may lead to moderate or low physical or high psychological dependence.

(F) The board may add or transfer a compound, mixture, preparation, or substance to schedule IV when it appears that it has a low potential for abuse relative to substances included in schedule III, and that it has a currently accepted medical use in treatment in this state, and that its abuse may lead to limited physical or psychological dependence relative to the substances included in schedule III.

(G) The board may add or transfer a compound, mixture, preparation, or substance to schedule V when it appears that it has lower potential for abuse than substances included in schedule IV, and that it has currently accepted medical use in treatment in this state, and that its abuse may lead to limited physical or psychological dependence relative to substances included in schedule IV.

(H) Even though a compound, mixture, preparation, or substance does not otherwise meet the criteria in this section for adding or transferring it to a schedule, the board may nevertheless add or transfer it to a schedule as an immediate precursor when all of the following apply:

(1) It is the principal compound used, or produced

primarily for use, in the manufacture of a controlled substance;

(2) It is an immediate chemical intermediary used or likely to be used in the manufacture of such a controlled substance;

(3) Its control is necessary to prevent, curtail, or limit the manufacture of the scheduled compound, mixture, preparation, or substance of which it is the immediate precursor.

(I) Authority to control under this section does not extend to distilled spirits, wine, or malt beverages, as those terms are defined or used in Chapter 4301. of the Revised Code.

(J) Authority to control under this section does not extend to any nonnarcotic substance if such substance may, under the Federal Food, Drug, and Cosmetic Act as defined in section 4729.02 of the Revised Code and the laws of this state, be lawfully sold over the counter without a prescription. Should a pattern of abuse develop for any nonnarcotic drug sold over the counter, the board may, by rule adopted in accordance with Chapter 119. of the Revised Code, after a public hearing and a documented study to determine that the substance actually meets the criteria listed in division (B) of this section, place such abused substance on a prescription basis.

(K)(1) A drug product containing ephedrine that is known as one of the following and is in the form specified shall not be considered a schedule V controlled substance:

(a) Amesec capsules;
(b) Bronitin tablets;
(c) Bronkotabs;
(d) Bronkolixir;
(e) Bronkaid tablets;
(f) Efedron nasal jelly;
(g) Guiaphed elixir;
(h) Haysma;
(i) Pazo hemorrhoid ointment and suppositories;
(j) Primatene "M" formula tablets;
(k) Primatene "P" formula tablets;
(l) Tedrigen tablets;
(m) Tedral tablets, suspension, and elixir;
(n) T.E.P.;
(o) Vatronol nose drops.

(2)(a) A product containing ephedrine shall not be considered a controlled substance if the product is a food product or dietary supplement that meets all of the following criteria:

(i) It contains, per dosage unit or serving, not more than the lesser of twenty-five milligrams of ephedrine alkaloids or the maximum amount of ephedrine alkaloids provided in applicable regulations adopted by the United States food and drug administration, and no other controlled substance.

(ii) It contains no hydrochloride or sulfate salts of ephedrine alkaloids.

(iii) It is packaged with a prominent label securely affixed to each package that states all of the following: the amount in milligrams of ephedrine in a serving or dosage unit; the amount of the food product or dietary supplement that constitutes a serving or dosage unit; that the maximum recommended dosage of ephedrine for a healthy adult human is the lesser of one hundred milligrams in a twenty-four-hour period for not more than twelve weeks or the maximum recommended dosage or period of use provided in applicable regulations adopted by the United States food and drug administration; and that improper use of the product may be hazardous to a person's health.

(b)(i) Subject to division (K)(2)(b)(ii) of this section, no person shall dispense, sell, or otherwise give a product described in division (K)(2)(a) of this section to any individual under eighteen years of age.

(ii) Division (K)(2)(b)(i) of this section does not apply to a physician or pharmacist who dispenses, sells, or otherwise gives a product described in division (K)(2)(a) of this section to an individual under eighteen years of age, to a parent or guardian of an individual under eighteen years of age who dispenses, sells, or otherwise gives a product of that nature to the individual under eighteen years of age, or to a person who, as authorized by the individual's parent or legal guardian, dispenses, sells, or otherwise gives a product of that nature to an individual under eighteen years of age.

(c) No person in the course of selling, offering for sale, or otherwise distributing a product described in division (K)(2)(a) of this section shall advertise or represent in any manner that the product causes euphoria, ecstasy, a "buzz" or "high," or an altered mental state; heightens sexual performance; or, because it contains ephedrine alkaloids, increased muscle mass.

(3) A drug product that contains the isomer pseudoephedrine, or any of its salts, optical isomers, or salts of optical isomers, shall not be considered a controlled substance if the drug product is labeled in a manner consistent with federal law or with the product's over-the-counter tentative final monograph or final monograph issued by the United States food and drug administration.

(4) At the request of any person, the board may except any product containing ephedrine not described in division (K)(1) or (2) of this section or any class of products containing ephedrine from being included as a schedule V controlled substance if it determines that the product or class of products does not contain any other controlled substance. The board shall make the determination in accordance with this section and by rule adopted in accordance with Chapter 119. of the Revised Code.

(L) As used in this section:

(1) "Food" has the same meaning as in section 3715.01 of the Revised Code;

(2) "Dietary supplement" has the meaning given in the "Federal Food, Drug, and Cosmetic Act," 108 Stat. 4327 (1994), 21 U.S.C.A. 321 (ff), as amended.

(3) "Ephedrine alkaloids" means ephedrine, pseudoephedrine, norephedrine, norpseudoephedrine, methylephedrine, and methylpseudoephedrine.

HISTORY: 136 v H 300 (Eff 7-1-76); 145 v H 391 (Eff 7-21-94); 146 v H 523. Eff 3-31-97.

Not analogous to former RC § 3719.44 (132 v S 74; 133 v H 1), repealed 136 v H 300, eff 7-1-76.

See provisions, §§ 3, 9 of HB 156 (145 v —) following RC § 3719.41.

§§ 3719.45 to 3719.51 Repealed, 136 v H 300, § 2 [132 v S 74; 133 v H 1; 133 v H 874; 134 v H 494]. Eff 7-1-76.

These sections concerned hallucinogens; harmful intoxicants, and drug dependent convicts.

§ 3719.61 Methadone maintenance.

Nothing in the laws dealing with drugs of abuse shall be construed to prohibit treatment of narcotic drug dependent persons by the continuing maintenance of their dependence through the administration of methadone in accordance with the rules adopted by the department of alcohol and drug addiction services under section 3793.11 of the Revised Code, when all of the following apply:

(A) The likelihood that any person undergoing maintenance treatment will be cured of his dependence on narcotic drugs is remote, the treatment is prescribed by a practitioner for the purpose of alleviating or controlling the patient's drug dependence, and the patient's prognosis while undergoing such treatment is at least a partial improvement in his asocial or antisocial behavior patterns;

(B) In the case of an inpatient in a hospital or clinic, the amount of the maintenance drug dispensed at any one time does not exceed the quantity necessary for a single dose, and such dose is administered to the patient immediately;

(C) In the case of an outpatient, the amount of the maintenance drug dispensed at any one time shall be determined by a practitioner with regard to the patient's progress in the treatment program, and the patient's needs for gainful employment, education, and responsible homemaking, provided, that in no event shall the dosage be greater than the amount permitted by federal law and rules adopted by the department pursuant to section 3793.11 of the Revised Code;

(D) The drug is not dispensed in any case to replace or supplement any part of a supply of the drug previously dispensed, or when there is reasonable cause to believe it will be used or disposed of unlawfully;

(E) The drug is dispensed through a program licensed and operated in accordance with section 3793.11 of the Revised Code.

HISTORY: 133 v H 874 (Eff 9-16-70); 134 v H 494 (Eff 7-12-72); 134 v H 521 (Eff 10-19-72); 136 v H 300 (Eff 7-1-76); 138 v H 900 (Eff 7-1-80); 143 v H 317 (Eff 10-10-89); 145 v H 385. Eff 7-19-94.

§ 3719.70 Informers; immunity from prosecution; sentences.

(A) When testimony, information, or other evidence in the possession of a person who uses, possesses, or traffics in any drug of abuse appears necessary to an investigation by law enforcement authorities into illicit sources of any drug of abuse, or appears necessary to successfully institute, maintain, or conclude a prosecution for any drug abuse offense, as defined in section 2925.01 of the Revised Code, a judge of the court of common pleas may grant to that person immunity from prosecution for any offense based upon the testimony, information, or other evidence furnished by that person, other than a prosecution of that person for giving false testimony, information, or other evidence.

(B)(1) When a person is convicted of any misdemeanor drug abuse offense, the court, in determining whether to suspend sentence or place the person on probation, shall take into consideration whether the person truthfully has revealed all information within the person's knowledge concerning illicit traffic in or use of drugs of abuse and, when required, has testified as to that information in any proceeding to obtain a search or arrest warrant against another or to prosecute another for any offense involving a drug of abuse. The information shall include, but is not limited to, the identity and whereabouts of accomplices, accessories, aiders, and abettors, if any, of the person or persons from whom any drug of abuse was obtained or to whom any drug of abuse was distributed, and of persons known or believed to be drug dependent persons, together with the location of any place or places where and the manner in which any drug of abuse is illegally cultivated, manufactured, sold, possessed, or used. The information also shall include all facts and circumstances surrounding any illicit traffic in or use of drugs of abuse of that nature.

(2) If a person otherwise is eligible for treatment in lieu of conviction and being ordered to a period of rehabilitation under section 2951.041 [2951.04.1] of the Revised Code as an offender who is a drug dependent person or is in danger of becoming a drug dependent person but the person has failed to cooperate with law enforcement authorities by providing them with the types of information described in division (B)(1) of this section, the person's lack of cooperation may be considered by the court under division (B) of section 2951.041 [2951.04.1] of the Revised Code in determining whether to stay all criminal proceedings and order the person to a requested period of rehabilitation.

(C) In the absence of a competent and voluntary waiver of the right against self-incrimination, no information or testimony furnished pursuant to division (B) of this section shall be used in a prosecution of the person furnishing it for any offense other than a prosecution of that person for giving false testimony, information, or other evidence.

HISTORY: 133 v H 874 (Eff 9-16-70); 136 v H 300 (Eff 7-1-76); 146 v S 2 (Eff 7-1-96); 146 v S 269. Eff 7-1-96.

§ 3719.81 Drug samples.

(A) A person may furnish another a sample of any drug of abuse, or of any drug or pharmaceutical preparation which would be hazardous to health or safety if used without the supervision of a practitioner, if all of the following apply:

(1) The sample is furnished by a manufacturer, manufacturer's representative, or wholesale dealer in pharmaceuticals to a practitioner, or is furnished by a practitioner to a patient for use as medication;

(2) The drug is in the original container in which it was placed by the manufacturer, and such container is plainly marked as a sample;

(3) Prior to its being furnished, the drug sample has been stored under the proper conditions to prevent its deterioration or contamination;

(4) If the drug is of a type which deteriorates with time, the sample container is plainly marked with the date beyond which the drug sample is unsafe to use, and such date has not expired on the sample furnished. Compliance with the labeling requirements of the Federal Food, Drug, and Cosmetics Act shall be deemed compliance with this section;

(5) The drug is distributed, stored, or discarded in such a way that the drug sample may not be acquired or used by any unauthorized person, or by any person, including a child, for whom it may present a health or safety hazard.

(B) Division (A) of this section does not apply to restrict the furnishing of any sample of a nonnarcotic substance if such substance may, under the "Federal Food, Drug, and Cosmetic Act," as defined in division (D)(1) of section 4729.02 of the Revised Code, and under the laws of this state, otherwise be lawfully sold over the counter without a prescription.

(C) The state board of pharmacy shall, pursuant to sections 119.01 to 119.13 of the Revised Code, adopt regulations necessary to give effect to this section.

HISTORY: 134 v H 521 (Eff 10-19-72); 136 v H 300. Eff 7-1-76.

The effective date is set by section 4 of HB 300.

§§ 3719.85 to 3719.87 Repealed, 138 v S 184, § 4 [138 v S 185]. Eff 6-20-84.

These sections concerned the therapeutic research program.

§ 3719.99 Penalties.

(A) Whoever violates section 3719.16 or 3719.161 [3719.16.1] of the Revised Code is guilty of a felony of the fifth degree. If the offender previously has been convicted of a violation of section 3719.16 or 3719.161 [3719.16.1] of the Revised Code or a drug abuse offense, a violation of section 3719.16 or 3719.161 [3719.16.1] of the Revised Code is a felony of the fourth degree. If the violation involves the sale, offer to sell, or possession of a schedule I or II controlled substance, with the exception of marihuana, and if the offender, as a result of the violation, is a major drug offender, division (D) of this section applies.

(B) Whoever violates division (C) or (D) of section 3719.172 [3719.17.2] of the Revised Code is guilty of a felony of the fifth degree. If the offender previously has been convicted of a violation of division (C) or (D) of section 3719.172 [3719.17.2] of the Revised Code or a drug abuse offense, a violation of division (C) or (D) of section 3719.172 [3719.17.2] of the Revised Code is a felony of the fourth degree. If the violation involves the sale, offer to sell, or possession of a schedule I or II controlled substance, with the exception of marihuana, and if the offender, as a result of the violation, is a major drug offender, division (D) of this section applies.

(C) Whoever violates section 3719.07 or 3719.08 of the Revised Code is guilty of a misdemeanor of the first degree. If the offender previously has been convicted of a violation of section 3719.07 or 3719.08 of the Revised Code or a drug abuse offense, a violation of section 3719.07 or 3719.08 of the Revised Code is a felony of the fifth degree. If the violation involves the sale, offer to sell, or possession of a schedule I or II controlled substance, with the exception of marihuana, and if the offender, as a result of the violation, is a major drug offender, division (D) of this section applies.

(D)(1) If an offender is convicted of or pleads guilty to a felony violation of section 3719.07, 3719.08, 3719.16, or 3719.161 [3719.16.1] or of division (C) or (D) of section 3719.172 [3719.17.2] of the Revised Code, if the violation involves the sale, offer to sell, or possession of a schedule I or II controlled substance, with the exception of marihuana, and if the offender, as a result of the violation, is a major drug offender, the court that sentences the offender, in lieu of the prison term authorized or required by division (A), (B), or (C) of this section and sections 2929.13 and 2929.14 of the Revised Code and in addition to any other sanction imposed for the offense under sections 2929.11 to 2929.18 of the Revised Code, shall impose upon the offender, in accordance with division (D)(3)(a) of section 2929.14 of the Revised Code, the mandatory prison term specified in that division and may impose an additional prison term under division (D)(3)(b) of that section.

(2) Notwithstanding any contrary provision of section 3719.21 of the Revised Code, the clerk of the court shall pay any fine imposed for a felony violation of section 3719.07, 3719.08, 3719.16, or 3719.161 [3719.16.1] or of division (C) or (D) of section 3719.172 [3719.17.2] of the Revised Code pursuant to division (A) of section 2929.18 of the Revised Code in accord-

ance with and subject to the requirements of division (F) of section 2925.03 of the Revised Code. The agency that receives the fine shall use the fine as specified in division (F) of section 2925.03 of the Revised Code.

(E) Whoever violates section 3719.05, 3719.06, 3719.13, or 3719.31 or division (B) or (E) of section 3719.172 [3719.17.2] of the Revised Code is guilty of a misdemeanor of the third degree. If the offender previously has been convicted of a violation of section 3719.05, 3719.06, 3719.13, or 3719.31 or division (B) or (E) of section 3719.172 [3719.17.2] of the Revised Code or a drug abuse offense, a violation of section 3719.05, 3719.06, 3719.13, or 3719.31 or division (B) or (E) of section 3719.172 [3719.17.2] of the Revised Code is a misdemeanor of the first degree.

(F) Whoever violates section 3719.30 of the Revised Code is guilty of a misdemeanor of the fourth degree. If the offender previously has been convicted of a violation of section 3719.30 of the Revised Code or a drug abuse offense, a violation of section 3719.30 of the Revised Code is a misdemeanor of the third degree.

(G) Whoever violates section 3719.32 or 3719.33 of the Revised Code is guilty of a minor misdemeanor.

(H) Whoever violates division (K)(2)(b) of section 3719.44 of the Revised Code is guilty of a felony of the fifth degree.

(I) Whoever violates division (K)(2)(c) of section 3719.44 of the Revised Code is guilty of a misdemeanor of the second degree.

(J) As used in this section, "major drug offender" has the same meaning as in section 2929.01 of the Revised Code.

HISTORY: 136 v H 300 (Eff 7-1-76); 146 v S 2 (Eff 7-1-96); 146 v S 269 (Eff 7-1-96); 146 v H 523. Eff 3-31-97.

Analogous to former RC § 3719.99 (Bureau of Code Revision, 10-1-53; 126 v 178; 128 v 1044; 132 v S 74; 133 v H 1; 133 v H 90; 133 v H 874; 134 v H 924; 134 v H 521), repealed, 136 v H 300, eff 7-1-76.

CHAPTER 3722: ADULT CARE FACILITIES

[§ 3722.15.1] § 3722.151 Criminal records check for prospective employees providing direct care to older adult.

(A) As used in this section:

(1) "Adult care facility" has the same meaning as in section 3722.01 of the Revised Code.

(2) "Applicant" means a person who is under final consideration for employment with an adult care facility in a full-time, part-time, or temporary position that involves providing direct care to an older adult. "Applicant" does not include a person who provides direct care as a volunteer without receiving or expecting to receive any form of remuneration other than reimbursement for actual expenses.

(3) "Criminal records check" and "older adult" have the same meanings as in section 109.572 [109.57.2] of the Revised Code.

(B)(1) Except as provided in division (I) of this section, the chief administrator of an adult care facility shall request that the superintendent of the bureau of criminal identification and investigation conduct a criminal records check with respect to each applicant. If the applicant does not present proof of having been a resident of this state for the five-year period immediately prior to the date the criminal records check is requested or provide evidence that within that five-year period the superintendent has requested information about the applicant from the federal bureau of investigation in a criminal records check, the chief administrator shall request that the superintendent obtain information from the federal bureau of investigation as part of the criminal records check of the applicant. Even if the applicant presents proof of having been a resident of this state for the five-year period, the chief administrator may request that the superintendent include information from the federal bureau of investigation in the criminal records check.

(2) A person required by division (B)(1) of this section to request a criminal records check shall do both of the following:

(a) Provide to each applicant a copy of the form prescribed pursuant to division (C)(1) of section 109.572 [109.57.2] of the Revised Code and a standard fingerprint impression sheet prescribed pursuant to division (C)(2) of that section, and obtain the completed form and impression sheet from the applicant;

(b) Forward the completed form and impression sheet to the superintendent of the bureau of criminal identification and investigation.

(3) An applicant provided the form and fingerprint impression sheet under division (B)(2)(a) of this section who fails to complete the form or provide fingerprint impressions shall not be employed in any position for which a criminal records check is required by this section.

(C)(1) Except as provided in rules adopted by the public health council in accordance with division (F) of this section, no adult care facility shall employ a person in a position that involves providing direct care to an older adult if the person has been convicted of or pleaded guilty to any of the following:

(a) A violation of section 2903.01, 2903.02, 2903.03, 2903.04, 2903.11, 2903.12, 2903.13, 2903.16, 2903.21, 2903.34, 2905.01, 2905.02, 2905.11, 2905.12, 2907.02, 2907.03, 2907.05, 2907.06, 2907.07, 2907.08, 2907.09, 2907.12,† 2907.25, 2907.31, 2907.32, 2907.321 [2907.32.1], 2907.322 [2907.32.2], 2907.323 [2907.32.3], 2911.01, 2911.02, 2911.11, 2911.12, 2911.13, 2913.02, 2913.03, 2913.04, 2913.11, 2913.21, 2913.31, 2913.40, 2913.43, 2913.47, 2913.51, 2919.25, 2921.36, 2923.12, 2923.13, 2923.161 [2923.16.1], 2925.02, 2925.03, 2925.11, 2925.13, 2925.22, 2925.23, or 3716.11 of the Revised Code.

(b) An existing or former law of this state, any other

state, or the United States that is substantially equivalent to any of the offenses listed in division (C)(1)(a) of this section.

(2) An adult care facility may employ an applicant conditionally prior to obtaining the results of a criminal records check regarding the individual. The facility shall request a criminal records check in accordance with division (B)(1) of this section not later than five business days after the individual begins conditional employment. The facility shall terminate the individual's employment if the results of the criminal records check, other than the results of any request for information from the federal bureau of investigation, are not obtained within the period ending sixty days after the date the request is made. Regardless of when the results of the criminal records check are obtained, if the results indicate that the individual has been convicted of or pleaded guilty to any of the offenses listed or described in division (C)(1) of this section, the facility shall terminate the individual's employment unless the facility chooses to employ the individual pursuant to division (F) of this section. Termination of employment under this division shall be considered just cause for discharge for purposes of division (D)(2) of section 4141.29 of the Revised Code if the individual makes any attempt to deceive the facility about the individual's criminal record.

(D)(1) Each adult care facility shall pay to the bureau of criminal identification and investigation the fee prescribed pursuant to division (C)(3) of section 109.572 [109.57.2] of the Revised Code for each criminal records check conducted pursuant to this section.

(2) An adult care facility may charge an applicant a fee not exceeding the amount the facility pays under division (D)(1) of this section. A facility may collect a fee only if it notifies the person at the time of initial application for employment of the amount of the fee and that, unless the fee is paid, the person will not be considered for employment.

(E) The report of any criminal records check conducted pursuant to a request made under this section is not a public record for the purposes of section 149.43 of the Revised Code and shall not be made available to any person other than the following:

(1) The individual who is the subject of the criminal records check or the individual's representative;

(2) The chief administrator of the facility requesting the criminal records check or the administrator's representative;

(3) The administrator of any other facility, agency, or program that provides direct care to older adults that is owned or operated by the same entity that owns or operates the adult care facility;

(4) A court, hearing officer, or other necessary individual involved in a case dealing with a denial of employment of the applicant.

(F) The public health council shall adopt rules in accordance with Chapter 119. of the Revised Code to implement this section. The rules shall specify circumstances under which an adult care facility may employ a person who has been convicted of or pleaded guilty to an offense listed or described in division (C)(1) of this section but meets personal character standards set by the council.

(G) The chief administrator of an adult care facility shall inform each individual, at the time of initial application for a position that involves providing direct care to an older adult, that the individual is required to provide a set of fingerprint impressions and that a criminal records check is required to be conducted if the individual comes under final consideration for employment.

(H) In a tort or other civil action for damages that is brought as the result of an injury, death, or loss to person or property caused by an individual who an adult care facility employs in a position that involves providing direct care to older adults, the following shall apply:

(1) If the facility employed the individual in good faith and reasonable reliance on the report of a criminal records check requested under this section, the facility shall not be found negligent solely because of its reliance on the report, even if the information in the report is determined later to have been incomplete or inaccurate;

(2) If the facility employed the individual in good faith on a conditional basis pursuant to division (C)(2) of this section, the facility shall not be found negligent solely because it employed the individual prior to receiving the report of a criminal records check requested under this section;

(3) If the facility in good faith employed the individual according to the personal character standards established in rules adopted under division (F) of this section, the facility shall not be found negligent solely because the individual prior to being employed had been convicted of or pleaded guilty to an offense listed or described in division (C)(1) of this section.

(I) The chief administrator is not required to request that the superintendent of the bureau of criminal identification and investigation conduct a criminal records check of an applicant if the applicant has been referred to the adult care facility by an employment service that supplies full-time, part-time, or temporary staff for positions involving the direct care of older adults and both of the following apply:

(1) The chief administrator receives from the employment service or the applicant a report of the results of a criminal records check regarding the applicant that has been conducted by the superintendent within the one-year period immediately preceding the applicant's referral;

(2) The report of the criminal records check demonstrates that the person has not been convicted of or pleaded guilty to an offense listed or described in division (C)(1) of this section.

HISTORY: 146 v S 160 (Eff 1-27-97); 147 v S 96. Eff 6-11-97.

† RC § 2907.12 repealed 9-3-96.

CHAPTER 3737: FIRE MARSHALL; FIRE SAFETY

§ 3737.28 Power to administer oaths; failure to cooperate.

The fire marshal or an assistant fire marshal may administer an oath to any person appearing as a witness before him. No witness shall refuse to be sworn or refuse to testify, or disobey an order of the marshal, or of an assistant marshal, or fail or refuse to produce a book, paper, or document concerning a matter under examination, or be guilty of contemptuous conduct after being summoned by such officer to appear before him to give testimony in relation to a matter or subject under investigation.

HISTORY: 137 v H 590. Eff 7-1-79.

Not analogous to former RC § 3737.28 (GC § 836-2; 102 v 430; 122 v 718; Bureau of Code Revision, 10-1-53), repealed 137 v H 590, § 2, eff 7-1-79. That section has been substantially incorporated into RC § 3737.45 (137 v H 590), eff 7-1-79.

The effective date is set by section 3 of HB 590.

§ 3737.51 Violations of fire code or order prohibited; civil penalties.

(A) No person shall knowingly violate any provision of the state fire code or any order made pursuant to it.

(B) Any person who has received a citation for a serious violation of the fire code or any order issued pursuant to it, shall be assessed a civil penalty of not more than one thousand dollars for each such violation.

(C) Any person who has received a citation for a violation of the fire code or any order issued pursuant to it, and such violation is specifically determined not to be of a serious nature, may be assessed a civil penalty of not more than one thousand dollars for each such violation.

(D) Any person who fails to correct a violation for which a citation has been issued within the period permitted for its correction, may be assessed a civil penalty of not more than one thousand dollars for each day during which such failure or violation continues.

(E) Any person who violates any of the posting requirements, as prescribed by division (C) of section 3737.42 of the Revised Code, shall be assessed a civil penalty of not more than one thousand dollars for each violation.

(F) Due consideration to the appropriateness of the penalty with respect to the gravity of the violation, the good faith of the person being charged, and the history of previous violations shall be given whenever a penalty is assessed under this chapter.

(G) For purposes of this section, a serious violation shall be considered to exist if there is a substantial probability that an occurrence causing death or serious physical harm to persons could result from a condition which exists, or from one or more practices, means, methods, operations or processes which have been adopted or are in use, unless the person did not and could not with the exercise of reasonable diligence, know of the presence of the violation.

(H) Civil penalties imposed by this chapter shall be paid to the fire marshal for deposit into the general revenue fund. Such penalties may be recovered in a civil action in the name of the state brought in the court of common pleas of the county where the violation is alleged to have occurred.

HISTORY: 137 v H 590. Eff 7-1-79.

The effective date is set by section 3 of HB 590.

§ 3737.61 Posting of arson laws.

The owner, operator, or lessee of any transient residential building shall post the provisions of sections 2909.02 and 2909.03 of the Revised Code in a conspicuous place in each room occupied by guests in such building. The owner, operator, or lessee of any nontransient residential building, institution, school, or place of assembly shall post the provisions of such sections in conspicuous places upon such premises. No person shall fail to comply with this section.

HISTORY: 137 v H 590. Eff 7-1-79.

The effective date is set by section 3 of HB 590.

§ 3737.62 Spreading of fires through negligence.

No person shall set, kindle, or cause to be set or kindled any fire, which through his negligence, spreads beyond its immediate confines to any structure, field, or wood lot.

HISTORY: 137 v H 590. Eff 7-1-79.

The effective date is set by section 3 of HB 590.

§ 3737.63 Duty upon discovery of unfriendly fire.

(A) The owner, operator, or lessee, an employee of any owner, operator, or lessee, an occupant, and any person in direct control of any building regulated under the Ohio building code, upon the discovery of an unfriendly fire, or upon receiving information that there is an unfriendly fire on the premises, shall immediately, and with all reasonable dispatch and diligence, call or otherwise notify the fire department concerning the fire, and shall spread an alarm immediately to all occupants of the building.

(B) For the purposes of this section, "unfriendly fire" means a fire of a destructive nature as distinguished from a controlled fire intended for a beneficial purpose.

(C) No person shall fail to comply with this section.

HISTORY: 137 v H 590. Eff 7-1-79.

The effective date is set by section 3 of HB 590.

§ 3737.64 Duty to disclose purpose of non-official inspection.

No person who is not a certified fire safety inspector shall act as such or hold himself out to be such, unless prior to commencing any inspection function, he discloses the purpose for which he is making such inspection and the fact that he is not employed by any state or local fire service or agency, and that he is not acting in an official capacity for any governmental subdivision or agency.

HISTORY: 137 v H 590. Eff 7-1-79.

The effective date is set by section 3 of HB 590.

§ 3737.65 Prohibitions concerning sale, use or servicing of fire protection equipment.

(A) No person shall sell, offer for sale, or use any fire protection or fire fighting equipment that does not meet the minimum standards established by the fire marshal in the state fire code.

(B) Except for public and private mobile fire trucks, no person shall service, test, repair, or install for profit any fire protection or fire fighting equipment without a certificate or a provisional certificate issued by the fire marshal.

(C) The fire marshal shall not issue a provisional certificate pursuant to division (B) of this section to any individual who is not enrolled in a bona fide apprenticeship training program registered with the apprenticeship council pursuant to section 4111.29 of the Revised Code or with the bureau of apprenticeship and training of the United States department of labor. A provisional certificate issued pursuant to this section authorizes an individual to engage in the activities permitted under division (B) of this section only if the individual:

(1) Remains enrolled in such an apprenticeship training program; and

(2) Is directly supervised by an individual who possesses a valid and current certificate issued pursuant to division (B) of this section for the activities in which the individual issued the provisional certificate is engaged and the certified individual directly supervising the individual issued the provisional certificate only supervises one provisional certificate holder.

HISTORY: 137 v H 590 (Eff 7-1-79); 143 v H 677 (Eff 11-7-90); 146 v S 162. Eff 10-29-95.

§ 3737.66 Qualifications for representation as fire fighter or prevention officer.

No person shall call himself, hold himself out as being, or act as a fireman, volunteer fireman, fire fighter, volunteer fire fighter, member of a fire department, chief of a fire department, or fire prevention officer unless at least one of the following applies:

(A) He is recognized as a fireman, volunteer fireman, fire fighter, volunteer fire fighter, member of a fire department, chief of a fire department, or fire prevention officer by the fire marshal or has received a certificate issued under former section 3303.07 or section 4765.55 of the Revised Code evidencing his satisfactory completion of a fire fighter training program and has been appointed by the board of fire district trustees, township, or municipal corporation or, in the case of a volunteer fire fighter, receives such a certificate within one year after his appointment;

(B) He is a member of a private fire company as defined in division (A)(2) of section 9.60 of the Revised Code and that company is providing fire protection in accordance with division (B), (C), or (D) of section 9.60 of the Revised Code.

HISTORY: 141 v H 552 (Eff 9-17-86); 144 v S 98. Eff 11-12-92.

§ 3737.73 Instruct pupils in fire drills and tornado safety precautions.

(A) No principal or person in charge of a public or private school or educational institution having an average daily attendance of fifty or more pupils, and no person in charge of any children's home or orphanage housing twenty or more minor persons, shall willfully neglect to instruct and train such children by means of drills or rapid dismissals at least once a month while such school, institution, or children's home is in operation, so that such children in a sudden emergency may leave the building in the shortest possible time without confusion. In the case of schools, no such person shall willfully neglect to keep the doors and exits of such building unlocked during school hours. The fire marshal may order the immediate installation of necessary fire gongs or signals in such schools, institutions, or children's homes and enforce this section.

(B) In conjunction with the drills or rapid dismissals required by division (A) of this section, principals or persons in charge of public or private primary and secondary schools, or educational institutions, shall instruct pupils in safety precautions to be taken in case of a tornado alert or warning. Such principals or persons in charge of such schools or institutions shall designate, in accordance with standards prescribed by the fire marshal, appropriate locations to be used to shelter pupils in case of a tornado, tornado alert, or warning.

(C) The fire marshal or his designee shall annually inspect each school or institution subject to division (B) of this section to ascertain whether the locations comply with the prescribed standards. Nothing in this section shall require a school or institution to construct or improve a facility or location for use as a shelter area.

(D) The fire marshal or his designee shall issue a warning to any person found in violation of division (A) or (B) of this section. The warning shall indicate the specific violation and a date by which such violation shall be corrected. No person shall fail to correct violations by the date indicated on a warning issued under this division.

HISTORY: GC § 12900; 99 v 231; 109 v 253; Bureau of Code

Revision, RC § 3737.29, 10-1-53; 136 v H 427 (Eff 1-30-76); RC § 3737.73, 137 v H 590 (Eff 7-1-79); 138 v S 18. Eff 7-1-79.

The effective date is set by section 3 of SB 18.

[§ 3737.88.1] § 3737.881 Certification of underground storage tank systems installers; training programs.

(A) The fire marshal shall certify underground storage tank systems installers who meet the standards for certification established in rules adopted under division (D)(1) of this section, pass the certification examination required by this division, and pay the certificate fee established in rules adopted under division (D)(5) of this section. Any individual who wishes to obtain certification as an installer shall apply to the fire marshal on a form prescribed by the fire marshal. The application shall be accompanied by the application and examination fees established in rules adopted under division (D)(5) of this section.

The fire marshal shall prescribe an examination designed to test the knowledge of applicants for certification as underground storage tank system[s] installers in the installation, repair, abandonment, and removal of those systems. The examination shall also test the applicants' knowledge and understanding of the requirements and standards established in rules adopted under sections 3737.88 and 3737.882 [3737.88.2] of the Revised Code pertaining to the installation, repair, abandonment, and removal of those systems.

Installer certifications issued under this division shall be renewed annually, upon submission of a certification renewal form prescribed by the fire marshal, provision of proof of successful completion of continuing education requirements, and payment of the certification renewal fee established in rules adopted under division (D)(5) of this section. In addition, the fire marshal may from time to time prescribe an examination for certification renewal and may require applicants to pass the examination and pay the fee established for it in rules adopted under division (D)(5) of this section.

The fire marshal may, in accordance with Chapter 119. of the Revised Code, deny, suspend, revoke, or refuse to renew an installer's certification or renewal thereof if he finds that any of the following applies:

(1) The applicant for certification or certificate holder fails to meet the standards for certification or renewal thereof under this section and rules adopted under it;

(2) The certification was obtained through fraud or misrepresentation;

(3) The certificate holder recklessly caused or permitted a person under his supervision to install, perform major repairs on site to, abandon, or remove an underground storage tank system in violation of the performance standards set forth in rules adopted under section 3737.88 or 3737.882 [3737.88.2] of the Revised Code.

As used in division (A)(3) of this section, "recklessly" has the same meaning as in section 2901.22 of the Revised Code.

(B) The fire marshal shall certify persons who sponsor training programs for underground storage tank system[s] installers who meet the criteria for certification established in rules adopted by the fire marshal under division (D)(4) of this section and pay the certificate fee established in rules adopted under division (D)(5) of this section. Any person who wishes to obtain certification to sponsor such a training program shall apply to the fire marshal on a form prescribed by him. Training program certificates issued under this division shall expire annually. Upon submission of a certification renewal application form prescribed by the fire marshal and payment of the application and certification renewal fees established in rules adopted under division (D)(5) of this section, the fire marshal shall issue a training program renewal certificate to the applicant.

The fire marshal may, in accordance with Chapter 119. of the Revised Code, deny an application for, suspend, or revoke a training program certificate or renewal thereof if he finds that the training program does not or will not meet the standards for certification established in rules adopted under division (D)(4) of this section.

(C) The fire marshal may conduct or cause to be conducted training programs for underground storage tank systems installers as he considers to be necessary or appropriate. The fire marshal is not subject to division (B) of this section with respect to training programs conducted by employees of the office of the fire marshal.

(D) The fire marshal shall adopt, and may amend and rescind, rules doing all of the following:

(1) Defining the activities that constitute supervision over the installation, performance of major repairs on site to, abandonment of, and removal of underground storage tank systems;

(2) Establishing standards and procedures for certification of underground storage tank systems installers;

(3) Establishing standards and procedures for continuing education for certification renewal;

(4) Establishing standards and procedures for certification of training programs for installers;

(5) Establishing fees for applications for certifications under this section, the examinations prescribed under division (A) of this section, the issuance and renewal of certificates under divisions (A) and (B) of this section, and attendance at training programs conducted by the fire marshal under division (C) of this section. Fees received under this section shall be credited to the underground storage tank administration fund created in section 3737.02 of the Revised Code and shall be used to defray the costs of implementing, administering, and enforcing this section and the rules adopted thereunder, conducting training sessions, and facilitating prevention of releases.

(6) That are necessary or appropriate for the imple-

mentation, administration, and enforcement of this section.

(E) Nothing in this section or the rules adopted under it prohibits an owner or operator of an underground storage tank system from installing, making major repairs on site to, abandoning, or removing an underground storage tank system under the supervision of an installer certified under division (A) of this section who is a full-time or part-time employee of the owner or operator.

(F) On and after the date one hundred eighty days after the effective date of this section, no person shall do any of the following:

(1) Install, make major repairs on site to, abandon, or remove an underground storage tank system unless the activity is performed under the supervision of a qualified individual who holds a valid installer certificate issued under division (A) of this section;

(2) Act in the capacity of providing supervision for the installation of, performance of major repairs on site to, abandonment of, or removal of an underground storage tank system unless the person holds a valid installer certificate issued under division (A) of this section;

(3) Except as provided in division (C) of this section, sponsor a training program for underground storage tank systems installers unless the person holds a valid training program certificate issued under division (B) of this section.

HISTORY: 143 v H 421. Eff 7-11-89.

[§ 3737.88.2] § 3737.882 Action to confirm or disprove suspected petroleum release; corrective actions; violations.

(A) If, after an examination or inspection, the fire marshal or an assistant fire marshal finds that a release of petroleum is suspected, he shall take such action as he considers necessary to ensure that a suspected release is confirmed or disproved and, if the occurrence of a release is confirmed, to correct the release. These actions may include one or more of the following:

(1) Issuance of a citation and order requiring the responsible person to undertake, in a manner consistent with the requirements of section 9003 of the "Resource Conservation and Recovery Act of 1976," 98 Stat. 3279, 42 U.S.C. 6991b, as amended, applicable regulations adopted thereunder, and rules adopted under division (B) of this section, such actions as are necessary to protect human health and the environment, including, without limitation, the investigation of a suspected release.

(2) Requesting the attorney general to bring a civil action for appropriate relief, including a temporary restraining order or preliminary or permanent injunction, in the court of common pleas of the county in which a suspected release is located or in which the release occurred, to obtain the corrective action necessary to protect human health and the environment. In granting any such relief, the court shall ensure that the terms of the temporary restraining order or injunction are sufficient to provide comprehensive corrective action to protect human health and the environment.

(3) Entry onto premises and undertaking corrective action with respect to a release of petroleum if, in his judgment, such action is necessary to protect human health and the environment. Any corrective action undertaken by the fire marshal or assistant fire marshal under division (A)(3) of this section shall be consistent with the requirements of sections 9003 and 9005 of the "Resource Conservation and Recovery Act of 1976," 98 Stat. 3279, 42 U.S.C. 6991b, and 98 Stat. 3284, 42 U.S.C. 6991e, respectively, as amended, applicable regulations adopted thereunder, and rules adopted under division (B) of this section.

(B) The fire marshal shall adopt, and may amend and rescind, such rules as he considers necessary to establish standards for corrective actions for suspected and confirmed releases of petroleum and standards for the recovery of costs incurred for undertaking corrective or enforcement actions with respect to such releases. The rules also shall include requirements for financial responsibility for the cost of corrective actions for and compensation of bodily injury and property damage incurred by third parties that are caused by releases of petroleum. Rules regarding financial responsibility shall, without limitation, require responsible persons to provide evidence that the parties guaranteeing payment of the deductible amount established under division (E) or (F) of section 3737.91 of the Revised Code are, at a minimum, secondarily liable for all corrective action and third-party liability costs incurred within the scope of the deductible amount. The rules shall be consistent with sections 9003 and 9005 of the "Resource Conservation and Recovery Act of 1976," 98 Stat. 3279, 42 U.S.C. 6991b, and 98 Stat. 3284, 42 U.S.C. 6991e, respectively, as amended, and applicable regulations adopted thereunder.

(C)(1) No person shall violate or fail to comply with a rule adopted under division (A) of section 3737.88 of the Revised Code or division (B) of this section, and no person shall violate or fail to comply with the terms of any order issued under division (A) of section 3737.88 of the Revised Code or division (A)(1) of this section.

(2) Whoever violates division (C)(1) of this section or division (F) of section 3737.881 [3737.88.1] of the Revised Code shall pay a civil penalty of not more than ten thousand dollars for each day that the violation continues. The fire marshal may, by order, assess a civil penalty under this division, or he may request the attorney general to bring a civil action for imposition of the civil penalty in the court of common pleas of the county in which the violation occurred. If the fire marshal determines that a responsible person is in violation of division (C)(1) of this section or division (F) of section 3737.881 [3737.88.1] of the Revised Code, the

fire marshal may request the attorney general to bring a civil action for appropriate relief, including a temporary restraining order or preliminary or permanent injunction, in the court of common pleas of the county in which the underground storage tank or, in the case of a violation of division (F)(3) of section 3737.881 [3737.88.1] of the Revised Code, the training program that is the subject of the violation is located. The court shall issue a temporary restraining order or an injunction upon a demonstration that a violation of division (C)(1) of this section or division (F) of section 3737.881 [3737.88.1] of the Revised Code has occurred or is occurring.

Any action brought by the attorney general under this division is a civil action, governed by the rules of civil procedure and other rules of practice and procedure applicable to civil actions.

(D) Orders issued under division (A) of section 3737.88 of the Revised Code and divisions (A)(1) and (C) of this section, and appeals thereof, are subject to and governed by Chapter 3745. of the Revised Code. Such orders shall be issued without the necessity for issuance of a proposed action under that chapter. For purposes of appeals of any such orders, the term "director" as used in Chapter 3745. of the Revised Code includes the fire marshal and an assistant fire marshal.

HISTORY: RC § 3737.88, 142 v H 171 (Eff 7-1-87); RC § 3737.88.2, 143 v H 421. Eff 7-11-89.

§ 3737.91 Financial assurance fund; fees; certificate of coverage.

(A) There is hereby created the petroleum underground storage tank financial assurance fund, which shall be in the custody of the treasurer of state, but is not a part of the state treasury. The fund shall consist of moneys from the following sources:

(1) All fees collected under divisions (B) and (F) of this section and all supplemental fees collected under division (C) of this section;

(2) Interest earned on moneys in the fund;

(3) Appropriations to the fund from the general revenue fund;

(4) The proceeds of revenue bonds issued under sections 3737.90 to 3737.948 [3737.94.8] of the Revised Code, provided that upon resolution of the petroleum underground storage tank release compensation board created in section 3737.90 of the Revised Code, all or part of those proceeds may be deposited into a separate account of the fund. Chapters 131. and 135. of the Revised Code do not apply to the establishment, deposit, investment, application, and safeguard of any such account and moneys in any such account.

(B) For the purposes of paying the costs of implementing and administering this section and sections 3737.90 and 3737.92 of the Revised Code and rules adopted under them; payment or reimbursement of corrective action costs under section 3737.92 of the Revised Code; compensating third parties for bodily injury or property damage under that section; and payment of principal and interest on revenue bonds issued under sections 3737.90 to 3737.948 [3737.94.8] of the Revised Code to raise capital for the fund, there is hereby assessed an annual petroleum underground storage tank financial assurance fee on each tank comprising an underground storage tank or an underground storage tank system that contains or has contained petroleum and for which a responsible person is required to demonstrate financial responsibility by rules adopted by the fire marshal under division (B) of section 3737.882 [3737.88.2] of the Revised Code. The fee assessed by this division shall be paid to the board by a responsible person for each tank that is subject to the fee. The fee shall be paid not later than the first day of July of each year, except that in 1989 the fee shall be paid by either the first day of September or ninety days after July 11, 1989, whichever is later. The fee is in addition to any fee established by the fire marshal under section 3737.88 of the Revised Code.

The amount of the annual fee due in 1989 and 1990 is one hundred fifty dollars per tank per year. In 1991 and subsequent years the board shall establish the amount of the annual fee in accordance with this division. Not later than the first day of April of 1991 and each subsequent year, the board, in consultation with the administrative agent of the fund with whom the board has entered into a contract under division (B)(3) of section 3737.90 of the Revised Code, if any, shall determine the amount of the annual fee to be assessed in that year and shall adopt rules in accordance with Chapter 119. of the Revised Code to establish the fee at that amount. The fee shall be established at an amount calculated to maintain the continued financial soundness of the fund, provided that if the unobligated balance of the fund exceeds forty-five million dollars on the date that an annual determination is made, the board may assess a fee in the year to which the determination applies only to the extent required in or by, or necessary to comply with covenants or other requirements in, revenue bonds issued under sections 3737.90 to 3737.948 [3737.94.8] of the Revised Code or in proceedings or other covenants or agreements related to such bonds. Not later than the first day of May of 1991 and each subsequent year, the board shall notify each responsible person by certified mail of the amount of the annual fee per tank due in that year. As used in this paragraph, "proceedings" has the same meaning as in section 133.01 of the Revised Code.

If a responsible person is both the owner and operator of a tank, he shall pay any annual fee assessed under this division in compliance with this division and the rules adopted thereunder. If the owner of the tank and the operator of the tank are not the same person, any annual fee assessed under this division in compliance with this division and the rules adopted thereunder shall be paid by one of the responsible persons; however, all such responsible persons are liable for noncompliance with this division.

(C) As necessary to maintain the financial soundness of the fund, the board, by rules adopted in accordance with Chapter 119. of the Revised Code, may at any time assess a supplemental petroleum underground storage tank financial assurance fee on tanks subject to the fee assessed under division (B) or (F) of this section in any fiscal year in which the board finds that the unobligated balance in the fund is less than fifteen million dollars. The board, in consultation with the fund's administrative agent, if any, shall establish the amount of the supplemental fee at an amount that will ensure an unobligated balance in the fund of at least fifteen million dollars at the end of the fiscal year in which the supplemental fee is assessed. Not less than thirty days before the date on which payment of the supplemental fee is due under the board's rules, the board shall notify each responsible person by certified mail of the amount of the supplemental fee and the date on which payment of the supplemental fee to the board is due.

If a responsible person is both the owner and operator of a tank, he shall pay any supplemental fee assessed under this division in compliance with this division and the rules adopted thereunder. If the owner of the tank and the operator of the tank are not the same person, any supplemental fee assessed under this division in compliance with this division and the rules adopted thereunder shall be paid by one of the responsible persons; however, all such responsible persons are liable for noncompliance with this division.

(D)(1) The board shall issue a certificate of coverage to any responsible person who has complied with both of the following:

(a) Paid the fee assessed under division (B) or (F) of this section;

(b) Demonstrated to the board financial responsibility in compliance with the rules adopted by the fire marshal under division (B) of section 3737.882 [3737.88.2] of the Revised Code for the deductible amount established under division (E) of this section or, when appropriate, the reduced deductible amount established under division (F) of this section. If the responsible person utilizes self-insurance as a financial responsibility mechanism, he shall provide the board with an affidavit in which the responsible party certifies that all documentation submitted to the board is true and accurate.

The certificate of coverage shall state the amount of coverage to which the responsible party is entitled from the fund pursuant to division (D)(3) of this section and the time period for which the certificate provides that coverage. An issued certificate of coverage is subject to the condition that the holder timely pay any supplemental fee assessed under division (C) of this section during the time that the certificate is in effect.

(2) The board shall not issue a certificate of coverage to any responsible person who fails to comply with divisions (D)(1)(a) and (b) of this section.

(3) The maximum disbursement from the fund for any single release of petroleum is the difference between the deductible amount established under division (E) of this section or, when appropriate, the reduced deductible amount established under division (F) of this section and one million dollars. The maximum disbursement from the fund during any fiscal year on behalf of any responsible person shall not exceed in the aggregate one million dollars less the deductible amount if the responsible person owns or operates not more than one hundred tanks comprising underground petroleum storage tanks or underground petroleum storage tank systems, shall not exceed in the aggregate two million dollars less the deductible amount if the responsible person owns or operates not more than two hundred such tanks, shall not exceed in the aggregate three million dollars less the deductible amount if the responsible person owns or operates not more than three hundred such tanks, and shall not exceed in the aggregate four million dollars less the deductible amount if the responsible person owns or operates more than three hundred such tanks. The maximum disbursement from the fund for any single release or for any fiscal year under this division does not in any manner limit the liability of a responsible person for a release of petroleum.

(E)(1) Except as otherwise provided in division (F) of this section, no responsible person is eligible to receive moneys from the fund under section 3737.92 of the Revised Code until he demonstrates to the board financial responsibility for the first fifty thousand dollars of the cost for corrective action for, and compensating third parties for bodily injury and property damage caused by, accidental releases of petroleum from an underground storage tank owned or operated by the responsible party. The fifty thousand dollar amount is the deductible amount for the purposes of this section and section 3737.92 of the Revised Code.

(2) The board, in consultation with the fund's administrative agent, if any, may, by rules adopted in accordance with Chapter 119. of the Revised Code, establish for any fiscal year a deductible amount that differs from fifty thousand dollars. The deductible amount established by the board shall be such an amount as to maintain the financial soundness of the fund. Any action of the board to establish a differing deductible amount or to alter a deductible amount previously established by it shall be taken concurrently with the establishment under division (B) of this section of the annual fee due on the first day of the fiscal year in which the deductible amount will apply. If the deductible amount established under this division differs from that in effect at the time of the board's action, the board shall notify each responsible person of the change by certified mail not later than the first day of May preceding the effective date of the change.

(F)(1) Any responsible person owning, or owning or

operating, a total of six or fewer petroleum underground storage tanks may elect in calendar years 1989 and 1990 to pay twice the amount of the per tank annual fee for each tank assessed under division (B) of this section in order to reduce the amount of the deductible established in division (E) of this section to the total amount of ten thousand dollars. The election shall be available only at the time of the payment of the annual fee and any supplemental fee. The election shall not be retroactively applied.

(2) Any responsible person owning, or owning or operating, a total of six or fewer petroleum underground storage tanks may elect in calendar year 1991 and in each subsequent year to pay an additional fee at an amount established by the board in addition to the per tank annual fee assessed under division (B) of this section in order to reduce the deductible amount established under division (E) of this section. In calendar year 1991 and in each subsequent year, the board shall establish the amount of the additional fee and the reduced deductible amount. In determining the amount of the additional fee and the reduced deductible amount, the board shall take into consideration the effect of the additional claims paid under section 3737.92 of the Revised Code to responsible persons making an election under division (F)(2) of this section and balance that consideration with such factors as the availability of liability insurance, the difficulty of proving financial responsibility pursuant to the rules adopted by the fire marshal under division (B) of section 3737.882 [3737.88.2] of the Revised Code, and the hardship created on small owners and operators of petroleum underground storage tanks by an increase in either the additional fee or the reduced deductible amount.

(3) Any responsible person owning, or owning or operating, a total of six or fewer petroleum underground storage tanks who elects to pay the additional fee under divisions (F)(1) and (2) of this section shall pay any per tank supplemental fee assessed under division (C) of this section.

(G) If the director of the fund determines that a responsible person has failed to comply with division (B), (C), or (F) of this section, the director of the fund shall notify each responsible person for the petroleum underground storage tank of the noncompliance. If, within thirty days after the notification, the responsible person fails to pay the applicable fee or any fee previously assessed upon the responsible person under this section, the director of the fund shall issue an order requiring the responsible person to pay all of the fees he owes to the fund and an additional late payment fee in the amount of one thousand dollars to the fund.

If a responsible person fails to comply with any order of the director of the fund within thirty days after the issuance of the order, the director shall notify the fire marshal of that noncompliance. Upon the request of the director of the fund, the attorney general may bring a civil action for appropriate relief, including a temporary restraining order or preliminary or permanent injunction, in the court of common pleas of the county in which the petroleum underground storage tank that is the subject of the order is located. The court shall issue an injunction upon a demonstration that a failure to comply with the director's order has occurred or is occurring.

Any orders issued by the director of the fund under this division may be appealed by the responsible person under division (F) of section 3737.92 of the Revised Code. For the purpose of an appeal of any order of the director of the fund, "determination" as used in that division includes any order of the director of the fund. The filing of a notice of appeal under this division does not operate as a stay of any order of the director of the fund.

HISTORY: 143 v H 421 (Eff 7-11-89); 144 v S 359. Eff 12-22-92.

§ 3737.93 Transferor of petroleum to give notice of registration requirements.

During the period commencing ninety days after the effective date of this section and ending on January 1, 1991, a person who transfers title to petroleum that is placed by the person directly into an underground storage tank of the transferee shall provide written notice to the transferee of the requirements for the registration of underground storage tanks established by rules adopted under sections 3737.88 and 3737.882 [3737.88.2] of the Revised Code.

No person shall fail to comply with this section.

HISTORY: 143 v H 421. Eff 7-11-89.

§ 3737.99 Penalties.

(A) Whoever violates section 3737.28 of the Revised Code may be summarily punished, by the officer concerned, by a fine of not more than one hundred dollars or commitment to the county jail until that person is willing to comply with the order of such officer.

(B) Except as a violation of section 2923.17 of the Revised Code involves subject matter covered by the state fire code and except as such a violation is covered by division (G) of this section, whoever violates division (A) of section 3737.51 of the Revised Code is guilty of a misdemeanor of the first degree.

(C) Whoever violates section 3737.61 of the Revised Code is guilty of a minor misdemeanor.

(D) Whoever violates section 3737.62 or 3737.64 of the Revised Code is guilty of a misdemeanor of the fourth degree.

(E) Whoever violates section 3737.63 or division (A) or (B) of section 3737.65 of the Revised Code is guilty of a misdemeanor of the third degree.

(F) Whoever violates division (D) of section 3737.73 of the Revised Code shall be fined not less than five nor more than twenty dollars.

(G) Whoever violates section 3737.66 of the Revised Code is guilty of a misdemeanor of the first degree.

(H) Whoever knowingly violates division (C) of section 3737.882 [3737.88.2] of the Revised Code is guilty of an unclassified felony and shall be fined not more than twenty-five thousand dollars or imprisoned for not more than fourteen months, or both. Whoever recklessly violates division (C) of section 3737.882 [3737.88.2] of the Revised Code is guilty of a misdemeanor of the first degree.

(I) Whoever knowingly violates division (F)(1), (2), or (3) of section 3737.881 [3737.88.1] or section 3737.93 of the Revised Code is guilty of a misdemeanor of the fourth degree.

(J) Whoever knowingly violates division (B) or (C) of section 3737.91 of the Revised Code is guilty of a misdemeanor of the second degree.

HISTORY: 137 v H 590 (Eff 7-1-79); 138 v S 18 (Eff 7-1-79); 141 v S 61 (Eff 5-30-86); 141 v H 552 (Eff 9-17-86); 141 v H 428 (Eff 12-23-86); 142 v H 171 (Eff 7-1-87); 143 v H 421 (Eff 7-11-89); 146 v S 2. Eff 7-1-96.

Analogous to former RC § 3737.99 (Bureau of Code Revision, 10-1-53; 125 v 903; 130 v 863; 133 v S 180; 136 v S 462; 136 v H 837; 137 v H 1), repealed 137 v H 590, § 2, eff 7-1-79.

The effective date is set by section 6 of SB 2.

CHAPTER 3743: FIREWORKS

§ 3743.01 Definitions.

As used in this chapter:

(A) "Beer" and "intoxicating liquor" have the same meanings as in section 4301.01 of the Revised Code.

(B) "Booby trap" means a small tube that has a string protruding from both ends, that has a friction-sensitive composition, and that is ignited by pulling the ends of the string.

(C) "Cigarette load" means a small wooden peg that is coated with a small quantity of explosive composition and that is ignited in a cigarette.

(D)(1) "1.3G fireworks" means display fireworks consistent with regulations of the United States department of transportation as expressed using the designation "division 1.3" in Title 49, Code of Federal Regulations.

(2) "1.4G fireworks" means consumer fireworks consistent with regulations of the United States department of transportation as expressed using the designation "division 1.4" in Title 49, Code of Federal Regulations.

(E) "Controlled substance" has the same meaning as in section 3719.01 of the Revised Code.

(F) "Fireworks" means any composition or device prepared for the purpose of producing a visible or an audible effect by combustion, deflagration, or detonation, except ordinary matches and except as provided in section 3743.80 of the Revised Code.

(G) "Fireworks plant" means all buildings and other structures in which the manufacturing of fireworks, or the storage or sale of manufactured fireworks by a manufacturer, takes place.

(H) "Highway" means any public street, road, alley, way, lane, or other public thoroughfare.

(I) "Licensed exhibitor of fireworks" or "licensed exhibitor" means a person licensed pursuant to sections 3743.50 to 3743.55 of the Revised Code.

(J) "Licensed manufacturer of fireworks" or "licensed manufacturer" means a person licensed pursuant to sections 3743.02 to 3743.08 of the Revised Code.

(K) "Licensed wholesaler of fireworks" or "licensed wholesaler" means a person licensed pursuant to sections 3743.15 to 3743.21 of the Revised Code.

(L) "List of licensed exhibitors" means the list required by division (C) of section 3743.51 of the Revised Code.

(M) "List of licensed manufacturers" means the list required by division (C) of section 3743.03 of the Revised Code.

(N) "List of licensed wholesalers" means the list required by division (C) of section 3743.16 of the Revised Code.

(O) "Manufacturing of fireworks" means the making of fireworks from raw materials, none of which in and of themselves constitute a fireworks, or the processing of fireworks.

(P) "Navigable waters" means any body of water susceptible of being used in its ordinary condition as a highway of commerce over which trade and travel is or may be conducted in the customary modes, but does not include a body of water that is not capable of navigation by barges, tugboats, and other large vessels.

(Q) "Novelties and trick noisemakers" include the following items:

(1) Devices that produce a small report intended to surprise the user, including, but not limited to, booby traps, cigarette loads, party poppers, and snappers;

(2) Snakes or glow worms;

(3) Smoke devices;

(4) Trick matches.

(R) "Party popper" means a small plastic or paper item that contains not more than sixteen milligrams of friction-sensitive explosive composition, that is ignited by pulling a string protruding from the item, and from which paper streamers are expelled when the item is ignited.

(S) "Processing of fireworks" means the making of fireworks from materials all or part of which in and of themselves constitute a fireworks, but does not include the mere packaging or repackaging of fireworks.

(T) "Railroad" means any railway or railroad that carries freight or passengers for hire, but does not include auxiliary tracks, spurs, and sidings installed and primarily used in serving a mine, quarry, or plant.

(U) "Retail sale" or "sell at retail" means a sale of fireworks to a purchaser who intends to use the fireworks, and not resell them.

(V) "Smoke device" means a tube or sphere that contains pyrotechnic composition that, upon ignition, produces white or colored smoke as the primary effect.

(W) "Snake or glow worm" means a device that consists of a pressed pellet of pyrotechnic composition that produces a large, snake-like ash upon burning, which ash expands in length as the pellet burns.

(X) "Snapper" means a small, paper-wrapped item that contains a minute quantity of explosive composition coated on small bits of sand, and that, when dropped, implodes.

(Y) "Trick match" means a kitchen or book match that is coated with a small quantity of explosive composition and that, upon ignition, produces a small report or a shower of sparks.

(Z) "Wire sparkler" means a sparkler consisting of a wire or stick coated with a nonexplosive pyrotechnic mixture that produces a shower of sparks upon ignition and that contains no more than one hundred grams of this mixture.

(AA) "Wholesale sale" or "sell at wholesale" means a sale of fireworks to a purchaser who intends to resell the fireworks so purchased.

(BB) "Licensed premises" means the real estate upon which a licensed manufacturer or wholesaler of fireworks conducts business.

(CC) "Licensed building" means a building on the licensed premises of a licensed manufacturer or wholesaler of fireworks that is approved for occupancy by the building official having jurisdiction.

HISTORY: 141 v S 61 (Eff 5-30-86); 147 v H 215. Eff 6-30-97.

Somewhat analogous to former RC § 3743.01 (GC § 5903-1; 108 v PtI, 334; Bureau of Code Revision, 10-1-53), repealed 137 v H 590, § 2, eff 7-1-79.

§ 3743.60 Unlicensed manufacturing prohibited; prohibited activities by manufacturer.

(A) No person shall manufacture fireworks in this state unless it is a licensed manufacturer of fireworks, and no person shall operate a fireworks plant in this state unless it has been issued a license as a manufacturer of fireworks for the particular fireworks plant.

(B) No person shall operate a fireworks plant in this state after its license as a manufacturer of fireworks for the particular fireworks plant has expired, been denied renewal, or been revoked, unless a new license has been obtained.

(C) No licensed manufacturer of fireworks, during the effective period of its licensure, shall construct, locate, or relocate any buildings or other structures on the premises of its fireworks plant, make any structural change or renovation in any building or other structure on the premises of its fireworks plant, or change the nature of its manufacturing of fireworks so as to include the processing of fireworks without first obtaining a written authorization from the fire marshal pursuant to division (B) of section 3743.04 of the Revised Code.

(D) No licensed manufacturer of fireworks shall manufacture fireworks, possess fireworks for sale at wholesale or retail, or sell fireworks at wholesale or retail, in a manner not authorized by division (C) of section 3743.04 of the Revised Code.

(E) No licensed manufacturer of fireworks shall knowingly fail to comply with the rules adopted by the fire marshal pursuant to section 3743.05 of the Revised Code or the requirements of section 3743.06 of the Revised Code.

(F) No licensed manufacturer of fireworks shall fail to maintain complete inventory, wholesale sale, and retail records as required by section 3743.07 of the Revised Code, or to permit inspection of these records or the premises of a fireworks plant pursuant to section 3743.08 of the Revised Code.

(G) No licensed manufacturer of fireworks shall fail to comply with an order of the fire marshal issued pursuant to division (B)(1) of section 3743.08 of the Revised Code, within the specified period of time.

(H) No licensed manufacturer of fireworks shall fail to comply with an order of the fire marshal issued pursuant to division (B)(2) of section 3743.08 of the Revised Code until the nonconformities are eliminated, corrected, or otherwise remedied or the seventy-two hour period specified in that division has expired, whichever first occurs.

(I) No person shall smoke or shall carry a pipe, cigarette, or cigar, or a match, lighter, other flame-producing item, or open flame on, or shall carry a concealed source of ignition into, the premises of a fireworks plant, except as smoking is authorized in specified lunchrooms or restrooms by a manufacturer pursuant to division (C) of section 3743.06 of the Revised Code.

(J) No person shall have possession or control of, or be under the influence of, any intoxicating liquor, beer, or controlled substance, while on the premises of a fireworks plant.

HISTORY: 141 v S 61 (Eff 5-30-86); 147 v H 215. Eff 6-30-97.

§ 3743.61 Restrictions on operation as wholesaler.

(A) No person, except a licensed manufacturer of fireworks engaging in the wholesale sale of fireworks as authorized by division (C)(2) of section 3743.04 of the Revised Code, shall operate as a wholesaler of fireworks in this state unless it is a licensed wholesaler of fireworks, or shall operate as a wholesaler of fireworks at any location in this state unless it has been issued a license as a wholesaler of fireworks for the particular location.

(B) No person shall operate as a wholesaler of fireworks at a particular location in this state after its license as a wholesaler of fireworks for the particular location has expired, been denied renewal, or been revoked, unless a new license has been obtained.

(C) No licensed wholesaler of fireworks, during the effective period of its licensure, shall perform any construction, or make any structural change or renovation, on the premises on which the fireworks are sold without first obtaining a written authorization from the fire marshal pursuant to division (B) of section 3743.17 of the Revised Code.

(D) No licensed wholesaler of fireworks shall possess fireworks for sale at wholesale or retail, or sell fireworks at wholesale or retail, in a manner not authorized by division (C) of section 3743.17 of the Revised Code.

(E) No licensed wholesaler of fireworks shall knowingly fail to comply with the rules adopted by the fire marshal pursuant to section 3743.18 or the requirements of section 3743.19 of the Revised Code.

(F) No licensed wholesaler of fireworks shall fail to maintain complete inventory, wholesale sale, and retail records as required by section 3743.20 of the Revised Code, or to permit inspection of these records or the premises of the wholesaler pursuant to section 3743.21 of the Revised Code.

(G) No licensed wholesaler of fireworks shall fail to comply with an order of the fire marshal issued pursuant to division (B)(1) of section 3743.21 of the Revised Code, within the specified period of time.

(H) No licensed wholesaler of fireworks shall fail to comply with an order of the fire marshal issued pursuant to division (B)(2) of section 3743.21 of the Revised Code until the nonconformities are eliminated, corrected, or otherwise remedied or the seventy-two hour period specified in that division has expired, whichever first occurs.

(I) No person shall smoke or shall carry a pipe, cigarette, or cigar, or a match, lighter, other flame-producing item, or open flame on, or shall carry a concealed source of ignition into, the premises of a wholesaler of fireworks, except as smoking is authorized in specified lunchrooms or restrooms by a wholesaler pursuant to division (D) of section 3743.19 of the Revised Code.

(J) No person shall have possession or control of, or be under the influence of, any intoxicating liquor, beer, or controlled substance, while on the premises of a wholesaler of fireworks.

HISTORY: 141 v S 61 (Eff 5-30-86); 147 v H 215. Eff 6-30-97.

§ 3743.63 Restrictions on purchasers.

(A) No person who resides in another state and purchases fireworks in this state shall obtain possession of the fireworks in this state unless the person complies with section 3743.44 of the Revised Code, provided that knowingly making a false statement on the fireworks purchaser form is not a violation of this section but is a violation of section 2921.13 of the Revised Code.

(B) No person who resides in another state and who purchases fireworks in this state shall obtain possession of fireworks in this state other than from a licensed manufacturer or wholesaler, or fail, when transporting the fireworks, to transport them directly out of this state within seventy-two hours after the time of their purchase. No such person shall give or sell to any other person in this state fireworks that the person has acquired in this state.

(C) No person who resides in this state and purchases fireworks in this state shall obtain possession of the fireworks in this state unless the person complies with section 3743.45 of the Revised Code, provided that knowingly making a false statement on the fireworks purchaser form is not a violation of this section but is a violation of section 2921.13 of the Revised Code.

(D) No person who resides in this state and who purchases fireworks in this state under section 3743.45 of the Revised Code shall obtain possession of fireworks in this state other than from a licensed manufacturer or licensed wholesaler, or fail, when transporting the fireworks, to transport them directly out of this state within forty-eight hours after the time of their purchase. No such person shall give or sell to any other person in this state fireworks that the person has acquired in this state.

HISTORY: 141 v S 61 (Eff 5-30-86); 146 v S 2. Eff 7-1-96.

The effective date is set by section 6 of SB 2.

§ 3743.64 Prohibited activities by exhibitors.

(A) No person shall conduct a fireworks exhibition in this state or act as an exhibitor of fireworks in this state unless the person is a licensed exhibitor of fireworks.

(B) No person shall conduct a fireworks exhibition in this state or act as an exhibitor of fireworks in this state after the person's license as an exhibitor of fireworks has expired, been denied renewal, or been revoked, unless a new license has been obtained.

(C) No licensed exhibitor of fireworks shall fail to comply with the rules adopted by the fire marshal pursuant to division (B) of section 3743.53 of the Revised Code or to comply with divisions (C) and (D) of that section.

(D) No licensed exhibitor of fireworks shall conduct a fireworks exhibition unless a permit has been secured for the exhibition pursuant to section 3743.54 of the Revised Code or if a permit so secured is revoked by a fire chief or fire prevention officer and police chief pursuant to that section.

(E) No licensed exhibitor of fireworks shall acquire fireworks for use at a fireworks exhibition other than in accordance with sections 3743.54 and 3743.55 of the Revised Code.

(F) No licensed exhibitor of fireworks or other person associated with the conduct of a fireworks exhibition shall have possession or control of, or be under the influence of, any intoxicating liquor, beer, or controlled substance while on the premises on which the exhibition is being conducted.

(G) No licensed exhibitor of fireworks shall permit an employee to assist the licensed exhibitor in conducting fireworks exhibitions unless the employee is registered with the fire marshal under section 3743.56 of the Revised Code.

HISTORY: 141 v S 61 (Eff 5-30-86); 147 v H 215. Eff 6-30-97.

§ 3743.65 Restrictions on possession, sale and use; disabling fire suppression system.

(A) No person shall possess fireworks in this state or shall possess for sale or sell fireworks in this state, except a licensed manufacturer of fireworks as authorized by sections 3743.02 to 3743.08 of the Revised Code, a licensed wholesaler of fireworks as authorized by sections 3743.15 to 3743.21 of the Revised Code, a shipping permit holder as authorized by section 3743.40 of the Revised Code, an out-of-state resident as authorized by section 3743.44 of the Revised Code, a resident of this state as authorized by section 3743.45 of the Revised Code, or a licensed exhibitor of fireworks as authorized by sections 3743.50 to 3743.55 of the Revised Code, and except as provided in section 3743.80 of the Revised Code.

(B) Except as provided in section 3743.80 of the Revised Code and except for licensed exhibitors of fireworks authorized to conduct a fireworks exhibition pursuant to sections 3743.50 to 3743.55 of the Revised Code, no person shall discharge, ignite, or explode any fireworks in this state.

(C) No person shall use in a theater or public hall, what is technically known as fireworks showers, or a mixture containing potassium chlorate and sulphur.

(D) No person shall sell fireworks of any kind to a person under eighteen years of age.

(E) No person shall advertise 1.4G fireworks for sale. A sign located on a seller's premises identifying the seller as a seller of fireworks is not the advertising of fireworks for sale.

(F) No person, other than a licensed manufacturer, licensed wholesaler, licensed exhibitor, or shipping permit holder, shall possess 1.3G fireworks in this state.

(G) Except as otherwise provided in division (K) of section 3743.06 and division (L) of section 3743.19 of the Revised Code, no person shall knowingly disable a fire suppression system as defined in section 3781.108 [3781.10.8] of the Revised Code on the premises of a fireworks plant of a licensed manufacturer of fireworks or on the premises of the business operations of a licensed wholesaler of fireworks.

HISTORY: 141 v S 61 (Eff 5-30-86); 142 v H 436 (Eff 6-14-88); 143 v H 111 (Eff 7-1-89); 146 v S 2 (Eff 7-1-96); 147 v H 215. Eff 6-30-97.

§ 3743.66 Limitations on shipping or transporting.

(A) No person shall transport fireworks in this state except in accordance with rules adopted by the fire marshal pursuant to section 3743.58 of the Revised Code.

(B) As used in this division, "fireworks" includes only 1.3G and 1.4G fireworks. No person shall ship fireworks into this state by mail, parcel post, or common carrier unless the person possesses a valid shipping permit issued under section 3743.40 of the Revised Code, and the fireworks are shipped directly to the holder of a license issued under section 3743.03, 3743.16, or 3743.51 of the Revised Code.

No person shall ship fireworks within this state by mail, parcel post, or common carrier unless the fireworks are shipped directly to the holder of a license issued under section 3743.03, 3743.16, or 3743.51 of the Revised Code.

HISTORY: 141 v S 61 (Eff 5-30-86); 147 v H 215. Eff 6-30-97.

§ 3743.68 Arrest of violators; seizure; forfeiture; distribution of fines.

(A) The fire marshal, an assistant fire marshal, or a certified fire safety inspector may arrest, or may cause the arrest of, any person whom the fire marshal, assistant fire marshal, or certified fire safety inspector finds in the act of violating, or who the fire marshal, assistant fire marshal, or certified fire safety inspector has reasonable cause to believe has violated, sections 3743.60 to 3743.66 of the Revised Code. Any arrest shall be made in accordance with statutory and constitutional provisions governing arrests by law enforcement officers.

(B) If the fire marshal, an assistant fire marshal, or certified fire safety inspector has probable cause to believe that fireworks are being manufactured, sold, possessed, transported, or used in violation of this chapter, the fire marshal, assistant fire marshal, or certified fire safety inspector may seize the fireworks. Any seizure of fireworks shall be made in accordance with statutory and constitutional provisions governing searches and seizures by law enforcement officers. The fire marshal's or certified fire safety inspector's office shall impound at the site or safely keep seized fireworks pending the time they are no longer needed as evidence. A sample of the seized fireworks is sufficient for evidentiary purposes. The remainder of the seized fireworks may be disposed of pursuant to an order from a court of competent jurisdiction after notice and a hearing.

Fireworks manufactured, sold, possessed, transported, or used in violation of this chapter shall be forfeited by the violator. The fire marshal's or certified fire safety inspector's office shall dispose of seized fireworks pursuant to the procedures specified in section 2933.41 of the Revised Code for the disposal of forfeited property by law enforcement agencies, and the fire marshal or that office is not liable for claims for the loss of or damages to the seized fireworks.

(C) This section does not affect the authority of a peace officer, as defined in section 2935.01 of the Revised Code, to make arrests for violations of this chapter or to seize fireworks manufactured, sold, possessed, transported, or used in violation of this chapter.

(D) Any fines imposed for a violation of this chapter relating to the sale, purchase, possession, or discharge of fireworks shall be distributed in the following manner if a municipal corporation, county, or township either filed or enforced the complaint regarding the violation. One-half of the amount of the fine shall be distributed to the municipal corporation, county, or township which filed the complaint regarding the violation and one-half of the amount of the fine shall be distributed to the municipal corporation, county, or township which enforced the complaint. If the same municipal corporation, county, or township both filed the complaint regarding the violation and enforced the complaint, the entire amount of the fine shall be distributed to that municipal corporation, county, or township.

HISTORY: 141 v S 61 (Eff 5-30-86); 147 v H 215. Eff 6-30-97.

§ 3743.70 Felony precludes license or permit.

The fire marshal shall not issue an initial license or permit under this chapter on or after the effective date of this section if the applicant for the license or permit, or any individual holding, owning, or controlling a five per cent or greater beneficial or equity interest in the applicant for the license or permit, has been convicted of or pleaded guilty to a felony under the laws of this state, another state, or the United States. The fire marshal shall revoke or deny renewal of a license or permit first issued under this chapter on or after the effective date of this section if the holder of the license or permit, or any individual holding, owning, or controlling a five per cent or greater beneficial or equity interest in the holder of the license or permit, is convicted of or pleads guilty to a felony under the laws of this state, another state, or the United States.

HISTORY: 147 v H 215. Eff 6-30-97.

The provisions of § 167 of HB 215 (147 v —) read as follows:

SECTION 167. The Fire Marshal shall not revoke or deny the renewal of a license or permit that was issued under Chapter 3743. of the Revised Code before the effective date of this act solely on the basis that the license or permit holder, or any individual holding, owning, or controlling a five per cent or greater beneficial or equity interest in the license or permit holder has been convicted of or pled guilty to a felony under the laws of this state, another state, or the United States before the effective date of this act, provided that there is no cause for revocation or denial of renewal pursuant to sections 3743.08, 3743.21, 3743.52, or 3743.54 of the Revised Code.

§ 3743.80 Exemptions from provisions.

This chapter does not prohibit or apply to the following:

(A) The manufacture, sale, possession, transportation, storage, or use in emergency situations, of pyrotechnic signaling devices and distress signals for marine, aviation, or highway use;

(B) The manufacture, sale, possession, transportation, storage, or use of fusees, torpedoes, or other signals necessary for the safe operation of railroads;

(C) The manufacture, sale, possession, transportation, storage, or use of blank cartridges in connection with theaters or shows, or in connection with athletics as signals or for ceremonial purposes;

(D) The manufacture for, the transportation, storage, possession, or use by, or sale to the armed forces of the United States and the militia of this state of pyrotechnic devices;

(E) The manufacture, sale, possession, transportation, storage, or use of toy pistols, toy canes, toy guns, or other devices in which paper or plastic caps containing twenty-five hundredths grains or less of explosive material are used, provided that they are constructed so that a hand cannot come into contact with a cap when it is in place for explosion, or apply to the manufacture, sale, possession, transportation, storage, or use of those caps;

(F) The manufacture, sale, possession, transportation, storage, or use of novelties and trick noisemakers, auto burglar alarms, or model rockets and model rocket motors designed, sold, and used for the purpose of propelling recoverable aero models;

(G) The manufacture, sale, possession, transportation, storage, or use of wire sparklers.

(H) The conduct of radio-controlled special effect exhibitions that use an explosive black powder charge of not more than one-quarter pound per charge, and that are not connected in any manner to propellant charges, provided that the exhibition complies with all of following:

(1) No explosive aerial display is conducted in the exhibition;

(2) The exhibition is separated from spectators by not less than two hundred feet;

(3) The person conducting the exhibition complies with regulations of the bureau of alcohol, tobacco, and firearms of the United States department of the treasury and the United States department of transportation with respect to the storage and transport of the explosive black powder used in the exhibition.

HISTORY: 141 v S 61 (Eff 5-30-86); 147 v H 215. Eff 6-30-97.

§ 3743.99 Penalties.

(A) Whoever violates division (A) or (B) of section 3743.60 of the Revised Code is guilty of a felony of the third degree.

(B) Whoever violates division (C) or (D) of section 3743.60, division (A), (B), (C), or (D) of section 3743.61, or division (A) or (B) of section 3743.64 of the Revised Code is guilty of a felony of the fourth degree.

(C) Whoever violates division (E), (F), (G), (H), (I), or (J) of section 3743.60, division (E), (F), (G), (H), (I), or (J) of section 3743.61, section 3743.63, division (C), (D), (E), (F), or (G) of section 3743.64, division (A), (B), (C), (D), or (F) of section 3743.65, or section 3743.66 of the Revised Code is guilty of a misdemeanor of the first degree. If the offender previously has been convicted of or pleaded guilty to a violation of division (I) of section 3743.60 or 3743.61 of the Revised Code, a violation of either of these divisions is a felony of the fifth degree.

(D) Whoever violates division (G) of section 3743.65 of the Revised Code is guilty of a felony of the fifth degree.

HISTORY: 141 v S 61 (Eff 5-30-86); 142 v H 436 (Eff 6-14-88); 146 v S 2 (Eff 7-1-96); 147 v H 215. Eff 6-30-97.

CHAPTER 3761: ASSEMBLIES; MOBS

§ 3761.12 Prohibition against conspiracy while wearing disguise.

No person shall unite with two or more others to commit a misdemeanor while wearing white caps, masks, or other disguise.

HISTORY: RS § 6895-1; 86 v 169; GC § 12810; Bureau of Code Revision. Eff 10-1-53.

§ 3761.16 Cordoning-off riot areas.

The chief administrative officer of a political subdivision with police powers, when engaged in suppressing a riot or when there is a clear and present danger of a riot, may cordon off any area or areas threatened by the riot and prohibit persons from entering the cordoned off area or areas except when carrying on necessary and legitimate pursuits and may prohibit the sale, offering for sale, dispensing, or transportation of firearms or other dangerous weapons, ammunition, dynamite, or other dangerous explosives in, to, or from the cordoned off areas.

HISTORY: 132 v H 753 (Eff 9-8-67); 146 v S 2. Eff 7-1-96.

The effective date is set by section 6 of SB 2.

§ 3761.99 Penalties.

Whoever violates section 3761.12 of the Revised Code is guilty of a felony of the fourth degree.

HISTORY: Bureau of Code Revision, 10-1-53; 131 v 897 (Eff 11-11-65); 132 v H 753 (Eff 9-8-67); 132 v H 996 (Eff 6-13-68); 136 v H 1 (Eff 6-13-75); 139 v S 199 (Eff 1-1-83); 146 v S 2. Eff 7-1-96.

The effective date is set by section 6 of SB 2.

CHAPTER 3767: NUISANCES

[DISORDERLY HOUSES]

§ 3767.01 Definitions.

As used in all sections of the Revised Code relating to nuisances:

(A) "Place" includes any building, erection, or place or any separate part or portion thereof or the ground itself;

(B) "Person" includes any individual, corporation, association, partnership, trustee, lessee, agent, or assignee;

(C) "Nuisance" means that which is defined and declared by statutes to be such and also means any place in or upon which lewdness, assignation, or prostitution is conducted, permitted, continued, or exists, or any place, in or upon which lewd, indecent, lascivious, or obscene films or plate negatives, film or plate positives, films designed to be projected on a screen for exhibition films, or glass slides either in negative or positive form designed for exhibition by projection on a screen, are photographed, manufactured, developed, screened, exhibited, or otherwise prepared or shown, and the personal property and contents used in conducting and maintaining any such place for any such purpose. This chapter shall not affect any newspaper, magazine, or other publication entered as second class matter by the post-office department.

HISTORY: GC § 6212-1; 107 v 514; 120 v 230; Bureau of Code Revision, 10-1-53; 129 v 1400. Eff 10-11-61.

§ 3767.02 Nuisance.

Any person, who uses, occupies, establishes, or conducts a nuisance, or aids or abets therein, and the owner, agent, or lessee of any interest in any such nuisance together with the persons employed in or in control of any such nuisance by any such owner, agent, or lessee is guilty of maintaining a nuisance and shall be enjoined as provided in sections 3767.03 to 3767.06, inclusive, of the Revised Code.

HISTORY: GC § 6212-2; 107 v 514, § 2; Bureau of Code Revision. Eff 10-1-53.

§ 3767.03 Abatement of nuisance; bond.

Whenever a nuisance exists, the attorney general; the village solicitor, city director of law, or other similar chief legal officer of the municipal corporation in which the nuisance exists; the prosecuting attorney of the county in which the nuisance exists; the law director of a township that has adopted the limited self-government form of government under Chapter 504. of the Revised Code; or any person who is a citizen of the country in which the nuisance exists may bring an action in equity in the name of the state, upon the relation of the attorney general; the village solicitor, city director of law, or other similar chief legal officer of the municipal corporation; the prosecuting attorney; the township law director; or the person, to abate the nuisance and to perpetually enjoin the person maintaining the nuisance from further maintaining it. If an action is instituted under this section by a person other than the prosecuting attorney; the village solicitor, city director of law, or other similar chief legal officer of the municipal corporation; the attorney general; or the township law director, the complainant shall execute a bond in the sum of not less than five hundred dollars, to the defendant, with good and sufficient surety to be approved by the court or clerk of the court, to secure to the defendant any damages the defendant may sustain and the reasonable attorney's fees the defendant may incur in defending the action if the action is wrongfully brought, not prosecuted to final judgment, is dismissed, or is not maintained, or if it is finally decided that an injunction should not have been granted. If it is finally decided that an injunction should not have been granted or if the action was wrongfully brought, not prosecuted to final judgment, dismissed, or not maintained, the defendant shall have recourse against the bond for all damages suffered, including damages to the defendant's property, person, or character, and for the reasonable attorney's fees incurred by the defendant in defending the action.

HISTORY: GC § 6212-3; 107 v 514, § 3; Bureau of Code Revision, 10-1-53; 144 v H 343 (Eff 6-1-92); 146 v H 501. Eff 11-6-96.

§ 3767.04 Procedure in injunction action.

(A) The civil action provided for in section 3767.03 of the Revised Code shall be commenced in the court of common pleas of the county in which the nuisance is located. At the commencement of the action, a complaint alleging the facts constituting the nuisance shall be filed in the office of the clerk of the court of common pleas.

(B)(1) After the filing of the complaint, an application for a temporary injunction may be filed with the court or a judge of the court. A hearing shall be held on the application within ten days after the filing.

(2) If an application for a temporary injunction is filed, the court or a judge of the court, on application of the complainant, may issue an ex parte restraining order restraining the defendant and all other persons from removing or in any manner interfering with the personal property and contents of the place where the nuisance is alleged to exist until the decision of the court or judge granting or refusing the requested temporary injunction and until the further order of the court. The restraining order may be served by handing it to and leaving a copy of it with any person who is in charge of the place where the nuisance is alleged to exist or who resides in that place, by posting a copy of it in a conspicuous place at or upon one or more of the principal doors or entrances to that place, or by both delivery and posting. The officer serving the restraining order forthwith shall make and return into court an inventory of the personal property and contents situated in and used in conducting or maintaining the nuisance. Any violation of the restraining order is a contempt of court, and, if the order is posted, its mutilation or removal while it remains in force is a contempt of court, provided the posted order contains a notice to that effect.

(3) A copy of the complaint, a copy of the application for the temporary injunction, and a notice of the time and place of the hearing on the application shall be served upon the defendant at least five days before the hearing. If the hearing then is continued on the motion of any defendant, the requested temporary injunction shall be granted as a matter of course. If, upon hearing, the allegations of the complaint are sustained to the satisfaction of the court or judge, the court or judge shall issue a temporary injunction without additional bond restraining the defendant and any other person from continuing the nuisance. Except as provided in division (C) of this section, if at the time of granting the temporary injunction it further appears that the person owning, in control, or in charge of the nuisance so enjoined had received five days' notice of the hearing and unless that person shows to the satisfaction of the court or judge that the nuisance complained of is abated or that he proceeded forthwith to enforce his rights under section 3767.10 of the Revised Code, the court or judge forthwith shall issue an order closing the place against its use for any purpose of lewdness, assignation, prostitution, or other prohibited conduct until a final decision is rendered on the complaint for the requested permanent injunction. Except as provided in division (C) of this section, the order closing the place also shall continue in effect for that further period any restraining order already issued under division (B)(2) of this section, or, if a restraining order was not so issued, the order closing the place shall include an order restraining for that further period the removal or interference with the personal property and contents located in the place. The order closing the place shall be served and an inventory of the personal property and contents situated in the place shall be made and filed as provided in division (B)(2) of this section for restraining orders.

(C) The owner of any real or personal property closed or restrained or to be closed or restrained may appear in the court of common pleas between the time of the filing of the complaint for the permanent injunction described in division (A) of this section and the hearing on the complaint, and, if all costs incurred are paid and if the owner of the real property files a bond with sureties approved by the clerk, in the full value of the real property as ascertained by the court or, in vacation, by the judge, and conditioned that the owner of the real property immediately will abate the nuisance and prevent it from being established or kept until the decision of the court or judge is rendered on the complaint for the permanent injunction, the court or judge in vacation, if satisfied of the good faith of the owner of the real property and of innocence on the part of any owner of the personal property of any knowledge of the use of the personal property as a nuisance and that, with reasonable care and diligence, the owner of the personal property could not have known of its use as a nuisance, shall deliver the real or personal property, or both, to the respective owners and discharge or refrain from issuing at the time of the hearing on the application for the temporary injunction any order closing the real property or restraining the removal or interference with the personal property. The release of any real or personal property under this division shall not release it from any judgment, lien, penalty, or liability to which it may be subjected.

HISTORY: GC § 6212-4; 107 v 514, § 4; Bureau of Code Revision, 10-1-53; 144 v H 343. Eff 6-1-92.

§ 3767.05 Priority of action; evidence; dismissal of citizen's complaint; costs; permanent injunction.

(A) The civil action provided for in section 3767.03 of the Revised Code shall be set down for trial and shall have precedence over all other cases except those involving crimes, election contests, or injunctions. In the civil action, evidence of the general reputation of the place where the nuisance is alleged to exist or an admission or finding of guilt of any person under the criminal laws against prostitution, lewdness, assignation, or other prohibited conduct at the place is admissible for the purpose of proving the existence of the nuisance and is prima-facie evidence of the nuisance and of knowledge of and of acquiescence and participation in the nuisance on the part of the person charged with maintaining it.

(B) If the complaint for the permanent injunction is filed by a person who is a citizen of the county, it shall not be dismissed unless the complainant and his attorney submit a sworn statement setting forth the reasons why the civil action should be dismissed and the dismissal is approved by the prosecuting attorney in writing or in open court. If the person who files the complaint for the permanent injunction is a citizen of the county, if that person refuses or otherwise fails to prosecute the complaint to judgment, and if the civil action is not dismissed pursuant to this division, then, with the approval of the court, the attorney general, the prosecuting attorney of the county in which the nuisance exists, or the village solicitor, city director of law, or other similar chief legal officer of the municipal corporation in which the nuisance exists, may be substituted for the complainant and prosecute the civil action to judgment.

(C) If the civil action is commenced by a person who is a citizen of the county where the nuisance is alleged to exist and the court finds that there were no reasonable grounds or cause for the civil action, the costs may be taxed to that person.

(D) If the existence of the nuisance is established upon the trial of the civil action, a judgment shall be entered that perpetually enjoins the defendant and any other person from further maintaining the nuisance at the place complained of and the defendant from maintaining the nuisance elsewhere.

HISTORY: GC § 6212-5; 107 v 514, § 5; Bureau of Code Revision, 10-1-53; 144 v H 343. Eff 6-1-92.

§ 3767.06 Order of abatement; removal of personal property and contents; attorney general nuisance abatement fund.

(A) If the existence of a nuisance is admitted or established in the civil action provided for in section 3767.03 of the Revised Code or in a criminal action, an order of abatement shall be included in the judgment entry under division (D) of section 3767.05 of the Revised Code. The order shall direct the removal from the place where the nuisance is found to exist of all personal property and contents used in conducting or maintaining the nuisance and not already released under authority of the court as provided in division (C) of section 3767.04 of the Revised Code and shall direct that the personal property or contents that belong to the defendants notified or appearing be sold, without appraisal, at a public auction to the highest bidder for cash. The order also shall require the renewal for one year of any bond furnished by the owner of the real property under section 3767.04 of the Revised Code; if a bond was not so furnished, shall continue for one year any closing order issued at the time of granting the temporary injunction; or, if a closing order was not then issued, shall include an order directing the effectual closing of the place where the nuisance is found to exist against its use for any purpose and keeping it closed for a period of one year unless sooner released. The owner of any place closed and not released under bond may appear and obtain a release in the manner and upon fulfilling the requirements provided in section 3767.04 of the Revised Code. The release of property under this division shall not release it from any judgment, lien, penalty, or liability to which it may be subject.

(B) Owners of unsold personal property or contents seized pursuant to division (A) of this section shall appear and claim the personal property or contents within ten days after the order of abatement is issued and prove to the satisfaction of the court their lack of any actual knowledge of the use of the personal property or contents in the conduct or maintenance of the nuisance and that with reasonable care and diligence they could not have known of that use. Every defendant in the action shall be presumed to have had knowledge of the general reputation of the place where the nuisance is found to exist. If an owner establishes the lack of actual or constructive knowledge of the use of his personal property or contents in the conduct or maintenance of the nuisance, the unsold personal property and contents shall be delivered to the owner. If an owner does not so establish, the personal property or contents shall be sold or otherwise disposed of as provided in division (A) of this section. For removing and selling the personal property and contents, the officer involved shall be entitled to charge and receive the same fees as he would for levying upon and selling similar property on execution. For closing the place where the nuisance is found to exist and keeping it closed, a reasonable sum shall be allowed by the court.

(C) There is hereby established in the state treasury the attorney general nuisance abatement fund. Except as otherwise provided in sections 3767.07 to 3767.11

of the Revised Code, all proceeds from the sale of personal property or contents seized pursuant to a civil action commenced or otherwise prosecuted by the attorney general under sections 3767.03 to 3767.11 of the Revised Code shall be deposited into the state treasury and credited to the fund. The attorney general shall use the fund solely to defray expenses and costs associated with those types of civil actions.

(D) All proceeds from the sale of personal property or contents seized pursuant to a civil action commenced or otherwise prosecuted under sections 3767.03 to 3767.11 of the Revised Code by a village solicitor, city director of law, or other similar chief legal officer of a municipal corporation initially shall be applied to the payment of the costs incurred in the prosecution of the civil action and the costs associated with the abatement and sale ordered pursuant to division (A) of this section, including, but not limited to, court costs, reasonable attorney's fees, and other litigation expenses incurred by the complainant. Except as otherwise provided in sections 3767.07 to 3767.11 of the Revised Code, any proceeds remaining after that initial application shall be deposited into the city or village treasury and credited to the general fund.

(E) All proceeds from the sale of personal property or contents seized pursuant to a civil action commenced or otherwise prosecuted under sections 3767.03 to 3767.11 of the Revised Code by a prosecuting attorney initially shall be applied to the payment of the costs incurred in the prosecution of the civil action and the costs associated with the abatement and sale ordered pursuant to division (A) of this section, including, but not limited to, court costs, reasonable attorney's fees, and other litigation expenses incurred by the complainant. Except as otherwise provided in sections 3767.07 to 3767.11 of the Revised Code, any proceeds remaining after that initial application shall be deposited into the county treasury and credited to the general fund.

(F) All proceeds from the sale of personal property or contents seized pursuant to a civil action commenced under sections 3767.03 to 3767.11 of the Revised Code by a person who is a citizen of the county where the nuisance is found to exist initially shall be applied to the payment of the costs incurred in the prosecution of the civil action and the costs associated with the abatement and sale ordered pursuant to division (A) of this section, including, but not limited to, court costs, reasonable attorney's fees, and other litigation expenses incurred by the complainant. Except as otherwise provided in sections 3767.07 to 3767.11 of the Revised Code, any proceeds remaining after that initial application shall be deposited into the county treasury and credited to the general fund.

HISTORY: GC § 6212-6; 107 v 514, § 6; Bureau of Code Revision, 10-1-53; 144 v H 343. Eff 6-1-92.

§ 3767.07 Court shall punish offender for violation of injunction or order.

In case of the violation of any injunction or closing order, granted under sections 3767.01 to 3767.11, inclusive, of the Revised Code, or of a restraining order or the commission of any contempt of court in proceedings under such sections, the court or, in vacation, a judge thereof, may summarily try and punish the offender. The trial may be had upon affidavits or either party may demand the production and oral examination of the witnesses.

HISTORY: GC § 6212-8; 107 v 514, § 8; Bureau of Code Revision. Eff 10-1-53.

§ 3767.08 Tax on nuisance.

Whenever a permanent injunction issues against any person for maintaining a nuisance, there shall be imposed upon said nuisance and against the person maintaining the same a tax of three hundred dollars. Such tax may not be imposed upon the personal property or against the owner thereof who has proved innocence as provided in section 3767.06 of the Revised Code, or upon the real property or against the owner thereof who shows to the satisfaction of the court or judge thereof at the time of the granting of the permanent injunction, that he has, in good faith, permanently abated the nuisance complained of. The imposition of said tax shall be made by the court as a part of the proceeding and the clerk of said court shall make and certify a return of the imposition of said tax thereon to the county auditor, who shall enter the same as a tax upon the property and against the persons upon which or whom the lien was imposed as and when other taxes are entered, and the same shall be and remain a perpetual lien upon all property, both personal and real, used for the purpose of maintaining said nuisance except as excepted in this section until fully paid. Any such lien imposed while the tax books are in the hands of the auditor shall be immediately entered therein. The payment of said tax shall not relieve the persons or property from any other taxes. The provisions of the laws relating to the collection of taxes in this state, the delinquency thereof, and sale of property for taxes shall govern in the collection of the tax prescribed in this section in so far as the same are applicable, and the said tax collected shall be applied in payment of any deficiency in the costs of the action and abatement on behalf of the state to the extent of such deficiency after the application thereto of the proceeds of the sale of personal property.

HISTORY: GC § 6212-9; 107 v 514, § 9; Bureau of Code Revision, 10-1-53; 134 v H 511. Eff 1-1-74.

§ 3767.09 Tax shall be imposed against owner of property.

When a nuisance is found to exist in any proceeding under sections 3767.01 to 3767.11, inclusive, of the Revised Code, and the owner or agent of such place whereon the same has been found to exist was not a party to such proceeding, and did not appear therein, the tax of three hundred dollars, imposed under section 3767.08 of the Revised Code, shall, nevertheless, be imposed against the persons served or appearing and against the property as set forth in this section. Before such tax is enforced against such property, the owner or agent thereof shall have appeared therein or shall be served with summons therein, and existing laws, regarding the service of process, shall apply to service in proceedings under sections 3767.01 to 3767.11, inclusive, of the Revised Code. The person in whose name the real estate affected by the action stands on the books of the county auditor for purposes of taxation is presumed to be the owner thereof, and in case of unknown persons having or claiming any ownership, right, title, or interest in property affected by the action, such may be made parties to the action by designating them in the petition as "all other persons unknown claiming any ownership, right, title, or interest in the property affected by the action." Service thereon may be had by publication in the manner prescribed in sections 2703.14 to 2703.19, inclusive, of the Revised Code. Any person having or claiming such ownership, right, title, or interest, and any owner or agent in behalf of himself and such owner may make defense thereto and have trial of his rights in the premises by the court; and if said cause has already proceeded to trial or to findings and judgment, the court shall, by order, fix the time and place of such further trial and shall modify, add to, or confirm such findings and judgment. Other parties to said action shall not be affected thereby.

HISTORY: GC § 6212-10; 107 v 514, § 10; Bureau of Code Revision. Eff 10-1-53.

§ 3767.10 Lease void if building used for lewd purposes.

If a tenant or occupant of a building or tenement, under a lawful title, uses such place for the purposes of lewdness, assignation, or prostitution, such use makes void the lease or other title under which he holds, at the option of the owner, and, without any act of the owner, causes the right of possession to revert and vest in such owner, who may without process of law make immediate entry upon the premises.

HISTORY: GC § 6212-12; 107 v 514, § 12; Bureau of Code Revision. Eff 10-1-53.

§ 3767.11 Procedure when nuisance established in criminal proceeding.

(A) If a nuisance is established in a criminal action, the prosecuting attorney, village solicitor, city director of law, or other similar chief legal officer shall proceed promptly under sections 3767.03 to 3767.11 of the Revised Code to enforce those sections. The finding of the defendant guilty in the criminal action, unless reversed or set aside, shall be conclusive against the defendant as to the existence of the nuisance in the civil action under those sections.

(B) Except for proceeds described in divisions (C) to (F) of section 3767.06 of the Revised Code, all moneys collected under sections 3767.03 to 3767.11 of the Revised Code shall be paid to the county treasurer.

HISTORY: GC § 6212-7; 107 v 514, § 7; Bureau of Code Revision, 10-1-53; 144 v H 343. Eff 6-1-92.

[OTHER NUISANCES]

§ 3767.12 Keeping a resort for thieves; prohibition.

A house or building used or occupied as a habitual resort for thieves, burglars, or robbers is a public nuisance, and the court may order such nuisance abated.

No person shall keep a house which is a habitual resort of thieves, burglars, or robbers. No person shall let a house to be so kept, or knowingly permit a house which he has let to be so kept.

HISTORY: RS § 6858a; 85 v 6; GC §§ 12453, 12454; Bureau of Code Revision. Eff 10-1-53.

§ 3767.13 Prohibitions.

(A) No person shall erect, continue, use, or maintain a building, structure, or place for the exercise of a trade, employment, or business, or for the keeping or feeding of an animal which, by occasioning noxious exhalations or noisome or offensive smells, becomes injurious to the health, comfort, or property of individuals or of the public.

(B) No person shall cause or allow offal, filth, or noisome substances to be collected or remain in any place to the damage or prejudice of others or of the public.

(C) No person shall unlawfully obstruct or impede the passage of a navigable river, harbor, or collection of water, or corrupt or render unwholesome or impure, a watercourse, stream, or water, or unlawfully divert such watercourse from its natural course or state to the injury or prejudice of others.

(D) Persons who are engaged in agriculture-related activities, as "agriculture" is defined in section 519.01 of the Revised Code, and who are conducting those activities outside a municipal corporation, in accordance with generally accepted agricultural practices, and in such a manner so as not to have a substantial, adverse effect on the public health, safety, or welfare are exempt from divisions (A) and (B) of this section, from any similar ordinances, resolutions, rules, or other enactments of a state agency or political subdivision, and from any ordinances, resolutions, rules, or other enactments of a state agency or political subdivision that prohibit excessive noise.

HISTORY: RS § 6921; S&C 441, 878, 880; 30 v 22, §§ 1, 2; 32

v 38; 54 v 130, §§ 1, 2; 72 v 112; GC § 12646; Bureau of Code Revision, 10-1-53; 139 v S 78. Eff 6-29-82.

§ 3767.14 Prohibition against throwing refuse, oil, or filth into lakes, streams, or drains.

No person shall intentionally throw, deposit, or permit to be thrown or deposited, coal dirt, coal slack, coal screenings, or coal refuse from coal mines, refuse or filth from a coal oil refinery or gasworks, or whey or filthy drainage from a cheese factory, into a river, lake, pond, or stream, or a place from which it may wash therein. No person shall cause or permit petroleum, crude oil, refined oil, or a compound, mixture, residuum of oil or filth from an oil well, oil tank, oil vat, or place of deposit of crude or refined oil, to run into or be poured, emptied, or thrown into a river, ditch, drain, or watercourse, or into a place from which it may run or wash therein. Prosecution for a violation of this section must be brought in the county in which such coal mine, coal oil refinery, gasworks, cheese factory, oil well, oil tank, oil vat, or place of deposit of crude or refined oil is situated.

HISTORY: RS § 6925; 73 v 87; 85 v 286; 87 v 351; 92 v 287; GC § 12647; Bureau of Code Revision. Eff 10-1-53.

§ 3767.15 Fine and costs are a lien.

The fine and costs imposed in division (D)[A]† of section 3767.99 of the Revised Code shall be a lien on such oil well, oil tank, oil refinery, oil vat, or place of deposit and the contents thereof until paid, and such oil well, oil tank, oil refinery, oil vat, or place of deposit and the contents thereof, may be sold for the payment of such fine and costs upon execution issued for that purpose.

HISTORY: RS § 6925; 73 v 87; 85 v 286; 87 v 351; 92 v 287; GC § 12648; Bureau of Code Revision. Eff 10-1-53.

† Section 3767.99 was revised (136 v S 71) effective 8-18-76 placing the penalty for violating § 3767.14 in division (A), but § 3767.15 has not been amended to refer to the appropriate division of the penalty section.

§ 3767.16 Prohibition against deposit of dead animals and offal upon land or water.

No person shall put the carcass of a dead animal or the offal from a slaughterhouse, butcher's establishment, packing house, or fish house, or spoiled meat, spoiled fish, or other putrid substance or the contents of a privy vault, upon or into a lake, river, bay, creek, pond, canal, road, street, alley, lot, field, meadow, public ground, market place or common. No owner or occupant of such place, shall knowingly permit such thing to remain therein to the annoyance of any citizen or neglect to remove or abate the nuisance occasioned thereby within twenty-four hours after knowledge of the existence thereof, or after notice thereof in writing from a township trustee or township highway superintendent, constable, or health commissioner of a city or general health district in which such nuisance exists or from a county commissioner of such county.

HISTORY: RS § 6923; S&S 500; S&C 878, 879; 30 v 22, § 3; 63 v 102; 85 v 268; 87 v 349; 93 v 298; 98 v 339; GC § 12649; Bureau of Code Revision. Eff 10-1-53.

§ 3767.17 Prohibition against obstructing township or county ditch.

No person shall willfully obstruct a ditch, drain, or watercourse constructed by order of a board of county commissioners or by a board of township trustees, or divert the water therefrom.

HISTORY: RS § 6926; 68 v 67, § 24; 72 v 150, §§ 1, 2; GC § 12653; Bureau of Code Revision. Eff 10-1-53.

§ 3767.18 Prohibition against defiling spring or well.

No person shall maliciously put a dead animal, carcass, or part thereof, or other putrid, nauseous, or offensive substance into, or befoul, a well, spring, brook, or branch of running water, or a reservoir of a water works, of which use is or may be made for domestic purposes.

HISTORY: RS § 6927; S&C 877; 70 v 12, § 2; GC § 12654; Bureau of Code Revision. Eff 10-1-53.

§ 3767.19 Prohibition against nuisances when near state institutions.

No person shall carry on the business of slaughtering, tallow chandlery, or the manufacturing of glue, soap, starch, or other article, the manufacture of which is productive of unwholesome or noxious odors in a building or place within one mile of a benevolent or correctional institution supported wholly or in part by the state. No person shall erect or operate, within one hundred twenty rods of such benevolent institution, a rolling mill, blast furnace, nail factory, copper-smelting works, petroleum oil refinery, or other works which may generate unwholesome or noxious odors or make loud noises, or which may annoy or endanger the health or prevent the recovery of the inmates of such institution. Each week such business is conducted, or works operated, constitutes a separate offense.

All property, real or personal, which is used with the knowledge of the owner thereof in violation of this section, shall be liable, without exemption, for the fines and costs assessed for such violation.

HISTORY: RS § 6924; S&S 53, 54; 62 v 137, §§ 1, 2, 3; 63 v 57; 63 v 96, §§ 1, 2; 95 v 592; GC §§ 12655, 12656; Bureau of Code Revision, 10-1-53; 125 v 903(1008) (Eff 10-1-53); 145 v H 571. Eff 10-6-94.

§ 3767.20 Repealed, 138 v H 361, § 2 [GC § 12652; 123 v 36; Bureau of Code Revision, 10-1-53]. Eff 7-14-80.

This section concerned disposal of garbage, refuse, or junk on public ways.

[§ 3767.20.1] § 3767.201 Destruction or removal of barriers along limited access highways prohibited; vehicles to enter and leave at designated intersections.

No person, firm or corporation shall cut, injure, remove, or destroy any fence or other barrier designed and erected to prevent traffic from entering or leaving a limited access highway without the permission of the director of transportation, except in a case of emergency where life or property is in danger. No person, firm, or corporation shall cause a vehicle of any character to enter or leave a limited access highway at any point other than intersections designated by the director for such purpose, except in a case of emergency where life or property is in danger.

HISTORY: 128 v 1217 (Eff 11-2-59); 135 v H 200. Eff 9-28-73.

§ 3767.21
Repealed, 138 v H 361, § 2 [GC § 12652-1; 123 v 36; Bureau of Code Revision, 10-1-53]. Eff 7-14-80.

This section concerned transportation of junk, refuse, or garbage upon public ways.

§ 3767.22 Exceptions.

Section 3767.16 of the Revised Code does not prohibit the deposit of the contents of privy vaults and catch basins into trenches or pits not less than three feet deep excavated in a lot, field, or meadow, with the consent of the owner, outside of the limits of a municipal corporation and not less than thirty rods distant from a dwelling, well or spring of water, lake, bay, pond, canal, run, creek, brook or stream of water, public road or highway, provided that such contents so deposited are forthwith covered with at least twelve inches of dry earth; nor prohibit the deposit of such contents in furrows, as specified for such trenches or pits, to be forthwith covered with dry earth by plowing or otherwise, and with the consent of the owner or occupant of the land in which such furrows are plowed.

The board of health of a city or a general health district may allow the contents of privy vaults and catch basins to be deposited within corporate limits into such trenches, pits, or furrows.

HISTORY: RS § 6923; S&S 500; S&C 878, 879; 30 v 22, § 3; 63 v 102; 85 v 268; 87 v 349; 93 v 298; 98 v 339; GC §§ 12650, 12651; Bureau of Code Revision. Eff 10-1-53.

§ 3767.23 Prosecution of corporations for nuisances; abatement.

Corporations may be prosecuted by indictment for violation of sections 3767.13 to 3767.29, inclusive, of the Revised Code, and in every case of conviction under such sections, the court shall adjudge that the nuisance described in the indictment be abated or removed within a time fixed, and, if it is of a recurring character, the defendant shall keep such nuisance abated.

HISTORY: RS § 6919; S&S 53; S&C 881; 54 v 130, § 3; 97 v 310; GC § 12657; Bureau of Code Revision, 10-1-53; 126 v 374. Eff 8-1-55.

§ 3767.24 Contempt proceedings.

If the defendant, convicted of a violation of sections 3767.13 to 3767.29, inclusive, of the Revised Code, fails, neglects, or refuses to abate the nuisance described in the indictment, as ordered by the court, or, if the nuisance is of a recurring character, and such defendant fails, neglects, or refuses to keep it abated, proceedings in contempt of court may be instituted against him and all others assisting in or conniving at the violation of such order, and the court may direct the sheriff to execute the order of abatement at the cost and expense of the defendant.

HISTORY: RS § 6919; S&S 53; S&C 881; 54 v 130, § 3; 97 v 310; GC § 12658; Bureau of Code Revision, 10-1-53; 126 v 374. Eff 8-1-55.

§ 3767.25 Venue.

An offense charged under sections 3767.13 to 3767.29, inclusive, of the Revised Code, shall be held to be committed in any county whose inhabitants are, or have been, aggrieved thereby. The continuance of such nuisance for five days after the prosecution thereof is begun is an additional offense.

HISTORY: RS § 6920; S&S 500; S&C 878; 30 v 22, §§ 1, 2, 3; 63 v 102; GC § 12659; Bureau of Code Revision, 10-1-53; 126 v 374. Eff 8-1-55.

§ 3767.26 Judgment for fine and costs.

A judgment for fine and costs rendered against a person or corporation for the violation of sections 3767.13 to 3767.29, inclusive, of the Revised Code, when the defendant has no property or has not a sufficient amount within the county upon which to levy to satisfy such judgment and costs, may be enforced and collected in the manner in which judgments are collected in civil cases.

HISTORY: RS § 6920c; 87 v 351; GC § 12660; Bureau of Code Revision, 10-1-53; 126 v 374. Eff 8-1-55.

§ 3767.27 Inspector of nuisances.

The board of county commissioners, whenever there is a violation of sections 3767.13 to 3767.29, inclusive, of the Revised Code, may employ and reasonably compensate one inspector of nuisances who shall be vested with police powers and authorized to examine all cases of violation of such sections.

HISTORY: RS § 6920a; 87 v 350; GC § 12661; Bureau of Code Revision, 10-1-53; 126 v 374. Eff 8-1-55.

§ 3767.28 Powers and duties of inspector.

For the purpose of examining cases of violations of sections 3767.13 to 3767.29, inclusive, of the Revised Code, and for obtaining evidence thereof, an inspector of nuisances may enter upon any premises in any county, and shall make a complaint, and institute prosecution, against any one violating such sections. The inspector shall not be required to give security for costs. The prosecuting attorney shall be the legal advisor of such inspector and the attorney in all such prosecutions.

HISTORY: RS §§ 6920a, 6920b; 87 v 350, 351; GC § 12662; Bureau of Code Revision, 10-1-53; 126 v 374. Eff 8-1-55.

§ 3767.29 Abandoned refrigerators.

No person shall abandon, discard, or knowingly permit to remain on premises under his control, in a place accessible to children, any abandoned or discarded icebox, refrigerator, or other airtight or semi-airtight container which has a capacity of one and one-half cubic feet or more and an opening of fifty square inches or more and which has a door or lid equipped with hinge, latch or other fastening device capable of securing such door or lid, without rendering said equipment harmless to human life by removing such hinges, latches or other hardware which may cause a person to be confined therein. This section shall not apply to an icebox, refrigerator or other airtight or semi-airtight container located in that part of a building occupied by a dealer, warehouseman or repairman.

HISTORY: 126 v 374. Eff 8-1-55.

§ 3767.30 Picketing during funeral or burial services.

Every citizen may freely speak, write, and publish his sentiments on all subjects, being responsible for the abuse of the right but no person shall picket, nor shall any association or corporation cause to be picketed, any residence, cemetery, funeral home, church, synagogue or other establishment within one hour before and during the conducting of an actual funeral or burial service at such place. No person shall picket, nor shall any association or corporation cause to be picketed, any funeral procession.

HISTORY: 127 v 242 (Eff 9-13-57); 129 v 582(818). Eff 1-10-61.

§ 3767.31 Repealed, 138 v H 361, § 2 [130 v 866]. Eff 7-14-80.

This section prohibited deposit of harmful objects in recreational waters.

§ 3767.32 Restrictions on depositing litter on public property, on private property owned by others and in state waters.

(A) No person, regardless of intent, shall deposit litter or cause litter to be deposited on any public property, on private property not owned by him, or in or on waters of the state unless one of the following applies:

(1) The person is directed to do so by a public official as part of a litter collection drive;

(2) Except as provided in division (B) of this section, the person deposits the litter in a litter receptacle in a manner that prevents its being carried away by the elements;

(3) The person is issued a permit or license covering the litter pursuant to Chapter 3734. or 6111. of the Revised Code.

(B) No person, without privilege to do so, shall knowingly deposit litter, or cause it to be deposited, in a litter receptacle located on any public property or on any private property not owned by him unless one of the following applies:

(1) The litter was generated or located on the property on which the litter receptacle is located;

(2) The person is directed to do so by a public official as part of a litter collection drive;

(3) The person is directed to do so by a person whom he reasonably believes to have the privilege to use the litter receptacle;

(4) The litter consists of any of the following:

(a) The contents of a litter bag or container of a type and size customarily carried and used in a motor vehicle;

(b) The contents of an ash tray of a type customarily installed or carried and used in a motor vehicle;

(c) Beverage containers and food sacks, wrappings, and containers of a type and in an amount that reasonably may be expected to be generated during routine commuting or business or recreational travel by a motor vehicle;

(d) Beverage containers, food sacks, wrappings, containers, and other materials of a type and in an amount that reasonably may be expected to be generated during a routine day by a person and deposited in a litter receptacle by a casual passerby.

(C)(1) As used in division (B)(1) of this section, "public property" includes any private property open to the public for the conduct of business, the provision of a service, or upon the payment of a fee but does not include any private property to which the public otherwise does not have a right of access.

(2) As used in division (B)(4) of this section, "casual passerby" means a person who does not have depositing litter in a litter receptacle as his primary reason for traveling to or by the property on which the litter receptacle is located.

(D) As used in this section:

(1) "Litter" means garbage, trash, waste, rubbish, ashes, cans, bottles, wire, paper, cartons, boxes, automobile parts, furniture, glass, or anything else of an unsightly or unsanitary nature.

(2) "Deposit" means to throw, drop, discard, or place.

(3) "Litter receptacle" means a dumpster, trash can,

trash bin, garbage can, or similar container in which litter is deposited for removal.

(E) This section may be enforced by any sheriff, deputy sheriff, police officer of a municipal corporation, police constable or officer of a township or township police district, wildlife officer, park officer, forest officer, preserve officer, conservancy district police officer, inspector of nuisances of a county, or any other law enforcement officer within his jurisdiction.

HISTORY: 132 v H 152 (Eff 9-21-67); 138 v H 361 (Eff 7-14-80); 142 v H 333 (Eff 10-20-87); 145 v H 114 (Eff 9-27-93); 145 v S 182. Eff 10-20-94.

§ 3767.33 Authorization for disposal of materials; injunction against disposal.

No zoning commission, municipal corporation, or other governmental authority, except the director of environmental protection acting pursuant to the powers granted to him in sections 6111.01 to 6111.08 of the Revised Code, may authorize the placing or disposal of materials in or upon the banks of a ditch, stream, river, or other watercourse after January 1, 1968, where such placing or disposal would be prohibited under the provisions of section 3767.32 of the Revised Code. Such placing or disposal may be enjoined by the common pleas court in the county in which the placing or disposal occurs, upon application by the prosecuting attorney of the county, the director of environmental protection, the director of health, or the attorney general.

HISTORY: 132 v H 152 (Eff 9-21-67); 134 v S 397. Eff 10-23-72.

§ 3767.34 Free rest room facilities.

(A) No person shall make available any rest room facility intended for multiple occupancy and which requires payment of money or any other thing of value for entry into the rest room facility, or for use of a toilet within, unless said person also makes available for use by the same sex, at the same location, an equal number of the same kind of rest room facilities, toilets, urinals, and washbowls free of charge.

(B) Rest room facilities having no more than one toilet and a washbowl, or having no more than one toilet, one urinal, and one washbowl, shall be exempt from the provisions of division (A) of this section if a key is made available immediately, or other means of access made available immediately, for any customer who requests use of the rest room facility or the toilet, urinal, or washbowl within.

(C) As used in divisions (A) and (B) of this section, "rest room facility" means any room or area containing one or more toilets, washbowls, or urinals; "multiple occupancy" means a rest room facility containing more than one toilet and one washbowl, or containing more than one toilet, one urinal, and one washbowl used for the purpose of eliminating human biological waste materials and commonly referred to as "lavatory," "toilet," "urinal," or "water closet."

HISTORY: 136 v S 71. Eff 8-18-76.

§ 3767.41 Buildings constituting public nuisance; action to enforce regulations; receivership.

(A) As used in this section:

(1) "Building" means, except as otherwise provided in this division, any building or structure that is used or intended to be used for residential purposes. "Building" includes, but is not limited to, a building or structure in which any floor is used for retail stores, shops, salesrooms, markets, or similar commercial uses, or for offices, banks, civic administration activities, professional services, or similar business or civic uses, and in which the other floors are used, or designed and intended to be used, for residential purposes. "Building" does not include any building or structure that is occupied by its owner and that contains three or fewer residential units.

(2) "Public nuisance" means a building that is a menace to the public health, welfare, or safety; that is structurally unsafe, unsanitary, or not provided with adequate safe egress; that constitutes a fire hazard, is otherwise dangerous to human life, or is otherwise no longer fit and habitable; or that, in relation to its existing use, constitutes a hazard to the public health, welfare, or safety by reason of inadequate maintenance, dilapidation, obsolescence, or abandonment.

(3) "Abate" or "abatement" in connection with any building means the removal or correction of any conditions that constitute a public nuisance and the making of any other improvements that are needed to effect a rehabilitation of the building that is consistent with maintaining safe and habitable conditions over its remaining useful life. "Abatement" does not include the closing or boarding up of any building that is found to be a public nuisance.

(4) "Interested party" means any owner, mortgagee, lienholder, tenant, or person that possesses an interest of record in any property that becomes subject to the jurisdiction of a court pursuant to this section, and any applicant for the appointment of a receiver pursuant to this section.

(5) "Neighbor" means any owner of property, including, but not limited to, any person who is purchasing property by land installment contract or under a duly executed purchase contract, that is located within five hundred feet of any property that becomes subject to the jurisdiction of a court pursuant to this section, and any occupant of a building that is so located.

(6) "Tenant" has the same meaning as in section 5321.01 of the Revised Code.

(B)(1) In any civil action to enforce any local building,

housing, air pollution, sanitation, health, fire, zoning, or safety code, ordinance, or regulation applicable to buildings, that is commenced in a court of common pleas, municipal court, housing or environmental division of a municipal court, or county court, or in any civil action for abatement commenced in a court of common pleas, municipal court, housing or environmental division of a municipal court, or county court, by a municipal corporation in which the building involved is located, by any neighbor, tenant, or by a nonprofit corporation that is duly organized and has as one of its goals the improvement of housing conditions in the county or municipal corporation in which the building involved is located, if a building is alleged to be a public nuisance, the municipal corporation, neighbor, tenant, or nonprofit corporation may apply in its complaint for an injunction or other order as described in division (C)(1) of this section, or for the relief described in division (C)(2) of this section, including, if necessary, the appointment of a receiver as described in divisions (C)(2) and (3) of this section, or for both such an injunction or other order and such relief. The municipal corporation, neighbor, tenant, or nonprofit corporation commencing the action is not liable for the costs, expenses, and fees of any receiver appointed pursuant to divisions (C)(2) and (3) of this section.

(2)(a) In a civil action described in division (B)(1) of this section, a copy of the complaint and a notice of the date and time of a hearing on the complaint shall be served upon the owner of the building and all other interested parties in accordance with the Rules of Civil Procedure. If certified mail service, personal service, or residence service of the complaint and notice is refused or certified mail service of the complaint and notice is not claimed, and if the municipal corporation, neighbor, tenant, or nonprofit corporation commencing the action makes a written request for ordinary mail service of the complaint and notice, or uses publication service, in accordance with the Rules of Civil Procedure, then a copy of the complaint and notice shall be posted in a conspicuous place on the building.

(b) The judge in a civil action described in division (B)(1) of this section shall conduct a hearing at least twenty-eight days after the owner of the building and the other interested parties have been served with a copy of the complaint and the notice of the date and time of the hearing in accordance with division (B)(2)(a) of this section.

(C)(1) If the judge in a civil action described in division (B)(1) of this section finds at the hearing required by division (B)(2) of this section that the building involved is a public nuisance, if the judge additionally determines that the owner of the building previously has not been afforded a reasonable opportunity to abate the public nuisance or has been afforded such an opportunity and has not refused or failed to abate the public nuisance, and if the complaint of the municipal corporation, neighbor, tenant, or nonprofit corporation commencing the action requested the issuance of an injunction as described in this division, then the judge may issue an injunction requiring the owner of the building to abate the public nuisance or issue any other order that the judge considers necessary or appropriate to cause the abatement of the public nuisance. If an injunction is issued pursuant to this division, the owner of the building involved shall be given no more than thirty days from the date of the entry of the judge's order to comply with the injunction, unless the judge, for good cause shown, extends the time for compliance.

(2) If the judge in a civil action described in division (B)(1) of this section finds at the hearing required by division (B)(2) of this section that the building involved is a public nuisance, if the judge additionally determines that the owner of the building previously has been afforded a reasonable opportunity to abate the public nuisance and has refused or failed to do so, and if the complaint of the municipal corporation, neighbor, tenant, or nonprofit corporation commencing the action requested relief as described in this division, then the judge shall offer any mortgagee, lienholder, or other interested party associated with the property on which the building is located, in the order of the priority of interest in title, the opportunity to undertake the work and to furnish the materials necessary to abate the public nuisance. Prior to selecting any interested party, the judge shall require the interested party to demonstrate the ability to promptly undertake the work and furnish the materials required, to provide the judge with a viable financial and construction plan for the rehabilitation of the building as described in division (D) of this section, and to post security for the performance of the work and the furnishing of the materials.

If the judge determines, at the hearing, that no interested party is willing or able to undertake the work and to furnish the materials necessary to abate the public nuisance, or if the judge determines, at any time after the hearing, that any party who is undertaking corrective work pursuant to this division cannot or will not proceed, or has not proceeded with due diligence, the judge may appoint a receiver pursuant to division (C)(3) of this section to take possession and control of the building.

(3)(a) The judge in a civil action described in division (B)(1) of this section shall not appoint any person as a receiver unless the person first has provided the judge with a viable financial and construction plan for the rehabilitation of the building involved as described in division (D) of this section and has demonstrated the capacity and expertise to perform the required work and to furnish the required materials in a satisfactory manner. An appointed receiver may be a financial institution that possesses an interest of record in the building or the property on which it is located, a nonprofit corporation as described in divisions (B)(1) and (C)(3)(b) of this section, including, but not limited to, a nonprofit corporation that commenced the action described in division (B)(1) of this section, or any other qualified property manager.

(b) To be eligible for appointment as a receiver, no part of the net earnings of a nonprofit corporation shall inure to the benefit of any private shareholder or individual. Membership on the board of trustees of a nonprofit corporation appointed as a receiver does not constitute the holding of a public office or employment within the meaning of sections 731.02 and 731.12 or any other section of the Revised Code and does not constitute a direct or indirect interest in a contract or expenditure of money by any municipal corporation. A member of a board of trustees of a nonprofit corporation appointed as a receiver shall not be disqualified from holding any public office or employment, and shall not forfeit any public office or employment, by reason of his membership on the board of trustees, notwithstanding any law to the contrary.

(D) Prior to ordering any work to be undertaken, or the furnishing of any materials, to abate a public nuisance under this section, the judge in a civil action described in division (B)(1) of this section shall review the submitted financial and construction plan for the rehabilitation of the building involved and, if it specifies all of the following, shall approve that plan:

(1) The estimated cost of the labor, materials, and any other development costs that are required to abate the public nuisance;

(2) The estimated income and expenses of the building and the property on which it is located after the furnishing of the materials and the completion of the repairs and improvements;

(3) The terms, conditions, and availability of any financing that is necessary to perform the work and to furnish the materials;

(4) If repair and rehabilitation of the building are found not to be feasible, the cost of demolition of the building or of the portions of the building that constitute the public nuisance.

(E) Upon the written request of any of the interested parties to have a building, or portions of a building, that constitute a public nuisance demolished because repair and rehabilitation of the building are found not to be feasible, the judge may order the demolition. However, the demolition shall not be ordered unless the requesting interested parties have paid the costs of demolition and, if any, of the receivership, and, if any, all notes, certificates, mortgages, and fees of the receivership.

(F) Before proceeding with his duties, any receiver appointed by the judge in a civil action described in division (B)(1) of this section may be required by the judge to post a bond in an amount fixed by the judge, but not exceeding the value of the building involved as determined by the judge.

The judge may empower the receiver to do any or all of the following:

(1) Take possession and control of the building and the property on which it is located, operate and manage the building and the property, establish and collect rents and income, lease and rent the building and the property, and evict tenants;

(2) Pay all expenses of operating and conserving the building and the property, including, but not limited to, the cost of electricity, gas, water, sewerage, heating fuel, repairs and supplies, custodian services, taxes and assessments, and insurance premiums, and hire and pay reasonable compensation to a managing agent;

(3) Pay pre-receivership mortgages or installments of them and other liens;

(4) Perform or enter into contracts for the performance of all work and the furnishing of materials necessary to abate, and obtain financing for the abatement of, the public nuisance;

(5) Pursuant to court order, remove and dispose of any personal property abandoned, stored, or otherwise located in or on the building and the property that creates a dangerous or unsafe condition or that constitutes a violation of any local building, housing, air pollution, sanitation, health, fire, zoning, or safety code, ordinance, or regulation;

(6) Obtain mortgage insurance for any receiver's mortgage from any agency of the federal government;

(7) Enter into any agreement and do those things necessary to maintain and preserve the building and the property and comply with all local building, housing, air pollution, sanitation, health, fire, zoning, or safety codes, ordinances, and regulations;

(8) Give the custody of the building and the property, and the opportunity to abate the nuisance and operate the property, to its owner or any mortgagee or lienholder of record;

(9) Issue notes and secure them by a mortgage bearing interest, and upon terms and conditions, that the judge approves. When sold or transferred by the receiver in return for valuable consideration in money, material, labor, or services, the notes or certificates shall be freely transferable. Any mortgages granted by the receiver shall be superior to any claims of the receiver. Priority among the receiver's mortgages shall be determined by the order in which they are recorded.

(G) A receiver appointed pursuant to this section is not personally liable except for misfeasance, malfeasance, or nonfeasance in the performance of the functions of his office.

(H)(1) The judge in a civil action described in division (B)(1) of this section may assess as court costs, the expenses described in division (F)(2) of this section, and may approve receiver's fees to the extent that they are not covered by the income from the property. Subject to that limitation, a receiver appointed pursuant to divisions (C)(2) and (3) of this section is entitled to receive fees in the same manner and to the same extent as receivers appointed in actions to foreclose mortgages.

(2)(a) Pursuant to the police powers vested in the state, all expenditures of a mortgagee, lienholder, or other interested party that has been selected pursuant to division (C)(2) of this section to undertake the work and to furnish the materials necessary to abate a public nuisance, and any expenditures in connection with the foreclosure of the lien created by this division, is a first lien upon the building involved and the property on which it is located and is superior to all prior and subsequent liens or other encumbrances associated with the building or the property, including, but not limited to, those for taxes and assessments, upon the occurrence of both of the following:

(i) The prior approval of the expenditures by, and the entry of a judgment to that effect by, the judge in the civil action described in division (B)(1) of this section;

(ii) The recordation of a certified copy of the judgment entry and a sufficient description of the property on which the building is located with the county recorder in the county in which the property is located within sixty days after the date of the entry of the judgment.

(b) Pursuant to the police powers vested in the state, all expenses and other amounts paid in accordance with division (F) of this section by a receiver appointed pursuant to divisions (C)(2) and (3) of this section, the amounts of any notes issued by the receiver in accordance with division (F) of this section, all mortgages granted by the receiver in accordance with that division, the fees of the receiver approved pursuant to division (H)(1) of this section, and any amounts expended in connection with the foreclosure of a mortgage granted by the receiver in accordance with division (F) of this section or with the foreclosure of the lien created by this division, are a first lien upon the building involved and the property on which it is located and are superior to all prior and subsequent liens or other encumbrances associated with the building or the property, including, but not limited to, those for taxes and assessments, upon the occurrence of both of the following:

(i) The approval of the expenses, amounts, or fees by, and the entry of a judgment to that effect by, the judge in the civil action described in division (B)(1) of this section; or the approval of the mortgages in accordance with division (F)(9) of this section by, and the entry of a judgment to that effect by, that judge;

(ii) The recordation of a certified copy of the judgment entry and a sufficient description of the property on which the building is located, or, in the case of a mortgage, the recordation of the mortgage, a certified copy of the judgment entry, and such a description, with the county recorder of the county in which the property is located within sixty days after the date of the entry of the judgment.

(c) Priority among the liens described in divisions (H)(2)(a) and (b) of this section shall be determined as described in division (I) of this section. Additionally, the creation pursuant to this section of a mortgage lien that is prior to or superior to any mortgage of record at the time the mortgage lien is so created, does not disqualify the mortgage of record as a legal investment under Chapter 1107. or 1151. or any other chapter of the Revised Code.

(I)(1) If a receiver appointed pursuant to divisions (C)(2) and (3) of this section files with the judge in the civil action described in division (B)(1) of this section a report indicating that the public nuisance has been abated, if the judge confirms that the receiver has abated the public nuisance, and if the receiver or any interested party requests the judge to enter an order directing the receiver to sell the building and the property on which it is located, the judge may enter that order after holding a hearing as described in division (I)(2) of this section and otherwise complying with that division.

(2) The receiver or interested party requesting an order as described in division (I)(1) of this section shall cause a notice of the date and time of a hearing on the request to be served on the owner of the building involved and all other interested parties in accordance with division (B)(2)(a) of this section. The judge in the civil action described in division (B)(1) of this section shall conduct the scheduled hearing. At the hearing, if the owner or any interested party objects to the sale of the building and the property, the burden of proof shall be upon the objecting person to establish, by a preponderance of the evidence, that the benefits of not selling the building and the property outweigh the benefits of selling them. If the judge determines that there is no objecting person, or if the judge determines that there is one or more objecting persons but no objecting person has sustained the burden of proof specified in this division, the judge may enter an order directing the receiver to offer the building and the property for sale upon terms and conditions that the judge shall specify.

(3) If a sale of a building and the property on which it is located is ordered pursuant to divisions (I)(1) and (2) of this section and if the sale occurs in accordance with the terms and conditions specified by the judge in his order of sale, then the receiver shall distribute the proceeds of the sale and the balance of any funds that the receiver may possess, after the payment of the costs of the sale, in the following order of priority and in the described manner:

(a) First, in satisfaction of any notes issued by the receiver pursuant to division (F) of this section, in their order of priority;

(b) Second, any unreimbursed expenses and other amounts paid in accordance with division (F) of this section by the receiver, and the fees of the receiver approved pursuant to division (H)(1) of this section;

(c) Third, all expenditures of a mortgagee, lienholder, or other interested party that has been selected pursuant to division (C)(2) of this section to undertake the work and to furnish the materials necessary to abate a public nuisance, provided that the expenditures were approved as described in division (H)(2)(a) of this section and provided that, if any such interested party subsequently became the receiver, its expenditures shall be paid prior to the expenditures of any of the other interested parties so selected;

(d) Fourth, the amount due for delinquent taxes, assessments, charges, penalties, and interest owed to this state or a political subdivision of this state, provided that, if the amount available for distribution pursuant to division (I)(3)(d) of this section is insufficient to pay the entire amount of those taxes, assessments, charges, penalties, and interest, the proceeds and remaining funds shall be paid to each claimant in proportion to the amount of those taxes, assessments, charges, penalties, and interest that each is due.

(e) The amount of any pre-receivership mortgages, liens, or other encumbrances, in their order of priority.

(4) Following a distribution in accordance with division (I)(3) of this section, the receiver shall request the judge in the civil action described in division (B)(1) of this section to enter an order terminating the receivership. If the judge determines that the sale of the building and the property on which it is located occurred in accordance with the terms and conditions specified by the judge in his order of sale under division (I)(2) of this section and that the receiver distributed the proceeds of the sale and the balance of any funds that the receiver possessed, after the payment of the costs of the sale, in accordance with division (I)(3) of this section, and if the judge approves any final accounting required of the receiver, the judge may terminate the receivership.

(J)(1) A receiver appointed pursuant to divisions (C)(2) and (3) of this section may be discharged at any time in the discretion of the judge in the civil action described in division (B)(1) of this section. The receiver shall be discharged by the judge as provided in division (I)(4) of this section, or when all of the following have occurred:

(a) The public nuisance has been abated;

(b) All costs, expenses, and approved fees of the receivership have been paid;

(c) Either all receiver's notes issued and mortgages granted pursuant to this section have been paid, or all the holders of the notes and mortgages request that the receiver be discharged.

(2) If a judge in a civil action described in division (B)(1) of this section determines that, and enters of record a declaration that, a public nuisance has been abated by a receiver, and if, within three days after the entry of the declaration, all costs, expenses, and approved fees of the receivership have not been paid in full, then, in addition to the circumstances specified in division (I) of this section for the entry of such an order, the judge may enter an order directing the receiver to sell the building involved and the property on which it is located. Any such order shall be entered, and the sale shall occur, only in compliance with division (I) of this section.

(K) The title in any building, and in the property on which it is located, that is sold at a sale ordered under division (I) or (J)(2) of this section shall be incontestable in the purchaser and shall be free and clear of all liens for delinquent taxes, assessments, charges, penalties, and interest owed to this state or any political subdivision of this state, that could not be satisfied from the proceeds of the sale and the remaining funds in the receiver's possession pursuant to the distribution under division (I)(3) of this section. All other liens and encumbrances with respect to the building and the property shall survive the sale, including, but not limited to, a federal tax lien notice properly filed in accordance with section 317.09 of the Revised Code prior to the time of the sale, and the easements and covenants of record running with the property that were created prior to the time of the sale.

(L)(1) Nothing in this section shall be construed as a limitation upon the powers granted to a court of common pleas, a municipal court or a housing or environmental division of a municipal court under Chapter 1901. of the Revised Code, or a county court under Chapter 1907. of the Revised Code.

(2) The monetary and other limitations specified in Chapters 1901. and 1907. of the Revised Code upon the jurisdiction of municipal and county courts, and of housing or environmental divisions of municipal courts, in civil actions do not operate as limitations upon any of the following:

(a) Expenditures of a mortgagee, lienholder, or other interested party that has been selected pursuant to division (C)(2) of this section to undertake the work and to furnish the materials necessary to abate a public nuisance;

(b) Any notes issued by a receiver pursuant to division (F) of this section;

(c) Any mortgage granted by a receiver in accordance with division (F) of this section;

(d) Expenditures in connection with the foreclosure of a mortgage granted by a receiver in accordance with division (F) of this section;

(e) The enforcement of an order of a judge entered pursuant to this section;

(f) The actions that may be taken pursuant to this section by a receiver or a mortgagee, lienholder, or other interested party that has been selected pursuant to division (C)(2) of this section to undertake the work and to furnish the materials necessary to abate a public nuisance.

(3) A judge in a civil action described in division

(B)(1) of this section, or the judge's successor in office, has continuing jurisdiction to review the condition of any building that was determined to be a public nuisance pursuant to this section.

HISTORY: 140 v H 706 (Eff 12-17-84); 143 v H 387 (Eff 7-18-90); 144 v H 200 (Eff 7-8-91); 146 v H 538. Eff 1-1-97.

The effective date is set by section 10 of HB 538.

§ 3767.99 Penalties.

(A) Whoever is guilty of contempt under sections 3767.01 to 3767.11 or violates section 3767.14 of the Revised Code is guilty of a misdemeanor of the first degree.

(B) Whoever violates section 3767.12 or 3767.29, or, being an association, violates section 3767.30 of the Revised Code is guilty of a misdemeanor of the fourth degree.

(C) Whoever violates section 3767.13, 3767.19, or 3767.32 or, being a natural person, violates section 3767.30 of the Revised Code is guilty of a misdemeanor of the third degree. The sentencing court may, in addition to or in lieu of the penalty provided in this division, require a person who violates section 3767.32 of the Revised Code to remove litter from any public or private property, or in or on waters of the state.

(D) Whoever violates section 3767.16, 3767.17, 3767.18, 3767.201 [3767.20.1], or 3767.34 of the Revised Code is guilty of a minor misdemeanor.

HISTORY: Bureau of Code Revision, 10-1-53; 127 v 242; 128 v 1217 (Eff 11-2-59); 129 v 1075 (Eff 9-25-61); 130 v 866 (Eff 1-23-63); 130 v 867 (Eff 9-30-63); 132 v H 152 (Eff 9-21-67); 133 v S 460 (Eff 9-3-70); 136 v S 71 (Eff 8-18-76); 138 v H 361. Eff 7-14-80.

CHAPTER 3770: STATE LOTTERY

§ 3770.08 Prohibitions.

(A) No person shall sell a lottery ticket at a price greater than that fixed by rule of the state lottery commission.

(B) No person other than a licensed lottery sales agent shall sell lottery tickets, but nothing in this section shall be construed to prevent any person from giving lottery tickets to another as a gift. A transfer of lottery tickets by any person which is made in connection with a marketing, promotional, or advertising program shall be deemed to be a gift for the purposes of this chapter.

(C) No person shall sell a lottery ticket to any person under eighteen years of age, and no person under eighteen years of age shall attempt to purchase a lottery ticket.

(D) No person, directly or indirectly, on behalf of self, or another, nor any organization, shall invite, solicit, demand, offer, or accept any payment, contribution, favor, or other consideration to influence the award, renewal, or retention of a lottery sales agent license.

(E) Except as otherwise provided in this division, no person shall sell lottery tickets on any fairgrounds during any annual exhibition conducted in accordance with Chapter 991. or 1711. of the Revised Code. "Fairgrounds" includes any land or property under the control or management of any agricultural society or of the Ohio expositions commission. This division does not apply to the sale of lottery tickets by the commission at the state fairground during the state fair.

HISTORY: 135 v H 990 (Eff 11-21-73); 137 v H 395 (Eff 11-28-77); 140 v H 665 (Eff 4-4-85); 146 v S 211. Eff 9-26-96.

§ 3770.99 Penalties.

(A) Whoever is prohibited from claiming a lottery prize award under division (A)(5) of section 3770.07 of the Revised Code and attempts to claim or is paid a lottery prize award is guilty of a minor misdemeanor, and shall provide restitution to the state lottery commission of any moneys erroneously paid as a lottery prize award to that person.

(B) Whoever violates division (C) of section 3770.071 [3770.07.1] or section 3770.08 of the Revised Code is guilty of a misdemeanor of the third degree.

HISTORY: 135 v H 990 (Eff 11-21-73); 146 v S 211. Eff 9-26-96.

CHAPTER 3773: BOXING; DISCHARGING FIREARMS; DUELING

§ 3773.05 Shooting upon, over, or near a cemetery.

No person shall, without permission from the proper officials, discharge a firearm upon or over a cemetery or within one hundred yards thereof, unless such person is upon his own land.

HISTORY: RS § 7037; S&S 69; 64 v 48; GC § 12818; Bureau of Code Revision. Eff 10-1-53.

§ 3773.06 Hunting or shooting game near township park.

No person shall hunt, shoot, or kill game within one-half mile of a township park.

The board of township park commissioners may grant permission to kill game not desired within the limits prohibited by this section.

HISTORY: RS § 6986-5; 90 v 175; GC § 12820; Bureau of Code Revision, 10-1-53; 135 v H 295. Eff 7-22-74.

§ 3773.07 Dueling.

No person shall fight a duel, be a second to a person who fights a duel, challenge another to fight a duel, accept a challenge to fight a duel, or knowingly be the bearer of such challenge.

HISTORY: RS § 6887; S&C 412; 33 v 33, § 25; GC § 12799; Bureau of Code Revision. Eff 10-1-53.

§ 3773.13 Suppression of prize fight.

When a sheriff has reason to believe that a fight or contention is about to take place in his county, he shall forthwith summon sufficient citizens of the county, suppress such fight or contention, and arrest all persons found at such prize fight violating the law and take them before a judge of the court of common pleas or magistrate.

HISTORY: GC § 13429-4; 113 v 123 (135), ch. 8, § 4; Bureau of Code Revision. Eff 10-1-53.

§ 3773.21 Discharge of firearm prohibited.

No person shall discharge a firearm on a lawn, park, pleasure ground, orchard, or other ground appurtenant to a schoolhouse, church, or an inhabited dwelling, the property of another, or a charitable institution. This section does not prevent or prohibit the owner thereof from discharging firearms upon his own enclosure.

HISTORY: RS § 6962; 71 v 148, § 4; GC § 12817; 107 v 641; Bureau of Code Revision, 10-1-53; 129 v 1625. Eff 10-18-61.

[§ 3773.21.1] § 3773.211 Discharge of firearm over highway prohibited.

No person shall discharge a firearm upon or over a public road or highway.

HISTORY: 129 v 1625. Eff 10-18-61.

§ 3773.99 Penalties.

(A) Whoever violates section 3773.05, 3773.06, 3773.21, or 3773.50 of the Revised Code is guilty of a misdemeanor of the fourth degree.

(B) Whoever violates section 3773.07 of the Revised Code is guilty of a felony of the fourth degree.

(C) Whoever violates section 3773.211 [3773.21.1], 3773.32, 3773.40, 3773.44, 3773.45, 3773.46, or 3773.47, division (A) of section 3773.54, or division (B) of section 3773.33 of the Revised Code is guilty of a misdemeanor of the first degree.

(D) Whoever violates section 3773.48 or 3773.49 of the Revised Code is guilty of a minor misdemeanor.

HISTORY: Bureau of Code Revision, 10-1-53; 126 v 392(404); 128 v 862 (Eff 10-1-59); 129 v 1625 (Eff 10-18-61); 134 v H 511 (Eff 1-1-74); 135 v H 59 (Eff 11-21-73); 135 v H 1041 (Eff 3-20-74); 136 v H 1 (Eff 6-13-75); 139 v S 60 (Eff 7-27-81); 140 v H 133 (Eff 9-27-83); 146 v S 240. Eff 9-3-96.

TITLE 39: INSURANCE

CHAPTER 3904: INSURANCE TRANSACTION INFORMATION STANDARDS

§ 3904.14 Obtaining information under false pretenses.

(A) No person shall knowingly obtain information under false pretenses about an individual from an insurance institution, agent, or insurance support organization.

(B) Whoever violates division (A) of this section is guilty of a felony of the fourth degree.

HISTORY: 145 v H 329. Eff 6-29-95.

The effective date is set by section 2 of HB 329.

CHAPTER 3937: CASUALTY INSURANCE; MOTOR VEHICLE INSURANCE

§ 3937.42 Duty to cooperate in investigation of fraudulent claims; use of information.

(A) The chief or head law enforcement officer of any federal, state, or local law enforcement agency or a prosecuting attorney of any county may request any insurance company, or agent authorized by the company to act on its behalf, that has investigated or is investigating a claim involving motor vehicle insurance to release any information in its possession relevant to the claim. The company or agent shall release the information that is requested in writing by the law enforcement officer.

(B) If an insurance company, or agent authorized by the company to act on its behalf, has reason to suspect that a loss involving a motor vehicle that is insured by the company is part of a fraudulent scheme to obtain control of motor vehicle insurance proceeds, the company or agent shall notify a law enforcement officer or a prosecuting attorney of any county having jurisdiction over the alleged fraud.

(C) An insurance company, or agent authorized by the company to act on its behalf, shall release any information requested in writing pursuant to division (A) of this section and cooperate with the officer or a prosecuting attorney of any county authorized to request the information. The company or agent shall take such action as may be reasonably requested of it by the officer or a prosecuting attorney of any county and shall permit any other person ordered by a court to inspect any information that is specifically requested by the court.

The information that may be requested pursuant to this section may include, but is not limited to, the following:

(1) Any insurance policy relevant to the claim under investigation and any application for such a policy;

(2) Policy premium payment records;

(3) History of previous motor vehicle claims made by the insured;

(4) Material relating to the investigation of the claim, including statements of any person, proof of loss, and any other relevant evidence.

(D) If the law enforcement officer or a prosecuting attorney of any county mentioned in division (A) of this section has received information pursuant to this section from an insurance company, or agent authorized by the company to act on its behalf, the officer or a prosecuting attorney of any county may release to, and share with, the insurance company or agent any information in his possession relative to the claim, upon the written request of the insurance company or agent.

(E) In the absence of fraud, recklessness, or malice, no insurance company, or agent authorized by the company to act on its behalf, is liable for damages in any civil action, including any action brought pursuant to section 1347.10 of the Revised Code for any oral or written statement made or any other action taken that is necessary to supply information required pursuant to this section.

(F) Except as otherwise provided in division (D) of this section, any officer or a prosecuting attorney of any county receiving any information furnished pursuant to this section shall hold the information in confidence and shall not disclose it to anyone except other law enforcement officers or agencies until its release is required pursuant to a criminal or civil proceeding.

(G) Any officer or a prosecuting attorney of any county referred to in division (A) of this section may testify as to any information in his possession regarding the claim referred to in that division in any civil action in which any person seeks recovery under a policy against an insurance company.

(H) As used in this section, "motor vehicle" has the same meaning as in section 4501.01 of the Revised Code.

(I)(1) No person shall purposely refuse to release any information requested pursuant to this section by an officer or a prosecuting attorney of any county authorized by division (A) of this section to request the information.

(2) No person shall purposely refuse to notify an appropriate law enforcement officer or a prosecuting attorney of any county of a loss required to be reported pursuant to division (B) of this section.

(3) No person shall purposely fail to hold in confidence information required to be held in confidence by division (F) of this section.

HISTORY: 140 v S 2. Eff 9-26-84.

§ 3937.99 Penalties.

(A) Whoever purposely violates sections 3937.01 to 3937.17 of the Revised Code shall be fined not more than five hundred dollars.

(B) Whoever violates division (I) of section 3937.42 of the Revised Code is guilty of a misdemeanor of the fourth degree.

HISTORY: Bureau of Code Revision, 10-1-53; 140 v S 2. Eff 9-26-84.

TITLE 41: LABOR AND INDUSTRY

CHAPTER 4112: CIVIL RIGHTS COMMISSION

§ 4112.01 Definitions.

(A) As used in this chapter:

(1) "Person" includes one or more individuals, partnerships, associations, organizations, corporations, legal representatives, trustees, trustees in bankruptcy, receivers, and other organized groups of persons. "Person" also includes, but is not limited to, any owner, lessor, assignor, builder, manager, broker, salesman, appraiser, agent, employee, lending institution, and the state and all political subdivisions, authorities, agencies, boards, and commissions of the state.

(2) "Employer" includes the state, any political subdivision of the state, any person employing four or more persons within the state, and any person acting directly or indirectly in the interest of an employer.

(3) "Employee" means an individual employed by any employer but does not include any individual employed in the domestic service of any person.

(4) "Labor organization" includes any organization that exists, in whole or in part, for the purpose of collective bargaining or of dealing with employers concerning grievances, terms or conditions of employment, or other mutual aid or protection in relation to employment.

(5) "Employment agency" includes any person regularly undertaking, with or without compensation, to procure opportunities to work or to procure, recruit, refer, or place employees.

(6) "Commission" means the Ohio civil rights commission created by section 4112.03 of the Revised Code.

(7) "Discriminate" includes segregate or separate.

(8) "Unlawful discriminatory practice" means any act prohibited by section 4112.02, 4112.021 [4112.02.1], or 4112.022 [4112.02.2] of the Revised Code.

(9) "Place of public accommodation" means any inn, restaurant, eating house, barbershop, public conveyance by air, land, or water, theater, store, other place for the sale of merchandise, or any other place of public accommodation or amusement of which the accommodations, advantages, facilities, or privileges are available to the public.

(10) "Housing accommodations" includes any building or structure, or portion of a building or structure, that is used or occupied or is intended, arranged, or designed to be used or occupied as the home residence, dwelling, dwelling unit, or sleeping place of one or more individuals, groups, or families whether or not living independently of each other; and any vacant land offered for sale or lease. "Housing accommodations" also includes any housing accommodations held or offered for sale or rent by a real estate broker, salesman, or agent, by any other person pursuant to authorization of the owner, by the owner, or by the owner's legal representative.

(11) "Restrictive covenant" means any specification limiting the transfer, rental, lease, or other use of any housing accommodations because of race, color, religion, sex, familial status, national origin, handicap, or ancestry, or any limitation based upon affiliation with or approval by any person, directly or indirectly, employing race, color, religion, sex, familial status, national origin, handicap, or ancestry as a condition of affiliation or approval.

(12) "Burial lot" means any lot for the burial of deceased persons within any public burial ground or cemetery, including, but not limited to, cemeteries owned and operated by municipal corporations, townships, or companies or associations incorporated for cemetery purposes.

(13) "Handicap" means a physical or mental impairment that substantially limits one or more major life activities, including the functions of caring for one's self, performing manual tasks, walking, seeing, hearing, speaking, breathing, learning, and working; a record of a physical or mental impairment; or being regarded as having a physical or mental impairment.

(14) Except as otherwise provided in section 4112.021 [4112.02.1] of the Revised Code, "age" means at least forty years old.

(15) "Familial status" means either of the following:

(a) One or more individuals who are under eighteen years of age and who are domiciled with a parent or guardian having legal custody of the individual or domiciled, with the written permission of the parent or guardian having legal custody, with a designee of the parent or guardian;

(b) Any person who is pregnant or in the process of securing legal custody of any individual who is under eighteen years of age.

(16)(a) Except as provided in division (A)(16)(b) of this section, "physical or mental impairment" includes any of the following:

(i) Any physiological disorder or condition, cosmetic disfigurement, or anatomical loss affecting one or more of the following body systems: neurological; musculoskeletal; special sense organs; respiratory, including speech organs; cardiovascular; reproductive; digestive; genito-urinary; hemic and lymphatic; skin; and endocrine;

(ii) Any mental or psychological disorder, including, but not limited to, mental retardation, organic brain syndrome, emotional or mental illness, and specific learning disabilities;

(iii) Diseases and conditions, including, but not limited to, orthopedic, visual, speech, and hearing impairments, cerebral palsy, autism, epilepsy, muscular dystrophy, multiple sclerosis, cancer, heart disease, diabetes, human immunodeficiency virus infection, mental retardation, emotional illness, drug addiction, and alcoholism.

(b) "Physical or mental impairment" does not include any of the following:

(i) Homosexuality and bisexuality;

(ii) Transvestism, transsexualism, pedophilia, exhibitionism, voyeurism, gender identity disorders not resulting from physical impairments, or other sexual behavior disorders;

(iii) Compulsive gambling, kleptomania, or pyromania;

(iv) Psychoactive substance use disorders resulting from current illegal use of a controlled substance.

(17) "Dwelling unit" means a single unit of residence for a family of one or more persons.

(18) "Common use areas" means rooms, spaces, or elements inside or outside a building that are made available for the use of residents of the building or their guests, and includes, but is not limited to, hallways, lounges, lobbies, laundry rooms, refuse rooms, mail rooms, recreational areas, and passageways among and between buildings.

(19) "Public use areas" means interior or exterior rooms or spaces of a privately or publicly owned building that are made available to the general public.

(20) "Controlled substance" has the same meaning as in section 3719.01 of the Revised Code.

(21) "Handicapped person" means a person with a handicap.

(22) "Handicapped tenant" means a tenant or prospective tenant who is a handicapped person.

(B) For the purposes of divisions (A) to (F) of section 4112.02 of the Revised Code, the terms "because of sex" and "on the basis of sex" include, but are not limited to, because of or on the basis of pregnancy, any illness arising out of and occurring during the course of a pregnancy, childbirth, or related medical conditions. Women affected by pregnancy, childbirth, or related medical conditions shall be treated the same for all employment-related purposes, including receipt of benefits under fringe benefit programs, as other persons not so affected but similar in their ability or inability to work, and nothing in division (B) of section 4111.17 of the Revised Code shall be interpreted to permit otherwise. This division shall not be construed to require an employer to pay for health insurance benefits for abortion, except where the life of the mother would be endangered if the fetus were carried to term or except where medical complications have arisen from the abortion, provided that nothing in this division precludes an employer from providing abortion benefits or otherwise affects bargaining agreements in regard to abortion.

HISTORY: 128 v 12 (Eff 7-29-59); 129 v 582 (860) (Eff 1-10-61); 129 v 1694 (Eff 10-24-61); 131 v 980 (Eff 10-30-65); 133 v H 47 (Eff 10-24-69); 133 v H 432 (Eff 11-12-69); 135 v H 610 (Eff 12-19-73); 136 v S 162 (Eff 7-23-76); 138 v H 230 (Eff 11-13-79); 138 v H 19 (Eff 1-10-80); 143 v H 314 (Eff 5-31-90); 144 v H 321. Eff 6-30-92.

CHAPTER 4163: ATOMIC ENERGY

§ 4163.07 Notification prior to shipment of nuclear materials into or through the state.

(A)(1) Prior to transporting any large quantity of special nuclear material or by-product material into or through the state, the carrier or shipper of the material shall notify the deputy director of the emergency management agency established under section 5502.22 of the Revised Code of the shipment. The notice shall be in writing and be sent by certified mail and shall include the name of the shipper; the name of the carrier; the type and quantity of the special nuclear material or by-product material; the transportation mode of the shipment; the proposed date and time of shipment of the material into or through the state; and the starting point, termination or exit point, scheduled route, and each alternate route, if any, of the shipment. In order to constitute effective notification under division (A)(1) of this section, notification shall be received by the deputy director at least forty-eight hours prior to entry of the shipment into the state.

(2) The carrier or shipper of any shipment subject to division (A)(1) of this section shall immediately notify the deputy director of any change in the date and time of the shipment or in the route of the shipment into or through the state.

(B) Upon receipt of a notice of any shipment of a large quantity of special nuclear material or by-product material into or through the state, the deputy director of the emergency management agency shall immediately notify the director of public safety, the director of environmental protection, the chairman of the public utilities commission, and the sheriff of each county along the proposed route, or any alternate route, of the shipment.

(C) The deputy director of the emergency management agency shall not disclose to any person other than those persons enumerated in division (B) of this section any information pertaining to any shipment of special nuclear material or by-product material prior to the time that the shipment is completed.

(D) This section does not apply to radioactive materials, other than by-products, shipped by or for the United States department of defense and United States department of energy. Nothing in this section shall require the disclosure of any defense information or restricted data as defined in the "Atomic Energy Act of 1954,"

68 Stat. 919, 42 U.S.C.A. 2011, as amended.

(E) No person shall transport or cause to be transported into or through the state any large quantity of special or by-product material without first providing the notice required in division (A) of this section.

HISTORY: 138 v S 208 (Eff 7-14-80); 142 v H 131 (Eff 6-29-88); 144 v S 98 (Eff 11-12-92); 146 v S 162. Eff 10-29-95.

§ 4163.99 Penalty.

Whoever violates division (E) of section 4163.07 of the Revised Code is guilty of a felony of the fourth degree. Each shipment made in violation of that division is a separate offense.

HISTORY: 138 v S 208 (Eff 7-14-80); 146 v S 2. Eff 7-1-96.

The effective date is set by section 6 of SB 2.

TITLE 43: LIQUOR

CHAPTER 4301: LIQUOR CONTROL LAW

§ 4301.01 Definitions.

(A) As used in the Revised Code:

(1) "Intoxicating liquor" and "liquor" include all liquids and compounds, other than beer as defined in division (B)(2) of this section, containing one-half of one per cent or more of alcohol by volume which are fit to use for beverage purposes, from whatever source and by whatever process produced, by whatever name called, and whether the same are medicated, proprietary, or patented. The phrase includes wine, as defined in division (B)(3) of this section even if it contains less than four per cent of alcohol by volume, mixed beverages, as defined in division (B)(4) of this section even if they contain less than four per cent of alcohol by volume, cider, as defined in division (B)(23) of this section, alcohol, and all solids and confections which contain any alcohol.

(2) Except as used in sections 4301.01 to 4301.20, 4301.22 to 4301.52, 4301.56, 4301.70, 4301.72, and 4303.01 to 4303.36 of the Revised Code, "sale" and "sell" include exchange, barter, gift, offer for sale, sale, distribution and delivery of any kind, and the transfer of title or possession of beer and intoxicating liquor either by constructive or actual delivery by any means or devices whatever, including the sale of beer or intoxicating liquor by means of a controlled access alcohol and beverage cabinet pursuant to section 4301.21 of the Revised Code. "Sale" and "sell" do not include the mere solicitation of orders for beer or intoxicating liquor from the holders of permits issued by the division of liquor control authorizing the sale of the beer or intoxicating liquor, but no solicitor shall solicit any such orders until the solicitor has been registered with the division pursuant to section 4303.25 of the Revised Code.

(3) "Vehicle" includes all means of transportation by land, by water, or by air, and everything made use of in any way for such transportation.

(B) As used in sections 4301.01 to 4301.74 of the Revised Code:

(1) "Alcohol" means ethyl alcohol, whether rectified or diluted with water or not, whatever its origin may be, and includes synthetic ethyl alcohol. "Alcohol" does not include denatured alcohol and wood alcohol.

(2) "Beer," "malt liquor," or "malt beverages" includes all brewed or fermented malt products containing one-half of one per cent or more of alcohol by volume but not more than six per cent of alcohol by weight.

(3) "Wine" includes all liquids fit to use for beverage purposes containing not less than one-half of one per cent of alcohol by volume and not more than twenty-one per cent of alcohol by volume, which is made from the fermented juices of grapes, fruits, or other agricultural products, except that as used in sections 4301.13, 4301.421 [4301.42.1], 4301.422 [4301.42.2], 4301.432 [4301.43.2], and 4301.44 of the Revised Code, and, for purposes of determining the rate of the tax that applies, division (B) of section 4301.43 of the Revised Code, "wine" does not include cider.

(4) "Mixed beverages" such as bottled and prepared cordials, cocktails, and highballs are products obtained by mixing any type of whiskey, neutral spirits, brandy, gin, or other distilled spirits with, or over, carbonated or plain water, pure juices from flowers and plants, and other flavoring materials. The completed product shall contain not less than one-half of one per cent of alcohol by volume and not more than twenty-one per cent of alcohol by volume.

(5) "Spirituous liquor" includes all intoxicating liquors containing more than twenty-one per cent of alcohol by volume.

(6) "Sealed container" means any container having a capacity of not more than one hundred twenty-eight fluid ounces, the opening of which is closed to prevent the entrance of air.

(7) "Person" includes firms and corporations.

(8) "Manufacture" includes all processes by which beer or intoxicating liquor is produced, whether by distillation, rectifying, fortifying, blending, fermentation, brewing, or in any other manner.

(9) "Manufacturer" means any person engaged in the business of manufacturing beer or intoxicating liquor.

(10) "Wholesale distributor" and "distributor" means a person engaged in the business of selling to retail dealers for purposes of resale.

(11) "Hotel" has the meaning set forth in section 3731.01 of the Revised Code, subject to the exceptions mentioned in section 3731.03 of the Revised Code.

(12) "Restaurant" means a place located in a permanent building provided with space and accommodations wherein, in consideration of the payment of money, hot meals are habitually prepared, sold, and served at noon and evening, as the principal business of the place. "Restaurant" does not include drugstores, confectionery stores, lunch stands, night clubs, and filling stations.

(13) "Club" means a corporation or association of individuals organized in good faith for social, recreational, benevolent, charitable, fraternal, political, patriotic, or athletic purposes, which is the owner, lessor, or occupant of a permanent building or part thereof operated solely for those purposes, membership in which entails the prepayment of regular dues, and includes the place so operated.

(14) "Night club" means a place operated for profit, where food is served for consumption on the premises

and one or more forms of amusement are provided or permitted for a consideration which may be in the form of a cover charge or may be included in the price of the food and beverages, or both, purchased by the patrons thereof.

(15) "At retail" means for use or consumption by the purchaser and not for resale.

(16) "Drugstore" means an establishment as defined in section 4729.27 of the Revised Code, which is under the management or control of a legally registered pharmacist.

(17) "Enclosed shopping center" means a group of retail sales and service business establishments that face into an enclosed mall, share common ingress, egress, and parking facilities, and are situated on a tract of land that contains an area of not less than five hundred thousand square feet. "Enclosed shopping center" also includes not more than one business establishment that is located within a free-standing building on such a tract of land, so long as the sale of beer and intoxicating liquor on the tract of land was approved in an election held under former section 4301.353 [4301.35.3] of the Revised Code.

(18) "Controlled access alcohol and beverage cabinet" means a closed container, either refrigerated, in whole or in part, or nonrefrigerated, access to the interior of which is restricted by means of a device which requires the use of a key, magnetic card, or similar device and from which beer, intoxicating liquor, other beverages, or food may be sold.

(19) "Residence district" means two or more contiguous election precincts located within the same county and also located within the same municipal corporation or within the unincorporated area of the same township, as described by a petition authorized by section 4301.33, 4301.332 [4301.33.2], 4303.29, or 4305.14 of the Revised Code.

(20) "Low-alcohol beverage" means any brewed or fermented malt product, or any product made from the fermented juices of grapes, fruits, or other agricultural products, that contains either no alcohol or less than one-half of one per cent of alcohol by volume. The beverages described in division (B)(20) of this section do not include a soft drink such as root beer, birch beer, or ginger beer.

(21) "Cider" means all liquids fit to use for beverage purposes that contain one-half of one per cent of alcohol by volume, but not more than six per cent of alcohol by weight that are made through the normal alcoholic fermentation of the juice of sound, ripe apples, including, without limitation, flavored, sparkling, or carbonated cider and cider made from pure condensed apple must.

HISTORY: 141 v H 428 (Eff 12-23-86); 142 v H 419 (Eff 7-31-87); 142 v H 562 (Eff 6-29-88); 143 v H 481 (Eff 7-1-89); 143 v S 131 (Eff 7-25-90); 143 v H 405 (Eff 4-11-91); 144 v H 340 (Eff 4-24-92); 145 v S 167 (Eff 11-1-94); 145 v S 209 (Eff 11-9-94); 146 v S 149 (Eff 11-21-95); 146 v H 239 (Eff 11-24-95); 146 v S 162 (Eff 7-1-97); 147 v H 390. Eff 7-21-97.

Analogous to former RC § 4301.01 (GC § 6064-1; 115 v Pt II, 118; 116 v 511; 117 v 628; Bureau of Code Revision, 10-1-53; 135 v S 339; 136 v H 928; 139 v H 357; 140 v S 74; 140 v H 37; 141 v H 39), repealed 141 v H 428, § 2, eff 12-23-86.

The provisions of § 5 of HB 390 (147 v —) read as follows:

SECTION 5. Section 4301.01 of the Revised Code is presented in this act [HB 390] as a composite of the section as amended by Sub. H.B. 239, Am. Sub. S.B. 149, and Am. Sub. S.B. 162 of the 121st General Assembly, with the new language of none of the acts shown in capital letters. ° ° ° This is in recognition of the principle stated in division (B) of section 1.52 of the Revised Code that such amendments are to be harmonized where not substantively irreconcilable and constitutes a legislative finding that such is the resulting version in effect prior to the effective date of this act.

The provisions of § 9 of SB 162 (146 v —) read as follows:

SECTION 9. On July 1, 1997, the functions of the Department of Liquor Control, except for the law enforcement functions transferred to the Department of Public Safety pursuant to Section 13 of this act, are abolished and all of its functions and assets, liabilities, equipment, and records, regardless of form or medium, are transferred to the Division of Liquor Control established in the Department of Commerce under section 121.08 of the Revised Code as amended by this act. On and after that date, the Division of Liquor Control in the Department of Commerce is thereupon and thereafter successor to, assumes the obligations of, and otherwise constitutes the continuation of the Department of Liquor Control.

Any business commenced but not completed by the Director or Department of Liquor Control on July 1, 1997, relating to the functions transferred under this section, shall be completed by the Superintendent or Division of Liquor Control in the same manner, and with the same effect, as if completed by the Director or Department of Liquor Control. No validation, cure, right, privilege, remedy, obligation, or liability is lost or impaired by reason of the transfer of functions required by this section, and each of these shall be administered by the Division of Liquor Control. All of the Department of Liquor Control's rules, orders, and determinations relating to the functions transferred under this section continue in effect as rules, orders, and determinations of the Division of Liquor Control until modified or rescinded by the Division. If necessary to ensure the integrity of the numbering of the Administrative Code, the Director of the Legislative Service Commission shall renumber the Department of Liquor Control's rules to reflect their transfer to the Division of Liquor Control.

Subject to the layoff provisions of sections 124.321 to 124.328 of the Revised Code, all employees of the Department of Liquor Control are transferred to the Division of Liquor Control.

Whenever the Director or Department of Liquor Control is referred to in any law, contract, or other document relating to the functions transferred under this section, the reference shall be deemed to refer to the Superintendent or Division of Liquor Control, whichever is appropriate.

No action or proceeding of the Director or Department of Liquor Control pending on the effective date of this section is affected by the transfer, and shall be prosecuted or defended in the name of the Superintendent or Division of Liquor Control. In all such actions or proceedings, the Superintendent or Division of Liquor Control, shall be substituted as a party upon application by the receiving entity to the court or other appropriate tribunal.

§ 4301.14 Rationing of liquor; purchase at retail by permit holder for resale prohibited.

(A) When the supply of spirituous liquor in this state is insufficient to meet the demands of ordinary trade, due to causes beyond the control of the superintendent of liquor control, the superintendent may establish rules which will insure the equitable distribution of such supplies of spirituous liquor as are available. The superintendent may institute and terminate such rules as conditions demand, and also make changes and alterations therein in accordance with specific needs.

(B) No permit holder or his employee or agent shall purchase at retail any spirituous liquor for resale or in the permit premises possess such liquor. The permit of any person, firm, partnership, or corporation violating this section, or employing an employee, or authorizing an agent who violates this section shall be suspended or revoked.

HISTORY: GC § 6064-8a; 120 v 66; Bureau of Code Revision, 10-1-53; 135 v H 496 (Eff 9-30-74); 146 v S 162. Eff 7-1-97.

The effective date is set by section 10 of SB 162.

See provisions, § 9 of SB 162 (146 v —) following RC § 4301.01.

§ 4301.15 Violation of rationing prohibited.

No person shall violate any rule issued by the superintendent of liquor control in pursuance of section 4301.14 of the Revised Code.

HISTORY: GC § 6064-8a; 120 v 66; Bureau of Code Revision, 10-1-53; 146 v S 162. Eff 7-1-97.

The effective date is set by section 10 of SB 162.

See provisions, § 9 of SB 162 (146 v —) following RC § 4301.01.

§ 4301.21 Restrictions on sale of beer or intoxicating liquor for consumption on premises.

The sale of beer or intoxicating liquor for consumption on the premises is subject to the following restrictions, in addition to those imposed by the rules and orders of the department or, beginning on July 1, 1997, the division of liquor control:

(A) Except as otherwise provided in this chapter, beer or intoxicating liquor may be served to a person not seated at a table unless there is reason to believe that the beer or intoxicating liquor so served will be consumed by a person under twenty-one years of age.

(B) Beer or intoxicating liquor may be served by a hotel in the room of a bona fide guest, and may be sold by a hotel holding a D-5a permit, or a hotel holding a D-3 or D-5 permit that otherwise meets all of the requirements for holding a D-5a permit, by means of a controlled access alcohol and beverage cabinet which shall be located only in the hotel room of a registered guest. A hotel may sell beer or intoxicating liquor as authorized by its permit to a registered guest by means of a controlled access alcohol and beverage cabinet in accordance with the following requirements:

(1) Only a person twenty-one years of age or older who is a guest registered to stay in a guestroom shall be provided a key, magnetic card, or other similar device necessary to obtain access to the contents of a controlled access alcohol and beverage cabinet in that guestroom.

(2) The hotel shall comply with section 4301.22 of the Revised Code in connection with the handling, restocking, and replenishing of the beer and intoxicating liquor in the controlled access alcohol and beverage cabinet.

(3) The hotel shall replenish or restock beer and intoxicating liquor in any controlled access alcohol and beverage cabinet only during the hours during which the hotel may serve or sell beer and intoxicating liquor.

(4) The registered guest shall verify in writing that he has read and understands the language which shall be posted on the controlled access alcohol and beverage cabinet as required by division (B)(5) of this section.

(5) A hotel authorized to sell beer and intoxicating liquor pursuant to division (B) of this section shall post on the controlled access alcohol and beverage cabinet, in conspicuous language, the following notice:

"The alcoholic beverages contained in this cabinet shall not be removed from the premises."

(6) The hotel shall maintain a record of each sale of beer or intoxicating liquor made by the hotel by means of a controlled access alcohol and beverage cabinet for any period in which the permit holder is authorized to hold the permit pursuant to sections 4303.26 and 4303.27 of the Revised Code and any additional period during which an applicant exercises its right to appeal a rejection by the department or division of liquor control to renew a permit pursuant to section 4303.271 [4303.27.1] of the Revised Code. The records maintained by the hotel shall comply with both of the following:

(a) Include the name, address, age, and signature of each hotel guest who is provided access by the hotel to a controlled access alcohol and beverage cabinet pursuant to division (B)(1) of this section;

(b) Be made available during business hours to authorized agents of the department or division of liquor control pursuant to division (A)(6) of section 4301.10 of the Revised Code or to liquor control investigators of the department of public safety pursuant to section 5502.26 of the Revised Code.

(7) The hotel shall observe all other applicable rules adopted by the department or division of liquor control and the liquor control commission.

(C) Neither the seller nor the liquor control commission by its regulations shall require the purchase of food with the purchase of beer or intoxicating liquor; nor shall the seller of beer or intoxicating liquor give away food of any kind in connection with the sale of beer or intoxicating liquor, except as authorized by rule of the liquor control commission.

(D) The seller shall not permit the purchaser to remove beer or intoxicating liquor so sold from the premises.

(E) A hotel authorized to sell beer and intoxicating liquor pursuant to division (B) of this section shall provide a registered guest with the opportunity to refuse to accept a key, magnetic card, or other similar device necessary to obtain access to the contents of a controlled access alcohol and beverage cabinet in that guest room. If a registered guest refuses to accept such key, magnetic card, or other similar device, the hotel shall not assess any charges on the registered guest for use of the controlled access alcohol and beverage cabinet in that guest room.

HISTORY: GC § 6064-21; 115 v PtII 118(139), § 21; Bureau of Code Revision, 10-1-53; 133 v H 558 (Eff 11-21-69); 135 v H 294 (Eff 11-21-73); 139 v H 357 (Eff 8-19-82); 142 v H 419 (Eff 7-31-87); 142 v H 562 (Eff 6-29-88); 146 v S 162. Eff 10-29-95.

See provisions, § 9 of SB 162 (146 v —) following RC § 4301.01.

§ 4301.22 Restrictions on sale of beer and liquor.

Sales of beer and intoxicating liquor under all classes of permits and from state liquor stores are subject to the following restrictions, in addition to those imposed by the rules or orders of the division of liquor control:

(A)(1) Except as otherwise provided in this chapter, no beer or intoxicating liquor shall be sold to any person under twenty-one years of age.

(2) No low-alcohol beverage shall be sold to any person under eighteen years of age. No permit issued by the division shall be suspended, revoked, or canceled because of a violation of division (A)(2) of this section.

(3) No intoxicating liquor shall be handled by any person under twenty-one years of age, except that a person eighteen years of age or older employed by a permit holder may handle or sell beer or intoxicating liquor in sealed containers in connection with wholesale or retail sales, and any person nineteen years of age or older employed by a permit holder may handle intoxicating liquor in open containers when acting in the capacity of a server in a hotel, restaurant, club, or night club, as defined in division (B) of section 4301.01 of the Revised Code, or in the premises of a D-7 permit holder. This section does not authorize persons under twenty-one years of age to sell intoxicating liquor across a bar. Any person employed by a permit holder may handle beer or intoxicating liquor in sealed containers in connection with manufacturing, storage, warehousing, placement, stocking, bagging, loading, or unloading, and may handle beer or intoxicating liquor in open containers in connection with cleaning tables or handling empty bottles or glasses.

(B) No permit holder and no agent or employee of a permit holder shall sell or furnish beer or intoxicating liquor to an intoxicated person.

(C) No intoxicating liquor shall be sold to any individual who habitually drinks intoxicating liquor to excess, or to whom the division has, after investigation, determined to prohibit the sale of such intoxicating liquor, because of cause shown by the husband, wife, father, mother, brother, sister, or other person dependent upon, or in charge of such individual, or by the mayor of any municipal corporation, or a township trustee of any township in which the individual resides. The order of the division in such case shall remain in effect until revoked by the division.

(D) No sales of intoxicating liquor shall be made after two-thirty a.m. on Sunday, except that intoxicating liquor may be sold on Sunday under authority of a permit which authorizes Sunday sale.

This section does not prevent a municipal corporation from adopting a closing hour for the sale of intoxicating liquor earlier than two-thirty a.m. on Sunday or to provide that no intoxicating liquor may be sold prior to that hour on Sunday.

(E) No holder of a permit shall give away any beer or intoxicating liquor of any kind at any time in connection with† permit holder's business.

(F) Except as otherwise provided in this division, no retail permit holder shall display or permit the display on the outside of any licensed retail premises, or on any lot of ground on which the licensed premises are situated, or on the exterior of any building of which said licensed premises are a part, any sign, illustration, or advertisement bearing the name, brand name, trade name, trade-mark, designation, or other emblem of or indicating the manufacturer, producer, distributor, place of manufacture, production, or distribution of any beer or intoxicating liquor. Signs, illustrations, or advertisements bearing the name, brand name, trade name, trade-mark, designation, or other emblem of or indicating the manufacturer, producer, distributor, place of manufacture, production, or distribution of beer or intoxicating liquor may be displayed and permitted to be displayed on the interior or in the show windows of any licensed premises, if the particular brand or type of product so advertised is actually available for sale on the premises at the time of such display. The liquor control commission shall determine by rule the size and character of such signs, illustrations, or advertisements.

(G) No retail permit holder shall possess on the licensed premises any barrel or other container from which beer is drawn, unless there is attached to the spigot or other dispensing apparatus the name of the manufacturer of the product contained therein, provided that where such beer is served at a bar the manufacturer's name or brand must appear in full view of the purchaser. The commission shall regulate the size and character of the devices provided for in this section.

(H) Except as otherwise provided in this division, no sale of any gift certificate shall be permitted whereby beer or intoxicating liquor of any kind is to be exchanged for such certificate, unless the gift certificate can be exchanged only for food, and beer or intoxicating liquor, for on-premises consumption and the value of the beer or intoxicating liquor for which the certificate can be exchanged does not exceed more than thirty per cent of the total value of the gift certificate. The sale of gift certificates for the purchase of beer, wine, or mixed beverages shall be permitted for the purchase of beer, wine, or mixed beverages for off-premises consumption. Limitations on the use of a gift certificate for the purchase of beer, wine, or mixed beverages for off-premises consumption may be expressed by clearly stamping or typing on the face of the certificate that the certificate may not be used for the purchase of beer, wine, or mixed beverages.

HISTORY: GC § 6064-22; 115 v PtII 118(140), § 22; 116 v 511(535); 117 v 628(644); Bureau of Code Revision, 10-1-53; 128 v 1282 (Eff 10-23-59); 129 v 1211 (Eff 10-7-61); 133 v H 616 (Eff 11-17-69); 134 v H 859 (Eff 4-28-72); 136 v H 158 (Eff 8-13-76); 139 v H 357 (Eff 8-19-82); 140 v S 74 (Eff 7-4-84); 142 v H 419 (Eff 7-31-87); 145 v S 82 (Eff 5-4-94); 145 v S 167 (Eff 11-1-94); 145 v S 209 (Eff 11-9-94); 146 v H 511, § 1 (Eff 8-20-96); 146 v S 162 (Eff 7-1-97); 146 v H 511, § 3. Eff 7-1-97.

† The word "the" was added in 146 v H 511, § 1, eff 8-20-96, division (E).

[§ 4301.25.1] § 4301.251 Emergency suspension of retail permits and retail sales.

Note: See following version effective 3-4-98.

When so ordered by the governor, the director or, beginning on July 1, 1997, the superintendent of liquor control shall immediately and without a hearing suspend, for a period of not less than twenty-four hours nor more than seventy-two hours, any retail beer or liquor permit issued under Chapters 4301. and 4303. of the Revised Code and the retail sales of spirituous liquor by any state liquor store or agency for premises within any area where the director or superintendent designates that civil disorder, looting, or rioting exists.

Such order of emergency suspension shall contain an identifiable description of the area in which such retail permits and sales by stores and agencies are suspended and shall specify the calendar date and hour of the beginning and the calendar date and hour of the ending of such suspension period. A written copy of such order shall be served upon the owner, operator, manager, agent, bartender, or clerk of such beer or liquor permit premises, upon the manager or clerk of a state liquor store, or upon the agent, manager, or clerk of a state liquor agency by any law enforcement agency or officer designated by the director or superintendent.

The law enforcement officer, upon serving such emergency suspension order, shall forthwith fill in and sign a return of service form provided by the director or superintendent of liquor control, on which the officer shall write the name and address of the permit premises or the state liquor store or agency, the name and title of the person on whom such suspension order was served, and the day, hour, and address at which such service was made.

Upon receipt of such copy of the emergency suspension order by the owner, operator, manager, agent, bartender, or clerk of such retail beer or liquor permit premises or the state liquor store or agency, no beer, intoxicating liquor, or spirituous liquor shall be permitted to be consumed or sold at or upon such permit premises or the state liquor store or agency.

Upon completion of the return of service form, the law enforcement officer shall cause it to be transmitted immediately to the nearest district office of the department or, beginning on July 1, 1997, the division of liquor control, where it shall be filed, recorded, and reported forthwith by telephone or teletype to the central office of the department or division of liquor control at Columbus.

Any subsequent order by the governor, to cancel or continue such order of emergency suspension or to diminish or expand the area of the last issued emergency suspension order, shall be processed and carried out in the same manner as that required for the issuance of the original order of emergency suspension.

HISTORY: 132 v H 345 (Eff 7-20-67); 146 v S 162. Eff 10-29-95.

See provisions, § 9 of SB 162 (146 v —) following RC § 4301.01.

[§ 4301.25.1] § 4301.251 Emergency suspension of retail permits and retail sales.

Note: See preceding version in effect until 3-4-98.

When so ordered by the governor, the director or, beginning on July 1, 1997, the superintendent of liquor control shall immediately and without a hearing suspend, for a period of not less than twenty-four hours nor more than seventy-two hours, any retail beer or liquor permit issued under Chapters 4301. and 4303. of the Revised Code and the retail sales of spirituous liquor by any state liquor store or agency for premises within any area where the director or superintendent designates that civil disorder, looting, or rioting exists.

Such order of emergency suspension shall contain an identifiable description of the area in which such retail permits and sales by stores and agencies are suspended and shall specify the calendar date and hour of the beginning and the calendar date and hour of the ending of such suspension period. A written copy of such order shall be served upon the owner, operator, manager, agent, bartender, or clerk of such beer or liquor permit premises, upon the manager or clerk of a state liquor store, or upon the agent, manager, or clerk of a state liquor agency by any law enforcement agency or officer designated by the director or superintendent.

The law enforcement officer, upon serving such emergency suspension order, shall forthwith fill in and sign a return of service form provided by the director or superintendent of liquor control, on which the officer shall write the name and address of the permit premises or the state liquor store or agency, the name and title of the person on whom such suspension order was served, and the day, hour, and address at which such service was made.

Upon receipt of such copy of the emergency suspension order by the owner, operator, manager, agent, bartender, or clerk of such retail beer or liquor permit premises or the state liquor store or agency, no beer, intoxicating liquor, or spirituous liquor shall be permitted to be consumed or sold at or upon such permit premises or the state liquor store or agency.

Upon completion of the return of service form, the law enforcement officer shall cause it to be transmitted immediately to the nearest district office of the department or, beginning on July 1, 1997, the division of liquor control, where it shall be filed, recorded, and reported forthwith by telephone or teletype to the central office of the department or division of liquor control.

Any subsequent order by the governor, to cancel or continue such order of emergency suspension or to diminish or expand the area of the last issued emergency suspension order, shall be processed and carried out in the same manner as that required for the issuance of the original order of emergency suspension.

HISTORY: 132 v H 345 (Eff 7-20-67); 146 v S 162 (Eff 10-29-95); 146 v H 60. Eff 3-4-98.

[SEIZURE AND SALE OF CONVEYANCES]

§ 4301.45 Seizure of illegally transported beer or intoxicating liquor and arrest of violator.

When any law enforcement officer discovers any person in the act of transporting in violation of law beer or intoxicating liquors in any wagon, buggy, automobile, watercraft, aircraft, or other vehicle, he shall seize all beer or intoxicating liquors found therein being transported contrary to law. Whenever beer or intoxicating liquors transported or possessed illegally are seized by a law enforcement officer, the officer shall take possession of the vehicle and team, or automobile, boat, watercraft, aircraft, or any other conveyance, and shall arrest any person in charge thereof. The law enforcement officer shall at once proceed against the person arrested under Chapters 4301. and 4303. of the Revised Code, in any court having jurisdiction of offenses under those chapters, but the vehicle or conveyance shall be returned to the owner upon execution by him of a valid bond with sufficient sureties, in a sum equal to the value of the property, which bond shall be approved by the law enforcement officer and shall be conditioned to return said property to the custody of said officer on the day of trial to abide by the judgment of the court. The court, upon conviction of the person so arrested, shall order the beer or intoxicating liquor that was not illegally manufactured to be forfeited to the state and disposed of under section 2933.41 of the Revised Code, and unless good cause to the contrary is shown by the owner, shall order a sale at public auction of the property seized, and the officer making the sale, after deducting the expenses of keeping the property, the fee for the seizure, and the cost of the sale, shall pay all liens, according to their priorities, which are established, by intervention or otherwise at said hearing or in other proceeding brought for said purpose, as being bona fide and as having been created without the lienor having any notice that the carrying vehicle was being used or was to be used for illegal transportation of beer or intoxicating liquor, and shall distribute the balance as money arising from fines and forfeited bonds under such chapters is distributed. The court, upon conviction of the person so arrested, shall order the beer or intoxicating liquor that was illegally manufactured to be destroyed.

All liens against property sold under this section shall be transferred from the property to the proceeds of the sale of the property. If no claimant is found for the team, vehicle, watercraft, aircraft, automobile, or other conveyance, the taking of the same, with its description, shall be advertised in some newspaper published in the city or county where taken, or if there is no newspaper published in such city or county, in a newspaper having circulation in the county, once a week for four weeks and by handbills posted in three public places near the place of seizure, and if no claimant appears within ten days after the last publication of the advertisement, the property shall be sold and the proceeds after deducting the expense and costs shall be distributed as if there were a claimant for said vehicle or conveyance.

HISTORY: GC § 6212-43; 108 v PtI 401, § 32; 109 v 95; 115 v PtII 118(158), § 62; Bureau of Code Revision, 10-1-53; 138 v S 50 (Eff 5-29-80); 146 v S 162. Eff 10-29-95.

See provisions, § 9 of SB 162 (146 v —) following RC § 4301.01.

[PROHIBITIONS]

§ 4301.47 Records required.

Every class A-1, A-2, and A-4 permit holder and each class B permit holder shall maintain and keep for a period of three years a record of the beer, wine, malt beverages, and mixed beverages purchased, distributed, or sold within this state by the permit holder, together with invoices, records, receipts, bills of lading, and other pertinent papers required by the tax commissioner and, upon demand by the tax commissioner, shall produce these records for a three-year period prior to the demand unless upon satisfactory proof it is shown that the non-production is due to causes beyond his control.

HISTORY: GC § 6064-45; 115 v PtII 118(153), § 45; 116 v PtII 89; Bureau of Code Revision, 10-1-53; 130 v 998 (Eff 1-1-64); 142 v H 231. Eff 10-5-87.

§ 4301.48 False entry upon invoice prohibited.

No person shall make any false entry upon an invoice or upon a container of beer, wine, or mixed beverages required to be made under this chapter and Chapters 4303. and 4307. of the Revised Code, or present any such false entry for the inspection of the tax commissioner.

HISTORY: GC § 6064-46; 115 v PtII 118(153), § 46; 116 v PtII 89; Bureau of Code Revision, 10-1-53; 139 v H 357 (Eff 10-1-82); 143 v S 188. Eff 3-20-90.

§ 4301.49 Interference with inspection prohibited.

No person shall prevent or hinder the tax commissioner from making a full inspection of any place where beer, wine, or mixed beverages subject to the tax imposed by section 4301.42, 4301.421 [4301.42.1], 4301.424 [4301.42.4], or 4301.43 of the Revised Code is manufactured, sold, or stored. No person shall prevent or hinder the full inspection of invoices, books, records, or papers required to be kept under this chapter and Chapters 4305. and 4307. of the Revised Code.

HISTORY: GC § 6064-47; 115 v PtII 118(153), § 47; 116 v PtII 89; Bureau of Code Revision, 10-1-53; 139 v H 357 (Eff 10-1-82); 143 v S 188 (Eff 3-20-90); 146 v S 188. Eff 7-19-95.

§ 4301.53 Search warrants; seizure and disposition of property.

The judge of a court of record may issue warrants to search a house, building, place, vehicle, watercraft, aircraft, or conveyance for beer, alcohol, or intoxicating liquor manufactured, possessed, stored, concealed, sold, furnished, given away, or transported in violation of Chapters 4301. and 4303. of the Revised Code, and the containers in which the same is found, or machinery, tools, implements, equipment, supplies, and materials used or kept for use in manufacturing beer or intoxicating liquor in violation of such chapters, and to seize any of such property and things found therein, together with the vehicle, watercraft, aircraft, or conveyance in which the same is found. The issuance of such warrants is subject in all respects to sections 2933.22 to 2933.27 of the Revised Code; except that any such vehicle, watercraft, aircraft, or other conveyance shall be returned to its owner upon execution by him of a bond with surety to the satisfaction of the liquor control investigator of the department of public safety or other law enforcement officer making the seizure in an equal amount to its value, conditioned upon its return to the custody of such officer on the day of trial to abide by the judgment of the court. Upon conviction of any violation of Chapters 4301. and 4303. of the Revised Code, any property found in the possession of the person convicted or the person's agent or employee shall be disposed of as provided in section 4301.45 of the Revised Code. If the accused is discharged by the judge or magistrate, such vehicle, watercraft, aircraft, or other conveyance shall be returned to its owner and any bond given pursuant to this section shall be canceled. If the accused is the holder of a permit issued under Chapters 4301. and 4303. of the Revised Code, any beer, intoxicating liquor, or alcohol seized shall be disposed of as provided in section 4301.29 of the Revised Code, and any other property seized shall be returned to its owner by the officer having the custody or possession of such property. If the accused is not the holder of such a permit in force at the time, any beer, intoxicating liquor, or alcohol that was not illegally manufactured shall be forfeited to the state and shall forthwith be disposed of under section 2933.41 of the Revised Code. Illegally manufactured beer, intoxicating liquor, or alcohol, and other property, except as provided in this section, shall be destroyed, and any such beer, intoxicating liquor, or alcohol, or other property is hereby declared to be a public nuisance.

HISTORY: GC § 6064-61; 115 v PtII 118(157), § 61; Bureau of Code Revision, 10-1-53; 138 v S 50 (Eff 5-29-80); 146 v S 162. Eff 10-29-95.

See provisions, § 9 of SB 162 (146 v —) following RC § 4301.01.

[ADDITIONAL PROHIBITIONS]

§ 4301.58 Actions prohibited without permit; unauthorized source of liquor.

(A) No person, by himself or herself or by the person's clerk, agent, or employee, who is not the holder of an A permit issued by the division of liquor control, in force at the time, and authorizing the manufacture of beer or intoxicating liquor, or who is not an agent or employee of the division authorized to manufacture such beer or intoxicating liquor, shall manufacture any beer or intoxicating liquor for sale, or shall manufacture spirituous liquor.

(B) No person, by himself or herself or by the person's clerk, agent, or employee, who is not the holder of a B, C, D, E, F, G, or I permit issued by the division, in force at the time, and authorizing the sale of beer, intoxicating liquor, or alcohol, or who is not an agent or employee of the division or the tax commissioner authorized to sell such beer, intoxicating liquor, or alcohol, shall sell, keep, or possess beer, intoxicating liquor, or alcohol for sale to any persons other than those authorized by Chapters 4301. and 4303. of the Revised Code to purchase any beer or intoxicating liquor, or sell any alcohol at retail. This division does not apply to or affect the sale or possession for sale of any low-alcohol beverage.

(C) No person, by himself or herself or by the person's clerk, agent, or employee, who is the holder of a permit issued by the division, shall sell, keep, or possess for sale any intoxicating liquor not purchased from the division or from the holder of a permit issued by the division authorizing the sale of such intoxicating liquor unless the same has been purchased with the special consent of the division. The division shall revoke the permit of any person convicted of a violation of division (C) of this section.

HISTORY: GC § 6064-54; 115 v PtII 118(155), § 54; 116 v

511(540); 117 v 628(651); Bureau of Code Revision, 10-1-53; 145 v S 209 (Eff 11-9-94); 146 v S 162. Eff 7-1-97.

The effective date is set by section 10 of SB 162.

See provisions, § 9 of SB 162 (146 v —) following RC § 4301.01.

§ 4301.59 Fraudulent misrepresentation prohibited.

No person, or his clerk, agent, or employee, shall make or issue any false or fraudulent statement, either orally or in writing, concerning the future value or use of any bonded warehouse receipt for spirituous liquor, or concerning the age, quality, quantity, ingredients, source, future value, or use of the spirituous liquor represented by such receipt for the purpose of promoting or inducing the sale or purchase of such receipt in this state.

HISTORY: GC § 6064-54a; 116 v 511(541); Bureau of Code Revision. Eff 10-1-53.

§ 4301.60 Illegal transportation prohibited.

No person, who is not the holder of an H permit, shall transport beer, intoxicating liquor, or alcohol in this state. This section does not apply to the transportation and delivery of beer, alcohol, or intoxicating liquor purchased or to be purchased from the holder of a permit issued by the division of liquor control, in force at the time, and authorizing the sale and delivery of the beer, alcohol, or intoxicating liquor so transported, or to the transportation and delivery of beer, intoxicating liquor, or alcohol purchased from the division or the tax commissioner, or purchased by the holder of an A or B permit outside this state and transported within this state by them in their own trucks for the purpose of sale under their permits.

HISTORY: GC § 6064-55; 115 v PtII 118(155), § 55; 117 v 628(651); Bureau of Code Revision, 10-1-53; 146 v S 162. Eff 7-1-97.

The effective date is set by section 10 of SB 162.

See provisions, § 9 of SB 162 (146 v —) following RC § 4301.01.

§ 4301.61 Repealed, 146 v S 2, § 6 [GC § 6064-56; 115 v PtII, 118 (156), § 56; 116 v 511(541); Bureau of Code Revision, 10-1-53; 140 v H 37]. Eff 7-1-96.

This section prohibited forging, altering, or counterfeiting labels.

§ 4301.62 Open container law.

(A) As used in this section:
(1) "Chauffeured limousine" means a vehicle registered under section 4503.24 of the Revised Code.

(2) "Street," "highway," and "motor vehicle" have the same meanings as in section 4511.01 of the Revised Code.

(B) No person shall have in the person's possession an opened container of beer or intoxicating liquor in any of the following circumstances:
(1) In a state liquor store;
(2) Except as provided in division (C) of this section, on the premises of the holder of any permit issued by the division of liquor control;
(3) In any other public place;
(4) Except as provided in division (D) of this section, while operating or being a passenger in or on a motor vehicle on any street, highway, or other public or private property open to the public for purposes of vehicular travel or parking;
(5) Except as provided in division (D) of this section, while being in or on a stationary motor vehicle on any street, highway, or other public or private property open to the public for purposes of vehicular travel or parking.

(C) A person may have in the person's possession an opened container of beer or intoxicating liquor that has been lawfully purchased for consumption on the premises where bought of a holder of an A-1-A, A-2, D-1, D-2, D-3, D-3a, D-4, D-4a, D-5, D-5a, D-5b, D-5c, D-5d, D-5e, D-5f, D-5g, D-5h, D-5i, D-7, E, F, or F-2 permit, or beer or intoxicating liquor consumed on the premises of a convention facility as provided in section 4303.201 [4303.20.1] of the Revised Code.

A person may have in the person's possession on an F liquor permit premises an opened container of beer or intoxicating liquor that was not purchased from the holder of the F permit if the premises for which the F permit is issued is a music festival and the holder of the F permit grants permission for such possession on the premises during the period for which the F permit is issued. As used in this division, "music festival" means a series of outdoor live musical performances, extending for a period of at least three consecutive days and located on an area of land of at least forty acres.

(D) This section does not apply to a person who pays all or a portion of the fee imposed for the use of a chauffeured limousine pursuant to a prearranged contract, or the guest of such a person, when all of the following apply:
(1) The person or guest is a passenger in the limousine;
(2) The person or guest is located in the limousine, but is not occupying a seat in the front compartment of the limousine where the operator of the limousine is located;
(3) The limousine is located on any street, highway, or other public or private property open to the public for purposes of vehicular travel or parking.

HISTORY: 145 v H 281 (Eff 7-2-93); 146 v S 39 (Eff 7-14-95); 146 v S 162 (Eff 7-1-97); 147 v S 85. Eff 5-15-97.

Analogous to former RC § 4301.62 (GC § 6064-57; 115 v PtII 118(156), § 57; 116 v. 511(541); 117 v 628(652); Bureau of Code

Revision, 10-1-53; 133 v H 150; 136 v H 613; 139 v H 357; 140 v H 502; 140 v H 711; 141 v H 359; 142 v H 562; 143 v S 131; 143 v H 405; 145 v H 152), repealed 145 v H 281, § 2, eff 7-2-93.

See provisions, § 9 of SB 162 (146 v —) following RC § 4301.01.

The provisions of § 3 of SB 85 (147 v —) read as follows:

SECTION 3. Section 4301.62 of the Revised Code is amended by this act and also by Am. Sub. S.B. 162 of the 121st General Assembly (effective July 1, 1997). The amendments of Am. Sub. S.B. 162 are included in this act in lower case to confirm the intention to retain them, but are not intended to be effective until July 1, 1997.

§ 4301.63 Persons under twenty-one not to purchase beer or intoxicating liquor.

Except as otherwise provided in this chapter, no person under the age of twenty-one years shall purchase beer or intoxicating liquor.

HISTORY: GC § 6064-57a; 118 v 691; Bureau of Code Revision, 10-1-53; 125 v 113 (Eff 10-2-53); 136 v H 315 (Eff 4-25-75); 139 v H 357 (Eff 8-19-82); 142 v H 419. Eff 7-31-87.

[§ 4301.63.1] § 4301.631 Underage person not to purchase or consume low-alcohol beverage.

(A) As used in this section, "underage person" means a person under eighteen years of age.

(B) No underage person shall purchase any low-alcohol beverage.

(C) No underage person shall order, pay for, share the cost of, or attempt to purchase any low-alcohol beverage.

(D) No person shall knowingly furnish any false information as to the name, age, or other identification of any underage person for the purpose of obtaining or with the intent to obtain any low-alcohol beverage for an underage person, by purchase or as a gift.

(E) No underage person shall knowingly show or give false information concerning the person's name, age, or other identification for the purpose of purchasing or otherwise obtaining any low-alcohol beverage in any place in this state.

(F) No person shall sell or furnish any low-alcohol beverage to, or buy any low-alcohol beverage for, an underage person, unless given by a physician in the regular line of his practice or given for established religious purposes, or unless the underage person is accompanied by a parent, spouse who is not an underage person, or legal guardian.

No permit issued by the division of liquor control shall be suspended, revoked, or canceled because of a violation of this division or division (G) of this section.

(G) No person who is the owner or occupant of any public or private place shall knowingly allow any underage person to remain in or on the place while possessing or consuming any low-alcohol beverage, unless the low-alcohol beverage is given to the person possessing or consuming it by that person's parent, spouse who is not an underage person, or legal guardian, and the parent, spouse who is not an underage person, or legal guardian is present when the person possesses or consumes the low-alcohol beverage.

An owner of a public or private place is not liable for acts or omissions in violation of this division that are committed by a lessee of that place, unless the owner authorizes or acquiesces in the lessee's acts or omissions.

(H) No underage person shall knowingly possess or consume any low-alcohol beverage in any public or private place, unless accompanied by a parent, spouse who is not an underage person, or legal guardian, or unless the low-alcohol beverage is given by a physician in the regular line of the physician's practice or given for established religious purposes.

(I) No parent, spouse who is not an underage person, or legal guardian of an underage person shall knowingly permit the underage person to violate this section.

HISTORY: 145 v S 209 (Eff 11-9-94); 146 v S 162. Eff 7-1-97.

Not analogous to former RC § 4301.631 (130 v 998; 139 v H 357), repealed 142 v H 419, § 2, eff 7-31-87.

The effective date is set by section 10 of SB 162.

See provisions, § 9 of SB 162 (146 v —) following RC § 4301.01.

[§ 4301.63.2] § 4301.632 Persons under twenty-one not to purchase or consume beer or intoxicating liquor.

Except as otherwise provided in this chapter, no person under the age of twenty-one years shall order, pay for, share the cost of, or attempt to purchase any beer or intoxicating liquor, or consume any beer or intoxicating liquor, either from a sealed or unsealed container or by the glass or by the drink, or possess any beer or intoxicating liquor, in any public or private place.

HISTORY: 130 v 998 (Eff 9-20-63); 142 v H 419 (Eff 7-31-87); 143 v H 22. Eff 8-1-89.

[§ 4301.63.3] § 4301.633 Misrepresentation to obtain beer or intoxicating liquor for person under twenty-one.

Except as otherwise provided in this chapter, no person shall knowingly furnish any false information as to the name, age, or other identification of any person under twenty-one years of age for the purpose of obtaining or with the intent to obtain, beer or intoxicating liquor for a person under twenty-one years of age, by purchase, or as a gift.

HISTORY: 130 v 999 (Eff 9-20-63); 139 v H 357 (Eff 8-19-82); 142 v H 419. Eff 7-31-87.

[§ 4301.63.4] § 4301.634 Misrepresentation by person under twenty-one.

Except as otherwise provided in this chapter, no person under the age of twenty-one years shall knowingly show or give false information concerning the person's name, age, or other identification for the purpose of purchasing or otherwise obtaining beer or intoxicating liquor in any place in this state where beer or intoxicating liquor is sold under a permit issued by the division of liquor control or sold by the division.

HISTORY: 130 v 999 (Eff 9-20-63); 139 v H 357 (Eff 8-19-82); 142 v H 419 (Eff 7-31-87); 146 v S 162. Eff 7-1-97.

The effective date is set by section 10 of SB 162.

See provisions, § 9 of SB 162 (146 v —) following RC § 4301.01.

[§ 4301.63.6] § 4301.636 Furnishing false identification card or driver's license.

(A)(1) No person shall manufacture, transfer, or distribute in any manner any identification card issued for the purpose of establishing a person's age that displays the great seal of the state of Ohio, the word "Ohio," "state," or "official," or any other designation that represents the card as the official identification card of Ohio, except for those cards issued pursuant to section 4507.50 of the Revised Code.

(2) No person shall manufacture, sell, or distribute in any manner for any compensation any identification card issued for the purpose of establishing a person's age that displays the great seal of the state of Ohio, the word "Ohio," "state," or "official," or any other designation that represents the card as the official identification card of Ohio, except for those cards issued pursuant to section 4507.50 of the Revised Code.

(B)(1) No person, other than the registrar of motor vehicles or a deputy registrar, shall manufacture, transfer, or distribute in any manner any card that displays the great seal of the state of Ohio, the word "Ohio," "state," "official," "chauffeur," "chauffeur's," "commercial driver," "commercial driver's," "driver," "driver's," "operator," or "operator's," or any other designation that represents the card as the official driver's license of the state.

(2) No person, other than the registrar of motor vehicles or a deputy registrar, shall manufacture, sell, or distribute in any manner for any compensation any card that displays the great seal of the state of Ohio, the word "Ohio," "state," "official," "chauffeur," "chauffeur's," "commercial driver," "commercial driver's," "driver," "driver's," "operator," or "operator's," or any other designation that represents the card as the official driver's license of the state.

HISTORY: 142 v H 419 (Eff 7-31-87); 143 v S 131. Eff 7-25-90.

Not analogous to former RC § 4301.63.6 (130 v 999), repealed 134 v H 109, eff 9-8-71.

[§ 4301.63.7] § 4301.637 Posting of warning cards as to underage persons and firearms.

(A) Except as otherwise provided in section 4301.691 [4301.69.1] of the Revised Code, every place in this state where beer, intoxicating liquor, or any low-alcohol beverage is sold for beverage purposes shall display at all times, in a prominent place on the premises thereof, a printed card, which shall be furnished by the division of liquor control and which shall read substantially as follows:

"WARNING TO PERSONS UNDER AGE
If you are under the age of 21
Under the statutes of the state of Ohio, if you order, pay for, share the cost of, or attempt to purchase, or possess or consume beer or intoxicating liquor in any public place, or furnish false information as to name, age, or other identification, you are subject to a fine of up to one thousand dollars, or imprisonment up to six months, or both.

If you are under the age of 18
Under the statutes of the state of Ohio, if you order, pay for, share the cost of, or attempt to purchase, or possess or consume, any type of beer or wine that contains either no alcohol or less than one-half of one per cent of alcohol by volume in any public place, or furnish false information as to name, age, or other identification, you are subject to a fine of up to two hundred fifty dollars or to imprisonment up to thirty days, or both."

No person shall be subject to any criminal prosecution or any proceedings before the division or the liquor control commission for failing to display this card. No permit issued by the division shall be suspended, revoked, or canceled because of the failure of the permit holder to display this card.

(B) Every place in this state for which a D permit has been issued under Chapter 4303. of the Revised Code shall be issued a printed card by the division that shall read substantially as follows:

"WARNING
If you are carrying a firearm
Under the statutes of Ohio, if you possess a firearm in any room in which liquor is being dispensed in premises for which a D permit has been issued under Chapter 4303. of the Revised Code, you may be guilty of a felony and may be subjected to a prison term of up to one year."

No person shall be subject to any criminal prosecution or any proceedings before the division or the liquor control commission for failing to display this card. No permit issued by the division shall be suspended, revoked, or canceled because of the failure of the permit holder to display this card.

HISTORY: 130 v 999 (Eff 9-20-63); 131 v 1047 (Eff 11-3-65); 132 v H 1 (Eff 2-21-67); 137 v S 49 (Eff 11-14-77); 139 v H 357 (Eff 8-19-82); 141 v H 51 (Eff 7-30-86); 141 v H 39 (Eff 2-21-87); 142 v H 419 (Eff 7-31-87); 145 v S 209 (Eff 11-9-94); 146 v S 2 (Eff 7-1-96); 146 v S 162. Eff 7-1-97.

See provisions, § 9 of SB 162 (146 v —) following RC § 4301.01.

Comment, Legislative Service Commission

° ° ° Sections 4301.637 and 4399.12 of the Revised Code

are amended by this act [Am. Sub. S.B. 162] (effective July 1, 1997) and also by Am. Sub. S.B. 2 of the 121st General Assembly (effective July 1, 1996). ° ° ° Comparison of these amendments in pursuance to section 1.52 of the Revised code discloses that they are not irreconcilable so that they are required by that section to be harmonized to give effect to each amendment.

[§ 4301.63.8] § 4301.638 No modification of other sections intended.

Sections 4301.632 [4301.63.2] to 4301.637 [4301.63.7] of the Revised Code shall not be deemed to modify or affect division (A) of section 4301.22 or section 4301.69 of the Revised Code.

HISTORY: 130 v 1000 (Eff 9-20-63); 142 v H 419. Eff 7-31-87.

[§ 4301.63.9] § 4301.639 Good faith acceptance of false identification.

No permit holder, his agent or employee, or any other person may be found guilty of a violation of any section of this chapter or any rule of the liquor control commission in which age is an element of the offense, if the liquor control commission or any court of record finds all of the following:

(A) That the person buying, at the time of so doing, exhibited to the permit holder, his agent or employee, or the other person a driver's or commercial driver's license or an identification card issued under sections 4507.50 to 4507.52 of the Revised Code showing that the person buying was then at least twenty-one years of age if he was buying beer as defined in section 4301.01 of the Revised Code or intoxicating liquor or that he was then at least eighteen years of age if he was buying any low-alcohol beverage;

(B) That the permit holder, his agent or employee, or the other person made a bona fide effort to ascertain the true age of the person buying by checking the identification presented, at the time of the purchase, to ascertain that the description on the identification compared with the appearance of the buyer and that the identification presented had not been altered in any way;

(C) That the permit holder, his agent or employee, or the other person had reason to believe that the person buying was of legal age.

In any hearing before the liquor control commission and in any action or proceeding before a court of record in which a defense is raised under this section, the registrar of motor vehicles or his deputy who issued an identification card under sections 4507.50 to 4507.52 of the Revised Code shall be permitted to submit certified copies of the records, in his possession, of such issuance in lieu of the testimony of the personnel of the bureau of motor vehicles at such hearing, action, or proceeding.

HISTORY: 134 v H 453 (Eff 9-28-72); 137 v H 90 (Eff 1-17-78); 143 v H 381 (Eff 7-1-89); 145 v S 209. Eff 11-9-94.

§ 4301.64 Prohibition against consumption in motor vehicle.

No person shall consume any beer or intoxicating liquor in a motor vehicle. This section does not apply to persons described in division (D) of section 4301.62 of the Revised Code.

HISTORY: GC § 6064-58; 115 v PtII 118(156), § 58; Bureau of Code Revision, 10-1-53; 130 v 1000 (Eff 7-11-63); 146 v S 39. Eff 7-14-95.

§ 4301.66 Obstructing search of premises prohibited.

No person shall hinder or obstruct any agent or employee of the department or, beginning on July 1, 1997, the division of liquor control, any liquor control investigator of the department of public safety, or any officer of the law, from making inspection or search of any place, other than a bona fide private residence, where beer or intoxicating liquor is possessed, kept, sold, or given away.

HISTORY: GC § 6064-63; 116 v 511(542); Bureau of Code Revision, 10-1-53; 139 v H 357 (Eff 10-1-82); 146 v S 162. Eff 10-29-95.

See provisions, § 9 of SB 162 (146 v —) following RC § 4301.01.

§ 4301.67 Illegal possession of intoxicating liquor prohibited.

No person shall have that person's possession of† any spirituous liquor, in excess of one liter, in one or more containers, which was not purchased at wholesale or retail from the division of liquor control or otherwise lawfully acquired pursuant to Chapters 4301. and 4303. of the Revised Code, or any other intoxicating liquor or beer, in one or more containers, which was not lawfully acquired pursuant to Chapters 4301. and 4303. of the Revised Code.

HISTORY: GC § 6064-64; 116 v 511(542); Bureau of Code Revision, 10-1-53; 128 v 1282 (Eff 10-23-59); 133 v H 638 (Eff 10-22-69); 139 v H 357 (Eff 10-1-82); 146 v S 149 (Eff 11-21-95); 146 v S 162. Eff 7-1-97.

Publisher's Note

The amendments made by SB 149 (146 v —) and SB 162 (147 v —) have been combined. Please see provisions of RC § 1.52.

The effective date is set by section 10 of SB 162.

See provisions, § 9 of SB 162 (146 v —) following RC § 4301.01.

† Wording is the result of combining SB 149 (146 v —) and SB 162 (146 v —).

§ 4301.68 Prohibition against sale or possession of diluted liquor and refilled containers.
(GC § 6064-68)

No person shall sell, offer for sale, or possess intoxicating liquor in any original container which has been diluted, refilled, or partly refilled.

HISTORY: GC § 6064-68; 119 v 217; Bureau of Code Revision. Eff 10-1-53.

§ 4301.69 Offenses involving underage persons.

(A) Except as otherwise provided in this chapter, no person shall sell beer or intoxicating liquor to an underage person, shall buy beer or intoxicating liquor for an underage person, or shall furnish it to an underage person, unless given by a physician in the regular line of his practice or given for established religious purposes or unless the underage person is accompanied by a parent, spouse who is not an underage person, or legal guardian.

In proceedings before the liquor control commission, no permit holder, or the employee or agent of a permit holder, charged with a violation of this division shall be charged, for the same offense, with a violation of division (A)(1) of section 4301.22 of the Revised Code.

(B) No person who is the owner or occupant of any public or private place shall knowingly allow any underage person to remain in or on the place while possessing or consuming beer or intoxicating liquor, unless the intoxicating liquor or beer is given to the person possessing or consuming it by that person's parent, spouse who is not an underage person, or legal guardian and the parent, spouse who is not an underage person, or legal guardian is present at the time of the person's possession or consumption of the beer or intoxicating liquor.

An owner of a public or private place is not liable for acts or omissions in violation of this division that are committed by a lessee of that place, unless the owner authorizes or acquiesces in the lessee's acts or omissions.

(C) No person shall engage or use accommodations at a hotel, inn, cabin, campground, or restaurant when he knows or has reason to know either of the following:

(1) That beer or intoxicating liquor will be consumed by an underage person on the premises of the accommodations that the person engages or uses, unless the person engaging or using the accommodations is the spouse of the underage person and who is not himself an underage person, or is the parent or legal guardian of all of the underage persons, who consume beer or intoxicating liquor on the premises and that person is on the premises at all times when beer or intoxicating liquor is being consumed by an underage person;

(2) That a drug of abuse will be consumed on the premises of the accommodations by any person, except a person who obtained the drug of abuse pursuant to a prescription issued by a practitioner and has the drug of abuse in the original container in which it was dispensed to the person.

(D)(1) No person is required to permit the engagement of accommodations at any hotel, inn, cabin, or campground by an underage person or for an underage person, if the person engaging the accomodations knows or has reason to know that the underage person is intoxicated, or that the underage person possesses any beer or intoxicating liquor and is not accompanied by a parent, spouse who is not an underage person, or legal guardian who is or will be present at all times when the beer or intoxicating liquor is being consumed by the underage person.

(2) No underage person shall knowingly engage or attempt to engage accommodations at any hotel, inn, cabin, or campground by presenting identification that falsely indicates that he is twenty-one years of age or older for the purpose of violating this section.

(E) No underage person shall knowingly possess or consume any beer or intoxicating liquor, in any public or private place, unless he is accompanied by a parent, spouse who is not an underage person, or legal guardian, or unless the beer or intoxicating liquor is given by a physician in the regular line of his practice or given for established religious purposes.

(F) No parent, spouse who is not an underage person, or legal guardian of a minor shall knowingly permit the minor to violate this section or section 4301.63, 4301.632 [4301.63.2], 4301.633 [4301.63.3], or 4301.634 [4301.63.4] of the Revised Code.

(G) The operator of any hotel, inn, cabin, or campground shall make the provisions of this section available in writing to any person engaging or using accommodations at the hotel, inn, cabin, or campground.

(H) As used in this section:

(1) "Drug of abuse" has the same meaning as in section 3719.011 [3719.01.1] of the Revised Code.

(2) "Hotel" has the same meaning as in section 3731.01 of the Revised Code.

(3) "Minor" means a person under the age of eighteen years.

(4) "Practitioner" and "prescription" have the same meanings as in section 3719.01 of the Revised Code.

(5) "Underage person" means a person under the age of twenty-one years.

HISTORY: RS § 6943; 63 v 149, § 2; GC § 12960; 113 v 495; 115 v Pt II, 118(161), § 62; 116 v 279; Bureau of Code Revision, 10-1-53; 132 v S 128 (Eff 11-24-67); 136 v H 315 (Eff 4-25-75); 139 v H 357 (Eff 8-19-82); 142 v H 419 (Eff 7-31-87); 142 v H 306 (Eff 6-9-88); 143 v H 22 (Eff 8-1-89); 145 v S 82. Eff 5-4-94.

The effective date is set by section 6 of SB 82.

[§ 4301.69.1] § 4301.691 Alternate prohibitions if federal mandate is no longer in force.

If the United States congress repeals the mandate established by the "Surface Transportation Assistance Act of 1982" relating to a national uniform drinking age of twenty-one or if a court of competent jurisdiction declares the mandate to be unconstitutional or otherwise invalid, then upon the certification by the secretary of state that this mandate has been repealed or invalidated, the following shall apply:

(A) Beer or intoxicating liquor may be served to a person not seated at a table unless there is reason to believe that the beer will be consumed by a person under nineteen years of age or that the intoxicating liquor will be consumed by a person under twenty-one years of age.

(B) No person under the age of twenty-one years shall purchase intoxicating liquor, nor shall a person under the age of nineteen years purchase beer.

(C) No person under the age of nineteen years shall order, pay for, share the cost of, or attempt to purchase any beer or intoxicating liquor, or consume any beer or intoxicating liquor, either from a sealed or unsealed container or by the glass or by the drink, in any public or private place, except as provided in section 4301.69 of the Revised Code.

(D) No person under the age of twenty-one years shall order, pay for, share the cost of, or attempt to purchase any intoxicating liquor, or consume any intoxicating liquor, either from a sealed or unsealed container or by the glass or by the drink, except as provided in section 4301.69 of the Revised Code.

(E) No person shall knowingly furnish any false information as to the name, age, or other identification of any person under twenty-one years of age for the purpose of obtaining or with the intent to obtain, beer or intoxicating liquor for a person under nineteen years of age, or intoxicating liquor for a person under twenty-one years of age, by purchase, or as a gift.

(F) No person under the age of nineteen years shall knowingly show or give false information concerning the person's name, age, or other identification for the purpose of purchasing or otherwise obtaining beer or intoxicating liquor in any place in this state where beer or intoxicating liquor is sold under a permit issued by the division of liquor control or sold by the division.

(G) No person under the age of twenty-one years shall knowingly show or give false information concerning the person's name, age, or other identification for the purpose of purchasing or otherwise obtaining intoxicating liquor in any place in this state where intoxicating liquor is sold under a permit issued by the division or sold by the division.

(H) No person shall sell intoxicating liquor to a person under the age of twenty-one years or sell beer to a person under the age of nineteen, or buy intoxicating liquor for, or furnish it to, a person under the age of twenty-one years, or buy beer for or furnish it to a person under the age of nineteen, unless given by a physician in the regular line of his practice, or by a parent or legal guardian.

In proceedings before the liquor control commission, no permit holder or the permit holder's employee or agent charged with a violation of this section shall, for the same offense, be charged with a violation of division (A)(1) of section 4301.22 of the Revised Code.

(I) No person who is the owner or occupant of any public or private place shall knowingly allow any person under the age of twenty-one to remain in or on the place while possessing or consuming intoxicating liquor, or knowingly allow any person under the age of nineteen to remain in or on the place while possessing or consuming beer, unless the intoxicating liquor or beer is given to the person possessing or consuming it by that person's parent or legal guardian and the parent or legal guardian is present at the time of the person's possession or consumption of the intoxicating liquor or beer.

(J) The division shall revise the warning sign required by section 4301.637 [4301.63.7] of the Revised Code so that the sign conforms to this section.

HISTORY: 142 v H 419 (Eff 7-31-87); 142 v H 306 (Eff 6-9-88); 143 v H 22 (Eff 8-1-89); 145 v S 82 (Eff 5-4-94); 146 v S 162. Eff 7-1-97.

The effective date is set by section 10 of SB 162.

See provisions, § 9 of SB 162 (146 v —) following RC § 4301.01.

§ 4301.70 Prohibition against violations not otherwise specified.

Any person who is subject to Chapter 4301., 4303., or 4307. of the Revised Code, in the transportation, possession, or sale of wine or mixed beverage subject to the taxes imposed by sections 4301.43 and 4301.432 [4301.43.2] of the Revised Code, and who violates such chapters or any lawful rule promulgated by the tax commissioner under such chapters, for the violation of which no penalty is otherwise provided, shall be fined as provided in division (A) of section 4301.99 of the Revised Code.

HISTORY: GC § 6064-50; 115 v Pt II, 118(154), § 50; 116 v Pt II, 89; Bureau of Code Revision, 10-1-53; 125 v 903(1024) (10-1-53); 139 v H 694 (Eff 11-15-81); 139 v H 357. Eff 10-1-82.

The effective date is set by section 6 of HB 357.

[NUISANCE]

§ 4301.73 Premises constituting nuisance; temporary injunction; abatement and closing orders.

Any room, house, building, boat, vehicle, structure, or place where beer or intoxicating liquor is manufactured, sold, bartered, possessed, or kept in violation of law, and all property kept and used in maintaining the same, and all property designed for the unlawful manufacture of beer or intoxicating liquor, and beer or intoxicating liquor contained in such room, house, building, boat, structure, or place is a common nuisance.

An action to enjoin such nuisance may be brought in the name of the state by the attorney general or by any prosecuting attorney of any county or any officer of the law of any municipal corporation or by the division of liquor control.†

Such action shall be brought and tried as an action in equity and may be brought in any court having jurisdiction to hear and determine equity cases. If it appears, by affidavits or otherwise, to the satisfaction of the court, or judge in vacation, that such nuisance exists, a temporary writ of injunction shall forthwith issue restraining the defendant from conducting or permitting the continuance of such nuisance until the conclusion of the trial. If a temporary injunction is prayed for, the court may issue an order restraining the defendant and all other persons from removing or in any way interfering with the beer or intoxicating liquor, property designed for the manufacture of beer or intoxicating liquors, fixtures, or other things, used in connection with the violation of this section, constituting such nuisance.

No bond shall be required in instituting such proceedings. The court need not find the property involved was being unlawfully used at the time of the hearing, but on finding that the material allegations of the petition are true, the court shall order that no beer or intoxicating liquors shall be manufactured, sold, bartered, possessed, kept, or stored in such room, house, building, structure, place, boat, or vehicle, or any part thereof.

Upon judgment of the court ordering such nuisance to be abated, the court may order that the room, house, building, structure, place, boat, or vehicle shall not be occupied or used for one year thereafter; but the court may permit it to be occupied or used if its owner, lessee, tenant, or occupant gives a bond with sufficient surety, to be approved by the court making the order, in the sum of not less than one thousand nor more than five thousand dollars, payable to the state, and conditioned that beer or intoxicating liquor will not thereafter be manufactured, sold, bartered, possessed, kept, stored, transported, or otherwise disposed of therein in violation of law, and that the person will pay all fines, costs, and damages that may be assessed for any such violation. For closing the premises and keeping them closed, a reasonable sum shall be allowed the officer by the court.

HISTORY: GC § 13195-1; 110 v 34; 115 v PtII 118(162), § 62; Bureau of Code Revision, 10-1-53; 145 v S 167 (Eff 11-1-94); 146 v S 162. Eff 7-1-97.

The effective date is set by section 10 of SB 162.

See provisions, § 9 of SB 162 (146 v —) following RC § 4301.01.

† The paragraph enacted in SB 167 (145 v), effective 11-1-94, does not appear in the amendment of RC § 4301.73 in SB 162 (146 v —), effective 7-1-97.

§ 4301.74 Procedure when injunction violated.

Any person subject to an injunction, temporary or permanent, granted pursuant to section 4301.73 of the Revised Code, shall obey such injunction. If such person violates such injunction, the court or in vacation a judge thereof, may summarily try and punish the violator. The proceedings for punishment for contempt shall be commenced by filing with the clerk of the court from which such injunction issued information under oath setting out the alleged facts constituting the violation, whereupon the court shall forthwith cause a warrant to issue under which the defendant shall be arrested. The trial may be had upon affidavits, or either party may demand the production and oral examination of the witnesses.

HISTORY: GC § 13195-3; 110 v 34; 115 v Pt II, 118(162), § 62; Bureau of Code Revision. Eff 10-1-53.

§ 4301.99 Penalties.

(A) Whoever violates section 4301.47, 4301.48, 4301.49, 4301.62, or 4301.70 or division (B) of section 4301.691 [4301.69.1] of the Revised Code is guilty of a minor misdemeanor.

(B) Whoever violates section 4301.15, division (A)(2) or (D) of section 4301.22, division (C), (D), (E), (F), (G), (H), or (I) of section 4301.631 [4301.63.1], or section 4301.64 or 4301.67 of the Revised Code is guilty of a misdemeanor of the fourth degree.

(C) Whoever violates division (D) of section 4301.21, or section 4301.251 [4301.25.1], 4301.58, 4301.59, 4301.60, 4301.632 [4301.63.2], 4301.633 [4301.63.3], 4301.66, 4301.68, or 4301.74, division (B), (C), (D), (E), or (F) of section 4301.69 of the Revised Code, or division (C), (D), (E), (F), (G), or (I) of section 4301.691 [4301.69.1] of the Revised Code is guilty of a misdemeanor of the first degree.

(D) Whoever violates division (B) of section 4301.14, or division (A)(1) or (3), (B), or (C) of section 4301.22 of the Revised Code is guilty of a misdemeanor of the third degree.

(E) Whoever violates section 4301.63 or division (B) of section 4301.631 [4301.63.1] of the Revised Code shall be fined not less than twenty-five nor more than one hundred dollars. The court imposing a fine for a violation of section 4301.63 or division (B) of section 4301.631 [4301.63.1] of the Revised Code may order that the fine be paid by the performance of public work at a reasonable hourly rate established by the court. The court shall designate the time within which the public work shall be completed.

(F)(1) Whoever violates section 4301.634 [4301.63.4] of the Revised Code is guilty of a misdemeanor of the first degree. If, in committing a first violation of that section, the offender presented to the permit holder or the permit holder's employee or agent a false, fictitious, or altered identification card, a false or fictitious driver's license purportedly issued by any state, or a driver's license issued by any state that has been altered, the offender is guilty of a misdemeanor of the first degree and shall be fined not less than two hundred fifty and not more than one thousand dollars, and may be sentenced to a term of imprisonment of not more than six months.

(2) On a second violation in which, for the second time, the offender presented to the permit holder or the permit holder's employee or agent a false, fictitious, or altered identification card, a false or fictitious driver's license purportedly issued by any state, or a driver's license issued by any state that has been altered, the offender is guilty of a misdemeanor of the first degree and shall be fined not less than five hundred nor more than one thousand dollars, and may be sentenced to a term of imprisonment of not more than six months. The court also may suspend the offender's driver's or commercial driver's license or permit or nonresident operating privilege or deny the offender the opportunity to be issued a driver's or commercial driver's license for a period not exceeding sixty days.

(3) On a third or subsequent violation in which, for the third or subsequent time, the offender presented to the permit holder or the permit holder's employee or agent a false, fictitious, or altered identification card, a false or fictitious driver's license purportedly issued by any state, or a driver's license issued by any state that has been altered, the offender is guilty of a misdemeanor of the first degree and shall be fined not less than five hundred nor more than one thousand dollars, and may be sentenced to a term of imprisonment of not more than six months. The court also shall suspend the offender's driver's or commercial driver's license or permit or nonresident operating privilege or deny the offender the opportunity to be issued a driver's or commercial driver's license for a period of ninety days, and the court may order that the suspension or denial remain in effect until the offender attains the age of twenty-one years. The court also may order the offender to perform a determinate number of hours of community service, with the court determining the actual number of hours and the nature of the community service the offender shall perform.

(G) Whoever violates section 4301.636 [4301.63.6] of the Revised Code is guilty of a felony of the fifth degree.

(H) Whoever violates division (A)(1) of section 4301.22 of the Revised Code is guilty of a misdemeanor, shall be fined not less than five hundred and not more than one thousand dollars, and, in addition to the fine, may be imprisoned for a definite term of not more than sixty days.

(I) Whoever violates division (A) of section 4301.69 or division (H) of section 4301.691 [4301.69.1] of the Revised Code is guilty of a misdemeanor, shall be fined not less than five hundred and not more than one thousand dollars, and, in addition to the fine, may be imprisoned for a definite term of not more than six months.

HISTORY: 135 v H 352 (Eff 9-30-74); 135 v H 496 (Eff 9-30-74); 136 v H 1 (Eff 6-13-75); 136 v H 158 (Eff 8-13-76); 137 v S 49 (Eff 11-14-77); 140 v S 74 (Eff 7-4-84); 142 v H 419 (Eff 7-31-87); 142 v H 562 (Eff 6-29-88); 142 v H 306 (Eff 6-9-88); 143 v S 131 (Eff 7-25-90); 145 v S 82 (Eff 5-4-94); 145 v S 209 (Eff 11-9-94); 146 v S 2. Eff 7-1-96.

Analogous to former RC § 4301.99 (Bureau of Code Revision, 10-1-53; 125 v 113; 126 v 324; 130 v 1000; 130 v 1003; 130 v 1002; 132 v H 345) repealed 135 v H 352 and H 496, eff 9-30-74.

The effective date is set by section 6 of SB 2.

[§ 4301.99.1] § 4301.991 Duty to send notice of conviction or acquittal.

Upon the trial of a permit holder, the permit holder's employee, or the permit holder's agent for a violation of sections 4301.01 to 4301.74 of the Revised Code occurring on the premises for which a permit issued by the department or, beginning on July 1, 1997, the division of liquor control is held by the permit holder, the magistrate or the clerk of the municipal court or of the court of common pleas shall, if the permit holder, the permit holder's employee, or the permit holder's agent is found guilty, within seven days after the sentence has been imposed mail a certified copy of the record of such conviction to the director of public safety, who shall forward a copy of that certified copy to the director or, beginning on July 1, 1997, the superintendent of liquor control.

If the permit holder, the permit holder's employee, or the permit holder's agent is found to be not guilty after a trial on the merits, the magistrate or clerk of the municipal court or of the court of common pleas shall within seven days mail a certified copy of the journal entry to the director or superintendent of liquor control and the permit holder shall not be cited to the liquor control commission for any alleged violations of law or rules based upon specifications contained in the indictment, information, or affidavit in the case.

HISTORY: 126 v 324 (Eff 10-4-55); 140 v S 72 (Eff 10-14-83); 146 v S 162. Eff 10-29-95.

See provisions, § 9 of SB 162 (146 v —) following RC § 4301.01.

CHAPTER 4399: PROHIBITORY PROVISIONS AND CRIMES

§ 4399.09 Keeping place where beer or intoxicating liquors are furnished in violation of law.

No person shall keep a place where beer or intoxicating liquors are sold, furnished, or given away in violation of law. The court, on conviction for a subsequent offense, shall order the place where such beer or intoxicating liquor is sold, furnished, or given away to be abated as a nuisance, or shall order the person convicted for such offense to give bond payable to the state in the sum of one thousand dollars, with sureties to the acceptance of the court, that such person will not sell, furnish, or give away beer or intoxicating liquor in violation of law, and will pay all fines, costs, and damages assessed against him for such violation. The giving away of beer or intoxicating liquors, or other device to evade this section, constitutes unlawful selling.

As used in this section, "beer" has the meaning set forth in section 4301.01 of the Revised Code.

HISTORY: RS § 6942; S&C 1431; 52 v 153; 92 v 55; 99 v 470; GC § 13195; Bureau of Code Revision, 10-1-53; 140 v S 74. Eff 7-4-84.

§ 4399.10 Intoxicating liquors shall not be sold in brothels.

No person shall sell, exchange, or give away intoxicating liquor in a brothel.

HISTORY: RS §§ 6943-5, 6943-6; GC § 13199; 88 v 567, § 2; Bureau of Code Revision. Eff 10-1-53.

§ 4399.11 Selling intoxicating liquors or keeping house of ill fame at certain places prohibited.

If a person is convicted of any violation of Title XLIII [43] of the Revised Code that involves the sale of intoxicating liquors at or within twelve hundred yards of the administration or main central building of the Columbus state hospital, Dayton state hospital, Athens state hospital, or Toledo state hospital, or within two miles of the place at which an agricultural fair is being held, or within one mile of a county children's home situated within one mile of a municipal corporation in which the sale of intoxicating liquors is prohibited by ordinance, the place in which the intoxicating liquors are sold shall be shut up and abated as a nuisance by order of the court upon conviction of its owner or keeper.

HISTORY: RS § 6946; S&C 68; 53 v 141, § 3; 71 v 82; 82 v 222; 84 v 70; 85 v 19; 88 v 603; 92 v 434; 93 v 341; GC § 13206; Bureau of Code Revision, 10-1-53; 137 v S 420 (Eff 7-24-78); 138 v H 965 (Eff 4-9-81); 146 v H 117 (Eff 9-29-95); 146 v S 2. Eff 7-1-96.

The effective date is set by section 6 of SB 2.

Comment, Legislative Service Commission

° ° ° Section ° ° ° 4399.11 of the Revised Code are [is] amended by this act [Am. Sub. S.B. 2] (effective July 1, 1996) and also by Am. Sub. H.B. 117 of the 121st General Assembly. ° ° ° Section 4399.12 of the Revised Code are [is] amended by this act [Am. Sub. S.B. 2] (effective July 1, 1996) and also by Am. Sub. S.B. 162 of the 121st General Assembly (effective July 1, 1997). ° ° ° Comparison of these amendments in pursuance of section 1.52 of the Revised Code discloses that they are not irreconcilable so that they are required by that section to be harmonized to give effect to each amendment.

§ 4399.12 Permit holders excepted.

No provision contained in Title XLIII [43] of the Revised Code that prohibits the sale of intoxicating liquors in any of the circumstances described in section 4399.11 of the Revised Code extends to or prevents the holder of an A, B, C-2, D-2, D-3, D-3a, D-4, D-4a, D-5, D-5a, D-5b, D-5e, D-5f, D-5g, D-5h, D-5i, G, or I permit issued by the division of liquor control from distributing or selling intoxicating liquor at the place of business described in the permit of the holder.

HISTORY: GC § 13207; 122 v 209; Bureau of Code Revision, 10-1-53; 140 v H 711 (Eff 7-1-85); 142 v H 562 (Eff 6-29-88); 143 v H 405 (Eff 4-11-91); 146 v S 2 (Eff 7-1-96); 146 v S 162. Eff 7-1-97.

See provisions, § 9 of SB 162 (146 v —) following RC § 4301.01.

See Comment, Legislative Service Commission following RC § 4399.11.

§ 4399.14 Use of intoxicating liquor in a public dance hall prohibited; exceptions.

No person who is the proprietor of any public dance hall, or who conducts, manages, or is in charge of any public dance hall, shall allow the use of any intoxicating liquor or the presence of intoxicated persons in such dance hall or on the premises on which such dance hall is located; but the prohibition against the use of any intoxicating liquor does not apply to establishments that are holders of a D-1, D-2, D-3, D-4, or D-5 permit whose principal business consists of conducting a hotel, a restaurant, a club, or a night club as defined by section 4301.01 of the Revised Code. No person who is the proprietor of any public dance hall, or who conducts, manages, or is in charge thereof, shall permit the presence at such public dance hall of any child younger than eighteen years of age, not accompanied by his father, mother, or legal guardian.

HISTORY: GC § 13393-1; 111 v 83; 116 v 511(547); Bureau of Code Revision. Eff 10-1-53.

§ 4399.15 Poisonously adulterated liquors.

No person, for the purpose of sale, shall adulterate spirituous, alcoholic, or malt liquor used or intended for drink or medicinal or mechanical purposes, with cocculus indicus, vitriol, grains of paradise, opium, alum, capsicum, copperas, laurel water, logwood, Brazilwood, cochineal, sugar of lead, aloes, glucose, tannic acid, or any other substance which is poisonous or injurious to health, or with a substance not a necessary ingredient in the manufacture thereof, or sell, offer, or keep for sale liquors so adulterated.

In addition to the penalties provided in division (E) of section 4399.99 of the Revised Code, a person convicted of violating this section shall pay all necessary costs and expenses incurred in inspecting and analyzing liquors so adulterated, sold, kept, or offered for sale.

HISTORY: RS § 7082; S&C 729; 52 v 108; 79 v 52; GC §§ 12676, 12677; Bureau of Code Revision, 10-1-53; 146 v S 2. Eff 7-1-96.

The effective date is set by section 6 of SB 2.

§ 4399.16 Tavern keeper permitting rioting or drunkenness.

No tavern keeper shall permit rioting, reveling, intoxication, or drunkenness in his house or on his premises.

HISTORY: RS § 6997; S&S 749; S&C 1430; 64 v 25; GC § 12813; Bureau of Code Revision. Eff 10-1-53.

§ 4399.17 Manufacturing or selling poisoned liquors.

No person shall use an active poison in the manufacture or preparation of intoxicating liquor or sell intoxicating liquor so manufactured or prepared.

HISTORY: RS § 7083; S&C 1436; 54 v 183; GC § 12675; Bureau of Code Revision. Eff 10-1-53.

§ 4399.18 Limitations on liability for acts of intoxicated person.

Notwithstanding division (A) of section 2307.60 of the Revised Code and except as otherwise provided in this section and in section 4399.01 of the Revised Code, a person, and the executor or administrator of the estate of a person, who suffers injury, death, or loss to person or property as a result of the actions or omissions of an intoxicated person do not have a cause of action against a liquor permit holder or an employee of a liquor permit holder who sold beer or intoxicating liquor to the intoxicated person unless the injury, death, or loss to person or property occurred on the liquor permit holder's premises or in a parking lot under the control of the liquor permit holder and was proximately caused by the negligence of the liquor permit holder or an employee of the liquor permit holder. A person has a cause of action against a liquor permit holder or an employee of a liquor permit holder for injury, death, or loss to person or property caused by the negligent actions or omissions of an intoxicated person occurring off the premises of the liquor permit holder or away from a parking lot under the liquor permit holder's control only when both of the following can be shown by a preponderance of the evidence:

(A) The liquor permit holder or an employee of the liquor permit holder knowingly sold an intoxicating beverage to at least one of the following:

(1) A noticeably intoxicated person in violation of division (B) of section 4301.22 of the Revised Code;

(2) A person in violation of division (C) of section 4301.22 of the Revised Code;

(3) A person in violation of section 4301.69 of the Revised Code.

(B) The person's intoxication proximately caused the injury, death, or loss to person or property.

Notwithstanding sections 4399.02 and 4399.05 of the Revised Code, a person, and the executor or administrator of the estate of a person, who suffers injury, death, or loss to person or property as a result of the actions or omissions of an intoxicated person do not have a cause of action against the owner of a building or premises who rents or leases the building or premises to a liquor permit holder against whom a cause of action may be brought under this section, except when the owner and the liquor permit holder are the same person.

HISTORY: 141 v H 759 (Eff 7-21-86); 146 v H 350. Eff 1-27-97.

§ 4399.99 Penalties.

(A) Whoever violates section 4399.16 of the Revised Code shall be fined not less than five nor more than one hundred dollars.

(B) Whoever violates section 4399.09 of the Revised Code shall be fined not less than one hundred nor more than five hundred dollars on a first offense and shall be fined not less than two hundred nor more than five hundred dollars on each subsequent offense.

(C) Whoever violates section 4399.10 of the Revised Code shall be fined not less than one hundred nor more than five hundred dollars and imprisoned not less than one nor more than six months.

(D) Whoever violates section 4399.14 of the Revised Code shall be fined not less than twenty-five nor more than five hundred dollars, imprisoned not more than six months, or both.

(E) Whoever violates section 4399.15 of the Revised Code shall be fined not less than twenty nor more than one hundred dollars, imprisoned not less than twenty nor more than sixty days, or both.

(F) Whoever violates section 4399.17 of the Revised Code is guilty of a felony of the fourth degree.

HISTORY: Bureau of Code Revision, 10-1-53; 133 v H 876 (Eff 8-25-70); 139 v S 199 (Eff 1-5-83); 146 v S 2. Eff 7-1-96.

The effective date is set by section 6 of SB 2.

TITLE 45: MOTOR VEHICLES—AERONAUTICS—WATERCRAFT

CHAPTER 4501: MOTOR VEHICLES—DEFINITIONS; GENERAL PROVISIONS

§ 4501.01 Definitions.

As used in this chapter and Chapters 4503., 4505., 4507., 4509., 4511., 4513., 4515., and 4517. of the Revised Code, and in the penal laws, except as otherwise provided:

(A) "Vehicles" means everything on wheels or runners, including motorized bicycles, but does not mean vehicles that are operated exclusively on rails or tracks or from overhead electric trolley wires and vehicles that belong to any police department, municipal fire department, or volunteer fire department, or that are used by such a department in the discharge of its functions.

(B) "Motor vehicle" means any vehicle, including manufactured homes and recreational vehicles, that is propelled or drawn by power other than muscular power or power collected from overhead electric trolley wires, except motorized bicycles, road rollers, traction engines, power shovels, power cranes, and other equipment used in construction work and not designed for or employed in general highway transportation, well-drilling machinery, ditch-digging machinery, farm machinery, trailers that are used to transport agricultural produce or agricultural production materials between a local place of storage or supply and the farm when drawn or towed on a public road or highway at a speed of twenty-five miles per hour or less, threshing machinery, hay-baling machinery, corn sheller, hammermill and agricultural tractors, machinery used in the production of horticultural, agricultural, and vegetable products, and trailers that are designed and used exclusively to transport a boat between a place of storage and a marina, or in and around a marina, when drawn or towed on a public road or highway for a distance of no more than ten miles and at a speed of twenty-five miles per hour or less.

(C) "Agricultural tractor" and "traction engine" mean any self-propelling vehicle that is designed or used for drawing other vehicles or wheeled machinery, but has no provisions for carrying loads independently of such other vehicles, and that is used principally for agricultural purposes.

(D) "Commercial tractor," except as defined in division (C) of this section, means any motor vehicle that has motive power and either is designed or used for drawing other motor vehicles, or is designed or used for drawing another motor vehicle while carrying a portion of the other motor vehicle or its load, or both.

(E) "Passenger car" means any motor vehicle that is designed and used for carrying not more than nine persons and includes any motor vehicle that is designed and used for carrying not more than fifteen persons in a ridesharing arrangement.

(F) "Collector's vehicle" means any motor vehicle or agricultural tractor or traction engine that is of special interest, that has a fair market value of one hundred dollars or more, whether operable or not, and that is owned, operated, collected, preserved, restored, maintained, or used essentially as a collector's item, leisure pursuit, or investment, but not as the owner's principal means of transportation. "Licensed collector's vehicle" means a collector's vehicle, other than an agricultural tractor or traction engine, that displays current, valid license tags issued under section 4503.45 of the Revised Code, or a similar type of motor vehicle that displays current, valid license tags issued under substantially equivalent provisions in the laws of other states.

(G) "Historical motor vehicle" means any motor vehicle that is over twenty-five years old and is owned solely as a collector's item and for participation in club activities, exhibitions, tours, parades, and similar uses, but that in no event is used for general transportation.

(H) "Noncommercial motor vehicle" means any motor vehicle, including a farm truck as defined in section 4503.04 of the Revised Code, that is designed by the manufacturer to carry a load of no more than one ton and is used exclusively for purposes other than engaging in business for profit.

(I) "Bus" means any motor vehicle that has motor power and is designed and used for carrying more than nine passengers, except any motor vehicle that is designed and used for carrying not more than fifteen passengers in a ridesharing arrangement.

(J) "Commercial car" means any motor vehicle that has motor power and is designed and used for carrying merchandise or freight, or that is used as a commercial tractor.

(K) "Bicycle" means every device, other than a tricycle that is designed solely for use as a play vehicle by a child, that is propelled solely by human power upon which any person may ride, and that has either two tandem wheels, or one wheel in front and two wheels in the rear, any of which is more than fourteen inches in diameter.

(L) "Motorized bicycle" means any vehicle that either has two tandem wheels or one wheel in the front and two wheels in the rear, that is capable of being pedaled, and that is equipped with a helper motor of not more than fifty cubic centimeters piston displacement that produces no more than one brake horsepower and is capable of propelling the vehicle at a speed of no greater than twenty miles per hour on a level surface.

(M) "Trailer" means any vehicle without motive power that is designed or used for carrying property or persons wholly on its own structure and for being drawn by a motor vehicle, and includes any such vehicle that is formed by or operated as a combination of a semitrailer and a vehicle of the dolly type such as that commonly known as a trailer dolly, a vehicle used to transport agricultural produce or agricultural production materials between a local place of storage or supply and the farm when drawn or towed on a public road or highway at a speed greater than twenty-five miles per hour, and a vehicle that is designed and used exclusively to transport a boat between a place of storage and a marina, or in and around a marina, when drawn or towed on a public road or highway for a distance of more than ten miles or at a speed of more than twenty-five miles per hour. "Trailer" does not include a manufactured home or travel trailer.

(N) "Noncommercial trailer" means any trailer, except a travel trailer or trailer that is used to transport a boat as described in division (B) of this section, but, where applicable, includes a vehicle that is used to transport a boat as described in division (M) of this section, that has a gross weight of no more than three thousand pounds, and that is used exclusively for purposes other than engaging in business for a profit.

(O) "Manufactured home" means any nonself-propelled vehicle transportable in one or more sections, which, in the traveling mode, is eight body feet or more in width or forty body feet or more in length or, when erected on site, is three hundred twenty or more square feet, and which is built on a permanent chassis and designed to be used as a dwelling with or without a permanent foundation when connected to the required utilities, and includes the plumbing, heating, air conditioning, and electrical systems contained therein. Calculations used to determine the number of square feet in a structure are based on the structure's exterior dimensions measured at the largest horizontal projections when erected on site. These dimensions include all expandable rooms, cabinets, and other projections containing interior space, but do not include bay windows.

(P) "Semitrailer" means any vehicle of the trailer type that does not have motive power and is so designed or used with another and separate motor vehicle that in operation a part of its own weight or that of its load, or both, rests upon and is carried by the other vehicle furnishing the motive power for propelling itself and the vehicle referred to in this division, and includes, for the purpose only of registration and taxation under those chapters, any vehicle of the dolly type, such as a trailer dolly, that is designed or used for the conversion of a semitrailer into a trailer.

(Q) "Recreational vehicle" means a vehicular portable structure that is designed and constructed to be used as a temporary dwelling for travel, recreational, and vacation uses and is classed as follows:

(1) "Travel trailer" means a nonself-propelled recreational vehicle that does not exceed an overall length of thirty-five feet, exclusive of bumper and tongue or coupling, and includes a tent-type fold-out camping trailer as defined in section 4517.01 of the Revised Code.

(2) "Motor home" means a self-propelled recreational vehicle that is constructed with permanently installed facilities for cold storage, cooking and consuming of food, and for sleeping.

(3) "Truck camper" means a nonself-propelled recreational vehicle that does not have wheels for road use and is designed to be placed upon and attached to a motor vehicle. "Truck camper" does not include truck covers that consist of walls and a roof, but do not have floors and facilities enabling them to be used as a dwelling.

(4) "Fifth wheel trailer" means a vehicle that is of such size and weight as to be movable without a special highway permit, that has a gross trailer area of four hundred square feet or less, that is constructed with a raised forward section that allows a bi-level floor plan, and that is designed to be towed by a vehicle equipped with a fifth-wheel hitch ordinarily installed in the bed of a truck.

(5) "Park trailer" means a vehicle that is commonly known as a park model recreational vehicle, meets the American national standard institute standard A119.5 (1988) for park trailers, is built on a single chassis, has a gross trailer area of four hundred square feet or less when set up, is designed for seasonal or temporary living quarters, and may be connected to utilities necessary for the operation of installed features and appliances.

(R) "Pneumatic tires" means tires of rubber and fabric or tires of similar material, that are inflated with air.

(S) "Solid tires" means tires of rubber or similar elastic material that are not dependent upon confined air for support of the load.

(T) "Solid tire vehicle" means any vehicle that is equipped with two or more solid tires.

(U) "Farm machinery" means all machines and tools that are used in the production, harvesting, and care of farm products, and includes trailers that are used to transport agricultural produce or agricultural production materials between a local place of storage or supply and the farm when drawn or towed on a public road or highway at a speed of twenty-five miles per hour or less.

(V) "Owner" includes any person, firm, or corporation other than a manufacturer or dealer that has title to a motor vehicle, except that in sections 4505.01 to 4505.19 of the Revised Code, "owner" includes in addition manufacturers and dealers.

(W) "Manufacturer" and "dealer" include all persons, firms, and corporations that are regularly engaged in the business of manufacturing, selling, displaying, offering for sale, or dealing in motor vehicles, at an established place of business that is used exclusively for the purpose of manufacturing, selling, displaying, offering for sale, or dealing in motor vehicles. A place of business that is used for manufacturing, selling, displaying, offering for sale, or dealing in motor vehicles shall be deemed to be used exclusively for those purposes even though snowmobiles or all-purpose vehicles are sold or displayed for sale thereat, even though farm machinery is sold or displayed for sale thereat, or even though repair, accessory, gasoline and oil, storage, parts, service, or paint departments are maintained thereat, or, in any county having a population of less than seventy-five thousand persons at the last federal census, even though a department in a place of business is used to dismantle, salvage, or rebuild motor vehicles by means of used parts, if such departments are operated for the purpose of furthering and assisting in the business of manufacturing, selling, displaying, offering for sale, or dealing in motor vehicles. Places of business or departments in a place of business used to dismantle, salvage, or rebuild motor vehicles by means of using used parts are not considered as being maintained for the purpose of assisting or furthering the manufacturing, selling, displaying, and offering for sale or dealing in motor vehicles.

(X) "Operator" includes any person who drives or operates a motor vehicle upon the public highways.

(Y) "Chauffeur" means any operator who operates a motor vehicle, other than a taxicab, as an employee for hire; or any operator whether or not the owner of a motor vehicle, other than a taxicab, who operates such vehicle for transporting, for gain, compensation, or profit, either persons or property owned by another. Any operator of a motor vehicle who is voluntarily involved in a ridesharing arrangement is not considered an employee for hire or operating such vehicle for gain, compensation, or profit.

(Z) "State" includes the territories and federal districts of the United States, and the provinces of Canada.

(AA) "Public roads and highways" for vehicles includes all public thoroughfares, bridges, and culverts.

(BB) "Manufacturer's number" means the manufacturer's original serial number that is affixed to or imprinted upon the chassis or other part of the motor vehicle.

(CC) "Motor number" means the manufacturer's original number that is affixed to or imprinted upon the engine or motor of the vehicle.

(DD) "Bill of sale" means the written statement or document of transfer or conveyance required prior to January 1, 1938, to be executed and delivered by the corporation, partnership, association, or person selling, giving away, transferring, or passing title to a motor vehicle.

(EE) "Distributor" means any person who is authorized by a motor vehicle manufacturer to distribute new motor vehicles to licensed motor vehicle dealers at an established place of business that is used exclusively for the purpose of distributing new motor vehicles to licensed motor vehicle dealers, except when the distributor also is a new motor vehicle dealer, in which case the distributor may distribute at the location of the distributor's licensed dealership.

(FF) "Ridesharing arrangement" means the transportation of persons in a motor vehicle where the transportation is incidental to another purpose of a volunteer driver and includes ridesharing arrangements known as carpools, vanpools, and buspools.

(GG) "Apportionable vehicle" means any vehicle that is used or intended for use in two or more international registration plan member jurisdictions that allocate or proportionally register vehicles, that is used for the transportation of persons for hire or designed, used, or maintained primarily for the transportation of property, and that meets any of the following qualifications:

(1) Is a power unit having a gross vehicle weight in excess of twenty-six thousand pounds;

(2) Is a power unit having three or more axles, regardless of the gross vehicle weight;

(3) Is a combination vehicle with a gross vehicle weight in excess of twenty-six thousand pounds.

"Apportionable vehicle" does not include recreational vehicles, vehicles displaying restricted plates, city pickup and delivery vehicles, buses used for the transportation of chartered parties, or vehicles owned and operated by the United States, this state, or any political subdivisions thereof.

(HH) "Chartered party" means a group of persons who contract as a group to acquire the exclusive use of a passenger-carrying motor vehicle at a fixed charge for the vehicle in accordance with the carrier's tariff, lawfully on file with the United States department of transportation, for the purpose of group travel to a specified destination or for a particular itinerary, either agreed upon in advance or modified by the chartered group after having left the place of origin.

(II) "International registration plan" means a reciprocal agreement of member jurisdictions that is endorsed by the American association of motor vehicle administrators, and that promotes and encourages the fullest possible use of the highway system by authorizing apportioned registration of fleets of vehicles and recognizing registration of vehicles apportioned in member jurisdictions.

(JJ) "Restricted plate" means a license plate that has a restriction of time, geographic area, mileage, or commodity, and includes license plates issued to farm trucks under division (K) of section 4503.04 of the Revised Code.

(KK) "Gross vehicle weight," with regard to any commercial car, trailer, semitrailer, or bus that is taxed at the rates established under section 4503.042 [4503.04.2] of the Revised Code, means the unladen weight of the vehicle fully equipped plus the maximum weight of the load to be carried on the vehicle.

(LL) "Combined gross vehicle weight" with regard to any combination of a commercial car, trailer, and semitrailer, that is taxed at the rates established under section 4503.042 [4503.04.2] of the Revised Code, means the total unladen weight of the combination of vehicles fully equipped plus the maximum weight of the load to be carried on that combination of vehicles.

(MM) "Chauffeured limousine" means a motor vehicle that is designed to carry nine or fewer passengers and is operated for hire on an hourly basis pursuant to a prearranged contract for the transportation of passengers on public roads and highways along a route under the control of the person hiring the vehicle and not over a defined and regular route. "Prearranged contract" means an agreement, made in advance of boarding, to provide transportation from a specific location in a chauffeured limousine at a fixed rate per hour or trip. "Chauffeured limousine" does not include any vehicle that is used exclusively in the business of funeral directing.

HISTORY: GC § 6290; 100 v 72; 103 v 763; 106 v 139; 108 v PtII, 1078; 110 v 135; 111 v 239; 114 v 173; 114 v 815; 115 v 454; 115 v PtII, 300; 116 v 286; 116 v 474; 117 v 680(691), § 23; 117 v 726; 123 v 513; 124 v 840; Bureau of Code Revision, 10-1-53; 125 v 268; 126 v 783 (Eff 9-30-55); 128 v 1170 (Eff 11-2-59); 130 v 1031 (Eff 9-16-63); 132 v H 684 (Eff 11-24-67); 133 v S 410 (Eff 11-25-69); 135 v S 108 (Eff 11-21-73); 135 v H 1161 (Eff 9-30-74); 136 v S 52 (Eff 9-15-75); 136 v S 56 (Eff 5-25-76); 136 v S 359 (Eff 8-27-76); 137 v H 1 (Eff 8-26-77); 137 v H 3 (Eff 1-1-79); 137 v S 100 (Eff 4-1-78); 137 v H 166 (Eff 3-7-78); 138 v H 1 (Eff 5-16-79); 138 v H 656 (Eff 1-1-80); 138 v H 1171 (Eff 10-24-80); 139 v H 53 (Eff 7-1-82); 140 v S 231 (Eff 9-20-84); 143 v H 422 (Eff 7-1-91); 143 v H 831 (Eff 7-17-90); 144 v H 282 (Eff 6-23-92); 144 v H 485 (Eff 10-7-92); 145 v S 191 (Eff 10-20-94); 147 v H 210 (Eff 3-31-97); 147 v S 60. Eff 10-21-97.

§ 4501.05 Duty of garage keepers.

Keepers of garages, parking lots, or other places where motor vehicles of any kind are stored or left for repair or for any other purpose, or any employee of any such person, who knows or becomes aware of the fact that any motor vehicle so stored or left has upon it, or in it, bullet marks, gunshot marks, blood stains, or marks or evidence of any crime, shall immediately report the facts to the police of a municipal corporation, a sheriff of the county, or a state highway patrol trooper.

Whoever violates this section shall forfeit not more than one hundred dollars, to be recovered on petition as in civil cases, filed by the prosecuting attorney, in the name of the state of Ohio, in the court of common pleas in the county in which such place is located.

HISTORY: GC § 13431-2; 113 v 123(139), ch 10, § 2; 117 v 432; Bureau of Code Revision, 10-1-53; 144 v S 144. Eff 8-8-91.

CHAPTER 4503: LICENSING OF MOTOR VEHICLES

§ 4503.05 Noncommercial motor vehicle restricted use.

No person shall use a motor vehicle registered as a noncommercial motor vehicle as defined in section 4501.01 of the Revised Code for other than the purposes set forth in that section.

HISTORY: 137 v H 166. Eff 3-7-78.

Analogous to former RC § 4503.05 (Bureau of Code Revision, 10-1-53; 129 v 1364), repealed 137 v H 166, § 2, eff 3-7-78.

§ 4503.13 Ineligibility due to outstanding municipal or county court arrest warrant.

(A) A municipal court or county court, at the court's discretion, may order the clerk of the court to send to the registrar of motor vehicles a report containing the name, address, and such other information as the registrar may require by rule, of any person for whom an arrest warrant has been issued by that court and is outstanding.

Upon receipt of such a report, the registrar shall enter the information contained in the report into the records of the bureau of motor vehicles. Neither the registrar nor any deputy registrar shall issue a certificate of registration for a motor vehicle owner or lessee, when a lessee is determinable under procedures established by the registrar under division (E) of this section, who is named in the report until the registrar receives notification from the municipal court or county court that there are no outstanding arrest warrants in the name of the person. The registrar also shall send a notice to the person who is named in the report, via regular first class mail sent to the person's last known address as shown in the records of the bureau, informing the person that neither the registrar nor any deputy registrar is permitted to issue a certificate of registration for a motor vehicle in the name of the person until the registrar receives notification that there are no outstanding arrest warrants in the name of the person.

(B) A clerk who reports an outstanding arrest warrant in accordance with division (A) of this section immediately shall notify the registrar when the warrant has been executed and returned to the issuing court or has been canceled. The clerk shall charge and collect from the person named in the executed or canceled arrest warrant a processing fee of fifteen dollars to cover the costs of the bureau in administering this section. The clerk shall transmit monthly all such processing fees to the registrar for deposit into the state bureau of motor vehicles fund created by section 4501.25 of the Revised Code.

Upon receipt of such notification, the registrar shall cause the report of that outstanding arrest warrant to be removed from the records of the bureau and, if there are no other outstanding arrest warrants issued by a municipal court or county court in the name of the person and the person otherwise is eligible to be issued a certificate of registration for a motor vehicle, the registrar or a deputy registrar may issue a certificate of registration for a motor vehicle in the name of the person named in the executed or canceled arrest warrant.

(C) Neither the registrar, any employee of the bureau, a deputy registrar, nor any employee of a deputy registrar is personally liable for damages or injuries resulting from any error made by a clerk in entering information contained in a report submitted to the registrar under this section.

(D) Any information submitted to the registrar by a clerk under this section shall be transmitted by means of an electronic data transfer system.

(E) The registrar shall determine the procedures and information necessary to implement this section in regard to motor vehicle lessees. Division (A) of this section shall not apply to cases involving a motor vehicle lessee until such procedures are established.

HISTORY: 147 v H 141. Eff 3-3-98.

Not analogous to former RC § 4503.13 (GC § 6294-2; 114 v 851, § 4; 116 v 286, § 6; 116 v 295; Bureau of Code Revision, 10-1-53; 131 v 1073; 135 v H 90), repealed 137 v H 3, § 2, eff 1-1-79.

The effective date is set by section 3 of HB 141.

[§ 4503.18.2] § 4503.182 Temporary licenses.

(A) Purchasers of motor vehicles upon application and proof of purchase of such vehicle, may be issued a temporary license placard or windshield sticker for such motor vehicles.

The purchaser of a vehicle applying for a temporary license placard or windshield sticker under this section shall execute an affidavit that he has not been issued previously during the current registration year a license plate registration that could legally be transferred to such vehicle.

Placards or windshield stickers shall be issued only for the applicant's use of such vehicle to enable him to legally operate the motor vehicle while proper title and license plate registration is being obtained and shall be displayed on no other motor vehicle.

Placards or windshield stickers issued under this section shall be valid for a period of thirty days from date of issuance and shall not be transferable or renewable.

The fee for such placards or windshield stickers shall be two dollars plus a fee of two dollars and twenty-five cents for each such placard issued by a deputy registrar.

(B) The registrar of motor vehicles may issue to a motorized bicycle dealer or a licensed motor vehicle dealer temporary license placards to be issued to purchasers for use on vehicles sold by such licensed dealer, in accordance with rules prescribed by the registrar. The dealer shall notify the registrar within forty-eight hours of proof of issuance on a form prescribed by the registrar.

The fee for each such placard issued by the registrar to such motor vehicle dealer shall be two dollars plus a fee of two dollars and twenty-five cents.

(C) The registrar of motor vehicles may, at his discretion, issue a temporary license placard. Such placard may be issued in the case of extreme hardship encountered by a citizen from this state or another state who has attempted to comply with all registration laws, but for extreme circumstances is unable to properly register his vehicle.

(D) Prior to July 1, 1985, the registrar shall adopt rules, in accordance with division (B) of section 111.15 of the Revised Code, to specify the procedures for reporting the information from applications for temporary license placards or windshield stickers and for providing the information from these applications to law enforcement agencies.

(E) As used in this section, "motorized bicycle dealer" means any person engaged in the business of selling at retail, displaying, offering for sale, or dealing in motorized bicycles who is not subject to section 4503.09 of the Revised Code.

HISTORY: 127 v 256 (Eff 9-4-57); 133 v H 207 (Eff 9-4-69); 134 v S 356 (Eff 1-14-72); 135 v S 471 (Eff 9-23-74); 136 v H 612 (Eff 7-9-76); 137 v H 3 (Eff 1-1-79) 139 v S 242 (Eff 1-1-83); 140 v S 169 (Eff 1-1-85); 140 v H 632 (Eff 3-28-85); 142 v S 1 (Eff 11-28-88); 143 v H 381 (Eff 7-1-89); 145 v H 154. Eff 6-30-93.

The provisions of § 12 of HB 154 (145 v —) read as follows:

SECTION 12. The fee increases of seventy-five cents contained in the amendments to sections 4503.10, 4503.102, 4503.12, 4503.182, 4506.08, 4507.24, 4507.50, and 4519.03 of the Revised Code shall take effect on August 1, 1993.

§ 4503.21 Display of license plates and validation stickers or temporary placard or windshield sticker.

No person who is the owner or operator of a motor vehicle shall fail to display in plain view on the front and rear of the motor vehicle the distinctive number and registration mark, including any county identification sticker and any validation sticker issued under sections 4503.19 and 4503.191 [4503.19.1] of the Revised Code, furnished by the director of public safety, except that a manufacturer of motor vehicles or dealer therein, the holder of an in transit permit, and the owner or operator of a motorcycle, motorized bicycle, manufactured home, trailer, or semitrailer shall display on the rear only. A motor vehicle that is issued two license plates shall display the validation sticker on the rear license plate. A commercial tractor that does not receive an apportioned license plate under the international registration plan shall be issued one license plate and one validation sticker, which license plate and validation sticker shall be displayed on the front of the commercial tractor. An apportioned vehicle receiving an apportioned license plate under the international registration plan shall display the license plate only on the front of a commercial tractor and on the rear of all other vehicles. All license plates shall be securely fastened so as not to swing, and shall not be covered by any material that obstructs their visibility.

No person to whom a temporary license placard or windshield sticker has been issued for the use of a motor vehicle under section 4503.182 [4503.18.2] of the Revised Code, and no operator of that motor vehicle, shall fail to display the temporary license placard in plain view from the rear of the vehicle either in the rear window or on an external rear surface of the motor vehicle, or fail to display the windshield sticker in plain view on the rear window of the motor vehicle. No temporary license placard or windshield sticker shall be covered by any material that obstructs its visibility.

HISTORY: GC § 12613; 99 v 540, § 9; 99 v 543, § 24; 103 v 763; 104 v 248; 115 v 108; 123 v 513; Bureau of Code Revision, 10-1-53; 125 v 127; 125 v 230; 126 v 717 (Eff 9-30-55); 130 v 1047 (Eff 1-23-63); 135 v H 90 (Eff 10-31-73); 140 v S 169 (Eff 1-1-85); 140 v S 231 (Eff 9-20-84); 140 v H 632 (Eff 3-28-85); 141 v H 428 (Eff 12-23-86); 142 v H 158 (Eff 9-10-87); 143 v H 831 (Eff 7-17-90); 143 v S 382 (Eff 12-31-90); 144 v S 98 (Eff 11-12-92); 147 v S 60. Eff 10-21-97.

§ 4503.22 Specifications for license plates.

The identification license plate shall consist of a placard upon the face of which shall appear the distinctive number assigned to the motor vehicle as provided in section 4503.19 of the Revised Code, in Arabic numerals or letters, or both. The dimensions of the numerals or letters and of each stroke shall be determined by the director of public safety. The license placard also shall contain the name of this state and the slogan "BIRTHPLACE OF AVIATION." The placard shall be made of steel and the background shall be treated with a reflective material that shall provide effective and dependable reflective brightness during the service period required of the placard. Specifications for the reflective and other materials and the design of the placard, the county identification stickers as provided by section 4503.19 of the Revised Code, and validation stickers as provided by section 4503.191 [4503.19.1] of the Revised Code, shall be adopted by the director as rules under sections 119.01 to 119.13 of the Revised Code. The identification license plate of motorized bicycles and of motor vehicles of the type commonly called "motorcycles" shall consist of a single placard, the size of which shall be prescribed by the director. The identification plate of a vehicle registered in accordance with the international registration plan shall contain the word "apportioned." The director may prescribe the type of placard, or means of fastening the placard, or both; the placard or means of fastening may be so designed and constructed as to render difficult the removal of the placard after it has been fastened to a motor vehicle.

HISTORY: GC § 6300; 100 v 73, § 10; 103 v 763; 107 v 546; 115 v 102; 116 v 286, § 9; 116 v 295; Bureau of Code Revision, 10-1-53; 125 v 127; 128 v 1173 (Eff 11-2-59); 131 v 1077 (Eff 9-9-65); 134 v H 727 (Eff 1-1-74); 135 v H 90 (Eff 10-31-73); 136 v H 1 (Eff 6-13-75); 137 v H 1 (Eff 8-26-77); 137 v H 3 (Eff 1-1-79); 139 v S 242 (Eff 1-1-83); 140 v S 169 (Eff 1-1-85); 143 v H 831 (Eff 7-17-90); 144 v S 98 (Eff 11-12-92); 145 v H 154 (Eff 6-30-93); 145 v H 687 (Eff 10-12-94); 146 v S 289. Eff 9-27-96.

[§ 4503.23.3] § 4503.233 Immobilization orders.

(A)(1) As used in this section, "vehicle owner" means either of the following:

(a) The person in whose name is registered, at the time of the offense, a vehicle that is subject to an immobilization and impound order issued under division (A)(2) of this section;

(b) A person to whom, at the time of the offense, the certificate of title to a vehicle has been assigned and who has not obtained a certificate of title to the vehicle in that person's name but who is deemed by the court as being the owner of the vehicle at the time of the offense for which the vehicle is subject to an immobilization and impoundment order issued under division (A)(2) of this section.

(2) If a court is required to order the immobilization of a vehicle for a specified period of time pursuant to division (B)(1) or (2), (C)(1) or (2), or (E)(1) of section 4507.99, pursuant to division (A)(2)(b) or (3)(b) of section 4511.99, pursuant to division (B)(1) or (2) or (C)(1) or (2) of section 4507.361 [4507.36.1], or pursuant to division (B)(2)(a) or (b) of section 4511.193 [4511.19.3] of the Revised Code, the court shall issue an immobilization order, subject to section 4503.235 [4503.23.5] of the Revised Code, in accordance with this division and for the period of time specified in the particular division, and the immobilization under the order shall be in accordance with this section. The court, at the time of sentencing the offender for the offense relative to which the immobilization order is issued or as soon thereafter as is practicable, shall give a copy of the order to the offender or the offender's counsel and to the vehicle owner or the vehicle owner's counsel. The court promptly shall send a copy of the order to the registrar on a form prescribed by the registrar and to the person or agency it designates to execute the order.

The order shall indicate the date on which it is issued, shall identify the vehicle that is subject to the order, and shall specify all of the following:

(a) The period of the immobilization;

(b) The place at which the court determines that the immobilization shall be carried out, provided that the court shall not determine and shall not specify that the immobilization is to be carried out at any place other than a commercially operated private storage lot, a place owned by a law enforcement or other government agency, or a place to which one of the following applies:

(i) The place is leased by or otherwise under the control of a law enforcement or other government agency.

(ii) The place is owned by the offender, the offender's

spouse, or a parent or child of the offender.

(iii) The place is owned by a private person or entity, and, prior to the issuance of the order, the private entity or person that owns the place, or the authorized agent of that private entity or person, has given express written consent for the immobilization to be carried out at that place.

(iv) The place is a public street or highway on which the vehicle is parked in accordance with the law.

(c) The person or agency designated by the court to execute the order, which shall be either the law enforcement agency that employs the law enforcement officer who seized the vehicle, a bailiff of the court, another person the court determines to be appropriate to execute the order, or the law enforcement agency with jurisdiction over the place of residence of the vehicle owner.

(3) The person or agency the court designates to immobilize the vehicle shall seize or retain that vehicle's license plates and forward them to the bureau of motor vehicles.

(4) In all cases, the vehicle owner shall be assessed an immobilization fee of one hundred dollars, and the immobilization fee shall be paid to the registrar before the vehicle may be released to the vehicle owner and that† Neither the registrar nor a deputy registrar shall will be permitted to† accept an application for the license plate registration of any motor vehicle in the name of the vehicle owner until the immobilization fee is paid.

(5) If the vehicle subject to the order is immobilized pursuant to the order and is found being operated upon any street or highway in this state during the immobilization period, it shall be seized, removed from the street or highway, and criminally forfeited and disposed of pursuant to section 4503.234 [4503.23.4] of the Revised Code.

(6) The registrar shall deposit the immobilization fee into the law enforcement reimbursement fund created by section 4501.19 of the Revised Code. Money in the fund shall be expended only as provided in division (A)(6) of this section. If the court designated in the order a court bailiff or another appropriate person other than a law enforcement officer to immobilize the vehicle, the amount of the fee deposited into the law enforcement reimbursement fund shall be paid out to the county treasury if the court that issued the order is a county court, to the treasury of the municipal corporation served by the court if the court that issued the order is a mayor's court, or to the city treasury of the legislative authority of the court, both as defined in section 1901.03 of the Revised Code, if the court that issued the order is a municipal court. If the court designated a law enforcement agency to immobilize the vehicle and if the law enforcement agency immobilizes the vehicle, the amount of the fee deposited into the law enforcement reimbursement fund shall be paid out to the law enforcement agency to reimburse the agency for the costs it incurs in obtaining immobilization equipment and, if required, in sending an officer or other person to search for and locate the vehicle specified in the immobilization order and to immobilize the vehicle.

In addition to the immobilization fee required to be paid under division (A)(4) of this section, the vehicle owner may be charged expenses or charges incurred in the removal and storage of the immobilized vehicle.

(B) If a court issues an immobilization order under division (A)(2) of this section, the person or agency designated by the court to execute the immobilization order promptly shall immobilize or continue the immobilization of the vehicle at the place specified by the court in the order. The registrar shall not authorize the release of the vehicle or authorize the issuance of new identification license plates for the vehicle at the end of the immobilization period the owner's† until the immobilization fee has been paid.

(C) Upon receipt of the license plates for a vehicle under this section, the registrar the registrar's† shall destroy the license plates. At the end of the immobilization period and upon the payment of the immobilization fee that must be paid under this section, the registrar shall authorize the release of the vehicle and authorize the issuance, upon the payment of the same fee as is required for the replacement of lost, mutilated, or destroyed license plates and certificates of registration, of new license plates and, if necessary, a new certificate of registration to the vehicle owner for the vehicle in question.

(D)(1) If a court issues an immobilization order under division (A) of this section, the immobilization period commences on the day on which the vehicle in question is immobilized. If the vehicle in question had been seized under section 4507.38 or 4511.195 [4511.19.5] of the Revised Code, the time between the seizure and the beginning of the immobilization period shall be credited against the immobilization period specified in the immobilization order issued under division (A) of this section. No vehicle that is impounded under this section is eligible to have special license plates of the type described in section 4503.231 [4503.23.1] of the Revised Code issued for that vehicle.

(2) If a court issues an immobilization order under division (A) of this section, if the vehicle subject to the order is immobilized under the order, and if the vehicle is found being operated upon any street or highway of this state during the immobilization period, it shall be seized, removed from the street or highway, and criminally forfeited, and disposed of pursuant to section 4503.234 [4503.23.4] of the Revised Code. No vehicle that is forfeited under this provision shall be considered contraband for purposes of section 2933.41, 2933.42, or 2933.43 of the Revised Code, but shall be held by the law enforcement agency that employs the officer who seized it for disposal in accordance with section 4503.234 [4503.23.4] of the Revised Code.

(3) If a court issues an immobilization order under

division (A) of this section, and if the vehicle is not claimed within seven days after the end of the period of immobilization or if the vehicle owner the owner's† has not paid the immobilization fee, the person or agency that immobilized the vehicle shall send a written notice to the vehicle owner at the vehicle owner's last known address informing the vehicle owner of the date on which the period of immobilization ended, that the owner's† the vehicle owner has twenty days after the date of the notice to pay the immobilization fee and obtain the release of the vehicle, and that if the owner's† the vehicle owner does not pay the fee and obtain the release of the vehicle within that twenty-day period, the vehicle will be forfeited under section 4503.234 [4503.23.4] of the Revised Code to the entity that is entitled to the immobilization fee.

(4) An owner of a motor vehicle that is subject to an immobilization order issued under division (A) of this section shall not sell the motor vehicle without approval of the court that issued the order. If such an owner wishes to sell such a the† motor vehicle during the immobilization period, the owner shall apply to the court that issued the immobilization order for permission to assign the title to the vehicle. If the court is satisfied that the sale will be in good faith and not for the purpose of circumventing the provisions of division (A)(2) of this section, it may certify its consent to the owner and to the registrar. Upon receipt of the court's consent, the registrar shall enter the court's notice in the owner's vehicle license plate registration record.

If, during a period of immobilization under an immobilization order issued under division (A) of this section, the title to the immobilized motor vehicle is transferred by the foreclosure of a chattel mortgage, a sale upon execution, the cancellation of a conditional sales contract, or an order of a court, the involved court shall notify the registrar of the action, and the registrar shall enter the court's notice in the owner's vehicle license plate registration record.

Nothing in this section shall be construed as requiring the registrar or the clerk of the court of common pleas to note upon the certificate of title records any prohibition regarding the sale of a motor vehicle.

(5) If the title to a motor vehicle that is subject to an immobilization order under division (A) of this section is assigned or transferred without court approval between the time of arrest of the person who was operating the vehicle at the time of the offense for which such an order is to be issued and the time of the actual immobilization of the vehicle, the court shall order that, for a period of two years from the date of the order, neither the registrar nor any deputy registrar shall accept an application for the registration of any motor vehicle in the name of the owner of the vehicle that was assigned or transferred without court approval. The court shall notify the registrar of the order on a form prescribed by the registrar for that purpose.

(E)(1) The court with jurisdiction over the case, after notice to all interested parties including lienholders, and after an opportunity for them to be heard, if the vehicle owner fails to appear in person, without good cause, or if the court finds that the vehicle owner does not intend to seek release of the vehicle at the end of the period of immobilization or that the vehicle owner is not or will not be able to pay the expenses and charges incurred in its removal and storage, may order that title to the vehicle be transferred, in order of priority, first into the name of the entity entitled to the immobilization fee under division (A)(6) of this section, next into the name of a lienholder, or lastly, into the name of the owner of the place of storage.

A lienholder that receives title under a court order shall do so on the condition that it pay any expenses or charges incurred in the vehicle's removal and storage. If the entity that receives title to the vehicle is the entity that is entitled to the immobilization fee under division (A)(6) of this section, it shall receive title on the condition that it pay any lien on the vehicle. The court shall not order that title be transferred to any person or entity other than the owner of the place of storage if the person or entity refuses to receive the title. Any person or entity that receives title may either keep title to the vehicle or may dispose of the vehicle in any legal manner that it considers appropriate, including assignment of the certificate of title to the motor vehicle to a salvage dealer or a scrap metal processing facility. The person or entity shall not transfer the vehicle to the person who is the vehicle's immediate previous owner.

If the person or entity assigns the motor vehicle to a salvage dealer or scrap metal processing facility, the person or entity shall send the assigned certificate of title to the motor vehicle to the clerk of the court of common pleas of the county in which the salvage dealer or scrap metal processing facility is located. The person or entity shall mark the face of the certificate of title with the words "FOR DESTRUCTION" and shall deliver a photocopy of the certificate of title to the salvage dealer or scrap metal processing facility for its records.

(2) Whenever a court issues an order under division (E)(1) of this section, the court also shall order removal of the license plates from the vehicle and cause them to be sent to the registrar if they have not already been sent to the registrar. Thereafter, no further proceedings shall take place under this section, but the vehicle owner remains liable for payment of the immobilization fee described in division (A)(4) of this section if an immobilization order previously had been issued by the court.

(3) Prior to initiating a proceeding under division (E)(1) of this section, and upon payment of the fee under division (B) of section 4505.14 of the Revised Code, any interested party may cause a search to be made of the public records of the bureau of motor vehicles or the clerk of the court of common pleas, to ascertain the identity of any lienholder of the vehicle. The initiating party shall furnish this information to the clerk of the court with jurisdiction over the case, and

the clerk shall provide notice to the vehicle owner, the defendant, any lienholder, and any other interested parties listed by the initiating party, at the last known address supplied by the initiating party, by certified mail or, at the option of the initiating party, by personal service or ordinary mail.

As used in this section, "interested party" includes the vehicle owner, all lienholders, the defendant, the owner of the place of storage, the person or entity that caused the vehicle to be removed, and the person or entity, if any, entitled to the immobilization fee under division (A)(6) of this section.

HISTORY: 144 v S 275 (Eff 9-1-93); 145 v S 62, §§ 1, 4 (Eff 9-1-93); 145 v H 154 (Eff 6-30-93); 145 v S 82 (Eff 5-4-94); 145 v H 236 (Eff 9-29-94); 145 v H 687 (Eff 10-12-94); 146 v H 353 (Eff 9-17-96); 146 v H 676. Eff 10-4-96.

Publisher's Note

The amendments made by HB 676 (146 v —) and HB 353 (146 v —) have been combined. Please see provisions of RC § 1.52.

† The wording is the result of combining HB 353 (146 v —) and HB 676 (146 v —).

[§ 4503.23.4] § 4503.234 Order of criminal forfeiture of vehicle; disposal of vehicle or proceeds of sale; registration of other vehicles in person's name.

(A) As used in this section, "vehicle owner" means the person in whose name is registered a vehicle that is subject to an order of forfeiture issued under this section.

(B) If a court is required by section 4503.233 [4503.-23.3], 4503.236 [4503.23.6], 4507.361 [4507.36.1], 4507.99, 4511.193 [4511.19.3], or 4511.99 of the Revised Code to order the criminal forfeiture of a vehicle, the order shall be issued and enforced in accordance with this division, subject to division (C) of this section and section 4503.235 [4503.23.5] of the Revised Code. An order of criminal forfeiture issued under this division shall authorize an appropriate law enforcement agency to seize the vehicle ordered criminally forfeited upon the terms and conditions that the court determines proper. No vehicle ordered criminally forfeited pursuant to this division shall be considered contraband for purposes of section 2933.41, 2933.42, or 2933.43 of the Revised Code, but shall be held by the law enforcement agency that employs the officer who seized it for disposal in accordance with this section. A forfeiture order may be issued only after the vehicle owner has been provided with an opportunity to be heard. The prosecuting attorney shall give the vehicle owner written notice of the possibility of forfeiture by sending a copy of the relevant uniform traffic ticket or other written notice to the vehicle owner not less than seven days prior to the date of issuance of the forfeiture order. A vehicle is subject to an order of criminal forfeiture pursuant to this division upon the conviction of the offender of or plea of guilty by the offender to a violation of division (A) of section 4503.236 [4503.23.6], division (B)(1) or (D)(2) of section 4507.02, section 4507.33, or division (A) of section 4511.19 of the Revised Code, or a municipal ordinance that is substantially equivalent to division (A) of section 4503.236 [4503.23.6], division (B)(1) or (D)(2) of section 4507.02, section 4507.33, or division (A) of section 4511.19 of the Revised Code.

(C)(1) Prior to the issuance of an order of criminal forfeiture pursuant to division (B) of this section, the law enforcement agency that employs the law enforcement officer who seized the vehicle shall conduct or cause to be conducted a search of the appropriate public records that relate to the vehicle and shall make or cause to be made reasonably diligent inquiries to identify any lienholder or any person or entity with an ownership interest in the vehicle. The court that is to issue the forfeiture order also shall cause a notice of the potential order relative to the vehicle and of the expected manner of disposition of the vehicle after its forfeiture to be sent to any lienholder or person who is known to the court to have any right, title, or interest in the vehicle. The court shall give the notice by certified mail, return receipt requested, or by personal service.

(2) No order of criminal forfeiture shall be issued pursuant to division (B) of this section if a lienholder or other person with an ownership interest in the vehicle establishes to the court, by a preponderance of the evidence after filing a motion with the court, that the lienholder or other person neither knew nor should have known after a reasonable inquiry that the vehicle would be used or involved, or likely would be used or involved, in the violation resulting in the issuance of the order of criminal forfeiture or the violation of the order of immobilization issued under section 4503.233 [4503.23.3] of the Revised Code, that the lienholder or other person did not expressly or impliedly consent to the use or involvement of the vehicle in that violation, and that the lien or ownership interest was perfected pursuant to law prior to the seizure of the vehicle under section 4503.236 [4503.23.6], 4507.38, or 4511.195 [4511.19.5] of the Revised Code. If the lienholder or holder of the ownership interest satisfies the court that these criteria have been met, the court shall preserve †the lienholder's or other person's lien or interest, and the court either shall return the vehicle to the holder, or shall order that the proceeds of any sale held pursuant to division (D) of this section be paid to the lienholder or holder of the interest less the costs of seizure, storage, and maintenance of the vehicle. The court shall not return a vehicle to a lienholder or a holder of an ownership interest under division (C)(2) of this section unless the lienholder or holder submits an affidavit to the court that states that the lienholder or holder will not return the vehicle to the person from whom the vehicle was seized pursuant to the order of criminal forfeiture or to any member of that person's family and will not otherwise knowingly permit that person or any member

of that person's family to obtain possession of the vehicle.

(3) No order of criminal forfeiture shall be issued pursuant to division (B) of this section if a person with an interest in the vehicle establishes to the court, by a preponderance of the evidence after filing a motion with the court, that the person neither knew nor should have known after a reasonable inquiry that the vehicle had been used or was involved in the violation resulting in the issuance of the order of criminal forfeiture or the violation of the order of immobilization issued under section 4503.233 [4503.23.3] of the Revised Code, that the person did not expressly or impliedly consent to the use or involvement of the vehicle in that violation, that the interest was perfected in good faith and for value pursuant to law between the time of the arrest of the offender and the final disposition of the criminal charge in question, and that the vehicle was in the possession of the vehicle owner at the time of the perfection of the interest. If the court is satisfied that the interest holder has met these criteria, the court shall preserve †the interest holder's interest, and the court either shall return the vehicle to the interest holder or order that the proceeds of any sale held pursuant to division (D) of this section be paid to the holder of the interest less the costs of seizure, storage, and maintenance of the vehicle. The court shall not return a vehicle to an interest holder under division (C)(3) of this section unless the holder submits an affidavit to the court stating that the holder will not return the vehicle to the person from whom the holder acquired the holder's interest, nor to any member of that person's family, and the holder will not otherwise knowingly permit that person or any member of that person's family to obtain possession of the vehicle.

(D) A vehicle ordered criminally forfeited to the state pursuant to division (B) of this section shall be disposed of as follows:

(1) It shall be given to the law enforcement agency that employs the law enforcement officer who seized the vehicle, if that agency desires to have it;

(2) If a vehicle is not disposed of pursuant to division (D)(1) of this section, the vehicle shall be sold, without appraisal, if the value of the vehicle is two thousand dollars or more as determined by publications of the national auto dealer's association, at a public auction to the highest bidder for cash. Prior to the sale, the prosecuting attorney in the case shall cause a notice of the proposed sale to be given in accordance with law. The court shall cause notice of the sale of the vehicle to be published in a newspaper of general circulation in the county in which the court is located at least seven days prior to the date of the sale. The proceeds of a sale under this division or division (G) of this section shall be applied in the following order:

(a) First, they shall be applied to the payment of the costs incurred in connection with the seizure, storage, and maintenance of, and provision of security for, the vehicle, any proceeding arising out of the forfeiture, and if any, the sale.

(b) Second, the remaining proceeds after compliance with division (D)(2)(a) of this section, shall be applied to the payment of the value of any lien or ownership interest in the vehicle preserved under division (C) of this section.

(c) Third, the remaining proceeds, after compliance with divisions (D)(2)(a) and (b) of this section, shall be applied to the appropriate funds in accordance with divisions (D)(1)(c) and (2) of section 2933.43 of the Revised Code, provided that the total of the amount so deposited under this division shall not exceed one thousand dollars. The remaining proceeds deposited under this division shall be used only for the purposes authorized by those divisions and division (D)(3)(a)(ii) of that section.

(d) Fourth, the remaining proceeds after compliance with divisions (D)(2)(a) and (b) of this section and after deposit of a total amount of one thousand dollars under division (D)(2)(c) of this section shall be applied so that fifty per cent of those remaining proceeds is paid into the reparation fund established by section 2743.191 [2743.19.1] of the Revised Code, twenty-five per cent is paid into the drug abuse resistance education programs fund created by division (L)(2)(e) of section 4511.191 [4511.19.1] of the Revised Code and shall be used only for the purposes authorized by division (L)(2)(e) of that section, and twenty-five per cent is applied to the appropriate funds in accordance with division (D)(1)(c) of section 2933.43 of the Revised Code. The proceeds deposited into any fund described in section 2933.43 of the Revised Code shall be used only for the purposes authorized by division (D)(1)(c), (2), and (3)(a)(ii) of that section.

(E) Notwithstanding any other provision of law, neither the registrar of motor vehicles nor any deputy registrar shall accept an application for the registration of any motor vehicle in the name of any person, or register any motor vehicle in the name of any person, if both of the following apply:

(1) Any vehicle registered in the person's name was criminally forfeited under division (B) of this section and section 4503.233 [4503.23.3], 4503.236 [4503.23.6], 4507.361 [4507.36.1], 4507.99, 4511.193 [4511.19.3], or 4511.99 of the Revised Code;

(2) Less than five years have expired since the issuance of the most recent order of criminal forfeiture issued in relation to a vehicle registered in the person's name.

(F) If a court is required by section 4503.233 [4503.23.3], 4507.361 [4507.36.1], 4507.99, 4511.193 [4511.19.3], or 4511.99 of the Revised Code to order the criminal forfeiture to the state of a vehicle, and the title to the motor vehicle is assigned or transferred, and division (C)(2) or (3) of this section applies, in addition to or independent of any other penalty established by law, the court may fine the offender the value of the vehicle as determined by publications of the national auto dealer's association. The proceeds from any fine imposed under division (F) of this section shall be distributed in accordance with division (D)(4) of this section.

(G) As used in division (D) of this section and divisions (D)(1)(c), (2), and (D)(3)(a)(ii) of section 2933.43 of the Revised Code in relation to proceeds of the sale of a vehicle under division (D) of this section, "prosecuting attorney" includes the prosecuting attorney, village solicitor, city director of law, or similar chief legal officer of a municipal corporation who prosecutes the case resulting in the conviction or guilty plea in question.††

(G) If the vehicle to be forfeited has an average retail value of less than two thousand dollars as determined by publications of the national auto dealer's association, no public auction is required to be held. In such a case, the court may direct that the vehicle be disposed of in any manner that it considers appropriate, including assignment of the certificate of title to the motor vehicle to a salvage dealer or a scrap metal processing facility. The court shall not transfer the vehicle to the person who is the vehicle's immediate previous owner.

If the court assigns the motor vehicle to a salvage dealer or scrap metal processing facility and the court is in possession of the certificate of title to the motor vehicle, it shall send the assigned certificate of title to the clerk of the court of common pleas of the county in which the salvage dealer or scrap metal processing facility is located. The court shall mark the face of the certificate of title with the words "FOR DESTRUCTION" and shall deliver a photocopy of the certificate of title to the salvage dealer or scrap metal processing facility for its records.

If the court is not in possession of the certificate of title to the motor vehicle, the court shall issue an order transferring ownership of the motor vehicle to a salvage dealer or scrap metal processing facility, send the order to the clerk of the court of common pleas of the county in which the salvage dealer or scrap metal processing facility is located, and send a photocopy of the order to the salvage dealer or scrap metal processing facility for its records. The clerk shall make the proper notations or entries in the clerk's records concerning the disposition of the motor vehicle.†††

HISTORY: 144 v S 275 (Eff 9-1-93); 145 v S 62, §§ 1, 4 (Eff 9-1-93); 145 v S 82 (Eff 5-4-94); 146 v H 353 (Eff 9-17-96); 146 v H 676. Eff 10-4-96.

Publisher's Note

The amendments made by HB 353 (146 v —) and HB 676 (146 v —) have been combined. Please see provisions of RC § 1.52.

† The amendments made in HB 676 (146 v —) in division (C)(3) uses the word "holder's."

†† This division (G) is the result of amendments by HB 676 (146 v —), effective 10-4-96.

††† This division (G) was enacted by HB 353 (146 v —), effective 9-17-96.

[§ 4503.23.5] § 4503.235 Protection of rights of innocent vehicle owners.

(A) As used in this section:

(1) "Vehicle owner" means the person in whose name is registered, at the time of the offense, a vehicle for which an immobilization order under section 4503.233 [4503.23.3] of the Revised Code or a forfeiture order under section 4503.234 [4503.23.4] of the Revised Code has been issued or will be issued.

(2) "Prosecutor" has the same meaning as in section 2935.01 of the Revised Code.

(B) No vehicle shall be immobilized under section 4503.233 [4503.23.3] of the Revised Code or forfeited under section 4503.234 [4503.23.4] of the Revised Code if all of the following apply:

(1) The person who was convicted of or pleaded guilty to a violation of division (A) of section 4503.236 [4503.23.6], division (B)(1) or (D)(2) of section 4507.02, section 4507.33, or division (A) of section 4511.19 of the Revised Code, or a municipal ordinance that is substantially equivalent to any of those Revised Code provisions that would be the basis of the order of immobilization or forfeiture, or the person who operated a vehicle that had been immobilized under an order of immobilization issued under section 4503.233 [4503.23.3] of the Revised Code, is not the owner of the vehicle that was used or involved in the offense or violation;

(2) The vehicle owner, prior to the issuance of the order of immobilization or forfeiture, files a motion with the court requesting that the order not be issued on the ground that the vehicle owner was innocent of any wrongdoing relative to the offense or violation;

(3) Any of the following applies:

(a) If the vehicle in question was leased or rented for a period of more than thirty days to the person who was convicted of or pleaded guilty to the offense in question or who committed the violation of the order of immobilization, the prosecutor in the case fails to establish to the court, at trial or subsequent to the filing of the motion and by a preponderance of the evidence, one or more of the following:

(i) That the person did not present the vehicle owner or an agent of the vehicle owner with a valid driver's or commercial driver's license or permit at the time the person leased or rented the vehicle;

(ii) That the person appeared to be under the influence of alcohol, a drug of abuse, or alcohol and a drug of abuse at the time the person leased or rented the vehicle;

(iii) That the vehicle owner knew or should have known after a reasonable inquiry that the vehicle was used or involved or likely to be used or involved in the offense or violation;

(iv) That the vehicle owner or the vehicle owner's agent expressly or impliedly consented to the use or involvement of the vehicle in the offense or violation.

(b) Except as otherwise provided in division (D) of this section, if the vehicle in question was not leased or rented to the person who was convicted of or pleaded guilty to the offense or who committed the violation of the order of immobilization, the prosecutor in the case fails to establish to the court, at trial or subsequent to the filing of the motion and by a preponderance of the evidence, one or more of the following:

(i) That the vehicle owner knew or should have known after a reasonable inquiry that the vehicle was used or involved or likely to be used or involved in the offense or violation;

(ii) That the vehicle owner or the vehicle owner's agent expressly or impliedly consented to the use or involvement of the vehicle in the offense or violation.

(c) The court determines that the immobilization or the forfeiture would be a substantial injustice to the vehicle owner.

(C) If a court has ordered a vehicle immobilized under section 4503.233 [4503.23.3] of the Revised Code or a vehicle criminally forfeited under section 4503.234 [4503.23.4] of the Revised Code, the vehicle owner shall be considered a party to the proceeding for purposes of Civil Rule 60.

(D) Sections 4503.233 [4503.23.3] and 4503.234 [4503.23.4] of the Revised Code do not apply to vehicles that are being rented or leased for a period of thirty days or less.

(E) Sections 4503.233 [4503.23.3] and 4503.234 [4503.23.4] of the Revised Code do not apply to a vehicle if it is shown that the vehicle is owned by the employer of the operator, that the employer and operator are different persons or entities, and that the employer shows that the employer is subject to and in full compliance with Chapter 4506. of the Revised Code.

HISTORY: 144 v S 275 (Eff 9-1-93); 145 v S 62, §§ 1, 4 (Eff 9-1-93); 145 v S 82 (Eff 5-4-94); 145 v H 687 (Eff 10-12-94); 146 v H 353. Eff 9-17-96.

[§ 4503.23.6] § 4503.236 Forfeiture for violation of immobilization order.

(A) No person shall operate a motor vehicle or permit the operation of a motor vehicle upon any public or private property used by the public for vehicular travel or parking knowing or having reasonable cause to believe that the motor vehicle has been ordered immobilized pursuant to an immobilization order issued under section 4503.233 [4503.23.3] of the Revised Code.

(B) A motor vehicle that is operated by a person during a violation of division (A) of this section shall be criminally forfeited in accordance with the procedures contained in section 4503.234 [4503.23.4] of the Revised Code, but such forfeiture is subject to section 4503.235 [4503.23.5] of the Revised Code.

HISTORY: 146 v H 353. Eff 9-17-96.

§ 4503.30 Display of placards issued to manufacturers, dealers or distributors.

Any placards issued by the registrar of motor vehicles and bearing the distinctive number assigned to a manufacturer, dealer, or distributor pursuant to section 4503.27 of the Revised Code may be displayed on any motor vehicle, other than commercial cars, or on any motorized bicycle owned by the manufacturer, dealer, or distributor, or lawfully in the possession or control of the manufacturer, or the agent or employee of the manufacturer, the dealer, or the agent or employee of the dealer, the distributor, or the agent or employee of the distributor, and shall be displayed on no other motor vehicle or motorized bicycle. A placard may be displayed on a motor vehicle, other than a commercial car, owned by a dealer when the vehicle is in transit from a dealer to a purchaser, when the vehicle is being demonstrated for sale or lease, or when the vehicle otherwise is being utilized by the dealer. A vehicle bearing a placard issued to a dealer under section 4503.27 of the Revised Code may be operated by the dealer, an agent or employee of the dealer, a prospective purchaser, or a third party operating the vehicle with the permission of the dealer.

Such placards may be displayed on commercial cars only when the cars are in transit from a manufacturer to a dealer, from a distributor to a dealer or distributor, or from a dealer to a purchaser, or when the cars are being demonstrated for sale or lease, and shall not be displayed when the cars are being used for delivery, hauling, transporting, or other commercial purpose.

HISTORY: GC § 6301-1a; 117 v 680(694), § 25; 118 v 486; Bureau of Code Revision, 10-1-53; 135 v H 1161 (Eff 9-30-74); 140 v S 169 (Eff 1-1-85); 146 v S 182. Eff 12-3-96.

[§ 4503.30.1] § 4503.301 Demonstration placards.

(A) A manufacturer, dealer, or distributor of motor vehicles may apply for a reasonable number of commercial car demonstration placards. The application shall show the make of commercial cars, commercial tractors, trailers, and semitrailers manufactured, dealt, or distributed in and shall show the taxing district in which the applicant's place of business is located.

Upon the filing of such application and the payment of an annual fee of five hundred dollars and appropriate postage as required by the registrar of motor vehicles, the registrar shall assign to the applicant a distinctive placard and number. Such placards shall be known as "commercial car demonstration placards," and shall expire on a date prescribed by the registrar. Upon the first application by any person for such placards, the registrar shall prorate the annual fee in accordance with section 4503.11 of the Revised Code; for all renewals or replacements of such placards, the registrar shall collect the full amount of the annual fee.

Commercial car demonstration placards may be displayed on commercial cars, commercial tractors, trailers and semitrailers owned by the manufacturer, dealer, or distributor, when those vehicles are operated by or being demonstrated to a prospective purchaser. In addition to the purposes permitted by section 4503.30 of the Revised Code, the placards provided for in this section may be displayed on vehicles operated or used for delivery, hauling, transporting, or any other lawful purpose. When such placards are used, the placards provided for in section 4503.30 of the Revised Code need not be displayed.

The operator of any commercial car, commercial tractor, trailer, or semitrailer displaying the placards provided for in this section, at all times, shall carry with the operator a letter from the manufacturer, dealer, or distributor authorizing the use of such manufacturer's, dealer's, or distributor's commercial car demonstration placards.

When such placards are used on any commercial car or commercial tractor, such power unit shall be considered duly registered and licensed for the purposes of section 4503.38 of the Revised Code.

(B) No manufacturer, dealer, or distributor of motor vehicles shall use the commercial car demonstration placard for purposes other than those authorized by this section.

HISTORY: 132 v S 272 (Eff 11-14-67); 135 v H 1161 (Eff 9-30-74); 147 v S 60. Eff 10-21-97.

§ 4503.44 Windshield placards, license plates and parking cards for walking-impaired persons; specially equipped vehicles.

(A) As used in this section and in section 4511.69 of the Revised Code:

(1) "Person with a disability that limits or impairs the ability to walk" means any person who, as determined by a physician or chiropractor, meets any of the following criteria:

(a) Cannot walk two hundred feet without stopping to rest;

(b) Cannot walk without the use of, or assistance from, a brace, cane, crutch, another person, prosthetic device, wheelchair, or other assistive device;

(c) Is restricted by a lung disease to such an extent that the person's forced (respiratory) expiratory volume for one second, when measured by spirometry, is less than one liter, or the arterial oxygen tension is less than sixty millimeters of mercury on room air at rest;

(d) Uses portable oxygen;

(e) Has a cardiac condition to the extent that the person's functional limitations are classified in severity as class III or class IV according to standards set by the American heart association;

(f) Is severely limited in the ability to walk due to an arthritic, neurological, or orthopedic condition;

(g) Is blind.

(2) "Organization" means any private organization or corporation, or any governmental board, agency, department, division, or office, that, as part of its business or program, transports persons with disabilities that limit or impair the ability to walk on a regular basis in a motor vehicle that has not been altered for the purpose of providing it with special equipment for use by handicapped persons. This definition does not apply to division (J) of this section.

(3) "Physician" means a person licensed to practice medicine or surgery or osteopathic medicine and surgery under Chapter 4731. of the Revised Code.

(4) "Chiropractor" means a person licensed to practice chiropractic under Chapter 4734. of the Revised Code.

(B) Any organization or person with a disability that limits or impairs the ability to walk may apply to the registrar of motor vehicles for a removable windshield placard or, if the person owns or leases a motor vehicle, the person may apply for the registration of any motor vehicle the person owns or leases. In addition to one or more sets of license plates or one placard, a person with a disability that limits or impairs the ability to walk shall be entitled to one additional placard. When a motor vehicle has been altered for the purpose of providing it with special equipment for a person with a disability that limits or impairs the ability to walk, but is owned or leased by someone other than such a person, the owner or lessee may apply to the registrar or a deputy registrar for registration under this section. The application for a removable windshield placard made by a person with a disability that limits or impairs the ability to walk or for registration of a motor vehicle owned or leased by such a person shall be accompanied by a signed statement from the applicant's personal physician or chiropractor certifying that the applicant meets at least one of the criteria contained in division (A)(1) of this section and that the disability is expected to continue for more than six consecutive months. The application for a removable windshield placard made by an organization shall be accompanied by such documentary evidence of regular transport of persons with disabilities that limit or impair the ability to walk by the organization as the registrar may require by rule and shall be completed in accordance with procedures that the registrar may require by rule. The application for registration of a motor vehicle that has been altered for the purpose of providing it with special equipment for a person with a disability that limits or impairs the ability to walk but is owned by someone other than such a person shall be accompanied by such documentary evidence of vehicle alterations as the registrar may require by rule.

(C) When an organization, a person with a disability that limits or impairs the ability to walk, or a person who does not have a disability that limits or impairs the ability to walk but owns a motor vehicle that has been altered for the purpose of providing it with special equipment for a person with a disability that limits or impairs the ability to walk first submits an application for registration of a motor vehicle under this section and every fifth year thereafter, the organization or person shall submit a signed statement from the applicant's personal physician or chiropractor or documentary evidence of vehicle alterations as provided in division (B) of this section, and also a power of attorney from the owner of the motor vehicle if the applicant leases the vehicle. Upon submission of these items, the registrar or deputy registrar shall issue to the applicant appropriate vehicle registration and a set of license plates and validation stickers, or validation stickers alone when required by section 4503.191 [4503.19.1] of the Revised Code. In addition to the letters and numbers ordinarily inscribed thereon, the license plates shall be imprinted with the international symbol of access. The license plates and validation stickers shall be issued upon payment of the regular license fee as prescribed under section 4503.04 of the Revised Code and any motor vehicle tax levied under Chapter 4504. of the Revised Code, and the payment of a service fee equal to the amount specified in division (D) or (G) of section 4503.10 of the Revised Code.

(D) Upon receipt of an application for a removable windshield placard and presentation of a signed statement from the applicant's personal physician or chiropractor as provided in division (B) of this section, if required, or presentation of documentary evidence of regular transport of persons with disabilities that limit or impair the ability to walk, if required, and, except as otherwise provided in division (F) of this section, payment of a fee of five dollars, and the payment of a service fee equal to the amount specified in division (D) or (G) of section 4503.10 of the Revised Code, the registrar or deputy registrar shall issue to the applicant a removable windshield placard, which shall bear the date of expiration on both sides of the placard, in numerals at least one inch in height, and printed in white on a blue-colored background, and shall be valid until expired, revoked, or surrendered. Every removable windshield placard shall expire on the last day of the month in the fifth year after the date it is issued. Removable windshield placards shall be renewable upon application as provided in division (B) of this section, and a service fee equal to the amount specified in division (D) or (G) of section 4503.10 of the Revised Code shall be charged for the renewal of a removable windshield placard. An additional renewal fee of five dollars shall be charged if the previous parking card or removable windshield placard expired more than six months prior to the date of application for renewal. The registrar shall provide the application form and shall determine the information to be included thereon. The registrar also shall determine the form and size of the removable windshield placard, the material of which it is to be made, and any other information to be included thereon, and shall adopt rules relating to the issuance, expiration, revocation, surrender, and proper display of such placards.

Nothing in this section shall be construed to require a person or organization to apply for a removable windshield placard or special license plates if the parking card or special license plates issued to the person or organization under prior law have not expired or been surrendered or revoked.

(E) Any person with a disability that limits or impairs the ability to walk may apply to the registrar or a deputy registrar for a temporary removable windshield placard. The application for a temporary removable windshield placard shall be accompanied by a signed statement from the applicant's personal physician or chiropractor certifying that the applicant meets at least one of the criteria contained in division (A)(1) of this section and that the disability is expected to continue for six consecutive months or less. Upon receipt of an application for a temporary removable windshield placard, presentation of the signed statement from the applicant's personal physician or chiropractor, payment of a fee of five dollars, and payment of a service fee equal to the amount specified in division (D) or (G) of section 4503.10 of the Revised Code, the registrar or deputy registrar shall issue to the applicant a temporary removable windshield placard. The temporary removable windshield placard shall be of the same size and form as the removable windshield placard, shall be printed in white on a red-colored background, shall bear the word "temporary" in letters of such size as the registrar shall prescribe, also shall bear the date of expiration on the front and back of the placard, in numerals at least one inch in height, and shall be valid until expired, surrendered, or revoked. The registrar shall provide the application form and shall determine the information to be included on it. The registrar also shall determine the material of which the temporary removable windshield placard is to be made and any other information to be included on the placard and shall adopt rules relating to the issuance, expiration, surrender, revocation, and proper display of those placards.

(F) If an applicant for a removable windshield placard or a temporary removable windshield placard is a veteran of the armed forces of the United States whose disability, as defined in division (A)(1) of this section, is service-connected, the registrar or deputy registrar, upon receipt of the application, presentation of a signed statement from the applicant's personal physician or chiropractor certifying the period for which the applicant's disability is expected to continue, and presentation of such documentary evidence that the disability is service-connected as the registrar may require by rule, but without the payment of any fee for issuance or of any service fee, shall issue the applicant a removable windshield placard or temporary removable windshield placard, as the case may be, that shall be valid until expired, surrendered, or revoked.

Upon a conviction of a violation of division (H), (I), or (J) of this section, the court shall report the conviction, and send the placard or parking card, if available, to the registrar, who shall thereupon revoke the privilege of using the placard or parking card and send notice in writing to the placardholder or cardholder at that holder's last known address as shown in the records of the bureau of motor vehicles, and the placardholder or cardholder shall return the placard or card if not previously surrendered to the court, to the registrar within ten days following mailing of the notice.

Whenever a person to whom a removable windshield placard or parking card has been issued moves to another state, the person shall surrender the placard or card to the registrar; and whenever an organization to which a placard or card has been issued changes its place of operation to another state, the organization shall surrender the placard or card to the registrar.

(G) Subject to the provisions of division (F) of section 4511.69 of the Revised Code, the operator of a motor vehicle displaying a removable windshield placard, temporary removable windshield placard, parking card, or the special license plates authorized by this section shall be entitled to park the motor vehicle in any special parking location reserved for persons with disabilities that limit or impair the ability to walk, also known as handicapped parking spaces or disability parking spaces.

(H) No person or organization that is not eligible under division (B) or (E) of this section shall willfully and falsely represent that the person or organization is so eligible.

No person or organization shall display license plates issued under this section unless the license plates have been issued for the vehicle on which they are displayed and are valid.

(I) No person or organization to which a removable windshield placard or temporary removable windshield placard is issued shall do either of the following:

(1) Display or permit the display of the placard on any motor vehicle when having reasonable cause to believe the motor vehicle is being used in connection with an activity that does not include providing transportation for persons with disabilities that limit or impair the ability to walk;

(2) Refuse to return or surrender the placard, when required.

(J)(1) No person or organization to which a parking card is issued shall do either of the following:

(a) Display or permit the display of the parking card on any motor vehicle when having reasonable cause to believe the motor vehicle is being used in connection with an activity that does not include providing transportation for a handicapped person;

(b) Refuse to return or surrender the parking card, when required.

(2) As used in division (J) of this section:

(a) "Handicapped person" means any person who has lost the use of one or both legs or one or both arms, who is blind, deaf, or so severely handicapped as to be unable to move about without the aid of crutches or a wheelchair, or whose mobility is restricted by a permanent cardiovascular, pulmonary, or other handicapping condition.

(b) "Organization" means any private organization or corporation, or any governmental board, agency, department, division, or office, that, as part of its business or program, transports handicapped persons on a regular basis in a motor vehicle that has not been altered for the purposes of providing it with special equipment for use by handicapped persons.

(K) If a removable windshield placard, temporary removable windshield placard, or parking card is lost, destroyed, or mutilated, the placardholder or cardholder may obtain a duplicate by doing both of the following:

(1) Furnishing suitable proof of the loss, destruction, or mutilation to the registrar;

(2) Paying a fee of five dollars for issuance, plus a service fee equal to the amount specified in division (D) or (G) of section 4503.10 of the Revised Code.

Any placardholder or cardholder losing a placard or card and, after obtaining a duplicate, finding the original, immediately shall surrender the original placard or card to the registrar.

(L) The registrar shall pay all fees received under this section for the issuance of removable windshield placards or temporary removable windshield placards or duplicate removable windshield placards or cards into the state treasury to the credit of the state bureau of motor vehicles fund created in section 4501.25 of the Revised Code.

(M) For purposes of enforcing this section, every peace officer is deemed to be an agent of the registrar. Any peace officer or any authorized employee of the bureau of motor vehicles who, in the performance of duties authorized by law, becomes aware of a person whose placard or parking card has been revoked pursuant to this section, may confiscate that placard or parking card and return it to the registrar. The registrar shall prescribe any forms used by law enforcement agencies in administering this section.

No peace officer, law enforcement agency employing a peace officer, or political subdivision or governmental agency employing a peace officer, and no employee of the bureau shall be liable in a civil action for damages or loss to persons arising out of the performance of any duty required or authorized by this section. As used in this division, "peace officer" has the same meaning as in division (B) of section 2935.01 of the Revised Code.

HISTORY: 138 v H 736 (Eff 10-16-80); 139 v H 48 (Eff 1-1-83); 140 v H 174 (Eff 9-30-83); 141 v H 201 (Eff 7-1-85); 141 v H 80 (Eff 5-26-86); 142 v H 12 (Eff 9-10-87); 142 v H 419 (Eff 7-1-87); 142 v H 708 (Eff 4-19-88); 143 v H 49 (Eff 2-14-90); 143 v H 737 (Eff 4-11-91); 145 v H 154 (Eff 6-30-93); 145 v H 687 (Eff 1-1-95); 146 v H 107 (Eff 6-30-95); 146 v S 2 (Eff 7-1-96); 146 v H 353. Eff 9-17-96.

Analogous to former RC § 4503.44 (137 v H 3), repealed 138 v H 736, § 2, eff 10-16-80. Former RC § 4503.44 was analogous to former RC § 4503.10.5 (136 v S 162; 137 v H 571), repealed 137 v H 3, § 2, eff 1-1-79.

§ 4503.99 Penalties.

(A) Whoever violates section 4503.05, 4503.11, or 4503.12, division (A) of section 4503.182 [4503.18.2], section 4503.28, 4503.44, 4503.46, or 4503.47, or division (C), (D), or (E) of section 4503.066 [4503.06.6] of the Revised Code is guilty of a misdemeanor of the fourth degree.

(B) Whoever violates section 4503.061 [4503.06.1], 4503.19, 4503.21, or 4503.34 of the Revised Code is guilty of a minor misdemeanor.

(C) Whoever violates division (B) of section 4503.182 [4503.18.2] of the Revised Code is guilty of a misdemeanor of the first degree.

(D) Whoever violates division (A) of section 4503.236 [4503.23.6] of the Revised Code is guilty of a misdemeanor of the second degree.

(E) Whoever violates section 4503.30, division (B) of section 4503.301 [4503.30.1], or section 4503.32 of the Revised Code is guilty of a misdemeanor of the third degree.

(F)(1) Whoever violates division (B) of section 4503.033 [4503.03.3] of the Revised Code shall be fined one thousand dollars.

(2) Whoever violates division (C) of section 4503.033 [4503.03.3] of the Revised Code shall be fined ten thousand dollars.

HISTORY: Bureau of Code Revision, 10-1-53; 127 v 256 (Eff 9-4-57); 127 v 725 (Eff 9-9-57); 129 v 1030 (Eff 9-1-61); 130 v 1050 (Eff 1-23-63); 132 v S 272 (Eff 11-14-67); 133 v H 207 (Eff 9-4-69); 136 v S 162 (Eff 7-23-76); 136 v H 837 (Eff 7-24-76); 137 v H 3 (Eff 1-1-79); 137 v S 441 (Eff 1-1-79); 138 v H 736 (Eff 10-16-80); 138 v H 553 (Eff 3-23-81); 139 v S 242 (Eff 1-1-83); 141 v H 500 (Eff 5-6-86); 141 v H 182 (Eff 3-13-87); 143 v S 382 (Eff 12-31-90); 145 v H 285 (Eff 3-2-94); 146 v H 353. Eff 9-17-96.

CHAPTER 4505: CERTIFICATE OF MOTOR VEHICLE TITLE LAW

§ 4505.01 Definitions.

(A) As used in this chapter:

(1) "Lien" includes, unless the context requires a different meaning, a security interest in a motor vehicle.

(2) "Motor vehicle" includes manufactured homes and recreational vehicles, and trailers and semitrailers whose weight exceeds four thousand pounds.

(B) The various certificates, applications, and assignments necessary to provide certificates of title for manufactured homes or recreational vehicles, and trailers and semitrailers whose weight exceeds four thousand pounds, shall be made upon forms prescribed by the registrar of motor vehicles.

HISTORY: GC § 6290-2a; 120 v 313; 124 v 217; Bureau of Code Revision, 10-1-53; 136 v S 359 (Eff 8-27-76); 140 v H 218 (Eff 5-24-84); 140 v S 231 (Eff 9-20-84); 141 v H 428 (Eff 12-23-86); 143 v H 381. Eff 7-1-89.

§ 4505.18 Operation or sale of motor vehicle without certificate of title.

No person shall:

(A) Operate in this state a motor vehicle for which a certificate of title is required without having such certificate in accordance with sections 4505.01 to 4505.21 of the Revised Code, or upon which the certificate of title has been canceled;

(B) Display or display for sale or sell as a dealer or acting on behalf of a dealer, a motor vehicle without having obtained a manufacturer's or importer's certificate or a certificate of title therefor as provided in sections 4505.01 to 4505.21 of the Revised Code;

(C) Fail to surrender any certificate of title or any certificate of registration or license plates upon cancellation of the same by the registrar of motor vehicles and notice thereof as prescribed in sections 4505.01 to 4505.21 of the Revised Code;

(D) Fail to surrender the certificate of title to the clerk of the court of common pleas as provided in sections 4505.01 to 4505.21 of the Revised Code, in case of the destruction or dismantling or change of a motor vehicle in such respect that it is not the motor vehicle described in the certificate of title;

(E) Violate any rules promulgated pursuant to sections 4505.01 to 4505.21 of the Revised Code.

(F) Except as otherwise provided in Chapter 4517. of the Revised Code, sell at wholesale a motor vehicle the ownership of which is not evidenced by an Ohio certificate of title, or the current certificate of title issued for the motor vehicle, or the manufacturer's certificate of origin, and all title assignments that evidence the seller's ownership of the motor vehicle, and an odometer disclosure statement that complies with section 4505.06 of the Revised Code and subchapter IV of the "Motor Vehicle Information and Cost Savings Act," 86 Stat. 961 (1972), 15 U.S.C. 1981.

This section does not apply to persons engaged in the business of warehousing or transporting motor vehicles for the purpose of salvage disposition.

HISTORY: GC § 6290-17; 117 v 373(387); 121 v 142; Bureau of Code Revision, 10-1-53; 129 v 1027 (Eff 9-18-61); 130 v 1052 (Eff 1-23-63); 130 v 1052 (Eff 8-19-63); 130 v PtII, H 5 (Eff 12-16-64); 141 v H 382 (Eff 3-19-87); 142 v S 10. Eff 8-13-87.

§ 4505.19 Offenses.

No person shall do any of the following:

(A) Procure or attempt to procure a certificate of title or a salvage certificate of title to a motor vehicle, or pass or attempt to pass a certificate of title, a salvage certificate of title, or any assignment thereof to a motor vehicle, knowing or having reason to believe that such motor vehicle or any part of the motor vehicle has been acquired through commission of a theft offense as defined in section 2913.01 of the Revised Code;

(B) Purport to sell or transfer a motor vehicle without delivering to the purchaser or transferee thereof a certificate of title, a salvage certificate of title, or a manufacturer's or importer's certificate thereto, assigned to such purchaser as provided for in this chapter;

(C) With intent to defraud, possess, sell, offer to sell, counterfeit, or supply a blank, forged, fictitious, counterfeit, stolen, or fraudulently or unlawfully obtained certificate of title, registration, bill of sale, or other instruments of ownership of a motor vehicle, or conspire to do any of the foregoing;

(D) Knowingly obtain goods, services, credit, or money by means of an invalid, fictitious, forged, counterfeit, stolen, or unlawfully obtained original or duplicate certificate of title, registration, bill of sale, or other instrument of ownership of a motor vehicle;

(E) Knowingly obtain goods, services, credit, or money by means of a certificate of title to a motor vehicle, which is required to be surrendered to the registrar of motor vehicles or the clerk of the court of common pleas as provided in this chapter.

HISTORY: GC § 6290-16; 117 v 373(387); Bureau of Code Revision, 10-1-53; 134 v H 84 (Eff 2-3-72); 134 v H 85 (Eff 9-22-72); 134 v H 511 (Eff 1-1-74); 140 v H 632 (Eff 3-28-85); 145 v H 687 (Eff 10-12-94); 146 v H 353. Eff 9-17-96.

§ 4505.99 Penalties.

(A) Whoever violates division (G) of section 4505.11 of the Revised Code shall be fined not more than one thousand dollars, imprisoned not more than six months, or both.

(B) Whoever violates division (F) of section 4505.11 or section 4505.111 [4505.11.1] of the Revised Code shall be fined not more than two thousand dollars or imprisoned not more than one year, or both.

(C) Whoever violates sections 4505.01 to 4505.21 of the Revised Code for which no penalty is otherwise provided in this section shall be fined not more than two hundred dollars, imprisoned not more than ninety days, or both.

(D) Whoever violates section 4505.19 of the Revised Code shall be fined not more than five thousand dollars or imprisoned in the county jail or workhouse not less than six months nor more than one year, or both, or in a state correctional institution not less than one nor more than five years.

(E) Whoever violates division (B)(1) or (C)(1) of section 4505.21 of the Revised Code is guilty of a misdemeanor of the first degree.

(F) Whoever violates division (B)(2) or (C)(2) of section 4505.21 of the Revised Code is guilty of a felony of the fifth degree.

HISTORY: Bureau of Code Revision, 10-1-53; 126 v 575 (Eff 10-6-65); 132 v H 555 (Eff 11-7-67); 134 v H 85 (Eff 9-22-72); 139 v H 102 (Eff 7-1-81); 139 v H 275 (Eff 8-1-81); 139 v H 671 (Eff 12-9-81); 140 v H 632 (Eff 3-28-85); 142 v S 10 (Eff 8-13-87); 145 v H 571 (Eff 10-6-94); 146 v S 2. Eff 7-1-96.

The effective date is set by section 6 of SB 2.

CHAPTER 4506: COMMERCIAL DRIVER'S LICENSING

§ 4506.01 Definitions.

As used in this chapter:

(A) "Alcohol concentration" means the concentration of alcohol in a person's blood, breath, or urine. When expressed as a percentage, it means grams of alcohol per the following:

(1) One hundred milliliters of blood;
(2) Two hundred ten liters of breath;
(3) One hundred milliliters of urine.

(B) "School bus" has the same meaning as in section 4511.01 of the Revised Code.

(C) "Commercial driver's license" means a license issued in accordance with this chapter that authorizes an individual to drive a commercial motor vehicle.

(D) "Commercial driver license information system" means the information system established pursuant to the requirements of the "Commercial Motor Vehicle Safety Act of 1986," 100 Stat. 3207-171, 49 U.S.C.A. App. 2701.

(E) "Commercial motor vehicle" means any motor vehicle designed or used to transport persons or property that meets any of the following qualifications:

(1) Any combination of vehicles with a combined gross vehicle weight rating of twenty-six thousand one pounds or more, provided the gross vehicle weight rating of the vehicle or vehicles being towed is in excess of ten thousand pounds;

(2) Any single vehicle with a gross vehicle weight rating of twenty-six thousand one pounds or more, or any such vehicle towing a vehicle having a gross vehicle weight rating that is not in excess of ten thousand pounds;

(3) Any single vehicle or combination of vehicles that is not a class A or class B vehicle, but that either is designed to transport sixteen or more passengers including the driver, or is placarded for hazardous materials;

(4) Any school bus with a gross vehicle weight rating of less than twenty-six thousand one pounds that is designed to transport fewer than sixteen passengers including the driver;

(5) Is transporting hazardous materials for which placarding is required by regulations adopted under the "Hazardous Materials Transportation Act," 88 Stat. 2156 (1975), 49 U.S.C.A. 1801, as amended;

(6) Any single vehicle or combination of vehicles that is designed to be operated and to travel on a public street or highway and is considered by the federal highway administration to be a commercial motor vehicle, including, but not limited to, a motorized crane, a vehi-

cle whose function is to pump cement, a rig for drilling wells, and a portable crane.

(F) "Controlled substance" means all of the following:

(1) Any substance classified as a controlled substance under the "Controlled Substances Act," 80 Stat. 1242 (1970), 21 U.S.C.A. 802(6), as amended;

(2) Any substance included in schedules I through V of 21 C.F.R. part 1308, as amended;

(3) Any drug of abuse.

(G) "Conviction" means an unvacated adjudication of guilt or a determination that a person has violated or failed to comply with the law in a court of original jurisdiction, an unvacated forfeiture of bail or collateral deposited to secure the person's appearance in court, the payment of a fine or court cost, or violation of a condition of release without bail, regardless of whether or not the penalty is rebated, suspended, or probated.

(H) "Disqualification" means withdrawal of the privilege to drive a commercial motor vehicle.

(I) "Drive" means to drive, operate, or be in physical control of a motor vehicle.

(J) "Driver" means any person who drives, operates, or is in physical control of a commercial motor vehicle or is required to have a commercial driver's license.

(K) "Driver's license" means a license issued by the bureau of motor vehicles that authorizes an individual to drive.

(L) "Drug of abuse" means any controlled substance, dangerous drug as defined in section 4729.02 of the Revised Code, or over-the-counter medication that, when taken in quantities exceeding the recommended dosage, can result in impairment of judgment or reflexes.

(M) "Employer" means any person, including the federal government, any state, and a political subdivision of any state, that owns or leases a commercial motor vehicle or assigns a person to drive such a motor vehicle.

(N) "Endorsement" means an authorization on a person's commercial driver's license that is required to permit the person to operate a specified type of commercial motor vehicle.

(O) "Felony" means any offense under federal or state law that is punishable by death or specifically classified as a felony under the law of this state, regardless of the penalty that may be imposed.

(P) "Foreign jurisdiction" means any jurisdiction other than a state.

(Q) "Gross vehicle weight rating" means the value specified by the manufacturer as the maximum loaded weight of a single or a combination vehicle. The gross vehicle weight rating of a combination vehicle is the gross vehicle weight rating of the power unit plus the gross vehicle weight rating of each towed unit.

(R) "Hazardous materials" means materials identified as such under regulations adopted under the "Hazardous Materials Transportation Act," 88 Stat. 2156 (1975), 49 U.S.C.A. 1801, as amended.

(S) "Motor vehicle" has the same meaning as in section 4511.01 of the Revised Code.

(T) "Out-of-service order" means a temporary prohibition against driving a commercial motor vehicle issued under this chapter or a similar law of another state or of a foreign jurisdiction.

(U) "Residence" means any person's residence determined in accordance with standards prescribed in rules adopted by the registrar.

(V) "Temporary residence" means residence on a temporary basis as determined by the registrar in accordance with standards prescribed in rules adopted by the registrar.

(W) "Serious traffic violation" means a conviction arising from the operation of a commercial motor vehicle that involves any of the following:

(1) A single charge of any speed that is in excess of the posted speed limit by an amount specified by the United States secretary of transportation and that the director of public safety designates as such by rule;

(2) Violation of section 4511.20, 4511.201 [4511.20.-1], or 4511.202 [4511.20.2] of the Revised Code or any similar ordinance or resolution, or of any similar law of another state or political subdivision of another state;

(3) Violation of a law of this state or an ordinance or resolution relating to traffic control, other than a parking violation, or of any similar law of another state or political subdivision of another state, that results in a fatal accident;

(4) Violation of any other law of this state or an ordinance or resolution relating to traffic control, other than a parking violation, that is determined to be a serious traffic violation by the United States secretary of transportation and the director designates as such by rule.

(X) "State" means a state of the United States and includes the District of Columbia.

(Y) "Tank vehicle" means any commercial motor vehicle that is designed to transport any liquid or gaseous materials within a tank that is either permanently or temporarily attached to the vehicle or its chassis, but does not include any portable tank having a rated capacity of less than one thousand gallons.

(Z) "United States" means the fifty states and the District of Columbia.

(AA) "Vehicle" has the same meaning as in section 4511.01 of the Revised Code.

(BB) "Peace officer" has the same meaning as in section 2935.01 of the Revised Code.

HISTORY: 143 v H 381 (Eff 7-1-89); 143 v H 88 (Eff 3-13-90); 143 v H 831 (Eff 7-17-90); 144 v S 98 (Eff 11-12-92); 145 v H 687 (Eff 10-12-94); 146 v S 2 (Eff 7-1-96); 146 v H 353 (Eff 9-17-96); 147 v S 60. Eff 10-21-97.

§ 4506.02 Exceptions to chapter.

(A) Nothing in this chapter applies to any person when engaged in the operation of any of the following:

(1) A farm truck;

(2) Fire equipment for a fire department, volunteer or nonvolunteer fire company, fire district, or joint fire district;

(3) A public safety vehicle used to provide transportation or emergency medical service for ill or injured persons;

(4) A recreational vehicle;

(5) A commercial motor vehicle within the boundaries of an eligible unit of local government, if the person is employed by the eligible unit of local government and is operating the commercial motor vehicle for the purpose of removing snow or ice from a roadway by plowing, sanding, or salting, but only if either the employee who holds a commercial driver's license issued under this chapter and ordinarily operates a commercial motor vehicle for these purposes is unable to operate the vehicle, or the employing eligible unit of local government determines that a snow or ice emergency exists that requires additional assistance.

Nothing contained in division (A)(5) of this section shall be construed as pre-empting or superseding any law, rule, or regulation of this state concerning the safe operation of commercial motor vehicles.

(B) As used in this section:

(1) "Eligible unit of local government" means a village, township, or county that has a population of not more than three thousand persons according to the most recent federal census.

(2) "Farm truck" means a truck controlled and operated by a farmer for use in the transportation to or from a farm, for a distance of no more than one hundred fifty miles, of products of the farm, including livestock and its products, poultry and its products, floricultural and horticultural products, and in the transportation to the farm, from a distance of no more than one hundred fifty miles, of supplies for the farm, including tile, fence, and every other thing or commodity used in agricultural, floricultural, horticultural, livestock, and poultry production, and livestock, poultry, and other animals and things used for breeding, feeding, or other purposes connected with the operation of the farm, when the truck is operated in accordance with this division and is not used in the operations of a motor transportation company or private motor carrier.

(3) "Public safety vehicle" has the same meaning as in divisions (E)(1) and (3) of section 4511.01 of the Revised Code.

(4) "Recreational vehicle" includes every vehicle that is defined as a recreational vehicle in section 4501.01 of the Revised Code and is used exclusively for purposes other than engaging in business for profit.

HISTORY: 143 v H 381 (Eff 7-1-89); 143 v H 831 (Eff 7-17-90); 146 v S 121. Eff 11-19-96.

§ 4506.03 Commercial driver's license or permit required.

(A) On and after April 1, 1992, the following shall apply:

(1) No person shall drive a commercial motor vehicle on a highway in this state unless he holds a valid commercial driver's license with proper endorsements for the motor vehicle being driven, issued by the registrar of motor vehicles, a valid examiner's commercial driving permit issued under section 4506.13 of the Revised Code, a valid restricted commercial driver's license and waiver for farm-related service industries issued under section 4506.24 of the Revised Code, or a valid commercial driver's license temporary instruction permit issued by the registrar and is accompanied by an authorized state driver's license examiner or tester or a person who has been issued and has in his immediate possession a current, valid commercial driver's license with proper endorsements for the motor vehicle being driven.

(2) No person shall be issued a commercial driver's license until he surrenders to the registrar of motor vehicles all valid licenses issued to him by another jurisdiction recognized by this state. All surrendered licenses shall be returned by the registrar to the issuing authority.

(3) No person who has been a resident of this state for thirty days or longer shall drive a commercial motor vehicle under the authority of a commercial driver's license issued by another jurisdiction.

(B) As used in this section and in section 4506.09 of the Revised Code, "tester" means a person or entity acting pursuant to a valid agreement entered into under division (B) of section 4506.09 of the Revised Code.

HISTORY: 143 v H 381 (Eff 7-1-89); 144 v H 485. Eff 7-8-92.

§ 4506.04 Prohibitions.

(A) No person shall do any of the following:

(1) Drive a commercial motor vehicle while having in his possession or otherwise under his control more than one valid driver's license issued by this state, any other state, or by a foreign jurisdiction;

(2) Drive a commercial motor vehicle on a highway in this state in violation of an out-of-service order, while his driving privilege is suspended, revoked, or canceled, or while he is subject to disqualification;

(3) Drive a motor vehicle on a highway in this state under authority of a commercial driver's license issued by another state or a foreign jurisdiction, after having been a resident of this state for thirty days or longer;

(4) Knowingly give false information in any application or certification required by section 4506.07 of the Revised Code.

(B) The department of public safety shall give every conviction occurring out of this state and notice of which is received after December 31, 1989, full faith and credit and treat it for sanctioning purposes under this chapter as though the conviction had occurred in this state.

HISTORY: 143 v H 381 (Eff 7-1-89); 144 v S 98. Eff 11-12-92.

§ 4506.05 Conditions for driving commercial motor vehicle.

Notwithstanding any other provision of law, a person

may drive a commercial motor vehicle on a highway in this state if all of the following conditions are met:

(A) He has a valid commercial driver's license or commercial driver's license temporary instruction permit issued by any state in accordance with the minimum standards adopted by the federal highway administration under the "Commercial Motor Vehicle Safety Act of 1986," 100 Stat. 3207-171, 49 U.S.C. App. 2701, for the issuance of commercial driver's licenses;

(B) His commercial driver's license or permit is not suspended, revoked, or canceled;

(C) He is not disqualified from driving a commercial motor vehicle;

(D) He is not subject to an out-of-service order.

HISTORY: 143 v H 381. Eff 7-1-89.

§ 4506.06 Issuance of temporary instruction permit; effect.

The registrar of motor vehicles, upon receiving an application for a commercial driver's temporary instruction permit, may issue the permit to any person who is at least eighteen years of age and holds a valid driver's license, other than a restricted license, issued under Chapter 4507. of the Revised Code. A commercial driver's temporary instruction permit shall not be issued for a period exceeding six months and only one renewal of a permit shall be granted in a two-year period.

The holder of a commercial driver's temporary instruction permit, unless otherwise disqualified, may drive a commercial motor vehicle when having the permit in the holder's actual possession and accompanied by a person who holds a valid commercial driver's license valid for the type of vehicle being driven and who occupies a seat beside the permit holder for the purpose of giving instruction in driving the motor vehicle.

HISTORY: 143 v H 381 (Eff 7-1-89); 143 v H 88 (Eff 3-13-90); 146 v H 353. Eff 9-17-96.

§ 4506.07 Form of application for license or permit; registration as elector or change of voting residence.

(A) Every application for a commercial driver's license, restricted commercial driver's license, or a commercial driver's temporary instruction permit, or a duplicate of such a license, shall be made upon a form approved and furnished by the registrar of motor vehicles. Except as provided in section 4506.24 of the Revised Code in regard to a restricted commercial driver's license, the application shall be signed by the applicant and shall contain the following information:

(1) The name, date of birth, social security account number, sex, general description including height, weight, and color of hair and eyes, current residence, duration of residence in this state, country of citizenship, and occupation;

(2) Whether the applicant previously has been licensed to operate a commercial motor vehicle or any other type of motor vehicle in another state or a foreign jurisdiction and, if so, when, by what state, and whether the license or driving privileges currently are suspended or revoked in any jurisdiction, or the applicant otherwise has been disqualified from operating a commercial motor vehicle, or is subject to an out-of-service order issued under this chapter or any similar law of another state or a foreign jurisdiction and, if so, the date of, locations involved, and reason for the suspension, revocation, disqualification, or out-of-service order;

(3) Whether the applicant is afflicted with or suffering from any physical or mental disability or disease that prevents him from exercising reasonable and ordinary control over a motor vehicle while operating it upon a highway or is or has been subject to any condition resulting in episodic impairment of consciousness or loss of muscular control and, if so, the nature and extent of the disability, disease, or condition, and the names and addresses of the physicians attending him;

(4) Whether the applicant has obtained a medical examiner's certificate as required by this chapter;

(5) Whether the applicant has pending a citation for violation of any motor vehicle law or ordinance except a parking violation and, if so, a description of the citation, the court having jurisdiction of the offense, and the date when the offense occurred;

(6) Whether the applicant wishes to certify willingness to make an anatomical donation under section 2108.04 of the Revised Code, which shall be given no consideration in the issuance of a license;

(7) On and after May 1, 1993, whether the applicant has executed a valid durable power of attorney for health care pursuant to sections 1337.11 to 1337.17 of the Revised Code or has executed a declaration governing the use or continuation, or the withholding or withdrawal, of life-sustaining treatment pursuant to Chapter 2133. of the Revised Code and, if the applicant has executed either type of instrument, whether he wishes his license to indicate that he has executed the instrument.

(B) Every applicant shall certify, on a form approved and furnished by the registrar, all of the following:

(1) That the motor vehicle in which the applicant intends to take the driving skills test is representative of the type of motor vehicle that the applicant expects to operate as a driver;

(2) That the applicant is not subject to any disqualification or out-of-service order, or license suspension, revocation, or cancellation, under the laws of this state, of another state, or of a foreign jurisdiction and does not have more than one driver's license issued by this or another state or a foreign jurisdiction;

(3) Any additional information, certification, or evidence that the registrar requires by rule in order to ensure that the issuance of a commercial driver's license to the applicant is in compliance with the law of this state and with federal law.

(C) Every applicant shall execute a form, approved and furnished by the registrar, under which the applicant consents to the release by the registrar of information from the applicant's driving record.

(D) The registrar or a deputy registrar shall, in accordance with section 3503.11 of the Revised Code, register as an elector any applicant for a commercial driver's license or for a renewal or duplicate of such a license under this chapter, if the applicant is eligible and wishes to be registered as an elector. The decision of an applicant whether to register as an elector shall be given no consideration in the decision of whether to issue him a license or a renewal or duplicate.

(E) The registrar or a deputy registrar shall, in accordance with section 3503.11 of the Revised Code, offer the opportunity of completing a notice of change of residence or change of name to any applicant for a commercial driver's license or for a renewal or duplicate of such a license who is a resident of this state, if the applicant is a registered elector who has changed his residence or name and has not filed such a notice.

HISTORY: 143 v H 381 (Eff 7-1-89); 144 v H 427 (Eff 10-8-92); 144 v H 485 (Eff 7-8-92); 145 v S 300. Eff 1-1-95.

The effective date is set by section 3 of SB 300.

§ 4506.08 Fees for applications; furnishing information on driving record.

(A) Each application for a commercial driver's license temporary instruction permit shall be accompanied by a fee of ten dollars; except as provided in division (B) of this section, each application for a commercial driver's license, restricted commercial driver's license, or renewal of such a license shall be accompanied by a fee of twenty-five dollars; and each application for a duplicate commercial driver's license shall be accompanied by a fee of ten dollars. In addition, the registrar of motor vehicles or deputy registrar may collect and retain an additional fee of no more than two dollars and twenty-five cents for each application for a commercial driver's license temporary instruction permit, commercial driver's license, renewal of a commercial driver's license, or duplicate commercial driver's license received by the registrar or deputy. No fee shall be charged for the annual issuance of a waiver for farm-related service industries pursuant to section 4506.24 of the Revised Code.

Each deputy registrar shall transmit the fees collected to the registrar at the time and in the manner prescribed by the registrar by rule. The registrar shall pay the fees into the state highway safety fund established in section 4501.06 of the Revised Code.

(B) Information regarding the driving record of any person holding a commercial driver's license issued by this state shall be furnished by the registrar, upon request and payment of a fee of three dollars, to the employer or prospective employer of such a person and to any insurer.

HISTORY: 143 v H 381 (Eff 7-1-89); 144 v H 134 (Eff 10-10-91); 144 v H 485 (Eff 7-8-92); 145 v H 154 (Eff 6-30-93); 146 v H 107 (Eff 6-30-95); 147 v S 60. Eff 10-21-97.

[§ 4506.08.1] § 4506.081 Request for donations to second chance trust fund.

In addition to the fees collected under section 4506.08 of the Revised Code, the registrar or deputy registrar of motor vehicles shall ask each person applying for or renewing a commercial driver's license, restricted commercial driver's license, or duplicate whether the person wishes to make a one-dollar voluntary contribution to the second chance trust fund established under section 2108.15 of the Revised Code. The registrar or deputy registrar shall also make available to the person informational material provided by the department of health on the importance of organ, tissue, and eye donation.

All donations collected under this section during each month shall be forwarded by the registrar or deputy registrar not later than the fifth day of the immediately following month to the treasurer of state, who shall deposit them in the second chance trust fund.

HISTORY: 146 v S 300. Eff 7-1-97.

The effective date is set by section 3 of SB 300.

§ 4506.09 Rules for qualification and testing of applicants.

(A) The registrar of motor vehicles, subject to approval by the director of public safety, shall adopt rules conforming with applicable standards adopted by the federal highway administration as regulations under the "Commercial Motor Vehicle Safety Act of 1986," 100 Stat. 3207-171, 49 U.S.C.A. App. 2701. The rules shall establish requirements for the qualification and testing of persons applying for a commercial driver's license, which shall be in addition to other requirements established by this chapter. Except as provided in division (B) of this section, the highway patrol shall supervise and conduct the testing of persons applying for a commercial driver's license.

(B) The director may adopt rules, in accordance with Chapter 119. of the Revised Code and applicable requirements of the federal highway administration, authorizing the skills test specified in this section to be administered by any person, by an agency of this or another state, or by an agency, department, or instrumentality of local government and establishing a maximum fee that may be charged by the other party, provided the skills test is the same that otherwise would be administered by this state and that the other party has entered into an agreement with the director that includes, without limitation, all of the following:

(1) Allows the director or his representative and the federal highway administration or its representative to conduct random examinations, inspections, and audits of the other party without prior notice;

(2) Requires the director or his representative to conduct on-site inspections of the other party at least annually;

(3) Requires that all examiners of the other party meet the same qualification and training standards as examiners of the department of public safety, to the extent necessary to conduct skills tests in the manner required by 49 C.F.R. 383.110 through 383.135;

(4) Requires either that state employees take, at least annually and as though the employees were test applicants, the tests actually administered by the other party, that the director test a sample of drivers who were examined by the other party to compare the test results, or that state employees accompany a test applicant during an actual test;

(5) Reserves to this state the right to take prompt and appropriate remedial action against testers of the other party if the other party fails to comply with standards of this state or federal standards for the testing program or with any other terms of the contract.

(C) The director shall enter into an agreement with the department of education authorizing the skills test specified in this section to be administered by the department at any location operated by the department for purposes of training and testing school bus drivers, provided that the agreement between the director and the department complies with the requirements of division (B) of this section. Skills tests administered by the department shall be limited to persons applying for a commercial driver's license with a school bus endorsement.

(D) The director shall adopt rules, in accordance with Chapter 119. of the Revised Code, authorizing waiver of the skills test specified in this section for any applicant for a commercial driver's license who meets all of the following requirements:

(1) Certifies that, during the two-year period immediately preceding his application for a commercial driver's license, all of the following apply:

(a) He has not had more than one license;

(b) He has not had any license suspended, revoked, or canceled;

(c) He has not had any convictions for any type of motor vehicle for the offenses for which disqualification is prescribed in section 4506.16 of the Revised Code;

(d) He has not had any violation of a state or local law relating to motor vehicle traffic control other than a parking violation arising in connection with any traffic accident and has no record of an accident in which he was at fault.

(2) Certifies and also provides evidence that he is regularly employed in a job requiring him to operate a commercial motor vehicle and that one of the following applies:

(a) He has previously taken and passed a skills test given by a state with a classified licensing and testing system in which the test was behind-the-wheel in a representative vehicle for his commercial driver's license classification;

(b) He has regularly operated, for at least two years immediately preceding his application for a commercial driver's license, a vehicle representative of the commercial motor vehicle he operates or expects to operate.

(E)(1) The department of public safety may charge and collect a divisible fee of fifty dollars for each skills test given as part of a commercial driver's license examination. The fee shall consist of ten dollars for the pretrip inspection portion of the test, ten dollars for the off-road maneuvering portion of the test, and thirty dollars for the on-road portion of the test.

(2) The director may require an applicant for a commercial driver's license who schedules an appointment with the highway patrol to take all portions of the skills test, to pay an appointment fee of fifty dollars at the time he schedules the appointment. If the applicant appears at the time and location specified for the appointment and takes all portions of the skills test during that appointment, the appointment fee shall serve as the skills test fee. If the applicant schedules an appointment with the highway patrol to take all portions of the skills test and fails to appear at the time and location specified for the appointment, no portion of the appointment fee shall be refunded. If the applicant schedules an appointment with the highway patrol to take all portions of the skills test and appears at the time and location specified for the appointment, but declines or is unable to take all portions of the skills test, the appointment fee shall serve as the skills test fee. If the applicant cancels a scheduled appointment forty-eight hours or more prior to the time of the appointment time, the applicant shall not forfeit his appointment fee.

An applicant for a commercial driver's license who schedules an appointment with the highway patrol to take one or more, but not all, portions of the skills test shall not be required to pay any appointment fee when scheduling such an appointment.

(3) All fees collected under division (E) of this section shall be deposited in the state highway safety fund.

(F) As used in this section, "skills test" means a test of an applicant's ability to drive the type of commercial motor vehicle for which he seeks a commercial driver's license by having the applicant drive such a motor vehicle while under the supervision of an authorized state driver's license examiner or tester.

HISTORY: 143 v H 381 (Eff 7-1-89); 143 v H 88 (Eff 3-13-90); 144 v S 98 (Eff 11-12-92); 145 v H 687. Eff 10-12-94.

§ 4506.10 Driver to be physically qualified; medical examination; restrictions on license.

(A) No person who holds a valid commercial driver's license shall drive a commercial motor vehicle unless he is physically qualified to do so. Each person who drives or expects to drive a commercial motor vehicle in interstate or foreign commerce or is otherwise subject to 49 C.F.R. 391, et seq., as amended, shall certify to the registrar of motor vehicles at the time of application for a commercial driver's license that he is in compliance with these standards. Any person who is not subject to 49 C.F.R. 391, et seq., as amended, also shall certify at the time of application that he is not subject to these standards.

(B) A person is qualified to drive a class B commercial motor vehicle with a school bus endorsement, if he has been certified as medically qualified in accordance with rules adopted by the department of education.

(C) Any medical examination required by this section shall be performed only by a person licensed under Chapter 4731. of the Revised Code to practice medicine or surgery or osteopathic medicine and surgery in this state, or licensed under any similar law of another state, except that any part of such an examination that pertains to visual acuity, field of vision, and the ability to recognize colors may be performed by a person licensed under Chapter 4725. of the Revised Code to practice optometry in this state, or licensed under any similar law of another state.

(D) Whenever good cause appears, the registrar, upon issuing a commercial driver's license under this chapter, may impose restrictions suitable to the licensee's driving ability with respect to the type of motor vehicle or special mechanical control devices required on a motor vehicle which the licensee may operate, or such other restrictions applicable to the licensee as the registrar determines to be necessary.

The registrar may either issue a special restricted license or may set forth such restrictions upon the usual license form.

The registrar, upon receiving satisfactory evidence of any violation of the restrictions of such license, may suspend or revoke the same.

The registrar, upon receiving satisfactory evidence that an applicant or holder of a commercial driver's license has violated division (A)(4) of section 4506.04 of the Revised Code and knowingly given false information in any application or certification required by section 4506.07 of the Revised Code, shall cancel the commercial driver's license of the person or any pending application from the person for a commercial driver's license or class D driver's license for a period of at least sixty days, during which time no application for a commercial driver's license or class D driver's license shall be received from the person.

HISTORY: 143 v H 381 (Eff 7-1-89); 143 v H 88. Eff 3-13-90.

§ 4506.11 Form and material of license; file of negatives.

(A) Every commercial driver's license shall be marked "commercial driver's license" or "CDL" and shall be of such material and so designed as to prevent its reproduction or alteration without ready detection, and, to this end, shall be laminated with a transparent plastic material. The commercial driver's license for licensees under twenty-one years of age shall have characteristics prescribed by the registrar of motor vehicles distinguishing it from that issued to a licensee who is twenty-one years of age or older. Every commercial driver's license shall contain all of the following information:

(1) The name and residence address of the licensee;
(2) A color photograph of the licensee;
(3) A physical description of the licensee, including sex, height, weight, and color of eyes and hair;
(4) The licensee's date of birth;
(5) The licensee's social security number and any number or other identifier the director of public safety considers appropriate and establishes by rules adopted under Chapter 119. of the Revised Code and in compliance with federal law;
(6) The licensee's signature;
(7) The classes of commercial motor vehicles the licensee is authorized to drive and any endorsements or restrictions relating to his driving of those vehicles;
(8) A space marked "blood type" in which the licensee may specify his blood type;
(9) The name of this state;
(10) The dates of issuance and of expiration of the license;
(11) If the licensee has certified willingness to make an anatomical donation under section 2108.04 of the Revised Code, any symbol chosen by the registrar of motor vehicles to indicate that the licensee has certified that willingness;
(12) On and after May 1, 1993, if the licensee has executed a durable power of attorney for health care or a declaration governing the use or continuation, or the withholding or withdrawal, of life-sustaining treatment and has specified that he wishes his license to indicate that he has executed either type of instrument, any symbol chosen by the registrar to indicate that the licensee has executed either type of instrument;
(13) Any other information the registrar considers advisable and requires by rule.

(B) The registrar may establish and maintain a file of negatives of photographs taken for the purposes of this section.

(C) Neither the registrar nor any deputy registrar shall issue a commercial driver's license to anyone under twenty-one years of age that does not have the characteristics prescribed by the registrar distinguishing it from the commercial driver's license issued to persons who are twenty-one years of age or older.

HISTORY: 143 v H 381 (Eff 7-1-89); 143 v S 131 (Eff 7-25-90); 144 v H 134 (Eff 10-10-91); 144 v H 427 (Eff 10-8-92); 144 v S 98 (Eff 11-12-92); 145 v H 580. Eff 12-9-94.

The provisions of § 4 of HB 580 (145 v —) read as follows:

SECTION 4. Section 4506.11 of the Revised Code is presented in this act as a composite of the section as amended by both Sub. H.B. 427 and Am. Sub. S.B. 98 of the 119th General Assembly, with the new language of neither of the acts shown in capital letters. This is in recognition of the principle stated in division (B) of section 1.52 of the Revised Code that such amendments are to be harmonized where not substantively irreconcilable and constitutes a legislative finding that such is

§ 4506.12 Classes of licenses; endorsements; restrictions.

(A) Commercial drivers' licenses shall be issued in the following classes and shall include any endorsements and restrictions that are applicable. Subject to any such endorsements and restrictions, the holder of a valid commercial driver's license may drive all commercial motor vehicles in the class for which that license is issued and all lesser classes of vehicles, except that he shall not operate a motorcycle unless he is licensed to do so under Chapter 4507. of the Revised Code.

(B) The classes of commercial drivers' licenses and the commercial motor vehicles that they authorize the operation of are as follows:

(1) Class A—any combination of vehicles with a combined gross vehicle weight rating of twenty-six thousand one pounds or more, if the gross vehicle weight rating of the vehicle or vehicles being towed is in excess of ten thousand pounds.

(2) Class B—any single vehicle with a gross vehicle weight rating of twenty-six thousand one pounds or more, or any such vehicle towing a vehicle having a gross vehicle weight rating that is not in excess of ten thousand pounds.

(3) Class C—any single vehicle, or combination of vehicles, that is not a class A or class B vehicle, but that either is designed to transport sixteen or more passengers, including the driver, or is placarded for hazardous materials and any school bus with a gross vehicle weight rating of less than twenty-six thousand one pounds that is designed to transport fewer than sixteen passengers including the driver.

(C) The following endorsements and restrictions apply to commercial drivers' licenses:

(1) H—authorizes the driver to drive a vehicle transporting hazardous materials;

(2) K—restricts the driver to only intrastate operation;

(3) L—restricts the driver to vehicles not equipped with air brakes;

(4) T—authorizes the driver to drive double and triple trailers;

(5) P—authorizes the driver to drive vehicles carrying passengers;

(6) P1—authorizes the driver to drive class A vehicles with fewer than fifteen passengers and all lesser classes of vehicles without restriction as to the number of passengers;

(7) P2—authorizes the driver to drive class A or B vehicles with fewer than fifteen passengers and all lesser classes of vehicles without restriction as to the number of passengers;

(8) P3—restricts the driver to driving class B school buses;

(9) P4—Restricts the driver to driving class C school buses designed to transport fewer than sixteen passengers including the driver.

(10) N—authorizes the driver to drive tank vehicles;

(11) S—authorizes the driver to drive school buses;

(12) X—authorizes the driver to drive tank vehicles transporting hazardous materials;

(13) W—restricts the driver to the operation of commercial motor vehicles in accordance with a waiver for farm-related service industries issued under section 4506.24 of the Revised Code.

(D) No person shall drive any commercial motor vehicle for which an endorsement is required under this section unless the proper endorsement appears on the person's commercial driver's license.

HISTORY: 143 v H 381 (Eff 7-1-89); 143 v H 88 (Eff 3-13-90); 143 v H 831 (Eff 7-17-90); 144 v H 485. Eff 7-8-92.

§ 4506.13 Examinations passed form; commercial driver license information system.

(A) The registrar may authorize the highway patrol to issue an examiner's commercial examinations passed form to an applicant who has passed the required examinations. The examiner's commercial examinations passed form shall be used, once it has been validated, to indicate the examinations taken and passed by the commercial driver's license applicant.

(B) Before issuing a commercial driver's license, the registrar of motor vehicles shall obtain information about the applicant's driving record through the commercial driver license information system, when available, and the national driver register. If the record check reveals information that the applicant claims is outdated, contested, or invalid, the registrar shall deny the application until the applicant can resolve the conflict.

Within ten days after issuing a commercial driver's license, the registrar shall notify the commercial driver license information system, when available, of that fact and shall provide all information required to ensure identification of the licensee.

HISTORY: 143 v H 381 (Eff 7-1-89); 143 v H 88 (Eff 3-13-90); 143 v H 831. Eff 7-17-90.

§ 4506.14 Expiration, renewal of license; notice of change of address.

(A) Commercial driver's licenses shall expire as follows:

(1) Except as provided in division (A)(3) of this section, each such license issued to replace an operator's or chauffeur's license shall expire on the original expiration date of the operator's or chauffeur's license and, upon renewal, shall expire on the licensee's birthday in the fourth year after the date of issuance.

(2) Except as provided in division (A)(3) of this section, each such license issued as an original license to

a person whose residence is in this state shall expire on the licensee's birthday in the fourth year after the date of issuance, and each such license issued to a person whose temporary residence is in this state shall expire in accordance with rules adopted by the registrar of motor vehicles. A license issued to a person with a temporary residence in this state is nonrenewable, but may be replaced with a new license within ninety days prior to its expiration upon the applicant's compliance with all applicable requirements.

(3) Each such license issued to replace the operator's or chauffeur's license of a person who is less than twenty-one years of age, and each such license issued as an original license to a person who is less than twenty-one years of age, shall expire on the licensee's twenty-first birthday.

(B) No commercial driver's license shall be issued for a period longer than four years and ninety days. Except as provided in section 4507.12 of the Revised Code, the registrar may waive the examination of any person applying for the renewal of a commercial driver's license issued under this chapter, provided that the applicant presents either an unexpired commercial driver's license or a commercial driver's license that has expired not more than six months prior to the date of application.

(C) Subject to the requirements of this chapter and except as provided in division (A)(2) of this section in regard to a person whose temporary residence is in this state, every commercial driver's license shall be renewable ninety days before its expiration upon payment of the fees required by section 4506.08 of the Revised Code. Each person applying for renewal of a commercial driver's license shall complete the application form prescribed by section 4506.07 of the Revised Code and shall provide all certifications required. If the person wishes to retain an endorsement authorizing the person to transport hazardous materials, the person shall take and successfully complete the written test for the endorsement.

(D) Each person licensed as a driver under this chapter shall notify the registrar of any change in the person's address within ten days following that change. The notification shall be in writing on a form provided by the registrar and shall include the full name, date of birth, license number, county of residence, social security number, and new address of the person.

HISTORY: 143 v H 381 (Eff 7-1-89); 143 v H 88 (Eff 3-13-90); 143 v S 382 (Eff 12-31-90); 144 v H 134 (Eff 10-10-91); 144 v S 98 (Eff 11-12-92); 145 v H 687 (Eff 10-12-94); 147 v S 60. Eff 10-21-97.

§ 4506.15 Alcohol and other prohibitions.

No person shall do any of the following:

(A) Drive a commercial motor vehicle while having a measurable or detectable amount of alcohol or of a controlled substance in his blood, breath, or urine;

(B) Drive a commercial motor vehicle while having an alcohol concentration of four-hundredths of one per cent or more;

(C) Drive a commercial motor vehicle while under the influence of a controlled substance;

(D) Knowingly leave the scene of an accident involving a commercial motor vehicle driven by the person;

(E) Use a commercial motor vehicle in the commission of a felony;

(F) Refuse to submit to a test under section 4506.17 of the Revised Code;

(G) Violate an out-of-service order issued under this chapter;

(H) Violate any prohibition described in divisions (B) to (G) of this section while transporting hazardous materials.

HISTORY: 143 v H 381 (Eff 7-1-89); 143 v H 88. Eff 3-13-90.

§ 4506.16 Disqualification of driver or placement out of service.

(A) Whoever violates division (A) of section 4506.15 of the Revised Code or a similar law of another state or a foreign jurisdiction, immediately shall be placed out-of-service for twenty-four hours, in addition to any disqualification required by this section and any other penalty imposed by the Revised Code.

(B) The registrar of motor vehicles shall disqualify any person from operating a commercial motor vehicle as follows:

(1) Upon a first conviction for a violation of divisions (B) to (G) of section 4506.15 of the Revised Code or a similar law of another state or a foreign jurisdiction, one year, in addition to any other penalty imposed by the Revised Code;

(2) Upon a first conviction for a violation of division (H) of section 4506.15 of the Revised Code or a similar law of another state or a foreign jurisdiction, three years, in addition to any other penalty imposed by the Revised Code;

(3) Upon a second conviction for a violation of divisions (B) to (G) of section 4506.15 of the Revised Code or a similar law of another state or a foreign jurisdiction, or any combination of such violations arising from two or more separate incidents, the person shall be disqualified for life or for any other period of time as determined by the United States secretary of transportation and designated by the director of public safety by rule, in addition to any other penalty imposed by the Revised Code;

(4) Upon conviction of a violation of division (E) of section 4506.15 of the Revised Code or a similar law of another state or a foreign jurisdiction in connection with the manufacture, distribution, or dispensing of a controlled substance or the possession with intent to manufacture, distribute, or dispense a controlled substance, the person shall be disqualified for life, in addition to any other penalty imposed by the Revised Code;

(5) Upon conviction of two serious traffic violations

involving the operation of a commercial motor vehicle by the person and arising from separate incidents occurring in a three-year period, the person shall be disqualified for sixty days, in addition to any other penalty imposed by the Revised Code;

(6) Upon conviction of three serious traffic violations involving the operation of a commercial motor vehicle by the person and arising from separate incidents occurring in a three-year period, the person shall be disqualified for one hundred twenty days, in addition to any other penalty imposed by the Revised Code.

(C) For the purposes of this section, conviction of a violation for which disqualification is required may be evidenced by any of the following:

(1) A judgment entry of a court of competent jurisdiction in this or any other state;

(2) An administrative order of a state agency of a state other than Ohio having statutory jurisdiction over commercial drivers;

(3) A computer record obtained from or through the commercial driver's license information system;

(4) A computer record obtained from or through a state agency of a state other than Ohio having statutory jurisdiction over commercial drivers or the records of commercial drivers.

(D) Any record described in division (C) of this section shall be deemed to be self-authenticating when it is received by the bureau of motor vehicles.

(E) When disqualifying a driver, the registrar shall cause the records of the bureau to be updated to reflect that action within ten days after it occurs.

(F) The registrar immediately shall notify a driver who is finally convicted of any offense described in section 4506.15 of the Revised Code or division (B)(4), (5), or (6) of this section and thereby is subject to disqualification, of the offense or offenses involved, of the length of time for which disqualification is to be imposed, and that the driver may request a hearing within thirty days of the mailing of the notice to show cause why the driver should not be disqualified from operating a commercial motor vehicle. If a request for such a hearing is not made within thirty days of the mailing of the notice, the order of disqualification is final. The registrar may designate hearing examiners who, after affording all parties reasonable notice, shall conduct a hearing to determine whether the disqualification order is supported by reliable evidence. The registrar shall adopt rules to implement this division.

(G) Any person who is disqualified from operating a commercial motor vehicle under this section may apply to the registrar for a driver's license to operate a motor vehicle other than a commercial motor vehicle, provided the person's commercial driver's license is not otherwise suspended or revoked. A person whose commercial driver's license is suspended or revoked shall not apply to the registrar for or receive a driver's license under Chapter 4507. of the Revised Code during the period of suspension or revocation.

HISTORY: 143 v H 381 (Eff 7-1-89); 144 v S 98 (Eff 11-12-92); 144 v S 275 (Eff 9-1-93); 145 v S 62, § 4 (Eff 9-1-93); 147 v S 60. Eff 10-21-97.

§ 4506.17 Implied consent to test; effect of refusal; immediate surrender of license; disqualification procedure.

(A) Any person who drives a commercial motor vehicle within this state shall be deemed to have given consent to a test or tests of the person's blood, breath, or urine for the purpose of determining the person's alcohol concentration or the presence of any controlled substance.

(B) A test or tests as provided in division (A) of this section may be administered at the direction of a peace officer having reasonable ground to stop or detain the person and, after investigating the circumstances surrounding the operation of the commercial motor vehicle, also having reasonable ground to believe the person was driving the commercial vehicle while having a measurable or detectable amount of alcohol or of a controlled substance in the person's blood, breath, or urine. Any such test shall be given within two hours of the time of the alleged violation.

(C) A person requested to submit to a test under division (A) of this section shall be advised by the peace officer requesting the test that a refusal to submit to the test will result in the person immediately being placed out-of-service for a period of twenty-four hours and being disqualified from operating a commercial motor vehicle for a period of not less than one year, and that the person is required to surrender the person's commercial driver's license to the peace officer.

(D) If a person refuses to submit to a test after being warned as provided in division (C) of this section or submits to a test that discloses the presence of a controlled substance or an alcohol concentration of four-hundredths of one per cent or more, the person immediately shall surrender the person's commercial driver's license to the peace officer. The peace officer shall forward the license, together with a sworn report, to the registrar of motor vehicles certifying that the test was requested pursuant to division (A) of this section and that the person either refused to submit to testing or submitted to a test that disclosed the presence of a controlled substance or an alcohol concentration of four-hundredths of one per cent or more. The form and contents of the report required by this section shall be established by the registrar by rule, but shall contain the advice to be read to the driver and a statement to be signed by the driver acknowledging that the driver has been read the advice and that the form was shown to the driver.

(E) Upon receipt of a sworn report from a peace officer as provided in division (D) of this section, the registrar shall disqualify the person named in the report from driving a commercial motor vehicle for the period described below:

(1) Upon a first incident, one year;

(2) Upon an incident of refusal or of a prohibited concentration of alcohol after one or more previous incidents of either refusal or of a prohibited concentration of alcohol, the person shall be disqualified for life or such lesser period as prescribed by rule by the registrar.

(F) A blood test given under this section shall comply with the applicable provisions of division (D) of section 4511.19 of the Revised Code and any physician, registered nurse, or qualified technician or chemist who withdraws blood from a person under this section, and any hospital, first-aid station, or clinic at which blood is withdrawn from a person pursuant to this section, is immune from criminal liability, and from civil liability that is based upon a claim of assault and battery or based upon any other claim of malpractice, for any act performed in withdrawing blood from the person.

(G) When a person submits to a test under this section, the results of the test, at the person's request, shall be made available to the person, the person's attorney, or the person's agent, immediately upon completion of the chemical test analysis. The person also may have an additional test administered by a physician, a registered nurse, or a qualified technician or chemist of the person's own choosing as provided in division (D) of section 4511.19 of the Revised Code for tests administered under that section, and the failure to obtain such a test has the same effect as in that division.

(H) No person shall refuse to immediately surrender the person's commercial driver's license to a peace officer when required to do so by this section.

(I) A peace officer issuing an out-of-service order or receiving a commercial driver's license surrendered under this section may remove or arrange for the removal of any commercial motor vehicle affected by the issuance of that order or the surrender of that license.

(J)(1) Except for civil actions arising out of the operation of a motor vehicle and civil actions in which the state is a plaintiff, no peace officer of any law enforcement agency within this state is liable in compensatory damages in any civil action that arises under the Revised Code or common law of this state for an injury, death, or loss to person or property caused in the performance of official duties under this section and rules adopted under this section, unless the officer's actions were manifestly outside the scope of the officer's employment or official responsibilities, or unless the officer acted with malicious purpose, in bad faith, or in a wanton or reckless manner.

(2) Except for civil actions that arise out of the operation of a motor vehicle and civil actions in which the state is a plaintiff, no peace officer of any law enforcement agency within this state is liable in punitive or exemplary damages in any civil action that arises under the Revised Code or common law of this state for any injury, death, or loss to person or property caused in the performance of official duties under this section of the Revised Code and rules adopted under this section, unless the officer's actions were manifestly outside the scope of the officer's employment or official responsibilities, or unless the officer acted with malicious purpose, in bad faith, or in a wanton or reckless manner.

(K) When disqualifying a driver, the registrar shall cause the records of the bureau of motor vehicles to be updated to reflect the disqualification within ten days after it occurs.

(L) The registrar immediately shall notify a driver who is subject to disqualification of the disqualification, of the length of the disqualification, and that the driver may request a hearing within thirty days of the mailing of the notice to show cause why the driver should not be disqualified from operating a commercial motor vehicle. If a request for such a hearing is not made within thirty days of the mailing of the notice, the order of disqualification is final. The registrar may designate hearing examiners who, after affording all parties reasonable notice, shall conduct a hearing to determine whether the disqualification order is supported by reliable evidence. The registrar shall adopt rules to implement this division.

(M) Any person who is disqualified from operating a commercial motor vehicle under this section may apply to the registrar for a driver's license to operate a motor vehicle other than a commercial motor vehicle, provided the person's commercial driver's license is not otherwise suspended or revoked. A person whose commercial driver's license is suspended or revoked shall not apply to the registrar for or receive a driver's license under Chapter 4507. of the Revised Code during the period of suspension or revocation.

HISTORY: 143 v H 381 (Eff 7-1-89); 143 v H 88 (Eff 3-13-90); 145 v S 82 (Eff 5-4-94); 147 v S 60. Eff 10-21-97.

§ 4506.18 Driver to give notice of out-of-state conviction.

Any driver who holds a commercial driver's license issued by this state and is convicted in another state or a foreign jurisdiction of violating any law or ordinance relating to motor vehicle traffic control, other than a parking violation, shall provide written notice of that conviction within thirty days after the date of conviction to the bureau of motor vehicles and to his employer in accordance with the provisions of 49 C.F.R. 383, subpart C, as amended.

HISTORY: 143 v H 381. Eff 7-1-89.

§ 4506.19 Provisions of 49 C.F.R. 383, subpart C.

The provisions of 49 C.F.R. 383, subpart C, as amended, shall apply to all commercial drivers or persons who apply for employment as commercial drivers. No person shall fail to make a report to his employer as required by this section.

HISTORY: 143 v H 381. Eff 7-1-89.

§ 4506.20 Duties of employer of driver.

(A) Each employer shall require every applicant for employment as a driver of a commercial motor vehicle to provide the information specified in section 4506.20 of the Revised Code.

(B) No employer shall knowingly permit or authorize any driver employed by him to drive a commercial motor vehicle during any period in which any of the following apply:

(1) The driver's commercial driver's license is suspended, revoked, or canceled by any state or a foreign jurisdiction;

(2) The driver has lost his privilege to drive, or currently is disqualified from driving, a commercial motor vehicle in any state or foreign jurisdiction;

(3) The driver is subject to an out-of-service order in any state or a foreign jurisdiction;

(4) The driver has more than one driver's license.

HISTORY: 143 v H 381. Eff 7-1-89.

§ 4506.21 Notice of conviction of nonresident licensee.

Within ten days after receiving a report of conviction of any nonresident holder of a commercial driver's license for a violation of a state law or local ordinance or resolution relating to traffic control, other than parking violations, committed in a commercial motor vehicle, the registrar of motor vehicles shall notify the driver licensing authority in the state that issued the nonresident's commercial driver's license of the conviction.

HISTORY: 143 v H 381. Eff 7-1-89.

§ 4506.22 Rules to carry out chapter; authority of public safety department, public utilities commission.

(A) The director of public safety and the registrar of motor vehicles, subject to approval by the director, may, in accordance with Chapter 119. of the Revised Code, adopt any rules necessary to carry out this chapter.

(B) The department of public safety may do all of the following:

(1) Enter into or make any agreements, arrangements, or declarations necessary to carry out this chapter;

(2) Charge a fee for all publications that is equal to the cost of printing the publications.

(C) Nothing in this chapter shall be construed to restrict the authority of the public utilities commission specified in Chapters 4921. and 4923. of the Revised Code regarding safety rules applicable to motor carriers.

HISTORY: 143 v H 381 (Eff 7-1-89); 144 v S 98 (Eff 11-12-92); 146 v S 162. Eff 10-29-95.

§ 4506.23 Duties of peace officer as to alcohol or drug offenders.

Within the jurisdictional limits of his appointing authority, any peace officer shall stop and detain any person found violating section 4506.15 of the Revised Code, without obtaining a warrant. When there is reasonable ground to believe that a violation of section 4506.15 of the Revised Code has been committed and a test or tests of the person's blood, breath, or urine is necessary, the peace officer shall take the person to an appropriate place for testing. If a person refuses to submit to a test after being warned as provided in division (C) of section 4506.17 of the Revised Code or submits to a test that discloses the presence of a controlled substance or an alcohol concentration of four-hundredths of one per cent or more, the peace officer shall require that the person immediately surrender his commercial driver's license to the peace officer.

As used in this section, "jurisdictional limits" means the limits within which a peace officer may arrest and detain a person without a warrant under section 2935.03 of the Revised Code, except that the superintendent and the troopers of the state highway patrol may stop and detain, without warrant, any person who, in the presence of the superintendent or any trooper, is engaged in the violation of this chapter.

HISTORY: 143 v H 381 (Eff 7-1-89); 143 v H 88 (Eff 3-13-90); 144 v S 144. Eff 8-8-91.

§ 4506.24 Restricted license and waiver for farm-related service industries.

(A) A restricted commercial driver's license and waiver for farm-related service industries may be issued by the registrar of motor vehicles to allow a person to operate a commercial motor vehicle during seasonal periods determined by the registrar and subject to the restrictions set forth in this section.

(B) Upon receiving an application for a restricted commercial driver's license under section 4506.07 of the Revised Code and payment of a fee as provided in section 4506.08 of the Revised Code, the registrar may issue such license to any person who meets all of the following requirements:

(1) Has at least one year of driving experience in any type of vehicle;

(2) Holds a valid driver's license, other than a restricted license, issued under Chapter 4507. of the Revised Code;

(3) Certifies that during the one-year period immediately preceding application, all of the following apply:

(a) The person has not had more than one license;

(b) The person has not had any license suspended, revoked, or canceled;

(c) The person has not had any convictions for any type of motor vehicle for the offenses for which disqualification is prescribed in section 4506.16 of the Revised Code;

(d) The person has not had any violation of a state or local law relating to motor vehicle traffic control other than a parking violation arising in connection with any traffic accident and has no record of an accident in which the person was at fault.

(4) Certifies and also provides evidence that the person is employed in one or more of the following farm-related service industries requiring the person to operate a commercial motor vehicle:

(a) Custom harvesters;
(b) Farm retail outlets and suppliers;
(c) Agri-chemical business;
(d) Livestock feeders.

(C) An annual waiver for farm-related service industries may be issued to authorize the holder of a restricted commercial driver's license to operate a commercial motor vehicle during seasonal periods designated by the registrar. The registrar shall determine the format of the waiver. The total number of days that a person may operate a commercial motor vehicle pursuant to a waiver for farm-related service industries shall not exceed one hundred eighty days in any twelve-month period. Each time the holder of a restricted commercial driver's license applies for a waiver for farm-related service industries, the registrar shall verify that the person meets all of the requirements set forth in division (B) of this section. The restricted commercial driver's license and waiver shall be carried at all times when a commercial motor vehicle is being operated by the holder of the license and waiver.

(D) The holder of a restricted commercial driver's license and valid waiver for farm-related service industries may operate a class B or C commercial motor vehicle subject to all of the following restrictions:

(1) The commercial motor vehicle is operated within a distance of no more than one hundred fifty miles of the employer's place of business or the farm currently being served;

(2) The operation of the commercial motor vehicle does not involve transporting hazardous materials for which placarding is required, except as follows:

(a) Diesel fuel in quantities of one thousand gallons or less;
(b) Liquid fertilizers in vehicles or implements of husbandry with total capacities of three thousand gallons or less;
(c) Solid fertilizers that are not transported with any organic substance.

(E) Except as otherwise provided in this section an applicant for or holder of a restricted commercial driver's license and waiver for farm-related service industries is subject to the provisions of this chapter. Divisions (A)(4) and (B)(1) of section 4506.07 and sections 4506.09 and 4506.10 of the Revised Code do not apply to an applicant for a restricted commercial driver's license and waiver.

HISTORY: 144 v H 485 (Eff 7-8-92); 147 v H 210. Eff 3-31-97.

§ 4506.99 Penalties.

(A) Whoever violates division (A) of section 4506.03, division (A)(1), (2), or (3) of section 4506.04, division (A) of section 4506.10, division (H) of section 4506.17, or section 4506.20 of the Revised Code is guilty of a misdemeanor of the first degree.

(B) Whoever violates division (A)(4) of section 4506.04 of the Revised Code is guilty of falsification, a misdemeanor of the first degree. In addition, the provisions of section 4507.19 of the Revised Code apply.

(C) Whoever violates division (C) of section 4506.11 or division (D) of section 4506.14 of the Revised Code is guilty of a minor misdemeanor.

(D) Whoever violates any provision of sections 4506.03 to 4506.20 of the Revised Code for which no penalty is otherwise provided in this section is guilty of a misdemeanor of the first degree.

HISTORY: 143 v H 381 (Eff 7-1-89); 143 v H 88 (Eff 3-13-90); 144 v H 134. Eff 10-10-91.

CHAPTER 4507: DRIVER'S LICENSE LAW

§ 4507.01 Definitions; deputy registrars; laminating equipment, materials.

(A) As used in this chapter, "motor vehicle," "motorized bicycle," "state," "owner," "operator," "chauffeur," and "highways" have the same meanings as in section 4501.01 of the Revised Code.

"Driver's license" means a class D license issued to any person to operate a motor vehicle or motor-driven cycle, other than a commercial motor vehicle, and includes "probationary license," "restricted license," and any operator's or chauffeur's license issued before January 1, 1990.

"Probationary license" means the license issued to any person between sixteen and eighteen years of age to operate a motor vehicle.

"Restricted license" means the license issued to any person to operate a motor vehicle subject to conditions or restrictions imposed by the registrar of motor vehicles.

"Commercial driver's license" means the license issued to a person under Chapter 4506. of the Revised Code to operate a commercial motor vehicle.

"Commercial motor vehicle" has the same meaning as in section 4506.01 of the Revised Code.

"Motorized bicycle license" means the license issued under section 4511.521 [4511.52.1] of the Revised Code to any person to operate a motorized bicycle including a "probationary motorized bicycle license."

"Probationary motorized bicycle license" means the license issued under section 4511.521 [4511.52.1] of the Revised Code to any person between fourteen and sixteen years of age to operate a motorized bicycle.

"Identification card" means a card issued under sections 4507.50 and 4507.51 of the Revised Code.

"Resident" means a person who, in accordance with standards prescribed in rules adopted by the registrar, resides in this state on a permanent basis.

"Temporary resident" means a person who, in accordance with standards prescribed in rules adopted by the registrar, resides in this state on a temporary basis.

(B) In the administration of this chapter and Chapter 4506. of the Revised Code, the registrar has the same authority as is conferred on the registrar by section 4501.02 of the Revised Code. Any act of an authorized deputy registrar of motor vehicles under direction of the registrar is deemed the act of the registrar.

To carry out this chapter, the registrar shall appoint such deputy registrars in each county as are necessary.

The registrar also shall provide at each place where an application for a driver's or commercial driver's license or identification card may be made the necessary equipment to take a color photograph of the applicant for such license or card as required under section 4506.11 or 4507.06 of the Revised Code, and to conduct the vision screenings required by section 4507.12 of the Revised Code, and equipment to laminate licenses, motorized bicycle licenses, and identification cards as required by sections 4507.13, 4507.52, and 4511.521 [4511.52.1] of the Revised Code.

The registrar shall assign one or more deputy registrars to any driver's license examining station operated under the supervision of the state highway patrol, whenever the registrar considers such assignment possible. Space shall be provided in the driver's license examining station for any such deputy registrar so assigned. The deputy registrars shall not exercise the powers conferred by such sections upon the registrar, unless they are specifically authorized to exercise such powers by such sections.

(C) No agent for any insurance company, writing automobile insurance, shall be appointed deputy registrar, and any such appointment is void. No deputy registrar shall in any manner solicit any form of automobile insurance, nor in any manner advise, suggest, or influence any licensee or applicant for license for or against any kind or type of automobile insurance, insurance company, or agent, nor have the deputy registrar's office directly connected with the office of any automobile insurance agent, nor impart any information furnished by any applicant for a license or identification card to any person, except the registrar. This division shall not apply to any nonprofit corporation appointed deputy registrar.

(D) The registrar shall immediately remove a deputy registrar who violates the requirements of this chapter.

(E) The registrar shall periodically solicit bids and enter into a contract for the provision of laminating equipment and laminating materials to the registrar and all deputy registrars. The registrar shall not consider any bid that does not provide for the supplying of both laminating equipment and laminating materials. The laminating materials selected shall contain a security feature so that any tampering with the laminating material covering a license or identification card is readily apparent. In soliciting bids and entering into a contract for the provision of laminating equipment and laminating materials, the registrar shall observe all procedures required by law.

HISTORY: GC § 6296-2; 116 v PtII, 33, § 2; Bureau of Code Revision, 10-1-53; 127 v 839 (Eff 9-16-57); 129 v 421 (Eff 10-19-61); 130 v 1053 (Eff 9-27-63); 132 v H 380 (Eff 1-1-68); 132 v S 43 (Eff 1-1-69); 135 v S 1 (Eff 1-1-74); 135 v S 313 (Eff 7-26-74); 136 v S 435 (Eff 8-24-76); 137 v S 100 (Eff 4-1-78); 140 v S 169 (Eff 1-1-85); 140 v H 58 (Eff 3-1-85); 141 v H 428 (Eff 12-23-86); 142 v S 1 (Eff 11-28-88); 143 v H 381 (Eff 7-1-89); 143 v S 131 (Eff 7-25-90); 147 v S 60. Eff 10-21-97.

[§ 4507.01.1] § 4507.011 Each deputy registrar to pay rental fee; registrar rental fund; facility rentals fund.

(A) Each deputy registrar assigned to a driver's license examining station by the registrar of motor vehicles as provided in section 4507.01 of the Revised Code shall remit to the superintendent of the state highway patrol a rental fee equal to the percentage of space occupied by the deputy registrar in the driver's license examining station multiplied by the rental fee paid for the entire driver's license examining station plus a pro rata share of all utility costs. All such moneys received by the superintendent shall be deposited in the state treasury to the credit of the registrar rental fund, which is hereby created. The moneys in the fund shall be used by the state highway patrol only to pay the rent and expenses of the driver's license examining stations. All investment earnings of the fund shall be credited to the fund.

(B) Each deputy registrar assigned to a bureau of motor vehicles' location shall reimburse the registrar a monthly building rental fee, including applicable utility charges. All such moneys received by the registrar shall be deposited into the state treasury to the credit of the facility rentals fund, which is hereby created. The moneys in the fund shall be used by the registrar to obtain or lease and maintain deputy registrar facilities. All investment earnings of the fund shall be credited to the fund.

HISTORY: 140 v H 58, § 1 (Eff 10-1-84); 140 v H 58, § 4 (Eff 3-1-85); 141 v H 201 (Eff 7-1-85); 141 v S 269 (Eff 3-13-86); 145 v H 154. Eff 6-30-93.

[§ 4507.01.2] § 4507.012 "Suspension" or "revocation" defined.

As used in the Revised Code, "suspension" or "revocation," when applied to a driver's license, means, unless the context clearly indicates otherwise, the withdrawal from a resident, temporary resident, or nonresident of the privilege to operate a motor vehicle upon a street or highway in this state. The withdrawal of the privilege from a person causes the person to be ineligible for the privilege during the entire period of the suspension or revocation and also includes any period during which the resident, temporary resident, or nonresident either has not paid any applicable driver's license reinstatement fee or has not complied with any other requirement governing license reinstatement.

HISTORY: 147 v S 60. Eff 10-21-97.

§ 4507.02 Operation without valid license prohibited; multiple licenses; impoundment of plates; special plates.

(A)(1) No person, except those expressly exempted under sections 4507.03, 4507.04, and 4507.05 of the Revised Code, shall operate any motor vehicle upon a highway or any public or private property used by the public for purposes of vehicular travel or parking in this state unless the person has a valid driver's license issued under this chapter or a commercial driver's license issued under Chapter 4506. of the Revised Code.

(2) No person shall permit the operation of a motor vehicle upon any public or private property used by the public for purposes of vehicular travel or parking knowing the operator does not have a valid driver's license issued to the operator by the registrar of motor vehicles under this chapter or a valid commercial driver's license issued under Chapter 4506. of the Revised Code.

(3) No person, except a person expressly exempted under sections 4507.03, 4507.04, and 4507.05 of the Revised Code, shall operate any motorcycle upon a highway or any public or private property used by the public for purposes of vehicular travel or parking in this state unless the person has a valid license as a motorcycle operator, that was issued upon application by the registrar under this chapter. The license shall be in the form of an endorsement, as determined by the registrar, upon a driver's or commercial driver's license, if the person has a valid license to operate a motor vehicle or commercial motor vehicle, or in the form of a restricted license as provided in section 4507.14 of the Revised Code, if the person does not have a valid license to operate a motor vehicle or commercial motor vehicle.

(4) No person shall receive a driver's license, or a motorcycle operator's endorsement of a driver's or commercial driver's license, unless and until the person surrenders to the registrar all valid licenses issued to the person by another jurisdiction recognized by this state. All surrendered licenses shall be returned by the registrar to the issuing authority, together with information that a license is now issued in this state. No person shall be permitted to have more than one valid license at any time.

(B)(1) No person, whose driver's or commercial driver's license or permit or nonresident's operating privilege has been suspended or revoked pursuant to Chapter 4509. of the Revised Code, shall operate any motor vehicle within this state, or knowingly permit any motor vehicle owned by the person to be operated by another person in the state, during the period of the suspension or revocation, except as specifically authorized by Chapter 4509. of the Revised Code. No person shall operate a motor vehicle within this state, or knowingly permit any motor vehicle owned by the person to be operated by another person in the state, during the period in which the person is required by section 4509.45 of the Revised Code to file and maintain proof of financial responsibility for a violation of section 4509.101 [4509.10.1] of the Revised Code, unless proof of financial responsibility is maintained with respect to that vehicle.

(2) No person shall operate any motor vehicle upon a highway or any public or private property used by the public for purposes of vehicular travel or parking in this state in violation of any restriction of the person's driver's or commercial driver's license imposed under division (D) of section 4506.10 or section 4507.14 of the Revised Code.

(C) No person, whose driver's or commercial driver's license or permit has been suspended pursuant to section 4511.191 [4511.19.1], section 4511.196 [4511.19.-6], or division (B) of section 4507.16 of the Revised Code, shall operate any motor vehicle within this state until the person has paid the license reinstatement fee required pursuant to division (L) of section 4511.191 [4511.19.1] of the Revised Code and the license or permit has been returned to the person or a new license or permit has been issued to the person.

(D)(1) No person, whose driver's or commercial driver's license or permit or nonresident operating privilege has been suspended or revoked under any provision of the Revised Code other than Chapter 4509. of the Revised Code or under any applicable law in any other jurisdiction in which the person's license or permit was issued, shall operate any motor vehicle upon the highways or streets within this state during the period of the suspension or within one year after the date of the revocation. No person who is granted occupational driving privileges by any court shall operate any motor vehicle upon the highways or streets in this state except in accordance with the terms of the privileges.

(2) No person, whose driver's or commercial driver's license or permit or nonresident operating privilege has been suspended under division (B) of section 4507.16 of the Revised Code, shall operate any motor vehicle upon the highways or streets within this state during the period of suspension. No person who is granted occupational driving privileges by any court shall operate any motor vehicle upon the highways or streets in this state except in accordance with the terms of those privileges.

(E) It is an affirmative defense to any prosecution

brought pursuant to division (B), (C), or (D) of this section that the alleged offender drove under suspension or in violation of a restriction because of a substantial emergency, provided that no other person was reasonably available to drive in response to the emergency.

(F)(1) If a person is convicted of a violation of division (B), (C), or (D) of this section, the trial judge of any court, in addition to or independent of, any other penalties provided by law or ordinance, shall impound the identification license plates of any motor vehicle registered in the name of the person. The court shall send the impounded license plates to the registrar, who may retain the license plates until the driver's or commercial driver's license of the owner has been reinstated or destroy them pursuant to section 4503.232 [4503.23.2] of the Revised Code.

If the license plates of a person convicted of a violation of division (B), (C), or (D) of this section have been impounded in accordance with the provisions of this division, the court shall notify the registrar of that action. The notice shall contain the name and address of the driver, the serial number of the driver's driver's or commercial driver's license, the serial numbers of the license plates of the motor vehicle, and the length of time for which the license plates have been impounded. The registrar shall record the data in the notice as part of the driver's permanent record.

(2) Any motor vehicle owner who has had the license plates of a motor vehicle impounded pursuant to division (F)(1) of this section may apply to the registrar, or to a deputy registrar, for special license plates which shall conform to the requirements of section 4503.231 [4503.23.1] of the Revised Code. The registrar or deputy registrar forthwith shall notify the court of the application and, upon approval of the court, shall issue special license plates to the applicant. Until the driver's or commercial driver's license of the owner is reinstated, any new license plates issued to the owner also shall conform to the requirements of section 4503.231 [4503.23.1] of the Revised Code.

The registrar or deputy registrar shall charge the owner of a vehicle the fees provided in section 4503.19 of the Revised Code for special license plates that are issued in accordance with this division, except upon renewal as specified in section 4503.10 of the Revised Code, when the regular fee as provided in section 4503.04 of the Revised Code shall be charged. The registrar or deputy registrar shall charge the owner of a vehicle the fees provided in section 4503.19 of the Revised Code whenever special license plates are exchanged, by reason of the reinstatement of the driver's or commercial driver's license of the owner, for those ordinarily issued.

(3) If an owner wishes to sell a motor vehicle during the time the special license plates provided under division (F)(2) of this section are in use, the owner may apply to the court that impounded the license plates of the motor vehicle for permission to transfer title to the motor vehicle. If the court is satisfied that the sale will be made in good faith and not for the purpose of circumventing the provisions of this section, it may certify its consent to the owner and to the registrar of motor vehicles who shall enter notice of the transfer of the title of the motor vehicle in the vehicle registration record.

If, during the time the special license plates provided under division (F)(2) of this section are in use, the title to a motor vehicle is transferred by the foreclosure of a chattel mortgage, a sale upon execution, the cancellation of a conditional sales contract, or by order of a court, the court shall notify the registrar of the action and the registrar shall enter notice of the transfer of the title to the motor vehicle in the vehicle registration record.

(G) This section is not intended to change or modify any provision of Chapter 4503. of the Revised Code with respect to the taxation of motor vehicles or the time within which the taxes on motor vehicles shall be paid.

HISTORY: GC § 6296-29; 116 v PtII, 33, § 29; Bureau of Code Revision, RC § 4507.38, 10-1-53; 130 v 1060 (Eff 10-10-63); 131 v 1087 (Eff 10-30-65); 132 v H 518 (Eff 12-14-67); 132 v S 451 (Eff 2-29-68); 139 v S 432 (Eff 3-16-83); RC § 4507.02, 141 v S 356 (Eff 9-24-86); 141 v S 262 (Eff 3-20-87); 142 v H 419 (Eff 7-1-87); 143 v H 381 (Eff 7-1-89); 143 v S 131 (Eff 7-25-90); 144 v S 275 (Eff 9-1-93); 145 v S 62, §§ 1, 4 (Eff 9-1-93); 145 v H 687 (Eff 10-12-94); 145 v S 20 (Eff 4-20-95); 147 v S 60. Eff 10-21-97.

Analogous in part to former RC § 4507.02 (GC § 6296-4; 116 v PtII, 33, § 4; Bureau of Code Revision, 10-1-53; 131 v 1081; 132 v H 380; 133 v H 636), repealed 141 v S 356, § 2, eff 9-24-86.

The provisions of § 1 of HB 248 (146 v —) read as follows:

SECTION 1. That Section 6 of Am. Sub. S.B. 20 of the 120th General Assembly be amended to read as follows:

"Sec. 6. Sections 4503.20, 4507.02, and 4509.45 of the Revised Code, as amended by Am. Sub. S.B. 20 of the 120th General Assembly, and sections 4509.102, and 4509.104 of the Revised Code, as enacted by that act, shall take effect April 20, 1995. Section 4509.101 of the Revised Code, as amended by Am. Sub. S.B. 20 of the 120th General Assembly, shall take effect April 20, 1995, except that division (E) of the section shall first apply October 20, 1995. Sections 4509.103 and 4513.022 of the Revised Code, as enacted by Am. Sub. S.B. 20 of the 120th General Assembly, shall take effect October 20, 1995."

[§ 4507.02.1] § 4507.021 Point system for license suspension.

(A) Every county court judge, mayor of a mayor's court, and clerk of a court of record shall keep a full record of every case in which a person is charged with any violation of sections 4511.01 to 4511.771 [4511.77.1], 4511.99, and 4513.01 to 4513.36 of the Revised Code, or of any other law or ordinance regulating the operation of vehicles, streetcars, and trackless trolleys on highways or streets.

A United States district court whose jurisdiction lies

within this state may keep a full record of every case in which a person is charged with any violation of sections 4511.01 to 4511.771 [4511.77.1], 4511.99, and 4513.01 to 4513.36 of the Revised Code, or of any other law or ordinance regulating the operation of vehicles, streetcars, and trackless trolleys on highways or streets located on federal property within this state.

(B) If a person is convicted of or forfeits bail in relation to a violation of any section listed in division (A) of this section or a violation of any other law or ordinance regulating the operation of vehicles, streetcars, and trackless trolleys on highways or streets, the county court judge, mayor of a mayor's court, or clerk, within ten days after the conviction or bail forfeiture, shall prepare and immediately forward to the bureau of motor vehicles an abstract, certified by the preparer to be true and correct, of the court record covering the case in which the person was convicted or forfeited bail.

If a person is convicted of or forfeits bail in relation to a violation of any section listed in division (A) of this section or a violation of any other law or ordinance regulating the operation of vehicles, streetcars, and trackless trolleys on highways or streets, a United States district court whose jurisdiction lies within this state, within ten days after the conviction or bail forfeiture, may prepare and immediately forward to the bureau an abstract, certified by the preparer to be true and correct, of the court record covering the case in which the person was convicted or forfeited bail.

(C)(1) Each abstract required by division (B) of this section shall be made upon a form approved and furnished by the bureau and shall include the name and address of the person charged, the number of the person's driver's or commercial driver's license, the registration number of the vehicle involved, the nature of the offense, the date of the offense, the date of hearing, the plea, the judgment, or whether bail was forfeited, and the amount of the fine or forfeiture.

If a United States district court whose jurisdiction lies within this state utilizes the provision contained in division (B) of this section and forwards an abstract to the bureau, on a form approved and furnished by the bureau, containing all the information prescribed in division (C)(1) of this section, the bureau shall accept and process the abstract in the same manner as it accepts and processes an abstract received from a county judge, mayor of a mayor's court, or clerk of a court of record.

(2)(a) If a person is charged with a violation of section 4511.19 of the Revised Code or a violation of any ordinance relating to operating a vehicle while under the influence of alcohol, a drug of abuse, or alcohol and a drug of abuse or relating to operating a vehicle with a prohibited concentration of alcohol in the blood, breath, or urine; if that charge is dismissed or reduced; if the person is convicted of or forfeits bail in relation to a violation of any other section of the Revised Code or of any ordinance that regulates the operation of vehicles, streetcars, and trackless trolleys on highways and streets but that does not relate to operating a vehicle while under the influence of alcohol, a drug of abuse, or alcohol and a drug of abuse or to operating a vehicle with a prohibited concentration of alcohol in the blood, breath, or urine; and if the violation of which the person was convicted or in relation to which the person forfeited bail arose out of the same facts and circumstances and the same act as did the charge that was dismissed or reduced, the abstract also shall set forth the charge that was dismissed or reduced, indicate that it was dismissed or reduced, and indicate that the violation resulting in the conviction or bail forfeiture arose out of the same facts and circumstances and the same act as did the charge that was dismissed or reduced.

(b) If a charge against a person of a violation of division (B)(1) or (D)(2) of section 4507.02 of the Revised Code or any municipal ordinance that is substantially equivalent to that division is dismissed or reduced and if the person is convicted of or forfeits bail in relation to a violation of any other section of the Revised Code or any other ordinance that regulates the operation of vehicles, streetcars, and trackless trolleys on highways and streets that arose out of the same facts and circumstances as did the charge that was dismissed or reduced, the abstract also shall set forth the charge that was dismissed or reduced, indicate that it was dismissed or reduced, and indicate that the violation resulting in the conviction or bail forfeiture arose out of the same facts and circumstances and the same act as did the charge that was dismissed or reduced.

(3) If a person was convicted of or pleaded guilty to a violation of division (B)(1) or (D)(2) of section 4507.02 of the Revised Code, a substantially equivalent municipal ordinance, section 4507.33 or division (A) of section 4511.19 of the Revised Code, or a municipal ordinance relating to operating a vehicle while under the influence of alcohol, a drug of abuse, or alcohol and a drug of abuse or with a prohibited concentration of alcohol in the blood, breath, or urine, and division (E) of section 4503.234 [4503.23.4] of the Revised Code prohibits the registrar of motor vehicles and all deputy registrars from accepting an application for the registration of, or registering, any motor vehicle in the name of that person, the abstract shall specifically set forth these facts and clearly indicate the date on which the order of criminal forfeiture was issued or would have been issued but for the operation of division (C) of section 4503.234 [4503.23.4] or section 4503.235 [4503.23.5] of the Revised Code. If the registrar receives an abstract containing this information relating to a person, the registrar, in accordance with sections 4503.12 and 4503.234 [4503.23.4] of the Revised Code, shall take all necessary measures to prevent the registrar's office or any deputy registrar from accepting from the person, for the period of time ending five years after the date on which the order was issued or would have been issued and as described in division (E) of section 4503.234 [4503.23.4] of the Revised Code, any new application for the regis-

tration of any motor vehicle in the name of the person.

(D)(1) Every court of record also shall forward to the bureau an abstract of the court record as described in division (C) of this section upon the conviction of any person of aggravated vehicular homicide or vehicular homicide or of a felony in the commission of which a vehicle was used.

A United States district court whose jurisdiction lies within this state also may forward to the bureau an abstract as described in division (C) of this section upon the conviction of any person of aggravated vehicular homicide or vehicular homicide or of a felony in the commission of which a vehicle was used.

(2)(a) If a child has been adjudicated an unruly or delinquent child or a juvenile traffic offender for having committed any act that if committed by an adult would be a drug abuse offense, as defined in section 2925.01 of the Revised Code, or any violation of division (B) of section 2917.11 or of section 4511.19 of the Revised Code, the court shall notify the bureau, by means of an abstract of the court record as described in divisions (B) and (C) of this section, within ten days after the adjudication.

(b) If a court requires a child as provided in division (D)(2)(a) of this section to attend a drug abuse or alcohol abuse education, intervention, or treatment program, the abstract required by that division and forwarded to the bureau also shall include the name and address of the operator of the program and the date that the child entered the program. If the child satisfactorily completes the program, the court, immediately upon receipt of such information, shall send to the bureau an updated abstract that also shall contain the date on which the child satisfactorily completed the program.

(E) The purposeful failure or refusal of the officer to comply with this section constitutes misconduct in office and is a ground for removal from the office.

(F) The bureau shall record within ten days and keep all abstracts received under this section at its main office and shall maintain records of convictions and bond forfeitures for any violation of law or ordinance regulating the operation of vehicles, streetcars, and trackless trolleys on highways and streets, except as to parking a motor vehicle. The bureau also shall record any abstract of a case involving a first violation of division (D) of section 4511.21 of the Revised Code, whether or not points are to be assessed therefor, in such a manner that it becomes a part of the person's permanent record and assists a court in monitoring the assessment of points under division (G) of this section.

(G) Every court of record or mayor's court before which a person is charged with a violation for which points are chargeable by this section shall assess and transcribe to the abstract of conviction report, furnished by the bureau, the number of points chargeable by this section in the correct space assigned on the reporting form. A United States district court whose jurisdiction lies within this state and before whom a person is charged with a violation for which points are chargeable by this section may assess and transcribe to the abstract of conviction report, furnished by the bureau, the number of points chargeable by this section in the correct space assigned on the reporting form. If the court so assesses and transcribes to the abstract of conviction report the number of points chargeable, the bureau shall record the points in the same manner as those assessed and transcribed by every court of record or mayor's court of this state. The points shall be assessed based on the following formula:

(1) Violation of division (B), (C), or (D) of section 4507.02 of the Revised Code or any ordinance prohibiting the operation of a motor vehicle while the driver's or commercial driver's license is under suspension or revocation .... 6 points

(2) Violation of section 2913.03 of the Revised Code, except the provisions relating to use or operation of an aircraft or motorboat, or any ordinance prohibiting the operation of a vehicle without the consent of the owner .... 6 points

(3) Aggravated vehicular homicide or vehicular homicide, when either involves the operation of a vehicle, streetcar, or trackless trolley on a highway or street.... .... 6 points

(4) Violation of division (A) of section 4511.19 of the Revised Code, any ordinance prohibiting the operation of a vehicle while under the influence of alcohol, a drug of abuse, or alcohol and a drug of abuse, or any ordinance substantially equivalent to division (A) of section 4511.19 of the Revised Code prohibiting the operation of a vehicle with a prohibited concentration of alcohol in the blood, breath, or urine .... 6 points

(5) Violation of section 4549.02 or 4549.021 [4549.02.1] of the Revised Code or any ordinance requiring the driver of a vehicle to stop and disclose identity at the scene of an accident .... 6 points

(6) Violation of section 2921.331 [2921.33.1] of the Revised Code or any ordinance prohibiting the willful fleeing or eluding of a police officer .... 6 points

(7) Any crime punishable as a felony under the motor vehicle laws of this state, or any other felony in the commission of which a motor vehicle was used .... 6 points

(8) Operating a motor vehicle in violation of a restriction imposed by a registrar .... 2 points

(9) Violation of section 4511.251 [4511.25.1] of the Revised Code or any ordinance prohibiting street racing .... 6 points

(10) Violation of section 4511.20 of the Revised Code or any ordinance prohibiting the operation of a motor vehicle in willful or wanton disregard of the safety of persons or property .... 4 points

(11) Violation of division (B) of section 4511.19 of the Revised Code or any ordinance substantially equivalent to that division prohibiting the operation of a vehicle with a prohibited concentration of alcohol in the blood, breath, or urine .... 4 points

(12) Violation of any law or ordinance pertaining to speed, except as otherwise provided in this section and in division (G) of section 4511.21 of the Revised Code .... 2 points

(13) Upon a first violation of a limitation under division (D) of section 4511.21 of the Revised Code at a speed in excess of seventy-five miles per hour .... 2 points

(14) Upon a second violation within one year of the first violation of a limitation under division (D) of section 4511.21 of the Revised Code, for each increment of five miles per hour in excess of the posted speed limit, exclusive of the first five miles per hour over the limitation .... 1 point

(15) Upon a third or subsequent violation within one year of the first violation of a limitation under division (D) of section 4511.21 of the Revised Code, for each increment of five miles per hour in excess of the posted speed limit, exclusive of the first five miles per hour over the limitation .... 2 points

(16) All other moving violations pertaining to the operation of motor vehicles reported under this section, except any violations of section 4513.263 [4513.26.3] of the Revised Code or any substantively comparable ordinance, or violations under Chapter 5577. of the Revised Code .... 2 points

(H) Upon receiving notification from the proper court, including a United States district court whose jurisdiction lies within this state, the bureau shall delete any points entered for bond forfeiture in the event the driver is acquitted of the offense for which bond was posted.

(I) In the event a person is convicted of, or forfeits bail for two or more offenses, arising out of the same facts, and points are chargeable for each of the offenses, points shall be charged for only the conviction or bond forfeiture for which the greater number of points is chargeable, and if the number of points chargeable for each offense is equal, only one offense shall be recorded and points charged therefor.

(J) Whenever the points charged against any person exceed five, the registrar shall forward to the person at the person's last known address, via regular mail, a warning letter listing the reported violations, along with the number of points charged for each, and outlining the suspension provision of this section.

(K) When, upon determination of the registrar, any person has charged against the person a total of not less than twelve points within a period of two years from the date of the first conviction within the two-year period, the registrar shall send written notification to the person at the person's last known address, that the person's driver's or commercial driver's license shall be suspended for six months, effective on the twentieth day after mailing the notice, unless the person files a petition in the municipal court or the county court, or in case such person is under the age of eighteen years, in the juvenile court, in whose jurisdiction such person resides, or in the case of a nonresident, in the Franklin county municipal court. By filing an appeal the person is agreeing to pay the cost of the proceedings and is alleging that the person can show cause why the person's driving privileges should not be suspended for a period of six months.

(L) Any person who has charged against the person more than five but not more than eleven points, for the purpose of obtaining a credit of two points against the total amount of points on the person's driving record, may enroll for one time only in a course of remedial driving instruction, as approved by the director of public safety. Such a credit, subject to successful completion of an approved remedial driving course taken at a time when more than five but not more than eleven points are charged against the person, shall be approved by the registrar.

(M) When the driving privileges of any person are suspended by any trial judge of any court of record pursuant to section 4507.16 of the Revised Code, and points are charged against the person under this section for the offense which resulted in the suspension, that period of suspension shall be credited against the time of any subsequent suspension under this section for which the points were considered in making the subsequent suspension.

When the driving privileges of a person are suspended pursuant to the "Assimilative Crimes Act," 102 Stat. 4381 (1988), 18 U.S.C.A. 13, as amended, by a United States district court whose jurisdiction lies within this state and the court utilizes the provision contained in division (B) of this section, and points are charged against the person under this section for the offense that resulted in the suspension, the period of suspension imposed by the district court shall be credited against the time of any subsequent suspension imposed under this section for which the points were considered in making the subsequent suspension.

(N) The registrar, upon written request of a licensee petitioning under division (K) of this section, shall furnish the licensee a copy of the registrar's record of the convictions and bond forfeitures of the person certified by the registrar. This record shall include the name, address, and birthdate of the person so charged; the number of the person's driver's or commercial driver's license; the name of the court in which each conviction or bail forfeiture took place; the nature of the offense; the date of hearing; the number of points charged against each conviction or bail forfeiture; and such other information as the registrar considers necessary. When the record includes not less than twelve points charged against the person within a two-year period, it is prima-facie evidence that the person is a repeat traffic offender and the person's driving privilege shall be suspended as provided in this section.

In hearing the matter and determining whether the person has shown cause why the person's driving privileges should not be suspended, the court shall decide the issue upon the record certified by the registrar and such additional relevant, competent, and material evidence as either the registrar or the person whose license is sought to be suspended submits.

In such proceedings, the registrar shall be represented by the prosecuting attorney of the county in which the person resides if the petition is filed in the county court, except where the petitioner is a resident of a city or village within the jurisdiction of a county court in which case the city director of law or village solicitor shall represent the registrar. If the petition is filed in the municipal court, the registrar shall be represented as provided in section 1901.34 of the Revised Code.

If the court finds from the evidence submitted that the person has failed to show cause why the person's driving privileges should not be suspended, then the court shall assess the cost of the proceeding against the person and shall impose the suspension provided in division (K) of this section or withhold the suspension, or part thereof, and provide such conditions or probation as the court deems proper. If the court finds that the person has shown cause why the person's driving privileges should not be suspended, the cost of the proceedings shall be paid out of the county treasury of the county in which the proceedings were held.

Any person whose license is suspended under this section is not entitled to apply for or receive a new license during the effective period of the suspension.

Upon termination of any suspension or other penalty imposed under this section involving surrender of a license or permit and upon request of the person whose license or permit was so suspended or surrendered, the registrar shall return the license or permit to the person upon determining that all provisions of section 4507.022 [4507.02.2] of the Revised Code have been met or shall reissue the person's license or permit under section 4507.54 of the Revised Code, if the registrar destroyed the license or permit under that section.

Any person whose license, permit, or privilege to operate a motor vehicle has been suspended as a repeat traffic offender under this section and who, during such suspension, drives any motor vehicle upon any highway is guilty of a misdemeanor of the first degree, and no court shall suspend the first three days of any such sentence.

(O) The privilege of driving a motor vehicle on the highways or streets of this state, given to nonresidents under section 4507.04 of the Revised Code, is subject to suspension by the registrar.

HISTORY: RC § 4507.40, 127 v 525 (Eff 6-22-57); 128 v 469 (Eff 11-10-59); 130 v 1061 (Eff 8-26-63); 130 v 1064 (Eff 10-10-63); 132 v S 37 (Eff 11-14-67); 132 v H 380 (Eff 1-1-68); 134 v H 1010 (Eff 9-22-72); 135 v S 325 (Eff 1-1-74); 135 v S 313 (Eff 7-26-74); 136 v S 65 (Eff 6-23-76); 136 v H 451 (Eff 1-3-77); 137 v H 219 (Eff 11-1-77); 139 v S 432 (Eff 3-16-83); 141 v S 54 (Eff 5-6-86); RC § 4507.02.1, 141 v S 356 (Eff 9-24-86); 141 v S 262 (Eff 3-20-87); 142 v H 493 (Eff 7-15-87); 142 v H 643 (Eff 3-17-89); 143 v H 329 (Eff 6-30-89); 143 v H 330 (Eff 6-30-89); 143 v H 381 (Eff 7-1-89); 143 v S 49 (Eff 11-3-89); 143 v S 131 (Eff 7-25-90); 144 v S 98 (Eff 11-12-92); 144 v S 331 (Eff 11-13-92); 144 v S 275 (Eff 9-1-93); 145 v S 62, §§ 1, 4 (Eff 9-1-93); 145 v S 82 (Eff 5-4-94); 145 v H 687 (Eff 10-12-94); 146 v H 107 (Eff 6-30-95); 146 v H 353 (Eff 9-17-96); 146 v H 438 (Eff 7-1-97); 147 v S 60. Eff 10-21-97.

The provisions of § 3 of SB 60 (147 v —) read as follows:

SECTION 3. ° ° ° Section 4507.021 of the Revised Code is presented in this act as a composite of the section as amended by both Am. Sub. H.B. 353 and Am. Sub. H.B. 438 of the 121st General Assembly, with the new language of neither of the acts shown in capital letters. Section 4507.16 of the Revised Code is presented in this act as a composite of the section as amended by Am. Sub. H.B. 353, Am. Sub. S.B. 166, Am. Sub. S.B. 269, and Am. Sub. H.B. 676 of the 121st General Assembly, with the new language of none of the acts shown in capital letters. ° ° ° This is in recognition of the principle stated in division (B) of section 1.52 of the Revised Code that such amendments are to be harmonized where not substantively irreconcilable and constitutes a legislative finding that such is the resulting version in effect prior to the effective date of this act.

[§ 4507.02.2] § 4507.022 Conditions for return of full driving privileges.

Any person whose driver's or commercial driver's license or permit is suspended, or who is put on probation or granted limited or occupational driving privileges, under section 4507.021 [4507.02.1] or division (E) of section 4507.16 of the Revised Code, is not eligible to retain the person's license, or to have the person's driving privileges reinstated, until each of the following has occurred:

(A) The person successfully completes a course of remedial driving instruction approved by the director of public safety, provided the person commences taking the course after the person's driver's or commercial driver's license or permit is suspended under section 4507.021 [4507.02.1] or division (E) of section 4507.16 of the Revised Code. A minimum of twenty-five per cent of the number of hours of instruction included in the course shall be devoted to instruction on driver attitude.

The course also shall devote a number of hours to instruction in the area of alcohol and drugs and the operation of motor vehicles. The instruction shall include, but not be limited to, a review of the laws governing the operation of a motor vehicle while under the influence of alcohol, drugs, or both, the dangers of operating a motor vehicle while under the influence of alcohol, drugs, or both, and other information relating to the operation of motor vehicles and the consumption of alcoholic beverages and use of drugs. The director, in consultation with the director of alcohol and drug addiction services, shall prescribe the content of the instruction. The number of hours devoted to the area of alcohol and drugs and the operation of motor vehicles shall comprise a minimum of twenty-five per cent of the number of hours of instruction included in the course.

(B) The person is examined in the manner provided for in section 4507.20 of the Revised Code, and found by the registrar of motor vehicles to be qualified to operate a motor vehicle;

(C) The person gives and maintains proof of financial responsibility, in accordance with section 4509.45 of the Revised Code.

HISTORY: RC § 4507.41, 129 v 238 (Eff 9-14-61); 131 v 1087 (Eff 10-30-65); 140 v H 278 (Eff 7-26-84); RC § 4507.02.2, 141 v S 356 (Eff 9-24-86); 143 v H 381 (Eff 7-1-89); 144 v S 98 (Eff 11-12-92); 145 v S 82 (Eff 5-4-94); 146 v H 353 (Eff 9-17-96); 147 v S 60. Eff 10-21-97.

[§ 4507.02.3] § 4507.023 Information furnished to tax commissioner to discover address.

The registrar of motor vehicles may furnish the name and social security number of any person whose driver's license or commercial driver's license has been suspended or revoked, or of any person whose certificate of registration and license plates are subject to impoundment, to the tax commissioner. The tax commissioner may return to the registrar the address of any such person as shown on the most recent return filed by that person under section 5747.08 of the Revised Code.

HISTORY: 143 v H 381. Eff 7-1-89.

§ 4507.03 Exemptions.

No person shall be required to obtain a driver's or commercial driver's license for the purpose of driving or operating a road roller, road machinery, or any farm tractor or implement of husbandry, temporarily drawn, moved, or propelled upon the highway.

Every person on active duty in the armed forces of the United States, when furnished with a driver's permit and when operating an official motor vehicle in connection with such duty, is exempt from the license requirements of Chapters 4506. and 4507. of the Revised Code.

Every person on active duty in the armed forces of the United States or in service with the peace corps, volunteers in service to America, or the foreign service of the United States is exempt from the license requirements of those chapters for the period of his active duty or service and for six months thereafter, provided the person was a licensee under those chapters at the time he commenced his active duty or service. The spouse or a dependent of any such person on active duty or in service also is exempt from the license requirements of those chapters for the period of the person's active duty or service and for six months thereafter, provided the spouse or dependent was a licensee under those chapters at the time the person commenced the active duty or service, and provided further that the person's active duty or service causes the spouse or dependent to relocate outside of this state during the period of the active duty or service.

This section does not prevent such a person or his spouse or dependent from making an application, as provided in division (C) of section 4507.10 of the Revised Code, for the renewal of a driver's license or motorcycle operator's endorsement or as provided in section 4506.14 of the Revised Code for the renewal of a commercial driver's license during the period of his active duty or service.

HISTORY: GC § 6296-5; 116 v Pt II, 33, § 5; 120 v 289; 124 v 42; Bureau of Code Revision, 10-1-53; 132 v H 57 (Eff 3-28-67); 134 v S 546 (Eff 10-16-72); 141 v H 165 (Eff 8-1-86); 142 v H 614 (Eff 3-17-89); 143 v H 381 (Eff 7-1-89); 145 v S 96. Eff 5-10-94.

§ 4507.04 Nonresident exemption.

Nonresidents, permitted to drive upon the highways of their own states, may operate any motor vehicle upon any highway in this state without examination or license under sections 4507.01 to 4507.39, inclusive, of the Revised Code, upon condition that such nonresidents may be required at any time or place to prove lawful possession, or their right to operate, such motor vehicle, and to establish proper identity.

HISTORY: GC § 6296-6; 116 v Pt II, 33, § 6; 119 v 701; Bureau of Code Revision. Eff 10-1-53.

§ 4507.05 Temporary instruction permit.

The registrar of motor vehicles, or the deputy registrar, upon receiving from any person an application for a temporary instruction permit for a driver's license, may issue such a permit entitling the applicant, while having the permit in his immediate possession, to drive a motor vehicle other than a commercial motor vehicle, upon the highways when accompanied by a licensed operator who is actually occupying a seat beside the driver. The registrar or a deputy registrar, upon receiving from any person an application for a temporary instruction permit to operate a motorcycle or motorized bicycle, may issue such a permit entitling the applicant, while having the permit in his immediate possession, to drive a motorcycle under restrictions determined by the registrar. Such permits shall be issued in the same manner as drivers' licenses, including the age requirements as provided under section 4507.08 of the Revised Code, upon forms to be furnished by the registrar, except that no photograph of the applicant shall be required on the permit, and that temporary instruction permits for motorized bicycles may be issued to persons fourteen or fifteen years old. No such permit shall be granted for a period to exceed six months.

Any person having in his possession a valid and current driver's license or motorcycle operator's license or endorsement issued to him by another jurisdiction recognized by this state is exempt from obtaining a temporary instruction permit for a driver's license, but shall submit to the regular examination in obtaining a driver's license or motorcycle operator's endorsement in this state. The registrar may adopt rules governing the use of such instruction permits.

HISTORY: GC § 6296-8; 116 v Pt II, 33, § 8; 119 v 701; 123 v 246; Bureau of Code Revision, 10-1-53; 128 v 1169 (Eff 11-2-59); 129 v 1490 (Eff 9-18-61); 131 v 1081 (Eff 10-30-65); 132 v H 380 (Eff 1-1-68); 132 v S 43 (Eff 1-1-69); 133 v H 1 (Eff 3-18-69); 140 v S 169 (Eff 1-1-85); 143 v H 381. Eff 7-1-89.

§ 4507.06 Application for license; voter registration.

(A)(1) Every application for a driver's license or motorcycle operator's license or endorsement, or duplicate of any such license or endorsement, shall be made upon the approved form furnished by the registrar of motor vehicles and shall be signed by the applicant.

Every application shall state the following:

(a) The applicant's name, date of birth, social security number if such has been assigned, sex, general description, including height, weight, color of hair, and eyes, residence address, including county of residence, duration of residence in this state, and country of citizenship;

(b) Whether the applicant previously has been licensed as an operator, chauffeur, driver, commercial driver, or motorcycle operator and, if so, when, by what state, and whether such license is suspended or revoked at the present time and, if so, the date of and reason for the suspension or revocation;

(c) Whether the applicant is now or ever has been afflicted with epilepsy, or whether the applicant now is suffering from any physical or mental disability or disease and, if so, the nature and extent of the disability or disease, giving the names and addresses of physicians then or previously in attendance upon the applicant;

(d) Whether an applicant for a duplicate driver's license, or duplicate license containing a motorcycle operator endorsement has pending a citation for violation of any motor vehicle law or ordinance, a description of any such citation pending, and the date of the citation;

(e) Whether the applicant wishes to certify willingness to make an anatomical gift under section 2108.04 of the Revised Code, which shall be given no consideration in the issuance of a license or endorsement;

(f) On and after May 1, 1993, whether the applicant has executed a valid durable power of attorney for health care pursuant to sections 1337.11 to 1337.17 of the Revised Code or has executed a declaration governing the use or continuation, or the withholding or withdrawal, of life-sustaining treatment pursuant to Chapter 2133. of the Revised Code and, if the applicant has executed either type of instrument, whether the applicant wishes the applicant's license to indicate that the applicant has executed the instrument.

(2) Every applicant for a driver's license shall be photographed in color at the time the application for the license is made. The application shall state any additional information that the registrar requires.

(B) The registrar or a deputy registrar, in accordance with section 3503.11 of the Revised Code, shall register as an elector any person who applies for a driver's license or motorcycle operator's license or endorsement under division (A) of this section, or for a renewal or duplicate of the license or endorsement, if the applicant is eligible and wishes to be registered as an elector. The decision of an applicant whether to register as an elector shall be given no consideration in the decision of whether to issue the applicant a license or endorsement, or a renewal or duplicate.

(C) The registrar or a deputy registrar, in accordance with section 3503.11 of the Revised Code, shall offer the opportunity of completing a notice of change of residence or change of name to any applicant for a driver's license or endorsement under division (A) of this section, or for a renewal or duplicate of the license or endorsement, if the applicant is a registered elector who has changed the applicant's residence or name and has not filed such a notice.

HISTORY: 141 v H 428 (Eff 12-23-86); 143 v H 381 (Eff 7-1-89); 143 v H 21 (Eff 3-27-91); 144 v H 427 (Eff 10-8-92); 145 v S 300 (Eff 1-1-95); 146 v H 353. Eff 9-17-96.

Analogous to former RC § 4507.06 (GC § 6296-9; 116 v Pt II, 33, § 9; 120 v 289; 123 v 246; Bureau of Code Revision, 10-1-53; 126 v 253; 132 v S 259; 132 v H 193; 132 v H 380; 132 v S 43; 132 v S 452; 132 v H 1007; 135 v S 313; 136 v H 650; 137 v S 125; 140 v H 183), repealed 141 v H 428, § 2, eff 12-23-86.

[§ 4507.06.1] § 4507.061 Restrictions where minor withdraws from school or is habitually absent.

(A) The registrar of motor vehicles shall record within ten days of receipt and keep at the main office of the bureau of motor vehicles all information provided to him by the superintendent of a school district in accordance with division (B) of section 3321.13 of the Revised Code.

(B) Whenever the registrar receives a notice under division (B) of section 3321.13 of the Revised Code, he shall suspend the temporary instruction permit or driver's license of the person who is the subject of the notice or, if the person has not been issued such a permit or license, the registrar shall deny to the person the issuance of a temporary instruction permit or driver's license. The requirements of the second paragraph of section 119.06 of the Revised Code do not apply to a suspension of a person's temporary instruction permit or driver's license or a denial of a person's opportunity to obtain a temporary instruction permit or driver's license by the registrar under this division.

(C) Upon suspending the temporary instruction permit or driver's license of any person or denying any person the opportunity to be issued such a license or permit as provided in division (B) of this section, the registrar immediately shall notify the person in writing of the suspension or denial and inform him that he may petition for a hearing as provided in division (E) of this section.

(D) Any person whose permit or license is suspended

under this section shall mail or deliver his permit or license to the registrar of motor vehicles within twenty days of notification of the suspension; however, the person's permit or license and his driving privileges shall be suspended immediately upon receipt of the notification. The registrar may retain the permit or license during the period of the suspension or he may destroy it under section 4507.54 of the Revised Code. Any such suspension of a person's permit or license or denial of a person's opportunity to obtain a permit or license under this section shall remain in effect until the person attains eighteen years of age or until it is terminated prior to the child's attainment of that age pursuant to division (F) of this section.

(E) Any person whose temporary instruction permit or driver's license has been suspended, or whose opportunity to obtain such a permit or license has been denied pursuant to this section, may file a petition in the juvenile court in whose jurisdiction the person resides alleging error in the action taken by the registrar of motor vehicles under division (B) of this section or alleging one or more of the matters within the scope of the hearing, as described in this division, or both. The petitioner shall notify the registrar and the superintendent of the school district who gave the notice to the registrar and juvenile judge under division (B) of section 3321.13 of the Revised Code of the filing of the petition and send them copies of the petition. The scope of the hearing is limited to the issues of whether the notice given by the superintendent to the registrar was in error and whether the suspension or denial of driving privileges will result in substantial hardship to the petitioner.

The registrar shall furnish the court a copy of the record created in accordance with division (A) of this section. The registrar and the superintendent shall furnish the court with any other relevant information required by the court.

In hearing the matter and determining whether the petitioner has shown that his temporary instruction permit or driver's license should not be suspended or that his opportunity to obtain such a permit or license should not be denied, the court shall decide the issue upon the information furnished by the registrar and the superintendent and any such additional evidence that the registrar, the superintendent, or the petitioner submits.

If the court finds from the evidence submitted that the petitioner has failed to show error in the action taken by the registrar under division (B) of this section and has failed to prove any of the matters within the scope of the hearing, then the court may assess the cost of the proceeding against the petitioner and shall uphold the suspension of his permit or license or the denial of his opportunity to obtain a permit or license. If the court finds that the petitioner has shown error in the action taken by the registrar under division (B) of this section or has proved one or more of the matters within the scope of the hearing, or both, the cost of the proceeding shall be paid out of the county treasury of the county in which the proceedings were held, and the suspension of the petitioner's permit or license or the denial of the person's opportunity to obtain a permit or license shall be terminated.

(F) The registrar shall cancel the record created under this section of any person who is the subject of a notice given under division (B) of section 3321.13 of the Revised Code and shall terminate the suspension of the person's permit or license or the denial of the person's opportunity to obtain a permit or license, if any of the following applies:

(1) The person is at least eighteen years of age.

(2) The person provides evidence, as the registrar shall require by rule, of receipt of a high school diploma or a general educational development certificate of high school equivalence.

(3) The superintendent of a school district informs the registrar that the notification of withdrawal, habitual absence without legitimate excuse, suspension, or expulsion concerning the person was in error.

(4) The suspension or denial was imposed subsequent to a notification given under division (B)(3) of section 3321.13 of the Revised Code, and the superintendent of a school district informs the registrar that the person in question has satisfied any terms or conditions established by the school as necessary to terminate the suspension or denial of driving privileges.

(5) The suspension or denial was imposed subsequent to a notification given under division (B)(1) of section 3321.13 of the Revised Code, and the superintendent of a school district informs the registrar that the person in question is now attending school or enrolled in and attending an approved program to obtain a diploma or its equivalent to the satisfaction of the school superintendent.

(6) The suspension or denial was imposed subsequent to a notification given under division (B)(2) of section 3321.13 of the Revised Code, the person has completed at least one semester or term of school after the one in which the notification was given, the person requests the superintendent of the school district to notify the registrar that the person no longer is habitually absent without legitimate excuse, the superintendent determines that the person has not been absent from school without legitimate excuse in the current semester or term, as determined under that division, for more than ten consecutive school days or for more than fifteen total school days, and the superintendent informs the registrar of that fact. If a person described in division (F)(6) of this section requests the superintendent of the school district to notify the registrar that the person no longer is habitually absent without legitimate excuse and the superintendent makes the determination described in this division, the superintendent shall provide the information described in division (F)(6) of this section to the registrar within five days after receiving the request.

(7) The suspension or denial was imposed subsequent to a notification given under division (B)(2) of section 3321.13 of the Revised Code, and the superintendent of a school district informs the registrar that the person in question has received an age and schooling certificate in accordance with section 3331.01 of the Revised Code.

(8) The person filed a petition in court under division (E) of this section and the court found that the person showed error in the action taken by the registrar under division (B) of this section or proved one or more of the matters within the scope of the hearing on the petition, as set forth in division (E) of this section, or both.

At the end of the suspension period under this section and upon the request of the person whose temporary instruction permit or driver's license was suspended, the registrar shall return the driver's license or permit to the person or reissue the person's license or permit under section 4507.54 of the Revised Code, if the registrar destroyed the suspended license or permit under that section.

HISTORY: 143 v H 204 (Eff 5-2-90); 145 v H 687. Eff 10-12-94.

§ 4507.07 Licenses of minors.

(A) The registrar of motor vehicles shall not grant the application of any minor under eighteen years of age for a probationary license or a restricted license, unless the application is signed by one of the minor's parents, the minor's guardian, another person having custody of the applicant, or, if there is no parent or guardian, a responsible person who is willing to assume the obligation imposed under this section.

At the time a minor under eighteen years of age submits an application for a license at a driver's license examining station, the adult who signs the application shall present identification establishing that the adult is the individual whose signature appears on the application. The registrar shall prescribe, by rule, the types of identification that are suitable for the purposes of this paragraph. If the adult who signs the application does not provide identification as required by this paragraph, the application shall not be accepted.

When a minor under eighteen years of age applies for a probationary license or a restricted license, the registrar shall give the adult who signs the application notice of the potential liability that may be imputed to the adult pursuant to division (B) of this section and notice of how the adult may prevent any liability from being imputed to the adult pursuant to that division.

(B) Any negligence, or willful or wanton misconduct, that is committed by a minor under eighteen years of age when driving a motor vehicle upon a highway shall be imputed to the person who has signed the application of the minor for a probationary license or restricted license, which person shall be jointly and severally liable with the minor for any damages caused by the negligence or the willful or wanton misconduct. This joint and several liability is not subject to division (D) of section 2315.19, division (F) of section 2315.20, or division (B) of section 2307.31 of the Revised Code with respect to a negligence or other tort claim that otherwise is subject to any of those sections.

There shall be no imputed liability imposed under this division if a minor under eighteen years of age has proof of financial responsibility with respect to the operation of a motor vehicle owned by the minor or, if the minor is not the owner of a motor vehicle, with respect to the minor's operation of any motor vehicle, in the form and in the amounts as required under Chapter 4509. of the Revised Code.

(C) Any person who has signed the application of a minor under eighteen years of age for a license subsequently may surrender to the registrar the license or temporary instruction permit of the minor and request that the license or permit be canceled. The registrar then shall cancel the license or temporary instruction permit, and the person who signed the application of the minor shall be relieved from the liability imposed by division (B) of this section.

(D) Any minor under eighteen years of age whose probationary license, restricted license, or temporary instruction permit is surrendered to the registrar by the person who signed the application for the license and whose license or temporary instruction permit subsequently is canceled by the registrar may obtain a new license or temporary instruction permit without having to undergo the examinations otherwise required by sections 4507.11 and 4507.12 of the Revised Code and without having to tender the fee for that license or temporary instruction permit, if the minor is able to produce another parent, guardian, other person having custody of the minor, or other adult, and that adult is willing to assume the liability imposed under division (B) of this section. That adult shall comply with the procedures contained in division (A) of this section.

HISTORY: GC § 6296-10; 116 v PtII, 33, § 10; 119 v 701; 120 v 289; Bureau of Code Revision, 10-1-53; 127 v 839 (Eff 9-16-57); 130 v 1054 (Eff 9-27-63); 132 v S 95 (Eff 11-24-67); 138 v H 522 (Eff 10-29-79); 142 v H 1 (Eff 1-5-88); 143 v H 71 (Eff 9-22-89); 146 v H 350. Eff 1-27-97.

The provisions of § 6(J) of HB 350 (146 v —) read as follows:

SECTION 6. ° ° °

(J) The amendments to sections 1775.14, 4171.10, and 4507.07 of the Revised Code made in this act shall apply only to tort actions involving claims of negligence or other tortious conduct that are commenced on or after the effective date of this act. ° ° °

§ 4507.08 Restrictions on issuance of license or temporary instruction permit.

Note: See following version, HB 141 (147 v —), effective 3-3-98.

No driver's license shall be issued to any person under eighteen years of age, except that a probationary license may be issued to a person over sixteen years of age and a restricted license may be issued to a person who is fourteen or fifteen years of age upon proof of hardship satisfactory to the registrar of motor vehicles. No probationary license shall be issued to any person under the age of eighteen who has been adjudicated an unruly or delinquent child or a juvenile traffic offender for having committed any act that if committed by an adult would be a drug abuse offense, as defined in section 2925.01 of the Revised Code, a violation of division (B) of section 2917.11, or a violation of division (A) of section 4511.19 of the Revised Code, unless the person has been required by the court to attend a drug abuse or alcohol abuse education, intervention, or treatment program specified by the court and has satisfactorily completed the program.

No temporary instruction permit or driver's license shall be issued to any person whose license has been suspended, during the period for which the license was suspended, nor to any person whose license has been revoked, under sections 4507.01 to 4507.39 of the Revised Code, until the expiration of one year after the license was revoked.

No temporary instruction permit or driver's license shall be issued to any person whose commercial driver's license is suspended under section 1905.201 [1905.20.1], 2301.374 [2301.37.4], 4507.16, 4507.34, 4507.99, 4511.191 [4511.19.1], or 4511.196 [4511.19.6] of the Revised Code or under any other provision of the Revised Code during the period of the suspension.

No temporary instruction permit or driver's license shall be issued to, or retained by:

(A) Any person who is an alcoholic, or is addicted to the use of controlled substances to the extent that the use constitutes an impairment to the person's ability to operate a motor vehicle with the required degree of safety;

(B) Any person who is under the age of eighteen and has been adjudicated an unruly or delinquent child or a juvenile traffic offender for having committed any act that if committed by an adult would be a drug abuse offense, as defined in section 2925.01 of the Revised Code, a violation of division (B) of section 2917.11, or a violation of division (A) of section 4511.19 of the Revised Code, unless the person has been required by the court to attend a drug abuse or alcohol abuse education, intervention, or treatment program specified by the court and has satisfactorily completed the program;

(C) Any person who, in the opinion of the registrar, is afflicted with or suffering from a physical or mental disability or disease that prevents the person from exercising reasonable and ordinary control over a motor vehicle while operating the vehicle upon the highways, except that a restricted license effective for six months may be issued to any person otherwise qualified who is or has been subject to any condition resulting in episodic impairment of consciousness or loss of muscular control and whose condition, in the opinion of the registrar, is dormant or is sufficiently under medical control that the person is capable of exercising reasonable and ordinary control over a motor vehicle. A restricted license effective for six months shall be issued to any person who is otherwise qualified who is subject to any condition which causes episodic impairment of consciousness or a loss of muscular control if the person presents a statement from a licensed physician that the person's condition is under effective medical control and the period of time for which the control has been continuously maintained, unless, thereafter, a medical examination is ordered and, pursuant thereto, cause for denial is found.

A person to whom a six-month restricted license has been issued shall give notice of the person's medical condition to the registrar on forms provided by the registrar and signed by the licensee's physician. The notice shall be sent to the registrar six months after the issuance of the license. Subsequent restricted licenses issued to the same individual shall be effective for six months.

(D) Any person who is unable to understand highway warnings or traffic signs or directions given in the English language;

(E) Any person making an application whose driver's license or driving privileges are under revocation or suspension in the jurisdiction where issued or any other jurisdiction, until the expiration of one year after the license was revoked or until the period of suspension ends. Any person whose application is denied under this division may file a petition in the municipal court or county court in whose jurisdiction the person resides agreeing to pay the cost of the proceedings and alleging that the conduct involved in the offense that resulted in suspension or revocation in the foreign jurisdiction would not have resulted in a suspension or revocation had the offense occurred in this state. If the petition is granted, petitioner shall notify the registrar of motor vehicles by a certified copy of the court's findings and a license shall not be denied under this division.

(F) Any person whose driver's or commercial driver's license or permit has been permanently revoked pursuant to division (C) of section 4507.16 of the Revised Code;

(G) Any person who is not a resident or temporary resident of this state.

HISTORY: GC § 6296-7; 116 v PtII, 33, § 7; 119 v 701; 120 v 289; 123 v 246; Bureau of Code Revision, 10-1-53; 127 v 839 (Eff 9-16-57); 127 v 789 (Eff 9-17-57); 128 v 539 (Eff 11-2-59); 129 v 582(896) (Eff 1-10-61); 129 v 1448 (Eff 10-25-61); 130 v 1057 (Eff 9-27-63); 130 v 1055 (Eff 10-10-63); 131 v 1084 (Eff 10-30-65); 131 v 1082 (Eff 11-9-65); 135 v S 1 (Eff 1-1-74); 135 v S 313 (Eff 7-26-74); 136 v H 300 (Eff 7-1-76); 137 v H 71 (Eff 8-26-77); 138 v H 328 (Eff 9-13-79); 138 v H 965 (Eff 4-9-81); 141 v S 262 (Eff 3-20-87); 142 v H 643 (Eff 3-17-89); 143 v H 329 (Eff 6-30-89); 143 v H 330 (Eff 6-30-89); 143 v H 381 (Eff 7-1-89); 144 v S 275 (Eff 9-1-93); 145 v S 62, §§ 1, 4 (Eff 9-1-93); 145 v S 82 (Eff 5-4-94); 146 v H 167 (Eff 5-15-97); 147 v S 60. Eff 10-21-97.

§ 4507.08 Restrictions on issuance of license or temporary instruction permit.

Note: See preceding version, SB 60 (147 v —), in effect until 3-3-98.

No driver's license shall be issued to any person under eighteen years of age, except that a probationary license may be issued to a person over sixteen years of age and a restricted license may be issued to a person who is fourteen or fifteen years of age upon proof of hardship satisfactory to the registrar of motor vehicles. No probationary license shall be issued to any person under the age of eighteen who has been adjudicated an unruly or delinquent child or a juvenile traffic offender for having committed any act that if committed by an adult would be a drug abuse offense, as defined in section 2925.01 of the Revised Code, a violation of division (B) of section 2917.11, or a violation of division (A) of section 4511.19 of the Revised Code, unless the person has been required by the court to attend a drug abuse or alcohol abuse education, intervention, or treatment program specified by the court and has satisfactorily completed the program.

No temporary instruction permit or driver's license shall be issued to any person whose license has been suspended, during the period for which the license was suspended, nor to any person whose license has been revoked, under sections 4507.01 to 4507.39 of the Revised Code, until the expiration of one year after the license was revoked.

No temporary instruction permit or driver's license shall be issued to any person whose commercial driver's license is suspended under section 1905.201 [1905.20.1], 2301.374 [2301.37.4], 4507.16, 4507.34, 4507.99, 4511.191 [4511.19.1], or 4511.196 [4511.19.6] of the Revised Code or under any other provision of the Revised Code during the period of the suspension.

No temporary instruction permit or driver's license shall be issued to any person when issuance is prohibited by division (A) of section 4507.091 [4507.09.1] of the Revised Code.

No temporary instruction permit or driver's license shall be issued to, or retained by:

(A) Any person who is an alcoholic, or is addicted to the use of controlled substances to the extent that the use constitutes an impairment to the person's ability to operate a motor vehicle with the required degree of safety;

(B) Any person who is under the age of eighteen and has been adjudicated an unruly or delinquent child or a juvenile traffic offender for having committed any act that if committed by an adult would be a drug abuse offense, as defined in section 2925.01 of the Revised Code, a violation of division (B) of section 2917.11, or a violation of division (A) of section 4511.19 of the Revised Code, unless the person has been required by the court to attend a drug abuse or alcohol abuse education, intervention, or treatment program specified by the court and has satisfactorily completed the program;

(C) Any person who, in the opinion of the registrar, is afflicted with or suffering from a physical or mental disability or disease that prevents the person from exercising reasonable and ordinary control over a motor vehicle while operating the vehicle upon the highways, except that a restricted license effective for six months may be issued to any person otherwise qualified who is or has been subject to any condition resulting in episodic impairment of consciousness or loss of muscular control and whose condition, in the opinion of the registrar, is dormant or is sufficiently under medical control that the person is capable of exercising reasonable and ordinary control over a motor vehicle. A restricted license effective for six months shall be issued to any person who is otherwise qualified who is subject to any condition that causes episodic impairment of consciousness or a loss of muscular control if the person presents a statement from a licensed physician that the person's condition is under effective medical control and the period of time for which the control has been continuously maintained, unless, thereafter, a medical examination is ordered and, pursuant thereto, cause for denial is found.

A person to whom a six-month restricted license has been issued shall give notice of the person's medical condition to the registrar on forms provided by the registrar and signed by the licensee's physician. The notice shall be sent to the registrar six months after the issuance of the license. Subsequent restricted licenses issued to the same individual shall be effective for six months.

(D) Any person who is unable to understand highway warnings or traffic signs or directions given in the English language;

(E) Any person making an application whose driver's license or driving privileges are under revocation or suspension in the jurisdiction where issued or any other jurisdiction, until the expiration of one year after the license was revoked or until the period of suspension ends. Any person whose application is denied under this division may file a petition in the municipal court or county court in whose jurisdiction the person resides agreeing to pay the cost of the proceedings and alleging that the conduct involved in the offense that resulted in suspension or revocation in the foreign jurisdiction would not have resulted in a suspension or revocation had the offense occurred in this state. If the petition is granted, petitioner shall notify the registrar by a certified copy of the court's findings and a license shall not be denied under this division.

(F) Any person whose driver's or commercial driver's license or permit has been permanently revoked pursuant to division (C) of section 4507.16 of the Revised Code.

HISTORY: GC § 6296-7; 116 v PtII, 33, § 7; 119 v 701; 120 v 289; 123 v 246; Bureau of Code Revision, 10-1-53; 127 v 839 (Eff 9-16-57); 127 v 789 (Eff 9-17-57); 128 v 539 (Eff 11-2-59); 129 v 582(896) (Eff 1-10-61); 129 v 1448 (Eff 10-25-61); 130 v 1057 (Eff 9-27-63); 130 v 1055 (Eff 10-10-63); 131 v 1084 (Eff 10-30-65); 131 v 1082 (Eff 11-9-65); 135 v S 1 (Eff 1-1-74); 135 v S 313 (Eff 7-26-74); 136 v H 300 (Eff 7-1-76); 137 v H 71 (Eff 8-26-77); 138 v H 328 (Eff 9-13-79); 138 v H 965 (Eff 4-9-81); 141 v S 262 (Eff 3-20-87); 142 v H 643 (Eff 3-17-89); 143 v H 329 (Eff 6-30-89); 143 v H 330 (Eff 6-30-89); 143 v H 381 (Eff 7-1-89); 144 v S 275 (Eff 9-1-93); 145 v S 62, §§ 1, 4 (Eff 9-1-93); 145 v S 82 (Eff 5-4-94); 146 v H 167 (Eff 5-15-97); 147 v S 60 (Eff 10-21-97); 147 v H 141. Eff 3-3-98.

The effective date is set by section 3 of HB 141.

[§ 4507.08.1] § 4507.081 Renewal of restricted drivers' licenses.

(A) Upon the expiration of a restricted license issued under division (C) of section 4507.08 of the Revised Code and submission of a statement as provided in division (C) of this section, the registrar of motor vehicles may issue a driver's license to the person to whom the restricted license was issued. A driver's license issued under this section shall, unless otherwise revoked, be effective for one year.

(B) A driver's license issued under this section may be renewed annually, for no more than three consecutive years, whenever the person to whom the license has been issued submits to the registrar, by certified mail and no sooner than thirty days prior to the expiration date of the license or renewal thereof, a statement as provided in division (C) of this section. A renewal of a driver's license shall, unless the license is otherwise revoked, be effective for one year following the expiration date of the license or renewal thereof, and shall be evidenced by a validation sticker. The renewal validation sticker shall be in a form prescribed by the registrar and shall be affixed to the license.

(C) No person may be issued a driver's license under this section, and no such driver's license may be renewed, unless the person presents a signed statement from a licensed physician that the person's condition is either dormant or under effective medical control, that the control has been maintained continuously for at least one year prior to the date on which application for the license is made, and that, if continued medication is prescribed to control the condition, the person may be depended upon to take the medication.

The statement shall be made on a form provided by the registrar, shall be in not less than duplicate, and shall contain such other information as the registrar considers necessary. The duplicate copy of the statement may be retained by the person requesting the license renewal and, when in his immediate possession and used in conjunction with the original license, shall entitle him to operate a motor vehicle during a period of no more than thirty days following the date of submission of the statement to the registrar, except when the registrar denies the request for the license renewal and so notifies the person.

(D) Whenever the registrar receives a statement indicating that the condition of a person to whom a driver's license has been issued under this section is no longer dormant or under effective medical control, the registrar shall revoke the person's driver's license.

(E) Nothing in this section shall require a person submitting a signed statement from a licensed physician to obtain a medical examination prior to the submission of the statement.

(F) Any person whose driver's license has been revoked under this section may apply for a subsequent restricted license according to the provisions of section 4507.08 of the Revised Code.

HISTORY: 137 v H 71 (Eff 8-26-77); 138 v H 328 (Eff 9-13-79); 140 v H 37 (Eff 6-22-84); 142 v H 643 (Eff 3-17-89); 143 v H 329 (Eff 6-30-89); 143 v H 381. Eff 7-1-89.

§ 4507.09 Expiration, renewal of license; notice of change of address.

Note: See following version, HB 141 (147 v —), effective 3-3-98.

(A) Except as provided in division (B) of this section, every driver's license issued to a resident of this state expires on the birthday of the applicant in the fourth year after the date it is issued and every driver's license issued to a temporary resident expires in accordance with rules adopted by the registrar of motor vehicles. In no event shall any license be issued for a period longer than four years and ninety days.

Subject to the requirements of section 4507.12 of the Revised Code, every driver's license issued to a resident is renewable at any time prior to its expiration and any license of a temporary resident is nonrenewable. A nonrenewable license may be replaced with a new license within ninety days prior to its expiration upon the applicant's compliance with all applicable requirements. No refund shall be made or credit given for the unexpired portion of the driver's license that is renewed. The registrar of motor vehicles shall notify each person whose driver's license has expired within forty-five days after the date of expiration. Notification shall be made by regular mail sent to the person's last known address as shown in the records of the bureau of motor vehicles. Failure to provide such notification shall not be construed as a renewal or extension of any license. For the purposes of this section, the date of birth of any applicant born on the twenty-ninth day of February shall be deemed to be the first day of March in any year in which there is no twenty-ninth day of February.

(B) Every driver's license or renewal of a driver's license issued to an applicant who is sixteen years of age or older, but less than twenty-one years of age, expires on the twenty-first birthday of the applicant, except that an applicant who applies no more than thirty days before the applicant's twenty-first birthday shall be issued a license in accordance with division (A) of this section.

(C) Each person licensed as a driver under this chapter shall notify the registrar of any change in the person's address within ten days following that change. The notification shall be in writing on a form provided by the registrar and shall include the full name, date of birth, license number, county of residence, social security number, and new address of the person.

HISTORY: GC § 6296-15; 116 v PtII, 33, § 15; 119 v 701; 123 v 246; Bureau of Code Revision, 10-1-53; 133 v H 113 (Eff 9-12-69); 136 v H 1337 (Eff 8-31-76); 137 v H 215 (Eff 12-12-78); 140 v H 58 (Eff 3-1-85); 143 v H 381 (Eff 7-1-89); 143 v H 88 (Eff 3-13-90); 144 v H 134 (Eff 10-10-91); 145 v S 96 (Eff 5-10-94); 146 v H 353 (Eff 9-17-96); 147 v S 60. Eff 10-21-97.

§ 4507.09 Expiration, renewal of license; notice of change of address.

Note: See preceding version, SB 60 (147 v —), in effect until 3-3-98.

(A) Except as provided in division (B) of this section, every driver's license expires on the birthday of the applicant in the fourth year after the date it is issued, but in no event shall any such license be issued for a period longer than four years.

Subject to the requirements of section 4507.12 of the Revised Code, every driver's license is renewable within sixty days prior to its expiration upon payment of the fees as required by law, except that any license of an Ohio resident who will be temporarily out-of-state is renewable at any time prior to its expiration. No refund shall be made or credit given for the unexpired portion of the driver's license that is renewed. The registrar of motor vehicles shall notify each person whose driver's license has expired within forty-five days after the date of expiration. Notification shall be made by regular mail sent to the person's last known address as shown in the records of the bureau of motor vehicles. Failure to provide such notification shall not be construed as a renewal or extension of any license. The registrar may issue rules permitting the use and display of drivers' licenses at any time not to exceed sixty days prior to the next succeeding birthday of the applicant. For the purposes of this section, the date of birth of any applicant born on the twenty-ninth day of February shall be deemed to be the first day of March in any year in which there is no twenty-ninth day of February.

The registrar may require an application for license renewal submitted by a resident who will be temporarily out-of-state to be accompanied by an affidavit, in a form prescribed by the registrar, certifying that the resident will be temporarily out-of-state at the time the resident's license will expire.

(B) Every driver's license or renewal of a driver's license issued to an applicant who is sixteen years of age or older, but less than twenty-one years of age, expires on the twenty-first birthday of the applicant.

(C) Each person licensed as a driver under this chapter shall notify the registrar of any change in the person's address within ten days following that change. The notification shall be in writing on a form provided by the registrar and shall include the full name, date of birth, license number, county of residence, social security number, and new address of the person.

(D) No driver's license shall be renewed when renewal is prohibited by division (A) of section 4507.091 [4507.09.1] of the Revised Code.

HISTORY: GC § 6296-15; 116 v PtII, 33, § 15; 119 v 701; 123 v 246; Bureau of Code Revision, 10-1-53; 133 v H 113 (Eff 9-12-69); 136 v H 1337 (Eff 8-31-76); 137 v H 215 (Eff 12-12-78); 140 v H 58 (Eff 3-1-85); 143 v H 381 (Eff 7-1-89); 143 v H 88 (Eff 3-13-90); 144 v H 134 (Eff 10-10-91); 145 v S 96 (Eff 5-10-94); 146 v H 353 (Eff 9-17-96); 147 v S 60 (Eff 10-21-97); 147 v H 141. Eff 3-3-98.

The effective date is set by section 3 of HB 141.

[§ 4507.09.1] § 4507.091 Ineligibility due to outstanding municipal or county court arrest warrant.

(A) A municipal court or county court, at the court's discretion, may order the clerk of the court to send to the registrar of motor vehicles a report containing the name, address, and such other information as the registrar may require by rule, of any person for whom an arrest warrant has been issued by that court and is outstanding.

Upon receipt of such a report, the registrar shall enter the information contained in the report into the records of the bureau of motor vehicles, and neither the registrar nor any deputy registrar shall issue a temporary instruction permit or driver's or commercial driver's license to the person named in the report, or renew the driver's or commercial driver's license of such person, until the registrar receives notification from the municipal court or county court that there are no outstanding arrest warrants in the name of the person. The registrar also shall send a notice to the person who is named in the report, via regular first class mail sent to the person's last known address as shown in the records of the bureau, informing the person that neither the registrar nor any deputy registrar is permitted to issue a temporary instruction permit or driver's or commercial driver's license to the person, or renew the driver's or commercial driver's license of the person, until the registrar receives notification that there are no outstanding arrest warrants in the name of the person.

(B) A clerk who reports an outstanding arrest warrant in accordance with division (A) of this section immediately shall notify the registrar when the warrant has been executed and returned to the issuing court or has been canceled. The clerk shall charge and collect from the person named in the executed or canceled arrest warrant a processing fee of fifteen dollars to cover the costs of the bureau in administering this section. The clerk shall transmit monthly all such processing fees to the registrar for deposit into the state bureau of motor vehicles fund created by section 4501.25 of the Revised Code.

Upon receipt of such notification, the registrar shall cause the report of that outstanding arrest warrant to be removed from the records of the bureau and, if there are no other outstanding arrest warrants issued by a municipal court or county court in the name of the person and the person otherwise is eligible to be issued a driver's or commercial driver's license or to have such a license renewed, the registrar or a deputy registrar may issue a driver's license or commercial driver's license to the person named in the executed or canceled arrest warrant, or renew the driver's or commercial driver's license of such person.

(C) Neither the registrar, any employee of the bureau, a deputy registrar, nor any employee of a deputy registrar is personally liable for damages or injuries resulting from any error made by a clerk in entering information contained in a report submitted to the registrar under this section.

(D) Any information submitted to the registrar by a clerk under this section shall be transmitted by means of an electronic data transfer system.

HISTORY: 147 v H 141. Eff 3-3-98.

The effective date is set by section 3 of HB 141.

§ 4507.10 Examination for license or endorsement; exceptions.

(A) The registrar of motor vehicles shall examine every applicant for a driver's license or motorcycle operator's endorsement before issuing any such license or endorsement.

(B) Except as provided in section 4507.12 of the Revised Code, the registrar may waive the examination of any person applying for the renewal of a driver's license, or motorcycle operator's endorsement issued under this chapter, provided that the applicant presents either an unexpired license or endorsement or a license or endorsement which has expired not more than six months prior to the date of application.

(C) The registrar may waive the examination of any person applying for the renewal of such license or endorsement who is on active duty in the military or naval forces of the United States, or in service with the peace corps, volunteers in service to America, or the foreign service of the United States if the applicant has no physical or mental disabilities that would affect the applicant's driving ability, had a valid Ohio driver's or commercial driver's license at the time the applicant commenced such active duty or service, and the applicant's license is not under suspension or revocation by this state or any other jurisdiction.

(D) Except as provided in section 4507.12 of the Revised Code, the registrar may waive the examination of any person applying for such license or endorsement who meets either of the following sets of qualifications:

(1) Has been on active duty in the military or naval forces of the United States, presents an honorable discharge certificate showing that the applicant has no physical or mental disabilities which would affect the applicant's driving ability, had a valid Ohio driver's or commercial driver's license at the time the applicant commenced such active duty, is not under a license suspension or revocation by this state or any other jurisdiction, and makes the application not more than six months after the date of discharge or separation;

(2) Was in service with the peace corps, volunteers in service to America, or the foreign service of the United States; presents such evidence of such service as the registrar prescribes showing that the applicant has no physical or mental disabilities that would affect applicant's driving ability; had a valid Ohio driver's or commercial driver's license at the time the applicant commenced such service, is not under a license suspension or revocation by this state or any other jurisdiction, and makes the application no more than six months after leaving the peace corps, volunteers, or foreign service.

HISTORY: GC § 6296-11; 116 v Pt II, 33, § 11; 119 v 701; 120 v 289; Bureau of Code Revision, 10-1-53; 132 v H 57 (Eff 3-28-67); 132 v H 380 (Eff 1-1-68); 134 v S 546 (Eff 10-16-72); 140 v H 58 (Eff 3-1-85); 142 v H 614 (Eff 3-17-89); 143 v H 381 (Eff 7-1-89); 145 v S 96 (Eff 5-10-94); 147 v S 60. Eff 10-21-97.

§ 4507.11 Examination for license; examiner's permit.

The registrar of motor vehicles shall conduct all necessary examinations of applicants for drivers' licenses, or motorcycle operators' endorsements. Such examination shall include a test of the applicant's knowledge of motor vehicle laws, including the laws on stopping for school buses, a test of his physical fitness to drive, and a test of his ability to understand highway traffic control devices. Such examination may be conducted in such a manner that applicants who are illiterate or limited in their knowledge of the English language may be tested by methods that would indicate to the examining officer that the applicant has a reasonable knowledge of motor vehicle laws and understands highway traffic control devices. Such applicant shall give an actual demonstration of his ability to exercise ordinary and reasonable control in the operation of a motor vehicle by driving the same under the supervision of an examining officer. An applicant for a motorcycle operator's endorsement shall give an actual demonstration of his ability to exercise ordinary and reasonable control in the operation of a motorcycle by driving the same under the supervision of an examining officer. Except as provided in section 4507.12 of the Revised Code, the registrar shall designate the highway patrol or any law enforcement body to supervise and conduct examinations for drivers' licenses and motorcycle operators' endorsements and shall provide the necessary rules and forms to properly conduct such examinations. The records of such examinations, together with the application for a driver's license or motorcycle operator's endorsement, shall be forwarded to the registrar by the deputy registrar, and, if in the opinion of the registrar the applicant is qualified to operate a motor vehicle, the registrar shall issue such license or endorsement.

The registrar may authorize the highway patrol or other designated law enforcement body to issue an examiner's driving permit to an applicant who has passed the required examination, permitting such applicant to operate a motor vehicle while the registrar is completing his investigation relative to such applicant's qualifications to receive a driver's license or motorcycle operator's endorsement. Such examiner's driving permit shall be in the immediate possession of the applicant while operating a motor vehicle and shall be effective until final action and notification has been given by the registrar, but in no event longer than sixty days from its date of issuance.

HISTORY: GC § 6296-12; 116 v Pt II, 33, § 12; 119 v 701; Bureau of Code Revision, 10-1-53; 129 v 1618 (Eff 10-25-61); 132 v H 380 (Eff 1-1-68); 133 v H 362 (Eff 6-23-70); 137 v S 389 (Eff 3-15-79); 140 v H 58 (Eff 3-1-85); 143 v H 381. Eff 7-1-89.

§ 4507.12 Vision screening prior to license renewal; retention of license upon failure.

(A) Except as provided in division (C) of section 4507.10 of the Revised Code, each person applying for the renewal of a driver's license shall submit to a screening of his vision before the license may be renewed. The vision screening shall be conducted at the office of the deputy registrar receiving the application for license renewal.

(B) When the results of a vision screening given under division (A) of this section indicate that the vision of the person examined meets the standards required for licensing, the deputy registrar may renew the person's driver's license at that time.

(C) When the results of a vision screening given under division (A) of this section indicate that the vision of the person screened may not meet the standards required for licensing, the deputy registrar shall not renew the person's driver's license at that time but shall refer the person to a driver's license examiner appointed by the superintendent of the state highway patrol under section 5503.21 of the Revised Code for a further examination of his vision. When a person referred to a driver's license examiner by a deputy registrar does not meet the vision standards required for licensing, the driver's license examiner shall retain the person's operator's or chauffeur's license and shall immediately notify the registrar of motor vehicles of that fact. No driver's license shall be issued to any such person, until the person's vision is corrected to meet the standards required for licensing and the person passes the vision screening required by this section. Any person who operates a motor vehicle on a highway, or on any public or private property used by the public for purposes of vehicular travel or parking, during the time his driver's license is held by a driver's license examiner under this division, shall be deemed to be operating a motor vehicle in violation of division (A) of section 4507.02 of the Revised Code.

(D) The registrar shall adopt rules and shall provide any forms necessary to properly conduct vision screenings at the office of a deputy registrar.

(E) No person conducting vision screenings under this section shall be personally liable for damages for injury or loss to persons or property and for death caused by the operation of a motor vehicle by any person whose driver's license was renewed by the deputy registrar under division (B) of this section.

HISTORY: 140 v H 58 (Eff 3-1-85); 141 v S 356 (Eff 9-24-86); 142 v S 1 (Eff 11-28-88); 143 v H 381. Eff 7-1-89.

Not analogous to former RC § 4507.12 (GC § 6296-14; 116 v Pt II, 33; 120 v 289; Bureau of Code Revision, 10-1-53); repealed 132 v S 43, § 2, eff 1-1-69.

§ 4507.13 Contents and characteristics of license; lamination.

(A) The registrar of motor vehicles shall issue a driver's license to every person licensed as an operator of motor vehicles other than commercial motor vehicles. No person licensed as a commercial motor vehicle driver under Chapter 4506. of the Revised Code need procure a driver's license, but no person shall drive any commercial motor vehicle unless licensed as a commercial motor vehicle driver.

Every driver's license shall bear on it the distinguishing number assigned to the licensee and shall contain the licensee's name, date of birth, social security number if such number has been assigned; the licensee's residence address and county of residence; a color photograph of the licensee; a brief description of the licensee for the purpose of identification; a facsimile of the signature of the licensee as it appears on the application for the license; a space marked "blood type" in which a licensee may specify the licensee's blood type; a notation, in a manner prescribed by the registrar, indicating any condition described in division (D) of section 4507.08 of the Revised Code to which the licensee is subject; on and after May 1, 1993, if the licensee has executed a durable power of attorney for health care or a declaration governing the use or continuation, or the withholding or withdrawal, of life-sustaining treatment and has specified that the licensee wishes the license to indicate that the licensee has executed either type of instrument, any symbol chosen by the registrar to indicate that the licensee has executed either type of instrument; and any additional information that the registrar requires by rule.

The driver's license for licensees under twenty-one years of age shall have characteristics prescribed by the registrar distinguishing it from that issued to a licensee who is twenty-one years of age or older, except that a driver's license issued to a person who applies no more than thirty days before the applicant's twenty-first birthday shall have the characteristics of a license issued to a person who is twenty-one year of age or older.

The driver's license issued to a temporary resident shall contain the word "nonrenewable" and shall have any additional characteristics prescribed by the registrar distinguishing it from a license issued to a resident.

Every driver's or commercial driver's license bearing a motorcycle operator's endorsement and every restricted license to operate a motor vehicle also shall bear the designation "novice," if the endorsement or license is issued to a person who is eighteen years of age or older and previously has not been licensed to operate a motorcycle by this state or another jurisdiction recognized by this state. The "novice" designation shall be effective for one year after the date of issuance of the motorcycle operator's endorsement or license.

Each license issued under this section shall be of such material and so designed as to prevent its reproduction or alteration without ready detection and, to this end, shall be laminated with a transparent plastic material.

(B) Except in regard to a driver's license issued to a person who applies no more than thirty days before the applicant's twenty-first birthday, neither the registrar nor any deputy registrar shall issue a driver's license to anyone under twenty-one years of age that does not have the characteristics prescribed by the registrar distinguishing it from the driver's license issued to persons who are twenty-one years of age or older.

HISTORY: GC § 6296-13; 116 v Pt II, 33, § 13; 119 v 701; 120 v 289; 123 v 246; Bureau of Code Revision, 10-1-53; 131 v 1087 (Eff 9-1-66); 132 v H 193 (Eff 12-11-67); 132 v S 43 (Eff 1-1-69); 132 v S 452 (Eff 1-1-69); 136 v H 650 (Eff 1-5-76); 137 v H 71 (Eff 8-26-77); 137 v H 115 (Eff 7-10-78); 138 v H 328 (Eff 9-13-79); 140 v H 183 (Eff 10-1-84); 142 v H 643 (Eff 3-17-89); 143 v

H 329 (Eff 6-30-89); 143 v H 381 (Eff 7-1-89); 143 v S 131 (Eff 7-25-90); 144 v H 134 (Eff 10-10-91); 144 v H 427 (Eff 10-8-92); 145 v H 580 (Eff 12-9-94); 147 v S 60. Eff 10-21-97.

§ 4507.14 Restrictions relating to driving ability.

The registrar of motor vehicles upon issuing a driver's license, a motorcycle operator's endorsement, a driver's license renewal, or the renewal of any other license issued under this chapter, whenever good cause appears, may impose restrictions suitable to the licensee's driving ability with respect to the type of or special mechanical control devices required on a motor vehicle which the licensee may operate, or such other restrictions applicable to the licensee as the registrar determines to be necessary.

When issuing a license to a person with impaired hearing, the registrar shall require that a motor vehicle operated by the person be equipped with two outside rear vision mirrors, one on the left side and the other on the right side.

The registrar either may issue a special restricted license or may set forth such restrictions upon the usual license form.

The registrar, upon receiving satisfactory evidence of any violation of the restrictions of such license, after an opportunity for a hearing in accordance with Chapter 119. of the Revised Code, may suspend the license for a period of six months.

HISTORY: GC § 6296-14a; 119 v 701; Bureau of Code Revision, 10-1-53; 132 v H 380 (Eff 1-1-68); 143 v H 381 (Eff 7-1-89); 147 v S 60. Eff 10-21-97.

[§ 4507.14.1] § 4507.141 Sun visor identification card for hearing-impaired persons.

(A) Any hearing-impaired person may apply to the registrar of motor vehicles for an identification card identifying the person as hearing-impaired. The application for a hearing-impaired identification card shall be accompanied by a signed statement from the applicant's personal physician certifying that the applicant is hearing-impaired. Upon receipt of the application for the identification card and the signed statement from the applicant's personal physician, and upon presentation by the applicant of his driver's or commercial driver's license or motorcycle operator's license and payment of a fee of five dollars, the registrar shall issue the applicant an identification card. A hearing-impaired person may also apply for a hearing-impaired identification card at the time he applies for a driver's or commercial driver's license or motorcycle operator's license or endorsement. Every hearing-impaired identification card shall expire on the same date that the cardholder's driver's or commercial driver's license or motorcycle operator's license expires.

(B) The hearing-impaired identification card shall be rectangular in shape, approximately the same size as an average motor vehicle sun visor, as determined by the registrar, to enable the identification card to be attached to a sun visor in a motor vehicle. The identification card shall contain the heading "Identification Card for the Hearing-impaired Driver" in boldface type, the name and signature of the hearing-impaired person to whom it is issued, an identifying number, and instructions on the actions the hearing-impaired person should take and the actions the person should refrain from taking in the event he is stopped by a law enforcement officer while operating the motor vehicle. The registrar shall determine the preferred manner in which a hearing-impaired motorcycle operator should carry or display the hearing-impaired identification card, and the color and composition of, and any other information to be included on, the identification card.

(C) As used in this section, "hearing-impaired" means a hearing loss of forty decibels or more in one or both ears.

HISTORY: 143 v H 581. Eff 7-13-90.

§ 4507.15 Courts of record; reports of convictions and forfeitures.

For the purpose of enforcing sections 4507.01 to 4507.39, inclusive, of the Revised Code, any court of record having criminal jurisdiction shall have county-wide jurisdiction within the county in which it is located to hear and finally determine cases arising under such sections. Such actions shall be commenced by the filing of an affidavit, and the right of trial by jury is preserved, but indictments are not required in misdemeanor cases arising under such sections. The registrar shall prepare and furnish blanks for the use of said court in making reports of said convictions and bond forfeitures.

HISTORY: GC § 6296-16; 116 v PtII 33, § 16; 119 v 701; Bureau of Code Revision, 10-1-53; 127 v 525. Eff 6-22-57.

[SUSPENSION OR REVOCATION]

§ 4507.16 Suspension or revocation of license by trial judge or mayor; ignition interlock order.

(A)(1) The trial judge of any court of record, in addition to or independent of all other penalties provided by law or by ordinance, shall suspend for not less than thirty days or more than three years or shall revoke the driver's or commercial driver's license or permit or nonresident operating privilege of any person who is convicted of or pleads guilty to any of the following:

(a) Perjury or the making of a false affidavit under this chapter, or any other law of this state requiring the registration of motor vehicles or regulating their operation on the highway;

(b) Any crime punishable as a felony under the motor vehicle laws of this state or any other felony in the commission of which a motor vehicle is used;

(c) Failing to stop and disclose identity at the scene of the accident when required by law or ordinance to do so;

(d) Street racing as defined in section 4511.251 [4511.25.1] of the Revised Code or any substantially similar municipal ordinance;

(e) Willfully eluding or fleeing a police officer;

(f) Trafficking in cigarettes with the intent to avoid payment of the cigarette tax under division (A) of section 5743.112 [5743.11.2] of the Revised Code;

(g) A violation of section 2903.06, 2903.07, or 2903.08 of the Revised Code or a municipal ordinance substantially similar to section 2903.07 of the Revised Code, unless the jury or judge as trier of fact in the case finds that the offender was under the influence of alcohol, a drug of abuse, or alcohol and a drug of abuse at the time of the commission of the offense.

If a person is convicted of or pleads guilty to a violation of section 2907.24 of the Revised Code, an attempt to commit a violation of that section, or a violation of or an attempt to commit a violation of a municipal ordinance that is substantially equivalent to that section and if the person, in committing or attempting to commit the violation, was in, was on, or used a motor vehicle, the trial judge of a court of record, in addition to or independent of all other penalties provided by law or ordinance, shall suspend for thirty days the person's driver's or commercial driver's license or permit.

The trial judge of any court of record, in addition to suspensions or revocations of licenses, permits, or privileges pursuant to this division and in addition to or independent of all other penalties provided by law or by ordinance, shall impose a suspended jail sentence not to exceed six months, if imprisonment was not imposed for the offense for which the person was convicted.

(2) If the trial judge of any court of record suspends or revokes the driver's or commercial driver's license or permit or nonresident operating privilege of a person who is convicted of or pleads guilty to any offense for which such suspension or revocation is provided by law or ordinance, in addition to all other penalties provided by law or ordinance, the judge may issue an order prohibiting the offender from registering, renewing, or transferring the registration of any vehicle during the period that the offender's license, permit, or privilege is suspended or revoked. The court promptly shall send a copy of the order to the registrar of motor vehicles.

Upon receipt of such an order, neither the registrar nor any deputy registrar shall accept any application for the registration, registration renewal, or transfer of registration of any motor vehicle owned or leased by the person named in the order during the period that the person's license, permit, or privilege is suspended or revoked, unless the registrar is properly notified by the court that the order of suspension or revocation has been canceled. When the period of suspension or revocation expires or the order is canceled, the registrar or deputy registrar shall accept the application for registration, registration renewal, or transfer of registration of the person named in the order.

(B) Except as otherwise provided in this section, the trial judge of any court of record and the mayor of a mayor's court, in addition to or independent of all other penalties provided by law or by ordinance, shall revoke the driver's or commercial driver's license or permit or nonresident operating privilege of any person who is convicted of or pleads guilty to a violation of division (A) of section 4511.19 of the Revised Code, of a municipal ordinance relating to operating a vehicle while under the influence of alcohol, a drug of abuse, or alcohol and a drug of abuse, or of a municipal ordinance that is substantially equivalent to division (A) of section 4511.19 of the Revised Code relating to operating a vehicle with a prohibited concentration of alcohol in the blood, breath, or urine or suspend the license, permit, or privilege as follows:

(1) Except when division (B)(2), (3), or (4) of this section applies and the judge or mayor is required to suspend or revoke the offender's license or permit pursuant to that division, the judge or mayor shall suspend the offender's driver's or commercial driver's license or permit or nonresident operating privilege for not less than six months nor more than three years.

(2) Subject to division (B)(4) of this section, if, within six years of the offense, the offender has been convicted of or pleaded guilty to one violation of division (A) or (B) of section 4511.19 of the Revised Code, a municipal ordinance relating to operating a vehicle while under the influence of alcohol, a drug of abuse, or alcohol and a drug of abuse, a municipal ordinance relating to operating a motor vehicle with a prohibited concentration of alcohol in the blood, breath, or urine, section 2903.04 of the Revised Code in a case in which the offender was subject to the sanctions described in division (D) of that section, section 2903.06, 2903.07, or 2903.08 of the Revised Code or a municipal ordinance that is substantially similar to section 2903.07 of the Revised Code in a case in which the jury or judge found that the offender was under the influence of alcohol, a drug of abuse, or alcohol and a drug of abuse, or a statute of the United States or of any other state or a municipal ordinance of a municipal corporation located in any other state that is substantially similar to division (A) or (B) of section 4511.19 of the Revised Code, the judge shall suspend the offender's driver's or commercial driver's license or permit or nonresident operating privilege for not less than one year nor more than five years.

(3) Subject to division (B)(4) of this section, if, within six years of the offense, the offender has been convicted of or pleaded guilty to two violations described in division (B)(2) of this section, or a statute of the United States or of any other state or a municipal ordinance of a municipal corporation located in any other state

that is substantially similar to division (A) or (B) of section 4511.19 of the Revised Code, the judge shall suspend the offender's driver's or commercial driver's license or permit or nonresident operating privilege for not less than one year nor more than ten years.

(4) If, within six years of the offense, the offender has been convicted of or pleaded guilty to three or more violations described in division (B)(2) of this section, a statute of the United States or of any other state or a municipal ordinance of a municipal corporation located in any other state that is substantially similar to division (A) or (B) of section 4511.19 of the Revised Code, or if the offender previously has been convicted of or pleaded guilty to a violation of division (A) of section 4511.19 of the Revised Code under circumstances in which the violation was a felony and regardless of when the violation and the conviction or guilty plea occurred, the judge shall suspend the offender's driver's or commercial driver's license or permit or nonresident operating privilege for a period of time set by the court but not less than three years, and the judge may permanently revoke the offender's driver's or commercial driver's license or permit or nonresident operating privilege.

(5) The filing of an appeal by a person whose driver's or commercial driver's license is suspended or revoked under division (B)(1), (2), (3), or (4) of this section regarding any aspect of the person's trial or sentence does not stay the operation of the suspension or revocation.

(C) The trial judge of any court of record or the mayor of a mayor's court, in addition to or independent of all other penalties provided by law or by ordinance, may suspend the driver's or commercial driver's license or permit or nonresident operating privilege of any person who violates a requirement or prohibition of the court imposed under division (F) of this section or division (G)(1) of section 2951.02 of the Revised Code as follows:

(1) For not more than one year, upon conviction for a first violation of the requirement or prohibition;

(2) For not more than five years, upon conviction for a second or subsequent violation of the requirement or prohibition during the same period of required use of an ignition interlock device that is certified pursuant to section 4511.83 of the Revised Code.

(D)(1) The trial judge of any court of record, in addition to or independent of all other penalties provided by law or by ordinance, shall permanently revoke the driver's or commercial driver's license or permit or nonresident operating privilege of any person who is convicted of or pleads guilty to a violation of section 2903.04 of the Revised Code in a case in which the offender is subject to the sanctions described in division (D) of that section, or of any person who is convicted of or pleads guilty to a violation of section 2903.06, 2903.07, or 2903.08 of the Revised Code or of a municipal ordinance that is substantially similar to section 2903.07 of the Revised Code if the jury or judge as trier of fact in the case in which the person is convicted finds that the offender was under the influence of alcohol, a drug of abuse, or alcohol and a drug of abuse, at the time of the commission of the offense.

(2) In addition to any prison term authorized or required by the section that establishes the offense and sections 2929.13 and 2929.14 of the Revised Code, and in addition to any other sanction imposed for the offense under the section that establishes the offense or sections 2929.11 to 2929.182 [2929.18.2] of the Revised Code, the court that sentences an offender who is convicted of or pleads guilty to a violation of section 2925.02, 2925.03, 2925.04, 2925.05, 2925.06, 2925.11, 2925.12, 2925.13, 2925.14, 2925.22, 2925.23, 2925.31, 2925.32, 2925.36, or 2925.37 of the Revised Code either shall revoke or, if it does not revoke, shall suspend for not less than six months or more than five years, as specified in the section that establishes the offense, the person's driver's or commercial driver's license or permit. If the person's driver's or commercial driver's license or permit is under suspension on the date the court imposes sentence upon the person, any revocation imposed upon the person that is referred to in division (D)(2) of this section shall take effect immediately. If the person's driver's or commercial driver's license or permit is under suspension on the date the court imposes sentence upon the person, any period of suspension imposed upon the person that is referred to in division (D)(2) of this section shall take effect on the next day immediately following the end of that period of suspension. If the person is sixteen years of age or older and is a resident of this state but does not have a current, valid Ohio driver's or commercial driver's license or permit, the court shall order the registrar to deny to the person the issuance of a driver's or commercial driver's license or permit for six months beginning on the date the court imposes a sentence upon the person. If the person has not attained the age of sixteen years on the date the court sentences the person for the violation, the period of denial shall commence on the date the person attains the age of sixteen years.

(E) Except as otherwise provided in this section, the trial judge of any court of record and the mayor of a mayor's court, in addition to or independent of all other penalties provided by law or ordinance, shall suspend for not less than sixty days nor more than two years the driver's or commercial driver's license or permit or nonresident operating privilege of any person who is convicted of or pleads guilty to a violation of division (B) of section 4511.19 of the Revised Code or of a municipal ordinance substantially equivalent to that division relating to operating a vehicle with a prohibited concentration of alcohol in the blood, breath, or urine.

(F) If a person's driver's or commercial driver's license or permit or nonresident operating privilege has been suspended pursuant to division (B) or (C) of this section or pursuant to division (F) of section 4511.191 [4511.19.1] of the Revised Code, and the person, within the preceding seven years, has been convicted of or pleaded guilty to three or more violations of division (A) or (B) of section 4511.19 of the Revised Code, a municipal ordinance relating to operating a vehicle while under the influence of alcohol, a drug of abuse, or alcohol and a drug of abuse, a municipal ordinance relating to operating a vehicle with a prohibited concentration of alcohol in the blood, breath, or urine, section 2903.04 of the Revised Code in a case in which the person was subject to the sanctions described in division (D) of that section, section 2903.06, 2903.07, or 2903.08 of the Revised Code or a municipal ordinance that is substantially similar to section 2903.07 of the Revised Code in a case in which the jury or judge found that the person was under the influence of alcohol, a drug of abuse, or alcohol and a drug of abuse, or a statute of the United States or of any other state or a municipal ordinance of a municipal corporation located in any other state that is substantially similar to division (A) or (B) of section 4511.19 of the Revised Code, the person is not entitled to request, and the judge or mayor shall not grant to the person, occupational driving privileges under this division. Any other person whose driver's or commercial driver's license or nonresident operating privilege has been suspended under any of those divisions may file a petition that alleges that the suspension would seriously affect the person's ability to continue the person's employment. The petition of a person whose license, permit, or privilege was suspended pursuant to division (F) of section 4511.191 [4511.19.1] of the Revised Code shall be filed in the court specified in division (I)(4) of that section, and the petition of a person whose license, permit, or privilege was suspended under division (B) or (C) of this section shall be filed in the municipal, county, mayor's, or in the case of a minor, juvenile court that has jurisdiction over the place of arrest. Upon satisfactory proof that there is reasonable cause to believe that the suspension would seriously affect the person's ability to continue the person's employment, the judge of the court or mayor of the mayor's court may grant the person occupational driving privileges during the period during which the suspension otherwise would be imposed, except that the judge or mayor shall not grant occupational driving privileges to any person who, within seven years of the filing of the petition, has been convicted of or pleaded guilty to three or more violations of division (A) or (B) of section 4511.19 of the Revised Code, a municipal ordinance relating to operating a vehicle while under the influence of alcohol, a drug of abuse, or alcohol and a drug of abuse, a municipal ordinance relating to operating a vehicle with a prohibited concentration of alcohol in the blood, breath, or urine, section 2903.04 of the Revised Code in a case in which the person was subject to the sanctions described in division (D) of that section, section 2903.06, 2903.07, or 2903.08 of the Revised Code or a municipal ordinance that is substantially similar to section 2903.07 of the Revised Code in a case in which the jury or judge found that the person was under the influence of alcohol, a drug of abuse, or alcohol and a drug of abuse, or a statute of the United States or of any other state or a municipal ordinance of a municipal corporation located in any other state that is substantially similar to division (A) or (B) of section 4511.19 of the Revised Code, shall not grant occupational driving privileges for employment as a driver of commercial motor vehicles to any person who is disqualified from operating a commercial motor vehicle under section 2301.374 [2301.37.4] or 4506.16 of the Revised Code, and shall not grant occupational driving privileges during any of the following periods of time:

(1) The first fifteen days of suspension imposed upon an offender whose license, permit, or privilege is suspended pursuant to division (B)(1) of this section or division (F)(1) of section 4511.191 [4511.19.1] of the Revised Code. On or after the sixteenth day of suspension, the court may grant the offender occupational driving privileges, but the court may provide that the offender shall not exercise the occupational driving privileges unless the vehicles the offender operates are equipped with ignition interlock devices.

(2) The first thirty days of suspension imposed upon an offender whose license, permit, or privilege is suspended pursuant to division (B)(2) of this section or division (F)(2) of section 4511.191 [4511.19.1] of the Revised Code. On or after the thirty-first day of suspension, the court may grant the offender occupational driving privileges, but the court may provide that the offender shall not exercise the occupational driving privileges unless the vehicles the offender operates are equipped with ignition interlock devices.

(3) The first one hundred eighty days of suspension imposed upon an offender whose license, permit, or privilege is suspended pursuant to division (B)(3) of this section or division (F)(3) of section 4511.191 [4511.19.1] of the Revised Code. The judge may grant occupational driving privileges to an offender who receives a suspension under either of those divisions on or after the one hundred eighty-first day of the suspension only if division (F) of this section does not prohibit the judge from granting the privileges and only if the judge, at the time of granting the privileges, also issues an order prohibiting the offender, while exercising the occupational driving privileges during the period commencing with the one hundred eighty-first day of suspension and ending with the first year of suspension, from operating any motor vehicle unless it is equipped with a certified ignition interlock device. After the first year of the suspension, the court may authorize the offender to continue exercising the occupational driving privileges in vehicles that are not equipped with ignition interlock devices. If the offender does not petition for occupational driving privileges until after the first year of suspension and if division (F) of this section does not prohibit the judge from granting the privileges,

the judge may grant the offender occupational driving privileges without requiring the use of a certified ignition interlock device.

(4) The first three years of suspension imposed upon an offender whose license, permit, or privilege is suspended pursuant to division (B)(4) of this section or division (F)(4) of section 4511.191 [4511.19.1] of the Revised Code. The judge may grant occupational driving privileges to an offender who receives a suspension under either of those divisions after the first three years of suspension only if division (F) of this section does not prohibit the judge from granting the privileges and only if the judge, at the time of granting the privileges, also issues an order prohibiting the offender from operating any motor vehicle, for the period of suspension following the first three years of suspension, unless the motor vehicle is equipped with a certified ignition interlock device.

(G) If a person's driver's or commercial driver's license or permit or nonresident operating privilege has been suspended under division (E) of this section, and the person, within the preceding seven years, has been convicted of or pleaded guilty to three or more violations of division (A) or (B) of section 4511.19 of the Revised Code, a municipal ordinance relating to operating a vehicle while under the influence of alcohol, a drug of abuse, or alcohol and a drug of abuse, a municipal ordinance relating to operating a vehicle with a prohibited concentration of alcohol in the blood, breath, or urine, section 2903.04 of the Revised Code in a case in which the person was subject to the sanctions described in division (D) of that section, section 2903.06, 2903.07, or 2903.08 of the Revised Code or a municipal ordinance that is substantially similar to section 2903.07 of the Revised Code in a case in which the jury or judge found that the person was under the influence of alcohol, a drug of abuse, or alcohol and a drug of abuse, or a statute of the United States or of any other state or a municipal ordinance of a municipal corporation located in any other state that is substantially similar to division (A) or (B) of section 4511.19 of the Revised Code, the person is not entitled to request, and the judge or mayor shall not grant to the person, occupational driving privileges under this division. Any other person whose driver's or commercial driver's license or nonresident operating privilege has been suspended under division (E) of this section may file a petition that alleges that the suspension would seriously affect the person's ability to continue the person's employment. The petition shall be filed in the municipal, county, or mayor's court that has jurisdiction over the place of arrest. Upon satisfactory proof that there is reasonable cause to believe that the suspension would seriously affect the person's ability to continue the person's employment, the judge of the court or mayor of the mayor's court may grant the person occupational driving privileges during the period during which the suspension otherwise would be imposed, except that the judge or mayor shall not grant occupational driving privileges to any person who, within seven years of the filing of the petition, has been convicted of or pleaded guilty to three or more violations of division (A) or (B) of section 4511.19 of the Revised Code, a municipal ordinance relating to operating a vehicle while under the influence of alcohol, a drug of abuse, or alcohol and a drug of abuse, a municipal ordinance relating to operating a vehicle with a prohibited concentration of alcohol in the blood, breath, or urine, section 2903.04 of the Revised Code in a case in which the person was subject to the sanctions described in division (D) of that section, section 2903.06, 2903.07, or 2903.08 of the Revised Code or a municipal ordinance that is substantially similar to section 2903.07 of the Revised Code in a case in which the jury or judge found that the person was under the influence of alcohol, a drug of abuse, or alcohol and a drug of abuse, or a statute of the United States or of any other state or a municipal ordinance of a municipal corporation located in any other state that is substantially similar to division (A) or (B) of section 4511.19 of the Revised Code, shall not grant occupational driving privileges for employment as a driver of commercial motor vehicles to any person who is disqualified from operating a commercial motor vehicle under section 4506.16 of the Revised Code, and shall not grant occupational driving privileges during the first sixty days of suspension imposed upon an offender whose driver's or commercial driver's license or permit or nonresident operating privilege is suspended pursuant to division (E) of this section.

(H)(1) After a driver's or commercial driver's license or permit has been suspended or revoked pursuant to this section, the judge of the court or mayor of the mayor's court that suspended or revoked the license or permit shall cause the offender to deliver the license or permit to the court. The judge, mayor, or clerk of the court or mayor's court, if the license or permit has been suspended or revoked in connection with any of the offenses listed in this section, forthwith shall forward it to the registrar with notice of the action of the court.

(2) Suspension of a commercial driver's license under this section shall be concurrent with any period of disqualification under section 2301.374 [2301.37.4] or 4506.16 of the Revised Code. No person who is disqualified for life from holding a commercial driver's license under section 4506.16 of the Revised Code shall be issued a driver's license under this chapter during the period for which the commercial driver's license was suspended under this section, and no person whose commercial driver's license is suspended under this section shall be issued a driver's license under this chapter during the period of the suspension.

(I) No judge shall suspend the first thirty days of suspension of a driver's or commercial driver's license or permit or a nonresident operating privilege required under division (A) of this section, no judge or mayor shall suspend the first six months of suspension required under division (B)(1) of this section, no judge shall suspend the first year of suspension required under division (B)(2) of this section, no judge shall suspend the first year of suspension required under division (B)(3) of this section, no judge shall suspend the first three years of suspension required under division (B)(4) of this section, no judge or mayor shall suspend the revocation required by division (D) of this section, and no judge or mayor shall suspend the first sixty days of suspension required under division (E) of this section, except that the court shall credit any period of suspension imposed pursuant to section 4511.191 [4511.19.1] or 4511.196 [4511.19.6] of the Revised Code against any time of suspension imposed pursuant to division (B) or (E) of this section as described in division (J) of this section.

(J) The judge of the court or mayor of the mayor's court shall credit any time during which an offender was subject to an administrative suspension of the offender's driver's or commercial driver's license or permit or nonresident operating privilege imposed pursuant to division (E) or (F) of section 4511.191 [4511.19.1] or a suspension imposed by a judge, referee, or mayor pursuant to division (B)(1) or (2) of section 4511.196 [4511.19.6] of the Revised Code against the time to be served under a related suspension imposed pursuant to this section.

(K) The judge or mayor shall notify the bureau of any determinations made, and of any suspensions or revocations imposed, pursuant to division (B) of this section.

(L)(1) If a court issues an ignition interlock order under division (F) of this section, the order shall authorize the offender during the specified period to operate a motor vehicle only if it is equipped with a certified ignition interlock device. The court shall provide the offender with a copy of an ignition interlock order issued under division (F) of this section, and the copy of the order shall be used by the offender in lieu of an Ohio driver's or commercial driver's license or permit until the registrar or a deputy registrar issues the offender a restricted license.

An order issued under division (F) of this section does not authorize or permit the offender to whom it has been issued to operate a vehicle during any time that the offender's driver's or commercial driver's license or permit is suspended or revoked under any other provision of law.

(2) The offender may present the ignition interlock order to the registrar or to a deputy registrar. Upon presentation of the order to the registrar or a deputy registrar, the registrar or deputy registrar shall issue the offender a restricted license. A restricted license issued under this division shall be identical to an Ohio driver's license, except that it shall have printed on its face a statement that the offender is prohibited during the period specified in the court order from operating any motor vehicle that is not equipped with a certified ignition interlock device, and except that the date of commencement and the date of termination of the period shall be indicated conspicuously upon the face of the license.

(3) As used in this section:
(a) "Ignition interlock device" has the same meaning as in section 4511.83 of the Revised Code.
(b) "Certified ignition interlock device" means an ignition interlock device that is certified pursuant to section 4511.83 of the Revised Code.

HISTORY: GC § 6296-17; 116 v PtII, 33, § 17; Bureau of Code Revision, 10-1-53; 125 v 367 (Eff 10-15-53); 132 v S 37 (Eff 11-14-67); 132 v H 380 (Eff 1-1-68); 133 v H 1 (Eff 3-18-69); 136 v H 300 (Eff 7-1-76); 137 v S 141 (Eff 11-11-77); 137 v H 469 (Eff 10-25-78); 139 v S 432 (Eff 3-16-83); 141 v S 262 (Eff 3-20-87); 142 v H 303 (Eff 10-20-87); 142 v H 429 (Eff 6-20-88); 143 v H 381 (Eff 7-1-89); 143 v S 131 (Eff 7-25-90); 143 v H 837 (Eff 7-25-90); 143 v S 258 (Eff 11-20-90); 144 v S 275 (Eff 9-1-93); 145 v S 62, §§ 1, 4 (Eff 9-1-93); 145 v H 377 (Eff 9-30-93); 145 v S 82 (Eff 5-4-94); 145 v H 236 (Eff 9-29-94); 146 v H 107 (Eff 6-30-96); 146 v S 2 (Eff 7-1-96); 146 v S 269, § 1 (Eff 7-1-96); 146 v H 353, § 1 (Eff 9-17-96); 146 v H 676, § 1 (Eff 10-4-96); 146 v S 166, § 1 (Eff 10-17-96); 146 v H 353, § 4 (Eff 5-15-97); 146 v S 269, § 8 (Eff 5-15-97); 146 v H 676, § 3 (Eff 5-15-97); 146 v S 166, § 6 (Eff 5-15-97); 147 v S 60. Eff 10-21-97.

See provisions, § 3 of SB 60 (147 v —) following RC § 4507.02.1.

[§ 4507.16.1] § 4507.161 Suspension of license of person mentally ill.

When any person having a driver's or commercial driver's license is adjudicated incompetent for the purpose of holding the license, as provided in section 5122.301 [5122.30.1] of the Revised Code, the probate judge shall order the license of such person delivered to the court. The court shall forward such license with notice of such adjudication to the registrar of motor vehicles. The registrar of motor vehicles shall suspend such license until receipt of written notice by the head of the hospital, or other agency which has or had custody of such person, that such person's mental illness is not an impairment to such person's ability to operate a motor vehicle, or upon receipt of notice from the adjudicating court that such person has been restored to competency by court decree.

HISTORY: 126 v 600 (Eff 9-30-55); 129 v 1448 (Eff 10-25-61); 130 v 1059 (Eff 10-10-63); 137 v H 725 (Eff 3-16-78); 143 v H 381. Eff 7-1-89.

[§ 4507.16.2] § 4507.162 Suspension of probationary license or temporary instruction permit.

(A) Except as provided in division (C) of this section, the registrar of motor vehicles shall suspend the probationary driver's license or restricted license issued to any person when the person, before reaching the person's eighteenth birthday, has been convicted of, pleaded guilty to, or been adjudicated in juvenile court of having committed any of the following:

(1) Three separate violations in any two-year period of section 2903.06, 2903.07, 2903.08, 2921.331 [2921.33.1], 4511.12, 4511.13, 4511.15, 4511.191 [4511.19.1], 4511.192 [4511.19.2], 4511.20, 4511.201 [4511.20.1], 4511.202 [4511.20.2], 4511.21, 4511.22, 4511.23, 4511.25 to 4511.48, 4511.57 to 4511.65, 4511.75, 4549.02, 4549.021 [4549.02.1], or 4549.03 of the Revised Code, section 2903.04 of the Revised Code in a case in which the person would have been subject to the sanctions described in division (D) of that section had the person been convicted of the violation of that section, or any municipal ordinances similarly relating to the offenses contained in those sections;

(2) One violation of section 4511.19 of the Revised Code or a substantially similar municipal ordinance.

Any person whose license is suspended under division (A) of this section shall mail or deliver the person's probationary driver's license or restricted license to the registrar within fourteen days of notification of the suspension. The registrar shall retain the license during the period of the suspension. A suspension pursuant to division (A)(1) of this section shall remain in effect until one year has elapsed since the date of suspension of the probationary driver's license or restricted license and a suspension pursuant to division (A)(2) of this section shall remain in effect until six months have elapsed since the date of the suspension. If the person's probationary driver's license or restricted license is under suspension on the date the court imposes sentence upon the person for a violation described in division (A)(2) of this section, the suspension shall take effect on the next day immediately following the end of that period of suspension. If the person is sixteen years of age or older and pleads guilty to or is convicted of a violation described in division (A)(2) of this section and the person does not have a current, valid probationary driver's license or restricted license, the registrar shall deny the issuance to the person of a probationary driver's license, restricted license, driver's license, or commercial driver's license, as the case may be, for six months beginning on the date the court imposes sentence upon the person for the violation. If the person has not attained the age of sixteen years on the date the court imposes sentence upon the person for the violation, the period of denial shall commence on the date the person attains the age of sixteen years.

(B) The registrar also shall suspend the temporary instruction permit or probationary driver's license of any person under the age of eighteen who has been adjudicated unruly, delinquent, or a juvenile traffic offender for having committed any act that if committed by an adult would be a drug abuse offense as defined in section 2925.01 of the Revised Code, or a violation of division (B) of section 2917.11 of the Revised Code until the person reaches the age of eighteen years or attends, at the discretion of the court, and satisfactorily completes a drug abuse or alcohol abuse education, intervention, or treatment program specified by the court. Any person whose temporary instruction permit or probationary driver's license is suspended under this division shall mail or deliver the person's permit or license to the registrar within fourteen days of notification of the suspension. The registrar shall retain the license during the period of the suspension.

(C) If a person is convicted of, pleads guilty to, or is adjudicated in juvenile court of having committed a third violation of sections 4511.12, 4511.13, 4511.15, 4511.20 to 4511.23, 4511.25, 4511.26 to 4511.48, 4511.57 to 4511.65, or 4511.75 of the Revised Code or any similar municipal ordinances within a two-year period, and the person, within the preceding seven years, has been convicted of, pleaded guilty to, or adjudicated in juvenile court of having committed three or more violations of division (A) or (B) of section 4511.19 of the Revised Code, a municipal ordinance relating to operating a vehicle while under the influence of alcohol, a drug of abuse, or alcohol and a drug of abuse, a municipal ordinance relating to operating a vehicle with a prohibited concentration of alcohol in the blood, breath, or urine, section 2903.04 of the Revised Code in a case in which the person was subject to the sanctions described in division (D) of that section, or section 2903.06, 2903.07, or 2903.08 of the Revised Code or a municipal ordinance that is substantially similar to section 2903.07 of the Revised Code in a case in which the jury or judge found that the person was under the influence of alcohol, a drug of abuse, or alcohol and a drug of abuse, the person is not entitled to request, and the court shall not grant to the person, occupational driving privileges under this division. For any other person who is convicted of, pleads guilty to, or is adjudicated in juvenile court of having committed a third violation of sections 4511.12, 4511.13, 4511.15, 4511.20 to 4511.23, 4511.25, 4511.26 to 4511.48, 4511.57 to 4511.65, or 4511.75 of the Revised Code or any similar municipal ordinances within a two-year period, the court in which the third conviction, finding, plea, or adjudication was made, upon petition of the person, may grant the person occupational driving privileges if the court finds that the person will reach the person's eighteenth birthday before the period of suspension required to be imposed under division (A)(1) of this section expires and further finds reasonable cause to believe that the suspension, if continued beyond the person's eighteenth birthday, will seriously affect the person's ability to continue in employment. The occupational driving privileges granted under this division shall be effective on the person's eighteenth birthday and during the period following such birthday for which the suspension would otherwise be imposed. A court shall not grant occupational driving privileges to any person who, within seven years of the filing of the petition, has been convicted of, pleaded guilty to, or adjudicated in juvenile court of having committed three or more violations of division (A) or (B) of section 4511.19 of the Revised Code, a municipal ordinance relating to operating a vehicle while under the influence of alcohol, a drug of abuse, or alcohol and a drug of abuse, a municipal ordinance relating to operating a vehicle with a prohibited concentration of alcohol in the blood, breath, or urine, section 2903.04 of the Revised Code in a case in which the person was subject to the sanctions described in division (D) of that section, or section 2903.06, 2903.07, or 2903.08 of the Revised Code or a municipal ordinance that is substantially similar to section 2903.07 of the Revised Code in a case in which the jury or judge found that the person was under the influence of alcohol, a drug of abuse, or alcohol and a drug of abuse. In granting occupational driving privileges, the court shall specify the times and places at which the person may drive and may impose any other conditions upon the person's use of a motor vehicle that the court considers reasonable and necessary.

A court that grants occupational driving privileges to a person under this division shall retain the person's probationary driver's license or restricted license during the period the license is suspended and also during the period for which occupational driving privileges are granted, and shall deliver to the person a permit card, in a form to be prescribed by the court, setting forth the date on which the occupational driving privileges will become effective, the times and places at which the person may drive, and any other conditions imposed upon the person's use of a motor vehicle.

The court immediately shall notify the registrar, in writing, of a grant of occupational driving privileges. The notification shall specify the date on which the occupational driving privileges will become effective, the times and places at which the person may drive, and any other conditions imposed upon the person's use of a motor vehicle. The registrar shall not suspend the probationary driver's license or restricted license of any person pursuant to division (A) of this section during any period for which the person has been granted occupational driving privileges as provided in this division, if the registrar has received the notification described in this division from the court.

(D) If a person who has been granted occupational driving privileges under division (C) of this section is convicted of, pleads guilty to, or is adjudicated in juvenile court of having committed, a violation of section 4507.02 of the Revised Code, or a fourth or subsequent violation of any of the other sections of the Revised Code listed in division (A)(1) of this section or any similar municipal ordinance during the period for which the person was granted occupational driving privileges, the court that granted the occupational driving privileges shall revoke them and cancel the person's permit card. The court or the clerk of the court immediately shall forward the person's probationary driver's license or restricted license together with written notification of the court's action to the registrar. Upon receipt of the license and notification, the registrar shall suspend the person's probationary driver's license or restricted license for a period of one year. The registrar shall retain the license during the period of suspension, and no further occupational driving privileges shall be granted during that period.

(E) No application for a driver's or commercial driver's license shall be received from any person whose probationary driver's license or restricted license has been suspended under this section until the suspension period has expired, a temporary instruction permit or commercial driver's license temporary instruction permit has been issued, and the applicant has submitted to the examination for a driver's license as provided for in section 4507.11 or a commercial driver's license as provided in Chapter 4506. of the Revised Code.

HISTORY: 127 v 839 (Eff 9-16-57); 128 v 539 (Eff 11-2-59); 129 v 1599 (Eff 10-11-61); 130 v 1060 (Eff 9-27-63); 132 v H 380 (Eff 1-1-68); 135 v S 1 (Eff 1-1-74); 140 v H 252 (Eff 4-4-85); 142 v H 643 (Eff 3-17-89); 143 v H 329 (Eff 6-30-89); 143 v H 330 (Eff 6-30-89); 143 v H 381 (Eff 7-1-89); 143 v S 49 (Eff 11-3-89); 143 v S 131 (Eff 7-25-90); 144 v S 275 (Eff 9-1-93); 145 v S 62, § 4 (Eff 9-1-93); 145 v H 377 (Eff 9-30-93); 145 v H 236 (Eff 9-29-94); 147 v S 60. Eff 10-21-97.

[§ 4507.16.3] § 4507.163 Underage persons using license to purchase liquor or beer.

(A) Any person of insufficient age to purchase intoxicating liquor or beer who, contrary to division (A) or (C) of section 4507.30 of the Revised Code, displays as proof that the person is of sufficient age to purchase intoxicating liquor or beer, a driver's or commercial driver's license, knowing the same to be fictitious, altered, or not the person's own, shall thereby forfeit the driving privileges authorized by the person's own driver's license, probationary driver's license, commercial driver's license, temporary instruction permit, or commercial driver's license temporary instruction permit and be denied the issuance or reissuance of any such license or permit by the registrar of motor vehicles for one year beginning with the date on which notification of such forfeiture and denial is mailed to the person by the registrar.

(B) In any prosecution, or in any proceeding before the liquor control commission, in which the defense authorized by section 4301.639 [4301.63.9] of the Revised Code is sustained, the clerk of the court in which the prosecution was had, or the clerk of the liquor control commission, shall certify to the registrar the facts ascertainable from the clerk's records evidencing violation of division (A) or (C) of section 4507.30 of the Revised Code by a person of insufficient age to purchase intoxicating liquor or beer, including in the certification the person's name and residence address.

(C) The registrar, upon receipt of the certification, shall suspend the person's license or permit to drive subject to review as provided in this section, and shall mail to the person, at the person's last known address, a notice of the suspension and of the hearing provided in division (D) of this section.

(D) Any person whose license or permit to drive has been suspended under this section, within twenty days of the mailing of the notice provided above, may file a petition in the municipal court or county court, or in case the person is under the age of eighteen years, in the juvenile court, in whose jurisdiction the person resides, agreeing to pay the cost of the proceedings, and alleging error by the registrar in the suspension of the license or permit to drive, or in one or more of the matters within the scope of the hearing as provided in this section, or both. The petitioner shall notify the registrar of the filing of the petition and send the registrar a copy thereof. The scope of the hearing shall be limited to whether a court of record did in fact find that the petitioner displayed, or, if the original proceedings were before the liquor control commission, whether the petitioner did in fact display, as proof that the person was of sufficient age to purchase intoxicating liquor or beer, a driver's or commercial driver's license knowing the same to be fictitious, altered, or not the person's own, and whether the person was at that time of insufficient age legally to make a purchase of intoxicating liquor or beer.

(E) In any hearing authorized by this section, the registrar shall be represented by the prosecuting attorney of the county where the petitioner resides.

(F) If the court finds from the evidence submitted that the person has failed to show error in the action by the registrar or in one or more of the matters within the scope of the hearing as limited in division (D) of this section, or both, the court shall assess the cost of the proceeding against the person and shall impose the suspension provided in divisions (A) and (C) of this section. If the court finds that the person has shown error in the action taken by the registrar, or in one or more of the matters within the scope of the hearing as limited in division (B) of this section, or both, the cost of the proceeding shall be paid out of the county treasury of the county in which the proceedings were held, and the suspension provided in divisions (A) and (C) of this section shall not be imposed. The court shall inform the registrar in writing of the action taken.

HISTORY: 134 v H 453 (Eff 9-28-72); 143 v H 381 (Eff 7-1-89); 147 v S 60. Eff 10-21-97.

[§ 4507.16.4] § 4507.164 Impoundment of license plates upon suspension or revocation of license; immobilization or criminal forfeiture of vehicle.

(A) Except as provided in divisions (C) to (E) of this section, when the license of any person is suspended or revoked pursuant to any provision of the Revised Code other than division (B) of section 4507.16 of the Revised Code, the trial judge may impound the identification license plates of any motor vehicle registered in the name of the person.

(B)(1) When the license of any person is suspended or revoked pursuant to division (B)(1) of section 4507.16 of the Revised Code, the trial judge of the court of record or the mayor of the mayor's court that suspended or revoked the license may impound the identification license plates of any motor vehicle registered in the name of the person.

(2) When the license of any person is suspended or revoked pursuant to division (B)(2) or (3) of section 4507.16 of the Revised Code, the trial judge of the court of record that suspended or revoked the license shall order the impoundment of the identification license plates of the motor vehicle the offender was operating at the time of the offense and the immobilization of that vehicle in accordance with section 4503.233 [4503.23.3] and division (A)(2) or (3) of section 4511.99 or division (B)(2)(a) or (b) of section 4511.193 [4511.19.3] of the Revised Code and may impound the identification license plates of any other motor vehicle registered in the name of the person whose license is suspended or revoked.

(3) When the license of any person is suspended or revoked pursuant to division (B)(4) of section 4507.16 of the Revised Code, the trial judge of the court of record that suspended or revoked the license shall order the criminal forfeiture to the state of the motor vehicle the offender was operating at the time of the offense in accordance with section 4503.234 [4503.23.4] and division (A)(4) of section 4511.99 or division (B)(2)(c) of section 4511.193 [4511.19.3] of the Revised Code and may impound the identification license plates of any other motor vehicle registered in the name of the person whose license is suspended or revoked.

(C)(1) When a person is convicted of or pleads guilty to a violation of division (D)(2) of section 4507.02 of the Revised Code or a substantially equivalent municipal ordinance and division (B)(1) or (2) of section 4507.99 or division (C)(1) or (2) of section 4507.36 of the Revised Code applies, the trial judge of the court of record or the mayor of the mayor's court that imposes sentence shall order the immobilization of the vehicle the person was operating at the time of the offense and the impoundment of its identification license plates in accordance with section 4503.233 [4503.23.3] and division (B)(1) or (2) of section 4507.99 or division (C)(1) or (2) of section 4507.361 [4507.36.1] of the Revised Code and may impound the identification license plates of any other vehicle registered in the name of that person.

(2) When a person is convicted of or pleads guilty to a violation of division (D)(2) of section 4507.02 of the Revised Code or a substantially equivalent municipal ordinance and division (B)(3) of section 4507.99 or division (C)(3) of section 4507.361 [4507.36.1] of the Revised Code applies, the trial judge of the court of record that imposes sentence shall order the criminal forfeiture to the state of the vehicle the person was operating at the time of the offense in accordance with section 4503.234 [4503.23.4] and division (B)(3) of section

4507.99 or division (C)(3) of section 4507.361 [4507.36.1] of the Revised Code and may impound the identification license plates of any other vehicle registered in the name of that person.

(D)(1) When a person is convicted of or pleads guilty to a violation of division (B)(1) of section 4507.02 of the Revised Code or a substantially equivalent municipal ordinance and division (C)(1) or (2) of section 4507.99 or division (B)(1) or (2) of section 4507.361 [4507.36.1] of the Revised Code applies, the trial judge of the court of record or the mayor of the mayor's court that imposes sentence shall order the immobilization of the vehicle the person was operating at the time of the offense and the impoundment of its identification license plates in accordance with section 4503.233 [4503.23.3] and division (C)(1) or (2) of section 4507.99 or division (B)(1) or (2) of section 4507.361 [4507.36.1] of the Revised Code and may impound the identification license plates of any other vehicle registered in the name of that person.

(2) When a person is convicted of or pleads guilty to a violation of division (B)(1) of section 4507.02 of the Revised Code or a substantially equivalent municipal ordinance and division (C)(3) of section 4507.99 or division (B)(3) of section 4507.361 [4507.36.1] of the Revised Code applies, the trial judge of the court of † that imposes sentence shall order the criminal forfeiture to the state of the vehicle the person was operating at the time of the offense in accordance with section 4503.234 [4503.23.4] and division (C)(3) of section 4507.99 or division (B)(3) of section 4507.361 [4507.36.1] of the Revised Code and may impound the identification license plates of any other vehicle registered in the name of that person.

(E)(1) When a person is convicted of or pleads guilty to a violation of section 4507.33 of the Revised Code and the person is sentenced pursuant to division (E)(1) of section 4507.99 of the Revised Code, the trial judge of the court of record or the mayor of the mayor's court that imposes sentence shall order the immobilization of the vehicle that was involved in the commission of the offense and the impoundment of its identification license plates in accordance with division (E)(1) of section 4507.99 and section 4503.233 [4503.23.3] of the Revised Code and may impound the identification license plates of any other vehicle registered in the name of that person.

(2) When a person is convicted of or pleads guilty to a violation of section 4507.33 of the Revised Code and the person is sentenced pursuant to division (E)(2) of section 4507.99 of the Revised Code, the trial judge of the court of record or the mayor of the mayor's court that imposes sentence shall order the criminal forfeiture to the state of the vehicle that was involved in the commission of the offense in accordance with division (E)(2) of section 4507.99 and section 4503.234 [4503.23.4] of the Revised Code and may impound the identification license plates of any other vehicle registered in the name of that person.

(F) Except as provided in section 4503.233 [4503.23.3] or 4503.234 [4503.23.4] of the Revised Code, when the certificate of registration, the identification license plates, or both have been impounded, division (F) of section 4507.02 of the Revised Code is applicable.

HISTORY: 132 v H 518 (Eff 12-14-67); 135 v S 313 (Eff 7-26-74); 140 v H 37 (Eff 6-22-84); 141 v S 356 (Eff 9-24-86); 142 v H 303 (Eff 10-20-87); 144 v S 275 (Eff 9-1-93); 145 v S 62, §§ 1, 4. Eff 9-1-93.

The effective date is set by section 3 of SB 62.

† The word "record" was not lined out in the unsigned printed version of SB 62 (145 v —), eff 9-1-93, but does appear on the tape from the State of Ohio Data Center.

[§ 4507.16.5] § 4507.165 Suspension for passing stopped school bus.

The trial judge of any court of record or mayor's court may, in addition to all other penalties provided by law, suspend for not more than one year the license of any person who is convicted of or pleads guilty to a violation of division (A) of section 4511.75 of the Revised Code.

When a driver's or commercial driver's license has been suspended under this section, the trial court shall cause the offender to deliver the license to the court, and the court or clerk of the court shall forthwith forward the license to the registrar of motor vehicles, together with notice of the action of the court.

HISTORY: 137 v S 389 (Eff 3-15-79); 143 v H 381. Eff 7-1-89.

[§ 4507.16.6] § 4507.166 Suspension for causing death while fleeing officer.

The trial judge of any court of record shall, in addition to or independent of all other penalties provided by law, suspend the driver's or commercial driver's license of any person who is convicted of or pleads guilty to causing the death of another, as the proximate result of operating a motor vehicle, while eluding or fleeing a police officer.

After the driver's or commercial driver's license has been suspended, the trial court shall cause the offender to deliver the license to the court, and the court or clerk of the court shall forthwith forward the license to the registrar of motor vehicles together with notice of the action of the court.

Such suspension shall be for a period of ten years and the registrar shall not issue to the offender another driver's or commercial driver's license during the effective date of such revocation.

The trial judge of any court of record shall suspend the driver's or commercial driver's license of any person who is convicted or pleads guilty under this section a second time, for the life of the offender.

HISTORY: 138 v H 116 (Eff 8-22-79); 141 v H 428 (Eff 12-23-86); 143 v H 381. Eff 7-1-89.

[§ 4507.16.7] § 4507.167† Revocation of probationary motorized bicycle license.

(A) The registrar of motor vehicles shall revoke the probationary motorized bicycle license issued to any person when the person has been convicted of, pleaded no contest to and been found guilty of, or pleaded guilty to, in any court of competent jurisdiction, or has been adjudicated in juvenile court of having committed, a violation of division (A) or (D) of section 4511.521 [4511.52.1] of the Revised Code, or of any other section of the Revised Code or similar municipal ordinance for which points are chargeable under section 4507.021 [4507.02.1] of the Revised Code.

(B) Any person whose license is revoked under this section shall mail or deliver his probationary motorized bicycle license to the registrar within fourteen days of notification of such revocation. The registrar shall retain such license during the period of revocation. Any such revocation shall remain in effect until the person reaches sixteen years of age.

(C) No application for a motorized bicycle license or probationary motorized bicycle license shall be received from any person whose probationary motorized bicycle license has been revoked under this section until the person reaches sixteen years of age.

HISTORY: RC § 4507.16.3†, 140 v S 169 (Eff 1-1-85); RC § 4507.16.7, 141 v H 356. Eff 9-24-86.

† Publisher's Note: This section was inadvertently numbered 4507.16.3 in Am. Sub. S.B. 169; it was renumbered to 4507.16.7 by H.B. 356.

[§ 4507.16.8] § 4507.168 Forfeiture of driver's license for failure to appear or pay fine; denial of vehicle registration.

(A) If a person who has a current valid Ohio driver's or commercial driver's license is charged with a violation of any provision in sections 4511.01 to 4511.76, section 4511.84, any provision in sections 4513.01 to 4513.65, or any provision in sections 4549.01 to 4549.65 of the Revised Code that is classified as a misdemeanor of the first, second, third, or fourth degree or with a violation of any municipal ordinance that is substantially comparable to any provision of any of these sections and if the person either fails to appear in court at the required time and place to answer the charge or pleads guilty to or is found guilty of the violation and fails within the time allowed by the court to pay the fine imposed by the court, the court shall declare the forfeiture of the person's license. Thirty days after the declaration of forfeiture, the court shall inform the registrar of motor vehicles of the forfeiture by entering information relative to the forfeiture on a form approved and furnished by the registrar and sending the form to the registrar. The court also shall forward the person's license, if it is in the possession of the court, to the registrar. The registrar shall suspend the person's driver's or commercial driver's license, send written notification to the person of the suspension at the person's last known address, and, if the person is in possession of the license, order the person to surrender the person's driver's or commercial driver's license to the registrar within forty-eight hours. No valid driver's or commercial driver's license shall be granted to the person after the suspension, unless the court having jurisdiction of the offense that led to the suspension orders that the forfeiture be terminated. The court shall so order if the person, after having failed to appear in court at the required time and place to answer the charge or after having pleaded guilty to or been found guilty of the violation and having failed within the time allowed by the court to pay the fine imposed by the court, thereafter appears to answer the charge and pays any fine imposed by the court or pays the fine originally imposed by the court. The court shall inform the registrar of the termination of the forfeiture by entering information relative to the termination on a form approved and furnished by the registrar and sending the form to the registrar. The court also shall charge and collect from the person a fifteen-dollar processing fee to cover the costs of the bureau of motor vehicles in administering this section. The clerk of the court shall transmit monthly all such processing fees to the registrar for deposit into the state bureau of motor vehicles fund created by section 4501.25 of the Revised Code.

(B) In addition to suspending the driver's or commercial driver's license of the person named in a declaration of forfeiture, the registrar, upon receipt from the court of the copy of the declaration of forfeiture, shall take any measures that may be necessary to ensure that neither the registrar nor any deputy registrar accepts any application for the registration or transfer of registration of any motor vehicle owned or leased by the person named in the declaration of forfeiture. However, for a motor vehicle leased by a person named in a declaration of forfeiture, the registrar shall not implement the preceding sentence until the registrar adopts procedures for that implementation under section 4503.39 of the Revised Code. The period of denial of registration or transfer shall continue until such time as the court having jurisdiction of the offense that led to the suspension of the person's driver's or commercial driver's license orders the forfeiture be terminated. Upon receipt by the registrar of an order terminating the forfeiture, the registrar also shall take any measures that may be necessary to permit the person to register a motor vehicle owned or leased by the person or to transfer the registration of such a motor vehicle, if the person later makes application to take such action and otherwise is eligible to register the motor vehicle or to transfer its registration.

The registrar shall not be required to give effect to any declaration of forfeiture or order terminating a forfeiture provided by a court under this section unless the information contained in the declaration or order is transmitted to the registrar by means of an electronic transfer system.

(C) The period of license suspension imposed pursuant to division (A) of this section is independent of any other period of license suspension that the court having jurisdiction over the offense may impose, and the period of license suspension imposed pursuant to that division and the period of denial relating to the issuance or transfer of a certificate of registration for a motor vehicle imposed pursuant to division (B) of this section remains in effect until the person pays any fine imposed by the court relative to the offense.

HISTORY: 143 v S 338 (Eff 11-28-90); 143 v S 285 (Eff 4-10-91); 144 v S 331 (Eff 11-13-92); 144 v S 275 (Eff 9-1-93); 145 v S 62, § 4 (Eff 9-1-93); 145 v H 687 (Eff 10-12-94); 146 v H 353 (Eff 9-17-96); 146 v S 121 (Eff 11-19-96); 147 v S 85. Eff 5-15-97.

[§ 4507.16.9] § 4507.169 Suspension or denial upon drug offense conviction under federal law or in another state or for OMVI offense in another state; application to minors; occupational driving privileges.

(A) The registrar of motor vehicles shall suspend for the period of time specified in this division the driver's or commercial driver's license or permit of, or deny for such period of time the issuance of a driver's or commercial driver's license or permit to, any person who is a resident of this state and is convicted of or pleads guilty to a violation of a statute of any other state or any federal statute that is substantially similar to section 2925.02, 2925.03, 2925.04, 2925.05, 2925.06, 2925.11, 2925.12, 2925.13, 2925.14, 2925.22, 2925.23, 2925.31, 2925.32, 2925.36, or 2925.37 of the Revised Code. Upon receipt of a report from a court, court clerk, or other official of any other state or from any federal authority that a resident of this state was convicted of or pleaded guilty to an offense described in this division, the registrar shall send a notice by regular first class mail to the person, at the person's last known address as shown in the records of the bureau of motor vehicles, informing the person of the suspension or denial, that the suspension or denial will take effect twenty-one days from the date of the notice, and that, if the person wishes to appeal the suspension or denial, the person must file a notice of appeal within twenty-one days of the date of the notice requesting a hearing on the matter. If the person requests a hearing, the registrar shall hold the hearing not more than forty days after receipt by the registrar of the notice of appeal. The filing of a notice of appeal does not stay the operation of the suspension or denial that must be imposed pursuant to this division. The scope of the hearing shall be limited to whether the person actually was convicted of or pleaded guilty to the offense for which the suspension or denial is to be imposed.

The period of suspension or denial the registrar is required to impose under this division shall end either on the last day of any period of suspension of the person's nonresident operating privilege imposed by the state or federal court located in the other state, or the date six months and twenty-one days from the date of the notice sent by the registrar to the person under this division, whichever is earlier.

The registrar shall subscribe to or otherwise participate in any information system or register, or enter into reciprocal and mutual agreements with other states and federal authorities, in order to facilitate the exchange of information with other states and the United States government regarding persons who plead guilty to or are convicted of offenses described in this division and therefore are subject to the suspension or denial described in this division.

(B) The registrar shall suspend for the period of time specified in this division the driver's or commercial driver's license or permit of, or deny for such period of time the issuance of a driver's or commercial driver's license or permit to, any person who is a resident of this state and is convicted of or pleads guilty to a violation of a statute of any other state or a municipal ordinance of a municipal corporation located in any other state that is substantially similar to section 4511.19 of the Revised Code. Upon receipt of a report from another state made pursuant to section 4507.60 of the Revised Code indicating that a resident of this state was convicted of or pleaded guilty to an offense described in this division, the registrar shall send a notice by regular first class mail to the person, at the person's last known address as shown in the records of the bureau of motor vehicles, informing the person of the suspension or denial, that the suspension or denial will take effect twenty-one days from the date of the notice, and that, if the person wishes to appeal the suspension or denial, the person must file a notice of appeal within twenty-one days of the date of the notice requesting a hearing on the matter. If the person requests a hearing, the registrar shall hold the hearing not more than forty days after receipt by the registrar of the notice of appeal. The filing of a notice of appeal does not stay the operation of the suspension or denial that must be imposed pursuant to this division. The scope of the hearing shall be limited to whether the person actually was convicted of or pleaded guilty to the offense for which the suspension or denial is to be imposed.

The period of suspension or denial the registrar is required to impose under this division shall end either on the last day of any period of suspension of the person's nonresident operating privilege imposed by the state or federal court located in the other state, or the date six months and twenty-one days from the date of the notice sent by the registrar to the person under this division, whichever is earlier.

(C) The registrar shall suspend for the period of time specified in this division the driver's or commercial driver's license or permit of, or deny for such period of time the issuance of a driver's or commercial driver's license or permit to, any child who is a resident of this state and is convicted of or pleads guilty to a violation of a statute of any other state or any federal statute that is substantially similar to section 2925.02, 2925.03, 2925.04, 2925.05, 2925.06, 2925.11, 2925.12, 2925.13, 2925.14, 2925.22, 2925.23, 2925.31, 2925.32, 2925.36, or 2925.37 of the Revised Code. Upon receipt of a report from a court, court clerk, or other official of any other state or from any federal authority that a child who is a resident of this state was convicted of or pleaded guilty to an offense described in this division, the registrar shall send a notice by regular first class mail to the child, at the child's last known address as shown in the records of the bureau of motor vehicles, informing the child of the suspension or denial, that the suspension or denial will take effect twenty-one days from the date of the notice, and that, if the child wishes to appeal the suspension or denial, the child must file a notice of appeal within twenty-one days of the date of the notice requesting a hearing on the matter. If the child requests a hearing, the registrar shall hold the hearing not more than forty days after receipt by the registrar of the notice of appeal. The filing of a notice of appeal does not stay the operation of the suspension or denial that must be imposed pursuant to this division. The scope of the hearing shall be limited to whether the child actually was convicted of or pleaded guilty to the offense for which the suspension or denial is to be imposed.

The period of suspension the registrar is required to impose under this division shall end either on the last day of any period of suspension of the child's nonresident operating privilege imposed by the state or federal court located in the other state, or the date six months and twenty-one days from the date of the notice sent by the registrar to the child under this division, whichever is earlier. If the child is a resident of this state who is sixteen years of age or older and does not have a current, valid Ohio driver's or commercial driver's license or permit, the notice shall inform the child that the child will be denied issuance of a driver's or commercial driver's license or permit for six months beginning on the date of the notice. If the child has not attained the age of sixteen years on the date of the notice, the notice shall inform the child that the period of denial of six months shall commence on the date the child attains the age of sixteen years.

The registrar shall subscribe to or otherwise participate in any information system or register, or enter into reciprocal and mutual agreements with other states and federal authorities, in order to facilitate the exchange of information with other states and the United States government regarding children who are residents of this state and plead guilty to or are convicted of offenses described in this division and therefore are subject to the suspension or denial described in this division.

(D) The registrar shall suspend for the period of time specified in this division the driver's or commercial driver's license or permit of, or deny for such period of time the issuance of a driver's or commercial driver's license or permit to, any child who is a resident of this state and is convicted of or pleads guilty to a violation of a statute of any other state or a municipal ordinance of a municipal corporation located in any other state that is substantially similar to section 4511.19 of the Revised Code. Upon receipt of a report from another state made pursuant to section 4507.60 of the Revised Code indicating that a child who is a resident of this state was convicted of or pleaded guilty to an offense described in this division, the registrar shall send a notice by regular first class mail to the child, at the child's last known address as shown in the records of the bureau of motor vehicles, informing the child of the suspension or denial, that the suspension or denial will take effect twenty-one days from the date of the notice, and that, if the child wishes to appeal the suspension or denial, the child must file a notice of appeal within twenty-one days of the date of the notice requesting a hearing on the matter. If the child requests a hearing, the registrar shall hold the hearing not more than forty days after receipt by the registrar of the notice of appeal. The filing of a notice of appeal does not stay the operation of the suspension or denial that must be imposed pursuant to this division. The scope of the hearing shall be limited to whether the child actually was convicted of or pleaded guilty to the offense for which the suspension or denial is to be imposed.

The period of suspension the registrar is required to impose under this division shall end either on the last day of any period of suspension of the child's nonresident operating privilege imposed by the state or federal court located in the other state, or the date six months and twenty-one days from the date of the notice sent by the registrar to the child under this division, whichever is earlier. If the child is a resident of this state who is sixteen years of age or older and does not have a current, valid Ohio driver's or commercial driver's license or permit, the notice shall inform the child that the child will be denied issuance of a driver's or commercial driver's license or permit for six months beginning on the date of the notice. If the child has not attained the age of sixteen years on the date of the notice, the notice shall inform the child that the period of denial of six months shall commence on the date the child attains the age of sixteen years.

(E) Any person whose license or permit has been suspended pursuant to division (B) or (D) of this section may file a petition in the municipal or county court, or in case the person is under eighteen years of age, the juvenile court, in whose jurisdiction the person resides, agreeing to pay the cost of the proceedings and alleging that the suspension would seriously affect the person's ability to continue the person's employment. Upon satisfactory proof that there is reasonable cause to believe that the suspension would seriously affect the person's ability to continue the person's employment, the judge may grant the person occupational driving privileges during the period during which the suspension otherwise would be imposed, except that the judge shall not grant occupational driving privileges for employment as a driver of a commercial motor vehicle to any person who would be disqualified from operating a commercial motor vehicle under section 4506.16 of the Revised Code if the violation had occurred in this state, or during any of the following periods of time:

(1) If the person has not been convicted within five years of the date of the offense giving rise to the suspension under this section of a violation of section 4511.19 of the Revised Code, of a municipal ordinance relating to operating a vehicle under the influence of alcohol, a drug of abuse, or alcohol and a drug of abuse, of a municipal ordinance relating to operating a motor vehicle with a prohibited concentration of alcohol in the blood, breath, or urine, of section 2903.04 of the Revised Code in a case in which the person was subject to the sanctions described in division (D) of that section, or of section 2903.06, 2903.07, or 2903.08 of the Revised Code or a municipal ordinance that is substantially similar to section 2903.07 of the Revised Code in a case in which the jury or judge found that the person was under the influence of alcohol, a drug of abuse, or alcohol and a drug of abuse, the first fifteen days of the suspension.

(2) If the person has been convicted only one time within five years of the date of the offense giving rise to the suspension under this section of a violation of section 4511.19 of the Revised Code, of a municipal ordinance relating to operating a vehicle under the influence of alcohol, a drug of abuse, or alcohol and a drug of abuse, of a municipal ordinance relating to operating a motor vehicle with a prohibited concentration of alcohol in the blood, breath, or urine, of section 2903.04 of the Revised Code in a case in which the person was subject to the sanctions described in division (D) of that section, or of section 2903.06, 2903.07, or 2903.08 of the Revised Code or a municipal ordinance that is substantially similar to section 2903.07 of the Revised Code in a case in which the jury or judge found that the person was under the influence of alcohol, a drug of abuse, or alcohol and a drug of abuse, the first thirty days of the suspension.

(3) If the person has been convicted two times within five years of the date of the offense giving rise to the suspension under this section of a violation of section 4511.19 of the Revised Code, of a municipal ordinance relating to operating a vehicle under the influence of alcohol, a drug of abuse, or alcohol and a drug of abuse, of a municipal ordinance relating to operating a motor vehicle with a prohibited concentration of alcohol in the blood, breath, or urine, of section 2903.04 of the Revised Code in a case in which the person was subject to the sanctions described in division (D) of that section, or of section 2903.06, 2903.07, or 2903.08 of the Revised Code or a municipal ordinance that is substantially similar to section 2903.07 of the Revised Code in a case in which the jury or judge found that the person was under the influence of alcohol, a drug of abuse, or alcohol and a drug of abuse, the first one hundred eighty days of the suspension.

(4) If the person has been convicted three or more times within five years of the date of the offense giving rise to the suspension under this section of a violation of section 4511.19 of the Revised Code, of a municipal ordinance relating to operating a vehicle under the influence of alcohol, a drug of abuse, or alcohol and a drug of abuse, of a municipal ordinance relating to operating a motor vehicle with a prohibited concentration of alcohol in the blood, breath, or urine, of section 2903.04 of the Revised Code in a case in which the person was subject to the sanctions described in division (D) of that section, or of section 2903.06, 2903.07, or 2903.08 of the Revised Code or a municipal ordinance that is substantially similar to section 2903.07 of the Revised Code in a case in which the jury or judge found that the person was under the influence of alcohol, a drug of abuse, or alcohol and a drug of abuse, no occupational driving privileges may be granted.

If a person petitions for occupational driving privileges under division (E) of this section, the registrar shall be represented by the county prosecutor of the county in which the person resides if the petition is filed in a juvenile court or county court, except that if the person resides within a city or village that is located within the jurisdiction of the county in which the petition is filed, the city director of law or village solicitor of that city or village shall represent the registrar. If the petition is filed in a municipal court, the registrar shall be represented as provided in section 1901.34 of the Revised Code.

In granting occupational driving privileges under division (E) of this section, the court may impose any condition it considers reasonable and necessary to limit the use of a vehicle by the person. The court shall deliver to the person a permit card, in a form to be prescribed by the court, setting forth the time, place, and other conditions limiting the person's use of a motor vehicle. The grant of occupational driving privileges shall be conditioned upon the person's having the permit in the person's possession at all times during which the person is operating a vehicle.

A person granted occupational driving privileges who operates a vehicle for other than occupational purposes, in violation of any condition imposed by the court or without having the permit in the person's possession, is guilty of a violation of division (D)(1) of section 4507.02 of the Revised Code.

(F) As used in divisions (C) and (D) of this section:

(1) "Child" means a person who is under the age of eighteen years, except that any person who violates a statute or ordinance described in division (C) or (D) of this section prior to attaining eighteen years of age shall be deemed a "child" irrespective of the person's age at the time the complaint or other equivalent document is filed in the other state or a hearing, trial, or other proceeding is held in the other state on the complaint or other equivalent document, and irrespective of the person's age when the period of license suspension or

denial prescribed in division (C) or (D) of this section is imposed.

(2) "Is convicted of or pleads guilty to" means, as it relates to a child who is a resident of this state, that in a proceeding conducted in a state or federal court located in another state for a violation of a statute or ordinance described in division (C) or (D) of this section, the result of the proceeding is any of the following:

(a) Under the laws that govern the proceedings of the court, the child is adjudicated to be or admits to being a delinquent child or a juvenile traffic offender for a violation described in division (C) or (D) of this section that would be a crime if committed by an adult;

(b) Under the laws that govern the proceedings of the court, the child is convicted of or pleads guilty to a violation described in division (C) or (D) of this section;

(c) Under the laws that govern the proceedings of the court, irrespective of the terminology utilized in those laws, the result of the court's proceedings is the functional equivalent of division (F)(2)(a) or (b) of this section.

HISTORY: 145 v H 377 (Eff 9-30-93); 146 v S 2 (Eff 7-1-96); 146 v H 353 (Eff 9-17-96); 147 v S 60. Eff 10-21-97.

[§ 4507.16.10] § 4507.1610 Suspension, revocation, cancellation or forfeiture by federal court.

If a United States district court whose jurisdiction lies within this state suspends, revokes, cancels, or forfeits the driver's or commercial driver's license or permit of any person pursuant to the "Assimilative Crimes Act," 102 Stat. 4381 (1988), 18 U.S.C.A. 13, as amended, that suspension, revocation, cancellation, or forfeiture is deemed to operate in the same manner and to have the same effect throughout this state as if it were imposed under the laws of this state by a judge of a court of record of this state. In such a case, if the United States district court observes the procedures prescribed by the Revised Code and utilizes the forms prescribed by the registrar of motor vehicles, the bureau of motor vehicles shall make the appropriate notation or record and shall take any other action that is prescribed or permitted by the Revised Code.

HISTORY: 146 v H 353. Eff 9-17-96.

Not analogous to former RC § 4507.16.10, amended and renumbered to RC § 4507.55 in 145 v H 687, eff 10-12-94.

[§ 4507.16.11] § 4507.1611 Suspension or revocation for violation of ordinance substantially similar to statute.

Except as may otherwise be provided in the Revised Code, whenever an offender is convicted of or pleads guilty to a violation of a municipal ordinance that is substantially similar to a provision of the Revised Code, and a court is permitted or required to suspend or revoke a person's driver's or commercial driver's license or permit for a violation of that provision, a court, in addition to any other penalties it is authorized by law to impose upon the offender, may suspend the offender's driver's or commercial driver's license or permit for the period of time the court determines appropriate, or may revoke the license or permit, but in no case shall the period of suspension imposed for the violation of the municipal ordinance exceed the period of suspension that is permitted or required to be imposed for the violation of the provision of the Revised Code to which the municipal ordinance is substantially similar.

HISTORY: 146 v H 510. Eff 9-19-96.

[§ 4507.16.12] § 4507.1612 Reinstatement fee after illegally conveying or possessing deadly weapon or dangerous ordnance on school premises.

The registrar shall not restore any operating privileges or reissue a probationary driver's license, restricted license, driver's license, or probationary commercial driver's license suspended under section 2923.122 [2923.12.2] of the Revised Code until the person whose license was suspended pays a reinstatement fee of thirty dollars to the bureau of motor vehicles.

The bureau of motor vehicles shall pay all fees collected under this section into the state treasury to the credit of the state bureau of motor vehicles fund created by section 4501.25 of the Revised Code.

HISTORY: 146 v H 124. Eff 9-30-97.

The effective date is set by section 3 of HB 124.

§ 4507.17 Effect of revocation of license.

Any person whose license is suspended or revoked under sections 4507.01 to 4507.39, inclusive, of the Revised Code, is not entitled to apply for or receive a new license during the effective dates of such suspension or revocation.

HISTORY: GC § 6296-21; 116 v Pt II, 33, § 21; Bureau of Code Revision, 10-1-53; 125 v 367. Eff 10-15-53.

§ 4507.18 Disposition of license while appeal proceedings are pending.

Any person whose driver's or commercial driver's license has been suspended or revoked under section 4507.16 of the Revised Code and who desires to retain the license during the pendency of an appeal, at the time sentence is pronounced, shall notify the court of record or mayor's court that suspended or revoked the license of his intention to appeal; whereupon the court, mayor, or clerk of the court shall retain the license until the appeal is perfected, and, if execution of sentence is stayed, the license shall be returned to the accused to be held by him during the pendency of the appeal.

If the appeal is not perfected or is dismissed or terminated in an affirmance of the conviction, then the license shall be taken up by the court, mayor, or clerk, at the time of putting sentence into execution, which court shall proceed in the same manner as if no appeal was taken.

HISTORY: GC § 6296-18; 116 v Pt II, 33, § 18; Bureau of Code Revision, 10-1-53; 142 v H 303 (Eff 10-20-87); 143 v H 381. Eff 7-1-89.

§ 4507.19 Suspension or cancellation of license.

The registrar of motor vehicles may suspend or cancel any driver's license upon determination that such license was obtained unlawfully, issued in error, or has been altered or willfully destroyed.

HISTORY: GC § 6296-18a; 119 v 701; Bureau of Code Revision, 10-1-53; 130 v 1060 (Eff 8-9-63); 143 v H 381. Eff 7-1-89.

§ 4507.20 Examination of licensee's competency.

The registrar of motor vehicles, upon determination that any person has more than seven points charged against him under section 4507.021 [4507.02.1] of the Revised Code, and is not subject to the provisions of section 4507.022 [4507.02.2] of the Revised Code, or, having good cause to believe that the holder of a driver's or commercial driver's license is incompetent or otherwise not qualified to be licensed, shall upon written notice of at least five days sent to the licensee's last known address, require him to submit to a driver's license examination or a physical examination, or both, or a commercial driver's license examination. Upon the conclusion of the examination the registrar may suspend or revoke the license of the person, or may permit him to retain the license, or may issue him a restricted license. Refusal or neglect of the licensee to submit to the examination is ground for suspension or revocation of his license.

HISTORY: GC § 6296-18b; 119 v 701; Bureau of Code Revision, 10-1-53; 129 v 1493 (Eff 9-9-61); 132 v H 135 (Eff 12-9-67); 141 v S 356 (Eff 9-24-86); 143 v H 381 (Eff 7-1-89); 144 v S 331. Eff 11-13-92.

§ 4507.21 Application for and issuance of license.

(A) Each applicant for a driver's license shall file an application in the office of the registrar of motor vehicles or of a deputy registrar. Each person under eighteen years of age applying for a driver's license issued in this state shall present satisfactory evidence of having successfully completed any one of the following:

(1) A driver education course approved by the state department of education.

(2) A driver training course approved by the director of public safety.

(3) A driver training course comparable to a driver education or driver training course described in division (A)(1) or (2) of this section and administered by a branch of the armed forces of the United States and completed by the applicant while residing outside this state for the purpose of being with or near any person serving in the armed forces of the United States.

If the registrar or deputy registrar determines that the applicant is entitled to the driver's license, it shall be issued. If the application shows that the applicant's license has been previously revoked or suspended, the deputy registrar shall forward the application to the registrar, who shall determine whether the license shall be granted.

All applications shall be filed in duplicate, and the deputy registrar issuing the license shall immediately forward to the office of the registrar the original copy of the application, together with the duplicate copy of the certificate, if issued. The registrar shall prescribe rules as to the manner in which the deputy registrar files and maintains the applications and other records. The registrar shall file every application for a driver's or commercial driver's license and index them by name and number, and shall maintain a suitable record of all licenses issued, all convictions and bond forfeitures, all applications for licenses denied, and all licenses which have been suspended or revoked.

(B) For purposes of section 2313.06 of the Revised Code, the registrar shall maintain accurate and current lists of the residents of each county who are eighteen years of age or older, have been issued, on and after January 1, 1984, driver's or commercial driver's licenses that are valid and current, and would be electors if they were registered to vote, regardless of whether they actually are registered to vote. The lists shall contain the names, addresses, dates of birth, duration of residence in this state, citizenship status, and social security numbers, if the numbers are available, of the licensees, and may contain any other information that the registrar considers suitable.

(C) Each person under eighteen years of age applying for a motorcycle operator's endorsement or a restricted license enabling him to operate a motorcycle shall present satisfactory evidence of having completed the courses of instruction in the motorcycle safety and education program described in section 4508.08 of the Revised Code or a comparable course of instruction administered by a branch of the armed forces of the United States and completed by the applicant while residing outside this state for the purpose of being with or near any person serving in the armed forces of the United States. If the registrar or deputy registrar then determines that the applicant is entitled to the endorsement or restricted license, it shall be issued.

HISTORY: GC § 6296-19; 116 v PtII 33, § 19; 119 v 701; Bureau of Code Revision, 10-1-53; 132 v H 380 (Eff 1-1-68); 135 v S 313 (Eff 7-26-74); 140 v H 183 (Eff 10-1-84); 141 v H 291 (Eff 3-11-87); 143 v H 381 (Eff 7-1-89); 144 v S 98 (Eff 11-12-92); 145 v S 96. Eff 5-10-94.

[§ 4507.21.2] § 4507.212 Statement of proof of financial responsibility.

(A) As used in this section, "motor vehicle" has the same meaning as in section 4509.01 of the Revised Code.

(B) An application for a driver's, commercial driver's, restricted, or probationary license, or renewal of such license shall contain a statement, to be signed by the applicant, that does all of the following:

(1) States that the applicant maintains, or has maintained on his behalf, proof of financial responsibility at the time of application, and will not operate a motor vehicle in this state, unless he maintains, or has maintained on his behalf, proof of financial responsibility;

(2) Contains a brief summary of the purposes and operation of section 4509.101 [4509.10.1] of the Revised Code, the rights and duties of the applicant under that section, and the penalties for violation of that section;

(3) Warns the applicant that the financial responsibility law does not prevent the possibility that the applicant may be involved in an accident with an owner or operator of a motor vehicle who is without proof of financial responsibility.

(C) The registrar of motor vehicles shall prescribe the form of the statement, and the manner in which the statement shall be presented to the applicant. The statement shall be designed to enable the applicant to retain a copy of it.

(D) Nothing within this section shall be construed to excuse a violation of section 4509.101 [4509.10.1] of the Revised Code.

(E) At the time a person submits an application for a driver's, commercial driver's, restricted, or probationary license, or renewal of such a license, the applicant also shall be furnished with a form that lists in plain language all the possible penalties to which the applicant could be subject for a violation of the financial responsibility law, including driver's license suspensions; all fees, including nonvoluntary compliance and reinstatement fees; and vehicle immobilization or impoundment. The applicant shall sign the form, which shall be submitted along with the application. The form shall be retained by the registrar or deputy registrar who issues the license or renewal or his successor for a period of two years from the date of issuance of the license or renewal. The registrar shall prescribe the manner in which the form shall be presented to the applicant, and the format of the form, which shall be such that the applicant can retain a copy of it.

HISTORY: 139 v S 250 (Eff 1-1-84); 140 v H 767 (Eff 8-1-84); 143 v H 381 (Eff 7-1-89); 145 v S 20. Eff 10-20-94.

§ 4507.22 Transmission of application with report of findings to registrar.

If the deputy registrar finds that an applicant is not entitled to an identification card or a driver's license, he shall transmit to the registrar of motor vehicles the original of the application together with the written report of his findings and recommendations in connection with such application. Upon receipt thereof, the registrar shall review the findings and recommendations and determine whether the application shall be granted, and report his findings to the deputy registrar and the applicant. If the registrar determines that the application should be granted, he shall thereupon notify the deputy registrar, who shall forthwith issue the license or card.

HISTORY: GC § 6296-20; 116 v Pt II, 33, § 20; Bureau of Code Revision, 10-1-53; 136 v S 435 (Eff 8-24-76); 143 v H 381. Eff 7-1-89.

[FEES; ORDERS]

§ 4507.23 License fees; lamination fees.

(A) Except as provided in division (H) of this section, each application for a temporary instruction permit and examination shall be accompanied by a fee of four dollars.

(B) Except as provided in division (H) of this section, each application for a driver's license made by a person who previously held such a license and whose license has expired not more than two years prior to the date of application, and who is required under this chapter to give an actual demonstration of the person's ability to drive, shall be accompanied by a fee of three dollars in addition to any other fees.

(C) Except as provided in divisions (E) and (H) of this section, each application for a driver's license, or motorcycle operator's endorsement, or renewal of a driver's license shall be accompanied by a fee of six dollars. Except as provided in division (H) of this section, each application for a duplicate driver's license shall be accompanied by a fee of two dollars and fifty cents. The duplicate driver's licenses issued under this section shall be distributed by the deputy registrar in accordance with rules adopted by the registrar of motor vehicles.

(D) Except as provided in division (H) of this section, each application for a motorized bicycle license or duplicate thereof shall be accompanied by a fee of two dollars and fifty cents.

(E) Except as provided in division (H) of this section, each application for a driver's license or renewal of a driver's license that will be issued to a person who is less than twenty-one years of age shall be accompanied by whichever of the following fees is applicable:

(1) If the person is sixteen years of age or older, but less than seventeen years of age, a fee of seven dollars and twenty-five cents;

(2) If the person is seventeen years of age or older, but less than eighteen years of age, a fee of six dollars;

(3) If the person is eighteen years of age or older, but less than nineteen years of age, a fee of four dollars and seventy-five cents;

(4) If the person is nineteen years of age or older, but less than twenty years of age, a fee of three dollars and fifty cents;

(5) If the person is twenty years of age or older, but less than twenty-one years of age, a fee of two dollars and twenty-five cents.

(F) Neither the registrar nor any deputy registrar shall charge a fee in excess of one dollar and fifty cents for laminating a driver's license or motorized bicycle license as required by sections 4507.13 and 4511.521 [4511.52.1] of the Revised Code. A deputy registrar laminating a driver's license or motorized bicycle license shall retain the entire amount of the fee charged for lamination, less the actual cost to the registrar of the laminating materials used for that lamination, as specified in the contract executed by the bureau for the laminating materials and laminating equipment. The deputy registrar shall forward the amount of the cost of the laminating materials to the registrar for deposit as provided in this section.

(G) At the time and in the manner provided by section 4503.10 of the Revised Code, the deputy registrar shall transmit the fees collected under divisions (A), (B), (C), (D), and (E), and those portions of the fees specified in and collected under division (F) of this section to the registrar. The registrar shall pay two dollars and fifty cents of each fee collected under divisions (A), (B), (C), (D), and (E)(1) to (4) of this section, and the entire fee collected under division (E)(5) of this section, into the state highway safety fund established in section 4501.06 of the Revised Code, and such fees shall be used for the sole purpose of supporting driver licensing activities. The remaining fees collected by the registrar under this section shall be paid into the state bureau of motor vehicles fund established in section 4501.25 of the Revised Code.

(H) A disabled veteran who has a service-connected disability rated at one hundred per cent by the veterans' administration may apply to the registrar or a deputy registrar for the issuance to that veteran, without the payment of any fee prescribed in this section, of any of the following items:

(1) A temporary instruction permit and examination;

(2) A new, renewal, or duplicate driver's or commercial driver's license;

(3) A motorcycle operator's endorsement;

(4) A motorized bicycle license or duplicate thereof;

(5) Lamination of a driver's license or motorized bicycle license as provided in division (F) of this section, if the circumstances specified in division (H)(5) of this section are met.

If the driver's license or motorized bicycle license of a disabled veteran described in division (H) of this section is laminated by a deputy registrar who is acting as a deputy registrar pursuant to a contract with the registrar that is in effect on the effective date of this amendment, the disabled veteran shall be required to pay the deputy registrar the lamination fee provided in division (F) of this section. If the driver's license or motorized bicycle license of such a disabled veteran is laminated by a deputy registrar who is acting as a deputy registrar pursuant to a contract with the registrar that is executed after the effective date of this amendment, the disabled veteran is not required to pay the deputy registrar the lamination fee provided in division (F) of this section.

A disabled veteran whose driver's license or motorized bicycle license is laminated by the registrar is not required to pay the registrar any lamination fee.

An application made under division (H) of this section shall be accompanied by such documentary evidence of disability as the registrar may require by rule.

HISTORY: GC § 6296-22; 116 v PtII, 33, § 22; 117 v 393; 119 v 701; 123 v 246; Bureau of Code Revision, 10-1-53; 125 v 1135; 129 v 381 (Eff 7-1-62); 132 v H 380 (Eff 1-1-68); 133 v H 113 (Eff 9-12-69); 137 v S 100 (Eff 4-1-78); 137 v S 393 (Eff 5-12-78); 137 v H 215 (Eff 12-12-78); 138 v H 204 (Eff 7-30-79); 140 v H 373 (Eff 9-19-83); 142 v H 171 (Eff 7-1-87); 142 v S 1 (Eff 11-28-88); 143 v H 381 (Eff 7-1-89); 143 v S 131 (Eff 7-25-90); 144 v H 134 (Eff 10-10-91); 145 v H 154 (Eff 6-30-93); 146 v H 107 (Eff 6-30-95); 146 v H 353 (Eff 9-17-96); 147 v H 144. Eff 10-14-97.

[§ 4507.23.1] § 4507.231 Request for donations to second chance trust fund.

In addition to the fees collected under section 4507.23 of the Revised Code, the registrar or deputy registrar of motor vehicles shall ask each person applying for or renewing a driver's license, motorcycle operator's endorsement, or duplicate whether the person wishes to make a one-dollar voluntary contribution to the second chance trust fund established under section 2108.15 of the Revised Code. The registrar or deputy registrar shall also make available to the person informational material provided by the department of health on the importance of organ, tissue, and eye donation.

All donations collected under this section during each month shall be forwarded by the registrar or deputy registrar not later than the fifth day of the immediately following month to the treasurer of state, who shall deposit them in the second chance trust fund.

HISTORY: 146 v S 300. Eff 7-1-97.

The effective date is set by section 3 of SB 300.

§ 4507.24 Fees for deputy registrars; portion paid to state highway safety fund.

(A) Except as provided in division (B) of this section, each deputy registrar may collect a fee not to exceed the following:

(1) Three dollars and twenty-five cents for each application for renewal of a driver's license received by the deputy registrar, when the applicant is required to submit to a screening of the applicant's vision under section 4507.12 of the Revised Code;

(2) Two dollars and twenty-five cents for each application for a driver's license, or motorized bicycle license, or for renewal of such a license, received by the deputy registrar, when the applicant is not required to submit to a screening of the applicant's vision under section 4507.12 of the Revised Code.

(B) The fees prescribed by division (A) of this section shall be in addition to the fee for a temporary instruction permit and examination, a driver's license, a motorized bicycle license, or duplicates thereof, and shall compensate the deputy registrar for the deputy registrar's services, for office and rental expense, and for costs as provided in division (C) of this section, as are necessary for the proper discharge of the deputy registrar's duties under sections 4507.01 to 4507.39 of the Revised Code.

A disabled veteran who has a service-connected disability rated at one hundred per cent by the veterans' administration is required to pay the applicable fee prescribed in division (A) of this section if the disabled veteran submits an application for a driver's license or motorized bicycle license or a renewal of either of these licenses to a deputy registrar who is acting as a deputy registrar pursuant to a contract with the registrar that is in effect on the effective date of this amendment. The disabled veteran also is required to submit with the disabled veteran's application such documentary evidence of disability as the registrar may require by rule.

A disabled veteran who submits an application described in this division is not required to pay either of the fees prescribed in division (A) of this section if the disabled veteran submits the application to a deputy registrar who is acting as a deputy registrar pursuant to a contract with the registrar that is executed after the effective date of this amendment. The disabled veteran still is required to submit with the disabled veteran's application such documentary evidence of disability as the registrar may require by rule.

A disabled veteran who submits an application described in this division directly to the registrar is not required to pay either of the fees prescribed in division (A) of this section if the disabled veteran submits with the disabled veteran's application such documentary evidence of disability as the registrar may require by rule.

(C) Each deputy registrar shall transmit to the registrar of motor vehicles, at such time and in such manner as the registrar shall require by rule, an amount of each fee collected under division (A)(1) of this section as shall be determined by the registrar. The registrar shall pay all such moneys so received into the state bureau of motor vehicles fund created in section 4501.25 of the Revised Code.

HISTORY: GC § 6296-23; 116 v PtII, 33, § 23; 119 v 701; 123 v 246; Bureau of Code Revision, 10-1-53; 132 v S 484 (Eff 6-11-68); 137 v H 3 (Eff 1-1-79); 137 v S 393 (Eff 5-12-78); 138 v H 656 (Eff 1-1-80); 139 v H 457 (Eff 2-11-82); 140 v H 58 (Eff 3-1-85); 141 v H 201 (Eff 7-1-85); 141 v S 269 (Eff 3-13-86); 142 v H 419 (Eff 7-1-87); 142 v S 1 (Eff 11-28-88); 143 v H 381 (Eff 7-1-89); 145 v H 154 (Eff 6-30-93); 146 v H 107 (Eff 6-30-95); 147 v H 144. Eff 10-14-97.

§ 4507.25 Records and proceedings of registrar.

(A) The registrar of motor vehicles may adopt and publish rules to govern his proceedings. All proceedings of the registrar shall be open to the public, and all documents in his possession shall be public records. He shall adopt a seal bearing the inscription: "Motor Vehicle Registrar of Ohio." The seal shall be affixed to all writs and authenticated copies of records, and when it has been so attached, such copies shall be received in evidence with the same effect as other public records. All courts shall take judicial notice of the seal.

(B) Upon the request of any person accompanied by a nonrefundable fee of two dollars per name, the registrar may furnish lists of names and addresses as they appear upon the applications for driver's licenses, provided that any further information contained in the applications shall not be disclosed. All the fees collected shall be paid by the registrar into the state treasury to the credit of the state bureau of motor vehicles fund established in section 4501.25 of the Revised Code.

This division does not apply to the list of qualified driver licensees required to be compiled and filed pursuant to section 2313.06 of the Revised Code.

HISTORY: GC § 6296-31; 116 v PtII, 33, § 31; Bureau of Code Revision, 10-1-53; 128 v 1176 (Eff 11-2-59); 129 v 381 (Eff 7-1-62); 139 v H 102 (Eff 7-1-81); 140 v H 183 (Eff 10-1-84); 146 v H 107. Eff 6-30-95.

§ 4507.26 Order of registrar subject to reversal or modification.

An order, except an order relating to a license as defined in section 119.01 of the Revised Code, made by the registrar of motor vehicles may be reversed, vacated, or modified by the court of common pleas of Franklin county, or by the court of common pleas in the county in which the party affected is a resident, or in which the matter complained of arose.

HISTORY: GC § 6296-32; 116 v Pt II, 33, § 32; 120 v 358(396), § 2; Bureau of Code Revision. Eff 10-1-53.

§ 4507.27 Reversal or modification of registrar's order by appeal.

A proceeding to obtain the reversal, vacation, or modification of an order of the registrar of motor vehicles shall be by appeal, notice of which shall be filed in the court of common pleas on or before the expiration of thirty days from date of entry of such order, by any party to the proceedings before the registrar. Such court shall set such appeal for hearing and take such testimony as is necessary to decide the matter. At least ten days'

§ 4507.28 Restrictions against interference of court.

No court may reverse, suspend, or delay any order made by the registrar of motor vehicles, or enjoin, restrain, or interfere with the registrar or a deputy registrar in the performance of official duties, except as provided in sections 4507.01 to 4507.39, inclusive, of the Revised Code.

HISTORY: GC § 6296-34; 116 v Pt II, 33, § 34; Bureau of Code Revision. Eff 10-1-53.

§ 4507.29 Prosecuting attorney to assist registrar.

Upon the request of the registrar of motor vehicles, the prosecuting attorney of the county in which any proceedings are pending, shall aid in any investigation, prosecution, hearing, or trial had under sections 4507.01 to 4507.39, of the Revised Code, and shall institute and prosecute such actions or proceedings for the enforcement of such sections, and for the punishment of all violations thereof, as the registrar directs.

HISTORY: GC § 6296-35; 116 v Pt II, 33, § 35; Bureau of Code Revision. Eff 10-1-53.

[PROHIBITIONS]

§ 4507.30 Prohibited acts.

No person shall:
(A) Display, or cause or permit to be displayed, or possess any identification card, driver's or commercial driver's license, temporary instruction permit, or commercial driver's license temporary instruction permit knowing the same to be fictitious, or to have been canceled, revoked, suspended, or altered;
(B) Lend to a person not entitled thereto, or knowingly permit him to use any identification card, driver's or commercial driver's license, temporary instruction permit, or commercial driver's license temporary instruction permit issued to the person so lending or permitting the use thereof;
(C) Display, or represent as one's own, any identification card, driver's or commercial driver's license, temporary instruction permit, or commercial driver's license temporary instruction permit not issued to the person so displaying the same;
(D) Fail to surrender to the registrar of motor vehicles, upon his demand, any identification card, driver's or commercial driver's license, temporary instruction permit, or commercial driver's license temporary instruction permit which has been suspended, canceled, or revoked;
(E) In any application for an identification card, driver's or commercial driver's license, temporary instruction permit, or commercial driver's license temporary instruction permit, or any renewal or duplicate thereof, knowingly conceal a material fact, or present any physician's statement required under section 4507.08 or 4507.081 [4507.08.1] of the Revised Code when knowing the same to be false or fictitious.

HISTORY: GC § 6296-24; 116 v Pt II, 33, § 24; Bureau of Code Revision, 10-1-53; 129 v 1491 (Eff 9-9-61); 136 v S 435 (Eff 8-24-76); 137 v H 71 (Eff 8-26-77); 143 v H 381. Eff 7-1-89.

§ 4507.31 Prohibition against permitting minor to operate vehicle.

No person shall cause or knowingly permit any minor under eighteen to drive a motor vehicle upon a highway as an operator, unless such minor has first obtained a license or permit to drive a motor vehicle under sections 4507.01 to 4507.39, inclusive, of the Revised Code.

HISTORY: GC § 6296-26; 116 v Pt II, 33, § 26; Bureau of Code Revision. Eff 10-1-53.

[§ 4507.32.1] § 4507.321 Employment of a minor to operate a taxicab prohibited.

Notwithstanding the definition of "chauffeur" in section 4501.01 of the Revised Code, no person shall employ, for the purpose of operating a taxicab, any minor under eighteen years of age.

HISTORY: 133 v S 410 (Eff 11-25-69); 140 v H 37. Eff 6-22-84.

§ 4507.33 Restrictions against owner lending vehicle for use of another.

No person shall authorize or knowingly permit a motor vehicle owned by him or under his control to be driven by any person if either of the following applies:
(A) The offender knows or has reasonable cause to believe the other person has no legal right to drive the motor vehicle;
(B) The offender knows or has reasonable cause to believe the other person's act of driving the motor vehicle would violate any prohibition contained in sections 4507.01 to 4507.39 of the Revised Code.

HISTORY: GC § 6296-28; 116 v PtII, 33, § 28; Bureau of Code Revision, 10-1-53; 144 v S 275 (Eff 9-1-93); 145 v S 62, § 4. Eff 9-1-93.

§ 4507.34 Suspension or revocation of license for reckless operation violation.

Whenever a person is found guilty under the laws of this state or under any ordinance of any political subdivision of this state, of operating a motor vehicle in violation of such laws or ordinances, relating to reckless

---

notice of the time and place of such hearing shall be given to the registrar.

HISTORY: GC § 6296-33; 116 v Pt II, 33, § 33; Bureau of Code Revision. Eff 10-1-53.

operation, the trial court of any court of record may, in addition to or independent of all other penalties provided by law, suspend for any period of time or revoke the driver's license or commercial driver's license of any person so convicted or pleading guilty to such offenses for any period that it determines, not to exceed one year.

Suspension of a commercial driver's license under this section shall be concurrent with any period of disqualification under section 2301.374 [2301.37.4] or 4506.16 of the Revised Code. No person who is disqualified for life from holding a commercial driver's license under section 4506.16 of the Revised Code shall be issued a driver's license under this chapter during the period for which the commercial driver's license was suspended under this section, and no person whose commercial driver's license is suspended under this section shall be issued a driver's license under this chapter during the period of the suspension.

HISTORY: GC § 6296-30; 116 v PtII, 33, § 30; Bureau of Code Revision, 10-1-53; 143 v H 381 (Eff 7-1-89); 144 v S 275 (Eff 9-1-93); 145 v S 62, § 4 (Eff 9-1-93); 146 v H 167. Eff 5-15-97.

The effective date is set by section 8(C) of HB 167.

§ 4507.35 Display of license.

The operator of a motor vehicle shall display his license, or furnish satisfactory proof that he has such license, upon demand of any peace officer or of any person damaged or injured in any collision in which such licensee may be involved. When a demand is properly made and the operator has his license on or about his person, he shall not refuse to display said license. Failure to furnish satisfactory evidence that such person is licensed under sections 4507.01 to 4507.30† of the Revised Code, when such person does not have his license on or about his person shall be prima-facie evidence of his not having obtained such license.

HISTORY: Bureau of Code Revision, 10-1-53; 143 v H 381. Eff 7-1-89.

† So in enrolled bill. Was "4507.39" intended?

Comment

This section is derived from GC § 6296-14. See also RC § 4507.12.

§ 4507.36 Prohibition against false statements.

No person shall knowingly make a false statement to any matter or thing required by sections 4507.01 to 4507.39, inclusive, of the Revised Code.

HISTORY: GC § 6296-25; 116 v Pt II, 33, § 25; 119 v 701; Bureau of Code Revision, 10-1-53; 126 v 253. Eff 9-13-55.

[§ 4507.36.1] § 4507.361 Additional sanctions for violating municipal ordinance concerning financial responsibility or OMVI suspension.

(A) The requirements and sanctions imposed by divisions (B) and (C) of this section are an adjunct to and derive from the state's exclusive authority over the registration and titling of motor vehicles and do not comprise a part of the criminal sentence to be imposed upon a person who violates a municipal ordinance that is substantially equivalent to division (B)(1) or (D)(2) of section 4507.02 of the Revised Code.

(B) If a person is convicted of or pleads guilty to a municipal ordinance that is substantially equivalent to division (B)(1) of section 4507.02 of the Revised Code, the court, in addition to and independent of any sentence that it imposes upon the offender for the offense, regardless of whether the vehicle the offender was operating at the time of the offense is registered in his name or in the name of another person, and subject to section 4503.235 [4503.23.5] of the Revised Code, shall do whichever of the following is applicable:

(1) If, within five years of the current offense, the offender has not been convicted of or pleaded guilty to a violation of division (B)(1) of section 4507.02 of the Revised Code or a municipal ordinance that is substantially equivalent to that division, the court shall order the immobilization for thirty days of the vehicle the offender was operating at the time of the offense and the impoundment for thirty days of the identification license plates of that vehicle.

(2) If, within five years of the current offense, the offender has been convicted of or pleaded guilty to one violation of division (B)(1) of section 4507.02 of the Revised Code or a municipal ordinance that is substantially equivalent to that division, the court shall order the immobilization for sixty days of the vehicle the offender was operating at the time of the offense and the impoundment for sixty days of the identification license plates of that vehicle.

(3) If, within five years of the current offense, the offender has been convicted of or pleaded guilty to two or more violations of division (B)(1) of section 4507.02 of the Revised Code or a municipal ordinance that is substantially equivalent to that division, the court shall order the criminal forfeiture to the state of the vehicle the offender was operating at the time of the offense. The order of criminal forfeiture shall be issued and enforced in accordance with section 4503.234 [4503.23.4] of the Revised Code.

(C) If a person is convicted of or pleads guilty to a municipal ordinance that is substantially equivalent to division (D)(2) of section 4507.02 of the Revised Code, the court, in addition to and independent of any sentence that it imposes upon the offender for the offense, regardless of whether the vehicle the offender was operating at the time of the offense is registered in his name or in the name of another person, and subject to section 4503.235 [4503.23.5] of the Revised Code, shall do whichever of the following is applicable:

(1) If, within five years of the current offense, the offender has not been convicted of or pleaded guilty to a violation of division (D)(2) of section 4507.02 of

the Revised Code or a municipal ordinance that is substantially equivalent to that division, the court shall order the immobilization for thirty days of the vehicle the offender was operating at the time of the offense and the impoundment for thirty days of the identification license plates of that vehicle.

(2) If, within five years of the current offense, the offender has been convicted of or pleaded guilty to one violation of division (D)(2) of section 4507.02 of the Revised Code or a municipal ordinance that is substantially equivalent to that division, the court shall order the immobilization for sixty days of the vehicle the offender was operating at the time of the offense and the impoundment for sixty days of the identification license plates of that vehicle.

(3) If, within five years of the current offense, the offender has been convicted of or pleaded guilty to two or more violations of division (D)(2) of section 4507.02 of the Revised Code or a municipal ordinance that is substantially equivalent to that division, the court shall order the criminal forfeiture to the state of the vehicle the offender was operating at the time of the offense.

(D) An order of criminal forfeiture issued pursuant to this section shall be issued and enforced in accordance with section 4503.234 [4503.23.4] of the Revised Code. An order for the immobilization and impoundment of a vehicle that issued pursuant to this section shall be issued and enforced in accordance with section 4503.233 [4503.23.3] of the Revised Code.

HISTORY: 145 v S 62. Eff 9-1-93.

The effective date is set by section 3 of SB 62.

§ 4507.38 Seizure of vehicle and license plates upon arrest for certain violations; motion for return or release; immobilization or forfeiture orders upon guilty plea or conviction.

(A) As used in this section:

(1) "Arrested person" means a person who is arrested for a violation of division (B)(1) or (D)(2) of section 4507.02 or section 4507.33 of the Revised Code, or a municipal ordinance that is substantially equivalent to any of those Revised Code provisions, and whose arrest results in a vehicle being seized under division (B) of this section.

(2) "Vehicle owner" means either of the following:

(a) The person in whose name is registered, at the time of the seizure, a vehicle that is seized under division (B) of this section;

(b) A person to whom the certificate of title to a vehicle that is seized under division (B) of this section has been assigned and who has not obtained a certificate of title to the vehicle in that person's name, but who is deemed by the court as being the owner of the vehicle at the time the vehicle was seized under division (B) of this section.

(3) "Interested party" includes the owner of a vehicle seized under this section, all lienholders of such a vehicle, the arrested person, the owner of the place of storage at which a vehicle seized under this section is stored, and the person or entity that caused the vehicle to be removed.

(B)(1) If a person is arrested for a violation of division (B)(1) or (D)(2) of section 4507.02 or section 4507.33 of the Revised Code, or a municipal ordinance that is substantially equivalent to any of those Revised Code provisions, the arresting officer or another officer of the law enforcement agency that employs the arresting officer, in addition to any action that the arresting officer is required or authorized to take by any other provision of law, shall seize the vehicle that the person was operating at the time of the alleged offense and its license plates. Except as otherwise provided in this division, the officer shall seize the vehicle and its license plates regardless of whether the vehicle is registered in the name of the arrested person or in the name of another person or entity. This section does not apply to or affect any rented or leased vehicle that is being rented or leased for a period of thirty days or less, except that a law enforcement agency that employs a law enforcement officer who makes an arrest of a type that is described in division (B)(1) of this section and that involves a rented or leased vehicle of this type shall notify, within twenty-four hours after the officer makes the arrest, the lessor or owner of the vehicle regarding the circumstances of the arrest and the location at which the vehicle may be picked up. At the time of the seizure of the vehicle, the law enforcement officer who made the arrest shall give the arrested person written notice that the vehicle and its license plates have been seized; that the vehicle either will be kept by the officer's law enforcement agency or will be immobilized at least until the person's initial appearance on the charge of the offense for which the arrest was made; that, at the initial appearance, the court in certain circumstances may order that the vehicle and license plates be released to the vehicle owner until the disposition of that charge; that, if the arrested person is convicted of that charge, the court generally must order the immobilization of the vehicle and the impoundment of its license plates or the forfeiture of the vehicle; and that, if the arrested person is not the vehicle owner, the arrested person immediately should inform the vehicle owner that the vehicle and its license plates have been seized and that the vehicle owner may be able to obtain their release at the initial appearance or thereafter.

(2) The arresting officer or a law enforcement officer of the agency that employs the arresting officer shall give written notice of the seizure to the court that will conduct the initial appearance of the arrested person. The notice shall be given when the charges are filed against the arrested person. Upon receipt of the notice, the court promptly shall determine whether the arrested person is the vehicle owner and whether there are any liens recorded on the certificate of title to the vehicle. If the court determines that the arrested person

is not the vehicle owner, it promptly shall send by regular mail written notice of the seizure of the motor vehicle to the vehicle owner and to all lienholders recorded on the certificate of title. The written notice to the vehicle owner and lienholders shall contain all of the information required by division (B)(1) of this section to be in a notice to be given to the arrested person and also shall specify the date, time, and place of the arrested person's initial appearance. The notice to the vehicle owner also shall state that if the vehicle is immobilized under division (a) of section 4503.233 [4503.23.3] of the Revised Code, seven days after the end of the period of immobilization a law enforcement agency will send the vehicle owner a notice, informing the owner that if the owner does not obtain the release of the vehicle in accordance with division (d)(3) of section 4503.233 [4503.23.3] of the Revised Code, the vehicle shall be forfeited. The notice also shall inform the vehicle owner that the owner may be charged expenses or charges incurred under this section and section 4503.233 [4503.23.3] of the Revised Code for the removal and storage of the vehicle.

The written notice that is given or delivered to the vehicle owner shall state that if the arrested person pleads guilty to or is convicted of the offense for which the arrested person was arrested and the court issues an immobilization and impoundment order relative to that vehicle, division (D)(4) of section 4503.233 [4503.23.3] of the Revised Code prohibits the vehicle from being sold during the period of immobilization without the prior approval of the court.

(3) At or before the initial appearance, the vehicle owner may file a motion requesting the court to order that the vehicle and its license plates be released to the vehicle owner. Except as provided in this division and subject to the payment of expenses or charges incurred in the removal and storage of the vehicle, the court, in its discretion, then may issue an order releasing the vehicle and its license plates to the vehicle owner. Such an order may be conditioned upon such terms as the court determines appropriate, including the posting of a bond in an amount determined by the court. If the arrested person is not the vehicle owner and if the vehicle owner is not present at the arrested person's initial appearance, and if the court believes that the vehicle owner was not provided with adequate notice of the initial appearance, the court, in its discretion, may allow the vehicle owner to file a motion within seven days of the initial appearance. If the court allows the vehicle owner to file such a motion after the initial appearance, the extension of time granted by the court does not extend the time within which the initial appearance is to be conducted. If the court issues an order for the release of the vehicle and its license plates, a copy of the order shall be made available to the vehicle owner. If the vehicle owner presents a copy of the order to the law enforcement agency that employs the law enforcement officer who arrested the person who was operating the vehicle, the law enforcement agency promptly shall release the vehicle and its license plates to the vehicle owner upon payment by the vehicle owner of any expenses or charges incurred in the removal or storage of the vehicle.

(4) A vehicle seized under division (B)(1) of this section either shall be towed to a place specified by the law enforcement agency that employs the arresting officer to be safely kept by the agency at that place for the time and in the manner specified in this section or shall be otherwise immobilized for the time and in the manner specified in this section. A law enforcement officer of that agency shall remove the identification license plates of the vehicle, and they shall be safely kept by the agency for the time and in the manner specified in this section. No vehicle that is seized and either towed or immobilized pursuant to this division shall be considered contraband for purposes of section 2933.41, 2933.42, or 2933.43 of the Revised Code. The vehicle shall not be immobilized at any place other than a commercially operated private storage lot, a place owned by a law enforcement or other government agency, or a place to which one of the following applies:

(a) The place is leased by or otherwise under the control of a law enforcement or other government agency.

(b) The place is owned by the arrested person, the arrested person's spouse, or a parent or child of the arrested person.

(c) The place is owned by a private person or entity, and, prior to the immobilization, the private entity or person that owns the place, or the authorized agent of that private entity or person, has given express written consent for the immobilization to be carried out at that place.

(d) The place is a public street or highway on which the vehicle is parked in accordance with the law.

(C)(1) A vehicle that is seized under division (B) of this section shall be safely kept at the place to which it is towed or otherwise moved by the law enforcement agency that employs the arresting officer until the initial appearance of the arrested person relative to the charge in question. The license plates of the vehicle that are removed pursuant to division (B) of this section shall be safely kept by the law enforcement agency that employs the arresting officer until at least the initial appearance of the arrested person relative to the charge in question.

The court also shall notify the arrested person, and the movant if the movant is not the arrested person, that if title to a motor vehicle that is subject to an order for criminal forfeiture under this section is assigned or transferred and division (C)(2) or (3) of section 4503.234 [4503.23.4] of the Revised Code applies, the court may fine the offender the value of the vehicle.†

(2)(a) If, at the initial appearance, the arrested person pleads guilty to the violation of division (B)(1) or (D)(2) of section 4507.02 or section 4507.33 of the Revised

Code, or a municipal ordinance that is substantially equivalent to any of those Revised Code provisions or pleads no contest to and is convicted of the violation, the court shall impose sentence upon the arrested person as provided by law or ordinance; the court, except as provided in this division and subject to section 4503.235 [4503.23.5] of the Revised Code, shall order the immobilization of the vehicle the arrested person was operating at the time of, or that was involved in, the offense and the impoundment of its license plates under section 4503.233 [4503.23.3] and section 4507.361 [4507.36.1] or 4507.99 of the Revised Code or the criminal forfeiture to the state of the vehicle under section 4503.234 [4503.23.4] and section 4507.361 [4507.36.1] or 4507.99 of the Revised Code, whichever is applicable; and the vehicle and its identification license plates shall not be returned or released to the vehicle owner. If the arrested person is not the vehicle owner and the vehicle owner the owner's† is not present at the arrested person's initial appearance and if the court believes that the vehicle owner was not provided adequate notice of the initial appearance, the court, in its discretion, may refrain for a period of time not exceeding seven days from ordering the immobilization of the vehicle and the impoundment of its license plates or the criminal forfeiture of the vehicle so that the vehicle owner may appear before the court to present evidence as to why the court should not order the immobilization of the vehicle and the impoundment of its license plates or the criminal forfeiture of the vehicle. If the court refrains from ordering the immobilization of the vehicle and the impoundment of its license plates or the criminal forfeiture of the vehicle, section 4503.235 [4503.23.5] of the Revised Code applies relative to the order of immobilization and impoundment or the order of forfeiture.

(b) If, at any time, the charge that the arrested person violated division (B)(1) or (D)(2) of section 4507.02 or section 4507.33 of the Revised Code, or a municipal ordinance that is substantially equivalent to any of those Revised Code provisions is dismissed for any reason, the court shall order that the vehicle seized at the time of the arrest and its license plates immediately be released to the vehicle owner the owner's† subject to the payment of expenses or charges incurred in the removal and storage of the vehicle.

(D) If a vehicle is seized under division (B) of this section and it is not returned to the vehicle owner pursuant to division (C) of this section, the vehicle and its license plates shall be retained until the final disposition of the charge in question. Upon the final disposition of that charge, the court shall do whichever of the following is applicable:

(1) If the arrested person is convicted of or pleads guilty to the violation of division (B)(1) or (D)(2) of section 4507.02 or section 4507.33 of the Revised Code, or a municipal ordinance that is substantially equivalent to any of those Revised Code provisions, the court shall impose sentence upon the arrested person as provided by law or ordinance and, subject to section 4503.235 [4503.23.5] of the Revised Code, shall order the immobilization of the vehicle the arrested person was operating at the time of, or that was involved in, the offense and the impoundment of its license plates under section 4503.233 [4503.23.3] and section 4507.361 [4507.36.1] or 4507.99 of the Revised Code or the criminal forfeiture of the vehicle under section 4503.234 [4503.23.4] and section 4507.361 [4507.36.1] or 4507.99 of the Revised Code, whichever is applicable.

(2) If the arrested person is found not guilty of the violation of division (B)(1) or (D)(2) of section 4507.02 or section 4507.33 of the Revised Code, or a municipal ordinance that is substantially equivalent to any of those Revised Code provisions, the court shall order that the vehicle and its license plates immediately be released to the vehicle owner upon the payment of any expenses or charges incurred in its removal and storage.

(3) If the charge that the arrested person violated division (B)(1) or (D)(2) of section 4507.02 or section 4507.33 of the Revised Code, or a municipal ordinance that is substantially equivalent to any of those Revised Code provisions is dismissed for any reason, the court shall order that the vehicle and its license plates immediately be released to the vehicle owner upon the payment of any expenses or charges incurred in its removal and storage.††

(E) If a vehicle is seized under division (B) of this section, the time between the seizure of the vehicle and either its release to the vehicle owner the owner's† pursuant to division (C) of this section or the issuance of an order of immobilization of the vehicle under section 4503.233 [4503.23.3] of the Revised Code shall be credited against the period of immobilization ordered by the court.

(F)(1) The vehicle owner may be charged expenses or charges incurred in the removal and storage of the immobilized vehicle. The court with jurisdiction over the case, after notice to all interested parties, including lienholders, and after an opportunity for them to be heard, if the vehicle owner fails to appear in person, without good cause, or if the court finds that the vehicle owner does not intend to seek release of the vehicle at the end of the period of immobilization under section 4503.233 [4503.23.3] of the Revised Code or that the vehicle owner is not or will not be able to pay the expenses and charges incurred in its removal and storage, may order that title to the vehicle be transferred, in order of priority, first into the name of the person or entity that removed it, next into the name of a lienholder, or lastly into the name of the owner of the place of storage.

Any lienholder that receives title under a court order shall do so on the condition that it pay any expenses or charges incurred in the vehicle's removal and storage. If the person or entity that receives title to the vehicle is the person or entity that removed it, the person or entity shall receive title on the condition that it pay any lien on the vehicle. The court shall not order that title be transferred to any person or entity other than the owner of the place of storage if the person or entity refuses to receive the title. Any person or entity that receives title either may keep title to the vehicle or may dispose of the vehicle in any legal manner that it considers appropriate, including assignment of the certificate of title to the motor vehicle to a salvage dealer or a scrap metal processing facility. The person or entity shall not transfer the vehicle to the person who is the vehicle's immediate previous owner.

If the person or entity assigns the motor vehicle to a salvage dealer or scrap metal processing facility, the person or entity shall send the assigned certificate of title to the motor vehicle to the clerk of the court of common pleas of the county in which the salvage dealer or scrap metal processing facility is located. The person or entity shall mark the face of the certificate of title with the words "FOR DESTRUCTION" and shall deliver a photocopy of the certificate of title to the salvage dealer or scrap metal processing facility for its records.

(2) Whenever a court issues an order under division (F)(1) of this section, the court also shall order removal of the license plates from the vehicle and cause them to be sent to the registrar if they have not already been sent to the registrar. Thereafter, no further proceedings shall take place under this section or under section 4503.233 [4503.23.3] of the Revised Code.

(3) Prior to initiating a proceeding under division (F)(1) of this section, and upon payment of the fee under division (B) of section 4505.14, any interested party may cause a search to be made of the public records of the bureau of motor vehicles or the clerk of the court of common pleas, to ascertain the identity of any lienholder of the vehicle. The initiating party shall furnish this information to the clerk of the court with jurisdiction over the case, and the clerk shall provide notice to the vehicle owner, the defendant, any lienholder, and any other interested parties listed by the initiating party, at the last known address supplied by the initiating party, by certified mail, or, at the option of the initiating party, by personal service or ordinary mail.

HISTORY: 144 v S 275 (Eff 9-1-93); 145 v S 62, §§ 1, 4 (Eff 9-1-93); 145 v H 236 (Eff 9-29-94); 145 v H 687 (Eff 10-12-94); 146 v H 353 (Eff 9-17-96); 146 v H 676. Eff 10-4-96.

Not analogous to former RC § 4507.38, renumbered RC § 4507.02 in 141 v S 356, eff 9-24-86.

Publisher's Note

The amendments made by HB 353 (146 v —) and HB 676 (146 v —) have been combined. Please see provisions of RC § 1.52.

† The language is the result of combining HB 353 (146 v —) and HB 676 (146 v —).

†† Division (D)(1), (2), (3) is presented as it appears in the HB 353 (146 v —) amendment.

§ 4507.45 Reinstatement fee in certain cases.

If a person's driver's license, commercial driver's license, or nonresident operating privilege is suspended, disqualified, or revoked for an indefinite period of time or for a period of at least ninety days, and if at the end of the period of suspension, disqualification, or revocation the person is eligible to have the license or privilege reinstated, the registrar of motor vehicles shall collect a reinstatement fee of thirty dollars when the person requests reinstatement. However, the registrar shall not collect the fee prescribed by this section if a different driver's license, commercial driver's license, or nonresident operating privilege reinstatement fee is prescribed by law.

HISTORY: 147 v H 210. Eff 3-31-97.

The effective date is set by section 20 of HB 210.

The provisions of § 25 of HB 210 (147 v —) read as follows:

SECTION 25. The reinstatement fee prescribed by section 4507.45 of the Revised Code and the fee increases prescribed by this act's amendments to section 4511.951 and division (L) of section 4511.191 of the Revised Code first apply on October 1, 1997.

§ 4507.50 Issuance of identification card or temporary card.

The registrar of motor vehicles or a deputy registrar, upon receipt of an application filed in compliance with section 4507.51 of the Revised Code by any person who is a resident or a temporary resident of this state and, except as otherwise provided in this section, is not licensed as an operator of a motor vehicle in this state or another licensing jurisdiction, and upon receipt of a fee of three dollars and fifty cents, shall issue an identification card to that person.

Any person who is a resident or temporary resident of this state whose Ohio driver's or commercial driver's license has been suspended or revoked, upon application in compliance with section 4507.51 of the Revised Code and payment of a fee of three dollars and fifty cents, may be issued a temporary identification card. The temporary identification card shall be identical to an identification card, except that it shall be printed on its face with a statement that the card is valid during the effective dates of the suspension or revocation of the cardholder's license, or until the birthday of the cardholder in the fourth year after the date on which it is issued, whichever is shorter. The cardholder shall surrender the identification card to the registrar or any deputy registrar before the cardholder's driver's or commercial driver's license is restored or reissued.

The deputy registrar shall be allowed a fee of two dollars and twenty-five cents for each identification card issued under this section. The fee allowed to the deputy registrar shall be in addition to the fee for issuing an identification card.

Neither the registrar nor any deputy registrar shall

charge a fee in excess of one dollar and fifty cents for laminating an identification card or temporary identification card. A deputy registrar laminating such a card shall retain the entire amount of the fee charged for lamination, less the actual cost to the registrar of the laminating materials used for that lamination, as specified in the contract executed by the bureau for the laminating materials and laminating equipment. The deputy registrar shall forward the amount of the cost of the laminating materials to the registrar for deposit as provided in this section.

The fee collected for issuing an identification card under this section, except the fee allowed to the deputy registrar, shall be paid into the state treasury to the credit of the state bureau of motor vehicles fund created in section 4501.25 of the Revised Code.

HISTORY: 136 v S 435 (Eff 8-24-76); 137 v H 3 (Eff 1-1-79); 137 v S 221 (Eff 11-23-77); 137 v H 90 (Eff 1-17-78); 138 v H 656 (Eff 1-1-80); 139 v H 457 (Eff 2-11-82); 141 v H 201 (Eff 7-1-85); 141 v S 269 (Eff 3-13-86); 141 v H 165 (Eff 8-1-86); 142 v H 419 (Eff 7-1-87); 142 v H 165 (Eff 6-29-88); 142 v S 1 (Eff 11-28-88); 143 v H 381 (Eff 7-1-89); 143 v S 131 (Eff 7-25-90); 145 v H 154 (Eff 6-30-93); 146 v H 107 (Eff 6-30-95); 147 v S 60. Eff 10-21-97.

[§ 4507.50.1] § 4507.501 Request for donation to second chance trust fund.

In addition to the fees collected under section 4507.50 of the Revised Code, the registrar or deputy registrar of motor vehicles shall ask each applicant for an identification card or duplicate under section 4507.51 of the Revised Code whether the person wishes to make a one-dollar voluntary contribution to the second chance trust fund established under section 2108.15 of the Revised Code. The registrar or deputy registrar shall also make available to the person informational material provided by the department of health on the importance of organ, tissue, and eye donation.

All donations collected under this section during each month shall be forwarded by the registrar or deputy registrar not later than the fifth day of the immediately following month to the treasurer of state, who shall deposit them in the second chance trust fund.

HISTORY: 146 v S 300. Eff 7-1-97.

The effective date is set by section 3 of SB 300.

§ 4507.51 Application for identification card.

(A)(1) Every application for an identification card or duplicate shall be made on a form furnished by the registrar of motor vehicles, shall be signed by the applicant, and by his parent or guardian if the applicant is under eighteen years of age, and shall contain the following information pertaining to the applicant: name, date of birth, sex, general description including the applicant's height, weight, hair color, and eye color, address, and at the option of the applicant, his social security number, his blood type, or his social security number and his blood type. The application form shall state that an applicant is not required to furnish his social security number or his blood type. The application shall also state whether an applicant wishes to certify willingness to make an anatomical gift under section 2108.04 of the Revised Code and shall include information about the requirements of that section that apply to persons who are less than eighteen years of age. The statement regarding willingness to make such a donation shall be given no consideration in the decision of whether to issue an identification card. Each applicant shall be photographed in color at the time of making application.

(2) On and after May 1, 1993, the application also shall state whether the applicant has executed a valid durable power of attorney for health care pursuant to sections 1337.11 to 1337.17 of the Revised Code or has executed a declaration governing the use or continuation, or the withholding or withdrawal, of life-sustaining treatment pursuant to Chapter 2133. of the Revised Code and, if the applicant has executed either type of instrument, whether he wishes his identification card to indicate that he has executed the instrument.

(3) The registrar or deputy registrar, in accordance with section 3503.11 of the Revised Code, shall register as an elector any person who applies for an identification card or duplicate if the applicant is eligible and wishes to be registered as an elector. The decision of an applicant whether to register as an elector shall be given no consideration in the decision of whether to issue him an identification card or duplicate.

(B) The application for an identification card or duplicate shall be filed in the office of the registrar or deputy registrar. Each applicant shall present documentary evidence as required by the registrar of his age and identity. Each applicant who did not enter his social security number on his application form, upon request, shall furnish the registrar or the deputy registrar with the applicant's social security number, if such a number has been assigned to the applicant, for purposes of determining whether a driver's or commercial driver's license has been issued under the same social security number. The registrar or deputy registrar shall not maintain the social security number as a part of the record or enter it on the application form. The applicant shall swear that all information given is true.

All applications for an identification card or duplicate shall be filed in duplicate, and if submitted to a deputy registrar, a copy shall be forwarded to the registrar. The registrar shall prescribe rules for the manner in which a deputy registrar is to file and maintain applications and other records. The registrar shall maintain a suitable, indexed record of all applications denied and cards issued or canceled.

HISTORY: 136 v S 435 (Eff 8-24-76); 137 v H 90 (Eff 1-17-78); 140 v S 302 (Eff 10-1-84); 142 v H 165 (Eff 6-29-88); 143 v H 381 (Eff 7-1-89); 143 v H 529 Eff (10-30-89); 143 v H 21 (Eff

3-27-91); 144 v H 427 (Eff 10-8-92); 145 v S 300. Eff 1-1-95.

The effective date is set by section 3 of SB 300.

§ 4507.52 Contents and characteristics; expiration; renewal; surrender; duplicate or replacement; cancellation; card not to be required.

Each identification card issued by the registrar of motor vehicles or a deputy registrar shall bear a distinguishing number assigned to the cardholder, and shall contain the following inscription:

"STATE OF OHIO IDENTIFICATION CARD

This card is not valid for the purpose of operating a motor vehicle. It is provided solely for the purpose of establishing the identity of the bearer described on the card, who currently is not licensed to operate a motor vehicle in the state of Ohio."

The identification card shall bear substantially the same information as contained in the application and as described in division (A)(1) of section 4507.51 of the Revised Code and shall contain the color photograph of the cardholder. On and after May 1, 1993, if the cardholder has executed a durable power of attorney for health care or a declaration governing the use or continuation, or the withholding or withdrawal, of life-sustaining treatment and has specified that the cardholder wishes the identification card to indicate that the cardholder has executed either type of instrument, the card also shall contain any symbol chosen by the registrar to indicate that the cardholder has executed either type of instrument. The card shall be sealed in transparent plastic or similar material and shall be so designed as to prevent its reproduction or alteration without ready detection.

The identification card for persons under twenty-one years of age shall have characteristics prescribed by the registrar distinguishing it from that issued to a person who is twenty-one years of age or older, except that an identification card issued to a person who applies no more than thirty days before the applicant's twenty-first birthday shall have the characteristics of an identification card issued to a person who is twenty-one years of age or older.

Every identification card issued to a resident of this state shall expire, unless canceled or surrendered earlier, on the birthday of the cardholder in the fourth year after the date on which it is issued. Every identification card issued to a temporary resident shall expire in accordance with rules adopted by the registrar and is nonrenewable, but may be replaced with a new identification card upon the applicant's compliance with all applicable requirements. A cardholder may renew the cardholder's identification card within ninety days prior to the day on which it expires by filing an application and paying the prescribed fee in accordance with section 4507.50 of the Revised Code.

If a cardholder applies for a driver's or commercial driver's license in this state or another licensing jurisdiction, the cardholder shall surrender the cardholder's identification card to the registrar or any deputy registrar before the license is issued.

If a card is lost, destroyed, or mutilated, the person to whom the card was issued may obtain a duplicate by doing both of the following:

(A) Furnishing suitable proof of the loss, destruction, or mutilation to the registrar or a deputy registrar;

(B) Filing an application and presenting documentary evidence under section 4507.51 of the Revised Code.

Any person who loses a card and, after obtaining a duplicate, finds the original, immediately shall surrender the original to the registrar or a deputy registrar.

A cardholder may obtain a replacement identification card that reflects any change of the cardholder's name by furnishing suitable proof of the change to the registrar or a deputy registrar and surrendering the cardholder's existing card.

When a cardholder applies for a duplicate or obtains a replacement identification card, the cardholder shall pay a fee of two dollars and fifty cents. A deputy registrar shall be allowed an additional fee of two dollars and twenty-five cents for issuing a duplicate or replacement identification card.

A duplicate or replacement identification card shall expire on the same date as the card it replaces.

The registrar shall cancel any card upon determining that the card was obtained unlawfully, issued in error, or was altered. The registrar also shall cancel any card that is surrendered to the registrar or to a deputy registrar after the holder has obtained a duplicate, replacement, or driver's or commercial driver's license.

No agent of the state or its political subdivisions shall condition the granting of any benefit, service, right, or privilege upon the possession by any person of an identification card. Nothing in this section shall preclude any publicly operated or franchised transit system from using an identification card for the purpose of granting benefits or services of the system.

No person shall be required to apply for, carry, or possess an identification card.

(C) Except in regard to an identification card issued to a person who applies no more than thirty days before the applicant's twenty-first birthday, neither the registrar nor any deputy registrar shall issue an identification card to a person under twenty-one years of age that does not have the characteristics prescribed by the registrar distinguishing it from the identification card issued to persons who are twenty-one years of age or older.

HISTORY: 136 v S 435 (Eff 8-24-76); 137 v H 90 (Eff 1-17-78); 142 v H 165 (Eff 6-29-88); 143 v H 381 (Eff 7-1-89); 143 v S 131 (Eff 7-25-90); 144 v H 134 (Eff 10-10-91); 144 v H 427 (Eff 10-8-92); 145 v H 580 (Eff 12-9-94); 146 v H 353 (Eff 9-17-96); 147 v S 60. Eff 10-21-97.

§ 4507.53 Release of digitalized photographic records.

Digitalized photographic records of the department

of public safety may be released only to state, local, or federal law enforcement agencies.

HISTORY: 145 v H 154. Eff 6-30-93.

Not analogous to former RC § 4507.53 (143 v S 71), repealed 143 v S 71, § 2, eff 11-2-91.

§ 4507.54 Destruction of license or permit; reissuance.

(A) Upon the receipt of any driver's license or commercial driver's license or permit that has been suspended, revoked, canceled, or forfeited under any provision of law, and notwithstanding any other provision of law that requires the registrar of motor vehicles to retain the license or permit, the registrar may destroy the license or permit.

(B) If, as authorized by division (A) of this section, the registrar destroys a license or permit that has been suspended, revoked, canceled, or forfeited, he shall reissue or authorize the reissuance of a new license or permit to the person to whom the destroyed license or permit originally was issued upon payment of a fee in the same amount as the fee specified in division (C) of section 4507.23 of the Revised Code for a duplicate license or permit and upon payment of a service fee in the same amount as specified in division (D) of section 4503.10 of the Revised Code if issued by a deputy registrar or in division (G) of that section if issued by the registrar.

This division applies only if the driver's license or commercial driver's license or permit that was destroyed would have been valid at the time the person applies for the duplicate license or permit. A duplicate driver's license or commercial driver's license or permit issued under this section shall bear the same expiration date that appeared on the license or permit it replaces.

HISTORY: 145 v H 687. Eff 10-12-94.

§ 4507.55 Destruction of license or permit after suspension under implied consent law; reissuance.

(A) Upon the receipt of any driver's or commercial driver's license or permit that has been revoked or suspended under section 4511.191 [4511.19.1] of the Revised Code, the registrar of motor vehicles, notwithstanding any other provision of law that purports to require him to retain the license or permit, may destroy the license or permit.

(B)(1) Subject to division (B)(2) of this section, if a driver's or commercial driver's license or permit that has been suspended under section 4511.191 [4511.19.1] of the Revised Code is delivered to the registrar and if the registrar destroys the license or permit under authority of division (A) of this section, the registrar shall reissue or authorize the reissuance of a driver's or commercial driver's license to the person, free of payment of any type of fee or charge, if either of the following applies:

(a) The person appeals the suspension of the license or permit at his initial appearance, pursuant to division (H) of section 4511.191 [4511.19.1] of the Revised Code, the judge of the court of record or the mayor of the mayor's court who conducts the initial appearance terminates the suspension, and the judge or mayor does not suspend the license or permit under section 4511.196 [4511.19.6] of the Revised Code;

(b) The person appeals the suspension of the license or permit at his initial appearance, pursuant to division (H) of section 4511.191 [4511.19.1] of the Revised Code, the judge of the court of record or the mayor of the mayor's court who conducts the initial appearance does not terminate the suspension, the person appeals the judge's or mayor's decision not to terminate the suspension that is made at the initial appearance, and upon appeal of the decision, the suspension is terminated.

(2) Division (B)(1) of this section applies only if the driver's or commercial driver's license that was destroyed would have been valid at the time in question, if it had not been destroyed as permitted by division (A) of this section.

(C) A driver's or commercial driver's license or permit issued to a person pursuant to division (B)(1) of this section shall bear the same expiration date as the expiration date that appeared on the license it replaces.

HISTORY: RC § 4507.16.10, 145 v S 62 (Eff 9-1-93); RC § 4507.55, 145 v H 687. Eff 10-12-94.

§ 4507.60 Driver license compact enacted.

The driver license compact is hereby enacted into law and entered into with all other jurisdictions legally joining therein in the form substantially as follows:

ARTICLE I
Findings and Declaration of Policy

(A) The party states find that:

(1) The safety of their streets and highways is materially affected by the degree of compliance with state and local ordinances relating to the operation of motor vehicles.

(2) Violation of such a law or ordinance is evidence that the violator engages in conduct which is likely to endanger the safety of persons and property.

(3) The continuance in force of a license to drive is predicated upon compliance with laws and ordinances relating to the operation of motor vehicles, in whichever jurisdiction the vehicle is operated.

(B) It is the policy of each of the party states to:

(1) Promote compliance with the laws, ordinances, and administrative rules and regulations relating to the operation of motor vehicles by their operators in each of the jurisdictions where such operators drive motor vehicles.

(2) Make the reciprocal recognition of licenses to drive and eligibility therefor more just and equitable by considering the over-all compliance with motor vehicle laws, ordinances, and administrative rules and regulations as a condition precedent to the continuance or issuance of any license by reason of which the licensee is authorized or permitted to operate a motor vehicle in any of the party states.

ARTICLE II
Definitions

As used in this compact:

(A) "State" means a state, territory, or possession of the United States, the District of Columbia, or the Commonwealth of Puerto Rico.

(B) "Home state" means the state that has issued and has the power to suspend or revoke the use of the license or permit to operate a motor vehicle.

(C) "Conviction" means a conviction of any offense related to the use or operation of a motor vehicle that is prohibited by state law, municipal ordinance, or administrative rule or regulation; or a forfeiture of bail, bond, or other security deposited to secure appearance by a person charged with having committed any such offense, and which conviction or forfeiture is required to be reported to the licensing authority.

ARTICLE III
Reports of Conviction

The licensing authority of a party state shall report each conviction of a person from another party state occurring within its jurisdiction to the licensing authority of the home state of the licensee. Such report shall clearly identify the person convicted; describe the violation specifying the section of the statute, code, or ordinance violated; identify the court in which action was taken; indicate whether a plea of guilty or not guilty was entered, or the security; and shall include any special findings made in connection therewith.

ARTICLE IV
Effect of Conviction

(A) The licensing authority in the home state, for the purpose of suspension, revocation, or limitation of the license to operate a motor vehicle, shall give the same effect to the conduct reported, pursuant to Article III of this compact, as it would if such conduct had occurred in the home state, in the case of convictions for:

(1) Manslaughter or negligent homicide resulting from the operation of a motor vehicle;

(2) Driving a motor vehicle while under the influence of intoxicating liquor or a narcotic drug, or under the influence of any other drug to a degree that renders the driver incapable of safely driving a motor vehicle;

(3) Any felony in the commission of which a motor vehicle is used;

(4) Failure to stop and render aid in the event of a motor vehicle accident resulting in the death or personal injury of another.

(B) As to other convictions, reported pursuant to Article III, the licensing authority in the home state shall give such effect to conduct as is provided by the laws of the home state.

(C) If the laws of a party state do not provide for offenses or violations denominated or described in precisely the words employed in subdivision (A) of this Article, such party state shall construe the denominations and descriptions appearing in subdivision (A) hereof as being applicable to and identifying those offenses or violations of a substantially similar nature, and the laws of such party state shall contain such provisions as may be necessary to ensure that full force and effect is given to this Article.

ARTICLE V
Applications for New Licenses

Upon application for a license to drive, the licensing authority in a party state shall ascertain whether the applicant has ever held, or is the holder of, a license to drive issued by any other party state. The licensing authority in the state where application is made shall not issue a license to drive to the applicant if:

(1) The applicant has held such a license, but the same has been suspended by reason, in whole or in part, of a violation and if such suspension period has not terminated.

(2) The applicant has held such a license, but the same has been revoked by reason, in whole or in part, of a violation; and if such revocation has not terminated, except that after the expiration of one year from the date the license was revoked, such person may make application for a new license if permitted by law. The licensing authority may refuse to issue a license to any such applicant if, after investigation, the licensing authority determines that it will not be safe to grant to such person the privilege of driving a motor vehicle on the public highways.

(3) The applicant is the holder of a license to drive issued by another party state and currently in force unless the applicant surrenders such license.

ARTICLE VI
Applicability of Other Laws

Except as expressly required by provisions of this compact, nothing contained herein shall be construed to affect the right of any party state to apply any of its other laws relating to licenses to drive to any person or circumstance, nor to invalidate or prevent any driver license agreement or other cooperative arrangement between a party state and a nonparty state.

ARTICLE VII
Compact Administrator and Interchange of Information

(A) The head of the licensing authority of each party state shall be the administrator of this compact for his state. The administrators, acting jointly, shall have the power to formulate all necessary and proper procedures for the exchange of information under this compact.

(B) The administrator of each party state shall furnish to the administrator of each other party state any information or documents reasonably necessary to facilitate the administration of this compact.

ARTICLE VIII
Entry Into Force and Withdrawal

(A) This compact shall enter into force and become effective as to any state when it has enacted the same into law.

(B) Any party state may withdraw from this compact by enacting a statute repealing the same, but no such withdrawal shall take effect until six months after the executive head of the withdrawing state has given notice of the withdrawal to the executive heads of all other party states. No withdrawal shall affect the validity or applicability by the licensing authorities of states remaining party to the compact of any report of conviction occurring prior to the withdrawal.

ARTICLE IX
Construction and Severability

This compact shall be liberally construed so as to effectuate the purposes thereof. The provisions of this compact shall be severable; and if any phrase, clause, sentence, or provision of this compact is declared to be contrary to the constitution of any party state or of the United States or the applicability thereof to any government, agency, person, or circumstance is held invalid, the validity of the remainder of this compact and the applicability thereof to any government, agency, person, or circumstance shall not be affected thereby. If this compact shall be held contrary to the constitution of any state party thereto, the compact shall remain in full force and effect as to the remaining states and in full force and effect as to the state affected as to all severable matters.

HISTORY: 142 v H 419. Eff 7-1-87.

Publisher's Note
According to Ohio Bureau of Motor Vehicles, as of March 12, 1996, the following states are members of the Driver's License Compact: Alabama, Alaska, Arizona, Arkansas, California, Colorado, Connecticut, Delaware, D.C., Florida, Hawaii, Idaho, Illinois, Indiana, Iowa, Kansas, Louisiana, Maine, Maryland, Minnesota, Mississippi, Missouri, Montana, Nebraska, Nevada, New Hampshire, New Jersey, New Mexico, New York, North Carolina, North Dakota, Ohio, Oklahoma, Oregon, Rhode Island, South Carolina, South Dakota, Tennessee, Texas, Utah, Vermont, Virginia, Washington, West Virginia, and Wyoming. For more up to date information, please call the Bureau of Motor Vehicles at (614) 752-7600.

§ 4507.61 Executive head and licensing authority specified.

(A) "Executive head" as used in Article VIII (b) of the compact set forth in section 4507.60 of the Revised Code with reference to this state means the governor.

(B) "Licensing authority" as used in Articles III, IV, V, and VII of the compact set forth in section 4507.60 of the Revised Code with reference to this state means the bureau of motor vehicles within the department of public safety.

HISTORY: 142 v H 419 (Eff 7-1-87); 144 v S 98. Eff 11-12-92.

§ 4507.62 Information or documents furnished to other states.

Pursuant to Article VII of the compact set forth in section 4507.60 of the Revised Code the bureau of motor vehicles shall furnish to the appropriate authorities of any other party state any information or documents reasonably necessary to facilitate the administration of Articles III, IV, and V of the compact set forth in section 4507.60 of the Revised Code.

HISTORY: 142 v H 419. Eff 7-1-87.

§ 4507.63 Reimbursement for compact administrator.

The compact administrator provided for in Article VII of the compact set forth in section 4507.60 of the Revised Code is not entitled to any additional compensation because of his services as administrator of the compact, but shall be reimbursed for travel and other necessary expenses incurred in the performance of his official duties thereunder as provided by law for other state officers.

HISTORY: 142 v H 419. Eff 7-1-87.

§ 4507.99 Penalties.

(A) Whoever violates division (B)(2) or (D)(1) of section 4507.02 of the Revised Code is guilty of driving under suspension or revocation or in violation of license restrictions, a misdemeanor of the first degree. Whoever violates division (C) of section 4507.02 of the Revised Code is guilty of driving without paying a license reinstatement fee, a misdemeanor of the first degree. Except as otherwise provided in division (D) of section 4507.162 [4507.16.2] of the Revised Code, the court, in addition to or independent of all other penalties provided by law, may suspend for a period not to exceed one year the driver's or commercial driver's license or permit or nonresident operating privilege of any person who pleads guilty to or is convicted of a violation of division (B)(2), (C), or (D)(1) of section 4507.02 of the Revised Code.

(B) Whoever violates division (D)(2) of section 4507.02 of the Revised Code is guilty of driving under OMVI suspension or revocation and shall be punished as provided in division (B)(1), (2), or (3) and divisions (B)(4) to (8) of this section.

(1) Except as otherwise provided in division (B)(2) or (3) of this section, driving under OMVI suspension

or revocation is a misdemeanor of the first degree, and the court shall sentence the offender to a term of imprisonment of not less than three consecutive days and may sentence the offender pursuant to section 2929.21 of the Revised Code to a longer term of imprisonment. As an alternative to the term of imprisonment required to be imposed by this division, but subject to division (B)(6) of this section, the court may sentence the offender to a term of not less than thirty consecutive days of electronically monitored house arrest as defined in division (A)(4) of section 2929.23 of the Revised Code. The period of electronically monitored house arrest shall not exceed six months. In addition, the court shall impose upon the offender a fine of not less than two hundred fifty and not more than one thousand dollars.

Regardless of whether the vehicle the offender was operating at the time of the offense is registered in the offender's name or in the name of another person, the court, in addition to or independent of any other sentence that it imposes upon the offender and subject to section 4503.235 [4503.23.5] of the Revised Code, shall order the immobilization for thirty days of the vehicle the offender was operating at the time of the offense and the impoundment for thirty days of the identification license plates of that vehicle. The order for immobilization and impoundment shall be issued and enforced in accordance with section 4503.233 [4503.23.3] of the Revised Code.

(2) If, within five years of the offense, the offender has been convicted of or pleaded guilty to one violation of division (D)(2) of section 4507.02 of the Revised Code or a municipal ordinance that is substantially equivalent to that division, driving under OMVI suspension or revocation is a misdemeanor, and the court shall sentence the offender to a term of imprisonment of not less than ten consecutive days and may sentence the offender to a longer definite term of imprisonment of not more than one year. As an alternative to the term of imprisonment required to be imposed by this division, but subject to division (B)(6) of this section, the court may sentence the offender to a term of not less than ninety consecutive days of electronically monitored house arrest as defined in division (A)(4) of section 2929.23 of the Revised Code. The period of electronically monitored house arrest shall not exceed one year. In addition, the court shall impose upon the offender a fine of not less than five hundred and not more than two thousand five hundred dollars.

Regardless of whether the vehicle the offender was operating at the time of the offense is registered in the offender's name or in the name of another person, the court, in addition to or independent of any other sentence that it imposes upon the offender and subject to section 4503.235 [4503.23.5] of the Revised Code, shall order the immobilization for sixty days of the vehicle the offender was operating at the time of the offense and the impoundment for sixty days of the identification license plates of that vehicle. The order for immobilization and impoundment shall be issued and enforced in accordance with section 4503.233 [4503.23.3] of the Revised Code.

(3) If, within five years of the offense, the offender has been convicted of or pleaded guilty to two or more violations of division (D)(2) of section 4507.02 of the Revised Code or a municipal ordinance that is substantially equivalent to that division, driving under OMVI suspension or revocation is guilty of a misdemeanor. The court shall sentence the offender to a term of imprisonment of not less than thirty consecutive days and may sentence the offender to a longer definite term of imprisonment of not more than one year. The court shall not sentence the offender to a term of electronically monitored house arrest as defined in division (A)(4) of section 2929.23 of the Revised Code. In addition, the court shall impose upon the offender a fine of not less than five hundred and not more than two thousand five hundred dollars.

Regardless of whether the vehicle the offender was operating at the time of the offense is registered in the offender's name or in the name of another person, the court, in addition to or independent of any other sentence that it imposes upon the offender and subject to section 4503.235 [4503.23.5] of the Revised Code, shall order the criminal forfeiture to the state of the vehicle the offender was operating at the time of the offense. The order of criminal forfeiture shall be issued and enforced in accordance with section 4503.234 [4503.23.4] of the Revised Code.

If title to a motor vehicle that is subject to an order for criminal forfeiture under this section is assigned or transferred and division (C)(2) or (3) of section 4503.234 [4503.23.4] of the Revised Code applies, in addition to or independent of any other penalty established by law, the court may fine the offender the value of the vehicle as determined by publications of the national auto dealer's association. The proceeds from any fine imposed under this division shall be distributed in accordance with division (D)(4) of section 4503.234 [4503.23.4] of the Revised Code.

(4) In addition to or independent of all other penalties provided by law or ordinance, the trial judge of any court of record or the mayor of a mayor's court shall suspend for a period not to exceed one year the driver's or commercial driver's license or permit or nonresident operating privilege of an offender who is sentenced under division (B)(1), (2), or (3) of this section.

(5) Fifty per cent of any fine imposed by a court under division (B)(1), (2), or (3) of this section shall be deposited into the county indigent driver's alcohol treatment fund or municipal indigent drivers alcohol treatment fund under the control of that court, as created by the county or municipal corporation pursuant to division (N) of section 4511.191 [4511.19.1] of the Revised Code.

(6) No court shall impose the alternative sentence of

not less than thirty consecutive days of electronically monitored house arrest permitted to be imposed by division (B)(1) of this section or the alternative sentence of a term of not less than ninety consecutive days of electronically monitored house arrest permitted to be imposed by division (B)(2) of this section, unless within sixty days of the date of sentencing, the court issues a written finding, entered into the record, that, due to the unavailability of space at the incarceration facility where the offender is required to serve the term of imprisonment imposed upon the offender, the offender will not be able to begin serving that term of imprisonment within the sixty-day period following the date of sentencing. If the court issues such a finding, the court may impose the alternative sentence comprised of or including electronically monitored house arrest permitted to be imposed by division (B)(1) or (2) of this section.

(7) An offender sentenced under this section to a period of electronically monitored house arrest shall be permitted work release during such period. The duration of the work release shall not exceed the time necessary each day for the offender to commute to and from the place of employment and the offender's home or other place specified by the sentencing court and the time actually spent under employment.

(8) Suspension of a commercial driver's license under this section shall be concurrent with any period of disqualification under section 2301.374 [2301.37.4] or 4506.16 of the Revised Code. No person who is disqualified for life from holding a commercial driver's license under section 4506.16 of the Revised Code shall be issued a driver's license under this chapter during the period for which the commercial driver's license was suspended under this section, and no person whose commercial driver's license is suspended under this section shall be issued a driver's license under this chapter during the period of the suspension.

(C) Whoever violates division (B)(1) of section 4507.02 of the Revised Code is guilty of driving under financial responsibility law suspension or revocation and shall be punished as provided in division (C)(1), (2), or (3) and division (C)(4) of this section.

(1) Except as otherwise provided in division (C)(2) or (3) of this section, driving under financial responsibility law suspension or revocation is a misdemeanor of the first degree.

Regardless of whether the vehicle the offender was operating at the time of the offense is registered in the offender's name or in the name of another person, the court, in addition to or independent of any other sentence that it imposes upon the offender and subject to section 4503.235 [4503.23.5] of the Revised Code, shall order the immobilization for thirty days of the vehicle the offender was operating at the time of the offense and the impoundment for thirty days of the identification license plates of that vehicle. The order for immobilization and impoundment shall be issued and enforced in accordance with section 4503.233 [4503.23.3] of the Revised Code.

(2) If, within five years of the offense, the offender has been convicted of or pleaded guilty to one violation of division (B)(1) of section 4507.02 of the Revised Code or a municipal ordinance that is substantially equivalent to that division, driving under financial responsibility law suspension or revocation is a misdemeanor of the first degree.

Regardless of whether the vehicle the offender was operating at the time of the offense is registered in the offender's name or in the name of another person, the court, in addition to or independent of any other sentence that it imposes upon the offender and subject to section 4503.235 [4503.23.5] of the Revised Code, shall order the immobilization for sixty days of the vehicle the offender was operating at the time of the offense and the impoundment for sixty days of the identification license plates of that vehicle. The order for immobilization and impoundment shall be issued and enforced in accordance with section 4503.233 [4503.23.3] of the Revised Code.

(3) If, within five years of the offense, the offender has been convicted of or pleaded guilty to two or more violations of division (B)(1) of section 4507.02 of the Revised Code or a municipal ordinance that is substantially equivalent to that division, driving under financial responsibility law suspension or revocation is a misdemeanor of the first degree.

Regardless of whether the vehicle the offender was operating at the time of the offense is registered in the offender's name or in the name of another person, the court, in addition to or independent of any other sentence that it imposes upon the offender and subject to section 4503.235 [4503.23.5] of the Revised Code, shall order the criminal forfeiture to the state of the vehicle the offender was operating at the time of the offense. The order of criminal forfeiture shall be issued and enforced in accordance with section 4503.234 [4503.23.4] of the Revised Code.

If title to a motor vehicle that is subject to an order for criminal forfeiture under this section is assigned or transferred and division (C)(2) or (3) of section 4503.234 [4503.23.4] of the Revised Code applies, in addition to or independent of any other penalty established by law, the court may fine the offender the value of the vehicle as determined by publications of the national auto dealer's association. The proceeds from any fine imposed under this division shall be distributed in accordance with division (D)(4) of section 4503.234 [4503.23.4] of the Revised Code.

(4) Except as otherwise provided in division (D) of section 4507.162 [4507.16.2] of the Revised Code, the court, in addition to or independent of all other penalties provided by law, may suspend for a period not to exceed one year the driver's or commercial driver's license or permit or nonresident operating privilege of an offender who is sentenced under division (C)(1), (2), or (3) of this section.

(5) The court shall not release a vehicle from the

immobilization ordered under division (C)(1) or (2) of this section unless the court is presented with current proof of financial responsibility with respect to that vehicle.

(D) Whoever violates division (A)(1) or (3) of section 4507.02 of the Revised Code by operating a motor vehicle when the offender's driver's or commercial driver's license has been expired for no more than six months is guilty of a minor misdemeanor. Whoever violates division (B) of section 4507.13 or division (C) of section 4507.52 of the Revised Code is guilty of a minor misdemeanor.

(E) Whoever violates section 4507.33 of the Revised Code is guilty of permitting the operation of a vehicle by a person with no legal right to operate a vehicle and shall be punished as provided in division (E)(1) or (2) of this section.

(1) Except as otherwise provided in division (E)(2) of this section, permitting the operation of a vehicle by a person with no legal right to operate a vehicle is a misdemeanor of the first degree. In addition to or independent of any other sentence that it imposes upon the offender and subject to section 4503.235 [4503.23.5] of the Revised Code, the court shall order the immobilization for thirty days of the vehicle involved in the offense and the impoundment for thirty days of the identification license plates of that vehicle. The order for immobilization and impoundment shall be issued and enforced in accordance with section 4503.233 [4503.23.3] of the Revised Code.

(2) If the offender previously has been convicted of or pleaded guilty to one or more violations of section 4507.33 of the Revised Code, permitting the operation of a vehicle by a person with no legal right to operate a vehicle is a misdemeanor of the first degree. In addition to or independent of any other sentence that it imposes upon the offender and subject to section 4503.235 [4503.23.5] of the Revised Code, the court shall order the criminal forfeiture to the state of the vehicle involved in the offense. The order of criminal forfeiture shall be issued and enforced in accordance with section 4503.234 [4503.23.4] of the Revised Code.

If title to a motor vehicle that is subject to an order for criminal forfeiture under this section is assigned or transferred and division (C)(2) or (3) of section 4503.234 [4503.23.4] of the Revised Code applies, in addition to or independent of any other penalty established by law, the court may fine the offender the value of the vehicle as determined by publications of the national auto dealer's association. The proceeds from any fine imposed under this division shall be distributed in accordance with division (D)(4) of section 4503.234 [4503.23.4] of the Revised Code.

(F) Except as provided in divisions (A) to (E) of this section and unless another penalty is provided by the laws of this state, whoever violates any provision of sections 4507.01 to 4507.081 [4507.08.1] or 4507.10 to 4507.37 of the Revised Code is guilty of a misdemeanor of the first degree.

(G) Whenever a person is found guilty of a violation of section 4507.32 of the Revised Code, the trial judge of any court of record, in addition to or independent of all other penalties provided by law or ordinance, may suspend for any period of time not exceeding three years or revoke the license of any person, partnership, association, or corporation, issued under section 4511.763 [4511.76.3] of the Revised Code.

(H) Whenever a person is found guilty of a violation of a traffic offense specified in Traffic Rule 13(B) that requires the person's appearance in court, the court shall require the person to verify the existence at the time of the offense of proof of financial responsibility covering the person's operation of the motor vehicle, or the motor vehicle if registered in the person's name, and notify the registrar pursuant to division (D) of section 4509.101 [4509.10.1] of the Revised Code if the person fails to verify the existence of such proof of financial responsibility.

HISTORY: Bureau of Code Revision, 10-1-53; 125 v 903(1025) (Eff 10-1-53); 131 v 1088 (Eff 9-1-65); 139 v S 432 (Eff 3-16-83); 140 v H 767 (Eff 8-1-84); 140 v H 252 (Eff 4-4-85); 141 v S 356 (Eff 9-24-86); 142 v H 643 (Eff 3-17-89); 143 v H 329 (Eff 6-30-89); 143 v S 102 (Eff 9-15-89); 143 v H 381 (Eff 7-1-89); 143 v H 88 (Eff 3-13-90); 143 v S 131 (Eff 7-25-90); 143 v H 837 (Eff 7-25-90); 144 v H 134 (Eff 10-10-91); 144 v H 725 (Eff 4-16-93); 144 v S 275 (Eff 9-1-93); 145 v S 62, §§ 1, 4 (Eff 9-1-93); 145 v S 82 (Eff 5-4-94); 145 v S 20 (Eff 10-20-94); 146 v S 2 (Eff 7-1-96); 146 v H 676, § 1 (Eff 10-4-96); 146 v H 676, § 6 (Eff 5-15-97); 146 v H 438. Eff 7-1-97.

The effective date is set by section 3 of HB 438.

Comment, Legislative Service Commission

Section 4507.99 of the Revised Code is amended by this act [Am. Sub. H.B. 438] and also by Am. Sub. H.B. 676 of the 121st General Assembly (effective July 1, 1997).† Comparison of these amendments in pursuance of section 1.52 of the Revised Code discloses that they are not irreconcilable so that they are required by that section to be harmonized to give effect to each amendment.

† The date corresponds to the version of RC § 4507.99 as amended by Am. Sub. H.B. 438.

CHAPTER 4509: FINANCIAL RESPONSIBILITY

[ACCIDENT REPORT]

§ 4509.06 Accident report concerning uninsured driver or owner.

(A) The driver of any motor vehicle which is in any manner involved in a motor vehicle accident within six months of the accident may forward a written report of the accident to the registrar of motor vehicles on a form prescribed by the registrar alleging that a driver or owner of any other vehicle involved in the accident was uninsured at the time of the accident.

(B) Upon receipt of the accident report, the registrar shall send a notice by regular mail to the driver and owner alleged to be uninsured requiring the person to give evidence that the person had proof of financial responsibility in effect at the time of the accident.

(C) Within thirty days after the mailing of the notice by the registrar, the driver of the vehicle alleged to be uninsured shall forward a report together with acceptable proof of financial responsibility to the registrar in a form prescribed by the registrar. The forwarding of the report by the owner of the motor vehicle involved in the accident is deemed compliance with this section by the driver. This section does not change or modify the duties of the driver or operator of a motor vehicle as set forth in section 4549.02 of the Revised Code.

(D) In accordance with sections 4509.01 to 4509.78 of the Revised Code, the registrar shall suspend the license of any person who fails to give acceptable proof of financial responsibility as required in this section.

HISTORY: GC § 6298-17; 124 v 563; Bureau of Code Revision, 10-1-53; 133 v H 131 (Eff 7-25-69); 147 v H 210. Eff 3-31-97.

The effective date is set by section 20 of HB 210.

§ 4509.07 Contents of accident report.

The report prescribed by the registrar of motor vehicles shall request only information sufficient to enable the registrar to administer and enforce the provisions of sections 4509.01 to 4509.78, inclusive of the Revised Code.

The driver or owner of a motor vehicle involved in an accident shall furnish such additional relevant information as the registrar requires.

HISTORY: GC §§ 6298-18, 6298-19; 124 v 563; Bureau of Code Revision, 10-1-53; 125 v 383. Eff 10-15-53.

§ 4509.08 Exception to report requirement.

A driver involved in a motor vehicle accident is not subject to section 4509.06 of the Revised Code if, during the time provided in such section, the driver is physically incapable of making a report, but in such event, the owner, if he were not the driver of the motor vehicle involved in the accident, shall within thirty days after learning of the accident make the report.

HISTORY: GC § 6298-20; 124 v 563; Bureau of Code Revision, 10-1-53; 133 v H 131. Eff 7-25-69.

§ 4509.09 Repealed, 147 v H 210, § 2 [GC § 6298-21; 124 v 563; Bureau of Code Revision. Eff 10-1-53]. Eff 3-31-97.

This section concerned suspension for failing to file an amended report.

The effective date is set by § 20 of HB 210.

§ 4509.10 Use of report.

The accident reports submitted pursuant to sections 4509.01 to 4509.78 of the Revised Code, shall be without prejudice to the person reporting and shall be for the confidential use of the registrar of motor vehicles, except that the registrar shall furnish a copy of such report to any person claiming to have been injured or damaged in a motor vehicle accident, or to his attorney, upon the receipt of a fee of one dollar and fifty cents for each search or report.

Motor vehicle accident reports shall not be subject to subpoena or be used as evidence in any trial, civil or criminal, arising out of the accident, except that in order to prove compliance or failure to comply with the accident reporting requirement the registrar shall furnish, upon demand of a court or any person who claims to have made an accident report, a certificate stating that a specified accident report has or has not been made to the registrar.

HISTORY: GC § 6298-22; 124 v 563; Bureau of Code Revision, 10-1-53; 125 v 383 (Eff 10-15-53); 139 v H 102. Eff 7-1-81.

[§ 4509.10.1] § 4509.101 Operation of motor vehicle without proof of financial responsibility prohibited; compliance fund.

(A)(1) No person shall operate, or permit the operation of, a motor vehicle in this state, unless proof of financial responsibility is maintained continuously throughout the registration period with respect to that vehicle, or, in the case of a driver who is not the owner, with respect to that driver's operation of that vehicle.

(2) Whoever violates division (A)(1) of this section shall be subject to the following civil penalties:

(a) Suspension of the person's operating privileges and impoundment of the person's license until the person complies with division (A)(5) of this section. The suspension shall be for a period of not less than ninety days except that if, within five years of the violation, the person's operating privileges are again suspended and the person's license is impounded one or more times for a violation of division (A)(1) of this section, the suspension shall be for a period of not less than one year. Except as provided by section 4509.105 [4509.10.5] of the Revised Code, the suspension is not subject to revocation, suspension, or occupational or other limited operating privileges.

(b) In addition to the suspension of an owner's license under division (A)(2)(a) of this section, the suspension of the rights of the owner to register the motor vehicle and the impoundment of the owner's certificate of registration and license plates until the owner complies with division (A)(5) of this section.

(3) A person to whom this state has issued a certificate of registration for a motor vehicle or a license to operate a motor vehicle or who is determined to have operated any motor vehicle or permitted the operation in this state of a motor vehicle owned by the person shall be required to verify the existence of proof of financial responsibility covering the operation of the motor vehicle or the person's operation of the motor vehicle under any of the following circumstances:

(a) The person or a motor vehicle owned by the person is involved in a traffic accident that requires the filing of an accident report under section 4509.06 of the Revised Code.

(b) The person receives a traffic ticket indicating that proof of the maintenance of financial responsibility was not produced upon the request of a peace officer or state highway patrol trooper made in accordance with division (D)(2) of this section.

(c) Whenever, in accordance with rules adopted by the registrar, the person is randomly selected by the registrar and requested to provide such verification.

(4) An order of the registrar that suspends and impounds a license or registration, or both, shall state the date on or before which the person is required to surrender the person's license or certificate of registration and license plates. The person is deemed to have surrendered the license or certificate of registration and license plates, in compliance with the order, if the person does either of the following:

(a) On or before the date specified in the order, personally delivers the license or certificate of registration and license plates, or causes the delivery of the items, to the registrar;

(b) Mails the license or certificate of registration and license plates to the registrar in an envelope or container bearing a postmark showing a date no later than the date specified in the order.

(5) The registrar shall not restore any operating privileges or registration rights suspended under this section, return any license, certificate of registration, or license plates impounded under this section, or reissue license plates under section 4503.232 [4503.23.2] of the Revised Code, if the registrar destroyed the impounded license plates under that section, or reissue a license under section 4507.54 of the Revised Code, if the registrar destroyed the suspended license under that section, unless the rights are not subject to suspension or revocation under any other law and unless the person, in addition to complying with all other conditions required by law for reinstatement of the operating privileges or registration rights, complies with all of the following:

(a) Pays a financial responsibility reinstatement fee of seventy-five dollars for the first violation of division (A)(1) of this section, two hundred fifty dollars for a second violation of that division, and five hundred dollars for a third or subsequent violation of that division;

(b) If the person has not voluntarily surrendered the license, certificate, or license plates in compliance with the order, pays a financial responsibility nonvoluntary compliance fee in an amount, not to exceed fifty dollars, determined by the registrar;

(c) Files and continuously maintains proof of financial responsibility under sections 4509.44 to 4509.65 of the Revised Code.

(B)(1) Every party required to file an accident report under section 4509.06 of the Revised Code also shall include with the report a document described in division (G)(1) of this section.

If the registrar determines, within forty-five days after the report is filed, that an operator or owner has violated division (A)(1) of this section, the registrar shall do all of the following:

(a) Order the impoundment, with respect to the motor vehicle involved, required under division (A)(2)(b) of this section, of the certificate of registration and license plates of any owner who has violated division (A)(1) of this section;

(b) Order the suspension required under division (A)(2)(a) of this section of the license of any operator or owner who has violated division (A)(1) of this section;

(c) Record the name and address of the person whose certificate of registration and license plates have been impounded or are under an order of impoundment, or whose license has been suspended or is under an order of suspension; the serial number of the person's license; the serial numbers of the person's certificate of registration and license plates; and the person's social security account number, if assigned, or, where the motor vehicle is used for hire or principally in connection with any established business, the person's federal taxpayer identification number. The information shall be recorded in such a manner that it becomes a part of the person's permanent record, and assists the registrar in monitoring compliance with the orders of suspension or impoundment.

(d) Send written notification to every person to whom the order pertains, at the person's last known address as shown on the records of the bureau. The person, within ten days after the date of the mailing of the notification, shall surrender to the registrar, in a manner set forth in division (A)(4) of this section, any certificate of registration and registration plates under an order of impoundment, or any license under an order of suspension.

(2) The registrar shall issue any order under division

(B)(1) of this section without a hearing. Any person adversely affected by the order, within ten days after the issuance of the order, may request an administrative hearing before the registrar, who shall provide the person with an opportunity for a hearing in accordance with this paragraph. A request for a hearing does not operate as a suspension of the order. The scope of the hearing shall be limited to whether the person in fact demonstrated to the registrar proof of financial responsibility in accordance with this section. The registrar shall determine the date, time, and place of any hearing, provided that the hearing shall be held, and an order issued or findings made, within thirty days after the registrar receives a request for a hearing. If requested by the person in writing, the registrar may designate as the place of hearing the county seat of the county in which the person resides or a place within fifty miles of the person's residence. The person shall pay the cost of the hearing before the registrar, if the registrar's order of suspension or impoundment is upheld.

(C) Any order of suspension or impoundment issued under this section or division (B) of section 4509.37 of the Revised Code may be terminated at any time if the registrar determines upon a showing of proof of financial responsibility that the operator or owner of the motor vehicle was in compliance with division (A)(1) of this section at the time of the traffic offense, motor vehicle inspection, or accident that resulted in the order against the person. A determination may be made without a hearing. This division does not apply unless the person shows good cause for the person's failure to present satisfactory proof of financial responsibility to the registrar prior to the issuance of the order.

(D)(1) For the purpose of enforcing this section, every peace officer is deemed an agent of the registrar. Any peace officer who, in the performance of the peace officer's duties as authorized by law, becomes aware of a person whose license is under an order of suspension, or whose certificate of registration and license plates are under an order of impoundment, pursuant to this section, may confiscate the license, certificate of registration, and license plates, and return them to the registrar.

(2) A peace officer shall request the owner or operator of a motor vehicle to produce proof of financial responsibility in a manner described in division (G) of this section at the time the peace officer acts to enforce the traffic laws of this state and during motor vehicle inspections conducted pursuant to section 4513.02 of the Revised Code.

(3) A peace officer shall indicate on every traffic ticket whether the person receiving the traffic ticket produced proof of the maintenance of financial responsibility in response to the officer's request under division (D)(2) of this section. The peace officer shall inform every person who receives a traffic ticket and who has failed to produce proof of the maintenance of financial responsibility that the person must submit proof to the traffic violations bureau with any payment of a fine and costs for the ticketed violation or, if the person is to appear in court for the violation, the person must submit proof to the court.

(4)(a) If a person who has failed to produce proof of the maintenance of financial responsibility appears in court for a ticketed violation, the court may permit the defendant to present evidence of proof of financial responsibility to the court at such time and in such manner as the court determines to be necessary or appropriate. The clerk of courts shall provide the registrar with the identity of any person who fails to submit proof of the maintenance of financial responsibility pursuant to division (D)(3) of this section.

(b) If a person who has failed to produce proof of the maintenance of financial responsibility also fails to submit that proof to the traffic violations bureau with payment of a fine and costs for the ticketed violation, the traffic violations bureau shall notify the registrar of the identity of that person.

(5)(a) Upon receiving notice from a clerk of courts or traffic violations bureau pursuant to division (D)(4) of this section, the registrar shall order the suspension of the license of the person required under division (A)(2)(a) of this section and the impoundment of the person's certificate of registration and license plates required under division (A)(2)(b) of this section, effective thirty days after the date of the mailing of notification. The registrar also shall notify the person that the person must present the registrar with proof of financial responsibility in accordance with this section, surrender to the registrar the person's certificate of registration, license plates, and license, or submit a statement subject to section 2921.13 of the Revised Code that the person did not operate or permit the operation of the motor vehicle at the time of the offense. Notification shall be in writing and shall be sent to the person at the person's last known address as shown on the records of the bureau of motor vehicles. The person, within fifteen days after the date of the mailing of notification, shall present proof of financial responsibility, surrender the certificate of registration, license plates, and license to the registrar in a manner set forth in division (A)(4) of this section, or submit the statement required under this section together with other information the person considers appropriate.

If the registrar does not receive proof or the person does not surrender the certificate of registration, license plates, and license, in accordance with this division, the registrar shall permit the order for the suspension of the license of the person and the impoundment of the person's certificate of registration and license plates to take effect.

(b) In the case of a person who presents, within the fifteen-day period, documents to show proof of financial responsibility, the registrar shall terminate the order of suspension and the impoundment of the registration and license plates required under division (A)(2)(b) of this section and shall send written notification to the person, at the person's last known address as shown on the records of the bureau.

(c) Any person adversely affected by the order of the registrar under division (D)(5)(a) or (b) of this section, within ten days after the issuance of the order, may request an administrative hearing before the registrar, who shall provide the person with an opportunity for a hearing in accordance with this paragraph. A request for a hearing does not operate as a suspension of the order. The scope of the hearing shall be limited to whether the person in fact demonstrated to the registrar proof of financial responsibility in accordance with this section. The registrar shall determine the date, time, and place of any hearing; provided, that the hearing shall be held, and an order issued or findings made, within thirty days after the registrar receives a request for a hearing. If requested by the person in writing, the registrar may designate as the place of hearing the county seat of the county in which the person resides or a place within fifty miles of the person's residence. Such person shall pay the cost of the hearing before the registrar, if the registrar's order of suspension or impoundment under division (D)(5)(a) or (b) of this section is upheld.

(6) A peace officer may charge an owner or operator of a motor vehicle with a violation of division (B)(1) of section 4507.02 of the Revised Code when the owner or operator fails to show proof of the maintenance of financial responsibility pursuant to a peace officer's request under division (D)(2) of this section, if a check of the owner or operator's driving record indicates that the owner or operator, at the time of the operation of the motor vehicle, is required to file and maintain proof of financial responsibility under section 4509.45 of the Revised Code for a previous violation of this chapter.

(7) Any forms used by law enforcement agencies in administering this section shall be prescribed, supplied, and paid for by the registrar.

(8) No peace officer, law enforcement agency employing a peace officer, or political subdivision or governmental agency that employs a peace officer shall be liable in a civil action for damages or loss to persons arising out of the performance of any duty required or authorized by this section.

(9) As used in this division and divisions (E) and (G) of this section, "peace officer" has the meaning set forth in section 2935.01 of the Revised Code.

(E) All fees, except court costs, collected under this section shall be paid into the state treasury to the credit of the financial responsibility compliance fund. The financial responsibility compliance fund shall be used exclusively to cover costs incurred by the bureau in the administration of this section and sections 4503.20, 4507.212 [4507.21.2], and 4509.81 of the Revised Code, and by any law enforcement agency employing any peace officer who returns any license, certificate of registration, and license plates to the registrar pursuant to division (C) of this section, except that the director of budget and management may transfer excess money from the financial responsibility compliance fund to the state bureau of motor vehicles fund if the registrar determines that the amount of money in the financial responsibility compliance fund exceeds the amount required to cover such costs incurred by the bureau or a law enforcement agency and requests the director to make the transfer.

All investment earnings of the financial responsibility compliance fund shall be credited to the fund.

(F) Chapter 119. of the Revised Code applies to this section only to the extent that any provision in that chapter is not clearly inconsistent with this section.

(G)(1) The registrar, court, traffic violations bureau, or peace officer may require proof of financial responsibility to be demonstrated by use of a standard form prescribed by the registrar. If the use of a standard form is not required, a person may demonstrate proof of financial responsibility under this section by presenting to the traffic violations bureau, court, registrar, or peace officer any of the following documents or a copy of the documents:

(a) A financial responsibility identification card as provided in section 4509.104 [4509.10.4] of the Revised Code;

(b) A certificate of proof of financial responsibility on a form provided and approved by the registrar for the filing of an accident report required to be filed under section 4509.06 of the Revised Code;

(c) A policy of liability insurance, a declaration page of a policy of liability insurance, or liability bond, if the policy or bond complies with section 4509.20 or sections 4509.49 to 4509.61 of the Revised Code;

(d) A bond or certification of the issuance of a bond as provided in section 4509.59 of the Revised Code;

(e) A certificate of deposit of money or securities as provided in section 4509.62 of the Revised Code;

(f) A certificate of self-insurance as provided in section 4509.72 of the Revised Code.

(2) If a person fails to demonstrate proof of financial responsibility in a manner described in division (G)(1) of this section, the person may demonstrate proof of financial responsibility under this section by any other method that the court or the bureau, by reason of circumstances in a particular case, may consider appropriate.

(3) A motor carrier certificated by the interstate commerce commission or by the public utilities commission may demonstrate proof of financial responsibility by providing a statement designating the motor carrier's operating authority and averring that the insurance coverage required by the certificating authority is in full force and effect.

(4)(a) A finding by the registrar or court that a person is covered by proof of financial responsibility in the form of an insurance policy or surety bond is not binding upon the named insurer or surety or any of its officers, employees, agents, or representatives and has no legal effect except for the purpose of administering this section.

(b) The preparation and delivery of a financial responsibility identification card or any other document authorized to be used as proof of financial responsibility under this division does not do any of the following:

(i) Create any liability or estoppel against an insurer or surety, or any of its officers, employees, agents, or representatives;

(ii) Constitute an admission of the existence of, or of any liability or coverage under, any policy or bond;

(iii) Waive any defenses or counterclaims available to an insurer, surety, agent, employee, or representative in an action commenced by an insured or third-party claimant upon a cause of action alleged to have arisen under an insurance policy or surety bond or by reason of the preparation and delivery of a document for use as proof of financial responsibility.

(c) Whenever it is determined by a final judgment in a judicial proceeding that an insurer or surety, which has been named on a document accepted by a court or the registrar as proof of financial responsibility covering the operation of a motor vehicle at the time of an accident or offense, is not liable to pay a judgment for injuries or damages resulting from such operation, the registrar, notwithstanding any previous contrary finding, shall forthwith suspend the operating privileges and registration rights of the person against whom the judgment was rendered as provided in division (A)(2) of this section.

(H) In order for any document described in division (G)(1)(b) of this section to be used for the demonstration of proof of financial responsibility under this section, the document shall state the name of the insured or obligor, the name of the insurer or surety company, and the effective and expiration dates of the financial responsibility, and designate by explicit description or by appropriate reference all motor vehicles covered which may include a reference to fleet insurance coverage.

(I) For purposes of this section, "owner" does not include a licensed motor vehicle leasing dealer as defined in section 4517.01 of the Revised Code, but does include a motor vehicle renting dealer as defined in section 4549.65 of the Revised Code. Nothing in this section or in section 4509.51 of the Revised Code shall be construed to prohibit a motor vehicle renting dealer from entering into a contractual agreement with a person whereby the person renting the motor vehicle agrees to be solely responsible for maintaining proof of financial responsibility, in accordance with this section, with respect to the operation, maintenance, or use of the motor vehicle during the period of the motor vehicle's rental.

(J) The purpose of this section is to require the maintenance of proof of financial responsibility with respect to the operation of motor vehicles on the highways of this state, so as to minimize those situations in which persons are not compensated for injuries and damages sustained in motor vehicle accidents. The general assembly finds that this section contains reasonable civil penalties and procedures for achieving this purpose.

(K) Nothing in this section shall be construed to be subject to section 4509.78 of the Revised Code.

(L) The registrar shall adopt rules in accordance with Chapter 119. of the Revised Code that are necessary to administer and enforce this section. The rules shall include procedures for the surrender of license plates upon failure to maintain proof of financial responsibility and provisions relating to reinstatement of registration rights, acceptable forms of proof of financial responsibility, and verification of the existence of financial responsibility during the period of registration.

HISTORY: 139 v S 250 (Eff 1-1-84); 140 v H 767 (Eff 8-1-84); 141 v H 201 (Eff 7-1-85); 141 v S 269 (Eff 3-13-86); 142 v H 419 (Eff 7-1-87); 143 v H 422 (Eff 7-1-91); 144 v S 331 (Eff 11-13-92); 144 v S 275 (Eff 9-1-93); 145 v S 62, § 4 (Eff 9-1-93); 145 v H 687 (Eff 10-12-94); 145 v S 20 (Eff 4-20-95); 146 v H 107 (Eff 6-30-95); 146 v H 353 (Eff 9-17-96); 146 v H 438 (Eff 7-1-97); 147 v H 215 (Eff 6-30-97); 147 v H 261. Eff 9-3-97.

The provisions of § 3 of HB 261 (147 v —) read as follows:

SECTION 3. Section 4509.101 of the Revised Code is presented in this act as a composite of the section as amended by both Am. Sub. H.B. 353 and Am. Sub. H.B. 438 of the 121st General Assembly, with the new language of neither of the acts shown in capital letters. This is in recognition of the principle stated in division (B) of section 1.52 of the Revised Code that such amendments are to be harmonized where not substantively irreconcilable and constitutes a legislative finding that such is the resulting version in effect prior to the effective date of this act.

[§ 4509.10.2] § 4509.102 Falsification.

No person who has knowingly failed to maintain proof of financial responsibility in accordance with section 4509.101 [4509.10.1] of the Revised Code shall produce any document with the purpose to mislead a peace officer upon the request of a peace officer for proof of financial responsibility made in accordance with division (D)(2) of section 4509.101 [4509.10.1] of the Revised Code. Any person who violates this division is guilty of falsification under section 2921.13 of the Revised Code.

HISTORY: 145 v S 20 (Eff 4-20-95); 146 v H 438. Eff 7-1-97.

The effective date is set by section 3 of HB 438.

[§ 4509.10.3] § 4509.103 Insurer to provide identification cards.

(A) Each insurer writing motor vehicle liability insurance in this state shall provide financial responsibility identification cards to every policyholder in this state to whom it has delivered or issued for delivery a motor vehicle liability insurance policy. A minimum of one financial responsibility identification card shall be issued for every motor vehicle insured under a motor vehicle liability insurance policy.

(B) A financial responsibility identification card shall be valid only for the policy period. The card shall be in a form prescribed by the registrar of motor vehicles. It shall disclose the policy period and shall contain such other information as required by the registrar.

HISTORY: 145 v S 20. Eff 4-20-95†.

The effective date is set by section 6 of SB 20.

† See provisions, § 1 of HB 248 (146 v —) following RC § 4507.02, for later effective date of 10-20-95.

The provisions of § 3 of HB 248 (146 v —) read as follows:

SECTION 3. In amending Section 6 of Am. Sub. S.B. 20 of the 120th General Assembly, the General Assembly finds that the intent of section 4509.103 of the Revised Code, as affected by the amendment of Section 6 of Am. Sub. S.B. 20 by this act, is to ensure that the financial responsibility identification cards required under section 4509.103 of the Revised Code are delivered by October 20, 1995, to all policyholders of insurers writing motor vehicle liability insurance in this state.

[§ 4509.10.4] § 4509.104 Warning that policy does not meet minimum amounts.

Any automobile insurance policy that does not provide liability coverage at the time of issuance of at least the minimum amounts provided under division (K) of section 4509.01 of the Revised Code for proof of financial responsibility shall contain a clear and conspicuous warning on the face of the policy stating the policy does not constitute proof of financial responsibility as required for the operation of a motor vehicle under division (A)(1) of section 4509.101 [4509.10.1] of the Revised Code.

HISTORY: 145 v S 20. Eff 4-20-95.

The effective date is set by section 6 of SB 20.

See provisions, § 1 of HB 248 (146 v —) following RC § 4507.02.

[§ 4509.10.5] § 4509.105 Occupational driving privileges for first time violators.

(A) Any person whose operating privileges have been suspended for a violation of division (A)(1) of section 4509.101 [4509.10.1] of the Revised Code, which suspension seriously affects the person's ability to continue employment, may petition the registrar of motor vehicles for occupational driving privileges. The person seeking occupational driving privileges shall file proof of financial responsibility with the petition.

(B) Upon receiving a petition pursuant to division (A) of this section, the registrar shall grant the petitioner occupational driving privileges if the registrar determines all of the following:

(1) The petitioner has filed current proof of financial responsibility with the registrar;

(2) The petitioner has not previously had operating privileges suspended for a violation of division (A)(1) of section 4509.101 [4509.10.1] of the Revised Code;

(3) The petitioner has not had a license or commercial driver's license suspended within the previous five years for repeated traffic offenses pursuant to division (K) of section 4507.021 [4507.02.1] of the Revised Code;

(4) The petitioner has not been convicted of any criminal or traffic violation within the previous five years for which six points are assessed under the formula provided in division (G) of section 4507.021 [4507.02.1] of the Revised Code;

(5) The petitioner's license is not subject to suspension for any other reason;

(6) The petitioner has paid or secured all damages caused while driving without proof of financial responsibility;

(7) The petitioner has paid all applicable financial responsibility reinstatement fees or financial responsibility nonvoluntary compliance fees.

(C) The occupational driving privileges granted pursuant to division (B) of this section shall not be granted during the first thirty days of the petitioner's license suspension.

(D) If a person's license plates have been surrendered or impounded pursuant to section 4509.101 [4509.10.1] of the Revised Code, the registrar shall make replacement license plates available upon granting occupational driving privileges pursuant to division (B) of this section.

(E) A person granted occupational driving privileges pursuant to this section shall continuously maintain proof of financial responsibility with the registrar for a period of five years from the date of suspension of operating privileges by the registrar.

(F) The petition filed pursuant to division (A) of this section shall be in a form prescribed by the registrar.

HISTORY: 147 v H 261. Eff 9-3-97.

[USE OF REPORT OR FINDINGS AT TRIAL]

§ 4509.30 Accident report and findings of registrar prohibited at trial.

The report required following a motor vehicle accident, the action taken by the registrar of motor vehicles pursuant to sections 4509.11 to 4509.291 [4509.29.1], inclusive, of the Revised Code, the findings of the registrar upon which such action is based, and the security filed as provided in such sections, shall not be referred to in any way and shall not be evidence of the negligence or due care of either party at the trial of any action to recover damages.

HISTORY: GC § 6298-41; 124 v 563; Bureau of Code Revision, 10-1-53; 128 v 1221. Eff 7-1-60.

[SUSPENSION OF REGISTRATION AND LICENSE; JUDGMENT]

§ 4509.31 Suspension of license and registration upon conviction; plea of guilty; or forfeiture of bail or collateral.

(A) Whenever the registrar of motor vehicles receives notice from a court of record or mayor's court that a person has been convicted of, pleads guilty to, or forfeits any bail or collateral deposited to secure an appearance for trial for any of the crimes listed in section 4507.16 of the Revised Code, the registrar shall suspend the driver's or commercial driver's license or permit or nonresident operating privilege of the person and the registration of all motor vehicles registered in the name of the person as the owner, except that the registrar shall not suspend the driver's or commercial driver's license or permit or nonresident operating privilege, and registration unless otherwise required by law in the event the person has given or immediately gives and thereafter maintains, for a period of three years, proof of financial responsibility with respect to all the motor vehicles registered by the person as the owner.

(B) Except as provided in division (L) of section 4511.191 [4511.19.1] of the Revised Code, division (A) of this section does not apply to any person who is convicted of, or pleads guilty to, a violation of section 4511.19 of the Revised Code, of a municipal ordinance relating to operating a vehicle while under the influence of alcohol, a drug of abuse, or alcohol and a drug of abuse, or of a municipal ordinance relating to operating a vehicle with a prohibited concentration of alcohol in the blood, breath, or urine, if the offender previously has not been convicted of a violation of section 4511.19 of the Revised Code, of a municipal ordinance relating to operating a vehicle while under the influence of alcohol, a drug of abuse, or alcohol and a drug of abuse or with a prohibited concentration of alcohol in the blood, breath, or urine, or of a statute of the United States or of any other state or a municipal ordinance of a municipal corporation located in any other state that is substantially similar to division (A) or (B) of section 4511.19 of the Revised Code, and the offender did not cause serious physical harm to a person other than the offender.

HISTORY: GC § 6298-42; 124 v 563; Bureau of Code Revision, 10-1-53; 125 v 381; 128 v 1221 (Eff 7-1-60); 133 v H 236 (Eff 10-22-69); 139 v S 432 (Eff 3-16-83); 141 v S 262 (Eff 3-20-87); 142 v H 303 (Eff 10-20-87); 143 v H 381 (Eff 7-1-89); 144 v S 275 (Eff 9-1-93); 145 v S 62, § 4 (Eff 9-1-93); 146 v H 353 (Eff 9-17-96); 147 v S 60. Eff 10-21-97.

§ 4509.32 Registration or license withheld.

If a person has no license but by final order or judgment of a court of record or mayor's court is convicted of, or forfeits any bail or collateral deposited to secure an appearance for trial for, any offense authorizing the revocation of license under section 4507.16 of the Revised Code, or for driving a motor vehicle upon the highways without being licensed to do so, or for driving an unregistered motor vehicle upon the highways, no motor vehicle shall continue to be registered or thereafter be registered in the name of the person as owner unless he gives and thereafter maintains proof of financial responsibility in accordance with section 4509.45 of the Revised Code; if the offense was an offense authorizing the revocation of license, no license shall be thereafter issued to such person for a period of two years following such conviction or bail forfeiture and not thereafter until the person gives and thereafter maintains proof of financial responsibility in accordance with section 4509.45 of the Revised Code.

HISTORY: GC § 6298-44; 124 v 563; Bureau of Code Revision, 10-1-53; 128 v 1221 (Eff 7-1-60); 131 v 1089 (Eff 11-4-65); 142 v H 303. Eff 10-20-87.

§ 4509.33 Suspension or revocation of nonresidents' operating privilege and registration.

If a nonresident by final order or judgment of a court of record or mayor's court is convicted of, or forfeits bail or collateral deposited to secure an appearance for trial for, any offense enumerated in section 4507.16 of the Revised Code, the registrar of motor vehicles shall suspend or revoke the privilege of the nonresident to operate a motor vehicle for the same period for which suspension or revocation of license by a court of record is authorized by section 4507.16 of the Revised Code. The suspension or revocation shall remain in effect until the expiration of the period so ordered and thereafter until the nonresident gives and thereafter maintains proof of financial responsibility in accordance with section 4509.45 of the Revised Code.

The registrar shall also suspend the privilege of the use in this state of every motor vehicle owned by the nonresident, except that the registrar shall not suspend the privilege if the owner has given or immediately gives and thereafter maintains proof of financial responsibility with respect to all motor vehicles owned by the nonresident. The registrar shall restore such privilege of a nonresident owner when the owner gives and thereafter maintains proof of financial responsibility in accordance with section 4509.45 of the Revised Code.

HISTORY: GC § 6298-45; 124 v 563; Bureau of Code Revision, 10-1-53; 128 v 1221 (Eff 7-1-60); 131 v 1090 (Eff 10-30-65); 142 v H 303. Eff 10-20-87.

§ 4509.34 Period of suspension or revocation.

(A) The suspension or revocation of a license referred to in sections 4509.291 [4509.29.1] and 4509.31 of the Revised Code shall remain in effect and the registrar of motor vehicles shall not issue to any person whose license is so suspended or revoked any new or renewal license until permitted under the motor vehicle laws, and not then until such person gives and thereafter maintains proof of financial responsibility in accordance with section 4509.45 of the Revised Code.

(B) The suspension of registration referred to in such sections shall remain in effect and the registrar shall not register or reregister in the name of any person whose registration is so suspended as owner of any motor vehicle, nor return or re-issue license plates for such vehicle, until such person gives and thereafter maintains proof of financial responsibility in accordance with section 4509.45 of the Revised Code.

HISTORY: GC § 6298-43; 124 v 563; Bureau of Code Revision, 10-1-53; 128 v 1221 (Eff 7-1-60); 131 v 1090. Eff 10-30-65.

[PROOF OF FINANCIAL RESPONSIBILITY]

§ 4509.44 Proof of financial responsibility required for registration.

No motor vehicle shall be or continue to be registered in the name of any person required to file proof of financial responsibility unless such proof is furnished and maintained in accordance with section 4509.45 of the Revised Code.

HISTORY: GC § 6298-58; 124 v 563(577); Bureau of Code Revision, 10-1-53; 131 v 1093. Eff 10-30-65.

§ 4509.45 Proof of financial responsibility.

Proof of financial responsibility when required under section 4507.022 [4507.02.2], 4509.101 [4509.10.1], 4509.32, 4509.33, 4509.34, 4509.38, 4509.40, 4509.42, or 4509.44 of the Revised Code may be given by filing any of the following:

(A) A financial responsibility identification card as provided in section 4509.104 [4509.10.4] of the Revised Code;

(B) A certificate of insurance as provided in section 4509.46 or 4509.47 of the Revised Code;

(C) A bond as provided in section 4509.59 of the Revised Code;

(D) A certificate of deposit of money or securities as provided in section 4509.62 of the Revised Code;

(E) A certificate of self-insurance, as provided in section 4509.72 of the Revised Code, supplemented by an agreement by the self-insurer that, with respect to accidents occurring while the certificate is in force, he will pay the same amounts that an insurer would have been obligated to pay under an owner's motor vehicle liability policy if it had issued such a policy to the self-insurer.

Such proof shall be filed and maintained for five years from the date of suspension of operating privileges by the registrar of motor vehicles.

HISTORY: GC § 6298-59; 124 v 563(577); Bureau of Code Revision, 10-1-53; 131 v 1093 (Eff 10-30-65); 139 v S 250 (Eff 1-1-84); 141 v S 356 (Eff 9-24-86); 145 v S 20. Eff 4-20-95.

The effective date is set by section 6 of SB 20.

§ 4509.74 Prohibition against failure to report accident.

No person shall fail to report a motor vehicle accident as required under the laws of this state.

HISTORY: GC § 6298-85; 124 v 563(583); Bureau of Code Revision. Eff 10-1-53.

§ 4509.75 Repealed, 146 v S 2, § 6 [GC § 6298-86; 124 v 563 (583); Bureau of Code Revisions, 10-1-53]. Eff 7-1-96.

This section prohibited giving false information concerning motor vehicle accidents.

§ 4509.77 Prohibition against failure to return license.

No person shall willfully fail to return a license or registration as required in section 4509.69 of the Revised Code.

HISTORY: GC § 6298-88; 124 v 563(584); Bureau of Code Revision. Eff 10-1-53.

§ 4509.78 General prohibition.

No person shall violate sections 4509.01 to 4509.78, inclusive, of the Revised Code for which no penalty is otherwise provided.

HISTORY: GC § 6298-89; 124 v 563(584); Bureau of Code Revision. Eff 10-1-53.

§ 4509.79 Liability insurance for motor vehicles used in a ridesharing arrangement.

(A) As used in this section, "ridesharing arrangement" means the transportation of persons in a motor vehicle where such transportation is incidental to another purpose of a volunteer driver and includes ridesharing arrangements known as carpools, vanpools, and buspools.

(B) Every owner registering as a passenger car a motor vehicle designed and used for carrying more than nine but not more than fifteen passengers or registering a bus under division (H)(8) of section 4503.04 of the Revised Code shall have in effect, whenever the motor vehicle is used in a ridesharing arrangement, a policy of liability insurance with respect to the motor vehicle in amounts and coverage no less than:

(1) One hundred thousand dollars because of bodily injury to or death of one person in any one accident;

(2) Three hundred thousand dollars because of bodily injury to or death of two or more persons in any one accident;

(3) Fifty thousand dollars because of injury to property of others in any one accident.

HISTORY: 139 v H 53 (Eff 7-1-82); 139 v S 331. Eff 5-21-82.

§ 4509.80 Requirements for chauffeured limousines.

(A) Every owner registering a chauffeured limousine shall furnish and maintain proof of financial responsibility with respect to the limousine by filing with the registrar of motor vehicles any of the following:

(1) A certificate of insurance as provided in section 4509.46 or 4509.47 of the Revised Code;

(2) A policy of liability insurance, a declaration page of a policy of liability insurance, or liability bond, if the policy or bond provides coverage in accordance with division (B) of this section and otherwise complies with sections 4509.49 to 4509.61 of the Revised Code, and if the policy or bond provides that such policy or bond shall not be canceled or terminated prior to not less than ten days after a written notice of cancellation or termination is filed with the registrar;

(3) A bond or certification of the issuance of a bond if the bond provides coverage in the amount of three hundred thousand dollars and otherwise complies with section 4509.59 of the Revised Code;

(4) A certificate of deposit of money or securities if the certificate of deposit provides coverage in the amount of three hundred thousand dollars and otherwise complies with section 4509.62 of the Revised Code;

(5) A certificate of self-insurance as provided in section 4509.72 of the Revised Code.

(B) As used in this section and section 4509.81 of the Revised Code, "proof of financial responsibility" means proof of ability to respond in damages for liability, on account of accidents occurring subsequent to the effective date of such proof, arising out of the ownership, maintenance, or use of a chauffeured limousine in the amount of one hundred thousand dollars because of bodily injury to or death of one person in any one accident, three hundred thousand dollars because of bodily injury to or death of two or more persons in any one accident, and fifty thousand dollars because of injury to property of others in any one accident.

(C) Upon the request of a law enforcement officer, the operator of any chauffeured limousine shall produce proof of compliance with this section. The law enforcement officer requesting such proof shall notify the registrar of any violation of this section. The notice to the registrar shall be on a form prescribed by the registrar and supplied by the registrar at the registrar's expense, and shall include the license plate number of the chauffeured limousine and any other information the registrar requires.

(D) The owner, or his designee, shall provide written notice to the registrar of cancellation or termination of the coverage required by this section not less than ten days prior to the effective date of cancellation, and, on or before the effective date of cancellation, shall voluntarily surrender the livery license plate sticker for the vehicle or vehicles for which the cancellation is effective. If the livery license plate sticker is timely and voluntarily surrendered, the registrar shall, upon the filing of proof of financial responsibility as required by this section, reinstate the livery registration of the vehicle and issue a current livery license plate sticker for the vehicle.

HISTORY: 143 v H 422. Eff 7-1-91.

The effective date is set by section 3 of HB 422.

§ 4509.81 Suspension of rights of owner of chauffeured limousine; impoundment.

(A) Upon receipt of a notification of violation as provided in division (C) of section 4509.80 of the Revised Code; upon failure of a timely surrender of the livery license plate sticker as required by division (D) of section 4509.80 of the Revised Code; or if the registrar of motor vehicles, upon receipt of notification from an insurer of the imminent cancellation or termination of coverage required by section 4509.80 of the Revised Code, fails to receive evidence of a continuation or substitution of coverage prior to the cancellation or termination date, the registrar shall order the immediate suspension of the rights of the owner of the chauffeured limousine described in the notice to register the limousine and the impoundment of the certificate of registration and registration plates for the limousine. The registrar shall notify the owner that the owner must surrender the certificate of registration and registration plates to the registrar. The notification shall be in writing and sent to the owner at the owner's last known address as shown in the records of the bureau of motor vehicles. Proceedings under this section are deemed special, summary statutory proceedings.

(B) The order of suspension and impoundment of a registration shall state the date on or before which the owner of the chauffeured limousine involved is required to surrender the certificate of registration and registration plates to the registrar. The owner shall be deemed to have surrendered the certificate of registration and registration plates if the owner causes the items to be delivered to the registrar on or before the date specified in the order or mails the items to the registrar in an envelope or container bearing a postmark showing a date no later than the date specified in the order.

(C) The registrar shall not restore any registration rights suspended under this section, return any certificate of registration or registration plates impounded under this section, or reissue registration plates under section 4503.232 [4503.23.2] of the Revised Code, if the registrar destroyed the impounded registration plates under that section, unless those rights are not subject to suspension or revocation under any other law and unless the owner complies with both of the following:

(1) Pays a financial responsibility reinstatement fee of thirty dollars. The reinstatement fee may be increased, upon approval of the controlling board, up to an amount not exceeding fifty dollars.

(2) Files and maintains proof of financial responsibility under section 4509.80 of the Revised Code.

(D) Any owner adversely affected by the order of the registrar under this section may, within ten days after the issuance of the order, request an administrative hearing before the registrar, who shall provide the owner with an opportunity for a hearing in accordance with this division. A request for a hearing does not operate as a suspension of the order unless the owner establishes to the satisfaction of the registrar that the operation of the owner's chauffeured limousine will be covered by proof of financial responsibility during the pendency of the appeal. The scope of the hearing shall be limited to whether the owner in fact demonstrated to the registrar proof of financial responsibility in accordance with section 4509.80 of the Revised Code. The registrar shall determine the date, time, and place of any hearing, provided that the hearing shall be held and an order issued or findings made within thirty days after the registrar receives a request for a hearing. If requested by the owner in writing, the registrar may designate as the place of hearing the county seat of the county in which the owner resides or a place within fifty miles of the owner's residence. The owner shall pay the cost of the hearing before the registrar, if the registrar's order of suspension or impoundment is upheld.

(E) Any order of suspension or impoundment issued under this section may be terminated at any time if the registrar determines upon a showing of proof of financial responsibility that the owner of the limousine was in compliance with section 4509.80 of the Revised Code at the time of the incident that resulted in the order against the owner. Such a determination may be made without a hearing.

(F) All fees collected under this section shall be paid into the state treasury to the credit of the financial responsibility compliance fund created by section 4509.101 [4509.10.1] of the Revised Code.

(G) Chapter 119. of the Revised Code applies to this section only to the extent that any provision in that chapter is not clearly inconsistent with this section.

(H)(1) Proof of financial responsibility may be demonstrated by any of the methods authorized in section 4509.80 of the Revised Code.

(2) Divisions (G)(4)(a) and (b) of section 4509.101 [4509.10.1] of the Revised Code apply to any finding by the registrar under this section that an owner is covered by proof of financial responsibility.

HISTORY: 143 v H 422 (Eff 7-1-91); 144 v S 331 (Eff 11-13-92); 144 v S 275 (Eff 9-1-93); 145 v S 62, § 4 (Eff 9-1-93); 145 v H 687 (Eff 10-12-94); 146 v H 438. Eff 7-1-97.

The effective date is set by section 3 of HB 438.

§ 4509.99 Penalties.

(A) Whoever violates section 4509.74 of the Revised Code shall be fined not more than one hundred dollars.

(B) Whoever violates section 4509.77 of the Revised Code shall be fined not more than five hundred dollars, imprisoned not more than thirty days, or both.

(C) Whoever violates section 4509.78 of the Revised Code shall be fined not more than five hundred dollars, imprisoned not more than ninety days, or both.

(D) Whoever violates section 4509.79 of the Revised Code shall be fined not more than five thousand dollars.

(E) Whoever violates section 4509.80 of the Revised Code is guilty of a misdemeanor of the first degree.

HISTORY: Bureau of Code Revision, 10-1-53; 139 v H 53 (Eff 7-1-82); 141 v S 356 (Eff 9-24-86); 143 v H 422 (Eff 7-1-91); 146 v S 2. Eff 7-1-96.

The effective date is set by section 6 of SB 2.

CHAPTER 4511: TRAFFIC LAWS—OPERATION OF MOTOR VEHICLES

§ 4511.01 Definitions.

As used in this chapter and in Chapter 4513. of the Revised Code:

(A) "Vehicle" means every device, including a motorized bicycle, in, upon, or by which any person or property may be transported or drawn upon a highway, except motorized wheelchairs, devices moved by power collected from overhead electric trolley wires, or used exclusively upon stationary rails or tracks, and devices other than bicycles moved by human power.

(B) "Motor vehicle" means every vehicle propelled or drawn by power other than muscular power or power collected from overhead electric trolley wires, except motorized bicycles, road rollers, traction engines, power shovels, power cranes, and other equipment used in construction work and not designed for or employed in general highway transportation, hole-digging machinery, well-drilling machinery, ditch-digging machinery, farm machinery, trailers used to transport agricultural produce or agricultural production materials between a local place of storage or supply and the farm when drawn or towed on a street or highway at a speed of twenty-five miles per hour or less, threshing machinery, hay-baling machinery, agricultural tractors and machinery used in the production of horticultural, floricultural, agricultural, and vegetable products, and trailers designed and used exclusively to transport a boat between a place of storage and a marina, or in and around a marina, when drawn or towed on a street or highway for a distance of no more than ten miles and at a speed of twenty-five miles per hour or less.

(C) "Motorcycle" means every motor vehicle, other than a tractor, having a saddle for the use of the operator and designed to travel on not more than three wheels in contact with the ground, including, but not limited to, motor vehicles known as "motor-driven cycle," "motor scooter," or "motorcycle" without regard to weight or brake horsepower.

(D) "Emergency vehicle" means emergency vehicles of municipal, township, or county departments or public utility corporations when identified as such as required by law, the director of public safety, or local authorities, and motor vehicles when commandeered by a police officer.

(E) "Public safety vehicle" means any of the following:

(1) Ambulances, including private ambulance companies under contract to a municipal corporation, township, or county, and private ambulances and nontransport vehicles bearing license plates issued under section 4503.49 of the Revised Code;

(2) Motor vehicles used by public law enforcement officers or other persons sworn to enforce the criminal and traffic laws of the state;

(3) Any motor vehicle when properly identified as required by the director of public safety, when used in response to fire emergency calls or to provide emergency medical service to ill or injured persons, and when operated by a duly qualified person who is a member of a volunteer rescue service or a volunteer fire department, and who is on duty pursuant to the rules or directives of that service. The state fire marshal shall be designated by the director of public safety as the certifying agency for all public safety vehicles described in division (E)(3) of this section.

(4) Vehicles used by fire departments, including motor vehicles when used by volunteer fire fighters responding to emergency calls in the fire department service when identified as required by the director of public safety.

Any vehicle used to transport or provide emergency medical service to an ill or injured person, when certified as a public safety vehicle, shall be considered a public safety vehicle when transporting an ill or injured person to a hospital regardless of whether such vehicle has already passed a hospital.

(5) Vehicles used by the commercial motor vehicle safety enforcement unit for the enforcement of orders and rules of the public utilities commission as specified in section 5503.34 of the Revised Code.

(F) "School bus" means every bus designed for carrying more than nine passengers which is owned by a public, private, or governmental agency or institution of learning and operated for the transportation of children to or from a school session or a school function, or owned by a private person and operated for compensation for the transportation of children to or from a school session or a school function, provided "school bus" does not include a bus operated by a municipally owned transportation system, a mass transit company operating exclusively within the territorial limits of a municipal corporation, or within such limits and the territorial limits of municipal corporations immediately contiguous to such municipal corporation, nor a common passenger carrier certified by the public utilities commission unless such bus is devoted exclusively to the transportation of children to and from a school session or a school function, and "school bus" does not include a van or bus used by a licensed child day-care center or type A family day-care home to transport children from the child day-care center or type A family day-care home to a school if the van or bus does not have more than fifteen children in the van or bus at any time.

(G) "Bicycle" means every device, other than a tricycle designed solely for use as a play vehicle by a child, propelled solely by human power upon which any person may ride having either two tandem wheels, or one wheel in the front and two wheels in the rear, any of which is more than fourteen inches in diameter.

(H) "Motorized bicycle" means any vehicle having either two tandem wheels or one wheel in the front and two wheels in the rear, that is capable of being pedaled and is equipped with a helper motor of not more than fifty cubic centimeters piston displacement which produces no more than one brake horsepower and is capable of propelling the vehicle at a speed of no greater than twenty miles per hour on a level surface.

(I) "Commercial tractor" means every motor vehicle having motive power designed or used for drawing other vehicles and not so constructed as to carry any load thereon, or designed or used for drawing other vehicles while carrying a portion of such other vehicles, or load thereon, or both.

(J) "Agricultural tractor" means every self-propelling vehicle designed or used for drawing other vehicles or wheeled machinery but having no provision for carrying loads independently of such other vehicles, and used principally for agricultural purposes.

(K) "Truck" means every motor vehicle, except trailers and semitrailers, designed and used to carry property.

(L) "Bus" means every motor vehicle designed for carrying more than nine passengers and used for the transportation of persons other than in a ridesharing arrangement, and every motor vehicle, automobile for hire, or funeral car, other than a taxicab or motor vehicle used in a ridesharing arrangement, designed and used for the transportation of persons for compensation.

(M) "Trailer" means every vehicle designed or used for carrying persons or property wholly on its own structure and for being drawn by a motor vehicle, including any such vehicle when formed by or operated as a combination of a "semitrailer" and a vehicle of the dolly type, such as that commonly known as a "trailer dolly," a vehicle used to transport agricultural produce or agricultural production materials between a local place of storage or supply and the farm when drawn or towed on a street or highway at a speed greater than twenty-five miles per hour, and a vehicle designed and used exclusively to transport a boat between a place of storage and a marina, or in and around a marina, when drawn or towed on a street or highway for a distance of more than ten miles or at a speed of more than twenty-five miles per hour.

(N) "Semitrailer" means every vehicle designed or used for carrying persons or property with another and separate motor vehicle so that in operation a part of its own weight or that of its load, or both, rests upon and is carried by another vehicle.

(O) "Pole trailer" means every trailer or semitrailer attached to the towing vehicle by means of a reach, pole, or by being boomed or otherwise secured to the towing vehicle, and ordinarily used for transporting long or irregular shaped loads such as poles, pipes, or structural members capable, generally, of sustaining themselves as beams between the supporting connections.

(P) "Railroad" means a carrier of persons or property operating upon rails placed principally on a private right-of-way.

(Q) "Railroad train" means a steam engine or an electric or other motor, with or without cars coupled thereto, operated by a railroad.

(R) "Streetcar" means a car, other than a railroad train, for transporting persons or property, operated upon rails principally within a street or highway.

(S) "Trackless trolley" means every car that collects its power from overhead electric trolley wires and that is not operated upon rails or tracks.

(T) "Explosives" means any chemical compound or mechanical mixture that is intended for the purpose of producing an explosion that contains any oxidizing and combustible units or other ingredients in such proportions, quantities, or packing that an ignition by fire, by friction, by concussion, by percussion, or by a detonator of any part of the compound or mixture may cause such a sudden generation of highly heated gases that the resultant gaseous pressures are capable of producing destructive effects on contiguous objects, or of destroying life or limb. Manufactured articles shall not be held to be explosives when the individual units contain explosives in such limited quantities, of such nature, or in such packing, that it is impossible to procure a simultaneous or a destructive explosion of such units, to the injury of life, limb, or property by fire, by friction, by concussion, by percussion, or by a detonator, such as fixed ammunition for small arms, firecrackers, or safety fuse matches.

(U) "Flammable liquid" means any liquid which has a flash point of seventy degrees Fahrenheit, or less, as determined by a tagliabue or equivalent closed cup test device.

(V) "Gross weight" means the weight of a vehicle plus the weight of any load thereon.

(W) "Person" means every natural person, firm, co-partnership, association, or corporation.

(X) "Pedestrian" means any natural person afoot.

(Y) "Driver or operator" means every person who drives or is in actual physical control of a vehicle, trackless trolley, or streetcar.

(Z) "Police officer" means every officer authorized to direct or regulate traffic, or to make arrests for violations of traffic regulations.

(AA) "Local authorities" means every county, municipal, and other local board or body having authority to adopt police regulations under the constitution and laws of this state.

(BB) "Street" or "highway" means the entire width between the boundary lines of every way open to the use of the public as a thoroughfare for purposes of vehicular travel.

(CC) "Controlled-access highway" means every street or highway in respect to which owners or occupants of abutting lands and other persons have no legal right of access to or from the same except at such points only and in such manner as may be determined by the public authority having jurisdiction over such street or highway.

(DD) "Private road or driveway" means every way or place in private ownership used for vehicular travel by the owner and those having express or implied permission from the owner but not by other persons.

(EE) "Roadway" means that portion of a highway improved, designed, or ordinarily used for vehicular travel, except the berm or shoulder. If a highway includes two or more separate roadways the term "roadway" means any such roadway separately but not all such roadways collectively.

(FF) "Sidewalk" means that portion of a street between the curb lines, or the lateral lines of a roadway, and the adjacent property lines, intended for the use of pedestrians.

(GG) "Laned highway" means a highway the roadway of which is divided into two or more clearly marked lanes for vehicular traffic.

(HH) "Through highway" means every street or highway as provided in section 4511.65 of the Revised Code.

(II) "State highway" means a highway under the jurisdiction of the department of transportation, outside the limits of municipal corporations, provided that the authority conferred upon the director of transportation in section 5511.01 of the Revised Code to erect state highway route markers and signs directing traffic shall not be modified by sections 4511.01 to 4511.79 and 4511.99 of the Revised Code.

(JJ) "State route" means every highway which is designated with an official state route number and so marked.

(KK) "Intersection" means:

(1) The area embraced within the prolongation or connection of the lateral curb lines, or, if none, then the lateral boundary lines of the roadways of two highways which join one another at, or approximately at, right angles, or the area within which vehicles traveling upon different highways joining at any other angle may come in conflict.

(2) Where a highway includes two roadways thirty feet or more apart, then every crossing of each roadway of such divided highway by an intersecting highway shall be regarded as a separate intersection. If an intersecting highway also includes two roadways thirty feet or more apart, then every crossing of two roadways of such highways shall be regarded as a separate intersection.

(3) The junction of an alley with a street or highway, or with another alley, shall not constitute an intersection.

(LL) "Crosswalk" means:

(1) That part of a roadway at intersections ordinarily included within the real or projected prolongation of property lines and curb lines or, in the absence of curbs, the edges of the traversable roadway;

(2) Any portion of a roadway at an intersection or elsewhere, distinctly indicated for pedestrian crossing by lines or other markings on the surface;

(3) Notwithstanding divisions (LL)(1) and (2) of this section, there shall not be a crosswalk where local authorities have placed signs indicating no crossing.

(MM) "Safety zone" means the area or space officially set apart within a roadway for the exclusive use of pedestrians and protected or marked or indicated by adequate signs as to be plainly visible at all times.

(NN) "Business district" means the territory fronting upon a street or highway, including the street or highway, between successive intersections within municipal corporations where fifty per cent or more of the frontage between such successive intersections is occupied by buildings in use for business, or within or outside municipal corporations where fifty per cent or more of the frontage for a distance of three hundred feet or more is occupied by buildings in use for business, and the character of such territory is indicated by official traffic control devices.

(OO) "Residence district" means the territory, not comprising a business district, fronting on a street or highway, including the street or highway, where, for a distance of three hundred feet or more, the frontage is improved with residences or residences and buildings in use for business.

(PP) "Urban district" means the territory contiguous to and including any street or highway which is built up with structures devoted to business, industry, or dwelling houses situated at intervals of less than one hundred feet for a distance of a quarter of a mile or more, and the character of such territory is indicated by official traffic control devices.

(QQ) "Traffic control devices" means all flaggers, signs, signals, markings, and devices placed or erected by authority of a public body or official having jurisdiction, for the purpose of regulating, warning, or guiding traffic, including signs denoting names of streets and highways.

(RR) "Traffic control signal" means any device, whether manually, electrically, or mechanically operated, by which traffic is alternately directed to stop, to proceed, to change direction, or not to change direction.

(SS) "Railroad sign or signal" means any sign, signal, or device erected by authority of a public body or official or by a railroad and intended to give notice of the presence of railroad tracks or the approach of a railroad train.

(TT) "Traffic" means pedestrians, ridden or herded animals, vehicles, streetcars, trackless trolleys, and other devices, either singly or together, while using any highway for purposes of travel.

(UU) "Right-of-way" means either of the following, as the context requires:

(1) The right of a vehicle, streetcar, trackless trolley, or pedestrian to proceed uninterruptedly in a lawful manner in the direction in which it or the individual is moving in preference to another vehicle, streetcar, trackless trolley, or pedestrian approaching from a different direction into its or the individual's path;

(2) A general term denoting land, property, or the interest therein, usually in the configuration of a strip,

acquired for or devoted to transportation purposes. When used in this context, right-of-way includes the roadway, shoulders or berm, ditch, and slopes extending to the right-of-way limits under the control of the state or local authority.

(VV) "Rural mail delivery vehicle" means every vehicle used to deliver United States mail on a rural mail delivery route.

(WW) "Funeral escort vehicle" means any motor vehicle, including a funeral hearse, while used to facilitate the movement of a funeral procession.

(XX) "Alley" means a street or highway intended to provide access to the rear or side of lots or buildings in urban districts and not intended for the purpose of through vehicular traffic, and includes any street or highway that has been declared an "alley" by the legislative authority of the municipal corporation in which such street or highway is located.

(YY) "Freeway" means a divided multi-lane highway for through traffic with all crossroads separated in grade and with full control of access.

(ZZ) "Expressway" means a divided arterial highway for through traffic with full or partial control of access with an excess of fifty per cent of all crossroads separated in grade.

(AAA) "Thruway" means a through highway whose entire roadway is reserved for through traffic and on which roadway parking is prohibited.

(BBB) "Stop intersection" means any intersection at one or more entrances of which stop signs are erected.

(CCC) "Arterial street" means any United States or state numbered route, controlled access highway, or other major radial or circumferential street or highway designated by local authorities within their respective jurisdictions as part of a major arterial system of streets or highways.

(DDD) "Ridesharing arrangement" means the transportation of persons in a motor vehicle where such transportation is incidental to another purpose of a volunteer driver and includes ridesharing arrangements known as carpools, vanpools, and buspools.

(EEE) "Motorized wheelchair" means any self-propelled vehicle designed for, and used by, a handicapped person and that is incapable of a speed in excess of eight miles per hour.

(FFF) "Child day-care center" and "type A family day-care home" have the same meanings as in section 5104.01 of the Revised Code.

HISTORY: GC § 6307-2; 119 v 766, § 2; 120 v 221; 124 v 514; Bureau of Code Revision, 10-1-53; 126 v 392(408) (Eff 3-17-55); 126 v 790 (Eff 9-14-55); 126 v 115 (Eff 10-1-56); 127 v 54 (Eff 8-27-57); 128 v 1270 (Eff 11-4-59); 129 v 1273 (Eff 10-26-61); 130 v 1068 (Eff 8-5-63); 130 v 1074 (Eff 10-10-63); 131 v 1094 (Eff 10-15-65); 132 v H 634 (Eff 11-24-67); 132 v H 380 (Eff 1-1-68); 132 v H 878 (Eff 12-14-67); 132 v S 451 (Eff 2-29-68); 135 v H 200 (Eff 9-23-73); 135 v S 108 (Eff 11-21-73); 135 v H 995 (Eff 1-1-75); 136 v H 338 (Eff 1-9-76); 136 v S 56 (Eff 5-25-76); 136 v H 235 (Eff 10-1-76); 137 v S 100 (Eff 4-1-78); 138 v S 9 (Eff 6-20-79); 139 v H 53 (Eff 7-1-82); 143 v H 258 (Eff 11-2-89); 143 v H 319 (Eff 7-2-90); 143 v S 272 (Eff 11-28-90); 143 v S 382 (Eff 12-31-90); 144 v H 485 (Eff 10-7-92); 144 v S 98 (Eff 11-12-92); 144 v H 356 (Eff 12-31-92); 146 v S 293. Eff 9-26-96.

[§ 4511.01.1] § 4511.011 Designation of freeway, expressway, and thruway.

The director of transportation, the board of county commissioners of a county, and the legislative authority of a municipality may, for highways under their jurisdiction, designate an existing highway in whole or in part as or included in a "freeway," "expressway," or "thruway."

HISTORY: 130 v 1080 (Eff 8-5-63); 135 v H 200. Eff 9-28-73.

§ 4511.03 Emergency vehicles to proceed cautiously past red or stop signal.

The driver of any emergency vehicle or public safety vehicle, when responding to an emergency call, upon approaching a red or stop signal or any stop sign shall slow down as necessary for safety to traffic, but may proceed cautiously past such red or stop sign or signal with due regard for the safety of all persons using the street or highway.

HISTORY: GC § 6307-4; 119 v 766, § 4; Bureau of Code Revision, 10-1-53; 132 v H 378. Eff 12-14-67.

§ 4511.04 Exceptions.

Sections 4511.01 to 4511.78, inclusive, section 4511.99, and sections 4513.01 to 4513.37, inclusive, of the Revised Code do not apply to persons, teams, motor vehicles, and other equipment while actually engaged in work upon the surface of a highway within an area designated by traffic control devices, but apply to such persons and vehicles when traveling to or from such work.

The drivers of snow plows, traffic line stripers, road sweepers, mowing machines, tar distributing vehicles, and other vehicles utilized in snow and ice removal or road surface maintenance, while engaged in work upon a highway, provided such vehicles are equipped with flashing lights and such other markings as are required by law, and such lights are in operation when the vehicles are so engaged shall be exempt from criminal prosecution for violations of sections 4511.22, 4511.25, 4511.26, 4511.27, 4511.28, 4511.30, 4511.31, 4511.33, 4511.35, and 4511.66 of the Revised Code. Such exemption shall not apply to such drivers when their vehicles are not so engaged. This section shall not exempt a driver of such equipment from civil liability arising from the violation of sections 4511.22, 4511.25, 4511.26, 4511.27, 4511.28, 4511.30, 4511.31, 4511.33, 4511.35, and 4511.66 of the Revised Code.

HISTORY: GC § 6307-4; 119 v 766, § 4; Bureau of Code Revision, 10-1-53; 133 v S 77. Eff 11-17-69.

[§ 4511.04.1] § 4511.041 Exceptions for emergency or public safety vehicle responding to emergency call.

Sections 4511.12, 4511.13, 4511.131 [4511.13.1], 4511.132 [4511.13.2], 4511.14, 4511.15, 4511.202 [4511.20.2], 4511.21, 4511.211 [4511.21.1], 4511.22, 4511.23, 4511.25, 4511.26, 4511.27, 4511.28, 4511.29, 4511.30, 4511.31, 4511.32, 4511.33, 4511.34, 4511.35, 4511.36, 4511.37, 4511.38, 4511.39, 4511.40, 4511.41, 4511.42, 4511.43, 4511.431 [4511.43.1], 4511.432 [4511.43.2], 4511.44, 4511.441 [4511.44.1], 4511.57, 4511.58, 4511.59, 4511.60, 4511.61, 4511.62, 4511.66, 4511.68, 4511.681 [4511.68.1], and 4511.69 of the Revised Code do not apply to the driver of an emergency vehicle or public safety vehicle if the emergency vehicle or public safety vehicle is responding to an emergency call, is equipped with and displaying at least one flashing, rotating, or oscillating light visible under normal atmospheric conditions from a distance of five hundred feet to the front of the vehicle and if the driver of the vehicle is giving an audible signal by siren, exhaust whistle, or bell. This section does not relieve the driver of an emergency vehicle or public safety vehicle from the duty to drive with due regard for the safety of all persons and property upon the highway.

HISTORY: 145 v H 149. Eff 5-20-93.

§ 4511.05 Persons riding or driving animals upon roadways.

Every person riding, driving, or leading an animal upon a roadway is subject to sections 4511.01 to 4511.78, inclusive, 4511.99, and 4513.01 to 4513.37, inclusive, of the Revised Code, applicable to the driver of a vehicle, except those provisions of such sections which by their nature are inapplicable.

HISTORY: GC § 6307-5; 119 v 766, § 5; Bureau of Code Revision. Eff 10-1-53.

[§ 4511.05.1] § 4511.051 Prohibitions on use of freeways.

No person, unless otherwise directed by a police officer, shall:

(A) As a pedestrian, occupy any space within the limits of the right-of-way of a freeway, except: in a rest area; on a facility that is separated from the roadway and shoulders of the freeway and is designed and appropriately marked for pedestrian use; in the performance of public works or official duties; as a result of an emergency caused by an accident or breakdown of a motor vehicle; or to obtain assistance;

(B) Occupy any space within the limits of the right-of-way of a freeway, with: an animal-drawn vehicle; a ridden or led animal; herded animals; a pushcart; a bicycle, except on a facility that is separated from the roadway and shoulders of the freeway and is designed and appropriately marked for bicycle use; a bicycle with motor attached; a motor driven cycle with a motor which produces not to exceed five brake horsepower; an agricultural tractor; farm machinery; except in the performance of public works or official duties.

HISTORY: 131 v 1099 (Eff 9-1-65); 132 v H 1 (Eff 2-21-67); 143 v H 258. Eff 11-2-89.

§ 4511.06 Uniform application and precedence of traffic law.

Sections 4511.01 to 4511.78, 4511.99, and 4513.01 to 4513.37 of the Revised Code shall be applicable and uniform throughout this state and in all political subdivisions and municipal corporations of this state. No local authority shall enact or enforce any rule in conflict with such sections, except that this section does not prevent local authorities from exercising the rights granted them by Chapter 4521. of the Revised Code and does not limit the effect or application of the provisions of that chapter.

HISTORY: GC § 6307-6; 119 v 766, § 6; Bureau of Code Revision, 10-1-53; 139 v H 707. Eff 1-1-83.

The effective date is set by section 3 of HB 707.

§ 4511.07 Local traffic regulations.

Sections 4511.01 to 4511.78, 4511.99, and 4513.01 to 4513.37 of the Revised Code do not prevent local authorities from carrying out the following activities with respect to streets and highways under their jurisdiction and within the reasonable exercise of the police power:

(A) Regulating the stopping, standing, or parking of vehicles, trackless trolleys, and streetcars;

(B) Regulating traffic by means of police officers or traffic control devices;

(C) Regulating or prohibiting processions or assemblages on the highways;

(D) Designating particular highways as one-way highways and requiring that all vehicles, trackless trolleys, and streetcars on the one-way highways be moved in one specific direction;

(E) Regulating the speed of vehicles, streetcars, and trackless trolleys in public parks;

(F) Designating any highway as a through highway and requiring that all vehicles, trackless trolleys, and streetcars stop before entering or crossing a through highway, or designating any intersection as a stop intersection and requiring all vehicles, trackless trolleys, and streetcars to stop at one or more entrances to the intersection;

(G) Regulating or prohibiting vehicles and trackless trolleys from passing to the left of safety zones;

(H) Regulating the operation of bicycles and requiring the registration and licensing of bicycles, including the requirement of a registration fee;

(I) Regulating the use of certain streets by vehicles, streetcars, or trackless trolleys.

No ordinance or regulation enacted under division (D), (E), (F), (G), or (I) of this section shall be effective until signs giving notice of the local traffic regulations are posted upon or at the entrance to the highway or part of the highway affected, as may be most appropriate.

Every ordinance, resolution, or regulation enacted under division (A) of this section shall be enforced in compliance with section 4511.071 [4511.07.1] of the Revised Code, unless the local authority that enacted it also enacted an ordinance, resolution, or regulation pursuant to division (A) of section 4521.02 of the Revised Code that specifies that a violation of it shall not be considered a criminal offense, in which case the ordinance, resolution, or regulation shall be enforced in compliance with Chapter 4521. of the Revised Code.

HISTORY: GC § 6307-7; 119 v 766; Bureau of Code Revision, 10-1-53; 129 v 1037 (Eff 8-11-61); 133 v S 452 (Eff 7-17-70); 135 v H 995 (Eff 1-1-75); 138 v S 257 (Eff 6-25-80); 139 v H 707. Eff 1-1-83.

The effective date is set by section 3 of HB 707.

[§ 4511.07.1] § 4511.071 Lessor under written lease may establish nonliability for violation.

(A) Except as provided in division (C) of this section, the owner of a vehicle shall be entitled to establish nonliability for prosecution for violation of an ordinance, resolution, or regulation enacted under division (A) of section 4511.07 of the Revised Code by proving the vehicle was in the care, custody, or control of a person other than the owner at the time of the violation pursuant to a written rental or lease agreement or affidavit providing that except for such agreement, no other business relationship with respect to the vehicle in question exists between the operator and owner.

(B) Proof that the vehicle was in the care, custody, or control of a person other than the owner shall be established by sending a copy of such written rental or lease agreement or affidavit to the prosecuting authority within thirty days from the date of receipt by the owner of the notice of violation. The furnishing of a copy of a written rental or lease agreement or affidavit shall be prima-facie evidence that a vehicle was in the care, custody, or control of a person other than the owner.

(C) This section does not apply to a violation of an ordinance, resolution, or regulation enacted under division (A) of section 4511.07 of the Revised Code if the ordinance, resolution, or regulation is one that is required to be enforced in compliance with Chapter 4521. of the Revised Code.

HISTORY: 138 v S 257 (Eff 6-25-80); 139 v H 707. Eff 1-1-83.

The effective date is set by section 3 of HB 707.

§ 4511.08 Use of private property for vehicular travel.

Sections 4511.01 to 4511.78, inclusive, 4511.99, and 4513.01 to 4513.37, inclusive, of the Revised Code do not prevent the owner of real property, used by the public for purposes of vehicular travel by permission of the owner and not as a matter of right, from prohibiting such use or from requiring additional conditions to those specified in such sections, or otherwise regulating such use as may seem best to such owner.

HISTORY: GC § 6307-8; 119 v 766, § 8; Bureau of Code Revision. Eff 10-1-53.

[TRAFFIC CONTROL DEVICES]

§ 4511.09 Uniform system of traffic control devices.

The department of transportation shall adopt a manual and specifications for a uniform system of traffic control devices, including signs denoting names of streets and highways, for use upon highways within this state.° Such uniform system shall correlate with, and so far as possible conform to, the system approved by the American Association of State Highway Officials.

HISTORY: GC § 6307-9; 119 v 766, § 9; Bureau of Code Revision, 10-1-53; 135 v H 200. Eff 9-28-73.

° The manual referred to is "Ohio Manual of Uniform Traffic Control Devices for Streets and Highways" prepared by the Ohio Department of Transportation, Bureau of Traffic, and for sale by the Bureau of Traffic, 25 S. Front Street, Columbus, Ohio 43215

[§ 4511.09.1] § 4511.091 Radar; authority of arresting officer.

The driver of any motor vehicle which has been checked by radar, or by any electrical or mechanical timing device to determine the speed of the motor vehicle over a measured distance of the highway or a measured distance of a private road or driveway and found to be in violation of any of the provisions of section 4511.21 or 4511.211 [4511.21.1] of the Revised Code, may be arrested until a warrant can be obtained, provided such officer has observed the recording of the speed of such motor vehicle by the radio microwaves, electrical or mechanical timing device, or has received a radio message from the officer who observed the speed of the motor vehicle recorded by the radio microwaves, electrical or mechanical timing device; provided, in case of an arrest based on such a message, such radio message has been dispatched immediately after the speed of the motor vehicle was recorded and the arresting officer is furnished a description of the motor vehicle for proper identification and the recorded speed.

HISTORY: 125 v 396; 129 v 582(898) (Eff 1-10-61); 130 v 1080 (Eff 10-10-63); 132 v H 380 (Eff 1-1-68); 143 v H 171. Eff 5-31-90.

§ 4511.10 Placing and maintaining traffic control devices.

The department of transportation may place and maintain traffic control devices, conforming to its manual and specifications, upon all state highways as are necessary to indicate and to carry out sections 4511.01 to 4511.78 and 4511.99 of the Revised Code, or to regulate, warn, or guide traffic.*

No local authority shall place or maintain any traffic control device upon any highway under the jurisdiction of the department except by permission of the director of transportation.

HISTORY: GC § 6307-10; 119 v 766, § 10; Bureau of Code Revision, 10-1-53; 135 v H 200. Eff 9-28-73.

* The manual referred to is "Ohio Manual of Uniform Traffic Control Devices for Streets and Highways" prepared by the Ohio Department of Transportation, Bureau of Traffic, and for sale by the Bureau of Traffic, 25 S. Front Street, Columbus, Ohio 43215.

§ 4511.11 Uniformity of traffic control devices.

(A) Local authorities in their respective jurisdictions shall place and maintain traffic control devices in accordance with the department of transportation manual and specifications for a uniform system of traffic control devices, adopted under section 4511.09 of the Revised Code, upon highways under their jurisdiction as are necessary to indicate and to carry out sections 4511.01 to 4511.76 and 4511.99 of the Revised Code, local traffic ordinances, or to regulate, warn, or guide traffic.

(B) The director of transportation may require to be removed any traffic control device that does not conform to the manual and specifications for a uniform system of traffic control devices on the extensions of the state highway system within municipal corporations.

(C) No village shall place or maintain any traffic control signal upon an extension of the state highway system within the village without first obtaining the permission of the director. The director may revoke the permission and may require to be removed any traffic control signal that has been erected without his permission on an extension of a state highway within a village, or that, if erected under a permit granted by the director, does not conform to the state manual and specifications, or that is not operated in accordance with the terms of the permit.

(D) All traffic control devices erected on a public road, street, or alley, shall conform to the state manual and specifications.

(E) No person, firm, or corporation shall sell or offer for sale to local authorities, any traffic control device that does not conform to the state manual and specifications, except by permission of the director.

(F) No local authority shall purchase or manufacture any traffic control device that does not conform to the state manual and specifications, except by permission of the director.

HISTORY: GC § 6307-11; 119 v 766, § 11; 121 v 684; Bureau of Code Revision, 10-1-53; 130 v 1081 (Eff 10-14-63); 130 v Pt2, H 5 (Eff 12-16-64); 131 v 1100 (Eff 11-1-65); 135 v H 200 (Eff 9-28-73); 143 v H 258 (Eff 11-2-89); 143 v H 162. Eff 6-28-90.

§ 4511.12 Obeying traffic control devices.

No pedestrian, driver of a vehicle, or operator of a streetcar or trackless trolley shall disobey the instructions of any traffic control device placed in accordance with this chapter, unless at the time otherwise directed by a police officer.

No provision of this chapter for which signs are required shall be enforced against an alleged violator if at the time and place of the alleged violation an official sign is not in proper position and sufficiently legible to be seen by an ordinarily observant person. Whenever a particular section of this chapter does not state that signs are required, that section shall be effective even though no signs are erected or in place.

HISTORY: GC § 6307-12; 119 v 766, § 12; 124 v 514; Bureau of Code Revision, 10-1-53; 143 v H 258. Eff 11-2-89.

§ 4511.13 Signal lights.

Whenever traffic is controlled by traffic control signals exhibiting different colored lights, or colored lighted arrows, successively one at a time or in combination, only the colors green, red, and yellow shall be used, except for special pedestrian signals carrying words or symbols, and said lights shall indicate and apply to drivers of vehicles, streetcars, and trackless trolleys, and to pedestrians as follows:

(A) Green indication:

(1) Vehicular traffic, streetcars, and trackless trolleys facing a circular green signal may proceed straight through or turn right or left unless a sign at such place prohibits either such turn. But vehicular traffic, streetcars, and trackless trolleys, including vehicles, streetcars, and trackless trolleys turning right or left, shall yield the right-of-way to other vehicles, streetcars, trackless trolleys, and pedestrians lawfully within the intersection or an adjacent crosswalk at the time such signal is exhibited.

(2) Vehicular traffic, streetcars, and trackless trolleys facing a green arrow signal, shown alone or in combination with another indication, may cautiously enter the intersection only to make the movement indicated by such arrow, or such other movement as is permitted by other indications shown at the same time. Such vehicular traffic, streetcars, and trackless trolleys shall yield the right-of-way to pedestrians lawfully within an adjacent crosswalk and to other traffic lawfully using the intersection.

(3) Unless otherwise directed by a pedestrian-control signal, as provided in section 4511.14 of the Revised Code, pedestrians facing any green signal, except when the sole green signal is a turn arrow, may proceed across the roadway within any marked or unmarked crosswalk.

(B) Steady yellow indication:

(1) Vehicular traffic, streetcars, and trackless trolleys facing a steady circular yellow or yellow arrow signal are thereby warned that the related green movement is being terminated or that a red indication will be exhibited immediately thereafter when vehicular traffic, streetcars, and trackless trolleys shall not enter the intersection.

(2) Pedestrians facing a steady circular yellow or yellow arrow signal, unless otherwise directed by a pedestrian-control signal as provided in section 4511.14 of the Revised Code, are thereby advised that there is insufficient time to cross the roadway before a red indication is shown and no pedestrian shall then start to cross the roadway.

(C) Steady red indication:

(1) Vehicular traffic, streetcars, and trackless trolleys facing a steady red signal alone shall stop at a clearly marked stop line, but if none, before entering the crosswalk on the near side of the intersection, or if none, then before entering the intersection and shall remain standing until an indication to proceed is shown except as provided in divisions (C)(2) and (3) of this section.

(2) Unless a sign is in place prohibiting a right turn as provided in division (C)(5) of this section, vehicular traffic, streetcars, and trackless trolleys facing a steady red signal may cautiously enter the intersection to make a right turn after stopping as required by division (C)(1) of this section. Such vehicular traffic, streetcars, and trackless trolleys shall yield the right-of-way to pedestrians lawfully within an adjacent crosswalk and to other traffic lawfully using the intersection.

(3) Unless a sign is in place prohibiting a left turn as provided in division (C)(5) of this section, vehicular traffic, streetcars, and trackless trolleys facing a steady red signal on a one-way street that intersects another one-way street on which traffic moves to the left may cautiously enter the intersection to make a left turn into the one-way street after stopping as required by division (C)(1) of this section, and yielding the right-of-way to pedestrians lawfully within an adjacent crosswalk and to other traffic lawfully using the intersection.

(4) Unless otherwise directed by a pedestrian-control signal as provided in section 4511.14 of the Revised Code, pedestrians facing a steady red signal alone shall not enter the roadway.

(5) Local authorities may by ordinance, or the director of transportation on state highways may, prohibit a right or a left turn against a steady red signal at any intersection, which shall be effective when signs giving notice thereof are posted at the intersection.

(D) In the event an official traffic-control signal is erected and maintained at a place other than an intersection, the provisions of this section shall be applicable except as to those provisions which by their nature can have no application. Any stop required shall be made at a sign or marking on the pavement indicating where the stop shall be made, but in the absence of any such sign or marking the stop shall be made at the signal.

HISTORY: GC § 6307-13; 119 v 766, § 13; 124 v 514; Bureau of Code Revision, 10-1-53; 130 v 1081 (Eff 8-9-63); 135 v S 263 (Eff 7-3-74); 135 v H 99 (Eff 7-1-75); 137 v H 171 (Eff 8-26-77); 140 v H 703. Eff 3-28-85.

[§ 4511.13.1] § 4511.131 Signals over reversible lanes.

When lane-use control signals are placed over individual lanes of a street or highway, said signals shall indicate and apply to drivers of vehicles and trackless trolleys as follows:

(A) A steady downward green arrow:

Vehicular traffic and trackless trolleys may travel in any lane over which a green arrow signal is shown.

(B) A steady yellow "X":

Vehicular traffic and trackless trolleys are warned to vacate in a safe manner any lane over which such signal is shown to avoid occupying that lane when a steady red "X" signal is shown.

(C) A flashing yellow "X":

Vehicular traffic and trackless trolleys may use with proper caution any lane over which such signal is shown for only the purpose of making a left turn.

(D) A steady red "X".[:]

Vehicular traffic and trackless trolleys shall not enter or travel in any lane over which such signal is shown.

HISTORY: 130 v 1083 (Eff 8-9-63); 135 v S 263. Eff 7-3-74.

[§ 4511.13.2] § 4511.132 Malfunctioning traffic signals.

The driver of a vehicle, streetcar, or trackless trolley who approaches an intersection where traffic is controlled by traffic control signals shall do all of the following, if the signal facing him either exhibits no colored lights or colored lighted arrows or exhibits a combination of such lights or arrows that fails to clearly indicate the assignment of right-of-way:

(A) Stop at a clearly marked stop line, but if none, stop before entering the crosswalk on the near side of the intersection, or, if none, stop before entering the intersection;

(B) Yield the right-of-way to all vehicles, streetcars, or trackless trolleys in the intersection or approaching on an intersecting road, if the vehicles, streetcars, or trackless trolleys will constitute an immediate hazard during the time the driver is moving across or within the intersection or junction of roadways;

(C) Exercise ordinary care while proceeding through the intersection.

HISTORY: 143 v S 44. Eff 7-25-89.

§ 4511.14 Pedestrian control signals.

Whenever special pedestrian control signals exhibiting the words "walk" or "don't walk," or the symbol of a walking person or an upraised palm are in place, such signals shall indicate the following instructions:

(A) "Walk" or the symbol of a walking person: Pedestrians facing such signal may proceed across the roadway in the direction of the signal and shall be given the right of way by the operators of all vehicles, streetcars, and trackless trolleys.

(B) "Don't walk" or the symbol of an upraised palm: No pedestrian shall start to cross the roadway in the direction of the signal.

(C) Nothing in this section shall be construed to invalidate the continued use of pedestrian control signals utilizing the word "wait" if those signals were installed prior to the effective date of this act.

HISTORY: GC § 6307-14; 119 v 766, § 14; 124 v 514; Bureau of Code Revision, 10-1-53; 140 v H 703. Eff 3-28-85.

§ 4511.15 Flashing traffic signals.

Whenever an illuminated flashing red or yellow traffic signal is used in a traffic signal or with a traffic sign it shall require obedience as follows:

(A) Flashing red stop signal: Operators of vehicles, trackless trolleys, and streetcars shall stop at a clearly marked stop line, but if none, before entering the crosswalk on the near side of the intersection, or if none, then at the point nearest the intersecting roadway where the driver has a view of approaching traffic on the intersecting roadway before entering it, and the right to proceed shall be subject to the rules applicable after making a stop at a stop sign.

(B) Flashing yellow caution signal: Operators of vehicles, trackless trolleys, and streetcars may proceed through the intersection or past such signal only with caution.

This section shall not apply at railroad grade crossings. Conduct of drivers of vehicles, trackless trolleys, and streetcars approaching railroad grade crossings shall be governed by sections 4511.61 and 4511.62 of the Revised Code.

HISTORY: GC § 6307-15; 119 v 766, § 15; Bureau of Code Revision, 10-1-53; 135 v H 995. Eff 1-1-75.

The effective date is set by section 3 of HB 995.

§ 4511.16 Prohibition against unauthorized signs and signals.

No person shall place, maintain, or display upon or in view of any highway any unauthorized sign, signal, marking, or device which purports to be, is an imitation of, or resembles a traffic control device or railroad sign or signal, or which attempts to direct the movement of traffic or hides from view or interferes with the effectiveness of any traffic control device or any railroad sign or signal, and no person shall place or maintain, nor shall any public authority permit, upon any highway any traffic sign or signal bearing thereon any commercial advertising. This section does not prohibit either the erection upon private property adjacent to highways of signs giving useful directional information and of a type that cannot be mistaken for traffic control devices or the erection upon private property of traffic control devices by the owner of real property in accordance with sections 4511.211 [4511.21.1], and 4511.432 [4511.43.2] of the Revised Code.

Every such prohibited sign, signal, marking, or device is a public nuisance, and the authority having jurisdiction over the highway may remove it or cause it to be removed.

HISTORY: GC § 6307-16; 119 v 766, § 16; Bureau of Code Revision, 10-1-53; 143 v H 171. Eff 5-31-90.

§ 4511.17 Tampering with sign, device or manhole cover; driving on freshly applied marking material.

No person, without lawful authority, shall do any of the following:

(A) Knowingly move, deface, damage, destroy, or otherwise improperly tamper with any traffic control device, any railroad sign or signal, or any inscription, shield, or insignia on the device, sign, or signal, or any part of the device, sign, or signal;

(B) Knowingly drive upon or over any freshly applied pavement marking material on the surface of a roadway while the marking material is in an undried condition and is marked by flags, markers, signs, or other devices intended to protect it;

(C) Knowingly move, damage, destroy, or otherwise improperly tamper with a manhole cover.

HISTORY: GC § 6307-17; 119 v 766, § 17; 121 v 684; Bureau of Code Revision, 10-1-53; 143 v H 162. Eff 6-28-90.

§ 4511.18 Possession or sale of sign or device prohibited.

(A) As used in this section, "traffic control device" means any sign, traffic control signal, or other device conforming to and placed or erected in accordance with the manual adopted under section 4511.09 of the Revised Code by authority of a public body or official having jurisdiction, for the purpose of regulating, warning, or guiding traffic, including signs denoting the names of streets and highways, but does not mean any pavement marking.

(B) No individual shall buy or otherwise possess, or sell, a traffic control device, except when one of the following applies:

(1) In the course of his employment by the state or a local authority for the express or implied purpose of manufacturing, providing, erecting, moving, or removing such a traffic control device;

(2) In the course of his employment by any manufacturer of traffic control devices other than a state or local authority;

(3) For the purpose of demonstrating the design and function of a traffic control device to state or local officials;

(4) When the traffic control device has been purchased from the state or a local authority at a sale of property that is no longer needed or is unfit for use;

(5) The traffic control device has been properly purchased from a manufacturer for use on private property and the person possessing the device has a sales receipt for the device or other acknowledgment of sale issued by the manufacturer.

(C) This section does not preclude, and shall not be construed as precluding, prosecution for theft in violation of section 2913.02 of the Revised Code or a municipal ordinance relating to theft, or for receiving stolen property in violation of section 2913.51 of the Revised Code or a municipal ordinance relating to receiving stolen property.

HISTORY: 143 v H 162. Eff 6-28-90.

Not analogous to former RC § 4511.18 (GC § 6307-18; 119 v 766; Bureau of Code Revision, 10-1-53; 132 v S 37), repealed 134 v H 511, § 2, eff 1-1-74.

[DRIVING WHILE INTOXICATED]

§ 4511.19 Driving while under the influence of alcohol or drugs or with certain concentration of alcohol in bodily substances; chemical analysis.

(A) No person shall operate any vehicle, streetcar, or trackless trolley within this state, if any of the following apply:

(1) The person is under the influence of alcohol, a drug of abuse, or alcohol and a drug of abuse;

(2) The person has a concentration of ten-hundredths of one per cent or more by weight of alcohol in his blood;

(3) The person has a concentration of ten-hundredths of one gram or more by weight of alcohol per two hundred ten liters of his breath;

(4) The person has a concentration of fourteen-hundredths of one gram or more by weight of alcohol per one hundred milliliters of his urine.

(B) No person under twenty-one years of age shall operate any vehicle, streetcar, or trackless trolley within this state, if any of the following apply:

(1) The person has a concentration of at least two-hundredths of one per cent but less than ten-hundredths of one per cent by weight of alcohol in his blood;

(2) The person has a concentration of at least two-hundredths of one gram but less than ten-hundredths of one gram by weight of alcohol per two hundred ten liters of his breath;

(3) The person has a concentration of at least twenty-eight one-thousandths of one gram but less than fourteen-hundredths of one gram by weight of alcohol per one hundred milliliters of his urine.

(C) In any proceeding arising out of one incident, a person may be charged with a violation of division (A)(1) and a violation of division (B)(1), (2), or (3) of this section, but he may not be convicted of more than one violation of these divisions.

(D)(1) In any criminal prosecution or juvenile court proceeding for a violation of this section, of a municipal ordinance relating to operating a vehicle while under the influence of alcohol, a drug of abuse, or alcohol and a drug of abuse, or of a municipal ordinance relating to operating a vehicle with a prohibited concentration of alcohol in the blood, breath, or urine, the court may admit evidence on the concentration of alcohol, drugs of abuse, or alcohol and drugs of abuse in the defendant's blood, breath, urine, or other bodily substance at the time of the alleged violation as shown by chemical analysis of the defendant's blood, urine, breath, or other bodily substance withdrawn within two hours of the time of the alleged violation.

When a person submits to a blood test at the request of a police officer under section 4511.191 [4511.19.1] of the Revised Code, only a physician, a registered nurse, or a qualified technician or chemist shall withdraw blood for the purpose of determining its alcohol, drug, or alcohol and drug content. This limitation does not apply to the taking of breath or urine specimens. A physician, a registered nurse, or a qualified technician or chemist may refuse to withdraw blood for the purpose of determining the alcohol, drug, or alcohol and drug content of the blood, if in his opinion the physical welfare of the person would be endangered by the withdrawing of blood.

Such bodily substance shall be analyzed in accordance with methods approved by the director of health by an individual possessing a valid permit issued by the director of health pursuant to section 3701.143 [3701.14.3] of the Revised Code.

(2) In a criminal prosecution or juvenile court proceeding for a violation of division (A) of this section, of a municipal ordinance relating to operating a vehicle while under the influence of alcohol, a drug of abuse, or alcohol and a drug of abuse, or of a municipal ordinance substantially equivalent to division (A) of this section relating to operating a vehicle with a prohibited concentration of alcohol in the blood, breath, or urine, if there was at the time the bodily substance was withdrawn a concentration of less than ten-hundredths of one per cent by weight of alcohol in the defendant's blood, less than ten-hundredths of one gram by weight of alcohol per two hundred ten liters of his breath, or less than fourteen-hundredths of one gram by weight of alcohol per one hundred milliliters of his urine, such fact may be considered with other competent evidence in determining the guilt or innocence of the defendant. This division does not limit or affect a criminal prosecution or juvenile court proceeding for a violation of division (B) of this section or of a municipal ordinance substantially equivalent to division (B) of this section relating to operating a vehicle with a prohibited concentration

of alcohol in the blood, breath, or urine.

(3) Upon the request of the person who was tested, the results of the chemical test shall be made available to him, his attorney, or his agent, immediately upon the completion of the chemical test analysis.

The person tested may have a physician, a registered nurse, or a qualified technician or chemist of his own choosing administer a chemical test or tests in addition to any administered at the request of a police officer, and shall be so advised. The failure or inability to obtain an additional chemical test by a person shall not preclude the admission of evidence relating to the chemical test or tests taken at the request of a police officer.

(4) Any physician, registered nurse, or qualified technician or chemist who withdraws blood from a person pursuant to this section, and any hospital, first-aid station, or clinic at which blood is withdrawn from a person pursuant to this section, is immune from criminal liability, and from civil liability that is based upon a claim of assault and battery or based upon any other claim that is not in the nature of a claim of malpractice, for any act performed in withdrawing blood from the person.

HISTORY: GC § 6307-19; 119 v 766, § 19; Bureau of Code Revision, 10-1-53; 125 v 461; 130 v 1083 (Eff 7-11-63); 132 v H 380 (Eff 1-1-68); 133 v H 874 (Eff 9-16-70); 134 v S 14 (Eff 12-3-71); 135 v H 995 (Eff 1-1-75); 139 v S 432 (Eff 3-16-83); 141 v S 262 (Eff 3-20-87); 143 v S 131 (Eff 7-25-90); 143 v S 131 (Eff 7-25-90); 143 v H 837 (Eff 7-25-90); 145 v S 82. Eff 5-4-94.

The effective date is set by section 6 of SB 82.

[§ 4511.19.1] § 4511.191 Implied consent.

(A) Any person who operates a vehicle upon a highway or any public or private property used by the public for vehicular travel or parking within this state shall be deemed to have given consent to a chemical test or tests of the person's blood, breath, or urine for the purpose of determining the alcohol, drug, or alcohol and drug content of the person's blood, breath, or urine if arrested for operating a vehicle while under the influence of alcohol, a drug of abuse, or alcohol and a drug of abuse or for operating a vehicle with a prohibited concentration of alcohol in the blood, breath, or urine. The chemical test or tests shall be administered at the request of a police officer having reasonable grounds to believe the person to have been operating a vehicle upon a highway or any public or private property used by the public for vehicular travel or parking in this state while under the influence of alcohol, a drug of abuse, or alcohol and a drug of abuse or with a prohibited concentration of alcohol in the blood, breath, or urine. The law enforcement agency by which the officer is employed shall designate which of the tests shall be administered.

(B) Any person who is dead or unconscious, or who is otherwise in a condition rendering the person incapable of refusal, shall be deemed not to have withdrawn consent as provided by division (A) of this section and the test or tests may be administered, subject to sections 313.12 to 313.16 of the Revised Code.

(C)(1) Any person under arrest for operating a vehicle while under the influence of alcohol, a drug of abuse, or alcohol and a drug of abuse or for operating a vehicle with a prohibited concentration of alcohol in the blood, breath, or urine shall be advised at a police station, or at a hospital, first-aid station, or clinic to which the person has been taken for first-aid or medical treatment, of both of the following:

(a) The consequences, as specified in division (E) of this section, of the person's refusal to submit upon request to a chemical test designated by the law enforcement agency as provided in division (A) of this section;

(b) The consequences, as specified in division (F) of this section, of the person's submission to the designated chemical test if the person is found to have a prohibited concentration of alcohol in the blood, breath, or urine.

(2)(a) The advice given pursuant to division (C)(1) of this section shall be in a written form containing the information described in division (C)(2)(b) of this section and shall be read to the person. The form shall contain a statement that the form was shown to the person under arrest and read to the person in the presence of the arresting officer and either another police officer, a civilian police employee, or an employee of a hospital, first-aid station, or clinic, if any, to which the person has been taken for first-aid or medical treatment. The witnesses shall certify to this fact by signing the form.

(b) The form required by division (C)(2)(a) of this section shall read as follows:

"You now are under arrest for operating a vehicle while under the influence of alcohol, a drug of abuse, or both alcohol and a drug of abuse and will be requested by a police officer to submit to a chemical test to determine the concentration of alcohol, drugs of abuse, or alcohol and drugs of abuse in your blood, breath, or urine.

If you refuse to submit to the requested test or if you submit to the requested test and are found to have a prohibited concentration of alcohol in your blood, breath, or urine, your driver's or commercial driver's license or permit or nonresident operating privilege immediately will be suspended for the period of time specified by law by the officer, on behalf of the registrar of motor vehicles. You may appeal this suspension at your initial appearance before the court that hears the charges against you resulting from the arrest, and your initial appearance will be conducted no later than five days after the arrest. This suspension is independent of the penalties for the offense, and you may be subject to other penalties upon conviction."

(D)(1) If a person under arrest as described in division (C)(1) of this section is not asked by a police officer to submit to a chemical test designated as provided in division (A) of this section, the arresting officer shall seize the Ohio or out-of-state driver's or commercial driver's license or permit of the person and immediately forward the seized license or permit to the court in which the arrested person is to appear on the charge for which the person was arrested. If the arrested person does not have the person's driver's or commercial driver's license or permit on his or her person or in his or her vehicle, the arresting officer shall order the arrested person to surrender it to the law enforcement agency that employs the officer within twenty-four hours after the arrest, and, upon the surrender, the officer's employing agency immediately shall forward the license or permit to the court in which the arrested person is to appear on the charge for which the person was arrested. Upon receipt of the license or permit, the court shall retain it pending the initial appearance of the arrested person and any action taken under section 4511.196 [4511.19.6] of the Revised Code.

If a person under arrest as described in division (C)(1) of this section is asked by a police officer to submit to a chemical test designated as provided in division (A) of this section and is advised of the consequences of the person's refusal or submission as provided in division (C) of this section and if the person either refuses to submit to the designated chemical test or the person submits to the designated chemical test and the test results indicate that the person's blood contained a concentration of ten-hundredths of one per cent or more by weight of alcohol, the person's breath contained a concentration of ten-hundredths of one gram or more by weight of alcohol per two hundred ten liters of the person's breath, or the person's urine contained a concentration of fourteen-hundredths of one gram or more by weight of alcohol per one hundred milliliters of the person's urine at the time of the alleged offense, the arresting officer shall do all of the following:

(a) On behalf of the registrar, serve a notice of suspension upon the person that advises the person that, independent of any penalties or sanctions imposed upon the person pursuant to any other section of the Revised Code or any other municipal ordinance, the person's driver's or commercial driver's license or permit or nonresident operating privilege is suspended, that the suspension takes effect immediately, that the suspension will last at least until the person's initial appearance on the charge that will be held within five days after the date of the person's arrest or the issuance of a citation to the person, and that the person may appeal the suspension at the initial appearance; seize the Ohio or out-of-state driver's or commercial driver's license or permit of the person; and immediately forward the seized license or permit to the registrar. If the arrested person does not have the person's driver's or commercial driver's license or permit on his or her person or in his or her vehicle, the arresting officer shall order the person to surrender it to the law enforcement agency that employs the officer within twenty-four hours after the service of the notice of suspension, and, upon the surrender, the officer's employing agency immediately shall forward the license or permit to the registrar.

(b) Verify the current residence of the person and, if it differs from that on the person's driver's or commercial driver's license or permit, notify the registrar of the change;

(c) In addition to forwarding the arrested person's driver's or commercial driver's license or permit to the registrar, send to the registrar, within forty-eight hours after the arrest of the person, a sworn report that includes all of the following statements:

(i) That the officer had reasonable grounds to believe that, at the time of the arrest, the arrested person was operating a vehicle upon a highway or public or private property used by the public for vehicular travel or parking within this state while under the influence of alcohol, a drug of abuse, or alcohol and a drug of abuse or with a prohibited concentration of alcohol in the blood, breath, or urine;

(ii) That the person was arrested and charged with operating a vehicle while under the influence of alcohol, a drug of abuse, or alcohol and a drug of abuse or with operating a vehicle with a prohibited concentration of alcohol in the blood, breath, or urine;

(iii) That the officer asked the person to take the designated chemical test, advised the person of the consequences of submitting to the chemical test or refusing to take the chemical test, and gave the person the form described in division (C)(2) of this section;

(iv) That the person refused to submit to the chemical test or that the person submitted to the chemical test and the test results indicate that the person's blood contained a concentration of ten-hundredths of one per cent or more by weight of alcohol, the person's breath contained a concentration of ten-hundredths of one gram or more by weight of alcohol per two hundred ten liters of the person's breath, or the person's urine contained a concentration of fourteen-hundredths of one gram or more by weight of alcohol per one hundred milliliters of the person's urine at the time of the alleged offense;

(v) That the officer served a notice of suspension upon the person as described in division (D)(1)(a) of this section.

(2) The sworn report of an arresting officer completed under division (D)(1)(c) of this section shall be given by the officer to the arrested person at the time of the arrest or sent to the person by regular first class mail by the registrar as soon thereafter as possible, but no later than fourteen days after receipt of the report. An arresting officer may give an unsworn report to the arrested person at the time of the arrest provided the report is complete when given to the arrested person and subsequently is sworn to by the arresting officer. As soon as possible, but no later than forty-eight hours after the arrest of the person, the arresting officer shall send a copy of the sworn report to the court in which

the arrested person is to appear on the charge for which the person was arrested.

(3) The sworn report of an arresting officer completed and sent to the registrar and the court under divisions (D)(1)(c) and (D)(2) of this section is prima-facie proof of the information and statements that it contains and shall be admitted and considered as prima-facie proof of the information and statements that it contains in any appeal under division (H) of this section relative to any suspension of a person's driver's or commercial driver's license or permit or nonresident operating privilege that results from the arrest covered by the report.

(E)(1) Upon receipt of the sworn report of an arresting officer completed and sent to the registrar and a court pursuant to divisions (D)(1)(c) and (D)(2) of this section in regard to a person who refused to take the designated chemical test, the registrar shall enter into the registrar's records the fact that the person's driver's or commercial driver's license or permit or nonresident operating privilege was suspended by the arresting officer under division (D)(1)(a) of this section and the period of the suspension, as determined under divisions (E)(1)(a) to (d) of this section. The suspension shall be subject to appeal as provided in this section and shall be for whichever of the following periods applies:

(a) If the arrested person, within five years of the date on which the person refused the request to consent to the chemical test, had not refused a previous request to consent to a chemical test of the person's blood, breath, or urine to determine its alcohol content, the period of suspension shall be one year. If the person is a resident without a license or permit to operate a vehicle within this state, the registrar shall deny to the person the issuance of a driver's or commercial driver's license or permit for a period of one year after the date of the alleged violation.

(b) If the arrested person, within five years of the date on which the person refused the request to consent to the chemical test, had refused one previous request to consent to a chemical test of the person's blood, breath, or urine to determine its alcohol content, the period of suspension or denial shall be two years.

(c) If the arrested person, within five years of the date on which the person refused the request to consent to the chemical test, had refused two previous requests to consent to a chemical test of the person's blood, breath, or urine to determine its alcohol content, the period of suspension or denial shall be three years.

(d) If the arrested person, within five years of the date on which the person refused the request to consent to the chemical test, had refused three or more previous requests to consent to a chemical test of the person's blood, breath, or urine to determine its alcohol content, the period of suspension or denial shall be five years.

(2) The suspension or denial imposed under division (E)(1) of this section shall continue for the entire one-year, two-year, three-year, or five-year period, subject to appeal as provided in this section and subject to termination as provided in division (K) of this section.

(F) Upon receipt of the sworn report of an arresting officer completed and sent to the registrar and a court pursuant to divisions (D)(1)(c) and (D)(2) of this section in regard to a person whose test results indicate that the person's blood contained a concentration of ten-hundredths of one per cent or more by weight of alcohol, the person's breath contained a concentration of ten-hundredths of one gram or more by weight of alcohol per two hundred ten liters of the person's breath, or the person's urine contained a concentration of fourteen-hundredths of one gram or more by weight of alcohol per one hundred milliliters of the person's urine at the time of the alleged offense, the registrar shall enter into the registrar's records the fact that the person's driver's or commercial driver's license or permit or nonresident operating privilege was suspended by the arresting officer under division (D)(1)(a) of this section and the period of the suspension, as determined under divisions (F)(1) to (4) of this section. The suspension shall be subject to appeal as provided in this section and shall be for whichever of the following periods that applies:

(1) Except when division (F)(2), (3), or (4) of this section applies and specifies a different period of suspension or denial, the period of the suspension or denial shall be ninety days.

(2) If the person has been convicted, within ten† years of the date the test was conducted, of one violation of division (A) or (B) of section 4511.19 of the Revised Code, a municipal ordinance relating to operating a vehicle while under the influence of alcohol, a drug of abuse, or alcohol and a drug of abuse, a municipal ordinance relating to operating a vehicle with a prohibited concentration of alcohol in the blood, breath, or urine, section 2903.04 of the Revised Code in a case in which the offender was subject to the sanctions described in division (D) of that section, or section 2903.06, 2903.07, or 2903.08 of the Revised Code or a municipal ordinance that is substantially similar to section 2903.07 of the Revised Code in a case in which the jury or judge found that at the time of the commission of the offense the offender was under the influence of alcohol, a drug of abuse, or alcohol and a drug of abuse, or a statute of the United States or of any other state or a municipal ordinance of a municipal corporation located in any other state that is substantially similar to division (A) or (B) of section 4511.19 of the Revised Code, the period of the suspension or denial shall be one year.

(3) If the person has been convicted, within ten† years of the date the test was conducted, of two violations of a statute or ordinance described in division (F)(2) of this section, the period of the suspension or denial shall be two years.

(4) If the person has been convicted, within ten†

years of the date the test was conducted, of more than two violations of a statute or ordinance described in division (F)(2) of this section, the period of the suspension or denial shall be three years.

(G)(1) A suspension of a person's driver's or commercial driver's license or permit or nonresident operating privilege under division (D)(1)(a) of this section for the period of time described in division (E) or (F) of this section is effective immediately from the time at which the arresting officer serves the notice of suspension upon the arrested person. Any subsequent finding that the person is not guilty of the charge that resulted in the person being requested to take, or in the person taking, the chemical test or tests under division (A) of this section affects the suspension only as described in division (H)(2) of this section.

(2) If a person is arrested for operating a vehicle while under the influence of alcohol, a drug of abuse, or alcohol and a drug of abuse or for operating a vehicle with a prohibited concentration of alcohol in the blood, breath, or urine and regardless of whether the person's driver's or commercial driver's license or permit or nonresident operating privilege is or is not suspended under division (E) or (F) of this section, the person's initial appearance on the charge resulting from the arrest shall be held within five days of the person's arrest or the issuance of the citation to the person, subject to any continuance granted by the court pursuant to division (H)(1) of this section regarding the issues specified in that division.

(H)(1) If a person is arrested for operating a vehicle while under the influence of alcohol, a drug of abuse, or alcohol and a drug of abuse or for operating a vehicle with a prohibited concentration of alcohol in the blood, breath, or urine and if the person's driver's or commercial driver's license or permit or nonresident operating privilege is suspended under division (E) or (F) of this section, the person may appeal the suspension at the person's initial appearance on the charge resulting from the arrest in the court in which the person will appear on that charge. If the person appeals the suspension at the person's initial appearance, the appeal does not stay the operation of the suspension. Subject to division (H)(2) of this section, no court has jurisdiction to grant a stay of a suspension imposed under division (E) or (F) of this section, and any order issued by any court that purports to grant a stay of any suspension imposed under either of those divisions shall not be given administrative effect.

If the person appeals the suspension at the person's initial appearance, either the person or the registrar may request a continuance of the appeal. Either the person or the registrar shall make the request for a continuance of the appeal at the same time as the making of the appeal. If either the person or the registrar requests a continuance of the appeal, the court may grant the continuance. The court also may continue the appeal on its own motion. The granting of a continuance applies only to the conduct of the appeal of the suspension and does not extend the time within which the initial appearance must be conducted, and the court shall proceed with all other aspects of the initial appearance in accordance with its normal procedures. Neither the request for nor the granting of a continuance stays the operation of the suspension that is the subject of the appeal.

If the person appeals the suspension at the person's initial appearance, the scope of the appeal is limited to determining whether one or more of the following conditions have not been met:

(a) Whether the law enforcement officer had reasonable ground to believe the arrested person was operating a vehicle upon a highway or public or private property used by the public for vehicular travel or parking within this state while under the influence of alcohol, a drug of abuse, or alcohol and a drug of abuse or with a prohibited concentration of alcohol in the blood, breath, or urine and whether the arrested person was in fact placed under arrest;

(b) Whether the law enforcement officer requested the arrested person to submit to the chemical test designated pursuant to division (A) of this section;

(c) Whether the arresting officer informed the arrested person of the consequences of refusing to be tested or of submitting to the test;

(d) Whichever of the following is applicable:

(i) Whether the arrested person refused to submit to the chemical test requested by the officer;

(ii) Whether the chemical test results indicate that the arrested person's blood contained a concentration of ten-hundredths of one per cent or more by weight of alcohol, the person's breath contained a concentration of ten-hundredths of one gram or more by weight of alcohol per two hundred ten liters of the person's breath, or the person's urine contained a concentration of fourteen-hundredths of one gram or more by weight of alcohol per one hundred milliliters of the person's urine at the time of the alleged offense.

(2) If the person appeals the suspension at the initial appearance, the judge or referee of the court or the mayor of the mayor's court shall determine whether one or more of the conditions specified in divisions (H)(1)(a) to (d) of this section have not been met. The person who appeals the suspension has the burden of proving, by a preponderance of the evidence, that one or more of the specified conditions has not been met. If during the appeal at the initial appearance the judge or referee of the court or the mayor of the mayor's court determines that all of those conditions have been met, the judge, referee, or mayor shall uphold the suspension, shall continue the suspension, and shall notify the registrar of the decision on a form approved by the registrar. Except as otherwise provided in division (H)(2) of this section, if the suspension is upheld or if the person does not appeal the suspension at the person's initial appearance under division (H)(1) of this

section, the suspension shall continue until the complaint alleging the violation for which the person was arrested and in relation to which the suspension was imposed is adjudicated on the merits by the judge or referee of the trial court or by the mayor of the mayor's court. If the suspension was imposed under division (E) of this section and it is continued under this division, any subsequent finding that the person is not guilty of the charge that resulted in the person being requested to take the chemical test or tests under division (A) of this section does not terminate or otherwise affect the suspension. If the suspension was imposed under division (F) of this section and it is continued under this division, the suspension shall terminate if, for any reason, the person subsequently is found not guilty of the charge that resulted in the person taking the chemical test or tests under division (A) of this section.

If, during the appeal at the initial appearance, the judge or referee of the trial court or the mayor of the mayor's court determines that one or more of the conditions specified in divisions (H)(1)(a) to (d) of this section have not been met, the judge, referee, or mayor shall terminate the suspension, subject to the imposition of a new suspension under division (B) of section 4511.196 [4511.19.6] of the Revised Code; shall notify the registrar of the decision on a form approved by the registrar; and, except as provided in division (B) of section 4511.196 [4511.19.6] of the Revised Code, shall order the registrar to return the driver's or commercial driver's license or permit to the person or to take such measures as may be necessary, if the license or permit was destroyed under section 4507.55 of the Revised Code, to permit the person to obtain a replacement driver's or commercial driver's license or permit from the registrar or a deputy registrar in accordance with that section. The court also shall issue to the person a court order, valid for not more than ten days from the date of issuance, granting the person operating privileges for that period of time.

If the person appeals the suspension at the initial appearance, the registrar shall be represented by the prosecuting attorney of the county in which the arrest occurred if the initial appearance is conducted in a juvenile court or county court, except that if the arrest occurred within a city or village within the jurisdiction of the county court in which the appeal is conducted, the city director of law or village solicitor of that city or village shall represent the registrar. If the appeal is conducted in a municipal court, the registrar shall be represented as provided in section 1901.34 of the Revised Code. If the appeal is conducted in a mayor's court, the registrar shall be represented by the city director of law, village solicitor, or other chief legal officer of the municipal corporation that operates that mayor's court.

(I)(1) If a person's driver's or commercial driver's license or permit or nonresident operating privilege has been suspended pursuant to division (E) of this section, and the person, within the preceding seven years, has refused three previous requests to consent to a chemical test of the person's blood, breath, or urine to determine its alcohol content or has been convicted of or pleaded guilty to three or more violations of division (A) or (B) of section 4511.19 of the Revised Code, a municipal ordinance relating to operating a vehicle while under the influence of alcohol, a drug of abuse, or alcohol and a drug of abuse, a municipal ordinance relating to operating a vehicle with a prohibited concentration of alcohol in the blood, breath, or urine, section 2903.04 of the Revised Code in a case in which the person was subject to the sanctions described in division (D) of that section, or section 2903.06, 2903.07, or 2903.08 of the Revised Code or a municipal ordinance that is substantially similar to section 2903.07 of the Revised Code in a case in which the jury or judge found that the person was under the influence of alcohol, a drug of abuse, or alcohol and a drug of abuse, or a statute of the United States or of any other state or a municipal ordinance of a municipal corporation located in any other state that is substantially similar to division (A) or (B) of section 4511.19 of the Revised Code, the person is not entitled to request, and the court shall not grant to the person, occupational driving privileges under this division. Any other person whose driver's or commercial driver's license or nonresident operating privilege has been suspended pursuant to division (E) of this section may file a petition requesting occupational driving privileges in the common pleas court, municipal court, county court, mayor's court, or, if the person is a minor, juvenile court with jurisdiction over the related criminal or delinquency case. The petition may be filed at any time subsequent to the date on which the notice of suspension is served upon the arrested person. The person shall pay the costs of the proceeding, notify the registrar of the filing of the petition, and send the registrar a copy of the petition.

In the proceedings, the registrar shall be represented by the prosecuting attorney of the county in which the arrest occurred if the petition is filed in the juvenile court, county court, or common pleas court, except that, if the arrest occurred within a city or village within the jurisdiction of the county court in which the petition is filed, the city director of law or village solicitor of that city or village shall represent the registrar. If the petition is filed in the municipal court, the registrar shall be represented as provided in section 1901.34 of the Revised Code. If the petition is filed in a mayor's court, the registrar shall be represented by the city director of law, village solicitor, or other chief legal officer of the municipal corporation that operates the mayor's court.

The court, if it finds reasonable cause to believe that suspension would seriously affect the person's ability to continue in the person's employment, may grant the person occupational driving privileges during the period of suspension imposed pursuant to division (E) of this section, subject to the limitations contained in this division and division (I)(2) of this section. The court may grant the occupational driving privileges, subject to the limitations contained in this division and division (I)(2) of this section, regardless of whether the person appeals the suspension at the person's initial appearance under division (H)(1) of this section or appeals the decision of the court made pursuant to the appeal conducted at the initial appearance, and, if the person has appealed the suspension or decision, regardless of whether the matter at issue has been heard or decided by the court. The court shall not grant occupational driving privileges to any person who, within seven years of the filing of the petition, has refused three previous requests to consent to a chemical test of the person's blood, breath, or urine to determine its alcohol content or has been convicted of or pleaded guilty to three or more violations of division (A) or (B) of section 4511.19 of the Revised Code, a municipal ordinance relating to operating a vehicle while under the influence of alcohol, a drug of abuse, or alcohol and a drug of abuse, a municipal ordinance relating to operating a vehicle with a prohibited concentration of alcohol in the blood, breath, or urine, section 2903.04 of the Revised Code in a case in which the person was subject to the sanctions described in division (D) of that section, or section 2903.06, 2903.07, or 2903.08 of the Revised Code or a municipal ordinance that is substantially similar to section 2903.07 of the Revised Code in a case in which the jury or judge found that the person was under the influence of alcohol, a drug of abuse, or alcohol and a drug of abuse, or a statute of the United States or of any other state or a municipal ordinance of a municipal corporation located in any other state that is substantially similar to division (A) or (B) of section 4511.19 of the Revised Code, and shall not grant occupational driving privileges for employment as a driver of commercial motor vehicles to any person who is disqualified from operating a commercial motor vehicle under section 2301.374 [2301.37.4] or 4506.16 of the Revised Code.

(2)(a) In granting occupational driving privileges under division (I)(1) of this section, the court may impose any condition it considers reasonable and necessary to limit the use of a vehicle by the person. The court shall deliver to the person a permit card, in a form to be prescribed by the court, setting forth the time, place, and other conditions limiting the defendant's use of a vehicle. The grant of occupational driving privileges shall be conditioned upon the person's having the permit in the person's possession at all times during which the person is operating a vehicle.

A person granted occupational driving privileges who operates a vehicle for other than occupational purposes, in violation of any condition imposed by the court, or without having the permit in the person's possession, is guilty of a violation of section 4507.02 of the Revised Code.

(b) The court may not grant a person occupational driving privileges under division (I)(1) of this section when prohibited by a limitation contained in that division or during any of the following periods of time:

(i) The first thirty days of suspension imposed upon a person who, within five years of the date on which the person refused the request to consent to a chemical test of the person's blood, breath, or urine to determine its alcohol content and for which refusal the suspension was imposed, had not refused a previous request to consent to a chemical test of the person's blood, breath, or urine to determine its alcohol content;

(ii) The first ninety days of suspension imposed upon a person who, within five years of the date on which the person refused the request to consent to a chemical test of the person's blood, breath, or urine to determine its alcohol content and for which refusal the suspension was imposed, had refused one previous request to consent to a chemical test of the person's blood, breath, or urine to determine its alcohol content;

(iii) The first year of suspension imposed upon a person who, within five years of the date on which the person refused the request to consent to a chemical test of the person's blood, breath, or urine to determine its alcohol content and for which refusal the suspension was imposed, had refused two previous requests to consent to a chemical test of the person's blood, breath, or urine to determine its alcohol content;

(iv) The first three years of suspension imposed upon a person who, within five years of the date on which the person refused the request to consent to a chemical test of the person's blood, breath, or urine to determine its alcohol content and for which refusal the suspension was imposed, had refused three or more previous requests to consent to a chemical test of the person's blood, breath, or urine to determine its alcohol content.

(3) The court shall give information in writing of any action taken under this section to the registrar.

(4) If a person's driver's or commercial driver's license or permit or nonresident operating privilege has been suspended pursuant to division (F) of this section, and the person, within the preceding seven years, has been convicted of or pleaded guilty to three or more violations of division (A) or (B) of section 4511.19 of the Revised Code, a municipal ordinance relating to operating a vehicle while under the influence of alcohol, a drug of abuse, or alcohol and a drug of abuse, a municipal ordinance relating to operating a vehicle with a prohibited concentration of alcohol in the blood, breath, or urine, section 2903.04 of the Revised Code in a case in which the person was subject to the sanctions described in division (D) of that section, or section 2903.06, 2903.07, or 2903.08 of the Revised Code or a municipal ordinance that is substantially similar to section 2903.07 of the Revised Code in a case in which the jury or judge found that the person was under the influence of alcohol, a drug of abuse, or alcohol and a drug of abuse, or a statute of the United States or of

any other state or a municipal ordinance of a municipal corporation located in any other state that is substantially similar to division (A) or (B) of section 4511.19 of the Revised Code, the person is not entitled to request, and the court shall not grant to the person, occupational driving privileges under this division. Any other person whose driver's or commercial driver's license or nonresident operating privilege has been suspended pursuant to division (F) of this section may file in the court specified in division (I)(1) of this section a petition requesting occupational driving privileges in accordance with section 4507.16 of the Revised Code. The petition may be filed at any time subsequent to the date on which the arresting officer serves the notice of suspension upon the arrested person. Upon the making of the request, occupational driving privileges may be granted in accordance with section 4507.16 of the Revised Code. The court may grant the occupational driving privileges, subject to the limitations contained in section 4507.16 of the Revised Code, regardless of whether the person appeals the suspension at the person's initial appearance under division (H)(1) of this section or appeals the decision of the court made pursuant to the appeal conducted at the initial appearance, and, if the person has appealed the suspension or decision, regardless of whether the matter at issue has been heard or decided by the court.

(J) When it finally has been determined under the procedures of this section that a nonresident's privilege to operate a vehicle within this state has been suspended, the registrar shall give information in writing of the action taken to the motor vehicle administrator of the state of the person's residence and of any state in which the person has a license.

(K) A suspension of the driver's or commercial driver's license or permit of a resident, a suspension of the operating privilege of a nonresident, or a denial of a driver's or commercial driver's license or permit for refusal to submit to a chemical test to determine the alcohol, drug, or alcohol and drug content of the person's blood, breath, or urine pursuant to division (E) of this section, shall be terminated by the registrar upon receipt of notice of the person's entering a plea of guilty to, or of the person's conviction after entering a plea of no contest under Criminal Rule 11 to, operating a vehicle while under the influence of alcohol, a drug of abuse, or alcohol and a drug of abuse or with a prohibited concentration of alcohol in the blood, breath, or urine, if the offense for which the plea is entered arose from the same incident that led to the suspension or denial.

The registrar shall credit against any judicial suspension of a person's driver's or commercial driver's license or permit or nonresident operating privilege imposed pursuant to division (B) or (E) of section 4507.16 of the Revised Code any time during which the person serves a related suspension imposed pursuant to division (E) or (F) of this section.

(L) At the end of a suspension period under this section, section 4511.196 [4511.19.6], or division (B) of section 4507.16 of the Revised Code and upon the request of the person whose driver's or commercial driver's license or permit was suspended and who is not otherwise subject to suspension, revocation, or disqualification, the registrar shall return the driver's or commercial driver's license or permit to the person upon the occurrence of all of the following:

(1) A showing by the person that the person had proof of financial responsibility, a policy of liability insurance in effect that meets the minimum standards set forth in section 4509.51 of the Revised Code, or proof, to the satisfaction of the registrar, that the person is able to respond in damages in an amount at least equal to the minimum amounts specified in section 4509.51 of the Revised Code.

(2) Payment by the person of a license reinstatement fee of two hundred eighty dollars to the bureau of motor vehicles, which fee shall be deposited in the state treasury and credited as follows:

(a) Seventy-five dollars shall be credited to the drivers' treatment and intervention fund, which is hereby established. The fund shall be used to pay the costs of driver treatment and intervention programs operated pursuant to sections 3793.02 and 3793.10 of the Revised Code. The director of alcohol and drug addiction services shall determine the share of the fund that is to be allocated to alcohol and drug addiction programs authorized by section 3793.02 of the Revised Code, and the share of the fund that is to be allocated to drivers' intervention programs authorized by section 3793.10 of the Revised Code.

(b) Fifty dollars shall be credited to the reparations fund created by section 2743.191 [2743.19.1] of the Revised Code.

(c) Twenty-five dollars shall be credited to the indigent drivers alcohol treatment fund, which is hereby established. Except as otherwise provided in division (L)(2)(c) of this section, moneys in the fund shall be distributed by the department of alcohol and drug addiction services to the county indigent drivers alcohol treatment funds, the county juvenile indigent drivers alcohol treatment funds, and the municipal indigent drivers treatment funds that are required to be established by counties and municipal corporations pursuant to division (N) of this section, and shall be used only to pay the cost of an alcohol and drug addiction treatment program attended by an offender or juvenile traffic offender who is ordered to attend an alcohol and drug addiction treatment program by a county, juvenile, or municipal court judge and who is determined by the county, juvenile, or municipal court judge not to have the means to pay for attendance at the program. Moneys in the fund that are not distributed to a county indigent drivers alcohol treatment fund, a county juvenile indigent drivers alcohol treatment fund, or a municipal indigent drivers alcohol treatment fund under division

(N) of this section because the director of alcohol and drug addiction services does not have the information necessary to identify the county or municipal corporation where the offender or juvenile offender was arrested may be transferred by the director of budget and management to the drivers' treatment and intervention fund, created in division (L)(2)(a) of this section, upon certification of the amount by the director of alcohol and drug addiction services.

(d) Fifty dollars shall be credited to the Ohio rehabilitation services commission established by section 3304.12 of the Revised Code, to the services for rehabilitation fund, which is hereby established. The fund shall be used to match available federal matching funds where appropriate, and for any other purpose or program of the commission to rehabilitate people with disabilities to help them become employed and independent.

(e) Fifty dollars shall be deposited into the state treasury and credited to the drug abuse resistance education programs fund, which is hereby established, to be used by the attorney general for the purposes specified in division (L)(2)(e) of this section.

(f) Thirty dollars shall be credited to the state bureau of motor vehicles fund created by section 4501.25 of the Revised Code.

The attorney general shall use amounts in the drug abuse resistance education programs fund to award grants to law enforcement agencies to establish and implement drug abuse resistance education programs in public schools. Grants awarded to a law enforcement agency under division (L)(2)(e) of this section shall be used by the agency to pay for not more than fifty per cent of the amount of the salaries of law enforcement officers who conduct drug abuse resistance education programs in public schools. The attorney general shall not use more than six per cent of the amounts the attorney general's office receives under division (L)(2)(e) of this section to pay the costs it incurs in administering the grant program established by division (L)(2)(e) of this section and in providing training and materials relating to drug abuse resistance education programs.

The attorney general shall report to the governor and the general assembly each fiscal year on the progress made in establishing and implementing drug abuse resistance education programs. These reports shall include an evaluation of the effectiveness of these programs.

(M) Suspension of a commercial driver's license under division (E) or (F) of this section shall be concurrent with any period of disqualification under section 2301.374 [2301.37.4] or 4506.16 of the Revised Code. No person who is disqualified for life from holding a commercial driver's license under section 4506.16 of the Revised Code shall be issued a driver's license under Chapter 4507. of the Revised Code during the period for which the commercial driver's license was suspended under division (E) or (F) of this section, and no person whose commercial driver's license is suspended under division (E) or (F) of this section shall be issued a driver's license under that chapter during the period of the suspension.

(N)(1) Each county shall establish an indigent drivers alcohol treatment fund, each county shall establish a juvenile indigent drivers alcohol treatment fund, and each municipal corporation in which there is a municipal court shall establish an indigent drivers alcohol treatment fund. All revenue that the general assembly appropriates to the indigent drivers alcohol treatment fund for transfer to a county indigent drivers alcohol treatment fund, a county juvenile indigent drivers alcohol treatment fund, or a municipal indigent drivers alcohol treatment fund, all portions of fees that are paid under division (L) of this section and that are credited under that division to the indigent drivers alcohol treatment fund in the state treasury for a county indigent drivers alcohol treatment fund, a county juvenile indigent drivers alcohol treatment fund, or a municipal indigent drivers alcohol treatment fund, and all portions of fines that are specified for deposit into a county or municipal indigent drivers alcohol treatment fund by section 4511.193 [4511.19.3] of the Revised Code shall be deposited into that county indigent drivers alcohol treatment fund, county juvenile indigent drivers alcohol treatment fund, or municipal indigent drivers alcohol treatment fund in accordance with division (N)(2) of this section. Additionally, all portions of fines that are paid for a violation of section 4511.19 of the Revised Code or division (B)(2) of section 4507.02 of the Revised Code, and that are required under division (A)(1) or (2) of section 4511.99 or division (B)(5) of section 4507.99 of the Revised Code to be deposited into a county indigent drivers alcohol treatment fund or municipal indigent drivers alcohol treatment fund shall be deposited into the appropriate fund in accordance with the applicable division.

(2) That portion of the license reinstatement fee that is paid under division (L) of this section and that is credited under that division to the indigent drivers alcohol treatment fund shall be deposited into a county indigent drivers alcohol treatment fund, a county juvenile indigent drivers alcohol treatment fund, or a municipal indigent drivers alcohol treatment fund as follows:

(a) If the suspension in question was imposed under this section, that portion of the fee shall be deposited as follows:

(i) If the fee is paid by a person who was charged in a county court with the violation that resulted in the suspension, the portion shall be deposited into the county indigent drivers alcohol treatment fund under the control of that court;

(ii) If the fee is paid by a person who was charged in a juvenile court with the violation that resulted in the suspension, the portion shall be deposited into the county juvenile indigent drivers alcohol treatment fund established in the county served by the court;

(iii) If the fee is paid by a person who was charged in a municipal court with the violation that resulted in the suspension, the portion shall be deposited into the municipal indigent drivers alcohol treatment fund under the control of that court.

(b) If the suspension in question was imposed under division (B) of section 4507.16 of the Revised Code, that portion of the fee shall be deposited as follows:

(i) If the fee is paid by a person whose license or permit was suspended by a county court, the portion shall be deposited into the county indigent drivers alcohol treatment fund under the control of that court;

(ii) If the fee is paid by a person whose license or permit was suspended by a municipal court, the portion shall be deposited into the municipal indigent drivers alcohol treatment fund under the control of that court.

(3) Expenditures from a county indigent drivers alcohol treatment fund, a county juvenile indigent drivers alcohol treatment fund, or a municipal indigent drivers alcohol treatment fund shall be made only upon the order of a county, juvenile, or municipal court judge and only for payment of the cost of the attendance at an alcohol and drug addiction treatment program of a person who is convicted of, or found to be a juvenile traffic offender by reason of, a violation of division (A) of section 4511.19 of the Revised Code or a substantially similar municipal ordinance, who is ordered by the court to attend the alcohol and drug addiction treatment program, and who is determined by the court to be unable to pay the cost of attendance at the treatment program. The board of alcohol, drug addiction, and mental health services established pursuant to section 340.02 of the Revised Code serving the alcohol, drug addiction, and mental health service district in which the court is located shall administer the indigent drivers alcohol treatment program of the court. When a court orders an offender or juvenile traffic offender to attend an alcohol and drug addiction treatment program, the board shall determine which program is suitable to meet the needs of the offender or juvenile traffic offender, and when a suitable program is located and space is available at the program, the offender or juvenile traffic offender shall attend the program designated by the board. A reasonable amount not to exceed five per cent of the amounts credited to and deposited into the county indigent drivers alcohol treatment fund, the county juvenile indigent drivers alcohol treatment fund, or the municipal indigent drivers alcohol treatment fund serving every court whose program is administered by that board shall be paid to the board to cover the costs it incurs in administering those indigent drivers alcohol treatment programs.

HISTORY: 132 v H 380 (Eff 1-1-68); 132 v S 512 (Eff 3-10-68); 133 v H 1 (Eff 3-18-69); 134 v H 792 (Eff 2-3-72); 136 v H 1 (Eff 6-13-75); 136 v H 451 (Eff 1-3-77); 137 v H 219 (Eff 11-1-77); 137 v H 469 (Eff 10-25-78); 139 v S 432 (Eff 3-16-83); 141 v H 201 (Eff 7-1-85); 141 v S 262 (Eff 3-20-87); 142 v H 303 (Eff 10-20-87); 142 v S 308 (Eff 3-14-89); 142 v H 643 (Eff 3-17-89); 143 v H 329 (Eff 6-30-89); 143 v H 381 (Eff 7-1-89); 143 v H 317 (Eff 10-10-89); 143 v S 131 (Eff 7-25-90); 143 v H 837 (Eff 7-25-90); 144 v S 275 (Eff 9-1-93); 145 v H 152 (Eff 7-1-93); 145 v S 62, §§ 1, 4 (Eff 9-1-93); 145 v S 82 (Eff 5-4-94); 145 v H 236 (Eff 9-29-94); 145 v H 687 (Eff 10-12-94); 146 v H 117 (Eff 6-30-95); 146 v S 2 (Eff 7-1-96); 146 v H 353, § 1 (Eff 9-17-96); 146 v S 166, § 1 (Eff 10-17-96); 146 v H 167 (Eff 5-15-97); 146 v H 353, § 4 (Eff 5-15-97); 146 v S 166, § 6 (Eff 5-15-97); 147 v S 85 (Eff 5-15-97); 147 v H 210 (Eff 6-30-97); 147 v S 60. Eff 10-21-97.

See provisions, § 25 of HB 210 (147 v —) following RC § 4507.45.

† Changed to six in SB 85 (147 v —).

[§ 4511.19.2] § 4511.192 Driving with suspended license.

(A) No person whose driver's or commercial driver's license or permit or nonresident operating privilege has been suspended under section 4511.191 [4511.19.1] or 4511.196 [4511.19.6] of the Revised Code shall operate a vehicle upon the highways or streets within this state.

(B) It is an affirmative defense to any prosecution brought pursuant to this section that the alleged offender drove under suspension because of a substantial emergency, provided that no other person was reasonably available to drive in response to the emergency.

HISTORY: 137 v S 381 (Eff 10-19-78); 139 v S 432 (Eff 3-16-83); 141 v S 262 (Eff 3-20-87); 143 v H 381 (Eff 7-1-89); 145 v S 62. Eff 9-1-93.

The effective date is set by section 3 of SB 62.

[§ 4511.19.3] § 4511.193 Deposit of $25 of fine for violating ordinance into indigent drivers alcohol treatment fund; vehicle immobilization or forfeiture orders based on prior convictions.

(A) Twenty-five dollars of any fine imposed for a violation of a municipal ordinance relating to operating a vehicle while under the influence of alcohol, a drug of abuse, or alcohol and a drug of abuse or relating to operating a vehicle with a prohibited concentration of alcohol in the blood, breath, or urine shall be deposited into the municipal or county indigent drivers alcohol treatment fund created pursuant to division (N) of section 4511.191 [4511.19.1] of the Revised Code in accordance with this section and section 733.40, divisions (A) and (B) of section 1901.024 [1901.02.4], division (F) of section 1901.31, or division (C) of section 1907.20 of the Revised Code. Regardless of whether the fine is imposed by a municipal court, a mayor's court, or a juvenile court, if the fine was imposed for a violation of an ordinance of a municipal corporation that is within the jurisdiction of a municipal court, the twenty-five dollars that is subject to this section shall be deposited into the indigent drivers alcohol treatment fund of the municipal corporation in which is located the municipal court that has jurisdiction over that municipal corporation. Regardless of whether the fine is imposed by a county court, a mayor's court, or a juvenile court, if the fine was imposed for a violation of an ordinance of a municipal corporation that is within the jurisdiction of a county court, the twenty-five dollars that is subject to this section shall be deposited into the indigent drivers alcohol treatment fund of the county in which is located the county court that has jurisdiction over that municipal corporation. The deposit shall be made in accordance with section 733.40, divisions (A) and (B) of section 1901.024 [1901.02.4], division (F) of section 1901.31, or division (C) of section 1907.20 of the Revised Code.

(B)(1) The requirements and sanctions imposed by divisions (B)(1) and (2) of this section are an adjunct to and derive from the state's exclusive authority over the registration and titling of motor vehicles and do not comprise a part of the criminal sentence to be imposed upon a person who violates a municipal ordinance relating to operating a vehicle while under the influence of alcohol, a drug of abuse, or alcohol and a drug of abuse or relating to operating a vehicle with a prohibited concentration of alcohol in the blood, breath, or urine.

(2) If a person is convicted of or pleads guilty to a municipal ordinance relating to operating a vehicle while under the influence of alcohol, a drug of abuse, or alcohol and a drug of abuse or relating to operating a vehicle with a prohibited concentration of alcohol in the blood, breath, or urine and if, within the period of time specified in division (B)(2)(a), (b), or (c) of this section, the offender has been convicted of or pleaded guilty to any violation of section 4511.19 of the Revised Code, a municipal ordinance relating to operating a vehicle while under the influence of alcohol, a drug of abuse, or alcohol and a drug of abuse, a municipal ordinance relating to operating a vehicle with a prohibited concentration of alcohol in the blood, breath, or urine, section 2903.04 of the Revised Code in a case in which the offender was subject to the sanctions described in division (D) of that section, section 2903.06, 2903.07, or 2903.08 of the Revised Code, or a municipal ordinance that is substantially similar to section 2903.07 of the Revised Code in a case in which the jury or judge found that the offender was under the influence of alcohol, a drug of abuse, or alcohol and a drug of abuse, a statute of the United States or of any other state or a municipal ordinance of a municipal corporation located in any other state that is substantially similar to division (A) or (B) of section 4511.19 of the Revised Code, or if the other circumstances described in division (B)(2)(c) of this section apply, the court, in addition to and independent of any sentence that it imposes upon the offender for the offense, regardless of whether the vehicle the offender was operating at the time of the offense is registered in the offender's name or in the name of another person, and subject to section 4503.235 [4503.23.5] of the Revised Code, shall do whichever of the following is applicable:

(a) Except as otherwise provided in division (B)(2)(c) of this section, if, within six years of the current offense, the offender has been convicted of or pleaded guilty to one violation described in division (B)(2) of this section, the court shall order the immobilization for ninety days of the vehicle the offender was operating at the time of the offense and the impoundment for ninety days of the license plates of that vehicle. The order for the immobilization and impoundment shall be issued and enforced in accordance with section 4503.233 [4503.23.3] of the Revised Code.

(b) Except as otherwise provided in division (B)(2)(c) of this section, if, within six years of the current offense, the offender has been convicted of or pleaded guilty to two violations described in division (B)(2) of this section, the court shall order the immobilization for one hundred eighty days of the vehicle the offender was operating at the time of the offense and the impoundment for one hundred eighty days of the license plates of that vehicle. The order for the immobilization and impoundment shall be issued and enforced in accordance with section 4503.233 [4503.23.3] of the Revised Code.

(c) If, within six years of the current offense, the offender has been convicted of or pleaded guilty to three or more violations described in division (B)(2) of this section, or if the offender previously has been convicted of or pleaded guilty to a violation of division (A) of section 4511.19 of the Revised Code under circumstances in which the violation was a felony and regardless of when the violation and the conviction or guilty plea occurred, the court shall order the criminal forfeiture to the state of the vehicle the offender was operating at the time of the offense. The order of criminal forfeiture shall be issued and enforced in accordance with section 4503.234 [4503.23.4] of the Revised Code.

HISTORY: 145 v S 62 (Eff 9-1-93); 146 v H 353 (Eff 9-17-96); 146 v S 166 (Eff 10-17-96); 147 v S 60. Eff 10-21-97.

The provisions of § 3 of SB 60 (147 v —) read as follows:

SECTION 3. ° ° ° Section 4511.193 of the Revised Code is presented in this act as a composite of the section as amended by both Am. Sub. H.B. 353 and Am. Sub. S.B. 166 of the 121st General Assembly, with the new language of neither of the acts shown in capital letters. Section 4511.195 of the Revised Code is presented in this act as a composite of the section as amended by Am. Sub. H.B. 353, Am. Sub. S.B. 166, and Am. Sub. H.B. 676 of the 121st General Assembly, with the new language of none of the acts shown in capital letters. This is in recognition of the principle stated in division (B) of section 1.52 of the Revised Code that such amendments are to be harmonized where not substantively irreconcilable and constitutes a legislative finding that such is the resulting version in effect prior to the effective date of this act.

[§ 4511.19.5] § 4511.195 Seizure and detention of vehicle where arrestee has prior conviction; return, immobilization or forfeiture after disposition of charge; rights of vehicle owner.

(A) As used in this section:

(1) "Vehicle operator" means a person who is op-

erating a vehicle at the time it is seized under division (B) of this section.

(2) "Vehicle owner" means either of the following:

(a) The person in whose name is registered, at the time of the seizure, a vehicle that is seized under division (B) of this section;

(b) A person to whom the certificate of title to a vehicle that is seized under division (B) of this section has been assigned and who has not obtained a certificate of title to the vehicle in that person's name, but who is deemed by the court as being the owner of the vehicle at the time the vehicle was seized under division (B) of this section.

(3) "Municipal OMVI ordinance" means any municipal ordinance prohibiting the operation of a vehicle while under the influence of alcohol, a drug of abuse, or alcohol and a drug of abuse or prohibiting the operation of a vehicle with a prohibited concentration of alcohol in the blood, breath, or urine.

(4) "Interested party" includes the owner of a vehicle seized under this section, all lienholders, the defendant, the owner of the place of storage at which a vehicle seized under this section is stored, and the person or entity that caused the vehicle to be removed.

(B)(1) If a person is arrested for a violation of division (A) of section 4511.19 of the Revised Code or of a municipal OMVI ordinance and, within six years of the alleged violation, the person previously has been convicted of or pleaded guilty to one or more violations of division (A) or (B) of section 4511.19 of the Revised Code, a municipal OMVI ordinance, section 2903.04 of the Revised Code in a case in which the offender was subject to the sanctions described in division (D) of that section, or section 2903.06, 2903.07, or 2903.08 of the Revised Code or a municipal ordinance that is substantially similar to section 2903.07 of the Revised Code in a case in which the jury or judge found that the offender was under the influence of alcohol, a drug of abuse, or alcohol and a drug of abuse, a statute of the United States or of any other state or a municipal ordinance of a municipal corporation located in any other state that is substantially similar to division (A) or (B) of section 4511.19 of the Revised Code, or if a person is arrested for a violation of division (A) of section 4511.19 of the Revised Code or of a municipal OMVI ordinance and the person previously has been convicted of or pleaded guilty to a violation of division (A) of section 4511.19 of the Revised Code under circumstances in which the violation was a felony, regardless of when the prior felony violation of division (A) of section 4511.19 of the Revised Code and the conviction or guilty plea occurred, the arresting officer or another officer of the law enforcement agency that employs the arresting officer, in addition to any action that the arresting officer is required or authorized to take by section 4511.191 [4511.19.1] of the Revised Code or by any other provision of law, shall seize the vehicle that the person was operating at the time of the alleged offense and its license plates. Except as otherwise provided in this division, the officer shall seize the vehicle and its license plates regardless of whether the vehicle is registered in the name of the person who was operating it or in the name of another person or entity. This section does not apply to or affect any rented or leased vehicle that is being rented or leased for a period of thirty days or less, except that a law enforcement agency that employs a law enforcement officer who makes an arrest of a type that is described in division (B)(1) of this section and that involves a rented or leased vehicle of this type shall notify, within twenty-four hours after the officer makes the arrest, the lessor or owner of the vehicle regarding the circumstances of the arrest and the location at which the vehicle may be picked up. At the time of the seizure of the vehicle, the law enforcement officer who made the arrest shall give the vehicle operator written notice that the vehicle and its license plates have been seized; that the vehicle either will be kept by the officer's law enforcement agency or will be immobilized at least until the operator's initial appearance on the charge of the offense for which the arrest was made; that, at the initial appearance, the court in certain circumstances may order that the vehicle and license plates be released to the vehicle owner until the disposition of that charge; that, if the vehicle operator is convicted of that charge, the court generally must order the immobilization of the vehicle and the impoundment of its license plates, or the forfeiture of the vehicle; and that, if the operator is not the vehicle owner, the operator immediately should inform the vehicle owner that the vehicle and its license plates have been seized and that the vehicle owner may be able to obtain their return or release at the initial appearance or thereafter.

(2) The arresting officer or a law enforcement officer of the agency that employs the arresting officer shall give written notice of the seizure to the court that will conduct the initial appearance of the vehicle operator. The notice shall be given when the charges are filed against the vehicle operator. Upon receipt of the notice, the court promptly shall determine whether the vehicle operator is the vehicle owner and whether there are any liens recorded on the certificate of title to the vehicle. If the court determines that the vehicle operator is not the vehicle owner, it promptly shall send by regular mail written notice of the seizure of the motor vehicle to the vehicle owner and to all lienholders recorded on the certificate of title. The written notice to the vehicle owner and lienholders shall contain all of the information required by division (B)(1) of this section to be in a notice to be given to the vehicle operator and also shall specify the date, time, and place of the vehicle operator's initial appearance. The notice to the vehicle owner also shall state that if the vehicle is immobilized under division (A) of section 4503.233 [4503.23.3] of the Revised Code, seven days after the end of the period of immobilization a law enforcement agency will send

the vehicle owner a notice, informing the vehicle owner that if the release of the vehicle is not obtained in accordance with division (D)(3) of section 4503.233 [4503.23.3] of the Revised Code, the vehicle shall be forfeited. The notice also shall inform the vehicle owner that the vehicle owner may be charged expenses or charges incurred under this section and section 4503.233 [4503.23.3] of the Revised Code for the removal and storage of the vehicle.

The written notice that is given to the vehicle operator or is sent or delivered to the vehicle owner if the vehicle owner is not the vehicle operator also shall state that if the vehicle operator pleads guilty to or is convicted of the offense for which the vehicle operator was arrested and the court issues an immobilization and impoundment order relative to that vehicle, division (D)(4) of section 4503.233 [4503.23.3] of the Revised Code prohibits the vehicle from being sold during the period of immobilization without the prior approval of the court.

Any such notice also shall state that if title to a motor vehicle that is subject to an order for criminal forfeiture under this section is assigned or transferred and division (C)(2) or (3) of section 4503.234 [4503.23.4] of the Revised Code applies, the court may fine the offender the value of the vehicle.

(3) At or before the initial appearance, the vehicle owner may file a motion requesting the court to order that the vehicle and its license plates be released to the vehicle owner. Except as provided in this division and subject to the payment of expenses or charges incurred in the removal and storage of the vehicle, the court, in its discretion, then may issue an order releasing the vehicle and its license plates to the vehicle owner. Such an order may be conditioned upon such terms as the court determines appropriate, including the posting of a bond in an amount determined by the court. If the vehicle operator is not the vehicle owner and if the vehicle owner is not present at the vehicle operator's initial appearance, and if the court believes that the vehicle owner was not provided with adequate notice of the initial appearance, the court, in its discretion, may allow the vehicle owner to file a motion within seven days of the initial appearance. If the court allows the vehicle owner to file such a motion after the initial appearance, the extension of time granted by the court does not extend the time within which the initial appearance is to be conducted. If the court issues an order for the release of the vehicle and its license plates, a copy of the order shall be made available to the vehicle owner. If the vehicle owner presents a copy of the order to the law enforcement agency that employs the law enforcement officer who arrested the person who was operating the vehicle, the law enforcement agency promptly shall release the vehicle and its license plates to the vehicle owner upon payment by the vehicle owner of any expenses or charges incurred in the removal and storage of the vehicle.

(4) A vehicle seized under division (B)(1) of this section either shall be towed to a place specified by the law enforcement agency that employs the arresting officer to be safely kept by the agency at that place for the time and in the manner specified in this section or shall be otherwise immobilized for the time and in the manner specified in this section. A law enforcement officer of that agency shall remove the identification license plates of the vehicle, and they shall be safely kept by the agency for the time and in the manner specified in this section. No vehicle that is seized and either towed or immobilized pursuant to this division shall be considered contraband for purposes of section 2933.41, 2933.42, or 2933.43 of the Revised Code. The vehicle shall not be immobilized at any place other than a commercially operated private storage lot, a place owned by a law enforcement agency or other government agency, or a place to which one of the following applies:

(a) The place is leased by or otherwise under the control of a law enforcement agency or other government agency.

(b) The place is owned by the vehicle operator, the vehicle operator's spouse, or a parent or child of the vehicle operator.

(c) The place is owned by a private person or entity, and, prior to the immobilization, the private entity or person that owns the place, or the authorized agent of that private entity or person, has given express written consent for the immobilization to be carried out at that place.

(d) The place is a street or highway on which the vehicle is parked in accordance with the law.

(C)(1) A vehicle that is seized under division (B) of this section shall be safely kept at the place to which it is towed or otherwise moved by the law enforcement agency that employs the arresting officer until the initial appearance of the vehicle operator relative to the charge in question. The license plates of the vehicle that are removed pursuant to division (B) of this section shall be safely kept by the law enforcement agency that employs the arresting officer until the initial appearance of the vehicle operator relative to the charge in question.

(2)(a) If, at the initial appearance, the vehicle operator pleads guilty to the violation of division (A) of section 4511.19 of the Revised Code or of the municipal OMVI ordinance or pleads no contest to and is convicted of the violation, the court shall impose sentence upon the vehicle operator as provided by law or ordinance; the court, except as provided in this division and subject to section 4503.235 [4503.23.5] of the Revised Code, shall order the immobilization of the vehicle and the impoundment of its license plates under section 4503.233 [4503.23.3] and section 4511.193 [4511.19.3] or 4511.99 of the Revised Code, or the criminal forfeiture of the vehicle under section 4503.234 [4503.23.4] and section 4511.193 [4511.19.3] or 4511.99 of the Revised Code, whichever is applicable; and the vehicle and its license plates shall not be returned or released to the vehicle owner. If the vehicle operator is not the vehicle owner and the vehicle owner is not present at the vehicle operator's initial appearance and if the court believes that the vehicle owner was not provided adequate notice of the initial appearance, the court, in its discretion, may refrain for a period of time not exceeding seven days from ordering the immobilization of the vehicle and the impoundment of its license plates, or the criminal forfeiture of the vehicle so that the vehicle owner may appear before the court to present evidence as to why the court should not order the immobilization of the vehicle and the impoundment of its license plates, or the criminal forfeiture of the vehicle. If the court refrains from ordering the immobilization of the vehicle and the impoundment of its license plates, or the criminal forfeiture of the vehicle, section 4503.235 [4503.23.5] of the Revised Code applies relative to the order of immobilization and impoundment, or the order of forfeiture.

(b) If, at any time, the charge that the vehicle operator violated division (A) of section 4511.19 of the Revised Code or the municipal OMVI ordinance is dismissed for any reason, the court shall order that the vehicle seized at the time of the arrest and its license plates immediately be released to the vehicle owner subject to the payment of expenses or charges incurred in the removal and storage of the vehicle.

(D) If a vehicle is seized under division (B) of this section and is not returned or released to the vehicle owner pursuant to division (C) of this section, the vehicle or its license plates shall be retained until the final disposition of the charge in question. Upon the final disposition of that charge, the court shall do whichever of the following is applicable:

(1) If the vehicle operator is convicted of or pleads guilty to the violation of division (A) of section 4511.19 of the Revised Code or of the municipal OMVI ordinance, the court shall impose sentence upon the vehicle operator as provided by law or ordinance and, subject to section 4503.235 [4503.23.5] of the Revised Code, shall order the immobilization of the vehicle the vehicle operator was operating at the time of, or that was involved in, the offense and the impoundment of its license plates under section 4503.233 [4503.23.3] and section 4511.193 [4511.19.3] or 4511.99 of the Revised Code, or the criminal forfeiture of the vehicle under section 4503.234 [4503.23.4] and section 4511.193 [4511.19.3] or 4511.99 of the Revised Code, whichever is applicable.

(2) If the vehicle operator is found not guilty of the violation of division (A) of section 4511.19 of the Revised Code or of the municipal OMVI ordinance, the court shall order that the vehicle and its license plates immediately be released to the vehicle owner upon the payment of any expenses or charges incurred in its removal and storage.

(3) If the charge that the vehicle operator violated division (A) of section 4511.19 of the Revised Code or the municipal OMVI ordinance is dismissed for any reason, the court shall order that the vehicle and its license plates immediately be released to the vehicle owner upon the payment of any expenses or charges incurred in its removal and storage.

(E) If a vehicle is seized under division (B) of this section, the time between the seizure of the vehicle and either its release to the vehicle owner under division (C) of this section or the issuance of an order of immobilization of the vehicle under section 4503.233 [4503.23.3] of the Revised Code shall be credited against the period of immobilization ordered by the court.

(F)(1) The vehicle owner may be charged expenses or charges incurred in the removal and storage of the immobilized vehicle. The court with jurisdiction over the case, after notice to all interested parties, including lienholders, and after an opportunity for them to be heard, if the vehicle owner fails to appear in person, without good cause, or if the court finds that the vehicle owner does not intend to seek release of the vehicle at the end of the period of immobilization under section 4503.233 [4503.23.3] of the Revised Code or that the vehicle owner is not or will not be able to pay the expenses and charges incurred in its removal and storage, may order that title to the vehicle be transferred, in order of priority, first into the name of the person or entity that removed it, next into the name of a lienholder, or lastly into the name of the owner of the place of storage.

Any lienholder that receives title under a court order shall do so on the condition that it pay any expenses or charges incurred in the vehicle's removal and storage. If the person or entity that receives title to the vehicle is the person or entity that removed it, the person or entity shall receive title on the condition that it pay any lien on the vehicle. The court shall not order that title be transferred to any person or entity other than the owner of the place of storage if the person or entity refuses to receive the title. Any person or entity that receives title either may keep title to the vehicle or may dispose of the vehicle in any legal manner that it considers appropriate, including assignment of the certificate of title to the motor vehicle to a salvage dealer or a scrap metal processing facility. The person or entity shall not transfer the vehicle to the person who is the vehicle's immediate previous owner.

If the person or entity assigns the motor vehicle to a salvage dealer or scrap metal processing facility, the person or entity shall send the assigned certificate of title to the motor vehicle to the clerk of the court of common pleas of the county in which the salvage dealer or scrap metal processing facility is located. The person or entity shall mark the face of the certificate of title with the words "for destruction" and shall deliver a photocopy of the certificate of title to the salvage dealer or scrap metal processing facility for its records.

(2) Whenever a court issues an order under division (F)(1) of this section, the court also shall order removal of the license plates from the vehicle and cause them to be sent to the registrar of motor vehicles if they have not already been sent to the registrar. Thereafter, no further proceedings shall take place under this section or under section 4503.233 [4503.23.3] of the Revised Code.

(3) Prior to initiating a proceeding under division (F)(1) of this section, and upon payment of the fee under division (B) of section 4505.14 of the Revised Code, any interested party may cause a search to be made of the public records of the bureau of motor vehicles or the clerk of the court of common pleas, to ascertain the identity of any lienholder of the vehicle. The initiating party shall furnish this information to the clerk of the court with jurisdiction over the case, and the clerk shall provide notice to the vehicle owner, the defendant, any lienholder, and any other interested parties listed by the initiating party, at the last known address supplied by the initiating party, by certified mail or, at the option of the initiating party, by personal service or ordinary mail.

HISTORY: 144 v S 275 (Eff 9-1-93); 145 v S 62, §§ 1, 4 (Eff 9-1-93); 145 v S 82 (Eff 5-4-94); 145 v H 236 (Eff 9-29-94); 145 v H 687 (Eff 10-12-94); 146 v H 353 (Eff 9-17-96); 146 v H 676 (Eff 10-4-96); 146 v S 166 (Eff 10-17-96); 147 v S 60. Eff 10-21-97.

See provisions, § 3 of SB 60 (147 v —) following RC § 4511.19.3.

[§ 4511.19.6] § 4511.196 Initial appearance; new suspension of license.

(A) If a person is arrested for operating a vehicle while under the influence of alcohol, a drug of abuse, or alcohol and a drug of abuse or for operating a vehicle with a prohibited concentration of alcohol in the blood, breath, or urine and regardless of whether the person's driver's or commercial driver's license or permit or nonresident operating privilege is or is not suspended under division (E) or (F) of section 4511.191 [4511.19.1] of the Revised Code, the person's initial appearance on the charge resulting from the arrest shall be held within five days of the person's arrest or the issuance of the citation to the person.

(B)(1) If a person is arrested as described in division (A) of this section, if the person's driver's or commercial driver's license or permit or nonresident operating privilege has been suspended under division (E) or (F) of section 4511.191 [4511.19.1] of the Revised Code in relation to that arrest, if the person appeals the suspension in accordance with division (H)(1) of that section, and if the judge, magistrate, or mayor terminates the suspension in accordance with division (H)(2) of that section, the judge, magistrate, or mayor may impose a new suspension of the person's license, permit, or nonresident operating privilege, notwithstanding the termination of the suspension imposed under division (E) or (F) of section 4511.191 [4511.19.1] of the Revised Code, if the judge, magistrate, or mayor determines that the person's continued driving will be a threat to public safety.

(2) If a person is arrested as described in division (A) of this section and if the person's driver's or commercial driver's license or permit or nonresident operating privilege has not been suspended under division (E) or (F) of section 4511.191 [4511.19.1] of the Revised Code in relation to that arrest, the judge, magistrate, or mayor may impose a suspension of the person's license, permit, or nonresident operating privilege if the judge, referee,† or mayor determines that the person's continued driving will be a threat to public safety.

(C) A suspension of a person's driver's or commercial driver's license or permit or nonresident operating privilege under division (B)(1) or (2) of this section shall continue until the complaint on the charge resulting from the arrest is adjudicated on the merits. A court that imposes a suspension under division (B)(2) of this section shall send the person's driver's license or permit to the registrar. If the court possesses the driver's or commercial driver's license or permit of a person in the category described in division (B)(2) of this section and the court does not impose a suspension under division (B)(2) of this section, the court shall return the license or permit to the person if the license or permit has not otherwise been suspended or revoked.

Any time during which the person serves a suspension of the person's driver's or commercial driver's license or permit or nonresident operating privilege that is imposed pursuant to division (B)(1) or (2) of this section shall be credited against any judicial suspension of the person's license, permit, or nonresident operating privilege that is imposed pursuant to division (B) of section 4507.16 of the Revised Code.

HISTORY: 145 v S 62 (Eff 9-1-93); 147 v S 60. Eff 10-21-97.

† So in enrolled bill, division (B)(2).

[RECKLESS OPERATION]

§ 4511.20 Reckless operation of vehicles.

No person shall operate a vehicle, trackless trolley, or streetcar on any street or highway in willful or wanton disregard of the safety of persons or property.

HISTORY: GC § 6307-20; 119 v 766, § 20; Bureau of Code Revision, 10-1-53; 132 v S 179 (Eff 12-13-67); 139 v S 432. Eff 3-16-83.

[§ 4511.20.1] § 4511.201 Reckless operation off streets and highways; competitive operation.

No person shall operate a vehicle, trackless trolley, or streetcar on any public or private property other than streets or highways, in willful or wanton disregard of the safety of persons or property.

This section does not apply to the competitive operation of vehicles on public or private property when the owner of such property knowingly permits such operation thereon.

HISTORY: 129 v 1637 (Eff 10-2-61); 132 v S 179 (Eff 12-13-67); 139 v S 432. Eff 3-16-83.

[§ 4511.20.2] § 4511.202 Operating a motor vehicle without reasonable control.

No person shall operate a motor vehicle, trackless trolley, or streetcar on any street, highway, or property open to the public for vehicular traffic without being in reasonable control of the vehicle, trolley, or streetcar.

HISTORY: 139 v S 432. Eff 3-16-83.

[SPEED REGULATIONS]

§ 4511.21 Speed limits.

(A) No person shall operate a motor vehicle, trackless trolley, or streetcar at a speed greater or less than is reasonable or proper, having due regard to the traffic, surface, and width of the street or highway and any other conditions, and no person shall drive any motor vehicle, trackless trolley, or streetcar in and upon any street or highway at a greater speed than will permit the person to bring it to a stop within the assured clear distance ahead.

(B) It is prima-facie lawful, in the absence of a lower limit declared pursuant to this section by the director of transportation or local authorities, for the operator of a motor vehicle, trackless trolley, or streetcar to operate the same at a speed not exceeding the following:

(1)(a) Twenty miles per hour in school zones during school recess and while children are going to or leaving school during the opening or closing hours, and when twenty miles per hour school speed limit signs are erected; except that, on controlled-access highways and expressways, if the right-of-way line fence has been erected without pedestrian opening, the speed shall be governed by division (B)(4) of this section and on freeways, if the right-of-way line fence has been erected without pedestrian opening, the speed shall be governed by divisions (B)(8) and (9) of this section. The end of every school zone may be marked by a sign indicating the end of the zone. Nothing in this section or in the manual and specifications for a uniform system of traffic control devices shall be construed to require school zones to be indicated by signs equipped with flashing or other lights, or giving other special notice of the hours in which the school zone speed limit is in effect.

(b) As used in this section and in section 4511.212 [4511.21.2] of the Revised Code, "school" means any school chartered under section 3301.16 of the Revised Code and any nonchartered school that during the preceding year filed with the department of education in compliance with rule 3301-35-08 of the Ohio Administrative Code, a copy of the school's report for the parents of the school's pupils certifying that the school meets Ohio minimum standards for nonchartered, nontax-supported schools and presents evidence of this filing to the jurisdiction from which it is requesting the establishment of a school zone.

(c) As used in this section, "school zone" means that portion of a street or highway passing a school fronting upon the street or highway that is encompassed by projecting the school property lines to the fronting street or highway, and also includes that portion of a state highway. Upon request from local authorities for streets and highways under their jurisdiction and that portion of a state highway under the jurisdiction of the director of transportation, the director may extend the traditional school zone boundaries. The distances in divisions (B)(1)(c)(i), (ii), and (iii) of this section shall not exceed three hundred feet per approach per direction and are bounded by whichever of the following distances or combinations thereof the director approves as most appropriate:

(i) The distance encompassed by projecting the school building lines normal to the fronting highway and extending a distance of three hundred feet on each approach direction;

(ii) The distance encompassed by projecting the school property lines intersecting the fronting highway and extending a distance of three hundred feet on each approach direction;

(iii) The distance encompassed by the special marking of the pavement for a principal school pupil crosswalk plus a distance of three hundred feet on each approach direction of the highway.

Nothing in this section shall be construed to invalidate the director's initial action on August 9, 1976, establishing all school zones at the traditional school zone boundaries defined by projecting school property lines, except when those boundaries are extended as provided in divisions (B)(1)(a) and (c) of this section.

(d) As used in this division, "crosswalk" has the meaning given that term in division (LL)(2) of section 4511.01 of the Revised Code.

The director may, upon request by resolution of the legislative authority of a municipal corporation, the board of trustees of a township, or a county board of mental retardation and developmental disabilities created pursuant to Chapter 5126. of the Revised Code, and upon submission by the municipal corporation, township, county board of such engineering, traffic, and other information as the director considers necessary, designate a school zone on any portion of a state route lying within the municipal corporation, lying within the unincorporated territory of the township, or lying adjacent to the property of a school that is operated by such county board, that includes a crosswalk customarily used by children going to or leaving a school during recess and opening and closing hours, whenever the distance, as measured in a straight line, from the school property line nearest the crosswalk to the nearest point of the crosswalk is no more than one thousand three hundred twenty feet. Such a school zone shall include the distance encompassed by the crosswalk and extending three hundred feet on each approach direction of the state route.

(2) Twenty-five miles per hour in all other portions of a municipal corporation, except on state routes outside business districts, through highways outside business districts, and alleys;

(3) Thirty-five miles per hour on all state routes or through highways within municipal corporations outside business districts, except as provided in divisions (B)(4) and (6) of this section;

(4) Fifty miles per hour on controlled-access highways and expressways within municipal corporations;

(5) Fifty-five miles per hour on highways outside of municipal corporations, other than freeways as provided in division (B)(12) of this section;

(6) Fifty miles per hour on state routes within municipal corporations outside urban districts unless a lower prima-facie speed is established as further provided in this section;

(7) Fifteen miles per hour on all alleys within the municipal corporation;

(8) Fifty-five miles per hour at all times on freeways with paved shoulders inside municipal corporations, other than freeways as provided in division (B)(12) of this section;

(9) Fifty-five miles per hour at all times on freeways outside municipal corporations, other than freeways as provided in division (B)(12) of this section;

(10) Fifty-five miles per hour at all times on all portions of freeways that are part of the interstate system and on all portions of freeways that are not part of the interstate system, but are built to the standards and specifications that are applicable to freeways that are part of the interstate system for operators of any motor vehicle weighing in excess of eight thousand pounds empty weight and any noncommercial bus;

(11) Fifty-five miles per hour for operators of any motor vehicle weighing eight thousand pounds or less empty weight and any commercial bus at all times on all portions of freeways that are part of the interstate system and that had such a speed limit established prior to October 1, 1995, and freeways that are not part of the interstate system, but are built to the standards and specifications that are applicable to freeways that are part of the interstate system and that had such a speed limit established prior to October 1, 1995, unless a higher speed limit is established under division (L) of this section;

(12) Sixty-five miles per hour for operators of any motor vehicle weighing eight thousand pounds or less empty weight and any commercial bus at all times on all portions of the following:

(a) Freeways that are part of the interstate system and that had such a speed limit established prior to October 1, 1995, and freeways that are not part of the interstate system, but are built to the standards and specifications that are applicable to freeways that are part of the interstate system and that had such a speed limit established prior to October 1, 1995;

(b) Freeways that are part of the interstate system and freeways that are not part of the interstate system but are built to the standards and specifications that are applicable to freeways that are part of the interstate system, and that had such a speed limit established under division (L) of this section;

(c) Rural, divided, multi-lane highways that are designated as part of the national highway system under the "National Highway System Designation Act of 1995," 109 Stat. 568, 23 U.S.C.A. 103, and that had such a speed limit established under division (M) of this section.

(C) It is prima-facie unlawful for any person to exceed any of the speed limitations in divisions (B)(1)(a), (2), (3), (4), (6), and (7) of this section, or any declared pursuant to this section by the director or local authorities and it is unlawful for any person to exceed any of the speed limitations in division (D) of this section. No person shall be convicted of more than one violation of this section for the same conduct, although violations of more than one provision of this section may be charged in the alternative in a single affidavit.

(D) No person shall operate a motor vehicle, trackless trolley, or streetcar upon a street or highway as follows:

(1) At a speed exceeding fifty-five miles per hour, except upon a freeway as provided in division (B)(12) of this section;

(2) At a speed exceeding sixty-five miles per hour upon a freeway as provided in division (B)(12) of this section except as otherwise provided in division (D)(3) of this section;

(3) If a motor vehicle weighing in excess of eight thousand pounds empty weight or a noncommercial bus as prescribed in division (B)(10) of this section, at a speed exceeding fifty-five miles per hour upon a freeway as provided in that division;

(4) At a speed exceeding the posted speed limit upon a freeway for which the director has determined and declared a speed limit of not more than sixty-five miles per hour pursuant to division (L)(2) or (M) of this section;

(5) At a speed exceeding sixty-five miles per hour upon a freeway for which such a speed limit has been established through the operation of division (L)(3) of this section;

(6) At a speed exceeding the posted speed limit upon a freeway for which the director has determined and declared a speed limit pursuant to division (I)(2) of this section.

(E) In every charge of violation of this section the affidavit and warrant shall specify the time, place, and speed at which the defendant is alleged to have driven, and in charges made in reliance upon division (C) of this section also the speed which division (B)(1)(a), (2), (3), (4), (6), or (7) of, or a limit declared pursuant to, this section declares is prima-facie lawful at the time and place of such alleged violation, except that in affidavits where a person is alleged to have driven at a greater speed than will permit the person to bring the vehicle to a stop within the assured clear distance ahead the affidavit and warrant need not specify the speed at which the defendant is alleged to have driven.

(F) When a speed in excess of both a prima-facie limitation and a limitation in division (D)(1), (2), (3), (4), (5), or (6) of this section is alleged, the defendant shall be charged in a single affidavit, alleging a single act, with a violation indicated of both division (B)(1)(a), (2), (3), (4), (6), or (7) of this section, or of a limit declared pursuant to this section by the director or local authorities, and of the limitation in division (D)(1), (2), (3), (4), (5), or (6) of this section. If the court finds a violation of division (B)(1)(a), (2), (3), (4), (6), or (7) of, or a limit declared pursuant to, this section has occurred, it shall enter a judgment of conviction under such division and dismiss the charge under division (D)(1), (2), (3), (4), (5), or (6) of this section. If it finds no violation of division (B)(1)(a), (2), (3), (4), (6), or (7) of, or a limit declared pursuant to, this section, it shall then consider whether the evidence supports a conviction under division (D)(1), (2), (3), (4), (5), or (6) of this section.

(G) Points shall be assessed for violation of a limitation under division (D) of this section only when the court finds the violation involved a speed of five miles per hour or more in excess of the posted speed limit.

(H) Whenever the director determines upon the basis of a geometric and traffic characteristic study that any speed limit set forth in divisions (B)(1)(a) to (D) of this section is greater or less than is reasonable or safe under the conditions found to exist at any portion of a street or highway under the jurisdiction of the director, the director shall determine and declare a reasonable and safe prima-facie speed limit, which shall be effective when appropriate signs giving notice of it are erected at the location.

(I)(1) Except as provided in divisions (I)(2) and (K) of this section, whenever local authorities determine upon the basis of an engineering and traffic investigation that the speed permitted by divisions (B)(1)(a) to (D) of this section, on any part of a highway under their jurisdiction, is greater than is reasonable and safe under the conditions found to exist at such location, the local authorities may by resolution request the director to determine and declare a reasonable and safe prima-facie speed limit. Upon receipt of such request the director may determine and declare a reasonable and safe prima-facie speed limit at such location, and if the director does so, then such declared speed limit shall become effective only when appropriate signs giving notice thereof are erected at such location by the local authorities. The director may withdraw the declaration of a prima-facie speed limit whenever in the director's opinion the altered prima-facie speed becomes unreasonable. Upon such withdrawal, the declared prima-facie speed shall become ineffective and the signs relating thereto shall be immediately removed by the local authorities.

(2) A local authority may determine on the basis of a geometric and traffic characteristic study that the speed limit of sixty-five miles per hour on a portion of a freeway under its jurisdiction that was established through the operation of division (L)(3) of this section is greater than is reasonable or safe under the conditions found to exist at that portion of the freeway. If the local authority makes such a determination, the local authority by resolution may request the director to determine and declare a reasonable and safe speed limit of not less than fifty-five miles per hour for that portion of the freeway. If the director takes such action, the declared speed limit becomes effective only when appropriate signs giving notice of it are erected at such location by the local authority.

(J) Local authorities in their respective jurisdictions may authorize by ordinance higher prima-facie speeds than those stated in this section upon through highways, or upon highways or portions thereof where there are no intersections, or between widely spaced intersections, provided signs are erected giving notice of the authorized speed, but local authorities shall not modify or alter the basic rule set forth in division (A) of this section or in any event authorize by ordinance a speed in excess of fifty miles per hour.

Alteration of prima-facie limits on state routes by local authorities shall not be effective until the alteration has been approved by the director. The director may withdraw approval of any altered prima-facie speed limits whenever in the director's opinion any altered prima-facie speed becomes unreasonable, and upon such withdrawal, the altered prima-facie speed shall become ineffective and the signs relating thereto shall be immediately removed by the local authorities.

(K)(1) As used in divisions (K)(1), (2), (3), and (4) of this section, "unimproved highway" means a highway consisting of any of the following:

(a) Unimproved earth;

(b) Unimproved graded and drained earth;

(c) Gravel.

(2) Except as otherwise provided in divisions (K)(4) and (5) of this section, whenever a board of township trustees determines upon the basis of an engineering and traffic investigation that the speed permitted by division (B)(5) of this section on any part of an unimproved highway under its jurisdiction and in the unincorporated territory of the township is greater than is reasonable or safe under the conditions found to exist

at the location, the board may by resolution declare a reasonable and safe prima-facie speed limit of fifty-five but not less than twenty-five miles per hour. An altered speed limit adopted by a board of township trustees under this division becomes effective when appropriate traffic control devices, as prescribed in section 4511.11 of the Revised Code, giving notice thereof are erected at the location, which shall be no sooner than sixty days after adoption of the resolution.

(3)(a) Whenever, in the opinion of a board of township trustees, any altered prima-facie speed limit established by the board under this division becomes unreasonable, the board may adopt a resolution withdrawing the altered prima-facie speed limit. Upon the adoption of such a resolution, the altered prima-facie speed limit becomes ineffective and the traffic control devices relating thereto shall be immediately removed.

(b) Whenever a highway ceases to be an unimproved highway and the board has adopted an altered prima-facie speed limit pursuant to division (K)(2) of this section, the board shall, by resolution, withdraw the altered prima-facie speed limit as soon as the highway ceases to be unimproved. Upon the adoption of such a resolution, the altered prima-facie speed limit becomes ineffective and the traffic control devices relating thereto shall be immediately removed.

(4)(a) If the boundary of two townships rests on the centerline of an unimproved highway in unincorporated territory and both townships have jurisdiction over the highway, neither of the boards of township trustees of such townships may declare an altered prima-facie speed limit pursuant to division (K)(2) of this section on the part of the highway under their joint jurisdiction unless the boards of township trustees of both of the townships determine, upon the basis of an engineering and traffic investigation, that the speed permitted by division (B)(5) of this section is greater than is reasonable or safe under the conditions found to exist at the location and both boards agree upon a reasonable and safe prima-facie speed limit of less than fifty-five but not less than twenty-five miles per hour for that location. If both boards so agree, each shall follow the procedure specified in division (K)(2) of this section for altering the prima-facie speed limit on the highway. Except as otherwise provided in division (K)(4)(b) of this section, no speed limit altered pursuant to division (K)(4)(a) of this section may be withdrawn unless the boards of township trustees of both townships determine that the altered prima-facie speed limit previously adopted becomes unreasonable and each board adopts a resolution withdrawing the altered prima-facie speed limit pursuant to the procedure specified in division (K)(3)(a) of this section.

(b) "Residential subdivision" means any platted territory outside the limits of a municipal corporation and fronting a highway, where, for a distance of three hundred feet or more, the frontage is improved with residences or residences and buildings in use for business, or where the entire length of the highway is less than three hundred feet long and the frontage is improved with residences or residences and buildings in use for business.

Whenever a board of township trustees finds upon the basis of an engineering and traffic investigation that the prima-facie speed permitted by division (B)(5) of this section on any part of a highway under its jurisdiction that is located in a commercial or residential subdivision, except on highways or portions thereof at the entrances to which vehicular traffic from the majority of intersecting highways is required to yield the right-of-way to vehicles on such highways in obedience to stop or yield signs or traffic control signals, is greater than is reasonable and safe under the conditions found to exist at the location, the board may by resolution declare a reasonable and safe prima-facie speed limit of less than fifty-five but not less than twenty-five miles per hour at the location. An altered speed limit adopted by a board of township trustees under this division shall become effective when appropriate signs giving notice thereof are erected at the location by the township. Whenever, in the opinion of a board of township trustees, any altered prima-facie speed limit established by it under this division becomes unreasonable, it may adopt a resolution withdrawing the altered prima-facie speed, and upon such withdrawal, the altered prima-facie speed shall become ineffective, and the signs relating thereto shall be immediately removed by the township.

(L)(1) Within one hundred twenty days of the effective date of this amendment, the director of transportation, based upon a geometric and traffic characteristic study of a freeway that is part of the interstate system or that is not part of the interstate system, but is built to the standards and specifications that are applicable to freeways that are part of the interstate system, in consultation with the director of public safety and, if applicable, the local authority having jurisdiction over a portion of such freeway, may determine and declare that the speed limit of less than sixty-five miles per hour established on such freeway or portion of freeway either is reasonable and safe or is less than that which is reasonable and safe.

(2) If the established speed limit for such a freeway or portion of freeway is determined to be less than that which is reasonable and safe, the director of transportation, in consultation with the director of public safety and, if applicable, the local authority having jurisdiction over the portion of freeway, shall determine and declare a reasonable and safe speed limit of not more than sixty-five miles per hour for that freeway or portion of freeway.

The director of transportation or local authority having jurisdiction over the freeway or portion of freeway shall erect appropriate signs giving notice of the speed limit at such location within one hundred fifty days of the effective date of this amendment. Such speed limit becomes effective only when such signs are erected at the location.

(3) If, within one hundred twenty days of the effective date of this amendment, the director of transportation does not make a determination and declaration of a reasonable and safe speed limit for a freeway or portion of freeway that is part of the interstate system or that is not part of the interstate system, but is built to the standards and specifications that are applicable to freeways that are part of the interstate system and that has a speed limit of less than sixty-five miles per hour, the speed limit on that freeway or portion of a freeway shall be sixty-five miles per hour. The director of transportation or local authority having jurisdiction over the freeway or portion of the freeway shall erect appropriate signs giving notice of the speed limit of sixty-five miles per hour at such location within one hundred fifty days of the effective date of this amendment. Such speed limit becomes effective only when such signs are erected at the location. A speed limit established through the operation of division (L)(3) of this section is subject to reduction under division (I)(2) of this section.

(M) Within three hundred sixty days after the effective date of this amendment, the director of transportation, based upon a geometric and traffic characteristic study of a rural, divided, multi-lane highway that has been designated as part of the national highway system under the "National Highway System Designation Act of 1995," 109 Stat. 568, 23 U.S.C.A. 103, in consultation with the director of public safety and, if applicable, the local authority having jurisdiction over a portion of the highway, may determine and declare that the speed limit of less than sixty-five miles per hour established on the highway or portion of highway either is reasonable and safe or is less than that which is reasonable and safe.

If the established speed limit for the highway or portion of highway is determined to be less than that which is reasonable and safe, the director of transportation, in consultation with the director of public safety and, if applicable, the local authority having jurisdiction over the portion of highway, shall determine and declare a reasonable and safe speed limit of not more than sixty-five miles per hour for that highway or portion of highway. The director of transportation or local authority having jurisdiction over the highway or portion of highway shall erect appropriate signs giving notice of the speed limit at such location within three hundred ninety days after the effective date of this amendment. The speed limit becomes effective only when such signs are erected at the location.

(N) As used in this section:

(1) "Interstate system" has the same meaning as in 23 U.S.C.A. 101.

(2) "Commercial bus" means a motor vehicle designed for carrying more than nine passengers and used for the transportation of persons for compensation.

(3) "Noncommercial bus" includes but is not limited to a school bus or a motor vehicle operated solely for the transportation of persons associated with a charitable or nonprofit organization.

HISTORY: GC § 6307-21; 119 v 766, § 21; 124 v 514; Bureau of Code Revision, 10-1-53; 126 v 115 (Eff 10-1-56); 127 v 931 (Eff 9-14-57); 128 v 1270 (Eff 11-4-59); 130 v 1083 (Eff 9-30-63); 130 v PtII, H 5 (Eff 12-16-64); 131 v 1101 (Eff 11-4-65); 132 v H 1 (Eff 2-21-67); 135 v H 200 (Eff 9-28-73); 136 v H 632 (Eff 6-27-75); 136 v H 1166 (Eff 8-9-76); 137 v H 587 (Eff 11-3-77); 138 v H 20 (Eff 8-29-79); 138 v H 32 (Eff 8-29-79); 138 v S 14 (Eff 10-25-79); 140 v S 37 (Eff 9-7-83); 141 v H 795 (Eff 8-29-86); 141 v S 356 (Eff 9-24-86); 141 v H 428 (Eff 12-23-86); 141 v H 666 (Eff 3-25-87); 142 v H 43 (Eff 7-31-87); 142 v H 493 (Eff 7-15-87); 143 v H 381 (Eff 7-1-89); 144 v H 96 (Eff 6-18-91); 144 v S 201 (Eff 8-19-92); 144 v S 301 (Eff 3-15-93); 146 v H 565. Eff 2-29-96.

The provisions of §§ 3, 4 of HB 565 (146 v —) read as follows:

SECTION 3. It is the intent of the General Assembly in amending section 4511.21 of the Revised Code to retain the speed limits established by that section at the limits and locations established prior to the repeal of the National Maximum Speed Limit Compliance Program in Pub. L. No. 104-59.

SECTION 4. Section 4511.21 of the Revised Code is presented in this act [Sub. H.B. 565] as a composite of the section as amended by both Am. Sub. S.B. 201 and Am. Sub. S.B. 301 of the 119th General Assembly, with the new language of neither of the acts shown in capital letters. This is in recognition of the principle stated in division (B) of section 1.52 of the Revised Code that such amendments are to be harmonized where not substantively irreconcilable and constitutes a legislative finding that such is the resulting version in effect prior to the effective date of this act.

[§ 4511.21.1] § 4511.211 Speed limit on private residential road or driveway.

(A) The owner of a private road or driveway located in a private residential area containing twenty or more dwelling units may establish a speed limit on the road or driveway by complying with all of the following requirements:

(1) The speed limit is not less than twenty-five miles per hour and is indicated by a sign that is in a proper position, is sufficiently legible to be seen by an ordinarily observant person, and meets the specifications for the basic speed limit sign included in the manual adopted by the department of transportation pursuant to section 4511.09 of the Revised Code;

(2) The owner has posted a sign at the entrance of the private road or driveway that is in plain view and clearly informs persons entering the road or driveway that they are entering private property, a speed limit has been established for the road or driveway, and the speed limit is enforceable by law enforcement officers under state law.

(B) No person shall operate a vehicle upon a private road or driveway as provided in division (A) of this section at a speed exceeding any speed limit established and posted pursuant to that division.

(C) When a speed limit is established and posted in accordance with division (A) of this section, any law enforcement officer may apprehend a person violating the speed limit of the residential area by utilizing any of the means described in section 4511.091 [4511.09.1] of the Revised Code or by any other accepted method of determining the speed of a motor vehicle and may stop and charge the person with exceeding the speed limit.

(D) Points shall be assessed for violation of a speed limit established and posted in accordance with division (A) of this section only when the violation involves a speed of five miles per hour or more in excess of the posted speed limit.

(E) As used in this section:

(1) "Owner" includes but is not limited to a person who holds title to the real property in fee simple, a condominium owners' association, a property owners' association, the board of directors or trustees of a private community, and a nonprofit corporation governing a private community.

(2) "Private residential area containing twenty or more dwelling units" does not include a Chautauqua assembly as defined in section 4511.90 of the Revised Code.

HISTORY: 143 v H 171. Eff 5-31-90.

Not analogous to former RC § 4511.21.1 (135 v H 1052), repealed, 136 v H 632, § 2, eff 6-27-75.

[§ 4511.21.2] § 4511.212 Complaint that local authority is not complying with school zone sign laws.

(A) As used in this section, "local authority" means the legislative authority of a municipal corporation, the board of trustees of a township, or the board of county commissioners of a county.

(B) The board of education or the chief administrative officer operating or in charge of any school may submit a written complaint to the director of transportation alleging that a local authority is not complying with section 4511.11 or divisions (B)(1)(a) to (d) of section 4511.21 of the Revised Code with regard to school zones. Upon receipt of such a complaint, the director shall review or investigate the facts of the complaint and discuss the complaint with the local authority and the board of education or chief administrative officer submitting the complaint. If the director finds that the local authority is not complying with section 4511.11 or divisions (B)(1)(a) to (d) of section 4511.21 of the Revised Code with regard to school zones, the director shall issue a written order requiring the local authority to comply by a specified date and the local authority shall comply with the order. If the local authority fails to comply with the order, the director shall implement the order and charge the local authority for the cost of the implementation. Any local authority being so charged shall pay to the state the amount charged. Any amounts received under this section shall be deposited into the state treasury to the credit of the highway operating fund created by section 5735.291 [5735.29.1] of the Revised Code.

HISTORY: 144 v S 201. Eff 8-19-92.

§ 4511.22 Slow speed.

(A) No person shall stop or operate a vehicle, trackless trolley, or street car at such a slow speed as to impede or block the normal and reasonable movement of traffic, except when stopping or reduced speed is necessary for safe operation or to comply with law.

(B) Whenever the director of transportation or local authorities determine on the basis of an engineering and traffic investigation that slow speeds on any part of a controlled-access highway, expressway, or freeway consistently impede the normal and reasonable movement of traffic, the director or such local authority may declare a minimum speed limit below which no person shall operate a motor vehicle, trackless trolley, or street car except when necessary for safe operation or in compliance with law. No minimum speed limit established hereunder shall be less than thirty miles per hour, greater than fifty miles per hour, nor effective until the provisions of section 4511.21 of the Revised Code, relating to appropriate signs, have been fulfilled and local authorities have obtained the approval of the director.

HISTORY: GC § 6307-22; 119 v 766, § 22; Bureau of Code Revision, 10-1-53; 127 v 51 (Eff 8-23-57); 135 v H 200 (Eff 9-28-73); 136 v H 632 (Eff 6-27-75); 144 v H 96. Eff 6-18-91.

§ 4511.23 Speed regulations on bridges.

No person shall operate a vehicle, trackless trolley, or streetcar over any bridge or other elevated structure constituting a part of a highway at a speed which is greater than the maximum speed that can be maintained with safety to such bridge or structure, when such structure is posted with signs as provided in this section.

The department of transportation upon request from any local authority shall, or upon its own initiative may, conduct an investigation of any bridge or other elevated structure constituting a part of a highway, and if it finds that such structure cannot with safety withstand traffic traveling at the speed otherwise permissible under sections 4511.01 to 4511.78 and 4511.99 of the Revised Code, the department shall determine and declare the maximum speed of traffic which such structure can withstand, and shall cause or permit suitable signs stating such maximum speed to be erected and maintained at a distance of at least one hundred feet before each end of such structure.

Upon the trial of any person charged with a violation of this section, proof of said determination of the maximum speed by the department and the existence of said signs shall constitute prima-facie evidence of the maximum speed which can be maintained with safety to such bridge or structure.

HISTORY: GC § 6307-23; 119 v 766, § 23; Bureau of Code Revision, 10-1-53; 135 v H 200. Eff 9-28-73.

§ 4511.24 Emergency vehicles excepted from speed limitations.

The prima-facie speed limitations set forth in section 4511.21 of the Revised Code do not apply to emergency vehicles or public safety vehicles when they are responding to emergency calls and are equipped with and displaying at least one flashing, rotating, or oscillating light visible under normal atmospheric conditions from a distance of five hundred feet to the front of the vehicle and when the drivers thereof sound audible signals by bell, siren, or exhaust whistle. This section does not relieve the driver of an emergency vehicle or public safety vehicle from the duty to drive with due regard for the safety of all persons using the street or highway.

HISTORY: GC § 6307-24; 119 v 766, § 24; Bureau of Code Revision, 10-1-53; 132 v H 378 (Eff 12-14-67); 135 v H 995. Eff 1-1-75.

The effective date is set by section 3 of HB 995.

[TRAFFIC RULES]

§ 4511.25 Lanes of travel upon roadways.

(A) Upon all roadways of sufficient width, a vehicle or trackless trolley shall be driven upon the right half of the roadway, except as follows:

(1) When overtaking and passing another vehicle proceeding in the same direction, or when making a left turn under the rules governing such movements;

(2) When an obstruction exists making it necessary to drive to the left of the center of the highway; provided, any person so doing shall yield the right of way to all vehicles traveling in the proper direction upon the unobstructed portion of the highway within such distance as to constitute an immediate hazard;

(3) When driving upon a roadway divided into three or more marked lanes for traffic under the rules applicable thereon;

(4) When driving upon a roadway designated and posted with signs for one-way traffic;

(5) When otherwise directed by a police officer or traffic control device.

(B) Upon all roadways any vehicle or trackless trolley proceeding at less than the normal speed of traffic at the time and place and under the conditions then existing shall be driven in the right-hand lane then available for traffic, or as close as practicable to the right-hand curb or edge of the roadway, except when overtaking and passing another vehicle or trackless trolley proceeding in the same direction or when preparing for a left turn.

(C) Upon any roadway having four or more lanes for moving traffic and providing for two-way movement of traffic, no vehicle or trackless trolley shall be driven to the left of the center line of the roadway, except when authorized by official traffic control devices designating certain lanes to the left of the center of the roadway for use by traffic not otherwise permitted to use the lanes, or except as permitted under division (A)(2) of this section.

Division (C) of this section shall not be construed as prohibiting the crossing of the center line in making a left turn into or from an alley, private road, or driveway.

HISTORY: GC § 6307-25; 119 v 766, § 25; Bureau of Code Revision, 10-1-53; 129 v 1032 (Eff 9-9-61); 130 v 1086 (Eff 6-10-63); 135 v H 995. Eff 1-1-75.

The effective date is set by section 3 of HB 995.

[§ 4511.25.1] § 4511.251 Street racing defined; prohibited on public highways.

(A) As used in this section and in sections 4507.021 [4507.02.1] and 4507.16 of the Revised Code, "street racing" means the operation of two or more vehicles from a point side by side at accelerating speeds in a competitive attempt to out-distance each other or the operation of one or more vehicles over a common selected course, from the same point to the same point, wherein timing is made of the participating vehicles involving competitive accelerations or speeds. Persons rendering assistance in any manner to such competitive use of vehicles shall be equally charged as the participants. The operation of two or more vehicles side by side either at speeds in excess of prima-facie lawful speeds established by divisions (B)(1)(a) to (B)(7) of section 4511.21 of the Revised Code or rapidly accelerating from a common starting point to a speed in excess of such prima-facie lawful speeds shall be prima-facie evidence of street racing.

(B) No person shall participate in street racing upon any public road, street, or highway in this state.

HISTORY: 128 v 469 (Eff 11-10-59); 138 v S 14 (Eff 10-25-79); 146 v H 107. Eff 6-30-95.

[§ 4511.25.2] § 4511.252 Closing of public roads for competitive racing.

In townships in this state composed entirely of islands, the legislative authority of a municipal corporation, the county commissioners of the county wherein such township is located, and the trustees of such township may, by joint consent, cause any road, street, or highway in said township, whether within or without the limits of a municipal corporation, excepting state highways, to be closed to public travel, except in cases of emergency, for periods of not to exceed twenty-four hours, and during such period such roads, streets, or highways so closed may be used for supervised sports car racing;

(A) Any competitive racing event to be held upon a public road, street, or highway shall be sponsored by a recognized responsible organization.

(B) Any race held pursuant to division (A) of this section shall be conducted under the rules and regulations of the Sports Car Clubs of America.

(C) Adequate barricades shall be maintained at all hazardous sections of the racing course, hazardous corners shall be provided with barricades in the form of bales of hay or similar material sufficient to check accidental deviations from the course, and spectators shall be prohibited from entering a designated zone within two hundred feet from such corner extending two hundred feet along the exit outside section of such corner.

(D) The sponsoring organization under division (A) of this section shall furnish public liability insurance in the amount of two hundred fifty thousand dollars because of bodily injury to or death of one person resulting from any one accident, in the amount of one million dollars because of bodily injury to or death of two or more persons in any one accident, and in the amount of fifty thousand dollars because of injury to property of others in any one accident.

HISTORY: 130 v 1086. Eff 5-1-63.

§ 4511.26 Vehicles traveling in opposite directions.

Operators of vehicles and trackless trolleys proceeding in opposite directions shall pass each other to the right, and upon roadways having width for not more than one line of traffic in each direction, each operator shall give to the other one-half of the main traveled portion of the roadway or as nearly one-half as is reasonably possible.

HISTORY: GC § 6307-26; 119 v 766(778), § 26; Bureau of Code Revision. Eff 10-1-53.

§ 4511.27 Rules governing overtaking and passing of vehicles.

The following rules govern the overtaking and passing of vehicles or trackless trolleys proceeding in the same direction:

(A) The operator of a vehicle or trackless trolley overtaking another vehicle or trackless trolley proceeding in the same direction shall, except as provided in division (C) of this section, signal to the vehicle or trackless trolley to be overtaken, shall pass to the left thereof at a safe distance, and shall not again drive to the right side of the roadway until safely clear of the overtaken vehicle or trackless trolley.

(B) Except when overtaking and passing on the right is permitted, the operator of an overtaken vehicle shall give way to the right in favor of the overtaking vehicle at the latter's audible signal, and he shall not increase the speed of his vehicle until completely passed by the overtaking vehicle.

(C) The operator of a vehicle or trackless trolley overtaking and passing another vehicle or trackless trolley proceeding in the same direction on a divided highway as defined in section 4511.35 of the Revised Code, a limited access highway as defined in section 5511.02 of the Revised Code, or a highway with four or more traffic lanes, is not required to signal audibly to the vehicle or trackless trolley being overtaken and passed.

HISTORY: GC § 6307-27; 119 v 766(778), § 27; Bureau of Code Revision, 10-1-53; 133 v S 289. Eff 11-6-69.

§ 4511.28 Permission to overtake and pass on the right.

(A) The driver of a vehicle or trackless trolley may overtake and pass upon the right of another vehicle or trackless trolley only under the following conditions:

(1) When the vehicle or trackless trolley overtaken is making or about to make a left turn;

(2) Upon a roadway with unobstructed pavement of sufficient width for two or more lines of vehicles moving lawfully in the direction being traveled by the overtaking vehicle.

(B) The driver of a vehicle or trackless trolley may overtake and pass another vehicle or trackless trolley only under conditions permitting such movement in safety. The movement shall not be made by driving off the roadway.

HISTORY: GC § 6307-28; 119 v 766(778), § 28; Bureau of Code Revision, 10-1-53; 135 v H 995. Eff 1-1-75.

§ 4511.29 Driving to left of center line.

No vehicle or trackless trolley shall be driven to the left of the center of the roadway in overtaking and passing traffic proceeding in the same direction, unless such left side is clearly visible and is free of oncoming traffic for a sufficient distance ahead to permit such overtaking and passing to be completely made, without interfering with the safe operation of any traffic approaching from the opposite direction or any traffic overtaken. In every event the overtaking vehicle or trackless trolley must return to an authorized lane of travel as soon as practicable and in the event the passing movement involves the use of a lane authorized for traffic approaching from the opposite direction, before coming within two hundred feet of any approaching vehicle.

HISTORY: GC § 6307-29; 119 v 766(778), § 29; Bureau of Code Revision, 10-1-53; 135 v H 995. Eff 1-1-75.

The effective date of is set by section 3 of HB 995.

§ 4511.30 Prohibition against driving upon left side of roadway.

No vehicle or trackless trolley shall be driven upon the left side of the roadway under the following conditions:

(A) When approaching the crest of a grade or upon a curve in the highway, where the operator's view is obstructed within such a distance as to create a hazard in the event traffic might approach from the opposite direction;

(B) When the view is obstructed upon approaching within one hundred feet of any bridge, viaduct, or tunnel;

(C) When approaching within one hundred feet of or traversing any intersection or railroad grade crossing.

This section does not apply to vehicles or trackless trolleys upon a one-way roadway, upon a roadway where traffic is lawfully directed to be driven to the left side, or under the conditions described in division (A)(2) of section 4511.25 of the Revised Code.

HISTORY: GC § 6307-30; 119 v 766(779), § 30; 120 v 221; Bureau of Code Revision, 10-1-53; 135 v H 995. Eff 1-1-75.

The effective date is set by section 3 of HB 995.

§ 4511.31 Hazardous zones.

The department of transportation may determine those portions of any state highway where overtaking and passing other traffic or driving to the left of the center or center line of the roadway would be especially hazardous, and may, by appropriate signs or markings on the highway, indicate the beginning and end of such zones. When such signs or markings are in place and clearly visible, every operator of a vehicle or trackless trolley shall obey the directions thereof, notwithstanding the distances set out in section 4511.30 of the Revised Code.

HISTORY: GC § 6307-31; 119 v 766(779), § 31; 124 v 514; Bureau of Code Revision, 10-1-53; 135 v H 200. Eff 9-28-73.

§ 4511.32 One-way highways and rotary traffic islands.

The department of transportation may designate any highway or any separate roadway under its jurisdiction for one-way traffic and shall erect appropriate signs giving notice thereof.

Upon a roadway designated and posted with signs for one-way traffic a vehicle shall be driven only in the direction designated.

A vehicle passing around a rotary traffic island shall be driven only to the right of such island.

HISTORY: GC § 6307-32; 119 v 766(779), § 32; Bureau of Code Revision, 10-1-53; 135 v H 200. Eff 9-28-73.

§ 4511.33 Rules for driving in marked lanes.

Whenever any roadway has been divided into two or more clearly marked lanes for traffic, or wherever within municipal corporations traffic is lawfully moving in two or more substantially continuous lines in the same direction, the following rules apply:

(A) A vehicle or trackless trolley shall be driven, as nearly as is practicable, entirely within a single lane or line of traffic and shall not be moved from such lane or line until the driver has first ascertained that such movement can be made with safety.

(B) Upon a roadway which is divided into three lanes and provides for two-way movement of traffic, a vehicle or trackless trolley shall not be driven in the center lane except when overtaking and passing another vehicle or trackless trolley where the roadway is clearly visible and such center lane is clear of traffic within a safe distance, or when preparing for a left turn, or where such center lane is at the time allocated exclusively to traffic moving in the direction the vehicle or trackless trolley is proceeding and is posted with signs to give notice of such allocation.

(C) Official signs may be erected directing specified traffic to use a designated lane or designating those lanes to be used by traffic moving in a particular direction regardless of the center of the roadway, and drivers of vehicles and trackless trolleys shall obey the directions of such signs.

(D) Official traffic control devices may be installed prohibiting the changing of lanes on sections of roadway and drivers of vehicles shall obey the directions of every such device.

HISTORY: GC § 6307-33; 119 v 766(779), § 33; Bureau of Code Revision, 10-1-53; 135 v H 995. Eff 1-1-75.

The effective date is set by section 3 of HB 995.

§ 4511.34 Space between moving vehicles.

The operator of a motor vehicle, streetcar, or trackless trolley shall not follow another vehicle, streetcar, or trackless trolley more closely than is reasonable and prudent, having due regard for the speed of such vehicle, streetcar, or trackless trolley, and the traffic upon and the condition of the highway.

The driver of any truck, or motor vehicle drawing another vehicle, when traveling upon a roadway outside a business or residence district shall maintain a sufficient space, whenever conditions permit, between such vehicle and another vehicle ahead so an overtaking motor vehicle may enter and occupy such space without danger. This paragraph does not prevent overtaking and passing nor does it apply to any lane specially designated for use by trucks.

Outside a municipal corporation, the driver of any truck, or motor vehicle when drawing another vehicle, while ascending to the crest of a grade beyond which the driver's view of the roadway is obstructed, shall not follow within three hundred feet of another truck, or motor vehicle drawing another vehicle. This paragraph shall not apply to any lane specially designated for use by trucks.

Motor vehicles being driven upon any roadway outside of a business or residence district in a caravan or motorcade, shall maintain a sufficient space between such vehicles so an overtaking vehicle may enter and occupy such space without danger. This paragraph shall not apply to funeral processions.

HISTORY: GC § 6307-34; 119 v 766(789), § 34; Bureau of Code Revision, 10-1-53; 126 v 113. Eff 9-30-55.

§ 4511.35 Divided roadways.

Whenever any highway has been divided into two roadways by an intervening space, or by a physical barrier, or clearly indicated dividing section so constructed as to impede vehicular traffic, every vehicle shall be driven only upon the right-hand roadway, and no vehicle shall be driven over, across, or within any such dividing space, barrier, or section, except through an opening, crossover, or intersection established by public authority. This section does not prohibit the occupancy of such dividing space, barrier, or section for the purpose of an emergency stop or in compliance with an order of a police officer.

HISTORY: GC § 6307-34a; 124 v 514; Bureau of Code Revision. Eff 10-1-53.

§ 4511.36 Rules for turns at intersections.

The driver of a vehicle intending to turn at an intersection shall be governed by the following rules:

(A) Approach for a right turn and a right turn shall be made as close as practicable to the right-hand curb or edge of the roadway.

(B) At any intersection where traffic is permitted to move in both directions on each roadway entering the intersection, an approach for a left turn shall be made in that portion of the right half of the roadway nearest the center line thereof and by passing to the right of such center line where it enters the intersection and after entering the intersection the left turn shall be made so as to leave the intersection to the right of the center line of the roadway being entered. Whenever practicable the left turn shall be made in that portion of the intersection to the left of the center of the intersection.

(C) At any intersection where traffic is restricted to one direction on one or more of the roadways, the driver of a vehicle intending to turn left at any such intersection shall approach the intersection in the extreme left-hand lane lawfully available to traffic moving in the direction of travel of such vehicle, and after entering the intersection the left turn shall be made so as to leave the intersection, as nearly as practicable, in the left-hand lane of the roadway being entered lawfully available to traffic moving in that lane.

The operator of a trackless trolley shall comply with divisions (A), (B), and (C) of this section wherever practicable.

The department of transportation and local authorities in their respective jurisdictions may cause markers, buttons, or signs to be placed within or adjacent to intersections and thereby require and direct that a different course from that specified in this section be traveled by vehicles, streetcars, or trackless trolleys, turning at an intersection, and when markers, buttons, or signs are so placed, no operator of a vehicle, streetcar, or trackless trolley shall turn such vehicle, streetcar, or trackless trolley at an intersection other than as directed and required by such markers, buttons, or signs.

HISTORY: GC § 6307-35; 119 v 766(780), § 35; 124 v 514; Bureau of Code Revision, 10-1-53; 135 v H 200. Eff 9-28-73.

§ 4511.37 Turning in roadway prohibited; exception for emergency or public safety vehicle.

(A) Except as provided in division (B) of this section, no vehicle shall be turned so as to proceed in the opposite direction upon any curve, or upon the approach to or near the crest of a grade, if the vehicle cannot be seen within five hundred feet by the driver of any other vehicle approaching from either direction.

(B) The driver of an emergency vehicle or public safety vehicle, when responding to an emergency call, may turn the vehicle so as to proceed in the opposite direction. This division applies only when the emergency vehicle or public safety vehicle is responding to an emergency call, is equipped with and displaying at least one flashing, rotating, or oscillating light visible under normal atmospheric conditions from a distance of five hundred feet to the front of the vehicle, and when the driver of the vehicle is giving an audible signal by siren, exhaust whistle, or bell. This division does not relieve the driver of an emergency vehicle or public safety vehicle from the duty to drive with due regard for the safety of all persons and property upon the highway.

HISTORY: GC § 6307-36; 119 v 766(781), § 36; Bureau of Code Revision, 10-1-53; 145 v H 149. Eff 5-20-93.

§ 4511.38 Rules for starting and backing vehicles.

No person shall start a vehicle, streetcar, or trackless trolley which is stopped, standing, or parked until such movement can be made with reasonable safety.

Before backing, operators of vehicles, streetcars, or trackless trolleys shall give ample warning, and while backing they shall exercise vigilance not to injure person or property on the street or highway.

No person shall back a motor vehicle on a freeway, except: in a rest area; in the performance of public works or official duties; as a result of an emergency caused by an accident or breakdown of a motor vehicle.

HISTORY: GC § 6307-37; 119 v 766(781), § 37; Bureau of Code Revision, 10-1-53; 131 v 1103. Eff 11-4-65.

§ 4511.39 Turn and stop signals.

No person shall turn a vehicle or trackless trolley or

move right or left upon a highway unless and until such person has exercised due care to ascertain that the movement can be made with reasonable safety nor without giving an appropriate signal in the manner hereinafter provided.

When required, a signal of intention to turn or move right or left shall be given continuously during not less than the last one hundred feet traveled by the vehicle or trackless trolley before turning.

No person shall stop or suddenly decrease the speed of a vehicle or trackless trolley without first giving an appropriate signal in the manner provided herein to the driver of any vehicle or trackless trolley immediately to the rear when there is opportunity to give a signal.

Any stop or turn signal required by this section shall be given either by means of the hand and arm, or by signal lights that clearly indicate to both approaching and following traffic intention to turn or move right or left, except that any motor vehicle in use on a highway shall be equipped with, and the required signal shall be given by, signal lights when the distance from the center of the top of the steering post of the left outside limit of the body, cab, or load of such motor vehicle exceeds twenty-four inches, or when the distance from the center of the top of the steering post of the rear limit of the body or load thereof exceeds fourteen feet, whether a single vehicle or a combination of vehicles.

The signal lights required by this section shall not be flashed on one side only on a disabled vehicle or trackless trolley, flashed as a courtesy or "do pass" signal to operators of other vehicles or trackless trolleys approaching from the rear, nor be flashed on one side only of a parked vehicle or trackless trolley except as may be necessary for compliance with this section.

HISTORY: GC § 6307-38; 119 v 766(781), § 38; 124 v 514(533); Bureau of Code Revision, 10-1-53; 125 v 460 (Eff 10-19-53); 135 v H 995. Eff 1-1-75.

The effective date is set by section 3 of HB 995.

§ 4511.40 Hand and arm signals.

(A) Except as provided in division (B) of this section, all signals required by sections 4511.01 to 4511.78 of the Revised Code, when given by hand and arm, shall be given from the left side of the vehicle in the following manner, and such signals shall indicate as follows:

(1) Left turn, hand and arm extended horizontally;

(2) Right turn, hand and arm extended upward;

(3) Stop or decrease speed, hand and arm extended downward.

(B) As an alternative to division (A)(2) of this section, a person operating a bicycle may give a right turn signal by extending the right hand and arm horizontally and to the right side of the bicycle.

HISTORY: GC § 6307-39; 119 v 766(782), § 39; Bureau of Code Revision, 10-1-53; 146 v H 461. Eff 9-10-96.

[RIGHT OF WAY]

§ 4511.41 Right-of-way at intersections.

(A) When two vehicles, including any trackless trolley or streetcar, approach or enter an intersection from different streets or highways at approximately the same time, the driver of the vehicle on the left shall yield the right-of-way to the vehicle on the right.

(B) The right-of-way rule declared in division (A) of this section is modified at through highways and otherwise as stated in Chapter 4511. of the Revised Code.

HISTORY: 135 v H 995 (Eff 1-1-75); 136 v H 1. Eff 6-13-75.

Analogous to former RC § 4511.41 (GC § 6307-40; 119 v 766(782), § 40; Bureau of Code Revision, 10-1-53; 128 v 1270), repealed 135 v H 995, eff 1-1-75.

§ 4511.42 Right-of-way when turning left.

The operator of a vehicle, streetcar, or trackless trolley intending to turn to the left within an intersection or into an alley, private road, or driveway shall yield the right of way to any vehicle, streetcar, or trackless trolley approaching from the opposite direction, whenever the approaching vehicle, streetcar, or trackless trolley is within the intersection or so close to the intersection, alley, private road, or driveway as to constitute an immediate hazard.

HISTORY: GC § 6307-41; 119 v 766(782), § 41; Bureau of Code Revision, 10-1-53; 130 v 1087 (Eff 6-27-63); 135 v H 995 (Eff 1-1-75); 137 v S 62. Eff 7-8-77.

§ 4511.43 Right-of-way at through highways; stop signs; yield signs.

(A) Except when directed to proceed by a law enforcement officer, every driver of a vehicle or trackless trolley approaching a stop sign shall stop at a clearly marked stop line, but if none, before entering the crosswalk on the near side of the intersection, or, if none, then at the point nearest the intersecting roadway where the driver has a view of approaching traffic on the intersecting roadway before entering it. After having stopped, the driver shall yield the right-of-way to any vehicle in the intersection or approaching on another roadway so closely as to constitute an immediate hazard during the time the driver is moving across or within the intersection or junction of roadways.

(B) The driver of a vehicle or trackless trolley approaching a yield sign shall slow down to a speed reasonable for the existing conditions and, if required for safety to stop, shall stop at a clearly marked stop line, but if none, before entering the crosswalk on the near side of the intersection, or, if none, then at the point nearest the intersecting roadway where the driver has a view of approaching traffic on the intersecting roadway before entering it. After slowing or stopping, the driver shall yield the right-of-way to any vehicle or trackless trolley in the intersection or approaching on another roadway so closely as to constitute an immediate hazard during the time the driver is moving across or within the intersection or junction of roadways. Whenever a driver is involved in a collision with a vehicle or trackless trolley in the intersection or junction of roadways, after driving past a yield sign without stopping, the collision shall be prima-facie evidence of the driver's failure to yield the right-of-way.

HISTORY: 135 v H 995. Eff 1-1-75.

Analogous to former RC § 4511.43 (GC § 6307-42; 119 v 766(782), § 42; Bureau of Code Revision, 10-1-53; 126 v 1119; 128 v 1270), repealed 135 v H 995, eff 1-1-75.

The effective date is set by section 3 of HB 995.

[§ 4511.43.1] § 4511.431 Stop at sidewalk area.

The driver of a vehicle or trackless trolley emerging from an alley, building, private road, or driveway within a business or residence district shall stop the vehicle or trackless trolley immediately prior to driving onto a sidewalk or onto the sidewalk area extending across the alley, building entrance, road, or driveway, or in the event there is no sidewalk area, shall stop at the point nearest the street to be entered where the driver has a view of approaching traffic thereon.

HISTORY: 135 v H 995. Eff 1-1-75.

The effective date is set by section 3 of HB 995.

[§ 4511.43.2] § 4511.432 Stop signs on private residential road or driveway.

(A) The owner of a private road or driveway located in a private residential area containing twenty or more dwelling units may erect stop signs at places where the road or driveway intersects with another private road or driveway in the residential area, in compliance with all of the following requirements:

(1) The stop sign is sufficiently legible to be seen by an ordinarily observant person and meets the specifications of and is placed in accordance with the manual adopted by the department of transportation pursuant to section 4511.09 of the Revised Code;

(2) The owner has posted a sign at the entrance of the private road or driveway that is in plain view and clearly informs persons entering the road or driveway that they are entering private property, stop signs have been posted and must be obeyed, and the signs are enforceable by law enforcement officers under state law. The sign required by division (A)(2) of this section, where appropriate, may be incorporated with the sign required by division (A)(2) of section 4511.211 [4511.21.1] of the Revised Code.

(B) Division (A) of section 4511.43 and section 4511.46 of the Revised Code shall be deemed to apply to the driver of a vehicle on a private road or driveway where a stop sign is placed in accordance with division (A) of this section and to a pedestrian crossing such a road or driveway at an intersection where a stop sign is in place.

(C) When a stop sign is placed in accordance with division (A) of this section, any law enforcement officer may apprehend a person found violating the stop sign and may stop and charge the person with violating the stop sign.

(D) As used in this section, and for the purpose of applying division (A) of section 4511.43 and section 4511.46 of the Revised Code to conduct under this section:

(1) "Intersection" means:

(a) The area embraced within the prolongation or connection of the lateral curb lines, or, if none, then the lateral boundary lines of the roadways of two private roads or driveways which join one another at, or approximately at, right angles, or the area within which vehicles traveling upon different private roads or driveways joining at any other angle may come in conflict.

(b) Where a private road or driveway includes two roadways thirty feet or more apart, then every crossing of two roadways of such private roads or driveways shall be regarded as a separate intersection.

(2) "Roadway" means that portion of a private road or driveway improved, designed, or ordinarily used for vehicular travel, except the berm or shoulder. If a private road or driveway includes two or more separate roadways, the term "roadway" means any such roadway separately but not all such roadways collectively.

(3) "Owner" and "private residential area containing twenty or more dwelling units" have the same meanings as in section 4511.211 [4511.21.1] of the Revised Code.

HISTORY: 143 v H 171. Eff 5-31-90.

§ 4511.44 Right-of-way on public highway.

The operator of a vehicle, streetcar, or trackless trolley about to enter or cross a highway from any place other than another roadway shall yield the right of way to all traffic approaching on the roadway to be entered or crossed.

HISTORY: GC § 6307-43; 119 v 766(782), § 43; Bureau of Code Revision, 10-1-53; 135 v H 995. Eff 1-1-75.

The effective date is set by section 3 of HB 995.

[§ 4511.44.1] § 4511.441 Pedestrian on sidewalk has right-of-way.

The driver of a vehicle shall yield the right-of-way to any pedestrian on a sidewalk.

HISTORY: 135 v H 995. Eff 1-1-75.

The effective date is set by section 3 of HB 995.

§ 4511.45 Right-of-way of public safety vehicles.

(A)(1) Upon the approach of a public safety vehicle, equipped with at least one flashing, rotating or oscillating light visible under normal atmospheric conditions from a distance of five hundred feet to the front of such vehicle and the driver is giving audible signal by siren, exhaust whistle, or bell, no driver of any other vehicle shall fail to yield the right of way, immediately drive to a position parallel to, and as close as possible to, the right edge or curb of the highway clear of any intersection, and stop and remain in such position until the public safety vehicle has passed, except when otherwise directed by a police officer.

(2) Upon the approach of a public safety vehicle, as stated in division (A)(1) of this section, no operator of any streetcar or trackless trolley shall fail to immediately stop the streetcar or trackless trolley clear of any intersection and keep it in that position until the public safety vehicle has passed, except when otherwise directed by a police officer.

(B) This section does not relieve the driver of a public safety vehicle from the duty to drive with due regard for the safety of all persons and property upon the highway.

HISTORY: GC § 6307-44; 119 v 766(782), § 44; 124 v 514; Bureau of Code Revision, 10-1-53; 132 v H 878 (Eff 12-14-67); 132 v S 451 (Eff 2-29-68); 145 v H 149. Eff 5-20-93.

[§ 4511.45.1] § 4511.451 Funeral procession has right of way.

As used in this section "funeral procession" means two or more vehicles accompanying a body of a deceased person in the daytime when each of such vehicles has its headlights lighted and is displaying a purple and white pennant attached to each vehicle in such a manner as to be clearly visible to traffic approaching from any direction.

Excepting public safety vehicles proceeding in accordance with section 4511.45 of the Revised Code or when directed otherwise by a police officer, pedestrians and the operators of all vehicles, street cars, and trackless trolleys shall yield the right of way to each vehicle which is a part of a funeral procession. Whenever the lead vehicle in a funeral procession lawfully enters an intersection the remainder of the vehicles in such procession may continue to follow such lead vehicle through the intersection notwithstanding any traffic control devices or right of way provisions of the Revised Code, provided the operator of each vehicle exercises due care to avoid colliding with any other vehicle or pedestrian upon the roadway.

No person shall operate any vehicle as a part of a funeral procession without having the headlights of such vehicle lighted and without displaying a purple and white pennant in such a manner as to be clearly visible to traffic approaching from any direction.

HISTORY: 126 v 632 (Eff 1-1-56); 132 v H 878. Eff 12-14-67.

[§ 4511.45.2] § 4511.452 Pedestrians yield right-of-way to public safety vehicle.

(A) Upon the immediate approach of a public safety vehicle, as stated in section 4511.45 of the Revised Code, every pedestrian shall yield the right-of-way to the public safety vehicle.

(B) This section shall not relieve the driver of a public safety vehicle from the duty to exercise due care to avoid colliding with any pedestrian.

HISTORY: 135 v H 995. Eff 1-1-75.

The effective date is set by section 3 of HB 995.

§ 4511.46 Pedestrian on crosswalk has right-of-way.

(A) When traffic control signals are not in place, not in operation, or are not clearly assigning the right-of-way, the driver of a vehicle, trackless trolley, or streetcar shall yield the right of way, slowing down or stopping if need be to so yield or if required by section 4511.132 [4511.13.2] of the Revised Code, to a pedestrian crossing the roadway within a crosswalk when the pedestrian is upon the half of the roadway upon which the vehicle is traveling, or when the pedestrian is approaching so closely from the opposite half of the roadway as to be in danger.

(B) No pedestrian shall suddenly leave a curb or other place of safety and walk or run into the path of a vehicle, trackless trolley, or streetcar which is so close as to constitute an immediate hazard.

(C) Division (A) of this section does not apply under the conditions stated in division (B) of section 4511.48 of the Revised Code.

(D) Whenever any vehicle, trackless trolley, or streetcar is stopped at a marked crosswalk or at any unmarked crosswalk at an intersection to permit a pedestrian to cross the roadway, the driver of any other vehicle, trackless trolley, or streetcar approaching from the rear shall not overtake and pass the stopped vehicle.

HISTORY: 135 v H 995 (Eff 1-1-75); 143 v S 44. Eff 7-25-89.

Analogous to former RC § 4511.46 (GC § 6307-45; 119 v 766; Bureau of Code Revision, 10-1-53), repealed 135 v H 995, eff 1-1-75.

§ 4511.47 Right of way yielded to blind person.

(A) As used in this section "blind person" or "blind pedestrian" means a person having not more than 20/200 visual acuity in the better eye with correcting lenses or visual acuity greater than 20/200 but with a limitation in the fields of vision such that the widest diameter of the visual field subtends an angle no greater than twenty degrees.

The driver of every vehicle shall yield the right of way to every blind pedestrian guided by a guide dog, or carrying a cane which is predominantly white or metallic in color, with or without a red tip.

(B) No person, other than a blind person, while on any public highway, street, alley, or other public thoroughfare shall carry a white or metallic cane, with or without a red tip.
HISTORY: GC §§ 6307-45a, 6307-45b, 6307-45c; 124 v 59; Bureau of Code Revision, 10-1-53; 133 v S 514. Eff 7-16-70.

§ 4511.48 Right-of-way yielded by pedestrian.

(A) Every pedestrian crossing a roadway at any point other than within a marked crosswalk or within an unmarked crosswalk at an intersection shall yield the right-of-way to all vehicles, trackless trolleys, or streetcars upon the roadway.
(B) Any pedestrian crossing a roadway at a point where a pedestrian tunnel or overhead pedestrian crossing has been provided shall yield the right of way to all traffic upon the roadway.
(C) Between adjacent intersections at which traffic control signals are in operation, pedestrians shall not cross at any place except in a marked crosswalk.
(D) No pedestrian shall cross a roadway intersection diagonally unless authorized by official traffic control devices; and, when authorized to cross diagonally, pedestrians shall cross only in accordance with the official traffic control devices pertaining to such crossing movements.
(E) This section does not relieve the operator of a vehicle, streetcar, or trackless trolley from exercising due care to avoid colliding with any pedestrian upon any roadway.
HISTORY: GC § 6307-46; 119 v 766(783), § 46; Bureau of Code Revision, 10-1-53; 135 v H 995. Eff 1-1-75.

The effective date is set by section 3 of HB 995.

[PEDESTRIANS]

[§ 4511.48.1] § 4511.481 Intoxicated or drugged pedestrian hazard on highway.

A pedestrian who is under the influence of alcohol or any drug of abuse, or any combination thereof, to a degree which renders himself a hazard shall not walk or be upon a highway.
HISTORY: 135 v H 995. Eff 1-1-75.

The effective date is set by section 3 of HB 995.

§ 4511.49 Pedestrians.

Pedestrians shall move, whenever practicable, upon the right half of crosswalks.
HISTORY: GC § 6307-47; 119 v 766(783), § 47; Bureau of Code Revision, 10-1-53; 135 v H 995. Eff 1-1-75.

The effective date is set by section 3 of HB 995.

[§ 4511.49.1] § 4511.491 Motorized wheelchair operators.

Every person operating a motorized wheelchair shall have all of the rights and duties applicable to a pedestrian that are contained in this chapter, except those provisions which by their nature can have no application.
HISTORY: 143 v S 272. Eff 11-28-90.

§ 4511.50 Pedestrian walking along highway.

(A) Where a sidewalk is provided and its use is practicable, it shall be unlawful for any pedestrian to walk along and upon an adjacent roadway.
(B) Where a sidewalk is not available, any pedestrian walking along and upon a highway shall walk only on a shoulder, as far as practicable from the edge of the roadway.
(C) Where neither a sidewalk nor a shoulder is available, any pedestrian walking along and upon a highway shall walk as near as practicable to an outside edge of the roadway, and, if on a two-way roadway, shall walk only on the left side of the roadway.
(D) Except as otherwise provided in sections 4511.13 and 4511.46 of the Revised Code, any pedestrian upon a roadway shall yield the right-of- way to all vehicles, trackless trolleys, or streetcars upon the roadway.
HISTORY: 135 v H 995. Eff 1-1-75.

Analogous to former RC § 4511.50 (GC § 6307-48; 119 v 766; Bureau of Code Revision, 10-1-53), repealed 135 v H 995, eff 1-1-75.

The effective date is set by section 3 of HB 995.

§ 4511.51 Prohibited solicitations by pedestrians; riding on outside of vehicle or in open cargo storage area or on tailgate.

(A) No person while on a roadway outside a safety zone shall solicit a ride from the driver of any vehicle.
(B)(1) Except as provided in division (B)(2) of this section, no person shall stand on a highway for the purpose of soliciting employment, business, or contributions from the occupant of any vehicle.
(2) The legislative authority of a municipal corporation, by ordinance, may authorize the issuance of a permit to a charitable organization to allow a person acting on behalf of the organization to solicit charitable contributions from the occupant of a vehicle by standing on a highway, other than a freeway as provided in division (A) of section 4511.051 [4511.05.1] of the Revised Code, that is under the jurisdiction of the municipal corporation. The permit shall be valid for only one period of time, which shall be specified in the permit, in any calendar year. The legislative authority also may specify the locations where contributions may be solicited and may impose any other restrictions on or requirements regarding the manner in which the solicita-

§ 4511.51.1   Ohio Criminal Law Handbook   1160

tions are to be conducted that the legislative authority considers advisable.

(3) As used in division (B)(2) of this section, "charitable organization" means an organization that has received from the internal revenue service a currently valid ruling or determination letter recognizing the tax-exempt status of the organization pursuant to section 501(c)(3) of the "Internal Revenue Code."

(C) No person shall hang onto or ride on the outside of any motor vehicle, streetcar, or trackless trolley while it is moving upon a roadway, except mechanics or test engineers making repairs or adjustments, or workers performing specialized highway or street maintenance or construction under authority of a public agency.

(D) No operator shall knowingly permit any person to hang onto, or ride on the outside of, any motor vehicle, streetcar, or trackless trolley while it is moving upon a roadway, except mechanics or test engineers making repairs or adjustments, or workers performing specialized highway or street maintenance or construction under authority of a public agency.

(E) No driver of a truck, trailer, or semitrailer shall knowingly permit any person who has not attained the age of sixteen years to ride in the unenclosed or unroofed cargo storage area of his vehicle if the vehicle is traveling faster than twenty-five miles per hour, unless either of the following applies:

(1) The cargo storage area of the vehicle is equipped with a properly secured seat to which is attached a seat safety belt that is in compliance with federal standards for an occupant restraining device as defined in division (A)(2) of section 4513.263 [4513.26.3] of the Revised Code, the seat and seat safety belt were installed at the time the vehicle was originally assembled, and the person riding in the cargo storage area is in the seat and is wearing the seat safety belt;

(2) An emergency exists that threatens the life of the driver or the person being transported in the cargo storage area of the truck, trailer, or semitrailer.

(F) No driver of a truck, trailer, or semitrailer shall permit any person, except for those workers performing specialized highway or street maintenance or construction under authority of a public agency, to ride in the cargo storage area or on a tailgate of his vehicle while the tailgate is unlatched.

HISTORY: GC § 6307-49; 119 v 776, § 49; 121 v 684; Bureau of Code Revision, 10-1-53; 135 v H 995 (Eff 1-1-75); 143 v H 8 (Eff 9-13-89); 145 v H 331. Eff 7-2-93.

[§ 4511.51.1] § 4511.511 Pedestrian on bridge or railroad crossing.

(A) No pedestrian shall enter or remain upon any bridge or approach thereto beyond the bridge signal, gate, or barrier after a bridge operation signal indication has been given.

(B) No pedestrian shall pass through, around, over, or under any crossing gate or barrier at a railroad grade crossing or bridge while the gate or barrier is closed or is being opened or closed.

HISTORY: 135 v H 995. Eff 1-1-75.

The effective date is set by section 3 of HB 995.

[BICYCLES, MOTORCYCLES AND SNOWMOBILES]

§ 4511.52 Bicycles.

Sections 4511.01 to 4511.78, inclusive, 4511.99, and 4513.01 to 4513.37, inclusive, of the Revised Code which are applicable to bicycles apply whenever a bicycle is operated upon any highway or upon any path set aside for the exclusive use of bicycles.

HISTORY: GC § 6307-50; 119 v 766(784), § 50; Bureau of Code Revision. Eff 10-1-53.

[§ 4511.52.1] § 4511.521 Rules governing operation of motorized bicycles.

(A) No person shall operate a motorized bicycle upon a highway or any public or private property used by the public for purposes of vehicular travel or parking, unless all of the following conditions are met:

(1) The person is fourteen or fifteen years of age and holds a valid probationary motorized bicycle license issued after the person has passed the test provided for in this section, or the person is sixteen years of age or older and holds either a valid commercial driver's license issued under Chapter 4506. or a driver's license issued under Chapter 4507. of the Revised Code or a valid motorized bicycle license issued after the person has passed the test provided for in this section, except that if a person is sixteen years of age, has a valid probationary motorized bicycle license and desires a motorized bicycle license, he is not required to comply with the testing requirements provided for in this section;

(2) The motorized bicycle is equipped in accordance with the rules adopted under division (B) of this section and is in proper working order;

(3) The person, if he is under eighteen years of age, is wearing a protective helmet on his head with the chin strap properly fastened and the motorized bicycle is equipped with a rear-view mirror.

(4) The person operates the motorized bicycle when practicable within three feet of the right edge of the roadway obeying all traffic rules applicable to vehicles.

(B) The director of public safety, subject to sections 119.01 to 119.13 of the Revised Code, shall adopt and promulgate rules concerning protective helmets, the equipment of motorized bicycles, and the testing and qualifications of persons who do not hold a valid driver's or commercial driver's license. The test shall be as near as practicable to the examination required for a motorcycle operator's endorsement under section 4507.11 of the Revised Code. The test shall also require the operator to give an actual demonstration of his ability to operate and control a motorized bicycle by driving one under the supervision of an examining officer.

(C) Every motorized bicycle license expires on the birthday of the applicant in the fourth year after the date it is issued, but in no event shall any motorized bicycle license be issued for a period longer than four years.

(D) No person operating a motorized bicycle shall carry another person upon the motorized bicycle.

(E) The protective helmet and rear-view mirror required by division (A)(3) of this section shall, on and after January 1, 1985, conform with rules adopted by the director under division (B) of this section.

(F) Each probationary motorized bicycle license or motorized bicycle license shall be laminated with a transparent plastic material.

HISTORY: 137 v S 100 (Eff 4-1-78); 137 v S 393 (Eff 5-12-78); 140 v S 169 (Eff 6-18-84); 140 v S 169, § 6 (Eff 1-1-85); 143 v H 381 (Eff 7-1-89); 143 v S 131 (Eff 7-25-90); 144 v S 98. Eff 11-12-92.

§ 4511.53 Rules for bicycles, motorcycles and snowmobiles.

For purposes of this section, "snowmobile" has the same meaning as given that term in section 4519.01 of the Revised Code.

A person operating a bicycle or motorcycle shall not ride other than upon the permanent and regular seat attached thereto, nor carry any other person upon such bicycle or motorcycle other than upon a firmly attached and regular seat thereon, nor shall any person ride upon a bicycle or motorcycle other than upon such a firmly attached and regular seat.

A person shall ride upon a motorcycle only while sitting astride the seat, facing forward, with one leg on each side of the motorcycle.

No person operating a bicycle shall carry any package, bundle, or article that prevents the driver from keeping at least one hand upon the handle bars.

No bicycle or motorcycle shall be used to carry more persons at one time than the number for which it is designed and equipped, nor shall any motorcycle be operated on a highway when the handle bars or grips are more than fifteen inches higher than the seat or saddle for the operator.

No person shall operate or be a passenger on a snowmobile or motorcycle without using safety glasses or other protective eye device. No person who is under the age of eighteen years, or who holds a motorcycle operator's endorsement or license bearing a "novice" designation that is currently in effect as provided in section 4507.13 of the Revised Code, shall operate a motorcycle on a highway, or be a passenger on a motorcycle, unless wearing a protective helmet on his head, and no other person shall be a passenger on a motorcycle operated by such a person unless similarly wearing a protective helmet. The helmet, safety glasses, or other protective eye device shall conform with regulations prescribed and promulgated by the director of public safety. The provisions of this paragraph or a violation thereof shall not be used in the trial of any civil action.

HISTORY: GC § 6307-51; 119 v 766(784); Bureau of Code Revision, 10-1-53; 132 v H 380 (Eff 1-1-68); 134 v H 214 (Eff 3-7-72); 135 v H 995 (Eff 1-1-75); 137 v H 115 (Eff 7-10-78); 144 v S 98. Eff 11-12-92.

§ 4511.54 Prohibition against attaching bicycles and sleds to vehicles.

No person riding upon any bicycle, coaster, roller skates, sled, or toy vehicle shall attach the same or himself to any streetcar, trackless trolley, or vehicle upon a roadway.

No operator shall knowingly permit any person riding upon any bicycle, coaster, roller skates, sled, or toy vehicle to attach the same or himself to any streetcar, trackless trolley, or vehicle while it is moving upon a roadway.

This section does not apply to the towing of a disabled vehicle.

HISTORY: GC § 6307-52; 119 v 776(784), § 52; 121 v 684; Bureau of Code Revision. Eff 10-1-53.

§ 4511.55 Riding bicycles; motorcycles abreast.

(A) Every person operating a bicycle upon a roadway shall ride as near to the right side of the roadway as practicable obeying all traffic rules applicable to vehicles and exercising due care when passing a standing vehicle or one proceeding in the same direction.

(B) Persons riding bicycles or motorcycles upon a roadway shall ride not more than two abreast in a single lane, except on paths or parts of roadways set aside for the exclusive use of bicycles or motorcycles.

HISTORY: GC § 6307-53; 119 v 766(784), § 53; Bureau of Code Revision, 10-1-53; 135 v H 995. Eff 1-1-75.

The effective date of H 995 is set by section 3 of the act.

§ 4511.56 Signal devices on bicycle.

(A) Every bicycle when in use at the times specified in section 4513.03 of the Revised Code, shall be equipped with the following:

(1) A lamp on the front that shall emit a white light visible from a distance of at least five hundred feet to the front;

(2) A red reflector on the rear of a type approved by the director of public safety that shall be visible from all distances from one hundred feet to six hundred feet to the rear when directly in front of lawful lower beams of head lamps on a motor vehicle;

(3) A lamp emitting a red light visible from a distance

of five hundred feet to the rear shall be used in addition to the red reflector;

(4) An essentially colorless reflector on the front of a type approved by the director;

(5) Either with tires with retroreflective sidewalls or with an essentially colorless or amber reflector mounted on the spokes of the front wheel and an essentially colorless or red reflector mounted on the spokes of the rear wheel. Each reflector shall be visible on each side of the wheel from a distance of six hundred feet when directly in front of lawful lower beams of head lamps on a motor vehicle. Retroreflective tires or reflectors shall be of a type approved by the director.

(B) No person shall operate a bicycle unless it is equipped with a bell or other device capable of giving a signal audible for a distance of at least one hundred feet, except that a bicycle shall not be equipped with nor shall any person use upon a bicycle any siren or whistle.

(C) Every bicycle shall be equipped with an adequate brake when used on a street or highway.

HISTORY: 135 v H 995 (Eff 1-1-75); 142 v H 412 (Eff 3-10-88); 144 v S 98. Eff 11-12-92.

Analogous to former RC § 4511.56 (GC § 6307-54; 119 v 766; Bureau of Code Revision, 10-1-53), repealed 135 v H 995, eff 1-1-75.

[STREETCARS]

§ 4511.57 Passing on left side of streetcar.

The driver of a vehicle shall not overtake and pass upon the left nor drive upon the left side of any streetcar proceeding in the same direction, whether such streetcar is in motion or at rest, except:

(A) When so directed by a police officer or traffic control device;

(B) When upon a one-way street;

(C) When upon a street where the tracks are so located as to prevent compliance with this section;

(D) When authorized by local authorities.

The driver of any vehicle when permitted to overtake and pass upon the left of a streetcar which has stopped for the purpose of receiving or discharging any passenger shall accord pedestrians the right of way.

HISTORY: GC § 6307-55; 119 v 766(785), § 55; Bureau of Code Revision. Eff 10-1-53.

§ 4511.58 Vehicle shall not pass streetcar discharging passengers; exception.

The driver of a vehicle overtaking upon the right any streetcar stopped for the purpose of receiving or discharging any passenger shall stop such vehicle at least five feet to the rear of the nearest running board or door of such streetcar and remain standing until all passengers have boarded such streetcar, or upon alighting therefrom have reached a place of safety, except that where a safety zone has been established, a vehicle need not be brought to a stop before passing any such streetcar or any trackless trolley, but may proceed past such streetcar or trackless trolley at a speed not greater than is reasonable and proper considering the safety of pedestrians.

HISTORY: GC § 6307-56; 119 v 766(785), § 56; Bureau of Code Revision. Eff 10-1-53.

§ 4511.59 Driving and turning in front of streetcars.

The driver of any vehicle proceeding upon any streetcar tracks in front of a streetcar shall remove such vehicle from the track as soon as practicable after signal from the operator of said streetcar.

The driver of a vehicle upon overtaking and passing a streetcar shall not turn in front of such streetcar unless such movement can be made in safety.

HISTORY: GC § 6307-57; 119 v 766(785), § 57; Bureau of Code Revision. Eff 10-1-53.

§ 4511.60 Driving through safety zone.

No vehicle shall at any time be driven through or within a safety zone.

HISTORY: GC § 6307-58; 119 v 766(785), § 58; Bureau of Code Revision. Eff 10-1-53.

[GRADE CROSSINGS]

§ 4511.61 Stop signs at grade crossings.

The department of transportation and local authorities in their respective jurisdictions, with the approval of the department, may designate dangerous highway crossings over railroad tracks whether on state, county, or township highways or on streets or ways within municipal corporations, and erect stop signs thereat. When such stop signs are erected, the operator of any vehicle, streetcar, or trackless trolley shall stop within fifty, but not less than fifteen, feet from the nearest rail of the railroad tracks and shall exercise due care before proceeding across such grade crossing.

HISTORY: GC § 6307-59; 119 v 766(786), § 59; Bureau of Code Revision, 10-1-53; 127 v 887 (Eff 9-16-57); 135 v H 200 (Eff 9-28-73); 135 v S 171. Eff 10-31-73.

§ 4511.62 Driver's duties relating to grade crossings.

(A)(1) Whenever any person driving a vehicle or trackless trolley approaches a railroad grade crossing, the person shall stop within fifty feet, but not less than fifteen feet from the nearest rail of the railroad if any of the following circumstances exist at the crossing:

(a) A clearly visible electric or mechanical signal device gives warning of the immediate approach of a train.

(b) A crossing gate is lowered.
(c) A flagperson gives or continues to give a signal of the approach or passage of a train.
(d) There is insufficient space on the other side of the railroad grade crossing to accommodate the vehicle or trackless trolley the person is operating without obstructing the passage of other vehicles, trackless trolleys, pedestrians, or railroad trains, notwithstanding any traffic control signal indication to proceed.
(e) An approaching train is emitting an audible signal or is plainly visible and is in hazardous proximity to the crossing.

(2) A person who is driving a vehicle or trackless trolley and who approaches a railroad grade crossing shall not proceed as long as any of the circumstances described in divisions (A)(1)(a) to (e) of this section exist at the crossing.

(B) No person shall drive any vehicle through, around, or under any crossing gate or barrier at a railroad crossing while the gate or barrier is closed or is being opened or closed unless the person is signaled by a law enforcement officer or flagperson that it is permissible to do so.

HISTORY: GC § 6307-60; 119 v 766(786), § 60; Bureau of Code Revision, 10-1-53; 135 v H 995 (Eff 1-1-75); 147 v S 60. Eff 10-21-97.

§ 4511.63 Vehicles required to stop at grade crossings.

(A) The operator of any motor vehicle or trackless trolley, carrying passengers, for hire, or of any school bus, or of any vehicle carrying explosives or flammable liquids as a cargo or as such part of a cargo as to constitute a hazard, before crossing at grade any track of a railroad, shall stop the vehicle or trackless trolley and, while so stopped he shall listen through an open door or open window and look in both directions along the track for any approaching train, and for signals indicating the approach of a train, and shall proceed only upon exercising due care after stopping, looking, and listening as required by this section. Upon proceeding, the operator of such a vehicle shall cross only in a gear that will ensure there will be no necessity for changing gears while traversing the crossing and shall not shift gears while crossing the tracks.

(B) This section does not apply at any of the following:
(1) Street railway grade crossings within a municipal corporation, or to abandoned tracks, spur tracks, side tracks, and industrial tracks when the public utilities commission has authorized and approved the crossing of the tracks without making the stop required by this section;
(2) Through June 30, 1995, a street railway grade crossing where out-of-service signs are posted in accordance with section 4955.37 of the Revised Code.

HISTORY: GC § 6307-61; 119 v 766(786), § 61; 124 v 514; Bureau of Code Revision, 10-1-53; 125 v 903(1025) (Eff 10-1-53); 145 v H 154. Eff 6-30-93.

§ 4511.64 Slow-moving vehicles or equipment crossing railroad tracks.

No person shall operate or move any crawler-type tractor, steam shovel, derrick, roller, or any equipment or structure having a normal operating speed of six or less miles per hour or a vertical body or load clearance of less than nine inches above the level surface of a roadway, upon or across any tracks at a railroad grade crossing without first complying with divisions (A) and (B) of this section.

(A) Before making any such crossing, the person operating or moving any such vehicle or equipment shall first stop the same, and while stopped he shall listen and look in both directions along such track for any approaching train and for signals indicating the approach of a train, and shall proceed only upon exercising due care.

(B) No such crossing shall be made when warning is given by automatic signal or crossing gates or a flagman or otherwise of the immediate approach of a railroad train or car.

If the normal sustained speed of such vehicle, equipment, or structure is not more than three miles per hour, the person owning, operating, or moving the same shall also give notice of such intended crossing to a station agent or superintendent of the railroad, and a reasonable time shall be given to such railroad to provide proper protection for such crossing. Where such vehicles or equipment are being used in constructing or repairing a section of highway lying on both sides of a railroad grade crossing, and in such construction or repair it is necessary to repeatedly move such vehicles or equipment over such crossing, one daily notice specifying when such work will start and stating the hours during which it will be prosecuted is sufficient.

HISTORY: GC § 6307-62; 119 v 766(786), § 62; Bureau of Code Revision. Eff 10-1-53.

[THROUGH HIGHWAYS]

§ 4511.65 Through highways.

(A) All state routes are hereby designated as through highways, provided that stop signs, yield signs, or traffic control signals shall be erected at all intersections with such through highways by the department of transportation as to highways under its jurisdiction and by local authorities as to highways under their jurisdiction, except as otherwise provided in this section. Where two or more state routes that are through highways intersect and no traffic control signal is in operation, stop signs or yield signs shall be erected at one or more entrances thereto by the department, except as otherwise provided in this section.

Whenever the director of transportation determines on the basis of an engineering and traffic investigation that stop signs are necessary to stop traffic on a through highway for safe and efficient operation, nothing in this section shall be construed to prevent such installations. When circumstances warrant, the director also may omit stop signs on roadways intersecting through highways under his jurisdiction. Before the director either installs or removes a stop sign under this division, he shall give notice, in writing, of that proposed action to the affected local authority at least thirty days before installing or removing the stop sign.

(B) Other streets or highways, or portions thereof, are hereby designated through highways if they are within a municipal corporation, if they have a continuous length of more than one mile between the limits of said street or highway or portion thereof, and if they have "stop" or "yield" signs or traffic control signals at the entrances of the majority of intersecting streets or highways. For purposes of this section, the limits of said street or highway or portion thereof shall be a municipal corporation line, the physical terminus of the street or highway, or any point on said street or highway at which vehicular traffic thereon is required by regulatory signs to stop or yield to traffic on the intersecting street, provided that in residence districts a municipal corporation may by ordinance designate said street or highway, or portion thereof, not to be a through highway and thereafter the affected residence district shall be indicated by official traffic control devices. Where two or more through highways designated under this division intersect and no traffic control signal is in operation, stop signs or yield signs shall be erected at one or more entrances thereto by the department or by local authorities having jurisdiction, except as otherwise provided in this section.

(C) The department or local authorities having jurisdiction need not erect stop signs at intersections they find to be so constructed as to permit traffic to safely enter a through highway without coming to a stop. Signs shall be erected at such intersections indicating that the operator of a vehicle shall yield the right-of-way to or merge with all traffic proceeding on the through highway.

(D) Local authorities with reference to highways under their jurisdiction may designate additional through highways and shall erect stop signs, yield signs, or traffic control signals at all streets and highways intersecting such through highways, or may designate any intersection as a stop or yield intersection and shall erect like signs at one or more entrances to such intersection.

HISTORY: GC § 6307-63; 119 v 766(787), § 63; Bureau of Code Revision, 10-1-53; 128 v 1270 (Eff 11-4-59); 131 v 1103 (Eff 10-15-65); 135 v H 200 (Eff 9-28-73); 136 v H 21 (Eff 12-30-75); 138 v H 290 (Eff 1-10-80); 143 v H 258. Eff 11-2-89.

[PARKING]

§ 4511.66 Prohibition against parking on highways.

Upon any highway outside a business or residence district no person shall stop, park, or leave standing any vehicle, whether attended or unattended, upon the paved or main traveled part of the highway if it is practicable to stop, park, or so leave such vehicle off the paved or main traveled part of said highway. In every event a clear and unobstructed portion of the highway opposite such standing vehicle shall be left for the free passage of other vehicles, and a clear view of such stopped vehicle shall be available from a distance of two hundred feet in each direction upon such highway.

This section does not apply to the driver of any vehicle which is disabled while on the paved or improved or main traveled portion of a highway in such manner and to such extent that it is impossible to avoid stopping and temporarily leaving the disabled vehicle in such position.

HISTORY: GC § 6307-64; 119 v 766(788), § 64; Bureau of Code Revision. Eff 10-1-53.

[§ 4511.66.1] § 4511.661 Condition when motor vehicle left unattended.

No person driving or in charge of a motor vehicle shall permit it to stand unattended without first stopping the engine, locking the ignition, removing the key from the ignition, effectively setting the parking brake, and, when the motor vehicle is standing upon any grade, turning the front wheels to the curb or side of the highway.

The requirements of this section relating to the stopping of the engine, locking of the ignition, and removing the key from the ignition of a motor vehicle shall not apply to an emergency vehicle or a public safety vehicle.

HISTORY: 135 v H 995 (Eff 1-1-75); 136 v H 763. Eff 8-6-76.

§ 4511.67 Police may remove illegally parked vehicle.

Whenever any police officer finds a vehicle standing upon a highway in violation of section 4511.66 of the Revised Code, such officer may move such vehicle, or require the driver or other person in charge of the vehicle to move the same, to a position off the paved or improved or main traveled part of such highway.

Whenever any police officer finds a vehicle unattended upon any highway, bridge, or causeway, or in any tunnel, where such vehicle constitutes an obstruction to traffic, such officer may provide for the removal of such vehicle to the nearest garage or other place of safety.

HISTORY: GC § 6307-65; 119 v 766(788), § 65; 121 v 684; Bureau of Code Revision. Eff 10-1-53.

§ 4511.68 Parking prohibitions.

No person shall stand or park a trackless trolley or vehicle, except when necessary to avoid conflict with other traffic or to comply with sections 4511.01 to 4511.78, inclusive, 4511.99, and 4513.01 to 4513.37, inclusive, of the Revised Code, or while obeying the directions of a police officer or a traffic control device, in any of the following places:

(A) On a sidewalk, except a bicycle;
(B) In front of a public or private driveway;
(C) Within an intersection;
(D) Within ten feet of a fire hydrant;
(E) On a crosswalk;
(F) Within twenty feet of a crosswalk at an intersection;
(G) Within thirty feet of, and upon the approach to, any flashing beacon, stop sign, or traffic control device;
(H) Between a safety zone and the adjacent curb or within thirty feet of points on the curb immediately opposite the ends of a safety zone, unless a different length is indicated by a traffic control device;
(I) Within fifty feet of the nearest rail of a railroad crossing;
(J) Within twenty feet of a driveway entrance to any fire station and, on the side of the street opposite the entrance to any fire station, within seventy-five feet of the entrance when it is properly posted with signs;
(K) Alongside or opposite any street excavation or obstruction when such standing or parking would obstruct traffic;
(L) Alongside any vehicle stopped or parked at the edge or curb of a street;
(M) Upon any bridge or elevated structure upon a highway, or within a highway tunnel;
(N) At any place where signs prohibit stopping;
(O) Within one foot of another parked vehicle;
(P) On the roadway portion of a freeway, expressway, or thruway.

HISTORY: GC § 6307-66; 119 v 766(788), § 66; 124 v 514; Bureau of Code Revision, 10-1-53; 130 v 1087. Eff 8-5-63.

[§ 4511.68.1] § 4511.681 Parking prohibitions on private property.

If an owner of private property posts on the property, in a conspicuous manner, a prohibition against parking on the property or conditions and regulations under which parking is permitted, no person shall do either of the following:

(A) Park a vehicle on the property without the owner's consent;
(B) Park a vehicle on the property in violation of any condition or regulation posted by the owner.

HISTORY: 139 v H 707 (Eff 1-1-83); 140 v H 112. Eff 10-4-84.

§ 4511.69 Parking near curb, facing direction of travel; locations and privileges for walking-impaired persons.

(A) Every vehicle stopped or parked upon a roadway where there is an adjacent curb shall be stopped or parked with the right-hand wheels of the vehicle parallel with and not more than twelve inches from the right-hand curb, unless it is impossible to approach so close to the curb; in such case the stop shall be made as close to the curb as possible and only for the time necessary to discharge and receive passengers or to load or unload merchandise. Local authorities may by ordinance permit angle parking on any roadway under their jurisdiction, except that angle parking shall not be permitted on a state route within a municipal corporation unless an unoccupied roadway width of not less than twenty-five feet is available for free moving traffic.

(B) Local authorities may by ordinance permit parking of vehicles with the left-hand wheels adjacent to and within twelve inches of the left-hand curb of a one-way roadway.

(C) No vehicle or trackless trolley shall be stopped or parked on a road or highway with the vehicle or trackless trolley facing in a direction other than the direction of travel on that side of the road or highway.

(D) Notwithstanding any statute or any rule, resolution, or ordinance adopted by any local authority, air compressors, tractors, trucks, and other equipment, while being used in the construction, reconstruction, installation, repair, or removal of facilities near, on, over, or under a street or highway, may stop, stand, or park where necessary in order to perform such work, provided a flagman is on duty or warning signs or lights are displayed as may be prescribed by the director of transportation.

(E) Special parking locations and privileges for persons with disabilities that limit or impair the ability to walk, also known as handicapped parking spaces or disability parking spaces, shall be provided and designated by all political subdivisions and by the state and all agencies and instrumentalities thereof at all offices and facilities, where parking is provided, whether owned, rented, or leased, and at all publicly owned parking garages. The locations shall be designated through the posting of an elevated sign, whether permanently affixed or movable, imprinted with the international symbol of access and shall be reasonably close to exits, entrances, elevators, and ramps. All elevated signs posted in accordance with this division and division (B) of section 3781.111 [3781.11.1] of the Revised Code shall be mounted on a fixed or movable post, and the distance from the ground to the top edge of the sign shall measure five feet.

(F) No person shall stop, stand, or park any motor vehicle at special parking locations provided under division (E) of this section or at special clearly marked parking locations provided in or on privately owned parking lots, parking garages, or other parking areas and designated in accordance with that division, unless one of the following applies:

(1) The motor vehicle is being operated by or for the transport of a person with a disability that limits or impairs the ability to walk and is displaying a valid removable windshield placard or special license plates;

(2) The motor vehicle is being operated by or for the transport of a handicapped person and is displaying a

parking card or special handicapped license plates.

(G) When a motor vehicle is being operated by or for the transport of a person with a disability that limits or impairs the ability to walk and is displaying a removable windshield placard or a temporary removable windshield placard or special license plates, or when a motor vehicle is being operated by or for the transport of a handicapped person and is displaying a parking card or special handicapped license plates, the motor vehicle shall be permitted to park for a period of two hours in excess of the legal parking period permitted by local authorities, except where local ordinances or police rules provide otherwise or where the vehicle is parked in such a manner as to be clearly a traffic hazard.

(H) No owner of an office, facility, or parking garage where special parking locations must be designated in accordance with division (E) of this section shall fail to properly mark the special parking locations as required by that division or fail to maintain the markings of the special locations, including the erection and maintenance of the fixed or movable signs.

(I) Nothing in this section shall be construed to require a person or organization to apply for a removable windshield placard or special license plates if the parking card or special license plates issued to the person or organization under prior law have not expired or been surrendered or revoked.

(J) As used in this section:

(1) "Handicapped person" means any person who has lost the use of one or both legs or one or both arms, who is blind, deaf, or so severely handicapped as to be unable to move without the aid of crutches or a wheelchair, or whose mobility is restricted by a permanent cardiovascular, pulmonary, or other handicapping condition.

(2) "Person with a disability that limits or impairs the ability to walk" has the same meaning as in section 4503.44 of the Revised Code.

(3) "Special license plates" and "removable windshield placard" mean any license plates or removable windshield placard or temporary removable windshield placard issued under section 4503.41 or 4503.44 of the Revised Code, and also mean any substantially similar license plates or removable windshield placard or temporary removable windshield placard issued by a state, district, country, or sovereignty.

HISTORY: GC § 6307-67; 119 v 766(789), § 67; 121 v 684; 124 v 514; Bureau of Code Revision, 10-1-53; 135 v H 200 (Eff 9-28-73); 136 v S 162 (Eff 7-23-76); 137 v H 652 (Eff 3-13-78); 139 v H 1 (Eff 8-5-81); 139 v H 48 (Eff 1-1-83); 139 v H 116 (Eff 7-5-82); 140 v H 174 (Eff 9-30-83); 142 v H 111 (Eff 4-27-88); 144 v H 73 (Eff 9-25-91); 144 v S 98 (Eff 11-12-92); 145 v H 687. Eff 1-1-95.

The effective date is set by section 4 of HB 687.

[PROHIBITIONS]

§ 4511.70 Obstruction and interference affecting view and control of driver.

(A) No person shall drive a vehicle or trackless trolley when it is so loaded, or when there are in the front seat such number of persons, as to obstruct the view of the driver to the front or sides of the vehicle or to interfere with the driver's control over the driving mechanism of the vehicle.

(B) No passenger in a vehicle or trackless trolley shall ride in such position as to interfere with the driver's view ahead or to the sides, or to interfere with his control over the driving mechanism of the vehicle.

(C) No person shall open the door of a vehicle on the side available to moving traffic unless and until it is reasonably safe to do so, and can be done without interfering with the movement of other traffic, nor shall any person leave a door open on the side of a vehicle available to moving traffic for a period of time longer than necessary to load or unload passengers.

HISTORY: GC § 6307-68; 119 v 766(789), § 68; Bureau of Code Revision, 10-1-53; 135 v H 995. Eff 1-1-75.

The effective date is set by section 3 of HB 995.

[§ 4511.70.1] § 4511.701 Occupancy while in motion prohibited.

No person shall occupy any travel trailer or nonself-propelled manufactured home while it is being used as a conveyance upon a street or highway.

HISTORY: 135 v S 205 (Eff 11-21-73); 140 v S 231. Eff 9-20-84.

§ 4511.71 Prohibition against driving upon closed highway.

No person shall drive upon, along, or across a street or highway, or any part thereof, which has been closed in the process of its construction, reconstruction, or repair, and posted with appropriate signs by the authority having jurisdiction to close such highway.

HISTORY: GC § 6307-69; 119 v 766(789), § 69; Bureau of Code Revision. Eff 10-1-53.

[§ 4511.71.1] § 4511.711 Driving upon sidewalk area.

No person shall drive any vehicle, other than a bicycle, upon a sidewalk or sidewalk area except upon a permanent or duly authorized temporary driveway.

Nothing in this section shall be construed as prohibiting local authorities from regulating the operation of bicycles within their respective jurisdictions.

HISTORY: 135 v H 995 (Eff 1-1-75); 136 v S 56. Eff 5-25-76.

[§ 4511.71.2] § 4511.712 Obstructing passage of other vehicles.

No driver shall enter an intersection or marked crosswalk or drive onto any railroad grade crossing unless there is sufficient space on the other side of the intersection, crosswalk, or grade crossing to accommodate the vehicle, streetcar, or trackless trolley he is operating without obstructing the passage of other vehicles, streetcars, trackless trolleys, pedestrians, or railroad trains, notwithstanding any traffic control signal indication to proceed.

HISTORY: 135 v H 995. Eff 1-1-75.

The effective date is set by section 3 of HB 995.

[§ 4511.71.3] § 4511.713 Paths exclusively for bicycles.

No person shall operate a motor vehicle, snowmobile, or all-purpose vehicle upon any path set aside for the exclusive use of bicycles, when an appropriate sign giving notice of such use is posted on the path.

Nothing in this section shall be construed to affect any rule of the director of natural resources governing the operation of motor vehicles, snowmobiles, all-purpose vehicles, and bicycles on lands under his jurisdiction.

HISTORY: 141 v H 311. Eff 3-11-87.

§ 4511.72 Following an emergency or public safety vehicle prohibited.

The driver of any vehicle, other than an emergency vehicle or public safety vehicle on official business, shall not follow any emergency vehicle or public safety vehicle traveling in response to an alarm closer than five hundred feet, or drive into or park such vehicle within the block where fire apparatus has stopped in answer to a fire alarm, unless directed to do so by a police officer or a fireman.

HISTORY: GC § 6307-70; 119 v 766(790), § 70; 124 v 514(525); Bureau of Code Revision, 10-1-53; 132 v H 878. Eff 12-14-67.

§ 4511.73 Driving over unprotected fire hose.

No streetcar, trackless trolley, or vehicle shall, without the consent of the fire department official in command, be driven over any unprotected hose of a fire department, when said hose is laid down on any street, private driveway, or streetcar track to be used at any fire or alarm of fire.

HISTORY: GC § 6307-71; 119 v 766(790), § 71; Bureau of Code Revision. Eff 10-1-53.

§ 4511.74 Prohibition against placing injurious material on highway.

(A) No person shall place or knowingly drop upon any part of a highway, lane, road, street, or alley any tacks, bottles, wire, glass, nails, or other articles which may damage or injure any person, vehicle, streetcar, trackless trolley, or animal traveling along or upon such highway, except such substances that may be placed upon the roadway by proper authority for the repair or construction thereof.

Any person who drops or permits to be dropped or thrown upon any highway any destructive or injurious material shall immediately remove the same.

Any person authorized to remove a wrecked or damaged vehicle, streetcar, or trackless trolley from a highway shall remove any glass or other injurious substance dropped upon the highway from such vehicle, streetcar, or trackless trolley.

No person shall place any obstruction in or upon a highway without proper authority.

(B) No person, with intent to cause physical harm to a person or a vehicle, shall place or knowingly drop upon any part of a highway, land, road, street, or alley any tacks, bottles, wire, glass, nails, or other articles which may damage or injure any person, vehicle, streetcar, trackless trolley, or animal traveling along or upon such highway, except such substances that may be placed upon the roadway by proper authority for the repair or construction thereof.

HISTORY: GC § 6307-72; 119 v 766(790), § 72; Bureau of Code Revision, 10-1-53; 140 v H 133. Eff 9-27-83.

[SCHOOL BUSES]

§ 4511.75 Stopping for school bus; signals.

(A) The driver of a vehicle, streetcar, or trackless trolley upon meeting or overtaking from either direction any school bus stopped for the purpose of receiving or discharging any school child or person attending programs offered by community boards of mental health and county boards of mental retardation and developmental disabilities shall stop at least ten feet from the front or rear of the school bus and shall not proceed until such school bus resumes motion, or until signaled by the school bus driver to proceed.

It is no defense to a charge under this division that the school bus involved failed to display or be equipped with an automatically extended stop warning sign as required by division (B) of this section.

(B) Every school bus shall be equipped with amber and red visual signals meeting the requirements of section 4511.771 [4511.77.1] of the Revised Code, and an automatically extended stop warning sign of a type approved by the state board of education, which shall be actuated by the driver of the bus whenever but only whenever the bus is stopped or stopping on the roadway for the purpose of receiving or discharging school children or persons attending programs offered by community boards of mental health and county boards of mental retardation and developmental disabilities. A school bus driver shall not actuate the visual signals or the stop warning sign in designated school bus loading areas where the bus is entirely off the roadway or at school buildings when children or persons attending programs offered by community boards of mental health and county boards of mental retardation and developmental disabilities are loading or unloading at curbside. The visual signals and stop warning sign shall be synchronized or otherwise operated as required by rule of the board.

(C) Where a highway has been divided into four or more traffic lanes, a driver of a vehicle, streetcar, or trackless trolley need not stop for a school bus approaching from the opposite direction which has stopped for the purpose of receiving or discharging any school child or persons attending programs offered by community boards of mental health and county boards of mental retardation and developmental disabilities. The driver of any vehicle, streetcar, or trackless trolley overtaking the school bus shall comply with division (A) of this section.

(D) School buses operating on divided highways or on highways with four or more traffic lanes shall receive and discharge all school children or persons attending programs offered by community boards of mental health and county boards of mental retardation and developmental disabilities on their residence side of the highway.

(E) No school bus driver shall start his bus until after any child or person attending programs offered by community boards of mental health and county boards of mental retardation and developmental disabilities who may have alighted therefrom has reached a place of safety on his residence side of the road.

HISTORY: GC § 6307-73; 119 v 766(790), § 73; 123 v 614; Bureau of Code Revision, 10-1-53; 125 v 167 (Eff 10-2-53); 135 v H 995 (Eff 1-1-75); 136 v H 369 (Eff 8-29-75); 137 v S 389 (Eff 3-15-79); 138 v S 160 (Eff 10-31-80); 140 v H 478. Eff 3-28-85.

[§ 4511.75.1] § 4511.751 Operator or person with first-hand knowledge to report violation; information; furnished upon issuance of plates.

As used in this section, "license plate" includes, but is not limited to, any temporary license placard issued under section 4503.182 [4503.18.2] of the Revised Code or similar law of another jurisdiction.

When the operator of a school bus believes that a motorist has violated division (A) of section 4511.75 of the Revised Code, the operator shall report the license plate number and a general description of the vehicle and of the operator of the vehicle to the law enforcement agency exercising jurisdiction over the area where the alleged violation occurred. The information contained in the report relating to the license plate number and to the general description of the vehicle and the operator of the vehicle at the time of the alleged violation may be supplied by any person with first-hand knowledge of the information. Information of which the operator of the school bus has first-hand knowledge also may be corroborated by any other person.

Upon receipt of the report of the alleged violation of division (A) of section 4511.75 of the Revised Code, the law enforcement agency shall conduct an investigation to attempt to determine or confirm the identity of the operator of the vehicle at the time of the alleged violation. If the identity of the operator at the time of the alleged violation is established, the reporting of the license plate number of the vehicle shall establish probable cause for the law enforcement agency to issue a citation for the violation of division (A) of section 4511.75 of the Revised Code. However, if the identity of the operator of the vehicle at the time of the alleged violation cannot be established, the law enforcement agency shall issue a warning to the owner of the vehicle at the time of the alleged violation, except in the case of a leased or rented vehicle when the warning shall be issued to the lessee at the time of the alleged violation.

The registrar of motor vehicles and deputy registrars shall, at the time of issuing license plates to any person, include with the license plate a summary of the requirements of division (A) of section 4511.75 of the Revised Code, the procedures of section 4507.165 [4507.16.5] of the Revised Code, and the penalty in division (G) of section 4511.99 of the Revised Code.

HISTORY: 137 v S 389 (Eff 3-15-79); 144 v H 130. Eff 10-10-91.

§ 4511.76 School bus construction, design, equipment, operation and licensing rules.

(A) The department of public safety, by and with the advice of the superintendent of public instruction, shall adopt and enforce rules relating to the construction, design, and equipment, including lighting equipment required by section 4511.771 [4511.77.1] of the Revised Code, of all school buses both publicly and privately owned and operated in this state.

(B) The department of education, by and with the advice of the director of public safety, shall adopt and enforce rules relating to the operation of all school buses both publicly and privately owned and operated in this state.

(C) No person shall operate a school bus within this state in violation of the rules of the department of education or the department of public safety. No person, being the owner thereof or having the supervisory responsibility therefor, shall permit the operation of a school bus within this state in violation of the rules of the department of education or the department of public safety.

(D) The department of public safety shall adopt and enforce rules relating to the issuance of a license under section 4511.763 [4511.76.3] of the Revised Code. The rules may relate to the moral character of the applicant; the condition of the equipment to be operated; the liability and property damage insurance carried by the applicant; the posting of satisfactory and sufficient bond; and such other rules as the director of public safety determines reasonably necessary for the safety of the pupils to be transported.

HISTORY: GC § 6307-74; 119 v 766(790), § 74; 122 v 284;

Bureau of Code Revision, 10-1-53; 126 v 392(412) (Eff 3-17-55); 129 v 1273 (Eff 10-26-61); 131 v 1105 (Eff 9-1-65); 132 v H 1 (Eff 2-21-67); 135 v H 995 (Eff 1-1-75); 144 v S 98 (Eff 11-12-92); 147 v S 60. Eff 10-21-97.

[§ 4511.76.1] § 4511.761 School bus inspection.

The state highway patrol shall inspect every school bus to ascertain whether its construction, design, and equipment comply with the regulations adopted pursuant to section 4511.76 of the Revised Code and all other provisions of law.

The superintendent of the state highway patrol shall adopt a distinctive inspection decal not less than twelve inches in size, and bearing the date of the inspection, which shall be affixed to the outside surface of each side of each school bus which upon such inspection is found to comply with the regulations adopted pursuant to section 4511.76 of the Revised Code. The appearance of said decal shall be changed from year to year as to shape and color in order to provide easy visual inspection.

No person shall operate, nor shall any person being the owner thereof or having supervisory responsibility therefor permit the operation of, a school bus within this state unless there are displayed thereon the decals issued by the state highway patrol bearing the proper date of inspection for the calendar year for which the inspection decals were issued.

HISTORY: 129 v 1273 (Eff 10-26-61); 131 v 1106 (Eff 9-1-65); 144 v S 98 (Eff 11-12-92); 145 v H 687. Eff 10-12-94.

[§ 4511.76.2] § 4511.762 School bus no longer used for school purposes.

(A) Except as provided in division (B) of this section, no person who is the owner of a bus that previously was registered as a school bus that is used or is to be used exclusively for purposes other than the transportation of children, shall operate the bus or permit it to be operated within this state unless the bus has been painted a color different from that prescribed for school buses by section 4511.77 of the Revised Code and painted in such a way that the words "stop" and "school bus" are obliterated.

(B) Any church bus that previously was registered as a school bus and is registered under section 4503.07 of the Revised Code may retain the paint color prescribed for school buses by section 4511.77 of the Revised Code if the bus complies with all of the following:

(1) The words "school bus" required by section 4511.77 of the Revised Code are covered or obliterated and the bus is marked on the front and rear with the words "church bus" painted in black lettering not less than ten inches in height;

(2) The automatically extended stop warning sign required by section 4511.75 of the Revised Code is removed and the word "stop" required by section 4511.77 of the Revised Code is covered or obliterated;

(3) The flashing red and amber lights required by section 4511.771 [4511.77.1] of the Revised Code are covered or removed;

(4) The inspection decal required by section 4511.761 [4511.76.1] of the Revised Code is covered or removed;

(5) The identification number assigned under section 4511.764 [4511.76.4] of the Revised Code and marked in black lettering on the front and rear of the bus is covered or obliterated.

HISTORY: 129 v 1273 (Eff 10-26-61); 147 v S 85. Eff 5-15-97.

[§ 4511.76.3] § 4511.763 Licensing by department of public safety.

No person, partnership, association, or corporation shall transport pupils to or from school on a school bus or enter into a contract with a board of education of any school district for the transportation of pupils on a school bus, without being licensed by the department of public safety.

HISTORY: 131 v 1106 (Eff 9-1-65); 144 v S 98 (Eff 11-12-92); 145 v H 687. Eff 10-12-94.

[§ 4511.76.4] § 4511.764 Registration and identification of school buses.

The superintendent of the state highway patrol shall require school buses to be registered, in the name of the owner, with the state highway patrol on forms and in accordance with regulations as the superintendent may adopt.

When the superintendent is satisfied that the registration has been completed, he shall assign an identifying number to each school bus registered in accordance with this section. The number so assigned shall be marked on the front and rear of the vehicle in black lettering not less than six inches in height and will remain unchanged as long as the ownership of that vehicle remains the same.

No person shall operate, nor shall any person, being the owner thereof or having supervisory responsibility therefor, permit the operation of a school bus within this state unless there is displayed thereon an identifying number in accordance with this section.

HISTORY: 131 v 1106 (Eff 9-22-65); 136 v H 1. Eff 6-13-75.

§ 4511.77 School bus marking.

No person shall operate, nor shall any person being the owner thereof or having supervisory responsibility therefor permit the operation of, a school bus within this state unless it is painted national school bus chrome number two and is marked on front and rear with the words "school bus" in black lettering not less than eight inches in height and on the rear of the bus with the word "stop" in black lettering not less than ten inches in height.

HISTORY: 129 v 1273. Eff 10-26-61.

Not analogous to former RC § 4511.77 (Bureau of Code Revision, 10-1-53; 125 v 903[1025]), repealed 128 v 469, eff 11-10-59.

[§ 4511.77.1] § 4511.771 Flashing red and amber lights.

Every school bus shall, in addition to any other equipment and distinctive markings required pursuant to sections 4511.76, 4511.761 [4511.76.1], 4511.764 [4511.76.4], and 4511.77 of the Revised Code, be equipped with signal lamps mounted as high as practicable, which shall display to the front two alternately flashing red lights and two alternately flashing amber lights located at the same level and to the rear two alternately flashing red lights and two alternately flashing amber lights located at the same level, and these lights shall be visible at five hundred feet in normal sunlight. The alternately flashing red lights shall be spaced as widely as practicable, and the alternately flashing amber lights shall be located next to them.

HISTORY: 135 v H 995 (Eff 1-1-75); 137 v S 389. Eff 3-15-79.

The provisions of § 4 of SB 389 (137 v —) read as follows:
SECTION 4. The cost of equipping school buses with amber visual signals that meet the requirements of section 4511.771 of the Revised Code and with automatically extended stop warning signs shall, in the case of all school buses that have been purchased without such equipment on them, be paid by the Bureau of Transportation Safety within the Department of Transportation out of federal money that the Bureau receives under the National Highway Safety Act to the extent that such federal money is available. No school district shall be required to equip school buses that have been purchased without such equipment prior to the effective date of this act unless federal funds are made available by the Bureau for this purpose.

[§ 4511.77.2] § 4511.772 Operator's seat belt.

On and after the effective date of this section, no person, school board, or governmental entity shall purchase, lease, or rent a new school bus unless the school bus has an occupant restraining device, as defined in section 4513.263 [4513.26.3] of the Revised Code, installed for use in its operator's seat.

HISTORY: 141 v S 54. Eff 5-6-86.

§ 4511.79 Driving with impaired alertness or ability; use of drugs.

(A) No person shall drive a "commercial motor vehicle" as defined in section 4506.01 of the Revised Code, or a "commercial car" or "commercial tractor," as defined in section 4501.01 of the Revised Code, while his ability or alertness is so impaired by fatigue, illness, or other causes that it is unsafe for him to drive such vehicle. No driver shall use any drug which would adversely affect his ability or alertness.

(B) No owner, as defined in section 4501.01 of the Revised Code, of a "commercial motor vehicle," "commercial car," or "commercial tractor," or a person employing or otherwise directing the driver of such vehicle, shall require or knowingly permit a driver in any such condition described in division (A) of this section to drive such vehicle upon any street or highway.

HISTORY: 130 v H 391 (Eff 10-10-63); 143 v H 381. Eff 7-1-89.

§ 4511.81 Child restraint system required; child highway safety fund.

(A) When any child who is in either or both of the following categories is being transported in a motor vehicle, other than a taxicab or public safety vehicle as defined in section 4511.01 of the Revised Code, that is registered in this state and is required by the United States department of transportation to be equipped with seat belts at the time of manufacture or assembly, the operator of the motor vehicle shall have the child properly secured in accordance with the manufacturer's instructions in a child restraint system that meets federal motor vehicle safety standards:

(1) A child who is less than four years of age;

(2) A child who weighs less than forty pounds.

(B) When any child who is in either or both of the following categories is being transported in a motor vehicle, other than a taxicab, that is registered in this state and is owned, leased, or otherwise under the control of a nursery school, kindergarten, or day-care center, the operator of the motor vehicle shall have the child properly secured in accordance with the manufacturer's instructions in a child restraint system that meets federal motor vehicle safety standards:

(1) A child who is less than four years of age;

(2) A child who weighs less than forty pounds.

(C) The director of public safety shall adopt such rules as are necessary to carry out this section.

(D) The failure of an operator of a motor vehicle to secure a child in a child restraint system as required by this section is not negligence imputable to the child, is not admissible as evidence in any civil action involving the rights of the child against any other person allegedly liable for injuries to the child, is not to be used as a basis for a criminal prosecution of the operator of the motor vehicle other than a prosecution for a violation of this section, and is not admissible as evidence in any criminal action involving the operator of the motor vehicle other than a prosecution for a violation of this section.

(E) This section does not apply when an emergency exists that threatens the life of any person operating a motor vehicle and to whom this section otherwise would apply or the life of any child who otherwise would be required to be restrained under this section.

(F) If a person who is not a resident of this state is charged with a violation of division (A) or (B) of this section and does not prove to the court, by a preponderance of the evidence, that his use or nonuse of a child restraint system was in accordance with the law of the state of which he is a resident, the court shall impose the fine levied by division (H)(2) of section 4511.99 of the Revised Code.

(G) There is hereby created in the state treasury the "child highway safety fund," consisting of those portions of every fine imposed pursuant to divisions (H)(1) and (2) of section 4511.99 of the Revised Code for violations of divisions (A) and (B) of this section, that are required to be forwarded to the treasurer of state for deposit in the fund. The money in the fund shall be used by the department of health only for the purpose of establishing and administering a child highway safety program. The purpose of the program shall be to educate the public about child restraint systems generally and the importance of their proper use. The program also shall include a process for providing child restraint systems to persons who meet the eligibility criteria established by the department, and a toll-free telephone number the public may utilize to obtain information about child restraint systems and their proper use.

The director of health, in accordance with Chapter 119. of the Revised Code, shall adopt any rules necessary to carry out this section, including rules establishing the criteria a person must meet in order to receive a child restraint system under the department's child restraint system program.

HISTORY: 139 v H 605 (Eff 3-7-83); 141 v S 54 (Eff 5-6-86); 141 v H 428 (Eff 12-23-86); 142 v S 53 (Eff 10-20-87); 144 v S 98 (Eff 11-12-92); 145 v H 381. Eff 6-23-94.

§ 4511.83 Ignition interlock devices.

(A) As used in this section:

(1) "Ignition interlock device" means a device that connects a breath analyzer to a motor vehicle's ignition system, that is constantly available to monitor the concentration by weight of alcohol in the breath of any person attempting to start that motor vehicle by using its ignition system, and that deters starting the motor vehicle by use of its ignition system unless the person attempting to so start the vehicle provides an appropriate breath sample for the device and the device determines that the concentration by weight of alcohol in the person's breath is below a preset level.

(2) "Offender with restricted driving privileges" means an offender who is subject to an order that was issued under division (F) of section 4507.16 of the Revised Code as a condition of the granting of occupational driving privileges or an offender whose driving privilege is restricted as a condition of probation pursuant to division (G) of section 2951.02 of the Revised Code.

(B)(1) Except in cases of a substantial emergency when no other person is reasonably available to drive in response to the emergency, no person shall knowingly rent, lease, or lend a motor vehicle to any offender with restricted driving privileges, unless the vehicle is equipped with a functioning ignition interlock device that is certified pursuant to division (D) of this section.

(2) Any offender with restricted driving privileges who rents, leases, or borrows a motor vehicle from another person shall notify the person who rents, leases, or lends the motor vehicle to the offender that the offender has restricted driving privileges and of the nature of the restriction.

(3) Any offender with restricted driving privileges who is required to operate a motor vehicle owned by the offender's employer in the course and scope of the offender's employment may operate that vehicle without the installation of an ignition interlock device, provided that the employer has been notified that the offender has restricted driving privileges and of the nature of the restriction and provided further that the offender has proof of the employer's notification in the offender's possession while operating the employer's vehicle for normal business duties. A motor vehicle owned by a business that is partly or entirely owned or controlled by an offender with restricted driving privileges is not a motor vehicle owned by an employer, for purposes of this division.

(C) If a court, pursuant to division (F) of section 4507.16 of the Revised Code, imposes the use of an ignition interlock device as a condition of the granting of occupational driving privileges, the court shall require the offender to provide proof of compliance to the court at least once quarterly or more frequently as ordered by the court in its discretion. If a court imposes the use of an ignition interlock device as a condition of probation under division (I) of section 2951.02 of the Revised Code, the court shall require the offender to provide proof of compliance to the court or probation officer prior to issuing any driving privilege or continuing the probation status. In either case in which a court imposes the use of such a device, the offender, at least once quarterly or more frequently as ordered by the court in its discretion, shall have the device inspected as ordered by the court for accurate operation and shall provide the results of the inspection to the court or, if applicable, to the offender's probation officer.

(D)(1) The director of public safety, upon consultation with the director of health and in accordance with Chapter 119. of the Revised Code, shall certify ignition interlock devices and shall publish and make available to the courts, without charge, a list of approved devices together with information about the manufacturers of the devices and where they may be obtained. The cost of obtaining the certification of an ignition interlock device shall be paid by the manufacturer of the device to the director of public safety and shall be deposited in the driver's treatment and intervention fund established by section 4511.191 [4511.19.1] of the Revised Code.

(2) The director of public safety, in accordance with Chapter 119. of the Revised Code, shall adopt and publish rules setting forth the requirements for obtaining the certification of an ignition interlock device. No ignition interlock device shall be certified by the director of public safety pursuant to division (D)(1) of this section unless it meets the requirements specified and published by the director in the rules adopted pursuant to this division. The requirements shall include provisions for setting a minimum and maximum calibration range and shall include, but shall not be limited to, specifications that the device complies with all of the following:

(a) It does not impede the safe operation of the vehicle.

(b) It has features that make circumvention difficult and that do not interfere with the normal use of the vehicle.

(c) It correlates well with established measures of alcohol impairment.

(d) It works accurately and reliably in an unsupervised environment.

(e) It is resistant to tampering and shows evidence of tampering if tampering is attempted.

(f) It is difficult to circumvent and requires premeditation to do so.

(g) It minimizes inconvenience to a sober user.

(h) It requires a proper, deep-lung breath sample or other accurate measure of the concentration by weight of alcohol in the breath.

(i) It operates reliably over the range of automobile environments.

(j) It is made by a manufacturer who is covered by product liability insurance.

(3) The director of public safety may adopt, in whole or in part, the guidelines, rules, regulations, studies, or independent laboratory tests performed and relied upon by other states, or their agencies or commissions, in the certification or approval of ignition interlock devices.

(4) The director of public safety shall adopt rules in accordance with Chapter 119. of the Revised Code for the design of a warning label that shall be affixed to each ignition interlock device upon installation. The label shall contain a warning that any person tampering, circumventing, or otherwise misusing the device is subject to a fine, imprisonment, or both and may be subject to civil liability.

(E)(1) No offender with restricted driving privileges, during any period that the offender is required to operate only a motor vehicle equipped with an ignition interlock device, shall request or permit any other person to breathe into the device or start a motor vehicle equipped with the device, for the purpose of providing the offender with an operable motor vehicle.

(2)(a) Except as provided in division (E)(2)(b) of this section, no person shall breathe into an ignition interlock device or start a motor vehicle equipped with an ignition interlock device for the purpose of providing an operable motor vehicle to an offender with restricted driving privileges.

(b) Division (E)(2)(a) of this section does not apply to an offender with restricted driving privileges who breathes into an ignition interlock device or starts a motor vehicle equipped with an ignition interlock device for the purpose of providing himself or herself with an operable motor vehicle.

(3) No unauthorized person shall tamper with or circumvent the operation of an ignition interlock device.

HISTORY: 142 v H 429 (Eff 6-20-88); 143 v S 131 (Eff 7-25-90); 143 v H 837 (Eff 7-25-90); 144 v S 98 (Eff 11-12-92); 145 v S 82 (Eff 5-4-94); 146 v S 2. Eff 7-1-96.

§ 4511.84 Earphones or earplugs on operator prohibited.

(A) No person shall operate a motor vehicle while wearing earphones over, or earplugs in, both ears. As used in this section, "earphones" means any headset, radio, tape player, or other similar device that provides the listener with radio programs, music, or other recorded information through a device attached to the head and that covers all or a portion of both ears. "Earphones" does not include speakers or other listening devices that are built into protective headgear.

(B) This section does not apply to:

(1) Any person wearing a hearing aid;

(2) Law enforcement personnel while on duty;

(3) Fire department personnel and emergency medical service personnel while on duty;

(4) Any person engaged in the operation of equipment for use in the maintenance or repair of any highway;

(5) Any person engaged in the operation of refuse collection equipment.

HISTORY: 143 v S 6. Eff 10-30-89.

§ 4511.85 Chauffeured limousines.

(A) The operator of a chauffeured limousine shall accept passengers only on the basis of prearranged contracts, as defined in division (GG) of section 4501.01 of the Revised Code, and shall not cruise in search of patronage unless the limousine is in compliance with any statute or ordinance governing the operation of taxicabs or other similar vehicles for hire.

(B) No person shall advertise or hold himself out as doing business as a limousine service or livery service or other similar designation unless each vehicle used by him to provide the service is registered in accordance with section 4503.24 of the Revised Code and is in compliance with section 4509.80 of the Revised Code.

HISTORY: 143 v H 422. Eff 7-1-91.

The effective date is set by section 3 of HB 422.

§ 4511.90 Application to streets within Chautauqua Assembly.

As used in this section, "Chautauqua assembly" means a corporation that is organized in this state for the purpose of holding Chautauqua assemblies or encouraging religion, art, science, literature, or the general dissemination of knowledge, or two or more of such purposes, and that occupies grounds and holds meetings or entertainments on the grounds for the purposes for which it is organized.

Chapters 4511. and 4513. of the Revised Code are applicable to streets within a Chautauqua assembly. A Chautauqua assembly is a local authority for the purposes of section 4511.07 of the Revised Code.

HISTORY: 138 v H 316 (Eff 10-26-79); 138 v H 948. Eff 5-22-80.

[NONRESIDENT VIOLATOR COMPACT OF 1977]

§ 4511.95 Nonresident violator compact.

The nonresident violator compact, hereinafter called "the compact," is hereby enacted into law and entered into with all other jurisdictions legally joining therein in the form substantially as follows:

"NONRESIDENT VIOLATOR COMPACT
Article I

Findings, Declaration of Policy and Purpose

(A) The party jurisdictions find that:

(1) In most instances, a motorist who is cited for a traffic violation in a jurisdiction other than his home jurisdiction:

(a) Must post collateral or bond to secure appearance for trial at a later date; or

(b) If unable to post collateral or bond, is taken into custody until the collateral or bond is posted; or

(c) Is taken directly to court for his trial to be held.

(2) In some instances, the motorist's driver's license may be deposited as collateral to be returned after he has complied with the terms of the citation.

(3) The purpose of the practices described in divisions (A)(1) and (2) of this article is to ensure compliance with the terms of a traffic citation by the motorist who, if permitted to continue on his way after receiving the traffic citation, could return to his home jurisdiction and disregard his duty under the terms of the traffic citation.

(4) A motorist receiving a traffic citation in his home jurisdiction is permitted, except for certain violations, to accept the citation from the officer at the scene of the violation and to immediately continue on his way after promising or being instructed to comply with the terms of the citation.

(5) The practice described in division (A)(1) of this article causes unnecessary inconvenience and, at times, a hardship for the motorist who is unable at the time to post collateral, furnish a bond, stand trial, or pay the fine, and thus is compelled to remain in custody until some arrangement can be made.

(6) The deposit of a driver's license as a bail bond, as described in division (A)(2) of this article, is viewed with disfavor.

(7) The practices described herein consume an undue amount of law enforcement time.

(B) It is the policy of the party jurisdictions to:

(1) Seek compliance with the laws, ordinances, and administrative rules and regulations relating to the operation of motor vehicles in each of the jurisdictions;

(2) Allow motorists to accept a traffic citation for certain violations and proceed on their way without delay whether or not the motorist is a resident of the jurisdiction in which the citation was issued;

(3) Extend cooperation to its fullest extent among the jurisdictions for obtaining compliance with the terms of a traffic citation issued in one jurisdiction to a resident of another jurisdiction;

(4) Maximize effective utilization of law enforcement personnel and assist court systems in the efficient disposition of traffic violations.

(C) The purpose of this compact is to:

(1) Provide a means through which the party jurisdictions may participate in a reciprocal program to effectuate the policies enumerated in division (B) of this article in a uniform and orderly manner;

(2) Provide for the fair and impartial treatment of traffic violators operating within party jurisdictions in recognition of the motorist's right of due process and the sovereign status of a party jurisdiction.

Article II

Definitions

(A) In the nonresident violator compact, the following words have the meaning indicated, unless the context requires otherwise.

(B)(1) "Citation" means any summons, ticket, or other official document issued by a police officer for a traffic violation containing an order which requires the motorist to respond.

(2) "Collateral" means any cash or other security deposited to secure an appearance for trial, following the issuance by a police officer of a citation for a traffic violation.

(3) "Court" means a court of law or traffic tribunal.

(4) "Driver's license" means any license or privilege to operate a motor vehicle issued under the laws of the home jurisdiction.

(5) "Home jurisdiction" means the jurisdiction that issued the driver's license of the traffic violator.

(6) "Issuing jurisdiction" means the jurisdiction in which the traffic citation was issued to the motorist.

(7) "Jurisdiction" means a state, territory, or possession of the United States, the District of Columbia, or the Commonwealth of Puerto Rico.

(8) "Motorist" means a driver of a motor vehicle operating in a party jurisdiction other than the home jurisdiction.

(9) "Personal recognizance" means an agreement by a motorist made at the time of issuance of the traffic citation that he will comply with the terms of that traffic citation.

(10) "Police officer" means any individual authorized by the party jurisdiction to issue a citation for a traffic violation.

(11) "Terms of the citation" means those options expressly stated upon the citation.

Article III
Procedure for Issuing Jurisdiction

(A) When issuing a citation for a traffic violation, a police officer shall issue the citation to a motorist who possesses a driver's license issued by a party jurisdiction and shall not, subject to the exceptions noted in division (B) of this article, require the motorist to post collateral to secure appearance, if the officer receives the motorist's signed, personal recognizance that he or she will comply with the terms of the citation.

(B) Personal recognizance is acceptable only if not prohibited by law. If mandatory appearance is required, it must take place immediately following issuance of the citation.

(C) Upon failure of a motorist to comply with the terms of a traffic citation, the appropriate official shall report the failure to comply to the licensing authority of the jurisdiction in which the traffic citation was issued. The report shall be made in accordance with procedures specified by the issuing jurisdiction and shall contain information as specified in the compact manual as minimum requirements for effective processing by the home jurisdiction.

(D) Upon receipt of the report, the licensing authority of the issuing jurisdiction shall transmit to the licensing authority in the home jurisdiction of the motorist the information in a form and content as contained in the compact manual.

(E) The licensing authority of the issuing jurisdiction may not suspend the privilege of a motorist for whom a report has been transmitted.

(F) The licensing authority of the issuing jurisdiction shall not transmit a report on any violation if the date of transmission is more than six months after the date on which the traffic citation was issued.

(G) The licensing authority of the issuing jurisdiction shall not transmit a report on any violation where the date of issuance of the citation predates the most recent of the effective dates of entry for the two jurisdictions affected.

Article IV
Procedures for Home Jurisdiction

(A) Upon receipt of a report of a failure to comply from the licensing authority of the issuing jurisdiction, the licensing authority of the home jurisdiction shall notify the motorist and initiate a suspension action, in accordance with the home jurisdiction's procedures, to suspend the motorist's driver's license until satisfactory evidence of compliance with the terms of the traffic citation has been furnished to the home jurisdiction licensing authority. Due process safeguards will be accorded.

(B) The licensing authority of the home jurisdiction shall maintain a record of actions taken and make reports to issuing jurisdictions as provided in the compact manual.

Article V
Applicability of Other Laws

Except as expressly required by provisions of this compact, nothing contained herein shall be construed to affect the right of any party jurisdiction to apply any of its other laws relating to licenses to drive to any person or circumstance, or to invalidate or prevent any driver license agreement or other cooperative arrangement between a party jurisdiction and nonparty jurisdiction.

Article VI
Compact Administrator Procedures

(A) For the purpose of administering the provisions of this compact and to serve as a governing body for the resolution of all matters relating to the operation of this compact, a board of compact administrators is established. The board shall be composed of one representative from each party jurisdiction to be known as the compact administrator. The compact administrator shall be appointed by the jurisdiction executive and will serve and be subject to removal in accordance with the laws of the jurisdiction he represents. A compact administrator may provide for the discharge of his duties and the performance of his functions as a board member by an alternate. An alternate may not be entitled to serve unless written notification of his identity has been given to the board.

(B) Each member of the board of compact administrators shall be entitled to one vote. No action of the board shall be binding unless taken at a meeting at which a majority of the total number of votes on the board are cast in favor. Action by the board shall be only at a meeting at which a majority of the party jurisdictions are represented.

(C) The board shall elect annually, from its membership, a chairman and a vice chairman.

(D) The board shall adopt bylaws, not inconsistent with the provisions of this compact or the laws of a party jurisdiction, for the conduct of its business and shall have the power to amend and rescind its bylaws.

(E) The board may accept for any of its purposes and functions under this compact any and all donations, and grants of money, equipment, supplies, materials, and services, conditional or otherwise, from any jurisdiction, the United States, or any other governmental agency, and may receive, utilize, and dispose of the same.

(F) The board may contract with, or accept services

or personnel from, any governmental or intergovernmental agency, person, firm, or corporation, or any private nonprofit organization or institution.

(G) The board shall formulate all necessary procedures and develop uniform forms and documents for administering the provisions of this compact. All procedures and forms adopted pursuant to board action shall be contained in the compact manual.

Article VII
Entry into Compact and Withdrawal

(A) This compact shall become effective when it has been adopted by at least two jurisdictions.

(B)(1) Entry into the compact shall be made by a resolution of ratification executed by the authorized officials of the applying jurisdiction and submitted to the chairman of the board.

(2) The resolution shall be in a form and content as provided in the compact manual and shall include statements that in substance are as follows:

(a) A citation of the authority by which the jurisdiction is empowered to become a party to this compact;

(b) Agreement to comply with the terms and provisions of the compact;

(c) That compact entry is with all jurisdictions then party to the compact and with any jurisdiction that legally becomes a party to the compact.

(3) The effective date of entry shall be specified by the applying jurisdiction, but it shall not be less than sixty days after notice has been given by the chairman of the board of compact administrators or by the secretariat of the board to each party jurisdiction that the resolution from the applying jurisdiction has been received.

(C) A party jurisdiction may withdraw from this compact by official written notice to the other party jurisdictions, but a withdrawal shall not take effect until ninety days after notice of withdrawal is given. The notice shall be directed to the compact administrator of each member jurisdiction. No withdrawal shall affect the validity of this compact as to the remaining party jurisdictions.

Article VIII
Exceptions

The provisions of this compact shall not apply to parking or standing violations, highway weight limit violations, and violations of law governing the transportation of hazardous materials.

Article IX
Amendments to the Compact

(A) This compact may be amended from time to time. Amendments shall be presented in resolution form to the chairman of the board of compact administrators and may be initiated by one or more party jurisdictions.

(B) Adoption of an amendment shall require endorsement of all party jurisdictions and shall become effective thirty days after the date of the last endorsement.

(C) Failure of a party jurisdiction to respond to the compact chairman within one hundred twenty days after receipt of the proposed amendment shall constitute endorsement.

Article X
Construction and Severability

This compact shall be liberally construed so as to effectuate the purposes stated herein. The provisions of this compact shall be severable and if any phrase, clause, sentence, or provision of this compact is declared to be contrary to the constitution of any party jurisdiction or of the United States or the applicability thereof to any government, agency, person, or circumstance, the compact shall not be affected thereby. If this compact shall be held contrary to the constitution of any jurisdiction party thereto, the compact shall remain in full force and effect as to the remaining jurisdictions and in full force and effect as to the jurisdiction affected as to all severable matters.

Article XI
Title

This compact shall be known as the Nonresident Violator Compact of 1977."

HISTORY: 140 v S 40. Eff 1-1-85.

[§ 4511.95.1] § 4511.951 License reinstatement fee; compact administrator.

(A) A fee of thirty dollars shall be charged by the registrar of motor vehicles for the reinstatement of any driver's license suspended pursuant to division (A) of Article IV of the compact enacted in section 4511.95 of the Revised Code.

(B) Pursuant to division (A) of Article VI of the nonresident violator compact of 1977 enacted in section 4511.95 of the Revised Code, the director of public safety shall serve as the compact administrator for Ohio.

HISTORY: 140 v S 40 (Eff 1-1-85); 144 v S 98 (Eff 11-12-92); 147 v H 210. Eff 3-31-97.

The effective date is set by section 20 of HB 210.

See provisions, § 25 of HB 210 (147 v —) following RC § 4507.45.

§ 4511.99 Penalties.

(A) Whoever violates division (A) of section 4511.19 of the Revised Code, in addition to the license suspension or revocation provided in section 4507.16 of the Revised Code and any disqualification imposed under section 4506.16 of the Revised Code, shall be punished as provided in division (A)(1), (2), (3), or (4) of this section.

(1) Except as otherwise provided in division (A)(2), (3), or (4) of this section, the offender is guilty of a misdemeanor of the first degree and the court shall sentence the offender to a term of imprisonment of

three consecutive days and may sentence the offender pursuant to section 2929.21 of the Revised Code to a longer term of imprisonment. In addition, the court shall impose upon the offender a fine of not less than two hundred and not more than one thousand dollars.

The court may suspend the execution of the mandatory three consecutive days of imprisonment that it is required to impose by this division, if the court, in lieu of the suspended term of imprisonment, places the offender on probation and requires the offender to attend, for three consecutive days, a drivers' intervention program that is certified pursuant to section 3793.10 of the Revised Code. The court also may suspend the execution of any part of the mandatory three consecutive days of imprisonment that it is required to impose by this division, if the court places the offender on probation for part of the three consecutive days; requires the offender to attend, for that part of the three consecutive days, a drivers' intervention program that is certified pursuant to section 3793.10 of the Revised Code; and sentences the offender to a term of imprisonment equal to the remainder of the three consecutive days that the offender does not spend attending the drivers' intervention program. The court may require the offender, as a condition of probation, to attend and satisfactorily complete any treatment or education programs that comply with the minimum standards adopted pursuant to Chapter 3793. of the Revised Code by the director of alcohol and drug addiction services, in addition to the required attendance at a drivers' intervention program, that the operators of the drivers' intervention program determine that the offender should attend and to report periodically to the court on the offender's progress in the programs. The court also may impose any other conditions of probation on the offender that it considers necessary.

Of the fine imposed pursuant to this division, twenty-five dollars shall be paid to an enforcement and education fund established by the legislative authority of the law enforcement agency in this state that primarily was responsible for the arrest of the offender, as determined by the court that imposes the fine. This share shall be used by the agency to pay only those costs it incurs in enforcing section 4511.19 of the Revised Code or a substantially similar municipal ordinance and in informing the public of the laws governing the operation of a motor vehicle while under the influence of alcohol, the dangers of operating a motor vehicle while under the influence of alcohol, and other information relating to the operation of a motor vehicle and the consumption of alcoholic beverages. Twenty-five dollars of the fine imposed pursuant to this division shall be deposited into the county indigent drivers alcohol treatment fund or municipal indigent drivers alcohol treatment fund under the control of that court, as created by the county or municipal corporation pursuant to division (N) of section 4511.191 [4511.19.1] of the Revised Code. The balance of the fine shall be disbursed as otherwise provided by law.

(2)(a) Except as otherwise provided in division (A)(4) of this section, if, within six years of the offense, the offender has been convicted of or pleaded guilty to one violation of division (A) or (B) of section 4511.19 of the Revised Code, a municipal ordinance relating to operating a vehicle while under the influence of alcohol, a drug of abuse, or alcohol and a drug of abuse, a municipal ordinance relating to operating a vehicle with a prohibited concentration of alcohol in the blood, breath, or urine, section 2903.04 of the Revised Code in a case in which the offender was subject to the sanctions described in division (D) of that section, section 2903.06, 2903.07, or 2903.08 of the Revised Code or a municipal ordinance that is substantially similar to section 2903.07 of the Revised Code in a case in which the jury or judge found that the offender was under the influence of alcohol, a drug of abuse, or alcohol and a drug of abuse, or a statute of the United States or of any other state or a municipal ordinance of a municipal corporation located in any other state that is substantially similar to division (A) or (B) of section 4511.19 of the Revised Code, the offender is guilty of a misdemeanor of the first degree and, except as provided in this division, the court shall sentence the offender to a term of imprisonment of ten consecutive days and may sentence the offender pursuant to section 2929.21 of the Revised Code to a longer term of imprisonment. As an alternative to the term of imprisonment required to be imposed by this division, but subject to division (A)(8) of this section, the court may impose upon the offender a sentence consisting of both a term of imprisonment of five consecutive days and not less than eighteen consecutive days of electronically monitored house arrest as defined in division (A) of section 2929.23 of the Revised Code. The five consecutive days of imprisonment and the period of electronically monitored house arrest shall not exceed six months. The five consecutive days of imprisonment do not have to be served prior to or consecutively with the period of electronically monitored house arrest.

In addition, the court shall impose upon the offender a fine of not less than three hundred and not more than one thousand five hundred dollars.

In addition to any other sentence that it imposes upon the offender, the court may require the offender to attend a drivers' intervention program that is certified pursuant to section 3793.10 of the Revised Code. If the officials of the drivers' intervention program determine that the offender is alcohol dependent, they shall notify the court, and the court shall order the offender to obtain treatment through an alcohol and drug addiction program authorized by section 3793.02 of the Revised Code. The cost of the treatment shall be paid by the offender.

Of the fine imposed pursuant to this division, thirty-five dollars shall be paid to an enforcement and education fund established by the legislative authority of the law enforcement agency in this state that primarily was responsible for the arrest of the offender, as determined by the court that imposes the fine. This share shall be used by the agency to pay only those costs it incurs in enforcing division (A) of section 4511.19 of the Revised Code or a substantially similar municipal ordinance and in informing the public of the laws governing the operation of a motor vehicle while under the influence of alcohol, the dangers of operating a motor vehicle while under the influence of alcohol, and other information relating to the operation of a motor vehicle and the consumption of alcoholic beverages. Sixty-five dollars of the fine imposed pursuant to this division shall be paid to the political subdivision responsible for housing the offender during the offender's term of incarceration. This share shall be used by the political subdivision to pay or reimburse incarceration costs it incurs in housing persons who violate section 4511.19 of the Revised Code or a substantially similar municipal ordinance and to pay for ignition interlock devices and electronic house arrest equipment for persons who violate that section, and shall be paid to the credit of the fund that pays the cost of the incarceration. Fifty dollars of the fine imposed pursuant to this division shall be deposited into the county indigent drivers alcohol treatment fund or municipal indigent drivers alcohol treatment fund under the control of that court, as created by the county or municipal corporation pursuant to division (N) of section 4511.191 [4511.19.1] of the Revised Code. The balance of the fine shall be disbursed as otherwise provided by law.

(b) Regardless of whether the vehicle the offender was operating at the time of the offense is registered in the offender's name or in the name of another person, the court, in addition to the penalties imposed under division (A)(2)(a) of this section and all other penalties provided by law and subject to section 4503.235 [4503.23.5] of the Revised Code, shall order the immobilization for ninety days of the vehicle the offender was operating at the time of the offense and the impoundment for ninety days of the identification license plates of that vehicle. The order for the immobilization and impoundment shall be issued and enforced in accordance with section 4503.233 [4503.23.3] of the Revised Code.

(3)(a) Except as otherwise provided in division (A)(4) of this section, if, within six years of the offense, the offender has been convicted of or pleaded guilty to two violations of division (A) or (B) of section 4511.19 of the Revised Code, a municipal ordinance relating to operating a vehicle while under the influence of alcohol, a drug of abuse, or alcohol and a drug of abuse, a municipal ordinance relating to operating a vehicle with a prohibited concentration of alcohol in the blood, breath, or urine, section 2903.04 of the Revised Code in a case in which the offender was subject to the sanctions described in division (D) of that section, section 2903.06, 2903.07, or 2903.08 of the Revised Code or a municipal ordinance that is substantially similar to section 2903.07 of the Revised Code in a case in which the jury or judge found that the offender was under the influence of alcohol, a drug of abuse, or alcohol and a drug of abuse, or a statute of the United States or of any other state or a municipal ordinance of a municipal corporation located in any other state that is substantially similar to division (A) or (B) of section 4511.19 of the Revised Code, except as provided in this division, the court shall sentence the offender to a term of imprisonment of thirty consecutive days and may sentence the offender to a longer definite term of imprisonment of not more than one year. As an alternative to the term of imprisonment required to be imposed by this division, but subject to division (A)(8) of this section, the court may impose upon the offender a sentence consisting of both a term of imprisonment of fifteen consecutive days and not less than fifty-five consecutive days of electronically monitored house arrest as defined in division (A) of section 2929.23 of the Revised Code. The fifteen consecutive days of imprisonment and the period of electronically monitored house arrest shall not exceed one year. The fifteen consecutive days of imprisonment do not have to be served prior to or consecutively with the period of electronically monitored house arrest.

In addition, the court shall impose upon the offender a fine of not less than five hundred and not more than two thousand five hundred dollars.

In addition to any other sentence that it imposes upon the offender, the court shall require the offender to attend an alcohol and drug addiction program authorized by section 3793.02 of the Revised Code. The cost of the treatment shall be paid by the offender. If the court determines that the offender is unable to pay the cost of attendance at the treatment program, the court may order that payment of the cost of the offender's attendance at the treatment program be made from that court's indigent drivers alcohol treatment fund.

Of the fine imposed pursuant to this division, one hundred twenty-three dollars shall be paid to an enforcement and education fund established by the legislative authority of the law enforcement agency in this state that primarily was responsible for the arrest of the offender, as determined by the court that imposes the fine. This share shall be used by the agency to pay only those costs it incurs in enforcing section 4511.19 of the Revised Code or a substantially similar municipal ordinance and in informing the public of the laws governing the operation of a motor vehicle while under the influence of alcohol, the dangers of operating a motor vehicle while under the influence of alcohol, and other information relating to the operation of a motor vehicle and the consumption of alcoholic beverages. Two hundred twenty-seven dollars of the fine imposed pursuant to this division shall be paid to the political subdivision responsible for housing the offender during the offender's term of incarceration. This share shall be used by the political subdivision to pay or reimburse incarceration costs it incurs in housing persons who violate division (A) of section 4511.19 of the Revised Code or a substantially similar municipal ordinance and to pay for ignition interlock devices and electronic house arrest equipment for persons who violate that section and shall be paid to the credit of the fund that pays the cost of incarceration. The balance of the fine shall be disbursed as otherwise provided by law.

(b) Regardless of whether the vehicle the offender was operating at the time of the offense is registered in the offender's name or in the name of another person, the court, in addition to the penalties imposed under division (A)(3)(a) of this section and all other penalties provided by law and subject to section 4503.235 [4503.23.5] of the Revised Code, shall order the immobilization for one hundred eighty days of the vehicle the offender was operating at the time of the offense and the impoundment for one hundred eighty days of the identification license plates of that vehicle. The order for the immobilization and impoundment shall be issued and enforced in accordance with section 4503.233 [4503.23.3] of the Revised Code.

(4)(a) If, within six years of the offense, the offender has been convicted of or pleaded guilty to three or more violations of division (A) or (B) of section 4511.19 of the Revised Code, a municipal ordinance relating to operating a vehicle while under the influence of alcohol, a drug of abuse, or alcohol and a drug of abuse, a municipal ordinance relating to operating a vehicle with a prohibited concentration of alcohol in the blood, breath, or urine, section 2903.04 of the Revised Code in a case in which the offender was subject to the sanctions described in division (D) of that section, section 2903.06, 2903.07, or 2903.08 of the Revised Code or a municipal ordinance that is substantially similar to section 2903.07 of the Revised Code in a case in which the jury or judge found that the offender was under the influence of alcohol, a drug of abuse, or alcohol and a drug of abuse, or a statute of the United States or of any other state or a municipal ordinance of a municipal corporation located in any other state that is substantially similar to division (A) or (B) of section 4511.19 of the Revised Code, or if the offender previously has been convicted of or pleaded guilty to a violation of division (A) of section 4511.19 of the Revised Code under circumstances in which the violation was a felony and regardless of when the violation and the conviction or guilty plea occurred, the offender is guilty of a felony of the fourth degree. The court shall sentence the offender in accordance with sections 2929.11 to 2929.19 of the Revised Code and shall impose as part of the sentence a mandatory term of local incarceration of sixty consecutive days of imprisonment in accordance with division (G)(1) of section 2929.13 of the Revised Code or a mandatory prison term of sixty consecutive days of imprisonment in accordance with division (G)(2) of that section, whichever is applicable. If the offender is required to serve a mandatory term of local incarceration of sixty consecutive days of imprisonment in accordance with division (G)(1) of section 2929.13 of the Revised Code, the court, pursuant to section 2929.17 of the Revised Code, may impose upon the offender a sentence that includes a term of electronically monitored house arrest, provided that the term of electronically monitored house arrest shall not commence until after the offender has served the mandatory term of local incarceration.

In addition to all other sanctions imposed, the court shall impose upon the offender, pursuant to section 2929.18 of the Revised Code, a fine of not less than seven hundred fifty nor more than ten thousand dollars.

In addition to any other sanction that it imposes upon the offender, the court shall require the offender to attend an alcohol and drug addiction program authorized by section 3793.02 of the Revised Code. The cost of the treatment shall be paid by the offender. If the court determines that the offender is unable to pay the cost of attendance at the treatment program, the court may order that payment of the cost of the offender's attendance at the treatment program be made from the court's indigent drivers alcohol treatment fund.

Of the fine imposed pursuant to this division, two hundred ten dollars shall be paid to an enforcement and education fund established by the legislative authority of the law enforcement agency in this state that primarily was responsible for the arrest of the offender, as determined by the court that imposes the fine. This share shall be used by the agency to pay only those costs it incurs in enforcing section 4511.19 of the Revised Code or a substantially similar municipal ordinance and in informing the public of the laws governing operation of a motor vehicle while under the influence of alcohol, the dangers of operation of a motor vehicle while under the influence of alcohol, and other information relating to the operation of a motor vehicle and the consumption of alcoholic beverages. Three hundred ninety dollars of the fine imposed pursuant to this division shall be paid to the political subdivision responsible for housing the offender during the offender's term of incarceration. This share shall be used by the political subdivision to pay or reimburse incarceration costs it incurs in housing persons who violate division (A) of section 4511.19 of the Revised Code or a substantially similar municipal ordinance and to pay for ignition interlock devices and electronic house arrest equipment for persons who violate that section, and shall be paid to the credit of the fund that pays the cost of incarceration. The balance of the fine shall be disbursed as otherwise provided by law.

(b) Regardless of whether the vehicle the offender was operating at the time of the offense is registered in the offender's name or in the name of another person, the court, in addition to the sanctions imposed under division (A)(4)(a) of this section and all other sanctions provided by law and subject to section 4503.235 [4503.23.5] of the Revised Code, shall order the criminal forfeiture to the state of the vehicle the offender was operating at the time of the offense. The order of criminal forfeiture shall be issued and enforced in accordance with section 4503.234 [4503.23.4] of the Revised Code.

(c) As used in division (A)(4)(a) of this section, "mandatory prison term" and "mandatory term of local incarceration" have the same meanings as in section 2929.01 of the Revised Code.

If title to a motor vehicle that is subject to an order for criminal forfeiture under this section is assigned or transferred and division (C)(2) or (3) of section 4503.234 [4503.23.4] of the Revised Code applies, in addition to or independent of any other penalty established by law, the court may fine the offender the value of the vehicle as determined by publications of the national auto dealer's association. The proceeds from any fine imposed under this division shall be distributed in accordance with division (D)(4) of section 4503.234 [4503.23.4] of the Revised Code.

(5)(a) Except as provided in division (A)(5)(b) of this section, upon a showing that imprisonment would seriously affect the ability of an offender sentenced pursuant to division (A)(1), (2), (3), or (4) of this section to continue the offender's employment, the court may authorize that the offender be granted work release from imprisonment after the offender has served the three, ten, or thirty consecutive days of imprisonment or the mandatory term of local incarceration of sixty consecutive days that the court is required by division (A)(1), (2), (3), or (4) of this section to impose. No court shall authorize work release from imprisonment during the three, ten, or thirty consecutive days of imprisonment or the mandatory term of local incarceration or mandatory prison term of sixty consecutive days that the court is required by division (A)(1), (2), (3), or (4) of this section to impose. The duration of the work release shall not exceed the time necessary each day for the offender to commute to and from the place of employment and the place of imprisonment and the time actually spent under employment.

(b) An offender who is sentenced pursuant to division (A)(2) or (3) of this section to a term of imprisonment followed by a period of electronically monitored house arrest is not eligible for work release from imprisonment, but that person shall be permitted work release during the period of electronically monitored house arrest. The duration of the work release shall not exceed the time necessary each day for the offender to commute to and from the place of employment and the offender's home or other place specified by the sentencing court and the time actually spent under employment.

(6) Notwithstanding any section of the Revised Code that authorizes the suspension of the imposition or execution of a sentence, the placement of an offender in any treatment program in lieu of imprisonment, or the use of a community control sanction for an offender convicted of a felony, no court shall suspend the ten or thirty consecutive days of imprisonment required to be imposed on an offender by division (A)(2) or (3) of this section, no court shall place an offender who is sentenced pursuant to division (A)(2), (3), or (4) of this section in any treatment program in lieu of imprisonment until after the offender has served the ten or thirty consecutive days of imprisonment or the mandatory term of local incarceration or mandatory prison term of sixty consecutive days required to be imposed pursuant to division (A)(2), (3), or (4) of this section, no court that sentences an offender under division (A)(4) of this section shall impose any sanction other than a mandatory term of local incarceration or mandatory prison term to apply to the offender until after the offender has served the mandatory term of local incarceration or mandatory prison term of sixty consecutive days required to be imposed pursuant to division (A)(4) of this section, and no court that imposes a sentence of imprisonment and a period of electronically monitored house arrest upon an offender under division (A)(2) or (3) of this section shall suspend any portion of the sentence or place the offender in any treatment program in lieu of imprisonment or electronically monitored house arrest. Notwithstanding any section of the Revised Code that authorizes the suspension of the imposition or execution of a sentence or the placement of an offender in any treatment program in lieu of imprisonment, no court, except as specifically authorized by division (A)(1) of this section, shall suspend the three consecutive days of imprisonment required to be imposed by division (A)(1) of this section or place an offender who is sentenced pursuant to division (A)(1) of this section in any treatment program in lieu of imprisonment until after the offender has served the three consecutive days of imprisonment required to be imposed pursuant to division (A)(1) of this section.

(7) No court shall sentence an offender to an alcohol treatment program pursuant to division (A)(1), (2), (3), or (4) of this section unless the treatment program complies with the minimum standards adopted pursuant to Chapter 3793. of the Revised Code by the director of alcohol and drug addiction services.

(8) No court shall impose the alternative sentence of a term of imprisonment of five consecutive days plus not less than eighteen consecutive days of electronically monitored house arrest permitted to be imposed by division (A)(2) of this section, or the alternative sentence of a term of imprisonment of fifteen consecutive days plus not less than fifty-five consecutive days of electronically monitored house arrest permitted to be imposed pursuant to division (A)(3) of this section, unless within sixty days of the date of sentencing, the court issues a written finding, entered into the record, that due to the unavailability of space at the incarceration facility where the offender is required to serve the term of imprisonment imposed upon the offender, the offender will not be able to commence serving the term of imprisonment

within the sixty-day period following the date of sentencing. If the court issues such a finding, the court may impose the alternative sentence comprised of a term of imprisonment and a term of electronically monitored house arrest permitted to be imposed by division (A)(2) or (3) of this section.

(B) Whoever violates section 4511.192 [4511.19.2], 4511.251 [4511.25.1], or 4511.85 of the Revised Code is guilty of a misdemeanor of the first degree. The court, in addition to or independent of all other penalties provided by law, may suspend for a period not to exceed one year the driver's or commercial driver's license or permit or nonresident operating privilege of any person who pleads guilty to or is convicted of a violation of section 4511.192 [4511.19.2] of the Revised Code.

(C) Whoever violates section 4511.63, 4511.76, 4511.761 [4511.76.1], 4511.762 [4511.76.2], 4511.764 [4511.76.4], 4511.77, or 4511.79 of the Revised Code is guilty of one of the following:

(1) Except as otherwise provided in division (C)(2) of this section, a minor misdemeanor.

(2) If the offender previously has been convicted of or pleaded guilty to one or more violations of section 4511.63, 4511.76, 4511.761 [4511.76.1], 4511.762 [4511.76.2], 4511.764 [4511.76.4], 4511.77, or 4511.79 of the Revised Code or a municipal ordinance that is substantially similar to any of those sections, a misdemeanor of the fourth degree.

(D)(1) Whoever violates any provision of sections 4511.01 to 4511.76 or section 4511.84 of the Revised Code, for which no penalty otherwise is provided in this section is guilty of one of the following:

(a) Except as otherwise provided in division (D)(1)(b), (1)(c), (2), or (3) of this section, a minor misdemeanor;

(b) If, within one year of the offense, the offender previously has been convicted of or pleaded guilty to one violation of any provision of sections 4511.01 to 4511.76 or section 4511.84 of the Revised Code for which no penalty otherwise is provided in this section or a municipal ordinance that is substantially similar to any provision of sections 4511.01 to 4511.76 or section 4511.84 of the Revised Code for which no penalty otherwise is provided in this section, a misdemeanor of the fourth degree;

(c) If, within one year of the offense, the offender previously has been convicted of or pleaded guilty to two or more violations of any provision described in division (D)(1)(b) of this section or any municipal ordinance that is substantially similar to any of those provisions, a misdemeanor of the third degree.

(2) When any person is found guilty of a first offense for a violation of section 4511.21 of the Revised Code upon a finding that the person operated a motor vehicle faster than thirty-five miles an hour in a business district of a municipal corporation, or faster than fifty miles an hour in other portions, or faster than thirty-five miles an hour while passing through a school zone during recess or while children are going to or leaving school during the opening or closing hours, the person is guilty of a misdemeanor of the fourth degree.

(3) Notwithstanding section 2929.21 of the Revised Code, upon a finding that such person operated a motor vehicle in a construction zone where a sign was then posted in accordance with section 4511.98 of the Revised Code, the court, in addition to all other penalties provided by law, shall impose a fine of two times the usual amount imposed for the violation. No court shall impose a fine of two times the usual amount imposed for the violation upon an offender who alleges, in an affidavit filed with the court prior to the offender's sentencing, that the offender is indigent and is unable to pay the fine imposed pursuant to this division, provided the court determines the offender is an indigent person and is unable to pay the fine.

(E) Whenever a person is found guilty in a court of record of a violation of section 4511.761 [4511.76.1], 4511.762 [4511.76.2], or 4511.77 of the Revised Code, the trial judge, in addition to or independent of all other penalties provided by law, may suspend for any period of time not exceeding three years, or revoke the license of any person, partnership, association, or corporation, issued under section 4511.763 [4511.76.3] of the Revised Code.

(F) Whoever violates division (E) or (F) of section 4511.51, division (A), (D), or (E) of section 4511.521 [4511.52.1], section 4511.681 [4511.68.1], division (A), (C), or (F) of section 4511.69, section 4511.772 [4511.77.2], or division (A) or (B) of section 4511.82 of the Revised Code is guilty of a minor misdemeanor.

(G) Whoever violates division (A) of section 4511.75 of the Revised Code may be fined an amount not to exceed five hundred dollars. A person who is issued a citation for a violation of division (A) of section 4511.75 of the Revised Code is not permitted to enter a written plea of guilty and waive the person's right to contest the citation in a trial, but instead must appear in person in the proper court to answer the charge.

(H)(1) Whoever is a resident of this state and violates division (A) or (B) of section 4511.81 of the Revised Code shall be punished as follows:

(a) Except as otherwise provided in division (H)(1)(b) of this section, the offender is guilty of a minor misdemeanor.

(b) If the offender previously has been convicted of or pleaded guilty to a violation of division (A) or (B) of section 4511.81 of the Revised Code or of a municipal ordinance that is substantially similar to either of those divisions, the offender is guilty of a misdemeanor of the fourth degree.

(2) Whoever is not a resident of this state, violates division (A) or (B) of section 4511.81 of the Revised Code, and fails to prove by a preponderance of the evidence that the offender's use or nonuse of a child restraint system was in accordance with the law of the state of which the offender is a resident is guilty of a

minor misdemeanor on a first offense; on a second or subsequent offense, that person is guilty of a misdemeanor of the fourth degree.

(3) Sixty-five per cent of every fine imposed pursuant to division (H)(1) or (2) of this section shall be forwarded to the treasurer of state for deposit in the "child highway safety fund" created by division (G) of section 4511.81 of the Revised Code. The balance of the fine shall be disbursed as otherwise provided by law.

(I) Whoever violates section 4511.202 [4511.20.2] of the Revised Code is guilty of operating a motor vehicle without being in control of it, a minor misdemeanor.

(J) Whoever violates division (B) of section 4511.74, division (B)(1), (2), or (3), (C), or (E)(1), (2), or (3) of section 4511.83 of the Revised Code is guilty of a misdemeanor of the first degree.

(K) Except as otherwise provided in this division, whoever violates division (E) of section 4511.11, division (A) or (C) of section 4511.17, or section 4511.18 of the Revised Code is guilty of a misdemeanor of the third degree. If a violation of division (A) or (C) of section 4511.17 of the Revised Code creates a risk of physical harm to any person, the offender is guilty of a misdemeanor of the first degree. A violation of division (A) or (C) of section 4511.17 of the Revised Code that causes serious physical harm to property that is owned, leased, or controlled by a state or local authority is a felony of the fifth degree.

(L) Whoever violates division (H) of section 4511.69 of the Revised Code shall be punished as follows:

(1) Except as otherwise provided in division (L)(2) of this section, the offender shall be issued a warning.

(2) If the offender previously has been convicted of or pleaded guilty to a violation of division (H) of section 4511.69 of the Revised Code or of a municipal ordinance that is substantially similar to that division, the offender shall not be issued a warning but shall be fined twenty-five dollars for each parking location that is not properly marked or whose markings are not properly maintained.

(M) Whoever violates division (A)(1) or (2) of section 4511.45 of the Revised Code is guilty of a misdemeanor of the fourth degree on a first offense; on a second offense within one year after the first offense, the person is guilty of a misdemeanor of the third degree; and on each subsequent offense within one year after the first offense, the person is guilty of a misdemeanor of the second degree.

(N)(1) Whoever violates division (B) of section 4511.19 of the Revised Code is guilty of operating a motor vehicle after under-age alcohol consumption and shall be punished as follows:

(a) Except as otherwise provided in division (N)(1)(b) of this section, the offender is guilty of a misdemeanor of the fourth degree.

(b) If, within one year of the offense, the offender has been convicted of or pleaded guilty to any violation of division (A) or (B) of section 4511.19 of the Revised Code, a municipal ordinance relating to operating a vehicle while under the influence of alcohol, a drug of abuse, or alcohol and a drug of abuse, a municipal ordinance relating to operating a vehicle with a prohibited concentration of alcohol in the blood, breath, or urine, section 2903.04 of the Revised Code in a case in which the offender was subject to the sanctions described in division (D) of that section, section 2903.06, 2903.07, or 2903.08 of the Revised Code or a municipal ordinance that is substantially similar to section 2903.07 of the Revised Code in a case in which the jury or judge found that the offender was under the influence of alcohol, a drug of abuse, or alcohol and a drug of abuse, or a statute of the United States or of any other state or a municipal ordinance of a municipal corporation located in any other state that is substantially similar to division (A) or (B) of section 4511.19 of the Revised Code, the offender is guilty of a misdemeanor of the third degree.

(2) In addition to or independent of all other penalties provided by law, the offender's driver's or commercial driver's license or permit or nonresident operating privilege shall be suspended in accordance with, and for the period of time specified in, division (E) of section 4507.16 of the Revised Code.

(O) Whoever violates section 4511.62 of the Revised Code is guilty of a misdemeanor of the fourth degree.

HISTORY: Bureau of Code Revision, 10-1-53; 125 v 461; 128 v 469 (Eff 11-10-59); 129 v 1273 (Eff 10-26-61); 130 v 1089 (Eff 10-10-63); 131 v 1109 (Eff 9-1-65); 131 v 1107 (Eff 9-22-65); 132 v H 1 (Eff 2-21-67); 132 v S 37 (Eff 11-14-67); 132 v H 380 (Eff 1-1-68); 134 v H 511 (Eff 1-1-74); 137 v H 652 (Eff 3-13-78); 137 v S 381 (Eff 10-19-78); 137 v S 389 (Eff 3-15-79); 139 v H 707 (Eff 1-1-83); 139 v H 605 (Eff 3-7-83); 139 v S 432 (Eff 3-16-83); 140 v H 133 (Eff 9-27-83); 140 v S 169, § 1 (Eff 6-18-84); 140 v S 169, § 3 (Eff 1-1-85); 140 v H 112 (Eff 10-4-84); 140 v H 460 (Eff 4-4-85); 141 v S 54 (Eff 5-6-86); 141 v S 262 (Eff 3-20-87); 142 v H 333 (Eff 10-20-87); 142 v S 53 (Eff 10-20-87); 142 v H 429 (Eff 6-20-88); 142 v H 708 (Eff 4-19-88); 143 v H 8 (Eff 9-13-89); 143 v H 381 (Eff 7-1-89); 143 v S 86 (Eff 10-30-89); 143 v S 49 (Eff 11-3-89); 143 v H 317 (Eff 10-10-89); 143 v H 162 (Eff 6-28-90); 143 v H 422 (Eff 7-1-91); 143 v S 131 (Eff 7-25-90); 143 v H 837 (Eff 7-25-90); 143 v S 382 (Eff 12-31-90); 144 v H 73 (Eff 9-25-91); 144 v H 130 (Eff 10-10-91); 144 v H 725 (Eff 4-16-93); 144 v S 275 (Eff 9-1-93); 145 v H 149 (Eff 5-20-93); 145 v S 62, §§ 1, 4 (Eff 9-1-93); 145 v S 82 (Eff 5-4-94); 145 v H 381 (Eff 6-23-94); 145 v H 247 (Eff 5-1-95); 146 v S 2 (Eff 7-1-96); 146 v H 353 (Eff 9-17-96); 146 v H 676 (Eff 10-4-96); 146 v S 166 (Eff 10-17-96); 146 v H 72 (Eff 3-18-97); 147 v S 60. Eff 10-21-97.

[§ 4511.99.1] § 4511.991 Three consecutive days defined.

As used in section 4511.99 of the Revised Code, three consecutive days means seventy-two consecutive hours.

HISTORY: 139 v S 432. Eff 3-16-83.

CHAPTER 4513: TRAFFIC LAWS—EQUIPMENT; LOADS

§ 4513.01 Definitions.

The definitions set forth in section 4511.01 of the Revised Code apply to sections 4513.01 to 4513.37, inclusive, of the Revised Code.

HISTORY: Bureau of Code Revision. Eff 10-1-53.

Comment

This section is derived from GC § 6307-2. It duplicates RC § 4511.01 to make the definitions apply to this section.

§ 4513.02 Unsafe vehicles, prohibition against operation; inspection by state highway patrol.

(A) No person shall drive or move, or cause or knowingly permit to be driven or moved, on any highway any vehicle or combination of vehicles which is in such unsafe condition as to endanger any person.

(B) When directed by any state highway patrol trooper, the operator of any motor vehicle shall stop and submit such motor vehicle to an inspection under division (B)(1) or (2) of this section, as appropriate, and such tests as are necessary.

(1) Any motor vehicle not subject to inspection by the public utilities commission shall be inspected and tested to determine whether it is unsafe or not equipped as required by law, or that its equipment is not in proper adjustment or repair, or in violation of the equipment provisions of Chapter 4513. of the Revised Code.

Such inspection shall be made with respect to the brakes, lights, turn signals, steering, horns and warning devices, glass, mirrors, exhaust system, windshield wipers, tires, and such other items of equipment as designated by the superintendent of the state highway patrol by rule or regulation adopted pursuant to sections 119.01 to 119.13 of the Revised Code.

Upon determining that a motor vehicle is in safe operating condition and its equipment in conformity with Chapter 4513. of the Revised Code, the inspecting officer shall issue to the operator an official inspection sticker, which shall be in such form as the superintendent prescribes except that its color shall vary from year to year.

(2) Any motor vehicle subject to inspection by the public utilities commission shall be inspected and tested in accordance with rules adopted by the commission. Upon determining that the vehicle and operator are in compliance with rules adopted by the commission, the inspecting officer shall issue to the operator an appropriate official inspection sticker.

(C) The superintendent of the state highway patrol, pursuant to sections 119.01 to 119.13 of the Revised Code, shall determine and promulgate standards for any inspection program conducted by a political subdivision of this state. These standards shall exempt licensed collector's vehicles and historical motor vehicles from inspection. Any motor vehicle bearing a valid certificate of inspection issued by another state or a political subdivision of this state whose inspection program conforms to the superintendent's standards, and any licensed collector's vehicle or historical motor vehicle which is not in a condition which endangers the safety of persons or property, shall be exempt from the tests provided in division (B) of this section.

(D) Every person, firm, association, or corporation which, in the conduct of its business, owns and operates not less than fifteen motor vehicles in this state and which, for the purpose of storing, repairing, maintaining, and servicing such motor vehicles, equips and operates one or more service departments within this state, may file with the superintendent of the state highway patrol applications for permits for such service departments as official inspection stations for its own motor vehicles. Upon receiving an application for each such service department, and after determining that it is properly equipped and has competent personnel to perform the inspections referred to in this section, the superintendent shall issue the necessary inspection stickers and permit to operate as an official inspection station. Any such person who has had one or more service departments so designated as official inspection stations may have his motor vehicles, excepting private passenger cars owned by him or his employees, inspected at such service department; and any motor vehicle bearing a valid certificate of inspection issued by such service department shall be exempt from the tests provided in division (B) of this section.

No permit for an official inspection station shall be assigned or transferred or used at any location other than therein designated, and every such permit shall be posted in a conspicuous place at the location designated.

(E) When any motor vehicle is found to be unsafe for operation, the inspecting officer may order it removed from the highway and not operated, except for purposes of removal and repair, until it has been repaired pursuant to a repair order as provided in division (F) of this section.

(F) When any motor vehicle is found to be defective or in violation of Chapter 4513. of the Revised Code, the inspecting officer may issue a repair order, in such form and containing such information as the superintendent shall prescribe, to the owner or operator of the motor vehicle. The owner or operator shall thereupon obtain such repairs as are required and shall, as directed by the inspecting officer, return the repair order together with proof of compliance with its provisions. When any motor vehicle or operator subject to rules of the public utilities commission fails the inspection, the inspecting officer shall issue an appropriate order to obtain compliance with such rules.

(G) Sections 4513.01 to 4513.37 of the Revised Code, with respect to equipment on vehicles, do not apply to implements of husbandry, road machinery, road rollers, or agricultural tractors except as made applicable to such articles of machinery.

HISTORY: GC § 6307-75; 119 v 766(791), § 75; Bureau of Code Revision, 10-1-53; 132 v H 380 (Eff 1-1-68); 136 v S 52 (Eff 9-15-75); 144 v S 144 (Eff 8-8-91); 144 v S 351 (Eff 7-1-92); 144 v S 301. Eff 3-15-93.

The provisions of § 3 of SB 301 (144 v —) read as follows:

SECTION 3. The amendment by this act of section 4513.02 of the Revised Code corrects an error that occurred in Am. Sub. S.B. 351 of the 119th General Assembly. As presented in Am. Sub. S.B. 351 for purposes of amendment, the then existing version of section 4513.02 of the Revised Code unintentionally omitted division (G) of that section. This act amends section 4513.02 of the Revised Code to restore the unintentionally omitted division to the law.

[§ 4513.02.1] § 4513.021 Maximum bumper height; modifying vehicle; disconnecting suspension system.

(A) As used in this section:

(1) "Passenger car" means any motor vehicle with motive power, designed for carrying ten persons or less, except a multipurpose passenger vehicle or motorcycle.

(2) "Multipurpose passenger vehicle" means a motor vehicle with motive power, except a motorcycle, designed to carry ten persons or less, that is constructed either on a truck chassis or with special features for occasional off-road operation.

(3) "Truck" means every motor vehicle, except trailers and semitrailers, designed and used to carry property and having a gross vehicle weight rating of ten thousand pounds or less.

(4) "Manufacturer" has the same meaning as in section 4501.01 of the Revised Code.

(5) "Gross vehicle weight rating" means the manufacturer's gross vehicle weight rating established for that vehicle.

(B) The director of public safety, in accordance with Chapter 119. of the Revised Code, shall adopt rules in conformance with standards of the vehicle equipment safety commission, that shall govern the maximum bumper height or, in the absence of bumpers and in cases where bumper heights have been lowered or modified, the maximum height to the bottom of the frame rail, of any passenger car, multipurpose passenger vehicle, or truck.

(C) No person shall operate upon a street or highway any passenger car, multipurpose passenger vehicle, or truck registered in this state that does not conform to the requirements of this section or to any applicable rule adopted pursuant to this section.

(D) No person shall modify any motor vehicle registered in this state in such a manner as to cause the vehicle body or chassis to come in contact with the ground, expose the fuel tank to damage from collision, or cause the wheels to come in contact with the body under normal operation, and no person shall disconnect any part of the original suspension system of the vehicle to defeat the safe operation of that system.

(E) Nothing contained in this section or in the rules adopted pursuant to this section shall be construed to prohibit either of the following:

(1) The installation upon a passenger car, multipurpose passenger vehicle, or truck registered in this state of heavy duty equipment, including shock absorbers and overload springs;

(2) The operation on a street or highway of a passenger car, multipurpose passenger vehicle, or truck registered in this state with normal wear to the suspension system if the normal wear does not adversely affect the control of the vehicle.

(F) This section and the rules adopted pursuant to it do not apply to any specially designed or modified passenger car, multipurpose passenger vehicle, or truck when operated off a street or highway in races and similar events.

HISTORY: 142 v H 447 (Eff 9-27-88); 144 v S 98. Eff 11-12-92.

Analogous in part to former RC § 4513.02.1 (135 v H 173), repealed 142 v H 447, § 2, eff 9-27-88.

[§ 4513.02.2] § 4513.022 Trooper may request proof of financial responsibility; indication on ticket; failure to produce proof.

(A) As part of the motor vehicle inspection conducted pursuant to section 4513.02 of the Revised Code, the state highway patrol trooper shall request that the owner or operator of the motor vehicle produce proof that the owner maintains or has maintained on the owner's behalf, proof of financial responsibility as required by section 4509.101 [4509.10.1] of the Revised Code.

(B) A state highway patrol trooper shall indicate on every traffic ticket issued pursuant to a motor vehicle inspection whether the person receiving the traffic ticket produced proof of the maintenance of financial responsibility in response to the state highway patrol trooper's request. The state highway patrol trooper shall inform every person who receives a traffic ticket and who has failed to produce proof of the maintenance of financial responsibility at the time of the motor vehicle inspection that the person must submit proof to the traffic violations bureau with any payment of a fine and costs for the ticketed violation or, if the person is to appear in court for the violation, the person must submit proof to the court.

(C)(1) If a person who has failed to produce proof of the maintenance of financial responsibility appears in court for a ticketed violation, the court may permit the defendant to present evidence of proof of financial responsibility to the court at such time and in such manner as the court determines to be necessary or appropriate. The clerk of courts shall provide the registrar with the identity of any person who fails to submit proof of the maintenance of financial responsibility pursuant to division (B) of this section.

(2) If a person who has failed to present proof of the maintenance of financial responsibility also fails to submit that proof to the traffic violations bureau, the traffic violations bureau shall notify the registrar of the identity of that person.

(3) Upon receiving notice from a clerk of courts or a traffic violation bureau pursuant to division (C) of this section, the registrar shall proceed against these persons under division (D) of section 4509.101 [4509.10.1] of the Revised Code in the same manner as the registrar proceeds against persons identified by the clerk of courts under division (D)(4) of section 4509.101 [4509.10.1] of the Revised Code.

(D) A state highway patrol trooper may charge an owner or operator of a motor vehicle with a violation if† division (B)(1) of section 4507.02 of the Revised Code when the operator fails to produce proof of the maintenance of financial responsibility upon the state highway patrol trooper's request under division (A) of this section, if a check of the owner or operator's driving record indicates that the owner or operator, at the time of the motor vehicle inspection, is required to file and maintain proof of financial responsibility under section 4509.45 of the Revised Code for a previous violation of Chapter 4509. of the Revised Code.

HISTORY: 145 v S 20 (Eff 10-20-95); 146 v H 248, § 1 (Eff 10-20-95); 146 v H 438. Eff 7-1-97.

The effective date is set by section 3 of HB 438.

† So in enrolled bill, division (D).

[EQUIPMENT]

§ 4513.03 Lighted lights required.

Every vehicle upon a street or highway within this state during the time from one-half hour after sunset to one-half hour before sunrise, and at any other time when there are unfavorable atmospheric conditions or when there is not sufficient natural light to render discernible persons, vehicles, and substantial objects on the highway at a distance of one thousand feet ahead, shall display lighted lights and illuminating devices as required by sections 4513.04 to 4513.37 of the Revised Code, for different classes of vehicles; except that every motorized bicycle shall display at such times lighted lights meeting the rules adopted by the director of public safety under section 4511.521 [4511.52.1] of the Revised Code. No motor vehicle, during such times, shall be operated upon a street or highway within this state using only parking lights as illumination.

Whenever in such sections a requirement is declared as to the distance from which certain lamps and devices shall render objects visible, or within which such lamps or devices shall be visible, such distance shall be measured upon a straight level unlighted highway under normal atmospheric conditions unless a different condition is expressly stated.

Whenever in such sections a requirement is declared as to the mounted height of lights or devices, it shall mean from the center of such light or device to the level ground upon which the vehicle stands.

HISTORY: GC § 6307-76; 119 v 766(791), § 76; Bureau of Code Revision, 10-1-53; 129 v 232 (Eff 9-21-61); 135 v H 272 (Eff 11-21-73); 137 v S 100 (Eff 4-1-78); 144 v S 98. Eff 11-12-92.

§ 4513.04 Headlights.

Every motor vehicle, other than a motorcycle, and every trackless trolley shall be equipped with at least two headlights with at least one near each side of the front of the motor vehicle or trackless trolley.

Every motorcycle shall be equipped with at least one and not more than two headlights.

HISTORY: GC § 6307-77; 119 v 766(792), § 77; Bureau of Code Revision. Eff 10-1-53.

§ 4513.05 Tail lights and illumination of rear license plate.

Every motor vehicle, trackless trolley, trailer, semitrailer, pole trailer, or vehicle which is being drawn at the end of a train of vehicles shall be equipped with at least one tail light mounted on the rear which, when lighted, shall emit a red light visible from a distance of five hundred feet to the rear, provided that in the case of a train of vehicles only the tail light on the rearmost vehicle need be visible from the distance specified.

Either a tail light or a separate light shall be so constructed and placed as to illuminate with a white light the rear registration plate, when such registration plate is required, and render it legible from a distance of fifty feet to the rear. Any tail light, together with any separate light for illuminating the rear registration plate, shall be so wired as to be lighted whenever the headlights or auxiliary driving lights are lighted, except where separate lighting systems are provided for trailers for the purpose of illuminating such registration plate.

HISTORY: GC § 6307-78; 119 v 766(792), § 78; Bureau of Code Revision. Eff 10-1-53.

§ 4513.06 Red reflectors required.

Every new motor vehicle sold after September 6, 1941, and operated on a highway, other than a commercial tractor, to which a trailer or semitrailer is attached shall carry at the rear, either as a part of the tail lamps or separately, two red reflectors meeting the requirements of this section, except that vehicles of the type mentioned in section 4513.07 of the Revised Code shall be equipped with reflectors as required by the regulations provided for in said section.

Every such reflector shall be of such size and characteristics and so maintained as to be visible at night from all distances within three hundred feet to fifty feet from such vehicle.

HISTORY: GC § 6307-79; 119 v 766(792), § 79; Bureau of Code Revision. Eff 10-1-53.

§ 4513.07 Safety lighting of commercial vehicles.

The director of public safety shall prescribe and promulgate regulations relating to clearance lights, marker lights, reflectors, and stop lights on busses, trackless trolleys, trucks, commercial tractors, trailers, semitrailers, and pole trailers, when operated upon any highway, and such vehicles shall be equipped as required by such regulations, and such equipment shall be lighted at all times mentioned in section 4513.03 of the Revised Code, except that clearance lights and side marker lights need not be lighted on any such vehicle when it is operated within a municipal corporation where there is sufficient light to reveal any person or substantial object on the highway at a distance of five hundred feet.

Such equipment shall be in addition to all other lights specifically required by sections 4513.03 to 4513.16 of the Revised Code.

Vehicles operated under the jurisdiction of the public utilities commission are not subject to this section.

HISTORY: GC § 6307-80; 119 v 766(793), § 80; Bureau of Code Revision, 10-1-53; 129 v 1180 (Eff 11-2-59); 144 v S 98. Eff 11-12-92.

[§ 4513.07.1] § 4513.071 Stop light regulations.

All motor vehicles when operated upon a highway shall be equipped with at least one stop light mounted on the rear of the vehicle which shall be actuated upon application of the service brake, and which may be incorporated with other rear lights. Such stop lights when actuated shall emit a red light visible from a distance of five hundred feet to the rear, provided that in the case of a train of vehicles only the stop lights on the rear-most vehicle need be visible from the distance specified.

Such stop lights when actuated shall give a steady warning light to the rear of a vehicle or train of vehicles to indicate the intention of the operator to diminish the speed of or stop a vehicle or train of vehicles.

When stop lights are used as required by this section, they shall be constructed or installed so as to provide adequate and reliable illumination and shall conform to the appropriate rules and regulations established under section 4513.19 of the Revised Code.

Historical motor vehicles as defined in section 4503.181 [4503.18.1] of the Revised Code are not subject to this section.

HISTORY: 134 v S 227. Eff 12-17-71.

§ 4513.08 Obscured lights on vehicles.

Whenever motor and other vehicles are operated in combination during the time that lights are required, any light, except tail lights, which by reason of its location on a vehicle of the combination would be obscured by another vehicle of the combination need not be lighted, but this section does not affect the requirement that lighted clearance lights be displayed on the front of the foremost vehicle required to have clearance lights or that all lights required on the rear of the rearmost vehicle of any combination shall be lighted.

HISTORY: GC § 6307-81; 119 v 766(793), § 81; Bureau of Code Revision. Eff 10-1-53.

§ 4513.09 Red light or flag required.

Whenever the load upon any vehicle extends to the rear four feet or more beyond the bed or body of such vehicle, there shall be displayed at the extreme rear end of the load, at the times specified in section 4513.03 of the Revised Code, a red light or lantern plainly visible from a distance of at least five hundred feet to the sides and rear. The red light or lantern required by this section is in addition to the red rear light required upon every vehicle. At any other time there shall be displayed at the extreme rear end of such load a red flag or cloth not less than sixteen inches square.

HISTORY: GC § 6307-82; 119 v 766(793), § 82; Bureau of Code Revision. Eff 10-1-53.

§ 4513.10 Lights on parked vehicles.

Except in case of an emergency, whenever a vehicle is parked or stopped upon a roadway open to traffic or a shoulder adjacent thereto, whether attended or unattended, during the times mentioned in section 4513.03 of the Revised Code, such vehicle shall be equipped with one or more lights which shall exhibit a white or amber light on the roadway side visible from a distance of five hundred feet to the front of such vehicle, and a red light visible from a distance of five hundred feet to the rear. No lights need be displayed upon any such vehicle when it is stopped or parked within a municipal corporation where there is sufficient light to reveal any person or substantial object within a distance of five hundred feet upon such highway. Any lighted headlights upon a parked vehicle shall be depressed or dimmed.

HISTORY: GC § 6307-83; 119 v 766(793), § 83; Bureau of Code Revision, 10-1-53; 128 v 1167. Eff 10-19-55.

§ 4513.11 Lamps, reflectors and emblems for animal-drawn or slow-moving vehicles.

(A) All vehicles other than bicycles, including animal-drawn vehicles and vehicles referred to in division (G) of section 4513.02 of the Revised Code, not specifically required to be equipped with lamps or other lighting devices by sections 4513.03 to 4513.10 of the Revised Code, shall, at the times specified in section 4513.03 of the Revised Code, be equipped with at least one lamp displaying a white light visible from a distance of not less than one thousand feet to the front of the vehicle, and also shall be equipped with two lamps displaying red light visible from a distance of not less than one thousand feet to the rear of the vehicle, or as an alternative, one lamp displaying a red light visible from a distance of not less than one thousand feet to the rear and two red reflectors visible from all distances of six hundred feet to one hundred feet to the rear when illuminated by the lawful lower beams of headlamps.

Lamps and reflectors required or authorized by this section shall meet standards adopted by the director of public safety.

(B) All boat trailers, farm machinery, and other machinery, including all road construction machinery, upon a street or highway, except when being used in actual construction and maintenance work in an area guarded by a flagperson, or where flares are used, or when operating or traveling within the limits of a construction area designated by the director of transportation, a city engineer, or the county engineer of the several counties, when such construction area is marked in accordance with requirements of the director and the manual of uniform traffic control devices, as set forth in section 4511.09 of the Revised Code, which is designed for operation at a speed of twenty-five miles per hour or less shall be operated at a speed not exceeding twenty-five miles per hour, and shall display a triangular slow-moving vehicle emblem (SMV). The emblem shall be mounted so as to be visible from a distance of not less than five hundred feet to the rear. The director of public safety shall adopt standards and specifications for the design and position of mounting the SMV emblem. The standards and specifications for SMV emblems referred to in this section shall correlate with and, so far as possible, conform with those approved by the American society of agricultural engineers.

As used in this division, "machinery" does not include any vehicle designed to be drawn by an animal.

(C) The use of the SMV emblem shall be restricted to animal-drawn vehicles, and to the slow-moving vehicles specified in division (B) of this section operating or traveling within the limits of the highway. Its use on slow-moving vehicles being transported upon other types of vehicles or on any other type of vehicle or stationary object on the highway is prohibited.

(D) No person shall sell, lease, rent, or operate any boat trailer, farm machinery, or other machinery defined as a slow-moving vehicle in division (B) of this section, except those units designed to be completely mounted on a primary power unit, which is manufactured or assembled on or after April 1, 1966, unless the vehicle is equipped with a slow-moving vehicle emblem mounting device as specified in division (B) of this section.

(E) Any boat trailer, farm machinery, or other machinery defined as a slow-moving vehicle in division (B) of this section, in addition to the use of the slow-moving vehicle emblem, may be equipped with a red flashing light that shall be visible from a distance of not less than one thousand feet to the rear at all times specified in section 4513.03 of the Revised Code. When a double-faced light is used, it shall display amber light to the front and red light to the rear.

In addition to the lights described in this division, farm machinery also may display a flashing, oscillating, or rotating amber light, as permitted by section 4513.17 of the Revised Code.

(F) Every animal-drawn vehicle upon a street or highway shall at all times be equipped in one of the following ways:

(1) With a slow-moving vehicle emblem complying with division (B) of this section;

(2) With alternate reflective material complying with rules adopted under this division;

(3) With both a slow-moving vehicle emblem and alternate reflective material as specified in this division.

The director of public safety, subject to Chapter 119. of the Revised Code, shall adopt rules establishing standards and specifications for the position of mounting of the alternate reflective material authorized by this division. The rules shall permit, as a minimum, the alternate reflective material to be black, gray, or silver in color. The alternate reflective material shall be mounted on the animal-drawn vehicle so as to be visible, at all times specified in section 4513.03 of the Revised Code, from a distance of not less than five hundred feet to the rear when illuminated by the lawful lower beams of headlamps.

(G) As used in this section, "boat trailer" means any vehicle designed and used exclusively to transport a boat between a place of storage and a marina, or in and around a marina, when drawn or towed on a street or highway for a distance of no more than ten miles and at a speed of twenty-five miles per hour or less.

HISTORY: GC § 6307-84; 119 v 766(794), § 84; Bureau of Code Revision, 10-1-53; 128 v 591 (Eff 11-2-59); 131 v 1110 (Eff 4-1-66); 132 v H 172 (Eff 9-26-67); 135 v H 200 (Eff 9-28-73); 135 v H 472 (Eff 1-1-75); 135 v H 995 (Eff 1-1-75); 136 v H 1 (Eff 6-13-75); 142 v H 52 (Eff 10-1-87); 142 v H 708 (Eff 4-19-88); 144 v H 485 (Eff 10-7-92); 144 v S 98 (Eff 11-12-92); 146 v S 121. Eff 11-19-96.

§ 4513.12 Spotlight and auxiliary driving lights.

Any motor vehicle may be equipped with not more than one spotlight and every lighted spotlight shall be so aimed and used upon approaching another vehicle that no part of the high-intensity portion of the beam will be directed to the left of the prolongation of the extreme left side of the vehicle, nor more than one hundred feet ahead of the vehicle.

Any motor vehicle may be equipped with not more

than three auxiliary driving lights mounted on the front of the vehicle. The director of public safety shall prescribe specifications for auxiliary driving lights and regulations for their use, and any such lights which do not conform to said specifications and regulations shall not be used.

HISTORY: GC § 6307-85; 119 v 766(794), § 85; Bureau of Code Revision, 10-1-53; 128 v 1180 (Eff 11-2-59); 144 v S 98. Eff 11-12-92.

§ 4513.13 Cowl, fender, and back-up lights.

Any motor vehicle may be equipped with side cowl or fender lights which shall emit a white or amber light without glare.

Any motor vehicle may be equipped with lights on each side thereof which shall emit a white or amber light without glare.

Any motor vehicle may be equipped with back-up lights, either separately or in combination with another light. No back-up lights shall be continuously lighted when the motor vehicle is in forward motion.

HISTORY: GC § 6307-86; 119 v 766(794), § 86; Bureau of Code Revision. Eff 10-1-53.

§ 4513.14 Two lights displayed.

At all times mentioned in section 4513.03 of the Revised Code at least two lighted lights shall be displayed, one near each side of the front of every motor vehicle and trackless trolley, except when such vehicle or trackless trolley is parked subject to the regulations governing lights on parked vehicles and trackless trolleys.

The director of public safety shall prescribe and promulgate regulations relating to the design and use of such lights and such regulations shall be in accordance with currently recognized standards.

HISTORY: GC § 6307-87; 119 v 766(794), § 87; Bureau of Code Revision, 10-1-53; 128 v 1180 (Eff 11-2-59); 144 v S 98. Eff 11-12-92.

§ 4513.15 Headlights required.

Whenever a motor vehicle is being operated on a roadway or shoulder adjacent thereto during the times specified in section 4513.03 of the Revised Code, the driver shall use a distribution of light, or composite beam, directed high enough and of sufficient intensity to reveal persons, vehicles, and substantial objects at a safe distance in advance of the vehicle, subject to the following requirements:

(A) Whenever a driver of a vehicle approaches an oncoming vehicle, such driver shall use a distribution of light, or composite beam, so aimed that the glaring rays are not projected into the eyes of the oncoming driver.

(B) Every new motor vehicle registered in this state, which has multiple-beam road lighting equipment shall be equipped with a beam indicator, which shall be lighted whenever the uppermost distribution of light from the headlights is in use, and shall not otherwise be lighted. Said indicator shall be so designed and located that, when lighted, it will be readily visible without glare to the driver of the vehicle.

HISTORY: GC § 6307-88; 119 v 766(795), § 88; Bureau of Code Revision. Eff 10-1-53.

§ 4513.16 Lights of less intensity.

Any motor vehicle may be operated under the conditions specified in section 4513.03 of the Revised Code when it is equipped with two lighted lights upon the front thereof capable of revealing persons and substantial objects seventy-five feet ahead, in lieu of lights required in section 4513.14 of the Revised Code, provided that such vehicle shall not be operated at a speed in excess of twenty miles per hour.

HISTORY: GC § 6307-89; 119 v 766(795), § 89; Bureau of Code Revision. Eff 10-1-53.

§ 4513.17 Number of lights permitted; direction of beam; flashing, oscillating or rotating lights.

(A) Whenever a motor vehicle equipped with headlights also is equipped with any auxiliary lights or spotlight or any other light on the front thereof projecting a beam of an intensity greater than three hundred candle power, not more than a total of five of any such lights on the front of a vehicle shall be lighted at any one time when the vehicle is upon a highway.

(B) Any lighted light or illuminating device upon a motor vehicle, other than headlights, spotlights, signal lights, or auxiliary driving lights, that projects a beam of light of an intensity greater than three hundred candle power, shall be so directed that no part of the beam will strike the level of the roadway on which the vehicle stands at a distance of more than seventy-five feet from the vehicle.

(C)(1) Flashing lights are prohibited on motor vehicles, except as a means for indicating a right or a left turn, or in the presence of a vehicular traffic hazard requiring unusual care in approaching, or overtaking or passing. This prohibition does not apply to emergency vehicles, road service vehicles servicing or towing a disabled vehicle, traffic line stripers, snow plows, rural mail delivery vehicles, vehicles as provided in section 4513.182 [4513.18.2] of the Revised Code, department of transportation maintenance vehicles, funeral hearses, funeral escort vehicles, and similar equipment operated by the department or local authorities, which shall be equipped with and display, when used on a street or highway for the special purpose necessitating such lights, a flashing, oscillating, or rotating amber light, but shall not display a flashing, oscillating, or rotating light of any other color, nor to vehicles or machinery permitted by section 4513.11 of the Revised Code to have a flashing red light.

(2) When used on a street or highway, farm machinery and vehicles escorting farm machinery may be equipped with and display a flashing, oscillating, or rotating amber light, and the prohibition contained in division (C)(1) of this section does not apply to such machinery or vehicles. Farm machinery also may display the lights described in section 4513.11 of the Revised Code.

(D) Except a person operating a public safety vehicle, as defined in division (E) of section 4511.01 of the Revised Code, or a school bus, no person shall operate, move, or park upon, or permit to stand within the right-of-way of any public street or highway any vehicle or equipment that is equipped with and displaying a flashing red or a flashing combination red and white light, or an oscillating or rotating red light, or a combination red and white oscillating or rotating light; and except a public law enforcement officer, or other person sworn to enforce the criminal and traffic laws of the state, operating a public safety vehicle when on duty, no person shall operate, move, or park upon, or permit to stand within the right-of-way of any street or highway any vehicle or equipment that is equipped with, or upon which is mounted, and displaying a flashing blue or a flashing combination blue and white light, or an oscillating or rotating blue light, or a combination blue and white oscillating or rotating light. This section does not prohibit the use of warning lights required by law or the simultaneous flashing of turn signals on disabled vehicles.

HISTORY: GC § 6307-90; 119 v 766(795), § 90; Bureau of Code Revision, 10-1-53; 126 v 790 (Eff 9-14-55); 127 v 54 (Eff 8-27-57); 128 v 591 (Eff 11-2-59); 131 v 1112 (Eff 4-1-66); 131 v 1113 (Eff 10-13-65); 132 v H 878 (Eff 12-14-67); 135 v H 956 (Eff 7-26-74); 136 v H 272 (Eff 1-1-76); 146 v S 121. Eff 11-19-96.

§ 4513.18 Standards for lights on snow removal equipment and oversize vehicles.

The director of transportation shall adopt standards and specifications applicable to headlights, clearance lights, identification and other lights, on snow removal equipment when operated on the highways, and on vehicles operating under special permits pursuant to section 4513.34 of the Revised Code, in lieu of the lights otherwise required on motor vehicles. Such standards and specifications may permit the use of flashing lights for purposes of identification on snow removal equipment, and oversize vehicles when in service upon the highways. The standards and specifications for lights referred to in this section shall correlate with and, so far as possible, conform with those approved by the American association of state highway officials.

It is unlawful to operate snow removal equipment on a highway unless the lights thereon comply with and are lighted when and as required by the standards and specifications adopted as provided in this section.

HISTORY: GC § 6307-90a; 124 v 514(525); Bureau of Code Revision, 10-1-53; 131 v 1113 (Eff 10-13-65); 132 v H 1 (Eff 2-21-67); 135 v H 200. Eff 9-28-73.

[§ 4513.18.1] § 4513.181 Standards and specifications for certain types of vehicles.

The director of public safety subject to the provisions of sections 119.01 to 119.13 of the Revised Code shall adopt standards and specifications applicable to rural mail delivery vehicles, state highway survey vehicles, and funeral escort vehicles. Such standards and specifications shall permit rural mail delivery vehicles, state highway survey vehicles, and funeral escort vehicles the use of flashing lights.

HISTORY: 126 v 790 (Eff 9-14-55); 127 v 54 (Eff 8-27-57); 144 v S 98. Eff 11-12-92.

[§ 4513.18.2] § 4513.182 Lights and sign on transportation for preschool children.

(A) No person shall operate any motor vehicle owned, leased, or hired by a nursery school, kindergarten, or day-care center, while transporting preschool children to or from such an institution unless the motor vehicle is equipped with and displaying two amber flashing lights mounted on a bar attached to the top of the vehicle, and a sign bearing the designation "caution—children," which shall be attached to the bar carrying the amber flashing lights in such a manner as to be legible to persons both in front of and behind the vehicle. The lights and sign shall meet standards and specifications adopted by the director of public safety. The director, subject to Chapter 119. of the Revised Code, shall adopt standards and specifications for the lights and sign, which shall include, but are not limited to, requirements for the color and size of lettering to be used on the sign, the type of material to be used for the sign, and the method of mounting the lights and sign so that they can be removed from a motor vehicle being used for purposes other than those specified in this section.

(B) No person shall operate a motor vehicle displaying the lights and sign required by this section for any purpose other than the transportation of preschool children as provided in this section.

HISTORY: 136 v H 272 (Eff 1-1-76); 144 v S 98. Eff 11-12-92.

§ 4513.19 Focus and aim of headlights.

No person shall use any lights mentioned in sections 4513.03 to 4513.18 of the Revised Code, upon any motor vehicle, trailer, or semitrailer unless said lights are equipped, mounted, and adjusted as to focus and aim in accordance with regulations which are prescribed by the director of public safety.

HISTORY: GC § 6307-91; 118 v 766(796), § 91; Bureau of Code Revision, 10-1-53; 128 v 1180 (Eff 11-2-59); 144 v S 98. Eff 11-12-92.

§ 4513.20 Brake equipment; specifications.

The following requirements govern as to brake equipment on vehicles:

(A) Every trackless trolley and motor vehicle, other than a motorcycle, when operated upon a highway shall be equipped with brakes adequate to control the movement of and to stop and hold such trackless trolley or motor vehicle, including two separate means of applying the brakes, each of which means shall be effective to apply the brakes to at least two wheels. If these two separate means of applying the brakes are connected in any way, then on such trackless trolleys or motor vehicles manufactured or assembled after January 1, 1942, they shall be so constructed that failure of any one part of the operating mechanism shall not leave the trackless trolley or motor vehicle without brakes on at least two wheels.

(B) Every motorcycle, when operated upon a highway shall be equipped with at least one adequate brake, which may be operated by hand or by foot.

(C) Every motorized bicycle shall be equipped with brakes meeting the rules adopted by the director of public safety under section 4511.521 [4511.52.1] of the Revised Code.

(D) Every trailer or semitrailer, except a pole trailer, of a gross weight of two thousand pounds or more, manufactured or assembled on or after January 1, 1942, when operated upon the highways of this state shall be equipped with brakes adequate to control the movement of and to stop and to hold such vehicle and so designed as to be applied by the driver of the towing motor vehicle from its cab, and said brakes shall be so designed and connected that, in case of a breakaway of the towed vehicle, the brakes shall be automatically applied.

(E) In any combination of motor-drawn trailers or semitrailers equipped with brakes, means shall be provided for applying the rearmost brakes in approximate synchronism with the brakes on the towing vehicle, and developing the required braking effort on the rearmost wheels at the fastest rate; or means shall be provided for applying braking effort first on the rearmost brakes; or both of the above means, capable of being used alternatively, may be employed.

(F) Every vehicle and combination of vehicles, except motorcycles and motorized bicycles, and except trailers and semitrailers of a gross weight of less than two thousand pounds, and pole trailers, shall be equipped with parking brakes adequate to hold the vehicle on any grade on which it is operated, under all conditions of loading, on a surface free from snow, ice, or loose material. The parking brakes shall be capable of being applied in conformance with the foregoing requirements by the driver's muscular effort or by spring action or by equivalent means. Their operation may be assisted by the service brakes or other source of power provided that failure of the service brake actuation system or other power assisting mechanism will not prevent the parking brakes from being applied in conformance with the foregoing requirements. The parking brakes shall be so designed that when once applied they shall remain applied with the required effectiveness despite exhaustion of any source of energy or leakage of any kind.

(G) The same brake drums, brake shoes and lining assemblies, brake shoe anchors, and mechanical brake shoe actuation mechanism normally associated with the wheel brake assemblies may be used for both the service brakes and the parking brakes. If the means of applying the parking brakes and the service brakes are connected in any way, they shall be so constructed that failure of any one part shall not leave the vehicle without operative brakes.

(H) Every trackless trolley, motor vehicle, or combination of motor-drawn vehicles shall be capable at all times and under all conditions of loading of being stopped on a dry, smooth, level road free from loose material, upon application of the service or foot brake, within the following specified distances, or shall be capable of being decelerated at a sustained rate corresponding to these distances:

(1) Trackless trolleys, vehicles, or combinations of vehicles having brakes on all wheels shall come to a stop in thirty feet or less from a speed of twenty miles per hour.

(2) Vehicles or combinations of vehicles not having brakes on all wheels shall come to a stop in forty feet or less from a speed of twenty miles per hour.

(I) All brakes shall be maintained in good working order and shall be so adjusted as to operate as equally as practicable with respect to the wheels on opposite sides of the trackless trolley or vehicle.

HISTORY: GC § 6307-92; 119 v 766(796), § 92; Bureau of Code Revision, 10-1-53; 130 v 1090 (Eff 7-25-63); 131 v 1114 (Eff 11-1-65); 132 v H 1 (Eff 2-21-67); 137 v S 100 (Eff 4-1-78); 138 v H 736 (Eff 10-16-80); 144 v S 98. Eff 11-12-92.

[§ 4513.20.1] § 4513.201 Brake fluid.

(A) No hydraulic brake fluid for use in motor vehicles shall be sold in this state if the brake fluid is below the minimum standard of specifications for heavy duty type brake fluid established by the society of automotive engineers and the standard of specifications established by 49 C.F.R. 571.116, as amended.

(B) All manufacturers, packers, or distributors of brake fluid selling such fluid in this state shall state on the containers that the brake fluid therein meets or exceeds the applicable minimum SAE standard of specifications and the standard of specifications established in 49 C.F.R. 571.116, as amended.

HISTORY: 129 v 1574 (Eff 1-1-62); 144 v S 98 (Eff 11-12-92); 147 v S 60. Eff 10-21-97.

[§ 4513.20.2] § 4513.202 Minimum standards for brakes and components.

(A) No brake lining, brake lining material, or brake lining assemblies for use as repair and replacement parts in motor vehicles shall be sold in this state if these items do not meet or exceed the minimum standard of specifications established by the society of automotive engineers and the standard of specifications established in 49 C.F.R. 571.105, as amended, and 49 C.F.R. 571.135, as amended.

(B) All manufacturers or distributors of brake lining, brake lining material, or brake lining assemblies selling these items for use as repair and replacement parts in motor vehicles shall state that the items meet or exceed the applicable minimum standard of specifications.

(C) As used in this section, "minimum standard of specifications" means a minimum standard for brake system or brake component performance that meets the need for motor vehicle safety and complies with the applicable SAE standards and recommended practices, and the federal motor vehicle safety standards that cover the same aspect of performance for any brake lining, brake lining material, or brake lining assemblies.

HISTORY: 134 v H 150 (Eff 9-8-71); 144 v S 98 (Eff 11-12-92); 147 v S 60. Eff 10-21-97.

§ 4513.21 Horns, sirens, and warning devices.

Every motor vehicle or trackless trolley when operated upon a highway shall be equipped with a horn which is in good working order and capable of emitting sound audible, under normal conditions, from a distance of not less than two hundred feet.

No motor vehicle or trackless trolley shall be equipped with, nor shall any person use upon a vehicle, any siren, whistle, or bell. Any vehicle may be equipped with a theft alarm signal device which shall be so arranged that it cannot be used as an ordinary warning signal. Every emergency vehicle shall be equipped with a siren, whistle, or bell, capable of emitting sound audible under normal conditions from a distance of not less than five hundred feet and of a type approved by the director of public safety. Such equipment shall not be used except when such vehicle is operated in response to an emergency call or is in the immediate pursuit of an actual or suspected violator of the law, in which case the driver of the emergency vehicle shall sound such equipment when it is necessary to warn pedestrians and other drivers of the approach thereof.

HISTORY: GC § 6307-93; 119 v 766(797), § 93; Bureau of Code Revision, 10-1-53; 135 v H 200 (Eff 9-28-73); 144 v S 98. Eff 11-12-92.

§ 4513.22 Mufflers; excessive smoke or gas.

Every motor vehicle and motorcycle with an internal combustion engine shall at all times be equipped with a muffler which is in good working order and in constant operation to prevent excessive or unusual noise, and no person shall use a muffler cutout, by-pass, or similar device upon a motor vehicle on a highway. Every motorcycle muffler shall be equipped with baffle plates.

No person shall own, operate, or have in his possession any motor vehicle or motorcycle equipped with a device for producing excessive smoke or gas, or so equipped as to permit oil or any other chemical to flow into or upon the exhaust pipe or muffler of such vehicle, or equipped in any other way to produce or emit smoke or dangerous or annoying gases from any portion of such vehicle, other than the ordinary gases emitted by the exhaust of an internal combustion engine under normal operation.

HISTORY: GC § 6307-94; 119 v 766(798), § 94; Bureau of Code Revision, 10-1-53; 132 v H 380 (Eff 1-1-68); 137 v H 115. Eff 7-10-78.

The 137 v H 115 amendment simply repeated the 132 v H 380 amendment.

[§ 4513.22.1] § 4513.221 Regulation of vehicle and engine noise in unincorporated areas.

(A) The board of county commissioners of any county, and the board of township trustees of any township subject to section 505.17 of the Revised Code, may regulate passenger car and motorcycle noise on streets and highways under their jurisdiction. Such regulations shall include maximum permissible noise limits measured in decibels, subject to the requirements of this section.

(B) Regulations establishing maximum permissible noise limits measured in decibels shall prohibit the operation, within the speed limits specified herein, of a passenger car or motorcycle of a type subject to registration at any time or under any condition of load, acceleration, or deceleration in such manner as to exceed the following maximum noise limits, based on a distance of not less than fifty feet from the center of the line of travel:

(1) For passenger cars:

(a) When operated at a speed of thirty-five miles per hour or less, a maximum noise limit of seventy decibels;

(b) When operated at a speed of more than thirty-five miles per hour, a maximum noise limit of seventy-nine decibels.

(2) For motorcycles:

(a) When operated at a speed of thirty-five miles per hour or less, a maximum noise limit of eighty-two decibels;

(b) When operated at a speed of more than thirty-five miles per hour, a maximum noise limit of eighty-six decibels.

(C) Maximum noise limits established pursuant to division (B) of this section shall be measured on the "A" scale of a standard sound level meter meeting the applicable requirements for a type 2 sound level meter as defined in American national standards institute standard S1.4 - 1983, or the most recent revision thereof. Measurement practices shall be in substantial conformity with standards and recommended practice established by the society of automotive engineers, including SAE standard J 986 A NOV81, SAE standard J 366 MAR85, SAE standard J 331 A, and such other standards and practices as may be approved by the federal government.

(D) No regulation enacted under division (B) of this section shall be effective until signs giving notice of the regulation are posted upon or at the entrance to the highway or part thereof affected, as may be most appropriate.

(E) A board of county commissioners of any county may regulate noise from passenger cars, motorcycles, or other devices using internal combustion engines in the unincorporated area of the county, and a board of township trustees may regulate such noise in the unincorporated area of the township, in any of the following ways:

(1) By prohibiting operating or causing to be operated any motor vehicle, agricultural tractor, motorcycle, all-purpose vehicle, or snowmobile not equipped with a factory-installed muffler or equivalent muffler in good working order and in constant operation;

(2) By prohibiting the removing or rendering inoperative, or causing to be removed or rendered inoperative, other than for purposes of maintenance, repair, or replacement, of any muffler;

(3) By prohibiting the discharge into the open air of exhaust of any stationary or portable internal combustion engine except through a factory-installed muffler or equivalent muffler in good working order and in constant operation;

(4) By prohibiting racing the motor of any vehicle described in division (E)(1) of this section in such a manner that the exhaust system emits a loud, cracking, or chattering noise unusual to its normal operation.

(F) Whoever violates any maximum noise limit established as provided in division (B) of this section or any of the prohibitions authorized in division (E) of this section is guilty of a minor misdemeanor. Fines collected under this section by the county shall be paid into the county general fund, and such fines collected by the township shall be paid into the township general fund.

No regulation adopted under this section shall apply to commercial racetrack operations.

HISTORY: 141 v H 131. Eff 6-26-86.

§ 4513.23 Rear view mirrors.

Every motor vehicle, motorcycle, and trackless trolley shall be equipped with a mirror so located as to reflect to the operator a view of the highway to the rear of such vehicle, motorcycle, or trackless trolley. Operators of vehicles, motorcycles, streetcars, and trackless trolleys shall have a clear and unobstructed view to the front and to both sides of their vehicles, motorcycles, streetcars, or trackless trolleys and shall have a clear view to the rear of their vehicles, motorcycles, streetcars, or trackless trolleys by mirror.

HISTORY: GC § 6307-95; 119 v 766(798), § 95; Bureau of Code Revision, 10-1-53; 132 v H 380. Eff 1-1-68.

§ 4513.24 Windshields and wipers.

(A) No person shall drive any motor vehicle on a street or highway in this state, other than a motorcycle or motorized bicycle, that is not equipped with a windshield.

(B) No person shall drive any motor vehicle, other than a bus, with any sign, poster, or other nontransparent material upon the front windshield, sidewings, side, or rear windows of such vehicle other than a certificate or other paper required to be displayed by law, except that there may be in the lower left-hand or right-hand corner of the windshield a sign, poster, or decal not to exceed four inches in height by six inches in width. No sign, poster, or decal shall be displayed in the front windshield in such a manner as to conceal the vehicle identification number for the motor vehicle when, in accordance with federal law, that number is located inside the vehicle passenger compartment and so placed as to be readable through the vehicle glazing without moving any part of the vehicle.

(C) The windshield on every motor vehicle, streetcar, and trackless trolley shall be equipped with a device for cleaning rain, snow, or other moisture from the windshield. The device shall be maintained in good working order and so constructed as to be controlled or operated by the operator of the vehicle, streetcar, or trackless trolley.

HISTORY: GC § 6307-96; 119 v 766(798), § 96; Bureau of Code Revision, 10-1-53; 143 v S 117 (Eff 10-26-89); 146 v H 353. Eff 9-17-96.

[§ 4513.24.1] § 4513.241 Restrictions on use of tinted glass and other vision obscuring materials.

(A) The director of public safety, in accordance with Chapter 119. of the Revised Code, shall adopt rules governing the use of tinted glass, and the use of transparent, nontransparent, translucent, and reflectorized materials in or on motor vehicle windshields, side windows, sidewings, and rear windows that prevent a person of normal vision looking into the motor vehicle from seeing or identifying persons or objects inside the motor vehicle.

(B) The rules adopted under this section may provide

for persons who meet either of the following qualifications:

(1) On the effective date of this section or of any rule adopted under this section, own a motor vehicle that does not conform to the requirements of this section or of any rule adopted under this section;

(2) Establish residency in this state and are required to register a motor vehicle that does not conform to the requirements of this section or of any rule adopted under this section.

(C) No person shall operate, on any highway or other public or private property open to the public for vehicular travel or parking, lease, or rent any motor vehicle that is registered in this state unless the motor vehicle conforms to the requirements of this section and of any applicable rule adopted under this section.

(D) No person shall install in or on any motor vehicle, any glass or other material that fails to conform to the requirements of this section or of any rule adopted under this section.

(E) No used motor vehicle dealer or new motor vehicle dealer, as defined in section 4517.01 of the Revised Code, shall sell any motor vehicle that fails to conform to the requirements of this section or of any rule adopted under this section.

(F) No reflectorized materials shall be permitted upon or in any front windshield, side windows, sidewings, or rear window.

(G) This section does not apply to the manufacturer's tinting or glazing of motor vehicle windows or windshields that is otherwise in compliance with or permitted by federal motor vehicle safety standard number two hundred five.

(H) With regard to any side window behind a driver's seat or any rear window other than any window on an emergency door, this section does not apply to any school bus used to transport a handicapped child pursuant to a special education program under Chapter 3323. of the Revised Code, whom it is impossible or impractical to transport by regular school bus in the course of regular route transportation provided by a school district. As used in this division, "handicapped child" and "special education program" have the same meanings as in section 3323.01 of the Revised Code.

(I) This section does not apply to any school bus that is to be sold and operated outside this state.

HISTORY: 141 v H 291 (Eff 3-11-88); 144 v S 98 (Eff 11-12-92); 145 v S 234. Eff 11-8-94.

[§ 4513.24.2] § 4513.242 Display of security decal on side window or sidewing.

Notwithstanding section 4513.24 and division (F) of section 4513.241 [4513.24.1] of the Revised Code or any rule adopted thereunder, a decal, whether reflectorized or not, may be displayed upon any side window or sidewing of a motor vehicle if all of the following are met:

(A) The decal is necessary for public or private security arrangements to which the motor vehicle periodically is subjected;

(B) The decal is no larger than is necessary to accomplish the security arrangements;

(C) The decal does not obscure the vision of the motor vehicle operator or prevent a person looking into the motor vehicle from seeing or identifying persons or objects inside the motor vehicle.

HISTORY: 147 v H 210. Eff 3-31-97.

The effective date is set by section 20 of HB 210.

§ 4513.25 Solid tire requirements.

Every solid tire, as defined in section 4501.01 of the Revised Code, on a vehicle shall have rubber or other resilient material on its entire traction surface at least one inch thick above the edge of the flange of the entire periphery.

HISTORY: GC § 6307-97; 119 v 766(798), § 97; Bureau of Code Revision. Eff 10-1-53.

§ 4513.26 Safety glass required.

No person shall sell any new motor vehicle nor shall any new motor vehicle be registered, and no person shall operate any motor vehicle, which is registered in this state and which has been manufactured or assembled on or after January 1, 1936, unless the motor vehicle is equipped with safety glass wherever glass is used in the windshields, doors, partitions, rear windows, and windows on each side immediately adjacent to the rear window.

"Safety glass" means any product composed of glass so manufactured, fabricated, or treated as substantially to prevent shattering and flying of the glass when it is struck or broken, or such other or similar product as may be approved by the registrar of motor vehicles.

Glass other than safety glass shall not be offered for sale, or sold for use in, or installed in any door, window, partition, or windshield that is required by this section to be equipped with safety glass.

HISTORY: GC § 6307-98; 119 v 766(798), § 98; Bureau of Code Revision, 10-1-53; 146 v H 353. Eff 9-17-96.

[§ 4513.26.1] § 4513.261 Directional signals.

No person shall sell any motor vehicle nor shall any motor vehicle be registered which has been manufactured or assembled on or after January 1, 1954, unless such vehicle is equipped with electrical or mechanical directional signals.

"Directional signals" means an electrical or mechanical signal device capable of clearly indicating an intention to turn either to the right or to the left and which shall be visible from both the front and rear.

All mechanical signal devices shall be self-illuminating devices when in use at the times mentioned in section 4513.03 of the Revised Code.

This section shall not apply to motorcycles or motor-driven cycles.

HISTORY: 125 v 456. Eff 10-19-53.

[§ 4513.26.2] § 4513.262 Installation and sale of seat safety belts required; definition.

As used in this section and in section 4513.263 [4513.26.3] of the Revised Code, the component parts of a "seat safety belt" include a belt, anchor attachment assembly, and a buckle or closing device.

(A) No person shall sell, lease, rent, or operate any passenger car, as defined in division (E) of section 4501.01 of the Revised Code, that is registered or to be registered in this state and that is manufactured or assembled on or after January 1, 1962, unless the passenger car is equipped with sufficient anchorage units at the attachment points for attaching at least two sets of seat safety belts to its front seat. Such anchorage units at the attachment points shall be of such construction, design, and strength to support a loop load pull of not less than four thousand pounds for each belt.

(B) No person shall sell, lease, or rent any passenger car, as defined in division (E) of section 4501.01 of the Revised Code, that is registered or to be registered in this state and that is manufactured or assembled on or after January 1, 1966, unless the passenger car has installed in its front seat at least two seat safety belt assemblies.

(C) After January 1, 1966, neither any seat safety belt for use in a motor vehicle nor any component part of any such seat safety belt shall be sold in this state unless the seat safety belt or the component part satisfies the minimum standard of specifications established by the society of automotive engineers for automotive seat belts and unless the seat safety belt or component part is labeled so as to indicate that it meets those minimum standard specifications.

(D) Each sale, lease, or rental in violation of this section constitutes a separate offense.

HISTORY: 129 v 1567 (Eff 9-23-61); 131 v 1115 (Eff 8-9-65); 141 v S 54. Eff 5-6-86.

[§ 4513.26.3] § 4513.263 Occupant restraining devices.

(A) As used in this section and in section 4513.99 of the Revised Code:

(1) "Automobile" means any commercial tractor, passenger car, commercial car, or truck that is required to be factory-equipped with an occupant restraining device for the operator or any passenger by regulations adopted by the United States secretary of transportation pursuant to the "National Traffic and Motor Vehicle Safety Act of 1966," 80 Stat. 719, 15 U.S.C.A. 1392.

(2) "Occupant restraining device" means a seat safety belt, shoulder belt, harness, or other safety device for restraining a person who is an operator of or passenger in an automobile and that satisfies the minimum federal vehicle safety standards established by the United States department of transportation.

(3) "Passenger" means any person in an automobile, other than its operator, who is occupying a seating position for which an occupant restraining device is provided.

(4) "Commercial tractor," "passenger car," and "commercial car" have the same meanings as in section 4501.01 of the Revised Code.

(5) "Vehicle" and "motor vehicle," as used in the definitions of the terms set forth in division (A)(4) of this section, have the same meanings as in section 4511.01 of the Revised Code.

(6) "Manufacturer" and "supplier" have the same meanings as in section 2307.71 of the Revised Code.

(7) "Tort action" means a civil action for damages for injury, death, or loss to person or property. "Tort action" includes a product liability claim but does not include a civil action for damages for a breach of contract or another agreement between persons.

(B) No person shall do any of the following:

(1) Operate an automobile on any street or highway unless that person is wearing all of the available elements of a properly adjusted occupant restraining device, or operate a school bus that has an occupant restraining device installed for use in its operator's seat unless that person is wearing all of the available elements of the device, as properly adjusted;

(2) Operate an automobile on any street or highway unless each passenger in the automobile who is subject to the requirement set forth in division (B)(3) of this section is wearing all of the available elements of a properly adjusted occupant restraining device;

(3) Occupy, as a passenger, a seating position on the front seat of an automobile being operated on any street or highway unless that person is wearing all of the available elements of a properly adjusted occupant restraining device;

(4) Operate a taxicab on any street or highway unless all factory-equipped occupant restraining devices in the taxicab are maintained in usable form.

(C) Division (B)(3) of this section does not apply to a person who is required by section 4511.81 of the Revised Code to be secured in a child restraint device. Division (B)(1) of this section does not apply to a person who is an employee of the United States postal service or of a newspaper home delivery service, during any period in which the person is engaged in the operation of an automobile to deliver mail or newspapers to addressees. Divisions (B)(1) and (3) of this section do not apply to a person who has an affidavit signed by a physician licensed to practice in this state under Chapter 4731. of the Revised Code or a chiropractor licensed to practice in this state under Chapter 4734. of the

Revised Code that states that the person has a physical impairment that makes use of an occupant restraining device impossible or impractical.

(D) Notwithstanding any provision of law to the contrary, no law enforcement officer shall cause an operator of an automobile being operated on any street or highway to stop the automobile for the sole purpose of determining whether a violation of division (B) of this section has been or is being committed or for the sole purpose of issuing a ticket, citation, or summons for a violation of that nature or causing the arrest of or commencing a prosecution of a person for a violation of that nature, and no law enforcement officer shall view the interior or visually inspect any automobile being operated on any street or highway for the sole purpose of determining whether a violation of that nature has been or is being committed.

(E) All fines collected for violations of division (B) of this section, or for violations of any ordinance or resolution of a political subdivision that is substantively comparable to that division, shall be forwarded to the treasurer of state for deposit as follows:

(1) Ten per cent shall be deposited into the seat belt education fund, which is hereby created in the state treasury, and shall be used by the department of public safety to establish a seat belt education program.

(2) Ten per cent shall be deposited into the elementary school program fund, which is hereby created in the state treasury, and shall be used by the department of public safety to establish and administer elementary school programs that encourage seat safety belt use.

(3) Until July 1, 1999, one per cent, and on and after July 1, 1999, two per cent shall be deposited into the Ohio ambulance licensing trust fund created by section 4766.05 of the Revised Code.

(4) Twenty-eight per cent shall be deposited into the emergency medical services fund, which is hereby created in the state treasury, and shall be used by the department of public safety for the administration of the division of emergency medical services and state board of emergency medical services.

(5) Until July 1, 1999, fifty-one per cent, and on and after July 1, 1999, fifty per cent shall be deposited into the emergency medical services grants fund, which is hereby created in the state treasury, and shall be used by the state board of emergency medical services to make grants, in accordance with section 4765.07 of the Revised Code and the rules that the board adopts under section 4765.11 of the Revised Code, to emergency medical service organizations for the training of their personnel, for the purchase of equipment, and to improve the availability, accessibility, and quality of emergency medical services in this state.

(F) The failure of a person to wear all of the available elements of a properly adjusted occupant restraining device in violation of division (B)(1) or (3) of this section or the failure of a person to ensure that each minor who is a passenger of an automobile being operated by that person is wearing all of the available elements of a properly adjusted occupant restraining device in violation of division (B)(2) of this section shall be considered by the trier of fact in a tort action as contributory negligence or other tortious conduct or considered for any other relevant purpose if the failure contributed to the harm alleged in the tort action and may diminish pursuant to section 2315.19 or 2315.20 of the Revised Code a recovery of compensatory damages in a tort action; shall not be used as a basis for a criminal prosecution of the person other than a prosecution for a violation of this section; and shall not be admissible as evidence in a criminal action involving the person other than a prosecution for a violation of this section.

HISTORY: 141 v S 54 (Eff 5-6-86); 141 v S 262 (Eff 3-20-87); 141 v H 428 (Eff 12-23-86); 142 v H 1 (Eff 1-5-88); 144 v H 118 (Eff 6-1-92); 144 v S 105 (Eff 6-23-92); 144 v S 98 (Eff 11-12-92); 145 v H 154 (Eff 6-30-93); 146 v H 350 (Eff 1-27-97); 147 v H 215. Eff 6-30-97.

Analogous to former RC § 4513.26.3 (129 v 1567), repealed, 131 v 1436, § 2, eff 8-9-65.

§ 4513.27 Requirements for extra signal equipment.

(A) No person shall operate any motor truck, trackless trolley, bus, or commercial tractor upon any highway outside the corporate limits of municipalities at any time from a half hour after sunset to a half hour before sunrise unless there is carried in such vehicle and trackless trolley, except as provided in division (B) of this section, the following equipment which shall be of the types approved by the director of transportation.

(1) At least three flares or three red reflectors or three red electric lanterns, each of which is capable of being seen and distinguished at a distance of five hundred feet under normal atmospheric conditions at night time;

(2) At least three red-burning fusees, unless red reflectors or red electric lanterns are carried;

(3) At least two red cloth flags, not less than twelve inches square, with standards to support them;

(4) The type of red reflectors shall comply with standards and specifications in effect on September 16, 1963 or later established by the interstate commerce commission and must be certified as meeting such standards by underwriter's laboratories.

(B) No person shall operate at the time and under the conditions stated in this section any motor vehicle used in transporting flammable liquids in bulk, or in transporting compressed flammable gases, unless there is carried in such vehicle three red electric lanterns or three red reflectors meeting the requirements stated in division (A) of this section. There shall not be carried in any such vehicle any flare, fusee, or signal produced by a flame.

(C) This section does not apply to any person who operates any motor vehicle in a work area designated by protection equipment devices that are displayed and used in accordance with the manual adopted by the department of transportation under section 4511.09 of the Revised Code.

HISTORY: GC § 6307-99; 119 v 766(799), § 99; 124 v 514(526); Bureau of Code Revision, 10-1-53; 130 v 1092 (Eff 9-16-63); 130 v Pt2, H 5 (Eff 12-16-64); 135 v H 200 (Eff 9-28-73); 143 v H 258. Eff 11-2-89.

§ 4513.28 Display of warning devices on disabled vehicles.

(A) Whenever any motor truck, trackless trolley, bus, commercial tractor, trailer, semi-trailer, or pole trailer is disabled upon the traveled portion of any highway or the shoulder thereof outside of any municipality, or upon any freeway, expressway, thruway and connecting, entering or exiting ramps within a municipality, at any time when lighted lamps are required on vehicles and trackless trolleys, the operator of such vehicle or trackless trolley shall display the following warning devices upon the highway during the time the vehicle or trackless trolley is so disabled on the highway except as provided in division (B) of this section:

(1) A lighted fusee shall be immediately placed on the roadway at the traffic side of such vehicle or trackless trolley, unless red electric lanterns or red reflectors are displayed.

(2) Within the burning period of the fusee and as promptly as possible, three lighted flares or pot torches, or three red reflectors or three red electric lanterns shall be placed on the roadway as follows:

(a) One at a distance of forty paces or approximately one hundred feet in advance of the vehicle;

(b) One at a distance of forty paces or approximately one hundred feet to the rear of the vehicle or trackless trolley except as provided in this section, each in the center of the lane of traffic occupied by the disabled vehicle or trackless trolley;

(c) One at the traffic side of the vehicle or trackless trolley.

(B) Whenever any vehicle used in transporting flammable liquids in bulk, or in transporting compressed flammable gases, is disabled upon a highway at any time or place mentioned in division (A) of this section, the driver of such vehicle shall display upon the roadway the following warning devices:

(1) One red electric lantern or one red reflector shall be immediately placed on the roadway at the traffic side of the vehicle;

(2) Two other red electric lanterns or two other red reflectors shall be placed to the front and rear of the vehicle in the same manner prescribed for flares in division (A) of this section.

(C) When a vehicle of a type specified in division (B) of this section is disabled, the use of flares, fusees, or any signal produced by flame as warning signals is prohibited.

(D) Whenever any vehicle or trackless trolley of a type referred to in this section is disabled upon the traveled portion of a highway or the shoulder thereof, outside of any municipality, or upon any freeway, expressway, thruway and connecting, entering or exiting ramps within a municipality, at any time when the display of fusees, flares, red reflectors, or electric lanterns is not required, the operator of such vehicle or trackless trolley shall display two red flags upon the roadway in the lane of traffic occupied by the disabled vehicle or trackless trolley, one at a distance of forty paces or approximately one hundred feet in advance of the vehicle or trackless trolley, and one at a distance of forty paces or approximately one hundred feet to the rear of the vehicle or trackless trolley, except as provided in this section.

(E) The flares, fusees, lanterns, red reflectors, and flags to be displayed as required in this section shall conform with the requirements of section 4513.27 of the Revised Code applicable thereto.

(F) In the event the vehicle or trackless trolley is disabled near a curve, crest of a hill, or other obstruction of view, the flare, flag, reflector, or lantern in that direction shall be placed as to afford ample warning to other users of the highway, but in no case shall it be placed less than forty paces or approximately one hundred feet nor more than one hundred twenty paces or approximately three hundred feet from the disabled vehicle or trackless trolley.

(G) This section does not apply to the operator of any vehicle in a work area designated by protection equipment devices that are displayed and used in accordance with the manual adopted by the department of transportation under section 4511.09 of the Revised Code.

HISTORY: GC § 6307-100; 119 v 766(800), § 100; Bureau of Code Revision, 10-1-53; 130 v 1092 (Eff 9-16-63); 143 v H 258. Eff 11-2-89.

§ 4513.29 Requirements for vehicles transporting explosives.

Any person operating any vehicle transporting explosives upon a highway shall at all times comply with the following requirements:

(A) Said vehicle shall be marked or placarded on each side and on the rear with the word "explosives" in letters not less than eight inches high, or there shall be displayed on the rear of such vehicle a red flag not less than twenty-four inches square marked with the word "danger" in white letters six inches high, or shall be marked or placarded in accordance with section 177.823 of the United States department of transportation regulations.

(B) Said vehicle shall be equipped with not less than two fire extinguishers, filled and ready for immediate use, and placed at convenient points on such vehicle.

(C) The director of transportation may promulgate such regulations governing the transportation of explosives and other dangerous articles by vehicles upon the highway as are reasonably necessary to enforce sections 4513.01 to 4513.37 of the Revised Code.

HISTORY: GC § 6307-101; 119 v 766(801), § 101; Bureau of Code Revision, 10-1-53; 133 v H 460 (Eff 10-22-69); 135 v H 200. Eff 9-28-73.

[LOADS]

§ 4513.30 Limitation of load extension on left side of vehicle.

No passenger-type vehicle shall be operated on a highway with any load carried on such vehicle which extends more than six inches beyond the line of the fenders on the vehicle's left side.

HISTORY: GC § 6307-102; 119 v 766(801), § 102; Bureau of Code Revision. Eff 10-1-53.

§ 4513.31 All loads shall be properly secured.

(A) No vehicle shall be driven or moved on any highway unless the vehicle is so constructed, loaded, or covered as to prevent any of its load from dropping, sifting, leaking, or otherwise escaping therefrom, except that sand or other substance may be dropped for the purpose of securing traction, or water or other substance may be sprinkled on a roadway in cleaning or maintaining the roadway.

(B) Except for a farm vehicle used to transport agricultural produce or agricultural production materials or a rubbish vehicle in the process of acquiring its load, no vehicle loaded with garbage, swill, cans, bottles, waste paper, ashes, refuse, trash, rubbish, waste, wire, paper, cartons, boxes, glass, solid waste, or any other material of an unsanitary nature that is susceptible to blowing or bouncing from a moving vehicle shall be driven or moved on any highway unless the load is covered with a sufficient cover to prevent the load or any part of the load from spilling onto the highway.

HISTORY: GC § 6307-103; 119 v 766(801), § 103; Bureau of Code Revision, 10-1-53; 142 v H 514. Eff 2-11-88.

§ 4513.32 Towing requirements.

When one vehicle is towing another vehicle, the drawbar or other connection shall be of sufficient strength to pull all the weight towed thereby, and the drawbar or other connection shall not exceed fifteen feet from one vehicle to the other, except the connection between any two vehicles transporting poles, pipe, machinery, or other objects of structural nature which cannot readily be dismembered.

When one vehicle is towing another and the connection consists only of a chain, rope, or cable, there shall be displayed upon such connection a white flag or cloth not less than twelve inches square.

In addition to such drawbar or other connection, each trailer and each semitrailer which is not connected to a commercial tractor by means of a fifth wheel shall be coupled with stay chains or cables to the vehicle by which it is being drawn. The chains or cables shall be of sufficient size and strength to prevent the towed vehicle's parting from the drawing vehicle in case the drawbar or other connection should break or become disengaged. In case of a loaded pole trailer, the connecting pole to the drawing vehicle shall be coupled to the drawing vehicle with stay chains or cables of sufficient size and strength to prevent the towed vehicle's parting from the drawing vehicle.

Every trailer or semitrailer, except pole and cable trailers and pole and cable dollies operated by a public utility as defined in section 5727.01 of the Revised Code, shall be equipped with a coupling device, which shall be so designed and constructed that the trailer will follow substantially in the path of the vehicle drawing it, without whipping or swerving from side to side. Vehicles used to transport agricultural produce or agricultural production materials between a local place of storage and supply and the farm, when drawn or towed on a street or highway at a speed of twenty-five miles per hour or less, and vehicles designed and used exclusively to transport a boat between a place of storage and a marina, or in and around a marina, when drawn or towed on a street or highway for a distance of no more than ten miles and at a speed of twenty-five miles per hour or less, shall have a drawbar or other connection, including the hitch mounted on the towing vehicle, which shall be of sufficient strength to pull all the weight towed thereby. Only one such vehicle used to transport agricultural produce or agricultural production materials as provided in this section may be towed or drawn at one time unless the towing vehicle is an agricultural tractor.

HISTORY: GC § 6307-104; 119 v 766(801), § 104; Bureau of Code Revision, 10-1-53; 132 v H 684 (Eff 11-24-67); 132 v H 1002 (Eff 6-3-68); 138 v H 1 (Eff 5-16-79); 144 v H 485. Eff 10-7-92.

§ 4513.33 Weighing vehicle; scales; alteration of weight limits by local authorities.

Any police officer having reason to believe that the weight of a vehicle and its load is unlawful may require the driver of said vehicle to stop and submit to a weighing of it by means of a compact, self-contained, portable, sealed scale specially adapted to determine the wheel loads of vehicles on highways; a sealed scale permanently installed in a fixed location, having a load-receiving element specially adapted to determining the wheel loads of highway vehicles; a sealed scale, permanently installed in a fixed location, having a load-receiving element specially adapted to determining the combined load of all wheels on a single axle or on successive axles of a highway vehicle, or a sealed scale adapted to weighing highway vehicles, loaded or unloaded. The driver of such vehicle shall, if necessary, be directed to proceed to the nearest available of such sealed scales to accomplish the weighing, provided such scales are within three miles of the point where such vehicle is stopped. Any vehicle stopped in accordance with this section may be held by the police officer for a reasonable time only to accomplish the weighing as prescribed by this section. All scales used in determining the lawful weight of a vehicle and its load shall be annually compared by a municipal, county, or state sealer with the state standards or standards approved by the state and such scales shall not be sealed if they do not conform to the state standards or standards approved by the state.

At each end of a permanently installed scale, there shall be a straight approach in the same plane as the platform, of sufficient length and width to insure the level positioning of vehicles during weight determinations.

During determination of weight by compact, self-contained, portable, sealed scales, specially adapted to determining the wheel loads of vehicles on highways, they shall always be used on terrain of sufficient length and width to accommodate the entire vehicle being weighed. Such terrain shall be level, or if not level, it shall be of such elevation that the difference in elevation between the wheels on any one axle does not exceed two inches and the difference in elevation between axles being weighed does not exceed one-fourth inch per foot of the distance between said axles.

In all determination of all weights, except gross weight, by compact, self-contained, portable sealed scales, specially adapted to determining the wheel loads of vehicles on highways, all succesive axles, twelve feet or less apart, shall be weighed simultaneously by placing one such scale under the outside wheel of each such axle. In determinations of gross weight by the use of compact, self-contained, portable sealed scales, specially adapted to determining the wheel loads of vehicles on highways, all axles shall be weighed simultaneously by placing one such scale under the outside wheel of each axle.

Whenever such officer upon weighing a vehicle and load determines that the weight is unlawful, he may require the driver to stop the vehicle in a suitable place and remain standing until such portion of the load is removed as is necessary to reduce the weight of such vehicle to the limit permitted under sections 5577.01 to 5577.14 of the Revised Code.

Whenever local authorities determine upon the basis of an engineering and traffic investigation that the weight limits permitted under sections 5577.01 to 5577.14 of the Revised Code, or the weight limits permitted when compact, self-contained, portable, sealed scales, specially adapted to determining the wheel loads of vehicles on highways, are used on any part of a state route under their jurisdiction is greater than is reasonable under the conditions found to exist at such location, the local authorities may, by resolution, request the director of transportation to determine and declare reasonable weight limits. Upon receipt of such request the director may determine and declare reasonable weight limits at such location, and if the director alters the weight limits set by sections 5577.01 to 5577.14 and this section of the Revised Code, then such altered weight limits shall become effective only when appropriate signs giving notice thereof are erected at such location by local authorities.

The director may withdraw his approval of any altered weight limit whenever, in his opinion, any altered weight limit becomes unreasonable, and upon such withdrawal the altered weight limit shall become ineffective, and the signs relating thereto shall be immediately removed by local authorities. Alteration of weight limits on state routes by local authorities is not effective until alteration has been approved by the director.

This section does not derogate or limit the power and authority conferred upon the director or boards of county commissioners by section 5577.07 of the Revised Code.

HISTORY: GC § 6307-105; 119 v 766(802), § 105; Bureau of Code Revision, 10-1-53; 130 v 1094 (Eff 8-19-63); 131 v 1116 (Eff 11-1-65); 132 v H 1 (Eff 2-21-67); 135 v H 200 (Eff 9-28-73); 136 v H 624. Eff 11-26-75.

§ 4513.34 Issuance of special permits.

The director of transportation with respect to all highways which are a part of the state highway system and local authorities with respect to highways under their jurisdiction may, upon application in writing and for good cause shown, issue a special permit in writing authorizing the applicant to operate or move a vehicle or combination of vehicles of a size or weight of vehicle or load exceeding the maximum specified in sections 5577.01 to 5577.09 of the Revised Code, or otherwise not in conformity with sections 4513.01 to 4513.37 of the Revised Code, upon any highway under the jurisdiction of the authority granting such permit. Notwithstanding sections 715.22 and 723.01 of the Revised Code, the holder of a special permit issued by the director under this section may move the vehicle or combination of vehicles described in such special permit on any highway which is a part of the state highway system, when the movement is partly within and partly without the corporate limits of a municipal corporation. No local authority shall require any other permit or license or charge any license fee or other charge against the holder of a permit for the movement of a vehicle or combination of vehicles on any highway that is a part of the state highway system. No holder of a permit issued by a local authority shall be required by the director to obtain a special permit for the movement of vehicles or combination of vehicles on highways within the jurisdiction of the local authority. Permits may be issued for any period of time, not to exceed one year, as the director in his discretion or a local authority in its discretion deems advisable or for the duration of any public construction project.

The application for a permit shall be in such form as the director or local authority prescribes. The director or local authority may prescribe a permit fee to be imposed and collected when any permit described in this section is issued. The permit fee may be in an amount sufficient to reimburse the director or local authority for the administrative costs incurred in issuing the permit, and also to cover the cost of the normal and expected damage caused to the roadway or a street or highway structure as the result of the operation of the nonconforming vehicle or combination of vehicles. The director, in accordance with Chapter 119. of the Revised Code, shall establish a schedule of fees for permits issued by the director under this section.

For the purposes of this section and of rules adopted by the director under this section, milk transported in bulk by vehicle is deemed a nondivisible load.

The director or local authority may issue or withhold a permit. If a permit is to be issued, the director or local authority may limit or prescribe conditions of operation for the vehicle, and may require the posting of a bond or other security conditioned upon the sufficiency of the permit fee to compensate for damage caused to the roadway or a street or highway structure.

Every permit shall be carried in the vehicle or combination of vehicles to which it refers and shall be open to inspection by any police officer or authorized agent of any authority granting the permit. No person shall violate any of the terms of a permit.

HISTORY: GC § 6307-106; 119 v 766(802), § 106; Bureau of Code Revision, 10-1-53; 131 v 1118 (Eff 9-28-65); 135 v H 200 (Eff 9-28-73); 142 v H 712 (Eff 9-9-88); 144 v S 223. Eff 9-30-92.

The effective date is set by section 3 of SB 223.

§ 4513.35 Disposition of moneys collected.

(A) All fines collected under sections 4511.01 to 4511.78, 4511.99, and 4513.01 to 4513.37 of the Revised Code shall be paid into the county treasury and, with the exception of that portion distributed under section 3375.53 of the Revised Code, shall be placed to the credit of the fund for the maintenance and repair of the highways within that county, except that:

(1) All fines for violations of division (B) of section 4513.263 [4513.26.3] shall be delivered to the treasurer of state as provided in division (E) of section 4513.263 [4513.26.3] of the Revised Code.

(2) All fines collected from, or moneys arising from bonds forfeited by, persons apprehended or arrested by state highway patrolmen shall be distributed as provided in section 5503.04 of the Revised Code.

(3)(a) Subject to division (E) of section 4513.263 [4513.26.3] of the Revised Code and except as otherwise provided in division (A)(3)(b) of this section, one-half of all fines collected from, and one-half of all moneys arising from bonds forfeited by, persons apprehended or arrested by a township constable or other township police officer shall be paid to the township treasury to be placed to the credit of the general fund.

(b) All fines collected from, and all moneys arising from bonds forfeited by, persons apprehended or arrested by a township constable or other township police officer pursuant to division (B)(2) of section 4513.39 of the Revised Code for a violation of section 4511.21 of the Revised Code or any other law, ordinance, or regulation pertaining to speed that occurred on a highway included as part of the interstate system, as defined in section 5516.01 of the Revised Code, shall be paid into the county treasury and be credited as provided in the first paragraph of this section.

(B) Notwithstanding any other provision of this section or of any other section of the Revised Code:

(1) All fines collected from, and all moneys arising from bonds forfeited by, persons arrested under division (E)(1) or (2) of section 2935.03 of the Revised Code are deemed to be collected, and to arise, from arrests made within the jurisdiction in which the arresting officer is appointed, elected, or employed, for violations of one of the sections or chapters of the Revised Code listed in division (E)(1) of that section and shall be distributed accordingly.

(2) All fines collected from, and all moneys arising from bonds forfeited by, persons arrested under division (E)(3) of section 2935.03 of the Revised Code are deemed to be collected, and to arise, from arrests made within the jurisdiction in which the arresting officer is appointed, elected, or employed, for violations of municipal ordinances that are substantially equivalent to one of the sections or one of the provisions of one of the chapters of the Revised Code listed in division(E)(1) of that section and shall be distributed accordingly.

HISTORY: GC § 6307-108; 119 v 766(803), § 108; Bureau of Code Revision, 10-1-53; 126 v 773 (Eff 10-5-55); 132 v H 24 (Eff 8-15-67); 141 v S 54 (Eff 5-6-86); 143 v H 171 (Eff 5-31-90); 143 v H 669 (Eff 1-10-91); 145 v H 687. Eff 10-12-94.

[MISCELLANEOUS PROVISIONS]

§ 4513.36 Prohibition against resisting officer.

No person shall resist, hinder, obstruct, or abuse any sheriff, constable, or other official while such official is attempting to arrest offenders under sections 4511.01 to 4511.78, inclusive, 4511.99, and 4513.01 to 4513.37, inclusive, of the Revised Code. No person shall interfere with any person charged under such sections with the enforcement of the law relative to public highways.

HISTORY: GC § 6307-109; 119 v 766(803), § 109; Bureau of Code Revision. Eff 10-1-53.

[§ 4513.36.1] § 4513.361 Furnishing false information to avoid citation.

No person shall knowingly present, display, or orally communicate a false name, social security number, or date of birth to a law enforcement officer who is in the process of issuing to the person a traffic ticket or complaint.

HISTORY: 144 v H 96. Eff 6-18-91.

§ 4513.37 Record of violations.

Every county court judge, mayor, and clerk of a court of record shall keep a full record of every case in which a person is charged with any violation of sections 4511.01 to 4511.78, section 4511.99, and sections 4513.01 to 4513.37 of the Revised Code, or of any other law or ordinance regulating the operation of vehicles, streetcars, and trackless trolleys on highways.

Within ten days after the conviction or forfeiture of bail of a person upon a charge of violating any of such sections or other law or ordinance regulating the operation of vehicles, streetcars, and trackless trolleys on highways, said judge, mayor, or clerk shall prepare and immediately forward to the department of public safety an abstract of the court record covering the case in which said person was convicted for forfeited bail, which abstract must be certified by the person required to prepare the same to be true and correct.

Said abstract shall be made upon a form approved and furnished by the department and shall include the name and address of the party charged, the number of his driver's or commercial driver's license, the registration number of the vehicle involved, the nature of the offense, the date of hearing, the plea, the judgment, or whether bail forfeited, and the amount of the fine or forfeiture.

Every court of record shall also forward a like report to the department upon the conviction of any person of manslaughter or other felony in the commission of which a vehicle was used.

The failure, refusal, or neglect of such officer to comply with this section constitutes misconduct in office and is ground for removal therefrom.

The department shall keep all abstracts received under this section at its main office.

HISTORY: GC § 6307-110; 119 v 766(804), § 110; Bureau of Code Revision, 10-1-53; 125 v 127 (140); 127 v 1039(1107) (Eff 1-1-58); 143 v H 381 (Eff 7-1-89); 144 v S 98. Eff 11-12-92.

§ 4513.38 Collector's or historical motor vehicle test exemptions.

No person shall be prohibited from owning or operating a licensed collector's vehicle or historical motor vehicle that is equipped with a feature of design, type of material, or article of equipment that was not in violation of any motor vehicle equipment law of this state or of its political subdivisions in effect during the calendar year the vehicle was manufactured, and no licensed collector's vehicle or historical motor vehicle shall be prohibited from displaying or using any such feature of design, type of material, or article of equipment.

No person shall be prohibited from owning or operating a licensed collector's vehicle or historical motor vehicle for failing to comply with an equipment provision contained in Chapter 4513. of the Revised Code or in any state rule that was enacted or adopted in a year subsequent to that in which the vehicle was manufactured, and no licensed collector's vehicle or historical motor vehicle shall be required to comply with an equipment provision enacted into Chapter 4513. of the Revised Code or adopted by state rule subsequent to the calendar year in which it was manufactured. No political subdivision shall require an owner of a licensed collector's vehicle or historical motor vehicle to comply with equipment provisions contained in laws or rules that were enacted or adopted subsequent to the calendar year in which the vehicle was manufactured, and no political subdivision shall prohibit the operation of a licensed collector's vehicle or historical motor vehicle for failure to comply with any such equipment laws or rules.

HISTORY: 136 v S 52. Eff 9-15-75.

Not analogous to former RC § 4513.38 [119 v 766(803)] (GC § 6307-107; Bureau of Code Revision, 10-1-53), repealed 125 v 903(1064), eff 10-1-53.

§ 4513.39 Power to make arrests on highways.

(A) The state highway patrol and sheriffs or their deputies shall exercise, to the exclusion of all other peace officers except within municipal corporations and except as specified in division (B) of this section and division (E) of section 2935.03 of the Revised Code, the power to make arrests for violations on all state highways, of sections 4503.11, 4503.21, 4511.14 to 4511.16, 4511.20 to 4511.23, 4511.26 to 4511.40, 4511.42 to 4511.48, 4511.58, 4511.59, 4511.62 to 4511.-71, 4513.03 to 4513.13, 4513.15 to 4513.22, 4513.24 to 4513.34, 4549.01, 4549.08 to 4549.12, and 4549.62 of the Revised Code.

(B) A member of the police force of a township police district created under section 505.48 of the Revised Code, and a township constable appointed pursuant to section 509.01 of the Revised Code, who has received a certificate from the Ohio peace officer training commission under section 109.75 of the Revised Code, shall exercise the power to make arrests for violations of those sections listed in division (A) of this section, other than sections 4513.33 and 4513.34 of the Revised Code, as follows:

(1) If the population of the township that created the township police district served by the member's police force or the township that is served by the township

constable is sixty thousand or less, the member or constable shall exercise that power on those portions of all state highways, except those highways included as part of the interstate system, as defined in section 5516.01 of the Revised Code, that are located within the township police district, in the case of a member of a township police district police force, or within the unincorporated territory of the township, in the case of a township constable;

(2) If the population of the township that created the township police district served by the member's police force or the township that is served by the township constable is greater than sixty thousand, the member or constable shall exercise that power on those portions of all state highways and highways included as part of the interstate highway system, as defined in section 5516.01 of the Revised Code, that are located within the township police district, in the case of a member of a township police district police force, or within the unincorporated territory of the township, in the case of a township constable.

HISTORY: GC § 6297; 119 v 810; Bureau of Code Revision, 10-1-53; 138 v H 207 (Eff 3-13-81); 139 v H 738 (Eff 6-25-82); 140 v H 632 (Eff 3-28-85); 143 v H 171 (Eff 5-31-90); 143 v H 669 (Eff 1-10-91); 145 v H 687 (Eff 10-12-94); 146 v H 670. Eff 12-2-96.

§ 4513.40 Warning sign before safety device at street crossing.

When a safety device has been installed in the traveled portion of a street at a railroad grade crossing for the protection of the traveling public, the municipal corporation shall place a warning sign not less than two hundred feet from the crossing. The driver of any vehicle shall place his vehicle under control at the location of said warning signs so as to be able to bring said vehicle to a complete stop at said safety device. Colliding with such safety device at the crossing is prima-facie evidence that the driver is a reckless driver.

HISTORY: GC § 591-1; 117 v 655; Bureau of Code Revision, 10-1-53; 125 v 903(1026). Eff 10-1-53.

§ 4513.41 Collector's agricultural tractor or traction engine test exemptions.

(A) No owner of a licensed collector's vehicle, a historical motor vehicle, or a collector's vehicle that is an agricultural tractor or traction engine shall be required to comply with an emission, noise control, or fuel usage provision contained in a law or rule of this state or its political subdivisions that was enacted or adopted subsequent to the calendar year in which the vehicle was manufactured.

(B) No person shall be prohibited from operating a licensed collector's vehicle, a historical motor vehicle, or a collector's vehicle that is an agricultural tractor or traction engine for failing to comply with an emission, noise control, or fuel usage law or rule of this state or its political subdivisions that was enacted or adopted subsequent to the calendar year in which his vehicle was manufactured.

(C) Except as provided in section 4505.061 [4505.06.1] of the Revised Code, no person shall be required to submit his collector's vehicle to a physical inspection prior to or in connection with an issuance of title to, or the sale or transfer of ownership of such vehicle, except that a police officer may inspect it to determine ownership.

In accordance with section 1.51 of the Revised Code, this section shall, without exception, prevail over any special or local provision of the Revised Code that requires owners or operators of collector's vehicles to comply with standards of emission, noise, fuel usage, or physical condition in connection with an issuance of title to, or the sale or transfer of ownership of such vehicle or part thereof.

HISTORY: 136 v S 52. Eff 9-15-75.

Not analogous to former RC § 4513.41 [131 v 1119], repealed 134 v H 24, eff 10-6-71.

§§ 4513.51, 4513.52, 4513.53

Repealed, 146 v H 23, § 1 [130 v 1095, 1102; 144 v S 98]. Eff 2-25-97.

These sections concerned the Vehicle Equipment Safety Compact, its creation and implementation.

The effective date is set by section 3 of HB 23.

The provisions of § 2 of HB 23 (146 v —) read as follows:

SECTION 2. Pursuant to Article IX(b) of the Vehicle Equipment Safety Compact, the Governor, within one month after the effective date of this act, shall give written notice of the withdrawal of Ohio from the Vehicle Equipment Safety Compact to the executive heads of all other states that are party to the compact.

§§ 4513.54, 4513.55, 4513.56

Repealed, 146 v H 23, § 1 [130 v 1102, 1103; 135 v H 173, § 3; 144 v S 98]. Eff 2-25-97.

These sections concerned the Vehicle Equipment Safety Compact, its creation and implementation.

The effective date is set by section 3 of HB 23.

See provisions, § 2 of HB 23 (146 v —) following Repeal note for RC § 4513.51.

§§ 4513.57, 4513.58 Repealed, 146 v H 23, § 1 [130 v 1103]. Eff 2-25-97.

These sections concerned the Vehicle Equipment Safety Compact, its creation and implementation.

The effective date is set by section 3 of HB 23.

See provisions, § 2 of HB 23 (146 v —) following Repeal note for RC § 4513.51.

[ABANDONED VEHICLES]

§ 4513.60 Sheriff or chief of police may order vehicle on private property into storage; private tow-away zone.

(A)(1) The sheriff of a county or chief of police of a municipal corporation, township, or township police district, within his respective territorial jurisdiction, upon complaint of any person adversely affected, may order into storage any motor vehicle, other than an abandoned junk motor vehicle as defined in section 4513.63 of the Revised Code, that has been left on private residential or private agricultural property for at least four hours without the permission of the person having the right to the possession of the property. The sheriff or chief of police, upon complaint of the owner of a repair garage or place of storage, may order into storage any motor vehicle, other than an abandoned junk motor vehicle, that has been left at the garage or place of storage for a longer period than that agreed upon. The place of storage shall be designated by the sheriff or chief of police. When ordering a motor vehicle into storage pursuant to this division, a sheriff or chief of police shall, whenever possible, arrange for the removal of such motor vehicle by a private tow truck operator or towing company. Subject to division (C) of this section, the owner of a motor vehicle that has been removed pursuant to this division may recover the vehicle only in accordance with division (E) of this section.

(2) Divisions (A)(1) to (3) of this section do not apply to any private residential or private agricultural property that is established as a private tow-away zone in accordance with division (B) of this section.

(3) As used in divisions (A)(1) and (2) of this section, "private residential property" means private property on which is located one or more structures that are used as a home, residence, or sleeping place by one or more persons, if no more than three separate households are maintained in the structure or structures. "Private residential property" does not include any private property on which is located one or more structures that are used as a home, residence, or sleeping place by two or more persons, if more than three separate households are maintained in the structure or structures.

(B)(1) The owner of private property may establish a private tow-away zone only if all of the following conditions are satisfied:

(a) The owner posts on his property a sign, that is at least eighteen inches by twenty-four inches in size, that is visible from all entrances to the property, and that contains at least all of the following information:

(i) A notice that the property is a private tow- away zone and that vehicles not authorized to park on the property will be towed away;

(ii) The telephone number of the person from whom a towed-away vehicle can be recovered, and the address of the place to which the vehicle will be taken and the place from which it may be recovered;

(iii) A statement that the vehicle may be recovered at any time during the day or night upon the submission of proof of ownership and the payment of a towing charge, in an amount not to exceed seventy dollars, and a storage charge, in an amount not to exceed eight dollars per twenty-four-hour period; except that the charge for towing shall not exceed one hundred dollars, and the storage charge shall not exceed twelve dollars per twenty-four-hour period, if the vehicle has a laden gross vehicle weight in excess of fifteen thousand pounds and is a truck, bus, or a combination of a commercial tractor and trailer or semitrailer.

(b) The place to which the towed vehicle is taken and from which it may be recovered is conveniently located, is well lighted, and is on or within a reasonable distance of a regularly scheduled route of one or more modes of public transportation, if any public transportation is available in the municipal corporation or township in which the private tow-away zone is located.

(2) If a vehicle is parked on private property that is established as a private tow-away zone in accordance with division (B)(1) of this section, without the consent of the owner of the property or in violation of any posted parking condition or regulation, the owner or his agent may remove, or cause the removal of, the vehicle, the owner and the operator of the vehicle shall be deemed to have consented to the removal and storage of the vehicle and to the payment of the towing and storage charges specified in division (B)(1)(a)(iii) of this section, and the owner, subject to division (C) of this section, may recover a vehicle that has been so removed only in accordance with division (E) of this section.

(3) If a municipal corporation requires tow trucks and tow truck operators to be licensed, no owner of private property located within the municipal corporation shall remove, or shall cause the removal and storage of, any vehicle pursuant to division (B)(2) of this section by an unlicensed tow truck or unlicensed tow truck operator.

(4) Divisions (B)(1) to (3) of this section do not affect or limit the operation of division (A) of this section or sections 4513.61 to 4513.65 of the Revised Code as they relate to property other than private property that is established as a private tow-away zone under division (B)(1) of this section.

(C) If the owner or operator of a motor vehicle that has been ordered into storage pursuant to division (A)(1) of this section or of a vehicle that is being removed under authority of division (B)(2) of this section arrives after the motor vehicle or vehicle has been prepared for removal but prior to its actual removal from the property, the owner or operator shall be given the opportunity to pay a fee of not more than one-half of the charge for the removal of motor vehicles under division (A)(1) of this section or of vehicles under division (B)(2) of this section, whichever is applicable, that normally is assessed by the person who has prepared the motor vehicle or vehicle for removal, in order to obtain release of the motor vehicle or vehicle. Upon payment of that fee, the motor vehicle or vehicle shall be released to the owner or operator, and upon its release, the owner or operator immediately shall move it so that:

(1) If the motor vehicle was ordered into storage pursuant to division (A)(1) of this section, it is not on the private residential or private agricultural property without the permission of the person having the right to possession of the property, or is not at the garage or place of storage without the permission of the owner, whichever is applicable.

(2) If the vehicle was being removed under authority of division (B)(2) of this section, it is not parked on the private property established as a private tow-away zone without the consent of the owner or in violation of any posted parking condition or regulation.

(D)(1) If an owner of private property that is established as a private tow-away zone in accordance with division (B)(1) of this section or the authorized agent of such an owner removes or causes the removal of a vehicle from that property under authority of division (B)(2) of this section, the owner or agent promptly shall notify the police department of the municipal corporation, township, or township police district in which the property is located, of the removal, the vehicle's license number, make, model, and color, the location from which it was removed, the date and time of its removal, the telephone number of the person from whom it may be recovered, and the address of the place to which it has been taken and from which it may be recovered.

(2) Each county sheriff and each chief of police of a municipal corporation, township, or township police district shall maintain a record of motor vehicles that he orders into storage pursuant to division (A)(1) of this section and of vehicles removed from private property in his jurisdiction that is established as a private tow-away zone of which he has received notice under division (D)(1) of this section. The record shall include an entry for each such motor vehicle or vehicle that identifies the motor vehicle's or vehicle's license number, make, model, and color, the location from which it was removed, the date and time of its removal, the telephone number of the person from whom it may be recovered, and the address of the place to which it has been taken and from which it may be recovered. Any information in the record that pertains to a particular motor vehicle or vehicle shall be provided to any person who, either in person or pursuant to a telephone call, identifies himself as the owner or operator of the motor vehicle or vehicle and requests information pertaining to its location.

(3) Any person who registers a complaint that is the basis of a sheriff's or police chief's order for the removal and storage of a motor vehicle under division (A)(1) of this section shall provide the identity of the law enforcement agency with which the complaint was registered to any person who identifies himself as the owner or operator of the motor vehicle and requests information pertaining to its location.

(E) The owner of a motor vehicle that is ordered into storage pursuant to division (A)(1) of this section or of a vehicle that is removed under authority of division (B)(2) of this section may reclaim it upon payment of any expenses or charges incurred in its removal, in an amount not to exceed seventy dollars, and storage, in an amount not to exceed eight dollars per twenty-four-hour period; except that the charge for towing shall not exceed one hundred dollars, and the storage charge shall not exceed twelve dollars per twenty-four-hour period, if the vehicle has a laden gross vehicle weight in excess of fifteen thousand pounds and is a truck, bus, or a combination of a commercial tractor and trailer or semitrailer. Presentation of proof of ownership, which may be evidenced by a certificate of title to the motor vehicle or vehicle shall also be required for reclamation of the vehicle. If a motor vehicle that is ordered into storage pursuant to division (A)(1) of this section remains unclaimed by the owner for thirty days, the procedures established by sections 4513.61 and 4513.62 of the Revised Code shall apply.

(F) No person shall remove, or cause the removal of, any vehicle from private property that is established as a private tow-away zone under division (B)(1) of this section other than in accordance with division (B)(2) of this section, and no person shall remove, or cause the removal of, any motor vehicle from any other private property other than in accordance with division (A)(1) of this section or sections 4513.61 to 4513.65 of the Revised Code.

HISTORY: 134 v H 24 (Eff 10-6-71); 135 v H 650 (Eff 7-9-74); 138 v S 257 (Eff 6-25-80); 140 v H 112 (Eff 10-4-84); 143 v S 285. Eff 4-10-91.

Analogous in part to former RC § 737.31.1 (131 v 276; 133 v H 13), and RC § 311.30 (131 v 208; 133 v S 218), both repealed 134 v H 24, eff 10-6-71.

§ 4513.61 Storage of vehicles in possession of law enforcement officers or left on public property; reclamation or disposal.

The sheriff of a county or chief of police of a municipal corporation, township, or township police district, within the sheriff's or chief's respective territorial jurisdiction, or a state highway patrol trooper, upon notification to the sheriff or chief of police of such action and of the location of the place of storage, may order into storage any motor vehicle, including an abandoned junk motor vehicle as defined in section 4513.63 of the Revised Code, that has come into the possession of the sheriff, chief of police, or state highway patrol trooper as a result of the performance of the sheriff's, chief's, or trooper's duties or that has been left on a public street or other property open to the public for purposes of vehicular travel, or upon or within the right-of-way of any road or highway, for forty-eight hours or longer without notification to the sheriff or chief of police of the reasons for leaving the motor vehicle in such place, except that when such a motor vehicle constitutes an obstruction to traffic it may be ordered into storage immediately. The sheriff or chief of police shall designate the place of storage of any motor vehicle so ordered removed.

The sheriff or chief of police immediately shall cause a search to be made of the records of the bureau of motor vehicles to ascertain the owner and any lienholder of a motor vehicle ordered into storage by the sheriff or chief of police, or by a state highway patrol trooper, and, if known, shall send or cause to be sent notice to the owner or lienholder at the owner's or lienholder's last known address by certified mail with return receipt requested, that the motor vehicle will be declared a nuisance and disposed of if not claimed within ten days of the date of mailing of the notice. The owner or lienholder of the motor vehicle may reclaim it upon payment of any expenses or charges incurred in its removal and storage, and presentation of proof of ownership, which may be evidenced by a certificate of title to the motor vehicle. If the owner or lienholder of the motor vehicle reclaims it after a search of the records of the bureau has been conducted and after notice has been sent to the owner or lienholder as described in this section, and the search was conducted by the owner of the place of storage or the owner's employee, and the notice was sent to the motor vehicle owner by the owner of the place of storage or the owner's employee, the owner or lienholder shall pay to the place of storage a processing fee of twenty-five dollars, in addition to any expenses or charges incurred in the removal and storage of the vehicle.

If the owner or lienholder makes no claim to the motor vehicle within ten days of the date of mailing of the notice, and if the vehicle is to be disposed of at public auction as provided in section 4513.62 of the Revised Code, the sheriff or chief of police shall file with the clerk of courts of the county in which the place of storage is located an affidavit showing compliance with the requirements of this section. Upon presentation of the affidavit, the clerk, without charge, shall issue a salvage certificate of title, free and clear of all liens and encumbrances, to the sheriff or chief of police. If the vehicle is to be disposed of to a motor vehicle salvage dealer or other facility as provided in section 4513.62 of the Revised Code, the sheriff or chief of police shall execute in triplicate an affidavit, as prescribed by the registrar of motor vehicles, describing the motor vehicle and the manner in which it was disposed of, and that all requirements of this section have been complied with. The sheriff or chief of police shall retain the original of the affidavit for the sheriff's or chief's records, and shall furnish two copies to the motor vehicle salvage dealer or other facility. Upon presentation of a copy of the affidavit by the motor vehicle salvage dealer, the clerk of courts shall issue to such owner a salvage certificate of title, free and clear of all liens and encumbrances.

Whenever a motor vehicle salvage dealer or other facility receives an affidavit for the disposal of a motor vehicle as provided in this section, the dealer or facility shall not be required to obtain an Ohio certificate of title to the motor vehicle in the dealer's or facility's own name if the vehicle is dismantled or destroyed and both copies of the affidavit are delivered to the clerk of courts.

HISTORY: 134 v H 24 (Eff 10-6-71); 135 v H 650 (Eff 7-9-74); 138 v S 257 (Eff 6-25-80); 141 v H 428 (Eff 12-23-86); 142 v S 10 (Eff 8-13-87); 142 v H 373 (Eff 10-9-89); 144 v S 144 (Eff 8-8-91); 146 v S 121 (Eff 11-19-96); 147 v S 60. Eff 10-21-97.

Analogous in part to former RC §§ 4513.41, 4513.42 (131 v 1119), and RC § 737.33.1 (127 v 285; 130 v 243; 133 v H 13), all repealed 134 v H 24, eff 10-6-71.

§ 4513.62 Disposal of unclaimed vehicles.

Unclaimed motor vehicles ordered into storage pursuant to division (A)(1) of section 4513.60 or section 4513.61 of the Revised Code shall be disposed of at the order of the sheriff of the county or the chief of police of the municipal corporation, township, or township police district to a motor vehicle salvage dealer or scrap metal processing facility as defined in section 4737.05 of the Revised Code, or to any other facility owned by or under contract with the county, municipal corporation, or township, for the disposal of such motor vehicles, or shall be sold by the sheriff, chief of police, or licensed auctioneer at public auction, after giving notice thereof by advertisement, published once a week for two successive weeks in a newspaper of general circulation in the county. Any moneys accruing from the disposition of an unclaimed motor vehicle that are in excess of the expenses resulting from the removal and storage of the vehicle shall be credited to the general fund of the county, the municipal corporation, or the township, as the case may be.

HISTORY: 134 v H 24 (Eff 10-6-71); 138 v S 257 (Eff 6-25-80); 140 v H 112 (Eff 10-4-84); 142 v S 10 (Eff 8-13-87); 142 v H 373. Eff 10-9-89.

Analogous to former RC § 737.31.2 (133 v H 13), repealed 134 v H 24, eff 10-6-71.

§ 4513.63 Photographing and recording information as to abandoned junk vehicles; disposal of vehicle.

"Abandoned junk motor vehicle" means any motor vehicle meeting all of the following requirements:

(A) Left on private property for forty-eight hours or

longer without the permission of the person having the right to the possession of the property, on a public street or other property open to the public for purposes of vehicular travel or parking, or upon or within the right-of-way of any road or highway, for forty-eight hours or longer;

(B) Three years old, or older;

(C) Extensively damaged, such damage including but not limited to any of the following: missing wheels, tires, motor, or transmission;

(D) Apparently inoperable;

(E) Having a fair market value of one thousand five hundred dollars or less.

The sheriff of a county or chief of police of a municipal corporation, township, or township police district, within the sheriff's or chief's respective territorial jurisdiction, or a state highway patrol trooper, upon notification to the sheriff or chief of police of such action, shall order any abandoned junk motor vehicle to be photographed by a law enforcement officer. The officer shall record the make of motor vehicle, the serial number when available, and shall also detail the damage or missing equipment to substantiate the value of one thousand five hundred dollars or less. The sheriff or chief of police shall thereupon immediately dispose of the abandoned junk motor vehicle to a motor vehicle salvage dealer as defined in section 4738.01 of the Revised Code or a scrap metal processing facility as defined in section 4737.05 of the Revised Code which is under contract to the county, township, or municipal corporation, or to any other facility owned by or under contract with the county, township, or municipal corporation for the destruction of such motor vehicles. The records and photograph relating to the abandoned junk motor vehicle shall be retained by the law enforcement agency ordering the disposition of such vehicle for a period of at least two years. The law enforcement agency shall execute in quadruplicate an affidavit, as prescribed by the registrar of motor vehicles, describing the motor vehicle and the manner in which it was disposed of, and that all requirements of this section have been complied with, and shall sign and file the same with the clerk of courts of the county in which the motor vehicle was abandoned. The clerk of courts shall retain the original of the affidavit for the clerk's files, shall furnish one copy thereof to the registrar, one copy to the motor vehicle salvage dealer or other facility handling the disposal of the vehicle, and one copy to the law enforcement agency ordering the disposal, who shall file such copy with the records and photograph relating to the disposal. Any moneys arising from the disposal of an abandoned junk motor vehicle shall be deposited in the general fund of the county, township, or the municipal corporation, as the case may be.

Notwithstanding section 4513.61 of the Revised Code, any motor vehicle meeting the requirements of divisions (C), (D), and (E) of this section which has remained unclaimed by the owner or lienholder for a period of ten days or longer following notification as provided in section 4513.61 of the Revised Code may be disposed of as provided in this section.

HISTORY: 134 v H 24 (Eff 10-6-71); 135 v H 650 (Eff 7-9-74); 136 v S 52 (Eff 9-15-75); 137 v H 865 (Eff 12-12-78); 138 v S 257 (Eff 6-25-80); 144 v S 144 (Eff 8-8-91); 144 v S 125 (Eff 4-16-93); 147 v S 60. Eff 10-21-97.

Analogous in part to former RC §§ 311.33, 737.31.3 (133 v H 920), 737.31.2 (133 v H 13), 311.30.1 (133 v S 218), repealed 134 v H 24, eff 10-6-71.

§ 4513.64 Willfully abandoning junk motor vehicle prohibited.

No person shall willfully leave an abandoned junk motor vehicle as defined in section 4513.63 of the Revised Code on private property for more than seventy-two hours without the permission of the person having the right to the possession of the property, or on a public street or other property open to the public for purposes of vehicular travel or parking, or upon or within the right-of-way of any road or highway, for forty-eight hours or longer without notification to the sheriff of the county or chief of police of the municipal corporation, township, or township police district of the reasons for leaving the motor vehicle in such place.

For purposes of this section, the fact that a motor vehicle has been so left without permission or notification is prima-facie evidence of abandonment.

Nothing contained in sections 4513.60, 4513.61, and 4513.63 of the Revised Code shall invalidate the provisions of municipal ordinances or township resolutions regulating or prohibiting the abandonment of motor vehicles on streets, highways, public property, or private property within municipal corporations or townships.

HISTORY: 134 v H 24 (Eff 10-6-71); 138 v S 257 (Eff 6-25-80); 144 v H 77. Eff 9-17-91.

Analogous to former RC §§ 311.34, 737.31.4 (133 v H 920), repealed 134 v H 24, eff 10-6-71.

§ 4513.65 Junk motor vehicle; collector's vehicle; storage; notice.

For purposes of this section, "junk motor vehicle" means any motor vehicle meeting the requirements of divisions (B), (C), (D), and (E) of section 4513.63 of the Revised Code that is left uncovered in the open on private property for more than seventy-two hours with the permission of the person having the right to the possession of the property, except if the person is operating a junk yard or scrap metal processing facility licensed under authority of sections 4737.05 to 4737.12 of the Revised Code, or regulated under authority of a political subdivision; or if the property on which the motor vehicle is left is not subject to licensure or regulation by any governmental authority, unless the person having the right to the possession of the property can establish that the motor vehicle is part of a bona fide commercial operation; or if the motor vehicle is a collector's vehicle.

No political subdivision shall prevent a person from storing or keeping, or restrict him in the method of storing or keeping, any collector's vehicle on private property with the permission of the person having the right to the possession of the property; except that a political subdivision may require a person having such permission to conceal, by means of buildings, fences, vegetation, terrain, or other suitable obstruction, any unlicensed collector's vehicle stored in the open.

The sheriff of a county, or chief of police of a municipal corporation, within his respective territorial jurisdiction, a state highway patrol trooper, a board of township trustees, the legislative authority of a municipal corporation, or the zoning authority of a township or a municipal corporation, may send notice, by certified mail with return receipt requested, to the person having the right to the possession of the property on which a junk motor vehicle is left, that within ten days of receipt of the notice, the junk motor vehicle either shall be covered by being housed in a garage or other suitable structure, or shall be removed from the property.

No person shall willfully leave a junk motor vehicle uncovered in the open for more than ten days after receipt of a notice as provided in this section. The fact that a junk motor vehicle is so left is prima-facie evidence of willful failure to comply with the notice, and each subsequent period of thirty days that a junk motor vehicle continues to be so left constitutes a separate offense.

HISTORY: 135 v H 635 (Eff 5-7-74); 136 v S 52 (Eff 9-15-75); 144 v S 144. Eff 8-8-91.

§ 4513.99 Penalties.

(A) Whoever violates division (C), (D), (E), or (F) of section 4513.241 [4513.24.1], section 4513.261 [4513.26.1], 4513.262 [4513.26.2], or 4513.36, or division (B)(3) of section 4513.60 of the Revised Code is guilty of a minor misdemeanor.

(B) Whoever violates section 4513.02 or 4513.021 [4513.02.1], or division (B)(4) of section 4513.263 [4513.26.3], or division (F) of section 4513.60 of the Revised Code is guilty of a minor misdemeanor on a first offense; on a second or subsequent offense such person is guilty of a misdemeanor of the third degree.

(C) Whoever violates sections 4513.03 to 4513.262 [4513.26.2] or 4513.27 to 4513.37 of the Revised Code, for which violation no penalty is otherwise provided, is guilty of a minor misdemeanor on a first offense; on a second offense within one year after the first offense, such person is guilty of a misdemeanor of the fourth degree; on each subsequent offense within one year after the first offense, such person is guilty of a misdemeanor of the third degree.

(D) Whoever violates section 4513.64 of the Revised Code is guilty of a minor misdemeanor, and shall also be assessed any costs incurred by the county, township, or municipal corporation in disposing of such abandoned junk motor vehicle, less any money accruing to the county, to the township, or to the municipal corporation from such disposal.

(E) Whoever violates section 4513.65 of the Revised Code is guilty of a minor misdemeanor on a first offense; on a second offense, such person is guilty of a misdemeanor of the fourth degree; on each subsequent offense, such person is guilty of a misdemeanor of the third degree.

(F) Whoever violates division (B)(1) of section 4513.263 [4513.26.3] of the Revised Code shall be fined twenty-five dollars.

(G) Whoever violates division (B)(3) of section 4513.263 [4513.26.3] of the Revised Code shall be fined fifteen dollars.

(H) Whoever violates section 4513.361 [4513.36.1] of the Revised Code is guilty of a misdemeanor of the first degree.

HISTORY: Bureau of Code Revision, 10-1-53; 125 v 903(1026); 125 v 456; 129 v 1567 (Eff 9-23-61); 132 v H 380 (Eff 1-1-68); 134 v H 24 (Eff 10-6-71); 135 v H 90 (Eff 10-31-73); 135 v H 173, § 1, 3 (Eff 1-1-74); 135 v H 635 (Eff 5-7-74); 138 v S 257 (Eff 6-25-80); 140 v H 112 (Eff 10-4-84); 141 v S 54 (Eff 5-6-86); 141 v H 291 (Eff 3-11-88); 144 v H 96 (Eff 6-18-91); 144 v H 118 (Eff 6-1-92); 144 v S 98. Eff 11-12-92.

CHAPTER 4549: MOTOR VEHICLE CRIMES

§ 4549.01 Stopping motor vehicle when signalled.

No person while operating a motor vehicle shall fail to slow down and stop said vehicle when signalled to do so upon meeting or overtaking a horse-drawn vehicle or person on horseback and to remain stationary until such vehicle or person has passed, provided such signal to stop is given in good faith, under circumstances of necessity, and only as often and for such length of time as is required for such vehicle or person to pass, whether it is approaching from the front or rear.

HISTORY: GC § 12605; 99 v 541, § 16; 99 v 543, § 25; Bureau of Code Revision. Eff 10-1-53.

§ 4549.02 Stopping after accident; exchange of identity and vehicle registration.

In case of accident to or collision with persons or property upon any of the public roads or highways, due to the driving or operation thereon of any motor vehicle, the person so driving or operating such motor vehicle, having knowledge of such accident or collision, shall immediately stop his motor vehicle at the scene of the accident or collision and shall remain at the scene of such accident or collision until he has given his name and address and, if he is not the owner, the name and address of the owner of such motor vehicle, together with the registered number of such motor vehicle, to any person injured in such accident or collision or to the operator, occupant, owner, or attendant of any motor vehicle damaged in such accident or collision, or to any police officer at the scene of such accident or collision.

In the event the injured person is unable to comprehend and record the information required to be given by this section, the other driver involved in such accident or collision shall forthwith notify the nearest police authority concerning the location of the accident or collision, and his name, address, and the registered number of the motor vehicle he was operating, and then remain at the scene of the accident or collision until a police officer arrives, unless removed from the scene by an emergency vehicle operated by a political subdivision or an ambulance.

If such accident or collision is with an unoccupied or unattended motor vehicle, the operator so colliding with such motor vehicle shall securely attach the information required to be given in this section, in writing, to a conspicuous place in or on said unoccupied or unattended motor vehicle.

HISTORY: GC § 12606; 99 v 541, § 16; 99 v 543, § 25; 113 v 76; Bureau of Code Revision, 10-1-53; 130 v 1111. Eff 8-19-63.

[§ 4549.02.1] § 4549.021 Stopping after accident involving injury to persons or property.

In case of accident or collision resulting in injury or damage to persons or property upon any public or private property other than public roads or highways, due to the driving or operation thereon of any motor vehicle, the person so driving or operating such motor vehicle, having knowledge of such accident or collision, shall stop, and, upon request of the person injured or damaged, or any other person, shall give such person his name and address, and, if he is not the owner, the name and address of the owner of such motor vehicle, together with the registered number of such motor vehicle, and, if available, exhibit his driver's or commercial driver's license.

If the owner or person in charge of such damaged property is not furnished such information, the driver of the motor vehicle involved in the accident or collision shall within twenty-four hours after such accident or collision, forward to the police department of the city or village in which such accident or collision occurred or if it occurred outside the corporate limits of a city or village to the sheriff of the county in which such accident or collision occurred the same information required to be given to the owner or person in control of such damaged property and give the date, time, and location of the accident or collision.

If the accident or collision is with an unoccupied or unattended motor vehicle, the operator so colliding with such motor vehicle shall securely attach the information required to be given in this section, in writing, to a conspicuous place in or on the unoccupied or unattended motor vehicle.

HISTORY: 130 v 1111 (Eff 9-30-63); 131 v 1132 (Eff 11-5-65); 143 v H 381. Eff 7-1-89.

§ 4549.03 Stopping after accident involving damage to realty.

The driver of any vehicle involved in an accident resulting in damage to real property, or personal property attached to such real property, legally upon or adjacent to a public road or highway shall immediately stop and take reasonable steps to locate and notify the owner or person in charge of such property of such fact, of his name and his address, and of the registration number of vehicle he is driving and shall, upon request and if available, exhibit his driver's or commercial driver's license.

If the owner or person in charge of such property cannot be located after reasonable search, the driver of the vehicle involved in the accident resulting in damage to such property shall, within twenty-four hours after such accident, forward to the police department of the city or village in which such accident or collision occurred or if it occurred outside the corporate limits of a city or village to the sheriff of the county in which such accident or collision occurred the same information required to be given to the owner or person in control of such property and give the location of the accident and a description of the damage insofar as it is known.

HISTORY: GC § 12606-1; 124 v 205; Bureau of Code Revision, 10-1-53; 131 v 1132 (Eff 11-5-65); 143 v H 381. Eff 7-1-89.

[§ 4549.04.2] § 4549.042 Illegal sale or possession of master key.

No person shall sell or otherwise dispose of a master key designed to fit more than one motor vehicle, knowing or having reasonable cause to believe such key will be used to commit a crime.

No person shall buy, receive, or have in his possession a master key designed to fit more than one motor vehicle, for the purpose of using such key to commit a crime.

HISTORY: 132 v H 591. Eff 12-14-67.

§ 4549.05 Officer may remove ignition key.

A law enforcement officer may remove the ignition key left in the ignition switch of an unlocked and unattended motor vehicle parked on a street or highway. The officer removing said key shall place notification upon the vehicle detailing his name and badge number, the place where said key may be reclaimed, and the procedure for reclaiming said key. The key shall be returned to the owner of the motor vehicle upon presentation of proof of ownership.

HISTORY: GC § 12619-1; 103 v 524; Bureau of Code Revision, 10-1-53; 133 v H 386 (Eff 10-30-69); 134 v H 511. Eff 1-1-74.

For provisions analogous to material deleted by HB 511 amendment, see now RC §§ 2913.02, 2913.51.

§ 4549.08 Unauthorized use of plate, number or identification mark.

No person shall operate or drive a motor vehicle upon the public roads and highways in this state if it displays a license plate or a distinctive number or identification mark that meets any of the following criteria:

(A) Is fictitious;

(B) Is a counterfeit or an unlawfully made copy of any distinctive number or identification mark;

(C) Belongs to another motor vehicle, provided that this section does not apply to a motor vehicle that is operated on the public roads and highways in this state when the motor vehicle displays license plates that originally were issued for a motor vehicle that previously was owned by the same person who owns the motor vehicle that is operated on the public roads and highways in this state, during the thirty-day period described in division (C) of section 4503.12 of the Revised Code.

A person who fails to comply with the transfer of registration provisions of section 4503.12 of the Revised Code and is charged with a violation of that section shall not be charged with a violation of this section.

HISTORY: GC § 12618; 99 v 543, § 26; 108 v PtII, 1078; 116 v 286, § 10; 116 v 295, § 3; Bureau of Code Revision, 10-1-53; 129 v 1030 (Eff 9-1-61); 130 v 1112 (Eff 1-23-63); 146 v H 353. Eff 9-17-96.

§ 4549.10 Operating without license plates.

No person shall operate or cause to be operated upon a public road or highway a motor vehicle of a manufacturer or dealer unless such vehicle carries and displays two placards, except as provided in section 4503.21 of the Revised Code issued by the director of public safety, bearing the registration number of its manufacturer or dealer.

HISTORY: GC § 12622; 99 v 543, § 24; 100 v 73, § 11; 115 v 109; Bureau of Code Revision, 10-1-53; 129 v 1492 (Eff 8-10-61); 144 v S 98. Eff 11-12-92.

§ 4549.11 Operating with number of former owner.

No person shall operate or drive upon the highways of this state a motor vehicle acquired from a former owner who has registered the same, while such vehicle displays the distinctive number or identification mark assigned to it upon its original registration.

HISTORY: GC § 12618-1; 108 v PtII 1078; Bureau of Code Revision. Eff 10-1-53.

§ 4549.12 Resident operating with number issued by foreign state.

No person who is the owner of a motor vehicle and a resident of this state shall operate or drive such motor vehicle upon the highways of this state, while it displays a distinctive number or identification mark issued by or under the authority of another state, without complying with the laws of this state relating to the registration and identification of motor vehicles.

HISTORY: GC § 12618-3; 108 v PtII 1078; Bureau of Code Revision. Eff 10-1-53.

§ 4549.13 Motor vehicles used by traffic officers.

Any motor vehicle used by a member of the state highway patrol or by any other peace officer, while said officer is on duty for the exclusive or main purpose of enforcing the motor vehicle or traffic laws of this state, provided the offense is punishable as a misdemeanor, shall be marked in some distinctive manner or color and shall be equipped with, but need not necessarily have in operation at all times, at least one flashing, oscillating, or rotating colored light mounted outside on top of the vehicle. The superintendent of the state highway patrol shall specify what constitutes such a distinctive marking or color for the state highway patrol.

HISTORY: GC § 12616; 118 v 271; Bureau of Code Revision, 10-1-53; 133 v H 625 (Eff 11-21-69); 138 v S 141. Eff 10-25-79.

Not analogous to former GC § 12616, repealed 116 v PtII 33(44), § 36.

§ 4549.14 Incompetency of officer as witness.

Any officer arresting, or participating or assisting in the arrest of, a person charged with violating the motor vehicle or traffic laws of this state, provided the offense is punishable as a misdemeanor, such officer being on duty exclusively or for the main purpose of enforcing such laws, is incompetent to testify as a witness in any prosecution against such arrested person if such officer at the time of the arrest was using a motor vehicle not marked in accordance with section 4549.13 of the Revised Code.

HISTORY: GC § 12616-1; 118 v 271, § 2; Bureau of Code Revision. Eff 10-1-53.

§ 4549.15 Uniform for traffic officers.

Every member of the state highway patrol and every other peace officer, while such officer is on duty for the exclusive or main purpose of enforcing motor vehicle or traffic laws of this state, provided the offense is punishable as a misdemeanor, shall wear a distinctive uniform. The superintendent of the patrol shall specify what constitutes such a distinctive uniform for the state highway patrol.

HISTORY: GC § 12616-2; 118 v 271, § 3; Bureau of Code

Revision, 10-1-53; 133 v H 625 (Eff 11-21-69); 138 v S 141. Eff 10-25-79.

§ 4549.16 Arresting officer as witness.

Any officer arresting, or participating or assisting in the arrest of, a person charged with violating the motor vehicle or traffic laws of this state, provided the offense is punishable as a misdemeanor, such officer being on duty exclusively or for the main purpose of enforcing such laws is incompetent to testify as a witness in any prosecution against such arrested person if such officer at the time of the arrest was not wearing a distinctive uniform in accordance with section 4549.15 of the Revised Code.

HISTORY: GC § 12616-3; 118 v 271, § 4; Bureau of Code Revision. Eff 10-1-53.

§ 4549.17 Restriction on local officers where only small portion of freeway located in their jurisdiction.

(A) No law enforcement officer employed by a law enforcement agency of a municipal corporation, township, or joint township police district shall issue any citation, summons, or ticket for a violation of section 4511.21 of the Revised Code or a substantially similar municipal ordinance or for a violation of section 5577.04 of the Revised Code or a substantially similar municipal ordinance, if all of the following apply:

(1) The citation, summons, or ticket would be issued for a violation described in division (A) of this section that occurs on a freeway that is part of the interstate system;

(2) The municipal corporation, township, or joint township police district that employs the law enforcement officer has less than eight hundred eighty yards of the freeway that is part of the interstate system within its jurisdiction;

(3) The law enforcement officer must travel outside the boundaries of the municipal corporation, township, or joint township police district that employs him in order to enter onto the freeway;

(4) The law enforcement officer travels onto the freeway for the primary purpose of issuing citations, summonses, or tickets for violations of section 4511.21 of the Revised Code or a substantially similar municipal ordinance or for violations of section 5577.04 of the Revised Code or a substantially similar municipal ordinance.

(B) As used in this section, "interstate system" has the same meaning as in section 5516.01 of the Revised Code.

HISTORY: 145 v H 687. Eff 10-12-94.

Not analogous to former RC § 4549.17 (RS § 4379-40; GC §§ 12626-12628; 99 v 544; Bureau of Code Revision, 10-1-53; 126 v 623), repealed 128 v 97, § 2, eff 1-1-60.

§ 4549.18 Display of certificates of registration.

The operator of a "commercial car" as defined in section 4501.01 of the Revised Code, when such car is required to be registered under the Revised Code, shall, when operating such commercial car, trailer, or semitrailer on the streets, roads, or highways of this state, display inside or on the vehicle the certificate of registration for such commercial car, trailer, or semitrailer provided for in section 4503.19 of the Revised Code, or shall carry such certificate on his person and display such certificate upon the demand of any state highway patrol trooper or other peace officer.

Every person operating a commercial car, trailer, or semitrailer required to be registered under the Revised Code, shall permit the inspection of the certificate of registration upon demand of the superintendent or any member of the state highway patrol or other peace officer of this state.

HISTORY: GC §§ 12630-1, 12630-2; 116 v PtII 155; Bureau of Code Revision, 10-1-53; 134 v H 1 (Eff 3-26-71); 143 v H 831 (Eff 7-17-90); 144 v S 144. Eff 8-8-91.

§ 4549.19 Enforcement of proceedings against violators.

Proceedings to enforce section 4549.18 of the Revised Code shall be brought in any court of record situated in the county in which the violation occurred, and all municipal courts shall have county-wide jurisdiction over such violations. Such actions shall be governed by section 4507.15 of the Revised Code. Commercial cars which are registered under the laws of another state, the owners of which are not residents of this state and which are operated in compliance with the laws of the state of their owner's residence, are not subject to this section and section 4549.18 of the Revised Code.

HISTORY: GC § 12630-3; 116 v PtII 155, § 3; Bureau of Code Revision. Eff 10-1-53.

§ 4549.31 Venue.

(A) Any person who as a part of a continuing course of criminal conduct commits auto theft offenses in more than one county may be indicted and tried for all such offenses in any county where one such offense was committed. It is prima-facie evidence of a continuing course of criminal conduct if an offender commits two or more auto theft offenses within a period of six months.

(B) As used in this section, "auto theft offense" means any of the following:

(1) A violation of section 4505.19, 4549.05, 4549.08, or 4549.62 of the Revised Code;

(2) A violation of a law of another state or the United States substantially equivalent to any offense listed in division (B)(1) of this section;

(3) A violation of a law of this or any other state, or

of the United States, of which an element is forging or altering a motor vehicle title or registration, or obtaining a motor vehicle or motor vehicle parts or accessories by theft or fraud, or wrongful conversion of a motor vehicle, or taking, operating, or keeping a motor vehicle without the consent of the owner, or receiving or disposing of a motor vehicle or motor vehicle parts or accessories knowing the same to have been unlawfully obtained.

HISTORY: 134 v H 101 (Eff 3-20-72); 136 v H 837 (Eff 5-25-76); 140 v H 632. Eff 3-28-85.

[ODOMETER ROLLBACK AND DISCLOSURE ACT]

§ 4549.41 Definitions.

As used in sections 4549.41 to 4549.51 of the Revised Code:

(A) "Person" includes an individual, corporation, government, governmental subdivision or agency, business trust, estate, trust, partnership, association, or cooperative or any other legal entity, whether acting individually or by their agents, officers, employees, or representatives.

(B) "Motor vehicle" means any vehicle driven or drawn by mechanical power for use on the public streets, roads, or highways.

(C) "Odometer" means an instrument for measuring and recording the total distance which a motor vehicle travels while in operation, including any cable, line, or other part necessary to make the instrument function properly. Odometer does not include any auxiliary odometer designed to be reset by the operator of a motor vehicle for the purpose of recording mileage on trips.

(D) "Transfer" means to change ownership of a motor vehicle by purchase, by gift, or, except as otherwise provided in this division, by any other means. A "transfer" does not include a change of ownership as a result of a bequest, under the laws of intestate succession, as a result of a surviving spouse's actions pursuant to section 2106.18 or 4505.10 of the Revised Code, as a result of the operation of section 2106.17 of the Revised Code, or in connection with the creation of a security interest.

(E) "Transferor" means the person involved in a transfer, who transfers ownership of a motor vehicle.

(F) "Transferee" means the person involved in a transfer, to whom the ownership of a motor vehicle is transferred.

(G) "Service" means to repair or replace an odometer which is not properly functioning.

HISTORY: 137 v S 78 (Eff 9-6-77); 140 v S 115 (Eff 10-14-83); 141 v H 382 (Eff 3-19-87); 143 v H 346 (Eff 5-31-90); 145 v H 458. Eff 7-20-94.

§ 4549.42 Tampering; notice of odometer repair.

(A) No person shall adjust, alter, change, tamper with, advance, set back, disconnect, or fail to connect, an odometer of a motor vehicle, or cause any of the foregoing to occur to an odometer of a motor vehicle with the intent to alter the number of miles registered on the odometer.

(B) Division (A) of this section does not apply to the disconnection of an odometer used for registering the mileage of any new motor vehicle being tested by the manufacturer prior to delivery to a franchise dealer.

(C) Nothing in this section shall prevent the service of an odometer, provided that after such service a completed form, captioned "notice of odometer repair", shall be attached to the left door frame of the motor vehicle by the person performing such repairs. Such notice shall contain, in bold-face type, the following information and statements:

"Notice of Odometer Repair

The odometer of this motor vehicle was repaired or replaced on . . . . (date of service).

The mileage registered on the odometer of this motor vehicle before repair was. . . . . (mileage).

The mileage registered on the odometer of this motor vehicle after repair is. . . . . (mileage).

....
(Repairman's signature)"

(D) No person shall intentionally remove or alter the notice required by division (C) of this section.

(E) If after the service of an odometer, the odometer can be set at the same mileage as before such service, the odometer shall be adjusted to reflect that mileage registered on the odometer of the motor vehicle before the service. If the odometer cannot be set at the same mileage as before such service, the odometer of the motor vehicle shall be adjusted to read "zero."

HISTORY: 137 v S 78. Eff 9-6-77.

§ 4549.43 Fraudulent device.

No person, with intent to defraud, shall advertise for sale, sell, use, or install on any part of any motor vehicle or an odometer in any motor vehicle any device which causes the odometer to register any mileage other than the actual mileage driven by the motor vehicle. For the purpose of this section the actual mileage driven is that mileage driven by the motor vehicle as registered by the odometer within the manufacturer's designed tolerance.

HISTORY: 137 v S 78. Eff 9-6-77.

§ 4549.44 Driving with nonfunctional odometer.

No person, with intent to defraud, shall operate a motor vehicle on any public street, road, or highway of this state knowing that the odometer of such vehicle is disconnected or nonfunctional.

A person's intent to defraud under this section may

be inferred from evidence of the circumstances of the vehicle's operation, including facts pertaining to the length of time or number of miles of operation with a nonfunctioning or disconnected odometer, and the fact that the person subsequently transferred the vehicle without disclosing the inoperative odometer to the transferee in violation of section 4549.45 of the Revised Code.

HISTORY: 137 v S 78 (Eff 9-6-77); 141 v H 382. Eff 3-19-87.

The effective date is set by section 3 of HB 382.

§ 4549.45 Notice of tampering or nonfunction.

No person shall transfer a motor vehicle if the person knows or recklessly disregards facts indicating that the odometer of the motor vehicle has been changed, tampered with, or disconnected, or has been in any other manner nonfunctional, to reflect a lesser mileage or use, unless that person gives clear and unequivocal notice of such tampering or nonfunction or of his reasonable belief of tampering or nonfunction, to the transferee in writing prior to the transfer. In a prosecution for violation of this section, evidence that a transferor or his agent has changed, tampered with, disconnected, or failed to connect the odometer of the motor vehicle constitutes prima-facie evidence of knowledge of the odometer's altered condition.

HISTORY: 137 v S 78 (Eff 9-6-77); 141 v H 382. Eff 3-19-87.

The effective date is set by section 3 of HB 382.

[§ 4549.45.1] § 4549.451 Auctioneer's statement.

No auctioneer licensed under Chapter 4707. of the Revised Code shall advertise for sale by means of any written advertisement, brochure, flyer, or other writing, any motor vehicle the auctioneer knows or has reason to believe has an odometer that has been changed, tampered with, or disconnected, or in any other manner has been nonfunctional, unless the listing or description of the vehicle contained in the written advertisement, brochure, flyer, or other writing contains one of the two following statements:

(A) "This motor vehicle has an odometer that has been changed, tampered with, or disconnected, or otherwise has been nonfunctional."

(B) "Nonactual odometer reading: warning - odometer discrepancy."

The statement selected by the auctioneer shall be printed in type identical in size to the other type used in the listing or description, and shall be located within the listing or description and not located as a footnote to the listing or description.

HISTORY: 147 v S 60. Eff 10-21-97.

§ 4549.46 Duties of transferor and dealer or wholesaler.

(A) No transferor shall fail to provide the true and complete odometer disclosures required by section 4505.06 of the Revised Code. The transferor of a motor vehicle is not in violation of this section's provisions requiring a true odometer reading if the odometer reading is incorrect due to a previous owner's violation of any of the provisions contained in sections 4549.42 to 4549.46 of the Revised Code, unless the transferor knows of or recklessly disregards facts indicating the violation.

(B) No dealer or wholesaler who acquires ownership of a motor vehicle shall accept any written odometer disclosure statement unless the statement is completed as required by section 4505.06 of the Revised Code.

(C) A motor vehicle leasing dealer may obtain a written odometer disclosure statement completed as required by section 4505.06 of the Revised Code from a motor vehicle lessee that can be used as prima-facie evidence in any legal action arising under sections 4549.41 to 4549.46 of the Revised Code.

HISTORY: 137 v S 78 (Eff 9-6-77); 140 v S 115 (Eff 10-14-83); 141 v H 382. Eff 3-19-87.

The effective date is set by section 3 of HB 382.

§ 4549.47 Attorney general investigates violations.

(A) If by his own inquiries or as a result of complaints, the attorney general has reason to believe that a person has engaged, is engaging, or is preparing to engage, in a violation of sections 4549.41 to 4549.46 of the Revised Code, he may investigate.

(B) For this purpose the attorney general may administer oaths, subpoena witnesses, adduce evidence, and require the production of relevant matter.

If the matter that the attorney general requires to be produced is located outside the state, he may designate representatives, including officials of the state in which the matter is located, to inspect the matter on his behalf, and he may respond to similar requests from officials of other states. The person subpoenaed may make the matter available to the attorney general at a convenient location within the state or pay the reasonable and necessary expenses for the attorney general or his representative to examine the matter at the place where it is located, provided that expenses shall not be charged to a party not subsequently found to have engaged in a violation of sections 4549.41 to 4549.46 of the Revised Code.

(C) At any time before the return day specified in the subpoena, or within twenty days after the subpoena has been served, whichever period is shorter, a petition to extend the return day, or to modify or quash the subpoena, stating good cause, may be filed in the court of common pleas in Franklin county or in the county where the person served resides or has his principal place of business.

(D) A person subpoenaed under this section shall comply with the terms of the subpoena unless otherwise provided by court order entered prior to the day for return contained in the subpoena or as extended by the court. If a person fails without lawful excuse to obey a subpoena or to produce relevant matter, the attorney general may apply to a court of common pleas and obtain an order doing any of the following:

(1) Adjudging the person in contempt of court;

(2) Granting injunctive relief to restrain the person from engaging in any conduct that violates sections 4549.41 to 4549.46 of the Revised Code;

(3) Granting injunctive relief to preserve or restore the status quo;

(4) Granting such other relief as may be required until the person obeys the subpoena.

If a person violates any order entered by a court under this section, the violation shall be punished as a violation of an injunction issued under division (A) of section 4549.48 of the Revised Code.

(E) The attorney general may request that an individual who refuses to testify or to produce relevant matter on the ground that the testimony or matter may incriminate him be ordered by the court to provide the testimony or matter. With the exception of a prosecution for perjury and an action for damages under section 4549.49 of the Revised Code, an individual who complies with a court order to provide testimony or matter, after asserting a privilege against self-incrimination to which he is entitled by law, shall not be subjected to a criminal proceeding on the basis of the testimony or matter required to be disclosed or testimony or matter discovered through that testimony or matter.

HISTORY: 137 v S 78. Eff 9-6-77.

§ 4549.48 Action to enjoin violation; penalty; remedies.

(A) Whenever it appears that a person has violated, is violating, or is about to violate any provision of sections 4549.41 to 4549.46 of the Revised Code, the attorney general may bring an action in the court of common pleas to enjoin the violation. Upon a showing of a violation of sections 4549.41 to 4549.46 of the Revised Code, a temporary restraining order, preliminary injunction, or permanent injunction shall be granted without bond. The court may impose a penalty of not more than five thousand dollars for each day of violation of a temporary restraining order, preliminary injunction, or permanent injunction issued under this section. The court may issue an order requiring the reimbursement of a consumer for any loss that results from a violation of sections 4549.41 to 4549.46 of the Revised Code, for the recovery of any amounts for which a violator is liable pursuant to division (A) of section 4549.49 of the Revised Code, for the appointment of a referee or receiver, for the sequestration of assets, for the rescission of transfers of motor vehicles, or granting any other appropriate relief. The court may award the attorney general all costs together with all expenses of his investigation and reasonable attorneys' fees incurred in the prosecution of the action, which shall be deposited in the consumer protection enforcement fund created by section 1345.51 of the Revised Code.

(B) In addition to the remedies otherwise provided by this section, the attorney general may request and the court shall impose a civil penalty of not less than one thousand nor more than two thousand dollars for each violation. A violation of any provision of sections 4549.41 to 4549.46 of the Revised Code shall, for purposes of this section, constitute a separate violation with respect to each motor vehicle or unlawful device involved, except that the maximum civil penalty shall not exceed one hundred thousand dollars for any related series of violations by a person. Civil penalties ordered pursuant to this division shall be paid as follows: one-fourth of the amount to the treasurer of the county in which the action is brought; three-fourths to the consumer protection enforcement fund created by section 1345.51 of the Revised Code.

(C) The remedies prescribed by this section are cumulative and concurrent with any other remedy, and the existence or exercise of one remedy does not prevent the exercise of any other remedy.

HISTORY: 137 v S 78 (Eff 9-6-77); 141 v H 382. Eff 3-19-87.

The effective date is set by section 3 of HB 382.

§ 4549.49 Liability to transferee.

(A) Any person who violates any requirement imposed by sections 4549.41 to 4549.46 of the Revised Code is liable to any transferee of the motor vehicle subsequent to the violation, in an amount equal to:

(1) Three times the amount of actual damages sustained or fifteen hundred dollars, whichever is greater; and

(2) In the case of any successful action to enforce the foregoing liability, the costs of the action together with reasonable attorneys' fees as determined by the court.

(B) An action to enforce any liability created under sections 4549.41 to 4549.46 of the Revised Code may be brought in a court of common pleas without regard to the amount in controversy, or in any other court of competent jurisdiction, within two years from the date on which the liability arises. For the purpose of this section, liability arises when the transferee discovers, or with due diligence should have discovered, the violation.

HISTORY: 137 v S 78. Eff 9-6-77.

§ 4549.50 Revocation or denial of license or permit; surety bond.

Violation of sections 4549.41 to 4549.46 of the Revised Code by any person licensed or granted a permit by this state as a dealer, wholesaler, distributor, salesman, or auction owner under Chapter 4517. of the

Revised Code, is prima-facie evidence of intent to defraud and constitutes cause for the revocation or denial of the license of such person to sell any motor vehicle in this state. Any person who violates sections 4549.41 to 4549.46 of the Revised Code, upon receiving notice from the registrar of motor vehicles or motor vehicle dealers board of the intent to revoke or suspend a license or permit, shall immediately post a surety bond with the registrar in favor of the state in the amount of twenty-five thousand dollars and shall maintain the bond while the license or permit is in effect. The bond shall be for the use, benefit, and protection of any transferee damaged by the licensee's or permitee's violation of sections 4549.41 to 4549.46 of the Revised Code or for the payment of civil penalties or costs resulting from enforcement actions. Any transferee claiming against the bond or the attorney general may maintain an action against the transferor or the surety, except that the surety is liable only for actual damages. The aggregate liability of the surety shall not exceed twenty-five thousand dollars. Any money unclaimed by transferees after two years from the date of the conviction of or judgment against the transferor shall be deposited in the consumer protection enforcement fund created by section 1345.51 of the Revised Code. The surety bond shall remain in effect until the license or permit is revoked or suspended by the motor vehicle dealers board pursuant to section 4517.33 of the Revised Code. Upon reinstatement of a license or permit that has been suspended, or upon reissuance of a license or permit after the period of revocation, the licensee or permit[t]ee shall post an additional surety bond in accordance with this section. The surety bond shall remain in effect during the period in which the licensee or permitee engages in business in the state.

HISTORY: 137 v. S 78 (Eff 9-6-77); 141 v H 382. Eff 3-19-87.

The effective date is set by section 3 of HB 382.

§ 4549.51 Additional remedies.

The remedies under sections 4549.41 to 4549.51 of the Revised Code are in addition to remedies otherwise available for the same conduct under federal, state, or local law.

HISTORY: 137 v S 78. Eff 9-6-77.

[TAMPERING WITH IDENTIFYING NUMBERS]

§ 4549.61 Definitions.

As used in sections 4549.61 to 4549.63 of the Revised Code, "vehicle identification number or derivative thereof" means any number or derivative of such a number that is embossed, engraved, etched, or otherwise marked on any vehicle or vehicle part by the manufacturer. "Vehicle identification number" also includes a duplicate vehicle identification number replaced upon a vehicle under the authority of the registrar of motor vehicles.

HISTORY: 140 v H 632. Eff 3-28-85.

§ 4549.62 Offenses involving tampering with identifying numbers to conceal identity of vehicle or part; replacement.

(A) No person shall, with purpose to conceal or destroy the identity of a vehicle or vehicle part, remove, deface, cover, alter, or destroy any vehicle identification number or derivative thereof on a vehicle or vehicle part.

(B) No person shall, with purpose to conceal or destroy the identity of a vehicle or a vehicle part, remove, deface, cover, alter, or destroy any identifying number that has been lawfully placed upon a vehicle or vehicle part by an owner of the vehicle or vehicle part, other than the manufacturer, for the purpose of deterring its theft and facilitating its recovery if stolen.

(C) No person shall, with purpose to conceal or destroy the identity of a vehicle or vehicle part, place a counterfeit vehicle identification number or derivative thereof upon the vehicle or vehicle part.

(D)(1) No person shall buy, offer to buy, sell, offer to sell, receive, dispose of, conceal, or, except as provided in division (D)(4) of this section, possess any vehicle or vehicle part with knowledge that the vehicle identification number or a derivative thereof has been removed, defaced, covered, altered, or destroyed in such a manner that the identity of the vehicle or part cannot be determined by a visual examination of the number at the site where the manufacturer placed the number.

(2)(a) A vehicle or vehicle part from which the vehicle identification number or a derivative thereof has been so removed, defaced, covered, altered, or destroyed shall be seized and forfeited under section 2933.41 of the Revised Code unless division (D)(3) or (4) of this section applies to the vehicle or part. If a derivative of the vehicle identification number has been removed, defaced, covered, altered, or destroyed in such a manner that the identity of the part cannot be determined, the entire vehicle is subject to seizure pending a determination of the original identity and ownership of the vehicle and parts of the vehicle, and the rights of innocent owners to reclaim the remainder or any part of the vehicle.

(b) The lawful owners of parts upon a vehicle that has been seized under this section and that is subject to forfeiture under section 2933.41 of the Revised Code are entitled to reclaim their respective parts upon satisfactory proof of all of the following:

(i) That the part is not needed for evidence in pending proceedings involving the vehicle or part and is not subject to forfeiture under section 2933.41 of the Revised Code;

(ii) That the original identity and ownership of the

part can be determined and that the claimant is the lawful owner of the part;

(iii) That no vehicle identification number or derivative of a vehicle identification number on the part has been destroyed or concealed in such a manner that the identity of the part cannot be determined from that number;

(iv) Payment of all costs of removing the part.

(3) Divisions (A), (B), and (D)(1) and (2) of this section do not apply to the good faith acquisition and disposition of vehicles and vehicle parts as junk or scrap in the ordinary course of business by a scrap metal processing facility as defined in division (E) of section 4737.05 of the Revised Code or by a motor vehicle salvage dealer licensed under Chapter 4738. of the Revised Code. This division (D)(3) does not create an element of an offense or an affirmative defense, or affect the burden of proceeding with the evidence or burden of proof in a criminal proceeding.

(4)(a) Divisions (D)(1) and (2) of this section do not apply to the possession of an owner, or the owner's insurer, who provides satisfactory evidence of all of the following:

(i) That the vehicle identification number or derivative thereof on the vehicle or part has been removed, defaced, covered, altered, or destroyed, after the owner acquired such possession, by another person without the consent of the owner, by accident or other casualty not due to the owner's purpose to conceal or destroy the identity of the vehicle or vehicle part, or by ordinary wear and tear;

(ii) That the person is the owner of the vehicle as shown on a valid certificate of title issued by this state or certificate of title or other lawful evidence of title issued in another state, in a clear chain of title beginning with the manufacturer;

(iii) That the original identity of the vehicle can be established in a manner that excludes any reasonable probability that the vehicle has been stolen from another person.

(b) The registrar of motor vehicles shall adopt rules under Chapter 119. of the Revised Code to permit an owner described in division (D)(4)(a) of this section, upon application and submission of satisfactory evidence to the registrar of motor vehicles, to obtain authority to replace the vehicle identification number under the supervision of a peace officer, trooper of the state highway patrol, or representative of the registrar. The rules shall be designed to restore the identification of the vehicle in a manner that will deter its theft and facilitate its marketability. Until such rules are adopted, the registrar shall follow the existing procedure for the replacement of vehicle identification numbers that have been established by the registrar, with such modifications as the registrar determines to be necessary or appropriate for the administration of the laws he is required to administer.

The registrar may issue a temporary permit to an owner of a motor vehicle who is described in division (D)(4)(a) of this section to authorize the owner to retain possession of the motor vehicle and to transfer title to the motor vehicle with the consent of the registrar.

(c) No owner described in division (D)(4)(a) of this section shall knowingly fail to apply to the registrar for authority to replace the vehicle identification number, within thirty days after the later of the following dates:

(i) The date of receipt by the applicant of actual knowledge of the concealment or destruction;

(ii) If the property has been stolen, the date thereafter upon which the applicant obtains possession of the vehicle or has been notified by a law enforcement agency that the vehicle has been recovered.

The requirement of division (D)(4)(c) of this section may be excused by the registrar for good cause shown.

HISTORY: 140 v H 632 (Eff 3-28-85); 144 v S 144. Eff 8-8-91.

§ 4549.63 Seizure of vehicle or parts.

(A) A law enforcement officer may seize and take possession of a vehicle or vehicle part if the officer has probable cause to believe that any vehicle identification number or derivative thereof on the vehicle or part has been removed, defaced, covered, altered, or destroyed in such a manner that the identity of the vehicle or part cannot be determined by visual examination of the number at the site where the manufacturer placed the number. The seizure shall be pursuant to a warrant, unless the circumstances are within one of the exceptions to the warrant requirement that have been established by the supreme court of the United States or of the supreme court of this state.

(B) A vehicle or vehicle part seized under division (A) of this section shall be held in custody pursuant to section 2933.41 of the Revised Code or any applicable municipal ordinance.

(C) A law enforcement officer who acts in good faith in the belief that the seizure of a vehicle or vehicle part is justified under division (A) of this section is immune from any civil or criminal liability for such seizure.

(D) The lawful owner of a vehicle or vehicle part seized under this section that is not needed as evidence and is not subject to forfeiture under division (D)(2) of section 4549.62 of the Revised Code may reclaim the property by submitting satisfactory proof of ownership to the law enforcement agency or court holding the property.

HISTORY: 140 v H 632. Eff 3-28-85.

§ 4549.65 Immunity of leasing or renting dealer believing that vehicle has been converted or stolen.

(A) As used in this section:

(1) "Motor vehicle leasing dealer" has the meaning set forth in division (M) of section 4517.01 of the Revised Code.

(2) "Motor vehicle renting dealer" means any person

engaged in the business of regularly making available, offering to make available, or arranging for another person to use a motor vehicle pursuant to a bailment, rental agreement, or other contractual arrangement for a period of less than thirty days under which a charge is made for its use at a periodic rate and the title to the motor vehicle is in a person other than the user, but does not mean a manufacturer or its affiliate renting to its employees or to dealers.

(B) A motor vehicle leasing dealer or a motor vehicle renting dealer and its officers, employees, agents, and representatives are not liable to a lessee or renter for damages or injuries sustained as a result of the lessee's or renter's being stopped, detained, arrested, or charged in connection with a theft offense involving the leased or rented motor vehicle if such dealer, its officers, employees, agents, or representatives act in good faith upon a reasonable belief that the motor vehicle was or is being converted or stolen or if both of the following apply:

(1) The lessee or renter did not return the motor vehicle at the time and place specified in the lease or rental contract;

(2) The lessee or renter failed to return the motor vehicle within twenty-four hours after the dealer, or an officer, employee, agent, or representative of the dealer has served a written notice upon the lessee or renter, requesting the return of the motor vehicle, at the lessee's or renter's address set forth in the lease or rental contract. Service may be by certified mail, return receipt requested, or by personal or residence service.

HISTORY: 140 v H 632. Eff 3-28-85.

§ 4549.99 Penalties.

(A) Whoever violates section 4549.01, 4549.10, 4549.11, or 4549.12 of the Revised Code is guilty of a minor misdemeanor on a first offense and a misdemeanor of the fourth degree on each subsequent offense.

(B) Whoever violates section 4549.02, 4549.021 [4549.02.1], or 4549.03 of the Revised Code is guilty of a misdemeanor of the first degree.

(C) Whoever violates section 4549.042 [4549.04.2] or sections 4549.41 to 4549.46 of the Revised Code is guilty of a felony of the fourth degree on a first offense and a felony of the third degree on each subsequent offense. The prosecuting attorney of the proper county, or the attorney general by information or complaint, may bring a criminal action in the courts of common pleas of this state, or in any other court of competent jurisdiction, to enforce the provisions of sections 4549.41 to 4549.51 of the Revised Code. The attorney general and the prosecuting attorney of the county in which a person licensed or granted a permit under Chapter 4517. of the Revised Code is convicted of, or pleads guilty to, a violation of sections 4549.41 to 4549.46 of the Revised Code shall report the conviction or guilty plea to the registrar of motor vehicles within five business days.

(D) Whoever violates section 4549.08 of the Revised Code is guilty of a misdemeanor of the fourth degree on a first offense and a misdemeanor of the third degree on each subsequent offense.

(E) Whoever violates section 4549.18 or division (D)(4)(c) of section 4549.62 of the Revised Code is guilty of a minor misdemeanor.

(F) Whoever violates division (A), (B), (C), or (D)(1) of section 4549.62 of the Revised Code is guilty of a felony of the fifth degree on a first offense and a felony of the fourth degree on each subsequent offense.

HISTORY: Bureau of Code Revision, 10-1-53; 129 v 366 (Eff 9-1-61); 130 v 1112 (Eff 9-30-63); 132 v H 591 (Eff 12-14-67); 134 v H 101 (Eff 3-20-72); 134 v H 511 (Eff 1-1-74); 137 v S 78 (Eff 9-6-77); 140 v H 632 (Eff 3-28-85); 141 v H 382 (Eff 3-19-87); 146 v S 2. Eff 7-1-96.

The effective date is set by section 6 of SB 2.

CHAPTER 4561: AERONAUTICS

§ 4561.01 Definitions.

As used in sections 4561.01 to 4561.151 [4561.15.1] of the Revised Code:

(A) "Aviation" means transportation by aircraft; operation of aircraft; the establishment, operation, maintenance, repair, and improvement of airports, landing fields, and other air navigation facilities; and all other activities connected therewith or incidental thereto.

(B) "Aircraft" means any contrivance used or designed for navigation or flight in the air, excepting a parachute or other contrivance for such navigation used primarily as safety equipment.

(C) "Airport" means any location either on land or water which is used for the landing and taking off of aircraft.

(D) "Landing field" means any location either on land or water of such size and nature as to permit the landing or taking off of aircraft with safety, and used for that purpose but not equipped to provide for the shelter, supply, or care of aircraft.

(E) "Air navigation facility" means any facility used, available for use, or designed for use in aid of navigation of aircraft, including airports, landing fields, facilities for the servicing of aircraft or for the comfort and accommodation of air travelers, and any structures, mechanisms, lights, beacons, marks, communicating systems, or other instrumentalities or devices used or useful as an aid to the safe taking off, navigation, and landing of aircraft, or to the safe and efficient operation or maintenance of an airport or landing field, and any combination of such facilities.

(F) "Air navigation hazard" means any structure, object of natural growth, or use of land, that obstructs the air space required for the flight of aircraft in landing or taking off at any airport or landing field, or that otherwise is hazardous to such landing or taking off.

(G) "Air navigation," "navigation of aircraft," or "navigate aircraft" means the operation of aircraft in the air space over this state.

(H) "Airman" means any individual who, as the person in command, or as pilot, mechanic, or member of the crew, engages in the navigation of aircraft.

(I) "Airway" means a route in the air space over and above the lands or waters of this state, designated by the Ohio aviation board as a route suitable for the navigation of aircraft.

(J) "Person" means any individual, firm, partnership, corporation, company, association, joint stock association, or body politic, and includes any trustee, receiver, assignee, or other similar representative thereof.

HISTORY: GC § 6310-38; 121 v 253; Bureau of Code Revision, Eff 10-1-53; 146 v S 2. Eff 7-1-96.

The effective date is set by section 6 of SB 2.

§ 4561.14 Prohibitions.

No person shall operate any aircraft in this state unless such person is the holder of a valid airman's license issued by the United States.

No person operating an aircraft within this state shall fail to exhibit such license for inspection upon the demand of any passenger on such aircraft, or fail to exhibit same for inspection upon the demand of any peace officer, member or employee of the department of transportation, or manager or person in charge of an airport or landing field within this state, prior to taking off or upon landing said aircraft.

No person shall operate an aircraft within this state unless such aircraft is licensed and registered by the United States; this section is inapplicable to the operation of military aircraft of the United States, aircraft of a state, territory, or possession of the United States, or aircraft licensed by a foreign country with which the United States has a reciprocal agreement covering the operation of such aircraft.

No person shall operate an aircraft within this state in violation of any air traffic rules in force under the laws of the United States or under sections 4561.01 to 4561.14 of the Revised Code, and the rules and regulations of the department adopted pursuant thereto.

HISTORY: GC § 6310-50; 121 v 253, § 13; Bureau of Code Revision, 10-1-53; 127 v 349 (Eff 9-17-57); 135 v S 96. Eff 8-22-73.

§ 4561.15 Unsafe operation of aircraft.

(A) No person shall commit any of the following acts:

(1) Carry passengers in an aircraft unless the person piloting the aircraft is a holder of a valid airman's certificate of competency in the grade of private pilot or higher issued by the United States; this division of this section is inapplicable to the operation of military aircraft of the United States, aircraft of a state, territory, or possession of the United States, or aircraft licensed by a foreign country with which the United States has a reciprocal agreement covering the operation of such aircraft.

(2) Operate an aircraft on the land or water or in the air space over this state in a careless or reckless manner that endangers any person or property, or with willful or wanton disregard for the rights or safety of others.

(3) Operate an aircraft on the land or water or in the air space over this state while under the influence of intoxicating liquor, controlled substances, or other habit-forming drugs.

(4) Tamper with, alter, destroy, remove, carry away, or cause to be carried away any object used for the marking of airports, landing fields, or other aeronautical facilities in this state, or in any way change the position or location of such markings, except by the direction of the proper authorities charged with the maintenance and operation of such facilities, or illegally possess any object used for such markings.

(B) Jurisdiction over any proceedings charging a violation of this section is limited to courts of record.

HISTORY: GC § 6310-50a; 122 v 72; Bureau of Code Revision, 10-1-53; 136 v H 300 (Eff 7-1-76); 146 v S 2. Eff 7-1-96.

The effective date is set by section 6 of SB 2.

§ 4561.16 Repealed, 146 v S 2, § 6 [Bureau of Code Revisions, 10-1-53]. Eff 7-1-96

This section prohibited unlawful use of aircraft of another.

§ 4561.24 Operation of motor vehicles on airport runways prohibited.

No person shall operate a motor vehicle upon any runway of an airport without prior approval of the person in charge of the airport when the airport has been certified as a commercial airport by the office of aviation.

Any person lending assistance to the operator or operation of a vehicle engaged in such activity shall be equally charged as the participants.

As used in this section, "motor vehicle" has the same meaning as in section 4501.01 of the Revised Code.

Airport vehicles and emergency and maintenance equipment are exempted from this section.

HISTORY: 133 v H 266 (Eff 8-28-69); 146 v H 572. Eff 9-17-96.

§ 4561.99 Penalties.

(A) Whoever violates sections 4561.01 to 4561.14 of the Revised Code shall be fined not more than five hundred dollars, imprisoned not more than ninety days, or both.

(B) Whoever violates section 4561.15 of the Revised Code shall be fined not more than five hundred dollars, imprisoned not more than six months, or both.

(C) Whoever violates section 4561.22 of the Revised Code shall be fined not more than one hundred dollars, imprisoned not more than thirty days, or both.

(D) Whoever violates section 4561.24 of the Revised Code shall be fined not less than one hundred nor more than five hundred dollars, imprisoned for not more than six months, or both, for a first offense and shall be fined not less than two hundred nor more than one thousand dollars, imprisoned for not more than one year, or both, for each subsequent offense.

(E) Whoever violates division (A)(1) or (2) of section 4561.31 of the Revised Code is guilty of a misdemeanor of the third degree. Each day of violation constitutes a separate offense.

(F) Whoever violates division (A)(3) or (B) of section 4561.31 of the Revised Code is guilty of a misdemeanor of the first degree. Each day of violation constitutes a separate offense.

HISTORY: Bureau of Code Revision, 10-1-53; 133 v H 266 (Eff 8-28-69); 144 v H 15 (Eff 10-15-91); 145 v H 571 (Eff 10-6-94); 146 v S 2. Eff 7-1-96.

The effective date is set by section 6 of SB 2.

TITLE 47:
OCCUPATIONS—PROFESSIONS

CHAPTER 4729: PHARMACISTS; DANGEROUS DRUGS

§ 4729.02 Definitions.

As used in this chapter:

(A) "Pharmacy" means any area, room, rooms, place of business, department, or portion of any of the foregoing, where prescriptions are filled or where drugs, dangerous drugs, or poisons are compounded, sold, offered, or displayed for sale, dispensed, or distributed to the public.

(B) To "practice pharmacy" means to interpret prescriptions, to compound or dispense drugs, dangerous drugs, and poisons, and related devices that under the "Federal Food, Drug, and Cosmetic Act" must be labeled for sale only on the order of a practitioner; to participate in drug selection pursuant to Chapter 3715. and section 4729.38 of the Revised Code; and to participate with practitioners in reviews of drug utilization.

(C) "Drug" means:

(1) Any article recognized in the official United States pharmacopeia, national formulary, or any supplement, intended for use in the diagnosis, cure, mitigation, treatment, or prevention of disease in man or other animals;

(2) Any other article intended for use in the diagnosis, cure, mitigation, treatment, or prevention of disease in man or other animals;

(3) Any article, other than food, intended to affect the structure or any function of the body of man or other animals;

(4) Any article intended for use as a component of any article specified in division (C)(1), (2), or (3) of this section; but does not include devices or their components, parts, or accessories.

(D) "Dangerous drug" means any of the following:

(1) Any drug to which either of the following applies:

(a) Under the "Federal Food, Drug, and Cosmetic Act" is required to bear a label containing the legend "Caution: Federal law prohibits dispensing without prescription" or "Caution: Federal law restricts this drug to use by or on the order of a licensed veterinarian" or any similar restrictive statement, or may be dispensed only upon a prescription;

(b) Under Chapter 3715. or 3719. of the Revised Code may be dispensed only upon a prescription;

(2) Any drug that contains a schedule V controlled substance and that is exempt from Chapter 3719. of the Revised Code or to which that chapter does not apply;

(3) Any drug intended for administration by injection into the human body other than through a natural orifice of the human body.

(E) "Federal drug abuse control laws" has the same meaning as in section 3719.01 of the Revised Code.

(F) "Federal Food, Drug, and Cosmetic Act," means the "Federal Food, Drug, and Cosmetic Act," 52 Stat. 1040 (1938), 21 U.S.C. 301, as amended.

(G) "Prescription" means an order for drugs or combinations or mixtures of drugs, written or signed by a practitioner or transmitted by a practitioner to a pharmacist by word of mouth, telephone, telegraph, or other means of communication and recorded in writing by the pharmacist.

(H) "Practitioner" means any of the following:

(1) A person who is licensed pursuant to Chapter 4715., 4725., 4731., or 4741. of the Revised Code and authorized by law to write prescriptions for drugs or dangerous drugs;

(2) A professional association, as defined in section 1785.01 of the Revised Code, organized by an individual who is, or a group of individuals who are, licensed pursuant to Chapter 4715., 4725., 4731., or 4741. of the Revised Code and authorized by law to write prescriptions for drugs or dangerous drugs, or a corporation-for-profit formed under Chapter 1701. of the Revised Code by an individual or group of individuals so licensed and authorized;

(3) A partnership of individuals who are licensed pursuant to Chapter 4715., 4725., 4731., or 4741. of the Revised Code and authorized by law to write prescriptions for drugs or dangerous drugs;

(4) A limited liability company formed under Chapter 1705. of the Revised Code for the purpose of rendering a professional service covered by Chapter 4715., 4725., 4731., or 4741. of the Revised Code, the members, employees, other agents, and, if applicable, managers of which are licensed or otherwise legally authorized to render the covered professional service in this state and are authorized by law to write prescriptions for drugs or dangerous drugs;

(5) An advanced practice nurse authorized under section 4723.56 of the Revised Code to prescribe drugs and therapeutic devices.

(I) "Poison" means any drug, chemical, or preparation likely to be deleterious or destructive to adult human life in quantities of four grams or less.

(J) "Sale" and "sell" include delivery, transfer, barter, exchange, or gift, or offer therefor, and each such transaction made by any person, whether as principal proprietor, agent, or employee.

(K) "Wholesale sale" and "sale at wholesale" mean any sale in which the purpose of the purchaser is to resell the article purchased or received by the purchaser.

(L) "Retail sale" and "sale at retail" mean any sale other than a wholesale sale or sale at wholesale.

(M) "Retail seller" means any person that sells any dangerous drug to consumers without assuming control over and responsibility for its administration. Mere advice or instructions regarding administration do not constitute control or establish responsibility.

(N) "Price information" means the price charged for a prescription for a particular drug product and, in an easily understandable manner, all of the following:

(1) The proprietary name of the drug product;

(2) The established (generic) name of the drug product;

(3) The strength of the drug product if the product contains a single active ingredient or if the drug product contains more than one active ingredient and a relevant strength can be associated with the product without indicating each active ingredient. The established name and quantity of each active ingredient are required if such a relevant strength cannot be so associated with a drug product containing more than one ingredient.

(4) The dosage form;

(5) The price charged for a specific quantity of the drug product. The stated price shall include all charges to the consumer, including, but not limited to, the cost of the drug product, professional fees, handling fees, if any, and a statement identifying professional services routinely furnished by the pharmacy. Any mailing fees and delivery fees may be stated separately without repetition. The information shall not be false or misleading.

(O) "Wholesale distributor of dangerous drugs" means a person engaged in the sale of dangerous drugs at wholesale and includes any agent or employee of such a person authorized by the person to engage in the sale of dangerous drugs at wholesale.

(P) "Manufacturer of dangerous drugs" means a person, other than a pharmacist, who manufactures dangerous drugs and who is engaged in the sale of those dangerous drugs within this state.

(Q) "Terminal distributor of dangerous drugs" means a person, other than a practitioner, who is engaged in the sale of dangerous drugs at retail, or any person, other than a wholesale distributor or a pharmacist, who has in the person's possession, custody, or control dangerous drugs for any purpose other than for the person's own use and consumption, and includes pharmacies, hospitals, nursing homes, and laboratories and all other persons who procure dangerous drugs for sale or other distribution by or under the supervision of a pharmacist or medical practitioner.

(R) "Promote to the public" means disseminating a representation to the public in any manner or by any means, other than by labeling, for the purpose of inducing, or that is likely to induce, directly or indirectly, the purchase of a dangerous drug at retail.

(S) "Person" includes any individual, partnership, association, limited liability company, or corporation, the state, any political subdivision of the state, and any district, department, or agency of the state or its political subdivisions.

(T) "Finished dosage form" has the same meaning as in division (A)(17) of section 3715.01 of the Revised Code.

(U) As used in section 4729.38 of the Revised Code, "manufacturer" means a person who manufactures, as defined in division (A)(18) of section 3715.01 of the Revised Code.

(V) "Generically equivalent drug" has the same meaning as in division (A)(20) of section 3715.01 of the Revised Code.

(W) "Animal shelter" means a facility operated by a humane society or any society organized under Chapter 1717. of the Revised Code or a dog pound operated pursuant to Chapter 955. of the Revised Code.

(X) "Food" has the same meaning as in section 3715.01 of the Revised Code.

HISTORY: GC § 1296-1; 121 v 681; Bureau of Code Revision, 10-1-53; 130 v 1140 (Eff 10-7-63); 134 v S 141 (Eff 12-31-71); 136 v H 300 (Eff 7-1-76); 136 v H 912 (Eff 10-1-76); 137 v H 1 (Eff 8-26-77); 137 v S 45 (Eff 1-1-78); 139 v S 4 (Eff 10-1-82); 140 v H 208 (Eff 9-20-84); 144 v S 110 (Eff 5-19-92); 145 v H 88 (Eff 6-29-94); 145 v S 74 (Eff 7-1-94); 145 v H 391 (Eff 7-21-94); 146 v H 162. Eff 1-1-97.

The effective date is set by section 3 of HB 162.

§ 4729.16 Grounds for disciplinary actions.

(A) The state board of pharmacy, after notice and hearing in accordance with Chapter 119. of the Revised Code, may revoke, suspend, place on probation, or refuse to grant or renew an identification card under this chapter, or may impose a monetary penalty or forfeiture not to exceed in severity any fine designated under the Revised Code for a similar offense, or in the case of a violation of a section of the Revised Code that does not bear a penalty, a monetary penalty or forfeiture of not more than five hundred dollars, if the board finds a pharmacist or pharmacy intern:

(1) Guilty of a felony or gross immorality;

(2) Guilty of dishonesty or unprofessional conduct in the practice of pharmacy;

(3) Addicted to or abusing liquor or drugs or impaired physically or mentally to such a degree as to render him unfit to practice pharmacy;

(4) Has been convicted of a misdemeanor related to, or committed in, the practice of pharmacy;

(5) Guilty of willfully violating, conspiring to violate, attempting to violate, or aiding and abetting the violation of any of the provisions of sections 3715.52 to 3715.72 or Chapter 2925., 3719., or 4729. of the Revised Code;

(6) Guilty of permitting anyone other than a pharmacist or pharmacy intern to practice pharmacy;

(7) Guilty of knowingly lending his name to an illegal practitioner of pharmacy or having professional connection with an illegal practitioner of pharmacy; or

(8) Guilty of dividing or agreeing to divide remuneration made in the practice of pharmacy with any other

individual, including, but not limited to, a practitioner or any owner, manager, or employee of a health care facility, residential care facility, or nursing home.

(B) Any individual whose identification card is revoked, suspended, or refused, shall return his identification card and certificate of registration to the offices of the state board of pharmacy within ten days after receipt of notice of such action.

(C) As used in this section:
"Unprofessional conduct in the practice of pharmacy" includes any of the following:

(1) Advertising or displaying signs that promote dangerous drugs to the public in a manner that is false or misleading;

(2) The sale of any drug for which a prescription from a practitioner is required, without having received a prescription for the drug;

(3) Willfully and knowingly filling prescriptions or selling drugs for false or forged prescriptions;

(4) Willfully and knowingly failing to maintain complete and accurate records of all controlled substances received or dispensed in compliance with federal laws and regulations and state laws and rules;

(5) Obtaining any remuneration by fraud, misrepresentation, or deception;

(6) Obtaining or attempting to obtain a license issued under Chapter 3715. or 4729. of the Revised Code from the state board of pharmacy by fraud, misrepresentation, or deception;

(7) Waiving the payment of all or any part of a deductible or copayment that an individual, pursuant to a health insurance or health care policy, contract, or plan that covers pharmaceutical services, would otherwise be required to pay for the services if the waiver is used as an enticement to a patient or group of patients to receive health care services from that provider.

(8) Advertising that a pharmacy, pharmacist, or pharmacist intern will waive the payment of all or any part of a deductible or copayment that an individual, pursuant to a health insurance or health care policy, contract, or plan that covers pharmaceutical services, would otherwise be required to pay for the services.

(D) Notwithstanding divisions (C)(7) and (8) of this section, sanctions shall not be imposed against any licensee who waives deductibles and copayments:

(1) In compliance with the health benefit plan that expressly allows such a practice. Waiver of the deductibles or copays shall be made only with the full knowledge and consent of the plan purchaser, payer, and third-party administrator. Such consent shall be made available to the board upon request.

(2) For professional services rendered to any other person licensed pursuant to this chapter to the extent allowed by this chapter and the rules of the board.

HISTORY: GC § 1307; 99 v 505, § 71; 103 v 487; 107 v 541; 120 v 358 (381), § 2; Bureau of Code Revision, 10-1-53; 127 v 162; 128 v 867 (Eff 10-19-59); 129 v 582 (918) (Eff 1-10-61); 132 v S 70 (Eff 9-14-67); 133 v H 1 (Eff 3-18-69); 134 v S 141 (Eff 12-31-71); 136 v H 300 (Eff 7-1-76); 140 v H 208 (Eff 9-20-84); 145 v S 279 (Eff 10-20-94); 146 v H 117. Eff 9-29-95.

The effective date is set by section 197 of HB 117.

§ 4729.25 Board shall enforce pharmacy laws.

(A) The state board of pharmacy shall enforce, or cause to be enforced, this chapter. If it has information that such sections have been violated, it shall investigate the matter, and take such action as it considers appropriate in accordance with its rules made and published pursuant to section 4729.26 of the Revised Code.

(B) Nothing in this chapter shall be construed to require the state board of pharmacy to enforce minor violations of this chapter if the board determines that the public interest is adequately served by a notice or warning to the alleged offender.

HISTORY: GC § 1313; 99 v 508, § 82; 103 v 304 (340); 107 v 148; 122 v 70; Bureau of Code Revision, 10-1-53; 130 v 1141 (Eff 10-14-63); 134 v S 141 (Eff 12-31-71); 140 v H 208. Eff 9-20-84.

§ 4729.26 Rules and regulations for enforcement; publication.

The state board of pharmacy is empowered to make such rules and regulations, subject to and in accordance with sections 119.01 to 119.13, inclusive, of the Revised Code, not inconsistent with the law, pertaining to the practice of pharmacy as may be necessary to carry out the purpose of and enforce sections 4729.01 to 4729.37, inclusive, of the Revised Code. Such rules and regulations shall be published and distributed by the board to each of its licensees.

HISTORY: GC § 12705-1; 121 v 681; Bureau of Code Revision, 10-1-53; 134 v S 141. Eff 12-31-71.

[§ 4729.26.1] § 4729.261 Rules regulating publication of dangerous drugs' price information.

The state board of pharmacy pursuant to section 4729.26 of the Revised Code may adopt rules regulating the publication of price information pertaining to dangerous drugs. Any rules adopted by the board pursuant to this section shall include, but not be limited to:

(A) Standards on the physical dimensions of the required books, loose-leaf notebooks, or similar compilation devices or leaflets;

(B) Lists of those dangerous drugs to be included on the required books, loose-leaf notebooks, or similar compilation devices or leaflets;

(C) A requirement that books, loose-leaf notebooks, or similar compilation devices or leaflets explicitly include such language as "our prices" that indicates that disclosed prices are uniquely those of the retail seller;

(D) A schedule for updating and maintaining as current the required books, loose-leaf notebooks, or similar compilation devices or leaflets.

HISTORY: 136 v H 912. Eff 10-1-76.

[§ 4729.26.2] § 4729.262 List of widely used dangerous drugs prepared.

The state board of pharmacy may annually prepare a poster displaying a list of the one hundred most widely used dangerous drugs. If the board prepares such a poster, it shall make the posters available without charge to any pharmacy in the state that requests them.

HISTORY: 136 v H 912. Eff 10-1-76.

[PROHIBITIONS]

§ 4729.27 Pharmacy must be conducted by legally registered pharmacist.

A person not a registered pharmacist, who owns, manages, or conducts a pharmacy as defined in section 4729.02 of the Revised Code, shall have in his employ, in full and actual charge of such pharmacy, a pharmacist registered under the laws of this state. Any registered pharmacist, who owns, manages, or conducts a pharmacy shall be personally in full and actual charge of such pharmacy, or shall have in his employ in full and actual charge of such pharmacy, a pharmacist registered under the laws of this state.

HISTORY: GC § 12705; 99 v 507, §§ 77, 78; 102 v 116; 108 v Pt II 1233; 121 v 681; Bureau of Code Revision, 10-1-53; 134 v S 141. Eff 12-31-71.

§ 4729.28 Unlawful selling of drugs.

No person who is not a registered pharmacist or a pharmacy intern under the personal supervision of a registered pharmacist shall compound, dispense, or sell drugs, dangerous drugs, and poisons.

HISTORY: GC § 12706; 99 v 507, §§ 77, 78; 108 v Pt II 1233; 121 v 681; Bureau of Code Revision, 10-1-53; 134 v S 141. Eff 12-31-71.

§ 4729.29 Exceptions to certain provisions.

(A) As used in this section:
(1) "Dentist" means a person licensed under Chapter 4715. of the Revised Code to practice dentistry.
(2) "Optometrist" means a person who is licensed to practice optometry and holds a valid therapeutic pharmaceutical agents certificate issued under Chapter 4725. of the Revised Code.
(3) "Physician" means a person holding a valid certificate issued under Chapter 4731. of the Revised Code authorizing the person to practice medicine and surgery, osteopathic medicine and surgery, or podiatry.
(4) "Veterinarian" means a person licensed under Chapter 4741. of the Revised Code to practice veterinarian medicine.
(5) "Advanced practice nurse" means an individual approved under section 4723.56 of the Revised Code to prescribe drugs and therapeutic devices.

(B) Divisions (A) and (B) of section 4729.02 and sections 4729.26, 4729.27, and 4729.28 of the Revised Code do not do either of the following:

(1) Apply to a dentist, optometrist, physician, veterinarian, or advanced practice nurse; prevent dentists, optometrists, physicians, or veterinarians from personally supplying their patients with such drugs as to the dentist, optometrist, physician, or veterinarian seem proper; or prevent an advanced practice nurse from personally supplying drugs and therapeutic devices in accordance with section 4723.561 [4723.56.1] of the Revised Code.

(2) Apply to the sale of oxygen, peritoneal dialysis solutions, or the sale of proprietary drugs or medicines by a retail dealer, in original packages when labeled as required by the "Federal Food, Drug, and Cosmetic Act," 52 Stat. 1040 (1938), 21 U.S.C.A. 301, as amended.

Nothing in this chapter prohibits a person who is certified to administer topical ocular pharmaceutical agents under Chapter 4725. of the Revised Code from purchasing, possessing, or administering topical ocular pharmaceutical agents in accordance with Chapter 4725. of the Revised Code.

HISTORY: GC § 12707; 99 v 507, § 79; 118 v 682; 121 v 681; Bureau of Code Revision, 10-1-53; 134 v S 141 (Eff 12-31-71); 140 v S 187 (Eff 6-14-84); 145 v H 391 (Eff 7-21-94); 146 v H 595 (Eff 10-16-96); 147 v H 215. Eff 6-30-97.

§ 4729.30 Certain preceding sections do not prohibit sale of Paris green.

Sections 4729.27 and 4729.28 of the Revised Code shall not prohibit a person from selling Paris green and other materials or compounds used exclusively for spraying and disinfecting when put up in bottles or boxes, bearing the name of a registered pharmacist or wholesale dealer, and labeled as required by section 3719.33 of the Revised Code or apply to or interfere with the exclusively wholesale business of a dealer.

HISTORY: GC § 12708; 99 v 507, § 79; 108 v PtI 427; Bureau of Code Revision. Eff 10-1-53.

§ 4729.31 Exceptions.

Sections 4729.27 and 4729.28 of the Revised Code shall not apply to, interfere with, or prohibit any person, firm, or corporation from selling completely denatured alcohol or wood alcohol.

HISTORY: GC § 12708-1; 110 v 294; Bureau of Code Revision. Eff 10-1-53.

§ 4729.32 Requirements for sale of denatured or wood alcohol in five gallon lots or more.

No person shall have in his possession, or dispense

or sell packages or containers of completely denatured alcohol or wood alcohol containing five wine gallons or more without having marked or stenciled thereon the name and address of the seller, the degree of proof of such alcohol, the formula number, and, in letters of not less than one inch in height, the words, "Completely Denatured Alcohol" or "Wood Alcohol," as the case may be, and the names of two or more antidotes for the same. This section, and sections 4729.33 and 3719.33 of the Revised Code shall not interfere with the transfer of such alcohol from storage tanks to other packages or containers, nor require the placing of such mark or stencil upon transportation tanks, nor the registration or placing of mark or stencil upon fuel tanks, automobile radiators, or similar containers for the final use or consumption of such alcohol and from which no further distribution thereof is made.

HISTORY: GC § 12708-2; 110 v 294; Bureau of Code Revision. Eff 10-1-53.

§ 4729.33 Requirements for sale of denatured or wood alcohol in less than five gallon lots.

No person shall dispense or sell completely denatured alcohol or wood alcohol in packages containing less than five wine gallons without having affixed thereto a label on which is printed or stenciled in plain, legible, red letters of equal prominence on a white background the words, "Completely Denatured Alcohol" or "Wood Alcohol," as the case may be, and in addition on the same label in red ink, under the skull and crossbones symbol, the word "POISON" together with the following statement: "Completely denatured alcohol, or wood alcohol is a violent poison. It cannot be applied externally to human or animal tissue without serious injurious results. It cannot be taken internally without inducing blindness and general physical decay ultimately resulting in death," and without having stamped, stenciled, or printed upon such label the name and address of the seller, the degree of proof, and the formula number thereof. Neither the word "pure" nor the single word "alcohol" alone shall appear on any label of completely denatured alcohol or wood alcohol.

HISTORY: GC § 12708-3; 110 v 294; Bureau of Code Revision. Eff 10-1-53.

§ 4729.34 Advertising.

No person shall dispense, sell, or offer for sale completely denatured alcohol or wood alcohol, or shall display a sign or use a label or advertise such alcohol having the word "pure" or the single word "alcohol" alone thereon, or shall fail to state the degree of proof of such alcohol, or to have the letters displaying or advertising "Completely Denatured Alcohol" or "Wood Alcohol" plain, legible, and of equal prominence.

HISTORY: GC § 12708-4; 110 v 294; Bureau of Code Revision. Eff 10-1-53.

§ 4729.35 Violation of drug laws as public nuisance.

The violation by a pharmacist or other person of any laws of Ohio or of the United States of America or of any rule of the board of pharmacy controlling the distribution of a drug of abuse as defined in section 3719.011 [3719.01.1] of the Revised Code or the commission of any act set forth in division (A) of section 4729.16 of the Revised Code, is hereby declared to be inimical, harmful, and adverse to the public welfare of the citizens of Ohio and to constitute a public nuisance. The attorney general, the prosecuting attorney of any county in which the offense was committed or in which the person committing the offense resides, or the state board of pharmacy may maintain an action in the name of the state to enjoin such person from engaging in such violation. Any action under this section shall be brought in the common pleas court of the county where the offense occurred or the county where the alleged offender resides.

HISTORY: 134 v S 141 (Eff 12-31-71); 134 v H 511 (Eff 1-1-74); 135 v H 716 (Eff 1-1-74); 140 v H 208. Eff 9-20-84.

Not analogous to former RC § 4729.35 [GC § 12709; 99 v 507; Bureau of Code Revision, 10-1-53], repealed 134 v S 141, § 2, eff 12-31-71.

This section was inadvertently repealed by H 511 (134 v —). This section shall be construed as a continuation of existing law.

§ 4729.36 Advertising prohibitions.

(A) No place except a pharmacy shall display any sign or advertise in any fashion, using the words "pharmacy," "drugs," "drug store," "drug store supplies," "pharmacist," "druggist," "pharmaceutical chemist," "apothecary," "drug sundries," "medicine," or any of these words or their equivalent, in any manner.

(B) A pharmacy or pharmacist making retail sales may advertise by name or therapeutic class the availability for sale or dispensing of any dangerous drug provided such advertising includes price information as defined in division (N) of section 4729.02 of the Revised Code.

HISTORY: 130 v 1141 (Eff 10-7-63); 134 v S 141 (Eff 12-31-71); 136 v H 912 (Eff 10-1-76); 137 v H 1 (Eff 8-26-77); 140 v H 208. Eff 9-20-84.

[§ 4729.36.1] § 4729.361 Retail seller to disclose price information.

(A) A retail seller of dangerous drugs shall disclose price information regarding dangerous drugs to any person requesting such information.

(B) Pursuant to division (A) of this section, a retail seller of dangerous drugs shall disclose price information in the following ways:

(1) By means of verbal disclosure on the premises of the retail seller to all persons requesting such information;

(2) By means of telephone to any person having a valid prescription, who identifies himself and requests such information.

(C) Price disclosure shall not be required for those schedule II controlled substances where lives or property could be endangered by such disclosure.

HISTORY: 136 v H 912. Eff 10-1-76.

§ 4729.37 Filling prescriptions; records.

A copy of an original prescription may only be filled in accordance with the rules and regulations adopted by the state board of pharmacy.

Prescriptions received by word of mouth, telephone, telegraph, or other means of communication shall be recorded in writing by the pharmacist and the record so made by the pharmacist shall constitute the original prescription to be filled by the pharmacist. All prescriptions shall be preserved on file at the pharmacy for a period of three years, subject to inspection by the proper officers of the law.

HISTORY: 130 v 1142 (Eff 10-7-63); 134 v S 141. Eff 12-31-71.

§ 4729.38 Generically equivalent drugs.

(A) Unless instructed otherwise by the person receiving the drug pursuant to the prescription, a pharmacist filling a prescription for a drug prescribed by its brand name may select a generically equivalent drug, as defined in section 3715.01 of the Revised Code, subject to the following conditions:

(1) The pharmacist shall not select a generically equivalent drug if the prescriber handwrites "dispense as written," or "D.A.W.," on the written prescription, or, when ordering a prescription orally, the prescriber specifies that the prescribed drug is medically necessary. These designations shall not be preprinted or stamped on the prescription. Division (A)(1) of this section does not preclude a reminder of the procedure required to prohibit the selection of a generically equivalent drug from being preprinted on the prescription.

(2) The pharmacist shall not select a generically equivalent drug unless its price to the purchaser is less than the price of the prescribed drug, and shall pass on as a savings to the purchaser, other than the state medical assistance program, the full amount of the retail price difference between the prescribed brand name drug and the generically equivalent drug. The amount paid for the generic drug under the state medical assistance program shall be as provided by federal regulation.

(3) The pharmacist, or the pharmacist's agent, assistant, or employee shall inform the person receiving the drug pursuant to the prescription of the selection of a lower cost generically equivalent drug, of the price difference between the brand name drug and the generically equivalent drug, and of the person's right to refuse the drug selected. Division (A)(3) of this section does not apply to any:

(a) Prescription that is billed to any agency, division, or department of this state which will reimburse the pharmacy;

(b) Prescriptions for patients of a hospital, nursing home, or similar patient care facility.

(B) Unless the prescriber instructs otherwise, the label for every drug dispensed shall include the drug's brand name, if any, or its generic name and the name of the distributor, using abbreviations if necessary. A pharmacist shall indicate on the container or its label the notation "generic substitution made" when dispensing at retail a generically equivalent drug for the brand name drug prescribed, and shall verbally notify the recipient that a generic substitution has been made. This requirement shall be in addition to all other labeling requirements of Chapter 3715. of the Revised Code.

(C) A pharmacist who selects a generically equivalent drug pursuant to this section assumes no greater liability for selecting the dispensed drug than would be incurred in filling a prescription for a drug prescribed by its brand name.

(D) The failure of a prescriber to restrict a prescription by specifying "dispense as written," or "D.A.W.," pursuant to division (A)(1) of this section shall not constitute evidence of the prescriber's negligence unless the prescriber had reasonable cause to believe that the health condition of the patient for whom the drug was intended warranted the prescription of a specific brand name drug and no other. No licensed prescriber shall be liable for civil damages or in any criminal prosecution arising from the interchange of a generically equivalent drug for a prescribed brand name drug by a pharmacist, unless the prescribed brand name drug would have reasonably caused the same loss, damage, injury, or death.

(E) Each terminal distributor shall prepare a list of generic and brand name drug products which may be selected as the drug product of choice. In compiling the list of generic and brand name drug products, the distributor shall rely on the drug product research, testing, information, and lists compiled by other pharmacies, states, the United States department of health and human services, and any other source which the distributor considers reliable. The list shall be available for review in the pharmacy on request of the public, the state board of pharmacy, or any practitioner. This list shall be revised following each addition, deletion, or modification. No drug interchange shall be made by a pharmacist unless the drug to be interchanged is on this list.

HISTORY: 139 v H 694. Eff 11-15-81.

Analogous to former RC § 4729.38 (137 v S 45), repealed 139 v H 694, eff 11-15-81.

[§ 4729.38.1] § 4729.381 Limitation on civil or criminal liability.

No licensed pharmacist shall be liable for civil damages or in any criminal prosecution arising from the dispensing of a drug based upon a formulary established by a practitioner in a hospital, health maintenance organization, or long-term care facility and requiring the pharmacist to dispense the particular drug.

HISTORY: 140 v H 208. Eff 9-20-84.

[DANGEROUS DRUGS]

§ 4729.51 Persons who may sell, purchase, distribute, or deliver dangerous drugs.

(A) No person other than a registered wholesale distributor of dangerous drugs shall possess for sale, sell, distribute, or deliver, at wholesale, dangerous drugs, except as follows:

(1) A pharmacist who is a licensed terminal distributor of dangerous drugs or who is employed by a licensed terminal distributor of dangerous drugs may make occasional sales of dangerous drugs at wholesale;

(2) A licensed terminal distributor of dangerous drugs having more than one establishment or place may transfer or deliver dangerous drugs from one establishment or place for which a license has been issued to the terminal distributor to another establishment or place for which a license has been issued to the terminal distributor if the license issued for each establishment or place is in effect at the time of the transfer or delivery.

(B)(1) No registered wholesale distributor of dangerous drugs shall possess for sale, or sell, at wholesale, dangerous drugs to any person other than the following:

(a) A practitioner;

(b) A registered wholesale distributor of dangerous drugs;

(c) A manufacturer of dangerous drugs;

(d) A licensed terminal distributor of dangerous drugs, subject to division (B)(2) of this section;

(e) Carriers or warehousers for the purpose of carriage or storage;

(f) Terminal or wholesale distributors of dangerous drugs who are not engaged in the sale of dangerous drugs within this state;

(g) An optometrist licensed under Chapter 4725. of the Revised Code who is certified to administer topical ocular pharmaceutical agents under that chapter for the purposes authorized by that chapter;

(h) An individual who holds a current license, certificate, or registration issued under Title 47 of the Revised Code and has been certified to conduct diabetes education by a national certifying body specified in rules adopted by the state board of pharmacy under section 4729.68 of the Revised Code, but only with respect to insulin that will be used for the purpose of diabetes education and only if diabetes education is within the individual's scope of practice under statutes and rules regulating the individual's profession.

(2) No registered wholesale distributor of dangerous drugs shall possess dangerous drugs for sale at wholesale, or sell such drugs at wholesale, to a licensed terminal distributor of dangerous drugs, except to:

(a) A terminal distributor who has a category I license, only dangerous drugs described in category I, as defined in division (A)(1) of section 4729.54 of the Revised Code;

(b) A terminal distributor who has a category II license, only dangerous drugs described in category I and category II, as defined in divisions (A)(1) and (2) of section 4729.54 of the Revised Code;

(c) A terminal distributor who has a category III license, dangerous drugs described in category I, category II, and category III, as defined in divisions (A)(1), (2), and (3) of section 4729.54 of the Revised Code;

(d) A terminal distributor who has a limited category I, II, or III license, only the dangerous drugs specified in the certificate furnished by the terminal distributor in accordance with section 4729.60 of the Revised Code.

(C)(1) Except as provided in division (C)(4) of this section, no person shall sell, at retail, dangerous drugs.

(2) Except as provided in division (C)(4) of this section, no person shall possess for sale, at retail, dangerous drugs.

(3) Except as provided in division (C)(4) of this section, no person shall possess dangerous drugs.

(4) Divisions (C)(1), (2), and (3) of this section do not apply to a registered wholesale distributor of dangerous drugs, a licensed terminal distributor of dangerous drugs, a practitioner, or a person who possesses, or possesses for sale or sells, at retail, a dangerous drug in accordance with Chapters 3719., 4715., 4729., 4731., and 4741. or section 4723.56 of the Revised Code.

Divisions (C)(1), (2), and (3) of this section do not apply to an individual who holds a current license, certificate, or registration issued under Title 47 of the Revised Code and has been certified to conduct diabetes education by a national certifying body specified in rules adopted by the state board of pharmacy under section 4729.68 of the Revised Code, but only to the extent that the individual possesses insulin or personally supplies insulin solely for the purpose of diabetes education and only if diabetes education is within the individual's scope of practice under statutes and rules regulating the individual's profession.

(D) No licensed terminal distributor of dangerous drugs shall purchase for the purpose of resale dangerous drugs from any person other than a registered wholesale distributor of dangerous drugs, except as follows:

(1) A licensed terminal distributor of dangerous drugs may make occasional purchases of dangerous drugs for resale from a pharmacist who is a licensed terminal distributor of dangerous drugs or who is employed by a licensed terminal distributor of dangerous drugs;

(2) A licensed terminal distributor of dangerous drugs having more than one establishment or place may transfer or receive dangerous drugs from one establishment or place for which a license has been issued to the

terminal distributor to another establishment or place for which a license has been issued to the terminal distributor if the license issued for each establishment or place is in effect at the time of the transfer or receipt.

(E) No licensed terminal distributor of dangerous drugs shall engage in the sale or other distribution of dangerous drugs at retail or maintain possession, custody, or control of dangerous drugs for any purpose other than the distributor's personal use or consumption, at any establishment or place other than that or those described in the license issued by the board of pharmacy to such terminal distributor.

(F) Nothing in this section shall do either of the following:

(1) Require a person engaged solely in the sale or other distribution, at wholesale, of drugs and supplies for veterinary use only, to be registered under sections 4729.50 to 4729.66 of the Revised Code;

(2) Prohibit the purchase or sale, at wholesale, of drugs and supplies for veterinary use only by a person engaged solely in the distribution of drugs and supplies for veterinary use only.

(G) Nothing in this section shall be construed to interfere with the performance of official duties by any law enforcement official authorized by municipal, county, state, or federal law to collect samples of any drug, regardless of its nature or in whose possession it may be.

HISTORY: 129 v 1376 (Eff 1-1-62); 133 v H 90 (Eff 11-19-69); 139 v S 4 (Eff 10-1-82); 140 v S 187 (Eff 6-14-84); 145 v H 391 (Eff 7-21-94); 146 v S 246 (Eff 11-6-96); 147 v H 215. Eff 6-30-97.

§ 4729.52 Registration as wholesale distributor.

(A) A person desiring to be registered as a wholesale distributor of dangerous drugs shall file with the executive director of the board of pharmacy a verified application containing such information as the board requires of the applicant relative to the qualifications for a wholesale distributor of dangerous drugs set forth in section 4729.53 of the Revised Code and the rules adopted pursuant thereto. The board shall register as a wholesale distributor of dangerous drugs each person who has submitted an application therefor and has paid the required registration fee if the board determines that the applicant meets the qualifications for a wholesale distributor of dangerous drugs set forth in section 4729.53 of the Revised Code and the rules adopted pursuant thereto.

(B) The board may register and issue to a nonresident person a registration certificate as a wholesale distributor of dangerous drugs if the person possesses a current and valid wholesale distributor of dangerous drugs registration certificate or license issued by another state that has qualifications for licensure or registration comparable to the registration requirements in this state and pays the required registration fee.

(C) All registration certificates issued pursuant to this section are effective for a period of twelve months from the first day of July of each year. A registration certificate shall be renewed annually by the board for a like period, pursuant to this section and the standard renewal procedure of Chapter 4745. of the Revised Code. A person desiring to renew a registration certificate shall submit an application for renewal and pay the required renewal fee before the first day of July each year.

(D) Each registration certificate and its application shall describe not more than one establishment or place where the registrant or applicant may engage in the sale of dangerous drugs at wholesale. No registration certificate shall authorize or permit the wholesale distributor of dangerous drugs named therein to engage in the sale of drugs at wholesale or to maintain possession, custody, or control of dangerous drugs for any purpose other than for the registrant's own use and consumption at any establishment or place other than that described in the certificate.

(E)(1) The registration fee is one hundred fifty dollars and shall accompany each application for registration. The registration renewal fee is one hundred fifty dollars and shall accompany each renewal application.

(2) A registration certificate that has not been renewed in any year by the first day of August may be reinstated upon payment of the renewal fee and a penalty fee of fifty-five dollars.

Renewal fees assessed under divisions (E)(1) and (2) of this section shall not be returned if the applicant fails to qualify for renewal.

(F) The registration of any person as a wholesale distributor of dangerous drugs subjects the person and the person's agents and employees to the jurisdiction of the board and to the laws of this state for the purpose of the enforcement of this chapter and the rules of the board. However, the filing of an application for registration as a wholesale distributor of dangerous drugs by, or on behalf of, any person or the registration of any person as a wholesale distributor of dangerous drugs shall not, of itself, constitute evidence that the person is doing business within this state.

HISTORY: 129 v 1376 (Eff 1-1-62); 132 v S 70 (Eff 9-14-67); 132 v H 911 (Eff 6-11-68); 133 v H 742 (Eff 11-21-69); 139 v H 694 (Eff 11-15-81); 144 v H 298 (Eff 7-26-91); 144 v S 193 (Eff 7-1-92); 146 v H 117 (Eff 6-30-95); 147 v H 215. Eff 6-30-97.

§ 4729.53 Requirements for registration.

(A) The board of pharmacy shall not register any person as a wholesale distributor of dangerous drugs unless the applicant for registration furnishes satisfactory proof to the board of pharmacy that he meets all of the following:

(1) That if the applicant has been convicted of a violation of any federal, state, or local law relating to drug samples, wholesale or retail drug distribution, or distribution of controlled substances or of a felony, or if a federal, state, or local governmental entity has sus-

pended or revoked any current or prior license or registration of the applicant for the manufacture or sale of any dangerous drugs, including controlled substances, the applicant, to the satisfaction of the board, assures that he has in place adequate safeguards to prevent the recurrence of any such violations;

(2) The applicant's past experience in the manufacture or distribution of dangerous drugs, including controlled substances, is acceptable to the board.

(3) The applicant is equipped as to land, buildings, equipment, and personnel to properly carry on the business of a wholesale distributor of dangerous drugs, including providing adequate security for and proper storage conditions and handling for dangerous drugs, and is complying with the requirements under this chapter and the rules adopted pursuant thereto for maintaining and making available records to properly identified board officials and federal, state, and local law enforcement agencies.

(4) Personnel employed by the applicant have the appropriate education or experience, as determined by the board, to assume responsibility for positions related to compliance with this chapter and the rules adopted pursuant thereto.

(5) The applicant has designated the name and address of a person to whom communications from the board may be directed and upon whom the notices and citations provided for in section 4729.56 of the Revised Code may be served.

(6) Adequate safeguards are assured to prevent the sale of dangerous drugs to any person other than those named in division (B) of section 4729.51 of the Revised Code.

(7) Any other requirement or qualification the board, by rule adopted in accordance with Chapter 119. of the Revised Code, considers relevant to and consistent with the public safety and health.

(B) The board may refuse to register or renew the registration certificate of any person if the board determines that the granting of the registration certificate or its renewal is not in the public interest.

HISTORY: 129 v 1376 (Eff 1-1-62); 136 v H 300 (Eff 7-1-76); 144 v S 193. Eff 7-1-92.

§ 4729.54 Licensing of terminal distributors.

(A) As used in this section:

(1) "Category I" means single-dose injections of intravenous fluids, including saline, Ringer's lactate, five per cent dextrose and distilled water, and other intravenous fluids or parenteral solutions included in this category by rule of the board of pharmacy, that have a volume of one hundred milliliters or more and that contain no added substances, or single-dose injections of epinephrine to be administered pursuant to sections 4765.38 and 4765.39 of the Revised Code.

(2) "Category II" means any dangerous drug that is not included in category I or III.

(3) "Category III" means any controlled substance that is contained in schedule I, II, III, IV, or V.

(4) "Emergency medical service organization" has the same meaning as in section 4765.01 of the Revised Code.

(5) "Person" includes an emergency medical service organization.

(6) "Schedule I, schedule II, schedule III, schedule IV, and schedule V" mean controlled substance schedules I, II, III, IV, and V, respectively, as established pursuant to section 3719.41 of the Revised Code and as amended.

(B) A person who desires to be licensed as a terminal distributor of dangerous drugs shall file with the executive director of the board of pharmacy a verified application that contains the following:

(1) Information that the board requires relative to the qualifications of a terminal distributor of dangerous drugs set forth in section 4729.55 of the Revised Code;

(2) A statement that the person wishes to be licensed as a category I, category II, category III, limited category I, limited category II, or limited category III terminal distributor of dangerous drugs;

(3) If the person wishes to be licensed as a limited category I, limited category II, or limited category III terminal distributor of dangerous drugs, a notarized list of the dangerous drugs that the person wishes to possess, have custody or control of, and distribute, which list shall also specify the purpose for which those drugs will be used and their source;

(4) If the person is an emergency medical service organization, the information that is specified in division (C)(1) of this section;

(5) Except for an emergency medical service organization, the identity of the one establishment or place at which the person intends to engage in the sale or other distribution of dangerous drugs at retail, and maintain possession, custody, or control of dangerous drugs for purposes other than the person's own use or consumption.

(C)(1) An emergency medical service organization that wishes to be licensed as a terminal distributor of dangerous drugs shall list in its application for licensure the following additional information:

(a) The units under its control that the organization determines will possess dangerous drugs for the purpose of administering emergency medical services in accordance with Chapter 4765. of the Revised Code;

(b) With respect to each such unit, whether the dangerous drugs that the organization determines the unit will possess are in category I, II, or III.

(2) An emergency medical service organization that is licensed as a terminal distributor of dangerous drugs shall file a new application for such licensure if there is any change in the number, or location of, any of its units or any change in the category of the dangerous drugs that any unit will possess.

(3) A unit listed in an application for licensure pursu-

ant to division (C)(1) of this section may obtain the dangerous drugs it is authorized to possess from its emergency medical service organization or, on a replacement basis, from a hospital pharmacy. If units will obtain dangerous drugs from a hospital pharmacy, the organization shall file, and maintain in current form, the following items with the pharmacist who is responsible for the hospital's terminal distributor of dangerous drugs license:

(a) A copy of its standing orders or protocol;

(b) A list of the personnel employed or used by the organization to provide emergency medical services in accordance with Chapter 4765. of the Revised Code, who are authorized to possess the drugs, which list also shall indicate the personnel who are authorized to administer the drugs.

(D) Each emergency medical service organization that applies for a terminal distributor of dangerous drugs license shall submit with its application the following:

(1) A notarized copy of its standing orders or protocol, which orders or protocol shall be signed by a physician and specify the dangerous drugs that its units may carry, expressed in standard dose units;

(2) A list of the personnel employed or used by the organization to provide emergency medical services in accordance with Chapter 4765. of the Revised Code.

An emergency medical service organization that is licensed as a terminal distributor shall notify the board immediately of any changes in its standing orders or protocol.

(E) There shall be six categories of terminal distributor of dangerous drugs licenses, which categories shall be as follows:

(1) Category I license. A person who obtains this license may possess, have custody or control of, and distribute only the dangerous drugs described in category I.

(2) Limited category I license. A person who obtains this license may possess, have custody or control of, and distribute only the dangerous drugs described in category I that were listed in the application for licensure.

(3) Category II license. A person who obtains this license may possess, have custody or control of, and distribute only the dangerous drugs described in category I and category II.

(4) Limited category II license. A person who obtains this license may possess, have custody or control of, and distribute only the dangerous drugs described in category I or category II that were listed in the application for licensure.

(5) Category III license. A person who obtains this license may possess, have custody or control of, and distribute the dangerous drugs described in category I, category II, and category III.

(6) Limited category III license. A person who obtains this license may possess, have custody or control of, and distribute only the dangerous drugs described in category I, category II, or category III that were listed in the application for licensure.

(F) Except for an application made on behalf of an animal shelter, if an applicant for licensure as a limited category I, II, or III terminal distributor of dangerous drugs intends to administer dangerous drugs to a person or animal, the applicant shall submit, with the application, a notarized copy of its protocol or standing orders, which protocol or orders shall be signed by a practitioner, specify the dangerous drugs to be administered, and list personnel who are authorized to administer the dangerous drugs in accordance with federal law or the law of this state. An application made on behalf of an animal shelter shall include a notarized list of the dangerous drugs to be administered to animals and the personnel who are authorized to administer the drugs to animals in accordance with section 4729.532 [4729.53.2] of the Revised Code. After obtaining a terminal distributor license, a licensee shall notify the board immediately of any changes in its protocol or standing orders, or in such personnel.

(G) Each applicant for licensure as a terminal distributor of dangerous drugs shall submit, with the application, a license fee determined as follows:

(1) For a category I or limited category I license, forty-five dollars;

(2) For a category II or limited category II license, one hundred twelve dollars and fifty cents;

(3) For a category III or limited category III license, one hundred fifty dollars.

Fees assessed under divisions (G)(1) to (3) of this section shall not be returned if the applicant fails to qualify for registration.

(H)(1) The board shall issue a terminal distributor of dangerous drugs license to each person who submits an application for such licensure in accordance with this section, pays the required license fee, is determined by the board to meet the requirements set forth in section 4729.55 of the Revised Code, and satisfies any other applicable requirements of this section.

(2) The license of a person other than an emergency medical service organization shall describe the one establishment or place at which the licensee may engage in the sale or other distribution of dangerous drugs at retail and maintain possession, custody, or control of dangerous drugs for purposes other than the licensee's own use or consumption. The one establishment or place shall be that which is described in the application for licensure.

No such license shall authorize or permit the terminal distributor of dangerous drugs named in it to engage in the sale or other distribution of dangerous drugs at retail or to maintain possession, custody, or control of dangerous drugs for any purpose other than the distributor's own use or consumption, at any establishment or place other than that described in the license, except that an agent or employee of an animal shelter may possess and use dangerous drugs in the course of business as provided in division (D) of section 4729.532 [4729.53.2] of the Revised Code.

(3) The license of an emergency medical service organization shall cover and describe all the units of the organization listed in its application for licensure.

(4) The license of every terminal distributor of dangerous drugs shall indicate, on its face, the category of licensure. If the license is a limited category I, II, or III license, it shall specify, and shall authorize the licensee to possess, have custody or control of, and distribute only, the dangerous drugs that were listed in the application for licensure.

(I) All licenses issued pursuant to this section shall be effective for a period of twelve months from the first day of January of each year. A license shall be renewed by the board for a like period, annually, according to the provisions of this section, and the standard renewal procedure of Chapter 4745. of the Revised Code. A person who desires to renew a license shall submit an application for renewal and pay the required fee on or before the thirty-first day of December each year. The fee required for the renewal of a license shall be the same as the fee paid for the license being renewed, and shall accompany the application for renewal.

A license that has not been renewed during December in any year and by the first day of February of the following year may be reinstated only upon payment of the required renewal fee and a penalty fee of fifty-five dollars.

(J)(1) No emergency medical service organization that is licensed as a terminal distributor of dangerous drugs shall fail to comply with division (C)(2) or (3) of this section.

(2) No emergency medical service organization that is licensed as a terminal distributor of dangerous drugs shall fail to comply with division (D) of this section.

(3) No licensed terminal distributor of dangerous drugs shall possess, have custody or control of, or distribute dangerous drugs that the terminal distributor is not entitled to possess, have custody or control of, or distribute by virtue of its category of licensure.

(4) No licensee that is required by division (F) of this section to notify the board of changes in its protocol or standing orders, or in personnel, shall fail to comply with that division.

HISTORY: 129 v 1376 (Eff 1-1-62); 132 v S 70 (Eff 9-14-67); 132 v H 911 (Eff 6-11-68); 133 v H 742 (Eff 11-21-69); 139 v H 694 (Eff 11-15-81); 139 v S 4 (Eff 10-1-82); 140 v S 19 (Eff 9-18-84); 144 v H 298 (Eff 7-26-91); 144 v S 98 (Eff 11-12-92); 145 v H 88 (Eff 6-29-94); 146 v H 117 (Eff 6-30-95); 147 v H 215. Eff 6-30-97.

§ 4729.55 Requirements for issuance of license.

(A) As used in this section:

(1) "Dentist" means a person licensed under Chapter 4715. of the Revised Code to practice dentistry.

(2) "Optometrist" means a person who is licensed to practice optometry and holds a valid therapeutic pharmaceutical agents certificate issued under Chapter 4725. of the Revised Code.

(3) "Physician" means a person holding a valid certificate issued under Chapter 4731. of the Revised Code authorizing the person to practice medicine and surgery, osteopathic medicine and surgery, or podiatry.

(4) "Veterinarian" means a person licensed under Chapter 4741. of the Revised Code to practice veterinary medicine.

(5) "Advanced practice nurse" means an individual approved under section 4723.56 of the Revised Code to prescribe drugs and therapeutic devices.

(B) No license shall be issued to an applicant for licensure as a terminal distributor of dangerous drugs unless the applicant has furnished satisfactory proof to the board of pharmacy that:

(1) The applicant is equipped as to land, buildings, and equipment to properly carry on the business of a terminal distributor of dangerous drugs within the category of licensure approved by the board.

(2) A pharmacist, dentist, optometrist, physician, veterinarian, advanced practice nurse, animal shelter licensed with the state board of pharmacy under section 4729.531 [4729.53.1] of the Revised Code, or a laboratory as defined in division (N) of section 3719.01 of the Revised Code shall maintain supervision and control over the possession and custody of dangerous drugs that may be acquired by or on behalf of the applicant.

(3) Adequate safeguards are assured to prevent the sale or other distribution of dangerous drugs by any person other than a pharmacist, dentist, optometrist, physician, veterinarian, or advanced practice nurse.

(4) If the applicant, or any agent or employee of the applicant, has been found guilty of violating section 4729.51 of the Revised Code, the "Federal Food, Drug and Cosmetic Act," 52 Stat. 1040 (1938), 21 U.S.C.A. 301, the federal narcotic law, sections 3715.01 to 3715.72, Chapter 2925., 3719., or 4729. of the Revised Code, or any rule of the board, adequate safeguards are assured to prevent the recurrence of the violation.

(5) In the case of an applicant who is a food processor or retail seller of food, the applicant shall maintain supervision and control over the possession and custody of nitrous oxide.

(6) In the case of an applicant who is a retail seller of oxygen in original packages labeled as required by the "Federal Food, Drug, and Cosmetic Act," the applicant shall maintain supervision and control over the possession, custody, and retail sale of the oxygen.

(7) If the application is made on behalf of an animal shelter, that at least one of the agents or employees of the animal shelter is certified in compliance with section 4729.532 [4729.53.2] of the Revised Code.

(8) In the case of an applicant who is a retail seller of peritoneal dialysis solutions in original packages la-

beled as required by the "Federal Food, Drug, and Cosmetic Act," 52 Stat. 1040 (1938), 21 U.S.C.A. 301, the applicant shall maintain supervision and control over the possession, custody, and retail sale of the peritoneal dialysis solutions.

HISTORY: 129 v 1376 (Eff 1-1-62); 136 v H 300 (Eff 7-1-76); 139 v S 4 (Eff 10-1-82); 145 v H 88 (Eff 6-29-94); 145 v H 391 (Eff 7-21-94); 146 v H 595 (Eff 10-16-96); 147 v H 215. Eff 6-30-97.

§ 4729.56 Suspension, revocation or refusal to review registration of wholesale distributor.

(A) In accordance with Chapter 119. of the Revised Code, the board of pharmacy may suspend, revoke, or refuse to renew any registration certificate issued to a wholesale distributor of dangerous drugs pursuant to section 4729.52 of the Revised Code or may impose a monetary penalty or forfeiture not to exceed in severity any fine designated under the Revised Code for a similar offense or one thousand dollars if the acts committed are not classified as an offense by the Revised Code for any of the following causes:

(1) Making any false material statements in an application for registration as a wholesale distributor of dangerous drugs;

(2) Violating any federal, state, or local drug law; any provision of this chapter or Chapter 2925., 3715., or 3719. of the Revised Code; or any rule of the board;

(3) A conviction of a felony;

(4) Ceasing to satisfy the qualifications for registration under section 4729.53 of the Revised Code or the rules of the board.

(B) Upon the suspension or revocation of the registration certificate of any wholesale distributor of dangerous drugs, the distributor shall immediately surrender his registration certificate to the board.

(C) If the board suspends, revokes, or refuses to renew any registration certificate issued to a wholesale distributor of dangerous drugs and determines that there is clear and convincing evidence of a danger of immediate and serious harm to any person, the board may place under seal all dangerous drugs owned by or in the possession, custody, or control of the affected wholesale distributor of dangerous drugs. Except as provided in this division, the board shall not dispose of the dangerous drugs sealed under this division until the wholesale distributor of dangerous drugs exhausts all of his appeal rights under Chapter 119. of the Revised Code. The court involved in such an appeal may order the board, during the pendency of the appeal, to sell sealed dangerous drugs that are perishable. The board shall deposit the proceeds of the sale with the court.

HISTORY: 129 v 1376 (Eff 1-1-62); 139 v H 135 (Eff 10-6-81); 144 v S 193. Eff 7-1-92.

§ 4729.57 Suspension or revocation of registration of terminal distributor.

(A) The board of pharmacy may suspend, revoke, or refuse to renew any license issued to a terminal distributor of dangerous drugs pursuant to section 4729.54 of the Revised Code or may impose a monetary penalty or forfeiture not to exceed in severity any fine designated under the Revised Code for a similar offense or one thousand dollars if the acts committed have not been classified as an offense by the Revised Code, for any of the following causes:

(1) Making any false material statements in an application for a license as a terminal distributor of dangerous drugs;

(2) Violating any rule of the board;

(3) Violating any provision of this chapter;

(4) Violating any provision of the "Federal Food, Drug, and Cosmetic Act," 52 Stat. 1040 (1938), 21 U.S.C. 301, or Chapter 3715. of the Revised Code;

(5) Violating any provision of the federal narcotic law or Chapter 2925. or 3719. of the Revised Code;

(6) Falsely or fraudulently promoting to the public a dangerous drug, except that nothing in this division prohibits a terminal distributor of dangerous drugs from furnishing information concerning a dangerous drug to a practitioner or another licensed terminal distributor;

(7) Ceasing to satisfy the qualifications of a terminal distributor of dangerous drugs set forth in section 4729.55 of the Revised Code.

(B)(1) Upon the suspension or revocation of a license issued to a terminal distributor of dangerous drugs or the refusal by the board to renew such a license, the distributor shall immediately surrender his license to the board.

(2) The board may place under seal all dangerous drugs that are owned by or in the possession, custody, or control of a terminal distributor at the time his license is suspended or revoked or at the time the board refuses to renew his license. Except as otherwise provided in this division, dangerous drugs so sealed shall not be disposed of, until appeal rights under Chapter 119. of the Revised Code have expired or an appeal filed pursuant to that chapter has been determined.

The court involved in an appeal filed pursuant to Chapter 119. of the Revised Code may order the board, during the pendency of the appeal, to sell sealed dangerous drugs that are perishable. The proceeds of such a sale shall be deposited with that court.

HISTORY: 129 v 1376 (Eff 1-1-62); 130 v 1143 (Eff 1-23-63); 134 v S 141 (Eff 12-31-71); 136 v H 300 (Eff 7-1-76); 139 v H 135 (Eff 10-6-81); 139 v S 4. Eff 10-1-82.

§ 4729.58 Renewal of license or registration.

The board of pharmacy, within thirty days after receipt of an application filed in the form and manner set forth in section 4729.52 or 4729.54 of the Revised Code for the issuance of a new license or registration certificate or the renewal of a license or registration certificate previously issued, shall notify the applicant therefor whether or not such license or registration certificate will be issued or renewed. If the board determines that such license or registration certificate will not be issued or renewed, such notice to the applicant shall set forth the reason or reasons that such license or registration certificate will not be issued or renewed.

HISTORY: 129 v 1376. Eff 1-1-62.

§ 4729.59 Roster of registered licensees.

The secretary of the board of pharmacy shall maintain a register of the names, addresses, and the date of registration of those persons to whom a registration certificate has been issued pursuant to section 4729.52 of the Revised Code and those persons to whom a license has been issued pursuant to section 4729.54 of the Revised Code. Such register shall be the property of the board and shall be open for public examination and inspection at all reasonable times, as the board may direct.

The board shall publish or make available to registered wholesale distributors and licensed terminal distributors of dangerous drugs, annually, and at such other times and in such manner as the board shall by regulation prescribe, a roster setting forth the names and addresses of those persons who have been registered by the board pursuant to section 4729.52 of the Revised Code and those persons who have been licensed pursuant to section 4729.54 of the Revised Code, those persons whose licenses or registration certificates have been suspended, revoked, or surrendered, and those persons whose licenses or registration certificates have not been renewed.

A written statement signed and verified by the secretary of the board in which it is stated that after diligent search of the register no record or entry of the issuance of a license or registration certificate to a person is found is admissible in evidence and constitutes presumptive evidence of the fact that such person is not a licensed terminal distributor or is not a registered wholesale distributor of dangerous drugs.

HISTORY: 129 v 1376. Eff 1-1-62.

§ 4729.60 Certificates required for purchasing drugs.

(A) Before a registered wholesale distributor of dangerous drugs may sell dangerous drugs at wholesale to any person other than a practitioner, a registered wholesale distributor of dangerous drugs, a manufacturer of dangerous drugs, a carrier or a warehouseman but only for the purpose of carriage or storage, or a terminal distributor of dangerous drugs who is not engaged in the sale of dangerous drugs within this state, such wholesale distributor shall obtain from the purchaser and the purchaser shall furnish to the wholesale distributor a certificate indicating that the purchaser is a licensed terminal distributor of dangerous drugs. The certificate shall be in the form that the board of pharmacy shall prescribe by regulation, and shall set forth the name of the licensee, the number of the license, a description of the place or establishment or each place or establishment for which the license was issued, the category of licensure, and, if the license is a limited category I, II, or III license, the dangerous drugs that the licensee is authorized to possess, have custody or control of, and distribute.

If no certificate is obtained or furnished before such sale, it shall be presumed that such sale of dangerous drugs by the wholesale distributor is in violation of division (B) of section 4729.51 of the Revised Code and such purchase of dangerous drugs by the purchaser is in violation of division (C) of section 4729.51 of the Revised Code. If a registered wholesale distributor of dangerous drugs obtains or is furnished such a certificate from a terminal distributor of dangerous drugs and relies on such certificate in selling dangerous drugs at wholesale to such terminal distributor of dangerous drugs, such wholesale distributor of dangerous drugs shall be deemed not to have violated division (B) of section 4729.51 of the Revised Code in making such sale.

(B) Before a licensed terminal distributor of dangerous drugs may purchase dangerous drugs at wholesale, such terminal distributor shall obtain from the seller and the seller shall furnish to the terminal distributor the number of the seller's registration certificate to engage in the sale of dangerous drugs at wholesale.

If no registration number is obtained or furnished before such purchase, it shall be presumed that such purchase of dangerous drugs by the terminal distributor is in violation of division (D) of section 4729.51 of the Revised Code and such sale of dangerous drugs by the seller is in violation of division (A) of section 4729.51 of the Revised Code. If a licensed terminal distributor of dangerous drugs obtains or is furnished a registration number from a wholesale distributor of dangerous drugs and relies on such registration number in purchasing dangerous drugs at wholesale from such wholesale distributor of dangerous drugs, such terminal distributor shall be deemed not to have violated division (D) of section 4729.51 of the Revised Code in making such purchase.

HISTORY: 129 v 1376 (Eff 1-1-62); 139 v S 4. Eff 10-1-82.

§ 4729.61 Fraudulent certificates; prohibition.

(A) No person shall make or cause to be made, or furnish or cause to be furnished to a wholesale distributor of dangerous drugs, a false certificate required to be furnished to a wholesale distributor of dangerous drugs by section 4729.60 of the Revised Code for the purchase of dangerous drugs at wholesale.

(B) No person shall make or cause to be made a false registration certificate of a wholesale distributor of dangerous drugs or a false or fraudulent license of a terminal distributor of dangerous drugs.

HISTORY: 129 v 1376 (Eff 1-1-62); 136 v H 300 (Eff 7-1-76); 146 v S 2. Eff 7-1-96.

The effective date is set by section 6 of SB 2.

§ 4729.62 Surrender of license.

If a wholesale distributor of dangerous drugs who has been registered ceases to engage in the sale of dangerous drugs at wholesale, or if a terminal distributor of dangerous drugs to whom a license has been issued ceases to engage in the sale of dangerous drugs at retail, such terminal or wholesale distributor of dangerous drugs shall notify the board of pharmacy of such fact and shall surrender such license or registration certificate to the board; provided, that on dissolution of a partnership by death, the surviving partner may operate under a license or registration certificate issued to the partnership until expiration, revocation, or suspension of such license or registration certificate, and the heirs or legal representatives of deceased persons, and receivers and trustees in bankruptcy appointed by any competent authority, may operate under the license or registration certificate issued to the persons succeeded in possession by such heir, representative, receiver, or trustee in bankruptcy until expiration, revocation, or suspension of such license or registration certificate.

HISTORY: 129 v 1376. Eff 1-1-62.

§ 4729.63 Enforcement.

Except as provided in division (B) of section 4729.25 of the Revised Code, the state board of pharmacy shall enforce, or cause to be enforced, sections 4729.51 to 4729.62 of the Revised Code. If it has information that such sections have been violated it shall investigate the matter and upon probable cause appearing file a complaint in an appropriate court for prosecution of the offender.

The attorney general, prosecuting attorney, or city director of law to whom the board reports any violation of sections 4729.51 to 4729.62 of the Revised Code shall cause appropriate proceedings to be instituted in the proper court without delay and to be prosecuted in the manner provided by law.

HISTORY: 129 v 1376 (Eff 1-1-62); 137 v H 219 (Eff 11-1-77); 140 v H 208. Eff 9-20-84.

§ 4729.64 Injunctions.

In addition to the remedies provided and irrespective of whether or not there exists an adequate remedy at law, the board of pharmacy may apply to the court of common pleas in the county where any of the provisions of sections 4729.51 to 4729.62 of the Revised Code are being violated or where any violation described in section 4729.35 of the Revised Code is occurring for a temporary or permanent injunction restraining any person from such violation.

HISTORY: 129 v 1376 (Eff 1-1-62); 140 v H 206. Eff 3-14-85.

§ 4729.65 Deposit of receipts; vouchers; excess fees.

(A) Except as provided in division (B) of this section, all receipts of the state board of pharmacy, from any source, shall be deposited into the state treasury to the credit of the occupational licensing and regulatory fund. All vouchers of the board shall be approved by the president or executive director of the board, or both, as authorized by the board. All initial issuance fees and renewal fees required by sections 4729.01 to 4729.54 of the Revised Code shall be payable by the applicant at the time of making application.

(B)(1) There is hereby created in the state treasury the board of pharmacy drug law enforcement fund. All moneys that are derived from any mandatory fines or forfeited bail to which the board may be entitled under Chapter 2925. or division (B)(5) of section 2925.42 of the Revised Code and all moneys that are derived from forfeitures of property to which the board may be entitled pursuant to Chapter 2925. of the Revised Code, section 2923.32, 2923.35, or 2933.43 of the Revised Code, any other section of the Revised Code, or federal law shall be deposited into the fund. Subject to division (B)(2) of this section, division (D)(2)(c) of section 2923.35, and divisions (D)(1)(c) and (3) of section 2933.43 of the Revised Code, the moneys in the fund shall be used solely to subsidize the drug law enforcement efforts of the board.

(2) Notwithstanding any contrary provision in the Revised Code, moneys that are derived from forfeitures of property pursuant to federal law and that are deposited into the board of pharmacy drug law enforcement fund in accordance with division (B)(1) of this section shall be used and accounted for in accordance with the applicable federal law, and the board otherwise shall comply with that law in connection with the moneys.

(C) All fines and forfeited bonds assessed and collected under prosecution or prosecution commenced in the enforcement of this chapter shall be paid to the executive director of the board within thirty days and by the executive director paid into the state treasury to the credit of the occupational licensing and regulatory fund. The board, subject to the approval of the controlling board and except for fees required to be established by the board at amounts "adequate" to cover designated expenses, may establish fees in excess of the amounts provided by this chapter, provided that such fees do not exceed the amounts permitted by this chapter by more than fifty per cent.

HISTORY: 129 v 1376 (Eff 1-1-62); 130 v 1144 (Eff 10-14-63); 132 v H 911 (Eff 6-11-68); 134 v S 141 (Eff 12-31-71); 136 v H 300 (Eff 7-1-76); 138 v H 204 (Eff 7-30-79); 139 v H 694 (Eff 7-1-82); 141 v H 201 (Eff 7-1-85); 142 v S 386 (Eff 3-29-88); 143 v H 266 (Eff 9-6-90); 143 v S 258 (Eff 11-20-90); 144 v S 218 (Eff

10-11-91); 145 v H 715 (Eff 7-22-94); 147 v H 215. Eff 9-29-97.

The effective date is set by section 222 of HB 215.

§ 4729.66 Rules and regulations.

The board of pharmacy may make such rules and regulations, subject to and in accordance with sections 119.01 to 119.13, inclusive, of the Revised Code, not inconsistent with the law pertaining to the purchase for resale, possession for sale, sale, and other distribution of dangerous drugs as may be necessary to carry out the purposes of and enforce sections 4729.51 to 4729.62, inclusive, of the Revised Code.

HISTORY: 129 v 1376. Eff 1-1-62.

§ 4729.99 Penalties.

(A) Whoever violates section 4729.16, division (A) or (B) of section 4729.38, or section 4729.57 of the Revised Code is guilty of a minor misdemeanor. Each day's violation constitutes a separate offense.

(B) Whoever violates section 4729.27, 4729.28, or 4729.36 of the Revised Code is guilty of a misdemeanor of the third degree. Each day's violation constitutes a separate offense. If the offender previously has been convicted of or pleaded guilty to a violation of this chapter, that person is guilty of a misdemeanor of the second degree.

(C) Whoever violates section 4729.32, 4729.33, or 4729.34 of the Revised Code is guilty of a misdemeanor.

(D) Whoever violates division (A), (B), (D), or (E) of section 4729.51 of the Revised Code is guilty of a misdemeanor of the first degree.

(E)(1) Whoever violates section 4729.37, division (C)(2) of section 4729.51, division (J) of section 4729.54, or section 4729.61 of the Revised Code is guilty of a felony of the fifth degree. If the offender previously has been convicted of or pleaded guilty to a violation of this chapter or a violation of Chapter 2925. or 3719. of the Revised Code, that person is guilty of a felony of the fourth degree.

(2) If an offender is convicted of or pleads guilty to a violation of section 4729.37, division (C) of section 4729.51, division (J) of section 4729.54, or section 4729.61 of the Revised Code, if the violation involves the sale, offer to sell, or possession of a schedule I or II controlled substance, with the exception of marihuana, and if the offender, as a result of the violation, is a major drug offender, as defined in section 2929.01 of the Revised Code, the court that sentences the offender, in lieu of the prison term authorized or required by division (E)(1) of this section and sections 2929.13 and 2929.14 of the Revised Code and in addition to any other sanction imposed for the offense under sections 2929.11 to 2929.181 [2929.18.1] of the Revised Code, shall impose upon the offender, in accordance with division (D)(3)(a) of section 2929.14 of the Revised Code, the mandatory prison term specified in that division and may impose an additional prison term under division (D)(3)(b) of that section.

(3) Notwithstanding any contrary provision of section 3719.21 of the Revised Code, the clerk of court shall pay any fine imposed for a violation of section 4729.37, division (C) of section 4729.51, division (J) of section 4729.54, or section 4729.61 of the Revised Code pursuant to division (A) of section 2929.18 of the Revised Code in accordance with and subject to the requirements of division (F) of section 2925.03 of the Revised Code. The agency that receives the fine shall use the fine as specified in division (F) of section 2925.03 of the Revised Code.

(F) Whoever violates section 4729.531 [4729.53.1] of the Revised Code or any rule adopted thereunder or section 4729.532 [4729.53.2] of the Revised Code is guilty of a misdemeanor of the first degree.

(G) Whoever violates division (C)(1) of section 4729.51 of the Revised Code is guilty of a felony of the fourth degree. If the offender has previously been convicted of or pleaded guilty to a violation of this chapter, or of a violation of Chapter 2925. or 3719. of the Revised Code, that person is guilty of a felony of the third degree.

(H) Whoever violates division (C)(3) of section 4729.51 of the Revised Code is guilty of a misdemeanor of the first degree. If the offender has previously been convicted of or pleaded guilty to a violation of this chapter, or of a violation of Chapter 2925. or 3719. of the Revised Code, that person is guilty of a felony of the fifth degree.

HISTORY: Bureau of Code Revision, 10-1-53; 127 v 162 (Eff 9-16-57); 129 v 1376 (Eff 1-1-62); 130 v 1145 (Eff 3-8-64); 133 v H 874 (Eff 9-16-70); 134 v S 141 (Eff 12-31-71); 136 v H 1 (Eff 6-13-75); 136 v H 300 (Eff 7-1-76); 137 v S 45 (Eff 1-1-78); 139 v H 694 (Eff 11-15-81); 139 v S 4 (Eff 10-1-82); 140 v H 208 (Eff 9-20-84); 145 v H 88 (Eff 6-29-94); 145 v H 391 (Eff 7-21-94); 146 v S 2. Eff 7-1-96.

The effective date is set by section 6 of SB 2.

The provisions of § 7 of SB 2 (146 v —) read in part as follows:

SECTION 7. ° ° ° Section 4729.99 of the Revised Code is presented in this act as a composite of the section as amended by both Sub. H.B. 88 and Sub. H.B. 391 of the 120th General Assembly, with the new language of neither of the acts shown in capital letters. ° ° ° This is in recognition of the principle stated in division (B) of section 1.52 of the Revised Code that such amendments are to be harmonized where not substantively irreconcilable and constitutes a legislative finding that such is the resulting version in effect prior to the effective date of this act.

CHAPTER 4749: PRIVATE INVESTIGATORS; SECURITY SERVICES

§ 4749.13 Prohibitions.

(A) No person shall engage in the business of private investigation, the business of security services, or both businesses in this state unless he is licensed pursuant to this chapter. Each day of continuing violation constitutes a separate offense. Nothing in this chapter shall be construed to require any employee of a class A, B, or C licensee to obtain a class A, B, or C license, provided that an employee shall be registered by a licensee when required by section 4749.06 of the Revised Code. Nothing in this chapter shall be construed to require a partner to be a class A, B, or C licensee except as provided in division (A)(3) of section 4749.03 of the Revised Code. Nothing in this chapter shall be construed to require a director, officer, or qualifying agent of a corporation to individually be a class A, B, or C licensee if the corporation is licensed pursuant to this chapter.

(B) No class A, B, or C licensee, or registered employee of a class A, B, or C licensee shall:

(1) Knowingly violate any provision of this chapter or any rule of the director of commerce adopted for the administration of this chapter;

(2) Knowingly make a false report with respect to any matter with which he is employed;

(3) Divulge any information acquired from or for a client to persons other than the client or his authorized agent without express authorization to do so or unless required by law;

(4) Knowingly accept employment which includes obtaining information intended for illegal purposes.

(C) No person shall knowingly authorize or permit another person to violate any provision of this chapter or any rule of the director of commerce adopted for the administration of this chapter.

(D) No person who is not licensed as a class A, B, or C licensee shall advertise that he is or otherwise hold himself out as a class A, B, or C licensee. This division does not prohibit registered employees from indicating in the course of authorized employment for a class A, B, or C licensee that they are authorized to engage in investigatory, security services activities, or both activities.

HISTORY: RC § 4749.10, 133 v H 341 (Eff 1-1-70); RC § 4749.13, 141 v H 402. Eff 11-27-85.

§ 4749.99 Penalties.

(A) Except as otherwise provided in this division, whoever violates division (A) of section 4749.13 of the Revised Code is guilty of a misdemeanor of the first degree. Whoever violates division (A) of section 4749.13 of the Revised Code and previously has been convicted of one or more violations of division (A) of that section is guilty of a felony of the fifth degree. If the offender previously has been convicted of two or more violations of division (A) of that section, the offender shall be fined ten thousand dollars and also may be imprisoned not more than one year.

(B) Whoever violates division (B), (C), or (D) of section 4749.13 of the Revised Code shall be fined not less than one hundred or more than one thousand dollars, imprisoned not more than one year, or both.

HISTORY: 133 v H 341 (Eff 1-1-70); 141 v H 402 (Eff 11-27-85); 144 v H 536 (Eff 11-5-92); 146 v S 2. Eff 7-1-96.

The effective date is set by section 6 of SB 2.

TITLE 49: PUBLIC UTILITIES
CHAPTER 4931: COMPANIES—TELEGRAPH; TELEPHONE

[DIVULGING MESSAGE]

§ 4931.26 Divulging telegraph message.

No person connected with a telegraph or messenger company, incorporated or unincorporated, operating a telegraph line or engaged in the business of receiving and delivering messages, shall willfully divulge the contents or the nature of the contents of a private communication entrusted to him for transmission or delivery, willfully refuse or neglect to transmit or deliver it, willfully delay its transmission or delivery, or willfully forge the name of the intended receiver to a receipt for such message, communication, or article of value entrusted to him by said company, with intent to injure, deceive, or defraud the sender or intended receiver thereof or such telegraph or messenger company, or to benefit himself or any other person.

HISTORY: RS § 3466; S&S 156; 62 v 72, § 10; 94 v 209; GC § 13388; Bureau of Code Revision. Eff 10-1-53.

§ 4931.27 Delaying telegraph message.

No telegraph operator of a railroad or telegraph company shall fail, on tender of the usual charge at regular commercial offices, to accept a telegram for transmission from any passenger delayed by an accident, or to send it forthwith to the person and point designated, without alteration, revision, or approval. If a violation of this section arises from obeying an order or rule of the employer of the telegraph operator, such employer shall repay him any fine imposed under division (B) of section 4931.99 of the Revised Code and costs.

HISTORY: RS § 3373-2; 88 v 429, § 3; GC § 13389; Bureau of Code Revision, 10-1-53; 144 v S 343. Eff 3-24-93.

§ 4931.28 Interfering with telegraph or telephone messages.

Except as authorized pursuant to sections 2933.51 to 2933.66 of the Revised Code, no person shall willfully and maliciously cut, break, tap, or make connection with a telegraph or telephone wire or read or copy in an unauthorized manner, a telegraphic message or communication from or upon a telegraph or telephone line, wire, or cable, so cut or tapped, or make unauthorized use thereof, or willfully and maliciously prevent, obstruct, or delay the sending, conveyance, or delivery of an authorized telegraphic message or communication by or through a line, cable, or wire, under the control of a telegraph or telephone company.

HISTORY: RS § 3467a; 89 v 52; 89 v 100; 90 v 346; 95 v 101; GC § 13402; Bureau of Code Revision, 10-1-53; 141 v S 222. Eff 3-25-87.

§ 4931.29 Divulging telephone communication.

No person connected with a telephone company, incorporated or unincorporated, operating a telephone line or engaged in the business of transmitting to, from, through, or in this state, telephone messages, in any capacity, shall willfully divulge a private telephone message or the nature of such message, or a private conversation between persons communicating over the wires of such company, or willfully delay the transmission of a telephonic message or communication, with intent to injure, deceive, or defraud the sender or receiver thereof or any other person, or any such telephone company, or to benefit himself or any other person.

HISTORY: 100 v 10; GC § 13419; Bureau of Code Revision. Eff 10-1-53.

§ 4931.30 Party lines to be yielded in emergencies.

No person shall willfully refuse immediately to yield or relinquish the use of a party line to another person for the purpose of permitting such other person to report a fire or summon law enforcement agencies, ambulance service, medical, or other aid in case of emergency.

No person shall ask for or request the use of a party line on the pretext that an emergency exists, knowing that no emergency exists.

Every telephone directory distributed after June 30, 1955 to the members of the general public in this state or in any portion thereof which lists the calling numbers of telephones of any telephone exchange located in this state shall contain a notice which explains the offenses provided for in this section, such notice to be printed in type which is not smaller than any other type on the same page and to be preceded by the word "warning" printed in type with at least equal prominence as other regulations or information on the same page; provided, that the provisions of this section do not apply to those directories distributed solely for business advertising purposes, commonly known as classified directories, nor to any telephone directory distributed or for which copy has been sent to the printer or is in the process of printing or distribution to the general public prior to June 30, 1955. Any person, firm, or corporation providing telephone service which distributes or causes to be distributed in this state one or more copies of a telephone directory which is subject to the provisions of this section and which willfully omits such notice is guilty of a violation of this section.

As used in this section:

(A) "Party line" means a subscribers' line telephone

circuit, to which two or more main telephone stations are connected, each station having a distinctive ring or telephone number.

(B) "Emergency" means a situation in which property or human life is in jeopardy and in which prompt summoning of aid is essential.

HISTORY: 126 v 74, (Eff 6-30-55); 129 v 582(928). Eff 1-10-61.

§ 4931.31 Threat or harassment in telephone communication prohibited; directory notice.

No person shall, while communicating with any other person over a telephone, threaten to do bodily harm or use or address to such other person any words or language of a lewd, lascivious, or indecent character, nature, or connotation for the sole purpose of annoying such other person; nor shall any person telephone any other person repeatedly or cause any person to be telephoned repeatedly for the sole purpose of harassing or molesting such other person or his family.

Any use, communication, or act prohibited by this section may be deemed to have occurred or to have been committed at either the place at which the telephone call was made or was received.

Every telephone directory distributed to the general public in this state which lists the calling numbers of telephones of any telephone exchange located in this state shall contain a notice which explains the offenses provided for in this section, such notice to be printed in type which is not smaller than the general body of the other type on the same page and to be preceded by the word "warning" printed in type with at least equal prominence as the headings of other regulations or information on the same page; provided, that the provision of this section shall not apply to those directories distributed solely for business advertising purposes, commonly known as classified directories, nor to any telephone directory distributed or for which a copy has been sent to the printer or is in the process of printing or distribution to the general public prior to August 14, 1959.

Any person, firm, or corporation providing telephone service which distributes or causes to be distributed in this state one or more copies of a telephone directory which is subject to the provisions of this section and which willfully omits such notice is guilty of a violation of this section.

HISTORY: 128 v 692 (Eff 8-14-59); 129 v 582(929). Eff 1-10-61.

§§ 4931.32, 4931.33 Repealed, 146 v S 2, § 6 [129 v 1306; 130 v 1164; 131 v 1195, 1196]. Eff 7-1-96.

These sections forbade fraudulent obtaining of telephone service and the making, possessing, or transferring devices designed for theft of telephone service.

§ 4931.55 Restrictions on transmitting advertising by facsimile device.

(A) As used in this section:

(1) "Advertisement" means a message or material intended to cause the sale of realty, goods, or services.

(2) "Facsimile device" means a device that electronically or telephonically receives and copies onto paper reasonable reproductions or facsimiles of documents and photographs through connection with a telephone network.

(3) "Pre-existing business relationship" does not include transmitting an advertisement to the owner's or lessee's facsimile device.

(B) No person shall transmit an advertisement to a facsimile device unless the person has received prior permission from the owner or, if the device is leased, from the lessee of the device to which the message is to be sent to transmit the advertisement; or the person has a pre-existing business relationship with such owner or lessee.

(C) When requested by the owner or lessee, the transmission shall occur between seven p.m. and five a.m.

This section applies to all such advertisements intended to be so transmitted within this state.

HISTORY: 144 v H 233. Eff 1-10-92.

§ 4931.99 Penalties.

(A) Whoever violates section 4931.24 or 4931.49 of the Revised Code is guilty of a misdemeanor of the fourth degree.

(B) Whoever violates section 4931.25, 4931.26, 4931.27, 4931.30, or 4931.31 of the Revised Code is guilty of a misdemeanor of the third degree.

(C) Whoever violates section 4931.28 of the Revised Code is guilty of a felony of the fourth degree.

(D) Whoever violates section 4931.29 or division (B) of section 4931.35 of the Revised Code is guilty of a misdemeanor in the first degree.

(E) Whoever violates division (E) of section 4931.49 of the Revised Code is guilty of a misdemeanor of the fourth degree on a first offense and a felony of the fifth degree on each subsequent offense.

(F) Whoever violates section 4931.55 of the Revised Code is guilty of a minor misdemeanor for a first offense and a misdemeanor of the first degree on each subsequent offense.

HISTORY: Bureau of Code Revision, 10-1-53; 126 v 74 (Eff 8-14-59); 129 v 1306 (Eff 9-14-61); 131 v 1197 (Eff 7-20-65); 131 v 1196 (Eff 7-20-65); 139 v S 199 (Eff 1-1-83); 139 v H 269 (Eff 1-5-83); 141 v H 491 (Eff 6-18-85); 144 v H 233 (Eff 1-10-92); 144 v S 343 (Eff 3-24-93); 146 v S 2. Eff 7-1-96.

The effective date is set by section 6 of SB 2.

CHAPTER 4933: COMPANIES—GAS; ELECTRIC; WATER; OTHERS

§ 4933.18 Tampering with utility equipment.

(A) In a prosecution for a theft offense, as defined in section 2913.01 of the Revised Code, that involves alleged tampering with a gas, electric, steam, or water meter, conduit, or attachment of a utility that has been disconnected by the utility, proof that a meter, conduit, or attachment of a utility has been tampered with is prima-facie evidence that the person who is obligated to pay for the service rendered through the meter, conduit, or attachment and is in possession or control of the meter, conduit, or attachment at the time the tampering occurred has caused the tampering with intent to commit a theft offense.

In a prosecution for a theft offense, as defined in section 2913.01 of the Revised Code, that involves the alleged reconnection of a gas, electric, steam, or water meter, conduit, or attachment of a utility that has been disconnected by the utility, proof that a meter, conduit, or attachment disconnected by a utility has been reconnected without the consent of the utility is prima-facie evidence that the person in possession or control of the meter, conduit, or attachment at the time of the reconnection has reconnected the meter, conduit, or attachment with intent to commit a theft offense.

(B) As used in this section:

(1) "Utility" means any electric light company, gas company, natural gas company, pipe-line company, water-works company, or heating or cooling company, as defined by division (A)(4), (5), (6), (7), (8), or (9) of section 4905.03 of the Revised Code, its lessees, trustees, or receivers, or any similar utility owned or operated by a political subdivision.

(2) "Tamper" means to interfere with, damage, or by-pass a utility meter, conduit, or attachment with the intent to impede the correct registration of a meter or the proper functions of a conduit or attachment so as to reduce the amount of utility service that is registered on the meter.

HISTORY: 137 v H 605 (Eff 8-18-78); 146 v S 2. Eff 7-1-96.

Analogous to former RC § 4933.18 (RS § 3560; S&S 160; 63 v 164, §§ 13, 14; GC § 9337; Bureau of Code Revision, 10-1-53), repealed 137 v H 605, eff 8-18-78.

The effective date is set by section 6 of SB 2.

§ 4933.19 Theft of utility service.

Electric light company, gas company, natural gas company, pipe-line company, water-works company, or heating or cooling company, as defined by division (A)(4), (5), (6), (7), (8), or (9) of section 4905.03 of the Revised Code, or its lessees, trustees, or receivers, and each similar utility owned or operated by a political subdivision shall notify its customers, on an annual basis, that tampering with or bypassing a meter constitutes a theft offense that could result in the imposition of criminal sanctions.

HISTORY: 137 v H 605 (Eff 8-18-78); 146 v S 2. Eff 7-1-96.

Analogous in part to former RC § 4933.19 (RS § 6860-1; 88 v 241, GC §§ 12512, 12513; Bureau of Code Revision, 10-1-53) renumbered 4933.20 in 137 v H 605, eff 8-18-78.

The effective date is set by section 6 of SB 2.

§ 4933.20 Tampering with gas pipes and apparatus.

No person shall maliciously open, close, adjust, or interfere with a valve, regulator, gauge, gate, disc, curb cock, stopcock, meter, or other regulating, operating, or measuring device or appliance in or attached to the wells, tanks, conduits, pipelines, mains, service pipes, house pipes, display pipes, or other pipes of a gas company or manufacturer or furnisher of gas with intent to cause the escape of gas or to injure or destroy such property. No person shall maliciously enlarge or alter a mixer furnished or approved by a gas company or manufacturer or furnisher of gas to or for a consumer of gas, or maliciously remove from its connection a mixer so furnished or approved. No person shall without express permission, consume for fuel the gas of a gas company or manufacturer or furnisher of gas without the use of a mixer so furnished or approved by such gas company or manufacturer or furnisher of gas, or tap, sever, or open a main or pipe used or intended for the transmission of gas, or connect with such main or pipe any other main or pipe. This section does not apply to an agent or employee, for that purpose, of the owner, manufacturer, or operator of the devices or appliances referred to in this section.

As used in this section, "gas" includes natural and artificial gas used for heating and illuminating purposes.

HISTORY: RS § 6860-1; 88 v 241; GC §§ 12512, 12513; Bureau of Code Revision, RC § 4933.19, 10-1-53; RC § 4933.20, 137 v H 605. Eff 8-18-78.

Not analogous to former RC § 4933.20 (RS § 3467a; 89 v 52; 89 v 100; 90 v 346; 95 v 101; GC § 12508; 111 v 58; Bureau of Code Revision, 10-1-53), repealed 137 v H 605, eff 8-18-78.

§ 4933.21 Interfering with electric wires.

No person shall willfully or maliciously injure, destroy, or intentionally permit to be injured or destroyed, disconnect, displace, cut, break, tap, ground, or make a connection with, or willfully or maliciously interfere with any pole, pier, cable, tower, or wire, legally erected, put, or strung, or electrical apparatus, appliance, or machinery used in the construction or operation of an electrical railway, electric light plant, or plant used in generating or transmitting electricity, or any meter, pipe, conduit, wire, line, post, lamp, burner, heater, machine, motor, or other appliance or apparatus used in the construction or operation of any such electrical railway or electrical plant. No person shall willfully or maliciously prevent any electric meter used in the construction or operation of any such electrical railway or electrical plant, from registering the quantity of electricity supplied, interfere with the proper action or just registration by such meter, alter the index in such meter, or, without the consent of the owner of such electrical railway or electrical plant, willfully or maliciously divert electric current from any such wire or otherwise willfully or maliciously use or cause to be used, without the consent of the owner of such electrical railway or electrical plant, electricity manufactured or distributed by any such electrical railway or electrical plant.

HISTORY: RS § 3467a; 89 v 52; 89 v 100; 90 v 346; 95 v 101; GC § 12507; 111 v 58; Bureau of Code Revision. Eff 10-1-53.

§ 4933.22 Tampering with hydrant, pipe, or meter.

No person shall maliciously open, close, adjust, or interfere with a fire hydrant, valve, regulator, gauge, gate, disc, curb cock, stopcock, meter, or other regulator, operating or measuring device, or appliance in or attached to the wells, tanks, reservoirs, conduits, pipes, mains, service pipes, house pipes, or other pipes or apparatus of a water company or furnisher of water, with intent to cause the escape of water or to injure or destroy such property. No person shall tap, sever, open, or make unauthorized connections with a main or pipe used or intended for the transmission of water. This section does not apply to the agent or employee for that purpose, of the owner or operator of the appliances referred to in this section, and does not apply to anything done by or under authority of any regularly constituted fire department.

HISTORY: GC § 12512-1; 108 v PtI 187; Bureau of Code Revision. Eff 10-1-53.

§ 4933.23 Interfering with pipes and meters.

No person shall willfully or maliciously injure or destroy, or intentionally permit to be injured or destroyed, cut, break, adjust, or interfere with any pipe, valve, regulator, gauge, gate, stopcock, trap, meter, or other regulating or measuring device or appliance used in the construction or operation of any plant furnishing or distributing hot water or steam for heating purposes. No person shall willfully or maliciously prevent any meter or other measuring device or appliance used in any such heating plant from duly registering the quantity of hot water or steam supplied. No person shall, without the consent of the owner of such heating plant, willfully or maliciously divert any hot water or steam from any pipe or other part of such heating plant or otherwise willfully or maliciously use or cause to be used, without the consent of the owner of such heating plant, hot water or steam supplied by any such heating plant.

HISTORY: GC § 12512-2; 111 v 59; Bureau of Code Revision. Eff 10-1-53.

§ 4933.24 Prohibition against interference with apparatus of sewage disposal companies.

No person shall maliciously open, close, adjust, or interfere with a valve, regulator, gauge, gate, disc, curb cock, stopcock, meter, or other regulator, operating or measuring device, or appliance in or attached to the tanks, conduits, pipes, mains, service pipes, house pipes, or other pipes or apparatus of a sewage disposal company, with intent to interfere with the flow of sewage, or to injure or destroy such property. No person shall tap, sever, open, or make unauthorized connections with a main or pipe used or intended for the transmission of sewage.

HISTORY: 129 v 501. Eff 9-19-61.

§ 4933.99 Penalties.

(A) Whoever violates section 4933.16 of the Revised Code is guilty of a misdemeanor of the third degree.

(B) Whoever violates section 4933.20, 4933.22, 4933.24, or 4933.25 of the Revised Code is guilty of a misdemeanor of the fourth degree.

(C) Whoever violates section 4933.21 or 4933.23 of the Revised Code is guilty of a misdemeanor of the first degree.

(D) Whoever violates division (E) of section 4933.28 of the Revised Code is guilty of a misdemeanor of the fourth degree. Each day of a violation of that division constitutes a separate offense.

HISTORY: Bureau of Code Revision, 10-1-53; 129 v 501 (Eff 9-19-61); 137 v H 271 (Eff 10-12-77); 137 v H 605 (Eff 8-18-78); 137 v H 1111 (Eff 1-12-79); 139 v S 199 (Eff 7-1-83); 140 v S 183 (Eff 9-26-84); 146 v S 2. Eff 7-1-96.

The effective date is set by section 6 of SB 2.

CHAPTER 4953: TRANSPORTATION TERMINAL COMPANIES

§ 4953.11 Authority to arrest.

The officers and agents of a union terminal company shall have the same authority to arrest and bring to justice pickpockets, thieves, persons who violate the public peace, persons who violate any rules and regulations posted as provided by section 4953.07 of the Revised Code, and persons who commit crimes and misdemeanors on the depot grounds, as constables possess within their respective townships.

HISTORY: RS § 3450; S&S 122; 65 v 63, § 3; GC § 9166; Bureau of Code Revision. Eff 10-1-53.

CHAPTER 4955: TRACKS; CROSSINGS

[§ 4955.20.1] § 4955.201 Abandonment of track; restoration of roadway.

(A) If the interstate commerce commission approves the abandonment of a railroad track that crosses a road or highway at grade, the railroad that owned the track immediately after the approval of the abandonment shall remove the track at the crossing and fill the space previously occupied by the rails with the same material that comprises the road or highway at the crossing. Upon completion of the work, the surface of the crossing where the rails previously were located shall be the same height as the surface of the road or highway abutting the crossing. The restored portion of the road or highway shall meet the construction standards applicable to the road or highway of which the restored portion is a part.

(B) No railroad shall fail to remove from a crossing the rails that comprise a track whose abandonment has been approved or fail to fill the space previously occupied by the rails as required by division (A) of this section.

HISTORY: 145 v H 154. Eff 6-30-93.

CHAPTER 4999: CRIMES RELATING TO RAILROADS

§ 4999.01 Drawing, driving, or moving vehicle on railroad track.

No person shall draw, drive, or cause to be moved any vehicle on or between the rails or tracks or on or along the graded roadway of a railroad without the knowledge and consent of the owner or controller of such railroad, unless compelled by necessity to do so. Whoever violates this section is guilty of a minor misdemeanor.

HISTORY: RS § 6872; S&S 268; S&C 419; 46 v 26; 60 v 17; GC § 12542; Bureau of Code Revision, 10-1-53; 144 v H 667. Eff 3-15-93.

§ 4999.02 Climbing upon railroad cars.

No person shall climb, jump, step, or stand upon, or cling or attach himself to, a locomotive, engine, or car upon the track of a railroad, unless in compliance with law or by permission under the rules of the corporation managing such railroad. Whoever violates this section is guilty of a minor misdemeanor.

HISTORY: RS § 6982; 74 v 202, §§ 1, 2; GC § 12543; Bureau of Code Revision, 10-1-53; 144 v H 667. Eff 3-15-93.

§ 4999.03 Riding or driving into enclosures of railroads.

No person shall, at a place other than a private crossing or for a purpose other than crossing a railroad, ride or drive a horse or other domestic animal into an enclosure of a railroad or knowingly permit such animal to go into or remain in such enclosure, or place feed, salt, or other thing within such enclosure to induce such animal to enter into it or upon the track of such railroad, or, while constructing a private crossing or crossing a railroad at a private crossing, permit a fence to remain down or open for a longer time than is necessary to construct or use such crossing. Whoever violates this section shall be fined not more than ten dollars or imprisoned for not less than ten nor more than thirty days. Each ten hours such animal is knowingly permitted to remain in such enclosure or upon such track is an additional offense. Such animal is not exempt from execution for a fine or costs imposed under this section.

HISTORY: RS § 6981; S&S 117; 65 v 194, §§ 1, 2; 72 v 32; GC §§ 12544, 12545; Bureau of Code Revision. Eff 10-1-53.

§ 4999.04 Duties of engineer.

(A) No person in charge of a locomotive shall do the following:

(1) Fail to bring the locomotive to a full stop at least two hundred feet before arriving at a crossing with another track, or proceed through the crossing before signaled to do so or before the way is clear;

(2) When approaching a grade crossing, fail to sound the locomotive whistle at frequent intervals, beginning no less than thirteen hundred twenty feet from such crossing and continuing until the locomotive has passed the crossing.

(B) Whoever violates this section is guilty of a misdemeanor of the fourth degree. If violation of this section causes physical harm to any person, whoever violates this section is guilty of a misdemeanor of the third degree.

HISTORY: 134 v H 511 (Eff 1-1-74); 137 v S 167. Eff 8-26-77.

Analogous to former RC § 4999.04 (RS § 6980; 69 v 49; 71 v 50; 85 v 112; GC §§ 12549, 12550; Bureau of Code Revision, 10-1-53), repealed 134 v H 511, § 2, eff 1-1-74.

§ 4999.05 Flagmen on railroads.

No person or company owning, operating, or controlling a railroad shall employ as a flagman, hostler, or assistant hostler, a person who cannot read, write, and speak the English language. Whoever violates this section shall be fined not less than five hundred nor more than one thousand dollars. This section does not apply to flagmen at street or highway crossings.

HISTORY: RS §§ 3365-17a, 3365-17b; 97 v 72, §§ 1, 2; GC § 12551; Bureau of Code Revision. Eff 10-1-53.

§ 4999.06 Running passenger trains with less than full crew.

No superintendent, trainmaster, or other employee of a railroad shall send or cause to be sent outside of yard limits, a passenger train of not more than five cars, any one of which carries passengers, with a crew consisting of less than one engineer, one fireman, one conductor, and one brakeman. If four of said cars are day coaches carrying passengers, or if in a train of more than five cars, three or more cars are day coaches carrying passengers, or if in a train of more than six cars, four cars carrying passengers, or if in a train of more than seven cars, two or more cars are carrying passengers, of [or] if any train, six or more cars are carrying passengers, such crew shall consist of at least one additional brakeman, regularly employed as such. When such train consists of more than two cars, either of which carries passengers, no such superintendent, trainmaster, or other employee shall require a brakeman to perform the duties of baggage master or express agent. Whoever violates this section shall be fined not less than twenty-five dollars for each offense.

For the purpose of this section, a combination mail or baggage and passenger car is a day coach, but straight dining cars and private cars are not cars carrying passengers.

This section does not apply to trains picking up a car between terminals in this state, or to cars propelled by electricity.

Mayors and county court judges have jurisdiction under this section. The public utilities commission shall enforce this section.

HISTORY: RS §§ 3365-33, 3365-34; 95 v 343; GC §§ 12553, 12555; 102 v 508; Bureau of Code Revision, 10-1-53; 132 v H 2 (Eff 2-14-67); 136 v H 205. Eff 1-1-76.

§ 4999.10 Constructing bridges over tracks.

No person, railroad company, private corporation, county, municipal corporation, or township shall violate any law relating to the height of bridges, viaducts, overhead roadways, footbridges, wires, or other structures constructed over the tracks of a railroad. Whoever violates this section shall be fined not less than one hundred nor more than one thousand dollars. Each day such structure or wire is permitted to so remain constitutes a separate offense.

HISTORY: RS § 3337-19; 91 v 365, § 2; GC § 12546; Bureau of Code Revision. Eff 10-1-53.

§ 4999.11 Mail cranes; livestock chutes.

No person or company owning, operating, or controlling a railroad shall erect or permit to be erected, place, or maintain along said railroad, a mail crane or livestock chute, any portion of which approaches nearer than eighteen inches to the nearest point of contact with the cab of the widest locomotive used on such railroad. Whoever violates this section shall be fined not less than five hundred nor more than one thousand dollars.

HISTORY: RS §§ 3365-19a, 3365-19b; 97 v 274, 275, §§ 1, 2; GC § 12552; Bureau of Code Revision. Eff 10-1-53.

§ 4999.13 Couplers and brakes on railroads.

No superintendent, conductor, or other officer or employee of a railroad company, shall refuse or neglect, upon receiving notice from the inspector appointed by the public utilities commission, of a defective coupler or brake, to have it repaired forthwith or, on receiving notice from such inspector condemning a car, tender, or engine, shall fail to put it out of service at the first freight division terminal. No superintendent, conductor, or other officer or employee shall violate any other law relating to automatic couplers and air brakes. Whoever violates this section shall be fined not less than twenty-five nor more than five hundred dollars. Such person is also personally liable for any injuries resulting to any employee from such violation.

HISTORY: RS § 3365-23i; 95 v 660; GC § 12562; Bureau of Code Revision. Eff 10-1-53.

§ 4999.16 Examination of employee for color blindness.

No railroad company shall contract to employ a person in a position which requires such person to distinguish form or color signals, unless within two years preceding such date he has been examined for color blindness, in the distinct colors in actual use by such company by a competent person employed and paid by such company, and has received a certificate that he is not disqualified for such position by color blindness in the colors used by the company. No such company shall fail to require such person to be re-examined at least once each two years at the expense of such company. This section does not prevent a railroad company from continuing in its employment an employee having defective sight when such defective sight can be fully remedied by the use of glasses or by other means satisfactory to the person making such examination. Whoever violates this section shall be fined one hundred dollars.

HISTORY: RS §§ 3365-9, 3365-10; 82 v 65; 85 v 58, §§ 1, 2; GC § 12548; Bureau of Code Revision. Eff 10-1-53.

§ 4999.17 Discipline or discharge of employee without hearing.

No railroad company, or its superintendent, or manager, employing any special agent, detective, or person commonly known as "spotter" for the purpose of investigating, obtaining, and reporting to the employer, its agent, superintendent, or manager, information concerning its employees, shall discipline or discharge any employee in its service, where such act of discipline or the discharge is based upon a report by such special agent, detective, or spotter, which report involves a question of integrity, honesty, or a breach of rules of the employer, unless such employer, its agent, superintendent, or manager, before disciplining or discharging such employee, grants such employee a fair opportunity to be heard in defense or explanation of the complaint against him, at which hearing said employer shall state specific charges on which said act or discharge is based and at which the accused employee has the right to furnish testimony in his defense.

Whoever violates this section shall be fined not less than fifty nor more than three hundred dollars or imprisoned not more than one year, or both. Such imprisonment, when imposed, shall be imposed upon the officers or agents of such company committing such offense.

HISTORY: GC §§ 12956-1, 12956-2; 107 v 603, §§ 1, 2; Bureau of Code Revision. Eff 10-1-53.

§ 4999.18 Demanding compensation when telegraph or telephone wires not working.

No officer, agent, or other person acting for or in behalf of a railroad company operating ten or more miles of its railroad for the carrying or transporting of passengers or freight over its railroad within this state which fails to erect and maintain telegraph or telephone wires in complete working order for use and operation along its railroad, with an office and proper means of communication by such wires at each of its principal railway stations, shall order, direct, advise, ask, demand, or receive compensation for transportation of passengers or freight. Whoever violates this section be fined not less than one hundred nor more than five hundred dollars or imprisoned for not less than thirty nor more than ninety days, or both.

HISTORY: RS § 3354-6; 93 v 89, § 2; GC § 12547; Bureau of Code Revision. Eff 10-1-53.

§ 4999.19 Diverting freight.

No agent of a railroad company shall knowingly divert or permit freight under his control to be diverted from the railroads over which it is ordered to be conveyed by the shipper of such freight. Whoever violates this section shall be fined not more than one hundred dollars or imprisoned not more than thirty days, or both.

HISTORY: RS § 3370; S&S 117; 58 v 74, § 3; GC § 13420; Bureau of Code Revision. Eff 10-1-53.

§ 4999.20 Maintenance of employee rights; penalty.

No railroad employee who has a seniority roster date on the effective date of the repeal of sections 4999.07 and 4999.08 of the Revised Code shall be removed from his employment or have his seniority rights or vacation or other fringe benefits reduced by reason of such repeal.

Any carrier which violates this section shall be fined not less than one hundred nor more than five thousand dollars. The public utilities commission shall enforce this section and prosecute any violations thereof.

HISTORY: 134 v H 464. Eff 6-15-72.

TITLE 51: PUBLIC WELFARE

CHAPTER 5101: DEPARTMENT OF HUMAN SERVICES—GENERAL PROVISIONS

§ 5101.31 Division of child support; spousal support enforcement; parent locator service agreement.

(A) As used in this section, "law enforcement entity" means a public entity that employs a law enforcement officer.

(B) The division of child support is hereby created in the department of human services. The division shall establish and administer a program of child support enforcement, which program shall meet the requirements of Title IV-D of the "Social Security Act," 88 Stat. 2351 (1975), 42 U.S.C. 651, as amended, and any rules adopted under Title IV-D. The program of child support enforcement shall include, but not be limited to, the location of absent parents, the establishment of parentage, the establishment and modification of child support orders and medical support orders, the enforcement of support orders, and the collection of support obligations.

The department shall charge an application fee of up to twenty-five dollars, as determined by rule adopted by the department pursuant to Chapter 119. of the Revised Code, for furnishing services under Title IV-D of the "Social Security Act," 88 Stat. 2351 (1975), 42 U.S.C. 651, as amended, to persons not participating in Ohio works first under Chapter 5107. of the Revised Code. The department shall adopt rules pursuant to Chapter 119. of the Revised Code authorizing counties, at their option, to waive the payment of the fee. The application fee, unless waived pursuant to rules adopted by the department pursuant to this section, shall be paid by those persons.

(C) The division of child support shall establish, by rule adopted pursuant to Chapter 119. of the Revised Code, a program of spousal support enforcement in conjunction with child support enforcement. The program shall conform, to the extent practicable, to the program for child support enforcement established pursuant to division (B) of this section.

(D) The department of human services shall enter into an agreement with the secretary of health and human services, as authorized by the "Parental Kidnapping Prevention Act of 1980," 94 Stat. 3572, 42 U.S.C. 663, as amended, under which the services of the parent locator service established pursuant to Title IV-D of the "Social Security Act," 88 Stat. 2351 (1975), 42 U.S.C. 651, as amended, shall be made available to this state for the purpose of determining the whereabouts of any absent parent or child in order to enforce a law with respect to the unlawful taking or restraint of a child, or to make or enforce a determination as to the allocation, between the parents of a child, of the parental rights and responsibilities for the care of a child and the designation of the residential parent and legal custodian of a child or otherwise as to the custody of a child.

(E) The division of child support shall not use any social security number made available to it under section 3705.07 of the Revised Code for any purpose other than child support enforcement.

(F) Except as provided by the rules adopted pursuant to this division, no person shall disclose information concerning applicants for and recipients of Title IV-D support enforcement program services provided by a child support enforcement agency. The department of human services shall adopt rules governing access to, and use and disclosure of, information concerning applicants for and recipients of Title IV-D support enforcement program services provided by a child support enforcement agency. The rules shall be consistent with the requirements of Title IV-D of the "Social Security Act," 88 Stat. 2351 (1975), 42 U.S.C. 651, as amended, and any rules adopted under Title IV-D.

(G)(1) Except as provided in division (G)(2) of this section, the department of human services shall have access to any information in the possession of any officer, board, commission, or agency of the state that would aid the department in locating an absent parent or child pursuant to division (D) of this section, unless release of the information is prohibited by federal law.

(2) The department of taxation, the bureau of motor vehicles, and a law enforcement entity shall provide information the division of child support requests from the department, bureau, or entity that will enable the division to locate a parent the division or a child support enforcement agency is seeking pursuant to child support enforcement activities. The department, bureau, or entity may provide such information to a child support enforcement agency at the agency's request or require the agency to request that the division of child support request the information for the agency. The division shall request the information from the department, bureau, or entity on the request of a child support enforcement agency.

The only information the department shall provide the division or an agency under this section is the name and address of a parent the division or agency is seeking. The information the bureau or entity shall provide to the division or an agency under this section is the information Title IV-D of the "Social Security Act" requires the division or agency be able to receive.

The division or agency shall reimburse the department, bureau, or entity for the cost of providing the information. If the division requests the information for an agency, the agency shall reimburse the division for reimbursing the department, bureau, or entity.

HISTORY: 137 v S 87 (Eff 1-1-79); 140 v S 321 (Eff 4-9-85); 141 v S 80 (Eff 10-1-85); 142 v H 242 (Eff 6-24-88); 143 v H 591 (Eff 4-12-90); 143 v H 514 (Eff 1-1-91); 143 v S 3 (Eff 4-11-91); 146 v H 167 (Eff 11-15-95); 147 v H 408. Eff 10-1-97.

Not analogous to former RC § 5101.31 (GC § 1849; 102 v 211; Bureau of Code Revision, 10-1-53), repealed 125 v 823, § 2, eff 7-1-54.

The effective date is set by section 26 of HB 408.

§ 5101.61 Duty to report abuse, neglect or exploitation of adult.

(A) As used in this section:

(1) "Senior service provider" means any person who provides care or services to a person who is an adult as defined in division (B) of section 5101.60 of the Revised Code.

(2) "Ambulatory health facility" means a nonprofit, public or proprietary freestanding organization or a unit of such an agency or organization that:

(a) Provides preventive, diagnostic, therapeutic, rehabilitative, or palliative items or services furnished to an outpatient or ambulatory patient, by or under the direction of a physician or dentist in a facility which is not a part of a hospital, but which is organized and operated to provide medical care to outpatients;

(b) Has health and medical care policies which are developed with the advice of, and with the provision of review of such policies, an advisory committee of professional personnel, including one or more physicians, one or more dentists, if dental care is provided, and one or more registered nurses;

(c) Has a medical director, a dental director, if dental care is provided, and a nursing director responsible for the execution of such policies, and has physicians, dentists, nursing, and ancillary staff appropriate to the scope of services provided;

(d) Requires that the health care and medical care of every patient be under the supervision of a physician, provides for medical care in a case of emergency, has in effect a written agreement with one or more hospitals and other centers or clinics, and has an established patient referral system to other resources, and a utilization review plan and program;

(e) Maintains clinical records on all patients;

(f) Provides nursing services and other therapeutic services in accordance with programs and policies, with such services supervised by a registered professional nurse, and has a registered professional nurse on duty at all times of clinical operations;

(g) Provides approved methods and procedures for the dispensing and administration of drugs and biologicals;

(h) Has established an accounting and record keeping system to determine reasonable and allowable costs;

(i) "Ambulatory health facilities" also includes an alcoholism treatment facility approved by the joint commission on accreditation of healthcare organizations as an alcoholism treatment facility or certified by the department of alcohol and drug addiction services, and such facility shall comply with other provisions of this division not inconsistent with such accreditation or certification.

(3) "Community mental health facility" means a facility which provides community mental health services and is included in the comprehensive mental health plan for the alcohol, drug addiction, and mental health service district in which it is located.

(4) "Community mental health service" means services, other than inpatient services, provided by a community mental health facility.

(5) "Home health agency" means an institution or a distinct part of an institution operated in this state which:

(a) Is primarily engaged in providing home health services;

(b) Has home health policies which are established by a group of professional personnel, including one or more duly licensed doctors of medicine or osteopathy and one or more registered professional nurses, to govern the home health services it provides and which includes a requirement that every patient must be under the care of a duly licensed doctor of medicine or osteopathy;

(c) Is under the supervision of a duly licensed doctor of medicine or doctor of osteopathy or a registered professional nurse who is responsible for the execution of such home health policies;

(d) Maintains comprehensive records on all patients;

(e) Is operated by the state, a political subdivision, or an agency of either, or is operated not for profit in this state and is licensed or registered, if required, pursuant to law by the appropriate department of the state, county, or municipality in which it furnishes services; or is operated for profit in this state, meets all the requirements specified in divisions (A)(5)(a) to (d) of this section, and is certified under Title XVIII of the "Social Security Act," 49 Stat. 620 (1935), 42 U.S.C. 301, as amended.

(6) "Home health service" means the following items and services, provided, except as provided in division (A)(6)(g) of this section, on a visiting basis in a place of residence used as the patient's home:

(a) Nursing care provided by or under the supervision of a registered professional nurse;

(b) Physical, occupational, or speech therapy ordered by the patient's attending physician;

(c) Medical social services performed by or under the supervision of a qualified medical or psychiatric social worker and under the direction of the patient's attending physician;

(d) Personal health care of the patient performed by aides in accordance with the orders of a doctor of medicine or osteopathy and under the supervision of a registered professional nurse;

(e) Medical supplies and the use of medical appliances;

(f) Medical services of interns and residents-in-training under an approved teaching program of a nonprofit hospital and under the direction and supervision of the patient's attending physician;

(g) Any of the foregoing items and services which:

(i) Are provided on an outpatient basis under arrangements made by the home health agency at a hospital or skilled nursing facility;

(ii) Involve the use of equipment of such a nature that the items and services cannot readily be made available to the patient in his place of residence, or which are furnished at the hospital or skilled nursing facility while he is there to receive any item or service involving the use of such equipment.

Any attorney, physician, osteopath, podiatrist, chiropractor, dentist, psychologist, any employee of a hospital as defined in section 3701.01 of the Revised Code, any nurse licensed under Chapter 4723. of the Revised Code, any employee of an ambulatory health facility, any employee of a home health agency, any employee of an adult care facility as defined in section 3722.01 of the Revised Code, any employee of a community alternative home as defined in section 3724.01 of the Revised Code, any employee of a nursing home, residential care facility, or home for the aging, as defined in section 3721.01 of the Revised Code, any senior service provider, any peace officer, coroner, clergyman, any employee of a community mental health facility, and any person engaged in social work or counseling having reasonable cause to believe that an adult is being abused, neglected, or exploited, or is in a condition which is the result of abuse, neglect, or exploitation shall immediately report such belief to the county department of human services. This section does not apply to employees of any hospital or public hospital as defined in section 5122.01 of the Revised Code.

(B) Any person having reasonable cause to believe that an adult has suffered abuse, neglect, or exploitation may report, or cause reports to be made of such belief to the department.

(C) The reports made under this section shall be made orally or in writing except that oral reports shall be followed by a written report if a written report is requested by the department. Written reports shall include:

(1) The name, address, and approximate age of the adult who is the subject of the report;

(2) The name and address of the individual responsible for the adult's care, if any individual is, and if he is known;

(3) The nature and extent of the alleged abuse, neglect, or exploitation of the adult;

(4) The basis of the reporter's belief that the adult has been abused, neglected, or exploited.

(D) Any person with reasonable cause to believe that an adult is suffering abuse, neglect, or exploitation who makes a report pursuant to this section or who testifies in any administrative or judicial proceeding arising from such a report, or any employee of the state or any of its subdivisions who is discharging responsibilities under section 5101.62 of the Revised Code shall be immune from civil or criminal liability on account of such investigation, report, or testimony, except liability for perjury, unless the person has acted in bad faith or with malicious purpose.

(E) No employer or any other person with the authority to do so shall discharge, demote, transfer, prepare a negative work performance evaluation, or reduce benefits, pay, or work privileges, or take any other action detrimental to an employee or in any way retaliate against an employee as a result of the employee's having filed a report under this section.

(F) Neither the written or oral report provided for in this section nor the investigatory report provided for in section 5101.62 of the Revised Code shall be considered a public record as defined in section 149.43 of the Revised Code. Information contained in the report shall upon request be made available to the adult who is the subject of the report, to agencies authorized by the department to receive information contained in the report, and to legal counsel for the adult.

HISTORY: 139 v H 694 (Eff 11-15-81); 141 v H 66 (Eff 3-6-86); 142 v S 124 (Eff 10-1-87); 143 v S 2 (Eff 11-1-89); 143 v H 253 (Eff 11-15-90); 143 v H 317 (Eff 10-10-89); 146 v H 117. Eff 9-29-95.

The effective date is set by section 197 of HB 117.

§ 5101.94 Repealed, 147 v H 408, § 2 [RC § 5101.91, 139 v S 530; RC § 5101.94, 146 v H 167]. Eff 10-1-97.

This section prohibited obtaining exemptions or benefits to which a person or employer was not entitled under former sections 5101.80 to 5101.94.

§ 5101.99 Penalties.

(A) Whoever violates division (A) or (B) of section 5101.61 of the Revised Code shall be fined not more than five hundred dollars.

(B) Whoever violates division (F) of section 5101.31 of the Revised Code shall be fined not more than five hundred dollars, or imprisoned not more than six months, or both.

(C) Whoever violates division (A) of section 5101.27 of the Revised Code is guilty of a misdemeanor of the first degree.

HISTORY: 139 v S 530 (Eff 1-1-83); 140 v H 37 (Eff 6-22-84); 142 v H 231 (Eff 10-5-87); 144 v H 298 (Eff 7-26-91); 146 v H 249 (Eff 7-17-95); 146 v H 167 (Eff 11-15-95); 147 v H 408. Eff 10-1-97.

The effective date is set by section 26 of HB 408.

CHAPTER 5104: CHILD DAY-CARE

[§ 5104.01.2] § 5104.012 Criminal records check and fingerprinting of prospective employees responsible for child; employment of certain offenders prohibited.

(A)(1) The administrator of a child day-care center or a type-A family day-care home and the provider of a certified type-B family day-care home shall request the superintendent of the bureau of criminal identification and investigation to conduct a criminal records check with respect to any applicant who has applied to the center, type-A home, or certified type-B home for employment as a person responsible for the care, custody, or control of a child. If the applicant does not present proof that the applicant has been a resident of this state for the five-year period immediately prior to the date upon which the criminal records check is requested or does not provide evidence that within that five-year period the superintendent has requested information about the applicant from the federal bureau of investigation in a criminal records check, the administrator or provider shall request that the superintendent obtain information from the federal bureau of investigation as a part of the criminal records check for the applicant. If the applicant presents proof that the applicant has been a resident of this state for that five-year period, the administrator or provider may request that the superintendent include information from the federal bureau of investigation in the criminal records check.

(2) A person required by division (A)(1) of this section to request a criminal records check shall provide to each applicant a copy of the form prescribed pursuant to division (C)(1) of section 109.572 [109.57.2] of the Revised Code, provide to each applicant a standard impression sheet to obtain fingerprint impressions prescribed pursuant to division (C)(2) of section 109.572 [109.57.2] of the Revised Code, obtain the completed form and impression sheet from each applicant, and forward the completed form and impression sheet to the superintendent of the bureau of criminal identification and investigation at the time the person requests a criminal records check pursuant to division (A)(1) of this section

(3) An applicant who receives pursuant to division (A)(2) of this section a copy of the form prescribed pursuant to division (C)(1) of section 109.572 [109.57.2] of the Revised Code and a copy of an impression sheet prescribed pursuant to division (C)(2) of that section and who is requested to complete the form and provide a set of fingerprint impressions shall complete the form or provide all the information necessary to complete the form and shall provide the impression sheet with the impressions of the applicant's fingerprints. If an applicant, upon request, fails to provide the information necessary to complete the form or fails to provide impressions of the applicant's fingerprints, the center, type-A home, or type-B home shall not employ that applicant for any position for which a criminal records check is required by division (A)(1) of this section.

(B)(1) Except as provided in rules adopted by the department of human services in accordance with division (E) of this section, no child day-care center, type-A family day-care home, or certified type-B family day-care home shall employ or contract with another entity for the services of a person as a person responsible for the care, custody, or control of a child if the person previously has been convicted of or pleaded guilty to any of the following:

(a) A violation of section 2903.01, 2903.02, 2903.03, 2903.04, 2903.11, 2903.12, 2903.13, 2903.16, 2903.21, 2903.34, 2905.01, 2905.02, 2905.05, 2907.02, 2907.03, 2907.04, 2907.05, 2907.06, 2907.07, 2907.08, 2907.09, 2907.21, 2907.22, 2907.23, 2907.25, 2907.31, 2907.32, 2907.321 [2907.32.1], 2907.322 [2907.32.2], 2907.323 [2907.32.3], 2911.01, 2911.02, 2911.11, 2911.12, 2919.12, 2919.22, 2919.24, 2919.25, 2923.12, 2923.13, 2923.161 [2923.16.1], 2925.02, 2925.03, 2925.04, 2925.05, 2925.06, or 3716.11 of the Revised Code, a violation of section 2905.04 of the Revised Code as it existed prior to July 1, 1996, a violation of section 2919.23 of the Revised Code that would have been a violation of section 2905.04 of the Revised Code as it existed prior to July 1, 1996, had the violation occurred prior to that date, a violation of section 2925.11 of the Revised Code that is not a minor drug possession offense, or felonious sexual penetration in violation of former section 2907.12 of the Revised Code;

(b) A violation of an existing or former law of this state, any other state, or the United States that is substantially equivalent to any of the offenses or violations described in division (B)(1)(a) of this section.

(2) A child day-care center, type-A family day-care home, or certified type-B family day-care home may employ an applicant conditionally until the criminal records check required by this section is completed and the center or home receives the results of the criminal records check. If the results of the criminal records check indicate that, pursuant to division (B)(1) of this section, the applicant does not qualify for employment, the center or home shall release the applicant from employment.

(C)(1) Each child day-care center, type-A family day-care home, and certified type-B family day-care home shall pay to the bureau of criminal identification and investigation the fee prescribed pursuant to division (C)(3) of section 109.572 [109.57.2] of the Revised Code for each criminal records check conducted in accordance with that section upon the request pursuant to division (A)(1) of this section of the administrator or provider of the center or home.

(2) A child day-care center, type-A family day-care home, and certified type-B family day-care home may

charge an applicant a fee for the costs it incurs in obtaining a criminal records check under this section. A fee charged under this division shall not exceed the amount of fees the center or home pays under division (C)(1) of this section. If a fee is charged under this division, the center or home shall notify the applicant at the time of the applicant's initial application for employment of the amount of the fee and that, unless the fee is paid, the center, type-A home, or type-B home will not consider the applicant for employment.

(D) The report of any criminal records check conducted by the bureau of criminal identification and investigation in accordance with section 109.572 [109.57.2] of the Revised Code and pursuant to a request under division (A)(1) of this section is not a public record for the purposes of section 149.43 of the Revised Code and shall not be made available to any person other than the applicant who is the subject of the criminal records check or the applicant's representative; the center, type-A home, or certified type-B home requesting the criminal records check or its representative; the state department of human services or a county department of human services; and any court, hearing officer, or other necessary individual involved in a case dealing with the denial of employment to the applicant.

(E) The department of human services shall adopt rules pursuant to Chapter 119. of the Revised Code to implement this section, including rules specifying circumstances under which a center or home may hire a person who has been convicted of an offense listed in division (B)(1) of this section but who meets standards in regard to rehabilitation set by the department.

(F) Any person required by division (A)(1) of this section to request a criminal records check shall inform each person, at the time of the person's initial application for employment, that the person is required to provide a set of impressions of the person's fingerprints and that a criminal records check is required to be conducted and satisfactorily completed in accordance with section 109.572 [109.57.2] of the Revised Code if the person comes under final consideration for appointment or employment as a precondition to employment for that position.

(G) As used in this section:

(1) "Applicant" means a person who is under final consideration for appointment to or employment in a position with a child day-care center, a type-A family day-care home, or a certified type-B family day-care home as a person responsible for the care, custody, or control of a child; an in-home aide certified pursuant to section 5104.12 of the Revised Code; or any person who would serve in any position with a child day-care center, a type-A family day-care home, or a certified type-B family day-care home as a person responsible for the care, custody, or control of a child pursuant to a contract with another entity.

(2) "Criminal records check" has the same meaning as in section 109.572 [109.57.2] of the Revised Code.

(3) "Minor drug possession offense" has the same meaning as in section 2925.01 of the Revised Code.

HISTORY: 145 v S 38 (Eff 10-29-93); 145 v H 694 (Eff 11-11-94); 146 v S 2 (Eff 7-1-96); 146 v S 269 (Eff 7-1-96); 146 v H 445. Eff 9-3-96.

Comment, Legislative Service Commission

Sections 5104.012, 5104.013, 5126.28, and 5153.111 of the Revised Code are amended by this act and also by Am. Sub. S.B. 269 of the 121st General Assembly. Comparison of these amendments in pursuance of section 1.52 of the Revised Code discloses that they are not irreconcilable so that they are required by that section to be harmonized to give effect to each amendment.

[§ 5104.01.3] § 5104.013 Criminal records check and fingerprinting of owner, licensee or administrator of facility; licensing of certain offenders prohibited.

(A)(1) The director of human services, as part of the process of licensure of child day-care centers and type-A family day-care homes, shall request the superintendent of the bureau of criminal identification and investigation to conduct a criminal records check with respect to the following persons:

(a) Any owner, licensee, or administrator of a child day-care center;

(b) Any owner, licensee, or administrator of a type-A family day-care home and any person eighteen years of age or older who resides in a type-A family day-care home.

(2) The director of a county department of human services, as part of the process of certification of type-B family day-care homes, shall request the superintendent of the bureau of criminal identification and investigation to conduct a criminal records check with respect to any authorized provider of a certified type-B family day-care home and any person eighteen years of age or older who resides in a certified type-B family day-care home.

(B) The director of human services or the director of a county department of human services shall provide to each person for whom a criminal records check is required under this section a copy of the form prescribed pursuant to division (C)(1) of section 109.572 [109.57.2] of the Revised Code and a standard impression sheet to obtain fingerprint impressions prescribed pursuant to division (C)(2) of that section, obtain the completed form and impression sheet from that person, and forward the completed form and impression sheet to the superintendent of the bureau of criminal identification and investigation.

(C) A person who receives pursuant to division (B) of this section a copy of the form and standard impression sheet described in that division and who is requested to complete the form and provide a set of fingerprint impressions shall complete the form or provide all the information necessary to complete the form and shall provide the impression sheet with the impressions of the person's fingerprints. If the person, upon request, fails to provide the information necessary to complete the form or fails to provide impressions of the person's fingerprints, the director may consider the failure as a reason to deny licensure or certification.

(D) Except as provided in rules adopted by the department of human services in accordance with division (G) of this section, the director of human services shall not grant a license to a child day-care center or type-A family day-care home and a county director of human services shall not certify a type-B family day-care home if a person for whom a criminal records check was required in connection with the center or home previously has been convicted of or pleaded guilty to any of the following:

(1) A violation of section 2903.01, 2903.02, 2903.03, 2903.04, 2903.11, 2903.12, 2903.13, 2903.16, 2903.21, 2903.34, 2905.01, 2905.02, 2905.05, 2907.02, 2907.03, 2907.04, 2907.05, 2907.06, 2907.07, 2907.08, 2907.09, 2907.21, 2907.22, 2907.23, 2907.25, 2907.31, 2907.32, 2907.321 [2907.32.1], 2907.322 [2907.32.2], 2907.323 [2907.32.3], 2911.01, 2911.02, 2911.11, 2911.12, 2919.12, 2919.22, 2919.24, 2919.25, 2923.12, 2923.13, 2923.161 [2923.16.1], 2925.02, 2925.03, 2925.04, 2925.05, 2925.06, or 3716.11 of the Revised Code, a violation of section 2905.04 as it existed prior to July 1, 1996, a violation of section 2919.23 of the Revised Code that would have been a violation of section 2905.04 of the Revised Code as it existed prior to July 1, 1996, had the violation been committed to that date, a violation of section 2925.11 of the Revised Code that is not a minor drug possession offense, or felonious sexual penetration in violation of former section 2907.12 of the Revised Code;

(2) A violation of an existing or former law of this state, any other state, or the United States that is substantially equivalent to any of the offenses or violations described in division (D)(1) of this section.

(E) Each child day-care center, type-A family day-care home, and type-B family day-care home shall pay to the bureau of criminal identification and investigation the fee prescribed pursuant to division (C)(3) of section 109.572 [109.57.2] of the Revised Code for each criminal records check conducted in accordance with that section upon a request made pursuant to division (A) of this section.

(F) The report of any criminal records check conducted by the bureau of criminal identification and investigation in accordance with section 109.572 [109.57.2] of the Revised Code and pursuant to a request made under division (A) of this section is not a public record for the purposes of section 149.43 of the Revised Code and shall not be made available to any person other than the person who is the subject of the criminal records check or the person's representative, the director of human services, the director of a county department of human services, the center, type-A home, or type-B home involved, and any court, hearing officer, or other necessary individual involved in a case dealing with a denial of licensure or certification related to the criminal records check.

(G) The department of human services shall adopt rules pursuant to Chapter 119. of the Revised Code to implement this section, including rules specifying exceptions to the prohibition in division (D) of this section for persons who have been convicted of an offense listed in that division but who meet standards in regard to rehabilitation set by the department.

(H) As used in this section:

(1) "Criminal records check" has the same meaning as in section 109.572 [109.57.2] of the Revised Code.

(2) "Minor drug possession offense" has the same meaning as in section 2925.01 of the Revised Code.

HISTORY: 145 v S 38 (Eff 10-29-93); 145 v H 694 (Eff 11-11-94); 146 v S 2 (Eff 7-1-96); 146 v S 269 (Eff 7-1-96); 146 v H 445. Eff 9-3-96.

See Comment, Legislative Service Commission following RC § 5104.01.2.

§ 5104.09 Certain offenders disqualified from day-care activities; statements of denial; discrimination in enrollment prohibited.

(A)(1) No individual who has been convicted of or pleaded guilty to a violation of section 2903.01, 2903.02, 2903.03, 2903.04, 2903.11, 2903.12, 2903.13, 2903.16, 2903.21, 2903.22, 2903.34, 2905.01, 2905.02, 2905.04,† 2905.05, 2905.11, 2907.02, 2907.03, 2907.04, 2907.05, 2907.06, 2907.07, 2907.08, 2907.09, 2907.21, 2907.22, 2907.23, 2907.25, 2907.31, 2907.32, 2907.321 [2907.32.1], 2907.322 [2907.32.2], 2907.323 [2907.32.3], 2909.02, 2909.03, 2909.04, 2909.05, 2911.01, 2911.02, 2911.11, 2911.12, 2917.01, 2917.02, 2917.03, 2917.31, 2919.12, 2919.24, 2919.25, 2921.03, 2921.34, 2921.35, 2923.12, 2923.13, 2923.161 [2923.16.1], 2919.22, 2925.02, 2925.03, 2925.04, 2925.05, 2925.06, or 3716.11 of the Revised Code, a violation of section 2925.11 of the Revised Code that is not a minor drug possession offense, as defined in section 2925.01 of the Revised Code, felonious sexual penetration in violation of former section 2907.12 of the Revised Code, or a violation of an existing or former law or ordinance of any municipal corporation, this state, any other state, or the United States that is substantially equivalent to any of those violations shall be certified as an in-home aide or be employed in any capacity in or own or operate a child day-care center, type A family day-care home, type B family day-care home, or certified type B family day-care home.

(2) Each employee of a child day-care center and type A home and every person eighteen years of age or older residing in a type A home shall sign a statement on forms prescribed by the director of human services attesting to the fact that the employee or resident person has not been convicted of or pleaded guilty to any offense set forth in division (A)(1) of this section and that no child has been removed from the employee's

or resident person's home pursuant to section 2151.353 [2151.35.3] of the Revised Code. Each licensee of a type A home shall sign a statement on a form prescribed by the director attesting to the fact that no person who resides at the type A home and who is under the age of eighteen has been adjudicated a delinquent child for committing a violation of any section listed in division (A)(1) of this section. The statements shall be kept on file at the center or type A home.

(3) Each in-home aide, each authorized provider, and every person eighteen years of age or older residing in a certified type B home shall sign a statement on forms prescribed by the director of human services attesting that the aide, provider, or resident person has not been convicted of or pleaded guilty to any offense set forth in division (A)(1) of this section and that no child has been removed from the aide's, provider's, or resident person's home pursuant to section 2151.353 [2151.35.3] of the Revised Code. Each authorized provider shall sign a statement on a form prescribed by the director attesting to the fact that no person who resides at the certified type B home and who is under the age of eighteen has been adjudicated a delinquent child for committing a violation of any section listed in division (A)(1) of this section. The statements shall be kept on file at the county department of human services.

(4) Each administrator and licensee of a center or type A home shall sign a statement on a form prescribed by the director of human services attesting that he has not been convicted of or pleaded guilty to any offense set forth in division (A)(1) of this section and that no child has been removed from the administrator's or licensee's home pursuant to section 2151.353 [2151.35.3] of the Revised Code. The statement shall be kept on file at the center or type A home.

(B) No in-home aide, no administrator, licensee, authorized provider, or employee of a center, type A home, or certified type B home, and no person eighteen years of age or older residing in a type A home or certified type B home shall withhold information from, or falsify information on, any statement required pursuant to division (A)(2), (3), or (4) of this section.

(C) No administrator, licensee, or child-care staff member shall discriminate in the enrollment of children in a child day-care center upon the basis of race, color, religion, sex, or national origin.

HISTORY: 141 v H 435 (Eff 9-1-86); 145 v S 38 (Eff 10-29-93); 146 v S 2 (Eff 7-1-96); 146 v H 445. Eff 9-3-96.

† RC § 2905.04 was repealed in SB 2 (146 v —), effective 7-1-96. See analogous provisions at 2905.01.

CHAPTER 5119: DEPARTMENT OF MENTAL HEALTH

§ 5119.57 System for tracking and monitoring after release of insanity acquittees or defendants found incompetent.

No later than January 1, 1998, the department of mental health, in conjunction with boards of alcohol, drug addiction, and mental health services and community mental health boards, shall develop a coordinated system for tracking and monitoring persons found not guilty by reason of insanity and committed pursuant to section 2945.40 of the Revised Code who have been granted a conditional release and persons found incompetent to stand trial and committed pursuant to section 2945.39 of the Revised Code who have been granted a conditional release. The system shall do all of the following:

(A) Centralize responsibility for the tracking of those persons;

(B) Develop uniformity in monitoring those persons;

(C) Develop a mechanism to allow prompt rehospitalization, reinstitutionalization, or detention when a violation of the conditional release or decompensation occurs.

HISTORY: 146 v S 285. Eff 7-1-97.

Not analogous to former RC § 5119.57 (125 v 859), repealed 184 v H 494, § 2, eff 7-12-72.

The effective date is set by section 4 of SB 285.

CHAPTER 5120: DEPARTMENT OF REHABILITATION AND CORRECTION

§ 5120.01 Director of rehabilitation and correction.

The director of rehabilitation and correction is the executive head of the department of rehabilitation and correction. All duties conferred on the various divisions and institutions of the department by law or by order of the director shall be performed under such rules and regulations as he prescribes, and shall be under his control. The director shall have power to control transfers of inmates between the several state institutions included under section 5120.05 of the Revised Code.

HISTORY: 134 v H 494. Eff 7-12-72.

The effective date set by section 3 of HB 494 (134 v 1845) was not applicable, and the constitutional provisions in Art. II, §§ 1c, 1d requiring the lapse of 90 days after filing the bill with the secretary of state prevails.

[§ 5120.01.1] § 5120.011 Sanctions where inmate's action is found to be frivolous or malicious.

(A) As used in this section, "civil action or appeal against a government entity or employee," "inmate," "political subdivision," and "employee" have the same meanings as in section 2969.21 of the Revised Code.

(B) The director of rehabilitation and correction may adopt rules under section 5120.01 of the Revised Code to implement the procedures described in sections 2323.51, 2969.22, and 2969.23 of the Revised Code.

(C) The director of rehabilitation and correction shall adopt rules that provide that, if an inmate files a civil action or appeal against a government entity or employee or files a civil action against the state, a political subdivision, or an employee in a federal court and if the court in which the action or appeal is filed dismisses the action or appeal pursuant to section 2969.24 of the Revised Code or the federal court finds the action to be frivolous under 28 U.S.C. 1915(d), the inmate shall be subject to one or more of the following sanctions:

(1) Extra work duty, without compensation, for not more than sixty days;

(2) The loss of commissary privileges for not more than sixty days;

(3) The loss of sundry-package privileges for one time in any calendar year;

(4) The loss of television privileges for not more than sixty days;

(5) The loss of radio privileges for not more than sixty days;

(6) The loss of recreational activity privileges for not more than sixty days.

HISTORY: 146 v H 455. Eff 10-17-96.

§ 5120.02 Assistant director of the department; powers and duties.

The assistant director of the department of rehabilitation and correction is hereby excepted from section 121.05 of the Revised Code. The assistant director shall exercise the powers and perform the duties which the director of correction may order and shall act as director in the absence or disability of the director, or in case of a vacancy in the position of director.

HISTORY: 134 v H 494. Eff 7-12-72.

See effective date provision following RC § 5120.01.

[§ 5120.02.1] § 5120.021 Application of provisions effective 7-1-96.

(A) Chapter 5120. of the Revised Code, as it existed prior to July 1, 1996, applies to a person upon whom a court imposed a term of imprisonment prior to July 1, 1996, and a person upon whom a court, on or after July 1, 1996, and in accordance with law existing prior to July 1, 1996, imposed a term of imprisonment for an offense that was committed prior to July 1, 1996.

(B) Chapter 5120. of the Revised Code, as it exists on and after the effective date of this section, applies to a person upon whom a court imposed a stated prison term for an offense committed on or after the effective date of this section.

HISTORY: 146 v S 2. Eff 7-1-96.

The effective date is set by section 6 of SB 2.

The provisions of § 5 of SB 2 (146 v —) read as follows:

SECTION 5. The provisions of the Revised Code in existence prior to July 1, 1996, shall apply to a person upon whom a court imposed a term of imprisonment prior to that date and to a person upon whom a court, on or after July 1, 1996, and in accordance with the law in existence prior to that date, imposed a term of imprisonment for an offense that was committed prior to that date.

The provisions of the Revised Code in existence on and after July 1, 1996, apply to a person who commits an offense on or after that date.

§ 5120.03 Change of use of institution; penal/reformatory distinction eliminated; privatization of facility.

(A) The director of rehabilitation and correction, by executive order and with the approval of the governor, may change the purpose for which any institution or place under the control of the department of rehabilitation and correction, is being used. The director may designate a new or another use for such institution, if the change of use and new designation has for its objective, improvement in the classification, segregation, care, education, cure, or rehabilitation of persons subject to the control of the department.

(B) The director of rehabilitation and correction, by executive order, issued on or before December 31, 1988, shall eliminate the distinction between penal institutions and reformatory institutions. Notwithstanding any provision of the Revised Code or the Administrative Code to the contrary, upon the issuance of the executive order, any distinction made between the types of prisoners sentenced to or otherwise assigned to the institutions under the control of the department shall be discontinued.

(C) The director may contract under section 9.06 of the Revised Code for the private operation and management of a facility under the control of the department. All inmates assigned to a facility operated and managed by a private contractor remain inmates in the care and custody of the department. The statutes, rules, and policies of the department may apply to the private contractor and any inmate assigned to a facility operated and managed by a private contractor as agreed to in the contract entered into under section 9.06 of the Revised Code.

HISTORY: 134 v H 494 (Eff 7-12-72); 142 v H 261 (Eff 11-1-87); 147 v H 215. Eff 9-29-97.

The effective date is set by section 222 of HB 215.

[§ 5120.03.1] § 5120.031 Pilot program of shock incarceration for eligible offenders.

(A) As used in this section:

(1) "Certificate of high school equivalence" means a statement that is issued by the state board of education or an equivalent agency of another state and that indi-

cates that its holder has achieved the equivalent of a high school education as measured by scores obtained on the tests of general educational development published by the American council on education.

(2) "Certificate of adult basic education" means a statement that is issued by the department of rehabilitation and correction through the Ohio central school system approved by the state board of education and that indicates that its holder has achieved a 6.0 grade level, or higher, as measured by scores of nationally standardized or recognized tests.

(3) "Deadly weapon" and "firearm" have the same meanings as in section 2923.11 of the Revised Code.

(4) "Eligible offender" means a person, other than one who is ineligible to participate in an intensive program prison under the criteria specified in section 5120.032 [5120.03.2] of the Revised Code, who has been convicted of or pleaded guilty to, and has been sentenced for, a felony.

(5) "Shock incarceration" means the program of incarceration that is established pursuant to the rules of the department of rehabilitation and correction adopted under this section.

(B)(1) The director of rehabilitation and correction, by rules adopted under Chapter 119. of the Revised Code, shall establish a pilot program of shock incarceration that may be used for eligible offenders who are sentenced to serve a term of imprisonment under the custody of the department of rehabilitation and correction and whom the department, subject to the approval of the sentencing judge, may permit to serve their sentence as a sentence of shock incarceration in accordance with this section.

(2) The rules for the pilot program shall require that the program be established at an appropriate state correctional institution designated by the director and that the program consist of both of the following for each eligible offender whom the department, with the approval of the sentencing judge, permits to serve the eligible offender's sentence as a sentence of shock incarceration:

(a) A period of imprisonment at that institution of ninety days that shall consist of a military style combination of discipline, physical training, and hard labor and substance abuse education, employment skills training, social skills training, and psychological treatment. During the ninety-day period, the department may permit an eligible offender to participate in a self-help program. Additionally, during the ninety-day period, an eligible offender who holds a high school diploma or a certificate of high school equivalence may be permitted to tutor other eligible offenders in the shock incarceration program. If an eligible offender does not hold a high school diploma or certificate of high school equivalence, the eligible offender may elect to participate in an education program that is designed to award a certificate of adult basic education or an education program that is designed to award a certificate of high school equivalence to those eligible offenders who successfully complete the education program, whether the completion occurs during or subsequent to the ninety-day period. To the extent possible, the department shall use as teachers in the education program persons who have been issued a license pursuant to sections 3319.22 to 3319.31 of the Revised Code, who have volunteered their services to the education program, and who satisfy any other criteria specified in the rules for the pilot project.

(b) Immediately following the ninety-day period of imprisonment, and notwithstanding any other provision governing the furlough or other early release of a prisoner from imprisonment, one of the following, as determined by the director:

(i) An intermediate, transitional type of detention for the period of time determined by the director and, immediately following the intermediate, transitional type of detention, a release under a post-release control sanction imposed in accordance with section 2967.28 of the Revised Code. The period of intermediate, transitional type of detention imposed by the director under this division may be in a halfway house, in a community-based correctional facility and program or district community-based correctional facility and program established under sections 2301.51 to 2301.56 of the Revised Code, or in any other facility approved by the director that provides for detention to serve as a transition between imprisonment in a state correctional institution and release from imprisonment.

(ii) A release under a post-release control sanction imposed in accordance with section 2967.28 of the Revised Code.

(3) The rules for the pilot program also shall include, but are not limited to, all of the following:

(a) Rules identifying the locations within the state correctional institution designated by the director that will be used for eligible offenders serving a sentence of shock incarceration;

(b) Rules establishing specific schedules of discipline, physical training, and hard labor for eligible offenders serving a sentence of shock incarceration, based upon the offender's physical condition and needs;

(c) Rules establishing standards and criteria for the department to use in determining which eligible offenders the department will permit to serve their sentence of imprisonment as a sentence of shock incarceration;

(d) Rules establishing guidelines for the selection of post-release control sanctions for eligible offenders;

(e) Rules establishing procedures for notifying sentencing courts of the performance of eligible offenders serving their sentences of imprisonment as a sentence of shock incarceration;

(f) Any other rules that are necessary for the proper conduct of the pilot program.

(C)(1) Subject to disapproval by the sentencing judge, if an eligible offender is sentenced to a term of imprisonment under the custody of the department, the department may permit the eligible offender to serve the sentence as a sentence of shock incarceration, in accordance with this section and the rules adopted under this section. At least three weeks prior to permitting an eligible offender to serve a sentence of shock incarceration, the department shall notify the sentencing judge of the proposed shock incarceration and of the fact that the judge may disapprove it. If the sentencing judge disapproves of shock incarceration for the eligible offender, the judge shall notify the department of the disapproval within ten days after receipt of the notice, and the department shall not permit the eligible offender to serve a sentence of shock incarceration. If the judge does not timely disapprove of shock incarceration for the eligible offender, the department may proceed with plans for the shock incarceration.

(2) If the department permits an eligible offender to serve the eligible offender's sentence of imprisonment as a sentence of shock incarceration and the eligible offender does not satisfactorily complete the entire period of imprisonment described in division (B)(2)(a) of this section, the offender shall be removed from the pilot program for shock incarceration and shall be required to serve the remainder of the offender's sentence of imprisonment imposed by the sentencing court as a regular term of imprisonment. If the eligible offender commences a period of post-release control described in division (B)(2)(b) of this section and violates the conditions of that post-release control, the eligible offender shall be subject to the provisions of sections 2967.15 and 2967.28 of the Revised Code regarding violation of post-release control sanctions.

(3) If an eligible offender's stated prison term expires at any time during the eligible offender's participation in the shock incarceration program, the adult parole authority shall terminate the eligible offender's participation in the program and shall issue to the eligible offender a certificate of expiration of the stated prison term.

(D) The director shall keep sentencing courts informed of the performance of eligible offenders serving their sentences of imprisonment as a sentence of shock incarceration, including, but not limited to, notice of eligible offenders who fail to satisfactorily complete their entire sentence of shock incarceration or who satisfactorily complete their entire sentence of shock incarceration.

(E) Within a reasonable period of time after November 20, 1990, the director shall appoint a committee to search for one or more suitable sites at which one or more programs of shock incarceration, in addition to the pilot program required by division (B)(1) of this section, may be established. The search committee shall consist of the director or the director's designee, as chairman; employees of the department of rehabilitation and correction appointed by the director; and any other persons that the director, in the director's discretion, appoints. In searching for such sites, the search committee shall give preference to any site owned by the state or any other governmental entity and to any existing structure that reasonably could be renovated, enlarged, converted, or remodeled for purposes of establishing such a program. The search committee shall prepare a report concerning its activities and, on the earlier of the day that is twelve months after the first day on which an eligible offender began serving a sentence of shock incarceration under the pilot program or January 1, 1992, shall file the report with the president and the minority leader of the senate, the speaker and the minority leader of the house of representatives, the members of the senate who were members of the senate judiciary committee in the 118th general assembly or their successors, and the members of the house of representatives who were members of the select committee to hear drug legislation that was established in the 118th general assembly or their successors. Upon the filing of the report, the search committee shall terminate. The report required by this division shall contain all of the following:

(1) A summary of the process used by the search committee in performing its duties under this division;

(2) A summary of all of the sites reviewed by the search committee in performing its duties under this division, and the benefits and disadvantages it found relative to the establishment of a program of shock incarceration at each such site;

(3) The findings and recommendations of the search committee as to the suitable site or sites, if any, at which a program of shock incarceration, in addition to the pilot program required by division (B)(1) of this section, may be established.

(F) The director periodically shall review the pilot program for shock incarceration required to be established by division (B)(1) of this section. The director shall prepare a report relative to the pilot program and, on the earlier of the day that is twelve months after the first day on which an eligible offender began serving a sentence of shock incarceration under the pilot program or January 1, 1992, shall file the report with the president and the minority leader of the senate, the speaker and the minority leader of the house of representatives, the members of the senate who were members of the senate judiciary committee in the 118th general assembly or their successors, and the members of the house of representatives who were members of the select committee to hear drug legislation that was established in the 118th general assembly or their successors. The pilot program shall not terminate at the time of the filing of the report, but shall continue in operation in accordance with this section. The report required by this division shall include all of the following:

(1) A summary of the pilot program as initially established, a summary of all changes in the pilot program made during the period covered by the report and the reasons for the changes, and a summary of the pilot program as it exists on the date of preparation of the report;

(2) A summary of the effectiveness of the pilot program, in the opinion of the director and employees of the department involved in its operation;

(3) An analysis of the total cost of the pilot program, of its cost per inmate who was permitted to serve a sentence of shock incarceration and who served the entire sentence of shock incarceration, and of its cost per inmate who was permitted to serve a sentence of shock incarceration;

(4) A summary of the standards and criteria used by the department in determining which eligible offenders were permitted to serve their sentence of imprisonment as a sentence of shock incarceration;

(5) A summary of the characteristics of the eligible offenders who were permitted to serve their sentence of imprisonment as a sentence of shock incarceration, which summary shall include, but not be limited to, a listing of every offense of which any such eligible offender was convicted or to which any such eligible offender pleaded guilty and in relation to which the eligible offender served a sentence of shock incarceration, and the total number of such eligible offenders who were convicted of or pleaded guilty to each such offense;

(6) A listing of the number of eligible offenders who were permitted to serve a sentence of shock incarceration and who did not serve the entire sentence of shock incarceration, and, to the extent possible, a summary of the length of the terms of imprisonment served by such eligible offenders after they were removed from the pilot program;

(7) A summary of the effect of the pilot program on overcrowding at state correctional institutions;

(8) To the extent possible, an analysis of the rate of recidivism of eligible offenders who were permitted to serve a sentence of shock incarceration and who served the entire sentence of shock incarceration;

(9) Recommendations as to legislative changes to the pilot program that would assist in its operation or that could further alleviate overcrowding at state correctional institutions, and recommendations as to whether the pilot program should be expanded.

HISTORY: 143 v S 258 (Eff 11-20-90); 145 v H 314 (Eff 9-29-94); 145 v H 571 (Eff 10-6-94); 146 v S 2 (Eff 7-1-96); 146 v S 269 (Eff 7-1-96); 146 v S 230. Eff 10-29-96.

Comment, Legislative Service Commission

° ° ° Sections ° ° ° 5120.032 of the Revised Code are amended by this act [Am. Sub. S.B. 269] and also by Am. Sub. S.B. 166 of the 121st General Assembly. ° ° ° Section 5120.031 of the Revised Code is amended by this act [Am. Sub. S.B. 269] and also by Am. Sub. S.B. 230 of the 121st General Assembly. Comparison of these amendments in pursuance of section 1.52 of the Revised Code discloses that they are not irreconcilable so that they are required by that section to be harmonized to give effect to each amendment.

[§ 5120.03.2] § 5120.032 Intensive program prisons.

(A) No later than January 1, 1998, the department of rehabilitation and correction shall develop and implement intensive program prisons for male and female prisoners other than prisoners described in division (B)(2) of this section. The intensive program prisons shall include institutions at which imprisonment of the type described in division (B)(2)(a) of section 5120.031 [5120.03.1] of the Revised Code is provided and prisons that focus on educational achievement, vocational training, alcohol and other drug abuse treatment, community service and conservation work, and other intensive regimens or combinations of intensive regimens.

(B)(1) Except as provided in division (B)(2) of this section, the department may place a prisoner in an intensive program prison established pursuant to division (A) of this section subject to the approval of the sentencing judge. At least three weeks prior to placing a prisoner in an intensive program prison, the department shall give notice of the placement and of the fact that the judge may disapprove the placement. If the judge disapproves the placement, the judge shall notify the department of the disapproval within ten days after receipt of the notice. If the judge timely disapproves the placement, the department shall not proceed with it. If the judge does not timely disapprove of the placement, the department may proceed with plans for it.

The department may reduce the stated prison term of a prisoner upon the prisoner's successful completion of a ninety-day period in an intensive program prison. A prisoner whose term has been so reduced shall be required to serve an intermediate, transitional type of detention followed by a release under post-release control sanctions or, in the alternative, shall be placed under post-release control sanctions, as described in division (B)(2)(b)(ii) of section 5120.031 [5120.03.1] of the Revised Code. In either case, the placement under post-release control sanctions shall be under terms set by the parole board in accordance with section 2967.28 of the Revised Code and shall be subject to the provisions of that section with respect to a violation of any post-release control sanction.

(2) A prisoner who is in any of the following categories is not eligible to participate in an intensive program prison established pursuant to division (A) of this section:

(a) The prisoner is serving a prison term for aggravated murder, murder, or a felony of the first or second degree or a comparable offense under the law in effect prior to the effective date of this section or the prisoner previously has been imprisoned for aggravated murder, murder, or a felony of the first or second degree or a comparable offense under the law in effect prior to the effective date of this section.

(b) The prisoner is serving a mandatory prison term, as defined in section 2929.01 of the Revised Code.

(c) The prisoner is serving a prison term for a felony of the third, fourth, or fifth degree that either is a sex offense, an offense betraying public trust, or an offense in which the prisoner caused or attempted to cause actual physical harm to a person, the prisoner is serving a prison term for a comparable offense under the law in effect prior to the effective date of this section, or the prisoner previously has been imprisoned for an offense of that type or a comparable offense under the law in effect prior to the effective date of this section.

(d) The prisoner is serving a mandatory prison term in prison for a fourth degree felony OMVI offense, as defined in section 2929.01 of the Revised Code, that was imposed pursuant to division (G)(2) of section 2929.13 of the Revised Code.

(C) Upon the implementation of intensive program prisons pursuant to division (A) of this section, the department at all times shall maintain intensive program prisons sufficient in number to reduce the prison terms of at least three hundred fifty prisoners who are eligible for reduction of their stated prison terms as a result of their completion of a regimen in an intensive program prison under this section.

HISTORY: 146 v S 2 (Eff 7-1-96); 146 v S 269 (Eff 7-1-96); 146 v S 166. Eff 10-17-96.

See Comment, Legislative Service Commission following RC § 5120.03.1.

[§ 5120.03.3] § 5120.033 Intensive program prisons for certain OMVI offenders.

(A) As used in this section, "fourth degree felony OMVI offense" has the same meaning as in section 2929.01 of the Revised Code.

(B) Within eighteen months after the effective date of this section, the department of rehabilitation and correction shall develop and implement intensive program prisons for male and female prisoners who are sentenced pursuant to division (G)(2) of section 2929.13 of the Revised Code to a mandatory prison term for a fourth degree felony OMVI offense. The intensive program prisons shall include prisons that focus on educational achievement, vocational training, alcohol and other drug abuse treatment, community service and conservation work, and other intensive regimens or combinations of intensive regimens.

(C) Except as provided in division (D) of this section, the department may place a prisoner who is sentenced to a mandatory prison term for a fourth degree felony OMVI offense in an intensive program prison established pursuant to division (B) of this section if the sentencing judge, upon notification by the department of its intent to place the prisoner in an intensive program prison, does not notify the department that the judge disapproves the placement. If the stated prison term imposed on a prisoner who is so placed is longer than the mandatory prison term that is required to be imposed on the prisoner, the department may reduce the stated prison term upon the prisoner's successful completion of the prisoner's mandatory prison term in an intensive program prison. A prisoner whose term has been so reduced shall be required to serve an intermediate, transitional type of detention followed by a release under post-release control sanctions or, in the alternative, shall be placed under post-release control sanctions, as described in division (B)(2)(b)(ii) of section 5120.031 [5120.03.1] of the Revised Code. In either case, the placement under post-release control sanctions shall be under terms set by the parole board in accordance with section 2967.28 of the Revised Code and shall be subject to the provisions of that section with respect to a violation of any post-release control sanction.

(D) A prisoner who is sentenced to a mandatory prison term for a fourth degree felony OMVI offense is not eligible to participate in an intensive program prison established under division (B) of this section if any of the following applies regarding the prisoner:

(1) In addition to the mandatory prison term for the fourth degree felony OMVI offense, the prisoner also is serving a prison term of a type described in division (B)(2)(a), (b), or (c) of section 5120.032 [5120.03.2] of the Revised Code.

(2) The prisoner previously has been imprisoned for an offense of a type described in division (B)(2)(a) or (c) of section 5120.032 [5120.03.2] of the Revised Code or a comparable offense under the law in effect prior to July 1, 1996.

(E) Intensive program prisons established under division (B) of this section are not subject to section 5120.032 [5120.03.2] of the Revised Code.

HISTORY: 146 v S 166. Eff 10-17-96.

§ 5120.04 Assignment of prisoner labor.

The department of rehabilitation and correction, with the approval of the governor and in accordance with rules adopted pursuant to division (B) of section 5145.03 of the Revised Code, may assign prisoners who are committed or transferred to institutions under the administration of the department to perform labor on any public work of the state.

HISTORY: 134 v H 494 (Eff 7-12-72); 138 v H 654. Eff 4-9-82.

The effective date is set by section 4 of HB 654.

§ 5120.05 Employees; management, naming of institutions; receipt of delinquent juveniles.

Except as otherwise provided as to appointments by chiefs of divisions, the director of rehabilitation and correction shall appoint the employees that are necessary for the efficient conduct of the department of rehabilitation and correction and shall prescribe their titles and duties. The department may maintain, operate, manage, and govern all state institutions for the custody, control, training, and rehabilitation of persons convicted of crime and sentenced to correctional institutions.

The department may designate correctional institutions by appropriate respective names.

The department may receive from the department of youth services any children in the custody of the department of youth services, committed to the department of rehabilitation and correction by the department of youth services, upon the terms and conditions that are agreed upon by the departments.

HISTORY: 134 v H 494 (Eff 7-12-72); 139 v H 440 (Eff 11-23-81); 145 v H 571. Eff 10-6-94.

[§ 5120.05.1] § 5120.051 Mentally ill or retarded inmates.

The department of rehabilitation and correction shall provide for the needs of mentally ill and mentally retarded persons who are incarcerated in state correctional institutions. The department may designate an institution or a unit within an institution for the custody, care, special training, treatment, and rehabilitation of mentally ill or mentally retarded persons.

HISTORY: RC § 5125.02, 139 v S 550 (Eff 11-26-82); RC § 5120.05.1, 145 v H 571 (Eff 10-6-94); 146 v S 310. Eff 6-20-96.

The effective date is determined by § 23 of SB 310 (146 v —).

§ 5120.06 Divisions of department of rehabilitation and correction.

The following divisions are hereby established in the department of rehabilitation and correction:

(A) The division of business administration;

(B) The division of parole and community services.

The director may establish other divisions and prescribe their powers and duties.

HISTORY: 134 v H 494. Eff 7-12-72.

See effective date provision following RC § 5120.01.

§ 5120.07 Division chiefs; requirements.

Each division established or authorized by section 5120.06 of the Revised Code shall consist of a chief and the officers and employees, including those in institutions, necessary for the performance of the functions assigned to it. The director of rehabilitation and correction shall supervise the work of each division and be responsible for the determination of general policies in the exercise of powers vested in the department and powers assigned to each division. The chief of each division shall be responsible to the director for the organization, direction, and supervision of the work of the division and the exercise of the powers and the performance of the duties of the department assigned to such division, and, with the approval of the director, may establish bureaus or other administrative units therein.

The director shall appoint the chief of each division, who shall be in the unclassified service and serve at the pleasure of the director. Appointment to the position of chief of a division shall be made from persons holding positions in the classified service in the department of rehabilitation and correction. A person so appointed shall retain the right to resume the position and status held by him in the classified service immediately prior to his appointment as chief of a division. Upon being relieved of his duties as chief of a division such person shall be reinstated to the position in the classified service held by him immediately prior to his appointment to the position of chief of a division, or to another position, certified by the director with approval of the department of administrative services as being substantially equal to such position. Service as a chief of a division shall be counted as service in the position in the classified service held by such person immediately preceding his appointment as chief of a division. When such person is reinstated to a position in the classified service, as provided in this section, he shall be entitled to all rights and emoluments accruing to such position during the time of his service as chief of a division.

The chief of each division shall be a person who has had special training and experience in the type of work with the performance of which the division is charged.

Each chief of the division, under the director, shall have entire executive charge of the division for which he is appointed. Subject to Chapter 124. of the Revised Code, and civil service regulations, the chief of the division shall, with the approval of the director, select and appoint the necessary employees and may remove such employees for cause.

HISTORY: 134 v H 494 (Eff 7-12-72); 137 v H 1. Eff 8-26-77.

[ELECTRONICALLY MONITORED EARLY RELEASE]

[§ 5120.07.1] § 5120.071 Definitions.

As used in sections 5120.071 [5120.07.1] to 5120.074 [5120.07.4] of the Revised Code:

(A) "Electronic monitoring device," "certified electronic monitoring device," "electronic monitoring system," and "certified electronic monitoring system" have the same meanings as in section 2929.23 of the Revised Code.

(B) "Electronically monitored early release" means a specified period of confinement during which an eligible offender is confined in or restricted to specified premises other than a correctional institution, during which period of confinement all of the following apply:

(1) The eligible offender wears, otherwise has attached to the eligible offender's person, or otherwise is subject to monitoring by a certified electronic monitoring device or is subject to monitoring by a certified electronic monitoring system.

(2) The eligible offender is required to remain in the eligible offender's home or in other premises that are approved and specified by the department of rehabilitation and correction during the specified period of confinement, except for periods of time during which the

eligible offender is at the eligible offender's place of employment or at other premises as authorized by the department.

(3) The eligible offender is subject to monitoring by a central system that monitors the certified electronic monitoring device that is attached to the eligible offender's person or that otherwise is used to monitor the eligible offender and that can monitor and determine the eligible offender's location at any time or at a designated point in time, or the eligible offender is required to participate in monitoring by a certified electronic monitoring system.

(4) The eligible offender is required by the department to report periodically to a person designated by the department.

(5) The eligible offender is subject to any other restrictions and requirements imposed by the department pursuant to its rules.

(6) For purposes of section 2967.193 [2967.19.3] of the Revised Code, the eligible offender is not to be considered as being confined in a state correctional institution and, during that specified period of confinement, is not entitled to earn any days of credit as a deduction from the eligible offender's sentence under section 2967.193 [2967.19.3] of the Revised Code.

(C) "Eligible offender" means an offender in the custody of the department of rehabilitation and correction who meets all of the following criteria:

(1) The offender has not been convicted of and did not plead guilty to an offense of violence.

(2) The offender did not, during the commission of the offense for which the offender is in the custody of the department, cause or attempt to cause physical harm to any person or make an actual threat of physical harm to any person with a deadly weapon.

(3) The offender was not convicted of and did not plead guilty to a specification of the type described in section 2941.141 [2941.14.1], 2941.144 [2941.14.4], or 2941.145 [2941.14.5] of the Revised Code charging the offender with having a firearm, or a firearm that is an automatic firearm or that is equipped with a firearm muffler or silencer, on or about the offender's person or under the offender's control while committing the offense for which the offender is in the custody of the department and was not convicted of and did not plead guilty to a specification of the type described in section 2941.146 [2941.14.6] of the Revised Code charging the offender with committing one of the offenses specified in that section by discharging a firearm from a motor vehicle of the type specified in that section.

(4) The offender has not been convicted of and has not pleaded guilty to a violation of section 2925.03, 2925.04, 2925.05, or 2925.06 of the Revised Code, and has not been convicted of and has not pleaded guilty to a violation of section 2925.11 of the Revised Code that is a violation other than a minor drug possession offense, as defined in section 2925.01 of the Revised Code.

(5) The offender has not been convicted of and has not pleaded guilty to a violation of Chapter 2907. of the Revised Code.

(6) The offender previously has not been convicted of or pleaded guilty to any felony for which, pursuant to sentence, the offender was confined for thirty days or more in a state correctional institution in this state or in a similar institution in any other state or the United States.

(7) The offender does not have more than six months of imprisonment to serve until the end of the offender's stated prison term, as defined in section 2929.01 of the Revised Code.

(D) "Central system" means a computerized system designed and operated to provide statewide electronic monitoring of eligible offenders who receive a period of electronically monitored early release.

(E) "Central system monitor" and "monitor" mean a person under contract with the department of rehabilitation and correction to design and operate the central system.

(F) "Electronically monitored early release contract" means a contract entered into by an eligible offender and the department of rehabilitation and correction in which the eligible offender agrees to do the following:

(1) Comply with all restrictions and requirements imposed by the department as conditions of receiving a period of electronically monitored early release;

(2) Pay any reasonable fee established by the department under division (G) of section 5120.073 [5120.07.3] of the Revised Code to the person and in the manner specified in the contract or, if the department determines under that division that the eligible offender is unable to pay for all or any part of the costs associated with receiving a period of electronically monitored early release, pay any part of the reasonable fee that the department does not waive under that division to the person and in the manner specified in the contract.

HISTORY: 144 v H 725 (Eff 4-16-93); 145 v H 571 (Eff 10-6-94); 146 v S 2. Eff 7-1-96.

The effective date is set by section 6 of SB 2.

[§ 5120.07.2] § 5120.072 Contract specifications for central system monitor; administration of statewide program.

(A) The division of parole and community services shall do all of the following:

(1) Prepare for use by the department contract specifications for a central system monitor. The specifications shall require the monitor to be capable of providing computerized electronic monitoring, or other electronic monitoring, of eligible offenders who receive a period of electronically monitored early release and to meet the criteria set forth in division (B) of section 5120.074 [5120.07.4] of the Revised Code. The department, at its discretion, may require the division to include in the specifications a requirement that the monitor, in accordance with division (G)(2) of section 5120.073 [5120.07.3] of the Revised Code, collect from each eligible offender who receives a period of electronically monitored early release any fee established under division (G)(1) of that section or may require the division to include in the specifications a requirement that the

monitor, in accordance with division (C)(2) of section 5120.073 [5120.07.3] of the Revised Code, provide the notice required by division (C)(1) of that section.

(2) Recommend rules for adoption by the department for the administration of a statewide program of electronically monitored early release in accordance with section 5120.073 [5120.07.3] of the Revised Code;

(3) Administer a statewide program of electronically monitored early release in accordance with section 5120.073 [5120.07.3] of the Revised Code;

(4) Administer the electronic detention fund established under section 5120.073 [5120.07.3] of the Revised Code;

(5) Perform any other duties that are assigned to the division by the director of the department.

(B) At the request of the chief of the division of parole and community services, the director of the department may require other employees of the department of rehabilitation and correction, including the parole officers of the adult parole authority, to perform specified duties related to the operation of the statewide program of electronically monitored early release.

HISTORY: 144 v H 725. Eff 4-16-93.

[§ 5120.07.3] § 5120.073 Statewide program of electronically monitored early release; effect of violation by releasee; electronic detention fund.

(A) The department of rehabilitation and correction shall establish a statewide program of electronically monitored early release for eligible offenders confined under its control and custody in state correctional institutions. The department shall adopt rules for the participation of eligible offenders in the statewide program of electronically monitored early release and for the administration of that program.

(B) The program of electronically monitored early release shall require that each eligible offender who receives a period of electronically monitored early release do all of the following:

(1) Wear, otherwise have attached to the eligible offender's person, or otherwise be subject to monitoring by a certified electronic monitoring device or participate in the operation of and monitoring by a certified electronic monitoring system;

(2) Remain in the eligible offender's home or other specified premises during the specified period of confinement in electronically monitored early release except for periods of time during which the eligible offender is at the eligible offender's place of employment or at other premises as authorized by the department;

(3) Be subject to monitoring by a central system that monitors the certified electronic monitoring device that is attached to the eligible offender's person or that otherwise is being used to monitor the eligible offender and that can monitor and determine the eligible offender's location at any time or at a designated point in time or abide by the requirements of a certified electronic monitoring system;

(4) Report periodically to a person designated by the department;

(5) Enter into an electronically monitored early release contract that includes a requirement that the eligible offender pay any reasonable fee established by the department under division (G) of this section to the person and in the manner specified in the contract or, if the department determines under that division that the eligible offender is unable to pay all or any part of the costs associated with receiving a period of electronically monitored early release, a requirement that the eligible offender pay any part of the reasonable fee that the department does not waive under that division to the person and in the manner specified in the contract;

(6) Comply with any other restrictions and requirements imposed by the department pursuant to its rules;

(7) Comply with any other requirements necessary to receive a period of electronically monitored early release.

(C)(1)(a) Unless the sentencing court disapproves in accordance with this division, at any time after an eligible offender who is sentenced to a term of imprisonment under the custody of the department actually has been delivered to the custody of the department, the department may permit the eligible offender to serve a portion of the eligible offender's sentence as a period of electronically monitored early release in accordance with this section and the rules adopted under this section. Subject to division (C)(2) of this section, at least three weeks before the department permits any eligible offender to serve a portion of the eligible offender's sentence as a period of electronically monitored early release, the department shall provide notice of the pendency of the electronically monitored early release to the court of common pleas in which the eligible offender was sentenced to the term of imprisonment, to the sheriff of the county in which the indictment against the eligible offender was found, to the chief law enforcement officer of any municipal corporation in which was committed the offense for which the eligible offender was sentenced to the term of imprisonment, and, if the victim of the offense of which the eligible offender was convicted or the victim's representative made a request for notification to the department pursuant to section 2930.16 of the Revised Code, to the victim or the victim's representative. The notice shall set forth the name of the eligible offender on whose behalf it is made, the offense of which the eligible offender was convicted, the time of the conviction, the term of imprisonment to which the eligible offender was sentenced, and the fact that the department intends to permit the eligible offender to serve a portion of the eligible offender's sentence as a period of electronically monitored early release. The notice to the court also shall inform the court that it may disapprove the pending grant of a period of electronically monitored early release for the eligible offender. The notice shall be provided to the victim or victim's representative at the address or telephone number provided by the victim or victim's representative.

(b) If the court of common pleas, upon receipt of the notice required by division (C)(1)(a) of this section, disapproves of the pending grant of a period of electronically monitored early release for the eligible offender, the court shall notify the department of the disapproval within ten days after receipt of the notice. If the court timely disapproves of the pending grant, the department shall not proceed with the grant of a period of electronically monitored early release for the eligible offender. If the court does not timely disapprove the pending grant, the department may proceed with plans for the period of electronically monitored early release for the eligible offender.

(c) The department shall not grant to any eligible offender a period of electronically monitored early release that exceeds six months. An eligible offender who is granted a period of electronically monitored early release is not entitled, during that specified period of confinement, to earn any days of credit as a deduction from the eligible offender's sentence under section 2967.193 [2967.19.3] of the Revised Code.

(2) The contract the department enters into with the central system monitor under section 5120.074 [5120.07.4] of the Revised Code may require the monitor to provide the notice that the department otherwise would be required to provide under division (C)(1)(a) of this section. If the contract requires the monitor to provide that notice, the monitor shall provide the notice described in division (C)(1)(a) of this section. The monitor shall provide the notice within the same period of time, shall provide it to the same persons, and shall include the same information in it as if the department had provided the notice under division (C)(1)(a) of this section. The department shall provide to the monitor all information that the monitor needs to provide the notice under this division.

(3) The failure of the department to comply with the notice requirements of division (C)(1)(a) of this section, or the failure of the central system monitor to comply with any notice requirements imposed upon the monitor by division (C)(2) of this section, does not give any rights or any grounds for appeal or post-conviction relief to the person serving the sentence.

(D) The rules adopted by the department pursuant to division (A) of this section shall include procedures and standards for all of the following:

(1) The training of appropriate personnel of the central system monitor and appropriate employees of the department of rehabilitation and correction and the adult parole authority to work with the central system and in all other relevant aspects of the statewide program of electronically monitored early release, including reporting and response procedures;

(2) The distribution, installation, and maintenance of the equipment necessary for the implementation of the program of electronically monitored early release;

(3) The determination of appropriate premises at which eligible offenders who receive a period of electronically monitored early release may reside or otherwise be present;

(4) A consistent statewide system of reporting and supervision that is sufficient for the department to adequately respond to reports made to the department by the central system monitor when an eligible offender requires investigation or other appropriate attention based upon reports received from the central system;

(5) A procedure for modifying or terminating, in accordance with division (B) of this section, an eligible offender's electronically monitored early release;

(6) A procedure for notifying courts, sheriffs, chief law enforcement officers, and crime victims or victims' representatives, when required pursuant to division (C)(1)(a) of this section, that the department intends to permit an eligible offender to serve a portion of the eligible offender's sentence as a period of electronically monitored early release;

(7) The granting of a period of electronically monitored early release in accordance with division (B) of this section.

(E) The department shall adopt any other rules necessary for the proper administration of sections 5120.071 [5120.07.1] to 5120.074 [5120.07.4] of the Revised Code.

(F)(1) If an eligible offender violates any of the restrictions or requirements imposed upon the eligible offender as part of the eligible offender's period of electronically monitored early release, the department may modify or terminate the eligible offender's electronically monitored early release and may return the eligible offender to the state correctional institution from which the eligible offender was granted electronically monitored early release.

(2) If an eligible offender violates any of the restrictions or requirements imposed upon the eligible offender as part of the eligible offender's period of electronically monitored early release and is returned to the state correctional institution from which the eligible offender was granted electronically monitored early release, the violation does not constitute cause for denial of credit for time served toward completion of the eligible offender's sentence of incarceration. This division does not permit the eligible offender to be awarded any days of credit as a deduction from the eligible offender's sentence of imprisonment under section 2967.193 [2967.19.3] of the Revised Code for any activity occurring during any time served on electronically monitored early release.

(3) If an eligible offender who has violated a restriction or requirement imposed upon the eligible offender as part of the eligible offender's period of electronically monitored early release is held, because of the violation, in a county, multicounty, municipal, municipal-county, or multicounty-municipal jail or workhouse or in a minimum security jail established under section 341.34 or

753.21 of the Revised Code, and if the period for which the eligible offender is held does not include a weekend or holiday and exceeds thirty-six hours or it includes a weekend or holiday and exceeds ninety-six hours, the department shall pay to the appropriate county or city treasury a per diem fee for the cost of housing the eligible offender from the time of the eligible offender's arrival at the facility. The department shall establish the fee to be paid under this division and shall base the fee upon the statewide average for the daily cost of housing a person in a similar facility.

(4) The department shall provide transportation from a local detention facility described in division (F)(3) of this section to a state correctional institution for any eligible offender who is returned to the state correctional institution upon the termination of the eligible offender's period of electronically monitored early release.

(G)(1) The department may establish a reasonable fee to cover the costs associated with receiving electronically monitored early release. The fee may include the actual costs of providing electronically monitored early release to an eligible offender and an additional amount to cover the costs of providing electronically monitored early release to eligible offenders whom the department determines are unable to pay for all or part of the costs associated with electronically monitored early release. If the department establishes a fee under this division, each eligible offender who receives a period of electronically monitored early release shall be required to pay the fee, except that the department may waive some or all of the fee for an eligible offender if the department determines the eligible offender is unable to pay all or any part of the costs associated with receiving the period of electronically monitored early release. If an eligible offender who receives a period of electronically monitored early release is required to pay a fee established under this division, the requirement shall be included in the electronically monitored early release contract.

(2)(a) Except as provided in division (G)(2)(b) of this section, if an eligible offender who receives a period of electronically monitored early release is required to pay a fee established under division (G)(1) of this section, the offender shall pay the fee to the department in the manner and at the time specified by the department. Upon receipt of the fee payment, the department shall deposit it into the electronic detention fund established under division (G)(3) of this section.

(b) The contract the department enters into with the central system monitor under section 5120.074 [5120.07.4] of the Revised Code may require the monitor to collect from each eligible offender who receives a period of electronically monitored early release any fee established under division (G)(1) of this section that the offender is required to pay. If the contract requires the monitor to collect the fee, the offender shall pay the fee to the monitor in the manner and at the time specified by the department, and the monitor shall accept the fee payments and transfer them to the department in accordance with the central system monitor contract. Upon receipt of the fee payment, the department shall deposit it into the electronic detention fund established under division (G)(3) of this section.

(c) If an eligible offender who receives a period of electronically monitored early release is required to pay a fee established under division (G)(1) of this section, the electronically monitored early release contract that sets forth the requirement also shall specify whether the eligible offender is to pay the fee to the department or to the central system monitor and the manner and time of payment.

(3) There is hereby created the electronic detention fund in the state treasury into which shall be deposited all fees paid by eligible offenders who receive a period of electronically monitored early release under this section and who are required as a condition of that program to pay the fee established by the department under division (G)(1) of this section and any other funds that may be appropriated by the general assembly for the program of electronically monitored early release. The electronic detention fund may be used only for the costs of the department associated with the program of electronically monitored early release, including the costs of electronically monitored early release for any eligible offender who is determined by the department to be unable to pay for all or part of the cost associated with the eligible offender's electronically monitored early release.

HISTORY: 144 v H 725 (Eff 4-16-93); 145 v H 571 (Eff 10-6-94); 145 v S 186 (Eff 10-12-94); 146 v S 2 (Eff 7-1-96); 146 v H 480. Eff 10-16-96.

[§ 5120.07.4] § 5120.074 Implementation of program; awarding of contract for central system monitor; periodic reviews and reports to legislature.

(A)(1) The department of rehabilitation and correction shall implement a statewide program of electronically monitored early release in accordance with section 5120.073 [5120.07.3] of the Revised Code.

(2) In accordance with Chapter 125. of the Revised Code, the department of rehabilitation and correction, through its division of parole and community services, shall prepare contract specifications and seek competitive bids for a central system monitor. The specifications shall require the monitor to provide computerized electronic monitoring or other electronic monitoring of eligible offenders who receive a period of electronically monitored early release and to meet the criteria set forth in division (B) of this section, shall require the monitor, at the discretion of the department and in accordance with division (G)(2) of section 5120.073 [5120.07.3] of the Revised Code, to collect from each eligible offender who receives a period of electronically monitored early release any fee established under division (G)(1) of that section, and shall require the monitor, at the discretion of the department and in accordance

with division (C)(2) of section 5120.073 [5120.07.3] of the Revised Code, to provide the notice required by division (C)(1)(a) of that section. The department shall provide each bidder for the central system monitor contract a copy of the list compiled under division (C) of section 2929.23 of the Revised Code from which the bidder shall select appropriate types of certified electronic monitoring devices or certified electronic monitoring systems for use in conjunction with the proposed central system monitor of the statewide program of electronically monitored early release established by the department. No bidder shall be a manufacturer of any certified electronic monitoring device or certified electronic monitoring system that is on the list compiled under division (C) of section 2929.23 of the Revised Code. Notwithstanding any other provision of law and notwithstanding any other practice it follows in relation to competitive bids, the department of administrative services shall perform all of its duties pertaining to the specifications for competitive bids for the central system monitor and all of its duties pertaining to the competitive bids for that monitor in a manner and within a period of time that enables the department of rehabilitation and correction to select a central system monitor within sixty days after the close of bidding for the central system monitor contract.

(B) The department of rehabilitation and correction shall use the following criteria in awarding the contract for the central system to the lowest responsive and responsible bidder:

(1) The bidder previously must have provided services and systems of a comparable complexity for other states or for political subdivisions of this state or other states.

(2) The bidder must be capable of doing all of the following:

(a) Administering a contract for monitoring services for two years and renewing the contract for an additional two years;

(b) Commencing the monitoring of a central system within a reasonable period of time as determined by the department;

(c) Providing adequate training to appropriate department of rehabilitation and correction personnel, adult parole authority parole officers, and other persons as determined necessary by the department in the use of the data received from the central system and related equipment and procedures;

(d) Providing technical support to department personnel involved in the administration of electronically monitored early release;

(e) Providing maintenance of the hardware involved in electronically monitored early release;

(f) Providing a central system that is capable of monitoring specified numbers of eligible offenders who receive electronically monitored early release;

(g) Monitoring the computer of the central system or the other means of electronic monitoring that is used in the system twenty-four hours each day and seven days each week to promptly detect unauthorized absences and late arrivals, to verify schedules by means of telephonic technology from a central system monitoring facility to the eligible offender, and to report each eligible offender's unauthorized absences, late arrivals, and deviations from schedule to the appropriate parole officer or other designated authority;

(h) Establishing a reporting system that employs a consistent statewide reporting format, regardless of any variation in the equipment used throughout the state by the department;

(i) Designing and operating a centralized data management system of sufficient detail to meet the reporting criteria of the department, including the capability to provide daily reports regarding each eligible offender's compliance with the requirements of the eligible offender's electronically monitored early release at a time no later than the following morning of each previous day.

(3) The bidder must demonstrate flexibility in the central system that is sufficient to accommodate multi-agency participation and the use of various types of electronic monitoring equipment.

(4) If the department includes within the contract specifications for a central system monitor a requirement that the monitor collect from each eligible offender who receives a period of electronically monitored early release any fee established under division (G)(1) of section 5120.073 [5120.07.3] of the Revised Code, the bidder must demonstrate a plan for complying with that requirement.

(5) If the department includes within the contract specifications for a central system monitor a requirement that the monitor provide, in accordance with division (C)(2) of section 5120.073 [5120.07.3] of the Revised Code, the notice required by division (C)(1) of that section, the bidder must demonstrate a plan for complying with that requirement.

(C) The costs of the implementation and operation of the statewide program of electronically monitored early release shall be paid from the moneys deposited in the electronic detention fund established by section 5120.073 [5120.07.3] of the Revised Code. Any additional costs of electronically monitored early release shall be paid from the general operating budget of the department of rehabilitation and correction as necessary.

(D) The director of rehabilitation and correction periodically shall review the statewide program of electronically monitored early release required to be established by section 5120.073 [5120.07.3] of the Revised Code. The director shall prepare a report relative to the program and shall file the report with the president and minority leader of the senate and with the speaker and minority leader of the house of representatives. In the first year of the program, the director shall file the report on a semi-annual basis, with the first report being filed at the end of the six-month period following the effective date of this section. In the second year of the program and in each year thereafter, the director shall file the report at the end of the fiscal year. The first report filed in the first year shall provide the status of the department's development and implementation of the status of the program. The second report filed in the first year and each report filed thereafter shall include all of the following:

(1) A summary of the effectiveness and availability of the statewide program of electronically monitored early release;

(2) An analysis of the total cost of the program and its cost per eligible offender compared to the total cost of incarceration in a state correctional institution;

(3) A summary of the characteristics of the eligible offenders who receive a period of electronically monitored early release, which summary shall include, but shall not be limited to, a summary of the offense for which each eligible offender was granted electronically monitored early release;

(4) A listing of the total number of eligible offenders who received a period of electronically monitored early release and who did not complete the specified time in the program and a summary of the reasons for failure to complete the program;

(5) A summary of the effect of the statewide program on overcrowding at state correctional institutions;

(6) Recommendations as to legislative changes to the statewide program that could further alleviate overcrowding at state correctional institutions and other recommendations that could improve the statewide program.

HISTORY: 144 v H 725 (Eff 4-16-93); 145 v H 571 (Eff 10-6-94); 146 v S 2. Eff 7-1-96.

The effective date is set by section 6 of SB 2.

§ 5120.08 Filing of bond of employees.

The department of rehabilitation and correction shall require any of its employees and each officer and employee of every institution under its control who may be charged with custody or control of any money or property belonging to the state or who is required to give bond, to give a surety company bond, properly conditioned, in a sum to be fixed by the department which when approved by the department, shall be filed in the office of the secretary of state. The cost of such bonds, when approved by the department, shall be paid from funds available for the department. The bonds required or authorized by this section may, in the discretion of the director of rehabilitation and correction, be individual, schedule, or blanket bonds.

HISTORY: 134 v H 494. Eff 7-12-72.

See effective date provision following RC § 5120.01.

§ 5120.09 Duties of division of business administration.

Under the supervision and control of the director of rehabilitation and correction, the division of business administration shall do all of the following:

(A) Submit the budgets for the several divisions of the department of rehabilitation and correction, as prepared by the respective chiefs of those divisions, to the director. The director, with the assistance of the chief of the division of business administration, shall compile a departmental budget that contains all proposals submitted by the chiefs of the divisions and shall forward the departmental budget to the governor with comments and recommendations that the director considers necessary.

(B) Maintain accounts and records and compile statistics that the director prescribes;

(C) Under the control of the director, coordinate and make the necessary purchases and requisitions for the department and its divisions, except as provided under section 5119.16 of the Revised Code;

(D) Administer within this state federal criminal justice acts that the governor requires the department to administer. In order to improve the criminal justice system of this state, the division of business administration shall apply for, allocate, disburse, and account for grants that are made available pursuant to those federal criminal justice acts and grants that are made available from other federal government sources, state government sources, or private sources. As used in this division, "criminal justice system" and "federal criminal justice acts" have the same meanings as in section 181.51 of the Revised Code.

(E) Audit the activities of governmental entities, persons as defined in section 1.59 of the Revised Code, and other types of nongovernmental entities that are financed in whole or in part by funds that the department allocates or disburses and that are derived from grants described in division (D) of this section;

(F) Enter into contracts, including contracts with federal, state, or local governmental entities, persons as defined in section 1.59 of the Revised Code, foundations, and other types of nongovernmental entities, that are necessary for the department to carry out its duties and that neither the director nor another section of the Revised Code authorizes another division of the department to enter;

(G) Exercise other powers and perform other duties that the director may assign to the division of business administration.

HISTORY: 134 v H 494 (Eff 7-12-72); 139 v H 1 (Eff 8-5-81); 140 v H 291 (Eff 7-1-83); 147 v H 215. Eff 9-29-97.

The effective date is set by section 222 of HB 215.

[§ 5120.09.1] § 5120.091 Education services fund.

There is hereby created in the state treasury the education services fund. The department of rehabilitation and correction shall deposit into the fund all state revenues it receives from the Ohio department of education. Any money in the fund shall solely be used to pay educational expenses incurred by the department.

HISTORY: 145 v H 715. Eff 7-22-94.

§ 5120.10 Minimum standards for jails; powers and duties of division of parole and community services.

(A)(1) The director of rehabilitation and correction, by rule, shall promulgate minimum standards for jails in Ohio, including minimum security jails dedicated under section 341.34 or 753.21 of the Revised Code. Whenever the director files a rule or an amendment to a rule in final form with both the secretary of state and the director of the legislative service commission pursuant to section 111.15 of the Revised Code, the director of rehabilitation and correction promptly shall send a copy of the rule or amendment, if the rule or amendment pertains to minimum jail standards, by ordinary mail to the political subdivisions or affiliations of political subdivisions that operate jails to which the standards apply.

(2) The rules promulgated in accordance with division (A)(1) of this section shall serve as criteria for the investigative and supervisory powers and duties vested by division (D) of this section in the division of parole and community services of the department of rehabilitation and correction or in another division of the department to which those powers and duties are assigned.

(B) The director may initiate an action in the court of common pleas of the county in which a facility that is subject to the rules promulgated under division (A)(1) of this section is situated to enjoin compliance with the minimum standards for jails or with the minimum standards and minimum renovation, modification, and construction criteria for minimum security jails.

(C) Upon the request of an administrator of a jail facility, the chief executive of a municipal corporation, or a board of county commissioners, the director of rehabilitation and correction or the director's designee shall grant a variance from the minimum standards for jails in Ohio for a facility that is subject to one of those minimum standards when the director determines that strict compliance with the minimum standards would cause unusual, practical difficulties or financial hardship, that existing or alternative practices meet the intent of the minimum standards, and that granting a variance would not seriously affect the security of the facility, the supervision of the inmates, or the safe, healthful operation of the facility. If the director or the director's designee denies a variance, the applicant may appeal the denial pursuant to section 119.12 of the Revised Code.

(D) The following powers and duties shall be exercised by the division of parole and community services unless assigned to another division by the director:

(1) The investigation and supervision of county and municipal jails, workhouses, minimum security jails, and other correctional institutions and agencies;

(2) The management and supervision of the adult parole authority created by section 5149.02 of the Revised Code;

(3) The review and approval of proposals for community-based correctional facilities and programs and district community-based correctional facilities and programs that are submitted pursuant to division (B) of section 2301.51 of the Revised Code;

(4) The distribution of funds made available to the division for purposes of assisting in the renovation, maintenance, and operation of community-based correctional facilities and programs and district community-based correctional facilities and programs in accordance with section 5120.112 [5120.11.2] of the Revised Code;

(5) The performance of the duty imposed upon the department of rehabilitation and correction in section 5149.31 of the Revised Code to establish and administer a program of subsidies to eligible municipal corporations, counties, and groups of contiguous counties for the development, implementation, and operation of community-based corrections programs;

(6) Licensing halfway houses and community residential centers for the care and treatment of adult offenders in accordance with section 2967.14 of the Revised Code;

(7) Contracting with a public or private agency or a department or political subdivision of the state that operates a licensed halfway house or community residential center for the provision of housing, supervision, and other services to parolees and probationers in accordance with section 2967.14 of the Revised Code.

Other powers and duties may be assigned by the director of rehabilitation and correction to the division of parole and community services. This section does not apply to the department of youth services or its institutions or employees.

HISTORY: 134 v H 494 (Eff 7-12-72); 139 v H 440 (Eff 11-23-81); 139 v S 23 (Eff 7-6-82); 143 v S 131 (Eff 7-25-90); 144 v S 351 (Eff 7-1-92); 145 v H 571 (Eff 10-6-94); 146 v H 480. Eff 10-16-96.

[§ 5120.10.1] § 5120.101 Repealed,

146 v H 480, § 2 [143 v S 131; 144 v H 298; 145 v H 152]. Eff 10-16-96.

This section concerned standards and criteria for minimum security misdemeanant jails. See now section 5120.10.

[HALFWAY HOUSE FACILITIES]

[§ 5120.10.2] § 5120.102 Definitions.

As used in sections 5120.102 [5120.10.2] to 5120.105 [5120.10.5] of the Revised Code:

(A) "Private, nonprofit organization" means a private association, organization, corporation, or other entity that is exempt from federal income taxation under section 501(a) and is described in section 501(c) of the "Internal Revenue Code of 1986," 100 stat. 2085, 26 U.S.C.A. 501, as amended.

(B) "Governmental agency" means a state agency; a municipal corporation, county, township, other political subdivision or special district in this state established by or pursuant to law, or a combination of those political subdivisions or special districts; the United States or a department, division, or agency of the United States; or an agency, commission, or authority established pursuant to an interstate compact or agreement.

(C) "State agency" means the state or one of its branches, offices, boards, commissions, authorities, departments, divisions, or other units or agencies of the state.

(D) "Halfway house organization" means a private, nonprofit organization or a governmental agency that provides programs or activities in areas directly concerned with housing offenders who are under the community supervision of the department of rehabilitation and correction or whom a court places in a halfway house pursuant to section 2929.16 of the Revised Code.

(E) "Halfway house facility" means a capital facility in this state to which all of the following apply:

(1) The construction of the capital facility is authorized or funded by the general assembly pursuant to division (C) of section 5120.105 [5120.10.5] of the Revised Code.

(2) The state owns or has a sufficient real property interest in the capital facility or in the site of the capital facility for a period of not less than the greater of the useful life of the capital facility, as determined by the director of budget and management using the guidelines for maximum maturities as provided under divisions (B), (C), and (E) of section 133.20 of the Revised Code and certified to the department of rehabilitation and correction and the Ohio building authority, or the final maturity of obligations issued by the Ohio building authority to finance the capital facility.

(3) The capital facility is managed directly by, or by contract with, the department of rehabilitation and correction and is used for housing offenders who are under the community supervision of the department of rehabilitation and correction or whom a court places in a halfway house pursuant to section 2929.16 of the Revised Code.

(F) "Construction" includes acquisition, demolition, reconstruction, alteration, renovation, remodeling, enlargement, improvement, site improvements, and related equipping and furnishing.

(G) "General building services" means general building services for a halfway house facility that include, but are not limited to, general custodial care, security, maintenance, repair, painting, decoration, cleaning, utilities, fire safety, grounds and site maintenance and upkeep, and plumbing.

(H) "Manage," "operate," or "management" means the provision of, or the exercise of control over the provision of, activities that relate to the housing of offenders in correctional facilities, including, but not limited to, providing for release services for offenders who are under the community supervision of the department of rehabilitation and correction, whom a court places in a halfway house pursuant to section 2929.16 of the Revised Code, and who reside in halfway house facilities.

HISTORY: 146 v H 117 (Eff 6-30-95); 146 v S 269. Eff 7-1-96.

Not analogous to former RC § 5120.10.2 (144 v H 298), repealed 145 v H 152, § 2, eff 7-1-93.

[§ 5120.10.3] § 5120.103 Grants for construction or renovation of halfway houses.

(A) To the extent that funds are available, the department of rehabilitation and correction, in accordance with this section and sections 5120.104 [5120.10.4] and 5120.105 [5120.10.5] of the Revised Code, may construct or provide for the construction of halfway house facilities for offenders whom a court places in a halfway house pursuant to section 2929.16 of the Revised Code or who are eligible for community supervision by the department of rehabilitation and correction .

(B) A halfway house organization that seeks to construct a halfway house facility described in division (A) of this section shall file an application with the director of rehabilitation and correction. The applicant shall submit with the application a plan that specifies all of the services that will be provided to offenders whom a court places in a halfway house pursuant to section 2929.16 of the Revised Code or who are eligible for community supervision by the department of rehabilitation and correction and who reside in the halfway house facility. Upon the submission of an application, the division of parole and community services shall review it and, if the division believes it is appropriate, shall submit a recommendation for its approval to the director. When the division submits a recommendation for approval of an application, the director may approve the application. The director shall not take action or fail to take action, or permit the taking of action or the failure to take action, with respect to halfway house facilities that would adversely affect the exclusion of interest on public obligations or on fractionalized interests in public obligations from gross income for federal income tax purposes, or the classification or qualification of the public obligations or the interest on or fractionalized interests in public obligations for, or their exemption from, other treatment under the Internal Revenue Code.

(C) The director of rehabilitation and correction and the halfway house organization may enter into an agreement establishing terms for the construction of the halfway house facility. Any terms so established shall conform to the terms of any covenant or agreement pertaining to an obligation from which the funds used for the construction of the halfway house facility are derived.

(D) The director of rehabilitation and correction, in

accordance with Chapter 119. of the Revised Code, shall adopt rules that specify procedures by which a halfway house organization may apply for construction of a halfway house facility under this section, procedures for the department to follow in considering an application, criteria for granting approval of an application, and any other rules that are necessary for the proper conduct of the construction of a halfway house facility.

HISTORY: 144 v H 904 (Eff 12-22-92); 146 v H 117 (Eff 9-29-95); 146 v S 2 (Eff 7-1-96); 146 v S 269. Eff 7-1-96.

The provisions of § 6 of SB 269 (146 v —) read in part as follows:

° ° ° Section 5120.103 of the Revised Code is presented in this act as a composite of the section as amended by both Am. Sub. H.B. 117 and Am. Sub. S.B. 2 of the 121st General Assembly, with the new language of neither of the acts shown in capital letters. This is in recognition of the principle stated in division (B) of section 1.52 of the Revised Code that such amendments are to be harmonized where not substantively irreconcilable and constitutes a legislative finding that the versions of those sections as so presented are the resulting versions in effect prior to the effective date of this act.

§ 5120.11 Bureau of examination and classification.

Within the department of rehabilitation and correction, there shall be established and maintained a bureau of examination and classification. The bureau shall conduct or provide for sociological, psychological, and psychiatric examination of each inmate of the correctional institutions. The examination shall be made as soon as possible after each inmate is admitted to any of the institutions, and further examinations may be made, if it is advisable. If the inmate is determined to be a mentally retarded or developmentally disabled person, as defined in section 5123.01 of the Revised Code, the bureau shall notify the sentencing court in writing of its determination within forty-five days after sentencing.

The bureau shall collect such social and other information as will aid in the interpretation of its examinations.

Subject to division (C) of section 5120.21 of the Revised Code, the bureau shall keep a record of the health, activities, and behavior of each inmate while the inmate is in the custody of the state. The records, including the findings and recommendations of the bureau, shall be made available to the adult parole authority for use in imposing post-release control sanctions under section 2967.28 of the Revised Code or any other section of the Revised Code, in granting parole, and in making parole, post-release, and rehabilitation plans for the inmate when the inmate leaves the institution, and to the department for its use in approving transfers of inmates from one institution to another.

HISTORY: 134 v H 494 (Eff 7-12-72); 137 v H 565 (Eff 11-1-78); 138 v S 297 (Eff 4-30-80); 138 v H 965 (Eff 4-9-81); 142 v S 94 (Eff 7-20-88); 143 v H 569 (Eff 7-1-91); 145 v H 571 (Eff 10-6-94); 146 v S 2 (Eff 7-1-96); 146 v S 269. Eff 7-1-96.

[§ 5120.11.1] § 5120.111 Rules and forms for community based correctional facilities.

With respect to community based correctional facilities and programs and district community based correctional facilities and programs authorized under section 2301.51 of the Revised Code, the department of rehabilitation and correction shall do all of the following:

(A) Adopt rules, under Chapter 119. of the Revised Code, that serve as criteria for the operation of community-based correctional facilities and programs and district community-based correctional facilities and programs approved in accordance with sections 2301.51 and 5120.10 of the Revised Code;

(B) Adopt rules, under Chapter 119. of the Revised Code, prescribing the minimum educational and experience requirements that must be satisfied by persons who staff and operate the facilities and programs;

(C) Adopt rules, under Chapter 119. of the Revised Code, governing the procedures for the submission of proposals for the establishment of community-based correctional facilities and programs and district community-based correctional facilities and programs to the division of parole and community services under division (B) of section 2301.51 of the Revised Code;

(D) Prescribe forms that are to be used by judicial corrections boards of community-based correctional facilities and programs and district community-based correctional facilities and programs in making application for state financial assistance under section 2301.56 of the Revised Code and that include a requirement that the applicant estimate the number of offenders that will be committed or referred to a facility and program and that the facility and program will serve in the year of application;

(E) Adopt rules, under Chapter 119. of the Revised Code, that prescribe the standards of operation and the training and qualifications of persons who staff and operate the facilities and programs and that must be satisfied for the facilities and programs to be eligible for state financial assistance. The standards prescribed shall include, but shall not be limited to, the minimum requirements that each proposal submitted for approval to the division of parole and community services, as contained in section 2301.52 of the Revised Code, must satisfy for approval.

(F) Through the division of parole and community services, accept and review proposals for the establishment of the facilities and programs and approve those proposals that satisfy the minimum requirements contained in section 2301.52 of the Revised Code; and administer the program for state financial assistance to the facilities and programs in accordance with section 5120.112 [5120.11.2] of the Revised Code.

HISTORY: 138 v H 1000 (Eff 4-9-81); 145 v H 571. Eff 10-6-94.

[§ 5120.11.2] § 5120.112 Application for state financial assistance to community-based corrections; agreement.

(A) The division of parole and community services

shall accept applications for state financial assistance for the renovation, maintenance, and operation of proposed and approved community-based correctional facilities and programs and district community-based correctional facilities and programs that are filed in accordance with section 2301.56 of the Revised Code. The division, upon receipt of an application for a particular facility and program, shall determine whether the application is in proper form, whether the applicant satisfies the standards of operation and training and qualifications of personnel that are prescribed by the department of rehabilitation and correction under section 5120.111 [5120.11.1] of the Revised Code, whether the applicant has established the facility and program, and, if the applicant has not at that time established the facility and program, whether the proposal of the applicant sufficiently indicates that the standards will be satisfied upon the establishment of the facility and program. If the division determines that the application is in proper form and that the applicant has satisfied or will satisfy the standards of the department, the division shall notify the applicant that it is qualified to receive state financial assistance for the facility and program under this section from moneys made available to the division for purposes of providing assistance to community-based correctional facilities and programs and district community-based correctional facilities and programs.

(B) The amount of state financial assistance that is granted to a qualified applicant under this section shall be determined by the division of parole and community services in accordance with this division. The division shall adopt a formula to determine the allocation of state financial assistance to qualified applicants. The formula shall provide for funding that is based upon a set fee to be paid to an applicant per person committed or referred in the year of application. In no case shall the set fee be greater than the average yearly cost of incarceration per inmate in all state correctional institutions, as defined in section 2967.01 of the Revised Code, as determined by the department of rehabilitation and correction.

The times and manner of distribution of state financial assistance to be granted to a qualified applicant under this section shall be determined by the division of parole and community services.

(C) No state financial assistance shall be distributed to a qualified applicant until an agreement concerning the assistance has been entered into by the director of rehabilitation and correction and the deputy director of the division of parole and community services on the part of the state, and by the chairman of the judicial corrections board of the community-based correctional facility and program or district community-based correctional facility and program to receive the financial assistance, whichever is applicable. The agreement shall be effective for a period of one year from the date of the agreement and shall specify all terms and conditions that are applicable to the granting of the assistance, including, but not limited to:

(1) The total amount of assistance to be granted for each community-based correctional facility and program or district community-based correctional facility and program, and the times and manner of the payment of the assistance;

(2) How persons who will staff and operate the facility and program are to be utilized during the period for which the assistance is to be granted, including descriptions of their positions and duties, their salaries and fringe benefits, and their job qualifications and classifications;

(3) A statement that none of the persons who will staff and operate the facility and program, including those who are receiving some or all of their salaries out of funds received by the facility and program as state financial assistance, are employees or are to be considered as being employees of the department of rehabilitation and correction, and a statement that the employees who will staff and operate that facility and program are employees of the facility and program;

(4) A list of the type of expenses, other than salaries of persons who will staff and operate the facility and program, for which the state financial assistance can be used, and a requirement that purchases made with funds received as state financial assistance be made through the use of competitive bidding;

(5) The accounting procedures that are to be used by the facility and program in relation to the state financial assistance;

(6) A requirement that the facility and program file quarterly reports, during the period that it receives state financial assistance, with the division of parole and community services, which reports shall be statistical in nature and shall contain that information required under a research design agreed upon by all parties to the agreement, for purposes of evaluating the facility and program;

(7) A requirement that the facility and program comply with all of the standards of operation and training and qualifications of personnel prescribed by the department under section 5120.111 [5120.11.1] of the Revised Code, and with all information submitted on its application;

(8) A statement that the facility and program will attempt to accept and treat at least fifteen per cent of the eligible adult felony offenders sentenced in the county or counties it serves during the period that it receives state financial assistance;

(9) A statement that the facility and program will make a reasonable effort to augment the funding received from the state.

(D)(1) No state financial assistance shall be distributed to a qualified applicant until its proposal for a community-based correctional facility and program or district community-based correctional facility and program has been approved by the division of parole and community services.

(2) State financial assistance may be denied to any

applicant if it fails to comply with the terms of any agreement entered into pursuant to division (C) of this section.

HISTORY: RC § 5149.06.1, 138 v H 1000 (Eff 4-9-81); 145 v H 152 (Eff 7-1-93); RC § 5120.11.2, 145 v H 571 (Eff 10-6-94); 145 v H 335. Eff 12-9-94.

The provisions of § 5 of HB 335 (145 v —) read as follows:

SECTION 5. The amendment and renumbering as indicated in parentheses by this act [HB 335] of section 5149.061 (5120.112) of the Revised Code is intended to affirm that this was the result intended by the General Assembly in Am. Sub. H.B. 571 of the 120th General Assembly. Am. Sub. H.B. 571 amended the section twice, once under its old number and once under its new number, and also declared the section to be repealed outright. The General Assembly did not intend to repeal the section outright but rather to renumber and amend it in the form as results from this act. The amendment and renumbering as indicated in parentheses of section 5149.061 (5120.112) of the Revised Code by this act combines, and is identical to, the amendment and renumbering of that section in Am. Sub. H.B. 571.

§ 5120.12 Director may lease, for oil and gas, real estate owned by state.

Note: See following version effective 3-4-98.

The director of rehabilitation and correction may lease, for oil and gas, any real estate owned by the state and placed under the supervision of the department of rehabilitation and correction, to any person, upon such terms and for such number of years, not more than forty, as will be for the best interest of the state. No such lease shall be agreed upon or entered into before the proposal to lease the property has been advertised once each week for four weeks in a newspaper of general circulation in the city of Columbus. Such lease shall be made with the person offering the best terms to the state.

The director, in such lease, may grant to such lessee the right to use so much of the surface of such land as may be reasonably necessary to carry on the work of prospecting for, extracting, piping, storing, and removing all oil or gas, and for depositing waste material and maintaining such buildings and constructions as are reasonably necessary for exploring or prospecting for such oil and gas.

All leases made under this section shall be prepared by the attorney general and approved by the governor. All moneys received from any such leases shall be paid into the state treasury to the credit of the general revenue fund.

HISTORY: 134 v H 494 (Eff 7-12-72); 141 v S 312. Eff 9-24-86.

§ 5120.12 Lease of real estate for oil and gas.

Note: See preceding version in effect until 3-4-98.

The director of rehabilitation and correction may lease, for oil and gas, any real estate owned by the state and placed under the supervision of the department of rehabilitation and correction, to any person, upon such terms and for such number of years, not more than forty, as will be for the best interest of the state. No such lease shall be agreed upon or entered into before the proposal to lease the property has been advertised once each week for four weeks in a newspaper of general circulation in the city where the central office of the department is located. Such lease shall be made with the person offering the best terms to the state.

The director, in such lease, may grant to such lessee the right to use so much of the surface of such land as may be reasonably necessary to carry on the work of prospecting for, extracting, piping, storing, and removing all oil or gas, and for depositing waste material and maintaining such buildings and constructions as are reasonably necessary for exploring or prospecting for such oil and gas.

All leases made under this section shall be prepared by the attorney general and approved by the governor. All moneys received from any such leases shall be paid into the state treasury to the credit of the general revenue fund.

HISTORY: 134 v H 494 (Eff 7-12-72); 141 v S 312 (Eff 9-24-86); 146 v H 60. Eff 3-4-98.

§ 5120.13 Acceptance of devise, grant, or bequest by department of rehabilitation and correction; trust funds for inmates.

(A) The department of rehabilitation and correction shall accept and hold on behalf of the state, if it is for the public interest, any grant, gift, devise, or bequest of money or property made to or for the use or benefit of any institution described in section 5120.05 of the Revised Code. The department shall keep such gift, grant, devise, or bequest as a distinct property or fund, and shall invest the same, if in money, in the manner provided by law. The department may deposit in a proper trust company or savings bank any fund left in trust during a specified life or lives, and shall adopt rules governing the deposit, transfer, withdrawal, or investment of such funds and the income thereof. Upon the expiration of any trust according to its terms, the department shall dispose of the funds or property held thereunder in the manner provided in the instrument creating the trust; except that, if the instrument creating the trust failed to make any terms of disposition, or if no trust was in evidence, then the decedent patient's, pupil's, or inmate's moneys, savings or commercial deposits, dividends or distributions, bonds, or any other interest bearing debt certificate or stamp issued by the United States government shall escheat to the state. All such unclaimed intangible personal property of a former inmate shall be retained by the managing officer in such institution for the period of one year during which time every possible effort shall be made to find that former inmate or that former inmate's legal representative. If, after a period of one year from the time such inmate has left such institution or has died, the managing officer is unable to locate the inmate or the inmate's legal representative, upon proper notice of such fact, the director of rehabilitation and correction shall at that time formulate in writing a method of disposition on the minutes of the department authorizing the managing officer of the institution to convert the same to cash to be paid into the treasury of the state to the credit of the general revenue fund. The department shall include in the annual report a statement of all such funds and property and the terms and conditions relating thereto.

Moneys or property deposited with managing officers of institutions by relatives, guardians, conservators, and friends for the special benefit of any inmate shall remain in the hands of such officers for use accordingly. Such funds shall be deposited in a personal deposit fund. Each such managing officer shall keep an itemized book account of the receipt and disposition thereof, which book shall be open at all times to the inspection of the department. The department shall adopt rules governing the deposit, transfer, withdrawal, or investment of such funds and the income thereof.

(B) Whenever an inmate confined in any state institution subject to the jurisdiction of the department dies, escapes, is discharged or paroled from the institution, or is placed on a term of post-release control under any section of the Revised Code and personal funds of the person remain in the hands of the managing officer of the institution and no demand is made upon the managing officer by the owner of the funds or the owner's legally appointed representative, the managing officer shall hold the funds in the personal deposit fund for a period of at least one year during which time the managing officer shall make every effort possible to locate the owner or the owner's legally appointed representative.

If, at the end of this period, no demand has been made for the funds, the managing officer shall dispose of the funds as follows:

(1) All moneys in a personal deposit fund in excess of ten dollars due for the support of an inmate shall be paid into the state's general revenue fund.

(2) All moneys in a personal deposit fund in excess of ten dollars not due for the support of an inmate shall be placed to the credit of the institution's local account designated as "industrial and entertainment" fund.

(3) All moneys less than ten dollars to the credit of an inmate shall be placed to the credit of the institution's local account designated as "industrial and entertainment" fund.

(C) Whenever an inmate in any state institution subject to the jurisdiction of the department dies, escapes, is discharged or paroled from the institution or is placed on a term of post-release control, and personal effects of the person remain in the hands of the managing officer of the institution, and no demand is made upon the managing officer by the owner of the property or the owner's legally appointed representative, the managing officer shall hold and dispose of such property as follows:

All the miscellaneous personal effects shall be held for a period of at least one year, during which time the managing officer shall make every effort possible to locate the owner or the owner's legal representative. If at the end of this period no demand has been made by the owner of the property or the owner's legal representative, the managing officer shall file with the county recorder of the county of commitment of the owner, all deeds, wills, contract mortgages, or assignments. The balance of the personal effects shall be sold at public auction after being duly advertised, and the funds turned over to the treasurer of state for credit to the general revenue fund. If any of the property is not of a type to be filed with the county recorder and is not salable at public auction, then the managing officer of the institution shall destroy the property.

HISTORY: 134 v H 494 (Eff 7-12-72); 137 v S 221 (Eff 11-23-77); 140 v H 250 (Eff 7-30-84); 146 v S 2. Eff 7-1-96.

The effective date is set by section 6 of SB 2.

[§ 5120.13.1] § 5120.131 Industrial and entertainment fund; commissary fund.

Each managing officer of an institution under the jurisdiction of the department of rehabilitation and correction as described in section 5120.05 of the Revised Code, with the approval of the director of the department of rehabilitation and correction, may establish local institution funds designated as follows:

(A) Industrial and entertainment fund created and maintained for the entertainment and welfare of the inmates of the institutions under the jurisdiction of the department. The director shall establish rules and regulations for the operation of the industrial and entertainment fund.

(B) Commissary fund created and maintained for the benefit of inmates in the institutions under the jurisdiction of the department.

Commissary revenue over and above operating costs and reserve shall be considered profits. All profits from the commissary fund operations shall be paid into the industrial and entertainment fund and used only for the entertainment and welfare of inmates. The director shall establish rules and regulations for the operation of the commissary fund.

HISTORY: 134 v H 494. Eff 7-12-72.

See effective date provision following RC § 5120.01.

[§ 5120.13.2] § 5120.132 Prisoner programs fund.

(A) There is hereby created in the state treasury the prisoner programs fund. The director of rehabilitation and correction shall deposit in the fund all moneys received by the department from commissions on telephone systems established for the use of prisoners. The money in the fund shall be used only to pay for the costs of the following:

(1) The purchase of material, supplies, and equipment used in any library program, educational program, religious program, recreational program, or pre-release

program operated by the department for the benefit of prisoners.

(2) The construction, alteration, repair, or reconstruction of buildings and structures owned by the department for use in any library program, educational program, religious program, recreational program, or pre-release program operated by the department for the benefit of prisoners;

(3) The payment of salary, wages, and other compensation to employees of the department who are employed in any library program, educational program, religious program, recreational program, or pre-release program operated by the department for the benefit of prisoners;

(4) The compensation to vendors that contract with the department for the provision of services for the benefit of prisoners in any library program, educational program, religious program, recreational program, or pre-release program operated by the department;

(5) The payment of prisoner release payments in an appropriate amount as determined pursuant to rule;

(6) The purchase of other goods and the payment of other services that are determined, in the discretion of the director, to be goods and services that may provide additional benefit to prisoners.

(B) The director shall establish rules for the operation of the prisoner programs fund.

HISTORY: 144 v S 351. Eff 7-1-92.

[§ 5120.13.3] § 5120.133 Transfer of prisoner's funds to satisfy judgment; exemptions.

(A) The department of rehabilitation and correction, upon receipt of a certified copy of the judgment of a court of record in an action in which a prisoner was a party that orders a prisoner to pay a stated obligation, may apply toward payment of the obligation money that belongs to a prisoner and that is in the account kept for the prisoner by the department. The department may transmit the prisoner's funds directly to the court for disbursement or may make payment in another manner as directed by the court. Except as provided in rules adopted under this section, when an amount is received for the prisoner's account, the department shall use it for the payment of the obligation and shall continue using amounts received for the account until the full amount of the obligation has been paid. No proceedings in aid of execution are necessary for the department to take the action required by this section.

(B) The department may adopt rules specifying a portion of an inmate's earnings or other receipts that the inmate is allowed to retain to make purchases from the commissary and that may not be used to satisfy an obligation pursuant to division (A) of this section. The rules shall not permit the application or disbursement of funds belonging to an inmate if those funds are exempt from execution, garnishment, attachment, or sale to satisfy a judgment or order pursuant to section 2329.66 of the Revised Code or to any other provision of law.

HISTORY: 145 v H 571. Eff 10-6-94.

§ 5120.14 Notice of escape of violent offender.

If a person who was convicted of or pleaded guilty to an offense of violence that is a felony escapes from a correctional institution in this state under the control of the department of rehabilitation and correction or otherwise escapes from the custody of the department, the department immediately after the escape shall cause notice of the escape to be published in a newspaper of general circulation in the county in which the institution from which the escape was made or to which the person was sentenced is located and in a newspaper of general circulation in each county in which the escaped person was indicted for an offense of violence that is a felony for which, at the time of the escape, he had been sentenced to that institution. The department also immediately shall give notice of the escape by telephone and in writing to the prosecuting attorney of each county in which the escaped person was indicted for an offense of violence that is a felony for which, at the time of the escape, he had been sentenced to that institution. Upon the apprehension of the escaped person, the department shall give notice of the apprehension by telephone and in writing to the same prosecuting attorneys who were given notice of the escape.

HISTORY: 142 v H 207 (Eff 9-24-87); 145 v H 571. Eff 10-6-94.

§ 5120.15 Regulation of admissions and discharge of inmates.

The department of rehabilitation and correction shall regulate the admission and discharge of inmates in the institutions described in section 5120.05 of the Revised Code.

HISTORY: 134 v H 494. Eff 7-12-72.

Publisher's Note

An attempt to amend this section in 138 v H 204, was disapproved by Governor Rhodes on 7-30-79.

See effective date provision following RC § 5120.01.

§ 5120.16 Examination, observation, and classification; assignment to institution; transfer.

(A) Persons sentenced to any institution, division, or place under the control of the department of rehabilitation and correction are committed to the control, care, and custody of the department. Subject to division (B) of this section, the director of rehabilitation and correction or the director's designee may direct that persons sentenced to the department, or to any institution or place within the department, shall first be conveyed to an appropriate facility established and maintained by the department for reception, examination, observation, and classification of the persons so sentenced. If a presentence investigation report was not prepared pursuant to section 2947.06 or 2951.03 of the Revised Code or Criminal Rule 32.2 regarding any person sentenced to the department or to any institution or place within the department, the director or the director's designee may order the department's field staff to conduct an offender background investigation and prepare an offender background investigation report regarding the person. The investigation and report shall be conducted in accordance with division (A) of section 2951.03 of the Revised Code and the report shall contain the same information as a presentence investigation report prepared pursuant to that section.

When the examination, observation, and classification of the person have been completed by the facility and a written report of the examination, observation, and classification is filed with the commitment papers, the director or the director's designee, subject to division (B) of this section, shall assign the person to a suitable state institution or place maintained by the state within the director's department or shall designate that the person is to be housed in a county, multicounty, municipal, municipal-county, or multicounty-municipal jail or workhouse, if authorized by section 5120.161 [5120.16.1] of the Revised Code, there to be confined, cared for, treated, trained, and rehabilitated until paroled, released in accordance with section 2967.20, 2967.23, or 2967.28 of the Revised Code, or otherwise released under the order of the court that imposed the person's sentence. No person committed by a probate court, a trial court pursuant to section 2945.40, 2945.401, or 2945.402 [2945.40.2] of the Revised Code subsequent to a finding of not guilty by reason of insanity, or a juvenile court shall be assigned to a state correctional institution.

If a person is sentenced, committed, or assigned for the commission of a felony to any one of the institutions or places maintained by the department or to a county, multicounty, municipal, municipal-county, or multicounty-municipal jail or workhouse, the department, by order duly recorded and subject to division (B) of this section, may transfer the person to any other institution, or, if authorized by section 5120.161 [5120.16.1] of the Revised Code, to a county, multicounty, municipal, municipal-county, or multicounty-municipal jail or workhouse.

(B) If the case of a child who is alleged to be a delinquent child is transferred for criminal prosecution to the appropriate court having jurisdiction of the offense pursuant to division (B) or (C) of section 2151.26 of the Revised Code, if the child is convicted of or pleads guilty to a felony in that case, if the child is sentenced to a prison term, as defined in section 2901.01 of the Revised Code, and if the child is under eighteen years of age when delivered to the custody of the department of rehabilitation and correction, all of the following apply regarding the housing of the child:

(1) Until the child attains eighteen years of age, subject to divisions (B)(2), (3), and (4) of this section, the department shall house the child in a housing unit in a state correctional institution separate from inmates who are eighteen years of age or older.

(2) The department is not required to house the child in the manner described in division (B)(1) of this section if the child does not observe the rules and regulations of the institution or the child otherwise creates a security risk by being housed separately.

(3) If the department receives too few inmates who are under eighteen years of age to fill a housing unit in a state correctional institution separate from inmates who are eighteen years of age or older, as described in division (B)(1) of this section, the department may house the child in a housing unit in a state correctional institution that includes both inmates who are under eighteen years of age and inmates who are eighteen years of age or older and under twenty-one years of age.

(4) Upon the child's attainment of eighteen years of age, the department may house the child with the adult population of the state correctional institution.

(C) The director or the director's designee shall develop a policy for dealing with problems related to infection with the human immunodeficiency virus. The policy shall include methods of identifying individuals committed to the custody of the department who are at high risk of infection with the virus, counseling these individuals, and, if it is determined to be medically appropriate, offering them the opportunity to be given an HIV test approved by the director of health pursuant to section 3701.241 [3701.24.1] of the Revised Code.

Arrangements for housing individuals diagnosed as having AIDS or an AIDS-related condition shall be made by the department based on security and medical considerations and in accordance with division (B) of this section, if applicable.

HISTORY: 134 v H 494 (Eff 7-12-72); 137 v H 565 (Eff 11-1-78); 138 v S 297 (Eff 4-30-80); 138 v H 900 (Eff 7-1-80); 138 v H 965 (Eff 4-9-81); 139 v S 199 (Eff 1-1-83); 142 v H 455 (Eff 7-20-87); 143 v S 2 (Eff 11-1-89); 144 v S 331 (Eff 11-13-92); 145 v H 571 (Eff 10-6-94); 146 v S 310 (Eff 6-20-96); 146 v S 2 (Eff 7-1-96); 146 v H 124 (Eff 3-31-97); 146 v S 285 (Eff 7-1-97); 147 v H 215. Eff 9-29-97.

The effective date is set by section 222 of HB 215.

[§ 5120.16.1] § 5120.161 Agreements with local authorities for housing of certain state prisoners.

(A) Except as provided in division (C) of this section, the department of rehabilitation and correction may enter into an agreement with any local authority operating a county, multicounty, municipal, municipal-county, or multicounty-municipal jail or workhouse, as described in section 307.93, 341.21, or 753.16 of the

Revised Code, for the housing in the jail or workhouse operated by the local authority of persons who are convicted of or plead guilty to a felony of the fourth or fifth degree if the person previously has not been convicted of or pleaded guilty to a felony and if the felony is not an offense of violence. The agreement shall specify a per diem fee that the department shall pay the local authority for each such person housed in the jail or workhouse pursuant to the agreement, shall set forth any other terms and conditions for the housing of such persons in the jail or workhouse, and shall indicate that the department, subject to the relevant terms and conditions set forth, may designate those persons to be housed at the jail or workhouse.

(B) A person designated by the department to be housed in a county, multicounty, municipal, municipal-county, or multicounty-municipal jail or workhouse that is the subject of an agreement entered into under division (A) of this section shall be conveyed by the department to that jail or workhouse and shall be kept at the jail or workhouse until the person's term of imprisonment expires, the person is pardoned, paroled, or placed under a post-release control sanction, or the person is transferred under the laws permitting the transfer of prisoners. The department shall pay the local authority that operates the jail or workhouse the per diem fee specified in the agreement for each such person housed in the jail or workhouse. Each such person housed in the jail or workhouse shall be under the direct supervision and control of the keeper, superintendent, or other person in charge of the jail or workhouse, but shall be considered for all other purposes to be within the custody of the department of rehabilitation and correction. Section 2967.193 [2967.19.3] of the Revised Code and all other provisions of the Revised Code that pertain to persons within the custody of the department that would not by their nature clearly be inapplicable apply to persons housed pursuant to this section.

(C) The department of rehabilitation and correction shall not enter into an agreement pursuant to division (A) of this section with any local authority unless the jail or workhouse operated by the authority complies with the Minimum Standards for Jails in Ohio.

(D) A court that sentences a person for a felony may include as the sentence or part of the sentence, in accordance with division (A) of section 2929.16 of the Revised Code and regardless of whether the jail or workhouse is the subject of an agreement entered into under division (A) of this section, a sanction that consists of a term of up to six months in a jail or workhouse or, if the offense is a fourth degree felony OMVI offense and the offender previously has not been convicted of a fourth degree felony OMVI offense, a sanction that consists of a term of up to one year in a jail less the mandatory term of local incarceration of sixty consecutive days imposed pursuant to division (G)(1) of section 2929.13 of the Revised Code.

(E) "Fourth degree felony OMVI offense" and "mandatory term of local incarceration" have the same meanings as in section 2929.01 of the Revised Code.

HISTORY: 139 v S 199 (Eff 1-1-83); 139 v H 269 (Eff 7-1-83); 142 v H 455 (Eff 7-20-87); 146 v S 2 (Eff 7-1-96); 146 v S 269 (Eff 7-1-96); 146 v H 72. Eff 3-18-97.

[§ 5120.16.2] § 5120.162 Agreement for transfer of children in custody of youth services department to correctional medical center.

(A) The department of rehabilitation and correction may enter into an agreement with the department of youth services pursuant to which the department of youth services may transfer to a correctional medical center established by the department of rehabilitation and correction children who are within its custody, who have an illness, physical condition, or other medical problem, and who apparently would benefit from diagnosis or treatment at the center for that illness, condition, or problem. Notwithstanding the fact that portions of the center may be used for the benefit of children in the custody of the department of youth services, the center shall be considered a facility of the department of rehabilitation and correction and shall be controlled and operated in accordance with the agreement and the provisions of this section. A child who is in the custody of the department of youth services and who is transferred to the center shall be considered as remaining in the custody of the department of youth services during the period of his diagnosis, treatment, or housing for diagnosis or treatment in the center.

During the development or renovation of a correctional medical center that is the subject of an agreement under this section, the department of rehabilitation and correction shall confer with the department of youth services to ensure that the center is planned and constructed or renovated to facilitate its use for the diagnosis or treatment of both prisoners in the custody of the department of rehabilitation and correction and children in the custody of the department of youth services who may be transferred to the center.

(B) All children who are in the custody of the department of youth services and who are transferred to a correctional medical center pursuant to an agreement under this section shall be housed in areas of the center that are totally separate and removed by sight and sound from all prisoners who are in the custody of the department of rehabilitation and correction and who are being diagnosed, treated, or housed for diagnosis or treatment in the center or who otherwise are in the center. For purposes of this division, children who are being diagnosed, treated, or housed for diagnosis or treatment in a building or wing of a building in which no prisoners in the custody of the department of rehabilitation and correction are being diagnosed, treated, or housed for diagnosis or treatment or otherwise are present are being housed totally separate from any prisoners who are in the custody of the department of rehabilitation and correction.

HISTORY: 144 v S 331. Eff 11-13-92.

§ 5120.17 Transfer of inmate to psychiatric hospital; discharge; parole; expiration of prison term.

(A) As used in this section:

(1) "Mental illness" means a substantial disorder of thought, mood, perception, orientation, or memory that grossly impairs judgment, behavior, capacity to recognize reality, or ability to meet the ordinary demands of life.

(2) "Mentally ill person subject to hospitalization" means a mentally ill person to whom any of the following applies because of the person's mental illness:

(a) The person represents a substantial risk of physical harm to the person as manifested by evidence of threats of, or attempts at, suicide or serious self-inflicted bodily harm.

(b) The person represents a substantial risk of physical harm to others as manifested by evidence of recent homicidal or other violent behavior, evidence of recent threats that place another in reasonable fear of violent behavior and serious physical harm, or other evidence of present dangerousness.

(c) The person represents a substantial and immediate risk of serious physical impairment or injury to the person as manifested by evidence that the person is unable to provide for and is not providing for the person's basic physical needs because of the person's mental illness and that appropriate provision for those needs cannot be made immediately available in the community.

(d) The person would benefit from treatment in a hospital for the person's mental illness and is in need of treatment in a hospital as manifested by evidence of behavior that creates a grave and imminent risk to substantial rights of others or the person.

(3) "Psychiatric hospital" means a facility that is operated by the department of rehabilitation and correction, is designated as a psychiatric hospital, is licensed by the department of mental health pursuant to section 5119.20 of the Revised Code, and is in substantial compliance with the standards set by the joint commission on accreditation of healthcare organizations.

(4) "Inmate patient" means an inmate who is admitted to a psychiatric hospital.

(5) "Admitted" to a psychiatric hospital means being accepted for and staying at least one night at the psychiatric hospital.

(6) "Treatment plan" means a written statement of reasonable objectives and goals for an inmate patient that is based on the needs of the inmate patient and that is established by the treatment team, with the active participation of the inmate patient and with documentation of that participation. "Treatment plan" includes all of the following:

(a) The specific criteria to be used in evaluating progress toward achieving the objectives and goals;

(b) The services to be provided to the inmate patient during the inmate patient's hospitalization;

(c) The services to be provided to the inmate patient after discharge from the hospital, including, but not limited to, housing and mental health services provided at the state correctional institution to which the inmate patient returns after discharge or community mental health services.

(7) "Mentally retarded person subject to institutionalization by court order" has the same meaning as in section 5123.01 of the Revised Code.

(B)(1) If the warden of a state correctional institution believes that an inmate should be transferred from the institution to a psychiatric hospital, the department shall hold a hearing to determine whether the inmate is a mentally ill person subject to hospitalization. The department shall conduct the hearing at the state correctional institution in which the inmate is confined, and the department shall provide qualified and independent assistance to the inmate for the hearing. An independent decision-maker provided by the department shall preside at the hearing and determine whether the inmate is a mentally ill person subject to hospitalization.

(2) Prior to the hearing held pursuant to division (B)(1) of this section, the warden shall give written notice to the inmate that the department is considering transferring the inmate to a psychiatric hospital, that it will hold a hearing on the proposed transfer at which the inmate may be present, that at the hearing the inmate has the rights described in division (B)(3) of this section, and that the department will provide qualified and independent assistance to the inmate with respect to the hearing. The department shall not hold the hearing until the inmate has received written notice of the proposed transfer and has had sufficient time to consult with the person appointed by the department to provide assistance to the inmate and to prepare for a presentation at the hearing.

(3) At the hearing held pursuant to division (B)(1) of this section, the department shall disclose to the inmate the evidence that it relies upon for the transfer and shall give the inmate an opportunity to be heard. Unless the independent decision-maker finds good cause for not permitting it, the inmate may present documentary evidence and the testimony of witnesses at the hearing and may confront and cross-examine witnesses called by the department.

(4) If the independent decision-maker does not find clear and convincing evidence that the inmate is a mentally ill person subject to hospitalization, the department shall not transfer the inmate to a psychiatric hospital but shall continue to confine the inmate in the same state correctional institution or in another state correctional institution that the department considers appropriate. If the independent decision-maker finds clear and convincing evidence that the inmate is a mentally

ill person subject to hospitalization, the decision-maker shall order that the inmate be transported to a psychiatric hospital for observation and treatment for a period of not longer than thirty days. After the hearing, the independent decision-maker shall submit to the department a written decision that states one of the findings described in division (B)(4) of this section, the evidence that the decision-maker relied on in reaching that conclusion, and, if the decision is that the inmate should be transferred, the reasons for the transfer.

(5) The director of rehabilitation and correction shall adopt rules setting forth guidelines for the procedures required under division (B) of this section.

(C)(1) If an independant decision-maker, pursuant to division (B)(4) of this section, orders an inmate transported to a psychiatric hospital, the staff of the psychiatric hospital shall examine the inmate patient when admitted to the psychiatric hospital as soon as practicable after the inmate patient arrives at the hospital and no later than twenty-four hours after the time of arrival. The attending physician responsible for the inmate patient's care shall give the inmate patient all information necessary to enable the patient to give a fully informed, intelligent, and knowing consent to the treatment the inmate patient will receive in the hospital. The attending physician shall tell the inmate patient the expected physical and medical consequences of any proposed treatment and shall give the inmate patient the opportunity to consult with another psychiatrist at the hospital and with the inmate advisor.

(2) No inmate patient who is transported to a psychiatric hospital pursuant to division (B)(4) of this section and who is in the physical custody of the department of rehabilitation and correction shall be subjected to any of the following procedures:

(a) Convulsive therapy;

(b) Major aversive interventions;

(c) Any unusually hazardous treatment procedures;

(d) Psychosurgery.

(D) The warden of the psychiatric hospital or the warden's designee shall ensure that an inmate patient hospitalized pursuant to this section receives or has all of the following:

(1) Receives sufficient professional care within twenty days of admission to ensure that an evaluation of the inmate patient's current status, differential diagnosis, probable prognosis, and description of the current treatment plan have been formulated and are stated on the inmate patient's official chart;

(2) Has a written treatment plan consistent with the evaluation, diagnosis, prognosis, and goals of treatment;

(3) Receives treatment consistent with the treatment plan;

(4) Receives periodic reevaluations of the treatment plan by the professional staff at intervals not to exceed thirty days;

(5) Is provided with adequate medical treatment for physical disease or injury;

(6) Receives humane care and treatment, including, without being limited to, the following:

(a) Access to the facilities and personnel required by the treatment plan;

(b) A humane psychological and physical environment;

(c) The right to obtain current information concerning the treatment program, the expected outcomes of treatment, and the expectations for the inmate patient's participation in the treatment program in terms that the inmate patient reasonably can understand;

(d) Opportunity for participation in programs designed to help the inmate patient acquire the skills needed to work toward discharge from the psychiatric hospital;

(e) The right to be free from unnecessary or excessive medication and from unnecessary restraints or isolation;

(f) All other rights afforded inmates in the custody of the department consistent with rules, policy, and procedure of the department.

(E) The department shall hold a hearing for the continued hospitalization of an inmate patient who is transported to a psychiatric hospital pursuant to division (B)(4) of this section prior to the expiration of the initial thirty-day period of hospitalization and, if necessary, at ninety-day intervals after the first hearing for continued hospitalization. An independent decision-maker shall conduct the hearings at the psychiatric hospital in which the inmate patient is confined. The inmate patient shall be afforded all of the rights set forth in this section for the hearing prior to transfer to the psychiatric hospital. A hearing for continued commitment is mandatory, and neither the department nor the inmate patient may waive the hearing.

If upon completion of the hearing the independent decision-maker does not find by clear and convincing evidence that the inmate patient is a mentally ill person subject to hospitalization, the independent decision-maker shall order the inmate patient's discharge from the psychiatric hospital. If the independent decision-maker finds by clear and convincing evidence that the inmate patient is a mentally ill person subject to hospitalization, the decision-maker shall order that the inmate patient remain at the psychiatric hospital for another period not to exceed ninety days.

If at any time prior to the expiration of the ninety-day period, the warden of the psychiatric hospital or the warden's designee determines that the treatment needs of the inmate patient could be met equally well in an available and appropriate less restrictive state correctional institution or unit, the warden or the warden's designee may discharge the inmate to that facility.

(F) An inmate patient is entitled to the credits toward the reduction of the inmate patient's stated prison term pursuant to Chapters 2967. and 5120. of the Revised Code under the same terms and conditions as if the inmate patient were in any other institution of the department of rehabilitation and correction.

(G) The adult parole authority may place an inmate patient on parole or under post-release control directly from a psychiatric hospital.

(H) If an inmate patient who is a mentally ill person subject to hospitalization is to be released from a psychiatric hospital because of the expiration of the inmate patient's stated prison term, the warden of the psychiatric hospital, at least fourteen days before the expiration date, may file an affidavit under section 5122.11 or 5123.71 of the Revised Code with the probate court in the county where the psychiatric hospital is located, alleging that the inmate patient is a mentally ill person subject to hospitalization by court order or a mentally retarded person subject to institutionalization by court order, whichever is applicable. The proceedings in the probate court shall be conducted pursuant to Chapter 5122. or 5123. of the Revised Code except as modified by this division.

Upon the request of the inmate patient, the probate court shall grant the inmate patient an initial hearing under section 5122.141 [5122.14.1] of the Revised Code or a probable cause hearing under section 5123.75 of the Revised Code before the expiration of the stated prison term. After holding a full hearing, the probate court shall make a disposition authorized by section 5122.15 or 5123.76 of the Revised Code before the date of the expiration of the stated prison term unless the court grants a continuance of the hearing at the request of the inmate patient or the inmate patient's counsel. No inmate patient shall be held in the custody of the department of rehabilitation and correction past the date of the expiration of the inmate patient's stated prison term.

(I) The department of rehabilitation and correction shall set standards for treatment provided to inmate patients, consistent where applicable with the standards set by the joint commission on accreditation of healthcare organizations.

(J) A certificate, application, record, or report that is made in compliance with this section and that directly or indirectly identifies an inmate or former inmate whose hospitalization has been sought under this section is confidential. No person shall disclose the contents of any certificate, application, record, or report of that nature unless one of the following applies:

(1) The person identified, or the person's legal guardian, if any, consents to disclosure, and the director of clinical services and psychiatry of the department of rehabilitation and correction determines that disclosure is in the best interests of the person.

(2) Disclosure is required by a court order signed by a judge.

(3) An inmate patient seeks access to the inmate patient's own psychiatric and medical records, unless access is specifically restricted in the treatment plan for clear treatment reasons.

(4) Hospitals and other institutions and facilities within the department of rehabilitation and correction may exchange psychiatric records and other pertinent information with other hospitals, institutions, and facilities of the department, but the information that may be released about an inmate patient is limited to medication history, physical health status and history, summary of course of treatment in the hospital, summary of treatment needs, and a discharge summary, if any.

(5) An inmate patient's family member who is involved in planning, providing, and monitoring services to the inmate patient may receive medication information, a summary of the inmate patient's diagnosis and prognosis, and a list of the services and personnel available to assist the inmate patient and family if the attending physician determines that disclosure would be in the best interest of the inmate patient. No disclosure shall be made under this division unless the inmate patient is notified of the possible disclosure, receives the information to be disclosed, and does not object to the disclosure.

(6) The department of rehabilitation and correction may exchange psychiatric hospitalization records, other mental health treatment records, and other pertinent information with county sheriffs' offices, hospitals, institutions, and facilities of the department of mental health and with community mental health agencies and boards of alcohol, drug addiction, and mental health services with which the department of mental health has a current agreement for patient care or services to ensure continuity of care. Disclosure under this division is limited to records regarding the inmate patient's medication history, physical health status and history, summary of course of treatment, summary of treatment needs, and a discharge summary, if any. No office, department, agency, or board shall disclose the records and other information unless one of the following applies:

(a) The inmate patient is notified of the possible disclosure and consents to the disclosure.

(b) The inmate patient is notified of the possible disclosure, an attempt to gain the consent of the inmate is made, and the office, department, agency, or board documents the attempt to gain consent, the inmate's objections, if any, and the reasons for disclosure in spite of the inmate's objections.

(7) Information may be disclosed to staff members designated by the director of rehabilitation and correction for the purpose of evaluating the quality, effectiveness, and efficiency of services and determining if the services meet minimum standards.

(K) The name of an inmate patient shall not be retained with the information obtained during the evaluations.

HISTORY: 146 v S 310 (Eff 6-20-96); 147 v S 52. Eff 9-3-97.

Not analogous to former RC § 5120.17 (GC § 1890-73; 117 v 550 (572), § 73; 119 v 616 (633); 121 v 423 (437); Bureau of Code Revision, RC § 5125.05, 10-1-53; 125 v 872; 130 v 1203; 134 v H 494; 137 v H 565; 138 v S 297; RC § 5120.17, 138 v H 900; 138 v H 965; 140 v H 37; 142 v S 156; 146 v S 2), repealed 146 v S 310, § 2, eff 6-20-96.

The provisions of § 19 of SB 310 (146 v —) read as follows:

SECTION 19. The version of section 5120.17 of the Revised Code that results from Am. Sub. S.B. 2 of the 121st General Assembly is hereby repealed. This repeal does not affect the repeal and reenactment of section 5120.17 of the Revised Code by Sections 1 and 2 of this act.

§ 5120.18 Classification of public buildings; purchase of articles to be used therein.

The department of rehabilitation and correction shall, with the advice and consent of the department of administrative services, classify public buildings, offices, and institutions and determine the kinds, patterns, designs, and qualities of articles to be manufactured for use therein, which shall be uniform for each class, so far as practicable.

Whenever the department of rehabilitation and correction gives written notice to the superintendent of purchases and printing, or other official having authority to purchase articles, that the department is prepared to supply such articles from any institution under its control, the superintendent or other official shall make any needed purchases of said articles from such institution, unless the chief officer thereof, or the department, having been requested to furnish such articles, gives notice in writing within thirty days from the date of the request, that such articles cannot be furnished.

If the superintendent requires such articles within thirty days from the day of making such request and so states upon the face of such request, the chief officer of such institution or the department of rehabilitation and correction shall forthwith advise the superintendent whether it will be able to furnish such articles within such time, the superintendent may purchase such articles in the open market as in other cases. This section does not apply to any officer, board, or agent of any municipal corporation which maintains an institution that produces or manufactures articles of the kind desired.

HISTORY: 134 v H 494 (Eff 7-12-72); 137 v H 1. Eff 8-26-77.

§ 5120.19 Cultivation and use of lands; transactions between institutions.

(A) The department of rehabilitation and correction, in accordance with rules adopted pursuant to division (B) of section 5145.03 of the Revised Code, shall determine and direct what lands belonging to institutions under its control shall be cultivated, the crops to be raised, and the use to be made of the land and crops, and may distribute the products among the different institutions. If the crops are distributed to institutions under the control of the department, the department shall keep records of the distributions and of the fair market value of the crops distributed. The department may sell any crops that are not necessary for the institutions under its control to any person. The money received from the sale of the crops shall be deposited in the services and agricultural fund created pursuant to section 5120.29 of the Revised Code.

The department may require institutions under its control, when they have proper lands and labor, to undertake intensive agriculture, may rent lands for the production of supplies for any of the institutions that have surplus labor, and may rent lands for the production of crops for sale, when it can be done to advantage.

The department shall pay and assign the prisoners who perform any labor pursuant to this division in accordance with the rules adopted pursuant to division (B) of section 5145.03 of the Revised Code.

(B) The department may direct the purchase of any materials, supplies, or other articles for any institution under its control from any other institution under its control at the reasonable market value, which value shall be fixed by the department. Payments for the articles shall be made as between institutions in the manner provided for payment for supplies.

HISTORY: 134 v H 494 (Eff 7-12-72); 138 v H 654 (Eff 4-9-82); 141 v H 201 (Eff 7-1-85); 142 v H 171. Eff 7-1-87.

§ 5120.20 Cooperation from agriculture and health departments and Ohio state university.

The department of agriculture, department of health, and Ohio state university shall cooperate with the department of rehabilitation and correction in making such cooperative tests as are necessary to determine the quality, strength, and purity of supplies, the value and use of farm lands, or conditions and needs of mechanical equipment.

HISTORY: 134 v H 494 (Eff 7-12-72); 136 v H 1. Eff 6-13-75.

§ 5120.21 Records; report on accident or injury or peculiar death.

(A) The department of rehabilitation and correction shall keep in its office, accessible only to its employees, except by the consent of the department or the order of the judge of a court of record, and except as provided in division (C) of this section, a record showing the name, residence, sex, age, nativity, occupation, condition, and date of entrance or commitment of every inmate in the several institutions governed by it. The record also shall include the date, cause, and terms of discharge and the condition of such person at the time of leaving, a record of all transfers from one institution to another, and, if such inmate is dead, the date and cause of death. These and other facts that the department requires shall be furnished by the managing officer of each institution within ten days after the commitment, entrance, death, or discharge of an inmate.

(B) In case of an accident or injury or peculiar death of an inmate, the managing officer shall make a special report to the department within twenty-four hours thereafter, giving the circumstances as fully as possible.

(C)(1) As used in this division, "medical record" means any document or combination of documents that pertains to the medical history, diagnosis, prognosis, or medical condition of a patient and that is generated and maintained in the process of medical treatment.

(2) A separate medical record of every inmate in an institution governed by the department shall be compiled, maintained, and kept apart from and independently of any other record pertaining to the inmate. Upon the signed written request of the inmate to whom the record pertains together with the written request of either a licensed attorney at law or a licensed physician designated by the inmate, the department shall make the inmate's medical record available to the designated attorney or physician. The record may be inspected or copied by the inmate's designated attorney or physician. The department may establish a reasonable fee for the copying of any medical record. If a physician concludes that presentation of all or any part of the medical record directly to the inmate will result in serious medical harm to the inmate, the physician shall so indicate on the medical record. An inmate's medical record shall be made available to a physician or to an attorney designated in writing by the inmate not more than once every twelve months.

(D) Except as otherwise provided by a law of this state or the United Sates,† the department and the officers of its institutions shall keep confidential and accessible only to its employees, except by the consent of the department or the order of a judge of a court of record, all of the following:

(1) Architectural, engineering, or construction diagrams, drawings, or plans of a correctional institution;

(2) Plans for hostage negotiation, for disturbance control, for the control and location of keys, and for dealing with escapes;

(3) Statements made by inmate informants;

(4) Records that are maintained by the department of youth services, that pertain to children in its custody, and that are released to the department of rehabilitation and correction by the department of youth services pursuant to section 5139.05 of the Revised Code.

(E) Except as otherwise provided by a law of this state or the United States, the department of rehabilitation and correction may release inmate records to the department of youth services or a court of record, and the department of youth services or the court of record may use those records for the limited purpose of carrying out the duties of the department of youth services or the court of record. Inmate records released by the department of rehabilitation and correction to the department of youth services or a court of record shall remain confidential and shall not be considered public records as defined in section 149.43 of the Revised Code.

(F) Except as otherwise provided in division (C) of this section, records of inmates committed to the department of rehabilitation and correction as well as records of persons under the supervision of the adult parole authority shall not be considered public records as defined in section 149.43 of the Revised Code.

HISTORY: 134 v H 494 (Eff 7-12-72); 142 v S 94 (Eff 7-20-88); 145 v H 571 (Eff 10-6-94); 146 v S 269. Eff 7-1-96.

† So in enrolled bill, division (D).

§ 5120.22 Property management duties of division of business administration.

The division of business administration shall examine the conditions of all buildings, grounds, and other property connected with the institutions under the control of the department of rehabilitation and correction, the methods of bookkeeping and storekeeping, and all matters relating to the management of such property. The division shall study and become familiar with the advantages and disadvantages of each as to location, freight rates, and efficiency of farm and equipment, for the purpose of aiding in the determination of the local and general requirements both for maintenance and improvements.

The division, with respect to the various types of state-owned housing under jurisdiction of the department, shall adopt, in accordance with section 111.15 of the Revised Code, rules governing maintenance of the housing and its usage by department personnel. The rules shall include a procedure for determining charges for rent and utilities, which the division shall assess against and collect from department personnel using the housing. All money collected for rent and utilities pursuant to the rules shall be deposited into the property receipts fund, which is hereby created in the state treasury. Money in the fund shall be used for any expenses necessary to provide housing of department employees, including but not limited to expenses for the acquisition, construction, operation, maintenance, repair, reconstruction, or demolition of land and buildings.

HISTORY: 134 v H 494 (Eff 7-12-72); 145 v H 152 (Eff 7-1-93); 146 v H 117. Eff 6-30-95.

§ 5120.23 Estimate of needed supplies made by correctional and penal institutions; disposition of money received.

(A) The department of rehabilitation and correction shall require proper officials of the state and its political subdivisions and of the institutions of the state and its political subdivisions, to report estimates for the ensuing year of the amount of supplies required by them, of the kinds that are produced by the state correctional and penal institutions. It may make rules for the reports and provide the manner in which the estimates shall be made.

(B) Any money that is received by the department of rehabilitation and correction from the state and its political subdivisions, any other state and its political subdivisions, the United States, or private persons for products and services produced by the state correctional and penal institutions shall be deposited in the services and agricultural fund or the Ohio penal industries manufacturing fund created pursuant to section 5120.29 of the Revised Code and shall be used and accounted for as provided in that section.

HISTORY: 134 v H 494 (Eff 7-12-72); 138 v H 654 (Eff 4-9-82); 142 v H 171. Eff 7-1-87.

§ 5120.24 Purchase of supplies; competitive bidding.

The department of administrative services shall purchase all supplies needed for the proper support and maintenance of the institutions under the control of the department of rehabilitation and correction in accordance with the competitive selection procedures of Chapter 125. of the Revised Code and such rules as the department of administrative services adopts. All bids shall be publicly opened on the day and hour and at the place specified in the advertisement.

Preference shall be given to bidders in localities wherein the institution is located if the price is fair and reasonable and not greater than the usual price. Bids not meeting the specifications shall be rejected.

The department of administrative services may require such security as it considers proper to accompany the bids and shall fix the security to be given by the contractor.

The department of administrative services may reject any or all bids and secure new bids, if for any reason it is considered to be in the best interest of the state to do so, and it may authorize the managing officer of any institution to purchase perishable goods and supplies for use in cases of emergency, in which cases such managing officer shall certify such fact in writing and the department of administrative services shall record the reasons for such purchase.

HISTORY: 134 v H 494 (Eff 7-12-72); 136 v S 430 (Eff 8-13-76); 142 v H 88 (Eff 1-1-88); 145 v H 152. Eff 7-1-93.

§ 5120.25 Books and accounts; department to prescribe form and method; audit.

The department of correction shall keep in its office a proper and complete set of books and accounts with each institution, which shall clearly show the nature and amount of every expenditure authorized and made at such institution, and which shall contain an account of all appropriations made by the general assembly and of all other funds, together with the disposition of such funds.

The department shall prescribe the form of vouchers, records, and methods of keeping accounts at each of the institutions, which shall be as nearly uniform as possible. The department may examine the records of each institution, at any time.

The department may authorize any of its bookkeepers, accountants, or employees to examine and check the records, accounts, and vouchers or take an inventory of the property of any institution, or do whatever is necessary, and pay the actual and reasonable expenses incurred in such service when an itemized account is filed and approved.

HISTORY: 134 v H 494. Eff 7-12-72.

See effective date provision following RC § 5120.01.

§ 5120.26 Use, custody, and insurance of funds.

(A) The treasurer of state shall have charge of all funds under the jurisdiction of the department of rehabilitation and correction and shall pay out the funds only in accordance with this chapter.

(B) The department shall cause to be furnished a contract of indemnity to cover all moneys and funds received by it or by its managing officers, employees, or agents while the moneys or funds are in the possession of the managing officers, employees, or agents. The funds are designated as follows:

(1) Funds that are due and payable to the treasurer of state as provided by Chapter 131. of the Revised Code;

(2) Funds that are held in trust by the managing officers, employees, or agents of the institution as local funds or accounts under the jurisdiction of the department.

The contract of indemnity shall be made payable to the state and the premium for the contract of indemnity may be paid from any of the moneys received for the use of the department under this chapter and Chapters 5121., 5123., and 5125. of the Revised Code.

(C) Moneys collected from various sources, such as the sale of goods, farm products, services, and all miscellaneous articles, shall be transmitted on or before Monday of each week to the treasurer of state and a detailed statement of the collections shall be made to the division of business administration by each managing officer. The receipts from manufacturing and service industries and agricultural products shall be used and accounted for as provided in section 5120.29 of the Revised Code.

HISTORY: 134 v H 494 (Eff 7-12-72); 137 v S 221 (Eff 11-23-77); 138 v H 654. Eff 4-9-82.

The effective date is set by section 4 of HB 654.

§ 5120.27 Industries to be carried on by institutions determined by department.

The department of rehabilitation and correction may assign among the correctional and penal institutions under its control and in accordance with the rules adopted pursuant to division (B) of section 5145.03 of the Revised Code, the industries to be carried on by the institutions, having due regard to the location and convenience of the industries, other institutions to be supplied, to the machinery in the institutions, and to the number and character of prisoners employed in the industries.

HISTORY: 134 v H 494 (Eff 7-12-72); 138 v H 654. Eff 4-9-82.

The effective date is set by section 4 of HB 654.

§ 5120.28 Prices fixed for labor, services, products and articles; disposition of money received.

(A) The department of rehabilitation and correction, subject to the approval of the office of budget and management, shall fix the prices at which all labor and services performed, all agricultural products produced, and all articles manufactured in correctional and penal institutions shall be furnished to the state, the political subdivisions of the state, and the public institutions of the state and the political subdivisions, and to private persons. The prices shall be uniform to all and not higher than the usual market price for like labor, products, services, and articles.

(B) Any money received by the department of rehabilitation and correction for labor and services performed and agricultural products produced shall be deposited into the services and agricultural fund created pursuant to division (A) of section 5120.29 of the Revised Code and shall be used and accounted for as provided in that section and division (B) of section 5145.03 of the Revised Code.

(C) Any money received by the department of rehabilitation and correction for articles manufactured in penal and correctional institutions shall be deposited into the Ohio penal industries manufacturing fund created pursuant to division (B) of section 5120.29 of the Revised Code and shall be used and accounted for as provided in that section and division (B) of section 5145.03 of the Revised Code.

HISTORY: 134 v H 494 (Eff 7-12-72); 137 v H 1 (Eff 8-26-77); 138 v H 654 (Eff 4-9-82); 142 v H 171. Eff 7-1-87.

§ 5120.29 Services and agricultural fund; penal industries manufacturing fund.

(A) There is hereby created, in the state treasury, the services and agricultural fund, which shall be used for the:

(1) Purchase of material, supplies, and equipment and the erection and extension of buildings used in service industries and agriculture;

(2) Purchase of lands and buildings necessary to carry on or extend the service industries and agriculture, upon the approval of the governor;

(3) Payment of compensation to employees necessary to carry on the service industries and agriculture;

(4) Payment of prisoners confined in state correctional institutions a portion of their earnings in accordance with rules adopted pursuant to section 5145.03 of the Revised Code.

(B) There is hereby created, in the state treasury, the Ohio penal industries manufacturing fund, which shall be used for the:

(1) Purchase of material, supplies, and equipment and the erection and extension of buildings used in manufacturing industries;

(2) Purchase of lands and buildings necessary to carry on or extend the manufacturing industries upon the approval of the governor;

(3) Payment of compensation to employees necessary to carry on the manufacturing industries;

(4) Payment of prisoners confined in state correctional institutions a portion of their earnings in accordance with rules adopted pursuant to section 5145.03 of the Revised Code.

(C) The department of rehabilitation and correction shall, in accordance with rules adopted pursuant to section 5145.03 of the Revised Code and subject to any pledge made as provided in division (D) of this section, place to the credit of each prisoner his earnings and pay the earnings so credited to the prisoner or his family.

(D) Receipts credited to the funds created in divisions (A) and (B) of this section constitute available receipts as defined in section 152.09 of the Revised Code, and may be pledged to the payment of bond service charges on obligations issued by the Ohio building authority pursuant to Chapter 152. of the Revised Code to construct, reconstruct, or otherwise improve capital facilities useful to the department. The authority may, with the consent of the department, provide in the bond proceedings for a pledge of all or such portion of receipts credited to the funds as the authority determines. The authority may provide in the bond proceedings for the transfer of receipts credited to the funds to the appropriate bond service fund or bond service reserve fund as required to pay the bond service charges when due, and any such provision for the transfer of receipts shall be controlling notwithstanding any other provision of law pertaining to such receipts.

All receipts received by the treasurer of state on account of the department and required by the applicable bond proceedings to be deposited, transferred, or credited to the bond service fund or bond service reserve fund established by such bond proceedings shall be transferred by the treasurer of state to such fund, whether or not such fund is in the custody of the treasurer of state, without necessity for further appropriation, upon receipt of notice from the Ohio building authority as prescribed in the bond proceedings. The authority may covenant in the bond proceedings that so long as any obligations are outstanding to which receipts credited to the fund are pledged, the state and the department shall neither reduce the prices charged pursuant to section 5120.28 of the Revised Code nor the level of manpower collectively devoted to the production of goods and services for which prices are set pursuant to section 5120.28 of the Revised Code, which covenant shall be controlling notwithstanding any other provision of law; provided, that no covenant shall require the general assembly to appropriate money derived from the levying of excises or taxes to purchase such goods and services or to pay rent or bond service charges.

HISTORY: 134 v H 494 (Eff 7-12-72); 138 v H 654 (Eff 4-9-82); 139 v H 530, § 1 (Eff 5-28-82); 139 v H 530, § 3 (Eff 4-9-82); 141 v H 201 (Eff 7-1-85); 142 v H 171 (Eff 7-1-87); 145 v H 571. Eff 10-6-94.

§ 5120.30 Investigations; director to have powers of county court judge; records; witness fees.

The department of rehabilitation and correction may make such investigations as are necessary in the performance of its duties and to that end the director of rehabilitation and correction shall have the same power as a judge of a county court to administer oaths and to enforce the attendance and testimony of witnesses and the production of books or papers.

The department shall keep a record of such investigations stating the time, place, charges or subject, witnesses summoned and examined, and its conclusions.

In matters involving the conduct of an officer, a stenographic report of the evidence shall be taken and a copy of such report, with all documents introduced, kept on file at the office of the department.

The fees of witnesses for attendance and travel shall be the same as in the court of common pleas, but no officer or employee of the institution under investigation is entitled to such fees.

Any judge of the probate court or of the court of common pleas, upon application of the department, may compel the attendance of witnesses, the production of books or papers, and the giving of testimony before the department, by a judgment for contempt or otherwise, in the same manner as in cases before said courts.

HISTORY: 134 v H 494 (Eff 7-12-72); 136 v H 390. Eff 8-6-76.

§ 5120.31 Appointment of competent agency or person; content of credentials.

The department of rehabilitation and correction may appoint and commission any competent agency or person, to serve without compensation, as a special agent, investigator, or representative to perform a designated duty for and in behalf of the department. Specific credentials shall be given by the department to each person so designated, and each credential shall state:

(A) The name;
(B) Agency with which such person is connected;
(C) Purpose of appointment;
(D) Date of expiration of appointment;
(E) Such information as the department considers proper.

HISTORY: 134 v H 494. Eff 7-12-72.

See effective date provision following RC § 5120.01.

§ 5120.32 Annual report; content.

In its annual report, the department of rehabilitation and correction shall include a complete financial statement of the various institutions under its control. The report shall state, as to each such institution, whether;

(A) The moneys appropriated have been economically and judiciously expended;
(B) The objects of the several institutions have been accomplished;
(C) The laws in relation to such institutions have been fully complied with;
(D) All parts of the state are equally benefited by said institutions.

Such annual report shall be accompanied by the reports of the managing officers and such other information and recommendations as the department considers proper.

HISTORY: 134 v H 494. Eff 7-12-72.

See effective date provision following RC § 5120.01.

§ 5120.33 List of employees; condition of state institutions; other statistics.

The annual report of the department of rehabilitation and correction shall include a list of the officers and agents employed, and the conditions of the state institutions under its control. Such report may include statistics and information in regard to correctional institutions of this or other states.

HISTORY: 134 v H 494. Eff 7-12-72.

See effective date provision following RC § 5120.01.

[§ 5120.33.1] § 5120.331 Report on time served by released inmates.

(A) Not later than the first day of April of each year, the department of rehabilitation and correction shall prepare an annual report covering the preceding calendar year that does all of the following:

(1) Indicates the total number of persons sentenced to any institution, division, or place under its control and management who are delivered within that calendar year to its custody and control;

(2) Indicates the total number of persons who, during that calendar year, were released from a prison term on any of the following bases:

(a) On judicial release under section 2929.20 of the Revised Code;
(b) On furlough under section 2967.26 of the Revised Code;
(c) On parole;

(d) Due to the expiration of the stated prison term imposed;

(e) On any basis not described in divisions (A)(2)(a) to (d) of this section.

(3) Lists each offense, by Revised Code section number and, if applicable, by designated name, for which at least one person who was released from a prison term in that calendar year was serving a prison term at the time of release;

(4) For each offense included in the list described in division (A)(3) of this section, indicates all of the following:

(a) The total number of persons released from a prison term in that calendar year who were serving a prison term for that offense at the time of release;

(b) The shortest, longest, and average prison term that had been imposed for that offense upon the persons described in division (A)(4)(a) of this section and that they were serving at the time of release;

(c) The shortest, longest, and average period of imprisonment actually served by the persons described in division (A)(4)(a) of this section under a prison term that had been imposed for that offense upon them and that they were serving at the time of release;

(d) The total number of persons released from a prison term in that calendar year under each of the bases for release set forth in division (A)(2) of this section who were serving a prison term for that offense at the time of release;

(e) The shortest, longest, and average prison term that had been imposed for that offense upon the persons in each category described in division (A)(4)(d) of this section and that they were serving at the time of release;

(f) The shortest, longest, and average period of imprisonment actually served by the persons in each category described in division (A)(4)(d) of this section under a prison term that had been imposed for that offense upon them and that they were serving at the time of release.

(B) No report prepared under division (A) of this section shall identify or enable the identification of any person released from a prison term in the preceding calendar year.

(C) Each annual report prepared under division (A) of this section shall be distributed to each member of the general assembly.

(D) As used in this section, "prison term" and "stated prison term" have the same meanings as in section 2929.01 of the Revised Code.

HISTORY: 142 v H 261 (Eff 11-1-87); 146 v S 2. Eff 7-1-96.

The effective date is set by section 6 of SB 2.

§ 5120.34 Internal management.

The department of rehabilitation and correction shall make rules for the nonpartisan management of the institutions under its control. Any officer or employee of the department or any officer or employee of any institution under its control, who, by solicitation or otherwise, exerts his influence, directly or indirectly, to induce any other officer or employee of any such institutions to adopt his political views or to favor any particular person, issue, or candidate for office shall be removed from his office or position, by the department in case of an officer or employee and by the governor in case of the director of rehabilitation and correction.

HISTORY: 134 v H 494 (Eff 7-12-72); 136 v H 617. Eff 11-7-75.

§ 5120.35 Suggestions of department in annual report.

In its annual report, the department of rehabilitation and correction shall make any suggestions or recommendations it considers wise for the more effectual accomplishment of the general purpose of Chapter 5120. of the Revised Code.

HISTORY: 134 v H 494. Eff 7-12-72.

See effective date provision following RC § 5120.01.

§ 5120.36 Executive, administrative, and fiscal supervision of institutions; powers of department.

The department of rehabilitation and correction, in addition to the powers expressly conferred, shall have all power and authority necessary for the full and efficient exercise of the executive, administrative, and fiscal supervision over the state institutions described in section 5120.05 of the Revised Code.

HISTORY: 134 v H 494. Eff 7-12-72.

See effective date provision following RC § 5120.01.

§ 5120.37 Information exchanges with human services department.

The department of rehabilitation and correction shall enter into an agreement with the department of human services to exchange or share information monthly concerning persons under the control or supervision of the department of rehabilitation and correction.

HISTORY: 147 v S 52. Eff 9-3-97.

Not analogous to former RC § 5120.37 (134 v H 494), repealed 145 v H 571, § 2, eff 10-6-94.

§ 5120.38 Managing officer; duties.

Subject to the rules and regulations of the department of rehabilitation and correction, each institution under the department's jurisdiction other than an institution operated pursuant to a contract entered into under section 9.06 of the Revised Code shall be under the control of a managing officer known as a superintendent or other appropriate title. Such managing officer shall be appointed by the director of the department of rehabilitation and correction and shall be in the unclassified service and serve at the pleasure of the director. Appointment to the position of managing officer shall be made from persons holding positions in the classified service in the department. A person so appointed shall retain the right to resume the position and status that the person held in the classified service immediately prior to the appointment. Upon being relieved of the person's duties as managing officer, such person shall be reinstated to the position in the classified service that the person held immediately prior to the appointment to the position of managing officer or to another position, certified by the director with approval of the state department of personnel as being substantially equal to such position. Service as a managing officer shall be counted as service in the position in the classified service held by such person immediately preceding the person's appointment as managing officer. A person who is reinstated to a position in the classified service, as provided in this section, shall be entitled to all rights and emoluments accruing to such position during the time of the person's service as managing officer.

The managing officer, under the director, shall have entire executive charge of the institution for which such managing officer is appointed. Subject to civil service rules and regulations, the managing officer shall appoint the necessary employees and the managing officer or the director may remove such employees for cause. A report of all appointments, resignations, and discharges shall be filed with the director at the close of each month.

After conference with the managing officer of each institution, the director shall determine the number of employees to be appointed to the various institutions.

HISTORY: 134 v H 494 (Eff 7-12-72); 147 v H 215. Eff 9-29-97.

The effective date is set by section 222 of HB 215.

§ 5120.39 Superintendent; qualifications; powers and duties.

Each superintendent of an institution under the control of the department of rehabilitation and correction shall be of good moral character and have skill, ability, and experience in his profession. He shall have control of the institution, and be responsible for the management thereof and for the service of all its employees. He shall appoint necessary teachers, attendants, nurses, servants, and other persons, assign their places and duties, and may discharge them, keeping a record thereof and reasons therefor.

HISTORY: 134 v H 494. Eff 7-12-72.

See effective date provision following RC § 5120.01.

§ 5120.40 Teacher qualifications.

All teachers employed in any institution under the jurisdiction of the department of rehabilitation and correction shall possess educator licenses or have the qualifications and approval that the superintendent of the Ohio central school system, after conference with the officers in charge of the several institutions, prescribes for the various particular types of service or service in the particular institutions.

HISTORY: 134 v H 494 (Eff 7-12-72); 138 v H 900 (Eff 7-1-80); 145 v H 571 (Eff 10-6-94); 146 v S 230. Eff 10-29-96.

§ 5120.41 Courses of study subject to approval of superintendent of public instruction.

The courses of study for the instruction and training of all persons in the correctional institutions under the control of the department of rehabilitation and correction shall be subject to the approval of the superintendent of public instruction.

HISTORY: 134 v H 494 (Eff 7-12-72); 145 v H 571. Eff 10-6-94.

§ 5120.42 Rules for proper execution of powers.

The department of rehabilitation and correction shall make rules for the proper execution of its powers and may require the performance of additional duties by the officers of the several institutions, so as to fully meet the requirements, intents, and purposes of Chapter 5120. of the Revised Code, and particularly those relating to making estimates and furnishing proper proof of the use made of all articles furnished or produced in such institutions. In case of an apparent conflict between the powers conferred upon any managing officer and those conferred by such sections upon the department, the presumption shall be conclusive in favor of the department.

HISTORY: 134 v H 494. Eff 7-12-72.

See effective date provision following RC § 5120.01.

[§ 5120.42.1] § 5120.421 Searches of visitors to correctional institutions.

(A) As used in this section:

(1) "Body cavity search" means an inspection of the anal or vaginal cavity of a person that is conducted visually, manually, by means of any instrument, apparatus, or object, or in any other manner.

(2) "Deadly weapon" and "dangerous ordnance" have the same meanings as in section 2923.11 of the Revised Code.

(3) "Drug of abuse" has the same meaning as in section 3719.011 [3719.01.1] of the Revised Code.

(4) "Intoxicating liquor" has the same meaning as in section 4301.01 of the Revised Code.

(5) "Strip search" means an inspection of the genitalia, buttocks, breasts, or undergarments of a person that is preceded by the removal or rearrangement of some or all of the person's clothing that directly covers the person's genitalia, buttocks, breasts, or undergarments

and that is conducted visually, manually, by means of any instrument, apparatus, or object, or in any other manner.

(B) For purposes of determining whether visitors to an institution under the control of the department of rehabilitation and correction are knowingly conveying, or attempting to convey, onto the grounds of the institution any deadly weapon, dangerous ordnance, drug of abuse, or intoxicating liquor in violation of section 2921.36 of the Revised Code, the department may adopt rules, pursuant to Chapter 119. of the Revised Code, that are consistent with this section.

(C) For the purposes described in division (B) of this section, visitors who are entering or have entered an institution under the control of the department of rehabilitation and correction may be searched by the use of a magnetometer or similar device, by a pat-down of the visitor's person that is conducted by a person of the same sex as that of the visitor, and by an examination of the contents of pockets, bags, purses, packages, and other containers proposed to be conveyed or already conveyed onto the grounds of the institution. Searches of visitors authorized by this division may be conducted without cause, but shall be conducted uniformly or by automatic random selection. Discriminatory or arbitrary selection searches of visitors are prohibited under this division.

(D) For the purposes described in division (B) of this section, visitors who are entering or have entered an institution under the control of the department of rehabilitation and correction may be searched by a strip or body cavity search, but only under the circumstances described in this division. In order for a strip or body cavity search to be conducted of a visitor, the highest officer present in the institution shall expressly authorize the search on the basis of a reasonable suspicion, based on specific objective facts and reasonable inferences drawn from those facts in the light of experience, that a visitor proposed to be so searched possesses, and intends to convey or already has conveyed, a deadly weapon, dangerous ordnance, drug of abuse, or intoxicating liquor onto the grounds of the institution in violation of section 2921.36 of the Revised Code.

Except as otherwise provided in this division, prior to the conduct of the strip or body cavity search, the highest officer present in the institution shall cause the visitor to be provided with a written statement that sets forth the specific objective facts upon which the proposed search is based. In the case of an emergency under which time constraints make it impossible to prepare the written statement before the conduct of the proposed search, the highest officer in the institution instead shall cause the visitor to be orally informed of the specific objective facts upon which the proposed search is based prior to its conduct, and shall cause the preparation of the written statement and its provision to the visitor within twenty-four hours after the conduct of the search. Both the highest officer present in the institution and the visitor shall retain a copy of a written statement provided in accordance with this division.

Any strip or body cavity search conducted pursuant to this division shall be conducted in a private setting by a person of the same sex as that of the visitor. Any body cavity search conducted under this division additionally shall be conducted by medical personnel.

This division does not preclude, and shall not be construed as precluding, a less intrusive search as authorized by division (C) of this section when reasonable suspicion as described in this division exists for a strip or body cavity search.

HISTORY: 143 v S 258. Eff 8-22-90.

[§ 5120.42.3] § 5120.423 Designation of additional exercise equipment and fighting skills programs to be denied to prisoners.

The department of rehabilitation and correction shall adopt rules in accordance with Chapter 119. of the Revised Code that designate devices and programs that, in addition to free weight exercise equipment as defined in sections 341.41, 753.31, and 5145.30 of the Revised Code and in addition to boxing, wrestling, and martial arts programs, would enable a person who uses a designated device or participates in a designated program to increase muscle mass and physical strength or to improve fighting skills.

HISTORY: 146 v H 152. Eff 10-4-96.

§ 5120.43 Occupational therapy.

Each managing officer of an institution under the department of rehabilitation and correction shall develop such occupations as shall promote the mental, moral, and physical improvement and happiness of the inmates and the department shall aid and encourage such activities so as best to advance the economical and efficient administration of all the institutions, but without prejudice to the primary needs of suitable education for the inmates.

HISTORY: 134 v H 494. Eff 7-12-72.

See effective date provision following RC § 5120.01.

§ 5120.44 Liberal construction.

Chapter 5120. of the Revised Code attempts:

(A) To provide humane and scientific treatment and care and the highest attainable degree of individual development for the dependent wards of the state;

(B) To provide for the delinquent, conditions of modern education and training that will restore the largest possible portion of them to useful citizenship;

(C) To promote the study of the causes of dependency and delinquency, and of mental, moral, and physical defects, with a view to cure and ultimate prevention;

(D) To secure by uniform and systematic management the highest attainable degree of economy in the administration of the state institutions.

Such sections shall be liberally construed to attain such purposes.

HISTORY: 134 v H 494. Eff 7-12-72.

See effective date provision following RC § 5120.01.

§ 5120.45 Burial of inmate dying in institution.

The state shall bear the expense of the burial of an inmate who dies in a state correctional institution, if the body is not claimed for interment at the expense of friends or relatives, or is not delivered for anatomical purposes or for the study of embalming in accordance with section 1713.34 of the Revised Code. When the expense is borne by the state, interment shall be in the institution cemetery or other place provided by the state. The managing officer of the institution shall provide at the grave of the person a metal, stone, or concrete marker on which shall be inscribed the name and age of the person and the date of death.

HISTORY: 138 v H 900 (Eff 7-1-80); 145 v H 571. Eff 10-6-94.

§ 5120.46 Appropriation of property.

When it is necessary for a state correctional institution to acquire any real estate, right-of-way, or easement in real estate in order to accomplish the purposes for which it was organized or is being conducted, and the department of rehabilitation and correction is unable to agree with the owner of the property upon the price to be paid therefor, the property may be appropriated in the manner provided for the appropriation of property for other state purposes.

HISTORY: 138 v H 900 (Eff 7-1-80); 145 v H 571. Eff 10-6-94.

§ 5120.47 Lease of capital facilities.

The department of rehabilitation and correction shall lease capital facilities constructed, reconstructed, otherwise improved, or financed by the Ohio building authority pursuant to Chapter 152. of the Revised Code for the use of the department, and may enter into any other agreements with the authority ancillary to the construction, reconstruction, improvement, financing, leasing, or operation of such capital facilities, including, but not limited to, any agreements required by the applicable bond proceedings authorized by Chapter 152. of the Revised Code. Such agreements shall not be subject to section 5120.24 of the Revised Code. Any lease of capital facilities authorized by this section shall be governed by division (D) of section 152.24 of the Revised Code.

HISTORY: 139 v H 530. Eff 5-28-82.

§ 5120.48 Apprehension of escapees.

If a prisoner escapes from a state correctional institution, the managing officer of the institution, after consultation with and upon the advice of appropriate law enforcement officials, shall assign and deploy into the community appropriate staff persons necessary to apprehend the prisoner. Correctional officers and officials may carry firearms when required in the discharge of their duties in apprehending, taking into custody, or transporting to a place of confinement a prisoner who has escaped from a state correctional institution.

HISTORY: 145 v H 571. Eff 10-6-94.

§ 5120.49 Rules for termination of parole board's control over certain sexually violent offenders.

The department of rehabilitation and correction, by rule adopted under Chapter 119. of the Revised Code, shall prescribe standards and guidelines to be used by the parole board in determining, pursuant to section 2971.04 of the Revised Code, whether it should terminate its control over an offender's service of a prison term imposed upon the offender for a sexually violent offense under division (A)(3) of section 2971.03 of the Revised Code. The rules shall include provisions that specify that the parole board may not terminate its control over an offender's service of a prison term imposed upon the offender under that division until after the offender has served the minimum term imposed as part of that prison term and until the parole board has determined that the offender does not represent a substantial risk of physical harm to others.

HISTORY: 146 v H 180. Eff 1-1-97.

The effective date is set by section 3 of HB 180.

The provisions of § 4 of HB 180 (146 v —) read in part as follows:

SECTION 4. ° ° ° 5120.49, 5120.61, 5149.03, and 5149.10 of the Revised Code, as amended or enacted in Sections 1 and 2 of this act, shall apply only to persons who commit an offense governed by those amended and enacted sections on or after the effective date of this act.

§ 5120.50 Interstate correction compact.

(A) The party states, desiring by common action to fully utilize and improve their programs for the confinement, treatment, and rehabilitation of various types of offenders, declare that it is the policy of each of the party states to provide institutional facilities and such programs on a basis of cooperation with one another, thereby serving the best interest of such offenders and of society and effecting economies in capital expenditures and operational costs. The purpose of this compact is to provide for the mutual development and execution of such programs of cooperation for the confinement, treatment, and rehabilitation of offenders with the most economical use of human and material resources.

(B) DEFINITIONS

As used in the compact, unless the context clearly requires otherwise:

(1) "State" means a state of the United States; the United States; a territory or possession of the United States; the District of Columbia; the Commonwealth of Puerto Rico.

(2) "Sending state" means a state party to this compact in which conviction or court commitment was had.

(3) "Receiving state" means a state party to this compact to which an inmate is sent for confinement other than a state in which conviction or court commitment was had.

(4) "Inmate" means a male or female offender who is committed, under sentence to or confined in a state penal or state reformatory institution.

(5) "Institution" means any state penal or state reformatory facility, including but not limited to a facility for the mentally ill or mentally defective, in which inmates as defined in division (B)(4) of this section may lawfully be confined.

(C) CONTRACTS

(1) Each party state may make one or more contracts with any one or more of the other party states for the confinement of inmates on behalf of a sending state in institutions situated within receiving states. Any such contract shall provide for:

(a) Its duration;

(b) Payments to be made to the receiving state by the sending state for inmate maintenance, extraordinary medical and dental expenses, and any participation in or receipt by inmates of rehabilitative or correctional services, facilities, programs, or treatment not reasonably included as part of normal maintenance;

(c) Participation in programs of inmate employment, if any; the disposition or crediting of any payments received by inmates on account thereof; and the crediting of proceeds from or disposal of any products resulting therefrom;

(d) Delivery and retaking of inmates;

(e) Such other matters as may be necessary and appropriate to fix the obligations, responsibilities, and rights of the sending and receiving states.

(2) The terms and provisions of this compact shall be a part of any contract entered into by the authority of or pursuant thereto, and nothing in any such contract shall be inconsistent therewith.

(D) PROCEDURES AND RIGHTS

(1) Whenever the duly constituted authorities in a state party to this compact, and which has entered into a contract pursuant to division (C) of this section, shall decide that confinement in, or transfer of an inmate to, an institution within the territory of another party state is necessary or desirable in order to provide adequate quarters and care, or an appropriate program of rehabilitation or treatment, said officials may direct that the confinement be within an institution within the territory of said other party state, the receiving state to act in that regard solely as agent for the sending state.

(2) No transfer shall take place pursuant to this compact unless one of the following has occurred: (a) the inmate has given his written consent to such transfer; (b) in the event the inmate does not consent to such transfer, a hearing shall be held and a record made indicating the reasons for said transfer.

(3) The appropriate officials of any state party to this compact shall have access, at all reasonable times, to any institution in which it has a contractual [contractual] right to confine inmates for the purpose of inspecting the facilities thereof and visiting such of its inmates as may be confined in the institution.

(4) Inmates confined in an institution pursuant to the terms of this compact shall at all times be subject to the jurisdiction of the sending state and may at any time be removed therefrom for transfer to a prison or other institution within the sending state, for transfer to another institution in which the sending state may have a contractual or other right to confine inmates, for release on probation or parole, for discharge, or for any other purpose permitted by the laws of the sending state; provided that the sending state shall continue to be obligated to such payments as may be required pursuant to the terms of any contract entered into under the terms of division (C) of this section.

(5) Each receiving state shall provide regular reports, no less than semiannually, to each sending state on the inmates of that sending state in institutions pursuant to this compact, including a conduct record of each inmate and certify said record to the official designated by the sending state, in order that each inmate may have official review of his or her record in determining and altering the disposition of said inmate in accordance with the law which may obtain in the sending state and in order that the same may be a source of information for the sending state.

(6) All inmates who may be confined in an institution pursuant to the provisions of this compact shall be treated in a reasonable and humane manner and shall be treated equally with such similar inmates of the receiving state as may be confined in the same institution. The fact of confinement in a receiving state shall not deprive any inmate so confined of any legal rights which said inmate would have had if confined in an appropriate institution of the sending state.

(7) Any hearing or hearings to which an inmate confined pursuant to this compact may be entitled by the laws of the sending state may be had before the appropriate authorities of the sending state, or of the receiving state if authorized by the sending state. The receiving state shall provide adequate facilities for such hearings as may be conducted by the appropriate officials of a sending state. In the event such hearing or hearings are had before officials of the receiving state, the governing law shall be that of the sending state and a record of the hearing or hearings as prescribed by the sending state shall be made. Said record together with any rec-

ommendations of the hearing officials shall be transmitted forthwith to the official or officials before whom the hearing would have been had if it had taken place in the sending state. In any and all proceedings had pursuant to the provisions of this division, the officials of the receiving state shall act solely as agents of the sending state and no final determination shall be made in any matter except by the appropriate officials of the sending state.

(8) Any inmate confined pursuant to this compact shall be released within the territory of the sending state unless the inmate, and the sending and receiving states, shall agree upon release in some other place. The sending state shall bear the cost of such return to its territory.

(9) Any inmate confined pursuant to the terms of this compact shall have any and all rights to participate in and derive any benefits, or incur or be relieved of any obligations, or have such obligations modified or his status changed on account of any action or proceeding in which he could have participated if confined in any appropriate institution of the sending state located within such state.

(10) The parent, guardian, trustee, or other person or persons entitled under the laws of the sending state to act for, advise, or otherwise function with respect to any inmate shall not be deprived of or restricted in his exercise of any power in respect of any inmate confined pursuant to the terms of this compact.

(E) ACTS NOT REVIEWABLE IN RECEIVING STATE: EXTRADITION

(1) Any decision of the sending state in respect of any matter over which it retains jurisdiction pursuant to this compact shall be conclusive upon and not reviewable within the receiving state, but if at the time the sending state seeks to remove an inmate from an institution in the receiving state there is pending against the inmate within such state any criminal charge or if the inmate is formally accused of having committed within such state a criminal offense, the inmate shall not be returned without the consent of the receiving state until discharged from prosecution or other form of proceeding, imprisonment or detention for such offense. The duly accredited officers of the sending state shall be permitted to transport inmates pursuant to this compact through any and all states party to this compact without interference.

(2) An inmate who escapes from an institution in which he is confined pursuant to this compact shall be deemed a fugitive from the sending state and from the state in which the institution is situated. In the case of an escape to a jurisdiction other than the sending or receiving state, the responsibility for institution of extradition or rendition proceedings shall be that of the sending state, but nothing contained herein shall be construed to prevent or affect the activities of officers and agencies of any jurisdiction directed toward the apprehension and return of an escapee.

(F) FEDERAL AID

Any state party to this compact may accept federal aid for use in connection with any institution or program, the use of which is or may be affected by this compact or any contract pursuant hereto. Any inmate in a receiving state pursuant to this compact may participate in any such federally aided program or activity for which the sending and receiving states have made contractual provision, provided that if such program or activity is not part of the customary correctional regimen, the express consent of the appropriate official of the sending state shall be required therefor.

(G) ENTRY INTO FORCE

This compact shall enter into force and become effective and binding upon the states so acting when it has been enacted into law by any two states. Thereafter, this compact shall enter into force and become effective and binding as to any other of said states upon similar action by such state.

(H) WITHDRAWAL AND TERMINATION

This compact shall continue in force and remain binding upon a party state until it shall have enacted a statute repealing the same and providing for the sending of formal written notice of withdrawal from the compact to the appropriate officials of all other party states. An actual withdrawal shall not take effect until one year after the notices provided in said statute have been sent. Such withdrawal shall not relieve the withdrawing state from its obligations assumed hereunder prior to the effective date of withdrawal. Before the effective date of withdrawal, a withdrawing state shall remove to its territory, at its own expense, such inmates as it may have confined pursuant to the provisions of this compact.

(I) OTHER ARRANGEMENTS UNAFFECTED

Nothing contained in this compact shall be construed to abrogate or impair any agreement or other arrangement which a party state may have with a nonparty state for the confinement, rehabilitation, or treatment of inmates nor to repeal any other laws of a party state authorizing the making of cooperative institutional arrangements.

(J) CONSTRUCTION AND SEVERABILITY

The provisions of this compact shall be liberally construed and shall be severable. If any phrase, clause, sentence, or provision of this compact is declared to be contrary to the constitution of any participating state or of the United States, or the applicability thereof to any government, agency, person, or circumstance is held invalid, the validity of the remainder of this compact and the applicability thereof to any government, agency, person, or circumstance shall not be affected thereby. If this compact shall be held contrary to the constitution of any state participating therein, the compact shall remain in full force and effect as to the remaining states and in full force and effect as to the state affected as to all severable matters.

(K) POWERS

The director of the department of rehabilitation and

correction is hereby authorized and directed to do all things necessary or incidental to the carrying out of the compact in every particular and he may in his discretion delegate this authority to the deputy director of the department of rehabilitation and correction.

HISTORY: 136 v H 47. Eff 12-28-76.

§ 5120.51 Population and cost impact statement for bill.

(A)(1) If the director of rehabilitation and correction determines that a bill introduced in the general assembly is likely to have a significant impact on the population of, or the cost of operating, any or all state correctional institutions under the administration of the department of rehabilitation and correction, the department shall prepare a population and cost impact statement for the bill, in accordance with division (A)(2) of this section.

(2) A population and cost impact statement required for a bill shall estimate the increase or decrease in the correctional institution population that likely would result if the bill were enacted, shall estimate, in dollars, the amount by which revenues or expenditures likely would increase or decrease if the bill were enacted, and briefly shall explain each of the estimates.

A population and cost impact statement required for a bill initially shall be prepared after the bill is referred to a committee of the general assembly in the house of origination but before the meeting of the committee at which the committee is scheduled to vote on whether to recommend the bill for passage. A copy of the statement shall be distributed to each member of the committee that is considering the bill and to the member of the general assembly who introduced it. If the bill is recommended for passage by the committee, the department shall update the statement before the bill is taken up for final consideration by the house of origination. A copy of the updated statement shall be distributed to each member of that house and to the member of the general assembly who introduced the bill. If the bill is passed by the house of origination and is introduced in the second house, the provisions of this division concerning the preparation, updating, and distribution of the statement in the house of origination also apply in the second house.

(B) The governor or any member of the general assembly, at any time, may request the department to prepare a population and cost impact statement for any bill introduced in the general assembly. Upon receipt of a request, the department promptly shall prepare a statement that includes the estimates and explanations described in division (A)(2) of this section and present a copy of it to the governor or member who made the request.

(C) In the preparation of a population and cost impact statement required by division (A) or (B) of this section, the department shall use a technologically sophisticated system capable of estimating future state correctional institution populations. The system shall have the capability to adjust its estimates based on actual and proposed changes in sentencing laws and trends, sentence durations, parole rates, crime rates, and any other data that affect state correctional institution populations. The department, in conjunction with the advisory committee appointed under division (E) of this section, shall review and update the data used in the system, not less than once every six months, to improve the accuracy of the system.

(D) At least once every six months, the department shall provide to the correctional institution inspection committee a copy of the estimates of state correctional institution populations obtained through use of the system described in division (C) of this section and a description of the assumptions regarding sentencing laws and trends, sentence durations, parole rates, crime rates, and other relevant data that were made by the department to obtain the estimates. Additionally, a copy of the estimates and a description of the assumptions made to obtain them shall be provided, upon reasonable request, to other legislative staff, including the staff of the legislative service commission and the legislative budget office of the legislative service commission, to the office of budget and management, and to the office of criminal justice services.

(E) The correctional institution inspection committee shall appoint an advisory committee to review the operation of the system for estimating future state correctional institution populations that is used by the department in the preparation of population cost impact statements pursuant to this section and to join with the department in its reviews and updating of the data used in the system under division (C) of this section. The advisory committee shall be comprised of at least one prosecuting attorney, at least one common pleas court judge, at least one public defender, at least one person who is a member or staff employee of the committee, and at least one representative of the office of criminal justice services.

HISTORY: 142 v S 94 (Eff 7-20-88); 144 v H 298 (Eff 7-26-91); 145 v H 152 (Eff 7-1-93); 145 v H 571. Eff 10-6-94.

§ 5120.52 Contract with political subdivision to provide sewage treatment services.

The department of rehabilitation and correction may enter into a contract with a political subdivision in which a state correctional institution is located under which the institution will provide sewage treatment services for the political subdivision if the institution has a sewage treatment facility with sufficient excess capacity to provide the services.

Any such contract shall include all of the following:

(A) Limitations on the quantity of sewage that the facility will accept that are compatible with the needs of the state correctional institution;

(B) The bases for calculating reasonable rates to be charged the political subdivision for sewage treatment services and for adjusting the rates;

(C) All other provisions the department considers necessary or proper to protect the interests of the state in the facility and the purpose for which it was constructed.

All amounts due the department under the contract shall be paid to the department by the political subdivision at the times specified in the contract. The department shall deposit all such amounts in the state treasury to the credit of the correctional institutions sewage treatment facility services fund, which is hereby created. The fund shall be used by the department to pay costs associated with operating and maintaining the sewage treatment facility.

HISTORY: 143 v S 330 (Eff 7-18-90); 145 v H 571. Eff 10-6-94.

§ 5120.53 Transfer or exchange of offender to foreign country pursuant to treaty.

(A) If a treaty between the United States and a foreign country provides for the transfer or exchange, from one of the signatory countries to the other signatory country, of convicted offenders who are citizens or nationals of the other signatory country, the governor, subject to and in accordance with the terms of the treaty, may authorize the director of rehabilitation and correction to allow the transfer or exchange of convicted offenders and to take any action necessary to initiate participation in the treaty. If the governor grants the director the authority described in this division, the director may take the necessary action to initiate participation in the treaty and, subject to and in accordance with division (B) of this section and the terms of the treaty, may allow the transfer or exchange to a foreign country that has signed the treaty of any convicted offender who is a citizen or national of that signatory country.

(B)(1) No convicted offender who is serving a term of imprisonment in this state for aggravated murder, murder, or a felony of the first or second degree, who is serving a mandatory prison term imposed under section 2925.03 or 2925.11 of the Revised Code in circumstances in which the court was required to impose as the mandatory prison term the maximum prison term authorized for the degree of offense committed, who is serving a term of imprisonment in this state imposed for an offense committed prior to the effective date of this amendment that was an aggravated felony of the first or second degree or that was aggravated trafficking in violation of division (A)(9) or (10) of section 2925.03 of the Revised Code, or who has been sentenced to death in this state shall be transferred or exchanged to another country pursuant to a treaty of the type described in division (A) of this section.

(2) If a convicted offender is serving a term of imprisonment in this state and the offender is a citizen or national of a foreign country that has signed a treaty of the type described in division (A) of this section, if the governor has granted the director of rehabilitation and correction the authority described in that division, and if the transfer or exchange of the offender is not barred by division (B)(1) of this section, the director or the director's designee may approve the offender for transfer or exchange pursuant to the treaty if the director or the designee, after consideration of the factors set forth in the rules adopted by the department under division (D) of this section and all other relevant factors, determines that the transfer or exchange of the offender is appropriate.

(C) Notwithstanding any provision of the Revised Code regarding the parole eligibility of, or the duration or calculation of a sentence of imprisonment imposed upon, an offender, if a convicted offender is serving a term of imprisonment in this state and the offender is a citizen or national of a foreign country that has signed a treaty of the type described in division (A) of this section, if the offender is serving an indefinite term of imprisonment, if the offender is barred from being transferred or exchanged pursuant to the treaty due to the indefinite nature of the offender's term of imprisonment, and if in accordance with division (B)(2) of this section the director of rehabilitation and correction or the director's designee approves the offender for transfer or exchange pursuant to the treaty, the parole board, pursuant to rules adopted by the director, shall set a date certain for the release of the offender. To the extent possible, the date certain that is set shall be reasonably proportionate to the indefinite term of imprisonment that the offender is serving. The date certain that is set for the release of the offender shall be considered only for purposes of facilitating the international transfer or exchange of the offender, shall not be viable or actionable for any other purpose, and shall not create any expectation or guarantee of release. If an offender for whom a date certain for release is set under this division is not transferred to or exchanged with the foreign country pursuant to the treaty, the date certain is null and void, and the offender's release shall be determined pursuant to the laws and rules of this state pertaining to parole eligibility and the duration and calculation of an indefinite sentence of imprisonment.

(D) If the governor, pursuant to division (A) of this section, authorizes the director of rehabilitation and correction to allow any transfer or exchange of convicted offenders as described in that division, the director shall adopt rules under Chapter 119. of the Revised Code to implement the provisions of this section. The rules shall include a rule that requires the director or the director's designee, in determining whether to approve a convicted offender who is serving a term of imprisonment in this state for transfer or exchange pursuant to a treaty of the type described in division (A) of this section, to consider all of the following factors:

(1) The nature of the offense for which the offender

is serving the term of imprisonment in this state;

(2) The likelihood that, if the offender is transferred or exchanged to a foreign country pursuant to the treaty, the offender will serve a shorter period of time in imprisonment in the foreign country than the offender would serve, if the offender is not transferred or exchanged to the foreign country pursuant to the treaty;

(3) The likelihood that, if the offender is transferred or exchanged to a foreign country pursuant to the treaty, the offender will return or attempt to return to this state after the offender has been released from imprisonment in the foreign country;

(4) The degree of any shock to the conscience of justice and society that will be experienced in this state if the offender is transferred or exchanged to a foreign country pursuant to the treaty;

(5) All other factors that the department determines are relevant to the determination.

HISTORY: 145 v S 242 (Eff 10-6-94); 146 v S 2. Eff 7-1-96.

The effective date is set by section 6 of SB 2.

§ 5120.55 Physician recruitment program.

(A) As used in this section, "physician" means an individual who is authorized under Chapter 4731. of the Revised Code to practice medicine and surgery, osteopathic medicine and surgery, or podiatry.

(B) The department of rehabilitation and correction may establish a physician recruitment program under which the department, by means of a contract entered into under division (C) of this section, agrees to repay all or part of the principal and interest of a government or other educational loan incurred by a physician who agrees to provide services to inmates of correctional institutions under the department's administration. To be eligible to participate in the program, a physician must have attended a school that was, during the time of attendance, a medical school or osteopathic medical school in this country accredited by the liaison committee on medical education or the American osteopathic association, a college of podiatry in this country recognized as being in good standing under section 4731.53 of the Revised Code, or a medical school, osteopathic medical school, or college of podiatry located outside this country that was acknowledged by the world health organization and verified by a member state of that organization as operating within that state's jurisdiction.

(C) The department shall enter into a contract with each physician it recruits under this section. Each contract shall include at least the following terms:

(1) The physician agrees to provide a specified scope of medical, osteopathic medical, or podiatric services to inmates of one or more specified state correctional institutions for a specified number of hours per week for a specified number of years.

(2) The department agrees to repay all or a specified portion of the principal and interest of a government or other educational loan taken by the physician for the following expenses to attend, for up to a maximum of four years, a school that qualifies the physician to participate in the program:

(a) Tuition;

(b) Other educational expenses for specific purposes, including fees, books, and laboratory expenses, in amounts determined to be reasonable in accordance with rules adopted under division (D) of this section;

(c) Room and board, in an amount determined to be reasonable in accordance with rules adopted under division (D) of this section.

(3) The physician agrees to pay the department a specified amount, which shall be no less than the amount already paid by the department pursuant to its agreement, as damages if the physician fails to complete the service obligation agreed to or fails to comply with other specified terms of the contract. The contract may vary the amount of damages based on the portion of the physician's service obligation that remains uncompleted.

(4) Other terms agreed upon by the parties.

The physician's lending institution or the Ohio board of regents may be a party to the contract. The contract may include an assignment to the department of the physician's duty to repay the principal and interest of the loan.

(D) If the department elects to implement the physician recruitment program, it shall adopt rules in accordance with Chapter 119. of the Revised Code that establish all of the following:

(1) Criteria for designating institutions for which physicians will be recruited;

(2) Criteria for selecting physicians for participation in the program;

(3) Criteria for determining the portion of a physician's loan which the department will agree to repay;

(4) Criteria for determining reasonable amounts of the expenses described in divisions (C)(2)(b) and (c) of this section;

(5) Procedures for monitoring compliance by physicians with the terms of their contracts;

(6) Any other criteria or procedures necessary to implement the program.

HISTORY: 144 v H 478 (Eff 1-14-93); 145 v H 571 (Eff 10-6-94); 146 v S 143 (Eff 3-5-96); 146 v H 627. Eff 12-2-96.

§ 5120.60 Office of victims' services.

(A) There is hereby created in the division of parole and community services the office of victims' services.

(B) The office shall provide assistance to victims of crime, victims' representatives designated under section 2930.02 of the Revised Code, and members of the victim's family. The assistance shall include, but not be limited to, providing information about the policies and procedures of the department of rehabilitation and correction and the status of offenders under the department's jurisdiction.

(C) The office shall also make available publications that will assist victims in contacting staff of the department about problems with offenders under the supervision of the adult parole authority or confined in state correctional institutions under the department's jurisdiction.

(D) The office shall employ a victims coordinator who shall administer the office's functions. The victims coordinator shall be in the unclassified civil service and report directly to the chief of the division.

(E) The office shall also employ at least three persons in the unclassified civil service whose primary duties shall be to help parole board hearing officers identify victims' issues and to make recommendations to the parole board in accordance with rules adopted by the department. The member of the parole board appointed pursuant to division (B) of section 5149.10 of the Revised Code shall approve the hiring of the employees of the office.

(F) The office shall coordinate its activities with the member of the parole board appointed pursuant to division (B) of section 5149.10 of the Revised Code. The victims coordinator and other employees of the office shall have full access to records of prisoners under the department's jurisdiction.

(G) As used in this section, "crime," "member of the victim's family," and "victim" have the meanings given in section 2930.01 of the Revised Code.

HISTORY: 146 v S 2. Eff 7-1-96.

The effective date is set by section 6 of SB 2.

§ 5120.61 Risk assessment reports for sexually violent predators.

(A)(1) Not later than ninety days after the effective date of this section, the department of rehabilitation and correction shall adopt standards that it will use under this section to assess a criminal offender who is convicted of or pleads guilty to a sexually violent offense and also is convicted of or pleads guilty to a sexually violent predator specification that was included in the indictment, count in the indictment, or information charging that offense. The department may periodically revise the standards.

(2) When the department is requested by the parole board or the court to provide a risk assessment report of the offender under section 2971.04 or 2971.05 of the Revised Code, it shall assess the offender and complete the assessment as soon as possible after the offender has commenced serving the prison term or term of life imprisonment without parole imposed under division (A) of section 2971.03 of the Revised Code. Thereafter, the department shall update a risk assessment report pertaining to an offender as follows:

(a) Periodically, in the discretion of the department, provided that each report shall be updated no later than two years after its initial preparation or most recent update;

(b) Upon the request of the parole board for use in determining pursuant to section 2971.04 of the Revised Code whether it should terminate its control over an offender's service of a prison term imposed upon the offender under division (A)(3) of section 2971.03 of the Revised Code;

(c) Upon the request of the court.

(3) After the department of rehabilitation and correction assesses an offender pursuant to division (A)(2) of this section, it shall prepare a report that contains its risk assessment for the offender or, if a risk assessment report previously has been prepared, it shall update the risk assessment report.

(4) The department of rehabilitation and correction shall provide each risk assessment report that it prepares or updates pursuant to this section regarding an offender to all of the following:

(a) The parole board for its use in determining pursuant to section 2971.04 of the Revised Code whether it should terminate its control over an offender's service of a prison term imposed upon the offender under division (A)(3) of section 2971.03 of the Revised Code, if the parole board has not terminated its control over the offender;

(b) The court for use in determining, pursuant to section 2971.05 of the Revised Code, whether to modify the requirement that the offender serve the entire prison term imposed upon the offender under division (A)(3) of section 2971.03 of the Revised Code in a state correctional institution, whether to revise any modification previously made, or whether to terminate the prison term;

(c) The prosecuting attorney who prosecuted the case, or the successor in office to that prosecuting attorney;

(d) The offender.

(B) When the department of rehabilitation and correction provides a risk assessment report regarding an offender to the parole board or court pursuant to division (A)(4)(a) or (b) of this section, the department, prior to the parole board's or court's hearing, also shall provide to the offender or to the offender's attorney of record a copy of the report and a copy of any other relevant documents the department possesses regarding the offender that the department does not consider to be confidential.

(C) As used in this section, "sexually violent offense" and "sexually violent predator specification" have the same meanings as in section 2971.01 of the Revised Code.

HISTORY: 146 v H 180. Eff 1-1-97.

The effective date is set by section 3 of HB 180.

See provisions, § 4 of HB 180 (146 v —) following RC § 5120.49.

CHAPTER 5122: HOSPITALIZATION OF MENTALLY ILL

§ 5122.01 Definitions.

As used in this chapter and Chapter 5119. of the Revised Code:

(A) "Mental illness" means a substantial disorder of thought, mood, perception, orientation, or memory that grossly impairs judgment, behavior, capacity to recognize reality, or ability to meet the ordinary demands of life.

(B) "Mentally ill person subject to hospitalization by court order" means a mentally ill person who, because of the person's illness:

(1) Represents a substantial risk of physical harm to self as manifested by evidence of threats of, or attempts at, suicide or serious self-inflicted bodily harm;

(2) Represents a substantial risk of physical harm to others as manifested by evidence of recent homicidal or other violent behavior, evidence of recent threats that place another in reasonable fear of violent behavior and serious physical harm, or other evidence of present dangerousness;

(3) Represents a substantial and immediate risk of serious physical impairment or injury to self as manifested by evidence that the person is unable to provide for and is not providing for the person's basic physical needs because of the person's mental illness and that appropriate provision for those needs cannot be made immediately available in the community; or

(4) Would benefit from treatment in a hospital for his mental illness and is in need of such treatment as manifested by evidence of behavior that creates a grave and imminent risk to substantial rights of others or himself.

(C)(1) "Patient" means, subject to division (C)(2) of this section, a person who is admitted either voluntarily or involuntarily to a hospital or other place under section 2945.39, 2945.40, 2945.401 [2945.40.1], or 2945.402 [2945.40.2] of the Revised Code subsequent to a finding of not guilty by reason of insanity or incompetence to stand trial or under this chapter, who is under observation or receiving treatment in such place.

(2) "Patient" does not include a person admitted to a hospital or other place under section 2945.39, 2945.40, 2945.401 [2945.40.1], or 2945.402 [2945.40.2] of the Revised Code to the extent that the reference in this chapter to patient, or the context in which the reference occurs, is in conflict with any provision of sections 2945.37 to 2945.402 [2945.40.2] of the Revised Code.

(D) "Licensed physician" means a person licensed under the laws of this state to practice medicine or a medical officer of the government of the United States while in this state in the performance of the person's official duties.

(E) "Psychiatrist" means a licensed physician who has satisfactorily completed a residency training program in psychiatry, as approved by the residency review committee of the American medical association, the committee on post-graduate education of the American osteopathic association, or the American osteopathic board of neurology and psychiatry, or who on July 1, 1989, has been recognized as a psychiatrist by the Ohio state medical association or the Ohio osteopathic association on the basis of formal training and five or more years of medical practice limited to psychiatry.

(F) "Hospital" means a hospital or inpatient unit licensed by the department of mental health under section 5119.20 of the Revised Code, and any institution, hospital, or other place established, controlled, or supervised by the department under Chapter 5119. of the Revised Code.

(G) "Public hospital" means a facility that is tax-supported and under the jurisdiction of the department of mental health.

(H) "Community mental health agency" means any agency, program, or facility with which a board of alcohol, drug addiction, and mental health services contracts to provide the mental health services listed in section 340.09 of the Revised Code.

(I) "Licensed clinical psychologist" means a person who holds a current valid psychologist license issued under section 4732.12 or 4732.15 of the Revised Code, and in addition, meets either of the following criteria:

(1) Meets the educational requirements set forth in division (B) of section 4732.10 of the Revised Code and has a minimum of two years' full-time professional experience, or the equivalent as determined by rule of the state board of psychology, at least one year of which shall be post-doctoral, in clinical psychological work in a public or private hospital or clinic or in private practice, diagnosing and treating problems of mental illness or mental retardation under the supervision of a psychologist who is licensed or who holds a diploma issued by the American board of professional psychology, or whose qualifications are substantially similar to those required for licensure by the state board of psychology when the supervision has occurred prior to enactment of laws governing the practice of psychology;

(2) Meets the educational requirements set forth in division (B) of section 4732.15 of the Revised Code and has a minimum of four years' full-time professional experience, or the equivalent as determined by rule of the state board of psychology, in clinical psychological work in a public or private hospital or clinic or in private practice, diagnosing and treating problems of mental illness or mental retardation under supervision, as set forth in division (I)(1) of this section.

(J) "Health officer" means any public health physician; public health nurse; or other person authorized by or designated by a city health district; a general health district; or a board of alcohol, drug addiction, and mental health services to perform the duties of a health officer under this chapter.

(K) "Chief clinical officer" means the medical director of a hospital, or a community mental health agency, or a board of alcohol, drug addiction, and mental health services, or, if there is no medical director, the licensed physician responsible for the treatment a hospital or community mental health agency provides. The chief clinical officer may delegate to the attending physician responsible for a patient's care the duties imposed on the chief clinical officer by this chapter. Within a community mental health agency, the chief clinical officer shall be designated by the governing body of the agency and shall be a licensed physician or licensed clinical psychologist who supervises diagnostic and treatment services. A licensed physician or licensed clinical psychologist designated by the chief clinical officer may perform the duties and accept the responsibilities of the chief clinical officer in his absence.

(L) "Working day" or "court day" means Monday, Tuesday, Wednesday, Thursday, and Friday, except when such day is a holiday.

(M) "Indigent" means unable without deprivation of satisfaction of basic needs to provide for the payment of an attorney and other necessary expenses of legal representation, including expert testimony.

(N) "Respondent" means the person whose detention, commitment, hospitalization, continued hospitalization or commitment, or discharge is being sought in any proceeding under this chapter.

(O) "Legal rights service" means the service established under section 5123.60 of the Revised Code.

(P) "Independent expert evaluation" means an evaluation conducted by a licensed clinical psychologist, psychiatrist, or licensed physician who has been selected by the respondent or his counsel and who consents to conducting the evaluation.

(Q) "Court" means the probate division of the court of common pleas.

(R) "Expunge" means:

(1) The removal and destruction of court files and records, originals and copies, and the deletion of all index references;

(2) The reporting to the person of the nature and extent of any information about him transmitted to any other person by the court;

(3) Otherwise insuring that any examination of court files and records in question shall show no record whatever with respect to the person;

(4) That all rights and privileges are restored, and that the person, the court, and any other person may properly reply that no such record exists, as to any matter expunged.

(S) "Residence" means a person's physical presence in a county with intent to remain there, except that:

(1) If a person is receiving a mental health service at a facility that includes nighttime sleeping accommodations, residence means that county in which the person maintained his primary place of residence at the time he entered the facility;

(2) If a person is committed pursuant to section 2945.38, 2945.39, 2945.40, 2945.401 [2945.40.1], or 2945.402 [2945.40.2] of the Revised Code, residence means the county where the criminal charges were filed.

When the residence of a person is disputed, the matter of residence shall be referred to the department of mental health for investigation and determination. Residence shall not be a basis for a board's denying services to any person present in the board's service district, and the board shall provide services for a person whose residence is in dispute while residence is being determined and for a person in an emergency situation.

(T) "Admission" to a hospital or other place means that a patient is accepted for and stays at least one night at the hospital or other place.

(U) "Prosecutor" means the prosecuting attorney, village solicitor, city director of law, or similar chief legal officer who prosecuted a criminal case in which a person was found not guilty by reason of insanity, who would have had the authority to prosecute a criminal case against a person if the person had not been found incompetent to stand trial, or who prosecuted a case in which a person was found guilty.

(V) "Treatment plan" means a written statement of reasonable objectives and goals for an individual established by the treatment team, with specific criteria to evaluate progress towards achieving those objectives. The active participation of the patient in establishing the objectives and goals shall be documented. The treatment plan shall be based on patient needs and include services to be provided to the patient while he is hospitalized and after he is discharged. The treatment plan shall address services to be provided upon discharge, including but not limited to housing, financial, and vocational services.

HISTORY: 129 v 1448 (1458) (Eff 10-25-61); 130 v 1190 (Eff 10-10-63); 133 v H 874 (Eff 9-16-70); 134 v H 494 (Eff 7-12-72); 136 v H 244 (Eff 8-26-76); 137 v H 1 (Eff 8-26-77); 137 v H 725 (Eff 3-16-78); 138 v S 297 (Eff 4-30-80); 138 v H 900 (Eff 7-1-80); 138 v H 965 (Eff 4-9-81); 142 v S 156 (Eff 7-1-89); 143 v H 317 (Eff 10-10-89); 146 v S 285. Eff 7-1-97.

Analogous to former RC § 5123.01.

The effective date is set by section 4 of SB 285.

[§ 5122.01.1] § 5122.011 Application to defendant found incompetent or to insanity acquittee.

The provisions of this chapter regarding hospitalization apply to a person who is found incompetent to stand trial or not guilty by reason of insanity and is committed pursuant to section 2945.39, 2945.40, 2945.401 [2945.40.1], or 2945.402 [2945.40.2] of the Revised Code to the extent that the provisions are not in conflict with any provision of sections 2945.37 to 2945.402 [2945.40.2] of the Revised Code. If a provision of this chapter is in conflict with a provision in sections 2945.37 to 2945.402 [2945.40.2] of the Revised Code regarding a person who has been so committed, the

provision in sections 2945.37 to 2945.402 [2945.40.2] of the Revised Code shall control regarding that person.
HISTORY: 146 v S 285. Eff 7-1-97.

The effective date is set by section 4 of SB 285.

§ 5122.02 Admission of voluntary patients.

(A) Except as provided in division (D) of this section, any person who is eighteen years of age or older and who is, appears to be, or believes self to be mentally ill may make written application for voluntary admission to the chief medical officer of a hospital.

(B) Except as provided in division (D) of this section, the application also may be made on behalf of a minor by a parent, a guardian of the person, or the person with custody of the minor, and on behalf of an adult incompetent person by the guardian or the person with custody of the incompetent person.

Any person whose admission is applied for under division (A) or (B) of this section may be admitted for observation, diagnosis, care, or treatment, in any hospital unless the chief clinical officer finds that hospitalization is inappropriate, and except that, in the case of a public hospital, no person shall be admitted without the authorization of the board of the person's county of residence.

(C) If a minor or person adjudicated incompetent due to mental illness whose voluntary admission is applied for under division (B) of this section is admitted, the court shall determine, upon petition by the legal rights service, private or otherwise appointed counsel, a relative, or one acting as next friend, whether the admission or continued hospitalization is in the best interest of the minor or incompetent.

The chief clinical officer shall discharge any voluntary patient who has recovered or whose hospitalization the officer determines to be no longer advisable and may discharge any voluntary patient who refuses to accept treatment consistent with the written treatment plan required by section 5122.27 of the Revised Code.

(D) A person who is found incompetent to stand trial or not guilty by reason of insanity and who is committed pursuant to section 2945.39, 2945.40, 2945.401 [2945.40.1], or 2945.402 [2945.40.2] of the Revised Code shall not voluntarily admit himself or herself or be voluntarily admitted to a hospital pursuant to this section until after the final termination of the commitment, as described in division (J) of section 2945.401 [2945.40.1] of the Revised Code.

HISTORY: 129 v 1448(1459) (Eff 10-25-61); 133 v H 874 (Eff 9-16-70); 134 v H 494 (Eff 7-12-72); 136 v H 244 (Eff 8-26-76); 137 v H 725 (Eff 3-16-78); 138 v S 297 (Eff 4-30-80); 138 v H 965 (Eff 4-9-81); 142 v S 156 (Eff 7-1-89); 146 v S 285. Eff 7-1-97.

Analogous to former RC §§ 5123.43 to 5123.45.

The effective date is set by section 4 of SB 285.

§ 5122.05 Admission and rights of involuntary patients.

(A) The chief clinical officer of a hospital may, and the chief clinical officer of a public hospital in all cases of psychiatric medical emergencies, shall receive for observation, diagnosis, care, and treatment any person whose admission is applied for under any of the following procedures:

(1) Emergency procedure, as provided in section 5122.10 of the Revised Code;

(2) Judicial procedure as provided in sections 2945.38, 2945.39, 2945.40, 2945.401 [2945.40.1], 2945.402 [2945.40.2], and 5122.11 to 5122.15 of the Revised Code.

Upon application for such admission, the chief clinical officer of a hospital immediately shall notify the board of the patient's county of residence. To assist the hospital in determining whether the patient is subject to involuntary hospitalization and whether alternative services are available, the board or an agency the board designates promptly shall assess the patient unless the board or agency already has performed such assessment, or unless the commitment is pursuant to section 2945.38, 2945.39, 2945.40, 2945.401 [2945.40.1], or 2945.402 [2945.40.2] of the Revised Code.

(B) No person who is being treated by spiritual means through prayer alone, in accordance with a recognized religious method of healing, may be involuntarily committed unless the court has determined that the person represents a substantial risk of impairment or injury to self or others;

(C) Any person who is involuntarily detained in a hospital or otherwise is in custody under this chapter, immediately upon being taken into custody, shall be informed and provided with a written statement that the person may do any of the following:

(1) Immediately make a reasonable number of telephone calls or use other reasonable means to contact an attorney, a licensed physician, or a licensed clinical psychologist, to contact any other person or persons to secure representation by counsel, or to obtain medical or psychological assistance, and be provided assistance in making calls if the assistance is needed and requested;

(2) Retain counsel and have independent expert evaluation of the person's mental condition and, if the person is unable to obtain an attorney or independent expert evaluation, be represented by court-appointed counsel or have independent expert evaluation of the person's mental condition, or both, at public expense if the person is indigent;

(3) Have a hearing to determine whether or not the person is a mentally ill person subject to hospitalization by court order.

HISTORY: 129 v 1448(1460) (Eff 10-25-61); 136 v H 244 (Eff 8-26-76); 137 v H 725 (Eff 3-16-78); 138 v S 297 (Eff 4-30-80); 142 v S 156 (Eff 7-1-89); 146 v S 310 (Eff 6-20-96); 146 v S 285. Eff 7-1-97.

The effective date is set by section 4 of SB 285.

§ 5122.11 Judicial hospitalization; temporary detention order.

Proceedings for the hospitalization of a person pursuant to sections 5122.11 to 5122.15 of the Revised Code shall be commenced by the filing of an affidavit in the manner and form prescribed by the department of mental health, by any person or persons with the court, either on reliable information or actual knowledge, whichever is determined to be proper by the court. This section does not apply to the hospitalization of a person pursuant to section 2945.39, 2945.40, 2945.401 [2945.40.1], or 2945.402 [2945.40.2] of the Revised Code.

The affidavit shall contain an allegation setting forth the specific category or categories under division (B) of section 5122.01 of the Revised Code upon which the jurisdiction of the court is based and a statement of alleged facts sufficient to indicate probable cause to believe that the person is a mentally ill person subject to hospitalization by court order. The affidavit may be accompanied, or the court may require that the affidavit be accompanied, by a certificate of a psychiatrist, or a certificate signed by a licensed clinical psychologist and a certificate signed by a licensed physician stating that the person who issued the certificate has examined the person and is of the opinion that the person is a mentally ill person subject to hospitalization by court order, or shall be accompanied by a written statement by the applicant, under oath, that the person has refused to submit to an examination by a psychiatrist, or by a licensed clinical psychologist and licensed physician.

Upon receipt of the affidavit, if a judge of the court or a referee who is an attorney at law appointed by the court has probable cause to believe that the person named in the affidavit is a mentally ill person subject to hospitalization by court order, the judge or referee may issue a temporary order of detention ordering any health or police officer or sheriff to take into custody and transport the person to a hospital or other place designated in section 5122.17 of the Revised Code, or may set the matter for further hearing.

The person may be observed and treated until the hearing provided for in section 5122.141 [5122.14.1] of the Revised Code. If no such hearing is held, the person may be observed and treated until the hearing provided for in section 5122.15 of the Revised Code.

HISTORY: 129 v 1448(1462) (Eff 10-25-61); 130 v 1193 (Eff 10-10-63); 134 v H 494 (Eff 7-12-72); 136 v H 244 (Eff 8-26-76); 138 v S 297 (Eff 4-30-80); 138 v H 900 (Eff 7-1-80); 138 v H 965 (Eff 4-9-81); 142 v S 156 (Eff 7-1-89); 146 v S 285. Eff 7-1-97.

Analogous to former RC § 5123.18.

The effective date is set by section 4 of SB 285.

§ 5122.15 Full hearing; disposition; mandatory hearing on continued commitment.

(A) Full hearings shall be conducted in a manner consistent with this chapter and with due process of law. The hearings shall be conducted by a judge of the probate court or a referee designated by a judge of the probate court and may be conducted in or out of the county in which the respondent is held. Any referee designated under this division shall be an attorney.

(1) With the consent of the respondent, the following shall be made available to counsel for the respondent:

(a) All relevant documents, information, and evidence in the custody or control of the state or prosecutor;

(b) All relevant documents, information, and evidence in the custody or control of the hospital in which the respondent currently is held, or in which the respondent has been held pursuant to this chapter;

(c) All relevant documents, information, and evidence in the custody or control of any hospital, facility, or person not included in division (A)(1)(a) or (b) of this section.

(2) The respondent has the right to attend the hearing and to be represented by counsel of the respondent's choice. The right to attend the hearing may be waived only by the respondent or counsel for the respondent after consultation with the respondent.

(3) If the respondent is not represented by counsel, is absent from the hearing, and has not validly waived the right to counsel, the court shall appoint counsel immediately to represent the respondent at the hearing, reserving the right to tax costs of appointed counsel to the respondent, unless it is shown that the respondent is indigent. If the court appoints counsel, or if the court determines that the evidence relevant to the respondent's absence does not justify the absence, the court shall continue the case.

(4) The respondent shall be informed that the respondent may retain counsel and have independent expert evaluation. If the respondent is unable to obtain an attorney, the respondent shall be represented by court-appointed counsel. If the respondent is indigent, court-appointed counsel and independent expert evaluation shall be provided as an expense under section 5122.43 of the Revised Code.

(5) The hearing shall be closed to the public, unless counsel for the respondent, with the permission of the respondent, requests that the hearing be open to the public.

(6) If the hearing is closed to the public, the court, for good cause shown, may admit persons who have a legitimate interest in the proceedings. If the respondent, the respondent's counsel, the designee of the director or of the chief clinical officer objects to the admission of any person, the court shall hear the objection and any opposing argument and shall rule upon the admission of the person to the hearing.

(7) The affiant under section 5122.11 of the Revised Code shall be subject to subpoena by either party.

(8) The court shall examine the sufficiency of all documents filed and shall inform the respondent, if present, and the respondent's counsel of the nature and content

of the documents and the reason for which the respondent is being detained, or for which the respondent's placement is being sought.

(9) The court shall receive only reliable, competent, and material evidence.

(10) Unless proceedings are initiated pursuant to section 5120.17 or 5139.08 of the Revised Code or proceedings are initiated regarding a resident of the service district of a board of alcohol, drug addiction, and mental health services that elects under division (B)(3)(b) of section 5119.62 of the Revised Code not to accept the amount allocated to it under division (B)(1) of that section, an attorney that the board designates shall present the case demonstrating that the respondent is a mentally ill person subject to hospitalization by court order. The attorney shall offer evidence of the diagnosis, prognosis, record of treatment, if any, and less restrictive treatment plans, if any. In proceedings pursuant to section 5120.17 or 5139.08 of the Revised Code and in proceedings in which the respondent is a resident of a service district of a board that elects under division (B)(3)(b) of section 5119.62 of the Revised Code not to accept the amount allocated to it under division (B)(1) of that section, the attorney general shall designate an attorney who shall present the case demonstrating that the respondent is a mentally ill person subject to hospitalization by court order. The attorney shall offer evidence of the diagnosis, prognosis, record of treatment, if any, and less restrictive treatment plans, if any.

(11) The respondent or the respondent's counsel has the right to subpoena witnesses and documents and to examine and cross-examine witnesses.

(12) The respondent has the right, but shall not be compelled, to testify, and shall be so advised by the court.

(13) On motion of the respondent or the respondent's counsel for good cause shown, or on the court's own motion, the court may order a continuance of the hearing.

(14) If the respondent is represented by counsel and the respondent's counsel requests a transcript and record, or if the respondent is not represented by counsel, the court shall make and maintain a full transcript and record of the proceeding. If the respondent is indigent and the transcript and record is made, a copy shall be provided to the respondent upon request and be treated as an expense under section 5122.43 of the Revised Code.

(15) To the extent not inconsistent with this chapter, the Rules of Civil Procedure are applicable.

(B) Unless, upon completion of the hearing the court finds by clear and convincing evidence that the respondent is a mentally ill person subject to hospitalization by court order, it shall order the respondent's discharge immediately.

(C) If, upon completion of the hearing, the court finds by clear and convincing evidence that the respondent is a mentally ill person subject to hospitalization by court order, the court shall order the respondent for a period not to exceed ninety days to any of the following:

(1) A hospital operated by the department of mental health if the respondent is committed pursuant to section 5139.08 of the Revised Code;

(2) A nonpublic hospital;

(3) The veterans' administration or other agency of the United States government;

(4) A board of alcohol, drug addiction, and mental health services or agency the board designates;

(5) Receive private psychiatric or psychological care and treatment;

(6) Any other suitable facility or person consistent with the diagnosis, prognosis, and treatment needs of the respondent.

(D) Any order made pursuant to division (C)(2), (3), (5), or (6) of this section shall be conditioned upon the receipt by the court of consent by the hospital, facility, agency, or person to accept the respondent.

(E) In determining the place to which, or the person with whom, the respondent is to be committed, the court shall consider the diagnosis, prognosis, preferences of the respondent and the projected treatment plan for the respondent and shall order the implementation of the least restrictive alternative available and consistent with treatment goals. If the court determines that the least restrictive alternative available that is consistent with treatment goals is inpatient hospitalization, the court's order shall so state.

(F) During such ninety-day period the hospital; facility; board of alcohol, drug addiction, and mental health services; agency the board designates; or person shall examine and treat the individual. If, at any time prior to the expiration of the ninety-day period, it is determined by the hospital, facility, board, agency, or person that the respondent's treatment needs could be equally well met in an available and appropriate less restrictive environment, both of the following apply:

(1) The respondent shall be released from the care of the hospital, agency, facility, or person immediately and shall be referred to the court together with a report of the findings and recommendations of the hospital, agency, facility, or person; and

(2) The hospital, agency, facility, or person shall notify the respondent's counsel or the attorney designated by a board of alcohol, drug addiction, and mental health services or, if the respondent was committed to a board or an agency designated by the board, it shall place the respondent in the least restrictive environment available consistent with treatment goals and notify the court and the respondent's counsel of the placement.

The court shall dismiss the case or order placement in the least restrictive environment.

(G)(1) Except as provided in divisions (G)(2) and (3) of this section, any person who has been committed under this section, or for whom proceedings for hospitalization have been commenced pursuant to section

5122.11 of the Revised Code, may apply at any time for voluntary admission to the hospital, facility, agency that the board designates, or person to which the person was committed. Upon admission as a voluntary patient the chief clinical officer of the hospital, agency, or other facility, or the person immediately shall notify the court, the patient's counsel, and the attorney designated by the board, if the attorney has entered the proceedings, in writing of that fact, and, upon receipt of the notice, the court shall dismiss the case.

(2) A person who is found incompetent to stand trial or not guilty by reason of insanity and who is committed pursuant to section 2945.39, 2945.40, 2945.401 [2945.40.1], or 2945.402 [2945.40.2] of the Revised Code shall not voluntarily commit the person pursuant to this section until after the final termination of the commitment, as described in division (J) of section 2945.401 [2945.40.1] of the Revised Code.

(H) If, at the end of the first ninety-day period or any subsequent period of continued commitment, there has been no disposition of the case, either by discharge or voluntary admission, the hospital, facility, board, agency, or person shall discharge the patient immediately, unless at least ten days before the expiration of the period the attorney the board designates or the prosecutor files with the court an application for continued commitment. The application of the attorney or the prosecutor shall include a written report containing the diagnosis, prognosis, past treatment, a list of alternative treatment settings and plans, and identification of the treatment setting that is the least restrictive consistent with treatment needs. The attorney the board designates or the prosecutor shall file the written report at least three days prior to the full hearing. A copy of the application and written report shall be provided to the respondent's counsel immediately.

The court shall hold a full hearing on applications for continued commitment at the expiration of the first ninety-day period and at least every two years after the expiration of the first ninety-day period.

Hearings following any application for continued commitment are mandatory and may not be waived.

Upon request of a person who is involuntarily committed under this section, or the person's counsel, that is made more than one hundred eighty days after the person's last full hearing, mandatory or requested, the court shall hold a full hearing on the person's continued commitment. Upon the application of a person involuntarily committed under this section, supported by an affidavit of a psychiatrist or licensed clinical psychologist, alleging that the person no longer is a mentally ill person subject to hospitalization by court order, the court for good cause shown may hold a full hearing on the person's continued commitment prior to the expiration of one hundred eighty days after the person's last full hearing. Section 5122.12 of the Revised Code applies to all hearings on continued commitment.

If the court, after a hearing for continued commitment finds by clear and convincing evidence that the respondent is a mentally ill person subject to hospitalization by court order, the court may order continued commitment at places specified in division (C) of this section.

(I) Unless the admission is pursuant to section 5120.17 or 5139.08 of the Revised Code, the chief clinical officer of the hospital or agency admitting a respondent pursuant to a judicial proceeding, within ten working days of the admission, shall make a report of the admission to the board of alcohol, drug addiction, and mental health services serving the respondent's county of residence.

(J) A referee appointed by the court may make all orders that a judge may make under this section and sections 5122.11 and 5122.141 [5122.14.1] of the Revised Code, except an order of contempt of court. The orders of a referee take effect immediately. Within fourteen days of the making of an order by a referee, a party may file written objections to the order with the court. The filed objections shall be considered a motion, shall be specific, and shall state their grounds with particularity. Within ten days of the filing of the objections, a judge of the court shall hold a hearing on the objections and may hear and consider any testimony or other evidence relating to the respondent's mental condition. At the conclusion of the hearing, the judge may ratify, rescind, or modify the referee's order.

(K) An order of the court under division (C), (H), or (J) of this section is a final order.

(L) Before a board, or an agency the board designates, may place an unconsenting respondent in an inpatient setting from a less restrictive placement, the board or agency shall do all of the following:

(1) Determine that the respondent is in immediate need of treatment in an inpatient setting because the respondent represents a substantial risk of physical harm to the respondent or others if allowed to remain in a less restrictive setting;

(2) On the day of placement in the inpatient setting or on the next court day, file with the court a motion for transfer to an inpatient setting or communicate to the court by telephone that the required motion has been mailed;

(3) Ensure that every reasonable and appropriate effort is made to take the respondent to the inpatient setting in the least conspicuous manner possible;

(4) Immediately notify the board's designated attorney and the respondent's attorney.

At the respondent's request, the court shall hold a hearing on the motion and make a determination pursuant to division (E) of this section within five days of the placement.

(M) Before a board, or an agency the board designates, may move a respondent from one residential placement to another, the board or agency shall consult with the respondent about the placement. If the respondent objects to the placement, the proposed placement and the need for it shall be reviewed by a qualified mental health professional who otherwise is not involved in the treatment of the respondent.

HISTORY: 129 v 1448(1464) (Eff 10-25-61); 130 v 1194 (Eff 10-10-63); 134 v H 494 (Eff 7-12-72); 136 v H 244 (Eff 8-26-76); 137 v H 725 (Eff 3-16-78); 138 v S 297 (Eff 4-30-80); 138 v H 900 (Eff 7-1-80); 138 v H 965 (Eff 4-9-81); 142 v S 156 (Eff 7-1-89); 143 v H 317 (Eff 10-10-89); 146 v S 310 (Eff 6-20-96); 146 v H 567 (Eff 10-29-96); 146 v S 285. Eff 7-1-97.

Analogous to former RC § 5123.23.

The effective date is set by section 4 of SB 285.

The provisions of § 3 of SB 285 (146 v —) read as follows:

SECTION 3. ° ° ° Section 5122.15 of the Revised Code is presented in this act as a composite of the section as amended by both Am. Sub. S.B. 310 and Sub. H.B. 567 of the 121st General Assembly, with the new language of neither of the acts shown in capital letters. This is in recognition of the principle stated in division (B) of section 1.52 of the Revised Code that such amendments are to be harmonized where not substantively irreconcilable and constitutes a legislative finding that such is the resulting version of those sections in effect prior to the effective date of this act.

§ 5122.21 Discharge of involuntary patients.

(A) The chief clinical officer shall as frequently as practicable, and at least once every thirty days, examine or cause to be examined every patient, and, whenever the chief clinical officer determines that the conditions justifying involuntary hospitalization or commitment no longer obtain, shall, except as provided in division (C)† of this section, discharge the patient not under indictment or conviction for crime and immediately make a report of the discharge to the department of mental health. The chief clinical officer may discharge a patient who is under indictment, sentence of imprisonment, or on probation or parole ten days after written notice of intent to discharge the patient has been given by personal service or certified mail, return receipt requested, to the court having criminal jurisdiction over the patient. Except when the patient was found not guilty by reason of insanity and his commitment is pursuant to section 2945.40 of the Revised Code, the chief clinical officer has final authority to discharge a patient who is under indictment, sentence of imprisonment, or on probation or parole.

(B) After a finding pursuant to section 5122.15 of the Revised Code that a person is a mentally ill person subject to hospitalization by court order, the chief clinical officer of the hospital or agency to which the person is ordered or to which the person is transferred under section 5122.20 of the Revised Code, may, except as provided in division (C)† of this section, grant a discharge without the consent or authorization of any court.

Upon discharge, the chief clinical officer shall notify the court that caused the judicial hospitalization of the discharge from the hospital.

HISTORY: 129 v 1448(1467) (Eff 10-25-61); 130 v 1197 (Eff 10-10-63); 132 v H 15 (Eff 10-1-67); 133 v H 1 (Eff 3-18-69); 134 v H 494 (Eff 7-12-72); 136 v H 244 (Eff 8-26-76); 137 v H 725 (Eff 3-16-78); 138 v S 297 (Eff 4-30-80); 138 v H 900 (Eff 7-1-80); 138 v H 965 (Eff 4-9-81); 142 v S 156 (Eff 7-1-89); 146 v S 285. Eff 7-1-97.

Analogous to former RC § 5123.50.

† Division (C) is deleted by SB 285 (146 v —).

The effective date is set by section 4 of SB 285.

§ 5122.26 Patient absent without leave.

(A) If a patient is absent without leave, on a verbal or written order issued within five days of the time of the unauthorized absence by the department of mental health, the chief clinical officer of the hospital from which the patient is absent without leave, or the court of either the county from which the patient was committed or in which the patient is found, any health or police officer or sheriff may take the patient into custody and transport the patient to the hospital in which the patient was hospitalized or to a place that is designated in the order. The officer immediately shall report such fact to the agency that issued the order.

The chief clinical officer of a hospital may discharge a patient who is under indictment, sentence of imprisonment, or on probation or parole and who has been absent without leave for more than thirty days, but shall give written notice of the discharge to the court with criminal jurisdiction over the patient. The chief clinical officer of a hospital may discharge any other patient who has been absent without leave for more than fourteen days.

The chief clinical officer shall take all proper measures for the apprehension of an escaped patient. The expense of the return of an escaped patient shall be borne by the hospital where the patient is hospitalized.

(B)(1) Subject to division (B)(2) of this section, no patient hospitalized under Chapter 5122. of the Revised Code whose absence without leave was caused or contributed to by his mental illness shall be subject to a charge of escape.

(2) Division (B)(1) of this section does not apply to any person who was hospitalized, institutionalized, or confined in a facility under an order made pursuant to or under authority of section 2945.37, 2945.371 [2945.37.1], 2945.38, 2945.39, 2945.40, 2945.401 [2945.40.1], or 2945.402 [2945.40.2] of the Revised Code and who escapes from the facility, from confinement in a vehicle for transportation to or from the facility, or from supervision by an employee of the facility that is incidental to hospitalization, institutionalization, or confinement in the facility and that occurs outside the facility, in violation of section 2921.34 of the Revised Code.

HISTORY: 129 v 1448(1469) (Eff 10-25-61); 134 v H 494 (Eff 7-12-72); 136 v H 244 (Eff 8-26-76); 137 v H 725 (Eff 3-16-78); 138 v H 900 (Eff 7-1-80); 142 v S 156 (Eff 7-1-89); 145 v H 42 (Eff 2-9-94); 146 v S 285. Eff 7-1-97.

Analogous to former RC § 5123.54.

The effective date is set by section 4 of SB 285.

§ 5122.30 Right to writ of habeas corpus.

Any person detained pursuant to this chapter or section 2945.39, 2945.40, 2945.401 [2945.40.1], or 2945.402 [2945.40.2] of the Revised Code shall be entitled to the writ of habeas corpus upon proper petition by self or by a friend to any court generally empowered to issue the writ of habeas corpus in the county in which the person is detained.

No person may bring a petition for a writ of habeas corpus that alleges that a person involuntarily detained pursuant to this chapter no longer is a mentally ill person subject to hospitalization by court order unless the person shows that the release procedures of division (H) of section 5122.15 of the Revised Code are inadequate or unavailable.

HISTORY: 129 v 1448(1470) (Eff 10-25-61); 136 v H 244 (Eff 8-26-76); 138 v H 965 (Eff 4-9-81); 146 v S 285. Eff 7-1-97.

The effective date is set by section 4 of SB 285.

§ 5122.31 Disclosure of information.

All certificates, applications, records, and reports made for the purpose of this chapter and sections 2945.38, 2945.39, 2945.40, 2945.401 [2945.40.1], and 2945.402 [2945.40.2] of the Revised Code, other than court journal entries or court docket entries, and directly or indirectly identifying a patient or former patient or person whose hospitalization has been sought under this chapter, shall be kept confidential and shall not be disclosed by any person except:

(A) If the person identified, or the person's legal guardian, if any, or if the person is a minor, the person's parent or legal guardian, consents, and if the disclosure is in the best interests of the person, as may be determined by the court for judicial records and by the chief clinical officer for medical records;

(B) When disclosure is provided for in this chapter or section 5123.60 of the Revised Code;

(C) That hospitals may release necessary medical information to insurers to obtain payment for goods and services furnished to the patient;

(D) Pursuant to a court order signed by a judge;

(E) That a patient shall be granted access to the patient's own psychiatric and medical records, unless access specifically is restricted in a patient's treatment plan for clear treatment reasons;

(F) That hospitals and other institutions and facilities within the department of mental health may exchange psychiatric records and other pertinent information with other hospitals, institutions, and facilities of the department, and with community mental health agencies and boards of alcohol, drug addiction, and mental health services with which the department has a current agreement for patient care or services. Records and information that may be released pursuant to this division shall be limited to medication history, physical health status and history, financial status, summary of course of treatment in the hospital, summary of treatment needs, and a discharge summary, if any.

(G) That a patient's family member who is involved in the provision, planning, and monitoring of services to the patient may receive medication information, a summary of the patient's diagnosis and prognosis, and a list of the services and personnel available to assist the patient and the patient's family, if the patient's treating physician determines that the disclosure would be in the best interests of the patient. No such disclosure shall be made unless the patient is notified first and receives the information and does not object to the disclosure.

(H) That community mental health agencies may exchange psychiatric records and certain other information with the board of alcohol, drug addiction, and mental health services and other agencies in order to provide services to a person involuntarily committed to a board. Release of records under this division shall be limited to medication history, physical health status and history, financial status, summary of course of treatment, summary of treatment needs, and discharge summary, if any.

(I) That information may be disclosed to the executor or the administrator of an estate of a deceased patient when the information is necessary to administer the estate;

(J) That records in the possession of the Ohio historical society may be released to the closest living relative of a deceased patient upon request of that relative;

(K) That information may be disclosed to staff members of the appropriate board or to staff members designated by the director of mental health for the purpose of evaluating the quality, effectiveness, and efficiency of services and determining if the services meet minimum standards. Information obtained during such evaluations shall not be retained with the name of any patient.

(L) That records pertaining to the patient's diagnosis, course of treatment, treatment needs, and prognosis shall be disclosed and released to the appropriate prosecuting attorney if the patient was committed pursuant to section 2945.38, 2945.39, 2945.40, 2945.401 [2945.40.1], or 2945.402 [2945.40.2] of the Revised Code, or to the attorney designated by the board for proceedings pursuant to involuntary commitment under this chapter.

(M) That the department of mental health may exchange psychiatric hospitalization records, other mental health treatment records, and other pertinent information with the department of rehabilitation and correction to ensure continuity of care for inmates who are receiving mental health services in an institution of the department of rehabilitation and correction. The department shall not disclose those records unless the inmate is notified, receives the information, and does not object to the disclosure. The release of records under this division is limited to records regarding an inmate's medication history, physical health status and history, summary of course of treatment, summary of treatment needs, and a discharge summary, if any.

(N) Before records are disclosed pursuant to divisions (C), (F), and (H) of this section, the custodian of the records shall attempt to obtain the patient's consent for the disclosure. No person shall reveal the contents of a medical record of a patient except as authorized by law.

HISTORY: 129 v 1448(1470) (Eff 10-25-61); 136 v H 244 (Eff 8-26-76); 137 v H 725 (Eff 3-16-78); 138 v H 900 (Eff 7-1-80); 142 v S 156 (Eff 7-1-89); 143 v H 317 (Eff 10-10-89); 146 v S 310 (Eff 6-20-96); 146 v S 285. Eff 7-1-97.

The effective date is set by section 4 of SB 285.

CHAPTER 5123: DEPARTMENT OF MENTAL RETARDATION AND DEVELOPMENTAL DISABILITIES

§ 5123.01 Definitions.

As used in this chapter:

(A) "Chief medical officer" means the licensed physician appointed by the managing officer of an institution for the mentally retarded with the approval of the director of mental retardation and developmental disabilities to provide medical treatment for residents of the institution.

(B) "Chief program director" means a person with special training and experience in the diagnosis and management of the mentally retarded, certified according to division (C) of this section in at least one of the designated fields, and appointed by the managing officer of an institution for the mentally retarded with the approval of the director to provide habilitation and care for residents of the institution.

(C) "Comprehensive evaluation" means a study including a sequence of observations and examinations of a person leading to conclusions and recommendations formulated jointly, with dissenting opinions if any, by a group of persons with special training and experience in the diagnosis and management of mentally retarded or developmentally disabled persons, which group shall include individuals who are professionally qualified in the fields of medicine, education, psychology, and social work, together with such other specialists as the individual case may require.

(D) "Education" means the process of formal training and instruction to facilitate the intellectual and emotional development of residents.

(E) "Habilitation" means the process by which the staff of the institution assists the resident in acquiring and maintaining those life skills that enable the resident to cope more effectively with the demands of the resident's own person and of the resident's environment and in raising the level of the resident's physical, mental, social, and vocational efficiency. Habilitation includes but is not limited to programs of formal, structured education and training.

(F) "Health officer" means any public health physician, public health nurse, or other person authorized or designated by a city or general health district.

(G) "Indigent person" means a person who is unable, without substantial financial hardship, to provide for the payment of an attorney and for other necessary expenses of legal representation, including expert testimony.

(H) "Institution" means a public or private facility, or a part of a public or private facility, that is licensed by the appropriate state department and is equipped to provide residential habilitation, care, and treatment for the mentally retarded.

(I) "Licensed physician" means a person who holds a valid certificate issued under Chapter 4731. of the Revised Code authorizing the person to practice medicine and surgery or osteopathic medicine and surgery, or a medical officer of the government of the United States while in the performance of the officer's official duties.

(J) "Managing officer" means a person who is appointed by the director of mental retardation and developmental disabilities to be in executive control of an institution for the mentally retarded under the jurisdiction of the department.

(K) "Mentally retarded person" means a person having significantly subaverage general intellectual functioning existing concurrently with deficiencies in adaptive behavior, manifested during the developmental period.

(L) "Mentally retarded person subject to institutionalization by court order" means a person eighteen years of age or older who is at least moderately mentally retarded and in relation to whom, because of the person's retardation, either of the following conditions exist:

(1) The person represents a very substantial risk of physical impairment or injury to self as manifested by evidence that the person is unable to provide for and is not providing for the person's most basic physical needs and that provision for those needs is not available in the community;

(2) The person needs and is susceptible to significant habilitation in an institution.

(M) "A person who is at least moderately mentally retarded" means a person who is found, following a comprehensive evaluation, to be impaired in adaptive behavior to a moderate degree and to be functioning at the moderate level of intellectual functioning in accordance with standard measurements as recorded in the most current revision of the manual of terminology and classification in mental retardation published by the American association on mental retardation.

(N) As used in this division, "substantial functional limitation," "developmental delay," and "established risk" have the meanings established pursuant to section 5123.011 [5123.01.1] of the Revised Code.

"Developmental disability" means a severe, chronic disability that is characterized by all of the following:

(1) It is attributable to a mental or physical impairment or a combination of mental and physical impairments, other than a mental or physical impairment solely caused by mental illness as defined in division (A) of section 5122.01 of the Revised Code.

(2) It is manifested before age twenty-two.

(3) It is likely to continue indefinitely.

(4) It results in one of the following:

(a) In the case of a person under three years of age, at least one developmental delay or an established risk;

(b) In the case of a person at least three years of age but under six years of age, at least two developmental delays or an established risk;

(c) In the case of a person six years of age or older, a substantial functional limitation in at least three of the following areas of major life activity, as appropriate for the person's age: self-care, receptive and expressive language, learning, mobility, self-direction, capacity for independent living, and, if the person is at least sixteen years of age, capacity for economic self-sufficiency.

(5) It causes the person to need a combination and sequence of special, interdisciplinary, or other type of care, treatment, or provision of services for an extended period of time that is individually planned and coordinated for the person.

(O) "Developmentally disabled person" means a person with a developmental disability.

(P) "State institution" means an institution that is tax-supported and under the jurisdiction of the department.

(Q) "Residence" and "legal residence" have the same meaning as "legal settlement," which is acquired by residing in Ohio for a period of one year without receiving general assistance prior to July 17, 1995, under former Chapter 5113. of the Revised Code, disability assistance under Chapter 5115. of the Revised Code, or assistance from a private agency that maintains records of assistance given. A person having a legal settlement in the state shall be considered as having legal settlement in the assistance area in which the person resides. No adult person coming into this state and having a spouse or minor children residing in another state shall obtain a legal settlement in this state as long as the spouse or minor children are receiving public assistance, care, or support at the expense of the other state or its subdivisions. For the purpose of determining the legal settlement of a person who is living in a public or private institution or in a home subject to licensing by the department of human services, the department of mental health, or the department of mental retardation and developmental disabilities, the residence of the person shall be considered as though the person were residing in the county in which the person was living prior to the person's entrance into the institution or home. Settlement once acquired shall continue until a person has been continuously absent from Ohio for a period of one year or has acquired a legal residence in another state. A woman who marries a man with legal settlement in any county immediately acquires the settlement of her husband. The legal settlement of a minor is that of the parents, surviving parent, sole parent, parent who is designated the residential parent and legal custodian by a court, other adult having permanent custody awarded by a court, or guardian of the person of the minor, provided that:

(1) A minor female who marries shall be considered to have the legal settlement of her husband and, in the case of death of her husband or divorce, she shall not thereby lose her legal settlement obtained by the marriage.

(2) A minor male who marries, establishes a home, and who has resided in this state for one year without receiving general assistance prior to July 17, 1995, under former Chapter 5113. of the Revised Code, disability assistance under Chapter 5115. of the Revised Code, or assistance from a private agency that maintains records of assistance given shall be considered to have obtained a legal settlement in this state.

(3) The legal settlement of a child under eighteen years of age who is in the care or custody of a public or private child caring agency shall not change if the legal settlement of the parent changes until after the child has been in the home of the parent for a period of one year.

No person, adult or minor, may establish a legal settlement in this state for the purpose of gaining admission to any state institution.

(R)(1) "Resident" means, subject to division (R)(2) of this section, a person who is admitted either voluntarily or involuntarily to an institution or other facility pursuant to section 2945.39, 2945.40, 2945.401 [2945.40.1], or 2945.402 [2945.40.2] of the Revised Code subsequent to a finding of not guilty by reason of insanity or incompetence to stand trial or under this chapter who is under observation or receiving habilitation and care in an institution.

(2) "Resident" does not include a person admitted to an institution or other facility under section 2945.39, 2945.40, 2945.401 [2945.40.1], or 2945.402 [2945.40.2] of the Revised Code to the extent that the reference in this chapter to resident, or the context in which the reference occurs, is in conflict with any provision of sections 2945.37 to 2945.402 [2945.40.2] of the Revised Code.

(S) "Respondent" means the person whose detention, commitment, or continued commitment is being sought in any proceeding under this chapter.

(T) "Working day" and "court day" mean Monday, Tuesday, Wednesday, Thursday, and Friday, except when such day is a legal holiday.

(U) "Prosecutor" means the prosecuting attorney, village solicitor, city director of law, or similar chief legal officer who prosecuted a criminal case in which a person was found not guilty by reason of insanity, who would have had the authority to prosecute a criminal case against a person if the person had not been found incompetent to stand trial, or who prosecuted a case in which a person was found guilty.

(V) "Court" means the probate division of the court of common pleas.

HISTORY: RC § 5123.68, 135 v S 336 (Eff 7-1-75); 138 v S 297 (Eff 4-30-80); RC § 5123.01, 138 v H 900 (Eff 7-1-80); 138 v H 965 (Eff 4-9-81); 139 v H 1 (Eff 8-5-81); 142 v H 231 (Eff 10-5-87); 143 v H 569 (Eff 7-1-91); 143 v S 3 (Eff 4-11-91); 144 v H 298 (Eff 7-26-91); 145 v S 21 (Eff 10-29-93); 145 v H 694 (Eff 11-11-94); 146 v H 249 (Eff 7-17-95); 146 v S 285. Eff 7-1-97.

Not analogous to former RC § 5123.01 (GC § 1890-19; 117 v 550; 121 v 423; Bureau of Code Revision, 10-1-53), repealed 129 v 1448(1483), § 2, eff 10-25-61.

The effective date is set by section 4 of SB 285.

[§ 5123.01.1] § 5123.011 Rules establishing certain definitions.

Note: See following version, SB 285 (146 v —), carrying the same number. That version will probably be renumbered later.

The director of mental retardation and developmental disabilities shall adopt rules in accordance with Chapter 119. of the Revised Code that establish definitions of "substantial functional limitation," "developmental delay," "established risk," "biological risk," and "environmental risk."

HISTORY: 143 v H 569 (Eff 11-11-91); 144 v S 156. Eff 1-10-92.

[§ 5123.01.1] § 5123.011 Application to defendant found incompetent or to insanity acquittee.

Note: See preceding version, SB 156 (144 v —), carrying the same section number. This version will probably be renumbered later.

The provisions of this chapter regarding institutionalization apply to a person who is found incompetent to stand trial or not guilty by reason of insanity and is committed pursuant to section 2945.39, 2945.40, 2945.401 [2945.40.1], or 2945.402 [2945.40.2] of the Revised Code to the extent that the provisions are not in conflict with any provision of sections 2945.37 to 2945.402 [2945.40.2] of the Revised Code. If a provision of this chapter is in conflict with a provision in sections 2945.37 to 2945.402 [2945.40.2] of the Revised Code regarding a person who has been so committed, the provision in sections 2945.37 to 2945.402 [2945.40.2] of the Revised Code shall control regarding that person.

HISTORY: 146 v S 285. Eff 7-1-97.

The effective date is set by section 4 of SB 285.

§ 5123.13 Special police officers for institutions.

(A) As used in this section, "felony" has the same meaning as in section 109.511 [109.51.1] of the Revised Code.

(B)(1) Subject to division (C) of this section, upon the recommendation of the director of mental retardation and developmental disabilities, the managing officer of an institution under the jurisdiction of the department of mental retardation and developmental disabilities may designate one or more employees to be special police officers of the department. The special police officers shall take an oath of office, wear the badge of office, and give bond for the proper and faithful discharge of their duties in an amount that the director requires.

(2) In accordance with section 109.77 of the Revised Code, the special police officers shall be required to complete successfully a peace officer basic training program approved by the Ohio peace officer training commission and to be certified by the commission. The cost of the training shall be paid by the department of mental retardation and developmental disabilities.

(3) Special police officers, on the premises of institutions under the jurisdiction of the department of mental retardation and developmental disabilities and subject to the rules of the department, shall protect the property of the institutions and the persons and property of patients in the institutions, suppress riots, disturbances, and breaches of the peace, and enforce the laws of the state and the rules of the department for the preservation of good order. They may arrest any person without a warrant and detain the person until a warrant can be obtained under the circumstances described in division (F) of section 2935.03 of the Revised Code.

(C)(1) The managing officer of an institution under the jurisdiction of the department of mental retardation and developmental disabilities shall not designate an employee as a special police officer of the department pursuant to division (B)(1) of this section on a permanent basis, on a temporary basis, for a probationary term, or on other than a permanent basis if the employee previously has been convicted of or has pleaded guilty to a felony.

(2)(a) The managing officer of an institution under the jurisdiction of the department of mental retardation and developmental disabilities shall terminate the employment as a special police officer of the department of an employee designated as a special police officer under division (B)(1) of this section if that employee does either of the following:

(i) Pleads guilty to a felony;

(ii) Pleads guilty to a misdemeanor pursuant to a negotiated plea agreement as provided in division (D) of section 2929.29 of the Revised Code in which the employee agrees to surrender the certificate awarded to that employee under section 109.77 of the Revised Code.

(b) The managing officer shall suspend from employment as a special police officer of the department an employee designated as a special police officer under division (B)(1) of this section if that employee is convicted, after trial, of a felony. If the special police officer files an appeal from that conviction and the conviction is upheld by the highest court to which the appeal is taken or if the special police officer does not file a timely appeal, the managing officer shall terminate the employment of that special police officer. If the special police officer files an appeal that results in that special police officer's acquittal of the felony or conviction of a misdemeanor, or in the dismissal of the felony charge against that special police officer, the managing officer shall reinstate that special police officer. A special police officer of the department who is reinstated under division (C)(2)(b) of this section shall not receive any back pay unless that special police officer's conviction of the felony was reversed on appeal, or the felony charge was dismissed, because the court found insufficient evidence to convict the special police officer of the felony.

(3) Division (C) of this section does not apply regarding an offense that was committed prior to January 1, 1997.

(4) The suspension from employment, or the termination of the employment, of a special police officer under division (C)(2) of this section shall be in accordance with Chapter 119. of the Revised Code.

HISTORY: 138 v H 900 (Eff 7-1-80); 139 v H 694 (Eff 11-15-81); 144 v S 49 (Eff 7-21-92); 145 v H 42 (Eff 2-9-94); 146 v H 566 (Eff 10-16-96); 146 v H 670. Eff 12-2-96.

Not analogous to former RC § 5123.13 (GC § 1890-16; 117 v 550; 119 v 616; 121 v 423; Bureau of Code Revision, 10-1-53; 125 v 864; 129 v 1448(1473); 120 v H 357; 133 v H 1; 134 v H 494) renumbered 5119.25 in 138 v H 900, eff 7-1-80.

Comment, Legislative Service Commission

° ° ° Section[s] 5123.13 of the Revised Code are [is] amended by this act [Sub. H.B. 670] and also by Am. Sub. H.B. 566 of the 121st General Assembly. ° ° ° Comparison of these amendments in pursuance of section 1.52 of the Revised Code discloses that they are not irreconcilable so that they are required by that section to be harmonized to give effect to each amendment.

§ 5123.14 Investigations by department.

The department of mental retardation and developmental disabilities may make such investigations as are necessary in the performance of its duties and to that end the director of mental retardation and developmental disabilities shall have the same power as a judge of a county court to administer oaths and to enforce the attendance and testimony of witnesses and the production of books or papers.

The department shall keep a record of such investigations stating the time, place, charges or subject, witnesses summoned and examined, and its conclusions.

In matters involving the conduct of an officer, a stenographic report of the evidence shall be taken and a copy of such report, with all documents introduced, kept on file at the office of the department.

The fees of witnesses for attendance and travel shall be the same as in the court of common pleas, but no officer or employee of the institution under investigation is entitled to such fees.

Any judge of the probate court or of the court of common pleas, upon application of the department, may compel the attendance of witnesses, the production of books or papers, and the giving of testimony before the department, by a judgment for contempt or otherwise, in the same manner as in cases before said courts.

HISTORY: 138 v H 900. Eff 7-1-80.

Not analogous to former RC § 5123.14 (GC § 1890-17; 117 v 550; 119 v 616; Bureau of Code Revision, 10-1-53; 129 v 1448(1473); 130 v 1201; 134 v H 494), repealed 138 v H 900, § 2, eff 7-1-80.

The effective date is set by section 3 of HB 900.

§ 5123.61 Duty to report abuse or neglect.

(A) As used in this section:

(1) "Mentally retarded or developmentally disabled adult" means a person who is eighteen years of age or older and is a mentally retarded or developmentally disabled person.

(2) "Law enforcement agency" means the state highway patrol, the police department of a municipal corporation, or a county sheriff.

(B) The department of mental retardation and developmental disabilities shall establish a registry office for the purpose of maintaining reports of abuse and neglect made to the department under this section and reports received from county boards of mental retardation and developmental disabilities under section 5126.31 of the Revised Code.

(C)(1) Any person listed in division (C)(2) of this section, having reason to believe that a mentally retarded or developmentally disabled adult has suffered any wound, injury, disability, or condition of such a nature as to reasonably indicate abuse or neglect of that adult, shall immediately report or cause reports to be made of such information to a law enforcement agency or to the county board of mental retardation and developmental disabilities, except that if the report concerns a resident of a facility operated by the department of mental retardation and developmental disabilities the report shall be made either to a law enforcement agency or to the department.

(2) All of the following persons are required to make a report under division (C)(1) of this section:

(a) Any physician, including a hospital intern or resident, any dentist, podiatrist, chiropractor, practitioner of a limited branch of medicine or surgery as defined in section 4731.15 of the Revised Code, hospital administrator or employee of a hospital, nurse licensed under

Chapter 4723. of the Revised Code, employee of an ambulatory health facility as defined in section 5101.61 of the Revised Code, employee of a home health agency, employee of an adult care facility licensed under Chapter 3722. of the Revised Code, or employee of a community mental health facility;

(b) Any school teacher or school authority, social worker, psychologist, attorney, peace officer, coroner, clergyman, or residents' rights advocate as defined in section 3721.10 of the Revised Code;

(c) A superintendent, board member, or employee of a county board of mental retardation and developmental disabilities; an administrator, board member, or employee of a residential facility licensed under section 5123.19 of the Revised Code; or an administrator, board member, or employee of any other public or private provider of services to a mentally retarded or developmentally disabled adult;

(d) A member of a citizen's advisory board established at an institution or branch institution of the department of mental retardation and developmental disabilities under section 5123.092 [5123.09.2] of the Revised Code;

(e) A person who renders spiritual treatment through prayer in accordance with the tenets of an organized religion acting in his official or professional capacity.

(3) The reporting requirements of this division do not apply to members of the legal rights service commission or to employees of the legal rights service.

(D) The reports required under division (C) of this section shall be made forthwith by telephone or in person and shall be followed by a written report. The reports shall contain the following:

(1) The names and addresses of the mentally retarded or developmentally disabled adult and his custodian, if known;

(2) The mentally retarded or developmentally disabled adult's age and the nature and extent of his injuries or physical neglect, including any evidence of previous injuries or physical neglect;

(3) Any other information which might be helpful in establishing the cause of the injury, abuse, or physical neglect.

(E) When a physician performing services as a member of the staff of a hospital or similar institution has reason to believe that a mentally retarded or developmentally disabled adult has suffered injury, abuse, or physical neglect, he shall notify the person in charge of the institution or his designated delegate, who shall make the necessary reports.

(F) Any person having reasonable cause to believe that a mentally retarded or developmentally disabled adult has suffered abuse or neglect may report the belief, or cause a report to be made, to a law enforcement agency or the county board of mental retardation and developmental disabilities, or, if the adult is a resident of a facility operated by the department of mental retardation and developmental disabilities, to a law enforcement agency or to the department.

(G)(1) Upon the receipt of a report concerning the possible nonaccidental infliction of a physical injury upon a mentally retarded or developmentally disabled adult, the law enforcement agency shall inform the county board of mental retardation and developmental disabilities or, if the adult is a resident of a facility operated by the department of mental retardation and developmental disabilities, the director of the department or his designee.

(2) On receipt of a report under this section, the department of mental retardation and developmental disabilities shall notify the law enforcement agency.

(3) When a county board of mental retardation and developmental disabilities receives a report under this section, the superintendent of the board or an individual he designates under division (H) of this section shall notify the law enforcement agency and the department of mental retardation and developmental disabilities.

(H) The superintendent of the board may designate an individual to be responsible for notifying the law enforcement agency and the department when the county board receives a report under this section.

(I) A mentally retarded or developmentally disabled adult about whom a report is made may be removed from his place of residence only by law enforcement officers who consider that his immediate removal is essential to protect him from further injury or abuse or in accordance with the order of a court made pursuant to section 5126.33 of the Revised Code.

(J) A law enforcement agency shall investigate each report of abuse or neglect made under this section. In addition, the department, in cooperation with law enforcement officials, shall investigate each report regarding a resident of a facility operated by the department to determine the circumstances surrounding the injury, the cause of the injury, and the person responsible. The department shall determine, with the registry office which shall be maintained by the department, whether prior reports have been made concerning the mentally retarded or developmentally disabled adult or other principals in the case. The department shall submit a report of its investigation, in writing, to the law enforcement agency, and with the consent of the adult, shall provide such protective services as are necessary to protect him. The law enforcement agency shall make a written report of its findings to the department.

If the adult is not a resident of a facility operated by the department, the county board of mental retardation and developmental disabilities shall review the report of abuse or neglect in accordance with sections 5126.30 to 5126.33 of the Revised Code and the law enforcement agency shall make the written report of its findings to the county board.

(K) Any person or any hospital, institution, school, health department, or agency participating in the making of reports pursuant to this section, any person participating as a witness in an administrative or judicial proceeding resulting from the reports, or any person or governmental entity that discharges responsibilities under sections 5126.31 to 5126.33 of the Revised Code shall be immune from any civil or criminal liability that might otherwise be incurred or imposed as a result of such actions except liability for perjury, unless the person or governmental entity has acted in bad faith or with malicious purpose.

(L) No employer or any person with the authority to do so shall discharge, demote, transfer, prepare a negative work performance evaluation, reduce pay or benefits, terminate work privileges, or take any other action detrimental to an employee or retaliate against an employee as a result of the employee's having made a report under this section. This division does not preclude an employer or person with authority from taking action with regard to an employee who has made a report under this section if there is another reasonable basis for the action.

(M) Reports made under this section are not public records as defined in section 149.43 of the Revised Code. Information contained in the reports on request shall be made available to the adult who is the subject of the report, to his legal counsel, and to agencies authorized to receive information in the report by the department or by a county board of mental retardation and developmental disabilities.

(N) Notwithstanding section 4731.22 of the Revised Code, the physician-patient privilege shall not be a ground for excluding evidence regarding a mentally retarded or developmentally disabled adult's injuries or physical neglect or the cause thereof in any judicial proceeding resulting from a report submitted pursuant to this section.

HISTORY RC § 5123.98, 135 v S 336 (Eff 7-1-75); 137 v H 219 (Eff 11-1-77); RC § 5123.61, 138 v H 900 (Eff 7-1-80); 141 v H 66 (Eff 3-6-86); 142 v H 403 (Eff 3-16-89); 143 v H 569 (Eff 7-1-91); 145 v S 21. Eff 10-29-93.

Not analogous to former RC § 5123.61 (GC § 1890-110; 117 v 581; 119 v 638; 121 v 442; Bureau of Code Revision, 10-1-53; 125 v 870), repealed 129 v 1448(1483), § 2, eff 10-25-61.

§ 5123.69 Voluntary admission.

(A) Except as provided in division (E) of this section, any person who is eighteen years of age or older and who is or believes self to be mentally retarded may make written application to the managing officer of any institution for voluntary admission. Except as provided in division (E) of this section, the application may be made on behalf of a minor by a parent or guardian, and on behalf of an adult adjudicated mentally incompetent by a guardian.

(B) The managing officer of an institution, with the concurrence of the chief program director, may admit a person applying pursuant to this section only after a comprehensive evaluation has been made of the person and only if the comprehensive evaluation concludes that the person is mentally retarded and would benefit significantly from admission.

(C) If application for voluntary admission of a minor or of a person adjudicated mentally incompetent is made by the parent or guardian of the minor or by the guardian of an incompetent and the minor or incompetent is admitted, the probate division of the court of common pleas shall determine, upon petition by the legal rights service, whether the voluntary admission or continued institutionalization is in the best interest of the minor or incompetent.

(D) The managing officer shall discharge any voluntary resident if, in the judgment of the chief program director, the results of a comprehensive examination indicate that institutionalization no longer is advisable. In light of the results of the comprehensive evaluation, the managing officer also may discharge any voluntary resident if, in the judgment of the chief program director, the discharge would contribute to the most effective use of the institution in the habilitation and care of the mentally retarded.

(E) A person who is found incompetent to stand trial or not guilty by reason of insanity and who is committed pursuant to section 2945.39, 2945.40, 2945.401 [2945.40.1], or 2945.402 [2945.40.2] of the Revised Code shall not voluntarily commit self pursuant to this section until after the final termination of the commitment, as described in division (J) of section 2945.401 [2945.40.1] of the Revised Code.

HISTORY: 135 v S 336 (Eff 7-1-75); 138 v S 297 (Eff 4-30-80); 146 v S 285. Eff 7-1-97.

The effective date is set by section 4 of SB 285.

[§ 5123.70.1] § 5123.701 Application for admission for short-term care.

(A) Except as provided in division (E) of this section, any person in the community who is eighteen years of age or older and who is or believes self to be mentally retarded may make written application to the managing officer of any institution for temporary admission for short-term care. The application may be made on behalf of a minor by a parent or guardian, and on behalf of an adult adjudicated mentally incompetent by a guardian.

(B) For purposes of this section, short-term care shall be defined to mean appropriate services provided to a person with mental retardation for no more than fourteen consecutive days and for no more than forty-two days in a fiscal year. When circumstances warrant, the fourteen-day period may be extended at the discretion of the managing officer. Short-term care is provided in a developmental center to meet the family's or caretaker's needs for separation from the person with mental retardation.

(C) The managing officer of an institution, with the concurrence of the chief program director, may admit a person for short-term care only after a medical examination has been made of the person and only if the managing officer concludes that the person is mentally retarded.

(D) If application for admission for short-term care of a minor or of a person adjudicated mentally incompetent is made by the minor's parent or guardian or by the incompetent's guardian and the minor or incompetent is admitted, the probate division of the court of common pleas shall determine, upon petition by the legal rights service, whether the admission for short-term care is in the best interest of the minor or the incompetent.

(E) A person who is found not guilty by reason of insanity shall not admit self to an institution for short-term care unless a hearing was held regarding the person pursuant to division (A) of section 2945.40 of the Revised Code and either of the following applies:

(1) The person was found at the hearing not to be a mentally retarded person subject to institutionalization by court order;

(2) The person was found at the hearing to be a mentally retarded person subject to institutionalization by court order, was involuntarily committed, and was finally discharged.

(F) The mentally retarded person, liable relatives, and guardians of mentally retarded persons admitted for respite care shall pay support charges in accordance with sections 5121.03 to 5121.07 of the Revised Code.

(G) At the conclusion of each period of short-term care, the person shall return to the person's family or caretaker. Under no circumstances shall a person admitted for short-term care according to this section remain in the institution after the period of short-term care unless the person is admitted according to section 5123.70, sections 5123.71 to 5123.76, or section 2945.38, 2945.39, 2945.40, 2945.401 [2945.40.1], or 2945.402 [2945.40.2] of the Revised Code.

HISTORY: 139 v H 694 (Eff 11-15-81); 146 v S 285. Eff 7-1-97.

The effective date is set by section 4 of SB 285.

§ 5123.76 Full hearing by probate judge, common pleas judge, or referee; disposition orders or discharge.

(A) The full hearing shall be conducted in a manner consistent with the procedures outlined in this chapter and with due process of law. The hearing shall be held by a judge of the probate division or, upon transfer by the judge of the probate division, by another judge of the court of common pleas, or a referee designated by the judge of the probate division. Any referee designated by the judge of the probate division must be an attorney.

(1) The following shall be made available to counsel for the respondent:

(a) All relevant documents, information, and evidence in the custody or control of the state or prosecutor;

(b) All relevant documents, information, and evidence in the custody or control of the institution, facility, or program in which the respondent currently is held or in which the respondent has been held pursuant to these proceedings;

(c) With the consent of the respondent, all relevant documents, information, and evidence in the custody or control of any institution or person other than the state.

(2) The respondent has the right to be represented by counsel of the respondent's choice and has the right to attend the hearing except if unusual circumstances of compelling medical necessity exist that render the respondent unable to attend and the respondent has not expressed a desire to attend.

(3) If the respondent is not represented by counsel and the court determines that the conditions specified in division (A)(2) of this section justify the respondent's absence and the right to counsel has not been validly waived, the court shall appoint counsel forthwith to represent the respondent at the hearing, reserving the right to tax costs of appointed counsel to the respondent unless it is shown that the respondent is indigent. If the court appoints counsel, or if the court determines that the evidence relevant to the respondent's absence does not justify the absence, the court shall continue the case.

(4) The respondent shall be informed of the right to retain counsel, to have independent expert evaluation, and, if indigent, to be represented by court appointed counsel and have expert independent evaluation at court expense.

(5) The hearing may be closed to the public unless counsel for the respondent requests that the hearing be open to the public.

(6) Unless objected to by the respondent, the respondent's counsel, or the designee of the director of mental retardation and developmental disabilities, the court, for good cause shown, may admit persons having a legitimate interest in the proceedings.

(7) The affiant under section 5123.71 of the Revised Code shall be subject to subpoena by either party.

(8) The court shall examine the sufficiency of all documents filed and shall inform the respondent, if present, and the respondent's counsel of the nature of the content of the documents and the reason for which the respondent is being held or for which the respondent's placement is being sought.

(9) The court shall receive only relevant, competent, and material evidence.

(10) The designee of the director shall present the evidence for the state. In proceedings under this chapter, the attorney general shall present the comprehensive evaluation, diagnosis, prognosis, record of habilitation and care, if any, and less restrictive habilitation plans, if any. The attorney general does not have a similar presentation responsibility in connection with a person who has been found not guilty by reason of insanity and who is the subject of a hearing under section 2945.40 of the Revised Code to determine whether the person is a mentally retarded person subject to institutionalization by court order.

(11) The respondent has the right to testify and the respondent or the respondent's counsel has the right to subpoena witnesses and documents and to present and cross-examine witnesses.

(12) The respondent shall not be compelled to testify and shall be so advised by the court.

(13) On motion of the respondent or the respondent's counsel for good cause shown, or upon the court's own motion, the court may order a continuance of the hearing.

(14) To an extent not inconsistent with this chapter, the Rules of Civil Procedure shall be applicable.

(B) Unless, upon completion of the hearing, the court finds by clear and convincing evidence that the respondent named in the affidavit is a mentally retarded person subject to institutionalization by court order, it shall order the respondent's discharge forthwith.

(C) If, upon completion of the hearing, the court finds by clear and convincing evidence that the respondent is a mentally retarded person subject to institutionalization by court order, the court may order the respondent's discharge or order the respondent, for a period not to exceed ninety days, to any of the following:

(1) A public institution, provided that commitment of the respondent to the institution will not cause the institution to exceed its licensed capacity determined in accordance with section 5123.19 of the Revised Code and provided that such a placement is indicated by the comprehensive evaluation report filed pursuant to section 5123.71 of the Revised Code;

(2) A private institution;

(3) A county mental retardation program;

(4) Receive private habilitation and care;

(5) Any other suitable facility, program, or the care of any person consistent with the comprehensive evaluation, diagnosis, prognosis, and habilitation needs of the respondent.

(D) Any order made pursuant to division (C)(2), (4), or (5) of this section shall be conditional upon the receipt by the court of consent by the facility, program, or person to accept the respondent.

(E) In determining the place to which, or the person with whom, the respondent is to be committed, the court shall consider the comprehensive evaluation, assessment, diagnosis, and projected habilitation plan for the respondent, and shall order the implementation of the least restrictive alternative available and consistent with habilitation goals.

(F) If, at any time it is determined by the director of the facility or program to which, or the person to whom, the respondent is committed that the respondent could be equally well habilitated in a less restrictive environment that is available, the following shall occur:

(1) The respondent shall be released by the director of the facility or program or by the person forthwith and referred to the court together with a report of the findings and recommendations of the facility, program, or person.

(2) The director of the facility or program or the person shall notify the respondent's counsel and the designee of the director of mental retardation and developmental disabilities.

(3) The court shall dismiss the case or order placement in the less restrictive environment.

(G)(1) Except as provided in divisions (G)(2) and (3) of this section,† any person who has been committed under this section may apply at any time during the ninety-day period for voluntary admission to an institution under section 5123.69 of the Revised Code. Upon admission of a voluntary resident, the managing officer immediately shall notify the court, the respondent's counsel, and the designee of the director in writing of that fact by mail or otherwise, and, upon receipt of the notice, the court shall dismiss the case.

(2) A person who is found incompetent to stand trial or not guilty by reason of insanity and who is committed pursuant to section 2945.39, 2945.40, 2945.401 [2945.40.1], or 2945.402 [2945.40.2] of the Revised Code shall not be voluntarily admitted to an institution pursuant to division (G)(1) of this section until after the termination of the commitment, as described in division (J) of section 2945.401 [2945.40.1] of the Revised Code.

(H) If, at the end of any commitment period, the resident has not already been discharged or has not requested voluntary admission status, the director of the facility or program, or the person to whose care the respondent has been committed, shall discharge the respondent forthwith, unless at least ten days before the expiration of that period the designee of the director of mental retardation and developmental disabilities or the prosecutor files an application with the court requesting continued commitment.

(1) An application for continued commitment shall include a written report containing a current comprehensive evaluation, a diagnosis, a prognosis, an account of progress and past habilitation, and a description of alternative habilitation settings and plans, including a habilitation setting that is the least restrictive setting consistent with the need for habilitation. A copy of the application shall be provided to respondent's counsel. The requirements for notice under section 5123.73 of the Revised Code and the provisions of divisions (A) to (E) of this section apply to all hearings on such applications.

(2) A hearing on the first application for continued commitment shall be held at the expiration of the first ninety-day period. The hearing shall be mandatory and may not be waived.

(3) Subsequent periods of commitment not to exceed one hundred eighty days each may be ordered by the court if the designee of the director of mental retardation and developmental disabilities files an application for continued commitment, after a hearing is held on the application or without a hearing if no hearing is requested and no hearing required under division

(H)(4) of this section is waived. Upon the application of a person involuntarily committed under this section, supported by an affidavit of a licensed physician alleging that the person is no longer a mentally retarded person subject to institutionalization by court order, the court for good cause shown may hold a full hearing on the person's continued commitment prior to the expiration of any subsequent period of commitment set by the court.

(4) A mandatory hearing shall be held at least every two years after the initial commitment.

(5) If the court, after a hearing upon a request to continue commitment, finds that the respondent is a mentally retarded person subject to institutionalization by court order, the court may make an order pursuant to divisions (C), (D), and (E) of this section.

(I) Notwithstanding the provisions of division (H) of this section, no person who is found to be a mentally retarded person subject to institutionalization by court order pursuant to division (L)(2) of section 5123.01 of the Revised Code shall be held under involuntary commitment for more than five years.

(J) The managing officer admitting a person pursuant to a judicial proceeding, within ten working days of the admission, shall make a report of the admission to the department.

HISTORY: 135 v S 336 (Eff 7-1-75); 138 v S 297 (Eff 4-30-80); 138 v H 900 (Eff 7-1-80); 138 v H 965 (Eff 4-9-81); 142 v H 231 (Eff 10-5-87); 145 v S 21 (Eff 10-29-93); 146 v H 567 (Eff 10-29-96); 146 v H 629 (Eff 3-13-97); 146 v S 285. Eff 7-1-97.

Publisher's Note

The amendments made by SB 285 (146 v —) and HB 629 (146 v —) have been combined. Please see provisions of RC § 1.52.

The effective date is set by section 4 of SB 285.

† Division (G)(3) was deleted by SB 285 (146 v —), eff 7-1-97.

CHAPTER 5126: COUNTY BOARDS OF MENTAL RETARDATION AND DEVELOPMENTAL DISABILITIES

§ 5126.28 Criminal records check and fingerprinting of prospective employees; employment of certain offenders prohibited.

(A) As used in this section:

(1) "Applicant" means a person who is under final consideration for appointment or employment in a position with a county board of mental retardation and developmental disabilities.

(2) "Criminal records check" has the same meaning as in section 109.572 [109.57.2] of the Revised Code.

(3) "Minor drug possession offense" has the same meaning as in section 2925.01 of the Revised Code.

(B) The superintendent of a county board of mental retardation and developmental disabilities shall request the superintendent of the bureau of criminal identification and investigation to conduct a criminal records check with respect to any applicant who has applied to the board for employment in any position, except that a county board superintendent is not required to request a criminal records check for an employee of the board who is being considered for a different position or is returning after a leave of absence or seasonal break in employment, as long as the superintendent has no reason to believe that the employee has committed any of the offenses listed or described in division (E) of this section.

If the applicant does not present proof that the applicant has been a resident of this state for the five-year period immediately prior to the date upon which the criminal records check is requested, the county board superintendent shall request that the superintendent of the bureau obtain information from the federal bureau of investigation as a part of the criminal records check for the applicant. If the applicant presents proof that the applicant has been a resident of this state for that five-year period, the county board superintendent may request that the superintendent of the bureau include information from the federal bureau of investigation in the criminal records check. For purposes of this division, an applicant may provide proof of residency in this state by presenting, with a notarized statement asserting that the applicant has been a resident of this state for that five-year period, a valid driver's license, notification of registration as an elector, a copy of an officially filed federal or state tax form identifying the applicant's permanent residence, or any other document the superintendent considers acceptable.

(C) The county board superintendent shall provide to each applicant a copy of the form prescribed pursuant to division (C)(2)† of section 109.572 [109.57.2] of the Revised Code, provide to each applicant a standard impression sheet to obtain fingerprint impressions prescribed pursuant to division (C)(2)† of section 109.572 [109.57.2] of the Revised Code, obtain the completed form and impression sheet from each applicant, and forward the completed form and impression sheet to the superintendent of the bureau of criminal identification and investigation at the time the criminal records check is requested.

Any applicant who receives pursuant to this division a copy of the form prescribed pursuant to division (C)(1) of section 109.572 [109.57.2] of the Revised Code and a copy of an impression sheet prescribed pursuant to division (C)(2) of that section and who is requested to complete the form and provide a set of fingerprint impressions shall complete the form or provide all the information necessary to complete the form and shall provide the impression sheet with the impressions of the applicant's fingerprints. If an applicant, upon request, fails to provide the information necessary to complete the form or fails to provide impressions of the applicant's fingerprints, the county board superintendent shall not employ that applicant.

(D) A county board superintendent may request any other state or federal agency to supply the board with a written report regarding the criminal record of each applicant. With regard to an applicant who becomes a board employee, if the employee holds an occupational or professional license or other credentials, the superintendent may request that the state or federal agency that regulates the employee's occupation or profession supply the board with a written report of any information pertaining to the employee's criminal record that the agency obtains in the course of conducting an investigation or in the process of renewing the employee's license or other credentials.

(E) Except as provided in division (K)(2) of this section and in rules adopted by the department of mental retardation and developmental disabilities in accordance with division (M) of this section, no county board of mental retardation and developmental disabilities shall employ a person to fill a position with the board who has been convicted of or pleaded guilty to any of the following:

(1) A violation of section 2903.01, 2903.02, 2903.03, 2903.04, 2903.11, 2903.12, 2903.13, 2903.16, 2903.21, 2903.34, 2905.01, 2905.02, 2905.05, 2907.02, 2907.03, 2907.04, 2907.05, 2907.06, 2907.07, 2907.08, 2907.09, 2907.21, 2907.22, 2907.23, 2907.25, 2907.31, 2907.32, 2907.321 [2907.32.1], 2907.322 [2907.32.2], 2907.323 [2907.32.3] 2911.01, 2911.02, 2911.11, 2911.12, 2919.12, 2919.22, 2919.24, 2919.25, 2923.12, 2923.13, 2923.161 [2923.16.1], 2925.02, 2925.03, 2925.04, 2925.05, 2925.06, or 3716.11 of the Revised Code, a violation of section 2905.04 of the Revised Code as it existed prior to July 1, 1996, a violation of section 2919.23 of the Revised Code that would have been a violation of section 2905.04 of the Revised Code as it existed prior to July 1, 1996, had the violation occurred prior to that date, a violation of section 2925.11 of the Revised Code that is not a minor drug possession offense, or felonious sexual penetration in violation of former section 2907.12 of the Revised Code;

(2) A felony contained in the Revised Code that is not listed in this division, if the felony bears a direct and substantial relationship to the duties and responsibilities of the position being filled;

(3) A violation of an existing or former law of this state, any other state, or the United States, if the offense is substantially equivalent to any of the offenses described in division (E)(1) or (2) of this section.

(F) Prior to employing an applicant, the county board superintendent shall require the applicant to submit a statement with the applicant's signature attesting that the applicant has not been convicted of or pleaded guilty to any of the offenses described in division (E) of this section. The superintendent also shall require the applicant to sign an agreement under which the applicant agrees to notify the superintendent if while employed by the board the person is ever formally charged for any of the offenses listed or described in division (E) of this section. The agreement shall inform the applicant that failure to report formal charges may result in being dismissed from employment.

(G) A county board of mental retardation and developmental disabilities shall pay to the bureau of criminal identification and investigation the fee prescribed pursuant to division (C)(2) of section 109.572 [109.57.2] of the Revised Code for each criminal records check requested and conducted pursuant to this section.

(H)(1) Any report obtained pursuant to this section is not a public record for purposes of section 149.43 of the Revised Code and shall not be made available to any person, other than the applicant who is the subject of the records check or criminal records check or the applicant's representative, the board requesting the records check or criminal records check or its representative, the department of mental retardation and developmental disabilities, and any court, hearing officer, or other necessary individual involved in a case dealing with the denial of employment to the applicant or the denial, suspension, or revocation of a certificate or evidence of registration under section 5126.25 of the Revised Code.

(2) An individual for whom a county board superintendent has obtained reports under this section may submit a written request to the county board to have copies of the reports sent to any state agency, entity of local government, or private entity. The individual shall specify in the request the entities to which the copies are to be sent. On receiving the request, the county board shall send copies of the reports to the entities specified.

A county board may request that a state agency, entity of local government, or private entity send copies to the board of any report regarding a records check or criminal records check that the entity possesses, if the county board obtains the written consent of the individual who is the subject of the report.

(I) Each county board superintendent shall request the registrar of motor vehicles to supply the superintendent with a certified abstract regarding the record of convictions for violations of motor vehicle laws of each applicant who will be required by the applicant's employment to transport individuals with mental retardation or developmental disabilities or to operate the board's vehicles for any other purpose. For each abstract provided under this section, the board shall pay the amount specified in section 4509.05 of the Revised Code.

(J) The county board superintendent shall provide each applicant with a copy of any report or abstract obtained about the applicant under this section. The superintendent also shall provide the department of mental retardation and developmental disabilities with a copy of each report or abstract obtained under this section.

(K)(1) The county board superintendent shall inform each person, at the time of the person's initial application for employment, that the person is required to provide a set of impressions of the person's fingerprints and that a criminal records check is required to be conducted and satisfactorily completed in accordance with section 109.572 [109.57.2] of the Revised Code if the person comes under final consideration for appointment or employment as a precondition to employment for that position.

(2) A board may employ an applicant pending receipt of reports requested under this section. The board shall terminate employment of any such applicant if it is determined from the reports that the applicant failed to inform the county board that the applicant had been convicted of or pleaded guilty to any of the offenses listed or described in division (E) of this section.

(L) The board may charge an applicant a fee for costs it incurs in obtaining reports, abstracts, or fingerprint impressions under this section. A fee charged under this division shall not exceed the amount of the fees the board pays under divisions (G) and (I) of this section. If a fee is charged under this division, the board shall notify the applicant of the amount of the fee at the time of the applicant's initial application for employment and that unless the fee is paid, the board will not consider the applicant for employment.

(M) The department of mental retardation and developmental disabilities shall adopt rules pursuant to Chapter 119. of the Revised Code to implement this section and section 5126.281 [5126.28.1] of the Revised Code, including rules specifying circumstances under which a county board or contracting entity may hire a person who has been convicted of an offense listed or described in division (E) of this section but who meets standards in regard to rehabilitation set by the department.

HISTORY: 144 v H 387 (Eff 5-4-92); 145 v S 38 (Eff 10-29-93); 145 v H 694 (Eff 11-11-94); 146 v S 2 (Eff 7-1-96); 146 v H 445 (Eff 9-3-96); 146 v S 269 (Eff 9-26-96); 146 v H 629. Eff 3-13-97.

† So in enrolled bill, division (C). Was (C)(1) intended?

The provisions of § 3 of HB 629 (146 v —) read as follows:

SECTION 3. Section 5126.28 of the Revised Code is presented in this act as a composite of the section as amended by both Am. Sub. H.B. 445 and Am. Sub. S.B. 269 of the 121st General Assembly, with the new language of neither of the acts shown in capital letters. This is in recognition of the principle stated in division (B) of section 1.52 of the Revised Code that such amendments are to be harmonized where not substantively irreconcilable and constitutes a legislative finding that such is the resulting version in effect prior to the effective date of this act.

[§ 5126.28.1] § 5126.281 Background investigations of prospective employees of contracting entities; restrictions on certain offenders.

(A) As used in this section, "contracting entity" means an entity under contract with a county board of mental retardation and developmental disabilities for the provision of direct services to individuals with mental retardation or a developmental disability.

(B) Each contracting entity shall conduct background investigations in the same manner county boards conduct investigations under section 5126.28 of the Revised Code of all persons under final consideration for employment with the contracting entity in a position that involves providing services directly to individuals with mental retardation or a developmental disability, except that a contracting entity is not required to request a criminal records check for a direct services employee of the entity who is being considered for a different direct services position or is returning after a leave of absence or seasonal break in employment, as long as the contracting entity has no reason to believe that the employee has committed any of the offenses listed or described in division (E) of section 5126.28 of the Revised Code. On request, the county board shall assist a contracting entity in obtaining reports from the bureau of criminal identification and investigation or any other state or federal agency and in obtaining abstracts from the registrar of motor vehicles.

(C) No contracting entity shall place a person in a position that involves providing services directly to individuals with mental retardation or a developmental disability if the person has been convicted of or pleaded guilty to any offense listed or described in division (E) of section 5126.28 of the Revised Code, unless the person meets the standards for rehabilitation established by rules adopted under section 5126.28 of the Revised Code.

(D) A contracting entity may place a person in a position that involves providing services directly to an individual with mental retardation or a developmental disability pending receipt of information concerning the person's background investigation from the bureau of criminal identification and investigation, the registrar of motor vehicles, or any other state or federal agency if the person submits to the contracting entity a statement with the person's signature that the person has not been convicted of or pleaded guilty to any of the offenses listed or described in division (E) of section 5126.28 of the Revised Code. No contracting entity shall fail to terminate the placement of such person if the contracting entity is informed that the person has been convicted of or pleaded guilty to any of the offenses listed or described in division (E) of section 5126.28 of the Revised Code.

(E) Prior to employing a person in a direct services position, the contracting entity shall require the person to submit a statement with the applicant's signature attesting that the applicant has not been convicted of or pleaded guilty to any of the offenses listed or described in division (E) of section 5126.28 of the Revised Code. The contracting entity also shall require the person to sign an agreement to notify the contracting entity if while employed by the entity the person is ever formally charged for any of the offenses listed or described in division (E) of section 5126.28 of the Revised Code. The agreement shall inform the person that failure to report formal charges may result in being dismissed from employment.

(F) A county board may take appropriate action against a contracting entity that violates this section, including terminating the contracting entity's contract with the board.

HISTORY: 145 v H 694 (Eff 11-11-94); 146 v H 629. Eff 3-13-97.

CHAPTER 5139: YOUTH SERVICES

§ 5139.21 Prohibition.

No person shall influence or attempt to influence any child under supervision of the department of youth services, to leave the institution or home in which he was placed, his home, or place of employment or to violate any of the conditions upon which he was released under supervision.

HISTORY: 130 v 1228 (Eff 10-7-63); 132 v H 491 (Eff 10-19-67); 139 v H 440. Eff 11-23-81.

§ 5139.99 Penalty.

Whoever violates section 5139.21 of the Revised Code shall be fined not less than ten nor more than five hundred dollars or imprisoned not more than one year, or both.

HISTORY: 130 v 1229. Eff 3-10-64.

CHAPTER 5145: PENITENTIARY

[SENTENCE; TERMINATION]

§ 5145.01 Duration of sentences.

Courts shall impose sentences to a state correctional institution for felonies pursuant to sections 2929.13 and 2929.14 of the Revised Code. All prison terms may be ended in the manner provided by law, but no prison term shall exceed the maximum term provided for the felony of which the prisoner was convicted as extended pursuant to section 2967.11 or 2967.28 of the Revised Code.

If a prisoner is sentenced for two or more separate felonies, the prisoner's term of imprisonment shall run as a concurrent sentence, except if the consecutive sentence provisions of sections 2929.14 and 2929.41 of the Revised Code apply. If sentenced consecutively, for the purposes of sections 5145.01 to 5145.27 of the Revised Code, the prisoner shall be held to be serving one continuous term of imprisonment.

If a court imposes a sentence to a state correctional institution for a felony of the fourth or fifth degree, the department of rehabilitation and correction, notwithstanding the court's designation of a state correctional institution as the place of service of the sentence, may designate that the person sentenced is to be housed in a county, multicounty, municipal, municipal-county, or multicounty-municipal jail or workhouse if authorized pursuant to section 5120.161 [5120.16.1] of the Revised Code.

If, through oversight or otherwise, a person is sentenced to a state correctional institution under a definite term for an offense for which a definite term of imprisonment is not provided by statute, the sentence shall not thereby become void, but the person shall be subject to the liabilities of such sections and receive the benefits thereof, as if the person had been sentenced in the manner required by this section.

As used in this section, "prison term" has the same meaning as in section 2929.01 of the Revised Code.

HISTORY: RS § 7388-6; 81 v 72; 81 v 186; 87 v 164, § 5; GC § 2166; 103 v 29; 109 v 64; 114 v 188; Bureau of Code Revision, 10-1-53; 129 v 1193 (Eff 10-26-61); 139 v S 199 (Eff 1-1-83); 140 v S 210 (Eff 7-1-83); 142 v H 455 (Eff 7-20-87); 145 v H 571 (Eff 10-6-94); 146 v S 2. Eff 7-1-96.

The effective date is set by section 6 of SB 2.

§ 5145.02 Repealed, 146 v S 2, § 2 [GC § 2166-1; 114 v 188, § 2; Bureau of Code Revision, 10-1-53; 139 v S 199]. Eff 7-1-96.

This section regulated termination of imprisonment.

The effective date is set by section 6 of SB 2.

§ 5145.21 Escaped convicts to be arrested and returned.

The warden of a state correctional institution shall arrest and again commit to the institution a convict who escapes from the institution and is found at large, whether the term for which he was sentenced to imprisonment has expired.

HISTORY: RS § 7404; S&C 918; 33 v 14, § 15; GC § 2186; Bureau of Code Revision, 10-1-53; 145 v H 571. Eff 10-6-94.

Publisher's Note

H.B. 571 (145 v —), effective 10-6-94 also purported to repeal this section. For related provisions, see section 5120.48.

CHAPTER 5149: ADULT PAROLE AUTHORITY

[§ 5149.10.1] § 5149.101 Petition for full board hearing on proposed parole; who may attend.

(A) A board hearing officer, a board member, or the office of victims' services may petition the board for a full board hearing that relates to the proposed parole of a prisoner. At a meeting of the board at which at least seven board members are present, a majority of those present shall determine whether a full board hearing shall be held.

(B) At a full board hearing that relates to the proposed parole of a prisoner and that has been petitioned for in accordance with division (A) of this section, the parole board shall permit the following persons to appear and to give testimony or to submit written statements:

(1) The prosecuting attorney of the county in which the indictment against the prisoner was found and members of any law enforcement agency that assisted in the prosecution of the offense;

(2) The judge of the court of common pleas who imposed the sentence of incarceration upon the prisoner, or the judge's successor;

(3) The victim of the offense for which the prisoner is serving the sentence or the victim's representative designated pursuant to section 2930.02 of the Revised Code.

(C) Except as otherwise provided in this division, a full board hearing of the parole board is not subject to section 121.22 of the Revised Code. The persons who may attend a full board hearing are the persons described in divisions (B)(1) to (3) of this section, and representatives of the press, radio and television stations, and broadcasting networks who are members of a generally recognized professional media organization.

At the request of a person described in division (B)(3) of this section, representatives of the news media described in this division shall be excluded from the hearing while that person is giving testimony at the hearing. The prisoner being considered for parole has no right to be present at the hearing, but may be represented by counsel or some other person designated by the prisoner.

If there is an objection at a full board hearing to a recommendation for the parole of a prisoner, the board may approve or disapprove the recommendation or defer its decision until a subsequent full board hearing. The board may permit interested persons other than those listed in this division and division (B) of this section to attend full board hearings pursuant to rules adopted by the adult parole authority.

(D) The adult parole authority shall adopt rules for the implementation of this section. The rules shall specify reasonable restrictions on the number of media representatives that may attend a hearing, based on considerations of space, and other procedures designed to accomplish an effective, orderly process for full board hearings.

HISTORY: 146 v S 2. Eff 7-1-96.

The effective date is set by section 6 of SB 2.

See provisions, § 5 of SB 2 (146 v —) following RC § 5120.02.1.

CHAPTER 5153: COUNTY CHILDREN'S SERVICES

[§ 5153.11.1] § 5153.111 Criminal records check and fingerprinting of prospective employees responsible for child; employment of certain offenders prohibited.

(A)(1) The executive director of a public children services agency shall request the superintendent of the bureau of criminal identification and investigation to conduct a criminal records check with respect to any applicant who has applied to the agency for employment as a person responsible for the care, custody, or control of a child. If the applicant does not present proof that the applicant has been a resident of this state for the five-year period immediately prior to the date upon which the criminal records check is requested or does not provide evidence that within that five-year period the superintendent has requested information about the applicant from the federal bureau of investigation in a criminal records check, the executive director shall request that the superintendent obtain information from the federal bureau of investigation as a part of the criminal records check for the applicant. If the applicant presents proof that the applicant has been a resident of this state for that five-year period, the executive director may request that the superintendent include information from the federal bureau of investigation in the criminal records check.

(2) Any person required by division (A)(1) of this section to request a criminal records check shall provide to each applicant a copy of the form prescribed pursuant to division (C)(1) of section 109.572 [109.57.2] of the Revised Code, provide to each applicant a standard impression sheet to obtain fingerprint impressions prescribed pursuant to division (C)(2) of section 109.572 [109.57.2] of the Revised Code, obtain the completed form and impression sheet from each applicant, and forward the completed form and impression sheet to the superintendent of the bureau of criminal identification and investigation at the time the person requests a criminal records check pursuant to division (A)(1) of this section.

(3) Any applicant who receives pursuant to division (A)(2) of this section a copy of the form prescribed

pursuant to division (C)(1) of section 109.572 [109.57.2] of the Revised Code and a copy of an impression sheet prescribed pursuant to division (C)(2) of that section and who is requested to complete the form and provide a set of fingerprint impressions shall complete the form or provide all the information necessary to complete the form and shall provide the impression sheet with the impressions of the applicant's fingerprints. If an applicant, upon request, fails to provide the information necessary to complete the form or fails to provide impressions of the applicant's fingerprints, that agency shall not employ that applicant for any position for which a criminal records check is required by division (A)(1) of this section.

(B)(1) Except as provided in rules adopted by the department of human services in accordance with division (E) of this section, no public children services agency shall employ a person as a person responsible for the care, custody, or control of a child if the person previously has been convicted of or pleaded guilty to any of the following:

(a) A violation of section 2903.01, 2903.02, 2903.03, 2903.04, 2903.11, 2903.12, 2903.13, 2903.16, 2903.21, 2903.34, 2905.01, 2905.02, 2905.05, 2907.02, 2907.03, 2907.04, 2907.05, 2907.06, 2907.07, 2907.08, 2907.09, 2907.21, 2907.22, 2907.23, 2907.25, 2907.31, 2907.32, 2907.321 [2907.32.1], 2907.322 [2907.32.2], 2907.323 [2907.32.3], 2911.01, 2911.02, 2911.11, 2911.12, 2919.12, 2919.22, 2919.24, 2919.25, 2923.12, 2923.13, 2923.161 [2923.16.1], 2925.02, 2925.03, 2925.04, 2925.05, 2925.06, or 3716.11 of the Revised Code, a violation of section 2905.04 of the Revised Code as it existed prior to July 1, 1996, a violation of section 2919.23 of the Revised Code that would have been a violation of section 2905.04 of the Revised Code as it existed prior to July 1, 1996, had the violation occurred prior to that date, a violation of section 2925.11 of the Revised Code that is not a minor drug possession offense, or felonious sexual penetration in violation of former section 2907.12 of the Revised Code;

(b) A violation of an existing or former law of this state, any other state, or the United States that is substantially equivalent to any of the offenses or violations described in division (B)(1)(a) of this section.

(2) A public children services agency may employ an applicant conditionally until the criminal records check required by this section is completed and the agency receives the results of the criminal records check. If the results of the criminal records check indicate that, pursuant to division (B)(1) of this section, the applicant does not qualify for employment, the agency shall release the applicant from employment.

(C)(1) Each public children services agency shall pay to the bureau of criminal identification and investigation the fee prescribed pursuant to division (C)(3) of section 109.572 [109.57.2] of the Revised Code for each criminal records check conducted in accordance with that section upon the request pursuant to division (A)(1) of this section of the executive director of the agency.

(2) A public children services agency may charge an applicant a fee for the costs it incurs in obtaining a criminal records check under this section. A fee charged under this division shall not exceed the amount of fees the agency pays under division (C)(1) of this section. If a fee is charged under this division, the agency shall notify the applicant at the time of the applicant's initial application for employment of the amount of the fee and that, unless the fee is paid, the agency will not consider the applicant for employment.

(D) The report of any criminal records check conducted by the bureau of criminal identification and investigation in accordance with section 109.572 [109.57.2] of the Revised Code and pursuant to a request under division (A)(1) of this section is not a public record for the purposes of section 149.43 of the Revised Code and shall not be made available to any person other than the applicant who is the subject of the criminal records check or the applicant's representative, the public children services agency requesting the criminal records check or its representative, and any court, hearing officer, or other necessary individual involved in a case dealing with the denial of employment to the applicant.

(E) The department of human services shall adopt rules pursuant to Chapter 119. of the Revised Code to implement this section, including rules specifying circumstances under which a public children services agency may hire a person who has been convicted of an offense listed in division (B)(1) of this section but who meets standards in regard to rehabilitation set by the department.

(F) Any person required by division (A)(1) of this section to request a criminal records check shall inform each person, at the time of the person's initial application for employment, that the person is required to provide a set of impressions of the person's fingerprints and that a criminal records check is required to be conducted and satisfactorily completed in accordance with section 109.572 [109.57.2] of the Revised Code if the person comes under final consideration for appointment or employment as a precondition to employment for that position.

(G) As used in this section:

(1) "Applicant" means a person who is under final consideration for appointment or employment in a position with the agency as a person responsible for the care, custody, or control of a child.

(2) "Criminal records check" has the same meaning as in section 109.572 [109.57.2] of the Revised Code.

(3) "Minor drug possession offense" has the same meaning as in section 2925.01 of the Revised Code.

HISTORY: 145 v S 38 (Eff 10-29-93); 145 v H 694 (Eff 11-11-94); 146 v S 2 (Eff 7-1-96); 146 v H 445 (Eff 9-3-96); 146 v S 269 (Eff 9-26-96); 147 v H 408. Eff 10-1-97.

The effective date is set by section 26 of HB 408.

TITLE 53: REAL PROPERTY

CHAPTER 5301: CONVEYANCES; ENCUMBRANCES

§ 5301.61 Improper removal of improvements from mortgaged realty.

No person having an interest in real property, buyer, lessee, tenant, or occupant of real property, knowing that such real property is mortgaged or the subject of a land contract, shall remove, or cause or permit the removal of any improvement or fixture from such real property without the consent of the mortgagee, vendor under the land contract, or other person authorized to give such consent.

HISTORY: 134 v H 511. Eff 1-1-74.

The effective date of H 511 is set by § 4 of the act.

§ 5301.99 Penalties.

(A) Any individual, corporation, or other business entity that violates section 5301.254 [5301.25.4] of the Revised Code shall be fined not less than five thousand dollars nor more than an amount equal to twenty-five per cent of the market value of the real property or mineral or mining rights about which information must be filed with the secretary of state pursuant to section 5301.254 [5301.25.4] of the Revised Code.

(B) Whoever violates section 5301.61 of the Revised Code is guilty of a misdemeanor of the first degree.

HISTORY: Bureau of Code Revision, 10-1-53; 134 v H 511 (Eff 1-1-74); 137 v S 508. Eff 3-19-79.

TITLE 55: ROADS—HIGHWAYS—BRIDGES

CHAPTER 5502: DEPARTMENT OF PUBLIC SAFETY

§ 5502.01 General duties of department.

(A) The department of public safety shall administer and enforce the laws relating to the registration, licensing, sale and operation of motor vehicles and the laws pertaining to the licensing of drivers of motor vehicles.

The department shall compile, analyze, and publish statistics relative to motor vehicle accidents and the causes thereof, prepare and conduct educational programs for the purpose of promoting safety in the operation of motor vehicles on the highways, assist the state board of education in the formulation of minimum standards for driver education courses of instruction, encourage driver instruction in the high schools of the state, and conduct research and studies for the purpose of promoting safety on the highways of this state.

(B) The department shall administer the laws and rules applicable to the division of state emergency medical services.

(C) The department shall administer and enforce the laws contained in Chapters 4301. and 4303. of the Revised Code and enforce the rules and orders of the liquor control commission pertaining to retail liquor permit holders.

(D) The department shall administer the laws governing the state emergency management agency and shall enforce all additional duties and responsibilities as prescribed in the Revised Code related to emergency management services.

(E) The department shall conduct investigations pursuant to Chapter 5101. of the Revised Code in support of the duty of the department of human services to administer food stamp programs throughout this state. The department of public safety shall conduct investigations necessary to protect the state's property rights and interests in the food stamp program.

(F) The department of public safety shall enforce compliance with orders and rules of the public utilities commission and applicable laws in accordance with Chapters 4919., 4921., and 4923. of the Revised Code regarding commercial motor vehicle transportation safety, economic, and hazardous materials requirements.

(G) Notwithstanding Chapter 4117. of the Revised Code, the department of public safety may establish requirements for its enforcement personnel that include standards of conduct, work rules and procedures, and criteria for eligibility as law enforcement personnel.

(H) The department shall administer, maintain, and operate the Ohio criminal justice network. The Ohio criminal justice network shall be a computer network that supports state and local criminal justice activities. The network shall be an electronic repository for various data, which may include arrest warrants, notices of persons wanted by law enforcement agencies, criminal records, prison inmate records, stolen vehicle records, vehicle operator's licenses, and vehicle registrations and titles.

HISTORY: 125 v 127 (Eff 10-2-53); 132 v H 380 (Eff 1-1-68); 144 v S 98 (Eff 11-12-92); 146 v S 162 (Eff 10-29-95); 147 v H 210. Eff 6-30-97.

The effective date is set by section 21 of HB 210.

The provisions of § 24 of SB 162 (146 v —) read as follows:

SECTION 24. This act is in no way intended to change, alter, or weaken the state's exclusive statewide authority to regulate, in a uniform manner, the manufacture, distribution, and sale of alcoholic beverages in this state as set forth in Title XLIII of the Ohio Revised Code; nor is this act intended in any way to derogate from the authority granted to this state by Amendment XXI to the United States Constitution. Any executive or legislative authority of a political subdivision has only such rights or powers with regard to the regulation of alcoholic beverages as are expressly granted under Title XLIII of the Ohio Revised Code. The legislative intent of this act in regard to the transfer of the Department of Liquor Control to the Departments of Commerce and Public Safety is merely to transfer and consolidate the administrative, licensing, and enforcement functions.

CHAPTER 5503: STATE HIGHWAY PATROL

§ 5503.01 Division of state highway patrol.

There is hereby created in the department of public safety a division of state highway patrol which shall be administered by a superintendent of the state highway patrol.

The superintendent shall be appointed by the director of public safety, and shall serve at the director's pleasure. The superintendent shall give bond for the faithful performance of the superintendent's official duties in such amount and with such security as the director approves.

The superintendent, with the approval of the director, may appoint any number of state highway patrol troopers and radio operators as are necessary to carry out sections 5503.01 to 5503.06 of the Revised Code, but the number of troopers shall not be less than eight hundred eighty. The number of radio operators shall not exceed eighty in number. Except as provided in this section, at the time of appointment, troopers shall be not less than twenty-one years of age, nor have reached thirty-five years of age. A person who is attending a training school for prospective state highway patrol troopers established under section 5503.05 of the

Revised Code and attains the age of thirty-five years during the person's period of attendance at that training school shall not be disqualified as over age and shall be permitted to continue to attend the training school as long as the person otherwise is eligible to do so. Such a person also remains eligible to be appointed a trooper. Any other person who attains or will attain the age of thirty-five years prior to the time of appointment shall be disqualified as over age.

At the time of appointment, troopers shall have been legal residents of Ohio for at least one year, except that this residence requirement may be waived by the superintendent.

If any state highway patrol troopers become disabled through accident or illness, the superintendent, with the approval of the director, shall fill any vacancies through the appointment of other troopers from a qualified list to serve during the period of the disability.

The superintendent and state highway patrol troopers shall be vested with the authority of peace officers for the purpose of enforcing the laws of the state that it is the duty of the patrol to enforce and may arrest, without warrant, any person who, in the presence of the superintendent or any trooper, is engaged in the violation of any such laws. The state highway patrol troopers shall never be used as peace officers in connection with any strike or labor dispute.

Each state highway patrol trooper and radio operator, upon appointment and before entering upon official duties, shall take an oath of office for faithful performance of the trooper's or radio operator's official duties and execute a bond in the sum of twenty-five hundred dollars, payable to the state and for the use and benefit of any aggrieved party who may have a cause of action against any trooper or radio operator for misconduct while in the performance of official duties. In no event shall the bond include any claim arising out of negligent operation of a motorcycle or motor vehicle used by a trooper or radio operator in the performance of official duties.

The superintendent shall prescribe a distinguishing uniform and badge which shall be worn by each state highway patrol trooper and radio operator while on duty, unless otherwise designated by the superintendent. No person shall wear the distinguishing uniform of the state highway patrol or the badge or any distinctive part of that uniform, except on order of the superintendent.

The superintendent, with the approval of the director, may appoint necessary clerks, stenographers, and employees.

HISTORY: GC § 1183; 121 v 455 (518); 123 v 862 (923); 124 v 711; Bureau of Code Revision, 10-1-53; 125 v 127 (142) (Eff 10-2-53); 126 v 621 (Eff 10-5-55); 129 v 1671 (1691); 131 v 1263 (Eff 11-11-65); 132 v H 1 (Eff 2-21-67); 132 v H 658 (Eff 3-20-68); 138 v H 165 (Eff 11-13-79); 144 v S 144 (Eff 8-8-91); 144 v S 98 (Eff 11-12-92); 147 v S 22. Eff 4-22-97.

§ 5503.02 Duties and powers of state highway patrol.

(A) The state highway patrol shall enforce the laws of the state relating to the titling, registration, and licensing of motor vehicles; enforce on all roads and highways, notwithstanding section 4513.39 of the Revised Code, the laws relating to the operation and use of vehicles on the highways; enforce and prevent the violation of the laws relating to the size, weight, and speed of commercial motor vehicles and all laws designed for the protection of the highway pavements and structures on the highways; investigate and enforce rules and laws of the public utilities commission governing the transportation of persons and property by motor carriers and report violations of such rules and laws to the commission; enforce against any motor transportation company as defined in section 4921.02 of the Revised Code, any contract carrier by motor vehicle as defined in section 4923.02 of the Revised Code, any private motor carrier as defined in section 4923.20 of the Revised Code, and any motor carrier as defined in section 4919.75 of the Revised Code those rules and laws that, if violated, may result in a forfeiture as provided in section 4905.83, 4919.99, 4921.99, or 4923.99 of the Revised Code; investigate and report violations of all laws relating to the collection of excise taxes on motor vehicle fuels; and regulate the movement of traffic on the roads and highways of the state, notwithstanding section 4513.39 of the Revised Code.

The patrol, whenever possible, shall determine the identity of the persons who are causing or who are responsible for the breaking, damaging, or destruction of any improved surfaced roadway, structure, sign, marker, guardrail, or other appurtenance constructed or maintained by the department of transportation and shall arrest the persons who are responsible for the breaking, damaging, or destruction and bring them before the proper officials for prosecution.

State highway patrol troopers shall investigate and report all motor vehicle accidents on all roads and highways outside of municipal corporations. The superintendent of the patrol or any state highway patrol trooper may arrest, without a warrant, any person, who is the driver of or a passenger in any vehicle operated or standing on a state highway, whom the superintendent or trooper has reasonable cause to believe is guilty of a felony, under the same circumstances and with the same power that any peace officer may make such an arrest.

The superintendent or any state highway patrol trooper may enforce the criminal laws on all state properties and state institutions, owned or leased by the state, and, when so ordered by the governor in the event of riot, civil disorder, or insurrection, may, pursuant to sections 2935.03 to 2935.05 of the Revised Code, arrest offenders against the criminal laws wherever they may be found within the state if the violations occurred upon, or resulted in injury to person or property on, state properties or state institutions, or under the conditions described in division (B) of this section.

(B) In the event of riot, civil disorder, or insurrection, or the reasonable threat of riot, civil disorder, or insurrection, and upon request, as provided in this section, of the sheriff of a county or the mayor or other chief executive of a municipal corporation, the governor may order the state highway patrol to enforce the criminal laws within the area threatened by riot, civil disorder, or insurrection, as designated by the governor, upon finding that law enforcement agencies within the counties involved will not be reasonably capable of controlling the riot, civil disorder, or insurrection and that additional assistance is necessary. In cities in which the sheriff is under contract to provide exclusive police services pursuant to section 311.29 of the Revised Code, in villages, and in the unincorporated areas of the county, the sheriff has exclusive authority to request the use of the patrol. In cities in which the sheriff does not exclusively provide police services, the mayor, or other chief executive performing the duties of mayor, has exclusive authority to request the use of the patrol.

The superintendent or any state highway patrol trooper may enforce the criminal laws within the area designated by the governor during the emergency arising out of the riot, civil disorder, or insurrection until released by the governor upon consultation with the requesting authority. State highway patrol troopers shall never be used as peace officers in connection with any strike or labor dispute.

When a request for the use of the patrol is made pursuant to this division, the requesting authority shall notify the law enforcement authorities in contiguous communities and the sheriff of each county within which the threatened area, or any part of the threatened area, lies of the request, but the failure to notify the authorities or a sheriff shall not affect the validity of the request.

(C) Any person who is arrested by the superintendent or a state highway patrol trooper shall be taken before any court or magistrate having jurisdiction of the offense with which the person is charged. Any person who is arrested or apprehended within the limits of a municipal corporation shall be brought before the municipal court or other tribunal of the municipal corporation.

(D)(1) State highway patrol troopers have the same right and power of search and seizure as other peace officers.

No state official shall command, order, or direct any state highway patrol trooper to perform any duty or service that is not authorized by law. The powers and duties conferred on the patrol are supplementary to, and in no way a limitation on, the powers and duties of sheriffs or other peace officers of the state.

(2)(a) A state highway patrol trooper, pursuant to the policy established by the superintendent of the state highway patrol under division (D)(2)(b) of this section, may render emergency assistance to any other peace officer who has arrest authority under section 2935.03 of the Revised Code, if both of the following apply:

(i) There is a threat of imminent physical danger to the peace officer, a threat of physical harm to another person, or any other serious emergency situation;

(ii) Either the peace officer requests emergency assistance or it appears that the peace officer is unable to request emergency assistance and the circumstances observed by the state highway patrol trooper reasonably indicate that emergency assistance is appropriate.

(b) The superintendent of the state highway patrol shall establish, within sixty days of August 8, 1991, a policy that sets forth the manner and procedures by which a state highway patrol trooper may render emergency assistance to any other peace officer under division (D)(2)(a) of this section. The policy shall include a provision that a state highway patrol trooper never be used as a peace officer in connection with any strike or labor dispute.

(3)(a) A state highway patrol trooper who renders emergency assistance to any other peace officer under the policy established by the superintendent pursuant to division (D)(2)(b) of this section shall be considered to be performing regular employment for the purposes of compensation, pension, indemnity fund rights, workers' compensation, and other rights or benefits to which the trooper may be entitled as incident to regular employment.

(b) A state highway patrol trooper who renders emergency assistance to any other peace officer under the policy established by the superintendent pursuant to division (D)(2)(b) of this section retains personal immunity from liability as specified in section 9.86 of the Revised Code.

(c) A state highway patrol trooper who renders emergency assistance under the policy established by the superintendent pursuant to division (D)(2)(b) of this section has the same authority as the peace officer for or with whom he is providing emergency assistance.

(E)(1) Subject to the availability of funds specifically appropriated by the general assembly for security detail purposes, the state highway patrol shall provide security as follows:

(a) For the governor;

(b) At the direction of the governor, for other officials of the state government of this state; officials of the state governments of other states who are visiting this state; officials of the United States government who are visiting this state; officials of the governments of foreign countries or their political subdivisions who are visiting this state; or other officials or dignitaries who are visiting this state, including, but not limited to, members of trade missions;

(c) For the capitol square, as defined in section 105.41 of the Revised Code;

(d) For other state property.

(2) To carry out the security responsibilities of the patrol listed in division (E)(1) of this section, the super-

intendent may assign state highway patrol troopers to a separate unit that is responsible for security details. The number of troopers assigned to particular security details shall be determined by the superintendent.

(3) The superintendent and any state highway patrol trooper, when providing security pursuant to division (E)(1)(a) or (b) of this section, have the same arrest powers as other peace officers to apprehend offenders against the criminal laws who endanger or threaten the security of any person being protected, no matter where the offense occurs.

The superintendent, any state highway patrol trooper, and any special police officer designated under section 5503.09 of the Revised Code, when providing security pursuant to division (E)(1)(c) of this section, shall enforce any rules governing capitol square adopted by the capitol square review and advisory board.

(F) The governor may order the state highway patrol to undertake major criminal investigations that involve state property interests. If an investigation undertaken pursuant to this division results in either the issuance of a no bill or the filing of an indictment, the superintendent shall file a complete and accurate report of the investigation with the president of the senate, the speaker of the house of representatives, the minority leader of the senate, and the minority leader of the house of representatives within fifteen days after the issuance of the no bill or the filing of an indictment. If the investigation does not have as its result any prosecutorial action, the superintendent shall, upon reporting this fact to the governor, file a complete and accurate report of the investigation with the president of the senate, the speaker of the house of representatives, the minority leader of the senate, and the minority leader of the house of representatives.

(G) The superintendent may purchase or lease real property and buildings needed by the patrol, negotiate the sale of real property owned by the patrol, rent or lease real property owned or leased by the patrol, and make or cause to be made repairs to all property owned or under the control of the patrol.

Sections 123.01 and 125.02 of the Revised Code do not limit the powers granted to the superintendent by this division.

HISTORY: GC § 1183-2; 121 v 455 (520); 122 v 531; Bureau of Code Revision, 10-1-53; 132 v H 996 (Eff 6-13-68); 134 v H 600 (Eff 3-3-72); 135 v H 200 (Eff 9-28-73); 135 v H 323 (Eff 10-31-73); 137 v S 221 (Eff 11-23-77); 138 v H 837 (Eff 3-23-81); 139 v H 694 (Eff 11-15-81); 142 v H 428 (Eff 9-26-88); 144 v S 144 (Eff 8-8-91); 144 v S 351 (Eff 7-1-92); 144 v S 381 (Eff 1-15-93); 145 v H 687 (Eff 10-12-94); 146 v H 117 (Eff 9-29-95); 146 v S 34. Eff 10-25-95.

Comment, Legislative Service Commission

Section 5503.02 of the Revised Code is amended by this act [Am. S.B. 34] and also Am. Sub. H.B. 117 of the 121st General Assembly. Comparison of these amendments in pursuance of section 1.52 of the Revised Code discloses that they are not irreconcilable so that they are required by that section to be harmonized to give effect to each amendment.

§ 5503.03 Equipment; rules; promotions.

The state highway patrol and the superintendent of the state highway patrol shall be furnished by the state with such vehicles, equipment, and supplies as the director of public safety deems necessary, all of which shall remain the property of the state and be strictly accounted for by each member of the patrol.

The patrol may be equipped with standardized and tested devices for weighing vehicles, and may stop and weigh any vehicle which appears to weigh in excess of the amounts permitted by sections 5577.01 to 5577.14 of the Revised Code.

The superintendent, with the approval of the director, shall prescribe rules for instruction and discipline, make all administrative rules, and fix the hours of duty for patrol officers. He shall divide the state into districts and assign members of the patrol to such districts in a manner that he deems proper. He may transfer members of the patrol from one district to another, and classify and rank members of the patrol. All promotions to a higher grade shall be made from the next lower grade. When a patrol officer is promoted by the superintendent, the officer's salary shall be increased to that of the lowest step in the pay range for the new grade which shall increase the officer's salary or wage by at least nine per cent of the base pay wherever possible.

HISTORY: GC § 1183-3; 121 v 455(521); Bureau of Code Revision, 10-1-53; 125 v 127(142) (10-2-53); 139 v H 694 (Eff 11-15-81); 144 v S 98. Eff 11-12-92.

§ 5503.04 Disposition of fines.

All fines collected from or moneys arising from bail forfeited by persons apprehended or arrested by state highway patrol troopers shall be paid forty-five per cent into the state treasury and fifty-five per cent into the treasury of the municipal corporation where the case is prosecuted, if in a mayor's court. If the prosecution is in a trial court outside a municipal corporation, or outside the territorial jurisdiction of a municipal court, the fines and moneys shall be paid fifty-five per cent into the county treasury. The fines and moneys paid into the state treasury shall be credited to the general revenue fund. The fines and moneys paid into a county treasury and the fines and moneys paid into the treasury of a municipal corporation shall be deposited one-half to the same fund and expended in the same manner as is the revenue received from the registration of motor vehicles, and one-half to the general fund of such county or municipal corporation.

If the prosecution is in a municipal court, forty-five per cent of the fines and moneys shall be paid into the state treasury to be credited to the general revenue fund, ten per cent shall be paid into the county treasury to be credited to the general fund of the county, and forty-five per cent shall be paid into the municipal treasury to be credited to the general fund of the municipal corporation. In the Auglaize county, Clermont county,

Crawford county, Hocking county, Jackson county, Lawrence county, Madison county, Miami county, Ottawa county, Portage county, and Wayne county municipal courts, that portion of money otherwise paid into the municipal treasury shall be paid into the county treasury.

The trial court shall make remittance of the fines and moneys as prescribed in this section, and at the same time as the remittance is made of the state's portion to the state treasury, the trial court shall notify the superintendent of the state highway patrol of the case and the amount covered by the remittance.

This section does not apply to fines for violations of division (B) of section 4513.263 [4513.26.3] of the Revised Code, or for violations of any municipal ordinance that is substantively comparable to that division, all of which shall be delivered to the treasurer of state as provided in division (E) of section 4513.263 [4513.26.3] of the Revised Code.

HISTORY: GC § 1183-4; 121 v 455(521); Bureau of Code Revision, 10-1-53; 126 v 773 (Eff 10-5-55); 129 v 1011 (Eff 1-1-62); 132 v H 361 (Eff 7-25-67); 136 v H 205 (Eff 1-1-76); 137 v S 221 (Eff 11-23-77); 137 v H 312 (Eff 1-1-78); 138 v H 1 (Eff 5-16-79); 138 v H 961 (Eff 9-29-80); 141 v S 54 (Eff 5-6-86); 142 v H 171 (Eff 7-1-87); 144 v H 200 (Eff 7-8-91); 144 v S 144 (Eff 8-8-91); 145 v H 21. Eff 2-4-94.

The provisions of § 6 of HB 21 (145 v —) read as follows:

SECTION 6. Section 5503.04 of the Revised Code is presented in this act as a composite of the section as amended by both Am. Sub. S.B. 144 and Am. Sub. H.B. 200 of the 119th General Assembly, with the new language of neither of the acts shown in capital letters. This is in recognition of the principle stated in division (B) of section 1.52 of the Revised Code that such amendments are to be harmonized where not substantively irreconcilable and constitutes a legislative finding that such is the resulting version in effect prior to the effective date of this act.

§ 5503.07 Misdemeanor arrests.

In addition to the powers and duties of the state highway patrol set forth in section 5503.02 of the Revised Code and subject to the limitations of section 5503.01 of the Revised Code, a state highway patrol trooper shall arrest any person found committing a misdemeanor within the bounds of rest areas or roadside parks within the limits of the right-of-way of interstate highways and other state highways, or in violation of section 5515.07 of the Revised Code in other areas within the limits of the right-of-way of interstate highways.

HISTORY: 130 v 1263 (Eff 9-20-63); 144 v S 144. Eff 8-8-91.

§ 5503.31 Authority on turnpike projects.

The state highway patrol shall have the same authority as is conferred upon it by section 5503.02 of the Revised Code with respect to the enforcement of state laws on other roads and highways and on other state properties, to enforce on all turnpike projects the laws of the state and the bylaws, rules, and regulations of the Ohio turnpike commission. The patrol, the superintendent of the patrol, and all state highway patrol troopers shall have the same authority to make arrests on all turnpike projects for violations of state laws and of bylaws, rules, and regulations of the Ohio turnpike commission as is conferred upon them by section 5503.02 of the Revised Code to make arrests on, and in connection with offenses committed on, other roads and highways and on other state properties.

HISTORY: 126 v 1036 (Eff 6-20-55); 144 v S 144. Eff 8-8-91.

CHAPTER 5589: OFFENSES RELATING TO HIGHWAYS

§ 5589.01 Obstructing public grounds, highway, street, or alley.

No person shall obstruct or encumber by fences, buildings, structures, or otherwise, a public ground, highway, street, or alley of a municipal corporation.

HISTORY: RS § 6921; S&C 441, 878, 880; 30 v 22, §§ 1, 2; 32 v 38; 54 v 130, §§ 1, 2; 72 v 112; GC § 13421; Bureau of Code Revision. Eff 10-1-53.

§ 5589.02 Altering or injuring marker or monument.

No person shall alter, deface, injure, or destroy any marker or monument placed along, upon, or near a public highway, by the proper authorities, to mark the boundaries thereof, or for any other purpose.

HISTORY: GC § 13421-4; 106 v 574(659), § 281; Bureau of Code Revision. Eff 10-1-53.

§ 5589.03 Refusal or neglect of officials to perform duty.

No county engineer, township trustee, or township highway superintendent shall willfully neglect, fail, or refuse to perform the duties of his office. Conviction for such neglect, failure, or refusal shall operate as a removal from office.

HISTORY: GC § 13421-5; 106 v 574(659), § 282; Bureau of Code Revision. Eff 10-1-53.

§ 5589.04 Repealed, 146 v S 2, § 6 [GC § 13421-6; 106 v 574(659), § 283; Bureau of Code Revision, 10-1-53]. Eff 7-1-96.

This section prohibited willful destruction or injury to bridge or culvert.

§ 5589.05 Interfering with drawbridge on Muskingum improvement.

No person, except a commissioner, engineer, superintendent, lock tender, bridge tender, or collector and without express direction or permission from one of them, shall open or interfere with a drawbridge on the Muskingum improvement.

HISTORY: RS § 218-216; GC § 12640; 76 v 187, § 12; Bureau of Code Revision. Eff 10-1-53.

§ 5589.06 Obstructing ditch, drain, or watercourse; duty of superintendent.

No person shall wrongfully obstruct any ditch, drain, or watercourse along, upon, or across a public highway, or divert any water from adjacent lands to or upon a public highway. Whenever the township highway superintendent learns of any obstruction of any ditch, drain, or watercourse along, upon, or across a public highway, or diversion of any water from adjacent lands to or upon a public highway, he shall notify the board of township trustees, which shall cause written notice thereof to be personally served upon the person, firm, or corporation, or upon any agent in charge of the property of the person, firm, or corporation causing such obstruction or diversion. Notice may be served by a constable of the proper township or any person authorized and deputed therefor by the board of township trustees, and shall describe and locate said obstruction or diversion and direct its immediate removal. If the person, company, or corporation does not within five days from the receipt of written notice proceed to remove such obstruction and complete the removal within a reasonable time, the township highway superintendent, upon the order of the board of township trustees, shall remove the obstruction. The expense incurred shall be paid in the first instance out of any money levied, collected, and available for highway purposes and shall then be collected from the person, company, or corporation by civil action by the board of township trustees, and paid into the highway fund of the township.

HISTORY: GC § 13421-7; 106 v 574(659), § 284; Bureau of Code Revision. Eff 10-1-53.

§ 5589.07 Failure to make levy or furnish estimates.

No person charged with the duty of making any levy or furnishing any estimates or budgets requesting any levy or allowance for the construction, improvement, maintenance, or repair of any public highway, bridge, or culvert shall fail to make such levy or allowance, or furnish such estimate, budget, or request.

HISTORY: GC § 13421-8; 106 v 574(660), § 285; Bureau of Code Revision. Eff 10-1-53.

§ 5589.08 Operating traction engines upon improved highways.

No person shall drive over the improved highways of the state, or any political subdivision thereof, a traction engine or tractor with tires or wheels equipped with ice picks, spuds, spikes, chains, or other projections of any kind extending beyond the cleats, or no person shall tow or in any way pull another vehicle over the improved highways of the state, or any political subdivision thereof, which towed or pulled vehicle has tires or wheels equipped with ice picks, spuds, spikes, chains or other projections of any kind. "Traction engine" or "tractor," as used in this section, applies to all self-propelling engines equipped with metal-tired wheels operated or propelled by any form of engine, motor, or mechanical power.

No municipal corporation, county, or township shall adopt, enforce, or maintain any ordinance, rule, or regulation contrary to or inconsistent with this section, or require of any person any license tax upon or registration fee for any traction engine, tractor, or trailer, or any permit or license to operate. Operators of traction engines or tractors shall have the same rights upon the public streets and highways as the drivers of any other vehicles, unless some other safe and convenient way is provided, and no public road open to traffic shall be closed to traction engines or tractors.

HISTORY: GC § 13421-12; 106 v 574(660), § 289; 107 v 652; Bureau of Code Revision, 10-1-53; 125 v 401. Eff 10-16-53.

[§ 5589.08.1] § 5589.081 Studded tires; prohibitions.

(A) For purposes of this section, "studded tire" means any tire designed for use on a vehicle, and equipped with metal studs or studs of wear-resisting material that project beyond the tread of the traction surface of the tire; and "motor vehicle," "street or highway," "public safety vehicle," and "school bus" have the same meaning as given those terms in section 4511.01 of the Revised Code.

(B) No person shall operate any motor vehicle, other than a public safety vehicle or school bus, that is equipped with studded tires on any street or highway in this state, except during the period extending from the first day of November of each year through the fifteenth day of April of the succeeding year.

(C) This section does not apply to the use of tire chains when there is snow or ice on the streets or highways where such chains are being used, or the immediate vicinity thereof.

HISTORY: 135 v H 398 (Eff 1-1-74); 136 v S 40. Eff 3-12-75.

§ 5589.09 Failure or neglect to drag road.

No person, charged with the duty of causing any unimproved or gravel road or part thereof to be dragged, shall willfully fail, neglect, or refuse to cause the same to be done, in such manner and within the time fixed by the sections of the Revised Code applicable thereto, or by the proper authority.

HISTORY: GC § 13421-13; 106 v 574(660), § 290; Bureau of Code Revision. Eff 10-1-53.

§ 5589.10 Digging, excavating, piling earth, or building fence on highway.

No person shall dig up, remove, excavate, or place any earth or mud upon any portion of any public highway or build a fence upon the same without authority to do so. Each day that such person continues to dig up, remove, or excavate any portion of the public highway constitutes a separate offense.

HISTORY: GC § 13421-14; 106 v 574(660), § 291; Bureau of Code Revision. Eff 10-1-53.

§ 5589.11 Failure or neglect to cut weeds, briers, or bushes.

No person, charged with the duty of cutting, destroying, or removing any weeds, briers, or bushes upon or along a public highway shall willfully fail, neglect, or refuse to cut, destroy, or remove such weeds, briers, or bushes as required in sections 5579.04 and 5579.08 of the Revised Code or on the order of the proper officials.

HISTORY: GC § 13421-15; 106 v 574(661), § 292; Bureau of Code Revision, 10-1-53; 140 v S 108. Eff 7-4-84.

§ 5589.12 Possession of tools belonging to state or county.

No person shall, without being authorized, have in his control or possession any equipment, tools, implements, or other property belonging to the state, county, or township.

HISTORY: GC § 13421-18; 106 v 574(661), § 295; Bureau of Code Revision. Eff 10-1-53.

§ 5589.13 Fines credited to maintenance and repair fund.

All fines collected for violations of sections 5589.02 to 5589.14, inclusive, of the Revised Code, shall be paid into the county treasury and placed to the credit of the fund for the maintenance and repair of the highways within such county.

HISTORY: GC § 13421-20; 106 v 574(661), § 297; Bureau of Code Revision. Eff 10-1-53.

§ 5589.14 Prosecution of offenses.

The prosecuting attorney shall prosecute all offenders under sections 5589.02 to 5589.13, inclusive, of the Revised Code, upon application of any official or individual filing any affidavit before any magistrate of the county charging an offense under such sections. This section shall not prevent the prosecuting attorney or any other official from prosecuting offenders under such sections upon his own initiative.

HISTORY: GC § 13421-22; 106 v 574(661), § 299; Bureau of Code Revision. Eff 10-1-53.

[RAILROADS]

§ 5589.21 Obstruction of roads by railroads.

No railroad company shall obstruct, or permit or cause to be obstructed a public street, road, or highway, by permitting a railroad car, locomotive, or other obstruction to remain upon or across it for longer than five minutes, to the hindrance or inconvenience of travelers or a person passing along or upon such street, road, or highways. No railroad company shall fail, at the end of each five minute period of obstruction of a public street, road, or highway, to cause such railroad car, locomotive, or other obstruction to be removed for sufficient time, not less than three minutes, to allow the passage of persons and vehicles waiting to cross.

This section does not apply to obstruction of a public street, road, or highway by a continuously moving through train or caused by circumstances wholly beyond the control of the railroad company, but does apply to other obstructions, including without limitation those caused by stopped trains and trains engaged in switching, loading, or unloading operations.

Upon the filing of an affidavit or complaint for violation of this section, summons shall be issued to the railroad company pursuant to division (B) of section 2935.10 of the Revised Code, which summons shall be served on the regular ticket or freight agent of the company in the county where the offense occurred.

HISTORY: RS § 4748; S&S 669; S&C 1311; GC § 7472; 65 v 14, § 31; Bureau of Code Revision, 10-1-53; 133 v S 5. Eff 9-4-69.

§ 5589.22 Damages.

A corporation or person shall be liable for all damages arising to a person from an obstruction or injury to a road or highway as provided by section 5589.21 of the Revised Code, which damage shall be recovered by an action at the suit of the board of township trustees of the township in which the offense is committed, or of any person suing therefor before a judge of a county court or judge of a municipal court having jurisdiction within the county where the offense is committed, or by indictment in the court of common pleas in the proper county. Each twenty-four hours the person or corporation, after being notified, permits such obstruction to remain, shall be an additional offense against such section.

HISTORY: RS § 4748; S&S 669; S&C 1311; GC § 7473; 65 v 14, § 31; Bureau of Code Revision, 10-1-53; 129 v 582(949). Eff 1-10-61.

§ 5589.23 Company liable for fines against employees.

A railroad company or other corporation, the servant, agent, or employee of which, in any manner, obstructs a public road or highway, shall pay all penalties which may be assessed against such servant, agent, or employee for obstructing it. The penalties may be enforced by execution issued against such corporation on the judgment rendered against the servant, agent, or employee.

HISTORY: RS § 4749; S&S 669; S&C 1311; GC § 7475; 65 v 14, § 32; Bureau of Code Revision. Eff 10-1-53.

§ 5589.24 Moneys collected.

All penalties collected under section 5589.21 of the Revised Code shall be paid to the township clerk of the township in which the offense was committed, and be applied by the board of township trustees to the improvement of roads and highways in such township.

HISTORY RS § 4748; S&S 669; S&C 1311; GC § 7474; 65 v 14, § 31; Bureau of Code Revision. Eff 10-1-53.

[OBSTRUCTIONS; SIGNS]

§ 5589.31 Construction of walk or ditch across highway.

No person, firm, or corporation shall construct a walk or dig a ditch across a public highway outside any municipal corporation without the consent of the director of transportation in the case of an intercounty or a state highway, county engineer in the case of a county road, or board of township trustees in the case of a township road.

HISTORY: GC § 7202; 106 v 574(618), § 159; 107 v 69(116); Bureau of Code Revision, 10-1-53; 135 v H 200. Eff 9-28-73.

§ 5589.32 Erection of advertising signs resembling those required of railroad companies.

No person, firm, or corporation shall erect, display, or maintain an advertising or other sign on, along, or near any public highway, in any county of this state, which resembles the highway crossing signs which steam and interurban railroads have erected, in compliance with section 4955.33 of the Revised Code, at the crossings of public roads and railroads.

The public utilities commission shall enforce this section, prosecute any violations thereof, and order the removal of any such prohibited sign.

The attorney general and the prosecuting attorney of any county shall carry into effect the orders of the commission made under this section and shall prosecute any violations of such orders.

Each day that any violation of this section continues constitutes a separate offense. The erection, display, or maintenance of each advertising or other sign referred to in this section, except as provided in section 4955.33 of the Revised Code, constitutes a separate offense.

HISTORY: GC §§ 7204-1-7204-3; 109 v 358, §§ 1 to 3; Bureau of Code Revision. Eff 10-1-53.

§ 5589.33 Advertising on public highway.

Except as provided in this section and in section 5515.04 of the Revised Code, no person shall place within the limits of the right-of-way or affix any sign, poster, or advertisement to any tree or utility pole within the right-of-way of any public highway outside of municipal corporations. No person, organization, corporation, or group shall place within the limits of the right-of-way any object as determined by the department of transportation to obscure sight distance.

Nothing in this section shall be construed to prohibit the erection and maintaining of notices of the existence and location of public utility facilities under or upon the highway and warnings against disturbing such facilities, or of notices that emergency or other public telephones are available for users of the highway at specified locations upon or near the highway.

HISTORY: 129 v 995 (Eff 10-25-61); 130 v 1294 (Eff 1-23-63); 135 v H 200. Eff 9-28-73.

§ 5589.99 Penalties.

(A) Whoever violates section 5589.01 of the Revised Code is guilty of a misdemeanor of the third degree.

(B) Whoever violates section 5589.02, 5589.03, 5589.05, 5589.06, 5589.08, 5589.081 [5589.08.1], 5589.09, 5589.11, 5589.12, 5589.21, 5589.32, or 5589.33 of the Revised Code is guilty of a minor misdemeanor.

(C) Whoever violates section 5589.07 or 5589.10 of the Revised Code is guilty of a misdemeanor of the fourth degree.

HISTORY: Bureau of Code Revision, 10-1-53; 129 v 995 (Eff 10-25-61); 133 v S 5 (Eff 9-4-69); 135 v H 398 (Eff 1-1-74); 146 v S 2. Eff 7-1-96.

The effective date is set by section 6 of SB 2.

CHAPTER 5591: COUNTY BRIDGES

§ 5591.42 Carrying capacity of bridges warning notice.

The board of county commissioners together with the county engineer or an engineer to be selected by the board, or the director of transportation, may ascertain the safe carrying capacity of the bridges on roads or highways under their jurisdiction. Where the safe carrying capacity of any such bridge is ascertained and found to be less than the load limit prescribed by sections 5577.01 to 5577.12 of the Revised Code, warning notice shall be conspicuously posted near each end of the bridge. The notice shall caution all persons against driving on the bridge a loaded conveyance of greater weight than the bridge's carrying capacity.

HISTORY: RS § 4944; S&C 193; 66 v 90; GC § 7572; 101 v 220; 119 v 182; Bureau of Code Revision, 10-1-53; 135 v H 200 (Eff 9-28-73); 139 v S 114 (Eff 10-27-81); 143 v H 258. Eff 11-2-89.

§ 5591.43 Arrest of certain persons on view.

A constable of a township, a marshal of a village, or a police officer of a city may arrest upon view, and without process, a person violating section 5591.42 of the Revised Code.

HISTORY: RS § 4945; 66 v 90, § 3; GC § 7573; Bureau of Code Revision. Eff 10-1-53.

§ 5591.44 Prosecutions.

Prosecution under sections 5591.42 and 5591.43 of the Revised Code shall be in the name of the state and be commenced within three months after the offense is committed. Sections 5591.33 to 5591.43 of the Revised Code do not take away from the board of county commissioners a right of action for damages, which it may have against a person for injury done to a bridge.

HISTORY: RS § 4946; 66 v 90, §§ 4, 5; GC § 7574; Bureau of Code Revision, 10-1-53; 143 v H 111. Eff 7-1-89.

Comment, Legislative Service Commission

This section was amended by Am. Sub. H.B. 111 of the 118th G.A. Its existing version, however, was not repealed by that act, as required by § 15(D) of Art. II, Ohio Constitution. Since the title, amending clause, and body of the act nevertheless indicate an intention to amend the section, it is presented here as having been amended by H.B. 111. The Code Revision Section of the Legislative Service Commission will propose legislation to confirm these amendments.

TITLE 57: TAXATION

CHAPTER 5705: TAX LEVY LAW

§ 5705.19 Resolution relative to tax levy in excess of ten-mill limitation.

This section does not apply to school districts or county school financing districts.

The taxing authority of any subdivision at any time and in any year, by vote of two-thirds of all the members of the taxing authority, may declare by resolution and certify the resolution to the board of elections not less than seventy-five days before the election upon which it will be voted that the amount of taxes that may be raised within the ten-mill limitation will be insufficient to provide for the necessary requirements of the subdivision and that it is necessary to levy a tax in excess of that limitation for any of the following purposes:

(A) For current expenses of the subdivision, except that the total levy for current expenses of a detention home district or district organized under section 2151.65 of the Revised Code shall not exceed two mills and that the total levy for current expenses of a combined district organized under sections 2151.34 and 2151.65 of the Revised Code shall not exceed four mills;

(B) For the payment of debt charges on certain described bonds, notes, or certificates of indebtedness of the subdivision issued subsequent to January 1, 1925;

(C) For the debt charges on all bonds, notes, and certificates of indebtedness issued and authorized to be issued prior to January 1, 1925;

(D) For a public library of, or supported by, the subdivision under whatever law organized or authorized to be supported;

(E) For a municipal university, not to exceed two mills over the limitation of one mill prescribed in section 3349.13 of the Revised Code;

(F) For the construction or acquisition of any specific permanent improvement or class of improvements that the taxing authority of the subdivision may include in a single bond issue;

(G) For the general construction, reconstruction, resurfacing, and repair of streets, roads, and bridges in municipal corporations, counties, or townships;

(H) For recreational purposes;

(I) For the purpose of providing and maintaining fire apparatus, appliances, buildings, or sites therefor, or sources of water supply and materials therefor, or the establishment and maintenance of lines of fire alarm telegraph, or the payment of permanent, part-time, or volunteer firefighters or fire-fighting companies to operate the same, including the payment of the firefighters employer's contribution required under section 742.34 of the Revised Code, or to purchase ambulance equipment, or to provide ambulance, paramedic, or other emergency medical services operated by a fire department or fire-fighting company;

(J) For the purpose of providing and maintaining motor vehicles, communications, and other equipment used directly in the operation of a police department, or the payment of salaries of permanent police personnel, including the payment of the police employer's contribution required under section 742.33 of the Revised Code, or the payment of the costs incurred by townships as a result of contracts made with other political subdivisions in order to obtain police protection, or to provide ambulance or emergency medical services operated by a police department;

(K) For the maintenance and operation of a county home;

(L) For community mental retardation and developmental disabilities programs and services pursuant to Chapter 5126. of the Revised Code, except that the procedure for such levies shall be as provided in section 5705.222 [5705.22.2] of the Revised Code;

(M) For regional planning;

(N) For a county's share of the cost of maintaining and operating schools, district detention homes, forestry camps, or other facilities, or any combination thereof established under section 2151.34 or 2151.65 of the Revised Code or both of those sections;

(O) For providing for flood defense, providing and maintaining a flood wall or pumps, and other purposes to prevent floods;

(P) For maintaining and operating sewage disposal plants and facilities;

(Q) For the purpose of purchasing, acquiring, constructing, enlarging, improving, equipping, repairing, maintaining, or operating, or any combination of the foregoing, a county transit system pursuant to sections 306.01 to 306.13 of the Revised Code, or to make any payment to a board of county commissioners operating a transit system or a county transit board pursuant to section 306.06 of the Revised Code;

(R) For the subdivision's share of the cost of acquiring or constructing any schools, forestry camps, detention homes, or other facilities, or any combination thereof under section 2151.34 or 2151.65 of the Revised Code or both of those sections;

(S) For the prevention, control, and abatement of air pollution;

(T) For maintaining and operating cemeteries;

(U) For providing ambulance service, emergency medical service, or both;

(V) For providing for the collection and disposal of garbage or refuse;

(W) For the payment of the police employer's contribution or the firefighters employer's contribution required under sections 742.33 and 742.34 of the Revised Code;

(X) For the construction and maintenance of a drainage improvement pursuant to section 6131.52 of the Revised Code;

(Y) For providing or maintaining senior citizens services or facilities as authorized by section 307.694 [307.69.4], 307.85, 505.70, 505.706 [505.70.6], or division (EE) of section 717.01 of the Revised Code;

(Z) For the provision and maintenance of zoological park services and facilities as authorized under section 307.76 of the Revised Code;

(AA) For the maintenance and operation of a free public museum of art, science, or history;

(BB) For the establishment and operation of a 9-1-1 system, as defined in section 4931.40 of the Revised Code;

(CC) For the purpose of acquiring, rehabilitating, or developing rail property or rail service. As used in this division, "rail property" and "rail service" have the same meanings as in section 4981.01 of the Revised Code. This division applies only to a county, township, or municipal corporation.

(DD) For the purpose of acquiring property for, constructing, operating, and maintaining community centers as provided for in section 755.16 of the Revised Code;

(EE) For the creation and operation of an office or joint office of economic development, for any economic development purpose of the office, and to otherwise provide for the establishment and operation of a program of economic development pursuant to sections 307.07 and 307.64 of the Revised Code;

(FF) For the purpose of acquiring, establishing, constructing, improving, equipping, maintaining, or operating, or any combination of the foregoing, a township airport, landing field, or other air navigation facility pursuant to section 505.15 of the Revised Code;

(GG) For the payment of costs incurred by a township as a result of a contract made with a county pursuant to section 505.263 [505.26.3] of the Revised Code in order to pay all or any part of the cost of constructing, maintaining, repairing, or operating a water supply improvement;

(HH) For a board of township trustees to acquire, other than by appropriation, an ownership interest in land, water, or wetlands, or to restore or maintain land, water, or wetlands in which the board has such an interest, not for purposes of recreation, but for the purposes of protecting and preserving the natural, scenic, open, or wooded condition of the land, water, or wetlands against modification or encroachment resulting from occupation, development, or other use;

(II) For the support by a county of a crime victim assistance program that is provided and maintained by a county agency or a private, nonprofit corporation or association under section 307.62 of the Revised Code;

(JJ) For any or all of the purposes set forth in division (I) or (J) of this section. This division applies only to a township.

(KK) For a countywide public safety communications system under section 307.63 of the Revised Code. This division applies only to counties.

(LL) For the support by a county of criminal justice services under section 307.45 of the Revised Code;

(MM) For the purpose of maintaining and operating a jail or other detention facility as defined in section 2921.01 of the Revised Code.

(NN) For purchasing, maintaining, or improving, or any combination of the foregoing, real estate on which to hold agricultural fairs. This division applies only to a county.

The resolution shall be confined to the purpose or purposes described in one division of this section, for which the revenue derived therefrom shall be applied. The existence in any other division of this section of authority to levy a tax for any part or all of the same purpose or purposes does not preclude the use of such revenues for any part of the purpose or purposes of the division under which the resolution is adopted.

The resolution shall specify the amount of the increase in rate that it is necessary to levy, the purpose thereof, and the number of years during which the increase in rate shall be in effect, which may or may not include a levy upon the duplicate of the current year. The number of years may be any number not exceeding five, except as follows:

(1) When the additional rate is for the payment of debt charges, the increased rate shall be for the life of the indebtedness.

(2) When the additional rate is any of the following, the increased rate shall be for a continuing period of time:

(a) For the current expenses for a detention home district, a district organized under section 2151.65 of the Revised Code, or a combined district organized under sections 2151.34 and 2151.65 of the Revised Code;

(b) For providing a county's share of the cost of maintaining and operating schools, district detention homes, forestry camps, or other facilities, or any combination thereof, established under section 2151.34 or 2151.65 of the Revised Code or under both of those sections.

(3) When the additional rate is for any of the following, the increased rate may be for a continuing period of time:

(a) For the purposes set forth in division (I), (J), (U), or (KK) of this section;

(b) For the maintenance and operation of a joint recreation district;

(c) A levy imposed by a township for the purposes set forth in division (G) of this section.

(4) When the increase is for the purpose set forth in division (D) or (CC) of this section, the tax levy may be for any specified number of years or for a continuing period of time, as set forth in the resolution.

(5) When the additional rate is for the purpose de-

scribed in division (Z) of this section, the increased rate shall be for any number of years not exceeding ten.

A levy for the purposes set forth in division (I), (J), or (U) of this section, and a levy imposed by a township for the purposes set forth in division (G) of this section, may be reduced pursuant to section 5705.261 [5705.26.1] or 5705.31 of the Revised Code. A levy for the purposes set forth in division (I), (J), or (U) of this section, and a levy imposed by a township for the purposes set forth in division (G) of this section, may also be terminated or permanently reduced by the taxing authority if it adopts a resolution stating that the continuance of the levy is unnecessary and the levy shall be terminated or that the millage is excessive and the levy shall be decreased by a designated amount.

A resolution of a detention home district, a district organized under section 2151.65 of the Revised Code, or a combined district organized under both sections 2151.34 and 2151.65 of the Revised Code may include both current expenses and other purposes, provided that the resolution shall apportion the annual rate of levy between the current expenses and other purpose or purposes. The apportionment need not be the same for each year of the levy, but the respective portions of the rate actually levied each year for the current expenses and the other purpose or purposes shall be limited by the apportionment.

Whenever a board of county commissioners, acting either as the taxing authority of its county or as the taxing authority of a sewer district or subdistrict created under Chapter 6117. of the Revised Code, by resolution declares it necessary to levy a tax in excess of the ten-mill limitation for the purpose of constructing, improving, or extending sewage disposal plants or sewage systems, the tax may be in effect for any number of years not exceeding twenty, and the proceeds thereof, notwithstanding the general provisions of this section, may be used to pay debt charges on any obligations issued and outstanding on behalf of the subdivision for the purposes enumerated in this paragraph, provided that any such obligations have been specifically described in the resolution.

The resolution shall go into immediate effect upon its passage, and no publication of the resolution is necessary other than that provided for in the notice of election.

When the electors of a subdivision have approved a tax levy under this section, the taxing authority of the subdivision may anticipate a fraction of the proceeds of the levy and issue anticipation notes in accordance with section 5705.191 [5705.19.1] or 5705.193 [5705.19.3] of the Revised Code.

HISTORY: GC § 5625-15; 112 v 391, § 15; 114 v 843; 115 v PtII, 412; 118 v 20; 118 v 248; 121 v 776; 122 v 75; Bureau of Code Revision, 10-1-53; 125 v 104; 125 v 713(799) (Eff 1-1-54); 126 v 882; 126 v 1126; 127 v 519; 128 v 574; 129 v 1209 (Eff 9-5-61); 130 v 1300 (Eff 8-19-63); 130 v PtII, 275 (Eff 12-16-64); 131 v 1316 (Eff 8-10-65); 131 v 1314 (Eff 10-25-65); 132 v H 1 (Eff 2-21-67); 132 v S 169 (Eff 10-25-67); 132 v 478 (Eff 11-14-67); 132 v S 350 (Eff 9-1-67); 133 v H 1 (Eff 3-18-69); 133 v H 769 (Eff 10-24-69); 133 v S 476 (Eff 8-31-70); 133 v H 1135 (Eff 9-16-70); 134 v S 370 (Eff 12-23-71); 134 v H 258 (Eff 1-27-72); 134 v H 1158 (Eff 3-31-73); 135 v S 44 (Eff 9-11-73); 135 v H 1173 (Eff 8-30-74); 136 v H 111 (Eff 8-31-76); 136 v H 920 (Eff 10-11-76); 136 v S 434 (Eff 1-17-77); 137 v H 277 (Eff 11-3-77); 137 v H 617 (Eff 1-13-78); 137 v S 58 (Eff 5-17-78); 137 v S 491 (Eff 7-13-78); 138 v H 36 (Eff 11-13-79); 138 v S 274 (Eff 8-7-80); 138 v H 850 (Eff 8-7-80); 138 v H 873 (Eff 10-6-80); 138 v S 160 (Eff 10-31-80); 138 v H 1062 (Eff 3-23-81); 138 v H 268 (Eff 4-9-81); 139 v H 1 (Eff 8-5-81); 139 v H 694 (Eff 11-15-81); 139 v S 550 (Eff 11-26-82); 140 v H 372 (Eff 11-8-83); 140 v H 56 (Eff 7-20-84); 140 v H 572 (Eff 9-26-84); 141 v H 203 (Eff 5-14-85); 141 v H 491 (Eff 6-18-85); 141 v S 289 (Eff 6-24-86); 142 v H 180 (Eff 6-29-88); 142 v S 318 (Eff 7-20-88); 142 v S 155 (Eff 6-24-88); 142 v H 661 (Eff 12-8-88); 143 v S 140 (Eff 10-2-89); 143 v H 173 (Eff 10-30-89); 143 v S 75 (Eff 3-1-90); 143 v H 717 (Eff 6-28-90); 143 v H 247 (Eff 11-30-90); 144 v S 32 (Eff 7-1-92); 144 v H 416 (Eff 8-3-92); 144 v H 791 (Eff 3-15-93); 144 v S 190 (Eff 4-16-93); 145 v H 184 (Eff 9-20-93); 145 v H 612 (Eff 7-19-94); 145 v H 677 (Eff 4-21-94); 146 v H 61 (Eff 10-25-95); 147 v H 117. Eff 9-3-97.

CONSTITUTION OF THE UNITED STATES

EFFECTIVE 1789

We the people of the United States, in Order to form a more perfect Union, establish Justice, insure domestic Tranquility, provide for the common defence, promote the general Welfare, and secure the Blessings of Liberty to ourselves and our Posterity, do ordain and establish this Constitution for the United States of America.

ARTICLE I

SECTION 1. All legislative Powers herein granted shall be vested in a Congress of the United States, which shall consist of a Senate and House of Representatives.

SECTION 2. The House of Representatives shall be composed of Members chosen every second Year by the People of the several States, and the Electors in each State shall have the Qualifications requisite for Electors of the most numerous Branch of the State Legislature.

No person shall be a Representative who shall not have attained to the Age of twenty five Years, and been seven Years a Citizen of the United States, and who shall not, when elected, be an Inhabitant of that State in which he shall be chosen.

Representatives and direct Taxes shall be apportioned among the several States which may be included within this Union, according to their respective Numbers, which shall be determined by adding to the whole Number of free Persons, including those bound to Service for a Term of Years, and excluding Indians not taxed, three fifths of all other Persons. The actual Enumeration shall be made within three Years after the first Meeting of the Congress of the United States, and within every subsequent term of ten Years, in such Manner as they shall by Law direct. The Number of Representatives shall not exceed one for every thirty Thousand, but each State shall have at Least one Representative; and until such enumeration shall be made, the State of New Hampshire shall be entitled to chuse three, Massachusetts eight, Rhode Island and Providence Plantations one, Connecticut five, New York six, New Jersey four, Pennsylvania eight, Delaware one, Maryland six, Virginia ten, North Carolina five, South Carolina five, and Georgia three.

When vacancies happen in the Representation from any State, the Executive Authority thereof shall issue Writs of Election to fill such Vacancies.

The House of Representatives shall chuse their Speaker and other Officers; and shall have the sole Power of Impeachment.

SECTION 3. The Senate of the United States shall be composed of two Senators from each State, chosen by the Legislature thereof, for six Years; and each Senator shall have one Vote.

Immediately after they shall be assembled in Consequence of the first Election, they shall be divided as equally as may be into three Classes. The Seats of the Senators of the first Class shall be vacated at the Expiration of the second Year, of the second Class at the Expiration of the fourth Year, and of the third Class at the Expiration of the sixth Year, so that one third may be chosen every second Year; and if Vacancies happen by Resignation, or otherwise, during the Recess of the Legislature of any State, the Executive thereof may make temporary Appointments until the next Meeting of the Legislature, which shall then fill such Vacancies.

No Person shall be a Senator who shall not have attained to the Age of thirty Years, and been nine Years a Citizen of the United States, and who shall not, when elected, be an Inhabitant of that State for which he shall be chosen.

The Vice President of the United States shall be President of the Senate, but shall have no Vote, unless they be equally divided.

The Senate shall chuse their other Officers, and also a President pro tempore, in the absence of the Vice President, or when he shall exercise the Office of President of the United States.

The Senate shall have the sole Power to try all Impeachment. When sitting for that Purpose, they shall be on Oath or Affirmation. When the President of the United States is tried, the Chief Justice shall preside: And no Person shall be convicted without the Concurrence of two thirds of the Members present.

Judgment in Cases of Impeachment shall not extend further than to removal from Office, and disqualification to hold and enjoy any Office of honor, Trust or Profit under the United States: but the Party convicted shall nevertheless be liable and subject to Indictment, Trial, Judgment and Punishment, according to Law.

SECTION 4. The Times, Places and Manner of holding Elections for Senators and Representatives, shall be prescribed in each State by the Legislature thereof; but the Congress may at any time by Law make or alter such Regulations, except as to the Places of Chusing Senators.

The Congress shall assemble at least once in every Year, and such Meeting shall be on the first Monday in December, unless they shall by Law appoint a different Day.

SECTION 5. Each House shall be the Judge of the Elections, Returns and Qualifications of its own Members, and a Majority of each shall constitute a Quorum to do Business; but a smaller Number may adjourn from day to day, and may be authorized to compel the

Attendance of Absent Members, in such Manner, and under such Penalties as each House may provide.

Each House may determine the Rules of its Proceedings, punish its Members for disorderly Behavior, and, with the Concurrence of two thirds, expel a Member.

Each House shall keep a Journal of its Proceedings, and from time to time publish the same, excepting such Parts as may in their Judgment require Secrecy; and the Yeas and Nays of the Members of either House on any question shall, at the Desire of one fifth of those Present, be entered on the Journal.

Neither House, during the Session of Congress, shall without the Consent of the other, adjourn for more than three days, nor to any other Place than that in which the two Houses shall be sitting.

SECTION 6. The Senators and Representatives shall receive a Compensation for their Services, to be ascertained by Law, and paid out of the Treasury of the United States. They shall in all Cases, except Treason, Felony and Breach of the Peace, be privileged from Arrest during their Attendance at the Session of their respective Houses, and in going to and returning from the same; and for any Speech or Debate in either House, they shall not be questioned in any other Place.

No Senator or Representative shall, during the Time for which he was elected, be appointed to any civil Office under the Authority of the United States, which shall have been created, or the Emoluments whereof shall have been encreased during such time; and no Person holding any Office under the United States, shall be a Member of either House during his Continuance in Office.

Ohio Constitution Comparison

Privilege from arrest, answering for speech or debate, Ohio Const. art. II, § 12.

SECTION 7. All Bills for raising Revenue shall originate in the House of Representatives; but the Senate may propose or concur with Amendments as on other Bills.

Every Bill which shall have passed the House of Representatives and the Senate, shall, before it become a Law, be presented to the President of the United States; If he approve he shall sign it, but if not he shall return it, with his Objections to that House in which it shall have originated, who shall enter the Objections at large on their Journal, and proceed to reconsider it. If after such Reconsideration two thirds of that House shall agree to pass the Bill, it shall be sent, together with the Objections, to the other House, by which it shall likewise be reconsidered, and if approved by two thirds of that House, it shall become a Law. But in all such Cases the Votes of both Houses shall be determined by Yeas and Nays, and the Names of the Persons voting for and against the Bill shall be entered on the Journal of each House respectively. If any Bill shall not be returned by the President within ten Days (Sundays excepted) after it shall have been presented to him, the Same shall be a Law, in like Manner as if he had signed it, unless the Congress by their Adjournment prevent its Return, in which Case it shall not be a Law.

Every Order, Resolution, or Vote to which the Concurrence of the Senate and House of Representatives may be necessary (except on a question of Adjournment) shall be presented to the President of the United States; and before the Same shall take Effect, shall be approved by him, or being disapproved by him, shall be repassed by two thirds of the Senate and House of Representatives, according to the Rules and Limitations prescribed in the Case of a Bill.

SECTION 8. The Congress shall have Power To lay and collect Taxes, Duties, Imposts and Excises, to pay the Debts and provide for the common Defence and general Welfare of the United States; but all Duties, Imposts and Excises shall be uniform throughout the United States;

To borrow Money on the Credit of the United States;

To regulate Commerce with foreign Nations, and among the several States, and with the Indian Tribes;

To establish an uniform Rule of Naturalization, and uniform Laws on the subject of Bankruptcies throughout the United States;

To coin Money, regulate the Value thereof, and of foreign Coin, and fix the Standard of Weights and Measures;

To provide for the Punishment of counterfeiting the Securities and current Coin of the United States;

To establish Post Offices and post Roads;

To promote the Progress of Science and useful Arts, by securing for limited Times to Authors and Inventors the exclusive Right to their respective Writings and Discoveries;

To constitute Tribunals inferior to the Supreme Court;

To define and punish Piracies and Felonies committed on the high Seas, and Offences against the Law of Nations;

To declare War, grant Letters of Marque and Reprisal, and make Rules concerning Captures on Land and Water;

To raise and support Armies, but no Appropriation of Money to that Use shall be for a longer Term than two Years;

To provide and maintain a Navy;

To make Rules for the Government and Regulation of the land and naval Forces;

To provide for calling forth the Militia to execute the Laws of the Union, suppress Insurrections and repel Invasions;

To provide for organizing, arming, and disciplining the Militia, and for governing such Part of them as may be employed in the Service of the United States, reserving to the States, respectively, the Appointment of the Officers, and the Authority of training the Militia according to the discipline prescribed by Congress.

To exercise exclusive Legislation in all Cases whatsoever, over such District (not exceeding ten Miles square) as may be, by Cession of particular States, and the Acceptance of Congress, become the Seat of the Government of the United States, and to exercise like Authority over all Places purchased by the Consent of the Legislature of the State in which the Same shall be, for the Erection of Forts, Magazines, Arsenals, dock-Yards, and other needful Buildings; — And

To make all Laws which shall be necessary and proper for carrying into Execution the foregoing Powers, and all other Powers vested by this Constitution in the Government of the United States, or in any Department or Officer thereof.

SECTION 9. The Migration or Importation of such Persons as any of the States now existing shall think proper to admit, shall not be prohibited by the Congress prior to the Year one thousand eight hundred and eight, but a Tax or duty may be imposed on such Importation, not exceeding ten dollars for each Person.

The privilege of the Writ of Habeas Corpus shall not be suspended, unless when in Cases of Rebellion or Invasion the public Safety may require it.

No Bill of Attainder or ex post facto Law shall be passed.

No capitation, or other direct, Tax shall be laid, unless in Proportion to the Census or Enumeration herein before directed to be taken.

No Tax or Duty shall be laid on Articles exported from any State.

No Preference shall be given by any Regulation of Commerce or Revenue to the Ports of one State over those of another; nor shall Vessels bound to, or from, one State, be obliged to enter, clear, or pay Duties in another.

No Money shall be drawn from the Treasury, but in Consequence of Appropriations made by Law; and a regular Statement and Account of the Receipts and Expenditures of all public Money shall be published from time to time.

No Title of Nobility shall be granted by the United States: And no Person holding any Office of Profit or Trust under them, shall, without the Consent of the Congress, accept of any present, Emolument, Office, or Title, of any kind whatever, from any King, Prince, or foreign State.

Ohio Constitution Comparison

Bills of attainder, Ohio Const. art. I, § 12.
Habeas corpus, Ohio Const. art. I, § 8.
Titles of nobility, Ohio Const. art. I, § 17.

SECTION 10. No State shall enter into any Treaty, Alliance, or Confederation; grant Letters of Marque or Reprisal; coin Money; emit Bills of Credit; make any Thing but gold and silver Coin a Tender in Payment of Debts; pass any Bill of Attainder, ex post facto Law, or Law impairing the Obligation of Contracts, or grant any Title of Nobility.

No State shall, without the Consent of the Congress, lay any Imposts or Duties on Imports or Exports, except what may be absolutely necessary for executing its inspection Laws: and the net Produce of all Duties and Imposts, laid by any State on Imports or Exports, shall be for the Use of the Treasury of the United States; and all such Laws shall be subject to the Revision and Control of the Congress.

No State shall, without the Consent of Congress, lay any duty of Tonnage, keep Troops, or Ships of War in time of Peace, enter into any Agreement or Compact with another State, or with a foreign Power, or engage in War, unless actually invaded, or in such imminent Danger as will not admit of delay.

Ohio Constitution Comparison

Bills of attainder, Ohio Const. art. I, § 12.
Ex post facto laws, Ohio Const. art II, § 28.
Laws impairing obligation of contract, Ohio Const. art. II, § 28.
Titles of nobility, Ohio Const. art. I, § 17.

ARTICLE II

SECTION 1. The executive Power shall be vested in a President of the United States of America. He shall hold his Office during the Term of four Years, and, together with the Vice President, chosen for the same Term, be elected, as follows

Each State shall appoint, in such Manner as the Legislature thereof may direct, a Number of Electors, equal to the whole Number of Senators and Representatives to which the State may be entitled in the Congress; but no Senator or Representative, or Person holding an Office of Trust or Profit under the United States, shall be appointed an Elector.

The Electors shall meet in their respective States, and vote by Ballot for two persons, of whom one at least shall not be an Inhabitant of the same State with themselves. And they shall make a List of all the Persons voted for, and of the Number of Votes for each; which List they shall sign and certify, and transmit sealed to the Seat of the Government of the United States, directed to the President of the Senate. The President of the Senate shall, in the Presence of the Senate and House of Representatives, open all the Certificates, and the Votes shall then be counted. The Person having the greatest Number of Votes shall be the President, if such Number be a Majority of the whole Number of Electors appointed; and if there be more than one who have such Majority, and have an equal Number of Votes, then the House of Representatives shall immediately chuse by Ballot one of them for President; and if no Person have a Majority, then from the five highest on the List the said House shall in like Manner chuse the President. But in chusing the President, the Votes shall be taken by States, the Representation from each State having one Vote; A quorum for this Purpose shall consist of a Member or Members from two thirds of the States, and a Majority of all the States shall be necessary to a Choice. In every Case, after the Choice of the President, the Person having the greatest Number of Votes of the Electors shall be the Vice President. But if there should remain two or more who have equal Votes, the Senate shall chuse from them by Ballot the Vice President.

The Congress may determine the Time of chusing the Electors, and the Day on which they shall give their Votes; which Day shall be the same throughout the United States.

No Person except a natural born Citizen, or a Citizen of the United States, at the time of the Adoption of this Constitution, shall be eligible to the Office of President; neither shall any Person be eligible to that Office who shall not have attained to the Age of thirty five Years, and been fourteen Years a Resident within the United States.

In Case of the Removal of the President from Office, or of his Death, Resignation, or Inability to Discharge the Powers and Duties of the said Office, the same shall devolve on the Vice President, and the Congress may by Law provide for the Case of Removal, Death, Resignation or Inability, both of the President and Vice President, declaring what Officer shall then act as President, and such Officer shall act accordingly, until the Disability be removed, or a President shall be elected.

The President shall, at stated Times, receive for his Services, a Compensation, which shall neither be encreased nor diminished during the Period for which he shall have been elected, and he shall not receive within that Period any other Emolument from the United States, or any of them.

Before he enter on the Execution of his Office, he shall take the following Oath or Affirmation: "I do solemnly swear (or affirm) that I will faithfully execute the Office of President of the United States, and will to the best of my Ability, preserve, protect and defend the Constitution of the United States."

SECTION 2. The President shall be Commander in Chief of the Army and Navy of the United States, and of the Militia of the several States, when called into the actual Service of the United States; he may require the Opinion, in writing, of the principal Officer in each of the executive Departments, upon any Subject relating to the Duties of their respective Offices, and he shall have Power to grant Reprieves and Pardons for Offences against the United States, except in Cases of Impeachment.

He shall have Power, by and with the Advice and Consent of the Senate, to make Treaties, provided two thirds of the Senators present concur; and he shall nominate, and by and with the Advice and Consent of the Senate, shall appoint Ambassadors, other public Ministers and Consuls, Judges of the Supreme Court, and all other Officers of the United States, whose Appointments are not herein otherwise provided for, and which shall be established by Law; but the Congress may by Law vest the Appointment of such inferior Officers, as they think proper, in the President alone, in the Courts of Law, or in the Heads of Departments.

The President shall have Power to fill up all Vacancies that may happen during the Recess of the Senate, by granting Commissions which shall expire at the End of their next Session.

Ohio Constitution Comparison

President as commander-in-chief of militia, Ohio Const. art. III, § 10.
Subordination of military to civilian authority, Ohio Const. art. I, § 4.

SECTION 3. He shall from time to time give to the Congress Information of the State of the Union, and recommend to their Consideration such Measures as he shall judge necessary and expedient; he may, on extraordinary Occasions, convene both Houses, or either of them, and in Cases of Disagreement between them, with Respect to the Time of Adjournment, he may adjourn them to such Time as he shall think proper; he shall receive Ambassadors and other public Ministers; he shall take Care that the Laws be faithfully executed, and shall Commission all the Officers of the United States.

SECTION 4. The President, Vice President and all civil Officers of the United States, shall be removed from Office on Impeachment for, and Conviction of, Treason, Bribery, or other high Crimes and Misdemeanors.

ARTICLE III

SECTION 1. The judicial Power of the United States, shall be vested in one Supreme Court, and in such inferior Courts as the Congress may from time to time ordain and establish. The Judges, both of the supreme and inferior Courts, shall hold their offices during good Behaviour, and shall, at stated Times, receive for their Services, a Compensation, which shall not be diminished during their Continuance in Office.

SECTION 2. The judicial Power shall extend to all Cases, in Law and Equity, arising under this Constitution, the Laws of the United States, and Treaties made, or which shall be made, under their authority; — to all Cases affecting Ambassadors, other public Ministers and Consuls; — to all Cases of admiralty and maritime Jurisdiction; — to Controversies to which the United States shall be a Party; — to Controversies between two or more States; — between a State and Citizens of another State; — between Citizens of different States; — between Citizens of the same State claiming Lands under Grants of different States, and between a State, or the Citizens thereof, and foreign States, Citizens or Subjects.

In all Cases affecting Ambassadors, other public Ministers and Consuls, and those in which a State shall be Party, the supreme Court shall have original Jurisdiction. In all the other Cases before mentioned, the supreme Court shall have appellate Jurisdiction, both as to Law and Fact, with such Exceptions, and under such Regulations as the Congress shall make.

The trial of all Crimes, except in Cases of Impeachment, shall be by Jury; and such Trial shall be held in the State where the said Crimes shall have been committed; but when not committed within any State, the Trial shall be at such Place or Places as the Congress may by Law have directed.

SECTION 3. Treason against the United States, shall

consist only in levying War against them, or in adhering to their Enemies, giving them Aid and Comfort. No Person shall be convicted of Treason unless on the Testimony of two Witnesses to the same overt Act, or on Confession in open Court.

The Congress shall have Power to declare the Punishment of Treason, but no Attainder of Treason shall work Corruption of Blood, or Forfeiture except during the Life of the Person attainted.

ARTICLE IV

SECTION 1. Full Faith and Credit shall be given in each State to the public Acts, Records, and judicial Proceedings of every other State. And the Congress may by general Laws prescribe the Manner in which such Acts, Records and Proceedings shall be proved, and the Effect thereof.

SECTION 2. The Citizens of each State shall be entitled to all Privileges and Immunities of Citizens in the several States.

A Person charged in any State with Treason, Felony, or other Crime, who shall flee from Justice, and be found in another State, shall on demand of the executive Authority of the State from which he fled, be delivered up, to be removed to the State having Jurisdiction of the Crime.

No Person held to Service or Labour in one State, under the Laws thereof, escaping into another, shall, in Consequence of any Law or Regulation therein, be discharged from such Service or Labour, but shall be delivered up on Claim of the Party to whom such Service or Labour may be due.

Ohio Constitution Comparison

Extradition proceedings, Ohio Const. art. I, § 12.

SECTION 3. New States may be admitted by the Congress into this Union, but no new State shall be formed or erected within the Jurisdiction of any other State; nor any State be formed by the Junction of two or more States, or parts of States, without the Consent of the Legislatures of the States concerned as well as of the Congress.

The Congress shall have Power to dispose of and make all needful Rules and Regulations respecting the Territory or other Property belonging to the United States, and nothing in this Constitution shall be so construed as to Prejudice any Claims of the United States, or of any particular State.

SECTION 4. The United States shall guarantee to every State in this Union a Republican Form of Government, and shall protect each of them against Invasion; and on Application of the Legislature, or of the Executive (when the Legislature cannot be convened) against domestic Violence.

ARTICLE V

The Congress, whenever two thirds of both Houses shall deem it necessary, shall propose Amendments to this Constitution, or, on the Application of the Legislatures of two thirds of the several States, shall call a Convention for proposing Amendments, which, in either Case, shall be valid to all Intents and Purposes, as part of this Constitution, when ratified by the Legislatures of three fourths of the several States, or by Conventions in three fourths thereof, as the one or the other Mode of Ratification may be proposed by the Congress; Provided that no Amendment which may be made prior to the Year One thousand eight hundred and eight shall in any Manner affect the first and fourth Clauses in the Ninth Section of the first Article; and that no State, without its Consent, shall be deprived of its equal Suffrage in the Senate.

ARTICLE VI

All Debts contracted and Engagements entered into, before the Adoption of this Constitution, shall be as valid against the United States under this Constitution, as under the Confederation.

This Constitution, and the Laws of the United States which shall be made in Pursuance thereof; and all Treaties made, or which shall be made, under the Authority of the United States, shall be the supreme Law of the Land; and the Judges in every State shall be bound thereby, any Thing in the Constitution or Laws of any State to the Contrary notwithstanding.

The Senators and Representatives before mentioned, and the Members of the several State Legislatures, and all executive and judicial Officers, both of the United States and of the several States, shall be bound by Oath or Affirmation, to support this Constitution; but no religious Test shall ever be required as a Qualification to any Office or public Trust under the United States.

ARTICLE VII

The Ratification of the Conventions of nine States shall be sufficient for the Establishment of this Constitution between the States so ratifying the Same.

Done in Convention by the Unanimous Consent of the States present the Seventeenth Day of September in the Year of our Lord one thousand seven hundred and Eighty seven and of the Independence of the United States of America the Twelfth. IN WITNESS whereof We have hereunto subscribed our Names.

G. WASHINGTON—Presidt.
and Deputy from Virginia

Attest.—WILLIAM JACKSON, Secretary.

New Hampshire.—John Langdon, Nicholas Gilman.

Massachusetts.—Nathaniel Gorham, Rufus King.

Connecticut.—Wm. Saml. Johnson, Roger Sherman.

New York.—Alexander Hamilton.

New Jersey.—Wil: Livingston, David Brearley, Wm. Paterson, Jona: Dayton.

Pennsylvania.—B. Franklin, Thomas Mifflin, Robt. Morris, Geo. Clymer, Thos. FitzSimons, Jared Ingersoll, James Wilson, Gouv Morris.

Delaware.—Geo: Read, Gunning Bedford Jun, John Dickinson, Richard Bassett, Jaco: Broom.

Maryland.—James McHenry Dan of St Thos. Jenifer, Danl. Carroll.

Virginia.—John Blair—James Madison, Jr.

North Carolina.—Wm. Blount, Richd. Dobbs Spaight, Hu Williamson.

South Carolina.—J. Rutledge, Charles Cotesworth Pinckney, Charles Pinckney, Pierce Butler.

Georgia.—William Few, Abr. Baldwin.

AMENDMENTS TO THE CONSTITUTION OF THE UNITED STATES

Articles in addition to, and amendments of the Constitution of the United States of America, proposed by Congress, and ratified by the Legislatures of the several States, pursuant to the fifth article of the original Constitution.

AMENDMENT I

Congress shall make no law respecting an establishment of religion, or prohibiting the free exercise thereof; or abridging the freedom of speech, or of the press; or the right of the people peaceably to assemble, and to petition the Government for a redress of grievances.

(Effective 1791)

Comparative Legislation

Freedom of speech, press, Ohio Const. art. I, § 11.
Rights of assembly petition, Ohio Const. art. I, § 3.

AMENDMENT II

A well regulated Militia, being necessary to the security of a free state, the right of the people to keep and bear Arms, shall not be infringed.

(Effective 1791)

Comparative Legislation

Ohio Const. art. I, § 4.

AMENDMENT III

No Soldier shall, in time of peace be quartered in any house, without the consent of the Owner, nor in time of war, but in a manner to be prescribed by law.

(Effective 1791)

Comparative Legislation

Ohio Const. art. I, § 13.

AMENDMENT IV

The right of the people to be secure in their persons, houses, papers, and effects, against unreasonable searches and seizures, shall not be violated, and no Warrants shall issue, but upon probable cause, supported by Oath or affirmation, and particularly describing the place to be searched, and the persons or things to be seized.

(Effective 1791)

Comparative Legislation

Ohio Const. art. I, § 14.

AMENDMENT V

No person shall be held to answer for a capital, or otherwise infamous crime, unless on a presentment or indictment of a Grand Jury, except in cases arising in the land or naval forces, or in the Militia, when in actual service in time of War or public danger; nor shall any person be subject for the same offence to be twice put in jeopardy of life or limb; nor shall be compelled in any criminal case to be a witness against himself, nor be deprived of life, liberty, or property, without due process of law; nor shall private property be taken for public use, without just compensation.

(Effective 1791)

Comparative Legislation

Compensation for taking for public use, Ohio Const. art. I, § 19.
Double jeopardy, Ohio Const. art. I, § 10.
Due process, art. I, § 16.
Indictment by grand jury, Ohio Const. art. I, § 10.
Self-incrimination, Ohio Const. art. I, § 10.

AMENDMENT VI

In all criminal prosecutions, the accused shall enjoy the right to a speedy and public trial, by an impartial jury of the State and district wherein the crime shall have been committed, which district shall have been previously ascertained by law, and to be informed of the nature and cause of the accusation; to be confronted with the witnesses against him; to have compulsory process for obtaining witnesses in his favor, and to have the Assistance of Counsel for his defence.

(Effective 1791)

Comparative Legislation

Compulsory process, Ohio Const. art. I, § 10.
Confronting witnesses, Ohio Const. art. I, § 10.
Nature of charge, Ohio Const. art. I, § 10.
Right to counsel, Ohio Const. art. I, § 10.
Right to trial by jury, Ohio Const. art. I, § 5.
Speedy and public trial by jury, Ohio Const. art. I, § 10.

AMENDMENT VII

In Suits at common law, where the value in controversy shall exceed twenty dollars, the right of trial by jury shall be preserved, and no fact tried by a jury, shall be otherwise reexamined in any Court of the United States, than according to the rules of the common law.

(Effective 1791)

Comparative Legislation

Ohio Const. art. I, § 5.

AMENDMENT VIII

Excessive bail shall not be required, nor excessive fines imposed, nor cruel and unusual punishments inflicted.

(Effective 1791)

Comparative Legislation

Ohio Const. art. I, § 9.

AMENDMENT IX

The enumeration in the Constitution, of certain

rights, shall not be construed to deny or disparage others retained by the people.
(Effective 1791)

Comparative Legislation

Ohio Const art. I, § 20.

AMENDMENT X

The powers not delegated to the United States by the Constitution, nor prohibited by it to the States, are reserved to the States respectively, or to the people.
(Effective 1791)

Comparative Legislation

Ohio Const. art. I, § 20.

AMENDMENT XI

The Judicial power of the United States shall not be construed to extend to any suit in law or equity, commenced or prosecuted against one of the United States by Citizens of another State, or by Citizens or Subjects of any Foreign State.
(Effective 1798)

AMENDMENT XII

The Electors shall meet in their respective states and vote by ballot for President and Vice President, one of whom, at least, shall not be an inhabitant of the same state with themselves; they shall name in their ballots the person voted for as President, and in distinct ballots the person voted for as Vice President, and they shall make distinct lists of all persons voted for as President, and of all persons voted for as Vice President, and of the number of votes for each, which lists they shall sign and certify, and transmit sealed to the seat of the government of the United States, directed to the President of the Senate;— The President of the Senate shall, in the presence of the Senate and House of Representatives; open all the certificates and the votes shall then be counted; — The person having the greatest number of votes for President, shall be the President, if such number be a majority of the whole number of Electors appointed; and if no person have such majority, then from the persons having the highest numbers not exceeding three on the list of those voted for as President, the House of Representatives shall choose immediately, by ballot, the President. But in choosing the President, the votes shall be taken by states, the representation from each state having one vote; a quorum for this purpose shall consist of a member or members from two-thirds of the states, and a majority of all the states shall be necessary to a choice. And if the House of Representatives shall not choose a President whenever the right of choice shall devolve upon them, before the fourth day of March next following, then the Vice President shall act as President, as in the case of the death or other constitutional disability of the President. — The person having the greatest number of votes as Vice President, shall be the Vice President, if such number be a majority of the whole number of Electors appointed, and if no person have a majority, then from the two highest numbers on the list, the Senate shall choose the Vice President; a quorum for the purpose shall consist of two-thirds of the whole number of Senators, and a majority of the whole number shall be necessary to a choice. But no person constitutionally ineligible to the office of President shall be eligible to that of Vice President of the United States.
(Effective 1804)

AMENDMENT XIII

SECTION 1. Neither slavery nor involuntary servitude, except as a punishment for crime whereof the party shall have been duly convicted, shall exist within the United States, or any place subject to their jurisdiction.

SECTION 2. Congress shall have power to enforce this article by appropriate legislation.
(Effective 1865)

Comparative Legislation

Ohio Const. art. I, § 6.

AMENDMENT XIV

SECTION 1. All persons born or naturalized in the United States, and subject to the jurisdiction thereof, are citizens of the United States and of the State wherein they reside. No State shall make or enforce any law which shall abridge the privileges or immunities of citizens of the United States; nor shall any State deprive any person of life, liberty, or property, without due process of law; nor deny to any person within its jurisdiction the equal protection of the laws.

SECTION 2. Representatives shall be apportioned among the several States according to their respective numbers, counting the whole number of persons in each State, excluding Indians not taxed. But when the right to vote at any election for the choice of electors for President and Vice President of the United States, Representatives in Congress, the Executive and Judicial officers of a State, or the members of the Legislature thereof, is denied to any of the male inhabitants of such State, being twenty-one years of age, and citizens of the United States, or in any way abridged, except for participation in rebellion, or other crime, the basis of representation therein shall be reduced in the proportion which the number of such male citizens shall bear to the whole number of male citizens twenty-one years of age in such State.

SECTION 3. No person shall be a Senator or Representative in Congress, or elector of President and Vice President, or hold any office, civil or military, under the United States, or under any State, who, having previously taken an oath, as a member of Congress, or as an officer of the United States, or as a member of any State legislature, or as an executive or judicial officer of any State, to support the Constitution of the United States, shall have engaged in insurrection or rebellion against the same, or given aid or comfort to the enemies thereof. But Congress may by a vote of two-thirds of each House, remove such disability.

Section 4. The validity of the public debt of the United States, authorized by law, including debts incurred for payment of pensions and bounties for services in suppressing insurrection or rebellion, shall not be questioned. But neither the United States nor any State shall assume or pay any debt or obligation incurred in aid of insurrection or rebellion against the United States, or any claim for the loss or emancipation of any slave; but all such debts, obligations and claims shall be held illegal and void.

Section 5. The Congress shall have power to enforce, by appropriate legislation, the provisions of this article.

(Effective 1868)

Comparative Legislation

Due process, Ohio Const. art. I, § 16.
Equal protection, Ohio Const. art. I, § 2.

AMENDMENT XV

Section 1. The right of citizens of the United States to vote shall not be denied or abridged by the United States or by any State on account of race, color, or previous condition of servitude.

Section 2. The Congress shall have power to enforce this article by appropriate legislation.

(Effective 1870)

AMENDMENT XVI

The Congress shall have power to lay and collect taxes on incomes, from whatever source derived, without apportionment among the several States, and without regard to any census or enumeration.

(Effective 1913)

Comparative Legislation

Taxation, Ohio Const. art. XII, §§ 3, 4, 5, 9.

AMENDMENT XVII

The Senate of the United States shall be composed of two Senators from each State, elected by the people thereof, for six years; and each Senator shall have one vote. The electors in each State shall have the qualifications requisite for electors of the most numerous branch of the State legislatures.

When vacancies happen in the representation of any State in the Senate, the executive authority of such State shall issue writs of election to fill such vacancies: *Provided,* That the legislature of any State may empower the executive thereof to make temporary appointments until the people fill the vacancies by election as the legislature may direct.

This amendment shall not be so construed as to affect the election or term of any Senator chosen before it becomes valid as part of the Constitution.

(Effective 1913)

Comparative Legislation

Vacancies, Ohio Const. art. II, § 11.

AMENDMENT XVIII

Section 1. After one year from the ratification of this article the manufacture, sale, or transportation of intoxicating liquors within, the importation thereof into, or the exportation thereof from the United States and all territory subject to the jurisdiction thereof for beverage purposes is hereby prohibited.

Section 2. The Congress and the several States shall have concurrent power to enforce this article by appropriate legislation.

Section 3. This article shall be inoperative unless it shall have been ratified as an amendment to the Constitution by the legislatures of the several States, as provided in the Constitution, within seven years from the date of the submission hereof to the States by the Congress.

(Effective 1919)

AMENDMENT XIX

The right of citizens of the United States to vote shall not be denied or abridged by the United States or by any State on account of sex.

Congress shall have power to enforce this article by appropriate legislation.

(Effective 1920)

Comparative Legislation

Elective franchise, Ohio Const. art. V, § 1.

AMENDMENT XX

Section 1. The terms of the President and Vice President shall end at noon on the 20th day of January, and the terms of Senators and Representatives at noon on the 3d day of January, of the years in which such terms would have ended if this article had not been ratified; and the terms of their successors shall then begin.

Section 2. The Congress shall assemble at least once in every year, and such meeting shall begin at noon on the 3d day of January, unless they shall by law appoint a different day.

Comparative Legislation

Rules of conduct, Ohio Const. art. II, § 8.

Section 3. If, at the time fixed for the beginning of the term of the President, the President elect shall have died, the Vice President elect shall become President. If a President shall not have been chosen before the time fixed for the beginning of his term, or if the President elect shall have failed to qualify, then the Vice President elect shall act as President until a President shall have qualified; and the Congress may by law provide for the case wherein neither a President elect nor a Vice President elect shall have qualified, declaring who shall then act as President, or the manner in which one who is to act shall be selected, and such person shall act accordingly until a President or Vice President shall have qualified.

SECTION 4. The Congress may by law provide for the case of the death of any of the persons from whom the House of Representatives may choose a President whenever the right of choice shall have devolved upon them, and for the case of the death of any of the persons from whom the Senate may choose a Vice President whenever the right of choice shall have devolved upon them.

SECTION 5. Sections 1 and 2 shall take effect on the 15th day of October following the ratification of this article.

SECTION 6. This article shall be inoperative unless it shall have been ratified as an amendment to the Constitution by the legislatures of three-fourths of the several States within seven years from the date of its submission.
(Effective 1933)

AMENDMENT XXI

SECTION 1. The eighteenth article of amendment to the Constitution of the United States is hereby repealed.

SECTION 2. The transportation or importation into any State, Territory, or possession of the United States for delivery or use therein of intoxicating liquors, in violation of the laws thereof, is hereby prohibited.

SECTION 3. This article shall be inoperative unless it shall have been ratified as an amendment to the Constitution by conventions in the several States, as provided in the Constitution, within seven years from the date of the submission hereof to the States by the Congress.
(Effective 1933)

AMENDMENT XXII

SECTION 1. No person shall be elected to the office of the President more than twice, and no person who has held the office of President, or acted as President, for more than two years of a term to which some other person was elected President shall be elected to the office of the President more than once. But this Article shall not apply to any person holding the office of President when this Article was proposed by the Congress, and shall not prevent any person who may be holding the office of President, or acting as President, during the term within which this Article becomes operative from holding the office of President or acting as President during the remainder of such term.

Comparative Legislation

Executive power, Ohio Const. art. III, § 2.

SECTION 2. This article shall be inoperative unless it shall have been ratified as an amendment to the Constitution by the legislatures of three-fourths of the several States within seven years from the date of its submission to the States by the Congress.
(Effective 1951)

AMENDMENT XXIII

SECTION 1. The District constituting the seat of Government of the United States shall appoint in such manner as the Congress may direct:

A number of electors of President and Vice President equal to the whole number of Senators and Representatives in Congress to which the District would be entitled if it were a State, but in no event more than the least populous State; they shall be in addition to those appointed by the States, but they shall be considered, for the purposes of the election of President and Vice President, to be electors appointed by a State; and they shall meet in the District and perform such duties as provided by the twelfth article of amendment.

SECTION 2. The Congress shall have power to enforce this article by appropriate legislation.
(Effective 1961)

AMENDMENT XXIV

SECTION 1. The right of citizens of the United States to vote in any primary or other election for President or Vice President, for electors for President or Vice President, or for Senator or Representative in Congress, shall not be denied or abridged by the United States or any State by reason of failure to pay any poll tax or other tax.

SECTION 2. The Congress shall have power to enforce this article by appropriate legislation.
(Effective 1964)

Comparative Legislation

Elective franchise, Ohio Const. art. V, § 1.

AMENDMENT XXV

SECTION 1. In case of the removal of the President from office or of his death or resignation, the Vice President shall become President.

SECTION 2. Whenever there is a vacancy in the office of the Vice President, the President shall nominate a Vice President who shall take office upon confirmation by a majority vote of both Houses of Congress.

SECTION 3. Whenever the President transmits to the President pro tempore of the Senate and the Speaker of the House of Representatives his written declaration that he is unable to discharge the powers and duties of his office, and until he transmits to them a written declaration to the contrary, such powers and duties shall be discharged by the Vice President as Acting President.

SECTION 4. Whenever the Vice President and a majority of either the principal officers of the executive departments or of such other body as Congress may by law provide, transmit to the President pro tempore of the Senate and the Speaker of the House of Representatives their written declaration that the President is unable to discharge the powers and duties of his office, the Vice President shall immediately assume the powers and duties of the office as Acting President.

Thereafter, when the President transmits to the President quo tempore of the Senate and the Speaker of the House of Representatives his written declaration that no inability exists, he shall resume the powers and duties of his office unless the Vice President and a majority of either the principal officers of the executive department or of such other body as Congress may by law provide, transmit within four days to the President pro tempore of the Senate and the Speaker of the House of Representatives their written declaration that the President is unable to discharge the powers and duties of his office. Thereupon Congress shall decide the issue, assembling within forty-eight hours for that purpose if not in session. If the Congress, within twenty-one days after receipt of the latter written declaration, or, if Congress is required to assemble, determines by two-thirds vote of both Houses that the President is unable to discharge the powers and duties of his office, the Vice President shall continue to discharge the same as Acting President; otherwise, the President shall resume the powers and duties of his office.

(Effective 1967)

Comparative Legislation

Vacancy, Ohio Const. art. III, § 17.

AMENDMENT XXVI

Section 1. The right of citizens of the United States, who are eighteen years of age or older, to vote shall not be denied or abridged by the United States or by any State on account of age.

Comparative Legislation

Elective franchise, Ohio Const. art. V, § 1.

Section 2. The Congress shall have power to enforce this article by appropriate legislation.

(Effective 1971)

AMENDMENT XXVII

No law, varying the compensation for the services of the Senators and Representatives, shall take effect, until an election of Representatives shall have intervened.

(Proposed 1789, Adopted 1992)

CONSTITUTION OF THE STATE OF OHIO
ADOPTED MARCH 10, 1851

SELECTED PROVISIONS INCLUDING LATEST AMENDMENTS EFFECTIVE MARCH 20, 1996

ARTICLE I: BILL OF RIGHTS

§ 1 Right to freedom and protection of property.

All men are, by nature, free and independent, and have certain inalienable rights, among which are those of enjoying and defending life and liberty, acquiring, possessing, and protecting property, and seeking and obtaining happiness and safety.

§ 2 Right to alter, reform, or abolish government, and repeal special privileges.

All political power is inherent in the people. Government is instituted for their equal protection and benefit, and they have the right to alter, reform, or abolish the same, whenever they may deem it necessary; and no special privileges or immunities shall ever be granted, that may not be altered, revoked, or repealed by the general assembly.

§ 3 Right to assemble together.

The people have the right to assemble together, in a peaceable manner, to consult for their common good; to instruct their representatives; and to petition the general assembly for the redress of grievances.

§ 4 Bearing arms; standing armies; subordination of military power.

The people have the right to bear arms for their defense and security; but standing armies, in time of peace, are dangerous to liberty, and shall not be kept up; and the military shall be in strict subordination to the civil power.

§ 5 Trial by jury; reform in civil jury system.

The right of trial by jury shall be inviolate, except that, in civil cases, laws may be passed to authorize the rendering of a verdict by the concurrence of not less than three-fourths of the jury.

(As amended September 3, 1912.)

§ 6 Slavery and involuntary servitude.

There shall be no slavery in this state; nor involuntary servitude, unless for the punishment of crime.

§ 7 Rights of conscience; education; necessity of religion and knowledge.

All men have a natural and indefeasible right to worship Almighty God according to the dictates of their own conscience. No person shall be compelled to attend, erect, or support any place of worship, or maintain any form of worship, against his consent; and no preference shall be given, by law, to any religious society; nor shall interference with the rights of conscience be permitted. No religious test shall be required, as a qualification for office, nor shall any person be incompetent to be a witness on account of his religious belief; but nothing herein shall be construed to dispense with oaths and affirmations. Religion, morality, and knowledge, however, being essential to good government, it shall be the duty of the general assembly to pass suitable laws to protect every religious denomination in the peaceable enjoyment of its own mode of public worship, and to encourage schools and the means of instruction.

§ 8 Writ of habeas corpus.

The privilege of the writ of habeas corpus shall not be suspended, unless, in cases of rebellion or invasion, the public safety require it.

§ 9 Bailable offenses; of bail, fine, and punishment.

All persons shall be bailable by sufficient sureties, except for capital offenses where the proof is evident or the presumption great. Excessive bail shall not be required; nor excessive fines imposed; nor cruel and unusual punishments inflicted.

§ 10 Trial of accused persons and their rights; depositions by state and comment on failure to testify in criminal cases.

Except in cases of impeachment, cases arising in the army and navy, or in the militia when in actual service in time of war or public danger, and cases involving offenses for which the penalty provided is less than imprisonment in the penitentiary, no person shall be held to answer for a capital, or otherwise infamous, crime, unless on presentment or indictment of a grand jury; and the number of persons necessary to constitute such grand jury and the number thereof necessary to concur in finding such indictment shall be determined by law. In any trial, in any court, the party accused shall be allowed to appear and defend in person and with counsel; to demand the nature and cause of the accusation against him, and to have a copy thereof; to meet the witnesses face to face, and to have compulsory process to procure the attendance of witnesses in his behalf, and a speedy public trial by an impartial jury of the county in which the offense is alleged to have been committed; but provision may be made by law for the taking of the deposition by the accused or by the state, to be used for or against the accused, of any witness whose attendance can not be had at the trial, always securing to the accused means and the opportunity to be present in person and with counsel at the taking of such deposition, and to examine the witness face to face as fully and in the same manner as if in court. No person shall be compelled, in any criminal case, to be a witness against himself; but his failure to testify may be considered by the court and jury and may be made the subject of comment by counsel. No person shall be twice put in jeopardy for the same offense.

(As amended September 1, 1912.)

§ 10a Rights of victims of crime.

Victims of criminal offenses shall be accorded fairness, dignity, and respect in the criminal justice process, and, as the general assembly shall define and provide by law, shall be accorded rights to reasonable and appropriate notice, information, access, and protection and to a meaningful role in the criminal justice process. This section does not confer upon any person a right to appeal or modify any decision in a criminal proceeding, does not abridge any other right guaranteed by the Constitution of the United States or this constitution, and does not create any cause of action for compensation or damages against the state, any political subdivision of the state, any officer, employee, or agent of the state or of any political subdivision, or any officer of the court.

(Adopted November 8, 1994)

§ 11 Freedom of speech and of the press; libel.

Every citizen may freely speak, write, and publish his sentiments on all subjects, being responsible for the abuse of the right; and no law shall be passed to restrain or abridge the liberty of speech, or of the press. In all criminal prosecutions for libel, the truth may be given in evidence to the jury, and if it shall appear to the jury, that the matter charged as libelous is true, and was published with good motives, and for justifiable ends, the party shall be acquitted.

§ 12 Transportation, etc., for crime.

No person shall be transported out of the state, for any offense committed within the same; and no conviction shall work corruption of blood, or forfeiture of estate.

§ 13 Quartering of troops.

No soldier shall, in time of peace, be quartered in any house, without the consent of the owner; nor, in time of war, except in the manner prescribed by law.

§ 14 Search warrants and general warrants.

The right of the people to be secure in their persons, houses, papers, and possessions, against unreasonable searches and seizures shall not be violated; and no warrant shall issue, but upon probable cause, supported by oath or affirmation, particularly describing the place to be searched and the person and things to be seized.

§ 15 No imprisonment for debt.

No person shall be imprisoned for debt in any civil action, on mesne or final process, unless in cases of fraud.

§ 16 Redress in courts.

All courts shall be open, and every person, for an injury done him in his land, goods, person, or reputation, shall have remedy by due course of law, and shall have justice administered without denial or delay.

[Suits against the state.] Suits may be brought against the state, in such courts and in such manner, as may be provided by law.

§ 17 Hereditary privileges, etc.

No hereditary emoluments, honors, or privileges, shall ever be granted or conferred by this state.

§ 18 Suspension of laws.

No power of suspending laws shall ever be exercised, except by the general assembly.

§ 19 Inviolability of private property.

Private property shall ever be held inviolate, but subservient to the public welfare. When taken in time of war or other public exigency, imperatively requiring its immediate seizure or for the purpose of making or repairing roads, which shall be open to the public, without charge, a compensation shall be made to the owner, in money, and in all other cases, where private property shall be taken for public use, a compensation therefor shall first be made in money, or first secured by a deposit of money; and such compensation shall be assessed by a jury, without deduction for benefits to any property of the owner.

§ 19a Damage for wrongful death.

The amount of damages recoverable by civil action in the courts for death caused by the wrongful act, neglect, or default of another, shall not be limited by law.

§ 20 Powers reserved to the people.

This enumeration of rights shall not be construed to impair or deny others retained by the people; and all powers, not herein delegated, remain with the people.

ARTICLE II: LEGISLATIVE

§ 39 Regulating expert testimony in criminal trials.

Laws may be passed for the regulation of the use of expert witnesses and expert testimony in criminal trials and proceedings.

(Adopted September 3, 1912.)

ARTICLE III: EXECUTIVE

§ 11 May grant reprieves, commutations, and pardons.

He shall have the power, after conviction, to grant reprieves, commutations, and pardons, for all crimes and offenses, except treason and cases of impeachment, upon such conditions as he may think proper; subject, however, to such regulations, as to the manner of applying for pardons, as may be prescribed by law. Upon conviction for treason, he may suspend the execution of the sentence, and report the case to the general assembly, at its next meeting, when the general assembly shall either pardon, commute the sentence, direct its execution, or grant a further reprieve. He shall communicate to the general assembly, at every regular session, each case of reprieve, commutation, or pardon granted, stating the name and crime of the convict, the sentence, its date, and the date of the commutation, pardon, or reprieve, with his reason therefor.

ARTICLE IV: JUDICIAL

§ 1 In whom judicial power vested.

The judicial power of the state is vested in a supreme court, courts of appeals, courts of common pleas and divisions thereof, and such other courts inferior to the supreme court as may from time to time be established by law.

(Amended May 7, 1968; Nov. 6, 1973; SJR No. 30.)

§ 2 The supreme court.

(A) The supreme court shall, until otherwise provided by law, consist of seven judges, who shall be known as the chief justice and justices. In case of the absence or disability of the chief justice, the judge having the period of longest total service upon the court shall be the acting chief justice. If any member of the court shall be unable, by reason of illness, disability or disqualification, to hear, consider and decide a cause or causes, the chief justice or the acting chief justice may direct any judge of any court of appeals to sit with the judges of the supreme court in the place and stead of the absent judge. A majority of the supreme court shall be necessary to constitute a quorum or to render a judgment.

(B)(1) The supreme court shall have original jurisdiction in the following:
(a) Quo warranto;
(b) Mandamus;
(c) Habeas corpus;
(d) Prohibition;
(e) Procedendo;
(f) In any cause on review as may be necessary to its complete determination;
(g) Admission to the practice of law, the discipline of persons so admitted, and all other matters relating to the practice of law.

(2) The supreme court shall have appellate jurisdiction as follows:
(a) In appeals from the courts of appeals as a matter of right in the following:
(i) Cases originating in the courts of appeals;
(ii) Cases involving questions arising under the constitution of the United States or of this state.
(b) In appeals from the courts of appeals in cases of felony on leave first obtained,
(c) In direct appeals from the courts of common pleas or other courts of record inferior to the court of appeals as a matter of right in cases in which the death penalty has been imposed;
(d) Such revisory jurisdiction of the proceedings of administrative officers or agencies as may be conferred by law;
(e) In cases of public or great general interest, the supreme court may direct any court of appeals to certify its record to the supreme court, and may review and affirm, modify, or reverse the judgment of the court of appeals;
(f) The supreme court shall review and affirm, modify, or reverse the judgment in any case certified by any court of appeals pursuant to section 3(B)(4) of this article.

(3) No law shall be passed or rule made whereby any

person shall be prevented from invoking the original jurisdiction of the supreme court.

(C) The decisions in all cases in the supreme court shall be reported, together with the reasons therefor.

(Amended May 7, 1968; November 8, 1994.)

§ 3 Court of appeals.

(A) The state shall be divided by law into compact appellate districts in each of which there shall be a court of appeals consisting of three judges. Laws may be passed increasing the number of judges in any district wherein the volume of business may require such additional judge or judges. In districts having additional judges, three judges shall participate in the hearing and disposition of each case. The court shall hold sessions in each county of the district as the necessity arises. The county commissioners of each county shall provide a proper and convenient place for the court of appeals to hold court.

(B)(1) The courts of appeals shall have original jurisdiction in the following:

(a) Quo warranto;
(b) Mandamus;
(c) Habeas corpus;
(d) Prohibition;
(e) Procedendo;
(f) In any cause on review as may be necessary to its complete determination.

(2) Courts of appeals shall have such jurisdiction as may be provided by law to review and affirm, modify, or reverse judgments or final orders of the courts of record inferior to the court of appeals within the district, except that courts of appeals shall not have jurisdiction to review on direct appeal a judgment that imposes a sentence of death. Courts of appeals shall have such appellate jurisdiction as may be provided by law to review and affirm, modify, or reverse final orders or actions of administrative officers or agencies.

(3) A majority of the judges hearing the cause shall be necessary to render a judgment. Judgments of the courts of appeals are final except as provided in section 2(B)(2) of this article. No judgment resulting from a trial by jury shall be reversed on the weight of the evidence except by the concurrence of all three judges hearing the cause.

(4) Whenever the judges of a court of appeals find that a judgment upon which they have agreed is in conflict with a judgment pronounced upon the same question by any other court of appeals of the state, the judges shall certify the record of the case to the supreme court for review and final determination.

(C) Laws may be passed providing for the reporting of cases in the courts of appeals.

(Adopted May 7, 1968. Former § 3 repealed and analogous provisions reenacted as § 4; Amended November 8, 1994.)

§ 4 Common pleas court.

(A) There shall be a court of common pleas and such divisions thereof as may be established by law serving each county of the state. Any judge of a court of common pleas or a division thereof may temporarily hold court in any county. In the interests of the fair, impartial, speedy, and sure administration of justice, each county shall have one or more resident judges, or two or more counties may be combined into districts having one or more judges resident in the district and serving the common pleas courts of all counties in the district, as may be provided by law. Judges serving a district shall sit in each county in the district as the business of the court requires. In counties or districts having more than one judge of the court of common pleas, the judges shall select one of their number to act as presiding judge, to serve at their pleasure. If the judges are unable because of equal division of the vote to make such selection, the judge having the longest total service on the court of common pleas shall serve as presiding judge until selection is made by vote. The presiding judge shall have such duties and exercise such powers as are prescribed by rule of the supreme court.

(B) The courts of common pleas and divisions thereof shall have such original jurisdiction over all justiciable matters and such powers of review of proceedings of administrative officers and agencies as may be provided by law.

(C) Unless otherwise provided by law, there shall be a probate division and such other divisions of the courts of common pleas as may be provided by law. Judges shall be elected specifically to such probate division and to such other divisions. The judges of the probate division shall be empowered to employ and control the clerks, employees, deputies, and referees of such probate division of the common pleas courts.

(Amended, effective Nov. 6, 1973; SJR No. 30. Adopted May 7, 1968. Former § 4 repealed.)

§ 5 Additional powers of supreme court; supervision; rule making.

(A)(1) In addition to all other powers vested by this article in the supreme court, the supreme court shall have general superintendence over all courts in the state. Such general superintending power shall be exercised by the chief justice in accordance with rules promulgated by the supreme court.

(2) The supreme court shall appoint an administrative director who shall assist the chief justice and who shall serve at the pleasure of the court. The compensation and duties of the administrative director shall be determined by the court.

(3) The chief justice or acting chief justice, as necessity arises, shall assign any judge of a court of common pleas or a division thereof temporarily to sit or hold court on any other court of common pleas or division thereof or any court of appeals or shall assign any judge

of a court of appeals temporarily to sit or hold court on any other court of appeals or any court of common pleas or division thereof and upon such assignment said judge shall serve in such assigned capacity until the termination of the assignment. Rules may be adopted to provide for the temporary assignment of judges to sit and hold court in any court established by law.

(B) The supreme court shall prescribe rules governing practice and procedure in all courts of the state, which rules shall not abridge, enlarge, or modify any substantive right. Proposed rules shall be filed by the court, not later than the fifteenth day of January, with the clerk of each house of the general assembly during a regular session thereof, and amendments to any such proposed rules may be so filed not later than the first day of May in that session. Such rules shall take effect on the following first day of July, unless prior to such day the general assembly adopts a concurrent resolution of disapproval. All laws in conflict with such rules shall be of no further force or effect after such rules have taken effect.

Courts may adopt additional rules concerning local practice in their respective courts which are not inconsistent with the rules promulgated by the supreme court. The supreme court may make rules to require uniform record keeping for all courts of the state, and shall make rules governing the admission to the practice of law and discipline of person so admitted.

(C) The chief justice of the supreme court or any judge of that court designated by him shall pass upon the disqualification of any judge of the courts of appeals or courts of common pleas or division thereof. Rules may be adopted to provide for the hearing of disqualification matters involving judges of courts established by law.

(Amended, effective Nov. 6, 1973; SJR No. 30. Adopted May 7, 1968.)

§ 20 Style of process, prosecution, and indictment.

The style of all process shall be, "The State of Ohio;" all prosecutions shall be carried on, in the name, and by the authority, of the state of Ohio; and all indictments shall conclude, "against the peace and dignity of the state of Ohio."

ARTICLE V: ELECTIVE FRANCHISE

§ 3 [Repealed, June 8, 1976.]

This section referred to the privilege from arrest of voters during elections.

§ 4 Forfeiture of elective franchise.

The General Assembly shall have power to exclude from the privilege of voting, or of being eligible to office, any person convicted of a felony.

(Amended, effective June 8, 1976; SJR No. 16.)

ARTICLE XVIII: MUNICIPAL CORPORATIONS

§ 3 Powers.

Municipalities shall have authority to exercise all powers of local self-government and to adopt and enforce within their limits such local police, sanitary and other similar regulations, as are not in conflict with general laws.

(Adopted September 3, 1912.)

§ 7 Home rule.

Any municipality may frame and adopt or amend a charter for its government and may, subject to the provisions of section 3 of this article, exercise thereunder all powers of local self-government.

(Adopted September 3, 1912.)

TIME TABLE IN CRIMINAL CASES
(Alphabetical Order)

ACQUITTAL — Crim. R. 29
Motion for Judgment of

An oral or written motion for judgment of acquittal is offered by the Defendant or by the court on its own motion:

a. *When* the State rests its case in chief.
b. *When* the Defense rests.
c. *When* all the evidence has been received.
d. After or renewed within *14* days following a jury's discharge *or* within such further time as the Court may fix during the 14 day period.

The Court *must* rule immediately on the motion offered at the close of the State's case.

The Court *may* reserve ruling on the motion offered at other authorized times and decide the same before or after submission of the case to the jury, after a guilty verdict or after a jury standing in disagreement is discharged.

ALIBI — Crim. R. 12.1
Written Notice Of

Shall be filed and served upon the Prosecuting Attorney *no later than 7 days before trial.*

APPEAL (Listed in case progression order)
Notice of Appeal—App. R. 4(B)

Defendant's notice of appeal shall be filed with the Trial Court Clerk within *30 days* of the date of the entry of the judgment or order appealed from. Where a Motion in Arrest of Judgment or a Motion for New Trial, other than on the grounds of newly discovered evidence is filed, the 30 day period commences to run from the journalization of the order denying the motion. A Motion for New Trial on the grounds of newly discovered evidence *does not extend* the 30 day period.

The Prosecution's Notice of Appeal in all cases except under Crim. R. 12(J) (a Trial Court order granting a Motion to Suppress Evidence) and Juv. R. 22(F) (a Juvenile Court order granting a Motion to Suppress Evidence) shall be filed *within 30 days* of the date of entry of the judgment or order appealed from. Appeal by the Prosecution from an order granting a Motion to Suppress Evidence is commenced by the filing of the Notice of Appeal with the Trial Court Clerk *within 7 days* from the date of entry of such order.

Motion For Leave To Appeal—App. R. 5.

After expiration of the 30-day period for filing a Notice of Appeal as of right, the Defendant may appeal only by leave of the court to which the appeal is taken. A Notice of Appeal must be filed concurrently with the Motion and a copy of the Notice must be filed in the Trial Court, also.

The prosecution may, *within 30 days* from the filing of the Motion for Leave to Appeal, file affidavits, parts of the record and brief or memorandum of law to refute the claims of the Defendant.

The Prosecution must file its Motion for Leave to Appeal *within 30 days* from the entry of the judgment or order appealed from.

The Defendant may *within 30 days thereafter* file affidavits, parts of the record, and a brief or memorandum of law to refute the claims of the Prosecution.

Application For Release On Bail—App. R. 8(B)

Application for release on bail and for suspension of execution of sentence after conviction shall be made *in the first instance* in the Trial Court.

Transcript Of Proceedings—App. R. 9(B)

At the time of filing the notice of appeal, Appellant shall order from the Court Reporter a complete or partial transcript of proceedings. Where appellant orders only a partial transcript of proceedings, he shall, *with his notice of appeal,* file and serve on appellee a description of the parts ordered and a statement of his assignments of error. Appellee, then, *within 10 days after service* of such statement, may serve on appellant a designation of additional parts to be included in the transcript of proceedings.

If the Appellant refuses or fails within *ten days after service* of the Appellee's designation to order such parts, the Appellee *within five days thereafter* shall either order the parts in writing or apply to the Court of Appeals for an order requiring Appellant to do so.

At the time of ordering, a party shall arrange for the payment to the reporter of the cost of the transcript.

Objections Or Amendments To Statement Of The Evidence Where A Transcript Of Proceedings Is Not Available—App. R. 9(C)

Objections or amendments shall be filed by appellee *within 10 days* after he is served with a copy of statement of the evidence.

Correction Or Modification Of Trial Court Record—App. R. 9(E)

Either before or after the record is transmitted to the Court of Appeals, the parties, by stipulation, or the trial court, may direct that an omission or misstatement be corrected.

Transmission Of The Record To Court of Appeals—App. R. 10

The record shall be transmitted to the Court of Appeals when the record is complete for purposes of the appeal, or when *40 days*, or *20 days* in an accelerated calendar case *have elapsed after the filing of the Notice of Appeal* and no extension has been granted. Where leave to appeal must be obtained, all time limits run from the filing of the journal entry granting leave.

Trial Court Extension—App. R. 10(C)

The Trial Court may extend the time for transmitting the record, provided the request for extension is filed within the *time originally prescribed* or within an *extension granted previously* except as provided by a local rule.

When The Record Is Deemed Complete—App. R. 10(B)

(1) When the transcript of proceedings is filed with the Clerk of the Trial Court.

(2) When a statement of the evidence or proceedings, pursuant to Rule 9(C), is settled and approved by the Trial Court, and filed with the Clerk of the Trial Court.

(3) When an agreed statement in lieu of the record, pursuant to Rule 9(D), is approved by the Trial Court, and filed with the Clerk of the Trial Court.

(4) Where Appellant, pursuant to Rule 9(B), designates that no part of the transcript of proceedings is to be included in the record or that no transcript is necessary for appeal, after the expiration of ten days following service of such designation upon Appellee, unless Appellee has within such time filed a designation of additional parts of the transcript to be included in the record.

(5) When forty days have elapsed after filing of the last Notice of Appeal, in an accelerated calendar case and there is no extension of time for transmission of the record.

(7) Where the Appellant fails to file either the docketing statement or the statement required by App. R. 9(B), ten days after filing the Notice of Appeal.

When Transmission Is Effected—App. R. 10(B)

Transmission is effected when the Trial Court Clerk mails or otherwise forwards the records to the Clerk of the Court of Appeals. The Trial Court Clerk shall note the date of transmission on the face of the record and shall note the transmission on the appearance docket.

Notice To Parties When Record Filed—App. R. 11(B)

The Clerk of the Court of Appeals shall *immediately* give notice to all parties of the date on which the trial court record was filed in the Court of Appeals.

Response By Appellant To Motion To Dismiss For Failure To File, Within Time, The Trial Court Record In The Court of Appeals—App. R. 11(C)

Appellant *may* respond to such motion within *10 days of service.*

Service By Mail—App. R. 13(C)

Service by mail is complete on mailing.

Additional Time After Service By Mail—App. R. 14(C)

Where service by mail is permitted and used, *3 days* shall be added to any prescribed period.

Computing Time—App. R. 14(A)

The day of the act, event or default from which the designated period of time begins to run *shall not be included* but the *last day* shall be included unless it is a Saturday, Sunday, or legal holiday, in which event, the period runs until the end of the next day which is not a Saturday, Sunday or legal holiday. But, where the time allowed or prescribed *is less than 7 days,* Saturdays, Sundays, and legal holidays *are not* included.

Enlargement Or Reduction Of Time—App. R. 14(B)

Except for the filing of a Notice of Appeal, the Court of Appeals may enlarge or reduce the prescribed time or permit an act to be done *after the expiration of such time.* The court may not enlarge or reduce the time for filing a notice of appeal or motion to certify pursuant to App. R. 25. Enlargement of time to file an application to reconsider pursuant to App. R. 26(A) shall not be granted except on a showing of extraordinary circumstances

Serving And Filing Briefs—App. R. 18

1. *Appellant shall* serve and file his Brief *within 20 days after* the date on which the Clerk has mailed the notice [required by Rule 11(B)] that the record has been filed. For accelerated calendar cases, *within 15 days* thereafter—App. R. 11.1.
2. *Appellee shall* serve and file his Brief *within 20 days after* service of the Brief of Appellant. For accelerated calendar cases, *within 15 days* thereafter—App. R. 11.1.
3. *Appellant may* serve and file a Reply Brief *within 10 days after* service of the Brief of Appellee. For accelerated calendar cases, Reply Briefs are prohibited unless ordered under order by the Court—App. R. 11.1.

NOTE: Counsel should be aware of App. R. 18(C)—Consequence of failure to file briefs.

Brief Of Amicus Curiae—App. R. 17

A Brief of an Amicus Curiae, unless all parties otherwise consent, shall be filed *within the time allowed* the party whose position the Brief supports, unless the Court extends such time and fixes the period when an opposing party may answer.

Argument Of Case—App. R. 21(B)

Each side is allowed 30 minutes for argument which time can be extended or reduced as the Court may order.

Argument On Motions—App. R. 21(G)

Oral argument *will not be heard* upon motions unless ordered by the Court.

Entry Of Judgment—App. R. 22(C)

Within 5 days from the Order, Decree or Judgment, Counsel for the prevailing party shall prepare and submit to opposing Counsel a proper journal entry *and within 5 days after* receipt of such entry, opposing Counsel shall approve or reject the entry and forward the same to Counsel for the prevailing party who shall immediately submit it to the Court.

NOTE: *App. R. 22(D)* authorizes the Court, *sua sponte,* to prepare and file its own Entry of Judgment.

Motion To Certify A Conflict—App. R. 25

A motion to certify a conflict under Article IV, Section 3(B)(4) of the Ohio Constitution shall be made in writing before the judgment or order of the court has been approved by the court and filed by the court with the clerk for journalization or within ten days after the announcement of the court's decision, whichever is the later. The filing of a motion to certify a conflict does not extend the time for filing a notice of appeal.

Parties opposing the motion must answer in writing within ten days after the filing of the motion.

The court of appeals shall rule upon a motion to certify within sixty days of its filing.

Application For Reconsideration—App. R. 26

Application for Reconsideration shall be filed *before* journalization of the Order or Judgment *or within 10 days* after the announcement of the Court's decision, *whichever is the later.* A party opposing the Application shall answer in writing *within 10 days* after the filing of the application. If an application for reconsideration under division (A) is filed with the court of appeals, the application shall be ruled upon within forty-five days of its filing.

Supreme Court Of Ohio, Appeal To

Institution of Appeal From Court of Appeals—Sup. Ct. R. II

To perfect an appeal from a court of appeals to the Supreme Court, other than in a certified conflict case (which is addressed in Sup. Ct. R. IV) the appellant shall file a notice of appeal within 45 days from the entry of the judgment being appealed.

APPEARANCE — Crim. R. 4(E)

One arrested with or without an arrest warrant having first been issued shall be brought before the Court having jurisdiction *without unnecessary delay.* The court shall proceed according to Crim. R. 5.

ARRAIGNMENT — Crim. R. 10(A)

Before being called upon to plead, a defendant shall be given a copy of the indictment, information or complaint.

ARREST — Crim. R. 4(E)(1)

With Arrest Warrant

A defendant shall be brought before the Court which issued the warrant, or before a court of record where the arrest takes place in another county *without unnecessary delay.*

Without An Arrest Warrant—Crim. R. 4(E)(2)

A defendant shall be brought before the Court having jurisdiction of the offense *without unnecessary delay.*

ARREST OF JUDGMENT — Crim. R. 34

Motion For

Shall be filed *within 14 days* after a verdict, or finding of guilty, or after plea of guilty or no contest, *or* within such time as the Court shall fix *within* the 14 day period.

ASSIGNMENT OF COUNSEL

Serious Offenses—Crim. R. 44(A)

Counsel shall be assigned for a defendant unable to obtain representation *at every stage of the proceedings, from his initial appearance before a court through appeal as of right,* unless Counsel is knowingly, intelligently and voluntarily waived.

Petty Offenses—Crim. R. 44(B)

Confinement may not be imposed unless Counsel is assigned for a defendant who desires representation *prior* to trial, unless counsel is knowingly, intelligently, and voluntarily waived.

BAIL

Amendments—Crim. R. 46(H)

At any time the judge who ordered release on bail on any condition may amend his order.

Hearing—Crim. R. 46(D)

Where a defendant is not released on his own recognizance or on an unsecured appearance bond or by complying with the Court's bail schedule in misdemeanor cases, he shall be given a hearing *without unnecessary delay* before a judge.

Where Summons Has Issued—Crim. R. 46(B)

Where a defendant appears pursuant to a summons, a judge *shall then* release him on his personal recognizance or upon the execution of an unsecured appearance bond.

BILL OF PARTICULARS — Crim. R. 7(E)

Amendment

A bill of particulars may be amended *at any time* subject to such conditions as justice requires.

Motion For—Crim. R. 7(E)

The written request shall be filed within *21 days after arraignment, but not later than 7 days before trial* or upon court order. But see R.C. § 2941.07, which states that the written request shall be filed *not less than 5 days before trial* or upon Court order.

CHANGE OF VENUE — Crim. R. 18(B)(1)

Motion For

The written motion shall be filed *within 35 days after arraignment* or *7 days before trial whichever is earlier*, or at such later, reasonable time as the Court may permit.

CLERICAL MISTAKES — Crim. R. 36

May be corrected at any time.

COMPLAINT — Crim. R. 4(E)(2)

One arrested without a warrant having first been issued shall be brought before the Court having jurisdiction of the offense and a complaint shall *without unnecessary delay be filed.*

COUNSEL, See Assignment of Counsel

DEFENSES AND MOTIONS — Crim. R. 12

Defects In Indictment, Information Or Complaint—Crim. R. 12(B)(2)

Those which show a lack of jurisdiction or the failure to charge an offense, shall be noticed by the Court *at any time.*

Failure To Raise Defenses Or Objections—Crim. R. 12(G)

Unless for good cause shown, the Court *extends the time for filing*, a failure to file *prior to trial* constitutes a waiver.

Mandatory Pre-Trial Motions—Crim. R. 12(B)

1. Defects in the institution of the prosecution.
2. Defects in the charge, except those which demonstrate that the Court is without jurisdiction or that no crime is charged.
3. Suppression of evidence.
4. Requests for discovery.
5. Requests for severance.

Pre-Trial Motions—When Made—Crim. R. 12(C)

All pre-trial motions *except* motions for Bill of Particulars and for Discovery *shall be filed within 35 days after arraignment or 7 days before trial, whichever is earlier* and, in the interest of justice, the Court may extend the time.

Ruling On Pre-Trial Motions—Crim. R. 12(E)

Except on a Change of Venue Motion, the Court must make a *timely ruling before trial.*

DEPOSITIONS — Crim. R. 15

Notice Of Taking—Crim. R. 15(B)

Reasonable written notice must be given to each opposing party of the time and place of the deposition by the party at whose instance the deposition is taken.

When Taken—Crim. R. 15(A)

At any time after the filing of the indictment, information or complaint.

DISABILITY OF JUDGE — Crim. R. 25

At any time, when it appears that the Judge before whom the trial has commenced is unable to proceed, a substitute judge who can adequately familiarize himself with the record may be designated to conclude the trial.

DISCHARGE — Crim. R. 5(B)(3)

Defendant's Motion At Preliminary Hearing

At the conclusion of the State's case, motion for discharge for failure of proof is proper.

DISCOVERY — Crim. R. 16

Defendant's Motion—When Made—Crim. R. 16(F)

The written motion shall be filed *within 21 days after arraignment or 7 days before trial whichever is earlier*, or at such later, reasonable time as the Court shall permit.

Failure To Comply—Crim. R. 16(E)(3)

At any time when it comes to the Court's attention that the order for discovery has not been observed, the court may make such order as it deems just.

In Camera Inspection Of Witness's Statement—Crim. R. 16(B)(1)(g) and Crim. R. 16(C)(1)(d)

Upon completion of the direct examination at trial of any witness except the defendant.

Prosecuting Attorney's Motion—When Made—Crim. R. 16(F)

The written motion shall be filed *within 7 days after defendant obtains discovery or 3 days before trial, whichever is earlier.*

Protective Order—Crim. R. 16(E)(1)

At any time, upon sufficient showing, the Court may order that discovery or inspection be denied, restricted or deferred, or make such other order as is appropriate.

GRAND JURY — Crim. R. 6

Challenges—When Made—Crim. R. 6(B)(1)

The array or an individual juror shall be challenged *before* the administration of the oath to the jurors.

Summoning Of Grand Juries—Crim. R. 6(A)

One or more Grand Juries may be summoned *at such time as the public interest requires.*

Term Of Service, Discharge And Excuse Of Juror—Crim. R. 6(G)

The Grand Jury shall serve until discharged, for *4 months, but not more than 9 months.* A juror may be excused and replaced, temporarily or permanently *at any time* for cause shown.

INDICTMENT, INFORMATION OR COMPLAINT — Crim. R. 7

Amendment—Crim. R. 7(D)

At any time, before, during or after trial, amendment is proper so long as there is no change in the name or identity of the crime charged.

Delivery Of Copy To Defendant—Crim. R. 10(A)

Before defendant is called upon to plead he shall receive a copy of the charge.

Dismissal—Crim. R. 7(A)

Where an indictment is waived, the offense may be prosecuted by information unless the indictment is filed *within 14 days after the date of the waiver.* Failure to file an information or indictment *within 14 days after the waiver date* operates as a dismissal of the complaint and a discharge of the defendant.

Secret Indictment—Crim. R. 6(E)

The Court may direct that an indictment shall be kept secret *until* the defendant is in custody or has been admitted to bail.

INSTRUCTIONS — Crim. R. 30

Action On Written Requests

Before closing argument the Court shall rule on requested instructions.

Cautionary Instructions

At the commencement and during the trial the Court may give instructions of law relating to procedure, credibility and weight of the evidence, duty and function of the jury and may acquaint the jury generally with the nature of the case.

Service Of Copies

Opposing parties shall receive copies of requests *at the time of making.*

Time For Filing Written Requests

At the *close of the evidence,* or at such earlier time during the trial as the Court reasonably directs.

Time For Objections To Charge

Objections shall specifically be made before the jury retires to deliberate.

JURY — Crim. R. 24

Challenge To Array—Crim. R. 24(E)

Either party may challenge the array of Petit Jurors before the examination commences.

Demand For—Crim. R. 23(A)

In petty offenses, where there is a right to trial by jury (R.C. § 2945.17 guarantees the right to trial by jury where the penalty is any possible confinement and/ or the possible fine is in excess of $100.00). Written demand shall be filed *not less than 10 days* prior to the date set for trial or on or before the *3rd day* following receipt of notice of the date set for trial, whichever is later.

Peremptory Challenges—Crim. R. 24(D)

Challenges without cause (3 for each party in misdemeanor cases, 4 for each party in felony cases and 6 for each party in capital cases) may be exercised after the minimum number of jurors (8 in misdemeanor cases and 12 in felony cases) have been passed for cause.

Poll—Crim. R. 31(D)

After a verdict is returned and *before* it is accepted, the jury may be polled by any party or the Court.

LIMITATIONS OF ACTION

Statute Of—R.C. § 2901.13

Prosecution shall be barred unless commenced within the following periods after an offense is committed:

1. For a *FELONY*, other than aggravated murder or murder, 6 YEARS.
2. For *ALL MISDEMEANORS*, other than minor misdemeanors, 2 YEARS.
3. For *MINOR MISDEMEANORS, 6 MONTHS.*

But, where the time has expired and the offense involves either *fraud* or *breach of a fiduciary duty,* prosecution is not barred until *1 YEAR* after discovery. *And* where the offense involves misconduct in office by a public servant, prosecution may be commenced at any time while the accused remains in office or *within 2 YEARS after he leaves office.*

NOTE: The time during which prosecution must be commenced *DOES NOT BEGIN TO RUN:*

1. Until all the elements of the crime have been committed,
2. Until the Corpus Delicti is discovered, or
3. Where the accused voluntarily avoids prosecution by flight or otherwise.
4. During any time a prosecution against the accused based on the same conduct is pending in this state.

NEW TRIAL — Crim. R. 33(B)

Motion For

The written New Trial Motion shall be filed within *14 days after verdict or court decision.* Where the Court finds by clear and convincing proof that unavoidable delay prevented a timely filing, the motion shall be filed *within 7 days from the Court finding of unavoidable delay.*

Newly Discovered Evidence—Crim. R. 33(B)

The written new trial motion alleging newly discovered evidence shall be filed within *120 days following the day when the verdict or court decision was rendered.* Where the Court finds by clear and convincing proof that unavoidable delay prevented a timely filing, the motion shall be filed *within 7 days from the Court finding of unavoidable delay.*

PLEA OF GUILTY — Crim. R. 32.1

Withdrawal Of Plea

A motion to withdraw a guilty plea may be made *only before* sentence is imposed or suspended.

Withdrawal Of No Contest Plea—Crim. R. 32.1

A motion to withdraw a no contest plea may be made *only before* sentence is imposed or suspended.

BUT to correct manifest injustice, the Court, *after sentence,* may permit the withdrawal of either plea.

PRELIMINARY HEARING — Crim. R. 5

Docketing—Crim. R. 5(B)(7)

The Clerk of Court shall, *within 7 days* from the hearing and finding of probable cause, file a transcript of the docket and copies of all original papers, pleading and documents with the Clerk of the Court in which defendant is to appear.

Extension Of Time For—Crim. R. 5(B)(1)

With the consent of the defendant and upon a showing of good cause, the time limits may be extended. Without the defendant's consent, time limits may be extended only as required by law, or upon a showing that extraordinary circumstances exist, and that delay is indispensable to the interest of justice.

Time When Hearing Shall Be Held—Crim. R. 5(B)(1) (See Time)

A Preliminary Hearing desired by the felony charged defendant shall be held *no later than 10 days following arrest or service of summons* if the defendant is in custody and *no later than 15 consecutive days following arrest or service of summons* if the defendant is not confined.

PRE-TRIAL CONFERENCE — Crim. R. 17.1

When Held

At any time after the filing of an indictment, information or complaint a pre-trial conference may be had *after* defendant is represented by Counsel.

Memorandum Of Agreed Matters

At the conclusion of the conference, the Court shall prepare and file a memorandum of agreed matters.

PROBATION — Crim. R. 32.2

Pre-Sentence Investigation—When Made

Before granting probation in felony cases, a pre-sentence investigation and report *must* be made. *Before* granting probation in misdemeanor cases, the court *may* order a presentence investigation and report.

Revocation—When—Crim. R. 32.3(A)

Only *after* a hearing at which defendant is present may probation be revoked.

SEARCH WARRANT — Crim. R. 41

Time For Return Of Warrant—Crim. R. 41(D)

The search warrant shall be returned *promptly* to a designated judge, accompanied by a written inventory of the property taken.

Time For Execution Of Warrant—Crim. R. 41(C)

The search warrant shall be executed and served *within 3 days* from the date of issuance, during the daytime (from the hours of 7:00 A.M. to 8:00 P.M.) unless the issuing Court authorizes otherwise.

SENTENCE — Crim. R. 32

Time For Imposition—Crim. R. 32(A)(1)

Sentence shall be imposed *without unnecessary delay, but not before* affording Counsel and the defendant the opportunity to be heard in mitigation.

Procedure Following Sentence—Crim. R. 32(A)(2)

After imposing sentence in a serious offense in which trial was had on a not guilty plea, the Court shall advise the defendant of all his appellate rights.

SERVICE — Crim. R. 49

Time For Filing—Crim. R. 49(C)

All papers required to be served upon a party shall be filed *simultaneously with or* immediately after service.

Time For Serving Motions: Affidavits—Crim. R. 45(D)

A written motion and notice of hearing thereof shall be served *not later than 7 days before the time specified for the hearing,* unless a different period is fixed by rule or order of the Court.

Opposing affidavits may be served *not less than 1 day before the hearing;* unless the Court permits them to be served at a later time.

SUBPOENA — Crim. R. 17

When Available To Indigent Defendant—Crim. R. 17(B)

At any time the Court shall order that a subpoena be issued for a necessary witness upon ex parte application of the indigent defendant.

SUMMONS — Crim. R. 4

When Service Of Summons Shall Be Made—Crim. R. 4(D)(4)

When the person serving summons is unable to serve

a copy of summons *within 28 days of the date of issuance,* he shall endorse that fact and the reasons therefor and return the summons and copies to the clerk.

SUPPRESSIONS OF EVIDENCE — Crim. R. 12

Appeal As Of Right By The State—Crim. R. 12(J)

The State's Notice of Appeal shall be filed *within 7 days* after the date of the order granting the motion to suppress evidence, with the Trial Court Clerk, and any such appeal shall be *diligently prosecuted.*

Time For Filing Motion For Suppression Of Evidence—Crim. R. 12(C)

Defendant's motion to suppress evidence and/or to return property shall be filed *within 35 days after arraignment or 7 days before trial,* whichever is earlier. The Court, in the interest of justice, may extend the times.

Return Of Tangible Property—Crim. R. 12(F)

An order granting a motion to suppress tangible evidence, where a return of the seized property is also ordered, is *stayed* pending appeal by the State.

TIME COMPUTATION

Computation—Crim. R. 45(A)

In computing time, the date of the act or event from which the designated period of time begins shall not be included. The last day is excluded if it is a Saturday, Sunday or legal holiday, in which event, the period runs until the end of the next day which is not a Saturday, Sunday or legal holiday. If the time prescribed *is less than 7 days,* intermediate Saturdays, Sundays and legal holidays *shall be excluded* in computation.

Credit For All Confinement—R.C. § 2967.191

The adult parole authority shall reduce the minimum and maximum sentence or the definite sentence of a prisoner by the total number of days that the prisoner was confined for any reason arising out of the offense for which he was convicted and sentenced, including confinement in lieu of bail while awaiting trial, confinement for examination to determine his competence to stand trial or sanity, confinement in a community based correctional facility and program or district community based correctional facility and program, and confinement while awaiting transportation to the place where he is to serve his sentence.

Enlargement Of Time—Crim. R. 45(B)

A. After the Expiration of Time

Time may be extended *after* the designated period has expired if the failure to act on time was the result of excusable delay or would result in injustice to the defendant, *EXCEPT:* The Court may not extend the time for:

1. Filing Motion for Acquittal.
2. Filing Motion for New Trial.
3. Filing Motion for Arrest of Judgment.
4. Demand for a Jury Trial.

B. Before Expiration of Time

With or without motion, for good cause shown, the Court may order the designated period either as determined by the criminal rule or fixed by the Court, extended.

TRIAL — R.C. § 2945.71

Misdemeanors

Minor Misdemeanor. Trial shall be had *within 30 days after arrest* or service of summons if the Court is *not* of record or if the crime charged is a *minor misdemeanor* pending in a Court of Record.

Misdemeanor. Where the crime charged is a *misdemeanor,* other than a minor misdemeanor, pending in a Court of Record, trial shall be had:

1. Within *45 days* after arrest or service of summons, if the misdemeanor charged is of the *3rd* or *4th* degree, *or* where the penalty is *not more* than *60 days* confinement.
2. Within *90 days* after arrest or service of summons, if the misdemeanor charged is of the *1st* or *2nd* degree *or* where the penalty is *more* than *60 days* confinement.

Felony

1. A preliminary hearing shall be had within 15 days from time of arrest, *but see Crim. R. 5(B)(1)* which provides that a preliminary hearing shall be scheduled within a reasonable time, but, in any event, *no later than 10 days* following arrest or service of summons if defendant is in custody and *no later than 15 consecutive days* following arrest or service of summons if he is not in custody.
2. *Trial* shall be had *within 270 days* following arrest.

NOTE: For both misdemeanors and felonies, each day of confinement shall be counted as *3 days.*

Trial Time Extension—R.C. § 2945.72

1. *Any period* during which the accused is unavailable for hearing or trial, by reason of other criminal proceedings against him, within or outside the state, by reason of his confinement in another state, or by reason of the pendency of extradition proceedings, provided that the prosecution exercises reasonable diligence to secure his availability;
2. *Any period* during which the accused is mentally incompetent to stand trial, or is physically incapable of standing trial;
3. *Any period* of delay necessitated by the accused's lack of counsel, provided that such delay is not occasioned by any lack of diligence in providing counsel to an indigent accused upon his request as required by law;

4. *Any period* of delay occasioned by the neglect or improper act of the accused;
5. *Any period* of delay necessitated by reason of a plea in bar or abatement, motion, proceeding, or action made or instituted by the accused;
6. *Any period* of delay necessitated by a removal or change of venue pursuant to law;
7. *Any period* during which trial is stayed pursuant to any express statutory requirement, or pursuant to an order of another Court competent to issue such order;
8. The *period of any continuance granted* on the accused's own motion, and the period of any reasonable continuance granted other than upon the accused's own motion.
9. Any period during which an appeal filed pursuant to R.C. § 2945.67 is pending.

NOTE: For Effect Of Failure To Bring To Trial, See: R.C. § 2945.73

Trial, Transfer For—Crim. R. 21

Within *14 days after* an indictment or information which charges only *misdemeanors* is filed in the Court of Common Pleas, the Administrative Judge of such Court may transfer it to the Court from which the bindover to the Grand Jury was made or to the Court of Record of the jurisdiction in which the offense was committed.

VENUE — *See* Change of Venue

WARRANT — Crim. R. 4

Appearance After Physical Arrest—Crim. R. 4(C)(1)

When the accused is physically arrested, he shall be brought before the Court which issued the warrant *without unnecessary delay.*

Delivery Of Copy Of Warrant—Crim. R. 4(D)(3)

A copy of the warrant shall be given to the defendant *as soon as possible.*

Issuance Of Warrant—Crim. R. 4(A)(1)

No warrant shall issue until it has been determined from the complaint, with or without affidavits attached thereto, that there is probable cause to believe that an offense has been committed and that defendant has committed it.

Return Of Warrant—Crim. R. 4(D)(4)

The officer executing a warrant shall make return thereof to the issuing Court before whom the defendant is brought.

OHIO RULES OF CRIMINAL PROCEDURE

Complete through July 1, 1997

For annotations and cases construing the Ohio Criminal Rules, see the
TITLE 29 VOLUME to PAGE'S OHIO REVISED CODE ANNOTATED

For text discussion of the Criminal Rules see **ANDERSON'S OHIO CRIMINAL PRACTICE AND PROCEDURE (3rd edition)**

Rule
1. Scope of rules: applicability; construction; exceptions
   (A) Applicability
   (B) Purpose and construction
   (C) Exceptions
2. Definitions
3. Complaint
4. Warrant or summons; arrest
   (A) Issuance
      (1) Upon complaint
      (2) By law enforcement officer with warrant
      (3) By law enforcement officer without a warrant
   (B) Multiple issuance; sanction
   (C) Warrant and summons: form
      (1) Warrant
      (2) Summons
   (D) Warrant or summons: execution or service; return
      (1) By whom
      (2) Territorial limits
      (3) Manner
      (4) Return
   (E) Arrest
      (1) Arrest upon warrant
      (2) Arrest without warrant
   (F) Release after arrest
4.1. Optional procedure in minor misdemeanor cases
   (A) Procedure in minor misdemeanor cases
   (B) Definition of minor misdemeanor
   (C) Form of citation
   (D) Duty of law enforcement officer
   (E) Fine schedule
   (F) Procedure upon failure to appear
   (G) Procedure where defendant does not enter a waiver
5. Initial appearance, preliminary hearing
   (A) Procedure upon initial appearance
   (B) Preliminary hearing in felony cases; procedure
6. The grand jury
   (A) Summoning grand juries
   (B) Objections to grand jury and to grand jurors
      (1) Challenges
      (2) Motion to dismiss
   (C) Foreman and deputy foreman
   (D) Who may be present
   (E) Secrecy of proceedings and disclosure
   (F) Finding and return of indictment
   (G) Discharge and excuse
   (H) Alternate grand jurors
7. The indictment and the information
   (A) Use of indictment or information
   (B) Nature and contents
   (C) Surplusage
   (D) Amendment of indictment, information or complaint

Rule
   (E) Bill of particulars
8. Joinder of offenses and defendants
   (A) Joinder of offenses
   (B) Joinder of defendants
9. Warrant or summons upon indictment or information
   (A) Issuance
   (B) Form of warrant and summons
      (1) Warrant
      (2) Summons
   (C) Execution or service; return
      (1) Execution or service
      (2) Return
10. Arraignment
    (A) Arraignment procedure
    (B) Presence of defendant
    (C) Explanation of rights
    (D) Joint arraignment
11. Pleas, rights upon plea
    (A) Pleas
    (B) Effect of guilty or no contest pleas
    (C) Pleas of guilty and no contest in felony cases
    (D) Misdemeanor cases involving serious offenses
    (E) Misdemeanor cases involving petty offenses
    (F) Negotiated plea in felony cases
    (G) Refusal of court to accept plea
    (H) Defense of insanity
12. Pleadings and motions before trial; defenses and objections
    (A) Pleadings and motions
    (B) Pretrial motions
    (C) Motion date
    (D) Notice by the prosecuting attorney of the intention to use evidence
       (1) At the discretion of the prosecuting attorney
       (2) At the request of the defendant
    (E) Ruling on motion
    (F) Return of tangible evidence
    (G) Effect of failure to raise defenses or objections
    (H) Effect of plea of no contest
    (I) Effect of determination
    (J) Appeal by state
12.1. Notice of alibi
13. Trial together of indictments or informations or complaints
14. Relief from prejudicial joinder
15. Deposition
    (A) When taken
    (B) Notice of taking
    (C) Attendance of defendant
    (D) Counsel
    (E) How taken
    (F) Use
    (G) Objections to admissibility

Rule
16. Discovery and inspection
    (A) Demand for discovery
    (B) Disclosure of evidence by the prosecuting attorney
        (1) Information subject to disclosure
        (2) Information not subject to disclosure
        (3) Grand jury transcripts
        (4) Witness list; no comment
    (C) Disclosure of evidence by the defendant
        (1) Information subject to disclosure
        (2) Information not subject to disclosure
        (3) Witness list; no comment
    (D) Continuing duty to disclose
    (E) Regulation of discovery
        (1) Protective orders
        (2) Time, place and manner of discovery and inspection
        (3) Failure to comply
    (F) Time of motions
17. Subpoena
    (A) For attendance of witnesses; form; issuance
    (B) Defendants unable to pay
    (C) For production of documentary evidence
    (D) Service
    (E) Subpoena for taking depositions; place of examination
    (F) Subpoena for a hearing or trial
    (G) Contempt
17.1. Pretrial conference
18. Venue and change of venue
    (A) General venue provision
    (B) Change of venue; procedure upon change of venue
        (1) Time of motion
        (2) Clerk's obligations upon change of venue
        (3) Additional counsel for prosecuting attorney
        (4) Appearance of defendant, witnesses
        (5) Expenses
19. Magistrates
    (A) Appointment
    (B) Powers and duties
    (C) Objections
20. Reserved
21. Transfer from common pleas court for trial
    (A) When permitted
    (B) Proceedings on transfer
22. Recording of proceedings
23. Trial by jury or by the court
    (A) Trial by jury
    (B) Number of jurors
    (C) Trial without a jury
24. Trial jurors
    (A) Examination of jurors
    (B) Challenge for cause
    (C) Peremptory challenges
    (D) Manner of exercising peremptory challenges
    (E) Challenge to array
    (F) Alternate jurors
    (G) Control of juries
        (1) Before submission of case to jury
        (2) After submission of case to jury
        (3) Separation in emergency
        (4) Duties of supervising officer
25. Disability of a judge
    (A) During trial
    (B) After verdict or finding of guilt

Rule
26. Substitution of photographs for physical evidence
27. Proof of official record; judicial notice: determination of foreign law
28. Reserved
29. Motion for acquittal
    (A) Motion for judgment of acquittal
    (B) Reservation of decision on motion
    (C) Motion after verdict or discharge of jury
30. Instructions
    (A) Instructions; error; record
    (B) Cautionary instructions
31. Verdict
    (A) Return
    (B) Several defendants
    (C) Conviction of lesser offense
    (D) Poll of jury
32. Sentence
    (A) Sentence
        (1) Imposition of sentence
        (2) Notification of right to appeal
    (B) Judgment
32.1. Withdrawal of guilty plea
32.2. Presentence investigation
    (A) When made
    (B) Report
    (C) Disclosure
    (D) Transmission of papers to custodian
32.3. Revocation of probation
    (A) Revocation hearing
    (B) Counsel
    (C) Confinement in petty offense cases
    (D) Waiver of counsel
33. New trial
    (A) Grounds
    (B) Motion for new trial; form, time
    (C) Affidavits required
    (D) Procedure when new trial granted
    (E) Invalid grounds for new trial
    (F) Motion for new trial not a condition for appellate review
34. Arrest of judgment
35. Post-Conviction Petition
36. Clerical mistakes
37–40. Reserved
41. Search and seizure
    (A) Authority to issue warrant
    (B) Property which may be seized with a warrant
    (C) Issuance and contents
    (D) Execution and return with inventory
    (E) Return of papers to clerk
    (F) Definition of property and daytime
42. Reserved
43. Presence of the defendant
    (A) Defendant's presence
    (B) Defendant excluded because of disruptive conduct
44. Assignment of counsel
    (A) Counsel in serious offenses
    (B) Counsel in petty offenses
    (C) Waiver of counsel
    (D) Assignment procedure
45. Time
    (A) Time: computation
    (B) Time: enlargement
    (C) Time: unaffected by expiration of term

Rule
- (D) Time: for motions; affidavits
- (E) Time: additional time after service by mail
46. Bail
- (A) Purpose of and right to bail
- (B) Pretrial release where summons issued
- (C) Preconviction release in serious offense cases
- (D) Preconviction release in petty offense cases
- (E) Release after conviction
- (F) Conditions of preconviction release; basis
- (G) Order
- (H) Amendments
- (I) Information need not be admissible
- (J) Continuation of bonds
- (K) Sanctions
- (L) Justification of sureties
- (M) Forfeiture of bonds
- (N) Exoneration
47. Motions
48. Dismissal
- (A) Dismissal by the state
- (B) Dismissal by the court
49. Service and filing of papers
- (A) Service: when required
- (B) Service: how made
- (C) Filing
50. Calendars
51. Exceptions unnecessary
52. Harmless error and plain error
- (A) Harmless error
- (B) Plain error
53. Reserved
54. Amendment of incorporated civil rules
55. Records
- (A) Criminal appearance docket
- (B) Files
- (C) Other books and records
- (D) Applicability to courts not of record
56. Reserved
57. Rule of court; procedure not otherwise specified
- (A) Rule of court
- (B) Procedure not otherwise specified
58. Forms
59. Effective date
- (A) Effective date of rules
- (B)–(O) Effective date of amendments
60. Title

APPENDIX OF FORMS

Form
- I. Complaint
- II. Complaint by prosecuting attorney upon affidavit
- III. Direction to issue summons
- IV. Clerk's memorandum of determination to issue summons upon complaint
- V. Prosecuting attorney's request for issuance of summons upon complaint
- VI. Summons upon/complaint/indictment/information
- VII. Warrant on complaint
- VIII. Clerk's memorandum of determination to issue summons upon indictment
- IX. Prosecuting attorney's request for issuance of summons upon/indictment/information
- X. Prosecuting attorney's request for issuance of warrant upon/indictment/information
- XI. Warrant upon/indictment/information
- XII. Summons in lieu of arrest without warrant, and complaint upon such summons
- XIII. Summons after arrest without warrant, and complaint upon each such summons
- XIV. Minor misdemeanor citation
- XV. Uniform petition form

RULE 1. Scope of Rules: Applicability; Construction; Exceptions

(A) Applicability. These rules prescribe the procedure to be followed in all courts of this state in the exercise of criminal jurisdiction, with the exceptions stated in division (C) of this rule.

(B) Purpose and construction. These rules are intended to provide for the just determination of every criminal proceeding. They shall be construed and applied to secure the fair, impartial, speedy, and sure administration of justice, simplicity in procedure, and the elimination of unjustifiable expense and delay.

(C) Exceptions. These rules, to the extent that specific procedure is provided by other rules of the Supreme Court or to the extent that they would by their nature be clearly inapplicable, shall not apply to procedure (1) upon appeal to review any judgment, order or ruling, (2) upon extradition and rendition of fugitives, (3) in cases covered by the Uniform Traffic Rules, (4) upon the application and enforcement of peace bonds, (5) in juvenile proceedings against a child as defined in Rule 2(D) of the Rules of Juvenile Procedure, (6) upon forfeiture of property for violation of a statute of this state, or (7) upon the collection of fines and penalties. Where any statute or rule provides for procedure by a general or specific reference to the statutes governing procedure in criminal actions, the procedure shall be in accordance with these rules.

Amended, eff 7-1-75; 7-1-96

RULE 2. Definitions

As used in these rules:

(A) "Felony" means an offense defined by law as a felony.

(B) "Misdemeanor" means an offense defined by law as a misdemeanor.

(C) "Serious offense" means any felony, and any misdemeanor for which the penalty prescribed by law includes confinement for more than six months.

(D) "Petty offense" means a misdemeanor other than a serious offense.

(E) "Judge" means judge of the court of common pleas, juvenile court, municipal court, or county court, or the mayor or mayor's court magistrate of a municipal corporation having a mayor's court.

(F) "Magistrate" means any person appointed by a court pursuant to Crim. R. 19. "Magistrate" does not include an official included within the definition of magistrate contained in section 2931.01 of the Revised Code, or a mayor's court magistrate appointed pursuant to section 1905.05 of the Revised Code.

(G) "Prosecuting attorney" means the attorney general of this state, the prosecuting attorney of a county, the law director, city solicitor, or other officer who prosecutes a criminal case on behalf of the state or a city, village, township, or other political subdivision, and the assistant or assistants of any of them. As used in Crim. R. 6, "prosecuting attorney" means the attorney general of this state, the prosecuting attorney of a county, and the assistant or assistants of either of them.

(H) "State" means this state, a county, city, village, township, other political subdivision, or any other entity of this state that may prosecute a criminal action.

(I) "Clerk of court" means the duly elected or appointed clerk of any court of record or the deputy clerk, and the mayor or mayor's court magistrate of a municipal corporation having a mayor's court.

(J) "Law enforcement officer" means a sheriff, deputy sheriff, constable, municipal police officer, marshal, deputy marshal, or state highway patrolman, and also means any officer, agent, or employee of the state or any of its agencies, instrumentalities, or political subdivisions, upon whom, by statute, the authority to arrest violators is conferred, when the officer, agent, or employee is acting within the limits of statutory authority. The definition of "law enforcement officer" contained in this rule shall not be construed to limit, modify, or expand any statutory definition, to the extent the statutory definition applies to matters not covered by the Rules of Criminal Procedure.

Amended, eff 7-1-76; 7-1-90

RULE 3. Complaint

The complaint is a written statement of the essential facts constituting the offense charged. It shall also state the numerical designation of the applicable statute or ordinance. It shall be made upon oath before any person authorized by law to administer oaths.

RULE 4. Warrant or Summons; Arrest

(A) Issuance.

(1) Upon complaint. If it appears from the complaint, or from an affidavit or affidavits filed with the complaint, that there is probable cause to believe that an offense has been committed, and that the defendant has committed it, a warrant for the arrest of the defendant, or a summons in lieu of a warrant, shall be issued by a judge, magistrate, clerk of court, or officer of the court designated by the judge, to any law enforcement officer authorized by law to execute or serve it.

The finding of probable cause may be based upon hearsay in whole or in part, provided there is a substantial basis for believing the source of the hearsay to be credible and for believing that there is a factual basis for the information furnished. Before ruling on a request for a warrant, the issuing authority may require the complainant to appear personally and may examine under oath the complainant and any witnesses. Such testimony shall be admissible at a hearing on a motion to suppress, if it was taken down by a court reporter or recording equipment.

The issuing authority shall issue a summons instead of a warrant upon the request of the prosecuting attorney, or when issuance of a summons appears reasonably calculated to assure the defendant's appearance.

(2) By law enforcement officer with warrant. In misdemeanor cases where a warrant has been issued to a law enforcement officer, he may, unless the issuing authority includes a prohibition against it in the warrant, issue a summons in lieu of executing the warrant by arrest, when issuance of a summons appears reasonably calculated to assure the defendant's appearance. The officer issuing such summons shall note on the warrant and the return that the warrant was executed by issuing summons, and shall also note the time and place the defendant must appear. No alias warrant shall be issued unless the defendant fails to appear in response to the summons, or unless subsequent to the issuance of summons it appears improbable that the defendant will appear in response thereto.

(3) By law enforcement officer without a warrant. In misdemeanor cases where a law enforcement officer is empowered to arrest without a warrant, he may issue a summons in lieu of making an arrest, when issuance of a summons appears reasonably calculated to assure the defendant's appearance. The officer issuing such summons shall file, or cause to be filed, a complaint describing the offense. No warrant shall be issued unless the defendant fails to appear in response to the summons, or unless subsequent to the issuance of summons it appears improbable that the defendant will appear in response thereto.

(B) Multiple issuance; sanction. More than one warrant or summons may issue on the same complaint. If the defendant fails to appear in response to summons, a warrant or alias warrant shall issue.

(C) Warrant and summons: form.

(1) Warrant. The warrant shall contain the name of the defendant or, if that is unknown, any name or description by which he can be identified with reasonable certainty. It shall describe the offense charged in the complaint, and shall state the numerical designation of the applicable statute or ordinance. A copy of the complaint shall be attached to the warrant. The warrant shall command that the defendant be arrested and

brought before the court issuing it without unnecessary delay.

(2) **Summons.** The summons shall be in the same form as the warrant, except that it shall not command that the defendant be arrested, but shall order the defendant to appear at a stated time and place and inform him that he may be arrested if he fails to appear at the time and place stated in the summons. A copy of the complaint shall be attached to the summons, except where an officer issues summons in lieu of making an arrest without a warrant, or where an officer issues summons after arrest without a warrant.

(D) **Warrant or summons: execution or service; return.**

(1) **By whom.** Warrants shall be executed and summons served by any officer authorized by law.

(2) **Territorial limits.** Warrants may be executed or summons may be served at any place within this state.

(3) **Manner.** Warrants, except as provided in subsection (A)(2), shall be executed by the arrest of the defendant. The officer need not have the warrant in his possession at the time of the arrest. In such case, he shall inform the defendant of the offense charged and of the fact that the warrant has been issued. A copy of the warrant shall be given to the defendant as soon as possible.

Summons may be served upon a defendant by delivering a copy to him personally, or by leaving it at his usual place of residence with some person of suitable age and discretion then residing therein, or, except when the summons is issued in lieu of executing a warrant by arrest, by mailing it to the defendant's last known address by certified mail with a return receipt requested. When service of summons is made by certified mail it shall be served by the clerk in the manner prescribed by Civil Rule 4.1(1). A summons to a corporation shall be served in the manner provided for service upon corporations in Civil Rules 4 through 4.2 and 4.6(A) and (B), except that the waiver provisions of Civil Rule 4(D) shall not apply. Summons issued under subsection (A)(2) in lieu of executing a warrant by arrest shall be served by personal or residence service. Summons issued under subsection (A)(3) in lieu of arrest and summons issued after arrest under subdivision (F) shall be served by personal service only.

(4) **Return.** The officer executing a warrant shall make return thereof to the issuing court before whom the defendant is brought pursuant to Rule 5. At the request of the prosecuting attorney, any unexecuted warrant shall be returned to the issuing court and cancelled by a judge of that court.

When the copy of the summons has been served, the person serving summons shall endorse that fact on the summons and return it to the clerk, who shall make the appropriate entry on the appearance docket.

When the person serving summons is unable to serve a copy of the summons within twenty-eight days of the date of issuance, he shall endorse that fact and the reasons therefore on the summons and return the summons and copies to the clerk, who shall make the appropriate entry on the appearance docket.

At the request of the prosecuting attorney, made while the complaint is pending, a warrant returned unexecuted and not cancelled, or a summons returned unserved, or a copy of either, may be delivered by the court to an authorized officer for execution or service.

(E) **Arrest.**

(1) **Arrest upon warrant.** Where under a warrant a person is arrested either in the county from which the warrant issued or in an adjoining county, the arresting officer shall, except as provided in division (F), bring the arrested person without unnecessary delay before the court that issued the warrant. Where the arrest occurs in any other county, the arrested person shall, except as provided in division (F), be brought without unnecessary delay before a court of record therein, having jurisdiction over such an offense, and he shall not be removed from that county until he has been given an opportunity to consult with an attorney, or another person of his choice, and to post bail to be determined by the judge or magistrate of that court. If he is not released, he shall then be removed from the county and brought before the court issuing the warrant, without unnecessary delay. If he is released, the release shall be on condition that he appear in the issuing court at a time and date certain for an initial appearance under Crim. R. 5.

(2) **Arrest without warrant.** Where a person is arrested without a warrant the arresting officer shall, except as provided in division (F), bring the arrested person without unnecessary delay before a court having jurisdiction of the offense, and shall file or cause to be filed a complaint describing the offense for which the person was arrested. Thereafter the court shall proceed in accordance with Crim. R. 5.

(F) **Release after arrest.** In misdemeanor cases where a person has been arrested with or without a warrant, the arresting officer, the officer in charge of the detention facility to which the person is brought or the superior of either officer, without unnecessary delay, may release the arrested person by issuing a summons when issuance of a summons appears reasonably calculated to assure the person's appearance. The officer issuing such summons shall note on the summons the time and place the person must appear and, if the person was arrested without a warrant, shall file or cause to be filed a complaint describing the offense. No warrant or alias warrant shall be issued unless the person fails to appear in response to the summons.

Amended, eff 7-1-75; 7-1-90

RULE 4.1. Optional Procedure in Minor Misdemeanor Cases

(A) **Procedure in minor misdemeanor cases.**

Notwithstanding Rule 3, Rule 5(A), Rule 10, Rule 11(A), Rule 11(E), Rule 22, Rule 43(A), and Rule 44, a court may establish the following procedure for all or particular minor misdemeanors other than offenses covered by the Uniform Traffic Rules.

(B) Definition of minor misdemeanor. A minor misdemeanor is an offense for which the potential penalty does not exceed a fine of fifty dollars. With respect to offenses committed on and after January 1, 1974, a minor misdemeanor is an offense for which the potential penalty does not exceed a fine of one hundred dollars.

(C) Form of citation. In minor misdemeanor cases a law enforcement officer may issue a citation. The citation shall: contain the name and address of the defendant; describe the offense charged; give the numerical designation of the applicable statute or ordinance; state the name of the law enforcement officer who issued the citation; and order the defendant to appear at a stated time and place.

The citation shall inform the defendant that, in lieu of appearing at the time and place stated, he may, within that stated time, appear personally at the office of the clerk of court and upon signing a plea of guilty and a waiver of trial pay a stated fine and stated costs, if any. The citation shall inform the defendant that, in lieu of appearing at the time and place stated, he may, within a stated time, sign the guilty plea and waiver of trial provision of the citation, and mail the citation and a check or money order for the total amount of the fine and costs to the violations bureau. The citation shall inform the defendant that he may be arrested if he fails to appear either at the clerk's office or at the time and place stated in the citation.

(D) Duty of law enforcement officer. A law enforcement officer who issues a citation shall complete and sign the citation form, serve a copy of the completed form upon the defendant and, without unnecessary delay, swear to and file the original with the court.

(E) Fine schedule. The court shall establish a fine schedule which shall list the fine for each minor misdemeanor, and state the court costs. The fine schedule shall be prominently posted in the place where violation fines are paid.

(F) Procedure upon failure to appear. When a defendant fails to appear, the court may issue a supplemental citation, or a summons or warrant under Rule 4. Supplemental citations shall be in the form prescribed by subdivision (C), but shall be issued and signed by the clerk and served in the same manner as a summons under Rule 4.

(G) Procedure where defendant does not enter a waiver. Where a defendant appears but does not sign a guilty plea and waiver of trial, the court shall proceed in accordance with Rule 5.

Amended, eff 7-1-78

RULE 5. Initial Appearance, Preliminary Hearing

(A) Procedure upon initial appearance. When a defendant first appears before a judge or magistrate, the judge or magistrate shall permit the accused or his counsel to read the complaint or a copy thereof, and shall inform the defendant:

(1) Of the nature of the charge against him;

(2) That he has a right to counsel and the right to a reasonable continuance in the proceedings to secure counsel, and, pursuant to Crim. R. 44, the right to have counsel assigned without cost to himself if he is unable to employ counsel;

(3) That he need make no statement and any statement made may be used against him;

(4) Of his right to a preliminary hearing in a felony case, when his initial appearance is not pursuant to indictment;

(5) Of his right, where appropriate, to jury trial and the necessity to make demand therefor in petty offense cases.

In addition, if the defendant has not been admitted to bail for a bailable offense, the judge or magistrate shall admit the defendant to bail as provided in these rules.

In felony cases the defendant shall not be called upon to plead either at the initial appearance or at a preliminary hearing.

In misdemeanor cases the defendant may be called upon to plead at the initial appearance. Where the defendant enters a plea the procedure established by Crim. R. 10 and Crim. R. 11 applies.

(B) Preliminary hearing in felony cases; procedure.

(1) In felony cases a defendant is entitled to a preliminary hearing unless waived in writing. If the defendant waives preliminary hearing, the judge or magistrate shall forthwith order the defendant bound over to the court of common pleas. If the defendant does not waive the preliminary hearing, the judge or magistrate shall schedule a preliminary hearing within a reasonable time, but in any event not later than ten consecutive days following arrest or service of summons if the defendant is in custody and not later than fifteen consecutive days following arrest or service of summons if he is not in custody. The preliminary hearing shall not be held, however, if the defendant is indicted. With the consent of the defendant and upon a showing of good cause, taking into account the public interest in the prompt disposition of criminal cases, time limits specified in this division may be extended. In the absence of such consent by the defendant, time limits may be extended only as required by law, or upon a showing that extraordinary circumstances exist and that delay is indispensable to the interests of justice.

(2) At the preliminary hearing the prosecuting attorney may state orally the case for the state, and shall then

proceed to examine witnesses and introduce exhibits for the state. The defendant and the judge or magistrate have full right of cross-examination, and the defendant has the right of inspection of exhibits prior to their introduction. The hearing shall be conducted under the rules of evidence prevailing in criminal trial generally.

(3) At the conclusion of the presentation of the state's case, defendant may move for discharge for failure of proof, and may offer evidence on his own behalf. If the defendant is not represented by counsel, the court shall advise him, prior to the offering of evidence on behalf of the defendant:

(a) That any such evidence, if unfavorable to him in any particular, may be used against him at later trial.

(b) That he may make a statement, not under oath, regarding the charge, for the purpose of explaining the facts in evidence.

(c) That he may refuse to make any statement, and such refusal may not be used against him at trial.

(d) That any statement he makes may be used against him at trial.

(4) Upon conclusion of all the evidence and the statement, if any, of the accused, the court shall do one of the following:

(a) Find that there is probable cause to believe the crime alleged or another felony has been committed and that the defendant committed it, and bind the defendant over to the court of common pleas of the county or any other county in which venue appears.

(b) Find that there is probable cause to believe that a misdemeanor was committed and that the defendant committed it, and retain the case for trial or order the defendant to appear for trial before an appropriate court.

(c) Order the accused discharged.

(5) Any finding requiring the accused to stand trial on any charge shall be based solely on the presence of substantial credible evidence thereof. No appeal shall lie from such decision and the discharge of defendant shall not be a bar to further prosecution.

(6) In any case in which the defendant is ordered to appear for trial for any offense other than the one charged the court shall cause a complaint charging such offense to be filed.

(7) Upon the conclusion of the hearing and finding, the court or the clerk of such court, shall, within seven days, complete all notations of appearance, motions, pleas, and findings on the criminal docket of the court, and shall transmit a transcript of the appearance docket entries, together with a copy of the original complaint and affidavits, if any, filed with the complaint, the journal or docket entry of reason for changes in the charge, if any, together with the order setting bail and the bail including any bail deposit, if any, filed, to the clerk of the court in which defendant is to appear. Such transcript shall contain an itemized account of the costs accrued.

Amended, eff 7-1-75; 7-1-76; 7-1-82; 7-1-90

RULE 6. The Grand Jury

(A) Summoning grand juries. The judge of the court of common pleas for each county, or the administrative judge of the general division in a multi-judge court of common pleas or a judge designated by him, shall order one or more grand juries to be summoned at such times as the public interest requires. The grand jury shall consist of nine members, including the foreman, plus not more than five alternates.

(B) Objections to grand jury and to grand jurors.

(1) Challenges. The prosecuting attorney, or the attorney for a defendant who has been held to answer in the court of common pleas, may challenge the array of jurors or an individual juror on the ground that the grand jury or individual juror was not selected, drawn, or summoned in accordance with the statutes of this state. Challenges shall be made before the administration of the oath to the jurors and shall be tried by the court.

(2) Motion to dismiss. A motion to dismiss the indictment may be based on objections to the array or on the lack of legal qualification of an individual juror, if not previously determined upon challenge. An indictment shall not be dismissed on the ground that one or more members of the grand jury were not legally qualified, if it appears from the record kept pursuant to subdivision (C) that seven or more jurors, after deducting the number not legally qualified, concurred in finding the indictment.

(C) Foreman and deputy foreman. The court may appoint any qualified elector or one of the jurors to be foreman and one of the jurors to be deputy foreman. The foreman shall have power to administer oaths and affirmations and shall sign all indictments. He or another juror designated by him shall keep a record of the number of jurors concurring in the finding of every indictment and shall upon the return of the indictment file the record with the clerk of court, but the record shall not be made public except on order of the court. During the absence or disqualification of the foreman, the deputy foreman shall act as foreman.

(D) Who may be present. The prosecuting attorney, the witness under examination, interpreters when needed and, for the purpose of taking the evidence, a stenographer or operator of a recording device may be present while the grand jury is in session, but no person other than the jurors may be present while the grand jury is deliberating or voting.

(E) Secrecy of proceedings and disclosure. Deliberations of the grand jury and the vote of any grand juror shall not be disclosed. Disclosure of other matters occurring before the grand jury may be made to the prosecuting attorney for use in the performance of his duties. A grand juror, prosecuting attorney, interpreter, stenographer, operator of a recording device, or typist who transcribes recorded testimony, may disclose matters occurring before the grand jury, other than the deliberations of a grand jury or the vote of a grand juror, but may disclose such matters only when so directed by the court preliminary to or in connection with a judicial proceeding, or when permitted by the court at the request of the defendant upon a showing that grounds may exist for a motion to dismiss the indictment because of matters occurring before the grand jury. No grand juror, officer of the court, or other person shall disclose that an indictment has been found against a person before such indictment is filed and the case docketed. The court may direct that an indictment shall be kept secret until the defendant is in custody or has been released pursuant to Rule 46. In that event the clerk shall seal the indictment, the indictment shall not be docketed by name until after the apprehension of the accused, and no person shall disclose the finding of the indictment except when necessary for the issuance of a warrant or summons. No obligation of secrecy may be imposed upon any person except in accordance with this rule.

(F) Finding and return of indictment. An indictment may be found only upon the concurrence of seven or more jurors. When so found the foreman or deputy foreman shall sign the indictment as foreman or deputy foreman. The indictment shall be returned by the foreman or deputy foreman to a judge of the court of common pleas and filed with the clerk who shall endorse thereon the date of filing and enter each case upon the appearance and trial dockets. If the defendant is in custody or has been released pursuant to Rule 46 and seven jurors do not concur in finding an indictment, the foreman shall so report to the court forthwith.

(G) Discharge and excuse. A grand jury shall serve until discharged by the court. A grand jury may serve for four months, but the court upon a showing of good cause by the prosecuting attorney may order a grand jury to serve more than four months but not more than nine months. The tenure and powers of a grand jury are not affected by the beginning or expiration of a term of court. At any time for cause shown the court may excuse a juror either temporarily or permanently, and in the latter event the court may impanel another eligible person in place of the juror excused.

(H) Alternate grand jurors. The court may order that not more than five grand jurors, in addition to the regular grand jury, be called, impanelled and sit as alternate grand jurors. Alternate grand jurors, in the order in which they are called, shall replace grand jurors who, prior to the time the grand jury votes on an indictment, are found to be unable or disqualified to perform their duties. Alternate grand jurors shall be drawn in the same manner, shall have the same qualifications, shall be subjected to the same examination and challenges, shall take the same oath, and shall have the same functions, powers, facilities, and privileges as the regular grand jurors. Alternate grand jurors may sit with the regular grand jury, but shall not be present when the grand jury deliberates and votes.

RULE 7. The Indictment and the Information

(A) Use of indictment or information. A felony that may be punished by death or life imprisonment shall be prosecuted by indictment. All other felonies shall be prosecuted by indictment, except that after a defendant has been advised by the court of the nature of the charge against the defendant and of the defendant's right to indictment, the defendant may waive that right in writing and in open court.

Where an indictment is waived, the offense may be prosecuted by information, unless an indictment is filed within fourteen days after the date of waiver. If an information or indictment is not filed within fourteen days after the date of waiver, the defendant shall be discharged and the complaint dismissed. This division shall not prevent subsequent prosecution by information or indictment for the same offense.

A misdemeanor may be prosecuted by indictment or information in the court of common pleas, or by complaint in courts inferior to the court of common pleas. An information may be filed without leave of court.

(B) Nature and contents. The indictment shall be signed, in accordance with Crim. R. 6 (C) and (F) and contain a statement that the defendant has committed a pubic offense specified in the indictment. The information shall be signed by the prosecuting attorney or in the name of the prosecuting attorney by an assistant prosecuting attorney and shall contain a statement that the defendant has committed a public offense specified in the information. The statement may be made in ordinary and concise language without technical averments or allegations not essential to be proved. The statement may be in the words of the applicable section of the statute, provided the words of that statute charge an offense, or in words sufficient to give the defendant notice of all the elements of the offense with which the defendant is charged. It may be alleged in a single count that the means by which the defendant committed the offense are unknown or that the defendant committed it by one or more specified means. Each count of the indictment or information shall state the numerical designation of the statute that the defendant is alleged to have violated. Error in the numerical designation or omission of the numerical designation shall not be ground for dismissal of the indictment or information, or for reversal of a conviction, if the error or omission did not prejudicially mislead the defendant.

(C) Surplusage. The court on motion of the defendant or the prosecuting attorney may strike surplusage from the indictment or information.

(D) Amendment of indictment, information, or complaint. The court may at any time before, during, or after a trial amend the indictment, information, complaint, or bill of particulars, in respect to any defect, imperfection, or omission in form or substance, or of any variance with the evidence, provided no change is made in the name or identity of the crime charged. If any amendment is made to the substance of the indictment, information, or complaint, or to cure a variance between the indictment, information, or complaint and the proof, the defendant is entitled to a discharge of the jury on the defendant's motion, if a jury has been impanelled, and to a reasonable continuance, unless it clearly appears from the whole proceedings that the defendant has not been misled or prejudiced by the defect or variance in respect to which the amendment is made, or that the defendant's rights will be fully protected by proceeding with the trial, or by a postponement thereof to a later day with the same or another jury. Where a jury is discharged under this division, jeopardy shall not attach to the offense charged in the amended indictment, information, or complaint. No action of the court in refusing a continuance or postponement under this division is reviewable except after motion to grant a new trial therefor is refused by the trial court, and no appeal based upon such action of the court shall be sustained nor reversal had unless, from consideration of the whole proceedings, the reviewing court finds that a failure of justice resulted.

(E) Bill of particulars. When the defendant makes a written request within twenty-one days after arraignment but not later than seven days before trial, or upon court order, the prosecuting attorney shall furnish the defendant with a bill of particulars setting up specifically the nature of the offense charge and of the conduct of the defendant alleged to constitute the offense. A bill of particulars may be amended at any time subject to such conditions as justice requires.

Amended, eff 7-1-93

RULE 8. Joinder of Offenses and Defendants

(A) Joinder of offenses. Two or more offenses may be charged in the same indictment, information or complaint in a separate count for each offense if the offenses charged, whether felonies or misdemeanors or both, are of the same or similar character, or are based on the same act or transaction, or are based on two or more acts or transactions connected together or constituting parts of a common scheme or plan, or are part of a course of criminal conduct.

(B) Joinder of defendants. Two or more defendants may be charged in the same indictment, information or complaint if they are alleged to have participated in the same act or transaction or in the same series of acts or transactions constituting an offense or offenses, or in the same course of criminal conduct. Such defendants may be charged in one or more counts together or separately, and all of the defendants need not be charged in each count.

RULE 9. Warrant or Summons Upon Indictment or Information

(A) Issuance. Upon the request of the prosecuting attorney the clerk shall forthwith issue a warrant for each defendant named in the indictment or in the information. The clerk shall issue a summons instead of a warrant where the defendant has been released pursuant to Rule 46 and is indicted for the same offense for which he was bound over pursuant to Rule 5. In addition, the clerk shall issue a summons instead of a warrant upon the request of the prosecuting attorney or by direction of the court.

Upon like request or direction, the clerk shall issue more than one warrant or summons for the same defendant. He shall deliver the warrant or summons to any officer authorized by law to execute or serve it. If a defendant fails to appear in response to summons, a warrant shall issue.

(B) Form of warrant and summons.

(1) Warrant. The form of the warrant shall be as provided in Rule 4(C)(1) except that it shall be signed by the court or clerk. It shall describe the offense charged in the indictment or information. A copy of the indictment or information shall be attached to the warrant which shall command that the defendant be arrested and brought before the court issuing the warrant without unnecessary delay.

(2) Summons. The summons shall be in the same form as the warrant, except that it shall not command that the defendant be arrested, but shall order the defendant to appear before the court at a stated time and place and inform him that he may be arrested if he fails to appear at the time and place stated in the summons. A copy of the indictment or information shall be attached to the summons.

(C) Execution or service; return.

(1) Execution or service. Warrants shall be executed or summons served as provided in Rule 4(D) and the arrested person shall be treated in accordance with Rule 4(E)(1).

(2) Return. The officer executing a warrant shall make return thereof to the court.

When the person serving summons is unable to serve a copy of the summons within twenty-eight days of the date of issuance, he shall endorse that fact and the reasons therefor on the summons and return the summons and copies to the clerk, who shall make the appropriate entry on the appearance docket.

At the request of the prosecuting attorney made at any time while the indictment or information is pending, a warrant returned unexecuted and not cancelled, or a summons returned unserved, or a copy thereof, may be delivered by the clerk to the sheriff or other authorized person for execution or service.

Amended, eff 7-1-75

RULE 10. Arraignment

(A) Arraignment procedure. Arraignment shall be conducted in open court, and shall consist of reading the indictment, information or complaint to the defendant, or stating to him the substance of the charge, and calling on him to plead thereto. The defendant may in open court waive the reading of the indictment, information, or complaint. The defendant shall be given a copy of the indictment, information, or complaint, or shall acknowledge receipt thereof, before being called upon to plead.

(B) Presence of defendant. The defendant must be present, except that the court, with the written consent of the defendant and the approval of the prosecuting attorney, may permit arraignment without the presence of the defendant, if a plea of not guilty is entered.

(C) Explanation of rights. When a defendant not represented by counsel is brought before a court and called upon to plead, the judge or magistrate shall cause him to be informed and shall determine that he understands all of the following:

(1) He has a right to retain counsel even if he intends to plead guilty, and has a right to a reasonable continuance in the proceedings to secure counsel.

(2) He has a right to counsel, and the right to a reasonable continuance in the proceeding to secure counsel, and, pursuant to Crim. R. 44, the right to have counsel assigned without cost to himself if he is unable to employ counsel.

(3) He has a right to bail, if the offense is bailable.

(4) He need make no statement at any point in the proceeding, but any statement made can and may be used against him.

(D) Joint arraignment. If there are multiple defendants to be arraigned, the judge or magistrate may by general announcement advise them of their rights as prescribed in this rule.

Amended, eff 7-1-90

RULE 11. Pleas, Rights Upon Plea

(A) Pleas. A defendant may plead not guilty, not guilty by reason of insanity, guilty or, with the consent of the court, no contest. A plea of not guilty by reason of insanity shall be made in writing by either the defendant or his attorney. All other pleas may be made orally. The pleas of not guilty and not guilty by reason of insanity may be joined. If a defendant refuses to plead, the court shall enter a plea of not guilty on behalf of the defendant.

(B) Effect of guilty or no contest pleas. With reference to the offense or offenses to which the plea is entered:

(1) The plea of guilty is a complete admission of the defendant's guilt.

(2) The plea of no contest is not an admission of defendant's guilt, but is an admission of the truth of the facts alleged in the indictment, information, or complaint and such plea or admission shall not be used against the defendant in any subsequent civil or criminal proceeding.

(3) When a plea of guilty or no contest is accepted pursuant to this rule, the court shall, except as provided in subsections (C)(3) and (4), proceed with sentencing under Rule 32.

(C) Pleas of guilty and no contest in felony cases.

(1) Where in a felony case the defendant is unrepresented by counsel the court shall not accept a plea of guilty or no contest unless the defendant, after being readvised that he has the right to be represented by retained counsel, or pursuant to Rule 44 by appointed counsel, waives this right.

(2) In felony cases the court may refuse to accept a plea of guilty or a plea of no contest, and shall not accept such plea without first addressing the defendant personally and:

(a) Determining that he is making the plea voluntarily, with understanding of the nature of the charge and of the maximum penalty involved, and, if applicable, that he is not eligible for probation.

(b) Informing him of and determining that he understands the effect of his plea of guilty or no contest, and that the court upon acceptance of the plea may proceed with judgment and sentence.

(c) Informing him and determining that he understands that by his plea he is waiving his rights to jury trial, to confront witnesses against him, to have compulsory process for obtaining witnesses in his favor, and to require the state to prove his guilt beyond a reasonable doubt at a trial at which he cannot be compelled to testify against himself.

(3) With respect to aggravated murder committed on and after January 1, 1974, the defendant shall plead separately to the charge and to each specification, if any. A plea of guilty or no contest to the charge waives the defendant's right to a jury trial, and before accepting such plea the court shall so advise the defendant and determine that he understands the consequences of such plea.

If the indictment contains no specification, and a plea of guilty or no contest to the charge is accepted, the court shall impose the sentence provided by law.

If the indictment contains one or more specifications, and a plea of guilty or no contest to the charge is accepted, the court may dismiss the specifications and impose sentence accordingly, in the interests of justice.

If the indictment contains one or more specifications which are not dismissed upon acceptance of a plea of guilty or no contest to the charge, or if pleas of guilty or no contest to both the charge and one or more specifications are accepted, a court composed of three judges shall: (a) determine whether the offense was aggravated murder or a lesser offense; and (b) if the offense is determined to have been a lesser offense, impose sentence accordingly; or (c) if the offense is determined to have been aggravated murder, proceed as provided by law to determine the presence or absence of the specified aggravating circumstances and of mitigating circumstances, and impose sentence accordingly.

(4) With respect to all other cases the court need not take testimony upon a plea of guilty or no contest.

(D) Misdemeanor cases involving serious offenses. In misdemeanor cases involving serious offenses the court may refuse to accept a plea of guilty or no contest, and shall not accept such plea without first addressing the defendant personally and informing him of the effect of the pleas of guilty, no contest, and not guilty and determining that he is making the plea voluntarily. Where the defendant is unrepresented by counsel the court shall not accept a plea of guilty or no contest unless the defendant, after being readvised that he has the right to be represented by retained counsel, or pursuant to Rule 44 by appointed counsel, waives this right.

(E) Misdemeanor cases involving petty offenses. In misdemeanor cases involving petty offenses the court may refuse to accept a plea of guilty or no contest, and shall not accept such plea without first informing the defendant of the effect of the pleas of guilty, no contest, and not guilty.

The counsel provisions of Rule 44(B) and (C) apply to this subdivision.

(F) Negotiated plea in felony cases. When, in felony cases, a negotiated plea of guilty or no contest to one or more offenses charged or to one or more other or lesser offenses is offered, the underlying agreement upon which the plea is based shall be stated on the record in open court.

(G) Refusal of court to accept plea. If the court refuses to accept a plea of guilty or no contest, the court shall enter a plea of not guilty on behalf of the defendant. In such cases neither plea shall be admissible in evidence nor be the subject of comment by the prosecuting attorney or court.

(H) Defense of insanity. The defense of not guilty by reason of insanity must be pleaded at the time of arraignment, except that the court for good cause shown shall permit such a plea to be entered at any time before trial.

Amended, eff 7-1-76; 7-1-80

RULE 12. Pleadings and Motions Before Trial: Defenses and Objections

(A) Pleadings and motions. Pleadings in criminal proceedings shall be the complaint, and the indictment or information, and the pleas of not guilty, not guilty by reason of insanity, guilty, and no contest. All other pleas, demurrers, and motions to quash, are abolished. Defenses and objections raised before trial which heretofore could have been raised by one or more of them shall be raised only by motion to dismiss or to grant appropriate relief, as provided in these rules.

(B) Pretrial motions. Prior to trial, any party may raise by motion any defense, objection, evidentiary issue, or request that is capable of determination without the trial of the general issue. The following must be raised before trial:

(1) Defenses and objections based on defects in the institution of the prosecution;

(2) Defenses and objections based on defects in the indictment, information, or complaint (other than failure to show jurisdiction in the court or to charge an offense, which objections shall be noticed by the court at any time during the pendency of the proceeding);

(3) Motions to suppress evidence, including but not limited to statements and identification testimony, on the ground that it was illegally obtained. Such motions shall be filed in the trial court only.

(4) Requests for discovery under Crim. R. 16;

(5) Requests for severance of charges or defendants under Crim. R. 14.

(C) Motion date. All pretrial motions except as provided in Rule 7(E) and Rule 16(F) shall be made within thirty-five days after arraignment or seven days before trial, whichever is earlier. The court in the interest of justice may extend the time for making pretrial motions.

(D) Notice by the prosecuting attorney of the intention to use evidence.

(1) **At the discretion of the prosecuting attorney.** At the arraignment or as soon thereafter as is practicable, the prosecuting attorney may give notice to the defendant of his intention to use specified evidence at trial, in order to afford the defendant an opportunity to raise objections to such evidence prior to trial under subsection (B)(3).

(2) **At the request of the defendant.** At the arraignment or as soon thereafter as is practicable the defendant may, in order to raise objections prior to trial under subsection (B)(3), request notice of the prosecuting attorney's intention to use evidence in chief at trial, which evidence the defendant is entitled to discover under Rule 16.

(E) Ruling on motion. The court may adjudicate a motion based upon briefs, affidavits, the proffer of testimony and exhibits, a hearing, or other appropriate means.

A motion made pursuant to divisions (B)(1) to (B)(5) of this rule shall be determined before trial. Any other motion made pursuant to division (B) of this rule shall be determined before trial whenever possible. Where the court defers ruling on any motion made by the prosecuting attorney before trial and makes a ruling adverse to the prosecuting attorney after the commencement of trial, and the ruling is appealed pursuant to law with the certification required by division (J) of this rule, the court shall stay the proceedings without discharging the jury or dismissing the charges.

Where factual issues are involved in determining a

motion, the court shall state its essential findings on the record.

(F) Return of tangible evidence. Where a motion to suppress tangible evidence is granted, the court upon request of the defendant shall order the property returned to the defendant if he is entitled to lawful possession thereof. Such order shall be stayed pending appeal by the state pursuant to Rule 12(J).

(G) Effect of failure to raise defenses or objections. Failure by the defendant to raise defenses or objections or to make requests which must be made prior to trial, at the time set by the court pursuant to subdivision (C), or prior to any extension thereof made by the court, shall constitute waiver thereof, but the court for good cause shown may grant relief from the waiver.

(H) Effect of plea of no contest. The plea of no contest does not preclude a defendant from asserting upon appeal that the trial court prejudicially erred in ruling on a pretrial motion, including a pretrial motion to suppress evidence.

(I) Effect of determination. If the court grants a motion to dismiss based on a defect in the institution of the prosecution or in the indictment, information, or complaint, it may also order that the defendant be held in custody or that his bail be continued for a specified time not exceeding fourteen days, pending the filing of a new indictment, information, or complaint. Nothing in this rule shall affect any statute relating to periods of limitations. Nothing in this rule shall affect the state's right to appeal an adverse ruling on a motion under subsections (B)(1) or (2), when such motion raises issues which were formerly raised pursuant to a motion to quash, a plea in abatement, a demurrer, or a motion in arrest of judgment.

(J) Appeal by state. When the state takes an appeal as provided by law, the prosecuting attorney shall certify that: (1) the appeal is not taken for the purpose of delay; and (2) the ruling on the motion or motions has rendered the state's proof with respect to the pending charge so weak in its entirety that any reasonable possibility of effective prosecution has been destroyed.

The appeal shall not be allowed unless the notice of appeal and the certification by the prosecuting attorney are filed with the clerk of the trial court within seven days after the date of the entry of the judgment or order granting the motion. Any appeal taken under this rule shall be prosecuted diligently.

If the defendant previously has not been released, the defendant shall, except in capital cases, be released from custody on his or her own recognizance pending appeal when the prosecuting attorney files the notice of appeal and certification.

This appeal shall take precedence over all other appeals.

If an appeal pursuant to this division results in an affirmance of the trial court, the state shall be barred from prosecuting the defendant for the same offense or offenses except upon a showing of newly discovered evidence that the state could not, with reasonable diligence, have discovered before filing of the notice of appeal.

Amended, eff 7-1-75; 7-1-80; 7-1-95

RULE 12.1. Notice of Alibi

Whenever a defendant in a criminal case proposes to offer testimony to establish an alibi on his behalf, he shall, not less than seven days before trial, file and serve upon the prosecuting attorney a notice in writing of his intention to claim alibi. The notice shall include specific information as to the place at which the defendant claims to have been at the time of the alleged offense. If the defendant fails to file such written notice, the court may exclude evidence offered by the defendant for the purpose of proving such alibi, unless the court determines that in the interest of justice such evidence should be admitted.

RULE 13. Trial Together of Indictments or Informations or Complaints

The court may order two or more indictments or informations or both to be tried together, if the offenses or the defendants could have been joined in a single indictment or information. The procedure shall be the same as if the prosecution were under such single indictment or information.

The court may order two or more complaints to be tried together, if the offenses or the defendants could have been joined in a single complaint. The procedure shall be the same as if the prosecution were under such single complaint.

RULE 14. Relief from Prejudicial Joinder

If it appears that a defendant or the state is prejudiced by a joinder of offenses or of defendants in an indictment, information, or complaint, or by such joinder for trial together of indictments, informations or complaints, the court shall order an election or separate trial of counts, grant a severance of defendants, or provide such other relief as justice requires. In ruling on a motion by a defendant for severance, the court shall order the prosecuting attorney to deliver to the court for inspection pursuant to Rule 16(B)(1)(a) any statements or confessions made by the defendants which the state intends to introduce in evidence at the trial.

When two or more persons are jointly indicted for a capital offense, each of such persons shall be tried separately, unless the court orders the defendants to be tried jointly, upon application by the prosecuting attorney or one or more of the defendants, and for good cause shown.

RULE 15. Deposition

(A) When taken. If it appears probable that a prospective witness will be unable to attend or will be prevented from attending a trial or hearing, and if it further appears that his testimony is material and that it is necessary to take his deposition in order to prevent a failure of justice, the court at any time after the filing of an indictment, information, or complaint shall upon motion of the defense attorney or the prosecuting attorney and notice to all the parties, order that his testimony be taken by deposition and that any designated books, papers, documents or tangible objects, not privileged, be produced at the same time and place.

If a witness is committed for failure to give bail or to appear to testify at a trial or hearing, the court on written motion of the witness and notice to the parties, may direct that his deposition be taken. After the deposition is completed, the court may discharge the witness.

(B) Notice of taking. The party at whose instance a deposition is to be taken shall give to every other party reasonable written notice of the time and place for taking the deposition. The notice shall state the name and address of each person to be examined. On motion of a party upon whom the notice is served, the court for cause shown may extend or shorten the time or fix the place of deposition.

(C) Attendance of defendant. The defendant shall have the right to attend the deposition. If he is confined the person having custody of the defendant shall be ordered by the court to take him to the deposition. The defendant may waive his right to attend the deposition, provided he does so in writing and in open court, is represented by counsel, and is fully advised of his right to attend by the court at a recorded proceeding.

(D) Counsel. Where a defendant is without counsel the court shall advise him of his right to counsel and assign counsel to represent him unless the defendant waives counsel or is able to obtain counsel. If it appears that a defendant at whose instance a deposition is to be taken cannot bear the expense thereof, the court may direct that all deposition expenses, including but not limited to travel and subsistence of the defendant's attorney for attendance at such examination together with a reasonable attorney fee, in addition to the compensation allowed for defending the defendant, and the expenses of the prosecuting attorney in the taking of such deposition, shall be paid out of public funds upon the certificate of the court making such order. Waiver of counsel shall be as prescribed in Rule 44(C).

(E) How taken. Depositions shall be taken in the manner provided in civil cases. The prosecution and defense shall have the right, as at trial, to full examination of witnesses. A deposition taken under this rule shall be filed in the court in which the action is pending.

(F) Use. At the trial or upon any hearing, a part or all of a deposition, so far as otherwise admissible under the rules of evidence, may be used if it appears: that the witness is dead; or, that the witness is out of the state, unless it appears that the absence of the witness was procured by the party offering the deposition; or that the witness is unable to attend or testify because of sickness or infirmity; or that the party offering the deposition has been unable to procure the attendance of the witness by subpoena. Any deposition may also be used by any party for the purpose of refreshing the recollection, or contradicting or impeaching the testimony of the deponent as a witness. If only a part of a deposition is offered in evidence by a party, any party may offer other parts.

(G) Objections to admissibility. Objections to receiving in evidence a deposition or a part thereof shall be made as provided in civil actions.

RULE 16. Discovery and Inspection

(A) Demand for discovery. Upon written request each party shall forthwith provide the discovery herein allowed. Motions for discovery shall certify that demand for discovery has been made and the discovery has not been provided.

(B) Disclosure of evidence by the prosecuting attorney.

(1) Information subject to disclosure.

(a) Statement of defendant or co-defendant. Upon motion of the defendant, the court shall order the prosecuting attorney to permit the defendant to inspect and copy or photograph any of the following which are available to, or within the possession, custody, or control of the state, the existence of which is known or by the exercise of due diligence may become known to the prosecuting attorney:

(i) Relevant written or recorded statements made by the defendant or co-defendant, or copies thereof;

(ii) Written summaries of any oral statement, or copies thereof, made by the defendant or co-defendant to a prosecuting attorney or any law enforcement officer;

(iii) Recorded testimony of the defendant or co-defendant before a grand jury.

(b) Defendant's prior record. Upon motion of the defendant the court shall order the prosecuting attorney to furnish defendant a copy of defendant's prior criminal record, which is available to or within the possession, custody or control of the state.

(c) Documents and tangible objects. Upon motion of the defendant the court shall order the prosecuting attorney to permit the defendant to inspect and copy or photograph books, papers, documents, photographs, tangible objects, buildings or places, or copies or portions thereof, available to or within the possession, custody or control of the state, and which are material to the preparation of his defense, or are intended for use by the prosecuting attorney as evidence at the trial, or were obtained from or belong to the defendant.

(d) Reports of examination and tests. Upon motion

of the defendant the court shall order the prosecuting attorney to permit the defendant to inspect and copy or photograph any results or reports of physical or mental examinations, and of scientific tests or experiments, made in connection with the particular case, or copies thereof, available to or within the possession, custody or control of the state, the existence of which is known or by the exercise of due diligence may become known to the prosecuting attorney.

(e) Witness names and addresses; record. Upon motion of the defendant, the court shall order the prosecuting attorney to furnish to the defendant a written list of the names and addresses of all witnesses whom the prosecuting attorney intends to call at trial, together with any record of prior felony convictions of any such witness, which record is within the knowledge of the prosecuting attorney. Names and addresses of witnesses shall not be subject to disclosure if the prosecuting attorney certifies to the court that to do so may subject the witness or others to physical or substantial economic harm or coercion. Where a motion for discovery of the names and addresses of witnesses has been made by a defendant, the prosecuting attorney may move the court to perpetuate the testimony of such witnesses in a hearing before the court, in which hearing the defendant shall have the right of cross-examination. A record of the witness' testimony shall be made and shall be admissible at trial as part of the state's case in chief, in the event the witness has become unavailable through no fault of the state.

(f) Disclosure of evidence favorable to defendant. Upon motion of the defendant before trial the court shall order the prosecuting attorney to disclose to counsel for the defendant all evidence, known or which may become known to the prosecuting attorney, favorable to the defendant and material either to guilt or punishment. The certification and the perpetuation provisions of subsection (B)(1)(e) apply to this subsection.

(g) In camera inspection of witness' statement. Upon completion of a witness' direct examination at trial, the court on motion of the defendant shall conduct an in camera inspection of the witness' written or recorded statement with the defense attorney and prosecuting attorney present and participating, to determine the existence of inconsistencies, if any, between the testimony of such witness and the prior statement.

If the court determines that inconsistencies exist, the statement shall be given to the defense attorney for use in cross-examination of the witness as to the inconsistencies.

If the court determines that inconsistencies do not exist the statement shall not be given to the defense attorney and he shall not be permitted to cross-examine or comment thereon.

Whenever the defense attorney is not given the entire statement, it shall be preserved in the records of the court to be made available to the appellate court in the event of an appeal.

(2) Information not subject to disclosure. Except as provided in subsections (B)(1)(a), (b), (d), (f), and (g), this rule does not authorize the discovery or inspection of reports, memoranda, or other internal documents made by the prosecuting attorney or his agents in connection with the investigation or prosecution of the case, or of statements made by witnesses or prospective witnesses to state agents.

(3) Grand jury transcripts. The discovery or inspection of recorded proceedings of a grand jury shall be governed by Rule 6(E) and subsection (B)(1)(a) of this rule.

(4) Witness list; no comment. The fact that a witness' name is on a list furnished under subsections (B)(1)(b) and (f), and that such witness is not called shall not be commented upon at the trial.

(C) Disclosure of evidence by the defendant.

(1) Information subject to disclosure.

(a) Documents and tangible objects. If on request or motion the defendant obtains discovery under subsection (B)(1)(c), the court shall, upon motion of the prosecuting attorney order the defendant to permit the prosecuting attorney to inspect and copy or photograph books, papers, documents, photographs, tangible objects, or copies or portions thereof, available to or within the possession, custody or control of the defendant and which the defendant intends to introduce in evidence at the trial.

(b) Reports of examinations and tests. If on request or motion the defendant obtains discovery under subsection (B)(1)(d), the court shall, upon motion of the prosecuting attorney, order the defendant to permit the prosecuting attorney to inspect and copy or photograph any results or reports of physical or mental examinations and of scientific tests or experiments made in connection with the particular case, or copies thereof, available to or within the possession or control of the defendant, and which the defendant intends to introduce in evidence at the trial, or which were prepared by a witness whom the defendant intends to call at the trial, when such results or reports relate to his testimony.

(c) Witness names and addresses. If on request or motion the defendant obtains discovery under subsection (B)(1)(e), the court shall, upon motion of the prosecuting attorney, order the defendant to furnish the prosecuting attorney a list of the names and addresses of the witnesses he intends to call at the trial. Where a motion for discovery of the names and addresses of witnesses has been made by the prosecuting attorney, the defendant may move the court to perpetuate the testimony of such witnesses in a hearing before the court in which hearing the prosecuting attorney shall have the right of cross-examination. A record of the witness' testimony shall be made and shall be admissible at trial as part of the defendant's case in chief in the event the witness has become unavailable through no fault of the defendant.

(d) In camera inspection of witness' statement. Upon completion of the direct examination, at trial, of a witness other than the defendant, the court on motion of the prosecuting attorney shall conduct an in camera inspection of the witness' written or recorded statement obtained by the defense attorney or his agents with the defense attorney and prosecuting attorney present and participating, to determine the existence of inconsistencies, if any, between the testimony of such witness and the prior statement.

If the court determines that inconsistencies exist the statement shall be given to the prosecuting attorney for use in cross-examination of the witness as to the inconsistencies.

If the court determines that inconsistencies do not exist the statement shall not be given to the prosecuting attorney, and he shall not be permitted to cross-examine or comment thereon.

Whenever the prosecuting attorney is not given the entire statement it shall be preserved in the records of the court to be made available to the appellate court in the event of an appeal.

(2) Information not subject to disclosure. Except as provided in subsections (C)(1)(b) and (d), this rule does not authorize the discovery or inspection of reports, memoranda, or other internal documents made by the defense attorney or his agents in connection with the investigation or defense of the case, or of statements made by witnesses or prospective witnesses to the defense attorney or his agents.

(3) Witness list; no comment. The fact that a witness' name is on a list furnished under subsection (C)(1)(c), and that the witness is not called shall not be commented upon at the trial.

(D) Continuing duty to disclose. If, subsequent to compliance with a request or order pursuant to this rule, and prior to or during trial, a party discovers additional matter which would have been subject to discovery or inspection under the original request or order, he shall promptly make such matter available for discovery or inspection, or notify the other party or his attorney or the court of the existence of the additional matter, in order to allow the court to modify its previous order, or to allow the other party to make an appropriate request for additional discovery or inspection.

(E) Regulation of discovery.

(1) Protective orders. Upon a sufficient showing the court may at any time order that the discovery or inspection be denied, restricted or deferred, or make such other order as is appropriate. Upon motion by a party the court may permit a party to make such showing, or part of such showing, in the form of a written statement to be inspected by the judge alone. If the court enters an order granting relief following such a showing, the entire text of the party's statement shall be sealed and preserved in the records of the court to be made available to the appellate court in the event of an appeal.

(2) Time, place and manner of discovery and inspection. An order of the court granting relief under this rule shall specify the time, place and manner of making the discovery and inspection permitted, and may prescribe such terms and conditions as are just.

(3) Failure to comply. If at any time during the course of the proceedings it is brought to the attention of the court that a party has failed to comply with this rule or with an order issued pursuant to this rule, the court may order such party to permit the discovery or inspection, grant a continuance, or prohibit the party from introducing in evidence the material not disclosed, or it may make such other order as it deems just under the circumstances.

(F) Time of motions. A defendant shall make his motion for discovery within twenty-one days after arraignment or seven days before the date of trial, whichever is earlier, or at such reasonable time later as the court may permit. The prosecuting attorney shall make his motion for discovery within seven days after defendant obtains discovery or three days before trial, whichever is earlier. The motion shall include all relief sought under this rule. A subsequent motion may be made only upon showing of cause why such motion would be in the interest of justice.

NOTE: The *PROPOSED* amendment to Crim. R. 16 published in *Ohio Official Reports* for comment in January 1995 and in *1995 Court Rules Bulletin* #2 did not go into effect.

RULE 17. Subpoena

(A) For attendance of witnesses; form; issuance. Every subpoena issued by the clerk shall be under the seal of the court, shall state the name of the court and the title of the action, and shall command each person to whom it is directed to attend and give testimony at a time and place therein specified. The clerk shall issue a subpoena, or a subpoena for the production of documentary evidence, signed and sealed but otherwise in blank, to a party requesting it, who shall fill it in and file a copy thereof with the clerk before service.

(B) Defendants unable to pay. The court shall order at any time that a subpoena be issued for service on a named witness upon an ex parte application of a defendant upon a satisfactory showing that the presence of the witness is necessary to an adequate defense and that the defendant is financially unable to pay the witness fees required by subdivision (D). If the court orders the subpoena to be issued the costs incurred by the process and the fees of the witness so subpoenaed shall be taxed as costs.

(C) For production of documentary evidence. A subpoena may also command the person to whom it is directed to produce the books, papers, documents or other objects designated therein; but the court, upon motion made promptly and in any event made at or before the time specified in the subpoena for compliance therewith, may quash or modify the subpoena if compliance would be unreasonable or oppressive. The court may direct that the books, papers, documents or other objects designated in the subpoena be produced before the court at a time prior to the trial or prior to the time they are offered in evidence, and may, upon their production, permit them or portions thereof to be inspected by the parties or their attorneys.

(D) Service. A subpoena may be served by a sheriff, bailiff, coroner, clerk of court, constable, marshal, or a deputy of any, by a municipal or township policeman, by an attorney at law or by any person designated by order of the court who is not a party and is not less than eighteen years of age. Service of a subpoena upon a person named therein shall be made by delivering a copy thereof to such person or by reading it to him in person or by leaving it at his usual place of residence, and by tendering to him upon demand the fees for one day's attendance and the mileage allowed by law. The person serving the subpoena shall file a return thereof with the clerk. If the witness being subpoenaed resides outside the county in which the court is located, the fees for one day's attendance and mileage shall be tendered without demand. The return may be forwarded through the postal service, or otherwise.

(E) Subpoena for taking depositions; place of examination. When the attendance of a witness before an official authorized to take depositions is required, the subpoena shall be issued by such person and shall command the person to whom it is directed to attend and give testimony at a time and place specified therein. The subpoena may command the person to whom it is directed to produce designated books, papers, documents, or tangible objects which constitute or contain evidence relating to any of the matters within the scope of the examination permitted by Rule 16.

A person whose deposition is to be taken may be required to attend an examination in the county wherein he resides or is employed or transacts his business in person, or at such other convenient place as is fixed by an order of court.

(F) Subpoena for a hearing or trial. At the request of any party, subpoenas for attendance at a hearing or trial shall be issued by the clerk of the court in which the hearing or trial is held. A subpoena requiring the attendance of a witness at a hearing or trial may be served at any place within this state.

(G) Contempt. Failure by any person without adequate excuse to obey a subpoena served upon him may be deemed a contempt of the court or officer issuing the subpoena.

RULE 17.1. Pretrial Conference

At any time after the filing of an indictment, information or complaint the court may, upon its own motion or the motion of any party, order one or more conferences to consider such matters as will promote a fair and expeditious trial. At the conclusion of a conference the court shall prepare and file a memorandum of the matters agreed upon. No admissions made by the defendant or his attorney at the conference shall be used against the defendant unless the admissions are reduced to writing and signed by the defendant and his attorney. The court shall not conduct pretrial conferences until the defendant is represented by counsel.

RULE 18. Venue and Change of Venue

(A) General venue provision. The venue of a criminal case shall be as provided by law.

(B) Change of venue; procedure upon change of venue. Upon the motion of any party or upon its own motion the court may transfer an action to any court having jurisdiction of the subject matter outside the county in which trial would otherwise be held, when it appears that a fair and impartial trial cannot be held in the court in which the action is pending.

(1) Time of motion. A motion under this rule shall be made within thirty-five days after arraignment or seven days before trial, whichever is earlier, or at such reasonable time later as the court may permit.

(2) Clerk's obligations upon change of venue. Where a change of venue is ordered the clerk of the court in which the cause is pending shall make copies of all of the papers in the action which, with the original complaint, indictment, or information, he shall transmit to the clerk of the court to which the action is sent for trial, and the trial and all subsequent proceedings shall be conducted as if the action had originated in the latter court.

(3) Additional counsel for prosecuting attorney. The prosecuting attorney of the political subdivision in which the action originated shall take charge of and try the case. The court to which the action is sent may on application appoint one or more attorneys to assist the prosecuting attorney in the trial, and allow the appointed attorneys reasonable compensation.

(4) Appearance of defendant, witnesses. Where a change of venue is ordered and the defendant is in custody, a warrant shall be issued by the clerk of the court in which the action originated, directed to the person having custody of the defendant commanding him to bring the defendant to the jail of the county to which the action is transferred, there to be kept until discharged. If the defendant on the date of the order changing venue is not in custody, the court in the order changing venue shall continue the conditions of release and direct the defendant to appear in the court to which the venue is changed. The court shall recognize the witnesses to appear before the court in which the accused is to be tried.

(5) Expenses. The reasonable expenses of the prosecuting attorney incurred in consequence of a change of venue, compensation of counsel appointed pursuant to Rule 44, the fees of the clerk of the court to which the venue is changed, the sheriff or bailiff, and of the jury shall be allowed and paid out of the treasury of the political subdivision in which the action originated.

RULE 19. Magistrates

(A) Appointment. A court other than a mayor's court may appoint one or more magistrates. A magistrate shall be an attorney admitted to practice in Ohio. The compensation for the services of a magistrate shall be fixed by the court. A person may serve as both a magistrate and a traffic referee. A magistrate may serve in more than one county or in two or more courts of the same criminal jurisdiction within the same county.

(B) Powers and Duties.

(1) Notwithstanding any contrary provisions of these rules and subject to limitations that may be established by the court, a court may refer to a magistrate and, upon such a reference, a magistrate may preside over the following proceedings and issue the appropriate orders:

(a) Initial appearances and preliminary hearings conducted pursuant to Crim. R. 5.

(b) Arraignments conducted pursuant to Crim. R. 10.

(c) Proceedings at which a plea may be entered in accordance with Crim. R. 11. A magistrate may accept and enter not guilty pleas in felony cases, and guilty, not guilty, and no contest pleas in misdemeanor cases. In no instance shall a magistrate make a determination of guilt or innocence, or recommend or impose a sentence.

(d) Pretrial conferences conducted pursuant to Crim. R. 17.1.

(e) Proceedings to establish bail pursuant to Crim. R. 46.

(f) Motions filed pursuant to Crim. R. 47 over which the magistrate has authority under these rules.

(2) The parties may secure the attendance of witnesses and the production of documents before a magistrate as provided in Crim. R. 17. If, without good cause, a person fails to appear and give testimony or fails to produce documentary evidence, the person may be subject to contempt proceedings as provided in Crim. R. 17(G).

(3) Any orders issued by a magistrate shall be made in writing and included in the record.

(C) Objections. Within seven days after the issuance of an order by a magistrate, a party may file objections to the order. Objections shall be made in writing and shall state, with particularity, the grounds for the objections. The objections shall be considered a motion and be heard by the judge to whom the case is assigned. Upon consideration of the objections, the judge may hear additional evidence and may affirm, reject, or modify the order of the magistrate.

Effective 7-1-90; 7-1-95

RULE 20. Reserved

RULE 21. Transfer From Common Pleas Court for Trial

(A) When permitted. Where an indictment or information charging only misdemeanors is filed in the court of common pleas, such court may retain the case for trial or the administrative judge may, within fourteen days after the indictment or information is filed with the clerk of the court of common pleas, transfer it to the court from which the bindover to the grand jury was made or to the court of record of the jurisdiction in which venue appears.

(B) Proceedings on transfer. When a transfer is ordered, the clerk of the court of common pleas shall transmit to the clerk of the court to which the case is transferred, the indictment, information, and all other papers in the case, or copies thereof, and any bail taken, and the prosecution shall continue in that jurisdiction.

RULE 22. Recording of Proceedings

In serious offense cases all proceedings shall be recorded.

In petty offense cases all waivers of counsel required by Rule 44(B) shall be recorded, and if requested by any party all proceedings shall be recorded.

Proceedings may be recorded in shorthand, or stenotype, or by any other adequate mechanical, electronic or video recording device.

RULE 23. Trial by Jury or by the Court

(A) Trial by jury. In serious offense cases the defendant before commencement of the trial may knowingly, intelligently and voluntarily waive in writing his right to trial by jury. Such waiver may also be made during trial with the approval of the court and the consent of the prosecuting attorney. In petty offense cases, where there is a right of jury trial, the defendant shall be tried by the court unless he demands a jury trial. Such demand must be in writing and filed with the clerk of court not less than ten days prior to the date set for trial, or on or before the third day following receipt of notice of the date set for trial, whichever is later. Failure to demand a jury trial as provided in this subdivision is a complete waiver of the right thereto.

(B) Number of jurors. In felony cases juries shall consist of twelve.

In misdemeanor cases juries shall consist of eight.

If a defendant is charged with a felony and with a misdemeanor or, if a felony and a misdemeanor involving different defendants are joined for trial, the jury shall consist of twelve.

(C) Trial without a jury. In a case tried without a

jury the court shall make a general finding.
Amended, eff 7-1-80

RULE 24. Trial Jurors

(A) **Examination of jurors.** Any person called as a juror for the trial of any cause shall be examined under oath or upon affirmation as to his qualifications. The court may permit the attorney for the defendant, or the defendant if appearing pro se, and the attorney for the state to conduct the examination of the prospective jurors or may itself conduct the examination. In the latter event, the court shall permit the state and defense to supplement the examination by further inquiry.

(B) **Challenge for cause.** A person called as a juror may be challenged for the following causes:

(1) That he has been convicted of a crime which by law renders him disqualified to serve on a jury.

(2) That he is a chronic alcoholic, or drug dependent person.

(3) That he was a member of the grand jury which found the indictment in the case.

(4) That he served on a petit jury drawn in the same cause against the same defendant, and such jury was discharged after hearing the evidence or rendering a verdict thereon which was set aside.

(5) That he served as a juror in a civil case brought against the defendant for the same act.

(6) That he has an action pending between him and the State of Ohio or the defendant.

(7) That he or his spouse is a party to another action then pending in any court in which an attorney in the cause then on trial is an attorney, either for or against him.

(8) That he has been subpoenaed in good faith as a witness in the case.

(9) That he is possessed of a state of mind evincing enmity or bias toward the defendant or the state; but no person summoned as a juror shall be disqualified by reason of a previously formed or expressed opinion with reference to the guilt or innocence of the accused, if the court is satisfied, from the examination of the juror or from other evidence, that he will render an impartial verdict according to the law and the evidence submitted to the jury at the trial.

(10) That he is related by consanguinity or affinity within the fifth degree to the person alleged to be injured or attempted to be injured by the offense charged, or to the person on whose complaint the prosecution was instituted; or to the defendant.

(11) That he is the person alleged to be injured or attempted to be injured by the offense charged, or the person on whose complaint the prosecution was instituted, or the defendant.

(12) That he is the employer or employee, or the spouse, parent, son, or daughter of the employer or employee, or the counsellor, agent, or attorney, of any person included in subsection (B)(11).

(13) That English is not his native language, and his knowledge of English is insufficient to permit him to understand the facts and the law in the case.

(14) That he is otherwise unsuitable for any other cause to serve as a juror.

The validity of each challenge listed in this subdivision shall be determined by the court.

(C) **Peremptory challenges.** In addition to challenges provided in subdivision (B), if there is one defendant, each party peremptorily may challenge three jurors in misdemeanor cases, four jurors in felony cases other than capital cases, and six jurors in capital cases. If there is more than one defendant, each defendant peremptorily may challenge the same number of jurors as if he were the sole defendant.

In any case where there are multiple defendants, the prosecuting attorney peremptorily may challenge a number of jurors equal to the total peremptory challenges allowed all defendants. In case of the consolidation of any indictments, informations or complaints for trial, such consolidated cases shall be considered, for purposes of exercising peremptory challenges, as though the defendants or offenses had been joined in the same indictment, information or complaint.

(D) **Manner of exercising peremptory challenges.** Peremptory challenges may be exercised after the minimum number of jurors allowed by the rules has been passed for cause and seated on the panel. Peremptory challenges shall be exercised alternately, with the first challenge exercised by the state. The failure of a party to exercise a peremptory challenge constitutes a waiver of that challenge. If all parties, alternately and in sequence, fail to exercise a peremptory challenge, the joint failure constitutes a waiver of all peremptory challenges.

A prospective juror peremptorily challenged by either party shall be excused and another juror shall be called who shall take the place of the juror excused and be sworn and examined as other jurors. The other party, if he has peremptory challenges remaining, shall be entitled to challenge any juror then seated on the panel.

(E) **Challenge to array.** The prosecuting attorney or the attorney for the defendant may challenge the array of petit jurors on the ground that it was not selected, drawn or summoned in accordance with law. A challenge to the array shall be made before the examination of the jurors pursuant to subdivision (A) and shall be tried by the court.

No array of petit jurors shall be set aside, nor shall any verdict in any case be set aside because the jury commissioners have returned such jury or any juror in any informal or irregular manner, if in the opinion of the court the irregularity is unimportant and insufficient to vitiate the return.

(F) **Alternate jurors.** The court may direct that not more than six jurors in addition to the regular jury be called and impanelled to sit as alternate jurors. Alternate jurors in the order in which they are called shall replace jurors who, prior to the time the jury retires to consider its verdict, become or are found to be unable or disqualified to perform their duties. Alternate jurors shall be drawn in the same manner, have the same qualifications, be subject to the same examination and challenges, take the same oath, and have the same functions, powers, facilities, and privileges as the regular jurors. An alternate juror who does not replace a regular juror shall be discharged after the jury retires to consider its verdict. Each party is entitled to one peremptory challenge in addition to those otherwise allowed if one or two alternate jurors are to be impanelled, two peremptory challenges if three or four alternate jurors are to be impanelled, and three peremptory challenges if five or six alternate jurors are to be impanelled. The additional peremptory challenges may be used against an alternate juror only, and the other peremptory challenges allowed by this rule may not be used against an alternate juror.

(G) Control of juries

(1) Before submission of case to jury. Before submission of a case to the jury, the court, upon its own motion or the motion of a party, may restrict the separation of jurors or may sequester the jury.

(2) After submission of case to jury.

(a) Misdemeanor cases. After submission of a misdemeanor case to the jury, the court, after giving cautionary instructions, may permit the separation of jurors.

(b) Non-capital felony cases. After submission of a non-capital felony case to the jury, the court, after giving cautionary instructions, may permit the separation of jurors during any period of court adjournment or may require the jury to remain under the supervision of an officer of the court.

(c) Capital cases. After submission of a capital case to the jury, the jury shall remain under the supervision of an officer of the court until a verdict is rendered or the jury is discharged by the court.

(3) Separation in emergency. Where the jury is sequestered or after a capital case is submitted to the jury, the court may, in an emergency and upon giving cautionary instructions, allow temporary separation of jurors.

(4) Duties of supervising officer. Where jurors are required to remain under the supervision of an officer of the court, the court shall make arrangements for their care, maintenance and comfort.

When the jury is in the care of an officer of the court and until the jury is discharged by the court, the officer may inquire whether the jury has reached a verdict, but shall not:

(a) Communicate any matter concerning jury conduct to anyone except the judge or;

(b) Communicate with the jurors or permit communications with jurors, except as allowed by court order.

Amended, eff 7-1-75

RULE 25. Disability of a Judge

(A) During trial. If for any reason the judge before whom a jury trial has commenced is unable to proceed with the trial, another judge designated by the administrative judge, or, in the case of a single-judge division, by the Chief Justice of the Supreme Court of Ohio, may proceed with and finish the trial, upon certifying in the record that he has familiarized himself with the record of the trial. If such other judge is satisfied that he cannot adequately familiarize himself with the record, he may in his discretion grant a new trial.

(B) After verdict or finding of guilt. If for any reason the judge before whom the defendant has been tried is unable to perform the duties of the court after a verdict or finding of guilt, another judge designated by the administrative judge, or, in the case of a single-judge division, by the Chief Justice of the Supreme Court of Ohio, may perform those duties. If such other judge is satisfied that he cannot perform those duties because he did not preside at the trial, he may in his discretion grant a new trial.

RULE 26. Substitution of Photographs for Physical Evidence

Physical property, other than contraband, as defined by statute, under the control of a Prosecuting Attorney for use as evidence in a hearing or trial should be returned to the owner at the earliest possible time. To facilitate the early return of such property, where appropriate, and by court order, photographs, as defined in Evid. R. 1001 (2), may be taken of the property and introduced as evidence in the hearing or trial. The admission of such photographs is subject to the relevancy requirements of Evid. R. 401, Evid. R. 402, Evid. R. 403, the authentication requirements of Evid. R. 901, and the best evidence requirements of Evid. R. 1002.

Effective, 7-1-81

RULE 27. Proof of Official Record; Judicial Notice: Determination of Foreign Law

The proof of official records provisions of Civil Rule 44, and the judicial notice and determination of foreign law provisions of Civil Rule 44.1 apply in criminal cases.

RULE 28. Reserved

RULE 29. Motion for Acquittal

(A) Motion for judgment of acquittal. The court on motion of a defendant or on its own motion, after the evidence on either side is closed, shall order the entry of a judgment of acquittal of one or more offenses charged in the indictment, information, or complaint, if the evidence is insufficient to sustain a conviction of such offense or offenses. The court may not reserve ruling on a motion for judgment of acquittal made at the close of the state's case.

(B) Reservation of decision on motion. If a motion for a judgment of acquittal is made at the close of all the evidence, the court may reserve decision on the motion, submit the case to the jury and decide the motion either before the jury returns a verdict, or after it returns a verdict of guilty, or after it is discharged without having returned a verdict.

(C) Motion after verdict or discharge of jury. If a jury returns a verdict of guilty or is discharged without having returned a verdict, a motion for judgment of acquittal may be made or renewed within fourteen days after the jury is discharged or within such further time as the court may fix during the fourteen day period. If a verdict of guilty is returned, the court may on such motion set aside the verdict and enter judgment of acquittal. If no verdict is returned, the court may enter judgment of acquittal. It shall not be a prerequisite to the making of such motion that a similar motion has been made prior to the submission of the case to the jury.

RULE 30. Instructions

(A) Instructions; error; record. At the close of the evidence or at such earlier time during the trial as the court reasonably directs, any party may file written requests that the court instruct the jury on the law as set forth in the requests. Copies shall be furnished to all other parties at the time of making the requests. The court shall inform counsel of its proposed action on the requests prior to counsel's arguments to the jury and shall give the jury complete instructions after the arguments are completed. The court also may give some or all of its instructions to the jury prior to counsel's arguments. The court need not reduce its instructions to writing.

On appeal, a party may not assign as error the giving or the failure to give any instructions unless the party objects before the jury retires to consider its verdict, stating specifically the matter objected to and the grounds of the objection. Opportunity shall be given to make the objection out of the hearing of the jury.

(B) Cautionary instructions. At the commencement and during the course of the trial, the court may give the jury cautionary and other instructions of law relating to trial procedure, credibility and weight of the evidence, and the duty and function of the jury and may acquaint the jury generally with the nature of the case.

Amended, eff 7-1-75; 7-1-82; 7-1-92

RULE 31. Verdict

(A) Return. The verdict shall be unanimous. It shall be in writing, signed by all jurors concurring therein, and returned by the jury to the judge in open court.

(B) Several defendants. If there are two or more defendants the jury at any time during its deliberations may return a verdict or verdicts with respect to a defendant or defendants as to whom it has agreed. If the jury cannot agree with respect to all, the defendant or defendants as to whom it does not agree may be tried again.

(C) Conviction of lesser offense. The defendant may be found not guilty of the offense charged but guilty of an attempt to commit it if such an attempt is an offense at law. When the indictment, information, or complaint charges an offense including degrees, or if lesser offenses are included within the offense charged, the defendant may be found not guilty of the degree charged but guilty of an inferior degree thereof, or of a lesser included offense.

(D) Poll of jury. When a verdict is returned and before it is accepted the jury shall be polled at the request of any party or upon the court's own motion. If upon the poll there is not unanimous concurrence, the jury may be directed to retire for further deliberation or may be discharged.

RULE 32. Sentence

(A) Sentence.

(1) Imposition of sentence. Sentence shall be imposed without unnecessary delay. Pending sentence, the court may commit the defendant or continue or alter the bail. Before imposing sentence the court shall afford counsel an opportunity to speak on behalf of the defendant and also shall address the defendant personally and ask if he or she wishes to make a statement in his or her own behalf or present any information in mitigation of punishment.

(2) Notification of right to appeal. After imposing sentence in a serious offense that has gone to trial on a plea of not guilty, the court shall advise the defendant of all of the following:

(a) That the defendant has a right to appeal;

(b) That if the defendant is unable to pay the cost of an appeal, the defendant has the right to appeal without payment;

(c) That if the defendant is unable to obtain counsel for an appeal, counsel will be appointed without cost;

(d) That if the defendant is unable to pay the costs of documents necessary to an appeal, the documents will be provided without cost;

(e) That the defendant has a right to have a notice of appeal timely filed on his or her behalf.

Upon defendant's request, the court shall forthwith appoint counsel for appeal.

(B) Judgment. A judgment of conviction shall set forth the plea, the verdict or findings, and the sentence. If the defendant is found not guilty or for any other reason is entitled to be discharged, the court shall render judgment accordingly. The judge shall sign the judgment and the clerk shall enter it on the journal. A judgment is effective only when entered on the journal by the clerk.

Amended, eff 7-1-92

RULE 32.1. Withdrawal of Guilty Plea

A motion to withdraw a plea of guilty or no contest may be made only before sentence is imposed or imposition of sentence is suspended; but to correct manifest injustice the court after sentence may set aside the judgment of conviction and permit the defendant to withdraw his plea.

RULE 32.2. Presentence Investigation

(A) When made. In felony cases the court shall, and in misdemeanor cases may, order a presentence investigation and report before granting probation.

(B) Report. The report of the presentence investigation shall state the defendant's prior criminal record, the circumstances of the offense, and such information about defendant's social history, employment record, financial ability and means, personal characteristics, family situation, and present physical and mental condition, as may be helpful in imposing or modifying sentence or providing rehabilitative or correctional treatment, and shall state such other information as may be required by the court. Whenever the court, probation officer, or investigator considers it advisable, the investigation may include a physical and mental examination of the defendant.

(C) Disclosure.

(1) Except in cases of aggravated murder, the report of the presentence investigation shall be confidential and need not be furnished to the defendant or his counsel or the prosecuting attorney unless the court, in its discretion, so orders.

(2) Any material disclosed to the defendant or his counsel shall also be disclosed to the prosecuting attorney.

(3) Any copies of the presentence investigation report made available to the defendant or his counsel and the prosecuting attorney shall be returned to the court, probation officer or investigator immediately following the imposition of sentence or the granting of probation. Copies of the presentence investigation report shall not be made by the defendant, his counsel, or the prosecuting attorney.

(D) Transmission of papers to custodian. If the defendant is committed to an institution or placed under custodial care or treatment under the supervision of a governmental agency, the court shall forward to the institution or custodian a copy of the report of any presentence investigation and any mental or physical examination, together with the entry of commitment or other appropriate entry. In addition, if the defendant is committed to a penal or reformatory institution, the court shall forward a statement of the number of days confinement which the defendant is entitled by law to have credited to his minimum and maximum sentence.

Amended, eff 7-1-76

RULE 32.3. Revocation of Probation

(A) Revocation hearing. The court shall not revoke probation except after a hearing at which the defendant shall be present and apprised of the grounds on which such action is proposed. The defendant may be admitted to bail pending such hearing.

(B) Counsel. The defendant shall have the right to be represented by retained counsel and shall be so advised. Where a defendant convicted of a serious offense is unable to obtain counsel, counsel shall be assigned to represent him, unless the defendant after being fully advised of his right to assigned counsel, knowingly, intelligently, and voluntarily waives his right to counsel. Where a defendant convicted of a petty offense is unable to obtain counsel, the court may assign counsel to represent him.

(C) Confinement in petty offense cases. If confinement after conviction was precluded by Rule 44(B), revocation of probation shall not result in confinement.

If confinement after conviction was not precluded by Rule 44(B), revocation of probation shall not result in confinement unless, at the revocation hearing, there is compliance with Rule 44(B).

(D) Waiver of counsel. Waiver of counsel shall be as prescribed in Rule 44(C).

RULE 33. New Trial

(A) Grounds. A new trial may be granted on motion of the defendant for any of the following causes affecting materially his substantial rights:

(1) Irregularity in the proceedings, or in any order or ruling of the court, or abuse of discretion by the court, because of which the defendant was prevented from having a fair trial;

(2) Misconduct of the jury, prosecuting attorney, or the witnesses for the state;

(3) Accident or surprise which ordinary prudence could not have guarded against;

(4) That the verdict is not sustained by sufficient evidence or is contrary to law. If the evidence shows the defendant is not guilty of the degree of crime for which he was convicted, but guilty of a lesser degree thereof, or of a lesser crime included therein, the court may modify the verdict or finding accordingly, without granting or ordering a new trial, and shall pass sentence on such verdict or finding as modified;

(5) Error of law occurring at the trial;

(6) When new evidence material to the defense is

discovered, which the defendant could not with reasonable diligence have discovered and produced at the trial. When a motion for a new trial is made upon the ground of newly discovered evidence, the defendant must produce at the hearing on the motion, in support thereof, the affidavits of the witnesses by whom such evidence is expected to be given, and if time is required by the defendant to procure such affidavits, the court may postpone the hearing of the motion for such length of time as is reasonable under all the circumstances of the case. The prosecuting attorney may produce affidavits or other evidence to impeach the affidavits of such witnesses.

(B) Motion for new trial; form, time. Application for a new trial shall be made by motion which, except for the cause of newly discovered evidence, shall be filed within fourteen days after the verdict was rendered, or the decision of the court where a trial by jury has been waived, unless it is made to appear by clear and convincing proof that the defendant was unavoidably prevented from filing his motion for a new trial, in which case the motion shall be filed within seven days from the order of the court finding that the defendant was unavoidably prevented from filing such motion within the time provided herein.

Motions for new trial on account of newly discovered evidence shall be filed within one hundred twenty days after the day upon which the verdict was rendered, or the decision of the court where trial by jury has been waived. If it is made to appear by clear and convincing proof that the defendant was unavoidably prevented from the discovery of the evidence upon which he must rely, such motion shall be filed within seven days from an order of the court finding that he was unavoidably prevented from discovering the evidence within the one hundred twenty day period.

(C) Affidavits required. The causes enumerated in subsection (A)(2) and (3) must be sustained by affidavit showing their truth, and may be controverted by affidavit.

(D) Procedure when new trial granted. When a new trial is granted by the trial court, or when a new trial is awarded on appeal, the accused shall stand trial upon the charge or charges of which he was convicted.

(E) Invalid grounds for new trial. No motion for a new trial shall be granted or verdict set aside, nor shall any judgment of conviction be reversed in any court because of:

(1) An inaccuracy or imperfection in the indictment, information, or complaint, provided that the charge is sufficient to fairly and reasonably inform the defendant of all the essential elements of the charge against him.

(2) A variance between the allegations and the proof thereof, unless the defendant is misled or prejudiced thereby;

(3) The admission or rejection of any evidence offered against or for the defendant, unless the defendant was or may have been prejudiced thereby;

(4) A misdirection of the jury, unless the defendant was or may have been prejudiced thereby;

(5) Any other cause, unless it affirmatively appears from the record that the defendant was prejudiced thereby or was prevented from having a fair trial.

(F) Motion for new trial not a condition for appellate review. A motion for a new trial is not a prerequisite to obtain appellate review.

RULE 34. Arrest of Judgment

The court on motion of the defendant shall arrest judgment if the indictment, information, or complaint does not charge an offense or if the court was without jurisdiction of the offense charged. The motion shall be made within fourteen days after verdict, or finding of guilty, or after plea of guilty or no contest, or within such further time as the court may fix during the fourteen day period.

When the judgment is arrested, the defendant shall be discharged, and his position with respect to the prosecution is as if the indictment, information, or complaint had not been returned or filed.

RULE 35. Post-Conviction Petition

(A) A petition for post-conviction relief pursuant to section 2953.21 of the Revised Code shall contain a case history, statement of facts, and separately identified grounds for relief. Each ground for relief shall not exceed three pages in length. (See recommended Form XV in Appendix of Forms.) A petition may be accompanied by an attachment of exhibits or other supporting materials. A trial court may extend the page limits provided in this rule, request further briefing on any ground for relief presented, or direct the petitioner to file a supplemental petition in the recommended form.

(B) The clerk of court immediately shall send a copy of the petition to the prosecuting attorney. Upon order of the trial court, the clerk of court shall duplicate all or any part of the record that the trial court requires.

(C) The trial court shall file its ruling upon a petition for post-conviction relief, including findings of fact and conclusions of law if required by law, not later than one hundred eighty days after the petition is filed.

Effective, 7-1-97

RULE 36. Clerical Mistakes

Clerical mistakes in judgments, orders, or other parts of the record, and errors in the record arising from oversight or omission, may be corrected by the court at any time.

RULE 37. Reserved

RULE 38. Reserved

RULE 39. Reserved

RULE 40. Reserved

RULE 41. Search and Seizure

(A) Authority to issue warrant. A search warrant authorized by this rule may be issued by a judge of a court of record to search and seize property located within the court's territorial jurisdiction, upon the request of a prosecuting attorney or a law enforcement officer.

(B) Property which may be seized with a warrant. A warrant may be issued under this rule to search for and seize any: (1) evidence of the commission of a criminal offense; or (2) contraband, the fruits of crime, or things otherwise criminally possessed; or (3) weapons or other things by means of which a crime has been committed or reasonably appears about to be committed.

(C) Issuance and contents. A warrant shall issue under this rule only on an affidavit or affidavits sworn to before a judge of a court of record and establishing the grounds for issuing the warrant. The affidavit shall name or describe the person to be searched or particularly describe the place to be searched, name or describe the property to be searched for and seized, state substantially the offense in relation thereto, and state the factual basis for the affiant's belief that such property is there located. If the judge is satisfied that probable cause for the search exists, he shall issue a warrant identifying the property and naming or describing the person or place to be searched. The finding of probable cause may be based upon hearsay in whole or in part, provided there is a substantial basis for believing the source of the hearsay to be credible and for believing that there is a factual basis for the information furnished. Before ruling on a request for a warrant, the judge may require the affiant to appear personally, and may examine under oath the affiant and any witnesses he may produce. Such testimony shall be admissible at a hearing on a motion to suppress if taken down by a court reporter or recording equipment, transcribed and made part of the affidavit. The warrant shall be directed to a law enforcement officer. It shall command the officer to search, within three days, the person or place named for the property specified. The warrant shall be served in the daytime, unless the issuing court, by appropriate provision in the warrant, and for reasonable cause shown, authorizes its execution at times other than daytime. The warrant shall designate a judge to whom it shall be returned.

(D) Execution and return with inventory. The officer taking property under the warrant shall give to the person from whom or from whose premises the property was taken a copy of the warrant and a receipt for the property taken, or shall leave the copy and receipt at the place from which the property was taken. The return shall be made promptly and shall be accompanied by a written inventory of any property taken. The inventory shall be made in the presence of the applicant for the warrant and the person from whose possession or premises the property was taken, if they are present, or in the presence of at least one credible person other than the applicant for the warrant or the person from whose possession or premises the property was taken, and shall be verified by the officer. The judge shall upon request deliver a copy of the inventory to the person from whom or from whose premises the property was taken and to the applicant for the warrant. Property seized under a warrant shall be kept for use as evidence by the court which issued the warrant or by the law enforcement agency which executed the warrant.

(E) Return of papers to clerk. The judge before whom the warrant is returned shall attach to the warrant a copy of the return, inventory, and all other papers in connection therewith and shall file them with the clerk.

(F) Definition of property and daytime. The term "property" is used in this rule to include documents, books, papers and any other tangible objects. The term "daytime" is used in this rule to mean the hours from 7:00 a.m. to 8:00 p.m.

RULE 42. Reserved

RULE 43. Presence of the Defendant

(A) Defendant's presence. The defendant shall be present at the arraignment and every stage of the trial, including the impaneling of the jury, the return of the verdict, and the imposition of sentence, except as otherwise provided by these rules. In all prosecutions, the defendant's voluntary absence after the trial has been commenced in his presence shall not prevent continuing the trial to and including the verdict. A corporation may appear by counsel for all purposes.

(B) Defendant excluded because of disruptive conduct. Where a defendant's conduct in the courtroom is so disruptive that the hearing or trial cannot reasonably be conducted with his continued presence, the hearing or trial may proceed in his absence, and judgment and sentence may be pronounced as if he were present. Where the court determines that it may be essential to the preservation of the constitutional rights of the defendant, it may take such steps as are required for the communication of the courtroom proceedings to the defendant.

RULE 44. Assignment of Counsel

(A) **Counsel in serious offenses.** Where a defendant charged with a serious offense is unable to obtain counsel, counsel shall be assigned to represent him at every stage of the proceedings from his initial appearance before a court through appeal as of right, unless the defendant, after being fully advised of his right to assigned counsel, knowingly, intelligently, and voluntarily waives his right to counsel.

(B) **Counsel in petty offenses.** Where a defendant charged with a petty offense is unable to obtain counsel, the court may assign counsel to represent him. When a defendant charged with a petty offense is unable to obtain counsel, no sentence of confinement may be imposed upon him, unless after being fully advised by the court, he knowingly, intelligently, and voluntarily waives assignment of counsel.

(C) **Waiver of counsel.** Waiver of counsel shall be in open court and the advice and waiver shall be recorded as provided in Rule 22. In addition, in serious offense cases the waiver shall be in writing.

(D) **Assignment procedure.** The determination of whether a defendant is able or unable to obtain counsel shall be made in a recorded proceeding in open court.

RULE 45. Time

(A) **Time: computation.** In computing any period of time prescribed or allowed by these rules, by the local rules of any court, by order of court, or by any applicable statute, the date of the act or event from which the designated period of time begins to run shall not be included. The last day of the period so computed shall be included, unless it is a Saturday, Sunday, or legal holiday, in which event the period runs until the end of the next day which is not Saturday, Sunday, or legal holiday. When the period of time prescribed or allowed is less than seven days, intermediate Saturdays, Sundays, and legal holidays shall be excluded in computation.

(B) **Time: enlargement.** When an act is required or allowed to be performed at or within a specified time, the court for cause shown may at any time in its discretion (1) with or without motion or notice, order the period enlarged if application therefor is made before expiration of the period originally prescribed or as extended by a previous order; or (2) upon motion permit the act to be done after expiration of the specified period, if the failure to act on time was the result of excusable neglect or would result in injustice to the defendant. The court may not extend the time for taking any action under Rule 23, Rule 29, Rule 33, and Rule 34 except to the extent and under the conditions stated in them.

(C) **Time: unaffected by expiration of term.** The period of time provided for the doing of any act or the taking of any proceeding is not affected or limited by the expiration of a term of court. The expiration of a term of court in no way affects the power of a court to do any act in a criminal proceeding.

(D) **Time: for motions; affidavits.** A written motion, other than one which may be heard ex parte, and notice of the hearing thereof, shall be served not later than seven days before the time specified for the hearing unless a different period is fixed by rule or order of the court. For cause shown such an order may be made on ex parte application. When a motion is supported by affidavit, the affidavit shall be served with the motion. Opposing affidavits may be served not less than one day before the hearing, unless the court permits them to be served at a later time.

(E) **Time: additional time after service by mail.** Whenever a party has the right or is required to do an act within a prescribed period after the service of a notice or other paper upon him, and the notice or other paper is served upon him by mail, three days shall be added to the prescribed period. This subdivision does not apply to responses to service of summons under Rule 4 and Rule 9.

RULE 46. Bail

(A) **Purpose of and right to bail.** The purpose of bail is to ensure that the defendant appears at all stages of the criminal proceedings. All persons are entitled to bail, except in capital cases where the proof is evident or the presumption great.

(B) **Pretrial release where summons issued.** Where summons has issued and the defendant has appeared, the judge or magistrate shall relase the defendant on personal recognizance or upon the execution of an unsecured appearance bond.

(C) **Preconviction release in serious offense cases.** Any person who is entitled to release under division (A) of this rule shall be released on personal recognizance or upon the execution of an unsecured appearance bond in an amount specified by the judge or magistrate, unless the judge or magistrate determines that release will not ensure the appearance of the person as required. Where a judge or magistrate so determines, he or she, either in lieu of or in addition to the preferred methods of release stated above, shall impose any of the following conditions of release that will reasonably ensure the appearance of the person for trial or, if no single condition ensures appearance, any combination of the following conditions:

(1) Place the person in the custody of a designated person or organization agreeing to supervise the person;

(2) Place restrictions on the travel, association, or place of abode of the person during the period of release;

(3) Require the execution of an appearance bond in a specified amount, and the deposit with the clerk of the court before which the proceeding is pending of

either twenty-five dollars or a sum of money equal to ten percent of the amount of the bond, whichever is greater. Ninety percent of the deposit shall be returned upon the performance of the conditions of the appearance bond;

(4) Require the execution of bail bond with sufficient solvent sureties, the execution of a bond secured by real estate in the county, or the deposit of cash or the securities allowed by law in lieu of a bond;

(5) Impose any other constitutional condition considered reasonably necessary to ensure appearance.

(D) Preconviction release in petty offense cases. A person arrested for a misdemeanor and not released pursuant to Crim. R. 4(F) shall be released by the clerk of court, or, if the clerk is not available, the officer in charge of the facility to which the person is brought, on the person's personal recognizance, or upon the execution of an unsecured appearance bond in the amount specified in the bail schedule established by the court. If the clerk or officer in charge of the facility determines pursuant to division (F) of this rule that release will not reasonably ensure appearance as required, the person shall be eligible for release by doing any of the following, at the person's option:

(1) Executing an appearance bond in the amount specified in the court's bail schedule, with a deposit of either twenty-five dollars or a sum of money equal to ten percent of the amount of the bond, whichever is greater. Ninety percent of the deposit shall be returned upon the performance of the conditions of the appearance bond;

(2) Posting a bond, in the amount specified in the court's bail schedule, that is guaranteed to the person as a policyholder of a casualty insurer, or as a member of a bona fide motorists' or travelers' organization;

(3) Executing a bail bond with sufficient solvent sureties, or executing a bond secured by real estate in the county, or depositing cash or the securities allowed by law in lieu of a bond in the amount specified in the court's bail schedule.

The court is not required to release a person on the person's own recognizance or upon the execution of an unsecured appearance bond if the person has a history of failure to appear when required in judicial proceedings or if the person's physical, mental, or emotional condition appears to indicate that the person may pose a danger to himself or others if released immediately. When a person is not released because of the person's physical, mental, or emotional condition, and it appears that the person's release into the temporary custody of a responsible relative, friend, or other person will obviate the danger to the person or others, the person shall be released into such temporary custody on the person making bail under division (D)(1), (2), or (3) of this rule.

If a person is not released on the person's own recognizance, upon the execution of an unsecured appearance bond, or pursuant to division (D)(1), (2), or (3) of this rule, the person shall be given a hearing without unnecessary delay before a judge or magistrate who shall determine the conditions of the person's release pursuant to division (C) of this rule.

Each court shall establish a bail schedule covering all misdemeanors including traffic offenses, either specifically, by type, by potential penalty, or by some other reasonable method of classification. Each court, by rule, shall establish a method whereby a person may make bail under division (D)(1) or (3) of this rule by the use of a credit card. The rule shall permit only credit cards of recognized and established issuers. No credit card transaction shall be permitted when a service charge is made against the court or clerk.

(E) Release after conviction.

(1) Serious offense cases. Except when a person has been sentenced to death, a person who has been convicted and is either awaiting sentence or has filed a notice of appeal shall be treated in accordance with the provision of division (C) of this rule unless the judge has reason to believe that no one or more conditions of release will reasonably ensure that the person will not flee or pose a danger to any other person or the community. If a risk of flight or danger is believed to exist, the person may be ordered detained.

(2) Petty offense cases. A person who has been convicted of a misdemeanor and is either awaiting sentence or has filed a notice of appeal shall be treated in accordance with the provision of division (C) of this rule.

(3) Bail or other conditions of release shall not be imposed, amended, or continued by order of a magistrate after conviction.

(F) Conditions of preconviction release; basis. In determining the conditions of release that will reasonably ensure appearance, the judge or magistrate, on the basis of available information, shall take into account the nature and circumstances of the offense charged, the weight of the evidence against the accused, and the accused's family ties, employment, financial resources, character and mental condition, length of residence in the community, record of convictions, and record of appearance at court proceedings, flight to avoid prosecution, or failure to appear at court proceedings.

(G) Order. The judge, magistrate, clerk, or officer who releases a person under this rule shall make an appropriate written order stating the conditions of release.

(H) Amendments. Subject to divisions (C) and (G) of this rule, a judge or magistrate ordering the release of a person on any condition specified in this rule may at any time amend the order to impose additional or different conditions of release.

(I) Information need not be admissible. Information stated in or offered in connection with any order entered pursuant to this rule need not conform to the rules pertaining to the admissibility of evidence in a court of law.

(J) Continuation of bonds. Unless application is made by the surety for discharge, the same bond shall continue as a matter of right until the return of a verdict or judgment by a jury or by the court on the issue of guilt or innocence. In the discretion of the trial judge and upon notice to the surety, the same bond may also continue after final disposition in the trial court and pending sentence or pending disposition of the case on review. Any provision of a bond or similar instrument that is contrary to this rule is void.

(K) Sanctions. Any person released pursuant to any provision of this rule who fails to appear before any court as required is subject to the punishment provided by law, and any bail given for the person's release shall be forfeited.

Any person released on personal recognizance shall, in addition, be considered to have been released pursuant to section 2937.29 of the Revised Code.

(L) Justification of sureties. Every surety, except a corporate surety licensed as provided by law, shall justify by affidavit, and may be required to describe in the affidavit, the property that the surety proposes as security and the encumbrances on it, the number and amount of other bonds and undertakings for bail entered into by the surety and remaining undischarged, and all of the surety's other liabilities. The surety shall provide other evidence of financial responsibility as the court or clerk may require. No bail bond shall be approved unless the surety or sureties appear, in the opinion of the court or clerk, to be financially responsible in at least the amount of the bond. No licensed attorney at law shall be a surety.

(M) Forfeiture of bonds. If there is a breach of condition of a bond, the court shall declare a forfeiture of the bail. Forfeiture proceedings shall be promptly enforced as provided by law.

(N) Exoneration. The obligor shall be exonerated as provided by law.

Amended, eff 7-1-90; 7-1-94

RULE 47. Motions

An application to the court for an order shall be by motion. A motion, other than one made during trial or hearing, shall be in writing unless the court permits it to be made orally. It shall state with particularity the grounds upon which it is made and shall set forth the relief or order sought. It shall be supported by a memorandum containing citations of authority, and may also be supported by an affidavit.

To expedite its business, the court may make provision by rule or order for the submission and determination of motions without oral hearing upon brief written statements of reasons in support and opposition.

RULE 48. Dismissal

(A) Dismissal by the state. The state may by leave of court and in open court file an entry of dismissal of an indictment, information, or complaint and the prosecution shall thereupon terminate.

(B) Dismissal by the court. If the court over objection of the state dismisses an indictment, information, or complaint, it shall state on the record its findings of fact and reasons for the dismissal.

RULE 49. Service and Filing of Papers

(A) Service: when required. Written notices, requests for discovery, designation of record on appeal, written motions other than those heard ex parte, and similar papers, shall be served upon each of the parties.

(B) Service: how made. Whenever under these rules or by court order service is required or permitted to be made upon a party represented by an attorney, the service shall be made upon the attorney unless service upon the party himself is ordered by the court. Service upon the attorney or upon the party shall be made in the manner provided in Civil Rule 5(B).

(C) Filing. All papers required to be served upon a party shall be filed simultaneously with or immediately after service. Papers filed with the court shall not be considered until proof of service is endorsed thereon or separately filed. The proof of service shall state the date and the manner of service and shall be signed and filed in the manner provided in Civil Rule 5(D).

RULE 50. Calendars

Criminal cases shall be given precedence over civil matters and proceedings.

RULE 51. Exceptions Unnecessary

An exception, at any stage or step of the case or matter, is unnecessary to lay a foundation for review, whenever a matter has been called to the attention of the court by objection, motion, or otherwise, and the court has ruled thereon.

RULE 52. Harmless Error and Plain Error

(A) Harmless error. Any error, defect, irregularity, or variance which does not affect substantial rights shall be disregarded.

(B) Plain error. Plain errors or defects affecting substantial rights may be noticed although they were not brought to the attention of the court.

RULE 53. Reserved

RULE 54. Amendment of Incorporated Civil Rules

An amendment to or rescission of any provision of

the Ohio Rules of Civil Procedure which has been incorporated by reference in these rules, shall, without the necessity of further action, be incorporated by reference in these rules unless the amendment or rescission specifies otherwise, effective on the effective date of the amendment or rescission.

RULE 55. Records

(A) Criminal appearance docket. The clerk shall keep a criminal appearance docket. Upon the commencment of a criminal action the clerk shall assign each action a number. This number shall be placed on the first page, and every continuation page, of the appearance docket which concerns the particular action. In addition this number and the names of the parties shall be placed on the case file and every paper filed in the action.

At the time the action is commenced the clerk shall enter in the appearance docket the names, except as provided in Rule 6(E), of the parties in full, the names of counsel and index the action by the name of each defendant. Thereafter the clerk shall chronologically note in the appearance docket all: process issued and returns, pleas and motions, papers filed in the action, orders, verdicts and judgments. The notations shall be brief but shall show the date of filing and the substance of each order, verdict and judgment.

An action is commenced for purposes of this rule by the earlier of, (a) the filing of a complaint, uniform traffic ticket, citation, indictment, or information with the clerk, or (b) the receipt by the clerk of the court of common pleas of a bind over order under Rule 5(B)(4)(a).

(B) Files. All papers filed in a case shall be filed in a separate file folder and on or after July 1, 1986 shall not exceed 8½ inches x 11 inches in size and without backing or cover.

(C) Other books and records. The clerk shall keep such other books and records as required by law and as the supreme court or other court may from time to time require.

(D) Applicability to courts not of record. In courts not of record the notations required by subdivision (A) shall be placed on a separate sheet or card kept in the file folder.

Amended, eff 7-1-85

RULE 56. Reserved

RULE 57. Rule of Court; Procedure Not Otherwise Specified

(A) Rule of court. (1) The expression "rule of court" as used in these rules means a rule promulgated by the Supreme Court or a rule concerning local practice adopted by another court that is not inconsistent with the rules promulgated by the Supreme Court and is filed with the Supreme Court.

(2) Local rules shall be adopted only after the court gives appropriate notice and an opportunity for comment. If the court determines that there is an immediate need for a rule, the court may adopt the rule without prior notice and opportunity for comment, but promptly shall afford notice and opportunity for comment.

(B) Procedure not otherwise specified. If no procedure is specifically prescribed by rule, the court may proceed in any lawful manner not inconsistent with these rules of criminal procedure, and shall look to the rules of civil procedure and to the applicable law if no rule of criminal procedure exists.

Amended, eff 7-1-94

RULE 58. Forms

The forms contained in the Appendix of Forms which the supreme court from time to time may approve are illustrative and not mandatory.

RULE 59. Effective Date

(A) Effective date of rules. These rules shall take effect on July 1, 1973, except for rules or portions of rules for which a later date is specified, which shall take effect on such later date. They govern all proceedings in actions brought after they take effect, and also all further proceedings in actions then pending, except to the extent that their application in a particular action pending when the rules take effect would not be feasible or would work injustice, in which event the former procedure applies.

(B) Effective date of amendments. The amendments submitted by the Supreme Court to the general assembly on January 10, 1975, shall take effect on July 1, 1975. They govern all proceedings in actions brought after they take effect and also all further proceedings in actions then pending, except to the extent that their application in a particular action pending when the amendments take effect would not be feasible or would work injustice, in which event the former procedure applies.

(C) Effective date of amendments. The amendments submitted by the Supreme Court to the general assembly on January 9, 1976 shall take effect on July 1, 1976. They govern all proceedings in actions brought after they take effect and also all further proceedings in actions then pending, except to the extent that their application in a particular action pending when the amendments take effect would not be feasible or would work injustice, in which event the former procedure applies.

(D) Effective date of amendments. The amendments submitted by the Supreme Court to the general assembly on January 12, 1978, and on April 28, 1978, shall take effect on July 1, 1978. They govern all proceedings in actions brought after they take effect and also all further proceedings in actions then pending, except to the extent that their application in a particular action pending when the amendments take effect would not be feasible or would work injustice, in which event the former procedure applies.

(E) Effective date of amendments. The amendments submitted by the Supreme Court to the general assembly on January 14, 1980, shall take effect on July 1, 1980. They govern all proceedings in actions brought after they take effect and also all further proceedings in actions then pending, except to the extent that their application in a particular action pending when the amendments take effect would not be feasible or would work injustice, in which event the former procedure applies.

(F) Effective date of amendments. The amendments submitted by the Supreme Court to the general assembly on January 14, 1981, and on April 29, 1981, shall take effect on July 1, 1981. They govern all proceedings in actions brought after they take effect and also all further proceedings in actions then pending, except to the extent that their application in a particular action pending when the amendments take effect would not be feasible or would work injustice, in which event the former procedure applies.

(G) Effective date of amendments. The amendments submitted by the Supreme Court to the general assembly on January 14, 1982 shall take effect on July 1, 1982. They govern all proceedings in actions brought after they take effect and also all further proceedings in actions then pending, except to the extent that their application in a particular action pending when the amendments take effect would not be feasible or would work injustice, in which event the former procedure applies.

(H) Effective date of amendments. The amendments submitted by the Supreme Court to the general assembly on December 24, 1984 and January 8, 1985 shall take effect on July 1, 1985. They govern all proceedings in actions brought after they take effect and also all further proceedings in actions then pending, except to the extent that their application in a particular action pending when the amendments take effect would not be feasible or would work injustice, in which event the former procedure applies.

(I) Effective date of amendments. The amendments submitted by the Supreme Court to the General Assembly on January 12, 1990 and further revised and submitted on April 16, 1990, shall take effect on July 1, 1990. They govern all proceedings in actions brought after they take effect and also all further proceedings in actions then pending, except to the extent that their application in a particular action pending when the amendments take effect would not be feasible or would work injustice, in which event the former procedure applies.

(J) Effective date of amendments. The amendments filed by the Supreme Court with the General Assembly on January 14, 1992 and further revised and filed on April 30, 1992, shall take effect on July 1, 1992. They govern all proceedings in actions brought after they take effect and also all further proceedings in actions then pending, except to the extent that their application in a particular action pending when the amendments take effect would not be feasible or would work injustice, in which event the former procedure applies.

(K) Effective date of amendments. The amendments submitted by the Supreme Court to the General Assembly on January 8, 1993 and further filed on April 30, 1993 shall take effect on July 1, 1993. They govern all proceedings in actions brought after they take effect and also all further proceedings in actions then pending, except to the extent that their application in a particular action pending when the amendments take effect would not be feasible or would work injustice, in which event the former procedure applies.

(L) Effective date of amendments. The amendments submitted by the Supreme Court to the General Assembly on January 14, 1994 shall take effect on July 1, 1994. They govern all proceedings in actions brought after they take effect and also all further proceedings in actions then pending, except to the extent that their application in a particular action pending when the amendments take effect would not be feasible or would work injustice, in which event the former procedure applies.

(M) Effective date of amendments. The amendments to rules 12 and 19 filed by the Supreme Court with the General Assembly on January 11, 1995 and refiled on April 25, 1995 shall take effect on July 1, 1995. They govern all proceedings in actions brought after they take effect and also all further proceedings in actions then pending, except to the extent that their application in a particular action pending when the amendments take effect would not be feasible or would work injustice, in which event the former procedure applies.

(N) Effective date of amendments. The amendments to Rule 1 filed by the Supreme Court with the General Assembly on January 5, 1996 and refiled on April 26, 1996 shall take effect on July 1, 1996. They govern all proceedings in actions brought after they take effect and also all further proceedings in actions then pending, except to the extent that their application in a particular action pending when the amendments take effect would not be feasible or would work injustice, in which event the former procedure applies.

(O) Effective date of amendments. The amendments to Rule 35 filed by the Supreme Court with the General Assembly on January 10, 1997 shall take effect on July 1, 1997. They govern all proceedings in actions brought after they take effect and also all further proceedings in actions then pending, except to the extent that their application in a particular action pending when the amendments take effect would not be feasible or would work injustice, in which event the former procedure applies.

Amended, eff 7-1-75; 7-1-76; 7-1-78; 7-1-80; 7-1-

82; 7-1-85; 7-1-90; 7-1-92; 7-1-93; 7-1-94; 7-1-95; 7-1-96; 7-1-97

RULE 60. Title

These rules shall be known as the Ohio Rules of Criminal Procedure and may be cited as "Criminal Rules" or "Crim. R. ___"

APPENDIX OF FORMS

(See Crim. R. 58)

The forms which follow are intended for illustration only. They are limited in number, there being no attempt to furnish a complete manual of forms.

Although the forms are for illustrative purposes, they have been drafted to conform to the policies expressed in the Criminal Rules.

In the illustrations, the Franklin County Court of Common Pleas and the Franklin County Municipal Court identifications have each been used with the forms to show the adjustments required at the two levels of adjudication.

FORM I

FRANKLIN COUNTY MUNICIPAL COURT
FRANKLIN COUNTY, OHIO

State of Ohio)
/City of Columbus/)
　　　　　　　　　　　　　　) NO._____
　　v.)
　　　　　　　　　　　　　　) COMPLAINT
_____)
name) (Rule 4)
　　　　　　　　　　　　　　)
_____)
address

Complainant being duly sworn states that _____C.D._____
　　　　　　　　　　　　　　　　　　　　　　　　　　　　defendant
at _____, County, Ohio on or about _____,
　　　　place
19___, _____
　　　　　　　　　　　　　state the essential facts
_____

in violation of _____.
　　　　　　state the numerical designation of the applicable statute or ordinance

　　　　　　　　　　　　　　A.B._____
　　　　　　　　　　　　　　Complainant

Sworn to and subscribed before me by _____ on
_____, 19___.

　　　　　　　　　　　　　　_____
　　　　　　　　　　　　　　/ Judge / Clerk / Deputy Clerk /
　　　　　　　　　　　　　　Franklin County Municipal Court
　　　　　　　　　　　　　　　　　　　　or

　　　　　　　　　　　　　　_____
　　　　　　　　　　　　　　Notary Public,
　　　　　　　　　　　　　　My Commission expires _____, 19___
　　　　　　　　　　　　　　/ Franklin County / State of Ohio /

FORM II

FRANKLIN COUNTY MUNICIPAL COURT
FRANKLIN COUNTY, OHIO

State of Ohio   )
/City of Columbus/   )   NO. _____
)
v.   )   COMPLAINT BY
)   PROSECUTING ATTORNEY
_____)   UPON AFFIDAVIT
name   )
)   (Rule 4)
)
_____)
address   )

Complainant prosecuting attorney being duly sworn states that _____
                                                                   name of affiant
has filed an affidavit, a copy of which is attached hereto, stating that _____
_____ C.D. _____ at _____, County, Ohio on or
                                         place
about _____, 19____, _____
                                         state the essential facts
_____
_____

Upon this affidavit complainant states that _____ C.D. _____ on or
                                                         defendant
about the above date and at the above place did violate _____
                                                         state the numerical designation
_____ .
of the applicable statute or ordinance

                              A.B. _____
                              Complainant, Title

Sworn to and subscribed before me by _____ A.B. _____
on _____, 19____.

                              _____
                              / Judge / Clerk / Deputy Clerk /
                              Franklin County Municipal Court

                                         or

                              _____
                              Notary Public,
                              My Commission expires _____, 19____
                              / Franklin County / State of Ohio /

FORM III

/FRANKLIN COUNTY MUNICIPAL COURT/
/COURT OF COMMON PLEAS/
FRANKLIN COUNTY, OHIO

State of Ohio)
/City of Columbus/)
)   NO._____

v.)
)   DIRECTION TO ISSUE SUMMONS

_____)
name   )   (Rules 4 and 9)

_____)
address)

TO _____
      / Clerk / Deputy Clerk /

Issue summons to an appropriate officer and direct him to make / personal service / residence service / certified mail service / upon _____C.D._____ at / the address
                                                                        defendant

stated in the caption of this direction./ _____
_____./
                        fill in address if different from caption

Special instructions for server: _____
_____
_____

                                           _____
                                           / Judge / Officer Designated by Judge(s) /
                                           Franklin County Municipal Court

                                                             or

                                           _____
                                           Judge
                                           Court of Common Pleas
                                           Franklin County, Ohio

FORM IV

FRANKLIN COUNTY MUNICIPAL COURT
FRANKLIN COUNTY, OHIO

State of Ohio)
/City of Columbus/)
)
) NO. _____
v.)
) CLERK'S MEMORANDUM
_____) OF DETERMINATION TO ISSUE
name) SUMMONS UPON COMPLAINT
)
) (Rule 4)
_____)
address)
)

It appearing that summons will reasonably assure the appearance of _____C.D._____
                                                                    defendant
summons shall issue:

/ to an appropriate officer and such officer shall be directed to make / personal service / residence service /.

/ by certified mail /

Service shall be at / the address stated in the caption of this notice / _____
_____.
fill in address if different from caption

Special instructions for server: _____
_____
_____

_____
/ Clerk / Deputy Clerk /
Franklin County Municipal Court

FORM V

FRANKLIN COUNTY MUNICIPAL COURT
FRANKLIN COUNTY, OHIO

State of Ohio)
/City of Columbus/) NO._____
)
v.) PROSECUTING ATTORNEY'S
) REQUEST FOR ISSUANCE OF
_____) SUMMONS UPON COMPLAINT
name)
) (Rule 4)
)
_____)
address)

TO _____
           / Clerk / Deputy Clerk /

A complaint has been filed against _____C.D._____
                                          defendant

Issue summons to an appropriate officer and direct him to make / personal service / residence service / certified mail service / upon defendant at / the address stated in the caption of this request. / _____
_____./
            fill in address if different from caption

Special instructions for server: _____
_____
_____

_____
                    Prosecuting Attorney, Title

FORM VI

/FRANKLIN COUNTY MUNICIPAL COURT/
/COURT OF COMMON PLEAS/
FRANKLIN COUNTY, OHIO

State of Ohio   )
/City of Columbus/   )   NO. _____
)
       v.   )   SUMMONS UPON / COMPLAINT /
)   INDICTMENT / INFORMATION /
_____   )
name   )
)
)
_____   )   (Rules 4 and 9)
address   )
)
)

TO _____ C.D. _____
                               defendant

A / complaint / indictment / information /, a copy of which is attached hereto, has been filed in the / Franklin County Municipal Court, 120 West Gay Street, Columbus, Ohio 43215, / Franklin County Court of Common Pleas, 410 South High Street, Columbus, Ohio 43215, / charging that you: _____
                                                   describe the offense
_____
and state the numerical designation of the applicable statute or ordinance
_____ .

You are hereby summoned and ordered to appear at _____
_____, / Franklin County Municipal Court, 120 West Gay
time, day, date, room
Street, Columbus, Ohio 43215. / Franklin County Court of Common Pleas, 410 South High Street, Columbus, Ohio 43215. /

If you fail to appear at the time and place stated above you may be arrested.

                              _____
                              / Judge / Officer Designated by Judge(s) /
                              / Clerk / Deputy Clerk /
                              Franklin County Municipal Court

                                            (or)

                              _____
                              / Judge / Clerk / Deputy Clerk /
                              Court of Common Pleas
                              Franklin County, Ohio

NOTICE TO DEFENDANT: For information regarding your duty to appear call
_____
fill in phone number(s)

CLERK'S INSTRUCTIONS TO SERVING OFFICER
FOR PERSONAL OR RESIDENCE SERVICE

TO _____
      officer other than clerk authorized to serve summons

Make / personal service / residence service / upon _____ defendant

at / the address stated in the caption of the summons. / _____

_____ ./
   fill in address for service if different from caption of summons

Special instructions for server: _____

_____

_____

_____
/ Clerk / Deputy Clerk /

• • • • • • • • • •

CLERK'S INSTRUCTIONS FOR
CERTIFIED MAIL SERVICE

TO _____
      clerk

Make certified mail service upon _____
      defendant

at / the address stated in the caption of the summons. / _____

_____ ./
   fill in address for service if different from caption of summons

Special instructions for server: _____

_____

_____.

_____
/ Clerk / Deputy Clerk /

RECEIPT OF SUMMONS BY SERVING AUTHORITY

First Receipt

Received this summons on _____, 19____,

at _____ o'clock ____ m.

_____
Officer
By _____
Title

Subsequent Receipt

Received this summons on _____, 19____,

at _____ o'clock ____ m.

_____
Officer
By _____
Title

Form VI   Ohio Criminal Law Handbook

RETURN OF SERVICE OF SUMMONS
(PERSONAL)

```
┌─────────────────────┐
│                     │
│       Fees          │
│   Mileage $ ____    │
│             ____    │
│             ____    │
│             ____    │
│             ____    │
│     Total $ ____    │
│                     │
└─────────────────────┘
```

I received this summons on _____, 19____,
at _____ o'clock, ____.m., and made personal
service of it upon _____
                                                    fill in name
by locating / him/her / and tendering a copy of the summons, a copy of the / complaint / indictment / information / and accompanying documents, on _____, 19____ .

Serving Officer, Title
Date return made: _____, 19____

• • • • • • • • • •

RETURN OF SERVICE OF SUMMONS
(RESIDENCE)

```
┌─────────────────────┐
│                     │
│       Fees          │
│   Mileage $ ____    │
│             ____    │
│             ____    │
│             ____    │
│             ____    │
│     Total $ ____    │
│                     │
└─────────────────────┘
```

I received this summons on _____, 19____,
at _____ o'clock, ____.m., and made residence
service of it upon _____
                                                      fill in name
by leaving, at / his/her / usual place of residence with _____ a person of suitable
                   fill in name
age and discretion then residing therein, a copy of the summons, a copy of the / complaint / indictment / information / and accompanying documents, on _____, 19____ .

Serving Officer, Title
Date return made: _____, 19____

RETURN OF SERVICE OF SUMMONS
(FAILURE OF SERVICE)

Fees
Mileage $ ____
____
____
____
Total $ ____

I received this summons on _____, 19 ___, at _____ o'clock, ___ .m., with instructions to make / personal service / residence service / upon

_____
fill in name

and I was unable to serve a copy of the summons upon / him/her / for the following reasons: _____

_____
_____
_____

_____
Serving Officer, Title
Date return made: _____, 19 ___

. . . .

RETURN OF SERVICE OF SUMMONS
(FAILURE OF SERVICE)

Fees
Mileage $ ____
____
____
____
Total $ ____

I received this summons on _____, 19 ___, at _____ o'clock, ___ .m., with instructions to make / personal service / residence service / upon

_____
fill in name

and I was unable to serve a copy of the summons upon / him/her / for the following reasons: _____

_____
_____
_____

_____
Serving Officer, Title
Date return made: _____, 19 ___

FORM VII
FRANKLIN COUNTY MUNICIPAL COURT
FRANKLIN COUNTY, OHIO

State of Ohio)
/City of Columbus/)
) NO. _____
v.)
) WARRANT ON COMPLAINT
_____)
name) (Rule 4)
)
_____)
address)

TO _____
               officer authorized to execute a warrant

A complaint, a copy of which is attached hereto, has been filed in this court charging _____

_____
describe the offense and state the numerical designation of the applicable statute or ordinance

You are ordered to arrest _____C.D._____ and bring / him/her / before
                                defendant
this court without unnecessary delay.

You / may / may not / issue summons in lieu of arrest under Rule 4(A)(2) or issue summons after arrest under Rule 4(F) because _____
                                                      state specific reasons if issuance of summons

_____
restricted

Special instructions to executing officer: _____

_____

_____

                                     _____
                                  Judge / Officer designated by Judge(s) /
                                        / Clerk / Deputy Clerk /
                                      Franklin County Municipal Court

SUMMONS ENDORSEMENT

See NOTE: Use only in appropriate case

This warrant was executed / by arrest and / by issuing the following summons:

TO _____ C.D. _____
                                     defendant

You are hereby summoned and ordered to appear at _____
                                                             time, day, date, room

Franklin County Municipal Court, 120 West Gay Street, Columbus, Ohio 43215.

If you fail to appear at the time and place stated above you may be arrested.

_____
Issuing Officer, Title
See Rule 4(A)(2), Rule 4(F) and Return Forms

NOTICE TO DEFENDANT: For information regarding your duty to appear call _____

_____
fill in telephone number(s)

. . . .

RECEIPT OF WARRANT BY EXECUTING AUTHORITY

First Receipt

Received this warrant on _____, 19 ___, at _____ o'clock ___.m.

_____
Officer
By _____
Title

Subsequent Receipt

Received this / alias / warrant on _____, 19 ___, at _____ o'clock ___.m.

_____
Officer
By _____
Title

RETURN OF EXECUTED WARRANT

```
        Fees
     Mileage $____
              ____
              ____
              ____
      Total $____
```

1. **Execution By Arrest**

   I received this warrant on _____, 19___,
   at ____ o'clock ____.m. On _____, 19___,
   I arrested _____ C.D. _____ and gave / him/
   her / a copy of this warrant with complaint attached
   and brought / him/her / to _____
   state the place

   _____
   Arresting Officer, Title

```
        Fees
     Mileage $____
              ____
              ____
              ____
      Total $____
```

2. **Execution By Issuance Of Summons Under Rule 4(A)(2) By Executing Officer**

   I received this warrant on _____, 19___, at
   ____ o'clock ____.m. On _____, 19___, I
   executed this warrant by issuing _____ C.D. _____
   a summons by / personal service / residence service /
   which ordered / him/her / to appear at _____
   time, day, date,
   _____, Franklin County Municipal Court,
   room
   120 West Gay Street, Columbus, Ohio, 43215. The
   summons was endorsed upon the warrant and accompanied by a copy of the complaint.

   _____
   Arresting Officer, Title

Fees
Mileage $ ____
____
____
____
Total $ ____

3. **Execution By Arrest And Issuance Of Summons Under Rule 4(F) By Arresting Officer**

I received this warrant on _____, 19 ____, at ____ o'clock ____.m. On _____, 19 ____, I arrested _____ C.D. _____ and after arrest I issued _____ C.D. _____ a summons by personal service which ordered / him/her / to appear at _____, Franklin County Municipal Court, 120 West Gay Street, Columbus, Ohio 43215. The summons was endorsed upon the warrant and accompanied by a copy of the complaint.

_____
Arresting-Issuing Officer, Title

4. **Execution By Arrest And Issuance Of Summons Under Rule 4(F) By Superior Of Arresting Officer**

On _____, 19 ____, _____ C.D. _____ was arrested by _____
                     name of arresting officer
and I issued _____ C.D. _____ a summons by personal service which ordered / him/her / to appear at _____
                     time, day, date, room
Franklin County Municipal Court, 120 West Gay Street, Columbus, Ohio 43215. The summons was endorsed upon the warrant and accompanied by a copy of the complaint.

_____
Issuing Officer, Title

RETURN OF UNEXECUTED WARRANT

Fees
Mileage $ ____
  ____
  ____
  ____
Total $ ____

I received this warrant on _____, 19____, at ____ o'clock ____.m. On _____, 19____, I attempted to execute this warrant but was unable to do so because _____
state specific reason or reasons and

_____
additional information regarding defendant's whereabouts

_____

_____
Executing Officer, Title

RETURN OF UNEXECUTED WARRANT

Fees
Mileage $ ____
  ____
  ____
  ____
Total $ ____

I received this warrant on _____, 19____, at ____ o'clock ____.m. On _____, 19____, I attempted to execute this warrant but was unable to do so because _____
state specific reason or reasons and

_____
additional information regarding defendant's whereabouts

_____

_____
Executing Officer, Title

FORM VIII

**COURT OF COMMON PLEAS
FRANKLIN COUNTY, OHIO**

State of Ohio   )
) NO. _____
v.   )
) CLERK'S MEMORANDUM OF
_____   ) DETERMINATION TO ISSUE
name   ) SUMMONS UPON INDICTMENT
)
_____   ) (Rule 9)
address   )

It appearing that defendant _____ was released pursuant to
                                        name
Rule 46 by the _____ on the same offense for which / he/she
                  bind-over court
/ was indicted in this court, summons shall issue: / to an appropriate officer and such officer shall be directed to make / personal service / residence service /.

/ by certified mail service /

Service shall be at / the address stated in the caption of this notice / _____
_____
                fill in address if different from caption
Special instructions for server: _____
_____
_____

_____
/ Clerk / Deputy Clerk /
Court of Common Pleas
Franklin County, Ohio

FORM IX

COURT OF COMMON PLEAS
FRANKLIN COUNTY, OHIO

State of Ohio   ) NO. _____
)
v.   ) PROSECUTING ATTORNEY'S
) REQUEST FOR ISSUANCE OF
_____) SUMMONS UPON/INDICTMENT
      name   ) /INFORMATION/
)
_____)   (Rule 9)
     address   )
)

TO _____
                    / Clerk / Deputy Clerk /

_____ C.D. _____ has been named a defendant in an / indictment returned by the grand jury / information filed by the prosecuting attorney. / Issue summons to an appropriate officer and direct him to make / personal service / residence service / certified mail service / upon defendant at / the address stated in the caption of this request./ _____
             fill in address if different from caption

Special instructions for server: _____
_____
_____

                                    _____
                                    Prosecuting Attorney, Title

FORM X

COURT OF COMMON PLEAS
FRANKLIN COUNTY, OHIO

State of Ohio   )
)   NO. _____
   v.   )
)   PROSECUTING ATTORNEY'S
_____)   REQUEST FOR ISSUANCE OF
name   )   WARRANT UPON
_____)   /INDICTMENT/INFORMATION/
address   )
)   (Rule 9)

TO: _____
                / Clerk / Deputy Clerk /

_____ has been named a defendant in an / indictment re-
        C.D.
      defendant
turned by the grand jury / information filed by the prosecuting attorney./

Issue a warrant to an appropriate officer and direct him to execute it upon _____
_____ / at the address stated in the caption of this request./
        C.D.
      defendant
_____./
        fill in address if different from caption

Special instructions for executing officer: _____
_____
_____

                                             _____
                                              Prosecuting Attorney, Title

Form XI   OHIO CRIMINAL LAW HANDBOOK   1400

FORM XI

COURT OF COMMON PLEAS
FRANKLIN COUNTY, OHIO

State of Ohio   )
)
    v.   )   NO. _____
)
)   WARRANT UPON/INDICTMENT/
_____   )   INFORMATION/
name   )
)   (Rule 9)
_____   )
address   )
)

TO _____
              officer authorized to execute warrant

An / indictment / information /, a copy of which is attached hereto has been filed in the Franklin County Court of Common Pleas, 410 South High Street, Columbus, Ohio 43215, charging _____ C.D. _____ with: _____
                                    defendant

_____
describe the offense and state the numerical designation of the applicable statute

_____

You are ordered to arrest _____ C.D. _____ and bring him before this
                                  defendant

court without unnecessary delay.

Special instructions to executing officer: _____

_____

_____

                                    _____
                                    / Judge / Clerk / Deputy Clerk /
                                    Court of Common Pleas
                                    Franklin County, Ohio

RECEIPT OF WARRANT BY EXECUTING AUTHORITY

First Receipt

Received this warrant on _____, 19____, at _____ o'clock ____.m.

_____
Officer

By _____
Title

Subsequent Receipt

Received this warrant on _____, 19____, at _____ o'clock ____.m.

_____
Officer

By _____
Title

· · · · · · · · · ·

RETURN OF EXECUTED WARRANT

Fees
Mileage $ ____
____
____
____
Total $ ____

I received this warrant on _____, 19____, at _____ o'clock ____.m. On _____, 19____, I arrested _____ C.D. _____, gave him/her a copy of this warrant with / indictment / information / attached and brought / him/her / to _____
state the place

_____
Arresting Officer, Title

RETURN OF UNEXECUTED WARRANT

Fees
Mileage $____
____
____
____
Total $____

I received this warrant on _____, 19___,
at _____ o'clock ___ .m. On _____, 19___,
I attempted to execute this warrant but was unable to do so because _____
                    state specific reason or reasons and

_____
        additional information regarding defendant's
_____
                      whereabouts
_____

_____
               Executing Officer, Title

· · · · · · · · · ·

RETURN OF UNEXECUTED WARRANT

Fees
Mileage $____
____
____
____
Total $____

I received this warrant on _____, 19___,
at _____ o'clock ___ .m. On _____, 19___,
I attempted to execute this warrant but was unable to do so because _____
                    state specific reason or reasons and

_____
        additional information regarding defendant's
_____
                      whereabouts
_____

_____
               Executing Officer, Title

FORM XII

FRANKLIN COUNTY MUNICIPAL COURT
FRANKLIN COUNTY, OHIO

State of Ohio)
/City of Columbus/)
)   SUMMONS NO. _____
v.)
)   CASE NO. _____
_____)
name of defendant)   SUMMONS IN LIEU OF ARREST
)   WITHOUT WARRANT, AND
_____)   COMPLAINT UPON SUCH
address)   SUMMONS
)
_____)   (Rule 4(A)(3))
age)

TO DEFENDANT:

SUMMONS

In lieu of immediate arrest upon a misdemeanor you are summoned and ordered to appear / at _____
                                time, day, date, room

Franklin County Municipal Court, 120 West Gay Street, Columbus, Ohio 43215. / before the Franklin County Juvenile Court, 50 East Mound Street, Columbus, Ohio 43215 at the time and place ordered by that court. / If you fail to appear at this time and place you may be arrested.

This summons served personally on the defendant on _____, 19____.

COMPLAINT

On _____, 19____, at _____
                                                                        place

you _____
       describe the offense charged and state the numerical
_____
       designation of the applicable statute or ordinance
_____
_____
_____

                                           _____
                                           Signature of Issuing-Charging
                                           Law Enforcement Officer

Being duly sworn the issuing-charging law enforcement officer states that he has read the above complaint and that it is true.

_____
Issuing-Charging Law Enforcement Officer

Sworn to and subscribed before me by _____
on _____, 19____.

_____
/ Judge / Clerk / Deputy Clerk
Franklin County Municipal Court

or

_____
Notary Public
My Commission Expires_____, 19____.
/ Franklin County / State of Ohio /

NOTICE TO DEFENDANT: The officer is not required to swear to the complaint upon your copy of the summons and complaint. He swears to the complaint on the copy he files with the court. You may obtain a copy of the sworn complaint before hearing time. You will be given a copy of the sworn complaint before or at the hearing. For information regarding your duty to appear call_____
fill in telephone number(s)

NOTICE TO DEFENDANT UNDER EIGHTEEN YEARS OF AGE: You must appear before the Franklin County Juvenile Court, 50 East Mound Street, Columbus, Ohio 43215, at the time and place determined by that Court. The Juvenile Court will notify you when and where to appear. This Summons and Complaint will be filed with the Juvenile Court. The Complaint may be used as a juvenile complaint. You may obtain a copy of the sworn complaint from the Juvenile Court before the Juvenile Court hearing. You will be given a copy of the sworn complaint before or at the Juvenile Court hearing. For information regarding your duty to appear at Juvenile Court call_____
fill in
_____
telephone number(s)

FORM XIII

FRANKLIN COUNTY MUNICIPAL COURT
FRANKLIN COUNTY, OHIO

State of Ohio   )
/City of Columbus/   )   SUMMONS NO._____
)
v.   )   CASE NO._____
)
_____   )   SUMMONS AFTER ARREST
name of defendant   )   WITHOUT WARRANT, AND
_____   )   COMPLAINT UPON EACH SUCH
address   )   SUMMONS
)
_____   )   (Rule 4(F))
age   )
)

TO DEFENDANT:

SUMMONS

In lieu of continued custody upon a misdemeanor arrest you are summoned and ordered to appear / at _____
            time, day, date, room
Franklin County Municipal Court, 120 West Gay Street, Columbus, Ohio 43215. / before the Franklin County Juvenile Court, 50 East Mound Street, Columbus, Ohio 43215 at the time and place ordered by that court. / If you fail to appear at this time and place you may be rearrested.

This summons served personally on the defendant on _____, 19____.

COMPLAINT

On _____, 19____, at _____
                                                    place
you _____
        describe the offense charged and state the numerical
        designation of the applicable statute or ordinance
_____
_____
_____

                                    _____
                                    Signature of Issuing-Charging
                                    Law Enforcement Officer

Being duly sworn the issuing-charging law enforcement officer states that he has read the above complaint and that it is true.

_____
Issuing-Charging Law Enforcement Officer

Sworn to and subscribed before me by _____
on _____, 19____.

_____
/ Judge / Clerk / Deputy Clerk /
Franklin County Municipal Court

or

_____
Notary Public
My Commission Expires _____, 19____.
/ Franklin County / State of Ohio /

NOTICE TO DEFENDANT: The officer is not required to swear to the complaint upon your copy of the summons and complaint. He swears to the complaint on the copy he files with the court. You may obtain a copy of the sworn complaint before hearing time. You will be given a copy of the sworn complaint before or at the hearing. For information regarding your duty to appear call _____
fill in telephone number(s)

NOTICE TO DEFENDANT UNDER EIGHTEEN YEARS OF AGE: You must appear before the Franklin County Juvenile Court, 50 East Mound Street, Columbus, Ohio 43215, at the time and place determined by that Court. The Juvenile Court will notify you when and where to appear. This Summons and Complaint will be filed with the Juvenile Court. The Complaint may be used as a juvenile complaint. You may obtain a copy of the sworn complaint from the Juvenile Court before the Juvenile Court hearing. You will be given a copy of the sworn complaint before or at the Juvenile Court hearing. For information regarding your duty to appear at Juvenile Court call _____
_____
fill in telephone number(s)

FORM XIV

FRANKLIN COUNTY MUNICIPAL COURT
FRANKLIN COUNTY, OHIO

State of Ohio
/City of Columbus/

    v.

_____
name of defendant

_____
address

_____
age

Citation No._____

Case No._____

MINOR MISDEMEANOR CITATION

(Rule 4.1)

TO DEFENDANT:

On _____, 19____, at _____
       date   place

You _____
                 describe the offense charged and state the

_____
numerical designation of the applicable statute or ordinance

_____

_____

_____

_____

You are ordered to appear at _____
                                   time, day, date, room

Franklin County Municipal Court, 120 West Gay Street, Columbus, Ohio 43215,/before the Franklin County Juvenile Court, 50 East Mound Street, Columbus, Ohio 43215, at the time and place ordered by that court. /

If you wish to contest this matter you must appear at the above time and place. In lieu of appearing at the above time and place you may, within the time stated above, appear personally at 120 West Gay Street, Columbus, Ohio 43215, Room 120, sign the guilty plea and waiver of trial which appear in this form, and pay a fine of $_____ and court

Form XIV OHIO CRIMINAL LAW HANDBOOK 1408

costs of $ _____ .

If you fail to appear at the time and place stated above you may be arrested.

This citation was served personally on the defendant.

_____
Signature of Issuing Law Enforcement Officer

Being duly sworn the issuing law enforcement officer states that he has read the citation and that it is true.

_____
Issuing Officer

Sworn to and subscribed before me by _____
on _____, 19____.

_____
/ Judge / Clerk / Deputy Clerk /

or

_____
Notary Public,
My Commission expires _____, 19 ___
Franklin County / State of Ohio /

NOTICE TO DEFENDANT: The officer is not required to swear to your copy of the citation and complaint. He swears to citation in the copy he files with the court. You may obtain a copy of the sworn citation before hearing time. You will be given a copy of the sworn citation before or at the hearing. For information regarding your duty to appear call _____
fill in telephone number(s)

NOTICE TO DEFENDANT UNDER EIGHTEEN YEARS OF AGE: The appearance, guilty plea, waiver and payment provisions of this form do not apply to you. You must appear before the Franklin County Juvenile Court, 50 East Mound Street, Columbus, Ohio 43215, at the time and place determined by that Court. The Juvenile Court will notify you when and where to appear. This citation will be filed with the Juvenile Court. The citation may be used as a juvenile complaint. You may obtain a copy of the sworn citation from the Juvenile Court before the Juvenile Court hearing. You will be given a copy of the sworn citation before or at the Juvenile Court hearing. For information regarding your duty to appear at Juvenile Court call _____

_____
fill in telephone number(s)

GUILTY PLEA, WAIVER OF TRIAL, PAYMENT OF FINE AND COSTS

I, the undersigned defendant, do hereby enter my written plea of guilty to the offense charged in this citation. I realize that by signing this guilty plea I admit my guilt of the offense charged and waive my right to contest the offense in a trial before the court. I plead guilty to the offense charged in the citation.

FINE _____   _____
                       Signature of Defendant

COST _____   _____
                       address

TOTAL _____
                       _____
RECEIPT NO. _____   Signature And Title Of Person Taking Guilty
                       Plea, Waiver And Payment

Form XV   OHIO CRIMINAL LAW HANDBOOK

FORM XV. UNIFORM PETITION FORM

IN THE COURT OF COMMON PLEAS
_____ COUNTY, OHIO

CASE NOS.: _____

_____

JUDGE: _____

STATE OF OHIO

    Plaintiff-Respondent

                                      POST-CONVICTION PETITION

-vs-

_____

    Defendant-Petitioner

I. CASE HISTORY

TRIAL:

Charge (include specifications)   Disposition

_____   _____

_____   _____

Date Sentenced: _____

Name of Attorney: _____

Was this conviction the result of a (circle one):   **Guilty Plea**   **No Contest Plea**   **Trial**

If the conviction resulted in a trial, what was the length of the trial?

_____

Appeal to Court of Appeals

Number or citation _____

Disposition _____

Name of Attorney _____

1411   Ohio Rules of Criminal Procedure   Form XV

Appeal to Supreme Court of Ohio

Number or citation _____

Disposition _____

Name of Attorney _____

HAS A POST-CONVICTION PETITION BEEN FILED BEFORE IN THIS CASE?

    YES   NO

If YES, attach a copy of the Petition and the Judgment Entry showing how it was disposed.

IF THIS IS NOT THE FIRST POST-CONVICTION PETITION, OR IT IS FILED OUTSIDE THE TIME LIMITS PROVIDED BY LAW, STATE THE REASONS WHY THE COURT SHOULD CONSIDER THIS PETITION: _____

_____

_____

_____

_____

OTHER RELEVANT CASE HISTORY: _____

_____

II. STATEMENT OF FACTS

III. GROUNDS FOR RELIEF

(each ground not to exceed three pages)

Ground for relief 1:   _____

                                       _____

                                       _____

                                       _____

                                       _____

Attached exhibit numbers which support ground for relief: _____
_____
_____

Legal authority (constitutional provisions, statutes, cases, rules, etc.) in support of ground for relief: _____
_____
_____
_____

_____
(name)

OHIO RULES OF EVIDENCE

Complete through July 1, 1996

For annotations and cases construing the Ohio Rules of Evidence, see the
TITLE 23 VOLUME to PAGE'S OHIO REVISED CODE ANNOTATED
For comprehensive text discussion see WEISSENBERGER'S OHIO EVIDENCE

ARTICLE I
GENERAL PROVISIONS

Rule
- 101. Scope of rules: applicability; privileges; exceptions
  - (A) Applicability
  - (B) Privileges
  - (C) Exceptions
- 102. Purpose and construction; supplementary principles
- 103. Rulings on evidence
  - (A) Effect of erroneous ruling
  - (B) Record of offer and ruling
  - (C) Hearing of jury
  - (D) Plain error
- 104. Preliminary questions
  - (A) Questions of admissibility generally
  - (B) Relevancy conditioned on fact
  - (C) Hearing of jury
  - (D) Testimony by accused
  - (E) Weight and credibility
- 105. Limited admissibility
- 106. Remainder of or related writings or recorded statements

ARTICLE II
JUDICIAL NOTICE

Rule
- 201. Judicial notice of adjudicative facts
  - (A) Scope of rule
  - (B) Kinds of facts
  - (C) When discretionary
  - (D) When mandatory
  - (E) Opportunity to be heard
  - (F) Time of taking notice
  - (G) Instructing jury

ARTICLE III
PRESUMPTIONS

Rule
- 301. Presumptions in general in civil actions and proceedings
- 302. [Reserved]

ARTICLE IV
RELEVANCY AND ITS LIMITS

Rule
- 401. Definition of "relevant evidence"
- 402. Relevant evidence generally admissible; irrelevant evidence inadmissible
- 403. Exclusion of relevant evidence on grounds of prejudice, confusion, or undue delay
  - (A) Exclusion mandatory
  - (B) Exclusion discretionary

Rule
- 404. Character evidence not admissible to prove conduct; exceptions; other crimes
  - (A) Character evidence generally
  - (B) Other crimes, wrongs or acts
- 405. Methods of proving character
  - (A) Reputation or opinion
  - (B) Specific instances of conduct
- 406. Habit; routine practice
- 407. Subsequent remedial measures
- 408. Compromise and offers to compromise
- 409. Payment of medical and similar expenses
- 410. Inadmissibility of pleas, offers of pleas, and related statements
- 411. Liability insurance

ARTICLE V
PRIVILEGES

Rule
- 501. General rule

ARTICLE VI
WITNESSES

Rule
- 601. General rule of competency
- 602. Lack of personal knowledge
- 603. Oath or affirmation
- 604. Interpreters
- 605. Competency of judge as witness
- 606. Competency of juror as witness
  - (A) At the trial
  - (B) Inquiry into validity of verdict or indictment
- 607. Who may impeach
- 608. Evidence of character and conduct of witness
  - (A) Opinion and reputation evidence of character
  - (B) Specific instances of conduct
- 609. Impeachment by evidence of conviction of crime
  - (A) General rule
  - (B) Time limit
  - (C) Effect of pardon, annulment, expungement, or certificate of rehabilitation
  - (D) Juvenile adjudications
  - (E) Pendency of appeal
  - (F) Methods of proof
- 610. Religious beliefs or opinions
- 611. Mode and order of interrogation and presentation
  - (A) Control by court
  - (B) Scope of cross-examination
  - (C) Leading questions
- 612. Writing used to refresh memory
- 613. Prior statements of witnesses
  - (A) Examining witness concerning prior statement
  - (B) Extrinsic evidence of prior inconsistent statement of witness

Rule
614. Calling and interrogation of witnesses by court
　　(A) Calling by court
　　(B) Interrogation by court
　　(C) Objections
615. Exclusion of witnesses
616. Bias of witness

ARTICLE VII
OPINIONS AND EXPERT TESTIMONY

Rule
701. Opinion testimony by lay witnesses
702. Testimony by experts
703. Bases of opinion testimony by experts
704. Opinion on ultimate issue
705. Disclosure of facts or data underlying expert opinion

ARTICLE VIII
HEARSAY

Rule
801. Definitions
　　(A) Statement
　　(B) Declarant
　　(C) Hearsay
　　(D) Statements which are not hearsay
802. Hearsay rule
803. Hearsay exceptions; availability of declarant immaterial
804. Hearsay exceptions; declarant unavailable
　　(A) Definition of unavailability
　　(B) Hearsay exceptions
805. Hearsay within hearsay
806. Attacking and supporting credibility of declarant
807. Hearsay exceptions; child statements in abuse cases

ARTICLE IX
AUTHENTICATION AND IDENTIFICATION

Rule
901. Requirement of authentication or identification
　　(A) General provision
　　(B) Illustrations
902. Self-authentication
903. Subscribing witness' testimony unnecessary

ARTICLE X
CONTENTS OF WRITINGS, RECORDINGS AND PHOTOGRAPHS

Rule
1001. Definitions
1002. Requirement of original
1003. Admissibility of duplicates
1004. Admissibility of other evidence of contents
1005. Public records
1006. Summaries
1007. Testimony or written admission of party
1008. Functions of court and jury

ARTICLE XI
MISCELLANEOUS RULES

Rule
1101. [Reserved]
1102. Effective date

Rule
　　(A) Effective date of rules
　　(B)-(H) Effective date of amendments
1103. Title

ARTICLE I
GENERAL PROVISIONS

RULE 101. Scope of Rules: Applicability; Privileges; Exceptions

(A) **Applicability.** These rules govern proceedings in the courts of this state, subject to the exceptions stated in division (C) of this rule.

(B) **Privileges.** The rule with respect to privileges applies at all stages of all actions, cases, and proceedings conducted under these rules.

(C) **Exceptions.** These rules (other than with respect to privileges) do not apply in the following situations:

(1) *Admissibility determinations.* Determinations prerequisite to rulings on the admissibility of evidence when the issue is to be determined by the court under Rule 104.

(2) *Grand jury.* Proceedings before grand juries.

(3) *Miscellaneous criminal proceedings.* Proceedings for extradition or rendition of fugitives; sentencing; granting or revoking probation; issuance of warrants for arrest, criminal summonses and search warrants; and proceedings with respect to release on bail or otherwise.

(4) *Contempt.* Contempt proceedings in which the court may act summarily.

(5) *Arbitration.* Proceedings for those mandatory arbitrations of civil cases authorized by the rules of superintendence and governed by local rules of court.

(6) *Other rules.* Proceedings in which other rules prescribed by the supreme court govern matters relating to evidence.

(7) *Special non-adversary statutory proceedings.* Special statutory proceedings of a non-adversary nature in which these rules would by their nature be clearly inapplicable.

(8) *Small claims division.* Proceedings in the small claims division of a county or municipal court.

(Amended, eff 7-1-90; 7-1-96)

RULE 102. Purpose and Construction; Supplementary Principles

The purpose of these rules is to provide procedures for the adjudication of causes to the end that the truth may be ascertained and proceedings justly determined. The principles of the common law of Ohio shall supplement the provisions of these rules, and the rules shall be construed to state the principles of the common law of Ohio unless the rule clearly indicates that a change is intended. These rules shall not supersede substantive statutory provisions.

(Amended, eff 7-1-96)

RULE 103. Rulings on Evidence

(A) Effect of erroneous ruling. Error may not be predicated upon a ruling which admits or excludes evidence unless a substantial right of the party is affected, and

(1) *Objection.* In case the ruling is one admitting evidence, a timely objection or motion to strike appears of record stating the specific ground of objection, if the specific ground was not apparent from the context; or

(2) *Offer of proof.* In case the ruling is one excluding evidence, the substance of the evidence was made known to the court by offer or was apparent from the context within which questions were asked. Offer of proof is not necessary if evidence is excluded during cross-examination.

(B) Record of offer and ruling. At the time of making the ruling, the court may add any other or further statement which shows the character of the evidence, the form in which it was offered, the objection made, and the ruling thereon. It may direct the making of an offer in question and answer form.

(C) Hearing of jury. In jury cases, proceedings shall be conducted, to the extent practicable, so as to prevent inadmissible evidence from being suggested to the jury by any means, such as making statements or offers of proof or asking questions in the hearing of the jury.

(D) Plain error. Nothing in this rule precludes taking notice of plain errors affecting substantial rights although they were not brought to the attention of the court.

RULE 104. Preliminary Questions

(A) Questions of admissibility generally. Preliminary questions concerning the qualification of a person to be a witness, the existence of a privilege, or the admissibility of evidence shall be determined by the court, subject to the provisions of subdivision (B). In making its determination it is not bound by the rules of evidence except those with respect to privileges.

(B) Relevancy conditioned on fact. When the relevancy of evidence depends upon the fulfillment of a condition of fact, the court shall admit it upon, or subject to, the introduction of evidence sufficient to support a finding of the fulfillment of the condition.

(C) Hearing of jury. Hearings on the admissibility of confessions shall in all cases be conducted out of the hearing of the jury. Hearings on other preliminary matters shall also be conducted out of the hearing of the jury when the interests of justice require.

(D) Testimony by accused. The accused does not, by testifying upon a preliminary matter, subject himself to cross-examination as to other issues in the case.

(E) Weight and credibility. This rule does not limit the right of a party to introduce before the jury evidence relevant to weight or credibility.

RULE 105. Limited Admissibility

When evidence which is admissible as to one party or for one purpose but not admissible as to another party or for another purpose is admitted, the court, upon request of a party, shall restrict the evidence to its proper scope and instruct the jury accordingly.

RULE 106. Remainder of or Related Writings or Recorded Statements

When a writing or recorded statement or part thereof is introduced by a party, an adverse party may require him at that time to introduce any other part or any other writing or recorded statement which is otherwise admissible and which ought in fairness to be considered contemporaneously with it.

ARTICLE II
JUDICIAL NOTICE

RULE 201. Judicial Notice of Adjudicative Facts

(A) Scope of rule. This rule governs only judicial notice of adjudicative facts; i.e., the facts of the case.

(B) Kinds of facts. A judicially noticed fact must be one not subject to reasonable dispute in that it is either (1) generally known within the territorial jurisdiction of the trial court or (2) capable of accurate and ready determination by resort to sources whose accuracy cannot reasonably be questioned.

(C) When discretionary. A court may take judicial notice, whether requested or not.

(D) When mandatory. A court shall take judicial notice if requested by a party and supplied with the necessary information.

(E) Opportunity to be heard. A party is entitled upon timely request to an opportunity to be heard as to the propriety of taking judicial notice and the tenor of the matter noticed. In the absence of prior notification, the request may be made after judicial notice has been taken.

(F) Time of taking notice. Judicial notice may be taken at any stage of the proceeding.

(G) Instructing jury. In a civil action or proceeding, the court shall instruct the jury to accept as conclusive any fact judicially noticed. In a criminal case, the court shall instruct the jury that it may, but is not required to, accept as conclusive any fact judicially noticed.

ARTICLE III
PRESUMPTIONS

RULE 301. Presumptions in General in Civil Actions and Proceedings

In all civil actions and proceedings not otherwise

provided for by statute enacted by the General Assembly or by these rules, a presumption imposes on the party against whom it is directed the burden of going forward with evidence to rebut or meet the presumption, but does not shift to such party the burden of proof in the sense of the risk of non-persuasion, which remains throughout the trial upon the party on whom it was originally cast.

RULE 302. [Reserved]

ARTICLE IV
RELEVANCY AND ITS LIMITS

RULE 401. Definition of "Relevant Evidence"

"Relevant evidence" means evidence having any tendency to make the existence of any fact that is of consequence to the determination of the action more probable or less probable than it would be without the evidence.

RULE 402. Relevant Evidence Generally Admissible; Irrelevant Evidence Inadmissible

All relevant evidence is admissible, except as otherwise provided by the Constitution of the United States, by the Constitution of the State of Ohio, by statute enacted by the General Assembly not in conflict with a rule of the Supreme Court of Ohio, by these rules, or by other rules prescribed by the Supreme Court of Ohio. Evidence which is not relevant is not admissible.

RULE 403. Exclusion of Relevant Evidence on Grounds of Prejudice, Confusion, or Undue Delay

(A) Exclusion mandatory. Although relevant, evidence is not admissible if its probative value is substantially outweighed by the danger of unfair prejudice, of confusion of the issues, or of misleading the jury.

(B) Exclusion discretionary. Although relevant, evidence may be excluded if its probative value is substantially outweighed by considerations of undue delay, or needless presentation of cumulative evidence.

(Amended, eff 7-1-96)

RULE 404. Character Evidence Not Admissible to Prove Conduct; Exceptions; Other Crimes

(A) Character evidence generally. Evidence of a person's character or a trait of his character is not admissible for the purpose of proving that he acted in conformity therewith on a particular occasion, subject to the following exceptions:

(1) *Character of accused.* Evidence of a pertinent trait of his character offered by an accused, or by the prosecution to rebut the same is admissible; however, in prosecutions for rape, gross sexual imposition, and prostitution, the exceptions provided by statute enacted by the General Assembly are applicable.

(2) *Character of victim.* Evidence of a pertinent trait of character of the victim of the crime offered by an accused, or by the prosecution to rebut the same, or evidence of a character trait of peacefulness of the victim offered by the prosecution in a homicide case to rebut evidence that the victim was the first aggressor is admissible; however, in prosecutions for rape, gross sexual imposition, and prostitution, the exceptions provided by statute enacted by the General Assembly are applicable.

(3) *Character of witness.* Evidence of the character of a witness on the issue of credibility is admissible as provided in Rules 607, 608, and 609.

(B) Other crimes, wrongs or acts. Evidence of other crimes, wrongs, or acts is not admissible to prove the character of a person in order to show that he acted in conformity therewith. It may, however, be admissible for other purposes, such as proof of motive, opportunity, intent, preparation, plan, knowledge, identity, or absence of mistake or accident.

RULE 405. Methods of Proving Character

(A) Reputation or opinion. In all cases in which evidence of character or a trait of character of a person is admissible, proof may be made by testimony as to reputation or by testimony in the form of an opinion. On cross-examination, inquiry is allowable into relevant specific instances of conduct.

(B) Specific instances of conduct. In cases in which character or a trait of character of a person is an essential element of a charge, claim, or defense, proof may also be made of specific instances of his conduct.

RULE 406. Habit; Routine Practice

Evidence of the habit of a person or of the routine practice of an organization, whether corroborated or not and regardless of the presence of eyewitnesses, is relevant to prove that the conduct of the person or organization on a particular occasion was in conformity with the habit or routine practice.

RULE 407. Subsequent Remedial Measures

When, after an event, measures are taken which, if taken previously, would have made the event less likely to occur, evidence of the subsequent measures is not admissible to prove negligence or culpable conduct in connection with the event. This rule does not require the exclusion of evidence of subsequent measures when offered for another purpose, such as proving ownership, control, or feasibility of precautionary measures, if controverted, or impeachment.

RULE 408. Compromise and Offers to Compromise

Evidence of (1) furnishing or offering or promising to furnish, or (2) accepting or offering or promising to accept, a valuable consideration in compromising or attempting to compromise a claim which was disputed as to either validity or amount, is not admissible to prove liability for or invalidity of the claim or its amount. Evidence of conduct or statements made in compromise negotiations is likewise not admissible. This rule does not require the exclusion of any evidence otherwise discoverable merely because it is presented in the course of compromise negotiations. This rule also does not require exclusion when the evidence is offered for another purpose, such as proving bias or prejudice of a witness, negativing a contention of undue delay, or proving an effort to obstruct a criminal investigation or prosecution.

RULE 409. Payment of Medical and Similar Expenses

Evidence of furnishing or offering or promising to pay medical, hospital, or similar expenses occasioned by an injury is not admissible to prove liability for the injury.

RULE 410. Inadmissibility of Pleas, Offers of Pleas, and Related Statements

(A) Except as provided in division (B) of this rule, evidence of the following is not admissible in any civil or criminal proceeding against the defendant who made the plea or who was a participant personally or through counsel in the plea discussions:

(1) A plea of guilty that later was withdrawn;

(2) A plea of no contest or the equivalent plea from another jurisdiction;

(3) A plea of guilty in a violations bureau;

(4) Any statement made in the course of any proceedings under Rule 11 of the Rules of Criminal Procedure or equivalent procedure from another jurisdiction regarding the foregoing pleas;

(5) Any statement made in the course of plea discussions in which counsel for the prosecuting authority or for the defendant was a participant and that do not result in a plea of guilty or that result in a plea of guilty later withdrawn.

(B) A statement otherwise inadmissible under this rule is admissible in either of the following:

(1) Any proceeding in which another statement made in the course of the same plea or plea discussions has been introduced and the statement should, in fairness, be considered contemporaneously with it;

(2) A criminal proceeding for perjury or false statement if the statement was made by the defendant under oath, on the record, and in the presence of counsel.

(Amended, eff 7-1-91)

RULE 411. Liability Insurance

Evidence that a person was or was not insured against liability is not admissible upon the issue whether he acted negligently or otherwise wrongfully. This rule does not require the exclusion of evidence of insurance against liability when offered for another purpose, such as proof of agency, ownership or control, if controverted, or bias or prejudice of a witness.

ARTICLE V
PRIVILEGES

RULE 501. General Rule

The privilege of a witness, person, state or political subdivision thereof shall be governed by statute enacted by the General Assembly or by principles of common law as interpreted by the courts of this state in the light of reason and experience.

ARTICLE VI
WITNESSES

RULE 601. General Rule of Competency

Every person is competent to be a witness except:

(A) Those of unsound mind, and children under ten years of age, who appear incapable of receiving just impressions of the facts and transactions respecting which they are examined, or of relating them truly.

(B) A spouse testifying against the other spouse charged with a crime except when either of the following applies:

(1) A crime against the testifying spouse or a child of either spouse is charged;

(2) The testifying spouse elects to testify.

(C) An officer, while on duty for the exclusive or main purpose of enforcing traffic laws, arresting or assisting in the arrest of a person charged with a traffic violation punishable as a misdemeanor where the officer at the time of the arrest was not using a properly marked motor vehicle as defined by statute or was not wearing a legally distinctive uniform as defined by statute.

(D) A person giving expert testimony on the issue of liability in any claim asserted in any civil action against a physician, podiatrist, or hospital arising out of the diagnosis, care, or treatment of any person by a physician or podiatrist, unless the person testifying is licensed to practice medicine and surgery, osteopathic medicine and surgery, or podiatric medicine and surgery by the state medical board or by the licensing authority of any state, and unless the person devotes at least one-half of his or her professional time to the active clinical practice in his or her field of licensure, or to its instruction in an accredited school. This division shall not prohibit other medical professionals who otherwise are competent to testify under these rules from giving expert testimony on the appropriate standard of care in their own profession in any claim asserted in any civil action against a physician, podiatrist, medical professional, or hospital arising out of the diagnosis, care, or treatment of any person.

(E) As otherwise provided in these rules.

(Amended, eff 7-1-91)

RULE 602. Lack of Personal Knowledge

A witness may not testify to a matter unless evidence is introduced sufficient to support a finding that he has personal knowledge of the matter. Evidence to prove personal knowledge may, but need not, consist of the testimony of the witness himself. This rule is subject to the provisions of Rule 703, relating to opinion testimony by expert witnesses.

RULE 603. Oath or Affirmation

Before testifying, every witness shall be required to declare that he will testify truthfully, by oath or affirmation administered in a form calculated to awaken his conscience and impress his mind with his duty to do so.

RULE 604. Interpreters

An interpreter is subject to the provisions of these rules relating to qualification as an expert and the administration of an oath or affirmation that he will make a true translation.

RULE 605. Competency of Judge as Witness

The judge presiding at the trial may not testify in that trial as a witness. No objection need be made in order to preserve the point.

RULE 606. Competency of Juror as Witness

(A) **At the trial.** A member of the jury may not testify as a witness before that jury in the trial of the case in which he is sitting as a juror. If he is called so to testify, the opposing party shall be afforded an opportunity to object out of the presence of the jury.

(B) **Inquiry into validity of verdict or indictment.** Upon an inquiry into the validity of a verdict or indictment, a juror may not testify as to any matter or statement occurring during the course of the jury's deliberations or to the effect of anything upon his or any other juror's mind or emotions as influencing him to assent to or dissent from the verdict or indictment or concerning his mental processes in connection therewith. A juror may testify on the question whether extraneous prejudicial information was improperly brought to the jury's attention or whether any outside influence was improperly brought to bear on any juror, only after some outside evidence of that act or event has been presented. However a juror may testify without the presentation of any outside evidence concerning any threat, any bribe, any attempted threat or bribe, or any improprieties of any officer of the court. His affidavit or evidence of any statement by him concerning a matter about which he would be precluded from testifying will not be received for these purposes.

RULE 607. Who May Impeach

The credibility of a witness may be attacked by any party except that the credibility of a witness may be attacked by the party calling the witness by means of a prior inconsistent statement only upon a showing of surprise and affirmative damage. This exception does not apply to statements admitted pursuant to Rules 801(D)(1)(a), 801(D)(2), or 803.

RULE 608. Evidence of Character and Conduct of Witness

(A) **Opinion and reputation evidence of character.** The credibility of a witness may be attacked or supported by evidence in the form of opinion or reputation, but subject to these limitations: (1) the evidence may refer only to character for truthfulness or untruthfulness, and (2) evidence of truthful character is admissible only after the character of the witness for truthfulness has been attacked by opinion or reputation evidence or otherwise.

(B) **Specific instances of conduct.** Specific instances of the conduct of a witness, for the purpose of attacking or supporting the witness's character for truthfulness, other than conviction of crime as provided in Evid.R. 609, may not be proved by extrinsic evidence. They may, however, in the discretion of the court, if clearly probative of truthfulness or untruthfulness, be inquired into on cross-examination of the witness (1) concerning the witness's character for truthfulness or untruthfulness, or (2) concerning the character for truthfulness or untruthfulness of another witness as to which character the witness being cross-examined has testified.

The giving of testimony by any witness, including an accused, does not operate as a waiver of the witness's privilege against self-incrimination when examined with respect to matters that relate only to the witness's character for truthfulness.

(Amended, eff 7-1-92)

RULE 609. Impeachment by Evidence of Conviction of Crime

(A) General rule. For the purpose of attacking the credibility of a witness:

(1) Subject to Evid. R. 403, evidence that a witness other than the accused has been convicted of a crime is admissible if the crime was punishable by death or imprisonment in excess of one year pursuant to the law under which the witness was convicted.

(2) Notwithstanding Evid. R. 403(A), but subject to Evid. R. 403(B), evidence that the accused has been convicted of a crime is admissible if the crime was punishable by death or imprisonment in excess of one year pursuant to the law under which the accused was convicted and if the court determines that the probative value of the evidence outweighs the danger of unfair prejudice of confusion of the issues, or of misleading the jury.

(3) Notwithstanding Evid. R. 403(A), but subject to Evid. R. 403(B), evidence that any witness, including an accused, has been convicted of a crime is admissible if the crime involved dishonesty or false statement, regardless of the punishment and whether based upon state or federal statute or local ordinance.

(B) Time limit. Evidence of a conviction under this rule is not admissible if a period of more than ten years has elapsed since the date of the conviction or of the release of the witness from the confinement, or the termination of probation, or shock probation, or parole, or shock parole imposed for that conviction, whichever is the later date, unless the court determines, in the interests of justice, that the probative value of the conviction supported by specific facts and circumstances substantially outweighs its prejudicial effect. However, evidence of a conviction more than ten years old as calculated herein, is not admissible unless the proponent gives to the adverse party sufficient advance written notice of intent to use such evidence to provide the adverse party with a fair opportunity to contest the use of such evidence.

(C) Effect of pardon, annulment, expungement, or certificate of rehabilitation. Evidence of a conviction is not admissible under this rule if (1) the conviction has been the subject of a pardon, annulment, expungement, certificate of rehabilitation, or other equivalent procedure based on a finding of the rehabilitation of the person convicted, and that person has not been convicted of a subsequent crime which was punishable by death or imprisonment in excess of one year, or (2) the conviction has been the subject of a pardon, annulment, expungement, or other equivalent procedure based on a finding of innocence.

(D) Juvenile adjudications. Evidence of juvenile adjudications is not admissible except as provided by statute enacted by the General Assembly.

(E) Pendency of appeal. The pendency of an appeal therefrom does not render evidence of a conviction inadmissible. Evidence of the pendency of an appeal is admissible.

(F) Methods of proof. When evidence of a witness's conviction of a crime is admissible under this rule, the fact of the conviction may be proved only by the testimony of the witness on direct or cross-examination, or by public record shown to the witness during his or her examination. If the witness denies that he or she is the person to whom the public record refers, the court may permit the introduction of additional evidence tending to establish that the witness is or is not the person to whom the public record refers.

(Amended, eff 7-1-91)

RULE 610. Religious Beliefs or Opinions

Evidence of the beliefs or opinions of a witness on matters of religion is not admissible for the purpose of showing that by reason of their nature his credibility is impaired or enhanced.

RULE 611. Mode and Order of Interrogation and Presentation

(A) Control by court. The court shall exercise reasonable control over the mode and order of interrogating witnesses and presenting evidence so as to (1) make the interrogation and presentation effective for the ascertainment of the truth, (2) avoid needless consumption of time, and (3) protect witnesses from harassment or undue embarrassment.

(B) Scope of cross-examination. Cross-examination shall be permitted on all relevant matters and matters affecting credibility.

(C) Leading questions. Leading questions should not be used on the direct examination of a witness except as may be necessary to develop his testimony. Ordinarily leading questions should be permitted on cross-examination. When a party calls a hostile witness, an adverse party, or a witness identified with an adverse party, interrogation may be by leading questions.

RULE 612. Writing Used to Refresh Memory

Except as otherwise provided in criminal proceedings

by Rule 16(B)(1)(g) and 16(C) (1)(d) of Ohio Rules of Criminal Procedure, if a witness uses a writing to refresh his memory for the purpose of testifying, either: (1) while testifying; or (2) before testifying, if the court in its discretion determines it is necessary in the interests of justice, an adverse party is entitled to have the writing produced at the hearing. He is also entitled to inspect it, to cross-examine the witness thereon, and to introduce in evidence those portions which relate to the testimony of the witness. If it is claimed that the writing contains matters not related to the subject matter of the testimony the court shall examine the writing *in camera*, excise any portions not so related, and order delivery of the remainder to the party entitled thereto. Any portion withheld over objections shall be preserved and made available to the appellate court in the event of an appeal. If a writing is not produced or delivered pursuant to order under this rule, the court shall make any order justice requires, except that in criminal cases when the prosecution elects not to comply, the order shall be one striking the testimony or, if the court in its discretion determines that the interests of justice so require, declaring a mistrial.

RULE 613. Prior Statements of Witnesses

(A) Examining witness concerning prior statement. In examining a witness concerning a prior statement made by him, whether written or not, the statement need not be shown nor its contents disclosed to him at that time, but on request the same shall be shown or disclosed to opposing counsel.

(B) Extrinsic evidence of prior inconsistent statement of witness. Extrinsic evidence of a prior inconsistent statement by a witness is not admissible unless the witness is afforded a prior opportunity to explain or deny the same and the opposite party is afforded an opportunity to interrogate him thereon, or the interests of justice otherwise require. This provision does not apply to admissions of a party-opponent as defined in Rule 801(D)(2).

RULE 614. Calling and Interrogation of Witnesses by Court

(A) Calling by court. The court may, on its own motion or at the suggestion of a party, call witnesses, and all parties are entitled to cross-examine witnesses thus called.

(B) Interrogation by court. The court may interrogate witnesses, in an impartial manner, whether called by itself or by a party.

(C) Objections. Objections to the calling of witnesses by the court or to interrogation by it may be made at the time or at the next available opportunity when the jury is not present.

RULE 615. Exclusion of Witnesses

At the request of a party the court shall order witnesses excluded so that they cannot hear the testimony of other witnesses, and it may make the order of its own motion. This rule does not authorize exclusion of (1) a party who is a natural person, or (2) an officer or employee of a party which is not a natural person designated as its representative by its attorney, or (3) a person whose presence is shown by a party to be essential to the presentation of his cause.

RULE 616. Bias of Witness

Bias, prejudice, interest, or any motive to misrepresent may be shown to impeach the witness either by examination of the witness or by extrinsic evidence.

(Effective 7-1-91)

ARTICLE VII
OPINIONS AND EXPERT TESTIMONY

RULE 701. Opinion Testimony by Lay Witnesses

If the witness is not testifying as an expert, his testimony in the form of opinions or inferences is limited to those opinions or inferences which are (1) rationally based on the perception of the witness and (2) helpful to a clear understanding of his testimony or the determination of a fact in issue.

RULE 702. Testimony by Experts

A witness may testify as an expert if all of the following apply:

(A) The witness' testimony either relates to matters beyond the knowledge or experience possessed by lay persons or dispels a misconception common among lay persons;

(B) The witness is qualified as an expert by specialized knowledge, skill, experience, training, or education regarding the subject matter of the testimony;

(C) The witness' testimony is based on reliable scientific, technical, or other specialized information. To the extent that the testimony reports the result of a procedure, test, or experiment, the testimony is reliable only if all of the following apply:

(1) The theory upon which the procedure, test, or experiment is based is objectively verifiable or is validly derived from widely accepted knowledge, facts, or principles;

(2) The design of the procedure, test, or experiment reliably implements the theory;

(3) The particular procedure, test, or experiment was

conducted in a way that will yield an accurate result.
(Amended, eff 7-1-94)

RULE 703. Bases of Opinion Testimony by Experts

The facts or data in the particular case upon which an expert bases an opinion or inference may be those perceived by him or admitted in evidence at the hearing.

RULE 704. Opinion on Ultimate Issue

Testimony in the form of an opinion or inference otherwise admissible is not objectionable solely because it embraces an ultimate issue to be decided by the trier of fact.

RULE 705. Disclosure of Facts or Data Underlying Expert Opinion

The expert may testify in terms of opinion or inference and give his reasons therefor after disclosure of the underlying facts or data. The disclosure may be in response to a hypothetical question or otherwise.

ARTICLE VIII
HEARSAY

RULE 801. Definitions

The following definitions apply under this article:

(A) Statement. A "statement" is (1) an oral or written assertion or (2) nonverbal conduct of a person, if it is intended by him as an assertion.

(B) Declarant. A "declarant" is a person who makes a statement.

(C) Hearsay. "Hearsay" is a statement, other than one made by the declarant while testifying at the trial or hearing, offered in evidence to prove the truth of the matter asserted.

(D) Statements which are not hearsay. A statement is not hearsay if:

(1) *Prior statement by witness.* The declarant testifies at the trial or hearing and is subject to cross-examination concerning the statement, and the statement is (a) inconsistent with his testimony, and was given under oath subject to cross-examination by the party against whom the statement is offered and subject to the penalty of perjury at a trial, hearing, or other proceeding, or in a deposition, or (b) consistent with his testimony and is offered to rebut an express or implied charge against him of recent fabrication or improper influence or motive, or (c) one of identification of a person soon after perceiving him, if the circumstances demonstrate the reliability of the prior identification.

(2) *Admission by party-opponent.* The statement is offered against a party and is (a) his own statement, in either his individual or a representative capacity, or (b) a statement of which he has manifested his adoption or belief in its truth, or (c) a statement by a person authorized by him to make a statement concerning the subject, or (d) a statement by his agent or servant concerning a matter within the scope of his agency or employment, made during the existence of the relationship, or (e) a statement by a co-conspirator of a party during the course and in furtherance of the conspiracy upon independent proof of the conspiracy.

RULE 802. Hearsay Rule

Hearsay is not admissible except as otherwise provided by the Constitution of the United States, by the Constitution of the State of Ohio, by statute enacted by the General Assembly not in conflict with a rule of the Supreme Court of Ohio, by these rules, or by other rules prescribed by the Supreme Court of Ohio.

RULE 803. Hearsay Exceptions; Availability of Declarant Immaterial

The following are not excluded by the hearsay rule, even though the declarant is available as a witness:

(1) *Present sense impression.* A statement describing or explaining an event or condition made while the declarant was perceiving the event or condition, or immediately thereafter unless circumstances indicate lack of trustworthiness.

(2) *Excited utterance.* A statement relating to a startling event or condition made while the declarant was under the stress of excitement caused by the event or condition.

(3) *Then existing, mental, emotional, or physical condition.* A statement of the declarant's then existing state of mind, emotion, sensation, or physical condition (such as intent, plan, motive, design, mental feeling, pain, and bodily health), but not including a statement of memory or belief to prove the fact remembered or believed unless it relates to the execution, revocation, identification, or terms of declarant's will.

(4) *Statements for purposes of medical diagnosis or treatment.* Statements made for purposes of medical diagnosis or treatment and describing medical history, or past or present symptoms, pain, or sensations, or the inception or general character of the cause or external source thereof insofar as reasonably pertinent to diagnosis or treatment.

(5) *Recorded recollection.* A memorandum or record concerning a matter about which a witness once had knowledge but now has insufficient recollection to enable him to testify fully and accurately, shown by the testimony of the witness to have been made or adopted when the matter was fresh in his memory and to reflect that knowledge correctly. If admitted, the memorandum or record may be read into evidence but may not

itself be received as an exhibit unless offered by an adverse party.

(6) *Records of regularly conducted activity.* A memorandum, report, record, or data compilation, in any form, of acts, events, or conditions, made at or near the time by, or from information transmitted by, a person with knowledge, if kept in the course of a regularly conducted business activity, and if it was the regular practice of that business activity to make the memorandum, report, record, or data compilation, all as shown by the testimony of the custodian or other qualified witness or as provided by Rule 901(B)(10), unless the source of information or the method or circumstances of preparation indicate lack of trustworthiness. The term "business" as used in this paragraph includes business, institution, association, profession, occupation, and calling of every kind, whether or not conducted for profit.

(7) *Absence of entry in record kept in accordance with the provisions of paragraph (6).* Evidence that a matter is not included in the memoranda, reports, records, or data compilations, in any form, kept in accordance with the provisions of paragraph (6), to prove the nonoccurence or nonexistence of the matter, if the matter was of a kind of which a memorandum, report, record, or data compilation was regularly made and preserved, unless the sources of information or other circumstances indicate lack of trustworthiness.

(8) *Public records and reports.* Records, reports, statements, or data compilations, in any form, of public offices or agencies, setting forth (a) the activities of the office or agency, or (b) matters observed pursuant to duty imposed by law as to which matters there was a duty to report, excluding, however, in criminal cases matters observed by police officers and other law enforcement personnel, unless offered by defendant, unless the sources of information or other circumstances indicate lack of trustworthiness.

(9) *Records of vital statistics.* Records or data compilations, in any form, of births, fetal deaths, deaths, or marriages, if the report thereof was made to a public office pursuant to requirement of law.

(10) *Absence of public record or entry.* To prove the absence of a record, report, statement, or data compilation, in any form, or the nonoccurence or nonexistence of a matter of which a record, report, statement, or data compilation, in any form, was regularly made and preserved by a public office or agency, evidence in the form of a certification in accordance with Rule 901(B)(10) or testimony, that diligent search failed to disclose the record, report, statement, or data compilation, or entry.

(11) *Records of religious organizations.* Statements of births, marriages, divorces, deaths, legitimacy, ancestry, relationship by blood or marriage, or other similar facts of personal or family history, contained in a regularly kept record of a religious organization.

(12) *Marriage, baptismal, and similar certificates.* Statements of fact contained in a certificate that the maker performed a marriage or other ceremony or administered a sacrament, made by a clergyman, public official, or other person authorized by the rules or practices of a religious organization or by law to perform the act certified, and purporting to have been issued at the time of the act or within a reasonable time thereafter.

(13) *Family records.* Statements of fact concerning personal or family history contained in family Bibles, genealogies, charts, engravings on rings, inscriptions on family portraits, engravings on urns, crypts, or tombstones, or the like.

(14) *Records of documents affecting an interest in property.* The record of a document purporting to establish or affect an interest in property, as proof of the content of the original recorded document and its execution and delivery by each person by whom it purports to have been executed, if the record is a record of a public office and an applicable statute authorizes the recording of documents of that kind in that office.

(15) *Statements in documents affecting an interest in property.* A statement contained in a document purporting to establish or affect an interest in property if the matter stated was relevant to the purpose of the document, unless dealings with the property since the document was made have been inconsistent with the truth of the statement or the purport of the document.

(16) *Statements in ancient documents.* Statements in a document in existence twenty years or more the authenticity of which is established.

(17) *Market reports, commercial publications.* Market quotations, tabulations, lists, directories, or other published compilations, generally used and relied upon by the public or by persons in particular occupations.

(18) *Reputation concerning personal or family history.* Reputation among members of his family by blood, adoption, or marriage or among his associates, or in the community, concerning a person's birth, adoption, marriage, divorce, death, legitimacy, relationship by blood, adoption, or marriage, ancestry, or other similar fact of his personal or family history.

(19) *Reputation concerning boundaries or general history.* Reputation in a community, arising before the controversy, as to boundaries of or customs affecting lands in the community, and reputation as to events of general history important to the community or state or nation in which located.

(20) *Reputation as to character.* Reputation of a person's character among his associates or in the community.

(21) *Judgment of previous conviction.* Evidence of a final judgment, entered after a trial or upon a plea of guilty (but not upon a plea of no contest or the equivalent plea from another jurisdiction), adjudging a person guilty of a crime punishable by death or imprisonment in excess of one year, to prove any fact essential to sustain the judgment, but not including, when offered by the Government in a criminal prosecution for pur-

poses other than impeachment, judgments against persons other than the accused. The pendency of an appeal may be shown but does not affect admissibility.

(22) *Judgment as to personal, family, or general history, or boundaries.* Judgments as proof of matters of personal, family or general history, or boundaries, essential to the judgment, if the same would be provable by evidence of reputation.

RULE 804. Hearsay Exceptions; Declarant Unavailable

(A) Definition of unavailability. "Unavailability as a witness" includes situations in which the declarant:

(1) is exempted by ruling of the court on the ground of privilege from testifying concerning the subject matter of the declarant's statement;

(2) persists in refusing to testify concerning the subject matter of the declarant's statement despite an order of the court to do so;

(3) testifies to a lack of memory of the subject matter of the declarant's statement;

(4) is unable to be present or to testify at the hearing because of death or then-existing physical or mental illness or infirmity; or

(5) is absent from the hearing and the proponent of the declarant's statement has been unable to procure the declarant's attendance (or in the case of a hearsay exception under division (B)(2), (3), or (4) of this rule, the declarant's attendance or testimony) by process or other reasonable means. A declarant is not unavailable as a witness if the declarant's exemption, refusal, claim of lack of memory, inability, or absence is due to the procurement or wrongdoing of the proponent of the declarant's statement for the purpose of preventing the witness from attending or testifying.

(B) Hearsay exceptions. The following are not excluded by the hearsay rule if the declarant is unavailable as a witness:

(1) *Former testimony.* Testimony given as a witness at another hearing of the same or a different proceeding, or in a deposition taken in compliance with law in the course of the same or another proceeding, if the party against whom the testimony is now offered, or, in a civil action or proceeding, a predecessor in interest, had an opportunity and similar motive to develop the testimony by direct, cross, or redirect examination. Testimony given at a preliminary hearing must satisfy the right to confrontation and exhibit indicia of reliability.

(2) *Statement under belief of impending death.* In a prosecution for homicide or in a civil action or proceeding, a statement made by a declarant, while believing that his or her death was imminent, concerning the cause or circumstances of what the declarant believed to be his or her impending death.

(3) *Statement against interest.* A statement that was at the time of its making so far contrary to the declarant's pecuniary or proprietary interest, or so far tended to subject the declarant to civil or criminal liability, or to render invalid a claim by the declarant against another, that a reasonable person in the declarant's position would not have made the statement unless the declarant believed it to be true. A statement tending to expose the declarant to criminal liability, whether offered to exculpate or inculpate the accused, is not admissible unless corroborating circumstances clearly indicate the truthworthiness of the statement.

(4) *Statement of personal or family history.* (a) A statement concerning the declarant's own birth, adoption, marriage, divorce, legitimacy, relationship by blood, adoption, or marriage, ancestry, or other similar fact of personal or family history, even though the declarant had no means of acquiring personal knowledge of the matter stated; or (b) a statement concerning the foregoing matters, and death also, of another person, if the declarant was related to the other by blood, adoption, or marriage or was so intimately associated with the other's family as to be likely to have accurate information concerning the matter declared.

(5) *Statement by a deceased or incompetent person.* The statement was made by a decedent or a mentally incompetent person, where (a) the estate or personal representative of the decedent's estate, or the guardian or trustee of the incompetent person is a party, and (b) the statement was made before the death or the development of the incompetency, and (c) the statement is offered to rebut testimony by an adverse party on a matter within the knowledge of the decedent or incompetent person.

(Amended, eff 7-1-81; 7-1-93)

RULE 805. Hearsay Within Hearsay

Hearsay included within hearsay is not excluded under the hearsay rule if each part of the combined statements conforms with an exception to the hearsay rule provided in these rules.

RULE 806. Attacking and Supporting Credibility of Declarant

When a hearsay statement, or a statement defined in Rule 801(D)(2), (c), (d), or (e), has been admitted in evidence, the credibility of the declarant may be attacked, and if attacked may be supported, by any evidence which would be admissible for those purposes if declarant had testified as a witness. Evidence of a statement or conduct by the declarant at any time, inconsistent with his hearsay statement, is not subject to any requirement that he may have been afforded an opportunity to deny or explain. If the party against whom a hearsay statement has been admitted calls the declarant as a witness, the party is entitled to examine him on the statement as if under cross-examination.

RULE 807. Hearsay Exceptions; Child Statements in Abuse Cases

(A) An out-of-court statement made by a child who is under twelve years of age at the time of trial or hearing describing any sexual act performed by, with, or on the child or describing any act of physical violence directed against the child is not excluded as hearsay under Evid. R. 802 if all of the following apply:

(1) The court finds that the totality of the circumstances surrounding the making of the statement provides particularized guarantees of trustworthiness that make the statement at least as reliable as statements admitted pursuant to Evid. R. 803 and 804. The circumstances must establish that the child was particularly likely to be telling the truth when the statement was made and that the test of cross-examination would add little to the reliability of the statement. In making its determination of the reliability of the statement, the court shall consider all of the circumstances surrounding the making of the statement, including but not limited to spontaneity, the internal consistency of the statement, the mental state of the child, the child's motive or lack of motive to fabricate, the child's use of terminology unexpected of a child of similar age, the means by which the statement was elicited, and the lapse of time between the act and the statement. In making this determination, the court shall not consider whether there is independent proof of the sexual act or act of physical violence.

(2) The child's testimony is not reasonably obtainable by the proponent of the statement.

(3) There is independent proof of the sexual act or act of physical violence.

(4) At least ten days before the trial or hearing, a proponent of the statement has notified all other parties in writing of the content of the statement, the time and place at which the statement was made, the identity of the witness who is to testify about the statement, and the circumstances surrounding the statement that are claimed to indicate its trustworthiness.

(B) The child's testimony is "not reasonably obtainable by the proponent of the statement" under division (A)(2) of this rule only if one or more of the following apply:

(1) The child refuses to testify concerning the subject matter of the statement or claims a lack of memory of the subject matter of the statement after a person trusted by the child, in the presence of the court, urges the child to both describe the acts described by the statement and to testify.

(2) The court finds all of the following:

(a) The child is absent from the trial or hearing;

(b) The proponent of the statement has been unable to procure the child's attendance or testimony by process or other reasonable means despite a good faith effort to do so;

(c) It is probable that the proponent would be unable to procure the child's testimony or attendance if the trial or hearing were delayed for a reasonable time.

(3) The court finds both of the following:

(a) The child is unable to testify at the trial or hearing because of death or then existing physical or mental illness or infirmity;

(b) The illness or infirmity would not improve sufficiently to permit the child to testify if the trial or hearing were delayed for a reasonable time.

The proponent of the statement has not established that the child's testimony or attendance is not reasonably obtainable if the child's refusal, claim of lack of memory, inability, or absence is due to the procurement or wrongdoing of the proponent of the statement for the purpose of preventing the child from attending or testifying.

(C) The court shall make the findings required by this rule on the basis of a hearing conducted outside the presence of the jury and shall make findings of fact, on the record, as to the bases for its ruling.

(Effective 7-1-91)

ARTICLE IX
AUTHENTICATION AND IDENTIFICATION

RULE 901. Requirement of Authentication or Identification

(A) **General provision.** The requirement of authentication or identification as a condition precedent to admissibility is satisfied by evidence sufficient to support a finding that the matter in question is what its proponent claims.

(B) **Illustrations.** By way of illustration only, and not by way of limitation, the following are examples of authentication or identification conforming with the requirements of this rule:

(1) *Testimony of witness with knowledge.* Testimony that a matter is what it is claimed to be.

(2) *Nonexpert opinion on handwriting.* Nonexpert opinion as to the genuineness of handwriting, based upon familiarity not acquired for purposes of the litigation.

(3) *Comparison by trier or expert witness.* Comparison by the trier of fact or by expert witness with specimens which have been authenticated.

(4) *Distinctive characteristics and the like.* Appearance, contents, substance, internal patterns, or other distinctive characteristics, taken in conjunction with circumstances.

(5) *Voice identification.* Identification of a voice, whether heard firsthand or through mechanical or electronic transmission or recording, by opinion based upon hearing the voice at any time under circumstances connecting it with the alleged speaker.

(6) *Telephone conversations.* Telephone conversations, by evidence that a call was made to the number

assigned at the time by the telephone company to a particular person or business, if (a) in the case of a person, circumstances, including self-identification, show the person answering to be the one called, or (b) in the case of a business, the call was made to a place of business and the conversation related to business reasonably transacted over the telephone.

(7) *Public records or reports.* Evidence that a writing authorized by law to be recorded or filed and in fact recorded or filed in a public office, or a purported public record, report, statement, or data compilation, in any form, is from the public office where items of this nature are kept.

(8) *Ancient documents or data compilation.* Evidence that a document or data compilation, in any form, (a) is in such condition as to create no suspicion concerning its authenticity, (b) was in a place where it, if authentic, would likely be, and (c) has been in existence twenty years or more at the time it is offered.

(9) *Process or system.* Evidence describing a process or system used to produce a result and showing that the process or system produces an accurate result.

(10) *Methods provided by statute or rule.* Any method of authentication or identification provided by statute enacted by the General Assembly not in conflict with a rule of the Supreme Court of Ohio or by other rules prescribed by the Supreme Court.

RULE 902. Self-Authentication

Extrinsic evidence of authenticity as a condition precedent to admissibility is not required with respect to the following:

(1) *Domestic public documents under seal.* A document bearing a seal purporting to be that of the United States, or of any State, district, Commonwealth, territory, or insular possession thereof, or the Panama Canal Zone, or the Trust Territory of the Pacific Islands, or of a political subdivision, department, officer, or agency thereof, and a signature purporting to be an attestation or execution.

(2) *Domestic public documents not under seal.* A document purporting to bear the signature in his official capacity of an officer or employee of any entity included in paragraph (1) hereof, having no seal, if a public officer having a seal and having official duties in the district or political subdivision of the officer or employee certifies under seal that the signer has the official capacity and that the signature is genuine.

(3) *Foreign public documents.* A document purporting to be executed or attested in his official capacity by a person authorized by the laws of a foreign country to make the execution or attestation, and accompanied by a final certification as to the genuineness of the signature and official position (a) of the executing or attesting person, or (b) of any foreign official whose certificate of genuineness of signature and official position relates to the execution or attestation or is in a chain of certificates of genuineness of signature and official position relating to the execution or attestation. A final certification may be made by a secretary of embassy or legation, consul general, consul, vice consul, or consular agent of the United States, or a diplomatic or consular official of the foreign country assigned or accredited to the United States. If reasonable opportunity has been given to all parties to investigate the authenticity and accuracy of official documents, the court may, for good cause shown, order that they be treated as presumptively authentic without final certification or permit them to be evidenced by an attested summary with or without final certification.

(4) *Certified copies of public records.* A copy of an official record or report or entry therein, or of a document authorized by law to be recorded or filed and actually recorded or filed in a public office, including data compilations in any form, certified as correct by the custodian or other person authorized to make the certification, by certificate complying with paragraph (1), (2), or (3) of this rule or complying with any law of a jurisdiction, state or federal, or rule prescribed by the Supreme Court of Ohio.

(5) *Official publications.* Books, pamphlets, or other publications purporting to be issued by public authority.

(6) *Newspapers and periodicals.* Printed materials purporting to be newspapers or periodicals, including notices and advertisements contained therein.

(7) *Trade inscriptions and the like.* Inscriptions, signs, tags, or labels purporting to have been affixed in the course of business and indicating ownership, control, or origin.

(8) *Acknowledged documents.* Documents accompanied by a certificate of acknowledgment executed in the manner provided by law by a notary public or other officer authorized by law to take acknowledgments.

(9) *Commercial paper and related documents.* Commercial paper, signatures thereon, and documents relating thereto to the extent provided by general commercial law.

(10) *Presumptions created by law.* Any signature, document, or other matter declared by any law of a jurisdiction, state or federal, to be presumptively or prima facie genuine or authentic.

RULE 903. Subscribing Witness' Testimony Unnecessary

The testimony of a subscribing witness is not necessary to authenticate a writing unless required by the laws of the jurisdiction whose laws govern the validity of the writing.

ARTICLE X
CONTENTS OF WRITINGS, RECORDINGS AND PHOTOGRAPHS

RULE 1001. Definitions

For purposes of this article the following definitions are applicable:

(1) *Writings and recordings.* "Writings" and "recordings" consist of letters, words, or numbers, or their equivalent, set down by handwriting, typewriting, printing, photostating, photographing, magnetic impulse, mechanical or electronic recording, or other forms of data compilation.

(2) *Photographs.* "Photographs" include still photographs, X-ray films, video tapes, and motion pictures.

(3) *Original.* An "original" of a writing or recording is the writing or recording itself or any counterpart intended to have the same effect by a person executing or issuing it. An "original" of a photograph includes the negative or any print therefrom. If data are stored in a computer or similar device, any printout or other output readable by sight, shown to reflect the data accurately, is an "original."

(4) *Duplicate.* A "duplicate" is a counterpart produced by the same impression as the original, or from the same matrix, or by means of photography, including enlargements and miniatures, or by mechanical or electronic re-recording, or by chemical reproduction, or by other equivalent techniques which accurately reproduce the original.

RULE 1002. Requirement of Original

To prove the content of a writing, recording, or photograph, the original writing, recording, or photograph is required, except as otherwise provided in these rules or by statute enacted by the General Assembly not in conflict with a rule of the Supreme Court of Ohio.

RULE 1003. Admissibility of Duplicates

A duplicate is admissible to the same extent as an original unless (1) a genuine question is raised as to the authenticity of the original or (2) in the circumstances it would be unfair to admit the duplicate in lieu of the original.

RULE 1004. Admissibility of Other Evidence of Contents

The original is not required, and other evidence of the contents of a writing, recording, or photograph is admissible if:

(1) *Originals lost or destroyed.* All originals are lost or have been destroyed, unless the proponent lost or destroyed them in bad faith; or

(2) *Original not obtainable.* No original can be obtained by any available judicial process or procedure; or

(3) *Original in possession of opponent.* At a time when an original was under the control of the party against whom offered, he was put on notice, by the pleadings or otherwise, that the contents would be a subject of proof at the hearing, and he does not produce the original at the hearing; or

(4) *Collateral matters.* The writing, recording, or photograph is not closely related to a controlling issue.

RULE 1005. Public Records

The contents of an official record, or of a document authorized to be recorded or filed and actually recorded or filed, including data compilations in any form if otherwise admissible, may be proved by copy, certified as correct in accordance with Rule 902, Civ. R. 44, Crim. R. 27 or testified to be correct by a witness who has compared it with the original. If a copy which complies with the foregoing cannot be obtained by the exercise of reasonable diligence, then other evidence of the contents may be given.

RULE 1006. Summaries

The contents of voluminous writings, recordings, or photographs which cannot conveniently be examined in court may be presented in the form of a chart, summary, or calculation. The originals, or duplicates, shall be made available for examination or copying, or both, by other parties at a reasonable time and place. The court may order that they be produced in court.

RULE 1007. Testimony or Written Admission of Party

Contents of writings, recordings, or photographs may be proved by the testimony or deposition of the party against whom offered or by his written admission, without accounting for the nonproduction of the original.

RULE 1008. Functions of Court and Jury

When the admissibility of other evidence of contents of writings, recordings, or photographs under these rules depends upon the fulfillment of a condition of fact, the question whether the condition has been fulfilled is ordinarily for the court to determine in accordance with the provisions of Rule 104. However, when an issue is raised (a) whether the asserted writing ever existed, or (b) whether another writing, recording, or photograph produced at the trial is the original, or (c) whether other evidence of contents correctly reflects the contents, the issue is for the trier of fact to determine as in the case of other issues of fact.

ARTICLE XI
MISCELLANEOUS RULES

RULE 1101. [Reserved]

RULE 1102. Effective Date

(A) Effective date of rules. These rules shall take effect on the first day of July, 1980. They govern all proceedings in actions brought after they take effect and also all further proceedings in actions then pending, except to the extent that in the opinion of the court their application in a particular action pending when the rules take effect would not be feasible or would work injustice, in which event former evidentiary principles apply.

(B) Effective date of amendments. The amendments submitted by the Supreme Court to the General Assembly on January 14, 1981, and on April 29, 1981, shall take effect on July 1, 1981. They govern all proceedings in actions brought after they take effect and also all further proceedings in actions then pending, except to the extent that their application in a particular action pending when the amendments take effect would not be feasible or would work injustice, in which event the former procedure applies.

(C) Effective date of amendments. The amendments submitted by the Supreme Court to the General Assembly on January 12, 1990, and further revised and submitted on April 16, 1990, shall take effect on July 1, 1990. They govern all proceedings in actions brought after they take effect and also further proceedings in actions then pending, except to the extent that their application in a particular action pending when the amendments take effect would not be feasible or would work injustice, in which event the former procedure applies.

(D) Effective date of amendments. The amendments submitted by the Supreme Court to the General Assembly on January 10, 1991 and further revised and submitted on April 29, 1991, shall take effect on July 1, 1991. They govern all proceedings in actions brought after they take effect and also all further proceedings in actions then pending, except to the extent that their application in a particular action pending when the amendments take effect would not be feasible or would work injustice, in which event the former procedure applies.

(E) Effective date of amendments. The amendments filed by the Supreme Court with the General Assembly on January 14, 1992 and further filed on April 30, 1992, shall take effect on July 1, 1992. They govern all proceedings in actions brought after they take effect and also all further proceedings in actions then pending, except to the extent that their application in a particular action pending when the amendments take effect would not be feasible or would work injustice, in which event the former procedure applies.

(F) Effective date of amendments. The amendments submitted by the Supreme Court to the General Assembly on January 8, 1993 and further filed on April 30, 1993 shall take effect on July 1, 1993. They govern all proceedings in actions brought after they take effect and also all further proceedings in actions then pending, except to the extent that their application in a particular action pending when the amendments take effect would not be feasible or would work injustice, in which event the former procedure applies.

(G) Effective date of amendments. The amendments submitted by the Supreme Court to the General Assembly on January 14, 1994 shall take effect on July 1, 1994. They govern all proceedings in actions brought after they take effect and also all further proceedings in actions then pending, except to the extent that their application in a particular action pending when the amendments take effect would not be feasible or would work injustice, in which event the former procedure applies.

(H) Effective date of amendments. The amendments to Rules 101, 102 and 403 filed by the Supreme Court with the General Assembly on January 5, 1996 and refiled on April 26, 1996 shall take effect on July 1, 1996. They govern all proceedings in actions brought after they take effect and also all further proceedings in actions then pending, except to the extent that their application in a particular action pending when the amendments take effect would not be feasible or would work injustice, in which event the former procedure applies.

(Amended, eff 7-1-81; 7-1-90; 7-1-91; 7-1-92; 7-1-93; 7-1-94; 7-1-96)

RULE 1103. Title

These rules shall be known as the Ohio Rules of Evidence and may be cited as "Evidence Rules" or "Evid. R."___.

OHIO RULES OF JUVENILE PROCEDURE

Complete through July 1, 1997

For annotations and cases construing the Ohio Juvenile Rules, see the
TITLE 21 VOLUME to PAGE'S OHIO REVISED CODE ANNOTATED
or the current edition of OHIO FAMILY LAW HANDBOOK

For text discussion of the Juvenile Rules see Volume 2 of
ANDERSON'S OHIO FAMILY LAW (2nd edition)

Rule
1. Scope of rules: applicability; construction; exceptions
    (A) Applicability
    (B) Construction
    (C) Exceptions
2. Definitions
3. Waiver of rights
4. Assistance of counsel; guardian ad litem
    (A) Assistance of counsel
    (B) Guardian ad litem; when appointed
    (C) Guardian ad litem as counsel
    (D) Appearance of attorneys
    (E) Notice to guardian ad litem
    (F) Withdrawal of counsel or guardian ad litem
    (G) Costs
5. [Reserved]
6. Taking into custody
    (A) [When]
    (B) Probable cause hearing
7. Detention and shelter care
    (A) Detention: standards
    (B) Priorities in placement prior to hearing
    (C) Initial procedure upon detention
    (D) Admission
    (E) Procedure after admission
    (F) Detention hearing
        (1) Hearing: time; notice
        (2) Hearing: advisement of rights
        (3) Hearing procedure
    (G) Rehearing
    (H) Separation from adults
    (I) Physical examination
    (J) Telephone and visitation rights
8. Filing by facsimile transmission
    (A) Procedure
    (B) Equipment
9. Intake
    (A) Court action to be avoided
    (B) Screening; referral
10. Complaint
    (A) Filing
    (B) Complaint: general form
    (C) Complaint: juvenile traffic offense
    (D) Complaint: permanent custody
    (E) Complaint: temporary custody
    (F) Complaint: long term foster care
    (G) Complaint: habeas corpus
11. Transfer to another county
    (A) Residence in another county; transfer optional
    (B) Proceedings in another county; transfer required
    (C) Adjudicatory hearing in county where complaint filed

Rule
    (D) Transfer of records
12. [Reserved]
13. Temporary disposition; temporary orders; emergency medical and surgical treatment
    (A) Temporary disposition
    (B) Temporary orders
    (C) Emergency medical and surgical treatment
    (D) Ex parte proceedings
    (E) Hearing; notice
    (F) Probable cause finding
    (G) Payment
14. Termination, extension or modification of temporary custody orders
    (A) Termination
    (B) Extension
    (C) Modification
15. Process: issuance, form
    (A) Summons: issuance
    (B) Summons: form
    (C) Summons: endorsement
    (D) Warrant: issuance
    (E) Warrant: form
16. Process: service
    (A) Summons: service, return
    (B) Warrant: execution; return
        (1) By whom
        (2) Territorial limits
        (3) Manner
        (4) Return
17. Subpoena
    (A) Form; issuance
    (B) Parties unable to pay
    (C) Service
    (D) Protection of persons subject to subpoenas
    (E) Duties in responding to subpoena
    (F) Sanctions
    (G) Privileges
    (H) Time
18. Time
    (A) Time: computation
    (B) Time: enlargement
    (C) Time: unaffected by expiration of term
    (D) Time: for motions; affidavits
    (E) Time: additional time after service by mail
19. Motions
20. Service and filing of papers when required subsequent to filing of complaint
    (A) Service: when required
    (B) Service: how made
    (C) Filing
21. Preliminary conferences

Rule
22. Pleadings and motions; defenses and objections
    (A) Pleadings and motions
    (B) Amendment of pleadings
    (C) Answer
    (D) Prehearing motions
    (E) Motion time
    (F) State's right to appeal upon granting a motion to suppress
23. Continuance
24. Discovery
    (A) Request for discovery
    (B) Order granting discovery: limitations; sanctions
    (C) Failure to comply
25. Depositions
26. [Reserved]
27. Hearings: general
    (A) General provisions
    (B) Special provisions
28. [Reserved]
29. Adjudicatory hearing
    (A) Scheduling the hearing
    (B) Advisement and findings at the commencement of the hearing
    (C) Entry of admission or denial
    (D) Initial procedure upon entry of an admission
    (E) Initial procedure upon entry of a denial
    (F) Procedure upon determination of the issues
30. Relinquishment of jurisdiction for purposes of criminal prosecution
    (A) Preliminary hearing
    (B) Mandatory transfer
    (C) Discretionary transfer
    (D) Notice
    (E) Retention of jurisdiction
    (F) Waiver of mental examination
    (G) Order of transfer
    (H) Release of child
31. [Reserved]
32. Social history; physical examination; mental examination; investigation involving the allocation of parental rights and responsibilities for the care of children
    (A) Social history and physical or mental examination: availability before adjudication
    (B) Limitations on preparation and use
    (C) Availability of social history or investigation report
    (D) Investigation: allocation of parental rights and responsibilities for the care of children; habeas corpus
33. [Reserved]
34. Dispositional hearing
    (A) Scheduling the hearing
    (B) Hearing procedure
    (C) Judgment
    (D) Dispositional orders
    (E) Protective supervision
    (F) Case plan
    (G) Modification of temporary order
    (H) Restraining orders
    (I) Bifurcation
    (J) Advisement of rights after hearing
35. Proceedings after judgment
    (A) Continuing jurisdiction; invoked by motion
    (B) Revocation of probation
    (C) Detention

Rule
36. Dispositional Review
    (A) Court review
    (B) Citizen's review board
    (C) Agency review
37. Recording of proceedings
    (A) Record of proceedings
    (B) Restrictions on use of recording or transcript
38. Voluntary surrender of custody
    (A) Temporary custody
    (B) Permanent custody
39. [Reserved]
40. Magistrates
    (A) Appointment
    (B) Compensation
    (C) Reference and powers
        (1) Order of reference
        (2) General powers
        (3) Power to enter orders
    (D) Proceedings
    (E) Decisions in referred matters
        (1) Magistrate's decision
        (2) Findings of fact and conclusions of law
        (3) Objections
        (4) Court's action on magistrate's decision
41. [Reserved]
42. Consent to marry
    (A) Application where parental consent not required
    (B) Contents of application
    (C) Application where female pregnant or delivered of child born out of wedlock
    (D) Contents of application
    (E) Investigation
    (F) Notice
    (G) Judgment
    (H) Certified copy
43. Reference to Ohio Revised Code
44. Jurisdiction unaffected
45. Rules by juvenile courts; procedure not otherwise specified
    (A) Local rules
    (B) Procedure not otherwise specified
46. Forms
47. Effective date
    (A) Effective date of rules
    (B)–(L) Effective date of amendments
48. Title

RULE 1. Scope of rules: applicability; construction; exceptions

(A) Applicability. These rules prescribe the procedure to be followed in all juvenile courts of this state in all proceedings coming within the jurisdiction of such courts, with the exceptions stated in subdivision (C).

(B) Construction. These rules shall be liberally interpreted and construed so as to effectuate the following purposes:

(1) to effect the just determination of every juvenile court proceeding by ensuring the parties a fair hearing and the recognition and enforcement of their constitutional and other legal rights;

(2) to secure simplicity and uniformity in procedure,

fairness in administration, and the elimination of unjustifiable expense and delay;

(3) to provide for the care, protection, and mental and physical development of children subject to the jurisdiction of the juvenile court, and to protect the welfare of the community; and

(4) to protect the public interest by treating children as persons in need of supervision, care and rehabilitation.

(C) Exceptions. These rules shall not apply to procedure (1) Upon appeal to review any judgment, order, or ruling; (2) Upon the trial of criminal actions; (3) Upon the trial of actions for divorce, annulment, legal separation, and related proceedings; (4) In proceedings to determine parent-child relationships, provided, however that appointment of counsel shall be in accordance with Rule 4(A) of the Rules of Juvenile Procedure; (5) In the commitment of the mentally ill and mentally retarded; (6) In proceedings under section 2151.85 of the Revised Code to the extent that there is a conflict between these rules and section 2151.85 of the Revised Code.

When any statute provides for procedure by general or specific reference to the statutes governing procedure in juvenile court actions, procedure shall be in accordance with these rules.

(Amended, eff 7-1-91; 7-1-94; 7-1-95)

RULE 2. Definitions

As used in these rules:

(A) "Abused child" has the same meaning as in section 2151.031 of the Revised Code.

(B) "Adjudicatory hearing" means a hearing to determine whether a child is a juvenile traffic offender, delinquent, unruly, abused, neglected, or dependent or otherwise within the jurisdiction of the court or whether temporary legal custody should be converted to permanent custody.

(C) "Agreement for temporary custody" means a voluntary agreement that is authorized by section 5103.15 of the Revised Code and transfers the temporary custody of a child to a public children services agency or a private child placing agency.

(D) "Child" means a person who is under the age of eighteen years except as it relates to transfer of jurisdiction pursuant to Juv. R. 30 for purposes of criminal prosecution. A child who violates a federal or state law or municipal ordinance prior to attaining eighteen years of age shall be considered a child irrespective of age at the time the complaint is filed or hearing is had.

(E) "Complaint" means the legal document that sets forth the allegations which form the basis for juvenile court jurisdiction.

(F) "Court proceeding" means all action taken by a court from the earlier of (1) the time a complaint is filed and (2) the time a person first appears before an officer of a juvenile court until the court relinquishes jurisdiction over such child.

(G) "Custodian" means a person who has legal custody of a child or a public children services agency or private child placing agency that has permanent, temporary, or legal custody of a child.

(H) "Delinquent child" has the same meaning as in section 2151.02 of the Revised Code.

(I) "Dependent child" has the same meaning as in section 2151.04 of the Revised Code.

(J) "Detention" means the temporary care of children in restricted facilities pending court adjudication or disposition.

(K) "Detention hearing" means a hearing to determine whether a child shall be held in detention or shelter care prior to or pending execution of a final dispositional order.

(L) "Dispositional hearing" means a hearing to determine what action shall be taken concerning a child who is within the jurisdiction of the court.

(M) "Guardian" means a person, association, or corporation that is granted authority by a probate court pursuant to Chapter 2111. of the Revised Code to exercise parental rights over a child to the extent provided in the court's order and subject to the residual parental rights of the child's parents.

(N) "Guardian ad litem" means a person appointed to protect the interests of a party in a juvenile court proceeding.

(O) "Hearing" means any portion of a juvenile court proceeding before the court, whether summary in nature or by examination of witnesses.

(P) "Indigent person" means a person who, at the time need is determined, is unable by reason of lack of property or income to provide for full payment of legal counsel and all other necessary expenses of representation.

(Q) "Juvenile court" means a division of the court of common pleas, or a juvenile court separately and independently created, that has jurisdiction under Chapter 2151 of the Revised Code.

(R) "Juvenile judge" means a judge of a court having jurisdiction under Chapter 2151 of the Revised Code.

(S) "Juvenile traffic offender" has the same meaning as in section 2151.021 of the Revised Code.

(T) "Legal custody" means a legal status that vests in the custodian the right to have physical care and control of the child and to determine where and with whom the child shall live, and the right and duty to protect, train, and discipline the child and provide the child with food, shelter, education, and medical care, all subject to any residual parental rights, privileges, and responsibilities. An individual granted legal custody shall exercise the rights and responsibilities personally unless otherwise authorized by any section of the Revised Code or by the court.

(U) "Long term foster care" means an order of a juvenile court pursuant to which both of the following apply:

(1) Legal custody of a child is given to a public children services agency or a private child placing agency without the termination of parental rights;

(2) The agency is permitted to make an appropriate placement of the child and enter into a written long-term foster care agreement with a foster care provider or with any other person or agency with whom the child is placed.

(V) "Mental examination" means an examination by a psychiatrist or psychologist.

(W) "Neglected child" has the same meaning as in section 2151.03 of the Revised Code.

(X) "Party" means a child who is the subject of a juvenile court proceeding, the child's spouse, if any, the child's parent or parents, or if the parent of a child is a child, the parent of that parent, in appropriate cases, the child's custodian, guardian, or guardian ad litem, the state, and any other person specifically designated by the court.

(Y) "Permanent custody" means a legal status that vests in a public children services agency or a private child placing agency, all parental rights, duties, and obligations, including the right to consent to adoption, and divests the natural parents or adoptive parents of any and all parental rights, privileges, and obligations, including all residual rights and obligations.

(Z) "Permanent surrender" means the act of the parents or, if a child has only one parent, of the parent of a child, by a voluntary agreement authorized by section 5103.15 of the Revised Code, to transfer the permanent custody of the child to a public children services agency or a private child placing agency.

(AA) "Person" includes an individual, association, corporation, or partnership and the state or any of its political subdivisions, departments, or agencies.

(BB) "Physical examination" means an examination by a physician.

(CC) "Private child placing agency means any association, as defined in section 5103.02 of the Revised Code that is certified pursuant to sections 5103.03 to 5103.05 of the Revised Code to accept temporary, permanent, or legal custody of children and place the children for either foster care or adoption.

(DD) "Public children services agency" means a children services board or a county department of human services that has assumed the administration of the children services function prescribed by Chapter 5153 of the Revised Code.

(EE) "Residence or legal settlement" means a location as defined by section 2151.06 of the Revised Code.

(FF) "Residual parental rights, privileges, and responsibilities" means those rights, privileges, and responsibilities remaining with the natural parent after the transfer of legal custody of the child, including but not limited to the privilege of reasonable visitation, consent to adoption, the privilege to determine the child's religious affiliation, and the responsibility for support.

(GG) "Rule of court" means a rule promulgated by the Supreme Court or a rule concerning local practice adopted by another court [that is not inconsistent with the rules promulgated by the Supreme Court and that is filed with the Supreme Court].

(HH) "Shelter care" means the temporary care of children in physically unrestricted facilities, pending court adjudication or disposition.

(II) "Social history" means the personal and family history of a child or any other party to a juvenile proceeding and may include the prior record of the person with the juvenile court or any other court.

(JJ) "Temporary custody" means legal custody of a child who is removed from the child's home, which custody may be terminated at any time at the discretion of the court or, if the legal custody is granted in an agreement for temporary custody, by the person or persons who executed the agreement.

(KK) "Unruly child" has the same meaning as in section 2151.022 of the Revised Code.

(LL) "Ward of court" means a child over whom the court assumes continuing jurisdiction.

(Amended, eff 7-1-94)

RULE 3. Waiver of rights

A child's right to be represented by counsel at a hearing conducted pursuant to Juv. R. 30 may not be waived. Other rights of a child may be waived with the permission of the court.

(Amended, eff 7-1-94)

RULE 4. Assistance of Counsel; Guardian Ad Litem

(A) Assistance of counsel. Every party shall have the right to be represented by counsel and every child, parent, custodian, or other person in loco parentis the right to appointed counsel if indigent. These rights shall arise when a person becomes a party to a juvenile court proceeding. When the complaint alleges that a child is an abused child, the court must appoint an attorney to represent the interests of the child. This rule shall not be construed to provide for a right to appointed counsel in cases in which that right is not otherwise provided for by constitution or statute.

(B) Guardian ad litem; when appointed. The court shall appoint a guardian ad litem to protect the interests of a child or incompetent adult in a juvenile court proceeding when:

(1) The child has no parent, guardian, or legal custodian;

(2) The interests of the child and the interests of the parent may conflict;

(3) The parent is under eighteen years of age or appears to be mentally incompetent;

(4) The court believes that the parent of the child is

not capable of representing the best interest of the child.

(5) Any proceeding involves allegations of abuse or neglect, voluntary surrender of permanent custody, or termination of parental rights as soon as possible after the commencement of such proceeding.

(6) There is an agreement for the voluntary surrender of temporary custody that is made in accordance with section 5103.15 of the Revised Code, and thereafter there is a request for extension of the voluntary agreement.

(7) Appointment is otherwise necessary to meet the requirements of a fair hearing.

(C) Guardian ad litem as counsel.

(1) When the guardian ad litem is an attorney admitted to practice in this state, the guardian may also serve as counsel to the ward providing no conflict between the roles exist[s].

(2) If a person is serving as guardian ad litem and as attorney for a ward and either that person or the court finds a conflict between the responsibilities of the role of attorney and that of guardian ad litem, the court shall appoint another person as guardian ad litem for the ward.

(3) If a court appoints a person who is not an attorney admitted to practice in this state to be a guardian ad litem, the court may appoint an attorney admitted to practice in this state to serve as attorney for the guardian ad litem.

(D) Appearance of attorneys. An attorney shall enter appearance by filing a written notice with the court or by appearing personally at a court hearing and informing the court of said representation.

(E) Notice to guardian ad litem. The guardian ad litem shall be given notice of all proceedings in the same manner as notice is given to other parties to the action.

(F) Withdrawal of counsel or guardian ad litem. An attorney or guardian ad litem may withdraw only with the consent of the court upon good cause shown.

(G) Costs. The court may fix compensation for the services of appointed counsel and guardians ad litem, tax the same as part of the costs and assess them against the child, the child's parents, custodian, or other person in loco parentis of such child.

(Amended, eff 7-1-76; 7-1-94; 7-1-95)

RULE 5. [Reserved]

RULE 6. Taking into custody

(A) [When.] A child may be taken into custody:
(1) pursuant to an order of the court;
(2) pursuant to the law of arrest;
(3) by a law enforcement officer or duly authorized officer of the court when any of the following conditions exist:

(a) There are reasonable grounds to believe that the child is suffering from illness or injury and is not receiving proper care, and the child's removal is necessary to prevent immediate or threatened physical or emotional harm;

(b) There are reasonable grounds to believe that the child is in immediate danger from the child's surroundings and that the child's removal is necessary to prevent immediate or threatened physical or emotional harm;

(c) There are reasonable grounds to believe that a parent, guardian, custodian, or other household member of the child has abused or neglected another child in the household, and that the child is in danger of immediate or threatened physical or emotional harm;

(d) There are reasonable grounds to believe that the child has run away from the child's parents, guardian, or other custodian;

(e) There are reasonable grounds to believe that the conduct, conditions, or surroundings of the child are endangering the health, welfare, or safety of the child; or

(f) During the pendency of court proceedings, there are reasonable grounds to believe that the child may abscond or be removed from the jurisdiction of the court or will not be brought to the court;

(g) A juvenile judge or designated magistrate has found that there is probable cause to believe any of the conditions set forth in division (A)(3)(a), (b), or (c) of this rule are present, has found that reasonable efforts have been made to notify the child's parents, guardian ad litem or custodian that the child may be placed into shelter care, except where notification would jeopardize the physical or emotional safety of the child or result in the child's removal from the court's jurisdiction, and has ordered ex parte, by telephone or otherwise, the taking of the child into custody.

(4) By the judge or designated magistrate ex parte pending the outcome of the adjudicatory and dispositional hearing in an abuse, neglect, or dependency proceeding, where it appears to the court that the best interest and welfare of the child require the immediate issuance of a shelter care order.

(B) Probable cause hearing. When a child is taken into custody pursuant to an ex parte emergency order pursuant to division (A)(3)(g) or (A)(4) of this rule, a probable cause hearing shall be held before the end of the next business day after the day on which the order is issued but not later than seventy-two hours after the issuance of the emergency order.

(Amended, eff 7-1-94; 7-1-96)

RULE 7. Detention and shelter care

(A) Detention: standards. A child taken into custody shall not be placed in detention or shelter care prior to final disposition unless any of the following apply:

(1) Detention or shelter care is required to protect the child from immediate or threatened physical or emotional harm;

(2) The child may abscond or be removed from the jurisdiction of the court;

(3) The child has no parent, guardian, custodian or other person able to provide supervision and care for the child and return the child to the court when required;

(4) An order for placement of the child in detention or shelter care has been made by the court.

(B) Priorities in placement prior to hearing. A person taking a child into custody shall, with all reasonable speed, do either of the following:

(1) Release the child to a parent, guardian, or other custodian;

(2) Where detention or shelter care appears to be required under the standards of division (A) of this rule, bring the child to the court or deliver the child to a place of detention or shelter care designated by the court.

(C) Initial procedure upon detention. Any person who delivers a child to a shelter or detention facility shall give the admissions officer at the facility a signed report stating why the child was taken into custody and why the child was not released to a parent, guardian or custodian, and shall assist the admissions officer, if necessary, in notifying the parent pursuant to division (E)(3) of this rule.

(D) Admission. The admissions officer in a shelter or detention facility, upon receipt of a child, shall review the report submitted pursuant to division (C) of this rule, make such further investigation as is feasible and do either of the following:

(1) Release the child to the care of a parent, guardian or custodian;

(2) Where detention or shelter care is required under the standards of division (A) of this rule, admit the child to the facility or place the child in some appropriate facility.

(E) Procedure after admission. When a child has been admitted to detention or shelter care the admissions officer shall do all of the following:

(1) Prepare a report stating the time the child was brought to the facility and the reasons the child was admitted;

(2) Advise the child of the right to telephone parents and counsel immediately and at reasonable times thereafter and the time, place, and purpose of the detention hearing;

(3) Use reasonable diligence to contact the child's parent, guardian, or custodian and advise that person of all of the following:

(a) The place of and reasons for detention;

(b) The time the child may be visited;

(c) The time, place, and purpose of the detention hearing;

(d) The right to counsel and appointed counsel in the case of indigency.

(F) Detention hearing.

(1) Hearing: time; notice. When a child has been admitted to detention or shelter care, a detention hearing shall be held promptly, not later than seventy-two hours after the child is placed in detention or shelter care or the next court day, whichever is earlier, to determine whether detention or shelter care is required. Reasonable oral or written notice of the time, place, and purpose of the detention hearing shall be given to the child and to the parents, guardian, or other custodian, if that person or those persons can be found.

(2) Hearing: advisement of rights. Prior to the hearing, the court shall inform the parties of the right to counsel and to appointed counsel if indigent and the child's right to remain silent with respect to any allegation of a juvenile traffic offense, delinquency, or unruliness.

(3) Hearing procedure. The court may consider any evidence, including the reports filed by the person who brought the child to the facility and the admissions officer, without regard to formal rules of evidence. Unless it appears from the hearing that the child's detention or shelter care is required under division (A) of this rule, the court shall order the child's release to a parent, guardian, or custodian. Whenever abuse, neglect, or dependency is alleged, the court shall determine whether there are any appropriate relatives of the child who are willing to be temporary custodians and, if so, appoint an appropriate relative as the temporary custodian of the child. The court shall make a reasonable efforts determination in accordance with Juv. R. 27(B)(1).

(G) Rehearing. If a parent, guardian, or custodian did not receive notice of the initial hearing and did not appear or waive appearance at the hearing, the court shall rehear the matter promptly. After a child is placed in shelter care or detention care, any party and the guardian ad litem of the child may file a motion with the court requesting that the child be released from detention or shelter care. Upon the filing of the motion, the court shall hold a hearing within seventy-two hours.

(H) Separation from adults. No child shall be placed in or committed to any prison, jail, lockup, or any other place where the child can come in contact or communication with any adult convicted of crime, under arrest, or charged with crime.

(I) Physical examination. The supervisor of a shelter or detention facility may provide for a physical examination of a child placed in the shelter or facility.

(J) Telephone and visitation rights. A child may telephone the child's parents and attorney immediately after being admitted to a shelter or detention facility and at reasonable times thereafter.

The child may be visited at reasonable visiting hours by the child's parents and adult members of the family, the child's pastor, and the child's teachers. The child may be visited by the child's attorney at any time.

(Amended, eff 7-1-94)

RULE 8. Filing by facsimile transmission

(A) Procedure. Any pleading, motion, or other paper may be filed by facsimile transmission only in the following manner:

(1) A document received by the clerk by facsimile transmission shall be accepted as the filed original provided an original writing complying with rules 7, 10, and 11 of the Rules of Civil Procedure, together with any necessary copies are mailed at the time of the facsimile transmission and received by the clerk within three days after transmission. Any signature on electronically transmitted pleadings or papers shall be considered that of the attorney or party it purports to be for all purposes. If it is established that the pleadings or papers were transmitted without authority, the court shall order the filing stricken.

(2) All required identification information shall be included on the cover page of the transmission including the case number, name of the judge or magistrate, or both, name of the parties, nature of the document, and number of pages including cover page. Papers transmitted without this information shall not be accepted as filed.

(3) No document shall be accepted as filed by facsimile transmission if it exceeds ten pages exclusive of the cover page or if it pertains to more than one case.

(4) Documents submitted by facsimile transmission will be considered filed only when the date and time has been stamped by the clerk. The date and time stamp produced by the clerk's facsimile machine shall constitute the date and time stamp of the clerk regardless of when actually received.

(5) All risk of filing by facsimile transmission remains with the filing party and, except as otherwise provided in this rule, facsimile filing shall be treated in the same manner as filing by mail.

(6) Fees for filing by facsimile transmission may be set by local rule of court. The local rule may provide for advance deposit or other acceptable means for payment.

(B) Equipment. No facsimile transmission will be permitted for filing unless the clerk maintains a facsimile machine that:

(1) is connected to a dedicated electronic circuit protected by a surge protector,

(2) is connected to a dedicated phone line,

(3) uses 20-pound bond paper,

(4) complies with Civ. R. 10(E),

(5) meets CCITT Group 3 specifications, and

(6) automatically places the date and time of receipt on the printed transmission.

(Effective 7-1-94; amended, eff 7-1-96)

RULE 9. Intake

(A) Court action to be avoided. In all appropriate cases formal action should be avoided and other community resources utilized to ameliorate situations brought to the attention of the court.

(B) Screening; referral. Information that a child is within the court's jurisdiction may be informally screened prior to the filing of a complaint to determine whether the filing of a complaint is in the best interest of the child and the public.

RULE 10. Complaint

(A) Filing. Any person having knowledge of a child who appears to be a juvenile traffic offender, delinquent, unruly, neglected, dependent, or abused may file a complaint with respect to the child in the juvenile court of the county in which the child has a residence or legal settlement, or in which the traffic offense, delinquency, unruliness, neglect, dependency, or abuse occurred.

Any person may file a complaint to have determined the custody of a child not a ward of another court of this state, and any person entitled to the custody of a child and unlawfully deprived of such custody may file a complaint requesting a writ of habeas corpus. Complaints concerning custody shall be filed in the county where the child is found or was last known to be.

Any person with standing may file a complaint for the determination of any other matter over which the juvenile court is given jurisdiction by section 2151.23 of the Revised Code. The complaint shall be filed in the county in which the child who is the subject of the complaint is found or was last known to be.

When a case concerning a child is transferred or certified from another court, the certification from the transferring court shall be considered the complaint. The juvenile court may order the certification supplemented upon its own motion or that of a party.

(B) Complaint: general form. The complaint, which may be upon information and belief, shall satisfy all of the following requirements:

(1) State in ordinary and concise language the essential facts that bring the proceeding within the jurisdiction of the court, and in juvenile traffic offense and delinquency proceedings, shall contain the numerical designation of the statute or ordinance alleged to have been violated;

(2) Contain the name and address of the parent, guardian, or custodian of the child or state that the name or address is unknown;

(3) Be made under oath.

(C) Complaint: juvenile traffic offense. A Uniform Traffic ticket shall be used as a complaint in juvenile traffic offense proceedings.

(D) Complaint: permanent custody. A complaint seeking permanent custody of a child shall state that permanent custody is sought.

(E) Complaint: temporary custody. A complaint

seeking temporary custody of a child shall state that temporary custody is sought.

(F) Complaint: long term foster care. A complaint seeking the placement of a child into long term foster care shall state that placement into long term foster care is sought.

(G) Complaint: habeas corpus. Where a complaint for a writ of habeas corpus involving the custody of a child is based on the existence of a lawful court order, a certified copy of the order shall be attached to the complaint.

(Amended, eff 7-1-75; 7-1-76; 7-1-94)

RULE 11. Transfer to another county

(A) Residence in another county; transfer optional. If the child resides in a county of this state and the proceeding is commenced in a court of another county, that court, on its own motion or a motion of a party, may transfer the proceeding to the county of the child's residence upon the filing of the complaint or after the adjudicatory or dispositional hearing for such further proceeding as required. The court of the child's residence shall then proceed as if the original complaint had been filed in that court. Transfer may also be made if the residence of the child changes.

(B) Proceedings in another county; transfer required. The proceedings shall be so transferred if other proceedings involving the child are pending in the juvenile court of the county of the child's residence.

(C) Adjudicatory hearing in county where complaint filed. Where either the transferring or receiving court finds that the interests of justice and the convenience of the parties so require, the adjudicatory hearing shall be held in the county wherein the complaint was filed. Thereafter the proceeding may be transferred to the county of the child's residence for disposition.

(D) Transfer of records. Certified copies of all legal and social records pertaining to the proceeding shall accompany the transfer.

(Amended, eff 7-1-94)

RULE 12. [Reserved]

RULE 13. Temporary disposition; temporary orders; emergency medical and surgical treatment

(A) Temporary disposition. Pending hearing on a complaint, the court may make such temporary orders concerning the custody or care of a child who is the subject of the complaint as the child's interest and welfare may require.

(B) Temporary orders.
(1) Pending hearing on a complaint, the judge or magistrate may issue temporary orders with respect to the relations and conduct of other persons toward a child who is the subject of the complaint as the child's interest and welfare may require.

(2) Upon the filing of an abuse, neglect, or dependency complaint, any party may by motion request that the court issue any of the following temporary orders to protect the best interest of the child:

(a) An order granting temporary custody of the child to a particular party;

(b) An order for the taking of the child into custody pending the outcome of the adjudicatory and dispositional hearings;

(c) An order granting, limiting, or eliminating visitation rights with respect to the child;

(d) An order for the payment of child support and continued maintenance of any medical, surgical, or hospital policies of insurance for the child that existed at the time of the filing of the complaint, petition, writ, or other document;

(e) An order requiring a party to vacate a residence that will be lawfully occupied by the child;

(f) An order requiring a party to attend an appropriate counseling program that is reasonably available to that party;

(g) Any other order that restrains or otherwise controls the conduct of any party which conduct would not be in the best interest of the child.

(3) The orders permitted by division (B)(2) of this rule may be granted ex parte if it appears that the best interest and welfare of the child require immediate issuance. If the court issues the requested ex parte order, the court shall hold a hearing to review the order within seventy-two hours after it is issued or before the end of the next court day after the day on which it is issued, whichever occurs first. The court shall appoint a guardian ad litem for the child prior to the hearing. The court shall give written notice of the hearing by means reasonably likely to result in the party's receiving actual notice and include all of the following:

(a) The date, time, and location of the hearing;

(b) The issues to be addressed at the hearing;

(c) A statement that every party to the hearing has a right to counsel and to court appointed counsel, if the party is indigent;

(d) The name, telephone number, and address of the person requesting the order;

(e) A copy of the order, except when it is not possible to obtain it because of the exigent circumstances in the case.

(4) The court may review any order under this rule at any time upon motion of any party for good cause shown or upon the motion of the court.

(5) If the court does not grant an ex parte order, the court shall hold a shelter care hearing on the motion within ten days after the motion is filed.

(C) Emergency medical and surgical treatment. Upon the certification of one or more reputable practicing physicians, the court may order such emergency medical and surgical treatment as appears to be immediately necessary for any child concerning whom a complaint has been filed.

(D) Ex parte proceedings. In addition to the ex parte proceeding described in division (B) of this rule, the court may proceed summarily and without notice under division (A), (B), or (C) of this rule, where it appears to the court that the interest and welfare of the child require that action be taken immediately.

(E) Hearing; notice. In addition to the procedures specified in division (B) of this rule and wherever possible, the court shall provide an opportunity for hearing before proceeding under division (D) of this rule. Where the court has proceeded without notice under division (D) of this rule, it shall give notice of the action it has taken to the parties and any other affected person and provide them an opportunity for a hearing concerning the continuing effects of the action.

(F) Probable cause finding. Upon the finding of probable cause at a shelter care hearing that a child is an abused child, the court may do any of the following:

(1) Upon motion by the court or of any party, issue reasonable protective orders with respect to the interviewing or deposition of the child;

(2) Order that the child's testimony be videotaped for preservation of the testimony for possible use in any other proceedings in the case;

(3) Set any additional conditions with respect to the child or the case involving the child that are in the best interest of the child.

(G) Payment. The court may order the parent, guardian, or custodian, if able, to pay for any emergency medical or surgical treatment provided pursuant to division (C) of this rule. The order of payment may be enforced by judgment, upon which execution may issue, and a failure to pay as ordered may be punished as contempt of court.

(Amended, eff 7-1-94; 7-1-96)

RULE 14. Termination, extension or modification of temporary custody orders

(A) Termination. Any temporary custody order issued shall terminate one year after the earlier of the date on which the complaint in the case was filed or the child was first placed into shelter care. A temporary custody order shall extend beyond a year and until the court issues another dispositional order, where any public or private agency with temporary custody, not later than thirty days prior to the earlier of the date for the termination of the custody order or the date set at the dispositional hearing for the hearing to be held pursuant to Division (A) of section 2151.415 of the Revised Code, files a motion requesting that any of the following orders of disposition be issued:

(1) An order that the child be returned home with custody to the child's parents, guardian, or custodian without any restrictions;

(2) An order for protective supervision;

(3) An order that the child be placed in the legal custody of a relative or other interested individual;

(4) An order terminating parental rights;

(5) An order for long term foster care;

(6) An order for the extension of temporary custody.

(B) Extension. Upon the filing of an agency's motion for the extension of temporary custody, the court shall schedule a hearing and give notice to all parties in accordance with these rules. The agency shall include in the motion an explanation of the progress on the case plan and of its expectations of reunifying the child with the child's family, or placing the child in a permanent placement, within the extension period. The court may extend the temporary custody order for a period of up to six months. Prior to the end of the extension period, the agency may request one additional extension of up to six months. The court shall grant either extension upon finding that it is in the best interest of the child, that there has been significant progress on the case plan, and that there is reasonable cause to believe that the child will be reunited with one of the child's parents or otherwise permanently placed within the period of extension. Prior to the end of either extension, the agency that received the extension shall file a motion and the court shall issue one of the orders of disposition set forth in division (A) of this rule. Upon the agency's motion or upon its own motion, the court shall conduct a hearing and issue an appropriate order of disposition.

(C) Modification. The court, upon its own motion or that of any party, shall conduct a hearing with notice to all parties to determine whether any order issued should be modified or terminated, or whether any other dispositional order set forth in division (A) should be issued. The court shall so modify or terminate any order in accordance with the best interest of the child.

(Effective 7-1-94)

RULE 15. Process: issuance, form

(A) Summons: issuance. After the complaint has been filed, the court shall cause the issuance of a summons directed to the child, the parents, guardian, custodian, or other person with whom the child may be living and any other persons who appear to the court to be proper or necessary parties. The summons shall require the parties to appear before the court at the time fixed to answer the allegations of the complaint. A child alleged to be abused, neglected, or dependent shall not be summoned unless the court so directs.

A summons issued for a child under fourteen years of age alleged to be delinquent, unruly, or a juvenile traffic offender shall be made by serving either the child's parents, guardian, custodian, or other person with whom the child lives or resides. If the person who has physical custody of the child or with whom the child resides is other than the parent or guardian, then the parents and guardian also shall be summoned. A copy of the complaint shall accompany the summons.

(B) Summons: form. The summons shall contain:

(1) The name of the party or person with whom the child may be or, if unknown, any name or description by which the party or person can be identified with reasonable certainty.

(2) A summary statement of the complaint and in juvenile traffic offense and delinquency proceedings the numerical designation of the applicable statute or ordinance.

(3) A statement that any party is entitled to be represented by an attorney and that upon request the court will appoint an attorney for an indigent party entitled to appointed counsel under Rule 4(A).

(4) An order to the party or person to appear at a stated time and place with a warning that the party or person may lose valuable rights or be subject to court sanction if the party or person fails to appear at the time and place stated in the summons.

(5) A statement that if a child is adjudicated abused, neglected, or dependent and the complaint seeks an order of permanent custody, an order of permanent custody would cause the parents, guardian, or legal custodian to be divested permanently of all parental rights and privileges.

(6) A statement that if a child is adjudicated abused, neglected, or dependent and the complaint seeks an order of temporary custody, an order of temporary custody will cause the removal of the child from the legal custody of the parents, guardian, or other custodian until the court terminates the order of temporary custody or permanently divests the parents of their parental rights.

(7) A statement that if the child is adjudicated abused, neglected, or dependent and the complaint seeks an order of long term foster care, an order of long term foster care will cause the removal of the child from legal custody of the parent, guardian, or other custodian.

(8) The name and telephone number of the court employee designated by the court to arrange for the prompt appointment of counsel for indigent persons.

(C) Summons: endorsement. The court may endorse upon the summons an order directed to the parents, guardian, or other person with whom the child may be, to appear personally and bring the child to the hearing.

(D) Warrant: issuance. If it appears that the summons will be ineffectual or the welfare of the child requires that the child be brought forthwith to the court, a warrant may be issued against the child. A copy of the complaint shall accompany the warrant.

(E) Warrant: form. The warrant shall contain the name of the child or, if that is unknown, any name or description by which the child can be identified with reasonable certainty. It shall contain a summary statement of the complaint and in juvenile traffic offense and delinquency proceedings the numerical designation of the applicable statute or ordinance. A copy of the complaint shall be attached to the warrant. The warrant shall command that the child be taken into custody and be brought before the court that issued the warrant without unnecessary delay.

(Amended, eff 7-1-94)

RULE 16. Process: service

(A) Summons: service, return. Except as otherwise provided in these rules, summons shall be served as provided in Civil Rules 4(A), (C) and (D), 4.1, 4.2, 4.3, 4.5 and 4.6. The summons shall direct the party served to appear at a stated time and place. Where service is by certified mail, the time shall not be less than seven days after the date of mailing.

Except as otherwise provided in this rule, when the residence of a party is unknown and cannot be ascertained with reasonable diligence, service shall be made by publication. Service by publication upon a non-custodial parent is not required in delinquent child or unruly child cases when the person alleged to have legal custody of the child has been served with summons pursuant to this rule, but the court may not enter any order or judgment against any person who has not been served with process or served by publication unless that person appears. Before service by publication can be made, an affidavit of a party or party's counsel shall be filed with the court. The affidavit shall aver that service of summons cannot be made because the residence of the person is unknown to the affiant and cannot be ascertained with reasonable diligence.

Upon the filing of the affidavit, the clerk shall serve notice by publication in a newspaper of general circulation in the county in which the complaint is filed. If no newspaper is published in that county, then publication shall be in a newspaper published in an adjoining county. The publication shall contain the name and address of the court, the case number, the name of the first party on each side, and the name and last known address, if any, of the person or persons whose residence is unknown. The publication shall also contain a summary statement of the object of the complaint and shall notify the person to be served that the person is required to appear at the time and place stated. The time stated shall not be less than fourteen days after the date of publication. The publication shall be published once and service shall be complete on the date of publication.

After the publication, the publisher or the publisher's agent shall file with the court an affidavit showing the fact of publication together with a copy of the notice of publication. The affidavit and copy of the notice shall constitute proof of service.

(B) Warrant: execution; return.

(1) By whom. The warrant shall be executed by any officer authorized by law.

(2) Territorial limits. The warrant may be executed at any place within this state.

(3) Manner. The warrant shall be executed by taking the party against whom it is issued into custody. The officer is not required to have possession of the warrant at the time it is executed, but in such case the officer shall inform the party of the complaint made and the fact that the warrant has been issued. A copy of the warrant shall be given to the person named in the warrant as soon as possible.

(4) Return. The officer executing a warrant shall make return thereof to the issuing court. Unexpected warrants shall upon request of the issuing court be returned to that court.

A warrant returned unexecuted and not cancelled or a copy thereof may, while the complaint is pending, be delivered by the court to an authorized officer for execution.

An officer executing a warrant shall take the person named therein without unnecessary delay before the court which issued the warrant.

(Amended, eff 7-1-94)

RULE 17. Subpoena

(A) Form; issuance.

(1) Every subpoena shall do all of the following:

(a) State the name of the court from which it is issued, the title of the action, and the case number;

(b) Command each person to whom it is directed, at a time and place specified in the subpoena, to do one or more of the following:

(i) Attend and give testimony at a trial, hearing, proceeding, or deposition;

(ii) Produce documents or tangible things at a trial, hearing, proceeding, or deposition;

(iii) Produce and permit inspection and copying of any designated documents that are in the possession, custody, or control of the person;

(iv) Produce and permit inspection and copying, testing, or sampling of any tangible things that are in the possession, custody, or control of the person.

(c) Set forth the text of divisions (D) and (E) of this rule.

A command to produce and permit inspection may be joined with a command to attend and give testimony, or may be issued separately.

(2) The clerk shall issue a subpoena, signed but otherwise in blank, to a party requesting it, who shall complete it before service. An attorney who has filed an appearance on behalf of a party in an action also may sign and issue a subpoena on behalf of the court in which the action is pending.

(3) If the issuing attorney modifies the subpoena in any way, the issuing attorney shall give prompt notice of the modifications to all other parties.

(B) Parties unable to pay. The court shall order at any time that a subpoena be issued for service on a named witness upon an ex parte application of a party and upon a satisfactory showing that the presence of the witness is necessary and that the party is financially unable to pay the witness fees required by division (C) of this rule. If the court orders the subpoena to be issued, the costs incurred by the process and the fees of the witness so subpoenaed shall be paid in the same manner that similar costs and fees are paid in case of a witness subpoenaed in behalf of the state in a criminal prosecution.

(C) Service. A subpoena may be served by a sheriff, bailiff, coroner, clerk of court, constable, probation officer, or a deputy of any, by an attorney or the attorney's agent, or by any person designated by order of the court who is not a party and is not less than eighteen years of age. Service of a subpoena upon a person named in the subpoena shall be made by delivering a copy of the subpoena to the person, by reading it to him or her in person, or by leaving it at the person's usual place of residence, and by tendering to the person upon demand the fees for one day's attendance and the mileage allowed by the law. The person serving the subpoena shall file a return of the subpoena with the clerk. If the witness being subpoenaed resides outside the county in which the court is located, the fees for one day's attendance and mileage shall be tendered without demand. The return may be forwarded through the postal service or otherwise.

(D) Protection of persons subject to subpoenas.

(1) A party or an attorney responsible for the issuance and service of a subpoena shall take reasonable steps to avoid imposing undue burden or expense on a person subject to that subpoena.

(2)(a) A person commanded to produce under division (A)(1)(b)(ii), (iii), or (iv) of this rule is not required to appear in person at the place of production or inspection unless commanded to attend and give testimony at a trial, hearing, proceeding, or deposition.

(b) Subject to division (E)(2) of this rule, a person commanded to produce under division (A)(1)(b)(ii), (iii), or (iv) of this rule may serve upon the party or attorney designated in the subpoena written objections to production. The objections must be served within fourteen days after service of the subpoena or before the time specified for compliance if that time is less than fourteen days after service. If objection is made, the party serving the subpoena shall not be entitled to production except pursuant to an order of the court that issued the subpoena. If objection has been made, the party serving the subpoena, upon notice to the person commanded to produce, may move at any time for an order to compel the production. An order to compel production shall protect any person who is not a party or an officer of a party from significant expense resulting from the production commanded.

(3) On timely motion, the court from which the subpoena was issued shall quash or modify the subpoena,

or order appearance or production only under specified conditions, if the subpoena does any of the following:

(a) Fails to allow reasonable time to comply;

(b) Requires disclosure of privileged or otherwise protected matter and no exception or waiver applies;

(c) Requires disclosure of a fact known or opinion held by an expert not retained or specially employed by any party in anticipation of litigation or preparation for trial if the fact or opinion does not describe specific events or occurrences in dispute and results from study by that expert that was not made at the request of any party;

(d) Subjects a person to undue burden.

(4) Before filing a motion pursuant to division (D)(3)(d) of this rule, a person resisting discovery under this rule shall attempt to resolve any claim of undue burden through discussions with the issuing attorney. A motion filed pursuant to division (D)(3)(d) of this rule shall be supported by an affidavit of the subpoenaed person or a certificate of that person's attorney of the efforts made to resolve any claim of undue burden.

(5) If a motion is made under division (D)(3)(c) or (D)(3)(d) of this rule, the court shall quash or modify the subpoena unless the party in whose behalf the subpoena is issued shows a substantial need for the testimony or material that cannot be otherwise met without undue hardship and assures that the person to whom the subpoena is addressed will be reasonably compensated.

(E) **Duties in responding to subpoena.**

(1) A person responding to a subpoena to produce documents shall, at the person's option, produce the documents as they are kept in the usual course of business or organized and labeled to correspond with the categories in the subpoena. A person producing documents pursuant to a subpoena for them shall permit their inspection and copying by all parties present at the time and place set in the subpoena for inspection and copying.

(2) When information subject to a subpoena is withheld on a claim that it is privileged or subject to protection as trial preparation materials, the claim shall be made expressly and shall be supported by a description of the nature of the documents, communications, or things not produced that is sufficient to enable the demanding party to contest the claim.

(F) **Sanctions.** Failure by any person without adequate excuse to obey a subpoena served upon that person may be a contempt of the court from which the subpoena issued. A subpoenaed person or that person's attorney who frivolously resists discovery under this rule may be required by the court to pay the reasonable expenses, including reasonable attorney's fees, of the party seeking the discovery. The court from which a subpoena was issued may impose upon a party or attorney in breach of the duty imposed by division (D)(1) of this rule an appropriate sanction, that may include, but is not limited to, lost earnings and reasonable attorney's fees.

(G) **Privileges.** Nothing in this rule shall be construed to authorize a party to obtain information protected by any privilege recognized by law or to authorize any person to disclose such information.

(H) **Time.** Nothing in this rule shall be construed to expand any other time limits imposed by rule or statute. All issues concerning subpoenas shall be resolved prior to the time otherwise set for hearing or trial.

(Amended, eff 7-1-94)

RULE 18. Time

(A) **Time: computation.** In computing any period of time prescribed or allowed by these rules, by the local rules of any court, by order of court, or by any applicable statute, the date of the act or event from which the designated period of time begins to run shall not be included. The last day of the period so computed shall be included, unless it is a Saturday, a Sunday, or a legal holiday, in which event the period runs until the end of the next day that is not a Saturday, a Sunday or a legal holiday. Such extension of time includes, but is not limited to, probable cause, shelter care, and detention hearings.

Except in the case of probable cause, shelter care, and detention hearings when the period of time prescribed or allowed is less than seven days, intermediate Saturdays, Sundays, and legal holidays shall be excluded in computation.

(B) **Time: enlargement.** When an act is required or allowed to be performed at or within a specified time, the court for cause shown may at any time in its discretion (1) with or without motion or notice, order the period enlarged if application therefor is made before expiration of the period originally prescribed or of that period as extended by a previous order, or (2) upon motion permit the act to be done after expiration of the specified period if the failure to act on time was the result of excusable neglect or would result in injustice to a party, but the court may not extend the time for taking any action under Rule 7(F)(1), Rule 22(F), Rule 29(A) and Rule 29(F)(2)(b), except to the extent and under the conditions stated in them.

(C) **Time: unaffected by expiration of term.** The period of time provided for the doing of any act or the taking of any proceeding is not affected or limited by the expiration of a term of court. The expiration of a term of court in no way affects the power of a court to do any act in a juvenile proceeding.

(D) **Time: for motions; affidavits.** A written motion, other than one which may be heard ex parte, and notice of the hearing thereof, shall be served not later than seven days before the time specified for the hearing unless a different period is fixed by rule or order of the court. For cause shown such an order may be made on ex parte application. When a motion is supported by affidavit, the affidavit shall be served with the motion, and opposing affidavits may be served not less than one day before the hearing unless the court permits them to be served at a later time.

(E) Time: additional time after service by mail. Whenever a party has the right or is required to do an act within a prescribed period after the service of a notice or other paper upon the person and the notice or other paper is served upon the person by mail, three days shall be added to the prescribed period. This division does not apply to service of summons.

(Amended, eff 7-1-94)

RULE 19. Motions

An application to the court for an order shall be by motion. A motion other than one made during trial or hearing shall be in writing unless the court permits it to be made orally. It shall state with particularity the grounds upon which it is made and shall set forth the relief or order sought. It shall be supported by a memorandum containing citations of authority and may be supported by an affidavit.

To expedite its business, unless otherwise provided by statute or rule, the court may make provision by rule or order for the submission and determination of motions without oral hearing upon brief written statements of reasons in support and opposition.

(Amended, eff 7-1-94)

RULE 20. Service and filing of papers when required subsequent to filing of complaint

(A) Service: when required. Written notices, requests for discovery, designation of record on appeal and written motions, other than those which are heard ex parte, and similar papers shall be served upon each of the parties.

(B) Service: how made. Whenever under these rules or by an order of the court service is required or permitted to be made upon a party represented by an attorney, the service shall be made upon the attorney unless service is ordered by the court upon the party. Service upon the attorney or upon the party shall be made in the manner provided in Civ. R. 5(B).

(C) Filing. All papers required to be served upon a party shall be filed simultaneously with or immediately after service. Papers filed with the court shall not be considered until proof of service is endorsed thereon or separately filed. The proof of service shall state the date and the manner of service and shall be signed and filed in the manner provided in Civil Rule 5(D).

(Amended, eff 7-1-94)

RULE 21. Preliminary conferences

At any time after the filing of a complaint, the court upon motion of any party or upon its own motion may order one or more conferences to consider such matters as will promote a fair and expeditious proceeding.

RULE 22. Pleadings and motions; defenses and objections

(A) Pleadings and motions. Pleadings in juvenile proceedings shall be the complaint and the answer, if any, filed by a party. A party may move to dismiss the complaint or for other appropriate relief.

(B) Amendment of pleadings. Any pleading may be amended at any time prior to the adjudicatory hearing. After the commencement of the adjudicatory hearing, a pleading may be amended upon agreement of the parties or, if the interests of justice require, upon order of the court. A complaint charging an act of delinquency may not be amended unless agreed by the parties, if the proposed amendment would change the name or identity of the specific violation of law so that it would be considered a change of the crime charged if committed by an adult. Where requested, a court order shall grant a party reasonable time in which to respond to an amendment.

(C) Answer. No answer shall be necessary. A party may file an answer to the complaint, which, if filed, shall contain specific and concise admissions or denials of each material allegation of the complaint.

(D) Prehearing motions. Any defense, objection or request which is capable of determination without hearing on the allegations of the complaint may be raised before the adjudicatory hearing by motion. The following must be heard before the adjudicatory hearing, though not necessarily on a separate date:

(1) Defenses or objections based on defects in the institution of the proceeding;

(2) Defenses or objections based on defects in the complaint (other than failure to show jurisdiction in the court or to charge an offense which objections shall be noticed by the court at any time during the pendency of the proceeding);

(3) Motions to suppress evidence on the ground that it was illegally obtained;

(4) Motions for discovery.

(E) Motion time. All prehearing motions shall be filed by the earlier of (1) seven days prior to hearing, or (2) ten days after the appearance of counsel. The court in the interest of justice may extend the time for making prehearing motions.

The court for good cause shown may permit a motion to suppress evidence under subsection (D)(3) to be made at the time such evidence is offered.

(F) State's right to appeal upon granting a motion to supress. In delinquency proceedings the state may take an appeal as of right from the granting of a motion to suppress evidence if, in addition to filing a notice of appeal, the prosecuting attorney certifies that

(1) the appeal is not taken for the purpose of delay and (2) the granting of the motion has rendered proof available to the state so weak in its entirety that any reasonable possibility of proving the complaint's allegations has been destroyed.

Such appeal shall not be allowed unless the notice of appeal and the certification by the prosecuting attorney are filed with the clerk of the juvenile court within seven days after the date of the entry of the judgment or order granting the motion. Any appeal which may be taken under this rule shall be diligently prosecuted.

A child in detention or shelter care may be released pending this appeal when the state files the notice of appeal and certification.

This appeal shall take precedence over all other appeals.

(Amended, eff 7-1-77; 7-1-94)

RULE 23. Continuance

Continuances shall be granted only when imperative to secure fair treatment for the parties.

RULE 24. Discovery

(A) Request for discovery. Upon written request, each party of whom discovery is requested shall, to the extent not privileged, produce promptly for inspection, copying, or photographing the following information, documents, and material in that party's custody, control, or possession:

(1) The names and last known addresses of each witness to the occurrence that forms the basis of the charge or defense;

(2) Copies of any written statements made by any party or witness;

(3) Transcriptions, recordings, and summaries of any oral statements of any party or witness, except the work product of counsel;

(4) Any scientific or other reports that a party intends to introduce at the hearing or that pertain to physical evidence that a party intends to introduce;

(5) Photographs and any physical evidence which a party intends to introduce at the hearing;

(6) Except in delinquency and unruly child proceedings, other evidence favorable to the requesting party and relevant to the subject matter involved in the pending action. In delinquency and unruly child proceedings, the prosecuting attorney shall disclose to respondent's counsel all evidence, known or that may become known to the prosecuting attorney, favorable to the respondent and material either to guilt or punishment.

(B) Order granting discovery: limitations; sanctions. If a request for discovery is refused, application may be made to the court for a written order granting the discovery. Motions for discovery shall certify that a request for discovery has been made and refused. An order granting discovery may make such discovery reciprocal for all parties to the proceeding, including the party requesting discovery. Notwithstanding the provisions of subdivision (A), the court may deny, in whole or part, or otherwise limit or set conditions on the discovery authorized by such subdivision, upon its own motion, or upon a showing by a party upon whom a request for discovery is made that granting discovery may jeopardize the safety of a party or, witness, or confidential informant, result in the production of perjured testimony or evidence, endanger the existence of physical evidence, violate a privileged communication, or impede the criminal prosecution of a minor as an adult or of an adult charged with an offense arising from the same transaction or occurrence.

(C) Failure to comply. If at any time during the course of the proceedings it is brought to the attention of the court that a person has failed to comply with an order issued pursuant to this rule, the court may grant a continuance, prohibit the person from introducing in evidence the material not disclosed, or enter such other order as it deems just under the circumstances.

(Amended, eff 7-1-94)

RULE 25. Depositions

The court upon good cause shown may grant authority to take the deposition of a party or other person upon such terms and conditions and in such manner as the court may fix.

RULE 26. [Reserved]

RULE 27. Hearings: general

(A) General provisions. The juvenile court may conduct its hearings in an informal manner and may adjourn its hearings from time to time. In the hearing of any case the general public may be excluded and only persons admitted who have a direct interest in the case.

All cases involving children shall be heard separate and apart from the trial of cases against adults. The court may excuse the attendance of the child at the hearing in neglect, dependency, or abuse cases. The court shall hear and determine all cases of children without a jury.

(B) Special provisions.

(1) In any proceeding involving abuse, neglect, or dependency at which the court removes a child from the child's home or continues the removal of a child from the child's home, or in a proceeding where the court orders detention, the court shall determine whether the person who filed the complaint in the case and removed the child from the child's home has custody of the child or will be given custody and has made reasonable efforts to do any of the following:

(a) Prevent the removal of the child from the child's home;

(b) Eliminate the continued removal of the child from the child's home;

(c) Make it possible for the child to return home.

(2) In a proceeding involving abuse, neglect, or dependency, the examination made by the court to determine whether a child is a competent witness shall comply with all of the following:

(a) Occur in an area other than a courtroom or hearing room;

(b) Be conducted in the presence of only those individuals considered necessary by the court for the conduct of the examination or the well being of the child;

(c) Be recorded in accordance with Juv. R. 37 or Juv. R. 40. The court may allow the prosecutor, guardian ad litem, or attorney for any party to submit questions for use by the court in determining whether the child is a competent witness.

(3) In a proceeding where a child is alleged to be an abused child, the court may order that the testimony of the child be taken by deposition in the presence of a judge or a magistrate. On motion of the prosecuting attorney, guardian ad litem, or a party, or in its own discretion, the court may order that the deposition be videotaped. All or part of the deposition is admissible in evidence where all of the following apply:

(a) It is filed with the clerk;

(b) Counsel for all parties had an opportunity and similar motive at the time of the taking of the deposition to develop the testimony by direct, cross, or redirect examination;

(c) The judge or magistrate determines there is reasonable cause to believe that if the child were to testify in person at the hearing, the child would experience emotional trauma as a result of the child's participation at the hearing.

(Amended, eff 7-1-76; 7-1-94; 7-1-96)

RULE 28. [Reserved]

RULE 29. Adjudicatory hearing

(A) Scheduling the hearing. The date for the adjudicatory hearing shall be set when the complaint is filed or as soon thereafter as is practicable. If the child who is the subject of the complaint is in detention or shelter care, the hearing shall be held not later than ten days after the filing of the complaint. Upon a showing of good cause, the adjudicatory hearing may be continued and detention or shelter care extended.

If the complaint alleges abuse, neglect, or dependency, the hearing shall be held no later than thirty days after the complaint is filed. For good cause shown, the adjudicatory hearing may extend beyond thirty days either for an additional ten days to allow any party to obtain counsel or for a reasonable time beyond thirty days to obtain service on all parties or complete any necessary evaluations. However, the adjudicatory hearing shall be held no later than sixty days after the complaint is filed.

The failure of the court to hold an adjudicatory hearing within any time period set forth in this rule does not affect the ability of the court to issue any order otherwise provided for in statute or rule and does not provide any basis for contesting the jurisdiction of the court or the validity of any order of the court.

(B) Advisement and findings at the commencement of the hearing. At the beginning of the hearing, the court shall do all of the following:

(1) Ascertain whether notice requirements have been complied with and, if not, whether the affected parties waive compliance;

(2) Inform the parties of the substance of the complaint, the purpose of the hearing, and possible consequences of the hearing, including the possibility that the cause may be transferred to the appropriate adult court under Juv. R. 30 where the complaint alleges that a child fifteen years of age or over is delinquent by conduct that would constitute a felony if committed by an adult;

(3) Inform unrepresented parties of their right to counsel and determine if those parties are waiving their right to counsel;

(4) Appoint counsel for any unrepresented party under Juv. R. 4(A) who does not waive the right to counsel;

(5) Inform any unrepresented party who waives the right to counsel of the right: to obtain counsel at any stage of the proceedings, to remain silent, to offer evidence, to cross-examine witnesses, and, upon request, to have a record of all proceedings made, at public expense if indigent.

(C) Entry of admission or denial. The court shall request each party against whom allegations are made in the complaint to admit or deny the allegations. A failure or refusal to admit the allegations shall be deemed a denial.

(D) Initial procedure upon entry of an admission. The court may refuse to accept an admission and shall not accept an admission without addressing the party personally and determining both of the following:

(1) The party is making the admission voluntarily with understanding of the nature of the allegations and the consequences of the admission;

(2) The party understands that by entering an admission the party is waiving the right to challenge the witnesses and evidence against the party, to remain silent, and to introduce evidence at the adjudicatory hearing.

The court may hear testimony, review documents, or make further inquiry, as it considers appropriate, or it may proceed directly to the action required by division (F) of this rule.

(E) Initial procedure upon entry of a denial. If a party denies the allegations, the court shall:

(1) Direct the prosecuting attorney or another attorney-at-law to assist the court by presenting evidence in support of the allegations of a complaint;

(2) Order the separation of witnesses, upon request of any party;

(3) Take all testimony under oath or affirmation in either question-answer or narrative form; and

(4) Determine the issues by proof beyond a reasonable doubt in juvenile traffic offense, delinquency, and unruly proceedings, by clear and convincing evidence in dependency, neglect, and child abuse proceedings, and by a preponderance of the evidence in all other cases.

(F) Procedure upon determination of the issues. Upon the determination of the issues, the court shall do one of the following:

(1) If the allegations of the complaint were not proved, dismiss the complaint;

(2) If the allegations of the complaint are admitted or proved, do one of the following:

(a) Enter an adjudication and proceed forthwith to disposition; or

(b) Enter an adjudication and continue the matter for disposition for not more than six months and may make appropriate temporary orders;

(c) Postpone judgment of adjudication for not more than six months;

(d) Dismiss the complaint if dismissal is in the best interest of the child and the community.

(3) Upon request make written findings of fact and conclusions of law pursuant to Civil Rule 52.

(4) Ascertain whether the child should remain or be placed in shelter care until the dispositional hearing in an abuse, neglect, or dependency proceeding. In making a shelter care determination, the court shall make written finding of facts with respect to reasonable efforts in accordance with the provisions in Juv. R. 27(B)(1) and to relative placement in accordance with Juv. R. 7(F)(3).

(Amended, eff 7-1-76; 7-1-94)

RULE 30. Relinquishment of jurisdiction for purposes of criminal prosecution

(A) Preliminary hearing. In any proceeding where the court considers the transfer of a case for criminal prosecution, the court shall hold a preliminary hearing to determine if there is probable cause to believe that the child committed the act alleged and that the act would be an offense if committed by an adult. The hearing may be upon motion of the court, the prosecuting attorney, or the child.

(B) Mandatory transfer. In any proceeding in which transfer of a case for criminal prosecution is required by statute upon a finding of probable cause, the order of transfer shall be entered upon a finding of probable cause.

(C) Discretionary transfer. In any proceeding in which transfer of a case for criminal prosecution is permitted, but not required, by statute, and in which probable cause is found at the preliminary hearing, the court shall continue the proceeding for full investigation. The investigation shall include a mental examination of the child by a public or private agency or by a person qualified to make the examination. When the investigation is completed, an amenability hearing shall be held to determine whether to transfer jurisdiction. The criteria for transfer shall be as provided by statute.

(D) Notice. Notice in writing of the time, place, and purpose of any hearing held pursuant to this rule shall be given to the state, the child's parents, guardian, or other custodian and the child's counsel at least three days prior to the hearing, unless written notice has been waived on the record.

(E) Retention of jurisdiction. If the court retains jurisdiction, it shall set the proceedings for hearing on the merits.

(F) Waiver of mental examination. The child may waive the mental examination required under division (C) of this rule. Refusal by the child to submit to a mental and physical examination or any part of the examination shall constitute a waiver of the examination.

(G) Order of transfer. The order of transfer shall state the reasons for transfer.

(H) Release of child. With respect to the transferred case, the juvenile court shall set the terms and conditions for release of the child in accordance with Crim. R. 46.

(Amended, eff 7-1-76; 7-1-94; 7-1-97)

RULE 31. [Reserved]

RULE 32. Social history; physical examination; mental examination; investigation involving the allocation of parental rights and responsibilities for the care of children

(A) Social history and physical or mental examination: availability before adjudication. The court may order and utilize a social history or physical or mental examination at any time after the filing of a complaint under any of the following circumstances:

(1) Upon the request of the party concerning whom the history or examination is to be made;

(2) Where transfer of a child for adult prosecution is an issue in the proceeding;

(3) Where a material allegation of a neglect, dependency, or abused child complaint relates to matters that a history or examination may clarify;

(4) Where a party's legal responsibility for the party's acts or the party's competence to participate in the proceedings is an issue;

(5) Where a physical or mental examination is re-

quired to determine the need for emergency medical care under Juv. R. 13; or

(6) Where authorized under Juv. R. 7(I).

(B) Limitations on preparation and use. Until there has been an admission or adjudication that the child who is the subject of the proceedings is a juvenile traffic offender, delinquent, unruly, neglected, dependent, or abused, no social history, physical examination or mental examination shall be ordered except as authorized under subdivision (A) and any social history, physical examination or mental examination ordered pursuant to subdivision (A) shall be utilized only for the limited purposes therein specified. The person preparing a social history or making a physical or mental examination shall not testify about the history or examination or information received in its preparation in any juvenile traffic offender, delinquency, or unruly child adjudicatory hearing, except as may be required in a hearing to determine whether a child should be transferred to an adult court for criminal prosecution.

(C) Availability of social history or investigation report. A reasonable time before the dispositional hearing, or any other hearing at which a social history or physical or mental examination is to be utilized, counsel shall be permitted to inspect any social history or report of a mental or physical examination. The court may, for good cause shown, deny such inspection or limit its scope to specified portions of the history or report. The court may order that the contents of the history or report, in whole or part, not be disclosed to specified persons. If inspection or disclosure is denied or limited, the court shall state its reasons for such denial or limitation to counsel.

(D) Investigation: allocation of parental rights and responsibilities for the care of children; habeas corpus. On the filing of a complaint for the allocation of parental rights and responsibilities for the care of children or for a writ of habeas corpus to determine the allocation of parental rights and responsibilities for the care of a child, or on the filing of a motion for change in the allocation of parental rights and responsibilities for the care of children, the court may cause an investigation to be made as to the character, health, family relations, past conduct, present living conditions, earning ability, and financial worth of the parties to the action. The report of the investigation shall be confidential, but shall be made available to the parties or their counsel upon written request not less than three days before hearing. The court may tax as costs all or any part of the expenses of each investigation.

(Amended, eff 7-1-73; 7-1-76; 7-1-91; 7-1-94)

RULE 33. [Reserved]

RULE 34. Dispositional hearing

(A) Scheduling the hearing. Where a child has been adjudicated as an abused, neglected, or dependent child, the court shall not issue a dispositional order until after it holds a separate dispositional hearing. The dispositional hearing for an adjudicated abused, neglected, or dependent child shall be held at least one day but not more than thirty days after the adjudicatory hearing is held. The dispositional hearing may be held immediately after the adjudicatory hearing if all parties were served prior to the adjudicatory hearing with all documents required for the dispositional hearing and all parties consent to the dispositional hearing being held immediately after the adjudicatory hearing. Upon the request of any party or the guardian ad litem of the child, the court may continue a dispositional hearing for a reasonable time not to exceed the time limit set forth in this division to enable a party to obtain or consult counsel. The dispositional hearing shall not be held more than ninety days after the date on which the complaint in the case was filed. If the dispositional hearing is not held within this ninety day period of time, the court, on its own motion or the motion of any party or the guardian ad litem of the child, shall dismiss the complaint without prejudice.

In all other juvenile proceedings, the dispositional hearing shall be held pursuant to Juv. R. 29(F)(2)(a) through (d) and the ninety day requirement shall not apply. Where the dispositional hearing is to be held immediately following the adjudicatory hearing, the court, upon the request of any party, shall continue the hearing for a reasonable time to enable the party to obtain or consult counsel.

(B) Hearing procedure. The hearing shall be conducted in the following manner:

(1) The judge or magistrate who presided at the adjudicatory hearing shall, if possible, preside;

(2) Except as provided in division (I) of this rule, the court may admit evidence that is material and relevant, including, but not limited to, hearsay, opinion, and documentary evidence;

(3) Medical examiners and each investigator who prepared a social history shall not be cross-examined, except upon consent of all parties, for good cause shown, or as the court in its discretion may direct. Any party may offer evidence supplementing, explaining, or disputing any information contained in the social history or other reports that may be used by the court in determining disposition.

(C) Judgment. After the conclusion of the hearing, the court shall enter an appropriate judgment within seven days. A copy of the judgment shall be given to any party requesting a copy. In all cases where a child is placed on probation, the child shall receive a written statement of the conditions of probation. If the judgment is conditional, the order shall state the conditions. If the child is not returned to the child's home, the court shall determine the school district that shall bear the cost of the child's education and may fix an amount of support to be paid by the responsible parent or from public funds.

(D) Dispositional orders. Where a child is adjudicated an abused, neglected, or dependent child, the court may make any of the following orders of disposition:

(1) Place the child in protective supervision;

(2) Commit the child to the temporary custody of a public or private agency, either parent, a relative residing within or outside the state, or a probation officer for placement in a certified foster home or approved foster care;

(3) Award legal custody of the child to either parent or to any other person who, prior to the dispositional hearing, files a motion requesting legal custody;

(4) Commit the child to the permanent custody of a public or private agency, if the court determines that the child cannot be placed with one of the child's parents within a reasonable time or should not be placed with either parent and determines that the permanent commitment is in the best interest of the child;

(5) Place the child in long-term foster care with a public or private agency if the agency requests the court for placement, if the court finds that long-term foster care is in the best interest of the child, and if the court finds that one of the following exists:

(a) The child because of physical, mental, or psychological problems or needs is unable to function in a family-like setting;

(b) The parents of the child have significant physical, mental or psychological problems and are unable to care for the child, adoption is not in the best interest of the child and the child retains a significant and positive relationship with a parent or relative;

(c) The child is sixteen years of age or older, has been counseled, is unwilling to accept or unable to adapt to a permanent placement and is in an agency program preparing the child for independent living.

(E) Protective supervision. If the court issues an order for protective supervision, the court may place any reasonable restrictions upon the child, the child's parents, guardian, or any other person including, but not limited to, any of the following:

(1) Ordering a party within forty-eight hours to vacate the child's home indefinitely or for a fixed period of time;

(2) Ordering a party, parent, or custodian to prevent any particular person from having contact with the child;

(3) Issuing a restraining order to control the conduct of any party.

(F) Case plan. As part of its dispositional order, the court shall journalize a case plan for the child. The agency required to maintain a case plan shall file the case plan with the court prior to the child's adjudicatory hearing but not later than thirty days after the earlier of the date on which the complaint in the case was filed or the child was first placed in shelter care. The plan shall specify what additional information, if any, is necessary to complete the plan and how the information will be obtained. All parts of the case plan shall be completed by the earlier of thirty days after the adjudicatory hearing or the date of the dispositional hearing for the child. If all parties agree to the content of the case plan and the court approves it, the court shall journalize the plan as part of its dispositional order. If no agreement is reached, the court, based upon the evidence presented at the dispositional hearing and the best interest of the child, shall determine the contents of the case plan and journalize it as part of the dispositional order for the child.

(G) Modification of temporary order. The department of human services or any other public or private agency or any party, other than a parent whose parental rights have been terminated, may at any time file a motion requesting that the court modify or terminate any order of disposition. The court shall hold a hearing upon the motion as if the hearing were the original dispositional hearing and shall give all parties and the guardian ad litem notice of the hearing pursuant to these rules. The court, on its own motion and upon proper notice to all parties and any interested agency, may modify or terminate any order of disposition.

(H) Restraining orders. In any proceeding where a child is made a ward of the court, the court may grant a restraining order controlling the conduct of any party if the court finds that the order is necessary to control any conduct or relationship that may be detrimental or harmful to the child and tend to defeat the execution of a dispositional order.

(I) Bifurcation; rules of evidence. Hearings to determine whether temporary orders regarding custody should be modified to orders for permanent custody shall be considered dispositional hearings and need not be bifurcated. The Rules of Evidence shall apply in hearings on motions for permanent custody.

(J) Advisement of rights after hearing. At the conclusion of the hearing, the court shall advise the child of the child's right to record expungement and, where any part of the proceeding was contested, advise the parties of their right to appeal.

(Amended, eff 7-1-94; 7-1-96)

RULE 35. Proceedings after judgment

(A) Continuing jurisdiction; invoked by motion. The continuing jurisdiction of the court shall be invoked by motion filed in the original proceeding, notice of which shall be served in the manner provided for the service of process.

(B) Revocation of probation. The court shall not revoke probation except after a hearing at which the child shall be present and apprised of the grounds on which revocation is proposed. The parties shall have the right to counsel and the right to appointed counsel where entitled pursuant to Juv. R. 4(A). Probation shall not be revoked except upon a finding that the child has violated a condition of probation of which the child had, pursuant to Juv. R. 34(C), been notified.

(C) Detention. During the pendency of proceedings under this rule, a child may be placed in detention in accordance with the provisions of Rule 7.

(Amended, eff 7-1-94)

RULE 36. Dispositional review

(A) Court review. A court that issues a dispositional order in an abuse, neglect, or dependency case may review the child's placement or custody arrangement, the case plan, and the actions of the public or private agency implementing that plan at any time. A court that issues a dispositional order shall hold a review hearing one year after the earlier of the date on which the complaint in the case was filed or the child was first placed into shelter care. The court shall schedule the review hearing at the time that it holds the dispositional hearing. The court shall hold a similar review hearing no later than every twelve months after the initial review hearing until the child is adopted, returned to the child's parents, or the court otherwise terminates the child's placement or custody arrangement. A hearing pursuant to section 2151.415 of the Revised Code shall take the place of the first review hearing. The court shall schedule each subsequent review hearing at the conclusion of the review hearing immediately preceding the review hearing to be scheduled. Review hearings may be conducted by a judge or magistrate.

(B) Citizens' review board. The court may appoint a citizens' review board to conduct review hearings, subject to the review and approval by the court.

(C) Agency review. Each agency required to prepare a case plan for a child shall complete a semiannual administrative review of the case plan no later than six months after the earlier of the date on which the complaint in the case was filed or the child was first placed in shelter care. After the first administrative review, the agency shall complete semiannual administrative reviews no later than every six months. The agency shall prepare and file a written summary of the semiannual administrative review that shall include an updated case plan. If the agency, parents, guardian, or custodian of the child and guardian ad litem stipulate to the revised case plan, the plan shall be signed by all parties and filed with the written summary of the administrative review no later than seven days after the completion of the administrative review. If the court does not object to the revised case plan, it shall journalize the case plan within fourteen days after it is filed with the court. If the court does not approve of the revised case plan or if the agency, parties, guardian ad litem, and the attorney of the child do not agree to the need for changes to the case plan and to all of the proposed changes, the agency shall file its written summary and request a hearing. The court shall schedule a review hearing to be held no later than thirty days after the filing of the case plan or written summary or both, if required. The court shall give notice of the date, time, and location of the hearing to all interested parties and the guardian ad litem of the child. The court shall take one of the following actions:

(1) Approve or modify the case plan based upon the evidence presented;

(2) Return the child home with or without protective supervision and terminate temporary custody or determine which agency shall have custody;

(3) If the child is in permanent custody determine what actions would facilitate adoption;

(4) Journalize the terms of the updated case plan.

(Effective 7-1-94; amended, eff 7-1-96)

RULE 37. Recording of proceedings

(A) Record of proceedings. The juvenile court shall make a record of adjudicatory and dispositional proceedings in abuse, neglect, dependent, unruly, and delinquent cases; permanent custody cases; and proceedings before magistrates. In all other proceedings governed by these rules, a record shall be made upon request of a party or upon motion of the court. The record shall be taken in shorthand, stenotype, or by any other adequate mechanical, electronic, or video recording device.

(B) Restrictions on use of recording or transcript. No public use shall be made by any person, including a party, of any juvenile court record, including the recording or a transcript of any juvenile court hearing, except in the course of an appeal or as authorized by order of the court.

(Amended, eff 7-1-96)

RULE 38. Voluntary surrender of custody

(A) Temporary custody.

(1) A person with custody of a child may enter into an agreement with any public or private children services agency giving the agency temporary custody for a period of up to thirty days without the approval of the juvenile court. The agency may request the court to grant a thirty day extension of the original agreement. The court may grant the original extension if it determines the extension to be in the best interest of the child. A case plan shall be filed at the same time the request for extension is filed. At the expiration of the original thirty day extension period, the agency may request the court to grant an additional thirty day extension. The court may grant the additional extension if it determines the extension is in the child's best interest. The agency shall file an updated case plan at the same time it files the request for additional extension. At the expiration of the additional thirty day extension period, or at the expiration of the original thirty day extension period if no additional thirty day extension was requested, the agency shall either return the child to the custodian or

file a complaint requesting temporary or permanent custody and a case plan.

(2) Notwithstanding division (A)(1) of this rule, the agreement may be for a period of sixty days if executed solely for the purpose of obtaining the adoption of a child less than six months of age. The agency may request the court to extend the temporary custody agreement for thirty days. A case plan shall be filed at the same time the request for extension is filed. At the expiration of the thirty day extension, the agency shall either return the child to the child's custodian or file a complaint with the court requesting temporary or permanent custody and a case plan.

(B) Permanent custody.

(1) A person with custody of a child may make an agreement with court approval surrendering the child into the permanent custody of a public children service agency or private child placing agency. A public children service agency shall request and a private child placing agency may request the juvenile court of the county in which the child had residence or legal settlement to approve the permanent surrender agreement. The court may approve the agreement if it determines it to be in the best interest of the child. The agency requesting the approval shall file a case plan at the same time it files its request for approval of the permanent surrender agreement.

(2) An agreement for the surrender of permanent custody of a child to a private service agency is not required to be approved by the court if the agreement is executed solely for the purpose of obtaining an adoption of a child who is less than six months of age on the date of the execution of the agreement.

One year after the agreement is entered and every subsequent twelve months after that date, the court shall schedule a review hearing if a final decree of adoption has not been entered for a child who is the subject of an agreement for the surrender of permanent custody.

(Effective 7-1-94)

RULE 39. [Reserved]

RULE 40. Magistrates

(A) Appointment. The court may appoint one or more magistrates. Magistrates first appointed on or after the effective date of this amendment shall be attorneys admitted to practice in Ohio. A magistrate appointed under this rule also may serve as a magistrate under Crim.R.19. The court shall not appoint as a magistrate any person who has contemporaneous responsibility for working with, or supervising the behavior of, children who are subject to dispositional orders of the appointing court or any other juvenile court.

(B) Compensation. The compensation of the magistrate shall be fixed by the court and no part of the compensation shall be taxed as costs.

(C) Reference and powers.

(1) Order of reference.

(a) The court by order may refer any of the following to a magistrate:

(i) pretrial or post-judgment motion or proceeding in any case;

(ii) the trial of any case not to be tried to a jury; and

(iii) upon the unanimous written consent of the parties, the trial of any case to be tried to a jury.

Except as provided in division (C)(1)(a)(iii) of this rule, the effect of a magistrate's order or decision is the same regardless of whether the parties have consented to the order of reference.

(b) An order of reference may be specific to a particular case or proceeding or may refer categories of motions, cases, or proceedings.

(c) The order of reference to a magistrate may do all of the following:

(i) Specify the magistrate's powers;

(ii) Direct the magistrate to report only upon particular issues, perform particular acts, or receive and report evidence only;

(iii) Fix the time and place for beginning and closing the hearings and for the filing of the magistrate's decision or order.

(2) General powers. Subject to the specifications stated in the order of reference, the magistrate shall regulate all proceedings in every hearing as if by the court and do all acts and take all measures necessary or proper for the efficient performance of the magistrate's duties under the order. The magistrate may do all of the following:

(a) Issue subpoenas for the attendance of witnesses and the production of evidence;

(b) Rule upon the admissibility of evidence, unless otherwise directed by the order of reference;

(c) Put witnesses under oath and examine them;

(d) Call the parties to the action and examine them under oath.

(e) In cases involving direct or indirect contempt of court, when necessary to obtain the alleged contemnor's presence for hearing, issue an attachment for the alleged contemnor and set bail to secure the alleged contemnor's appearance. In determining bail, the magistrate shall consider the conditions of release prescribed in Crim.R.46.

(3) Power to enter orders.

(a) Pretrial orders. Unless otherwise specified in the order of reference, the magistrate may enter orders effective without judicial approval in pretrial proceedings under Civ.R.16, in discovery proceedings under Civ.R.26 to 37, Juv.R.24 and 25, and in the following situations:

(i) Appointment of an attorney or guardian ad litem pursuant to Juv.R.4 and 29(B)(4);

(ii) Taking a child into custody pursuant to Juv.R.6;

(iii) Detention hearings pursuant to Juv.R.7;
(iv) Temporary orders pursuant to Juv.R.13;
(v) Extension of temporary orders pursuant to Juv.R.14;
(vi) Summons and warrants pursuant to Juv.R.15;
(vii) Preliminary conferences pursuant to Juv.R.21;
(viii) Continuances pursuant to Juv.R.23;
(ix) Deposition orders pursuant to Juv.R.27(B)(3);
(x) Orders for social histories, physical and mental examinations pursuant to Juv.R.32;
(xi) Other orders as necessary to regulate the proceedings.

(b) Appeal of pretrial orders. Any person may appeal to the court from any order of a magistrate entered under division (C)(3)(a) of this rule by filing a motion to set the order aside, stating the party's objections with particularity. The motion shall be filed no later than ten days after the magistrate's order is entered. The pendency of a motion to set aside does not stay the effectiveness of the magistrate's order unless the magistrate or the court grants a stay.

(c) Contempt in the magistrate's presence. In cases of contempt in the presence of the magistrate, the magistrate may impose an appropriate civil or criminal contempt sanction. Contempt sanctions under division (C)(3)(c) of this rule may be imposed only by a written order that recites the facts and certifies that the magistrate saw or heard the conduct constituting contempt. The contempt order shall be filed and a copy provided by the clerk to the appropriate judge of the court forthwith. The contemnor may by motion obtain immediate review of the magistrate's contempt order by a judge, or the judge or magistrate may set bail pending judicial review.

(d) Other orders. Unless prohibited by the order of reference, magistrates shall continue to be authorized to enter orders when authority to enter orders is specifically conveyed by statute or rule to magistrates or referees.

(e) Form of magistrate's orders. All orders of a magistrate shall be in writing, signed by the magistrate, identified as a magistrate's order in the caption, filed with the clerk, and served on all parties or their attorneys.

(D) Proceedings.
(1) All proceedings before the magistrate shall be in accordance with these rules and any applicable statutes, as if before the court.
(2) Except as otherwise provided by law and notwithstanding the provisions of Juv.R.37, all proceedings before magistrates shall be recorded in accordance with procedures established by the court.

(E) Decisions in referred matters. Unless specifically required by the order of reference, a magistrate is not required to prepare any report other than the magistrate's decision. Except as to matters on which magistrates are permitted by division (C)(3) of this rule to enter orders without judicial approval, all matters referred to magistrates shall be decided as follows:

(1) Magistrate's decision. The magistrate promptly shall conduct all proceedings necessary for decision of referred matters. The magistrate shall then prepare, sign, and file a magistrate's decision of the referred matter with the clerk, who shall serve copies on all parties or their attorneys.

(2) Findings of fact and conclusions of law. If any party makes a request for findings of fact and conclusions of law under Civ.R.52 or if findings and conclusions are otherwise required by law or by the order of reference, the magistrate's decision shall include findings of fact and conclusions of law. If the request under Civ.R.52 is made after the magistrate's decision is filed, the magistrate shall include the findings of fact and conclusions of law in an amended magistrate's decision.

(3) Objections.
(a) Time for filing. Within fourteen days of the filing of a magistrate's decision, a party may file written objections to the decision. If any party timely files objections, any other party also may file objections not later than ten days after the first objections are filed. If a party makes a request for findings of fact and conclusions of law under Civ.R.52, the time for filing objections begins to run when the magistrate files a decision including findings of fact and conclusions of law.

(b) Form of objections. Objections shall be specific and state with particularity the grounds of objection. If the parties stipulate in writing that the magistrate's findings of fact shall be final, they may only object to errors of law in the magistrate's decision. Any objection to a finding of fact shall be supported by a transcript of all the evidence submitted to the magistrate relevant to that fact or an affidavit of the evidence if a transcript is not available. A party shall not assign as error on appeal the court's adoption of any finding of fact or conclusion of law unless the party has objected to that finding or conclusion under this rule.

(4) Court's action on magistrate's decision.
(a) When effective. The magistrate's decision shall be effective when adopted by the court as noted in the journal record. The court may adopt the magistrate's decision if no written objections are filed unless it determines that there is an error of law or other defect on the face of the magistrate's decision.

(b) Consideration of objections. Except as provided herein, upon consideration of any objections, the court may adopt, reject, or modify the magistrate's decision, hear additional evidence, recommit the matter to the magistrate with instructions, or hear the matter itself. In delinquency, unruly, or juvenile traffic offender cases, the court may hear additional evidence or hear the matter itself only with the consent of the child. The court may refuse to consider additional evidence proffered upon objections unless the objecting party demonstrates that with reasonable diligence the party could not have produced that evidence for the magistrate's consideration.

(c) **Permanent and interim orders.** The court may adopt a magistrate's decision and enter judgment without waiting for timely objections by the parties, but the filing of timely written objections shall operate as an automatic stay of execution of that judgment until the court disposes of those objections and vacates, modifies, or adheres to the judgment previously entered. The court may make an interim order on the basis of a magistrate's decision without waiting for or ruling on timely objections by the parties where immediate relief is justified. An interim order shall not be subject to the automatic stay caused by the filing of timely objections. An interim order shall not extend more than twenty-eight days from the date of its entry unless, within that time and for good cause shown, the court extends the interim order for an additional twenty-eight days.

(Amended, eff 7-1-75; 7-1-85; 7-1-92; 7-1-95)

RULE 41. [Reserved]

RULE 42. Consent to marry

(A) Application where parental consent not required. When a minor desires to contract matrimony and has no parent, guardian, or custodian whose consent to the marriage is required by law, the minor shall file an application under oath in the county where the female resides requesting that the judge of the juvenile court give consent and approbation in the probate court for such marriage.

(B) Contents of application. The application required by division (A) of this rule shall contain all of the following:

(1) The name and address of the person for whom consent is sought;

(2) The age of the person for whom consent is sought;

(3) The reason why consent of a parent is not required;

(4) The name and address, if known, of the parent, where the minor alleges that parental consent is unnecessary because the parent has neglected or abandoned the child for at least one year immediately preceding the application.

(C) Application where female pregnant or delivered of child born out of wedlock. Where a female is pregnant or delivered of a child born out of wedlock and the parents of such child seek to marry even though one or both of them is under the minimum age prescribed by law for persons who may contract marriage, such persons shall file an application under oath in the county where the female resides requesting that the judge of the juvenile court give consent in the probate court to such marriage.

(D) Contents of application. The application required by subdivision (C) shall contain:

(1) The name and address of the person or persons for whom consent is sought;

(2) The age of such person;

(3) An indication of whether the female is pregnant or has already been delivered;

(4) An indication of whether or not any applicant under eighteen years of age is already a ward of the court; and

(5) Any other facts which may assist the court in determining whether to consent to such marriage.

If pregnancy is asserted, a certificate from a physician verifying pregnancy shall be attached to the application. If an illegitimate child has been delivered, the birth certificate of such child shall be attached.

The consent to the granting of the application by each parent whose consent to the marriage is required by law shall be indorsed on the application.

(E) Investigation. Upon receipt of an application under subdivision (C), the court shall set a date and time for hearing thereon at its earliest convenience and shall direct that an inquiry be made as to the circumstances surrounding the applicants.

(F) Notice. If neglect or abandonment is alleged in an application under subdivision (A) and the address of the parent is known, the court shall cause notice of the date and time of hearing to be served upon such parent.

(G) Judgment. If the court finds that the allegations stated in the application are true, and that the granting of the application is in the best interest of the applicants, the court shall grant the consent and shall make the applicant referred to in subdivision (C) a ward of the court.

(H) Certified copy. A certified copy of the judgment entry shall be transmitted to the probate court.

(Amended, eff 7-1-80; 7-1-94)

RULE 43. Reference to Ohio Revised Code

A reference in these rules to a section of the Revised Code shall mean the section as amended from time to time including the enactment of additional sections, the numbers of which are subsequent to the section referred to in the rules.

(Effective 7-1-94)

RULE 44. Jurisdiction unaffected

These rules shall not be construed to extend or limit the jurisdiction of the juvenile court.

RULE 45. Rules by juvenile courts; procedure not otherwise specified

(A) Local rules. The juvenile court may adopt rules concerning local practice that are not inconsistent with these rules. Local rules shall be adopted only after the court gives appropriate notice and an opportunity for comment. If the court determines that there is an immediate need for a rule, the court may adopt the rule without prior notice and opportunity for comment but promptly shall afford notice and opportunity for comment. Local rules shall be filed with the Supreme Court.

(B) Procedure not otherwise specified. If no procedure is specifically prescribed by these rules or local rule, the court shall proceed in any lawful manner not inconsistent with these rules or local rule.

(Amended, eff 7-1-94)

RULE 46. Forms

The forms contained in the Appendix of Forms which the supreme court from time to time may approve are illustrative and not mandatory.

RULE 47. Effective date

(A) Effective date of rules. These rules shall take effect on the first day of July, 1972. They govern all proceedings in actions brought after they take effect and also all further proceedings in actions then pending, except to the extent that their application in a particular action pending when the rules take effect would not be feasible or would work injustice, in which event the former procedure applies.

(B) Effective date of amendments. The amendments submitted by the Supreme Court to the General Assembly on January 12, 1973, shall take effect on the first day of July, 1973. They govern all proceedings in actions brought after they take effect and also all further proceedings in actions then pending, except to the extent that their application in a particular action pending when the amendments take effect would not be feasible or would work injustice, in which event the former procedure applies.

(C) Effective date of amendments. The amendments submitted by the Supreme Court to the General Assembly on January 10, 1975, and on April 29, 1975, shall take effect on July 1, 1975. They govern all proceedings in actions brought after they take effect and also all further proceedings in actions then pending, except to the extent that their application in a particular action pending when the amendments take effect would not be feasible or would work injustice, in which event the former procedure applies.

(D) Effective date of amendments. The amendments submitted by the Supreme Court to the General Assembly on January 9, 1976 shall take effect on July 1, 1976. They govern all proceedings in actions brought after they take effect and also all further proceedings in actions then pending, except to the extent that their application in a particular action pending when the amendments take effect would not be feasible or would work injustice, in which event the former procedure applies.

(E) Effective date of amendments. The amendments submitted by the Supreme Court to the General Assembly on January 14, 1980, shall take effect on July 1, 1980. They govern all proceedings in actions brought after they take effect and also all further proceedings in actions then pending, except to the extent that their application in a particular action pending when the amendments take effect would not be feasible or would work injustice, in which event the former procedure applies.

(F) Effective date of amendments. The amendments submitted by the Supreme Court to the General Assembly on December 24, 1984 and January 8, 1985 shall take effect on July 1, 1985. They govern all proceedings in actions brought after they take effect and also all further proceedings in actions then pending, except to the extent that their application in a particular action pending when the amendments take effect would not be feasible or would work injustice, in which event the former procedure applies.

(G) Effective date of amendments. The amendments submitted by the Supreme Court to the General Assembly on January 10, 1991 shall take effect on July 1, 1991. They govern all proceedings in actions brought after they take effect and also all further proceedings in actions then pending, except to the extent that their application in a particular action pending when the amendments take effect would not be feasible or would work injustice, in which event the former procedure applies.

(H) Effective date of amendments. The amendments filed by the Supreme Court with the General Assembly on January 14, 1992 and further filed on April 30, 1992, shall take effect on July 1, 1992. They govern all proceedings in actions brought after they take effect and also all future proceedings in actions then pending, except to the extent that their application in a particular action pending when the amendments take effect would not be feasible or would work injustice, in which event the former procedure applies.

(I) Effective date of amendments. The amendments filed by the Supreme Court with the General Assembly on January 14, 1994 shall take effect on July 1, 1994. They govern all proceedings in actions brought after they take effect and also all future proceedings in actions then pending, except to the extent that their application in a particular action pending when the amendments take effect would not be feasible or would work injustice, in which event the former procedure applies.

(J) Effective date of amendments. The amendments to Rules 1, 4, and 40 filed by the Supreme Court with the General Assembly on January 11, 1995 and further revised and filed on April 25, 1995 shall take effect on July 1, 1995. They govern all proceedings in actions brought after they take effect and also all further proceedings in actions then pending, except to the extent that their application in a particular action pending when the amendments take effect would not be feasible or would work injustice, in which event the former procedure applies.

(K) Effective date of amendments. The amendments to Rules 6, 8, 13, 27, 34, 36, and 37 filed by the Supreme Court with the General Assembly on January 5, 1996 and refiled on April 26, 1996 shall take effect on July 1, 1996. They govern all proceedings in actions brought after they take effect and also all further proceedings in actions then pending, except to the extent that their application in a particular action pending when the amendments take effect would not be feasible or would work injustice, in which event the former procedure applies.

(L) Effective date of amendments. The amendments to Rule 30 filed by the Supreme Court with the General Assembly on January 10, 1997 shall take effect on July 1, 1997. They govern all proceedings in actions brought after they take effect and also all further proceedings in actions then pending, except to the extent that their application in a particular action pending when the amendments take effect would not be feasible or would work injustice, in which event the former procedure applies.

(Amended, eff 7-1-73; 7-1-75; 7-1-76; 7-1-80; 7-1-85; 7-1-91; 7-1-92; 7-1-94; 7-1-95; 7-1-96; 7-1-97)

RULE 48. Title

These rules shall be known as Ohio Rules of Juvenile Procedure and may be cited as "Juvenile Rules" or "Juv. R. ___."

OHIO TRAFFIC RULES

Complete through July 1, 1997

For annotations and cases construing the Ohio Traffic Rules, see the
TITLE 45 VOLUME to PAGE'S OHIO REVISED CODE ANNOTATED
For a more complete discussion of Ohio Traffic Law, see ANDERSON'S OHIO TRAFFIC LAW HANDBOOK

Temporary Provisions

Rule
1. Scope of rules; applicability; authority and construction
   (A) Applicability
   (B) Authority and construction
2. Definitions
3. Complaint and summons; form; use
   (A) Traffic complaint and summons
   (B) Traffic complaint and summons form
   (C) Use of ticket
   (D) Issuance of tickets to enforcement agency
   (E) Duty of law enforcement officer
4. Bail and security
   (A) Posting of bail; depositing of security
   (B) Bail and security procedure
5. Joinder of offense and defendants; consolidation for trial; relief prejudicial joinder
6. Summons, warrants: form, service and execution
   (A) Form
   (B) Service and execution
7. Procedure upon failure to appear
   (A) Issuance of summons, warrant
   (B) Issuance of notice to nonresident
   (C) Effect of waiting periods and bail forfeiture
8. Arraignment
   (A) Arraignment time
   (B) Arraignment procedure
   (C) Presence of defendant
   (D) Explanation of rights
   (E) Joint arraignment
9. Jury demand
   (A) Jury demand
   (B) Jury demands in mayor's court
   (C) Transfer
10. Pleas; rights upon plea
    (A) Pleas
    (B) Effect of guilty or no contest plea
    (C) Misdemeanor cases involving serious offenses
    (D) Misdemeanor cases involving petty offenses
    (E) Refusal of court to accept plea
    (F) Immediate trial
11. Pleadings and motions before plea and trial; defenses and objections
    (A) Pleadings and motions
    (B) Motions before plea and trial
    (C) Motion date
    (D) Disclosure of evidence by prosecuting attorney
    (E) Ruling on motion
    (F) Effect of failure to raise defenses or objections
    (G) Effect of plea of no contest
    (H) Effect of determination
    (I) State's right of appeal
12. Receipt of guilty plea
13. Traffic violations bureau

Rule
   (A) Establishment and operation of traffic violations bureau
   (B) Authority of violations bureau
   (C) Schedule of fines
   (D) Defendant's appearance, plea and waiver of trial
   (E) Records
   (F) Hours of operation; personnel
14. Magistrates
15. Violation of rules
    (A) Failure to apply rules
    (B) Improper disposition of ticket
16. Judicial conduct
17. Traffic case scheduling
    (A) Separate trial
    (B) Arraignment and trial by traffic division
    (C) Arraignment and trial by traffic session
    (D) Single-judge courts
18. Continuances
19. Rule of court
20. Procedure not otherwise specified
21. Forms
22. Review commission
    (A) Duties of review commission
    (B) Appointment, term and membership
    (C) Meetings
23. Title
24. Effective date
    (A) Effective date of rules
    (B) Use of tickets conforming to prior rules
25. Effective date of amendments

APPENDIX OF FORMS
Multi-Count Uniform Traffic Ticket

Court Record
Defendant's Copy
Abstract of Court Record
Enforcement Agency Record

TEMPORARY PROVISION

Notwithstanding Traffic Rule 3, the Akron Municipal Court, Berea Municipal Court, Licking County Municipal Court, Newton Falls Municipal Court, Parma Municipal Court, Brown County Court, Broadview Heights Mayor's Court, Moraine Mayor's Court, North Royalton Mayor's Court, and the Ohio Highway Patrol are authorized to use the modified version of the Uniform Traffic Ticket approved by the Supreme Court Traffic Rules Review Commission in all moving traffic cases. The modified version of the Uniform Traffic Ticket shall be used by these courts and the Highway Patrol beginning on a date no earlier than April 1, 1996. The use of the modified Uniform Traffic Ticket shall continue for a period of six months from the date on which it is first used in the individual courts or by the Highway Patrol or until such time as the existing supplies of modified Uniform Traffic Tickets are exhausted by the issuing law enforcement agencies. As used in the Ohio Traffic Rules and defined by Traffic Rule 2, "traffic ticket" shall include the modified version of the Uniform Traffic Ticket used pursuant to this provision.

(Effective 4-1-96; amended, eff 10-15-96)

TEMPORARY PROVISION

Notwithstanding Traffic Rule 3, the Bowling Green Municipal Court is authorized to develop and use a modified version of the Uniform Traffic Ticket in all moving traffic cases. The modified version of the Uniform Traffic Ticket shall be used by the Bowling Green Municipal Court beginning on a date not later than three months from October 21, 1991 and its use shall terminate one year from the date on which it is first used. As used in the Ohio Traffic Rules and defined by Traffic Rule 2, "traffic ticket" shall include the modified version of the Uniform Traffic Ticket developed and used by the Bowling Green Municipal court pursuant to this provision.

(Effective 10-21-91)

RULE 1. Scope of rules; applicability; authority and construction

(A) Applicability. These rules prescribe the procedure to be followed in all courts of this state in traffic cases and supersede the "Ohio Rules of Practice and Procedure in Traffic Cases For All Courts Inferior To Common Pleas" effective January 1, 1969, and as amended on January 4, 1971, and December 7, 1972.

(B) Authority and construction. These rules are promulgated pursuant to authority granted the Supreme Court by R.C. § 2935.17 and § 2937.46. They shall be construed and applied to secure the fair, impartial, speedy and sure administration of justice, simplicity and uniformity in procedure, and the elimination of unjustifiable expense and delay.

RULE 2. Definitions

As used in these rules:

"Traffic case" means all proceedings involving violations of laws, ordinances and regulations governing the operation and use of vehicles, conduct of pedestrians in relation thereto, and governing weight, dimension, loads or equipment or vehicles drawn or moved on highways and bridges.

"Traffic ticket" means the traffic complaint and summons described in Rule 3 and which appears in the Appendix of Forms.

"Highway" includes "street" and "alley."

"Petty offense" means an offense for which the penalty prescribed by law includes confinement for six months or less.

"Serious offense" means an offense for which the penalty prescribed by law includes confinement for more than six months.

"Court" means municipal court, county court, juvenile court, police court and mayor's court.

"Judge" means judge of the municipal court, county court, juvenile court, mayor's court and police court.

"Prosecuting attorney" means the attorney general of this state, the prosecuting attorney of a county, the law director, city solicitor, or other officer who prosecutes a criminal case on behalf of the state or a city, village, township, or other political subdivision, and the assistant or assistants of any of them.

"State" means this state, a county, city, village, township, other political subdivision or any other entity of this state which may prosecute a criminal action.

"Clerk of court" means the duly elected or appointed clerk of any court of record or police court, or the deputy of any of them, and the mayor of a municipal corporation having a mayor's court.

"Review Commission" means the committee appointed by the Supreme Court to study and consider the application and administration of these rules.

RULE 3. Complaint and summons; form; use

(A) Traffic complaint and summons. In traffic cases, the complaint and summons shall be the "Ohio Uniform Traffic Ticket" as set out in the Appendix of Forms.

(B) Traffic complaint and summons form. The Ohio Uniform Traffic Ticket shall consist of four sheets, padded together and bound at the top or bottom edge. Each sheet shall be four and one-fourth inches in width and nine and one-half inches in length from a perforation below the binding to the bottom edge. The first sheet shall be white and the second sheet shall be canary yellow. Where an additional copy is needed by an agency, it may be added. The first and second sheets shall be at least fifteen pound paper.

The first sheet shall be the court record.

The second sheet shall be the abstract of court record for the Bureau of Motor Vehicles as required by Section 4507.021 [4507.02.1] of the Revised Code. The second sheet may be omitted from the Ticket if the court reports violations to the Bureau by electronic or other means acceptable to the Bureau.

The third sheet shall be the defendant's copy.

The fourth sheet shall be the enforcement agency record.

A wrap-around may be added to the first sheet. The issuing authority may use the front and back of the wrap-around for any data or information it may require.

Each ticket sheet shall be perforated tab bound at the edge or end with carbon paper interleaved so that all carbon paper is securely bound to the tab and removable with it, or shall be on treated paper so that marking from the top sheet is transferred legibly to successive sheets in the group.

(C) **Use of ticket.** The Ohio Uniform Traffic Ticket shall be used in all moving traffic cases, but its use for parking and equipment violations is optional in each local jurisdiction. Any ticket properly issued to a law enforcement officer shall be accepted for filing and disposition in any court having jurisdiction over the offense alleged. An officer may include more than one alleged violation on a single ticket provided the alleged violations are numbered sequentially on the face of the ticket. An officer who completes a ticket at the scene of an alleged offense shall not be required to rewrite or type a new complaint as a condition of filing the ticket, unless the original complaint is illegible or does not state an offense. If a new complaint is executed, a copy shall be served upon defendant as soon as possible.

(D) **Issuance of tickets to enforcement agency.** The judge in a single-judge court, and the administrative judge in multi-judge courts, shall designate the issuing authority for tickets and prescribe the conditions of issuance and accountability. The issuing authority may be the clerk of the court, the violations clerk, or the enforcement agency of the municipality.

When a single enforcement agency, except the State Highway Patrol, regularly has cases in more than one court, the ticket used by the agency shall be issued through the court for adults in the most populous area in the jurisdiction of the agency. Tickets used by the State Highway Patrol shall be issued by the Superintendent of the State Highway Patrol.

(E) **Duty of law enforcement officer.** A law enforcement officer who issues a ticket shall complete and sign the ticket, serve a copy of the completed ticket upon defendant, and, without unnecessary delay, file the court copy with the court.

The officer shall notify defendant that if defendant does not appear at the time and place stated in the citation or comply with division (C) of section 2935.26 of the Revised Code, defendant's license will be cancelled, defendant will not be eligible for the reissuance of the license or the issuance of a new license for one year after cancellation, and defendant will be subject to any applicable criminal penalties.

(Amended, eff 8-4-80; 2-26-90; 11-28-90; 6-1-92)

RULE 4. Bail and security

(A) **Posting of bail; depositing of security.** The posting of bail or the depositing of security is for the purpose of securing appearance or compliance with R.C. § 2935.26(C) only. The forfeiture of the bail or security is not a substitute for appearance in court, compliance with R.C. § 2935.26(C), and payment of penalty imposed on pleas of finding of guilty.

(B) **Bail and security procedure.** Criminal Rule 46 governs bail in traffic cases. In addition, the provisions of R.C. § 2937.221 and R.C. § 2935.27 apply in traffic cases.

(Amended, eff 8-4-80)

RULE 5. Joinder of offense and defendants; consolidation for trial; relief prejudicial joinder

Criminal Rules 8, 13 and 14 govern joinder of offenses and defendants, consolidation of cases for trial and relief from prejudicial joinder in traffic cases.

RULE 6. Summons, warrants: form, service and execution

(A) **Form.** The form of summons and warrants, other than the ticket, shall be as prescribed in Criminal Rule 4.

(B) **Service and execution.** Summons, other than the ticket, and warrants shall be served and executed as prescribed by Criminal Rule 4.

RULE 7. Procedure upon failure to appear

(A) **Issuance of summons, warrant.** When a defendant fails to appear pursuant to a ticket issued to him, the court shall issue a supplemental summons or warrant.

If a supplemental summons is not served or a warrant is not executed within twenty-eight days of receipt by the serving officer, the court may place the case in a file of cases disposed of subject to being reopened. Where bond is forfeited such disposition shall be reported to the Registrar of Motor Vehicles. For all other purposes, including disposition reports, the cases shall be reported as disposed of, subject to being reopened, if defendant subsequently appears or is apprehended.

(B) **Issuance of notice to nonresident.** When a nonresident of this state fails to appear pursuant to a supplemental summons or a warrant issued under division (A), the court may send by ordinary mail to defendant's address as it appears on the ticket, or the summons or warrant return, a notice ordering defendant to appear at a specified time and place.

If defendant fails to appear or answer within twenty-eight days after the date of mailing of the notice, the court shall place the case in the file of cases disposed of subject to being reopened.

The mailing of notice in parking cases is discretionary with the court.

(C) **Effect of waiting periods and bail forfeiture.** The waiting period prescribed in division (A) does not affect forfeiture of bail.

If there is a breach of a condition of bail, the court shall declare a forfeiture of bail. Forfeiture proceedings shall be promptly enforced as provided by law.

If defendant fails to appear at the time and place specified on the citation and fails to comply with division (C) of Section 2935.26 of the Revised Code, or fails to comply with or satisfy any judgment of the court within the time allowed, the court shall declare the forfeiture of defendant's license. Thirty days after the declaration, the court shall forward a copy of the declaration to the Registrar of Motor Vehicles for cancellation in accordance with division (D) of Section 2935.27 of the Revised Code. If the defendant deposits a sum of money or other security with the court, the deposit immediately shall be forfeited to the court if he fails to appear or comply with division (C) of Section 2935.26 of the Revised Code.

(Amended, eff 8-4-80; 11-28-90)

RULE 8. Arraignment

(A) Arraignment time. Where practicable, every defendant shall be arraigned before contested matters are taken up. Trial may be conducted immediately following arraignment.

(B) Arraignment procedure. Arraignment shall be conducted in open court and shall consist of reading the complaint to the defendant, or stating to him the substance of the charge, and calling on him to plead thereto. The defendant shall be given a copy of the complaint, or shall acknowledge receipt thereof, before being called upon to plead and may in open court waive the reading of the complaint.

(C) Presence of defendant. The defendant must be present at the arraignment, but the court may allow the defendant to enter a not guilty plea at the clerk's office in person, by his attorney in person, or by his attorney by mail, within four days after receipt of the ticket by the defendant.

(D) Explanation of rights. Before calling upon a defendant to plead at arraignment the judge shall cause him to be informed and shall determine that defendant knows and understands:

(1) That he has a right to counsel and the right to a reasonable continuance in the proceedings to secure counsel, and, pursuant to Criminal Rule 44, the right to have counsel assigned without cost to himself if he is unable to employ counsel;

(2) That he has a right to bail as provided in Rule 4;

(3) That he need make no statement at any point in the proceeding; but any statement made may be used against him;

(4) That he has, where such right exists, a right to jury trial and that he must, in petty offense cases, make a demand for a jury pursuant to Criminal Rule 23;

(5) That if he is convicted a record of the conviction will be sent to the Bureau of Motor Vehicles and become a part of his driving record.

(E) Joint arraignment. If there are multiple defendants to be arraigned, the judge may advise, or cause them to be advised, of their rights by general announcement.

RULE 9. Jury demand

(A) Jury demand. Jury demands shall be made pursuant to Criminal Rule 23.

(B) Jury demands in mayor's court. Where, in a mayor's court, a defendant is entitled to a jury trial and a jury demand is made pursuant to Criminal Rule 23, the mayor shall transfer the case pursuant to subdivision (C).

If a jury demand is not made pursuant to Criminal Rule 23, and the defendant waives his right to a jury trial in writing, a mayor may try the case if (1) his compensation as a judge is not directly dependent upon criminal case convictions, or (2) he is not the chief executive and administrative officer of the municipality and as such responsible for the financial condition of the municipality. Guilty and no contest pleas may be taken by any mayor, including mayors whose compensation as a judge is directly dependent upon criminal case convictions and mayors who as chief executive and administrative officer of the municipality are responsible for the financial condition of the municipality.

(C) Transfer. Where transfer is required, the mayor's court shall make a written order directing the defendant to appear at the transferee court, continuing the same bail, if any, and making appearance before the transferee court as a condition of bail, if any. Upon transfer, the mayor's court shall transmit to the clerk of the transferee court the ticket and all other papers in the case, and any bail taken in the case.

Upon receipt of such papers the clerk of the transferee court shall set the case for trial and shall notify the defendant by ordinary mail of his trial date.

RULE 10. Pleas; rights upon plea

(A) Pleas. A defendant may plead not guilty, guilty or, with the consent of the court, no contest. All pleas may be made orally. If a defendant refuses to plead, the court shall enter a plea of not guilty on behalf of the defendant.

(B) Effect of guilty or no contest plea. With reference to the offense or offenses to which the plea is entered:

(1) The plea of guilty is a complete admission of the defendant's guilt.

(2) The plea of no contest is not an admission of defendant's guilt, but is an admission of the truth of the facts alleged in the complaint and such plea or admission shall not be used against the defendant in any subsequent civil or criminal proceeding.

(3) When a plea of guilty or no contest is accepted pursuant to this rule, the court shall proceed with sentencing under Criminal Rule 32.

(C) Misdemeanor cases involving serious offenses. In misdemeanor cases involving serious offenses, the court may refuse to accept a plea of guilty or no contest and shall not accept such plea without first addressing the defendant personally and informing him of the effect of the pleas of guilty, no contest, and not guilty and determining that he is making the plea voluntarily. Where the defendant is unrepresented by counsel, the court shall not accept a plea of guilty or no contest unless the defendant, after being readvised that he has a right to be represented by retained counsel, or pursuant to Criminal Rule 44 by appointed counsel, waives this right.

(D) Misdemeanor cases involving petty offenses. In misdemeanor cases involving petty offenses, except those processed in a traffic violations bureau, the court may refuse to accept a plea of guilty or no contest and shall not accept such pleas without first informing the defendant of the effect of the plea of guilty, no contest, and not guilty.

The counsel provisions of Criminal Rule 44(B), (C) and (D) apply to this subdivision.

(E) Refusal of court to accept plea. If the court refuses to accept a plea of guilty or no contest, the court shall enter a plea of not guilty on behalf of the defendant. In such cases neither plea shall be admissible in evidence not be the subject of comment by the prosecuting attorney or court.

(F) Immediate trial. Upon written consent of defendant and the prosecuting attorney, trial may be conducted immediately after the acceptance of a plea at arraignment. If the defendant seeks a continuance, or demands a jury trial where such right exists, the court shall cause the case to be set for trial.

RULE 11. Pleadings and motions before plea and trial: defenses and objections

(A) Pleadings and motions. Pleadings in traffic cases shall be the complaint, the pleas of not guilty, guilty, and no contest. Defenses and objections shall be raised before plea and trial by motion to dismiss or to grant appropriate relief.

(B) Motions before plea and trial. Any defense, objection, or request which is capable of determination without the trial of the general issue may be raised before plea or trial by motion.

(1) The following defenses and objections must be raised before plea:

(a) Defenses and objections based in defects in the institution of the prosecution;

(b) Defenses and objections based on defects in the complaint other than failure to show jurisdiction in the court or to charge an offense, which objections shall be notices by the court at any time during the pendency of the proceeding.

(2) The following motions and requests must be made before trial:

(a) Motions to suppress evidence, including but not limited to identification testimony, on the ground that it was illegally obtained;

(b) Requests and motions for discovery under Criminal Rule 16;

(c) Motions for severance of charges or of defendants under Criminal Rule 14.

(C) Motion date. Pre-plea motions shall be made before or at arraignment.

All pretrial motions, except as provided in Criminal Rule 16(F), shall be made within thirty-five days after arraignment or seven days before trial, whichever is earlier. The court, in the interest of justice, may extend the time for making pre-plea or pretrial motions.

(D) Disclosure of evidence by prosecuting attorney. At the arraignment, or as soon thereafter as is practicable, the defendant may, in order to raise objections prior to trial under subsection (B)(2), request notice of the prosecuting attorney's intention to use evidence in chief at trial, which evidence the defendant is entitled to discover under Criminal Rule 16.

(E) Ruling on motion. A motion made before trial, other than a motion for change of venue, shall be timely determined before trial. Where factual issues are involved in determining a motion, the court shall state its essential findings on the record.

(F) Effect of failure to raise defenses or objections. Failure by the defendant to raise defenses or objections or to make motions and requests which must be made prior to plea, trial, or at the time set by the court pursuant to subdivision (C), or prior to any extension thereof made by the court, shall constitute waiver thereof, but the court for good cause shown may grant relief from the waiver.

(G) Effect of plea of no contest. The plea of no contest does not preclude a defendant from asserting upon appeal that the trial court prejudicially erred in ruling on a pretrial motion, including a pretrial motion to suppress evidence.

(H) Effect of determination. If the court grants a motion to dismiss based in a defect in the institution of the prosecution or in the complaint, the court shall dismiss the case unless the prosecuting attorney can, pursuant to Criminal Rule 7(D), amend the complaint.

(I) State's right of appeal. The state, pursuant to Criminal Rule 12(J), may take an appeal as of right in cases where the defendant is charged with an offense listed in Rule 13(B)(1) and (3).

RULE 12. Receipt of guilty plea

The pleas of guilty and no contest shall be received only by personal appearance of the defendant in open court, except that, the plea of guilty may be received in accordance with Rule 13 at a regularly established traffic violations bureau. Upon the showing of exceptional circumstances by written motion, a court may receive a guilty or no contest plea in such manner as it deems just.

The receipt of a plea contrary to the provisions of these rules is forbidden.

RULE 13. Traffic violations bureau

(A) Establishment and operation of traffic violations bureau. Each court, other than the juvenile division of the court of common pleas, shall establish a traffic violations bureau. The court shall appoint its clerk as violations clerk. If there is no clerk, the court shall appoint any appropriate person of the municipality or county in which the court sits. The violations bureau and violations clerk shall be under the direction and control of the court. Fines and costs shall be paid to, receipted by, and accounted for by the violations clerk.

The violations bureau shall accept appearance, waiver of trial, plea of guilty, and payment of fine and costs for offenses within its authority.

(B) Authority of violations bureau. All traffic offenses except those listed in division (B)(1) to (9) of this rule may be disposed of by a traffic violations bureau. The following traffic offenses shall not be processed by a traffic violations bureau:

(1) Indictable offenses;

(2) Operating a motor vehicle while under the influence of alcohol or any drug of abuse;

(3) Leaving the scene of an accident;

(4) Driving while under suspension or revocation of a driver's or commercial driver's license;

(5) Driving without being licensed to drive, except where the driver's or commercial driver's license had been expired for six months or less;

(6) A third moving traffic offense within a twelve-month period;

(7) Failure to stop and remain standing upon meeting or overtaking a school bus stopped on the highway for the purpose of receiving or discharging a school child;

(8) Willfully eluding or fleeing a police officer;

(9) Drag racing.

(C) Schedule of fines. The court shall establish and publish a schedule of fines and costs for all offenses. The schedule shall be distributed to all law enforcement agencies operating within the jurisdiction of the court and shall be prominently displayed at the place in the violations bureau where fines are paid.

(D) Defendant's appearance, plea and waiver of trial. Within seven days after the date of issuance of the ticket, a defendant charged with an offense that can be processed by a traffic violations bureau may do either of the following:

(1) Appear in person at the traffic violations bureau, sign a plea of guilty and waiver of trial provision of the ticket, and pay the total amount of the fine and costs;

(2) Sign the guilty plea and waiver of trial provision of the ticket and mail the ticket and a check, money order, or other approved form of payment for the total amount of the fine and costs to the traffic violations bureau.

Remittance by mail of the fine and costs to the traffic violations bureau constitutes a guilty plea and waiver of trial whether or not the guilty plea and waiver of trial provision of the ticket are signed by the defendant.

(E) Records. All cases processed in the violations bureau shall be numbered and recorded for identification and statistical purposes. In any statistical reports required by law, the number of cases disposed of by the violations bureau shall be listed separately from those disposed of in open court.

(F) Hours of operation; personnel. The court shall appoint a law enforcement officer as a deputy violations bureau clerk to act as violations clerk when the violations clerk is not on duty.

(Amended, eff 8-4-80; 2-26-90; 11-1-94; 7-1-97)

RULE 14. Magistrates

(A) A court may appoint one or more magistrates for the purpose of receiving pleas, statements in explanation and in mitigation of sentence, and recommending penalty to be imposed, subject to exception taken by defendant and subject to confirmation by the court. Except as provided in division (D) of this rule, a defendant shall not be required to appear before a magistrate in lieu of appearance before a judge in open court, but may elect to appear before a magistrate.

(B) A magistrate shall be an attorney admitted to practice in Ohio. A magistrate shall be provided with court room accommodations resembling as nearly as possible traffic court rooms.

(C) A court may provide for the reference of contested cases to a magistrate for adjudication and written decision. Objections may be filed pursuant to division (E)(3) of Rule 53 of the Rules of Civil Procedure and, if filed, shall be considered by the court pursuant to division (E)(4)(b) of that rule. Except as provided in division (D) of this rule, contested cases shall not be referred to a magistrate without the written consent of the defendant.

(D) An alleged juvenile traffic offender may be required to appear before a magistrate. The written consent of the alleged juvenile traffic offender or his or her parent, guardian, or custodian shall not be required.

(Amended, eff 9-1-96)

RULE 15. Violation of rules

(A) Failure to apply rules. Any willful failure to apply these rules, including the failure to amend or rescind inconsistent local court rules or the continued participation in practices expressly forbidden in these rules, by a judge, clerk or other personnel may be considered a contempt of the Supreme Court and may be punished as such. Proceedings in contempt under this rule can be instituted only with leave of the Supreme Court.

(B) Improper disposition of ticket. Any person who

disposes of a ticket, or who solicits or knowingly aids in the disposition of a ticket, in any manner other than that authorized by these rules may be proceeded against for criminal contempt in the manner provided by law.

(Amended, eff 8-4-80)

RULE 16. Judicial conduct

The Code of Judicial Conduct as adopted by the Supreme Court applies to all judges except mayors.

Canons 1, 2, 3A, 3B, 3C, 3D and 4 of the Code of Judicial Conduct apply to mayors. It shall be the obligation of each mayor to conduct his court and his professional and personal relationships in accordance with the same standards as are required of judges of courts of record.

RULE 17. Traffic case scheduling

(A) Separate trial. Traffic cases shall be tried separately from other cases except upon good cause shown.

(B) Arraignment and trial by traffic division. Where a court sits in divisions and one division is designated as traffic court, all traffic defendants shall, where practicable, be arraigned and tried in such division.

(C) Arraignment and trial by traffic session. Where a court not sitting in separate divisions designates a particular session as a traffic session, traffic defendants shall, where practicable, be arraigned and tried at such session.

(D) Single-judge courts. In single-judge courts, traffic cases shall, where practicable, be called before nontraffic cases. Uncontested traffic cases shall be disposed of first and contested cases scheduled for later hearing.

RULE 18. Continuances

Continuances shall be granted only upon a written motion which states the grounds for the requested continuance.

When a court grants a continuance, it shall set a definite date for the hearing or trial.

RULE 19. Rule of court

The expression "rule of court" as used in these rules means a rule promulgated by the Supreme Court or a rule concerning local practice adopted by another court and filed with the Supreme Court. Local rules shall be supplementary to and consistent with these rules. Each court shall publish its local rules, distribute them within its jurisdiction, and keep copies for inspection.

RULE 20. Procedure not otherwise specified

If no procedure is specifically prescribed by these rules, the Rules of Criminal Procedure and the applicable law apply.

RULE 21. Forms

The forms contained in the Appendix of Forms are mandatory, except that additional copies of any portions of the ticket may be made. The reverse of the enforcement agency record shall be made in the form prescribed by the issuing authority.

RULE 22. Review commission

(A) Duties of review commission. All comments and suggestions concerning the application, administration, and amendment of these rules, including the Appendix of Forms, shall be submitted to the Review Commission. The Review Commission shall consider all comments and suggestions and submit its recommendations to the Supreme Court.

(B) Appointment, term and membership. The Review Commission shall be appointed by the Supreme Court and shall be composed of thirteen members who shall serve without compensation, but who may be reimbursed for expenses incurred in the performance of their duties. All appointments to the Review Commission shall be for three-year terms, except that the Superintendent of the State Highway Patrol, the Chairman of the Traffic Law Committee of the Ohio State Bar Association, and the Director of the Department of Public Safety shall serve on the Review Commission for as long as the person holds the position of Superintendent of the State Highway Patrol, Chairman of the Traffic Law Committee of the Ohio State Bar Association, or Director of the Department of Public Safety. Their successors shall become members of the Review Commission on the day they assume the position of Superintendent of the State Highway Patrol, Chairman of the Traffic Law Committee of the Ohio State Bar Association, or Director of Public Safety. The Director of the Department of Public Safety may designate an individual to represent the Department on the Commission, and the designation shall be in effect for as long as the Director holds the position of Director of the Department of Public Safety.

The membership of the Commission shall include: a court of common pleas judge, a municipal court judge, a county court judge, a municipal court clerk, the Superintendent of the State Highway Patrol, the Chairman of the Traffic Law Committee of the Ohio State Bar Association, and the Director of the Department of Public Safety or his or her designee. The Chairman of the Commission shall be designated by the Supreme Court and shall serve for a period of three years.

(C) Meetings. The Review Commission shall meet upon the call of the chairman. Meetings may be held anywhere in Ohio.

(Amended, eff 7-27-88; 12-5-89; 9-19-94)

RULE 23. Title

These rules shall be known as the Ohio Traffic Rules and may be cited as "Traffic Rules" or Traf. R. . . ."

RULE 24. Effective date

(A) Effective date of rules. These rules take effect on January 1, 1975. They govern all proceedings in actions brought after they take effect, and also all further proceedings in actions then pending, except to the extent that their application in a particular action pending when the rules take effect would not be feasible or would work injustice, in which event the former procedure applies.

(B) Use of tickets conforming to prior rules. Traffic tickets conforming to the requirements of the "Ohio Rules of Practice and Procedure in Traffic Cases For All Courts Inferior to Common Pleas" may be used after the effective date of these rules.

After the effective date of these rules, issuing authorities shall order only tickets conforming to these rules.

RULE 25. Effective date of amendments

(A) The amendments to these rules and the Uniform Traffic Ticket adopted by the Supreme Court of Ohio on June 17, 1980, shall take effect on August 4, 1980.

(B) The amendments to the Uniform Traffic Ticket shall take effect on September 15, 1985. The amendment to Traffic Rule 22 shall take effect on July 27, 1988.

(C) The amendment to Traffic Rule 22, adopted by the Supreme Court on December 5, 1989, shall take effect on December 5, 1989.

(D) The amendments to Traffic Rules 3, 13, and 25, and the Uniform Traffic Ticket, adopted by the Supreme Court of Ohio on February 13, 1990, shall take effect on February 26, 1990.

(E) The amendments to Traffic Rules 3 and 7, adopted by the Supreme Court of Ohio on November 20, 1990, shall take effect on November 28, 1990.

(F) The amendments to Traffic Rule 3 and to the "Reverse of Defendant's Copy" of the Uniform Traffic Ticket, adopted by the Supreme Court of Ohio on March 16, 1992, shall take effect on June 1, 1992.

(G) The amendments to Traffic Rule 22, adopted by the Supreme Court of Ohio on August 17, 1994, shall take effect on September 19, 1994. The amendment to Traffic Rule 13 and to the Uniform Traffic Ticket, adopted by the Supreme Court of Ohio on August 17, 1994, shall take effect on November 1, 1994.

(H) The amendments to Traffic Rule 14, adopted by the Supreme Court of Ohio on July 10, 1996, shall take effect on September 1, 1996.

(I)(1) The amendments to Traffic Rule 13, adopted by the Supreme Court of Ohio on March 31, 1997, shall take effect on July 1, 1997.

(2) The amendments to the Uniform Traffic Ticket, adopted by the Supreme Court of Ohio on March 31, 1997, shall take effect on July 1, 1997. Through June 30, 1998, jurisdictions may use tickets printed in the format that was authorized prior to July 1, 1997. All tickets ordered for use on or after July 1, 1997 and all tickets used on or after July 1, 1998 shall conform to the format of the July 1, 1997 Uniform Traffic Ticket.

APPENDIX OF FORMS

(Amended, eff 8-4-80; 9-15-85; 2-26-90; 6-1-92; 11-1-94; 7-1-97)

MULTI-COUNT UNIFORM TRAFFIC TICKET

COMMISSION COMMENTARY (July 1, 1997 Amendments)

The Supreme Court Traffic Rules Review Commission has developed the following Multi-Count Uniform Traffic Ticket. This ticket will significantly change the way in which traffic offenses are processed in the State of Ohio.

The Commission's comments are intended to provide an overview of the major changes, both in information and layout, to assist in understanding the new form. The Commission has worked with the input of law enforcement, judges, the Ohio Bureau of Motor Vehicles, and court personnel to solve most of the issues raised in the devising of this type of ticket. Separate comments for each side of the Multi-Count Uniform Traffic Ticket, which will be referred to as UTT.

Training, Implementation, and General Comment

Although all jurisdictions are required to use the basic UTT, some courts might not use the Face of Court Record or paper Abstract, while other might use the Face of Court Record but not the paper Abstract.

Training on the new UTT will be of great importance. Although there are a number of changes, after some relatively basic training the forms can be implemented without a significant shock in changing from the pre July 1, 1997 version of the UTT.

In the Commission's work, many issues have been raised regarding inclusion or exclusion of language, information, and what would go best in what locations. Many of the issues which may be raised as training proceeds will be primarily issues that can be resolved in training and actual use of the ticket.

Face of Court Record

The new Face of Court Record provides for the ability to write up to six separate traffic citations on one traffic ticket. The Face of Court Record is identical to the face of Defendant's copy and the Enforcement Agency Record front copy.

The Driver's Identification Information is substantially similar to the previous UTT, although certain information items, such as eye glasses and driving restrictions were deleted. Boxes are printed for officer compliance with S.B. 20, to indicate whether Financial Responsibility Proof is shown at time of the traffic stop, to provide a record for the Court System on S.B. 20 compliance.

The Citation Section consists of six separate boxes, four of which identify specific types of offenses. The two remaining boxes would be for other offenses. The Statutory Code Box provides for a check-off as to whether Ordinance, State Code, or Turnpike Rule is being cited. The Speed Section includes identification for all of the various speed measurement devices currently in use in the State of Ohio. The OMVI Section would be for the writing of one of the two potential OMVI charges, with a second OMVI charge being written in one of the other offense sections. The Driver's License Section would deal with all license-related charges, whether DUS, NOL, or restriction type offenses. The Safety Belt Section would address all belt or restraint offenses.

The Weather and Pavement information is similar to current traffic ticket forms. The UTT would not be used for the citing of non-traffic criminal charges in a traffic stop, which would be written under a separate criminal citation form. The information above the Defendant's Summons would be completed to indicate whether another complaint exists, as well as the total number of offenses being cited on the ticket for the Court to match up the total number of offenses which the officer has written. The Defendant's Summons is similar to the current Defendant's Summons.

Reverse of Court Record

The Reverse of Court Record is a significant departure from the current Reverse of Court Record, primarily so that up to six citations could be resolved on one document. The proposed Reverse of Court Record retains all of the necessary information from the current Reverse of Court Copy, but redesigns the layout to enable for information to be recorded efficiently.

The "Court Action: Orders" Section of the old ticket is replaced by the new section with bail and rescheduling information. The Bail Section enables the court to record the bail status of the Defendant, whether released without bail or bail being set, including the type of bond, and the Depositor's identification information. The Continuance Section enables space to be allotted for sufficient continuances of cases with new dates indicated, including check-off boxes for the various Failure to Appear Sanctions available under Traffic Rule 7, including License Forfeiture for Failure to Appear.

The Court Entry Section enables a court to take pleas on and dispose of up to six charges on one form. Defendant's pleas, findings and sentencing are handled vertically for each charge, as indicated (court will use "G, NG, NC" for plea and finding notations). The initial plea in each respective charge would be indicated by a "G/NG/NC" designation with a comparable finding code in the finding box. The fine would be noted and imposed for each particular offense in its appropriate box as would any jail days imposed. Any suspended costs, fines, or jail would be noted in the appropriate boxes.

Additional space is provided for limited sentencing parameters for certain mandatory OMVI issues. A 72-Hour Program box in noted. Sections include not only driver's license suspension information, but information regarding modified privileges when granted. The Court Section also provides the waiver approval so that waiver could be checked off and signed by the Judicial Official by checking the box and signing off.

The Clerk's Use Section includes all the appropriate financial information needed by the clerks, including the breaking out of local and state costs for accounting purposes. The Check Box Section provides check-off process for the waiver process and also appropriate S.B. 20 information as to the showing or failing to show of insurance proof.

The Commission acknowledges that on this page, and others, that space is at a premium. In the implementation of the UTT, fine point pens should almost certainly be used on all writing on the documents to enable all print to be read. Notwithstanding the limitations, sufficient space would be available for all necessary entries. The form in no way precludes the addition of any other forms or entries which a court may use in conjunction with the Reverse of Court Record, but this Reverse of Court Record provides a simple one-write system for a court to use, if desired.

Reverse of Defendant's Copy

The current Reverse of Defendant's Copy has been revised to not only include currently required information, but to incorporate a new warning on S.B. 20 compliance.

The language throughout the Defendant's copy is substantially similar to current language, except syntax has been changed, now referring to multiple offenses on the citation, and to also note the changes in Traffic Rule 13(B) effective November 1, 1994. It also includes the warning of License Cancellation and Forfeiture for Failure to Appear or Pay Fines. On the bottom, the clerk's receipt signature on the waiver form was eliminated, as this would be kept on the Reverse of Court Record form with receipts being separately given to the defendant.

The center of Reverse of Defendant's Copy contains a new insurance warning to place all traffic violators on notice regarding mandatory insurance showing under S.B. 20. The sections that were block lettered were do so to identify in bolder type the sanctions and warnings, to place all defendants on notice of the requirements of S.B. 20. Although the form has a blank line for filling in information as to the courts, this information could be pre-printed in the space provided to eliminate the officer having to fill in this information.

Abstract of Court Record

The Abstract of Court Record is the manual copy that is sent to the Bureau of Motor Vehicles (BMV) for the processing of necessary conviction and other information to the BMV. Many courts currently are on computer to computer information transfer to the BMV, and it may well be that all courts eventually will report electronically. This form would be used by those courts that manually report their information to the BMV.

The top two-thirds of the Abstract of Court Record is identical to the Face of Court Record with the identifying information of original charges and driver's identification information. The court code and case number identifies the court sending the Abstract. The "No FR" boxes are to identify to the BMV those situations where there has not been compliance with S.B. 20, which the clerk reports to the BMV.

The Box Section would list, vertically, for each of the offenses for which BMV requires reporting the various information items in the required BMV format, including the plea, points assessed and the BMV offense code. A Section for Reduced Offenses is also present, based upon the required reporting of reduction of OMVI and DUS offenses, regardless of disposition, to the BMV. Child Restraint convictions are included in the BMV reporting based upon current law which require escalated fines based upon prior Child Restraint convictions. The two blank boxes would be for the two charges that would come from the "other offense" boxes.

The License Information Section provides a check-off to notify the BMV of any driver's license suspension, including indication for modified driving privileges, and to indicate the charge for which the suspension was imposed. In the event of a license forfeiture, the Abstract would be accompanied by a BMV form 2528. The other information box is to provide that the clerk could send additional information. This would be dome [sic] on the reverse side of the paper Abstract by placing the information on the back side, which will be blank. The checking of this box will advise the BMV to check for additional information on the reverse side.

Reverse of Enforcement Agency Record

This is the Reverse Side of the Enforcement Agency's copy of the basic ticket. This side provides an information and tracking process for the Enforcement Agency to track court action on the case and to provide the officer with space for limited notes as to the offense at the time of citation, including identification of witnesses. The bottom of the form is to provide information location to the officer for PUCO and weight citations, so that the information may be preserved.

Ohio Traffic Rules

FACE OF COURT RECORD

REVERSE OF COURT RECORD

Ohio Criminal Law Handbook

UTT — 1464

FACE OF DEFENDANT'S COPY

_____ COURT _____ COUNTY, OHIO

STATE OF OHIO
☐ City ☐ Village ☐ Township
TICKET NO. _____
CASE NO. _____

NAME _____
STREET _____
CITY, STATE _____ ZIP _____
LICENSE ISSUED MO. ____ YR. ____ EXPIRES BIRTHDATE 19____ STATE ____
SSN ___-___-___ D.O.B. MO.____ DAY____ YR.____

RACE	SEX	HEIGHT	WEIGHT	HAIR	EYES	FINANCIAL RESPONSIBILITY PROOF SHOWN
						☐ Yes ☐ No

LICENSE NO. _____
Lic. Class _____ DOT # _____ ☐ Does Not Apply

TO DEFENDANT: COMPLAINT

ON _____, 19___ AT _____ M. YOU/OPERATED/PARKED/WALKED/ A
☐ Pass ☐ Comm. ☐ Cycle ☐ Over 26001 ☐ Bus ☐ Haz. Mat.
VEHICLE: YR. ____ MAKE ____ BODY TYPE ____
COLOR ____ LIC. ____ STATE ____
UPON A PUBLIC HIGHWAY, NAMELY ____
AT/BETWEEN ____ (M.P.)
IN THE ____ OF ____ IN ____
COUNTY (NO. ____), STATE OF OHIO AND COMMITTED THE FOLLOWING OFFENSE(S).

SPEED: ____ MPH in ____ MPH zone	☐ ORC ☐ ORD ☐ T.P.
☐ Over limits ☐ Unsafe for cond. ☐ ACDA ☐ Radar ☐ Air ☐ VASCAR ☐ Pace ☐ Laser ☐ Stationary ☐ Moving	
OMVI: ☐ Under the influence of alcohol/drug of abuse ☐ Prohibited blood alcohol concentration ____ BAC ☐ Blood ☐ Breath ☐ Urine ☐ Refused	☐ ORC ☐ ORD ☐ T.P.
DRIVER LICENSE: ☐ None ☐ Revoked ☐ Suspended ☐ Not on person Expired: ☐ 6 mos. or less ☐ Over 6 mos. Suspension Type ____	☐ ORC ☐ ORD ☐ T.P.
SAFETY BELT — Failure to wear ☐ Driver ☐ Passenger ☐ Child Restraint	☐ ORC ☐ ORD ☐ T.P.
OTHER OFFENSE ____	☐ ORC ☐ ORD ☐ T.P.
OTHER OFFENSE ____	☐ ORC ☐ ORD ☐ T.P.

☐ DRIVER LICENSE HELD ☐ VEHICLE SEIZED   ARREST CODE ____
☐ PAVEMENT: ☐ Dry ☐ Wet ☐ Snow ☐ Icy # of Lanes ____ ☐ Const. Zone
☐ VISIBILITY: ☐ Clear ☐ Cloudy ☐ Dusk ☐ Night
☐ WEATHER: ☐ Rain ☐ Snow ☐ Fog ☐ No Adverse
☐ TRAFFIC: ☐ Heavy ☐ Moderate ☐ Light ☐ None
☐ AREA: ☐ Business ☐ Rural ☐ Residential ☐ Industry ☐ School
☐ CRASH: ☐ Yes ☐ No ☐ Almost Caused ☐ Injury ☐ Non-Injury ☐ Fatal
☐ Crash Report Number: ____
☐ REMARKS ____

ACCOMPANYING CRIMINAL CHARGE ☐ Yes ☐ No   TOTAL # OFFENSES ____

TO DEFENDANT: SUMMONS ☐ PERSONAL APPEARANCE REQUIRED

You are summoned and ordered to appear at ____ Court ____ at ____ M.,
____, 19____. If you fail to appear at this time and place you may be arrested or your license may be cancelled.
This summons served personally on the defendant on ____, 19____.
The issuing-charging law enforcement officer states under the penalties of perjury and falsification that he/she has read the above complaint and that it is true.

| Issuing-Charging Law Enforcement Officer | Court Code | Unit | Post | Dist. |

NOTE: ISSUING OFFICER BE SURE TO VERIFY ADDRESS, IF DIFFERENT FROM LICENSE ADDRESS WRITE PRESENT ADDRESS IN SPACE PROVIDED   OSHP HP7

OHP0080   10-006000   (REVISION 9-1-96)   DEFENDANT'S COPY   [B6305]

REVERSE OF DEFENDANT'S COPY

TO DEFENDANT: READ THIS MATERIAL CAREFULLY

☐ **PERSONAL APPEARANCE REQUIRED.** If the officer marked this block on the face of the ticket, you must appear in court. Your appearance in court is required because the offenses cannot be processed by a traffic violations bureau.

FAILURE TO APPEAR AND/OR PAY. The posting of bail or depositing your license as bond is to secure your appearance in court or the processing of the offenses through a traffic violations bureau. It is not a payment of fines or costs. If you do not appear at the time and place stated in the citation or if you do not timely process this citation through a traffic violations bureau, your license will be cancelled. Also, a warrant may be issued for your arrest and you may be subject to additional criminal penalties.

OFFENSES THAT MAY NOT BE PROCESSED BY TRAFFIC VIOLATIONS BUREAU: The following offenses require court appearance and may not be processed by a traffic violations bureau:

Any indictable offense; Operating a motor vehicle under the influence of alcohol or any drug of abuse; Leaving scene of accident; Driving while under suspension or revocation of driver's or commercial driver's license; Driving without being licensed to drive, except where the driver's or commercial driver's license has been expired for six months or less; A third moving traffic offense within 12 months; Passing a standing school bus; Willfully eluding or fleeing a police officer; Drag racing.

☐ **WAIVERABLE THROUGH TRAFFIC VIOLATIONS BUREAU.** If you are charged with offenses other than those listed above, you may, within seven days after the day you receive the ticket, plead guilty to the offenses charged and dispose of the case without court appearance by:

(1) appearing personally at the traffic violations bureau, signing the waiver printed below and paying the fines and costs or
(2) signing the waiver printed below and mailing it and a check, money order, or other approved payment for the total of the fines and costs to the traffic violations bureau at the following address:

Address of traffic violations bureau ____

____

MAKE CHECK OR MONEY ORDER PAYABLE TO: ____

INSURANCE WARNING. UNDER OHIO LAW YOU ARE REQUIRED TO SHOW PROOF OF FINANCIAL RESPONSIBILITY OR INSURANCE. If you did not do so at the time of receiving this ticket, you must submit proof of insurance when you appear in court on these offenses. IF YOU DO NOT SUBMIT THE REQUIRED PROOF, YOUR DRIVER'S LICENSE WILL BE SUSPENDED AND YOU MAY BE SUBJECT TO ADDITIONAL FEES AND INSURANCE SANCTIONS. If you have any questions regarding the proof filing, you may call the traffic violations bureau at the telephone indicated.

INFORMATION: For information regarding your duty to appear or the amount of fines and costs, call:

____
fill in telephone number(s)

CONTESTED CASE; COURT APPEARANCE REQUIRED. If you desire to contest the offenses or if court appearance is required, you must appear at the time and place stated in the summons.

NOTICE TO DEFENDANT UNDER EIGHTEEN YEARS OF AGE. You must appear before the Juvenile Court at the time and place determined by that Court. The Juvenile Court will notify you when and where to appear. This ticket will be filed with the Juvenile Court and may be used as a juvenile complaint. For information regarding your duty to appear at Juvenile Court call:

____
fill in telephone number(s)

Address of Juvenile Court ____

GUILTY PLEAS, WAIVER OF TRIAL, PAYMENT OF FINES AND COSTS
I, the undersigned defendant, do hereby enter my written pleas of guilty to the offenses charged in this ticket. I realize that by signing these guilty pleas, I admit my guilt of the offenses charged and waive my right to contest the offenses in a trial before the court or jury. Further, I realize that a record of this plea will be sent to the Ohio Bureau of Motor Vehicles. I have not been convicted of, pleaded guilty to, or forfeited bond for two or more prior moving traffic offenses within the last 12 months. I plead guilty to the offense(s) charged.

FINES ____
Costs ____   Signature of Defendant ____
Total ____   Address ____

ABSTRACT OF COURT RECORD

REVERSE OF ABSTRACT

[blank]

ENFORCEMENT AGENCY RECORD

REVERSE OF AGENCY RECORD

VICTIMS OF CRIME REPARATIONS APPLICATION

Court of Claims of Ohio

CAPITOL SQUARE OFFICE BUILDING
65 EAST STATE STREET, SUITE 1100
COLUMBUS, OHIO 43215
1-800-824-8263

**INFORMATION ABOUT
COMPENSATION FOR VICTIMS OF CRIME**

YOUR APPLICATION MUST BE RECEIVED AND FILE STAMPED BY THE COURT OF CLAIMS OR THE APPROPRIATE COMMON PLEAS COURT WITHIN ONE YEAR AFTER THE DATE OF THE CRIMINALLY INJURIOUS CONDUCT (CRIME)
Failure to file within one year will result in the denial of your claim.

Reparations applications are required to be filed within one year after the crime occurred.

In general, the crime must be reported to the police within 72 hours after the crime occurred.

Awards of reparations may be reduced or denied if the claimant or victim does not fully cooperate with appropriate law enforcement agencies.

Awards of reparations are limited to losses that are caused by personal injury or death resulting from the crime. PROPERTY loss or damage is not covered under the program.

Awards of reparations are limited to actual losses which have not been and cannot be recouped from other sources.

A claim may be denied if the personal injury or death was caused by a motor vehicle, unless the driver of the vehicle intended to cause personal injury or death, or was using the vehicle to flee after committing a felony.

A person seeking an award may choose whether or not to be represented by an attorney. An attorney who represents an applicant for an award of reparations cannot charge the applicant for the services rendered in relation to that representation, but is required to apply to the Court of Claims for payment for the representation.

**INSTRUCTIONS FOR COMPLETING AND FILING
A VICTIMS OF CRIME REPARATIONS APPLICATION
ARE ON THE REVERSE SIDE OF THIS PAGE**

INSTRUCTIONS FOR COMPLETING AND FILING A VICTIMS OF CRIME REPARATIONS APPLICATION

YOUR APPLICATION MUST BE RECEIVED AND FILE STAMPED BY THE COURT OF CLAIMS OR THE APPROPRIATE COMMON PLEAS COURT WITHIN ONE YEAR AFTER THE DATE OF THE CRIMINALLY INJURIOUS CONDUCT (CRIME).
Failure to file within one year will result in the denial of your claim.
UNDER LIMITED CIRCUMSTANCES an application may be initiated by completing the first page and signing the form.
HOWEVER, you will be required to provide additional information in the future. This process will cause substantial delay!

Applications may be submitted without the aid of an attorney. If an attorney does assist in applying for an award of reparations, the attorney cannot charge the claimant attorney fees, but may apply to the Court for payment of attorney fees.

Separate sets 1, 2, 3 and 4 before filling out form. No carbon is required.

Use a typewriter or ball point pen to complete each page. TYPE OR PRINT LEGIBLY. If there is not enough space on the form for required information, continue the information on a blank sheet of paper. Identify each continuation with the number of the line continued. Attach the continuation sheets to the Reparations Application.

Make one legible photo or machine copy of all supporting documents. Attach these COPIES to the Reparations Application. KEEP THE ORIGINALS — RETAIN THEM FOR YOUR RECORDS.

Supporting documents should include:
- bills for expenses caused by the incident, whether paid or unpaid
- medical reports, prepared and signed by the person treating the victim
- receipts of reimbursements from collateral sources

If the victim died as a result of the criminally injurious conduct (crime), the following should also be submitted:
- The victim's death certificate
- The victim's marriage certificate
- Birth certificates for each of the victim's minor children

Sign all four copies of set 4 of the application.

Enclose a filing fee of $7.50 in the form of a MONEY ORDER made out to the Court of Claims of Ohio, or submit a signed affidavit of indigency in place of the filing fee. Applications submitted without a filing fee or an affidavit of indigency will NOT be processed.

File all copies of the completed and signed application, the filing fee and the copies of all supporting documents with:

Court of Claims of Ohio
CAPITOL SQUARE OFFICE BUILDING
65 EAST STATE STREET, SUITE 1100
COLUMBUS, OHIO 43215
1-800-824-8263

or file the completed and signed application and filing fee with the Clerk of the appropriate Common Pleas Court. If you are a resident of Ohio, you may file in the Common Pleas Court of the county in which the criminally injurious conduct (crime) occurred.

The filing of a Reparations Application is the beginning of a legal process; do not expect an immediate payment of money. You must prove eligibility and loss. The office of the Attorney General will check the information stated in the application and contact the individuals and organizations listed therein. You will be informed of the progress of the application and the actions you must take. Failure to respond to notices and requests could result in the dismissal of your claim. Awards of reparations are limited to losses that are caused by physical injury resulting from criminally injurious conduct. Property loss or damage is not covered under this program.

Claimant has the responsibility to immediately report changes of addess in writing to the Court. The Court MUST be able to contact the claimant. Failure to make the Court aware of changes in the claimant's address may result in the dismissal of claimant's case.

For public awareness of this program, completion of Line 67a is requested. This response in no way affects the final determination of your claim.

Keep these instructions for your records.

VC-1X REV. 3/87

COURT OF CLAIMS OF OHIO
Victims of Crime Division
Capitol Square Office Building
65 East State Street, Suite 1100
Columbus, Ohio 43215
1-800-824-8263

SET 1 — Separate sets 1, 2, 3 and 4 before filling out.

OFFICE USE ONLY
C.P. CASE NUMBER

☐ Filing Fee Paid
☐ Affidavit of Indigency

No carbon required.
TYPE OR PRINT LEGIBLY.

Reparations Application

SAMPLE

1. VICTIM NAME FIRST-MIDDLE INITIAL-LAST   MAIDEN NAME
2. PRESENT ADDRESS-STREET
3. CITY   COUNTY
4. STATE   ZIP
5. PHONE—HOME   6. WORK
7. SOC. SEC NUMBER   8. BIRTHDATE
9. SEX ☐ MALE ☐ FEMALE   10. MARITAL STATUS ☐ WIDOW(ER) ☐ SINGLE ☐ MARRIED ☐ SEPARATED ☐ DIVORCED

11. CLAIMANT NAME (IF VICTIM CHECK ☐ GO TO LINE 20)
12. STREET
13. CITY   COUNTY
14. STATE   ZIP
15. PHONE—HOME   16. WORK
17. SOC. SEC NUMBER   18. BIRTHDATE
19. RELATIONSHIP TO VICTIM

20. VICTIM'S ADDRESS AT TIME OF INJURY (IF SAME CHECK HERE ☐ GO TO LINE 23.)
STREET
21. CITY   COUNTY
22. STATE   ZIP

23. LIST ALL OTHER ADDRESSES OF VICTIM DURING 10 YEARS PRIOR TO INJURY
CITY   COUNTY   STATE   DATES
24. CITY   COUNTY   STATE   DATES
25. CITY   COUNTY   STATE   DATES

26. DATE OF INJURY MO DAY YR
27. TIME OF INJURY : ☐ AM : ☐ PM
28. ADDRESS OR LOCATION WHERE INJURY OCCURRED (INCLUDE COUNTY)

29. CRIME REPORTED TO: LAW ENFORCEMENT AGENCY   STREET   CITY   STATE   ZIP
30. DATE CRIME REPORTED MO DAY YR
31. TIME REPORTED : ☐ AM : ☐ PM
32. WHO NOTIFIED LAW ENFORCEMENT AGENCY?   NAME   ADDRESS

33. IF NOT REPORTED WITHIN 72 HOURS, WHY NOT?

Use additional sheet if necessary

34. SUSPECTED OFFENDERS   STREET   CITY   STATE   ZIP

Use additional sheet if necessary

DISTRIBUTION: WHITE & CANARY TO Court of Claims; PINK To Common Pleas Court; GOLDENROD To Claimant.
VC-1A REV. 2/92
PAGE 1 of 4

Form

OHIO CRIMINAL LAW HANDBOOK

1472

COURT OF CLAIMS OF OHIO

SET 2
Separate sets 1, 2, 3 and 4 before filling out.

35. WITNESSES TO CRIME	STREET	CITY	STATE	ZIP	PHONE ( )
					PHONE ( )
					PHONE ( )
					PHONE ( )
	Use additional sheet if necessary				PHONE ( )

36. DESCRIBE WHAT HAPPENED

Use additional sheet if necessary

37. DESCRIBE PARTS OF BODY INJURED AND TYPE OF INJURY

Use additional sheet if necessary

SAMPLE

38. PERSON OR HOSPITAL GIVING EMERGENCY CARE	NAME	STREET	CITY	STATE	ZIP
39. PHYSICIAN OR DENTIST TREATING THIS INJURY	NAME	STREET	CITY	STATE	ZIP
40. SECOND PHYSICIAN OR DENTIST TREATING THIS INJURY	NAME	STREET	CITY	STATE	ZIP

41. HOSPITALIZED? ☐ YES ☐ NO	HOSPITAL NAME	DATES HOSPITALIZED	
42. STREET	CITY	STATE	ZIP
43. SECOND HOSPITAL NAME		DATES HOSPITALIZED	
44. STREET	CITY	STATE	ZIP

45. IS VICTIM DECEASED? ☐ YES ☐ NO	IF YES, ATTACH: VICTIM'S DEATH CERTIFICATE VICTIM'S MARRIAGE CERTIFICATE BIRTH CERTIFICATES FOR VICTIM'S MINOR CHILDREN IF NO, GO TO NEXT PAGE	46. DATE OF DEATH	47. AUTOPSY PERFORMED? ☐ YES ☐ NO
48. IF AUTOPSY, WHERE PERFORMED	STREET	CITY	STATE	ZIP
49. PHYSICIAN AT TIME OF DEATH	STREET	CITY	STATE	ZIP
50. FUNERAL DIRECTOR	STREET	CITY	STATE	ZIP
51. EXECUTOR(TRIX) OR ADMINISTRATOR(TRIX) OF DECEDENT'S ESTATE	NAME	STREET	CITY	STATE	ZIP	PHONE ( )

DISTRIBUTION: WHITE & CANARY To Court of Claims; PINK To Common Pleas Court; GOLDENROD To Claimant.

VC-18 REV. 2/92

PAGE 2 of 4

COURT OF CLAIMS OF OHIO

SET 3 — Separate sets 1, 2, 3 and 4 before filling out.

52. VICTIM'S EMPLOYMENT STATUS IMMEDIATELY PRIOR TO INJURY
☐ GAINFULLY EMPLOYED FOR SALARY, WAGES, OR OTHER REMUNERATION AT $ _____ GROSS PER WEEK
☐ NOT GAINFULLY EMPLOYED FOR SALARY, WAGES, OR OTHER REMUNERATION

53. EMPLOYER AT TIME OF INJURY | STREET | CITY | STATE | ZIP

54. DID VICTIM LOSE TIME FROM WORK? ☐ YES ☐ NO — DATES OF TIME LOST

55. DID VICTIM LOSE WAGES DUE TO THE INJURY? ☐ YES ☐ NO — TOTAL WAGES LOST AND NOT REIMBURSED $

56. EXPENSES INCURRED AS A RESULT OF THE INJURY (ATTACH COPIES OF BILLS, RETAIN ORIGINALS)

AMOUNT	TO WHOM OWED	STREET	CITY	STATE	TYPE OF EXPENSE	DATE INCURRED MO / DAY / YR
$						
$						
$						
$						
$						
$						

Use additional sheet if necessary

57. ARE MEDICAL OR LOSS OF INCOME BENEFITS AVAILABLE FROM ANY SOURCE OTHER THAN UNDER THE VICTIMS OF CRIME ACT?
CHECK "YES" OR "NO" BOXES FOR ALL SOURCES LISTED

YES NO
☐ ☐ OFFENDER
☐ ☐ BLUE CROSS/BLUE SHIELD — CONTRACT NO. OR ID. NO. _____
☐ ☐ OTHER HEALTH/MAJOR MED. — POLICY NO. _____

YES NO
☐ ☐ MEDICARE
☐ ☐ MEDICAID
☐ ☐ WELFARE — WELFARE CASE NO. _____
☐ ☐ SOC. SEC.

YES NO
☐ ☐ VETERANS' ADMINISTRATION
☐ ☐ WORKERS' COMPENSATION
☐ ☐ EMPLOYER'S WAGE CONTINUATION PROGRAM
☐ ☐ LIFE INSURANCE
☐ ☐ OTHER _____

ENTER IDENTIFYING INFORMATION BELOW FOR ANY BOX CHECKED YES, EVEN IF AMOUNT IS PRESENTLY UNKNOWN.

BENEFITS RECEIVED OR AVAILABLE (e.g. Blue Cross, Medicare, etc.)

AMOUNT	SOURCE	STREET	CITY	STATE	ZIP	DATE RECEIVED MO / DAY / YR
$						
$						
$						

Use additional sheet if necessary

58. HAS A CIVIL ACTION BEEN FILED AGAINST THE OFFENDER AS A RESULT OF THIS INJURY ☐ YES ☐ NO
IF YES, NAME OF COURT _____ CASE NO. _____ AMOUNT OF SETTLEMENT OR JUDGMENT _____

59. HAS THE VICTIM BEEN ARRESTED FOR, OR CONVICTED OF, ANY FELONY WITHIN 10 YEARS PRIOR TO THE INJURY? ☐ YES ☐ NO

	DATE	CITY	COUNTY	STATE
☐ ARRESTED				
☐ CONVICTED				

DISTRIBUTION: WHITE & CANARY TO Court of Claims; PINK To Common Pleas Court; GOLDENROD To Claimant.
VC-1C REV. 2/92

Form — Ohio Criminal Law Handbook — 1474

COURT OF CLAIMS OF OHIO

SET 4 — Separate sets 1, 2, 3 and 4 before filling out.

60. SPOUSE OF VICTIM

61. STREET | CITY | STATE | ZIP | PHONE

62. LIST ALL MINOR CHILDREN OF VICTIM WHETHER OR NOT THEY WERE DEPENDENT UPON THE VICTIM. ALSO LIST ALL DEPENDENTS OF VICTIM

NAME	ADDRESS IF DIFFERENT FROM LINES 2-4	RELATIONSHIP TO VICTIM	DATE OF BIRTH (MO/DAY/YR)	AMOUNT OF SUPPORT

Use additional sheet if necessary

SAMPLE

63. GUARDIAN OF CHILDREN | STREET | CITY | STATE | ZIP | PHONE

64. COURT-APPOINTED ☐ YES ☐ NO IF YES, ATTACH LETTERS OF AUTHORITY

65. I, the claimant, hereby state UNDER THE PENALTIES OF PERJURY AND FALSIFICATION that this application of four pages has been prepared or read by me and that the information given herein, including any attached bills, records or certificates, is true and complete.

I hereby authorize any person (including any physician), organization, law enforcement or government agency to release to the Ohio Attorney General or the Ohio Court of Claims, upon their request, a copy of any report, document, record, criminal record or other information (including tax information or returns) in any way relating to my claim for an award of reparations. This authorization or a copy hereof shall be valid for a period of two years without any further consent by me.

_____ Date   _____ Claimant's Signature

SIGN AND DATE EACH COPY OF THIS PAGE

65a. HOW DID YOU FIND OUT ABOUT THE VICTIMS OF CRIME PROGRAM?
☐ Police ☐ Advocate Group ☐ Victims Assistance Program ☐ Prosecutor's Office ☐ Attorneys
☐ Radio/TV/Newspaper ☐ Hospital/Doctor ☐ Friends/Family ☐ Other (Explain) _____

66. You are not required to have an attorney assist in submitting your application. However, if an attorney does assist you, the attorney must also sign this application. The attorney cannot charge attorney fees for representing you in this application, but may apply to the Court for attorney fees.

Pursuant to Civil Rule 11, I state that I have read the Reparations Application; that to the best of my knowledge, information, and belief there is good ground to support it. I further state that I have read Section 2743.65 of the Ohio Revised Code concerning attorney fees.

ATTORNEY'S NAME: _____

ADDRESS: _____

Attorney's Signature _____

TELEPHONE: _____

SOC. SEC. OR TAX I.D. NO: _____

DISTRIBUTION: WHITE & CANARY TO Court of Claims; PINK To Common Pleas Court; GOLDENROD To Claimant.

VC-1D REV. 2/82
PAGE 4 of 4

Funds for an award of reparations are provided, in part, by a grant awarded by the Office for Victims of Crime, Office of Justice Programs, U.S. Department of Justice.

1475 RULES OF THE COURT OF CLAIMS Form

COURT OF CLAIMS OF OHIO
Capitol Square Office Building
65 East State Street
Suite 1100
Columbus, Ohio 43215

Supplemental Reparations Application

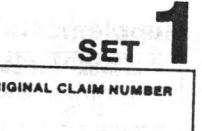

SET 1

ORIGINAL CLAIM NUMBER

TYPE OR PRINT LEGIBLY. Separate sets 1 and 2 before filling out. NO carbon required. List all expenses since last award.

1. VICTIM NAME FIRST - MIDDLE - LAST	11. CLAIMANT NAME (If victim, check here ☐ and go to Line 20)
2. PRESENT ADDRESS - STREET	12. STREET
3. CITY / COUNTY	13. CITY / COUNTY
4. STATE / ZIP	14. STATE / ZIP
5. PHONE - HOME / 6. WORK	15. PHONE - HOME / 16. WORK
7. SOC. SEC. NUMBER / 8. BIRTHDATE	17. SOC. SEC. NUMBER
9. SEX ☐ MALE ☐ FEMALE 10. MARITAL STATUS ☐ WIDOW(ER) ☐ SINGLE ☐ MARRIED ☐ SEPARATED ☐ DIVORCED	19. RELATIONSHIP TO VICTIM

20. VICTIM'S ADDRESS AT TIME OF INJURY (If same, check here ☐ and go to Line 23)
STREET

23. LIST ALL OTHER ADDRESSES OF VICTIM DURING 10 YEARS PRIOR TO INJURY
CITY / COUNTY / STATE / DATES

| 21. CITY / COUNTY | 24. CITY / COUNTY / STATE / DATES |
| 22. STATE / ZIP | 25. CITY / COUNTY / STATE / DATES |

26. HAS THE VICTIM BEEN ARRESTED FOR, OR CONVICTED OF, ANY FELONY WITHIN 10 YEARS PRIOR TO THE INJURY? ☐ YES ☐ NO
☐ ARRESTED   DATE   CITY   COUNTY   STATE
☐ CONVICTED

27. ADDITIONAL EXPENSES INCURRED AS A RESULT OF THE INJURY (Attach copies of bills, retain originals)

AMOUNT	TO WHOM OWED	STREET	CITY	STATE	TYPE OF EXPENSE	DATE INCURRED MO / DAY / YR
$						
$						
$						
$						
$						
$						
$						
$						

USE ADDITIONAL SHEET IF NECESSARY

DISTRIBUTION: WHITE & CANARY to Court of Claims; PINK to Claimant
VC 2A REV. 3/87
Page 1 of 2

Supplemental Reparations Application

SET 2

28. VICTIM'S EMPLOYMENT STATUS IMMEDIATELY PRIOR TO INJURY	☐ GAINFULLY EMPLOYED FOR SALARY WAGES, OR OTHER REMUNERATION AT	GROSS PER WEEK	☐ NOT GAINFULLY EMPLOYED FOR SALARY, WAGES, OR OTHER REMUNERATION.
29. EMPLOYER AT TIME OF INJURY	STREET	CITY	STATE ZIP

30. DID VICTIM LOSE MORE TIME FROM WORK?	☐ YES ☐ NO	DATES OF TIME LOST
31. DID VICTIM LOSE MORE WAGES DUE TO THE INJURY?	☐ YES ☐ NO	TOTAL WAGES LOST (AND NOT REIMBURSED)

32. ARE MEDICAL OR LOSS OF INCOME BENEFITS AVAILABLE FROM ANY SOURCE OTHER THAN UNDER THE VICTIMS OF CRIME ACT? CHECK "YES" or "NO" BOXES FOR ALL SOURCES LISTED

	YES NO		YES NO		YES NO	
	☐ ☐	OFFENDER	☐ ☐	MEDICARE	☐ ☐	VETERAN'S ADMINISTRATION
	☐ ☐	BLUE CROSS/BLUE SHIELD CONTRACT NO. OR ID. NO.	☐ ☐	MEDICAID	☐ ☐	WORKERS' COMPENSATION
			☐ ☐	WELFARE	☐ ☐	EMPLOYER'S WAGE CONTINUATION PROGRAM
			WELFARE CASE NO.			
	☐ ☐	OTHER HEALTH/MAJOR MED POLICY NO.	☐ ☐	SOC. SEC.	☐ ☐	LIFE INSURANCE
					☐ ☐	OTHER

ENTER IDENTIFYING INFORMATION BELOW FOR ANY BOX CHECKED YES, EVEN IF AMOUNT IS PRESENTLY UNKNOWN.

BENEFITS RECEIVED OR AVAILABLE (e.g., Blue Cross, Medicare, etc.)

AMOUNT	SOURCE	STREET	CITY	STATE	ZIP	DATE RECEIVED MO DATE YR
$						
$						
$						

Use additional sheet if necessary

SAMPLE

33. HAS A CIVIL ACTION BEEN FILED AGAINST THE OFFENDER AS A RESULT OF THIS INJURY ☐ YES ☐ NO
IF YES, NAME OF COURT _____ CASE NO. _____ AMOUNT OF SETTLEMENT OR JUDGMENT _____

34. I, the claimant, hereby state UNDER THE PENALTIES OF PERJURY AND FALSIFICATION that this application of two pages has been prepared or read by me and that the information given herein, including any attached bills, records or certificates, is true and complete.

I hereby authorize any person (including any physician), organization, law enforcement or governmental agency to release to the Ohio Attorney General or the Ohio Court of Claims, upon their request, a copy of any report, document, record, criminal record or other information (including tax information or returns) in any way relating to my claim for an award of reparations. This authorization or a copy hereof shall be valid for a period of one year without any further consent by me.

Date _____ Claimant's Signature _____

SIGN AND DATE **EACH COPY** OF THIS PAGE

35. You are not required to have an attorney assist in submitting your application. However, if an attorney does assist you, the attorney must also sign this application. The attorney cannot charge attorney fees for representing you in this application, but may apply to the Court for attorney fees.

Pursuant to Civil Rule 11, I state that I have read the Reparations Application; that to the best of my knowledge, information, and belief there is good ground to support it. I further state that I have read Section 2743.65 of the Ohio Revised Code concerning attorney fees.

ATTORNEY'S NAME: _____

ADDRESS: _____

Attorney's Signature _____

TELEPHONE: _____

SOC. SEC. OR TAX I.D. NO. _____

DISTRIBUTION: WHITE & CANARY to Court of Claims; PINK to Claimant
VC 28 REV 3/87
Page 2 of 2

COURT OF CLAIMS OF OHIO
Victims of Crime Division
Capitol Square Office Building
65 East State Street, Suite 1100
Columbus, Ohio 43215

INDIGENCY STATEMENT

VICTIM _____

CLAIMANT _____   CLAIM NO. _____

    I, Claimant, state under the penalties of perjury and falsification that I am indigent and that payment of the $7.50 filing fee would create a financial hardship for me.

_____
Claimant's Signature

_____
Date

Under R.C. 2921.11 and R.C. 2929.11 perjury is a felony of the third degree and punishable by imprisonment for one to ten years and fine up to $5,000.00. Under R.C. 2921.13 and R.C. 2929.21 falsification is a misdemeanor of the first degree and punishable by imprisonment for six months and fine up to $1,000.00.

SELECTED RULES OF SUPERINTENDENCE FOR THE COURTS OF OHIO

Effective July 1, 1997

Rule
10. Notifying Law Enforcement Agencies of Criminal or Civil Protection Orders
18. Minor Misdemeanors: Violations Bureau—Municipal and County Courts
20. Appointment of Counsel for Indigent Defendants in Capital Cases—Courts of Common Pleas
21. Appointment of Counsel for Indigent Defendants in Capital Cases—Courts of Appeal
22. Verification of Indigency
36. Designation of Trial Attorney; Assignment System
39. Case Time Limits

RULE 10. Notifying Law Enforcement Agencies of Criminal or Civil Protection Orders.

Upon issuance of a civil or criminal protection order by a court pursuant to section 2919.26(E)(2) or 3113.31 of the Revised Code, the court shall complete Form 10-A. Form 10-A and a copy of the order shall be filed by the court with the local law enforcement agency for entry in the Law Enforcement Automation Data System and statewide dissemination.

Commentary (July 1, 1997)

This rule was adopted, effective July 1, 1996, and implements R.C. 2919.26 and 3113.31.

FORM 10-A
PROTECTION ORDER NOTICE TO
LAW ENFORCEMENT AUTOMATION DATA SYSTEMS

OHP DATA ONLY #EPO

SUBJECT NAME _____
                    (LAST)   (FIRST)   (M.I.)

ADDRESS _____

SSN _____ DOB _____

PHYSICAL DESCRIPTION:

HGT_____ WGT_____ HAIR_____ EYES_____ RACE_____ SEX_____

VEHICLE LICENSE NO. _____

BRADY HANDGUN DISQUALIFIERS [18 U.S.C. Sec. 922(d)(8)]
(REQUIRES ALL "YES" TO DISQUALIFY HANDGUN PURCHASE)
* Does order protect intimate partner or child?   YES NO
* Did Defendant have opportunity to participate in hearing regarding order? YES NO
* Does order find defendant a credible threat or explicitly prohibit physical force? YES NO

CASE NO. _____ COURT CODE No. _____   BRADY DISQUALIFIED?

                                                                                  YES ☐
                                                                                  NO ☐

PUR/2   ☐ R.C.2919.26   ☐ R.C.3113.31   UNKNOWN ☐

DATE OF ORDER _____ EXPIRATION OF ORDER _____

NAME OF JUDGE _____

MIS/ PROTECTED PERSON(S) _____

Authorized by _____ Date _____
(circle one)   Judge   Magistrate   Clerk

May be reproduced locally.

RULE 18. Minor Misdemeanors: Violations Bureau—Municipal and County Courts.

Each municipal and county court shall establish a violations bureau for minor misdemeanors utilizing the citation system and procedure set forth in Criminal Rule 4.1.

Commentary (July 1, 1997)

Only nonsubstantive changes were made to former M.C. Sup. R. 11 in the 1997 amendments to this rule.

A minor misdemeanor is any offense specifically classified as such or any unclassified offense for which the only penalty is a fine not exceeding one hundred dollars. R.C. 2901.02.

Crim. R. 4.1 provides that a court may establish a violations bureau for all or particular minor misdemeanors. Thus, each court, by local rule, must specify that all or particular minor misdemeanors are to be processed by violations bureau.

Crim. R. 4.1 specifies the form of citation to be used and that the citation "* * * shall inform the defendant that, in lieu of appearing at the time and place stated, he may, within that stated time, appear personally at the office of the clerk of court and upon signing a plea of guilty and a waiver of trial pay a stated fine and stated costs, if any."

Crim. R. 4.1(E) requires the court to establish a fine schedule listing the fines and court costs for each minor misdemeanor. The fine schedule is to be prominently posted at the place violation fines are paid.

RULE 20. Appointment of Counsel for Indigent Defendants in Capital Cases—Courts of Common Pleas.

I. Applicability.

(A) This rule shall apply in cases where an indigent defendant has been charged with or convicted of an offense for which the death penalty can be or has been imposed.

(B) The provisions for the appointment of counsel set forth in this rule apply only in cases where the defendant is indigent, counsel is not privately retained by or for the defendant, and the death penalty can be or has been imposed upon the defendant. This rule does not apply in the case of a juvenile defendant who is indicted for a "capital offense" but because of his or her age cannot be sentenced to death.

(C) If the defendant is entitled to the appointment of counsel, the court shall appoint two attorneys certified pursuant to this rule. If the defendant engages one privately retained attorney, the court shall not appoint a second attorney pursuant to this rule.

(D) The provisions of this rule apply in addition to the reporting requirements created by section 2929.021 of the Revised Code.

II. Qualifications for certification as counsel for indigent defendants in capital cases.

(A) **Trial counsel.** (1) At least two attorneys shall be appointed by the court to represent an indigent defendant charged with an offense for which the death penalty may be imposed. At least one of the appointed counsel must maintain a law office in Ohio and have experience in Ohio criminal trial practice.

The counsel appointed shall be designated "lead counsel" and "co-counsel."

(2) Lead counsel shall satisfy all of the following:

(a) Be admitted to the practice of law in Ohio or admitted to practice *pro hac vice*;

(b) Have at least five years of civil or criminal litigation or appellate experience;

(c) Have specialized training, as approved by the committee, on subjects that will assist counsel in the defense of persons accused of capital crimes in the two-year period prior to making application;

(d) Have at least one of the following qualifications:

(i) Experience as "lead counsel" in the jury trial of at least one capital case;

(ii) Experience as "co-counsel" in the trial of at least two capital cases;

(e) Have at least one of the following qualifications:

(i) Experience as "lead counsel" in the jury trial of at least one murder or aggravated murder case;

(ii) Experience as "lead counsel" in ten or more criminal or civil jury trials, at least three of which were felony jury trials;

(iii) Experience as "lead counsel" in either: three murder or aggravated murder jury trials; one murder or aggravated murder jury trial and three felony jury trials; or three aggravated or first- or second-degree felony jury trials in a court of common pleas in the three years prior to making application.

(3) Co-counsel shall satisfy all of the following:

(a) Be admitted to the practice of law in Ohio or admitted to practice *pro hac vice*;

(b) Have at least three years of civil or criminal litigation or appellate experience;

(c) Have specialized training, as approved by the committee, on subjects that will assist counsel in the defense of persons accused of capital crimes in the two years prior to making application;

(d) Have at least one of the following qualifications:

(i) Experience as "co-counsel" in one murder or aggravated murder trial;

(ii) Experience as "lead counsel" in one first-degree felony jury trial;

(iii) Experience as "lead" or "co-counsel" in at least two felony jury or civil jury trials in a court of common pleas in the three years prior to making application.

(4) As used in this rule, "trial" means a case concluded with a judgment of acquittal under Criminal Rule 29 or submission to the trial court or jury for decision and verdict.

(B) **Appellate counsel.** (1) At least two attorneys shall be appointed by the court to appeal cases where the trial court has imposed the death penalty on an indigent defendant. At least one of the appointed counsel shall maintain a law office in Ohio.

(2) Appellate counsel shall satisfy all of the following:

(a) Be admitted to the practice of law in Ohio or admitted to practice *pro hac vice*;

(b) Have at least three years of civil or criminal litigation or appellate experience;

(c) Have specialized training, as approved by the Committee, on subjects that will assist counsel in the defense of persons accused of capital crimes in the two years prior to making application;

(d) Have specialized training, as approved by the Committee, on subjects that will assist counsel in the appeal of cases in which the death penalty was imposed in the two years prior to making application;

(e) Have experience as counsel in the appeal of at least three felony convictions in the three years prior to making application.

(C) Exceptional circumstances. If an attorney does not satisfy the requirements of divisions (A)(2), (A)(3), or (B)(2) of this section, the attorney may be certified as lead counsel, co-counsel, or appellate counsel if it can be demonstrated to the satisfaction of the Committee that competent representation will be provided to the defendant. In so determining, the Committee may consider the following:

(a) Specialized training on subjects that will assist counsel in the trial or appeal of cases in which the death penalty may be or was imposed;

(b) Experience in the trial or appeal of criminal or civil cases;

(c) Experience in the investigation, preparation, and litigation of capital cases that were resolved prior to trial;

(d) Any other relevant considerations.

(D) Savings clause. Attorneys certified by the Committee prior to January 1, 1991 may maintain their certification by complying with the requirements of Section VII of this rule, notwithstanding the requirements of Sections II(A)(2)(d), II(A)(3)(b) and (d), and II(B)(2)(d) as amended effective January 1, 1991.

III. Committee on the appointment of counsel for indigent defendants in capital cases.

(A) There shall be a Committee on the Appointment of Counsel for Indigent Defendants in Capital Cases.

(B) Appointment of Committee members. The Committee shall be composed of five attorneys. Three members shall be appointed by a majority vote of all members of the Supreme Court of Ohio; one shall be appointed by the Ohio State Bar Association; and one shall be appointed by the Ohio Public Defender Commission.

(C) Eligibility for appointment to the Committee. Each member of the Committee shall satisfy all of the following qualifications:

(1) Be admitted to the practice of law in Ohio;

(2) Have represented criminal defendants for not less than five years;

(3) Demonstrate a knowledge of the law and practice of capital cases;

(4) Currently not serving as a prosecuting attorney, city director of law, village solicitor, or similar officer or their assistant or employee, or an employee of any court.

(D) Overall composition. The overall composition of the Committee shall meet both of the following criteria:

(1) No more than two members shall reside in the same county;

(2) No more than one shall be a judge.

(E) Terms; vacancies. The term of office for each member shall be five years, each term beginning on the first day of January. Members shall be eligible for reappointment. Vacancies shall be filled in the same manner as original appointments. Any member appointed to fill a vacancy occurring prior to the expiration of a term shall hold office for the remainder of the term.

(F) Election of chair. The Committee shall elect a chair and such other officers as are necessary. The officers shall serve for two years and may be reelected to additional terms.

(G) Powers and duties of the Committee. The Committee shall do all of the following:

(1) Prepare and notify attorneys of procedures for applying for certification to be appointed counsel for indigent defendants in capital cases;

(2) Periodically provide all common pleas and appellate court judges and the Ohio Public Defender with a list of all attorneys who are certified to be appointed counsel for indigent capital defendants;

(3) Periodically review the list of certified counsel, all court appointments given to attorneys in capital cases, and the result and status of those cases;

(4) Develop criteria and procedures for retention of certification including, but not limited to, mandatory continuing legal education on the defense and appeal of capital cases;

(5) Expand, reduce, or otherwise modify the list of certified attorneys as appropriate and necessary in accord with division (G)(4) of this section;

(6) Review and approve specialized training programs on subjects that will assist counsel in the defense and appeal of capital cases;

(7) Recommend to the Supreme Court of Ohio amendments to this rule or any other rule or statute relative to the defense or appeal of capital cases.

(H) Meetings. The Committee shall meet at the call of the chair, at the request of a majority of the members, or at the request of the Supreme Court of Ohio. A quorum consists of three members. A majority of the Committee is necessary for the Committee to elect a chair and take any other action.

(I) Compensation. All members of the Committee shall receive equal compensation in an amount to be established by the Supreme Court of Ohio.

IV. Procedures for court appointments of counsel.

(A) Appointing counsel. Only counsel who have been certified by the Committee shall be appointed to represent indigent defendants charged with or convicted of an offense for which the death penalty may be or has been imposed. Each court may adopt local rules establishing qualifications in addition to and not in conflict with those established by this rule. Appointments of counsel for these cases should be distributed as widely as possible among the certified attorneys in the jurisdiction of the appointing court.

(B) Workload of appointed counsel.

(1) In appointing counsel, the court shall consider the nature and volume of the workload of the prospective counsel to ensure that counsel, if appointed, could direct sufficient attention to the defense of the case and provide competent representation to the defendant.

(2) Attorneys accepting appointments shall provide each client with competent representation in accordance with constitutional and professional standards. Appointed counsel shall not accept workloads that, by reason of their excessive size, interfere with the rendering of competent representation or lead to the breach of professional obligations.

(C) Notice to the Committee.

(1) Within two weeks of appointment, the appointing court shall notify the Committee secretary of the appointment on a form prescribed by the Committee. The notice shall include all of the following:

(a) The court and the judge assigned to the case;

(b) The case name and number;

(c) A copy of the indictment;

(d) The names, business addresses, telephone numbers, and Sup. R. 20 certification of all attorneys appointed;

(e) Any other information considered relevant by the Committee or appointing court.

(2) Within two weeks of disposition, the trial court shall notify the Committee secretary of the disposition of the case on a form prescribed by the Committee. The notice shall include all of the following:

(a) The outcome of the case;

(b) The title and section of the Revised Code of any crimes to which the defendant pleaded or was found guilty;

(c) The date of dismissal, acquittal, or that sentence was imposed;

(d) The sentence, if any;

(e) A copy of the judgment entry reflecting the above;

(f) If the death penalty was imposed, the name of counsel appointed to represent the defendant on appeal.

(g) Any other information considered relevant by the Committee or trial court.

(D) Support services. The appointing court shall provide appointed counsel, as required by Ohio law or the federal Constitution, federal statutes, and professional standards, with the investigator, mitigation specialists, mental health professional, and other forensic experts and other support services reasonably necessary or appropriate for counsel to prepare for and present an adequate defense at every stage of the proceedings including, but not limited to, determinations relevant to competency to stand trial, a not guilty by reason of insanity plea, cross-examination of expert witnesses called by the prosecution, disposition following conviction, and preparation for and presentation of mitigating evidence in the sentencing phase of the trial.

V. Monitoring; removal.

(A) The appointing court should monitor the performance of assigned counsel to ensure that the defendant is receiving competent representation. If there is compelling evidence before any court, trial or appellate, that an attorney has ignored basic responsibilities of providing competent counsel, which results in prejudice to the defendant's case, the court, in addition to any other action it may take, shall report this evidence to the Committee, which shall accord the attorney an opportunity to be heard.

(B) Complaints concerning the performance of attorneys assigned in the trials or appeals of indigent defendants in capital cases shall be reviewed by the Committee pursuant to the provisions of Section III(G)(3), (4), and (5) of this rule.

VI. Programs for specialized training.

(A) Programs for specialized training in the defense of persons charged with a capital offense.

(1) To be approved by the Committee, a death penalty trial seminar shall include instruction devoted to the investigation, preparation, and presentation of a death penalty trial.

(2) The curriculum for an approved death penalty trial seminar should include, but is not limited to, specialized training in the following areas:

(a) An overview of current developments in death penalty litigation;

(b) Death penalty voir dire;

(c) Trial phase presentation;

(d) Use of experts in the trial and penalty phase;

(e) Investigation, preparation, and presentation of mitigation;

(f) Preservation of the record;

(g) Counsel's relationship with the accused and the accused's family;

(h) Death penalty appellate and post-conviction litigation in state and federal courts.

(B) Programs for specialized training in the appeal of cases in which the death penalty has been imposed.

(1) To be approved by the Committee, a death penalty appeals seminar shall include instruction devoted to the appeal of a case in which the death penalty has been imposed.

(2) The curriculum for an approved death penalty appeal seminar should include, but is not limited to, specialized training in the following areas:

(a) An overview of current developments in death penalty law;

(b) Completion, correction, and supplementation of the record on appeal;
(c) Reviewing the record for unique death penalty issues;
(d) Motion practice for death penalty appeals;
(e) Preservation and presentation of constitutional issues;
(f) Preparing and presenting oral argument;
(g) Unique aspects of death penalty practice in the courts of appeals, the Supreme Court of Ohio, and the United States Supreme Court;
(h) The relationship of counsel with the appellant and the appellant's family during the course of the appeals.
(i) Procedure and practice in collateral litigation, extraordinary remedies, state post-conviction litigation, and federal habeas corpus litigation.

(C) The sponsor of a death penalty seminar shall apply for approval from the Committee at least sixty days before the date of the proposed seminar. An application for approval shall include the curriculum for the seminar and include biographical information of each member of the seminar faculty.

(D) The Committee shall obtain a list of attendees from the Supreme Court Commission on Continuing Legal Education that shall be used to verify attendance at and grant Sup. R. 20 credit for each Committee-approved seminar. Credit for purposes of this rule shall be granted to instructors using the same ratio provided in Rule X of the Supreme Court Rules for the Government of the Bar of Ohio.

(E) The Committee may grant credit under this rule for attendance at programs other than those described in divisions (A) and (B) of this section. Application for credit may be made by the program sponsor or any program attendee, and may be made prior to or after completion of the program.

VII. Standards for retention of Sup. R. 20 certification.

(A)(1) To retain certification, an attorney who has previously been certified by the Committee shall complete at least twelve hours of Committee-approved specialized training every two years. To maintain certification as lead counsel or co-counsel, at least six of the twelve hours shall be devoted to instruction in the trial of capital cases. To maintain certification as appellate counsel, at least six of the twelve hours shall be devoted to instruction in the appeal of capital cases.

(2) On the first day of July of each year, the Committee shall review the list of certified counsel and revoke the certification of any attorney who has not complied with the specialized training requirements of this rule. An attorney whose certification has been revoked shall not be eligible to accept future appointment as counsel for an indigent defendant charged with or convicted of an offense for which the death penalty can be or has been imposed.

(B) An out-of-state seminar providing specialized training on subjects that will assist counsel in the defense of persons accused of capital crimes or in the appeal of cases in which the death penalty was imposed may be approved by the Committee. Applications for approval may be submitted by the seminar sponsor or a seminar attendee and shall include the curriculum for the seminar, biographical information on the faculty, and proof of attendance.

(C) An attorney who has previously been certified but whose certification has been revoked for failure to comply with the specialized training requirements of this rule must, in order to regain certification, submit a new application that demonstrates that the attorney has completed twelve hours of Committee-approved specialized training in the two year period prior to making application for recertification.

VIII. Reserved.

IX. Effective date.

(A) The effective date of this rule shall be October 1, 1987.

(B) The amendments to Section II(A)(5)(b), Section III(B)(2), and to the Subcommittee Comments following Section II of this Rule adopted by the Supreme Court of Ohio on June 28, 1989, shall be effective on July 1, 1989.

(C) The amendments to Sections I(A)(2), I(A)(3), I(B), and II, and the addition of Sections I(C) and IV, adopted by the Supreme Court of Ohio on December 11, 1990, shall be effective on January 1, 1991.

(D) The amendments to this rule adopted by the Supreme Court of Ohio on April 19, 1995, shall take effect on July 1, 1995.

Commentary (July 1, 1997)

This rule is identical to former C.P. Sup. R. 65.

RULE 21. Appointment of Counsel for Indigent Defendants in Capital Cases—Courts of Appeal.

(A) Applicability. This rule shall apply in appeals of cases where the trial court has imposed the death penalty on an indigent defendant. The appointment of counsel and notice requirements shall be in accordance with this rule and Sup. R. 20.

(B) Procedures for court appointments of counsel.

(1) Appointing counsel. Only attorneys who have been certified as appellate counsel pursuant to Sup. R. 20 shall be appointed as appellate counsel where the trial court has imposed the death penalty on an indigent defendant. Each appellate court may adopt local rules establishing qualifications in addition to and not in conflict with those established by Sup. R. 20. Appointments of counsel for these cases should be distributed as widely as possible among the certified attorneys in the jurisdiction of the appointing court.

(2) Workload of appointed counsel. In appointing

counsel, the court shall consider the nature and volume of the workload of the prospective counsel to ensure that counsel, if appointed, can direct sufficient attention to the appeal of the case and provide competent representation to the defendant. Attorneys accepting appointments shall provide each client with competent representation in accordance with constitutional and professional standards. Appointed counsel shall not accept workloads that, by reason of their excessive size, interfere with the rendering of competent representation or lead to the breach of professional obligations.

(C) **Notice of the appointment of counsel.** Within two weeks of appointment, the appellate court shall notify the Committee secretary of the appointment of appellate counsel on a form prescribed by the Committee. If appellate counsel are appointed by the trial court, the notice is not required. The notice shall include all of the following:

(1) The case name and number;

(2) The names, business addresses, telephone numbers, and certification pursuant to Sup. R. 20 of counsel appointed to represent the defendant on appeal;

(3) Any other information considered relevant by the Committee or appointing court.

(D) **Notice of disposition of the appeal.** Within two weeks of disposition of the appeal, the appellate court shall notify the Committee secretary of the disposition of the appeal on a form prescribed by the Committee. The notice shall include all of the following:

(1) The case name and number;

(2) The names, business addresses, telephone numbers, and certification pursuant to Sup. R. 20 of counsel who represented the defendant on appeal;

(3) The disposition of the appeal;

(4) If the death sentence was affirmed, the names, addresses, telephone numbers, and certification pursuant to Sup. R. 20 of counsel who were appointed to represent the defendant on appeal to the Supreme Court of Ohio;

(5) Any other information considered relevant by the Committee or appellate court.

Commentary (July 1, 1997)

This rule is identical to former C.A. Sup. R. 6.

RULE 22. Verification of Indigency.

Where required by law to appoint counsel to represent indigent defendants in cases for which the county will apply to the Ohio Public Defender Commission for reimbursement of costs, the court shall require the applicant to complete the financial disclosure form. The court shall follow rules promulgated by the Commission pursuant to division (B)(1) of section 120.03 of the Revised Code as guidelines to determine indigency and standards of indigency.

Commentary (July 1, 1997)

This is a new rule added in the 1997 amendments to the Rules of Superintendence. The rule is intended to facilitate compliance with the statutes and administrative rules relative to the appointment of counsel for indigent defendants in criminal cases.

RULE 36. Designation of Trial Attorney; Assignment System.

(A) **Designation of trial attorney.** In civil cases the attorney who is to try the case shall be designated as trial attorney on all pleadings. In criminal cases, except felonies, the attorney who is to try the case, upon being retained or appointed, shall notify the court that he or she is the trial attorney by filing a written statement with the clerk of the court.

(B)(1) **Individual assignment system.** As used in these rules, "individual assignment system" means the system in which, upon the filing in or transfer to the court or a division of the court, a case immediately is assigned by lot to a judge of the division, who becomes primarily responsible for the determination of every issue and proceeding in the case until its termination. All preliminary matters, including requests for continuances, shall be submitted for disposition to the judge to whom the case has been assigned or, if the assigned judge is unavailable, to the administrative judge. The individual assignment system ensures all of the following:

(a) Judicial accountability for the processing of individual cases;

(b) Timely processing of cases through prompt judicial control over cases and the pace of litigation;

(c) Random assignment of cases to judges of the division through an objective and impartial system that ensures the equitable distribution of cases between or among the judges of the division.

(2) Each multi-judge general, domestic relations, and juvenile division of the court of common pleas shall adopt the individual assignment system for the assignment of all cases to judges of the division. Each multi-judge municipal or county court shall adopt the individual assignment system for the assignment of all cases to the judges of that court, except as otherwise provided in division (C) of this rule. Modifications to the individual assignment system may be adopted to provide for the redistribution of cases involving the same criminal defendant, parties, family members, or subject-matter. Any modifications shall satisfy divisions (B)(1)(a) to (c) of this rule and be adopted by local rule of court.

(C) **Assignment system.** In each multi-judge municipal or county court, cases may be assigned to an individual judge or to a particular session of court pursuant to the following system:

(1) **Particular session.** A particular session of court is one in which cases are assigned by subject category rather than by the individual assignment system. The following subject categories shall be disposed of by particular session:

(a) Civil cases in which a motion for default judgment is made;
(b) Criminal cases in which a plea of guilty or no contest is entered;
(c) Initial appearance in criminal cases;
(d) Preliminary hearings in criminal cases;
(e) Criminal cases in which an immediate trial is conducted upon initial appearance;
(f) Small claims cases;
(g) Forcible entry and detainer cases in which the right to trial by jury is waived or not demanded.

(2) Assignment. Cases not subject to assignment in a particular session shall be assigned using the individual assignment system. Civil cases shall be assigned under division (C)(2) of this rule when an answer is filed or when a motion, other than one for default judgment, is filed. Criminal cases shall be assigned under division (C)(2) of this rule when a plea of not guilty is entered.

(3) Duration of assignment to particular session. The administrative judge shall equally apportion particular session assignments among all judges. A judge shall not be assigned to a particular session of court for more than two consecutive weeks.

(D) Assignment of refiled cases. In any instance where a previously filed and dismissed case is refiled, that case shall be reassigned to the judge originally assigned by lot to hear it unless, for good cause shown, that judge is precluded from hearing the case.

(E) Assignment—new judicial positions. After the date of election, but prior to the first day of the term of a new judicial position, the administrative judge of a court or division through a random selection of pending cases shall equitably reassign cases pending in the court or division between or among the judges of the court or division and shall create a docket similar to a representative docket. Reassignment shall be completed in a manner consistent with this rule and may exclude criminal cases and cases scheduled for trial. Any matters arising in cases assigned to the docket for the new judicial position prior to the date on which the judge elected to that position takes office shall be resolved by the administrative judge or assigned to another judge.

Commentary (July 1, 1997)

This rule merges the provisions of former C.P. Sup. R. 4 and M.C. Sup. R. 3 into a single rule governing the assignment of cases pursuant to the individual assignment system.

Rule 36(A) Designation of trial attorney

Rule 36(A) requires attorneys who are to serve as trial counsel in either civil or criminal cases to notify the court of that fact. Notification in civil cases is accomplished by designation of the trial attorney on all pleadings. In criminal cases, immediately upon being retained or appointed, the trial attorney is required to file a written notification of the attorney's retention or appointment with the clerk of court.

Rule 36(B)(1) Individual assignment

The individual assignment system is defined by the rule as a system whereby, upon the filing or transfer of a civil case, or upon arraignment in a criminal case, the case is immediately assigned to a judge of the court. The rule sets forth three purposes of the individual assignment system. All multi-judge divisions of the court of common pleas and all multi-judge municipal and county courts, except as provided in division (C)(2) of the rule, are required to adopt the individual assignment system. Courts or divisions are permitted to deviate from the individual assignment system only if the modifications satisfy the three stated purposes of the system and are adopted by local rule of court pursuant to Rule 5. Permissible modifications include the assignment and consideration of cases involving the same criminal defendant, parties, family members, or subject-matter.

The distinguishing feature of the individual assignment system is that it places responsibility upon one judge for the disposition of cases. Once a case is assigned to a judge under this system, all matters pertaining to the case are to be submitted to that judge for determination. An exception is made where that judge is unavailable. In that instance, the administrative judge may act in the assigned judge's absence.

Under Rule 36(B), the administrative judge is responsible for the assignment of cases to the individual judges of the court. Assignment may be made by the administrative judge personally or by court personnel at the administrative judge's direction. All assignments of cases to individual judges must be made by lot.

The purpose of the random assignment, by lot, of cases is to avoid judge-shopping on the part of counsel and to distribute the cases equitably among the judges. "Lot" mandates an assignment arbitrated by chance; the determination must be fortuitous, wholly uncontrolled.

Assignment to the judges of the division in an established order of rotation does not comply with the rule, even if the order of rotation is altered periodically.

An acceptable method of assignment is a form of drawing from a pool of the names of the judges, using paper, balls, or other objects as lots or counter. The pea pool system or the bingo cage are examples. To be an assignment by lot, the entire base of the number of judges in the division must be utilized in each assignment.

A computer may be used for lot selection as long as random assignment is maintained.

Assignment by lot can be systematized. Judges can be identified by number. Those numbers can then be arranged in random order by chance over any given range of numbers. The greater the range, the greater the validity of the arrangement. The range of numbers might well represent the total of three years or so of filings. Slips of paper are then printed with serial control numbers on the front and a line for writing in a case number upon assignment. The judges' numbers are printed in the order of their lot determination on the back of the serially arranged slips. The slips are then padded so that the judges' numbers may not be seen. The evidence of the selection or printing list shall not be revealed. When a case is to be assigned, a slip is removed, the case number written on it, the code number of an individual judge is revealed, and a control sheet maintained.

The practice of making no assignment until "X" number of cases have accumulated when there are "X" number of judges, merely provides for assignment by lot within a very small control and the operation of chance is minimized. That method is only a modified form of rotation and is not assignment by lot.

Once a case is assigned to an individual judge, by lot, it may be reassigned or transferred to another judge by order of the administrative judge. See the Instructions for Preparation concerning the proper use and reporting of transfers.

Although many ancillary matters, and in fact the entire case, frequently may be handled by a magistrate, the assignment system mandates responsibility for every case be affixed to a judge. The assigned judge's report form will reflect action taken by the magistrate.

See Rule 43(E) and its commentary concerning how the numbering system is geared to the record keeping requirements of the individual assignment system.

Rule 36(C) Assignment system

In multi-judge municipal and county courts, Rule 36(C) establishes a dual system for the assignment of cases. Under this system, certain types of cases are processed in a court session, designated particular session, presided over by a judge or magistrate for a specified period of time. Other types of cases are assigned to an individual judge pursuant to the individual assignment system.

Rule 36(C)(1) and (2) Particular session; assignment

The types of cases designated in division (C)(1) for disposition in particular sessions of court are high volume cases that may be processed by a judge or magistrate at a single session. The rule does not preclude the processing of types of cases, other than those listed, that are susceptible to disposition in particular sessions.

Cases that may not be processed by particular session are civil cases where an answer is filed or a motion, other than one for default judgment, is filed and criminal cases in which a plea of not guilty is entered. These cases are to be assigned pursuant to the individual assignment system at the time the answer, motion, or plea is filed or made.

Rule 36(C)(3) Duration of assignment to particular session

Assignments to particular session are to be equally divided among the judges of the court and are to be limited to two-week periods. The two week limitation accommodates the individual assignment system, and allows each judge adequate time to work on the cases individually assigned to the judge. Judges should not be assigned to a particular session or a series of particular sessions for more than two consecutive weeks.

Rule 36(D) Assignment of refiled cases

To promote judicial economy and discourage judge-shopping, this division mandates that all dismissed and subsequently refiled cases be reassigned to the originally assigned judge. An exception exists for circumstances in which the original judge is barred from hearing the refiled case.

Rule 36(E) Assignment—new judicial positions.

This provision governs the reassignment of pending cases where a new judicial position is added to the court or division. Reassignment of cases must be random, equitable, and accomplished in a manner consistent with the principles set forth in division (B)(1) of the rule. In effect, a random selection system must be used, rather than culling cases from pending dockets. Certain dockets or portions of dockets may be created through the individual assignment system. This method may be particularly useful in assigning criminal cases. The process set forth in division (E) should facilitate the creation of a balanced docket with a minimum disruption of the pending caseload of the court or division.

RULE 39. Case Time Limits.

(A) Appellate and civil case time limits. The time limits for disposition of appellate and civil cases shall be as indicated on the Supreme Court report forms.

(B) Criminal case time limits. (1) In common pleas court, all criminal cases shall be tried within six months of the date of arraignment on an indictment or information. In municipal and county court, all criminal cases shall be tried within the time provided in Chapter 2945. of the Revised Code. Whenever a hearing or trial time is extended or shortened pursuant to section 2945.72 of the Revised Code or Criminal Rule 5 or 45, the judge shall state the reason for the change in an order and journalize the order.

(2) Grand jury proceedings. When an accused has been bound over to a grand jury and no final action is taken by the grand jury within sixty days after the date of the bindover, the court or the administrative judge of the court shall dismiss the charge unless for good cause shown the prosecuting attorney is granted a continuance for a definite period of time.

(3) Felony preliminary hearing. A preliminary hearing in a felony case shall be held within one month of the date of arrest or the date of issuance of the summons.

(4) Sentencing. Provided the defendant in a criminal case is available, the court shall impose sentence or hold a sentencing hearing with all parties present within fifteen days of the verdict or finding of guilt or receipt of a completed pre-sentence investigation report. Any failure to meet this time standard shall be reported to the administrative judge, who shall take the necessary corrective action. In a single judge division, the failure shall be reported by the judge to the Court Statistical Reporting Section, which shall refer the matter to the Chief Justice for corrective action.

(5) Post-conviction relief petitions; death penalty cases. All post-conviction relief petitions filed in death penalty cases shall be ruled upon within one hundred eighty days of the date of filing. In any month where a post-conviction relief petition in a death penalty case is filed, pending, or terminated, the administrative judge shall submit the Post-Conviction Relief Petition Report detailing the status of the petition.

(C) Reporting. Any failure to comply with the time limits specified in this rule, and the reason for the failure, shall be reported immediately to the administrative judge, who shall take the necessary corrective action. In a single-judge court or division, the failure shall be reported by the judge to the Court Statistical Reporting Section. The Section shall report to the Chief

Justice, who may take such action as may be necessary to cause the delinquent case to be tried forthwith.

Commentary (July 1, 1997)

Rule 39 consolidates the time limits contained in former C.P. Sup. R. 8 and 8.01 and M.C. Sup. R. 5. The provisions of C.P. Sup. R. 8.01(B) have been moved to Rule 42. Division (B)(5) is a new time guideline and reporting requirement.

The time limits applicable to criminal cases are for the purpose of facilitating the prompt disposition of criminal cases. These time limits in no way affect the statutorily mandated limits contained in R.C. 2945.71. However, the failure to dispose of cases within these time guidelines may result in intervention by the Chief Justice. While the administrative guidelines set out in Rule 8(B) are keyed to the date of arraignment, the requirement of R.C. 2945.71 begins to run from the date of arrest.

Although criminal cases are not reported as filed on Common Pleas Form A until the accused is arraigned on an indictment or information, the responsibility of the court of common pleas for the processing of the case beings upon receipt of the papers in the case pursuant to Crim. R. 5(B)(7). When no final action has been taken by a grand jury within sixty days after bindover, the court or administrative judge should dismiss the charge unless the prosecutor is, for good cause, granted a continuance. The key date for purposes of division (B)(2) is the date of bindover. Thus, the summoning of a grand jury under Crim. R. 8 should not be unduly delayed. Although R.C. 2945.71 does not mandate a time limit for completion of the grand jury process, the statutory time limit runs from the date of arrest, including time taken in the grand jury process.

The dismissal contemplated by division (B)(2) is not a dismissal with prejudice.

Crim. R. 5(B)(1) provides time guidelines for preliminary hearings only. Crim. R. 5(A)(2) and 5(B)(1) each contain provisions pertaining to the extension of preliminary hearing time limits. Crim. R. 45(A) explains the method to be used in computing time. Crim. R. 45(B) provides for the enlargement or reduction of time provisions.

Division (B)(1) provides for the journalization of all actions taken pursuant to section 2945.72 of the Revised Code, Crim. R. 5(A)(2), 5(B)(1) or 45(B), which either extend or shorten the time periods provided in section 2945.71 of the Revised Code or Crim. R. 5. The journal entry must include the fact of the extension or shortening of time and a statement of the reasons therefor to provide a record should any question arise concerning compliance with section 2945.71 of the Revised Code.

Rule 39(B)(4) Sentencing

If the defendant is available, the court must take action within fifteen days of the verdict or finding of guilty or within fifteen days of the receipt of a completed presentence investigation report. This action may be to impose sentence, to place on probation, or to hold a hearing on the report.

Although R.C. 2945.71 is satisfied if the accused is brought to trial within the appropriate period from arrest, the Form A report keys termination to the sentencing or granting of probation. Thus, the six month guidelines contained on the report form includes any period of time between the commencement of trial and the imposition of sentence.

Failure to meet the time standard of this section must be reported to the administrative judge for corrective action. In a single judge division, any failure is to be reported to the Court Statistical Reporting Section of the Supreme Court.

The fifteen day time limit of division (B)(4) should not be confused with the requirement of Rule 7 that the journal entry be made within thirty days of the judgment.

Rule 39(B)(5) Post-conviction relief petitions; death penalty cases

Prior to July 1997, no reporting requirements existed for post-conviction relief petitions, and these petitions were treated as motions in previously terminated cases. In view of the public policies reflected by the November 1994 constitutional amendment abolishing intermediate appeals in death penalty cases and legislation affecting post-conviction relief actions (Am. Sub. S.B. 4 of the 121st General Assembly, effective September 21, 1995), it is imperative that courts provide timely consideration of death penalty cases and ensuing post-conviction relief petitions in those cases. To assist in the management of post-conviction relief petitions in death penalty cases, division (B)(5) of this rule establishes a one hundred eighty day time guideline for the disposition of these petitions and provides for the monthly reporting of the status of the petitions. The one hundred eighty day time guideline is identical to the guideline contained in Rule 35 of the Ohio Rules of Criminal Procedure, effective July 1, 1997.

Although the assigned judge is ultimately responsible for the termination of the case and is so designated on the report form, the administrative judge is responsible for tracking and reporting the status of these petitions.

Rule 39(C) Reporting

The time limits imposed by this rule are for administrative purposes only. Failure to comply with these time limits does not give rise to the sanctions imposed by R.C. 2945.73. However, failure to dispose of cases within these time limits may result in the intervention of the administrative judge and the Chief Justice.

The reports required by this rule should be submitted monthly to the administrative judge or the Court Statistical Reporting Section. A case should be listed on this report for each month during which it is delinquent.

Although no specific form is prescribed for this report, it should contain, at a minimum, the style of the case, the offense charged, the date of its filing, an explanation of the delay in disposition, and the date on which it is anticipated that the case will be completed.

Failure to meet the time standard of this section must be reported to the administrative judge for corrective action. In a single-judge division, any failure is to be reported to the Court Statistical Reporting Section of the Supreme Court.

GENERAL INDEX

References are to Revised Code Section numbers;
Crim. R. refers to the Criminal Rules; EvR refers to the Evidence Rules;
Juv. R. refers to the Juvenile Rules; SupR refers to the Superintendence Rules; Traf. R. refers to the Traffic Rules

ABANDONED BUILDING, 3767.41

ABANDONMENT
attempt, of, as affirmative defense, 2923.01
child, of, 2919.21
child, of, jurisdiction of county court judge, 2931.02
conspiracy, of, 2923.01
court order, in violation of, 2919.21
parent, of, when prohibited, 2919.21
property, of, disposal by law enforcement agency, 2933.41
prosecution, of, for consideration, prohibited, 2921.21
spouse, of, prohibited, 2919.21

ABATEMENT
nuisance, of—*see* NUISANCES
plea in, abolished, Crim. R. 12
    trial time extended by, 2945.72

ABDUCTION, 2905.02

ABETTING—*see* COMPLICITY, 2923.03

ABORTION
abortion manslaughter, 2919.13
abortion trafficking, 2919.14
complaint, 2151.85
consent form, 2317.56
defined, 2919.11
dilation and extraction procedure—
    civil liability, 2307.51
    criminal liability, 2919.15
discipline by state medical board, 2317.56
information to be provided to woman prior to, 2317.56
medical emergency or necessity, 2317.56
post-viability abortion—
    civil liability, 2307.52
    definitions, 2919.16
    failure to perform viability testing, 2919.18
    terminating or attempting to terminate human pregnancy after viability, 2919.17
publication of information materials by state agencies, 2317.56
unlawful, 2919.12
unmarried minor may seek without notice to parent, guardian or custodian, 2151.85

ABSENT WITNESS
deposition of, use of, Crim. R. 15
preservation of testimony of, 2945.49

ABUSE
child, of, 2919.22—*see also* CHILD
corpse, of, 2927.01
discretion, of, as cause for new trial, 2945.79
drug, 2925.11—*see also* DRUG
patient, resident of care facility, 2903.33 et seq

ABUSING HARMFUL INTOXICANTS, 2925.31

ACCIDENT
as cause for new trial, Crim. R. 33; 2945.79
hampering officer, fireman, etc., at, 2917.13

ACCOMPLICE
property subject of attempt, loses possession right, 2933.41

ACCUSED—*see* DEFENDANT

ACKNOWLEDGEMENTS
peace officer, by, 2935.08.1

ACQUITTAL
convict, of another offense, serves remaining sentence, 2941.43
higher offense, of, effect re lesser included offenses, 2943.09
motion for judgment of, Crim. R. 29
one count, of, not acquittal of any other, 2941.04

ACTION, CRIMINAL
commencement, docketing, of, Crim. R. 55

ACT, OVERT, RE CONSPIRACY, 2923.01

ACTUAL INCARCERATION—*see also* SENTENCE, *at* mandatory prison term
driving under the influence, 4511.99, 4511.99.1

ADMINISTER, DEFINED, 3719.01

ADMINISTRATIVE
judge, to appoint substitute judge, Crim. R. 25
orders, right of appeal from, 2953.02
release, 2967.01, 2967.17

ADMISSIBILITY—*see also* EVIDENCE
depositions, of, Crim. R. 15
pleas of guilty, no contest, not accepted by court, Crim. R. 11

ADMISSION
pretrial conference, by defense at, when used, Crim. R. 17.1

ADOPTION
hearings to be closed; confidentiality, 3107.17
penalty, 3107.99

ADOPTIVE PARENT
abandonment, nonsupport, of, 2919.21

ADULT CABARETS
appeals, 503.57
application for permit, 503.54
definitions, 503.51
deposit, use of fees, 503.58
duty to obtain permit, 503.53
expiration of permit, 503.54
notice of orders, 503.57
penalties, 503.59
procedure for adopting regulations, amendments, 503.52
prohibitions, 503.53
reasons for denial or revocation of permit, 503.55
   hearing not required, 503.57
records of proceedings, 503.57
requirements that may be imposed on cabaret, 503.56
resolution to regulate, require registration, 503.52

ADULT CARE FACILITIES
criminal records check for certain employees, 3722.15.1
   access to records, 2950.08, 2953.32
   procedure for checking, 109.57, 109.57.2

ADULTERATION AND MISBRANDING
contaminating substance for human consumption or use, 2927.24
jurisdiction of county court, 2931.02
spreading false report of contamination, 2927.24

ADVERTISING
drug paraphernalia, 2925.14
facsimile device, transmitting to, 4931.55
obscene material, performance, of, as pandering, 2907.32
property held by law enforcement agency, for owner, 2933.41

AFFIDAVIT
charging misdemeanor, when process need not issue, 2935.10
charging one as fugitive from justice, extradition purposes, 2963.11
dead bodies, search for, 2933.30
degree, elements, of offense charged, effect of omitting, 2945.75
forms re, 2935.19
   authority of supreme court to prescribe, 2935.17

AFFIDAVIT—Continued
initiating prosecution, procedure, 2935.09, 2935.10
motions may be supported by, Crim. R. 47
new trial, re, Crim. R. 33; 2945.81
nonconsensual entry, waiver of statutory precondition for, 2933.23.1
preliminary hearing transcript, to accompany, Crim. R. 5
prosecution by, misdemeanors, 2941.35
search warrant, for, Crim. R. 41; 2933.23
surety of bail, of, Crim. R. 46; 2937.24
venue change, original transmitted to receiving court, 2931.29
warrant, arrest filed with complaint re, Crim. R. 4
warrantless arrest for misdemeanor, 2935.05

AFFINITY, RELATION BY
jurors, of, to party, challenge for, Crim. R. 24

AFFIRMATION
falsification, re offense of, 2921.13
jurors to be examined under, Crim. R. 24
perjury, re, 2921.11

AGE
aggravated murder prosecution, effect on, 2929.02.2, 2929.02.3, 2929.03, 2929.05
corruption of a minor, effect on, 2907.04
endangering children, 2919.22
firearms, re sale, furnishing of, 2923.21
importuning, effect on, 2907.07
matter harmful to juveniles—
   displaying, 2907.31.1
   disseminating, 2907.31
nudity-oriented performance involving minor, 2909.32.3
obscenity, pandering, 2907.32
   minor, involving, 2907.32.1
ordnance, dangerous, for license, 2923.18
prostitution—
   compelling, 2907.21
   promoting, 2907.22
rape, effect on, 2907.02
service of subpoena, re, Crim. R. 17
sexual imposition, effect on, 2907.05, 2907.06
sexual penetration, effect on, 2907.12
sexually oriented material involving a minor, pandering, 2907.32.2
pandering, 2907.32.2

AGED, AID FOR
falsification to obtain, 2921.13

AGENT
improperly handling infections, 2917.47
organization, of, when may prosecute for offense, 2901.24
personating government, 2913.44

AGGRAVATED OFFENSES—*see* particular offense

AIDS, HIV
blood, contaminated, selling or donating, 2927.13
engaging in prostitution after positive test, 2907.25
engaging in solicitation after positive test, 2907.24
harassment by inmate, 2921.38
loitering to engage in solicitation after positive test, 2907.24.1
testing of accused for, 2907.27, 2907.28

AIRCRAFT
communications, disrupting, 2909.04
defraud, hiring to, 2913.41
disorderly conduct, operating while drunk, drugged, is not, 2917.11
endangering craft or airport operations, 2909.08
homicide by, 2903.07
   aggravated, 2903.06
operating under influence of controlled substance, 4561.15
structure, as occupied, re arson, 2909.01
unauthorized use of, 2913.03
used in transaction involving contraband, construed contraband, 2933.42
   seizure of; notice, disposition, 2933.43
venue when offense, element committed in, 2901.11
weapon, carrying concealed, aboard, 2923.12

ALARMS, MAKING FALSE, 2917.32

ALCOHOL, ALCOHOLICS—*see also* INTOXICATED
challenge of juror, as, Crim. R. 24
commitment of, 2935.33
felony sentencing consideration, 2929.12
firearm, dangerous ordnance—
   possession by chronic, prohibited, 2923.13
   relief from disability re, void for chronic, 2923.14
request to health care provider for results of alcohol test for use in criminal proceedings, 2317.02, 2317.02.2
treatment, 2929.51, 2935.33, 2951.04, 2951.04.1
watercraft, operating under influence of, 1547.11, 1547.99

ALCOHOL AND DRUG ADDICTION SERVICES DEPARTMENT
duty to report abuse, neglect or exploitation of patient, 5101.61
juveniles, related forfeiture used for programs, 2933.44

ALIAS WARRANT, Crim. R. 4

ALIBI, NOTICE OF, Crim. R. 12.1; 2945.58

ALTERNATE JURORS, Crim. R. 24—*see also* JURORS

AMENDMENT
bill of particulars, of, effect, Crim. R. 7; 2941.30
civil rules, of, Crim. R. 54
complaint, of, effect, Crim. R. 7
indictment, information, of, Crim. R. 7; 2941.30
release order, of, Crim. R. 46
statute, of, 1.58

AMMUNITION
interstate transactions in, when permissible, 2923.22

ANABOLIC STEROIDS
abuse, 2925.11
athletic facilities, posting in, 3707.50
illegal administration or distribution, 2925.06
schools, posting in, 3313.75.2
trafficking, 2925.03

ANIMALS
assaulting police dog or horse or handicapped assistance dog, 2921.32.1
carcasses, 3767.16, 3767.18
   exceptions, 3767.22
cruelty to, 2931.02
   humane society may employ attorney, 2931.18
dogfighting, animal fighting, offenses re, 959.15, 959.16, 959.99
escaped; duty to report, 2927.21
running at large, 951.01, 951.02, 951.99

ANTIQUE
simulating object to resemble, prohibited, 2913.32
value of, re theft offense, 2913.61

APPEAL
abatement plea, of issues formerly raised by, Crim. R. 12
applicability of Criminal Rules to, exception, Crim. R. 1
arrest of judgment motion, re issues in, Crim. R. 12
capital cases, in—
   judgment affirmed, procedure, 2953.07
   no release pending, Crim. R. 12
constitutional provisions re jurisdiction of supreme court and courts of appeals, Art. IV, §§ 2, 3 OC
costs of—
   appeal cost oversight committee, 2953.08
   defendant entitled to, without paying, Crim. R. 32; 2941.51
   documents necessary for, provided to indigent, Crim. R. 32
counsel—
   assignment of, for defendant, Crim. R. 32, 44
   indigents, for, Crim. R. 32
court of appeals, to, 2953.02
demurrer, of issues formerly raised by, Crim. R. 12
designation of record on, service of, Crim. R. 49

APPEAL—*Continued*
dismissal of charge, from, by state, Crim. R. 12
dispositions of, procedure, 2953.07
habeas corpus proceedings, re, 2725.02, 2725.26
new trial, motion for, re, Crim. R. 33
notice of—
    defendant entitled to timely filing of, Crim. R. 32
ordinance, conviction of violation of, 2953.02
preliminary hearing finding requiring trial, no, Crim. R. 5
probation, from order of, 2951.10
quash, of issues formerly raised by motion to, Crim. R. 12
release after notice of, Crim. R. 46
sentence—
    contrary to law, of, 2953.07
    defendant to be advised of right to, at, Crim. R. 32
    felony, grounds for, 2953.08
state, by, 2945.67
    felony sentence, 2953.08
    reversal of conviction, in appellate court, to next higher court, 2953.14
    suppress, granting of motion, of, Crim. R. 12
statement, preserving in court records for—
    defendant, by, Crim. R. 16
    denial, deferring, restricting discovery, by counsel re, Crim. R. 16
    prosecuting attorney, by, Crim. R. 16
    suppress, motion to, re, Crim. R. 12
supreme court of Ohio, to, 2953.02
transcript of proceedings, Crim. R. 32

APPEARANCE
bond, Crim. R. 46 *et seq*
docket, Crim. R. 55
initial, Crim. R. 5

APPLICABILITY OF RULES OF CRIMINAL PROCEDURE, Crim. R. 1

APPREHENSION OF CRIMINAL
law enforcement officer, failing to make, 2921.44
means of avoiding, providing, 2921.32
warning of impending, 2921.32

APPROPRIATION
exceeding, creating deficiency, by public official, 2921.44

ARBITRATOR, AS PUBLIC SERVANT, 2921.02

ARRAIGNMENT
explanation of rights, Crim. R. 10
presence of defendant, at, Crim. R. 10
procedure at, Crim. R. 10; 2937.03 *et seq*, 2943.01 *et seq*

ARRAY, CHALLENGE TO, Crim. R. 24

ARREST, Crim. R. 4; 2935.01 *et seq*
bureau of criminal identification and investigation investigator, by, 109.54.1
criminal justice network, 5502.01
domestic violence offenses, 2935.03, 2935.03.2
forcible entry of dwelling, to effect, 2935.12
highways, on, power to make, 4513.39
pardon or parole violator, of, 2941.46
private citizen, by, 2935.04, 2935.04.1, 2935.06, 2935.07
probationer, of, 2941.46, 2951.08, 2951.09
resisting, 2921.33
rights of arrestee, 2935.14, 2935.20
sham legal process, 2921.52
warrantless, Crim. R. 4; 2935.03, 2935.05
    arrestee to be informed of cause, 2935.07
    felony drug abuse offenses, re, 2935.03
    fugitive from justice, of, 2963.12
    warrant to issue, 2935.08
warrant, with, Crim. R. 4
    after indictment, 2941.36, 2941.37
    escape after jury sworn, 2941.38
    extradition proceedings, 2963.07, 2963.19
    outstanding municipal or county court—
        driver's license ineligibility, 4507.09.1

ARREST OF JUDGMENT, Crim. R. 34; 2947.02 *et seq*
appeal of issues formerly raised by motion for, Crim. R. 12

ARSON AND RELATED OFFENSES, 2909.01 *et seq*
aggravated arson, 2909.02
arson, 2909.03
criminal damaging or endangering, 2909.06
criminal mischief, 2909.07
definitions, re, 2909.01
determining property value or amount of physical harm, 2909.11
reimbursement by offender for costs incurred by agency in investigation, prosecution of offense, 2929.28
restitution, 2929.11, 2929.21
vandalism, 2909.05

ART WORK
desecration of, 2927.11

ASSAULT, 2903.11 *et seq*
police dog or horse or handicapped assistance dog, 2921.32.1
vehicular, 2903.08

ASSEMBLY, RIGHT OF, Art. I, § 3 OC

ASSIGNMENT OF COUNSEL—*see* COUNSEL

ATHLETIC FACILIITES
anabolic steroids, notice re
    colleges, 3345.41

ATHLETIC FACILIITES—*Continued*
anabolic steroids, notice re—*Continued*
   private and public, 3707.50
   schools, 3313.75.2
   universities, 3345.41

ATTEMPT, 2923.02
conviction of, after not guilty verdict, Crim. R. 31
defendant may be found guilty of, when such attempt is an offense at law, 2945.74
included offense, as, Crim. R. 31
killing, while attempting certain crimes, as aggravating circumstance, 2929.04

ATTENDANCE
defendant, of—*see* PRESENCE OF DEFENDANT
witness, of, civil procedure to govern, 2945.46

ATTORNEY—*see also* COUNSEL
assignment—
   capital cases, SupR 20, SupR 21, SupR 22
   designation of trial attorney, SupR 36(A)
conviction of, or dismissal of charge on technical or procedural grounds, 2929.17
drug offense, convicted of, 2925.38
grand jury, disclosure of matters before, when, Crim. R. 6
intimidation, 2921.03, 2921.04
retaliation against, 2921.05
service of papers on, when, how made, Crim. R. 49
subpoena, service, return by, Crim. R. 17
surety on bail, may not be, Crim. R. 46

ATTORNEY-CLIENT PRIVILEGE, 2317.02, 2317.02.1, 2921.22

ATTORNEY GENERAL
advancement of state actions on docket, 109.20
annual report, 109.21
antitrust section, 109.82
   attorney for political subdivisions, 109.81
   arrest authority of, investigator, 109.54.1
assistant attorney general—
   appointment, 109.03
   duties, 109.03
auditor of state may request action to secure compliance, 117.42
audit revealing shortage in office of, 117.31
bill of exceptions, may file, 2945.67
bond, 109.06
building contract enforcement, 153.20
bureau of criminal identification and investigation—
   DNA laboratory, database, 109.57.3, 109.99
   chiefs of police, duties to take fingerprints, 109.60
   cooperation, interstate, national and international, 109.62
   coordination of law enforcement activities, 109.55
   creation, 109.51

ATTORNEY GENERAL—*Continued*
bureau of criminal identification, etc.—*Continued*
   descriptions, fingerprints, and photographs sent to bureau by sheriffs and chiefs of police, 109.61
   DNA laboratory, database, 109.57.3, 109.99
   emergency assistance, 109.54.1
   equipment, 109.53
   felony precludes or terminates employment as investigator or special agent, 109.51.1
   fingerprint impression sheet, superintendent to prepare, 109.58
   furnishings, 109.53
   intergovernmental cooperation, 109.54
   investigator assistance to law enforcement officer, 109.54.1
   operations, 109.52
   records—
      descriptive measurement, 109.59
      fingerprint impression, 109.59
   reports, sheriffs and chiefs of police, 109.60
   sex offender registration duties, 2950.13—*see also* SEXUAL PREDATORS, HABITUAL SEX OFFENDERS, SEXUALLY ORIENTED OFFENDERS
   sex offenders, duties re—*see* SEXUAL PREDATORS, HABITUAL SEX OFFENDERS, SEXUALLY ORIENTED OFFENDERS
   sheriff's duty to take fingerprints, 109.60
   superintendent of bureau and assistants may testify in court, 109.63
   superintendent of bureau, duties, 109.57
   training local law enforcement authorities, 109.56
charitable bingo, duties re—*see* BINGO
charitable trusts administration, 109.23 *et seq*
   administration, acts prohibited, 109.23.1
   amendment of trust, 109.23.2
   assistants, 109.33
   charitable trust, defined, 109.23
   enforcement, 109.24
   fees, 109.31
   information, 109.29
   moneys paid into charitable foundations fund, 109.32
   notice to attorney general, 109.30
   notice to beneficiaries after probate of will, 109.30
   penalty, 109.99
   proceedings, necessary parties, 109.25
   register, 109.26
   register, inspection, 109.28
   rules, 109.27
   trustee's report, 109.31
chief counsel, appointment, duties, 109.03
children, criminal records check and fingerprinting of persons having frequent contact with, 109.57.2
claims special account, 109.08.1
contracts, forms 109.15
costs, security not required from state, 109.19
court order fund, 109.11.1

ATTORNEY GENERAL—Continued
crisis intervention training for peace officers, 109.74.1
domestic violence training, 109.74.3
duties, 109.02
election, 109.01
employees, 109.05
escheat matters, attorney general as agent, 109.41
expositions commission duties, 109.12.2
firearm requalification programs, 109.74.3, 109.80.1
first assistant, 109.04
Franklin county, suits may be brought, 109.16
general assembly may require written opinions, 109.13
health care, nonprofit entities to obtain approval for certain transfers, 109.34, 109.35, 109.99
investigation of abuse or neglect of care facility patient, 109.86
investigation of demand for extradition, 2963.04
land title review, opinion, 109.12.1
legal advisor—
    boards, 109.12
    state officers, 109.12
lobbying violations, may investigate, 101.79
medicaid, investigations, 109.85
missing children, duties re, 109.64, 109.65
money laundering investigations, 1315.54
obscenity laws, compilation and distribution, 109.40
official bonds, actions, 109.09
organized crime, may investigate, 109.83, 177.01 et seq
peace officer training council—see PEACE OFFICER TRAINING COUNCIL
periodic information bulletin concerning missing children, 109.64
pleadings, verification, 109.19
post-audit action to recover public money or property, 117.30, 117.35
powers re grand jury, 2939.10
problem resolution officers re taxes, 109.08.2
prosecuting attorneys, attorney general may advise, 109.14
quo warranto proceedings, 109.10
registers shall be kept, 109.22
salary, 141.01
service by publication, 109.18
special counsel, 109.07
    claims, collections, 109.08, 109.08.1
special grand jury, duties as to, 2939.17
state officer or employee, duty to defend in civil action, 109.36-109.36.6
victims of crime—
    assistance programs, 109.91, 109.92
    bill of rights pamphlet, 109.42, 2743.19.1
    neighborhood organization may employ attorney to assist crime victims, 122.95
workers' compensation investigations, 109.84
writs, other counties, 109.17
written opinions, general assembly may require, 109.13

AUCTION, PUBLIC
firearm, sold by law enforcement agency at, when, 2933.41
unclaimed, forfeited property, may be sold by, 2933.41

AUTHORITY, RESISTING LAWFUL, 2921.35

AUTOPSY, CORONER'S DUTIES AS TO, 313.09, 313.12.1-313.13

BAD TIME
added to prison term for violation, 2929.01, 2967.11

BAIL, Crim. R. 46
additional court costs added to, 2949.09.1
amount of, 2937.23
appeal, 2953.03
appeal to supreme court, procedure, 2953.09, 2953.10
arraignment, provision for, to be made upon, 2937.03
arrest upon warrant, after, Crim. R. 4
bond—
    deposition of witness committed for failure to give, Crim. R. 15
constitutional provisions, re, Art. I, § 9 OC
domestic violence cases; consideration in setting, 2919.25.1, 2937.23
extradition proceedings, 2963.14-2963.16
firearms, relief from disability re, as grounds for, 2923.14
forfeit of, procedure, 2937.35 et seq
initial appearance, judge shall admit to, on, Crim. R. 5
menacing by stalking, 2903.21.2
misdemeanor cases, 2935.15
motion for new trial, 2953.03
notice of appeal, 2953.03
probation revocation hearing, prior to, Crim. R. 32.3
purpose of, 2937.22
receipt for, 2937.22
release of, 2937.40
return of, 2937.41
sentencing, pending, court may admit to, Crim. R. 32
stalking, menacing by, 2903.21.2
surety for, oath, affidavit, 2937.24
transfer from common pleas court for trial, re, Crim. R. 21
unbailable offenses, procedure, 2937.32
upon charge of misdemeanor or violation of ordinance, 2935.10

BAILIFF
criminal, 2301.15-2301.17
subpoena, service, return by, Crim. R. 17
venue change, fees re, originating jurisdiction pays, Crim. R. 18; 2931.31

BANKS—CRIMES AND PROHIBITED ACTIVITIES
concealment of assets, 1127.13

BANKS—CRIMES, ETC.—*Continued*
false communications, 1127.09
falsifications, forgery, counterfeiting, 1127.08
impeding official, 1127.13
penalties, 1127.99

BARGAINING, PLEA, Crim. R. 11

BARRIERS TO LIMITED ACCESS HIGHWAYS, 3767.20.1

BATTERED WOMAN SYNDROME
evaluation of mental condition, 2945.37.1
generally, 2901.06
NGRI—
    evaluation, relevant to, 2945.39
    evidence relevant to determination, 2945.39.2

BATTERY, SEXUAL, 2907.03—*see also* SEXUAL BATTERY

BEER
keeping place where sold or furnished illegally, 4399.09
restriction on sale of, 4301.21, 4301.22

BETTING—*see also* GAMBLING AND RELATED OFFENSES
bookmaking, 2915.02
cheating, 2915.05
defined, 2915.01
gaming, public, when prohibited, 2915.04
livelihood, as, prohibited, 2915.02

BICYCLES, MOTORIZED
rules for operating, 4511.52.1

BICYCLES, TRAFFIC LAWS RE, 4511.52 *et seq*

BIGAMY, 2919.01

BILL OF INFORMATION—*see* INDICTMENTS, INFORMATIONS

BILL OF LADING, VALUE RE THEFT OF, 2913.61

BILL OF PARTICULARS, Crim. R. 7; 2941.07
amending, Crim. R. 7; 2941.30

BINGO
amusement only, exempted from provisions, 2915.12
application for license, 2915.08
definitions re, 2915.01
persons prohibited from being game operators, 2915.11
records to be kept, 2915.10
rules for conducting, 2915.09
senior centers, at, 173.12.1
who may conduct or advertise, 2915.07

BIRDS, LIVE, TRAPSHOOTING OF, 959.17, 959.99

BLACKJACK, 2923.20

BLIND PERSONS
aid for, falsification to obtain, 2921.13
guide dogs, assaulting, 2921.32.1

BLOCK PARENT SYMBOL, UNAUTHORIZED USE OF, 2917.46

BLOOD, CONTAMINATED, SELLING OR DONATING, 2927.13

BODY CAVITY SEARCH, 2933.32

BOND
appearance, Crim. R. 46
bail, Crim. R. 46
county officials, of, prosecuting attorney to prepare, certify, 309.11
misdemeanors, Crim. R. 46
peace, Crim. R. 1; 2933.01 *et seq*
prosecuting attorney to give, 309.03
traffic arrests, in, driver's license as, 2937.22.1

BOOKMAKING, 2915.02
defined, 2915.01

BOOKS, PAPERS
deposition, order to produce at, Crim. R. 15
discovery, inspection re—
    defendant, from, Crim. R. 16
    prosecuting attorney, from, Crim. R. 16
search warrant, as property re, Crim. R. 41
subpoena, for production of, Crim. R. 17

BRANDS, ANIMAL, ALTERATION OF, 959.12, 959.99

BRASS KNUCKLES, 2923.20

BREAKING AND ENTERING, 2911.13

BREATHALYZER, 4511.19

BRIBERY, 2921.02
contract, public, effect of unlawful interest in, 2921.42
disqualification from public office forever, *(political)* party officials, public servants, upon conviction of, 2921.02
syndicate, criminal, commission by, 2923.04
witness in official proceeding, 2921.02

BRIDGE, LOAD LIMITS OF, 5591.42-5591.44, 5591.99

BROADCASTING BY RADIO, INFORMATION OF CRIME, 2935.32

BROTHEL
evidence of reputation of, admissible re, 2907.26
management, establishment, control of, promoting prostitution, 2907.22
minor under 16, inducing, procuring re, 2907.22
procuring, enticing, soliciting another to patronize as, 2907.23

BUILDING AND LOAN ASSOCIATIONS—*see* SAVINGS AND LOAN ASSOCIATIONS

BUILDINGS
abandoned, 3767.41
definition (*re nuisance*), 3767.41
discovery, inspection of, Crim. R. 16
gambling house, 2915.03, 2915.04
lease, void, 3767.10
lewd purposes, used for, 3767.10
nuisance, constituting, 3767.41
obscenity laws, premises used to violate, 2907.37
receivership, 3767.41
structure, occupied, as, re arson, 2909.01
thieves, resort for, 3767.12

BULK AMOUNT, DEFINED, 2925.01

BURDEN OF PROOF, 2901.05

BUREAU OF NARCOTICS AND DANGEROUS DRUGS, DEFINED, 3719.01

BURGLARY, 2911.11, 2911.12
conspiracy, re, 2923.01
murder during, committing, as aggravating circumstance, 2929.04
tools, possession of, prohibited, 2923.24

BURIAL
marker, place, desecration of, 2909.05

BURNS, DUE TO INCENDIARY DEVICE, ETC., REPORTING, 2921.22

BUSINESS
obstructing official, 2921.31
vandalism to property used in, 2909.05

BUTCHER'S ESTABLISHMENT, 3767.16, 3767.22

CABLE TELEVISION
action by system owner or operator for damages, 2307.62
definitions, 2901.01, 2913.01
possession or sale of unauthorized devices, 2913.04.1

CALENDAR, PRECEDENCE TO CRIMINAL CASES, Crim. R. 50

CANDIDATE FOR PUBLIC OFFICE
assassination of, as aggravating circumstance, 2929.04
defined, 2921.01

CANNON, WHEN NOT DANGEROUS ORDNANCE, 2923.11

CAPITAL OFFENSE—*see also* DEATH PENALTY
appeal re, no release from custody pending, Crim. R. 12
appointment of counsel for indigents, SupR 20, SupR 21, SupR 22
bail in, when not entitled to, Crim. R. 46
charge when committed prior to 1-1-74, 2929.61
defined, 2901.02
guilty plea, court to take testimony upon, Crim. R. 11
joinder of defendants re, when, Crim. R. 14; 2945.20
judgment affirmed by appellate court, procedure, 2953.07
jurors, re—
peremptory challenges, Crim. R. 24; 2945.21
no-contest plea, court to take testimony upon, Crim. R. 11
reimbursement of public defender, 120.35
time of execution, 2947.08

CARDS, PLAYING, AS GAMBLING DEVICE, 2915.01

CARE FACILITY
abuse, neglect of patient or resident, 2903.34
definitions re, 2903.33
false complaint prohibited, 2903.35
license revocation upon conviction, 2903.37
protection for person filing complaint, 2903.36

CARRIERS, WHEN MAY POSSESS DANGEROUS ORDNANCE, 2923.17

CASE FILE
docket number and names of parties, placed upon, Crim. R. 55

CAUSE
challenge to juror for, Crim. R. 24; 2945.25 *et seq*
new trial, for, Crim. R. 33; 2945.79, 2945.83
time—
enlargement by court of, for, Crim. R. 45
service of motion, hearing notice, extended for, Crim. R. 45

CAUSTIC MATERIAL, CRIMINAL DAMAGING, ENDANGERING BY, 2909.06

CEMETERY
burial marker, place, desecration of, 2909.05

CEMETERY—*Continued*
shooting, 3773.05

CHALLENGES TO JURORS
array, to, Crim. R. 24
cause, for, Crim. R. 24; 2945.25 *et seq*
grand jury array or individual jurors, to, Crim. R. 6
peremptory, Crim. R. 24; 2945.22
    capital offense, Crim. R. 24; 2945.21
    magistrate courts, 2938.06

CHANGE OF VENUE, Crim. R. 18; 2901.12, 2931.29 *et seq*

CHARACTER
defendant, of—
    evidence as to, rules, 2945.56 *et seq*
probation, favoring, indicating offender unlikely to repeat, 2951.02
release, conditions of, effect on, Crim. R. 46

CHARGE
defendant to be informed of, at initial appearance, Crim. R. 5
offense committed prior to 1-1-74; third or fourth degree felony committed between 1-1-74 and 7-1-83, 2929.61

CHARGE TO JURY, Crim. R. 30
grand jurors, to, 2939.07
magistrate court, presumption of innocence, reasonable doubt, 2938.08
procedure, 2945.10, 2945.11
proof beyond reasonable doubt to be defined in, 2901.05

CHEATING, RE GAMBLING, CONTEST, 2915.05

CHECKS
blank, theft of, as aggravating circumstance, 2913.71
passing bad, 2913.11
recording credit card, telephone, or social security number, 1349.17, 1349.99

CHEESE FACTORY, REFUSE FROM, 3767.14

CHILD—*see also* JUVENILE COURTS; MINOR
abandonment, nonsupport of, 2919.21
    jurisdiction of county court judge, re, 2931.02
abuse or neglect, 2919.22
    child in domestic violence or homeless shelter, 2151.42.2
    false reports, 2921.14
    reporting, 2151.42.1
aid to dependent, falsification to obtain, 2913.21
contributing to unruliness or delinquency of, 2919.24
corruption of, 2907.04
criminal records check and fingerprinting of employees

CHILD—*Continued*
    responsible for out-of-home child care and prospective adoptive or foster parents, 2151.86
criminal records check and fingerprinting of persons having frequent contact with, 109.57.2
custody of, interference with, 2919.23
custody, permanent; motion by agency for; hearing, 2151.41.3, 2151.41.4
day-care centers, homes, 5104.01.2, 5104.01.3, 5104.09
    criminal records check of persons having contact with, prohibition of certain offenders, 5104.01.2, 5104.01.3
death of, autopsy required, 313.12-313.13
defined, 1.59
endangering, 2919.22
enticement into motor vehicle, 2905.05
head start agencies, criminal records check of persons having contact with, prohibition of certain offenders, 3301.32
importuning of, 2907.07
liability for torts, 3109.09, 3109.10
mentally, physically handicapped, failure to support, alternative remedy, 3113.06, 3113.99
missing, report of; definitions, 2901.30
    cooperation between law enforcement and U.S. attorney general, 2901.31
    improper solicitation for contributions to distribute information re, 2901.32
    parental locator service agreement, 5101.31
murder of as aggravating circumstance, 2903.01, 2929.04, 2941.14
nonsupport of, 2919.21
    jurisdiction of county court judge re, 2931.02
offenses against, humane society may employ attorney, 2931.18
pandering obscenity involving, 2907.32.1
preschool programs, criminal records check of persons having contact with, prohibition of certain offenders, 3301.54.1
rape of, under 13, 2907.02
    life imprisonment for, 2907.02
sexual imposition on, under 13, 2907.05
sexual penetration of, 2907.12
spiritual treatment through prayer, when not endangering, 2919.22
statements of, in abuse cases, EvR 807
support orders, 3113.21.5-3113.21.8
temporary commitment of abused, neglected or dependent child; initial plan; comprehensive reunification plan, 2151.41.2
victim, testifying by deposition, videotaping or televising, 2945.48.1
    bureau of criminal identification and investigation, duties, 109.54
    juvenile court proceedings, 2151.35.11
    preliminary hearing, use at, 2937.11, 2937.15
    statement not hearsay, EvR 807

CHILD—*Continued*
victim, testifying by deposition—*Continued*
   trial, use at, 2945.49

CHILDREN SERVICES, COUNTY
criminal records check for job applicants, employment of certain offenders prohibited, 5153.11.1

CIGARETTES
illegal sale, distribution of, 2927.02

CITATION
minor misdemeanor, for, Crim. Form XIV, 2935.26, 2935.27
minor misdemeanors, as optional procedure re, Crim. R. 4.1
Ohio Rules of Criminal Procedure, style of, Crim. R. 60
prosecution commenced when issued, exception, 2901.13

CITIZEN'S ARREST, 2935.04, 2935.04.1, 2935.06, 2935.07

CITY DIRECTOR OF LAW
assistants for, 733.51
duties as to suits, 733.53
employees, appointment of—
  persons associated in the private practice of law, 2921.42, 2921.42.1
  officers, to serve as legal counsel and attorney for, 733.51
opinions, duty to give, 733.54
prosecutes criminal cases in municipal court, 1901.34
prosecuting attorney in mayor's courts, to serve as, 733.51, 733.52
prosecution of officers, council members, for malfeasance, 733.73
removal of municipal officers, council members, by probate court, duties as to, 733.72, 733.73

CIVIL RECOVERY FOR CRIMINAL ACT, 2307.60, 2307.61

CIVIL RIGHTS
convicted felons, of, 2961.01
interfering with, 2921.45
probation, parole, conditional pardon, effect on, 2951.09, 2961.01

CIVIL RULES
amendment of, effect, Crim. R. 54

CLERGYMAN NOT REQUIRED TO REPORT CRIME, WHEN, 2921.22

CLERK OF COURT
criminal records, duties as to, Crim R. 55

CLERK OF COURT—*Continued*
defined, Crim. R. 2
docket, duties re, Crim. R. 55
indictment, grand jury, 2939.22
  filed with, Crim. R. 6
  report re jurors concurring in, filed with, Crim. R. 6
  sealed, duties re, Crim. R. 6
jury trial, demand for, filed with, Crim. R. 23
preliminary hearing, duties re, Crim. R. 5
release on bail, duties re—
  deposit of cash with, before, Crim. R. 46
  misdemeanor cases, in, by, Crim. R. 46
  order stating conditions of, by, written, Crim. R. 46
search warrant, papers, copies filed with, Crim. R. 41
subpoena, duties re, Crim. R. 17; 2945.45
  grand jury witnesses, 2939.12
summons, duties re, Crim. R. 9
surety, evidence re financial responsibility, may require, Crim. R. 46
transfer from common pleas court for trial, duties re, Crim. R. 21
venue change, duties re, Crim. R. 18; 2931.31
warrant, duties re, Crim. R. 9

COAL
mine, refuse from, 3767.14
oil refinery, refuse from, 3767.14

CODICILS
offenses involving, allegations necessary in indictment or information, 2941.22

COERCION, 2905.12
corrupt activity, engaging in pattern of, 2923.31 *et seq*
murder, aggravated, as mitigating circumstance re, 2929.04

COIN MACHINES
defined, re theft, fraud, 2913.01
slugs, use in, to defraud, 2913.33
tampering with, 2911.32
tobacco products, 2907.02

COLLEGES, ANABOLIC STEROIDS, NOTICE RE, 3345.41

COLLEGES AND UNIVERSITIES
sex offenders in area, notices re, 2950.11

COMMENCEMENT OF ACTION
defined, Crim. R. 55

COMMENT
defendant's failure to testify, 2945.43
guilty plea, no contest plea, not accepted by court, on, Crim. R. 11
witnesses, on list, on failure to call, Crim. R. 16

COMMERCIAL DRIVERS, 4506.01 et seq—see also DRIVER'S LICENSE
alcohol or drug offenses, 4506.15
   disqualification, placement out of service, 4506.16
   duties of peace officer, 4506.23
   implied consent to test, surrender of license, 4506.17
application for license or permit, 4506.07
   fees, 4506.08
   request for donation to second chance trust fund, 4506.08.1
change of address notice, 4506.14
classes of licenses, 4506.12
conditions for driving commercial vehicle, 4506.05
definitions, 4506.01
disqualification, placement out of service, 4506.16
driver to be physically qualified, 4506.10
driving record, furnishing to employer, insurer, 4506.08
employer of driver, duties, 4506.20
   driving record furnished to, 4506.08
examiner's permit, 4506.13
exceptions to chapter, 4506.02
fees, 4506.08
license information system, 4506.13
license or permit required, 4506.13
   endorsements, 4506.13
   expiration, renewal, 4506.14
   form, material of, 4506.11
   reinstatement fee in certain cases, 4507.45
   restrictions, 4506.10, 4506.12
medical examination, 4506.10
nonresident license, notice of violation, 4506.21
out-of-state convictions, driver to give notice, 4506.18
penalties, 4506.99
prohibitions, 4506.04, 4506.15
public safety department authority, 4506.22
public utilities commission authority, 4506.22
restricted—see specific topics, this entry
rules for qualification, testing of applicants
rules to carry out chapter, 4506.22
temporary instruction permit, 4506.06
voter registration or change of address, 4506.07

COMMITMENT
entry, presentence report to accompany, Crim. R. 32.2
forms, 2937.45
mental hospital, to, procedure, 2945.37 et seq

COMMON LAW
offenses, abrogated, 2901.03

COMMON PLEAS COURT
firearm possession, disability re, relief by, 2923.14
immunity from prosecution, may grant, 2945.44
jurisdiction, 2931.03
property, forfeited, unclaimed, to order disposal of, 2933.41
transfer from, for trial, Crim. R. 21

COMMUNICATIONS, DISRUPTING, 2909.04

COMMUNITY RESIDENTIAL CENTER
parolee may be required to reside in, 2967.14

COMMUTATION OF SENTENCE
application for, 2967.07
conditional, governor may grant, 2967.04
defined, 2967.01
notice of pendency of, to be sent to judge, prosecuting attorney, 2967.12
procedure, 2967.03, 2967.04
warrant of, 2967.06

COMPELLING ACCEPTANCE OF OBJECTIONABLE MATERIALS, 2907.34

COMPELLING PROSTITUTION, 2907.21

COMPENSATION, SOLICITING, RECEIVING IMPROPER, 2921.43

COMPETENCY OF WITNESSES, 2945.42

COMPETENCY TO STAND TRIAL, 2945.37
application of mental retardation department provisions, 5123.01.1, 5123.69
application of R.C. Chapter 5122, 5122.01.01, 5122.02, 5122.05, 5122.11, 5122.15
continuing jurisdiction of court, 2945.40.1
definitions, 2945.37, 2945.39.1, 5122.01, 5123.01
disclosure of information, 5122.31
disposition of defendant after hearing, sentence reduction for confinement for evaluation, 2945.38
escape, 2921.01, 2921.34, 5122.26
evaluation of mental condition, 2945.37.1
habeas corpus, 5122.30
proceedings after expiration of maximum time for treatment 2945.39
system of tracking, monitoring after release, 5119.57

COMPLAINT
amendment of, Crim. R. 7
appearance, initial, counsel, accused may read at, Crim. R. 5
arraignment, re, Crim. R. 10
arrest of judgment, for defect in, Crim. R. 34
contents, Crim. R. 3
defects in—see DEFENSES, OBJECTIONS, PRETRIAL
defined, Crim. R. 3
degree of offense in, effect of omitting, 2945.75
dismissal of—
   court, by, Crim. R. 48
   state, by, Crim. R. 48
elements of offense in, effect of omitting, 2945.75
forms, Crim. Form I, II
joinder in—
   defendants, of, Crim. R. 8
   offenses, of, Crim. R. 8

COMPLAINT—*Continued*
joinder in—*Continued*
  prejudicial, relief from, Crim. R. 14
misdemeanor prosecuted by, in inferior court, Crim. R. 7
oath, made upon, Crim. R. 3
pleading, as, Crim. R. 12
preliminary hearing—
  court, filed at instance of, after, when, Crim. R. 5
  transcript, copy of original with, Crim. R. 5
summons—
  copy of, attached to, when, Crim. R. 4
  issued upon, when, Crim. R. 4
  warrant, filed after issuance in lieu of, Crim. R. 4
venue change, original transmitted to receiving court, Crim. R. 18; 2931.29
warrant, arrest—
  arrest without, filed after, Crim. R. 4
  copy attached to, Crim. R. 4
  issuance upon, Crim. R. 4

COMPLICITY, 2923.03
conviction of attempt or conspiracy, precludes conviction of other, 2923.01, 2923.02
habitual sex offender, re, 2950.01
innocent or irresponsible person, causing to commit offense as, 2923.03
jurisdiction over—
  out of state, when committed, 2901.11
  state, when committed in, 2901.11
venue of—
  out of state, when committed, 2901.12
  state, when committed in, 2901.12

COMPOUNDING A CRIME, 2921.21

COMPUTATION OF TIME, Crim. R. 4.5—*see also* TIME

COMPUTER SYSTEMS, SERVICES
contraband, when considered, 2901.01
definitions re, 2913.01
disposition of property held by law enforcement, 2933.41
tampering with records, 2913.42
theft of, 2913.02
unauthorized use of, 2913.04
venue for trial of offenses re, 2901.12

CONCEALED WEAPON, CARRYING, 2923.12—*see also* FIREARMS, DANGEROUS ORDNANCE

CONCURRENT SENTENCES, 2929.41

CONDUCT
disorderly, 2917.11
disruptive, by defendant, exclusion for, Crim. R. 43

CONFERENCE, PRETRIAL, Crim. R. 17.1

CONFESSIONS
severance of defendants, considered re motion for, Crim. R. 14

CONFINEMENT—*see also* IMPRISONMENT
commitment, awaiting, credit for, 2967.19.1
effect on time within which hearing or trial must be held, 2945.71
intermittent service of sentence of, 2929.51
reimbursement of costs of—
  felonies, 2929.18
  misdemeanors, 2929.22.3, 2949.11.1
right to counsel, when possibility of sentence of, Crim. R. 32.3, 44
state, in another, re extending time for trial, 2945.72
trial, awaiting, credit for, on sentence, 2967.19.1

CONSANGUINITY, RELATION BY
challenge for cause, of juror re, Crim. R. 24

CONSECUTIVE SENTENCES, 2929.41

CONSENT
implied, to intoxication tests, 4511.19.1
theft, re—
  beyond scope of express, implied, 2913.02
  without, 2913.02
unauthorized use of property, re, 2913.04
vehicle, use without, 2913.03

CONSENT AGREEMENT, VIOLATING, 2919.27

CONSERVATION LAWS
jurisdiction of county court judge, re, 2931.02

CONSPIRACY, 2923.01
civil rights, by public servant to deprive of, 2921.45
complicity, re, 2923.03
corrupt activity, engaging in pattern of, 2923.31 *et seq*
disguise, while wearing, 3761.12, 3761.99
gambling offense, re, 2915.01
habitual sex offender, re, 2950.01
jurisdiction over—
  out of state, when committed, 2901.11
  state, when committed in, 2901.11
offense of violence, as, 2901.01
property subject of, conspirator loses right to, 2933.41
theft offense, re, 2913.01
venue of, 2901.12

CONSTABLES
arrest by, 509.10
as law enforcement officer, 2901.01
bond of, 509.02
compensation of, 509.01
confinement of misdemeanant, duties as to, 2949.08

CONSTABLES—*Continued*
designation of, 509.01
duties of, 509.05
fees of, 509.15
forfeiture, 509.13
moneys, payment of, 509.12
powers of, 509.05
process, 509.07-509.11
removal of, 509.01
sheriff, aid of, 509.06
special, when provided, 2931.06
subpoena service, return, by, Crim. R. 17
writ, time of receiving, 509.08

CONSTITUTION OF OHIO (*Provisions Relevant to Criminal Law*)
assembly, right of, Art. I, § 3 OC
bail, provisions for, Art. I, § 9 OC
bear arms, right to, Art. I, § 4 OC
convict's forfeiture of elective franchise, Art. V, § 4 OC
courts, redress in, Art. I, § 16 OC
cruel and unusual punishment, prohibited, Art. I, § 9 OC
death, wrongful, Art. I, § 19a OC
debt, imprisonment for, Art. I, § 15 OC
expert witnesses, in criminal trials, laws regulating, Art. II, § 39 OC
freedom of speech, press, Art. I, § 11 OC
freedom, right to, Art. I, § 1 OC
government, right to alter, etc., Art. I, § 2 OC
habeas corpus, Art. I, § 5 OC
indictment, right to, Art. I, § 10 OC
involuntary servitude, Art. I, § 6 OC
judiciary, Art. IV, OC
jury trial, right to, Art. I, § 5 OC
municipalities, police powers, home-rule provision, Art. XVIII, §§ 3, 7 OC
people, powers reserved to, Art. I, § 20 OC
private property, Art. I, §§ 1, 19 OC
privileges, hereditary, prohibited, Art. I, § 17
religion, freedom of, Art. I, § 7
reprieves, commutations, pardons, Art. III, § 11 OC
rights, inalienable, Art. I, § 1 OC
search warrants, provisions re, Art. I, § 14 OC
schools, encouragement of, Art. I, § 7 OC
slavery, Art. I, § 6 OC
style of process, prosecution, indictment, Art. IV, § 20 OC
suspension of laws, Art. I, § 18 OC
trial, rights at, Art. I, § 10 OC
troops, quartering of, Art. I, § 13 OC

CONSTRUCTION OF STATUTES, RULES, Crim. R. 1; 2901.04—*see also* STATUTES

CONTAMINATING SUBSTANCE FOR HUMAN CONSUMPTION OR USE, 2927.24

CONTEMPT
abrogation of common law offenses does not affect court's power re, 2901.03
acts constituting, 2705.01, 2705.02
alternate remedy, 2705.10
appeal, 2705.09
bail—
 forfeited when, 2705.07
 right of accused to, 2705.04
direct, 2705.01
garnishee, 2715.31
grand jury proceedings, re, 2939.15
hearing, 2705.03
imprisonment—
 release from, 2705.08
 when, 2705.06
indirect, 2705.02 et seq
juvenile court—
 powers of juvenile court re, 2151.21
 subpoena, failure to obey, re, JuvR 17(G)
punishment, 2705.01, 2705.05
subpoena, failure to obey, re, Crim. R. 17(G)
support, action for failure to pay, 2705.03.1, 2705.05

CONTEST, ATHLETIC, ETC., CORRUPTING, 2915.05, 2915.06

CONTINUANCE
arraignment, at, to secure counsel, Crim. R. 10
complaint, upon amendment of, when, Crim. R. 7
indictment, information, upon amendment of, when, Crim. R. 7
initial appearance, at, to secure counsel, Crim. R. 5
procedure, 2937.21, 2945.02
when trial time extended for, 2945.72

CONTRABAND, 2901.01, 2933.42
disposition of property held by law enforcement, 2933.41 et seq
forfeiture provisions not affecting, 2925.44
possession of, transactions in, prohibited; property used in transaction construed contraband, 2933.42
search warrant to seize, Crim. R. 41
seizure of property used in transaction involving contraband; notice, disposition of, 2933.43

CONTRACT, PUBLIC, UNLAWFUL INTEREST IN, 2921.42
county, by, prosecuting attorney to protect interests of county, 309.12

CONTRIBUTIONS
soliciting of, re missing children, 2901.32

CONTROLLED SUBSTANCES, 2925.01 et seq, 3719.01 et seq
counterfeit, offenses involving, 2925.37
police, sales by, 3719.14.1

CONVEYANCE OF REAL PROPERTY
fraudulent, to defraud creditors, 2913.45

CONVEYANCE OF WEAPONS OR DANGEROUS ORDNANCE ONTO SCHOOL PREMISES, 2923.12.2

CONVICT—*see also* ESCAPE; PENITENTIARIES
civil rights of felons, generally, 2961.01
delivery to penal or reformatory institution, 2949.12
dereliction of duty re, by officer in charge of detention facility, 2921.44
disposition of, after trial on another offense, 2941.43
DNA tests, 2901.07—*see also* DNA TESTS
escaped, time absent not to be counted toward sentence, 2949.07
escape of, mileage and expenses for recapturing officer, 2941.44
forfeiture of elective franchise, Art. V, § 4 OC
furloughs for employment, education, to trustworthy, 2967.26
imminent danger of death of, may be released, 2967.05
indictment of, 2941.39
labor of, terms, 2947.15
may be transferred to other institution, 2967.21
probation revocation hearing, attendance at, 2951.13
removal for sentence or trial, 2941.40
request for trial on pending charges, by, 2941.40.1
subpoena of, procedure, 2945.47, 2945.48
to be confined after removal, 2941.42
warrant for removal for sentence or trial, 2941.41
witness, material, not to be confined with, 2937.18

CONVICTION
disabilities re, unconditional pardon removes, 2967.04
felony, of, effect on civil rights, 2961.01
    elective franchise, Art. V, § 4 OC
firearm, dangerous ordnance, possession of, prohibited, 2923.13
    relief from disability re, 2923.14
juror, of, re challenge for cause, Crim. R. 24
prior—
    admissible even if record expunged, 2953.32
    juvenile adjudication as, 2901.08
    procuring, prostitution, soliciting, when admissible re, 2907.26
    proof of, 2945.75
    repeat offender, as prima facie evidence re, 2929.01
    sex offenses, of, when makes offender habitual, 2950.01
    sufficient pleading of, in indictment or information, 2941.11

CORONER
autopsies, duties as to, 313.12.1-313.13
cause of death, conclusiveness of determination of, 313.19

CORONER—*Continued*
firearms belonging to certain decedents, to deliver to sheriff or police chief, 313.14.1
how long must hold dead body, 313.15
investigation of death, may request further, 313.09
recordkeeping duties of, 313.09, 313.10
subpoena of witnesses, powers as to, Crim. R. 17; 313.17
testing for toxic substances for law enforcement purposes, 313.21

CORPORATIONS—*see also* CORRUPT ACTIVITY
attorney-client privilege, re, 2317.02.1
contractor, public, owning, controlling shares in—
    affidavit by public servant re, where filed, 2921.42
    limited to 5% of outstanding shares, by public servant, 2921.42
counsel, may appear by, for all purposes, Crim. R. 43
criminal liability, 2901.23, 2929.31
indictment of, sufficient identification in, 2941.09
nuisance cases—*see* NUISANCES
ordnance, dangerous, permit, license application by, 2923.18
service on, Crim. R. 4

CORPSE, ABUSE OF, 2927.01

CORPUS DELICTI
statute of limitation, does not run while undiscovered, 2901.13

CORRECTIONAL INSTITUTIONS
assaults of guards, visitors etc., 2903.13
DNA testing, 2901.07—*see also* DNA TESTS
municipal—
    access to exercise equipment, participation in fighting skills program, 753.31
    contracts for private operation, management, of correctional facilities, 9.06

CORROSIVE MATERIAL, CRIMINAL DAMAGING, ENDANGERING BY, 2909.06

CORRUPT ACTIVITY, 2923.31 *et seq*
civil proceedings for relief from violation, 2923.34
conduct constituting, 2923.31, 2923.32
definitions, 2923.31
engaging in pattern of, 2923.32
felony sanctions, 2929.13
ill-gotten enterprise, property investments, 2923.32
    disposition of forfeited property, 2923.35
    filing of corrupt activity lien notice; lis pendens, 2923.36
    motion to preserve reachability of property subject to forfeiture, 2923.33
immunity of witness turning state's evidence, 2945.44
penalties—
    civil, 2923.34
    criminal; fines, forfeitures, 2923.32

CORRUPTING ANOTHER WITH DRUGS, 2925.02

CORRUPTION OF MINOR, 2907.04

COSTS AND FEES
additional, imposed by court, 2949.09.1, 2949.09.2
appeal, of—
   counsel for defendant, appointment of, without, Crim. R. 32
   defendant entitled to, without payment of, Crim. R. 32
   documents necessary for, to defendant without, Crim. R. 32
arraignment, right of defendant to counsel without, Crim. R. 10
assignment of offender's payments toward satisfaction of, 2949.11.1
convicted felon to pay, 2949.14 *et seq*
conviction, of, pardon does not release from, 2961.01
costs of confinement—*see* CONFINEMENT
examination of victim of sex offense, 2907.28
habeas corpus proceedings, in, 2725.28
initial appearance, at, counsel assigned without, Crim. R. 5
judgment of conviction, to be entered in, 2335.11
judgment to include, 2947.23
jurors, of, to be included in sentence, 2947.23
limitation on total reimbursement by state, 2949.20.1
preliminary hearing, of, itemized account in transcript, Crim. R. 5
probation fees, 2949.11.1, 2951.02.1
reversal of judgment, state to pay, 2949.20
security for, to be furnished by complainant, 2935.21
subpoena, of, defendant unable to pay, Crim. R. 17
venue change, of, originating county to pay, Crim. R. 18; 2931.31
when state to pay, 2949.19, 2949.20
witnesses, material, re detention of, 2937.18
   subpoena, re, Crim. R. 17

COUNSEL—*see also* ATTORNEY
appeal, for, appointment for defendant without cost, Crim. R. 32
appearance, initial—
   continuance to secure, right to reasonable, Crim. R. 5
   cost, assigned without, if unable to employ, Crim. R. 5
arraignment, at, right to, Crim. R. 10; 2937.03
arrest, right to, upon, 2935.14, 2935.20
assignment of, Crim. R. 44
   delay in, when extends time for trial, 2945.72
   payment for defense of indigent, 2941.51
assist prosecutor, appointment to, 2941.63
corporation may appear by, for all purposes, Crim. R. 43
deposition, re, Crim. R. 15; 2945.52, 2945.53

COUNSEL—*Continued*
names of, entered in appearance docket, Crim. R. 55
preliminary hearing, defendant at, without, effect, Crim. R. 5
probation revocation hearing, re, Crim. R. 32.3
service of papers on, when, Crim. R. 49
waiver of, recorded, re petty offenses, Crim. R. 22

COUNTERFEITING
trademarks—*see* TRADEMARK COUNTERFEITING; TRADEMARKS

COUNTY
crime victim assistance programs, 307.62, 5705.19
officers, bonds of, duties of prosecuting attorney as to, 309.11
prosecuting attorney to serve as legal adviser for county officers, 309.09

COUNTY BOARD OF MENTAL RETARDATION AND DEVELOPMENTAL DISABILITIES
background investigations of prospective employees of contracting entities, restrictions on certain offenders, 5126.28.1
criminal records check, employment of certain offenders prohibited, 5126.28

COUNTY COMMISSIONERS
convict labor, to set terms of, 2947.15
payment of counsel to assist prosecutor, 2941.63
workhouse, contract for use of, 2947.19

COUNTY COURTS
arrest warrants, outstanding—
   driver's license ineligibility, 4507.09.1
   vehicle registration ineligibility, 4503.13
fines, disposition of, 2931.08 *et seq*
jurisdiction of judge of, 2931.02

COUNTY JAIL
grand jury's duties as to, 2939.21
industry program, sentencing court to determine eligibility for—
   felony, 2929.16
   misdemeanor, 2929.21

COUNTY TREASURY, FINES TO BE PAID INTO, 2949.11

COURTHOUSE, COURTROOM FACILITY
conveyance, possession or control of deadly weapon or dangerous ordnance, 2923.12.3

COURTS
appeals, of—
   appointment of counsel to assist prosecutor, 2941.63
   constitutional provisions re, Art. IV, § 3 OC

COURTS—*Continued*
appeals, of—*Continued*
  immunity from prosecution, power to grant to witness, 2945.44
  review of judgments, final orders, of inferior courts, right to, 2953.02
common pleas, of—
  counsel to assist prosecutor, of, 2941.63
  county jail, duties as to, 2939.21
  grand jury, summoning, 2939.17
  immunity from prosecution, may grant to witness, 2945.44
  presiding judge to receive notice of pendency of pardon, commutation, parole, 2967.12
defined, 2931.01
not of record, notation to be kept, Crim. R. 55

CRACK COCAINE—*see also* DRUG OFFENSES
defined, 2925.01, 2929.01
possession, 2925.11

CREDIT
coercion, threat to impair, as, 2905.12
defrauding creditors, 2913.45
extortionate extension of, 2905.21-2905.24
extortion, threat to impair, as, 2905.11
falsification to obtain, 2921.13

CREDIT CARDS
bail, use to make, Crim. R. 46
definition, 2913.01
misuse of, 2913.21
numbers, recording when check is presented, 1349.17, 1349.99
receiving stolen, 2913.71
theft of, 2913.71
value, re misuse of, to be found in verdict, 2913.61

CREDITORS, DEFRAUDING, 2913.45

CRIME
compounding, 2921.21
failure to report, 2921.22
organized, engaging in, 2923.31 *et seq*

CRIMINAL ACTION
commencement, docketing, numbering of, Crim. R. 55
employer's duty when employee subpoenaed to, 2945.45.1

CRIMINAL CHILD ENTICEMENT, 2905.05

CRIMINAL DAMAGING OR ENDANGERING, 2909.06

CRIMINAL INTENT—*see* INTENT

CRIMINAL JUSTICE NETWORK, 5502.01

CRIMINAL JUSTICE SERVICES
office of, state supervisory board, metropolitan agencies, 181.51-181.56

CRIMINAL MISCHIEF, 2909.07

CRIMINAL RECORDS CHECK
employees responsible for out-of-home child care, 2151.86
persons having frequent contact with children, 109.57.2
prospective adoptive or foster parents, 2151.86

CRIMINAL SENTENCING COUNCIL, 181.21, 181.26

CRIMINAL SIMULATION, 2913.32

CRIMINAL SYNDICATES, 2923.04 (*repealed, eff. 1-1-86; see now* CORRUPT ACTIVITY, 2923.31 *et seq*)

CRIMINAL TRESPASS, 2911.21

CRISIS INTERVENTION
trained officer to interview victim of sex offense, 2907.30

CROSS-EXAMINATION
death penalty hearing, of offender, at, 2929.03
preliminary hearing, of witnesses at, Crim. R. 5
statement of witness on—
  defense counsel, by, Crim. R. 16
  prosecutor, by, Crim. R. 16

CROWD SAFETY, 2917.40

CULPABILITY, CRIMINAL, 2901.21, 2901.22

CULTIVATE, DEFINED RE DRUG OFFENSES, 2925.01

CULVERT, OFFENSES INVOLVING
generally, 3767.16
highway, along, 5589.04

CURFEW
felony offender, 2929.01, 2929.17

CUSTODY
interference with, 2919.23
permanent, motion by agency for, 2151.41.3, 2151.41.4
temporary, of abused, neglected or dependent child, 2151.41.2

DAMAGING, ENDANGERING, CRIMINAL, 2909.06

DANGEROUS OFFENDER
imprisonment of—
    felony, favors longer term of, 2929.12
    misdemeanor, favors imposing, 2929.22
probation for, prohibited, 2951.02

DAY-CARE
sex offender in area, notice to home or center, 2950.11

DAYTIME, RE SEARCH WARRANT
defined, Crim. R. 41
execution in, exception, Crim. R. 41

DEAD ANIMALS—see NUISANCES

DEAD BODIES
autopsy, disposition of, 313.13 et seq
disinterment of, 313.18
report finding of, duty to, 2921.22
search for, 2933.41

DEADLY FORCE
defined, 2901.01
riot, use by officer to suppress, when permissible, 2917.05

DEADLY WEAPONS—see FIREARMS; DANGEROUS ORDNANCE; WEAPONS

DEATH—see also DEATH PENALTY
cause of, conclusiveness of coroner's verdict, 313.19
certificate, coroner's duties re, 313.09, 313.19
defined, 2108.30
duty to report, 2921.22
indictment for causing, manner, means not required in, 2941.14
physician's duty to report suspicious or unusual, 313.12
representation in lurid detail, as matter harmful to juveniles, 2907.01
risk of, as serious physical harm to person, 2901.01
sentence of, no release on bail after, Crim. R. 46
witness, of, use of deposition upon, Crim. R. 15; 2945.49

DEATH PENALTY—see also MURDER, AGGRAVATED
appellate review, 2929.05, 2953.02, 2953.07
    suspension of sentence, 2953.09, 2953.10
capital offense, defined, 2901.02
conveyance to penitentiary for, 2949.21
convict, for another offense, how executed upon, 2941.43
disposition of body, costs, 2949.26
escape, rearrest, execution, 2949.27
inquiring into sanity, suspension of execution, 2949.28 et seq
mitigating circumstances, 2929.04

DEATH PENALTY—Continued
postconviction relief—
    appointed counsel, 120.06, 120.16, 120.26, 120.33, 2953.21
    petitions, SupR 39
pregnant prisoner, 2949.31
procedure for carrying out, 2949.22
time of execution, 2949.23
vacated upon appeal, procedure, 2929.06
warden or deputy warden to be paid, 2949.23
warrant, return of, 2949.24
who may attend execution, 2949.25

DEBT, EVIDENCE OF, VALUE RE CRIMINAL ACT, 1.07

DECEPTION
credit card, procuring issuance by, 2913.21
dangerous drugs, to obtain, 2925.22
defined, 2913.01
hostelry, livery, to obtain rental of, 2913.41
sale of dairy products, food, drink, drugs, medicine, in, 2931.02
theft, by, 2913.02
trespass, criminal, authorization obtained by, no defense, 2911.21
writing, securing by, 2913.43

DECLARATORY JUDGMENT RE OBSCENITY, 2907.36

DECREE
abandonment, nonsupport of dependent, in violation of, 2919.21
power of courts to enforce by contempt or otherwise, 2901.03

DEFECTS
initiation of prosecution, indictment, etc., in—see DEFENSES, OBJECTIONS, PRETRIAL

DEFENDANT
presence of, when required, Crim. R. 43—see also PRESENCE OF DEFENDANT
testifying or failing to testify at trial, 2945.43

DEFENSES—see also DEFENSES, OBJECTIONS, PRETRIAL
affirmative—
    abortion, unlawful, 2919.12
    attempt charge, re, 2923.02
    bigamy, re, 2919.01
    burden of advancing, on accused, 2901.05
    coercion charge, to, 2905.12
    complicity, to charge of, 2923.03
    compounding a crime, re, 2921.21
    conspiracy, re charge of, 2923.01
    custody, re interference with, 2919.23

DEFENSES—*Continued*
affirmative—*Continued*
  defined, 2901.05
  dependents, re nonsupport of, 2919.21
  escape, re, 2921.34
  firearm, re improper handling in motor vehicle, 2923.12, 2923.16
  impossibility, re attempt, 2923.02
  juveniles, re disseminating matter harmful to, 2907.31
  obscenity, pandering, to charge of, 2907.32
  property, re unauthorized use of, 2913.03, 2913.04
  vehicle, re unauthorized use of, 2913.03
  weapons, re carrying concealed, 2923.12
insanity, 2901.01, 2945.39.1
murder, aggravated, mental deficiency, psychosis as, re, 2929.04
organizational offense, due diligence of representative as, 2901.23

DEFENSES, OBJECTIONS, PRETRIAL, Crim. R. 12
appeal by state, right of, re, Crim. R. 12
effect of granting motion to dismiss, Crim. R. 12
time—
  pretrial motions, for making, Crim. R. 12
waiver of, for failure to raise timely, Crim. R. 12

DEFINITIONS
abduction, 2905.02
abortion, 2919.11
acts—
  involuntary, 2901.21
  knowingly, 2901.22
  negligently, 2901.22
  overt, substantial, re conspiracy, 2923.01
  purposely, 2901.22
  recklessly, 2901.22
  voluntary, re conspiracy, 2923.01
acute alcohol intoxication, 2935.33
affirmative defense, 2901.05
aid law enforcement officer, failure to, 2921.23
alarms, making false, 2917.32
alcoholic, 2935.33
alternative residential facility, 2929.01
and, 1.02
another, 1.02
anything of value, 1.03
arrest, resisting, 2921.33
arson, re, 2909.01
  aggravated, 2909.02
assault, 2903.13
  aggravated, 2903.12
  felonious, 2903.11
  negligent, 2903.14
attempt, 2923.02
authority, resistance to lawful, 2921.35
bad time, 2929.01

DEFINITIONS—*Continued*
bail forfeiture, 2953.31
basic supervision, 2929.01
bet, 2915.01
bigamy, 2919.01
body cavity search, 2933.32
bond, 1.02
bookmaking, 2915.01
  facilitating, 2915.02
breaking and entering, 2911.13
bribery, 2921.02
burglary, 2911.12
  aggravated, 2911.11
burn injury, 2921.22
cable television service, 2913.01
campaign committee, 2921.01
candidate for public office, 2921.01
capital offense, 2901.02
caretaker, 2903.10
certified electronic monitoring device, 2929.23
certified grievance committee, 2925.01
chance—
  game of, 2915.01
    facilitating, 2915.02
    profit, game, scheme for, 2915.01
  scheme of, 2915.01
    facilitating, 2915.02
cheating, 2915.05
checks, passing bad, 2913.11
child, 1.59
  endangering, 2919.22
civil rights, interfering with, 2921.45
clerk of court, Crim. R. 2; 2931.01
coercion, 2905.12
coin machine, 2913.01
  tampering with, 2911.32
commence, criminal action, Crim. R. 55
community control sanction, 2929.01
commutation of sentence, 2967.01
compensation, soliciting, receiving improper, 2921.43
complaint, Crim. R. 3
complicity, 2923.03
compounding a crime, 2921.21
computers, re, 2913.01
conduct, pattern of, 2903.21.1
conspiracy, 2923.01
contraband, 2909.01, 2933.42
contract, public, re having unlawful interest in, 2921.42
contributions, 2921.01
corpse, abuse of, 2927.01
corrupt activity; definitions re, 2923.31
corruption of minor, 2907.04
counterfeit controlled substances, 2925.01
court, 2931.01
credit card, 2913.01
credit cards, misuse of, 2913.21
creditors, defrauding, 2913.45
crime—
  compounding a, 2921.21

DEFINITIONS—*Continued*
crime—*Continued*
   report, failure to, 2921.22
criminally injurious conduct, 2929.01
culpability, 2901.21
curfew, 2929.01
custody, interference with, 2919.23
damaging, criminal, 2909.06
dangerous ordnance, 2923.11
data, 2913.01
day reporting, 2929.01
daytime, re search warrants, Crim. R. 41
deadly force, 2901.01
deadly weapon, 2923.11
death, 2108.30
deception, 2913.01
deceptive (re: insurance fraud), 2913.47
defense, affirmative, 2901.05
defraud, 2913.01
delinquent child, 2951.02
dependents, nonsupport of, 2919.21
deprive, 2913.01
desecration, 2927.11
detention, 2921.01
   facility, 2921.01
device—
   explosive, 2923.11
   incendiary, 2923.11
disability from firearm possession, 2923.13
   relief from, 2923.14
disciplinary counsel, 2925.01
disorderly conduct, 2917.11
disperse, failure to, 2917.04
domestic violence, re, 2919.25
doubt, reasonable, proof beyond, 2901.05
drug and alcohol use monitoring, 2929.01
drug offenses, re, 2925.01
drug paraphernalia, 2925.14
drug treatment program, 2929.01
duty, dereliction of, 2921.44
economic loss, 2929.01
electronic monitoring device, 2929.23
electronic monitoring system, 2929.23
electronically monitored early release, 2929.23
electronically monitored house arrest, 2929.23
electronically monitored house detention, 2929.23
eligible offender, 2929.23
emergency, misconduct at, 2917.13
emergency personnel, 2909.01
endangering—
   children, 2919.22
   criminal, 2909.06
escape, 2921.34
   aiding, 2921.35
evidence, tampering with, 2921.12
explosive device, 2923.11
extortion, 2905.11
facsimile devices, 4931.55

DEFINITIONS—*Continued*
fair market value, 2909.11, 2913.61
falsification, 2921.13
fax machines—*see* facsimile devices
federal drug abuse control laws, 2925.01
felony, Crim. R. 2; 2901.02
financial institution, 2925.41
firearm, 2923.11
   automatic, 2923.11
   disability, no possession while under, 2923.13
   interstate transactions in, permitted, 2923.22
   intoxicated, use while, 2923.15
   minor, improperly furnishing to, 2923.21
   motor vehicle, improperly handling in, 2923.16
   prosecution re, immunity from, 2923.23
   relief from disability re, 2923.14
   sawed-off, 2923.11
   semi-automatic, 2923.11
   surrender of, voluntary, 2923.23
   unloaded, 2923.16
first offender, 2953.31
force, 2901.01
   deadly, 2901.01
foreign jurisdiction (juvenile proceedings), 2151.26
forge, 2913.01
forgery, 2913.31
fraud, re, 2913.01
   medicaid, 2913.40
fresh pursuit, 2935.29
functionally impaired person, 2903.10
gain access, 2913.01
gambling, 2915.02
   device, 2915.01
   house, operating a, 2915.03
   offense, 2915.01
   re, 2915.01
gaming, public, 2915.04
habitual sex offender, 2950.01
halfway house, 2929.01
handgun, 2923.11
harassment, telephone, 2917.21
hazing, 2903.31
homicide—
   negligent, 2903.05
   vehicular, 2903.07
     aggravated, 2903.06
hospital, re abortion, 2919.11
hostelry, defrauding, 2913.41
house arrest, 2929.01
identification card, 2913.31
impersonate, 2921.51
importuning, 2907.07
imprisoned, 1.05
incendiary device, 2923.11
indecency, public, 2907.09
indefinite commitment, 2947.24
insanity, 2901.01, 2945.39.1
intensive supervision, 2929.01

DEFINITIONS—*Continued*
intimidation, 2921.03
investigatory work product, 2953.32.1
jail, 2929.01
judge, Crim. R. 2; 2931.01
justice—
    obstructing, 2921.32
    public administration, re offenses against, 2921.01
juvenile, 2907.01
    drug offenses, re, 2925.01
    material, performance harmful to, 2907.01
juvenile court, relative to, 2151.01.1
kidnapping, 2905.01
land or premises, re criminal trespass, 2911.21
law enforcement officer, Crim. R. 2; 2901.01
license violation report, 2929.01
livery, defrauding, 2913.41
magistrate, 2931.01
major drug offender, 2929.01
mandatory prison term, 2929.01
manslaughter—
    involuntary, 2903.04
    voluntary, 2903.03
market value, fair—
    arson, vandalism, etc., 2909.11
    theft offense, re, 2913.61
massage, 503.40
massage establishment, 503.40
masseur, 503.40
masseuse, 503.40
material, 2907.01
    juveniles, harmful to, 2907.01
    obscene, 2907.01
    perjury, re, 2921.11
medicaid fraud, 2913.40
meeting, disturbing a lawful, 2917.12
menacing, 2903.22
    aggravated, 2903.21
    stalking, by, 2903.21.1
mental distress, 2903.21.1
mind, of unsound, 1.02
minor, improperly furnishing firearms to, 2923.21
minor misdemeanor, Crim. R. 4.1; 2901.02
mischief, criminal, 2909.07
misdemeanor, Crim. R. 2; 2901.02
monitored time, 2929.01
murder, 2903.02
    aggravated, 2903.01
nudity, 2907.01
nuisance cases, 3767.01
oath, 1.59
obscene material, performance, 2907.01
occupied structure, 2909.01
offender, various categories of—
    dangerous, 2929.01
    generally, 2929.01
    habitual sex, 2950.01
    major drug, 2929.01

DEFINITIONS—*Continued*
offender, various categories of—*Continued*
    repeat, 2929.01
offense, 2935.01
    petty, Crim. R. 2
    serious, Crim. R. 2
    violence, of, 2901.01
officer—
    law enforcement, Crim. R. 2; 2901.01
        aid, failure to, 2921.23
    peace, 2935.01
    personating, 2913.44
official—
    business, obstructing, 2921.31
    party, 2921.01
    proceeding, 2921.01
    public, 2921.01
or, 1.02
ordnance, dangerous, 2923.11
organization, 2901.23
organized crime, engaging in, 2923.04 (*repealed, eff. 1-1-86; see now* CORRUPT ACTIVITY, 2923.31 *et seq*)
owner, 2913.01
panic, inducing, 2917.31
pardon, 2967.01
    unconditional pardon, 2967.04
parole, 2967.01
parolee, 2967.01
patient abuse, neglect, 2903.33
peace officer, 2921.51, 2935.01
pecuniary value, 2923.31
penalties, re, 2929.01
performance, 2907.01
    harmful to juveniles, 2907.01
    obscene, 2907.01
perjury, 2921.11
person, 1.02, 1.59, 2923.31
    nuisance cases, 3767.01
personal property, 2923.31
petty offense, Crim. R. 2
physical harm—
    persons, to, 2901.01
        serious, 2901.01
    property, to, 2901.01
        serious, 2901.01
place (*re nuisance*), 3767.01
political subdivision, 2909.01
population, 1.59
premises, re criminal trespass, 2911.21
prison, 2929.01
prison term, 2929.01
private policeman, 2921.51
privilege, 2901.01
proceeding, official, 2921.01
procuring, 2907.23
professional license, 2925.01
professionally licensed person, 2925.01

DEFINITIONS—*Continued*
proof beyond a reasonable doubt, 2901.05
property, 2901.01
    re forfeiture for drug abuse offenses, 2925.41
    re search warrants, Crim. R. 41
prosecuting attorney, Crim. R. 2; 2935.01
prostitute, 2907.01
prostitution, 2907.25
    compelling, 2907.21
    promoting, 2907.22
public—
    candidate for, office, 2921.01
    contract, 2921.42
    official, 2921.01
    servant, 2921.01
    services, disrupting, 2909.04
racketeering, 2923.31
rape, 2907.02
real property, 2923.31
reasonable doubt, 2901.05
receiving stolen property, 2913.51
records, tampering with, 2913.42
registered mail, 1.02
repeat violent offender, 2929.01
report crime, failure to, 2921.22
reprieve, 2967.01
restraint, unlawful, 2905.03
riot, 2917.03
    aggravated, 2917.02
    suppress, justifiable use of force to, 2917.05
risk, 2901.01
    substantial, 2901.01
robbery, 2911.02
    aggravated, 2911.01
rule, 1.59
rule of court, Crim. R. 57
safecracking, 2911.31
sanction, 2929.01
school, 2925.01
school building, 2925.01
school premises, 2925.01
sentence, 2929.01
serious offense, Crim. R. 2
serious physical harm to—
    persons, 2901.01
    property, 2901.01
servant, public, 2921.01
services (*re theft*), 2913.01
sex—
    offender, habitual, 2950.01
    offense, 2950.01
sexual—
    activity, 2907.01
    battery, 2907.03
    conduct, 2907.01
    contact, 2907.01
    excitement, 2907.01
    imposition, 2907.06
        gross, 2907.05

DEFINITIONS—*Continued*
sexual—*Continued*
    predator, 2929.01
sexual or genital area, re: massage establishments, etc., 503.40
sexually oriented offense, 2950.01
simulation, criminal, 2913.32
slugs, 2913.01
    making, using, 2913.33
soliciting, 2907.24
stalking, menacing by, 2903.21.1
state, Crim. R. 2; 2901.11, 2909.01
stated prison term, 2929.01
statutory precondition for nonconsensual entry, 2933.23.1
strip search, 2933.32
structure, occupied, 2909.01
substantial risk, 2901.01
swear, 1.59
tampering with evidence, 2921.12
telephone harassment, 2917.21
theft, 2913.02
    fraud, re, 2913.01
    grand, 2913.02
    offense, 2913.01
    office, in, 2921.41
    petty, 2913.02
threat—
    coercion, re, 2905.12
    extortion, re, 2905.11
time, standard, 1.04
tools, criminal, possession of, 2923.24
traffic control device, 4511.18
trespass—
    aggravated, 2911.21.1
    criminal, 2911.21
trustee, 2923.31
unconditional pardon, 2967.04
undertaking, 1.02
unloaded firearm, 2923.16
utter, 2913.01
value—
    anything of, 1.03
    fair market, 2909.11, 2913.61
vandalism, 2909.05
vehicle, unauthorized use of, 2913.03
vending machine, tobacco product, 2927.02
victim-offender mediation, 2929.01
violence—
    inciting to, 2917.01
    offense of, 2901.01
voluntary—
    conspiracy, re, 2923.01
    surrender of firearm, dangerous ordnance, 2923.23
voyeurism, 2907.08
weapon—
    carrying concealed, 2923.12
    deadly, 2923.11

DEFINITIONS—*Continued*
week, 1.44
wheelchair, motorized, 4511.01
whoever, 1.02
will, 1.59
writing, 1.59, 2913.01
   deception, securing by, 2913.43
written, 1.59
year, 1.44
zip-gun, 2923.11

DEFRAUD
arson, damage to property by fire or explosive, with intent to, 2909.03
cheating, to, 2915.05
checks, passing bad, to, 2913.11
coin machine, tampering with, to, 2911.32
computer system or service; denial of authorized access to, 2913.81
contract, public, unlawful interest in, 2921.42
credit cards, use to, 2913.21
creditors, to, 2913.45
defined, 2913.01
forgery to, 2913.31
insurance fraud, 2913.47
hostelry, 2913.41
livery, 2913.41
medical assistance program, to obtain benefits, 2913.40
officer, personating to, 2913.44
records, by tampering with, 2913.42
simulation, to, 2913.32
slugs, use to, 2913.33

DEGREE
falsification to obtain, written, 2921.13
offense, of—
   verdict, re—
      guilty, to state, effect of omitting, 2945.75
      modification of, 2945.79
   when additional element makes offense more serious, procedure, 2945.75

DEMAND
discovery, for, written, Crim. R. 16
extradition, for, procedure, 2963.03 *et seq*
jury trial, for, Crim. R. 23

DEMURRER
abolished, Crim. R. 12
appeal of issues formerly raised by, Crim. R. 12
hearing on, 2941.62
overruled, accused may plead, 2941.61
when, 2941.57

DEPENDENTS, NONSUPPORT OF, 2919.21
county to contribute to support of dependent when defendant confined, 3113.11
failure to comply with order, arrest, 3113.08

DEPENDENTS, NONSUPPORT OF—*Continued*
maintenance cost of county ward, failure to pay, 3113.06, 3113.07
personal earnings, withholding to pay support, 3113.21
suspension of sentence upon posting of bond, 3113.04
trustee, provisions re, 3113.09 *et seq*

DEPORTATION
administrative release to deported parolee, 2967.17

DEPOSITIONS, Crim. R. 15; 2945.50 *et seq*
child victim—*see* CHILD
subpoena for taking, Crim. R. 17

DEPOSIT OF CASH RE RELEASE, Crim. R. 46

DEPRIVE
civil rights, of, by public servant, 2921.45
defined, re theft, fraud, 2913.01

DEPUTY FOREMAN OF GRAND JURY, Crim. R. 6

DERELICTION OF DUTY, 2921.44

DESECRATION, 2927.11

DESTRUCTIVE DEVICE
license to deal in, possession by permitted, 2923.17
ordnance, dangerous, when not, 2923.11

DETAINERS, INTERSTATE AGREEMENT ON, 2963.30 *et seq*
time for trial computation, not affected by, 2945.71

DETENTION
defined, 2921.01
escape from, 2921.34, 2921.35
facility—
   conveying weapons, drugs or liquor into, 2921.36, 2921.37
   defined, 2921.01
   dereliction of duty by officer in charge, 2921.44
   DNA testing, 2901.07—*see also* DNA TESTS
   murder by prisoner in, as aggravating circumstance, 2929.04
   possessing deadly weapon while under, 2923.13.1, 2929.41
   riot by prisoner in, aggravated, sentence served consecutively, 2929.41
witness, of material, 2937.18

DEVICES
destructive—
   license to deal in, possession permissible by, 2923.17
   ordnance, dangerous, when not, 2923.11
explosive—
   defined, 2923.11
   license or permit for, 2923.18

DEVICES—*Continued*
facsimile—*see* FACSIMILE DEVICES
gambling—
    defined, 2915.01
    possession, control, operation of, prohibited, 2915.02
incendiary—
    defined, 2923.11
    ordnance, as dangerous, 2923.11
    reporting burns caused by, 2921.22
safety, as zip-gun, when, 2923.11
tools, criminal, as, 2923.24
traffic control, 4511.18

DICE, AS GAMBLING DEVICE, 2915.01

DILATION AND EXTRACTION—*see* ABORTION

DIPLOMA, WRITTEN FALSIFICATION TO OBTAIN, 2921.13

DISABILITY
firearms, dangerous ordnance, re, 2923.13
    immunity from prosecution re, 2923.23
    relief from, 2923.14
    unlawful transaction in weapons, re, 2923.20
judge, of, procedure, Crim. R. 25
pardon, unconditional, removes civil, 2967.04

DISABLED, AID TO, FALSIFICATION TO OBTAIN, 2921.13

DISABLED PERSON, DUTY TO, 2305.41-2305.49

DISASTER, HAMPERING OFFICER, FIREMAN, ETC., AT, 2917.13

DISCHARGE
defendant, of—
    arrest of judgment, after, Crim. R. 34
    evidence insufficient to put upon defense, 2945.15
    indictment, information, not filed within 14 days of waiver of, Crim. R. 7
grand jury, of, Crim. R. 6
joint defendant, of, re immunity, 2945.15
jury, of—
    amendment of complaint, indictment, information, re, effect, Crim. R. 7; 2941.30
    causes for, 2945.36
    failure to agree on verdict, re, Crim. R. 31
    motion for judgment of acquittal, re, Crim. R. 29
preliminary hearing, at, of accused—
    court, by, Crim. R. 5
    motion for, at close of state's evidence, Crim. R. 5
    prosecution, not bar to further, Crim. R. 5
surety, of, on bail bond, Crim. R. 46
trial delay, of accused, for, 2945.73
witness of, after deposition taken, Crim. R. 15

DISCIPLINARY MEASURES, RE CHILD ENDANGERING, 2919.22

DISCLOSURE
confidential information, of, 2921.24
defendant, by, Crim. R. 16
grand jury proceedings, of, when, Crim. R. 6
peace officer's home address, 2921.24, 2921.25
presentence investigation, of, Crim. R. 32.2
prosecuting attorney, by, Crim. R. 16

DISCOVERY, Crim. R. 16
defendant, by—
    evidence favorable to, Crim. R. 16
grand jury—
    testimony of defendant, co-defendant before, of, Crim. R. 16
    transcript of proceedings, of, Crim. R. 16

DISCRETION
abuse of, new trial for, Crim. R. 33; 2945.79
probation, of court, re, 2951.02

DISCRIMINATION
ethnic intimidation—*see* ETHNIC INTIMIDATION
felony sentencing, 2929.11

DISEASES
improperly handling infectious agents, 1917.47
venereal, 2907.27
    notification to victim of sex offenses, 2151.14, 2907.30

DISFIGUREMENT, AS SERIOUS PHYSICAL HARM, 2901.01

DISFRANCHISEMENT, CONVICTED FELONS, OF, 2961.01

DISGUISE
conspiracy while wearing, 3761.12, 3761.99

DISINTERMENT, 313.18

DISMISSAL, Crim. R. 48
affidavit or complaint, of motion for, 2937.04, 2937.05
indictment, information, of, for error in designation of statute, Crim. R. 7
preliminary hearing, re delay, 2945.73

DISMISS, MOTION TO
bail, custody, continued pending correction of defects re, Crim. R. 12
defenses, pretrial, raised by, Crim. R. 12
indictment, re, grand jury—
    disclosure of matters before, re, when, Crim. R. 6
    objections to array or to individual jurors, Crim. R. 6

DISORDERLY CONDUCT, 2917.11
alcoholic treatment center, commitment to, 2935.33
riot, when constitutes, 2917.03
  aggravated, 2917.02

DISPENSE, DEFINED RE DRUG OFFENSES, 3719.01

DISPERSE, FAILURE TO, 2917.04

DISPLAYING MATTER HARMFUL TO JUVENILES, 2907.31.1

DISQUALIFICATION OF JUDGE OR MAGISTRATE OF INFERIOR COURT, 2937.20

DISRUPTING PUBLIC SERVICES, 2909.04

DISRUPTIVE CONDUCT, EXCLUSION OF DEFENDANT FOR, Crim. R. 43

DISSEMINATING MATTER HARMFUL TO JUVENILES, 2907.31

DISTRIBUTE, DEFINED RE DANGEROUS DRUGS, 3719.01

DISTRIBUTOR
cigarettes, tobacco products—
  illegal sale, distribution of, 2927.02
controlled substances; drugs—
  terminal, false or forged license for, 2925.23
  theft to obtain, 2925.23
  wholesale, false or forged registration certificate, for, 2925.23
  theft of, 2925.23

DISTURBING A LAWFUL MEETING, 2917.12

DITCH, OBSTRUCTING OR DIVERTING, 3767.16
highway, along, 5589.04

DIVERSION PROGRAMS, PRETRIAL, 2935.36

DNA TESTS
database, 109.57.3, 109.99
juvenile delinquents, 2151.31.5
laboratory, 109.57.3, 109.99
offender sentenced to incarceration, 2901.07
public records disclosure exemption, 109.43

DOCKET, Crim. R. 55

DOCUMENTS, DISCOVERY
subpoena for, Crim. R. 17
  deposition, re order to produce at, Crim. R. 15

DOCUMENTS, ILLEGAL PROCESSING OF DRUG, 2925.23

DOGFIGHTING, 959.16, 959.99

DOGS
assaulting police dog or handicapped assistance dog, 2921.32.1
biting person, duties after, 955.26.1
capture, obstructing, 955.24
confinement of, 955.22, 955.22.1, 955.26, 955.39
killing, when permitted, 955.28
penalties, 955.99
quarantine, 955.26, 955.39
registration of, 955.01
tags to be worn, 955.10
transfer of ownership, 955.11

DOMESTIC VIOLENCE, 2919.25, 3113.31, 3113.32
anti-stalking protection order, 2903.21.3
arrest for, 2935.03, 2935.03.2
bail, considerations in setting, 2919.25.1, 2937.23
consent agreements, 3113.31
duty of certain persons to report, 2921.22
orders to present offenses against complainant or his ward, child, or property, 2945.04
out-of-state protection orders, 2919.27.2
probation provisions, 2933.16
protection orders, notice to law enforcement agencies, SupR 10
shelters for victims, 3113.33-3113.39
  abused child living in, 2151.42.2
  additional marriage license fee to support, 3113.34
  annual reports by shelters, compilation by attorney general, 3113.39
  definitions, 3113.33
  deposit of unallocated funds in state treasury, applications to attorney general for assistance, 3113.37
  determination of last known address of admittee, 3113.40
  priorities for allocating funds, 3113.38
  shelter may apply to county for release of fees, 3113.35, 3113.36
temporary protection order, 2919.26
  evaluation of violator's mental condition, 2919.27.1
  violation of, as offense, 2919.27
victim's rights pamphlet to include information, 109.42

DOUBLE JEOPARDY, DEFENSE OF
misdemeanors, plea of, 2937.06, 2937.08
plea of, procedure, 2943.05 *et seq*

DOUBT, REASONABLE, 2901.05—*see also* REASONABLE DOUBT

DRAG RACING, PROHIBITED, 4511.25.1, 4511.99

DRAIN, OBSTRUCTING, 5589.06

DRIVE BY SHOOTING
specification in indictment, 2941.14.6

DRIVER'S LICENSE—*see also* **COMMERCIAL DRIVERS**
additional sanctions for violating municipal ordinance concerning financial responsibility or OMVI suspensions, 4507.36.1
age requirements, 4507.08
alcoholic, drug addict; license not issued to, 4507.08
another's; displaying as one's own, prohibited, 4507.30
application, 4507.06, 4507.21
    concealing facts in, prohibited, 4507.30
    fees, 4507.23, 4507.24
    filing; indexing of, 4507.21
    names, addresses of applicants filed by registrar; fee for list of, 4507.25
    previously suspended or revoked license, procedure when, 4507.21
    probationary, for minor, 4507.07
    prohibited while license suspended or revoked, 4507.17
    request for donation to second chance trust fund, 4507.23.1
arrest warrant, ineligibility due to outstanding municipal or county court, 4507.09.1
automobile insurance, connection with, by deputy registrar assigned to licensing station, prohibited, 4507.01
blank, offenses concerning, 2913.71
bond, use as, 2937.22.1
chauffeur—*see* **COMMERCIAL DRIVERS**
contents, 4507.13
criminal justice network, 5502.01
deaf persons, restrictions re, 4507.14
definitions, re, 4507.01
digitalized photographic records, release of, 4507.53
disability, physical, mental; license not issued, when, 4507.08
display upon demand of peace officer required, 4507.35
driver license compact, 4507.60-4507.63
duplicate, application for, 4507.06
epileptic, restricted license, 4507.08, 4507.08.1
examination of licensee's competency by registrar, 4507.20
    after suspension under point system for traffic offenses, 4507.02.2
    examiners' permit, 4507.11
    exceptions, 4507.10
    facilities at deputy registrar's office, 4503.03.1
examination special account, 4507.24
expiration dates; renewal, 4507.09
failure to appear or pay fine, cancellation for, 4507.16.8
false statements re, prohibited, 4507.36
fees, 4507.23 et seq
    deputy registrars', 4507.24

DRIVER'S LICENSE—*Continued*
fees—*Continued*
    names, addresses of applicants on file with registrar, for, 4507.25
fictitious, altered, cancelled, display, possession prohibited, 4507.30
free replacement or permit or license lost due to crime, 4507.24.1
hearing-impaired persons, sun visor identification for, 4507.14.1
information furnished to tax commissioner to discover address, 4507.02.3
issuance, 4507.21, 4507.22
jurisdiction of actions re, 4507.15
lending to person not entitled to use; permitting another's use of; prohibited, 4507.30
lending vehicle to unlicensed driver prohibited, 4507.33
liability for minor's negligence imputed to person signing application, 4507.07
liquor laws, suspension for use of false license to violate, 4507.16.3
minor's, 4507.07
    cancellation upon request of person signing application, 4507.07
    driver education course completion required, 4507.21
    liability for minor's negligence, misconduct imputed to person signing application, 4507.07
    permitting unlicensed minor to drive prohibited, 4507.31
    restrictions on issuance, 4507.08
    revocation, grounds, 4507.16.2
    school, withdrawal/absenteeism, 4507.06.1
motorcycle license—
    examination, 4507.11
    "novice" designation, 4507.13
motorized bicycle (moped) license, 4507.01
non-English-speaking persons, 4507.08
notice of license expiration, 4507.09
out-of-state licensed drivers—
    license revoked, suspended, denial of Ohio license, when; action re, 4507.08
    nonresidents, Ohio license not required, 4507.04
    surrender of license prior to issuance of Ohio license, 4507.02
penalties, 4507.99
point system, 4507.02.1
prohibited acts re, 4507.30
prosecuting attorney to aid registrar in investigations, prosecutions, 4507.29
refusal; review by registrar, 4507.22
registrar; deputies—
    point system for traffic offenses, duties, re, 4507.02.1
    powers, duties re; fees, 4507.01
    reversal, modification of registrar's order re, 4507.26-4507.28
    review of refused applications, 4507.22
registrar rental special fund, 4507.01.1

DRIVER'S LICENSE—*Continued*
renewal, 4507.09
    restricted licenses, 4507.08.1
required, for motor vehicle, motorcycle operation on public, private property, 4507.02
    exceptions, 4507.03, 4507.04
restrictions on issuance, 4507.08
    falsified physician's statement to obtain restricted license prohibited, 4507.30
    registrar, imposed by, 4507.14
    renewal of restricted licenses, 4507.08.1
snowmobile, all purpose vehicle operation, when required for, 4519.44
surrender of suspended or revoked license, failure re, 4507.30
suspension, revocation, cancellation—
    accident, failure to make security deposit required after; suspension for, 4509.17, 4509.18, 4509.26, 4509.29.1
    accident report, failure to file, for, 4509.09
    alteration or destruction of license, for, 4507.19
    causing death while fleeing police, suspension for, 4507.16
    conviction, guilty plea to certain offenses, for, 4507.16
        appeal, disposition of license during, 4507.18
        proof of financial responsibility required to reinstate after, 4509.31, 4509.32
    destruction of license after, 4507.54, 4507.55
    driving after, prohibited, 4507.02
    driving while intoxicated, refusal to take blood alcohol tests; for, 4511.19.1, 4511.19.2
    drug offense conviction under federal law or in another state or for OMVI offense in another state; application to minors, 4507.16.9
    effect, 4507.17
    epileptic's restricted license, when, 4507.08.1
    failure to appear/comply, 2935.27, 4507.16.8
    federal court, by, 4507.16.10
    financial responsibility, proof of; when required to avoid or reinstate after, 4509.31-4509.34
        return of license to registrar, when, 4509.09, 4509.77
    illegally conveying or possessing deadly weapon or dangerous ordnance on school premises, 2923.12.2, 4507.16.12
    intoxicating liquor, beer, use of false license to purchase illegally; suspension for; hearing re, 4507.16.3
    license plates, registration impounded during, 4507.02, 4507.16.4
    mentally ill person adjudicated incompetent, of, 4507.16.1
    minor's license cancelled upon request of person signing application, 4507.07
    minor's probationary or restricted license revocation, 4507.16.2
    point system for traffic offenses, 4507.02.1
    reckless operation, for, 4507.34

DRIVER'S LICENSE—*Continued*
suspension, revocation, cancellation—*Continued*
    re-examination for return of license after suspension under point system, 4507.02.2
    reinstatement fee in certain cases, 4507.45
    school bus, stopped; suspension for passing, 4507.16.5
    suspension or revocation defined, 4507.01.2
    unlawfully obtained; erroneously issued, 4507.19
    use as bond, 2937.22.1
    violating ordinance substantially similar to statute, 4507.16.11
temporary instruction permit, 4507.05
test, 4507.11
unlicensed driver, lending vehicle to, prohibited, 4507.33
vision screening prior to renewal, 4507.12
voter registration of applicant, 4507.06

DRIVING UNDER INFLUENCE OF ALCOHOL OR DRUG, 4511.19-4511.19.6
additional sanctions for violating municipal ordinance, 4507.36.1
advice form to be read to arrestee, 4511.19.1
county, municipal indigent drivers alcohol treatment funds, 4507.99, 4511.19.1, 4511.99
disorderly conduct, is not, 2917.11
driver's license suspension for, 4507.16, 4511.19.6
driver's license suspension for refusal to take BAC tests, 4511.19.1
driving after, prohibited, 4511.19.2
endangering children, 2919.22
ignition interlock as a condition of probative, implied consent to BAC tests, 4511.19.1
impoundment, immobilization, forfeiture of vehicle, 4503.23.3-4503.23.5
    municipal ordinance, violation of, 4511.19.3
initial appearance, 4511.19.6
intensive program prisons, 5120.03.3
prior conviction, arrestee with, seizure of vehicle, 4511.19.5
recognizance, requirements of, 2937.28.1
request to health care provider for results of alcohol or drug test for use in criminal proceedings, 2317.02, 2317.02.2

DRUG ADDICTION AND TREATMENT
drug treatment program—
    defined, 2929.01
    felony sanctions, 2929.13

DRUGS AND DRUG OFFENSES, 2925.01 *et seq*
abuse, 2925.11
    disorderly conduct, operating vehicle during, is not, 2917.11
    drug of abuse, defined, 3719.01.1
    felony sentencing considerations, 2929.12
    offense, defined, 2925.01

DRUGS AND DRUG OFFENSES—*Continued*
abuse—*Continued*
   permitting, 2925.13
conspiracy, re drug offenses, 2923.01
contaminating substance for human consumption or use, 2927.24
conveying into detention facility or institution, 2921.36, 2921.37
corrupting another with, 2925.02
counterfeit controlled substance—
   definition, 2925.01
   offenses, re, 2925.37
dangerous, ch. 4729.
dependent person—
   challenge to juror, as, Crim. R. 24
   conditional probation for treatment, of, 2951.04
   firearms, disabilities re, 2923.13, 2923.14
   person in danger of becoming, defined, 3719.01.1
   treatment in lieu of conviction, 2951.04.1
destroyed by law enforcement agency, when, 2933.41
firearm, dangerous ordnance—
   possession after conviction, indictment re, when prohibited, 2923.13
   possession while under the influence of, 2923.15
   relief from disability re, 2923.14
forfeiture of property—*see* FORFEITURE *at* drug abuse offenses, for
funding of drug or marihuana trafficking, 2925.05
illegal administration or distribution of anabolic steroids, 2925.06
illegal manufacturing of drugs or cultivation of marihuana, 2925.04
informant rewards, immunity, 309.08, 3719.70—*see also* INFORMANTS
livestock involving, 2925.09
major drug offender—
   defined, 2929.01
   specification in indictment, 2941.14.10
medical, scientific use, by law enforcement agency, 2933.41
motor vehicle, operation under influence of, 4511.19, 4511.99
narcotic, 3719.01 *et seq*
offenses, 2925.01 *et seq*
organized crime investigations commission jurisdiction, 177.01
paraphernalia, 2925.14
possession, 2925.11
rape, use in preventing resistance re, 2907.02
request to health care provider for results of drug test for use in criminal proceedings, 2317.02, 2317.02.2
schedules, 3719.41
spreading false report of contamination, 2927.24
theft of, 2925.21
trafficking in, 2925.03
unapproved drugs, 2925.04

DUELING, 3773.07

DURESS, AS MITIGATING CIRCUMSTANCE RE AGGRAVATED MURDER, 2929.04

DUTY
dereliction of, 2921.44
fiduciary, of, prosecutions limited for breach of, 2901.13
legal, 2901.04, 2901.23
   out of state, omission to perform, jurisdiction, 2901.11
omission to perform, 2901.21

EAVESDROPPING—*see also* WIRETAPPING, ELECTRONIC SURVEILLANCE
voyeurism, as, 2907.08

EDUCATION—*see* SCHOOL

ELECTIONS
offenses and penalties, 3599.01 *et seq*
   absent voter's ballot, offenses pertaining to, 3599.21
   ballot box, illegal possession of, 3599.24
   ballots—
      alteration of, 3599.33
      custody of, and papers, 3599.23
      failure to keep, secret, 3599.20
      offenses pertaining to, 3599.21
      possession of, illegal, 3599.24
      printing of, offenses pertaining to, 3599.22
      tampering with, 3599.26
   bribery, 3599.01, 3599.02
   campaign contributions and expenditures, 3599.45
   communications purporting to be from board of elections, 3599.43
   congregating at polls, 3599.30
   corporations, prohibited use of funds by, 3599.03
   custody of ballots and papers, 3599.23
   demanding pledges, 3599.10
   destroying or mutilating petitions, 3599.15
   destroying records in contest cases, 3599.34
   election falsification, 3599.36
   employers—
      corporate political activities, 3599.03, 3599.03.1
      influence by, 3599.05
      interference with voting, 3599.06
   failure of officer to assist election officials, 3599.31
   failure to enforce law, election officials, 3599.32
   false affidavit, 3599.36
   falsely signing petitions, 3599.13
   false records, possession of, 3599.29
   false registration, 3599.11
   false signatures, 3599.28
   false statements on form, 3599.11
   falsification, elections, 3599.36
   fraudulent writing on poll books, 3599.33
   fraud, violation of act constitutes, 3599.42
   illegal voting, 3599.12
   impersonating delegate or committeeman, 3599.35
   inducing illegal voting, 3599.25

ELECTIONS—*Continued*
offenses and penalties—*Continued*
  influencing electors, 3599.02
  interfering with election, 3599.24
  intimidating election officers, 3599.24
  judges and clerks, failure of, to perform duties, 3599.17, 3599.19
  loitering, 3599.24
  medicaid provider, accepting contribution from, 3599.45
  misconduct of board members or employees, 3599.16
  misrepresenting contents of petition, 3599.14
  multiple voting, 3599.12
  newspaper publications, 3599.08
  party representatives, 3599.35
  paying for votes, 3599.04
  penalties not otherwise provided, 3599.40
  perjury, 3599.36
  pledges, demanding, 3599.10
  pollbooks, illegal possession of, 3599.24
  possession of false records, 3599.29
  prima facie case of fraud, 3599.42
  printing of ballots, 3599.22
  procedure in booth, 3599.19
  prohibiting inspection of election records, 3599.16.1
  proxy may not be issued, 3599.35
  refusal to testify, 3599.37
  registrars, misconduct of, 3599.18
  registration form, destroying or failing to return, 3599.11
  second offense, 3599.39
  secret ballot, 3599.20
  supplies, removal from polling place, 3599.24
  tampering with voting machines, 3599.27
  testify, refusal to, 3599.37
  violating witness shall testify, 3599.41
  wearing of badge, sign, etc., 3599.38

ELECTORAL FRANCHISE, EFFECT OF FELONY CONVICTION ON, 2961.01

ELECTRICITY
value of stolen service, 2913.61

ELECTRONICALLY MONITORED HOUSE ARREST, 2929.23
assignment of offender's payments to pay costs, 2949.11.1
defined, 2929.01
sanctions for felony, 2929.17

ELECTRONIC BENEFIT TRANSFERS
criminal violations, 2913.46

ELECTRONIC SURVEILLANCE—*see* WIRETAPPING, ELECTRONIC SURVEILLANCE

ELEMENTS OF OFFENSE
affidavit, complaint, indictment, information, must be stated in, 2945.75

ELEMENTS OF OFFENSE—*Continued*
guilty verdict shall state, effect of omitting, 2945.75

EMBEZZLEMENT, 2913.02
prima facie evidence of, what constitutes, 2945.64

EMERGENCY
false alarms, making, re, 2917.32
law enforcement officers, firemen, rescue personnel, impairing ability of, to respond to, 2909.04
misconduct at, 2917.13
paroles due to overcrowding, 2967.18

EMPLOYEE
organization, of, when may be prosecuted for offense, 2901.24
subpoenaed before grand jury; employer may not penalize, 2939.12.1
subpoenaed to criminal proceeding; employer may not penalize, 2945.45.1

EMPLOYER
crime victims, prohibited actions of employers, 2930.18

EMPLOYMENT
presentence report, record of defendant's, in, Crim. R. 32.2
release on bail, based on, Crim. R. 46

ENDANGERING
aircraft or airport operations, 2909.08
child, 2919.22—*see also* CHILD
child victim of; testimony by deposition, videotape, closed circuit TV, 2907.41
criminal, 2909.06

ENGINE NOISE, TOWNSHIP MAY MAKE REGULATIONS FOR, 505.17

ENTICEMENT
child, of, into motor vehicle, 2905.05

ENTRY
commitment, of, to accompany presentence report, Crim. R. 32.2
dismissal, of, filed by state, Crim. R. 48
judgment, of, by clerk, Crim. R. 32
  prior conviction proved by, 2945.75
nonconsensual, statutory precondition for, 2933.23.1

ERROR
appeal, re—
  instructions, re, only if objected to, Crim. R. 30
clerical, Crim. R. 36
harmless, disregarded, Crim. R. 52
law, of, new trial for, Crim. R. 33; 2945.79
plain, court may notice, Crim. R. 52

ESCAPE, 2921.34
after jury sworn, arrest warrant to issue, 2941.38
aiding, 2921.35
   person on detainer, 2963.34
before confinement, resentencing upon capture, 2949.06
convict, of, arrest and return, 5120.48
death sentence, convict under, of, procedure, 2949.27
detainer, person on, of, 2963.34
duty to give notice, add, 2930.16
facility, from, officer negligently allowing, 2921.44
notice of, 341.01.1
prosecution of furloughee or releasee, 2967.15
removal to county for sentence or trial, after, 2941.40
sentence of confinement, for, 2929.14
time absent not counted toward sentence, 2949.07
voids request for trial, 2941.40.1

ETHNIC INTIMIDATION, 2927.12

EVIDENCE, 2945.41 *et seq*
acquittal, motion for judgment of, when insufficient to put upon defense, Crim. R. 29
admissibility of videotaped testimony of child victim of sex offense, 2907.41
alibi, of, excluded for failure to file notice of, Crim. R. 12.1
destroying physical, of crime, re obstructing justice, 2921.32
drug prosecutions, laboratory analysis reports by both parties provided, 2925.51
embezzlement, what constitutes prima facie proof of, 2945.64
firearm, dangerous ordnance, application for relief from disability re, evidence derived not admissible, 2923.23
newly discovered, as grounds for new trial, Crim. R. 33; 2945.79
photographs, substitution for physical evidence, Crim. R. 26
property held as, Crim. R. 41; 2933.41
rules of civil, when applicable, 2945.41
same or similar acts, proof of, 2945.59
sufficiency of, motion for new trial not necessary to obtain appellate review, Crim. R. 33; 2945.-83.1
tampering with, 2921.12

EVIDENCE, RULES OF
admissibility, EvR 104, 105
authentication, EvR 901, 902, 903
best evidence rule, EvR 1002
   duplicate, EvR 1003
bias of witness, EvR 616
character evidence, EvR 404, 405, 608
child statements in abuse cases, EvR 807
competency, EvR 601
   judge, EvR 605

EVIDENCE, RULES OF—*Continued*
competency—*Continued*
   juror, EvR 606
construction, EvR 102
definitions—
   declarant, EvR 801
   hearsay, EvR 801
   photograph, EvR 1001
   recording, EvR 1001
   relevant evidence, EvR 401
   statement, EvR 801
   writing, EvR 1001
effective date, EvR 1102
expert witness—
   opinion, EvR 703, 704
   testimony, EvR 702
   underlying facts, EvR 705
habit, EvR 406
hearsay—
   child statements in abuse cases, EvR 807
   credibility of declarant, EvR 806
   definitions, EvR 801
   exceptions, EvR 803, 804
   rule, EvR 802
   within hearsay, EvR 805
impeachment, EvR 607, 608, 609
insurance, EvR 411
interpreter, EvR 604
interrogation—
   court, EvR 614
   mode, EvR 611
judicial notice, EvR 201
oath, EvR 603
offers to compromise, EvR 408
opinion testimony—
   expert witness, EvR 703, 704, 705
   lay witness, EvR 701
past recollection recorded, EvR 803
personal knowledge, lack of, EvR 602
pleas, offers of pleas, EvR 410
present memory refreshed, EvR 612
presumptions, EvR 301
prior conviction of crime, EvR 404, 609
prior statements, EvR 613
privileges, EvR 101, 501
relevancy, EvR 402, 403
   conditional, EvR 104
religious belief, EvR 610
res gestae, EvR 803
rulings, EvR 103
scope of rules, EvR 101
separation of witnesses, EvR 615
settlements, EvR 408, 409
spouse, competency of, EvR 601
subsequent remedial measures, EvR 407
title, EvR 1103
writings, recordings, and photographs—
   admission of party, EvR 1007

EVIDENCE, RULES OF—*Continued*
writings, recordings, and photographs—*Continued*
  definitions, EvR 1001
  duplicates, EvR 1003
  function of court and jury, EvR 1008
  original required, EvR 1002
  other evidence of contents, EvR 1004
  public records, EvR 1005
  remainder of writings, EvR 106
  summaries, EvR 1006

EXAMINATION
discovery re reports of—
  defendant, from, Crim. R. 16
  prosecuting attorney, from, Crim. R. 16
jurors, of, Crim. R. 24; 2945.27
presentence investigation, re, Crim. R. 32.2
psychiatric, before sentencing—
  death penalty, re, 2929.03
sentence to be reduced by time confined for sanity examination, 2967.19.1
sex offense victim, of, 2907.28, 2907.29

EXCEPTIONS
applicability of criminal rules, to, Crim. R. 1
ruling or motions, etc., unnecessary, Crim. R. 51; 2945.09
  magistrate courts, 2938.09

EXCUSABLE NEGLECT, ACT PERMITTED AFTER TIME, FOR, Crim. R. 45

EXCUSE
affirmative defense, as, 2901.05
imprisonment for felony, as criterion re, 2929.12
probation, as factor favoring, 2951.02

EXECUTION OF SENTENCE—*see also* DEATH PENALTY; SENTENCE
suspension of, re appeal, 2949.02, 2949.03, 2953.03, 2953.09, 2953.10
when not appealed, 2949.05

EXHIBITS
preliminary hearing, at, Crim. R. 5

EXONERATION OF SURETY (BAIL BOND), Crim. R. 46

EXPERT WITNESS—*see also* EVIDENCE, RULES OF
constitutional basis for laws regulating, Art. II, § 39 OC

EXPLOSION—*see also* EXPLOSIVES
alarm, false, re impending, 2917.32
arson, by, 2909.03
damaging, endangering, criminal, by, 2909.06
panic, inducing by false report of impending, 2917.31

EXPLOSIVES
devices, defined, 2923.11
farmers, when granted license, permit to possess, 2923.18
illegally manufacturing or processing, 2923.17
industrial use, license, permit to possess, 2923.18
license for, 2923.17, 2923.18
ordnance, as dangerous, 2923.11
vehicles, transporting, 4513.29

EXPUNGEMENT, SEALING OF RECORD
after dismissal of proceedings or not guilty verdict, 2953.51 *et seq*
multiple offenses from same act, 2953.61
sealing of record of first offender, 2953.31 *et seq*

EXTENSION OF TIME—*see also* TIME
excusable neglect, as ground for, Crim. R. 45
hearing or trial, for, 2945.72

EXTORTION, 2905.11—*see also* COERCION
extension of credit, re, 2905.21-2905.24

EXTRADITION, 2963.01 *et seq*
applicability of Criminal Rules, to, Crim. R. 1
proceedings re, extends time for trial, 2945.72

FACILITY, DETENTION—*see* DETENTION

FACSIMILE DEVICES
transmitting advertising to, 4931.55

FAILURE
aid law enforcement officer, to, 2921.23
  extradition proceedings, re, 2963.08
crime, to report, 2921.22
disperse, to, 2917.04
order or signal of officer, to obey, 2921.33.1
testify, to, by defendant, 2945.43

FAIR HOUSING RIGHTS, INTERFERENCE WITH, 2927.03

FAIR TRIAL, RE NEW TRIAL, Crim. R. 33

FALSE ALARM, MAKING, 2917.32

FALSE IMPRISONMENT, 2905.03

FALSE REPORT OF CHILD ABUSE OR NEGLECT, 2921.14

FALSE REPORT OF CONTAMINATION, SPREADING, 2927.24

FALSE STATEMENTS
intimidation by filing, recording or using false writing, 2921.03

FALSIFICATION, 2921.13
drug documents, re, 2925.23

FAMILY, OFFENSES AGAINST, 2919.01 *et seq*
abortion, 2919.11 *et seq*
bigamy, 2919.01
child, endangering, 2919.22
contributing to delinquency of, 2919.24
custody, interference with, 2919.23
dependents, nonsupport of, 2919.21
domestic violence, 2919.25 *et seq*

FAX MACHINES—*see* FACSIMILE DEVICES

FEEDS
commercial, offenses, jurisdiction of county court judge, 2931.02

FELONIOUS ASSAULT, 2903.11

FELONY
bail, re—
    conditions of, Crim. R. 46
    conviction, after, Crim. R. 46
civil rights lost upon conviction of, 2961.01
classification of offenses, re, 2901.02
concurrently, misdemeanor sentence to be served with, 2929.41
costs, convicted felon to pay, 2949.14 *et seq*
defined, Crim. R. 2
drug abuse offense, defined, 2925.01
joinder of defendants, re, Crim. R. 8; 2945.13, 2945.15
joinder of offenses, re, Crim. R. 8
jury trial, re right to—
    number of jurors, Crim. R. 23
    peremptory challenges, Crim. R. 24
limitation of prosecutions for, six years, 2901.13
murder while committing felony, 2903.01
    aggravating circumstance, as, 2929.04
    death penalty, fine for, 2903.01, 2929.02
negotiated plea to, underlying agreement to be stated in open court, Crim. R. 11
offense committed prior to 1-1-74; third or fourth degree felony committed between 1-1-74 and 7-1-83, 2929.61
parole, early, if no prior conviction for, 2967.31
penalties for, 2929.11, 2929.12
    definite term of imprisonment, 2929.13
    fine, imposition of, 2929.14
    specification required in indictment for imposition of certain, 2941.14.1-2941.14.3
peremptory challenges, re, Crim. R. 24
preliminary hearing, re, Crim. R. 5—*see also* PRELIMINARY HEARING
presentence investigation, re, mandatory, Crim. R. 32.2
probation, investigation before, 2951.03
procedure on charge of, 2937.09 *et seq*
sentencing criteria for third or fourth degree, 2929.13

FELONY—*Continued*
trial, time for—
    arrest, within 270 days after, 2945.71
    discharge of accused for delay in holding, 2945.73
        nolle prosequi, has same effect as, 2945.73
    extension of, reasons for, 2945.72

FESTIVAL SEATING
prohibited, 2917.40

FIDUCIARY
creditors, in behalf of, nondisclosure to, 2913.45
duty, breach of, limitation of prosecutions for, 2901.13

FIGHTING, AS DISORDERLY CONDUCT, 2917.11

FILTH, 3767.13—*see also* NUISANCES

FINAL RELEASE, BY ADULT PAROLE AUTHORITY, 2967.01, 2967.16

FINANCIAL RESPONSIBILITY—*see* MOTOR VEHICLES, *at* financial responsibility laws re

FINE
applicability of rules to, exception re, Crim. R. 1
confinement in satisfaction of, 2947.14
county treasury, to be paid into, 2949.11
felony drug offenses, mandatory minimum for, 2925.03
felony, for, 2929.11
forfeited property not available to pay, 2925.44
imposition of, for felony, 2929.14
installment payments of, court may permit, 2929.51
jury trial, potential, effect on right to, 2945.17
minor misdemeanors, for, posting of schedule re, Crim. R. 4.1
misdemeanor, for, 2929.21
organization, against, for offenses by, 2929.31
suspension of, 2929.51

FIRE
alarm, making false, 2917.32
arson, 2909.01 *et seq*—*see also* ARSON AND RELATED OFFENSES
code, 505.37.3, 505.37.4
communications, disrupting, 2909.04
criminal mischief, 2909.07
damaging, endangering, criminal, by, 2909.06
department, city, ch. 737
duty upon discovering unfriendly, 3737.63
hampering officer, fireman, etc., at, 2917.13
hydrant, tampering with, 4933.22
negligent spreading of fire, 3737.62, 3737.99
panic, inducing by false report re, 2917.31
public buildings, examination of, 737.34-737.37, 737.99

FIREARMS, DANGEROUS ORDNANCE, 2923.11 *et seq*

FIREARMS, DANGEROUS, ETC.—*Continued*
automatic, muffled, or silenced—
  effect on sentence, 2929.22
  specification required, 2941.14.1, 2941.14.4
carrying concealed, 2923.12
cemetery, discharging near, 3773.05
courthouse or courtroom facility, conveyance, possession or control in, 2923.12.3
defined, 2923.11
disability re, possession, use, under, 2923.13
discharge in certain places prohibited, 3773.21
discharging at or into habitation or school, 2923.16.1
discharging over or upon road or highway, 3773.21.1
disposition of, by law enforcement agency, 2933.41
falsification in connection with purchase, 2921.13
felony sentencing considerations, 2929.14
immunity from prosecution, re, 2923.23
interstate transactions in, 2923.22
intoxicated, carrying, use while, 2923.15
liquor, premises; possession of, prohibited, 2923.12.1
minor, improperly furnishing to, 2923.21
motor vehicle—
  carrying concealed in, 2923.12
  improperly handling in, 2923.16
ordnance, dangerous, as, 2923.11
receiving stolen, 2913.51
relief from disability re, 2923.14
specification in indictment or information, 2941.14.1, 2941.14.5
  automatic or equipped with muffler or silencer, 2941.14.4
  discharge from motor vehicle, 2941.14.6
theft of, 2913.02
  report to law enforcement authorities required, 2923.20
transactions in, unlawful, 2923.20
  interstate transactions in, lawful, 2923.22
underage purchase of, 2923.21.1

FIRE MARSHAL
arson—
  transient residential building, posting of arson law required, 3737.61
    penalty, 3737.99
false representation as fire fighter, 3737.66, 3737.99
fire protection and fire fighting equipment—
  prohibitions, 3737.65
fire safety inspector—
  impersonating prohibited, 3737.64, 3737.99
fireworks—*see* FIREWORKS
licenses, permits certificates—
  dangerous ordnance, explosives, file of, 2923.18
oaths, failure to cooperate, 3737.28
petroleum underground storage tanks—*see* PETROLEUM UNDERGROUND STORAGE TANKS
schools, fire drills, tornado safety, 3737.73, 3737.99
underground petroleum storage tanks, 3737.99

FIREMEN
assaulting, 2903.13
hampering performance of, at emergency, 2917.13
riot, suppressing by justifiable force, 2917.05

FIREWORKS
advertising for sale prohibited, 3743.65
arrest of violators, 3743.68
definitions, 3743.01
discharging prohibited, 3743.65
exemptions from provisions, 3743.80
exhibitor's, prohibited activities, 3743.64
felony precludes license or permit, 3743.70
fines, distribution of, 3743.68
manufacturer's license—
  manufacturing without, 3743.60
  prohibited activities, 3743.60
  purchaser's form, 3743.65
minors, sales to, 3743.65
possession, restrictions on, 3743.65
purchasers—
  duties of, restrictions, 3743.63
  form, false statements, 3743.65
sales—
  class C fireworks to residents, 3743.63, 3743.65
  manufacturer, by, 3743.65
  minors, to, 3743.65
  nonresidents to, 3743.63, 3743.65
  wholesaler's, 3743.65
seizure and forfeiture, 3743.68
shipping or transporting, rules, 3743.66
wholesaler's license—
  prohibited activities, 3743.61
  purchaser's form, 3743.65
  unlicensed operation, 3743.61

FIRST OFFENDER, SEALING OF RECORD OF, 2953.31 *et seq*

FISH HOUSES, 3767.16, 3767.22

FLAG, U.S., OHIO, DESECRATING, 2927.11

FLIGHT
avoid prosecution, to—*see also* ESCAPE
  kidnapping to facilitate, 2905.01
  limitation statute, tolls, 2901.13
  murder during, as aggravating circumstance, 2924.04

FLOOD, CRIMINAL DAMAGING, ENDANGERING BY, 2909.06

FOOD
contaminating substance for human consumption or use, 2927.24
placing drug or harmful object or substance in, 3716.11
spreading false report of contamination, 2927.24

FOOD STAMPS, COUPONS
illegal use of; trafficking in, 2913.46

FORCE
defined, 2901.01
rape, use to effect, 2907.02
riot, use in suppressing, justifiable, 2917.05

FORCIBLE ENTRY OF DWELLING, TO EFFECT ARREST, 2935.12

FOREIGN LAW
determination of, Crim. R. 27

FOREIGN STATE REQUESTING WITNESS, 2939.25 et seq

FOREMAN OF GRAND JURY, Crim. R. 6
indorsement of indictment, 2939.20
oath to witnesses, to administer, 2939.13
report to court when indictment not found, 2939.23
to be appointed, 2939.06

FORFEITED PROPERTY, DISPOSITION OF, BY LAW ENFORCEMENT AGENCY, 2933.41

FORFEITURE
bail, of, 2937.35 et seq
  appearance, for failure to make, as required, Crim. R. 46
  condition of release, for breach of, Crim. R. 46
contraband, property used in committing offense, 2933.42, 2933.43
drug abuse offenses, for—
  civil action, 2925.43
  contesting, 2925.45
  contraband, 2925.44
  conviction, pursuant to, 2925.42
  custodian, duties of, 2925.44
  definitions, 2925.41
  disposition of property, 2925.44
  fine, property not available to pay, 2925.44
  security interest, unsatisfied, 2925.44
  title to property, 2925.44
property, of, applicability of rules to, Crim. R. 1
vehicle—
  criminal, 4503.23.4, 4503.23.5
  immobilization order violation, 4503.23.6, 4503.99

FORGE, DEFINED RE THEFT, FRAUD, 2913.01

FORGERY, 2913.31—*see also* CRIMINAL SIMULATION, 2913.32
identification cards, 2913.31
  official, false, 4301.63.6
indictment for, sufficient when, 2941.15 et seq

FORMER ACQUITTAL, CONVICTION, AS PLEA, 2943.03, 2943.05 et seq
what is, is not, former acquittal, 2943.07, 2943.08

FORMS, Crim. R. 58

FOSTER HOMES—*see* JUVENILE COURTS

FRANCHISE
denied for failure to accept objectionable material, 2907.34

FRAUD—*see* DEFRAUD

FRESH PURSUIT—*see also* SEARCH AND SEIZURE
authority of foreign police, 2935.30
defined, 2935.29
hearing and arrest, 2935.31

FUGITIVE
firearm, dangerous ordnance, re—
  possession by, prohibited, 2923.13
  relief from disability re, void if becomes, 2923.14
justice, from—*see* EXTRADITION, 2963.01 et seq

FUNCTIONALLY IMPAIRED PERSON
assaulting, 2903.13
defined, 2903.10
failing to provide for, 2903.16

FUNERAL SERVICES, PICKETING DURING, 3767.30

FURLOUGHS FOR TRUSTWORTHY PRISONERS, 2967.26

GAMBLING AND RELATED OFFENSES, 2915.01 et seq—*see also* BINGO
cheating, 2915.05
corrupting sports, 2915.05
definitions, 2915.01
gambling, 2915.02
house, operating a, 2915.03
public gaming, 2915.04

GAMING, PUBLIC, 2915.04

GARAGE KEEPER
crime, evidence of, shall report, 4501.05

GARBAGE, OFFENSES INVOLVING, 3767.32, 3767.33

GAS
poison, criminal damaging, endangering by, 2909.06
tear, use as criminal mischief, 2909.07
works as nuisance, 3767.14

GENDER, USAGE IN CODE, 1.43

GENERAL ASSEMBLY
special grand jury, may request, 2939.17

GOOD BEHAVIOR
consecutive indeterminate sentences, parole time diminished for, 2967.25
probation, as condition of, 2951.02
sentence, diminution of, 2967.19 et seq

GOVERNMENT AGENCY
appropriation, annual, public official exceeding, 2921.44
contract with, unlawful interest in, 2921.42
records of, tampering with, 2913.42
riot, to impede function of, 2917.03
theft of property of, by public official, 2921.41

GOVERNOR
assassination of, as aggravating circumstance, 2929.04
constitutional powers re reprieves, commutations, pardons, Art. III, § 11 OC
extradition, duties, powers, re, 2963.01 et seq
pardon, conditional, by, 2967.04
release of convict in imminent danger of death, may order, 2967.05
reprieve by, 2967.01, 2967.07 et seq
special grand jury, may request, 2939.17

GRAND JURY, Crim. R. 6; 2939.01 et seq
constitutional provisions re, Art. I, § 10 OC
employer's duty when employee subpoenaed before, 2939.12.1
insanity of defendant, may inform judge of, 2945.37
jail inspection, 2939.21
special, 2939.17
time limit, SupR 39

GRAND THEFT, 2913.02—see also THEFT AND RELATED OFFENSES

GROSS SEXUAL IMPOSITION, 2907.05

GROUP HOME—see CARE FACILITY

GUARDIAN
endangering children by, 2919.22
interference with custody of, 2919.22
mental institution inmate, case review, request by, 2947.27.1
sexual battery by, 2907.03

GUILTY PLEA
arraignment, at, form, Crim. R. 10; 2943.03, 2943.04
arrest of judgment motion filed after, Crim. R. 39
entering of, 2937.06
felonies, procedure, 2937.09

GUILTY PLEA—Continued
misdemeanors, procedure, 2937.07
negotiated—
    coercion, does not constitute crime of, by prosecutor, 2905.12
    felonies, re, Crim. R. 11
notice to defendant, 2943.03.1

GUILTY VERDICT
acquittal, motion for, after, Crim. R. 29
degree of offense, re, least if omitted in, 2945.75
elements of offense, effect of omitting from, 2945.75

GUN CONTROL ACT OF 1968
destructive devices, license under, effect, 2923.17
interstate firearm transactions governed by, 2923.22
ordnance, dangerous, destructive device exception under, not, 2923.11

HABEAS CORPUS, 2725.01 et seq
bail provisions, re, 2725.18, 2725.19
civil liability for offenses re, 2725.27
clerk, refusing to issue writ, 2725.21
constitutional provision for, Art. I, § 8 OC
contents of writ, 2725.09
continuance for cause, 2725.16
courts authorized to grant, 2725.02
designation of prisoner, 2725.08
discharge of prisoner, 2725.17
execution and return of writ, 2725.12
failure to obey writ, penalty, 2725.22
fees and costs, re, 2725.28
form of writ when prisoner not in custody of an officer, 2725.10
imprisonment out of state, prohibited, 2725.25
issuance of writ, 2725.07
jurisdiction over inmates of state institutions, 2725.03
    mental institutions, 2945.35
persons entitled to, 2725.01
petition for, form, contents, 2725.04
record of proceedings, 2725.26
reimprisonment for same offense prohibited where writ granted, 2725.23
return, as evidence or plea, 2725.20
return of writ, contents of, 2725.14, 2725.15
return of writ to another judge, 2725.13
service of writ, 2725.11
transfer of custody, prohibited, 2725.24
when writ must be granted, 2725.06
when writ not to be granted, 2725.05

HABITUAL SEX OFFENDER, 2950.01 et seq—see also SEXUAL PREDATORS, HABITUAL SEX OFFENDERS, SEXUALLY ORIENTED OFFENDERS

HALFWAY HOUSE
adult parole authority may pay costs, 2967.14

HALFWAY HOUSE—*Continued*
defined, 2929.01
release of prisoner in, 2967.23
residential sanction, as, 2923.16
status as imprisonment, 1.05

HANDGUN—*see also* FIREARMS, DANGEROUS ORDNANCE
defined, 2923.11
minor under 21, sale to, prohibited, 2923.21

HARASSMENT
by inmate, 2921.38
telephone, 2917.21

HARBOR, BEFOULING OR OBSTRUCTING, 3767.13, 3767.16
exceptions, 3767.22

HARBORING CRIMINAL, 2921.32

HARDSHIP, UNDUE
felon, dependents of, fine must not cause to, 2929.12
misdemeanant, dependents of, fine must not cause to, 2929.22
murderer, dependents of, fine must not cause to, 2929.02
probation, favoring, when imprisonment would entail, 2951.02

HARMFUL INTOXICANT
abusing, 2925.31
defined, 2925.01
distributing to minor, 2925.32
improperly dispensing or distributing nitrous oxide, 2925.32
possessing nitrous oxide in motor vehicle, 2925.33

HARMLESS ERROR
disregarded, to be, Crim. R. 52

HAZING, 2903.31

HEAD START PROGRAMS
criminal records check for employees responsible for children, employment of certain offenders prohibited, 3301.32

HEALTH
care, nonprofit entities to obtain approval for certain transactions, 109.34, 109.35, 109.99

HEARING
extradition proceedings, right to, 2963.09
firearm disability relief application, on, 2923.14
insanity verdict, re mental institution commitment, when, 2945.39
new trial, on motion for, Crim. R. 33

HEARING—*Continued*
probation revocation, re, Crim. R. 32.3
suppress, on motion to—*see* SUPPRESS, MOTION TO
time for filing motions, affidavits re, Crim. R. 45
time for, unavailability of accused, when extends, 2945.72

HEARSAY
exception to permit videotaped preliminary hearing testimony or deposition where child under 11 is victim of sex offense, 2907.41
search, arrest, warrants, use re, Crim. R. 4, 41

HEIRLOOM, VALUE RE THEFT OFFENSE, 2913.61

HIGHWAY PATROL
law enforcement officer, 2901.01

HIGHWAYS
arrest on, 4513.39
barriers on limited access, 3767.20.1
bridge or culvert, destroying or injuring, 5589.04
marker or monument, injuring or altering, 5589.02
obstructing, 5589.01, 5589.10, 5589.31
penalties, 5589.99
prosecution of offenses, 5589.14
railroad, obstruction by, 5589.21-5589.24
signs, 5589.32, 5589.33
traction engines, operation of, 5589.08
weeds, failure to cut, 5589.11

HISTORY
prisoner, of—
 parole criterion, as, 2967.31
 probation criterion, as, 2951.02

HIV—*see* AIDS, HIV

HOLIDAY, LEGAL, RE TIME COMPUTATION, Crim. R. 45

HOME SOLICITATION SALES
contract in writing required, contents, 1345.23
cooling-off period, 1345.23
notice of cancellation, 1345.23
 form, 1345.24
 seller must retain; penalty, 1345.99

HOMICIDE, 2903.01 *et seq*
indictments re, necessary allegations in, 2941.14
jurisdiction re, 2901.11
negligent, 2903.05
vehicular, 2903.07
 aggravated, 2903.06

HORSES
assaulting police horse, 2921.32.1
hiring, to defraud, 2913.41
servicing mare in public street, 959.19, 959.99
tails, cutting off, 959.14, 959.99

HOSPICE CARE PROGRAMS
criminal records check for certain employees, 3712.09
   access to records, 2950.08, 2953.32
   procedure for checking, 109.57, 109.57.2

HOSPITALS
defined, re drugs, 3719.01
examination of sex offense victims, 2907.29
nonprofit, to obtain approval for certain transactions, 109.34, 109.35, 109.99
patient abuse, neglect in care facility, 2903.33 *et seq*
report of crime by, when not required, 2921.22
sexual battery of patient by supervisor, 2907.03

HOSTAGE, KIDNAPPING TO HOLD AS, 2905.01

HOSTELRY, DEFRAUDING, 2913.41

HOUSE—*see also* BUILDINGS
arrest, electronically monitored, 2929.23
concealed weapon, carrying in, 2923.12
gambling, operating a, 2915.03—*see also* GAMBLING AND RELATED OFFENSES
structure, as occupied, re arson, 2909.01

HOUSING RIGHTS, INTERFERENCE WITH, 2927.03

HUFFING—*see* HARMFUL INTOXICANT

HUMANE SOCIETY
when may employ attorney at public expense, 2931.18

HUMAN SERVICES DEPARTMENT, STATE
abuse of adult, duty to report, 5101.61
parent locator service agreement, 5101.31
penalty, 5101.99

HUNTING, OFFENSES RE
minor, may furnish with firearms for, 2923.21
park, near, 3773.06

HUSBAND AND WIFE, COMPETENCY AS WITNESSES, 2945.42

HYPODERMICS
defined, 3719.01
offenses re, 2925.12, 2925.14, 3719.17.2

IDENTIFICATION CARD
definition, 2913.31
disabled person, 2305.41-2305.49

IDENTIFICATION CARD—*Continued*
false official, 4301.63.6
forged, offenses involving, 2913.31
nondrivers, 4507.50, 4507.51, 4507.52
request for donation to second chance trust fund, 4507.50.1

IDENTIFICATION OF ACCUSED BY WITNESS, 2945.55

ILLEGAL CONVEYANCE OF DEADLY WEAPON OR DANGEROUS ORDNANCE INTO COURTHOUSE; ILLEGAL POSSESSION OR CONTROL IN COURTHOUSE, 2923.12.3

ILLEGAL CONVEYANCE OF DEADLY WEAPONS OR DANGEROUS ORDNANCE ONTO SCHOOL PREMISES, 2923.12.2

ILLEGAL POSSESSION OF AN OBJECT INDISTINGUISHABLE FROM A FIREARM ON SCHOOL PREMISES, 2923.12.2

IMMUNITY
owner, lessee or renter of realty, to self-defense of property, 2305.40
sex offender registration, notification, 2950.12

IMMUNITY FROM PROSECUTION
civil suit, of, against extradited person, 2963.23
coercion charge, re, grant of, 2905.12
felony of violence, after indictment, how obtained, 2923.23
firearm, dangerous ordnance, for unlawful possession of, 2923.23
special grand jury witness, 2939.17
witnesses turning state's evidence, of, 2945.44

IMPEACHMENT OF WITNESS
deposition, use for, Crim. R. 15

IMPERSONATING
peace officer, state official or private policeman, 2921.51
personating a law enforcement officer or agency official, 2913.44

IMPORTUNING, 2907.07
habitual sex offender re, with minor under 13, 2950.01

IMPOSITION, SEXUAL, 2907.06
gross, 2907.05
habitual sex offender, re, 2950.01

IMPOSSIBILITY
attempt, re, 2923.02
conspiracy, re, 2923.01

IMPOUNDMENT, IMMOBILIZATION, FORFEITURE ORDERS
forfeiture, criminal, 4503.23.4
   disposal of vehicle or proceeds, 4503.23.4
   registration of other vehicles, 4503.23.4
immobilization and impoundment—
   forfeiture of vehicle, 4503.23.3
   immobilization fee, 4503.23.3
   issuance of new identification license plates, 4503.23.3
   law enforcement reimbursement fund, 4503.23.3
   release of vehicle, 4503.23.3
innocent owner, rights protected, 4503.23.5

IMPRISONED, 1.05

IMPRISONMENT—*see also* CONFINEMENT
concurrently served sentences for, 2929.41
consecutively served sentences for, minimum aggregate term, 2929.41
convict, of, for another offense, how served, 2941.43
DNA testing, 2901.07—*see also* DNA TESTS
electronically monitored house arrest, 2929.23
felony, for, 2929.11
   concurrently served with, for misdemeanor, where, 2929.41
   consecutive serving, 2929.41
   dangerous offender, favors longer term for, 2929.12
   fine for—
      burden of payment, as criterion re, 2929.12
      in addition to, when, 2929.12
   firearm, automatic, muffled, or silenced, 2929.72, 2941.14.1, 2941.14.4
   first degree, 4 to 25 years, 2929.11
   fourth degree, 6 months to 5 years, 2929.11
   harm, serious, neither caused, threatened, effect, 2929.12
   history, character, condition, offender's, as criteria re, 2929.12
   induced, facilitated by victim, as criterion re, 2929.12
   justification, excuse for offense, as criterion re, 2929.12
   minimum term of, other criteria re, 2929.12
   more than one year, as, 2901.02
   nature, circumstance of offense, as criteria re, 2929.12
   parole from, when eligible for, 2967.13
   probationer, parolee, escapee, by, consecutively serving terms, 2929.41
   protection, public, need for, as criterion re, 2929.12
   provocation, strong, offender under, as criterion re, 2929.12
   record, offender's good past, as criterion re, 2929.12
   recur, offense unlikely to, as criterion re, 2929.12
   rehabilitation, correction, offender's need for, as criterion re, 2929.12
   repeat offender, favors longer term for, 2929.12
   resources, ability of offender, as criterion re, 2929.12

IMPRISONMENT—*Continued*
felony, for—*Continued*
   risk offender will repeat, as criterion re, 2929.12
   second degree, 2 to 15 years, 2929.11
   shorter minimum term of, criteria favoring, 2929.12
   suspension of sentence re, 2929.51
   third degree, 1 to 10 years, 2929.11
   treatment, rehabilitative, corrective, favorable response to, effect, 2929.12
fine—
   felony, for—
      burden of payment, as criterion re, 2929.12
      in addition to, when, 2929.12
      in lieu of, how credit computed, 2947.20
      in satisfaction of fine; maximum commitment, 2947.14
firearm disability relief, release from, ground for, 2923.14
house arrest, electronically monitored, 2929.23
intermittent confinement, sentence served in—
   felony, for, as condition of probation, when, 2929.51
   misdemeanor, for, 2929.51
life—
   murder, for aggravated, 2929.02
      criteria, 2929.04
      fine in addition to, when, 2929.02
      indictment, no aggravating circumstances in, requires, 2929.03
      mitigating circumstances, when court finds present, 2929.03
      parole from, eligible after 15 years, 2967.13
   parole from, when eligible for, 2967.13
   rape of minor under 13, for, 2907.02
misdemeanor, for, 2929.21
   concurrently served with, for felony, where, 2929.41
   consecutive serving, 2929.41
   dangerous offender, favors imposing, 2929.22
   definite term, 2929.21
   discharge from jail for trial delay—
      bar to further criminal proceedings re, as, 2945.73
      fine for minor, re, after term of, 2945.73
      maximum term for most serious, after serving, 2945.73
   fine for—
      burden of payment, as criterion re, 2929.22
      in addition to, 2929.21, 2929.22
      in lieu of, how credit computed, 2947.20
   first degree, of—
      maximum of six months, 2929.21
      minimum of one year, served consecutively, where, 2929.41
   fourth degree, of, 30 days maximum, 2929.21
   history, character, condition, offender's, as criteria re, 2929.22
   imposing, other criteria re, 2929.22
   less than one year, as, 2901.02
   nature, circumstance of offense, as criteria re, 2929.22

IMPRISONMENT—*Continued*
misdemeanor, for—*Continued*
    protection, public, need for, as criterion re, 2929.22
    rehabilitation, correction, offender's need for, as criterion re, 2929.22
    repeat offender, favors imposing, 2929.22
    resources, ability of offender, as criterion re, 2929.22
    risk offender will repeat, as criterion re, 2929.22
    second degree, of, 90 days maximum, 2929.21
    shorter minimum term for felony, criteria, effect, 2929.12, 2929.22
    suspension of sentence re, 2929.51—*see also* SENTENCE
    third degree, of, 60 days maximum, 2929.21
    trial re, time for, effect on, 2945.71
motor vehicles, for operating under influence, 4511.99
murder, for, 2903.02, 2929.02
    aggravated—
        fine in addition to, when, 2929.02
        hire, gain, re, fine in addition to, 2929.02
        life, 2929.02
        syndicate, re criminal, fine in addition to, 2929.02
        consecutively serving, 20 years aggregate minimum term, 2929.41
    fifteen years to life, 2929.02
    fine in addition to, when, 2929.02
    hire, gain, re, fine in addition to, 2929.02
    syndicate, re criminal, fine in addition to, 2929.02
overnight, for, sentence served during, 2929.51
probation instead of—
    correction, rehabilitation need, as factor against, 2951.02
    hardship on offender, undue, when would entail, 2951.02
rape of minor under 13, for, 2907.02
reimburse cost of confinement, 2929.15
repeat offender after, prima facie evidence of, 2929.01
shock incarceration, 2929.11, 5120.03.1
suspension of sentence of, 2929.51—*see also* SENTENCE
trial, awaiting, credit for, on sentence, 2967.19.1
weekends, on, sentence served during, 2929.51

INCAPACITATION, AS SERIOUS PHYSICAL HARM, 2901.01

INCAPACITY, PHYSICAL, OF DEFENDANT, EXTENDS TRIAL TIME, 2945.72

INCENDIARY DEVICE
defined, 2923.11
ordnance, as dangerous, 2923.11
reporting burns caused by, 2921.22

INCITING TO VIOLENCE, 2917.01

INDECENCY, PUBLIC, 2907.09
habitual sex offender, re, 2950.01

INDICTMENTS, INFORMATIONS, Crim. R. 7; 2941.01 *et seq*
aggravating circumstance, alleging, 2945.75
amendment of, Crim. R. 7; 2941.30
arraignment, re, Crim. R. 10; 2943.01 *et seq*
constitutional provisions re style of, Art. IV, § 20 OC
constitutional right to, unless waived, Art. I, § 10 OC
dismissal of, Crim. R. 7, 48
firearm specification—*see* FIREARMS, DANGEROUS ORDNANCE
"secret" indictment, 2939.18
sham legal process, 2921.52

INDIGENTS
appointment of counsel in capital cases, SupR 20-22
right to counsel, Crim. R. 44
    depositions re, 2945.53
    payment of counsel, 2941.51
    petition to vacate judgment, re, 2953.21 *et seq*
transcript to be furnished for appeal, 2953.03

INDUSTRY PROGRAM, COUNTY JAIL
sentencing court to determine eligibility for, 2929.16
    felons, 2929.16
    misdemeanants, 2929.21

INFECTIOUS AGENTS
improperly handling, 2917.47

INFORMANTS
drug prosecutions, immunity from prosecution, 3719.70

INJUNCTION
nuisance—*see* NUISANCE
obscene material or performance, 2907.37—*see also* OBSCENE MATERIAL, PERFOMANCE

INMATE—*see* CONVICT; PRISONER

INNKEEPER, DEFRAUDING, 2913.41

INNOCENCE, PRESUMPTION OF, 2901.05

INSANITY—*see* NOT GUILTY BY REASON OF INSANITY

INSTITUTION
conveying weapons, drugs or liquor into, 2921.36
mental—*see* MENTAL INSTITUTION
presentence report, commitment entry to, Crim. R. 32.2
statement of days credited to sentence, sent to, Crim. R. 32.2
state penal, reformatory—
    custody of inmate, interference with, 2919.23
    felony, imprisoned for, in, 1.05
    riot by inmate of—*see* RIOT AND RELATED OFFENSES
    sentences to—*see* SENTENCE

INSTRUCTIONS, Crim. R. 30
murder, re aggravated, penalty not mentioned in, 2929.03

INSTRUMENTS, POSSESSING DRUG ABUSE, 2925.12

INSURANCE
false pretenses, obtaining information under, 3904.14
health insurance claims for prisoners, 2947.20

INSURANCE FRAUD, 2913.47
duty to cooperate in criminal investigation, 3937.42, 3937.99

INSURANCE, MOTOR VEHICLE—*see* MOTOR VEHICLES, *at* financial responsibility laws re

INTENT
criminal tools, to use, 2923.24
defraud to, alleging, proving, 2941.19

INTERCEPTION OF WIRE OR ORAL COMMUNICATIONS—*see* WIRETAPPING, ELECTRONIC SURVEILLANCE

INTERFERENCE WITH FAIR HOUSING RIGHTS, 2927.03

INTERFERING WITH ACTION TO ISSUE OR MODIFY SUPPORT ORDER, 2919.23.1

INTERPRETER, RE GRAND JURY
disclosure of matters before, when, Crim. R. 6
present when in session, may be, Crim. R. 6

INTERSTATE AGREEMENT ON DETAINERS, 2963.30 *et seq*

INTIMIDATION, 2921.03
crime victim or witness, of, 2921.04
ethnic, 2927.12
prisoner in detention facility, of, duty to prevent, 2921.44
public servant, party official, attorney or witness involved in civil action, 2921.03
victim, attorney or witness in criminal case, 2921.04, 2945.04

INTOXICANTS, ABUSING HARMFUL, 2925.31

INTOXICATED—*see also* ALCOHOL, ALCOHOLICS
disorderly conduct while, 2917.11
firearm, dangerous ordnance, carrying, use while, 2923.15
sale, furnishing, lending to person who is, 2923.20

INTOXICATED—*Continued*
persons, commitment of, 2935.33

INTOXICATING LIQUOR
alternate prohibitions if federal mandate repealed, 4301.69.1
conveying into detention facility or institution, 2921.36, 2921.37
jurisdiction of municipal court, 2931.04
minors, offenses concerning, 4301.63 *et seq*
offenses, jurisdiction of county court judge, 2931.02
premises where served; possession of firearm prohibited, 2923.12.1
search warrants for, 4301.53
unlawful sale, necessary allegations in indictment, 2941.20

INVENTORY OF PROPERTY TAKEN UNDER SEARCH WARRANT, Crim. R. 41

INVESTIGATION
drug abuse, re, immunity from prosecution in return for testimony, 3719.70
evidence, tampering with, 2921.12
felony, of, examination of witnesses re, 2935.23
immunity from prosecution, for state's witness re, 2945.44
presentence, Crim. R. 32.2; 2951.03—*see also* PRESENTENCE INVESTIGATION

INVESTIGATOR, PERSONATING, 2913.44

INVOLUNTARY MANSLAUGHTER, 2903.03

INVOLUNTARY SERVITUDE—*see* SERVITUDE, INVOLUNTARY

ISOMER, DEFINED, 3719.01

JAILS
access to exercise equipment, participation in fighting skills program, 341.41
administrator for, 341.05
assaults of guards, visitors etc., 2903.13
commissary; fund, 341.24
contracts for private operation, management of correctional facilities, 9.06, 341.35
conveying weapon, drug or liquor into, 2921.36, 2921.37
cook, 341.20
defined, 2929.01
DNA testing, 2901.07—*see also* DNA TESTS
escape, notice of, 341.01.1
exercise equipment, prisoner access to, 341.41
fighting skills programs, participation in, 341.41
female prisoners, 341.20
health insurance claims, submission of, 341.19.1
inspection by grand jury, 2939.21

JAILS—Continued
minimum standards—
   copies of, 341.07
   revision of, 341.08
minors, 341.11
misdemeanant minimum security, 341.34, 753.21
misdemeanor, imprisonment for, in, 1.05, 2949.08
Ohio, prisoners of, 341.21
operational policies and procedures, 341.02
other jails, use of, 341.12-341.18
prisoner reimbursement policy, 341.06
prisoner rules of conduct, 341.02, 341.07
probation, six-month term in, as condition of, 2929.51
register, 341.02
reimbursement by convict, 341.19
religious work in, 341.22
sentence to workhouse, for jailable offense, 2947.18
separation of prisoners, 341.09, 341.10
sheriff to have charge of, 341.01
sheriff to visit, 341.04
temporary confinement in, person committed to workhouse, 2947.22
United States, prisoners of, 341.21
welfare work in, 341.22
work camps, rehabilitation, 341.31-341.33
workhouse—
   absence of, 341.23
   regulations generally, ch. 753

JOINDER
defendants, of, Crim. R. 8
   arraignment of, Crim. R. 10
   capital cases, Crim. R. 14; 2945.20
   felonies, 2945.13, 2945.15
offenses, of, Crim. R. 8
severance, Crim. R. 14

JOYRIDING, 2913.03

JUDGE
additional, magistrate courts, 2938.03
defined, Crim. R. 2; 2931.01
disability of, Crim. R. 25
disqualification of inferior court judge, 2937.20
judgment signed by, Crim. R. 32

JUDGMENT
acquittal, of, motion for, Crim. R. 29—*see also* ACQUITTAL, *at* motion for judgment of
arrest of, Crim. R. 34; 2947.02 *et seq*
bail bond continues until, by court, Crim. R. 46
conviction of—
   certified copy of entry proves, 2945.75
   set aside after sentence, court may, Crim. R. 32.1
copy of, commitment to workhouse, on, 2947.21
costs and jury fees to be included in, 2947.23
criminal fine or judgment for state, 2929.25
entry of, by clerk, Crim. R. 32

JUDGMENT—Continued
judge, signed by, Crim. R. 32
mistakes in, clerical, correction of, Crim. R. 36
presence of defendant at, when not required, Crim. R. 43
sham legal process, 2921.52
when court shall pronounce, 2947.07

JUDICIAL NOTICE OF CERTAIN LAW, Crim. R. 27

JUDICIAL NOTICE OF STATUTE, 2941.12

JUDICIAL RELEASE
reduction of felony prison term, 2929.20, 2930.17, 5120.33.1

JURISDICTION, 2901.11
arrest of judgment, for lack of—*see* ARREST OF JUDGMENT
common pleas courts, 2931.03
county courts, 2931.02
disputed territory, over offense committed in, 2901.11
escape, lack of, when affirmative defense re, 2921.34
homicide, re, 2901.11
magistrate courts, territorial, 2938.10
multi-state, out-of-state acts, re, 2901.11
municipal courts, 2931.04
objection for failure to show in court, Crim. R. 12
search warrants, re, Crim. R. 41
venue change, of receiving court, same as originating, 2931.29

JURORS, Crim. R. 24
alternate, Crim. R. 24; 2945.29
capital cases, 2945.18 *et seq*
challenges—
   array, to, Crim. R. 24
   cause, for, Crim. R. 24; 2945.25 *et seq*
   peremptory, Crim. R. 24; 2945.21 *et seq*
examination of, Crim. R. 24; 2945.27
grand jury—*see* GRAND JURY; JURY
medical attendance for, 2945.30
number of, Crim. R. 24
servant, public, as, 2921.01

JURY—*see also* JURORS; JURY TRIAL
challenges to array, Crim. R. 24
death sentence, to decide sanity or pregnancy of convict under, 2949.32
defendant's failure to testify, may consider, 2945.43
discharge of—*see* DISCHARGE, *at* jury, of
fees, of, to be included in sentence, 2947.23
grand—*see* GRAND JURY
instructions to, Crim. R. 30; 2945.10, 2945.11
keeping and conduct of, after case submitted, 2945.33
misconduct of, as grounds for new trial, Crim. R. 33; 2945.79

JURY—*Continued*
municipal courts, in, provisions for, 1901.24, 1901.25
oath, form, 2945.28
papers, may have while deliberating, 2945.35
poll of, re verdict, Crim. R. 31; 2945.77
presence of defendant at impaneling of, Crim. R. 43
sanity inquiry, for, 2945.37 *et seq*
separation of, procedure, 2945.31 *et seq*
venue change, fees re, originating county pays, Crim. R. 18; 2931.31
verdict of—*see* VERDICT
view of premises by, 2945.16

JURY TRIAL—*see also* JURORS; JURY
demand for, waiver of, Crim. R. 23
magistrate courts, right to, in, 2938.04 *et seq*
right to, 2945.17
   constitutional basis of, Art. I, § 5 OC
   guilty, no contest plea, waives, Crim. R. 11
   initial appearance, defendant to be informed of, at, Crim. R. 5
   waiver of right to, Crim. R. 23; 2945.05

JUSTICE, OBSTRUCTING, 2921.32

JUSTICE, PUBLIC ADMINISTRATION, OFFENSES AGAINST, 2921.01 *et seq*
arrest, resisting, 2921.33
authority, resistance to lawful, 2921.35
bribery, 2921.02
civil rights, interfering with, 2921.45
compensation, soliciting, receiving improper, 2921.43
compounding a crime, 2921.21
contract, public, having unlawful interest in, 2921.42
conveying weapon, drug or liquor into detention facility, 2921.36, 2921.37
duty, dereliction of, 2921.44
escape, 2921.34
   aiding, 2921.35
evidence, tampering with, 2921.12
failure to report a crime, 2921.22
falsification, 2921.13
information disclosed, 2921.24, 2921.25
intimidation, 2921.03
   crime victim or witness, 2921.04
law enforcement officer, failure to aid, 2921.23
obstructing justice, 2921.32
official business, obstructing, 2921.31
perjury, 2921.11
theft in office, 2921.41

JUSTIFICATION
affirmative defense, as, 2901.05
imprisonment for felony, as criterion re, 2929.12
probation, as factor favoring, 2951.02
sureties, of, Crim. R. 46

JUVENILE COURTS
abandonment—
   consent to marriage, effect re, Juv.R. 42

JUVENILE COURTS—*Continued*
abused child—
   defined, 2151.03.1
   disposition of, 2151.35.3
   living in domestic violence or homeless shelter, 2151.42.2
abuse of child—
   criminal offense, as, 2919.22
   duty to report, investigation, 2151.42.1
adjudicatory hearing—
   county other than residence, when held in, Juv. R. 11
   defined, Juv.R. 2
   hearings generally, Juv.R. 27
adults—
   affidavit of charges, arrest, trial in juvenile court or bindover to grand jury, 2151.43
   appeal, 2151.52
   bail, 2151.46
   commitment to women's reformatory instead of jail or workhouse, 2151.48
   complaint against, juvenile judge to order to be filed, when, 2151.44
   county to contribute to support of dependent children of, when, 2151.51
   defined, 2151.01.1
   extradition of, 2151.45
   jury trial, 2151.47
   suspension of sentence, 2151.49, 2151.50
answer, Juv.R. 22
appeal—
   adult, of conviction, by, 2151.52
   advisement of right to, Juv.R. 34
   motion to suppress, from granting of, by state, Juv.R. 22
applicability of rules, exceptions, Juv.R. 1
arrest—
   child, of, when, 2151.31
   rights of child upon, 2151.35.2
auditor of county—
   district detention home, duties re, 2151.34.14
   juvenile court, duty re, 2151.13
   juvenile facility, duties re, 2151.79
bail—
   adults, re, 2151.46
bequests—
   juvenile facility, for, 2151.67
bindover, Juv.R. 30; 2151.26
   adult, of, to grand jury, 2151.43
certified foster home, 2151.01.1
child—
   defined, Juv.R. 2; 2151.01.1
children services board—
   report of abuse or neglect, duties re, 2151.42.1
citation of rule, Juv.R. 48
commit—
   defined, 2151.01.1
commitment—
   jurisdiction of juvenile court after, 2151.38

JUVENILE COURTS—*Continued*
commitment—*Continued*
    reports required after, 2151.37
    support, liability for, after, 2151.36
complaint, 2151.27
    adult, juvenile judge to order to be filed against, when, 2151.44
    certification from transferring court, as, Juv.R. 10
    copy to accompany summons, Juv.R. 15
    defined, Juv.R. 2
    form, generally, Juv.R. 10
    habeas corpus, for writ of, Juv.R. 10
    permanent custody, for, Juv.R. 10
    pleading, as, Juv.R. 22
    records, request for, 2151.14.1
    screening, referral, before filing, Juv.R. 9
    traffic offense, juvenile, for, Juv.R. 10
    who may file, where, Juv.R. 10
computerization of clerk's office, fees for, 2151.54.1
consent to marry, by court, Juv.R. 42
construction—
    Chapter 2151., of, 2151.01
construction of rules, Juv.R. 1
contempt—
    powers of juvenile court re, 2151.21
    subpoena, failure to obey, Juv.R. 17
continuance, Juv.R. 23; 2151.22
    failure to comply with discovery order, for, Juv.R. 24
continuing jurisdiction, Juv.R. 35
contributing to delinquency, etc., 2919.24
cooperation with court—
    duty of county, township, municipal officials, 2151.40
costs, 2151.54
    appointed counsel, guardian ad litem, services of, as, Juv.R. 4
    investigation re custody, as, Juv.R. 32
    school district to pay costs of education, when, Juv.R. 34; 2151.35.7
county commissioners—
    dependent children of person in workhouse or jail, to contribute to support of, 2151.51
    district detention homes, duties re, 2151.34 *et seq*
    extradition expenses, to pay re juvenile proceedings, 2151.45
    juvenile court, powers, duties re—
        appropriation for expenses, 2151.09
        separate building and site for, purchase or lease of, 2151.10
        separate room for hearings, to provide, 2151.24
    juvenile facilities (schools, forestry camps, etc.), may provide, 2151.65 *et seq*
    support of committed child, duty re, 2151.36
court action to be avoided, Juv.R. 9
court proceeding—
    defined, Juv.R. 2
criminal prosecution, transfer for, Juv.R. 30; 2151.26

JUVENILE COURTS—*Continued*
criminal records check and fingerprinting of employees responsible for out-of-home child care and prospective adoptive or foster parents, 2151.86
custodian—
    defined, Juv.R. 2; 2151.01.1
custody (*see also* commitment, *herein*)—
    complaint to have determined, Juv.R. 10
    comprehensive reunification plan, 2151.41.2
    detention during pendency of proceedings after judgment, Juv.R. 35
    detention hearing, notice of rights re, right to rehearing, Juv.R. 7
    detention, shelter care, when permitted, initial procedure upon, Juv.R. 7
    inducing child to leave, 2919.24
    investigation re, Juv.R. 32
    legal, defined, 2151.01.1
    medical examination, Juv.R. 7
    permanent custody, 2151.41.3, 2151.41.4
    permanent, defined, 2151.01.1
    place of detention, 2151.31.2
    procedure upon taking into, 2151.31, 2151.31.1
    review of, 2151.41.7
    rights of child upon being taken into, 2151.35.2
    separation from adults, Juv.R. 7; 2151.31.2, 2151.34
    taking into, when permitted, Juv.R. 6
    telephone and visitation rights, Juv.R. 7
    temporary, defined, 2151.01.1
    termination of permanent, application for, 2151.38
    when child may be taken into, 2151.31
Cuyahoga County juvenile court
    administrative judge, 2153.03, 2153.08
    appeal from, 2153.17
    bailiffs, 2153.11
    bond, judges to give, 2153.10
    clerk of, administrative judge is, 2153.08
    contempt powers, 2153.13
    election of judges, 2153.02, 2153.03
    employees, 2153.08
        compensation of, 2153.09
    established, 2153.01
    facilities for, expenses of, 2153.07
    jurisdiction, 2153.16
    qualifications of judges, 2153.02
    removal of judge from office, 2153.06
    rules of practice, 2153.15
    seal of court, 2153.14
    term of court, 2153.12
    vacancies, additional judges, 2153.05
    vacation, modification of judgments, powers re, 2153.15
definitions, Juv.R. 2
    abused child, 2151.03.1
    adequate parental care, 2151.01.1
    adjudicatory hearing, Juv.R. 2
    adults, 2151.01.1

JUVENILE COURTS—*Continued*
definitions—*Continued*
  chapter 2151, re, 2151.01.1
  child, Juv.R. 2; 2151.01.1
  child without proper parental care, 2151.05
  commit, 2151.01.1
  complaint, Juv.R. 2
  court proceeding, Juv.R. 2
  custodian, Juv.R. 2; 2151.01.1
  delinquent child, 2151.02
  dependent child, 2151.04
  detention, Juv.R. 2; 2151.01.1
  detention hearing, Juv.R. 2
  dispositional hearing, Juv.R. 2
  foster home, 2151.01.1
    approved foster care, 2151.01.1
    certified foster home, 2151.01.1
  guardian, Juv.R. 2; 2151.01.1
  guardian ad litem, Juv.R. 2
  hearing, Juv.R. 2
  indigent person, Juv.R. 2
  juvenile court, Juv.R. 2; 2151.01.1
  juvenile judge, Juv.R. 2; 2151.01.1
  juvenile traffic offender, 2151.02.1
  legal custody, 2151.01.1
  mental examination, Juv.R. 2
  neglected child, 2151.03
  organization, 2151.01.1
    certified organization, 2151.01.1
  party, Juv.R. 2
  permanent custody, 2151.01.1
  person, Juv.R. 2
  physical examination, Juv.R. 2
  private child placing agency, 2151.01.1
  probation, 2151.01.1
  protective supervision, 2151.01.1
  residual parental rights, 2151.01.1
  rule of court, Juv.R. 2
  shelter, 2151.01.1
  shelter care, Juv.R. 2
  social history, Juv.R. 2
  temporary custody, 2151.01.1
  unruly child, 2151.02.2
  ward of court, Juv.R. 2
delinquency—
  contributing to, 2919.24
  DNA testing, 2151.31.5—*see also* DNA TESTS
  employee not to be penalized for being subpoenaed to proceeding, 2151.21.1
  felony sentencing consideration, 2929.12
    consideration prior to release, 2967.28
  firearm, purchase of, 2151.02, 2923.21.1
  forfeiture orders, 2923.32, 2923.35, 2925.44, 2933.41, 2933.44
  gifts, bequests, to prevent, administered by juvenile judge, 2151.11
  juvenile court employees may be assigned to work against, 2151.11

JUVENILE COURTS—*Continued*
delinquency—*Continued*
  liability of parent or guardian for subsequent acts of, 2151.41.1
  schedule of fines and costs, 2151.35.12
  status of adjudication or prior conviction, 2901.08
delinquent child—
  defined, 2151.02
  disposition of, 2151.35.5
department of public welfare—
  charges of nonsupport, re aid recipient, 2151.43
  commitment to, effect on jurisdiction of court, 2151.38
  committed child, duties re, 2151.36
  placement of children from other states, duties re, 2151.39
  report of abuse or neglect of child, to, investigation, 2151.42.1
dependency—
  contributing to, 2919.24
dependent child—
  defined, 2151.04
  disposition of, 2151.35.3
deposition, Juv.R. 25
  subpoena for, Juv.R. 17
detention (*see also* custody, *herein*)—
  defined, Juv.R. 2; 2151.01.1
detention hearing, Juv.R. 7; 2151.31.4
  defined, Juv.R. 2
detention home—
  school district to pay educational costs, 2151.35.7
detention homes, district, 2151.34 *et seq*
discovery, Juv.R. 24
dispositional hearing, Juv.R. 34
  defined, Juv.R. 2
effective date—
  rules, amendments, of, Juv.R. 47
emergency medical, surgical treatment, Juv.R. 13; 2151.33
examination, physical, mental, Juv.R. 32; 2151.53
expungement of record, 2151.35.8
  advisement of right to, Juv.R. 34
extradition—
  county commissioners to pay expenses re, 2151.45
fees and costs, 2151.54
  schedule of fines and costs, 2151.35.12
filing of papers, Juv.R. 20
fingerprints—
  restriction re child, 2151.31.3
forfeiture—*see* FORFEITURE
forms—
  illustrative, not mandatory, Juv.R. 46
foster home—
  defined, 2151.01.1
  placement in home in another county, 2151.55
  zoning, 2151.41.8
gifts—
  juvenile facility, for, 2151.67

JUVENILE COURTS—Continued
guardian—
    defined, Juv.R. 2
guardian ad litem, Juv.R. 4 et seq
    defined, Juv.R. 2
    when appointed, 2151.28.1
habeas corpus—
    complaint re custody of child, Juv.R. 10
    investigation re, Juv.R. 32
Hamilton County—
    juvenile court judges in, 2151.08
hearings, Juv.R. 27
    adjudicatory (see adjudicatory hearing, herein)
    defined, Juv.R. 2
    detention, Juv.R. 7; 2151.31.4
    dispositional, Juv.R. 34; 2151.41.5
    generally, 2151.35
    permanent custody, 2151.41.5
    probation revocation, Juv.R. 35
    referee, before, Juv.R. 40
    review, 2151.41.7
    separate room for, 2151.24
    summons for, 2151.28
indigent person—
    defined, Juv.R. 2
interstate compact on juveniles, 2151.56 et seq
interstate compact on placement of children, 2151.39
investigation—
    consent to marriage, re, Juv.R. 42
    custody, habeas corpus, re, Juv.R. 32
judgment, Juv.R. 34
    consent to marriage, re, Juv.R. 42
jurisdiction, 2151.23
    continuing, to be invoked, Juv.R. 35
    permanent custody, effect of grant of, 2151.38
    unaffected by Rules, Juv.R. 44
jury trial—
    adults, 2151.47
juvenile court, 2151.07
    additional judge for, 2151.07
    appropriation for expenses of, 2151.10
    assignment of employees to work against delinquency, 2151.11
    bond—
        employees, may be required of, 2151.12
        judge to give when acting as clerk, 2151.12
    clerk of, 2151.12
    defined, Juv.R. 2; 2151.01.1
    employees, duties, compensation, etc., 2151.13
    gifts, bequests, to combat delinquency, to administer, 2151.11
    Hamilton County, judges in, 2151.08
    jurisdiction of, 2151.23
    probation powers (see probation, herein)
    records, annual report, 2151.18
    separate building and site may be purchased or leased, 2151.09
    separate room for hearings, 2151.24

JUVENILE COURTS—Continued
juvenile court—Continued
    term, continuances, location of sessions, 2151.22
juvenile facilities (schools, forestry camps, etc.)—
    single-county, joint-county, 2151.65 et seq
juvenile judge—
    defined, Juv.R. 2; 2151.01.1
juvenile traffic offender—
    defined, 2151.02.1
    disposition of, 2151.35.6
marriage—
    consent to, by judge, Juv.R. 42
medical treatment, emergency, Juv.R. 13 et seq; 2151.33
mental examination (see also examination, physical, mental, herein)—
    defined, Juv.R. 2; 2151.53
mentally ill, retarded child—
    hospitalization by court order, 2151.23
motions, Juv.R. 19
    discovery, for, Juv.R. 24
    prehearing, Juv.R. 22
    time re, Juv.R. 18
neglect—
    consent to marriage, effect re, Juv.R. 42
    contributing to, 2919.24
    duty to report, investigation, 2151.42.1
neglected child—
    defined, 2151.03
    disposition of, 2151.35.3
notice—
    detention hearing, of, Juv.R. 7
    temporary disposition, orders, emergency medical, surgical treatment of child, Juv.R. 13
organization—
    defined, 2151.01.1
out-of-state children—
    placement in state, 2151.39
papers—
    service, filing, of, Juv.R. 20
party—
    defined, Juv.R. 2
permanent custody—
    application for termination of, 2151.38
    defined, 2151.01.1
person—
    defined, Juv.R. 2
photographs—
    restrictions re child, 2151.31.3
physical examination (see also examination, physical, mental, herein)—
    defined, Juv.R. 2; 2151.53
placement options for abused, neglected, dependent, or unruly child, 2151.33.1
pleadings, Juv.R. 22
pregnancy—
    consent to marriage, re, Juv.R. 42
preliminary conferences, Juv.R. 21
private child placing agency, 2151.01.1

JUVENILE COURTS—*Continued*
probation—
    contract for supervisory services, 2151.15.1
    defined, 2151.01.1
    department, 2151.14, 2151.15
    revocation of, Juv.R. 35
    written statement of conditions, Juv.R. 34
procedure not otherwise specified, Juv.R. 45
process—
    issuance, form, Juv.R. 15
    service of, Juv.R. 16
proper parental care, child without—
    defined, 2151.05
prosecuting attorney—
    appeal from granting of motion to suppress, Juv.R. 22
    juvenile court, to prosecute adult in, when, 2151.44
    juvenile hearings, duties re, 2151.40
protective supervision—
    defined, 2151.01.1
recording of proceedings, Juv.R. 37
    advisement of right re, Juv.R. 29
records, annual report, 2151.18
referees, 2151.16
    proceedings before, Juv.R. 40
reimbursement of court for costs of children in custody of court, 2151.15.2
report—
    abuse or neglect, of, 2151.42.1
    institution receiving or desiring to receive children, required of, 2151.37
residence—
    child has same as parent or guardian, 2151.06
restraining order, Juv.R. 34
    parent, guardian, custodian, re, 2151.35.9
revocation of probation, Juv.R. 35
right to counsel, Juv.R. 4; 2151.35.2
    adjudicatory hearing, advisement of, at, Juv.R. 29
    dispositional hearing, at, Juv.R. 34
    probation revocation hearing, at, Juv.R. 35
    summons to state, Juv.R. 15
rule of court—
    defined, Juv.R. 2
rules—
    juvenile court may make own, 2151.17
runaways—
    authority to take into custody, 2151.31
    Interstate Compact on Juveniles, 2151.56 *et seq*
school district—
    educational costs, to pay, when, 2151.35.7
screening, referral, before filing complaint, Juv.R. 9
seal of court, 2151.20
service—
    papers, of, on all parties, Juv.R. 20
    subpoena, of, Juv.R. 17
    summons, of, Juv.R. 16
service of process, 2151.19
    manner of, 2151.29

JUVENILE COURTS—*Continued*
shelter—
    defined, 2151.01.1
shelter care—
    defined, Juv.R. 2
social history—
    defined, Juv.R. 2
    placement of children from other states, required re, 2151.39
    prepared during detention, 2151.34
    report, Juv.R. 32
statement—
    discovery of, Juv.R. 24
subpoena, Juv.R. 17
summons, 2151.28
    issuance, form, Juv.R. 15
    manner of serving, 2151.29
    service, return, of, Juv.R. 16
superintendent—
    juvenile facility, of, 2151.70
support—
    county welfare department to bring charges re, when, 2151.43
    failure to, 2919.21
    liability re, 2151.36
    marital status disregarded, 2151.23.1
    suspension of sentence for agreement to pay, 2151.49, 2151.50
suppress, motion to, Juv.R. 22
tax levy—
    district detention home, for, 2151.34.12, 2151.34.13
    juvenile facility, for, 2151.66, 2151.77, 2151.78
temporary custody—
    defined, 2151.01.1
temporary disposition, 2151.33
    order, Juv.R. 13
term of court, 2151.22
time, Juv.R. 18
title—
    rules, of, Juv.R. 48
transfer—
    county of residence, to, Juv.R. 11
    criminal prosecution, for, Juv.R. 30; 2151.26
    juvenile court of another county to, Juv.R. 11; 2151.27.1
    juvenile court, to, where arrested child brought before other court, 2151.25
treasurer of county—
    juvenile court salaries, expenses, to pay, 2151.13
    juveniles, cost of interstate transportation of, to pay, 2151.54
    support of child, to pay, 2151.36
trustees—
    juvenile facility, for, 2151.68 *et seq*
unruliness—
    contributing to, 2919.24
unruly child—
    defined, 2151.02.2

JUVENILE COURTS—Continued
unruly child—Continued
  disposition of, 2151.35.4
waiver of rights, Juv.R. 3
ward of court—
  defined, Juv.R. 2
warrant, 2151.30
  execution, return, Juv.R. 16
  issuance, form, Juv.R. 15
witnesses—
  discovery, protection of, from, Juv.R. 24
  request for discovery of names, addresses of, Juv.R. 24
  subpoena of, Juv.R. 17
youth commission—
  commitment to, effect on jurisdiction of court, 2151.38
  district detention home, financial assistance to, 2151.34.16
  examination of child re transfer for criminal prosecution, Juv.R. 30
  juvenile facilities (schools, forestry camps, etc.), may aid county to establish, 2151.65.1 et seq

JUVENILES—see also CHILD; MINOR
defined, 2907.01
delinquent, possession of firearm, dangerous ordnance, 2923.13
  relief from disability re, 2923.14
drug paraphernalia, sale of, 2925.14
matter harmful to, 2907.31 et seq
  deception to obtain, 2907.33
  displaying, 2907.31.1
  disseminating, 2907.31
schedule of fines and costs, 2151.35.12
status of adjudication as prior conviction, 2901.08
traffic offender—
  indigent drivers alcohol treatment fund, 4511.19.1

KEY, IGNITION, REMOVAL BY OFFICER PERMITTED, WHEN, 4549.05

KIDNAPPING, 2905.01 et seq
conspiracy to commit, 2923.01
murder, during, as aggravating circumstance, 2929.04
sexual motivation—see SEX OFFENSES

KNIFE, 2923.20
ballistic, 2923.11

KNOWINGLY
attempt, as sufficient culpability re, 2923.02
culpability, when sufficient for, 2901.22
defined, 2901.22

LABELS, RE CONTROLLED SUBSTANCES, DANGEROUS DRUGS
false or forged, making or affixing to drug container, 2925.23

LABOR
convict, 2947.15

LABORATORY, DEFINED RE DRUGS, 3719.01

LANGUAGE
abusive, as disorderly conduct, 2917.11

LAUGHING GAS—see HARMFUL INTOXICANT

LAW ENFORCEMENT EMBLEM
unlawful display, 2913.44.1

LAW ENFORCEMENT OFFICER
address, disclosure of, prohibited, 2921.24, 2921.25
assistance by bureau of criminal identification and investigation investigator, 109.54.1
child support enforcement, providing of information, 5101.31
defined, Crim. R. 2; 2901.01
dereliction of duty, by, 2921.44
disarming or attempting to disarm, 109.57, 2911.01, 2929.14, 2929.20
emblem display, 2913.44.1
failure to aid, 2921.23
firearm, loaded, may carry in motor vehicle, 2923.16
murder of, as aggravating circumstance, 2929.04
ordnance, dangerous, possession by, when permissible, 2923.17
personating, 2913.44, 2921.51
property held by, disposition of, Crim. R. 41; 2933.41
riot, suppressing by force, justifiable, 2917.05
sham legal process, 2921.52
weapons, when may carry concealed, 2923.13

LEGAL AID SOCIETIES
financial assistance to, 120.51 et seq

LEGAL ASSISTANCE FOUNDATION, 120.52.1—see also LEGAL AID SOCIETIES

LESSER INCLUDED OFFENSES
defendant may be convicted of, 2945.74
verdict, effect re, Crim. R. 31, 33
  modification of, 2945.79

LICENSE
dangerous ordnance, re, 2923.17, 2923.18
driver's—see DRIVER'S LICENSE
falsification to obtain, 2921.13
motor vehicle, ch. 4503
plate, motor vehicle—
  theft of, receiving stolen, 2913.71
professional—see PROFESSIONAL LICENSE
revocation of, pawnbrokers, certain dealers, upon conviction of receiving stolen property, 2961.03
terminal distributor of dangerous drugs—
  false, forged, 2925.23

LICENSE—*Continued*
terminal distributor of dangerous drugs—*Continued*
theft to obtain, 2925.23

LIEUTENANT GOVERNOR, ASSASSINATING, AS AGGRAVATING CIRCUMSTANCE, 2929.04

LIFE IMPRISONMENT
felonious sexual penetration, 2907.12
murder, for, 2929.02
  criteria re, 2929.04
  indictment, no aggravating circumstances in, 2929.03
  mitigating circumstances, when court finds present, 2929.03
  verdict of guilty, 2929.03
parole eligibility re, 2967.13
rape, for, 2907.02

LIMA STATE HOSPITAL—*see also* **MENTAL INSTITUTION**
commitment to, upon determination of insanity, 2945.37 *et seq*

LIMITATION OF PROSECUTIONS, 2901.13

LIQUOR—*see also* **INTOXICATING LIQUOR**
conveyances, seizure of, 4301.45
conviction, notification of, 4301.99.1
definitions, 4301.01
diluted or refilled, sale or possession prohibited, 4301.68, 4301.99
drunkenness, tavern keeper not to permit, 4399.16, 4399.99
false entry on invoice or container prohibited, 4301.48
firearm, possession of in liquor permit premises, 2923.12, 2923.12.1, 4301.63.7
injunction, violation of, 4301.99.1
inspection, interference with, 4301.49
keeping place where sold in violation of law, 4399.09, 4399.99
miscellaneous offenses re, 4301.70, 4301.71
motor vehicle, consumption in, prohibited, 4301.64, 4301.99
nuisance, place of sale as, 4301.73
open container prohibited, 4301.62
permit, activities prohibited without, 4301.58, 4301.99
poisoned, 4399.15, 4399.17, 4399.99
possession, illegal, when, 4301.67, 4301.99
purchase of spiritous liquor at retail by permit holder for resale, 4301.14
rationing of spiritous liquor, 4301.14, 4301.15
record keeping by permit holders, 4301.47
restrictions on sale, 4301.21, 4301.22, 4301.99
riot, civil disorder, etc., emergency suspension during, 4301.25.1
sale at certain places prohibited, 4399.10 *et seq*, 4399.99

LIQUOR—*Continued*
search of premises where sold, obstruction of, 4301.66, 4301.99
transportation, unlawful, 4301.60
underage persons—
  low-alcohol beverage, purchase or consumption, 4301.22, 4301.63.1, 4301.99
  prohibitions on, 4301.63 *et seq*, 4301.99
  sale to, prohibited, 4301.69, 4301.99
unlawful sale of, allegations necessary in indictment, 2941.20

LITTER, OFFENSES INVOLVING, 3767.32, 3767.33

LIVE ENTERTAINMENT PERFORMANCE
crowd safety restrictions, 2917.40

LIVERY, DEFRAUDING, 2913.41

LIVESTOCK
dangerous drug offenses involving, 2925.09
running at large, 951.01, 951.02, 951.99
value re theft of, 2913.61

LOAN SHARKING, 2905.21-2905.24
as pattern of corrupt activity, 2923.31 *et seq*

LOCKER ROOMS
anabolic steroids, notice re—
  athletic facilities, public and private, 3707.50
  colleges, 3345.41
  schools, 3313.75.2
  universities, 3345.41

LOITERING
engage in solicitation, to, 2907.24.1

LORAN, INTERRUPTING, IMPAIRING, 2909.04

LOST
firearms, report to law enforcement authorities required, 2923.22
ordnance, dangerous—
  fire marshal, state, report copy to, 2923.18
  law enforcement authorities, report to required, 2923.23
property, held by law enforcement agency, disposition of, 2933.41

LOTTERY, STATE, 3770.01 *et seq*—*see also* **GAMBLING**
bribery; penalty, 3770.08, 3770.99
fairgrounds, sale at, 3770.08
person under eighteen, sale to prohibited; penalty, 3770.08, 3770.99
sale at greater price prohibited; penalty, 3770.08, 3770.99

LOTTERY, STATE—*Continued*
sale by unauthorized person prohibited; penalty, 3770.08, 3770.99

MACHINES, COIN—*see* COIN MACHINES

MAGISTRATE COURTS, 2938.01 *et seq*

MAGISTRATE, DEFINED, 2931.01

MANDATORY SENTENCING—*see* SENTENCE, *at* actual incarceration, of

MANSLAUGHTER
indictment re, manner, means of death not required in, 2941.14
involuntary, 2903.04
voluntary, 2903.03

MARIHUANA
cultivation, 2925.04
defined, 3719.01
finding of trafficking, 2925.05
possession, prohibited, 2925.11
sale of paraphernalia for use of to juvenile, 2925.14
sale, prohibited, 2925.03
trafficking in, 2925.03

MARKER, DESECRATION OF, 2927.11

MARKET VALUE, FAIR
arson, vandalism, defined re, 2909.11

MARSHAL
subpoena service, return by, Crim. R. 17
village, 737.15-737.20

MASSAGE ESTABLISHMENTS
definitions, 503.40
fees, deposit and use of, 503.49
inspections, 503.47
masseur or masseuse—
  defined, 503.40
  penalties, 503.50
  permit, application for, 503.45
  permit, denial of, 503.46
  permit, display of, 503.47
  physical examinations, 503.47
penalties, 503.50
permit—
  application for, 503.40
  denial of, 503.44
  display of, 503.47
  expiration of, 503.43
prohibitions, 503.42
township may regulate, 503.41

MASSEURS AND MASSEUSES—*see* MASSAGE ESTABLISHMENTS

MASS MURDER, AS AGGRAVATING CIRCUMSTANCE, 2929.04

MASTER, AS PUBLIC SERVANT, 2921.01

MASTER CAR KEY, OFFENSES RE, 4549.04.2

MASTURBATION
indecency, public, as, 2907.09
juveniles, when material, performance displaying harmful to, 2907.01
obscene material, performance, as, 2907.01

MATERIAL, OBSCENE—*see* OBSCENE MATERIAL, PERFORMANCE

MATERIAL WITNESS, 2937.18

MAYOR
law enforcement officer, as, 2901.01
mayor's court, ch. 1905
special patrolmen appointed by, 2901.01

MEDIATION, MEDIATORS
disclosure of mediation communication, 2717.02.3
victim-offender, 2929.01, 2929.17

MEDICAID FRAUD, 2913.40

MEDICAID FRAUD FORFEITURES
definitions, 2933.71
disposal of property, use of proceeds, 2933.74
filing of lien notice, 2933.75
hearing, forfeiture order, 2933.73
informants, award to, 2933.74
order to preserve reachability of property, 2933.72
petition by innocent person claiming interest in property, 2933.73
post-conviction orders to preserve rights of state or innocent person, 2933.72, 2933.74
settlement of claims, 2933.74
temporary restraining orders, 2933.72
trustees of forfeitable property, 2933.75

MEETING, DISTURBING LAWFUL, 2917.12

MEGAN'S LAW—*see* SEXUAL PREDATORS, HABITUAL SEX OFFENDERS, SEXUALLY ORIENTED OFFENDERS

MEMORANDA
motions supported by, containing citations of authority, Crim. R. 47
pretrial conference, of matters agreed on, by court, Crim. R. 17.1

MENACING, 2903.22
aggravated, 2903.21
extortion, as, 2905.11

MENTAL DEFICIENCY, AS MITIGATING CIRCUMSTANCE RE MURDER, 2929.04

MENTAL EXAMINATION
presentence, Crim. R. 32.2
violator of anti-stalking protection order, 2903.21.5
violator of protection order issued re domestic violence, of, 2919.27.1

MENTAL ILLNESS
firearm, dangerous ordnance, possession under, prohibited, 2923.13
  relief from disability re, void if adjudicated, 2923.14
serious physical harm, as infliction of, 2901.01
trial time extended re, 2945.72

MENTAL INSTITUTION—*see also* **LIMA STATE HOSPITAL**
custody of inmate, interference with, 2919.23
verdict of insanity, commitment under, 2945.39

MENTALLY ILL PAROLEES, 2967.22

MENTAL RETARDATION AND DEVELOPMENTAL DISABILITIES DEPARTMENT
abuse or neglect of mentally retarded adult, report, investigation, 5123.61
investigation by department, 5123.14
special police officers for institutions, 5123.13

MENTAL STATES, CULPABLE, 2901.21, 2901.22

METHADONE, 3719.61

MINOR—*see also* **CHILD; JUVENILES**
bail forfeit proceedings, minority not a defense, 2937.38
consent to examination as sex offense victim, may, 2907.29
convicted of felony, delivery to reformatory, 2949.12
corruption of, 2907.04
  habitual sex offender, re, 2950.01
firearm—
  improperly furnishing to, 2923.21
  purchase by, 2923.21.1
importuning of—*see* **IMPORTUNING**
intoxicating liquor, furnishing to, 4301.63 *et seq*
liability of parents, 3109.09, 3109.10
lottery, state—
  sale of tickets to prohibited, 3770.08
nude photos or performance, use of, 2907.32.3
pandering material, performance including minor—
  obscene, 2907.32.1
  sexually oriented, 2907.32.2

MINOR—*Continued*
pandering obscenity involving, 2907.32.1
prostitution of—
  compelling, when under 16, 2907.21
  promoting, under 16, 2907.22
recognizance of, 2937.17, 2937.18

MINOR MISDEMEANOR
attempt to commit, not an offense, 2923.02
citation, issuance for, 2935.26, 2935.27
fine for—
  maximum of $100, 2929.21
  organization, re, 2929.31
jury trial, no right to, re, 2945.17
limitation of prosecutions for, six months, 2901.13
offense, classified as, 2901.02
optional procedure, re, Crim. R. 4.1
repeat offender, not applicable re, 2929.01
trial, within 15 days after arrest, summons, 2945.71
  discharge re delay, 2945.73
    bar to further proceedings, as, 2945.73
violations bureau, municipal and county courts, SupR 18

MISCHIEF, CRIMINAL, 2909.07

MISCONDUCT
emergency, at—*see* **EMERGENCY**
juror, prosecutor, witness, of, as grounds for new trial, Crim. R. 33; 2945.79
public transportation system, involving, 2917.41

MISDEMEANOR
appeal of conviction of, recognizance to be given before suspension of execution of sentence, 2953.12
bail, re—*see* **BAIL**
classification of offenses, re, 2901.02
complaint, prosecuted by, in inferior court, Crim. R. 7
confinement for, 2949.08
defined, Crim. R. 2
joinder of, with felony, other misdemeanor, Crim. R. 8
jury trial re—*see* **JURORS; JURY; JURY TRIAL**
limitation of prosecutions for, two years, 2901.13
minor—*see* **MINOR MISDEMEANOR**
penalties, 2929.21, 2929.22, 2929.41, 2929.51
pleas to—*see* **PLEAS**
presentence investigation re, discretionary, Crim. R. 32.2
prosecution by affidavit, 2941.35
  indictment, information, complaint, by, Crim. R. 7
recognizance may be demanded upon conviction of, 2947.16, 2947.17
trial for, time limits re, 2945.71, 2945.72, 2945.73
trial in absentia for, 2945.12

MISJOINDER, Crim. R. 14; 2941.28

MISTAKE, CLERICAL, Crim. R. 36

MITIGATING CIRCUMSTANCES, RE AGGRAVATED MURDER, 2929.03, 2929.04

MITIGATION OF SENTENCE, Crim. R. 32; 2947.06

MODERN COURTS AMENDMENT, Art. IV, § 5 OC

MONEY LAUNDERING TRANSACTION REPORTING, 1315.51-1315.55
corrupt activity, as, 2923.31
definitions, 1315.51
duty to report transactions, keep records, 1315.53
investigation, 1315.54
liberal construction of provisions, 1315.52
penalties, 1315.99
prohibitions, 1315.53, 1315.55
wiretapping provisions, 2933.51

MOTIONS
acquittal, for judgment of, Crim. R. 29
affidavit, may be supported by, Crim. R. 47
applications to court for orders, to be by, Crim. R. 47
arrest of judgment, for—*see* ARREST OF JUDGMENT
defenses, objections, pretrial to be raised by, Crim. R. 12—*see also* DEFENSES, OBJECTIONS, PRETRIAL
discharge, for—*see* DISCHARGE
generally, Crim. R. 47
grounds upon which made, shall state, Crim. R. 47
guilty plea, for withdrawal of, time for, Crim. R. 32.1—*see also* GUILTY PLEA
indictment, to dismiss, bases for, Crim. R. 6—*see also* INDICTMENTS, INFORMATIONS
leave to appeal, for, 2953.06
new trial, for—*see* NEW TRIAL
quash, to, abolished, Crim. R. 12; 2941.54, 2941.62
service of, written, on each party, Crim. R. 49
suppress, to—*see* SUPPRESS, MOTION TO
venue, for change of, Crim. R. 18
writing, in, when shall be, Crim. R. 47

MOTORBOAT—*see* WATERCRAFT, OFFENSES RE
abandoned, 4513.60-4513.65

MOTORCYCLES, TRAFFIC LAWS RE, 4511.53

MOTOR VEHICLES—*see also* TRAFFIC LAWS
alcohol—
  consumption of, while in, 4301.64, 4301.99
  operating under influence of, 4511.19, 4511.99—*see also* DRIVING UNDER INFLUENCE
abandoned, 4513.61-4513.65

MOTOR VEHICLES—*Continued*
assured clear distance, 4511.21
bicycles, motorized, rules for operating, 4511.52.1
brakes, 4513.20-4513.20.2
chauffered limousines, regulation of, 4511.85
collector's exemptions for, 4513.38.41
commercial vehicle, driving with impaired alertness, 4511.79
crimes, 4549.01 *et seq*
decal, security, display on side window or sidewing, 4513.24.2
defraud, hiring to, 2913.41
directional signals, 4513.26.1
drag racing of, 4511.25.1, 4511.99
driver's license, for—*see* DRIVER'S LICENSE
drug of abuse, operating under influence of, 4511.19, 4511.99
earphones prohibited, 4511.84
engine noise, township may regulate, 505.17
enticement of child into, 2905.05
equipment, ch. 4513
explosives, transporting, 4513.29
financial responsibility laws re—
  accident report—
    contents, 4509.07
    duty to make, 4509.06
    exception to requirement, 4509.08
    failure to make, 4509.10.1, 4509.74, 4509.99
    use of, 4509.10
  additional sanctions for violating municipal ordinance, 4507.36.1
  chauffered limousines, 4509.80, 4509.81
  false information, giving of, 4509.10.2, 4509.99
  highway patrol trooper may request proof of, 4513.02.2
  insurer to provide identification cards, 4509.10.3
  insurer to warn when policy does not meet minimum amounts, 4509.10.4
  license, failure to return, 4509.77, 4509.99
  offenses, 4507.99
  proof of—
    generally, 4509.45
    suspension for failure to furnish, 4509.30-4509.34
    registration, required for, 4509.44
  suspended license, operating vehicle with, 4511.19.2
firearms, discharge from, 2941.14.6
firearms, improperly handling in, 2923.16
forfeiture of—
  drug offenses, 2925.13
  other offenses, 4507.16.4, 4507.37, 4507.99
garage keepers—
  crime, evidence of, shall report, 4501.05
glass, safety, 4513.26
historical, exemptions for, 4513.38, 4513.41
homicide by, 2903.07
  aggravated, 2903.06
horns, 4513.21
ignition interlock device, 2951.02, 4507.16, 4511.83, 4511.99

MOTOR VEHICLES—*Continued*
junk, disposal of by law enforcement agency, 2933.41
key—
   ignition, officer may remove, 4549.05
   master, possession of illegal, 4549.04.2, 4549.99
law enforcement emblem, unlawful display on, 2913.44.1
license plates—
   impoundment, 4507.16.4, 4507.37, 4507.99
   licensing generally, ch. 4503
   loads, ch. 4513
   operating without or with unauthorized, 4549.08, 4549.10, 4549.99
   parking, township may regulate, 505.17
   theft of, receiving stolen, 2913.71
lights, 4513.03-4513.19
loads, ch. 4513
mirrors, 4513.23
mufflers, 4513.22
nitrous oxide, possession in, 2925.33
noise, 4513.22, 4513.22.1
odometer—*see* ODOMETER ROLLBACK AND DISCLOSURE ACT
railroads, offenses concerning, 4999.01, 4999.03
receiving stolen motor vehicle, 2913.51
reckless driving of, 4511.20, 4511.20.1
registration—
   certificates—
      display of, 4549.18, 4549.99
      financial responsibility, 4509.44
      impoundment, 4507.16.4, 4507.37, 4507.99
      number of former owner or foreign state, 4549.11, 4549.12, 4549.99
safety compact, equipment, 4513.51 *et seq*
school zones, 4511.21, 4511.21.2
seat belts, 4513.26.2, 4513.26.3
smoke, 4513.22
speed limits, 4511.21 *et seq*
storage fees, payment of, 2913.82
tampering with identifying numbers, 4549.61 *et seq*
temporary license or windshield sticker, failure to display, 4503.21, 4503.99
theft of, 2913.71
theft offender to pay towing or storage costs, 2913.82
tires, solid, 4513.25
title, certificate of—
   blank, theft of, receiving stolen, 2913.71
   offenses re, 4505.19, 4505.99
   sale or operation of vehicle without, 4505.18, 4505.99
towing, 4513.32
towing fees, payment of, 2913.82
unauthorized use of, 2913.03
used in transaction involving contraband, construed contraband, 2933.42
   seizure of; notice, disposition, 2933.43
venue when offense, element of, committed in, 2901.12
warning devices, 4513.21, 4513.27, 4513.28
weapon, carrying concealed in, when permissible, 2923.12

MOTOR VEHICLES—*Continued*
weighing, 4513.33
windows, 4513.24, 4513.24.1, 4513.26
windshields, 4513.24, 4513.24.1, 4513.26
wipers, 4513.24

MULTIPLE COUNTS—*see also* JOINDER
when defendant can be convicted of only one, or more than one, 2941.25

MULTIPLE DEFENDANTS—*see* JOINDER, *at* defendants, of

MULTIPLE SENTENCES, 2929.41

MUNICIPAL CORPORATIONS, 715.48-715.67
probation services fund, 737.41

MUNICIPAL COURT
arrest warrants, outstanding—
   driver's license ineligibility, 4507.01.1
   vehicle registration ineligibility, 4503.13
criminal jurisdiction of, 1901.20, 2931.04, 2931.04.1
jury, provisions for, 1901.24, 1901.25
procedure in, 1901.21
prosecuting attorney, in, 1901.34
writs and process, issuance of, 1901.23

MURDER, 2903.02—*see also* MURDER, AGGRAVATED
attempt to commit, 2923.02
conspiracy to commit, 2923.01
felony, classified as, 2901.02
indictment, for, manner, means of causing death, not required in, 2941.14
limitation of prosecution, re, none, 2901.13
offense, classified as, 2901.02
penalties for, 2929.02
   organizations, 2929.31
probation, prohibited, 2951.02
sexual predators—*see* SEXUAL PREDATORS, HABITUAL SEX OFFENDERS, SEXUALLY ORIENTED OFFENDERS

MURDER, AGGRAVATED, 2903.01—*see also* DEATH PENALTY
age of offender, 2929.02.2, 2929.02.3, 2929.03, 2929.05
attempt to commit, 2923.02
capital offense, as, 2901.02—*see also* CAPITAL OFFENSE
conspiracy to commit, 2923.01
death sentence vacated upon appeal, procedure after, 2929.06
felony—
   classified as, 2901.02
   murder, during commission of, 2903.01
indictment for, 2941.14

MURDER, AGGRAVATED—*Continued*
indigent defendant, costs of necessary services, 2929.02.4
limitation of prosecution for, none, 2901.13
mitigating circumstances, 2929.03, 2929.04
notice to Ohio supreme court of indictment for, with specifications, further notice, 2929.02.1
parole eligibility, 2967.13
penalties for, 2929.02-2929.04
　organizations, 2929.31
pleas re, Crim. R. 11
prior conviction as aggravating circumstance, 2929.02.2, 2929.04
probation for, prohibited, 2951.02
sexual predators—*see* SEXUAL PREDATORS, HABITUAL SEX OFFENDERS, SEXUALLY ORIENTED OFFENDERS
specifications, 2903.01

MUSEUM PIECE
desecration of, 2927.11
firearm as, when sold at public auction, 2933.41
ordnance, dangerous, as, when not, 2923.11
value of, re theft offense, 2913.61

NAMES
case file, criminal docket, names of parties, counsel to be placed on, Crim. R. 55

NEGLECT
delay caused by accused extends trial time, 2945.72
dependents, of, 2919.21
excusable, re permitting act after time for, Crim. R. 45
patient, resident of care facility, 2903.33 *et seq*

NEGLIGENT ASSAULT, 2903.14

NEGLIGENT HOMICIDE, 2903.05—*see also* HOMICIDE

NEGLIGENTLY, 2901.22

NEGOTIABLE INSTRUMENTS—*see also* CHECKS
blank, theft of, receiving stolen, 2913.71
theft of, value re, 2913.61

NEGOTIATED PLEA, Crim. R. 11

NEIGHBORS
sex offender notification—*see* SEXUAL PREDATORS, HABITUAL SEX OFFENDERS, SEXUALLY ORIENTED OFFENDERS

NETWORK, CRIMINAL JUSTICE, 5502.01

NEWLY DISCOVERED EVIDENCE, AS GROUNDS FOR NEW TRIAL, Crim. R. 33; 2945.79

NEWS SOURCE, PRIVILEGED, RE MAKING CRIME REPORT, 2921.22

NEW TRIAL, Crim. R. 33
causes for—
　what are, 2945.79
　what are not, 2945.83
courts inferior to common pleas, procedure, 2931.15
motion for, procedure, 2945.80 *et seq*
　bail, effect on, 2953.03

NITROUS OXIDE—*see* HARMFUL INTOXICANT

NO CONTEST PLEA, 2937.06, 2937.07
felony, to, Crim. R. 11
negotiated, Crim. R. 11
notice to defendant, 2943.03.1

NOLLE PROSEQUI, Crim. R. 48
dismissal for delay, as, re felony, 2945.73
leave of court necessary, 2941.33
record not to be made, when, 2941.31

NON-PROBATIONABLE OFFENSES—(*Former* 2951.04, *see now* 2951.02)

NONSUPPORT OF DEPENDENTS, 2919.21

NOTARY PUBLIC, FALSIFICATION IN STATEMENT BEFORE, 2921.13

NOT GUILTY
finding of, judgment to be entered, Crim. R. 32
plea—*see* PLEAS
sealing of record after finding, 2953.51 *et seq*
verdict—*see* VERDICT

NOT GUILTY BY REASON OF INSANITY
application of mental retardation department provisions, 5123.01.1, 5123.69, 5123.70.1, 5123.76
application of R.C. Chapter 5122, 5122.01.1, 5122.02, 5122.05, 5122.11, 5122.15, 5122.21
battered woman syndrome testimony, 2945.39.2
conditional release, 2945.40.2
continuing jurisdiction of court, termination of commitment on change in conditions, 2945.40.1
definitions, 2901.01, 2945.37, 2945.39.1, 5122.01, 5123.01
escape provisions, 2921.01, 2921.34, 5122.26
evolutions of mental condition upon plea of, 2945.37.1
habeas corpus, 5122.30
plea, 2943.03, Crim. R. 11
procedure upon acquittal, 2945.40
system of tracking, monitoring after release, 5119.57

NOTICE
alibi, of intended use of, Crim. R. 12.1
appeal, of—*see* APPEAL, *at* notice of

NOTICE—*Continued*
custody interference, to authorities, as defense re, 2919.23
depositions, re, Crim. R. 15
early release of aggravated felon by parole authority, to prosecuting attorney, 2967.12.1
evidence, of intention to use, by prosecutor, Crim. R. 12
firearm disability relief, revocation by court upon, 2923.14
judicial—*see* JUDICIAL NOTICE OF CERTAIN LAW; JUDICIAL NOTICE OF STATUTE
lien, corrupt activity, 2923.36
pendency of pardon, commutation, parole, to be sent to judge, prosecuting attorney, 2967.12
property held by law enforcement agency, to owner, 2933.41
service of, written, on each party, Crim. R. 49
surety, to, re continuation of bail bond, Crim. R. 46
theft of services, re rate for, as value, 2913.61
time re, Crim. R. 45
victim, to—
  access to information re sentencing, probation, parole of offender; by court, 2943.04.1, 2945.07
  invitation to submit impact statement prior to parole; by parole authority, 2967.03, 2967.12
  trial date, or other final disposition; by prosecuting attorney, 2937.08.1

NUCLEAR MATERIALS, TRANSPORTING, 4163.07, 4163.99

NUDITY—*see also* OBSCENE MATERIAL, PERFORMANCE
defined, 2907.01
juveniles—
  when material, performance which displays is harmful to, 2907.01
  when photos of or performance using is illegal, 2907.32.3
obscene material, performance, when display is, 2907.01

NUISANCES
abandoned building, 3767.41
abatement, 3767.03—*see also* injunction, *this entry*
agriculture, persons engaged in, 3767.13
animal carcasses, 3767.16, 3767.18
  exceptions, 3767.22
authorization for disposal of litter, 3767.33
barriers to limited access highways, 3767.20.1
bond, 3767.03
building—
  abandoned, 3767.41
  definition, 3767.41
  gambling house, 2915.03, 2915.04
  lease, void, 3767.10
  lewd purposes, used for, 3767.10

NUISANCES—*Continued*
building—*Continued*
  nuisance, constituting, 3767.41
  obscenity laws, premises used to violate, 2907.37
  receivership, 3767.41
  thieves, resort for, 3767.12
burglars, resort for, 3767.12
butcher's establishment—
  exceptions, 3767.22
  violations, 3767.16
cheese factory, refuse from, 3767.14
coal mine, refuse from, 3767.14
coal oil refinery, refuse from, 3767.14
contempt proceedings, 3767.24
corporations—
  judgment for fine and costs, 3767.26
  prosecution of, 3767.23
definitions, 3767.01—*see also* specific terms
ditch, obstructing or diverting, 3767.17
  highway, along, 5589.04
environmental protection, director of, 3767.33
filth—*see also* specific entries
  general prohibition, 3767.13
fish house—
  exceptions, 3767.22
  violations, 3767.16
funeral services, picketing during, 3767.30
gambling house as, 2915.03, 2915.04
gasworks, refuse from, 3767.14
harbor, obstructing or befouling, 3767.13, 3767.16
  exceptions, 3767.22
highways, limited access, barriers, 3767.20.1
injunction—
  costs, 3767.05, 3767.11
  criminal proceeding, nuisance established in, 3767.11
  evidence, 3767.05
  general provision, 3767.02
  judgment, 3767.06
  order, 3767.06
  priority of action, 3767.05
  procedure, 3767.04
  violation of, 3767.07
inspector of, 3767.27, 3767.28
liquor, place of sale as, 4301.73
litter—
  exception, 3767.33
  violations, 3767.32
obscenity laws, premises used to violate, 2907.37
oil refinery—
  lien on, 3767.15
  refuse from, 3767.14
oil tank—
  lien on, 3767.15
  refuse from, 3767.14
oil well—
  lien on, 3767.15
  refuse from, 3767.14
packing house—
  exceptions, 3767.22

NUISANCES—*Continued*
packing house—*Continued*
    violations, 3767.16
penalties, 3767.99
person defined, 3767.01
place defined, 3767.01
prohibition, general, 3767.02
refrigerators, abandoned, 3767.28
reservoir, befouling, 3767.18
rest room facilities, 3767.34
river—
    befouling, 3767.13, 3767.14, 3767.16
        exceptions, 3767.22
    obstructing or diverting, 3767.13.2
robbers, resort for, 3767.12
slaughterhouse—
    exceptions, 3767.22
    violations, 3767.16
smells, 3767.13
spring, befouling, 3767.18
state institutions, near, 3767.19
tax on, 3767.08, 3767.09
thieves, resort for, 3767.12
venue, 3767.25—*see also* specific offenses
waste, infectious, 3734.02.3-3734.02.6
watercourse—
    befouling, 3767.13, 3767.14, 3767.16
        exceptions, 3767.22
    obstructing or diverting, 3767.13
well, befouling, 3767.18

NUMBER
action, criminal, of, re clerk's filing of, Crim. R. 55
character witnesses, of, 2945.57
jurors, of, Crim. R. 24
    alternate, Crim. R. 24
    grand jury, Crim. R. 6; 2939.02
    indictment, concurring in, 2939.20
    magistrate court, 2938.06
    peremptory challenges, of, Crim. R. 24; 2945.21, 2945.22

NURSE
crime, duty to report, 2921.22
defined, 3719.01

NURSING HOME—*see* CARE FACILITY

OATH OR AFFIRMATION
administration by peace officer, 2935.08.1
complaint made upon, Crim. R. 3
death penalty, statement of offender under, effect, 2929.03
defined, 1.59
falsification, irregularly administered, no defense re, 2921.13
grand jurors, by, 2939.06
    alternate jurors, of, Crim. R. 6

OATH OR AFFIRMATION—*Continued*
grand jurors, by—*Continued*
    challenges to array, before administered to, Crim. R. 6
    foreman, administered by, Crim. R. 6
grand jury witnesses, 2939.13
jury, by, 2945.28
    alternate jurors, Crim. R. 24
    examination under, Crim. R. 24
officers of court, re separation of jury, 2945.32
ordnance, dangerous, permit, license application under, 2923.18
perjury, false statement under, as, 2921.11
    administered irregularly, no defense, 2921.11
search warrant affiant, witnesses, examination under, Crim. R. 41
secrecy, of, grand jury stenographer, 2939.11
subpoena, by server of, 2945.45
surety for bail, of, 2937.24

OBJECTIONS
depositions, to admission of, Crim. R. 15
exceptions re, Crim. R. 51; 2945.09
instruction, to, Crim. R. 30
pretrial—*see* DEFENSES, OBJECTIONS, PRETRIAL

OBSCENE MATERIAL, PERFORMANCE
compelling acceptance of, 2907.34
declaratory judgment re, 2907.36
defined, 2907.01
destruction of, by law enforcement agency, when, 2933.41
injunction against, 2907.37
juveniles, harmful to—*see* JUVENILES, *at* matter harmful to
minor, involving, 2907.32.1
nuisance, premises used re, as, 2907.37
pandering, 2907.32
presumptions re, 2907.35
violence, cruelty, displaying, as, 2907.01

OBSTRUCTING JUSTICE, 2921.32

OBSTRUCTING OFFICIAL BUSINESS, 2921.31

OCCUPATION
property used in, vandalism to, 2909.05

OCCUPIED STRUCTURE—*see* STRUCTURE, OCCUPIED

ODOMETER ROLLBACK AND DISCLOSURE ACT, 4549.41-4549.51
auctioneer's statement, 4549.45.1
dealer's, salesperson's, etc., license revocation for violation, 4549.50
definitions, 4549.41

ODOMETER ROLLBACK, ETC.—*Continued*
device altering mileage recorded by, prohibited; penalty, 4549.43, 4549.99
disclosure, failure to provide prohibited; penalty, 4549.46, 4549.99
injunction; other remedies, 4549.48
liability of violator to transferee; action to enforce, 4549.49
nonfunctioning odometer, operating with intent to defraud; penalty, 4549.44, 4549.99
notice of tampering or nonfunction required; penalty, 4549.45, 4549.99
remedies, 4549.48, 4549.51
repair, notice of, 4549.42
tampering prohibited; penalty, 4549.42, 4549.99
violations investigated by attorney general, 4549.47

OFFENDERS—*see also* CONVICTS; DEFENDANTS, CRIMINAL
recovery of profits—*see* RECOVERY OF OFFENDER'S PROFITS
sentence—*see* PENALTIES; SENTENCE

OFFENSE OF VIOLENCE—*see also* OFFENSES
arrest without warrant for, upon reasonable ground, 2935.03
corrupt activity, as pattern of, 2923.31 *et seq*
defined, 2901.01
domestic—*see* DOMESTIC VIOLENCE
extortion, threat to commit as, 2905.11
firearm, dangerous ordnance—
  possession of, after conviction, indictment for, when prohibited, 2923.13
  relief from disability re possession of, how obtained, 2923.14
inciting to violence, re, 2917.01
indefinite term, 2929.12
panic, inducing by threatening, 2917.31
repeat offender, re, prima-facie evidence of, 2929.01
report re, failure to make, when prohibited, 2921.22
riot, aggravated, disorderly conduct to commit, as, 2917.02
specification that offender is repeat violent offender, 2941.14.9

OFFENSES—*see also* OFFENSE OF VIOLENCE
arrest of judgment for failure to charge, Crim. R. 34
capital—*see* CAPITAL OFFENSE
classification of, 2901.02
committed prior to 1-1-74; third or fourth degree felony committed between 1-1-74 and 7-1-83, 2929.61
common law, abrogated, 2901.03
construction of sections defining, 2901.04
culpability, re, 2901.21, 2901.22
degree of—
  affidavit, complaint, indictment, information, must state in, 2945.75

OFFENSES—*Continued*
degree of—*Continued*
  guilty verdict shall state, effect of omitting, 2945.75
family, against, 2919.01 *et seq*—*see also* FAMILY, OFFENSES AGAINST
joinder of, Crim. R. 13
relief from, Crim. R. 14
justice, against, 2921.01 *et seq*
lesser included—*see* LESSER INCLUDED OFFENSES
profits from; recovery of, 2969.01 *et seq*

OFFICE, PUBLIC—*see* PUBLIC, *at* office

OFFICER
dereliction of duty, by, 2921.44
law enforcement—*see* LAW ENFORCEMENT OFFICER
organization, corporation, of, when personally liable, 2901.24
personating, 2913.44

OFFICIAL
business, obstructing, 2921.31
political party, of—
  bribery, re, 2921.02
  defined, 2921.01
  intimidation of, 2921.03
proceeding—*see* PROCEEDING, OFFICIAL
public—*see* PUBLIC, *at* official
record, proof of, Crim. R. 27

OIL
coal, refinery, 3767.14
refinery, tanks, well as nuisance, 3767.14, 3767.15

OPEN CONTAINER, 4301.62

OPERATING A MOTOR VEHICLE AFTER UNDER-AGE ALCOHOL CONSUMPTION, 4511.19

OPIATE, DEFINED, 3719.01

OPIUM POPPY, DEFINED, 3719.01

ORDER OF COURT
sham legal process, 2921.52

ORDERS
abandonment, nonsupport of dependent, in violation of, 2919.21
docketing of, Crim. R. 55
mistakes, clerical, in, correcting, Crim. R. 36
protection—*see* PROTECTION ORDERS
sanctions to enforce, 2901.03—*see also* CONTEMPT

ORDINANCES, MUNICIPAL
appeal from conviction, re, right to, 2953.02
gambling offense, re, 2915.01
habitual sex offender, 2950.01
numerical designation of, in complaint, Crim. R. 3
offense of violence, as violation of, 2901.01
theft offenses, re, 2913.01
violation of—
    costs and fees to be included in judgment, 2947.23
    jurisdiction of municipal court, 2931.04.1
    suspension of execution of sentence, for, 2949.02, 2949.03

ORDNANCE, DANGEROUS, 2923.11 et seq—see also FIREARMS, DANGEROUS ORDNANCE
secure, failure to, 2923.19

ORGANIZED CRIME—see also CORRUPT ACTIVITY
commission fund, 177.01.1
control act of 1970, explosives license, permit, re, 2923.17
investigation and prosecution, 177.01 et seq

OWNER, DEFINED RE THEFT, FRAUD, 2913.01

PACKING HOUSE, 3767.16, 3767.22

PAIN, INFLICTION OF, AS SERIOUS PHYSICAL HARM, 2901.01

PANDERING OBSCENITY, 2907.32—see also OBSCENE MATERIAL, PERFORMANCE
involving a minor, 2907.32.1

PANIC, INDUCING, 2917.31

PAPERS
deposition, order to produce at, Crim. R. 15
discovery, inspection re—
    defendant, from, Crim. R. 16
    prosecuting attorney, from, Crim. R. 16
docketing, filing, re, Crim. R. 55
service, filing of, Crim. R. 49
subpoena for production of, re, Crim. R. 17

PARDON
adult parole authority, duties of, re, 2967.02
application for, 2967.07
application of provisions effective 7-1-96, 2967.02.1
arrest of violator of, 2941.46
civil rights of felon under conditional, 2961.01
conditional, 2967.04
    additional conditions, searches, 2967.13.1
defined, 2967.01
firearm disability relief application, set out in, 2923.14
governor's authority, OConst III:11, 2967.02

PARDON—Continued
notice of pendency of, to be sent to judge, prosecuting attorney, 2967.12
post-release control sanctions for certain offenders, 2967.28
probation, violation of previous, as factor against, 2951.02
procedure, 2967.03
unconditional, 2967.04
violation of, procedure, 2967.15
warrant of, 2967.06

PARENT
abandonment, nonsupport of aged, infirm, 2919.21
block parent symbol, unauthorized use, 2917.46
education neglect, 2919.22.2
endangering child, 2919.22
interference with custody, by, 2919.23
liability for children's acts, 2151.41.1, 3109.09, 3109.10
sexual battery, by, 2907.03

PAROLE—see also PAROLE AUTHORITY, ADULT
additional conditions, searches during, 2967.13.1
administrative release of parole violator, 2967.17
application of provisions effective 7-1-96, 2967.02.1
arrest of violator, report re, 2941.46
bad time added to prison term for violation, 2929.01, 2967.11
civil rights of felon during, 2961.01
condition of, generally, 2301.30
defined, 2967.01
emergency, due to overcrowding, 2967.18
final release from, 2967.16
firearm disability, relief from, 2923.14
mentally ill parolees, 2967.22
notice of pendency of, to be sent to judge, prosecutor, 2967.12
petition for full board hearing on proposed parole, 5149.10.1
post-release control sanctions for certain offenders, 2967.28
probation, department of, generally, 2301.27-2301.32
probation, violation of previous, as factor against, 2951.02
rules infraction board at each institution, 2967.11
sentence for new felony during, served consecutively, 2929.41
sexual offenders, certain—see SEXUAL PREDATORS, HABITUAL SEX OFFENDERS, SEXUALLY ORIENTED OFFENDERS
supervision of, agreement for, 2301.32
time eligible for, 2967.13
violation of—
    administrative release re, 2967.17
    arrest, 2301.31
    generally, 2301.30
    procedure, 2967.15
    violator defined, 2967.01

PAROLE AUTHORITY, ADULT, 2967.02
arrest of probationer, by officer of, 2951.08
halfway house or community residential center, powers re, 2967.14
notice to—
  prosecuting attorney of early release of aggravated felon, 2967.12.1
  victim, to invite impact statement prior to granting parole, 2967.03, 2967.12
supervision of probationers, by, 2951.05, 2951.06

PAROLEE
arrest of, 2941.46, 2951.08, 2967.15
defined, 2967.01

PARTICULARS, BILL OF—*see* BILL OF PARTICULARS

PARTNERSHIPS
property of, allegations necessary in indictment or information, 2941.21

PARTY OFFICIAL—*see* OFFICIAL, *at* political party, of

PASSING BAD CHECKS, 2913.11

PATERNITY
interfering with the establishment of, 3111.29, 3111.99

PATIENT ABUSE, NEGLECT
definitions, 2903.33
false complaint, 2903.35
license revocation, 2903.37
prohibited actions, 2903.34
protection for person filing complaint, 2903.36

PEACE BOND, WARRANTS, 2933.01 *et seq*
application of Criminal Rules to, Crim. R. 1

PEACE OFFICER—*see also* LAW ENFORCEMENT OFFICER
administration of oaths, acknowledgment of documents, 2935.08.1
assaulting, 2903.13
defined, 2935.01
felony conviction, effect, 109.77
guilty plea to felony or conviction, negotiated misdemeanor plea, 2929.29

PEACE OFFICER TRAINING COUNCIL
authority, 109.73
bailiffs, deputy bailiffs, public defender investigators, 109.75.1
certificate necessary for appointment, prohibition, 109.77
certification as special policeman, 109.78
civil service provision, not to exempt officers, 109.76

PEACE OFFICER, ETC.—*Continued*
conservancy district law enforcement officers, 109.71, 109.77
costs, 109.78
created, 109.71
crisis intervention, 109.71, 109.73, 109.74.1, 109.74.2, 109.77, 109.79
executive director, powers and duties, 109.75
meetings, 109.72
members, 109.71
missing children, child abuse and neglect cases, 109.74.1
peace officer defined, 109.71
penalty, 109.99
procedure for accepting guilty plea to felony or after conviction, negotiated misdemeanor pleas, 2929.29
rules and regulations, attorney general may adopt and promulgate, 109.74
sheriffs, basic training course, continuing education, 109.75.2, 109.80
terms, 109.72
training academy, 109.79
undercover drug agents may attend schools, 109.75.1

PEACE, PUBLIC, OFFENSES AGAINST, 2917.01 *et seq*
alarm, making false, 2917.32
disorderly conduct, 2917.11
disperse, failure to, 2917.04
emergency, misconduct at, 2917.13
meeting, disturbing a lawful, 2917.12
panic, inducing, 2917.31
riot, 2917.03
  aggravated, 2917.02
  justifiable use of force to suppress, 2917.05
telephone harassment, 2917.21
violence, inciting to, 2917.01

PENALTIES, 2929.01 *et seq*
actual incarceration, as—
  drug offenses, 2925.01
  specification in indictment required for imposition of, 2941.14.1
applicability of Criminal Rules to, Crim. R. 1
assignment of offender's payment to pay costs, 2949.11.1
construction of sections defining, 2901.04
definite term of imprisonment, 2929.13
fines, financial sanctions—
  additional fine up to $1,000,000 for certain offenders, 2929.25—*see also* VICTIMS OF CRIME *at* crime victim recovery fund
  collection of judgment in favor of state, 2929.25
  felony, for, 2929.11, 2929.18, 2929.18.1, 2929.19
  imposition of, for felony, 2929.14
  withholding or deduction orders, 2929.18.1
guilty, no contest plea, defendant must understand maximum, Crim. R. 11

PENALTIES—*Continued*
indefinite term; specification required in indictment for imposition of, 2929.12
jury trial, effect on right to, 2945.11
juvenile court fines and costs, schedule of, 2151.35.12
organizational, 2929.31
    personal accountability re, 2901.24

PENITENTIARIES
duration of sentence, 5145.01
erroneous sentence to, procedure, 2967.20
escapees, arrest and return, 5145.21
termination of sentence, 5145.02
type of institution where sentence to be served, 2929.22.1

PEN REGISTERS—*see* WIRETAPPING, ELECTRONIC SURVEILLANCE

PEREMPTORY CHALLENGES
alternate jurors, to, Crim. R. 24
capital cases, Crim. R. 24; 2945.21
manner of exercising, Crim. R. 24; 2945.23
number of, Crim. R. 24

PERFORMANCE, OBSCENE—*see* OBSCENE MATERIAL, PERFORMANCE

PERJURY, 2921.11
immunity from prosecution, does not include, 2945.44
indictment, information, for, 2941.18

PERMIT
drugs, re—*see* DRUG
explosive devices, possession permissible under, 2923.17
falsification to obtain, 2921.13
ordnance, dangerous, to possess, 2923.18

PERSONATING AN OFFICER, 2913.44, 2921.51

PERSONS
defined, 1.59
    re controlled substances, 3719.01

PETITION
offenses concerning, 731.36, 731.38-731.40, 731.99
vacation of judgment, for, 2953.21 *et seq*

PETROLEUM UNDERGROUND STORAGE TANKS
action to confirm or disprove release, 3737.88.2
certification of systems installers, training programs, 3737.88.1
corrective actions, 3737.88.2
financial assurance fund, fees, certificate of coverage, 3737.91
purposes, claims for reimbursement, 3737.92

PETROLEUM UNDERGROUND, ETC.—*Continued*
penalties, 3737.99
transferor of petroleum to give notice of registration requirements, 3737.93

PETTY OFFENSES
assignment of counsel, re, Crim. R. 44
defined, Crim. R. 2
guilty, no contest plea to, procedure, Crim. R. 11
probation revocation hearing, re, Crim. R. 32.3
recording of proceedings re, Crim. R. 22
right to jury re, Crim. R. 5, 23
theft, 2913.02

PHARMACY, PHARMACIST
contaminating substance for human consumption or use, 2927.24
dangerous drugs, ch. 4729
defined, 3719.01
jurisdiction of county court judge, 2931.02
spreading false report of contamination, 2927.24

PHONOGRAPH RECORD, CRIMINAL SIMULATION OF, 2913.32

PHOTOGRAPH
criminal simulation of, 2913.32
discovery re—
    defendant, from, Crim. R. 16
    prosecuting attorney, from, Crim. R. 16
minors, involving; prohibitions, exceptions—
    nudity, 2907.32.3
    obscenity, 2907.32.1
    sexually oriented, 2907.32.2
physical evidence, as substitute for, Crim. R. 26

PHYSICAL EXAMINATION
presentence, Crim. R. 32.2
search of body cavity, 2933.32

PHYSICAL HARM
child, to, substantial risk of, when prohibited, 2919.22
kidnapping to inflict serious, prohibited, 2905.01
persons, to—
    alarm involving, making false, prohibited, 2917.32
    arson, as aggravated, when, prohibited, 2909.02
    burglary, aggravated, as, prohibited, 2911.11
    damaging, endangering, criminal, as, first degree misdemeanor, 2909.06
    death, risk of, as serious, 2901.01
    defined, 2901.01
    disfigurement, permanent, temporary, as serious, 2901.01
    disorderly conduct, risk as, prohibited, 2917.11
    disperse, failure to, likelihood re, 2917.04
    escape, no risk of, as affirmative defense, 2921.34
    felony, lack of, as criterion re imprisonment for, 2929.12

PHYSICAL HARM—*Continued*
persons, to—*Continued*
  impairing protection from, prohibited, 2909.04
  incapacity, permanent, temporary, as serious, 2901.01
  mental illness as serious, 2901.01
  misdemeanor, fine, imprisonment for, as criterion re, 2929.22
  ordinance, municipal, violation as offense of violence, 2901.01
  pain, suffering, as serious, 2901.01
  probation, did not cause, threaten, factor favoring, 2951.02
  report to officer, failure to make, prohibited, 2921.22
  riot, risk of, force used to suppress, 2917.05
  robbery, aggravated, when, prohibited, 2911.01
  serious, defined, 2901.01
prisoner in detention facility, to, must prevent, 2921.44
property, to—
  alarm involving, making false, prohibited, 2917.32
  arson—
    aggravated, as, when, prohibited, 2909.02
    consent of owner, without, prohibited, 2909.03
    defraud, to, risk of, as, prohibited, 2909.03
  damaging, endangering, criminal, as, when, prohibited, 2909.06
  defined, 2901.01
  disorderly conduct, risk as, prohibited, 2917.11
  disperse, failure to, likelihood re, 2917.04
  escape, no risk of, as affirmative defense, 2921.34
  felony, lack of, as criterion re imprisonment for, 2929.12
  impairing protection from, prohibited, 2909.04
  misdemeanor, fine, imprisonment for, as criterion re, 2929.22
  probation, did not cause, threaten, factor favoring, 2951.02
  repair, requiring substantial, as serious, 2901.01
  serious, defined, 2901.01
  use, prevention, interference with, as serious, 2901.01
  value—
    arson, related offenses, how determined, 2909.11
    serious, substantial loss of, as, 2901.01
  vandalism, as, when, prohibited, 2909.05
  wear, tear, normal, excluded, 2901.01

PHYSICIAN
abortion, 2919.11 *et seq*
gunshot, stab wound, burn, failure to report, 2921.22
suspicious or unusual manner of death, duty to notify coroner, 313.12

PLAIN ERROR, Crim. R. 52

PLEA BARGAINING
advice as to possible extension of felony prison term, 2943.03.2

PLEA BARGAINING—*Continued*
felony, re, underlying agreement to be stated in open court, Crim. R. 11

PLEADINGS, Crim. R. 12

PLEAS, Crim. R. 11; 2937.06, 2943.03
abatement, in, 2941.55, 2941.56, 2941.60, 2941.62
  abolished, Crim. R. 12
  appeal of issues formerly raised by, Crim. R. 12
  trial time extended re, 2945.72
advice as to possible extension of felony prison term, 2943.03.2
appearance, at initial, Crim. R. 5
arraignment, at, Crim. R. 10
capital cases, Crim. R. 11
form of, 2943.04
guilty—*see* GUILTY PLEA
negotiated, Crim. R. 11
no contest—*see* NO CONTEST PLEA
not guilty—
  arraignment, defendant absent from, entered, Crim. R. 10
  form re, 2943.03, 2943.04
  felonies, 2937.09
  misdemeanors, 2937.06, 2937.08
not guilty by reason of insanity—*see* NOT GUILTY BY REASON OF INSANITY PLEA
preliminary hearing, at, Crim. R. 5

PLURAL, INCLUDES SINGULAR, 1.43

POISONS, OFFENSES RE
animals, of, 959.03, 959.99
contaminating substance for human consumption or use, 2927.24
criminal damaging, endangering, by, 2909.06
spreading false report of contamination, 2927.24

POLICE AND POLICE DEPARTMENTS—*see also* LAW ENFORCEMENT OFFICER
auxiliary officers—
  law enforcement officers, as, 2901.01
city, ch. 737
communications of, disrupting, 2909.04
controlled substance, sales of, 3719.14.1
dogs, horses, assaulting, 2921.32.1
municipal, jurisdiction of, 715.50
registration of sex offenders—*see* SEXUAL PREDATORS, HABITUAL SEX OFFENDERS, SEXUALLY ORIENTED OFFENDERS
subpoena, service, return, by, Crim. R. 17
township, 505.48-505.55

POLITICAL CAMPAIGN
contribution, public servant improperly soliciting, 2921.43
theft of funds by official, 2921.41

POLITICAL PARTIES
intimidation of official involved in civil action, 2921.03
retaliation against official involved in civil or criminal action, 2921.05

POLITICAL PARTY OFFICIAL—*see also* OFFICIAL, *at* political party, of
intimidation of, 2921.03

POLL OF JURY, RE VERDICT, Crim. R. 31; 2945.77

POPPY STRAW, DEFINED, 3719.01

POPULATION, DEFINED, 1.59

POSSESSION, AS VOLUNTARY ACT, 2901.21

POSSESS, POSSESSION
defined, re drugs, 2925.01

POST-CONVICTION REMEDIES
death penalty cases, SupR 39
first offender, sealing of record of, 2953.31 *et seq*
vacation of sentence, 2953.21 *et seq*

POULTRY, VALUE RE THEFT OF, 2913.61

PRACTITIONER, RE CONTROLLED SUBSTANCES, DRUGS
defined, 3719.01

PRECEDENCE OF CRIMINAL CASES, ON COURT CALENDAR, Crim. R. 50; 2945.02

PREDATORS, SEXUAL—*see* SEXUAL PREDATORS, HABITUAL SEX OFFENDERS, SEXUALLY ORIENTED OFFENDERS

PREGNANCY
abortion—*see* ABORTION
drug abuse offender, of, 2925.11
prisoner under death sentence of, 2949.31

PREJUDICE—*see* DISCRIMINATION

PREJUDICIAL ERROR
plain, Crim. R. 52

PRELIMINARY HEARING, Crim. R. 5; 2937.01 *et seq*
plea at, Crim. R. 5
right to, informed of, at initial appearance, Crim. R. 5
time limits re, 2945.71 *et seq*, SupR 39
videotaped testimony, deposition of child victim of sex offense, 2945.48.1

PREMISES, VIEW OF BY JURY, 2945.16

PRESCRIPTION
deception re, 2925.22
defined, 3719.01
false or forged, 2925.23
theft of prescription, prescription blank, 2925.23

PRESENCE OF DEFENDANT, Crim. R. 43
arraignment, at, Crim. R. 10
probation revocation hearing, at, Crim. R. 32.3

PRESENTENCE INVESTIGATION, Crim. R. 32.2
death penalty, re, 2929.03
felony case, 2951.03
mitigation, 2947.06

PRESIDENT, ASSASSINATION OF, AS AGGRAVATING CIRCUMSTANCE, 2929.04

PRESS, FREEDOM OF, Art. I, § 11 OC

PRESUMPTIONS
bail, capital case exclusion, Crim. R. 46
checks, re passing bad, 2913.11
child, unborn, viability, 2919.17
hostelry, re defrauding of, 2913.41
innocence of, 2901.05
 magistrate courts, 2938.08
livery, re defrauding of, 2913.41
obscenity, re, 2907.35
sanity, of, where no insanity plea made, Crim. R. 11

PRETRIAL CONFERENCE, Crim. R. 17.1

PRETRIAL DEFENSES, OBJECTIONS—*see* DEFENSES, OBJECTIONS, PRETRIAL

PRETRIAL DIVERSION PROGRAMS, 2935.36

PRIEST-PENITENT PRIVILEGE, RE REPORTING CRIME, 2921.22

PRIOR CONVICTION—*see* CONVICTION, *at* prior

PRISONS AND PRISONERS
civil action against governmental entity or employee, 2969.21-2969.27
 claims subject to grievance system, 2969.26
 clerk of court to collect fees, expenses, 2969.23
 deductions from inmate account, procedures generally, 2969.22
 definitions, 2969.21
 grounds for dismissal of action or appeal, 2969.24
 inmate affidavit as to prior actions, 2969.25
 multiple actions by inmate, 2969.25
 sanctions when action is frivolous or malicious, 5120.01.1
 waiver of prepayment, 2969.25
child support withholding from earnings, 3113.16
conveying weapon, drug or liquor into, 2921.36, 2921.37

PRISONS AND PRISONERS—*Continued*
criminal justice network information, 5502.01
harassment by inmate, 2921.38
health insurance claims, 2947.20
transfer of, on change of venue, 2931.30

PRIVACY
voyeurism, as invasion of, 2907.08

PRIVATE INVESTIGATORS AND SECURITY GUARD PROVIDERS
penalty, 4749.99
prohibitions, 4749.13

PRIVILEGE
communications and acts, re, 2317.02, 2317.02.1
defined, 2901.01
report of crime, re making, 2921.22

PROBABLE CAUSE
arrest warrant, for issuance of, Crim. R. 4
intoxicated, to believe, re disorderly conduct, 2917.11
preliminary hearing, finding of, at, Crim. R. 5
search warrant, re, Crim. R. 41; 2933.22

PROBATION, 2951.01 *et seq*
adult parole authority, duties of, re, 2967.02
application of 7-1-96 amendments, 2951.01.1
arrest during, 2941.46, 2951.08, 2967.15
civil rights of felon during, 2961.01
coercion charge, re, 2905.12
conditional, upon treatment for drug dependency, (*former* 2951.04, *see now* 2951.02)
conditions of, generally, 2301.30
county or multicounty department or contract for services, 2301.27
  agreements with adult parole authority to provide services, 2301.32
  arrest of parolees, 2301.31
  arrest of probationer, 2951.08
  court placement of offender under control, supervision, 2951.05
  duties generally, 2301.30
  offender may be ordered to pay monthly probation fee, 2949.11.1, 2951.02.1
  rules, 2301.29
  supervision of persons on probation or parole or conditionally pardoned, 2301.28
court to consider defendant's cooperation in revealing information, 3719.70
criteria re, 2951.02
department of, generally, 2301.27-2301.32
fees, offender may be charged monthly, 2949.11.1, 2951.02.1
firearm—
  carrying by probation officer, 109.80.1-109.80.3, 1901.33, 2301.27
  disability re, relief from, 2923.14
  offense committed with, prohibited, 2951.02

PROBATION—*Continued*
municipal court probation department, 1901.33
  probation services fund, 737.41
non-probationable offenses, (*former* 2951.04, *see now* 2951.02)
report in mitigation of sentence, duties as to, 2947.06
revocation of, Crim. R. 32.3; 2951.09, 2951.13
searches during, 2951.02
sentence for new felony during, served consecutively, 2929.41
supervision, agreement for, 2301.32
suspension of sentence re, 2929.51
venereal disease treatment as condition of, 2907.27
violations of conditions, 2301.31

PROCEDURAL LAW
construction of statutes re, 2901.04

PROCEEDING, OFFICIAL
defined, 2921.01
evidence re, tampering with, 2921.12
falsification in, 2921.13
perjury, false statement in, as, 2921.11
trial time, extending, 2945.72

PROCESS
constitutional provisions re style of, Art. IV, § 20 OC
criminal docket, re, Crim. R. 55
inducing person to elude legal, 2921.32
prosecution commenced when issued, exception, 2901.13
quashing of, tolls limitation period, 2901.13
using sham legal, 2921.52

PROCESSION, DISTURBING, 2917.12

PROCURING, 2907.23
rules of evidence re, 2907.26

PROFESSION
theft of equipment, supplies re, value of, 2913.61
vandalism to property used in, 2909.05

PROFESSIONAL LICENSE
defined, 2925.01
drug offenses, notice of, 2925.38
notice to licensing board upon conviction or dismissal on procedural or technical grounds, 2929.17

PROFITS, RECOVERY OF OFFENDER'S, 2969.01 *et seq*

PROMOTING PROSTITUTION, 2907.22—*see also* PROSTITUTION, *at* promoting

PROPERTY
defined, 1.59, 2901.01
depriving another of—
  defined, 2913.01

PROPERTY—Continued

depriving another of—Continued
theft, as, 2913.02
forfeited, held by law enforcement agency, disposition, 2933.41
jurisdiction re out-of-state taking, retaining, 2901.11
law enforcement agency, held by, disposition, 737.29-737.33, 2933.41
physical harm to, defined, 2901.01
serious, defined, 2901.01
receiving stolen, 2913.51—*see also* RECEIVING STOLEN PROPERTY
search warrants for—*see* SEARCH AND SEIZURE
unauthorized use of, 2913.03, 2913.04
value of, 2913.61

PROSECUTING ATTORNEY—*see also* PROSECUTION

alibi, notice of, to be served on, Crim. R. 12.1
appeal by, 2945.67
  motion to suppress, re, Crim. R. 12
arraignment, may approve defendant's absence from, Crim. R. 10
assistants, clerks, stenographers, appointment, compensation of, 309.06
  persons who are associated in the private practice of law, 309.06, 2921.42, 2921.42.1
bill of particulars, to furnish defendant—*see* BILL OF PARTICULARS
capital offense, joinder of defendants, application for, Crim. R. 14
coercion charge, discretion, re, 2905.12
comment by—
  defendant's failure to testify, on, 2945.43
  plea, on, when prohibited, Crim. R. 11
  witness, on failure to call, Crim. R. 16
coroner's records, reports, to be furnished to, 313.09
death penalty for aggravated murder, duties re, 2929.03
defined, Crim. R. 2; 2935.01
discovery, re, Crim. R. 16—*see also* DISCOVERY
dismissal, role in, Crim. R. 48
drug analysis reports, duties re, 2925.51
election of, 309.01
evidence, notice of intention to use, by, Crim. R. 12
extradition—
  investigation of demand for, by, 2963.04
  requisition for return of fugitive, by, 2963.21
firearm disability relief application, duties re, 2923.14
grand jury, 2939.10
  challenge to array, jurors, by, Crim. R. 6
  disclosure of matters before, to, when, Crim. R. 6
  present when in session, may be, Crim. R. 6
  tenure extended upon recommendation of, Crim. R. 6
indictment—
  signed by, or assistant, Crim. R. 7
  surplusage, struck upon motion of, Crim. R. 7
information—
  signed by, or assistant, Crim. R. 6

PROSECUTING ATTORNEY—Continued

information—Continued
  surplusage, struck upon motion of, Crim. R. 7
jurors—*see also* JURORS
  array, challenge to, by, Crim. R. 24
  examination by, Crim. R. 24
  peremptory challenges by—*see* PEREMPTORY CHALLENGES
jury trial waiver, with consent of, Crim. R. 23
legal adviser to county, township officers, to serve as, 309.09
misconduct of, as grounds for new trial, Crim. R. 33; 2945.79
notice of appeal, motion for leave to appeal, copy to be served on, 2953.06
notice of conviction of board of education employee of certain crimes, 3319.20
notice of pendency of pardon, commutation, parole, to receive, 2967.12
officer, law enforcement, as, 2901.01
powers, duties of, 309.08
preliminary hearing, duties re, Crim. R. 5
presentence report, disclosure to, Crim. R. 32.2
protection of public funds, duties as to, 309.12
qualifications of candidate for, 309.02
rebuttal, by—
  defendant's character evidence, of, 2945.56
removal of, for misconduct, 309.05
report annually—
  attorney general, to, 309.15
  county commissioners, to, 309.16
sealed records, inspection of, 2953.32
search warrant, issued upon request of, Crim. R. 41
secret service officers, may appoint, 309.07
severance of defendants, duties re, Crim. R. 14
summons—
  unserved, request for service of, by, Crim. R. 4
  warrant, in lieu of, on request of, Crim. R. 4
summons upon indictment, information, Crim. R. 9
timber, state-owned, duty to protect, 309.14
venue change, duties, re, Crim. R. 18; 2931.29, 2931.31
videotaping of testimony of child victim of sex offense; request for, procedures, 2907.41
warrant, arrest, unexecuted, duties re, Crim. R. 4
warrant upon indictment, information, Crim. R. 9; 2941.36 *et seq*

PROSECUTION—*see also* PROSECUTING ATTORNEY

abandoning, agreeing to, for consideration, 2921.21
appeal by, 2945.67
coercion, instituting, threatening as, 2905.12
commenced, how, 2901.13
defects in instituting—*see* DEFENSES, OBJECTIONS, PRETRIAL
flight to avoid, tolls limitation period, 2901.13—*see also* FLIGHT
immunity from—*see* IMMUNITY FROM PROSECUTION

PROSECUTION—*Continued*
indictment, information, by—*see* INDICTMENTS, INFORMATIONS
limitation of, 2901.13
offense committed prior to 1-1-74; third or fourth degree felony committed between 1-1-74 and 7-1-83, 2929.61
private attorney, by, in magistrate courts, 2938.13
proof, burden of, upon, 2901.05
to be in name of state of Ohio, Art. IV, § 20 OC
transfer from common pleas court, after, Crim. R. 21
wrong county, in, procedure for transfer, 2945.08

PROSTITUTE—*see also* PROCURING; PROSTITUTION; SOLICITING
defining, 2907.01

PROSTITUTION, 2907.25—*see also* PROCURING; PROSTITUTE; SOLICITING
compelling, 2907.21
  conspiracy to commit, facilitate, 2923.01
engaging in after positive HIV test, 2907.25
payment for medical examination and test of victim or accused, 2907.28
promoting, 2907.22
  conspiracy to commit, 2923.01
  syndicate, criminal, engaging in, 2923.04
rules of evidence in prosecutions re, 2907.26
testing of accused for venereal disease and HIV, 2907.27

PROTECTION ORDERS
anti-stalking—
  generally, 2903.21.3, 2919.26
  mental condition, evaluation of violator's, 2903.21.5
  violating, 2903.21.4
generally, 2919.26
violating, 2919.27

PROVOCATION
imprisonment for felony, criterion re, 2929.12
murder, aggravated, as mitigating circumstance re, 2929.04
probation, criterion re, 2951.02

PRURIENT INTEREST
juveniles, when material, performance appealing to, harmful to, 2907.01
obscene material, performance appealing to, when, 2907.01

PSYCHOLOGIST
client privilege, re, making crime report, 2921.22
report in mitigation of sentence, by, 2941.06

PUBLIC
administration, offenses against, 2921.01 *et seq*—*see also* JUSTICE, PUBLIC ADMINISTRATION, OFFENSES AGAINST
contract, 2921.42

PUBLIC—*Continued*
defender, 120.01 *et seq*
defender, state, reimbursement of counties, 2949.17 *et seq*
  report to legislature, budget and management of money needed for next biennium, 2949.20.1
gaming, 2915.04
health, offenses against, jurisdiction of county court re, 2931.02
indecency, 2907.09—*see also* INDECENCY, PUBLIC
office—
  bribery conviction, when disqualifies from, 2921.02
  compensation, soliciting, receiving improper, disqualifies from, 2921.43
  theft in, conviction disqualifies from, 2921.41
official—
  appropriation, annual, creating deficiency in, 2921.44
  contract, public, having unlawful interest in, 2921.42
  defined, 2921.01
  servant, public, as, 2921.01
  theft in office, by, 2921.41
records, 149.43
safety, department of, Ch. 737
servant—
  bribery, re, 2921.02—*see also* BRIBERY
  civil rights, interfering with, 2921.45
  compensation, soliciting, receiving improper, 2921.43
  contract, public, having unlawful interest in, 2921.42
  defined, 2921.01
  dereliction of duty, by, 2921.44
  intimidation, of, 2921.03
  limitation of prosecutions for misconduct in office, 2901.13
  office, public, conviction disqualifies from, 2921.41
  retaliation against, 2921.05
  theft in office, by, 2921.41
services, disrupting, 2909.04
transportation system, misconduct involving, 2917.41
utilities—
  electric wires, interfering with, 4933.21
  sewage disposal company, interfering with apparatus, 4933.24
  steam or heating plant, offenses re, 4933.23
  tampering with equipment of, 4933.18
  tampering with gas pipes and apparatus, 4933.20
  tampering with hydrant, or water pipe or meter, 4933.22
  theft of service of, 4933.19
  value of stolen electric service, 2913.61

PURPOSE
bail, of, Crim. R. 46
culpability, when sufficient, 2901.22
organization, as element of offense by, 2901.23
Rules of Criminal Procedure, of, Crim. R. 1

PURPOSELY
attempt, as sufficient culpability re, 2923.02

PURPOSELY—*Continued*
defined, 2901.22

PURSUIT POLICY, 2935.03.1

PYRAMID SALES PLANS, 1333.91-1333.95, 1333.99

QUASH
motion to—
  abolished, Crim. R. 12
  appeal of issues formerly raised by, Crim. R. 12
  hearing on, 2941.62
  when, 2941.54
subpoena for production of documents etc., court may, Crim. R. 17

RADAR, INTERRUPTING, IMPAIRING, 2909.04

RADIO
broadcasting information re crime, 2935.32
interrupting, impairing, 2909.04

RADIOACTIVE MATERIAL, CRIMINAL DAMAGING, ENDANGERING BY, 2909.06

RAILROADS
abandonment of track, restoration of roadway, 4955.20.1, 4955.99
animals, allowing into enclosures of, 4999.03
brakes, 4999.13
bridges over, constructing, 4999.10
cars—
  as occupied structures (re arson), 2909.01
  climbing on, 4999.02
chute, livestock, 4999.11
color blindness, testing for, 4999.16
couplers, 4999.13
crane, mail, 4999.11
crew of passenger train, 4999.06
discipline and discharge of employees, 4999.17
driving vehicles on, 4999.01
employee rights, maintenance of, 4999.20
enclosures of, riding or driving into, 4999.03
engineer, duties of, 4999.04
flagmen, 4999.05
freight, diverting, 4999.19
highway, obstructing, 5589.21-5589.24
procedure for taking tracks out of service, 4955.37, 4955.99
vehicular homicide, 2903.07
  aggravated, 2903.06
wires inoperative, demanding compensation for, 4999.18

RAPE, 2907.02
habitual sex offender, re, 2950.01
murder, committing during, as aggravating circumstance of, 2929.04
venereal disease examination, treatment re, 2907.27

RAPE—*Continued*
victim to be interviewed by crisis intervention trained officer, 2907.30

RATIFICATION
previous false statement, of—
  falsification, as, 2921.13
  perjury, 2921.11
vehicle, unauthorized use of, as affirmative defense, 2913.03

REAL PROPERTY
bail bond secured by—
  felonies, Crim. R. 46
  misdemeanors, Crim. R. 46
damage to by traffic law violator; name to be provided to owner, 2935.28
improper removal of fixtures from property, 5301.61, 5301.99

REASONABLE DOUBT, 2901.05
defined, jury instruction, 2901.05
guilty, no contest pleas, waive requiring proof beyond, Crim. R. 11
magistrate courts, charge on, in, 2938.08
specifications re aggravated murder, to be proved beyond, 2929.03, 2929.04

RECEIPT
property taken under search warrant, for, Crim. R. 41

RECEIVING STOLEN PROPERTY, 2913.51
degree of offense when certain property involved, 2913.71
pawnbrokers, certain dealers, to lose license upon conviction of, 2961.03
value of—
  jury, court, as part of guilty verdict, finding, to determine, 2913.61
  penalty, effect on, 2913.51

RECKLESS DRIVING, 4511.20, 4511.20.1, 4511.20.2

RECKLESSLY, DEFINED, 2901.22

RECKLESSNESS, 2901.21
sufficient when statute does not specify degree of culpability, 2901.22

RECOGNIZANCE, 2937.22 *et seq*
appeal, for, 2937.28, 2937.30
  reduction or increase of, 2949.04
arrest for failure to appear after release on, 2937.43
court may request upon conviction for misdemeanor, 2947.16, 2947.17
felony cases, in, Crim. R. 46
firearm disability relief, release on, as grounds for, 2923.14

RECOGNIZANCE—*Continued*
minors, of, 2937.17, 2937.18
misdemeanors, re, Crim. R. 46; 2935.15
  necessary before suspension of execution of sentence for appeal, 2953.12
peace, to keep, 2937.44
preliminary hearing transcript, order setting, in, Crim. R. 5
statutory provisions, when deemed pursuant to, Crim. R. 46
summons, issuance, appearance, after, Crim. R. 46
venue change, re, 2931.30
witness, for, 2937.16, 2937.18, 2941.48

RECOLLECTION, REFRESHING, OF WITNESS, Crim. R. 15

RECORD
controlled substances, drugs, re—
  hypodermics, re, 3719.17.2
coroner's, 313.09, 313.10
discovery of defendant's prior, from prosecutor, Crim. R. 16
errors, clerical, in, Crim. R. 36
habeas corpus proceedings, re, 2725.26
official, proof of, Crim. R. 27
public, 149.43
sealing of—
  first offender, 2953.31 *et seq*
  person found not guilty, 2953.51 *et seq*
tampering with, 2913.42—*see also* TAMPERING, *at* evidence, with

RECORDING OF PROCEEDINGS, Crim. R. 22
arrest warrant, testimony re issuance, Crim. R. 4
grand jury, re, Crim. R. 6
search warrant, testimony re issuance, Crim. R. 41

RECORDING TAPE, CRIMINAL SIMULATION OF, 2913.32

RECOVERY OF OFFENDER'S PROFITS
administration of fund, 2969.04
declaratory judgment to determine application to contract, 2969.03
definitions, 2969.01
distributions to victims, 2969.04
payment of proceeds of contract with offender or person into fund, 2969.02
payment of unexpended funds to person from whom obtained, 2969.05

REENACTMENT OF STATUTE, EFFECT, 1.58

REFORMATORY INSTITUTIONS, Ch. 753

REFRESHING RECOLLECTION OF WITNESS, Crim. R. 15

REFRIGERATORS, ABANDONED, 3767.28

REFUSAL TO TESTIFY, BY GRAND JURY WITNESS, PROCEDURE, 2939.14, 2939.15

REGIONAL TRANSIT AUTHORITIES
law enforcement, 306.35, 2935.03
  felony precludes or terminates employment as officer, 306.35.2

REGISTRATION
falsification to obtain, 2921.13
firearms, 2923.17
motor vehicles—*see* MOTOR VEHICLES
sex offenders—*see* SEXUAL PREDATORS, HABITUAL SEX OFFENDERS, SEXUALLY ORIENTED OFFENDERS

REGISTRY NUMBER, DEFINED, 3719.01

REHABILITATION
drug dependent persons, 2951.04, 2951.04.1
felony, criterion re fine, imprisonment for, 2929.12
fine, suspension of, as basis for, 2929.51
misdemeanor, criterion re fine, imprisonment for, 2929.22
probation, criterion re, 2951.02

REHABILITATION AND CORRECTION DEPARTMENT, 5120.01 *et seq*
accident, injury or peculiar death of inmate, report by managing officer, 5120.21
admission and discharge of inmates, to regulate, 5120.15
agreement for transfer of children in custody of youth services department to correctional medical center, 5120.16.2
agreements to house certain persons in jail or workhouse, 5120.16.1
AIDS policy, 5120.16
annual report, financial statement, 5120.32, 5120.33, 5120.35
application of provisions effective 7-1-96, 5120.02.1
appropriation of property, by, 5120.46
assistant director, status, powers, duties generally, 5120.02
bond required of certain officers and employees, 5120.08
books and accounts for each institution, audit, inventory, 5120.25
bureau of examination and classification, 5120.11
burial of inmate dying in institution, 5120.45
capital facilities, lease of, 5120.47
change of purpose of institution, 5120.03
classification of buildings as to manufacturing use, 5120.18
commissary fund at each institution, 5120.13.1
community and district community based correctional facilities and programs—
rules and forms, 5120.11.1

REHAB. & CORR. DEPT.—*Continued*
conflict in apparent powers of managing officer, department, 5120.42
contracts for private operation, management of correctional facilities, 9.06
courses of study in institutions, 5120.41
cultivation of lands, 5120.19, 5120.20
director, powers and duties generally, 5120.01
  same power as judge of county court, 5120.30
divisions of, 5120.06
  business administration, 5120.09, 5120.22
  organization generally, chiefs, 5120.07
  parole and community services, 5120.10
DNA testing, 2901.07—*see also* DNA TESTS
education services fund, 5120.09.1
electronically monitored early release, 5120.07.1-5120.07.4
employees, appointment generally, 5120.05
escapees, provisions for apprehension, 5120.48
escape of violent offender, notice of, 5120.14
executive, administrative, fiscal powers over institutions, 5120.36
exercise equipment and fighting skills programs denied to prisoners, 5120.42.3
fund, prisoner programs, 5120.13.2
funds and property of inmates, 5120.13
funds, indemnity contract, treasurer of state to have custody, 5120.26
funds of prisoner, transfer to pay judgment, 5120.13.3
gifts and bequests to institutions, 5120.13
halfway houses, grants for construction or renovation, 5120.10.3
HIV policy, 5120.16
improper politicking by officer or employee, 5120.34
industrial and entertainment fund at each institution, 5120.13.1
information exchanges with human services department, 5120.37
initial examination, classification and assignment to institution, 5120.16
inspection committee of legislative service commission, 2967.18, 5120.10.1, 5120.10.2, 5120.51, 5145.16.2
institutions managed by, 5120.05
intensive program prisons, 5120.03.2
  OMVI offenders, 5120.03.3
interstate correction compact, 5120.50
investigations, 5120.30
  special agents, credentials, 5120.31
jails, minimum standards set by director, 5120.10
managing officers of institutions, 5120.38, 5120.39
  estimates and proof of use of articles produced, 5120.42
manufacturing and industries, department to determine for each institution, 5120.18, 5120.27
manufacturing fund, 5120.29
mentally ill or retarded prisoners in need of treatment, transfer and discharge of, 5120.17
minimum security misdemeanent jails, 5120.10.1

REHAB. & CORR. DEPT.—*Continued*
naming of institutions, 5120.05
nonpartisan management of institutions, rules for, 5120.34
occupational therapy, 5120.43
oil and gas leases, 5120.12
penal industries manufacturing fund, 5120.29
penal/reformatory distinction eliminated, 5120.03
physician recruitment program, 5120.55
population and cost impact statement for bills introduced in general assembly, 5120.51
prices for manufactured items and inmate labor, setting, 5120.28
prisoner programs fund, 5120.13.2
purchases of supplies, 5120.18, 5120.19, 5120.24
  contract secured through competitive bidding, 5120.24
purposes of Chapter 5120., liberal construction, 5120.44
records concerning inmates, 5120.21
report on time served by released inmates, 5120.33.1
rules for proper execution of department's powers, 5120.42
rules infraction board for each institution, 2967.11
sanction for frivolous or malicious action, 5120.01.1
searches, visitor, 5120.42.1
separate medical records for inmates, 5120.21
services and agricultural fund, 5120.23, 5120.29
sewage treatment services, contract to provide, 5120.52
sexually violent offenders—
  risk assessment reports, 5120.61
  rules for termination of parole board's control over, 5120.49
shock incarceration pilot program, 5120.03.1
state and local officials to estimate need for prison-made supplies, 5120.23
teachers employed by, qualifications, 5120.40
transfer of inmates between institutions, 5120.01, 5120.16
transfer or exchange of offender to foreign county pursuant to treaty, 5120.53
victims' services office, 5120.60, 5149.10.1
wages paid to inmates, 5120.28, 5120.29
youth services, acceptance of children from, 5120.05

REIMBURSEMENT
cost of confinement in workhouse, by convicted person, 2947.19
  hearing on ability to pay, 2929.15
costs of investigation and prosecution, by convicted person—
  arson and related offenses, 2929.28
  corrupt activity, engaging in pattern of; court order, 2923.32

RELEASE—*see also* BAIL; PAROLE; PROBATION; RECOGNIZANCE
falsification to obtain, 2921.13

RELIEF
falsification to obtain, 2921.13

RELIEF—*Continued*
sought, to be set forth in motion, Crim. R. 47

REMORSE
felony sentencing considerations, 2929.12

RENEWAL OF ACQUITTAL MOTION, Crim. R. 29

RENUNCIATION
attempt, of, 2923.02
complicity, of, 2923.03
conspiracy, of, 2923.01

RENTAL PROPERTY
evidence of intent to commit theft, 2913.41, 2913.72

REPARATION
felon, by, fine must not prevent, 2929.12
misdemeanant, by, fine must not prevent, 2929.22
murderer, by, fine must not prevent, 2929.02
probation—
  criterion favoring, as, 2951.02

REPEAT OFFENDER
defined, 2929.01
felony, criterion re fine, imprisonment for, 2929.12
felony sentencing considerations, 2929.14
misdemeanor, criterion re fine, imprisonment for, 2929.22
murder, as aggravating circumstance re, 2929.04
pre-trial diversion program ineligibility, 2935.36
probation, criterion re, 2951.02
specification that offender is repeat violent offender, 2941.14.9

REPORT
crime, of, failure to make, 2921.22
  garage keepers, 4501.05
discovery, re—
  laboratory analysis of evidence, re drug prosecution, provisions re, 2925.51
escaped animals; duty in certain cases, 2927.21
falsification of written, required by law, 2921.13
mitigation of sentence, in, 2947.06
ordnance, dangerous—
  lost, stolen, of—
    fire marshal, state, copy to, duties re, 2923.18
    law enforcement authorities, to, required, 2923.20
    possession of unlawful, immunity from prosecution for, 2923.23
panic, including by false, 2917.31
presentence examination of—*see* PRESENTENCE INVESTIGATION
specification that offender is repeat violent offender, 2941.14.9

REPRIEVE
application for, 2967.07

REPRIEVE—*Continued*
confinement of prisoner during, 2967.10
defined, 2967.01
governor may grant, 2967.08
procedure, 2967.03
warrant of, 2967.09

RESCUE PERSONNEL
burn, gunshot, stab wound, failure to report, 2921.22
emergency, hampering at, 2917.13
impairing response to emergency, 2909.04

RESEARCH, LICENSE TO POSSESS DANGEROUS ORDNANCE FOR, 2923.18

RESERVOIR, BEFOULING, 3767.18

RESIDENCE IN COMMUNITY, RELEASE BASED ON, Crim. R. 46

RESISTANCE TO LAWFUL AUTHORITY, 2921.35
traffic offenses, 4513.36

RESISTING ARREST, 2921.33
traffic offenses, 4513.36

RESTITUTION
assignment of offender's payments toward satisfaction of, 2949.11.1
coercion charge, re, as condition of probation, 2905.12
felon, by, fine must not prevent, 2929.12
felony conviction, 2929.11, 2929.18
misdemeanant, by, fine must not prevent, 2929.22
probation, offender will make, as factor favoring, 2951.02
sex offenses, withholding from government deferred compensation or public retirement system payment, 2907.15
victim of certain offenses may accept, rather than prosecute, 2921.21

RESTRAINT
child, excessive physical, of, 2919.22
unlawful, 2905.03

REST ROOM FACILITIES, 3767.34

RETALIATION, 2921.05

RETIREMENT BENEFITS, FALSIFICATION TO OBTAIN, 2921.13

RETROACTIVE APPLICATION OF CRIMINAL RULES, Crim. R. 59

RETURN
arrest warrant, of, Crim. R. 4
  indictment, information, upon, after execution of, Crim. R. 9

RETURN—*Continued*
bail—
    deposit, 90% of, upon appearance bond performance, Crim. R. 46
    verdict, of, bond continues until, Crim. R. 46
falsification of written, required by law, 2921.13
indictment, of, by grand jury foreman, Crim. R. 6
search warrant, of, Crim. R. 41
subpoena service, of, filed with clerk, Crim. R. 17
summons, of—*see* SUMMONS
verdict, of, Crim. R. 31

REVERSAL, BY APPELLATE COURT
error in designating statute in indictment, information, for, Crim. R. 7
state may appeal to next higher court, 2953.14

REVIEW
judgments, final orders, of—*see also* APPEAL
    bail bond may be continued pending, Crim. R. 46
    exceptions not necessary for, Crim. R. 51

REVISED CODE, REENACTMENT OF, 1.01

REVOCATION
license, of, upon conviction for receiving stolen property, 2961.03
probation, parole, of, Crim. R. 32.3; 2951.08, 2951.09, 2951.13

RIDICULE
coercion, subjecting person to, as, 2905.12
extortion, subjecting person to, as, 2905.11

RIFLES, INTERSTATE TRANSACTIONS RE, 2923.22

RIGHTS
appeal, to, 2953.02
appearance, initial, informed of, at, Crim. R. 5
arms, to bear, Art. I, § 4 OC
arraignments, explanation of, at, Crim. R. 10
    multiple defendants, Crim. R. 10
arrestee, of, 2935.14, 2935.20
    constitutional provisions re, Art. I, § 10 OC
assembly, of, Art. I, § 3 OC
civil—*see* CIVIL RIGHTS
counsel to—*see* COUNSEL

RIOT AND RELATED OFFENSES, 2917.01 *et seq*
aggravated, 2917.02
cordoning off area, 3761.16, 3761.99
disorderly conduct—*see* DISORDERLY CONDUCT
force, use by officer, fireman, in suppressing, 2917.05
special patrolmen for, 2901.01

RISK
defined, 2901.01

RISK—*Continued*
physical harm to persons, of serious—
    death, as, 2901.01
    ordinance, municipal, violation of, offense of violence, as, 2901.01
probation, offender will repeat, as factor against, 2951.02
repeat offender, of—
    felony, re, fine, imprisonment for, 2929.12
    misdemeanor, re, fine, imprisonment for, 2929.22
    parole, early, as criterion re, 2967.31
substantial, defined, 2901.01

RIVER
befouling, 3767.13, 3767.14, 3767.16
    exceptions, 3767.22
obstructing or diverting, 3767.13

ROBBERY, 2911.02
aggravated, 2911.01
conspiracy to commit, 2923.01
murder, committing during, as aggravating circumstance re, 2929.04

ROULETTE WHEEL, AS GAMBLING DEVICE, 2915.01

RULES
conformity of videotaped testimony, deposition of child victim of sex offense, 2907.41
court, of—
    defined, Crim. R. 57
criminal procedure, of—
    construction of, 2901.04
    scope of coverage, Crim. R. 1
evidence, of, 2945.51
    magistrate courts, 2938.15
infraction board, each prison, 2967.11
powers of Supreme Court of Ohio, re, Art. IV, § 5 OC

RULING
exception unnecessary to, re objections, motions, Crim. R. 51
new trial, as grounds for, Crim. R. 33

SAFECRACKING, 2911.31

SALE DEFINED RE CONTROLLED SUBSTANCE, 3719.01

SAME OR SIMILAR ACT, PROOF OF, 2945.59

SAMPLE DRUG
defined, 2925.01
illegal dispensing of, 2925.36

SANITY
inquiry into, 2945.37 *et seq*
presumption of, where no insanity plea, Crim. R. 11

SAVINGS AND LOAN ASSOCIATIONS
civil liability of officers for violations of, 1153.01 *et seq*
excessive dividend, declaration of, prohibited, 1153.03
miscellaneous offenses by officers of, 1153.01
reports, failure to make, 1153.06
solicitation of business, unlawful, 1153.06

SCATOLOGICAL INTEREST, MATERIAL APPEALING TO, 2907.01

SCENE OF OFFENSE, VIEW OF BY JURY, 2945.16

SCHEDULES I, II, III, IV, V CONTROLLED SUBSTANCES
amendment of—
    state board of pharmacy, by, 3719.44
    United States attorney general, by, 3719.43
defined, 3719.01
listed, 3719.41
schedule III, 3719.16.1

SCHOOL
actions against parents of minors who damage or steal property, 3109.09
anabolic steroids, notice re, 3313.75
arson, re, 2909.03
busses, traffic laws re, 4511.75 *et seq*, 4511.99
bus, suspension for passing stopped, 4507.16.5
driver's license, effect of withdrawal or absenteeism on, 4507.06.1
exclusion, permanent, 3301.12.1, 3313.66-3313.66.2
failure to send child to school; penalty, 3321.38, 3321.99
notices to board as to sex offenders in area, 2950.11
parental education neglect, 2919.22.2
psychologist-client privilege, re, duty to report crime, 2921.22
sealing of criminal record, effect on expulsion, 2933.52
searches, 3313.20
suspension generally, 3313.66-3313.66.2
weapons offenses, 2923.12.2

SCOPE OF RULES, Crim. R. 1

SEALING OF RECORD
first offender, of, 2953.31 *et seq*
person found not guilty, 2953.51 *et seq*

SEAL OF COURT, SUBPOENA ISSUED UNDER, Crim. R. 17

SEARCH AND SEIZURE—*see also* SUPPRESS, MOTION TO
constitutional protections re, Art. I, § 14 OC
delinquent child on probation subject to, 2151.35.5, 2151.41.1
interception of wire or oral communications—*see* INTERCEPTION OF WIRE OR ORAL COMMUNICATIONS

SEARCH AND SEIZURE—*Continued*
nonconsensual entry, 2933.23.1, 2935.12
parole, conditional pardon or other release, during, 2967.13.1
probationer subject to, 2951.02
sexually violent predators after release or modification of term, 2971.07
sham legal process, 2921.52
strip search, 2933.32
warrants, Crim. R. 41; 2933.21 *et seq*

SECONDHAND DEALERS
license revocation, upon conviction of receiving stolen property, 2961.03

SECRECY, RE GRAND JURY PROCEEDINGS, INDICTMENTS, Crim. R. 6; 2939.07, 2939.10, 2939.18, 2939.19, 2939.22

SECRET SERVICE OFFICER
appointed by prosecuting attorney, 309.07
law enforcement officer, as, 2901.01

SECURING WRITINGS BY DECEPTION, 2913.43

SECURITIES
bail, deposited in lieu of bond—
    felonies, Crim. R. 46
    misdemeanors, Crim. R. 46
contract, public, unlawful interest re, investing in, 2921.42
theft of, value re, 2913.61

SELF-DEFENSE
battered woman syndrome, 2901.06

SELF-INCRIMINATION
constitutional privilege against, Art. I, § 10 OC
guilty, no contest plea, waives privilege, Crim. R. 11

SENIOR CENTERS, BINGO GAMES AT, 173.12.1

SENTENCE, Crim. R. 32—*see also* PENALTIES
actual incarceration, of—
    drug offenses, re, 2925.01
    sex offenses, re, 2907.10 (*repealed, eff. 7-1-83*)
    specification of having firearm while committing felony, 2941.14.1
appeal from—
    imposed contrary to law, 2953.07
bad time added to prison term for violation, 2929.01, 2967.11
capital offense, for, 2929.03
commutation of, 2967.01, 2967.02 *et seq*
confinement re—*see* CONFINEMENT; IMPRISONMENT
convict, of, for subsequent offense, 2941.43
costs and jury fees to be included in, 2947.23

SENTENCE—*Continued*
death penalty, of—*see* DEATH PENALTY
execution of, when not appealed, 2949.05
felony, for—
    community residential sanctions, 2929.16
    considerations in imposing sentence, 2929.12, 2929.13, 2929.14
    criminal sentencing commission impact reports, 181.25
    financial sanctions, restitution, 2929.18, 2929.18.1
    grounds for appeal by defendant or prosecutor, 2953.08
    hearing, 2929.19
    judicial release, reduction of prison term, 2929.20, 2930.17, 5120.33.1
    nonresidential sanctions, 2929.17
    purpose of sentencing, discrimination prohibited, 2929.11
    sanctions where prison term not required, 2929.15
guilty, no contest plea—
    court may proceed with, after, Crim. R. 11
    when entered, Crim. R. 11
    withdraw, motion to, before, Crim. R. 32.1
imposition of—
    without unnecessary delay, Crim. R. 32
industry program, county jail; sentencing court to determine eligibility for, 2929.16
    felons, 2929.16
    misdemeanants, 2929.21
institution where sentence to be served, type of, 2929.22.1
life imprisonment, of—*see* LIFE IMPRISONMENT
mandatory prison term—
    automatic firearm, firearm muffler, or silencer, 2929.72, 2941.14.4
    defined, 2929.01
        drug offenses, 2925.01
    discharging firearm from motor vehicle, 2941.14.6
    firearm offenses generally, 2929.71, 2941.14.1, 2941.14.5
    sexually violent predators, 2971.01
misdemeanor, for, criteria re, 2929.22
mitigation of, procedure for receiving evidence on, 2947.06
modification of, 2929.51
multiple counts, upon conviction of, 2941.25
multiple sentences, 2929.41
presence of defendant at imposition of, Crim. R. 43
pre-sentence investigation, Crim. R. 32.2
psychiatric examination prior to, for certain offenses, 2947.25
reduction of, 2947.15.1, 2967.19.1
sexually violent predators—*see* SEXUAL PREDATORS, HABITUAL SEX OFFENDERS, SEXUALLY ORIENTED OFFENDERS
sham legal process, 2921.52
state criminal sentencing council, 181.21-181.26
suspension of, 2949.01 *et seq*

SENTENCE—*Continued*
time for imposing a holding hearing, SupR 39
vacating, setting aside, procedure for, 2953.21 *et seq*
victim impact statement, 2947.05.1
workhouse, to, for jail offense, when, 2947.18

SEQUESTRATION OF JURORS, Crim. R. 24; 2945.31 *et seq*

SERIOUS OFFENSES
assignment of counsel re, Crim. R. 44
defined, Crim. R. 2
guilty or no contest plea, procedure for taking re, Crim. R. 11
recording of all proceedings re, required, Crim. R. 22
sentence for, defendant's right to appeal after, Crim. R. 32

SERIOUS PHYSICAL HARM
persons, to, 2901.01
property, to, 2901.01

SERVANT, PUBLIC—*see* PUBLIC, *at* servant

SERVICE
alibi notice, of, on prosecutor, Crim. R. 12.1
certified mail, of summons by, Crim. R. 4
citation for minor misdemeanors, of, Crim. R. 4.1
corporation, of summons on, Crim. R. 4
filing of papers, and, Crim. R. 49
how made, Crim. R. 49
misdemeanor, re, withdrawal after 2 years' failure to serve complaint, 2935.10
subpoena, of, Crim. R. 17
summons, of, Crim. R. 4
    indictment, information, upon, Crim. R. 9
time for, Crim. R. 45
when required, Crim. R. 49

SERVICES
credit cards, misuse to obtain, 2913.21—*see also* CREDIT CARDS
defined, re theft, fraud, 2913.01
depriving another of—
    defined, 2913.01
    theft, as, 2913.02—*see also* THEFT AND RELATED OFFENSES
disrupting public, 2909.04
value of, re theft offense, 2913.02, 2913.61

SERVITUDE, INVOLUNTARY
abduction to hold another in, 2905.02
kidnapping to hold another in, 2905.01

SEVERANCE
charges, of, pretrial request for, Crim. R. 12
defendants, of, Crim. R. 14
    pretrial request for, Crim. R. 12

SEWAGE DISPOSAL COMPANY
interfering with apparatus, 4933.24

SEX OFFENDER, HABITUAL, 2950.01 et seq

SEX OFFENSES, 2907.01 et seq—see also SEXUAL PREDATORS, HABITUAL SEX OFFENDERS, SEXUALLY ORIENTED OFFENDERS
AIDS, HIV testing of accused, 2907.27, 2907.28—see also AIDS, HIV
disease, notification to victim, 2151.14, 2907.30
examination of victim, 2907.28, 2907.29
   interview by crisis intervention officer, 2907.30
medical tests, mandatory, 2907.27
minor; producing, pandering material, performance—
   nudity oriented, 2907.32.3
   obscene, 2907.32.1
   sexually oriented, 2907.32.2
names, details re, may be suppressed, 2907.11
repeat offender, re, prima-facie evidence of, 2929.01
solicitation, 2907.24—see also SOLICITING
specification of sexual motivation in indictment, 2941.14.7
videotaping of testimony of child victim under 11, 2945.48.1
withholding of restitution from government deferred compensation or public retirement system payment, 2907.15

SEXUAL ACTIVITY
defined, 2907.01
hire, for—see PROSTITUTION
juveniles, when material, performance displaying harmful to, 2907.01
juveniles—
   pandering sexually oriented matter including, 2907.32.1 et seq
   when material, performance which displays is harmful to, 2907.01
kidnapping to engage in involuntary, 2905.01
massage establishments, etc.—see MASSAGE ESTABLISHMENTS
obscene material, performance, when display of is, 2907.01

SEXUAL BATTERY, 2907.03
habitual sex offender re, 2950.01
venereal disease, examination, treatment re, 2907.27

SEXUAL CONDUCT, DEFINED, 2907.01

SEXUAL CONTACT, DEFINED, 2907.01

SEXUAL EXCITEMENT, DEFINED, 2907.01

SEXUAL IMPOSITION, 2907.06—see also IMPOSITION, SEXUAL

SEXUAL PENETRATION, 2907.12

SEXUAL PREDATORS, HABITUAL SEX OFFENDERS, SEXUALLY ORIENTED OFFENDERS, 2950.01 et seq
classification as sexual predator, 2950.09
definitions, 2950.01
determination that offender is habitual, 2950.09
divulging confidential information, 2953.35, 2953.54
DNA testing, 2901.07
duties of attorney general, 2950.13
duty to register, 2950.04, 2950.07
felony sentencing considerations generally, 2929.13
immunity, 2950.12
information provided to crime bureaus prior to release, 2950.14
legislative determinations, intent to provide information to protect public safety, 2950.02
misdemeanor penalties, 2929.21
notice of change of address, 2950.05
notice to offender of duty to register and update address, 2950.03
notice to victim of offender's registration or change of information, 2950.10, 2950.13
periodic verification of current address, 2950.06
persons authorized to inspect information, records, 2950.08
persons to be notified within geographical area, 2950.11
sentencing hearing, 2929.19, 2950.09
sentencing of sexually violent predators, 2971.01 et seq
   aggravated murder penalties, 2929.03, 2971.03
   appeal of sentence, grounds, 2953.08
   application of chapter, 2971.07
   definitions, 2929.01, 2971.01
   determination of specification by court or jury, 2971.02
   escape, 2921.34
   furlough ineligibility, 2967.26
   imposition of definite term, 2929.14
   ineligibility for earning days of credit, 2967.19.3
   multiple sentences, 2929.41
   murder penalties, 2929.02, 2971.03
   notice of early release, 2967.12.1
   notice of parole board's termination of control, 2967.12
   notices given to victim, 2930.16
   overcrowding emergency, ineligibility for release, 2967.18
   parole ineligibility, 2967.13
   resentencing after vacation of death or life imprisonment without parole sentence, 2929.06
   sentencing with specification, 2971.03
   specification in indictment, 2941.14.8
   termination of parole board control after minimum term, 2971.04
      detention for violation of conditions or for likely additional offense, 2971.06
      hearing on modification or termination, 2971.05

SEXUAL PREDATORS, ETC.—*Continued*
sentencing of sexually violent—*Continued*
   termination of parole board control—*Continued*
      notice, 2967.12
      warrantless searches, 2971.07
specification in indictment of sexual motivation, 2941.14.7

SHAM LEGAL PROCESS, 2921.52

SHELTERS
domestic violence—*see* DOMESTIC VIOLENCE

SHERIFF—*see also* JAILS; LAW ENFORCEMENT OFFICER
absence, 311.03
annual report, 311.16
books, etc. delivered to successor, 311.13-311.15
bond, 311.02
car-marking, 311.25-311.28.1
cashbook, 311.11
commitment to workhouse, duties as to, 2947.21
confinement of misdemeanant, duties as to, 2949.08
contracts to provide service, 311.29
convicted felon liable for costs, duties as to, 2949.15, 2949.16
convicted felons, to deliver to institution, 2949.12, 2949.13, 2949.17
convict under death sentence, to deliver to penitentiary, 2949.21
court, adjournment, of, 311.23
depositions of confined defendants, duties as to, 2945.51
deputy, 311.04, 311.05
disability, 311.03
education, continuing, 311.01
execution, foreign, 311.10
execution of fines, duties as to, 2949.10, 2949.11
fees, 311.17-311.21
jails—*see* JAILS
office, location of, 311.06
ordnance, dangerous—
   license, temporary permit application to, 2923.18
   transaction in, copy of record to, 2923.20
penalties, 311.99
process—
   execution and return of, 311.08
   service of, 311.22
prisoners, convicts, labor of, rehabilitation of, duties as to, 2947.15
probation revocation hearing for convict, duties as to, 2951.13
qualifications, 311.01
registration of sex offenders—*see* SEXUAL PREDATORS, HABITUAL SEX OFFENDERS, SEXUALLY ORIENTED OFFENDERS
removal of convict for sentence or trial, duties as to, 2941.41 *et seq*

SHERIFF—*Continued*
subpoenas, duties as to, Crim. R. 17; 2945.45, 2945.47
successor, 311.13-311.15
training, basic, 311.01
uniforms, 311.25-311.28.1
vendors, transient, 311.37
venue change, originating county to pay fees of, Crim. R. 18; 2931.31
warrant for recapture of escapee, 2949.06
warrant upon indictment, information, execution by, Crim. R. 9
writs, orders, to indorse day, hour upon, 311.09

SHOPLIFTERS, DETENTION OF, 2935.04.1, 2935.06, 2935.07

SILENCER
specification in indictment or information, 2941.14.4

"SIMILAR ACTS" STATUTE, RE PROOF OF MOTIVE, 2945.59

SIMULATION, CRIMINAL, 2913.32

SINGULAR, INCLUDES PLURAL, 1.43

SLAUGHTERHOUSES, 3767.16, 3767.22

SLOT MACHINE, AS GAMBLING DEVICE, 2915.01

SLUGS
defined, re theft, fraud, 2913.01
making, using, 2913.33

SMELLS AS NUISANCES, 3767.13

SOCIAL SECURITY NUMBER
recording when check is presented, 1349.17, 1349.99

SOLICITING
after positive HIV test, 2907.24
contributions, re missing children, 2901.32
improper compensation, 2921.43
loitering to engage in, 2907.24.1
sexual activity for hire, 2907.24—*see also* PROCURING, 2907.23
   rules of evidence re, 2907.26
testing of accused for veneral disease and HIV, 2907.27, 2907.28

SON OF SAM LAW—*see* RECOVERY OF OFFENDER'S PROFITS

SPECIAL GRAND JURY, 2939.17

SPECIFICATIONS IN INDICTMENT, Crim. R. 11
actual incarceration; required for imposition of—
   firearm, automatic, muffled or silenced, 2941.14.1, 2941.14.4
   firearm, possession of, 2941.14.1
offender is major drug offender, 2941.14.10
offender is repeat violent offender, 2941.14.9
prior offense, 2941.11
sexual motivation, 2941.14.7
sexually violent predator, 2941.14.8, 2971.02, 2971.03

SPEECH, FREEDOM OF, Art. I, § 11 OC

SPIRITUAL TREATMENT OF CHILD, WHEN NOT ENDANGERING, 2919.22

SPORTS, CORRUPTING, 2915.05

SPOUSE, ABANDONMENT, NONSUPPORT OF, 2919.21

SPOUSE, COMPETENCY AS WITNESS, EvR 601

SPOUSE, DEFINED RE SEX OFFENSES, 2907.01

SPREADING A FALSE REPORT OF CONTAMINATION, 2927.24

SPRING, BEFOULING, 3767.18

STALKING, MENACING BY, 2903.21.1
arrest and detention, 2925.03
bail, 2903.21.2
protection orders—
   generally, 2903.21.3, 2919.26
repeat offenders, 2903.21.1., 2903.21.2

STANDARD PHARMACEUTICAL REFERENCE MANUAL, DEFINED, 2925.01

STARTER'S PISTOL, AS ZIP-GUN, 2923.11

STATE—*see also* PROSECUTING ATTORNEY; PUBLIC, *at* official, etc.
construction of code, strict, against, 2901.04
defined, Crim. R. 2; 2901.11
dismissal of indictment, information, by, Crim. R. 48
flag, desecration of, 2927.11
highway patrol, 5503.01 *et seq*—*see also* LAW ENFORCEMENT OFFICER
   duties and powers, 5503.02
   misdemeanor arrests, by, 5503.07
   turnpikes, re, 5503.31 *et seq*
institution, nuisance near, 3767.19
jurisdiction of, 2901.11
lottery, 3770.08, 3770.99

STATEMENT
appeal, preserved in court records for—
   defendant, by, Crim. R. 16
   prosecuting attorney, by, Crim. R. 16
appearance, at initial, Crim. R. 5
arraignment, at, Crim. R. 10
cross-examination of witness re—
   defendant, by, Crim. R. 16
   prosecuting attorney, by, Crim. R. 16
death penalty, of offender, re, 2929.03
discovery, re, Crim. R. 16
falsification, as, when, 2921.13
perjury, as, when, 2921.11
preliminary hearing, by defendant at, Crim. R. 5
sentence, before, defendant may make, Crim. R. 32
severance of defendants, considered re motion for, Crim. R. 14

STATE'S EVIDENCE, WITNESS TURNING, 2945.44

STATUTE OF LIMITATIONS, 2901.13

STATUTES
amendment, reenactment—
   intended to be continuation of prior, 1.54
   prospective application, 1.58
   reference to part of statute applies to, 1.55
amendments to be reconciled if possible, 1.52
"and" may be read "or," vice versa, 1.02
applicability of sections, 1.41-1.59
"certified mail" includes "registered mail," 1.02
change in judicial construction, retroactive effect, 1.22
complaint, designation in, Crim. R. 3
constitutions, compliance with intended, 1.47
correction of nonsubstantive errors, intent, 1.30
definitions of words used in—*see* DEFINITIONS
designation as the "Revised Code," 1.01
effective date, 1.15
enrolled act language prevails in conflicts, 1.53
entire, intended to be effective, 1.47
gender, words of one include the other, 1.43
General Code, relationship to Revised Code, 1.01, 1.23; Appendix Volume, Part Four
general, special, local provisions, relationship, 1.51
headings, title chapter and section, not part of law, 1.01
indictment, information re, Crim. R. 7
intentions in enacting, 1.47
irreconcilable statutes or amendments, 1.52
just and reasonable result intended, 1.47
legislative intent, considerations courts to apply in determining, 1.49
limitations, of, 2901.13
prospective, presumption re, 1.48
"registered mail" includes "certified mail," 1.02
remedial laws, liberal construction, 1.11
   special provisions to govern, 1.12
repeal of repealing statute, effect, 1.57

STATUTES—*Continued*
repeal, prospective effect, 1.58
result feasible of execution intended, 1.47
section references, construction, 1.23
series of numbers or letters includes first and last, 1.56
severability of provisions if part held invalid, 1.50
singular includes plural, and vice versa, 1.43
tense, words in present include the future, 1.43
time, computation, 1.14, 1.45
words and phrases to be read in context; common or technical use, 1.42
words govern figures in expressing number, 1.46

STAY, AS EXTENDING TIME FOR TRIAL, 2945.72

STENOGRAPHER, GRAND JURY, Crim. R. 6; 2939.11

STEROIDS, ANABOLIC, OFFENSES INVOLVING, 2925.03
abuse, 2925.11
athletic facilities, posting in, 3707.50
schools, posting in, 3313.75.2
trafficking, 2925.03

STINK BOMB, USE AS CRIMINAL MISCHIEF, 2909.07

STOLEN PROPERTY
law enforcement agency, held by, disposition of, 2933.41
receiving, 2913.51—*see also* RECEIVING STOLEN PROPERTY

STREETCARS, TRAFFIC LAWS RE, 4511.57 *et seq*

STRICT LIABILITY, 2901.21
organizations, re, 2901.23

STRIP SEARCH, 2933.32

STRUCTURE, OCCUPIED
arson, re, 2909.02
burglary, re, 2911.11, 2911.12
defined, 2909.01
vandalism to, 2909.05

SUBPOENA, Crim. R. 17
convict, for, 2945.47, 2945.48
coroner may issue, 313.17
depositions—
 use as evidence, when party unable to subpoena witness, Crim. R. 15
documentary evidence, for production of, 2937.19
employer's duty, employee's rights re appearance at criminal proceeding, 2945.45.1
re appearance before grand jury, 2939.12.1

SUBPOENA—*Continued*
felony witness, of, before arrest, 2935.23
general use, for attendance of witnesses at trial, 2945.45
grand jury proceedings, re, 2939.12
juror, of, as grounds for challenge for cause, of, Crim. R. 24
sham legal process, 2921.52

SUDDEN INFANT DEATH SYNDROME, AUTOPSY REQUIRED, 313.12-313.13

SUICIDE, PHYSICIAN'S DUTY TO REPORT TO CORONER, 313.12

SUMMONS
arrest, release after, upon issuance of, Crim. R. 4
bail after appearance pursuant to, Crim. R. 46
citation, minor misdemeanors, after defendant's non-appearance re, Crim. R. 4.1
complaint, re, Crim. R. 4
contents, form of, Crim. R. 4, 9; 2935.18
corporation, to, Crim. R. 4
failure to appear re, 2935.11
forms, Crim. Forms III, IV, V, VII, VIII, IX, XII, XIII
indictment, information, upon, Crim. R. 9
issuance of—
 by whom, Crim. R. 4
 multiple, on same complaint, Crim. R. 4
misdemeanor, upon affidavit charging, 2935.10
prosecution commenced when issued, exception, 2901.13
sham legal process, 2921.52
sheriff to execute and return, 311.08
to state substance of charge, 2935.10
trial, re time for, 2945.71

SUNDAY
effect on time computation, Crim. R. 45

SUPPORT
dependents, of, 2919.21
order, interfering with action to issue or modify, 2919.23.1
order to withhold earnings, 3113.21 *et seq*

SUPPRESS, MOTION TO—*see also* SEARCH AND SEIZURE
appeal by state, from granting of, Crim. R. 12; 2945.67
 return of property stayed pending appeal, Crim. R. 12
arrest warrant, when testimony re admissible, Crim. R. 4
no contest plea does not affect appeal re, Crim. R. 12
pretrial, must be raised, Crim. R. 12
search warrant testimony, admissible at hearing on, Crim. R. 41
wiretapping, etc. 2933.63

SUPREME COURT OF OHIO
appeal to, 2945.67, 2953.08 *et seq*
books, records kept by clerk, powers re, Crim. R. 55
constitutional provisions re, Art. IV, § 2 OC
criminal sentencing council, 181.21-181.26
forms approved by, illustrative, not mandatory, Crim. R. 58
immunity from prosecution, power to grant to witness, 2945.44
local rules of court, to be filed with, Crim. R. 57
right of appeal to, 2953.02
rule-making powers of, Art. IV, § 5 OC

SURPLUSAGE IN INDICTMENT, INFORMATION, COURT MAY STRIKE, Crim. R. 7

SURPRISE
new trial, as grounds for, Crim. R. 33; 2945.79

SURVEILLANCE, ELECTRONIC—*see* WIRETAPPING, ELECTRONIC SURVEILLANCE

SWEAR, DEFINED, 1.59

SWITCHBLADE KNIFE, WHEN MAY MANUFACTURE, SELL, POSSESS, 2923.20

SYNDICATE, CRIMINAL—*see* CORRUPT ACTIVITY, 2923.31 *et seq*

SYRINGE, OFFENSES RE, 2925.12

TAMPERING
coin machines, with—*see* COIN MACHINES
contaminating substance for human consumption or use, 2927.24
evidence, with, 2921.12
gas pipes and apparatus, 4933.20
records, with, 2913.42
spreading false report of contamination, 2927.24
utility equipment, with, 4933.18
wiretapping, re, 2933.59

TEAR GAS, USE AS CRIMINAL MISCHIEF, 2909.07

TELEGRAPH
delaying message, 4931.27
divulging message, 4931.26
interrupting, impairing, 2909.04, 4931.28

TELEPHONE
divulging message, 4931.29
facsimile devices—*see* FACSIMILE DEVICES
harassment, 2917.21, 4931.31
interrupting, impairing, 2909.04, 4931.28

TELEPHONE—*Continued*
number, recording when check is presented, 1349.17, 1349.99
party lines, 4931.30
penalties, 4931.99
threat, 4931.31
value re theft of services of, 2913.61
wiretapping—*see* WIRETAPPING, ELECTRONIC SURVEILLANCE

TELEVISION
closed broadcast, videotaping testimony of child victim of sex offense, 2907.41
interrupting, impairing, 2909.04

TENSE OF VERB, USAGE IN CODE, 1.43

TERM OF COURT
time computation unaffected by expiration of, Crim. R. 45

TESTIMONY—*see also* WITNESS
complicity, of accomplice re, uncorroborated, insufficient, 2923.01
conspiracy, of co-conspirator re, uncorroborated, insufficient, 2923.01
perjury, necessary to prove, 2921.11
videotaping, recording; procedures when sex offense victim is child under 11, 2907.41

TESTS, DISCOVERY RE REPORTS OF
defendant, from, Crim. R. 16
prosecuting attorney, from, Crim. R. 16

THEFT AND RELATED OFFENSES, 2913.01 *et seq*
arrest without warrant for, upon reasonable ground, 2935.03
breaking, entering unoccupied structure to commit, 2911.13
burglary in attempting to commit, 2911.12
aggravated, 2911.11
civil action by victim, 2307.60, 2307.61
coin machines, tampering with, to commit, 2911.32
computer services, 2913.81—*see also* general theft and fraud provisions, 2913.01 *et seq*
degree of offense, when certain kinds of property involved, 2913.71
drugs, of, 2925.21
grand, 2913.02
motor vehicle—
offender to pay towing or storage costs, 2913.82
multiple offenses, 2913.61
offense, 2913.01
office, in, 2921.41
prosecution for, victim may abandon upon restitution, 2921.21

THEFT AND RELATED—*Continued*
receiving stolen property, re—*see* RECEIVING STOLEN PROPERTY
rental property, evidence of intent, 2913.41, 2913.72
repeat offender, re, 2929.01
robbery in attempt to commit, 2911.02
    aggravated, 2911.01
syndicate, criminal, re—*see* CORRUPT ACTIVITY
utility service, of, 4933.19
value of property, services re, 2913.61

THREAT
defined—
    coercion, re, 2905.12
    extortion, re, 2905.11
disorderly conduct, as, 2917.11
panic, inducing by, 2917.31
theft by, 2913.02

TICKET
gambling device, as, 2915.01
municipal corporations may regulate sales, 715.48
theft offense, value re, 2913.61

TIMBER
state-owned, prosecuting attorney's duties re, 309.14

TIME
acquittal, re motion for judgment of, Crim. R. 29
alibi notice, for filing, service on prosecutor, Crim. R. 12.1
appeal—
    as of right, for, 2953.05
arrest of judgment, re motion for, Crim. R. 34; 2947.03
bill of particulars, for defendant to request, Crim. R. 7; 2941.07
charge offense, failure to, for objection re, Crim. R. 12
commission of offense prior to 1-1-74; third or fourth degree felony between 1-1-74 and 7-1-83, 2929.61
computation of, generally, Crim. R. 45
criminal cases, 2945.71-2945.73, SupR 39
depositions, re, Crim. R. 15
discovery, re motion for, Crim. R. 16
enlargement of, Crim. R. 45
escaped, while, not to be counted toward sentence, 2949.07
excusable neglect, act permitted after, for, Crim. R. 45
execution, of, 2947.08, 2949.23
fines, for payment of, two years maximum, 2929.51
grand jury—
    challenges to array, jurors, for, Crim. R. 6
    discharge of, by court, for, Crim. R. 6
    summoning, for, Crim. R. 6
guilty plea, for withdrawal of, Crim. R. 32.1
hearing, re, Crim. R. 45; 2945.71 *et seq*
indictment, waiver of, re, Crim. R. 7
insanity plea, for making, Crim. R. 11

TIME—*Continued*
instructions to jury, re, Crim. R. 30
jury trial, re demand, waiver of, Crim. R. 23
motions, generally re. Crim. R. 45
new trial, re motion for, Crim. R. 33; 2945.80
no contest plea, for withdrawal of, Crim. R. 32.1
obscenity declaratory judgment action, re, 2907.36
obscenity injunction action, re, 2907.37
parole, re eligibility for, 2967.13
    consecutive indeterminate sentences, diminished for good behavior, 2967.25
    early release from, criteria, 2967.31
    final release from, 2967.16
    good behavior, reduced for, how computed, 2967.19, 2967.19.2, 2967.25
preliminary hearing, for, Crim. R. 5; 2945.71 *et seq*
presentence investigation, for, Crim. R. 32.2
pretrial conferences, for, Crim. R. 17.1
pretrial motions, for, Crim. R. 12
prosecution attorney—
    appeal certification, notice, by, Crim. R. 12
    evidence, for notice of intention to use, by, Crim. R. 12
search warrant, re, Crim. R. 41
sentence, of, reduced by pretrial confinement, 2967.19.1
service, re, Crim. R. 45—*see* SERVICE
subpoena, re, Crim. R. 17
summons upon indictment, information, for service of, Crim. R. 9
suspension of sentence of imprisonment, for, 2929.51
term of court, unaffected by expiration of, Crim. R. 45
trial, for, 2945.71 *et seq*, SupR 39
venue, for filing motion to change, Crim. R. 18
withdrawal of summons, warrant, for, 2935.10

TIRES, STUDDED, 5589.08.1

TITLE
certificate of, for motor vehicle—*see* MOTOR VEHICLES, *at* title, certificate of
rules of criminal procedure, of, Crim. R. 60

TOBACCO PRODUCTS
illegal sale, distribution of, 2927.02

TOKEN
gambling device, as, when, 2915.01
theft of, for admission, transportation, value re, 2913.61

TOOLS
device, substance, instrument, article as criminal, when, 2923.24
indictment, information, how described in, 2941.17
industrial, as zip gun, when, 2923.11
possessing criminal, 2923.24

TORTURE
child under 18, of, as endangering, 2919.22

TORTURE—*Continued*
juveniles, when material, performance displaying harmful to, 2907.01

TOTALIZER, AS GAMBLING DEVICE, 2915.01

TOWNSHIP
answer, hearing, judgment, appeal, 504.07
building code, 505.73-505.77, 505.99
citation, 504.06
fines, 504.05
law director—
  employment of persons associated in private practice of law, 2921.42, 2921.42.1
limited self-government, generally, 504.04
massage establishments, etc., regulation of—*see* MASSAGE ESTABLISHMENTS
police, 505.48-505.55
prosecuting attorney to serve as legal adviser for township officers, 309.09

TRADE, VANDALISM TO PROPERTY USED IN, 2909.04

TRADEMARK COUNTERFEITING, 2913.34

TRAFFICKING
drugs, in—
  affirmative defenses to, 2925.03
  aggravated, 2925.03
  conspiracy to commit, 2923.01
food stamps, in, 2913.46
marihuana, in, 2925.03

TRAFFIC LAWS
animals, riding or driving on roadways, 4511.05, 4511.99
application in Chautauqua assembly, 4511.90
arrests on highways, power to make, 4513.39
bail schedule, re, Crim. R. 46
  driver's license as bond, 2937.22.1
bicycles, re, 4511.52 *et seq*
door of motor vehicle open on traffic side, re, 4511.70
drag-racing prohibited, 4511.25.1
driver's license, re—*see* DRIVER'S LICENSE
duties upon leaving vehicle unattended, 4511.66.1
emergency vehicle, at stop light or sign, re, 4511.03, 4511.99
emergency vehicle, following, prohibited, 4511.72
exceptions from certain traffic laws, 4511.04.1
exemptions, for highway workers, 4511.04
fire hose, unprotected, driving over prohibited, 4511.73
freeways, prohibitions on use of, 4511.05.1, 4511.99
grade crossings, re, 4511.61 *et seq*, 4511.99
handicapped, parking for, nonhandicapped prohibited, 4511.69
injurious material on highway, placing, prohibited, 4511.74
  restriction on local officers where only small portion of freeway located in their jurisdiction, 4549.17

TRAFFIC LAWS—*Continued*
intersections and crosswalks, driver shall not enter unless space on other side, 4511.71.2
intersections, turns at, rules for, 4511.36
intoxicated, driving while, 4511.19—*see also* DRIVING UNDER INFLUENCE
lessor may establish non-liability for violations, 4511.07.1
local, 4511.07
motorcycles, re, 4511.53
nonresident violator compact, 4511.95 *et seq*
officer resisting, 2921.33.1, 4513.36, 4511.99, 4513.99
parking, re, 4511.66 *et seq*
passing of vehicles, re, 4511.27 *et seq*
pedestrians, 4511.49 *et seq*
penalty, 4511.99
"three consecutive days" defined, 4511.99.1
police officer, compliance with order of, 4511.02, 4511.99
private property, use of, for vehicular traffic, 4511.08
private roads, 4511.09.1, 4511.16, 4511.21.1, 4511.43.2
property subject of, used to violate, right to possession of not lost, 2933.41
racing, competitive, re, 4511.25.2
radar, 4511.09.1
reckless operation, 4511.20, 4511.20.1, 4511.20.2, 4511.99
repeat offender, not applicable re, 2929.01
right-of-way, re, 4511.41 *et seq*
school busses, re, 4511.75 *et seq*, 4511.99
sidewalk, driving on, prohibited, 4511.71.1
space between moving vehicles, re, 4511.34
speed regulations, re, 4511.21 *et seq*, 4511.99
streetcars, re, 4511.57 *et seq*
supreme court's authority to set uniform procedure, 2937.46
through highways, re, 4511.65
traffic control devices, re, 4511.09 *et seq*, 4511.99
trailer, occupying while on highway, prohibited, 4511.70.1
turn and stop signals, re, 4511.39, 4511.40
uniform application of, 4511.06
view of driver, obstructed by passenger or load, 4511.70
violator who damages real property; name to be provided to owner, 2935.28

TRAFFIC RULES OF PROCEDURE
arraignment, Traf. R. 8, 17
bail, Traf. R. 4, 7
complaint, Traf. R. 3
continuance, Traf. R. 18
definitions, Traf. R. 2
failure to appear, Traf. R. 7
forms, Traf. R. 6, 21
guilty plea, Traf. R. 12, 13
joinder, Traf. R. 5
judicial conduct, Traf. R. 16
jury demand, Traf. R. 9

TRAFFIC RULES OF PROCEDURE—*Continued*
motions, Traf. R. 11
pleas, Traf. R. 10, 11, 12
referees, Traf. R. 14
rules—
   amendments, Traf. R. 25
   applicability, Traf. R. 1
   court, Traf. R. 19
   effective date, Traf. R. 24
   review commission, Traf. R. 22
   title, Traf. R. 23
   violations, Traf. R. 15
scheduling, Traf. R. 17
service, Traf. R. 6
summons, Traf. R. 3, 6, 7
Traffic Violations Bureau, Traf. R. 13
warrant, Traf. R. 6, 7

TRANSCRIPT
grand jury proceedings, of—
   not subject to discovery, Crim. R. 16
preliminary hearing, of, Crim. R. 5; 2937.15
search warrant testimony, of, part of affidavit re, Crim. R. 41

TRANSFER FROM COMMON PLEAS COURT FOR TRIAL, Crim. R. 21

TRANSFER OF PROCEEDINGS—*see* CHANGE OF VENUE

TRANSPORTATION
criminal, furnishing with, prohibited, 2921.32
public, interrupting, impairing, 2909.04
   misconduct involving, 2917.41
utility, value re theft of services of, 2913.61

TRASH, OFFENSES INVOLVING, 3767.32, 3767.33

TREATMENT, RE DRUGS
in lieu of conviction, 2951.04.1
probation, as condition of, 2951.04

TREES
injuring, 901.5
state-owned, prosecuting attorney's duties re, 309.14

TRESPASS
aggravated, 2911.21.1
criminal, 2911.21

TRIAL, 2945.01 *et seq*
confinement awaiting, credit for, on sentence, 2967.19.1
continuances, procedure, 2945.02
docket, indictment entered on, by clerk, Crim. R. 6
in absentia, 2945.12
   magistrate courts, 2938.12

TRIAL—*Continued*
inmate of jail or workhouse, of, 2941.45
judge, effect of disability during, Crim. R. 25
jury, by—*see* JURY TRIAL
magistrate courts, in, procedure, 2938.01 *et seq*
murder to escape, as aggravating circumstance, 2929.04
new—*see* NEW TRIAL
order of proceedings at, 2945.10
presence of defendant at, Crim. R. 43
sham legal process, 2921.52
time for, 2945.71 *et seq*
transfer from common pleas court for, Crim. R. 21
rules, of evidence, civil, when applicable, 2945.41
wrong county, in, procedure, 2945.08

UNAUTHORIZED USE
block parent symbol, of, 2917.46
property, of, 2913.04
vehicle, of, 2913.03

UNEMPLOYMENT COMPENSATION, FALSIFICATION TO OBTAIN, 2921.13

UNION TERMINAL COMPANIES
authority to arrest, 4953.11

UNIT DOSE, DEFINED, 2925.01

UNIVERSITIES, ANABOLIC STEROIDS, NOTICE RE, 3345.41

UNLAWFUL RESTRAINT, 2905.03

USURY, CRIMINAL, 2905.21-2905.24

UTILITIES—*see* PUBLIC, *at* utilities

UTTER
defined, re theft, fraud, 2913.01
forged writing, 2913.31
records, after tampering with, 2913.42
simulated object, to, 2913.32

VACATION OF JUDGMENT (SENTENCE), 2953.21 *et seq*

VALUE
arson, related offenses, re, how determined, 2909.11
effect on degree of offense—*see* specific offense
theft, related offenses, re property services, 2913.61
vandalism, re, 2909.11
written instrument or evidence of debt, 1.07

VANDALISM, 2909.05
value of property re, how determined, 2909.11

VARIANCE
allegations, proof, between, when new trial for, Crim. R. 33

VARIANCE—*Continued*
amendment of indictment, Crim. R. 7
effect, 2941.26
harmless, disregarded, Crim. R. 52

VEHICLE—*see* MOTOR VEHICLES

VENDING MACHINES—*see* COIN MACHINES

VENDORS, TRANSIENT, 311.37, 715.64

VENEREAL DISEASE, EXAMINATION, TREATMENT, FOR, 2907.27

VENIRE
capital cases, in, 2945.18, 2945.19
magistrate courts, in, 2938.14

VENUE, Crim. R. 18; 2901.12
change of—*see* CHANGE OF VENUE
nuisance cases, 3767.25—*see also* NUISANCES

VERDICT, Crim. R. 31
bail bond continues until return of, Crim. R. 46
disability of judge after, effect, Crim. R. 25
docket, criminal, chronologically noted in, Crim. R. 55
guilty, of, degree, elements of offense to be stated in, effect of omitting, 2945.75
insanity, not guilty by reason of, 2945.39
judgment of conviction, to be stated in, Crim. R. 32
jury or court to determine amount of controlled substance involved, 2925.03
modification to lesser degree, 2945.79
murder, aggravated, of guilty of, procedure upon, 2929.03
poll of jury, re, Crim. R. 31; 2945.77
presence of defendant at, Crim. R. 43
recording of, 2945.78
to be in writing, signed by jurors, 2945.17.1
value of property—
 arson, related offenses, re, 2909.11
 theft offenses, re, 2913.61
 vandalism, re, 2909.11

VESSELS—*see* WATERCRAFT, OFFENSES RE

VICE PRESIDENT, ASSASSINATION OF, AS AGGRAVATING CIRCUMSTANCE, 2929.04

VICTIMS OF CRIME, OConst I:10a; 2930.01 *et seq*
attorney general education fund, 109.93
bill of rights pamphlet, 109.42, 2743.19.1, 2930.04
character evidence, admissibility, EvR 404(A)
concealment of victim's address, phone number, similar identifying facts, 149.43, 2930.07
conflict between Chapter 2930., other statutes, 2930.19
county assistance programs, 307.62, 5705.19

VICTIMS OF CRIME—*Continued*
crime victims assistance office, advisory board, 109.91, 109.92
crime victim's recovery fund, 2969.11-2969.14
 administration, 2969.12
 created, 2929.25
 crediting of moneys collected and intent, 2969.13
 definitions, 2969.11
 disposition of residue of account, 2969.14
 distributions to victims, 2969.12
 payment of cost of imprisonment and incarceration from unexpended funds, 2969.14
defendant's right to respond to statements, 2930.14
definitions, 2930.01
effect of violations of rights, 2930.19
elderly or disabled, effect on sentence, 2929.11, 2929.12, 2929.21, 2929.22
electronically monitored early release of offender, 2930.16, 5120.07.3
employer of victims, prohibited actions, 2930.18
incarcerated victims, 2930.19
intimidation or violence directed at, 2921.04
 orders prohibiting, 2945.04
 revocation of bond or recognizance, 2930.05
investigating law enforcement agency, information furnished by, 2930.04
juvenile offenders—
 sex offenses, 2151.14
 victim impact statement, 2151.35.5
 victim 65 or disabled, 2151.26, 2151.35.5
liability for violation of rights, 2930.19
mediation, victim-offender, 2929.01, 2929.17
minimization of unwanted contact between prosecution and defense sides at proceedings, 2930.10
misdemeanor sentencing, consideration of victim's statement, 2929.22
notice to victim—
 acquittal or conviction, 2930.12
 appeal by defendant, 2930.15
 arrest of defendant, pretrial release, 2930.05
 changes in information previously furnished, 2930.03
 court proceedings as scheduled, 2930.06
 death of incarcerated defendant, 2930.16
 defendant's incarceration after conviction, 2930.16
 escape of defendant, 309.18, 2930.16
 furlough of defendant, 2930.16, 2967.26, 2967.27
 means of giving, 2930.03
 pre-trial diversion program, 2935.36
 release of defendant after conviction, 2930.16, 2967.03, 2967.12
 sex offender's registration or change of information, 2950.10
 substantial delay in prosecution, opportunity to object, 2930.08
office of criminal justice services assistance, 181.51-181.56
office of victims' services, 5120.60, 5149.10.1
pardon, parole or other release of offender, notice, opportunity to object, 2930.16, 2967.03, 2967.12

VICTIMS OF CRIME—Continued
presence at proceedings generally, 2930.09
presentence investigation report, inclusion of victim's statement, 2930.12, 2930.13, 2951.03
pre-trial diversion program consideration, opportunity to object, 2935.36
property of victim, return or retention, 2930.11
prosecutor's duty to seek compliance with rights, 2930.19
prosecutor to confer with victim, provide information, 2930.06
recovery of offender's profits—see RECOVERY OF OFFENDER'S PROFITS
reparation awards, notice of right to apply, 2929.14, 2930.04
representative of victim, exercise of rights by generally, 2930.02
restitution—see RESTITUTION
retaliation against, 2921.05
reversal of conviction, victim's rights upon, 2930.15
sex offenses—
    counseling services, confidentiality of information, 2921.22
    evidence of victim's sexual history, 2907.02, 2907.05
    interview by crisis intervention officer, notice of defendant's communicable disease, 2907.30
    medical examination, hospital emergency services, 2907.28, 2907.29
shock probation, statement prior to, 2930.17
statement prior to sentencing, defendant's response, 2930.14
victim's impact statement, 2947.05.1
    address, phone number of preparer furnished to victim, 2930.12
    fine for felony, consideration in imposing, 2929.14
    juvenile court, 2151.35.5
    minimum term of imprisonment for felony, consideration, 2929.12
    victim's written or oral statement to preparer, 2930.13

VIDEOTAPE
child victim testimony—see CHILD
criminal simulation of, 2913.32

VIEW OF PREMISES BY JURY, 2945.16

VIOLATION OF PARDON, PAROLE AND PROBATION—see PARDON; PAROLE; PROBATION

VIOLENCE—see also OFFENSE OF VIOLENCE
disorderly conduct, as, 2917.11
domestic—see DOMESTIC VIOLENCE
inciting to, 2917.01
juvenile, when material, performance displaying harmful to, 2907.01

VIOLENCE—Continued
obscene material, performance, when display of is, 2907.01
riot, as—see RIOT AND RELATED OFFENSES

VOID JUDGMENTS, VACATION OF SENTENCE, PETITION FOR, 2953.21 et seq

VOLUNTARINESS
guilty, no contest pleas, of, Crim. R. 11

VOLUNTARY MANSLAUGHTER, 2903.03

VOYEURISM, 2907.08
habitual sex offender, re, 2950.01

WAIVER
arraignment, of reading indictment, information, complaint at, Crim. R. 10
deposition, re, attendance by defendant at, of right to, Crim. R. 15
jury trial, of right to, Crim. R. 23; 2945.05
minor misdemeanors, of trial re, Crim. R. 4.1
peremptory challenges, of, Crim. R. 24
preliminary hearing, of, Crim. R. 5
pretrial defenses, objections, requests, by not making, Crim. R. 12
    defects in indictment, 2941.59

WARDEN
removal of convict for sentence or trial, duties as to, 2941.41 et seq

WARRANT—see also SEARCH AND SEIZURE, at warrants; WARRANT FOR ARREST
change of venue, re transfer of custody, 2931.30
death sentence, re, 2949.24
failure to serve without delay, as dereliction of duty, 2921.44
forms, Crim. Form VII, X, XI
interception (of wire or oral communication), 2933.53-2933.66
pardon, commutation, of, 2967.06
peace—see PEACE BOND, WARRANTS
recapture for, of one escaping after sentence and before confinement, 2949.06
removal of convict for sentence or trial, 2941.41
    trial time unaffected by, 2945.71
reprieve, of, 2967.09
upon indictment or information, Crim. R. 9
wiretapping, etc.—see WIRETAPPING, ELECTRONIC SURVEILLANCE

WARRANT FOR ARREST, Crim. R. 4
affidavit, complaint, issuance upon, 2935.10
after indictment, 2941.36, 2941.37
arrest pursuant to, procedure after, 2935.13

WARRANT FOR ARREST—*Continued*
charging misdemeanor, when may be withdrawn, 2935.10
citation, minor misdemeanor, after defendant's nonappearance re, Crim. R. 4.1
copy of, sent by telegraph, teletype, etc., 2935.24
escape after jury sworn, 2941.38
extradition proceedings, re, 2963.07, 2963.19
failure to appear after release on own recognizance, 2937.43
prosecution commenced when issued, exception, 2901.13

WASTE, INFECTIOUS—*see* NUISANCES

WATERCOURSE
befouling, 3767.13, 3767.14, 3767.16
  exceptions, 3767.22
obstructing or diverting, 3767.13

WATERCRAFT, OFFENSES RE, 1547.01 *et seq*—
  see also MOTOR VEHICLES
especially hazardous condition, authority of officer, 1547.07.1
felony precludes employment as officer, 1547.52.3
personal flotation devices, insufficient, 1547.07.1
used in transaction involving contraband, construed contraband, 2933.42
  seizure of; notice, disposition, 2933.43

WEAPON—*see also* FIREARMS, DANGEROUS ORDNANCE
conveying into detention facility or institution, 2921.36, 2921.37
criminal, providing with, 2921.32
deadly—
  burglary, aggravated, possession as, 2911.11
  courthouse or courtroom facility, conveyance, possession or control in, 2923.12.3
  defined, 2923.11
  possession while under detention, 2923.13.1, 2929.41
  riot, aggravated, possession as, 2917.02
  robbery, aggravated, possession as, 2911.01
  trafficking, unlawful transactions in, 2923.20
    as corrupt activity, 2923.31
schools and school functions, 2923.12.2
specification that offender had a firearm while committing offense, 2941.14.1
specification upon second offense that either was offense of violence, 2941.14.3

WEEK, DEFINED, 1.44

WEIGHT OF EVIDENCE
motion for new trial, not necessary for appeal on, 2945.83.1

WELL, BEFOULING, 3767.18

WHEELCHAIR, MOTORIZED, 4511.49.1

WHOLESALER OF CONTROLLED SUBSTANCE, DANGEROUS DRUG
defined, 3719.01

WILDLIFE DIVISION
division, jurisdiction of, 1531.07
polluting state land or water, 1531.29
propagation and preservation—
  protection of species threatened with statewide extinction, 1531.25
prosecutions and penalties—
  action to recover possession or value of wild animal, 1531.20.1
  consequences of conviction; failure to pay fine, 1531.23
  penalties, 1531.99
state ownership of wild animals, 1531.02

WILLS
defined, 1.59
indictment, information, re, necessary allegations in, 2941.22
unrevoked, tampering with, 2913.42

WIRETAPPING, ELECTRONIC SURVEILLANCE, 2933.51-2933.77
appeals by state, 2933.63
application for extension of warrant, 2933.55
application for interception warrant, 2933.53
civil, criminal actions for violations, 2933.65
conditions for issuance of warrant, finding of objective, 2933.54
conditions for receiving results in evidence or disclosure, 2933.62
constitutions, conformance of proceedings to, 2933.66
contents, sealing, disclosure, retention of warrant, 2933.56
definitions, 2933.51
divulgence of content of communication by provider of electronic communication service, 2933.52.1
execution of warrant or oral order, tampering, disclosure of document, 2933.59
giving warning of possible surveillance, 2933.59.1
immunity of persons assisting, 2933.58.1, 2933.77
instructions to investigative officers, procedure for interception, 2933.58
interception concerning other than designated offense, 2933.55
interception of wire, oral or electronic communication prohibited, exceptions, 2933.52
motion for inspection of materials, 2933.61
motion to suppress evidence, 2933.63
oral order for interception without warrant, 2933.57
pen register or trap and trace device, 2933.76, 2933.77
persons providing information, facilities or technical assistance, 2933.58.1, 2933.77

WIRETAPPING, ETC.—*Continued*
powers of common pleas court judge, 2933.52.2
reports by judges, prosecuting attorneys, 2933.60
service of inventory on interested persons, 2933.61
territorial validity of warrant, 2933.58
training of investigative officers, 2933.64

WITHDRAWAL OF REQUEST FOR JURY TRIAL, MAGISTRATE COURTS, 2938.05

WITNESS
absent, deceased, preservation of testimony of, 2945.49—see also DEPOSITIONS
attendance of, civil procedure to govern, 2945.46
bias of, EvR 616
bribery of, 2921.02
character testimony, 2945.57
competency of, 2317.01, 2945.42
coroner may subpoena, 313.17
court may discharge joint defendant to serve as witness, 2945.15
criminal proceedings, minimization of unwanted contact between opposing sides, 2930.10
defendant may testify, when, 2945.43
deposing—*see* DEPOSITIONS
fees, 2335.08
felony, to, subpoena examination before arrest re, 2935.23
grand jury—
    employer may not penalize employee, 2939.12.1
    may be present during session of, Crim. R. 6
    refusal to testify, procedure, 2939.14, 2939.15
    to give oath, 2939.13
identification of defendant, re, 2945.55
immunity from prosecution, 2945.44
    special grand jury, re, 2939.17
intimidation of, 2921.03, 2921.04
    court order to cease, 2945.04
material, provisions for compulsory attendance, 2937.18
misconduct of, as cause for new trial, Crim. R. 33; 2945.79
out-of-state, procedure, 2939.25 *et seq*
preliminary hearing, at, Crim. R. 5
prosecution, abandoning by, state not bound by, 2921.21
recognizance, re, 2937.16, 2937.18, 2937.44, 2941.48
record of conviction of prior felony, discovery from prosecutor, Crim. R. 16

WITNESS—*Continued*
search warrant, judge may examine before issuance, Crim. R. 41
subpoena of, 2935.23, 2937.18, 2945.45—*see also* SUBPOENA
    employer may not penalize employee, 2945.45.1
venue change, recognized to appear re, 2931.30

WOMEN, INFANTS AND CHILDREN PROGRAM
illegal use of benefits, 2913.46

WORKERS' COMPENSATION
falsification to obtain, 2921.13
fraud, 2913.48

WORKHOUSE—*see also* JAILS
commitment to, 2947.21
county commissioners may contract for use of, 2947.19
misdemeanant, confinement in, 1.05, 2949.08
person sentenced to, temporary confinement in county jail, 2947.22
probation, six-month term in, as condition of, 2929.51
regulation generally, ch. 753
sentence to for jail offense, 2947.18
trial of inmate of, for another offense, 2941.45

WORSHIP, DESECRATION OF PLACE OF, 2927.11

WRIT
execution, of, convicted felon to pay costs, 2949.15

WRITING
defined, re theft, fraud, 2913.01
forgery of—*see* FORGERY
securing by deception, 2913.43
    value of, re, 2913.61
        effect on penalty, 2913.43

WRITTEN, DEFINED, 1.59

YEAR, DEFINED, 1.44

YOUTH SERVICES DEPARTMENT
assaulting guards, visitors etc., 2903.13
influencing child to violate terms of placement or release; penalty, 5139.21, 5139.99

ZIP-GUN, 2923.11